Beckett COLLECTIBLE

GAMING ALMANAC

A COMPREHENSIVE PRICE GUIDE TO GAMING AND NON-SPORTS CARDS

7TH EDITION • 2017

Manufactured in the United States of America
Published by Beckett Media LLC

4635 McEwen Road, Dallas, TX 75244, (972) 991-6657
www.beckett.com

First Printing
ISBN 9781887432078

FEATURES

PRICE GUIDES

Beckett COLLECTIBLE GAMING ALMANAC 7H EDITION 2017

A COMPREHENSIVE PRICE GUIDE TO GAMING AND NON-SPORTS CARDS

EDITORIAL

Elliot Ross - **Managing Editor / Design**

COLLECTIBLES DATA PUBLISHING

Brian Fleischer - **Manager | Sr. Market Analyst**

Lloyd Almonguera, Ryan Altubar, Matt Bible, Jeff Camay, Steve Dalton, Justin Grunert, Junel Magale, Ian McDaries, Eric Norton, Kristian Redulla, Arsenio Tan, Paul Wirth, Sam Zimmer - **Price Guide Staff**

ADVERTISING

Bill Dumas - **Advertising Director**
bdumas@beckett.com, 972.448.9147
Priscilla Torres - **Advertising Sales**
ptorres@beckett.com 972-448-9131
Thomas Carroll - **Ad Traffic/Production Coordinator**
tcarroll@beckett.com, 972.448.9181

BECKETT GRADING SERVICES

Jeromy Murray - **Director**
4635 McEwen Road, Dallas, TX 75244
jmurray@beckett.com
Grading Sales - 972-448-9188 | grading@beckett.com

BECKETT GRADING SALES/SHOW STAFF

Dallas Office
4635 McEwen, Dallas, TX 75244
Derek Ficken
dficken@beckett.com • 972.448.9144

New York Office
135 W 50th St, 14th Floor, New York, NY 10020
Charles Stabile - **Northeast Regional Sales Manager**
cstabile@beckett.com
212.375.6760

California Office
22840 Savi Ranch Parkway #200, Yorba Linda, CA 92887
Michael Gardner - **Western Regional Sales Manager**
mgardner@beckett.com • Office: 714-200-1934
Fax: 714-388-3741

Asia Office
Seoul, Korea
Dongwoon Lee - **Asia/Pacific Sales Manager**
dongwoonl@beckett.com
Cell +82.10.6826.6868

BECKETT AUCTION SERVICES

Traci Kaplan - **Auctions Manager**
tkaplan@beckett.com 972.448.9040
Daniel Moscoso - Digital Studio

OPERATIONS

Amit Sharma - **Manager-Business Analytics**
Alberto Chavez - **Sr. Logistics & Facilities Manager**

EDITORIAL, PRODUCTION & SALES OFFICE

4635 McEwen Road, Dallas TX 75244
972.991.6657 www.beckett.com

Letters the Editor:
4635 McEwen Rd., Dallas, TX, 75244

CUSTOMER SERVICE

Beckett Media, LLC
4635 Mc Ewen Road. Dallas, TX 75244
Subscriptions, Address Changes, Renewals, Missing or Damaged Copies - 866.287.9383 • 239.653.0225 Foreign Inquires
subscriptions@beckett.com

Price Guide Inquiries
customerservice@beckett.com
239.280.2348

Back Issues www.beckettmedia.com
Books, Merchandise, Reprints 239.280.2380

Dealer Sales 239.280.2380 dealers@beckett.com

Beckett Media, LLC
Sandeep Dua - **President**
Kevin Isaacson - **Beckett Conferences**
Bill Sutherland - **Senior Director**
Sushmita Gulabani - **Global Head, Branding and Marketing**

Magic: the Gathering HOT LIST

Here's a quick look at the hottest cards from the latest Magic the Gathering sets

ELDRITCH MOON

LILIANA, THE LAST HOPE

GRIM FLAYER

EMRAKUL, THE PROMISED END

TAMIYO, FIELD RESEARCHER

ISHKANAH, GRAFWIDOW

ETERNAL MASTERS

FORCE OF WILL

MANA CRYPT

SNEAK ATTACK

VAMPIRIC TUTOR

NATURAL ORDER

SHADOWS OVER INNISTRAD

AVACYN, THE PURIFIER

NAHIRI, THE HARBINGER

ARLINN KORD

SORIN, GRIM NEMESIS

JACE, UNRAVELER OF SECRETS

Magic: The Gathering 2016 Year in Review

It has been a great year for Magic: The Gathering product releases. With 4 Booster sets, 2 Duel Decks, 1 From the Vault, 4 Specialty Sets and a Holiday Gift Box, there was more than enough to collect throughout the year. Enjoy this visial tour through the past year of Magic: The Gathering.

BOOSTER BOXES

- Oath of the Gatewatch
- Shadows over Innistrad
- Eldritch Moon
- Kaladesh

Continued on page 20

COMMAND & CONQUER

PLANESWALKING COMMANDERS COME TO THE TABLE

By Elliot Ross | Editor

The Commander format expanded once again back in 2014 with a whole new cycle of offerings from Wizards of the Coast. The format has now officially reached a cult classic status withing the Magic community, so much so that there is an entire generation of Magic players that only play Commander. There have been five decks released in the 2014 version of Commander, one for each color instead of the multicolored wedge decks from the past entries in the series. Many people feel that monocolored decks take away from the fun of Commander. Whether that is true or not will remain to be seen but can really be put to the test by exploring these decks. Aside from each being monocolored, these decks now each contain a Planeswalker as the featured commander. Generally Planeswalkers have not been used as commanders because of their high casting cost and their effects typically do not make them good commanders. Yet these five new Planeswalkers were designed specifically for the Commander format. While some still feel they are too limited, expensive, and lack the fun of a traditional legendary commander, we are generally in favor of giving players as many options as possible. This is where this set excels. These cards may not be for everyone, but fit the right sweet spot for some players who wanted more monocolored support and Planeswalker options in the Commander format.

OFFERINGS

THE NEW COMMANDERS

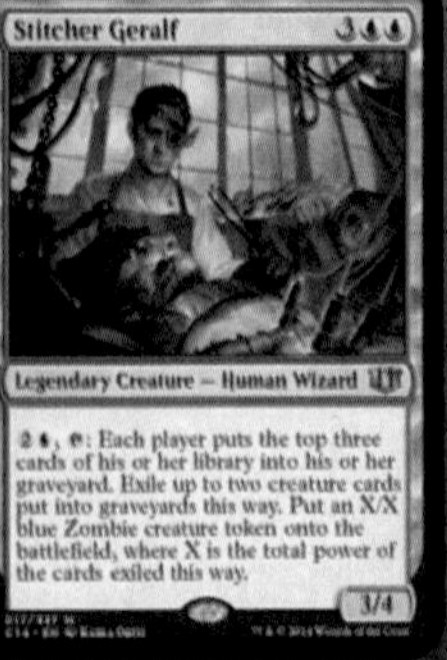

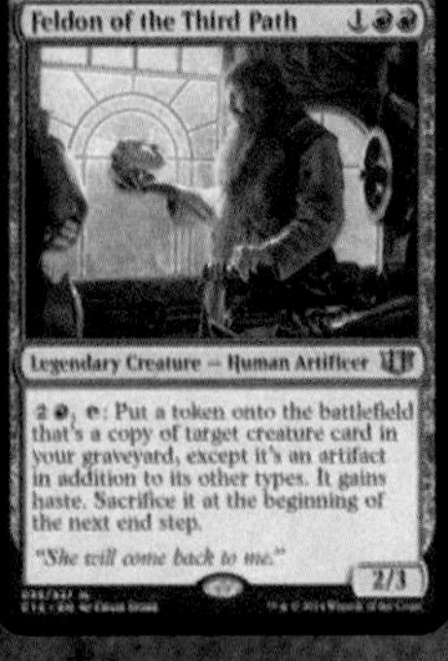

THE RULES OF COMMAND

Anybody can make a Commander deck from their own cards. Here's how it works!

Commander Deck Construction

Commander decks are exactly 100 cards, including the deck's commander.

The deck's commander must be a legendary creature.

Other than basic lands, each card must have a different English name.

A commander's color identity includes its colors, as defined by its mana cost or characteristic-defining abilities, and also the colors of any colored mana symbols in its rules text.

The colors of colored mana symbols found only in reminder text aren't part of a commander's color identity.

A card can't be included in your deck if any mana symbol in its mana cost or rules text is a color not in your commander's color identity. A card also can't be included in your deck if it has a characteristic-defining ability defining it to be a color not in your commander's color identity.

A card with one or more basic land types can't be included in your deck if it could produce mana of a color not in your commander's color identity.

During the game, if mana would be added to your mana pool that isn't a color in your commander's color identity, that much colorless mana is added to your mana pool instead.

Color identity is established before the game begins.

Using Your Commander

Commanders often appear on the battlefield multiple times throughout the game.

Your commander begins the game in the command zone, a game area created for the Commander format and now also used for nontraditional _Magic_ cards (vanguard, plane, and scheme cards) and for emblems created by planeswalkers. The other 99 cards are shuffled and become your library.

You may cast your commander from the command zone. Each time you do this, it costs {2} more to cast for each time you previously cast it from the command zone that game.

If your commander would be put into your graveyard from anywhere or be exiled from anywhere, you may choose to put it into the command zone instead.

In addition to the normal rules regarding winning and losing the game, the Commander format adds this additional rule: A player that's been dealt 21 or more combat damage by the same commander over the course of the game loses the game.

Players should keep track of combat damage dealt to them by each commander over the course of the game.

This rule includes a player's own commander, who can deal combat damage to its owner if the commander is controlled by another player or if combat damage gets redirected to that player.

Alternate Mulligan Rule

The Commander variant uses an alternate mulligan rule. Each time a player takes a mulligan, rather than shuffling his or her entire hand of cards into his or her library, that player exiles any number of cards from his or her hand. Then the player draws a number of cards equal to one less than the number of cards he or she exiled this way. Once a player keeps an opening hand, that player shuffles all cards he or she exiled this way into his or her library.

Leaving the Game

Unlike two-player games, multiplayer games can continue after a player leaves the game (because that player lost the game or conceded).

When a player leaves the game, all permanents, spells, and other cards owned by that player also leave the game.

If that player controlled any abilities or copies of spells that were waiting to resolve, they cease to exist.

If that player controlled any permanents owned by another player, the effects that gave control of them to the player who left end. If that doesn't give control of them to a different player (perhaps because they entered the battlefield under the control of the player who left), they're exiled.

Rules/Banned List Courtesy of WOTC and mtgcommander.net

COMMANDER BANNED LIST

The following cards are generally considered banned from the Commander format. Even with just one in your deck, these cards still break the game!

Ancestral Recall
Balance
Biorhythm
Black Lotus
Channel
Coalition Victory
Emrakul, the Aeons Torn
Fastbond
Gifts Ungiven
Griselbrand
Karakas
Library of Alexandria
Limited Resources
Metalworker
Mox Emerald
Mox Jet
Mox Pearl
Mox Ruby
Mox Sapphire
Painter's Servant
Panoptic Mirror
Primeval Titan
Protean Hulk
Recurring Nightmare
Sundering Titan
Sway of the Stars
Time Vault
Time Walk
Tinker
Tolarian Academy
Trade Secrets
Upheaval
Worldfire
Yawgmoth's Bargain

Yu-Gi-Oh! HOTLIST

Here's a quick look at the hottest cards from the latest Yu-Gi-Oh! sets

DARK SIDE OF DIMENSIONS:

1. BLUE-EYES ALTERNATIVE WHITE DRAGON

2. GOLD GADGET

3. SILVER GADGET

4. CHOCOLATE MAGICIAN GIRL

5. CHAOS FORM

2016 MEGA TINS:

1. SOLEMN STRIKE

2. CYBER DRAGON INFINITY

3. TWIN TWISTERS

4. PAINFUL DECISION

5. ODD-EYES VORTEX DRAGON

DARK ILLUSION:

1. POT OF DESIRES

2. DARK MAGICAL CIRCLE

3. MAGICIAN NAVIGATION

4. CORAL DRAGON

5. THE HIDDEN CITY

Yu-gi-oh! Year in Review

Great Year, Great Products 2016

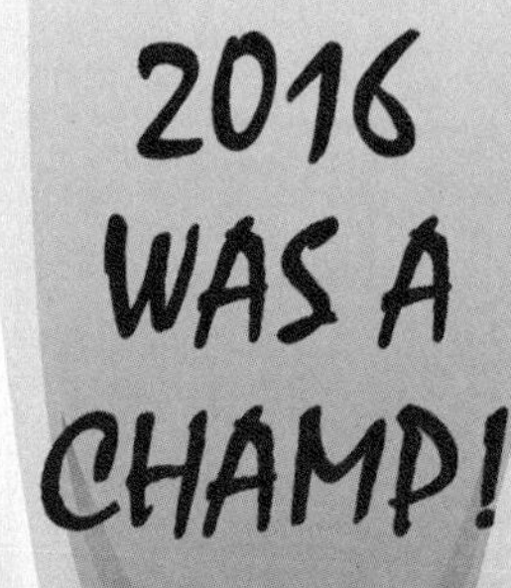

It has been a great year for Yu-Gi-Oh! product releases. With 8 Booster sets, 2 Deluxe Editions, only 1 tin (but boy what a tin!), 1 Duelist Pack, 1 Starter, 4 Structure Decks, and 3 Special Releases, there was more than enough to collect throughout the year. Enjoy this visial tour through the past year of Yu-Gi-Oh!.

BOOSTERS:

Breakers of Shadow • Wing Raiders • Millenium Pack
Shining Victories • Dark Side of Dimensions
The Dark Illusion • Dragons of Legend
Invasion: Vengeance

DELUXE EDITIONS:

- Breakers of Shadow
- Shining Victories

TINS:

- 2016 Mega-Tins

DUELIST PACKS:

- Rivals of the Pharaoh

STARTER:

- Yuya

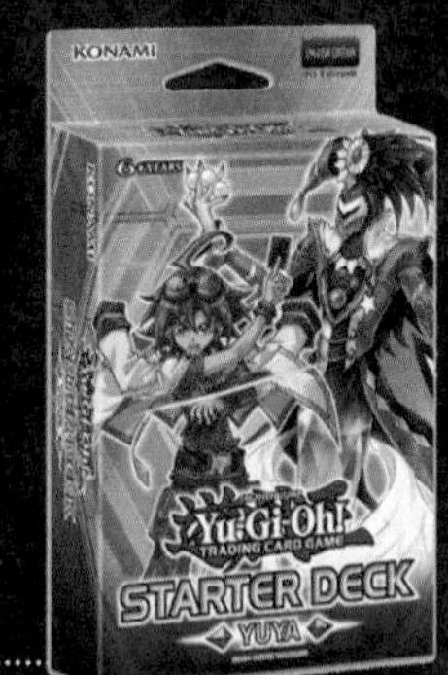

STRUCTURE DECKS:

- Emperor of Darkness
- Rise of True Dragons
- Yugi Muto
- Seto Kaiba

SPECIALTY BOXES:

- Premium Gold: Infinite Gold
- OTS Tournament Pack
- Legendary Decks II

Force of Will

HOT LIST

Here's a quick look at the hottest cards from the latest Force of Will sets

VALKYRIA CHRONICLES

1. ALFONS AVCLAIR

2. SELVARIA'S LANCE

3. COURAGEOUS STAND

4. KURT IRVING

5. ISARA GUNTHER

PROMOS

1. CHESHIRE CAT, THE GRINNING REMNANT

2. LITTLE RED, THE PURE STONE

3. MAGIC STONE OF HEARTH'S CORE

4. ISHTAR, THE GREAT GODDESS OF KINDNESS

5. ZERO, THE FLASHING MAGE-WARRIOR

THE MILLENNIA OF AGES

1. NYARLATHOTEP, THE USURPER

2. MILEST, THE INVISIBLE GHOSTLY FLAME

3. MOOJDART, THE QUEEN OF FANTASY WORLD

4. KAGUYA, THE TALE OF THE BAMBOO CUTTER

5. GRUSBALESTA, THE KEEPER OF MAGIC STONES

SPECIALTY SETS

- Eternal Masters
- Commander 2016
- Conspiracy: Take the Crown

SHADOWS OVER INNISTRAD: THE GIFT BOX

FROM THE VAULT: LORE

DUEL DECKS: BLESSED VS. CURSED

NISSA VS. OB NIXILIS

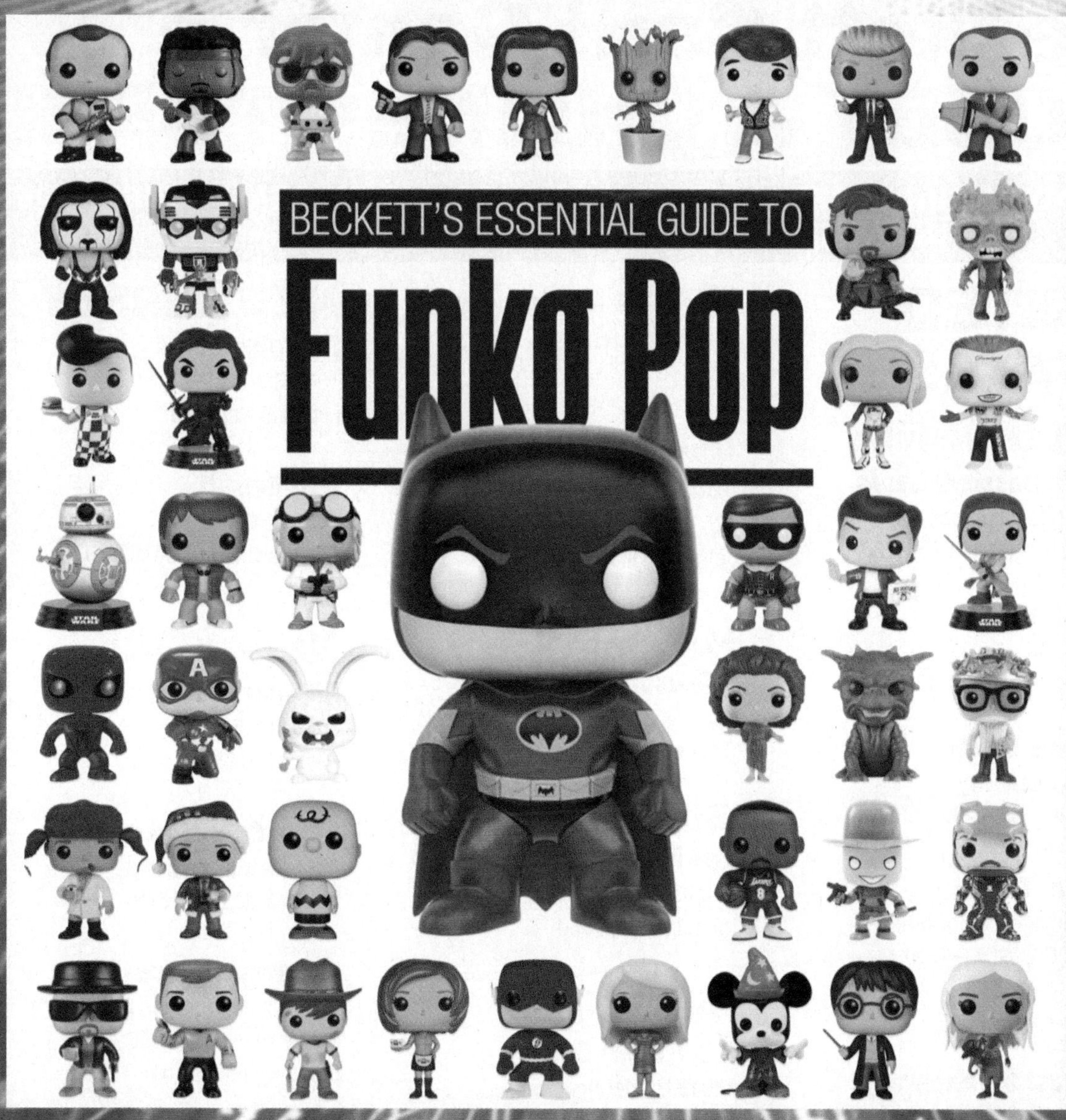
BECKETT'S ESSENTIAL GUIDE TO
Funko Pop

Beckett Card Gamer
HOBBY & ONLINE STORES

UNITED STATES

CALIFORNIA

Lefty's Baseball Cards
1859 El Camino Real
Burlingame CA, 94010-3220

Bill's Bullpen
207 4th St
Hollister CA, 95023-3923

Ardillo's Cards
2001 S Coast Hwy
Oceanside CA, 92054-6555

All Star Cards
8781 Cuyamaca St Suite 5
Santee CA, 92071-4216

FLORIDA

Not Just Cardboard
116 N 14th St
Leesburg FL, 34748

GEORGIA

Champion Sportscards & Collectibles
800 Ernest W Barrett Pkwy NW
Suite 352
Kennesaw GA, 30144

Book End
6041 North Henry Blvd Ste C
Stockbridge GA, 30281

ILLINOIS

The Baseball Card King
16030 Lincoln Hwy Unit 1
Plainfield IL, 60586

KFL Sales
714 Cottage St
Shorewood IL, 60404-9023

INDIANA

Hockeyman's
125 E Maple St
Jeffersonville IN, 47130

MASSACHUSETTS

"Newsbreak, Inc"
Route 6 Target Plaza
Swansea MA, 2777

G2 Sports Cards and Memorabilia
6 South Main Street
Uxbridge MA, 1569

MICHIGAN

S & F Sport Cards
26019 Lorelei Dr
Flat Rock MI, 48134-9422

Stadium Cards & Comics
2061 Golfside Dr
Ypsilanti MI, 48197-1303

MISSOURI

Central Missouri Sportscards
408 S Bishop Ave
Rolla MO, 65401-4311

MISSISSIPPI

Gulf Coast Cards & Sports Memo
2600 Beach Blvd
Biloxi MS, 39531-4606

NEW JERSEY

RC Collectibles
1060 Route 22W
Lebanon NJ, 8833

Tem Dee
5051 Rt 42
Turnersville NJ, 08012-1703

NEW YORK

All Sports
3649 Erie Blvd E
Dewitt NY, 13214

Royal Collectibles
9611 Metropolitan Ave
Forest Hills NY, 11375

Montasy Comics
"70-17 Austin Street, 2nd floor"
Forest Hills NY, 11375
montasycomics.com

Two Brothers DVD and Memorabilia
51 Railroad Avenue
Lake Ronkonkoma NY, 11779

Montasy Chapter 2
"431 5th Avenue, 2nd floor"
New York NY, 10016
montasycomics.com

A&S Sports LLC
825 Carman Ave
Westbury NY, 11590

OKLAHOMA

S & S Sportscards
2012 W Washington St
Broken Arrow OK, 74012

One Stop Anime
123 24th Ave NW
Norman OK, 73069

PENNSYLVANIA

Don's Sports Cards
101 Maple St
Athens PA, 18810-1621

Sports Cards Etc
5629 B Steubenville Pike
Mc Kees Rocks PA, 15136-1415

Steel City Collectibles - Ross Park Mall
1000 Ross Park Mall Drive
Pittsburgh PA, 15237
www.steelcitycollectibles.com

SOUTH DAKOTA

Heroes Sports Cards & Games
2425 A Mt. Rushmore Road
Rapid City SD, 57701
southdakotasbest@hotmail.com

Heroes Sports Cards & Games
513 Main Street
Rapid City SD, 57701
southdakotasbest@hotmail.com

TENNESSEE

B & M Amusement Company
5036 Highway 58 Suite D
Chattanooga TN, 37416-1843

3 R Baseball Cards
55 Flea Market
Manchester TN, 37355

TEXAS

Rick's Collectibles
3556 N 6th St
Abilene TX, 79603

Card Traders Of Austin
8650 Spicewood Springs Rd Suite 128
Austin TX, 78759-4323

VIRGINIA

Blowout Cards - The Fantastic Store
14508 Lee Rd - Unit F
Chantilly VA, 20151
Blowoutcards.com

Branded Memorabilia
10408 Fairfax Blvd
Fairfax VA, 22023

Jerseys Cards And Comics
1818 Todds Ln Suite G
Hampton VA, 23666-3139

Heroes Sports Cards
519 N Witchduck Rd
Virginia Beach VA, 23462

VERMONT

Main Street Sportscards
325 Main St Suite 7
Winnoski VT, 5404

WASHINGTON

Knutsen's Northwest Sports-cards
3816 Bridgeport Way West
University Place WA, 98466

Ron's Coin & Collectibles
6 North 3rd St
Yakima WA, 98901-2703

WISCONSIN

Noble Knight Games
2242 Kennedy Rd
Janesville WI, 53545

Globe News
1430 Tower Ave
Superior WI, 54880-1526

ONLINE

Blowout Cards
Blowoutcards.com

Steel City Collectibles
steelcitycollect.com

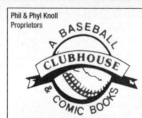

MAGIC: THE GATHERING

HOW TO USE AND CONDITION GUIDE

WHAT'S LISTED
This Beckett Price Guide includes products that are produced by Wizards of the Coast or by licensed manufacturers.

WHAT THE COLUMNS MEAN
The LO and HI columns reflect a range of current retail selling prices and are listed in U.S. dollars. The HI column represents the typical full retail selling price while the LO column represents the lowest price one could expect to find through extensive shopping. Both columns represent the same condition for the card listed. Keep in mind that market conditions can change quickly up or down based on extreme levels of demand. The published HI and LO column prices in this issue are a single snapshot in time and cannot be exact for every card listed.

ONLY A REFERENCE
The data and pricing information contained within this publication is intended for reference only. Beckett's goal is to provide the most accurate and verifiable information in the industry. However, Beckett cannot guarantee the accuracy of all data published and typographical errors occasionally occur. Buyers and sellers of Magic cards should be aware of this and handle their personal transactions at their own risk. If you discover an error or misprint in this issue, please notify us via email at nonsports@beckett.com

MULTIPLIERS
Some parallel Foil sets are listed with multipliers to provide values of unlisted cards. Multiplier ranges (i.e. 1X to 2X HI) apply only to the HI column. Example: If basic-issue card A lists for $2 to $4, and the multiplier is "1X to 2X HI", then the parallel version of card A or the insert card in question is valued at $4 to $8. Please note the term "basic card" used in the Price Guide refers to a standard regular-issue card. A "basic card" cannot be an insert or parallel card.

CARD CONDITION
The value of your card is dependent on the condition or "grade" of your card. Prices in this issue reflect the highest raw condition (i.e. not professionally graded by a third party) of the card most commonly found at shows, shops, on the Internet, and right out of the pack for brand new releases. This generally means Near Mint-Mint condition for all Magic cards. Use the following chart as a guide to estimate the value of your cards in a variety of conditions using the prices found in this issue.

CARD GRADES

Mint (MT) – A card with no wear or flaws. The card has four perfect corners, 60/40 or better centering from top to bottom and from left to right, original gloss, smooth edges and original color borders. A Mint card does not have print spots, color or focus imperfections.

Near Mint-Mint (NRMT-MT) – A card with one minor flaw. Any one of the following would lower a Mint card to Near Mint-Mint: one corner with a slight touch of wear, barely noticeable print spots, color or focus imperfections. This card must have a 60/40 or better centering in both directions, original gloss, smooth edges and original color borders.

Near Mint (NRMT) – A card with one minor flaw. Any one of the following would lower a Mint card to Near Mint: one very slightly scuffed corner or two or four corners with slight touches of wear, 70/30 to 60/40 centering, slightly rough edges, minor print spots, color or focus imperfections. This card must have original gloss and original color borders.

Excellent-Mint (EXMT) – A card with two or three slightly worn corners with centering no worse than 80/20. The card may have no more than two of the following slightly rough edges, very slightly discolored borders, minor print spots, color or focus imperfections. The card must have original gloss.

Excellent (EX) – (a.k.a. SP or Slightly Played.) A card with four slightly worn corners and centering is no worse than 80/20. The card may have a small amount of original gloss lost, rough edges, slightly discolored borders and minor print spots, color or focus imperfections.

Very Good (VG) – A card that has been handled but not abused slightly worn corners with slight layering, slight notching on edges, a significant amount of gloss lost from the surface but no scuffing and moderate discoloration of borders. The card may have a few light creases.

Good (G), Fair (F), Poor (P) – (a.k.a. HP or Heavily Played) A well-worn, mishandled or abused card badly worn corners, lots of scuffing, most or all original gloss missing, seriously discolored borders, moderate or heavy creases, and one or more serious flaws. The grade of Good, Fair or Poor depends on the severity of wear and flaws. Good, Fair and Poor cards generally are used only as fillers.

Special Note: The most widely used grades are defined here. Obviously, many cards will not perfectly match one of the definitions. Therefore, categories between the major grades known as in-between grades are used, such as Good to Very Good (G-VG), Very Good to Excellent (VG-EX), and Excellent-Mint to Near Mint (EXMT-NRMT). Such grades indicate a card with all qualities of the lower category but with at least a few qualities if the higher category.

LEGEND
C - Common Card
C1 - Common Card appeared one time on the press sheet
C2 - Common Card appeared two times on the press sheet
C3 - Common Card appeared three times on the press sheet
C4 - Common Card appeared four times on the press sheet

U - Uncommon Card
U1 - Uncommon Card appeared one time on the press sheet
U2 - Uncommon Card appeared two times on the press sheet
U3 - Uncommon Card appeared three times on the press sheet

R - Rare Card
M - Mythic Rare Card
TR - Timeshifted Rare Card

FOIL - Parallel card. These cards have a special foil-coated film (usually shiny), which separates it from its twin.

MAGIC SETS AND SYMBOLS

All set symbols are located on the right side of every card underneath the card's artwork. Some of the early Core sets did not carry a symbol.

Core Sets
Alpha Edition
Beta Edition
Unlimited Edition
Revised Edition
Fourth Edition
Fifth Edition
Sixth Edition
Seventh Edition
Eighth Edition
Ninth Edition
Tenth Edition
Magic 2010 (M10)
Magic 2011 (M11)
Magic 2012 (M12)
Magic 2013 (M13)
Magic 2014 (M14)
Magic 2015 (M15)
Magic Origins

Expansion Sets
Arabian Nights
Antiquities
Legends
The Dark
Fallen Empires
Ice Age
Homelands
Alliances
Mirage
Visions
Weatherlight
Tempest
Stronghold
Exodus
Urza's Saga
Urza's Legacy
Urza's Destiny
Mercadian Masques
Nemesis
Prophecy
Invasion
Planeshift
Apocalypse
Odyssey
Torment
Judgment
Onslaught
Legions
Scourge
Mirrodin
Darksteel
Fifth Dawn
Champions of Kamigawa
Betrayers of Kamigawa
Saviors of Kamigawa
Ravnica
Guildpact
Dissension
Coldsnap
Time Spiral
Timeshifted
Planar Chaos
Future Sight
Lorwyn
Morningtide
Shadowmoor
Eventide
Shards of Alara
Conflux
Alara Reborn
Zendikar
Worldwake
Rise of the Eldrazi
Scars of Mirrodin
Mirrodin Besieged
New Phyrexia
Innistrad
Dark Ascension
Avacyn Restored
Return to Ravnica
Gatecrash
Dragon's Maze
Theros
Born of the Gods
Journey into Nyx
Khans of Tarkir
Fate Reforged
Dragons of Tarkir
Battle for Zendikar
Eldritch Moon

Starter Sets
Portal
Portal Second Age
Portal Three Kingdoms
Starter 1999
Starter 2000

Special Sets
Chronicles
Vanguard
Unglued
Unhinged
Planechase 2009
Archenemy
Commander 2011
Planechase 2012
Commander's Arsenal
Modern Masters 2013
Commander 2013
Conspiracy
Commander 2014
Modern Masters 2015
Eternal Masters

From the Vault
From The Vault: Dragons
From The Vault: Exiled
From The Vault: Relics
From The Vault: Legends
From The Vault: Realms
From The Vault: Twenty
From The Vault: Annihilation
From the Vault: Angels
From the Vault: Lore

Duel Decks
Elves vs. Goblins
Jace vs. Chandra
Divine vs. Demonic
Garruk vs. Liliana
Phyrexia vs. The Coalition
Elspeth vs. Tezzeret
Knights vs. Dragons
Ajani vs. Nicol Bolas
Venser vs. Koth
Izzet vs. Golgari
Sorin vs. Tibalt
Heroes vs. Monsters
Jace vs. Vraska
Speed vs. Cunning
Duel Decks Anthology
Elspeth vs. Kiora
Zendikar vs. Eldrazi

MAGIC: THE GATHERING

Magic price guide brought to you by www.pwccauctions.com

1993 Magic The Gathering Alpha

COMPLETE SET (295)	60000.00	100000.00
BOOSTER BOX (36 PACKS)	180000.00	300000.00
BOOSTER PACK (15 CARDS)	5000.00	8000.00
STARTER DECK BOX (10 DECKS)	100000.00	120000.00
STARTER DECK (60 CARDS)	10000.00	12000.00

RELEASED ON AUGUST 5, 1993
LARGE ROUNDED CORNERS WITH BLACK BORDERS.
NO COPYRIGHT DATE AND NAME OF ILLUSTRATOR AT THE BOTTOM.

1 Air Elemental U :B:	6.00	15.00
2 Ancestral Recall R :B:	2500.00	4000.00
3 Animate Artifact U :B:	2.00	5.00
4 Animate Dead U :K:	35.00	60.00
5 Animate Wall R :W:	100.00	200.00
6 Ankh of Mishra R :A:	180.00	230.00
7 Armageddon R :W:	250.00	320.00
8 Aspect of Wolf R :G:	60.00	120.00
9 Bad Moon R :K:	160.00	250.00
10 Badlands R :L:	800.00	1000.00
11 Balance R :W:	200.00	280.00
12 Basalt Monolith U :A:	20.00	45.00
13 Bayou R :L:	1100.00	1300.00
14 Benalish Hero C :W:	1.25	3.00
15 Berserk U :G:	140.00	200.00
16 Birds of Paradise R :G:	650.00	800.00
17 Black Knight U :K:	20.00	40.00
18 Black Lotus R :A:	15000.00	20000.00
19 Black Vise U :A:	60.00	100.00
20 Black Ward U :W:	3.00	8.00
21 Blaze of Glory R :W:	50.00	80.00
22 Blessing R :W:	60.00	80.00
23 Blue Elemental Blast C :B:	8.00	20.00
24 Blue Ward U :W:	5.00	12.00
25 Bog Wraith U :K:	2.50	5.00
26 Braingeyser R :B:	170.00	230.00
27 Burrowing U :R:	5.00	12.00
28 Camouflage U :G:	5.00	12.00
29 Castle U :W:	6.00	15.00
30 Celestial Prism U :A:	3.00	8.00
31 Channel U :G:	15.00	30.00
32 Chaos Orb R :A:	500.00	650.00
33 Chaoslace R :R:	35.00	70.00
34 Circle of Protection: Blue C :W:	2.00	5.00
35 Circle of Protection: Green C :W:	2.00	5.00
36 Circle of Protection: Red C :W:	5.00	12.00
37 Circle of Protection: White C :W:	2.00	5.00
38 Clockwork Beast R :A:	60.00	100.00
39 Clone U :B:	15.00	30.00
40 Cockatrice R :G:	50.00	100.00
41 Consecrate Land U :W:	10.00	25.00
42 Conservator U :A:	8.00	20.00
43 Contract from Below R :K:	60.00	120.00
44 Control Magic U :B:	15.00	30.00
45 Conversion U :W:	5.00	12.00
46 Copper Tablet U :A:	10.00	25.00
47 Copy Artifact R :B:	200.00	300.00
48 Counterspell U :B:	110.00	180.00
49 Craw Wurm C :G:	6.00	15.00
50 Creature Bond C :B:	3.00	8.00
51 Crusade R :W:	110.00	160.00
52 Crystal Rod U :A:	6.00	15.00
53 Cursed Land U :K:	6.00	15.00
54 Cyclopean Tomb R :A:	150.00	200.00
55 Dark Ritual C :K:	30.00	60.00
56 Darkpact R :K:	25.00	45.00
57 Death Ward C :W:	4.00	10.00
58 Deathgrip U :K:	8.00	20.00
59 Deathlace R :K:	60.00	120.00
60 Demonic Attorney R :K:	70.00	120.00
61 Demonic Hordes R :K:	120.00	180.00
62 Demonic Tutor U :K:	160.00	250.00
63 Dingus Egg R :A:	60.00	110.00
64 Disenchant C :W:	10.00	25.00
65 Disintegrate C :R:	5.00	12.00
66 Disrupting Scepter R :A:	180.00	250.00
67 Dragon Whelp U :R:	25.00	50.00
68 Drain Life C :K:	5.00	12.00
69 Drain Power R :B:	80.00	150.00
70 Drudge Skeletons C :K:	2.00	5.00
71 Dwarven Demolition Team U :R:	10.00	25.00
72 Dwarven Warriors C :R:	1.50	4.00
73 Earth Elemental U :R:	4.00	10.00
74 Earthbind C :R:	2.50	6.00
75 Earthquake R :R:	110.00	180.00
76 Elvish Archers R :G:	150.00	200.00
77 Evil Presence U :K:	6.00	15.00
78 False Orders C :R:	5.00	12.00
79 Farmstead R :W:	60.00	120.00
80 Fastbond R :G:	225.00	310.00
81 Fear C :K:	1.50	4.00
82 Feedback U :B:	4.00	10.00
83 Fire Elemental U :R:	6.00	15.00
84 Fireball C :R:	8.00	20.00
85 Firebreathing C :R:	4.00	10.00
86 Flashfires U :R:	4.00	10.00
87 Flight C :B:	1.50	4.00
88 Fog C :G:	5.00	12.00
89 Force of Nature R :G:	140.00	180.00
90 Forcefield R :A:	500.00	650.00
91 Forest v1 C :L:	4.00	10.00
92 Forest v2 C :L:	4.00	10.00
93 Fork R :R:	200.00	350.00
94 Frozen Shade C :K:	4.00	10.00
95 Fungusaur R :G:	60.00	120.00
96 Gaea's Liege R :G:	100.00	150.00
97 Gauntlet of Might R :A:	300.00	450.00
98 Giant Growth C :G:	3.00	8.00
99 Giant Spider C :G:	1.00	2.50
100 Glasses of Urza U :A:	4.00	10.00
101 Gloom U :K:	3.00	8.00
102 Goblin Balloon Brigade U :R:	3.00	8.00
103 Goblin King R :R:	100.00	150.00
104 Granite Gargoyle R :R:	80.00	120.00
105 Gray Ogre C :R:	1.25	3.00
106 Green Ward U :W:	3.00	8.00
107 Grizzly Bears C :G:	.75	2.00
108 Guardian Angel C :W:	2.00	5.00
109 Healing Salve C :W:	.75	2.00
110 Helm of Chatzuk R :A:	80.00	120.00
111 Hill Giant C :R:	2.00	5.00
112 Hive, The R :A:	30.00	60.00
113 Holy Armor C :W:	.60	1.50
114 Holy Strength C :W:	2.00	5.00
115 Howl from Beyond C :K:	3.00	8.00
116 Howling Mine R :A:	200.00	300.00
117 Hurloon Minotaur C :R:	2.00	5.00
118 Hurricane U :G:	6.00	12.00
119 Hypnotic Specter U :K:	60.00	120.00
120 Ice Storm U :G:	30.00	60.00
121 Icy Manipulator U :A:	120.00	200.00
122 Illusionary Mask R :A:	150.00	250.00
123 Instill Energy U :G:	6.00	15.00
124 Invisibility C :B:	2.50	6.00
125 Iron Star U :A:	8.00	20.00
126 Ironclaw Orcs C :R:	1.25	3.00
127 Ironroot Treefolk C :G:	1.25	3.00
128 Island Sanctuary R :W:	40.00	80.00
129 Island v1 C :L:	5.00	12.00
130 Island v2 C :L:	5.00	12.00
131 Ivory Cup U :A:	3.00	8.00
132 Jade Monolith R :A:	70.00	110.00
133 Jade Statue U :A:	10.00	25.00
134 Jayemdae Tome R :A:	300.00	450.00
135 Juggernaut U :A:	15.00	30.00
136 Jump C :B:	1.25	3.00
137 Karma U :W:	5.00	12.00
138 Keldon Warlord U :R:	6.00	15.00
139 Kormus Bell R :A:	18.00	40.00
140 Kudzu R :G:	15.00	30.00
141 Lance U :W:	2.00	5.00
142 Ley Druid U :G:	6.00	15.00
143 Library of Leng U :A:	15.00	30.00
144 Lich R :K:	200.00	400.00
145 Lifeforce U :G:	3.00	8.00
146 Lifelace R :G:	80.00	150.00
147 Lifetap U :B:	2.00	6.00
148 Lightning Bolt C :R:	140.00	200.00
149 Living Artifact R :G:	140.00	200.00
150 Living Lands R :G:	60.00	120.00
151 Living Wall U :A:	8.00	20.00
152 Llanowar Elves C :G:	15.00	30.00
153 Lord of Atlantis R :B:	200.00	400.00
154 Lord of the Pit R :K:	200.00	300.00
155 Lure U :G:	6.00	15.00
156 Magical Hack R :B:	60.00	100.00
157 Mahamoti Djinn R :B:	200.00	400.00
158 Mana Flare R :R:	80.00	150.00
159 Mana Short R :B:	80.00	150.00
160 Mana Vault R :A:	400.00	700.00
161 Manabarbs R :R:	60.00	100.00
162 Meekstone R :A:	120.00	200.00
163 Merfolk of the Pearl Trident C :B:	2.50	6.00
164 Mesa Pegasus C :W:	2.50	6.00
165 Mind Twist R :K:	175.00	350.00
166 Mons's Goblin Raiders C :R:	3.00	8.00
167 Mountain v1 C :L:	4.00	10.00
168 Mountain v2 C :L:	4.00	10.00
169 Mox Emerald R :A:	2000.00	3500.00
170 Mox Jet R :A:	1800.00	3000.00
171 Mox Pearl R :A:	1800.00	3000.00
172 Mox Ruby R :A:	1500.00	2500.00
173 Mox Sapphire R :A:	1500.00	2500.00
174 Natural Selection R :G:	60.00	120.00
175 Nether Shadow R :K:	160.00	220.00
176 Nettling Imp U :K:	10.00	25.00
177 Nevinyrral's Disk R :A:	400.00	600.00
178 Nightmare R :K:	120.00	200.00
179 Northern Paladin R :W:	80.00	150.00
180 Obsianus Golem U :A:	8.00	20.00
181 Orcish Artillery U :R:	20.00	45.00
182 Orcish Oriflamme U :R:	8.00	20.00
183 Paralyze C :K:	4.00	10.00
184 Pearled Unicorn C :W:	2.50	6.00
185 Personal Incarnation R :W:	80.00	200.00
186 Pestilence C :K:	5.00	12.00
187 Phantasmal Forces U :B:	10.00	25.00
188 Phantasmal Terrain C :B:	3.00	8.00
189 Phantom Monster U :B:	6.00	15.00
190 Pirate Ship R :B:	60.00	100.00
191 Plague Rats C :K:	3.00	8.00
192 Plains v1 C :L:	4.00	10.00
193 Plains v2 C :L:	4.00	10.00
194 Plateau R :L:	500.00	800.00
195 Power Leak C :B:	1.50	4.00
196 Power Sink C :B:	10.00	25.00
197 Power Surge R :R:	80.00	150.00
198 Prodigal Sorcerer C :B:	4.00	10.00
199 Psionic Blast U :B:	60.00	100.00
200 Psychic Venom C :B:	3.00	8.00
201 Purelace R :W:	80.00	150.00
202 Raging River R :R:	120.00	220.00
203 Raise Dead C :K:	3.00	8.00
204 Red Elemental Blast C :R:	35.00	70.00
205 Red Ward U :W:	4.00	10.00
206 Regeneration C :G:	3.00	8.00
207 Regrowth U :G:	35.00	70.00
208 Resurrection U :W:	10.00	25.00
209 Reverse Damage R :W:	70.00	120.00
210 Righteousness R :W:	50.00	90.00
211 Roc of Kher Ridges R :R:	60.00	120.00
212 Rock Hydra R :R:	120.00	200.00
213 Rod of Ruin U :A:	4.00	10.00
214 Royal Assassin R :K:	150.00	300.00
215 Sacrifice U :K:	2.00	5.00
216 Samite Healer C :W:	2.00	5.00
217 Savannah Lions R :W:	200.00	300.00
218 Savannah R :L:	800.00	1000.00
219 Scathe Zombies C :K:	3.00	8.00
220 Scavenging Ghoul U :K:	5.00	12.00
221 Scrubland R :L:	800.00	1300.00
222 Scryb Sprites C :G:	3.00	8.00
223 Sea Serpent C :B:	1.50	4.00
224 Sedge Troll R :R:	120.00	160.00
225 Sengir Vampire U :K:	20.00	40.00
226 Serra Angel U :W:	120.00	200.00
227 Shanodin Dryads C :G:	.75	2.00
228 Shatter C :R:	3.00	8.00
229 Shivan Dragon R :R:	800.00	1200.00
230 Simulacrum U :K:	8.00	20.00
231 Sinkhole C :K:	40.00	80.00
232 Siren's Call U :B:	5.00	12.00
233 Sleight of Mind R :B:	100.00	150.00
234 Smoke R :R:	180.00	250.00
235 Sol Ring U :A:	150.00	220.00
236 Soul Net U :A:	6.00	15.00
237 Spell Blast C :B:	4.00	10.00
238 Stasis R :B:	180.00	220.00
239 Steal Artifact U :B:	8.00	20.00
240 Stone Giant U :R:	4.00	10.00
241 Stone Rain C :R:	8.00	20.00
242 Stream of Life C :G:	3.00	8.00
243 Sunglasses of Urza R :A:	80.00	120.00
244 Swamp v1 C :L:	4.00	10.00
245 Swamp v2 C :L:	4.00	10.00
246 Swords to Plowshares U :W:	130.00	200.00
247 Taiga R :L:	900.00	1400.00
248 Terror C :K:	8.00	20.00
249 Thicket Basilisk U :G:	5.00	12.00
250 Thoughtlace R :B:	90.00	150.00
251 Throne of Bone U :A:	6.00	15.00
252 Timber Wolves R :G:	60.00	120.00
253 Time Vault R :A:	800.00	1200.00
254 Time Walk R :B:	1800.00	2500.00
255 Timetwister R :B:	1200.00	2000.00
256 Tranquility C :G:	4.00	10.00
257 Tropical Island R :L:	1600.00	2200.00
258 Tsunami U :G:	15.00	30.00
259 Tundra R :L:	1800.00	3000.00
260 Tunnel U :R:	6.00	15.00
261 Twiddle C :B:	6.00	15.00
262 Two-Headed Giant of Foriys R :R:	80.00	150.00
263 Underground Sea R :L:	4000.00	5500.00
264 Unholy Strength C :K:	5.00	12.00
265 Unsummon C :B:	3.00	8.00
266 Uthden Troll U :R:	10.00	25.00
267 Verduran Enchantress R :G:	60.00	120.00
268 Vesuvan Doppelganger R :B:	200.00	400.00
269 Veteran Bodyguard R :W:	50.00	100.00
270 Volcanic Eruption R :B:	35.00	70.00
271 Wall of Air U :B:	6.00	15.00
272 Wall of Bone U :K:	5.00	12.00
273 Wall of Brambles U :G:	6.00	15.00
274 Wall of Fire U :R:	6.00	15.00
275 Wall of Ice U :G:	5.00	12.00
276 Wall of Stone U :R:	6.00	15.00
277 Wall of Swords U :W:	6.00	15.00
278 Wall of Water U :B:	6.00	15.00
279 Wall of Wood C :G:	5.00	12.00
280 Wanderlust U :G:	8.00	20.00
281 War Mammoth C :G:	6.00	15.00
282 Warp Artifact R :K:	120.00	200.00
283 Water Elemental U :B:	5.00	12.00
284 Weakness C :K:	3.00	8.00
285 Web R :G:	80.00	150.00
286 Wheel of Fortune R :R:	400.00	600.00
287 White Knight U :W:	20.00	40.00
288 White Ward U :W:	6.00	15.00
289 Wild Growth C :G:	1.50	4.00
290 Will-O'-The-Wisp R :K:	180.00	300.00
291 Winter Orb R :A:	280.00	350.00
292 Wooden Sphere U :A:	5.00	12.00
293 Word of Command R :K:	200.00	400.00
294 Wrath of God R :W:	300.00	450.00
295 Zombie Master R :K:	120.00	200.00

1993 Magic The Gathering Beta

COMPLETE SET (302)	12000.00	25000.00
BOOSTER BOX (36 PACKS)	15000.00	18000.00
BOOSTER PACK (15 CARDS)	375.00	550.00
STARTER DECK BOX (10 DECKS)	12000.00	15000.00
STARTER DECK	900.00	1500.00

RELEASED ON OCTOBER 15, 1993
BLACK BORDERS AND NO COPYRIGHT DATE
NAME OF ILLUSTRATOR AT THE BOTTOM

1 Air Elemental U :B:	6.00	15.00
2 Ancestral Recall R :B:	1800.00	3000.00
3 Animate Artifact U :B:	2.00	5.00
4 Animate Dead U :K:	20.00	40.00
5 Animate Wall R :W:	8.00	20.00
6 Ankh of Mishra R :A:	65.00	100.00
7 Armageddon R :W:	180.00	250.00
8 Aspect of Wolf R :G:	30.00	60.00
9 Bad Moon R :K:	60.00	100.00
10 Badlands R :L:	500.00	800.00
11 Balance R :W:	180.00	250.00
12 Basalt Monolith U :A:	10.00	25.00
13 Bayou R :L:	1000.00	1300.00
14 Benalish Hero C :W:	1.00	2.50
15 Berserk U :G:	100.00	150.00
16 Birds of Paradise R :G:	350.00	600.00
17 Black Knight U :K:	8.00	20.00
18 Black Lotus R :A:	8000.00	12000.00
19 Black Vise U :A:	30.00	50.00
20 Black Ward U :W:	1.50	4.00
21 Blaze of Glory R :W:	15.00	30.00
22 Blessing R :W:	30.00	45.00
23 Blue Elemental Blast C :B:	2.50	6.00
24 Blue Ward U :W:	2.50	6.00
25 Bog Wraith U :K:	2.00	5.00
26 Braingeyser R :B:	130.00	180.00
27 Burrowing U :R:	1.50	4.00
28 Camouflage U :G:	4.00	10.00
29 Castle U :W:	3.00	8.00
30 Celestial Prism U :A:	1.50	4.00
31 Channel U :G:	10.00	25.00
32 Chaos Orb R :A:	250.00	400.00
33 Chaoslace R :R:	25.00	50.00
34 Circle of Protection Black C :W:	1.50	4.00
35 Circle of Protection Blue C :W:	1.50	4.00
36 Circle of Protection Green C :W:	1.50	4.00
37 Circle of Protection Red C :W:	2.00	5.00
38 Circle of Protection White C :W:	1.50	4.00
39 Clockwork Beast R :A:	25.00	45.00
40 Clone U :B:	10.00	25.00
41 Cockatrice R :G:	30.00	55.00
42 Consecrate Land U :W:	3.00	8.00
43 Conservator U :A:	1.00	2.50
44 Contract from Below R :K:	10.00	25.00
45 Control Magic U :B:	10.00	25.00
46 Conversion U :W:	2.00	5.00
47 Copper Tablet U :A:	3.00	8.00
48 Copy Artifact R :B:	180.00	240.00
49 Counterspell U :B:	100.00	160.00
50 Craw Wurm C :G:	2.00	5.00
51 Creature Bond C :B:	1.00	2.50
52 Crusade R :W:	80.00	150.00
53 Crystal Rod U :A:	1.00	2.50
54 Cursed Land U :K:	4.00	10.00
55 Cyclopean Tomb R :A:	60.00	100.00
56 Dark Ritual C :K:	20.00	40.00
57 Darkpact R :K:	30.00	60.00
58 Death Ward C :W:	1.00	2.50
59 Deathgrip U :K:	3.00	8.00
60 Deathlace R :K:	30.00	60.00
61 Demonic Attorney R :K:	25.00	50.00
62 Demonic Hordes R :K:	120.00	160.00
63 Demonic Tutor U :K:	120.00	180.00
64 Dingus Egg R :A:	35.00	60.00
65 Disenchant C :W:	5.00	12.00
66 Disintegrate C :R:	2.50	6.00
67 Disrupting Scepter R :A:	120.00	160.00
68 Dragon Whelp U :R:	6.00	15.00
69 Drain Life C :K:	1.50	4.00
70 Drain Power R :B:	45.00	70.00
71 Drudge Skeletons C :K:	1.50	4.00
72 Dwarven Demolition Team U :R:	3.00	8.00
73 Dwarven Warriors C :R:	.75	2.00
74 Earth Elemental U :R:	2.00	5.00
75 Earthbind C :R:	1.50	4.00
76 Earthquake R :R:	100.00	140.00
77 Elvish Archers R :G:	60.00	100.00
78 Evil Presence U :K:	2.50	6.00
79 False Orders C :R:	1.00	2.50
80 Farmstead R :W:	15.00	30.00
81 Fastbond R :G:	180.00	240.00
82 Fear C :K:	1.00	2.50
83 Feedback U :B:	2.00	5.00
84 Fire Elemental U :R:	2.50	6.00
85 Fireball C :R:	6.00	15.00
86 Firebreathing C :R:	1.00	2.50
87 Flashfires U :R:	3.00	8.00
88 Flight C :B:	1.50	4.00
89 Fog C :G:	3.00	8.00
90 Force of Nature R :G:	50.00	80.00
91 Forcefield R :A:	350.00	500.00
92 Forest (blue) C :L:	4.00	10.00
93 Forest (black) C :L:	4.00	10.00
94 Forest (with trail) v3 C :L:	4.00	10.00
95 Fork R :R:	180.00	250.00
96 Frozen Shade C :K:	1.00	2.50
97 Fungusaur R :G:	35.00	60.00
98 Gaea's Liege R :G:	15.00	30.00
99 Gauntlet of Might R :A:	300.00	400.00
100 Giant Growth C :G:	5.00	12.00
101 Giant Spider C :G:	1.50	4.00
102 Glasses of Urza U :A:	6.00	15.00
103 Gloom U :K:	5.00	12.00
104 Goblin Balloon Brigade U :R:	4.00	10.00
105 Goblin King R :R:	40.00	80.00
106 Granite Gargoyle R :R:	60.00	100.00
107 Gray Ogre C :R:	.75	2.00
108 Green Ward U :W:	1.50	4.00
109 Grizzly Bears C :G:	1.50	4.00
110 Guardian Angel C :W:	1.50	4.00
111 Healing Salve C :W:	1.25	3.00
112 Helm of Chatzuk R :A:	10.00	25.00
113 Hill Giant C :R:	1.00	2.50
114 Hive, The R :A:	30.00	60.00
115 Holy Armor C :W:	.75	2.00
116 Holy Strength C :W:	1.50	4.00
117 Howl from Beyond C :K:	2.00	5.00
118 Howling Mine R :A:	120.00	200.00
119 Hurloon Minotaur C :R:	.75	2.00
120 Hurricane U :G:	8.00	20.00
121 Hypnotic Specter U :K:	30.00	60.00
122 Ice Storm U :G:	20.00	35.00
123 Icy Manipulator U :A:	50.00	75.00
124 Illusionary Mask R :A:	120.00	200.00
125 Instill Energy U :G:	3.00	8.00
126 Invisibility C :B:	2.00	5.00
127 Iron Star U :A:	2.50	6.00
128 Ironclaw Orcs C :R:	1.50	4.00
129 Ironroot Treefolk C :G:	1.50	4.00
130 Island Sanctuary R :W:	40.00	60.00
131 Island v1 C :L:	5.00	12.00
132 Island v2 C :L:	5.00	12.00
133 Island v3 C :L:	5.00	12.00
134 Ivory Cup U :A:	2.00	5.00
135 Jade Monolith R :A:	15.00	30.00
136 Jade Statue U :A:	6.00	15.00
137 Jayemdae Tome R :A:	300.00	400.00
138 Juggernaut U :A:	12.00	25.00
139 Jump C :B:	1.50	1.00
140 Karma U :W:	1.50	4.00
141 Keldon Warlord U :R:	4.00	8.00
142 Kormus Bell R :A:	9.00	15.00
143 Kudzu R :G:	6.00	15.00
144 Lance U :W:	3.00	6.00
145 Ley Druid U :G:	3.00	2.00
146 Library of Leng U :A:	4.00	10.00
147 Lich R :K:	40.00	75.00
148 Lifeforce U :G:	3.00	2.00
149 Lifelace R :G:	8.00	20.00
150 Lifetap U :B:	3.00	6.00
151 Lightning Bolt C :R:	10.00	40.00
152 Living Artifact R :G:	8.00	20.00
153 Living Lands R :G:	9.00	18.00
154 Living Wall U :A:	2.50	3.00
155 Llanowar Elves C :G:	3.00	8.00
156 Lord of Atlantis R :B:	25.00	50.00
157 Lord of the Pit R :K:	35.00	80.00
158 Lure U :G:	.80	2.00
159 Magical Hack R :B:	10.00	20.00
160 Mahamoti Djinn R :B:	30.00	50.00
161 Mana Flare R :R:	25.00	60.00
162 Mana Short R :B:	25.00	50.00
163 Mana Vault R :A:	60.00	350.00
164 Manabarbs R :R:	8.00	20.00
165 Meekstone R :A:	20.00	40.00
166 Merfolk of the Pearl Trident C :B:	1.50	1.00
167 Mesa Pegasus C :W:	.40	1.00
168 Mind Twist R :K:	65.00	130.00
169 Mons's Goblin Raiders C :R:	1.50	1.00
170 Mountain v1 C :L:	1.50	4.00
171 Mountain v2 C :L:	1.50	3.00
172 Mountain v3 C :L:	1.50	6.00
173 Mox Emerald R :A:	800.00	1500.00
174 Mox Jet R :A:	1600.00	2500.00
175 Mox Pearl R :A:	450.00	1500.00
176 Mox Ruby R :A:	850.00	1800.00
177 Mox Sapphire R :A:	1800.00	3000.00
178 Natural Selection R :G:	25.00	40.00
179 Nether Shadow R :K:	18.00	35.00
180 Nettling Imp U :K:	2.00	5.00
181 Nevinyrral's Disk R :A:	75.00	250.00
182 Nightmare R :K:	30.00	60.00
183 Northern Paladin R :W:	18.00	35.00
184 Obsianus Golem U :A:	.80	2.00
185 Orcish Artillery U :R:	4.00	8.00
186 Orcish Oriflamme U :R:	4.00	8.00
187 Paralyze C :K:	1.50	1.00
188 Pearled Unicorn C :W:	.40	1.00
189 Personal Incarnation R :W:	9.00	18.00
190 Pestilence C :K:	2.50	1.50

191 Phantasmal Forces U :B: 3.00 6.00
192 Phantasmal Terrain C :B: .40 1.00
193 Phantom Monster U :B: 1.00 2.00
194 Pirate Ship R :B: 9.00 18.00
195 Plague Rats C :K: 2.50 5.00
196 Plains v1 C :L: 1.50 4.00
197 Plains v2 C :L: 1.50 3.00
198 Plains v3 C :L: 1.50 3.00
199 Plateau R :L: 350.00 550.00
200 Power Leak C :B: .40 1.00
201 Power Sink C :B: 2.00 4.00
202 Power Surge R :R: 9.00 15.00
203 Prodigal Sorcerer C :B: 2.50 5.00
204 Psionic Blast U :B: 8.00 20.00
205 Psychic Venom C :B: 1.50 3.00
206 Purelace R :W: 6.00 15.00
207 Raging River R :R: 20.00 40.00
208 Raise Dead C :K: .40 1.00
209 Red Elemental Blast C :R: 5.00 10.00
210 Red Ward U :W: 1.00 2.00
211 Regeneration C :G: 1.50 3.00
212 Regrowth U :G: 15.00 40.00
213 Resurrection U :W: 3.00 6.00
214 Reverse Damage R :W: 10.00 20.00
215 Righteousness R :W: 10.00 20.00
216 Roc of Kher Ridges R :R: 6.00 15.00
217 Rock Hydra R :R: 15.00 30.00
218 Rod of Ruin U :A: 1.00 2.00
219 Royal Assassin R :K: 50.00 100.00
220 Sacrifice U :K: .80 2.00
221 Samite Healer C :W: 1.50 3.00
222 Savannah Lions R :W: 300.00 550.00
223 Savannah R :L: 350.00 700.00
224 Scathe Zombies C :K: .40 1.00
225 Scavenging Ghoul U :K: 3.00 6.00
226 Scrubland R :L: 1000.00 1800.00
227 Scryb Sprites C :G: 1.50 3.00
228 Sea Serpent C :B: .40 1.00
229 Sedge Troll R :R: 10.00 25.00
230 Sengir Vampire U :K: 8.00 20.00
231 Serra Angel U :W: 20.00 50.00
232 Shanodin Dryads C :G: .40 1.00
233 Shatter C :R: .50 1.25
234 Shivan Dragon R :R: 125.00 250.00
235 Simulacrum U :K: 1.25 3.00
236 Sinkhole C :K: 20.00 50.00
237 Siren's Call U :B: .80 2.00
238 Sleight of Mind R :B: 8.00 20.00
239 Smoke R :R: 8.00 20.00
240 Sol Ring U :A: 60.00 120.00
241 Soul Net U :A: .80 2.00
242 Spell Blast C :B: .40 1.00
243 Stasis R :B: 30.00 80.00
244 Steal Artifact U :B: 1.00 2.50
245 Stone Giant U :R: .80 2.00
246 Stone Rain C :R: .80 2.00
247 Stream of Life C :G: .40 1.00
248 Sunglasses of Urza R :A: 6.00 15.00
249 Swamp v1 C :L: 2.00 5.00
250 Swamp v2 C :L: 2.00 5.00
251 Swamp v3 C :L: 3.00 8.00
252 Swords to Plowshares U :W: 50.00 100.00
253 Taiga R :L: 400.00 1300.00
254 Terror C :K: 1.50 4.00
255 Thicket Basilisk U :G: 1.00 2.50
256 Thoughtlace R :B: 8.00 20.00
257 Throne of Bone U :A: .80 2.00
258 Timber Wolves R :G: 8.00 20.00
259 Time Vault R :A: 600.00 1100.00
260 Time Walk R :B: 1400.00 2200.00
261 Timetwister R :B: 600.00 1600.00
262 Tranquility C :G: .40 1.00
263 Tropical Island R :L: 1100.00 1600.00
264 Tsunami U :G: 1.25 3.00
265 Tundra R :L: 1200.00 2000.00
266 Tunnel U :R: .80 2.00
267 Twiddle C :B: .40 1.00
268 Two-Headed Giant of Foriys R :R: 20.00 50.00
269 Underground Sea R :L: 1600.00 2500.00
270 Unholy Strength C :K: .80 2.00
271 Unsummon C :B: .80 2.00
272 Uthden Troll U :R: .80 2.00
273 Verduran Enchantress R :G: 20.00 50.00
274 Vesuvan Doppelganger R :B: 50.00 100.00
275 Veteran Bodyguard R :W: 10.00 25.00
276 Volcanic Eruption R :B: 8.00 20.00
277 Volcanic Island R :L: 2200.00 2700.00
278 Wall of Air U :B: .80 2.00
279 Wall of Bone U :K: .80 2.00
280 Wall of Brambles U :G: .80 2.00
281 Wall of Fire U :R: .80 2.00
282 Wall of Ice U :G: .80 2.00
283 Wall of Stone U :R: .80 2.00
284 Wall of Swords U :W: .80 2.00
285 Wall of Water U :B: .60 1.50
286 Wall of Wood C :G: .40 1.00
287 Wanderlust U :G: .60 1.50
288 War Mammoth C :G: .40 1.00
289 Warp Artifact R :K: 6.00 15.00
290 Water Elemental U :B: .80 2.00
291 Weakness C :K: .40 1.00
292 Web R :G: 6.00 15.00
293 Wheel of Fortune R :R: 150.00 300.00
294 White Knight U :W: 6.00 15.00
295 White Ward U :W: .80 2.00
296 Wild Growth C :G: 1.00 2.50
297 Will-O'-The-Wisp R :K: 25.00 60.00
298 Winter Orb R :A: 25.00 60.00
299 Wooden Sphere U :A: .80 2.00
300 Word of Command R :K: 30.00 80.00
301 Wrath of God R :W: 125.00 250.00
302 Zombie Master R :K: 20.00 50.00

1993 Magic The Gathering Collector's Edition

COMPLETE SET (302) 1200.00 2000.00
BOOSTER BOX
BOOSTER PACK
*INTERNATIONAL: SAME VALUE
RELEASED IN DECEMBER 1993
1 Air Elemental U :B: .20 .50
2 Ancestral Recall R :B: 60.00 120.00
3 Animate Artifact U :B: .15 .40
4 Animate Dead U :K: 2.00 5.00
5 Animate Wall R :W: .40 1.00
6 Ankh of Mishra R :A: 1.50 4.00
7 Armageddon R :W: 1.50 4.00
8 Aspect of Wolf R :G: .50 1.25
9 Bad Moon R :K: 1.00 2.50
10 Badlands R :L: 25.00 60.00
11 Balance R :W: 2.00 5.00
12 Basalt Monolith U :A: .75 2.00
13 Bayou R :L: 25.00 60.00
14 Benalish Hero C :W: .30 .75
15 Berserk U :G: 20.00 50.00
16 Birds of Paradise R :G: 8.00 20.00
17 Black Knight U :K: 1.00 2.50
18 Black Lotus R :A: 500.00 750.00
19 Black Vise U :A: 1.00 2.50
20 Black Ward U :W: .20 .50
21 Blaze of Glory R :W: 1.00 2.50
22 Blessing R :W: .40 1.00
23 Blue Elemental Blast C :B: .30 .75
24 Blue Ward U :W: .20 .50
25 Bog Wraith U :K: .25 .60
26 Braingeyser R :B: 1.50 4.00
27 Burrowing U :R: .25 .60
28 Camouflage U :G: .20 .50
29 Castle U :W: .25 .60
30 Celestial Prism U :A: .20 .50
31 Channel U :G: .75 2.00
32 Chaos Orb R :A: 6.00 15.00
33 Chaoslace R :R: .40 1.00
34 Circle of Protection Black C :W: .12 .30
35 Circle of Protection Blue C :W: .12 .30
36 Circle of Protection Green C :W: .12 .30
37 Circle of Protection Red C :W: .12 .30
38 Circle of Protection White C :W: .12 .30
39 Clockwork Beast R :A: .50 1.25
40 Clone U :B: 1.50 4.00
41 Cockatrice R :G: .40 1.00
42 Consecrate Land U :W: .20 .50
43 Conservator U :A: .20 .50
44 Contract from Below R :K: .40 1.00
45 Control Magic U :B: 1.25 3.00
46 Conversion U :W: .20 .50
47 Copper Tablet U :A: .25 .60
48 Copy Artifact R :B: 3.00 8.00
49 Counterspell U :B: 2.00 5.00
50 Craw Wurm C :G: .12 .30
51 Creature Bond C :B: .12 .30
52 Crusade R :W: 1.00 2.50
53 Crystal Rod U :A: .25 .60
54 Cursed Land U :K: .25 .60
55 Cyclopean Tomb R :A: 3.00 8.00
56 Dark Ritual C :K: 2.50 6.00
57 Darkpact R :K: .60 1.50
58 Death Ward C :W: .12 .30
59 Deathgrip U :K: .20 .50
60 Deathlace R :K: .40 1.00
61 Demonic Attorney R :K: .30 .75
62 Demonic Hordes R :K: .75 2.00
63 Demonic Tutor U :K: 10.00 25.00
64 Dingus Egg R :A: .40 1.00
65 Disenchant C :W: .50 1.25
66 Disintegrate C :R: .20 .50
67 Disrupting Scepter R :A: .40 1.00
68 Dragon Whelp U :R: .75 2.00
69 Drain Life C :K: .20 .50
70 Drain Power R :B: .40 1.00
71 Drudge Skeletons C :K: .12 .30
72 Dwarven Demolition Team U :R: .25 .60
73 Dwarven Warriors C :R: .12 .30
74 Earth Elemental U :R: .20 .50
75 Earthbind C :R: .20 .50
76 Earthquake R :R: 1.00 2.50
77 Elvish Archers R :G: .40 1.00
78 Evil Presence U :K: .25 .60
79 False Orders C :R: .25 .60
80 Farmstead R :W: .40 1.00
81 Fastbond R :G: 2.50 6.00
82 Fear C :K: .12 .30
83 Feedback U :B: .20 .50
84 Fire Elemental U :R: .25 .60
85 Fireball C :R: .50 1.25
86 Firebreathing C :R: .12 .30
87 Flashfires U :R: .25 .60
88 Flight C :B: .12 .30
89 Fog C :G: .15 .40
90 Force of Nature R :G: .60 1.50
91 Forcefield R :A: 12.00 30.00
92 Forest (blue) C :L: .50 1.25
93 Forest (black) C :L: .50 1.25
94 Forest (with trail) v3 C :L: .50 1.25
95 Fork R :R: 3.00 8.00
96 Frozen Shade C :K: .12 .30
97 Fungusaur R :G: .40 1.00
98 Gaea's Liege R :G: .60 1.50
99 Gauntlet of Might R :A: 20.00 50.00
100 Giant Growth C :G: .25 .60
101 Giant Spider C :G: .25 .60
102 Glasses of Urza U :A: .20 .50
103 Gloom U :K: .20 .50
104 Goblin Balloon Brigade U :R: .20 .50
105 Goblin King R :R: 1.00 2.50
106 Granite Gargoyle R :R: .40 1.00
107 Gray Ogre C :R: .12 .30
108 Green Ward U :W: .20 .50
109 Grizzly Bears C :G: .25 .60
110 Guardian Angel C :W: .12 .30
111 Healing Salve C :W: .12 .30
112 Helm of Chatzuk R :A: .50 1.25
113 Hill Giant C :R: .12 .30
114 Hive, The R :A: .40 1.00
115 Holy Armor C :W: .12 .30
116 Holy Strength C :W: .12 .30
117 Howl from Beyond C :K: .12 .30
118 Howling Mine R :A: 2.00 5.00
119 Hurloon Minotaur C :R: .15 .40
120 Hurricane U :G: .25 .60
121 Hypnotic Specter U :K: 3.00 8.00
122 Ice Storm U :G: 2.50 6.00
123 Icy Manipulator U :A: 1.50 4.00
124 Illusionary Mask R :A: 8.00 20.00
125 Instill Energy U :G: .30 .75
126 Invisibility C :B: .12 .30
127 Iron Star U :A: .15 .40
128 Ironclaw Orcs C :R: .12 .30
129 Ironroot Treefolk C :G: .12 .30
130 Island Sanctuary R :W: .40 1.00
131 Island v1 C :L: .50 1.25
132 Island v2 C :L: .50 1.25
133 Island v3 C :L: .50 1.25
134 Ivory Cup U :A: .25 .60
135 Jade Monolith R :A: .60 1.50
136 Jade Statue U :A: 1.50 4.00
137 Jayemdae Tome R :A: .40 1.00
138 Juggernaut U :A: .50 1.25
139 Jump C :B: .15 .40
140 Karma U :W: .20 .50
141 Keldon Warlord U :R: .20 .50
142 Kormus Bell R :A: .50 1.25
143 Kudzu R :G: .40 1.00
144 Lance U :W: .30 .75
145 Ley Druid U :G: .20 .50
146 Library of Leng U :A: .40 1.00
147 Lich R :K: 3.00 8.00
148 Lifeforce U :G: .25 .60
149 Lifelace R :G: .40 1.00
150 Lifetap U :B: .20 .50
151 Lightning Bolt C :R: 4.00 10.00
152 Living Artifact R :G: .40 1.00
153 Living Lands R :G: .40 1.00
154 Living Wall U :A: .20 .50
155 Llanowar Elves C :G: 1.00 2.50
156 Lord of Atlantis R :B: 1.50 4.00
157 Lord of the Pit R :K: 1.00 2.50
158 Lure U :G: .30 .75
159 Magical Hack R :B: .40 1.00
160 Mahamoti Djinn R :B: .40 1.00
161 Mana Flare R :R: 1.25 3.00
162 Mana Short R :B: .75 2.00
163 Mana Vault R :A: 5.00 12.00
164 Manabarbs R :R: .50 1.25
165 Meekstone R :A: .75 2.00
166 Merfolk of the Pearl Trident C :B: .15 .40
167 Mesa Pegasus C :W: .12 .30
168 Mind Twist R :K: 3.00 8.00
169 Mons's Goblin Raiders C :R: .12 .30
170 Mountain v1 C :L: .40 1.00
171 Mountain v2 C :L: .40 1.00
172 Mountain v3 C :L: .40 1.00
173 Mox Emerald R :A: 80.00 150.00
174 Mox Jet R :A: 80.00 150.00
175 Mox Pearl R :A: 60.00 120.00
176 Mox Ruby R :A: 80.00 150.00
177 Mox Sapphire R :A: 80.00 150.00
178 Natural Selection R :G: 1.25 3.00
179 Nether Shadow R :K: 1.50 4.00
180 Nettling Imp U :K: .30 .75
181 Nevinyrral's Disk R :A: 2.50 6.00
182 Nightmare R :K: 1.00 2.50
183 Northern Paladin R :W: .40 1.00
184 Obsianus Golem U :A: .25 .60
185 Orcish Artillery U :R: .20 .50
186 Orcish Oriflamme U :R: .20 .50
187 Paralyze C :K: .12 .30
188 Pearled Unicorn C :W: .12 .30
189 Personal Incarnation R :W: .50 1.25
190 Pestilence C :K: .12 .30
191 Phantasmal Forces U :B: .25 .60
192 Phantasmal Terrain C :B: .12 .30
193 Phantom Monster U :B: .20 .50
194 Pirate Ship R :B: .40 1.00
195 Plague Rats C :K: .12 .30
196 Plains v1 C :L: .40 1.00
197 Plains v2 C :L: .40 1.00
198 Plains v3 C :L: .40 1.00
199 Plateau R :L: 25.00 60.00
200 Power Leak C :B: .12 .30
201 Power Sink C :B: .12 .30
202 Power Surge R :R: .50 1.25
203 Prodigal Sorcerer C :B: .25 .60
204 Psionic Blast U :B: 1.50 4.00
205 Psychic Venom C :B: .12 .30
206 Purelace R :W: .40 1.00
207 Raging River R :R: 1.00 2.50
208 Raise Dead C :K: .12 .30
209 Red Elemental Blast C :R: .75 2.00
210 Red Ward U :W: .25 .60
211 Regeneration C :G: .12 .30
212 Regrowth U :G: 3.00 8.00
213 Resurrection U :W: .20 .50
214 Reverse Damage R :W: .40 1.00
215 Righteousness R :W: .40 1.00
216 Roc of Kher Ridges R :R: .40 1.00
217 Rock Hydra R :R: .40 1.00
218 Rod of Ruin U :A: .20 .50
219 Royal Assassin R :K: 1.50 4.00
220 Sacrifice U :K: .25 .60
221 Samite Healer C :W: .12 .30
222 Savannah Lions R :W: 2.00 5.00
223 Savannah R :L: 30.00 80.00
224 Scathe Zombies C :K: .25 .60
225 Scavenging Ghoul U :K: .20 .50
226 Scrubland R :L: 25.00 60.00
227 Scryb Sprites C :G: .12 .30
228 Sea Serpent C :B: .12 .30
229 Sedge Troll R :R: .40 1.00
230 Sengir Vampire U :K: 1.00 2.50
231 Serra Angel U :W: 4.00 10.00
232 Shanodin Dryads C :G: .12 .30
233 Shatter C :R: .12 .30
234 Shivan Dragon R :R: 3.00 8.00
235 Simulacrum U :K: .20 .50
236 Sinkhole C :K: 12.00 30.00
237 Siren's Call U :B: .20 .50
238 Sleight of Mind R :B: .40 1.00
239 Smoke R :R: .40 1.00
240 Sol Ring U :A: 10.00 25.00
241 Soul Net U :A: .20 .50
242 Spell Blast C :B: .12 .30
243 Stasis R :B: 1.50 4.00
244 Steal Artifact U :B: .20 .50
245 Stone Giant U :R: .20 .50
246 Stone Rain C :R: .20 .50
247 Stream of Life C :G: .12 .30
248 Sunglasses of Urza R :A: .40 1.00
249 Swamp v1 C :L: .50 1.25
250 Swamp v2 C :L: .50 1.25
251 Swamp v3 C :L: .50 1.25
252 Swords to Plowshares U :W: 2.50 6.00
253 Taiga R :L: 30.00 80.00
254 Terror C :K: .75 2.00
255 Thicket Basilisk U :G: .20 .50
256 Thoughtlace R :B: .40 1.00
257 Throne of Bone U :A: .20 .50
258 Timber Wolves R :G: .40 1.00
259 Time Vault R :A: 20.00 50.00
260 Time Walk R :B: 100.00 200.00
261 Timetwister R :B: 50.00 100.00
262 Tranquility C :G: .25 .60
263 Tropical Island R :L: 30.00 80.00
264 Tsunami U :G: .20 .50
265 Tundra R :L: 50.00 100.00
266 Tunnel U :R: .25 .60
267 Twiddle C :B: .12 .30
268 Two-Headed Giant of Foriys R :R: .75 2.00
269 Underground Sea R :L: 100.00 200.00
270 Unholy Strength C :K: .20 .50
271 Unsummon C :B: .12 .30
272 Uthden Troll U :R: .20 .50
273 Verduran Enchantress R :G: .40 1.00
274 Vesuvan Doppelganger R :B: 2.00 5.00
275 Veteran Bodyguard R :W: .40 1.00
276 Volcanic Eruption R :B: .40 1.00
277 Volcanic Island R :L: 60.00 120.00
278 Wall of Air U :B: .20 .50
279 Wall of Bone U :K: .25 .60
280 Wall of Brambles U :G: .25 .60
281 Wall of Fire U :R: .20 .50
282 Wall of Ice U :G: .20 .50
283 Wall of Stone U :R: .20 .50
284 Wall of Swords U :W: .25 .60
285 Wall of Water U :B: .30 .75
286 Wall of Wood C :G: .12 .30
287 Wanderlust U :G: .25 .60
288 War Mammoth C :G: .12 .30
289 Warp Artifact R :K: .40 1.00
290 Water Elemental U :B: .20 .50
291 Weakness C :K: .12 .30
292 Web R :G: .40 1.00
293 Wheel of Fortune R :R: 10.00 25.00
294 White Knight U :W: 1.25 3.00
295 White Ward U :W: .20 .50
296 Wild Growth C :G: .40 1.00
297 Will-O'-The-Wisp R :K: 1.00 2.50
298 Winter Orb R :A: 3.00 8.00
299 Wooden Sphere U :A: .20 .50
300 Word of Command R :K: 5.00 12.00
301 Wrath of God R :W: 6.00 15.00
302 Zombie Master R :K: 1.50 4.00

1993 Magic The Gathering Unlimited

COMPLETE SET (302) 6000.00 10000.00
BOOSTER BOX (36 PACKS) 5400.00 7500.00
BOOSTER PACK (15 CARDS) 150.00 250.00
STARTER DECK BOX (10 DECKS) 4000.00 5500.00
STARTER DECK (60 CARDS) 500.00 650.00
RELEASED ON DECEMBER 15, 1993
WHITE BORDERS AND NO COPYRIGHT DATE
NAME OF ILLUSTRATOR AT THE BOTTOM
EDGES ON INNER COLORED BORDERS HAVE A BEVELED LOOK TO THEM
1 Air Elemental U :B: .20 .50
2 Ancestral Recall R :B: 800.00 1500.00
3 Animate Artifact U :B: .20 .50
4 Animate Dead U :K: 1.25 3.00
5 Animate Wall R :W: 1.00 2.50
6 Ankh of Mishra R :A: 2.00 5.00
7 Armageddon R :W: 4.00 10.00
8 Aspect of Wolf R :G: 1.25 3.00
9 Bad Moon R :K: 4.00 10.00
10 Badlands R :L: 75.00 150.00
11 Balance R :W: 3.00 8.00
12 Basalt Monolith U :A: 1.25 3.00
13 Bayou R :L: 100.00 200.00
14 Benalish Hero C :W: .10 .25
15 Berserk U :G: 25.00 60.00
16 Birds of Paradise R :G: 15.00 40.00
17 Black Knight U :K: .75 2.00
18 Black Lotus R :A: 3800.00 5000.00
19 Black Vise U :A: .75 2.00
20 Black Ward U :W: .20 .50
21 Blaze of Glory R :W: 4.00 10.00
22 Blessing R :W: 1.00 2.50
23 Blue Elemental Blast C :B: .25 .60
24 Blue Ward U :W: .20 .50
25 Bog Wraith U :K: .20 .50
26 Braingeyser R :B: 4.00 10.00
27 Burrowing U :R: .20 .50
28 Camouflage U :G: .50 1.25
29 Castle U :W: .20 .50
30 Celestial Prism U :A: .20 .50
31 Channel U :G: .50 1.25
32 Chaos Orb R :A: 50.00 100.00
33 Chaoslace R :R: .75 2.00
34 Circle of Protection: Black C :W: .10 .25
35 Circle of Protection: Blue C :W: .10 .25
36 Circle of Protection: Green C :W: .10 .25
37 Circle of Protection: Red C :W: .10 .25
38 Circle of Protection: White C :W: .10 .25
39 Clockwork Beast R :A: .75 2.00
40 Clone U :B: .75 2.00
41 Cockatrice R :G: 2.50 6.00
42 Consecrate Land U :W: .40 1.00
43 Conservator U :A: .20 .50
44 Contract from Below R :K: 1.00 2.50
45 Control Magic U :B: .75 2.00
46 Conversion U :W: .20 .50
47 Copper Tablet U :A: .40 1.00
48 Copy Artifact R :B: 4.00 10.00
49 Counterspell U :B: 2.00 5.00
50 Craw Wurm C :G: .10 .25
51 Creature Bond C :B: .10 .25
52 Crusade R :W: 7.50 15.00
53 Crystal Rod U :A: .20 .50
54 Cursed Land U :K: .50 1.00
55 Cyclopean Tomb R :A: 8.00 20.00
56 Dark Ritual C :K: 2.00 4.00
57 Darkpact R :K: .75 2.00
58 Death Ward C :W: .25 .50
59 Deathgrip U :K: .20 .50
60 Deathlace R :K: 2.50 5.00
61 Demonic Attorney R :K: .75 2.00
62 Demonic Hordes R :K: 9.00 18.00
63 Demonic Tutor U :K: 8.00 20.00
64 Dingus Egg R :A: 2.50 5.00
65 Disenchant C :W: .20 .50
66 Disintegrate C :R: .50 1.00
67 Disrupting Scepter R :A: 1.25 3.00
68 Dragon Whelp U :R: 1.50 3.00
69 Drain Life C :K: .10 .25
70 Drain Power R :B: 4.00 8.00
71 Drudge Skeletons C :K: .10 .25
72 Dwarven Demolition Team U :R: 1.00 2.00
73 Dwarven Warriors C :R: .10 .25
74 Earth Elemental U :R: .50 1.00
75 Earthbind C :R: .10 .25
76 Earthquake R :R: 5.00 10.00
77 Elvish Archers R :G: 2.00 5.00
78 Evil Presence U :K: 1.00 2.00
79 False Orders C :R: .10 .25
80 Farmstead R :W: 1.50 3.00
81 Fastbond R :G: 5.00 12.00
82 Fear C :K: .10 .25
83 Feedback U :B: .20 .50
84 Fire Elemental U :R: .20 .50
85 Fireball C :R: .25 .60
86 Firebreathing C :R: .10 .25
87 Flashfires U :R: .20 .50
88 Flight C :B: .10 .25
89 Fog C :G: .10 .25
90 Force of Nature R :G: 3.00 8.00
91 Forcefield R :A: 60.00 120.00
92 Forest v1 C :L: .25 .60
93 Forest v2 C :L: .25 .60
94 Forest v3 C :L: .25 .60
95 Fork R :R: 6.00 15.00
96 Frozen Shade C :K: .10 .25
97 Fungusaur R :G: .75 2.00
98 Gaea's Liege R :G: 2.00 5.00
99 Gauntlet of Might R :A: 75.00 150.00
100 Giant Growth C :G: .20 .50
101 Giant Spider C :G: .10 .25
102 Glasses of Urza U :A: .20 .50
103 Gloom U :K: .20 .50
104 Goblin Balloon Brigade U :R: .30 .75
105 Goblin King R :R: 2.50 6.00
106 Granite Gargoyle R :R: 1.50 4.00
107 Gray Ogre C :R: .10 .25
108 Green Ward U :W: .20 .50
109 Grizzly Bears C :G: .10 .25
110 Guardian Angel C :W: .10 .25
111 Healing Salve C :W: .10 .25
112 Helm of Chatzuk R :A: .75 2.00
113 Hill Giant C :R: .10 .25
114 Hive, The R :A: 1.25 3.00
115 Holy Armor C :W: .10 .25
116 Holy Strength C :W: .10 .25
117 Howl from Beyond C :K: .10 .25
118 Howling Mine R :A: 5.00 12.00
119 Hurloon Minotaur C :R: .10 .25
120 Hurricane U :G: .40 1.00
121 Hypnotic Specter U :K: 2.00 5.00
122 Ice Storm U :G: 4.00 10.00
123 Icy Manipulator U :A: 4.00 10.00
124 Illusionary Mask R :A: 25.00 60.00
125 Instill Energy U :G: .40 1.00
126 Invisibility C :B: .10 .25
127 Iron Star U :A: .20 .50
128 Ironclaw Orcs C :R: .10 .25
129 Ironroot Treefolk C :G: .10 .25
130 Island Sanctuary R :W: 1.25 3.00
131 Island v1 C :L: .40 1.00
132 Island v2 C :L: .50 1.00
133 Island v3 C :L: .40 1.00
134 Ivory Cup U :A: .50 1.00
135 Jade Monolith R :A: 1.00 2.50
136 Jade Statue U :A: 6.00 12.00
137 Jayemdae Tome R :A: 1.25 3.00
138 Juggernaut U :A: 3.50 7.00
139 Jump C :B: .10 .25
140 Karma U :W: 2.00 4.00
141 Keldon Warlord U :R: .30 .75
142 Kormus Bell R :A: 2.50 5.00
143 Kudzu R :G: 1.00 2.50
144 Lance U :W: .50 1.00
145 Ley Druid U :G: .20 .50
146 Library of Leng U :A: 1.00 2.00
147 Lich R :K: 10.00 25.00
148 Lifeforce U :G: .50 1.00
149 Lifelace R :G: .75 2.00
150 Lifetap U :B: .50 1.00
151 Lightning Bolt C :R: 1.25 3.00
152 Living Artifact R :G: 2.50 5.00
153 Living Lands R :G: .75 2.00
154 Living Wall U :A: 1.50 3.00
155 Llanowar Elves C :G: .30 .75
156 Lord of Atlantis R :B: 4.00 8.00
157 Lord of the Pit R :K: 2.50 6.00
158 Lure U :G: 2.00 4.00
159 Magical Hack R :B: 1.00 2.50
160 Mahamoti Djinn R :B: 7.50 15.00
161 Mana Flare R :R: 3.00 8.00
162 Mana Short R :B: 5.00 10.00
163 Mana Vault R :A: 5.00 12.00
164 Manabarbs R :R: 2.50 5.00
165 Meekstone R :A: 3.00 8.00
166 Merfolk of the Pearl Trident C :B: .25 .50
167 Mesa Pegasus C :W: .10 .25
168 Mind Twist R :K: 10.00 20.00
169 Mons's Goblin Raiders C :R: .10 .25
170 Mountain v1 C :L: .25 .50
171 Mountain v2 C :L: .30 .75
172 Mountain v3 C :L: .25 .50
173 Mox Emerald R :A: 550.00 1100.00
174 Mox Jet R :A: 700.00 1200.00
175 Mox Pearl R :A: 425.00 850.00
176 Mox Ruby R :A: 550.00 1100.00
177 Mox Sapphire R :A: 1600.00 2100.00
178 Natural Selection R :G: 10.00 20.00
179 Nether Shadow R :K: 3.00 8.00
180 Nettling Imp U :K: 1.00 2.00
181 Nevinyrral's Disk R :A: 5.00 12.00
182 Nightmare R :K: 9.00 18.00
183 Northern Paladin R :W: 7.50 15.00

184 Obsianus Golem U :A: .20 .50
185 Orcish Artillery U :R: .50 1.00
186 Orcish Oriflamme U :R: 1.00 2.00
187 Paralyze C :K: .10 .25
188 Pearled Unicorn C :W: .25 .50
189 Personal Incarnation R :W: 2.50 5.00
190 Pestilence C :K: .10 .25
191 Phantasmal Forces U :B: 1.00 2.00
192 Phantasmal Terrain C :B: .50 1.00
193 Phantom Monster U :B: 2.00 5.00
194 Pirate Ship R :B: 2.00 4.00
195 Plague Rats C :K: .25 .50
196 Plains v1 C :L: .25 .60
197 Plains v2 C :L: .25 .50
198 Plains v3 C :L: .25 .50
199 Plateau R :L: 60.00 120.00
200 Power Leak C :B: .25 .50
201 Power Sink C :B: .25 .50
202 Power Surge R :R: 1.00 2.50
203 Prodigal Sorcerer C :B: .50 1.00
204 Psionic Blast U :B: 12.00 25.00
205 Psychic Venom C :B: .10 .25
206 Purelace R :W: 2.00 4.00
207 Raging River R :R: 10.00 20.00
208 Raise Dead C :K: .10 .25
209 Red Elemental Blast C :R: 1.00 2.00
210 Red Ward U :W: 1.00 2.00
211 Regeneration C :G: .10 .25
212 Regrowth U :G: 3.50 7.00
213 Resurrection U :W: 1.00 2.00
214 Reverse Damage R :W: 1.25 3.00
215 Righteousness R :W: 3.50 7.00
216 Roc of Kher Ridges R :R: 3.00 6.00
217 Rock Hydra R :R: 1.50 4.00
218 Rod of Ruin U :A: .50 1.00
219 Royal Assassin R :K: 12.00 25.00
220 Sacrifice U :K: .20 .50
221 Samite Healer C :W: .25 .50
222 Savannah Lions R :L: 10.00 20.00
223 Savannah R :W: 3.00 8.00
224 Scathe Zombies C :K: .25 .50
225 Scavenging Ghoul U :K: .20 .50
226 Scrubland R :L: 60.00 120.00
227 Scryb Sprites C :G: .10 .25
228 Sea Serpent C :B: .10 .25
229 Sedge Troll R :R: 1.25 3.00
230 Sengir Vampire U :K: 1.00 2.50
231 Serra Angel U :W: 1.50 4.00
232 Shanodin Dryads C :G: .10 .25
233 Shatter C :R: .10 .25
234 Shivan Dragon R :R: 8.00 20.00
235 Simulacrum U :K: .25 .60
236 Sinkhole C :K: 10.00 25.00
237 Siren's Call U :B: .20 .50
238 Sleight of Mind R :B: .75 2.00
239 Smoke R :R: 1.00 2.50
240 Sol Ring U :A: 6.00 15.00
241 Soul Net U :A: .20 .50
242 Spell Blast C :B: .10 .25
243 Stasis R :B: 3.00 8.00
244 Steal Artifact U :B: .25 .60
245 Stone Giant U :R: .20 .50
246 Stone Rain C :R: .10 .25
247 Stream of Life C :G: .10 .25
248 Sunglasses of Urza R :A: 1.25 3.00
249 Swamp v1 C :L: .25 .60
250 Swamp v2 C :L: .25 .60
251 Swamp v3 C :L: .30 .75
252 Swords to Plowshares U :W: 2.50 6.00
253 Taiga R :L: 60.00 120.00
254 Terror C :K: .25 .60
255 Thicket Basilisk U :G: .20 .50
256 Thoughtlace R :B: .75 2.00
257 Throne of Bone U :A: .20 .50
258 Timber Wolves R :G: 1.00 2.50
259 Time Vault R :A: 200.00 400.00
260 Time Walk R :B: 750.00 1400.00
261 Timetwister R :B: 300.00 650.00
262 Tranquility C :G: .10 .25
263 Tropical Island R :L: 150.00 300.00
264 Tsunami U :G: .25 .60
265 Tundra R :L: 150.00 300.00
266 Tunnel U :R: .20 .50
267 Twiddle C :B: .10 .25
268 Two-Headed Giant of Foriys R :R: 5.00 12.00
269 Underground Sea R :L: 200.00 400.00
270 Unholy Strength C :K: .10 .25
271 Unsummon C :B: .10 .25
272 Uthden Troll U :R: .20 .50
273 Verduran Enchantress R :G: 1.25 3.00
274 Vesuvan Doppelganger R :B: 6.00 15.00
275 Veteran Bodyguard R :W: 1.50 4.00
276 Volcanic Eruption R :B: 3.00 6.00
277 Volcanic Island R :L: 200.00 400.00
278 Wall of Air U :B: 1.50 3.00
279 Wall of Bone U :K: .20 .50
280 Wall of Brambles U :G: .50 1.00
281 Wall of Fire U :R: .20 .50
282 Wall of Ice U :G: 1.00 2.00
283 Wall of Stone U :R: .20 .50
284 Wall of Swords U :W: .50 1.00
285 Wall of Water U :B: .20 .50
286 Wall of Wood C :G: .50 1.00
287 Wanderlust U :G: .20 .50
288 War Mammoth C :G: .20 .50
289 Warp Artifact R :K: .75 2.00
290 Water Elemental U :B: 1.00 2.00
291 Weakness C :K: .10 .25
292 Web R :G: 2.50 5.00
293 Wheel of Fortune R :R: 12.00 30.00
294 White Knight U :W: 3.00 6.00
295 White Ward U :W: .20 .50
296 Wild Growth C :G: .10 .25
297 Will-O'-The-Wisp R :K: 4.00 10.00
298 Winter Orb R :A: 3.00 8.00
299 Wooden Sphere U :A: .20 .50
300 Word of Command R :K: 20.00 50.00
301 Wrath of God R :W: 8.00 20.00
302 Zombie Master R :K: 3.00 8.00

1993 Magic The Gathering Arabian Nights

COMPLETE SET (92) 500.00 1000.00
BOOSTER BOX (60 PACKS) 8000.00 10000.00
BOOSTER PACK (8 CARDS) 140.00 235.00
RELEASED ON DECEMBER 15, 1993
WITH VARIATIONS THERE ARE 92 CARDS
1 Abu Jafar U3 :W: 1.50 4.00
2 Aladdin U2 :R: 2.50 6.00
3 Aladdin's Lamp U2 :A: 2.00 5.00
4 Aladdin's Ring U2 :A: 2.00 5.00
5 Ali Baba U3 :R: .75 2.00
6 Ali from Cairo U2 :R: 15.00 40.00
7 Army of Allah (dark 1) C3 :W: .75 2.00
8 Army of Allah (light 1) C1 :W: .75 2.00
9 Bazaar of Baghdad U3 :L: 175.00 350.00
10 Bird Maiden (dark 1) C2 :R: .20 .50
11 Bird Maiden (light 1) C2 :R: .20 .50
12 Bottle of Suleiman U2 :A: 1.25 3.00
13 Brass Man U3 :A: .75 2.00
14 Camel C5 :W: .25 .60
15 City in a Bottle U2 :A: 5.00 12.00
16 City of Brass U3 :L: 25.00 60.00
17 Cuombajj Witches C4 :K: .25 .60
18 Cyclone U3 :G: .60 1.50
19 Dancing Scimitar U2 :A: 2.00 5.00
20 Dandan C4 :B: .20 .50
21A Desert C11 :L: .40 1.00
21B Desert (mirage variant) C11 :L:
22 Desert Nomads C4 :R: .20 .50
23 Desert Twister U3 :G: 2.50 6.00
24 Diamond Valley U2 :L: 50.00 100.00
25 Drop of Honey U2 :G: 20.00 50.00
26 Ebony Horse U2 :A: 1.00 2.50
27 Elephant Graveyard U2 :L: 1.25 3.00
28 El-Hajjaj U2 :K: 12.00 30.00
29 Erg Raiders (dark 1) C3 :K: .25 .60
30 Erg Raiders (light 1) C2 :K: .25 .60
31 Erhnam Djinn U2 :G: 6.00 15.00
32 Eye for an Eye U3 :W: 1.00 2.50
33 Fishliver Oil (dark 1) C3 :B: .20 .50
34 Fishliver Oil (light 1) C1 :B: .20 .50
35 Flying Carpet U3 :A: .60 1.50
36 Flying Men C5 :B: .50 1.25
37 Ghazban Ogre C4 :G: .30 .75
38 Giant Tortoise (dark 1) C3 :B: .20 .50
39 Giant Tortoise (light 1) C1 :B: .30 .75
40 Guardian Beast U2 :K: 20.00 50.00
41 Hasran Ogress (dark mana) C3 :K: .20 .50
42 Hasran Ogress (light mana) C2 :K: .20 .50
43 Hurr Jackal C4 :R: .20 .50
44 Ifh-Biff Efreet U2 :G: 5.00 12.00
45 Island Fish Jasconius U2 :B: 1.25 3.00
46 Island of Wak-Wak U2 :L: 15.00 40.00
47 Jandor's Ring U2 :A: 1.00 2.50
48 Jandor's Saddlebags U2 :A: 1.00 2.50
49 Jeweled Bird U3 :A: .60 1.50
50 Jihad U2 :W: 12.00 30.00
51 Junun Efreet U2 :K: 1.50 4.00
52 Juzam Djinn U2 :K: 110.00 225.00
53 Khabal Ghoul U3 :K: 8.00 20.00
54 King Suleiman U2 :W: 12.00 25.00
55 Kird Ape C5 :R: 1.25 3.00
56 Library of Alexandria U3 :L: 150.00 300.00
57 Magnetic Mountain U3 :R: .60 1.50
58 Merchant Ship U3 :B: 3.50 7.00
59 Metamorphosis C4 :G: .20 .50
60 Mijae Djinn U2 :R: 4.00 8.00
61 Moorish Cavalry (dark 2) C4 :W: .20 .50
62 Moorish Cavalry (light 2) C1 :W: 1.00 2.00
63 Mountain C1 :L: 15.00 40.00
64 Nafs Asp (dark 1) C3 :G: 1.00 2.00
65 Nafs Asp (light 1) C2 :G: .20 .50
66 Oasis U4 :L: 2.50 5.00
67 Old Man of the Sea U2 :B: 15.00 40.00
68 Oubliette (dark 1) C2 :K: 2.50 5.00
69 Oubliette (light 1) C2 :K: 4.00 10.00
70 Piety (dark 1) C3 :W: 1.00 2.00
71 Piety (light 1) C1 :W: .30 .75
72 Pyramids U2 :A: 4.00 10.00
73 Repentant Blacksmith U2 :W: 1.25 3.00
74 Ring of Maruf U2 :A: 8.00 20.00
75 Rukh Egg (dark 3) C3 :R: 1.00 2.50
76 Rukh Egg (light 3) C1 :R: 1.50 4.00
77 Sandals of Abdallah U3 :A: 1.00 2.50
78 Sandstorm C4 :G: .20 .50
79 Serendib Djinn U2 :B: 8.00 20.00
80 Serendib Efreet U2 :B: 12.00 30.00
81 Shahrazad U2 :W: 15.00 40.00
82 Sindbad U3 :B: .75 2.00
83 Singing Tree U2 :G: 8.00 20.00
84 Sorceress Queen U3 :K: 3.00 8.00
85 Stone-Throwing Devils (dark mana) C3 :K: 1.25 3.00
86 Stone-Throwing Devils (light mana) C1 :K: 1.50 4.00
87 Unstable Mutation C5 :B: .20 .50
88 War Elephant (dark 3) C3 :W: .20 .50
89 War Elephant (light 3) C1 :W: .30 .75
90 Wyluli Wolf (dark 1) C4 :G: .30 .75
91 Wyluli Wolf (light 1) C1 :G: .75 2.00
92 Ydwen Efreet U2 :R: 4.00 10.00

1994 Magic The Gathering Antiquities

COMPLETE SET (100) 450.00 600.00
BOOSTER BOX (60 PACKS) 1600.00 2000.00
BOOSTER PACK (8 CARDS) 35.00 45.00
RELEASED ON MARCH 15, 1994
1 Amulet of Kroog C4 :A: .10 .25
2 Argivian Archaeologist U1 :W: 6.00 15.00
3 Argivian Blacksmith C4 :W: .10 .25
4 Argothian Pixies C4 :G: .10 .25
5 Argothian Treefolk C4 :G: .10 .25
6 Armageddon Clock U2 :A: .30 .75
7 Artifact Blast C4:R: .10 .25
8 Artifact Possession C4:K: .10 .25
9 Artifact Ward C4:W: .10 .25
10 Ashnod's Altar U2 :A: 1.50 4.00
11 Ashnod's Battle Gear U2 :A: .15 .40
12 Ashnod's Transmogrant U3 :A: .15 .40
13 Atog C4 :R: .15 .40
14 Battering Ram C4 :A: .10 .25
15 Bronze Tablet U1 :A: .40 1.00
16 Candelabra of Tawnos U1 :A: 175.00 350.00
17 Circle of Protection: Artifacts U3 :W: .40 1.00
18 Citanul Druid U3 :G: .25 .60
19 Clay Statue C4 :A: .10 .25
20 Clockwork Avian U1 :A: .60 1.50
21 Colossus of Sardia U1 :A: 1.25 3.00
22 Coral Helm U1 :A: .30 .75
23 Crumble C4 :G: .10 .25
24 Cursed Rack C1 :A: .25 .60
25 Damping Field U3 :W: .15 .40
26 Detonate U3 :R: .15 .40
27 Drafna's Restoration C4 :B: .10 .25
28 Dragon Engine C4 :A: .10 .25
29 Dwarven Weaponsmith U3 :R: .15 .40
30 Energy Flux U3 :B: .50 1.25
31 Feldon's Cane C1 :A: .75 2.00
32 Gaea's Avenger U1 :G: 1.50 4.00
33 Gate to Phyrexia U3 :K: 2.50 6.00
34 Goblin Artisans U3 :R: .15 .40
35 Golgothian Sylex U1 :A: .75 2.00
36 Grapeshot Catapult C4 :A: .10 .25
37 Haunting Wind U3 :K: .15 .40
38 Hurkyl's Recall U1 :B: 10.00 25.00
39 Ivory Tower U3 :A: 1.25 3.00
40 Jalum Tome U2 :A: .25 .60
41 Martyrs of Korlis U3 :W: .15 .40
42 Mightstone U3 :A: .15 .40
43 Millstone U3 :A: .75 2.00
44 Mishra's Factory, autumn U1 :L: 8.00 20.00
45 Mishra's Factory, spring C1 :L: 3.00 8.00
46 Mishra's Factory, summer U1 :L: 12.00 30.00
47 Mishra's Factory, winter U1 :L: 30.00 80.00
48 Mishra's War Machine U1 :A: .40 1.00
49 Mishra's Workshop U1 :L: 300.00 600.00
50 Obelisk of Undoing U1 :A: .40 1.00
51 Onulet U3 :A: .15 .40
52 Orcish Mechanics C4 :R: .10 .25
53 Ornithopter C4 :A: .60 1.50
54 Phyrexian Gremlins C4 :K: .10 .25
55 Power Artifact U3 :B: 8.00 20.00
56 Powerleech U3 :G: .15 .40
57 Priest of Yawgmoth C 4:K: .10 .25
58 Primal Clay U3 :A: .15 .40
59 Rack, The U3 :A: .15 .40
60 Rakalite U3 :A: .10 .25
61 Reconstruction C4 :B: .10 .25
62 Reverse Polarity C4 :W: .25 .60
63 Rocket Launcher U3 :A: .10 .25
64 Sage of Lat-Nam C4 :B: .75 2.00
65 Shapeshifter U1 :A: 6.00 15.00
66 Shatterstorm U1 :R: .10 .25
67 Staff of Zegon C4 :A: 5.00 12.00
68 Strip Mine, horizon, even stripe U1 :L: 3.00 8.00
69 Strip Mine, horizon, uneven stripe U1 :L: 6.00 15.00
70 Strip Mine, no horizon C1 :L: 4.00 10.00
71 Strip Mine, small tower in forest U1 :L: 1.50 4.00
72 Su-Chi U3 :A: .10 .25
73 Tablet of Epityr C4 :A: 8.00 20.00
74 Tawnos's Coffin U1 :A: .15 .40
75 Tawnos's Wand U3 :A: .15 .40
76 Tawnos's Weaponry U3 :A: .50 1.25
77 Tetravus U1 :A: 2.00 5.00
78 Titania's Song U3 :G: .15 .40
79 Transmute Artifact U3 :B: 15.00 40.00
80 Triskelion U1 :A: 3.00 8.00
81 Urza's Avenger U1 :A: 1.00 2.50
82 Urza's Chalice C4 :A: .10 .25
83 Urza's Mine, clawed sphere C2 :L: .60 1.50
84 Urza's Mine, mouth C1 :L: .75 2.00
85 Urza's Mine, pulley C1 :L: 1.00 2.50
86 Urza's Mine, tower C2 :L: .60 1.50
87 Urza's Miter U1 :A: 1.25 3.00
88 Urza's Power Plant, bug C2 :L: .60 1.50
89 Urza's Power Plant, columns C1 :L: 1.00 2.50
90 Urza's Power Plant, rock in pot C1 :L: .75 2.00
91 Urza's Power Plant, sphere C2 :L: .60 1.50
92 Urza's Tower, forest C2 :L: .75 2.00
93 Urza's Tower, mountains C1 :L: .75 2.00
94 Urza's Tower, plains C1 :L: 1.00 2.50
95 Urza's Tower, shore C1 :L: 1.50 4.00
96 Wall of Spears U3 :A: .15 .40
97 Weakstone U3 :A: .15 .40
98 Xenic Poltergeist U3 :K: .15 .40
99 Yawgmoth Demon U3 :K: 1.00 2.50
100 Yotian Soldier C4 :A: .10 .25

1994 Magic The Gathering Revised Edition

COMPLETE SET (306) 500.00 900.00
BOOSTER BOX (36 PACKS) 450.00 600.00
BOOSTER PACK (15 CARDS) 15.00 20.00
STARTER DECK BOX 400.00 500.00
STARTER DECK 40.00 55.00
RELEASED ON APRIL 15, 1994
ALSO KNOWN AS 3RD EDITION
WHITE BORDERS AND NO COPYRIGHT DATE
PALE COLORS AND NAME OF ILLUSTRATOR AT THE BOTTOM.
NO BEVELED EDGES INSIDE THE COLORED BORDERS.
1 Air Elemental U :B: .15 .40
2 Aladdin's Lamp R :A: .25 .60
3 Aladdin's Ring R :A: .25 .60
4 Animate Artifact U :B: .15 .40
5 Animate Dead U :K: .40 1.00
6 Animate Wall R :W: .25 .60
7 Ankh of Mishra R :A: .25 .60
8 Armageddon Clock R :A: 1.00 2.50
9 Armageddon R :W: .25 .60
10 Aspect of Wolf R :G: .25 .60
11 Atog C :R: .08 .20
12 Bad Moon R :K: .60 1.50
13 Badlands R :L: 30.00 80.00
14 Balance R :W: .50 1.25
15 Basalt Monolith U :A: .30 .75
16 Bayou R :L: 80.00 150.00
17 Benalish Hero C :W: .08 .20
18 Birds of Paradise R :G: 1.50 4.00
19 Black Knight U :K: .15 .40
20 Black Vise U :A: .25 .60
21 Black Ward U :W: .15 .40
22 Blessing R :W: .25 .60
23 Blue Elemental Blast C :B: .15 .40
24 Blue Ward U :W: .15 .40
25 Bog Wraith U :K: .15 .40
26 Bottle of Suleiman R :A: .25 .60
27 Braingeyser R :B: .80 2.00
28 Brass Man U :A: .15 .40
29 Burrowing U :R: .15 .40
30 Castle U :W: .15 .40
31 Celestial Prism U :A: .15 .40
32 Channel U :G: .25 .60
33 Chaoslace R :R: .25 .60
34 Circle of Protection Black C :W: .08 .20
35 Circle of Protection Blue C :W: .08 .20
36 Circle of Protection Green C :W: .08 .20
37 Circle of Protection Red C :W: .15 .40
38 Circle of Protection White C :W: .08 .20
39 Clockwork Beast R :A: .25 .60
40 Clone U :B: .25 .60
41 Cockatrice R :G: .25 .60
42 Conservator U :A: .15 .40
43 Contract from Below R :K: .25 .60
44 Control Magic U :B: .25 .60
45 Conversion U :W: .15 .40
46 Copy Artifact R :B: 2.00 5.00
47 Counterspell U :B: .40 1.00
48 Craw Wurm C :G: .08 .20
49 Creature Bond C :B: .08 .20
50 Crumble U :G: .15 .40
51 Crusade R :W: .40 1.00
52 Crystal Rod U :A: .50 1.00
53 Cursed Land U :K: .15 .40
54 Dancing Scimitar R :A: .50 1.00
55 Dark Ritual C :K: .30 .75
56 Darkpact R :K: .50 1.00
57 Death Ward C :W: .08 .20
58 Deathgrip U :K: .50 1.00
59 Deathlace R :K: .25 .60
60 Demonic Attorney R :K: .50 1.00
61 Demonic Hordes R :K: .40 1.00
62 Demonic Tutor U :K: 6.00 15.00
63 Desert Twister U :G: .15 .40
64 Dingus Egg R :A: 1.00 2.00
65 Disenchant C :W: .15 .40
66 Disintegrate C :R: .50 1.00
67 Disrupting Scepter R :A: .25 .60
68 Dragon Engine R :A: 1.00 2.00
69 Dragon Whelp U :R: .15 .40
70 Drain Life C :K: .15 .30
71 Drain Power R :B: .25 .60
72 Drudge Skeletons C :K: .15 .30
73 Dwarven Warriors C :R: .08 .20
74 Dwarven Weaponsmith U :R: .50 1.00
75 Earth Elemental U :R: .15 .40
76 Earthbind C :R: .15 .30
77 Earthquake R :R: .25 .60
78 Ebony Horse R :A: .50 1.00
79 El-Hajjaj R :K: .25 .60
80 Elvish Archers R :G: 1.50 3.00
81 Energy Flux U :B: .15 .40
82 Erg Raiders C :K: .15 .30
83 Evil Presence U :K: .15 .40
84 Eye for an Eye R :W: 1.00 2.00
85 Farmstead R :W: .25 .60
86 Fastbond R :G: 1.50 4.00
87 Fear C :K: .08 .20
88 Feedback U :B: .50 1.00
89 Fire Elemental U :R: .15 .40
90 Fireball C :R: .50 1.00
91 Firebreathing C :R: .08 .20
92 Flashfires U :R: 1.00 2.00
93 Flight C :B: .08 .20
94 Flying Carpet R :A: .75 1.50
95 Fog C :G: .08 .20
96 Force of Nature R :G: 1.50 3.00
97 Forest v1 C :L: .15 .40
98 Forest v2 C :L: .15 .30
99 Forest v3 C :L: .15 .40
100 Fork R :R: 2.00 5.00
101 Frozen Shade C :K: .08 .20
102 Fungusaur R :G: 1.00 2.00
103 Gaea's Liege R :G: .25 .60
104 Giant Growth C :G: .08 .20
105 Giant Spider C :G: .15 .30
106 Glasses of Urza U :A: .50 1.00
107 Gloom U :K: .15 .40
108 Goblin Balloon Brigade U :R: 1.00 2.00
109 Goblin King R :R: 2.00 4.00
110 Granite Gargoyle R :R: .25 .60
111 Gray Ogre C :R: .08 .20
112 Green Ward U :W: .50 1.00
113 Grizzly Bears C :G: .08 .20
114 Guardian Angel C :W: .15 .30
115 Healing Salve C :W: .08 .20
116 Helm of Chatzuk R :A: .25 .60
117 Hill Giant C :R: .15 .30
118 Hive, The R :A: 1.00 2.00
119 Holy Armor C :W: .08 .20
120 Holy Strength C :W: .15 .30
121 Howl from Beyond C :K: .15 .30
122 Howling Mine R :A: .80 2.00
123 Hurkyl's Recall R :B: 2.00 5.00
124 Hurloon Minotaur C :R: .15 .30
125 Hurricane U :G: .15 .40
126 Hypnotic Specter U :K: 6.00 12.00
127 Instill Energy U :G: .15 .40
128 Iron Star U :A: .15 .40
129 Ironroot Treefolk C :G: .15 .30
130 Island Fish Jasconius R :B: 1.00 2.00
131 Island Sanctuary R :W: .25 .60
132 Island v1 C :L: .15 .30
133 Island v2 C :L: .15 .30
134 Island v3 C :L: .30 .75
135 Ivory Cup U :A: .50 1.00
136 Ivory Tower R :A: .60 1.50
137 Jade Monolith R :A: .25 .60
138 Jandor's Ring R :A: 1.00 2.00
139 Jandor's Saddlebags R :A: 1.00 2.00
140 Jayemdae Tome R :A: .25 .60
141 Juggernaut U :A: 1.50 3.00
142 Jump C :B: .15 .30
143 Karma U :W: .15 .40
144 Keldon Warlord U :R: 1.00 2.00
145 Kird Ape C :R: .50 1.00
146 Kormus Bell R :A: .25 .60
147 Kudzu R :G: 1.00 2.00
148 Lance U :W: .50 1.00
149 Ley Druid U :G: .15 .40
150 Library of Leng U :A: .50 1.00
151 Lifeforce U :G: .50 1.00
152 Lifelace R :G: .25 .60
153 Lifetap U :B: .50 1.00
154 Lightning Bolt C :R: .60 1.50
155 Living Artifact R :G: .25 .60
156 Living Lands R :G: 1.00 2.00
157 Living Wall U :A: .50 1.00
158 Llanowar Elves C :G: .15 .40
159 Lord of Atlantis R :B: 1.50 4.00
160 Lord of the Pit R :K: 1.50 3.00
161 Lure U :G: .15 .40
162 Magical Hack R :B: 1.00 2.00
163 Magnetic Mountain R :R: 1.00 2.00
164 Mahamoti Djinn R :B: .25 .60
165 Mana Flare R :R: .80 2.00
166 Mana Short R :B: 2.00 4.00
167 Mana Vault R :A: 2.00 5.00
168 Manabarbs R :R: 1.00 2.00
169 Meekstone R :A: 1.50 3.00
170 Merfolk of the Pearl Trident C :B: .08 .20
171 Mesa Pegasus C :W: .15 .30
172 Mijae Djinn R :R: 1.00 2.00
173 Millstone R :A: .25 .60
174 Mind Twist R :K: 1.25 3.00
175 Mishra's War Machine R :A: 1.00 2.00
176 Mons's Goblin Raiders C :R: .08 .20
177 Mountain v1 C :L: .15 .30
178 Mountain v2 C :L: .15 .30
179 Mountain v3 C :L: .15 .40
180 Nether Shadow R :K: 1.25 3.00
181 Nettling Imp U :K: .50 1.00
182 Nevinyrral's Disk R :A: 1.00 2.50
183 Nightmare R :K: 3.50 7.00
184 Northern Paladin R :W: .25 .60
185 Obsianus Golem U :A: .15 .40
186 Onulet R :A: 1.00 2.00
187 Orcish Artillery U :R: .50 1.00
188 Orcish Oriflamme U :R: .15 .40
189 Ornithopter U :A: 1.00 2.00
190 Paralyze C :K: .15 .30
191 Pearled Unicorn C :W: .08 .20
192 Personal Incarnation R :W: .25 .60
193 Pestilence C :K: .15 .30
194 Phantasmal Forces U :B: .15 .40
195 Phantasmal Terrain C :B: .15 .30
196 Phantom Monster U :B: .15 .40
197 Pirate Ship R :B: .25 .60
198 Plague Rats C :K: .15 .30
199 Plains v1 C :L: .15 .30
200 Plains v2 C :L: .25 .60
201 Plains v3 C :L: .15 .30
202 Plateau R :L: 25.00 60.00
203 Power Leak C :B: .08 .20
204 Power Sink C :B: .08 .20
205 Power Surge R :R: 1.00 2.00
206 Primal Clay R :A: .25 .60
207 Prodigal Sorcerer C :B: .15 .30
208 Psychic Venom C :B: .08 .20
209 Purelace R :W: 1.00 2.00
210 Rack, The U :A: .60 1.50
211 Raise Dead C :K: .15 .30
212 Reconstruction C :B: .08 .20
213 Red Elemental Blast C :R: .15 .30
214 Red Ward U :W: .15 .40
215 Regeneration C :G: .15 .30
216 Regrowth U :G: .50 1.25
217 Resurrection U :W: .50 1.00
218 Reverse Damage R :W: .25 .60
219 Reverse Polarity U :W: .50 1.00
220 Righteousness R :W: .25 .60
221 Roc of Kher Ridges R :R: 2.00 4.00
222 Rock Hydra R :R: .25 .60
223 Rocket Launcher R :A: 1.50 3.00
224 Rod of Ruin U :A: .15 .40
225 Royal Assassin R :K: 5.00 10.00
226 Sacrifice U :K: .15 .40
227 Samite Healer C :W: .15 .30
228 Savannah Lions R :W: 30.00 80.00
229 Savannah R :L: 40.00 80.00
230 Scathe Zombies C :K: .08 .20
231 Scavenging Ghoul U :K: .50 1.00
232 Scrubland R :L: 30.00 80.00
233 Scryb Sprites C :G: .08 .20
234 Sea Serpent C :B: .08 .20
235 Sedge Troll R :R: 2.00 4.00
236 Sengir Vampire U :K: .25 .60
237 Serendib Efreet R :B: 3.00 6.00
238 Serra Angel U :W: .25 .60
239 Shanodin Dryads C :G: .15 .30
240 Shatter C :R: .08 .20
241 Shatterstorm U :R: 1.00 2.00
242 Shivan Dragon R :R: .40 1.00
243 Simulacrum U :K: .50 1.00
244 Siren's Call U :B: .15 .40
245 Sleight of Mind R :B: 1.00 2.00
246 Smoke R :R: .25 .60
247 Sol Ring U :A: 2.00 5.00
248 Sorceress Queen R :K: .25 .60
249 Soul Net U :A: .50 1.00
250 Spell Blast C :B: .08 .20
251 Stasis R :B: .60 1.50
252 Steal Artifact U :B: .15 .40
253 Stone Giant U :R: .50 1.00
254 Stone Rain C :R: .08 .20
255 Stream of Life C :G: .15 .30
256 Sunglasses of Urza R :A: .25 .60
257 Swamp v1 C :L: .15 .40
258 Swamp v2 C :L: .25 .60
259 Swamp v3 C :L: .25 .60
260 Swords to Plowshares U :W: 1.00 2.50
261 Taiga R :L: 25.00 60.00
262 Terror C :K: .15 .40
263 Thicket Basilisk U :G: .15 .40
264 Thoughtlace R :B: .25 .60
265 Throne of Bone U :A: .15 .40
266 Timber Wolves R :G: .25 .60
267 Titania's Song R :G: .25 .60
268 Tranquility C :G: .08 .20
269 Tropical Island R :L: 100.00 200.00
270 Tsunami U :G: .15 .40
271 Tundra R :L: 100.00 200.00
272 Tunnel U :R: .15 .40
273 Underground Sea R :L: 150.00 300.00
274 Unholy Strength C :K: .08 .20
275 Unstable Mutation C :B: .08 .20
276 Unsummon C :B: .08 .20
277 Uthden Troll U :R: .15 .40
278 Verduran Enchantress R :G: .25 .60
279 Vesuvan Doppelganger R :B: 1.25 3.00

280 Veteran Bodyguard R :W: .25 .60
281 Volcanic Eruption R :B: .25 .60
282 Volcanic Island R :L: 125.00 250.00
283 Wall of Air U :B: .15 .40
284 Wall of Bone U :K: .15 .40
285 Wall of Brambles U :G: .15 .40
286 Wall of Fire U :R: .15 .40
287 Wall of Ice U :G: .15 .40
288 Wall of Stone U :R: .15 .40
289 Wall of Swords U :W: .15 .40
290 Wall of Water U :B: .15 .40
291 Wall of Wood C :G: .08 .20
292 Wanderlust U :G: .15 .40
293 War Mammoth C :G: .08 .20
294 Warp Artifact R :K: .25 .60
295 Water Elemental U :B: .15 .40
296 Weakness C :K: .08 .20
297 Web R :G: .25 .60
298 Wheel of Fortune R :R: 8.00 20.00
299 White Knight U :W: .15 .40
300 White Ward U :W: .15 .40
301 Wild Growth C :G: .15 .40
302 Will-O'-The-Wisp R :K: .60 1.50
303 Winter Orb R :A: 1.00 2.50
304 Wooden Sphere U :A: .15 .40
305 Wrath of God R :W: 1.50 4.00
306 Zombie Master R :K: .80 2.00

1994 Magic The Gathering Legends

COMPLETE SET (310) 1500.00 1800.00
BOOSTER BOX (36 PACKS) 1500.00 2000.00
BOOSTER PACKS (15 CARDS) 42.00 58.00
ITALIAN BOOSTER BOX 600.00 700.00
RELEASED ON JUNE 15, 1994
1 Abomination U :K: .20 .50
2 Abyss, The R :K: 100.00 200.00
3 Acid Rain R :B: 5.00 12.00
4 Active Volcano C :R: .12 .30
5 Adun Oakenshield R :D: 15.00 40.00
6 Adventurers' Guildhouse U :L: .30 .75
7 Ærathi Berserker U :R: .20 .50
8 Aisling Leprechaun C :G: .12 .30
9 Akron Legionnaire R :W: .75 2.00
10 Al-abara's Carpet R :A: 2.00 5.00
11 Alabaster Potion C :W: .12 .30
12 Alchor's Tomb R :A: 1.25 3.00
13 All Hallow's Eve R :K: 15.00 40.00
14 Amrou Kithkin C :W: .12 .30
15 Angelic Voices R :W: 1.25 3.00
16 Angus Mackenzie R :D: 30.00 80.00
17 Anti-Magic Aura C :B: .12 .30
18 Arboria U :G: 1.00 2.50
19 Arcades Sabboth R :D: 3.00 8.00
20 Arena of the Ancients R :A: 1.50 4.00
21 Avoid Fate C :G: .40 1.00
22 Axelrod Gunnarson R :D: 1.00 2.50
23 Ayesha Tanaka R :D: .75 2.00
24 Azure Drake U :B: .20 .50
25 Backdraft U :R: .20 .50
26 Backfire U :B: .20 .50
27 Barbary Apes C :G: .12 .30
28 Barktooth Warbeard U :D: .20 .50
29 Bartel Runeaxe R :D: 2.00 5.00
30 Beasts of Bogardan U :R: .20 .50
31 Black Mana Battery U :A: .30 .75
32 Blazing Effigy C :R: .12 .30
33 Blight U :K: .60 1.50
34 Blood Lust U :R: .60 1.50
35 Blue Mana Battery U :A: .20 .50
36 Boomerang C :B: .20 .50
37 Boris Devilboon R :D: 2.50 6.00
38 Brine Hag U :B: .20 .50
39 Bronze Horse R :A: .75 2.00
40 Brute, The C :R: .12 .30
41 Carrion Ants R :K: 1.25 3.00
42 Cat Warriors C :G: .12 .30
43 Cathedral of Serra U :L: .40 1.00
44 Caverns of Despair R :R: 1.50 4.00
45 Chain Lightning C :R: 6.00 15.00
46 Chains of Mephistopheles R :K: 175.00 350.00
47 Chromium R :D: 4.00 10.00
48 Cleanse R :W: 3.00 8.00
49 Clergy of the Holy Nimbus C :W: .12 .30
50 Cocoon U :G: .20 .50
51 Concordant Crossroads R :G: 8.00 20.00
52 Cosmic Horror R :K: .75 2.00
53 Craw Giant U :G: .20 .50
54 Crevasse U :R: .20 .50
55 Crimson Kobolds C :R: .40 1.00
56 Crimson Manticore R :R: .60 1.50
57 Crookshank Kobolds C :R: .40 1.00
58 Cyclopean Mummy C :K: .12 .30
59 Dakkon Blackblade R :D: 5.00 12.00
60 Darkness C :K: 1.00 2.50
61 D'Avenant Archer C :W: .12 .30
62 Deadfall U :G: .20 .50
63 Demonic Torment U :K: .20 .50
64 Devouring Deep C :B: .12 .30
65 Disharmony R :R: 2.00 5.00
66 Divine Intervention R :W: 4.00 10.00
67 Divine Offering C :W: .12 .30
68 Divine Transformation R :W: 1.25 3.00
69 Dream Coat U :B: .20 .50
70 Durkwood Boars C :G: .12 .30
71 Dwarven Song U :R: .20 .50
72 Elder Land Wurm R :W: 1.50 4.00
73 Elder Spawn R :B: .75 2.00
74 Elven Riders R :G: .75 2.00
75 Emerald Dragonfly C :G: .12 .30
76 Enchanted Being C :W: .12 .30
77 Enchantment Alteration C :B: .12 .30
78 Energy Tap C :B: .12 .30
79 Equinox C :W: .12 .30
80 Eternal Warrior U :R: .20 .50
81 Eureka R :G: 50.00 100.00
82 Evil Eye of Orms-By-Gore U :K: .30 .75
83 Fallen Angel U :K: .75 2.00
84 Falling Star R :R: 1.50 4.00
85 Feint C :R: .12 .30
86 Field of Dreams R :B: 2.00 5.00
87 Fire Sprites C :G: .12 .30
88 Firestorm Phoenix R :R: 2.50 6.00
89 Flash Counter C :B: .12 .30
90 Flash Flood C :B: .12 .30
91 Floral Spuzzem U :G: .20 .50
92 Force Spike C :B: .25 .60
93 Forethought Amulet R :A: 1.00 2.50
94 Fortified Area U :W: .20 .50
95 Frost Giant U :R: .20 .50
96 Gabriel Angelfire R :D: 2.00 5.00
97 Gaseous Form C :B: .12 .30
98 Gauntlets of Chaos R :A: .75 2.00
99 Ghosts of the Damned C :K: .12 .30
100 Giant Slug C :K: .12 .30
101 Giant Strength C :R: .12 .30
102 Giant Turtle C :G: .12 .30
103 Glyph of Delusion C :B: .12 .30
104 Glyph of Destruction C :R: .12 .30
105 Glyph of Doom C :K: .12 .30
106 Glyph of Life C :W: .12 .30
107 Glyph of Reincarnation C :G: .12 .30
108 Gosta Dirk R :D: 1.25 3.00
109 Gravity Sphere R :R: 4.00 10.00
110 Great Defender U :W: .20 .50
111 Great Wall U :W: .20 .50
112 Greater Realm of Preservation U :W: .20 .50
113 Greed R :K: 1.25 3.00
114 Green Mana Battery U :A: .20 .50
115 Gwendlyn Di Corci R :D: 10.00 25.00
116 Halfdane R :D: 3.00 8.00
117 Hammerheim U :L: .60 1.50
118 Hazezon Tamar R :D: 15.00 40.00
119 Headless Horseman C :K: .12 .30
120 Heaven's Gate U :W: .20 .50
121 Hell Swarm C :K: .12 .30
122 Hellfire R :K: 4.00 10.00
123 Hell's Caretaker R :K: 5.00 12.00
124 Holy Day C :W: .20 .50
125 Horn of Deafening R :A: .75 2.00
126 Hornet Cobra C :G: .12 .30
127 Horror of Horrors U :K: .20 .50
128 Hunding Gjornersen U :D: .20 .50
129 Hyperion Blacksmith U :R: .20 .50
130 Ichneumon Druid U :G: .20 .50
131 Immolation C :R: .12 .30
132 Imprison R :K: 1.25 3.00
133 In the Eye of Chaos R :B: 20.00 50.00
134 Indestructible Aura C :W: .12 .30
135 Infernal Medusa U :K: .60 1.50
136 Infinite Authority R :W: 1.00 2.50
137 Invoke Prejudice R :B: 60.00 120.00
138 Ivory Guardians U :W: .20 .50
139 Jacques le Vert R :D: 2.00 5.00
140 Jasmine Boreal U :D: .20 .50
141 Jedit Ojanen U :D: .40 1.00
142 Jerrard of the Closed Fist U :D: .20 .50
143 Johan R :D: 1.25 3.00
144 Jovial Evil R :K: 2.00 5.00
145 Juxtapose R :B: .60 1.50
146 Karakas U :L: 80.00 150.00
147 Kasimir the Lone Wolf U :D: .20 .50
148 Keepers of the Faith C :W: .12 .30
149 Kei Takahashi R :D: .75 2.00
150 Killer Bees R :G: 2.00 5.00
151 Kismet U :W: .75 2.00
152 Knowledge Vault R :A: 1.25 3.00
153 Kobold Drill Sergeant U :R: 1.25 3.00
154 Kobold Overlord R :R: 5.00 12.00
155 Kobold Taskmaster U :R: .75 2.00
156 Kobolds of Kher Keep C :R: .60 1.50
157 Kry Shield U :A: .20 .50
158 Lady Caleria R :D: 1.50 4.00
159 Lady Evangela R :D: 5.00 12.00
160 Lady of the Mountain, The U :D: .20 .50
161 Lady Orca U :D: .20 .50
162 Land Equilibrium R :B: 20.00 50.00
163 Land Tax U :W: 8.00 20.00
164 Land's Edge R :R: 1.00 2.50
165 Lesser Werewolf U :K: .30 .75
166 Life Chisel U :A: .30 .75
167 Life Matrix R :A: 1.25 3.00
168 Lifeblood R :W: 1.00 2.50
169 Living Plane R :G: 12.00 30.00
170 Livonya Silone R :D: 2.50 6.00
171 Lord Magnus U :D: .30 .75
172 Lost Soul C :K: .12 .30
173 Mana Drain U :B: 100.00 200.00
174 Mana Matrix R :A: 3.00 8.00
175 Marble Priest U :A: .20 .50
176 Marhault Elsdragon U :D: .20 .50
177 Master of the Hunt R :G: 2.50 6.00
178 Mirror Universe R :A: 15.00 40.00
179 Moat R :W: 150.00 300.00
180 Mold Demon R :K: 1.25 3.00
181 Moss Monster C :G: .12 .30
182 Mountain Stronghold U :L: .20 .50
183 Mountain Yeti U :R: .20 .50
184 Nebuchadnezzar R :D: 1.50 4.00
185 Nether Void R :K: 80.00 150.00
186 Nicol Bolas R :D: 6.00 15.00
187 North Star R :A: 1.50 4.00
188 Nova Pentacle R :A: 2.00 5.00
189 Osai Vultures C :W: .12 .30
190 Palladia-Mors R :D: 3.00 8.00
191 Part Water U :B: .20 .50
192 Pavel Maliki U :D: .20 .50
193 Pendelhaven U :L: 2.50 6.00
194 Petra Sphinx R :W: .75 2.00
195 Pit Scorpion C :K: .12 .30
196 Pixie Queen R :G: 2.00 5.00
197 Planar Gate R :A: 3.00 8.00
198 Pradesh Gypsies U :G: .20 .50
199 Presence of the Master U :W: .50 1.25
200 Primordial Ooze U :R: .20 .50
201 Princess Lucrezia U :D: .20 .50
202 Psionic Entity R :B: .60 1.50
203 Psychic Purge C :B: .12 .30
204 Puppet Master U :B: .20 .50
205 Pyrotechnics C :R: .12 .30
206 Quagmire U :K: .20 .50
207 Quarum Trench Gnomes R :R: .75 2.00
208 Rabid Wombat U :G: .40 1.00
209 Radjan Spirit U :G: .20 .50
210 Raging Bull C :R: .12 .30
211 Ragnar R :D: 1.50 4.00
212 Ramirez DePietro U :D: .30 .75
213 Ramses Overdark R :D: 3.00 8.00
214 Rapid Fire R :W: .75 2.00
215 Rasputin Dreamweaver R :D: 15.00 40.00
216 Rebirth R :G: .60 1.50
217 Recall R :B: 2.00 5.00
218 Red Mana Battery U :A: .30 .75
219 Reincarnation U :G: .75 2.00
220 Relic Barrier U :A: .20 .50
221 Relic Bind U :B: .20 .50
222 Remove Enchantments C :W: .12 .30
223 Remove Soul C :B: .12 .30
224 Reset U :B: 8.00 20.00
225 Revelation R :G: .75 2.00
226 Reverberation R :B: 1.25 3.00
227 Righteous Avengers U :W: .20 .50
228 Ring of Immortals R :A: 2.00 5.00
229 Riven Turnbull U :D: .20 .50
230 Rohgahh of Kher Keep R :D: 4.00 10.00
231 Rubinia Soulsinger R :D: 3.00 8.00
232 Rust C :G: .12 .30
233 Sea Kings' Blessing U :B: .20 .50
234 Seafarer's Quay U :L: .20 .50
235 Seeker U :W: .20 .50
236 Segovian Leviathan U :B: .20 .50
237 Sentinel R :A: 1.00 2.50
238 Serpent Generator R :A: 1.25 3.00
239 Shelkin Brownie C :G: .12 .30
240 Shield Wall U :W: .20 .50
241 Shimian Night Stalker U :K: .20 .50
242 Silhouette U :B: .20 .50
243 Sir Shandlar of Eberyn U :D: .20 .50
244 Sivitri Scarzam U :D: .20 .50
245 Sol'kanar the Swamp King R :D: 2.50 6.00
246 Spectral Cloak U :B: .20 .50
247 Spinal Villain R :R: 5.00 12.00
248 Spirit Link U :W: .75 2.00
249 Spirit Shackle C :K: .12 .30
250 Spiritual Sanctuary R :W: 1.00 2.50
251 Stangg R :D: 1.00 2.50
252 Storm Seeker U :G: .50 1.25
253 Storm World R :R: 2.00 5.00
254 Subdue C :G: .12 .30
255 Sunastian Falconer U :D: .30 .75
256 Sword of the Ages R :A: 4.00 10.00
257 Sylvan Library U :G: 15.00 40.00
258 Sylvan Paradise U :G: .20 .50
259 Syphon Soul C :K: .12 .30
260 Tabernacle at Pendrell Vale R :L: 350.00 700.00
261 Takklemaggot U :K: .20 .50
262 Telekinesis R :B: 2.50 6.00
263 Teleport R :B: .60 1.50
264 Tempest Efreet R :R: .60 1.50
265 Tetsuo Umezawa R :D: 8.00 20.00
266 Thunder Spirit R :W: 6.00 15.00
267 Time Elemental R :B: 2.00 5.00
268 Tobias Andrion U :D: .20 .50
269 Tolaria U :L: .20 .50
270 Tor Wauki U :D: .20 .50
271 Torsten Von Ursus U :D: .20 .50
272 Touch of Darkness U :K: .20 .50
273 Transmutation C :K: .12 .30
274 Triassic Egg R :A: .75 2.00
275 Tuknir Deathlock R :D: 1.25 3.00
276 Tundra Wolves C :W: .12 .30
277 Typhoon R :G: 1.00 2.50
278 Undertow U :B: .20 .50
279 Underworld Dreams U :K: 3.00 8.00
280 Unholy Citadel U :L: .20 .50
281 Untamed Wilds U :G: .20 .50
282 Urborg U :L: 1.25 3.00
283 Ur-Drago R :D: 1.25 3.00
284 Vaevictis Asmadi R :D: 4.00 10.00
285 Vampire Bats C :K: .12 .30
286 Venarian Gold C :B: .12 .30
287 Visions U :W: .20 .50
288 Voodoo Doll R :A: .60 1.50
289 Walking Dead C :K: .12 .30
290 Wall of Caltrops C :W: .12 .30
291 Wall of Dust U :R: .20 .50
292 Wall of Earth C :R: .12 .30
293 Wall of Heat C :R: .12 .30
294 Wall of Light U :W: .30 .75
295 Wall of Opposition R :R: .60 1.50
296 Wall of Putrid Flesh U :K: .30 .75
297 Wall of Shadows C :K: .12 .30
298 Wall of Tombstones U :K: .20 .50
299 Wall of Vapor C :B: .12 .30
300 Wall of Wonder U :B: .20 .50
301 Whirling Dervish U :G: .50 1.25
302 White Mana Battery U :A: .20 .50
303 Willow Satyr R :G: 5.00 12.00
304 Winds of Change U :R: 1.50 4.00
305 Winter Blast R :G: 1.00 2.50
306 Wolverine Pack C :G: .12 .30
307 Wood Elemental R :G: 1.25 3.00
308 Wretched, The R :K: 3.00 8.00
309 Xira Arien R :D: 2.50 6.00
310 Zephyr Falcon C :B: .12 .30

1994 Magic The Gathering The Dark

COMPLETE SET (119) 120.00 135.00
BOOSTER BOX (60 PACKS) 375.00 500.00
BOOSTER PACK (8 CARDS) 10.00 15.00
RELEASED ON AUGUST 15, 1994
1 Amnesia U2 :B: .25 .60
2 Angry Mob U2 :W: .15 .40
3 Apprentice Wizard U1 :B: .40 1.00
4 Ashes to Ashes C3 :K: .15 .40
5 Ball Lightning U1 :R: 2.00 5.00
6 Banshee U2 :K: .15 .40
7 Barl's Cage U1 :A: .15 .40
8 Blood Moon U1 :R: 10.00 25.00
9 Blood of the Martyr U2 :W: .15 .40
10 Bog Imp C3 :K: .08 .20
11 Bog Rats C3 :K: .08 .20
12 Bone Flute U2 :A: .15 .40
13 Book of Rass U2 :A: .15 .40
14 Brainwash C3 :W: .08 .20
15 Brothers of Fire U2 :R: .15 .40
16 Carnivorous Plant C3 :G: .08 .20
17 Cave People U2 :R: .15 .40
18 City of Shadows U1 :L: 1.50 4.00
19 Cleansing U1 :W: .40 1.00
20 Coal Golem U2 :A: .15 .40
21 Curse Artifact U2 :K: .15 .40
22 Dance of Many U1 :B: .40 1.00
23 Dark Heart of the Wood C3 :D: .08 .20
24 Dark Sphere U2 :A: .25 .60
25 Deep Water C3 :B: .08 .20
26 Diabolic Machine U2 :A: .15 .40
27 Drowned C3 :B: .08 .20
28 Dust to Dust C3 :W: .08 .20
29 Eater of the Dead U2 :K: .25 .60
30 Electric Eel U2 :B: .15 .40
31 Elves of Deep Shadow U2 :G: .40 1.00
32 Erosion C3 :B: .08 .20
33 Eternal Flame U1 :R: .15 .40
34 Exorcist U1 :W: .50 1.25
35 Fallen, The U2 :K: .15 .40
36 Fasting U2 :W: .15 .40
37 Fellwar Stone U2 :A: .40 1.00
38 Festival C3 :W: .08 .20
39 Fire and Brimstone U2 :W: .15 .40
40 Fire Drake U2 :R: .15 .40
41 Fissure C3 :R: .08 .20
42 Flood U2 :B: .15 .40
43 Fountain of Youth U2 :A: .15 .40
44 Frankenstein's Monster U1 :K: .40 1.00
45 Gaea's Touch C3 :G: .15 .40
46 Ghost Ship C3 :B: .08 .20
47 Giant Shark C3 :B: .08 .20
48 Goblin Caves C3 :R: .15 .40
49 Goblin Digging Team C3 :R: .08 .20
50 Goblin Hero C3 :R: .08 .20
51 Goblin Rock Sled C3 :R: .08 .20
52 Goblin Shrine C3 :R: .15 .30
53 Goblin Wizard U1 :R: 3.00 8.00
54 Goblins of the Flarg C3 :R: .15 .30
55 Grave Robbers U1 :K: .15 .40
56 Hidden Path U1 :G: 1.00 2.00
57 Holy Light C3 :W: .08 .20
58 Inferno U1 :R: 2.00 4.00
59 Inquisition C3 :K: .08 .20
60 Knights of Thorn U1 :W: 1.50 3.00
61 Land Leeches C3 :G: .08 .20
62 Leviathan U1 :B: 2.50 5.00
63 Living Armor U2 :A: .15 .40
64 Lurker U1 :G: .50 1.00
65 Mana Clash U1 :R: .25 .60
66 Mana Vortex U1 :B: 1.50 3.00
67 Marsh Gas C3 :K: .08 .20
68 Marsh Goblins C3 :D: .15 .30
69 Marsh Viper C3 :G: .08 .20
70 Martyr's Cry U1 :W: .25 .60
71 Maze of Ith C1 :L: 8.00 20.00
72 Merfolk Assassin U2 :B: .25 .60
73 Mind Bomb U1 :B: .25 .60
74 Miracle Worker C3 :W: .08 .20
75 Morale C3 :W: .08 .20
76 Murk Dwellers C3 :K: .08 .20
77 Nameless Race U1 :K: .15 .40
78 Necropolis U2 :A: .15 .40
79 Niall Silvain U1 :G: .25 .60
80 Orc General U2 :R: .15 .40
81 People of the Woods U2 :G: .15 .40
82 Pikemen C3 :W: .08 .20
83 Preacher U1 :W: 2.00 5.00
84 Psychic Allergy U1 :B: .25 .60
85 Rag Man U1 :K: .25 .60
86 Reflecting Mirror U2 :A: .15 .40
87 Riptide C3 :B: .08 .20
88 Runesword U2 :A: .15 .40
89 Safe Haven U1 :L: .40 1.00
90 Savaen Elves C3 :G: .08 .20
91 Scarecrow U2 :A: .15 .40
92 Scarwood Bandits U1 :G: .25 .60
93 Scarwood Goblins C3 :D: .08 .20
94 Scarwood Hag U2 :G: .15 .40
95 Scavenger Folk C3 :G: .08 .20
96 Season of the Witch U1 :K: .40 1.00
97 Sisters of the Flame U2 :R: .15 .40
98 Skull of Orm U2 :A: .25 .60
99 Sorrow's Path U1 :L: .25 .60
100 Spitting Slug U2 :G: .15 .40
101 Squire C3 :W: .08 .20
102 Standing Stones U2 :A: .15 .40
103 Stone Calendar U1 :A: .75 2.00
104 Sunken City C3 :B: .08 .20
105 Tangle Kelp U2 :B: .15 .40
106 Tivadar's Crusade U2 :W: .40 1.00
107 Tormod's Crypt U2 :A: 1.00 2.50
108 Tower of Coireall U2 :A: .15 .40
109 Tracker U1 :G: .25 .60
110 Uncle Istvan U2 :K: .15 .40
111 Venom C3 :G: .08 .20
112 Wand of Ith U2 :A: .15 .40
113 War Barge U2 :A: .15 .40
114 Water Wurm C3 :B: .08 .20
115 Whippoorwill U2 :G: .15 .40
116 Witch Hunter U1 :W: .25 .60
117 Word of Binding C3 :K: .08 .20
118 Worms of the Earth U1 :K: .40 1.00
119 Wormwood Treefolk U1 :G: .25 .60

1994 Magic The Gathering Fallen Empires

COMPLETE SET (187) 15.00 40.00
BOOSTER BOX (60 PACKS) 85.00 125.00
BOOSTER PACK (8 CARDS) 125.00 180.00
RELEASED ON NOVEMBER 15, 1994
1 Aeolipile U :A: .25 .60
2 Armor Thrull v1 C :K: .08 .20
3 Armor Thrull v2 C :K: .08 .20
4 Armor Thrull v3 C :K: .08 .20
5 Armor Thrull v4 C :K: .08 .20
6 Balm of Restoration U :A: .25 .60
7 Basal Thrull v1 C :K: .08 .20
8 Basal Thrull v2 C :K: .08 .20
9 Basal Thrull v3 C :K: .08 .20
10 Basal Thrull v4 C :K: .15 .40
11 Bottomless Vault U :L: .30 .75
12 Brassclaw Orcs v1 C :R: .08 .20
13 Brassclaw Orcs v2 C :R: .08 .20
14 Brassclaw Orcs v3 C :R: .08 .20
15 Brassclaw Orcs v4 C :R: .08 .20
16 Breeding Pit U :K: .15 .40
17 Combat Medic v1 C :W: .08 .20
18 Combat Medic v2 C :W: .08 .20
19 Combat Medic v3 C :W: .08 .20
20 Combat Medic v4 C :W: .08 .20
21 Conch Horn U :A: .25 .60
22 Deep Spawn U :B: .15 .40
23 Delif's Cone C :A: .08 .20
24 Delif's Cube U :A: .25 .60
25 Derelor U :K: .25 .60
26 Draconian Cylix U :A: .25 .60
27 Dwarven Armorer U :R: .25 .60
28 Dwarven Catapult U :R: .15 .40
29 Dwarven Hold U :L: .30 .75
30 Dwarven Lieutenant U :R: .15 .40
31 Dwarven Ruins U :L: .15 .40
32 Dwarven Soldier v1 C :R: .08 .20
33 Dwarven Soldier v2 C :R: .08 .20
34 Dwarven Soldier v3 C :R: .08 .20
35 Ebon Praetor U :K: .25 .60
36 Ebon Stronghold U :L: .15 .40
37 Elven Fortress v1 C :G: .08 .20
38 Elven Fortress v2 C :G: .08 .20
39 Elven Fortress v3 C :G: .08 .20
40 Elven Fortress v4 C :G: .08 .20
41 Elven Lyre U :A: .25 .60
42 Elvish Farmer U :G: .50 1.25
43 Elvish Hunter v1 C :G: .08 .20
44 Elvish Hunter v2 C :G: .08 .20
45 Elvish Hunter v3 C :G: .08 .20
46 Elvish Scout v1 C :G: .08 .20
47 Elvish Scout v2 C :G: .08 .20
48 Elvish Scout v3 C :G: .08 .20
49 Farrelite Priest U :W: .15 .40
50 Farrel's Mantle U :W: .15 .40
51 Farrel's Zealot v1 C :W: .08 .20
52 Farrel's Zealot v2 C :W: .08 .20
53 Farrel's Zealot v3 C :W: .08 .20
54 Feral Thallid U :G: .15 .40
55 Fungal Bloom U :G: .30 .75
56 Goblin Chirurgeon v1 C :R: .15 .40
57 Goblin Chirurgeon v2 C :R: .15 .40
58 Goblin Chirurgeon v3 C :R: .15 .40
59 Goblin Flotilla U :R: .25 .60
60 Goblin Grenade v1 C :R: .25 .60
61 Goblin Grenade v2 C :R: .25 .60
62 Goblin Grenade v3 C :R: .25 .60
63 Goblin Kites U :R: .15 .40
64 Goblin War Drums v1 C :R: .08 .20
65 Goblin War Drums v2 C :R: .15 .40
66 Goblin War Drums v3 C :R: .15 .40
67 Goblin War Drums v4 C :R: .08 .20
68 Goblin Warrens U :R: 1.00 2.00
69 Hand of Justice U :W: .25 .60
70 Havenwood Battleground U :L: .50 1.00
71 Heroism U :W: .15 .40
72 High Tide v1 C :B: .30 .75
73 High Tide v2 C :B: .30 .75
74 High Tide v3 C :B: .30 .75
75 Hollow Trees U :L: .30 .75
76 Homarid v1 C :B: .08 .20
77 Homarid v2 C :B: .08 .20
78 Homarid v3 C :B: .08 .20
79 Homarid v4 C :B: .08 .20
80 Homarid Shaman U :B: .25 .60
81 Homarid Spawning Bed U :B: .15 .40
82 Homarid Warrior v1 C :B: .08 .20
83 Homarid Warrior v2 C :B: .08 .20
84 Homarid Warrior v3 C :B: .08 .20
85 Hymn to Tourach v1 C :K: .60 1.50
86 Hymn to Tourach v2 C :K: .40 1.00
87 Hymn to Tourach v3 C :K: .50 1.25
88 Hymn to Tourach v4 C :K: .50 1.25
89 Icatian Infantry v1 C :W: .08 .20
90 Icatian Infantry v2 C :W: .08 .20
91 Icatian Infantry v3 C :W: .08 .20
92 Icatian Infantry v4 C :W: .08 .20
93 Icatian Javelineers v1 C :W: .15 .40
94 Icatian Javelineers v2 C :W: .08 .20
95 Icatian Javelineers v3 C :W: .15 .40
96 Icatian Lieutenant U :W: .25 .60
97 Icatian Moneychanger v1 C :W: .08 .20
98 Icatian Moneychanger v2 C :W: .15 .40
99 Icatian Moneychanger v3 C :W: .08 .20
100 Icatian Phalanx U :W: .15 .40
101 Icatian Priest U :W: .15 .40
102 Icatian Scout v1 C :W: .08 .20
103 Icatian Scout v2 C :W: .08 .20
104 Icatian Scout v3 C :W: .08 .20
105 Icatian Scout v4 C :W: .08 .20
106 Icatian Skirmishers U :W: .25 .60
107 Icatian Store U :L: .25 .60
108 Icatian Town U :W: .25 .60
109 Implements of Sacrifice U :A: .25 .60
110 Initiates of the Ebon Hand v1 C :K: .08 .20
111 Initiates of the Ebon Hand v2 C :K: .08 .20
112 Initiates of the Ebon Hand v3 C :K: .08 .20
113 Merseine v1 C :B: .08 .20
114 Merseine v2 C :B: .08 .20
115 Merseine v3 C :B: .08 .20
116 Merseine v4 C :B: .08 .20
117 Mindstab Thrull v1 C :K: .08 .20
118 Mindstab Thrull v2 C :K: .08 .20
119 Mindstab Thrull v3 C :K: .08 .20
120 Necrite v1 C :K: .08 .20
121 Necrite v2 C :K: .08 .20
122 Necrite v3 C :K: .08 .20
123 Night Soil v1 C :G: .08 .20
124 Night Soil v2 C :G: .08 .20
125 Night Soil v3 C :G: .08 .20
126 Orcish Captain U :R: .15 .40
127 Orcish Spy v1 C :R: .08 .20
128 Orcish Spy v2 C :R: .08 .20
129 Orcish Spy v3 C :R: .08 .20
130 Orcish Veteran v1 C :R: .08 .20
131 Orcish Veteran v2 C :R: .08 .20
132 Orcish Veteran v3 C :R: .08 .20
133 Orcish Veteran v4 C :R: .08 .20
134 Order of Leitbur v1 C :W: .15 .40
135 Order of Leitbur v2 C :W: .08 .20
136 Order of Leitbur v3 C :W: .15 .40
137 Order of the Ebon Hand v1 C :K: .08 .20
138 Order of the Ebon Hand v2 C :K: .08 .20
139 Order of the Ebon Hand v3 C :K: .15 .40
140 Orgg U :R: .25 .60
141 Raiding Party U :R: .15 .40
142 Rainbow Vale U :L: .25 .60

Card	Low	High
143 Ring of Renewal U :A:	.25	.60
144 River Merfolk U :B:	.25	.60
145 Ruins of Trokair U :L:	.15	.40
146 Sand Silos U :L:	.30	.75
147 Seasinger U :B:	.15	.40
148 Soul Exchange U :K:	.25	.60
149 Spirit Shield U :A:	.25	.60
150 Spore Cloud v1 C :G:	.15	.40
151 Spore Cloud v2 C :G:	.15	.40
152 Spore Cloud v3 C :G:	.08	.20
153 Spore Flower U :G:	.25	.60
154 Svyelunite Priest U :B:	.15	.40
155 Svyelunite Temple U :L:	.15	.40
156 Thallid v1 C :G:	.08	.20
157 Thallid v2 C :G:	.15	.40
158 Thallid v3 C :G:	.08	.20
159 Thallid v4 C :G:	.15	.40
160 Thallid Devourer U :G:	.15	.40
161 Thelonite Druid U :G:	.15	.40
162 Thelonite Monk U :G:	.25	.60
163 Thelon's Chant U :G:	.15	.40
164 Thelon's Curse U :G:	.25	.60
165 Thorn Thallid v1 C :G:	.08	.20
166 Thorn Thallid v2 C :G:	.08	.20
167 Thorn Thallid v3 C :G:	.08	.20
168 Thorn Thallid v4 C :G:	.08	.20
169 Thrull Champion U :K:	.25	.60
170 Thrull Retainer U :K:	.15	.40
171 Thrull Wizard U :K:	.15	.40
172 Tidal Flats v1 C :B:	.08	.20
173 Tidal Flats v2 C :B:	.08	.20
174 Tidal Flats v3 C :B:	.08	.20
175 Tidal Influence U :B:	.15	.40
176 Tourach's Chant U :K:	.15	.40
177 Tourach's Gate U :K:	.25	.60
178 Vodalian Knights U :B:	.25	.60
179 Vodalian Mage v1 C :B:	.08	.20
180 Vodalian Mage v2 C :B:	.08	.20
181 Vodalian Mage v3 C :B:	.08	.20
182 Vodalian Soldiers v1 C :B:	.08	.20
183 Vodalian Soldiers v2 C :B:	.08	.20
184 Vodalian Soldiers v3 C :B:	.08	.20
185 Vodalian Soldiers v4 C :B:	.08	.20
186 Vodalian War Machine U :B:	.25	.60
187 Zelyon Sword U :A:	.25	.60

1994 Magic The Gathering Summer Edition

Item	Low	High
COMPLETE SET (306)	125000.00	250000.00
BOOSTER PACK (15 CARDS)	2000.00	2200.00

RELEASED IN APRIL 1994
ALSO KNOWN AS EDGAR OR SUMMER REVISED.
WHITE BORDERS WITH 1994 COPYRIGHT DATE BEFORE ARTIST'S NAME.
PALE COLORS AND NAME OF ILLUSTRATOR AT THE BOTTOM.
NO BEVELED EDGES INSIDE THE COLORED BORDERS.

Card	Low	High
1 Air Elemental U :B:	250.00	400.00
2 Aladdin's Lamp R :A:	800.00	1000.00
3 Aladdin's Ring R :A:	800.00	1000.00
4 Animate Artifact U :B:	150.00	300.00
5 Animate Dead U :K:	400.00	600.00
6 Animate Wall R :W:	800.00	1000.00
7 Ankh of Mishra R :A:	950.00	1200.00
8 Armageddon Clock R :A:	550.00	800.00
9 Armageddon R :W:	1750.00	2000.00
10 Aspect of Wolf R :G:	550.00	800.00
11 Atog C :R:	100.00	200.00
12 Bad Moon R :K:	850.00	1100.00
13 Badlands R :L:	2500.00	3000.00
14 Balance R :W:	2000.00	2500.00
15 Basalt Monolith U :A:	500.00	750.00
16 Bayou R :L:	2350.00	2800.00
17 Benalish Hero C :W:	120.00	250.00
18 Birds of Paradise R :G:	3300.00	3800.00
19 Black Knight U :K:	400.00	600.00
20 Black Vise U :A:	1450.00	1700.00
21 Black Ward U :W:	100.00	200.00
22 Blessing R :W:	750.00	950.00
23 Blue Elemental Blast C :B:	100.00	200.00
24 Blue Ward U :W:	150.00	300.00
25 Bog Wraith U :K:	120.00	250.00
26 Bottle of Suleiman R :A:	800.00	1000.00
27 Braingeyser R :B:	1750.00	2000.00
28 Brass Man U :A:	150.00	300.00
29 Burrowing U :R:	100.00	200.00
30 Castle U :W:	120.00	250.00
31 Celestial Prism U :A:	120.00	250.00
32 Channel U :G:	550.00	800.00
33 Chaoslace R :R:	550.00	800.00
34 Circle of Protection Black C :W:	150.00	300.00
35 Circle of Protection Blue C :W:	100.00	200.00
36 Circle of Protection Green C :W:	100.00	200.00
37 Circle of Protection Red C :W:	300.00	450.00
38 Circle of Protection White C :W:	100.00	200.00
39 Clockwork Beast R :A:	850.00	1100.00
40 Clone U :B:	550.00	800.00
41 Cockatrice R :G:	800.00	1000.00
42 Conservator U :A:	100.00	200.00
43 Contract from Below R :K:	1400.00	1600.00
44 Control Magic U :B:	550.00	800.00
45 Conversion U :W:	150.00	300.00
46 Copy Artifact R :B:	950.00	1200.00
47 Counterspell U :B:	1850.00	2200.00
48 Craw Wurm C :G:	120.00	250.00
49 Creature Bond C :B:	80.00	150.00
50 Crumble U :G:	200.00	350.00
51 Crusade R :W:	1000.00	1250.00
52 Crystal Rod U :A:	200.00	350.00
53 Cursed Land U :K:	150.00	300.00
54 Dancing Scimitar R :A:	800.00	1000.00
55 Dark Ritual C :K:	800.00	1000.00
56 Darkpact R :K:	550.00	800.00
57 Death Ward C :W:	120.00	250.00
58 Deathgrip U :K:	150.00	300.00
59 Deathlace R :K:	800.00	1000.00
60 Demonic Attorney R :K:	750.00	950.00
61 Demonic Hordes R :K:	1400.00	1600.00
62 Demonic Tutor U :K:	2700.00	3400.00
63 Desert Twister U :G:	150.00	300.00
64 Dingus Egg R :A:	700.00	900.00
65 Disenchant C :W:	400.00	600.00
66 Disintegrate C :R:	250.00	400.00
67 Disrupting Scepter R :A:	800.00	1000.00
68 Dragon Engine R :A:	950.00	1200.00
69 Dragon Whelp U :R:	250.00	400.00
70 Drain Life C :K:	350.00	500.00
71 Drain Power R :B:	550.00	800.00
72 Drudge Skeletons C :K:	100.00	200.00
73 Dwarven Warriors C :R:	100.00	200.00
74 Dwarven Weaponsmith U :R:	100.00	200.00
75 Earth Elemental U :R:	120.00	250.00
76 Earthbind C :R:	80.00	150.00
77 Earthquake R :R:	850.00	1100.00
78 Ebony Horse R :A:	800.00	1000.00
79 El-Hajjaj R :K:	550.00	800.00
80 Elvish Archers R :G:	800.00	1000.00
81 Energy Flux U :B:	150.00	300.00
82 Erg Raiders C :K:	100.00	200.00
83 Evil Presence U :K:	150.00	300.00
84 Eye for an Eye R :W:	850.00	1100.00
85 Farmstead R :W:	800.00	1000.00
86 Fastbond R :G:	1900.00	2300.00
87 Fear C :K:	100.00	200.00
88 Feedback U :B:	150.00	300.00
89 Fire Elemental U :R:	120.00	250.00
90 Fireball C :R:	250.00	400.00
91 Firebreathing C :R:	80.00	150.00
92 Flashfires U :R:	120.00	250.00
93 Flight C :B:	80.00	150.00
94 Flying Carpet R :A:	550.00	800.00
95 Fog C :G:	80.00	150.00
96 Force of Nature R :G:	950.00	1200.00
97 Forest v1 C :L:	250.00	400.00
98 Forest v2 C :L:	250.00	400.00
99 Forest v3 C :L:	250.00	400.00
100 Fork R :R:	2000.00	2500.00
101 Frozen Shade C :K:	100.00	200.00
102 Fungusaur R :G:	450.00	700.00
103 Gaea's Liege R :G:	450.00	700.00
104 Giant Growth C :G:	250.00	400.00
105 Giant Spider C :G:	80.00	150.00
106 Glasses of Urza U :A:	120.00	250.00
107 Gloom U :K:	250.00	400.00
108 Goblin Balloon Brigade U :R:	150.00	300.00
109 Goblin King R :R:	950.00	1200.00
110 Granite Gargoyle R :R:	700.00	900.00
111 Gray Ogre C :R:	100.00	200.00
112 Green Ward U :W:	120.00	250.00
113 Grizzly Bears C :G:	100.00	200.00
114 Guardian Angel C :W:	100.00	200.00
115 Healing Salve C :W:	100.00	200.00
116 Helm of Chatzuk R :A:	550.00	800.00
117 Hill Giant C :R:	80.00	150.00
118 Hive, The R :A:	300.00	450.00
119 Holy Armor C :W:	100.00	200.00
120 Holy Strength C :W:	100.00	200.00
121 Howl from Beyond C :K:	100.00	200.00
122 Howling Mine R :A:	1200.00	1400.00
123 Hurkyl's Recall R :B:	1750.00	2000.00
124 Hurloon Minotaur C :R:	100.00	200.00
125 Hurricane U :G:	6500.00	8000.00
126 Hypnotic Specter U :K:	1100.00	1300.00
127 Instill Energy U :G:	150.00	300.00
128 Iron Star U :A:	150.00	300.00
129 Ironroot Treefolk C :G:	80.00	150.00
130 Island Fish Jasconius R :B:	800.00	1000.00
131 Island Sanctuary R :W:	700.00	900.00
132 Island v1 C :L:	400.00	600.00
133 Island v2 C :L:	400.00	600.00
134 Island v3 C :L:	400.00	600.00
135 Ivory Cup U :A:	150.00	300.00
136 Ivory Tower R :A:	950.00	1200.00
137 Jade Monolith R :A:	950.00	1200.00
138 Jandor's Ring R :A:	950.00	1200.00
139 Jandor's Saddlebags R :A:	950.00	1200.00
140 Jayemdae Tome R :A:	950.00	1200.00
141 Juggernaut U :A:	250.00	400.00
142 Jump C :B:	80.00	150.00
143 Karma U :W:	150.00	300.00
144 Keldon Warlord U :R:	150.00	300.00
145 Kird Ape C :R:	450.00	700.00
146 Kormus Bell R :A:	550.00	800.00
147 Kudzu R :G:	350.00	500.00
148 Lance U :W:	120.00	250.00
149 Ley Druid U :G:	150.00	300.00
150 Library of Leng U :A:	120.00	250.00
151 Lifeforce U :G:	120.00	250.00
152 Lifelace R :G:	800.00	1000.00
153 Lifetap U :B:	150.00	300.00
154 Lightning Bolt C :R:	800.00	1000.00
155 Living Artifact R :G:	800.00	1000.00
156 Living Lands R :G:	800.00	1000.00
157 Living Wall U :A:	120.00	250.00
158 Llanowar Elves C :G:	550.00	800.00
159 Lord of Atlantis R :B:	1400.00	1600.00
160 Lord of the Pit R :K:	1400.00	1600.00
161 Lure U :G:	150.00	300.00
162 Magical Hack R :B:	800.00	1000.00
163 Magnetic Mountain R :R:	800.00	1000.00
164 Mahamoti Djinn R :B:	1300.00	1500.00
165 Mana Flare R :R:	1300.00	1500.00
166 Mana Short R :B:	1300.00	1500.00
167 Mana Vault R :A:	4600.00	5000.00
168 Manabarbs R :R:	550.00	800.00
169 Meekstone R :A:	550.00	800.00
170 Merfolk of the Pearl Trident C :B:	100.00	200.00
171 Mesa Pegasus C :W:	100.00	200.00
172 Mijae Djinn R :R:	550.00	800.00
173 Millstone R :A:	1200.00	1400.00
174 Mind Twist R :K:	4100.00	4500.00
175 Mishra's War Machine R :A:	800.00	1000.00
176 Mons's Goblin Raiders C :R:	100.00	200.00
177 Mountain v1 C :L:	200.00	350.00
178 Mountain v2 C :L:	200.00	350.00
179 Mountain v3 C :L:	200.00	350.00
180 Nether Shadow R :K:	950.00	1200.00
181 Nettling Imp U :K:	120.00	250.00
182 Nevinyrral's Disk R :A:	1500.00	1800.00
183 Nightmare R :K:	1450.00	1750.00
184 Northern Paladin R :W:	550.00	800.00
185 Obsianus Golem U :A:	150.00	300.00
186 Onulet R :A:	850.00	1100.00
187 Orcish Artillery U :R:	150.00	300.00
188 Orcish Oriflamme U :R:	200.00	350.00
189 Ornithopter U :A:	350.00	500.00
190 Paralyze C :K:	100.00	200.00
191 Pearled Unicorn C :W:	100.00	200.00
192 Personal Incarnation R :W:	800.00	1000.00
193 Pestilence C :K:	100.00	200.00
194 Phantasmal Forces U :B:	150.00	300.00
195 Phantasmal Terrain C :B:	80.00	150.00
196 Phantom Monster U :B:	120.00	250.00
197 Pirate Ship R :B:	800.00	1000.00
198 Plague Rats C :K:	100.00	200.00
199 Plains v1 C :L:	250.00	400.00
200 Plains v2 C :L:	250.00	400.00
201 Plains v3 C :L:	250.00	400.00
202 Plateau R :L:	2600.00	3200.00
203 Power Leak C :B:	80.00	150.00
204 Power Sink C :B:	80.00	150.00
205 Power Surge R :R:	550.00	800.00
206 Primal Clay R :A:	800.00	1000.00
207 Prodigal Sorcerer C :B:	100.00	200.00
208 Psychic Venom C :B:	100.00	200.00
209 Purelace R :W:	950.00	1200.00
210 Rack, The U :A:	80.00	1000.00
211 Raise Dead C :K:	100.00	200.00
212 Reconstruction C :B:	100.00	200.00
213 Red Elemental Blast C :R:	350.00	500.00
214 Red Ward U :W:	150.00	300.00
215 Regeneration C :G:	100.00	200.00
216 Regrowth U :G:	1450.00	1750.00
217 Resurrection U :W:	350.00	500.00
218 Reverse Damage R :W:	800.00	1000.00
219 Reverse Polarity U :W:	150.00	300.00
220 Righteousness R :W:	800.00	1000.00
221 Roc of Kher Ridges R :R:	800.00	1000.00
222 Rock Hydra R :R:	800.00	1000.00
223 Rocket Launcher R :A:	550.00	800.00
224 Rod of Ruin U :A:	120.00	250.00
225 Royal Assassin R :K:	1800.00	2100.00
226 Sacrifice U :K:	150.00	300.00
227 Samite Healer C :W:	100.00	200.00
228 Savannah Lions R :W:	1550.00	1900.00
229 Savannah R :L:	2600.00	3200.00
230 Scathe Zombies C :K:	100.00	200.00
231 Scavenging Ghoul U :K:	150.00	300.00
232 Scrubland R :L:	2500.00	3000.00
233 Scryb Sprites C :G:	80.00	150.00
234 Sea Serpent C :B:	80.00	150.00
235 Sedge Troll R :R:	550.00	800.00
236 Sengir Vampire U :K:	700.00	900.00
237 Serendib Efreet R :B:	9000.00	12000.00
238 Serra Angel U :W:	2000.00	2500.00
239 Shanodin Dryads C :G:	100.00	200.00
240 Shatter C :R:	100.00	200.00
241 Shatterstorm U :R:	350.00	500.00
242 Shivan Dragon R :R:	5400.00	6000.00
243 Simulacrum U :K:	150.00	300.00
244 Siren's Call U :B:	150.00	300.00
245 Sleight of Mind R :B:	550.00	800.00
246 Smoke R :R:	550.00	800.00
247 Sol Ring U :A:	2350.00	2800.00
248 Sorceress Queen R :K:	550.00	800.00
249 Soul Net U :A:	150.00	300.00
250 Spell Blast C :B:	100.00	200.00
251 Stasis R :B:	1450.00	1700.00
252 Steal Artifact U :B:	150.00	300.00
253 Stone Giant U :R:	150.00	300.00
254 Stone Rain C :R:	350.00	500.00
255 Stream of Life C :G:	100.00	200.00
256 Sunglasses of Urza R :A:	550.00	800.00
257 Swamp v1 C :L:	300.00	450.00
258 Swamp v2 C :L:	300.00	450.00
259 Swamp v3 C :L:	300.00	450.00
260 Swords to Plowshares U :W:	1750.00	2000.00
261 Taiga R :L:	2350.00	2800.00
262 Terror C :K:	350.00	500.00
263 Thicket Basilisk U :G:	150.00	300.00
264 Thoughtlace R :B:	800.00	1000.00
265 Throne of Bone U :A:	150.00	300.00
266 Timber Wolves R :G:	800.00	1000.00
267 Titania's Song R :G:	800.00	1000.00
268 Tranquility C :G:	100.00	200.00
269 Tropical Island R :L:	3600.00	4000.00
270 Tsunami U :G:	150.00	300.00
271 Tundra R :L:	4100.00	4500.00
272 Tunnel U :R:	150.00	300.00
273 Underground Sea R :L:	7500.00	10000.00
274 Unholy Strength C :K:	150.00	300.00
275 Unstable Mutation C :B:	100.00	200.00
276 Unsummon C :B:	150.00	300.00
277 Uthden Troll U :R:	150.00	300.00
278 Verduran Enchantress R :G:	800.00	1000.00
279 Vesuvan Doppelganger R :B:	2500.00	3000.00
280 Veteran Bodyguard R :W:	800.00	1000.00
281 Volcanic Eruption R :B:	800.00	1000.00
282 Volcanic Island R :L:	6000.00	6500.00
283 Wall of Air U :B:	150.00	300.00
284 Wall of Bone U :K:	150.00	300.00
285 Wall of Brambles U :G:	150.00	300.00
286 Wall of Fire U :R:	150.00	300.00
287 Wall of Ice U :G:	150.00	300.00
288 Wall of Stone U :R:	150.00	300.00
289 Wall of Swords U :W:	150.00	300.00
290 Wall of Water U :B:	150.00	300.00
291 Wall of Wood C :G:	100.00	200.00
292 Wanderlust U :G:	150.00	300.00
293 War Mammoth C :G:	100.00	200.00
294 Warp Artifact R :K:	550.00	800.00
295 Water Elemental U :B:	150.00	300.00
296 Weakness C :K:	100.00	200.00
297 Web R :G:	350.00	500.00
298 Wheel of Fortune R :R:	2500.00	3000.00
299 White Knight U :W:	350.00	500.00
300 White Ward U :W:	150.00	300.00
301 Wild Growth C :G:	150.00	300.00
302 Will-O'-The-Wisp R :K:	1300.00	1500.00
303 Winter Orb R :A:	1300.00	1500.00
304 Wooden Sphere U :A:	150.00	300.00
305 Wrath of God R :W:	2500.00	3000.00
306 Zombie Master R :K:	800.00	1000.00

1995 Magic The Gathering 4th Edition

Item	Low	High
COMPLETE SET (378)	80.00	150.00
BOOSTER BOX (36 PACKS)	175.00	225.00
BOOSTER PACK (15 CARDS)	5.00	7.00
STARTER DECK BOX (10 DECKS)	100.00	150.00
STARTER DECK	13.00	17.00

*ALT: 1.2X TO 3X BASIC CARDS
RELEASED ON APRIL 15, 1995
WHITE BORDERS AND A 1995 COPYRIGHT DATE

Card	Low	High
1 Abomination U :K:	.15	.40
2 Air Elemental U :B:	.15	.40
3 Alabaster Potion C :W:	.08	.20
4 Aladdin's Lamp R :A:	.25	.60
5 Aladdin's Ring R :A:	.25	.60
6 Ali Baba U :R:	.15	.40
7 Amrou Kithkin C :W:	.08	.20
8 Amulet of Kroog C :A:	.08	.20
9 Angry Mob U :W:	.15	.40
10 Animate Artifact U :B:	.15	.40
11 Animate Dead U :K:	.40	1.00
12 Animate Wall R :W:	.25	.60
13 Ankh of Mishra R :A:	.25	.60
14 Apprentice Wizard C :B:	.08	.20
15 Armageddon R :W:	1.00	2.50
16 Armageddon Clock R :A:	.25	.60
17 Ashes to Ashes U :K:	.15	.40
18 Ashnod's Battle Gear U :A:	.15	.40
19 Aspect of Wolf R :G:	.25	.60
20 Backfire U :B:	.15	.40
21 Bad Moon R :K:	.60	1.50
22 Balance R :W:	.60	1.50
23 Ball Lightning R :R:	.75	2.00
24 Battering Ram C :A:	.08	.20
25 Benalish Hero C :W:	.08	.20
26 Bird Maiden C :R:	.08	.20
27 Birds of Paradise R :G:	1.50	4.00
28 Black Knight U :K:	.15	.40
29 Black Mana Battery R :A:	.25	.60
30 Black Vise U :A:	.25	.60
31 Black Ward U :W:	.15	.40
32 Blessing R :W:	.25	.60
33 Blight U :K:	.25	.60
34 Blood Lust C :R:	.08	.20
35 Blue Elemental Blast C :B:	.15	.40
36 Blue Mana Battery R :A:	.25	.60
37 Blue Ward U :W:	.15	.40
38 Bog Imp C :K:	.08	.20
39 Bog Wraith U :K:	.15	.40
40 Bottle of Suleiman R :A:	.25	.60
41 Brainwash C :W:	.08	.20
42 Brass Man U :A:	.15	.40
43 Bronze Tablet R :A:	.25	.60
44 Brothers of Fire C :R:	.08	.20
45 Brute, The C :R:	.08	.20
46 Burrowing U :R:	.15	.40
47 Carnivorous Plant C :G:	.08	.20
48 Carrion Ants U :K:	.15	.40
49 Castle U :W:	.15	.40
50 Cave People U :R:	.15	.40
51 Celestial Prism U :A:	.15	.40
52 Channel U :G:	1.00	2.00
53 Chaoslace R :R:	.25	.60
54 Circle of Protection Artifacts U :W:	.50	1.00
55 Circle of Protection Black C :W:	.08	.20
56 Circle of Protection Blue C :W:	.08	.20
57 Circle of Protection Green C :W:	.15	.40
58 Circle of Protection Red C :W:	.08	.20
59 Circle of Protection: White C :W:	.08	.20
60 Clay Statue C :A:	.08	.20
61 Clockwork Avian R :A:	.25	.60
62 Clockwork Beast R :A:	1.00	2.00
63 Cockatrice R :G:	.25	.60
64 Colossus of Sardia R :A:	1.50	3.00
65 Conservator U :A:	.15	.40
66 Control Magic U :B:	.25	.60
67 Conversion U :W:	.15	.40
68 Coral Helm R :A:	.25	.60
69 Cosmic Horror R :K:	.25	.60
70 Counterspell U :B:	.40	1.00
71 Craw Wurm C :G:	.08	.20
72 Creature Bond C :B:	.08	.20
73 Crimson Manticore R :R:	.25	.60
74 Crumble U :G:	.15	.40
75 Crusade R :W:	.40	1.00
76 Crystal Rod U :A:	.15	.40
77 Cursed Land U :K:	.15	.40
78 Cursed Rack U :A:	.15	.40
79 Cyclopean Mummy C :K:	.08	.20
80 Dancing Scimitar R :A:	.25	.60
81 Dark Ritual C :K:	.30	.75
82 Death Ward C :W:	.08	.20
83 Deathgrip U :K:	.15	.40
84 Deathlace R :K:	.25	.60
85 Desert Twister U :G:	.15	.40
86 Detonate U :R:	.15	.40
87 Diabolic Machine U :A:	.15	.40
88 Dingus Egg R :A:	.25	.60
89 Disenchant C :W:	.15	.40
90 Disintegrate C :R:	.15	.30
91 Disrupting Scepter R :A:	.25	.60
92 Divine Transformation U :W:	.15	.40
93 Dragon Engine R :A:	.25	.60
94 Dragon Whelp U :R:	.15	.40
95 Drain Life C :K:	.08	.20
96 Drain Power R :B:	.25	.60
97 Drudge Skeletons C :K:	.08	.20
98 Durkwood Boars C :G:	.08	.20
99 Dwarven Warriors C :R:	.08	.20
100 Earth Elemental U :R:	.25	.50
101 Earthquake R :R:	.25	.60
102 Ebony Horse R :A:	.25	.60
103 Elder Land Wurm R :W:	.25	.60
104 El-Hajjaj R :K:	.25	.60
105 Elven Riders U :G:	.25	.50
106 Elvish Archers R :G:	.25	.60
107 Energy Flux U :B:	.15	.40
108 Energy Tap C :B:	.08	.20
109 Erg Raiders C :K:	.08	.20
110 Erosion C :B:	.08	.20
111 Eternal Warrior C :R:	.08	.20
112 Evil Presence U :K:	.25	.50
113 Eye for an Eye R :W:	.25	.60
114 Fear C :K:	.08	.20
115 Feedback U :B:	.15	.40
116 Fellwar Stone U :A:	.25	.60
117 Fire Elemental U :R:	.15	.40
118 Fireball C :R:	.15	.40
119 Firebreathing C :R:	.08	.20
120 Fissure C :R:	.08	.20
121 Flashfires U :R:	.25	.50
122 Flight C :B:	.08	.20
123 Flood C :B:	.08	.20
124 Flying Carpet R :A:	.25	.60
125 Fog C :G:	.08	.20
126 Force of Nature R :G:	2.00	4.00
127 Forest v1 C :L:	.25	.60
128 Forest v2 C :L:	.25	.60
129 Forest v3 C :L:	.15	.40
130 Fortified Area C :W:	.08	.20
131 Frozen Shade C :K:	.08	.20
132 Fungusaur R :G:	.25	.60
133 Gaea's Liege R :G:	1.00	2.00
134 Gaseous Form C :B:	.08	.20
135 Ghost Ship U :B:	.15	.40
136 Giant Growth C :G:	.08	.20
137 Giant Spider C :G:	.08	.20
138 Giant Strength C :R:	.08	.20
139 Giant Tortoise C :B:	.08	.20
140 Glasses of Urza U :A:	.15	.40
141 Gloom U :K:	.15	.40
142 Goblin Balloon Brigade U :R:	.50	1.00
143 Goblin King R :R:	.40	1.00
144 Goblin Rock Sled C :R:	.08	.20
145 Grapeshot Catapult C :A:	.08	.20
146 Gray Ogre C :R:	.08	.20
147 Greed R :K:	.25	.60
148 Green Mana Battery R :A:	1.50	3.00
149 Green Ward U :W:	.15	.40
150 Grizzly Bears C :G:	.08	.20
151 Healing Salve C :W:	.08	.20
152 Helm of Chatzuk R :A:	.25	.60
153 Hill Giant C :R:	.08	.20
154 Hive, The R :A:	.25	.60
155 Holy Armor C :W:	.08	.20
156 Holy Strength C :W:	.08	.20
157 Howl from Beyond C :K:	.08	.20
158 Howling Mine R :A:	.75	2.00
159 Hurkyl's Recall R :B:	2.00	5.00
160 Hurloon Minotaur C :R:	.08	.20
161 Hurr Jackal R :R:	.25	.60
162 Hurricane U :G:	.15	.40
163 Hypnotic Specter U :K:	.30	.75
164 Immolation C :R:	.08	.20
165 Inferno R :R:	1.50	3.00
166 Instill Energy U :G:	.50	1.00
167 Iron Star U :A:	.15	.40
168 Ironclaw Orcs C :R:	.08	.20
169 Ironroot Treefolk C :G:	.15	.30
170 Island v1 C :L:	.25	.60
171 Island v2 C :L:	.25	.60
172 Island v3 C :L:	.15	.40
173 Island Fish Jasconius R :B:	.25	.60
174 Island Sanctuary R :W:	.25	.60
175 Ivory Cup U :A:	.15	.40
176 Ivory Tower R :A:	.60	1.50
177 Jade Monolith R :A:	.25	.60
178 Jandor's Saddlebags R :A:	1.00	2.00
179 Jayemdae Tome R :A:	.25	.60
180 Jump C :B:	.08	.20
181 Junún Efreet U :K:	.25	.50
182 Karma U :W:	.15	.40
183 Keldon Warlord U :R:	.15	.40
184 Killer Bees U :G:	.25	.60
185 Kismet U :W:	.15	.40
186 Kormus Bell R :A:	.25	.60
187 Land Leeches C :G:	.08	.20
188 Land Tax R :W:	6.00	12.00
189 Leviathan R :B:	1.50	3.00
190 Ley Druid U :G:	.15	.40
191 Library of Leng U :A:	.25	.60
192 Lifeforce U :G:	.15	.40
193 Lifelace R :G:	1.00	2.00
194 Lifetap U :B:	.25	.50
195 Lightning Bolt C :R:	.60	1.50
196 Living Artifact R :G:	.25	.60
197 Living Lands R :G:	1.00	2.00
198 Llanowar Elves C :G:	.15	.40
199 Lord of Atlantis R :B:	1.50	4.00
200 Lord of the Pit R :K:	.25	.60
201 Lost Soul C :K:	.08	.20
202 Lure U :G:	.25	.50
203 Magical Hack R :B:	.25	.60
204 Magnetic Mountain R :R:	.25	.60
205 Mahamoti Djinn R :B:	1.50	3.00
206 Mana Clash R :R:	.25	.60
207 Mana Flare R :R:	.75	2.00
208 Mana Short R :B:	.30	.75
209 Mana Vault R :A:	2.50	6.00
210 Manabarbs R :R:	1.00	2.00
211 Marsh Gas C :K:	.15	.30
212 Marsh Viper C :G:	.08	.20
213 Meekstone R :A:	.60	1.50
214 Merfolk of the Pearl Trident C :B:	.15	.30
215 Mesa Pegasus C :W:	.08	.20
216 Millstone R :A:	.25	.60
217 Mind Bomb U :B:	.25	.50
218 Mind Twist R :K:	1.25	3.00
219 Mishra's Factory U :L:	.60	1.50
220 Mishra's War Machine R :A:	.25	.60
221 Mons's Goblin Raiders C :R:	.08	.20
222 Morale C :W:	.08	.20
223 Mountain v1 C :L:	.25	.60
224 Mountain v2 C :L:	.25	.60
225 Mountain v3 C :L:	.15	.40
226 Murk Dwellers C :K:	.15	.30
227 Nafs Asp C :G:	.08	.20
228 Nether Shadow R :K:	1.25	3.00
229 Nevinyrral's Disk R :A:	1.25	3.00
230 Nightmare R :K:	.25	.60
231 Northern Paladin R :W:	1.00	2.00
232 Oasis U :L:	.15	.40
233 Obsianus Golem U :A:	.15	.40
234 Onulet R :A:	.25	.60
235 Orcish Artillery U :R:	.15	.40
236 Orcish Oriflamme U :R:	.15	.40
237 Ornithopter U :A:	1.00	2.00
238 Osai Vultures U :W:	.15	.40
239 Paralyze C :K:	.08	.20
240 Pearled Unicorn C :W:	.08	.20
241 Personal Incarnation R :W:	.25	.60
242 Pestilence C :K:	.08	.20
243 Phantasmal Forces U :B:	.15	.40
244 Phantasmal Terrain C :B:	.08	.20
245 Phantom Monster U :B:	.15	.40

246 Piety C :W:	.15	.30
247 Pikemen C :W:	.08	.20
248 Pirate Ship R :B:	.25	.60
249 Pit Scorpion C :K:	.25	.50
250 Plague Rats C :K:	.08	.20
251 Plains (ver. 1) C :L:	.25	.60
252 Plains (ver. 2) C :L:	.25	.60
253 Plains (ver. 3) C :L:	.25	.60
254 Power Leak C :B:	.08	.20
255 Power Sink C :B:	.08	.20
256 Power Surge R :R:	.25	.60
257 Pradesh Gypsies C :G:	.08	.20
258 Primal Clay R :A:	.25	.60
259 Prodigal Sorcerer C :B:	.08	.20
260 Psionic Entity R :B:	.25	.60
261 Psychic Venom C :B:	.15	.30
262 Purelace R :W:	.25	.60
263 Pyrotechnics U :R:	.15	.40
264 Rack, The U :A:	.75	2.00
265 Radjan Spirit U :G:	.15	.40
266 Rag Man R :K:	.25	.60
267 Raise Dead C :K:	.08	.20
268 Rebirth R :G:	.25	.60
269 Red Elemental Blast C :R:	.15	.40
270 Red Mana Battery R :A:	.25	.60
271 Red Ward U :W:	.25	.50
272 Regeneration C :G:	.08	.20
273 Relic Bind R :B:	.50	1.00
274 Reverse Damage R :W:	.25	.60
275 Righteousness R :W:	.25	.60
276 Rod of Ruin U :A:	.15	.40
277 Royal Assassin R :K:	.40	1.00
278 Samite Healer C :W:	.08	.20
279 Sandstorm C :G:	.15	.30
280 Savannah Lions R :W:	.30	.75
281 Scathe Zombies C :K:	.08	.20
282 Scavenging Ghoul U :K:	.15	.40
283 Scryb Sprites C :G:	.15	.30
284 Sea Serpent C :B:	.08	.20
285 Seeker C :W:	.15	.30
286 Segovian Leviathan U :B:	.15	.40
287 Sengir Vampire U :K:	2.00	4.00
288 Serra Angel U :W:	.25	.60
289 Shanodin Dryads C :G:	.08	.20
290 Shapeshifter U :A:	.15	.40
291 Shatter C :R:	.15	.30
292 Shivan Dragon R :R:	.25	.60
293 Simulacrum U :K:	.25	.50
294 Sindbad U :B:	.15	.40
295 Siren's Call U :B:	.15	.40
296 Sisters of the Flame C :R:	.08	.20
297 Sleight of Mind R :B:	.25	.60
298 Smoke R :R:	.25	.60
299 Sorceress Queen R :K:	.25	.60
300 Soul Net U :A:	.15	.40
301 Spell Blast C :B:	.15	.30
302 Spirit Link U :W:	.15	.40
303 Spirit Shackle U :K:	.25	.50
304 Stasis R :B:	.60	1.50
305 Steal Artifact U :B:	.15	.40
306 Stone Giant U :R:	.15	.40
307 Stone Rain C :R:	.15	.30
308 Stream of Life C :G:	.08	.20
309 Strip Mine U :L:	1.50	4.00
310 Sunglasses of Urza R :A:	.25	.60
311 Sunken City C :B:	.15	.30
312 Swamp v1 C :L:	.25	.60
313 Swamp v2 C :L:	.15	.30
314 Swamp v3 C :L:	.25	.60
315 Swords to Plowshares U :W:	1.00	2.50
316 Sylvan Library R :G:	8.00	20.00
317 Tawnos's Wand U :A:	.25	.50
318 Tawnos's Weaponry U :A:	.15	.40
319 Tempest Efreet R :R:	.25	.60
320 Terror C :K:	.15	.40
321 Tetravus R :A:	1.00	2.00
322 Thicket Basilisk U :G:	.15	.40
323 Thoughtlace R :B:	.25	.60
324 Throne of Bone U :A:	.15	.40
325 Timber Wolves R :G:	.15	.30
326 Time Elemental R :B:	.25	.60
327 Titania's Song R :G:	.25	.60
328 Tranquility C :G:	.08	.20
329 Triskelion R :A:	.25	.60
330 Tsunami U :G:	.15	.40
331 Tundra Wolves C :W:	.08	.20
332 Tunnel U :R:	.15	.40
333 Twiddle C :B:	.15	.40
334 Uncle Istvan U :K:	.15	.40
335 Unholy Strength C :K:	.08	.20
336 Unstable Mutation C :B:	.08	.20
337 Unsummon C :B:	.08	.20
338 Untamed Wilds U :G:	.15	.40
339 Urza's Avenger R :A:	.25	.60
340 Uthden Troll U :R:	.15	.40
341 Vampire Bats C :K:	.08	.20
342 Venom C :G:	.08	.20
343 Verduran Enchantress R :G:	.25	.60
344 Visions U :W:	.15	.40
345 Volcanic Eruption R :B:	.25	.60
346 Wall of Air U :B:	.15	.40
347 Wall of Bone U :K:	.15	.40
348 Wall of Brambles U :G:	.15	.40
349 Wall of Dust U :R:	.15	.40
350 Wall of Fire U :R:	.15	.40
351 Wall of Ice U :G:	.15	.40
352 Wall of Spears C :A:	.08	.20
353 Wall of Stone U :R:	.15	.40
354 Wall of Swords U :W:	.15	.40
355 Wall of Water U :B:	.15	.40
356 Wall of Wood C :G:	.08	.20
357 Wanderlust U :G:	.15	.40
358 War Mammoth C :G:	.08	.20
359 Warp Artifact R :K:	.25	.60
360 Water Elemental U :B:	.15	.40
361 Weakness C :K:	.08	.20
362 Web R :G:	.25	.60
363 Whirling Dervish U :G:	.15	.40
364 White Knight U :W:	.25	.60
365 White Mana Battery R :A:	.25	.60
366 White Ward U :W:	.15	.40
367 Wild Growth C :G:	.15	.40
368 Will-O'-The-Wisp R :K:	.60	1.50
369 Winds of Change R :R:	1.00	2.50
370 Winter Blast U :G:	.15	.40
371 Winter Orb R :A:	1.25	3.00
372 Wooden Sphere U :A:	.15	.40
373 Word of Binding C :K:	.08	.20
374 Wrath of God R :W:	1.50	4.00
375 Xenic Poltergeist R :K:	.25	.60
376 Yotian Soldier C :A:	.08	.20
377 Zephyr Falcon C :B:	.08	.20
378 Zombie Master R :K:	.75	2.00

1995 Magic The Gathering Ice Age

COMPLETE SET (383)	175.00	200.00
BOOSTER BOX (36 PACKS)	175.00	190.00
BOOSTER PACK (15 CARDS)	6.00	8.00
STARTER DECK BOX (10 DECKS)	150.00	165.00
STARTER DECK	15.00	20.00
RELEASED ON JUNE 15, 1995		
1 Abyssal Specter U :K:	.50	1.00
2 Adarkar Sentinel U :A:	.50	1.00
3 Adarkar Unicorn C :W:	.15	.30
4 Adarkar Wastes R :L:	4.00	8.00
5 Aegis of the Meek R :A:	1.00	2.00
6 Aggression U :R:	.50	1.00
7 Altar of Bone R :D:	1.25	2.50
8 Amulet of Quoz R :A:	1.25	2.50
9 Anarchy U :R:	1.00	2.00
10 Arctic Foxes C :W:	.15	.30
11 Arcum's Sleigh U :A:	.25	.50
12 Arcum's Weathervane U :A:	.25	.50
13 Arcum's Whistle U :A:	.25	.50
14 Arenson's Aura C :W:	.15	.30
15 Armor of Faith C :W:	.15	.30
16 Arnjlot's Ascent C :B:	.15	.30
17 Ashen Ghoul U :K:	.50	1.00
18 Aurochs C :G:	.15	.30
19 Avalanche U :R:	.25	.50
20 Balduvian Barbarians C :R:	.15	.30
21 Balduvian Bears C :G:	.15	.30
22 Balduvian Conjurer U :B:	.50	1.00
23 Balduvian Hydra R :R:	1.50	3.00
24 Balduvian Shaman C :B:	.15	.30
25 Barbarian Guides C :R:	.15	.30
26 Barbed Sextant C :A:	.15	.30
27 Baton of Morale U :A:	.50	1.00
28 Battle Cry U :W:	.50	1.00
29 Battle Frenzy C :R:	.15	.30
30 Binding Grasp U :B:	.50	1.00
31 Black Scarab U :W:	.50	1.00
32 Blessed Wine C :W:	.15	.30
33 Blinking Spirit R :W:	2.00	4.00
34 Blizzard R :G:	1.50	3.00
35 Blue Scarab U :W:	.50	1.00
36 Bone Shaman C :R:	.15	.30
37 Brainstorm C :B:	1.00	2.00
38 Brand of Ill Omen R :R:	1.00	2.00
39 Breath of Dreams U :B:	.50	1.00
40 Brine Shaman C :K:	.15	.30
41 Brown Ouphe C :G:	.15	.30
42 Brushland R :L:	3.50	7.00
43 Burnt Offering C :K:	.15	.30
44 Call to Arms R :W:	1.00	2.00
45 Caribou Range R :W:	1.00	2.00
46 Celestial Sword R :A:	1.00	2.00
47 Centaur Archer U :D:	.50	1.00
48 Chaos Lord R :R:	1.00	2.00
49 Chaos Moon R :R:	1.00	2.00
50 Chromatic Armor R :D:	1.00	2.00
51 Chub Toad C :G:	.15	.30
52 Circle of Protection Black C :W:	.15	.30
53 Circle of Protection Blue C :W:	.15	.30
54 Circle of Protection Green C :W:	.15	.30
55 Circle of Protection Red C :W:	.15	.30
56 Circle of Protection White C :W:	.15	.30
57 Clairvoyance C :B:	.15	.30
58 Cloak of Confusion C :K:	.15	.30
59 Cold Snap U :W:	.50	1.00
60 Conquer U :R:	.50	1.00
61 Cooperation C :W:	.15	.30
62 Counterspell C :B:	1.00	2.00
63 Crown of the Ages R :A:	1.00	2.00
64 Curse of Marit Lage R :R:	1.00	2.00
65 Dance of the Dead U :K:	1.50	3.00
66 Dark Banishing C :K:	.15	.30
67 Dark Ritual C :K:	.50	1.00
68 Death Ward C :W:	.15	.30
69 Deflection R :B:	1.50	3.00
70 Demonic Consultation U :K:	1.00	2.00
71 Despotic Scepter R :A:	1.50	3.00
72 Diabolic Vision U :D:	.50	1.00
73 Dire Wolves C :G:	.15	.30
74 Disenchant C :W:	.15	.30
75 Dread Wight R :K:	1.00	2.00
76 Dreams of the Dead U :B:	.50	1.00
77 Drift of the Dead U :K:	.50	1.00
78 Drought U :W:	.50	1.00
79 Dwarven Armory R :R:	1.00	2.00
80 Earthlink R :D:	1.00	2.00
81 Earthlore C :G:	.15	.30
82 Elder Druid R :G:	1.00	2.00
83 Elemental Augury R :D:	1.50	3.00
84 Elkin Bottle R :A:	1.00	2.00
85 Elvish Healer C :W:	.15	.30
86 Enduring Renewal R :W:	3.50	7.00
87 Energy Storm R :W:	1.50	3.00
88 Enervate C :B:	.15	.30
89 Errant Minion C :B:	.15	.30
90 Errantry C :R:	.15	.30
91 Essence Filter C :G:	.15	.30
92 Essence Flare C :B:	.15	.30
93 Essence Vortex U :D:	.25	.50
94 Fanatical Fever U :G:	.25	.50
95 Fear C :K:	.15	.30
96 Fiery Justice R :D:	1.00	2.00
97 Fire Covenant U :D:	.25	.50
98 Flame Spirit U :R:	.25	.50
99 Flare C :R:	.15	.30
100 Flooded Woodlands R :D:	1.00	2.00
101 Flow of Maggots R :K:	1.00	2.00
102 Folk of the Pines C :G:	.15	.30
103 Forbidden Lore R :G:	1.50	3.00
104 Force Void U :B:	.50	1.00
105 Forest v1 L :L:	.25	.50
106 Forest v2 L :L:	.25	.50
107 Forest v3 L :L:	.25	.50
108 Forgotten Lore U :G:	.50	1.00
109 Formation R :W:	1.50	3.00
110 Foul Familiar C :K:	.15	.30
111 Foxfire C :G:	.15	.30
112 Freyalise Supplicant U :G:	.50	1.00
113 Freyalise's Charm U :G:	.50	1.00
114 Freyalise's Winds R :G:	1.00	2.00
115 Fumarole U :D:	.50	1.00
116 Fylgja C :W:	.15	.30
117 Fyndhorn Bow U :A:	.50	1.00
118 Fyndhorn Brownie C :G:	.15	.30
119 Fyndhorn Elder U :G:	.50	1.00
120 Fyndhorn Elves C :G:	1.00	2.00
121 Fyndhorn Pollen R :G:	1.50	3.00
122 Game of Chaos R :R:	1.50	3.00
123 Gangrenous Zombies C :K:	.15	.30
124 Gaze of Pain C :K:	.15	.30
125 General Jarkeld R :W:	1.00	2.00
126 Ghostly Flame R :D:	1.50	3.00
127 Giant Growth C :G:	.15	.30
128 Giant Trap Door Spider U :D:	.50	1.00
129 Glacial Chasm U :L:	.50	1.00
130 Glacial Crevasses R :R:	1.50	3.00
131 Glacial Wall U :B:	.50	1.00
132 Glaciers R :D:	1.50	3.00
133 Goblin Lyre R :A:	1.50	3.00
134 Goblin Mutant U :R:	.50	1.00
135 Goblin Sappers C :R:	.15	.30
136 Goblin Ski Patrol C :R:	.15	.30
137 Goblin Snowman U :R:	.50	1.00
138 Gorilla Pack C :G:	.15	.30
139 Gravebind R :K:	1.50	3.00
140 Green Scarab U :W:	.50	1.00
141 Grizzled Wolverine C :R:	.15	.30
142 Hallowed Ground U :W:	.50	1.00
143 Halls of Mist R :L:	1.00	2.00
144 Heal C :W:	.15	.30
145 Hecatomb R :K:	2.00	4.00
146 Hematite Talisman U :A:	.50	1.00
147 Hipparion U :W:	.50	1.00
148 Hoar Shade C :K:	.15	.30
149 Hot Springs R :G:	1.50	3.00
150 Howl from Beyond C :K:	.15	.30
151 Hurricane U :G:	.50	1.00
152 Hyalopterous Lemure U :K:	.50	1.00
153 Hydroblast C :B:	.15	.30
154 Hymn of Rebirth U :D:	.50	1.00
155 Ice Cauldron R :A:	1.50	3.00
156 Ice Floe U :L:	.50	1.00
157 Iceberg U :B:	.50	1.00
158 Icequake U :K:	.50	1.00
159 Icy Manipulator U :A:	2.00	4.00
160 Icy Prison R :B:	1.50	3.00
161 Illusionary Forces C :B:	1.00	2.00
162 Illusionary Presence R :B:	.50	1.00
163 Illusionary Terrain U :B:	.15	.30
164 Illusionary Wall C :B:	.15	.30
165 Illusions of Grandeur R :B:	3.50	7.00
166 Imposing Visage C :R:	.15	.30
167 Incinerate C :R:	.50	1.00
168 Infernal Darkness R :K:	1.00	2.00
169 Infernal Denizen R :K:	1.00	2.00
170 Infinite Hourglass R :A:	1.00	2.00
171 Infuse C :B:	.15	.30
172 Island v1 L :L:	.25	.50
173 Island v2 L :L:	.25	.50
174 Island v3 L :L:	.25	.50
175 Jester's Cap R :A:	3.00	6.00
176 Jester's Mask R :A:	2.00	4.00
177 Jeweled Amulet U :A:	.50	1.00
178 Johtull Wurm U :G:	.50	1.00
179 Jokulhaups R :R:	2.00	4.00
180 Juniper Order Druid C :G:	.15	.30
181 Justice U :W:	.50	1.00
182 Karplusan Forest R :L:	2.50	5.00
183 Karplusan Giant U :R:	.50	1.00
184 Karplusan Yeti R :R:	1.50	3.00
185 Kelsinko Ranger C :W:	.15	.30
186 Kjeldoran Dead C :K:	.15	.30
187 Kjeldoran Elite Guard U :W:	.50	1.00
188 Kjeldoran Frostbeast U :D:	.50	1.00
189 Kjeldoran Guard C :W:	.15	.30
190 Kjeldoran Knight R :W:	1.00	2.00
191 Kjeldoran Phalanx R :W:	1.00	2.00
192 Kjeldoran Royal Guard R :W:	1.00	2.00
193 Kjeldoran Skycaptain U :W:	.50	1.00
194 Kjeldoran Skyknight C :W:	.15	.30
195 Kjeldoran Warrior C :W:	.15	.30
196 Knight of Stromgald U :K:	.50	1.00
197 Krovikan Elementalist U :K:	.50	1.00
198 Krovikan Fetish C :K:	.15	.30
199 Krovikan Sorcerer C :B:	.15	.30
200 Krovikan Vampire U :K:	1.00	2.00
201 Land Cap R :L:	1.00	2.00
202 Lapis Lazuli Talisman U :A:	.50	1.00
203 Lava Burst C :R:	.25	.50
204 Lava Tubes R :L:	1.00	2.00
205 Legions of Lim-Dûl C :K:	.15	.30
206 Leshrac's Rite U :K:	.50	1.00
207 Leshrac's Sigil U :K:	.50	1.00
208 Lhurgoyf R :G:	2.00	4.00
209 Lightning Blow R :W:	1.50	3.00
210 Lim-Dûl's Cohort C :K:	.15	.30
211 Lim-Dûl's Hex U :K:	.50	1.00
212 Lost Order of Jarkeld R :W:	1.50	3.00
213 Lure U :G:	.50	1.00
214 Maddening Wind U :G:	.50	1.00
215 Magus of the Unseen R :B:	1.00	2.00
216 Malachite Talisman U :A:	.50	1.00
217 Marton Stromgald R :R:	2.00	4.00
218 Melee U :R:	.50	1.00
219 Melting U :R:	.50	1.00
220 Mercenaries R :W:	1.00	2.00
221 Merieke Ri Berit R :D:	1.00	2.00
222 Mesmeric Trance R :B:	1.00	2.00
223 Meteor Shower C :R:	.15	.30
224 Mind Ravel C :K:	.15	.30
225 Mind Warp U :K:	.50	1.00
226 Mind Whip R :K:	1.00	2.00
227 Minion of Leshrac R :K:	1.50	3.00
228 Minion of Tevesh Szat R :K:	1.00	2.00
229 Mistfolk C :B:	.15	.30
230 Mole Worms U :K:	.50	1.00
231 Monsoon R :D:	1.50	3.00
232 Moor Fiend C :K:	.15	.30
233 Mountain v1 L :L:	.25	.50
234 Mountain v2 L :L:	.25	.50
235 Mountain v3 L :L:	.25	.50
236 Mountain Goat C :R:	.15	.30
237 Mountain Titan R :D:	1.50	3.00
238 Mudslide R :R:	1.50	3.00
239 Musician R :B:	1.50	3.00
240 Mystic Might R :B:	1.50	3.00
241 Mystic Remora C :B:	.15	.30
242 Nacre Talisman U :A:	.50	1.00
243 Naked Singularity R :A:	1.50	3.00
244 Nature's Lore U :G:	.50	1.00
245 Necropotence R :K:	3.00	6.00
246 Norritt C :K:	.15	.30
247 Oath of Lim-Dûl R :K:	1.50	3.00
248 Onyx Talisman U :A:	.50	1.00
249 Orcish Cannoneers U :R:	.50	1.00
250 Orcish Conscripts C :R:	.15	.30
251 Orcish Farmer C :R:	.15	.30
252 Orcish Healer U :R:	.50	1.00
253 Orcish Librarian R :R:	1.50	3.00
254 Orcish Lumberjack C :R:	.15	.30
255 Orcish Squatters R :R:	1.50	3.00
256 Order of the Sacred Torch R :W:	1.00	2.00
257 Order of the White Shield U :W:	.50	1.00
258 Pale Bears R :G:	1.00	2.00
259 Panic C :R:	.15	.30
260 Pentagram of the Ages R :A:	1.00	2.00
261 Pestilence Rats C :K:	.15	.30
262 Phantasmal Mount U :B:	.50	1.00
263 Pit Trap U :A:	.50	1.00
264 Plains v1 L :L:	.25	.50
265 Plains v2 L :L:	.25	.50
266 Plains v3 L7 :L:	.25	.50
267 Polar Kraken R :B:	2.00	4.00
268 Portent C :B:	.15	.30
269 Power Sink C :B:	.15	.30
270 Pox R :K:	2.00	4.00
271 Prismatic Ward C :W:	.15	.30
272 Pygmy Allosaurus R :G:	2.00	4.00
273 Pyknite C :G:	.15	.30
274 Pyroblast C :R:	.15	.30
275 Pyroclasm U :R:	1.50	3.00
276 Rally C :W:	.15	.30
277 Ray of Command C :B:	.15	.30
278 Ray of Erasure C :B:	.15	.30
279 Reality Twist R :B:	1.00	2.00
280 Reclamation R :D:	1.00	2.00
281 Red Scarab U :W:	.50	1.00
282 Regeneration C :G:	.15	.30
283 Rime Dryad C :G:	.15	.30
284 Ritual of Subdual R :G:	1.00	2.00
285 River Delta R :L:	1.00	2.00
286 Runed Arch R :A:	1.00	2.00
287 Sabretooth Tiger C :R:	.15	.30
288 Sacred Boon U :W:	.25	.50
289 Scaled Wurm C :G:	.25	.50
290 Sea Spirit U :B:	.50	1.00
291 Seizures C :K:	.15	.30
292 Seraph R :W:	2.00	4.00
293 Shambling Strider C :G:	.15	.30
294 Shatter C :R:	.15	.30
295 Shield Bearer C :W:	.15	.30
296 Shield of the Ages U :A:	.50	1.00
297 Shyft R :B:	1.00	2.00
298 Sibilant Spirit R :B:	2.00	4.00
299 Silver Erne U :B:	.50	1.00
300 Skeleton Ship R :D:	1.50	3.00
301 Skull Catapult U :A:	.50	1.00
302 Sleight of Mind U :B:	.50	1.00
303 Snow Devil C :B:	.15	.30
304 Snow Fortress R :A:	1.50	3.00
305 Snow Hound U :W:	.50	1.00
306 Snowblind R :G:	1.00	2.00
307 Snow-Covered Forest L :L:	.25	.50
308 Snow-Covered Island L :L:	.25	.50
309 Snow-Covered Mountain L :L:	.25	.50
310 Snow-Covered Plains L :L:	.25	.50
311 Snow-Covered Swamp L :L:	.50	1.00
312 Snowfall C :B:	.25	.50
313 Soldevi Golem R :A:	1.00	2.00
314 Soldevi Machinist U :B:	.50	1.00
315 Soldevi Simulacrum U :A:	.50	1.00
316 Songs of the Damned C :K:	.15	.30
317 Soul Barrier U :B:	.50	1.00
318 Soul Burn C :K:	.15	.30
319 Soul Kiss C :K:	.15	.30
320 Spectral Shield U :D:	.50	1.00
321 Spoils of Evil R :K:	1.00	2.00
322 Spoils of War R :K:	1.00	2.00
323 Staff of the Ages R :A:	1.00	2.00
324 Stampede R :G:	1.00	2.00
325 Stench of Evil U :K:	.50	1.00
326 Stone Rain C :R:	.15	.30
327 Stone Spirit U :R:	.50	1.00
328 Stonehands C :R:	.15	.30
329 Storm Spirit R :D:	1.00	2.00
330 Stormbind R :D:	2.00	4.00
331 Stromgald Cabal R :K:	1.00	2.00
332 Stunted Growth R :G:	2.00	4.00
333 Sulfurous Springs R :L:	3.50	7.00
334 Sunstone U :A:	.50	1.00
335 Swamp v1 L :L:	.25	.50
336 Swamp v2 L :L:	.25	.50
337 Swamp v3 L :L:	.25	.50
338 Swords to Plowshares U :W:	2.50	5.00
339 Tarpan C :G:	.15	.30
340 Thermokarst U :G:	1.00	2.00
341 Thoughtleech U :G:	.50	1.00
342 Thunder Wall U :B:	.50	1.00
343 Timberline Ridge R :L:	1.00	2.00
344 Time Bomb R :A:	1.50	3.00
345 Tinder Wall C :G:	.15	.30
346 Tor Giant C :R:	.15	.30
347 Total War R :R:	1.50	3.00
348 Touch of Death C :K:	.15	.30
349 Touch of Vitae U :G:	.50	1.00
350 Trailblazer R :G:	1.00	2.00
351 Underground River R :L:	2.50	5.00
352 Updraft U :B:	.50	1.00
353 Urza's Bauble U :A:	.50	1.00
354 Veldt R :L:	1.00	2.00
355 Venomous Breath U :G:	.50	1.00
356 Vertigo U :R:	.50	1.00
357 Vexing Arcanix R :A:	1.50	3.00
358 Vibrating Sphere R :A:	1.00	2.00
359 Walking Wall U :A:	.50	1.00
360 Wall of Lava U :R:	.50	1.00
361 Wall of Pine Needles U :G:	.50	1.00
362 Wall of Shields U :A:	.50	1.00
363 War Chariot U :A:	.50	1.00
364 Warning C :W:	.15	.30
365 Whalebone Glider U :A:	.50	1.00
366 White Scarab U :W:	.50	1.00
367 Whiteout U :G:	.50	1.00
368 Wiitigo R :G:	1.00	2.00
369 Wild Growth C :G:	.15	.30
370 Wind Spirit U :B:	1.00	2.00
371 Wings of Aesthir U :D:	.50	1.00
372 Winter's Chill R :B:	1.50	3.00
373 Withering Wisps U :K:	.50	1.00
374 Woolly Mammoths C :G:	.15	.30
375 Woolly Spider C :G:	.15	.30
376 Word of Blasting U :R:	.50	1.00
377 Word of Undoing C :B:	.15	.30
378 Wrath of Marit Lage R :B:	1.00	2.00
379 Yavimaya Gnats U :G:	.50	1.00
380 Zuran Enchanter C :B:	.15	.30
381 Zuran Orb U :A:	2.00	4.00
382 Zuran Spellcaster C :B:	.15	.30
383 Zur's Weirding R :B:	1.50	3.00

1995 Magic The Gathering Homelands

COMPLETE SET (140)	30.00	60.00
BOOSTER BOX (60 PACKS)	70.00	100.00
BOOSTER PACK (8 CARDS)	2.50	3.25
RELEASED IN OCTOBER 15, 1995		
1 Abbey Gargoyles U :W:	.50	1.00
2 Abbey Matron v1 C :W:	.15	.30
3 Abbey Matron v2 C :W:	.15	.30
4 AEther Storm U :B:	.25	.50
5 Aliban's Tower v1 C :R:	.15	.30
6 Aliban's Tower v2 C :R:	.15	.30
7 Ambush C :R:	.15	.30
8 Ambush Party v1 C :R:	.15	.30
9 Ambush Party v2 C :R:	.15	.30
10 Anaba Ancestor U :R:	1.00	2.00
11 Anaba Bodyguard v1 C :R:	.15	.30
12 Anaba Bodyguard v2 C :R:	.15	.30
13 Anaba Shaman v1 C :R:	.15	.30
14 Anaba Shaman v2 C :R:	.15	.30
15 Anaba Spirit Crafter U :R:	.50	1.00
16 An-Havva Constable U :G:	.50	1.00
17 An-Havva Inn U :G:	.50	1.00
18 An-Havva Township U :L:	.50	1.00
19 An-Zerrin Ruins U :R:	.50	1.00
20 Apocalypse Chime U :A:	.50	1.00
21 Autumn Willow U :G:	1.00	2.00
22 Aysen Abbey U :L:	.25	.50
23 Aysen Bureaucrats v1 C :W:	.15	.30
24 Aysen Bureaucrats v2 C :W:	.15	.30
25 Aysen Crusader U :W:	.50	1.00
26 Aysen Highway U :W:	.50	1.00
27 Baki's Curse U :B:	.50	1.00
28 Baron Sengir U :K:	5.00	10.00
29 Beast Walkers U :W:	.50	1.00
30 Black Carriage U :K:	.50	1.00
31 Broken Visage U :K:	.50	1.00
32 Carapace v1 C :G:	.15	.30
33 Carapace v2 C :G:	.15	.30
34 Castle Sengir U :L:	.50	1.00
35 Cemetery Gate v1 C :K:	.15	.30
36 Cemetery Gate v2 C :K:	.15	.30
37 Chain Stasis U :B:	.50	1.00
38 Chandler U :R:	.25	.50
39 Clockwork Gnomes C :A:	.15	.30
40 Clockwork Steed C :A:	.15	.30
41 Clockwork Swarm C :A:	.15	.30
42 Coral Reef C :B:	.15	.30
43 Dark Maze v1 C :B:	.15	.30
44 Dark Maze v2 C :B:	.15	.30
45 Daughter of Autumn U :G:	.50	1.00
46 Death Speakers U :W:	.25	.50
47 Didgeridoo U :A:	1.50	3.00
48 Drudge Spell U :K:	.50	1.00
49 Dry Spell v1 C :K:	.15	.30
50 Dry Spell v2 C :K:	.15	.30
51 Dwarven Pony U :R:	.50	1.00
52 Dwarven Sea Clan U :R:	.50	1.00
53 Dwarven Trader v1 C :R:	.15	.30
54 Dwarven Trader v2 C :R:	.15	.30
55 Ebony Rhino C :A:	.15	.30
56 Eron the Relentless U :R:	.50	1.00
57 Evaporate U :R:	.50	1.00
58 Faerie Noble U :G:	1.50	3.00
59 Feast of the Unicorn v1 C :K:	.15	.30
60 Feast of the Unicorn v2 C :K:	.15	.30
61 Feroz's Ban U :A:	.50	1.00
62 Folk of An-Havva v1 C :G:	.15	.30
63 Folk of An-Havva v2 C :G:	.15	.30
64 Forget U :B:	.50	1.00
65 Funeral March C :K:	.15	.30
66 Ghost Hounds U :K:	.25	.50
67 Giant Albatross v1 C :B:	.15	.30
68 Giant Albatross v2 C :B:	.15	.30
69 Giant Oyster U :B:	.25	.50
70 Grandmother Sengir U :K:	1.50	3.00
71 Greater Werewolf U :K:	.25	.50
72 Hazduhr the Abbot U :W:	.50	1.00
73 Headstone C :K:	.15	.30
74 Heart Wolf U :R:	.50	1.00
75 Hungry Mist v1 C :G:	.15	.30
76 Hungry Mist v2 C :G:	.15	.30
77 Ihsan's Shade U :K:	1.00	2.00
78 Irini Sengir U :K:	.50	1.00
79 Ironclaw Curse U :R:	.50	1.00
80 Jinx C :B:	.15	.30
81 Joven U :R:	.25	.50
82 Joven's Ferrets C :G:	.25	.50
83 Joven's Tools U :A:	.25	.50
84 Koskun Falls U :K:	.50	1.00
85 Koskun Keep U :L:	.25	.50
86 Labyrinth Minotaur v1 C :B:	.15	.30
87 Labyrinth Minotaur v2 C :B:	.15	.30

88 Leaping Lizard C :G: .15 .30
89 Leeches U :W: .50 1.00
90 Mammoth Harness U :G: .50 1.00
91 Marjhan U :B: .50 1.00
92 Memory Lapse v1 C :B: .15 .30
93 Memory Lapse v2 C :B: .15 .30
94 Merchant Scroll C :B: 1.50 3.00
95 Mesa Falcon v1 C :W: .15 .30
96 Mesa Falcon v2 C :W: .15 .30
97 Mystic Decree U :B: 1.00 2.00
98 Narwhal U :B: .50 1.00
99 Orcish Mine U :R: .25 .50
100 Primal Order U :G: 1.00 2.00
101 Prophecy U :W: .25 .50
102 Rashka the Slayer U :W: .25 .50
103 Reef Pirates v1 C :B: .15 .30
104 Reef Pirates v2 C :B: .15 .30
105 Renewal C :G: .15 .30
106 Retribution U :R: .25 .50
107 Reveka, Wizard Savant U :B: 1.00 2.00
108 Root Spider U :G: .25 .50
109 Roots U :G: .25 .50
110 Roterothopter C :A: .15 .30
111 Rysorian Badger U :G: .50 1.00
112 Samite Alchemist v1 C :W: .15 .30
113 Samite Alchemist v2 C :W: .15 .30
114 Sea Sprite U :B: .50 1.00
115 Sea Troll U :B: .50 1.00
116 Sengir Autocrat U :K: 1.50 3.00
117 Sengir Bats v1 C :K: .15 .30
118 Sengir Bats v2 C :K: .15 .30
119 Serra Aviary U :W: 1.00 2.00
120 Serra Bestiary U :W: .25 .50
121 Serra Inquisitors U :W: .25 .50
122 Serra Paladin C :W: .15 .30
123 Serrated Arrows C :A: .15 .30
124 Shrink v1 C :G: .15 .30
125 Shrink v2 C :G: .15 .30
126 Soraya the Falconer U :W: 1.00 2.00
127 Spectral Bears U :G: .50 1.00
128 Timmerian Fiends U :K: .50 1.00
129 Torture v1 C :K: .15 .30
130 Torture v2 C :K: .15 .30
131 Trade Caravan v1 C :W: .15 .30
132 Trade Caravan v2 C :W: .15 .30
133 Truce U :W: 1.00 2.00
134 Veldrane of Sengir U :K: 1.00 2.00
135 Wall of Kelp U :B: 1.50 3.00
136 Willow Faerie v1 C :G: .15 .30
137 Willow Faerie v2 C :G: .15 .30
138 Willow Priestess U :G: 1.50 3.00
139 Winter Sky U :R: .50 1.00
140 Wizards' School U :L: .50 1.00

1996 Magic The Gathering Alliances

COMPLETE SET (199) 120.00 130.00
BOOSTER BOX (45 PACKS) 190.00 250.00
BOOSTER PACK (12 CARDS) 5.00 8.00
RELEASED ON JUNE 10, 1996
1 Aesthir Glider v1 C :A: .15 .30
2 Aesthir Glider v2 C :A: .15 .30
3 Agent of Stromgald v1 C :R: .15 .30
4 Agent of Stromgald v2 C :R: .15 .30
5 Arcane Denial v1 C :B: 1.00 2.00
6 Arcane Denial v2 C :B: 1.00 2.00
7 Ashnod's Cylix R :A: 1.00 2.00
8 Astrolabe v1 C :A: .15 .30
9 Astrolabe v2 C :A: .15 .30
10 Awesome Presence v1 C :B: .15 .30
11 Awesome Presence v2 C :B: .15 .30
12 Balduvian Dead U :K: .25 .50
13 Balduvian Horde R :R: 2.50 5.00
14 Balduvian Trading Post R :L: 1.50 3.00
15 Balduvian War-Makers v1 C :R: .15 .30
16 Balduvian War-Makers v2 C :R: .15 .30
17 Benthic Explorers v1 C :B: .15 .30
18 Benthic Explorers v2 C :B: .15 .30
19 Bestial Fury v1 C :R: .15 .30
20 Bestial Fury v2 C :R: .15 .30
21 Bounty of the Hunt U :G: .50 1.00
22 Browse U :B: .50 1.00
23 Burnout U :R: .50 1.00
24 Carrier Pigeons v1 C :W: .15 .30
25 Carrier Pigeons v2 C :W: .15 .30
26 Casting of Bones v1 C :K: .15 .30
27 Casting of Bones v2 C :K: .15 .30
28 Chaos Harlequin R :R: 1.00 2.00
29 Contagion U :K: 1.00 2.00
30 Deadly Insect v1 U :G: .25 .50
31 Deadly Insect v2 U :G: .25 .50
32 Death Spark U :R: .25 .50
33 Diminishing Returns R :B: 1.50 3.00
34 Diseased Vermin U :K: .50 1.00
35 Dystopia R :K: 1.00 2.00
36 Elvish Bard U :G: .25 .50
37 Elvish Ranger v1 C :G: .15 .30
38 Elvish Ranger v2 C :G: .15 .30
39 Elvish Spirit Guide U :G: 3.00 6.00
40 Energy Arc U :D: .25 .50
41 Enslaved Scout v1 C :R: .15 .30
42 Enslaved Scout v2 C :R: .15 .30
43 Errand of Duty v1 C :W: .15 .30
44 Errand of Duty v2 C :W: .15 .30
45 Exile R :W: 1.50 3.00
46 False Demise v1 U :B: .50 1.00
47 False Demise v2 U :B: .50 1.00
48 Fatal Lore R :K: 1.00 2.00
49 Feast or Famine v1 U :K: .50 1.00
50 Feast or Famine v2 U :K: .50 1.00
51 Fevered Strength v1 C :K: .15 .30
52 Fevered Strength v2 C :K: .15 .30
53 Floodwater Dam R :A: 1.00 2.00
54 Force of Will U :B: 50.00 100.00
55 Foresight v1 C :B: .15 .30
56 Foresight v2 C :B: .15 .30
57 Fyndhorn Druid v1 C :G: .15 .30
58 Fyndhorn Druid v2 C :G: .15 .30
59 Gargantuan Gorilla R :G: 1.00 2.00
60 Gift of the Woods v1 C :G: .15 .30
61 Gift of the Woods v2 C :G: .15 .30
62 Gorilla Berserkers v1 C :G: .15 .30
63 Gorilla Berserkers v2 C :G: .15 .30
64 Gorilla Chieftain v1 C :G: .15 .30
65 Gorilla Chieftain v2 C :G: .15 .30
66 Gorilla Shaman v1 U :R: .50 1.00
67 Gorilla Shaman v2 U :R: .50 1.00
68 Gorilla War Cry v1 C :R: .15 .30
69 Gorilla War Cry v2 C :R: .15 .30
70 Guerrilla Tactics v1 C :R: .15 .30
71 Guerrilla Tactics v2 C :R: .15 .30
72 Gustha's Scepter R :A: 1.50 3.00
73 Hail Storm U :G: .25 .50
74 Heart of Yavimaya R :L: 1.00 2.00
75 Helm of Obedience R :A: 1.50 3.00
76 Inheritance U :W: .25 .50
77 Insidious Bookworms v1 C :K: .15 .30
78 Insidious Bookworms v2 C :K: .15 .30
79 Ivory Gargoyle R :W: 1.50 3.00
80 Juniper Order Advocate U :W: .25 .50
81 Kaysa R :G: 1.50 3.00
82 Keeper of Tresserhorn R :K: 1.00 2.00
83 Kjeldoran Escort v1 C :W: .15 .30
84 Kjeldoran Escort v2 C :W: .15 .30
85 Kjeldoran Home Guard U :W: .50 1.00
86 Kjeldoran Outpost R :L: 3.00 6.00
87 Kjeldoran Pride v1 C :W: .15 .30
88 Kjeldoran Pride v2 C :W: .15 .30
89 Krovikan Horror R :K: 1.50 3.00
90 Krovikan Plague U :K: .25 .50
91 Lake of the Dead R :L: 4.00 8.00
92 Lat-Nam's Legacy v1 C :B: .15 .30
93 Lat-Nam's Legacy v2 C :B: .15 .30
94 Library of Lat-Nam R :B: 1.00 2.00
95 Lim-Dûl's High Guard v1 C :K: .15 .30
96 Lim-Dûl's High Guard v2 C :K: .15 .30
97 Lim-Dûl's Paladin U :D: 1.00 2.00
98 Lim-Dûl's Vault U :D: 1.00 2.00
99 Lodestone Bauble R :A: 1.00 2.00
100 Lord of Tresserhorn R :D: 1.50 3.00
101 Martyrdom v1 C :W: .15 .30
102 Martyrdom v2 C :W: .15 .30
103 Misfortune R :D: 1.00 2.00
104 Mishra's Groundbreaker U :A: .25 .50
105 Misinformation U :K: .25 .50
106 Mystic Compass U :A: .25 .50
107 Nature's Blessing U :D: .30 .75
108 Nature's Chosen U :G: .50 1.00
109 Nature's Wrath R :G: 1.50 3.00
110 Noble Steeds v1 C :W: .15 .30
111 Noble Steeds v2 C :W: .15 .30
112 Omen of Fire R :R: 1.00 2.00
113 Phantasmal Fiend v1 C :K: .15 .30
114 Phantasmal Fiend v2 C :K: .15 .30
115 Phantasmal Sphere R :B: 1.00 2.00
116 Phelddagrif R :D: 1.00 2.00
117 Phyrexian Boon v1 C :K: .15 .30
118 Phyrexian Boon v2 C :K: .15 .30
119 Phyrexian Devourer R :A: 1.00 2.00
120 Phyrexian Portal R :A: 1.00 2.00
121 Phyrexian War Beast v1 C :A: .15 .30
122 Phyrexian War Beast v2 C :A: .15 .30
123 Pillage U :R: 1.00 2.00
124 Primitive Justice U :R: .50 1.00
125 Pyrokinesis U :R: 1.00 2.00
126 Reinforcements v1 C :W: .15 .30
127 Reinforcements v2 C :W: .15 .30
128 Reprisal v1 U :W: .25 .50
129 Reprisal v2 U :W: .25 .50
130 Ritual of the Machine R :K: 1.00 2.00
131 Rogue Skycaptain R :R: 1.00 2.00
132 Royal Decree R :W: 1.00 2.00
133 Royal Herbalist v1 C :W: .15 .30
134 Royal Herbalist v2 C :W: .15 .30
135 Scarab of the Unseen U :A: .25 .50
136 Scars of the Veteran U :W: .30 .75
137 School of the Unseen U :L: .25 .50
138 Seasoned Tactician U :W: .25 .50
139 Sheltered Valley R :L: 1.00 2.00
140 Shield Sphere U :A: 1.50 3.00
141 Sol Grail R :A: 1.00 2.00
142 Soldevi Adnate v1 C :K: .15 .30
143 Soldevi Adnate v2 C :K: .15 .30
144 Soldevi Digger R :A: 1.50 3.00
145 Soldevi Excavations R :L: 1.00 2.00
146 Soldevi Heretic v1 C :B: .15 .30
147 Soldevi Heretic v2 C :B: .15 .30
148 Soldevi Sage v1 C :B: .15 .30
149 Soldevi Sage v2 C :B: .15 .30
150 Soldevi Sentry v1 C :A: .15 .30
151 Soldevi Sentry v2 C :A: .15 .30
152 Soldevi Steam Beast v1 C :A: .15 .30
153 Soldevi Steam Beast v2 C :A: .15 .30
154 Soldier of Fortune U :R: .50 1.00
155 Spiny Starfish U :B: .25 .50
156 Splintering Wind R :G: 1.00 2.00
157 Stench of Decay v1 C :K: .15 .30
158 Stench of Decay v2 C :K: .15 .30
159 Storm Cauldron R :A: 1.00 2.00
160 Storm Crow v1 C :B: .15 .30
161 Storm Crow v2 C :B: .15 .30
162 Storm Elemental U :B: .25 .50
163 Storm Shaman v1 C :R: .15 .30
164 Storm Shaman v2 C :R: .15 .30
165 Stromgald Spy U :K: .25 .50
166 Suffocation U :B: .25 .50
167 Surge of Strength U :D: .25 .50
168 Sustaining Spirit R :W: 1.00 2.00
169 Swamp Mosquito v1 C :K: .15 .30
170 Swamp Mosquito v2 C :K: .15 .30
171 Sworn Defender R :W: 1.00 2.00
172 Taste of Paradise v1 C :G: .15 .30
173 Taste of Paradise v2 C :G: .15 .30
174 Thawing Glaciers R :L: 3.50 7.00
175 Thought Lash R :B: 1.50 3.00
176 Tidal Control R :B: 1.50 3.00
177 Tornado R :G: 1.00 2.00
178 Undergrowth v1 C :G: .15 .30
179 Undergrowth v2 C :G: .15 .30
180 Unlikely Alliance U :W: .50 1.00
181 Urza's Engine R :A: 1.00 2.00
182 Varchild's Crusader v1 C :R: .15 .30
183 Varchild's Crusader v2 C :R: .15 .30
184 Varchild's War-Riders R :R: 1.50 3.00
185 Veteran's Voice v1 C :R: .15 .30
186 Veteran's Voice v2 C :R: .15 .30
187 Viscerid Armor v1 C :B: .15 .30
188 Viscerid Armor v2 C :B: .15 .30
189 Viscerid Drone U :B: .25 .50
190 Wandering Mage R :D: 1.00 2.00
191 Whip Vine v1 C :G: .15 .30
192 Whip Vine v2 C :G: .15 .30
193 Whirling Catapult R :A: 1.00 2.00
194 Wild Aesthir v1 C :W: .15 .30
195 Wild Aesthir v2 C :W: .15 .30
196 Winter's Night R :D: 1.00 2.00
197 Yavimaya Ancients v1 C :G: .15 .30
198 Yavimaya Ancients v2 C :G: .15 .30
199 Yavimaya Ants U :G: .50 1.00

1996 Magic The Gathering Mirage

COMPLETE SET (350) 110.00 150.00
BOOSTER BOX (36 PACKS) 175.00 200.00
BOOSTER PACK (15 CARDS) 7.00 9.00
STARTER DECK BOX 100.00 140.00
STARTER DECK 12.00 18.00
RELEASED ON OCTOBER 7, 1996
1 Abyssal Hunter R :K: 1.00 2.00
2 Acidic Dagger R :A: 1.00 2.00
3 Afiya Grove R :G: 1.00 2.00
4 Afterlife U :W: .25 .50
5 Agility C :R: .15 .30
6 Alarum C :W: .15 .30
7 Aleatory U :R: .25 .50
8 Amber Prison R :A: 1.00 2.00
9 Amulet of Unmaking R :A: 1.00 2.00
10 Ancestral Memories R :B: 1.00 2.00
11 Armor of Thorns C :G: .15 .30
12 Armorer Guildmage C :R: .15 .30
13 Ashen Powder R :K: 1.00 2.00
14 Asmira, Holy Avenger R :D: 1.00 2.00
15 Auspicious Ancestor R :W: 1.00 2.00
16 Azimaet Drake C :B: .15 .30
17 Bad River U :L: .50 1.00
18 Barbed Foliage U :G: .25 .50
19 Barbed-Back Wurm U :K: .25 .50
20 Barreling Attack R :R: 1.00 2.00
21 Basalt Golem U :A: .25 .50
22 Bay Falcon C :B: .15 .30
23 Bazaar of Wonders R :B: 1.00 2.00
24 Benevolent Unicorn C :W: .15 .30
25 Benthic Djinn R :D: 1.00 2.00
26 Binding Agony C :K: .15 .30
27 Blighted Shaman U :K: .25 .50
28 Blind Fury U :R: .25 .50
29 Blinding Light U :W: .25 .50
30 Blistering Barrier C :R: .15 .30
31 Bone Harvest C :K: .15 .30
32 Bone Mask R :A: 1.00 2.00
33 Boomerang C :B: .15 .30
34 Breathstealer C :K: .15 .30
35 Brushwagg R :G: 1.50 3.00
36 Builder's Bane C :R: .15 .30
37 Burning Palm Efreet U :R: .25 .50
38 Burning Shield Askari C :R: .15 .30
39 Cadaverous Bloom R :D: 2.00 4.00
40 Cadaverous Knight C :K: .50 1.00
41 Canopy Dragon R :G: 2.00 4.00
42 Carrion R :K: 1.00 2.00
43 Catacomb Dragon R :K: 3.50 7.00
44 Celestial Dawn R :W: 1.25 2.50
45 Cerulean Wyvern U :B: .25 .50
46 Chaos Charm C :R: .15 .30
47 Chaosphere R :R: 1.00 2.00
48 Charcoal Diamond U :A: .50 1.00
49 Chariot of the Sun U :A: .50 1.00
50 Choking Sands C :K: .15 .30
51 Cinder Cloud U :R: .25 .50
52 Circle of Despair R :D: 1.00 2.00
53 Civic Guildmage C :W: .15 .30
54 Cloak of Invisibility C :B: .15 .30
55 Consuming Ferocity U :R: .25 .50
56 Coral Fighters U :B: .25 .50
57 Crash of Rhinos C :G: .15 .30
58 Crimson Hellkite R :R: 2.50 5.00
59 Crimson Roc U :R: .25 .50
60 Crypt Cobra U :K: 1.50 3.00
61 Crystal Golem U :A: .25 .50
62 Crystal Vein U :L: .50 1.00
63 Cursed Totem R :A: 1.00 2.00
64 Cycle of Life R :G: .50 1.00
65 Daring Apprentice R :B: 1.00 2.00
66 Dark Banishing C :K: .15 .30
67 Dark Ritual C :K: 1.00 2.00
68 Dazzling Beauty C :W: .25 .50
69 Decomposition U :G: .25 .50
70 Delirium U :D: .50 1.00
71 Dirtwater Wraith C :K: .15 .30
72 Discordant Spirit R :D: 1.00 2.00
73 Disempower C :W: .15 .30
74 Disenchant C :W: .15 .30
75 Dissipate U :B: 2.00 4.00
76 Divine Offering C :W: .15 .30
77 Divine Retribution R :W: 1.00 2.00
78 Drain Life C :K: .50 1.00
79 Dread Specter U :K: .25 .50
80 Dream Cache C :B: .15 .30
81 Dream Fighter C :B: .15 .30
82 Dwarven Miner U :R: .25 .50
83 Dwarven Nomad C :R: .15 .30
84 Early Harvest R :G: 3.50 7.00
85 Ebony Charm C :K: .15 .30
86 Ekundu Cyclops C :R: .15 .30
87 Ekundu Griffin C :W: .15 .30
88 Elixir of Vitality U :A: .25 .50
89 Emberwilde Caliph R :D: 1.00 2.00
90 Emberwilde Djinn R :R: 1.50 3.00
91 Energy Bolt R :D: 1.00 2.00
92 Energy Vortex R :B: 1.00 2.00
93 Enfeeblement C :K: .15 .30
94 Enlightened Tutor U :W: 4.00 8.00
95 Ersatz Gnomes U :A: .50 1.00
96 Ether Well U :B: .25 .50
97 Ethereal Champion R :W: 1.50 3.00
98 Fallow Earth U :G: .50 1.00
99 Favorable Destiny U :W: .50 1.00
100 Femeref Archers U :G: .50 1.00
101 Femeref Healer C :W: .15 .30
102 Femeref Knight C :W: .15 .30
103 Femeref Scouts C :W: .15 .30
104 Feral Shadow C :K: .15 .30
105 Fetid Horror C :K: .15 .30
106 Final Fortune R :R: 1.00 2.00
107 Fire Diamond U :A: .25 .50
108 Firebreathing C :R: .15 .30
109 Flame Elemental U :R: .25 .50
110 Flare C :R: .15 .30
111 Flash R :B: 1.00 2.00
112 Flood Plain U :L: .50 1.00
113 Floodgate U :B: .50 1.00
114 Fog C :G: .15 .30
115 Foratog U :G: .50 1.00
116 Forbidden Crypt R :K: 1.00 2.00
117 Forest A L :L: .25 .50
118 Forest B L :L: .25 .50
119 Forest C L :L: .25 .50
120 Forest D L :L: .25 .50
121 Forsaken Wastes R :K: 1.50 3.00
122 Frenetic Efreet R :D: 1.00 2.00
123 Giant Mantis C :G: .15 .30
124 Gibbering Hyenas C :G: .15 .30
125 Goblin Elite Infantry C :R: .50 1.00
126 Goblin Scouts U :R: .50 1.00
127 Goblin Soothsayer U :R: .50 1.00
128 Goblin Tinkerer C :R: .15 .30
129 Granger Guildmage C :G: .15 .30
130 GrassLands U :L: .25 .50
131 Grave Servitude C :K: .15 .30
132 Gravebane Zombie C :K: .15 .30
133 Grim Feast R :D: 1.00 2.00
134 Grinning Totem R :A: 1.00 2.00
135 Hakim, Loreweaver R :B: 1.00 2.00
136 Hall of Gemstone R :G: 1.00 2.00
137 Hammer of Bogardan R :R: 3.00 6.00
138 Harbinger of Night R :K: 1.50 3.00
139 Harbor Guardian U :D: .25 .50
140 Harmattan Efreet U :B: .25 .50
141 Haunting Apparition U :D: .25 .50
142 Hazerider Drake U :D: .25 .50
143 Healing Salve C :W: .15 .30
144 Hivis of the Scale R :R: 1.50 3.00
145 Horrible Hordes U :A: .25 .50
146 Igneous Golem U :A: .25 .50
147 Illicit Auction R :R: 1.00 2.00
148 Illumination U :W: .25 .50
149 Incinerate C :R: 1.50 3.00
150 Infernal Contract R :K: 1.00 2.00
151 Iron Tusk Elephant U :W: .25 .50
152 Island A L :L: .25 .50
153 Island B L :L: .25 .50
154 Island C L :L: .25 .50
155 Island D L :L: .25 .50
156 Ivory Charm C :W: .15 .30
157 Jabari's Influence R :W: 1.00 2.00
158 Jolrael's Centaur C :G: .15 .30
159 Jolt C :B: .15 .30
160 Jungle Patrol R :G: 1.00 2.00
161 Jungle Troll U :D: .25 .50
162 Jungle Wurm C :G: .15 .30
163 Kaervek's Hex U :K: .25 .50
164 Kaervek's Purge U :D: .25 .50
165 Kaervek's Torch C :R: .15 .30
166 Karoo Meerkat U :G: .25 .50
167 Kukemssa Pirates R :B: 1.00 2.00
168 Kukemssa Serpent C :B: .15 .30
169 Lead Golem U :A: .50 1.00
170 Leering Gargoyle R :D: 1.00 2.00
171 Lightning Reflexes C :R: .15 .30
172 Lion's Eye Diamond R :A: 5.00 10.00
173 Locust Swarm U :G: .50 1.00
174 Lure of Prey R :G: 1.00 2.00
175 Malignant Growth R :D: 1.00 2.00
176 Mana Prism U :A: .50 1.00
177 Mangara's Blessing U :W: .50 1.00
178 Mangara's Equity U :W: .50 1.00
179 Mangara's Tome R :A: 1.50 3.00
180 Marble Diamond U :A: .50 1.00
181 Maro R :G: 1.50 3.00
182 Meddle U :B: .50 1.00
183 Melesse Spirit U :W: 1.50 3.00
184 Memory Lapse C :B: .15 .30
185 Merfolk Raiders C :B: .15 .30
186 Merfolk Seer C :B: .15 .30
187 Mind Bend U :B: 1.00 2.00
188 Mind Harness U :B: .50 1.00
189 Mindbender Spores R :G: 1.00 2.00
190 Mire Shade U :K: .50 1.00
191 Misers' Cage R :A: 1.50 3.00
192 Mist Dragon R :B: 2.00 4.00
193 Moss Diamond U :A: .50 1.00
194 Mountain A L :L: .25 .50
195 Mountain B L :L: .25 .50
196 Mountain C L :L: .25 .50
197 Mountain D L :L: .25 .50
198 Mountain Valley U :L: .50 1.00
199 Mtenda Griffin U :W: .50 1.00
200 Mtenda Herder C :W: .15 .30
201 Mtenda Lion C :G: .15 .30
202 Mystical Tutor U :B: 2.50 5.00
203 Natural Balance R :G: 1.00 2.00
204 Nettletooth Djinn U :G: .50 1.00
205 Noble Elephant C :W: .15 .30
206 Nocturnal Raid U :K: .25 .50
207 Null Chamber R :W: 1.00 2.00
208 Pacifism C :W: .15 .30
209 Painful Memories U :K: .25 .50
210 Patagia Golem U :A: .50 1.00
211 Paupers' Cage R :A: 1.00 2.00
212 Pearl Dragon R :W: 1.50 3.00
213 Phyrexian Dreadnought R :A: 5.00 10.00
214 Phyrexian Purge R :D: 1.50 3.00
215 Phyrexian Tribute R :K: 1.50 3.00
216 Phyrexian Vault U :A: .50 1.00
217 Plains A L :L: .25 .50
218 Plains B L :L: .25 .50
219 Plains C L :L: .25 .50
220 Plains D L :L: .25 .50
221 Political Trickery R :B: 1.00 2.00
222 Polymorph R :B: 1.00 2.00
223 Power Sink C :B: .15 .30
224 Preferred Selection R :G: 1.00 2.00
225 Prismatic Boon U :D: .50 1.00
226 Prismatic Circle C :W: .15 .30
227 Prismatic Lace R :B: 1.50 3.00
228 Psychic Transfer R :B: 1.00 2.00
229 Purgatory R :D: 1.50 3.00
230 Purraj of Urborg R :K: 1.50 3.00
231 Pyric Salamander C :R: .15 .30
232 Quirion Elves C :G: .15 .30
233 Radiant Essence U :D: .25 .50
234 Raging Spirit C :R: .15 .30
235 Rampant Growth C :G: .15 .30
236 Rashida Scalebane R :W: 1.50 3.00
237 Ravenous Vampire U :K: .50 1.00
238 Ray of Command C :B: .15 .30
239 Razor Pendulum R :A: 1.00 2.00
240 Reality Ripple C :B: .15 .30
241 Reckless Embermage R :R: 1.00 2.00
242 Reflect Damage R :D: 1.50 3.00
243 Regeneration C :G: .15 .30
244 Reign of Chaos U :R: .50 1.00
245 Reign of Terror U :K: .50 1.00
246 Reparations R :D: 1.50 3.00
247 Restless Dead C :K: .15 .30
248 Ritual of Steel C :W: .15 .30
249 Rock Basilisk R :D: 1.00 2.00
250 Rocky Tar Pit U :L: .50 1.00
251 Roots of Life U :G: .50 1.00
252 Sabertooth Cobra C :G: .25 .50
253 Sacred Mesa R :W: 1.50 3.00
254 Sand Golem U :A: .25 .50
255 Sandbar Crocodile C :B: .15 .30
256 Sandstorm C :G: .15 .30
257 Sapphire Charm C :B: .15 .30
258 Savage Twister U :D: .50 1.00
259 Sawback Manticore R :D: 1.00 2.00
260 Sea Scryer C :B: .15 .30
261 Sealed Fate U :D: .25 .50
262 Searing Spear Askari C :R: .15 .30
263 Seedling Charm C :G: .15 .30
264 Seeds of Innocence R :G: 1.50 3.00
265 Serene Heart C :G: .15 .30
266 Sewer Rats C :K: .15 .30
267 Shadow Guildmage C :K: .15 .30
268 Shadowbane U :W: .25 .50
269 Shallow Grave R :K: 1.00 2.00
270 Shaper Guildmage C :B: .15 .30
271 Shauku, Endbringer R :K: 1.50 3.00
272 Shauku's Minion U :D: .50 1.00
273 Shimmer R :B: 1.50 3.00
274 Sidar Jabari R :W: 1.50 3.00
275 Sirocco U :R: .50 1.00
276 Skulking Ghost C :K: .15 .30
277 Sky Diamond U :A: .50 1.00
278 Soar C :B: .15 .30
279 Soul Echo R :W: 1.50 3.00
280 Soul Rend U :K: .25 .50
281 Soulshriek C :K: .25 .50
282 Spatial Binding U :D: .25 .50
283 Spectral Guardian R :W: 1.50 3.00
284 Spirit of the Night R :K: 6.00 12.00
285 Spitting Earth C :R: .15 .30
286 Stalking Tiger C :G: .15 .30
287 Stone Rain C :R: .15 .30
288 Stupor U :K: .25 .50
289 Subterranean Spirit R :R: 1.50 3.00
290 Sunweb R :W: 1.50 3.00
291 Superior Numbers U :G: .25 .50
292 Suq'Ata Firewalker U :B: 1.50 3.00
293 Swamp A L :L: .25 .50
294 Swamp B L :L: .25 .50
295 Swamp C L :L: .25 .50
296 Swamp D L :L: .25 .50
297 Tainted Specter R :K: 1.00 2.00
298 Talruum Minotaur C :R: .15 .30
299 Taniwha R :B: 1.00 2.00
300 Teeka's Dragon R :A: 4.00 8.00
301 Teferi's Curse C :B: .15 .30
302 Teferi's Drake C :B: .15 .30
303 Teferi's Imp R :B: 1.50 3.00
304 Teferi's Isle R :L: 1.50 3.00
305 Telim'Tor R :R: 1.50 3.00
306 Telim'Tor's Darts U :A: .25 .50
307 Telim'Tor's Edict R :R: 1.00 2.00
308 Teremko Griffin C :W: .15 .30
309 Thirst C :B: .15 .30
310 Tidal Wave U :B: .25 .50
311 Tombstone Stairwell R :K: 1.00 2.00
312 Torrent of Lava R :R: 1.00 2.00
313 Tranquil Domain C :G: .15 .30
314 Tropical Storm U :G: .25 .50
315 Uktabi Faerie C :G: .15 .30
316 Uktabi Wildcats R :G: 1.50 3.00
317 Unerring Sling U :A: .50 1.00
318 Unfulfilled Desires R :D: 1.00 2.00
319 Unseen Walker U :G: .50 1.00
320 Unyaro Bee Sting U :G: .50 1.00
321 Unyaro Griffin U :W: .50 1.00
322 Urborg Panther C :K: .15 .30
323 Vaporous Djinn U :B: .25 .50
324 Ventifact Bottle R :A: 1.50 3.00
325 Viashino Warrior C :R: .15 .30
326 Vigilant Martyr U :W: .50 1.00
327 Village Elder C :G: .15 .30
328 Vitalizing Cascade U :D: .50 1.00
329 Volcanic Dragon R :R: 3.00 6.00
330 Volcanic Geyser U :R: .50 1.00
331 Waiting in the Weeds R :G: 1.50 3.00
332 Wall of Corpses C :K: .15 .30
333 Wall of Resistance C :W: .15 .30
334 Wall of Roots C :G: .15 .30
335 Ward of Lights C :W: .15 .30
336 Warping Wurm R :D: 1.50 3.00
337 Wave Elemental U :B: .25 .50
338 Wellspring R :D: .25 .50
339 Wild Elephant C :G: .15 .30
340 Wildfire Emissary U :R: .25 .50
341 Windreaper Falcon U :D: .25 .50
342 Withering Boon U :K: .25 .50
343 Worldly Tutor U :G: 4.00 8.00
344 Yare R :W: 1.50 3.00
345 Zebra Unicorn U :D: .25 .50
346 Zhalfirin Commander U :W: .50 1.00
347 Zhalfirin Knight C :W: .15 .30
348 Zirilan of the Claw R :R: 2.00 4.00
349 Zombie Mob U :K: .50 1.00
350 Zuberi, Golden Feather R :W: 1.00 2.00

1997 Magic The Gathering Visions

COMPLETE SET (167)	100.00	175.00
BOOSTER BOX (36 PACKS)	175.00	250.00
BOOSTER PACK (15 CARDS)	5.00	8.00
RELEASED ON FEBRUARY 3, 1997		
1 Aku Djinn R :K:	1.25	3.00
2 Anvil of Bogardan R :A:	2.00	5.00
3 Archangel R :W:	2.50	6.00
4 Army Ants U :D:	.40	1.00
5 Betrayal C :B:	.15	.30
6 Blanket of Night U :K:	.60	1.50
7 Bogardan Phoenix R :R:	1.50	4.00
8 Brass-Talon Chimera U :A:	.40	1.00
9 Breathstealer's Crypt R :D:	1.25	3.00
10 Breezekeeper C :B:	.15	.30
11 Brood of Cockroaches U :K:	.40	1.00
12 Bull Elephant C :G:	.15	.30
13 Chronatog R :B:	1.50	4.00
14 City of Solitude R :G:	1.50	4.00
15 Cloud Elemental C :B:	.15	.30
16 Coercion C :K:	.15	.30
17 Coral Atoll U :L:	.40	1.00
18 Corrosion R :D:	.75	2.00
19 Creeping Mold U :G:	.40	1.00
20 Crypt Rats C :K:	.15	.30
21 Daraja Griffin U :W:	.40	1.00
22 Dark Privilege C :K:	.15	.30
23 Death Watch C :K:	.15	.30
24 Desertion R :B:	1.50	4.00
25 Desolation U :K:	.40	1.00
26 Diamond Kaleidoscope R :A:	1.25	3.00
27 Dormant Volcano U :L:	.40	1.00
28 Dragon Mask U :A:	.40	1.00
29 Dream Tides U :B:	.40	1.00
30 Dwarven Vigilantes C :R:	.15	.30
31 Elephant Grass U :G:	.40	1.00
32 Elkin Lair R :R:	.75	2.00
33 Elven Cache C :G:	.15	.30
34 Emerald Charm C :G:	.40	1.00
35 Equipoise R :W:	.75	2.00
36 Everglades U :L:	.40	1.00
37 Eye of Singularity R :W:	.75	2.00
38 Fallen Askari C :K:	.15	.30
39 Femeref Enchantress R :D:	1.25	3.00
40 Feral Instinct C :G:	.15	.30
41 Fireblast C :R:	.30	.75
42 Firestorm Hellkite R :D:	1.50	4.00
43 Flooded Shoreline R :B:	1.25	3.00
44 Forbidden Ritual R :K:	1.25	3.00
45 Foreshadow U :B:	.40	1.00
46 Freewind Falcon C :W:	.15	.30
47 Funeral Charm C :K:	.15	.30
48 Giant Caterpillar C :G:	.15	.30
49 Goblin Recruiter U :R:	1.50	4.00
50 Goblin Swine-Rider C :R:	.15	.30
51 Gossamer Chains C :W:	.15	.30
52 Griffin Canyon R :L:	.75	2.00
53 Guiding Spirit R :D:	.75	2.00
54 Hearth Charm C :R:	.15	.30
55 Heat Wave U :R:	.75	2.00
56 Helm of Awakening U :A:	1.25	3.00
57 Honorable Passage U :W:	.75	2.00
58 Hope Charm C :W:	.15	.30
59 Hulking Cyclops U :R:	.40	1.00
60 Impulse C :B:	.20	.50
61 Infantry Veteran C :W:	.15	.30
62 Infernal Harvest C :K:	.15	.30
63 Inspiration C :B:	.15	.30
64 Iron-Heart Chimera U :A:	.40	1.00
65 Jamuraan Lion C :W:	.15	.30
66 Juju Bubble U :A:	.40	1.00
67 Jungle Basin U :L:	.40	1.00
68 Kaervek's Spite R :K:	1.25	3.00
69 Karoo U :L:	.40	1.00
70 Katabatic Winds R :G:	1.25	3.00
71 Keeper of Kookus C :R:	.15	.30
72 King Cheetah C :G:	.15	.30
73 Knight of the Mists C :B:	.15	.30
74 Knight of Valor C :W:	.15	.30
75 Kookus R :R:	1.25	3.00
76 Kyscu Drake U :G:	.75	2.00
77 Lead-Belly Chimera U :A:	.40	1.00
78 Lichenthrope R :G:	1.25	3.00
79 Lightning Cloud R :R:	.75	2.00
80 Longbow Archer U :W:	1.50	4.00
81 Magma Mine U :A:	.75	2.00
82 Man-o'-War C :B:	.40	1.00
83 Matopi Golem U :A:	.40	1.00
84 Miraculous Recovery U :W:	.40	1.00
85 Mob Mentality U :R:	.40	1.00
86 Mortal Wound C :G:	.15	.30
87 Mundungu U :D:	.40	1.00
88 Mystic Veil C :B:	.15	.30
89 Natural Order R :G:	2.50	6.00
90 Necromancy U :K:	1.25	3.00
91 Necrosavant R :K:	2.50	6.00
92 Nekrataal U :K:	.75	2.00
93 Ogre Enforcer R :R:	.75	2.00
94 Ovinomancer U :B:	.40	1.00
95 Panther Warriors C :G:	.15	.30
96 Parapet C :W:	.15	.30
97 Peace Talks U :W:	.40	1.00
98 Phyrexian Marauder R :A:	1.00	2.50
99 Phyrexian Walker C :A:	.15	.30
100 Pillar Tombs of Aku R :K:	.75	2.00
101 Prosperity U :B:	1.25	3.00
102 Pygmy Hippo R :D:	1.25	3.00
103 Python C :K:	.15	.30
104 Quicksand U :L:	.75	2.00
105 Quirion Druid R :G:	1.50	4.00
106 Quirion Ranger C :G:	.15	.30
107 Raging Gorilla C :R:	.15	.30
108 Rainbow Efreet R :B:	1.50	4.00
109 Relentless Assault R :R:	2.50	6.00
110 Relic Ward U :W:	.40	1.00
111 Remedy C :W:	.15	.30
112 Resistance Fighter C :W:	.15	.30
113 Retribution of the Meek R :W:	.75	2.00
114 Righteous Aura C :W:	.15	.30
115 Righteous War R :D:	.75	2.00
116 River Boa C :G:	.60	1.50
117 Rock Slide C :R:	.15	.30
118 Rowen R :G:	1.50	4.00
119 Sands of Time R :A:	.75	2.00
120 Scalebane's Elite U :D:	.40	1.00
121 Shimmering Efreet U :B:	.40	1.00
122 Shrieking Drake C :B:	.15	.30
123 Simoon U :D:	.40	1.00
124 Sisay's Ring C :A:	.15	.30
125 Snake Basket R :A:	1.25	3.00
126 Solfatara C :R:	.15	.30
127 Song of Blood C :R:	.15	.30
128 Spider Climb C :G:	.15	.30
129 Spitting Drake U :R:	.40	1.00
130 Squandered Resources R :D:	2.00	5.00
131 Stampeding Wildebeests U :G:	.40	1.00
132 Suleiman's Legacy R :D:	.75	2.00
133 Summer Bloom U :G:	.40	1.00
134 Sun Clasp C :W:	.15	.30
135 Suq'Ata Assassin U :K:	.40	1.00
136 Suq'Ata Lancer C :R:	.15	.30
137 Talruum Champion C :R:	.15	.30
138 Talruum Piper U :R:	.40	1.00
139 Tar Pit Warrior C :K:	.15	.30
140 Teferi's Honor Guard U :W:	.40	1.00
141 Teferi's Puzzle Box R :A:	1.50	4.00
142 Teferi's Realm R :B:	1.50	4.00
143 Tempest Drake U :D:	.40	1.00
144 Three Wishes R :B:	1.25	3.00
145 Time and Tide U :B:	.40	1.00
146 Tin-Wing Chimera U :A:	.40	1.00
147 Tithe R :W:	2.50	6.00
148 Tremor C :R:	.15	.30
149 Triangle of War R :A:	1.25	3.00
150 Uktabi Orangutan U :G:	.75	2.00
151 Undiscovered Paradise R :L:	3.00	8.00
152 Undo C :B:	.15	.30
153 Urborg Mindsucker C :K:	.15	.30
154 Vampiric Tutor R :K:	12.00	30.00
155 Vampirism U :K:	.75	2.00
156 Vanishing C :B:	.15	.30
157 Viashino Sandstalker U :R:	.75	2.00
158 Viashivan Dragon R :D:	2.00	5.00
159 Vision Charm C :B:	.15	.30
160 Wake of Vultures C :K:	.15	.30
161 Wand of Denial R :A:	1.50	4.00
162 Warrior's Honor C :W:	.15	.30
163 Warthog C :G:	.15	.30
164 Waterspout Djinn U :B:	.75	2.00
165 Wicked Reward C :K:	.15	.30
166 Wind Shear U :G:	.40	1.00
167 Zhalfirin Crusader R :W:	1.25	3.00

1997 Magic The Gathering 5th Edition

COMPLETE SET (434)	190.00	250.00
BOOSTER BOX (36 PACKS)	140.00	185.00
BOOSTER PACK (15 CARDS)	4.50	6.00
STARTER DECK BOX (10 DECKS)	120.00	150.00
STARTER DECK	12.00	15.00
RELEASED ON MARCH 24, 1997		
WHITE BORDERS AND A 1997 COPYRIGHT DATE		
1 Abbey Gargoyles U :W:	.50	1.00
2 Abyssal Specter U :K:	.50	1.00
3 Adarkar Wastes R :L:	3.50	7.00
4 Aether Storm U :B:	.50	1.00
5 Air Elemental U :B:	.50	1.00
6 Akron Legionnaire R :W:	1.00	2.00
7 Alabaster Potion C :W:	.15	.30
8 Aladdin's Ring R :A:	1.50	3.00
9 Ambush Party C :R:	.15	.30
10 Amulet of Kroog C :A:	.15	.30
11 Angry Mob U :W:	.25	.50
12 An-Havva Constable R :G:	1.50	3.00
13 Animate Dead U :K:	2.00	4.00
14 Animate Wall R :W:	1.50	3.00
15 Ankh of Mishra R :A:	1.50	3.00
16 Anti-Magic Aura U :B:	.50	1.00
17 Arenson's Aura U :W:	.50	1.00
18 Armageddon R :W:	3.00	6.00
19 Armor of Faith C :W:	.15	.30
20 Ashes to Ashes U :K:	.25	.50
21 Ashnod's Altar U :A:	.50	1.00
22 Ashnod's Transmogrant C :A:	.15	.30
23 Aspect of Wolf R :G:	2.00	4.00
24 Atog U :R:	1.00	2.00
25 Aurochs C :G:	.15	.30
26 Aysen Bureaucrats C :W:	.15	.30
27 Azure Drake U :B:	.25	.50
28 Bad Moon R :K:	4.00	8.00
29 Ball Lightning R :R:	3.00	6.00
30 Barbed Sextant C :A:	.15	.30
31 Barl's Cage R :A:	1.50	3.00
32 Battering Ram C :A:	.15	.30
33 Benalish Hero C :W:	.15	.30
34 Binding Grasp U :B:	.50	1.00
35 Bird Maiden C :R:	.15	.30
36 Birds of Paradise R :G:	5.00	10.00
37 Black Knight U :K:	1.00	2.00
38 Blessed Wine C :W:	.15	.30
39 Blight U :K:	.50	1.00
40 Blinking Spirit R :W:	1.50	3.00
41 Blood Lust C :R:	.15	.30
42 Bog Imp C :K:	.15	.30
43 Bog Rats C :K:	.15	.30
44 Bog Wraith U :K:	.25	.50
45 Boomerang C :B:	.15	.30
46 Bottle of Suleiman R :A:	1.50	3.00
47 Bottomless Vault R :L:	1.50	3.00
48 Brainstorm C :B:	.50	1.00
49 Brainwash C :W:	.15	.30
50 Brassclaw Orcs C :R:	.15	.30
51 Breeding Pit U :K:	1.00	2.00
52 Broken Visage R :K:	1.00	2.00
53 Brothers of Fire C :R:	.15	.30
54 Brushland R :L:	3.50	7.00
55 Brute, The C :R:	.15	.30
56 Carapace C :G:	.15	.30
57 Caribou Range R :W:	1.00	2.00
58 Carrion Ants U :K:	.50	1.00
59 Castle U :W:	.25	.50
60 Cat Warriors C :G:	.15	.30
61 Cave People U :R:	.50	1.00
62 Chub Toad C :G:	.15	.30
63 City of Brass R :L:	3.50	7.00
64 Clay Statue C :A:	.15	.30
65 Cloak of Confusion C :K:	.15	.30
66 Clockwork Beast R :A:	2.00	4.00
67 Clockwork Steed U :A:	.25	.50
68 Cockatrice R :G:	2.00	4.00
69 Colossus of Sardia R :A:	2.00	4.00
70 Conquer U :R:	.50	1.00
71 CoP: Artifacts U :W:	.50	1.00
72 CoP: Black C :W:	.15	.30
73 CoP: Blue C :W:	.15	.30
74 CoP: Green C :W:	.15	.30
75 CoP: Red C :W:	.15	.30
76 CoP: White C :W:	.15	.30
77 Coral Helm R :A:	1.50	3.00
78 Counterspell C :B:	1.00	2.00
79 Craw Giant U :G:	.50	1.00
80 Craw Wurm C :G:	.15	.30
81 Crimson Manticore R :R:	2.00	4.00
82 Crown of the Ages R :A:	1.50	3.00
83 Crumble U :G:	.50	1.00
84 Crusade R :W:	3.00	6.00
85 Crystal Rod U :A:	.25	.50
86 Cursed Land U :K:	.50	1.00
87 D'Avenant Archer C :W:	.15	.30
88 Dance of Many R :B:	1.50	3.00
89 Dancing Scimitar R :A:	1.00	2.00
90 Dandân C :B:	.15	.30
91 Dark Maze C :B:	.15	.30
92 Dark Ritual C :K:	.75	1.50
93 Death Speakers C :W:	.15	.30
94 Death Ward C :W:	.15	.30
95 Deathgrip U :K:	.50	1.00
96 Deflection R :B:	2.00	4.00
97 Derelor R :K:	1.00	2.00
98 Desert Twister U :G:	.50	1.00
99 Detonate U :R:	.50	1.00
100 Diabolic Machine U :A:	.50	1.00
101 Dingus Egg R :A:	1.50	3.00
102 Disenchant C :W:	.25	.50
103 Disintegrate C :R:	.25	.50
104 Disrupting Scepter R :A:	1.50	3.00
105 Divine Offering C :W:	.15	.30
106 Divine Transformation U :W:	.50	1.00
107 Dragon Engine R :A:	1.50	3.00
108 Drain Life C :K:	.50	1.00
109 Drain Power R :B:	1.50	3.00
110 Drudge Skeletons C :K:	.15	.30
111 Durkwood Boars C :G:	.15	.30
112 Dust to Dust U :W:	1.00	2.00
113 Dwarven Catapult U :R:	.25	.50
114 Dwarven Hold R :L:	1.50	3.00
115 Dwarven Ruins U :L:	.50	1.00
116 Dwarven Soldier C :R:	.15	.30
117 Dwarven Warriors C :R:	.15	.30
118 Earthquake R :R:	2.00	4.00
119 Ebon Stronghold U :L:	.50	1.00
120 Elder Druid R :G:	1.00	2.00
121 Elkin Bottle R :A:	1.50	3.00
122 Elven Riders U :G:	.25	.50
123 Elvish Archers R :G:	2.00	4.00
124 Energy Flux U :B:	1.00	2.00
125 Enervate C :B:	.15	.30
126 Erg Raiders C :K:	.15	.30
127 Errantry C :R:	.15	.30
128 Eternal Warrior C :R:	.15	.30
129 Evil Eye of Orms-by-Gore U :K:	.30	.75
130 Evil Presence U :K:	1.00	2.00
131 Eye for an Eye R :W:	2.00	4.00
132 Fallen Angel U :K:	.50	1.00
133 Fear C :K:	.15	.30
134 Feedback U :B:	.25	.50
135 Feldon's Cane U :A:	2.00	4.00
136 Fellwar Stone U :A:	1.00	2.00
137 Feroz's Ban R :A:	2.00	4.00
138 Fire Drake U :R:	.25	.50
139 Fireball C :R:	.25	.50
140 Firebreathing C :R:	.15	.30
141 Flame Spirit U :R:	.25	.50
142 Flare C :R:	.15	.30
143 Flashfires U :R:	.50	1.00
144 Flight C :B:	.15	.30
145 Flood C :B:	.15	.30
146 Flying Carpet R :A:	1.00	2.00
147 Fog C :G:	.15	.30
148 Force of Nature R :G:	2.50	5.00
149 Force Spike C :B:	.25	.50
150 Forest L :L:	.50	1.00
151 Forget R :B:	1.00	2.00
152 Fountain of Youth U :A:	.50	1.00
153 Foxfire C :G:	.15	.30
154 Frozen Shade C :K:	.25	.50
155 Funeral March C :K:	.15	.30
156 Fungusaur R :G:	1.50	3.00
157 Fyndhorn Elder U :G:	.50	1.00
158 Game of Chaos R :R:	1.50	3.00
159 Gaseous Form C :B:	.15	.30
160 Gauntlets of Chaos R :A:	1.00	2.00
161 Ghazbán Ogre C :G:	.50	1.00
162 Giant Growth C :G:	.50	1.00
163 Giant Spider C :G:	.15	.30
164 Giant Strength C :R:	.15	.30
165 Glacial Wall U :B:	.25	.50
166 Glasses of Urza U :A:	.50	1.00
167 Gloom U :K:	.50	1.00
168 Goblin Digging Team C :R:	.15	.30
169 Goblin Hero C :R:	.15	.30
170 Goblin King R :R:	2.50	5.00
171 Goblin War Drums C :R:	.15	.30
172 Goblin Warrens R :R:	1.50	3.00
173 Grapeshot Catapult C :A:	.15	.30
174 Greater Realm of Preservation U :W:	.25	.50
175 Greater Werewolf U :K:	.25	.50
176 Grizzly Bears C :G:	.15	.30
177 Havenwood Battleground U :L:	.50	1.00
178 Heal C :W:	.15	.30
179 Healing Salve C :W:	.15	.30
180 Hecatomb R :K:	2.00	4.00
181 Helm of Chatzuk R :A:	1.00	2.00
182 Hill Giant C :R:	.15	.30
183 Hipparion C :W:	.15	.30
184 Hive, The R :A:	1.50	3.00
185 Hollow Trees R :L:	1.50	3.00
186 Holy Strength C :W:	.15	.30
187 Homarid Warrior C :B:	.15	.30
188 Howl from Beyond C :K:	.15	.30
189 Howling Mine R :A:	3.50	7.00
190 Hungry Mist C :G:	.15	.30
191 Hurkyl's Recall R :B:	1.50	3.00
192 Hurloon Minotaur C :R:	.15	.30
193 Hurricane U :G:	.50	1.00
194 Hydroblast U :B:	.50	1.00
195 Icatian Phalanx U :W:	.50	1.00
196 Icatian Scout C :W:	.15	.30
197 Icatian Store R :L:	1.50	3.00
198 Icatian Town R :W:	1.50	3.00
199 Ice Floe U :L:	.50	1.00
200 Imposing Visage C :R:	.15	.30
201 Incinerate C :R:	.50	1.00
202 Inferno R :R:	1.50	3.00
203 Infinite Hourglass R :A:	1.50	3.00
204 Initiates of the Ebon Hand C :K:	.15	.30
205 Instill Energy U :G:	.50	1.00
206 Iron Star U :A:	.50	1.00
207 Ironclaw Curse R :R:	1.50	3.00
208 Ironclaw Orcs C :R:	.15	.30
209 Ironroot Treefolk C :G:	.15	.30
210 Island L :L:	.25	.50
211 Island Sanctuary R :W:	1.50	3.00
212 Ivory Cup U :A:	.50	1.00
213 Ivory Guardians U :W:	.25	.50
214 Jade Monolith R :A:	1.50	3.00
215 Jalum Tome R :A:	1.00	2.00
216 Jandor's Saddlebags R :A:	1.50	3.00
217 Jayemdae Tome R :A:	1.00	2.00
218 Jester's Cap R :A:	3.00	6.00
219 Johtull Wurm U :G:	.25	.50
220 Jokulhaups R :R:	2.00	4.00
221 Joven's Tools U :A:	.25	.50
222 Justice U :W:	.25	.50
223 Juxtapose R :B:	1.50	3.00
224 Karma U :W:	.50	1.00
225 Karplusan Forest R :L:	3.50	7.00
226 Keldon Warlord U :R:	.50	1.00
227 Killer Bees U :G:	.75	1.50
228 Kismet U :W:	.50	1.00
229 Kjeldoran Dead C :K:	.15	.30
230 Kjeldoran Royal Guard R :W:	1.50	3.00
231 Kjeldoran Skycaptain U :W:	.50	1.00
232 Knight of Stromgald U :K:	.50	1.00
233 Krovikan Fetish C :K:	.15	.30
234 Krovikan Sorcerer C :B:	.15	.30
235 Labyrinth Minotaur C :B:	.15	.30
236 Leshrac's Rite U :K:	.50	1.00
237 Leviathan R :B:	1.50	3.00
238 Ley Druid C :G:	.15	.30
239 Lhurgoyf R :G:	2.00	4.00
240 Library of Leng U :A:	1.00	2.00
241 Lifeforce U :G:	.50	1.00
242 Lifetap U :B:	.25	.50
243 Living Artifact R :G:	1.50	3.00
244 Living Lands R :G:	1.50	3.00
245 Llanowar Elves C :G:	.50	1.00
246 Lord of Atlantis R :B:	2.00	4.00
247 Lord of the Pit R :K:	2.50	5.00
248 Lost Soul C :K:	.15	.30
249 Lure U :G:	.50	1.00
250 Magical Hack R :B:	2.00	4.00
251 Magus of the Unseen R :B:	1.00	2.00
252 Mana Clash R :R:	1.00	2.00
253 Mana Flare R :R:	3.00	6.00
254 Mana Vault R :A:	2.50	5.00
255 Manabarbs R :R:	1.50	3.00
256 Marsh Viper C :G:	.15	.30
257 Meekstone R :A:	2.00	4.00
258 Memory Lapse C :B:	.15	.30
259 Merfolk of the Pearl Trident C :B:	.15	.30
260 Mesa Falcon C :W:	.15	.30
261 Mesa Pegasus C :W:	.15	.30
262 Millstone R :A:	3.00	6.00
263 Mind Bomb U :B:	.50	1.00
264 Mind Ravel C :K:	.15	.30
265 Mind Warp U :K:	.50	1.00
266 Mindstab Thrull C :K:	.15	.30
267 Mole Worms U :K:	.25	.50
268 Mons's Goblin Raiders C :R:	.15	.30
269 Mountain Goat C :R:	.15	.30
270 Mountain L :L:	.50	1.00
271 Murk Dwellers C :K:	.15	.30
272 Nature's Lore C :G:	.15	.30
273 Necrite C :K:	.15	.30
274 Necropotence R :K:	3.00	6.00
275 Nether Shadow R :K:	1.50	3.00
276 Nevinyrral's Disk R :A:	4.00	8.00
277 Nightmare R :K:	2.50	5.00
278 Obelisk of Undoing R :A:	1.00	2.00
279 Orcish Artillery U :R:	.25	.50
280 Orcish Captain U :R:	.25	.50
281 Orcish Conscripts C :R:	.15	.30
282 Orcish Farmer C :R:	.15	.30
283 Orcish Oriflamme U :R:	.50	1.00
284 Orcish Squatters R :R:	1.50	3.00
285 Order of the Sacred Torch R :W:	1.50	3.00
286 Order of the White Shield U :W:	.50	1.00
287 Orgg R :R:	1.50	3.00
288 Ornithopter U :A:	1.00	2.00
289 Panic C :R:	.15	.30
290 Paralyze C :K:	.15	.30
291 Pearled Unicorn C :W:	.15	.30
292 Pentagram of the Ages R :A:	1.50	3.00
293 Personal Incarnation R :W:	1.50	3.00
294 Pestilence C :K:	.15	.30
295 Phantasmal Forces U :B:	.15	.30
296 Phantasmal Terrain C :B:	.15	.30
297 Phantom Monster U :B:	.50	1.00
298 Pikemen C :W:	.15	.30
299 Pirate Ship R :B:	1.50	3.00
300 Pit Scorpion C :K:	.25	.50
301 Plague Rats C :K:	.25	.50
302 Plains L :L:	.25	.50
303 Portent C :B:	.15	.30
304 Power Sink U :B:	.50	1.00
305 Pox R :K:	1.50	3.00
306 Pradesh Gypsies C :G:	.15	.30
307 Primal Clay R :A:	1.50	3.00
308 Primal Order R :G:	1.50	3.00
309 Primordial Ooze U :R:	.25	.50
310 Prismatic Ward C :W:	.15	.30
311 Prodigal Sorcerer C :B:	.15	.30
312 Psychic Venom C :B:	.15	.30
313 Pyroblast U :R:	.50	1.00
314 Pyrotechnics U :R:	1.00	2.00
315 Rabid Wombat U :G:	.50	1.00
316 Radjan Spirit U :G:	.50	1.00
317 Rag Man R :K:	1.50	3.00
318 Raise Dead C :K:	.15	.30
319 Ray of Command C :B:	.15	.30
320 Recall R :B:	1.50	3.00
321 Reef Pirates C :B:	.15	.30
322 Regeneration C :G:	.15	.30
323 Remove Soul C :B:	.15	.30
324 Repentant Blacksmith C :W:	.15	.30
325 Reverse Damage R :W:	1.50	3.00
326 Righteousness R :W:	1.50	3.00
327 Rod of Ruin U :A:	.50	1.00
328 Ruins of Trokair U :L:	.50	1.00
329 Sabretooth Tiger C :R:	.15	.30
330 Sacred Boon U :W:	.50	1.00
331 Samite Healer C :W:	.15	.30
332 Sand Silos R :L:	1.50	3.00
333 Scaled Wurm C :G:	.15	.30
334 Scathe Zombies C :K:	.15	.30
335 Scavenger Folk C :G:	.15	.30
336 Scryb Sprites C :G:	.15	.30
337 Sea Serpent C :B:	.15	.30
338 Sea Spirit U :B:	.50	1.00
339 Sea Sprite U :B:	.50	1.00
340 Seasinger U :B:	.50	1.00
341 Segovian Leviathan U :B:	.50	1.00
342 Sengir Autocrat R :K:	2.00	4.00
343 Seraph R :W:	3.00	6.00
344 Serpent Generator R :A:	2.00	4.00
345 Serra Bestiary U :W:	.25	.50
346 Serra Paladin U :W:	.50	1.00
347 Shanodin Dryads C :G:	.15	.30
348 Shapeshifter U :A:	.50	1.00
349 Shatter C :R:	.50	1.00
350 Shatterstorm U :R:	1.00	2.00
351 Shield Bearer C :W:	.15	.30
352 Shield Wall C :W:	.15	.30
353 Shivan Dragon R :R:	3.00	6.00
354 Shrink C :G:	.15	.30
355 Sibilant Spirit R :B:	1.50	3.00
356 Skull Catapult U :A:	1.00	2.00
357 Sleight of Mind R :B:	1.50	3.00
358 Smoke R :R:	1.50	3.00
359 Sorceress Queen R :K:	2.00	4.00
360 Soul Barrier C :B:	.15	.30
361 Soul Net U :A:	.25	.50
362 Spell Blast C :B:	.15	.30
363 Spirit Link U :W:	.50	1.00
364 Stampede R :G:	1.50	3.00
365 Stasis R :B:	2.50	5.00
366 Steal Artifact U :B:	.25	.50
367 Stone Giant U :R:	.50	1.00
368 Stone Rain C :R:	.50	1.00
369 Stone Spirit U :R:	.25	.50
370 Stream of Life C :G:	.25	.50
371 Stromgald Cabal R :K:	1.50	3.00
372 Sulfurous Springs R :L:	3.00	6.00
373 Svyelunite Temple U :L:	.50	1.00
374 Swamp L :L:	.50	1.00
375 Sylvan Library R :G:	3.50	7.00
376 Tarpan C :G:	.15	.30
377 Tawnos's Weaponry U :A:	.50	1.00
378 Terror C :K:	.15	.30
379 Thicket Basilisk U :G:	.25	.50
380 Throne of Bone U :A:	1.00	2.00
381 Thrull Retainer U :K:	.50	1.00
382 Time Bomb R :A:	1.50	3.00
383 Time Elemental R :B:	2.00	4.00
384 Titania's Song R :G:	1.50	3.00
385 Torture C :K:	.15	.30
386 Touch of Death C :K:	.15	.30
387 Tranquility C :G:	.15	.30
388 Truce R :W:	1.50	3.00
389 Tsunami U :G:	.50	1.00
390 Tundra Wolves C :W:	.15	.30
391 Twiddle C :B:	.15	.30
392 Underground River R :L:	4.00	8.00
393 Unholy Strength C :K:	.15	.30
394 Unstable Mutation C :B:	.25	.50
395 Unsummon C :B:	.25	.50
396 Untamed Wilds U :G:	.25	.50
397 Updraft C :B:	.15	.30
398 Urza's Avenger R :A:	1.50	3.00
399 Urza's Bauble U :A:	.50	1.00
400 Urza's Mine C :L:	.50	1.00
401 Urza's Power Plant C :L:	.50	1.00
402 Urza's Tower C :L:	.50	1.00
403 Vampire Bats C :K:	.15	.30
404 Venom C :G:	.25	.50
405 Verduran Enchantress R :G:	1.50	3.00
406 Vodalian Soldiers C :B:	.15	.30
407 Wall of Air U :B:	.50	1.00
408 Wall of Bone U :K:	.50	1.00
409 Wall of Brambles U :G:	.50	1.00
410 Wall of Fire U :R:	.50	1.00
411 Wall of Spears C :A:	.15	.30
412 Wall of Stone U :R:	.30	.75
413 Wall of Swords U :W:	.50	1.00
414 Wanderlust U :G:	.50	1.00
415 War Mammoth C :G:	.15	.30
416 Warp Artifact R :K:	1.50	3.00
417 Weakness C :K:	.15	.30
418 Whirling Dervish U :G:	.50	1.00
419 White Knight U :W:	1.00	2.00
420 Wild Growth C :G:	.15	.30
421 Wind Spirit U :B:	.50	1.00
422 Winds of Change R :R:	1.50	3.00
423 Winter Blast U :G:	.50	1.00
424 Winter Orb R :A:	2.50	5.00
425 Wolverine Pack U :G:	.50	1.00
426 Wooden Sphere U :A:	.50	1.00
427 Word of Blasting U :R:	.50	1.00
428 Wrath of God R :W:	4.00	10.00
429 Wretched, The R :K:	1.50	3.00
430 Wyluli Wolf R :G:	1.00	2.00
431 Xenic Poltergeist R :K:	1.50	3.00
432 Zephyr Falcon C :B:	.15	.30
433 Zombie Master R :K:	2.00	4.00
434 Zur's Weirding R :B:	1.00	2.00

1997 Magic The Gathering Weatherlight

Card	Low	High
COMPLETE SET (167)	75.00	150.00
BOOSTER BOX (36 PACKS)	175.00	250.00
BOOSTER PACK (15 CARDS)	5.00	7.00
RELEASED ON JUNE 9, 1997		
1 Abduction U :B:	.40	1.00
2 Abeyance R :W:	1.50	4.00
3 Abjure C :B:	.15	.30
4 Aboroth R :G:	1.25	3.00
5 Abyssal Gatekeeper C :K:	.15	.30
6 AEther Flash U :R:	.40	1.00
7 Agonizing Memories U :K:	.40	1.00
8 Alabaster Dragon R :W:	1.50	4.00
9 Alms C :W:	.15	.30
10 Ancestral Knowledge R :B:	.75	2.00
11 Angelic Renewal C :W:	.15	.30
12 Apathy C :B:	.15	.30
13 Arctic Wolves U :G:	.40	1.00
14 Ardent Militia C :W:	.15	.30
15 Argivian Find U :W:	.40	1.00
16 Argivian Restoration U :B:	.40	1.00
17 Aura of Silence U :W:	.60	1.50
18 Avizoa R :B:	.75	2.00
19 Barishi U :G:	.40	1.00
20 Barrow Ghoul C :K:	.15	.30
21 Benalish Infantry C :W:	.15	.30
22 Benalish Knight C :W:	.15	.30
23 Benalish Missionary C :W:	.15	.30
24 Betrothed of Fire C :R:	.15	.30
25 Bloodrock Cyclops C :R:	.15	.30
26 Blossoming Wreath C :G:	.15	.30
27 Bogardan Firefiend C :R:	.15	.30
28 Boiling Blood C :R:	.15	.30
29 Bone Dancer R :K:	1.50	4.00
30 Bosium Strip R :A:	1.50	4.00
31 Briar Shield C :G:	.40	1.00
32 Bubble Matrix R :A:	1.50	4.00
33 Buried Alive U :K:	1.50	4.00
34 Call of the Wild R :G:	1.25	3.00
35 Chimeric Sphere U :A:	.40	1.00
36 Choking Vines C :G:	.15	.30
37 Cinder Giant U :R:	.40	1.00
38 Cinder Wall C :R:	.15	.30
39 Circling Vultures U :K:	.40	1.00
40 Cloud Djinn U :B:	.40	1.00
41 Coils of the Medusa C :K:	.15	.30
42 Cone of Flame U :R:	.40	1.00
43 Debt of Loyalty R :W:	1.25	3.00
44 Dense Foliage R :G:	.75	2.00
45 Desperate Gambit U :R:	.75	2.00
46 Dingus Staff U :A:	.40	1.00
47 Disrupt C :B:	.15	.30
48 Doomsday R :K:	1.25	3.00
49 Downdraft U :G:	.40	1.00
50 Duskrider Falcon C :W:	.15	.30
51 Dwarven Berserker C :R:	.15	.30
52 Dwarven Thaumaturgist R :R:	1.25	3.00
53 Empyrial Armor C :W:	.15	.30
54 Ertai's Familiar R :B:	1.25	3.00
55 Fallow Wurm U :G:	.40	1.00
56 Familiar Ground U :G:	.75	2.00
57 Fatal Blow C :K:	.15	.30
58 Fervor R :R:	1.25	3.00
59 Festering Evil U :K:	.40	1.00
60 Fire Whip C :R:	.15	.30
61 Firestorm R :R:	2.00	5.00
62 Fit of Rage C :R:	.15	.30
63 Fledgling Djinn C :K:	.15	.30
64 Flux C :B:	.15	.30
65 Fog Elemental C :B:	.15	.30
66 Foriysian Brigade U :W:	.40	1.00
67 Fungus Elemental R :G:	1.25	3.00
68 Gaea's Blessing U :G:	1.50	4.00
69 Gallowbraid R :K:	1.25	3.00
70 Gemstone Mine U :L:	2.00	5.00
71 Gerrard's Wisdom U :W:	.75	2.00
72 Goblin Bomb R :R:	1.50	4.00
73 Goblin Grenadiers U :R:	.40	1.00
74 Goblin Vandal C :R:	.15	.30
75 Guided Strike C :W:	.15	.30
76 Harvest Wurm C :G:	.15	.30
77 Haunting Misery C :K:	.15	.30
78 Heart of Bogardan R :R:	1.25	3.00
79 Heat Stroke R :R:	.75	2.00
80 Heavy Ballista C :W:	.15	.30
81 Hidden Horror U :K:	.60	1.50
82 Hurloon Shaman U :R:	.40	1.00
83 Infernal Tribute R :K:	.75	2.00
84 Inner Sanctum R :W:	.75	2.00
85 Jabari's Banner U :A:	.40	1.00
86 Jangling Automaton C :A:	.15	.30
87 Kithkin Armor C :W:	.15	.30
88 Lava Hounds U :R:	.60	1.50
89 Lava Storm C :R:	.15	.30
90 Liege of the Hollows R :G:	1.25	3.00
91 Llanowar Behemoth U :G:	.40	1.00
92 Llanowar Druid C :G:	.15	.30
93 Llanowar Sentinel C :G:	.15	.30
94 Lotus Vale R :L:	4.00	10.00
95 Mana Chains C :B:	.15	.30
96 Mana Web R :A:	1.50	4.00
97 Manta Ray C :B:	.15	.30
98 Maraxus of Keld R :R:	1.25	3.00
99 Master of Arms U :W:	.40	1.00
100 Merfolk Traders C :B:	.15	.30
101 Mind Stone C :A:	.15	.30
102 Mischievous Poltergeist U :K:	.40	1.00
103 Mistmoon Griffin U :W:	.40	1.00
104 Morinfen R :K:	.75	2.00
105 Mwonvuli Ooze R :G:	.75	2.00
106 Nature's Kiss C :G:	.15	.30
107 Nature's Resurgence R :G:	1.50	4.00
108 Necratog U :K:	.40	1.00
109 Noble Benefactor U :B:	.40	1.00
110 Null Rod R :A:	2.50	6.00
111 Odylic Wraith U :K:	.75	2.00
112 Ophidian C :B:	.15	.30
113 Orcish Settlers U :R:	.40	1.00
114 Paradigm Shift R :B:	.75	2.00
115 Peacekeeper R :W:	1.50	4.00
116 Pendrell Mists R :B:	1.25	3.00
117 Phantom Warrior U :B:	.40	1.00
118 Phantom Wings C :B:	.15	.30
119 Phyrexian Furnace U :A:	1.50	4.00
120 Psychic Vortex R :B:	1.50	4.00
121 Razortooth Rats C :K:	.15	.30
122 Redwood Treefolk C :G:	.15	.30
123 Relearn U :B:	.40	1.00
124 Revered Unicorn U :W:	.40	1.00
125 Roc Hatchling U :R:	.40	1.00
126 Rogue Elephant C :G:	.40	1.00
127 Sage Owl C :B:	.15	.30
128 Sawtooth Ogre C :R:	.15	.30
129 Scorched Ruins R :L:	1.25	3.00
130 Serenity R :W:	1.25	3.00
131 Serra's Blessing U :W:	.75	2.00
132 Serrated Biskelion U :A:	.40	1.00
133 Shadow Rider C :K:	.15	.30
134 Shattered Crypt C :K:	.15	.30
135 Soul Shepherd C :W:	.15	.30
136 Southern Paladin R :W:	1.50	4.00
137 Spinning Darkness C :K:	.75	2.00
138 Steel Golem U :A:	.40	1.00
139 Strands of Night U :K:	.40	1.00
140 Straw Golem U :A:	.40	1.00
141 Striped Bears C :G:	.15	.30
142 Sylvan Hierophant U :G:	.40	1.00
143 Tariff R :W:	1.50	4.00
144 Teferi's Veil U :B:	.40	1.00
145 Tendrils of Despair C :K:	.15	.30
146 Thran Forge U :A:	.40	1.00
147 Thran Tome R :A:	1.50	4.00
148 Thunderbolt C :R:	.15	.30
149 Thundermare R :R:	1.50	4.00
150 Timid Drake U :B:	.40	1.00
151 Tolarian Drake C :B:	.15	.30
152 Tolarian Entrancer R :B:	1.25	3.00
153 Tolarian Serpent R :B:	1.50	4.00
154 Touchstone U :A:	.40	1.00
155 Tranquil Grove R :G:	1.50	4.00
156 Uktabi Efreet C :G:	.15	.30
157 Urborg Justice R :K:	1.50	4.00
158 Urborg Stalker R :K:	1.25	3.00
159 Veteran Explorer U :G:	.40	1.00
160 Vitalize C :G:	.15	.30
161 Vodalian Illusionist U :B:	.40	1.00
162 Volunteer Reserves U :W:	.40	1.00
163 Wave of Terror R :K:	1.50	4.00
164 Well of Knowledge R :A:	1.25	3.00
165 Winding Canyons R :L:	1.50	4.00
166 Xanthic Statue R :A:	1.25	3.00
167 Zombie Scavengers C :K:	.15	.30

1997 Magic The Gathering Tempest

Card	Low	High
COMPLETE SET (335)	200.00	300.00
BOOSTER BOX (36 PACKS)	350.00	500.00
BOOSTER PACK (15 CARDS)	10.00	15.00
STARTER DECK BOX (12 DECKS)	200.00	300.00
STARTER DECK	20.00	25.00
RELEASED ON OCTOBER 13, 1997		
1 Abandon Hope U :K:	.20	.50
2 Advance Scout C :W:	.15	.30
3 Aftershock C :R:	.15	.30
4 Altar of Dementia R :A:	2.50	6.00
5 Aluren R :G:	3.00	8.00
6 Ancient Runes U :R:	.40	1.00
7 Ancient Tomb U :L:	1.25	3.00
8 Angelic Protector U :W:	.40	1.00
9 Anoint C :W:	.15	.30
10 Apes of Rath U :G:	.20	.50
11 Apocalypse R :R:	1.25	3.00
12 Armor Sliver U :W:	.75	2.00
13 Armored Pegasus C :W:	.15	.30
14 Auratog R :W:	1.50	4.00
15 Avenging Angel R :W:	1.50	4.00
16 Barbed Sliver U :R:	.75	2.00
17 Bayou Dragonfly C :G:	.15	.30
18 Bellowing Fiend R :K:	.75	2.00
19 Benthic Behemoth R :B:	1.25	3.00
20 Blood Frenzy C :R:	.15	.30
21 Blood Pet C :K:	.15	.30
22 Boil U :R:	.75	2.00
23 Booby Trap R :A:	1.50	4.00
24 Bottle Gnomes U :A:	.60	1.50
25 Bounty Hunter R :K:	2.00	5.00
26 Broken Fall C :G:	.15	.30
27 Caldera Lake R :L:	1.25	3.00
28 Canopy Spider C :G:	.15	.30
29 Canyon Drake R :R:	.40	1.00
30 Canyon Wildcat C :R:	.15	.30
31 Capsize C :B:	.40	1.00
32 Carrionette R :K:	1.25	3.00
33 Chaotic Goo R :R:	.75	2.00
34 Charging Rhino U :G:	.40	1.00
35 Chill U :B:	1.50	4.00
36 Choke U :G:	.40	1.00
37 Cinder Marsh U :L:	.40	1.00
38 Circle of Protection Black C :W:	.15	.30
39 Circle of Protection Blue C :W:	.15	.30
40 Circle of Protection Green C :W:	.15	.30
41 Circle of Protection Red C :W:	.15	.30
42 Circle of Protection Shadow C :W:	.15	.30
43 Circle of Protection White C :W:	.15	.30
44 Clergy en-Vec C :W:	.15	.30
45 Clot Sliver C :K:	.40	1.00
46 Cloudchaser Eagle C :W:	.15	.30
47 Coercion C :K:	.15	.30
48 Coffin Queen R :K:	2.00	5.00
49 Coiled Tinviper C :A:	.15	.30
50 Cold Storage R :A:	1.25	3.00
51 Commander Greven il-Vec R :K:	2.00	5.00
52 Corpse Dance R :K:	2.50	6.00
53 Counterspell C :B:	.75	2.00
54 Crazed Armodon R :G:	.75	2.00
55 Crown of Flames C :R:	.15	.30
56 Cursed Scroll R :A:	5.00	12.00
57 Dark Banishing C :K:	.15	.30
58 Dark Ritual C :K:	.40	1.00
59 Darkling Stalker C :K:	.15	.30
60 Dauthi Embrace U :K:	.40	1.00
61 Dauthi Ghoul U :K:	.40	1.00
62 Dauthi Horror C :K:	.15	.30
63 Dauthi Marauder C :K:	.15	.30
64 Dauthi Mercenary U :K:	.40	1.00
65 Dauthi Mindripper U :K:	.40	1.00
66 Dauthi Slayer C :K:	.40	1.00
67 Deadshot R :R:	.75	2.00
68 Death Pits of Rath R :K:	1.50	4.00
69 Diabolic Edict C :K:	1.25	3.00
70 Dirtcowl Wurm R :G:	.60	1.50
71 Disenchant C :W:	.15	.30
72 Dismiss U :B:	.60	1.50
73 Disturbed Burial C :K:	.15	.30
74 Dracoplasm R :D:	.75	2.00
75 Dread of Night U :K:	.40	1.00
76 Dream Cache C :B:	.15	.30
77 Dregs of Sorrow R :K:	.75	2.00
78 Duplicity R :B:	.75	2.00
79 Earthcraft R :G:	8.00	20.00
80 Echo Chamber R :A:	.75	2.00
81 Eladamri, Lord of Leaves R :G:	5.00	12.00
82 Eladamri's Vineyard R :G:	1.50	4.00
83 Elite Javelineer C :W:	.15	.30
84 Elven Warhounds R :G:	.75	2.00
85 Elvish Fury C :G:	.15	.30
86 Emerald Medallion R :A:	2.50	6.00
87 Emmessi Tome R :A:	.75	2.00
88 Endless Scream C :K:	.15	.30
89 Energizer R :A:	.75	2.00
90 Enfeeblement C :K:	.15	.30
91 Enraging Licid U :R:	.20	.50
92 Ertai's Meddling R :B:	.75	2.00
93 Escaped Shapeshifter R :B:	.75	2.00
94 Essence Bottle U :A:	.40	1.00
95 Evincar's Justice C :K:	.15	.30
96 Excavator U :A:	.20	.50
97 Extinction R :K:	1.50	4.00
98 Fevered Convulsions R :K:	1.25	3.00
99 Field of Souls R :W:	.75	2.00
100 Fighting Drake U :B:	.20	.50
101 Firefly U :R:	.20	.50
102 Fireslinger C :R:	.15	.30
103 Flailing Drake U :G:	.20	.50
104 Flickering Ward U :W:	.75	2.00
105 Flowstone Giant C :R:	.15	.30
106 Flowstone Salamander U :R:	.40	1.00
107 Flowstone Sculpture R :A:	1.25	3.00
108 Flowstone Wyvern R :R:	.75	2.00
109 Fool's Tome R :A:	.75	2.00
110 Forest L :L:	.15	.30
111 Frog Tongue C :G:	.15	.30
112 Fugitive Druid R :G:	1.25	3.00
113 Furnace of Rath R :R:	2.00	5.00
114 Fylamarid U :B:	.40	1.00
115 Gallantry U :W:	.40	1.00
116 Gaseous Form C :B:	.15	.30
117 Gerrard's Battle Cry R :W:	.75	2.00
118 Ghost Town U :L:	.40	1.00
119 Giant Crab C :B:	.15	.30
120 Giant Strength C :R:	.15	.30
121 Goblin Bombardment U :R:	.75	2.00
122 Gravedigger C :K:	.15	.30
123 Grindstone R :A:	3.00	8.00
124 Hand to Hand R :R:	1.25	3.00
125 Hanna's Custody R :W:	1.25	3.00
126 Harrow U :G:	.40	1.00
127 Havoc U :R:	.40	1.00
128 Heart Sliver C :R:	.40	1.00
129 Heartwood Dryad C :G:	.15	.30
130 Heartwood Giant R :G:	.75	2.00
131 Heartwood Treefolk U :G:	.40	1.00
132 Helm of Possession R :A:	1.25	3.00
133 Hero's Resolve C :W:	.15	.30
134 Horned Sliver U :G:	1.50	4.00
135 Horned Turtle C :B:	.15	.30
136 Humility R :W:	3.00	8.00
137 Imps' Taunt U :K:	.40	1.00
138 Insight U :B:	.40	1.00
139 Interdict U :B:	.40	1.00
140 Intuition R :B:	15.00	40.00
141 Invulnerability U :W:	.40	1.00
142 Island L :L:	.15	.30
143 Jackal Pup U :R:	1.50	4.00
144 Jet Medallion R :A:	3.00	8.00
145 Jinxed Idol R :A:	1.25	3.00
146 Kezzerdrix R :K:	1.25	3.00
147 Kindle C :R:	.20	.50
148 Knight of Dawn U :W:	.40	1.00
149 Knight of Dusk U :K:	.40	1.00
150 Krakilin U :G:	.40	1.00
151 Leeching Licid U :K:	.40	1.00
152 Legacy's Allure U :B:	.40	1.00
153 Legerdemain U :B:	.40	1.00
154 Light of Day U :W:	.75	2.00
155 Lightning Blast C :R:	.20	.50
156 Lightning Elemental C :R:	.15	.30
157 Living Death R :K:	2.00	5.00
158 Lobotomy U :D:	.40	1.00
159 Lotus Petal C :A:	1.25	3.00
160 Lowland Giant C :R:	.15	.30
161 Maddening Imp R :K:	.75	2.00
162 Magmasaur R :R:	.75	2.00
163 Magnetic Web R :A:	.75	2.00
164 Mana Severance R :B:	2.00	5.00
165 Manakin C :A:	.15	.30
166 Manta Riders C :B:	.15	.30
167 Marble Titan R :W:	.75	2.00
168 Marsh Lurker C :K:	.15	.30
169 Master Decoy C :W:	.15	.30
170 Mawcor R :B:	.75	2.00
171 Maze of Shadows U :L:	.40	1.00
172 Meditate R :B:	2.50	6.00
173 Metallic Sliver C :A:	.40	1.00
174 Mindwhip Sliver U :K:	.75	2.00
175 Minion of the Wastes R :K:	1.25	3.00
176 Mirri's Guile R :G:	2.00	5.00
177 Mnemonic Sliver U :B:	.75	2.00
178 Mogg Cannon U :A:	.20	.50
179 Mogg Conscripts C :R:	.15	.30
180 Mogg Fanatic C :R:	.75	2.00
181 Mogg Hollows U :L:	.40	1.00
182 Mogg Raider C :R:	.15	.30
183 Mogg Squad U :R:	.40	1.00
184 Mongrel Pack R :G:	1.25	3.00
185 Mountain L :L:	.15	.30
186 Mounted Archers C :W:	.15	.30
187 Muscle Sliver C :G:	.75	2.00
188 Natural Spring C :G:	.15	.30
189 Nature's Revolt R :G:	1.25	3.00
190 Needle Storm U :G:	.40	1.00
191 No Quarter R :R:	.75	2.00
192 Nurturing Licid U :G:	.40	1.00
193 Opportunist U :R:	.40	1.00
194 Oracle en-Vec R :W:	1.25	3.00
195 Orim, Samite Healer R :W:	1.25	3.00
196 Orim's Prayer U :W:	.75	2.00
197 Overrun U :G:	1.25	3.00
198 Pacifism C :W:	.15	.30
199 Pallimud R :R:	.75	2.00
200 Patchwork Gnomes U :A:	.40	1.00
201 Pearl Medallion R :A:	3.00	8.00
202 Pegasus Refuge R :W:	1.25	3.00
203 Perish U :K:	.75	2.00
204 Phyrexian Grimoire R :A:	.75	2.00
205 Phyrexian Hulk U :A:	.40	1.00
206 Phyrexian Splicer U :A:	.40	1.00
207 Pincher Beetles C :G:	.15	.30
208 Pine Barrens R :L:	.75	2.00
209 Pit Imp C :K:	.15	.30
210 Plains L :L:	.15	.30
211 Power Sink C :B:	.15	.30
212 Precognition R :B:	.75	2.00
213 Propaganda U :B:	1.25	3.00
214 Puppet Strings U :A:	.40	1.00
215 Quickening Licid U :W:	.40	1.00
216 Rain of Tears U :K:	.40	1.00
217 Rampant Growth C :G:	.15	.30
218 Ranger en-Vec U :D:	.40	1.00
219 Rathi Dragon R :R:	3.00	8.00
220 Rats of Rath C :K:	.15	.30
221 Reality Anchor C :G:	.15	.30
222 Reanimate U :K:	2.50	6.00
223 Reap U :G:	.20	.50
224 Reckless Spite U :K:	.40	1.00
225 Recycle R :G:	1.50	4.00
226 Reflecting Pool R :L:	4.00	10.00
227 Renegade Warlord U :R:	.40	1.00
228 Repentance U :W:	.40	1.00
229 Respite C :G:	.15	.30
230 Rolling Thunder C :R:	.15	.30
231 Root Maze R :G:	1.25	3.00
232 Rootbreaker Wurm C :G:	.15	.30
233 Rootwalla C :G:	.15	.30
234 Rootwater Depths U :L:	.40	1.00
235 Rootwater Diver U :B:	.40	1.00
236 Rootwater Hunter C :B:	.15	.30
237 Rootwater Matriarch R :B:	.75	2.00
238 Rootwater Shaman R :B:	.75	2.00
239 Ruby Medallion R :A:	2.50	6.00
240 Sacred Guide R :W:	1.25	3.00
241 Sadistic Glee C :K:	.15	.30
242 Safeguard R :W:	.75	2.00
243 Salt Flats R :L:	.75	2.00
244 Sandstone Warrior C :R:	.15	.30
245 Sapphire Medallion R :A:	4.00	10.00
246 Sarcomancy R :K:	2.50	6.00
247 Scabland R :L:	.75	2.00
248 Scalding Tongs R :A:	1.50	4.00
249 Scorched Earth R :R:	1.25	3.00
250 Scragnoth U :G:	.40	1.00
251 Screeching Harpy U :K:	.40	1.00
252 Scroll Rack R :A:	3.00	8.00
253 Sea Monster C :B:	.15	.30
254 Searing Touch U :R:	.40	1.00
255 Seeker of Skybreak C :G:	.15	.30
256 Segmented Wurm U :D:	.40	1.00
257 Selenia, Dark Angel R :D:	2.00	5.00
258 Serene Offering U :W:	.40	1.00
259 Servant of Volrath C :K:	.15	.30
260 Shadow Rift C :B:	.15	.30
261 Shadowstorm U :R:	.40	1.00
262 Shatter C :R:	.15	.30
263 Shimmering Wings C :B:	.15	.30
264 Shocker R :R:	1.25	3.00
265 Sky Spirit U :D:	.40	1.00
266 Skyshroud Condor U :B:	.40	1.00
267 Skyshroud Elf C :G:	.15	.30
268 Skyshroud Forest R :L:	1.25	3.00
269 Skyshroud Ranger C :G:	.15	.30
270 Skyshroud Troll C :G:	.15	.30
271 Skyshroud Vampire U :K:	.40	1.00
272 Soltari Crusader U :W:	.40	1.00
273 Soltari Emissary R :W:	1.25	3.00
274 Soltari Foot Soldier C :W:	.15	.30
275 Soltari Guerrillas R :D:	1.25	3.00
276 Soltari Lancer C :W:	.15	.30
277 Soltari Monk U :W:	1.25	3.00
278 Soltari Priest U :W:	1.25	3.00
279 Soltari Trooper C :W:	.15	.30
280 Souldrinker U :K:	.40	1.00
281 Spell Blast C :B:	.15	.30
282 Spike Drone C :G:	.15	.30
283 Spinal Graft C :K:	.15	.30
284 Spirit Mirror R :W:	.75	2.00
285 Spontaneous Combustion U :D:	.40	1.00
286 Squee's Toy C :A:	.15	.30
287 Stalking Stones U :L:	.40	1.00
288 Starke of Rath R :R:	.75	2.00
289 Static Orb R :A:	2.00	5.00
290 Staunch Defenders U :W:	.40	1.00
291 Steal Enchantment U :B:	.40	1.00
292 Stinging Licid U :B:	.40	1.00
293 Stone Rain C :R:	.15	.30
294 Storm Front U :G:	.40	1.00
295 Stun C :R:	.15	.30
296 Sudden Impact U :R:	.40	1.00
297 Swamp (4 versions) L :L:	.15	.30
298 Tahngarth's Rage U :R:	.40	1.00
299 Talon Sliver C :W:	.40	1.00
300 Telethopter U :A:	.40	1.00
301 Thalakos Dreamsower U :B:	.40	1.00
302 Thalakos Lowlands U :L:	.40	1.00
303 Thalakos Mistfolk C :B:	.15	.30
304 Thalakos Seer C :B:	.15	.30
305 Thalakos Sentry C :B:	.15	.30
306 Thumbscrews R :A:	.75	2.00
307 Time Ebb C :B:	.15	.30
308 Time Warp R :B:	3.00	8.00
309 Tooth and Claw R :R:	1.25	3.00
310 Torture Chamber R :A:	.75	2.00
311 Tradewind Rider R :B:	2.00	5.00
312 Trained Armodon C :G:	.15	.30
313 Tranquility C :G:	.15	.30
314 Trumpeting Armodon U :G:	.20	.50
315 Twitch C :B:	.15	.30
316 Unstable Shapeshifter R :B:	.75	2.00
317 Vec Townships U :L:	.40	1.00
318 Verdant Force R :G:	.60	1.50
319 Verdigris U :G:	.20	.50
320 Vhati il-Dal R :D:	1.25	3.00
321 Volrath's Curse C :B:	.15	.30
322 Wall of Diffusion C :R:	.15	.30
323 Warmth U :W:	.20	.50
324 Wasteland U :L:	30.00	60.00
325 Watchdog U :A:	.20	.50
326 Whim of Volrath R :B:	1.25	3.00
327 Whispers of the Muse U :B:	.40	1.00
328 Wild Wurm U :R:	.40	1.00
329 Wind Dancer U :B:	.20	.50
330 Wind Drake C :B:	.15	.30
331 Winds of Rath R :W:	1.50	4.00
332 Winged Sliver C :B:	.75	2.00
333 Winter's Grasp U :G:	.75	2.00
334 Wood Sage R :D:	.75	2.00
335 Worthy Cause U :W:	1.25	3.00

1998 Magic The Gathering Stronghold

Card	Low	High
COMPLETE SET (143)	100.00	175.00
BOOSTER BOX (36 PACKS)	200.00	300.00
BOOSTER PACK (15 CARDS)	5.00	8.00
STARTER DECK BOX (12 DECKS)	175.00	250.00
STARTER DECK	15.00	20.00
RELEASED ON MARCH 2, 1998		
1 Acidic Sliver U :D:	1.25	3.00
2 Amok R :R:	.75	2.00
3 Awakening R :G:	.75	2.00
4 Bandage C :W:	.15	.30
5 Bottomless Pit U :K:	.20	.50
6 Brush With Death C :K:	.15	.30
7 Bullwhip U :A:	.20	.50
8 Burgeoning R :G:	1.25	3.00
9 Calming Licid U :W:	.20	.50
10 Cannibalize C :K:	.15	.30
11 Cardassid R :G:	.75	2.00
12 Change of Heart C :W:	.15	.30
13 Cloud Spirit C :B:	.15	.30
14 Constant Mists U :G:	.75	2.00
15 Contemplation U :W:	.40	1.00
16 Contempt C :B:	.15	.30
17 Conviction C :W:	.15	.30
18 Convulsing Licid U :R:	.20	.50
19 Corrupting Licid U :K:	.20	.50
20 Craven Giant C :R:	.15	.30
21 Crossbow Ambush C :G:	.15	.30
22 Crovax, The Cursed R :K:	1.25	3.00
23 Crystalline Sliver U :D:	3.00	8.00
24 Dauthi Trapper U :K:	.40	1.00
25 Death Stroke C :K:	.15	.30
26 Dream Halls R :B:	1.25	3.00
27 Dream Prowler C :B:	.15	.30
28 Duct Crawler C :R:	.15	.30
29 Dungeon Shade C :K:	.15	.30
30 Elven Rite U :G:	.20	.50
31 Endangered Armodon C :G:	.15	.30
32 Ensnaring Bridge R :A:	5.00	12.00
33 Evacuation R :B:	1.50	4.00
34 Fanning the Flames U :R:	.60	1.50
35 Flame Wave U :R:	.60	1.50
36 Fling C :R:	.75	2.00
37 Flowstone Blade C :R:	.15	.30
38 Flowstone Hellion U :R:	.40	1.00
39 Flowstone Mauler R :R:	.75	2.00
40 Flowstone Shambler C :R:	.15	.30
41 Foul Imp C :K:	.15	.30
42 Furnace Spirit C :R:	.15	.30
43 Gliding Licid U :B:	.40	1.00
44 Grave Pact R :K:	3.00	8.00
45 Hammerhead Shark C :B:	.15	.30
46 Heartstone U :A:	.75	2.00
47 Heat of Battle U :R:	.40	1.00
48 Hermit Druid R :G:	.75	2.00
49 Hesitation U :B:	.40	1.00
50 Hibernation Sliver U :D:	.75	2.00
51 Hidden Retreat R :W:	.75	2.00
52 Honor Guard C :W:	.15	.30
53 Horn of Greed R :A:	2.00	5.00
54 Hornet Cannon U :A:	.20	.50
55 Intruder Alarm R :B:	3.00	8.00
56 Invasion Plans R :R:	.75	2.00
57 Jinxed Ring R :A:	1.25	3.00
58 Lab Rats C :K:	.15	.30
59 Lancers en-Kor U :W:	.20	.50
60 Leap C :B:	.15	.30
61 Lowland Basilisk C :G:	.15	.30
62 Mana Leak C :B:	1.25	3.00
63 Mask of the Mimic U :B:	.75	2.00
64 Megrim U :K:	1.25	3.00
65 Mind Games C :B:	.15	.30
66 Mind Peel U :K:	.40	1.00
67 Mindwarper R :K:	.75	2.00
68 Mob Justice C :R:	.15	.30
69 Mogg Bombers C :R:	.15	.30
70 Mogg Flunkies C :R:	.15	.30
71 Mogg Infestation R :R:	1.25	3.00
72 Mogg Maniac U :R:	.75	2.00
73 Morgue Thrull C :K:	.15	.30
74 Mortuary R :K:	1.25	3.00
75 Mox Diamond R :A:	15.00	40.00
76 Mulch C :G:	.15	.30
77 Nomads en-Kor C :W:	.40	1.00
78 Overgrowth C :G:	.15	.30
79 Portcullis R :A:	1.25	3.00
80 Primal Rage U :G:	.75	2.00
81 Provoke C :G:	.15	.30
82 Pursuit of Knowledge R :W:	1.25	3.00
83 Rabid Rats C :K:	.15	.30
84 Ransack U :B:	.40	1.00
85 Rebound U :B:	.75	2.00
86 Reins of Power R :B:	.75	2.00
87 Revenant R :K:	.75	2.00
88 Rolling Stones R :W:	.75	2.00
89 Ruination R :R:	.75	2.00
90 Sacred Ground R :W:	1.50	4.00
91 Samite Blessing C :W:	.15	.30
92 Scapegoat U :W:	.40	1.00
93 Seething Anger C :R:	.15	.30

94 Serpent Warrior C :K: .15 .30
95 Shaman en-Kor R :W: .60 1.50
96 Shard Phoenix R :R: 1.50 4.00
97 Shifting Wall U :A: .75 2.00
98 Shock C :R: .15 .30
99 Silt C :B: .15 .30
100 Silver Wyvern R :B: .75 2.00
101 Skeleton Scavengers R :K: 1.25 3.00
102 Skyshroud Archer C :G: .15 .30
103 Skyshroud Falcon C :W: .15 .30
104 Skyshroud Troopers C :G: .15 .30
105 Sliver Queen R :D: 25.00 50.00
106 Smite C :W: .15 .30
107 Soltari Champion R :W: 1.25 3.00
108 Spike Breeder R :G: 1.25 3.00
109 Spike Colony C :G: .15 .30
110 Spike Feeder U :G: .75 2.00
111 Spike Soldier U :G: .40 1.00
112 Spike Worker C :G: .15 .30
113 Spindrift Drake C :B: .15 .30
114 Spined Sliver U :D: .75 2.00
115 Spined Wurm C :G: .15 .30
116 Spirit en-Kor C :W: .15 .30
117 Spitting Hydra R :R: .40 1.00
118 Stronghold Assassin R :K: .75 2.00
119 Stronghold Taskmaster U :K: .40 1.00
120 Sword of the Chosen R :A: 1.25 3.00
121 Temper U :W: .40 1.00
122 Tempting Licid U :G: .20 .50
123 Thalakos Deceiver R :B: 1.50 4.00
124 Tidal Surge C :B: .15 .30
125 Tidal Warrior C :B: .15 .30
126 Torment C :K: .15 .30
127 Tortured Existence C :K: .40 1.00
128 Venerable Monk C :W: .15 .30
129 Verdant Touch R :G: 1.25 3.00
130 Victual Sliver U :D: 1.25 3.00
131 Volrath's Gardens R :G: .75 2.00
132 Volrath's Laboratory R :A: .75 2.00
133 Volrath's Shapeshifter R :B: 1.50 4.00
134 Volrath's Stronghold R :L: 10.00 25.00
135 Walking Dream U :B: .40 1.00
136 Wall of Blossoms U :G: 1.25 3.00
137 Wall of Essence U :W: .40 1.00
138 Wall of Razors U :R: .40 1.00
139 Wall of Souls U :K: 1.25 3.00
140 Wall of Tears U :B: .40 1.00
141 Warrior Angel R :W: 1.50 4.00
142 Warrior en-Kor U :W: .75 2.00
143 Youthful Knight C :W: .15 .30

1998 Magic The Gathering Exodus

COMPLETE SET (143) 100.00 175.00
BOOSTER BOX 200.00 300.00
BOOSTER PACK 7.00 9.00
THEME DECK 15.00 20.00
RELEASED ON JUNE 15, 1998
1 Allay C :W: .20 .50
2 Angelic Blessing C :W: .15 .30
3 Cataclysm R :W: 2.50 6.00
4 Charging Paladin C :W: .15 .30
5 Convalescence R :W: 1.50 4.00
6 Exalted Dragon R :W: 1.50 4.00
7 High Ground U :W: .40 1.00
8 Keeper of the Light U :W: .40 1.00
9 Kor Chant C :W: .15 .30
10 Limited Resources R :W: 1.50 4.00
11 Oath of Lieges R :W: 1.25 3.00
12 Paladin en-Vec R :W: 1.25 3.00
13 Peace of Mind U :W: .40 1.00
14 Pegasus Stampede U :W: .40 1.00
15 Penance U :W: .40 1.00
16 Reaping the Rewards C :W: .15 .30
17 Reconnaissance U :W: .40 1.00
18 Shackles C :W: .15 .30
19 Shield Mate C :W: .15 .30
20 Soltari Visionary C :W: .15 .30
21 Soul Warden C :W: .15 .30
22 Standing Troops C :W: .15 .30
23 Treasure Hunter U :W: .40 1.00
24 Wall of Nets R :W: 1.50 4.00
25 Welkin Hawk C :W: .15 .30
26 Zealots en-Dal U :W: .40 1.00
27 AEther Tide C :B: .15 .30
28 Cunning C :B: .15 .30
29 Curiosity U :B: .60 1.50
30 Dominating Licid R :B: 1.50 4.00
31 Ephemeron R :B: .75 2.00
32 Equilibrium R :B: 1.25 3.00
33 Ertai, Wizard Adept R :B: 3.00 8.00
34 Fade Away C :B: .15 .30
35 Forbid U :B: .75 2.00
36 Keeper of the Mind U :B: .40 1.00
37 Killer Whale U :B: .40 1.00
38 Mana Breach U :B: .40 1.00
39 Merfolk Looter C :B: .20 .50
40 Mind Over Matter R :B: 3.00 8.00
41 Mirozel U :B: .40 1.00
42 Oath of Scholars R :B: 1.25 3.00
43 Robe of Mirrors C :B: .15 .30
44 Rootwater Mystic C :B: .15 .30
45 School of Piranha C :B: .15 .30
46 Scrivener U :B: .40 1.00
47 Thalakos Drifters R :B: 1.25 3.00
48 Thalakos Scout C :B: .15 .30
49 Theft of Dreams C :B: .15 .30
50 Treasure Trove U :B: .40 1.00
51 Wayward Soul C :B: .15 .30
52 Whiptongue Frog C :B: .15 .30
53 Carnophage C :K: .40 1.00
54 Cat Burglar C :K: .15 .30
55 Culling the Weak C :K: .40 1.00
56 Cursed Flesh C :K: .15 .30
57 Dauthi Cutthroat U :K: .75 2.00
58 Dauthi Jackal C :K: .15 .30
59 Dauthi Warlord U :K: .75 2.00
60 Death's Duet C :K: .15 .30
61 Entropic Specter R :K: .75 2.00
62 Fugue U :K: .40 1.00
63 Grollub C :K: .15 .30
64 Hatred R :K: 2.50 6.00
65 Keeper of the Dead U :K: .40 1.00
66 Mind Maggots U :K: .40 1.00
67 Nausea C :K: .20 .50
68 Necrologia U :K: .40 1.00
69 Oath of Ghouls R :K: 1.25 3.00
70 Pit Spawn R :K: 1.25 3.00
71 Plaguebearer R :K: 1.25 3.00
72 Recurring Nightmare R :K: 6.00 15.00
73 Scare Tactics C :K: .15 .30
74 Slaughter U :K: .40 1.00
75 Spike Cannibal U :K: .40 1.00
76 Thrull Surgeon C :K: .15 .30
77 Vampire Hounds C :K: .15 .30
78 Volrath's Dungeon R :K: .75 2.00
79 Anarchist C :R: .15 .30
80 Cinder Crawler C :R: .15 .30
81 Dizzying Gaze C :R: .15 .30
82 Fighting Chance R :R: 1.25 3.00
83 Flowstone Flood U :R: .20 .50
84 Furnace Brood C :R: .15 .30
85 Keeper of the Flame U :R: .40 1.00
86 Mage il-Vec C :R: .15 .30
87 Maniacal Rage C :R: .15 .30
88 Mogg Assassin U :R: .75 2.00
89 Monstrous Hound R :R: .75 2.00
90 Oath of Mages R :R: 1.25 3.00
91 Ogre Shaman R :R: .75 2.00
92 Onslaught C :R: .15 .30
93 Pandemonium R :R: .60 1.50
94 Paroxysm U :R: .40 1.00
95 Price of Progress U :R: .75 2.00
96 Raging Goblin C :R: .15 .30
97 Ravenous Baboons R :R: .75 2.00
98 Reckless Ogre C :R: .15 .30
99 Sabertooth Wyvern U :R: .40 1.00
100 Scalding Salamander U :R: .40 1.00
101 Seismic Assault R :R: 1.50 4.00
102 Shattering Pulse C :R: .20 .50
103 Sonic Burst C :R: .15 .30
104 Spellshock U :R: .40 1.00
105 Avenging Druid C :G: .15 .30
106 Bequeathal C :G: .20 .50
107 Cartographer U :G: .40 1.00
108 Crashing Boars U :G: .40 1.00
109 Elven Palisade U :G: .20 .50
110 Elvish Berserker C :G: .20 .50
111 Jackalope Herd C :G: .15 .30
112 Keeper of the Beasts U :G: .40 1.00
113 Manabond R :G: 1.25 3.00
114 Mirri, Cat Warrior R :G: .75 2.00
115 Oath of Druids R :G: 3.00 8.00
116 Plated Rootwalla C :G: .15 .30
117 Predatory Hunger C :G: .15 .30
118 Pygmy Troll C :G: .15 .30
119 Rabid Wolverines C :G: .15 .30
120 Reclaim C :G: .15 .30
121 Resuscitate U :G: .20 .50
122 Rootwater Alligator C :G: .15 .30
123 Skyshroud Elite U :G: .75 2.00
124 Skyshroud War Beast R :G: 1.25 3.00
125 Song of Serenity U :G: .40 1.00
126 Spike Hatcher R :G: 1.25 3.00
127 Spike Rogue U :G: .20 .50
128 Spike Weaver R :G: 2.00 5.00
129 Survival of the Fittest R :G: 12.00 30.00
130 Wood Elves C :G: .15 .30
131 Coat of Arms R :A: 4.00 10.00
132 Erratic Portal R :A: 1.25 3.00
133 Medicine Bag U :A: .40 1.00
134 Memory Crystal R :A: 1.25 3.00
135 Mindless Automaton R :A: 1.50 4.00
136 Null Brooch R :A: 1.50 4.00
137 Skyshaper U :A: .40 1.00
138 Spellbook U :A: .75 2.00
139 Sphere of Resistance R :A: 2.00 5.00
140 Thopter Squadron R :A: .75 2.00
141 Transmogrifying Licid U :A: .40 1.00
142 Workhorse R :A: 1.25 3.00
143 City of Traitors R :L: 25.00 50.00

1998 Magic The Gathering Urza's Saga

COMPLETE SET (350) 375.00 500.00
BOOSTER BOX (36 PACKS) 350.00 500.00
BOOSTER PACK (15 CARDS) 15.00 20.00
STARTER DECK BOX (12 DECKS) 150.00 200.00
STARTER DECK 15.00 20.00
RELEASED ON OCTOBER 12, 1998
1 Absolute Grace U :W: .75 2.00
2 Absolute Law U :W: .75 2.00
3 Angelic Chorus R :W: 4.00 10.00
4 Angelic Page C :W: .15 .30
5 Brilliant Halo C :W: .15 .30
6 Catastrophe R :W: 1.50 4.00
7 Clear U :W: .40 1.00
8 Congregate C :W: .40 1.00
9 Defensive Formation U :W: .40 1.00
10 Disciple of Grace C :W: .15 .30
11 Disciple of Law C :W: .15 .30
12 Disenchant C :W: .40 1.00
13 Elite Archers R :W: .75 2.00
14 Faith Healer R :W: .75 2.00
15 Glorious Anthem R :W: 3.00 8.00
16 Healing Salve C :W: .15 .30
17 Herald of Serra R :W: 1.50 4.00
18 Humble U :W: .40 1.00
19 Intrepid Hero R :W: 2.50 5.00
20 Monk Idealist U :W: .40 1.00
21 Monk Realist C :W: .15 .30
22 Opal Acrolith U :W: .20 .50
23 Opal Archangel R :W: 2.50 5.00
24 Opal Caryatid C :W: .15 .30
25 Opal Gargoyle C :W: .15 .30
26 Opal Titan R :W: 1.25 3.00
27 Pacifism C :W: .15 .30
28 Pariah R :W: 1.50 4.00
29 Path of Peace C :W: .15 .30
30 Pegasus Charger C :W: .15 .30
31 Planar Birth R :W: 1.25 3.00
32 Presence of the Master U :W: .40 1.00
33 Redeem U :W: .40 1.00
34 Remembrance R :W: 1.25 3.00
35 Rune of Protection Artifacts U :W: .20 .50
36 Rune of Protection Black C :W: .15 .30
37 Rune of Protection Blue C :W: .15 .30
38 Rune of Protection Green C :W: .15 .30
39 Rune of Protection Lands R :W: .15 .30
40 Rune of Protection Red C :W: .15 .30
41 Rune of Protection White C :W: .15 .30
42 Sanctum Custodian C :W: .15 .30
43 Sanctum Guardian U :W: .30 .75
44 Seasoned Marshal U :W: .40 1.00
45 Serra Avatar R :W: 2.00 5.00
46 Serra Zealot C :W: .15 .30
47 Serra's Embrace U :W: .75 2.00
48 Serra's Hymn U :W: .40 1.00
49 Serra's Liturgy R :W: 1.25 3.00
50 Shimmering Barrier U :W: .40 1.00
51 Silent Attendant C :W: .15 .30
52 Songstitcher U :W: .40 1.00
53 Soul Sculptor R :W: 1.50 4.00
54 Voice of Grace U :W: .75 2.00
55 Voice of Law U :W: .75 2.00
56 Waylay U :W: .40 1.00
57 Worship R :W: .75 2.00
58 Academy Researchers U :B: .20 .50
59 Annul C :B: .40 1.00
60 Arcane Laboratory U :B: .75 2.00
61 Attunement R :B: .75 2.00
62 Back to Basics R :B: 2.00 5.00
63 Barrin's Codex R :A: .75 2.00
64 Catalog C :B: .15 .30
65 Cloak of Mists C :B: .15 .30
66 Confiscate U :B: .40 1.00
67 Coral Merfolk C :B: .15 .30
68 Curfew C :B: .15 .30
69 Disruptive Student C :B: .15 .30
70 Douse U :B: .40 1.00
71 Drifting Djinn R :B: 1.50 4.00
72 Enchantment Alteration U :B: .40 1.00
73 Energy Field R :B: 1.50 4.00
74 Exhaustion U :B: .40 1.00
75 Fog Bank U :B: .75 2.00
76 Gilded Drake R :B: 8.00 20.00
77 Great Whale R :B: 1.50 4.00
78 Hermetic Study C :B: .15 .30
79 Hibernation U :B: .60 1.50
80 Horseshoe Crab C :B: .15 .30
81 Imaginary Pet R :B: 1.25 3.00
82 Launch C :B: .15 .30
83 Lilting Refrain U :B: .40 1.00
84 Lingering Mirage U :B: .40 1.00
85 Morphling R :B: 3.00 8.00
86 Pendrell Drake C :B: .15 .30
87 Pendrell Flux C :B: .15 .30
88 Peregrine Drake U :B: .40 1.00
89 Power Sink C :B: .15 .30
90 Power Taint C :B: .15 .30
91 Recantation R :B: 1.25 3.00
92 Rescind C :B: .15 .30
93 Rewind C :B: .15 .30
94 Sandbar Merfolk C :B: .15 .30
95 Sandbar Serpent U :B: .20 .50
96 Show and Tell R :B: 2.50 6.00
97 Somnophore R :B: 1.25 3.00
98 Spire Owl C :B: .15 .30
99 Stern Proctor U :B: .40 1.00
100 Stroke of Genius R :B: 4.00 10.00
101 Sunder R :B: .75 2.00
102 Telepathy U :B: .40 1.00
103 Time Spiral R :B: 6.00 15.00
104 Tolarian Winds C :B: .60 1.50
105 Turnabout U :B: 1.25 3.00
106 Veil of Birds C :B: .15 .30
107 Veiled Apparition U :B: .40 1.00
108 Veiled Crocodile R :B: 1.25 3.00
109 Veiled Sentry U :B: .40 1.00
110 Veiled Serpent C :B: .15 .30
111 Windfall U :B: .40 1.00
112 Wizard Mentor C :B: .15 .30
113 Zephid R :B: 1.25 3.00
114 Zephid's Embrace U :B: .40 1.00
115 Abyssal Horror R :K: .75 2.00
116 Befoul C :K: .15 .30
117 Bereavement U :K: .20 .50
118 Blood Vassal C :K: .15 .30
119 Bog Raiders C :K: .15 .30
120 Breach C :K: .15 .30
121 Cackling Fiend C :K: .15 .30
122 Carrion Beetles C :K: .15 .30
123 Contamination R :K: 2.50 5.00
124 Corrupt C :K: .15 .30
125 Crazed Skirge U :K: .40 1.00
126 Dark Hatchling R :K: 1.50 4.00
127 Dark Ritual C :K: .15 .30
128 Darkest Hour R :K: 1.50 4.00
129 Despondency C :K: .15 .30
130 Diabolic Servitude U :K: .60 1.50
131 Discordant Dirge R :K: .75 2.00
132 Duress C :K: 2.50 5.00
133 Eastern Paladin R :K: 1.50 4.00
134 Exhume C :K: .15 .30
135 Expunge C :K: .15 .30
136 Flesh Reaver U :K: .40 1.00
137 Hollow Dogs C :K: .15 .30
138 Ill-Gotten Gains R :K: 1.25 3.00
139 Looming Shade C :K: .15 .30
140 Lurking Evil R :K: 1.25 3.00
141 Mana Leech U :K: .40 1.00
142 No Rest for the Wicked U :K: .40 1.00
143 Oppression R :K: 1.25 3.00
144 Order of Yawgmoth U :K: .40 1.00
145 Parasitic Bond U :K: .40 1.00
146 Persecute R :K: 3.00 8.00
147 Pestilence C :K: .15 .30
148 Phyrexian Ghoul C :K: .15 .30
149 Planar Void U :K: 1.25 3.00
150 Priest of Gix U :K: .75 2.00
151 Rain of Filth U :K: .40 1.00
152 Ravenous Skirge C :K: .15 .30
153 Reclusive Wight U :K: .40 1.00
154 Reprocess R :K: 1.25 3.00
155 Sanguine Guard U :K: .20 .50
156 Sicken C :K: .15 .30
157 Skirge Familiar U :K: .40 1.00
158 Skittering Skirge C :K: .15 .30
159 Sleeper Agent R :K: 1.50 4.00
160 Spined Fluke U :K: .40 1.00
161 Tainted Æther R :K: 1.50 4.00
162 Unnerve C :K: .15 .30
163 Unworthy Dead C :K: .15 .30
164 Vampiric Embrace U :K: .75 2.00
165 Vebulid R :K: 1.25 3.00
166 Victimize U :K: .75 2.00
167 Vile Requiem U :K: .40 1.00
168 Western Paladin R :K: 1.50 4.00
169 Witch Engine R :K: .75 2.00
170 Yawgmoth's Edict U :K: .40 1.00
171 Yawgmoth's Will R :K: 6.00 15.00
172 Acidic Soil U :R: .20 .50
173 Antagonism R :R: .75 2.00
174 Arc Lightning C :R: .15 .30
175 Bedlam R :R: 1.50 4.00
176 Brand R :R: 1.25 3.00
177 Bravado C :R: .15 .30
178 Bulwark R :R: 1.25 3.00
179 Crater Hellion R :R: 2.50 5.00
180 Destructive Urge U :R: .60 1.50
181 Disorder U :R: .40 1.00
182 Dromosaur C :R: .15 .30
183 Electryte R :R: 1.25 3.00
184 Falter C :R: .15 .30
185 Fault Line R :R: 1.25 3.00
186 Fiery Mantle C :R: .15 .30
187 Fire Ants U :R: .40 1.00
188 Gamble R :R: 2.50 5.00
189 Goblin Cadets U :R: .75 2.00
190 Goblin Lackey U :R: 4.00 10.00
191 Goblin Matron C :R: 1.25 3.00
192 Goblin Offensive U :R: .75 2.00
193 Goblin Patrol C :R: .40 1.00
194 Goblin Raider C :R: .15 .30
195 Goblin Spelunkers C :R: .15 .30
196 Goblin War Buggy C :R: .20 .50
197 Guma U :R: .40 1.00
198 Headlong Rush C :R: .15 .30
199 Heat Ray C :R: .15 .30
200 Jagged Lightning U :R: .40 1.00
201 Lay Waste C :R: .15 .30
202 Lightning Dragon R :R: 2.00 5.00
203 Meltdown U :R: .75 2.00
204 Okk R :R: 1.25 3.00
205 Outmaneuver U :R: .40 1.00
206 Rain of Salt U :R: .40 1.00
207 Raze C :R: .15 .30
208 Reflexes C :R: .15 .30
209 Retromancer C :R: .15 .30
210 Rumbling Crescendo R :R: 1.25 3.00
211 Scald U :R: .40 1.00
212 Scoria Wurm R :R: 1.50 4.00
213 Scrap C :R: .15 .30
214 Shivan Raptor U :R: .40 1.00
215 Shiv's Embrace U :R: .40 1.00
216 Shivan Gorge R :L: 1.50 4.00
217 Shower of Sparks C :R: .15 .30
218 Sneak Attack R :R: 15.00 40.00
219 Steam Blast U :R: .40 1.00
220 Sulfuric Vapors R :R: 1.50 4.00
221 Thundering Giant U :R: .40 1.00
222 Torch Song U :R: .40 1.00
223 Viashino Outrider C :R: .15 .30
224 Viashino Runner C :R: .15 .30
225 Viashino Sandswimmer R :R: 1.50 4.00
226 Viashino Weaponsmith C :R: .15 .30
227 Vug Lizard U :R: .40 1.00
228 Wildfire R :R: .75 2.00
229 Abundance R :G: 1.25 3.00
230 Acridian C :G: .15 .30
231 Albino Troll U :G: .75 2.00
232 Anaconda U :G: .20 .50
233 Argothian Elder U :G: .75 2.00
234 Argothian Enchantress R :G: 5.00 12.00
235 Argothian Swine C :G: .15 .30
236 Argothian Wurm R :G: 2.50 6.00
237 Blanchwood Armor U :G: .75 2.00
238 Blanchwood Treefolk C :G: .15 .30
239 Bull Hippo U :G: .20 .50
240 Carpet of Flowers U :G: .40 1.00
241 Cave Tiger C :G: .15 .30
242 Child of Gaea R :G: 2.50 5.00
243 Citanul Centaurs R :G: 1.25 3.00
244 Citanul Hierophants R :G: 1.25 3.00
245 Cradle Guard U :G: .40 1.00
246 Crosswinds U :G: .40 1.00
247 Elvish Herder C :G: .75 2.00
248 Elvish Lyrist C :G: .15 .30
249 Endless Wurm R :G: 2.50 6.00
250 Exploration R :G: 10.00 25.00
251 Fecundity U :G: 1.25 3.00
252 Fertile Ground C :G: .15 .30
253 Fortitude C :G: .15 .30
254 Gaea's Bounty C :G: .15 .30
255 Gaea's Embrace U :G: .75 2.00
256 Gorilla Warrior C :G: .15 .30
257 Greater Good R :G: 4.00 10.00
258 Greener Pastures R :G: 1.25 3.00
259 Hawkeater Moth U :G: .40 1.00
260 Hidden Ancients U :G: .40 1.00
261 Hidden Guerrillas U :G: .40 1.00
262 Hidden Herd R :G: 1.25 3.00
263 Hidden Predators R :G: 1.50 4.00
264 Hidden Spider C :G: .15 .30
265 Hidden Stag R :G: 1.25 3.00
266 Hush C :G: .15 .30
267 Lull C :G: .15 .30
268 Midsummer Revel R :G: 1.25 3.00
269 Pouncing Jaguar C :G: .40 1.00
270 Priest of Titania C :G: 2.50 5.00
271 Rejuvenate C :G: .15 .30
272 Retaliation U :G: .40 1.00
273 Sporogenesis R :G: 1.25 3.00
274 Spreading Algae U :G: .40 1.00
275 Symbiosis C :G: .15 .30
276 Titania's Boon U :G: .40 1.00
277 Titania's Chosen U :G: 1.50 4.00
278 Treefolk Seedlings U :G: .40 1.00
279 Treetop Rangers C :G: .15 .30
280 Venomous Fangs C :G: .40 1.00
281 Vernal Bloom R :G: 2.50 6.00
282 War Dance U :G: .40 1.00
283 Whirlwind R :G: 1.25 3.00
284 Wild Dogs C :G: .15 .30
285 Winding Wurm C :G: .15 .30
286 Barrin, Master Wizard R :B: .75 2.00
287 Cathodion U :A: .40 1.00
288 Chimeric Staff R :A: 1.50 4.00
289 Citanul Flute R :A: 1.25 3.00
290 Claws of Gix U :A: .40 1.00
291 Copper Gnomes R :A: 1.25 3.00
292 Crystal Chimes U :A: .40 1.00
293 Dragon Blood U :A: .40 1.00
294 Endoskeleton U :A: .20 .50
295 Fluctuator R :A: 3.00 8.00
296 Grafted Skullcap R :A: 1.50 4.00
297 Hopping Automaton U :A: .40 1.00
298 Karn, Silver Golem R :A: 3.00 8.00
299 Lifeline R :A: 2.50 6.00
300 Lotus Blossom R :A: 1.50 4.00
301 Metrognome R :A: 1.25 3.00
302 Mishra's Helix R :A: 2.50 5.00
303 Mobile Fort U :A: .20 .50
304 Noetic Scales R :A: 1.25 3.00
305 Phyrexian Colossus R :A: 1.25 3.00
306 Phyrexian Processor R :A: 3.00 8.00
307 Pit Trap U :A: .30 .75
308 Purging Scythe R :A: .75 2.00
309 Smokestack R :A: 2.50 6.00
310 Temporal Aperture R :A: 1.25 3.00
311 Thran Turbine U :A: .40 1.00
312 Umbilicus R :A: 1.50 4.00
313 Urza's Armor U :A: .60 1.50
314 Voltaic Key U :A: 1.25 3.00
315 Wall of Junk U :A: .40 1.00
316 Whetstone R :A: 1.50 4.00
317 Wirecat U :A: .40 1.00
318 Worn Powerstone U :A: .75 2.00
319 Blasted Landscape U :L: .40 1.00
320 Drifting Meadow C :L: .15 .30
321 Gaea's Cradle R :L: 60.00 120.00
322 Phyrexian Tower R :L: 1.50 4.00
323 Polluted Mire C :L: .15 .30
324 Remote Isle C :L: .15 .30
325 Serra's Sanctum R :L: 3.00 8.00
326 Shivan Hellkite R :R: 3.00 8.00
327 Slippery Karst C :L: .15 .30
328 Smoldering Crater C :L: .15 .30
329 Thran Quarry R :L: 3.00 8.00
330 Tolarian Academy R :L: 12.00 30.00
331 Plains L :L: .20 .50
332 Plains L :L: .20 .50
333 Plains L :L: .20 .50
334 Plains L :L: .20 .50
335 Island L :L: .20 .50
336 Island L :L: .20 .50
337 Island L :L: .20 .50
338 Island L :L: .20 .50
339 Swamp L :L: .20 .50
340 Swamp L :L: .20 .50
341 Swamp L :L: .20 .50
342 Swamp L :L: .20 .50
343 Mountain L :L: .20 .50
344 Mountain L :L: .20 .50
345 Mountain L :L: .20 .50
346 Mountain L :L: .20 .50
347 Forest L :L: .20 .50
348 Forest L :L: .20 .50
349 Forest L :L: .20 .50
350 Forest L :L: .20 .50

1999 Magic The Gathering Urza's Legacy

COMPLETE SET (143) 100.00 150.00
BOOSTER BOX (36 PACKS) 300.00 400.00
BOOSTER PACK (15 CARDS)* 8.00 12.00
*FOIL: 1X TO 2X BASIC CARDS
RELEASED ON FEBRUARY 15, 1999
1 Angelic Curator C :W: .15 .30
2 Blessed Reversal R :W: 1.50 4.00
3 Burst of Energy C :W: .15 .30
4 Cessation C :W: .15 .30
5 Defender of Law C :W: .15 .30
6 Devout Harpist C :W: .15 .30
7 Erase C :W: .15 .30
8 Expendable Troops C :W: .15 .30
9 Hope and Glory U :W: .30 .75
10 Iron Will C :W: .15 .30
11 Karmic Guide R :W: 1.25 3.00
12 Knighthood U :W: .20 .50
13 Martyr's Cause U :W: .20 .50
14 Mother of Runes U :W: 1.25 3.00
15 Opal Avenger R :W: 1.50 4.00
16 Opal Champion C :W: .15 .30
17 Peace and Quiet U :W: .20 .50
18 Planar Collapse R :W: 1.25 3.00
19 Purify R :W: 1.25 3.00
20 Radiant, Archangel R :W: .50 1.00
21 Radiant's Dragoons U :W: .50 1.00
22 Radiant's Judgment C :W: .15 .30
23 Sustainer of the Realm U :W: .20 .50
24 Tragic Poet C :W: .15 .30
25 Anthroplasm R :B: 1.25 3.00
26 Archivist R :B: 1.50 4.00
27 Aura Flux C :B: .15 .30
28 Bouncing Beebles C :B: .15 .30
29 Cloud of Faeries C :B: .15 .30
30 Delusions of Mediocrity R :B: 1.50 4.00
31 Fleeting Image R :B: .75 2.00
32 Frantic Search C :B: .15 .30
33 Intervene C :B: .15 .30
34 King Crab U :B: .20 .50
35 Levitation U :B: .20 .50
36 Miscalculation C :B: .15 .30
37 Opportunity U :B: .50 1.00
38 Palinchron R :B: 4.00 10.00
39 Raven Familiar U :B: .50 1.00
40 Rebuild U :B: .75 2.00
41 Second Chance R :B: 1.50 4.00
42 Slow Motion C :B: .15 .30
43 Snap C :B: .15 .30
44 Thornwind Faeries C :B: .15 .30
45 Tinker U :B: 1.50 4.00
46 Vigilant Drake C :B: .15 .30
47 Walking Sponge U :B: .20 .50
48 Weatherseed Faeries C :B: .15 .30
49 Bone Shredder U :K: .50 1.00
50 Brink of Madness R :K: 1.25 3.00
51 Engineered Plague U :K: .75 2.00
52 Eviscerator R :K: 1.25 3.00

53 Fog of Gnats C :K: .15 .30
54 Giant Cockroach C :K: .15 .30
55 Lurking Skirge R :K: 1.25 3.00
56 No Mercy R :K: 2.50 6.00
57 Ostracize C :K: .15 .30
58 Phyrexian Broodlings C :K: .15 .30
59 Phyrexian Debaser C :K: .15 .30
60 Phyrexian Defiler U :K: .20 .50
61 Phyrexian Denouncer C :K: .15 .30
62 Phyrexian Plaguelord R :K: 1.50 4.00
63 Phyrexian Reclamation U :K: .50 1.00
64 Plague Beetle C :K: .15 .30
65 Rank and File U :K: .20 .50
66 Sick and Tired C :K: .15 .30
67 Sleeper's Guile C :K: .15 .30
68 Subversion R :K: 1.25 3.00
69 Swat C :K: .15 .30
70 Tethered Skirge U :K: .20 .50
71 Treacherous Link U :K: .20 .50
72 Unearth C :K: .15 .30
73 About Face C :R: .15 .30
74 Avalanche Riders U :R: .75 2.00
75 Defender of Chaos C :R: .15 .30
76 Ghitu Fire-Eater U :R: .50 1.00
77 Ghitu Slinger C :R: .15 .30
78 Ghitu War Cry U :R: .20 .50
79 Goblin Medics C :R: .15 .30
80 Goblin Welder R :R: 4.00 10.00
81 Granite Grip C :R: .15 .30
82 Impending Disaster R :R: 1.25 3.00
83 Last-Ditch Effort U :R: .20 .50
84 Lava Axe C :R: .15 .30
85 Molten Hydra R :R: 1.50 4.00
86 Parch C :R: .15 .30
87 Pygmy Pyrosaur C :R: .15 .30
88 Pyromancy R :R: .75 2.00
89 Rack and Ruin U :R: .75 2.00
90 Rivalry R :R: .75 2.00
91 Shivan Phoenix R :R: 1.50 4.00
92 Sluggishness C :R: .15 .30
93 Viashino Bey C :R: .15 .30
94 Viashino Cutthroat U :R: .20 .50
95 Viashino Heretic U :R: .50 1.00
96 Viashino Sandscout C :R: .15 .30
97 Bloated Toad U :G: .15 .30
98 Crop Rotation C :G: .15 .30
99 Darkwatch Elves U :G: .20 .50
100 Defense of the Heart R :G: 6.00 15.00
101 Deranged Hermit R :G: 5.00 12.00
102 Gang of Elk U :G: .20 .50
103 Harmonic Convergence U :G: .20 .50
104 Hidden Gibbons R :G: 1.50 4.00
105 Lone Wolf U :G: .20 .50
106 Might of Oaks R :G: 1.00 2.50
107 Multani, Maro-Sorcerer R :G: 1.00 2.50
108 Multani's Acolyte C :G: .15 .30
109 Multani's Presence U :G: .20 .50
110 Rancor C :G: 1.25 3.00
111 Repopulate C :G: .15 .30
112 Silk Net C :G: .15 .30
113 Simian Grunts C :G: .15 .30
114 Treefolk Mystic C :G: .15 .30
115 Weatherseed Elf C :G: .15 .30
116 Weatherseed Treefolk R :G: 1.50 4.00
117 Wing Snare U :G: .20 .50
118 Yavimaya Granger C :G: .15 .30
119 Yavimaya Scion C :G: .15 .30
120 Yavimaya Wurm C :G: .15 .30
121 Angel's Trumpet U :A: .50 1.00
122 Beast of Burden R :A: 1.50 4.00
123 Crawlspace R :A: 1.50 4.00
124 Damping Engine R :A: 1.25 3.00
125 Defense Grid R :A: 2.00 5.00
126 Grim Monolith R :A: 10.00 25.00
127 Iron Maiden R :A: 1.25 3.00
128 Jhoira's Toolbox U :A: .30 .75
129 Memory Jar R :A: 1.50 4.00
130 Quicksilver Amulet R :A: 3.00 8.00
131 Ring of Gix R :A: .75 2.00
132 Scrapheap R :A: .75 2.00
133 Thran Lens R :A: 1.25 3.00
134 Thran War Machine R :A: .20 .50
135 Thran Weaponry R :A: 1.50 4.00
136 Ticking Gnomes U :A: .20 .50
137 Urza's Blueprints R :A: 1.50 4.00
138 Wheel of Torture R :A: 1.50 4.00
139 Faerie Conclave U :L: .75 2.00
140 Forbidding Watchtower U :L: .40 1.00
141 Ghitu Encampment U :L: .75 2.00
142 Spawning Pool U :L: .50 1.00
143 Treetop Village U :L: 1.25 3.00

1999 Magic The Gathering 6th Edition

COMPLETE SET (350) 200.00 300.00
BOOSTER BOX (36 PACKS) 120.00 170.00
BOOSTER PACK (15 CARDS) 4.50 5.50
STARTER DECK BOX (12 DECKS) 100.00 150.00
STARTER DECK 10.00 16.00
RELEASED ON APRIL, 28 1999
1 Animate Wall R :W: 1.00 2.00
2 Archangel R :W: 4.00 8.00
3 Ardent Militia U :W: .25 .50
4 Armageddon R :W: 4.00 8.00
5 Armored Pegasus C :W: .15 .30
6 Castle U :W: .25 .50
7 Celestial Dawn R :W: 1.50 3.00
8 Circle of Protection Black C :W: .15 .30
9 Circle of Protection Blue C :W: .15 .30
10 Circle of Protection Green C :W: .15 .30
11 Circle of Protection Red C :W: .15 .30
12 Circle of Protection White C :W: .15 .30
13 Crusade R :W: 3.00 6.00
14 Daring Apprentice R :B: 1.50 3.00
15 Dancing Scimitar R :A: 1.50 3.00
16 Disenchant C :W: .15 .30
17 Divine Transformation U :W: .50 1.00
18 Ekundu Griffin C :W: .25 .50
19 Enlightened Tutor U :W: 4.00 8.00
20 Ethereal Champion R :W: 1.00 2.00
21 Exile R :W: 2.50 5.00
22 Healing Salve C :W: .15 .30
23 Heavy Ballista U :W: .25 .50
24 Hero's Resolve C :W: .25 .50
25 Icatian Town R :W: 1.50 3.00
26 Infantry Veteran C :W: .15 .30
27 Kismet U :W: .50 1.00
28 Kjeldoran Royal Guard R :W: 1.50 3.00
29 Light of Day U :W: 1.00 2.00
30 Longbow Archer U :W: .50 1.00
31 Mesa Falcon C :W: .15 .30
32 Order of the Sacred Torch R :W: 1.50 3.00
33 Pacifism C :W: .25 .50
34 Pearl Dragon R :W: 2.00 4.00
35 Regal Unicorn C :W: .15 .30
36 Remedy C :W: .15 .30
37 Reprisal U :W: .50 1.00
38 Resistance Fighter C :W: .15 .30
39 Reverse Damage R :W: 1.50 3.00
40 Samite Healer C :W: .15 .30
41 Serenity R :W: 1.50 3.00
42 Serra's Blessing U :W: 2.50 5.00
43 Spirit Link U :W: .25 .50
44 Standing Troops C :W: .15 .30
45 Staunch Defenders U :W: .50 1.00
46 Sunweb R :W: 1.50 3.00
47 Tariff R :W: 1.00 2.00
48 Tundra Wolves C :W: .15 .30
49 Unyaro Griffin U :W: .25 .50
50 Venerable Monk C :W: .15 .30
51 Wall of Swords U :W: .25 .50
52 Warmth U :W: .25 .50
53 Warrior's Honor C :W: .15 .30
54 Wrath of God R :W: 7.50 15.00
55 Abduction U :B: .50 1.00
56 Air Elemental U :B: .50 1.00
57 Ancestral Memories R :B: .50 1.00
58 Boomerang C :B: .25 .50
59 Browse U :B: .50 1.00
60 Chill U :B: 2.50 5.00
61 Counterspell C :B: 1.00 2.00
62 D'Avenant Archer C :W: .15 .30
63 Deflection R :B: 1.50 3.00
64 Desertion R :B: 2.00 4.00
65 Diminishing Returns R :B: 1.50 3.00
66 Dream Cache C :B: .15 .30
67 Flash R :B: 1.00 2.00
68 Flight C :B: .15 .30
69 Fog Elemental C :B: .15 .30
70 Forget R :B: 1.00 2.00
71 Gaseous Form C :B: .15 .30
72 Glacial Wall U :B: .25 .50
73 Harmattan Efreet U :B: .25 .50
74 Horned Turtle C :B: .15 .30
75 Insight U :B: .50 1.00
76 Inspiration C :B: .15 .30
77 Juxtapose R :B: 1.50 3.00
78 Library of Lat-Nam R :B: 1.00 2.00
79 Lord of Atlantis R :B: 2.00 4.00
80 Mana Short R :B: 2.00 4.00
81 Memory Lapse C :B: .25 .50
82 Merfolk of the Pearl Trident C :B: .15 .30
83 Mystical Tutor U :B: 2.00 4.00
84 Phantasmal Terrain C :B: .15 .30
85 Phantom Warrior U :B: .50 1.00
86 Polymorph R :B: 1.50 3.00
87 Power Sink U :B: .50 1.00
88 Prodigal Sorcerer C :B: .15 .30
89 Prosperity U :B: 1.00 2.00
90 Psychic Transfer R :B: 1.00 2.00
91 Psychic Venom C :B: .15 .30
92 Recall R :B: 2.00 4.00
93 Relearn U :B: .50 1.00
94 Remove Soul C :B: .25 .50
95 Sage Owl C :B: .25 .50
96 Sea Monster C :B: .15 .30
97 Segovian Leviathan U :B: .25 .50
98 Sibilant Spirit R :B: 1.00 2.00
99 Soldevi Sage U :B: .25 .50
100 Spell Blast C :B: .15 .30
101 Storm Crow C :B: .15 .30
102 Tidal Surge C :B: .15 .30
103 Unsummon C :B: .15 .30
104 Vodalian Soldiers C :B: .15 .30
105 Wall of Air U :B: .50 1.00
106 Wind Drake C :B: .15 .30
107 Wind Spirit U :B: .15 .30
108 Zur's Weirding R :B: 1.00 2.00
109 Abyssal Hunter R :K: 1.00 2.00
110 Abyssal Specter U :K: .25 .50
111 Agonizing Memories U :K: .25 .50
112 Ashen Powder R :K: 1.00 2.00
113 Blight U :K: .25 .50
114 Blighted Shaman U :K: .25 .50
115 Blood Pet C :K: .25 .50
116 Bog Imp C :K: .15 .30
117 Bog Rats C :K: .15 .30
118 Bog Wraith U :K: .25 .50
119 Coercion C :K: .15 .30
120 Derelor R :K: 1.50 3.00
121 Doomsday R :K: 2.00 4.00
122 Dread of Night U :K: .50 1.00
123 Drudge Skeletons C :K: .15 .30
124 Dry Spell C :K: .15 .30
125 Enfeeblement C :K: .15 .30
126 Evil Eye of Orms-by-Gore U :K: .50 1.00
127 Fallen Angel R :K: 2.00 4.00
128 Fatal Blow C :K: .25 .50
129 Fear C :K: .15 .30
130 Feast of the Unicorn C :K: .15 .30
131 Feral Shadow C :K: .15 .30
132 Forbidden Crypt R :K: 1.50 3.00
133 Gravebane Zombie U :K: .50 1.00
134 Gravedigger C :K: .15 .30
135 Greed R :K: 1.50 3.00
136 Hecatomb R :K: 1.50 3.00
137 Hidden Horror U :K: .25 .50
138 Howl from Beyond C :K: .15 .30
139 Infernal Contract R :K: 1.00 2.00
140 Kjeldoran Dead C :K: .15 .30
141 Leshrac's Rite U :K: .25 .50
142 Lost Soul C :K: .15 .30
143 Mind Warp U :K: .25 .50
144 Mischievous Poltergeist U :K: .25 .50
145 Necrosavant R :K: 1.00 2.00
146 Nightmare R :K: 2.00 4.00
147 Painful Memories C :K: .15 .30
148 Perish U :K: 1.00 2.00
149 Pestilence U :K: .25 .50
150 Python C :K: .15 .30
151 Rag Man R :K: 1.50 3.00
152 Raise Dead C :K: .15 .30
153 Razortooth Rats C :K: .25 .50
154 Scathe Zombies C :K: .15 .30
155 Sengir Autocrat R :K: 1.50 3.00
156 Strands of Night U :K: .50 1.00
157 Stromgald Cabal R :K: 1.00 2.00
158 Stupor U :K: .50 1.00
159 Syphon Soul C :K: .50 1.00
160 Terror C :K: .25 .50
161 Vampiric Tutor R :K: 12.00 25.00
162 Zombie Master R :K: 3.00 6.00
163 Aether Flash U :R: .15 .30
164 Anaba Bodyguard C :R: .15 .30
165 Anaba Shaman C :R: .15 .30
166 Balduvian Barbarians C :R: .15 .30
167 Balduvian Horde R :R: 2.00 4.00
168 Blaze U :R: .50 1.00
169 Boil U :R: .50 1.00
170 Burrowing U :R: .25 .50
171 Conquer U :R: .50 1.00
172 Crimson Hellkite R :R: 3.00 6.00
173 Earthquake R :R: 1.00 2.00
174 Fervor R :R: 2.00 4.00
175 Final Fortune R :R: 1.50 3.00
176 Fire Elemental U :R: .50 1.00
177 Firebreathing C :R: .15 .30
178 Fit of Rage C :R: .15 .30
179 Flame Spirit C :R: .15 .30
180 Flashfires U :R: .25 .50
181 Giant Strength C :R: .15 .30
182 Goblin Digging Team C :R: .15 .30
183 Goblin Elite Infantry C :R: .15 .30
184 Goblin Hero C :R: .15 .30
185 Goblin King R :R: 2.00 4.00
186 Goblin Recruiter U :R: 1.50 3.00
187 Goblin Warrens R :R: .15 .30
188 Hammer of Bogardan R :R: 3.00 6.00
189 Hulking Cyclops U :R: .25 .50
190 Illicit Auction R :R: 1.00 2.00
191 Inferno R :R: 1.50 3.00
192 Jokulhaups R :R: 2.00 4.00
193 Lightning Blast C :R: .50 1.00
194 Manabarbs R :R: 1.00 2.00
195 Mountain L :L: .25 .50
196 Orcish Artillery U :R: .25 .50
197 Orcish Oriflamme U :R: .25 .50
198 Pillage U :R: .50 1.00
199 Pyrotechnics C :R: .15 .30
200 Raging Goblin C :R: .15 .30
201 Reckless Embermage R :R: 1.50 3.00
202 Relentless Assault R :R: 2.00 4.00
203 Sabretooth Tiger C :R: .15 .30
204 Shatter C :R: .15 .30
205 Shatterstorm R :R: 1.50 3.00
206 Shock C :R: .15 .30
207 Spitting Drake U :R: .25 .50
208 Spitting Earth C :R: .15 .30
209 Stone Rain C :R: .15 .30
210 Talruum Minotaur C :R: .15 .30
211 Tremor C :R: .15 .30
212 Vertigo U :R: .25 .50
213 Viashino Warrior C :R: .15 .30
214 Volcanic Dragon R :R: 3.00 6.00
215 Volcanic Geyser U :R: .50 1.00
216 Wall of Fire U :R: .50 1.00
217 Birds of Paradise R :G: 9.00 18.00
218 Call of the Wild R :G: 1.50 3.00
219 Cat Warriors C :G: .15 .30
220 Creeping Mold U :G: .25 .50
221 Dense Foliage R :G: 1.00 2.00
222 Early Harvest R :G: 2.00 4.00
223 Elder Druid R :G: 1.00 2.00
224 Elven Cache C :G: .25 .50
225 Elven Riders U :G: .50 1.00
226 Elvish Archers R :G: 1.50 3.00
227 Fallow Earth U :G: .25 .50
228 Familiar Ground U :G: .25 .50
229 Femeref Archers U :G: .25 .50
230 Fog C :G: .15 .30
231 Fyndhorn Brownie C :G: .15 .30
232 Fyndhorn Elder U :G: .50 1.00
233 Giant Growth C :G: .15 .30
234 Giant Spider C :G: .15 .30
235 Gorilla Chieftain C :G: .15 .30
236 Grizzly Bears C :G: .15 .30
237 Hurricane R :G: .25 .50
238 Living Lands R :G: 1.50 3.00
239 Llanowar Elves C :G: .50 1.00
240 Lure U :G: .50 1.00
241 Maro R :G: 2.00 4.00
242 Nature's Resurgence R :G: 1.50 3.00
243 Panther Warriors C :G: .15 .30
244 Pradesh Gypsies C :G: .15 .30
245 Radjan Spirit U :G: .25 .50
246 Rampant Growth C :G: .25 .50
247 Redwood Treefolk C :G: .15 .30
248 Regeneration C :G: .15 .30
249 River Boa U :G: 1.00 2.00
250 Rowen R :G: 1.50 3.00
251 Scaled Wurm C :G: .15 .30
252 Shanodin Dryads C :G: .15 .30
253 Stalking Tiger C :G: .15 .30
254 Stream of Life C :G: .25 .50
255 Summer Bloom U :G: .50 1.00
256 Thicket Basilisk U :G: .50 1.00
257 Trained Armodon C :G: .15 .30
258 Tranquil Grove R :G: 1.50 3.00
259 Tranquility C :G: .15 .30
260 Uktabi Orangutan U :G: 1.00 2.00
261 Uktabi Wildcats R :G: 1.00 2.00
262 Unseen Walker U :G: .25 .50
263 Untamed Wilds U :G: .15 .30
264 Verduran Enchantress R :G: 1.00 2.00
265 Vitalize C :G: .15 .30
266 Waiting in the Weeds R :G: 1.00 2.00
267 Warthog U :G: .25 .50
268 Wild Growth C :G: .15 .30
269 Worldly Tutor U :G: 2.50 5.00
270 Wyluli Wolf R :G: 1.00 2.00
271 Aladdin's Ring R :A: 1.00 2.50
272 Amber Prison R :A: 1.00 2.00
273 Ankh of Mishra R :A: 1.50 3.00
274 Ashnod's Altar U :A: .50 1.00
275 Bottle of Suleiman R :A: 1.50 3.00
276 Charcoal Diamond U :A: .25 .50
277 Crystal Rod U :A: .25 .50
278 Cursed Totem R :A: 1.50 3.00
279 Daraja Griffin U :W: .25 .50
280 Dingus Egg R :A: 1.50 3.00
281 Disrupting Scepter R :A: .50 1.00
282 Dragon Engine R :A: 1.50 3.00
283 Dragon Mask U :A: .50 1.00
284 Fire Diamond U :A: .50 1.00
285 Flying Carpet R :A: 1.50 3.00
286 Fountain of Youth U :A: .50 1.00
287 Glasses of Urza U :A: .25 .50
288 Grinning Totem R :A: 1.50 3.00
289 The Hive R :A: 1.00 2.00
290 Howling Mine R :A: 3.00 6.00
291 Iron Star U :A: .25 .50
292 Ivory Cup U :A: .25 .50
293 Jade Monolith R :A: 1.50 3.00
294 Jalum Tome R :A: 1.00 2.00
295 Jayemdae Tome R :A: 1.00 2.00
296 Lead Golem U :A: .25 .50
297 Mana Prism U :A: .50 1.00
298 Marble Diamond U :A: .15 .30
299 Meekstone R :A: 1.50 3.00
300 Millstone R :A: 2.00 4.00
301 Moss Diamond U :A: .25 .50
302 Mystic Compass U :A: .25 .50
303 Obsianus Golem U :A: .25 .50
304 Ornithopter U :A: 1.00 2.00
305 Patagia Golem U :A: .25 .50
306 Pentagram of the Ages R :A: 1.00 2.00
307 Phyrexian Vault U :A: .50 1.00
308 Primal Clay R :A: 1.00 2.00
309 Rod of Ruin U :A: .25 .50
310 Skull Catapult U :A: .25 .50
311 Sky Diamond U :A: .25 .50
312 Snake Basket R :A: 2.50 5.00
313 Soul Net U :A: .25 .50
314 Storm Cauldron R :A: 1.00 2.00
315 Teferi's Puzzle Box R :A: 1.50 3.00
316 Throne of Bone U :A: .25 .50
317 Wand of Denial R :A: 1.00 2.00
318 Wooden Sphere U :A: .25 .50
319 Adarkar Wastes R :L: 3.00 6.00
320 Brushland R :L: 3.00 6.00
321 City of Brass R :L: 4.00 8.00
322 Crystal Vein U :L: .50 1.00
323 Dwarven Ruins U :L: .50 1.00
324 Ebon Stronghold U :L: .50 1.00
325 Havenwood Battleground U :L: .50 1.00
326 Karplusan Forest R :L: 4.00 8.00
327 Ruins of Trokair U :L: .50 1.00
328 Sulfurous Springs R :L: 3.00 6.00
329 Svyelunite Temple U :L: .50 1.00
330 Underground River R :L: 4.00 8.00
331 Plains L :L: .25 .50
332 Plains L :L: .25 .50
333 Plains L :L: .25 .50
334 Plains L :L: .25 .50
335 Island L :L: .25 .50
336 Island L :L: .25 .50
337 Island L :L: .25 .50
338 Island L :L: .25 .50
339 Swamp L :L: .25 .50
340 Swamp L :L: .25 .50
341 Swamp L :L: .25 .50
342 Swamp L :L: .25 .50
343 Mountain Goat C :R: .15 .30
344 Mountain L :L: .25 .50
345 Mountain L :L: .25 .50
346 Mountain L :L: .25 .50
347 Forest L :L: .25 .50
348 Forest L :L: .25 .50
349 Forest L :L: .25 .50
350 Forest L :L: .25 .50

1999 Magic The Gathering Urza's Destiny

COMPLETE SET (143) 100.00 150.00
BOOSTER BOX (36 PACKS) 250.00 350.00
BOOSTER PACK (15 CARDS) 8.00 11.00
*FOIL: 1X TO 2X BASIC CARDS
RELEASED ON JUNE 7, 1999
1 Academy Rector R :W: 8.00 20.00
2 Archery Training U :W: .40 1.00
3 Capashen Knight C :W: .15 .30
4 Capashen Standard C :W: .15 .30
5 Capashen Templar C :W: .15 .30
6 False Prophet R :W: 1.50 4.00
7 Fend Off C :W: .15 .30
8 Field Surgeon C :W: .15 .30
9 Flicker R :W: 1.25 3.00
10 Jasmine Seer U :W: .40 1.00
11 Mask of Law and Grace C :W: .15 .30
12 Master Healer R :W: 1.50 4.00
13 Opalescence R :W: 1.50 4.00
14 Reliquary Monk C :W: .15 .30
15 Replenish R :W: 6.00 15.00
16 Sanctimony U :W: .75 2.00
17 Scent of Jasmine C :W: .15 .30
18 Scour U :W: .40 1.00
19 Serra Advocate U :W: .40 1.00
20 Solidarity C :W: .15 .30
21 Tethered Griffin R :W: 1.25 3.00
22 Tormented Angel C :W: .15 .30
23 Voice of Duty U :W: .40 1.00
24 Voice of Reason U :W: .40 1.00
25 Wall of Glare C :W: .15 .30
26 Aura Thief R :B: 1.50 4.00
27 Blizzard Elemental R :B: 1.25 3.00
28 Brine Seer U :B: .40 1.00
29 Bubbling Beebles C :B: .15 .30
30 Disappear U :B: .40 1.00
31 Donate R :B: 2.00 5.00
32 Fatigue C :B: .15 .30
33 Fledgling Osprey C :B: .15 .30
34 Illuminated Wings C :B: .15 .30
35 Iridescent Drake U :B: .40 1.00
36 Kingfisher C :B: .15 .30
37 Mental Discipline C :B: .15 .30
38 Metathran Elite U :B: .40 1.00
39 Metathran Soldier C :B: .15 .30
40 Opposition R :B: 2.50 6.00
41 Private Research U :B: .40 1.00
42 Quash U :B: 1.00 2.50
43 Rayne, Academy Chancellor R :B: .75 2.00
44 Rescue C :B: .15 .30
45 Scent of Brine C :B: .15 .30
46 Sigil of Sleep C :B: .15 .30
47 Telepathic Spies C :B: .15 .30
48 Temporal Adept R :B: 1.50 4.00
49 Thieving Magpie U :B: .75 2.00
50 Treachery R :B: 5.00 12.00
51 Apprentice Necromancer R :K: 1.25 3.00
52 Attrition R :K: 1.50 4.00
53 Body Snatcher R :K: 1.25 3.00
54 Bubbling Muck C :K: .15 .30
55 Carnival of Souls R :K: .75 2.00
56 Chime of Night C :K: .15 .30
57 Disease Carriers C :K: .15 .30
58 Dying Wail C :K: .15 .30
59 Encroach U :K: .40 1.00
60 Eradicate U :K: 1.00 2.50
61 Festering Wound U :K: .40 1.00
62 Lurking Jackals U :K: .40 1.00
63 Nightshade Seer U :K: .40 1.00
64 Phyrexian Monitor C :K: .15 .30
65 Phyrexian Negator R :K: 1.50 4.00
66 Plague Dogs U :K: .40 1.00
67 Rapid Decay R :K: 1.50 4.00
68 Ravenous Rats C :K: .15 .30
69 Scent of Nightshade C :K: .15 .30
70 Skittering Horror C :K: .15 .30
71 Slinking Skirge C :K: .15 .30
72 Soul Feast U :K: .40 1.00
73 Squirming Mass C :K: .15 .30
74 Twisted Experiment C :K: .15 .30
75 Yawgmoth's Bargain R :K: 1.25 3.00
76 Aether Sting U :R: .40 1.00
77 Bloodshot Cyclops R :R: 1.50 4.00
78 Cinder Seer U :R: .40 1.00
79 Colos Yearling C :R: .15 .30
80 Covetous Dragon R :R: .75 2.00
81 Flame Jet C :R: .15 .30
82 Goblin Berserker U :R: .40 1.00
83 Goblin Festival R :R: 1.50 4.00
84 Goblin Gardener C :R: .15 .30
85 Goblin Marshal R :R: 1.50 4.00
86 Goblin Masons C :R: .15 .30
87 Hulking Ogre C :R: .15 .30
88 Impatience R :R: .75 2.00
89 Incendiary U :R: .40 1.00
90 Keldon Champion U :R: .40 1.00
91 Keldon Vandals C :R: .15 .30
92 Landslide U :R: .40 1.00
93 Mark of Fury C :R: .15 .30
94 Reckless Abandon C :R: .15 .30
95 Repercussion R :R: 1.50 4.00
96 Scent of Cinder C :R: .15 .30
97 Sowing Salt U :R: .40 1.00
98 Trumpet Blast C :R: .15 .30
99 Wake of Destruction R :R: 1.50 4.00
100 Wild Colos C :R: .15 .30
101 Ancient Silverback R :G: 1.50 4.00
102 Compost U :G: .75 2.00
103 Elvish Lookout C :G: .15 .30
104 Elvish Piper R :G: 4.00 10.00
105 Emperor Crocodile R :G: 1.50 4.00
106 Gamekeeper U :G: .40 1.00
107 Goliath Beetle C :G: .15 .30
108 Heart Warden C :G: .15 .30
109 Hunting Moa U :G: .40 1.00
110 Ivy Seer U :G: .40 1.00
111 Magnify C :G: .15 .30
112 Marker Beetles C :G: .15 .30
113 Momentum U :G: .40 1.00
114 Multani's Decree C :G: .15 .30
115 Pattern of Rebirth R :G: 2.00 5.00
116 Plated Spider C :G: .15 .30
117 Plow Under R :G: 1.50 4.00
118 Rofellos's Gift C :G: .15 .30
119 Rofellos, Llanowar Emissary R :G: 8.00 20.00
120 Scent of Ivy C :G: .15 .30
121 Splinter U :G: .75 2.00
122 Taunting Elf C :G: .15 .30
123 Thorn Elemental R :G: .75 2.00
124 Yavimaya Elder C :G: .15 .30
125 Yavimaya Enchantress U :G: .75 2.00
126 Braidwood Cup U :A: .40 1.00
127 Braidwood Sextant U :A: .40 1.00
128 Brass Secretary U :A: .40 1.00
129 Caltrops U :A: .40 1.00
130 Extruder U :A: .40 1.00
131 Fodder Cannon U :A: .40 1.00
132 Junk Diver R :A: 1.25 3.00
133 Mantis Engine U :A: .40 1.00
134 Masticore R :A: 2.00 5.00
135 Metalworker R :A: 6.00 15.00
136 Powder Keg R :A: 1.00 2.50
137 Scrying Glass R :A: 1.50 4.00
138 Storage Matrix R :A: 1.25 3.00
139 Thran Dynamo U :A: 1.25 3.00
140 Thran Foundry U :A: .40 1.00
141 Thran Golem R :A: 1.50 4.00
142 Urza's Incubator R :A: 4.00 10.00
143 Yavimaya Hollow R :L: 1.50 4.00

1999 Magic The Gathering Mercadian Masques

COMPLETE SET (350) 150.00 200.00
BOOSTER BOX (36 PACKS) 150.00 250.00
BOOSTER PACK (15 CARDS) 4.50 8.00
THEME DECK BOX (12 DECKS) 100.00 125.00
THEME DECK 9.00 13.00
FAT PACK 60.00 100.00
*FOIL: 1X TO 2X BASIC CARDS
RELEASED ON OCTOBER 4, 1999
1 Afterlife U :W: .20 .50
2 Alabaster Wall C :W: .15 .30
3 Armistice R :W: .75 2.00
4 Arrest U :W: .40 1.00
5 Ballista Squad U :W: .40 1.00
6 Charm Peddler C :W: .15 .30
7 Charmed Griffin U :W: .40 1.00

8 Cho-Arrim Alchemist R :W: 1.25 3.00
9 Cho-Arrim Bruiser R :W: .75 2.00
10 Cho-Arrim Legate U :W: .40 1.00
11 Cho-Manno's Blessing C :W: .15 .30
12 Cho-Manno, Revolutionary R :W: 1.25 3.00
13 Common Cause R :W: .75 2.00
14 Cornered Market R :W: .75 2.00
15 Crackdown R :W: 1.25 3.00
16 Crossbow Infantry C :W: .15 .30
17 Devout Witness C :W: .15 .30
18 Disenchant C :W: .15 .30
19 Fountain Watch R :W: 1.50 4.00
20 Fresh Volunteers C :W: .15 .30
21 Honor the Fallen R :W: 1.25 3.00
22 Ignoble Soldier U :W: .40 1.00
23 Inviolability C :W: .15 .30
24 Ivory Mask R :W: 2.00 5.00
25 Jhovall Queen R :W: 1.25 3.00
26 Jhovall Rider U :W: .20 .50
27 Last Breath U :W: .40 1.00
28 Moment of Silence C :W: .15 .30
29 Moonlit Wake U :W: .40 1.00
30 Muzzle C :W: .15 .30
31 Nightwind Glider C :W: .15 .30
32 Noble Purpose U :W: .75 2.00
33 Orim's Cure C :W: .15 .30
34 Pious Warrior C :W: .15 .30
35 Ramosian Captain U :W: .40 1.00
36 Ramosian Commander U :W: .40 1.00
37 Ramosian Lieutenant C :W: .15 .30
38 Ramosian Rally C :W: .15 .30
39 Ramosian Sergeant C :W: .15 .30
40 Ramosian Sky Marshal R :W: .75 2.00
41 Rappelling Scouts R :W: .75 2.00
42 Renounce U :W: .40 1.00
43 Revered Elder C :W: .15 .30
44 Reverent Mantra R :W: .40 1.00
45 Righteous Aura U :W: .20 .50
46 Righteous Indignation U :W: .20 .50
47 Security Detail R :W: .75 2.00
48 Soothing Balm C :W: .15 .30
49 Spiritual Focus R :W: .75 2.00
50 Steadfast Guard C :W: .15 .30
51 Story Circle U :W: 1.25 3.00
52 Task Force C :W: .15 .30
53 Thermal Glider C :W: .15 .30
54 Tonic Peddler U :W: .20 .50
55 Trap Runner U :W: .20 .50
56 Wave of Reckoning R :W: .75 2.00
57 Wishmonger U :W: .40 1.00
58 Aerial Caravan R :B: .75 2.00
59 Balloon Peddler C :B: .15 .30
60 Blockade Runner C :B: .15 .30
61 Brainstorm C :B: 1.50 4.00
62 Bribery R :B: 8.00 20.00
63 Buoyancy C :B: .15 .30
64 Chambered Nautilus U :B: .40 1.00
65 Chameleon Spirit U :B: .40 1.00
66 Charisma R :B: 2.50 6.00
67 Cloud Sprite C :B: .15 .30
68 Coastal Piracy U :B: .75 2.00
69 Counterspell C :B: .75 2.00
70 Cowardice R :B: 1.25 3.00
71 Customs Depot U :B: .40 1.00
72 Darting Merfolk C :B: .15 .30
73 Dehydration C :B: .15 .30
74 Diplomatic Escort U :B: .40 1.00
75 Diplomatic Immunity C :B: .40 1.00
76 Drake Hatchling C :B: .15 .30
77 Embargo R :B: .75 2.00
78 Energy Flux U :B: 1.50 4.00
79 Extravagant Spirit R :B: .75 2.00
80 False Demise U :B: .40 1.00
81 Glowing Anemone U :B: .20 .50
82 Gush C :B: .15 .30
83 High Seas U :B: .40 1.00
84 Hoodwink C :B: .15 .30
85 Indentured Djinn U :B: .40 1.00
86 Karn's Touch R :B: .40 1.00
87 Misdirection R :B: 10.00 25.00
88 Misstep C :B: .15 .30
89 Overtaker R :B: .75 2.00
90 Port Inspector C :B: .15 .30
91 Rishadan Airship C :B: .15 .30
92 Rishadan Brigand R :B: .75 2.00
93 Rishadan Cutpurse C :B: .15 .30
94 Rishadan Footpad U :B: .40 1.00
95 Sailmonger U :B: .20 .50
96 Sand Squid R :B: .75 2.00
97 Saprazzan Bailiff R :B: .75 2.00
98 Saprazzan Breaker U :B: .20 .50
99 Saprazzan Heir R :B: 1.25 3.00
100 Saprazzan Legate U :B: .20 .50
101 Saprazzan Outrigger C :B: .15 .30
102 Saprazzan Raider C :B: .15 .30
103 Shoving Match U :B: .20 .50
104 Soothsaying U :B: .60 1.50
105 Squeeze R :B: .75 2.00
106 Statecraft R :B: .75 2.00
107 Stinging Barrier C :B: .15 .30
108 Thwart U :B: .75 2.00
109 Tidal Bore C :B: .15 .30
110 Tidal Kraken R :B: 1.50 4.00
111 Timid Drake U :B: .20 .50
112 Trade Routes R :B: 1.50 4.00
113 War Tax U :B: .40 1.00
114 Waterfront Bouncer C :B: .15 .30
115 Alley Grifters C :K: .15 .30
116 Black Market R :K: .75 2.00
117 Bog Smugglers C :K: .15 .30
118 Bog Witch C :K: .15 .30
119 Cackling Witch U :K: .40 1.00
120 Cateran Brute C :K: .15 .30
121 Cateran Enforcer U :K: .40 1.00
122 Cateran Kidnappers U :K: .40 1.00
123 Cateran Overlord R :K: 1.50 4.00
124 Cateran Persuader C :K: .15 .30
125 Cateran Slaver R :K: .75 2.00
126 Cateran Summons U :K: .40 1.00
127 Conspiracy R :K: 1.25 3.00
128 Corrupt Official R :K: .75 2.00
129 Dark Ritual C :K: .40 1.00
130 Deathgazer U :K: .40 1.00
131 Deepwood Ghoul C :K: .15 .30
132 Deepwood Legate U :K: .40 1.00
133 Delraich R :K: 1.50 4.00
134 Enslaved Horror U :K: .40 1.00
135 Extortion R :K: 1.25 3.00
136 Forced March R :K: .75 2.00
137 Ghoul's Feast U :K: .20 .50
138 Haunted Crossroads U :K: .75 2.00
139 Highway Robber C :K: .15 .30
140 Instigator R :K: .75 2.00
141 Insubordination C :K: .15 .30
142 Intimidation U :K: .60 1.50
143 Larceny U :K: .75 2.00
144 Liability R :K: .75 2.00
145 Maggot Therapy C :K: .15 .30
146 Midnight Ritual R :K: 1.25 3.00
147 Misshapen Fiend C :K: .15 .30
148 Molting Harpy U :K: .40 1.00
149 Nether Spirit R :K: 2.00 5.00
150 Notorious Assassin R :K: .75 2.00
151 Pretender's Claim U :K: .40 1.00
152 Primeval Shambler U :K: .40 1.00
153 Putrefaction U :K: .40 1.00
154 Quagmire Lamprey U :K: .40 1.00
155 Rain of Tears U :K: .40 1.00
156 Rampart Crawler C :K: .15 .30
157 Rouse C :K: .15 .30
158 Scandalmonger U :K: .20 .50
159 Sever Soul C :K: .15 .30
160 Silent Assassin R :K: .40 1.00
161 Skulking Fugitive C :K: .15 .30
162 Snuff Out C :K: .15 .30
163 Soul Channeling C :K: .15 .30
164 Specter's Wail C :K: .15 .30
165 Strongarm Thug U :K: .20 .50
166 Thrashing Wumpus R :K: 1.25 3.00
167 Undertaker C :K: .15 .30
168 Unmask R :K: 2.00 5.00
169 Unnatural Hunger R :K: .75 2.00
170 Vendetta C :K: .15 .30
171 Wall of Distortion C :K: .15 .30
172 Arms Dealer U :R: .40 1.00
173 Battle Rampart C :R: .15 .30
174 Battle Squadron R :R: .75 2.00
175 Blaster Mage C :R: .15 .30
176 Blood Hound R :R: .75 2.00
177 Blood Oath R :R: 1.25 3.00
178 Brawl R :R: .75 2.00
179 Cave Sense C :R: .15 .30
180 Cave-In R :R: 1.50 4.00
181 Cavern Crawler C :R: .15 .30
182 Ceremonial Guard C :R: .15 .30
183 Cinder Elemental U :R: .40 1.00
184 Close Quarters U :R: .40 1.00
185 Crag Saurian R :R: .75 2.00
186 Crash C :R: .15 .30
187 Flailing Manticore R :R: .75 2.00
188 Flailing Ogre U :R: .20 .50
189 Flailing Soldier C :R: .15 .30
190 Flaming Sword C :R: .15 .30
191 Furious Assault C :R: .15 .30
192 Gerrard's Irregulars C :R: .15 .30
193 Hammer Mage U :R: .20 .50
194 Hired Giant U :R: .40 1.00
195 Kris Mage C :R: .15 .30
196 Kyren Glider C :R: .15 .30
197 Kyren Legate U :R: .40 1.00
198 Kyren Negotiations U :R: .40 1.00
199 Kyren Sniper C :R: .15 .30
200 Lava Runner R :R: 1.25 3.00
201 Lightning Hounds C :R: .15 .30
202 Lithophage R :R: 1.25 3.00
203 Lunge C :R: .15 .30
204 Magistrate's Veto U :R: .40 1.00
205 Mercadian Atlas R :A: 1.25 3.00
206 Ogre Taskmaster U :R: .20 .50
207 Pulverize R :R: 1.25 3.00
208 Puppet's Verdict R :R: .75 2.00
209 Robber Fly U :R: .40 1.00
210 Rock Badger U :R: .40 1.00
211 Seismic Mage R :R: .75 2.00
212 Shock Troops C :R: .15 .30
213 Sizzle C :R: .15 .30
214 Squee, Goblin Nabob R :R: 2.50 6.00
215 Stone Rain C :R: .15 .30
216 Tectonic Break R :R: .75 2.00
217 Territorial Dispute R :R: .75 2.00
218 Thieves' Auction R :R: .75 2.00
219 Thunderclap C :R: .15 .30
220 Tremor C :R: .15 .30
221 Two-Headed Dragon R :R: 1.50 4.00
222 Uphill Battle U :R: .20 .50
223 Volcanic Wind U :R: .40 1.00
224 War Cadence U :R: .40 1.00
225 Warmonger U :R: .40 1.00
226 Warpath U :R: .40 1.00
227 Wild Jhovall C :R: .15 .30
228 Word of Blasting U :R: .40 1.00
229 Ancestral Mask C :G: .40 1.00
230 Bifurcate R :G: 1.25 3.00
231 Boa Constrictor U :G: .40 1.00
232 Briar Patch U :G: .40 1.00
233 Caller of the Hunt R :G: 1.25 3.00
234 Caustic Wasps U :G: .40 1.00
235 Clear the Land R :G: 1.25 3.00
236 Collective Unconscious R :G: 1.25 3.00
237 Dawnstrider R :G: .75 2.00
238 Deadly Insect C :G: .15 .30
239 Deepwood Drummer C :G: .15 .30
240 Deepwood Elder R :G: .75 2.00
241 Deepwood Tantiv U :G: .40 1.00
242 Deepwood Wolverine C :G: .15 .30
243 Desert Twister U :G: .40 1.00
244 Erithizon R :G: 1.25 3.00
245 Ferocity C :G: .15 .30
246 Food Chain R :G: 2.50 6.00
247 Foster R :G: .75 2.00
248 Game Preserve R :G: .75 2.00
249 Giant Caterpillar C :G: .15 .30
250 Groundskeeper U :G: .40 1.00
251 Horned Troll C :G: .15 .30
252 Howling Wolf C :G: .15 .30
253 Hunted Wumpus U :G: .40 1.00
254 Invigorate C :G: .15 .30
255 Land Grant C :G: .15 .30
256 Ley Line U :G: .40 1.00
257 Lumbering Satyr U :G: .20 .50
258 Lure U :G: .20 .50
259 Megatherium R :G: .75 2.00
260 Natural Affinity R :G: 1.25 3.00
261 Pangosaur R :G: .75 2.00
262 Revive U :G: .40 1.00
263 Rushwood Dryad C :G: .15 .30
264 Rushwood Elemental R :G: 2.00 5.00
265 Rushwood Herbalist C :G: .15 .30
266 Rushwood Legate U :G: .20 .50
267 Saber Ants U :G: .40 1.00
268 Sacred Prey C :G: .15 .30
269 Silverglade Elemental C :G: .15 .30
270 Silverglade Pathfinder U :G: .20 .50
271 Snake Pit U :G: .40 1.00
272 Snorting Gahr C :G: .15 .30
273 Spidersilk Armor C :G: .15 .30
274 Spontaneous Generation R :G: 1.25 3.00
275 Squall C :G: .15 .30
276 Squallmonger U :G: .20 .50
277 Stamina U :G: .75 2.00
278 Sustenance U :G: .20 .50
279 Tiger Claws C :G: .15 .30
280 Tranquility C :G: .15 .30
281 Venomous Breath U :G: .20 .50
282 Venomous Dragonfly C :G: .15 .30
283 Vernal Equinox R :G: .75 2.00
284 Vine Dryad R :G: 1.50 4.00
285 Vine Trellis C :G: .15 .30
286 Assembly Hall R :A: .75 2.00
287 Barbed Wire U :A: .40 1.00
288 Bargaining Table R :A: 1.25 3.00
289 Credit Voucher U :A: .40 1.00
290 Crenellated Wall U :A: .40 1.00
291 Crooked Scales R :A: .75 2.00
292 Crumbling Sanctuary R :A: 1.25 3.00
293 Distorting Lens R :A: 1.25 3.00
294 Eye of Ramos R :A: .75 2.00
295 General's Regalia R :A: .75 2.00
296 Heart of Ramos R :A: .75 2.00
297 Henge Guardian U :A: .40 1.00
298 Horn of Plenty R :A: .75 2.00
299 Horn of Ramos R :A: 1.25 3.00
300 Iron Lance U :A: .40 1.00
301 Jeweled Torque U :A: .40 1.00
302 Kyren Archive R :A: .75 2.00
303 Kyren Toy R :A: .75 2.00
304 Magistrate's Scepter R :A: 2.00 5.00
305 Mercadian Bazaar U :L: .40 1.00
306 Mercadia's Downfall U :R: .40 1.00
307 Monkey Cage R :A: 1.25 3.00
308 Panacea U :A: .20 .50
309 Power Matrix R :A: 1.50 4.00
310 Puffer Extract U :A: .40 1.00
311 Rishadan Pawnshop R :A: .75 2.00
312 Skull of Ramos R :A: .75 2.00
313 Tooth of Ramos R :A: .75 2.00
314 Toymaker U :A: .20 .50
315 Worry Beads R :A: .75 2.00
316 Dust Bowl R :L: 3.00 8.00
317 Fountain of Cho U :L: .20 .50
318 Henge of Ramos U :L: .40 1.00
319 Hickory Woodlot C :L: .15 .30
320 High Market R :L: 1.25 3.00
321 Mercadian Lift R :A: 1.25 3.00
322 Peat Bog C :L: .15 .30
323 Remote Farm C :L: .15 .30
324 Rishadan Port R :L: 40.00 80.00
325 Rushwood Grove U :L: .40 1.00
326 Sandstone Needle C :L: .15 .30
327 Saprazzan Cove U :L: .40 1.00
328 Saprazzan Skerry C :L: .15 .30
329 Subterranean Hangar U :L: .20 .50
330 Tower of the Magistrate R :L: 1.25 3.00
331 Plains C :L: .15 .30
332 Plains C :L: .15 .30
333 Plains C :L: .15 .30
334 Plains C :L: .15 .30
335 Island C :L: .15 .30
336 Island C :L: .15 .30
337 Island C :L: .15 .30
338 Island C :L: .15 .30
339 Swamp C :L: .15 .30
340 Swamp C :L: .15 .30
341 Swamp C :L: .15 .30
342 Swamp C :L: .15 .30
343 Mountain C :L: .15 .30
344 Mountain C :L: .15 .30
345 Mountain C :L: .15 .30
346 Mountain C :L: .15 .30
347 Forest C :L: .20 .50
348 Forest C :L: .20 .50
349 Forest C :L: .20 .50
350 Forest C :L: .20 .50

2000 Magic The Gathering Nemesis

COMPLETE SET (143) 75.00 90.00
BOOSTER BOX (36 PACKS) 90.00 125.00
BOOSTER PACK (15 CARDS) 3.75 4.50
STARTER DECK BOX (12 DECKS) 90.00 125.00
STARTER DECK 10.00 12.50
FAT PACK 40.00 50.00
*FOIL: 1X TO 2X BASIC CARDS
RELEASED ON FEBRUARY 14, 2000
1 Angelic Favor U :W: .20 .50
2 Avenger en-Dal R :W: 1.00 2.00
3 Blinding Angel R :W: 4.00 8.00
4 Chieftain en-Dal U :W: .20 .50
5 Defender en-Vec C :W: .12 .30
6 Defiant Falcon C :W: .12 .30
7 Defiant Vanguard U :W: .50 1.00
8 Fanatical Devotion C :W: .12 .30
9 Lashknife C :W: .12 .30
10 Lawbringer C :W: .12 .30
11 Lightbringer C :W: .12 .30
12 Lin Sivvi, Defiant Hero R :W: 3.00 6.00
13 Netter en-Dal C :W: .12 .30
14 Noble Stand U :W: .20 .50
15 Off Balance C :W: .12 .30
16 Oracle's Attendants R :W: 1.00 2.00
17 Parallax Wave R :W: 2.00 4.00
18 Seal of Cleansing C :W: .12 .30
19 Silkenfist Fighter C :W: .12 .30
20 Silkenfist Order U :W: .20 .50
21 Sivvi's Ruse U :W: .20 .50
22 Sivvi's Valor R :W: 1.00 2.00
23 Spiritual Asylum R :W: 1.00 2.00
24 Topple C :W: .12 .30
25 Voice of Truth U :W: .50 1.00
26 Accumulated Knowledge C :B: 1.00 2.00
27 Ather Barrier R :B: .50 1.00
28 Air Bladder C :B: .12 .30
29 Cloudskate C :B: .12 .30
30 Daze C :B: .12 .30
31 Dominate U :B: .50 1.00
32 Ensnare U :B: .50 1.00
33 Infiltrate C :B: .12 .30
34 Jolting Merfolk U :B: .20 .50
35 Oraxid C :B: .12 .30
36 Pale Moon R :B: 1.00 2.00
37 Parallax Tide R :B: 2.00 4.00
38 Rising Waters R :B: 1.50 3.00
39 Rootwater Commando C :B: .12 .30
40 Rootwater Thief R :B: 4.00 8.00
41 Seahunter R :B: 1.00 2.00
42 Seal of Removal C :B: .12 .30
43 Sliptide Serpent R :B: 1.00 2.00
44 Sneaky Homunculus C :B: .12 .30
45 Harvest Mage C :G: .12 .30
45 Stronghold Biologist U :B: .50 1.00
46 Stronghold Machinist U :B: .50 1.00
47 Stronghold Zeppelin U :B: .20 .50
48 Submerge U :B: .20 .50
49 Trickster Mage C :B: .12 .30
50 Wandering Eye C :B: .12 .30
51 Ascendant Evincar R :K: 2.50 5.00
52 Battlefield Percher U :K: .20 .50
53 Belbe's Percher C :K: .12 .30
54 Carrion Wall U :K: .20 .50
55 Dark Triumph U :K: .20 .50
56 Death Pit Offering R :K: 2.00 4.00
57 Divining Witch R :K: 1.00 2.00
58 Massacre U :K: .20 .50
59 Mind Slash U :K: .20 .50
60 Mind Swords C :K: .12 .30
61 Murderous Betrayal R :K: 1.00 2.00
62 Parallax Dementia C :K: .12 .30
63 Parallax Nexus R :K: 1.00 2.00
64 Phyrexian Driver C :K: .12 .30
65 Phyrexian Prowler U :K: .50 1.00
66 Plague Witch C :K: .12 .30
67 Rathi Fiend U :K: .50 1.00
68 Rathi Intimidator C :K: .12 .30
69 Rath's Edge R :L: 1.00 2.00
70 Seal of Doom C :K: .12 .30
71 Spineless Thug C :K: .12 .30
72 Spiteful Bully C :K: .12 .30
73 Stronghold Discipline C :K: .12 .30
74 Vicious Hunger C :K: .12 .30
75 Volrath the Fallen R :K: 2.50 5.00
76 Ancient Hydra U :R: .20 .50
77 Arc Mage U :R: .20 .50
78 Bola Warrior C :R: .12 .30
79 Downhill Charge C :R: .12 .30
80 Flame Rift C :R: .12 .30
81 Flowstone Crusher C :R: .12 .30
82 Flowstone Overseer R :R: 1.00 2.00
83 Flowstone Slide R :R: 1.00 2.00
84 Flowstone Strike C :R: .12 .30
85 Flowstone Surge U :R: .20 .50
86 Flowstone Wall C :R: .12 .30
87 Laccolith Grunt C :R: .12 .30
88 Laccolith Rig C :R: .12 .30
89 Laccolith Titan R :R: 1.00 2.00
90 Laccolith Warrior U :R: .20 .50
91 Laccolith Whelp C :R: .12 .30
92 Mana Cache R :R: 1.00 2.00
93 Mogg Alarm U :R: .20 .50
94 Mogg Salvage U :R: .20 .50
95 Mogg Toady C :R: .12 .30
96 Moggcatcher R :R: 1.00 2.00
97 Rupture U :R: .20 .50
98 Seal of Fire C :R: .12 .30
99 Shrieking Mogg R :R: 1.00 2.00
100 Stronghold Gambit R :R: 1.00 2.00
101 Animate Land U :G: .50 1.00
102 Blastoderm C :G: .12 .30
103 Coiling Woodworm U :G: .20 .50
104 Fog Patch C :G: .12 .30
106 Mossdog C :G: .12 .30
107 Nesting Wurm U :G: .50 1.00
108 Overlaid Terrain R :G: 1.00 2.00
109 Pack Hunt R :G: 1.00 2.00
110 Refreshing Rain U :G: .50 1.00
111 Reverent Silence C :G: .12 .30
112 Rhox R :G: 2.00 4.00
113 Saproling Burst R :G: 2.00 4.00
114 Saproling Cluster R :G: 1.50 3.00
115 Seal of Strength C :G: .12 .30
116 Skyshroud Behemoth R :G: 1.50 3.00
117 Skyshroud Claim C :G: .12 .30
118 Skyshroud Cutter C :G: .12 .30
119 Skyshroud Poacher R :G: 2.50 5.00
120 Skyshroud Ridgeback C :G: .12 .30
121 Skyshroud Sentinel C :G: .12 .30
122 Stampede Driver U :G: .20 .50
123 Treetop Bracers C :G: .12 .30
124 Wild Mammoth U :G: .20 .50
125 Woodripper U :G: .20 .50
126 Belbe's Armor U :A: .20 .50
127 Belbe's Portal R :A: 2.00 4.00
128 Complex Automaton R :A: 1.00 2.00
129 Eye of Yawgmoth R :A: 1.00 2.00
130 Flint Golem U :A: .20 .50
131 Flowstone Armor U :A: .20 .50
132 Flowstone Thopter U :A: .20 .50
133 Kill Switch R :A: 1.00 2.00
134 Parallax Inhibitor R :A: 1.00 2.00
135 Predator, Flagship R :A: 2.00 4.00
136 Rackling U :A: .50 1.00
137 Rejuvenation Chamber U :A: .50 1.00
138 Rusting Golem U :A: .20 .50
139 Tangle Wire R :A: 5.00 10.00
140 Viseling U :A: .50 1.00
141 Kor Haven R :L: 1.50 3.00
142 Rathi Assassin R :K: 2.00 4.00
143 Terrain Generator U :L: .50 1.00

2000 Magic The Gathering Prophecy

COMPLETE SET (143) 50.00 100.00
BOOSTER BOX (36 PACKS) 100.00 150.00
BOOSTER PACK (15 CARDS) 4.00 5.00
STARTER DECK BOX (12 DECKS) 120.00 175.00
STARTER DECK 15.00 20.00
FAT PACK 30.00 60.00
*FOIL: .8X TO 2X BASIC CARDS
RELEASED ON JUNE 5, 2000
1 Abolish U :W: .50 1.00
2 Aura Fracture C :W: .12 .30
3 Avatar of Hope R :W: 4.00 8.00
4 Blessed Wind R :W: 1.50 3.00
5 Celestial Convergence R :W: 1.00 2.00
6 Diving Griffin C :W: .12 .30
7 Entangler U :W: 1.00 2.00
8 Excise C :W: .12 .30
9 Flowering Field U :W: .20 .50
10 Glittering Lion U :W: .30 .75
11 Glittering Lynx C :W: .12 .30
12 Jeweled Spirit R :W: 1.00 2.00
13 Mageta the Lion R :W: 2.00 4.00
14 Mageta's Boon C :W: .12 .30
15 Mercenary Informer R :W: 1.00 2.00
16 Mine Bearer C :W: .12 .30
17 Mirror Strike U :W: .50 1.00
18 Reveille Squad U :W: .50 1.00
19 Rhystic Circle C :W: .12 .30
20 Rhystic Shield C :W: .12 .30
21 Samite Sanctuary R :W: 1.00 2.00
22 Sheltering Prayers R :W: 1.00 2.00
23 Shield Dancer U :W: .20 .50
24 Soul Charmer C :W: .12 .30
25 Sword Dancer U :W: .20 .50
26 Trenching Steed C :W: .12 .30
27 Troubled Healer C :W: .12 .30
28 Alexi's Cloak C :B: .12 .30
29 Alexi, Zephyr Mage R :B: 1.50 3.00
30 Avatar of Will R :B: 3.00 6.00
31 Coastal Hornclaw C :B: .12 .30
32 Denying Wind R :B: 1.50 3.00
33 Excavation U :B: .20 .50
34 Foil U :B: 1.00 2.00
35 Gulf Squid C :B: .12 .30
36 Hazy Homunculus C :B: .12 .30
37 Heightened Awareness R :B: 1.00 2.00
38 Mana Vapors U :B: .50 1.00
39 Overburden R :B: 1.50 3.00
40 Psychic Theft R :B: 1.00 2.00
41 Quicksilver Wall U :B: .20 .50
42 Rethink C :B: .12 .30
43 Rhystic Deluge C :B: .12 .30
44 Rhystic Scrying U :B: .50 1.00
45 Rhystic Study C :B: .12 .30
46 Ribbon Snake C :B: .12 .30
47 Shrouded Serpent R :B: 1.00 2.00
48 Spiketail Drake U :B: .50 1.00
49 Spiketail Hatchling C :B: .12 .30
50 Stormwatch Eagle C :B: .12 .30
51 Sunken Field U :B: .20 .50
52 Troublesome Spirit R :B: 1.00 2.00
53 Windscouter U :B: .20 .50
54 Withdraw C :B: .12 .30
55 Agent of Shauku C :K: .12 .30
56 Avatar of Woe R :K: 10.00 20.00
57 Bog Elemental R :K: 1.00 2.00
58 Bog Glider C :K: .12 .30
59 Chilling Apparition U :K: .50 1.00
60 Coffin Puppets R :K: 1.00 2.00
61 Death Charmer C :K: .12 .30
62 Despoil C :K: .12 .30
63 Endbringer's Revel U :K: .20 .50
64 Fen Stalker C :K: .12 .30
65 Flay C :K: .12 .30
66 Greel's Caress C :K: .12 .30
67 Greel, Mind Raker R :K: 1.50 3.00
68 Infernal Genesis R :K: 1.00 2.00
69 Nakaya Shade U :K: .20 .50
70 Noxious Field U :K: .20 .50
71 Outbreak U :K: .20 .50
72 Pit Raptor U :K: .20 .50
73 Plague Fiend C :K: .12 .30
74 Plague Wind R :K: 2.00 4.00
75 Rebel Informer R :K: 1.00 2.00
76 Rhystic Syphon U :K: .20 .50
77 Rhystic Tutor R :K: 2.00 4.00
78 Soul Strings C :K: .12 .30
79 Steal Strength C :K: .12 .30
80 Wall of Vipers U :K: .20 .50
81 Whipstitched Zombie C :K: .12 .30
82 Avatar of Fury R :R: 4.00 8.00
83 Barbed Field U :R: .20 .50
84 Branded Brawlers C :R: .12 .30
85 Brutal Suppression U :R: .20 .50
86 Citadel of Pain U :R: .50 1.00
87 Devastate C :R: .12 .30
88 Fault Riders C :R: .12 .30
89 Fickle Efreet R :R: 1.00 2.00
90 Flameshot U :R: .20 .50
91 Inflame C :R: .12 .30
92 Keldon Arsonist U :R: .20 .50
93 Keldon Berserker C :R: .12 .30
94 Keldon Firebombers R :R: 1.00 2.00
95 Latulla's Orders C :R: .12 .30
96 Latulla, Keldon Overseer R :R: 2.00 4.00
97 Lesser Gargadon U :R: .20 .50
98 Panic Attack C :R: .12 .30
99 Rhystic Lightning C :R: .12 .30
100 Ridgeline Rager C :R: .12 .30
101 Scoria Cat U :R: .20 .50
102 Search for Survivors R :R: 1.00 2.00
103 Searing Wind R :R: 1.00 2.00
104 Spur Grappler C :R: .12 .30
105 Task Mage Assembly R :R: 1.00 2.00
106 Veteran Brawlers R :R: 1.50 3.00
107 Whip Sergeant U :R: .50 1.00
108 Zerapa Minotaur C :R: .12 .30
109 Avatar of Might R :G: 4.00 8.00
110 Calming Verse C :G: .12 .30
111 Darba U :G: .20 .50

112 Dual Nature R :G: 1.00 2.00
113 Elephant Resurgence R :G: 1.00 2.00
114 Forgotten Harvest R :G: 1.00 2.00
115 Jolrael's Favor C :G: .12 .30
116 Jolrael, Empress of Beasts R :G: 2.00 4.00
117 Living Terrain U :G: .20 .50
118 Marsh Boa C :G: .12 .30
119 Mungha Wurm R :G: 1.00 2.00
120 Pygmy Razorback C :G: .12 .30
121 Rib Cage Spider C :G: .12 .30
122 Root Cage U :G: .20 .50
123 Silt Crawler C :G: .12 .30
124 Snag U :G: .20 .50
125 Spitting Spider U :G: .20 .50
126 Spore Frog C :G: .12 .30
127 Squirrel Wrangler R :G: 2.00 4.00
128 Thresher Beast C :G: .12 .30
129 Thrive C :G: .12 .30
130 Verdant Field U :G: .20 .50
131 Vintara Elephant C :G: .12 .30
132 Vintara Snapper U :G: .20 .50
133 Vitalizing Wind R :G: 2.00 4.00
134 Wild Might C :G: .12 .30
135 Wing Storm U :G: .20 .50
136 Chimeric Idol U :A: 1.00 2.00
137 Copper-Leaf Angel R :A: 2.00 4.00
138 Hollow Warrior U :A: .20 .50
139 Keldon Battlewagon R :A: 1.00 2.00
140 Well of Discovery R :A: 1.00 2.00
141 Well of Life U :A: .50 1.00
142 Rhystic Cave U :L: .50 1.00
143 Wintermoon Mesa R :L: 1.00 2.00

2000 Magic The Gathering Invasion

COMPLETE SET (340) 175.00 225.00
BOOSTER BOX (36 PACKS) 125.00 165.00
BOOSTER PACK (15 CARDS) 4.00 6.00
STARTER DECK BOX (12 DECKS) 110.00 160.00
STARTER DECK 15.00 20.00
FAT PACK 35.00 40.00
*FOIL: 1X TO 2X BASIC CARDS
RELEASED ON OCTOBER 2, 2000
1 Alabaster Leech R :W: 1.50 3.00
2 Angel of Mercy U :W: .50 1.00
3 Ardent Soldier C :W: .12 .30
4 Atalya, Samite Master R :W: 1.50 3.00
5 Benalish Emissary U :W: .50 1.00
6 Benalish Heralds U :W: .50 1.00
7 Benalish Lancer C :W: .12 .30
8 Benalish Trapper C :W: .12 .30
9 Blinding Light U :W: .50 1.00
10 Capashen Unicorn C :W: .12 .30
11 Crimson Acolyte C :W: .12 .30
12 Crusading Knight R :W: 2.00 4.00
13 Death or Glory R :W: 1.50 3.00
14 Dismantling Blow C :W: .12 .30
15 Divine Presence R :W: 1.50 3.00
16 Fight or Flight R :W: 1.50 3.00
17 Glimmering Angel C :W: .12 .30
18 Global Ruin R :W: 1.50 3.00
19 Harsh Judgment R :W: 1.50 3.00
20 Holy Day C :W: .12 .30
21 Liberate U :W: .50 1.00
22 Obsidian Acolyte C :W: .12 .30
23 Orim's Touch C :W: .12 .30
24 Pledge of Loyalty U :W: .50 1.00
25 Prison Barricade C :W: .12 .30
26 Protective Sphere C :W: .12 .30
27 Pure Reflection R :W: 1.50 3.00
28 Rampant Elephant C :W: .12 .30
29 Razorfoot Griffin C :W: .12 .30
30 Restrain C :W: .12 .30
31 Reviving Dose C :W: .12 .30
32 Rewards of Diversity U :W: .50 1.00
33 Reya Dawnbringer R :W: 10.00 20.00
34 Rout R :W: 2.50 5.00
35 Ruham Djinn U :W: .50 1.00
36 Samite Ministration U :W: .50 1.00
37 Shackles C :W: .12 .30
38 Spirit of Resistance R :W: 1.50 3.00
39 Spirit Weaver U :W: .50 1.00
40 Strength of Unity C :W: .12 .30
41 Sunscape Apprentice C :W: .12 .30
42 Sunscape Master R :W: 2.00 4.00
43 Teferi's Care U :W: .50 1.00
44 Wayfaring Giant U :W: .50 1.00
45 Winnow R :W: 1.00 2.00
46 Barrin's Unmaking C :B: .12 .30
47 Blind Seer R :B: 1.50 3.00
48 Breaking Wave R :B: 1.00 2.00
49 Collective Restraint R :B: 1.50 3.00
50 Crystal Spray R :B: 1.50 3.00
51 Disrupt U :B: .50 1.00
52 Distorting Wake R :B: 1.50 3.00
53 Dream Thrush C :B: .12 .30
54 Empress Galina R :B: 1.00 2.00
55 Essence Leak U :B: .50 1.00
56 Exclude C :B: .12 .30
57 Fact or Fiction U :B: 3.00 6.00
58 Faerie Squadron C :B: .12 .30
59 Mana Maze R :B: 1.50 3.00
60 Manipulate Fate U :B: .50 1.00
61 Metathran Aerostat R :B: 1.00 2.00
62 Metathran Transport U :B: .50 1.00
63 Metathran Zombie C :B: .12 .30
64 Opt C :B: .12 .30
65 Phantasmal Terrain C :B: .12 .30
66 Probe C :B: .12 .30
67 Prohibit C :B: .12 .30
68 Psychic Battle R :B: 1.00 2.00
69 Rainbow Crow U :B: .50 1.00
70 Repulse C :B: .12 .30
71 Sapphire Leech R :B: 1.50 3.00
72 Shimmering Wings C :B: .12 .30
73 Shoreline Raider C :B: .12 .30
74 Sky Weaver U :B: .50 1.00
75 Stormscape Apprentice C :B: .12 .30
76 Stormscape Master R :B: 1.50 3.00
77 Sway of Illusion U :B: .50 1.00
78 Teferi's Response R :B: 1.50 3.00
79 Temporal Distortion R :B: 1.50 3.00
80 Tidal Visionary C :B: .12 .30
81 Tolarian Emissary U :B: .50 1.00
82 Tower Drake C :B: .12 .30
83 Traveler's Cloak C :B: .12 .30
84 Vodalian Hypnotist U :B: .50 1.00
85 Vodalian Merchant C :B: .12 .30
86 Vodalian Serpent C :B: .12 .30
87 Wash Out U :B: .50 1.00
88 Well-Laid Plans R :B: .50 1.00
89 Worldly Counsel C :B: .12 .30
90 Zanam Djinn U :B: .50 1.00
91 Addle U :K: .20 .50
92 Agonizing Demise C :K: .12 .30
93 Andradite Leech R :K: 1.00 2.00
94 Annihilate U :K: .50 1.00
95 Bog Initiate C :K: .12 .30
96 Cremate U :K: .20 .50
97 Crypt Angel R :K: 1.50 3.00
98 Cursed Flesh C :K: .12 .30
99 Defiling Tears U :K: .50 1.00
100 Desperate Research R :K: 1.50 3.00
101 Devouring Strossus R :K: 2.00 4.00
102 Do or Die R :K: 1.50 3.00
103 Dredge U :K: .50 1.00
104 Duskwalker C :K: .12 .30
105 Exotic Curse C :K: .12 .30
106 Firescreamer C :K: .12 .30
107 Goham Djinn U :K: .50 1.00
108 Hate Weaver U :K: .50 1.00
109 Hypnotic Cloud C :K: .12 .30
110 Marauding Knight R :K: 1.50 3.00
111 Mourning C :K: .12 .30
112 Nightscape Apprentice C :K: .12 .30
113 Nightscape Master R :K: 2.00 4.00
114 Phyrexian Battleflies C :K: .12 .30
115 Phyrexian Delver R :K: 1.00 2.00
116 Phyrexian Infiltrator R :K: 1.00 2.00
117 Phyrexian Reaper C :K: .12 .30
118 Phyrexian Slayer C :K: .12 .30
119 Plague Spitter U :K: .50 1.00
120 Ravenous Rats C :K: .12 .30
121 Reckless Spite U :K: .50 1.00
122 Recover C :K: .12 .30
123 Scavenged Weaponry C :K: .12 .30
124 Soul Burn C :K: .12 .30
125 Spreading Plague R :K: 1.00 2.00
126 Tainted Well C :K: .12 .30
127 Trench Wurm U :K: .50 1.00
128 Tsabo's Assassin R :K: 1.50 3.00
129 Tsabo's Decree R :K: 2.00 4.00
130 Twilight's Call R :K: 1.50 3.00
131 Urborg Emissary U :K: .50 1.00
132 Urborg Phantom C :K: .12 .30
133 Urborg Shambler U :K: .50 1.00
134 Urborg Skeleton C :K: .12 .30
135 Yawgmoth's Agenda R :K: 1.50 3.00
136 Ancient Kavu C :R: .12 .30
137 Bend or Break R :R: 1.50 3.00
138 Breath of Darigaaz U :R: .20 .50
139 Callous Giant R :R: 1.50 3.00
140 Chaotic Strike U :R: .20 .50
141 Collapsing Borders R :R: 1.00 2.00
142 Crown of Flames C :R: .12 .30
143 Firebrand Ranger U :R: .12 .30
144 Ghitu Fire R :R: 1.50 3.00
145 Goblin Spy U :R: .50 1.00
146 Halam Djinn U :R: .50 1.00
147 Hooded Kavu C :R: .12 .30
148 Kavu Aggressor C :R: .12 .30
149 Kavu Monarch R :R: 2.00 4.00
150 Kavu Runner U :R: .50 1.00
151 Kavu Scout C :R: .12 .30
152 Lightning Dart U :R: .50 1.00
153 Loafing Giant R :R: 1.50 3.00
154 Mages' Contest R :R: 1.50 3.00
155 Maniacal Rage C :R: .12 .30
156 Obliterate R :R: 3.00 6.00
157 Overload C :R: .12 .30
158 Pouncing Kavu C :R: .12 .30
159 Rage Weaver U :R: .50 1.00
160 Rogue Kavu C :R: .12 .30
161 Ruby Leech R :R: 1.50 3.00
162 Savage Offensive C :R: .12 .30
163 Scarred Puma C :R: .12 .30
164 Scorching Lava C :R: .12 .30
165 Searing Rays U :R: .50 1.00
166 Shivan Emissary U :R: .50 1.00
167 Shivan Harvest U :R: .50 1.00
168 Skittish Kavu U :R: .50 1.00
169 Skizzik R :R: 3.00 6.00
170 Slimy Kavu C :R: .12 .30
171 Stand or Fall R :R: 1.50 3.00
172 Stun C :R: .12 .30
173 Tectonic Instability R :R: 1.50 3.00
174 Thunderscape Apprentice C :R: .12 .30
175 Thunderscape Master R :R: 1.50 3.00
176 Tribal Flames C :R: .12 .30
177 Turf Wound C :R: .12 .30
178 Urza's Rage R :R: 5.00 10.00
179 Viashino Grappler C :R: .12 .30
180 Zap C :R: .12 .30
181 Aggressive Urge C :G: .12 .30
182 Bind R :G: 1.50 3.00
183 Blurred Mongoose R :G: 2.00 4.00
184 Canopy Surge U :G: .20 .50
185 Elfhame Sanctuary U :G: .50 1.00
186 Elvish Champion R :G: 4.00 8.00
187 Explosive Growth C :G: .12 .30
188 Fertile Ground C :G: .12 .30
189 Harrow C :G: .12 .30
190 Jade Leech R :G: 2.00 4.00
191 Kavu Chameleon U :G: .50 1.00
192 Kavu Climber C :G: .12 .30
193 Kavu Lair R :G: 1.50 3.00
194 Kavu Titan R :G: 2.00 4.00
195 Llanowar Cavalry C :G: .12 .30
196 Llanowar Elite C :G: .12 .30
197 Llanowar Vanguard C :G: .12 .30
198 Might Weaver U :G: 1.50 3.00
199 Molimo, Maro-Sorcerer R :G: 2.00 4.00
200 Nomadic Elf C :G: .12 .30
201 Pincer Spider C :G: .12 .30
202 Pulse of Llanowar U :G: .50 1.00
203 Quirion Elves C :G: .12 .30
204 Quirion Sentinel C :G: .12 .30
205 Quirion Trailblazer C :G: .12 .30
206 Restock R :G: 1.50 3.00
207 Rooting Kavu U :G: .50 1.00
208 Saproling Infestation R :G: 2.00 4.00
209 Saproling Symbiosis R :G: 2.00 4.00
210 Scouting Trek U :G: .50 1.00
211 Serpentine Kavu C :G: .12 .30
212 Sulam Djinn U :G: .50 1.00
213 Tangle U :G: 1.00 2.00
214 Thicket Elemental R :G: 2.00 4.00
215 Thornscape Apprentice C :G: .12 .30
216 Thornscape Master R :G: 2.00 4.00
217 Tranquility C :G: .12 .30
218 Treefolk Healer U :G: .50 1.00
219 Utopia Tree R :G: 2.50 5.00
220 Verdeloth the Ancient R :G: 2.00 4.00
221 Verduran Emissary U :G: .50 1.00
222 Vigorous Charge C :G: .12 .30
223 Wallop U :G: .50 1.00
224 Wandering Stream C :G: .12 .30
225 Whip Silk C :G: .12 .30
226 Absorb R :D: 4.00 8.00
227 AEther Rift R :D: 1.50 3.00
228 Angelic Shield U :D: .50 1.00
229 Armadillo Cloak C :D: .12 .30
230 Armored Guardian R :D: 1.00 2.00
231 Artifact Mutation R :D: 2.00 4.00
232 Aura Mutation R :D: 1.50 3.00
233 Aura Shards U :D: .50 1.00
234 Backlash U :D: .50 1.00
235 Barrin's Spite R :D: 1.00 2.00
236 Blazing Specter R :D: 2.50 5.00
237 Captain Sisay R :D: 2.00 4.00
238 Cauldron Dance U :D: .50 1.00
239 Charging Troll U :D: .50 1.00
240 Cinder Shade U :D: .50 1.00
241 Coalition Victory R :D: 2.00 4.00
242 Crosis's Attendant U :A: .50 1.00
243 Darigaaz's Attendant U :A: .50 1.00
244 Dromar, the Banisher R :D: 4.00 8.00
245 Dueling Grounds R :D: 2.00 4.00
246 Fires of Yavimaya U :D: .50 1.00
247 Frenzied Tilling C :D: .12 .30
248 Galina's Knight C :D: .12 .30
249 Hanna, Ship's Navigator R :D: 2.00 4.00
250 Heroes' Reunion U :D: .50 1.00
251 Horned Cheetah U :D: .50 1.00
252 Hunting Kavu U :D: .50 1.00
253 Kangee, Aerie Keeper R :D: 1.50 3.00
254 Llanowar Knight C :D: .12 .30
255 Lobotomy U :D: .50 1.00
256 Meteor Storm R :D: 1.50 3.00
257 Noble Panther R :D: 2.00 4.00
258 Ordered Migration U :D: .50 1.00
259 Overabundance R :D: 1.50 3.00
260 Plague Spores C :D: .12 .30
261 Pyre Zombie R :D: 2.00 4.00
262 Raging Kavu R :D: 1.50 3.00
263 Reckless Assault R :D: 1.50 3.00
264 Recoil C :D: .12 .30
265 Reviving Vapors U :D: .50 1.00
266 Riptide Crab U :D: .50 1.00
267 Rith's Attendant U :A: .50 1.00
268 Sabertooth Nishoba R :D: 2.00 4.00
269 Samite Archer U :D: .50 1.00
270 Seer's Vision U :D: .50 1.00
271 Shivan Zombie C :D: .12 .30
272 Simoon U :D: .50 1.00
273 Sleeper's Robe U :D: .50 1.00
274 Slinking Serpent U :D: .50 1.00
275 Smoldering Tar U :D: .50 1.00
276 Spinal Embrace R :D: 1.50 3.00
277 Stalking Assassin R :D: 1.50 3.00
278 Sterling Grove U :D: 1.00 2.00
279 Teferi's Moat R :D: 2.00 4.00
280 Treva's Attendant U :A: .50 1.00
281 Tsabo Tavoc R :D: 2.00 4.00
282 Undermine R :D: 5.00 10.00
283 Urborg Drake U :D: .50 1.00
284 Vicious Kavu U :D: .50 1.00
285 Vile Consumption R :D: 1.50 3.00
286 Vodalian Zombie C :D: .12 .30
287 Void R :D: 1.00 2.00
288 Voracious Cobra U :D: .50 1.00
289 Wings of Hope C :D: .12 .30
290 Yavimaya Barbarian C :D: .12 .30
291 Yavimaya Kavu U :D: .50 1.00
292 Stand/Deliver (Deliver) U :B: .50 1.00
292 Stand/Deliver (Stand) U :W: .50 1.00
293 Spite/Malice (Malice) U :K: .50 1.00
293 Spite/Malice (Spite) U :B: .50 1.00
294 Pain/Suffering (Suffering) U :R: .50 1.00
294 Pain/Suffering (Pain) U :K: .50 1.00
295 Assault/Battery (Battery) U :G: .50 1.00
295 Assault/Battery (Assault) U :R: .50 1.00
296 Wax/Wane (Wax) U :G: .50 1.00
296 Wax/Wane (Wane) U :W: .50 1.00
297 Alloy Golem U :A: .12 .30
298 Bloodstone Cameo U :A: .20 .50
299 Chromatic Sphere U :A: .50 1.00
300 Crosis, the Purger R :D: 4.00 8.00
301 Darigaaz, the Igniter R :D: 4.00 8.00
302 Drake-Skull Cameo U :A: .50 1.00
303 Dromar's Attendant U :A: .50 1.00
304 Juntu Stakes R :A: 1.50 3.00
305 Lotus Guardian R :A: 1.00 2.00
306 Phyrexian Altar R :A: 1.00 2.00
307 Phyrexian Lens R :A: 1.00 2.00
308 Planar Portal R :A: 2.00 4.00
309 Power Armor U :A: .50 1.00
310 Rith, the Awakener R :D: 5.00 10.00
311 Seashell Cameo U :A: .50 1.00
312 Sparring Golem U :A: .50 1.00
313 Tek R :A: 2.00 4.00
314 Tigereye Cameo U :A: .50 1.00
315 Treva, the Renewer R :D: 4.00 8.00
316 Troll-Horn Cameo U :A: .50 1.00
317 Tsabo's Web R :A: 2.00 4.00
318 Urza's Filter R :A: 1.00 2.00
319 Ancient Spring C :L: .12 .30
320 Archaeological Dig U :L: .50 1.00
321 Coastal Tower U :L: 1.00 2.00
322 Elfhame Palace U :L: 1.00 2.00
323 Geothermal Crevice C :L: .12 .30
324 Irrigation Ditch C :L: .12 .30
325 Keldon Necropolis R :L: 1.50 3.00
326 Salt Marsh U :L: 1.00 2.00
327 Shivan Oasis U :L: 1.00 2.00
328 Sulfur Vent C :L: .12 .30
329 Tinder Farm C :L: .12 .30
330 Urborg Volcano U :L: 1.00 2.00
331 Plains C :L: .12 .30
332 Plains C :L: .12 .30
333 Plains C :L: .12 .30
334 Plains C :L: .12 .30
335 Island C :L: .12 .30
336 Island C :L: .12 .30
337 Island C :L: .12 .30
338 Island C :L: .12 .30
339 Swamp C :L: .12 .30
340 Swamp C :L: .12 .30
341 Swamp C :L: .12 .30
342 Swamp C :L: .12 .30
343 Mountain C :L: .12 .30
344 Mountain C :L: .12 .30
345 Mountain C :L: .12 .30
346 Mountain C :L: .12 .30
347 Forest C :L: .12 .30
348 Forest C :L: .12 .30
349 Forest C :L: .12 .30
350 Forest C :L: .12 .30

2001 Magic The Gathering Planeshift

COMPLETE SET (143) 75.00 110.00
BOOSTER BOX (36 PACKS) 100.00 160.00
BOOSTER PACK (15 CARDS) 4.50 5.50
THEME DECK BOX 100.00 125.00
THEME DECK 10.00 13.50
FAT PACK 40.00 50.00
*FOIL: 1X TO 2X BASIC CARDS
RELEASED ON FEBRUARY 5, 2001
1 Aura Blast C :W: .12 .30
2 Aurora Griffin C :W: .12 .30
3 Disciple of Kangee C :W: .12 .30
4 Dominaria's Judgment R :W: 2.00 3.00
5 Guard Dogs U :W: .50 1.00
6 Heroic Defiance C :W: .12 .30
7 Hobble C :W: .12 .30
8 Honorable Scout C :W: .12 .30
9 Lashknife Barrier U :W: .50 1.00
10 March of Souls R :W: 1.00 2.00
11 Orim's Chant R :W: 18.00 22.00
12 Planeswalker's Mirth R :W: 1.50 3.00
13 Pollen Remedy C :W: .12 .30
14 Samite Elder R :W: 2.00 3.00
15 Samite Pilgrim C :W: .12 .30
16 Sunscape Battlemage U :W: .20 .50
17 Sunscape Familiar C :W: .12 .30
18 Surprise Deployment U :W: .20 .50
19 Voice of All U :W: 1.00 2.00
20 Allied Strategies U :B: .50 1.00
21 Arctic Merfolk C :B: .12 .30
22 Confound C :B: .12 .30
23 Dralnu's Pet R :B: 1.50 3.00
24 Ertai's Trickery U :B: .50 1.00
25 Escape Routes C :B: .12 .30
26 Gainsay U :B: .50 1.00
27 Hunting Drake C :B: .12 .30
28 Planar Overlay R :B: 1.50 3.00
29 Planeswalker's Mischief R :B: 1.50 3.00
30 Rushing River C :B: .12 .30
31 Sea Snidd C :B: .12 .30
32 Shifting Sky U :B: .50 1.00
33 Sisay's Ingenuity C :B: .12 .30
34 Sleeping Potion C :B: .12 .30
35 Stormscape Battlemage U :B: .20 .50
36 Stormscape Familiar C :B: .12 .30
37 Sunken Hope R :B: 2.00 3.00
38 Waterspout Elemental R :B: 1.50 3.00
39 Bog Down C :K: .12 .30
40 Dark Suspicions R :K: 2.00 4.00
41 Death Bomb C :K: .12 .30
42 Diabolic Intent R :K: 2.00 3.00
43 Exotic Disease U :K: .20 .50
44 Maggot Carrier C :K: .12 .30
44 Lord of the Undead R :K: 3.50 6.00
46 Morgue Toad C :K: .12 .30
47 Nightscape Battlemage U :K: .20 .50
48 Nightscape Familiar C :K: .12 .30
49 Noxious Vapors U :K: .50 1.00
50 Phyrexian Bloodstock C :K: .12 .30
51 Phyrexian Scuta R :K: 3.50 6.00
52 Planeswalker's Scorn R :K: 1.50 3.00
53 Shriek of Dread C :K: .12 .30
54 Sinister Strength C :K: .12 .30
55 Slay U :K: .50 1.00
56 Volcano Imp C :K: .12 .30
57 Warped Devotion U :K: .50 1.00
58 Caldera Kavu C :R: .12 .30
59 Deadapult R :R: 1.00 2.00
60 Flametongue Kavu U :R: 3.00 5.00
61 Goblin Game R :R: 2.00 4.00
62 Implode U :R: .20 .50
63 Insolence C :R: .12 .30
64 Kavu Recluse C :R: .12 .30
65 Keldon Mantle C :R: .12 .30
66 Magma Burst C :R: .12 .30
67 Mire Kavu C :R: .12 .30
68 Mogg Jailer U :R: .50 1.00
69 Mogg Sentry R :R: 2.00 4.00
70 Planeswalker's Fury R :R: 2.00 4.00
71 Singe C :R: .12 .30
72 Slingshot Goblin C :R: .12 .30
73 Strafe U :R: .20 .50
74 Tahngarth, Talruum Hero R :R: 1.00 2.00
77 Alpha Kavu U :G: .50 1.00
78 Amphibious Kavu C :G: .12 .30
79 Falling Timber C :G: .12 .30
80 Gaea's Herald R :G: 2.00 3.00
81 Gaea's Might C :G: .12 .30
82 Magnigoth Treefolk R :G: 2.00 3.00
83 Mirrorwood Treefolk U :G: .50 1.00
84 Multani's Harmony U :G: .50 1.00
85 Nemata, Grove Guardian R :G: 2.00 4.00
86 Planeswalker's Favor R :G: 1.50 3.00
87 Primal Growth C :G: .12 .30
88 Pygmy Kavu C :G: .12 .30
89 Quirion Dryad R :G: 2.00 4.00
90 Quirion Explorer C :G: .12 .30
91 Root Greevil C :G: .12 .30
92 Skyshroud Blessing U :G: .50 1.00
93 Stone Kavu C :G: .12 .30
94 Thornscape Battlemage U :G: .20 .50
95 Thornscape Familiar C :G: .12 .30
96 Ancient Spider R :D: 1.00 2.00
97 Cavern Harpy C :D: .12 .30
98 Cloud Cover R :D: 2.00 3.00
99 Crosis's Charm U :D: .20 .50
100 Darigaaz's Charm U :D: .20 .50
101 Daring Leap C :D: .12 .30
102 Destructive Flow R :D: 1.00 2.00
103 Doomsday Specter R :D: 2.00 4.00
104 Dralnu's Crusade R :D: 1.00 2.00
105 Dromar's Charm U :D: .50 1.00
106 Eladamri's Call R :D: 3.00 5.00
107 Ertai, the Corrupted R :D: 1.50 3.00
108 Fleetfoot Panther U :D: .50 1.00
109 Gerrard's Command C :D: .12 .30
110 Horned Kavu C :D: .12 .30
111 Hull Breach C :D: .12 .30
112 Keldon Twilight R :D: 1.00 2.00
113 Lava Zombie C :D: .12 .30
114 Malicious Advice C :D: .12 .30
115 Marsh Crocodile U :D: .50 1.00
116 Meddling Mage R :D: 18.00 20.00
117 Natural Emergence R :D: 1.50 3.00
118 Phyrexian Tyranny R :D: 1.50 3.00
119 Questing Phelddagrif R :D: 1.00 2.00
120 Radiant Kavu R :D: 1.00 2.00
121 Razing Snidd U :D: .20 .50
122 Rith's Charm U :D: .50 1.00
123 Sawtooth Loon U :D: .20 .50
124 Shivan Wurm R :D: 4.00 7.00
125 Silver Drake C :D: .12 .30
126 Sparkcaster U :D: .20 .50
127 Steel Leaf Paladin C :D: .12 .30
128 Terminate C :D: .30 .75
129 Treva's Charm U :D: .50 1.00
130 Urza's Guilt R :D: 1.50 3.00
131 Draco R :A: 4.00 8.00
132 Mana Cylix U :A: .50 1.00
133 Skyship Weatherlight R :A: 1.50 3.00
134 Star Compass U :A: .20 .50
135 Stratadon U :A: .50 1.00
136 Crosis's Catacombs U :L: 1.00 2.00
137 Darigaaz's Caldera U :L: 1.00 2.00
138 Dromar's Cavern U :L: 1.00 2.00
139 Forsaken City R :L: 2.00 3.00
140 Meteor Crater R :L: 1.50 3.00
141 Rith's Grove U :L: .75 1.50
142 Terminal Moraine U :L: .20 .50
143 Treva's Ruins U :L: 1.00 2.00

2001 Magic The Gathering 7th Edition

COMPLETE SET (350) 140.00 200.00
BOOSTER BOX (36 PACKS) 120.00 140.00
BOOSTER PACK (15 CARDS) 4.00 6.00
STARTER DECK 6.00 10.00
THEME DECK BOX (15 DECKS) 70.00 90.00
*FOIL: 1X TO 2X BASIC CARDS
RELEASED ON APRIL 11, 2001
1 Angelic Page C :W: .12 .30
2 Ardent Militia U :W: .20 .50
3 Blessed Reversal R :W: 1.00 2.00
4 Breath of Life U :W: .50 1.00
5 Castle U :W: .20 .50
6 Circle of Protection Black C :W: .12 .30
7 Circle of Protection Blue C :W: .12 .30
8 Circle of Protection Green C :W: .12 .30
9 Circle of Protection Red C :W: .12 .30
10 Circle of Protection White C :W: .12 .30
11 Cloudchaser Eagle C :W: .12 .30
12 Crossbow Infantry C :W: .12 .30
13 Disenchant C :W: .12 .30
14 Eager Cadet C :W: .12 .30
15 Elite Archers R :W: 1.00 2.00
16 Gerrard's Wisdom U :W: .20 .50
17 Glorious Anthem R :W: 3.00 6.00
18 Healing Salve C :W: .12 .30
19 Heavy Ballista U :W: .20 .50
20 Holy Strength C :W: .12 .30
21 Honor Guard C :W: .12 .30
22 Intrepid Hero R :W: 2.00 4.00
23 Kjeldoran Royal Guard R :W: 1.00 2.00
24 Knight Errant C :W: .12 .30
25 Knighthood U :W: .50 1.00
26 Longbow Archer U :W: .50 1.00
27 Master Healer R :W: 1.00 2.00
28 Northern Paladin R :W: 1.00 2.00
29 Pacifism C :W: .12 .30
30 Pariah R :W: 2.50 5.00
31 Purify R :W: 1.00 2.00
32 Razorfoot Griffin C :W: .12 .30
33 Reprisal U :W: .50 1.00
34 Reverse Damage R :W: 1.00 2.00
35 Rolling Stones R :W: 1.00 2.00
36 Sacred Ground R :W: 2.00 4.00
37 Sacred Nectar C :W: .12 .30
38 Samite Healer C :W: .12 .30
39 Sanctimony U :W: .20 .50
40 Seasoned Marshal U :W: .20 .50
41 Serra Advocate U :W: .20 .50
42 Serra Angel R :W: 3.00 6.00
43 Serra's Embrace U :W: .50 1.00
44 Shield Wall C :W: .12 .30
45 Skyshroud Falcon C :W: .12 .30
46 Southern Paladin R :W: 1.25 2.50
47 Spirit Link U :W: .50 1.00
48 Standing Troops C :W: .12 .30
49 Starlight U :W: .20 .50
50 Staunch Defenders U :W: .50 1.00
51 Sunweb R :W: 1.50 3.00
52 Sustainer of the Realm U :W: .20 .50
53 Venerable Monk C :W: .12 .30
54 Vengeance U :W: .20 .50
55 Wall of Swords U :W: .50 1.00
56 Worship R :W: 4.00 8.00
57 Wrath of God R :W: 10.00 20.00
58 Air Elemental U :B: .20 .50
59 Ancestral Memories R :B: 1.00 2.00
60 Arcane Laboratory U :B: .50 1.00
61 Archivist R :B: .50 1.00

62 Baleful Stare U :B:	.20	.50
63 Benthic Behemoth R :B:	1.00	2.00
64 Boomerang C :B:	.12	.30
65 Confiscate U :B:	.20	.50
66 Coral Merfolk C :B:	.12	.30
67 Counterspell C :B:	1.00	2.00
68 Daring Apprentice R :B:	1.00	2.00
69 Deflection R :B:	1.00	2.00
70 Delusions of Mediocrity R :B:	1.00	2.00
71 Equilibrium R :B:	1.00	2.00
72 Evacuation R :B:	1.00	2.00
73 Fighting Drake U :B:	.20	.50
74 Fleeting Image R :B:	1.00	2.00
75 Flight C :B:	.20	.50
76 Force Spike C :B:	.50	1.00
77 Giant Octopus C :B:	.12	.30
78 Glacial Wall U :B:	.20	.50
79 Hibernation U :B:	.20	.50
80 Horned Turtle C :B:	.12	.30
81 Inspiration C :B:	1.00	2.00
82 Levitation U :B:	.20	.50
83 Lord of Atlantis R :B:	2.00	4.00
84 Mahamoti Djinn R :B:	2.00	4.00
85 Mana Breach U :B:	.20	.50
86 Mana Short R :B:	1.50	3.00
87 Mawcor R :B:	1.00	2.00
88 Memory Lapse C :B:	.12	.30
89 Merfolk Looter U :B:	.50	1.00
90 Merfolk of the Pearl Trident C :B:	.12	.30
91 Opportunity U :B:	.20	.50
92 Opposition R :B:	2.50	5.00
93 Phantom Warrior U :B:	.20	.50
94 Prodigal Sorcerer C :B:	.12	.30
95 Remove Soul C :B:	.12	.30
96 Sage Owl C :B:	.12	.30
97 Sea Monster C :B:	.12	.30
98 Sleight of Hand C :B:	.12	.30
99 Steal Artifact U :B:	.20	.50
100 Storm Crow C :B:	.20	.50
101 Telepathic Spies C :B:	.12	.30
102 Telepathy U :B:	.50	1.00
103 Temporal Adept R :B:	2.00	4.00
104 Thieving Magpie U :B:	.20	.50
105 Tolarian Winds C :B:	.12	.30
106 Treasure Trove U :B:	.20	.50
107 Twiddle C :B:	.12	.30
108 Unsummon C :B:	.12	.30
109 Vigilant Drake C :B:	.12	.30
110 Vizzerdrix R :B:	1.00	2.00
111 Wall of Air U :B:	.50	1.00
112 Wall of Wonder R :B:	1.00	2.00
113 Wind Dancer U :B:	.20	.50
114 Wind Drake C :B:	.12	.30
115 Abyssal Horror R :K:	1.00	2.00
116 Abyssal Specter U :K:	.20	.50
117 Agonizing Memories U :K:	.20	.50
118 Befoul U :K:	.20	.50
119 Bellowing Fiend R :K:	1.00	2.00
120 Bereavement U :K:	.20	.50
121 Blood Pet C :K:	.12	.30
122 Bog Imp C :K:	.12	.30
123 Bog Wraith U :K:	.20	.50
124 Corrupt C :K:	.12	.30
125 Crypt Rats U :K:	.50	1.00
126 Dakmor Lancer U :K:	.20	.50
127 Dark Banishing C :K:	.12	.30
128 Darkest Hour R :K:	1.50	3.00
129 Dregs of Sorrow R :K:	1.00	2.00
130 Drudge Skeletons C :K:	.12	.30
131 Duress C :K:	1.25	2.50
132 Eastern Paladin R :K:	1.00	2.00
133 Engineered Plague U :K:	1.25	2.50
134 Fallen Angel R :K:	2.00	4.00
135 Fear C :K:	.12	.30
136 Foul Imp U :K:	.20	.50
137 Fugue U :K:	.12	.30
138 Giant Cockroach C :K:	.12	.30
139 Gravedigger C :K:	.12	.30
140 Greed R :K:	1.00	2.00
141 Hollow Dogs C :K:	.12	.30
142 Howl from Beyond C :K:	.12	.30
143 Infernal Contract R :K:	1.00	2.00
144 Leshrac's Rite U :K:	.20	.50
145 Looming Shade C :K:	.12	.30
146 Megrim U :K:	1.00	2.00
147 Mind Rot C :K:	.12	.30
148 Nausea C :K:	.12	.30
149 Necrologia U :K:	.20	.50
150 Nightmare R :K:	2.50	5.00
151 Nocturnal Raid U :K:	.20	.50
152 Oppression R :K:	1.00	2.00
153 Ostracize C :K:	.12	.30
154 Persecute R :K:	3.00	6.00
155 Plague Beetle C :K:	.12	.30
156 Rag Man R :K:	1.00	2.00
157 Raise Dead C :K:	.12	.30
158 Razortooth Rats C :K:	.12	.30
159 Reprocess R :K:	1.00	2.00
160 Revenant R :K:	1.00	2.00
161 Scathe Zombies C :K:	.20	.50
162 Serpent Warrior C :K:	.12	.30
163 Soul Feast U :K:	.50	1.00
164 Spineless Thug C :K:	.12	.30
165 Strands of Night U :K:	.20	.50
166 Stronghold Assassin R :K:	1.00	2.00
167 Tainted AEther R :K:	1.50	3.00
168 Unholy Strength C :K:	.12	.30
169 Wall of Bone U :K:	.50	1.00
170 Western Paladin R :K:	1.00	2.00
171 Yawgmoth's Edict U :K:	.20	.50
172 AEther Flash U :R:	.20	.50
173 Balduvian Barbarians C :R:	.12	.30
174 Bedlam R :R:	1.50	3.00
175 Blaze U :R:	.50	1.00
176 Bloodshot Cyclops R :R:	1.00	2.00
177 Boil U :R:	.50	1.00
178 Crimson Hellkite R :R:	2.00	4.00
179 Disorder U :R:	.20	.50
180 Earthquake R :R:	1.00	2.00
181 Fervor R :R:	1.00	2.00
182 Final Fortune R :R:	1.50	3.00
183 Fire Elemental U :R:	.20	.50
184 Ghitu Fire-Eater U :R:	.20	.50
185 Goblin Chariot C :R:	.12	.30
186 Goblin Digging Team C :R:	.12	.30
187 Goblin Elite Infantry C :R:	.12	.30
188 Goblin Gardener C :R:	.12	.30
189 Goblin Glider U :R:	.20	.50
190 Goblin King R :R:	2.00	4.00
191 Goblin Matron U :R:	.50	1.00
192 Goblin Raider C :R:	.12	.30
193 Goblin Spelunkers C :R:	.12	.30
194 Goblin War Drums U :R:	.20	.50
195 Granite Grip C :R:	.12	.30
196 Hill Giant C :R:	.12	.30
197 Impatience R :R:	1.00	2.00
198 Inferno R :R:	1.00	2.00
199 Lava Axe C :R:	.12	.30
200 Lightning Blast C :R:	.12	.30
201 Lightning Elemental C :R:	.12	.30
202 Mana Clash R :R:	1.00	2.00
203 Ogre Taskmaster U :R:	.20	.50
204 Okk R :R:	1.00	2.00
205 Orcish Artillery U :R:	.20	.50
206 Orcish Oriflamme U :R:	.20	.50
207 Pillage U :R:	1.50	3.00
208 Pygmy Pyrosaur C :R:	.12	.30
209 Pyroclasm U :R:	1.50	3.00
210 Pyrotechnics U :R:	.20	.50
211 Raging Goblin C :R:	.12	.30
212 Reckless Embermage R :R:	1.00	2.00
213 Reflexes C :R:	.12	.30
214 Relentless Assault R :R:	.50	1.00
215 Sabretooth Tiger C :R:	.12	.30
216 Seismic Assault R :R:	1.00	2.00
217 Shatter C :R:	.12	.30
218 Shivan Dragon R :R:	3.00	6.00
219 Shock C :R:	.12	.30
220 Spitting Earth C :R:	.12	.30
221 Stone Rain C :R:	.20	.50
222 Storm Shaman U :R:	.20	.50
223 Sudden Impact U :R:	.20	.50
224 Trained Orgg R :R:	1.00	2.00
225 Tremor C :R:	.12	.30
226 Volcanic Hammer C :R:	.12	.30
227 Wall of Fire U :R:	.50	1.00
228 Wildfire R :R:	2.00	4.00
229 Anaconda U :G:	.20	.50
230 Ancient Silverback R :G:	1.00	2.00
231 Birds of Paradise R :G:	9.00	18.00
232 Blanchwood Armor U :G:	1.00	2.00
233 Bull Hippo U :G:	.20	.50
234 Canopy Spider C :G:	.12	.30
235 Compost U :G:	.50	1.00
236 Creeping Mold U :G:	.50	1.00
237 Early Harvest R :G:	3.00	6.00
238 Elder Druid R :G:	1.00	2.00
239 Elvish Archers R :G:	1.50	3.00
240 Elvish Champion R :G:	3.00	6.00
241 Elvish Lyrist U :G:	.20	.50
242 Elvish Piper R :G:	5.00	10.00
243 Familiar Ground U :G:	.20	.50
244 Femeref Archers U :G:	.12	.30
245 Fog C :G:	.12	.30
246 Fyndhorn Elder U :G:	.50	1.00
247 Gang of Elk U :G:	.50	1.00
248 Giant Growth C :G:	.12	.30
249 Giant Spider C :G:	.12	.30
250 Gorilla Chieftain C :G:	.12	.30
251 Grizzly Bears C :G:	.12	.30
252 Hurricane R :G:	1.00	2.00
253 Llanowar Elves C :G:	.50	1.00
254 Lone Wolf C :G:	.12	.30
255 Lure U :G:	.20	.50
256 Maro R :G:	1.00	2.00
257 Might of Oaks R :G:	2.50	5.00
258 Monstrous Growth C :G:	.12	.30
259 Nature's Resurgence R :G:	1.00	2.00
260 Nature's Revolt R :G:	1.00	2.00
261 Pride of Lions U :G:	.50	1.00
262 Rampant Growth C :G:	.12	.30
263 Reclaim C :G:	.50	1.00
264 Redwood Treefolk C :G:	.12	.30
265 Regeneration C :G:	.12	.30
266 Rowen R :G:	1.00	2.00
267 Scavenger Folk U :G:	.20	.50
268 Seeker of Skybreak C :G:	.20	.50
269 Shanodin Dryads C :G:	.12	.30
270 Spined Wurm C :G:	.12	.30
271 Squall C :G:	.12	.30
272 Stream of Life C :G:	.20	.50
273 Thorn Elemental R :G:	2.00	4.00
274 Thoughtleech U :G:	.50	1.00
275 Trained Armodon C :G:	.12	.30
276 Tranquility C :G:	.12	.30
277 Treefolk Seedlings U :G:	.20	.50
278 Uktabi Wildcats R :G:	1.00	2.00
279 Untamed Wilds U :G:	.20	.50
280 Verduran Enchantress R :G:	1.50	3.00
281 Vernal Bloom R :G:	2.50	5.00
282 Wild Growth C :G:	.12	.30
283 Wing Snare U :G:	.20	.50
284 Wood Elves C :G:	.12	.30
285 Yavimaya Enchantress U :G:	.20	.50
286 Aladdin's Ring R :A:	1.50	3.00
287 Beast of Burden R :A:	1.50	3.00
288 Caltrops U :A:	.20	.50
289 Charcoal Diamond U :A:	.20	.50
290 Coat of Arms R :A:	7.50	15.00
291 Crystal Rod U :A:	.20	.50
292 Dingus Egg R :A:	1.00	2.00
293 Disrupting Scepter R :A:	1.00	2.00
294 Ensnaring Bridge R :A:	2.00	4.00
295 Feroz's Ban R :A:	.50	1.00
296 Fire Diamond U :A:	.50	1.00
297 Flying Carpet R :A:	1.00	2.00
298 Grafted Skullcap R :A:	1.00	2.00
299 Grapeshot Catapult U :A:	.20	.50
300 Howling Mine R :A:	2.50	5.00
301 Iron Star U :A:	.20	.50
302 Ivory Cup U :A:	.20	.50
303 Jalum Tome R :A:	1.00	2.00
304 Jandor's Saddlebags R :A:	1.00	2.00
305 Jayemdae Tome R :A:	1.00	2.00
306 Marble Diamond U :A:	.20	.50
307 Meekstone R :A:	1.50	3.00
308 Millstone R :A:	1.50	3.00
309 Moss Diamond U :A:	.20	.50
310 Patagia Golem U :A:	.20	.50
311 Phyrexian Colossus R :A:	2.00	4.00
312 Phyrexian Hulk U :A:	.20	.50
313 Pit Trap U :A:	.20	.50
314 Rod of Ruin U :A:	.20	.50
315 Sisay's Ring U :A:	.20	.50
316 Sky Diamond U :A:	.20	.50
317 Soul Net U :A:	.50	1.00
318 Spellbook U :A:	.50	1.00
319 Static Orb R :A:	1.50	3.00
320 Storm Cauldron R :A:	1.00	2.00
321 Teferi's Puzzle Box R :A:	1.50	3.00
322 Throne of Bone U :A:	.20	.50
323 Wall of Spears U :A:	.20	.50
324 Wooden Sphere U :A:	.20	.50
325 Adarkar Wastes R :L:	3.00	6.00
326 Brushland R :L:	3.00	6.00
327 City of Brass R :L:	4.00	8.00
328 Forest L :L:	.20	.50
329 Forest L :L:	.20	.50
330 Forest L :L:	.50	1.00
331 Forest L :L:	.50	1.00
332 Island L :L:	.20	.50
333 Island L :L:	.20	.50
334 Island L :L:	.20	.50
335 Island L :L:	.20	.50
336 Karplusan Forest R :L:	4.00	8.00
337 Mountain L :L:	.20	.50
338 Mountain L :L:	.20	.50
339 Mountain L :L:	.20	.50
340 Mountain L :L:	.20	.50
341 Plains L :L:	.20	.50
342 Plains L :L:	.20	.50
343 Plains L :L:	.20	.50
344 Plains L :L:	.20	.50
345 Sulfurous Springs R :L:	3.00	6.00
346 Swamp L :L:	.20	.50
347 Swamp L :L:	.20	.50
348 Swamp L :L:	.20	.50
349 Swamp L :L:	.20	.50
350 Underground River R :L:	5.00	10.00

2001 Magic The Gathering Apocalypse

COMPLETE SET (143)	75.00	110.00
BOOSTER BOX (36 PACKS)	175.00	225.00
BOOSTER PACK (15 CARDS)	5.00	7.00
THEME DECK BOX	110.00	150.00
THEME DECK	12.00	15.00
FAT PACK	30.00	60.00
*FOIL: 1X TO 2X BASIC CARDS		
RELEASED ON JUNE 4, 2001		
1 Angelfire Crusader C :W:	.12	.30
2 Coalition Flag U :W:	.50	1.00
3 Coalition Honor Guard C :W:	.12	.30
4 Dega Disciple C :W:	.12	.30
5 Dega Sanctuary U :W:	.50	1.00
6 Degavolver R :W:	1.50	3.00
7 Diversionary Tactics U :W:	.50	1.00
8 Divine Light C :W:	.12	.30
9 Enlistment Officer U :W:	.20	.50
10 False Dawn R :W:	1.00	2.50
11 Gerrard Capashen R :W:	1.50	3.00
12 Haunted Angel U :W:	.50	1.00
13 Helionaut C :W:	.12	.30
14 Manacles of Decay C :W:	.12	.30
15 Orim's Thunder C :W:	.12	.30
16 Shield of Duty and Reason C :W:	.12	.30
17 Spectral Lynx R :W:	2.00	4.00
18 Standard Bearer C :W:	.12	.30
19 Ceta Disciple C :B:	.12	.30
20 Ceta Sanctuary U :B:	.50	1.00
21 Cetavolver R :B:	1.50	3.00
22 Coastal Drake C :B:	.12	.30
23 Evasive Action U :B:	.50	1.00
24 Ice Cave R :B:	1.00	2.00
25 Index C :B:	.12	.30
26 Jaded Response C :B:	.12	.30
27 Jilt C :B:	.12	.30
28 Living Airship C :B:	.12	.30
29 Reef Shaman C :B:	.12	.30
30 Shimmering Mirage C :B:	.12	.30
31 Tidal Courier U :B:	.30	.75
32 Unnatural Selection R :B:	2.00	4.00
33 Vodalian Mystic U :B:	.50	1.00
34 Whirlpool Drake U :B:	.50	1.00
35 Whirlpool Rider C :B:	.12	.30
36 Whirlpool Warrior R :B:	1.50	3.00
37 Day/Night U :W:/:K:	.50	1.00
38 Desolation Angel R :K:	2.50	5.00
39 Foul Presence U :K:	.20	.50
40 Grave Defiler U :K:	.50	1.00
41 Last Caress C :K:	.12	.30
42 Mind Extraction C :K:	.12	.30
43 Mournful Zombie C :K:	.12	.30
44 Necra Disciple C :K:	.12	.30
45 Necra Sanctuary U :K:	.50	1.00
46 Necravolver R :K:	1.00	2.00
47 Phyrexian Arena R :K:	3.00	6.00
48 Phyrexian Gargantua U :K:	.30	.75
49 Phyrexian Rager C :K:	.12	.30
50 Planar Despair R :K:	1.00	2.00
51 Quagmire Druid C :K:	.12	.30
52 Suppress U :K:	.30	.75
53 Urborg Uprising C :K:	.12	.30
54 Zombie Boa C :K:	.12	.30
55 Bloodfire Colossus R :R:	2.00	4.00
56 Bloodfire Dwarf C :R:	.12	.30
57 Bloodfire Infusion C :R:	.12	.30
58 Bloodfire Kavu U :R:	.50	1.00
59 Desolation Giant R :R:	1.00	2.00
60 Dwarven Landslide C :R:	.12	.30
61 Dwarven Patrol U :R:	.50	1.00
62 Goblin Ringleader U :R:	1.50	3.00
63 Illuminate U :R:	.50	1.00
64 Kavu Glider C :R:	.12	.30
65 Minotaur Tactician C :R:	.12	.30
66 Raka Disciple C :R:	.12	.30
67 Raka Sanctuary U :R:	.30	.75
68 Rakavolver R :R:	1.00	2.00
69 Smash C :R:	.12	.30
70 Tahngarth's Glare C :R:	.12	.30
71 Tundra Kavu C :R:	.12	.30
72 Wild Research R :R:	1.50	3.00
73 Ana Disciple C :G:	.12	.30
74 Ana Sanctuary U :G:	.50	1.00
75 Anavolver R :G:	1.50	3.00
76 Bog Gnarr C :G:	.12	.30
77 Gaea's Balance U :G:	.50	1.00
78 Glade Gnarr C :G:	.12	.30
79 Kavu Howler U :G:	.50	1.00
80 Kavu Mauler R :G:	1.50	3.00
81 Lay of the Land C :G:	.12	.30
82 Penumbra Bobcat C :G:	.12	.30
83 Penumbra Kavu U :G:	.30	.75
84 Penumbra Wurm R :G:	2.00	4.00
85 Savage Gorilla C :G:	.12	.30
86 Strength of Night C :G:	.12	.30
87 Sylvan Messenger U :G:	.50	1.00
88 Symbiotic Deployment R :G:	1.00	2.00
89 Tranquil Path C :G:	.12	.30
90 Urborg Elf C :G:	.12	.30
91 AEther Mutation U :D:	.20	.50
92 Captain's Maneuver U :D:	.50	1.00
93 Consume Strength C :D:	.12	.30
94 Cromat R :D:	1.50	3.00
95 Death Grasp R :D:	2.00	4.00
96 Death Mutation U :D:	.50	1.00
97 Ebony Treefolk U :D:	.50	1.00
98 Fervent Charge R :D:	1.50	3.00
99 Flowstone Charger U :D:	.20	.50
100 Fungal Shambler R :D:	1.50	3.00
101 Gaea's Skyfolk C :D:	.12	.30
102 Gerrard's Verdict U :D:	.50	1.00
103 Goblin Legionnaire C :D:	.12	.30
104 Goblin Trenches R :D:	2.00	4.00
105 Guided Passage R :D:	1.00	2.00
106 Jungle Barrier U :D:	.50	1.00
107 Last Stand R :D:	1.00	2.50
108 Lightning Angel R :D:	2.50	5.00
109 Llanowar Dead C :D:	.12	.30
110 Martyrs' Tomb U :D:	.50	1.00
111 Minotaur Illusionist U :D:	.50	1.00
112 Mystic Snake R :D:	2.50	5.00
113 Overgrown Estate R :D:	1.00	2.00
114 Pernicious Deed R :D:	7.50	15.00
115 Powerstone Minefield R :D:	2.00	4.00
116 Prophetic Bolt R :D:	1.00	2.00
117 Putrid Warrior C :D:	.12	.30
118 Quicksilver Dagger C :D:	.12	.30
119 Razorfin Hunter C :D:	.12	.30
120 Soul Link C :D:	.12	.30
121 Spiritmonger R :D:	6.00	12.00
122 Squee's Embrace C :D:	.12	.30
123 Squee's Revenge U :D:	.20	.50
124 Suffocating Blast R :D:	1.50	3.00
125 Temporal Spring C :D:	.12	.30
126 Vindicate R :D:	6.00	12.00
127 Yavimaya's Embrace R :D:	1.00	2.50
128 Fire/Ice U :R:/:B:	1.50	3.00
129 Illusion/Reality U :B:/:G:	.50	1.00
130 Death/Life U :G:/:K:	.50	1.00
131 Dead Ringers C :K:	.12	.30
132 Chaos/Order U :R:/:W:	.50	1.00
133 Brass Herald U :A:	.50	1.00
134 Dodecapod U :A:	.50	1.00
135 Dragon Arch U :A:	1.00	2.00
136 Emblazoned Golem U :A:	.50	1.00
137 Legacy Weapon R :A:	1.50	3.00
138 Mask of Intolerance R :A:	1.00	2.00
139 Battlefield Forge R :L:	5.00	10.00
140 Caves of Koilos R :L:	5.00	10.00
141 Llanowar Wastes R :L:	5.00	10.00
142 Shivan Reef R :L:	6.00	12.00
143 Yavimaya Coast R :L:	5.00	10.00

2001 Magic The Gathering Odyssey

COMPLETE SET (350)	125.00	200.00
BOOSTER BOX (36 PACKS)	100.00	120.00
BOOSTER PACK (15 CARDS)	4.00	5.00
THEME DECK BOX	75.00	100.00
THEME DECK	9.00	12.00
FAT PACK	30.00	40.00
*FOIL: 1X TO 2X BASIC CARDS		
RELEASED ON OCTOBER 1, 2001		
1 Aegis of Honor R :W:	2.00	4.00
2 Ancestral Tribute R :W:	1.00	2.00
3 Angelic Wall C :W:	.12	.30
4 Animal Boneyard U :W:	.50	1.00
5 Auramancer C :W:	.12	.30
6 Aven Archer U :W:	.50	1.00
7 Aven Cloudchaser C :W:	.12	.30
8 Aven Flock C :W:	.12	.30
9 Aven Shrine R :W:	1.00	2.00
10 Balancing Act R :W:	1.50	3.00
11 Beloved Chaplain U :W:	.50	1.00
13 Cantivore R :W:	1.00	2.00
14 Cease-Fire C :W:	.12	.30
15 Confessor C :W:	.12	.30
16 Dedicated Martyr C :W:	.12	.30
17 Delaying Shield R :W:	1.00	2.00
18 Devoted Caretaker R :W:	2.00	4.00
19 Divine Sacrament R :W:	2.00	4.00
20 Dogged Hunter R :W:	1.00	2.50
21 Earnest Fellowship R :W:	1.50	3.00
22 Embolden C :W:	.12	.30
23 Gallantry U :W:	.50	1.00
24 Graceful Antelope R :W:	1.00	2.00
25 Hallowed Healer C :W:	.12	.30
26 Karmic Justice R :W:	1.50	3.00
27 Kirtar's Desire C :W:	.12	.30
28 Kirtar's Wrath R :W:	2.00	4.00
29 Lieutenant Kirtar R :W:	2.00	4.00
30 Life Burst C :W:	.12	.30
31 Luminous Guardian U :W:	.50	1.00
32 Master Apothecary R :W:	1.50	3.00
33 Mystic Crusader R :W:	2.00	4.00
34 Mystic Penitent U :W:	.50	1.00
35 Mystic Visionary C :W:	.12	.30
36 Mystic Zealot C :W:	.12	.30
37 Blessed Orator U :W:	.50	1.00
37 Nomad Decoy U :W:	.50	1.00
38 Patrol Hound C :W:	.12	.30
39 Pianna, Nomad Captain R :W:	2.00	4.00
40 Pilgrim of Justice C :W:	.12	.30
41 Pilgrim of Virtue C :W:	.12	.30
42 Ray of Distortion C :W:	.12	.30
43 Resilient Wanderer U :W:	.20	.50
44 Sacred Rites C :W:	.12	.30
45 Second Thoughts C :W:	.12	.30
46 Shelter C :W:	.12	.30
47 Soulcatcher U :W:	.50	1.00
48 Sphere of Duty U :W:	.20	.50
49 Sphere of Grace U :W:	.50	1.00
50 Sphere of Law U :W:	.20	.50
51 Sphere of Reason U :W:	.20	.50
52 Sphere of Truth U :W:	.50	1.00
53 Spiritualize U :W:	.20	.50
54 Tattoo Ward U :W:	.20	.50
55 Testament of Faith U :W:	.20	.50
56 Tireless Tribe C :W:	.12	.30
57 Wayward Angel R :W:	2.00	4.00
58 Aboshan's Desire C :B:	.12	.30
59 Aboshan, Cephalid Emperor R :B:	2.00	4.00
60 AEther Burst C :B:	.12	.30
61 Amugaba R :B:	1.50	3.00
62 Aura Graft U :B:	.20	.50
63 Aven Fisher C :B:	.12	.30
64 Aven Smokeweaver U :B:	.50	1.00
65 Aven Windreader C :B:	.12	.30
66 Balshan Beguiler U :B:	.50	1.00
67 Balshan Griffin U :B:	.50	1.00
68 Bamboozle U :B:	.50	1.00
69 Battle of Wits R :B:	1.50	3.00
70 Careful Study C :B:	.12	.30
71 Cephalid Broker U :B:	.50	1.00
72 Cephalid Looter C :B:	.12	.30
73 Cephalid Retainer R :B:	1.50	3.00
74 Cephalid Scout C :B:	.12	.30
75 Cephalid Shrine R :B:	1.00	2.00
76 Chamber of Manipulation U :B:	.50	1.00
77 Cognivore R :B:	1.50	3.00
78 Concentrate U :B:	.50	1.00
79 Cultural Exchange R :B:	1.00	2.00
80 Deluge U :B:	.20	.50
81 Dematerialize C :B:	.12	.30
82 Divert R :B:	1.00	2.00
83 Dreamwinder C :B:	.12	.30
84 Escape Artist C :B:	.12	.30
85 Extract R :B:	2.00	4.00
86 Fervent Denial U :B:	.20	.50
87 Immobilizing Ink C :B:	.12	.30
88 Laquatus's Creativity U :B:	.50	1.00
89 Patron Wizard R :B:	2.00	4.00
90 Pedantic Learning R :B:	1.50	3.00
91 Peek C :B:	.12	.30
92 Persuasion R :B:	1.50	3.00
93 Phantom Whelp C :B:	.12	.30
94 Predict U :B:	.20	.50
95 Psionic Gift C :B:	.12	.30
96 Pulsating Illusion U :B:	.50	1.00
97 Puppeteer U :B:	.50	1.00
98 Repel C :B:	.12	.30
99 Rites of Refusal C :B:	.12	.30
100 Scrivener C :B:	.12	.30
101 Shifty Doppelganger R :B:	1.00	2.00
102 Standstill U :B:	2.50	5.00
103 Syncopate C :B:	.12	.30
104 Think Tank U :B:	.20	.50
105 Thought Devourer R :B:	1.00	2.00
106 Thought Eater U :B:	.20	.50
107 Thought Nibbler C :B:	.12	.30
108 Time Stretch R :B:	2.50	5.00
109 Touch of Invisibility C :B:	.12	.30
110 Traumatize R :B:	7.50	15.00
111 Treetop Sentinel U :B:	.20	.50
112 Unifying Theory R :B:	1.00	2.00
113 Upheaval R :B:	4.00	8.00
114 Words of Wisdom C :B:	.12	.30
115 Afflict C :K:	.12	.30
116 Bloodcurdler R :K:	1.00	2.00
117 Braids, Cabal Minion R :K:	2.50	5.00
118 Buried Alive U :K:	1.50	3.00
119 Cabal Inquisitor C :K:	.12	.30
120 Cabal Patriarch R :K:	1.50	3.00
121 Cabal Shrine R :K:	1.00	2.00
122 Caustic Tar U :K:	.50	1.00
123 Childhood Horror U :K:	.50	1.00
124 Coffin Purge C :K:	.12	.30
125 Crypt Creeper C :K:	.12	.30
126 Cursed Monstrosity R :K:	1.50	3.00
127 Decaying Soil R :K:	1.00	2.00
128 Decompose U :K:	.50	1.00
129 Diabolic Tutor U :K:	1.50	3.00
130 Dirty Wererat C :K:	.12	.30
131 Dusk Imp C :K:	.12	.30
132 Entomb R :K:	4.00	8.00
133 Execute U :K:	.50	1.00
134 Face of Fear U :K:	.50	1.00
135 Famished Ghoul U :K:	.50	1.00
136 Filthy Cur C :K:	.12	.30
137 Fledgling Imp C :K:	.12	.30
138 Frightcrawler C :K:	.12	.30
139 Ghastly Demise C :K:	.12	.30
140 Gravedigger C :K:	.12	.30
141 Gravestorm R :K:	2.00	4.00
142 Haunting Echoes R :K:	6.00	12.00
143 Hint of Insanity R :K:	1.00	2.00
144 Infected Vermin U :K:	.50	1.00
145 Innocent Blood C :K:	.12	.30
146 Last Rites C :K:	.12	.30
147 Malevolent Awakening U :K:	.20	.50
148 Mind Burst C :K:	.12	.30
149 Mindslicer R :K:	2.00	4.00
150 Morbid Hunger C :K:	.12	.30
151 Morgue Theft C :K:	.12	.30
152 Mortivore R :K:	2.50	5.00
153 Nefarious Lich R :K:	1.50	3.00
154 Overeager Apprentice C :K:	.12	.30
155 Painbringer U :K:	.50	1.00
156 Patriarch's Desire C :K:	.12	.30
157 Repentant Vampire R :K:	2.00	4.00
158 Rotting Giant U :K:	.20	.50
159 Sadistic Hypnotist U :K:	.20	.50
160 Screams of the Damned U :K:	.20	.50
161 Skeletal Scrying U :K:	.50	1.00
162 Skull Fracture U :K:	.50	1.00
163 Stalking Bloodsucker R :K:	1.50	3.00
164 Tainted Pact R :K:	2.00	4.00
165 Tombfire R :K:	1.50	3.00

166 Traveling Plague R :K: 1.50 3.00
167 Whispering Shade C :K: .12 .30
168 Zombie Assassin C :K: .12 .30
169 Zombie Cannibal C :K: .12 .30
170 Zombie Infestation U :K: 1.00 2.00
171 Zombify U :K: 1.00 2.00
172 Acceptable Losses C :R: .12 .30
173 Anarchist C :R: .12 .30
174 Ashen Firebeast R :R: 1.50 3.00
175 Barbarian Lunatic C :R: .12 .30
176 Bash to Bits U :R: .50 1.00
177 Battle Strain U :R: .20 .50
178 Blazing Salvo C :R: .12 .30
179 Bomb Squad R :R: .50 1.00
180 Burning Sands R :R: 1.50 3.00
181 Chainflinger C :R: .12 .30
182 Chance Encounter R :R: 1.00 2.00
183 Demolish U :R: .50 1.00
184 Demoralize C :R: .12 .30
185 Dwarven Grunt C :R: .12 .30
186 Dwarven Recruiter U :R: .50 1.00
187 Dwarven Shrine R :R: 1.00 2.00
188 Dwarven Strike Force U :R: .50 1.00
189 Earth Rift C :R: .12 .30
190 Ember Beast C :R: .12 .30
191 Engulfing Flames U :R: .50 1.00
192 Epicenter R :R: 1.00 2.00
193 Firebolt C :R: .12 .30
194 Flame Burst C :R: .12 .30
195 Frenetic Ogre U :R: .50 1.00
196 Halberdier C :R: .12 .30
197 Impulsive Maneuvers R :R: 1.00 2.00
198 Kamahl's Desire C :R: .12 .30
199 Kamahl, Pit Fighter R :R: 3.00 6.00
200 Lava Blister U :R: .50 1.00
201 Liquid Fire U :R: .50 1.00
202 Mad Dog C :R: .12 .30
203 Magma Vein U :R: .20 .50
204 Magnivore R :R: 1.00 2.00
205 Mine Layer R :R: 1.50 3.00
206 Minotaur Explorer U :R: .50 1.00
207 Molten Influence R :R: 2.00 4.00
208 Mudhole R :R: 1.50 3.00
209 Need for Speed R :R: 1.50 3.00
210 Obstinate Familiar R :R: 1.50 3.00
211 Pardic Firecat C :R: .12 .30
212 Pardic Miner R :R: 1.50 3.00
213 Pardic Swordsmith C :R: .12 .30
214 Price of Glory U :R: .20 .50
215 Reckless Charge C :R: .12 .30
216 Recoup U :R: .50 1.00
217 Rites of Initiation C :R: .12 .30
218 Savage Firecat R :R: 1.50 3.00
219 Scorching Missile C :R: .12 .30
220 Seize the Day R :R: 1.50 3.00
221 Shower of Coals U :R: .50 1.00
222 Spark Mage U :R: .20 .50
223 Steam Vines U :R: .50 1.00
224 Thermal Blast C :R: .12 .30
225 Tremble C :R: .12 .30
226 Volcanic Spray U :R: .50 1.00
227 Volley of Boulders R :R: 1.00 2.00
228 Whipkeeper U :R: .20 .50
229 Bearscape R :G: 2.00 4.00
230 Beast Attack U :G: .50 1.00
231 Call of the Herd R :G: 5.00 10.00
232 Cartographer C :G: .12 .30
233 Chatter of the Squirrel C :G: .12 .30
234 Chlorophant R :G: 1.50 3.00
235 Crashing Centaur U :G: .20 .50
236 Deep Reconnaissance U :G: .50 1.00
237 Diligent Farmhand C :G: .12 .30
238 Druid Lyrist C :G: .12 .30
239 Druid's Call U :G: .50 1.00
240 Elephant Ambush C :G: .12 .30
241 Gorilla Titan U :G: .50 1.00
242 Ground Seal R :G: 2.00 4.00
243 Holistic Wisdom R :G: 2.00 4.00
244 Howling Gale U :G: .50 1.00
245 Ivy Elemental R :G: 2.00 4.00
246 Krosan Archer C :G: .12 .30
247 Krosan Avenger C :G: .12 .30
248 Krosan Beast R :G: 2.00 4.00
249 Leaf Dancer C :G: .12 .30
250 Metamorphic Wurm U :G: .50 1.00
251 Moment's Peace C :G: .12 .30
252 Muscle Burst C :G: .12 .30
253 Nantuko Disciple C :G: .12 .30
254 Nantuko Elder U :G: .50 1.00
255 Nantuko Mentor R :G: 1.50 3.00
256 Nantuko Shrine R :G: 1.50 3.00
257 New Frontiers R :G: 2.00 4.00
258 Nimble Mongoose U :G: .50 1.00
259 Nut Collector R :G: 2.50 5.00
260 Overrun U :G: 1.00 2.00
261 Piper's Melody U :G: .20 .50
262 Primal Frenzy C :G: .12 .30
263 Rabid Elephant C :G: .12 .30
264 Refresh C :G: .12 .30
265 Rites of Spring C :G: .12 .30
266 Roar of the Wurm U :G: 1.50 3.00
267 Seton's Desire C :G: .12 .30
268 Seton, Krosan Protector R :G: 1.50 3.00
269 Simplify C :G: .12 .30
270 Skyshooter U :G: .20 .50
271 Spellbane Centaur R :G: 2.00 4.00
272 Springing Tiger C :G: .12 .30
273 Squirrel Mob R :G: 2.50 5.00
274 Squirrel Nest U :G: 2.50 5.00
275 Still Life U :G: .50 1.00
276 Stone-Tongue Basilisk R :G: 2.00 4.00
277 Sylvan Might U :G: .50 1.00
278 Terravore R :G: 2.00 4.00
279 Twigwalker U :G: .20 .50
280 Verdant Succession R :G: 2.00 4.00
281 Vivify U :G: .50 1.00
282 Werebear C :G: .12 .30
283 Wild Mongrel C :G: .12 .30
284 Woodland Druid C :G: .12 .30
285 Zoologist R :G: 1.00 2.00
286 Atogatog R :D: 1.50 3.00
287 Decimate R :D: 1.50 3.00
288 Iridescent Angel R :D: 5.00 10.00
289 Lithatog U :D: .50 1.00
290 Mystic Enforcer R :D: 3.00 6.00
291 Phantatog U :D: .50 1.00
292 Psychatog U :D: 2.00 4.00
293 Sarcatog U :D: .50 1.00
294 Shadowmage Infiltrator R :D: 5.00 10.00
295 Thaumatog U :D: .20 .50
296 Vampiric Dragon R :D: 5.00 10.00
297 Catalyst Stone R :A: 1.50 3.00
298 Charmed Pendant R :A: 1.00 2.50
299 Darkwater Egg U :A: .50 1.00
300 Junk Golem R :A: 1.00 2.00
301 Limestone Golem U :A: .50 1.00
302 Millikin U :A: .50 1.00
303 Mirari R :A: 6.00 12.00
304 Mossfire Egg U :A: .50 1.00
305 Otarian Juggernaut R :A: 1.50 3.00
306 Patchwork Gnomes U :A: .50 1.00
307 Sandstone Deadfall U :A: .20 .50
308 Shadowblood Egg U :A: .50 1.00
309 Skycloud Egg U :A: .50 1.00
310 Steamclaw U :A: .20 .50
311 Sungrass Egg U :A: .50 1.00
312 Abandoned Outpost C :L: .12 .30
313 Barbarian Ring U :L: .50 1.00
314 Bog Wreckage C :L: .12 .30
315 Cabal Pit U :L: .50 1.00
316 Centaur Garden U :L: .20 .50
317 Cephalid Coliseum U :L: .50 1.00
318 Crystal Quarry R :L: 2.50 5.00
319 Darkwater Catacombs R :L: 2.00 4.00
320 Deserted Temple R :L: 1.50 3.00
321 Mossfire Valley R :L: 2.00 4.00
322 Nomad Stadium U :L: .50 1.00
323 Petrified Field R :L: 1.50 3.00
324 Ravaged Highlands C :L: .12 .30
325 Seafloor Debris C :L: .12 .30
326 Shadowblood Ridge R :L: 2.00 4.00
327 Skycloud Expanse R :L: 2.00 4.00
328 Sungrass Prairie R :L: 2.00 4.00
329 Tarnished Citadel R :L: 1.00 2.00
330 Timberland Ruins C :L: .12 .30
331 Plains v1 C :L: .12 .30
332 Plains v2 C :L: .12 .30
333 Plains v3 C :L: .12 .30
334 Plains v4 C :L: .12 .30
335 Island v1 C :L: .12 .30
336 Island v2 C :L: .12 .30
337 Island v3 C :L: .12 .30
338 Island v4 C :L: .12 .30
339 Swamp v1 C :L: .12 .30
340 Swamp v2 C :L: .12 .30
341 Swamp v3 C :L: .12 .30
342 Swamp v4 C :L: .12 .30
343 Mountain v1 C :L: .12 .30
344 Mountain v2 C :L: .12 .30
345 Mountain v3 C :L: .12 .30
346 Mountain v4 C :L: .12 .30
347 Forest v1 C :L: .12 .30
348 Forest v2 C :L: .12 .30
349 Forest v3 C :L: .12 .30
350 Forest v4 C :L: .12 .30

2002 Magic The Gathering Torment

COMPLETE SET (143) 80.00 125.00
BOOSTER BOX (36 PACKS) 120.00 185.00
BOOSTER PACK (15 CARDS) 4.50 6.50
THEME DECK BOX 120.00 170.00
THEME DECK 12.00 17.00
*FOIL: 1X TO 2X BASIC CARDS 125.00 180.00
RELEASED ON FEBRUARY 4, 2002
1 Angel of Retribution R :W: 2.00 4.00
2 Aven Trooper C :W: .10 .30
3 Cleansing Meditation U :W: .20 .50
4 Equal Treatment U :W: .20 .50
5 Floating Shield C :W: .10 .30
7 Hypochondria U :W: .20 .50
8 Major Teroh R :W: 2.00 4.00
9 Militant Monk C :W: .10 .30
10 Morningtide R :W: 1.50 3.00
11 Mystic Familiar C :W: .10 .30
12 Pay No Heed C :W: .10 .30
13 Possessed Nomad R :W: 1.50 3.00
14 Reborn Hero R :W: 2.00 4.00
15 Spirit Flare C :W: .10 .30
16 Stern Judge U :W: .30 .75
17 Strength of Isolation U :W: .20 .50
18 Teroh's Faithful C :W: .10 .30
19 Teroh's Vanguard U :W: .20 .50
20 Transcendence R :W: 1.00 2.00
21 Vengeful Dreams R :W: 1.50 3.00
22 Alter Reality R :B: 1.50 3.00
23 Ambassador Laquatus R :B: 2.50 5.00
24 Aquamoeba C :B: .10 .30
25 Balshan Collaborator U :B: .20 .50
26 Breakthrough U :B: .20 .50
27 Cephalid Aristocrat C :B: .10 .30
28 Cephalid Illusionist U :B: .20 .50
29 Cephalid Sage U :B: .20 .50
30 Cephalid Snitch C :B: .10 .30
31 Cephalid Vandal R :B: 1.00 2.00
32 Churning Eddy C :B: .10 .30
33 Circular Logic U :B: 2.50 5.00
34 Compulsion U :B: .75 1.50
35 Coral Net C :B: .10 .30
36 Deep Analysis C :B: .10 .30
37 False Memories R :B: 1.50 3.00
38 Ghostly Wings C :B: .10 .30
39 Hydromorph Guardian C :B: .10 .30
40 Hydromorph Gull U :B: .20 .50
41 Liquify C :B: .10 .30
42 Llawan, Cephalid Empress R :B: 1.50 3.00
43 Obsessive Search C :B: .10 .30
44 Plagiarize R :B: 2.00 4.00
45 Possessed Aven R :B: 1.50 3.00
46 Retraced Image R :B: 1.50 3.00
47 Skywing Aven C :B: .10 .30
48 Stupefying Touch U :B: .20 .50
49 Turbulent Dreams R :B: 1.00 2.00
50 Boneshard Slasher U :K: .20 .50
51 Cabal Ritual C :K: .10 .30
52 Frantic Purification C :W: .10 .30
52 Cabal Surgeon C :K: .10 .30
53 Cabal Torturer C :K: .10 .30
54 Carrion Rats C :K: .10 .30
55 Carrion Wurm U :K: .20 .50
56 Chainer's Edict U :K: 2.00 4.00
57 Chainer, Dementia Master R :K: 2.50 5.00
58 Crippling Fatigue C :K: .10 .30
59 Dawn of the Dead R :K: 1.50 3.00
60 Faceless Butcher C :K: .10 .30
61 Gloomdrifter U :K: .20 .50
62 Gravegouger C :K: .10 .30
63 Grotesque Hybrid U :K: .20 .50
64 Hypnox R :K: 2.50 5.00
65 Ichorid R :K: 3.00 6.00
66 Insidious Dreams R :K: 2.00 4.00
67 Laquatus's Champion R :K: 3.00 6.00
68 Last Laugh R :K: 1.00 2.00
69 Mesmeric Fiend C :K: .10 .30
70 Mind Sludge U :K: .50 1.00
71 Mortal Combat R :K: 1.50 3.00
72 Mortiphobia U :K: .20 .50
73 Mutilate R :K: 4.00 8.00
74 Nantuko Shade R :K: 7.00 14.00
75 Organ Grinder C :K: .10 .30
76 Psychotic Haze C :K: .10 .30
77 Putrid Imp C :K: .10 .30
78 Rancid Earth C :K: .10 .30
79 Restless Dreams C :K: .10 .30
80 Sengir Vampire R :K: 2.50 5.00
81 Shade's Form C :K: .10 .30
82 Shambling Swarm R :K: 2.00 4.00
83 Sickening Dreams U :K: .50 1.00
84 Slithery Stalker U :K: .20 .50
85 Soul Scourge C :K: .10 .30
86 Strength of Lunacy U :K: .20 .50
87 Unhinge C :K: .10 .30
88 Waste Away C :K: .10 .30
89 Zombie Trailblazer U :K: .50 1.00
90 Accelerate C :R: .10 .30
91 Balthor the Stout R :R: 1.50 3.00
92 Barbarian Outcast C :R: .10 .30
93 Crackling Club C :R: .10 .30
94 Crazed Firecat U :R: .20 .50
95 Devastating Dreams R :R: 1.50 3.00
96 Enslaved Dwarf C :R: .10 .30
97 Fiery Temper C :R: .10 .30
98 Flaming Gambit U :R: .50 1.00
99 Flash of Defiance C :R: .10 .30
100 Grim Lavamancer R :R: 6.00 12.00
101 Hell-Bent Raider R :R: 2.00 4.00
102 Kamahl's Sledge C :R: .10 .30
103 Longhorn Firebeast C :R: .10 .30
104 Overmaster R :R: 1.00 2.00
105 Pardic Arsonist U :R: .20 .50
106 Pardic Collaborator U :R: .20 .50
107 Pardic Lancer C :R: .10 .30
108 Petradon R :R: 1.50 3.00
109 Petravark C :R: .10 .30
110 Pitchstone Wall U :R: .20 .50
111 Possessed Barbarian R :R: 1.50 3.00
112 Pyromania U :R: .20 .50
113 Radiate R :R: 2.50 5.00
114 Skullscorch R :R: 3.00 5.00
115 Sonic Seizure C :R: .10 .30
116 Temporary Insanity U :R: .20 .50
117 Violent Eruption U :R: .75 1.50
118 Acorn Harvest C :G: .10 .30
119 Anurid Scavenger U :G: .20 .50
120 Arrogant Wurm U :G: 1.50 3.00
121 Basking Rootwalla C :G: .10 .30
122 Centaur Chieftain U :G: .20 .50
123 Centaur Veteran C :G: .10 .30
124 Dwell on the Past U :G: .50 1.00
125 Far Wanderings C :G: .10 .30
126 Gurzigost R :G: 2.00 4.00
127 Insist R :G: 1.50 3.00
128 Invigorating Falls C :G: .10 .30
129 Krosan Constrictor C :G: .10 .30
130 Krosan Restorer C :G: .10 .30
131 Nantuko Blightcutter R :G: 1.50 3.00
132 Nantuko Calmer C :G: .10 .30
133 Nantuko Cultivator R :G: 1.50 3.00
134 Narcissism U :G: .20 .50
135 Nostalgic Dreams R :G: 2.00 4.00
136 Parallel Evolution R :G: 2.50 5.00
137 Possessed Centaur R :G: 1.50 3.00
138 Seton's Scout U :G: .20 .50
139 Cabal Coffers U :L: 4.00 8.00
140 Tainted Field U :L: 1.00 2.00
141 Tainted Isle U :L: 1.00 2.00
142 Tainted Peak U :L: 1.00 2.00
143 Tainted Wood U :L: 1.00 2.00

2002 Magic The Gathering Judgment

COMPLETE SET (143) 75.00 125.00
BOOSTER BOX (36 PACKS) 100.00 120.00
BOOSTER PACK (15 CARDS) 3.50 4.00
THEME DECK BOX 140.00 200.00
THEME DECK 15.00 20.00
FAT PACK 40.00 50.00
*FOIL: 1X TO 2X BASIC CARDS
RELEASED ON MAY 27, 2002
1 Ancestor's Chosen U :W: .50 1.00
3 Battle Screech U :W: .50 1.00
4 Battlewise Aven C :W: .10 .30
5 Benevolent Bodyguard C :W: .10 .30
6 Border Patrol C :W: .10 .30
7 Cagemail C :W: .10 .30
8 Chastise U :W: .50 1.00
9 Commander Eesha R :W: 2.00 4.00
10 Funeral Pyre C :W: .10 .30
11 Glory R :W: 2.00 4.00
12 Golden Wish R :W: 1.50 3.00
13 Guided Strike C :W: .10 .30
14 Lead Astray C :W: .10 .30
15 Nomad Mythmaker R :W: 1.50 3.00
16 Phantom Flock U :W: .50 1.00
17 Phantom Nomad C :W: .10 .30
18 Prismatic Strands C :W: .10 .30
19 Pulsemage Advocate R :W: 1.50 3.00
20 Ray of Revelation C :W: .10 .30
21 Selfless Exorcist R :W: 1.50 3.00
22 Shieldmage Advocate C :W: .10 .30
23 Silver Seraph R :W: 2.50 5.00
24 Solitary Confinement R :W: 2.00 4.00
25 Soulcatchers' Aerie U :W: .50 1.00
26 Spirit Cairn U :W: .75 1.50
27 Spurnmage Advocate U :W: .20 .50
28 Suntail Hawk C :W: .10 .30
29 Test of Endurance R :W: 3.00 6.00
30 Trained Pronghorn C :W: .10 .30
31 Unquestioned Authority U :W: .50 1.00
32 Valor U :W: .50 1.00
33 Vigilant Sentry C :W: .10 .30
34 Aven Fogbringer C :B: .10 .30
35 Cephalid Constable R :B: 1.50 3.00
36 Cephalid Inkshrouder U :B: .50 1.00
37 Cunning Wish R :B: 8.00 15.00
38 Defy Gravity C :B: .10 .30
39 Envelop C :B: .10 .30
40 Flash of Insight U :B: .20 .50
41 Grip of Amnesia C :B: .10 .30
42 Hapless Researcher C :B: .10 .30
43 Keep Watch C :B: .10 .30
44 Laquatus's Disdain U :B: .20 .50
45 Lost in Thought C :B: .10 .30
46 Mental Note C :B: .10 .30
47 Mirror Wall C :B: .10 .30
48 Mist of Stagnation R :B: 1.00 2.00
49 Quiet Speculation U :B: .50 1.00
50 Scalpelexis R :B: 2.00 4.00
51 Spelljack R :B: 2.00 4.00
52 Telekinetic Bonds R :B: 1.50 3.00
53 Web of Inertia U :B: .50 1.00
54 Wonder U :B: 1.25 2.50
55 Wormfang Behemoth R :B: 1.25 2.50
56 Wormfang Crab U :B: .20 .50
57 Wormfang Drake C :B: .10 .30
58 Wormfang Manta R :B: 1.00 2.00
59 Wormfang Newt C :B: .10 .30
60 Wormfang Turtle U :B: .50 1.00
61 Balthor the Defiled R :K: 2.00 4.00
62 Cabal Therapy U :K: 3.50 7.00
63 Cabal Trainee C :K: .10 .30
64 Death Wish R :K: 1.00 2.00
65 Earsplitting Rats C :K: .10 .30
66 Filth U :K: .20 .50
67 Grave Consequences U :K: .50 1.00
68 Guiltfeeder R :K: 2.00 4.00
69 Masked Gorgon R :K: 1.50 3.00
70 Morality Shift R :K: 1.00 2.00
71 Rats' Feast C :K: .10 .30
72 Stitch Together U :K: .75 1.50
73 Sutured Ghoul R :K: 1.50 3.00
74 Toxic Stench C :K: .10 .30
75 Treacherous Vampire U :K: .50 1.00
76 Treacherous Werewolf C :K: .10 .30
77 Anger U :R: 1.00 2.00
78 Arcane Teachings C :R: .10 .30
79 Barbarian Bully C :R: .10 .30
8 Aven Warcraft U :W: .20 .50
80 Book Burning C :R: .10 .30
81 Breaking Point R :R: 2.50 5.00
82 Browbeat U :R: 2.00 4.00
83 Burning Wish R :R: 4.00 8.00
84 Dwarven Bloodboiler R :R: 1.00 2.00
85 Dwarven Driller U :R: .50 1.00
86 Dwarven Scorcher C :R: .10 .30
87 Ember Shot C :R: .10 .30
88 Firecat Blitz U :R: .20 .50
89 Flaring Pain C :R: .10 .30
90 Fledgling Dragon R :R: 3.00 6.00
91 Goretusk Firebeast C :R: .10 .30
92 Infectious Rage U :R: .20 .50
93 Jeska, Warrior Adept R :R: 1.50 3.00
94 Lava Dart C :R: .10 .30
95 Liberated Dwarf C :R: .10 .30
96 Lightning Surge R :R: 1.50 3.00
97 Planar Chaos U :R: .20 .50
98 Shaman's Trance R :R: 1.00 2.00
99 Soulgorger Orgg U :R: .20 .50
100 Spellgorger Barbarian C :R: .10 .30
101 Swelter U :R: .20 .50
102 Swirling Sandstorm C :R: .10 .30
103 Worldgorger Dragon R :R: 3.00 6.00
104 Anurid Barkripper C :G: .10 .30
105 Anurid Swarmsnapper U :G: .20 .50
106 Battlefield Scrounger C :G: .10 .30
107 Brawn U :G: .50 1.00
108 Canopy Claws C :G: .10 .30
109 Centaur Rootcaster C :G: .10 .30
110 Crush of Wurms R :G: 2.00 4.00
111 Elephant Guide U :G: .75 1.50
112 Epic Struggle R :G: 1.50 3.00
113 Erhnam Djinn R :G: 2.00 4.00
114 Exoskeletal Armor U :G: .50 1.00
115 Folk Medicine C :G: .10 .30
116 Forcemage Advocate U :G: .20 .50
117 Genesis R :G: 3.50 7.00
118 Giant Warthog C :G: .10 .30
119 Grizzly Fate U :G: .50 1.00
120 Harvester Druid C :G: .10 .30
121 Ironshell Beetle C :G: .10 .30
122 Krosan Reclamation U :G: .50 1.00
123 Krosan Wayfarer C :G: .10 .30
124 Living Wish R :G: 6.00 12.00
125 Nantuko Tracer C :G: .10 .30
126 Nullmage Advocate C :G: .10 .30
127 Phantom Centaur U :G: 1.00 2.00
128 Phantom Nantuko R :G: 1.50 3.00
129 Phantom Tiger C :G: .10 .30
130 Seedtime R :G: 2.00 4.00
131 Serene Sunset U :G: .20 .50
132 Sudden Strength C :G: .10 .30
133 Sylvan Safekeeper R :G: 1.50 3.00
134 Thriss, Nantuko Primus R :G: 1.50 3.00
135 Tunneler Wurm U :G: .20 .50
136 Venomous Vines C :G: .10 .30
137 Anurid Brushhopper R :D: 2.50 5.00
138 Hunting Grounds R :D: 1.50 3.00
139 Mirari's Wake R :D: 4.00 8.00
140 Phantom Nishoba R :D: 3.00 6.00
141 Krosan Verge U :L: .50 1.00
142 Nantuko Monastery U :L: .50 1.00
143 Riftstone Portal U :L: .50 1.00

2002 Magic The Gathering Onslaught

COMPLETE SET (350) 150.00 250.00
BOOSTER BOX 85.00 100.00
BOOSTER PACK 3.50 4.00
THEME DECK BOX 90.00 110.00
THEME DECK 10.00 14.00
FAT PACK 40.00 50.00
*FOIL: 1X TO 2X BASIC CARDS
RELEASED ON OCTOBER 7, 2002
1 Akroma's Blessing U :W: .50 1.00
2 Akroma's Vengeance R :W: 3.00 6.00
3 Ancestor's Prophet R :W: 1.50 3.00
4 Astral Slide U :W: 1.00 2.00
5 Aura Extraction U :W: .20 .50
6 Aurification R :W: 1.00 2.00
7 Aven Brigadier R :W: 2.00 4.00
8 Aven Soulgazer U :W: .20 .50
9 Battlefield Medic C :W: .10 .30
10 Catapult Master R :W: 1.00 2.00
11 Catapult Squad U :W: .20 .50
12 Chain of Silence U :W: .20 .50
13 Circle of Solace R :W: 1.50 3.00
14 Convalescent Care R :W: 1.50 3.00
15 Crowd Favorites U :W: .20 .50
16 Crown of Awe C :W: .10 .30
17 Crude Rampart U :W: .20 .50
18 Daru Cavalier C :W: .10 .30
19 Daru Healer C :W: .10 .30
20 Daru Lancer C :W: .10 .30
21 Daunting Defender C :W: .10 .30
22 Dawning Purist U :W: .20 .50
23 Defensive Maneuvers C :W: .10 .30
24 Demystify C :W: .10 .30
25 Disciple of Grace C :W: .10 .30
26 Dive Bomber C :W: .10 .30
27 Doubtless One U :W: 1.00 2.00
28 Exalted Angel R :W: 10.00 20.00
29 Foothill Guide C :W: .10 .30
30 Glarecaster R :W: 1.50 3.00
31 Glory Seeker C :W: .10 .30
32 Grassland Crusader C :W: .10 .30
33 Gravel Slinger C :W: .10 .30
34 Gustcloak Harrier C :W: .10 .30
35 Gustcloak Runner C :W: .10 .30
36 Gustcloak Savior R :W: 1.50 3.00
37 Gustcloak Sentinel U :W: .20 .50
38 Gustcloak Skirmisher U :W: .20 .50
39 Harsh Mercy R :W: 2.00 4.00
40 Improvised Armor U :W: .20 .50
41 Inspirit U :W: .20 .50
42 Ironfist Crusher U :W: .20 .50
43 Jareth, Leonine Titan R :W: 4.00 8.00
43 Cabal Archon U :K: .50 1.00
44 Mobilization R :W: 3.00 6.00
45 Nova Cleric U :W: .20 .50
46 Oblation R :W: 1.50 3.00
47 Pacifism C :W: .10 .30
48 Pearlspear Courier U :W: .20 .50
49 Piety Charm C :W: .10 .30
50 Renewed Faith C :W: .10 .30
51 Righteous Cause U :W: .50 1.00
52 Sandskin C :W: .10 .30
53 Shared Triumph R :W: 2.50 5.00
54 Shieldmage Elder U :W: .50 1.00
55 Sigil of the New Dawn R :W: 2.00 4.00
56 Sunfire Balm U :W: .20 .50
57 True Believer R :W: 2.50 5.00
58 Unified Strike C :W: .10 .30
59 Weathered Wayfarer R :W: 2.00 4.00
60 Whipcorder U :W: .50 1.00
61 Words of Worship R :W: 1.50 3.00
62 Airborne Aid C :B: .10 .30
63 Annex U :B: .50 1.00
64 Aphetto Alchemist U :B: 1.00 2.00
65 Aphetto Grifter U :B: .20 .50
66 Arcanis the Omnipotent R :B: 3.00 6.00
67 Artificial Evolution R :B: 1.50 3.00
68 Ascending Aven C :B: .10 .30
69 Aven Fateshaper U :B: .20 .50
70 Backslide C :B: .10 .30
71 Blatant Thievery R :B: 1.50 3.00
72 Callous Oppressor R :B: 1.50 3.00
73 Chain of Vapor U :B: .50 1.00
74 Choking Tethers C :B: .10 .30
75 Clone R :B: 2.00 4.00
76 Complicate U :B: .50 1.00
77 Crafty Pathmage C :B: .10 .30
78 Crown of Ascension C :B: .10 .30
79 Discombobulate U :B: .50 1.00
80 Dispersing Orb U :B: .20 .50
81 Disruptive Pitmage C :B: .10 .30
82 Essence Fracture U :B: .20 .50
83 Fleeting Aven U :B: .20 .50
84 Future Sight R :B: 2.50 5.00
85 Ghosthelm Courier U :B: .20 .50
86 Graxiplon U :B: .20 .50
87 Imagecrafter C :B: .10 .30
88 Information Dealer C :B: .10 .30
89 Ixidor's Will C :B: .10 .30
90 Ixidor, Reality Sculptor R :B: 2.00 4.00
91 Mage's Guile C :B: .10 .30
92 Meddle U :B: .20 .50
93 Mistform Dreamer C :B: .10 .30
94 Mistform Mask C :B: .10 .30
95 Mistform Mutant U :B: .20 .50
96 Mistform Shrieker U :B: .20 .50
97 Mistform Skyreaver R :B: 1.50 3.00
98 Mistform Stalker U :B: .20 .50
99 Mistform Wall C :B: .10 .30
100 Nameless One U :B: .50 1.00
101 Peer Pressure R :B: 1.50 3.00
102 Psychic Trance R :B: 1.50 3.00
103 Quicksilver Dragon R :B: 3.00 6.00
104 Read the Runes R :B: 1.50 3.00
105 Reminisce U :B: .50 1.00
106 Riptide Biologist C :B: .10 .30
107 Riptide Chronologist U :B: .50 1.00
108 Riptide Entrancer R :B: 1.25 2.50
109 Riptide Shapeshifter U :B: .20 .50
110 Rummaging Wizard U :B: .50 1.00
111 Sage Aven C :B: .10 .30
112 Screaming Seahawk C :B: .10 .30
113 Sea's Claim C :B: .10 .30
114 Slipstream Eel C :B: .10 .30
115 Spy Network C :B: .10 .30
116 Standardize R :B: 1.50 3.00
117 Supreme Inquisitor R :B: 2.00 4.00

118 Trade Secrets R :B: 1.50 3.00
119 Trickery Charm C :B: .10 .30
120 Voidmage Prodigy R :B: 3.00 6.00
121 Wheel and Deal R :B: 2.00 4.00
122 Words of Wind R :B: 1.50 3.00
123 Accursed Centaur C :K: .10 .30
124 Anurid Murkdiver C :K: .10 .30
125 Aphetto Dredging C :K: .10 .30
126 Aphetto Vulture U :K: .20 .50
127 Blackmail U :K: .75 1.50
128 Boneknitter U :K: .50 1.00
130 Cabal Executioner U :K: .20 .50
131 Cabal Slaver U :K: .20 .50
132 Chain of Smog U :K: .20 .50
133 Cover of Darkness R :K: 2.00 4.00
134 Crown of Suspicion C :K: .10 .30
135 Cruel Revival C :K: .10 .30
136 Death Match R :K: 1.50 3.00
137 Death Pulse U :K: .20 .50
138 Dirge of Dread C :K: .10 .30
139 Disciple of Malice C :K: .10 .30
140 Doomed Necromancer R :K: 2.00 4.00
141 Ebonblade Reaper R :K: 2.00 4.00
142 Endemic Plague R :K: 1.50 3.00
143 Entrails Feaster R :K: 1.50 3.00
144 Fade from Memory U :K: .50 1.00
145 Fallen Cleric C :K: .10 .30
146 False Cure R :K: 2.00 4.00
147 Feeding Frenzy U :K: .20 .50
148 Festering Goblin C :K: .10 .30
149 Frightshroud Courier U :K: .20 .50
150 Gangrenous Goliath R :K: 1.50 3.00
151 Gluttonous Zombie U :K: .20 .50
152 Gravespawn Sovereign R :K: 2.00 4.00
153 Grinning Demon R :K: 3.00 6.00
154 Haunted Cadaver C :K: .10 .30
155 Head Games R :K: 1.00 2.00
156 Headhunter U :K: .20 .50
157 Infest U :K: 1.00 2.00
158 Misery Charm C :K: .10 .30
159 Nantuko Husk C :K: .10 .30
160 Oversold Cemetery R :K: 3.00 6.00
161 Patriarch's Bidding R :K: 4.00 8.00
162 Profane Prayers C :K: .10 .30
163 Prowling Pangolin U :K: .20 .50
164 Rotlung Reanimator R :K: 4.00 8.00
165 Screeching Buzzard C :K: .10 .30
166 Severed Legion C :K: .10 .30
167 Shade's Breath U :K: .20 .50
168 Shepherd of Rot C :K: .10 .30
169 Silent Specter R :K: 1.50 3.00
170 Smother U :K: 1.00 2.00
171 Soulless One U :K: 1.00 2.00
172 Spined Basher C :K: .10 .30
173 Strongarm Tactics R :K: 1.50 3.00
174 Swat C :K: .10 .30
175 Syphon Mind C :K: .10 .30
176 Syphon Soul C :K: .10 .30
177 Thrashing Mudspawn U :K: .20 .50
178 Undead Gladiator R :K: 2.00 4.00
179 Visara the Dreadful R :K: 6.00 12.00
180 Walking Desecration U :K: .20 .50
181 Withering Hex U :K: .20 .50
182 Words of Waste R :K: 1.50 3.00
183 Wretched Anurid C :K: .10 .30
184 AEther Charge U :R: .50 1.00
185 Aggravated Assault R :R: 1.25 2.50
186 Airdrop Condor U :R: .20 .50
187 Avarax U :R: .50 1.00
188 Battering Craghorn C :R: .10 .30
189 Blistering Firecat R :R: 4.00 8.00
190 Break Open C :R: .10 .30
191 Brightstone Ritual C :R: .10 .30
192 Butcher Orgg R :R: 1.50 3.00
193 Chain of Plasma U :R: .20 .50
194 Charging Slateback C :R: .10 .30
195 Commando Raid U :R: .20 .50
196 Crown of Fury C :R: .10 .30
197 Custody Battle U :R: .20 .50
198 Dragon Roost R :R: 2.50 5.00
199 Dwarven Blastminer U :R: .50 1.00
200 Embermage Goblin U :R: .50 1.00
201 Erratic Explosion C :R: .10 .30
202 Fever Charm C :R: .10 .30
203 Flamestick Courier U :R: .20 .50
204 Goblin Machinist U :R: .20 .50
205 Goblin Piledriver R :R: 8.00 15.00
206 Goblin Pyromancer R :R: 1.50 3.00
207 Goblin Sharpshooter R :R: 5.00 10.00
208 Goblin Sky Raider C :R: .10 .30
209 Goblin Sledder C :R: .10 .30
210 Goblin Taskmaster C :R: .10 .30
211 Grand Melee R :R: 1.00 2.00
212 Gratuitous Violence R :R: 2.00 4.00
213 Insurrection R :R: 1.50 3.00
214 Kaboom! R :R: 1.50 3.00
215 Lavamancer's Skill C :R: .10 .30
216 Lay Waste C :R: .10 .30
217 Lightning Rift U :R: .50 1.00
218 Mana Echoes R :R: 1.50 3.00
219 Menacing Ogre R :R: 1.50 3.00
220 Nosy Goblin C :R: .10 .30
221 Pinpoint Avalanche C :R: .10 .30
222 Reckless One U :R: .75 1.50
223 Risky Move R :R: 1.50 3.00
224 Rorix Bladewing R :R: 4.00 8.00
225 Searing Flesh U :R: .50 1.00
226 Shaleskin Bruiser U :R: .20 .50
227 Shock C :R: .10 .30
228 Skirk Commando C :R: .10 .30
229 Skirk Fire Marshal R :R: 2.00 4.00
230 Skirk Prospector C :R: .10 .30
231 Skittish Valesk U :R: .20 .50
232 Slice and Dice U :R: 1.00 2.00
233 Snapping Thragg U :R: .50 1.00
234 Solar Blast C :R: .10 .30
235 Sparksmith C :R: .10 .30
236 Spitfire Handler U :R: .20 .50
237 Spurred Wolverine C :R: .10 .30
238 Starstorm R :R: 3.00 6.00
239 Tephraderm R :R: 1.50 3.00
240 Thoughtbound Primoc U :R: .20 .50
241 Threaten U :R: .50 1.00
242 Thunder of Hooves U :R: .20 .50
243 Wave of Indifference C :R: .10 .30
244 Words of War R :R: 1.50 3.00
245 Animal Magnetism R :G: 1.25 2.50
246 Barkhide Mauler C :G: .10 .30
247 Biorhythm R :G: 2.00 4.00
248 Birchlore Rangers C :G: .10 .30
249 Bloodline Shaman U :G: .20 .50
250 Broodhatch Nantuko U :G: .20 .50
251 Centaur Glade U :G: .50 1.00
252 Chain of Acid U :G: .20 .50
253 Crown of Vigor C :G: .10 .30
254 Elven Riders U :G: .50 1.00
255 Elvish Guidance C :G: .10 .30
256 Elvish Pathcutter C :G: .10 .30
257 Elvish Pioneer C :G: .10 .30
258 Elvish Scrapper U :G: .50 1.00
259 Elvish Vanguard R :G: 2.00 4.00
260 Elvish Warrior C :G: .10 .30
261 Enchantress's Presence R :G: 2.00 4.00
262 Everglove Courier U :G: .20 .50
263 Explosive Vegetation U :G: .50 1.00
264 Gigapede R :G: 1.50 3.00
265 Heedless One U :G: 2.00 4.00
266 Hystrodon R :G: 1.00 2.00
267 Invigorating Boon U :G: .20 .50
268 Kamahl's Summons U :G: .50 1.00
269 Kamahl, Fist of Krosa R :G: 4.00 8.00
270 Krosan Colossus R :G: 2.00 4.00
271 Krosan Groundshaker U :G: .20 .50
272 Krosan Tusker C :G: .10 .30
273 Leery Fogbeast C :G: .10 .30
274 Mythic Proportions R :G: 1.50 3.00
275 Naturalize C :G: .10 .30
276 Overwhelming Instinct U :G: .20 .50
277 Primal Boost U :G: .20 .50
278 Ravenous Baloth R :G: 5.00 10.00
279 Run Wild U :G: .50 1.00
280 Serpentine Basilisk U :G: .20 .50
281 Silklash Spider R :G: 2.00 4.00
282 Silvos, Rogue Elemental R :G: 4.00 8.00
283 Snarling Undorak C :G: .10 .30
284 Spitting Gourna C :G: .10 .30
285 Stag Beetle R :G: 1.50 3.00
286 Steely Resolve R :G: 2.50 5.00
287 Symbiotic Beast U :G: .20 .50
288 Symbiotic Elf C :G: .10 .30
289 Symbiotic Wurm R :G: 2.00 4.00
290 Taunting Elf C :G: .10 .30
291 Tempting Wurm R :G: 1.50 3.00
292 Towering Baloth U :G: .20 .50
293 Treespring Lorian C :G: .10 .30
294 Tribal Unity U :G: .50 1.00
295 Venomspout Brackus U :G: .20 .50
296 Vitality Charm C :G: .10 .30
297 Voice of the Woods R :G: 2.50 5.00
298 Wall of Mulch U :G: .20 .50
299 Weird Harvest R :G: 1.50 3.00
300 Wellwisher C :G: .10 .30
301 Wirewood Elf C :G: .10 .30
302 Wirewood Herald C :G: .10 .30
303 Wirewood Pride C :G: .10 .30
304 Wirewood Savage C :G: .10 .30
305 Words of Wilding R :G: 1.50 3.00
306 Cryptic Gateway R :A: 2.00 4.00
307 Doom Cannon R :A: 1.50 3.00
308 Dream Chisel R :A: 1.50 3.00
309 Riptide Replicator R :A: 2.50 5.00
310 Slate of Ancestry R :A: 2.00 4.00
311 Tribal Golem R :A: 1.50 3.00
312 Barren Moor C :L: .10 .30
313 Bloodstained Mire R :L: 10.00 20.00
314 Contested Cliffs R :L: 2.00 4.00
315 Daru Encampment U :L: .50 1.00
316 Flooded Strand R :L: 10.00 20.00
317 Forgotten Cave C :L: .10 .30
318 Goblin Burrows U :L: .50 1.00
319 Grand Coliseum R :L: 3.00 6.00
320 Lonely Sandbar C :L: .10 .30
321 Polluted Delta R :L: 10.00 20.00
322 Riptide Laboratory R :L: 1.50 3.00
323 Seaside Haven U :L: .20 .50
324 Secluded Steppe C :L: .10 .30
325 Starlit Sanctum U :L: 1.00 2.00
326 Tranquil Thicket C :L: .10 .30
327 Unholy Grotto R :L: 2.00 4.00
328 Windswept Heath R :L: 7.00 14.00
329 Wirewood Lodge U :L: 1.25 2.50
330 Wooded Foothills R :L: 8.00 15.00
331 Plains C :L: .10 .30
332 Plains C :L: .10 .30
333 Plains C :L: .10 .30
334 Plains C :L: .10 .30
335 Island C :L: .10 .30
336 Island C :L: .10 .30
337 Island C :L: .10 .30
338 Island C :L: .10 .30
339 Swamp C :L: .10 .30
340 Swamp C :L: .10 .30
341 Swamp C :L: .10 .30
342 Swamp C :L: .10 .30
343 Mountain C :L: .10 .30
344 Mountain C :L: .10 .30
345 Mountain C :L: .10 .30
346 Mountain C :L: .10 .30
347 Forest C :L: .10 .30
348 Forest C :L: .10 .30
349 Forest C :L: .10 .30
350 Forest C :L: .10 .30

2003 Magic The Gathering Legions

COMPLETE SET (145) 75.00 125.00
BOOSTER BOX (36 PACKS) 120.00 140.00
BOOSTER PACK (12 CARDS) 4.00 5.00
THEME DECK BOX 125.00 150.00
THEME DECK 7.00 14.00
FAT PACK 38.00 45.00
*FOIL: .75X TO 2X BASIC CARDS
RELEASED ON FEBRUARY 3, 2003
1 Akroma, Angel of Wrath R :W: 15.00 30.00
2 Akroma's Devoted U :W: .50 1.00
3 Aven Redeemer C :W: .10 .30
4 Aven Warhawk U :W: .20 .50
5 Beacon of Destiny R :W: 1.50 3.00
6 Celestial Gatekeeper R :W: 1.50 3.00
7 Cloudreach Cavalry U :W: .20 .50
8 Daru Mender U :W: .20 .50
9 Daru Sanctifier C :W: .10 .30
10 Daru Stinger C :W: .10 .30
11 Defender of the Order R :W: 1.00 2.00
12 Deftblade Elite C :W: .10 .30
13 Essence Sliver R :W: 3.00 6.00
14 Gempalm Avenger C :W: .10 .30
15 Glowrider R :W: 1.50 3.00
16 Liege of the Axe U :W: .20 .50
17 Lowland Tracker C :W: .10 .30
18 Planar Guide R :W: 1.50 3.00
19 Plated Sliver C :W: .10 .30
20 Starlight Invoker C :W: .10 .30
21 Stoic Champion U :W: .20 .50
22 Sunstrike Legionnaire R :W: 1.50 3.00
23 Swooping Talon U :W: .20 .50
24 Wall of Hope C :W: .10 .30
25 Ward Sliver U :W: 1.50 3.00
26 Whipgrass Entangler C :W: .10 .30
27 White Knight U :W: .75 1.50
28 Windborn Muse R :W: 2.00 4.00
29 Wingbeat Warrior C :W: .10 .30
30 Aven Envoy C :B: .10 .30
31 Cephalid Pathmage C :B: .10 .30
32 Chromeshell Crab R :B: 2.00 4.00
33 Covert Operative C :B: .10 .30
34 Crookclaw Elder U :B: .20 .50
35 Dermoplasm R :B: 1.00 2.00
36 Dreamborn Muse R :B: 1.50 3.00
37 Echo Tracer C :B: .10 .30
38 Fugitive Wizard C :B: .10 .30
39 Gempalm Sorcerer U :B: .20 .50
40 Glintwing Invoker C :B: .10 .30
41 Keeneye Aven C :B: .10 .30
42 Keeper of the Nine Gales R :B: 1.00 2.00
43 Master of the Veil U :B: .20 .50
43 Embalmed Brawler C :K: .10 .30
44 Merchant of Secrets C :B: .10 .30
45 Mistform Seaswift C :B: .10 .30
46 Mistform Sliver C :B: .10 .30
47 Mistform Ultimus R :B: 1.00 2.00
48 Mistform Wakecaster U :B: .20 .50
49 Primoc Escapee U :B: .20 .50
50 Riptide Director R :B: 1.50 3.00
51 Riptide Mangler R :B: 1.50 3.00
52 Shifting Sliver U :B: .50 1.00
53 Synapse Sliver R :B: 2.00 4.00
54 Voidmage Apprentice C :B: .10 .30
55 Wall of Deceit U :B: .20 .50
56 Warped Researcher U :B: .20 .50
57 Weaver of Lies R :B: 1.00 2.00
58 Willbender U :B: .50 1.00
59 Aphetto Exterminator U :K: .20 .50
60 Bane of the Living R :K: 1.50 3.00
61 Blood Celebrant C :K: .10 .30
62 Corpse Harvester U :K: .20 .50
63 Crypt Sliver C :K: .10 .30
64 Dark Supplicant U :K: .50 1.00
65 Deathmark Prelate U :K: .20 .50
66 Drinker of Sorrow R :K: 1.00 2.00
67 Dripping Dead C :K: .10 .30
68 Earthblighter U :K: .20 .50
70 Gempalm Polluter C :K: .10 .30
71 Ghastly Remains R :K: 1.50 3.00
72 Goblin Turncoat C :K: .10 .30
73 Graveborn Muse R :K: 1.00 2.00
74 Havoc Demon R :K: 1.50 3.00
75 Hollow Specter R :K: 1.50 3.00
76 Infernal Caretaker C :K: .10 .30
77 Noxious Ghoul U :K: 1.00 2.00
78 Phage the Untouchable R :K: 5.00 10.00
79 Scion of Darkness R :K: 4.00 8.00
80 Skinthinner C :K: .10 .30
81 Smokespew Invoker C :K: .10 .30
82 Sootfeather Flock C :K: .10 .30
83 Spectral Sliver U :K: .50 1.00
84 Toxin Sliver R :K: 4.00 8.00
85 Vile Deacon C :K: .10 .30
86 Withered Wretch U :K: 1.00 2.00
87 Zombie Brute U :K: .20 .50
88 Blade Sliver U :R: 1.00 2.00
89 Bloodstoke Howler C :R: .10 .30
90 Clickslither R :R: 1.00 2.00
91 Crested Craghorn C :R: .10 .30
92 Flamewave Invoker C :R: .10 .30
93 Frenetic Raptor U :R: .20 .50
94 Gempalm Incinerator U :R: .75 1.50
95 Goblin Assassin U :R: .20 .50
96 Goblin Clearcutter U :R: .20 .50
97 Goblin Dynamo U :R: .20 .50
98 Goblin Firebug C :R: .10 .30
99 Goblin Goon R :R: 2.00 4.00
100 Goblin Grappler C :R: .10 .30
101 Goblin Lookout C :R: .10 .30
102 Hunter Sliver C :R: .10 .30
103 Imperial Hellkite R :R: 2.00 4.00
104 Kilnmouth Dragon R :R: 4.00 8.00
105 Lavaborn Muse R :R: 1.50 3.00
106 Macetail Hystrodon C :R: .10 .30
107 Magma Sliver R :R: 2.50 5.00
108 Ridgetop Raptor U :R: .20 .50
109 Rockshard Elemental R :R: 1.50 3.00
110 Shaleskin Plower C :R: .10 .30
111 Skirk Alarmist R :R: 1.00 2.00
112 Skirk Drill Sergeant U :R: .50 1.00
113 Skirk Marauder C :R: .10 .30
114 Skirk Outrider C :R: .10 .30
115 Unstable Hulk R :R: 1.00 2.00
116 Warbreak Trumpeter U :R: .20 .50
117 Berserk Murlodont C :G: .10 .30
118 Branchsnap Lorian U :G: .20 .50
119 Brontotherium U :G: .20 .50
120 Brood Sliver R :G: 3.00 6.00
121 Caller of the Claw R :G: 2.00 4.00
122 Canopy Crawler U :G: .20 .50
123 Defiant Elf C :G: .10 .30
124 Elvish Soultiller R :G: 1.50 3.00
125 Enormous Baloth U :G: .20 .50
126 Feral Throwback R :G: 1.00 2.00
127 Gempalm Strider U :G: .20 .50
128 Glowering Rogon C :G: .10 .30
129 Hundroog C :G: .10 .30
130 Krosan Cloudscraper R :G: 4.00 8.00
131 Krosan Vorine C :G: .10 .30
132 Nantuko Vigilante C :G: .10 .30
133 Needleshot Gourna C :G: .10 .30
134 Patron of the Wild C :G: .10 .30
135 Primal Whisperer R :G: 1.00 2.00
136 Quick Sliver C :G: .10 .30
137 Root Sliver U :G: .50 1.00
138 Seedborn Muse R :G: 4.00 8.00
139 Stonewood Invoker C :G: .10 .30
140 Timberwatch Elf C :G: .10 .30
141 Totem Speaker U :G: .20 .50
142 Tribal Forcemage R :G: 1.50 3.00
143 Vexing Beetle R :G: 1.00 2.00
144 Wirewood Channeler U :G: 1.50 3.00
145 Wirewood Hivemaster U :G: 1.50 3.00

2003 Magic The Gathering Scourge

COMPLETE SET (143) 90.00 140.00
BOOSTER BOX (36 PACKS) 80.00 120.00
BOOSTER PACK (15 CARDS) 3.50 4.00
THEME DECK BOX 90.00 110.00
THEME DECK 10.00 12.00
FAT PACK 25.00 30.00
*FOIL: .75X TO 2X BASIC CARDS
RELEASED ON MAY 26, 2003
1 Ageless Sentinels R :W: 1.50 3.00
2 Astral Steel C :W: .10 .30
3 Aven Farseer C :W: .10 .30
4 Aven Liberator C :W: .10 .30
5 Daru Spiritualist C :W: .10 .30
6 Daru Warchief U :W: 1.00 2.00
7 Dawn Elemental R :W: 2.00 4.00
8 Decree of Justice R :W: 4.00 8.00
9 Dimensional Breach R :W: 1.50 3.00
10 Dragon Scales C :W: .10 .30
11 Dragonstalker U :W: .30 .75
12 Eternal Dragon R :W: 6.00 12.00
13 Exiled Doomsayer R :W: 1.50 3.00
14 Force Bubble R :W: 1.50 3.00
15 Frontline Strategist C :W: .10 .30
16 Gilded Light U :W: .50 1.00
17 Guilty Conscience C :W: .10 .30
18 Karona, False God R :D: 2.00 4.00
19 Noble Templar C :W: .10 .30
20 Rain of Blades U :W: .20 .50
21 Recuperate C :W: .10 .30
22 Reward the Faithful U :W: .20 .50
23 Silver Knight U :W: 1.00 2.00
24 Trap Digger R :W: 1.50 3.00
25 Wing Shards U :W: 1.00 2.00
26 Wipe Clean C :W: .10 .30
27 Zealous Inquisitor C :W: .10 .30
28 Aphetto Runecaster U :B: .50 1.00
29 Brain Freeze U :B: 2.00 4.00
30 Coast Watcher C :B: .10 .30
31 Day of the Dragons R :B: 2.50 5.00
32 Decree of Silence R :B: 2.00 4.00
33 Dispersal Shield C :B: .10 .30
34 Dragon Wings C :B: .10 .30
35 Faces of the Past R :B: 1.50 3.00
36 Frozen Solid C :B: .10 .30
37 Hindering Touch C :B: .10 .30
38 Long-Term Plans U :B: .20 .50
39 Mercurial Kite C :B: .10 .30
40 Metamorphose U :B: .20 .50
41 Mind's Desire R :B: 2.00 4.00
42 Mischievous Quanar R :B: 1.00 2.00
43 Mistform Warchief U :B: .20 .50
44 Parallel Thoughts R :B: 1.00 2.00
45 Pemmin's Aura U :B: 1.00 2.00
46 Raven Guild Initiate C :B: .10 .30
47 Raven Guild Master R :B: 4.00 8.00
48 Riptide Survivor U :B: .20 .50
49 Rush of Knowledge C :B: .10 .30
50 Scornful Egotist C :B: .10 .30
51 Elvish Aberration U :G: .50 1.00
51 Shoreline Ranger C :B: .10 .30
52 Stifle R :B: 4.00 8.00
53 Temporal Fissure C :B: .10 .30
54 Thundercloud Elemental U :B: .30 .75
55 Bladewing's Thrall U :K: .20 .50
56 Cabal Conditioning R :K: 1.00 2.00
57 Cabal Interrogator U :K: .50 1.00
58 Call to the Grave R :K: 3.00 6.00
59 Carrion Feeder C :K: .10 .30
60 Chill Haunting U :K: .30 .75
61 Clutch of Undeath C :K: .10 .30
62 Consumptive Goo R :K: 1.50 3.00
63 Death's-Head Buzzard C :K: .10 .30
64 Decree of Pain R :K: 2.00 4.00
65 Dragon Shadow C :K: .10 .30
66 Fatal Mutation U :K: .20 .50
67 Final Punishment R :K: 1.50 3.00
68 Lethal Vapors R :K: 2.00 4.00
69 Lingering Death C :K: .10 .30
70 Nefashu R :K: 1.50 3.00
71 Putrid Raptor U :K: .20 .50
72 Reaping the Graves C :K: .10 .30
73 Skulltap C :K: .10 .30
74 Soul Collector R :K: 2.00 4.00
75 Tendrils of Agony U :K: .75 1.50
76 Twisted Abomination C :K: .10 .30
77 Unburden C :K: .10 .30
78 Undead Warchief U :K: 1.00 2.50
79 Unspeakable Symbol U :K: .20 .50
80 Vengeful Dead C :K: .10 .30
81 Zombie Cutthroat C :K: .10 .30
82 Bonethorn Valesk C :R: .10 .30
83 Carbonize U :R: .20 .50
84 Chartooth Cougar C :R: .10 .30
85 Decree of Annihilation R :R: 3.00 6.00
86 Dragon Breath C :R: .10 .30
87 Dragon Mage R :R: 2.50 4.00
88 Dragon Tyrant R :R: 3.00 6.00
89 Dragonspeaker Shaman U :R: 1.00 2.00
90 Dragonstorm R :R: 2.50 5.00
91 Enrage U :R: .20 .50
92 Extra Arms U :R: .20 .50
93 Form of the Dragon R :R: 2.50 5.00
94 Goblin Brigand C :R: .10 .30
95 Goblin Psychopath U :R: .30 .75
96 Goblin War Strike C :R: .10 .30
97 Goblin Warchief U :R: 2.00 4.00
98 Grip of Chaos R :R: 1.00 2.00
99 Misguided Rage C :R: .10 .30
100 Pyrostatic Pillar U :R: .20 .50
101 Rock Jockey C :R: .10 .30
102 Scattershot C :R: .10 .30
103 Siege-Gang Commander R :R: 3.00 6.00
104 Skirk Volcanist U :R: .20 .50
105 Spark Spray C :R: .10 .30
106 Sulfuric Vortex R :R: 2.00 4.00
107 Torrent of Fire C :R: .10 .30
108 Uncontrolled Infestation C :R: .10 .30
109 Accelerated Mutation C :G: .10 .30
110 Alpha Status U :G: 1.00 2.00
111 Ambush Commander R :G: 2.50 5.00
112 Ancient Ooze R :G: 2.00 4.00
113 Break Asunder C :G: .10 .30
114 Claws of Wirewood U :G: .30 .75
115 Decree of Savagery R :G: 1.50 3.00
116 Divergent Growth C :G: .10 .30
117 Dragon Fangs C :G: .10 .30
119 Fierce Empath C :G: .10 .30
120 Forgotten Ancient R :G: 4.00 8.00
121 Hunting Pack U :G: .20 .50
122 Krosan Drover C :G: .10 .30
123 Krosan Warchief U :G: .75 1.50
124 Kurgadon U :G: .20 .50
125 One with Nature U :G: .50 1.00
126 Primitive Etchings R :G: 1.50 3.00
127 Root Elemental R :G: 1.50 3.00
128 Sprouting Vines C :G: .10 .30
129 Titanic Bulvox C :G: .10 .30
130 Treetop Scout C :G: .10 .30
131 Upwelling R :G: 2.00 4.00
132 Wirewood Guardian C :G: .10 .30
133 Wirewood Symbiote U :G: .50 1.00
134 Woodcloaker C :G: .10 .30
135 Xantid Swarm R :G: 2.00 4.00
136 Bladewing the Risen R :D: 2.00 4.00
137 Edgewalker U :D: .75 1.50
138 Karona's Zealot U :W: .20 .50
139 Sliver Overlord R :D: 4.00 8.00
140 Ark of Blight U :A: .50 1.00
141 Proteus Machine U :A: .30 .75
142 Stabilizer R :A: 1.00 2.00
143 Temple of the False God U :L: .50 1.00

2003 Magic The Gathering 8th Edition

COMPLETE SET (356) 150.00 250.00
BOOSTER BOX (36 PACKS) 80.00 125.00
BOOSTER PACK (15 CARDS) 3.50 4.00
THEME DECK BOX 125.00 140.00
THEME DECK 8.00 10.00
*FOIL: .75X TO 2X BASIC CARDS
RELEASED ON JULY 28, 2003
1 Angel of Mercy U :W: .50 1.00
2 Angelic Page C :W: .10 .30
3 Ardent Militia U :W: .50 1.00
4 Avatar of Hope R :W: 1.50 3.00
5 Aven Cloudchaser C :W: .10 .30
6 Aven Flock C :W: .10 .30
7 Blessed Reversal R :W: 1.50 3.00
8 Blinding Angel R :W: 4.00 8.00
9 Chastise U :W: .20 .50
10 Circle of Protection: Black U :W: .20 .50
11 Circle of Protection: Blue U :W: .20 .50
12 Circle of Protection: Green U :W: .20 .50
13 Circle of Protection: Red U :W: .20 .50
14 Circle of Protection: White U :W: .20 .50
15 Crossbow Infantry C :W: .10 .30
16 Demystify C :W: .10 .30
17 Diving Griffin C :W: .10 .30
18 Elite Archers R :W: 1.50 3.00
19 Elite Javelineer U :W: .20 .50
20 Glorious Anthem R :W: 3.00 6.00
21 Glory Seeker C :W: .10 .30
22 Healing Salve C :W: .10 .30
23 Holy Day C :W: .10 .30
24 Holy Strength C :W: .10 .30
25 Honor Guard C :W: .10 .30
26 Intrepid Hero R :W: 2.00 4.00
27 Ivory Mask R :W: 3.00 6.00
28 Karma U :W: .20 .50
29 Master Decoy C :W: .10 .30
30 Master Healer R :W: 1.00 2.00
31 Noble Purpose R :W: 1.50 3.00
32 Oracle's Attendants R :W: 1.00 2.00
33 Pacifism C :W: .10 .30
34 Peach Garden Oath U :W: .20 .50
35 Rain of Blades U :W: .20 .50
36 Razorfoot Griffin C :W: .10 .30
37 Redeem C :W: .10 .30
38 Rolling Stones R :W: 1.50 3.00
39 Sacred Ground R :W: 2.00 4.00
40 Sacred Nectar C :W: .10 .30
41 Samite Healer C :W: .10 .30
42 Sanctimony U :W: .20 .50
43 Savannah Lions R :W: 3.00 6.00
44 Seasoned Marshal U :W: .10 .30
45 Serra Angel R :W: 4.00 8.00
46 Solidarity C :W: .10 .30
47 Spirit Link U :W: .20 .50
48 Standing Troops C :W: .10 .30
49 Staunch Defenders U :W: .20 .50
50 Story Circle R :W: 2.00 4.00
51 Suntail Hawk C :W: .10 .30
52 Sunweb R :W: 1.00 2.00
53 Sword Dancer U :W: .20 .50
54 Tundra Wolves C :W: .10 .30
55 Venerable Monk C :W: .10 .30
56 Wall of Swords U :W: .20 .50
57 Worship R :W: 3.00 6.00
58 Wrath of God R :W: 8.00 15.00
59 Air Elemental U :B: .20 .50
60 Archivist R :B: 1.00 2.00
61 Aven Fisher C :B: .10 .30
62 Balance of Power R :B: 2.00 4.00
63 Boomerang C :B: .10 .30
64 Bribery R :B: 5.00 10.00
65 Catalog C :B: .10 .30
66 Coastal Hornclaw C :B: .10 .30
67 Coastal Piracy R :B: 1.00 2.00
68 Concentrate U :B: .20 .50
69 Confiscate U :B: .20 .50

Card	Low	High
70 Coral Eel C :B:	.10	.30
71 Cowardice R :B:	1.50	3.00
72 Curiosity U :B:	.20	.50
73 Daring Apprentice R :B:	1.50	3.00
74 Deflection R :B:	2.00	4.00
75 Dehydration C :B:	.10	.30
76 Evacuation R :B:	1.50	3.00
77 Fighting Drake U :B:	.20	.50
78 Flash Counter C :B:	.10	.30
79 Fleeting Image R :B:	1.50	3.00
80 Flight C :B:	.10	.30
81 Fugitive Wizard C :B:	.10	.30
82 Hibernation U :B:	.20	.50
83 Horned Turtle C :B:	.10	.30
84 Index C :B:	.10	.30
85 Inspiration C :B:	.10	.30
86 Intruder Alarm R :B:	2.00	4.00
87 Invisibility U :B:	.20	.50
88 Mahamoti Djinn R :B:	2.00	4.00
89 Mana Leak C :B:	.10	.30
90 Merchant of Secrets C :B:	.10	.30
91 Merchant Scroll U :B:	.20	.50
92 Mind Bend R :B:	1.50	3.00
93 Phantom Warrior U :B:	.20	.50
94 Puppeteer U :B:	.20	.50
95 Remove Soul C :B:	.10	.30
96 Rewind U :B:	.50	1.00
97 Sage of Lat-Nam R :B:	1.50	3.00
98 Sage Owl C :B:	.10	.30
99 Sea Monster C :B:	.10	.30
S1 Eager Cadet C :W:	.75	1.50
S2 Vengeance U :W:	4.00	8.00
S3 Giant Octopus C :B:	.50	1.00
S5 Vizzerdrix R :B:	.50	1.00
S6 Enormous Baloth U :G:	.20	.50
S7 Silverback Ape U :G:	.75	1.50
100 Shifting Sky R :B:	1.50	3.00
101 Sneaky Homunculus C :B:	.10	.30
102 Spiketail Hatchling U :B:	.20	.50
103 Steal Artifact U :B:	.20	.50
104 Storm Crow C :B:	.10	.30
105 Telepathy U :B:	.20	.50
106 Temporal Adept R :B:	2.00	4.00
107 Thieving Magpie U :B:	.20	.50
108 Tidal Kraken R :B:	2.00	4.00
109 Trade Routes R :B:	1.00	2.00
110 Treasure Trove U :B:	.20	.50
111 Twiddle C :B:	.10	.30
112 Unsummon C :B:	.10	.30
113 Wall of Air U :B:	.20	.50
114 Wind Drake C :B:	.10	.30
115 Wrath of Marit Lage U :B:	.20	.50
116 Zur's Weirding R :B:	1.50	3.00
117 Abyssal Specter U :K:	.20	.50
118 Ambition's Cost U :K:	.20	.50
119 Bog Imp C :K:	.10	.30
120 Bog Wraith U :K:	.50	1.00
121 Carrion Wall U :K:	.20	.50
122 Coercion C :K:	.10	.30
123 Dark Banishing C :K:	.10	.30
124 Death Pit Offering R :K:	1.50	3.00
125 Death Pits of Rath R :K:	1.50	3.00
126 Deathgazer U :K:	.20	.50
127 Deepwood Ghoul C :K:	.10	.30
128 Diabolic Tutor U :K:	1.00	2.00
129 Drudge Skeletons C :K:	.10	.30
130 Dusk Imp C :K:	.10	.30
131 Eastern Paladin R :K:	1.00	2.00
132 Execute U :K:	.20	.50
133 Fallen Angel R :K:	2.00	4.00
134 Fear C :K:	.10	.30
135 Giant Cockroach C :K:	.10	.30
136 Gluttonous Zombie U :K:	.20	.50
137 Grave Pact R :K:	5.00	10.00
138 Gravedigger C :K:	.10	.30
139 Larceny R :K:	1.00	2.00
140 Looming Shade C :K:	.10	.30
141 Lord of the Undead R :K:	3.00	6.00
142 Maggot Carrier C :K:	.10	.30
143 Megrim U :K:	.20	.50
144 Mind Rot C :K:	.10	.30
145 Mind Slash U :K:	.20	.50
146 Mind Sludge U :K:	.20	.50
147 Murderous Betrayal R :K:	1.00	2.00
148 Nausea C :K:	.10	.30
149 Nekrataal U :K:	.20	.50
150 Nightmare R :K:	2.00	4.00
151 Persecute R :K:	3.00	6.00
152 Phyrexian Arena R :K:	3.00	6.00
153 Phyrexian Plaguelord R :K:	2.00	4.00
154 Plague Beetle C :K:	.10	.30
155 Plague Wind R :K:	2.00	4.00
156 Primeval Shambler U :K:	.20	.50
157 Raise Dead C :K:	.10	.30
158 Ravenous Rats C :K:	.10	.30
159 Royal Assassin R :K:	5.00	10.00
160 Scathe Zombies C :K:	.10	.30
161 Serpent Warrior C :K:	.10	.30
162 Sever Soul U :K:	.20	.50
163 Severed Legion C :K:	.10	.30
164 Slay U :K:	.20	.50
165 Soul Feast U :K:	.20	.50
166 Spineless Thug C :K:	.10	.30
167 Swarm of Rats U :K:	.20	.50
168 Underworld Dreams R :K:	6.00	12.00
169 Unholy Strength C :K:	.10	.30
170 Vampiric Spirit R :K:	1.50	3.00
171 Vicious Hunger C :K:	.10	.30
172 Warped Devotion R :K:	1.00	2.00
173 Western Paladin R :K:	1.00	2.00
174 Zombify U :K:	.20	.50
175 Anaba Shaman C :R:	.10	.30
176 Balduvian Barbarians C :R:	.10	.30
177 Blaze U :R:	.50	1.00
178 Blood Moon R :R:	2.00	4.00
179 Bloodshot Cyclops R :R:	2.00	4.00
180 Boil U :R:	.50	1.00
181 Canyon Wildcat C :R:	.10	.30
182 Cinder Wall C :R:	.10	.30
183 Demolish U :R:	.20	.50
184 Dwarven Demolition Team U :R:	.20	.50
185 Enrage U :R:	.20	.50
186 Flashfires U :R:	.20	.50
187 Furnace of Rath R :R:	2.00	4.00
188 Goblin Chariot C :R:	.10	.30
189 Goblin Glider U :R:	.20	.50
190 Goblin King R :R:	2.00	4.00
191 Goblin Raider C :R:	.10	.30
192 Guerrilla Tactics U :R:	.20	.50
193 Hammer of Bogardan R :R:	4.00	8.00
194 Hill Giant C :R:	.10	.30
195 Hulking Cyclops U :R:	.20	.50
196 Inferno R :R:	1.50	3.00
197 Lava Axe C :R:	.10	.30
198 Lava Hounds R :R:	1.50	3.00
199 Lesser Gargadon U :R:	.20	.50
200 Lightning Blast U :R:	.20	.50
201 Lightning Elemental C :R:	.10	.30
202 Mana Clash R :R:	1.50	3.00
203 Mogg Sentry R :R:	1.50	3.00
204 Obliterate R :R:	2.50	5.00
205 Ogre Taskmaster U :R:	.20	.50
206 Okk R :R:	1.00	2.00
207 Orcish Artillery U :R:	.20	.50
208 Orcish Spy C :R:	.10	.30
209 Panic Attack C :R:	.10	.30
210 Pyroclasm U :R:	1.00	2.00
211 Pyrotechnics U :R:	.20	.50
212 Raging Goblin C :R:	.10	.30
213 Reflexes C :R:	.10	.30
214 Relentless Assault R :R:	1.00	2.00
215 Ridgeline Rager C :R:	.10	.30
216 Rukh Egg R :R:	2.00	4.00
217 Sabretooth Tiger C :R:	.10	.30
218 Searing Wind R :R:	2.00	4.00
219 Seismic Assault R :R:	1.00	2.00
220 Shatter C :R:	.10	.30
221 Shivan Dragon R :R:	4.00	8.00
222 Shock C :R:	.10	.30
223 Shock Troops C :R:	.10	.30
224 Sizzle C :R:	.10	.30
225 Stone Rain C :R:	.10	.30
226 Sudden Impact U :R:	.20	.50
227 Thieves' Auction R :R:	1.00	2.00
228 Tremor C :R:	.10	.30
229 Two-Headed Dragon R :R:	5.00	10.00
230 Viashino Sandstalker U :R:	.20	.50
231 Volcanic Hammer C :R:	.10	.30
232 Wall of Stone U :R:	.20	.50
233 Birds of Paradise R :G:	8.00	15.00
234 Blanchwood Armor U :G:	.50	1.00
235 Call of the Wild R :G:	1.50	3.00
236 Canopy Spider C :G:	.10	.30
237 Choke U :G:	.20	.50
238 Collective Unconscious R :G:	1.00	2.00
239 Craw Wurm C :G:	.10	.30
240 Creeping Mold U :G:	.20	.50
241 Elvish Champion R :G:	3.00	6.00
242 Elvish Lyrist U :G:	.50	1.00
243 Elvish Pioneer C :G:	.10	.30
244 Elvish Piper R :G:	5.00	10.00
245 Elvish Scrapper U :G:	.20	.50
246 Emperor Crocodile R :G:	2.00	4.00
247 Fecundity U :G:	.50	1.00
248 Fertile Ground C :G:	.10	.30
249 Foratog U :G:	.20	.50
250 Fungusaur R :G:	1.00	2.00
251 Fyndhorn Elder U :G:	.20	.50
252 Gaea's Herald R :G:	1.50	3.00
253 Giant Badger C :G:	.10	.30
254 Giant Growth C :G:	.10	.30
255 Giant Spider C :G:	.10	.30
256 Grizzly Bears C :G:	.10	.30
257 Horned Troll C :G:	.10	.30
258 Hunted Wumpus U :G:	.20	.50
259 Lhurgoyf R :G:	1.50	3.00
260 Living Terrain U :G:	.20	.50
261 Llanowar Behemoth U :G:	.20	.50
262 Lone Wolf C :G:	.10	.30
263 Lure U :G:	.20	.50
264 Maro R :G:	1.00	2.00
265 Might of Oaks R :G:	2.00	4.00
266 Monstrous Growth C :G:	.10	.30
267 Moss Monster C :G:	.10	.30
268 Nantuko Disciple C :G:	.10	.30
269 Natural Affinity R :G:	1.50	3.00
270 Naturalize C :G:	.10	.30
271 Norwood Ranger C :G:	.10	.30
272 Plow Under R :G:	5.00	10.00
273 Primeval Force R :G:	1.00	2.00
274 Rampant Growth C :G:	.10	.30
275 Regeneration C :G:	.10	.30
276 Revive U :G:	.20	.50
277 Rhox R :G:	1.50	3.00
278 Rushwood Dryad C :G:	.10	.30
279 Spined Wurm C :G:	.10	.30
280 Spitting Spider U :G:	.20	.50
281 Spreading Algae U :G:	.20	.50
282 Stream of Life U :G:	.20	.50
283 Thorn Elemental R :G:	2.00	4.00
284 Trained Armodon C :G:	.10	.30
285 Verduran Enchantress R :G:	1.50	3.00
286 Vernal Bloom R :G:	2.50	5.00
287 Vine Trellis C :G:	.10	.30
288 Wing Snare U :G:	.20	.50
289 Wood Elves C :G:	.10	.30
290 Yavimaya Enchantress U :G:	.20	.50
291 Aladdin's Ring R :A:	1.00	2.00
292 Beast of Burden R :A:	1.00	2.00
293 Brass Herald R :A:	1.00	2.00
294 Coat of Arms R :A:	6.00	12.00
295 Crystal Rod U :A:	.20	.50
296 Defense Grid R :A:	2.00	4.00
297 Dingus Egg R :A:	1.00	2.00
298 Disrupting Scepter R :A:	1.00	2.00
299 Distorting Lens R :A:	1.00	2.00
300 Ensnaring Bridge R :A:	4.00	8.00
301 Flying Carpet R :A:	1.00	2.00
302 Fodder Cannon U :A:	.20	.50
303 Howling Mine R :A:	3.00	6.00
304 Iron Star U :A:	.20	.50
305 Ivory Cup U :A:	.20	.50
306 Jayemdae Tome R :A:	1.00	2.00
307 Millstone R :A:	1.50	3.00
308 Patagia Golem U :A:	.20	.50
309 Phyrexian Colossus R :A:	2.00	4.00
310 Phyrexian Hulk U :A:	.20	.50
311 Planar Portal R :A:	2.00	4.00
312 Rod of Ruin U :A:	.20	.50
313 Skull of Orm R :A:	1.50	3.00
314 Spellbook U :A:	.20	.50
315 Star Compass U :A:	.20	.50
316 Teferi's Puzzle Box R :A:	1.50	3.00
317 Throne of Bone U :A:	.20	.50
318 Urza's Armor R :A:	1.50	3.00
319 Vexing Arcanix R :A:	1.00	2.00
320 Wall of Spears U :A:	.20	.50
321 Wooden Sphere U :A:	.20	.50
322 City of Brass R :L:	4.00	8.00
323 Coastal Tower U :L:	.50	1.00
324 Elfhame Palace U :L:	.50	1.00
325 Salt Marsh U :L:	.20	.50
326 Shivan Oasis U :L:	.20	.50
327 Urborg Volcano U :L:	.20	.50
328 Urza's Mine U :L:	.20	.50
329 Urza's Power Plant U :L:	.20	.50
330 Urza's Tower U :L:	.20	.50
331 Plains L :L:	.10	.30
332 Plains L :L:	.10	.30
333 Plains L :L:	.10	.30
334 Plains L :L:	.10	.30
335 Island L :L:	.10	.30
336 Island L :L:	.10	.30
337 Island L :L:	.10	.30
338 Island L :L:	.10	.30
339 Swamp L :L:	.10	.30
340 Swamp L :L:	.10	.30
341 Swamp L :L:	.10	.30
342 Swamp L :L:	.10	.30
343 Mountain L :L:	.10	.30
344 Mountain L :L:	.10	.30
345 Mountain L :L:	.10	.30
346 Mountain L :L:	.10	.30
347 Forest L :L:	.10	.30
348 Forest L :L:	.10	.30
349 Forest L :L:	.10	.30
350 Forest L :L:	.10	.30

2003 Magic The Gathering Mirrodin

Item	Low	High
COMPLETE SET (306)	125.00	200.00
BOOSTER BOX (36 PACKS)	80.00	110.00
BOOSTER PACK (15 CARDS)	3.50	4.00
STARTER BOX (12 DECKS)	80.00	125.00
STARTER DECK	10.00	13.00
FAT PACK	30.00	38.00

*FOIL: .75X TO 2X BASIC CARDS
RELEASED OCTOBER 3, 2003

Card	Low	High
1 Altar's Light U :W:	.50	1.00
2 Arrest C :W:	.10	.30
3 Auriok Bladewarden U :W:	.50	1.00
4 Auriok Steelshaper R :W:	2.00	4.00
5 Auriok Transfixer C :W:	.10	.30
6 Awe Strike C :W:	.10	.30
7 Blinding Beam C :W:	.10	.30
8 Leonin Abunas R :W:	2.50	5.00
9 Leonin Den-Guard C :W:	.10	.30
10 Leonin Elder C :W:	.10	.30
11 Leonin Skyhunter U :W:	1.00	2.00
12 Loxodon Mender C :W:	.10	.30
13 Loxodon Peacekeeper R :W:	1.50	3.00
14 Loxodon Punisher R :W:	1.00	2.00
15 Luminous Angel R :W:	2.00	4.00
16 Raise the Alarm C :W:	.10	.30
17 Razor Barrier C :W:	.10	.30
18 Roar of the Kha U :W:	.20	.50
19 Rule of Law R :W:	1.50	3.00
20 Second Sunrise R :W:	2.00	4.00
21 Skyhunter Cub C :W:	.10	.30
22 Skyhunter Patrol C :W:	.10	.30
23 Slith Ascendant U :W:	.20	.50
24 Solar Tide R :W:	1.50	3.00
25 Soul Nova U :W:	.20	.50
26 Sphere of Purity C :W:	.10	.30
27 Taj-Nar Swordsmith U :W:	.20	.50
28 Tempest of Light U :W:	.20	.50
29 Annul C :B:	.10	.30
30 Assert Authority U :B:	.50	1.00
31 Broodstar R :B:	2.50	5.00
32 Disarm C :B:	.10	.30
33 Domineer U :B:	.20	.50
34 Dream's Grip C :B:	.10	.30
35 Fabricate U :B:	1.00	2.00
36 Fatespinner R :B:	1.50	3.00
37 Inertia Bubble C :B:	.10	.30
38 Looming Hoverguard U :B:	.20	.50
39 Lumengrid Augur R :B:	1.00	2.00
40 Lumengrid Sentinel U :B:	.20	.50
41 Lumengrid Warden C :B:	.10	.30
42 March of the Machines R :B:	3.00	6.00
43 Neurok Familiar C :B:	.10	.30
44 Neurok Spy C :B:	.10	.30
45 Override C :B:	.10	.30
46 Psychic Membrane U :B:	.20	.50
47 Quicksilver Elemental R :B:	1.00	2.00
48 Regress C :B:	.10	.30
49 Shared Fate R :B:	1.50	3.00
50 Slith Strider U :B:	.20	.50
51 Somber Hoverguard C :B:	.10	.30
52 Temporal Cascade R :B:	1.50	3.00
53 Thirst for Knowledge U :B:	1.00	2.00
54 Thoughtcast C :B:	.20	.50
55 Vedalken Archmage R :B:	1.50	3.00
56 Wanderguard Sentry C :B:	.10	.30
57 Barter in Blood U :K:	.50	1.00
58 Betrayal of Flesh U :K:	.30	.75
59 Chimney Imp C :K:	.10	.30
60 Consume Spirit C :K:	.10	.30
61 Contaminated Bond C :K:	.10	.30
62 Disciple of the Vault C :K:	.10	.30
63 Dross Harvester R :K:	1.50	3.00
64 Dross Prowler C :K:	.10	.30
65 Flayed Nim U :K:	.20	.50
66 Grim Reminder R :K:	1.00	2.00
67 Irradiate C :K:	.10	.30
68 Moriok Scavenger C :K:	.10	.30
69 Necrogen Mists R :K:	1.50	3.00
70 Nim Devourer R :K:	1.00	2.00
71 Nim Lasher C :K:	.10	.30
72 Nim Shambler U :K:	.20	.50
73 Nim Shrieker C :K:	.10	.30
74 Promise of Power R :K:	1.50	3.00
75 Reiver Demon R :K:	2.50	5.00
76 Relic Bane U :K:	.20	.50
77 Slith Bloodletter U :K:	.20	.50
78 Spoils of the Vault R :K:	1.50	3.00
79 Terror C :K:	.10	.30
80 Vermiculos R :K:	1.00	2.00
81 Wail of the Nim C :K:	.10	.30
82 Wall of Blood U :K:	.20	.50
83 Woebearer U :K:	.20	.50
84 Wrench Mind C :K:	.10	.30
85 Arc-Slogger R :R:	2.50	5.00
86 Atog U :R:	.50	1.00
87 Confusion in the Ranks R :R:	1.50	3.00
88 Detonate U :R:	.50	1.00
89 Electrostatic Bolt C :R:	.20	.50
90 Fiery Gambit R :R:	1.00	2.00
91 Fists of the Anvil C :R:	.10	.30
92 Forge Armor U :R:	.20	.50
93 Fractured Loyalty U :R:	.20	.50
94 Goblin Striker C :R:	.10	.30
95 Grab the Reins U :R:	.50	1.00
96 Incite War C :R:	.10	.30
97 Krark-Clan Shaman C :R:	.10	.30
98 Krark's Thumb R :A:	1.00	2.00
99 Mass Hysteria R :R:	1.50	3.00
100 Megatog R :R:	2.00	4.00
101 Molten Rain C :R:	.10	.30
102 Ogre Leadfoot C :R:	.10	.30
103 Rustmouth Ogre U :R:	.30	.75
104 Seething Song C :R:	.10	.30
105 Shatter C :R:	.10	.30
106 Shrapnel Blast U :R:	1.00	2.00
107 Slith Firewalker U :R:	1.00	2.00
108 Spikeshot Goblin C :R:	.10	.30
109 Trash for Treasure R :R:	1.50	3.00
110 Vulshok Battlemaster R :R:	1.00	2.00
111 Vulshok Berserker C :R:	.10	.30
112 War Elemental R :R:	1.50	3.00
113 Battlegrowth C :G:	.10	.30
114 Bloodscent U :G:	.50	1.00
115 Brown Ouphe U :G:	.50	1.00
116 Copperhoof Vorrac R :G:	1.00	2.00
117 Creeping Mold U :G:	.20	.50
118 Deconstruct C :G:	.10	.30
119 Fangren Hunter C :G:	.10	.30
120 Glissa Sunseeker R :G:	2.00	4.00
121 Groffskithur C :G:	.10	.30
122 Hum of the Radix R :G:	1.50	3.00
123 Journey of Discovery C :G:	.10	.30
124 Living Hive R :G:	1.50	3.00
125 Molder Slug R :G:	2.00	4.00
126 One Dozen Eyes U :G:	.20	.50
127 Plated Slagwurm R :G:	1.50	3.00
128 Predator's Strike C :G:	.10	.30
129 Slith Predator U :G:	.20	.50
130 Sylvan Scrying U :G:	.50	1.00
131 Tel-Jilad Archers C :G:	.10	.30
132 Tel-Jilad Chosen C :G:	.10	.30
133 Tel-Jilad Exile C :G:	.10	.30
134 Tooth and Nail R :G:	4.00	8.00
135 Troll Ascetic R :G:	5.00	10.00
136 Trolls of Tel-Jilad U :G:	.20	.50
137 Turn to Dust C :G:	.10	.30
138 Viridian Joiner C :G:	.10	.30
139 Viridian Shaman U :G:	.50	1.00
140 Wurmskin Forger C :G:	.10	.30
141 AEther Spellbomb C :A:	.10	.30
142 Alpha Myr C :A:	.10	.30
143 Altar of Shadows R :A:	1.50	3.00
144 Banshee's Blade U :A:	.50	1.00
145 Blinkmoth Urn R :A:	1.00	2.00
146 Bonesplitter C :A:	.10	.30
147 Bosh, Iron Golem R :A:	2.00	4.00
148 Bottle Gnomes U :A:	.50	1.00
149 Cathodion U :A:	.50	1.00
150 Chalice of the Void R :A:	2.50	5.00
151 Chromatic Sphere C :A:	.10	.30
152 Chrome Mox R :A:	10.00	20.00
153 Clockwork Beetle C :A:	.10	.30
154 Clockwork Condor C :A:	.10	.30
155 Clockwork Dragon R :A:	2.00	4.00
156 Clockwork Vorrac U :A:	.20	.50
157 Cobalt Golem C :A:	.10	.30
158 Copper Myr C :A:	.10	.30
159 Crystal Shard U :A:	.10	.30
160 Culling Scales R :A:	1.00	2.00
161 Damping Matrix R :A:	2.00	4.00
162 Dead-Iron Sledge U :A:	.20	.50
163 Dragon Blood U :A:	.50	1.00
164 Dross Scorpion C :A:	.10	.30
165 Duplicant R :A:	2.50	5.00
166 Duskworker U :A:	.20	.50
167 Elf Replica C :A:	.10	.30
168 Empyrial Plate R :A:	2.00	4.00
169 Extraplanar Lens R :A:	2.50	5.00
170 Farsight Mask U :A:	.20	.50
171 Fireshrieker U :A:	1.00	2.00
172 Frogmite C :A:	.10	.30
173 Galvanic Key C :A:	.10	.30
174 Gate to the Æther R :A:	1.50	3.00
175 Gilded Lotus R :A:	3.00	6.00
176 Goblin Charbelcher R :A:	2.50	5.00
177 Goblin Dirigible U :A:	.20	.50
178 Goblin Replica C :A:	.10	.30
179 Goblin War Wagon C :A:	.10	.30
180 Gold Myr C :A:	.10	.30
181 Golem-Skin Gauntlets U :A:	.50	1.00
182 Granite Shard U :A:	.20	.50
183 Grid Monitor R :A:	2.00	4.00
184 Heartwood Shard U :A:	.20	.50
185 Hematite Golem C :A:	.10	.30
186 Icy Manipulator U :A:	1.00	2.00
187 Iron Myr C :A:	.10	.30
188 Isochron Scepter U :A:	4.00	8.00
189 Jinxed Choker R :A:	1.00	2.00
190 Krark-Clan Grunt C :R:	.10	.30
191 Leaden Myr C :A:	.10	.30
192 Leonin Bladetrap U :A:	.20	.50
193 Leonin Scimitar C :A:	.10	.30
194 Leonin Sun Standard R :A:	1.50	3.00
195 Leveler R :A:	1.50	3.00
196 Liar's Pendulum R :A:	1.00	2.00
197 Lifespark Spellbomb C :A:	.10	.30
198 Lightning Coils R :A:	2.00	4.00
199 Lightning Greaves U :A:	1.00	2.00
200 Lodestone Myr R :A:	1.50	3.00
201 Loxodon Warhammer U :A:	1.00	2.00
202 Malachite Golem C :A:	.10	.30
203 Mask of Memory U :A:	.20	.50
204 Mesmeric Orb R :A:	1.50	3.00
205 Mind's Eye R :A:	1.50	3.00
206 Mindslaver R :A:	4.00	8.00
207 Mindstorm Crown U :A:	.20	.50
208 Mirror Golem U :A:	.20	.50
209 Mourner's Shield U :A:	.20	.50
210 Myr Adapter C :A:	.10	.30
211 Myr Enforcer C :A:	.10	.30
212 Myr Incubator R :A:	2.00	4.00
213 Myr Mindservant U :A:	.20	.50
214 Myr Prototype U :A:	.20	.50
215 Myr Retriever U :A:	1.00	2.00
216 Necrogen Spellbomb C :A:	.10	.30
217 Needlebug U :A:	.20	.50
218 Neurok Hoversail C :A:	.10	.30
219 Nightmare Lash R :A:	1.00	2.00
220 Nim Replica C :A:	.10	.30
221 Nuisance Engine U :A:	.20	.50
222 Oblivion Stone R :A:	4.00	8.00
223 Omega Myr C :A:	.10	.30
224 Ornithopter U :A:	1.00	2.00
225 Pearl Shard U :A:	.20	.50
226 Pentavus R :A:	1.50	3.00
227 Pewter Golem C :A:	.10	.30
228 Platinum Angel R :A:	8.00	15.00
229 Power Conduit U :A:	.50	1.00
230 Proteus Staff R :A:	1.50	3.00
231 Psychogenic Probe R :A:	1.00	2.00
232 Pyrite Spellbomb C :A:	.10	.30
233 Quicksilver Fountain R :A:	1.00	2.00
234 Rust Elemental U :A:	.20	.50
235 Rustspore Ram U :A:	.20	.50
236 Scale of Chiss-Goria C :A:	.10	.30
237 Scrabbling Claws U :A:	.20	.50
238 Sculpting Steel R :A:	2.00	4.00
239 Scythe of the Wretched R :A:	1.50	3.00
240 Serum Tank U :A:	.20	.50
241 Silver Myr C :A:	.10	.30
242 Skeleton Shard U :A:	.20	.50
243 Slagwurm Armor C :A:	.10	.30
244 Soldier Replica C :A:	.10	.30
245 Solemn Simulacrum R :A:	4.00	8.00
246 Soul Foundry R :A:	2.00	4.00
247 Spellweaver Helix R :A:	1.50	3.00
248 Steel Wall C :A:	.10	.30
249 Sun Droplet U :A:	.50	1.00
250 Sunbeam Spellbomb C :A:	.10	.30
251 Sword of Kaldra R :A:	3.00	6.00
252 Synod Sanctum U :A:	.20	.50
253 Talisman of Dominance U :A:	.50	1.00
254 Talisman of Impulse U :A:	.20	.50
255 Talisman of Indulgence U :A:	.20	.50
256 Talisman of Progress U :A:	.50	1.00
257 Talisman of Unity U :A:	.20	.50
258 Tanglebloom C :A:	.10	.30
259 Tangleroot R :A:	1.00	2.00
260 Tel-Jilad Stylus U :A:	.20	.50
261 Thought Prison U :A:	.20	.50
262 Timesifter R :A:	1.50	3.00
263 Titanium Golem C :A:	.10	.30
264 Tooth of Chiss-Goria C :A:	.10	.30
265 Tower of Champions R :A:	1.00	2.00
266 Tower of Eons R :A:	1.50	3.00
267 Tower of Fortunes R :A:	1.50	3.00
268 Tower of Murmurs R :A:	1.50	3.00
269 Triskelion R :A:	2.00	4.00
270 Viridian Longbow C :A:	.10	.30
271 Vorrac Battlehorns C :A:	.10	.30
272 Vulshok Battlegear U :A:	.20	.50
273 Vulshok Gauntlets C :A:	.10	.30
274 Welding Jar C :A:	.10	.30
275 Wizard Replica C :A:	.10	.30
276 Worldslayer R :A:	1.50	3.00
277 Yotian Soldier C :A:	.10	.30
278 Ancient Den C :L:	.10	.30
279 Blinkmoth Well U :L:	.50	1.00
280 Cloudpost C :L:	.10	.30
281 Glimmervoid R :L:	5.00	10.00
282 Great Furnace C :L:	.20	.50
283 Seat of the Synod C :L:	.20	.50
284 Stalking Stones U :L:	.20	.50
285 Tree of Tales C :L:	.10	.30
286 Vault of Whispers C :L:	.10	.30
287 Plains L :L:	.10	.30
288 Plains L :L:	.10	.30
289 Plains L :L:	.10	.30
290 Plains L :L:	.10	.30
291 Island L :L:	.10	.30
292 Island L :L:	.10	.30
293 Island L :L:	.10	.30
294 Island L :L:	.10	.30
295 Swamp L :L:	.10	.30
296 Swamp L :L:	.10	.30
297 Swamp L :L:	.10	.30
298 Swamp L :L:	.10	.30
299 Mountain L :L:	.10	.30
300 Mountain L :L:	.10	.30
301 Mountain L :L:	.10	.30
302 Mountain L :L:	.10	.30
303 Forest L :L:	.10	.30
304 Forest L :L:	.10	.30
305 Forest L :L:	.10	.30
306 Forest L :L:	.10	.30

2004 Magic The Gathering Darksteel

Item	Low	High
COMPLETE SET (165)	125.00	200.00
BOOSTER BOX (36 PACKS)	150.00	250.00
BOOSTER PACK (15 CARDS)	4.50	8.00
FAT PACK	30.00	60.00

*FOIL: .75X TO 2X BASIC CARDS
RELEASED ON FEBRUARY 6, 2004

Card	Low	High
1 Auriok Glaivemaster C :W:	.10	.25
2 Echoing Calm C :W:	.10	.25
3 Emissary of Hope U :W:	.20	.50
5 Leonin Battlemage U :W:	.20	.50
6 Leonin Shikari R :W:	1.50	4.00
7 Loxodon Mystic C :W:	.10	.25

8 Metal Fatigue C :W: .10 .25
9 Pristine Angel R :W: 1.50 4.00
10 Pteron Ghost C :W: .10 .25
11 Pulse of the Fields R :W: .40 1.00
12 Purge U :W: .20 .50
13 Ritual of Restoration C :W: .10 .25
14 Soulscour R :W: .30 .75
15 Steelshaper Apprentice R :W: .30 .75
16 Stir the Pride U :W: .20 .50
17 Test of Faith U :W: .20 .50
18 Turn the Tables R :W: .30 .75
19 Carry Away U :B: .20 .50
20 Chromescale Drake R :B: .30 .75
21 Echoing Truth C :B: .30 .75
22 Hoverguard Observer U :B: .20 .50
23 Last Word R :B: .40 1.00
24 Machinate C :B: .10 .25
25 Magnetic Flux C :B: .10 .25
26 Neurok Prodigy C :B: .10 .25
27 Neurok Transmuter U :B: .20 .50
28 Psychic Overload U :B: .20 .50
29 Pulse of the Grid R :B: .30 .75
30 Quicksilver Behemoth C :B: .10 .25
31 Reshape R :B: .60 1.50
32 Retract R :B: .30 .75
33 Second Sight U :B: .20 .50
34 Synod Artificer R :B: .30 .75
35 Vedalken Engineer C :B: .10 .25
36 Vex C :B: .10 .25
37 AEther Snap R :K: .30 .75
38 Burden of Greed C :K: .10 .25
39 Chittering Rats C :K: .10 .25
40 Death Cloud R :K: 1.00 2.50
41 Echoing Decay C :K: .10 .25
42 Emissary of Despair U :K: .20 .50
43 Essence Drain C :K: .10 .25
44 Greater Harvester R :K: .30 .75
45 Grimclaw Bats C :K: .10 .25
46 Hunger of the Nim C :K: .10 .25
47 Mephitic Ooze R :K: .30 .75
48 Murderous Spoils U :K: .20 .50
49 Nim Abomination U :K: .20 .50
50 Pulse of the Dross R :K: .30 .75
51 Scavenging Scarab C :K: .10 .25
52 Screams from Within U :K: .20 .50
53 Scrounge U :K: .20 .50
54 Shriveling Rot R :K: .30 .75
55 Barbed Lightning C :R: .10 .25
56 Crazed Goblin C :R: .10 .25
57 Dismantle U :R: .20 .50
58 Drooling Ogre C :R: .10 .25
59 Echoing Ruin C :R: .10 .25
60 Fireball U :R: .20 .50
61 Flamebreak R :R: .75 2.00
62 Furnace Dragon R :R: .30 .75
63 Hallow C :W: .10 .25
63 Goblin Archaeologist U :R: .20 .50
64 Inflame C :R: .10 .25
65 Krark-Clan Stoker C :R: .10 .25
66 Pulse of the Forge R :R: .40 1.00
67 Savage Beating R :R: .40 1.00
68 Shunt R :R: .30 .75
69 Slobad, Goblin Tinkerer R :R: .30 .75
70 Tears of Rage U :R: .20 .50
71 Unforge C :R: .10 .25
72 Vulshok War Boar U :R: .20 .50
73 Ageless Entity R :G: .50 1.25
74 Echoing Courage C :G: .10 .25
75 Fangren Firstborn R :G: .40 1.00
76 Infested Roothold U :G: .20 .50
77 Karstoderm U :G: .20 .50
78 Nourish C :G: .10 .25
79 Oxidize U :G: .20 .50
80 Pulse of the Tangle R :G: .30 .75
81 Reap and Sow C :G: .10 .25
82 Rebuking Ceremony R :G: .30 .75
83 Roaring Slagwurm R :G: .30 .75
84 Stand Together U :G: .20 .50
85 Tangle Spider C :G: .10 .25
86 Tanglewalker U :G: .20 .50
87 Tel-Jilad Outrider C :G: .10 .25
88 Tel-Jilad Wolf C :G: .10 .25
89 Viridian Acolyte C :G: .10 .25
90 Viridian Zealot R :G: .75 2.00
91 AEther Vial U :A: 6.00 15.00
92 Angel's Feather U :A: .20 .50
93 Arcane Spyglass C :A: .10 .25
94 Arcbound Bruiser C :A: .10 .25
95 Arcbound Crusher U :A: .40 1.00
96 Arcbound Fiend U :A: .20 .50
97 Arcbound Hybrid C :A: .10 .25
98 Arcbound Lancer U :A: .20 .50
99 Arcbound Overseer R :A: 1.00 2.50
100 Arcbound Ravager R :A: 10.00 25.00
101 Arcbound Reclaimer R :A: .50 1.25
102 Arcbound Slith U :A: .30 .75
103 Arcbound Stinger C :A: .10 .25
104 Arcbound Worker C :A: .20 .50
105 Auriok Siege Sled U :A: .20 .50
106 Chimeric Egg U :A: .20 .50
107 Coretapper U :A: .40 1.00
108 Darksteel Brute U :A: .20 .50
109 Darksteel Colossus R :A: 2.50 6.00
110 Darksteel Forge R :A: 5.00 12.00
111 Darksteel Gargoyle U :A: .20 .50
112 Darksteel Ingot C :A: .30 .75
113 Darksteel Pendant C :A: .10 .25
114 Darksteel Reactor R :A: 1.25 3.00
115 Death-Mask Duplicant U :A: .20 .50
116 Demon's Horn U :A: .20 .50
117 Dragon's Claw U :A: .20 .50
118 Drill-Skimmer C :A: .10 .25
119 Dross Golem C :A: .10 .25
120 Eater of Days R :A: .40 1.00
121 Gemini Engine R :A: .30 .75
122 Genesis Chamber U :A: .40 1.00
123 Geth's Grimoire U :A: .20 .50
124 Heartseeker R :A: .40 1.00
125 Juggernaut U :A: .20 .50
126 Kraken's Eye U :A: .20 .50
127 Leonin Bola C :A: .10 .25
128 Lich's Tomb R :A: .30 .75
129 Memnarch R :A: 2.50 6.00
130 Mycosynth Lattice R :A: 3.00 8.00
131 Myr Landshaper C :A: .10 .25
132 Myr Matrix R :A: 1.50 4.00
133 Myr Moonvessel C :A: .10 .25
134 Nemesis Mask U :A: .20 .50
135 Oxidda Golem C :A: .10 .25
136 Panoptic Mirror R :A: 1.50 4.00
137 Razor Golem C :A: .10 .25
138 Serum Powder R :A: .50 1.25
139 Shield of Kaldra R :A: 2.00 5.00
140 Skullclamp U :A: 1.25 3.00
141 Spawning Pit U :A: .20 .50
142 Specter's Shroud U :A: .20 .50
143 Spellbinder R :A: .30 .75
144 Spincrusher U :A: .20 .50
145 Spire Golem C :A: .10 .25
146 Sundering Titan R :A: 1.25 3.00
147 Surestrike Trident U :A: .20 .50
148 Sword of Fire and Ice R :A: 20.00 40.00
149 Sword of Light and Shadow R :A: 15.00 30.00
150 Talon of Pain U :A: .20 .50
151 Tangle Golem C :A: .10 .25
152 Thought Dissector R :A: .30 .75
153 Thunderstaff U :A: .20 .50
154 Trinisphere R :A: 1.25 3.00
155 Ur-Golem's Eye C :A: .10 .25
156 Voltaic Construct U :A: .20 .50
157 Vulshok Morningstar C :A: .10 .25
158 Wand of the Elements R :A: .30 .75
159 Well of Lost Dreams R :A: 1.00 2.50
160 Whispersilk Cloak C :A: .30 .75
161 Wirefly Hive U :A: .20 .50
162 Wurm's Tooth U :A: .20 .50
163 Blinkmoth Nexus R :L: 6.00 15.00
164 Darksteel Citadel C :L: .60 1.50
165 Mirrodin's Core U :L: .40 1.00

2004 Magic The Gathering Fifth Dawn

COMPLETE SET (165) 100.00 175.00
BOOSTER BOX (36 PACKS) 125.00 200.00
BOOSTER PACK (15 CARDS) 3.50 6.00
THEME DECK 10.00 15.00
FAT PACK 30.00 50.00
*FOIL: .75X TO 2X BASIC CARDS
RELEASED ON JUNE 4, 2004

1 Abuna's Chant C :W: .10 .25
2 Armed Response C :W: .10 .25
3 Auriok Champion R :W: 2.00 5.00
4 Auriok Salvagers U :W: .25 .60
5 Auriok Windwalker R :W: .30 .75
6 Beacon of Immortality R :W: 1.50 4.00
7 Bringer of the White Dawn R :W: .75 2.00
8 Circle of Protection: Artifacts U :W: .20 .50
9 Leonin Squire C :W: .10 .25
10 Loxodon Anchorite C :W: .10 .25
11 Loxodon Stalwart U :W: .20 .50
12 Raksha Golden Cub R :W: .75 2.00
13 Retaliate R :W: .30 .75
14 Roar of Reclamation R :W: .30 .75
15 Skyhunter Prowler C :W: .10 .25
16 Skyhunter Skirmisher U :W: .25 .60
17 Stand Firm C :W: .10 .25
18 Stasis Cocoon C :W: .10 .25
19 Steelshaper's Gift U :W: 2.00 5.00
20 Vanquish U :W: .20 .50
21 Acquire R :B: 1.00 2.50
22 Advanced Hoverguard C :B: .10 .25
23 Artificer's Intuition R :B: .30 .75
24 Beacon of Tomorrows R :B: 1.00 2.50
25 Blinkmoth Infusion R :B: .30 .75
26 Bringer of the Blue Dawn R :B: 1.25 3.00
27 Condescend C :B: .25 .60
28 Disruption Aura U :B: .20 .50
30 Eyes of the Watcher U :B: .20 .50
31 Fold into Æther U :B: .20 .50
32 Hoverguard Sweepers R :B: .25 .60
33 Into Thin Air C :B: .10 .25
34 Plasma Elemental U :B: .20 .50
35 Qumulox U :B: .20 .50
36 Serum Visions C :B: .60 1.50
37 Spectral Shift R :B: .25 .60
38 Thought Courier C :B: .10 .25
39 Trinket Mage C :B: .25 .60
40 Vedalken Mastermind U :B: .25 .60
41 Beacon of Unrest R :K: 1.50 4.00
42 Blind Creeper C :K: .10 .25
43 Bringer of the Black Dawn R :K: .75 2.00
44 Cackling Imp C :K: .10 .25
45 Desecration Elemental R :K: .30 .75
46 Devour in Shadow U :K: .20 .50
47 Dross Crocodile C :K: .10 .25
48 Early Frost C :B: .10 .25
48 Ebon Drake U :K: .20 .50
49 Endless Whispers R :K: .30 .75
50 Fill with Fright C :K: .10 .25
51 Fleshgrafter C :K: .10 .25
52 Lose Hope C :K: .10 .25
53 Mephidross Vampire R :K: 3.00 8.00
54 Moriok Rigger R :K: .30 .75
55 Night's Whisper U :K: .60 1.50
56 Nim Grotesque U :K: .20 .50
57 Plunge into Darkness R :K: .50 1.25
58 Relentless Rats U :K: .60 1.50
59 Shattered Dreams U :K: .20 .50
60 Vicious Betrayal C :K: .10 .25
61 Beacon of Destruction R :R: .40 1.00
62 Bringer of the Red Dawn R :R: .60 1.50
63 Cosmic Larva R :R: .30 .75
64 Feedback Bolt U :R: .20 .50
65 Furnace Whelp U :R: .25 .60
66 Goblin Brawler C :R: .10 .25
67 Granulate R :R: .30 .75
68 Ion Storm R :R: .30 .75
69 Iron-Barb Hellion U :R: .20 .50
70 Krark-Clan Engineers U :R: .20 .50
71 Krark-Clan Ogre C :R: .10 .25
72 Magma Giant R :R: .25 .60
73 Magma Jet U :R: 1.50 4.00
74 Magnetic Theft U :R: .20 .50
75 Mana Geyser C :R: .10 .25
76 Rain of Rust C :R: .10 .25
77 Reversal of Fortune R :R: .25 .60
78 Screaming Fury C :R: .10 .25
79 Spark Elemental C :R: .25 .60
80 Vulshok Sorcerer C :R: .10 .25
81 All Suns' Dawn R :G: .40 1.00
82 Beacon of Creation R :G: 1.25 3.00
83 Bringer of the Green Dawn R :G: .60 1.50
84 Channel the Suns U :G: .30 .75
85 Dawn's Reflection C :G: .10 .25
86 Eternal Witness U :G: 2.00 5.00
87 Fangren Pathcutter U :G: .20 .50
88 Ferocious Charge C :G: .10 .25
89 Joiner Adept R :G: .75 2.00
90 Ouphe Vandals U :G: .20 .50
91 Rite of Passage R :G: .30 .75
92 Rude Awakening R :G: .40 1.00
93 Sylvok Explorer C :G: .10 .25
94 Tangle Asp C :G: .10 .25
95 Tel-Jilad Justice U :G: .20 .50
96 Tel-Jilad Lifebreather C :G: .10 .25
97 Tornado Elemental R :G: .50 1.25
98 Tyrranax C :G: .10 .25
99 Viridian Lorebearers U :G: .20 .50
100 Viridian Scout C :G: .10 .25
101 Anodet Lurker C :A: .10 .25
102 Arachnoid U :A: .20 .50
103 Arcbound Wanderer U :A: .20 .50
104 Avarice Totem U :A: .20 .50
105 Baton of Courage C :A: .10 .25
106 Battered Golem C :A: .10 .25
107 Blasting Station U :A: .60 1.50
108 Chimeric Coils U :A: .20 .50
109 Clearwater Goblet R :A: .40 1.00
110 Clock of Omens U :A: .25 .60
111 Composite Golem U :A: .25 .60
112 Conjurer's Bauble C :A: .10 .25
113 Cranial Plating C :A: .75 2.00
114 Crucible of Worlds R :A: 10.00 25.00
115 Door to Nothingness R :A: .75 2.00
116 Doubling Cube R :A: 1.50 4.00
117 Energy Chamber U :A: .75 2.00
118 Engineered Explosives R :A: 6.00 15.00
119 Ensouled Scimitar U :A: .20 .50
120 Eon Hub R :A: .50 1.25
121 Etched Oracle U :A: .25 .60
122 Ferropede U :A: .20 .50
123 Fist of Suns R :A: .75 2.00
124 Gemstone Array U :A: .25 .60
125 Goblin Cannon U :A: .20 .50
126 Grafted Wargear U :A: .50 1.25
127 Grinding Station U :A: .25 .60
128 Guardian Idol U :A: .25 .60
129 Healer's Headdress C :A: .10 .25
130 Heliophial C :A: .10 .25
131 Helm of Kaldra R :A: 2.00 5.00
132 Horned Helm C :A: .10 .25
133 Infused Arrows U :A: .20 .50
134 Krark-Clan Ironworks U :A: .40 1.00
135 Lantern of Insight U :A: .20 .50
136 Lunar Avenger U :A: .20 .50
137 Mycosynth Golem R :A: 5.00 12.00
138 Myr Quadropod C :A: .10 .25
139 Myr Servitor C :A: .30 .75
140 Neurok Stealthsuit C :A: .10 .25
141 Opaline Bracers C :A: .10 .25
142 Paradise Mantle U :A: 1.25 3.00
143 Pentad Prism C :A: .10 .25
144 Possessed Portal R :A: .25 .60
145 Razorgrass Screen C :A: .10 .25
146 Razormane Masticore R :A: .30 .75
147 Relic Barrier U :A: .25 .60
148 Salvaging Station R :A: .30 .75
149 Sawtooth Thresher C :A: .10 .25
150 Silent Arbiter R :A: 1.25 3.00
151 Skullcage U :A: .20 .50
152 Skyreach Manta C :A: .10 .25
153 Solarion R :A: .40 1.00
154 Sparring Collar C :A: .10 .25
155 Spinal Parasite U :A: .20 .50
156 Staff of Domination R :A: 2.50 6.00
157 Summoner's Egg R :A: .40 1.00
158 Summoning Station R :A: .40 1.00
159 Suncrusher R :A: .25 .60
160 Suntouched Myr C :A: .10 .25
161 Synod Centurion U :A: .20 .50
162 Thermal Navigator C :A: .10 .25
163 Vedalken Orrery R :A: 2.00 5.00
164 Vedalken Shackles R :A: 8.00 20.00
165 Wayfarer's Bauble C :A: .10 .25

2004 Magic The Gathering Champions of Kamigawa

COMPLETE SET (307) 125.00 200.00
BOOSTER BOX (36 PACKS) 175.00 250.00
BOOSTER PACK (15 CARDS) 5.00 8.00
THEME DECK 9.00 12.00
*FOIL: .75X TO 2X BASIC CARDS
RELEASED ON OCTOBER 1, 2004

1 Blessed Breath C :W: .10 .25
2 Bushi Tenderfoot U :W: .25 .60
3 Cage of Hands C :W: .10 .25
4 Call to Glory C :W: .10 .25
5 Candles' Glow U :W: .20 .50
6 Cleanfall U :W: .25 .60
7 Devoted Retainer C :W: .10 .25
8 Eight-and-a-Half-Tails R :W: 1.50 4.00
9 Ethereal Haze C :W: .10 .25
10 Ghostly Prison U :W: 1.50 4.00
11 Harsh Deceiver C :W: .10 .25
12 Hikari, Twilight Guardian R :W: .30 .75
13 Hold the Line R :W: .30 .75
14 Honden of Cleansing Fire U :W: .30 .75
15 Horizon Seed U :W: .20 .50
16 Hundred-Talon Kami C :W: .10 .25
17 Indomitable Will C :W: .10 .25
18 Innocence Kami U :W: .20 .50
19 Isamaru, Hound of Konda R :W: 1.25 3.00
20 Kabuto Moth C :W: .10 .25
21 Kami of Ancient Law C :W: .10 .25
22 Kami of Old Stone U :W: .20 .50
23 Kami of the Painted Road C :W: .10 .25
24 Kami of the Palace Fields U :W: .20 .50
25 Kitsune Blademaster C :W: .10 .25
26 Kitsune Diviner C :W: .10 .25
27 Kitsune Healer C :W: .10 .25
28 Kitsune Mystic R :W: .30 .75
29 Kitsune Riftwalker C :W: .10 .25
30 Konda's Hatamoto U :W: 1.25 3.00
31 Konda's Banner R :A: .25 .60
32 Lantern Kami C :W: .10 .25
33 Masako the Humorless R :W: .30 .75
34 Mothrider Samurai C :W: .10 .25
35 Myojin of Cleansing Fire R :W: .60 1.50
36 Nagao, Bound by Honor U :W: .25 .60
37 Otherworldly Journey U :W: .25 .60
38 Pious Kitsune C :W: .10 .25
39 Quiet Purity C :W: .10 .25
40 Reciprocate U :W: .25 .60
41 Reverse the Sands R :W: .30 .75
42 Samurai Enforcers U :W: .25 .60
43 Samurai of the Pale Curtain U :W: .30 .75
44 Sensei Golden-Tail R :W: .40 1.00
45 Silent-Chant Zubera C :W: .10 .25
46 Takeno, Samurai General R :W: .30 .75
47 Terashi's Cry C :W: .10 .25
48 Vassal's Duty R :W: .30 .75
49 Vigilance C :W: .10 .25
50 Yosei, the Morning Star R :W: 3.00 8.00
51 Aura of Dominion U :B: .20 .50
53 Callous Deceiver C :B: .10 .25
54 Consuming Vortex C :B: .10 .25
55 Counsel of the Soratami C :B: .10 .25
56 Cut the Tethers U :B: .20 .50
57 Dampen Thought U :B: .25 .60
58 Eerie Procession U :B: .25 .60
59 Eye of Nowhere C :B: .10 .25
60 Field of Reality C :B: .10 .25
61 Floating-Dream Zubera C :B: .10 .25
62 Gifts Ungiven R :B: 5.00 12.00
63 Graceful Adept U :B: .25 .60
64 Guardian of Solitude U :B: .20 .50
65 Hinder U :B: .40 1.00
66 Hisoka's Guard C :B: .30 .75
67 Hisoka, Minamo Sensei R :B: .10 .25
68 Hisoka's Defiance C :B: .10 .25
69 Honden of Seeing Winds U :B: .30 .75
70 Jushi Apprentice R :B: .30 .75
71 Kami of Twisted Reflection C :B: .10 .25
72 Keiga, the Tide Star R :B: 2.50 6.00
73 Lifted by Clouds C :B: .10 .25
74 Meloku the Clouded Mirror R :B: .75 2.00
75 Myojin of Seeing Winds R :B: .30 .75
76 Mystic Restraints C :B: .10 .25
77 Part the Veil R :B: .30 .75
78 Peer Through Depths C :B: .30 .75
79 Petals of Insight U :B: .25 .60
8 Azami, Lady of Scrolls R :B: .75 2.00
80 Psychic Puppetry C :B: .10 .25
81 Reach Through Mists C :B: .10 .25
82 Reweave R :B: .30 .75
83 River Kaijin C :B: .10 .25
84 Sift Through Sands C :B: .10 .25
85 Sire of the Storm U :B: .25 .60
86 Soratami Cloudskater C :B: .10 .25
87 Soratami Mirror-Guard C :B: .10 .25
88 Soratami Mirror-Mage U :B: .20 .50
89 Soratami Rainshaper C :B: .10 .25
90 Soratami Savant U :B: .25 .60
91 Soratami Seer U :B: .20 .50
92 Squelch U :B: .25 .60
93 Student of Elements U :B: .20 .50
94 Swirl the Mists R :B: .30 .75
95 Teller of Tales R :B: .10 .25
96 Thoughtbind C :B: .10 .25
97 Time Stop R :B: .50 1.25
98 The Unspeakable R :B: .30 .75
99 Uyo, Silent Prophet R :B: .30 .75
100 Wandering Ones C :B: .10 .25
101 Ashen-Skin Zubera C :K: .10 .25
102 Befoul C :K: .10 .25
103 Blood Speaker U :K: .25 .60
104 Bloodthirsty Ogre U :K: .25 .60
105 Cranial Extraction R :K: .75 2.00
106 Cruel Deceiver C :K: .10 .25
107 Cursed Ronin C :K: .10 .25
108 Dance of Shadows U :K: .25 .60
109 Deathcurse Ogre C :K: .10 .25
110 Devouring Greed C :K: .10 .25
111 Distress C :K: .10 .25
112 Gibbering Kami C :K: .10 .25
113 Gutwrencher Oni U :K: .25 .60
114 He Who Hungers R :K: .30 .75
115 Hideous Laughter U :K: .25 .60
116 Honden of Night's Reach U :K: .25 .60
117 Horobi, Death's Wail R :K: .30 .75
118 Iname, Death Aspect R :K: .30 .75
119 Kami of Lunacy U :K: .20 .50
120 Kami of the Waning Moon C :K: .10 .25
121 Kiku, Night's Flower R :K: .40 1.00
122 Kokusho, the Evening Star R :K: 4.00 10.00
123 Kuro, Pitlord R :K: .30 .75
124 Marrow-Gnawer R :K: 1.50 4.00
125 Midnight Covenant C :K: .10 .25
126 Myojin of Night's Reach R :K: .75 2.00
127 Nezumi Bone-Reader U :K: .25 .60
128 Nezumi Cutthroat C :K: .10 .25
129 Nezumi Graverobber U :K: .30 .75
130 Nezumi Ronin C :K: .10 .25
131 Nezumi Shortfang R :K: 1.25 3.00
132 Night Dealings R :K: .30 .75
133 Night of Souls' Betrayal R :K: .30 .75
134 Numai Outcast U :K: .20 .50
135 Oni Possession U :K: .20 .50
136 Painwracker Oni U :K: .20 .50
137 Pull Under C :K: .10 .25
138 Rag Dealer C :K: .10 .25
139 Ragged Veins C :K: .10 .25
140 Rend Flesh C :K: .25 .60
141 Rend Spirit C :K: .10 .25
142 Scuttling Death C :K: .10 .25
143 Seizan, Perverter of Truth R :K: .30 .75
144 Soulless Revival C :K: .10 .25
145 Struggle for Sanity U :K: .20 .50
146 Swallowing Plague U :K: .20 .50
147 Thief of Hope U :K: .25 .60
148 Villainous Ogre C :K: .10 .25
149 Waking Nightmare C :K: .10 .25
150 Wicked Akuba C :K: .10 .25
151 Akki Avalanchers C :R: .10 .25
152 Akki Coalflinger U :R: .20 .50
153 Akki Lavarunner R :R: .30 .75
154 Akki Rockspeaker C :R: .10 .25
155 Akki Underminer U :R: .25 .60
156 Battle-Mad Ronin C :R: .10 .25
157 Ben-Ben, Akki Hermit R :R: .30 .75
158 Blind with Anger U :R: .25 .60
159 Blood Rites U :R: .20 .50
160b Brothers Yamazaki U :R: .30 .75
160a Brothers Yamazaki U :R: .30 .75
161 Brutal Deceiver C :R: .10 .25
162 Crushing Pain C :R: .10 .25
163 Desperate Ritual C :R: .40 1.00
164 Devouring Rage C :R: .10 .25
165 Earthshaker U :R: .20 .50
166 Ember-Fist Zubera C :R: .10 .25
167 Frostwielder C :R: .10 .25
168 Glacial Ray C :R: .10 .25
169 Godo, Bandit Warlord R :R: .75 2.00
170 Hanabi Blast U :R: .20 .50
171 Hearth Kami C :R: .10 .25
172 Honden of Infinite Rage U :R: .25 .60
173 Initiate of Blood U :R: .20 .50
174 Kami of Fire's Roar C :R: .10 .25
175 Kiki-Jiki, Mirror Breaker R :R: 6.00 15.00
176 Kumano's Pupils U :R: .20 .50
177 Kumano, Master Yamabushi R :R: .30 .75
178 Lava Spike C :R: 1.25 3.00
179 Mana Seism U :R: .20 .50
180 Mindblaze R :R: .30 .75
181 Myojin of Infinite Rage R :R: .40 1.00
182 Ore Gorger U :R: .20 .50
183 Pain Kami U :R: .20 .50
184 Ronin Houndmaster C :R: .10 .25
185 Ryusei, the Falling Star R :R: .75 2.00
186 Shimatsu the Bloodcloaked R :R: .30 .75
187 Sideswipe U :R: .20 .50
188 Sokenzan Bruiser C :R: .10 .25
189 Soul of Magma C :R: .10 .25
190 Soulblast R :R: .30 .75
191 Stone Rain C :R: .10 .25
192 Strange Inversion U :R: .20 .50
193 Through the Breach R :R: 2.50 6.00
194 Tide of War R :R: .30 .75
195 Uncontrollable Anger C :R: .10 .25
196 Unearthly Blizzard C :R: .10 .25
197 Unnatural Speed C :R: .10 .25
198 Yamabushi's Flame C :R: .10 .25
199 Yamabushi's Storm C :R: .10 .25
200 Zo-Zu the Punisher R :R: .30 .75
201 Azusa, Lost but Seeking R :G: 2.00 5.00
202 Budoka Gardener R :G: .40 1.00
203 Burr Grafter C :G: .10 .25
204 Commune with Nature C :G: .10 .25
205 Dosan the Falling Leaf R :G: .30 .75
206 Dripping-Tongue Zubera C :G: .10 .25
207 Feast of Worms U :G: .20 .50
208 Feral Deceiver C :G: .10 .25
209 Gale Force U :G: .20 .50
210 Glimpse of Nature R :G: 8.00 20.00
211 Hana Kami U :G: .25 .60
212 Heartbeat of Spring R :G: .60 1.50
213 Honden of Life's Web U :G: .25 .60
214 Humble Budoka C :G: .10 .25
215 Iname, Life Aspect R :G: .30 .75
216 Joyous Respite C :G: .10 .25
217 Jugan, the Rising Star R :G: 1.25 3.00
218 Jukai Messenger C :G: .10 .25
219 Kami of the Hunt C :G: .10 .25
220 Kashi-Tribe Reaver U :G: .25 .60
221 Kashi-Tribe Warriors C :G: .10 .25
222 Kodama of the North Tree R :G: .40 1.00
223 Kodama of the South Tree R :G: .30 .75
224 Kodama's Might C :G: .10 .25
225 Kodama's Reach C :G: .30 .75
226 Lure U :G: .25 .60
227 Matsu-Tribe Decoy C :G: .10 .25
228 Moss Kami C :G: .10 .25
229 Myojin of Life's Web R :G: 1.25 3.00
230 Nature's Will R :G: .30 .75
231 Orbweaver Kumo U :G: .20 .50
232 Order of the Sacred Bell C :G: .10 .25
233 Orochi Eggwatcher U :G: .25 .60
234 Orochi Leafcaller C :G: .10 .25
235 Orochi Ranger C :G: .10 .25
236 Orochi Sustainer C :G: .10 .25
237 Rootrunner U :G: .20 .50
238 Sachi, Daughter of Seshiro U :G: .25 .60
239 Sakura-Tribe Elder C :G: .40 1.00
240 Serpent Skin C :G: .10 .25
241 Seshiro the Anointed R :G: .60 1.50
242 Shisato, Whispering Hunter R :G: .30 .75
243 Soilshaper U :G: .20 .50
244 Sosuke, Son of Seshiro U :G: .25 .60
245 Strength of Cedars U :G: .20 .50
246 Thousand-legged Kami U :G: .20 .50
247 Time of Need U :G: .30 .75
248 Venerable Kumo C :G: .10 .25
249 Vine Kami C :G: .10 .25
250 Wear Away C :G: .10 .25
251 General's Kabuto R :A: .75 2.00
252 Hair-Strung Koto R :A: .30 .75
253 Hankyu U :A: .20 .50
254 Honor-Worn Shaku U :A: .20 .50
255 Imi Statue R :A: .30 .75
256 Jade Idol U :A: .20 .50
257 Journeyer's Kite R :A: 1.25 3.00
258 Junkyo Bell R :A: .30 .75
259 Konda, Lord of Eiganjo R :W: 1.25 3.00
260 Kusari-Gama R :A: .30 .75
261 Long-Forgotten Gohei R :A: .30 .75
262 Moonring Mirror R :A: .30 .75
263 Nine-Ringed Bo U :A: .20 .50
264 No-Dachi U :A: .25 .60
265 Oathkeeper, Takeno's Daisho R :A: .30 .75
266 Orochi Hatchery R :A: .30 .75
267 Reito Lantern U :A: .25 .60
268 Sensei's Divining Top U :A: 6.00 15.00
269 Shell of the Last Kappa R :A: .30 .75
270 Tatsumasa, the Dragon's Fang R :A: 1.00 2.50
271 Tenza, Godo's Maul U :A: .25 .60
272 Uba Mask R :A: .30 .75
273 Boseiju, Who Shelters All R :L: 2.00 5.00
274 Cloudcrest Lake U :L: .25 .60

275 Eiganjo Castle R :L:	.75	2.00
276 Forbidden Orchard R :L:	2.50	6.00
277 Hall of the Bandit Lord R :L:	.50	1.25
278 Lantern-Lit Graveyard U :L:	.25	.60
279 Minamo, School at Water's Edge R :L:	2.00	5.00
280 Okina, Temple to the Grandfathers R :L:	.40	1.00
281 Pinecrest Ridge U :L:	.25	.60
282 Shinka, the Bloodsoaked Keep R :L:	.40	1.00
283 Shizo, Death's Storehouse R :L:	1.50	4.00
284 Tranquil Garden U :L:	.25	.60
285 Untaidake, the Cloud Keeper R :L:	.30	.75
286 Waterveil Cavern U :L:	.25	.60
287 Plains L :L:	.10	.25
288 Plains L :L:	.10	.25
289 Plains L :L:	.10	.25
290 Plains L :L:	.10	.25
291 Island L :L:	.10	.25
292 Island L :L:	.10	.25
293 Island L :L:	.10	.25
294 Island L :L:	.10	.25
295 Swamp L :L:	.10	.25
296 Swamp L :L:	.10	.25
297 Swamp L :L:	.10	.25
298 Swamp L :L:	.10	.25
299 Mountain L :L:	.10	.25
300 Mountain L :L:	.10	.25
301 Mountain L :L:	.10	.25
302 Mountain L :L:	.10	.25
303 Forest L :L:	.10	.25
304 Forest L :L:	.10	.25
305 Forest L :L:	.10	.25
306 Forest L :L:	.10	.25

2005 Magic The Gathering Betrayers of Kamigawa

COMPLETE SET (165)	75.00	150.00
BOOSTER BOX (36 PACKS)	150.00	200.00
BOOSTER PACK (15 CARDS)	4.00	6.00
THEME DECK	10.00	25.00
FAT PACK	40.00	80.00
*FOIL: .75X TO 2X BASIC CARDS		
RELEASED ON FEBRUARY 4, 2005		
1 Day of Destiny R :W:	.30	.75
2 Empty-Shrine Kannushi U :W:	.12	.30
3 Faithful Squire U :W:	.10	.25
4 Final Judgment R :W:	1.25	3.00
5 Genju of the Fields U :W:	.20	.50
6 Heart of Light C :W:	.08	.20
7 Hokori, Dust Drinker R :W:	.40	1.00
8 Hundred-Talon Strike C :W:	.08	.20
9 Indebted Samurai U :W:	.20	.50
10 Kami of False Hope C :W:	.08	.20
11 Kami of Tattered Shoji C :W:	.08	.20
12 Kami of the Honored Dead U :W:	.10	.25
13 Kentaro, the Smiling Cat R :W:	.30	.75
14 Kitsune Palliator U :W:	.10	.25
15 Mending Hands C :W:	.08	.20
16 Moonlit Strider C :W:	.08	.20
17 Opal-Eye, Konda's Yojimbo R :W:	.40	1.00
18 Oyobi, Who Split the Heavens R :W:	.25	.60
19 Patron of the Kitsune R :W:	.25	.60
20 Scour U :W:	.12	.30
21 Shining Shoal R :W:	.40	1.00
22 Silverstorm Samurai C :W:	.08	.20
23 Split-Tail Miko C :W:	.08	.20
24 Takeno's Cavalry C :W:	.08	.20
25 Tallowisp U :W:	.15	.40
26 Terashi's Grasp C :W:	.08	.20
27 Terashi's Verdict U :W:	.10	.25
28 Ward of Piety U :W:	.10	.25
29 Waxmane Baku C :W:	.08	.20
30 Yomiji, Who Bars the Way R :W:	.25	.60
31 Callow Jushi U :B:	.10	.25
32 Chisei, Heart of Oceans R :B:	.25	.60
33 Disrupting Shoal R :B:	2.00	5.00
34 Floodbringer C :B:	.08	.20
35 Genju of the Falls U :B:	.15	.40
36 Heed the Mists U :B:	.10	.25
37 Higure, the Still Wind R :B:	.75	2.00
38 Jetting Glasskite U :B:	.10	.25
39 Kaijin of the Vanishing Touch U :B:	.12	.30
40 Kira, Great Glass-Spinner R :B:	8.00	20.00
41 Minamo Sightbender U :B:	.10	.25
42 Minamo's Meddling C :B:	.08	.20
43 Mistblade Shinobi C :B:	.10	.25
44 Ninja of the Deep Hours C :B:	.20	.50
45 Patron of the Moon R :B:	.30	.75
46 Phantom Wings C :B:	.08	.20
47 Quash U :B:	.20	.50
48 Quillmane Baku C :B:	.08	.20
49 Reduce to Dreams R :B:	.25	.60
50 Ribbons of the Reikai C :B:	.08	.20
51 Shimmering Glasskite C :B:	.08	.20
52 Soratami Mindsweeper U :B:	.10	.25
53 Stream of Consciousness U :B:	.10	.25
54 Sway of the Stars R :B:	.25	.60
55 Teardrop Kami C :B:	.08	.20
56 Threads of Disloyalty R :B:	2.00	5.00
57 Toils of Night and Day C :B:	.08	.20
58 Tomorrow, Azami's Familiar R :B:	.25	.60
59 Veil of Secrecy C :B:	.08	.20
60 Walker of Secret Ways U :B:	.25	.60
61 Iwamori of the Open Fist R :G:	.30	.75
61 Bile Urchin C :K:	.08	.20
62 Blessing of Leeches C :K:	.08	.20
63 Call for Blood C :K:	.08	.20
64 Crawling Filth C :K:	.08	.20
65 Eradicate U :K:	.30	.75
66 Genju of the Fens U :K:	.12	.30
67 Goryo's Vengeance R :K:	2.00	5.00
68 Hero's Demise R :K:	.30	.75
69 Hired Muscle U :K:	.10	.25
70 Horobi's Whisper C :K:	.08	.20
71 Ink-Eyes, Servant of Oni R :K:	5.00	12.00
72 Kyoki, Sanity's Eclipse R :K:	.25	.60
73 Mark of the Oni U :K:	.10	.25
74 Nezumi Shadow-Watcher U :K:	.10	.25
75 Ogre Marauder U :K:	.15	.40
76 Okiba-Gang Shinobi C :K:	.10	.25
77 Patron of the Nezumi R :K:	.25	.60
78 Psychic Spear C :K:	.08	.20
79 Pus Kami U :K:	.10	.25
80 Scourge of Numai U :K:	.10	.25
81 Shirei, Shizo's Caretaker R :K:	.60	1.50
82 Sickening Shoal R :K:	.40	1.00
83 Skullmane Baku C :K:	.08	.20
84 Skullsnatcher C :K:	.08	.20
85 Stir the Grave C :K:	.08	.20
86 Takenuma Bleeder C :K:	.08	.20
87 Three Tragedies U :K:	.10	.25
88 Throat Slitter U :K:	.50	1.25
89 Toshiro Umezawa R :K:	.30	.75
90 Yukora, the Prisoner R :K:	.25	.60
91 Akki Blizzard-Herder C :R:	.08	.20
92 Akki Raider U :R:	.10	.25
93 Ashen Monstrosity U :R:	.10	.25
94 Aura Barbs U :R:	.10	.25
95 Blademane Baku C :R:	.08	.20
96 Blazing Shoal R :R:	1.50	4.00
97 Clash of Realities R :R:	.25	.60
98 Crack the Earth C :R:	.08	.20
99 Cunning Bandit U :R:	.10	.25
100 First Volley C :R:	.08	.20
101 Flames of the Blood Hand U :R:	.60	1.50
102 Frost Ogre C :R:	.08	.20
103 Frostling C :R:	.08	.20
104 Fumiko the Lowblood R :R:	.50	1.25
105 Genju of the Spires U :R:	.30	.75
106 Goblin Cohort C :R:	.08	.20
107 Heartless Hidetsugu R :R:	.30	.75
108 In the Web of War R :R:	.30	.75
109 Ire of Kaminari C :R:	.08	.20
110 Ishi-Ishi, Akki Crackshot R :R:	.25	.60
111 Kumano's Blessing C :R:	.08	.20
112 Mannichi, the Fevered Dream R :R:	.25	.60
113 Ogre Recluse U :R:	.10	.25
114 Overblaze U :R:	.10	.25
115 Patron of the Akki R :R:	.25	.60
116 Ronin Cliffrider U :R:	.10	.25
117 Shinka Gatekeeper C :R:	.08	.20
118 Sowing Salt U :R:	.12	.30
119 Torrent of Stone C :R:	.08	.20
120 Twist Allegiance R :R:	.25	.60
121 Body of Jukai U :G:	.10	.25
122 Budoka Pupil U :G:	.10	.25
123 Child of Thorns C :G:	.08	.20
124 Enshrined Memories R :G:	.30	.75
125 Forked-Branch Garami U :G:	.10	.25
126 Genju of the Cedars U :G:	.15	.40
127 Gnarled Mass C :G:	.08	.20
128 Harbinger of Spring C :G:	.08	.20
129 Isao, Enlightened Bushi R :G:	.30	.75
131 Kodama of the Center Tree R :G:	.25	.60
132 Lifegift R :G:	.50	1.25
133 Lifespinner U :G:	.12	.30
134 Loam Dweller U :G:	.10	.25
135 Mark of Sakiko U :G:	.12	.30
136 Matsu-Tribe Sniper C :G:	.08	.20
137 Nourishing Shoal R :G:	.25	.60
138 Patron of the Orochi R :G:	1.00	2.50
139 Petalmane Baku C :G:	.08	.20
140 Roar of Jukai C :G:	.08	.20
141 Sakiko, Mother of Summer R :G:	.30	.75
142 Sakura-Tribe Springcaller C :G:	.08	.20
143 Scaled Hulk C :G:	.08	.20
144 Shizuko, Caller of Autumn R :G:	.25	.60
145 Sosuke's Summons U :G:	.30	.75
146 Splinter U :G:	.15	.40
147 Traproot Kami C :G:	.08	.20
148 Unchecked Growth U :G:	.10	.25
149 Uproot C :G:	.08	.20
150 Vital Surge C :G:	.08	.20
151 Genju of the Realm R :D:	.60	1.50
152 Baku Altar R :A:	.25	.60
153 Blinding Powder U :A:	.20	.50
154 Mirror Gallery R :A:	1.50	4.00
155 Neko-Te R :A:	.50	1.25
156 Orb of Dreams R :A:	.30	.75
157 Ornate Kanzashi R :A:	.25	.60
158 Ronin Warclub U :A:	.15	.40
159 Shuko U :A:	.20	.50
160 Shuriken U :A:	.20	.50
161 Slumbering Tora R :A:	.25	.60
162 That Which Was Taken R :A:	1.50	4.00
163 Umezawa's Jitte R :A:	8.00	20.00
164 Gods' Eye, Gate to the Reikai U :L:	.20	.50
165 Tendo Ice Bridge R :L:	1.25	3.00

2005 Magic The Gathering Saviors of Kamigawa

COMPLETE SET (165)	75.00	150.00
BOOSTER BOX (36 PACKS)	100.00	150.00
BOOSTER PACK (15 CARDS)	3.00	5.00
THEME DECK	5.00	10.00
FAT PACK	25.00	50.00
*FOIL: .75X TO 2X BASIC CARDS		
RELEASED ON JUNE 3, 2005		
1 AEther Shockwave U :W:	.10	.25
2 Araba Mothrider C :W:	.08	.20
3 Celestial Kirin R :W:	.30	.75
4 Charge Across the Araba U :W:	.10	.25
5 Cowed by Wisdom C :W:	.08	.20
6 Curtain of Light C :W:	.08	.20
7 Descendant of Kiyomaro U :W:	.10	.25
8 Eiganjo Free-Riders U :W:	.10	.25
9 Enduring Ideal R :W:	.75	2.00
10 Ghost-Lit Redeemer U :W:	.20	.50
11 Hail of Arrows U :W:	.10	.25
12 Hand of Honor U :W:	.50	1.25
13 Inner-Chamber Guard U :W:	.20	.50
14 Kataki, War's Wage R :W:	2.50	6.00
15 Kitsune Bonesetter C :W:	.08	.20
16 Kitsune Dawnblade C :W:	.08	.20
17 Kitsune Loreweaver C :W:	.08	.20
18 Kiyomaro, First to Stand R :W:	.25	.60
19 Michiko Konda, Truth Seeker R :W:	1.25	3.00
20 Moonwing Moth C :W:	.08	.20
21 Nikko-Onna U :W:	.10	.25
22 Plow Through Reito C :W:	.08	.20
23 Presence of the Wise U :W:	.10	.25
24 Promise of Bunrei R :W:	.75	2.00
25 Pure Intentions R :W:	.25	.60
26 Reverence R :W:	.30	.75
27 Rune-Tail, Kitsune Ascendant R :W:	1.25	3.00
28 Shinen of Stars' Light C :W:	.08	.20
29 Spiritual Visit C :W:	.08	.20
30 Torii Watchward C :W:	.08	.20
31 Cloudhoof Kirin R :B:	.25	.60
32 Cut the Earthly Bond C :B:	.08	.20
33 Descendant of Soramaro C :B:	.08	.20
34 Dreamcatcher C :B:	.08	.20
35 Erayo, Soratami Ascendant R :B:	3.00	8.00
36 Eternal Dominion R :B:	1.00	2.50
37 Evermind U :B:	.10	.25
38 Freed from the Real C :B:	.20	.50
39 Ghost-Lit Warder U :B:	.10	.25
40 Ideas Unbound C :B:	.20	.50
41 Kaho, Minamo Historian R :B:	.40	1.00
42 Kami of the Crescent Moon R :B:	.60	1.50
43 Kiri-Onna U :B:	.10	.25
44 Meishin, the Mind Cage R :B:	.30	.75
45 Minamo Scrollkeeper C :B:	.08	.20
46 Moonbow Illusionist C :B:	.08	.20
47 Murmurs from Beyond C :B:	.08	.20
48 Oboro Envoy U :B:	.10	.25
49 Oboro, Palace in the Clouds R :L:	1.00	2.50
50 Oppressive Will C :B:	.08	.20
51 Overwhelming Intellect U :B:	.20	.50
52 Rushing-Tide Zubera U :B:	.10	.25
53 Sakashima the Impostor R :B:	2.00	5.00
54 Secretkeeper U :B:	.10	.25
55 Shape Stealer U :B:	.20	.50
56 Shifting Borders U :B:	.10	.25
57 Shinen of Flight's Wings C :B:	.08	.20
58 Soramaro, First to Dream R :B:	.25	.60
58 Haru-Onna U :G:	.08	.20
59 Trusted Advisor U :B:	.10	.25
60 Twincast R :B:	1.25	3.00
61 Akuta, Born of Ash R :K:	.25	.60
62 Choice of Damnations R :K:	1.00	2.50
63 Death Denied C :K:	.08	.20
64 Death of a Thousand Stings C :K:	.08	.20
65 Deathknell Kami C :K:	.08	.20
66 Deathmask Nezumi C :K:	.08	.20
67 Exile into Darkness U :K:	.10	.25
68 Footsteps of the Goryo U :K:	.20	.50
69 Ghost-Lit Stalker U :K:	.10	.25
70 Gnat Miser C :K:	.08	.20
71 Hand of Cruelty U :K:	.30	.75
72 Infernal Kirin R :K:	.30	.75
73 Kagemaro, First to Suffer R :K:	.60	1.50
74 Kagemaro's Clutch C :K:	.08	.20
75 Kami of Empty Graves C :K:	.08	.20
76 Kemuri-Onna U :K:	.10	.25
77 Kiku's Shadow U :K:	.20	.50
78 Kuon, Ogre Ascendant R :K:	.25	.60
79 Kuro's Taken C :K:	.08	.20
80 Locust Miser U :K:	.20	.50
81 Maga, Traitor to Mortals R :K:	.50	1.25
82 Measure of Wickedness U :K:	.10	.25
83 Neverending Torment R :K:	.30	.75
84 One with Nothing R :K:	.30	.75
85 Pain's Reward R :K:	.30	.75
86 Raving Oni-Slave C :K:	.08	.20
87 Razorjaw Oni U :K:	.10	.25
88 Shinen of Fear's Chill C :K:	.08	.20
89 Sink into Takenuma C :K:	.08	.20
90 Skull Collector U :K:	.10	.25
91 Adamaro, First to Desire R :R:	.25	.60
92 Akki Drillmaster C :R:	.08	.20
93 Akki Underling C :R:	.08	.20
94 Barrel Down Sokenzan C :R:	.08	.20
95 Burning-Eye Zubera U :R:	.10	.25
96 Captive Flame U :R:	.10	.25
97 Feral Lightning U :R:	.10	.25
98 Gaze of Adamaro U :R:	.10	.25
99 Ghost-Lit Raider U :R:	.10	.25
100 Glitterfang C :R:	.08	.20
101 Godo's Irregulars U :R:	.10	.25
102 Hidetsugu's Second Rite R :R:	.50	1.25
103 Homura, Human Ascendant R :R:	.50	1.25
104 Iizuka the Ruthless R :R:	.30	.75
105 Inner Fire C :R:	.08	.20
106 Into the Fray C :R:	.08	.20
107 Jiwari, the Earth Aflame R :R:	.25	.60
108 Oni of Wild Places U :R:	.10	.25
109 Path of Anger's Flame C :R:	.08	.20
110 Rally the Horde R :R:	.25	.60
111 Ronin Cavekeeper C :R:	.08	.20
112 Shinen of Fury's Fire C :R:	.08	.20
113 Skyfire Kirin R :R:	.25	.60
114 Sokenzan Renegade U :R:	.08	.20
115 Sokenzan Spellblade C :R:	.08	.20
116 Spiraling Embers C :R:	.08	.20
117 Sunder from Within U :R:	.10	.25
118 Thoughts of Ruin R :R:	.30	.75
119 Undying Flames R :R:	.25	.60
120 Yuki-Onna U :R:	.10	.25
121 Arashi, the Sky Asunder R :G:	.50	1.25
122 Ayumi, the Last Visitor R :G:	.30	.75
123 Bounteous Kirin R :G:	.25	.60
124 Briarknit Kami U :G:	.20	.50
125 Dense Canopy U :G:	.10	.25
126 Descendant of Masumaro U :G:	.10	.25
127 Dosan's Oldest Chant C :G:	.08	.20
128 Elder Pine of Jukai C :G:	.08	.20
129 Endless Swarm R :G:	.30	.75
130 Fiddlehead Kami C :G:	.08	.20
131 Ghost-Lit Nourisher U :G:	.10	.25
133 Inner Calm, Outer Strength C :G:	.08	.20
134 Kami of the Tended Garden U :G:	.10	.25
135 Kashi-Tribe Elite U :G:	.25	.60
136 Masumaro, First to Live R :G:	.30	.75
137 Matsu-Tribe Birdstalker C :G:	.08	.20
138 Molting Skin U :G:	.10	.25
139 Nightsoil Kami C :G:	.08	.20
140 O-Naginata U :A:	.25	.60
141 Promised Kannushi C :G:	.08	.20
142 Reki, the History of Kamigawa R :G:	.30	.75
143 Rending Vines C :G:	.08	.20
144 Sakura-Tribe Scout C :G:	.10	.25
145 Sasaya, Orochi Ascendant R :G:	.30	.75
146 Seed the Land R :G:	.30	.75
147 Seek the Horizon U :G:	.20	.50
148 Sekki, Seasons' Guide R :G:	.40	1.00
149 Shinen of Life's Roar C :G:	.08	.20
150 Stampeding Serow U :G:	.10	.25
151 Iname as One R :D:	.30	.75
152 Ashes of the Fallen R :A:	.25	.60
153 Blood Clock R :A:	.30	.75
154 Ebony Owl Netsuke U :A:	.20	.50
155 Ivory Crane Netsuke U :A:	.10	.25
156 Manriki-Gusari U :A:	.60	1.50
157 Oboro Breezecaller C :B:	.08	.20
158 Pithing Needle R :A:	1.50	4.00
159 Scroll of Origins R :A:	.25	.60
160 Soratami Cloud Chariot U :A:	.10	.25
161 Wine of Blood and Iron R :A:	.25	.60
162 Mikokoro, Center of the Sea R :L:	2.00	5.00
163 Miren, the Moaning Well R :L:	2.50	6.00
164 Okina Nightwatch C :G:	.08	.20
165 Tomb of Urami R :L:	.30	.75

2005 Magic The Gathering 9th Edition

COMPLETE SET (350)	125.00	200.00
BOOSTER BOX (36 PACKS)	100.00	175.00
BOOSTER PACK (15 CARDS)	3.00	5.00
FAT PACK	50.00	80.00
*FOIL: .75X TO 2X BASIC CARDS		
RELEASED ON JULY 29, 2005		
1 Angel of Mercy U :W:	.15	.40
2 Angelic Blessing C :W:	.08	.20
3 Aven Cloudchaser C :W:	.08	.20
4 Aven Flock C :W:	.08	.20
5 Ballista Squad U :W:	.10	.25
6 Blessed Orator U :W:	.10	.25
7 Blinding Angel R :W:	1.25	3.00
8 Blinking Spirit R :W:	.30	.75
9 Chastise U :W:	.15	.40
10 Circle of Protection: Black U :W:	.10	.25
11 Circle of Protection: Red U :W:	.20	.50
12 Crossbow Infantry C :W:	.08	.20
13 Demystify C :W:	.08	.20
14 Foot Soldiers C :W:	.08	.20
15 Gift of Estates U :W:	.75	2.00
16 Glorious Anthem R :W:	1.00	2.50
18 Holy Day C :W:	.10	.25
19 Holy Strength C :W:	.08	.20
20 Honor Guard C :W:	.08	.20
21 Infantry Veteran C :W:	.08	.20
22 Inspirit U :W:	.10	.25
23 Ivory Mask R :W:	.75	2.00
24 Kami of Old Stone U :W:	.10	.25
25 Leonin Skyhunter U :W:	.20	.50
26 Marble Titan R :W:	.30	.75
27 Master Decoy C :W:	.08	.20
28 Master Healer R :W:	.25	.60
29 Mending Hands C :W:	.08	.20
30 Oracle's Attendants R :W:	.25	.60
31 Pacifism C :W:	.08	.20
32 Paladin en-Vec R :W:	.75	2.00
33 Peace of Mind U :W:	.10	.25
34 Pegasus Charger C :W:	.08	.20
35 Reverse Damage R :W:	.40	1.00
36 Righteousness R :W:	.25	.60
37 Sacred Ground R :W:	.40	1.00
38 Sacred Nectar C :W:	.08	.20
39 Samite Healer C :W:	.08	.20
40 Sanctum Guardian U :W:	.10	.25
41 Savannah Lions R :W:	.75	2.00
42 Seasoned Marshal U :W:	.10	.25
43 Serra Angel R :W:	.60	1.50
44 Serra's Blessing U :W:	.60	1.50
45 Skyhunter Prowler C :W:	.08	.20
46 Soul Warden U :W:	.40	1.00
47 Spirit Link U :W:	.20	.50
48 Story Circle R :W:	.75	2.00
49 Suntail Hawk C :W:	.08	.20
50 Tempest of Light U :W:	.10	.25
51 Venerable Monk C :W:	.08	.20
52 Veteran Cavalier C :W:	.08	.20
53 Warrior's Honor C :W:	.08	.20
54 Weathered Wayfarer R :W:	2.00	5.00
55 Worship R :W:	1.25	3.00
56 Wrath of God R :W:	4.00	10.00
57 Zealous Inquisitor U :W:	.10	.25
58 Air Elemental U :B:	.10	.25
59 Annex U :B:	.15	.40
60 Archivist R :B:	.40	1.00
61 Aven Fisher C :B:	.08	.20
62 Aven Windreader C :B:	.08	.20
63 Azure Drake U :B:	.10	.25
64 Baleful Stare U :B:	.10	.25
65 Battle of Wits R :B:	.40	1.00
66 Boomerang C :B:	.08	.20
67 Clone R :B:	.40	1.00
68 Confiscate U :B:	.15	.40
69 Counsel of the Soratami C :B:	.08	.20
70 Cowardice R :B:	.25	.60
71 Crafty Pathmage C :B:	.08	.20
72 Daring Apprentice R :B:	.30	.75
73 Dehydration C :B:	.08	.20
74 Dream Prowler U :B:	.10	.25
75 Evacuation R :B:	.75	2.00
76 Exhaustion U :B:	.20	.50
77 Fishliver Oil C :B:	.08	.20
78 Fleeting Image R :B:	.25	.60
79 Flight C :B:	.08	.20
80 Fugitive Wizard C :B:	.08	.20
81 Horned Turtle C :B:	.08	.20
82 Imaginary Pet R :B:	.30	.75
83 Levitation U :B:	.10	.25
84 Lumengrid Warden C :B:	.08	.20
85 Mahamoti Djinn R :B:	.25	.60
86 Mana Leak C :B:	.40	1.00
87 Mind Bend R :B:	.25	.60
88 Phantom Warrior U :B:	.10	.25
89 Plagiarize R :B:	.30	.75
90 Polymorph R :B:	.60	1.50
91 Puppeteer U :B:	.10	.25
92 Reminisce U :B:	.15	.40
93 Remove Soul C :B:	.08	.20
94 Rewind U :B:	.50	1.25
95 Sage Aven C :B:	.08	.20
96 Sea Monster C :B:	.08	.20
97 Sea's Claim C :B:	.08	.20
98 Sift C :B:	.08	.20
99 Sleight of Hand C :B:	.60	1.50
100 Storm Crow C :B:	.08	.20
101 Telepathy U :B:	.10	.25
102 Temporal Adept R :B:	.60	1.50
103 Thieving Magpie U :B:	.10	.25
104 Thought Courier U :B:	.10	.25
105 Tidal Kraken R :B:	.50	1.25
106 Tidings U :B:	.30	.75
107 Time Ebb C :B:	.08	.20
108 Trade Routes R :B:	.30	.75
109 Traumatize R :B:	1.00	2.50
110 Treasure Trove U :B:	.10	.25
111 Wanderguard Sentry C :B:	.08	.20
112 Wind Drake C :B:	.08	.20
113 Withering Gaze U :B:	.10	.25
114 Zur's Weirding R :B:	.30	.75
115 Blackmail U :K:	.40	1.00
116 Glory Seeker C :W:	.08	.20
116 Bog Imp C :K:	.08	.20
117 Bog Wraith U :K:	.10	.25
118 Coercion C :K:	.08	.20
119 Consume Spirit U :K:	.10	.25
120 Contaminated Bond C :K:	.08	.20
121 Cruel Edict U :K:	.50	1.25
122 Dark Banishing C :K:	.08	.20
123 Death Pits of Rath R :K:	.40	1.00
124 Deathgazer U :K:	.10	.25
125 Diabolic Tutor U :K:	.50	1.25
126 Drudge Skeletons U :K:	.10	.25
127 Enfeeblement C :K:	.08	.20
128 Execute U :K:	.10	.25
129 Fear C :K:	.08	.20
130 Festering Goblin C :K:	.08	.20
131 Final Punishment R :K:	.30	.75
132 Foul Imp C :K:	.08	.20
133 Giant Cockroach C :K:	.08	.20
134 Gluttonous Zombie U :K:	.10	.25
135 Grave Pact R :K:	2.50	6.00
136 Gravedigger C :K:	.08	.20
137 Hell's Caretaker R :K:	1.25	3.00
138 Highway Robber C :K:	.08	.20
139 Hollow Dogs C :K:	.08	.20
140 Horror of Horrors U :K:	.10	.25
141 Hypnotic Specter R :K:	1.00	2.50
142 Looming Shade C :K:	.08	.20
143 Lord of the Undead R :K:	4.00	10.00
144 Megrim U :K:	.50	1.25
145 Mind Rot C :K:	.08	.20
146 Mindslicer R :K:	.50	1.25
147 Mortivore R :K:	.75	2.00
148 Nantuko Husk U :K:	.10	.25
149 Nekrataal U :K:	.20	.50
150 Nightmare R :K:	.40	1.00
151 Persecute R :K:	.75	2.00
152 Phyrexian Arena R :K:	1.50	4.00
153 Phyrexian Gargantua U :K:	.10	.25
154 Plague Beetle C :K:	.08	.20
155 Plague Wind R :K:	.75	2.00
156 Raise Dead C :K:	.08	.20
157 Ravenous Rats C :K:	.08	.20
158 Razortooth Rats C :K:	.08	.20
159 Royal Assassin R :K:	.60	1.50
160 Scathe Zombies C :K:	.08	.20
161 Sengir Vampire R :K:	.50	1.25
162 Serpent Warrior C :K:	.08	.20
163 Slay U :K:	.10	.25
164 Soul Feast U :K:	.10	.25
165 Spineless Thug C :K:	.08	.20
166 Swarm of Rats U :K:	.20	.50
167 Underworld Dreams R :K:	.75	2.00
168 Unholy Strength C :K:	.08	.20
169 Will-o'-the-Wisp R :K:	1.25	3.00
170 Yawgmoth Demon R :K:	.30	.75
171 Zombify U :K:	.60	1.50
172 Anaba Shaman C :R:	.08	.20
173 Anarchist U :R:	.10	.25
174 Balduvian Barbarians C :R:	.08	.20
175 Blaze U :R:	.20	.50
176 Blood Moon R :R:	2.50	6.00
177 Bloodfire Colossus R :R:	.25	.60
178 Boiling Seas U :R:	.15	.40
179 Demolish U :R:	.10	.25
180 Enrage U :R:	.10	.25
181 Firebreathing C :R:	.08	.20
182 Flame Wave U :R:	.15	.40
183 Flashfires U :R:	.10	.25
184 Flowstone Crusher U :R:	.10	.25
185 Flowstone Shambler C :R:	.08	.20
186 Flowstone Slide R :R:	.25	.60
187 Form of the Dragon R :R:	.50	1.25
188 Furnace of Rath R :R:	.60	1.50
189 Goblin Balloon Brigade U :R:	.10	.25
190 Goblin Brigand C :R:	.08	.20
191 Goblin Chariot C :R:	.08	.20
192 Goblin King R :R:	.75	2.00
193 Goblin Mountaineer C :R:	.08	.20
194 Goblin Piker C :R:	.08	.20
195 Goblin Sky Raider C :R:	.08	.20
196 Guerrilla Tactics U :R:	.10	.25
197 Hill Giant C :R:	.08	.20
198 Karplusan Yeti R :R:	.25	.60
199 Kird Ape U :R:	.60	1.50
200 Lava Axe C :R:	.08	.20
201 Lightning Elemental C :R:	.08	.20
202 Magnivore R :R:	.40	1.00
203 Mana Clash R :R:	.30	.75
204 Mogg Sentry R :R:	.30	.75
205 Ogre Taskmaster U :R:	.10	.25
206 Orcish Artillery U :R:	.10	.25
207 Panic Attack C :R:	.08	.20
208 Pyroclasm U :R:	.40	1.00
209 Raging Goblin C :R:	.08	.20
210 Rathi Dragon R :R:	.50	1.25
211 Reflexes C :R:	.08	.20
212 Relentless Assault R :R:	.30	.75
213 Rogue Kavu C :R:	.08	.20
214 Rukh Egg R :R:	.40	1.00
215 Sandstone Warrior C :R:	.08	.20
216 Seething Song C :R:	.75	2.00
217 Shard Phoenix R :R:	.40	1.00
218 Shatter C :R:	.08	.20
219 Shivan Dragon R :R:	.50	1.25
220 Shock C :R:	.10	.25
221 Stone Rain C :R:	.08	.20
222 Sudden Impact U :R:	.10	.25
223 Threaten U :R:	.15	.40
224 Thundermare R :R:	.50	1.25
225 Viashino Sandstalker U :R:	.10	.25
226 Volcanic Hammer C :R:	.08	.20
227 Whip Sergeant U :R:	.10	.25
228 Wildfire R :R:	.50	1.25

Card	Low	High
229 Anaconda U :G:	.10	.25
230 Ancient Silverback R :G:	.30	.75
231 Biorhythm R :G:	.50	1.25
232 Blanchwood Armor U :G:	.50	1.25
233 Craw Wurm C :B:	.08	.20
234 Creeping Mold U :G:	.10	.25
235 Early Harvest R :G:	.60	1.50
236 Elvish Bard U :G:	.10	.25
237 Elvish Berserker C :G:	.08	.20
238 Elvish Champion R :G:	2.00	5.00
239 Elvish Piper R :G:	2.50	6.00
240 Elvish Warrior C :G:	.08	.20
241 Emperor Crocodile R :G:	.25	.60
242 Force of Nature R :G:	.30	.75
243 Giant Growth C :G:	.08	.20
244 Giant Spider C :G:	.08	.20
245 Greater Good R :G:	1.50	4.00
246 Grizzly Bears C :G:	.08	.20
247 Groundskeeper U :G:	.10	.25
248 Hunted Wumpus U :G:	.10	.25
249 Kavu Climber C :G:	.08	.20
250 King Cheetah U :G:	.10	.25
251 Ley Druid U :G:	.10	.25
252 Llanowar Behemoth U :G:	.10	.25
253 Llanowar Elves C :G:	.20	.50
254 Maro R :G:	.40	1.00
255 Might of Oaks R :G:	.50	1.25
256 Natural Affinity R :G:	.40	1.00
257 Natural Spring C :G:	.08	.20
258 Naturalize C :G:	.08	.20
259 Needle Storm U :G:	.10	.25
260 Norwood Ranger C :G:	.08	.20
261 Order of the Sacred Bell C :G:	.08	.20
262 Overgrowth C :G:	.08	.20
263 Rampant Growth C :G:	.08	.20
264 Reclaim C :G:	.08	.20
265 Regeneration U :G:	.10	.25
266 River Bear U :G:	.10	.25
267 Rootbreaker Wurm U :G:	.10	.25
268 Rootwalla C :G:	.08	.20
269 Scaled Wurm C :G:	.08	.20
270 Seedborn Muse R :G:	2.00	5.00
271 Silklash Spider R :G:	.60	1.50
272 Stream of Life U :G:	.10	.25
273 Summer Bloom U :G:	.40	1.00
274 Trained Armodon C :G:	.08	.20
275 Tree Monkey C :G:	.08	.20
276 Treetop Bracers C :G:	.08	.20
277 Utopia Tree R :G:	.75	2.00
278 Verdant Force R :G:	.75	2.00
279 Verduran Enchantress R :G:	.40	1.00
280 Viridian Shaman U :G:	.10	.25
281 Web U :G:	.10	.25
282 Weird Harvest R :G:	.60	1.50
283 Wood Elves C :G:	.10	.25
284 Yavimaya Enchantress U :G:	.15	.40
285 Zodiac Monkey C :G:	.08	.20
286 Aladdin's Ring R :A:	.25	.60
287 Angel's Feather U :A:	.10	.25
288 Beast of Burden R :A:	.40	1.00
289 Booby Trap R :A:	.50	1.25
290 Bottle Gnomes U :A:	.10	.25
291 Coat of Arms R :A:	2.00	5.00
292 Dancing Scimitar U :A:	.10	.25
293 Defense Grid R :A:	.75	2.00
294 Demon's Horn U :A:	.15	.40
295 Disrupting Scepter R :A:	.25	.60
296 Dragon's Claw U :A:	.20	.50
297 Fellwar Stone U :A:	.20	.50
298 Howling Mine R :A:	1.25	3.00
299 Icy Manipulator U :A:	.30	.75
300 Jade Statue R :A:	.25	.60
301 Jester's Cap R :A:	1.00	2.50
302 Kraken's Eye U :A:	.10	.25
303 Loxodon Warhammer R :A:	1.00	2.50
304 Millstone R :A:	.50	1.25
305 Ornithopter U :A:	.50	1.25
306 Phyrexian Hulk U :A:	.10	.25
307 Rod of Ruin U :A:	.10	.25
308 Slate of Ancestry R :A:	.60	1.50
309 Spellbook U :A:	.20	.50
310 Storage Matrix R :A:	.40	1.00
311 Tanglebloom U :A:	.10	.25
312 Teferi's Puzzle Box R :A:	.60	1.50
313 Thran Golem R :A:	.30	.75
314 Ur-Golem's Eye U :A:	.10	.25
315 Vulshok Morningstar U :A:	.10	.25
316 Wurm's Tooth U :A:	.10	.25
317 Adarkar Wastes R :L:	1.00	2.50
318 Battlefield Forge R :L:	1.00	2.50
319 Brushland R :L:	.75	2.00
320 Caves of Koilos R :L:	1.00	2.50
321 Karplusan Forest R :L:	1.00	2.50
322 Llanowar Wastes R :L:	1.25	3.00
323 Quicksand U :L:	.15	.40
324 Shivan Reef R :L:	2.00	5.00
325 Sulfurous Springs R :L:	.75	2.00
326 Underground River R :L:	1.25	3.00
327 Urza's Mine U :L:	.60	1.50
328 Urza's Power Plant U :L:	.60	1.50
329 Urza's Tower U :L:	.60	1.50
330 Yavimaya Coast R :L:	1.25	3.00
331 Plains L :L:	.08	.20
332 Plains L :L:	.08	.20
333 Plains L :L:	.08	.20
334 Plains L :L:	.08	.20
335 Island L :L:	.08	.20
336 Island L :L:	.08	.20
337 Island L :L:	.08	.20
338 Island L :L:	.08	.20
339 Swamp L :L:	.08	.20
340 Swamp L :L:	.08	.20
341 Swamp L :L:	.08	.20
342 Swamp L :L:	.08	.20
343 Mountain L :L:	.08	.20
344 Mountain L :L:	.08	.20
345 Mountain L :L:	.08	.20
346 Mountain L :L:	.08	.20
347 Forest L :L:	.08	.20
348 Forest L :L:	.08	.20
349 Forest L :L:	.08	.20
350 Forest L :L:	.08	.20
S01 Coral Eel C :B:	.08	.20
S02 Eager Cadet C :W:	.08	.20
S03 Enormous Baloth U :G:	.15	.40
S04 Giant Octopus C :B:	.10	.25
S05 Goblin Raider C :R:	.08	.20
S06 Index C :B:	.20	.50
S07 Spined Wurm C :G:	.08	.20
S08 Vengeance U :W:	.10	.25
S09 Vizzerdrix R :B:	.25	.60

2005 Magic The Gathering Ravnica: City of Guilds

Card	Low	High
COMPLETE SET (306)	125.00	200.00
BOOSTER BOX (36 PACKS)	300.00	400.00
BOOSTER PACK (15 CARDS)	9.00	12.00
THEME DECK	20.00	30.00
FAT PACK	175.00	250.00
*FOIL: .75X TO 2X BASIC CARDS		
RELEASED OCTOBER 7, 2005		
1 Auratouched Mage U :W:	.12	.30
2 Bathe in Light U :W:	.12	.30
3 Benevolent Ancestor C :W:	.08	.20
4 Blazing Archon R :W:	1.25	3.00
5 Boros Fury-Shield C :W:	.08	.20
6 Caregiver C :W:	.08	.20
7 Chant of Vitu-Ghazi U :W:	.12	.30
8 Concerted Effort R :W:	1.00	2.50
9 Conclave Equenaut C :W:	.08	.20
10 Conclave Phalanx U :W:	.12	.30
11 Conclave's Blessing C :W:	.08	.20
12 Courier Hawk C :W:	.08	.20
13 Devouring Light U :W:	.20	.50
14 Divebomber Griffin U :W:	.12	.30
15 Dromad Purebred C :W:	.08	.20
16 Faith's Fetters C :W:	.12	.30
17 Festival of the Guildpact U :W:	.12	.30
18 Flickerform R :W:	.25	.60
19 Gate Hound C :W:	.08	.20
20 Ghosts of the Innocent R :W:	.25	.60
21 Hour of Reckoning R :W:	.30	.75
22 Hunted Lammasu R :W:	.25	.60
23 Leave No Trace C :W:	.08	.20
24 Light of Sanction R :W:	.25	.60
25 Loxodon Gatekeeper R :W:	.30	.75
26 Nightguard Patrol C :W:	.08	.20
27 Oathsworn Giant U :W:	.20	.50
28 Sandsower U :W:	.12	.30
29 Screeching Griffin C :W:	.08	.20
30 Seed Spark U :W:	.12	.30
31 Suppression Field U :W:	.20	.50
32 Three Dreams R :W:	.30	.75
33 Twilight Drover R :W:	.75	2.00
34 Veteran Armorer C :W:	.08	.20
35 Votary of the Conclave C :W:	.08	.20
36 Wojek Apothecary U :W:	.12	.30
37 Wojek Siren C :W:	.08	.20
38 Belltower Sphinx U :B:	.12	.30
39 Cerulean Sphinx R :B:	.25	.60
40 Compulsive Research C :B:	.12	.30
41 Convolute C :B:	.08	.20
42 Copy Enchantment R :B:	1.25	3.00
43 Dizzy Spell C :B:	.08	.20
44 Drake Familiar C :B:	.08	.20
45 Dream Leash R :B:	.25	.60
46 Drift of Phantasms C :B:	.12	.30
47 Ethereal Usher U :B:	.12	.30
48 Eye of the Storm R :B:	.25	.60
49 Flight of Fancy C :B:	.08	.20
50 Flow of Ideas U :B:	.12	.30
51 Followed Footsteps R :B:	1.50	4.00
52 Grayscaled Gharial C :B:	.08	.20
53 Grozoth R :B:	.30	.75
54 Halcyon Glaze U :B:	.12	.30
55 Hunted Phantasm R :B:	.40	1.00
56 Induce Paranoia C :B:	.08	.20
57 Lore Broker U :B:	.12	.30
58 Mark of Eviction U :B:	.12	.30
59 Mnemonic Nexus U :B:	.12	.30
60 Muddle the Mixture C :B:	.30	.75
61 Peel from Reality C :B:	.08	.20
62 Quickchange C :B:	.08	.20
63 Remand U :B:	3.00	8.00
64 Snapping Drake C :B:	.08	.20
65 Spawnbroker R :B:	.25	.60
66 Stasis Cell C :B:	.08	.20
67 Surveilling Sprite C :B:	.08	.20
68 Tattered Drake C :B:	.08	.20
69 Telling Time U :B:	.20	.50
70 Terraformer C :B:	.08	.20
71 Tidewater Minion C :B:	.08	.20
72 Tunnel Vision R :B:	.40	1.00
73 Vedalken Dismisser C :B:	.08	.20
74 Vedalken Entrancer C :B:	.08	.20
75 Wizened Snitches U :B:	.12	.30
76 Zephyr Spirit C :B:	.08	.20
77 Blood Funnel R :K:	.25	.60
78 Brainspoil C :K:	.08	.20
79 Carrion Howler U :K:	.12	.30
80 Clinging Darkness C :K:	.08	.20
81 Dark Confidant R :K:	25.00	50.00
82 Darkblast U :K:	.25	.60
83 Dimir House Guard C :K:	.08	.20
84 Dimir Machinations U :K:	.20	.50
85 Disembowel C :K:	.08	.20
86 Empty the Catacombs R :K:	.25	.60
87 Golgari Thug U :K:	.75	2.00
88 Helldozer R :K:	.50	1.25
89 Hex R :K:	.30	.75
90 Hunted Horror R :K:	.75	2.00
91 Infectious Host C :K:	.08	.20
92 Keening Banshee U :K:	.12	.30
93 Last Gasp C :K:	.08	.20
94 Mausoleum Turnkey U :K:	.12	.30
95 Moonlight Bargain R :K:	.25	.60
96 Mortipede C :K:	.08	.20
97 Necromantic Thirst C :K:	.30	.75
98 Necroplasm R :K:	.30	.75
99 Netherborn Phalanx U :K:	.12	.30
100 Nightmare Void U :K:	.12	.30
101 Ribbons of Night U :K:	.12	.30
102 Roofstalker Wight C :K:	.08	.20
103 Sadistic Augermage C :K:	.08	.20
104 Sewerdreg C :K:	.08	.20
105 Shred Memory C :K:	.08	.20
106 Sins of the Past R :K:	.25	.60
107 Stinkweed Imp C :K:	.20	.50
108 Strands of Undeath C :K:	.08	.20
109 Thoughtpicker Witch C :K:	.08	.20
110 Undercity Shade U :K:	.12	.30
111 Vigor Mortis U :K:	.12	.30
112 Vindictive Mob U :K:	.12	.30
113 Woebringer Demon R :K:	.25	.60
114 Barbarian Riftcutter C :R:	.08	.20
115 Blockbuster U :R:	.12	.30
116 Breath of Fury R :R:	.25	.60
117 Char R :R:	.40	1.00
118 Cleansing Beam U :R:	.12	.30
119 Coalhauler Swine C :R:	.08	.20
12 Bloodbond March R :D:	.25	.60
120 Dogpile C :R:	.08	.20
121 Excruciator R :R:	.25	.60
122 Fiery Conclusion C :R:	.08	.20
123 Flame Fusillade R :R:	.25	.60
124 Flash Conscription U :R:	.12	.30
125 Frenzied Goblin U :R:	.12	.30
126 Galvanic Arc C :R:	.08	.20
127 Goblin Fire Fiend C :R:	.08	.20
128 Goblin Spelunkers C :R:	.08	.20
129 Greater Forgeling U :R:	.12	.30
130 Hammerfist Giant R :R:	.25	.60
131 Hunted Dragon R :R:	.50	1.25
132 Incite Hysteria C :R:	.08	.20
133 Indentured Oaf U :R:	.12	.30
134 Instill Furor U :R:	.12	.30
135 Mindmoil R :R:	.25	.60
136 Molten Sentry R :R:	.25	.60
137 Ordruun Commando C :R:	.08	.20
138 Rain of Embers C :R:	.08	.20
139 Reroute U :R:	.12	.30
140 Sabertooth Alley Cat C :R:	.08	.20
141 Seismic Spike C :R:	.08	.20
142 Sell-Sword Brute C :R:	.08	.20
143 Smash C :R:	.08	.20
144 Sparkmage Apprentice C :R:	.08	.20
145 Stoneshaker Shaman U :R:	.12	.30
146 Surge of Zeal C :R:	.08	.20
147 Torpid Moloch C :R:	.08	.20
148 Viashino Fangtail C :R:	.08	.20
149 Viashino Slasher C :R:	.08	.20
150 Warp World R :R:	.08	.20
151 War-Torch Goblin C :R:	.25	.60
152 Wojek Embermage U :R:	.12	.30
153 Birds of Paradise R :G:	2.50	6.00
154 Bramble Elemental C :G:	.08	.20
155 Carven Caryatid U :G:	.20	.50
156 Chord of Calling R :G:	5.00	12.00
157 Civic Wayfinder C :G:	.08	.20
158 Doubling Season R :G:	15.00	30.00
159 Dowsing Shaman U :G:	.12	.30
160 Dryad's Caress C :G:	.08	.20
161 Elves of Deep Shadow C :G:	.08	.20
162 Elvish Skysweeper C :G:	.08	.20
163 Farseek C :G:	.08	.20
164 Fists of Ironwood C :G:	.08	.20
165 Gather Courage C :G:	.08	.20
166 Golgari Brownscale C :G:	.08	.20
167 Golgari Grave-Troll R :G:	1.50	4.00
168 Goliath Spider U :G:	.12	.30
169 Greater Mossdog C :G:	.08	.20
170 Hunted Troll R :G:	.30	.75
171 Ivy Dancer U :G:	.12	.30
172 Life from the Loam R :G:	6.00	15.00
173 Moldervine Cloak U :G:	.20	.50
174 Nullmage Shepherd U :G:	.20	.50
175 Overwhelm U :G:	.12	.30
176 Perilous Forays U :G:	.12	.30
177 Primordial Sage R :G:	.30	.75
178 Recollect U :G:	.12	.30
179 Rolling Spoil U :G:	.12	.30
180 Root-Kin Ally U :G:	.12	.30
181 Scatter the Seeds C :G:	.08	.20
182 Scion of the Wild R :G:	.25	.60
183 Siege Wurm C :G:	.08	.20
184 Stone-Seeder Hierophant C :G:	.08	.20
185 Sundering Vitae C :G:	.08	.20
186 Transluminant C :G:	.08	.20
187 Trophy Hunter U :G:	.12	.30
188 Ursapine R :G:	.25	.60
189 Vinelasher Kudzu R :G:	.50	1.25
190 Agrus Kos, WojekVeteran R :D:	.25	.60
191 Autochthon Wurm R :D:	.40	1.00
193 Boros Swiftblade U :D:	.20	.50
194 Brightflame R :D:	.30	.75
195 Chorus of the Conclave R :D:	.25	.60
196 Circu, Dimir Lobotomist R :D:	2.00	5.00
197 Clutch of the Undercity U :D:	.20	.50
198 Congregation at Dawn U :D:	.30	.75
199 Consult the Necrosages C :D:	.08	.20
200 Dark Heart of the Wood U :D:	.12	.30
201 Dimir Cutpurse R :D:	.50	1.25
202 Dimir Doppelganger R :D:	1.00	2.50
203 Dimir Infiltrator C :D:	.08	.20
204 Drooling Groodion U :D:	.12	.30
205 Firemane Angel R :D:	.60	1.50
206 Flame-Kin Zealot U :D:	.20	.50
207 Glare of Subdual R :D:	.50	1.25
208 Glimpse the Unthinkable R :D:	6.00	15.00
209 Golgari Germination U :D:	.20	.50
210 Golgari Rotwurm C :D:	.08	.20
211 Grave-Shell Scarab R :D:	.30	.75
212 Guardian of Vitu-Ghazi C :D:	.08	.20
213 Lightning Helix U :D:	1.25	3.00
214 Loxodon Hierarch R :D:	.60	1.50
215 Mindleech Mass R :D:	.40	1.00
216 Moroii U :D:	.12	.30
217 Perplex C :D:	.12	.30
218 Phytohydra R :D:	.60	1.50
219 Pollenbright Wings U :D:	.12	.30
220 Psychic Drain U :D:	.25	.60
221 Putrefy U :D:	.60	1.50
222 Rally the Righteous C :D:	.08	.20
223 Razia's Purification R :D:	.30	.75
224 Razia, Boros Archangel R :D:	.60	1.50
225 Savra, Queen of the Golgari R :D:	.40	1.00
226 Searing Meditation R :D:	.30	.75
227 Seeds of Strength C :D:	.08	.20
228 Selesnya Evangel C :D:	.08	.20
229 Selesnya Sagittars U :D:	.12	.30
230 Shambling Shell C :D:	.08	.20
231 Sisters of Stone Death R :D:	.50	1.25
232 Skyknight Legionnaire C :D:	.08	.20
233 Sunhome Enforcer U :D:	.12	.30
234 Szadek, Lord of Secrets R :D:	.40	1.00
235 Thundersong Trumpeter C :D:	.08	.20
236 Tolsimir Wolfblood R :D:	.60	1.50
237 Twisted Justice U :D:	.12	.30
238 Vulturous Zombie R :D:	.60	1.50
239 Watchwolf U :D:	.40	1.00
240 Woodwraith Corrupter R :D:	.25	.60
241 Woodwraith Strangler C :D:	.08	.20
242 Boros Guildmage U :R::W:	.12	.30
243 Boros Recruit C :R::W:	.08	.20
244 Centaur Safeguard C :G::W:	.08	.20
245 Dimir Guildmage U :B::K:	.20	.50
246 Gaze of the Gorgon C :K::G:	.08	.20
247 Gleancrawler R :K::G:	.50	1.25
248 Golgari Guildmage U :K::G:	.12	.30
249 Lurking Informant C :B::K:	.08	.20
250 Master Warcraft R :R::W:	.40	1.00
251 Privileged Position R :G::W:	4.00	10.00
252 Selesnya Guildmage U :G::W:	.12	.30
253 Shadow of Doubt R :B::K:	.30	.75
254 Bloodletter Quill R :A:	.25	.60
255 Boros Signet C :A:	.12	.30
256 Bottled Cloister R :A:	.25	.60
257 Cloudstone Curio R :A:	1.25	3.00
258 Crown of Convergence R :A:	.25	.60
259 Cyclopean Snare U :A:	.12	.30
260 Dimir Signet C :A:	.12	.30
261 Glass Golem U :A:	.12	.30
262 Golgari Signet C :A:	.12	.30
263 Grifter's Blade U :A:	.12	.30
264 Junktroller U :A:	.12	.30
265 Leashling U :A:	.12	.30
266 Nullstone Gargoyle R :A:	.25	.60
267 Pariah's Shield R :A:	.75	2.00
268 Peregrine Mask U :A:	.12	.30
269 Plague Boiler R :A:	.25	.60
270 Selesnya Signet C :A:	.12	.30
271 Spectral Searchlight U :A:	.20	.50
272 Sunforger R :A:	.50	1.25
273 Terrarion C :A:	.08	.20
274 Voyager Staff U :A:	.12	.30
275 Boros Garrison C :L:	.20	.50
276 Dimir Aqueduct C :L:	.30	.75
277 Duskmantle,HouseofShadow U :L:	.12	.30
278 Golgari Rot Farm C :L:	.25	.60
279 Overgrown Tomb R :L:	8.00	20.00
280 Sacred Foundry R :L:	6.00	15.00
281 Selesnya Sanctuary C :L:	.20	.50
282 Sunhome,Fortress U :L:	.20	.50
283 Svogthos,Restless Tomb U :L:	.12	.30
284 Temple Garden R :L:	8.00	20.00
285 Vitu-Ghazi, City-Tree U :L:	.20	.50
286 Watery Grave R :L:	8.00	20.00
287 Plains C :L:	.08	.20
288 Plains C :L:		
289 Plains C :L:		
290 Plains C :L:		
291 Island C :L:	.08	.20
292 Island C :L:		
293 Island C :L:		
294 Island C :L:		
295 Swamp C :L:	.08	.20
296 Swamp C :L:		
297 Swamp C :L:		
298 Swamp C :L:		
299 Mountain C :L:	.08	.20
300 Mountain C :L:		
301 Mountain C :L:		
302 Mountain C :L:		
303 Forest C :L:	.08	.20
304 Forest C :L:		
305 Forest C :L:		
306 Forest C :L:		

2006 Magic The Gathering Guildpact

Card	Low	High
COMPLETE SET (165)	100.00	175.00
BOOSTER BOX (36 PACKS)	175.00	300.00
BOOSTER PACK (15 CARDS)	5.00	10.00
THEME DECK	10.00	20.00
FAT PACK	40.00	80.00
*FOIL: .75X TO 2X BASIC CARDS		
RELEASED FEBRUARY 3, 2006		
1 Absolver Thrull C :W:	.10	.20
2 Belfry Spirit U :W:	.12	.30
3 Benediction of Moons C :W:	.10	.20
4 Droning Bureaucrats U :W:	.12	.30
5 Ghost Warden C :W:	.10	.20
6 Ghostway R :W:	1.00	2.50
7 Graven Dominator R :W:	.25	.60
8 Guardian's Magemark C :W:	.10	.20
9 Harrier Griffin U :W:	.12	.30
10 Leyline of the Meek R :W:	1.00	2.50
11 Lionheart Maverick C :W:	.10	.20
12 Martyred Rusalka U :W:	.12	.30
13 Order of the Stars U :W:	.15	.40
14 Shadow Lance U :W:	.12	.30
15 Shrieking Grotesque C :W:	.10	.20
16 Sinstriker's Will U :W:	.12	.30
17 Skyrider Trainee C :W:	.10	.20
18 Spelltithe Enforcer R :W:	.25	.60
19 Storm Herd R :W:	.40	1.00
20 To Arms! U :W:	.15	.40
21 Withstand C :W:	.10	.20
22 AEtherplasm U :B:	.15	.40
23 Crystal Seer C :B:	.10	.20
24 Drowned Rusalka U :B:	.12	.30
25 Frazzle U :B:	.12	.30
26 Gigadrowse C :B:	.10	.20
27 Hatching Plans R :B:	.30	.75
28 Infiltrator's Magemark C :B:	.10	.20
29 Leyline of Singularity R :B:	.40	1.00
30 Mimeofacture R :B:	.25	.60
31 Quicken R :B:	.30	.75
32 Repeal C :B:	.15	.40
33 Runeboggle C :B:	.10	.20
34 Sky Swallower R :B:	.30	.75
35 Steamcore Weird C :B:	.10	.20
36 Stratozeppelid U :B:	.12	.30
37 Thunderheads U :B:	.12	.30
38 Torch Drake C :B:	.10	.20
39 Train of Thought C :B:	.12	.30
40 Vacuumelt U :B:	.12	.30
41 Vedalken Plotter U :B:	.12	.30
42 Vertigo Spawn U :B:	.12	.30
43 Abyssal Nocturnus R :K:	.40	1.00
44 Caustic Rain U :K:	.12	.30
45 Cremate C :K:	.10	.20
46 Cry of Contrition C :K:	.10	.20
47 Cryptwailing U :K:	.12	.30
48 Daggerclaw Imp U :K:	.12	.30
49 Douse in Gloom C :K:	.10	.20
50 Exhumer Thrull U :K:	.12	.30
51 Hissing Miasma U :K:	.15	.40
52 Leyline of the Void R :K:	1.00	2.50
53 Necromancer's Magemark C :K:	.10	.20
54 Orzhov Euthanist C :K:	.10	.20
55 Ostiary Thrull C :K:	.10	.20
56 Plagued Rusalka U :K:	.15	.40
57 Poisonbelly Ogre C :K:	.10	.20
58 Restless Bones C :K:	.10	.20
59 Revenant Patriarch U :K:	.12	.30
60 Sanguine Praetor R :K:	.25	.60
61 Seize the Soul R :K:	.25	.60
62 Skeletal Vampire R :K:	6.00	1.50
63 Smogsteed Rider U :K:	.12	.30
64 Bloodscale Prowler C :R:	.10	.20
65 Fencer's Magemark C :R:	.10	.20
66 Ghor-Clan Bloodscale U :R:	.12	.30
67 Hypervolt Grasp U :R:	.12	.30
68 Leyline of Lightning R :R:	.30	.75
69 Living Inferno R :R:	.25	.60
70 Ogre Savant C :R:	.12	.30
71 Parallectric Feedback R :R:	.30	.75
72 Pyromatics C :R:	.10	.20
73 Rabble-Rouser U :R:	.12	.30
74 Scorched Rusalka U :R:	.15	.40
75 Shattering Spree U :R:	1.50	4.00
76 Siege of Towers R :R:	.25	.60
77 Skarrgan Firebird R :R:	.25	.60
78 Tin Street Hooligan C :R:	.10	.20
79 Battering Wurm U :G:	.12	.30
80 Beastmaster's Magemark C :G:	.10	.20
81 Bioplasm R :G:	.25	.60
82 Crash Landing U :G:	.12	.30
83 Dryad Sophisticate U :G:	.15	.40
84 Earth Surge R :G:	.25	.60
85 Gatherer of Graces U :G:	.12	.30
86 Ghor-Clan Savage C :G:	.10	.20
87 Gristleback U :G:	.12	.30
88 Gruul Nodorog C :G:	.10	.20
89 Gruul Scrapper C :G:	.10	.20
90 Leyline of Lifeforce R :G:	.40	1.00
91 Petrified Wood-Kin R :G:	.25	.60
92 Predatory Focus U :G:	.12	.30
93 Primeval Light U :G:	.15	.40
94 Silhana Ledgewalker C :G:	.15	.40
95 Silhana Starfletcher C :G:	.10	.20
96 Skarrgan Pit-Skulk C :G:	.10	.20
97 Starved Rusalka U :G:	.12	.30
98 Wildsize C :G:	.10	.20
99 Wurmweaver Coil R :G:	.25	.60
100 Agent of Masks U :D:	.15	.40
101 Angel of Despair R :D:	2.50	6.00
102 Blind Hunter C :D:	.10	.20
103 Borborygmos R :D:	.30	.75
104 Burning-Tree Bloodscale C :D:	.10	.20
105 Burning-Tree Shaman R :D:	6.00	1.50
106 Castigate C :D:	.10	.20
107 Cerebral Vortex R :D:	.30	.75
108 Conjurer's Ban U :D:	.15	.40
109 Culling Sun R :D:	.30	.75
110 Dune-Brood Nephilim R :D:	.30	.75
111 Electrolyze U :D:	.40	1.00
112 Feral Animist U :D:	.12	.30
113 Gelectrode U :D:	6.00	1.50
114 Ghost Council of Orzhova R :D:	6.00	1.50
115 Glint-Eye Nephilim R :D:	.30	.75
116 Goblin Flectomancer U :D:	.12	.30
117 Ink-Treader Nephilim R :D:	.30	.75
118 Invoke the Firemind R :D:	.30	.75
119 Izzet Chronarch C :D:	.10	.20
120 Killer Instinct R :D:	.25	.60
121 Leap of Flame C :D:	.10	.20
122 Mortify U :D:	6.00	1.50
123 Nivix, Aerie of the Firemind U :L:	.12	.30
124 Orzhov Pontiff R :D:	.40	1.00
125 Pillory of the Sleepless C :D:	.12	.30
126 Rumbling Slum R :D:	.40	1.00
127 Savage Twister U :D:	.25	.60
128 Scab-Clan Mauler C :D:	.10	.20
129 Schismotivate U :D:	.12	.30
130 Skarrgan Skybreaker U :D:	.12	.30
131 Souls of the Faultless U :D:	.40	1.00
132 Stitch in Time R :D:	6.00	1.50
133 Streetbreaker Wurm C :D:	.10	.20
134 Teysa, Orzhov Scion R :D:	.40	1.00
135 Tibor and Lumia R :D:	.40	1.00
136 Ulasht, the Hate Seed R :D:	.30	.75
137 Wee Dragonauts C :D:	.12	.30
138 Witch-Maw Nephilim R :D:	.30	.75
139 Wreak Havoc U :D:	.30	.75
140 Yore-Tiller Nephilim R :D:	.30	.75
141 Debtors' Knell R :D:	4.00	10.00
142 Djinn Illuminatus R :D:	6.00	1.50
143 Giant Solifuge R :D:	6.00	1.50
144 Gruul Guildmage U :D:	.15	.40
145 Izzet Guildmage U :D:	.30	.75
146 Mourning Thrull C :D:	.10	.20
147 Orzhov Guildmage U :D:	.15	.40
148 Petrahydrox C :D:	.10	.20
149 Wild Cantor C :D:	.10	.20
150 Gruul Signet C :A:	.10	.20
151 Gruul War Plow R :A:	.30	.75
152 Izzet Signet C :A:	.10	.20
153 Mizzium Transreliquat R :A:	.30	.75
154 Moratorium Stone R :A:	.30	.75
155 Orzhov Signet C :A:	.10	.20
156 Sword of the Paruns R :A:	.30	.75
157 Godless Shrine R :L:	8.00	20.00
158 Gruul Turf C :L:	.15	.40
159 Izzet Boilerworks C :L:	.30	.75
160 Niv-Mizzet, the Firemind R :D:	6.00	15.00
161 Orzhov Basilica C :L:	.15	.40

Card	Low	High
162 Orzhova, the Church of Deals U :L:	.12	.30
163 Skarrg, the Rage Pits U :L:	.15	.40
164 Steam Vents R :L:	10.00	25.00
165 Stomping Ground R :L:	8.00	20.00

2006 Magic The Gathering Dissension

Card	Low	High
COMPLETE SET (180)	100.00	200.00
BOOSTER BOX (36 PACKS)	175.00	250.00
BOOSTER PACK (15 CARDS)	5.00	8.00
THEME DECK	10.00	20.00
FAT PACK	50.00	80.00
*FOIL: .75X TO 2X BASIC CARDS		
RELEASED ON MAY 5, 2006		
1 Aurora Eidolon C :W:	.08	.20
2 Azorius Herald U :W:	.20	.50
3 Beacon Hawk C :W:	.08	.20
4 Blessing of the Nephilim U :W:	.20	.50
5 Brace for Impact U :W:	.10	.25
6 Carom C :W:	.08	.20
7 Celestial Ancient R :W:	.50	1.25
8 Condemn U :W:	.50	1.25
9 Freewind Equenaut C :W:	.08	.20
10 Guardian of the Guildpact C :W:	.08	.20
11 Haazda Exonerator C :W:	.08	.20
12 Haazda Shield Mate R :W:	.25	.60
13 Mistral Charger U :W:	.10	.25
14 Paladin of Prahv U :W:	.10	.25
15 Proclamation of Rebirth R :W:	3.00	8.00
16 Proper Burial R :W:	.50	1.25
17 Soulsworn Jury C :W:	.08	.20
18 Steeling Stance C :W:	.08	.20
19 Stoic Ephemera U :W:	.10	.25
20 Valor Made Real C :W:	.08	.20
21 Wakestone Gargoyle R :W:	.25	.60
22 Court Hussar U :B:	.20	.50
23 Cytoplast Manipulator R :B:	1.00	2.50
24 Enigma Eidolon C :B:	.08	.20
25 Govern the Guildless R :B:	.25	.60
26 Helium Squirter C :B:	.08	.20
27 Novijen Sages R :B:	.40	1.00
28 Ocular Halo C :B:	.08	.20
29 Plaxmanta U :B:	.20	.50
30 Psychic Possession R :B:	.40	1.00
31 Silkwing Scout C :B:	.08	.20
32 Skyscribing U :B:	.10	.25
33 Spell Snare U :B:	5.00	12.00
34 Tidespout Tyrant R :B:	1.00	2.50
35 Vigean Graftmage U :B:	.20	.50
36 Vision Skeins C :B:	.08	.20
37 Writ of Passage C :B:	.08	.20
38 Bond of Agony U :K:	.40	1.00
39 Brain Pry U :K:	.10	.25
40 Crypt Champion U :K:	.20	.50
41 Delirium Skeins C :K:	.08	.20
42 Demon's Jester C :K:	.08	.20
43 Drekavac U :K:	.10	.25
44 Enemy of the Guildpact C :K:	.08	.20
45 Entropic Eidolon C :K:	.08	.20
46 Infernal Tutor R :K:	4.00	10.00
47 Macabre Waltz C :K:	.08	.20
48 Nettling Curse C :K:	.08	.20
49 Nightcreep U :K:	.10	.25
50 Nihilistic Glee R :K:	.25	.60
51 Ragamuffyn U :K:	.10	.25
52 Ratcatcher R :K:	.50	1.25
53 Seal of Doom C :K:	.08	.20
54 Slaughterhouse Bouncer C :K:	.08	.20
55 Slithering Shade U :K:	.10	.25
56 Unliving Psychopath R :K:	.40	1.00
57 Vesper Ghoul C :K:	.08	.20
58 Wit's End R :K:	.25	.60
59 Cackling Flames C :R:	.08	.20
60 Demonfire R :R:	.75	2.00
61 Flame-Kin War Scout U :R:	.10	.25
62 Flaring Flame-Kin U :R:	.20	.50
63 Gnat Alley Creeper U :R:	.10	.25
64 Ignorant Bliss U :R:	.20	.50
65 Kill-Suit Cultist C :R:	.08	.20
66 Kindle the Carnage U :R:	.10	.25
67 Ogre Gatecrasher C :R:	.08	.20
68 Psychotic Fury C :R:	.08	.20
69 Rakdos Pit Dragon R :R:	1.00	2.50
70 Sandstorm Eidolon C :R:	.08	.20
71 Seal of Fire C :R:	.10	.25
72 Squealing Devil U :R:	.10	.25
73 Stalking Vengeance R :R:	.50	1.25
74 Stormscale Anarch R :R:	.25	.60
75 Taste for Mayhem C :R:	.08	.20
76 Utvara Scalper C :R:	.08	.20
77 War's Toll R :R:	.40	1.00
78 Weight of Spires U :R:	.10	.25
79 Whiptail Moloch C :R:	.08	.20
80 Aquastrand Spider C :G:	.08	.20
81 Cytoplast Root-Kin R :G:	.75	2.00
82 Cytospawn Shambler C :G:	.08	.20
83 Elemental Resonance R :G:	.40	1.00
84 Fertile Imagination U :G:	.10	.25
85 Flash Foliage U :G:	.10	.25
86 Indrik Stomphowler U :G:	.20	.50
87 Loaming Shaman R :G:	.60	1.50
88 Might of the Nephilim U :G:	.20	.50
89 Patagia Viper U :G:	.10	.25
90 Protean Hulk R :G:	1.25	3.00
91 Simic Basilisk U :G:	.10	.25
92 Simic Initiate C :G:	.08	.20
93 Simic Ragworm C :G:	.08	.20
94 Sporeback Troll C :G:	.08	.20
95 Sprouting Phytohydra R :G:	.50	1.25
96 Stomp and Howl U :G:	.10	.25
97 Street Savvy C :G:	.08	.20
98 Thrive C :G:	.08	.20
99 Utopia Sprawl C :G:	.20	.50
100 Verdant Eidolon C :G:	.08	.20
101 AEthermage's Touch R :W: :B:	.40	1.00
102 Anthem of Rakdos R :K: :R:	.40	1.00
103 Assault Zeppelid C :G: :B:	.08	.20
104 Azorius AEthermage U :W: :B:	.10	.25
105 Azorius First-Wing C :W: :B:	.08	.20
106 Azorius Ploy U :W: :B:	.10	.25
107 Coiling Oracle C :G: :B:	.30	.75
108 Cytoshape R :G: :B:	.50	1.25
109 Dread Slag R :K: :R:	.25	.60
110 Experiment Kraj R :G: :B:	.60	1.50
111 Gobhobbler Rats C :K: :R:	.08	.20
112 Grand Arbiter Augustin IV R :W: :B:	4.00	10.00
113 Hellhole Rats U :K: :R:	.20	.50
114 Isperia the Inscrutable R :W: :B:	.25	.60
115 Jagged Poppet U :K: :R:	.10	.25
116 Leafdrake Roost U :G: :B:	.10	.25
117 Lyzolda, the Blood Witch R :K: :R:	.40	1.00
118 Momir Vig, Simic Visionary R :G: :B:	1.50	4.00
119 Omnibian R :G: :B:	.40	1.00
120 Overrule C :W: :B:	.08	.20
121 Pain Magnification U :K: :R:	.20	.50
122 Palliation Accord U :W: :B:	.10	.25
123 Plaxcaster Frogling U :G: :B:	.50	1.25
124 Plumes of Peace C :W: :B:	.08	.20
125 Pride of the Clouds R :W: :B:	1.00	2.50
126 Rain of Gore R :K: :R:	.60	1.50
127 Rakdos Augermage R :K: :R:	.40	1.00
128 Rakdos Ickspitter C :K: :R:	.08	.20
129 Rakdos the Defiler R :K: :R:	.75	2.00
130 Simic Sky Swallower R :G: :B:	1.25	3.00
131 Sky Hussar U :W: :B:	.30	.75
132 Swift Silence R :W: :B:	.25	.60
133 Trygon Predator U :G: :B:	1.50	4.00
134 Twinstrike U :K: :R:	.10	.25
135 Vigean Hydropon C :G: :B:	.08	.20
136 Vigean Intuition U :G: :B:	.10	.25
137 Voidslime R :G: :B:	2.00	5.00
138 Windreaver R :W: :B:	.40	1.00
139 Wrecking Ball C :K: :R:	.08	.20
140 Avatar of Discord R :K: :R:	1.00	2.50
141 Azorius Guildmage U :W: :B:	.30	.75
142 Biomantic Mastery R :G: :B:	.40	1.00
143 Dovescape R :K: :B:	.60	1.50
144 Minister of Impediments C :W: :B:	.08	.20
145 Rakdos Guildmage U :K: :R:	.20	.50
146 Riot Spikes C :K: :R:	.08	.20
147 Shielding Plax C :G: :B:	.08	.20
148 Simic Guildmage U :G: :B:	.30	.75
149 Bound // Determined R :K: :G:	.40	1.00
150 Crime // Punishment R :W: :K:	.75	2.00
151 Hide // Seek R :R: :W:	.75	2.00
152 Hit // Run U :K: :R:	.20	.50
153 Odds // Ends R :B: :R:	.50	1.25
154 Pure // Simple U :R: :G:	.20	.50
155 Research // Development R :G: :B:	.50	1.25
156 Rise // Fall U :B: :K:	.20	.50
157 Supply // Demand U :G: :W:	.30	.75
158 Trial // Error U :W: :B:	.10	.25
159 Azorius Signet C :A:	.20	.50
160 Bronze Bombshell R :A:	.50	1.25
161 Evolution Vat R :A:	.40	1.00
162 Magewright's Stone U :A:	.20	.50
163 Muse Vessel R :A:	.40	1.00
164 Rakdos Riteknife R :A:	.25	.60
165 Rakdos Signet C :A:	.08	.20
166 Simic Signet C :A:	.08	.20
167 Skullmead Cauldron U :A:	.10	.25
168 Transguild Courier U :A:	.20	.50
169 Walking Archive R :A:	.40	1.00
170 Azorius Chancery C :L:	.40	1.00
171 Blood Crypt R :L:	8.00	20.00
172 Breeding Pool R :L:	12.00	30.00
173 Ghost Quarter U :L:	1.00	2.50
174 Hallowed Fountain R :L:	12.00	30.00
175 Novijen, Heart of Progress U :L:	.20	.50
176 Pillar of the Paruns R :L:	1.50	4.00
177 Prahv, Spires of Order U :L:	.20	.50
178 Rakdos Carnarium C :L:	.30	.75
179 Rix Maadi, Dungeon Palace U :L:	.10	.25
180 Simic Growth Chamber C :L:	.30	.75

2006 Magic The Gathering Coldsnap

Card	Low	High
COMPLETE SET (155)	75.00	125.00
BOOSTER BOX (36 PACKS)	125.00	175.00
BOOSTER PACK (15 CARDS)	4.00	6.00
FAT PACK	40.00	80.00
*FOIL: .75X TO 2X BASIC CARDS		
RELEASED ON JULY 21, 2006		
1 Adarkar Valkyrie R :W:	4.00	10.00
26 Adarkar Windform U :B:	.10	.25
101 Allosaurus Rider R :G:	.40	1.00
143 Arctic Flats U :L:	.50	1.25
102 Arctic Nishoba U :G:	.10	.25
27 Arcum Dagsson R :B:	.75	2.00
103 Aurochs Herd C :G:	.08	.20
51 Balduvian Fallen U :K:	.10	.25
28 Balduvian Frostwaker U :B:	.10	.25
76 Balduvian Rage U :R:	.10	.25
77 Balduvian Warlord U :R:	.10	.25
126 Blizzard Specter U :D:	.60	1.50
104 Boreal Centaur C :G:	.08	.20
105 Boreal Druid C :G:	.10	.25
2 Boreal Griffin C :W:	.08	.20
144 Boreal Shelf U :L:	.50	1.25
78 Braid of Fire R :R:	3.00	8.00
106 Brooding Saurian R :G:	.25	.60
107 Bull Aurochs C :G:	.08	.20
52 Chill to the Bone C :K:	.08	.20
53 Chilling Shade C :K:	.08	.20
136 Coldsteel Heart U :A:	.50	1.25
29 Commandeer R :B:	1.25	3.00
30 Controvert U :B:	.10	.25
31 Counterbalance U :B:	3.00	8.00
3 Cover of Winter R :W:	.25	.60
79 Cryoclasm U :R:	.20	.50
4 Darien, King of Kjeldor R :W:	1.50	4.00
145 Dark Depths R :L:	8.00	20.00
54 Deathmark U :K:	.20	.50
127 Deepfire Elemental U :D:	.10	.25
128 Diamond Faerie R :D:	.20	.50
55 Disciple of Tevesh Szat C :K:	.08	.20
32 Drelnoch C :B:	.08	.20
80 Earthen Goo U :R:	.10	.25
56 Feast of Flesh C :K:	.08	.20
5 Field Marshal R :W:	2.50	6.00
33 Flashfreeze U :B:	.20	.50
108 Freyalise's Radiance U :G:	.10	.25
146 Frost Marsh U :L:	.60	1.50
34 Frost Raptor C :B:	.08	.20
109 Frostweb Spider C :G:	.08	.20
35 Frozen Solid C :B:	.08	.20
81 Fury of the Horde R :R:	.25	.60
129 Garza Zol, Plague Queen R :D:	.50	1.25
57 Garza's Assassin R :K:	.20	.50
6 Gelid Shackles C :W:	.08	.20
7 Glacial Plating U :W:	.10	.25
82 Goblin Furrier C :R:	.08	.20
83 Goblin Rimerunner C :R:	.08	.20
84 Greater Stone Spirit U :R:	.10	.25
58 Grim Harvest C :K:	.08	.20
59 Gristle Grinner U :K:	.10	.25
60 Gutless Ghoul C :K:	.08	.20
61 Haakon, Stromgald Scourge R :K:	3.00	8.00
36 Heidar, Rimewind Master R :B:	.20	.50
62 Herald of Leshrac R :K:	.60	1.50
110 Hibernation's End R :G:	.30	.75
147 Highland Weald U :L:	.40	1.00
85 Icefall C :R:	.08	.20
111 Into the North C :G:	.08	.20
137 Jester's Scepter R :A:	.50	1.25
37 Jokulmorder R :B:	.20	.50
8 Jotun Grunt U :W:	1.00	2.50
9 Jotun Owl Keeper U :W:	.10	.25
130 Juniper Order Ranger U :D:	.75	2.00
86 Karplusan Minotaur R :R:	.25	.60
112 Karplusan Strider U :G:	.10	.25
87 Karplusan Wolverine C :R:	.08	.20
10 Kjeldoran Gargoyle U :W:	.10	.25
11 Kjeldoran Javelineer C :W:	.08	.20
12 Kjeldoran Outrider C :W:	.08	.20
13 Kjeldoran War Cry C :W:	.08	.20
38 Krovikan Mist C :B:	.30	.75
63 Krovikan Rot U :K:	.10	.25
64 Krovikan Scoundrel C :K:	.08	.20
39 Krovikan Whispers U :B:	.10	.25
88 Lightning Serpent R :R:	.75	2.00
89 Lightning Storm U :R:	.10	.25
90 Lovisa Coldeyes R :R:	.30	.75
14 Luminesce U :W:	.10	.25
91 Magmatic Core U :R:	.10	.25
92 Martyr of Ashes C :R:	.08	.20
65 Martyr of Bones C :K:	.08	.20
40 Martyr of Frost C :B:	.08	.20
15 Martyr of Sands C :W:	.30	.75
113 Martyr of Spores C :G:	.08	.20
138 Mishra's Bauble U :A:	.50	1.25
148 Mouth of Ronom U :L:	.30	.75
114 Mystic Melting U :G:	.10	.25
115 Ohran Viper R :G:	2.00	5.00
93 Ohran Yeti C :R:	.08	.20
94 Orcish Bloodpainter C :R:	.08	.20
116 Panglacial Wurm R :G:	1.25	3.00
41 Perilous Research U :B:	.20	.50
66 Phobian Phantasm U :K:	.10	.25
67 Phyrexian Etchings R :K:	.20	.50
139 Phyrexian Ironfoot U :A:	.20	.50
140 Phyrexian Snowcrusher U :A:	.10	.25
141 Phyrexian Soulgorger R :A:	.25	.60
117 Resize U :G:	.10	.25
68 Rime Transfusion U :K:	.10	.25
69 Rimebound Dead C :K:	.08	.20
42 Rimefeather Owl R :B:	.20	.50
118 Rimehorn Aurochs U :G:	.10	.25
95 Rimescale Dragon R :R:	.60	1.50
43 Rimewind Cryomancer U :B:	.10	.25
44 Rimewind Taskmage C :B:	.08	.20
96 Rite of Flame C :R:	1.50	4.00
119 Ronom Hulk C :G:	.08	.20
45 Ronom Serpent C :B:	.08	.20
16 Ronom Unicorn C :W:	.08	.20
46 Rune Snag C :B:	.50	1.25
149 Scrying Sheets R :L:	1.25	3.00
131 Sek'Kuar, Deathkeeper R :D:	.30	.75
120 Shape of the Wiitigo R :G:	.20	.50
121 Sheltering Ancient U :G:	.20	.50
122 Simian Brawler C :G:	.08	.20
97 Skred C :R:	.10	.25
155 Snow-Covered Forest C :L:	.30	.75
152 Snow-Covered Island C :L:	.40	1.00
154 Snow-Covered Mountain C :L:	.40	1.00
151 Snow-Covered Plains C :L:	.30	.75
153 Snow-Covered Swamp C :L:	.30	.75
70 Soul Spike R :K:	.30	.75
123 Sound the Call C :G:	.08	.20
17 Squall Drifter C :W:	.08	.20
98 Stalking Yeti U :R:	.10	.25
124 Steam Spitter U :G:	.10	.25
71 Stromgald Crusader U :K:	1.25	3.00
18 Sun's Bounty C :W:	.08	.20
19 Sunscour R :W:	.40	1.00
47 Surging AEther C :B:	.08	.20
72 Surging Dementia C :K:	.08	.20
99 Surging Flame C :R:	.08	.20
125 Surging Might C :G:	.08	.20
20 Surging Sentinels C :W:	.08	.20
48 Survivor of the Unseen C :B:	.08	.20
21 Swift Maneuver C :W:	.08	.20
132 Tamanoa R :D:	.30	.75
49 Thermal Flux C :B:	.08	.20
100 Thermopod C :R:	.08	.20
142 Thrumming Stone R :A:	3.00	8.00
150 Tresserhorn Sinks U :L:	.40	1.00
73 Tresserhorn Skyknight U :K:	.10	.25
22 Ursine Fylgja U :W:	.10	.25
133 Vanish into Memory U :D:	.10	.25
50 Vexing Sphinx R :B:	.30	.75
74 Void Maw R :K:	.20	.50
23 Wall of Shards U :W:	.20	.50
24 White Shield Crusader U :W:	.20	.50
134 Wilderness Elemental U :D:	.10	.25
25 Woolly Razorback R :W:	.25	.60
75 Zombie Musher C :K:	.08	.20
135 Zur the Enchanter R :D:	1.50	4.00

2006 Magic The Gathering Time Spiral

Card	Low	High
COMPLETE SET (301)	100.00	175.00
BOOSTER BOX (36 PACKS)	150.00	200.00
BOOSTER PACK (15 CARDS)	4.00	6.00
THEME DECK	8.00	15.00
FAT PACK	40.00	60.00
*FOIL: .75X TO 2X BASIC CARDS		
RELEASED ON OCTOBER 6, 2006		
1 Amrou Scout C :W:	.10	.20
2 Amrou Seekers C :W:	.10	.20
3 Angel's Grace R :W:	2.50	6.00
4 Benalish Cavalry C :W:	.10	.20
5 Castle Raptors C :W:	.10	.20
6 Cavalry Master U :W:	.12	.30
7 Celestial Crusader U :W:	.20	.50
8 Children of Korlis C :W:	.10	.20
9 Chronosavant R :W:	.25	.60
10 Cloudchaser Kestrel C :W:	.10	.20
11 D'Avenant Healer C :W:	.10	.20
12 Detainment Spell C :W:	.10	.20
13 Divine Congregation C :W:	.10	.20
14 Duskrider Peregrine U :W:	.12	.30
15 Errant Doomsayers C :W:	.10	.20
16 Evangelize R :W:	.25	.60
17 Flickering Spirit C :W:	.10	.20
18 Foriysian Interceptor C :W:	.10	.20
19 Fortify C :W:	.10	.20
20 Gaze of Justice C :W:	.10	.20
21 Griffin Guide U :W:	.15	.40
22 Gustcloak Cavalier U :W:	.12	.30
23 Icatian Crier C :W:	.10	.20
24 Ivory Giant C :W:	.10	.20
25 Jedit's Dragoons C :W:	.10	.20
26 Knight of the Holy Nimbus U :W:	.20	.50
27 Magus of the Disk R :W:	.60	1.50
28 Mangara of Corondor R :W:	1.25	3.00
29 Momentary Blink C :W:	.20	.50
30 Opal Guardian R :W:	.25	.60
31 Outrider en-Kor U :W:	.12	.30
32 Pentarch Paladin R :W:	1.00	2.50
33 Pentarch Ward C :W:	.15	.40
34 Plated Pegasus U :W:	.12	.30
35 Pull from Eternity U :W:	.12	.30
36 Pulmonic Sliver R :W:	1.25	3.00
37 Quilled Sliver U :W:	.15	.40
38 Restore Balance R :W:	.75	2.00
39 Return to Dust U :W:	.25	.60
40 Serra Avenger R :W:	3.00	8.00
41 Sidewinder Sliver C :W:	.10	.20
42 Spirit Loop U :W:	.40	1.00
43 Temporal Isolation C :W:	.10	.20
44 Tivadar of Thorn R :W:	.25	.60
45 Watcher Sliver C :W:	.10	.20
46 Weathered Bodyguards R :W:	.25	.60
47 Zealot il-Vec C :W:	.10	.20
48 Ancestral Vision R :B:	2.00	5.00
49 Bewilder C :B:	.10	.20
50 Brine Elemental U :B:	.12	.30
51 Cancel C :B:	.10	.20
52 Careful Consideration U :B:	.12	.30
53 Clockspinning C :B:	.15	.40
54 Coral Trickster C :B:	.10	.20
55 Crookclaw Transmuter C :B:	.10	.20
56 Deep-Sea Kraken R :B:	1.25	3.00
57 Draining Whelk R :B:	1.00	2.50
58 Dream Stalker C :B:	.10	.20
59 Drifter il-Dal C :B:	.10	.20
60 Errant Ephemeron C :B:	.10	.20
61 Eternity Snare C :B:	.10	.20
62 Fathom Seer C :B:	.12	.30
63 Fledgling Mawcor U :B:	.12	.30
64 Fool's Demise U :B:	.15	.40
65 Ixidron R :B:	.30	.75
66 Looter il-Kor C :B:	.10	.20
67 Magus of the Jar R :B:	.25	.60
68 Moonlace R :B:	.25	.60
69 Mystical Teachings C :B:	.20	.50
70 Ophidian Eye C :B:	.10	.20
71 Paradox Haze U :B:	1.25	3.00
72 Psionic Sliver R :B:	.30	.75
73 Riftwing Cloudskate U :B:	.12	.30
74 Sage of Epityr C :B:	.12	.30
75 Screeching Sliver C :B:	.10	.20
76 Shadow Sliver C :B:	.10	.20
77 Slipstream Serpent C :B:	.10	.20
78 Snapback C :B:	.10	.20
79 Spell Burst U :B:	.15	.40
80 Spiketail Drakeling C :B:	.10	.20
81 Sprite Noble R :B:	.30	.75
82 Stormcloud Djinn U :B:	.12	.30
83 Teferi, Mage of Zhalfir R :B:	2.50	6.00
84 Telekinetic Sliver U :B:	.20	.50
85 Temporal Eddy C :B:	.10	.20
86 Think Twice C :B:	.15	.40
87 Tolarian Sentinel C :B:	.10	.20
88 Trickbind R :B:	2.00	5.00
89 Truth or Tale U :B:	.15	.40
90 Vesuvan Shapeshifter R :B:	1.25	3.00
91 Viscerid Deepwalker C :B:	.10	.20
92 Voidmage Husher U :B:	.15	.40
93 Walk the Aeons R :B:	.60	1.50
94 Wipe Away U :B:	.20	.50
95 Assassinate C :K:	.10	.20
96 Basal Sliver C :K:	.10	.20
97 Call to the Netherworld C :K:	.10	.20
98 Corpulent Corpse C :K:	.10	.20
99 Curse of the Cabal R :K:	.30	.75
100 Cyclopean Giant C :K:	.10	.20
101 Dark Withering C :K:	.10	.20
102 Deathspore Thallid C :K:	.10	.20
103 Demonic Collusion R :K:	.30	.75
104 Dread Return U :K:	.75	2.00
105 Drudge Reavers C :K:	.10	.20
106 Endrek Sahr, Master Breeder R :K:	.30	.75
107 Evil Eye of Urborg U :K:	.12	.30
108 Faceless Devourer U :K:	.12	.30
109 Fallen Ideal U :K:	.12	.30
110 Feebleness C :K:	.10	.20
111 Gorgon Recluse C :K:	.10	.20
112 Haunting Hymn U :K:	.12	.30
113 Liege of the Pit R :K:	.25	.60
114 Lim-Dûl the Necromancer R :K:	1.25	3.00
115 Living End R :K:	1.50	4.00
116 Magus of the Mirror R :K:	.25	.60
117 Mana Skimmer C :K:	.10	.20
118 Mindlash Sliver C :K:	.10	.20
119 Mindstab C :K:	.10	.20
120 Nether Traitor R :K:	2.00	5.00
121 Nightshade Assassin U :K:	.12	.30
122 Phthisis U :K:	.12	.30
123 Pit Keeper C :K:	.10	.20
124 Plague Sliver R :K:	.30	.75
125 Premature Burial U :K:	.12	.30
126 Psychotic Episode C :K:	.10	.20
127 Sangrophage C :K:	.10	.20
128 Sengir Nosferatu R :K:	.25	.60
129 Skittering Monstrosity U :K:	.12	.30
130 Skulking Knight C :K:	.10	.20
131 Smallpox U :K:	.30	.75
132 Strangling Soot C :K:	.10	.20
133 Stronghold Overseer R :K:	.30	.75
134 Sudden Death U :K:	.20	.50
135 Sudden Spoiling R :K:	1.50	4.00
136 Tendrils of Corruption C :K:	.10	.20
137 Traitor's Clutch C :K:	.10	.20
138 Trespasser il-Vec C :K:	.10	.20
139 Urborg Syphon-Mage C :K:	.10	.20
140 Vampiric Sliver U :K:	.20	.50
141 Viscid Lemures C :K:	.10	.20
142 AEtherflame Wall C :R:	.10	.20
143 Ancient Grudge C :R:	.15	.40
144 Barbed Shocker U :R:	.15	.40
145 Basalt Gargoyle U :R:	.12	.30
146 Blazing Blade Askari C :R:	.10	.20
147 Bogardan Hellkite R :R:	1.50	4.00
148 Bogardan Rager C :R:	.10	.20
149 Bonesplitter Sliver C :R:	.10	.20
150 Coal Stoker C :R:	.10	.20
151 Conflagrate U :R:	.12	.30
152 Empty the Warrens C :R:	.30	.75
153 Firemaw Kavu U :R:	.12	.30
154 Flamecore Elemental C :R:	.10	.20
155 Flowstone Channeler C :R:	.10	.20
156 Fortune Thief R :R:	.25	.60
157 Fury Sliver U :R:	.20	.50
158 Ghitu Firebreathing C :R:	.10	.20
159 Goblin Skycutter C :R:	.10	.20
160 Grapeshot C :R:	.30	.75
161 Greater Gargadon R :R:	1.50	4.00
162 Ground Rift C :R:	.10	.20
163 Ib Halfheart, Goblin Tactician R :R:	.25	.60
164 Ignite Memories U :R:	.15	.40
165 Ironclaw Buzzardiers C :R:	.10	.20
166 Jaya Ballard, Task Mage R :R:	.30	.75
167 Keldon Halberdier C :R:	.10	.20
168 Lightning Axe C :R:	.10	.20
169 Magus of the Scroll R :R:	.25	.60
170 Mogg War Marshal C :R:	.40	1.00
171 Norin the Wary R :R:	.25	.60
172 Orcish Cannonade C :R:	.10	.20
173 Pardic Dragon R :R:	.25	.60
174 Plunder C :R:	.10	.20
175 Reiterate R :R:	1.25	3.00
176 Rift Bolt C :R:	1.25	3.00
177 Sedge Sliver R :R:	1.00	2.50
178 Subterranean Shambler C :R:	.10	.20
179 Sudden Shock U :R:	.20	.50
180 Sulfurous Blast U :R:	.15	.40
181 Tectonic Fiend U :R:	.12	.30
182 Thick-Skinned Goblin U :R:	.12	.30
183 Two-Headed Sliver C :R:	.10	.20
184 Undying Rage U :R:	.15	.40
185 Viashino Bladescout C :R:	.10	.20
186 Volcanic Awakening U :R:	.12	.30
187 Wheel of Fate R :R:	1.25	3.00
188 Word of Seizing R :R:	.25	.60
189 AEther Web C :G:	.10	.20
190 Ashcoat Bear C :G:	.10	.20
191 Aspect of Mongoose U :G:	.20	.50
192 Chameleon Blur C :G:	.10	.20
193 Durkwood Baloth C :G:	.10	.20
194 Durkwood Tracker U :G:	.12	.30
195 Fungus Sliver R :G:	.30	.75
196 Gemhide Sliver C :G:	.40	1.00
197 Glass Asp C :G:	.10	.20
198 Greenseeker C :G:	.10	.20
199 Havenwood Wurm C :G:	.10	.20
200 Herd Gnarr C :G:	.10	.20
201 Hypergenesis R :G:	2.00	5.00
202 Krosan Grip U :G:	1.50	4.00
203 Magus of the Candelabra R :G:	.60	1.50
204 Might of Old Krosa U :G:	.20	.50
205 Might Sliver U :G:	.30	.75
206 Molder C :G:	.10	.20
207 Mwonvuli Acid-Moss C :G:	.15	.40
208 Nantuko Shaman C :G:	.10	.20
209 Pendelhaven Elder U :G:	.12	.30
210 Penumbra Spider C :G:	.10	.20
211 Phantom Wurm U :G:	.12	.30
212 Primal Forcemage U :G:	.15	.40
213 Savage Thallid C :G:	.10	.20
214 Scarwood Treefolk C :G:	.10	.20
215 Scryb Ranger U :G:	.25	.60
216 Search for Tomorrow C :G:	.10	.20
217 Spectral Force R :G:	.25	.60
218 Spike Tiller R :G:	.25	.60
219 Spinneret Sliver C :G:	.10	.20
220 Sporesower Thallid U :G:	.25	.60
221 Sprout C :G:	.10	.20
222 Squall Line R :G:	.25	.60
223 Stonewood Invocation R :G:	.25	.60
224 Strength in Numbers C :G:	.10	.20
225 Thallid Germinator C :G:	.10	.20
226 Thallid Shell-Dweller C :G:	.10	.20
227 Thelon of Havenwood R :G:	.30	.75
228 Thelonite Hermit R :G:	.30	.75
229 Thrill of the Hunt C :G:	.10	.20
230 Tromp the Domains U :G:	.12	.30
231 Unyaro Bees R :G:	.25	.60
232 Verdant Embrace R :G:	.30	.75
233 Wormwood Dryad C :G:	.10	.20
234 Wurmcalling R :G:	.25	.60
235 Yavimaya Dryad U :G:	.15	.40
236 Dementia Sliver U :D:	.15	.40
237 Dralnu, Lich Lord R :D:	.75	2.00
238 Firewake Sliver U :D:	.15	.40
239 Ghostflame Sliver U :D:	.15	.40
240 Harmonic Sliver U :D:	.75	2.00
241 Ith, High Arcanist R :D:	.40	1.00
242 Kaervek the Merciless R :D:	.30	.75
243 Mishra, Artificer Prodigy R :D:	.30	.75
244 Opaline Sliver U :D:	.20	.50
245 Saffi Eriksdotter R :D:	.75	2.00
246 Scion of the Ur-Dragon R :D:	1.25	3.00
247 Stonebrow, Krosan Hero R :D:	.25	.60
248 Assembly-Worker U :A:	.12	.30
249 Brass Gnat C :A:	.10	.20
250 Candles of Leng R :A:	.25	.60
251 Chromatic Star C :A:	.15	.40
252 Chronatog Totem U :A:	.12	.30
253 Clockwork Hydra U :A:	.12	.30

254 Foriysian Totem U :A: .12 .30
255 Gauntlet of Power R :A: 4.00 10.00
256 Hivestone R :A: .40 1.00
257 Jhoira's Timebug C :A: .10 .20
258 Locket of Yesterdays U :A: .12 .30
259 Lotus Bloom R :A: 4.00 10.00
260 Paradise Plume U :A: .12 .30
261 Phyrexian Totem U :A: .15 .40
262 Prismatic Lens C :A: .10 .20
263 Sarpadian Empires, Vol. VII R :A: .25 .60
264 Stuffy Doll R :A: 3.00 8.00
265 Thunder Totem U :A: .12 .30
266 Triskelavus R :A: .25 .60
267 Venser's Sliver C :A: .10 .20
268 Weatherseed Totem U :A: .12 .30
269 Academy Ruins R :L: 4.00 10.00
270 Calciform Pools U :L: .20 .50
271 Dreadship Reef U :L: .25 .60
272 Flagstones of Trokair R :L: 3.00 8.00
273 Fungal Reaches U :L: .20 .50
274 Gemstone Caverns R :L: .75 2.00
275 Kher Keep R :L: .60 1.50
276 Molten Slagheap U :L: .15 .40
277 Saltcrusted Steppe U :L: .20 .50
278 Swarmyard R :L: 1.50 4.00
279 Terramorphic Expanse C :L: .20 .50
280 Urza's Factory U :L: .25 .60
281 Vesuva R :L: 6.00 15.00
282 Plains L :L: .10 .20
283 Plains L :L: .10 .20
284 Plains L :L: .10 .20
285 Plains L :L: .10 .20
286 Island L :L: .10 .20
287 Island L :L: .10 .20
288 Island L :L: .10 .20
289 Island L :L: .10 .20
290 Swamp L :L: .10 .20
291 Swamp L :L: .10 .20
292 Swamp L :L: .10 .20
293 Swamp L :L: .10 .20
294 Mountain L :L: .10 .20
295 Mountain L :L: .10 .20
296 Mountain L :L: .10 .20
297 Mountain L :L: .10 .20
298 Forest L :L: .10 .20
299 Forest L :L: .10 .20
300 Forest L :L: .10 .20
301 Forest L :L: .10 .20

2006 Magic The Gathering Time Spiral Timeshifted

COMPLETE SET (121) 50.00 100.00
TR = TIMESHIFTED RARE
ACCORDING TO WOTC, THE TR ARE 50% RARER THAN THE TIME SPIRAL RARES WITHIN THE BOOSTERS.
*FOIL: .75X TO 2X BASIC CARDS
1 Akroma, Angel of Wrath TR :W: 4.00 10.00
2 Auratog TR :W: .25 .60
3 Celestial Dawn TR :W: .25 .60
4 Consecrate Land TR :W: .10 .25
5 Defiant Vanguard TR :W: .10 .25
6 Disenchant TR :W: .25 .60
7 Enduring Renewal TR :W: .40 1.00
8 Essence Sliver TR :W: 1.50 4.00
9 Honorable Passage TR :W: .10 .25
10 Icatian Javelineers TR :W: .10 .25
11 Moorish Cavalry TR :W: .10 .25
12 Resurrection TR :W: .20 .50
13 Sacred Mesa TR :W: .30 .75
14 Soltari Priest TR :W: .50 1.25
15 Squire TR :W: .10 .25
16 Valor TR :W: .10 .25
17 Witch Hunter TR :W: .15 .40
18 Zhalfirin Commander TR :W: .10 .25
19 Dandan TR :B: .10 .25
20 Flying Men TR :B: .30 .75
21 Ghost Ship TR :B: .10 .25
22 Giant Oyster TR :B: .10 .25
23 Leviathan TR :B: .15 .40
24 Lord of Atlantis TR :B: 3.00 8.00
25 Merfolk Assassin TR :B: .10 .25
26 Mistform Ultimus TR :B: .20 .50
27 Ovinomancer TR :B: .10 .25
28 Pirate Ship TR :B: .15 .40
29 Prodigal Sorcerer TR :B: .10 .25
30 Psionic Blast TR :B: 1.00 2.50
31 Sindbad TR :B: .10 .25
32 Stormscape Familiar TR :B: .15 .40
33 Unstable Mutation TR :B: .10 .25
34 Voidmage Prodigy TR :B: .50 1.25
35 Whispers of the Muse TR :B: .10 .25
36 Willbender TR :B: .20 .50
37 Avatar of Woe TR :K: 2.00 5.00
38 Bad Moon TR :K: 1.25 3.00
39 Conspiracy TR :K: .40 1.00
40 Darkness TR :K: 1.25 3.00
41 Dauthi Slayer TR :K: .20 .50
42 Evil Eye of Orms-by-Gore TR :K: .10 .25
43 Faceless Butcher TR :K: .10 .25
44 Funeral Charm TR :K: .30 .75
45 Sengir Autocrat TR :K: .15 .40
46 Shadow Guildmage TR :K: .10 .25
47 Soul Collector TR :K: .50 1.25
48 Stupor TR :K: .30 .75
49 Swamp Mosquito TR :K: .10 .25
50 Twisted Abomination TR :K: .10 .25
51 Uncle Istvan TR :K: .10 .25
52 Undead Warchief TR :K: 2.50 6.00
53 Undertaker TR :K: .10 .25
54 Withered Wretch TR :R: :K: .30 .75
55 Avalanche Riders TR :R: .50 1.25
56 Browbeat TR :R: 1.25 3.00
57 Desolation Giant TR :R: .20 .50
58 Disintegrate TR :R: .20 .50
59 Dragon Whelp TR :R: .15 .40
60 Dragonstorm TR :R: 2.00 5.00
61 Eron the Relentless TR :R: .10 .25
62 Fiery Temper TR :R: .20 .50
63 Fire Whip TR :R: .10 .25
64 Goblin Snowman TR :R: .10 .25
65 Kobold Taskmaster TR :R: .15 .40
66 Orcish Librarian TR :R: .15 .40
67 Orgg TR :R: .15 .40
68 Pandemonium TR :R: .60 1.50
69 Suq'Ata Lancer TR :R: .10 .25
70 Tribal Flames TR :R: .15 .40
71 Uthden Troll TR :R: .10 .25
72 Wildfire Emissary TR :R: .10 .25
73 Avoid Fate TR :G: .40 1.00
74 Call of the Herd TR :G: .50 1.25
75 Cockatrice TR :G: .15 .40
76 Craw Giant TR :G: .10 .25
77 Gaea's Blessing TR :G: .75 2.00
78 Gaea's Liege TR :G: .20 .50
79 Hail Storm TR :G: .10 .25
80 Hunting Moa TR :G: .10 .25
81 Jolrael, Empress of Beasts TR :G: .15 .40
82 Krosan Cloudscraper TR :G: .40 1.00
83 Scragnoth TR :G: .10 .25
84 Spike Feeder TR :G: .10 .25
85 Spitting Slug TR :G: .10 .25
86 Thallid TR :G: .10 .25
87 Thornscape Battlemage TR :G: .10 .25
88 Verdeloth the Ancient TR :G: .40 1.00
89 Wall of Roots TR :G: .40 1.00
90 Whirling Dervish TR :G: .10 .25
91 Coalition Victory TR :D: .25 .60
92 Fiery Justice TR :D: .20 .50
93 Jasmine Boreal TR :D: .10 .25
94 Lightning Angel TR :D: .50 1.25
95 Merieke Ri Berit TR :D: .25 .60
96 Mystic Enforcer TR :D: .40 1.00
97 Mystic Snake TR :D: 1.00 2.50
98 Nicol Bolas TR :D: .60 1.50
99 Shadowmage Infiltrator TR :D: 1.00 2.50
100 Sol'kanar the Swamp King TR :D: .20 .50
101 Spined Sliver TR :D: .15 .40
102 Stormbind TR :D: .20 .50
103 Teferi's Moat TR :D: .40 1.00
104 Vhati il-Dal TR :D: .20 .50
105 Void TR :D: .20 .50
106 Assault // Battery TR :R: :G: .10 .25
107 Claws of Gix TR :A: .15 .40
108 Dodecapod TR :A: .10 .25
109 Feldon's Cane TR :A: .40 1.00
110 Grinning Totem TR :A: .20 .50
111 Mindless Automaton TR :A: .15 .40
112 Mirari TR :A: .75 2.00
113 The Rack TR :A: .75 2.00
114 Serrated Arrows TR :A: .15 .40
115 Tormod's Crypt TR :A: 1.25 3.00
116 War Barge TR :A: .10 .25
117 Arena TR :L: .20 .50
118 Desert TR :L: .30 .75
119 Gemstone Mine TR :L: 2.00 5.00
120 Pendelhaven TR :L: .60 1.50
121 Safe Haven TR :L: .20 .50

2007 Magic The Gathering Planar Chaos

COMPLETE SET (165) 75.00 125.00
BOOSTER BOX (36 PACKS) 150.00 250.00
BOOSTER PACK (15 CARDS) 5.00 8.00
THEME DECK 8.00 15.00
FAT PACK 30.00 60.00
*FOIL: .75X TO 2X BASIC CARDS
RELEASED ON FEBRUARY 2, 2007
1 Aven Riftwatcher C :W: .10 .25
2 Benalish Commander R :W: .60 1.50
3 Crovax, Ascendant Hero R :W: .40 1.00
4 Dawn Charm C :W: .20 .50
5 Dust Elemental R :W: .25 .60
6 Ghost Tactician C :W: .10 .25
7 Heroes Remembered R :W: .25 .60
8 Magus of the Tabernacle R :W: .25 .60
9 Mantle of Leadership U :W: .15 .40
10 Pallid Mycoderm C :W: .10 .25
11 Poultice Sliver C :W: .10 .25
12 Rebuff the Wicked U :W: .50 1.25
13 Retether R :W: .25 .60
14 Riftmarked Knight U :W: .15 .40
15 Saltblast U :W: .15 .40
16 Saltfield Recluse C :W: .10 .25
17 Serra's Boon U :W: .15 .40
18 Shade of Trokair C :W: .10 .25
19 Stonecloaker U :W: .20 .50
20 Stormfront Riders U :W: .15 .40
21 Voidstone Gargoyle R :W: .25 .60
22 Whitemane Lion C :W: .10 .25
23 Calciderm U :W: .20 .50
24 Malach of the Dawn U :W: .15 .40
25 Mana Tithe C :W: .20 .50
26 Mesa Enchantress R :W: .25 .60
27 Mycologist U :W: .15 .40
28 Porphyry Nodes R :W: .25 .60
29 Revered Dead C :W: .10 .25
30 Sinew Sliver C :W: .20 .50
31 Sunlance C :W: .10 .25
32 Aeon Chronicler R :B: .40 1.00
33 Aquamorph Entity C :B: .10 .25
34 Auramancer's Guise U :B: .15 .40
35 Body Double R :B: .75 2.00
36 Braids, Conjurer Adept R :B: .25 .60
37 Chronozoa R :B: .60 1.50
38 Dichotomancy R :B: .25 .60
39 Dismal Failure U :B: .15 .40
40 Dreamscape Artist C :B: .10 .25
41 Erratic Mutation C :B: .10 .25
42 Jodah's Avenger U :B: .15 .40
43 Magus of the Bazaar R :B: .25 .60
44 Pongify U :B: .20 .50
45 Reality Acid C :B: .10 .25
46 Shaper Parasite C :B: .10 .25
47 Spellshift R :B: .25 .60
48 Synchronous Sliver C :B: .10 .25
49 Tidewalker U :B: .15 .40
50 Timebender U :B: .15 .40
51 Veiling Oddity C :B: .10 .25
52 Venarian Glimmer U :B: .15 .40
53 Wistful Thinking C :B: .10 .25
54 Frozen AEther U :B: .25 .60
55 Gossamer Phantasm C :B: .10 .25
56 Merfolk Thaumaturgist C :B: .10 .25
57 Ovinize U :B: .15 .40
58 Piracy Charm C :B: .10 .25
59 Primal Plasma C :B: .10 .25
60 Riptide Pilferer U :B: .15 .40
61 Serendib Sorcerer R :B: .25 .60
62 Serra Sphinx R :B: .40 1.00
63 Big Game Hunter U :K: .20 .50
64 Blightspeaker C :K: .10 .25
65 Brain Gorgers C :K: .10 .25
66 Circle of Affliction U :K: .15 .40
67 Cradle to Grave C :K: .10 .25
68 Dash Hopes C :K: .20 .50
69 Deadly Grub C :K: .10 .25
70 Enslave U :K: .20 .50
71 Extirpate R :K: 3.00 8.00
72 Imp's Mischief R :K: .25 .60
73 Magus of the Coffers R :K: .40 1.00
74 Midnight Charm C :K: .10 .25
75 Mirri the Cursed R :K: 1.00 2.50
76 Muck Drubb U :K: .15 .40
77 Phantasmagorian U :K: .20 .50
78 Ridged Kusite C :K: .10 .25
79 Roiling Horror R :K: .25 .60
80 Spitting Sliver C :K: .10 .25
81 Temporal Extortion R :K: 1.00 2.50
82 Treacherous Urge U :K: .15 .40
83 Waning Wurm U :K: .15 .40
84 Bog Serpent C :K: .10 .25
85 Damnation R :K: 10.00 25.00
86 Dunerider Outlaw U :K: .15 .40
87 Kor Dirge U :K: .15 .40
88 Melancholy C :K: .10 .25
89 Null Profusion R :K: .25 .60
90 Rathi Trapper C :K: .10 .25
91 Shrouded Lore U :K: .15 .40
92 Vampiric Link C :K: .20 .50
93 AEther Membrane U :R: .20 .50
94 Akroma, Angel of Fury R :R: 1.25 3.00
95 Battering Sliver C :R: .10 .25
96 Detritivore R :R: .25 .60
97 Dust Corona C :R: .10 .25
98 Fatal Frenzy R :R: .25 .60
99 Firefright Mage C :R: .10 .25
100 Fury Charm C :R: .10 .25
101 Hammerheim Deadeye U :R: .15 .40
102 Keldon Marauders C :R: .20 .50
103 Lavacore Elemental U :R: .15 .40
104 Magus of the Arena R :R: .25 .60
105 Needlepeak Spider C :R: .10 .25
106 Shivan Meteor U :R: .20 .50
107 Stingscourger C :R: .10 .25
108 Sulfur Elemental U :R: .40 1.00
109 Timecrafting U :R: .15 .40
110 Torchling R :R: .25 .60
111 Volcano Hellion R :R: .25 .60
112 Boom // Bust R :R: .60 1.50
113 Dead // Gone C :R: .10 .25
114 Rough // Tumble U :R: .20 .50
115 Blood Knight U :R: .30 .75
116 Brute Force C :R: .15 .40
117 Molten Firebird R :R: .25 .60
118 Prodigal Pyromancer C :R: .10 .25
119 Pyrohemia U :R: .20 .50
120 Reckless Wurm U :R: .20 .50
121 Shivan Wumpus R :R: .40 1.00
122 Simian Spirit Guide C :R: .25 .60
123 Skirk Shaman C :R: .10 .25
124 Ana Battlemage U :G: .15 .40
125 Citanul Woodreaders C :G: .10 .25
126 Deadwood Treefolk U :G: .15 .40
127 Evolution Charm C :G: .10 .25
128 Fungal Behemoth R :G: .25 .60
129 Giant Dustwasp C :G: .10 .25
130 Hunting Wilds U :G: .15 .40
131 Jedit Ojanen of Efrava R :G: .25 .60
132 Kavu Predator U :G: .75 2.00
133 Life and Limb R :G: .25 .60
134 Magus of the Library R :G: .25 .60
135 Mire Boa C :G: .15 .40
136 Pouncing Wurm U :G: .15 .40
137 Psychotrope Thallid U :G: .30 .75
138 Reflex Sliver C :G: .10 .25
139 Sophic Centaur U :G: .15 .40
140 Timbermare R :G: .25 .60
141 Uktabi Drake C :G: .10 .25
142 Utopia Vow C :G: .10 .25
143 Vitaspore Thallid C :G: .10 .25
144 Wild Pair R :G: .50 1.25
145 Essence Warden C :G: .25 .60
146 Fa'adiyah Seer C :G: .10 .25
147 Gaea's Anthem R :G: 1.00 2.50
148 Groundbreaker R :G: .75 2.00
149 Harmonize U :G: .75 2.00
150 Healing Leaves C :G: .10 .25
151 Hedge Troll U :G: .15 .40
152 Keen Sense U :G: .20 .50
153 Seal of Primordium C :G: .10 .25
154 Cautery Sliver U :D: .20 .50
155 Darkheart Sliver U :D: .20 .50
156 Dormant Sliver U :D: .20 .50
157 Frenetic Sliver U :D: .15 .40
158 Intet, the Dreamer R :D: .40 1.00
159 Necrotic Sliver U :D: .40 1.00
160 Numot, the Devastator R :D: .60 1.50
161 Oros, the Avenger R :D: .25 .60
162 Radha, Heir to Keld R :D: .30 .75
163 Teneb, the Harvester R :D: .60 1.50
164 Vorosh, the Hunter R :D: .40 1.00
165 Urborg, Tomb of Yawgmoth R :L: 8.00 20.00

2007 Magic The Gathering Future Sight

COMPLETE SET (180) 200.00 275.00
BOOSTER BOX (36 PACKS) 200.00 350.00
BOOSTER PACK (15 CARDS) 6.00 10.00
THEME DECK 8.00 15.00
FAT PACK 40.00 80.00
*FOIL: .75X TO 2X BASIC CARDS
RELEASED ON MAY 4, 2007
1 Angel of Salvation R :W: .25 .60
2 Augur il-Vec C :W: .10 .25
3 Barren Glory R :W: .25 .60
3 Marshaling Cry C :W: .10 .25
4 Chronomantic Escape U :W: .15 .40
5 Dust of Moments U :W: .15 .40
6 Even the Odds U :W: .15 .40
7 Gift of Granite C :W: .10 .25
8 Intervention Pact R :W: .40 1.00
9 Judge Unworthy C :W: .10 .25
10 Knight of Sursi C :W: .10 .25
11 Lost Auramancers U :W: .15 .40
12 Magus of the Moat R :W: 1.00 2.50
13 Magus of the Vineyard R :G: .25 .60
14 Saltskitter C :W: .10 .25
15 Samite Censer-Bearer C :W: .10 .25
16 Scout's Warning R :W: .25 .60
17 Spirit en-Dal U :W: .15 .40
18 Aven Mindcensor U :W: 1.25 3.00
19 Blade of the Sixth Pride C :W: .10 .25
20 Bound in Silence U :W: .15 .40
21 Daybreak Coronet R :W: 1.25 3.00
22 Goldmeadow Lookout U :W: .15 .40
23 Imperial Mask R :W: .25 .60
24 Lucent Liminid C :W: .10 .25
25 Lumithread Field C :W: .10 .25
26 Lymph Sliver C :W: .10 .25
27 Mistmeadow Skulk U :W: .15 .40
28 Oriss, Samite Guardian R :W: .30 .75
29 Patrician's Scorn C :W: .10 .25
30 Ramosian Revivalist U :W: .15 .40
31 Seht's Tiger R :W: .25 .60
32 Aven Augur C :B: .10 .25
33 Cloudseeder U :B: .15 .40
34 Cryptic Annelid U :B: .15 .40
35 Delay U :B: .25 .60
36 Foresee C :B: .10 .25
37 Infiltrator il-Kor C :B: .10 .25
38 Leaden Fists C :B: .10 .25
39 Maelstrom Djinn R :B: .25 .60
40 Magus of the Future R :B: .50 1.25
41 Mystic Speculation U :B: .25 .60
42 Pact of Negation R :B: 8.00 20.00
43 Reality Strobe U :B: .15 .40
44 Take Possession R :B: .30 .75
45 Unblinking Bleb C :B: .10 .25
46 Venser's Diffusion C :B: 2.00 5.00
47 Venser, Shaper Savant R :B: .25 .60
48 Arcanum Wings U :B: .15 .40
49 Blind Phantasm C :B: .10 .25
50 Bonded Fetch U :B: .15 .40
51 Linessa, Zephyr Mage R :B: .25 .60
52 Logic Knot C :B: .10 .25
54 Narcomoeba U :B: 1.00 2.50
55 Nix R :B: .25 .60
56 Sarcomite Myr C :B: .10 .25
57 Second Wind U :B: .15 .40
58 Shapeshifter's Marrow R :B: .25 .60
59 Spellweaver Volute R :B: .25 .60
60 Spin into Myth U :B: .15 .40
61 Vedalken AEthermage C :B: .10 .25
62 Whip-Spine Drake C :B: .10 .25
63 Augur of Skulls C :K: .10 .25
64 Cutthroat il-Dal C :K: .10 .25
65 Festering March U :K: .15 .40
66 Gibbering Descent R :K: .25 .60
67 Grave Peril C :K: .10 .25
68 Ichor Slick C :K: .10 .25
69 Lost Hours C :K: .10 .25
70 Magus of the Abyss R :K: .25 .60
72 Nihilith R :K: .25 .60
73 Oblivion Crown C :K: .10 .25
74 Pooling Venom U :K: .15 .40
75 Putrid Cyclops C :K: .10 .25
76 Shimian Specter R :K: .75 2.00
77 Skirk Ridge Exhumer U :K: .15 .40
78 Slaughter Pact R :K: 1.25 3.00
79 Stronghold Rats U :K: .15 .40
80 Bitter Ordeal R :K: .60 1.50
81 Bridge from Below R :K: 8.00 20.00
82 Death Rattle C :K: .10 .25
83 Deepcavern Imp C :K: .10 .25
84 Fleshwrither U :K: .15 .40
85 Frenzy Sliver C :K: .10 .25
86 Grave Scrabbler C :K: .10 .25
87 Korlash, Heir to Blackblade R :K: 2.50 6.00
88 Mass of Ghouls C :K: .10 .25
89 Snake Cult Initiation U :K: .15 .40
90 Street Wraith U :K: .75 2.00
91 Tombstalker R :K: 4.00 10.00
92 Witch's Mist U :K: .15 .40
93 Yixlid Jailer U :K: .15 .40
94 Arc Blade U :R: .15 .40
95 Bogardan Lancer C :R: .10 .25
96 Char-Rumbler U :R: .15 .40
97 Emberwilde Augur C :R: .10 .25
98 Fatal Attraction C :R: .10 .25
99 Gathan Raiders C :R: .10 .25
100 Haze of Rage U :R: .15 .40
101 Magus of the Moon R :R: 2.50 6.00
103 Pact of the Titan R :R: .75 2.00
104 Pyromancer's Swath R :R: .75 2.00
105 Riddle of Lightning C :R: .10 .25
106 Rift Elemental C :R: .10 .25
107 Scourge of Kher Ridges R :R: .75 2.00
108 Shivan Sand-Mage U :R: .15 .40
109 Sparkspitter U :R: .15 .40
110 Bloodshot Trainee U :R: .15 .40
111 Boldwyr Intimidator U :R: .15 .40
112 Emblem of the Warmind U :R: .15 .40
113 Flowstone Embrace C :R: .10 .25
114 Fomori Nomad C :R: .10 .25
115 Ghostfire C :R: .10 .25
116 Grinning Ignus C :R: .10 .25
117 Henchfiend of Ukor C :R: .10 .25
118 Homing Sliver C :R: .10 .25
119 Shah of Naar Isle R :R: .25 .60
120 Skizzik Surger U :R: .15 .40
121 Steamflogger Boss R :R: .30 .75
122 Storm Entity U :R: .15 .40
123 Tarox Bladewing R :R: .25 .60
124 Thunderblade Charge R :R: .25 .60
125 Cyclical Evolution U :G: .15 .40
126 Force of Savagery R :G: .25 .60
127 Heartwood Storyteller R :G: .30 .75
128 Kavu Primarch C :G: .10 .25
129 Llanowar Augur C :G: .10 .25
130 Llanowar Empath C :G: .10 .25
131 Llanowar Mentor U :G: .25 .60
133 Petrified Plating C :G: .10 .25
134 Quiet Disrepair C :G: .10 .25
135 Ravaging Riftwurm U :G: .15 .40
136 Riftsweeper U :G: .15 .40
137 Rites of Flourishing R :G: .40 1.00
138 Sprout Swarm C :G: .10 .25
139 Summoner's Pact R :G: 4.00 10.00
140 Utopia Mycon U :G: .50 1.25
141 Wrap in Vigor C :G: .10 .25
142 Baru, Fist of Krosa R :G: .25 .60
143 Centaur Omenreader U :G: .15 .40
144 Edge of Autumn C :G: .10 .25
145 Imperiosaur U :G: .15 .40
147 Nacatl War-Pride U :G: .15 .40
148 Nessian Courser C :G: .10 .25
149 Phosphorescent Feast U :G: .15 .40
150 Quagnoth R :G: .25 .60
151 Spellwild Ouphe U :G: .15 .40
152 Sporoloth Ancient C :G: .10 .25
153 Tarmogoyf R :G: 75.00 125.00
154 Thornweald Archer C :G: .15 .40
155 Virulent Sliver C :G: .15 .40
156 Glittering Wish R :D: .60 1.50
157 Jhoira of the Ghitu R :D: 1.50 4.00
158 Sliver Legion R :D: 4.00 10.00
159 Akroma's Memorial R :A: 6.00 15.00
160 Cloud Key R :A: 1.25 3.00
161 Coalition Relic R :A: 1.50 4.00
162 Epochrasite R :A: .60 1.50
163 Sliversmith U :A: .15 .40
164 Soultether Golem U :A: .15 .40
165 Sword of the Meek U :A: .75 2.00
166 Veilstone Amulet R :A: .25 .60
167 Darksteel Garrison R :A: .25 .60
168 Whetwheel R :A: .25 .60
169 Dakmor Salvage U :L: .30 .75
170 Keldon Megaliths U :L: .15 .40
171 Llanowar Reborn U :L: .25 .60
172 New Benalia U :L: .15 .40
173 Tolaria West U :L: .75 2.00
174 Dryad Arbor U :L: 1.50 4.00
175 Graven Cairns R :L: 1.25 3.00
176 Grove of the Burnwillows R :L: 5.00 12.00
177 Horizon Canopy R :L: 3.00 8.00
178 Nimbus Maze R :L: 1.00 2.50
179 River of Tears R :L: 1.00 2.50
180 Zoetic Cavern U :L: .15 .40
97 Mesmeric Sliver C :B: .10 .25
98 Minions' Murmurs U :K: .15 .40
100 Molten Disaster R :R: .25 .60
101 Muraganda Petroglyphs R :G: .25 .60

2007 Magic The Gathering 10th Edition

COMPLETE SET (383) 125.00 200.00
BOOSTER BOX (36 PACKS) 200.00 250.00
BOOSTER PACK (15 CARDS) 6.00 8.00
*FOIL: .75X TO 2X BASIC CARDS
RELEASED ON JULY 14, 2007
1 Ancestor's Chosen U :W: .20 .50
2 Angel of Mercy U :W: .20 .50
3 Angelic Chorus R :W: .10 .25
4 Angelic Wall C :W: 1.50 4.00
5 Angel's Feather U :A: .20 .50
6 Aura of Silence U :W: .60 1.50
7 Aven Cloudchaser C :W: .10 .25
8 Ballista Squad U :W: .20 .50
9 Bandage C :W: .10 .25
10 Beacon of Immortality R :W: 2.00 5.00
11 Benalish Knight C :W: .10 .25
12 Cho-Manno, Revolutionary R :W: .40 1.00
13 Condemn U :W: .40 1.00
14 Demystify C :W: .10 .25
15 Field Marshal R :W: 2.50 6.00
16 Ghost Warden C :W: .10 .25
17 Glorious Anthem R :W: 1.25 3.00
18 Hail of Arrows U :W: .20 .50
19 Heart of Light C :W: .10 .25
20 High Ground U :W: .20 .50
21 Holy Day C :W: .25 .60
22 Holy Strength C :W: .10 .25
23 Honor Guard C :W: .10 .25
24 Icatian Priest U :W: .20 .50
25 Kjeldoran Royal Guard R :W: .30 .75
26 Loxodon Mystic C :W: .10 .25
27 Loyal Sentry R :W: .40 1.00
28 Luminesce U :W: .20 .50
29 Mobilization R :W: 1.25 3.00
30 Nomad Mythmaker R :W: .60 1.50
31 Pacifism C :W: .10 .25
32 Paladin en-Vec R :W: .75 2.00
33 Pariah R :W: 1.50 4.00
34 Reviving Dose C :W: .10 .25
35 Reya Dawnbringer R :W: 2.50 6.00
36 Righteousness R :W: .30 .75
37 Rule of Law U :W: .40 1.00
38 Samite Healer C :W: .10 .25
39 Serra Angel R :W: .40 1.00
40 Serra's Embrace U :W: .25 .60
41 Skyhunter Patrol C :W: .10 .25
42 Skyhunter Prowler C :W: .10 .25
43 Skyhunter Skirmisher U :W: .20 .50
44 Soul Warden U :W: .30 .75
45 Spirit Link U :W: .25 .60
46 Spirit Weaver U :W: .20 .50
47 Starlight Invoker U :W: .20 .50
48 Steadfast Guard C :W: .10 .25
49 Story Circle R :W: .75 2.00
50 Suntail Hawk C :W: .10 .25
51 Tempest of Light U :W: .20 .50
52 Treasure Hunter U :W: .20 .50
53 True Believer R :W: 1.25 2.50
54 Tundra Wolves C :W: .10 .25
55 Venerable Monk C :W: .10 .25
56 Voice of All R :W: .60 1.50
57 Wall of Swords U :W: .20 .50
58 Warrior's Honor C :W: .10 .25
59 Wild Griffin C :W: .10 .25
60 Windborn Muse R :W: .75 2.00
61 Wrath of God R :W: 6.00 15.00
62 Youthful Knight C :W: .10 .25
63 Academy Researchers U :B: .20 .50
64 Air Elemental U :B: .20 .50
65 Ambassador Laquatus R :B: .60 1.50
66 Arcanis the Omnipotent R :B: 2.00 5.00
67 Aura Graft U :B: .20 .50
68 Aven Fisher C :B: .10 .25
69 Aven Windreader C :B: .10 .25
70 Boomerang C :B: .20 .50

71 Cancel C :B: .20 .50
72 Cephalid Constable R :B: .30 .75
73 Clone R :B: .40 1.00
74 Cloud Elemental C :B: .10 .25
75 Cloud Sprite C :B: .10 .25
76 Counsel of the Soratami C :B: .10 .25
77 Crafty Pathmage C :B: .10 .25
78 Dehydration C :B: .10 .25
79 Deluge U :B: .20 .50
80 Denizen of the Deep R :B: .30 .75
81 Discombobulate U :B: .20 .50
82 Dreamborn Muse R :B: .30 .75
83 Evacuation R :B: 1.25 3.00
84 Flashfreeze U :B: .30 .75
85 Fog Elemental U :B: .20 .50
86 Fugitive Wizard C :B: .10 .25
87 Horseshoe Crab C :B: .10 .25
88 Hurkyl's Recall R :B: 1.25 3.00
89 Lumengrid Warden C :B: .10 .25
90 Mahamoti Djinn R :B: .30 .75
91 March of the Machines R :B: .30 .75
92 Merfolk Looter C :B: .10 .25
93 Mind Bend R :B: .30 .75
94 Peek C :B: .10 .25
95 Persuasion U :B: .25 .60
96 Phantom Warrior U :B: .25 .60
97 Plagiarize R :B: .30 .75
98 Puppeteer U :B: .20 .50
99 Reminisce U :B: .20 .50
100 Remove Soul C :B: .10 .25
101 Robe of Mirrors C :B: .10 .25
102 Rootwater Commando C :B: .10 .25
103 Rootwater Matriarch R :B: .60 1.50
104 Sage Owl C :B: .10 .25
105 Scalpelexis R :B: .30 .75
106 Sea Monster C :B: .10 .25
107 Shimmering Wings C :B: .10 .25
108 Sift C :B: .10 .25
109 Sky Weaver U :B: .20 .50
110 Snapping Drake C :B: .10 .25
111 Spiketail Hatchling U :B: .20 .50
112 Sunken Hope R :B: .30 .75
113 Telepathy U :B: .20 .50
114 Telling Time U :B: .30 .75
115 Thieving Magpie U :B: .20 .50
116 Tidings U :B: .40 1.00
117 Time Stop R :B: .75 2.00
118 Time Stretch R :B: 2.00 5.00
119 Traumatize R :B: 1.25 2.50
120 Twincast R :B: 1.25 3.00
121 Twitch C :B: .10 .25
122 Unsummon C :B: .10 .25
123 Vedalken Mastermind U :B: .20 .50
124 Wall of Air U :B: .20 .50
125 Afflict C :K: .10 .25
126 Agonizing Memories U :K: .20 .50
127 Ascendant Evincar R :K: .75 2.00
128 Assassinate C :K: .10 .25
129 Beacon of Unrest R :K: 1.50 4.00
130 Bog Wraith U :K: .20 .50
131 Consume Spirit U :K: .20 .50
132 Contaminated Bond C :K: .10 .25
133 Cruel Edict U :K: .60 1.50
134 Deathmark U :K: .25 .60
135 Diabolic Tutor U :K: .50 1.25
136 Distress C :K: .10 .25
137 Doomed Necromancer R :K: 1.25 2.50
138 Dross Crocodile C :K: .10 .25
139 Drudge Skeletons U :K: .20 .50
140 Dusk Imp C :K: .10 .25
141 Essence Drain C :K: .10 .25
142 Fear C :K: .10 .25
143 Festering Goblin C :K: .10 .25
144 Grave Pact R :K: 2.50 6.00
145 Graveborn Muse R :K: .50 1.25
146 Gravedigger C :K: .10 .25
147 Hate Weaver U :K: .20 .50
148 Head Games R :K: .30 .75
149 Hidden Horror U :K: .20 .50
150 Highway Robber C :K: .10 .25
151 Hypnotic Specter R :K: 1.25 3.00
152 Knight of Dusk U :K: .25 .60
153 Looming Shade C :K: .10 .25
154 Lord of the Pit R :K: .30 .75
155 Lord of the Undead R :K: 6.00 15.00
156 Mass of Ghouls C :K: .10 .25
157 Megrim U :K: .40 1.00
158 Midnight Ritual R :K: .30 .75
159 Mind Rot C :K: .10 .25
160 Mortal Combat R :K: .30 .75
161 Mortivore R :K: .75 2.00
162 Nantuko Husk U :K: .20 .50
163 Nekrataal U :K: .25 .60
164 Nightmare R :K: .30 .75
165 No Rest for the Wicked U :K: .20 .50
166 Phage the Untouchable R :K: 2.50 6.00
167 Phyrexian Rager C :K: .10 .25
168 Plague Beetle C :K: .10 .25
169 Plague Wind R :K: 1.25 3.00
170 Rain of Tears U :K: .25 .60
171 Ravenous Rats C :K: .10 .25
172 Recover C :K: .10 .25
173 Relentless Rats U :K: .75 2.00
174 Royal Assassin R :K: .75 2.00
175 Scathe Zombies C :K: .10 .25
176 Sengir Vampire R :K: .50 1.25
177 Severed Legion C :K: .10 .25
178 Sleeper Agent R :K: .30 .75
179 Soul Feast U :K: .20 .50
180 Spineless Thug C :K: .10 .25
181 Stronghold Discipline U :K: .20 .50
182 Terror C :K: .25 .60
183 Thrull Surgeon U :K: .20 .50
184 Underworld Dreams R :K: 1.25 2.50
185 Unholy Strength C :K: .10 .25
186 Vampire Bats C :K: .10 .25
187 Anaba Bodyguard C :R: .10 .25
188 Arcane Teachings U :R: .20 .50
189 Beacon of Destruction R :R: .50 1.25
190 Blaze U :R: .25 .60
191 Bloodfire Colossus R :R: .30 .75
192 Bloodrock Cyclops C :R: .10 .25
193 Bogardan Firefiend C :R: .10 .25
194 Cone of Flame U :R: .20 .50
195 Cryoclasm U :R: .40 1.00
196 Demolish C :R: .10 .25
197 Dragon Roost R :R: .60 1.50
198 Duct Crawler C :R: .10 .25
199 Earth Elemental U :R: .20 .50
200 Firebreathing C :R: .10 .25
201 Fists of the Anvil C :R: .10 .25
202 Flamewave Invoker U :R: .20 .50
203 Flowstone Slide R :R: .30 .75
204 Furnace of Rath R :R: .60 1.50
205 Furnace Whelp U :R: .20 .50
206 Goblin Elite Infantry C :R: .10 .25
207 Goblin King R :R: 1.25 3.00
208 Goblin Lore U :R: .40 1.00
209 Goblin Piker C :R: .10 .25
210 Goblin Sky Raider C :R: .10 .25
211 Guerrilla Tactics U :R: .20 .50
212 Hill Giant C :R: .10 .25
213 Incinerate C :R: .30 .75
214 Kamahl, Pit Fighter R :R: .30 .75
215 Lava Axe C :R: .10 .25
216 Lavaborn Muse R :R: .30 .75
217 Lightning Elemental C :R: .10 .25
218 Manabarbs R :R: .30 .75
219 Mogg Fanatic U :R: .60 1.50
220 Orcish Artillery U :R: .20 .50
221 Prodigal Pyromancer C :R: .10 .25
222 Pyroclasm U :R: .40 1.00
223 Rage Weaver U :R: .20 .50
224 Raging Goblin C :R: .10 .25
225 Relentless Assault R :R: .30 .75
226 Rock Badger C :R: .10 .25
227 Scoria Wurm R :R: .30 .75
228 Seismic Assault R :R: 1.25 2.50
229 Shatterstorm U :R: .30 .75
230 Shivan Dragon R :R: .30 .75
231 Shivan Hellkite R :R: .40 1.00
232 Shock C :R: .20 .50
233 Shunt R :R: .30 .75
234 Siege-Gang Commander R :R: 1.25 2.50
235 Smash C :R: .10 .25
236 Soulblast R :R: .30 .75
237 Spark Elemental U :R: .40 1.00
238 Spitting Earth C :R: .10 .25
239 Squee, Goblin Nabob R :R: 2.00 5.00
240 Stun C :R: .10 .25
241 Sudden Impact U :R: .20 .50
242 Threaten U :R: .20 .50
243 Thundering Giant U :R: .20 .50
244 Uncontrollable Anger C :R: .10 .25
245 Viashino Runner C :R: .10 .25
246 Viashino Sandscout C :R: .10 .25
247 Wall of Fire U :R: .20 .50
248 Warp World R :R: .30 .75
249 Abundance R :G: .40 1.00
250 Aggressive Urge C :G: .10 .25
251 Avatar of Might R :G: .40 1.00
252 Birds of Paradise R :G: 2.50 6.00
253 Blanchwood Armor U :G: .50 1.25
254 Canopy Spider C :G: .10 .25
255 Civic Wayfinder C :G: .10 .25
256 Commune with Nature C :G: .10 .25
257 Craw Wurm C :G: .10 .25
258 Creeping Mold U :G: .20 .50
259 Elven Riders U :G: .20 .50
260 Elvish Berserker C :G: .10 .25
261 Elvish Champion R :G: 2.50 6.00
262 Elvish Piper R :G: 3.00 8.00
263 Enormous Baloth U :G: .20 .50
264 Femeref Archers U :G: .20 .50
265 Gaea's Herald R :G: .40 1.00
266 Giant Growth C :G: .10 .25
267 Giant Spider C :G: .10 .25
268 Grizzly Bears C :G: .10 .25
269 Hunted Wumpus U :G: .20 .50
270 Hurricane R :G: .30 .75
271 Joiner Adept R :G: 1.25 3.00
272 Karplusan Strider U :G: .20 .50
273 Kavu Climber C :G: .10 .25
274 Llanowar Elves C :G: .30 .75
275 Llanowar Sentinel C :G: .10 .25
276 Lure U :G: .20 .50
277 Might of Oaks R :G: .30 .75
278 Might Weaver U :G: .20 .50
279 Mirri, Cat Warrior R :G: .50 1.25
280 Molimo, Maro-Sorcerer R :G: .30 .75
281 Natural Spring C :G: .10 .25
282 Naturalize C :G: .10 .25
283 Overgrowth C :G: .20 .50
284 Overrun U :G: .30 .75
285 Pincher Beetles C :G: .10 .25
286 Primal Rage U :G: .60 1.50
287 Quirion Dryad R :G: .60 1.50
288 Rampant Growth C :G: .20 .50
289 Recollect U :G: .20 .50
290 Regeneration U :G: .20 .50
291 Rhox R :G: .30 .75
292 Root Maze R :G: .30 .75
293 Rootwalla C :G: .10 .25
294 Rushwood Dryad C :G: .10 .25
295 Scion of the Wild R :G: .30 .75
296 Seedborn Muse R :G: 2.50 6.00
297 Skyshroud Ranger C :G: .20 .50
298 Spined Wurm C :G: .10 .25
299 Stalking Tiger C :G: .10 .25
300 Stampeding Wildebeests U :G: .20 .50
301 Sylvan Basilisk U :G: .25 .60
302 Sylvan Scrying U :G: .40 1.00
303 Tangle Spider U :G: .20 .50
304 Treetop Bracers C :G: .20 .50
305 Troll Ascetic R :G: 1.25 2.50
306 Upwelling R :G: .30 .75
307 Verdant Force R :G: .75 2.00
308 Viridian Shaman U :G: .25 .60
309 Wall of Wood C :G: .10 .25
310 Yavimaya Enchantress U :G: .25 .60
311 Angelic Blessing C :W: .20 .50
312 Bottle Gnomes U :A: .20 .50
313 Chimeric Staff R :A: .30 .75
314 Chromatic Star U :A: .25 .60
315 Citanul Flute R :A: .40 1.00
316 Coat of Arms R :A: 2.50 6.00
317 Colossus of Sardia R :A: .30 .75
318 Composite Golem U :A: .20 .50
319 Crucible of Worlds R :A: 15.00 30.00
320 Demon's Horn U :A: .20 .50
321 Doubling Cube R :A: 2.00 5.00
322 Dragon's Claw U :A: .25 .60
323 Fountain of Youth U :A: .20 .50
324 The Hive R :A: .30 .75
325 Howling Mine R :A: 1.50 4.00
326 Icy Manipulator U :A: .30 .75
327 Jayemdae Tome R :A: .30 .75
328 Juggernaut U :A: .20 .50
329 Kraken's Eye U :A: .20 .50
330 Legacy Weapon R :A: .40 1.00
331 Leonin Scimitar U :A: .20 .50
332 Loxodon Warhammer R :A: 1.25 3.00
333 Mantis Engine U :A: .20 .50
334 Millstone R :A: .40 1.00
335 Mind Stone U :A: .40 1.00
336 Ornithopter U :A: .40 1.00
337 Phyrexian Vault U :A: .20 .50
338 Pithing Needle R :A: 1.50 4.00
339 Platinum Angel R :A: 2.00 5.00
340 Razormane Masticore R :A: .40 1.00
341 Rod of Ruin U :A: .20 .50
342 Sculpting Steel R :A: 2.00 5.00
343 Spellbook U :A: .25 .60
344 Steel Golem U :A: .20 .50
345 Whispersilk Cloak U :A: .40 1.00
346 Wurm's Tooth U :A: .20 .50
347 Adarkar Wastes R :L: 1.25 3.00
348 Battlefield Forge R :L: 1.25 2.50
349 Brushland R :L: .75 2.00
350 Caves of Koilos R :L: 1.25 3.00
351 Faerie Conclave U :L: .75 2.00
352 Forbidding Watchtower U :L: .30 .75
353 Ghitu Encampment U :L: .30 .75
354 Karplusan Forest R :L: 1.25 3.00
355 Llanowar Wastes R :L: 1.25 3.00
356 Quicksand U :L: .20 .50
357 Shivan Reef R :L: 2.50 6.00
358 Spawning Pool U :L: .25 .60
359 Sulfurous Springs R :L: 1.25 3.00
360 Terramorphic Expanse C :L: .25 .60
361 Treetop Village U :L: 1.25 2.50
362 Underground River R :L: 1.50 4.00
363 Yavimaya Coast R :L: 1.50 4.00
364 Plains :L: .20 .50
365 Plains :L: .20 .50
366 Plains :L: .20 .50
367 Plains :L: .20 .50
368 Island :L: .20 .50
369 Island :L: .20 .50
370 Island :L: .20 .50
371 Island :L: .20 .50
372 Swamp :L: .20 .50
373 Swamp :L: .20 .50
374 Swamp :L: .20 .50
375 Swamp :L: .20 .50
376 Mountain :L: .20 .50
377 Mountain :L: .20 .50
378 Mountain :L: .20 .50
379 Mountain :L: .20 .50
380 Forest :L: .20 .50
381 Forest :L: .20 .50
382 Forest :L: .20 .50
383 Forest :L: .20 .50

2007 Magic The Gathering Lorwyn

COMPLETE SET (301) 250.00 350.00
BOOSTER BOX (36 PACKS) 300.00 500.00
BOOSTER PACK (15 CARDS) 8.00 15.00
*FOIL: .75X TO 2X BASIC CARDS
RELEASED ON OCTOBER 12, 2007

1 Ajani Goldmane R :W: 4.00 10.00
2 Arbiter of Knollridge R :W: .25 .60
3 Austere Command R :W: 1.50 4.00
4 Avian Changeling C :W: .10 .25
5 Battle Mastery U :W: .40 1.00
6 Brigid, Hero of Kinsbaile R :W: .40 1.00
7 Burrenton Forge-Tender U :W: .20 .50
8 Cenn's Heir C :W: .10 .25
9 Changeling Hero U :W: .20 .50
10 Cloudgoat Ranger U :W: .20 .50
11 Crib Swap U :W: .30 .75
12 Dawnfluke C :W: .10 .25
13 Entangling Trap U :W: .15 .40
14 Favor of the Mighty R :W: .25 .60
15 Galepowder Mage R :W: .40 1.00
16 Goldmeadow Dodger C :W: .10 .25
17 Goldmeadow Harrier C :W: .10 .25
18 Goldmeadow Stalwart U :W: .20 .50
19 Harpoon Sniper U :W: .12 .30
20 Hillcomber Giant C :W: .10 .25
21 Hoofprints of the Stag R :W: .40 1.00
22 Judge of Currents C :W: .12 .30
23 Kinsbaile Balloonist C :W: .10 .25
24 Kinsbaile Skirmisher C :W: .10 .25
25 Kithkin Greatheart C :W: .10 .25
26 Kithkin Harbinger U :W: .20 .50
27 Kithkin Healer C :W: .10 .25
28 Knight of Meadowgrain U :W: 1.25 3.00
29 Lairwatch Giant C :W: .10 .25
30 Militia's Pride R :W: .50 1.25
31 Mirror Entity R :W: 4.00 10.00
32 Neck Snap C :W: .10 .25
33 Oaken Brawler C :W: .10 .25
34 Oblivion Ring C :W: .25 .60
35 Plover Knights C :W: .10 .25
36 Pollen Lullaby U :W: .20 .50
37 Purity R :W: .50 1.25
38 Sentry Oak U :W: .12 .30
39 Shields of Velis Vel C :W: .10 .25
40 Soaring Hope C :W: .10 .25
41 Springjack Knight C :W: .10 .25
42 Summon the School U :W: .20 .50
43 Surge of Thoughtweft C :W: .12 .30
44 Thoughtweft Trio R :W: .40 1.00
45 Triclopean Sight C :W: .10 .25
46 Veteran of the Depths U :W: .12 .30
47 Wellgabber Apothecary C :W: .10 .25
48 Wispmare C :W: .12 .30
49 Wizened Cenn U :W: .20 .50
50 Aethersnipe C :B: .10 .25
51 Amoeboid Changeling C :B: .10 .25
52 Aquitect's Will C :B: .10 .25
53 Benthicore U :B: .12 .30
54 Broken Ambitions C :B: .12 .30
55 Captivating Glance U :B: .12 .30
56 Cryptic Command R :B: 20.00 40.00
57 Deeptread Merrow C :B: .10 .25
58 Drowner of Secrets U :B: .20 .50
59 Ego Erasure U :B: .12 .30
60 Ethereal Whiskergill U :B: .12 .30
61 Faerie Harbinger U :B: .12 .30
62 Faerie Trickery C :B: .12 .30
63 Fallowsage U :B: .15 .40
64 Familiar's Ruse U :B: .12 .30
65 Fathom Trawl R :B: .25 .60
66 Forced Fruition R :B: .75 2.00
67 Glen Elendra Pranksters U :B: .12 .30
68 Glimmerdust Nap C :B: .10 .25
69 Guile R :B: .40 1.00
70 Inkfathom Divers C :B: .10 .25
71 Jace Beleren R :B: 4.00 10.00
72 Merrow Commerce U :B: .40 1.00
73 Merrow Harbinger U :B: .20 .50
74 Merrow Reejerey U :B: 1.25 3.00
75 Mistbind Clique R :B: 1.25 3.00
76 Mulldrifter C :B: .15 .40
77 Paperfin Rascal C :B: .10 .25
78 Pestermite C :B: .40 1.00
79 Ponder C :B: .40 1.00
80 Protective Bubble C :B: .10 .25
81 Ringskipper C :B: .10 .25
82 Scattering Stroke U :B: .12 .30
83 Scion of Oona R :B: 3.00 8.00
84 Sentinels of Glen Elendra C :B: .10 .25
85 Shapesharer R :B: .75 2.00
86 Silvergill Adept U :B: .40 1.00
87 Silvergill Douser C :B: .10 .25
88 Sower of Temptation R :B: 4.00 10.00
89 Spellstutter Sprite C :B: .40 1.00
90 Stonybrook Angler C :B: .10 .25
91 Streambed Aquitects C :B: .10 .25
92 Surgespanner R :B: .25 .60
93 Tideshaper Mystic C :B: .10 .25
94 Turtleshell Changeling U :B: .12 .30
95 Wanderwine Prophets R :B: .25 .60
96 Whirlpool Whelm C :B: .10 .25
97 Wings of Velis Vel C :B: .10 .25
98 Zephyr Net C :B: .10 .25
99 Black Poplar Shaman C :K: .10 .25
100 Bog Hoodlums C :K: .10 .25
101 Boggart Birth Rite C :K: .10 .25
102 Boggart Harbinger U :K: .20 .50
103 Boggart Loggers C :K: .10 .25
104 Boggart Mob R :K: .40 1.00
105 Cairn Wanderer R :K: .60 1.50
106 Colfenor's Plans R :K: .25 .60
107 Dread R :K: 1.25 3.00
108 Dreamspoiler Witches R :K: .25 .60
109 Exiled Boggart C :K: .10 .25
110 Eyeblight's Ending C :K: .12 .30
111 Facevaulter C :K: .10 .25
112 Faerie Tauntings C :K: .20 .50
113 Final Revels U :K: .12 .30
114 Fodder Launch U :K: .25 .60
115 Footbottom Feast U :K: .12 .30
116 Ghostly Changeling C :K: .12 .30
117 Hoarder's Greed U :K: .12 .30
118 Hornet Harasser R :K: .25 .60
119 Hunter of Eyeblights C :K: .12 .30
120 Knucklebone Witch U :K: .50 1.25
121 Liliana Vess R :K: 4.00 10.00
122 Lys Alana Scarblade R :K: .25 .60
123 Mad Auntie R :K: .60 1.50
124 Makeshift Mannequin U :K: .25 .60
125 Marsh Flitter R :K: .25 .60
126 Moonglove Winnower U :K: .12 .30
127 Mournwhelk U :K: .12 .30
128 Nameless Inversion C :K: .12 .30
129 Nath's Buffoon C :K: .10 .25
130 Nectar Faerie R :K: .25 .60
131 Nettlevine Blight C :K: .25 .60
132 Nightshade Stinger U :K: .12 .30
133 Oona's Prowler R :K: 1.00 2.50
134 Peppersmoke C :K: .12 .30
135 Profane Command R :K: 1.50 4.00
136 Prowess of the Fair C :K: .20 .50
137 Quill-Slinger Boggart R :K: .10 .25
138 Scarred Vinebreeder U :K: .12 .30
139 Shriekmaw C :K: .40 1.00
140 Skeletal Changeling C :K: .10 .25
141 Spiderwig Boggart U :K: .12 .30
142 Squeaking Pie Sneak C :K: .15 .40
143 Thieving Sprite C :K: .10 .25
144 Thorntooth Witch U :K: .12 .30
145 Thoughtseize R :K: 35.00 70.00
146 Warren Pilferers C :K: .10 .25
147 Weed Strangle C :K: .10 .25
148 Adder-Staff Boggart C :R: .10 .25
149 Ashling the Pilgrim R :R: .40 1.00
150 Ashling's Prerogative R :R: .25 .60
151 Axegrinder Giant C :R: .10 .25
152 Blades of Velis Vel C :R: .10 .25
153 Blind-Spot Giant C :R: .10 .25
154 Boggart Forager C :R: .10 .25
155 Boggart Shenanigans U :R: .25 .60
156 Boggart Sprite-Chaser C :R: .10 .25
157 Caterwauling Boggart C :R: .10 .25
158 Ceaseless Searblades U :R: .12 .30
159 Chandra Nalaar R :R: 1.50 4.00
160 Changeling Berserker U :R: .12 .30
161 Consuming Bonfire C :R: .12 .30
162 Crush Underfoot U :R: .12 .30
163 Faultgrinder C :R: .10 .25
164 Fire-Belly Changeling C :R: .10 .25
165 Flamekin Bladewhirl U :R: .25 .60
166 Flamekin Brawler C :R: .10 .25
167 Flamekin Harbinger U :R: .75 2.00
168 Flamekin Spitfire U :R: .12 .30
169 Giant Harbinger U :R: .20 .50
170 Giant's Ire C :R: .10 .25
171 Glarewielder U :R: .12 .30
172 Goatnapper U :R: .12 .30
173 Hamletback Goliath R :R: .25 .60
174 Hearthcage Giant U :R: .12 .30
175 Heat Shimmer R :R: .25 .60
176 Hostility R :R: .40 1.00
177 Hurly-Burly C :R: .10 .25
178 Incandescent Soulstoke R :R: 1.25 3.00
179 Incendiary Command R :R: .60 1.50
180 Ingot Chewer C :R: .12 .30
181 Inner-Flame Acolyte C :R: .10 .25
182 Inner-Flame Igniter U :R: .12 .30
183 Lash Out C :R: .12 .30
184 Lowland Oaf C :R: .10 .25
185 Mudbutton Torchrunner C :R: .10 .25
186 Needle Drop C :R: .10 .25
187 Nova Chaser R :R: 1.25 3.00
188 Rebellion of the Flamekin U :R: .12 .30
189 Smokebraider C :R: .12 .30
190 Soulbright Flamekin C :R: .10 .25
191 Stinkdrinker Daredevil C :R: .10 .25
192 Sunrise Sovereign R :R: .25 .60
193 Tar Pitcher U :R: .12 .30
194 Tarfire C :R: .12 .30
195 Thundercloud Shaman U :R: .12 .30
196 Wild Ricochet R :R: .40 1.00
197 Battlewand Oak C :G: .10 .25
198 Bog-Strider Ash C :G: .10 .25
199 Briarhorn U :G: .20 .50
200 Changeling Titan U :G: .20 .50
201 Cloudcrown Oak C :G: .10 .25
202 Cloudthresher R :G: .40 1.00
203 Dauntless Dourbark R :G: 1.50 4.00
204 Elvish Branchbender C :G: .10 .25
205 Elvish Eulogist C :G: .10 .25
206 Elvish Handservant C :G: .10 .25
207 Elvish Harbinger U :G: .75 2.00
208 Elvish Promenade U :G: 1.50 4.00
209 Epic Proportions R :G: .25 .60
210 Eyes of the Wisent R :G: .40 1.00
211 Fertile Ground C :G: .12 .30
212 Fistful of Force C :G: .10 .25
213 Garruk Wildspeaker R :G: 4.00 10.00
214 Gilt-Leaf Ambush C :G: .10 .25
215 Gilt-Leaf Seer C :G: .10 .25
216 Guardian of Cloverdell U :G: .12 .30
217 Heal the Scars C :G: .12 .30
218 Hunt Down C :G: .10 .25
219 Immaculate Magistrate R :G: 4.00 10.00
220 Imperious Perfect U :G: 3.00 8.00
221 Incremental Growth U :G: .12 .30
222 Jagged-Scar Archers U :G: 1.00 2.50
223 Kithkin Daggerdare C :G: .10 .25
224 Kithkin Mourncaller U :G: .12 .30
225 Lace with Moonglove C :G: .10 .25
226 Lammastide Weave U :G: .12 .30
227 Leaf Gilder C :G: .12 .30
228 Lignify C :G: .10 .25
229 Lys Alana Huntmaster C :G: .10 .25
230 Masked Admirers R :G: .40 1.00
231 Nath's Elite C :G: .10 .25
232 Oakgnarl Warrior C :G: .10 .25
233 Primal Command R :G: 2.00 5.00
234 Rootgrapple C :G: .10 .25
235 Seedguide Ash U :G: .12 .30
236 Spring Cleaning C :G: .10 .25
237 Sylvan Echoes U :G: .12 .30
238 Timber Protector R :G: 3.00 8.00
239 Treefolk Harbinger U :G: .60 1.50
240 Vigor R :G: 6.00 15.00
241 Warren-Scourge Elf C :G: .10 .25
242 Woodland Changeling C :G: .10 .25
243 Woodland Guidance U :G: .10 .25
244 Wren's Run Packmaster R :G: 1.00 2.50
245 Wren's Run Vanquisher U :G: .40 1.00
246 Brion Stoutarm R :W: :R: .40 1.00
247 Doran, the Siege Tower R :W: :K: :G: 2.50 6.00
248 Gaddock Teeg R :W: :G: 3.00 8.00
249 Horde of Notions R :W: :B: :K: :R: :G: .40 1.00
250 Nath of the Gilt-Leaf R :K: :G: .60 1.50
251 Sygg, River Guide R :W: :B: .40 1.00
252 Wort, Boggart Auntie R :K: :R: .75 2.00
253 Wydwen, the Biting Gale R :B: :K: .40 1.00
254 Colfenor's Urn R :A: .25 .60
255 Deathrender R :A: 3.00 8.00
256 Dolmen Gate R :A: 1.50 4.00
257 Herbal Poultice C :A: .10 .25
258 Moonglove Extract C :A: .10 .25
259 Rings of Brighthearth R :A: 2.00 5.00
260 Runed Stalactite C :A: .10 .25
261 Springleaf Drum C :A: .40 1.00
262 Thorn of Amethyst R :A: 1.25 3.00
263 Thousand-Year Elixir R :A: 2.50 6.00
264 Twinning Glass R :A: .25 .60
265 Wanderer's Twig C :A: .10 .25
266 Ancient Amphitheater R :L: .30 .75
267 Auntie's Hovel R :L: 1.00 2.50
268 Gilt-Leaf Palace R :L: 1.25 3.00
269 Howltooth Hollow R :L: .30 .75
270 Mosswort Bridge R :L: 1.25 3.00
271 Secluded Glen R :L: 1.00 2.50
272 Shelldock Isle R :L: .40 1.00
273 Shimmering Grotto C :L: .12 .30
274 Spinerock Knoll R :L: .60 1.50
275 Vivid Crag U :L: .30 .75
276 Vivid Creek U :L: .40 1.00
277 Vivid Grove U :L: .30 .75
278 Vivid Marsh U :L: .30 .75
279 Vivid Meadow U :L: .30 .75
280 Wanderwine Hub R :L: 1.25 3.00
281 Windbrisk Heights R :L: 2.00 5.00
282 Plains C :L: .20 .50
283 Plains C :L: .20 .50
284 Plains C :L: .20 .50
285 Plains C :L: .20 .50
286 Island C :L: .20 .50
287 Island C :L: .20 .50
288 Island C :L: .20 .50
289 Island C :L: .20 .50
290 Swamp C :L: .20 .50
291 Swamp C :L: .20 .50
292 Swamp C :L: .20 .50
293 Swamp C :L: .20 .50
294 Mountain C :L: .20 .50
295 Mountain C :L: .20 .50
296 Mountain C :L: .20 .50

297 Mountain C :L: .20 .50
298 Forest C :L: .20 .50
299 Forest C :L: .20 .50
300 Forest C :L: .20 .50
301 Forest C :L: .20 .50

2008 Magic The Gathering Morningtide

COMPLETE SET (150) 120.00 200.00
BOOSTER BOX (36 PACKS) 175.00 275.00
BOOSTER PACK (15 CARDS) 5.00 8.00
THEME DECK 10.00 20.00
FAT PACK 40.00 80.00
*FOIL: .75X TO 2X BASIC CARDS
RELEASED ON FEBRUARY 1, 2008
1 Ballyrush Banneret C :W: .15 .40
2 Battletide Alchemist R :W: .25 .60
3 Burrenton Bombardier C :W: .10 .25
4 Burrenton Shield-Bearers C :W: .10 .25
5 Cenn's Tactician U :W: .20 .50
6 Changeling Sentinel C :W: .10 .25
7 Coordinated Barrage C :W: .10 .25
8 Daily Regimen U :W: .15 .40
9 Feudkiller's Verdict R :W: .25 .60
10 Forfend C :W: .10 .25
11 Graceful Reprieve U :W: .15 .40
12 Idyllic Tutor R :W: 2.50 6.00
13 Indomitable Ancients R :W: .60 1.50
14 Kinsbaile Borderguard R :W: .60 1.50
15 Kinsbaile Cavalier R :W: 1.50 4.00
16 Kithkin Zephyrnaut C :W: .10 .25
17 Meadowboon U :W: .15 .40
18 Mosquito Guard C :W: .10 .25
19 Order of the Golden Cricket C :W: .10 .25
20 Preeminent Captain R :W: 2.50 6.00
21 Redeem the Lost U :W: .15 .40
22 Reveillark R :W: 2.00 5.00
23 Shinewend C :W: .10 .25
24 Stonehewer Giant R :W: 2.50 6.00
25 Stonybrook Schoolmaster C :W: .10 .25
26 Swell of Courage U :W: .15 .40
27 Wandering Graybeard U :W: .15 .40
28 Weight of Conscience C :W: .10 .25
29 Declaration of Naught R :B: .25 .60
30 Dewdrop Spy C :B: .10 .25
31 Disperse C :B: .10 .25
32 Distant Melody C :B: .10 .25
33 Fencer Clique C :B: .10 .25
34 Floodchaser C :B: .10 .25
35 Grimoire Thief R :B: 1.25 3.00
36 Ink Dissolver C :B: .10 .25
37 Inspired Sprite U :B: .15 .40
38 Knowledge Exploitation R :B: .25 .60
39 Latchkey Faerie C :B: .10 .25
40 Merrow Witsniper C :B: .10 .25
41 Mind Spring R :B: .25 .60
42 Mothdust Changeling C :B: .10 .25
43 Negate C :B: .15 .40
44 Nevermaker U :B: .15 .40
45 Notorious Throng R :B: .25 .60
46 Research the Deep U :B: .15 .40
47 Sage of Fables U :B: .20 .50
48 Sage's Dousing U :B: .20 .50
49 Sigil Tracer R :B: .40 1.00
50 Slithermuse R :B: .25 .60
51 Stonybrook Banneret C :B: .20 .50
52 Stream of Unconsciousness C :B: .10 .25
53 Supreme Exemplar R :B: .25 .60
54 Thieves' Fortune U :B: .15 .40
55 Vendilion Clique R :B: 12.00 30.00
56 Waterspout Weavers U :B: .15 .40
57 Auntie's Snitch R :K: .25 .60
58 Bitterblossom R :K: 6.00 15.00
59 Blightsoil Druid C :K: .10 .25
60 Earwig Squad R :K: .60 1.50
61 Fendeep Summoner R :K: .25 .60
62 Festercreep C :K: .10 .25
63 Final-Sting Faerie C :K: .10 .25
64 Frogtosser Banneret C :K: .10 .25
65 Maralen of the Mornsong R :K: .30 .75
66 Mind Shatter R :K: .25 .60
67 Moonglove Changeling C :K: .10 .25
68 Morsel Theft C :K: .10 .25
69 Nightshade Schemers U :K: .15 .40
70 Noggin Whack U :K: .20 .50
71 Offalsnout U :K: .15 .40
72 Oona's Blackguard U :K: .20 .50
73 Pack's Disdain C :K: .10 .25
74 Prickly Boggart C :K: .10 .25
75 Pulling Teeth C :K: .10 .25
76 Revive the Fallen U :K: .15 .40
77 Scarblade Elite R :K: .25 .60
78 Squeaking Pie Grubfellows C :K: .10 .25
79 Stenchskipper R :K: .25 .60
80 Stinkdrinker Bandit U :K: .15 .40
81 Violet Pall C :K: .10 .25
82 Warren Weirding U :K: .10 .25
83 Weed-Pruner Poplar C :K: .10 .25
84 Weirding Shaman R :K: .25 .60
85 Boldwyr Heavyweights R :R: .25 .60
86 Boldwyr Intimidator U :R: .15 .40
87 Borderland Behemoth R :R: .25 .60
88 Brighthearth Banneret C :R: .10 .25
89 Countryside Crusher R :R: 1.00 2.50
90 Fire Juggler C :R: .10 .25
91 Hostile Realm C :R: .10 .25
92 Kindled Fury C :R: .10 .25
93 Lightning Crafter R :R: .75 2.00
94 Lunk Errant C :R: .10 .25
95 Mudbutton Clanger C :R: .10 .25
96 Pyroclast Consul U :R: .15 .40
97 Rage Forger U :R: .15 .40
98 Release the Ants U :R: .15 .40
99 Rivals' Duel U :R: .15 .40
100 Roar of the Crowd C :R: .10 .25
101 Seething Pathblazer C :R: .10 .25
102 Sensation Gorger R :R: .25 .60
103 Shard Volley C :R: .15 .40
104 Shared Animosity R :R: .25 .60
105 Spitebellows U :R: .15 .40
106 Stingmoggie C :R: .10 .25
107 Stomping Slabs U :R: .15 .40
108 Sunflare Shaman C :R: .10 .25
109 Taurean Mauler R :R: .75 2.00
110 Titan's Revenge R :R: .25 .60
111 Vengeful Firebrand R :R: .25 .60
112 War-Spike Changeling C :R: .20 .50
113 Ambassador Oak C :G: .10 .25
114 Bosk Banneret C :G: .15 .40
115 Bramblewood Paragon U :G: .60 1.50
116 Chameleon Colossus R :G: 1.50 4.00
117 Cream of the Crop R :G: .25 .60
118 Deglamer C :G: .10 .25
119 Earthbrawn C :G: .10 .25
120 Elvish Warrior C :G: .10 .25
121 Everbark Shaman C :G: .10 .25
122 Fertilid C :G: .10 .25
123 Game-Trail Changeling C :G: .10 .25
124 Gilt-Leaf Archdruid R :G: .40 1.00
125 Greatbow Doyen R :G: .25 .60
126 Heritage Druid U :G: 1.00 2.50
127 Hunting Triad U :G: .15 .40
128 Leaf-Crowned Elder R :G: 1.50 4.00
129 Luminescent Rain C :G: .10 .25
130 Lys Alana Bowmaster C :G: .10 .25
131 Orchard Warden U :G: .15 .40
132 Reach of Branches R :G: .25 .60
133 Recross the Paths U :G: .15 .40
134 Reins of the Vinesteed C :G: .10 .25
135 Rhys the Exiled R :G: .60 1.50
136 Scapeshift R :G: 1.50 4.00
137 Unstoppable Ash R :G: .30 .75
138 Walker of the Grove U :G: .15 .40
139 Winnower Patrol C :G: .10 .25
140 Wolf-Skull Shaman U :G: .25 .60
141 Cloak and Dagger U :A: .20 .50
142 Diviner's Wand U :A: .15 .40
143 Door of Destinies R :A: 4.00 10.00
144 Obsidian Battle-Axe U :A: .20 .50
145 Thornbite Staff U :A: .15 .40
146 Veteran's Armaments U :A: .20 .50
147 Murmuring Bosk R :L: 2.00 5.00
148 Mutavault R :L: 12.00 30.00
149 Primal Beyond R :L: .60 1.50
150 Rustic Clachan R :L: .30 .75

2008 Magic The Gathering Shadowmoor

COMPLETE SET (301) 150.00 225.00
BOOSTER BOX (36 PACKS) 150.00 225.00
BOOSTER PACK (15 CARDS) 5.00 8.00
THEME DECK 20.00 40.00
FAT PACK 50.00 100.00
*FOIL: .75X TO 2X BASIC CARDS
RELEASED ON MAY 2, 2008
1 Apothecary Initiate C :W: .10 .25
2 Armored Ascension U :W: .15 .40
3 Ballynock Cohort C :W: .10 .25
4 Barrenton Medic C :W: .10 .25
5 Boon Reflection R :W: 1.25 3.00
6 Goldenglow Moth C :W: .10 .25
7 Greater Auramancy R :W: 2.50 6.00
8 Inquisitor's Snare C :W: .10 .25
9 Kithkin Rabble U :W: .15 .40
10 Kithkin Shielddare C :W: .10 .25
11 Last Breath C :W: .15 .40
12 Mass Calcify R :W: .40 1.00
13 Mine Excavation C :W: .10 .25
14 Mistmeadow Skulk U :W: .15 .40
15 Niveous Wisps C :W: .10 .25
16 Order of Whiteclay R :W: .30 .75
17 Pale Wayfarer U :W: .15 .40
18 Prison Term U :W: .25 .60
19 Resplendent Mentor U :W: .15 .40
20 Rune-Cervin Rider C :W: .10 .25
21 Runed Halo R :W: 1.25 3.00
22 Safehold Sentry C :W: .10 .25
23 Spectral Procession U :W: 1.25 3.00
24 Strip Bare C :W: .10 .25
25 Twilight Shepherd R :W: 1.00 2.50
26 Windbrisk Raptor R :W: .25 .60
27 Woeleecher C :W: .10 .25
28 Advice from the Fae U :B: .15 .40
29 Biting Tether U :B: .15 .40
30 Briarberry Cohort C :B: .10 .25
31 Cerulean Wisps C :B: .10 .25
32 Consign to Dream C :B: .10 .25
33 Counterbore R :B: .40 1.00
34 Cursecatcher U :B: 1.50 4.00
35 Deepchannel Mentor U :B: .20 .50
36 Drowner Initiate C :B: .10 .25
37 Faerie Swarm U :B: .15 .40
38 Flow of Ideas U :B: .15 .40
39 Ghastly Discovery C :B: .10 .25
40 Isleback Spawn R :B: .25 .60
41 Kinscaer Harpoonist C :B: .10 .25
42 Knacksaw Clique R :B: .25 .60
43 Leech Bonder U :B: .15 .40
44 Merrow Wavebreakers C :B: .10 .25
45 Parapet Watchers C :B: .10 .25
46 Prismwake Merrow C :B: .10 .25
47 Puca's Mischief R :B: .25 .60
48 Put Away C :B: .10 .25
49 River Kelpie R :B: .25 .60
50 Savor the Moment R :B: .50 1.25
51 Sinking Feeling C :B: .10 .25
52 Spell Syphon C :B: .10 .25
53 Thought Reflection R :B: .30 .75
54 Whimwader C :B: .10 .25
55 Aphotic Wisps C :K: .10 .25
56 Ashenmoor Cohort C :K: .10 .25
57 Beseech the Queen U :K: .60 1.50
58 Blowfly Infestation U :K: .15 .40
59 Cinderbones C :K: .10 .25
60 Cinderhaze Wretch C :K: .10 .25
61 Corrosive Mentor U :K: .15 .40
62 Corrupt U :K: .15 .40
63 Crowd of Cinders U :K: .15 .40
64 Disturbing Plot C :K: .10 .25
65 Dusk Urchins R :K: .40 1.00
66 Faerie Macabre C :K: .15 .40
67 Gloomlance C :K: .10 .25
68 Hollowborn Barghest R :K: .25 .60
69 Hollowsage U :K: .15 .40
70 Incremental Blight U :K: .15 .40
71 Loch Korrigan C :K: .10 .25
72 Midnight Banshee R :K: .60 1.50
73 Plague of Vermin R :K: .25 .60
74 Polluted Bonds R :K: .40 1.00
75 Puppeteer Clique R :K: .60 1.50
76 Rite of Consumption C :K: .10 .25
77 Sickle Ripper C :K: .10 .25
78 Smolder Initiate C :K: .10 .25
79 Splitting Headache C :K: .10 .25
80 Torture C :K: .10 .25
81 Wound Reflection R :K: .30 .75
82 Blistering Dieflyn C :R: .10 .25
83 Bloodmark Mentor U :R: .15 .40
84 Bloodshed Fever C :R: .10 .25
85 Boggart Arsonists C :R: .10 .25
86 Burn Trail C :R: .10 .25
87 Cragganwick Cremator R :R: .25 .60
88 Crimson Wisps C :R: .10 .25
89 Deep-Slumber Titan R :R: .25 .60
90 Elemental Mastery R :R: .30 .75
91 Ember Gale C :R: .10 .25
92 Flame Javelin U :R: .40 1.00
93 Furystoke Giant R :R: .25 .60
94 Horde of Boggarts U :R: .15 .40
95 Inescapable Brute C :R: .10 .25
96 Intimidator Initiate C :R: .10 .25
97 Jaws of Stone U :R: .15 .40
98 Knollspine Dragon R :R: .40 1.00
99 Knollspine Invocation R :R: .25 .60
100 Mudbrawler Cohort C :R: .10 .25
101 Power of Fire C :R: .10 .25
102 Puncture Bolt C :R: .10 .25
103 Pyre Charger U :R: .15 .40
104 Rage Reflection R :R: .30 .75
105 Rustrazor Butcher C :R: .10 .25
106 Slinking Giant U :R: .15 .40
107 Smash to Smithereens C :R: .30 .75
108 Wild Swing U :R: .15 .40
109 Crabapple Cohort C :G: .10 .25
110 Devoted Druid C :G: .20 .50
111 Dramatic Entrance R :G: .30 .75
112 Drove of Elves U :G: .75 2.00
113 Farhaven Elf C :G: .15 .40
114 Flourishing Defenses U :G: .15 .40
115 Foxfire Oak C :G: .10 .25
116 Gleeful Sabotage C :G: .10 .25
117 Gloomwidow U :G: .15 .40
118 Gloomwidow's Feast C :G: .10 .25
119 Howl of the Night Pack U :G: .15 .40
120 Hungry Spriggan C :G: .10 .25
121 Juvenile Gloomwidow C :G: .10 .25
122 Mana Reflection R :G: 2.50 6.00
123 Mossbridge Troll R :G: .30 .75
124 Nurturer Initiate C :G: .10 .25
125 Presence of Gond C :G: .10 .25
126 Prismatic Omen R :G: 1.50 4.00
127 Raking Canopy U :G: .15 .40
128 Roughshod Mentor U :G: .15 .40
129 Spawnwrithe R :G: .25 .60
130 Toil to Renown C :G: .10 .25
131 Tower Above U :G: .15 .40
132 Viridescent Wisps C :G: .10 .25
133 Wildslayer Elves C :G: .10 .25
134 Witherscale Wurm R :G: .25 .60
135 Woodfall Primus R :G: 3.00 8.00
136 AEthertow C :W: :B: .10 .25
137 Ashenmoor Gouger U :K: :R: .15 .40
138 Ashenmoor Liege R :K: :R: 1.50 4.00
139 Augury Adept R :W: :B: .60 1.50
140 Barkshell Blessing C :G: :W: .10 .25
141 Barrenton Cragtreads C :W: :B: .10 .25
142 Boartusk Liege R :R: :G: 1.50 4.00
143 Boggart Ram-Gang U :R: :G: .60 1.50
144 Cemetery Puca R :B: :K: .30 .75
145 Cultbrand Cinder C :K: :R: .10 .25
146 Curse of Chains C :W: :B: .10 .25
147 Dawnglow Infusion U :G: :W: .15 .40
148 Demigod of Revenge R :K: :R: 2.50 6.00
149 Deus of Calamity R :R: :G: 1.50 4.00
150 Din of the Fireherd R :K: :R: .25 .60
151 Dire Undercurrents R :B: :K: .30 .75
152 Dream Salvage U :B: :K: .15 .40
153 Elvish Hexhunter C :G: :W: .10 .25
154 Emberstrike Duo C :K: :R: .10 .25
155 Enchanted Evening R :W: :B: .60 1.50
156 Everlasting Torment R :K: :R: .75 2.00
157 Fate Transfer C :B: :K: .10 .25
158 Firespout U :R: :G: .75 2.00
159 Fists of the Demigod C :K: :R: .10 .25
160 Fossil Find U :R: :G: .15 .40
161 Fracturing Gust R :G: :W: .50 1.25
162 Fulminator Mage R :K: :R: 1.50 4.00
163 Ghastlord of Fugue R :B: :K: 1.25 3.00
164 Giantbaiting C :R: :G: .10 .25
165 Glamer Spinners U :W: :B: .15 .40
166 Glen Elendra Liege R :B: :K: 1.50 4.00
167 Godhead of Awe R :W: :B: .75 2.00
168 Gravelgill Axeshark C :B: :K: .10 .25
169 Gravelgill Duo C :B: :K: .10 .25
170 Grief Tyrant U :K: :R: .15 .40
171 Guttural Response U :R: :G: .40 1.00
172 Heartmender R :G: :W: .50 1.25
173 Helm of the Ghastlord C :B: :K: .10 .25
174 Impromptu Raid R :R: :G: .25 .60
175 Inkfathom Infiltrator U :B: :K: .30 .75
176 Inkfathom Witch U :B: :K: .15 .40
177 Kitchen Finks U :G: :W: 4.00 10.00
178 Kulrath Knight U :K: :R: .40 1.00
179 Loamdragger Giant C :R: :G: .10 .25
180 Manaforge Cinder C :K: :R: .10 .25
181 Manamorphose C :R: :G: 1.00 2.50
182 Medicine Runner C :G: :W: .10 .25
183 Memory Plunder R :B: :K: .60 1.50
184 Memory Sluice C :B: :K: .30 .75
185 Mercy Killing U :G: :W: .20 .50
186 Merrow Grimeblotter U :B: :K: .15 .40
187 Mirrorweave R :W: :B: .40 1.00
188 Mistmeadow Witch U :W: :B: .15 .40
189 Morselhoarder C :R: :G: .10 .25
190 Mudbrawler Raiders C :R: :G: .10 .25
191 Murderous Redcap U :K: :R: .50 1.25
192 Old Ghastbark C :G: :W: .10 .25
193 Oona, Queen of the Fae R :B: :K: 2.00 5.00
194 Oona's Gatewarden C :B: :K: .10 .25
195 Oracle of Nectars R :G: :W: .75 2.00
196 Oversoul of Dusk R :G: :W: 1.25 3.00
197 Plumeveil U :W: :B: .30 .75
198 Poison the Well C :K: :R: .10 .25
199 Puresight Merrow U :W: :B: .15 .40
200 Raven's Run Dragoon C :G: :W: .10 .25
201 Reknit U :G: :W: .15 .40
202 Repel Intruders U :W: :B: .15 .40
203 Rhys the Redeemed R :G: :W: 3.00 8.00
204 River's Grasp U :B: :K: .15 .40
205 Rosheen Meanderer R :R: :G: .25 .60
206 Runes of the Deus C :R: :G: .10 .25
207 Safehold Duo C :G: :W: .10 .25
208 Safehold Elite C :G: :W: .10 .25
209 Safewright Quest C :G: :W: .10 .25
210 Scar C :K: :R: .10 .25
211 Scarscale Ritual C :B: :K: .10 .25
212 Scuzzback Marauders C :R: :G: .10 .25
213 Scuzzback Scrapper C :R: :G: .10 .25
214 Seedcradle Witch U :G: :W: .15 .40
215 Shield of the Oversoul C :G: :W: .30 .75
216 Silkbind Faerie C :W: :B: .10 .25
217 Somnomancer C :W: :B: .10 .25
218 Sootstoke Kindler C :K: :R: .10 .25
219 Sootwalkers C :K: :R: .10 .25
220 Spiteflame Witch U :K: :R: .15 .40
221 Spiteful Visions R :K: :R: .30 .75
222 Steel of the Godhead C :W: :B: .20 .50
223 Swans of Bryn Argoll R :W: :B: 1.00 2.50
224 Sygg, River Cutthroat R :B: :K: .75 2.00
225 Tattermunge Duo C :R: :G: .10 .25
226 Tattermunge Maniac U :R: :G: .20 .50
227 Tattermunge Witch U :R: :G: .15 .40
228 Thistledown Duo C :W: :B: .10 .25
229 Thistledown Liege R :W: :B: .60 1.50
230 Thoughtweft Gambit U :W: :B: .15 .40
231 Torpor Dust C :B: :K: .10 .25
232 Torrent of Souls U :K: :R: .15 .40
233 Traitor's Roar C :K: :R: .10 .25
234 Turn to Mist C :W: :B: .10 .25
235 Tyrannize R :K: :R: .25 .60
236 Valleymaker R :R: :G: .25 .60
237 Vexing Shusher R :R: :G: 1.25 3.00
238 Wanderbrine Rootcutters C :B: :K: .10 .25
239 Wasp Lancer U :B: :K: .15 .40
240 Wheel of Sun and Moon R :G: :W: 1.50 4.00
241 Wilt-Leaf Cavaliers U :G: :W: .40 1.00
242 Wilt-Leaf Liege R :G: :W: 2.00 5.00
243 Worldpurge R :W: :B: .25 .60
244 Wort, the Raidmother R :R: :G: .40 1.00
245 Zealous Guardian C :W: :B: .10 .25
246 Blazethorn Scarecrow C :A: .10 .25
247 Blight Sickle C :A: .10 .25
248 Cauldron of Souls R :A: .75 2.00
249 Chainbreaker C :A: .10 .25
250 Elsewhere Flask C :A: .10 .25
251 Gnarled Effigy U :A: .15 .40
252 Grim Poppet R :A: .30 .75
253 Heap Doll U :A: .15 .40
254 Illuminated Folio U :A: .15 .40
255 Lockjaw Snapper U :A: .15 .40
256 Lurebound Scarecrow U :A: .15 .40
257 Painter's Servant R :A: 2.50 6.00
258 Pili-Pala C :A: .15 .40
259 Rattleblaze Scarecrow C :A: .10 .25
260 Reaper King R :A: 1.50 4.00
261 Revelsong Horn U :A: .15 .40
262 Scrapbasket C :A: .10 .25
263 Scuttlemutt C :A: .15 .40
264 Tatterkite U :A: .15 .40
265 Thornwatch Scarecrow C :A: .10 .25
266 Trip Noose U :A: .15 .40
267 Umbral Mantle U :A: .15 .40
268 Watchwing Scarecrow C :A: .10 .25
269 Wicker Warcrawler U :A: .15 .40
270 Wingrattle Scarecrow C :A: .10 .25
271 Fire-Lit Thicket R 1.50 4.00
272 Forest L .10 .25
273 Forest L .10 .25
274 Forest L .10 .25
275 Forest L .10 .25
276 Graven Cairns R 1.50 4.00
277 Island L .10 .25
278 Island L .10 .25
279 Island L .10 .25
280 Island L .10 .25
281 Leechridden Swamp U .20 .50
282 Madblind Mountain U .15 .40
283 Mistveil Plains U .30 .75
284 Moonring Island U .15 .40
285 Mountain L .10 .25
286 Mountain L .10 .25
287 Mountain L .10 .25
288 Mountain L .10 .25
289 Mystic Gate R 2.50 6.00
290 Plains L .10 .25
291 Plains L .10 .25
292 Plains L .10 .25
293 Plains L .10 .25
294 Reflecting Pool R 4.00 10.00
295 Sapseep Forest U .15 .40
296 Sunken Ruins R 2.50 6.00
297 Swamp L .10 .25
298 Swamp L .10 .25
299 Swamp L .10 .25
300 Swamp L .10 .25
301 Wooded Bastion R 1.50 4.00

2008 Magic The Gathering Eventide

COMPLETE SET (180) 150.00 250.00
BOOSTER BOX (36 PACKS) 100.00 175.00
BOOSTER PACK (15 CARDS) 3.50 5.00
THEME DECK 10.00 20.00
FAT PACK 40.00 80.00
*FOIL: .75X TO 2X BASIC CARDS
RELEASED ON JULY 25, 2008
1 Archon of Justice R :W: .40 1.00
2 Ballynock Trapper C :W: .10 .25
3 Cenn's Enlistment C :W: .10 .25
4 Endless Horizons R :W: .60 1.50
5 Endure U :W: .15 .40
6 Flickerwisp U :W: .40 1.00
7 Hallowed Burial R :W: 1.25 3.00
8 Kithkin Spellduster C :W: .10 .25
9 Kithkin Zealot C :W: .10 .25
10 Light from Within R :W: .75 2.00
11 Loyal Gyrfalcon U :W: .15 .40
12 Patrol Signaler U :W: .15 .40
13 Recumbent Bliss C :W: .10 .25
14 Spirit of the Hearth R :W: .40 1.00
15 Springjack Shepherd U :W: .20 .50
16 Suture Spirit U :W: .15 .40
17 Banishing Knack C :B: .10 .25
18 Cache Raiders U :B: .15 .40
19 Dream Fracture U :B: .25 .60
20 Dream Thief C :B: .10 .25
21 Glamerdye R :B: .25 .60
22 Glen Elendra Archmage R :B: 3.00 8.00
23 Idle Thoughts U :B: .15 .40
24 Indigo Faerie U :B: .15 .40
25 Inundate R :B: .25 .60
26 Merrow Levitator C :B: .10 .25
27 Oona's Grace C :B: .10 .25
28 Razorfin Abolisher U :B: .15 .40
29 Sanity Grinding R :B: 1.25 3.00
30 Talonrend U :B: .15 .40
31 Wake Thrasher R :B: 1.50 4.00
32 Wilderness Hypnotist C :B: .10 .25
33 Ashling, the Extinguisher R :K: .75 2.00
34 Creakwood Ghoul U :K: .15 .40
35 Crumbling Ashes U :K: .25 .60
36 Lingering Tormentor U :K: .15 .40
37 Merrow Bonegnawer C :K: .10 .25
38 Necroskitter R :K: 2.00 5.00
39 Needle Specter R :K: .40 1.00
40 Nightmare Incursion R :K: .25 .60
41 Raven's Crime C :K: .10 .25
42 Smoldering Butcher C :K: .10 .25
43 Soot Imp U :K: .15 .40
44 Soul Reap C :K: .10 .25
45 Soul Snuffers U :K: .25 .60
46 Syphon Life U :K: .15 .40
47 Talara's Bane C :K: .10 .25
48 Umbra Stalker R :K: .25 .60
49 Chaotic Backlash U :R: .15 .40
50 Cinder Pyromancer C :R: .10 .25
51 Duergar Cave-Guard U :R: .15 .40
52 Fiery Bombardment R :R: .25 .60
53 Flame Jab C :R: .10 .25
54 Hatchet Bully U :R: .15 .40
55 Hateflayer R :R: .30 .75
56 Heartlash Cinder C :R: .10 .25
57 Hotheaded Giant C :R: .10 .25
58 Impelled Giant U :R: .15 .40
59 Outrage Shaman U :R: .15 .40
60 Puncture Blast C :R: .10 .25
61 Rekindled Flame R :R: .25 .60
62 Stigma Lasher R :R: 1.25 3.00
63 Thunderblust R :R: .40 1.00
64 Unwilling Recruit U :R: .20 .50
65 Aerie Ouphes C :G: .10 .25
66 Bloom Tender R :G: 1.50 4.00
67 Duskdale Wurm U :G: .15 .40
68 Helix Pinnacle R :G: .75 2.00
69 Marshdrinker Giant U :G: .15 .40
70 Monstrify C :G: .10 .25
71 Nettle Sentinel C :G: .25 .60
72 Phosphorescent Feast U :G: .15 .40
73 Primalcrux R :G: 2.00 5.00
74 Regal Force R :G: 2.50 6.00
75 Savage Conception U :G: .15 .40
76 Swirling Spriggan U :G: .15 .40
77 Talara's Battalion R :G: 1.50 4.00
78 Tilling Treefolk C :G: .10 .25
79 Twinblade Slasher U :G: .25 .60
80 Wickerbough Elder C :G: .10 .25
81 Balefire Liege R :R: :W: 2.00 5.00
82 Battlegate Mimic C :R: :W: .10 .25
83 Batwing Brume U :W: :K: .30 .75
84 Beckon Apparition C :W: :K: .15 .40
85 Belligerent Hatchling U :R: :W: .20 .50
86 Bloodied Ghost U :W: :K: .15 .40
87 Call the Skybreaker R :B: :R: .30 .75
88 Canker Abomination U :K: :G: .15 .40
89 Cankerous Thirst U :K: :G: .15 .40
90 Cauldron Haze U :W: :K: .20 .50
91 Clout of the Dominus C :B: :R: .10 .25
92 Cold-Eyed Selkie R :G: :B: 2.00 5.00
93 Crackleburr R :B: :R: .60 1.50
94 Crag Puca U :B: :R: .15 .40
95 Creakwood Liege R :K: :G: 3.00 8.00
96 Deathbringer Liege R :W: :K: 5.00 12.00
97 Deity of Scars R :K: :G: .75 2.00
98 Desecrator Hag C :K: :G: .10 .25
99 Divinity of Pride R :W: :K: 4.00 10.00
100 Dominus of Fealty R :B: :R: 1.25 3.00
101 Doomgape R :K: :G: .75 2.00
102 Double Cleave C :R: :W: .10 .25
103 Drain the Well C :K: :G: .10 .25
104 Duergar Assailant C :R: :W: .10 .25
105 Duergar Hedge-Mage U :R: :W: .20 .50
106 Duergar Mine-Captain U :R: :W: .15 .40
107 Edge of the Divinity C :W: :K: .15 .40
108 Evershrike R :W: :K: .50 1.25
109 Fable of Wolf and Owl R :G: :B: .60 1.50
110 Favor of the Overbeing C :G: :B: .10 .25
111 Figure of Destiny R :R: :W: 3.00 8.00
112 Fire at Will C :R: :W: .10 .25
113 Gift of the Deity C :K: :G: .10 .25
114 Gilder Bairn U :G: :B: .60 1.50
115 Grazing Kelpie C :G: :B: .10 .25
116 Groundling Pouncer U :G: :B: .15 .40
117 Gwyllion Hedge-Mage U :W: :K: .15 .40
118 Hag Hedge-Mage U :K: :G: .15 .40
119 Harvest Gwyllion C :W: :K: .10 .25
120 Hearthfire Hobgoblin U :R: :W: .30 .75
121 Hobgoblin Dragoon C :R: :W: .10 .25
122 Inside Out C :B: :R: .10 .25
123 Invert the Skies U :G: :B: .15 .40
124 Mindwrack Liege R :B: :R: .75 2.00
125 Mirror Sheen R :B: :R: .30 .75
126 Moonhold U :R: :W: .15 .40
127 Murkfiend Liege R :G: :B: 2.00 5.00
128 Nightsky Mimic C :W: :K: .10 .25
129 Nip Gwyllion C :W: :K: .10 .25
130 Nobilis of War R :R: :W: .60 1.50
131 Noggle Bandit C :B: :R: .10 .25
132 Noggle Bridgebreaker C :B: :R: .10 .25
133 Noggle Hedge-Mage U :B: :R: .15 .40
134 Noggle Ransacker U :B: :R: .15 .40

135 Noxious Hatchling U :K: :G: .25 .60
136 Nucklavee U :B: :R: .15 .40
137 Odious Trow C :K: :G: .10 .25
138 Overbeing of Myth R :G: :B: 1.00 2.50
139 Pyrrhic Revival R :W: :K: .30 .75
140 Quillspike U :K: :G: .30 .75
141 Rendclaw Trow C :K: :G: .10 .25
142 Restless Apparition U :W: :K: .15 .40
143 Rise of the Hobgoblins R :R: :W: 1.00 2.50
144 Riverfall Mimic C :B: :R: .10 .25
145 Sapling of Colfenor R :K: :G: .60 1.50
146 Scourge of the Nobilis C :R: :W: .10 .25
147 Selkie Hedge-Mage U :G: :B: .15 .40
148 Shorecrasher Mimic C :G: :B: .10 .25
149 Shrewd Hatchling U :B: :R: .20 .50
150 Slippery Bogle C :G: :B: .10 .25
151 Snakeform C :G: :B: .10 .25
152 Spitemare U :R: :W: .25 .60
153 Splitting Image R :G: :B: .60 1.50
154 Stalker Hag U :K: :G: .15 .40
155 Stillmoon Cavalier R :W: :K: 2.50 6.00
156 Stream Hopper C :B: :R: .10 .25
157 Sturdy Hatchling U :G: :B: .15 .40
158 Trapjaw Kelpie C :G: :B: .10 .25
159 Unmake C :W: :K: .40 1.00
160 Unnerving Assault U :B: :R: .15 .40
161 Voracious Hatchling U :W: :K: .30 .75
162 Waves of Aggression R :R: :W: .30 .75
163 Wistful Selkie U :G: :B: .15 .40
164 Woodlurker Mimic C :K: :G: .10 .25
165 Worm Harvest R :K: :G: .40 1.00
166 Altar Golem R :A: .30 .75
167 Antler Skulkin C :A: .10 .25
168 Fang Skulkin C :A: .10 .25
169 Hoof Skulkin C :A: .10 .25
170 Jawbone Skulkin C :A: .10 .25
171 Leering Emblem R :A: .25 .60
172 Scarecrone R :A: 1.25 3.00
173 Shell Skulkin C :A: .10 .25
174 Ward of Bones R :A: .30 .75
175 Cascade Bluffs R :L: 4.00 10.00
176 Fetid Heath R :L: 5.00 12.00
177 Flooded Grove R :L: 3.00 8.00
178 Rugged Prairie R :L: 3.00 8.00
179 Springjack Pasture R :L: .60 1.50
180 Twilight Mire R :L: 3.00 8.00

2008 Magic The Gathering Shards of Alara

COMPLETE SET (249) 125.00 200.00
BOOSTER BOX (36 PACKS) 100.00 150.00
BOOSTER PACK (15 CARDS) 3.50 5.00
THEME DECK 10.00 15.00
FAT PACK 30.00 60.00
*FOIL: .75X TO 2X BASIC CARDS
RELEASED ON OCTOBER 3, 2008
1 Akrasan Squire C :W: .20 .50
2 Angel's Herald U :W: .20 .50
3 Angelic Benediction U :W: .20 .50
4 Angelsong C :W: .10 .25
5 Bant Battlemage U :W: .20 .50
6 Battlegrace Angel R :W: 1.25 3.00
7 Cradle of Vitality R :W: .60 1.50
8 Dispeller's Capsule C :W: .10 .25
9 Elspeth, Knight-Errant M :W: 12.00 30.00
10 Ethersworn Canonist R :W: 4.00 10.00
11 Excommunicate C :W: .08 .20
12 Guardians of Akrasa C :W: .10 .25
13 Gustrider Exuberant C :W: .10 .25
14 Invincible Hymn R :W: .25 .60
15 Knight of the Skyward Eye C :W: .10 .25
16 Knight of the White Orchid R :W: 1.50 4.00
17 Knight-Captain of Eos R :W: .30 .75
18 Marble Chalice C :W: .10 .25
19 Metallurgeon U :W: .20 .50
20 Oblivion Ring C :W: .60 1.50
21 Ranger of Eos R :W: 2.00 5.00
22 Resounding Silence C :W: .10 .25
22 Crumbling Necropolis U :L: .75 2.00
23 Rockcaster Platoon U :W: .20 .50
24 Sanctum Gargoyle C :W: .10 .25
25 Scourglass R :W: .60 1.50
26 Sighted-Caste Sorcerer C :W: .10 .25
27 Sigiled Paladin U :W: .40 1.00
28 Soul's Grace C :W: .10 .25
29 Sunseed Nurturer U :W: .20 .50
30 Welkin Guide C :W: .10 .25
31 Yoked Plowbeast C :W: .10 .25
32 Call to Heel C :B: .10 .25
33 Cancel C :B: .10 .25
34 Cathartic Adept C :B: .10 .25
35 Cloudheath Drake C :B: .10 .25
36 Coma Veil C :B: .10 .25
37 Courier's Capsule C :B: .10 .25
38 Covenant of Minds R :B: .25 .60
39 Dawnray Archer U :B: .20 .50
40 Esper Battlemage U :B: .20 .50
41 Etherium Astrolabe U :B: .20 .50
42 Etherium Sculptor C :B: .75 2.00
43 Fatestitcher U :B: .20 .50
44 Filigree Sages U :B: .20 .50
45 Gather Specimens R :B: .30 .75
46 Jhessian Lookout C :B: .10 .25
47 Kathari Screecher C :B: .10 .25
48 Kederekt Leviathan R :B: .25 .60
49 Master of Etherium R :B: 2.50 6.00
50 Memory Erosion R :B: 1.50 4.00
51 Mindlock Orb R :B: .30 .75
52 Outrider of Jhess C :B: .10 .25
53 Protomatter Powder U :B: .20 .50
54 Resounding Wave C :B: .10 .25
55 Sharding Sphinx R :B: .30 .75
56 Skill Borrower R :B: .30 .75
57 Spell Snip C :B: .10 .25
58 Sphinx's Herald U :B: .20 .50
59 Steelclad Serpent C :B: .10 .25
60 Tezzeret the Seeker M :B: 4.00 10.00
61 Tortoise Formation C :B: .10 .25
62 Vectis Silencers C :B: .10 .25
63 Ad Nauseam R :K: .60 1.50
64 Archdemon of Unx R :K: .30 .75
65 Banewasp Affliction C :K: .10 .25
66 Blister Beetle C :K: .10 .25
67 Bone Splinters C :K: .10 .25
68 Corpse Connoisseur U :K: .20 .50
69 Cunning Lethemancer R :K: .30 .75
70 Death Baron R :K: 6.00 15.00
71 Deathgreeter C :K: .10 .25
72 Demon's Herald U :K: .20 .50
73 Dreg Reaver C :K: .10 .25
74 Dregscape Zombie C :K: .10 .25
75 Executioner's Capsule C :K: .10 .25
76 Fleshbag Marauder U :K: .20 .50
77 Glaze Fiend C :K: .10 .25
78 Grixis Battlemage U :K: .20 .50
79 Immortal Coil R :K: .30 .75
80 Infest U :K: .25 .60
81 Onyx Goblet C :K: .10 .25
82 Puppet Conjurer U :K: .20 .50
83 Resounding Scream C :K: .10 .25
84 Salvage Titan R :K: .30 .75
85 Scavenger Drake U :K: .20 .50
86 Shadowfeed C :K: .10 .25
87 Shore Snapper C :K: .10 .25
88 Skeletal Kathari C :K: .10 .25
89 Tar Fiend R :K: .25 .60
90 Undead Leotau C :K: .10 .25
91 Vein Drinker R :K: .30 .75
92 Viscera Dragger C :K: .10 .25
93 Bloodpyre Elemental C :R: .10 .25
94 Bloodthorn Taunter C :R: .20 .50
95 Caldera Hellion R :R: .30 .75
96 Crucible of Fire R :R: 1.50 4.00
97 Dragon Fodder C :R: .20 .50
98 Dragon's Herald U :R: .20 .50
99 Exuberant Firestoker U :R: .20 .50
100 Flameblast Dragon R :R: .50 1.25
101 Goblin Assault R :R: .60 1.50
102 Goblin Mountaineer C :R: .10 .25
103 Hell's Thunder R :R: 2.00 5.00
104 Hissing Iguanar C :R: .10 .25
105 Incurable Ogre C :R: .10 .25
106 Jund Battlemage U :R: .20 .50
107 Lightning Talons C :R: .10 .25
108 Magma Spray C :R: .10 .25
109 Predator Dragon R :R: .40 1.00
110 Resounding Thunder C :R: .10 .25
111 Ridge Rannet C :R: .10 .25
112 Rockslide Elemental U :R: .20 .50
113 Scourge Devil U :R: .20 .50
114 Skeletonize U :R: .20 .50
115 Soul's Fire C :R: .10 .25
116 Thorn-Thrash Viashino C :R: .20 .50
117 Thunder-Thrash Elder U :R: .20 .50
118 Viashino Skeleton C :R: .10 .25
119 Vicious Shadows R :R: .25 .60
120 Vithian Stinger C :R: .10 .25
121 Volcanic Submersion C :R: .10 .25
122 Where Ancients Tread R :R: .25 .60
123 Algae Gharial U :G: .20 .50
124 Behemoth's Herald U :G: .20 .50
125 Cavern Thoctar C :G: .10 .25
126 Court Archers C :G: .10 .25
127 Cylian Elf C :G: .10 .25
128 Druid of the Anima C :G: .10 .25
129 Drumhunter U :G: .20 .50
130 Elvish Visionary C :G: .12 .30
131 Feral Hydra R :G: .30 .75
132 Gift of the Gargantuan C :G: .10 .25
133 Godtoucher C :G: .10 .25
134 Jungle Weaver C :G: .10 .25
135 Keeper of Progenitus R :G: .30 .75
136 Lush Growth C :G: .10 .25
137 Mighty Emergence U :G: .20 .50
138 Manaplasm R :G: .25 .60
139 Mosstodon C :G: .10 .25
140 Mycoloth R :G: 2.00 5.00
141 Naturalize C :G: .10 .25
142 Naya Battlemage U :G: .20 .50
143 Ooze Garden R :G: .30 .75
144 Resounding Roar C :G: .10 .25
145 Rhox Charger U :G: .20 .50
146 Sacellum Godspeaker R :G: .25 .60
147 Savage Hunger C :G: .10 .25
148 Skullmulcher R :G: .25 .60
149 Soul's Might C :G: .10 .25
150 Spearbreaker Behemoth R :G: .30 .75
151 Topan Ascetic U :G: .20 .50
152 Wild Nacatl C :G: .20 .50
153 Agony Warp C :D: .10 .25
154 Ajani Vengeant M :D: 2.50 6.00
155 Bant Charm U :D: .50 1.25
156 Blightning C :D: .60 1.50
157 Blood Cultist U :D: .20 .50
158 Branching Bolt C :D: .10 .25
159 Brilliant Ultimatum R :D: .30 .75
160 Broodmate Dragon R :D: 1.50 4.00
161 Bull Cerodon U :D: .20 .50
162 Carrion Thrash C :D: .10 .25
163 Clarion Ultimatum R :D: .30 .75
164 Cruel Ultimatum R :D: .60 1.50
165 Deft Duelist C :D: .10 .25
166 Empyrial Archangel M :D: 2.50 6.00
167 Esper Charm U :D: .50 1.25
168 Fire-Field Ogre U :D: .20 .50
169 Goblin Deathraiders C :D: .10 .25
170 Godsire M :D: 2.50 6.00
171 Grixis Charm U :D: .20 .50
172 Hellkite Overlord M :D: 4.00 10.00
173 Hindering Light C :D: .20 .50
174 Jhessian Infiltrator U :D: .25 .60
175 Jund Charm U :D: .20 .50
176 Kederekt Creeper C :D: .10 .25
177 Kiss of the Amesha U :D: .20 .50
178 Kresh the Bloodbraided M :D: .75 2.00
179 Mayael the Anima M :D: 1.00 2.50
180 Naya Charm U :D: .20 .50
181 Necrogenesis U :D: .20 .50
182 Prince of Thralls M :D: 1.25 3.00
183 Punish Ignorance R :D: .30 .75
184 Qasali Ambusher U :D: .20 .50
185 Rafiq of the Many M :D: 2.50 6.00
186 Rakeclaw Gargantuan C :D: .10 .25
187 Realm Razer R :D: .30 .75
188 Rhox War Monk U :D: .25 .60
189 Rip-Clan Crasher C :D: .10 .25
190 Sangrite Surge U :D: .20 .50
191 Sarkhan Vol M :D: 6.00 15.00
192 Sedraxis Specter R :D: .40 1.00
193 Sedris, the Traitor King M :D: 1.00 2.50
194 Sharuum the Hegemon M :D: 1.50 4.00
195 Sigil Blessing C :D: .10 .25
196 Sphinx Sovereign M :D: .60 1.50
197 Sprouting Thrinax U :D: .25 .60
198 Steward of Valeron C :D: .20 .50
199 Stoic Angel R :D: .75 2.00
200 Swerve U :D: .25 .60
201 Thoughtcutter Agent U :D: .20 .50
202 Tidehollow Sculler U :D: .40 1.00
203 Tidehollow Strix C :D: .20 .50
204 Titanic Ultimatum R :D: .25 .60
205 Tower Gargoyle U :D: .20 .50
206 Violent Ultimatum R :D: .30 .75
207 Waveskimmer Aven C :D: .10 .25
208 Windwright Mage C :D: .10 .25
209 Woolly Thoctar U :D: .50 1.25
210 Lich's Mirror M :A: 1.00 2.50
211 Minion Reflector R :A: .30 .75
212 Obelisk of Bant C :A: .10 .25
213 Obelisk of Esper C :A: .10 .25
214 Obelisk of Grixis C :A: .10 .25
215 Obelisk of Jund C :A: .10 .25
216 Obelisk of Naya C :A: .10 .25
217 Quietus Spike R :A: 1.50 4.00
218 Relic of Progenitus C :A: .60 1.50
219 Sigil of Distinction R :A: .30 .75
220 Arcane Sanctum U :L: 1.00 2.50
221 Bant Panorama C :L: .10 .25
223 Esper Panorama C :L: .10 .25
224 Grixis Panorama C :L: .12 .30
225 Jund Panorama C :L: .10 .25
226 Jungle Shrine U :L: .60 1.50
227 Naya Panorama C :L: .10 .25
228 Savage Lands U :L: .75 2.00
229 Seaside Citadel U :L: .75 2.00
230 Plains L :L: .10 .25
231 Plains L :L: .10 .25
232 Plains L :L: .10 .25
233 Plains L :L: .10 .25
234 Island L :L: .10 .25
235 Island L :L: .10 .25
236 Island L :L: .10 .25
237 Island L :L: .10 .25
238 Swamp L :L: .10 .25
239 Swamp L :L: .10 .25
240 Swamp L :L: .10 .25
241 Swamp L :L: .10 .25
242 Mountain L :L: .10 .25
243 Mountain L :L: .10 .25
244 Mountain L :L: .10 .25
245 Mountain L :L: .10 .25
246 Forest L :L: .10 .25
247 Forest L :L: .10 .25
248 Forest L :L: .10 .25
249 Forest L :L: .10 .25

2009 Magic The Gathering Conflux

COMPLETE SET (145) 100.00 175.00
BOOSTER BOX (36 PACKS) 200.00 300.00
BOOSTER PACK (15 CARDS) 6.00 10.00
THEME DECK 15.00 30.00
FAT PACK 75.00 125.00
*FOIL: .75X TO 2X BASIC CARDS
RELEASED ON FEBRUARY 6, 2009
1 Aerie Mystics U :W: .20 .50
2 Asha's Favor C :W: .10 .25
3 Aven Squire C :W: .10 .25
4 Aven Trailblazer C :W: .10 .25
5 Celestial Purge U :W: .25 .60
6 Court Homunculus C :W: .10 .25
7 Darklit Gargoyle C :W: .10 .25
8 Gleam of Resistance C :W: .10 .25
9 Lapse of Certainty C :W: .10 .25
10 Mark of Asylum R :W: .40 1.00
11 Martial Coup R :W: 1.50 4.00
12 Mirror-Sigil Sergeant M :W: .75 2.00
13 Nacatl Hunt-Pride U :W: .20 .50
14 Paragon of the Amesha U :W: .20 .50
15 Path to Exile U :W: 3.00 8.00
16 Rhox Meditant C :W: .10 .25
17 Scepter of Dominance R :W: .30 .75
18 Sigil of the Empty Throne R :W: .75 2.00
19 Valiant Guard C :W: .10 .25
20 Wall of Reverence R :W: 1.25 3.00
21 Brackwater Elemental C :B: .10 .25
22 Constricting Tendrils C :B: .10 .25
23 Controlled Instincts U :B: .20 .50
24 Cumber Stone U :B: .20 .50
25 Esperzoa U :B: .25 .60
26 Ethersworn Adjudicator M :B: 2.50 6.00
27 Faerie Mechanist C :B: .10 .25
28 Frontline Sage C :B: .10 .25
29 Grixis Illusionist C :B: .10 .25
30 Inkwell Leviathan R :B: 1.25 3.00
31 Master Transmuter R :B: 4.00 10.00
32 Parasitic Strix C :B: .10 .25
33 Scepter of Insight R :B: .30 .75
34 Scornful AEther-Lich U :B: .20 .50
35 Telemin Performance R :B: .60 1.50
36 Traumatic Visions C :B: .10 .25
37 Unsummon C :B: .10 .25
38 View from Above U :B: .20 .50
39 Worldly Counsel C :B: .10 .25
40 Absorb Vis C :K: .20 .50
41 Corrupted Roots U :K: .20 .50
42 Drag Down C :K: .10 .25
43 Dreadwing U :K: .20 .50
44 Extractor Demon R :K: .40 1.00
45 Fleshformer U :K: .20 .50
46 Grixis Slavedriver U :K: .20 .50
47 Infectious Horror C :K: .10 .25
48 Kederekt Parasite R :K: .40 1.00
49 Nyxathid R :K: .75 2.00
50 Pestilent Kathari C :K: .10 .25
51 Rotting Rats C :K: .10 .25
52 Salvage Slasher C :K: .10 .25
53 Scepter of Fugue R :K: .40 1.00
54 Sedraxis Alchemist C :K: .20 .50
55 Voices from the Void U :K: .20 .50
56 Wretched Banquet C :K: .10 .25
57 Yoke of the Damned C :K: .10 .25
58 Banefire R :R: 1.50 4.00
59 Bloodhall Ooze R :R: .30 .75
60 Canyon Minotaur C :R: .10 .25
61 Dark Temper C :R: .10 .25
62 Dragonsoul Knight U :R: .20 .50
63 Fiery Fall C :R: .10 .25
64 Goblin Razerunners R :R: .40 1.00
65 Hellspark Elemental U :R: .75 2.00
66 Ignite Disorder U :R: .20 .50
67 Kranioceros C :R: .10 .25
68 Maniacal Rage C :R: .10 .25
69 Molten Frame C :R: .10 .25
70 Quenchable Fire C :R: .10 .25
71 Rakka Mar R :R: .40 1.00
72 Toxic Iguanar C :R: .10 .25
73 Viashino Slaughtermaster U :R: .20 .50
74 Volcanic Fallout U :R: .75 2.00
75 Voracious Dragon R :R: .40 1.00
76 Wandering Goblins C :R: .10 .25
77 Worldheart Phoenix R :R: .30 .75
78 Beacon Behemoth C :G: .10 .25
79 Cliffrunner Behemoth R :G: .40 1.00
80 Cylian Sunsinger R :G: .40 1.00
81 Ember Weaver C :G: .10 .25
82 Filigree Fracture U :G: .20 .50
83 Gluttonous Slime U :G: .20 .50
84 Matca Rioters C :G: .10 .25
85 Might of Alara C :G: .10 .25
86 Nacatl Savage C :G: .10 .25
87 Noble Hierarch R :G: 20.00 50.00
88 Paleoloth R :G: .40 1.00
89 Sacellum Archers U :G: .20 .50
90 Scattershot Archer C :G: .10 .25
91 Shard Convergence U :G: .20 .50
92 Soul's Majesty R :G: .30 .75
93 Spore Burst U :G: .20 .50
94 Sylvan Bounty C :G: .10 .25
95 Thornling M :G: 1.00 2.50
96 Tukatongue Thallid C :G: .10 .25
97 Wild Leotau C :G: .10 .25
98 Apocalypse Hydra M :D: 4.00 10.00
99 Blood Tyrant R :D: .40 1.00
100 Charnelhoard Wurm R :D: .40 1.00
101 Child of Alara M :D: .75 2.00
102 Conflux M :D: .75 2.00
103 Countersquall U :D: .50 1.25
104 Elder Mastery U :D: .20 .50
105 Esper Cormorants C :D: .10 .25
106 Exploding Borders C :D: .10 .25
107 Fusion Elemental U :D: .25 .60
108 Giltspire Avenger R :D: .40 1.00
109 Goblin Outlander C :D: .10 .25
110 Gwafa Hazid, Profiteer R :D: .30 .75
111 Hellkite Hatchling U :D: .25 .60
112 Jhessian Balmgiver U :D: .20 .50
113 Knight of the Reliquary R :D: 6.00 15.00
114 Knotvine Mystic U :D: .30 .75
115 Maelstrom Archangel M :D: 6.00 15.00
116 Magister Sphinx R :D: .40 1.00
117 Malfegor M :D: .75 2.00
118 Meglonoth R :D: .40 1.00
119 Nacatl Outlander C :D: .10 .25
120 Nicol Bolas, Planeswalker M :D: 6.00 15.00
121 Progenitus M :D: 8.00 20.00
122 Rhox Bodyguard C :D: .10 .25
123 Scarland Thrinax U :D: .20 .50
124 Shambling Remains U :D: .30 .75
125 Skyward Eye Prophets U :D: .20 .50
126 Sludge Strider U :D: .20 .50
127 Sphinx Summoner R :D: .60 1.50
128 Suicidal Charge C :D: .10 .25
129 Vagrant Plowbeasts U :D: .20 .50
130 Valeron Outlander C :D: .10 .25
131 Vectis Agents C :D: .10 .25
132 Vedalken Outlander C :D: .10 .25
133 Zombie Outlander C :D: .10 .25
134 Armillary Sphere C :A: .10 .25
135 Bone Saw C :A: .10 .25
136 Font of Mythos R :A: 3.00 8.00
137 Kaleidostone C :A: .10 .25
138 Mana Cylix C :A: .10 .25
139 Manaforce Mace U :A: .20 .50
140 Obelisk of Alara R :A: .40 1.00
141 Ancient Ziggurat U :L: .75 2.00
142 Exotic Orchard R :L: .75 2.00
143 Reliquary Tower U :L: 2.00 5.00
144 Rupture Spire C :L: .25 .60
145 Unstable Frontier U :L: .20 .50

2009 Magic The Gathering Alara Reborn

COMPLETE SET (145) 100.00 175.00
BOOSTER BOX (36 PACKS) 175.00 250.00
BOOSTER PACK (15 CARDS) 5.00 8.00
THEME DECK 10.00 20.00
FAT PACK 50.00 100.00
*FOIL: .75X TO 2X BASIC CARDS
RELEASED ON APRIL 30, 2009
1 Ardent Plea U :W: :B: .25 .60
2 Aven Mimeomancer R :W: :B: .30 .75
3 Ethercaste Knight C :W: :B: .10 .25
4 Ethersworn Shieldmage C :W: :B: .10 .25
5 Fieldmist Borderpost C :W: :B: .20 .50
6 Filigree Angel R :W: :B: .40 1.00
7 Glassdust Hulk C :W: :B: .10 .25
8 Meddling Mage R :W: :B: 2.50 6.00
9 Offering to Asha C :W: :B: .10 .25
10 Sanctum Plowbeast C :W: :B: .10 .25
11 Shield of the Righteous U :W: :B: .20 .50
12 Sovereigns of Lost Alara R :W: :B: .75 2.00
13 Stormcaller's Boon C :W: :B: .10 .25
14 Talon Trooper C :W: :B: .10 .25
15 Unbender Tine U :W: :B: .20 .50
16 Wall of Denial U :W: :B: .75 2.00
17 Architects of Will C :B: :K: .10 .25
18 Brainbite C :B: :K: .10 .25
19 Deny Reality C :B: :K: .10 .25
20 Etherium Abomination C :B: :K: .10 .25
21 Illusory Demon U :B: :K: .20 .50
22 Jhessian Zombies C :B: :K: .10 .25
23 Kathari Remnant U :B: :K: .20 .50
24 Lich Lord of Unx R :B: :K: 2.50 6.00
25 Mask of Riddles U :B: :K: .20 .50
26 Mind Funeral U :B: :K: 2.00 5.00
27 Mistvein Borderpost C :B: :K: .20 .50
28 Nemesis of Reason R :B: :K: 3.00 8.00
29 Soul Manipulation C :B: :K: .10 .25
30 Soulquake R :B: :K: .30 .75
31 Time Sieve R :B: :K: 1.00 2.50
32 Vedalken Ghoul C :B: :K: .10 .25
33 Anathemancer U :D: .30 .75
34 Bituminous Blast U :K: :R: .30 .75
35 Breath of Malfegor C :K: :R: .10 .25
36 Deathbringer Thoctar R :K: :R: .30 .75
37 Defiler of Souls M :K: :R: .75 2.00
38 Demonic Dread C :K: :R: .10 .25
39 Demonspine Whip U :K: :R: .20 .50
40 Igneous Pouncer C :K: :R: .10 .25
41 Kathari Bomber C :K: :R: .10 .25
42 Lightning Reaver R :K: :R: .40 1.00
43 Monstrous Carabid C :K: :R: .10 .25
44 Sanity Gnawers U :K: :R: .20 .50
45 Singe-Mind Ogre C :K: :R: .10 .25
46 Terminate C :K: :R: .60 1.50
47 Thought Hemorrhage R :K: :R: .60 1.50
48 Veinfire Borderpost C :K: :R: .20 .50
49 Blitz Hellion R :R: :G: .30 .75
50 Bloodbraid Elf U :R: :G: 1.25 3.00
51 Colossal Might C :R: :G: .10 .25
52 Deadshot Minotaur C :R: :G: .10 .25
53 Dragon Broodmother M :R: :B: 5.00 12.00
54 Firewild Borderpost C :R: :G: .10 .25
55 Godtracker of Jund C :R: :G: .10 .25
56 Gorger Wurm C :R: :G: .10 .25
57 Mage Slayer U :R: :G: .25 .60
58 Predatory Advantage R :R: :G: .30 .75
59 Rhox Brute C :R: :G: .10 .25
60 Spellbreaker Behemoth R :R: :G: .75 2.00
61 Valley Rannet C :R: :G: .10 .25
62 Vengeful Rebirth U :R: :G: .20 .50
63 Violent Outburst C :R: :G: .10 .25
64 Vithian Renegades U :R: :G: .20 .50
65 Behemoth Sledge U :G: :W: .60 1.50
66 Captured Sunlight C :G: :W: .10 .25
67 Dauntless Escort R :G: :W: .75 2.00
68 Enlisted Wurm U :G: :W: .20 .50
69 Grizzled Leotau C :G: :W: .10 .25
70 Knight of New Alara R :G: :W: .60 1.50
71 Knotvine Paladin R :G: :W: .40 1.00
72 Leonin Armorguard C :G: :W: .10 .25
73 Mycoid Shepherd R :G: :W: .30 .75
74 Pale Recluse C :G: :W: .10 .25
75 Qasali Pridemage C :G: :W: .60 1.50
76 Reborn Hope U :G: :W: .20 .50
77 Sigil Captain U :G: :W: .20 .50
78 Sigil of the Nayan Gods C :G: :W: .10 .25
79 Sigiled Behemoth C :G: :W: .10 .25
80 Wildfield Borderpost C :G: :W: .20 .50
81 Identity Crisis R :W: :B: .30 .75
82 Necromancer's Covenant R :W: :K: .30 .75
83 Tainted Sigil U :W: :B: .20 .50
84 Vectis Dominator C :W: :K: .10 .25
85 Zealous Persecution U :W: :K: .30 .75
86 Cloven Casting R :B: :R: .30 .75
87 Double Negative U :B: :R: .20 .50
88 Magefire Wings C :B: :R: .10 .25
89 Skyclaw Thrash U :B: :R: .20 .50
90 Spellbound Dragon R :B: :R: .30 .75
91 Lord of Extinction M :K: :G: 5.00 12.00
92 Maelstrom Pulse R :K: :G: 6.00 15.00
93 Marrow Chomper U :K: :G: .20 .50
94 Morbid Bloom U :B: :G: .20 .50
95 Putrid Leech C :K: :G: .20 .50
96 Cerodon Yearling C :R: :W: .10 .25
97 Fight to the Death R :R: :W: .30 .75
98 Glory of Warfare R :R: :W: .40 1.00
99 Intimidation Bolt U :R: :W: .20 .50
101 Lorescale Coatl U :G: :B: .40 1.00
102 Nulltread Gargantuan U :G: :B: .25 .60
103 Sages of the Anima R :G: :B: .30 .75
104 Vedalken Heretic R :G: :B: .30 .75
105 Winged Coatl C :G: :B: .10 .25
106 Enigma Sphinx R :D: .30 .75
107 Esper Sojourners C :D: .10 .25
108 Etherwrought Page U :D: .20 .50
109 Sen Triplets M :D: 6.00 15.00
110 Sphinx of the Steel Wind M :D: 4.00 10.00
111 Drastic Revelation U :D: .20 .50
112 Grixis Sojourners C :D: .10 .25
113 Thraximundar M :D: 5.00 12.00
114 Unscythe, Killer of Kings R :D: .40 1.00
115 Dragon Appeasement U :D: .20 .50
116 Jund Sojourners C :D: .10 .25
117 Karrthus, Tyrant of Jund M :D: 4.00 10.00
118 Lavalanche R :D: .30 .75
119 Madrush Cyclops R :D: .30 .75
120 Gloryscale Viashino U :D: .20 .50
121 Mayael's Aria R :D: .75 2.00
100 Stun Sniper U :R: :W: .20 .50
122 Naya Sojourners C :D: .10 .25
123 Retaliator Griffin R :D: .30 .75
124 Uril, the Miststalker M :D: 2.50 6.00
125 Bant Sojourners C :D: .10 .25
126 Finest Hour R :D: .60 1.50
127 Flurry of Wings U :D: .20 .50
128 Jenara, Asura of War M :D: 4.00 10.00
129 Wargate R :D: .60 1.50
130 Maelstrom Nexus M :D: 2.50 6.00
131 Arsenal Thresher C :W: :K: :B: .10 .25
132 Esper Stormblade C :W: :K: :B: .10 .25
133 Thopter Foundry U :W: :K: :B: .40 1.00
134 Grixis Grimblade C :B: :R: :K: .20 .50
135 Sewn-Eye Drake C :B: :R: :K: .10 .25
136 Slave of Bolas U :B: :R: :K: .20 .50
137 Giant Ambush Beetle U :K: :G: :R: .20 .50
138 Jund Hackblade C :K: :G: :R: .10 .25
139 Sangrite Backlash C :K: :G: :R: .10 .25
140 Marisi's Twinclaws U :R: :W: :G: .20 .50
141 Naya Hushblade C :R: :W: :G: .10 .25
142 Trace of Abundance C :R: :W: :G: .20 .50
143 Bant Sureblade C :G: :B: :W: .10 .25
144 Crystallization C :G: :B: :W: .10 .25
145 Messenger Falcons U :G: :B: :W: .20 .50

2009 Magic The Gathering Alara Reborn

2009 Magic The Gathering Magic 2010

COMPLETE SET (234)	100.00	175.00
BOOSTER BOX (36 PACKS)	75.00	125.00
BOOSTER PACK (15 CARDS)	3.00	4.00
THEME DECK	10.00	20.00
FAT PACK	60.00	120.00
*FOIL: .75X TO 2X BASIC CARDS		
RELEASED ON JULY 17, 2009		
1 Ajani Goldmane M :W:	6.00	15.00
2 Angel's Mercy C :W:	.10	.25
3 Armored Ascension U :W:	.20	.50
4 Baneslayer Angel M :W:	6.00	15.00
5 Blinding Mage C :W:	.10	.25
6 Captain of the Watch R :W:	2.00	5.00
7 Celestial Purge U :W:	.20	.50
8 Divine Verdict C :W:	.10	.25
9 Elite Vanguard U :W:	.30	.75
10 Excommunicate C :W:	.10	.25
11 Glorious Charge C :W:	.10	.25
12 Griffin Sentinel C :W:	.10	.25
13 Guardian Seraph R :W:	.30	.75
14 Harm's Way U :W:	.30	.75
15 Holy Strength C :W:	.10	.25
16 Honor of the Pure R :W:	1.50	4.00
17 Indestructibility R :W:	.40	1.00
18 Lifelink C :W:	.10	.25
19 Lightwielder Paladin R :W:	.30	.75
20 Mesa Enchantress R :W:	.30	.75
21 Open the Vaults R :W:	.30	.75
22 Pacifism C :W:	.10	.25
23 Palace Guard C :W:	.10	.25
24 Planar Cleansing R :W:	.30	.75
25 Razorfoot Griffin C :W:	.10	.25
26 Rhox Pikemaster U :W:	.20	.50
27 Righteousness U :W:	.20	.50
28 Safe Passage C :W:	.10	.25
29 Serra Angel U :W:	.30	.75
30 Siege Mastodon C :W:	.10	.25
31 Silence R :W:	.60	1.50
32 Silvercoat Lion C :W:	.10	.25
33 Solemn Offering C :W:	.10	.25
34 Soul Warden C :W:	.20	.50
35 Stormfront Pegasus C :W:	.10	.25
36 Tempest of Light U :W:	.20	.50
37 Undead Slayer U :W:	.20	.50
38 Veteran Armorsmith C :W:	.10	.25
39 Veteran Swordsmith C :W:	.10	.25
40 Wall of Faith C :W:	.10	.25
41 White Knight U :W:	.20	.50
42 Air Elemental U :B:	.20	.50
43 Alluring Siren U :B:	.20	.50
44 Cancel C :B:	.10	.25
45 Clone R :B:	.30	.75
46 Convincing Mirage C :B:	.10	.25
47 Coral Merfolk C :B:	.10	.25
48 Disorient C :B:	.10	.25
49 Divination C :B:	.10	.25
50 Djinn of Wishes R :B:	.30	.75
51 Essence Scatter C :B:	.10	.25
52 Fabricate U :B:	.40	1.00
53 Flashfreeze U :B:	.20	.50
54 Hive Mind R :B:	.40	1.00
55 Horned Turtle C :B:	.10	.25
56 Ice Cage C :B:	.10	.25
57 Illusionary Servant C :B:	.10	.25
58 Jace Beleren M :B:	4.00	10.00
59 Jump C :B:	.10	.25
60 Levitation U :B:	.20	.50
61 Merfolk Looter C :B:	.10	.25
62 Merfolk Sovereign R :B:	.30	.75
63 Mind Control U :B:	.30	.75
64 Mind Spring R :B:	.30	.75
65 Negate C :B:	.10	.25
66 Phantom Warrior U :B:	.20	.50
67 Polymorph R :B:	.40	1.00
68 Ponder C :B:	.40	1.00
69 Sage Owl C :B:	.10	.25
70 Serpent of the Endless Sea C :B:	.10	.25
71 Sleep U :B:	.30	.75
72 Snapping Drake C :B:	.10	.25
73 Sphinx Ambassador M :B:	.60	1.50
74 Telepathy U :B:	.20	.50
75 Time Warp M :B:	6.00	15.00
76 Tome Scour C :B:	.10	.25
77 Traumatize R :B:	.60	1.50
78 Twincast R :B:	1.00	2.50
79 Unsummon C :B:	.10	.25
80 Wall of Frost U :B:	.20	.50
81 Wind Drake C :B:	.10	.25
82 Zephyr Sprite C :B:	.10	.25
83 Acolyte of Xathrid C :K:	.10	.25
84 Assassinate C :K:	.10	.25
85 Black Knight U :K:	.30	.75
86 Bog Wraith U :K:	.20	.50
87 Cemetery Reaper R :K:	1.50	4.00
88 Child of Night C :K:	.10	.25
89 Consume Spirit U :K:	.20	.50
90 Deathmark U :K:	.30	.75
91 Diabolic Tutor U :K:	.30	.75
92 Disentomb C :K:	.10	.25
93 Doom Blade C :K:	.20	.50
94 Dread Warlock C :K:	.10	.25
95 Drudge Skeletons C :K:	.10	.25
96 Duress C :K:	.20	.50
97 Gravedigger C :K:	.10	.25
98 Haunting Echoes R :K:	.40	1.00
99 Howling Banshee U :K:	.20	.50
100 Hypnotic Specter R :K:	.75	2.00
101 Kelinore Bat C :K:	.10	.25
102 Liliana Vess M :K:	6.00	15.00
103 Looming Shade C :K:	.10	.25
104 Megrim U :K:	.30	.75
105 Mind Rot C :K:	.10	.25
106 Mind Shatter R :K:	.30	.75
107 Nightmare R :K:	.30	.75
108 Relentless Rats U :K:	.60	1.50
109 Rise from the Grave U :K:	.20	.50
110 Royal Assassin R :K:	.30	.75
111 Sanguine Bond R :K:	2.00	5.00
112 Sign in Blood C :K:	.20	.50
113 Soul Bleed C :K:	.10	.25
114 Tendrils of Corruption C :K:	.10	.25
115 Underworld Dreams R :K:	.60	1.50
116 Unholy Strength C :K:	.10	.25
117 Vampire Aristocrat C :K:	.10	.25
118 Vampire Nocturnus M :K:	5.00	12.00
119 Wall of Bone U :K:	.20	.50
120 Warpath Ghoul C :K:	.10	.25
121 Weakness C :K:	.10	.25
122 Xathrid Demon M :K:	.40	1.00
123 Zombie Goliath C :K:	.10	.25
124 Act of Treason U :R:	.20	.50
125 Ball Lightning R :R:	1.25	3.00
126 Berserkers of Blood Ridge C :R:	.10	.25
127 Bogardan Hellkite M :R:	.75	2.00
128 Burning Inquiry C :R:	.10	.25
129 Burst of Speed C :R:	.10	.25
130 Canyon Minotaur C :R:	.10	.25
131 Capricious Efreet R :R:	.30	.75
132 Chandra Nalaar M :R:	2.50	6.00
133 Dragon Whelp U :R:	.20	.50
134 Earthquake R :R:	.40	1.00
135 Fiery Hellhound C :R:	.10	.25
136 Fireball U :R:	.20	.50
137 Firebreathing C :R:	.10	.25
138 Goblin Artillery U :R:	.20	.50
139 Goblin Chieftain R :R:	.60	1.50
140 Goblin Piker C :R:	.10	.25
141 Ignite Disorder U :R:	.20	.50
142 Inferno Elemental U :R:	.20	.50
143 Jackal Familiar C :R:	.10	.25
144 Kindled Fury C :R:	.10	.25
145 Lava Axe C :R:	.10	.25
146 Lightning Bolt C :R:	.40	1.00
147 Lightning Elemental C :R:	.10	.25
148 Magma Phoenix R :R:	.30	.75
149 Manabarbs R :R:	.30	.75
150 Panic Attack C :R:	.10	.25
151 Prodigal Pyromancer U :R:	.20	.50
152 Pyroclasm U :R:	.30	.75
153 Raging Goblin C :R:	.10	.25
154 Seismic Strike C :R:	.10	.25
155 Shatter C :R:	.10	.25
156 Shivan Dragon R :R:	.30	.75
157 Siege-Gang Commander R :R:	.75	2.00
158 Sparkmage Apprentice C :R:	.10	.25
159 Stone Giant U :R:	.20	.50
160 Trumpet Blast C :R:	.10	.25
161 Viashino Spearhunter C :R:	.10	.25
162 Wall of Fire U :R:	.20	.50
163 Warp World R :R:	.30	.75
164 Yawning Fissure C :R:	.10	.25
165 Acidic Slime U :G:	.20	.50
166 Ant Queen R :G:	.30	.75
167 Awakener Druid U :G:	.20	.50
168 Birds of Paradise R :G:	2.00	5.00
169 Borderland Ranger C :G:	.10	.25
170 Bountiful Harvest C :G:	.10	.25
171 Bramble Creeper C :G:	.10	.25
172 Centaur Courser C :G:	.10	.25
173 Craw Wurm C :G:	.10	.25
174 Cudgel Troll U :G:	.20	.50
175 Deadly Recluse C :G:	.20	.50
176 Elvish Archdruid R :G:	.75	2.00
177 Elvish Piper R :G:	5.00	12.00
178 Elvish Visionary C :G:	.20	.50
179 Emerald Oryx C :G:	.10	.25
180 Enormous Baloth U :G:	.20	.50
181 Entangling Vines C :G:	.10	.25
182 Fog C :G:	.10	.25
183 Garruk Wildspeaker M :G:	4.00	10.00
184 Giant Growth C :G:	.10	.25
185 Giant Spider C :G:	.10	.25
186 Great Sable Stag R :G:	.60	1.50
187 Howl of the Night Pack U :G:	.20	.50
188 Kalonian Behemoth R :G:	.40	1.00
189 Llanowar Elves C :G:	.20	.50
190 Lurking Predators R :G:	.40	1.00
191 Master of the Wild Hunt M :G:	8.00	20.00
192 Might of Oaks R :G:	.30	.75
193 Mist Leopard C :G:	.10	.25
194 Mold Adder U :G:	.20	.50
195 Naturalize C :G:	.10	.25
196 Nature's Spiral U :G:	.20	.50
197 Oakenform C :G:	.10	.25
198 Overrun U :G:	.30	.75
199 Prized Unicorn U :G:	.20	.50
200 Protean Hydra M :G:	.60	1.50
201 Rampant Growth C :G:	.10	.25
202 Regenerate C :G:	.10	.25
203 Runeclaw Bear C :G:	.10	.25
204 Stampeding Rhino C :G:	.10	.25
205 Windstorm U :G:	.20	.50
206 Angel's Feather U :A:	.20	.50
207 Coat of Arms R :A:	3.00	8.00
208 Darksteel Colossus M :A:	3.00	8.00
209 Demon's Horn U :A:	.20	.50
210 Dragon's Claw U :A:	.20	.50
211 Gorgon Flail U :A:	.30	.75
212 Howling Mine R :A:	1.25	3.00
213 Kraken's Eye U :A:	.20	.50
214 Magebane Armor R :A:	.30	.75
215 Mirror of Fate R :A:	.30	.75
216 Ornithopter U :A:	.30	.75
217 Pithing Needle R :A:	1.50	4.00
218 Platinum Angel M :A:	4.00	10.00
219 Rod of Ruin U :A:	.20	.50
220 Spellbook U :A:	.20	.50
221 Whispersilk Cloak U :A:	.30	.75
222 Wurm's Tooth U :A:	.20	.50
223 Dragonskull Summit R :L:	1.50	4.00
224 Drowned Catacomb R :L:	3.00	8.00
225 Gargoyle Castle R :L:	.40	1.00
226 Glacial Fortress R :L:	2.00	5.00
227 Rootbound Crag R :L:	2.00	5.00
228 Sunpetal Grove R :L:	1.50	4.00
229 Terramorphic Expanse C :L:	.10	.25
230 Plains C :L:	.10	.25
231 Plains C :L:	.10	.25
232 Plains C :L:	.10	.25
233 Plains C :L:	.10	.25
234 Island C :L:	.10	.25
235 Island C :L:	.10	.25
236 Island C :L:	.10	.25
237 Island C :L:	.10	.25
238 Swamp C :L:	.10	.25
239 Swamp C :L:	.10	.25
240 Swamp C :L:	.10	.25
241 Swamp C :L:	.10	.25
242 Mountain C :L:	.10	.25
243 Mountain C :L:	.10	.25
244 Mountain C :L:	.10	.25
245 Mountain C :L:	.10	.25
246 Forest C :L:	.10	.25
247 Forest C :L:	.10	.25
248 Forest C :L:	.10	.25
249 Forest C :L:	.10	.25

2009 Magic The Gathering Zendikar

COMPLETE SET (234)	100.00	175.00
BOOSTER BOX (36 PACKS)	350.00	450.00
BOOSTER PACK (15 CARDS)	10.00	15.00
THEME DECK	15.00	30.00
FAT PACK	200.00	300.00
*FOIL: .75X TO 2X BASIC CARDS		
RELEASED ON OCTOBER 2, 2009		
1 Armament Master R :W:	.30	.75
2 Arrow Volley Trap U :W:	.12	.30
3 Bold Defense C :W:	.10	.25
4 Brave the Elements U :W:	.40	1.00
5 Caravan Hurda C :W:	.10	.25
6 Celestial Mantle R :W:	1.25	3.00
7 Cliff Threader C :W:	.08	.20
8 Conqueror's Pledge R :W:	.75	2.00
9 Day of Judgment R :W:	1.00	2.50
10 Devout Lightcaster R :W:	.30	.75
11 Emeria Angel R :W:	.75	2.00
12 Felidar Sovereign M :W:	3.00	8.00
13 Iona, Shield of Emeria M :W:	10.00	25.00
14 Journey to Nowhere C :W:	.12	.30
15 Kabira Evangel R :W:	.40	1.00
16 Kazandu Blademaster U :W:	.30	.75
17 Kor Aeronaut U :W:	.20	.50
18 Kor Cartographer C :W:	.08	.20
19 Kor Duelist U :W:	.20	.50
20 Kor Hookmaster C :W:	.08	.20
21 Kor Outfitter C :W:	.10	.25
22 Kor Sanctifiers C :W:	.12	.30
23 Kor Skyfisher C :W:	.20	.50
24 Landbind Ritual U :W:	.20	.50
25 Luminarch Ascension R :W:	1.25	3.00
26 Makindi Shieldmate C :W:	.10	.25
27 Narrow Escape C :W:	.10	.25
28 Nimbus Wings C :W:	.10	.25
29 Noble Vestige C :W:	.08	.20
30 Ondu Cleric C :W:	.10	.25
31 Pillarfield Ox C :W:	.10	.25
32 Pitfall Trap U :W:	.20	.50
33 Quest for the Holy Relic U :W:	.40	1.00
34 Shepherd of the Lost U :W:	.20	.50
35 Shieldmate's Blessing C :W:	.10	.25
36 Steppe Lynx C :W:	.20	.50
37 Sunspring Expedition C :W:	.10	.25
38 Windborne Charge U :W:	.20	.50
39 World Queller R :W:	.30	.75
40 Aether Figment U :B:	.20	.50
41 Archive Trap R :B:	1.25	3.00
42 Archmage Ascension R :B:	.30	.75
43 Caller of Gales C :B:	.10	.25
44 Cancel C :B:	.10	.25
45 Cosi's Trickster R :B:	.30	.75
46 Gomazoa U :B:	.20	.50
47 Hedron Crab U :B:	.75	2.00
48 Into the Roil C :B:	.30	.75
49 Ior Ruin Expedition C :B:	.10	.25
50 Kraken Hatchling C :B:	.10	.25
51 Lethargy Trap C :B:	.10	.25
52 Living Tsunami U :B:	.20	.50
53 Lorthos, the Tidemaker M :B:	.75	2.00
54 Lullmage Mentor R :B:	.30	.75
55 Merfolk Seastalkers U :B:	.20	.50
56 Merfolk Wayfinder U :B:	.20	.50
57 Mindbreak Trap M :B:	2.00	5.00
58 Paralyzing Grasp C :B:	.08	.20
59 Quest for Ancient Secrets U :B:	.20	.50
60 Reckless Scholar C :B:	.10	.25
61 Rite of Replication R :B:	2.00	5.00
62 Roil Elemental R :B:	.40	1.00
63 Sea Gate Loremaster R :B:	.30	.75
64 Seascape Aerialist U :B:	.20	.50
65 Shoal Serpent C :B:	.10	.25
66 Sky Ruin Drake C :B:	.10	.25
67 Spell Pierce C :B:	.50	1.25
68 Sphinx of Jwar Isle R :B:	.40	1.00
69 Sphinx of Lost Truths R :B:	.30	.75
70 Spreading Seas C :B:	.30	.75
71 Summoner's Bane U :B:	.20	.50
72 Tempest Owl C :B:	.10	.25
73 Trapfinder's Trick C :B:	.10	.25
74 Trapmaker's Snare U :B:	.20	.50
75 Umara Raptor C :B:	.10	.25
76 Welkin Tern C :B:	.10	.25
77 Whiplash Trap C :B:	.10	.25
78 Windrider Eel C :B:	.10	.25
79 Bala Ged Thief R :K:	.30	.75
80 Blood Seeker C :K:	.10	.25
81 Blood Tribute R :K:	.40	1.00
82 Bloodchief Ascension R :K:	1.25	3.00
83 Bloodghast R :K:	5.00	12.00
84 Bog Tatters C :K:	.10	.25
85 Crypt Ripper C :K:	.10	.25
86 Desecrated Earth C :K:	.08	.20
87 Disfigure C :K:	.10	.25
88 Feast of Blood U :K:	.30	.75
89 Gatekeeper of Malakir U :K:	.60	1.50
90 Giant Scorpion C :K:	.10	.25
91 Grim Discovery C :K:	.10	.25
92 Guul Draz Specter R :K:	.30	.75
93 Guul Draz Vampire C :K:	.10	.25
94 Hagra Crocodile C :K:	.10	.25
95 Hagra Diabolist U :K:	.20	.50
96 Halo Hunter R :K:	.30	.75
97 Heartstabber Mosquito C :K:	.08	.20
98 Hideous End C :K:	.12	.30
99 Kalitas, Bloodchief of Ghet M :K:	3.00	8.00
100 Malakir Bloodwitch R :K:	.75	2.00
101 Marsh Casualties U :K:	.20	.50
102 Mind Sludge U :K:	.20	.50
103 Mindless Null C :K:	.08	.20
104 Mire Blight C :K:	.10	.25
105 Needlebite Trap U :K:	.20	.50
106 Nimana Sell-Sword C :K:	.10	.25
107 Ob Nixilis, the Fallen M :K:	2.50	6.00
108 Quest for the Gravelord U :K:	.20	.50
109 Ravenous Trap U :K:	.20	.50
110 Sadistic Sacrament R :K:	.60	1.50
111 Sorin Markov M :K:	8.00	20.00
112 Soul Stair Expedition C :K:	.10	.25
113 Surrakar Marauder C :K:	.10	.25
114 Vampire Hexmage U :K:	.40	1.00
115 Vampire Lacerator C :K:	.10	.25
116 Vampire Nighthawk U :K:	.75	2.00
117 Vampire's Bite C :K:	.10	.25
118 Bladetusk Boar C :R:	.10	.25
119 Burst Lightning C :R:	.30	.75
120 Chandra Ablaze M :R:	4.00	10.00
121 Demolish C :R:	.10	.25
122 Electropotence R :R:	.25	.60
123 Elemental Appeal R :R:	.30	.75
124 Geyser Glider U :R:	.20	.50
125 Goblin Bushwhacker C :R:	.20	.50
126 Goblin Guide R :R:	4.00	10.00
127 Goblin Ruinblaster U :R:	.20	.50
128 Goblin Shortcutter C :R:	.08	.20
129 Goblin War Paint C :R:	.10	.25
130 Hellfire Mongrel U :R:	.20	.50
131 Hellkite Charger R :R:	.40	1.00
132 Highland Berserker C :R:	.10	.25
133 Inferno Trap U :R:	.12	.30
134 Kazuul Warlord R :R:	.30	.75
135 Lavaball Trap R :R:	.30	.75
136 Magma Rift C :R:	.10	.25
137 Mark of Mutiny U :R:	.20	.50
138 Molten Ravager C :R:	.08	.20
139 Murasa Pyromancer U :R:	.20	.50
140 Obsidian Fireheart M :R:	.75	2.00
141 Plated Geopede C :R:	.20	.50
142 Punishing Fire U :R:	.20	.50
143 Pyromancer Ascension R :R:	1.50	4.00
144 Quest for Pure Flame U :R:	.20	.50
145 Ruinous Minotaur C :R:	.10	.25
146 Runeflare Trap U :R:	.20	.50
147 Seismic Shudder C :R:	.10	.25
148 Shatterskull Giant C :R:	.10	.25
149 Slaughter Cry C :R:	.10	.25
150 Spire Barrage C :R:	.10	.25
151 Torch Slinger C :R:	.10	.25
152 Tuktuk Grunts C :R:	.10	.25
153 Unstable Footing U :R:	.20	.50
154 Warren Instigator M :R:	3.00	8.00
155 Zektar Shrine Expedition C :R:	.10	.25
156 Baloth Cage Trap U :G:	.15	.40
157 Baloth Woodcrasher U :G:	.20	.50
158 Beast Hunt C :G:	.10	.25
159 Beastmaster Ascension R :G:	.75	2.00
160 Cobra Trap U :G:	.20	.50
161 Frontier Guide U :G:	.20	.50
162 Gigantiform R :G:	.30	.75
163 Grazing Gladehart C :G:	.10	.25
164 Greenweaver Druid U :G:	.20	.50
165 Harrow C :G:	.20	.50
166 Joraga Bard C :G:	.10	.25
167 Khalni Heart Expedition C :G:	.12	.30
168 Lotus Cobra M :G:	3.00	8.00
169 Mold Shambler C :G:	.10	.25
170 Nissa Revane M :G:	6.00	15.00
171 Nissa's Chosen C :G:	.20	.50
172 Oracle of Mul Daya R :G:	3.00	8.00
173 Oran-Rief Recluse C :G:	.10	.25
174 Oran-Rief Survivalist C :G:	.12	.30
175 Predatory Urge R :G:	.30	.75
176 Primal Bellow U :G:	.20	.50
177 Quest for the Gemblades U :G:	.20	.50
178 Rampaging Baloths M :G:	1.50	4.00
179 Relic Crush C :G:	.10	.25
180 River Boa U :G:	.20	.50
181 Savage Silhouette C :G:	.10	.25
182 Scute Mob R :G:	.75	2.00
183 Scythe Tiger C :G:	.10	.25
184 Summoning Trap R :G:	.75	2.00
185 Tajuru Archer U :G:	.20	.50
186 Tanglesap C :G:	.10	.25
187 Terra Stomper R :G:	.40	1.00
188 Territorial Baloth C :G:	.10	.25
189 Timbermaw Larva C :G:	.10	.25
190 Turntimber Basilisk U :G:	.20	.50
191 Turntimber Ranger R :G:	.30	.75
192 Vastwood Gorger C :G:	.10	.25
193 Vines of Vastwood C :G:	.30	.75
194 Zendikar Farguide C :G:	.10	.25
195 Adventuring Gear C :A:	.10	.25
196 Blade of the Bloodchief R :A:	1.25	3.00
197 Blazing Torch U :A:	.20	.50
198 Carnage Altar U :A:	.20	.50
199 Eldrazi Monument M :A:	3.00	8.00
200 Eternity Vessel M :A:	.75	2.00
201 Expedition Map C :A:	.30	.75
202 Explorer's Scope C :A:	.10	.25
203 Grappling Hook R :A:	.30	.75
204 Hedron Scrabbler C :A:	.10	.25
205 Khalni Gem U :A:	.20	.50
206 Spidersilk Net C :A:	.10	.25
207 Stonework Puma C :A:	.10	.25
208 Trailblazer's Boots U :A:	.20	.50
209 Trusty Machete U :A:	.20	.50
210 Akoum Refuge U :L:	.30	.75
211 Arid Mesa R :L:	20.00	50.00
212 Crypt of Agadeem R :L:	.40	1.00
213 Emeria, the Sky Ruin R :L:	2.50	6.00
214 Graypelt Refuge U :L:	.30	.75
215 Jwar Isle Refuge U :L:	.30	.75
216 Kabira Crossroads C :L:	.10	.25
217 Kazandu Refuge U :L:	.20	.50
218 Magosi, the Waterveil R :L:	.30	.75
219 Marsh Flats R :L:	15.00	40.00
220 Misty Rainforest R :L:	35.00	70.00
221 Oran-Rief, the Vastwood R :L:	1.00	2.50
222 Piranha Marsh C :L:	.08	.20
223 Scalding Tarn R :L:	40.00	80.00
224 Sejiri Refuge U :L:	.30	.75
225 Soaring Seacliff C :L:	.10	.25
226 Teetering Peaks C :L:	.20	.50
227 Turntimber Grove C :L:	.10	.25
228 Valakut, the Molten Pinnacle R :L:	.75	2.00
229 Verdant Catacombs R :L:	20.00	50.00
230 Plains C :L:	.12	.30
231 Plains C :L:		
232 Plains C :L:		
233 Plains C :L:		
234 Island C :L:	.12	.30
235 Island C :L:		
236 Island C :L:		
237 Island C :L:		
238 Swamp C :L:	.60	1.50
239 Swamp C :L:		
240 Swamp C :L:		
241 Swamp C :L:		
242 Mountain C :L:	.60	1.50
243 Mountain C :L:		
244 Mountain C :L:		
245 Mountain C :L:		
246 Forest C :L:	.60	1.50
247 Forest C :L:		
248 Forest C :L:		
249 Forest C :L:		
250 Plains C :L:		
251 Plains C :L:		
252 Plains C :L:		
253 Plains C :L:		
254 Island C :L:		
255 Island C :L:		
256 Island C :L:		
257 Island C :L:		
258 Swamp C :L:		
259 Swamp C :L:		
260 Swamp C :L:		
261 Swamp C :L:		
262 Mountain C :L:		
263 Mountain C :L:		
264 Mountain C :L:		
265 Mountain C :L:		
266 Forest C :L:		
267 Forest C :L:		
268 Forest C :L:		
269 Forest C :L:		

2010 Magic The Gathering Worldwake

COMPLETE SET (145)	125.00	200.00
BOOSTER BOX (36 PACKS)	450.00	600.00
BOOSTER PACK (15 CARDS)	12.00	20.00
THEME DECK	15.00	30.00
FAT PACK	200.00	300.00
*FOIL: .75X TO 2X BASIC CARDS		
RELEASED ON FEBRUARY 2, 2010		
1 Admonition Angel M :W:	2.00	5.00
2 Apex Hawks C :W:	.20	.50
3 Archon of Redemption R :W:	.60	1.50
4 Battle Hurda C :W:	.10	.25
5 Fledgling Griffin C :W:	.10	.25
6 Guardian Zendikon C :W:	.10	.25
7 Hada Freeblade U :W:	.30	.75
8 Iona's Judgment C :W:	.10	.25
9 Join the Ranks C :W:	.20	.50
10 Kitesail Apprentice C :W:	.10	.25
11 Kor Firewalker U :W:	.75	2.00
12 Lightkeeper of Emeria U :W:	.20	.50
13 Loam Lion U :W:	.40	1.00
14 Marsh Threader C :W:	.10	.25
15 Marshal's Anthem R :W:	.60	1.50
16 Perimeter Captain U :W:	.40	1.00
17 Refraction Trap U :W:	.40	1.00
18 Rest for the Weary C :W:	.20	.50
19 Ruin Ghost U :W:	.40	1.00
20 Stoneforge Mystic R :W:	10.00	25.00
21 Talus Paladin R :W:	.75	2.00
22 Terra Eternal R :W:	.60	1.50
23 Veteran's Reflexes C :W:	.10	.25
24 Aether Tradewinds C :L:	.10	.25
25 Calcite Snapper C :B:	.10	.25
26 Dispel C :B:	.30	.75
27 Enclave Elite C :B:	.10	.25
28 Goliath Sphinx R :B:	.60	1.50
29 Halimar Excavator C :B:	.10	.25
30 Horizon Drake U :B:	.20	.50
31 Jace, Mind Sculptor M :L:	50.00	100.00
32 Jwari Shapeshifter R :B:	.75	2.00
33 Mysteries of the Deep C :B:	.10	.25
34 Permafrost Trap U :B:	.20	.50
35 Quest for Ula's Temple R :B:	.60	1.50
36 Sejiri Merfolk U :B:	.40	1.00
37 Selective Memory R :B:	.60	1.50
38 Spell Contortion U :B:	.40	1.00
39 Surrakar Banisher C :B:	.10	.25
40 Thada Adel, Acquisitor R :B:	.60	1.50
41 Tideforce Elemental U :B:	.20	.50
42 Treasure Hunt C :B:	.20	.50
43 Twitch C :B:	.10	.25
44 Vapor Snare U :B:	.40	1.00
45 Voyager Drake U :B:	.20	.50
46 Wind Zendikon C :B:	.10	.25
47 Abyssal Persecutor M :K:	3.00	8.00
48 Agadeem Occultist R :K:	.60	1.50
49 Anowon, the Ruin Sage R :K:	1.50	4.00
50 Bloodhusk Ritualist U :K:	.30	.75
51 Bojuka Brigand C :K:	.10	.25
52 Brink of Disaster C :K:	.10	.25
53 Butcher of Malakir R :K:	.60	1.50
54 Caustic Crawler U :K:	.30	.75
55 Corrupted Zendikon C :K:	.10	.25
56 Dead Reckoning C :K:	.10	.25
57 Death's Shadow R :K:	.60	1.50
58 Jagwasp Swarm C :K:	.10	.25
59 Kalastria Highborn R :K:	2.50	6.00
60 Mire's Toll C :K:	.10	.25
61 Nemesis Trap U :K:	.30	.75
62 Pulse Tracker C :K:	.30	.75
63 Quag Vampires C :K:	.10	.25
64 Quest for the Nihil Stone R :K:	.60	1.50
65 Ruthless Cullblade C :K:	.10	.25
66 Scrib Nibblers U :K:	.20	.50
67 Shoreline Salvager U :K:	.20	.50
68 Smother U :K:	.40	1.00
69 Tomb Hex C :K:	.10	.25
70 Urge to Feed U :K:	.40	1.00
71 Akoum Battlesinger C :R:	.10	.25
72 Bazaar Trader R :R:	.60	1.50
73 Bull Rush C :R:	.10	.25

Card	Low	High
74 Chain Reaction R :R:	.60	1.50
75 Claws of Valakut C :R:	.10	.25
76 Comet Storm M :R:	1.00	2.50
77 Cosi's Ravager C :R:	.10	.25
78 Crusher Zendikon C :R:	.10	.25
79 Cunning Sparkmage U :R:	.30	.75
80 Deathforge Shaman U :R:	.20	.50
81 Dragonmaster Outcast M :R:	6.00	15.00
82 Goblin Roughrider C :R:	.10	.25
83 Grotag Thrasher C :R:	.10	.25
84 Kazuul, Tyrant R :R:	.60	1,50
85 Mordant Dragon R :R:	.60	1.50
86 Quest for the Goblin Lord U :R:	.40	1.00
87 Ricochet Trap U :R:	.40	1.00
88 Roiling Terrain C :R:	.10	.25
89 Rumbling Aftershocks U :R:	.20	.50
90 Searing Blaze C :R:	.30	.75
91 Skitter of Lizards C :R:	.10	.25
92 Slavering Nulls U :R:	.40	1.00
93 Stone Idol Trap R :R:	.60	1.50
94 Tuktuk Scrapper U :R:	.40	1.00
95 Arbor Elf C :G:	.30	.75
96 Avenger of Zendikar M :G:	3.00	8.00
97 Bestial Menace U :G:	.30	.75
98 Canopy Cover U :G:	.30	.75
99 Explore C :G:	.40	1.00
R1 Rules Tip: Allies and Quests	.10	.25
R2 Rules Tip: Landfall	.10	.25
R3 Rules Tip: Lands Alive	.10	.25
R4 Rules Tip: Multikicker	.10	.25
R5 Rules Tip: Traps	.10	.25
T1 Token: Construct	.10	.25
T2 Token: Dragon	.10	.25
T3 Token: Elephant	.10	.25
T4 Token: Ogre	.10	.25
T5 Token: Plant	.10	.25
T6 Token: Soldier Ally	.10	.25
100 Feral Contest C :G:	.10	.25
101 Gnarlid Pack C :G:	.10	.25
102 Grappler Spider C :G:	.10	.25
103 Graypelt Hunter C :G:	.10	.25
104 Groundswell C :G:	.20	.50
105 Harabaz Druid R :G:	.75	2.00
106 Joraga Warcaller R :G:	3.00	8.00
107 Leatherback Baloth U :G:	.30	.75
108 Nature's Claim C :G:	.30	.75
109 Omnath, Locus M :G:	4.00	10.00
110 Quest for Renewal U :G:	.40	1.00
111 Slingbow Trap U :G:	.40	1.00
112 Snapping Creeper C :G:	.10	.25
113 Strength of the Tajuru R :G:	.60	1.50
114 Summit Apes U :G:	.40	1.00
115 Terastodon R :G:	.75	2.00
116 Vastwood Animist U :G:	.40	1.00
117 Vastwood Zendikon C :G:	.10	.25
118 Wolfbriar Elemental R :G:	.75	2.00
119 Novablast Wurm M :W: :G:	1.50	4.00
120 Wrexial, Risen Deep M :B: :K:	.75	2.00
121 Amulet of Vigor R	.75	2.00
122 Basilisk Collar R	3.00	8.00
123 Everflowing Chalice U	1.00	2.50
124 Hammer of Ruin U	.30	.75
125 Hedron Rover C	.20	.50
126 Kitesail C	.10	.25
127 Lodestone Golem R	.75	2.00
128 Pilgrim's Eye C	.10	.25
129 Razor Boomerang U	.40	1.00
130 Seer's Sundial R	.60	1.50
131 Walking Atlas C	.10	.25
132 Bojuka Bog C	.20	.50
133 Celestial Colonnade R	6.00	15.00
134 Creeping Tar Pit R	5.00	12.00
135 Dread Statuary U	.20	.50
136 Eye of Ugin M	4.00	10.00
137 Halimar Depths C	.30	.75
138 Khalni Garden C	.30	.75
139 Lavaclaw Reaches R	1.50	4.00
140 Quicksand C	.20	.50
141 Raging Ravine R	3.00	8.00
142 Sejiri Steppe C	.20	.50
143 Smoldering Spires C	.20	.50
144 Stirring Wildwood R	1.00	2.50
145 Tectonic Edge U	2.50	6.00

2010 Magic The Gathering Rise of the Eldrazi

Card	Low	High
COMPLETE SET (248)	225.00	300.00
BOOSTER BOX (36 PACKS)	350.00	450.00
BOOSTER PACK (15 CARDS)	10.00	15.00
THEME DECK	20.00	40.00
FAT PACK	75.00	125.00
*FOIL: .75X TO 2X BASIC CARDS		
RELEASED ON APRIL 23, 2010		
1 All Is Dust M	8.00	20.00
2 Artisan of Kozilek U	.20	.50
3 Eldrazi Conscription R	4.00	10.00
4 Emrakul, Aeons Torn M :A:	20.00	50.00
5 Evolving Wilds C	.20	.50
6 Keening Stone R	.60	1.50
7 Hedron Matrix R	.30	.75
8 Kozilek, Butcher M :A:	20.00	50.00
9 Ogre's Cleaver U	.20	.50
10 Runed Servitor U	.20	.50
11 Skittering Invasion U	.20	.50
12 Ulamog, the Infinite M	15.00	40.00
13 Sphinx-Bone Wand R	.30	.75
14 Affa Guard Hound U :W:	.20	.50
15 Caravan Escort C :W:	.10	.25
16 Dawnglare Invoker C :W:	.10	.25
17 Deathless Angel R :W:	.60	1.50
18 Demystify C :W:	.10	.25
19 Eland Umbra C :W:	.10	.25
20 Emerge Unscathed U :W:	.20	.50
21 Gideon Jura M :W:	5.00	12.00
22 Glory Seeker C :W:	.10	.25
23 Guard Duty C :W:	.10	.25
24 Harmless Assault C :W:	.10	.25
25 Hedron-Field Purists R :W:	.30	.75
26 Hyena Umbra C :W:	.20	.50
27 Ikiral Outrider C :W:	.10	.25
28 Kabira Vindicator U :W:	.20	.50
29 Knight of Cliffhaven C :W:	.10	.25
30 Kor Line-Slinger C :W:	.10	.25
31 Kor Spiritdancer R :W:	.75	2.00
32 Lightmine Field R :W:	.30	.75
33 Linvala, Keeper M :W:	15.00	40.00
34 Lone Missionary C :W:	.10	.25
35 Luminous Wake U :W:	.20	.50
36 Makindi Griffin C :W:	.10	.25
37 Mammoth Umbra U :W:	.20	.50
38 Near-Death Exp R :W:	.30	.75
39 Nomads' Assembly R :W:	.30	.75
40 Oust U :W:	.20	.50
41 Puncturing Light C :W:	.10	.25
42 Repel the Darkness C :W:	.10	.25
43 Smite C :W:	.10	.25
44 Soulbound Guardians U :W:	.20	.50
45 Soul's Attendant C :W:	.20	.50
46 Stalwart Shield-Bearers C :W:	.10	.25
47 Student of Warfare R :W:	2.00	5.00
48 Survival Cache U :W:	.20	.50
49 Time of Heroes U :W:	.20	.50
50 Totem-Guide Hartebeest C :W:	.10	.25
51 Transcendent Master M :W:	3.00	8.00
52 Umbra Mystic R :W:	.30	.75
53 Wall of Omens U :W:	.60	1.50
54 Aura Finesse C :B:	.10	.25
55 Cast Through Time M :B:	.40	1.00
56 Champion's Drake C :B:	.10	.25
57 Coralhelm Commander R :B:	2.00	5.00
58 Crab Umbra U :B:	.20	.50
59 Deprive C :B:	.20	.50
60 Distortion Strike C :B:	.20	.50
61 Domestication U :B:	.20	.50
62 Dormant Gomazoa R :B:	.30	.75
63 Drake Umbra U :B:	.20	.50
64 Echo Mage R :B:	.60	1.50
65 Eel Umbra C :B:	.10	.25
66 Enclave Cryptologist U :B:	.20	.50
67 Fleeting Distraction C :B:	.10	.25
68 Frostwind Invoker C :B:	.10	.25
69 Gloomhunter C :B:	.10	.25
70 Gravitational Shift R :B:	.30	.75
71 Guard Gomazoa U :B:	.20	.50
72 Hada Spy Patrol U :B:	.20	.50
73 Halimar Wavewatch C :B:	.10	.25
74 Induce Despair C :B:	.10	.25
75 Inquisition of Kozilek U :B:	3.00	8.00
76 Jwari Scuttler C :B:	.10	.25
77 Lay Bare C :B:	.10	.25
78 Lighthouse Chrono M :B:	4.00	10.00
79 Merfolk Observer C :B:	.10	.25
80 Merfolk Skyscout U :B:	.20	.50
81 Mnemonic Wall C :B:	.10	.25
82 Narcolepsy C :B:	.10	.25
83 Null Champion C :B:	.10	.25
84 Phantasmal Abomination U :B:	.20	.50
85 Reality Spasm U :B:	.20	.50
86 Recurring Insight R :B:	.30	.75
87 Regress C :B:	.10	.25
88 Renegade Doppelganger R :B:	.30	.75
89 Sea Gate Oracle C :B:	.20	.50
90 See Beyond C :B:	.20	.50
91 Shared Discovery C :B:	.10	.25
92 Skywatcher Adept C :B:	.10	.25
93 Sphinx of Magosi R :B:	.30	.75
94 Surrakar Spellblade R :B:	.30	.75
95 Training Grounds R :B:	.75	2.00
96 Unified Will U :B:	.20	.50
97 Venerated Teacher C :B:	.10	.25
98 Arrogant Bloodlord U :K:	.20	.50
99 Baneful Omen R :K:	.30	.75
100 Bloodrite Invoker C :K:	.10	.25
101 Bloodthrone Vampire C :K:	.10	.25
102 Cadaver Imp C :K:	.10	.25
103 Consume the Meek R :K:	.40	1.00
104 Consuming Vapors R :K:	.40	1.00
105 Contaminated Ground C :K:	.10	.25
106 Corpsehatch U :K:	.20	.50
107 Curse of Wizardry U :K:	.20	.50
108 Death Cultist C :K:	.10	.25
109 Demonic Appetite C :K:	.10	.25
110 Drana, Klstria Bldchf R :K:	1.25	3.00
111 Dread Drone C :K:	.10	.25
112 Escaped Null U :K:	.20	.50
113 Essence Feed C :K:	.10	.25
114 Guul Draz Assassin R :K:	2.00	5.00
115 Hellcarver Demon M :K:	.40	1.00
116 Last Kiss C :K:	.10	.25
117 Mortician Beetle R :K:	.30	.75
118 Nighthaze C :K:	.10	.25
119 Nirkana Cutthroat U :K:	.20	.50
120 Nirkana Revenant M :K:	6.00	15.00
121 Pawn of Ulamog U :K:	.20	.50
122 Perish the Thought C :K:	.10	.25
123 Pestilence Demon R :K:	.30	.75
124 Repay In Kind R :K:	.30	.75
125 Shrivel C :K:	.10	.25
126 Skeletal Wurm U :K:	.20	.50
127 Suffer the Past U :K:	.20	.50
128 Thought Gorger R :K:	.30	.75
129 Vendetta C :K:	.10	.25
130 Virulent Swipe U :K:	.20	.50
131 Zof Shade C :K:	.10	.25
132 Zulaport Enforcer C :K:	.10	.25
133 Akoum Boulderfoot U :R:	.20	.50
134 Battle Rampart C :R:	.10	.25
135 Battle-Rattle Shaman C :R:	.10	.25
136 Brimstone Mage U :R:	.20	.50
137 Brood Birthing C :R:	.10	.25
138 Conquering Manticore R :R:	.30	.75
139 Devastating Summons R :R:	.30	.75
140 Disaster Radius R :R:	.30	.75
141 Emrakul's Hatcher C :R:	.10	.25
142 Explosive Revelation U :R:	.20	.50
143 Fissure Vent C :R:	.10	.25
144 Flame Slash C :R:	.10	.25
145 Forked Bolt U :R:	.20	.50
146 Goblin Arsonist C :R:	.10	.25
147 Goblin Tunneler C :R:	.10	.25
148 Grotag Siege-Runner C :R:	.10	.25
149 Heat Ray C :R:	.10	.25
150 Hellion Eruption R :R:	.30	.75
151 Kargan Dragonlord M :R:	3.00	8.00
152 Kiln Fiend C :R:	.20	.50
153 Lagac Lizard C :R:	.10	.25
154 Lavafume Invoker C :R:	.10	.25
155 Lord of Shatter Pass R :R:	.30	.75
156 Lust for War U :R:	.20	.50
157 Magmaw R :R:	.30	.75
158 Ogre Sentry C :R:	.10	.25
159 Rage Nimbus R :R:	.30	.75
160 Raid Bombardment C :R:	.10	.25
161 Rapacious One U :R:	.20	.50
162 Soulsurge Elemental U :R:	.20	.50
163 Spawning Breath C :R:	.10	.25
164 Splinter Twin R :R:	6.00	15.00
165 Staggershock C :R:	.20	.50
166 Surreal Memoir U :R:	.20	.50
167 Traitorous Instinct U :R:	.20	.50
168 Tuktuk the Explorer R :R:	.40	1.00
169 Valakut Fireboar U :R:	.20	.50
170 Vent Sentinel C :R:	.10	.25
171 World at War R :R:	.30	.75
172 Wrap in Flames C :R:	.10	.25
173 Ancient Stirrings C :G:	.10	.25
174 Aura Gnarlid C :G:	.10	.25
175 Awakening Zone R :G:	1.00	2.50
176 Bala Ged Scorpion C :G:	.10	.25
177 Bear Umbra R :G:	.60	1.50
178 Beastbreaker of Bala Ged U :G:	.20	.50
179 Boar Umbra U :G:	.20	.50
180 Bramblesnap U :G:	.20	.50
181 Broodwarden U :G:	.20	.50
182 Daggerback Basilisk C :G:	.10	.25
183 Gelatinous Genesis R :G:	.30	.75
184 Gigantomancer R :G:	.30	.75
185 Gravity Well U :G:	.20	.50
186 Growth Spasm C :G:	.20	.50
187 Haze Frog C :G:	.10	.25
188 Irresistible Prey U :G:	.20	.50
189 Jaddi Lifestrider U :G:	.20	.50
190 Joraga Treespeaker U :G:	1.00	2.50
191 Kazandu Tuskcaller R :G:	.30	.75
192 Khalni Hydra M :G:	6.00	15.00
193 Kozilek's Predator C :G:	.20	.50
194 Leaf Arrow C :G:	.10	.25
195 Living Destiny C :G:	.10	.25
196 Might of the Masses C :G:	.10	.25
197 Momentous Fall R :G:	.60	1.50
198 Mul Daya Channelers R :G:	.40	1.00
199 Naturalize C :G:	.10	.25
200 Nema Siltlurker C :G:	.10	.25
201 Nest Invader C :G:	.20	.50
202 Ondu Giant C :G:	.10	.25
203 Overgrown Battlement C :G:	.20	.50
204 Pelakka Wurm U :G:	.20	.50
205 Prey's Vengeance U :G:	.20	.50
206 Realms Uncharted R :G:	.40	1.00
207 Snake Umbra C :G:	.10	.25
208 Spider Umbra C :G:	.10	.25
209 Sporecap Spider C :G:	.10	.25
210 Stomper Cub C :G:	.10	.25
211 Tajuru Preserver R :G:	.30	.75
212 Vengevine M :G:	6.00	15.00
213 Wildheart Invoker C :G:	.10	.25
214 Sarkhan the Mad M :K: :R:	3.00	8.00
215 Angelheart Vial R	.30	.75
216 Dreamstone Hedron U	.20	.50
217 Enatu Golem U	.20	.50
218 Hand of Emrakul C	.10	.25
219 It That Betrays R	6.00	15.00
220 Not Of This World U	.20	.50
221 Pathrazer of Ulamog U	.20	.50
222 Pennon Blade U	.20	.50
223 Prophetic Prism C	.10	.25
224 Reinforced Bulwark C	.10	.25
225 Spawnsire of Ulamog R	.60	1.50
226 Ulamog's Crusher C	.20	.50
227 Warmonger's Chariot U	.20	.50
228 Eldrazi Temple R :L:	1.50	4.00
229 Plains (a) L	.10	.25
230 Plains (b) L	.10	.25
231 Plains (c) L	.10	.25
232 Plains (d) L	.10	.25
233 Island (a) L	.10	.25
234 Island (b) L	.10	.25
235 Island (c) L	.10	.25
236 Island (d) L	.10	.25
237 Swamp (a) L	.10	.25
238 Swamp (b) L	.10	.25
239 Swamp (c) L	.10	.25
240 Swamp (d) L	.10	.25
241 Mountain (a) L	.10	.25
242 Mountain (b) L	.10	.25
243 Mountain (c) L	.10	.25
244 Mountain (d) L	.10	.25
245 Forest (a) L	.20	.50
246 Forest (b) L	.10	.25
247 Forest (c) L	.10	.25
248 Forest (d) L	.10	.25
R2 Rules Tip: Eldrazi Abilities	.10	.25
R3 Rules Tip: Levelers	.10	.25
R4 Rules Tip: Rebound	.10	.25
R5 Rules Tip: Totem Armor	.10	.25
T3 Token: Hellion	.10	.25
T1b Token: Eldrazi Spawn (Mark Tedin)	.10	.25
T4 Token: Ooze	.10	.25
T2 Token: Elemental	.10	.25
T5 Token: Tuktuk the Returned	.10	.25
R1 Rules Tip: Eldrazi	.10	.25
T1a Token: Eldrazi Spawn (Aleksi Briclot)	.10	.25
T1c Token: Eldrazi Spawn (Veronique Meignaud)	.10	.25

2010 Magic The Gathering Magic 2011

Card	Low	High
COMPLETE SET (249)	75.00	150.00
BOOSTER BOX (36 PACKS)	75.00	125.00
BOOSTER PACK (15 CARDS)	3.00	5.00
THEME DECK	8.00	12.00
FAT PACK	30.00	50.00
*FOIL: .75X TO 2X BASIC CARDS		
RELEASED ON JULY 16, 2010		
1 Ajani Goldmane M :W:	6.00	15.00
2 Ajani's Mantra C :W:	.10	.25
3 Ajani's Pridemate U :W:	.40	1.00
4 Angelic Arbiter R :W:	.30	.75
5 Armored Ascension U :W:	.20	.50
6 Assault Griffin C :W:	.10	.25
7 Baneslayer Angel M :W:	6.00	15.00
8 Blinding Mage C :W:	.10	.25
9 Celestial Purge U :W:	.20	.50
10 Cloud Crusader C :W:	.10	.25
11 Condemn U :W:	.30	.75
12 Day of Judgment R :W:	1.25	3.00
13 Elite Vanguard U :W:	.20	.50
14 Excommunicate C :W:	.10	.25
15 Goldenglow Moth C :W:	.10	.25
16 Holy Strength C :W:	.10	.25
17 Honor of the Pure R :W:	1.50	4.00
18 Infantry Veteran C :W:	.10	.25
19 Inspired Charge C :W:	.10	.25
20 Knight Exemplar R :W:	1.50	4.00
21 Leyline of Sanctity R :W:	8.00	20.00
22 Mighty Leap C :W:	.10	.25
23 Pacifism C :W:	.10	.25
24 Palace Guard C :W:	.10	.25
25 Roc Egg U :W:	.20	.50
26 Safe Passage C :W:	.10	.25
27 Serra Angel U :W:	.20	.50
28 Serra Ascendant R :W:	5.00	12.00
29 Siege Mastodon C :W:	.10	.25
30 Silence R :W:	.40	1.00
31 Silvercoat Lion C :W:	.10	.25
32 Solemn Offering C :W:	.10	.25
33 Squadron Hawk C :W:	.40	1.00
34 Stormfront Pegasus C :W:	.10	.25
35 Sun Titan M :W:	2.50	6.00
36 Tireless Missionaries C :W:	.10	.25
37 Vengeful Archon R :W:	.30	.75
38 Warlord's Axe U	.20	.50
39 White Knight U :W:	.20	.50
40 Wild Griffin C :W:	.10	.25
41 Aether Adept C :B:	.10	.25
42 Air Servant U :B:	.20	.50
43 Alluring Siren U :B:	.20	.50
44 Armored Cancrix C :B:	.10	.25
45 Augury Owl C :B:	.10	.25
46 Azure Drake U :B:	.20	.50
47 Call to Mind U :B:	.20	.50
48 Cancel C :B:	.10	.25
49 Clone R :B:	.40	1.00
50 Cloud Elemental C :B:	.10	.25
51 Conundrum Sphinx R :B:	.40	1.00
52 Diminish C :B:	.10	.25
53 Flashfreeze U :B:	.20	.50
54 Foresee C :B:	.10	.25
55 Frost Titan M :B:	1.50	4.00
56 Harbor Serpent C :B:	.10	.25
57 Ice Cage C :B:	.10	.25
58 Jace Beleren M :B:	4.00	10.00
59 Jace's Erasure C :B:	.10	.25
60 Jace's Ingenuity U :B:	.20	.50
61 Leyline of Anticipation R :B:	.60	1.50
62 Mana`Leak C :B:	.40	1.00
63 Maritime Guard C :B:	.10	.25
64 Mass Polymorph R :B:	.30	.75
65 Merfolk Sovereign R :B:	.40	1.00
66 Merfolk Spy C :B:	.10	.25
67 Mind Control U :B:	.20	.50
68 Negate C :B:	.10	.25
69 Phantom Beast C :B:	.10	.25
70 Preordain C :B:	.40	1.00
71 Redirect R :B:	.40	1.00
72 Scroll Thief C :B:	.10	.25
73 Sleep U :B:	.20	.50
74 Stormtide Leviathan R :B:	.40	1.00
75 Time Reversal M :B:	.60	1.50
76 Tome Scour C :B:	.10	.25
77 Traumatize R :B:	1.25	3.00
78 Unsummon C :B:	.10	.25
79 Wall of Frost U :B:	.20	.50
80 Water Servant U :B:	.20	.50
81 Assassinate C :K:	.10	.25
82 Barony Vampire C :K:	.10	.25
83 Black Knight U :K:	.20	.50
84 Blood Tithe C :K:	.10	.25
85 Bloodthrone Vampire C :K:	.10	.25
86 Bog Raiders C :K:	.10	.25
87 Captivating Vampire R :K:	4.00	10.00
88 Child of Night C :K:	.10	.25
89 Corrupt U :K:	.20	.50
90 Dark Tutelage R :K:	.40	1.00
91 Deathmark U :K:	.20	.50
92 Demon of Death's Gate M :K:	2.50	6.00
93 Diabolic Tutor U :K:	.30	.75
94 Disentomb C :K:	.10	.25
95 Doom Blade C :K:	.20	.50
96 Duress C :K:	.20	.50
97 Grave Titan M :K:	4.00	10.00
98 Gravedigger C :K:	.10	.25
99 Haunting Echoes R :K:	.40	1.00
100 Howling Banshee U :K:	.20	.50
101 Leyline of the Void R :K:	.75	2.00
102 Liliana Vess M :K:	5.00	12.00
103 Liliana's Caress U :K:	.75	2.00
104 Liliana's Specter C :K:	.10	.25
105 Mind Rot C :K:	.10	.25
106 Nantuko Shade R :K:	.60	1.50
107 Necrotic Plague C :K:	.30	.75
108 Nether Horror C :K:	.20	.50
109 Nightwing Shade C :K:	.10	.25
110 Phylactery Lich R :K:	.60	1.50
111 Quag Sickness C :K:	.10	.25
112 Rssmblng Skltn U :K:	.20	.50
113 Relentless Rats U :K:	.60	1.50
114 Rise from the Grave U :K:	.20	.50
115 Rotting Legion C :K:	.10	.25
116 Royal Assassin R :K:	.40	1.00
117 Sign in Blood C :K:	.20	.50
118 Stabbing Pain C :K:	.10	.25
119 Unholy Strength C :K:	.10	.25
120 Viscera Seer C :K:	.10	.25
121 Act of Treason U :R:	.20	.50
122 Ancient Hellkite R :R:	.30	.75
123 Arc Runner C :R:	.10	.25
124 Berserkers of Blood Ridge C :R:	.10	.25
125 Bloodcrazed Goblin C :R:	.10	.25
126 Canyon Minotaur C :R:	.10	.25
127 Chandra Nalaar M :R:	3.00	8.00
128 Chandra's Outrage C :R:	.10	.25
129 Chandra's Spitfire U :R:	.20	.50
130 Combust U :R:	.20	.50
131 Cyclops Gladiator R :R:	.30	.75
132 Demolish C :R:	.10	.25
133 Destructive Force R :R:	.40	1.00
134 Earth Servant U :R:	.20	.50
135 Ember Hauler U :R:	.30	.75
136 Fiery Hellhound C :R:	.10	.25
137 Fire Servant U :R:	.30	.75
138 Fireball U :R:	.20	.50
139 Fling C :R:	.10	.25
140 Goblin Balloon Brigade C :R:	.10	.25
141 Goblin Chieftain R :R:	.60	1.50
142 Goblin Piker C :R:	.10	.25
143 Goblin Tunneler C :R:	.10	.25
144 Hoarding Dragon R :R:	.30	.75
145 Incite C :R:	.10	.25
146 Inferno Titan M :R:	2.00	5.00
147 Lava Axe R :R:	.10	.25
148 Leyline of Punishment R :R:	.40	1.00
149 Lightning Bolt C :R:	.60	1.50
150 Magma Phoenix R :R:	.30	.75
151 Manic Vandal C :R:	.10	.25
152 Prodigal Pyromancer U :R:	.20	.50
153 Pyretic Ritual C :R:	.10	.25
154 Pyroclasm U :R:	.30	.75
155 Reverberate R :R:	.40	1.00
156 Shiv's Embrace U :R:	.20	.50
157 Thunder Strike C :R:	.10	.25
158 Volcanic Strength C :R:	.10	.25
159 Vulshok Berserker C :R:	.10	.25
160 Wild Evocation R :R:	.30	.75
161 Acidic Slime U :G:	.20	.50
162 Autumn's Veil U :G:	.20	.50
163 Awakener Druid U :B:	.20	.50
164 Back to Nature U :G:	.20	.50
165 Birds of Paradise R :G:	2.50	6.00
166 Brindle Boar C :G:	.10	.25
167 Cudgel Troll U :G:	.20	.50
168 Cultivate C :G:	.30	.75
169 Dryad's Favor C :G:	.10	.25
170 Duskdale Wurm U :G:	.20	.50
171 Elvish Archdruid R :G:	.60	1.50
172 Fauna Shaman R :G:	2.50	6.00
173 Fog C :G:	.10	.25
174 Gaea's Revenge M :G:	.75	2.00
175 Garruk Wildspeaker M :G:	4.00	10.00
176 Garruk's Companion C :G:	.10	.25
177 Garruk's Packleader U :G:	.20	.50
178 Giant Growth C :G:	.10	.25
179 Giant Spider C :G:	.10	.25
180 Greater Basilisk C :G:	.10	.25
181 Hornet Sting C :G:	.10	.25
182 Hunters' Feast C :G:	.10	.25
183 Leyline of Vitality R :G:	.40	1.00
184 Llanowar Elves C :G:	.20	.50
185 Mitotic Slime R :G:	.40	1.00
186 Naturalize C :G:	.10	.25
187 Nature's Spiral U :G:	.20	.50
188 Obstinate Baloth U :G:	.60	1.50
189 Ovrwlmng Stmpd R :G:	.60	1.50
190 Plummet C :G:	.10	.25
191 Primal Cocoon C :G:	.10	.25
192 Primeval Titan M :G:	8.00	20.00
193 Prized Unicorn U :G:	.20	.50
194 Protean Hydra R :G:	.40	1.00
195 Runeclaw Bear C :G:	.10	.25
196 Sacred Wolf C :G:	.10	.25
197 Spined Wurm C :G:	.10	.25
198 Sylvan Ranger C :G:	.10	.25
199 Wall of Vines C :G:	.10	.25
200 Yavimaya Wurm C :G:	.10	.25
201 Angel's Feather U	.20	.50
202 Brittle Effigy R	.40	1.00
203 Crystal Ball U	.30	.75
204 Demon's Horn U	.20	.50
205 Dragon's Claw U	.20	.50
206 Elixir of Immortality U	.40	1.00
207 Gargoyle Sentinel U	.20	.50
208 Jinxed Idol R	.30	.75
209 Juggernaut U	.20	.50
210 Kraken's Eye U	.20	.50
211 Ornithopter U	.40	1.00
212 Platinum Angel M	4.00	10.00
213 Sorcerer's Strongbox U	.20	.50
214 Steel Overseer R	4.00	10.00
215 Stone Golem U	.20	.50
216 Sword of Vengeance R	.60	1.50
217 Temple Bell R	.40	1.00
218 Triskelion R	.30	.75
219 Voltaic Key U	.40	1.00
220 War Priest of Thune U :W:	.20	.50
221 Whispersilk Cloak U	.30	.75
222 Wurm's Tooth U	.20	.50
223 Dragonskull Summit R :L:	2.00	5.00
224 Drowned Catacomb R :L:	3.00	8.00
225 Glacial Fortress R :L:	1.50	4.00
226 Mystifying Maze R :L:	.40	1.00
227 Rootbound Crag R :L:	2.00	5.00
228 Sunpetal Grove R :L:	1.50	4.00
229 Terramorphic Expanse C :L:	.20	.50
230 Plains L :L:	.10	.25
231 Plains - B L :L:	.10	.25
232 Plains - C L :L:	.10	.25
233 Plains - D L :L:	.10	.25
234 Island L :L:	.10	.25
235 Island - B L :L:	.10	.25
236 Island - C L :L:	.10	.25
237 Island - D L :L:	.10	.25
238 Swamp L :L:	.10	.25
239 Swamp - B L :L:	.10	.25
240 Swamp - C L :L:	.10	.25
241 Swamp - D L :L:	.10	.25
242 Mountain L :L:	.10	.25
243 Mountain - B L :L:	.10	.25
244 Mountain - C L :L:	.10	.25
245 Mountain - D L :L:	.10	.25
246 Forest - A L :L:	.10	.25
247 Forest - B L :L:	.10	.25
248 Forest - C L :L:	.10	.25
249 Forest - D L :L:	.10	.25
R1 Rules Tip: Planeswalker Cards	.10	.25
R2 Rules Tip: Parts of the Turn	.10	.25
R3 Rules Tip: Deathtouch	.10	.25
R4 Rules Tip: Tokens and Counters	.10	.25
R5 Rules Tip: Building a Deck	.10	.25
R6 Rules Tip: Limited Play	.10	.25

R7 Rules Tip: The Stack .10 .25
R8 Rules Tip: Gatherer Card Database .10 .25
R9 Rules Tip: Leylines .10 .25
T1 Token: Avatar .10 .25
T2 Token: Bird .10 .25
T3 Token: Zombie .10 .25
T4 Token: Beast .10 .25
T5 Token: Ooze (2/2) .10 .25
T6 Token: Ooze (1/1) .10 .25

2010 Magic The Gathering Scars of Mirrodin

COMPLETE SET (249) 150.00 250.00
BOOSTER BOX (36 PACKS) 75.00 150.00
BOOSTER PACK (15 CARDS) 3.50 5.00
FAT PACK 30.00 50.00
*FOIL: .75X TO 2X BASIC CARDS
RELEASED ON OCTOBER 1, 2010
1 Abuna Acolyte U :W: .20 .50
2 Arrest C :W: .10 .25
3 Auriok Edgewright U :W: .20 .50
4 Auriok Sunchaser C :W: .10 .25
5 Dispense Justice U :W: .20 .50
6 Elspeth Tirel M :W: 6.00 15.00
7 Fulgent Distraction C :W: .10 .25
8 Ghalma's Warden C :W: .10 .25
9 Glimmerpoint Stag U :W: .20 .50
10 Glint Hawk C :W: .10 .25
11 Indomitable Archangel M :W: 1.25 3.00
12 Kemba, Kha Regent R :W: .30 .75
13 Kemba's Skyguard C :W: .10 .25
14 Leonin Arbiter R :W: .40 1.00
15 Loxodon Wayfarer C :W: .10 .25
16 Myrsmith U :W: .20 .50
17 Razor Hippogriff U :W: .20 .50
18 Revoke Existence C :W: .10 .25
19 Salvage Scout C :W: .10 .25
20 Seize the Initiative C :W: .10 .25
21 Soul Parry C :W: .10 .25
22 Sunblast Angel R :W: .40 1.00
23 Sunspear Shikari C :W: .10 .25
24 Tempered Steel R :W: 1.50 4.00
25 True Conviction R :W: .40 1.00
26 Vigil for the Lost U :W: .20 .50
27 Whitesun's Passage C :W: .10 .25
28 Argent Sphinx R :B: .30 .75
29 Bonds of Quicksilver C :B: .10 .25
30 Darkslick Drake U :B: .20 .50
31 Disperse C :B: .10 .25
32 Dissipation Field R :B: .60 1.50
33 Grand Architect R :B: 1.25 3.00
34 Halt Order U :B: .20 .50
35 Inexorable Tide R :B: .30 .75
36 Lumengrid Drake C :B: .10 .25
37 Neurok Invisimancer C :B: .10 .25
38 Plated Seastrider C :B: .10 .25
39 Quicksilver Gargantuan M :B: .60 1.50
40 Riddlesmith U :B: .20 .50
41 Scrapdiver Serpent C :B: .10 .25
42 Screeching Silcaw C :B: .10 .25
43 Shape Anew R :B: .30 .75
44 Sky-Eel School C :B: .10 .25
45 Steady Progress C :B: .10 .25
46 Stoic Rebuttal C :B: .20 .50
47 Thrummingbird U :B: .30 .75
48 Trinket Mage U :B: .20 .50
49 Turn Aside C :B: .10 .25
50 Twisted Image U :B: .20 .50
51 Vault Skyward C :B: .10 .25
52 Vedalken Certarch C :B: .10 .25
53 Volition Reins U :B: .30 .75
54 Blackcleave Goblin C :K: .10 .25
55 Bleak Coven Vampires C :K: .10 .25
56 Blistergrub C :K: .10 .25
57 Carnifex Demon R :K: .30 .75
58 Contagious Nim C :K: .10 .25
59 Corrupted Harvester U :K: .20 .50
60 Dross Hopper C :K: .10 .25
61 Exsanguinate U :K: .40 1.00
62 Flesh Allergy U :K: .20 .50
63 Fume Spitter C :K: .10 .25
64 Geth, Lord of the Vault M :K: 2.00 5.00
65 Grasp of Darkness C :K: .10 .25
66 Hand of the Praetors R :K: 1.25 3.00
67 Ichor Rats U :K: .20 .50
68 Instill Infection C :K: .10 .25
69 Memoricide R :K: .75 2.00
70 Moriok Reaver C :K: .10 .25
71 Necrogen Scudder U :K: .20 .50
72 Necrotic Ooze R :K: 1.00 2.50
73 Painful Quandary R :K: .30 .75
74 Painsmith U :K: .10 .25
75 Plague Stinger C :K: .10 .25
76 Psychic Miasma C :K: .10 .25
77 Relic Putrescence C :K: .10 .25
78 Skinrender U :K: .30 .75
79 Skithiryx, the Blight M :K: 3.00 8.00
80 Tainted Strike C :K: .10 .25
81 Arc Trail U :R: .60 1.50
82 Assault Strobe C :R: .10 .25
83 Barrage Ogre U :R: .20 .50
84 Blade-Tribe Berserkers C :R: .10 .25
85 Bloodshot Trainee U :R: .20 .50
86 Cerebral Eruption R :R: .30 .75
87 Embersmith U :R: .20 .50
88 Ferrovore C :R: .10 .25
89 Flameborn Hellion C :R: .10 .25
90 Furnace Celebration U :R: .20 .50
91 Galvanic Blast C :R: .30 .75
92 Goblin Gaveleer C :R: .10 .25
93 Hoard-Smelter Dragon R :R: .30 .75
94 Koth of the Hammer M :R: 5.00 12.00
95 Kuldotha Phoenix R :R: .30 .75
96 Kuldotha Rebirth C :R: .10 .25
97 Melt Terrain C :R: .10 .25
98 Molten Psyche R :R: .30 .75
99 Ogre Geargrabber U :R: .20 .50
100 Oxidda Daredevil C :R: .10 .25
101 Oxidda Scrapmelter U :R: .20 .50
102 Scoria Elemental C :R: .10 .25
103 Shatter C :R: .10 .25
104 Spikeshot Elder R :R: .75 2.00
105 Tunnel Ignus R :R: .40 1.00
106 Turn to Slag C :R: .10 .25
107 Vulshok Heartstoker C :R: .10 .25
108 Acid Web Spider U :G: .20 .50
109 Alpha Tyrranax C :G: .10 .25
110 Asceticism R :G: 3.00 8.00
111 Bellowing Tanglewurm U :G: .20 .50
112 Blight Mamba C :G: .10 .25
113 Blunt the Assault C :G: .10 .25
114 Carapace Forger C :G: .10 .25
115 Carrion Call U :G: .20 .50
116 Copperhorn Scout C :G: .10 .25
117 Cystbearer C :G: .10 .25
118 Engulfing Slagwurm R :G: .30 .75
119 Ezuri, Renegade Leader R :G: 1.00 2.50
120 Ezuri's Archers C :G: .10 .25
121 Ezuri's Brigade R :G: .60 1.50
122 Genesis Wave R :G: .75 2.00
123 Liege of the Tangle M :G: 1.25 3.00
124 Lifesmith U :G: .20 .50
125 Molder Beast C :G: .10 .25
126 Putrefax R :G: .40 1.00
127 Slice in Twain U :G: .20 .50
128 Tangle Angler U :G: .20 .50
129 Tel-Jilad Defiance C :G: .10 .25
130 Tel-Jilad Fallen C :G: .10 .25
131 Untamed Might C :G: .10 .25
132 Viridian Revel U :G: .20 .50
133 Wing Puncture C :G: .20 .50
134 Withstand Death C :G: .10 .25
135 Venser, the Sojourner M :G: 4.00 10.00
136 Accorder's Shield C .10 .25
137 Argentum Armor R 1.00 2.50
138 Auriok Replica C .10 .25
139 Barbed Battlegear U .20 .50
140 Bladed Pinions C .10 .25
141 Chimeric Mass R .40 1.00
142 Chrome Steed C .10 .25
143 Clone Shell U .20 .50
144 Contagion Clasp U .40 1.00
145 Contagion Engine R .75 2.00
146 Copper Myr C .10 .25
147 Corpse Cur C .10 .25
148 Culling Dais U .20 .50
149 Darksteel Axe U .20 .50
150 Darksteel Juggernaut R .30 .75
151 Darksteel Myr U .30 .75
152 Darksteel Sentinel U .20 .50
153 Echo Circlet C .10 .25
154 Etched Champion R 2.50 6.00
155 Flight Spellbomb C .10 .25
156 Glint Hawk Idol C .10 .25
157 Gold Myr C .10 .25
158 Golden Urn C .10 .25
159 Golem Artisan U .20 .50
160 Golem Foundry C .10 .25
161 Golem's Heart U .20 .50
162 Grafted Exoskeleton U .20 .50
163 Grindclock R .30 .75
164 Heavy Arbalest U .20 .50
165 Horizon Spellbomb C .10 .25
166 Ichorclaw Myr C .30 .75
167 Infiltration Lens U .40 1.00
168 Iron Myr C .10 .25
169 Kuldotha Forgemaster R .40 1.00
170 Leaden Myr C .10 .25
171 Liquimetal Coating U .20 .50
172 Livewire Lash R .40 1.00
173 Lux Cannon M 1.25 3.00
174 Memnite U .60 1.50
175 Mimic Vat R 1.25 3.00
176 Mindslaver M .75 2.00
177 Molten-Tail Mast M .75 2.00
178 Moriok Replica C .10 .25
179 Mox Opal M 20.00 50.00
180 Myr Battlesphere R .75 2.00
181 Myr Galvanizer U .40 1.00
182 Myr Propagator R .30 .75
183 Myr Reservoir R .30 .75
184 Necrogen Censer C .10 .25
185 Necropede U .30 .75
186 Neurok Replica C .10 .25
187 Nihil Spellbomb C .30 .75
188 Nim Deathmantle R .30 .75
189 Origin Spellbomb C .10 .25
190 Palladium Myr U .40 1.00
191 Panic Spellbomb C .10 .25
192 Perilous Myr C .20 .50
193 Platinum Emperion M 3.00 8.00
194 Precursor Golem R .40 1.00
195 Prototype Portal R .40 1.00
196 Ratchet Bomb R 2.00 5.00
197 Razorfield Thresher C .10 .25
198 Rust Tick U .20 .50
199 Rusted Relic U .20 .50
200 Saberclaw Golem C .10 .25
201 Semblance Anvil R .60 1.50
202 Silver Myr C .10 .25
203 Snapsail Glider C .10 .25
204 Soliton C .10 .25
205 Steel Hellkite R .75 2.00
206 Strata Scythe R .30 .75
207 Strider Harness C .10 .25
208 Sword of Body M 5.00 12.00
209 Sylvok Lifestaff C .10 .25
210 Sylvok Replica C .10 .25
211 Throne of Geth U .20 .50
212 Tower of Calamities R .30 .75
213 Trigon of Corruption U .20 .50
214 Trigon of Infestation U .20 .50
215 Trigon of Mending U .20 .50
216 Trigon of Rage U .20 .50
217 Trigon of Thought U .20 .50
218 Tumble Magnet C .20 .50
219 Vector Asp C .10 .25
220 Venser's Journal R .75 2.00
221 Vulshok Replica C .10 .25
222 Wall of Tanglecord C .10 .25
223 Wurmcoil Engine M 10.00 25.00
224 Blackcleave Cliffs R 3.00 8.00
225 Copperline Gorge R 3.00 8.00
226 Darkslick Shores R 4.00 10.00
227 Glimmerpost C .10 .25
228 Razorverge Thicket R 4.00 10.00
229 Seachrome Coast R 3.00 8.00
230 Plains L .10 .25
231 Plains L .10 .25
232 Plains L .10 .25
233 Plains L .10 .25
234 Island L .10 .25
235 Island L .10 .25
236 Island L .10 .25
237 Island L .10 .25
238 Swamp L .10 .25
239 Swamp L .10 .25
240 Swamp L .10 .25
241 Swamp L .10 .25
242 Mountain L .10 .25
243 Mountain L .10 .25
244 Mountain L .10 .25
245 Mountain L .10 .25
246 Forest L .10 .25
247 Forest L .10 .25
248 Forest L .10 .25
249 Forest L .10 .25
PC Poison Counter .10 .25
R1 Rules Tip: Infect .10 .25
R2 Rules Tip: Metalcraft .10 .25
R3 Rules Tip: Proliferate .10 .25
R4 Rules Tip: Imprint .10 .25
R5 Rules Tip: Poison and Emblems .10 .25
T1 Token: Cat .10 .25
T2 Token: Soldier .10 .25
T3 Token: Goblin .10 .25
T4 Token: Insect .10 .25
T5 Token: Wolf .10 .25
T6 Token: Golem .10 .25
T7 Token: Myr .10 .25
T8 Token: Wurm (Deathtouch) .10 .25
T9 Token: Wurm (Lifelink) .10 .25

2011 Magic The Gathering Mirrodin Besieged

COMPLETE SET (155) 75.00 150.00
BOOSTER BOX (36 PACKS) 100.00 150.00
BOOSTER PACK (16 CARDS) 3.00 5.00
*FOIL: .75X TO 2X BASIC CARDS
RELEASED ON FEBRUARY 4, 2011
1 Accorder Paladin U :W: .30 .75
2 Ardent Recruit C :W: .10 .25
3 Banishment Decree C :W: .10 .25
4 Choking Fumes U :W: .20 .50
5 Divine Offering C :W: .20 .50
6 Frantic Salvage C :W: .10 .25
7 Gore Vassal U :W: .20 .50
8 Hero of Bladehold M :W: 5.00 12.00
9 Kemba's Legion U :W: .20 .50
10 Leonin Relic-Warder U :W: .20 .50
11 Leonin Skyhunter C :W: .30 .75
12 Loxodon Partisan C :W: .10 .25
13 Master's Call C :W: .40 1.00
14 Mirran Crusader R :W: 3.00 8.00
15 Phyrexian Rebirth R :W: .40 1.00
16 Priests of Norn C :W: .10 .25
17 Tine Shrike C :W: .10 .25
18 Victory's Herald R :W: .40 1.00
19 White Sun's Zenith R :W: .75 2.00
20 Blue Sun's Zenith R :B: .60 1.50
21 Consecrated Sphinx M :B: 6.00 15.00
22 Corrupted Conscience U :B: .20 .50
23 Cryptoplasm R :B: .40 1.00
24 Distant Memories R :B: .40 1.00
25 Fuel for the Cause C :B: .10 .25
26 Mirran Spy C :B: .10 .25
27 Mitotic Manipulation R :B: .40 1.00
28 Neurok Commando U :B: .20 .50
29 Oculus C :B: .10 .25
30 Quicksilver Geyser C :B: .10 .25
31 Serum Raker C :B: .10 .25
32 Spire Serpent C :B: .10 .25
33 Steel Sabotage C :B: .10 .25
34 Treasure Mage U :B: .30 .75
35 Turn the Tide C :B: .10 .25
36 Vedalken Anatomist U :B: .20 .50
37 Vedalken Infuser U :B: .20 .50
38 Vivisection C :B: .10 .25
39 Black Sun's Zenith R :K: 2.00 5.00
40 Caustic Hound C :K: .10 .25
41 Flensermite C :K: .10 .25
42 Flesh-Eater Imp U :K: .20 .50
43 Go for the Throat U :K: 1.25 3.00
44 Gruesome Encore U :K: .20 .50
45 Horrifying Revelation C :K: .10 .25
46 Massacre Wurm M :K: 2.50 6.00
47 Morbid Plunder C :K: .10 .25
48 Nested Ghoul U :K: .20 .50
49 Phyresis C :K: .10 .25
50 Phyrexian Crusader R :K: 2.50 6.00
51 Phyrexian Rager C :K: .10 .25
52 Phyrexian Vatmother R :K: .75 2.00
53 Sangromancer R :K: .75 2.00
54 Scourge Servant C :K: .10 .25
55 Septic Rats U :K: .20 .50
56 Spread the Sickness C :K: .20 .50
57 Virulent Wound C :K: .10 .25
58 Blisterstick Shaman C :R: .10 .25
59 Burn the Impure C :R: .10 .25
60 Concussive Bolt C :R: .10 .25
61 Crush C :R: .10 .25
62 Galvanoth R :R: .40 1.00
63 Gnathosaur C :R: .10 .25
64 Goblin Wardriver U :R: .40 1.00
65 Hellkite Igniter R :R: .40 1.00
66 Hero of Oxid Ridge M :R: 1.50 4.00
67 Into the Core U :R: .20 .50
68 Koth's Courier C :R: .10 .25
69 Kuldotha Flamefiend U :R: .20 .50
70 Kuldotha Ringleader C :R: .10 .25
71 Metallic Mastery U :R: .20 .50
72 Ogre Resister C :R: .10 .25
73 Rally the Forces C :R: .10 .25
74 Red Sun's Zenith R :R: .75 2.00
75 Slagstorm R :R: .40 1.00
76 Spiraling Duelist U :R: .20 .50
77 Blightwidow C :G: .10 .25
78 Creeping Corrosion R :G: .40 1.00
79 Fangren Marauder C :G: .10 .25
80 Glissa's Courier C :G: .10 .25
81 Green Sun's Zenith R :G: 5.00 12.00
82 Lead the Stampede U :G: .30 .75
83 Melira's Keepers U :G: .20 .50
84 Mirran Mettle C :G: .10 .25
85 Phyrexian Hydra R :G: .40 1.00
86 Pistus Strike C :G: .10 .25
87 Plaguemaw Beast U :G: .20 .50
88 Praetor's Counsel M :G: .75 2.00
89 Quilled Slagwurm U :G: .20 .50
90 Rot Wolf C :G: .10 .25
91 Tangle Mantis C :G: .10 .25
92 Thrun, the Last Troll M :G: 6.00 15.00
93 Unnatural Predation C :G: .10 .25
94 Viridian Corrupter U :G: .20 .50
95 Viridian Emissary C :G: .40 1.00
96 Glissa, the Traitor M :K: :G: 1.50 4.00
97 Tezzeret, Agent of Bolas M :B: :K: 8.00 20.00
98 Bladed Sentinel C .10 .25
99 Blightsteel Colossus M 6.00 15.00
100 Bonehoard R .60 1.50
101 Brass Squire U .30 .75
102 Copper Carapace C .10 .25
103 Core Prowler U .20 .50
104 Darksteel Plate R 2.50 6.00
105 Decimator Web R .40 1.00
106 Dross Ripper C .10 .25
107 Flayer Husk C .10 .25
108 Gust-Skimmer C .10 .25
109 Hexplate Golem C .10 .25
110 Ichor Wellspring C .10 .25
111 Knowledge Pool R .40 1.00
112 Lumengrid Gargoyle U .20 .50
113 Magnetic Mine R .40 1.00
114 Mirrorworks R .40 1.00
115 Mortarpod U .40 1.00
116 Myr Sire C .10 .25
117 Myr Turbine R 1.00 2.50
118 Myr Welder R .40 1.00
119 Peace Strider U .20 .50
120 Phyrexian Digester C .10 .25
121 Phyrexian Juggernaut U .20 .50
122 Phyrexian Revoker R 1.00 2.50
123 Pierce Strider U .20 .50
124 Piston Sledge U .20 .50
125 Plague Myr U .60 1.50
126 Psychosis Crawler R .40 1.00
127 Razorfield Rhino C .10 .25
128 Rusted Slasher C .10 .25
129 Shimmer Myr R .40 1.00
130 Shriekhorn C .10 .25
131 Signal Pest U .60 1.50
132 Silverskin Armor U .20 .50
133 Skinwing U .20 .50
134 Sphere of the Suns U .75 2.00
135 Spin Engine C .10 .25
136 Spine of Ish Sah R .40 1.00
137 Strandwalker U .20 .50
138 Sword of Feast and Famine M 12.00 30.00
139 Tangle Hulk C .10 .25
140 Thopter Assembly R .40 1.00
141 Titan Forge R .40 1.00
142 Training Drone C .10 .25
143 Viridian Claw U .20 .50
144 Contested War Zone R .40 1.00
145 Inkmoth Nexus R 5.00 12.00
146 Plains L .10 .25
147 Plains L .10 .25
148 Island L .10 .25
149 Island L .10 .25
150 Swamp L .10 .25
151 Swamp L .10 .25
152 Mountain L .10 .25
153 Mountain L .10 .25
154 Forest L .10 .25
155 Forest L .10 .25
PC Poison Counter .10 .25
R1 Rules Tip: Battle Cry .10 .25
R2 Rules Tip: Metalcraft Imprint .10 .25
R3 Rules Tip: Living Weapon .10 .25
R4 Rules Tip: Infect .10 .25
R5 Rules Tip: Proliferate .10 .25
T1 Token: Germ .10 .25
T2 Token: Zombie .10 .25
T3 Token: Golem .10 .25
T4 Token: Horror .10 .25
T5 Token: Thopter .10 .25

2011 Magic The Gathering Magic 2012

COMPLETE SET (249) 125.00 250.00
BOOSTER BOX (36 PACKS) 75.00 125.00
BOOSTER PACK (15 CARDS) 3.00 4.00
*FOIL: .75X TO 2X BASIC CARDS
RELEASED ON JULY 15, 2011
1 Aegis Angel R :W: .40 1.00
2 Alabaster Mage U :W: .20 .50
3 Angelic Destiny M :W: 6.00 15.00
4 Angel's Mercy C :W: .10 .25
5 Arbalest Elite U :W: .20 .50
6 Archon of Justice R :W: .40 1.00
7 Armored Warhorse C :W: .10 .25
8 Assault Griffin C :W: .10 .25
9 Auramancer C :W: .10 .25
10 Benalish Veteran C :W: .10 .25
11 Celestial Purge U :W: .20 .50
12 Day of Judgment R :W: 1.25 3.00
13 Demystify C :W: .10 .25
14 Divine Favor C :W: .10 .25
15 Elite Vanguard U :W: .20 .50
16 Gideon Jura M :W: 5.00 12.00
17 Gideon's Avenger R :W: .60 1.50
18 Gideon's Lawkeeper C :W: .10 .25
19 Grand Abolisher R :W: 3.00 8.00
20 Griffin Rider C :W: .10 .25
21 Griffin Sentinel C :W: .10 .25
22 Guardians' Pledge C :W: .10 .25
23 Honor of the Pure R :W: 1.25 3.00
24 Lifelink C :W: .10 .25
25 Mesa Enchantress R :W: .40 1.00
26 Mighty Leap C :W: .10 .25
27 Oblivion Ring U :W: .60 1.50
28 Pacifism C :W: .10 .25
29 Peregrine Griffin C :W: .10 .25
30 Personal Sanctuary R :W: .40 1.00
31 Pride Guardian C :W: .10 .25
32 Roc Egg U :W: .20 .50
33 Serra Angel U :W: .20 .50
34 Siege Mastodon C :W: .10 .25
35 Spirit Mantle U :W: .40 1.00
36 Stave Off C :W: .10 .25
37 Stonehorn Dignitary C :W: .10 .25
38 Stormfront Pegasus C :W: .10 .25
39 Sun Titan M :W: 2.50 6.00
40 Timely Reinforcements U :W: 1.00 2.50
41 AEther Adept C :B: .10 .25
42 Alluring Siren U :B: .20 .50
43 Amphin Cutthroat C :B: .10 .25
44 Aven Fleetwing C :B: .10 .25
45 Azure Mage U :B: .20 .50
46 Belltower Sphinx U :B: .20 .50
47 Cancel C :B: .10 .25
48 Chasm Drake C :B: .10 .25
49 Coral Merfolk C :B: .10 .25
50 Divination C :B: .10 .25
51 Djinn of Wishes R :B: .40 1.00
52 Flashfreeze U :B: .20 .50
53 Flight C :B: .10 .25
54 Frost Breath C :B: .10 .25
55 Frost Titan M :B: 1.50 4.00
56 Harbor Serpent C :B: .10 .25
57 Ice Cage C :B: .10 .25
58 Jace, Memory Adept M :B: 6.00 15.00
59 Jace's Archivist R :B: .75 2.00
60 Jace's Erasure C :B: .10 .25
61 Levitation U :B: .20 .50
62 Lord of the Unreal R :B: .75 2.00
63 Mana Leak C :B: .40 1.00
64 Master Thief U :B: .20 .50
65 Merfolk Looter C :B: .10 .25
66 Merfolk Mesmerist C :B: .10 .25
67 Mind Control U :B: .20 .50
68 Mind Unbound R :B: .40 1.00
69 Negate C :B: .10 .25
70 Phantasmal Bear C :B: .10 .25
71 Phantasmal Dragon U :B: .20 .50
72 Phantasmal Image R :B: 6.00 15.00
73 Ponder C :B: .60 1.50
74 Redirect R :B: .60 1.50
75 Skywinder Drake C :B: .10 .25
76 Sphinx of Uthuun R :B: .40 1.00
77 Time Reversal M :B: .60 1.50
78 Turn to Frog U :B: .20 .50
79 Unsummon C :B: .10 .25
80 Visions of Beyond R :B: 1.00 2.50
81 Blood Seeker C :K: .10 .25
82 Bloodlord of Vaasgoth M :K: 1.25 3.00
83 Bloodrage Vampire C :K: .10 .25
84 Brink of Disaster C :K: .10 .25
85 Call to the Grave R :K: .60 1.50
86 Cemetery Reaper R :K: 1.50 4.00
87 Child of Night C :K: .10 .25
88 Consume Spirit U :K: .20 .50
89 Dark Favor C :K: .10 .25
90 Deathmark U :K: .20 .50
91 Devouring Swarm C :K: .10 .25
92 Diabolic Tutor U :K: .40 1.00
93 Disentomb C :K: .10 .25
94 Distress C :K: .10 .25
95 Doom Blade C :K: .20 .50
96 Drifting Shade C :K: .10 .25
97 Duskhunter Bat C :K: .10 .25
98 Grave Titan M :K: 4.00 10.00
99 Gravedigger C :K: .10 .25
100 Hideous Visage C :K: .10 .25
101 Mind Rot C :K: .10 .25
102 Monomania R :K: .40 1.00
103 Onyx Mage U :K: .20 .50
104 Reassembling Skeleton U :K: .20 .50
105 Royal Assassin R :K: .40 1.00
106 Rune-Scarred Demon R :K: 1.00 2.50
107 Sengir Vampire U :K: .20 .50
108 Smallpox U :K: .40 1.00
109 Sorin Markov M :K: 6.00 15.00
110 Sorin's Thirst C :K: .10 .25
111 Sorin's Vengeance R :K: .60 1.50
112 Sutured Ghoul R :K: .40 1.00
113 Taste of Blood C :K: .10 .25
114 Tormented Soul C :K: .10 .25
115 Vampire Outcasts U :K: .20 .50
116 Vengeful Pharaoh R :K: .75 2.00
117 Warpath Ghoul C :K: .10 .25
118 Wring Flesh C :K: .10 .25
119 Zombie Goliath C :K: .10 .25
120 Zombie Infestation U :K: .40 1.00
121 Act of Treason C :R: .10 .25
122 Blood Ogre C :R: .10 .25
123 Bonebreaker Giant C :R: .10 .25
124 Chandra, the Firebrand M :R: 4.00 10.00
125 Chandra's Outrage C :R: .10 .25
126 Chandra's Phoenix R :R: 2.50 6.00
127 Circle of Flame U :R: .20 .50
128 Combust U :R: .20 .50
129 Crimson Mage U :R: .20 .50
130 Fiery Hellhound C :R: .10 .25
131 Fireball U :R: .20 .50
132 Firebreathing C :R: .10 .25
133 Flameblast Dragon R :R: .40 1.00
134 Fling C :R: .10 .25
135 Furyborn Hellkite M :R: 2.00 5.00
136 Goblin Arsonist C :R: .10 .25
137 Goblin Bangchuckers U :R: .20 .50
138 Goblin Chieftain R :R: .60 1.50
139 Goblin Fireslinger C :R: .10 .25
140 Goblin Grenade U :R: .40 1.00
141 Goblin Piker C :R: .10 .25
142 Goblin Tunneler C :R: .10 .25
143 Goblin War Paint C :R: .10 .25
144 Gorehorn Minotaurs C :R: .10 .25
145 Grim Lavamancer R :R: 2.00 5.00
146 Incinerate C :R: .40 1.00
147 Inferno Titan M :R: 1.00 2.50
148 Lava Axe C :R: .10 .25
149 Lightning Elemental C :R: .10 .25
150 Manabarbs R :R: .40 1.00
151 Manic Vandal C :R: .10 .25
152 Reverberate R :R: .40 1.00
153 Scrambleverse R :R: .40 1.00
154 Shock C :R: .10 .25
155 Slaughter Cry C :R: .10 .25

Card	Low	High
156 Stormblood Berserker U :R:	.60	1.50
157 Tectonic Rift U :R:	.20	.50
158 Volcanic Dragon U :R:	.20	.50
159 Wall of Torches C :R:	.10	.25
160 Warstorm Surge R :R:	.40	1.00
161 Acidic Slime U :G:	.20	.50
162 Arachnus Spinner R :G:	.40	1.00
163 Arachnus Web C :G:	.10	.25
164 Autumn's Veil U :G:	.20	.50
165 Birds of Paradise R :G:	2.00	5.00
166 Bountiful Harvest C :G:	.10	.25
167 Brindle Boar C :G:	.10	.25
168 Carnage Wurm U :G:	.20	.50
169 Cudgel Troll U :G:	.20	.50
170 Doubling Chant R :G:	.40	1.00
171 Dungrove Elder R :G:	2.00	5.00
172 Elvish Archdruid R :G:	.75	2.00
173 Fog C :G:	.10	.25
174 Garruk, Primal Hunter M :G:	6.00	15.00
175 Garruk's Companion C :G:	.10	.25
176 Garruk's Horde R :G:	.40	1.00
177 Giant Spider C :G:	.10	.25
178 Gladecover Scout C :G:	.10	.25
179 Greater Basilisk C :G:	.10	.25
180 Hunter's Insight U :G:	.20	.50
181 Jade Mage U :G:	.20	.50
182 Llanowar Elves C :G:	.10	.25
183 Lure U :G:	.20	.50
184 Lurking Crocodile C :G:	.10	.25
185 Naturalize C :G:	.10	.25
186 Overrun U :G:	.20	.50
187 Plummet C :G:	.10	.25
188 Primeval Titan M :G:	8.00	20.00
189 Primordial Hydra M :G:	4.00	10.00
190 Rampant Growth C :G:	.10	.25
191 Reclaim C :G:	.10	.25
192 Rites of Flourishing R :G:	.40	1.00
193 Runeclaw Bear C :G:	.10	.25
194 Sacred Wolf C :G:	.10	.25
195 Skinshifter R :G:	.75	2.00
196 Stampeding Rhino C :G:	.10	.25
197 Stingerfling Spider U :G:	.20	.50
198 Titanic Growth C :G:	.10	.25
199 Trollhide C :G:	.10	.25
200 Vastwood Gorger C :G:	.10	.25
201 Adaptive Automaton R	1.50	4.00
202 Angel's Feather U	.20	.50
203 Crown of Empires U	.20	.50
204 Crumbling Colossus U	.20	.50
205 Demon's Horn U	.20	.50
206 Dragon's Claw U	.20	.50
207 Druidic Satchel R	.60	1.50
208 Elixir of Immortality U	.40	1.00
209 Greatsword U	.20	.50
210 Kite Shield U	.20	.50
211 Kraken's Eye U	.20	.50
212 Manalith C	.20	.50
213 Pentavus R	.40	1.00
214 Quicksilver Amulet R	3.00	8.00
215 Rusted Sentinel U	.20	.50
216 Scepter of Empires U	.20	.50
217 Solemn Simulacrum R	4.00	10.00
218 Sundial of the Infinite R	.60	1.50
219 Swiftfoot Boots U	.75	2.00
220 Thran Golem U	.20	.50
221 Throne of Empires R	.40	1.00
222 Worldslayer R	.40	1.00
223 Wurm's Tooth U	.20	.50
224 Buried Ruin U	.40	1.00
225 Dragonskull Summit R	2.00	5.00
226 Drowned Catacomb R	3.00	8.00
227 Glacial Fortress R	2.00	5.00
228 Rootbound Crag R	2.00	5.00
229 Sunpetal Grove R	2.50	6.00
230 Plains L	.10	.25
231 Plains L	.10	.25
232 Plains L	.10	.25
233 Plains L	.10	.25
234 Island L	.10	.25
235 Island L	.10	.25
236 Island L	.10	.25
237 Island L	.10	.25
238 Swamp L	.10	.25
239 Swamp L	.10	.25
240 Swamp L	.10	.25
241 Swamp L	.10	.25
242 Mountain L	.10	.25
243 Mountain L	.10	.25
244 Mountain L	.10	.25
245 Mountain L	.10	.25
246 Forest L	.10	.25
247 Forest L	.10	.25
248 Forest L	.10	.25
249 Forest L	.10	.25
T1 Token: Bird	.10	.25
T2 Token: Soldier	.10	.25
T3 Token: Zombie	.10	.25
T4 Token: Beast	.10	.25
T5 Token: Saproling	.10	.25
T6 Token: Wurm	.10	.25
T7 Token: Pentavite	.10	.25

2011 Magic The Gathering New Phyrexia

Card	Low	High
COMPLETE SET (175)	60.00	120.00
BOOSTER BOX (36 PACKS)	100.00	175.00
BOOSTER PACK (15 CARDS)	3.00	6.00
*FOIL: .75X TO 2X BASIC CARDS		
RELEASED ON MAY 13, 2011		
1 Karn Liberated M	20.00	50.00
2 Apostle's Blessing C :W:	.10	.25
3 Auriok Survivors U :W:	.20	.50
4 Blade Splicer R :W:	1.00	2.50
5 Cathedral Membrane U :W:	.20	.50
6 Chancellor of the Annex R :W:	.60	1.50
7 Dispatch U :W:	1.00	2.50
8 Due Respect U :W:	.20	.50
9 Elesh Norn, Grand Cenobite M :W:	12.00	30.00
10 Exclusion Ritual U :W:	.20	.50
11 Forced Worship C :W:	.10	.25
12 Inquisitor Exarch U :W:	.20	.50
13 Lost Leonin C :W:	.10	.25
14 Loxodon Convert C :W:	.10	.25
15 Marrow Shards U :W:	.40	1.00
16 Master Splicer U :W:	.20	.50
17 Norn's Annex R :W:	.75	2.00
18 Phyrexian Unlife R :W:	.60	1.50
19 Porcelain Legionnaire C :W:	.10	.25
20 Puresteel Paladin R :W:	1.50	4.00
21 Remember the Fallen C :W:	.10	.25
22 Sensor Splicer C :W:	.10	.25
23 Shattered Angel U :W:	.20	.50
24 Shriek Raptor C :W:	.10	.25
25 Suture Priest C :W:	.10	.25
26 War Report C :W:	.10	.25
27 Argent Mutation U :B:	.20	.50
28 Arm with AEther U :B:	.40	1.00
29 Blighted Agent C :B:	.10	.25
30 Chained Throatseeker C :B:	.10	.25
31 Chancellor of the Spires R :B:	.60	1.50
32 Corrupted Resolve U :B:	.40	1.00
33 Deceiver Exarch U :B:	.40	1.00
34 Defensive Stance C :B:	.10	.25
35 Gitaxian Probe C :B:	.60	1.50
36 Impaler Shrike C :B:	.10	.25
37 Jin-Gitaxias, Core Augur M :B:	4.00	10.00
38 Mental Misstep U :B:	.60	1.50
39 Mindculling U :B:	.60	1.50
40 Numbing Dose C :B:	.10	.25
41 Phyrexian Ingester R :B:	.60	1.50
42 Phyrexian Metamorph R :B:	4.00	10.00
43 Psychic Barrier C :B:	.10	.25
44 Psychic Surgery R :B:	.60	1.50
45 Spined Thopter C :B:	.10	.25
46 Spire Monitor C :B:	.10	.25
47 Tezzeret's Gambit U :B:	.75	2.00
48 Vapor Snag C :B:	.75	2.00
49 Viral Drake U :B:	.20	.50
50 Wing Splicer U :B:	.20	.50
51 Xenograft R :B:	.60	1.50
52 Blind Zealot C :K:	.10	.25
53 Caress of Phyrexia U :K:	.40	1.00
54 Chancellor of the Dross R :K:	1.00	2.50
55 Dementia Bat C :K:	.10	.25
56 Despise U :K:	1.00	2.50
57 Dismember U :K:	1.50	4.00
58 Enslave U :K:	.20	.50
59 Entomber Exarch U :K:	.20	.50
60 Evil Presence C :K:	.10	.25
61 Geth's Verdict C :K:	.40	1.00
62 Glistening Oil R :K:	.60	1.50
63 Grim Affliction C :K:	.10	.25
64 Ichor Explosion U :K:	.20	.50
65 Life's Finale R :K:	1.00	2.50
66 Mortis Dogs C :K:	.10	.25
67 Parasitic Implant C :K:	.10	.25
68 Phyrexian Obliterator M :K:	15.00	40.00
69 Pith Driller C :K:	.10	.25
70 Postmortem Lunge U :K:	.20	.50
71 Praetor's Grasp R :K:	.75	2.00
72 Reaper of Sheoldred U :K:	.20	.50
73 Sheoldred, Whispering One M :K:	4.00	10.00
74 Surgical Extraction R :K:	4.00	10.00
75 Toxic Nim C :K:	.10	.25
76 Vault Skirge C :K:	.20	.50
77 Whispering Specter U :K:	.75	2.00
78 Act of Aggression U :R:	.40	1.00
79 Artillerize C :R:	.10	.25
80 Bludgeon Brawl R :R:	.60	1.50
81 Chancellor of the Forge R :R:	.60	1.50
82 Fallen Ferromancer U :R:	.20	.50
83 Flameborn Viron C :R:	.10	.25
84 Furnace Scamp C :R:	.10	.25
85 Geosurge U :R:	.20	.50
86 Gut Shot U :R:	.60	1.50
87 Invader Parasite R :R:	.60	1.50
88 Moltensteel Dragon R :R:	.75	2.00
89 Ogre Menial C :R:	.10	.25
90 Priest of Urabrask U :R:	.60	1.50
91 Rage Extractor U :R:	.20	.50
92 Razor Swine C :R:	.10	.25
93 Ruthless Invasion C :R:	.10	.25
94 Scrapyard Salvo C :R:	.10	.25
95 Slag Fiend R :R:	.40	1.00
96 Slash Panther C :R:	.10	.25
97 Tormentor Exarch U :R:	.20	.50
98 Urabrask the Hidden M :R:	2.00	5.00
99 Victorious Destruction C :R:	.10	.25
100 Volt Charge C :R:	.10	.25
101 Vulshok Refugee U :R:	.40	1.00
102 Whipflare U :R:	1.00	2.50
103 Beast Within U :G:	1.50	4.00
104 Birthing Pod R :G:	5.00	12.00
105 Brutalizer Exarch U :G:	.20	.50
106 Chancellor of the Tangle R :G:	.60	1.50
107 Corrosive Gale U :G:	.60	1.50
108 Death-Hood Cobra C :G:	.10	.25
109 Fresh Meat R :G:	.60	1.50
110 Glissa's Scorn C :G:	.10	.25
111 Glistener Elf C :G:	.10	.25
112 Greenhilt Trainee U :G:	.20	.50
113 Leeching Bite C :G:	.10	.25
114 Maul Splicer C :G:	.10	.25
115 Melira, Sylvok Outcast R :G:	1.25	3.00
116 Mutagenic Growth C :G:	.10	.25
117 Mycosynth Fiend U :G:	.20	.50
118 Noxious Revival U :G:	1.00	2.50
119 Phyrexian Swarmlord R :G:	.60	1.50
120 Rotted Hystrix C :G:	.10	.25
121 Spinebiter U :G:	.20	.50
122 Thundering Tanadon C :G:	.10	.25
123 Triumph of the Hordes U :G:	.40	1.00
124 Viridian Betrayers C :G:	.10	.25
125 Viridian Harvest C :G:	.10	.25
126 Vital Splicer U :G:	.20	.50
127 Vorinclex, Voice of Hunger M :G:	4.00	10.00
128 Jor Kadeen, the Prevailer R :W/R:	.75	2.00
129 Alloy Myr U	.60	1.50
130 Batterskull M	10.00	25.00
131 Blinding Souleater C	.10	.25
132 Caged Sun R	1.50	4.00
133 Conversion Chamber U	.20	.50
134 Darksteel Relic U	.20	.50
135 Etched Monstrosity M	1.00	2.50
136 Gremlin Mine C	.10	.25
137 Hex Parasite R	.40	1.00
138 Hovermyr C	.10	.25
139 Immolating Souleater C	.10	.25
140 Insatiable Souleater C	.10	.25
141 Isolation Cell U	.20	.50
142 Kiln Walker U	.20	.50
143 Lashwrithe R	.40	1.00
144 Mindcrank U	.60	1.50
145 Mycosynth Wellspring C	.10	.25
146 Myr Superion R	1.25	3.00
147 Necropouncer U	.20	.50
148 Omen Machine R	.60	1.50
149 Pestilent Souleater C	.10	.25
150 Phyrexian Hulk C	.10	.25
151 Pristine Talisman C	.10	.25
152 Shrine of Boundless Growth U	.20	.50
153 Shrine of Burning Rage U	.40	1.00
154 Shrine of Limitless Power U	.20	.50
155 Shrine of Loyal Legions U	.75	2.00
156 Shrine of Piercing Vision U	.20	.50
157 Sickleslicer U	.40	1.00
158 Soul Conduit R	.60	1.50
159 Spellskite R	6.00	15.00
160 Surge Node U	.40	1.00
161 Sword of War and Peace M	12.00	30.00
162 Torpor Orb R	1.25	3.00
163 Trespassing Souleater C	.10	.25
164 Unwinding Clock R	1.00	2.50
165 Phyrexia's Core U	.40	1.00
166 Plains L	.10	.25
167 Plains L	.10	.25
168 Island L	.10	.25
169 Island L	.10	.25
170 Swamp L	.10	.25
171 Swamp L	.10	.25
172 Mountain L	.10	.25
173 Mountain L	.10	.25
174 Forest L	.10	.25
175 Forest L	.10	.25
PC Poison Counter	.10	.25
R1 Rules Tip: Phyrexian Mana	.10	.25
R2 Rules Tip: Living Weapon	.10	.25
R3 Rules Tip: Infect	.10	.25
R4 Rules Tip: Proliferate	.10	.25
T1 Token: Beast	.10	.25
T2 Token: Goblin	.10	.25
T3 Token: Golem	.10	.25
T4 Token: Myr	.10	.25

2011 Magic The Gathering Innistrad

Card	Low	High
COMPLETE SET (277)	200.00	275.00
BOOSTER BOX (36 PACKS)	75.00	150.00
BOOSTER PACK (15 CARDS)	3.00	6.00
*FOIL: .75X TO 2X BASIC CARDS		
RELEASED ON SEPTEMBER 30, 2011		
1 Abbey Griffin C :W:	.10	.25
2 Angel of Flight Alabaster R :W:	.40	1.00
3 Angelic Overseer M :W:	1.50	4.00
4 Avacynian Priest C :W:	.10	.25
5 Bonds of Faith C :W:	.10	.25
6 Champion of the Parish R :W:	3.00	8.00
7 Chapel Geist C :W:	.10	.25
8 Cloistered Youth/Unholy Fiend U :W: :K:	.20	.50
9 Dearly Departed R :W:	.40	1.00
10 Divine Reckoning R :W:	.60	1.50
11 Doomed Traveler C :W:	.30	.75
12 Elder Cathar C :W:	.10	.25
13 Elite Inquisitor R :W:	.75	2.00
14 Feeling of Dread C :W:	.10	.25
15 Fiend Hunter U :W:	.50	1.25
16 Gallows Warden U :W:	.20	.50
17 Geist-Honored Monk R :W:	.75	2.00
18 Ghostly Possession C :W:	.10	.25
19 Intangible Virtue U :W:	.75	2.00
20 Mausoleum Guard U :W:	.20	.50
21 Mentor of the Meek R :W:	1.00	2.50
22 Midnight Haunting U :W:	.50	1.25
23 Mikaeus, the Lunarch M :W:	2.00	5.00
24 Moment of Heroism C :W:	.10	.25
25 Nevermore R :W:	.75	2.00
26 Paraselene U :W:	.20	.50
27 Purify the Grave U :W:	.20	.50
28 Rally the Peasants U :W:	.20	.50
29 Rebuke C :W:	.10	.25
30 Selfless Cathar C :W:	.10	.25
31 Silverchase Fox C :W:	.30	.75
32 Slayer of the Wicked U :W:	.20	.50
33 Smite the Monstrous C :W:	.10	.25
34 Spare from Evil C :W:	.10	.25
35 Spectral Rider U :W:	.20	.50
36 Stony Silence R :W:	.60	1.50
37 Thraben Purebloods C :W:	.10	.25
38 Thraben Sentry/Thraben Militia C :W:	.10	.25
39 Unruly Mob C :W:	.10	.25
40 Urgent Exorcism C :W:	.10	.25
41 Village Bell-Ringer C :W:	.10	.25
42 Voiceless Spirit C :W:	.10	.25
43 Armored Skaab C :B:	.10	.25
44 Back from the Brink R :B:	.40	1.00
45 Battleground Geist U :B:	.20	.50
46 Cackling Counterpart R :B:	.60	1.50
47 Civilized Scholar/Homicidal Brute U :B: :R:	.20	.50
48 Claustrophobia C :B:	.10	.25
49 Curiosity U :B:	.30	.75
50 Curse of the Bloody Tome C :B:	.10	.25
51 Delver of Secrets/Insectile Aberration C :B:	.50	1.25
52 Deranged Assistant C :B:	.10	.25
53 Dissipate U :B:	.60	1.50
54 Dream Twist C :B:	.10	.25
55 Forbidden Alchemy C :B:	.40	1.00
56 Fortress Crab C :B:	.10	.25
57 Frightful Delusion C :B:	.10	.25
58 Grasp of Phantoms U :B:	.20	.50
59 Hysterical Blindness C :B:	.10	.25
60 Invisible Stalker U :B:	.60	1.50
61 Laboratory Maniac R :B:	.60	1.50
62 Lantern Spirit U :B:	.20	.50
63 Lost in the Mist C :B:	.10	.25
64 Ludevic's Test Subject/Ludevic's Abomination R :B:	.75	2.00
65 Makeshift Mauler C :B:	.10	.25
66 Memory's Journey U :B:	.20	.50
67 Mindshrieker R :B:	1.00	2.50
68 Mirror-Mad Phantasm M :B:	1.00	2.50
69 Moon Heron C :B:	.10	.25
70 Murder of Crows U :B:	.30	.75
71 Rooftop Storm R :B:	.50	1.25
72 Runic Repetition U :B:	.20	.50
73 Selhoff Occultist C :B:	.10	.25
74 Sensory Deprivation C :B:	.10	.25
75 Silent Departure C :B:	.10	.25
76 Skaab Goliath U :B:	.20	.50
77 Skaab Ruinator M :B:	1.50	4.00
78 Snapcaster Mage R :B:	12.00	30.00
79 Spectral Flight C :B:	.10	.25
80 Stitched Drake C :B:	.10	.25
81 Stitcher's Apprentice C :B:	.10	.25
82 Sturmgeist R :B:	.40	1.00
83 Think Twice C :B:	.20	.50
84 Undead Alchemist R :B:	.60	1.50
85 Abattoir Ghoul U :K:	.20	.50
86 Altar's Reap C :K:	.10	.25
87 Army of the Damned M :K:	1.50	4.00
88 Bitterheart Witch U :K:	.20	.50
89 Bloodgift Demon R :K:	1.00	2.50
90 Bloodline Keeper/Lord of Lineage R :K:	2.50	6.00
91 Brain Weevil C :K:	.10	.25
92 Bump in the Night C :K:	.10	.25
93 Corpse Lunge C :K:	.10	.25
94 Curse of Death's Hold R :K:	.60	1.50
95 Curse of Oblivion C :K:	.10	.25
96 Dead Weight C :K:	.10	.25
97 Diregraf Ghoul U :K:	.50	1.25
98 Disciple of Griselbrand U :K:	.20	.50
99 Endless Ranks of the Dead R :K:	1.00	2.50
100 Falkenrath Noble U :K:	.20	.50
101 Ghoulcaller's Chant C :K:	.10	.25
102 Ghoulraiser C :K:	.10	.25
103 Gruesome Deformity C :K:	.10	.25
104 Heartless Summoning R :K:	1.25	3.00
105 Liliana of the Veil M :K:	30.00	60.00
106 Manor Skeleton C :K:	.10	.25
107 Markov Patrician C :K:	.10	.25
108 Maw of the Mire C :K:	.10	.25
109 Moan of the Unhallowed U :K:	.20	.50
110 Morkrut Banshee U :K:	.20	.50
111 Night Terrors C :K:	.10	.25
112 Reaper from the Abyss M :K:	.75	2.00
113 Rotting Fensnake C :K:	.10	.25
114 Screeching Bat/Stalking Vampire U :K:	.20	.50
115 Sever the Bloodline R :K:	.60	1.50
116 Skeletal Grimace C :K:	.10	.25
117 Skirsdag High Priest R :K:	.75	2.00
118 Stromkirk Patrol C :K:	.10	.25
119 Tribute to Hunger U :K:	.40	1.00
120 Typhoid Rats C :K:	.10	.25
121 Unbreathing Horde R :K:	1.00	2.50
122 Unburial Rites U :K:	.50	1.25
123 Vampire Interloper C :K:	.10	.25
124 Victim of Night C :K:	.10	.25
125 Village Cannibals U :K:	.20	.50
126 Walking Corpse C :K:	.10	.25
127 Ancient Grudge C :R:	.10	.25
128 Ashmouth Hound C :R:	.10	.25
129 Balefire Dragon M :R:	1.00	2.50
130 Blasphemous Act R :R:	.60	1.50
131 Bloodcrazed Neonate C :R:	.10	.25
132 Brimstone Volley C :R:	.40	1.00
133 Burning Vengeance U :R:	.30	.75
134 Charmbreaker Devils R :R:	.40	1.00
135 Crossway Vampire C :R:	.10	.25
136 Curse of Stalked Prey R :R:	.60	1.50
137 Curse of the Nightly Hunt U :R:	.20	.50
138 Curse of the Pierced Heart C :R:	.10	.25
139 Desperate Ravings U :R:	.20	.50
140 Devil's Play R :R:	.60	1.50
141 Falkenrath Marauders R :R:	.60	1.50
142 Feral Ridgewolf C :R:	.10	.25
143 Furor of the Bitten C :R:	.10	.25
144 Geistflame C :R:	.20	.50
145 Hanweir Watchkeep/Bane of Hanweir U :R:	.20	.50
146 Harvest Pyre C :R:	.10	.25
147 Heretic's Punishment R :R:	.40	1.00
148 Infernal Plunge C :R:	.10	.25
149 Instigator Gang/Wildblood Pack R :R:	.60	1.50
150 Into the Maw of Hell U :R:	.20	.50
151 Kessig Wolf C :R:	.10	.25
152 Kruin Outlaw/Terror of Kruin Pass R :R:	.75	2.00
153 Night Revelers C :R:	.10	.25
154 Nightbird's Clutches C :R:	.10	.25
155 Past in Flames M :R:	1.50	4.00
156 Pitchburn Devils C :R:	.10	.25
157 Rage Thrower U :R:	.20	.50
158 Rakish Heir U :R:	.40	1.00
159 Reckless Waif/Merciless Predator U :R:	.50	1.25
160 Riot Devils C :R:	.10	.25
161 Rolling Temblor U :R:	.20	.50
162 Scourge of Geier Reach U :R:	.20	.50
163 Skirsdag Cultist U :R:	.30	.75
164 Stromkirk Noble R :R:	.60	1.50
165 Tormented Pariah/Rampaging Werewolf C :R:	.10	.25
166 Traitorous Blood C :R:	.30	.75
167 Vampiric Fury C :R:	.10	.25
168 Village Ironsmith/Ironfang C :R:	.10	.25
169 Ambush Viper C :G:	.10	.25
170 Avacyn's Pilgrim C :G:	.10	.25
171 Boneyard Wurm U :G:	.30	.75
172 Bramblecrush U :G:	.20	.50
173 Caravan Vigil C :G:	.10	.25
174 Creeping Renaissance R :G:	.40	1.00
175 Darkthicket Wolf C :G:	.10	.25
176 Daybreak Ranger/Nightfall Predator R :G:	1.25	3.00
177 Elder of Laurels R :G:	.40	1.00
178 Essence of the Wild M :G:	.60	1.50
179 Festerhide Boar C :G:	.10	.25
180 Full Moon's Rise U :G:	.30	.75
181 Garruk Relentless Garruk, the Veil-Cursed M :K: :G:	6.00	15.00
182 Gatstaf Shepherd/Gatstaf Howler U :G:	.20	.50
183 Gnaw to the Bone C :G:	.10	.25
184 Grave Bramble C :G:	.10	.25
185 Grizzled Outcasts/Krallenhorde Wantons C :G:	.10	.25
186 Gutter Grime R :G:	.40	1.00
187 Hamlet Captain U :G:	.20	.50
188 Hollowhenge Scavenger U :G:	.30	.75
189 Kessig Cagebreakers R :G:	.60	1.50
190 Kindercatch C :G:	.10	.25
191 Lumberknot U :G:	.20	.50
192 Make a Wish U :G:	.20	.50
193 Mayor of Avabruck/Howlpack Alpha R :G:	1.00	2.50
194 Moldgraf Monstrosity R :G:	.40	1.00
195 Moonmist C :G:	.20	.50
196 Mulch C :G:	.10	.25
197 Naturalize C :G:	.10	.25
198 Orchard Spirit C :G:	.10	.25
199 Parallel Lives R :G:	1.50	4.00
200 Prey Upon C :G:	.10	.25
201 Ranger's Guile C :G:	.10	.25
202 Somberwald Spider C :G:	.10	.25
203 Spider Spawning U :G:	.20	.50
204 Spidery Grasp C :G:	.30	.75
205 Splinterfright R :G:	.60	1.50
206 Travel Preparations C :G:	.10	.25
207 Tree of Redemption M :G:	1.25	3.00
208 Ulvenwald Mystics/Ulvenwald Primordials U :G:	.20	.50
209 Villagers of Estwald/Howlpack of Estwald C :G:	.10	.25
210 Woodland Sleuth C :G:	.10	.25
211 Wreath of Geists U :G:	.20	.50
212 Evil Twin R :B: :K:	.60	1.50
213 Geist of Saint Traft M :W: :B:	10.00	25.00
214 Grimgrin, Corpse-Born M :B: :K:	1.50	4.00
215 Olivia Voldaren M :K: :R:	2.50	6.00
216 Blazing Torch C	.10	.25
217 Butcher's Cleaver U	.20	.50
218 Cellar Door U	.20	.50
219 Cobbled Wings C	.10	.25
220 Creepy Doll R	.40	1.00
221 Demonmail Hauberk U	.20	.50
222 Galvanic Juggernaut U	.20	.50
223 Geistcatcher's Rig U	.60	1.50
224 Ghoulcaller's Bell C	.10	.25
225 Graveyard Shovel U	.20	.50
226 Grimoire of the Dead M	1.50	4.00
227 Inquisitor's Flail U	.20	.50
228 Manor Gargoyle R	.40	1.00
229 Mask of Avacyn U	.30	.75
230 One-Eyed Scarecrow C	.10	.25
231 Runechanter's Pike R	1.00	2.50
232 Sharpened Pitchfork U	.20	.50
233 Silver-Inlaid Dagger U	.20	.50
234 Traveler's Amulet C	.10	.25
235 Trepanation Blade U	.30	.75
236 Witchbane Orb R	.60	1.50
237 Wooden Stake C	.30	.75
238 Clifftop Retreat R	3.00	8.00
239 Gavony Township R	1.25	3.00
240 Ghost Quarter U	.60	1.50
241 Hinterland Harbor R	3.00	8.00
242 Isolated Chapel R	3.00	8.00
243 Kessig Wolf Run R	1.50	4.00
244 Moorland Haunt R	.40	1.00
245 Nephalia Drownyard R	.60	1.50
246 Shimmering Grotto C	.10	.25
247 Stensia Bloodhall R	.40	1.00
248 Sulfur Falls R	3.00	8.00
249 Woodland Cemetery R	3.00	8.00
250 Plains L	.10	.25
251 Plains L	.10	.25
252 Plains L	.10	.25
253 Island L	.10	.25
254 Island L	.10	.25
255 Island L	.10	.25
256 Swamp L	.10	.25
257 Swamp L	.10	.25
258 Swamp L	.10	.25
259 Mountain L	.10	.25
260 Mountain L	.10	.25
261 Mountain L	.10	.25
262 Forest L	.10	.25
263 Forest L	.10	.25
264 Forest L	.10	.25
CL Checklist	.10	.25
T1 Token: Angel	.10	.25
T2 Token: Spirit	.10	.25
T3 Token: Homunculus	.10	.25
T4 Token: Demon	.10	.25
T5 Token: Vampire	.10	.25
T6 Token: Wolf BLACK	.10	.25
T7 Token: Zombie	.10	.25
T8 Token: Zombie	.10	.25
T9 Token: Zombie	.10	.25
T10 Token: Ooze	.10	.25
T11 Token: Spider	.10	.25
T12 Token: Wolf GREEN	.10	.25

2012 Magic The Gathering Dark Ascension

Card	Low	High
COMPLETE SET (158)	75.00	150.00
BOOSTER BOX (36 PACKS)	75.00	150.00
BOOSTER PACK (15 CARDS)	3.00	5.00
*FOIL: .75X TO 2X BASIC CARDS		
RELEASED ON FEBRUARY 3, 2012		
1 Archangel's Light M :W:	1.00	2.50
2 Bar the Door C :W:	.10	.25
3 Break of Day C :W:	.10	.25
4 Burden of Guilt C :W:	.10	.25
5 Curse of Exhaustion U :W:	.20	.50
6 Elgaud Inquisitor C :W:	.10	.25
7 Faith's Shield U :W:	.20	.50
8 Gather the Townsfolk C :W:	.10	.25
9 Gavony Ironwright U :W:	.20	.50
10 Hollowhenge Spirit U :W:	.20	.50
11 Increasing Devotion R :W:	.60	1.50
12 Lingering Souls U :W:	.20	.50
13 Loyal Cathar/Unhallowed Cathar C :W: :K:	.10	.25
14 Midnight Guard C :W:	.10	.25
15 Niblis of the Mist C :W:	.10	.25
16 Niblis of the Urn U :W:	.20	.50
17 Ray of Revelation C :W:	.10	.25
18 Requiem Angel R :W:	.60	1.50
19 Sanctuary Cat C :W:	.10	.25
20 Seance R :W:	.60	1.50
21 Silverclaw Griffin C :W:	.10	.25
22 Skillful Lunge C :W:	.10	.25
23 Sudden Disappearance R :W:	.60	1.50
24 Thalia, Guardian of Thraben R :W:	3.00	8.00
25 Thraben Doomsayer R :W:	.60	1.50
26 Thraben Heretic U :W:	.20	.50
27 Artful Dodge C :L:	.10	.25
28 Beguiler of Wills M :L:	1.00	2.50
29 Bone to Ash C :L:	.10	.25
30 Call to the Kind:R: R :L:	.60	1.50
31 Chant of the Skifsang C :L:	.10	.25
32 Chill of Foreboding U :L:	.20	.50

33 Counterlash R :L: .60 1.50
34 Curse of Echoes R :L: .60 1.50
35 Divination C :L: .10 .25
36 Dungeon Geists R :B: .60 1.50
37 Geralf's Mindcrusher R :L: .60 1.50
38 Griptide C :L: .10 .25
39 Havengul Runebinder R :L: .60 1.50
40 Headless Skaab C :L: .10 .25
41 Increasing Confusion R :L: 1.00 2.50
42 Mystic Retrieval U :L: .20 .50
43 Nephalia Seakite C :L: .10 .25
44 Niblis of the Breath U :L: .20 .50
45 Relentless Skaabs U :L: .20 .50
46 Saving Grasp C :L: .10 .25
47 Screeching Skaab C :L: .10 .25
48 Secrets of the Dead U :L: .20 .50
49 Shriekgeist C :L: .10 .25
50 Soul Seizer/Ghastly Haunting U :L: .20 .50
51 Stormbound Geist C :L: .10 .25
52 Thought Scour C :L: .10 .25
53 Tower Geist U :L: .20 .50
54 Black Cat C :K: .10 .25
55 Chosen of Markov/Markov's Servant C :K: .10 .25
56 Curse of Misfortunes R :K: .60 1.50
57 Curse of Thirst U :K: .20 .50
58 Deadly Allure U :K: .20 .50
59 Death's Caress C :K: .10 .25
60 Falkenrath Torturer C :K: .10 .25
61 Farbog Boneflinger U :K: .20 .50
62 Fiend of the Shadows R :K: .60 1.50
63 Geralf's Messenger R :K: 2.50 6.00
64 Gravecrawler R :K: 4.00 10.00
65 Gravepurge C :K: .10 .25
66 Gruesome Discovery C :K: .10 .25
67 Harrowing Journey U :K: .20 .50
68 Highborn Ghoul C :K: .10 .25
69 Increasing Ambition R :K: .60 1.50
70 Mikaeus, the Unhallowed M :K: 3.00 8.00
71 Ravenous Demon/Archdemon of Greed R :K: .60 1.50
72 Reap the Seagraf C :K: .10 .25
73 Sightless Ghoul C :K: .10 .25
74 Skirsdag Flayer U :K: .20 .50
75 Spiteful Shadows C :K: .10 .25
76 Tragic Slip C :K: .10 .25
77 Undying Evil C :K: .10 .25
78 Vengeful Vampire U :K: .20 .50
79 Wakedancer U :K: .20 .50
80 Zombie Apocalypse R :K: .60 1.50
81 Afflicted Deserter/Werewolf Ransacker U :R: .20 .50
82 Alpha Brawl R :R: .60 1.50
83 Blood Feud U :R: .20 .50
84 Burning Oil U :R: .20 .50
85 Curse of Bloodletting R :R: 1.00 2.50
86 Erdwal Ripper C :R: .10 .25
87 Faithless Looting C :R: .10 .25
88 Fires of Undeath C :R: .10 .25
89 Flayer of the Hatebound R :R: .60 1.50
90 Fling C :R: .10 .25
91 Forge Devil C :R: .10 .25
92 Heckling Fiends U :R: .20 .50
93 Hellrider R :R: 1.00 2.50
94 Hinterland Hermit/Hinterland Scourge C :R: .10 .25
95 Increasing Vengeance R :R: .60 1.50
96 Markov Blademaster R :R: .60 1.50
97 Markov Warlord U :R: .20 .50
98 Mondronen Shaman/Tovolar's Magehunter R :R: .60 1.50
99 Moonveil Dragon M :R: 1.50 4.00
100 Nearheath Stalker C :R: .10 .25
101 Pyreheart Wolf U :R: .20 .50
102 Russet Wolves C :R: .10 .25
103 Scorch the Fields C :R: .10 .25
104 Shatte:R: Perception U :R: .20 .50
105 Talons of Falkenrath C :R: .10 .25
106 Torch Fiend C :R: .10 .25
107 Wrack with Madness C :R: .10 .25
108 Briarpack Alpha U :G: .20 .50
109 Clinging Mists C :G: .10 .25
110 Crushing Vines C :G: .10 .25
111 Dawntreader Elk C :G: .10 .25
112 Deranged Outcast R :G: .60 1.50
113 Favor of the Woods C :G: .10 .25
114 Feed the Pack R :G: .60 1.50
115 Ghoultree R :G: .60 1.50
116 Gravetiller Wurm U :G: .20 .50
117 Grim Flowering U :G: .20 .50
118 Hollowhenge Beast C :G: .10 .25
119 Hunger of the Howlpack C :G: .10 .25
120 Increasing Savagery R :G: 1.00 2.50
121 Kessig Recluse C :G: .10 .25
122 Lambholt Elder/Silverpelt Werewolf U :G: .20 .50
123 Lost in the Woods R :G: .60 1.50
124 Predator Ooze R :G: 2.00 5.00
125 Scorned Villager/Moonscarred Werewolf C :G: .10 .25
126 Somberwald Dryad C :G: .10 .25
127 Strangleroot Geist U :G: .20 .50
128 Tracker's Instincts U :G: .20 .50
129 Ulvenwald Bear C :G: .10 .25
130 Village Survivors U :G: .20 .50
131 Vorapede M :G: 1.50 4.00
132 Wild Hunger C :G: .10 .25
133 Wolfbitten Captive/Krallenhorde Killer R :G: .60 1.50
134 Young Wolf C :G: .10 .25
135 Diregraf Captain U :L: :K: .20 .50
136 Drogskol Captain U :W: :L: .20 .50
137 Drogskol Reaver M :W: :L: 1.50 4.00
138 Falkenrath Aristocrat M :K: :R: 3.00 8.00
139 Havengul Lich M :L: :K: 2.00 5.00
140 Huntmaster of the Fells :Ravager of the Fells M :R: :G: 4.00 10.00
141 Immerwolf U :R: :G: .20 .50
142 Sorin, Lord of Innistrad M :W: :K: 4.00 10.00
143 Stromkirk Captain U :K: :R: .20 .50
144 Altar of the Lost U .20 .50
145 Avacyn's Collar U .20 .50
146 Chalice of Life/Chalice of Death U .20 .50
147 Elbrus, the Binding Blade Withengar Unbound M :K: 3.00 8.00
148 Executioner's Hood C .10 .25
149 Gratdigger's Cage R 1.50 4.00
150 Heavy Mattock C .10 .25
151 Helvault M 1.00 2.50
152 Jar of Eyeballs R .60 1.50
153 Warden of the Wall U .20 .50
154 Wolfhunter's Quiver U .20 .50
155 Evolving Wilds C .10 .25
156 Grim Backwoods R .60 1.50
157 Haunted Fengraf C .10 .25
158 Vault of the Archangel R 1.25 3.00
CL Checklist .10 .25
T1 Token: Human .10 .25
T2 Token: Vampire .10 .25
T3 Emblem: Sorin, Lord of Innistrad .10 .25

2012 Magic The Gathering Avacyn Restored

COMPLETE SET (244) 150.00 250.00
BOOSTER BOX (36 PACKS) 75.00 125.00
BOOSTER PACK (15 CARDS) 3.00 4.00
*FOIL: .75X TO 2X BASIC CARDS
RELEASED ON MAY 4, 2012
1 Angel of Glory's Rise R :W: .75 2.00
2 Angel of Jubilation R :W: 2.00 5.00
3 Angel's Mercy C :W: .10 .25
4 Angelic Wall C :W: .10 .25
5 Archangel U :W: .20 .50
6 Avacyn, Angel of Hope M :W: 4.00 10.00
7 Banishing Stroke U :W: .20 .50
8 Builder's Blessing U :W: .20 .50
9 Call to Serve U :W: .20 .50
10 Cathars' Crusade R :W: 1.00 2.50
11 Cathedral Sanctifier C :W: .10 .25
12 Cloudshift C :W: .10 .25
13 Commander's Authority U :W: .20 .50
14 Cursebreak C :W: .10 .25
15 Defang C :W: .10 .25
16 Defy Death U :W: .20 .50
17 Devout Chaplain U :W: .20 .50
18 Divine Deflection R :W: .40 1.00
19 Emancipation Angel U :W: .20 .50
20 Entreat the Angels M :W: 6.00 15.00
21 Farbog Explorer C :W: .10 .25
22 Goldnight Commander U :W: .20 .50
23 Goldnight Redeemer U :W: .20 .50
24 Herald of War R :W: 1.00 2.50
25 Holy Justiciar U :W: .20 .50
26 Leap of Faith C :W: .10 .25
27 Midnight Duelist C :W: .10 .25
28 Midvast Protector C :W: .10 .25
29 Moonlight Geist C :W: .10 .25
30 Moorland Inquisitor C :W: .10 .25
31 Nearheath Pilgrim U :W: .20 .50
32 Restoration Angel R :W: 3.00 8.00
33 Riders of Gavony R :W: .75 2.00
34 Righteous Blow C :W: .10 .25
35 Seraph of Dawn C :W: .10 .25
36 Silverblade Paladin R :W: 1.00 2.50
37 Spectral Gateguards C :W: .10 .25
38 Terminus R :W: 2.50 6.00
39 Thraben Valiant C :W: .10 .25
40 Voice of the Provinces C :W: .10 .25
41 Zealous Strike C :W: .10 .25
42 Alchemist's Apprentice C :B: .10 .25
43 Amass the Components C :B: .10 .25
44 Arcane Melee R :B: .40 1.00
45 Captain of the Mists R :B: .40 1.00
46 Crippling Chill C :B: .10 .25
47 Deadeye Navigator R :B: .40 1.00
48 Devastation Tide R :B: .40 1.00
49 Dreadwaters C :B: .10 .25
50 Elgaud Shieldmate C :B: .10 .25
51 Favorable Winds U :B: .20 .50
52 Fettergeist U :B: .20 .50
53 Fleeting Distraction C :B: .10 .25
54 Galvanic Alchemist C :B: .10 .25
55 Geist Snatch C :B: .10 .25
56 Ghostform C :B: .10 .25
57 Ghostly Flicker C :B: .10 .25
58 Ghostly Touch U :B: .20 .50
59 Gryff Vanguard C :B: .10 .25
60 Havengul Skaab C :B: .10 .25
61 Infinite Reflection R :B: .40 1.00
62 Into the Void U :B: .20 .50
63A Latch Seeker U :B: .20 .50
63B Latch Seeker U :B: FULL ART 2.00 5.00
64 Lone Revenant R :B: .40 1.00
65 Lunar Mystic R :B: .40 1.00
66 Mass Appeal U :B: .20 .50
67 Mist Raven C :B: .10 .25
68 Misthollow Griffin M :B: 1.00 2.50
69 Nephalia Smuggler U :B: .20 .50
70 Outwit C :B: .10 .25
71 Peel from Reality C :B: .10 .25
72 Rotcrown Ghoul C :B: .10 .25
73 Scrapskin Drake C :B: .10 .25
74 Second Guess U :B: .20 .50
75 Spectral Prison C :B: .10 .25
76 Spirit Away R :B: .40 1.00
77 Stern Mentor U :B: .20 .50
78 Stolen Goods R :B: .75 2.00
79 Tamiyo, the Moon Sage M :B: 8.00 20.00
80 Tandem Lookout U :B: .20 .50
81 Temporal Mastery M :B: 6.00 15.00
82 Vanishment U :B: .20 .50
83 Wingcrafter C :B: .10 .25
84 Appetite for Brains U :K: .20 .50
85 Barter in Blood U :K: .20 .50
86 Blood Artist U :K: .20 .50
87 Bloodflow Connoisseur C :K: .10 .25
88 Bone Splinters C :K: .10 .25
89 Butcher Ghoul C :K: .10 .25
90 Corpse Traders U :K: .20 .50
91 Crypt Creeper C :K: .10 .25
92 Dark Impostor R :K: .75 2.00
93 Death Wind C :K: .10 .25
94 Demonic Rising R :K: .40 1.00
95 Demonic Taskmaster U :K: .20 .50
96 Demonlord of Ashmouth R :K: .60 1.50
97 Descent into Madness M :K: 1.00 2.50
98 Dread Slaver R :K: .40 1.00
99 Driver of the Dead C :K: .10 .25
100 Essence Harvest C :K: .10 .25
101 Evernight Shade U :K: .20 .50
102 Exquisite Blood R :K: .75 2.00
103 Ghoulflesh C :K: .10 .25
104 Gloom Surgeon R :K: .40 1.00
105 Grave Exchange C :K: .10 .25
106 Griselbrand M :K: 12.00 30.00
107 Harvester of Souls R :K: 1.00 2.50
108 Homicidal Seclusion U :K: .20 .50
109 Human Frailty U :K: .20 .50
110 Hunted Ghoul C :K: .10 .25
111A Killing Wave R :K: .75 2.00
111B Killing Wave R :K: FULL ART 6.00 15.00
112 Maalfeld Twins U :K: .20 .50
113 Marrow Bats U :K: .20 .50
114 Mental Agony C :K: .10 .25
115 Necrobite C :K: .10 .25
116 Polluted Dead C :K: .10 .25
117 Predator's Gambit C :K: .10 .25
118 Renegade Demon C :K: .10 .25
119 Searchlight Geist C :K: .10 .25
120 Soulcage Fiend C :K: .10 .25
121 Treacherous Pit-Dweller R :K: .75 2.00
122 Triumph of Cruelty U :K: .20 .50
123 Undead Executioner C :K: .10 .25
124 Unhallowed Pact C :K: .10 .25
125 Aggravate U :R: .20 .50
126 Archwing Dragon R :R: 1.00 2.50
127 Banners Raised C :R: .10 .25
128 Battle Hymn C :R: .10 .25
129 Bonfire of the Damned M :R: 5.00 12.00
130 Burn at the Stake R :R: .75 2.00
131 Dangerous Wager C :R: .10 .25
132 Demolish C :R: .10 .25
133 Dual Casting R :R: .60 1.50
134 Falkenrath Exterminator U :R: .20 .50
135 Fervent Cathar C :R: .10 .25
136 Gang of Devils U :R: .20 .50
137 Guise of Fire C :R: .10 .25
138 Hanweir Lancer C :R: .10 .25
139 Havengul Vampire U :R: .20 .50
140 Heirs of Stromkirk C :R: .10 .25
141 Hound of Griselbrand R :R: .40 1.00
142 Kessig Malcontents U :R: .20 .50
143 Kruin Striker C :R: .10 .25
144 Lightning Mauler U :R: .20 .50
145 Lightning Prowess U :R: .20 .50
146 Mad Prophet C :R: .10 .25
147 Malicious Intent C :R: .10 .25
148 Malignus M :R: 1.00 2.50
149 Pillar of Flame C :R: .10 .25
150 Raging Poltergeist C :R: .10 .25
151 Reforge the Soul R :R: 1.00 2.50
152 Riot Ringleader C :R: .10 .25
153 Rite of Ruin R :R: .40 1.00
154 Rush of Blood U :R: .20 .50
155 Scalding Devil C :R: .10 .25
156 Somberwald Vigilante C :R: .10 .25
157 Stonewright U :R: .20 .50
158 Thatcher Revolt C :R: .10 .25
159 Thunderbolt C :R: .10 .25
160 Thunderous Wrath U :R: .20 .50
161 Tibalt, the Fiend-Blooded M :R: 1.50 4.00
162 Tyrant of Discord R :R: .40 1.00
163 Uncanny Speed C :R: .10 .25
164 Vexing Devil R :R: 6.00 15.00
165 Vigilante Justice U :R: .20 .50
166 Zealous Conscripts R :R: .40 1.00
167 Abundant Growth C :G: .10 .25
168 Blessings of Nature U :G: .20 .50
169 Borderland Ranger C :G: .10 .25
170 Bower Passage U :G: .20 .50
171 Champion of Lambholt R :G: .75 2.00
172 Craterhoof Behemoth M :G: 5.00 12.00
173 Descendants' Path R :G: 1.00 2.50
174 Diregraf Escort C :G: .10 .25
175 Druid's Familiar U :G: .20 .50
176 Druids' Repository R :G: .75 2.00
177 Eaten by Spiders U :G: .20 .50
178 Flowering Lumberknot C :G: .10 .25
179 Geist Trappers C :G: .10 .25
180 Gloomwidow U :G: .20 .50
181 Grounded C :G: .10 .25
182 Howlgeist U :G: .20 .50
183 Joint Assault C :G: .10 .25
184 Lair Delve C :G: .10 .25
185 Natural End C :G: .10 .25
186 Nettle Swine C :G: .10 .25
187 Nightshade Peddler C :G: .10 .25
188 Pathbreaker Wurm C :G: .10 .25
189 Primal Surge M :G: 1.25 3.00
190 Rain of Thorns U :G: .20 .50
191 Revenge of the Hunted R :G: .40 1.00
192 Sheltering Word C :G: .10 .25
193 Snare the Skies C :G: .10 .25
194 Somberwald Sage R :G: .60 1.50
195 Soul of the Harvest R :G: .40 1.00
196 Terrifying Presence C :G: .10 .25
197 Timberland Guide C :G: .10 .25
198 Triumph of Ferocity U :G: .20 .50
199 Trusted Forcemage C :G: .10 .25
200 Ulvenwald Tracker R :G: .40 1.00
201 Vorstclaw U :G: .20 .50
202 Wandering Wolf C :G: .10 .25
203 Wild Defiance R :G: .75 2.00
204 Wildwood Geist C :G: .10 .25
205 Wolfir Avenger U :G: .20 .50
206 Wolfir Silverheart R :G: 1.00 2.50
207 Yew Spirit U :G: .20 .50
208 Bruna, Alabaster M :W/B: 1.50 4.00
209 Gisela, Goldnight M :W/R: 5.00 12.00
210 Sigarda, Herons M :W/G: 6.00 15.00
211 Angel's Tomb U .20 .50
212 Angelic Armaments U .20 .50
213 Bladed Bracers C .10 .25
214 Conjurer's Closet R .40 1.00
215 Gallows at Willow Hill R .40 1.00
216 Haunted Guardian U .20 .50
217 Moonsilver Spear R .75 2.00
218 Narstad Scrapper C .10 .25
219 Otherworld Atlas R .40 1.00
220 Scroll of Avacyn C .10 .25
221 Scroll of Griselbrand C .10 .25
222 Tormentor's Trident U .20 .50
223 Vanguard's Shield C .10 .25
224 Vessel of Endless Rest U .20 .50
225 Alchemist's Refuge R .60 1.50
226 Cavern of Souls R 12.00 30.00
227 Desolate Lighthouse R .40 1.00
228 Seraph Sanctuary C .10 .25
229 Slayers' Stronghold R .40 1.00
230 Plains L .10 .25
231 Plains L .10 .25
232 Plains L .10 .25
233 Island L .10 .25
234 Island L .10 .25
235 Island L .10 .25
236 Swamp L .10 .25
237 Swamp L .10 .25
238 Swamp L .10 .25
239 Mountain L .10 .25
240 Mountain L .10 .25
241 Mountain L .10 .25
242 Forest L .10 .25
243 Forest L .10 .25
244 Forest L .10 .25
T1 Token: Angel .10 .25
T2 Token: Human .10 .25
T3 Token: Spirit WHITE .10 .25
T4 Token: Spirit BLUE .10 .25
T5 Token: Demon .10 .25
T6 Token: Zombie .10 .25
T7 Token: Human .10 .25
T8 Emblem: Tamiyo, The Moon Sage .10 .25

2012 Magic The Gathering Magic 2013

COMPLETE SET (260) 200.00 350.00
BOOSTER BOX (36 PACKS) 80.00 120.00
BOOSTER PACK (15 CARDS) 3.00 4.50
*FOIL: .75X TO 2X BASIC CARDS
RELEASED ON JULY 26, 2012
1 Ajani, Caller of the Pride M :W: 6.00 15.00
2 Ajani's Sunstriker C :W: .10 .25
3 Angel's Mercy C :W: .10 .25
4 Angelic Benediction U :W: .20 .50
5 Attended Knight C :W: .10 .25
6 Aven Squire C :W: .10 .25
7 Battleflight Eagle C :W: .10 .25
8 Captain of the Watch R :W: .75 2.00
9 Captain's Call C :W: .10 .25
10 Crusader of Odric U :W: .40 1.00
11 Divine Favor C :W: .10 .25
12 Divine Verdict C :W: .10 .25
13 Erase C :W: .10 .25
14 Faith's Reward R :W: .60 1.50
15 Glorious Charge C :W: .10 .25
16 Griffin Protector C :W: .10 .25
17 Guardian Lions C :W: .10 .25
18 Guardians of Akrasa C :W: .10 .25
19 Healer of the Pride U :W: .20 .50
20 Intrepid Hero R :W: .60 1.50
21 Knight of Glory U :W: .30 .75
22 Oblivion Ring U :W: .50 1.25
23 Odric, Master Tactician R :W: 1.50 4.00
24 Pacifism C :W: .10 .25
25 Pillarfield Ox C :W: .10 .25
26 Planar Cleansing R :W: .60 1.50
27 Prized Elephant U :W: .20 .50
28 Rain of Blades U :W: .20 .50
29 Rhox Faithmender R :W: .75 2.00
30 Safe Passage C :W: .10 .25
31 Serra Angel U :W: .20 .50
32 Serra Avatar M :W: 2.00 5.00
33 Serra Avenger R :W: 1.50 4.00
34 Show of Valor C :W: .10 .25
35 Silvercoat Lion C :W: .10 .25
36 Sublime Archangel M :W: 6.00 15.00
37 Touch of the Eternal R :W: .60 1.50
38 War Falcon C :W: .10 .25
39 War Priest of Thune U :W: .20 .50
40 Warclamp Mastiff C :W: .10 .25
41 Archaeomancer C :B: .10 .25
42 Arctic Aven U :B: .20 .50
43 Augur of Bolas U :B: .50 1.25
44 Battle of Wits R :B: .60 1.50
45 Clone R :B: .60 1.50
46 Courtly Provocateur U :B: .20 .50
47 Divination C :B: .10 .25
48 Downpour C :B: .10 .25
49 Encrust C :B: .10 .25
50 Essence Scatter C :B: .10 .25
51 Faerie Invaders C :B: .10 .25
52 Fog Bank U :B: .40 1.00
53 Harbor Serpent C :B: .10 .25
54 Hydrosurge C :B: .10 .25
55 Index C :B: .10 .25
56 Jace, Memory Adept M :B: 6.00 15.00
57 Jace's Phantasm U :B: .75 2.00
58 Kraken Hatchling C :B: .10 .25
59 Master of the Pearl Trident R :B: 2.50 6.00
60 Merfolk of the Pearl Trident C :B: .10 .25
61 Mind Sculpt C :B: .10 .25
62 Negate C :B: .10 .25
63 Omniscience M :B: 4.00 10.00
64 Redirect R :B: .60 1.50
65 Rewind U :B: .30 .75
66 Scroll Thief C :B: .10 .25
67 Sleep U :B: .20 .50
68 Spelltwine R :B: .60 1.50
69 Sphinx of Uthuun R :B: .60 1.50
70 Stormtide Leviathan R :B: .60 1.50
71 Switcheroo U :B: .20 .50
72 Talrand, Sky Summoner R :B: 1.50 4.00
73 Talrand's Invocation U :B: .20 .50
74 Tricks of the Trade C :B: .10 .25
75 Unsummon C :B: .10 .25
76 Vedalken Entrancer C :B: .10 .25
77 Void Stalker R :B: .75 2.00
78 Watercourser C :B: .10 .25
79 Welkin Tern C :B: .10 .25
80 Wind Drake C :B: .10 .25
81 Blood Reckoning U :K: .20 .50
82 Bloodhunter Bat C :K: .10 .25
83 Bloodthrone Vampire C :K: .10 .25
84 Cower in Fear U :K: .20 .50
85 Crippling Blight C :K: .10 .25
86 Dark Favor C :K: .10 .25
87 Diabolic Revelation R :K: .60 1.50
88 Disciple of Bolas R :K: 1.50 4.00
89 Disentomb C :K: .10 .25
90 Duress C :K: .10 .25
91 Duskmantle Prowler U :K: .20 .50
92 Duty-Bound Dead C :K: .10 .25
93 Essence Drain C :K: .10 .25
94 Giant Scorpion C :K: .10 .25
95 Harbor Bandit U :K: .20 .50
96 Knight of Infamy U :K: .30 .75
97 Liliana of the Dark Realms M :K: 5.00 12.00
98 Liliana's Shade C :K: .10 .25
99 Mark of the Vampire C :K: .10 .25
100 Mind Rot C :K: .10 .25
101 Murder C :K: .10 .25
102 Mutilate R :K: 1.25 3.00
103 Nefarox, Overlord of Grixis R :K: 1.00 2.50
104 Phylactery Lich R :K: .60 1.50
105 Public Execution U :K: .20 .50
106 Ravenous Rats C :K: .10 .25
107 Rise from the Grave U :K: .20 .50
108 Servant of Nefarox C :K: .10 .25
109 Shimian Specter R :K: .60 1.50
110 Sign in Blood C :K: .10 .25
111 Tormented Soul C :K: .10 .25
112 Vampire Nighthawk U :K: .60 1.50
113 Vampire Nocturnus M :K: 3.00 8.00
114 Veilborn Ghoul U :K: .20 .50
115 Vile Rebirth C :K: .10 .25
116 Walking Corpse C :K: .10 .25
117 Wit's End R :K: .60 1.50
118 Xathrid Gorgon R :K: .60 1.50
119 Zombie Goliath C :K: .10 .25
120 Arms Dealer U :R: .20 .50
121 Bladetusk Boar C :R: .10 .25
122 Canyon Minotaur C :R: .10 .25
123 Chandra, the Firebrand M :R: 2.50 6.00
124 Chandra's Fury C :R: .10 .25
125 Cleaver Riot U :R: .20 .50
126 Craterize C :R: .10 .25
127 Crimson Muckwader U :R: .20 .50
128 Dragon Hatchling C :R: .10 .25
129 Fervor R :R: .60 1.50
130 Fire Elemental C :R: .10 .25
131 Firewing Phoenix R :R: .60 1.50
132 Flames of the Firebrand U :R: .40 1.00
133 Furnace Whelp U :R: .20 .50
134 Goblin Arsonist C :R: .10 .25
135 Goblin Battle Jester C :R: .10 .25
136 Hamletback Goliath R :R: .60 1.50
137 Kindled Fury C :R: .10 .25
138 Krenko, Mob Boss R :R: 2.00 5.00
139 Krenko's Command C :R: .10 .25
140 Magmaquake R :R: .75 2.00
141 Mark of Mutiny U :R: .20 .50
142 Mindclaw Shaman U :R: .20 .50
143 Mogg Flunkies C :R: .10 .25
144 Reckless Brute C :R: .10 .25
145 Reverberate R :R: .60 1.50
146 Rummaging Goblin C :R: .10 .25
147 Searing Spear C :R: .10 .25
148 Slumbering Dragon R :R: 1.25 3.00
149 Smelt C :R: .10 .25
150 Thundermaw Hellkite M :R: 12.00 30.00
151 Torch Fiend U :R: .20 .50
152 Trumpet Blast C :R: .10 .25
153 Turn to Slag C :R: .10 .25
154 Volcanic Geyser U :R: .20 .50
155 Volcanic Strength C :R: .10 .25
156 Wall of Fire C :R: .10 .25
157 Wild Guess C :R: .10 .25
158 Worldfire M :R: .75 2.00
159 Acidic Slime U :G: .20 .50
160 Arbor Elf C :G: .10 .25
161 Bond Beetle C :G: .10 .25
162 Boundless Realms R :G: .60 1.50
163 Bountiful Harvest C :G: .10 .25
164 Centaur Courser C :G: .10 .25
165 Deadly Recluse C :G: .10 .25
166 Duskdale Wurm U :G: .20 .50
167 Elderscale Wurm M :G: 2.00 5.00
168 Elvish Archdruid R :G: .60 1.50
169 Elvish Visionary C :G: .10 .25
170 Farseek C :G: .10 .25
171 Flinthoof Boar U :G: .30 .75
172 Fog C :G: .10 .25
173 Fungal Sprouting U :G: .20 .50
174 Garruk, Primal Hunter M :G: 6.00 15.00
175 Garruk's Packleader U :G: .20 .50
176 Ground Seal R :G: .60 1.50
177 Mwonvuli Beast Tracker U :G: .30 .75
178 Naturalize C :G: .10 .25
179 Plummet C :G: .10 .25
180 Predatory Rampage R :G: .60 1.50
181 Prey Upon C :G: .10 .25
182 Primal Huntbeast C :G: .10 .25
183 Primordial Hydra M :G: 4.00 10.00
184 Quirion Dryad R :G: .60 1.50
185 Rancor U :G: 1.00 2.50
186 Ranger's Path C :G: .10 .25
187 Revive U :G: .20 .50
188 Roaring Primadox U :G: .20 .50
189 Sentinel Spider C :G: .10 .25
190 Serpent's Gift C :G: .10 .25
191 Silklash Spider R :G: .60 1.50
192 Spiked Baloth C :G: .10 .25
193 Thragtusk R :G: 1.50 4.00
194 Timberpack Wolf C :G: .10 .25
195 Titanic Growth C :G: .10 .25
196 Vastwood Gorger C :G: .10 .25
197 Yeva, Nature's Herald R :G: .60 1.50
198 Yeva's Forcemage C :G: .10 .25
199 Nicol Bolas, Planeswalker M :B/K/R: 3.00 8.00
200 Akroma's Memorial M 5.00 12.00
201 Chronomaton U .20 .50
202 Clock of Omens U .20 .50
203 Door to Nothingness R .60 1.50
204 Elixir of Immortality U .25 .60
205 Gem of Becoming U .25 .60
206 Gilded Lotus R 2.00 5.00
207 Jayemdae Tome U .20 .50
208 Kitesail U .20 .50
209 Phyrexian Hulk U .20 .50
210 Primal Clay U .20 .50
211 Ring of Evos Isle U .25 .60
212 Ring of Kalonia U .25 .60
213 Ring of Thune U .25 .60
214 Ring of Valkas U .25 .60
215 Ring of Xathrid U .25 .60
216 Sands of Delirium R .75 2.00

217 Staff of Nin R .60 1.50
218 Stuffy Doll R 1.25 3.00
219 Tormod's Crypt U .75 2.00
220 Trading Post R .75 2.00
221 Cathedral of War R 1.50 4.00
222 Dragonskull Summit R 2.00 5.00
223 Drowned Catacomb R 2.00 5.00
224 Evolving Wilds C .10 .25
225 Glacial Fortress R 1.25 3.00
226 Hellion Crucible R .75 2.00
227 Reliquary Tower U .75 2.00
228 Rootbound Crag R 1.25 3.00
229 Sunpetal Grove R 2.00 5.00
230 Plains L .10 .25
231 Plains L .10 .25
232 Plains L .10 .25
233 Plains L .10 .25
234 Island L .10 .25
235 Island L .10 .25
236 Island L .10 .25
237 Island L .10 .25
238 Swamp L .10 .25
239 Swamp L .10 .25
240 Swamp L .10 .25
241 Swamp L .10 .25
242 Mountain L .10 .25
243 Mountain L .10 .25
244 Mountain L .10 .25
245 Mountain L .10 .25
246 Forest L .10 .25
247 Forest L .10 .25
248 Forest L .10 .25
249 Forest L .10 .25
T1 Token: Cat .10 .25
T2 Token: Goat .10 .25
T3 Token: Soldier .10 .25
T4 Token: Drake .10 .25
T5 Token: Zombie .10 .25
T6 Token: Goblin .10 .25
T7 Token: Hellion .10 .25
T8 Token: Beast .10 .25
T9 Token: Saproling .10 .25
T10 Token: Wurm .10 .25
T11 Emblem: Liliana of the Dark Realms .10 .25

2012 Magic the Gathering Return to Ravnica

COMPLETE SET (287) 175.00 300.00
BOOSTER BOX (36 PACKS) 80.00 120.00
BOOSTER PACK (15 CARDS) 3.00 4.00
*FOIL: .75X TO 2X BASIC CARDS
RELEASED ON OCTOBER 5, 2012
1 Angel of Serenity M :W: 3.00 8.00
2 Armory Guard C :W: .10 .25
3 Arrest U :W: .20 .50
4 Avenging Arrow C :W: .10 .25
5 Azorius Arrester C :W: .10 .25
6 Azorius Justiciar U :W: .20 .50
7 Bazaar Krovod U :W: .20 .50
8 Concordia Pegasus C :W: .10 .25
9 Ethereal Armor C :W: .10 .25
10 Eyes in the Skies C :W: .10 .25
11 Fencing Ace U :W: .20 .50
12 Keening Apparition C :W: .10 .25
13 Knightly Valor C :W: .10 .25
14 Martial Law R :W: .40 1.00
15 Palisade Giant R :W: .40 1.00
16 Phantom General U :W: .20 .50
17 Precinct Captain R :W: .75 2.00
18 Rest in Peace R :W: 1.00 2.50
19 Rootborn Defenses C :W: .10 .25
20 Security Blockade U :W: .20 .50
21 Selesnya Sentry C :W: .10 .25
22 Seller of Songbirds C :W: .10 .25
23 Soul Tithe U :W: .20 .50
24 Sphere of Safety U :W: .20 .50
25 Sunspire Griffin C :W: .10 .25
26 Swift Justice C :W: .10 .25
27 Trained Caracal C :W: .10 .25
28 Trostani's Judgment C :W: .10 .25
29 Aquus Steed U :B: .20 .50
30 Blustersquall U :B: .20 .50
31 Cancel C :B: .10 .25
32 Chronic Flooding C :B: .10 .25
33 Conjured Currency R :B: .40 1.00
34 Crosstown Courier C :B: .10 .25
35 Cyclonic Rift R :B: 1.50 4.00
36 Dispel C :B: .10 .25
37 Doorkeeper C :B: .10 .25
38 Downsize C :B: .10 .25
39 Faerie Impostor U :B: .20 .50
40 Hover Barrier U :B: .20 .50
41 Inaction Injunction C :B: .10 .25
42 Inspiration C :B: .10 .25
43 Isperia's Skywatch C :B: .10 .25
44 Jace, Architect M :B: 10.00 25.00
45 Mizzium Skin C :B: .10 .25
46 Paralyzing Grasp C :B: .10 .25
47 Psychic Spiral U :B: .20 .50
48 Runewing C :B: .10 .25
49 Search the City R :B: .40 1.00
50 Skyline Predator U :B: .20 .50
51 Soulsworn Spirit U :B: .20 .50
52 Sphinx of the Chimes R :B: .40 1.00
53 Stealer of Secrets C :B: .10 .25
54 Syncopate U :B: .20 .50
55 Tower Drake C :B: .10 .25
56 Voidwielder C :B: .10 .25
57 Assassin's Strike U :K: .20 .50
58 Catacomb Slug C :K: .10 .25
59 Cremate C :K: .10 .25
60 Daggerdrome Imp C :K: .10 .25
61 Dark Revenant U :K: .20 .50
62 Dead Reveler C :K: .10 .25
63 Desecration Demon R :K: 1.25 3.00
64 Destroy the Evidence C :K: .10 .25
65 Deviant Glee C :K: .10 .25
66 Drainpipe Vermin C :K: .10 .25
67 Grave Betrayal R :K: .40 1.00
68 Grim Roustabout C :K: .10 .25
69 Launch Party C :K: .10 .25
70 Mind Rot C :K: .10 .25
71 Necropolis Regent M :K: .75 2.00
72 Ogre Jailbreaker C :K: .10 .25
73 Pack Rat R :K: .40 1.00
74 Perilous Shadow C :K: .10 .25
75 Sewer Shambler C :K: .10 .25
76 Shrieking Affliction U :K: .20 .50
77 Slum Reaper U :K: .20 .50
78 Stab Wound C :K: .10 .25
79 Tavern Swindler U :K: .20 .50
80 Terrus Wurm C :K: .10 .25
81 Thrill-Kill Assassin U :K: .20 .50
82 Ultimate Price U :K: .40 1.00
83 Underworld Connections R :K: .60 1.50
84 Zanikev Locust U :K: .20 .50
85 Annihilating Fire C :R: .10 .25
86 Ash Zealot R :R: 2.50 6.00
87 Batterhorn C :R: .10 .25
88 Bellows Lizard C :R: .10 .25
89 Bloodfray Giant U :R: .20 .50
90 Chaos Imps R :R: .40 1.00
91 Cobblebrute C :R: .10 .25
92 Dynacharge C :R: .10 .25
93 Electrickery C :R: .10 .25
94 Explosive Impact C :R: .10 .25
95 Goblin Rally U :R: .20 .50
96 Gore-House Chainwalker C :R: .10 .25
97 Guild Feud R :R: .40 1.00
98 Guttersnipe U :R: .50 1.25
99 Lobber Crew C :R: .10 .25
100 Minotaur Aggressor U :R: .20 .50
101 Mizzium Mortars R :R: 1.50 4.00
102 Pursuit of Flight C :R: .10 .25
103 Pyroconvergence U :R: .20 .50
104 Racecourse Fury U :R: .20 .50
105 Splatter Thug C :R: .10 .25
106 Street Spasm U :R: .20 .50
107 Survey the Wreckage C :R: .10 .25
108 Tenement Crasher C :R: .10 .25
109 Traitorous Instinct C :R: .10 .25
110 Utvara Hellkite M :R: 1.00 2.50
111 Vandalblast U :R: .20 .50
112 Viashino Racketeer C :R: .10 .25
113 Aerial Predation C :G: .10 .25
114 Archweaver U :G: .20 .50
115 Axebane Guardian C :G: .10 .25
116 Axebane Stag C :G: .10 .25
117 Brushstrider U :G: .20 .50
118 Centaur's Herald C :G: .10 .25
119 Chorus of Might C :G: .10 .25
120 Deadbridge Goliath R :G: .40 1.00
121 Death's Presence R :G: .40 1.00
122 Drudge Beetle C :G: .10 .25
123 Druid's Deliverance C :G: .10 .25
124 Gatecreeper Vine C :G: .10 .25
125 Giant Growth C :G: .10 .25
126 Gobbling Ooze U :G: .20 .50
127 Golgari Decoy U :G: .20 .50
128 Horncaller's Chant C :G: .10 .25
129 Korozda Monitor C :G: .10 .25
130 Mana Bloom R :G: .40 1.00
131 Oak Street Innkeeper U :G: .20 .50
132 Rubbleback Rhino C :G: .10 .25
133 Savage Surge U :G: .20 .50
134 Seek the Horizon U :G: .20 .50
135 Slime Molding U :G: .20 .50
136 Stonefare Crocodile C :G: .10 .25
137 Towering Indrik C :G: .10 .25
138 Urban Burgeoning C :G: .10 .25
139 Wild Beastmaster R :G: .40 1.00
140 Worldspine Wurm M :G: 1.00 2.50
141 Abrupt Decay R :K/G: 3.00 8.00
142 Archon of the Triumvirate R :W: :B: .40 1.00
143 Armada Wurm M :W: :G: 1.50 4.00
144 Auger Spree C :K: :R: .10 .25
145 Azorius Charm U :W: :B: .50 1.25
146 Call of the Conclave U :W: :G: .40 1.00
147 Carnival Hellsteed R :K: :R: .40 1.00
148 Centaur Healer C :W: :G: .10 .25
149 Chemister's Trick C :B: :R: .10 .25
150 Collective Blessing R :W: :G: .40 1.00
151 Common Bond C :W: :G: .10 .25
152 Corpsejack Menace R :K: :G: .75 2.00
153 Counterflux R :B: :R: .75 2.00
154 Coursers' Accord C :W: :G: .10 .25
155 Detention Sphere R :W: :B: 1.50 4.00
156 Dramatic Rescue C :W: :B: .10 .25
157 Dreadbore R :K: :R: 2.00 5.00
158a Dreg Mangler U :K: :G: .40 1.00
158b Dreg Mangler ALT ART 1.50 4.00
159 Epic Experiment M :B: :R: 1.25 3.00
160 Essence Backlash C :B: :R: .10 .25
161 Fall of the Gavel U :W: :B: .20 .50
162 Firemind's Foresight R :B: :R: .40 1.00
163 Goblin Electromancer C :B: :R: .10 .25
164 Golgari Charm U :K: :G: .20 .50
165 Grisly Salvage C :K: :G: .10 .25
166 Havoc Festival R :K: :R: .40 1.00
167 Hellhole Flailer U :K: :R: .20 .50
168 Heroes' Reunion U :W: :G: .20 .50
169 Hussar Patrol C :W: :B: .10 .25
170 Hypersonic Dragon R :B: :R: .40 1.00
171 Isperia, Supreme M :W/B: 1.25 3.00
172 Izzet Charm U :B: :R: .40 1.00
173 Izzet Staticaster U :B: :R: .20 .50
174 Jarad, Golgari M :K/G: .75 2.00
175 Jarad's Orders R :K: :G: .40 1.00
176 Korozda Guildmage U :K: :G: .20 .50
177 Lotleth Troll R :K: :G: 1.50 4.00
178 Loxodon Smiter R :W: :G: 2.00 5.00
179 Lyev Skyknight U :W: :B: .20 .50
180 Mercurial Chemister R :B: :R: .40 1.00
181 New Prahv Guildmage U :W: :B: .20 .50
182 Nivix Guildmage U :B: :R: .20 .50
183 Niv-Mizzet M :B/R: 2.00 5.00
184 Rakdos Charm U :K: :R: .20 .50
185 Rakdos Ragemutt U :K: :R: .20 .50
186 Rakdos Ringleader U :K: :R: .20 .50
187 Rakdos, Lord of Riots M :K: :R: 2.00 5.00
188 Rakdos's Return M :K: :R: 2.50 6.00
189 Righteous Authority R :W: :B: .40 1.00
190 Risen Sanctuary U :W: :G: .20 .50
191 Rites of Reaping U :K: :G: .20 .50
192 Rix Maadi Guildmage U :K: :R: .20 .50
193 Search Warrant C :W: :B: .10 .25
194 Selesnya Charm U :W: :G: .50 1.25
195 Skull Rend C :K: :R: .10 .25
196 Skymark Roc U :W: :B: .20 .50
197 Slaughter Games R :K: :R: .75 2.00
198 Sluiceway Scorpion C :K: :G: .10 .25
199 Spawn of Rix Maadi C :K: :R: .10 .25
200 Sphinx's Revelation M :W: :B: 10.00 25.00
201 Supreme Verdict R :W: :B: 2.50 6.00
202 Teleportal U :B: :R: .20 .50
203 Thoughtflare U :B: :R: .20 .50
204 Treasured Find U :K: :G: .20 .50
205 Trestle Troll C :K: :G: .10 .25
206 Trostani, Selesnya's M :W/G: 3.00 8.00
207 Vitu-Ghazi Guildmage U :W: :G: .20 .50
208 Vraska the Unseen M :K: :G: 4.00 10.00
209 Wayfaring Temple R :W: :G: .60 1.50
210 Azor's Elocutors R :W: :B: .40 1.00
211 Blistercoil Weird U :B: :R: .20 .50
212 Cryptborn Horror R :K: :R: .40 1.00
213 Deathrite Shaman R :K: :G: 6.00 15.00
214 Dryad Militant U :W: :G: .40 1.00
215 Frostburn Weird C :B: :R: .10 .25
216 Golgari Longlegs C :K: :G: .10 .25
217 Growing Ranks R :W: :G: .75 2.00
218 Judge's Familiar U :W: :B: .40 1.00
219 Nivmagus Elemental R :B: :R: .60 1.50
220 Rakdos Cackler U :K: :R: .40 1.00
221 Rakdos Shred-Freak C :K: :R: .10 .25
222 Slitherhead U :K: :G: .20 .50
223 Sundering Growth C :W: :G: .10 .25
224 Vassal Soul C :W: :B: .10 .25
225 Azorius Keyrune U .20 .50
226 Chromatic Lantern R 2.00 5.00
227 Civic Saber U .20 .50
228 Codex Shredder U .20 .50
229 Golgari Keyrune U .20 .50
230 Izzet Keyrune U .20 .50
231 Pithing Needle R .60 1.50
232 Rakdos Keyrune U .20 .50
233 Selesnya Keyrune U .20 .50
234 Street Sweeper U .20 .50
235 Tablet of the Guilds U .20 .50
236 Volatile Rig R .40 1.00
237 Azorius Guildgate C .10 .25
238 Blood Crypt R 6.00 15.00
239 Golgari Guildgate C .10 .25
240 Grove of the Guardian R .40 1.00
241 Hallowed Fountain R 5.00 12.00
242 Izzet Guildgate C .10 .25
243 Overgrown Tomb R 6.00 15.00
244 Rakdos Guildgate C .10 .25
245 Rogue's Passage U .20 .50
246 Selesnya Guildgate C .10 .25
247 Steam Vents R 4.00 10.00
248 Temple Garden R 6.00 15.00
249 Transguild Promenade C .10 .25
250 Plains L .10 .25
251 Plains L .10 .25
252 Plains L .10 .25
253 Plains L .10 .25
254 Plains L .10 .25
255 Island L .10 .25
256 Island L .10 .25
257 Island L .10 .25
258 Island L .10 .25
259 Island L .10 .25
260 Swamp L .10 .25
261 Swamp L .10 .25
262 Swamp L .10 .25
263 Swamp L .10 .25
264 Swamp L .10 .25
265 Mountain L .10 .25
266 Mountain L .10 .25
267 Mountain L .10 .25
268 Mountain L .10 .25
269 Mountain L .10 .25
270 Forest L .10 .25
271 Forest L .10 .25
272 Forest L .10 .25
273 Forest L .10 .25
274 Forest L .10 .25
T1 Bird .20 .50
T2 Knight .20 .50
T3 Soldier .20 .50
T4 Assassin .60 1.50
T5 Dragon .60 1.50
T6 Goblin .20 .50
T7 Centaur .20 .50
T8 Ooze .20 .50
T9 Rhino .20 .50
T10 Saproling .20 .50
T11 Wurm .60 1.50
T12 Elemental .40 1.00

2013 Magic The Gathering Gatecrash

COMPLETE SET (249) 175.00 300.00
BOOSTER BOX (36 PACKS) 60.00 80.00
BOOSTER PACK (15 CARDS) 2.00 3.00
*FOIL: .75X TO 2X BASIC CARDS
RELEASED ON FEBRUARY 1, 2013
1 Aerial Maneuver C :W: .10 .25
2 Angelic Edict C :W: .20 .50
3 Angelic Skirmisher R :W: .60 1.50
4 Assault Griffin C :W: .10 .25
5 Basilica Guards C :W: .10 .25
6 Blind Obedience R :W: 2.50 6.00
7 Boros Elite U :W: .20 .50
8 Court Street Denizen C :W: .10 .25
9 Daring Skyjek C :W: .10 .25
10 Debtor's Pulpit U :W: .20 .50
11 Dutiful Thrull C :W: .10 .25
12 Frontline Medic R :W: 3.00 8.00
13 Gideon, Champion of Justice M :W: 4.00 10.00
14 Guardian of the Gateless U :W: .20 .50
15 Guildscorn Ward C :W: .10 .25
16 Hold the Gates U :W: .20 .50
17 Holy Mantle U :W: .20 .50
18 Knight of Obligation U :W: .20 .50
19 Knight Watch C :W: .10 .25
20 Luminate Primordial R :W: .40 1.00
21 Murder Investigation U :W: .20 .50
22 Nav Squad Commandos C :W: .10 .25
23 Righteous Charge U :W: .20 .50
24 Shielded Passage C :W: .10 .25
25 Smite C :W: .10 .25
26 Syndic of Tithes C :W: .10 .25
27 Urbis Protector U :W: .20 .50
28 Zarichi Tiger C :W: .10 .25
29 AEtherize U :B: .20 .50
30 Agoraphobia U :B: .20 .50
31 Clinging Anemones C :B: .10 .25
32 Cloudfin Raptor C :B: .10 .25
33 Diluvian Primordial R :B: .40 1.00
34 Enter the Infinite M :B: 1.25 3.00
35 Frilled Oculus C :B: .20 .50
36 Gridlock U :B: .20 .50
37 Hands of Binding C :B: .10 .25
38 Incursion Specialist U :B: .20 .50
39 Keymaster Rogue C :B: .10 .25
40 Last Thoughts C :B: .10 .25
41 Leyline Phantom C :B: .10 .25
42 Metropolis Sprite C :B: .10 .25
43 Mindeye Drake U :B: .20 .50
44 Rapid Hybridization U :B: .20 .50
45 Realmwright R :B: .75 2.00
46 Sage's Row Denizen C :B: .10 .25
47 Sapphire Drake U :B: .20 .50
48 Scatter Arc C :B: .10 .25
49 Simic Fluxmage U :B: .20 .50
50 Simic Manipulator R :B: .60 1.50
51 Skygames C :B: .10 .25
52 Spell Rupture C :B: .10 .25
53 Stolen Identity R :B: .40 1.00
54 Totally Lost C :B: .10 .25
55 Voidwalk U :B: .20 .50
56 Way of the Thief C :B: .10 .25
57 Balustrade Spy C :K: .10 .25
58 Basilica Screecher C :K: .10 .25
59 Contaminated Ground C :K: .10 .25
60 Corpse Blockade C :K: .10 .25
61 Crypt Ghast R :K: 1.25 3.00
62 Death's Approach C :K: .10 .25
63 Devour Flesh C :K: .10 .25
64 Dying Wish U :K: .20 .50
65 Gateway Shade U :K: .20 .50
66 Grisly Spectacle C :K: .10 .25
67 Gutter Skulk C :K: .10 .25
68 Horror of the Dim C :K: .10 .25
69 Illness in the Ranks U :K: .20 .50
70 Killing Glare U :K: .20 .50
71 Lord of the Void M :K: 1.25 3.00
72 Mental Vapors U :K: .20 .50
73 Midnight Recovery C :K: .20 .50
74 Ogre Slumlord R :K: .40 1.00
75 Sepulchral Primordial R :K: .40 1.00
76 Shadow Alley Denizen C :K: .10 .25
77 Shadow Slice C :K: .10 .25
78 Slate Street Ruffian C :K: .10 .25
79 Smog Elemental U :K: .20 .50
80 Syndicate Enforcer C :K: .10 .25
81 Thrull Parasite U :K: .20 .50
82 Undercity Informer U :K: .20 .50
83 Undercity Plague R :K: .40 1.00
84 Wight of Precinct Six U :K: .20 .50
85 Act of Treason C :R: .10 .25
86 Bomber Corps C :R: .10 .25
87 Cinder Elemental U :R: .20 .50
88 Crackling Perimeter U :R: .20 .50
89 Ember Beast C :R: .10 .25
90 Firefist Striker U :R: .20 .50
91 Five-Alarm Fire R :R: .40 1.00
92 Foundry Street Denizen C :R: .10 .25
93 Furious Resistance C :R: .10 .25
94 Hellkite Tyrant M :R: 1.00 2.50
95 Hellraiser Goblin U :R: .20 .50
96 Homing Lightning U :R: .20 .50
97 Legion Loyalist R :R: 2.50 6.00
98 Madcap Skills C :R: .10 .25
99 Mark for Death U :R: .20 .50
100 Massive Raid C :R: .10 .25
101 Molten Primordial R :R: .40 1.00
102 Mugging C :R: .10 .25
103 Ripscale Predator U :R: .20 .50
104 Scorchwalker C :R: .10 .25
105 Skinbrand Goblin C :R: .10 .25
106 Skullcrack U :R: .75 2.00
107 Structural Collapse C :R: .10 .25
108 Tin Street Market C :R: .10 .25
109 Towering Thunderfist C :R: .10 .25
110 Viashino Shanktail U :R: .20 .50
111 Warmind Infantry C :R: .10 .25
112 Wrecking Ogre R :R: .40 1.00
113 Adaptive Snapjaw C :G: .10 .25
114 Alpha Authority U :G: .20 .50
115 Burst of Strength C :G: .10 .25
116 Crocanura C :G: .10 .25
117 Crowned Ceratok U :G: .20 .50
118 Disciple of the Old Ways C :G: .10 .25
119 Experiment One U :G: .30 .75
120 Forced Adaptation C :G: .10 .25
121 Giant Adephage M :G: 1.25 3.00
122 Greenside Watcher C :G: .10 .25
123 Gyre Sage R :G: 1.00 2.50
124 Hindervines U :G: .20 .50
125 Ivy Lane Denizen C :G: .10 .25
126 Miming Slime U :G: .20 .50
127 Naturalize C :G: .10 .25
128 Ooze Flux R :G: .40 1.00
129 Predator's Rapport C :G: .10 .25
130 Rust Scarab U :G: .20 .50
131 Scab-Clan Charger C :G: .10 .25
132 Serene Remembrance U :G: .20 .50
133 Skarrg Goliath R :G: .40 1.00
134 Slaughterhorn C :G: .10 .25
135 Spire Tracer C :G: .10 .25
136 Sylvan Primordial R :G: .75 2.00
137 Tower Defense U :G: .20 .50
138 Verdant Haven C :G: .10 .25
139 Wasteland Viper U :G: .20 .50
140 Wildwood Rebirth C :G: .10 .25
141 Alms Beast R :W: :K: .40 1.00
142 Assemble the Legion R :W: :R: .75 2.00
143 Aurelia, the Warleader M :W: :R: 4.00 10.00
144 Aurelia's Fury M :W: :R: 2.50 6.00
145 Bane Alley Broker U :B: :K: .20 .50
146 Biovisionary R :B: :G: .40 1.00
147 Borborygmos Enraged M :R: :G: 1.50 4.00
148 Boros Charm U :W: :R: 1.50 4.00
149 Call of the Nightwing U :B: :K: .20 .50
150 Cartel Aristocrat U :W: :K: .20 .50
151 Clan Defiance R :R: :G: 1.25 3.00
152 Consuming Aberration R :B: :K: .75 2.00
153 Deathpact Angel M :W: :K: 2.00 5.00
154 Dimir Charm U :B: :K: .30 .75
155 Dinrova Horror U :B: :K: .20 .50
156 Domri Rade M :R: :G: 8.00 20.00
157 Drakewing Krasis C :B: :G: .10 .25
158 Duskmantle Guildmage U :B: :K: .20 .50
159 Duskmantle Seer M :B: :K: 3.00 8.00
160 Elusive Krasis U :B: :G: .20 .50
161 Executioner's Swing C :W: :K: .10 .25
162 Fathom Mage R :B: :G: .60 1.50
163 Firemane Avenger R :W: :R: 1.25 3.00
164 Fortress Cyclops U :W: :R: .20 .50
165 Foundry Champion R :W: :R: .40 1.00
166 Frenzied Tilling U :R: :G: .20 .50
167 Ghor-Clan Rampager U :R: :G: .30 .75
168 Ground Assault U :R: :G: .20 .50
169 Gruul Charm U :R: :G: .20 .50
170 Gruul Ragebeast R :R: :G: .40 1.00
171 High Priest of Penance R :W: :K: 1.25 3.00
172 Hydroform C :B: :G: .10 .25
173 Kingpin's Pet C :W: :K: .10 .25
174 Lazav, Dimir Mastermind M :B: :K: 3.00 8.00
175 Martial Glory C :W: :R: .10 .25
176 Master Biomancer M :B: :G: 4.00 10.00
177 Merciless Eviction R :W: :K: .75 2.00
178 Mind Grind R :B: :K: 1.25 3.00
179 Mortus Strider C :B: :K: .10 .25
180 Mystic Genesis R :B: :G: .40 1.00
181 Nimbus Swimmer U :B: :G: .20 .50
182 Obzedat, Ghost Council M :W: :K: 5.00 12.00
183 One Thousand Lashes U :W: :K: .20 .50
184 Ordruun Veteran U :W: :R: .20 .50
185 Orzhov Charm U :W: :K: .40 1.00
186 Paranoid Delusions C :B: :K: .10 .25
187 Primal Visitation C :R: :G: .10 .25
188 Prime Speaker Zegana M :B: :G: 5.00 12.00
189 Psychic Strike C :B: :K: .10 .25
190 Purge the Profane C :W: :K: .10 .25
191 Rubblehulk R :R: :G: .40 1.00
192 Ruination Wurm C :R: :G: .10 .25
193 Shambleshark C :B: :G: .10 .25
194 Signal the Clans R :R: :G: .60 1.50
195 Simic Charm U :B: :G: .40 1.00
196 Skarrg Guildmage U :R: :G: .20 .50
197 Skyknight Legionnaire C :W: :R: .10 .25
198 Soul Ransom R :B: :K: .60 1.50
199 Spark Trooper R :W: :R: 1.25 3.00
200 Sunhome Guildmage U :W: :R: .20 .50
201 Treasury Thrull R :W: :K: .40 1.00
202 Truefire Paladin U :W: :R: .20 .50
203 Unexpected Results R :B: :G: .75 2.00
204 Urban Evolution U :B: :G: .20 .50
205 Vizkopa Confessor U :W: :K: .20 .50
206 Vizkopa Guildmage U :W: :K: .20 .50
207 Whispering Madness R :B: :K: .60 1.50
208 Wojek Halberdiers C :W: :R: .10 .25
209 Zameck Guildmage U :B: :G: .20 .50
210 Zhur-Taa Swine C :R: :G: .10 .25
211 Arrows of Justice U :W: :R: .20 .50
212 Beckon Apparition C :W: :K: .10 .25
213 Biomass Mutation R :B: :G: .40 1.00
214 Bioshift C :B: :G: .10 .25
215 Boros Reckoner R :W: :R: 8.00 20.00
216 Burning-Tree Emissary U :R: :G: .60 1.50
217 Coerced Confession U :B: :K: .20 .50
218 Deathcult Rogue C :B: :K: .10 .25
219 Gift of Orzhova U :W: :K: .20 .50
220 Immortal Servitude R :W: :K: .75 2.00
221 Merfolk of the Depths U :B: :G: .20 .50
222 Nightveil Specter R :B: :K: .75 2.00
223 Pit Fight C :R: :G: .10 .25
224 Rubblebelt Raiders R :R: :G: .75 2.00
225 Shattering Blow C :W: :R: .10 .25
226 Armored Transport C .10 .25
227 Boros Keyrune U .20 .50
228 Dimir Keyrune U .20 .50
229 Glaring Spotlight R .75 2.00
230 Gruul Keyrune U .20 .50
231 Illusionist's Bracers R .75 2.00
232 Millennial Gargoyle C .10 .25
233 Orzhov Keyrune U .20 .50
234 Prophetic Prism C .10 .25
235 Razortip Whip C .10 .25
236 Riot Gear C .10 .25
237 Simic Keyrune U .20 .50
238 Skyblinder Staff C .10 .25
239 Boros Guildgate C .20 .50
240 Breeding Pool R 6.00 15.00
241 Dimir Guildgate C .10 .25
242 Godless Shrine R 6.00 15.00
243 Gruul Guildgate C .10 .25
244 Orzhov Guildgate C .10 .25
245 Sacred Foundry R 8.00 20.00
246 Simic Guildgate C .10 .25
247 Stomping Ground R 5.00 12.00
248 Thespian's Stage R 2.00 5.00
249 Watery Grave R 6.00 15.00
T1 Angel .10 .25
T2 Rat .10 .25
T3 Frog Lizard .10 .25
T4 Cleric .60 1.50
T5 Horror .10 .25
T6 Soldier .10 .25
T7 Spirit .10 .25
T8 Emblem: Domri Rade .40 1.00

2013 Magic The Gathering Commander Oversized Foil

COMPLETE SET (158) 175.00 250.00
*FOIL: .75X TO 2X BASIC CARDS
RELEASED ON MAY 3, 2013
1 Boros Mastiff C :W: .10 .25
2 Haazda Snare Squad C :W: .10 .25
3 Lyev Decree C :W: .10 .25
4 Maze Sentinel C :W: .10 .25
5 Renounce the Guilds R :W: .50 1.25
6 Riot Control C :W: .10 .25
7 Scion of Vitu-Ghazi R :W: .40 1.00
8 Steeple Roc C :W: .10 .25
9 Sunspire Gatekeepers C :W: .10 .25

Card	Low	High
10 Wake the Reflections C :W:	.10	.25
11 AEtherling R :B:	1.50	4.00
12 Hidden Strings C :B:	.10	.25
13 Maze Glider C :B:	.10	.25
14 Mindstatic C :B:	.10	.25
15 Murmuring Phantasm C :B:	.10	.25
16 Opal Lake Gatekeepers C :B:	.10	.25
17 Runner's Bane C :B:	.10	.25
18 Trait Doctoring R :B:	.30	.75
19 Uncovered Clues C :B:	.10	.25
20 Wind Drake C :B:	.10	.25
21 Bane Alley Blackguard C :K:	.10	.25
22 Blood Scrivener R :K:	1.50	4.00
23 Crypt Incursion C :K:	.10	.25
24 Fatal Fumes C :K:	.10	.25
25 Hired Torturer C :K:	.10	.25
26 Maze Abomination C :K:	.10	.25
27 Pontiff of Blight R :K:	.30	.75
28 Rakdos Drake C :K:	.10	.25
29 Sinister Possession C :K:	.10	.25
30 Ubul Sar Gatekeepers C :K:	.10	.25
31 Awe for the Guilds C :R:	.10	.25
32 Clear a Path C :R:	.10	.25
33 Maze Rusher C :R:	.10	.25
34 Possibility Storm R :R:	.30	.75
35 Punish the Enemy C :R:	.10	.25
36 Pyrewild Shaman R :R:	.50	1.25
37 Riot Piker C :R:	.10	.25
38 Rubblebelt Maaka C :R:	.10	.25
39 Smelt-Ward Gatekeepers C :R:	.10	.25
40 Weapon Surge C :R:	.10	.25
41 Battering Krasis C :G:	.10	.25
42 Kraul Warrior C :G:	.10	.25
43 Maze Behemoth C :G:	.10	.25
44 Mending Touch C :G:	.10	.25
45 Mutant's Prey C :G:	.10	.25
46 Phytoburst C :G:	.10	.25
47 Renegade Krasis R :G:	.30	.75
48 Saruli Gatekeepers C :G:	.10	.25
49 Skylasher R :G:	.75	2.00
50 Thrashing Mossdog C :G:	.10	.25
51 Advent of the Wurm R :W/G:	3.00	8.00
52 Armored Wolf-Rider C :W/G:	.10	.25
53 Ascended Lawmage U :W/B:	.15	.40
54 Beetleform Mage C :B/G:	.10	.25
55 Blast of Genius U :B/R:	.15	.40
56 Blaze Commando U :W/R:	.15	.40
57 Blood Baron of Vizkopa M :W/K:	4.00	10.00
58 Boros Battleshaper R :W/R:	.30	.75
59 Bred for the Hunt U :B/G:	.15	.40
60 Bronzebeak Moa U :W/G:	.15	.40
61 Carnage Gladiator U :K/R:	.15	.40
62 Council of the Absolute M :W/B:	1.50	4.00
63 Deadbridge Chant M :K/G:	3.00	8.00
64 Debt to the Deathless U :W/K:	.15	.40
65 Deputy of Acquittals C :W/B:	.10	.25
66 Dragonshift R :B/R:	.30	.75
67 Drown in Filth C :K/G:	.10	.25
68 Emmara Tandris R :W/G:	.30	.75
69 Exava, Rakdos Blood Witch R :K/R:	.60	1.50
70 Feral Animist U :R/G:	.15	.40
71 Fluxcharger U :B/R:	.15	.40
72 Gaze of Granite R :K/G:	.75	2.00
73 Gleam of Battle U :W/R:	.15	.40
74 Goblin Test Pilot U :B/R:	.15	.40
75 Gruul War Chant U :R/G:	.15	.40
76 Haunter of Nightveil U :B/K:	.15	.40
77 Jelenn Sphinx U :W/B:	.15	.40
78 Korozda Gorgon U :K/G:	.15	.40
79 Krasis Incubation U :B/G:	.15	.40
80 Lavinia of the Tenth R :W/B:	.40	1.00
81 Legion's Initiative M :W/R:	3.00	8.00
82 Master of Cruelties M :K/R:	3.00	8.00
83 Maw of the Obzedat U :W/K:	.15	.40
84 Melek, Izzet Paragon R :B/R:	.30	.75
85 Mirko Vosk, Mind Drinker R :B/K:	.50	1.25
86 Morgue Burst C :K/R:	.10	.25
87 Nivix Cyclops C :B/R:	.10	.25
88 Notion Thief R :B/K:	1.00	2.50
89 Obzedat's Aid R :W/K:	.60	1.50
90 Pilfered Plans C :B/K:	.10	.25
91 Plasm Capture R :B/G:	1.25	3.00
92 Progenitor Mimic M :B/G:	2.00	5.00
93 Putrefy U :K/G:	.30	.75
94 Ral Zarek M :B/R:	6.00	15.00
95 Reap Intellect M :B/K:	.60	1.50
96 Render Silent R :W/B:	1.00	2.50
97 Restore the Peace U :W/B:	.15	.40
98 Rot Farm Skeleton U :K/G:	.15	.40
99 Ruric Thar, the Unbowed R :R/G:	.60	1.50
100 Savageborn Hydra M :R/G:	2.00	5.00
101 Scab-Clan Giant U :R/G:	.15	.40
102 Showstopper U :K/R:	.15	.40
103 Sin Collector U :W/K:	.30	.75
104 Sire of Insanity R :K/R:	1.50	4.00
105 Species Gorger U :B/G:	.15	.40
106 Spike Jester U :K/R:	.15	.40
107 Tajic, Blade of the Legion R :W/R:	1.00	2.50
108 Teysa, Envoy of Ghosts R :W/K:	.50	1.25
109 Tithe Drinker C :W/K:	.10	.25
110 Trostani's Summoner U :W/G:	.15	.40
111 Unflinching Courage U :W/G:	.30	.75
112 Varolz, the Scar-Striped R :K/G:	1.50	4.00
113 Viashino Firstblade C :W/R:	.10	.25
114 Voice of Resurgence M :W/G:	20.00	40.00
115 Vorel of the Hull Clade R :B/G:	.60	1.50
116 Warleader's Helix U :W/R:	.30	.75
117 Warped Physique U :B/K:	.15	.40
118 Woodlot Crawler U :B/K:	.15	.40
119 Zhur-Taa Ancient R :R/G:	.30	.75
120 Zhur-Taa Druid C :R/G:	.10	.25
121 Alive/Well U :G/W:	.15	.40
122 Armed/Dangerous U :R/G:	.15	.40
123 Beck/Call R :B/G/W:	1.00	2.50
124 Breaking/Entering R :B/K/R:	.50	1.25
125 Catch/Release R :B/R/W:	.30	.75
126 Down/Dirty U :K/G:	.15	.40
127 Far/Away U :B/K:	.30	.75
128 Flesh/Blood R :K/G/R:	.30	.75
129 Give/Take U :G/B:	.15	.40
130 Profit/Loss U :W/K:	.15	.40
131 Protect/Serve U :W/B:	.15	.40
132 Ready/Willing R :W/G/K:	.60	1.50
133 Toil/Trouble U :K/R:	.15	.40
134 Turn/Burn U :B/R:	.30	.75
135 Wear/Tear U :R/W:	.15	.40
136 Azorius Cluestone C	.10	.25
137 Boros Cluestone C	.10	.25
138 Dimir Cluestone C	.10	.25
139 Golgari Cluestone C	.10	.25
140 Gruul Cluestone C	.10	.25
141 Izzet Cluestone C	.10	.25
142 Orzhov Cluestone C	.10	.25
143 Rakdos Cluestone C	.10	.25
144 Selesnya Cluestone C	.10	.25
145 Simic Cluestone C	.10	.25
146 Azorius Guildgate C	.10	.25
147 Boros Guildgate C	.10	.25
148 Dimir Guildgate C	.10	.25
149 Golgari Guildgate C	.10	.25
150 Gruul Guildgate C	.10	.25
151 Izzet Guildgate C	.10	.25
152 Maze's End M	1.25	3.00
153 Orzhov Guildgate C	.10	.25
154 Rakdos Guildgate C	.10	.25
155 Selesnya Guildgate C	.10	.25
156 Simic Guildgate C	.10	.25
T1 Bird	.10	.25
T2 Elemental	.10	.25

2013 Magic The Gathering Magic 2014

Card	Low	High
COMPLETE SET (249)	200.00	300.00
BOOSTER BOX (36 PACKS)	80.00	90.00
BOOSTER PACK (15 CARDS)	3.00	4.00
FAT PACK	40.00	60.00
*FOIL: .75X TO 2X BASIC CARDS		
1 Ajani, Caller of the Pride M :W:	3.00	8.00
2 Ajani's Chosen R :W:	.30	.75
3 Angelic Accord U :W:	.20	.50
4 Angelic Wall C :W:	.10	.25
5 Archangel of Thune M :W:	12.00	30.00
6 Auramancer C :W:	.10	.25
7 Banisher Priest U :W:	.30	.75
8 Blessing U :W:	.15	.40
9 Bonescythe Sliver R :W:	1.25	3.00
10 Brave the Elements U :W:	.20	.50
11 Capashen Knight C :W:	.10	.25
12 Celestial Flare C :W:	.10	.25
13 Charging Griffin C :W:	.10	.25
14 Congregate U :W:	.15	.40
15 Dawnstrike Paladin C :W:	.10	.25
16 Devout Invocation M :W:	1.00	2.50
17 Divine Favor C :W:	.10	.25
18 Fiendslayer Paladin R :W:	3.00	8.00
19 Fortify C :W:	.10	.25
20 Griffin Sentinel C :W:	.10	.25
21 Hive Stirrings C :W:	.10	.25
22 Imposing Sovereign R :W:	1.50	4.00
23 Indestructibility R :W:	.30	.75
24 Master of Diversion C :W:	.10	.25
25 Pacifism C :W:	.10	.25
26 Path of Bravery R :W:	.60	1.50
27 Pay No Heed C :W:	.10	.25
28 Pillarfield Ox C :W:	.10	.25
29 Planar Cleansing R :W:	.30	.75
30 Sentinel Sliver C :W:	.10	.25
31 Seraph of the Sword R :W:	.60	1.50
32 Serra Angel U :W:	.15	.40
33 Show of Valor C :W:	.10	.25
34 Siege Mastodon C :W:	.10	.25
35 Silence R :W:	.40	1.00
36 Solemn Offering C :W:	.10	.25
37 Soulmender C :W:	.10	.25
38 Steelform Sliver U :W:	.20	.50
39 Stonehorn Chanter U :W:	.15	.40
40 Suntail Hawk C :W:	.10	.25
41 Wall of Swords U :W:	.15	.40
42 Air Servant U :B:	.15	.40
43 Archaeomancer C :B:	.10	.25
44 Armored Cancrix C :B:	.10	.25
45 Cancel C :B:	.10	.25
46 Claustrophobia C :B:	.10	.25
47 Clone R :B:	.30	.75
48 Colossal Whale R :B:	.30	.75
49 Coral Merfolk C :B:	.10	.25
50 Dismiss into Dream R :B:	.30	.75
51 Disperse C :B:	.10	.25
52 Divination C :B:	.10	.25
53 Domestication R :B:	.30	.75
54 Elite Arcanist R :B:	.40	1.00
55 Essence Scatter C :B:	.10	.25
56 Frost Breath C :B:	.10	.25
57 Galerider Sliver R :B:	1.50	4.00
58 Glimpse the Future U :B:	.15	.40
59 Illusionary Armor U :B:	.15	.40
60 Jace, Memory Adept M :B:	3.00	8.00
61 Jace's Mindseeker R :B:	.30	.75
62 Merfolk Spy C :B:	.10	.25
63 Messenger Drake C :B:	.10	.25
64 Negate C :B:	.10	.25
65 Nephalia Seakite C :B:	.10	.25
66 Opportunity U :B:	.15	.40
67 Phantom Warrior U :B:	.15	.40
68 Quicken R :B:	.40	1.00
69 Scroll Thief C :B:	.10	.25
70 Seacoast Drake C :B:	.10	.25
71 Sensory Deprivation C :B:	.10	.25
72 Spell Blast U :B:	.15	.40
73 Tidebinder Mage R :B:	.60	1.50
74 Time Ebb C :B:	.10	.25
75 Tome Scour C :B:	.10	.25
76 Trained Condor C :B:	.10	.25
77 Traumatize R :B:	.40	1.00
78 Wall of Frost U :B:	.15	.40
79 Warden of Evos Isle U :B:	.15	.40
80 Water Servant U :B:	.15	.40
81 Windreader Sphinx M :B:	.75	2.00
82 Zephyr Charge C :B:	.10	.25
83 Accursed Spirit C :K:	.10	.25
84 Altar's Reap C :K:	.10	.25
85 Artificer's Hex U :K:	.15	.40
86 Blightcaster U :K:	.15	.40
87 Blood Bairn C :K:	.10	.25
88 Bogbrew Witch R :K:	.30	.75
89 Child of Night C :K:	.10	.25
90 Corpse Hauler C :K:	.10	.25
91 Corrupt U :K:	.15	.40
92 Dark Favor C :K:	.10	.25
93 Dark Prophecy R :K:	.40	1.00
94 Deathgaze Cockatrice C :K:	.10	.25
95 Diabolic Tutor U :K:	.15	.40
96 Doom Blade U :K:	.15	.40
97 Duress C :K:	.10	.25
98 Festering Newt C :K:	.10	.25
99 Gnawing Zombie U :K:	.15	.40
100 Grim Return R :K:	.60	1.50
101 Lifebane Zombie R :K:	3.00	8.00
102 Liliana of the Dark Realms M :K:	2.50	6.00
103 Liliana's Reaver R :K:	.60	1.50
104 Liturgy of Blood C :K:	.10	.25
105 Mark of the Vampire C :K:	.10	.25
106 Mind Rot C :K:	.10	.25
107 Minotaur Abomination C :K:	.10	.25
108 Nightmare R :K:	.30	.75
109 Nightwing Shade C :K:	.10	.25
110 Quag Sickness C :K:	.10	.25
111 Rise of the Dark Realms M :K:	1.25	3.00
112 Sanguine Bond R :K:	.75	2.00
113 Sengir Vampire U :K:	.15	.40
114 Shadowborn Apostle C :K:	.10	.25
115 Shadowborn Demon M :K:	3.00	8.00
116 Shrivel C :K:	.10	.25
117 Syphon Sliver R :K:	.60	1.50
118 Tenacious Dead U :K:	.15	.40
119 Undead Minotaur C :K:	.10	.25
120 Vampire Warlord U :K:	.15	.40
121 Vile Rebirth C :K:	.10	.25
122 Wring Flesh C :K:	.10	.25
123 Xathrid Necromancer R :K:	3.00	8.00
124 Academy Raider C :R:	.10	.25
125 Act of Treason C :R:	.10	.25
126 Awaken the Ancient R :R:	.30	.75
127 Barrage of Expendables U :R:	.15	.40
128 Battle Sliver U :R:	.20	.50
129 Blur Sliver C :R:	.10	.25
130 Burning Earth R :R:	1.25	3.00
131 Canyon Minotaur C :R:	.10	.25
132 Chandra, Pyromaster M :R:	6.00	15.00
133 Chandra's Outrage C :R:	.10	.25
134 Chandra's Phoenix R :R:	.60	1.50
135 Cyclops Tyrant C :R:	.10	.25
136 Demolish C :R:	.10	.25
137 Dragon Egg U :R:	.15	.40
138 Dragon Hatchling C :R:	.10	.25
139 Flames of the Firebrand U :R:	.15	.40
140 Fleshpulper Giant U :R:	.15	.40
141 Goblin Diplomats R :R:	.40	1.00
142 Goblin Shortcutter C :R:	.10	.25
143 Lava Axe C :R:	.10	.25
144 Lightning Talons C :R:	.10	.25
145 Marauding Maulhorn C :R:	.10	.25
146 Mindsparker R :R:	.75	2.00
147 Molten Birth U :R:	.15	.40
148 Ogre Battledriver R :R:	1.25	3.00
149 Pitchburn Devils C :R:	.10	.25
150 Regathan Firecat C :R:	.10	.25
151 Scourge of Valkas M :R:	2.50	6.00
152 Seismic Stomp C :R:	.10	.25
153 Shiv's Embrace U :R:	.15	.40
154 Shivan Dragon R :R:	.30	.75
155 Shock C :R:	.10	.25
156 Smelt C :R:	.10	.25
157 Striking Sliver C :R:	.10	.25
158 Thorncaster Sliver R :R:	.60	1.50
159 Thunder Strike C :R:	.10	.25
160 Volcanic Geyser U :R:	.15	.40
161 Wild Guess C :R:	.10	.25
162 Wild Ricochet R :R:	.30	.75
163 Young Pyromancer U :R:	.75	2.00
164 Advocate of the Beast C :G:	.10	.25
165 Bramblecrush U :G:	.15	.40
166 Briarpack Alpha U :G:	.15	.40
167 Brindle Boar C :G:	.10	.25
168 Deadly Recluse C :G:	.10	.25
169 Elvish Mystic C :G:	.20	.50
170 Enlarge U :G:	.15	.40
171 Fog C :G:	.10	.25
172 Garruk, Caller of Beasts M :G:	8.00	20.00
173 Garruk's Horde R :G:	.30	.75
174 Giant Growth C :G:	.10	.25
175 Giant Spider C :G:	.10	.25
176 Gladecover Scout C :G:	.10	.25
177 Groundshaker Sliver C :G:	.10	.25
178 Howl of the Night Pack U :G:	.15	.40
179 Hunt the Weak C :G:	.10	.25
180 Into the Wilds R :G:	.40	1.00
181 Kalonian Hydra M :G:	10.00	25.00
182 Kalonian Tusker U :G:	.20	.50
183 Lay of the Land C :G:	.10	.25
184 Manaweft Sliver U :G:	.60	1.50
185 Megantic Sliver R :G:	.60	1.50
186 Naturalize C :G:	.10	.25
187 Oath of the Ancient Wood R :G:	.30	.75
188 Plummet C :G:	.10	.25
189 Predatory Sliver C :G:	.40	1.00
190 Primeval Bounty M :G:	3.00	8.00
191 Ranger's Guile C :G:	.10	.25
192 Rootwalla C :G:	.10	.25
193 Rumbling Baloth C :G:	.10	.25
194 Savage Summoning R :G:	1.00	2.50
195 Scavenging Ooze R :G:	6.00	15.00
196 Sporemound C :G:	.10	.25
197 Trollhide C :G:	.10	.25
198 Vastwood Hydra R :G:	.40	1.00
199 Verdant Haven C :G:	.10	.25
200 Voracious Wurm U :G:	.20	.50
201 Windstorm U :G:	.15	.40
202 Witchstalker R :G:	2.00	5.00
203 Woodborn Behemoth U :G:	.15	.40
204 Accorder's Shield U	.15	.40
205 Bubbling Cauldron U	.15	.40
206 Darksteel Forge M	1.50	4.00
207 Darksteel Ingot U	.15	.40
208 Door of Destinies R	1.25	3.00
209 Elixir of Immortality U	.15	.40
210 Fireshrieker U	.15	.40
211 Guardian of the Ages R	.30	.75
212 Haunted Plate Mail R	.40	1.00
213 Millstone U	.15	.40
214 Pyromancer's Gauntlet R	.30	.75
215 Ratchet Bomb R	.60	1.50
216 Ring of Three Wishes M	1.00	2.50
217 Rod of Ruin U	.15	.40
218 Sliver Construct C	.10	.25
219 Staff of the Death Magus U	.15	.40
220 Staff of the Flame Magus U	.15	.40
221 Staff of the Mind Magus U	.15	.40
222 Staff of the Sun Magus U	.15	.40
223 Staff of the Wild Magus U	.15	.40
224 Strionic Resonator R	.75	2.00
225 Trading Post R	.30	.75
226 Vial of Poison U	.15	.40
227 Encroaching Wastes U	.20	.50
228 Mutavault R	8.00	20.00
229 Shimmering Grotto U	.15	.40
230 Plains L	.10	.25
231 Plains L	.10	.25
232 Plains L	.10	.25
233 Plains L	.10	.25
234 Island L	.10	.25
235 Island L	.10	.25
236 Island L	.10	.25
237 Island L	.10	.25
238 Swamp L	.10	.25
239 Swamp L	.10	.25
240 Swamp L	.10	.25
241 Swamp L	.10	.25
242 Mountain L	.10	.25
243 Mountain L	.10	.25
244 Mountain L	.10	.25
245 Mountain L	.10	.25
246 Forest L	.10	.25
247 Forest L	.10	.25
248 Forest L	.10	.25
249 Forest L	.10	.25
T1 Sliver	.10	.25
T2 Angel	.10	.25
T3 Cat	.10	.25
T4 Goat	.20	.50
T5 Zombie	.10	.25
T6 Dragon	.10	.25
T7 Elemental	.10	.25
T8 Elemental	.10	.25
T9 Beast	.10	.25
T10 Saprolig	.10	.25
T11 Wolf	.10	.25
T12 Emblem: Liliana of the Dark Realms	.40	1.00
T13 Emblem: Garruk, Caller of Beasts	.75	2.00

2013 Magic The Gathering Theros

Card	Low	High
COMPLETE SET (262)	200.00	300.00
BOOSTER BOX (36 PACKS)	60.00	90.00
BOOSTER PACK (15 CARDS)	3.00	4.00
*FOIL: .75X TO 2X BASIC CARDS		
RELEASED ON SEPTEMBER 27, 2013		
1 Battlewise Valor C :W:	.10	.25
2 Cavalry Pegasus C :W:	.10	.25
3 Celestial Archon R :W:	.30	.75
4 Chained to the Rocks R :W:	1.25	3.00
5 Chosen by Heliod C :W:	.10	.25
6 Dauntless Onslaught U :W:	.20	.50
7 Decorated Griffin U :W:	.15	.40
8 Divine Verdict C :W:	.10	.25
9 Elspeth, Sun's Champion M :W:	20.00	40.00
10 Ephara's Warden C :W:	.10	.25
11 Evangel of Heliod U :W:	.15	.40
12 Fabled Hero R :W:	.60	1.50
13 Favored Hoplite U :W:	.15	.40
14 Gift of Immortality R :W:	.40	1.00
15 Glare of Heresy U :W:	.20	.50
16 Gods Willing C :W:	.10	.25
17 Heliod, God of the Sun M :W:	4.00	10.00
18 Heliod's Emissary U :W:	.15	.40
19 Hopeful Eidolon C :W:	.10	.25
20 Hundred-Handed One R :W:	.30	.75
21 Lagonna-Band Elder C :W:	.10	.25
22 Last Breath C :W:	.10	.25
23 Leonin Snarecaster C :W:	.10	.25
24 Observant Alseid C :W:	.10	.25
25 Ordeal of Heliod U :W:	.20	.50
26 Phalanx Leader U :W:	.30	.75
27 Ray of Dissolution C :W:	.10	.25
28 Scholar of Athreos C :W:	.10	.25
29 Setessan Battle Priest C :W:	.10	.25
30 Setessan Griffin C :W:	.10	.25
31 Silent Artisan C :W:	.10	.25
32 Soldier of the Pantheon R :W:	1.25	3.00
33 Spear of Heliod R :W:	1.00	2.50
34 Traveling Philosopher C :W:	.10	.25
35 Vanquish the Foul U :W:	.15	.40
36 Wingsteed Rider C :W:	.10	.25
37 Yoked Ox C :W:	.10	.25
38 Annul C :B:	.10	.25
39 Aqueous Form C :B:	.10	.25
40 Artisan of Forms R :B:	.40	1.00
41 Benthic Giant C :B:	.10	.25
42 Bident of Thassa R :B:	.30	.75
43 Breaching Hippocamp C :B:	.10	.25
44 Coastline Chimera C :B:	.10	.25
45 Crackling Triton C :B:	.10	.25
46 Curse of the Swine R :B:	.40	1.00
47 Dissolve U :B:	.40	1.00
48 Fate Foretold C :B:	.10	.25
49 Gainsay U :B:	.15	.40
50 Griptide C :B:	.15	.40
51 Horizon Scholar U :B:	.15	.40
52 Lost in a Labyrinth C :B:	.10	.25
53 Master of Waves M :B:	2.50	6.00
54 Meletis Charlatan R :B:	.30	.75
55 Mnemonic Wall C :B:	.10	.25
56 Nimbus Naiad C :B:	.10	.25
57 Omenspeaker C :B:	.10	.25
58 Ordeal of Thassa U :B:	.15	.40
59 Prescient Chimera C :B:	.10	.25
60 Prognostic Sphinx R :B:	.40	1.00
61 Sea God's Revenge U :B:	.15	.40
62 Sealock Monster U :B:	.15	.40
63 Shipbreaker Kraken R :B:	.30	.75
64 Stymied Hopes C :B:	.10	.25
65 Swan Song R :B:	1.00	2.50
66 Thassa, God of the Sea M :B:	6.00	15.00
67 Thassa's Bounty C :B:	.10	.25
68 Thassa's Emissary U :B:	.15	.40
69 Triton Fortune Hunter U :B:	.15	.40
70 Triton Shorethief C :B:	.10	.25
71 Triton Tactics U :B:	.20	.50
72 Vaporkin C :B:	.10	.25
73 Voyage's End C :B:	.10	.25
74 Wavecrash Triton C :B:	.10	.25
75 Abhorrent Overlord R :K:	.30	.75
76 Agent of the Fates R :K:	.60	1.50
77 Asphodel Wanderer C :K:	.10	.25
78 Baleful Eidolon C :K:	.10	.25
79 Blood-Toll Harpy C :K:	.10	.25
80 Boon of Erebos C :K:	.10	.25
81 Cavern Lampad C :K:	.10	.25
82 Cutthroat Maneuver U :K:	.15	.40
83 Dark Betrayal U :K:	.15	.40
84 Disciple of Phenax C :K:	.10	.25
85 Erebos, God of the Dead M :K:	3.00	8.00
86 Erebos's Emissary U :K:	.15	.40
87 Felhide Minotaur C :K:	.10	.25
88 Fleshmad Steed C :K:	.10	.25
89 Gray Merchant of Asphodel C :K:	.10	.25
90 Hero's Downfall R :K:	2.50	6.00
91 Hythonia the Cruel M :K:	.60	1.50
92 Insatiable Harpy U :K:	.15	.40
93 Keepsake Gorgon U :K:	.15	.40
94 Lash of the Whip C :K:	.10	.25
95 Loathsome Catoblepas C :K:	.10	.25
96 March of the Returned C :K:	.10	.25
97 Mogis's Marauder U :K:	.15	.40
98 Nighthowler R :K:	.40	1.00
99 Ordeal of Erebos U :K:	.15	.40
100 Pharika's Cure C :K:	.10	.25
101 Read the Bones C :K:	.10	.25
102 Rescue from the Underworld U :K:	.20	.50
103 Returned Centaur C :K:	.10	.25
104 Returned Phalanx C :K:	.10	.25
105 Scourgemark C :K:	.10	.25
106 Sip of Hemlock C :K:	.10	.25
107 Thoughtseize R :K:	8.00	20.00
108 Tormented Hero U :K:	.20	.50
109 Viper's Kiss C :K:	.10	.25
110 Whip of Erebos R :K:	.75	2.00
111 Akroan Crusader C :R:	.10	.25
112 Anger of the Gods R :R:	2.50	6.00
113 Arena Athlete U :R:	.15	.40
114 Borderland Minotaur C :R:	.10	.25
115 Boulderfall C :R:	.10	.25
116 Coordinated Assault U :R:	.15	.40
117 Deathbellow Raider C :R:	.10	.25
118 Demolish C :R:	.10	.25
119 Dragon Mantle C :R:	.10	.25
120 Ember Swallower R :R:	.30	.75
121 Fanatic of Mogis U :R:	.15	.40
122 Firedrinker Satyr R :R:	.50	1.25
123 Flamespeaker Adept U :R:	.15	.40
124 Hammer of Purphoros R :R:	.75	2.00
125 Ill-Tempered Cyclops C :R:	.10	.25
126 Labyrinth Champion R :R:	.30	.75
127 Lightning Strike C :R:	.20	.50
128 Magma Jet U :R:	.75	2.00
129 Messenger's Speed C :R:	.10	.25
130 Minotaur Skullcleaver C :R:	.10	.25
131 Ordeal of Purphoros U :R:	.15	.40
132 Peak Eruption U :R:	.15	.40
133 Portent of Betrayal C :R:	.10	.25
134 Priest of Iroas C :R:	.10	.25
135 Purphoros, God of the Forge M :R:	8.00	20.00
136 Purphoros's Emissary U :R:	.15	.40
137 Rage of Purphoros C :R:	.10	.25
138 Rageblood Shaman R :R:	.40	1.00
139 Satyr Rambler C :R:	.10	.25
140 Spark Jolt C :R:	.10	.25
141 Spearpoint Oread C :R:	.10	.25
142 Stoneshock Giant U :R:	.15	.40
143 Stormbreath Dragon M :R:	12.00	30.00
144 Titan of Eternal Fire R :R:	.30	.75
145 Titan's Strength C :R:	.10	.25
146 Two-Headed Cerberus C :R:	.10	.25
147 Wild Celebrants C :R:	.10	.25
148 Agent of Horizons C :G:	.10	.25
149 Anthousa, Setessan Hero R :G:	.30	.75
150 Arbor Colossus R :G:	.30	.75
151 Artisan's Sorrow U :G:	.15	.40
152 Boon Satyr R :G:	1.00	2.50
153 Bow of Nylea R :G:	1.00	2.50
154 Centaur Battlemaster U :G:	.20	.50
155 Commune with the Gods C :G:	.10	.25
156 Defend the Hearth C :G:	.10	.25
157 Fade into Antiquity C :G:	.30	.75
158 Feral Invocation C :G:	.10	.25
159 Hunt the Hunter U :G:	.15	.40
160a Karametra's Acolyte U :G:	.15	.40
160b Karametra's Alcolyte ALT ART	2.00	5.00
161 Leafcrown Dryad C :G:	.10	.25
162 Mistcutter Hydra R :G:	1.00	2.50
163 Nemesis of Mortals U :G:	.20	.50
164 Nessian Asp C :G:	.10	.25
165 Nessian Courser C :G:	.10	.25
166 Nylea, God of the Hunt M :G:	3.00	8.00
167 Nylea's Disciple C :G:	.10	.25
168 Nylea's Emissary U :G:	.15	.40
169 Nylea's Presence C :G:	.10	.25
170 Ordeal of Nylea U :G:	.15	.40
171 Pheres-Band Centaurs C :G:	.10	.25
172 Polukranos, World Eater M :G:	2.50	6.00
173 Reverent Hunter R :G:	.40	1.00
174 Satyr Hedonist C :G:	.10	.25
175 Satyr Piper U :G:	.15	.40
176 Savage Surge C :G:	.10	.25
177 Sedge Scorpion C :G:	.10	.25
178 Shredding Winds C :G:	.10	.25
179 Staunch-Hearted Warrior C :G:	.10	.25
180 Sylvan Caryatid R :G:	2.00	5.00
181 Time to Feed C :G:	.10	.25
182 Voyaging Satyr C :G:	.10	.25
183 Vulpine Goliath C :G:	.10	.25
184 Warriors' Lesson U :G:	.15	.40
185 Akroan Hoplite U :W: :R:	.15	.40
186 Anax and Cymede R :W: :R:	.40	1.00
187 Ashen Rider M :W: :K:	1.50	4.00
188 Ashiok, Nightmare Weaver M :B: :K:	10.00	25.00
189 Battlewise Hoplite U :W: :B:	.15	.40
190 Chronicler of Heroes U :W: :G:	.15	.40
191 Daxos of Meletis R :W: :B:	.60	1.50

192 Destructive Revelry U :R: :G: .30 .75
193 Fleecemane Lion R :W: :G: 4.00 10.00
194 Horizon Chimera U :B: :G: .15 .40
195 Kragma Warcaller U :K: :R: .15 .40
196 Medomai the Ageless M :W: :B: 1.25 3.00
197 Pharika's Mender U :K: :G: .15 .40
198 Polis Crusher R :R: :G: .40 1.00
199 Prophet of Kruphix R :B: :G: .75 2.00
200 Psychic Intrusion R :B: :K: .40 1.00
201 Reaper of the Wilds R :K: :G: .75 2.00
202 Sentry of the Underworld U :W: :K: .15 .40
203 Shipwreck Singer U :B: :K: .15 .40
204 Spellheart Chimera U :B: :R: .30 .75
205 Steam Augury R :B: :R: .75 2.00
206 Triad of Fates R :W: :K: .40 1.00
207 Tymaret, the Murder King R :K: :R: .40 1.00
208 Underworld Cerberus M :K: :R: 1.50 4.00
209 Xenagos, the Reveler M :R: :G: 8.00 20.00
210 Akroan Horse R .30 .75
211 Anvilwrought Raptor U .15 .40
212 Bronze Sable C .10 .25
213 Burnished Hart U .15 .40
214 Colossus of Akros R .30 .75
215 Flamecast Wheel U .15 .40
216 Fleetfeather Sandals C .10 .25
217 Guardians of Meletis C .10 .25
218 Opaline Unicorn C .10 .25
219 Prowler's Helm U .15 .40
220 Pyxis of Pandemonium R .30 .75
221 Traveler's Amulet C .10 .25
222 Witches' Eye U .15 .40
223 Nykthos, Shrine to Nyx R 2.50 6.00
224 Temple of Abandon R 1.50 4.00
225 Temple of Deceit R 2.00 5.00
226 Temple of Mystery R 1.50 4.00
227 Temple of Silence R 2.00 5.00
228 Temple of Triumph R 2.00 5.00
229 Unknown Shores C .10 .25
230 Plains L .10 .25
231 Plains L .10 .25
232 Plains L .10 .25
233 Plains L .10 .25
234 Island L .10 .25
235 Island L .10 .25
236 Island L .10 .25
237 Island L .10 .25
238 Swamp L .10 .25
239 Swamp L .10 .25
240 Swamp L .10 .25
241 Swamp L .10 .25
242 Mountain L .10 .25
243 Mountain L .10 .25
244 Mountain L .10 .25
245 Mountain L .10 .25
246 Forest L .10 .25
247 Forest L .10 .25
248 Forest L .10 .25
249 Forest L .10 .25
T1 Cleric .20 .50
T2 Soldier (white) .10 .25
T3 Soldier (white) .10 .25
T4 Bird .20 .50
T5 Elemental .20 .50
T6 Harpy .10 .25
T7 Soldier (red) .10 .25
T8 Boar .10 .25
T9 Satyr .30 .75
T10 Golem .20 .50
T11 Emblem: Elspeth, Sun's Champion 1.25 3.00

2014 Magic The Gathering Born of the Gods

COMPLETE SET (176) 150.00 225.00
BOOSTER BOX (36 PACKS) 60.00 90.00
BOOSTER PACK (15 CARDS) 3.00 4.00
*FOIL: .75X TO 2X BASIC CARDS
RELEASED ON FEBRUARY 7, 2014
1 Acolyte's Reward U :W: .10 .30
2 Akroan Phalanx U :W: .10 .30
3 Akroan Skyguard C :W: .10 .25
4 Archetype of Courage U :W: .40 1.00
5 Brimaz, King of Oreskos M :W: 4.00 10.00
6 Dawn to Dusk U :W: .10 .30
7 Eidolon of Countless Battles R :W: .40 1.00
8 Elite Skirmisher C :W: .10 .25
9 Ephara's Radiance C :W: .10 .25
10 Excoriate C :W: .10 .25
11 Fated Retribution R :W: .15 .40
12 Ghostblade Eidolon U :W: .10 .30
13 Glimpse the Sun God U :W: .10 .30
14 God-Favored General U :W: .10 .30
15 Great Hart C :W: .10 .25
16 Griffin Dreamfinder C :W: .10 .25
17 Hero of Iroas R :W: .40 1.00
18 Hold at Bay C :W: .10 .25
19 Loyal Pegasus C :W: .10 .25
20 Mortal's Ardor C :W: .10 .25
21 Nyxborn Shieldmate C :W: .10 .25
22 Oreskos Sun Guide C :W: .10 .25
23 Ornitharch U :W: .10 .30
24 Plea for Guidance R :W: .15 .40
25 Revoke Existence C :W: .10 .25
26 Silent Sentinel R :W: .15 .40
27 Spirit of the Labyrinth R :W: .40 1.00
28 Sunbond U :W: .20 .60
29 Vanguard of Brimaz U :W: .10 .30
30 Aerie Worshippers U :B: .10 .30
31 Arbiter of the Ideal R :B: .15 .40
32 Archetype of Imagination U :B: .10 .30
33 Chorus of the Tides C :B: .10 .25
34 Crypsis C :B: .10 .25
35 Deepwater Hypnotist C :B: .10 .25
36 Divination C :B: .10 .25
37 Eternity Snare U :B: .10 .30
38 Evanescent Intellect C :B: .10 .25
39 Fated Infatuation R :B: .15 .40
40 Flitterstep Eidolon U :B: .10 .30
41 Floodtide Serpent C :B: .10 .25
42 Kraken of the Straits U :B: .10 .30
43 Meletis Astronomer U :B: .10 .30
44 Mindreaver R :B: .15 .40
45 Nullify C :B: .10 .25
46 Nyxborn Triton C :B: .10 .25
47 Oracle's Insight U :B: .10 .30
48 Perplexing Chimera R :B: .15 .40
49 Retraction Helix C :B: .10 .25
50 Siren of the Fanged Coast U :B: .10 .30
51 Sphinx's Disciple C :B: .10 .25
52 Stratus Walk C :B: .10 .25
53 Sudden Storm C :B: .10 .25
54 Thassa's Rebuff U :B: .10 .30
55 Tromokratis R :B: .15 .40
56 Vortex Elemental U :B: .10 .30
57 Whelming Wave R :B: .15 .40
58 Archetype of Finality U :K: .10 .30
59 Ashiok's Adept U :K: .10 .30
60 Asphyxiate C :K: .10 .25
61 Bile Blight U :K: .10 .30
62 Black Oak of Odunos U :K: .10 .30
63 Champion of Stray Souls M :K: .20 .60
64 Claim of Erebos C :K: .10 .25
65 Drown in Sorrow U :K: .10 .30
66 Eater of Hope R :K: .15 .40
67 Eye Gouge C :K: .10 .25
68 Fate Unraveler R :K: .15 .40
69 Fated Return R :K: .15 .40
70 Felhide Brawler C :K: .10 .25
71 Forlorn Pseudamma U :K: .10 .30
72 Forsaken Drifters C :K: .10 .25
73 Gild R :K: .15 .40
74 Grisly Transformation C :K: .10 .25
75 Herald of Torment R :K: .15 .40
76 Marshmist Titan C :K: .10 .25
77 Necrobite C :K: .10 .25
78 Nyxborn Eidolon C :K: .10 .25
79 Odunos River Trawler U :K: .10 .30
80 Pain Seer R :K: .15 .40
81 Sanguimancy U :K: .10 .30
82 Servant of Tymaret C :K: .10 .25
83 Shrike Harpy U :K: .10 .30
84 Spiteful Returned U :K: .10 .30
85 Warchanter of Mogis C :K: .10 .25
86 Weight of the Underworld C :K: .10 .25
87 Akroan Conscriptor U :R: .10 .30
88 Archetype of Aggression U :R: .10 .30
89 Bolt of Keranos C :R: .10 .25
90 Cyclops of One-Eyed Pass C :R: .10 .25
91 Epiphany Storm C :R: .10 .25
92 Everflame Eidolon U :R: .10 .30
93 Fall of the Hammer C :R: .10 .25
94 Fated Conflagration R :R: .15 .40
95 Fearsome Temper C :R: .10 .25
96 Felhide Spiritbinder R :R: .15 .40
97 Flame-Wreathed Phoenix M :R: .40 1.00
98 Forgestoker Dragon R :R: .15 .40
99 Impetuous Sunchaser C :R: .10 .25
100 Kragma Butcher C :R: .10 .25
101 Lightning Volley U :R: .10 .30
102 Nyxborn Rollicker C :R: .10 .25
103 Oracle of Bones R :R: .15 .40
104 Pharagax Giant C :R: .10 .25
105 Pinnacle of Rage U :R: .10 .30
106 Reckless Reveler C :R: .10 .25
107 Rise to the Challenge C :R: .10 .25
108 Satyr Firedancer R :R: .20 .60
109 Satyr Nyx-Smith U :R: .10 .30
110 Scouring Sands C :R: .10 .25
111 Searing Blood U :R: .20 .60
112 Stormcaller of Keranos U :R: .10 .30
113 Thunder Brute U :R: .10 .30
114 Thunderous Might U :R: .10 .30
115 Whims of the Fates R :R: .15 .40
116 Archetype of Endurance U :G: .20 .60
117 Aspect of Hydra C :G: .10 .25
118 Charging Badger C :G: .10 .25
119 Courser of Kruphix R :G: 1.50 4.00
120 Culling Mark C :G: .10 .25
121 Fated Intervention R :G: .15 .40
122 Graverobber Spider U :G: .10 .30
123 Hero of Leina Tower R :G: .15 .40
124 Hunter's Prowess R :G: .15 .40
125 Karametra's Favor C :G: .10 .25
126 Mischief and Mayhem U :G: .10 .30
127 Mortal's Resolve C :G: .10 .25
128 Nessian Demolok U :G: .10 .30
129 Nessian Wilds Ravager R :G: .15 .40
130 Noble Quarry U :G: .10 .30
131 Nyxborn Wolf C :G: .10 .25
132 Peregrination U :G: .10 .30
133 Pheres-Band Raiders U :G: .10 .30
134 Pheres-Band Tromper C :G: .10 .25
135 Raised by Wolves U :G: .10 .30
136 Satyr Wayfinder C :G: .10 .25
137 Scourge of Skola Vale R :G: .15 .40
138 Setessan Oathsworn C :G: .10 .25
139 Setessan Starbreaker C :G: .10 .25
140 Skyreaping U :G: .10 .30
141 Snake of the Golden Grove C :G: .10 .25
142 Swordwise Centaur C :G: .10 .25
143 Unravel the AEther U :G: .10 .30
144 Chromanticore M :W: :B: :K: :R: :G: .50 1.25
145 Ephara, God of the Polis M :W: :B: 1.00 2.50
146 Ephara's Enlightenment U :W: :B: .10 .30
147 Fanatic of Xenagos U :R: :G: .10 .30
148 Karametra, God of Harvests M :W: :G: 2.00 5.00
149 Kiora, the Crashing Wave M :B: :G: 1.25 3.00
150 Kiora's Follower U :B: :G: .10 .30
151 Mogis, God of Slaughter M :K: :R: 2.50 6.00
152 Phenax, God of Deception M :B: :K: 2.50 6.00
153 Ragemonger U :K: :R: .10 .30
154 Reap What Is Sown U :W: :G: .10 .30
155 Siren of the Silent Song U :B: :K: .10 .30
156 Xenagos, God of Revels M :R: :G: 3.00 8.00
157 Astral Cornucopia R .15 .40
158 Gorgon's Head U .10 .30
159 Heroes' Podium R .15 .40
160 Pillar of War U .10 .30
161 Siren Song Lyre U .10 .30
162 Springleaf Drum U .50 1.25
163 Temple of Enlightenment R 1.00 2.50
164 Temple of Malice R 1.00 2.50
165 Temple of Plenty R 1.00 2.50
T1 Bird (white) .10 .25
T2 Cat Soldier .10 .25
T3 Soldier .10 .25
T4 Bird (blue) .10 .25
T5 Kraken 1.50 2.00
T6 Zombie .10 .25
T7 Elemental .10 .25
T8 Centaur .10 .25
T9 Wolf .10 .25
T10 Gold .10 .25
T11 Emblem: Kiora, the Crashing Wave .75 2.00

2014 Magic The Gathering Journey into Nyx

COMPLETE SET (165) 80.00 200.00
BOOSTER BOX (36 PACKS) 50.00 120.00
BOOSTER PACK (15 CARDS) 2.00 5.00
*FOIL: 1X TO 2.5X BASIC CARDS
RELEASED ON MAY 2, 2014
1 Aegis of the Gods R :W: 1.25 3.00
2 Ajani's Presence C :W: .10 .25
3 Akroan Mastiff C :W: .10 .25
4 Armament of Nyx C :W: .10 .25
5 Banishing Light U :W: .75 2.00
6 Dawnbringer Charioteers R :W: .40 1.00
7 Deicide R :W: 1.50 4.00
8 Dictate of Heliod R :W: .40 1.00
9 Eagle of the Watch C :W: .10 .25
10 Eidolon of Rhetoric U :W: .20 .50
11 Font of Vigor C :W: .10 .25
12 Godsend M :W: 6.00 12.00
13 Harvestguard Alseids C :W: .10 .25
14 Lagonna-Band Trailblazer C :W: .10 .25
15 Launch the Fleet R :W: .75 2.00
16 Leonin Iconoclast U :W: .20 .50
17 Mortal Obstinacy C :W: .10 .25
18 Nyx-Fleece Ram U :W: .20 .50
19 Oppressive Rays C :W: .10 .25
20 Oreskos Swiftclaw C :W: .10 .25
21 Phalanx Formation U :W: .20 .50
22 Quarry Colossus U :W: .20 .50
23 Reprisal U :W: .20 .50
24 Sightless Brawler U :W: .20 .50
25 Skybind R :W: .40 1.00
26 Skyspear Cavalry U :W: .20 .50
27 Stonewise Fortifier C :W: .10 .25
28 Supply-Line Cranes C :W: .10 .25
29 Tethmos High Priest U :W: .20 .50
30 Aerial Formation C :B: .10 .25
31 Battlefield Thaumaturge R :B: 1.25 3.00
32 Cloaked Siren C :B: .10 .25
33 Countermand C :B: .10 .25
34 Crystalline Nautilus U :B: .20 .50
35 Dakra Mystic U :B: .20 .50
36 Daring Thief R :B: .40 1.00
37 Dictate of Kruphix R :B: .75 2.00
38 Font of Fortunes C :B: .10 .25
39 Godhunter Octopus C :B: .10 .25
40 Hour of Need U :B: .20 .50
41 Hubris C :B: .10 .25
42 Hypnotic Siren R :B: .60 1.50
43 Interpret the Signs U :B: .20 .50
44 Kiora's Dismissal U :B: .20 .50
45 Pin to the Earth C :B: .10 .25
46 Polymorphous Rush R :B: .40 1.00
47 Pull from the Deep U :B: .20 .50
48 Riptide Chimera U :B: .20 .50
49 Rise of Eagles U :B: .20 .50
50 Sage of Hours M :B: 2.00 5.00
51 Scourge of Fleets R :B: .40 1.00
52 Sigiled Starfish C :B: .10 .25
53 Thassa's Devourer C :B: .10 .25
54 Thassa's Ire U :B: .20 .50
55 Triton Cavalry U :B: .20 .50
56 Triton Shorestalker C :B: .10 .25
57 War-Wing Siren C :B: .10 .25
58 Whitewater Naiads U :B: .20 .50
59 Agent of Erebos U :K: .20 .50
60 Aspect of Gorgon C :K: .10 .25
61 Bloodcrazed Hoplite C :K: .10 .25
62 Brain Maggot U :K: .20 .50
63 Cast into Darkness C :K: .10 .25
64 Cruel Feeding C :K: .10 .25
65 Dictate of Erebos R :K: 1.25 3.00
66 Doomwake Giant R :K: .40 1.00
67 Dreadbringer Lampads C :K: .10 .25
68 Extinguish All Hope R :K: .40 1.00
69 Feast of Dreams C :K: .10 .25
70 Felhide Petrifier U :K: .20 .50
71 Font of Return C :K: .10 .25
72 Gnarled Scarhide U :K: .20 .50
73 Grim Guardian C :K: .10 .25
74 King Macar, the Gold-Cursed R :K: .60 1.50
75 Master of the Feast R :K: 2.00 5.00
76 Nightmarish End U :K: .20 .50
77 Nyx Infusion C :K: .10 .25
78 Pharika's Chosen C :K: .10 .25
79 Returned Reveler C :K: .10 .25
80 Ritual of the Returned U :K: .20 .50
81 Rotted Hulk U :K: .20 .50
82 Silence the Believers R :K: .60 1.50
83 Spiteful Blow U :K: .20 .50
84 Squelching Leeches U :K: .20 .50
85 Thoughtrender Lamia U :K: .20 .50
86 Tormented Thoughts U :K: .20 .50
87 Worst Fears M :K: 1.00 2.50
88 Akroan Line Breaker U :R: .20 .50
89 Bearer of the Heavens R :R: .40 1.00
90 Bladetusk Boar C :R: .10 .25
91 Blinding Flare U :R: .20 .50
92 Cyclops of Eternal Fury U :R: .20 .50
93 Dictate of the Twin Gods R :R: .40 1.00
94 Eidolon of the Great Revel R :R: 1.25 3.00
95 Flamespeaker's Will C :R: .10 .25
96 Flurry of Horns C :R: .10 .25
97 Font of Ire C :R: .10 .25
98 Forgeborn Oreads U :R: .20 .50
99 Gluttonous Cyclops C :R: .10 .25
100 Harness by Force R :R: .40 1.00
101 Knowledge and Power U :R: .20 .50
102 Lightning Diadem C :R: .10 .25
103 Magma Spray C :R: .10 .25
104 Mogis's Warhound U :R: .20 .50
105 Pensive Minotaur C :R: .10 .25
106 Prophetic Flamespeaker M :R: 3.00 8.00
107 Riddle of Lightning U :R: .20 .50
108 Rollick of Abandon U :R: .20 .50
109 Rouse the Mob C :R: .10 .25
110 Satyr Hoplite C :R: .10 .25
111 Sigiled Skink C :R: .10 .25
112 Spawn of Thraxes R :R: .40 1.00
113 Spite of Mogis U :R: .20 .50
114 Starfall C :R: .10 .25
115 Twinflame R :R: .40 1.00
116 Wildfire Cerberus U :R: .20 .50
117 Bassara Tower Archer U :G: .20 .50
118 Colossal Heroics U :G: .20 .50
119 Consign to Dust U :G: .20 .50
120 Desecration Plague C :G: .10 .25
121 Dictate of Karametra R :G: .40 1.00
122 Eidolon of Blossoms R :G: 1.00 2.50
123 Font of Fertility C :G: .10 .25
124 Golden Hind C :G: .10 .25
125 Goldenhide Ox U :G: .20 .50
126 Heroes' Bane R :G: .40 1.00
127 Humbler of Mortals C :G: .10 .25
128 Hydra Broodmaster R :G: .60 1.50
129 Kruphix's Insight C :G: .10 .25
130 Market Festival C :G: .10 .25
131 Nature's Panoply C :G: .10 .25
132 Nessian Game Warden U :G: .20 .50
133 Oakheart Dryads C :G: .10 .25
134 Pheres-Band Thunderhoof C :G: .10 .25
135 Pheres-Band Warchief R :G: .40 1.00
136 Ravenous Leucrocota C :G: .10 .25
137 Renowned Weaver C :G: .10 .25
138 Reviving Melody U :G: .20 .50
139 Satyr Grovedancer C :G: .10 .25
140 Setessan Tactics R :G: .40 1.00
141 Solidarity of Heroes U :G: .20 .50
142 Spirespine U :G: .20 .50
143 Strength from the Fallen U :G: .20 .50
144 Swarmborn Giant U :G: .20 .50
145 Ajani, Mentor of Heroes M :M: 15.00 25.00
146 Athreos, God of Passage M :M: 15.00 25.00
147 Desperate Stand U :M: .20 .50
148 Disciple of Deceit U :M: .20 .50
149 Fleetfeather Cockatrice U :M: .20 .50
150 Iroas, God of Victory M :M: 3.00 8.00
151 Keranos, God of Storms M :M: 3.00 8.00
152 Kruphix, God of Horizons M :M: 3.00 8.00
153 Nyx Weaver U :M: .20 .50
154 Pharika, God of Affliction M :M: 2.50 6.00
155 Revel of the Fallen God R :M: .40 1.00
156 Stormchaser Chimera U :M: .20 .50
157 Underworld Coinsmith U :M: .20 .50
158 Armory of Iroas U .20 .50
159 Chariot of Victory U .20 .50
160 Deserter's Quarters U .20 .50
161 Gold-Forged Sentinel U .20 .50
162 Hall of Triumph R .60 1.50
163 Mana Confluence R 10.00 20.00
164 Temple of Epiphany R 2.50 6.00
165 Temple of Malady R 2.50 6.00
T1 Sphinx Token T .10 .25
T2 Zombie Token T .30 .75
T3 Minotaur Token T .10 .25
T4 Hydra Token T .10 .25
T5 Spider Token T .10 .25

2014 Magic The Gathering Magic 2015 Core Set

COMPLETE SET (301) 60.00 150.00
BOOSTER BOX (36 PACKS) 80.00 90.00
BOOSTER PACK (15 CARDS) 3.00 4.00
*FOIL: 1X TO 2.5X BASIC CARDS
RELEASED ON JULY 28, 2014
1 Ajani Steadfast M :W: 12.00 30.00
2 Ajani's Pridemate U :W: .40 1.00
3 Avacyn, Guardian Angel R :W: .40 1.00
4 Battle Mastery U :W: .20 .50
5 Boonweaver Giant U :W: .20 .50
6 Congregate U :W: .20 .50
7 Constricting Sliver U :W: .60 1.50
8 Dauntless River Marshal U :W: .20 .50
9 Devouring Light U :W: .40 1.00
10 Divine Favor C :W: .10 .25
11 Ephemeral Shields C :W: .10 .25
12 First Response U :W: .20 .50
13 Geist of the Moors U :W: .20 .50
14 Heliod's Pilgrim C :W: .10 .25
15 Hushwing Gryff R :W: .40 1.00
16 Kinsbaile Skirmisher C :W: .10 .25
17 Marked by Honor C :W: .10 .25
18 Mass Calcify R :W: .40 1.00
19 Meditation Puzzle C :W: .10 .25
20 Midnight Guard C :W: .10 .25
21 Oppressive Rays C :W: .10 .25
22 Oreskos Swiftclaw C :W: .10 .25
23 Paragon of New Dawns U :W: .20 .50
24 Pillar of Light C :W: .10 .25
25 Preeminent Captain R :W: .40 1.00
26 Raise the Alarm C :W: .10 .25
27 Razorfoot Griffin C :W: .10 .25
28 Resolute Archangel R :W: .40 1.00
29 Return to the Ranks R :W: .40 1.00
30 Sanctified Charge C :W: .10 .25
31 Selfless Cathar C :W: .10 .25
32 Seraph of the Masses U :W: .20 .50
33 Solemn Offering C :W: .10 .25
34 Soul of Theros M :W: 3.00 8.00
35 Soulmender C :W: .10 .25
36 Spectra Ward R :W: .40 1.00
37 Spirit Bonds R :W: .40 1.00
38 Sungrace Pegasus C :W: .10 .25
39 Tireless Missionaries C :W: .10 .25
40 Triplicate Spirits C :W: .10 .25
41 Wall of Essence U :W: .20 .50
42 Warden of the Beyond U :W: .20 .50
43 Aeronaut Tinkerer C :B: .10 .25
44 AEtherspouts R :B: .40 1.00
45 Amphin Pathmage C :B: .10 .25
46 Chasm Skulker R :B: .40 1.00
47 Chief Engineer R :B: .40 1.00
48 Chronostutter C :B: .10 .25
49 Coral Barrier C :B: .10 .25
50 Diffusion Sliver U :B: .40 1.00
51 Dissipate U :B: .40 1.00
52 Divination C :B: .10 .25
53 Encrust C :B: .10 .25
54 Ensoul Artifact U :B: .50 1.25
55 Frost Lynx C :B: .10 .25
56 Fugitive Wizard C :B: .10 .25
57 Glacial Crasher C :B: .10 .25
58 Hydrosurge C :B: .10 .25
59 Illusory Angel U :B: .20 .50
60 Into the Void U :B: .20 .50
61 Invisibility C :B: .10 .25
62 Jace, the Living Guildpact M :B: 8.00 20.00
63 Jace's Ingenuity U :B: .20 .50
64 Jalira, Master Polymorphist R :B: .40 1.00
65 Jorubai Murk Lurker U :B: .20 .50
66 Kapsho Kitefins U :B: .20 .50
67 Master of Predicaments R :B: .40 1.00
68 Mercurial Pretender R :B: .40 1.00
69 Military Intelligence U :B: .20 .50
70 Mind Sculpt C :B: .10 .25
71 Negate C :B: .10 .25
72 Nimbus of the Isles C :B: .10 .25
73 Paragon of Gathering Mists U :B: .20 .50
74 Peel from Reality C :B: .10 .25
75 Polymorphist's Jest R :B: .40 1.00
76 Quickling U :B: .20 .50
77 Research Assistant C :B: .10 .25
78 Soul of Ravnica M :B: 1.25 3.00
79 Statute of Denial C :B: .10 .25
80 Stormtide Leviathan R :B: .40 1.00
81 Turn to Frog U :B: .20 .50
82 Void Snare C :B: .10 .25
83 Wall of Frost U :B: .20 .50
84 Welkin Tern C :B: .10 .25
85 Accursed Spirit C :K: .10 .25
86 Black Cat C :K: .10 .25
87 Blood Host U :K: .20 .50
88 Carrion Crow C :K: .10 .25
89 Caustic Tar U :K: .20 .50
90 Child of Night C :K: .10 .25
91 Covenant of Blood C :K: .10 .25
92 Crippling Blight C :K: .10 .25
93 Cruel Sadist R :K: .40 1.00
94 Endless Obedience U :K: .40 1.00
95 Eternal Thirst C :K: .10 .25
96 Feast on the Fallen U :K: .20 .50
97 Festergloom C :K: .10 .25
98 Flesh to Dust C :K: .10 .25
99 Gravedigger C :K: .10 .25
100 In Garruk's Wake R :K: .40 1.00
101 Indulgent Tormentor R :K: .40 1.00
102 Leeching Sliver U :K: .20 .50
103 Liliana Vess M :K: 6.00 15.00
104 Mind Rot C :K: .10 .25
105 Necrobite C :K: .10 .25
106 Necrogen Scudder U :K: .20 .50
107 Necromancer's Assistant C :K: .10 .25
108 Necromancer's Stockpile R :K: .40 1.00
109 Nightfire Giant U :K: .20 .50
110 Ob Nixilis, Unshackled R :K: .40 1.00
111 Paragon of Open Graves U :K: .20 .50
112 Rotfeaster Maggot C :K: .10 .25
113 Shadowcloak Vampire C :K: .10 .25
114 Sign in Blood C :K: .10 .25
115 Soul of Innistrad M :K: 1.25 3.00
116 Stab Wound C :K: .10 .25
117 Stain the Mind R :K: .40 1.00
118 Typhoid Rats C :K: .10 .25
119 Ulcerate U :K: .20 .50
120 Unmake the Graves C :K: .10 .25
121 Wall of Limbs U :K: .20 .50
122 Waste Not R :K: .40 1.00
123 Witch's Familiar C :K: .10 .25
124 Xathrid Slyblade U :K: .20 .50
125 Zof Shade C :K: .10 .25
126 Act on Impulse U :R: .20 .50
127 Aggressive Mining R :R: .40 1.00
128 Altac Bloodseeker U :R: .20 .50
129 Belligerent Sliver U :R: .50 1.25
130 Blastfire Bolt C :R: .10 .25
131 Borderland Marauder C :R: .10 .25
132 Brood Keeper U :R: .20 .50
133 Burning Anger R :R: .40 1.00
134 Chandra, Pyromaster M :R: 12.00 30.00
135 Circle of Flame U :R: .20 .50
136 Clear a Path C :R: .10 .25
137 Cone of Flame U :R: .20 .50
138 Crowd's Favor C :R: .10 .25
139 Crucible of Fire R :R: .40 1.00
140 Forge Devil C :R: .10 .25
141 Foundry Street Denizen C :R: .10 .25
142 Frenzied Goblin U :R: .20 .50
143 Generator Servant C :R: .10 .25
144 Goblin Kaboomist R :R: .40 1.00
145 Goblin Rabblemaster R :R: .40 1.00
146 Goblin Roughrider C :R: .10 .25
147 Hammerhand C :R: .10 .25
148 Heat Ray C :R: .10 .25
149 Hoarding Dragon R :R: .40 1.00
150 Inferno Fist C :R: .10 .25
151 Kird Chieftain U :R: .20 .50
152 Krenko's Enforcer C :R: .10 .25
153 Kurkesh, Onakke Ancient R :R: .40 1.00
154 Lava Axe C :R: .10 .25
155 Lightning Strike C :R: .10 .25
156 Might Makes Right U :R: .20 .50
157 Miner's Bane C :R: .10 .25
158 Paragon of Fierce Defiance U :R: .20 .50
159 Rummaging Goblin C :R: .10 .25
160 Scrapyard Mongrel C :R: .10 .25
161 Shrapnel Blast U :R: .20 .50
162 Siege Dragon R :R: .40 1.00
163 Soul of Shandalar M :R: 12.00 30.00
164 Stoke the Flames U :R: .20 .50
165 Thundering Giant C :R: .10 .25
166 Torch Fiend C :R: .10 .25
167 Wall of Fire C :R: .10 .25
168 Ancient Silverback U :G: .20 .50
169 Back to Nature U :G: .40 1.00
170 Carnivorous Moss-Beast C :G: .10 .25
171 Charging Rhino C :G: .10 .25
172 Chord of Calling R :G: .40 1.00
173 Elvish Mystic C :G: .40 1.00
174 Feral Incarnation U :G: .20 .50
175 Gather Courage U :G: .20 .50
176 Genesis Hydra R :G: .40 1.00
177 Hornet Nest R :G: .40 1.00
178 Hornet Queen R :G: .40 1.00
179 Hunt the Weak C :G: .10 .25

180 Hunter's Ambush C :G: .10 .25
181 Invasive Species C :G: .10 .25
182 Kalonian Twingrove R :G: .40 1.00
183 Life's Legacy R :G: .40 1.00
184 Living Totem U :G: .20 .50
185 Naturalize C :G: .10 .25
186 Netcaster Spider C :G: .10 .25
187 Nissa's Expedition U :G: .20 .50
188 Nissa, Worldwaker M :G: 12.00 30.00
189 Overwhelm U :G: .20 .50
190 Paragon of Eternal Wilds U :G: .20 .50
191 Phytotitan R :G: .40 1.00
192 Plummet C :G: .10 .25
193 Ranger's Guile C :G: .10 .25
194 Reclamation Sage U :G: .20 .50
195 Restock R :G: .40 1.00
196 Roaring Primadox U :G: .20 .50
197 Runeclaw Bear C :G: .10 .25
198 Satyr Wayfinder C :G: .10 .25
199 Shaman of Spring C :G: .10 .25
200 Siege Wurm C :G: .10 .25
201 Soul of Zendikar M :G: 2.00 5.00
202 Sunblade Elf U :G: .20 .50
203 Titanic Growth C :G: .10 .25
204 Undergrowth Scavenger C :G: .10 .25
205 Venom Sliver U :G: .20 .50
206 Verdant Haven C :G: .10 .25
207 Vineweft C :G: .10 .25
208 Wall of Mulch U :G: .20 .50
209 Yisan, the Wanderer Bard R :G: .40 1.00
210 Garruk, Apex Predator M :K: :G: 15.00 40.00
211 Sliver Hivelord M :D: 8.00 20.00
212 Avarice Amulet R .40 1.00
213 Brawler's Plate U .20 .50
214 Bronze Sable C .10 .25
215 The Chain Veil M 2.50 6.00
216 Gargoyle Sentinel U .20 .50
217 Grindclock R .40 1.00
218 Haunted Plate Mail R .40 1.00
219 Hot Soup U .20 .50
220 Juggernaut U .20 .50
221 Meteorite U .20 .50
222 Obelisk of Urd R .40 1.00
223 Ornithopter U .20 .50
224 Perilous Vault M 4.00 10.00
225 Phyrexian Revoker R .40 1.00
226 Profane Memento U .20 .50
227 Rogue's Gloves U .20 .50
228 Sacred Armory U .20 .50
229 Scuttling Doom Engine R .40 1.00
230 Shield of the Avatar R .40 1.00
231 Soul of New Phyrexia M 6.00 15.00
232 Staff of the Death Magus U .20 .50
233 Staff of the Flame Magus U .20 .50
234 Staff of the Mind Magus U .20 .50
235 Staff of the Sun Magus U .20 .50
236 Staff of the Wild Magus U .20 .50
237 Tormod's Crypt U .20 .50
238 Tyrant's Machine C .10 .25
239 Will-Forged Golem C .10 .25
240 Battlefield Forge R .40 1.00
241 Caves of Koilos R .40 1.00
242 Darksteel Citadel U .60 1.50
243 Evolving Wilds C .10 .25
244 Llanowar Wastes R .40 1.00
245 Radiant Fountain C .10 .25
246 Shivan Reef R .40 1.00
247 Sliver Hive R .40 1.00
248 Urborg, Tomb of Yawgmoth R .40 1.00
249 Yavimaya Coast R .40 1.00
250 Plains L .10 .25
251 Plains L .10 .25
252 Plains L .10 .25
253 Plains L .10 .25
254 Island L .10 .25
255 Island L .10 .25
256 Island L .10 .25
257 Island L .10 .25
258 Swamp L .10 .25
259 Swamp L .10 .25
260 Swamp L .10 .25
261 Swamp L .10 .25
262 Mountain L .10 .25
263 Mountain L .10 .25
264 Mountain L .10 .25
265 Mountain L .10 .25
266 Forest L .10 .25
267 Forest L .10 .25
268 Forest L .10 .25
269 Forest L .10 .25
270 Aegis Angel R :W: .40 1.00
271 Divine Verdict C :W: .40 1.00
272 Inspired Charge C :W: .10 .25
273 Serra Angel U :W: .20 .50
274 Cancel C :B: .60 1.50
275 Mahamoti Djinn R :B: .40 1.00
276 Nightmare R :K: .40 1.00
277 Sengir Vampire U :K: .20 .50
278 Walking Corpse C :K: .10 .25
279 Furnace Whelp U :R: .75 2.00
280 Seismic Strike C :R: .10 .25
281 Shivan Dragon R :R: .40 1.00
282 Centaur Courser C :G: .50 1.25
283 Garruk's Packleader U :G: 1.00 2.50
284 Terra Stomper R :G: .40 1.00
P1 Garruk the Slayer (Oversize) S :K: :G: 4.00 10.00
P1 Garruk, the Slayer P 2.00 5.00
T1 Soldier Token :W: .30 .75
T2 Spirit Token :W: .40 1.00
T3 Squid Token :B: .50 1.25
T4 Beast Token :K: .20 .50
T5 Zombie Token :K: .40 1.00
T6 Dragon Token :R: .30 .75
T7 Goblin Token :R: .40 1.00
T9 Insect Token :G: 1.00 2.50
T8 Beast Token :G: .40 1.00
T10 Treefolk Warrior Token :G: .60 1.50
T11 Wolf Token :G: .60 1.50
T12 Emblem - Ajani Steadfast 1.25 3.00
T13 Emblem - Garruk, Apex Predator 1.25 3.00
T14 Land Mine .50 1.25
T15 Sliver Token .40 1.00

2014 Magic The Gathering Khans of Tarkir

COMPLETE SET (282) 100.00 250.00
BOOSTER BOX (36 PACKS) 80.00 100.00
BOOSTER PACK (15 CARDS) 3.00 5.00
*FOIL: .75X TO 2X BASIC CARDS
RELEASED ON SEPTEMBER 26, 2014
3 Ainok Bond-Kin C :W: .10 .25
4 Alabaster Kirin C :W: .10 .25
7 Defiant Strike C :W: .10 .25
9 Erase C :W: .10 .25
10 Feat of Resistance C :W: .10 .25
11 Firehoof Cavalry C :W: .10 .25
14 Jeskai Student C :W: .10 .25
15 Kill Shot C :W: .10 .25
16 Mardu Hateblade C :W: .10 .25
17 Mardu Hordechief C :W: .10 .25
19 Rush of Battle C :W: .10 .25
20 Sage-Eye Harrier C :W: .10 .25
21 Salt Road Patrol C :W: .10 .25
23 Siegecraft C :W: .10 .25
24 Smite the Monstrous C :W: .10 .25
31 Wingmate Roc M :W: 4.00 10.00
8 End Hostilities R :W: 1.00 2.50
12 Herald of Anafenza R :W: .40 1.00
13 High Sentinels of Arashin R :W: .40 1.00
18 Master of Pearls R :W: .40 1.00
1 Abzan Battle Priest U :W: .20 .50
2 Abzan Falconer U :W: .20 .50
5 Brave the Sands U :W: .20 .50
6 Dazzling Ramparts U :W: .20 .50
22 Seeker of the Way U :W: .20 .50
25 Suspension Field U :W: .20 .50
26 Take Up Arms U :W: .20 .50
27 Timely Hordemate U :W: .20 .50
28 Venerable Lammasu U :W: .20 .50
29 War Behemoth U :W: .20 .50
30 Watcher of the Roost U :W: .20 .50
33 Cancel C :B: .10 .25
35 Crippling Chill C :B: .10 .25
37 Disdainful Stroke C :B: .10 .25
39 Embodiment of Spring C :B: .10 .25
40 Force Away C :B: .10 .25
41 Glacial Stalker C :B: .10 .25
44 Jeskai Windscout C :B: .10 .25
47 Monastery Flock C :B: .10 .25
48 Mystic of the Hidden Way C :B: .10 .25
52 Scaldkin C :B: .10 .25
55 Singing Bell Strike C :B: .10 .25
57 Taigam's Scheming C :B: .10 .25
59 Treasure Cruise C :B: .10 .25
61 Weave Fate C :B: .10 .25
62 Wetland Sambar C :B: .10 .25
63 Whirlwind Adept C :B: .10 .25
34 Clever Impersonator M :B: 6.00 15.00
49 Pearl Lake Ancient M :B: .75 2.00
36 Dig Through Time R :B: 2.00 5.00
42 Icy Blast R :B: .40 1.00
45 Kheru Spellsnatcher R :B: .40 1.00
58 Thousand Winds R :B: .40 1.00
32 Blinding Spray U :B: .20 .50
38 Dragon's Eye Savants U :B: .20 .50
43 Jeskai Elder U :B: .20 .50
46 Mistfire Weaver U :B: .20 .50
50 Quiet Contemplation U :B: .20 .50
51 Riverwheel Aerialists U :B: .20 .50
53 Scion of Glaciers U :B: .20 .50
54 Set Adrift U :B: .20 .50
56 Stubborn Denial U :B: .20 .50
60 Waterwhirl U :B: .20 .50
65 Bitter Revelation C :K: .10 .25
68 Debilitating Injury C :K: .10 .25
70 Disowned Ancestor C :K: .10 .25
71 Dutiful Return C :K: .10 .25
76 Kheru Dreadmaw C :K: .10 .25
77 Krumar Bond-Kin C :K: .10 .25
78 Mardu Skullhunter C :K: .10 .25
80 Molting Snakeskin C :K: .10 .25
84 Rakshasa's Secret C :K: .10 .25
86 Rite of the Serpent C :K: .10 .25
87 Rotting Mastodon C :K: .10 .25
75 Shambling Attendants C :K: .10 .25
90 Sidisi's Pet C :K: .10 .25
91 Sultai Scavenger C :K: .10 .25
93 Throttle C :K: .10 .25
94 Unyielding Krumar C :K: .10 .25
72 Empty the Pits M :K: 1.50 4.00
66 Bloodsoaked Champion R :K: 3.00 8.00
73 Grim Haruspex R :K: .40 1.00
82 Necropolis Fiend R :K: .40 1.00
85 Retribution of the Ancients R :K: .40 1.00
64 Bellowing Saddlebrute U :K: .20 .50
67 Dead Drop U :K: .20 .50
69 Despise U :K: .20 .50
74 Gurmag Swiftwing U :K: .20 .50
75 Kheru Bloodsucker U :K: .20 .50
79 Mer-Ek Nightblade U :K: .20 .50
81 Murderous Cut U :K: .20 .50
83 Raiders' Spoils U :K: .20 .50
88 Ruthless Ripper U :K: .20 .50
92 Swarm of Bloodflies U :K: .20 .50
95 Act of Treason C :R: .10 .25
96 Ainok Tracker C :R: .10 .25
98 Arrow Storm C :R: .10 .25
100 Barrage of Boulders C :R: .10 .25
101 Bloodfire Expert C :R: .10 .25
102 Bloodfire Mentor C :R: .10 .25
103 Bring Low C :R: .10 .25
105 Canyon Lurkers C :R: .10 .25
114 Leaping Master C :R: .10 .25
117 Mardu Warshrieker C :R: .10 .25
120 Shatter C :R: .10 .25
121 Summit Prowler C :R: .10 .25
122 Swift Kick C :R: .10 .25
123 Tormenting Voice C :R: .10 .25
124 Trumpet Blast C :R: .10 .25
125 Valley Dasher C :R: .10 .25
99 Ashcloud Phoenix M :R: 2.00 5.00
119 Sarkhan, the Dragonspeaker M :R: 10.00 25.00
106 Crater's Claws R :R: .50 1.25
108 Dragon-Style Twins R :R: .40 1.00
112 Howl of the Horde R :R: .40 1.00
113 Jeering Instigator R :R: .40 1.00
97 Arc Lightning U :R: .20 .50
104 Burn Away U :R: .20 .50
107 Dragon Grip U :R: .20 .50
109 Goblinslide U :R: .20 .50
110 Horde Ambusher U :R: .20 .50
111 Hordeling Outburst U :R: .40 1.00
115 Mardu Blazebringer U :R: .20 .50
116 Mardu Heart-Piercer U :R: .20 .50
118 Monastery Swiftspear U :R: .40 1.00
126 War-Name Aspirant U :R: .20 .50
158 Woolly Loxodon C :G: .10 .25
157 Windstorm U :G: .20 .50
127 Alpine Grizzly C :G: .10 .25
128 Archers' Parapet C :G: .10 .25
129 Awaken the Bear C :G: .10 .25
131 Dragonscale Boon C :G: .10 .25
132 Feed the Clan C :G: .10 .25
135 Highland Game C :G: .10 .25
137 Hooting Mandrills C :G: .10 .25
139 Kin-Tree Warden C :G: .10 .25
140 Longshot Squad C :G: .10 .25
142 Naturalize C :G: .10 .25
146 Sagu Archer C :G: .10 .25
147 Savage Punch C :G: .10 .25
148 Scout the Borders C :G: .10 .25
151 Smoke Teller C :G: .10 .25
155 Tusked Colossodon C :G: .10 .25
136 Hooded Hydra M :G: 1.25 3.00
149 See the Unwritten M :G: 1.50 4.00
133 Hardened Scales R :G: .40 1.00
141 Meandering Towershell R :G: .40 1.00
144 Rattleclaw Mystic R :G: 2.00 5.00
154 Trail of Mystery R :G: .40 1.00
130 Become Immense U :G: .20 .50
134 Heir of the Wilds U :G: .20 .50
138 Incremental Growth U :G: .20 .50
143 Pine Walker U :G: .20 .50
145 Roar of Challenge U :G: .20 .50
150 Seek the Horizon U :G: .20 .50
152 Sultai Flayer U :G: .20 .50
153 Temur Charger U :G: .20 .50
156 Tuskguard Captain U :G: .20 .50
202 Sorin, Solemn Visitor M :D: 10.00 25.00
210 Utter End R :D: 1.50 4.00
159 Abomination of Gudul C :D: .10 .25
160 Abzan Ascendancy R :D: .75 2.00
161 Abzan Charm U :D: .20 .50
162 Abzan Guide C :D: .10 .25
163 Anafenza, the Foremost M :D: 2.00 5.00
164 Ankle Shanker R :D: .40 1.00
165 Armament Corps U :D: .20 .50
166 Avalanche Tusker R :D: .40 1.00
167 Bear's Companion U :D: .20 .50
168 Butcher of the Horde R :D: 1.50 4.00
169 Chief of the Edge U :W: :K: .20 .50
170 Chief of the Scale U :W: :K: .20 .50
171 Crackling Doom R :D: .75 2.00
172 Death Frenzy U :K: :G: .20 .50
173 Deflecting Palm R :R: :W: .60 1.50
174 Duneblast R :D: .40 1.00
175 Efreet Weaponmaster C :D: .10 .25
176 Flying Crane Technique R :D: .40 1.00
177 Highspire Mantis U :R: :W: .20 .50
178 Icefeather Aven U :G: :B: .50
179 Ivorytusk Fortress R :D: .40 1.00
180 Jeskai Ascendancy R :D: 2.00 5.00
181 Jeskai Charm U :D: .50
182 Kheru Lich Lord R :D: .40 1.00
183 Kin-Tree Invocation U :K: :G: .20 .50
184 Mantis Rider R :D: 2.50 6.00
185 Mardu Ascendancy R :D: .40 1.00
186 Mardu Charm U :D: .20 .50
187 Mardu Roughrider U :D: .20 .50
188 Master the Way U :B: :R: .20 .50
189 Mindswipe R :B: :R: 1.00
190 Narset, Enlightened Master M :D: 1.50 4.00
191 Ponyback Brigade C :D: .10 .25
192 Rakshasa Deathdealer R :K: :G: .60 1.50
193 Rakshasa Vizier R :D: 1.00
194 Ride Down U :R: :W: .20 .50
195 Sage of the Inward Eye R :D: .40 1.00
196 Sagu Mauler R :G: :B: .40 1.00
197 Savage Knuckleblade R :D: 1.25 3.00
198 Secret Plans U :G: :B: .20 .50
199 Sidisi, Brood Tyrant M :D: 2.50 6.00
200 Siege Rhino R :D: 2.00 5.00
201 Snowhorn Rider C :D: .10 .25
203 Sultai Ascendancy R :D: .40 1.00
204 Sultai Charm U :D: .20 .50
205 Sultai Soothsayer U :D: .20 .50
206 Surrak Dragonclaw M :D: 3.00 8.00
207 Temur Ascendancy R :D: .40 1.00
208 Temur Charm U :D: .20 .50
209 Trap Essence R :D: .40 1.00
211 Villainous Wealth R :D: 1.00
212 Warden of the Eye U :D: .20 .50
213 Winterflame U :B: :R: .20 .50
214 Zurgo Helmsmasher M :D: .75 2.00
266 Forest (267) L .10 .25
267 Forest (268) L .10 .25
268 Forest (269) L .10 .25
269 Forest L .10 .25
234 Frontier Bivouac U :L: .10 .25
254 Island (255) L .10 .25
255 Island (256) L .10 .25
256 Island (257) L .10 .25
257 Island L .10 .25
262 Mountain (263) L .10 .25
263 Mountain (264) L .10 .25
264 Mountain (265) L .10 .25
265 Mountain L .10 .25
238 Opulent Palace U :L: .20 .50
250 Plains (251) L .10 .25
251 Plains (252) L .10 .25
252 Plains (253) L .10 .25
253 Plains L .10 .25
241 Sandsteppe Citadel U :L: .20 .50
258 Swamp (259) L .10 .25
259 Swamp (260) L .10 .25
260 Swamp (261) L .10 .25
261 Swamp L .10 .25
215 Abzan Banner C .10 .25
216 Altar of the Brood R .40 1.00
229 Bloodfell Caves C .10 .25
230 Bloodstained Mire R 5.00 12.00
231 Blossoming Sands C .10 .25
217 Briber's Purse U .20 .50
218 Cranial Archive U .20 .50
232 Dismal Backwater C .10 .25
219 Dragon Throne of Tarkir R .40 1.00
233 Flooded Strand R 6.00 15.00
220 Ghostfire Blade R .40 1.00
221 Heart-Piercer Bow U .20 .50
222 Jeskai Banner C .10 .25
235 Jungle Hollow C .10 .25
223 Lens of Clarity C .10 .25
224 Mardu Banner C .10 .25
236 Mystic Monastery U .20 .50
237 Nomad Outpost U .20 .50
239 Polluted Delta R 6.00 15.00
240 Rugged Highlands C .10 .25
242 Scoured Barrens C .10 .25
225 Sultai Banner C .10 .25
243 Swiftwater Cliffs C .10 .25
226 Temur Banner C .10 .25
244 Thornwood Falls C .10 .25
245 Tomb of the Spirit Dragon U .20 .50
246 Tranquil Cove C .10 .25
227 Ugin's Nexus M .50 1.25
247 Wind-Scarred Crag C .10 .25
248 Windswept Heath R 6.00 15.00
228 Witness of the Ages U .20 .50
249 Wooded Foothills R 5.00 12.00
E1 Emblem - Sarkhan, the Dragonspeaker E .50 1.25
E2 Emblem - Sorin, Solemn Visitor E .60 1.50
T1 Bird Token T :W: .10 .25
T2 Spirit Token T :W: .10 .25
T3 Warrior Token (Pike) T :W: .10 .25
T4 Warrior Token (Sword & Shield) T :W: .10 .25
T5 Vampire Token T :K: .30 .75
T6 Zombie Token T :K: .10 .25
T7 Goblin Token T :R: .10 .25
T8 Bear Token T :G: .10 .25
T9 Snake Token T :G: .10 .25
T10 Spirit Warrior Token T :B: :G: .10 .25
T11 Morph Reminder Card T .10 .25

2015 Magic The Gathering Fate Reforged

COMPLETE SET (189) 50.00 120.00
BOOSTER BOX (36 PACKS) 80.00 90.00
BOOSTER PACK (15 CARDS) 3.00 4.00
FAT PACK 20.00 30.00
*FOIL: .75X TO 2X BASIC CARDS
RELEASED ON JANUARY 23, 2015
1 Ugin, the Spirit Dragon M 18.00 22.00
2 Abzan Advantage C :W: .10 .25
3 Abzan Runemark C :W: .10 .25
4 Abzan Skycaptain C :W: .10 .25
5 Arashin Cleric C :W: .10 .25
6 Aven Skirmisher C :W: .10 .25
7 Channel Harm U :W: .10 .30
8 Citadel Siege R :W: .15 .40
9 Daghatar the Adamant R :W: .15 .40
10 Dragon Bell Monk C :W: .10 .25
11 Dragonscale General R :W: .15 .40
12 Elite Scaleguard U :W: .10 .30
13 Great-Horn Krushok C :W: .10 .25
14 Honor's Reward U :W: .10 .30
15 Jeskai Barricade U :W: .10 .30
16 Lightform U :W: .10 .30
17 Lotus-Eye Mystics U :W: .10 .30
18 Mardu Woe-Reaper U :W: .10 .30
19 Mastery of the Unseen R :W: .15 .40
20 Monastery Mentor M :W: 9.50 11.00
21 Pressure Point C :W: .10 .25
22 Rally the Ancestors R :W: .20 .60
23 Sage's Reverie U :W: .10 .30
24 Sandblast C :W: .10 .25
25 Sandsteppe Outcast C :W: .10 .25
26 Soul Summons C :W: .10 .25
27 Soulfire Grand Master M :W: 2.00 2.50
28 Valorous Stance U :W: .10 .30
29 Wandering Champion U :W: .10 .30
30 Wardscale Dragon U :W: .10 .30
31 Aven Surveyor C :B: .10 .25
32 Cloudform U :B: .10 .30
33 Enhanced Awareness C :B: .10 .25
34 Fascination U :B: .10 .30
35 Frost Walker U :B: .10 .30
36 Jeskai Infiltrator R :B: .15 .40
37 Jeskai Runemark C :B: .10 .25
38 Jeskai Sage C :B: .10 .25
39 Lotus Path Djinn C :B: .10 .25
40 Marang River Prowler U :B: .10 .30
41 Mindscour Dragon U :B: .10 .30
42 Mistfire Adept U :B: .10 .30
43 Monastery Siege R :B: .20 .60
44 Neutralizing Blast U :B: .10 .30
45 Rakshasa's Disdain C :B: .10 .25
46 Reality Shift U :B: .10 .30
47 Refocus C :B: .10 .25
48 Renowned Weaponsmith U :B: .10 .30
49 Rite of Undoing U :B: .10 .30
50 Sage-Eye Avengers R :B: .15 .40
51 Shifting Loyalties U :B: .10 .30
52 Shu Yun, the Silent Tempest R :B: .15 .40
53 Sultai Skullkeeper C :B: .10 .25
54 Supplant Form R :B: .15 .40
55 Temporal Trespass M :B: 1.25 1.50
56 Torrent Elemental M :B: .50 .75
57 Whisk Away C :B: .10 .25
58 Will of the Naga C :B: .10 .25
59 Write into Being C :B: .10 .25
60 Alesha's Vanguard C :K: .10 .25
61 Ancestral Vengeance C :K: .10 .25
62 Archfiend of Depravity R :K: .20 .60
63 Battle Brawler U :K: .10 .30
64 Brutal Hordechief M :K: .75 1.25
65 Crux of Fate R :K: .40 .75
66 Dark Deal U :K: .10 .30
67 Diplomacy of the Wastes U :K: .10 .30
68 Douse in Gloom C :K: .10 .25
69 Fearsome Awakening U :K: .10 .30
70 Ghastly Conscription M :K: .20 .60
71 Grave Strength U :K: .10 .30
72 Gurmag Angler C :K: .10 .25
73 Hooded Assassin C :K: .10 .25
74 Mardu Shadowspear U :K: .10 .30
75 Mardu Strike Leader R :K: .15 .40
76 Merciless Executioner U :K: .10 .30
77 Noxious Dragon U :K: .10 .30
78 Orc Sureshot U :K: .10 .30
79 Palace Siege R :K: .15 .40
80 Qarsi High Priest U :K: .10 .30
81 Reach of Shadows C :K: .10 .25
82 Sibsig Host C :K: .10 .25
83 Sibsig Muckdraggers U :K: .10 .30
84 Soulflayer R :K: .15 .40
85 Sultai Emissary C :K: .10 .25
86 Sultai Runemark C :K: .10 .25
87 Tasigur, the Golden Fang R :K: 2.00 2.50
88 Tasigur's Cruelty C :K: .10 .25
89 Typhoid Rats C :K: .10 .25
90 Alesha, Who Smiles at Death R :R: .15 .40
91 Arcbond R :R: .15 .40
92 Bathe in Dragonfire C :R: .10 .25
93 Bloodfire Enforcers U :R: .10 .30
94 Break Through the Line U :R: .10 .30
95 Collateral Damage C :R: .10 .25
96 Defiant Ogre C :R: .10 .25
97 Dragonrage U :R: .10 .30
98 Fierce Invocation C :R: .10 .25
99 Flamerush Rider R :R: .15 .40
100 Flamewake Phoenix R :R: .15 .40
101 Friendly Fire U :R: .10 .30
102 Goblin Heelcutter C :R: .10 .25
103 Gore Swine C :R: .10 .25
104 Humble Defector U :R: .10 .30
105 Hungering Yeti U :R: .10 .30
106 Lightning Shrieker C :R: .10 .25
107 Mardu Runemark C :R: .10 .25
108 Mardu Scout C :R: .10 .25
109 Mob Rule R :R: .15 .40
110 Outpost Siege R :R: .20 .60
111 Pyrotechnics U :R: .10 .30
112 Rageform U :R: .10 .30
113 Shaman of the Great Hunt M :R: .50 .75
114 Shockmaw Dragon U :R: .10 .30
115 Smoldering Efreet C :R: .10 .25
116 Temur Battle Rage C :R: .20 .60
117 Vaultbreaker U :R: .10 .30
118 Wild Slash U :R: .10 .30
119 Abzan Beastmaster U :G: .10 .30
120 Abzan Kin-Guard U :G: .10 .30
121 Ainok Guide C :G: .10 .25
122 Ambush Krotiq C :G: .10 .25
123 Arashin War Beast U :G: .10 .30
124 Archers of Qarsi C :G: .10 .25
125 Battlefront Krushok U :G: .10 .30
126 Cached Defenses U :G: .10 .30
127 Destructor Dragon U :G: .10 .30
128 Feral Krushok C :G: .10 .25
129 Formless Nurturing C :G: .10 .25
130 Frontier Mastodon C :G: .10 .25
131 Frontier Siege R :G: .15 .40
132 Fruit of the First Tree U :G: .10 .30
133 Hunt the Weak C :G: .10 .25
134 Map the Wastes C :G: .10 .25
135 Return to the Earth C :G: .10 .25
136 Ruthless Instincts U :G: .10 .30
137 Sandsteppe Mastodon R :G: .15 .40
138 Shamanic Revelation R :G: .15 .40
139 Sudden Reclamation U :G: .10 .30
140 Temur Runemark C :G: .10 .25
141 Temur Sabertooth U :G: .10 .30
142 Temur War Shaman R :G: .15 .40
143 Warden of the First Tree M :G: .50 .75
144 Whisperer of the Wilds C :G: .10 .25
145 Whisperwood Elemental M :G: .50 .75
146 Wildcall R :G: .15 .40
147 Winds of Qal Sisma U :G: .10 .30
148 Yasova Dragonclaw R :G: .15 .40
149 Atarka, World Render R :M: .20 .60
150 Cunning Strike C :M: .10 .25
151 Dromoka, the Eternal R :M: .15 .40
152 Ethereal Ambush C :M: .10 .25
153 Grim Contest C :M: .10 .25
154 Harsh Sustenance C :M: .10 .25
155 Kolaghan, the Storm's Fury R :M: .20 .60
156 Ojutai, Soul of Winter R :M: .15 .40
157 Silumgar, the Drifting Death R :M: .20 .60
158 War Flare C :M: .10 .25
159 Goblin Boom Keg U .10 .30
160 Hero's Blade U .10 .30
161 Hewed Stone Retainers U .10 .30
162 Pilgrim of the Fires U .10 .30
163 Scroll of the Masters R .15 .40
164 Ugin's Construct U .10 .30
165 Bloodfell Caves C .10 .25
166 Blossoming Sands C .10 .25
167 Crucible of the Spirit Dragon R .15 .40
168 Dismal Backwater C .10 .25
169 Jungle Hollow C .10 .25
170 Rugged Highlands C .10 .25
171 Scoured Barrens C .10 .25
172 Swiftwater Cliffs C .10 .25
173 Thornwood Falls C .10 .25
174 Tranquil Cove C .10 .25
175 Wind-Scarred Crag C .10 .25
176 Plains L .10 .25
177 Plains L .10 .25
178 Island L .10 .25
179 Island L .10 .25
180 Swamp L .10 .25
181 Swamp L .10 .25
182 Mountain L .10 .25
183 Mountain L .10 .25
184 Forest L .10 .25
185 Forest L .10 .25
FRF-T1 Monk T :W: .10 .25
FRF-T2 Spirit T :W: .10 .25
FRF-T3 Warrior T :K: .10 .25
FRF-T4 Manifest Overlay T .10 .25

2015 Magic The Gathering Dragons of Tarkir

Card	Low	High
COMPLETE SET (264)	100.00	200.00
BOOSTER BOX (36 PACKS)	80.00	90.00
BOOSTER PACK (15 CARDS)	3.00	4.00
FAT PACK	15.00	25.00
*FOIL: .75X TO 2X BASIC CARDS		
RELEASED ON MARCH 27, 2015		
2 Anafenza, Kin-Tree Spirit R :W:	1.50	2.00
3 Arashin Foremost R :W:	.75	2.00
4 Artful Maneuver C :W:	.10	.25
5 Aven Sunstriker U :W:	.10	.30
6 Aven Tactician C :W:	.10	.25
7 Battle Mastery U :W:	.10	.30
8 Center Soul C :W:	.10	.25
9 Champion of Arashin C :W:	.10	.25
10 Dragon Hunter U :W:	.10	.30
11 Dragon's Eye Sentry C :W:	.10	.25
12 Dromoka Captain U :W:	.10	.30
13 Dromoka Dunecaster C :W:	.10	.25
14 Dromoka Warrior C :W:	.10	.25
15 Echoes of the Kin Tree U :W:	.10	.30
16 Enduring Victory C :W:	.10	.25
17 Fate Forgotten C :W:	.10	.25
18 Glaring Aegis C :W:	.10	.25
19 Gleam of Authority R :W:	.40	1.00
20 Graceblade Artisan U :W:	.10	.30
21 Great Teacher's Decree U :W:	.10	.30
22 Herald of Dromoka C :W:	.10	.25
23 Hidden Dragonslayer R :W:	.50	.75
24 Lightwalker C :W:	.10	.25
25 Misthoof Kirin C :W:	.10	.25
26 Myth Realized R :W:	1.50	4.00
27 Ojutai Exemplars M :W:	.75	1.00
28 Orator of Ojutai U :W:	.10	.30
29 Pacifism C :W:	.10	.25
30 Profound Journey R :W:	.40	1.00
31 Radiant Purge R :W:	.40	1.00
32 Resupply C :W:	.10	.25
33 Sandcrafter Mage C :W:	.10	.25
34 Sandstorm Charger C :W:	.10	.25
35 Scale Blessing U :W:	.10	.30
36 Secure the Wastes R :W:	2.75	3.50
37 Shieldhide Dragon U :W:	.10	.30
38 Silkwrap U :W:	.50	1.25
39 Strongarm Monk U :W:	.10	.30
40 Student of Ojutai C :W:	.10	.25
41 Sunscorch Regent R :W:	.40	.75
42 Surge of Righteousness U :W:	.10	.30
43 Territorial Roc C :W:	.10	.25
44 Ancient Carp C :B:	.10	.25
45 Anticipate C :B:	.10	.25
46 Belltoll Dragon R :B:	.40	1.00
47 Blessed Reincarnation R :B:	.40	1.00
48 Clone Legion M :B:	.50	.75
49 Contradict C :B:	.10	.25
50 Dance of the Skywise U :B:	.10	.30
51 Dirgur Nemesis C :B:	.10	.25
52 Dragonlord's Prerogative R :B:	.40	1.00
53 Elusive Spellfist C :B:	.10	.25
54 Encase in Ice U :B:	.10	.30
55 Glint C :B:	.10	.25
56 Gudul Lurker U :B:	.10	.30
57 Gurmag Drowner C :B:	.10	.25
58 Icefall Regent R :B:	.50	.75
59 Illusory Gains R :B:	.40	1.00
60 Learn from the Past U :B:	.10	.30
61 Living Lore R :B:	.40	1.00
62 Mirror Mockery R :B:	.40	1.00
63 Monastery Loremaster C :B:	.10	.25
64 Mystic Meditation C :B:	.10	.25
65 Negate C :B:	.10	.25
66 Ojutai Interceptor C :B:	.10	.25
67 Ojutai's Breath C :B:	.10	.25
68 Ojutai's Summons C :B:	.10	.25
69 Palace Familiar C :B:	.10	.25
70 Profaner of the Dead R :B:	.40	1.00
71 Qarsi Deceiver U :B:	.10	.30
72 Reduce in Stature C :B:	.10	.25
73 Shorecrasher Elemental M :B:	.50	.75
74 Sidisi's Faithful C :B:	.10	.25
75 Sight Beyond Sight U :B:	.10	.30
76 Silumgar Sorcerer U :B:	.10	.30
77 Silumgar Spell-Eater U :B:	.10	.30
78 Silumgar's Scorn U :B:	.20	.60
79 Skywise Teachings U :B:	.10	.30
80 Stratus Dancer R :B:	.50	.80
81 Taigam's Strike C :B:	.10	.25
82 Updraft Elemental C :B:	.10	.25
83 Void Squall U :B:	.10	.30
84 Youthful Scholar U :B:	.10	.30
85 Zephyr Scribe C :B:	.10	.25
86 Acid-Spewer Dragon U :K:	.10	.30
87 Ambuscade Shaman U :K:	.10	.30
88 Blood-Chin Fanatic R :K:	.40	1.00
89 Blood-Chin Rager U :K:	.10	.30
90 Butcher's Glee C :K:	.10	.25
91 Coat with Venom C :K:	.10	.25
92 Corpseweft R :K:	.40	1.00
93 Damnable Pact R :K:	.40	1.00
94 Deadly Wanderings U :K:	.10	.30
95 Death Wind U :K:	.10	.30
96 Deathbringer Regent R :K:	.40	1.00
97 Defeat C :K:	.10	.25
98 Duress C :K:	.10	.25
99 Dutiful Attendant C :K:	.10	.25
100 Flatten C :K:	.10	.25
101 Foul Renewal R :K:	.40	1.00
102 Foul-Tongue Invocation U :K:	.10	.30
103 Foul-Tongue Shriek C :K:	.10	.25
104 Gravepurge C :K:	.10	.25
105 Hand of Silumgar C :K:	.10	.25
106 Hedonist's Trove R :K:	.40	1.00
107 Kolaghan Skirmisher C :K:	.10	.25
108 Marang River Skeleton U :K:	.10	.30
109 Marsh Hulk C :K:	.10	.25
110 Mind Rot C :K:	.10	.25
111 Minister of Pain U :K:	.10	.30
112 Pitiless Horde R :K:	.40	1.00
113 Qarsi Sadist C :K:	.10	.25
114 Rakshasa Gravecaller U :K:	.10	.30
115 Reckless Imp C :K:	.10	.25
116 Risen Executioner M :K:	3.00	3.50
117 Self-Inflicted Wound U :K:	.10	.30
118 Shambling Goblin C :K:	.10	.25
119 Sibsig Icebreakers C :K:	.10	.25
120 Sidisi, Undead Vizier R :K:	2.40	3.00
121 Silumgar Assassin R :K:	.40	1.00
122 Silumgar Butcher C :K:	.10	.25
123 Ukud Cobra U :K:	.10	.30
124 Ultimate Price U :K:	.10	.30
125 Virulent Plague U :K:	.10	.30
126 Vulturous Aven C :K:	.10	.25
127 Wandering Tombshell C :K:	.10	.25
128 Atarka Efreet C :R:	.10	.25
129 Atarka Pummeler U :R:	.10	.30
130 Berserkers' Onslaught R :R:	.40	1.00
131 Commune with Lava R :R:	.40	1.00
132 Crater Elemental R :R:	.40	1.00
133 Descent of the Dragons M :R:	1.50	2.00
134 Draconic Roar U :R:	.20	.60
135 Dragon Fodder C :R:	.10	.25
136 Dragon Tempest R :R:	.75	1.00
137 Dragon Whisperer M :R:	.75	1.25
138 Dragonlord's Servant U :R:	.10	.30
139 Hardened Berserker C :R:	.10	.25
140 Impact Tremors C :R:	.10	.25
141 Ire Shaman R :R:	.40	1.00
142 Kindled Fury C :R:	.10	.25
143 Kolaghan Aspirant C :R:	.10	.25
144 Kolaghan Forerunners U :R:	.10	.30
145 Kolaghan Stormsinger C :R:	.10	.25
146 Lightning Berserker U :R:	.20	.60
147 Lose Calm C :R:	.10	.25
148 Magmatic Chasm C :R:	.10	.25
149 Qal Sisma Behemoth U :R:	.10	.30
150 Rending Volley U :R:	.40	1.00
151 Roast U :R:	.50	1.25
152 Sabertooth Outrider C :R:	.10	.25
153 Sarkhan's Rage C :R:	.10	.25
154 Sarkhan's Triumph U :R:	.10	.30
155 Screamreach Brawler C :R:	.10	.25
156 Seismic Rupture U :R:	.10	.30
157 Sprinting Warbrute C :R:	.10	.25
158 Stormcrag Elemental U :R:	.10	.30
159 Stormwing Dragon U :R:	.10	.30
160 Summit Prowler C :R:	.10	.25
161 Tail Slash C :R:	.10	.25
162 Thunderbreak Regent R :R:	1.50	2.00
163 Tormenting Voice C :R:	.10	.25
164 Twin Bolt C :R:	.10	.25
165 Vandalize C :R:	.10	.25
166 Volcanic Rush C :R:	.10	.25
167 Volcanic Vision R :R:	.40	1.00
168 Warbringer U :R:	.10	.30
169 Zurgo Bellstriker R :R:	.50	.75
170 Aerie Bowmasters C :G:	.10	.25
171 Ainok Artillerist C :G:	.10	.25
172 Ainok Survivalist U :G:	.10	.30
173 Assault Formation R :G:	1.00	1.50
174 Atarka Beastbreaker C :G:	.10	.25
175 Avatar of the Resolute R :G:	.75	1.00
176 Circle of Elders U :G:	.10	.30
177 Collected Company R :G:	10.00	13.00
178 Colossodon Yearling C :G:	.10	.25
179 Conifer Strider C :G:	.10	.25
180 Deathmist Raptor M :G:	1.75	2.50
181 Den Protector R :G:	1.50	2.25
182 Display of Dominance U :G:	.10	.30
183 Dragon-Scarred Bear C :G:	.10	.25
184 Dromoka's Gift U :G:	.10	.30
185 Epic Confrontation C :G:	.10	.25
186 Explosive Vegetation U :G:	1.00	2.50
187 Foe-Razer Regent R :G:	.40	1.00
188 Glade Watcher C :G:	.10	.25
189 Guardian Shield-Bearer C :G:	.10	.25
190 Herdchaser Dragon U :G:	.10	.30
191 Inspiring Call U :G:	.10	.30
192 Lurking Arynx U :G:	.10	.30
193 Naturalize C :G:	.10	.25
194 Obscuring Aether R :G:	.40	1.00
195 Pinion Feast C :G:	.10	.25
196 Press the Advantage U :G:	.10	.30
197 Revealing Wind C :G:	.10	.25
198 Salt Road Ambushers U :G:	.10	.30
199 Salt Road Quartermasters U :G:	.10	.30
200 Sandsteppe Scavenger C :G:	.10	.25
201 Scaleguard Sentinels U :G:	.10	.30
202 Segmented Krotiq C :G:	.10	.25
203 Servant of the Scale C :G:	.10	.25
204 Shaman of Forgotten Ways M :G:	2.00	3.00
205 Shape the Sands C :G:	.10	.25
206 Sheltered Aerie C :G:	.10	.25
207 Sight of the Scalelords U :G:	.10	.30
208 Stampeding Elk Herd C :G:	.10	.25
209 Sunbringer's Touch R :G:	.40	1.00
210 Surrak, the Hunt Caller R :G:	2.00	5.00
211 Tread Upon C :G:	.10	.25
212 Arashin Sovereign R :M:	.40	1.00
213 Atarka's Command R :M:	4.50	5.50
214 Boltwing Marauder R :M:	.40	1.00
215 Cunning Breezedancer U :M:	.10	.30
216 Dragonlord Atarka M :M:	5.00	7.00
217 Dragonlord Dromoka M :M:	4.00	5.00
218 Dragonlord Kolaghan M :M:	2.50	3.25
219 Dragonlord Ojutai M :M:	3.50	5.50
220 Dragonlord Silumgar M :M:	4.00	5.50
221 Dromoka's Command R :M:	3.00	4.00
222 Enduring Scalelord U :M:	.10	.30
223 Harbinger of the Hunt R :M:	.40	1.00
224 Kolaghan's Command R :M:	5.00	7.00
225 Narset Transcendent M :M:	6.50	8.00
226 Necromaster Dragon R :M:	.40	1.00
227 Ojutai's Command R :M:	1.25	1.50
228 Pristine Skywise R :M:	.40	1.00
229 Ruthless Deathfang U :M:	.10	.30
230 Sarkhan Unbroken M :M:	3.75	4.50
231 Savage Ventmaw U :M:	.10	.30
232 Silumgar's Command R :M:	.75	2.00
233 Swift Warkite U :M:	.10	.30
263 Forest (263) L :L:	.10	.25
264 Forest (264) L :L:	.10	.25
262 Forest L :L:	.10	.25
254 Island (254) L :L:	.10	.25
255 Island (255) L :L:	.10	.25
253 Island L :L:	.10	.25
260 Mountain (260) L :L:	.10	.25
261 Mountain (261) L :L:	.10	.25
259 Mountain L :L:	.10	.25
251 Plains (251) L :L:	.10	.25
252 Plains (252) L :L:	.10	.25
250 Plains L :L:	.10	.25
257 Swamp (257) L :L:	.10	.25
258 Swamp (258) L :L:	.10	.25
256 Swamp L :L:	.10	.25
234 Ancestral Statue C	.10	.25
235 Atarka Monument U	.10	.30
236 Custodian of the Trove C	.10	.25
237 Dragonloft Idol U	.10	.30
238 Dromoka Monument U	.10	.30
248 Evolving Wilds C	.10	.25
239 Gate Smasher U	.10	.30
249 Haven of the Spirit Dragon R	.75	1.25
240 Keeper of the Lens C	.10	.25
241 Kolaghan Monument U	.10	.30
242 Ojutai Monument U	.10	.30
1 Scion of Ugin U	.10	.30
243 Silumgar Monument U	.10	.30
244 Spidersilk Net C	.10	.25
245 Stormrider Rig U	.10	.30
246 Tapestry of the Ages U	.10	.30
247 Vial of Dragonfire C	.10	.25
E1 Emblem - Narset	.10	.25
T1 Warrior Token :W:	.10	.25
T2 Djinn Monk Token :B:	.10	.25
T3 Zombie Horror Token :K:	.10	.25
T4 Zombie Token :K:	.10	.25
T5 Dragon Token :R:	.25	.60
T6 Goblin Token :R:	.10	.25
T7 Morph Token	.10	.25

2015 Magic The Gathering Battle for Zendikar

Card	Low	High
COMPLETE SET (299)	120.00	250.00
BOOSTER BOX (36 PACKS)	80.00	100.00
BOOSTER PACK (15 CARDS)	2.50	6.00
RELEASED ON OCTOBER 2, 2015		
1 Bane of Bala Ged U	.10	.30
2 Blight Herder R	.40	1.00
3 Breaker of Armies U	.10	.30
4 Conduit of Ruin R	.50	1.25
5 Deathless Behemoth U	.10	.30
6 Desolation Twin R	.40	1.00
7 Eldrazi Devastator C	.10	.25
8 Endless One R	.40	1.00
9 Gruesome Slaughter R	.40	1.00
10 Kozilek's Channeler C	.10	.25
11 Oblivion Sower M	1.25	2.00
12 Ruin Processor C	.10	.25
13 Scour from Existence C	.10	.25
14 Titan's Presence U	.10	.30
15 Ulamog, the Ceaseless Hunger M	10.00	13.00
16 Ulamog's Despoiler U	.10	.30
17 Void Winnower M	1.50	2.00
18 Angel of Renewal U :W:	.10	.30
19 Angelic Gift C :W:	.10	.25
20 Cliffside Lookout C :W:	.10	.25
21 Courier Griffin C :W:	.10	.25
22 Emeria Shepherd R :W:	.40	1.00
23 Encircling Fissure U :W:	.10	.30
24 Expedition Envoy U :W:	.10	.30
25 Felidar Cub C :W:	.10	.25
26 Felidar Sovereign R :W:	.40	1.00
27 Fortified Rampart C :W:	.10	.25
28 Ghostly Sentinel C :W:	.10	.25
29 Gideon, Ally of Zendikar M :W:	15.00	20.00
30 Gideon's Reproach C :W:	.10	.25
31 Hero of Goma Fada R :W:	.40	1.00
32 Inspired Charge C :W:	.10	.25
33 Kitesail Scout C :W:	.10	.25
34 Kor Bladewhirl U :W:	.10	.30
35 Kor Castigator C :W:	.10	.25
36 Kor Entanglers U :W:	.10	.30
37 Lantern Scout R :W:	.40	1.00
38 Lithomancer's Focus C :W:	.10	.25
39 Makindi Patrol C :W:	.10	.25
40 Ondu Greathorn C :W:	.10	.25
41 Ondu Rising U :W:	.10	.30
42 Planar Outburst R :W:	.40	1.00
43 Quarantine Field M :W:	.75	1.00
44 Retreat to Emeria U :W:	.10	.30
45 Roil's Retribution U :W:	.10	.30
46 Serene Steward U :W:	.10	.30
47 Shadow Glider C :W:	.10	.25
48 Sheer Drop C :W:	.10	.25
49 Smite the Monstrous C :W:	.10	.25
50 Stasis Snare U :W:	.40	1.00
51 Stone Haven Medic C :W:	.10	.25
52 Tandem Tactics C :W:	.10	.25
53 Unified Front U :W:	.10	.30
54 Adverse Conditions U :B:	.10	.30
55 Benthic Infiltrator C :B:	.10	.25
56 Cryptic Cruiser U :B:	.10	.30
57 Drowner of Hope R :B:	.40	1.00
58 Eldrazi Skyspawner C :B:	.10	.25
59 Horribly Awry U :B:	.10	.30
60 Incubator Drone C :B:	.10	.25
61 Mist Intruder C :B:	.10	.25
62 Murk Strider C :B:	.10	.25
63 Oracle of Dust C :B:	.10	.25
64 Ruination Guide U :B:	.10	.30
65 Salvage Drone C :B:	.10	.25
66 Spell Shrivel C :B:	.10	.25
67 Tide Drifter U :B:	.10	.30
68 Ulamog's Reclaimer U :B:	.10	.30
69 Anticipate C :B:	.10	.25
70 Brilliant Spectrum C :B:	.10	.25
71 Cloud Manta C :B:	.10	.25
72 Clutch of Currents C :B:	.10	.25
73 Coastal Discovery U :B:	.10	.30
74 Coralhelm Guide C :B:	.10	.25
75 Dampening Pulse U :B:	.10	.30
76 Dispel C :B:	.10	.25
77 Exert Influence R :B:	.40	1.00
78 Guardian of Tazeem R :B:	.40	1.00
79 Halimar Tidecaller U :B:	.10	.30
80 Part the Waterveil M :B:	2.50	4.00
81 Prism Array R :B:	.40	1.00
82 Retreat to Coralhelm U :B:	.10	.30
83 Roilmage's Trick C :B:	.10	.25
84 Rush of Ice C :B:	.10	.25
85 Scatter to the Winds R :B:	.75	2.00
86 Tightening Coils C :B:	.10	.25
87 Ugin's Insight R :B:	.40	1.00
88 Wave-Wing Elemental C :B:	.10	.25
89 Windrider Patrol U :B:	.10	.30
90 Complete Disregard C :K:	.10	.25
91 Culling Drone C :K:	.10	.25
92 Dominator Drone C :K:	.10	.25
93 Grave Birthing C :K:	.10	.25
94 Grip of Desolation U :K:	.10	.30
95 Mind Raker C :K:	.10	.25
96 Silent Skimmer C :K:	.10	.25
97 Skitterskin U :K:	.10	.30
98 Sludge Crawler C :K:	.10	.25
99 Smothering Abomination R :K:	.40	1.00
100 Swarm Surge C :K:	.10	.25
101 Transgress the Mind U :K:	.75	2.00
102 Wasteland Strangler R :K:	.40	1.00
103 Altar's Reap C :K:	.10	.25
104 Bloodbond Vampire U :K:	.10	.30
105 Bone Splinters C :K:	.10	.25
106 Carrier Thrall U :K:	.10	.30
107 Defiant Bloodlord R :K:	.40	1.00
108 Demon's Grasp C :K:	.10	.25
109 Drana, Liberator of Malakir M :K:	4.00	6.00
110 Dutiful Return C :K:	.10	.25
111 Geyserfield Stalker C :K:	.10	.25
112 Guul Draz Overseer R :K:	.40	1.00
113 Hagra Sharpshooter U :K:	.10	.30
114 Kalastria Healer C :K:	.10	.25
115 Kalastria Nightwatch C :K:	.10	.25
116 Malakir Familiar U :K:	.10	.30
117 Mire's Malice C :K:	.10	.25
118 Nirkana Assassin C :K:	.10	.25
119 Ob Nixilis Reignited M :K:	4.50	6.50
120 Painful Truths R :K:	.40	1.00
121 Retreat to Hagra U :K:	.10	.30
122 Rising Miasma U :K:	.10	.30
123 Ruinous Path R :K:	1.50	2.00
124 Vampiric Rites U :K:	.10	.30
125 Voracious Null C :K:	.10	.25
126 Zulaport Cutthroat U :K:	.40	1.00
127 Barrage Tyrant R :R:	.40	1.00
128 Crumble to Dust U :R:	.10	.30
129 Kozilek's Sentinel C :R:	.10	.25
130 Molten Nursery U :R:	.10	.30
131 Nettle Drone C :R:	.10	.25
132 Processor Assault U :R:	.10	.30
133 Serpentine Spike R :R:	.40	1.00
134 Touch of the Void C :R:	.10	.25
135 Turn Against U :R:	.10	.30
136 Vestige of Emrakul C :R:	.10	.25
137 Vile Aggregate U :R:	.10	.30
138 Akoum Firebird M :R:	.20	.30
139 Akoum Hellkite R :R:	.40	1.00
140 Akoum Stonewaker U :R:	.10	.30
141 Belligerent Whiptail C :R:	.10	.25
142 Boiling Earth C :R:	.10	.25
143 Chasm Guide U :R:	.10	.30
144 Dragonmaster Outcast M :R:	1.75	2.25
145 Firemantle Mage U :R:	.10	.30
146 Goblin War Paint C :R:	.10	.25
147 Lavastep Raider C :R:	.10	.25
148 Makindi Sliderunner C :R:	.10	.25
149 Ondu Champion C :R:	.10	.25
150 Outnumber C :R:	.10	.25
151 Radiant Flames R :R:	1.25	3.00
152 Reckless Cohort C :R:	.10	.25
153 Retreat to Valakut U :R:	.10	.30
154 Rolling Thunder U :R:	.10	.30
155 Shatterskull Recruit C :R:	.10	.25
156 Stonefury C :R:	.10	.25
157 Sure Strike C :R:	.10	.25
158 Tunneling Geopede U :R:	.10	.30
159 Valakut Invoker C :R:	.10	.25
160 Valakut Predator C :R:	.10	.25
161 Volcanic Upheaval C :R:	.10	.25
162 Zada, Hedron Grinder R :R:	.40	1.00
163 Blisterpod C :G:	.10	.25
164 Brood Monitor U :G:	.10	.30
165 Call the Scions C :G:	.10	.25
166 Eyeless Watcher C :G:	.10	.25
167 From Beyond R :G:	.75	2.00
168 Unnatural Aggression C :G:	.10	.25
169 Void Attendant U :G:	.10	.30
170 Beastcaller Savant R :G:	.40	1.00
171 Broodhunter Wurm C :G:	.10	.25
172 Earthen Arms C :G:	.10	.25
173 Giant Mantis C :G:	.10	.25
174 Greenwarden of Murasa M :G:	.75	1.00
175 Infuse with the Elements U :G:	.10	.30
176 Jaddi Offshoot U :G:	.10	.30
177 Lifespring Druid C :G:	.10	.25
178 Murasa Ranger U :G:	.10	.30
179 Natural Connection C :G:	.10	.25
180 Nissa's Renewal R :G:	.40	1.00
181 Oran-Rief Hydra R :G:	.40	1.00
182 Oran-Rief Invoker C :G:	.10	.25
183 Plated Crusher U :G:	.10	.30
184 Plummet C :G:	.10	.25
185 Reclaiming Vines C :G:	.10	.25
186 Retreat to Kazandu U :G:	.10	.30
187 Rot Shambler U :G:	.10	.30
188 Scythe Leopard U :G:	.10	.30
189 Seek the Wilds C :G:	.10	.25
190 Snapping Gnarlid C :G:	.10	.25
191 Swell of Growth C :G:	.10	.25
192 Sylvan Scrying U :G:	.10	.30
193 Tajuru Beastmaster C :G:	.10	.25
194 Tajuru Stalwart C :G:	.10	.25
195 Tajuru Warcaller U :G:	.10	.30
196 Territorial Baloth C :G:	.10	.25
197 Undergrowth Champion M :G:	1.00	1.50
198 Woodland Wanderer R :G:	.75	2.00
199 Brood Butcher R :M:	.40	1.00
200 Brutal Expulsion R :M:	.40	1.00
201 Catacomb Sifter U :M:	.10	.30
202 Dust Stalker R :M:	.40	1.00
203 Fathom Feeder R :M:	.40	1.00
204 Forerunner of Slaughter U :M:	.10	.30
205 Herald of Kozilek U :M:	.10	.30
206 Sire of Stagnation M :M:	.75	1.00
207 Ulamog's Nullifier U :M:	.10	.30
208 Angelic Captain R :M:	.40	1.00
209 Bring to Light R :M:	1.25	3.00
210 Drana's Emissary U :M:	.20	.75
211 Grove Rumbler U :M:	.10	.30
212 Grovetender Druids U :M:	.10	.30
213 Kiora, Master of the Depths M :M:	2.00	3.00
214 March from the Tomb R :M:	.40	1.00
215 Munda, Ambush Leader R :M:	.40	1.00
216 Noyan Dar, Roil Shaper R :M:	.40	1.00
217 Omnath, Locus of Rage M :M:	1.00	1.50
218 Resolute Blademaster U :M:	.10	.30
219 Roil Spout U :M:	.10	.30
220 Skyrider Elf U :M:	.10	.30
221 Veteran Warleader R :M:	.40	1.00
222 Aligned Hedron Network R :A:	.75	2.00
223 Hedron Archive U :A:	.15	.45
224 Hedron Blade C :A:	.10	.25
225 Pathway Arrows U :A:	.10	.30
226 Pilgrim's Eye U :A:	.10	.30
227 Slab Hammer U :A:	.10	.30
228 Ally Encampment R :L:	.40	1.00
229 Blighted Cataract U :L:	.10	.30
230 Blighted Fen U :L:	.10	.30
231 Blighted Gorge U :L:	.10	.30
232 Blighted Steppe U :L:	.10	.30
233 Blighted Woodland U :L:	.10	.30
234 Canopy Vista R :L:	2.25	2.75
235 Cinder Glade R :L:	2.25	2.75
236 Evolving Wilds C :L:	.10	.25
237 Fertile Thicket C :L:	.10	.25
238 Looming Spires C :L:	.10	.25
239 Lumbering Falls R :L:	1.00	1.50
240 Mortuary Mire C :L:	.10	.25
241 Prairie Stream R :L:	2.50	3.50
242 Sanctum of Ugin R :L:	1.00	1.50
243 Sandstone Bridge C :L:	.10	.25
244 Shambling Vent R :L:	2.25	2.75
245 Shrine of the Forsaken Gods R :L:	.50	.75
246 Skyline Cascade C :L:	.10	.25
247 Smoldering Marsh R :L:	2.50	3.00
248 Spawning Bed U :L:	.10	.30
249 Sunken Hollow R :L:	2.00	2.50
T6 Kor Ally T	.10	.30
T8 Dragon Token T	.10	.30
T2 Eldrazi Scion Izzy T	.10	.30
T4 Eldrazi Scion Velinov T	.10	.30
T1 Eldrazi Token T	.10	.30
T3 Eldrazi Scion Nelson T	.10	.30
T7 Octopus Token T	.10	.30
T5 Knight Ally T	.10	.30
T9 Elemental Token T	.10	.30
T10 Plant T	.10	.30
T11 Elemental Token T	.10	.30
T12 Gideon, Ally of Zendikar Emblem T	.10	.30
T13 Ob Nixilis Reignited T	.10	.30
T14 Kiora, Master of the Depths T	.10	.30
250a Plains L :L:	.10	.25
250b Plains Full Art L :L:	.10	.25
251a Plains L :L:	.10	.25
251b Plains Full Art L :L:	.10	.25
252a Plains L :L:	.10	.25
252b Plains Full Art L :L:	.10	.25
253a Plains L :L:	.10	.25
253b Plains Full Art L :L:	.10	.25
254a Plains L :L:	.10	.25
254b Plains Full Art L :L:	.10	.25
255a Island L :L:	.10	.25
255b Island Full Art L :L:	.10	.25
256a Island L :L:	.10	.25
256b Island Full Art L :L:	.10	.25
257a Island L :L:	.10	.25
257b Island Full Art L :L:	.10	.25
258a Island L :L:	.10	.25
258b Island Full Art L :L:	.10	.25
259a Island L :L:	.10	.25
259b Island Full Art L :L:	.10	.25
260a Swamp L :L:	.10	.25
260b Swamp Full Art L :L:	.10	.25
261a Swamp L :L:	.10	.25
261b Swamp Full Art L :L:	.10	.25
262a Swamp L :L:	.10	.25
262b Swamp Full Art L :L:	.10	.25
263a Swamp L :L:	.10	.25
263b Swamp Full Art L :L:	.10	.25
264a Swamp L :L:	.10	.25
264b Swamp Full Art L :L:	.10	.25
265a Mountain L :L:	.10	.25
265b Mountain Full Art L :L:	.10	.25
266a Mountain L :L:	.10	.25
266b Mountain Full Art L :L:	.10	.25
267a Mountain L :L:	.10	.25
267b Mountain Full Art L :L:	.10	.25
268a Mountain L :L:	.10	.25
268b Mountain Full Art L :L:	.10	.25
269a Mountain L :L:	.10	.25
269b Mountain Full Art L :L:	.10	.25
270a Forest L :L:	.10	.25
270b Forest Full Art L :L:	.10	.25
271a Forest L :L:	.10	.25
271b Forest Full Art L :L:	.10	.25
272a Forest L :L:	.10	.25
272b Forest Full Art L :L:	.10	.25
273a Forest L :L:	.10	.25
273b Forest Full Art L :L:	.10	.25
274a Forest L :L:	.10	.25
274b Forest Full Art L :L:	.10	.25

2015 Magic The Gathering Battle for Zendikar Foil

Card	Low	High
COMPLETE SET (299)	300.00	600.00
*FOIL: .75X TO 2X BASIC CARDS		
1 Bane of Bala Ged U	1.00	2.50
2 Blight Herder R	.75	2.00
3 Breaker of Armies U	.20	.75
4 Conduit of Ruin R	1.50	4.00
5 Deathless Behemoth U	.20	.75
6 Desolation Twin R	.75	2.00
7 Eldrazi Devastator C	.10	.30
8 Endless One R	2.50	5.00
9 Gruesome Slaughter R	.75	2.00
10 Kozilek's Channeler C	.10	.30
11 Oblivion Sower M	3.00	6.00
12 Ruin Processor C	.10	.30

13 Scour from Existence C	1.00	2.50
14 Titan's Presence U	.50	1.25
15 Ulamog, the Ceaseless Hunger M	25.00	45.00
16 Ulamog's Despoiler U	.20	.75
17 Void Winnower M	4.00	8.00
18 Angel of Renewal U :W:	.20	.75
19 Angelic Gift C :W:	.10	.30
20 Cliffside Lookout C :W:	.10	.30
21 Courier Griffin C :W:	.10	.30
22 Emeria Shepherd R :W:	.75	2.00
23 Encircling Fissure U :W:	.20	.75
24 Expedition Envoy U :W:	.50	1.25
25 Felidar Cub C :W:	.10	.30
26 Felidar Sovereign R :W:	.75	2.00
27 Fortified Rampart C :W:	.10	.30
28 Ghostly Sentinel C :W:	.10	.30
29 Gideon, Ally of Zendikar M :W:	18.00	30.00
30 Gideon's Reproach C :W:	.10	.30
31 Hero of Goma Fada R :W:	.75	2.00
32 Inspired Charge C :W:	.10	.30
33 Kitesail Scout C :W:	.10	.30
34 Kor Bladewhirl U :W:	.20	.75
35 Kor Castigator C :W:	.10	.30
36 Kor Entanglers U :W:	.20	.75
37 Lantern Scout R :W:	.75	2.00
38 Lithomancer's Focus C :W:	.10	.30
39 Makindi Patrol C :W:	.10	.30
40 Ondu Greathorn C :W:	.10	.30
41 Ondu Rising U :W:	.20	.75
42 Planar Outburst R :W:	.75	2.00
43 Quarantine Field M :W:	2.00	4.00
44 Retreat to Emeria U :W:	.20	.75
45 Roil's Retribution U :W:	.20	.75
46 Serene Steward U :W:	.20	.75
47 Shadow Glider C :W:	.10	.30
48 Sheer Drop C :W:	.10	.30
49 Smite the Monstrous C :W:	.10	.30
50 Stasis Snare U :W:	1.00	2.50
51 Stone Haven Medic C :W:	.10	.30
52 Tandem Tactics C :W:	.10	.30
53 Unified Front U :W:	.20	.75
54 Adverse Conditions U :B:	.20	.75
55 Benthic Infiltrator C :B:	.10	.30
56 Cryptic Cruiser U :B:	.20	.75
57 Drowner of Hope R :B:	.75	2.00
58 Eldrazi Skyspawner C :B:	1.50	4.00
59 Horribly Awry U :B:	.60	1.50
60 Incubator Drone C :B:	.10	.30
61 Mist Intruder C :B:	.10	.30
62 Murk Strider C :B:	.10	.30
63 Oracle of Dust C :B:	.10	.30
64 Ruination Guide U :B:	.50	1.25
65 Salvage Drone C :B:	.10	.30
66 Spell Shrivel C :B:	.20	.60
67 Tide Drifter U :B:	.20	.75
68 Ulamog's Reclaimer U :B:	.20	.75
69 Anticipate C :B:	.40	1.00
70 Brilliant Spectrum C :B:	.10	.30
71 Cloud Manta C :B:	.10	.30
72 Clutch of Currents C :B:	.10	.30
73 Coastal Discovery U :B:	.20	.75
74 Coralhelm Guide C :B:	.10	.30
75 Dampening Pulse U :B:	.20	.75
76 Dispel C :B:	2.00	5.00
77 Exert Influence R :B:	.75	2.00
78 Guardian of Tazeem R :B:	.75	2.00
79 Halimar Tidecaller U :B:	.20	.75
80 Part the Waterveil M :B:	5.00	10.00
81 Prism Array R :B:	.75	2.00
82 Retreat to Coralhelm U :B:	.20	.75
83 Roilmage's Trick C :B:	.10	.30
84 Rush of Ice C :B:	.10	.30
85 Scatter to the Winds R :B:	2.50	6.00
86 Tightening Coils C :B:	.10	.30
87 Ugin's Insight R :B:	.75	2.00
88 Wave-Wing Elemental C :B:	.10	.30
89 Windrider Patrol U :B:	.20	.75
90 Complete Disregard C :K:	.10	.30
91 Culling Drone C :K:	.10	.30
92 Dominator Drone C :K:	.10	.30
93 Grave Birthing C :K:	.10	.30
94 Grip of Desolation U :K:	.20	.75
95 Mind Raker C :K:	.10	.30
96 Silent Skimmer C :K:	.10	.30
97 Skitterskin U :K:	.20	.75
98 Sludge Crawler C :K:	.10	.30
99 Smothering Abomination R :K:	.75	2.00
100 Swarm Surge C :K:	.10	.30
101 Transgress the Mind U :K:	1.50	4.00
102 Wasteland Strangler R :K:	1.50	4.00
103 Altar's Reap C :K:	.10	.30
104 Bloodbond Vampire U :K:	.20	.75
105 Bone Splinters C :K:	.10	.30
106 Carrier Thrall U :K:	.20	.75
107 Defiant Bloodlord R :K:	.75	2.00
108 Demon's Grasp C :K:	.10	.30
109 Drana, Liberator of Malakir M :K:	6.00	12.00
110 Dutiful Return C :K:	.10	.30
111 Geyserfield Stalker C :K:	.10	.30
112 Guul Draz Overseer R :K:	.75	2.00
113 Hagra Sharpshooter U :K:	.20	.75
114 Kalastria Healer C :K:	.40	1.00
115 Kalastria Nightwatch C :K:	.10	.30
116 Malakir Familiar U :K:	.20	.75
117 Mire's Malice C :K:	.10	.30
118 Nirkana Assassin C :K:	.10	.30
119 Ob Nixilis Reignited M :K:	8.00	20.00
120 Painful Truths R :K:	3.00	7.00
121 Retreat to Hagra U :K:	.20	.75
122 Rising Miasma U :K:	.20	.75
123 Ruinous Path R :K:	1.50	3.00
124 Vampiric Rites U :K:	.20	.75
125 Voracious Null C :K:	.10	.30
126 Zulaport Cutthroat U :K:	2.00	4.00
127 Barrage Tyrant R :R:	.75	2.00
128 Crumble to Dust U :R:	2.50	6.00
129 Kozilek's Sentinel C :R:	.10	.30
130 Molten Nursery U :R:	.20	.75
131 Nettle Drone C :R:	.10	.30
132 Processor Assault U :R:	.20	.75
133 Serpentine Spike R :R:	.75	2.00
134 Touch of the Void C :R:	.10	.30
135 Turn Against U :R:	.20	.75
136 Vestige of Emrakul C :R:	.10	.30
137 Vile Aggregate U :R:	1.00	2.50
138 Akoum Firebird M :R:	.50	1.25
139 Akoum Hellkite R :R:	.75	2.00
140 Akoum Stonewaker U :R:	.20	.75
141 Belligerent Whiptail C :R:	.10	.30
142 Boiling Earth C :R:	.10	.30
143 Chasm Guide U :R:	.20	.75
144 Dragonmaster Outcast M :R:	3.00	7.00
145 Firemantle Mage U :R:	.20	.75
146 Goblin War Paint C :R:	.10	.30
147 Lavastep Raider C :R:	.10	.30
148 Makindi Sliderunner C :R:	.10	.30
149 Ondu Champion C :R:	.10	.30
150 Outnumber C :R:	.10	.30
151 Radiant Flames R :R:	2.50	6.00
152 Reckless Cohort C :R:	.10	.30
153 Retreat to Valakut U :R:	.20	.75
154 Rolling Thunder U :R:	.20	.75
155 Shatterskull Recruit C :R:	.10	.30
156 Stonefury C :R:	.10	.30
157 Sure Strike C :R:	.10	.30
158 Tunneling Geopede U :R:	.20	.75
159 Valakut Invoker C :R:	.10	.30
160 Valakut Predator C :R:	.10	.30
161 Volcanic Upheaval C :R:	.10	.30
162 Zada, Hedron Grinder R :R:	.75	2.00
163 Blisterpod C :G:	.60	1.50
164 Brood Monitor U :G:	.20	.75
165 Call the Scions C :G:	.10	.30
166 Eyeless Watcher C :G:	.10	.30
167 From Beyond R :G:	1.25	3.00
168 Unnatural Aggression C :G:	.10	.30
169 Void Attendant U :G:	.20	.75
170 Beastcaller Savant R :G:	.75	2.00
171 Broodhunter Wurm C :G:	.10	.30
172 Earthen Arms C :G:	.10	.30
173 Giant Mantis C :G:	.10	.30
174 Greenwarden of Murasa M :G:	3.00	7.00
175 Infuse with the Elements U :G:	.20	.75
176 Jaddi Offshoot U :G:	.20	.75
177 Lifespring Druid C :G:	.10	.30
178 Murasa Ranger U :G:	.20	.75
179 Natural Connection C :G:	.10	.30
180 Nissa's Renewal R :G:	.75	2.00
181 Oran-Rief Hydra R :G:	.75	2.00
182 Oran-Rief Invoker C :G:	.10	.30
183 Plated Crusher U :G:	.20	.75
184 Plummet C :G:	.10	.30
185 Reclaiming Vines C :G:	.10	.30
186 Retreat to Kazandu U :G:	.20	.75
187 Rot Shambler U :G:	.20	.75
188 Scythe Leopard U :G:	.20	.75
189 Seek the Wilds C :G:	.10	.30
190 Snapping Gnarlid C :G:	.10	.30
191 Swell of Growth C :G:	.20	.60
192 Sylvan Scrying U :G:	2.00	5.00
193 Tajuru Beastmaster C :G:	.10	.30
194 Tajuru Stalwart C :G:	.10	.30
195 Tajuru Warcaller U :G:	.20	.75
196 Territorial Baloth C :G:	.10	.30
197 Undergrowth Champion M :G:	2.00	5.00
198 Woodland Wanderer R :G:	1.50	4.00
199 Brood Butcher R :M:	.75	2.00
200 Brutal Expulsion R :M:	.75	2.00
201 Catacomb Sifter U :M:	.20	.75
202 Dust Stalker R :M:	.75	2.00
203 Fathom Feeder R :M:	2.00	5.00
204 Forerunner of Slaughter U :M:	.20	.75
205 Herald of Kozilek U :M:	.50	1.25
206 Sire of Stagnation M :M:	2.50	5.00
207 Ulamog's Nullifier U :M:	.20	.75
208 Angelic Captain R :M:	.75	2.00
209 Bring to Light R :M:	2.50	6.00
210 Drana's Emissary U :M:	1.00	2.50
211 Grove Rumbler U :M:	.20	.75
212 Grovetender Druids U :M:	.20	.75
213 Kiora, Master of the Depths M :M:	5.00	10.00
214 March from the Tomb R :M:	.75	2.00
215 Munda, Ambush Leader R :M:	.75	2.00
216 Noyan Dar, Roil Shaper R :M:	.75	2.00
217 Omnath, Locus of Rage M :M:	5.00	10.00
218 Resolute Blademaster U :M:	.20	.75
219 Roil Spout U :M:	.20	.75
220 Skyrider Elf U :M:	.20	.75
221 Veteran Warleader R :M:	.75	2.00
222 Aligned Hedron Network R :A:	1.50	4.00
223 Hedron Archive U :A:	2.00	5.00
224 Hedron Blade C :A:	.10	.30
225 Pathway Arrows U :A:	.20	.75
226 Pilgrim's Eye U :A:	.20	.75
227 Slab Hammer U :A:	.20	.75
228 Ally Encampment R :L:	1.25	3.00
229 Blighted Cataract U :L:	.60	1.50
230 Blighted Fen U :L:	.20	.75
231 Blighted Gorge U :L:	.20	.75
232 Blighted Steppe U :L:	.20	.75
233 Blighted Woodland U :L:	1.00	2.50
234 Canopy Vista R :L:	3.00	7.00
235 Cinder Glade R :L:	3.00	7.00
236 Evolving Wilds C :L:	.50	1.25
237 Fertile Thicket C :L:	.10	.30
238 Looming Spires C :L:	.10	.30
239 Lumbering Falls R :L:	2.50	5.00
240 Mortuary Mire C :L:	.50	1.25
241 Prairie Stream R :L:	3.00	6.00
242 Sanctum of Ugin R :L:	2.50	5.00
243 Sandstone Bridge C :L:	.10	.30
244 Shambling Vent R :L:	6.00	10.00
245 Shrine of the Forsaken Gods R :L:	1.50	3.00
246 Skyline Cascade C :L:	.10	.30
247 Smoldering Marsh R :L:	3.00	7.00
248 Spawning Bed U :L:	.20	.75
249 Sunken Hollow R :L:	3.00	7.00
250a Plains L :L:	.10	.30
250b Plains Full Art L :L:	2.50	6.00
251a Plains L :L:	.10	.30
251b Plains Full Art L :L:	2.50	6.00
252a Plains L :L:	.10	.30
252b Plains Full Art L :L:	2.50	6.00
253a Plains L :L:	.10	.30
253b Plains Full Art L :L:	2.50	6.00
254a Plains L :L:	.10	.30
254b Plains Full Art L :L:	2.50	6.00
255a Island L :L:	.10	.30
255b Island Full Art L :L:	2.50	6.00
256a Island L :L:	.10	.30
256b Island Full Art L :L:	2.50	6.00
257a Island L :L:	.10	.30
257b Island Full Art L :L:	2.50	6.00
258a Island L :L:	.10	.30
258b Island Full Art L :L:	2.50	6.00
259a Island L :L:	.10	.30
259b Island Full Art L :L:	2.50	6.00
260a Swamp L :L:	.10	.30
260b Swamp Full Art L :L:	2.50	6.00
261a Swamp L :L:	.10	.30
261b Swamp Full Art L :L:	2.50	6.00
262a Swamp L :L:	.10	.30
262b Swamp Full Art L :L:	2.50	6.00
263a Swamp L :L:	.10	.30
263b Swamp Full Art L :L:	2.50	6.00
264a Swamp L :L:	.10	.30
264b Swamp Full Art L :L:	2.50	6.00
265a Mountain L :L:	.10	.30
265b Mountain Full Art L :L:	2.50	6.00
266a Mountain L :L:	.10	.30
266b Mountain Full Art L :L:	2.50	6.00
267a Mountain L :L:	.10	.30
267b Mountain Full Art L :L:	2.50	6.00
268a Mountain L :L:	.10	.30
268b Mountain Full Art L :L:	2.50	6.00
269a Mountain L :L:	.10	.30
269b Mountain Full Art L :L:	2.50	6.00
270a Forest L :L:	.10	.30
270b Forest Full Art L :L:	2.50	6.00
271a Forest L :L:	.10	.30
271b Forest Full Art L :L:	2.50	6.00
272a Forest L :L:	.10	.30
272b Forest Full Art L :L:	2.50	6.00
273a Forest L :L:	.10	.30
273b Forest Full Art L :L:	2.50	6.00
274a Forest L :L:	.10	.30
274b Forest Full Art L :L:	2.50	6.00

2016 Magic The Gathering Oath of the Gatewatch

COMPLETE SET (184)	100.00	140.00
BOOSTER BOX	90.00	110.00
BOOSTER PACK	3.00	5.00
UNLISTED C	.05	.15
UNLISTED U	.05	.15
UNLISTED R	.10	.20
RELEASED ON JANUARY 22, 2016		
1 Deceiver of Form R	.10	.20
2 Eldrazi Mimic R	.50	.75
3 Endbringer R	.30	.50
4 Kozilek, the Great Distortion M	3.50	4.00
5 Kozilek's Pathfinder C	.05	.15
6 Matter Reshaper R	3.00	3.50
7 Reality Smasher R	3.25	4.00
8 Spatial Contortion U	.05	.15
9 Thought-Knot Seer R	5.00	6.00
10 Walker of the Wastes U	.05	.15
11 Warden of Geometries C	.05	.15
12 Warping Wail U	.25	.40
13 Eldrazi Displacer R :W:	3.50	4.25
14 Affa Protector C :W:	.05	.15
15 Allied Reinforcements U :W:	.05	.15
16 Call the Gatewatch R :W:	.20	.30
17 Dazzling Reflection C :W:	.05	.15
18 Expedition Raptor C :W:	.05	.15
19 General Tazri M :W:	.60	1.00
20 Immolating Glare U :W:	.05	.15
21 Iona's Blessing U :W:	.05	.15
22 Isolation Zone C :W:	.05	.15
23 Kor Scythemaster C :W:	.05	.15
24 Kor Sky Climber C :W:	.05	.15
25 Linvala, the Preserver M :W:	2.25	2.75
26 Make a Stand U :W:	.05	.15
27 Makindi Aeronaut C :W:	.05	.15
28 Mighty Leap C :W:	.05	.15
29 Munda's Vanguard R :W:	.05	.15
30 Oath of Gideon R :W:	.30	.50
31 Ondu War Cleric C :W:	.05	.15
32 Relief Captain U :W:	.05	.15
33 Searing Light C :W:	.05	.15
34 Shoulder to Shoulder C :W:	.05	.15
35 Spawnbinder Mage C :W:	.05	.15
36 Steppe Glider U :W:	.05	.15
37 Stone Haven Outfitter R :W:	.40	.60
38 Stoneforge Acolyte U :W:	.05	.15
39 Wall of Resurgence U :W:	.05	.15
40 Abstruse Interference C	.05	.15
41 Blinding Drone C :B:	.05	.15
42 Cultivator Drone C :B:	.05	.15
43 Deepfathom Skulker R :B:	.10	.20
44 Dimensional Infiltrator R :B:	.15	.25
45 Gravity Negator C :B:	.05	.15
46 Prophet of Distortion U :B:	.05	.15
47 Slip Through Space C :B:	.05	.15
48 Thought Harvester U :B:	.05	.15
49 Void Shatter U :B:	.10	.20
50 Ancient Crab C :B:	.05	.15
51 Comparative Analysis C :B:	.05	.15
52 Containment Membrane C :B:	.05	.15
53 Crush of Tentacles M :B:	1.50	2.25
54 Cyclone Sire U :B:	.05	.15
55 Gift of Tusks U :B:	.05	.15
56 Grip of the Roil U :B:	.05	.15
57 Hedron Alignment R :B:	.05	.15
58 Jwar Isle Avenger C :B:	.05	.15
59 Negate C :B:	.05	.15
60 Oath of Jace R :B:	.30	.50
61 Overwhelming Denial R :B:	.10	.20
62 Roiling Waters U :B:	.05	.15
63 Sphinx of the Final Word M :B:	.60	1.00
64 Sweep Away C :B:	.05	.15
65 Umara Entangler C :B:	.05	.15
66 Unity of Purpose U :B:	.05	.15
67 Bearer of Silence R :K:	.20	.30
68 Dread Defiler R :K:	.05	.15
69 Essence Depleter U :K:	.05	.15
70 Flaying Tendrils U :K:	.05	.15
71 Havoc Sower U :K:	.05	.15
72 Inverter of Truth M :K:	.60	1.00
73 Kozilek's Shrieker C :K:	.05	.15
74 Kozilek's Translator C :K:	.05	.15
75 Oblivion Strike C :K:	.05	.15
76 Reaver Drone U :K:	.05	.15
77 Sifter of Skulls R :K:	.10	.20
78 Sky Scourer C :K:	.05	.15
79 Slaughter Drone C :K:	.05	.15
80 Unnatural Endurance C :K:	.05	.15
81 Visions of Brutality U :K:	.05	.15
82 Witness the End C :K:	.05	.15
83 Corpse Churn C :K:	.05	.15
84 Drana's Chosen R :K:	.10	.20
85 Grasp of Darkness U :K:	.60	1.00
86 Kalitas, Traitor of Ghet M :K:	18.00	21.00
87 Malakir Soothsayer U :K:	.05	.15
88 Null Caller U :K:	.05	.15
89 Remorseless Punishment R :K:	.15	.25
90 Tar Snare C :K:	.05	.15
91 Untamed Hunger C :K:	.05	.15
92 Vampire Envoy C :K:	.05	.15
93 Zulaport Chainmage C :K:	.05	.15
94 Consuming Sinkhole C :R:	.05	.15
95 Eldrazi Aggressor C :R:	.05	.15
96 Eldrazi Obligator R :R:	.15	.25
97 Immobilizer Eldrazi U :R:	.05	.15
98 Kozilek's Return M :R:	9.00	11.00
99 Maw of Kozilek C :R:	.05	.15
100 Reality Hemorrhage C :R:	.05	.15
101 Akoum Flameseeker C :R:	.05	.15
102 Boulder Salvo C :R:	.05	.15
103 Brute Strength C :R:	.05	.15
104 Chandra, Flamecaller M :R:	8.00	9.00
105 Cinder Hellion C :R:	.05	.15
106 Devour in Flames U :R:	.05	.15
107 Embodiment of Fury U :R:	.05	.15
108 Expedite C :R:	.05	.15
109 Fall of the Titans R :R:	.20	.30
110 Goblin Dark-Dwellers R :R:	1.25	1.50
111 Goblin Freerunner C :R:	.05	.15
112 Kazuul's Toll Collector U :R:	.05	.15
113 Oath of Chandra R :R:	.15	.25
114 Press into Service U :R:	.05	.15
115 Pyromancer's Assault U :R:	.05	.15
116 Reckless Bushwhacker U :R:	.40	.60
117 Sparkmage's Gambit C :R:	.05	.15
118 Tears of Valakut U :R:	.05	.15
119 Tyrant of Valakut R :R:	.05	.15
120 Zada's Commando C :R:	.05	.15
121 Birthing Hulk U :G:	.05	.15
122 Ruin in Their Wake U :G:	.05	.15
123 Scion Summoner C :G:	.05	.15
124 Stalking Drone C :G:	.05	.15
125 Vile Redeemer R :G:	.05	.15
126 World Breaker M :G:	3.50	4.25
127 Baloth Pup U :G:	.05	.15
128 Bonds of Mortality U :G:	.05	.15
129 Canopy Gorger C :G:	.05	.15
130 Elemental Uprising C :G:	.05	.15
131 Embodiment of Insight U :G:	.05	.15
132 Gladehart Cavalry R :G:	.05	.15
133 Harvester Troll U :G:	.05	.15
134 Lead by Example C :G:	.05	.15
135 Loam Larva C :G:	.05	.15
136 Natural State C :G:	.05	.15
137 Netcaster Spider C :G:	.05	.15
138 Nissa, Voice of Zendikar M :G:	6.00	7.00
139 Nissa's Judgment U :G:	.05	.15
140 Oath of Nissa R :G:	2.25	2.75
141 Pulse of Murasa C :G:	.05	.15
142 Saddleback Lagac C :G:	.05	.15
143 Seed Guardian U :G:	.05	.15
144 Sylvan Advocate R :G:	4.00	4.50
145 Tajuru Pathwarden C :G:	.05	.15
146 Vines of the Recluse C :G:	.05	.15
147 Zendikar Resurgent R :G:	.40	.60
148 Flayer Drone U :M:	.05	.15
149 Mindmelter U :M:	.05	.15
150 Void Grafter U :M:	.05	.15
151 Ayli, Eternal Pilgrim R :M:	.50	.75
152 Baloth Null U :M:	.05	.15
153 Cliffhaven Vampire U :M:	.05	.15
154 Joraga Auxiliary U :M:	.05	.15
155 Jori En, Ruin Diver R :M:	.20	.30
156 Mina and Denn, Wildborn R :M:	.30	.50
157 Reflector Mage U :M:	.75	1.15
158 Relentless Hunter U :M:	.05	.15
159 Stormchaser Mage U :M:	.30	.50
160 Weapons Trainer U :M:	.05	.15
161 Bone Saw C :A:	.05	.15
162 Captain's Claws R :A:	.30	.50
163 Chitinous Cloak U :A:	.05	.15
164 Hedron Crawler C :A:	.05	.15
165 Seer's Lantern C :A:	.05	.15
166 Stoneforge Masterwork R :A:	.50	.75
167 Strider Harness U :A:	.05	.15
168 Cinder Barrens U :L:	.05	.15
169 Corrupted Crossroads R :L:	.20	.30
170 Crumbling Vestige C :L:	.05	.15
171 Hissing Quagmire R :L:	3.00	3.25
172 Holdout Settlement C :L:	.05	.15
173 Meandering River U :L:	.05	.15
174 Mirrorpool M :L:	1.25	2.00
175 Needle Spires R :L:	1.25	1.50
176 Ruins of Oran-Rief R :L:	.15	.25
177 Sea Gate Wreckage R :L:	.40	.60
178 Submerged Boneyard U :L:	.05	.15
179 Timber Gorge U :L:	.05	.15
180 Tranquil Expanse U :L:	.05	.15
181 Unknown Shores C :L:	.05	.15
182 Wandering Fumarole R :L:	2.75	3.15
183b Wastes C :L:	.20	.30
183 Wastes C :L:	.50	1.00
184b Wastes C :L:	.20	.30
184 Wastes C :L:	.50	.75
T1 Eldrazi Scion 1	.05	.15
T2 Eldrazi Scion 2	.05	.15
T3 Eldrazi Scion 3	.05	.15
T4 Eldrazi Scion 4	.05	.15
T5 Eldrazi Scion 5	.05	.15
T6 Eldrazi Scion 6	.05	.15
T7 Angel Token	.05	.15
T8 Zombie Token	.05	.15
T9 Elemental Token (Red)	.05	.15
T10 Elemental Token (Green)	.05	.15
T11 Plant Token	.05	.15

2016 Magic The Gathering Shadows over Innistrad

COMPLETE SET (297)	150.00	200.00
BOOSTER BOX (36 PACKS)	90.00	150.00
BOOSTER PACK (15 PACKS)	2.50	4.00
RELEASED ON APRIL 8, 2016		
1 Always Watching R :W:	1.25	2.00
2 Angel of Deliverance R :W:	.10	.20
3 Angelic Purge C :W:	.05	.15
4 Apothecary Geist C :W:	.05	.15
5 Archangel Avacyn	16.00	20.00
Avacyn the Purifier M		
6 Avacynian Missionaries	.05	.15
Lunarch Inquisitors U		
7 Bound by Moonsilver U :W:	.05	.15
8 Bygone Bishop R :W:	.75	1.25
9 Cathar's Companion C :W:	.05	.15
10 Chaplain's Blessing C :W:	.05	.15
11 Dauntless Cathar C :W:	.05	.15
12 Declaration in Stone R :W:	3.75	4.25
13 Descend upon the Sinful M :W:	.75	1.15
14 Devilthorn Fox C :W:	.05	.15
15 Drogskol Cavalry R :W:	.10	.20
16 Eerie Interlude R :W:	.30	.50
17 Emissary of the Sleepless C :W:	.05	.15
18 Ethereal Guidance C :W:	.05	.15
19 Expose Evil C :W:	.05	.15
20 Gryff's Boon U :W:	.10	.20
21 Hanweir Militia Captain	.75	1.00
Westvale Cult Leader R		
22 Hope Against Hope U :W:	.05	.15
23 Humble the Brute U :W:	.05	.15
24 Inquisitor's Ox C :W:	.05	.15
25 Inspiring Captain C :W:	.05	.15
26 Militant Inquisitor C :W:	.05	.15
27 Moorland Drifter C :W:	.05	.15
28 Nahiri's Machinations U :W:	.05	.15
29 Nearheath Chaplain U :W:	.05	.15
30 Not Forgotten U :W:	.05	.15
31 Odric, Lunarch Marshal R :W:	.40	.60
32 Open the Armory U :W:	.15	.25
33 Paranoid Parish-Blade U :W:	.05	.15
34 Pious Evangel	.05	.15
Wayward Disciple U		
35 Puncturing Light C :W:	.05	.15
36 Reaper of Flight Moonsilver U :W:	.05	.15
37 Silverstrike U :W:	.05	.15
38 Spectral Shepherd U :W:	.05	.15
39 Stern Constable C :W:	.05	.15
40 Strength of Arms C :W:	.05	.15
41 Survive the Night C :W:	.05	.15
42 Tenacity U :W:	.05	.15
43 Thalia's Lieutenant R :W:	2.25	3.00
44 Thraben Inspector C :W:	.05	.15
45 Topplegeist U :W:	.05	.15
46 Town Gossipmonger	.10	.20
Incited Rabble U		
47 Unruly Mob C :W:	.05	.15
48 Vessel of Ephemera C :W:	.05	.15
49 Aberrant Researcher	.05	.15
Perfected Form U		
50 Broken Concentration U :B:	.05	.15
51 Catalog C :B:	.05	.15
52 Compelling Deterrence U :B:	.05	.15
53 Confirm Suspicions R :B:	.10	.20
54 Daring Sleuth	.05	.15
Bearer of Overwhelming Truths U		
55 Deny Existence C :B:	.05	.15
56 Drownyard Explorers C :B:	.05	.15
57 Drunau Corpse Trawler U :B:	.05	.15
58 Engulf the Shore R :B:	.60	1.00
59 Epiphany at the Drownyard R :B:	.15	.25
60 Erdwal Illuminator U :B:	.05	.15
61 Essence Flux U :B:	.05	.15
62 Fleeting Memories U :B:	.05	.15
63 Forgotten Creation R :B:	.20	.30
64 Furtive Homunculus C :B:	.05	.15
65 Geralf's Masterpiece M :B:	.60	1.00
66 Ghostly Wings C :B:	.05	.15
67 Gone Missing C :B:	.05	.15
68 Invasive Surgery U :B:	.05	.15
69 Jace, Unraveler of Secrets M :B:	4.50	5.25
70 Jace's Scrutiny C :B:	.05	.15
71 Just the Wind C :B:	.05	.15
72 Lamplighter of Selhoff C :B:	.05	.15
73 Manic Scribe U :B:	.05	.15
74 Nagging Thoughts C :B:	.05	.15
75 Nephalia Moondrakes R :B:	.50	.75
76 Niblis of Dusk C :B:	.05	.15
77 Ongoing Investigation U :B:	.05	.15
78 Pieces of the Puzzle C :B:	.05	.15
79 Pore Over the Pages U :B:	.05	.15
80 Press for Answers C :B:	.05	.15
81 Rattlechains R :B:	1.00	1.50
82 Reckless Scholar U :B:	.05	.15
83 Rise from the Tides U :B:	.05	.15
84 Seagraf Skaab C :B:	.05	.15
85 Silburlind Snapper C :B:	.05	.15
86 Silent Observer C :B:	.05	.15
87 Sleep Paralysis C :B:	.05	.15
88 Startled Awake	1.25	1.75
Persistent Nightmare M		
89 Stitched Mangler C :B:	.05	.15
90 Stitchwing Skaab U :B:	.05	.15
91 Stormrider Spirit C :B:	.05	.15
92 Thing in the Ice	4.25	4.75
Awoken Horror R		
93 Trail of Evidence U :B:	.05	.15
94 Uninvited Geist	.05	.15
Unimpeded Trespasser U		
95 Vessel of Paramnesia C :B:	.05	.15
96 Welcome to the Fold R :B:	.50	.15
97 Accursed Witch	.05	.15
Infectious Curse U		
98 Alms of the Vein C :K:	.05	.15
99 Asylum Visitor R :K:	.75	1.00
100 Behind the Scenes U :K:	.05	.15
101 Behold the Beyond M :K:	.50	.75
102 Biting Rain U :K:	.05	.15
103 Call the Bloodline U :K:	.05	.15
104 Creeping Dread U :K:	.05	.15
105 Crow of Dark Tidings C :K:	.05	.15

106 Dead Weight C :K:	.05	.15
107 Diregraf Colossus R :K:	1.25	2.00
108 Elusive Tormentor	.10	.20
Insidious Mist R		
109 Ever After R :K:	.40	.60
110 Farbog Revenant C :K:	.05	.15
111 From Under the Floorboards R :K:	.25	.35
112 Ghoulcaller's Accomplice C :K:	.05	.15
113 Ghoulsteed U :K:	.05	.15
114 Gisa's Bidding U :K:	.05	.15
115 Grotesque Mutation C :K:	.05	.15
116 Heir of Falkenrath	.40	.60
Heir to the Night U		
117 Hound of the Farbogs C :K:	.05	.15
118 Indulgent Aristocrat U :K:	.05	.15
119 Kindly Stranger	.05	.15
Demon-Possessed Witch U		
120 Liliana's Indignation U :K:	.05	.15
121 Macabre Waltz C :K:	.05	.15
122 Markov Dreadknight R :K:	.10	.20
123 Merciless Resolve C :K:	.05	.15
124 Mindwrack Demon M :K:	1.75	2.25
125 Morkrut Necropod U :K:	.05	.15
126 Murderous Compulsion C :K:	.05	.15
127 Olivia's Bloodsworn U :K:	.05	.15
128 Pale Rider of Trostad U :K:	.05	.15
129 Pick the Brain U :K:	.05	.15
130 Rancid Rats C :K:	.05	.15
131 Relentless Dead M :K:	9.00	11.00
132 Rottenheart Ghoul C :K:	.05	.15
133 Sanitarium Skeleton C :K:	.05	.15
134 Shamble Back C :K:	.05	.15
135 Sinister Concoction U :K:	.05	.15
136 Stallion of Ashmouth C :K:	.05	.15
137 Stromkirk Mentor C :K:	.05	.15
138 Throttle C :K:	.05	.15
139 To the Slaughter R :K:	1.25	3.00
140 Tooth Collector U :K:	.05	.15
141 Triskaidekaphobia R :K:	.50	.75
142 Twins of Maurer Estate C :K:	.05	.15
143 Vampire Noble C :K:	.05	.15
144 Vessel of Malignity C :K:	.05	.15
145 Avacyn's Judgment R :R:	.30	.50
146 Bloodmad Vampire C :R:	.05	.15
147 Breakneck Rider	.05	.15
Neck Breaker U		
148 Burn from Within R :R:	.15	.25
149 Convicted Killer	.05	.15
Branded Howler C		
150 Dance with Devils U :R:	.05	.15
151 Devils' Playground R :R:	.50	.15
152 Dissension in the Ranks U :R:	.05	.15
153 Dual Shot C :R:	.05	.15
154 Ember-Eye Wolf C :R:	.05	.15
155 Falkenrath Gorger R :R:	1.00	1.50
156 Fiery Temper C :R:	.10	.20
157 Flameblade Angel R :R:	.50	.15
158 Gatstaf Arsonists	.05	.15
Gatstaf Ravagers C		
159 Geier Reach Bandit	.40	.60
Vildin-Pack Alpha R		
160 Geistblast U :R:	.05	.15
161 Gibbering Fiend U :R:	.05	.15
162 Goldnight Castigator M :R:	1.25	2.00
163 Harness the Storm R :R:	.10	.20
164 Howlpack Wolf C :R:	.05	.15
165 Hulking Devil C :R:	.05	.15
166 Incorrigible Youths U :R:	.05	.15
167 Inner Struggle U :R:	.05	.15
168 Insolent Neonate C :R:	.10	.20
169 Kessig Forgemaster	.05	.15
Flameheart Werewolf U		
170 Lightning Axe U :R:	.40	.60
171 Mad Prophet U :R:	.05	.15
172 Magmatic Chasm C :R:	.05	.15
173 Malevolent Whispers U :R:	.05	.15
174 Pyre Hound C :R:	.05	.15
175 Ravenous Bloodseeker U :R:	.05	.15
176 Reduce to Ashes C :R:	.05	.15
177 Rush of Adrenaline C :R:	.05	.15
178 Sanguinary Mage C :R:	.05	.15
179 Scourge Wolf R :R:	.10	.20
180 Senseless Rage C :R:	.05	.15
181 Sin Prodder R :R:	.40	.60
182 Skin Invasion	.05	.15
Skin Shedder U		
183 Spiteful Motives U :R:	.05	.15
184 Stensia Masquerade U :R:	.05	.15
185 Structural Distortion C :R:	.05	.15
186 Tormenting Voice C :R:	.05	.15
187 Ulrich's Kindred U :R:	.05	.15
188 Uncaged Fury C :R:	.05	.15
189 Vessel of Volatility C :R:	.05	.15
190 Village Messenger	.30	.50
Moonrise Intruder U		
191 Voldaren Duelist C :R:	.05	.15
192 Wolf of Devil's Breach M :R:	.30	.50
193 Aim High C :G:	.05	.15
194 Autumnal Gloom	.05	.15
Ancient of the Equinox U		
195 Briarbridge Patrol U :G:	.05	.15
196 Byway Courier C :G:	.05	.15
197 Clip Wings C :G:	.05	.15
198 Confront the Unknown C :G:	.05	.15
199 Crawling Sensation U :G:	.05	.15
200 Cryptolith Rite R :G:	1.00	1.50
201 Cult of the Waxing Moon U :G:	.05	.15
202 Deathcap Cultivator R :G:	.30	.50
203 Duskwatch Recruiter	1.75	2.25
Krallenhorde Howler U		
204 Equestrian Skill C :G:	.05	.15
205 Fork in the Road C :G:	.05	.15
206 Gloomwidow U :G:	.05	.15
207 Graf Mole U :G:	.05	.15
208 Groundskeeper U :G:	.05	.15
209 Hermit of the Natterknolls	.05	.15
Lone Wolf of the Natterknolls U		
210 Hinterland Logger	.05	.15
Timber Shredder C		
211 Howlpack Resurgence U :G:	.25	.40
212 Inexorable Blob R :G:	.10	.20
213 Intrepid Provisioner C :G:	.05	.15
214 Kessig Dire Swine C :G:	.05	.15
215 Lambholt Pacifist	.50	.75
Lambholt Butcher U		
216 Loam Dryad C :G:	.05	.15
217 Might Beyond Reason C :G:	.05	.15
218 Moldgraf Scavenger C :G:	.05	.15
219 Moonlight Hunt U :G:	.15	.25
220 Obsessive Skinner U :G:	.05	.15
221 Pack Guardian U :G:	.05	.15
222 Quilled Wolf C :G:	.05	.15
223 Rabid Bite C :G:	.05	.15
224 Root Out C :G:	.05	.15
225 Sage of Ancient Lore	.10	.20
Werewolf of Ancient Hunger R		
226 Seasons Past M :G:	1.25	1.75
227 Second Harvest R :G:	.30	.50
228 Silverfur Partisan R :G:	.50	.75
229 Solitary Hunter	.05	.15
One of the Pack C		
230 Soul Swallower R :G:	.10	.20
231 Stoic Builder C :G:	.05	.15
232 Thornhide Wolves C :G:	.05	.15
233 Tireless Tracker R :G:	4.00	5.00
234 Traverse the Ulvenwald R :G:	3.25	4.00
235 Ulvenwald Hydra M :G:	1.00	1.50
236 Ulvenwald Mysteries U :G:	.05	.15
237 Vessel of Nascency C :G:	.05	.15
238 Veteran Cathar U :G:	.05	.15
239 Watcher in the Web C :G:	.05	.15
240 Weirding Wood U :G:	.05	.15
241 Altered Ego R :G:B:	.20	.30
242 Anguished Unmaking R :W:K:	1.00	1.50
243 Arlinn Kord	7.00	9.00
Arlinn, Embraced by the Moon M		
244 Fevered Visions R :B:R:	1.75	2.25
245 The Gitrog Monster M :K:G:	2.00	2.50
246 Invocation of Saint Traft R :W:B:	.10	.20
247 Nahiri, the Harbinger M :R:W:	16.00	20.00
248 Olivia, Mobilized for War M :K:R:	4.25	5.00
249 Prized Amalgam R :B:K:	3.00	3.75
250 Sigarda, Heron's Grace M :G:W:	1.25	1.75
251 Sorin, Grim Nemesis M :W:K:	6.00	7.50
252 Brain in a Jar R :A:	.30	.50
253 Corrupted Grafstone R :A:	.20	.30
254 Epitaph Golem U :A:	.05	.15
255 Explosive Apparatus C :A:	.05	.15
256 Harvest Hand	.05	.15
Scrounged Scythe U		
257 Haunted Cloak U :A:	.05	.15
258 Magnifying Glass U :A:	.05	.15
259 Murderer's Axe U :A:	.05	.15
260 Neglected Heirloom	.05	.15
Ashmouth Blade U		
261 Runaway Carriage U :A:	.05	.15
262 Shard of Broken Glass C :A:	.05	.15
263 Skeleton Key U :A:	.05	.15
264 Slayer's Plate R :A:	.10	.20
265 Tamiyo's Journal R :A:	.40	.60
266 Thraben Gargoyle	.05	.15
Stonewing Antagonizer U		
267 True-Faith Censer C :A:	.05	.15
268 Wicker Witch C :A:	.05	.15
269 Wild-Field Scarecrow U :A:	.05	.15
270 Choked Estuary R :L:	1.50	2.00
271 Drownyard Temple R :L:	.30	.50
272 Foreboding Ruins R :L:	1.75	2.25
273 Forsaken Sanctuary U :L:	.05	.15
274 Fortified Village R :L:	1.50	2.00
275 Foul Orchard U :L:	.05	.15
276 Game Trail R :L:	1.50	2.00
277 Highland Lake U :L:	.10	.20
278 Port Town R :L:	1.50	2.00
279 Stone Quarry U :L:	.05	.15
280 Warped Landscape C :L:	.05	.15
281 Westvale Abbey	3.50	4.00
Ormendahl Profane Prince R		
282 Woodland Stream U :L:	.05	.15
283 Plains L :L:	.10	.25
284 Plains L :L:	.10	.25
285 Plains L :L:	.10	.25
286 Island L :L:	.10	.25
287 Island L :L:	.10	.25
288 Island L :L:	.10	.25
289 Swamp L :L:	.10	.25
290 Swamp L :L:	.10	.25
291 Swamp L :L:	.10	.25
292 Mountain L :L:	.10	.25
293 Mountain L :L:	.10	.25
294 Mountain L :L:	.10	.25
295 Forest L :L:	.10	.25
296 Forest L :L:	.10	.25
297 Forest L :L:	.10	.25
CH1 Checklist Card 1 T	.05	.15
CH2 Checklist Card 2 T	.05	.15
T1 Angel Token T	.20	.30
T2 Human Soldier Token T	.05	.15
T3 Spirit Token T	.05	.15
T4 Vampire Knight Token T	.15	.25
T5 Zombie Token T	.05	.15
T6 Devil Token T	.05	.15
T7 Insect Token T	.05	.15
T8 Ooze Token T	.05	.15
T9 Wolf Token T	.05	.15
T10 Human Cleric Token T	.50	.75
T11 Clue Token (11) T	.05	.15
T12 Clue Token (12) T	.05	.15
T13 Clue Token (13) T	.05	.15
T14 Clue Token (14) T	.05	.15
T15 Clue Token (15) T	.05	.15
T16 Clue Token (16) T	.05	.15
T17 Emblem - Arlinn Kord T	.30	.50
T18 Emblem - Jace, Unraveler of Secrets T	.30	.50

2016 Magic The Gathering Eldritch Moon

COMPLETE SET (205 CARDS)	170.00	220.00
BOOSTER BOX (36 PACKS)	90.00	120.00
BOOSTER PACK (15 CARDS)	2.50	6.00
RELEASED ON JULY 22, 2016		
1 Abundant Maw U	.05	.15
2 Decimator of the Provinces MR	2.50	3.00
3 Distended Mindbender R	1.25	1.75
4 Drownyard Behemoth U	.05	.15
5 Elder Deep Fiend R	3.00	4.00
6 Emrakul the Promised End MR	17.00	20.00
7 Eternal Scourge R	.20	.30
8 It of the Horrid Swarm C	.05	.15
9 Lashweed Lurker U	.05	.15
10 Mockery of Nature U	.05	.15
11 Vexing Scuttler U	.05	.15
12 Wretched Gryff C	.05	.15
13 Blessed Alliance U	.15	.25
14 Borrowed Grace C	.05	.15
15 Bruna, The Fading Light R	1.00	1.25
16 Choking Restraints C	.05	.15
17 Collective Effort R	.60	.80
18 Courageous Outrider U	.05	.15
19 Dawn Gryff C	.05	.15
20 Deploy the Gatewatch MR	1.00	1.25
21 Desperate Sentry C	.05	.15
22 Drogskol Shieldmate U	.05	.15
23 Extricator of Sin, Extricator of Flesh U	.05	.15
24 Faith Unbroken U	.05	.15
25 Faith Bearer Paladin C	.05	.15
26 Fiend Binder C	.05	.15
27 Geist of the Lonely Vigil U	.05	.15
28 Gisela, the Broken Blade MR	8.00	10.00
29 Give No Ground U	.05	.15
30 Guardian of Pilgrims C	.05	.15
31 Ironclad Slayer C	.05	.15
32 Ironwrights Cleansing C	.05	.15
33 Lone Rider, It That Rides as One U	.25	.40
34 Long Road Home U	.05	.15
35 Lunarch Mantle C	.05	.15
36 Peace of Mind U	.05	.15
37 Providence R	.10	.20
38 Repel the Abominable U	.05	.15
39 Sanctifier of Souls R	.10	.20
40 Selfless Spirit R	3.75	4.25
41 Sigardas Aid R	1.00	1.50
42 Sigardian Priest C	.05	.15
43 Spectral Reserves C	.05	.15
44 Steadfast Cathar C	.05	.15
45 Subjugator Angel U	.05	.15
46 Thalia Heretic Cathar R	2.75	3.50
47 Thalias Lancers R	.45	.65
48 Thraben Standard Bearer C	.05	.15
49 Advanced Stitchwing U	.05	.15
50 Chilling Grasp U	.05	.15
51 Coax from the Blind Eternities R	.20	.30
52 Contingency Plan C	.05	.15
53 Convolute C	.05	.15
54 Curious Homunculus, Voracious Reader U	.20	.30
55 Displace C	.05	.15
56 Docent of Perfection, Final Iteration R	.25	.40
57 Drag Under C	.05	.15
58 Enlightened Maniac C	.05	.15
59 Exultant Cultist C	.05	.15
60 Fogwalker C	.05	.15
61 Fortunes Favor U	.05	.15
62 Geist of the Archives U	.05	.15
63 Grizzled Angler, Grisly Anglerfish U	.05	.15
64 Identity Thief R	.10	.20
65 Imprisoned in the Moon R	.40	.60
66 Ingenious Skaab C	.05	.15
67 Laboratory Brute C	.05	.15
68 Lunar Force U	.05	.15
69 Mausoleum Wanderer R	1.25	1.75
70 Mind's Dilation MR	.80	1.15
71 Nebelgast Herald U	.10	.20
72 Niblis of Frost R	.30	.50
73 Scour the Laboratory U	.05	.15
74 Spontaneous Mutation C	.05	.15
75 Summary Dismissal R	1.00	1.50
76 Take Inventory C	.05	.15
77 Tattered Haunter C	.05	.15
78 Turn Aside C	.05	.15
79 Unsubstantiate U	.30	.50
80 Wharf Infiltrator R	.20	.30
81 Boon of Emrakul C	.05	.15
82 Borrowed Malevolence C	.05	.15
83 Cemetery Recruitment C	.05	.15
84 Certain Death C	.05	.15
85 Collective Brutality R	3.00	3.75
86 Cryptbreaker R	1.25	1.75
87 Dark Salvation R	.40	.60
88 Dusk Feaster U	.05	.15
89 Gavony Unhallowed C	.05	.15
90 Graf Harvest U	.05	.15
91 Graf Rats C	.05	.15
92 Haunted Dead U	.15	.25
93 Liliana, the Last Hope MR	38.00	42.00
94 Lilianas Elite U	.05	.15
95 Markov Crusader U	.05	.15
96 Midnight Scavengers C	.05	.15
97 Murder U	.10	.20
98 Noosegraf Mob R	.10	.20
99 Oath of Liliana R	.30	.50
100 Olivias Dragoon C	.05	.15
101 Prying Questions C	.05	.15
102 Rise from the Grave U	.05	.15
103 Ruthless Disposal U	.05	.15
104 Skirsdag Supplicant C	.05	.15
105 Strange Augmentation C	.05	.15
106 Stromkirk Condemned R	.60	1.00
107 Succumb to Temptation C	.05	.15
108 Thraben Foulbloods C	.05	.15
109 Tree of Perdition MR	2.75	3.50
110 Vampire Cutthroat U	.05	.15
111 Voldaren Pariah, Abolisher of Bloodlines R	1.25	1.75
112 Wailing Ghoul C	.05	.15
113 Weirded Vampire C	.05	.15
114 Whispers of Emrakul U	.15	.25
115 Aandon Reason U	.05	.15
116 Alchemists Greeting C	.05	.15
117 Assembled Alphas R	.10	.20
118 Bedlam Reveler R	2.50	3.15
119 Blood Mist U	.05	.15
120 Bold Impaler C	.05	.15
121 Borrowed Hostility C	.05	.15
122 Brazen Wolves C	.05	.15
123 Collective Defiance R	4.75	5.50
124 Conduit of Storms, Conduit of Emrakul U	.05	.15
125 Deranged Whelp U	.05	.15
126 Distmper of the Blood C	.05	.15
127 Falkenrath Reaver C	.05	.15
128 Furyblade Vampire U	.05	.15
129 Galvanic Bombardment C	.05	.15
130 Hanweir Garrison R	1.50	2.00
131 Harmless Offering R	.30	.50
132 Impetuous Devils R	.10	.20
133 Incendiary Flow U	.60	1.00
134 Insatiable Gorgers U	.05	.15
135 Make Mischief C	.05	.15
136 Mirrorwing Dragon MR	1.75	2.00
137 Nahiris Wrath MR	2.00	2.50
138 Otherworldy Outburst C	.05	.15
139 Prophetic Ravings C	.05	.15
140 Savage Alliance U	.05	.15
141 Shreds of Sanity U	.05	.15
142 Smoldering Werewolf, Erupting Dreadwolf U	.05	.15
143 Spreading Flames U	.05	.15
144 Stensia Banquet C	.05	.15
145 Stensia Innkeeper C	.05	.15
146 Stromkirk Occulist R	.20	.30
147 Thermo Alchemist C	.05	.15
148 Vildin Pack Outcast, Dronepack kindred C	.05	.15
149 Weaver of Lightning U	.05	.15
150 Backwoods Survivalists C	.05	.15
151 Bloodbriar C	.05	.15
152 Clear Shot U	.05	.15
153 Crop Sigil U	.05	.15
154 Crossroads Consecrator C	.05	.15
155 Eldritch Evolution R	4.50	5.25
156 Emrakuls Evangel R	.10	.20
157 Emrakuls Influence U	.05	.15
158 Foul Emissary U	.05	.15
159 Gnarlwood Dryad U	.30	.50
160 Grapple with the Past C	.05	.15
161 Hamlet Captain U	.05	.15
162 Ishkanah, Grafwidow MR	8.00	10.00
163 Kessig Prowler, Sinuous Predator U	.15	.25
164 Noose Constrictor U	.10	.20
165 Permeating Mass R	.20	.30
166 Prey Upon C	.05	.15
167 Primal Druid C	.05	.15
168 Shrill Howler, Howling Chorus U	.05	.15
169 Somberwald Stag U	.05	.15
170 Spirit of the Hunt R	.20	.30
171 Splendid Reclamation R	1.00	1.25
172 Springsage Ritual C	.05	.15
173 Swift Spinner C	.05	.15
174 Tangleclaw Werewolf, Fibrous Entangler U	.05	.15
175 Ulvenwald Captive, Ulvenwald Abomination C	.05	.15
176 Ulvenwald Observer R	.10	.20
177 Waxing Moon C	.05	.15
178 Wolfkin Bond C	.05	.15
179 Woodcutters Grit C	.05	.15
180 Woodland Patrol C	.05	.15
181 Bloodhall Priest R	.30	.50
182 Campaign of Vengeance U	.05	.15
183 Gisa and Geralf MR	2.00	2.50
184 Grim Flayer MR	17.00	20.00
185 Herons Grace Champion R	.20	.30
186 Mercurial Geists U	.05	.15
187 Mournwillow U	.05	.15
188 Ride Down U	.05	.15
189 Spell Queller R	6.75	8.00
190 Tamiyo Field Researcher MR	9.00	11.00
191 Ulrich of the Krallenhorde, Ulrich, Uncontested Alpha MR	1.25	1.75
192 Cathars Shield U	.05	.15
193 Cryptolith Fragment, Aurora of Emrakul U	.05	.15
194 Cultists Staff C	.05	.15
195 Field Creeper C	.05	.15
196 Geist Fueled Scarecrow U	.05	.15
197 Lupine Prototype R	.40	.60
198 Slayers Cleaver U	.05	.15
199 Soul Separator R	.10	.20
200 Stitchers Graft R	.10	.20
201 Terrarion C	.05	.15
202 Thirsting Axe U	.05	.15
203 Geier Reach Sanitarium R	.50	.75
204 Hanweir Battlements R	.60	.80
205 Nephalia Academy U	.05	.15

2016 Magic The Gathering Eldritch Moon Foil

COMPLETE SET (205 CARDS)	500.00	1000.00
1 Abundant Maw U	.40	1.00
2 Decimator of the Provinces MR	8.00	20.00
3 Distended Mindbender R	5.00	12.00
4 Drownyard Behemoth U	.40	1.00
5 Elder Deep Fiend R	6.00	15.00
6 Emrakul the Promised End MR	40.00	70.00
7 Eternal Scourge R	3.00	8.00
8 It of the Horrid Swarm C	.25	.75
9 Lashweed Lurker U	.40	1.00
10 Mockery of Nature U	.40	1.00
11 Vexing Scuttler U	.40	1.00
12 Wretched Gryff C	.25	.75
13 Blessed Alliance U	2.00	5.00
14 Borrowed Grace C	.25	.75
15 Bruna, The Fading Light R	8.00	20.00
16 Choking Restraints C	.25	.75
17 Collective Effort R	4.00	10.00
18 Courageous Outrider U	.40	1.00
19 Dawn Gryff C	.25	.75
20 Deploy the Gatewatch MR	8.00	20.00
21 Desperate Sentry C	.25	.75
22 Drogskol Shieldmate U	.40	1.00
23 Extricator of Sin, Extricator of Flesh U	.40	1.00
24 Faith Unbroken U	.40	1.00
25 Faith Bearer Paladin C	.25	.75
26 Fiend Binder C	.25	.75
27 Geist of the Lonely Vigil U	.40	1.00
28 Gisela, the Broken Blade MR	40.00	70.00
29 Give No Ground U	.40	1.00
30 Guardian of Pilgrims C	.25	.75
31 Ironclad Slayer C	.25	.75
32 Ironwrights Cleansing C	.25	.75
33 Lone Rider, It That Rides as One U	2.50	6.00
34 Long Road Home U	.40	1.00
35 Lunarch Mantle C	.25	.75
36 Peace of Mind U	.40	1.00
37 Providence R	1.50	4.00
38 Repel the Abominable U	.40	1.00
39 Sanctifier of Souls R	1.50	4.00
40 Selfless Spirit R	5.00	12.00
41 Sigardas Aid R	6.00	15.00
42 Sigardian Priest C	.25	.75
43 Spectral Reserves C	.25	.75
44 Steadfast Cathar C	.25	.75
45 Subjugator Angel U	.25	.75
46 Thalia Heretic Cathar R	20.00	35.00
47 Thalias Lancers R	1.50	4.00
48 Thraben Standard Bearer C	.25	.75
49 Advanced Stitchwing U	.40	1.00
50 Chilling Grasp U	.40	1.00
51 Coax from the Blind Eternities R	2.50	6.00
52 Contingency Plan C	.25	.75
53 Convolute C	.25	.75
54 Curious Homunculus, Voracious Reader U	5.00	12.00
55 Displace C	.25	.75
56 Docent of Perfection, Final Iteration R	1.50	4.00
57 Drag Under C	.25	.75
58 Enlightened Maniac C	.25	.75
59 Exultant Cultist C	.25	.75
60 Fogwalker C	.25	.75
61 Fortunes Favor U	.40	1.00
62 Geist of the Archives U	.40	1.00
63 Grizzled Angler, Grisly Anglerfish U	.40	1.00
64 Identity Thief R	1.50	4.00
65 Imprisoned in the Moon R	3.00	8.00
66 Ingenious Skaab C	.25	.75
67 Laboratory Brute C	.25	.75
68 Lunar Force U	.40	1.00
69 Mausoleum Wanderer R	6.00	15.00
70 Mind's Dilation MR	6.00	15.00
71 Nebelgast Herald U	.40	1.00
72 Niblis of Frost R	1.50	4.00
73 Scour the Laboratory U	.40	1.00
74 Spontaneous Mutation C	.25	.75
75 Summary Dismissal R	1.50	4.00
76 Take Inventory C	.25	.75
77 Tattered Haunter C	.25	.75
78 Turn Aside C	.25	.75
79 Unsubstantiate U	5.00	12.00
80 Wharf Infiltrator R	1.50	4.00
81 Boon of Emrakul C	.25	.75
82 Borrowed Malevolence C	.25	.75
83 Cemetery Recruitment C	.25	.75
84 Certain Death C	.25	.75
85 Collective Brutality R	4.00	10.00
86 Cryptbreaker R	5.00	12.00
87 Dark Salvation R	1.50	4.00
88 Dusk Feaster U	.40	1.00
89 Gavony Unhallowed C	.25	.75
90 Graf Harvest U	.40	1.00
91 Graf Rats C	.25	.75
92 Haunted Dead U	.40	1.00
93 Liliana, the Last Hope MR	40.00	70.00
94 Lilianas Elite U	.40	1.00
95 Markov Crusader U	.40	1.00
96 Midnight Scavengers C	.25	.75
97 Murder U	2.50	6.00
98 Noosegraf Mob R	1.50	4.00
99 Oath of Liliana R	3.00	8.00
100 Olivias Dragoon C	.25	.75
101 Prying Questions C	.25	.75
102 Rise from the Grave U	.40	1.00
103 Ruthless Disposal U	.40	1.00
104 Skirsdag Supplicant C	.25	.75
105 Strange Augmentation C	.25	.75
106 Stromkirk Condemned R	3.00	8.00
107 Succumb to Temptation C	.25	.75
108 Thraben Foulbloods C	.25	.75
109 Tree of Perdition MR	10.00	25.00
110 Vampire Cutthroat U	.40	1.00
111 Voldaren Pariah, Abolisher of Bloodlines R	1.50	4.00
112 Wailing Ghoul C	.25	.75
113 Weirded Vampire C	.25	.75
114 Whispers of Emrakul U	3.00	8.00
115 Aandon Reason U	.40	1.00
116 Alchemists Greeting C	.25	.75
117 Assembled Alphas R	1.50	4.00
118 Bedlam Reveler R	6.00	15.00
119 Blood Mist U	.40	1.00
120 Bold Impaler C	.25	.75
121 Borrowed Hostility C	.25	.75
122 Brazen Wolves C	.25	.75
123 Collective Defiance R	2.50	6.00
124 Conduit of Storms, Conduit of Emrakul U	.40	1.00
125 Deranged Whelp U	.40	1.00
126 Distmper of the Blood C	.25	.75
127 Falkenrath Reaver C	.25	.75
128 Furyblade Vampire U	.40	1.00
129 Galvanic Bombardment C	.25	.75
130 Hanweir Garrison R	6.00	15.00
131 Harmless Offering R	3.00	8.00
132 Impetuous Devils R	1.50	4.00
133 Incendiary Flow U	2.00	5.00
134 Insatiable Gorgers U	.40	1.00
135 Make Mischief C	.25	.75
136 Mirrorwing Dragon MR	8.00	20.00
137 Nahiris Wrath MR	6.00	15.00
138 Otherworldy Outburst C	.25	.75
139 Prophetic Ravings C	.25	.75
140 Savage Alliance U	.40	1.00
141 Shreds of Sanity U	.40	1.00
142 Smoldering Werewolf, Erupting Dreadwolf U	.40	1.00
143 Spreading Flames U	.40	1.00
144 Stensia Banquet C	.25	.75
145 Stensia Innkeeper C	.25	.75
146 Stromkirk Occulist R	1.50	4.00
147 Thermo Alchemist C	.25	.75
148 Vildin Pack Outcast, Dronepack kindred C	.25	.75
149 Weaver of Lightning U	.40	1.00
150 Backwoods Survivalists C	.25	.75
151 Bloodbriar C	.25	.75
152 Clear Shot U	.40	1.00
153 Crop Sigil U	.40	1.00
154 Crossroads Consecrator C	.25	.75
155 Eldritch Evolution R	15.00	30.00
156 Emrakuls Evangel R	1.50	4.00
157 Emrakuls Influence U	.40	1.00
158 Foul Emissary U	.40	1.00
159 Gnarlwood Dryad U	.40	1.00
160 Grapple with the Past C	.25	.75
161 Hamlet Captain U	.40	1.00
162 Ishkanah, Grafwidow MR	30.00	60.00
163 Kessig Prowler, Sinuous Predator U	.40	1.00
164 Noose Constrictor U	.40	1.00
165 Permeating Mass R	2.50	6.00
166 Prey Upon C	.25	.75

167 Primal Druid C .25 .75
168 Shrill Howler, Howling Chorus U .40 1.00
169 Somberwald Stag U .40 1.00
170 Spirit of the Hunt R 1.50 4.00
171 Splendid Reclamation R 6.00 15.00
172 Springsage Ritual C .25 .75
173 Swift Spinner C .25 .75
174 Tangleclaw Werewolf, Fibrous Entangler U .40 1.00
175 Ulvenwald Captive, Ulvenwald Abomination C .25 .75
176 Ulvenwald Observer R 1.50 4.00
177 Waxing Moon C .25 .75
178 Wolfkin Bond C .25 .75
179 Woodcutters Grit C .25 .75
180 Woodland Patrol C .25 .75
181 Bloodhall Priest R 2.00 5.00
182 Campaign of Vengeance U .40 1.00
183 Gisa and Geralf MR 8.00 20.00
184 Grim Flayer MR 15.00 30.00
185 Herons Grace Champion R 2.50 6.00
186 Mercurial Geists U .40 1.00
187 Mournwillow U .40 1.00
188 Ride Down U .40 1.00
189 Spell Queller R 15.00 30.00
190 Tamiyo Field Researcher MR 50.00 80.00
191 Ulrich of the Krallenhorde, Ulrich, Uncontested Alpha MR 10.00 25.00
192 Cathars Shield U .40 1.00
193 Cryptolith Fragment, Aurora of Emrakul U .40 1.00
194 Cultists Staff C .25 .75
195 Field Creeper C .25 .75
196 Geist Fueled Scarecrow U .40 1.00
197 Lupine Prototype R 5.00 12.00
198 Slayers Cleaver U .40 1.00
199 Soul Separator R 1.50 4.00
200 Stitchers Graft R 1.50 4.00
201 Terrarion C .25 .75
202 Thirsting Axe U .40 1.00
203 Geier Reach Sanitarium R 5.00 12.00
204 Hanweir Battlements R 5.00 12.00
205 Nephalia Academy U 5.00 12.00

1997 Magic The Gathering Portal

COMPLETE SET (222) 200.00 300.00
BOOSTER BOX (36 PACKS) 120.00 160.00
BOOSTER PACK (15 CARDS) 5.00 7.00
RELEASED ON JUNE 1, 1997
1 Alabaster Dragon R :W: 4.00 8.00
2 Alluring Scent R :G: 1.50 3.00
3 Anaconda v1 C :G: .50 1.00
4 Anaconda v2 U :G: .25 .50
5 Ancestral Memories R :B: 2.00 4.00
6 Angelic Blessing C :W: .15 .30
7 Archangel R :W: 5.00 10.00
8 Ardent Militia U :W: .25 .50
9 Armageddon R :W: 5.00 10.00
10 Armored Pegasus C :W: .15 .30
11 Arrogant Vampire U :K: .50 1.00
12 Assassin's Blade U :K: .50 1.00
13 Balance of Power R :B: 2.00 4.00
14 Baleful Stare U :B: .50 1.00
15 Bee Sting U :G: .25 .50
16 Blaze v1 C :R: .50 1.00
17 Blaze v2 U :R: .50 1.00
18 Blessed Reversal R :W: 2.00 4.00
19 Blinding Light R :W: 2.00 4.00
20 Bog Imp C :K: .15 .30
21 Bog Raiders C :K: .15 .30
22 Bog Wraith U :K: .25 .50
23 Boiling Seas U :R: .50 1.00
24 Border Guard C :W: .15 .30
25 Breath of Life C :W: .15 .30
26 Bull Hippo U :G: .25 .50
27 Burning Cloak C :R: .15 .30
28 Capricious Sorcerer R :B: 2.00 4.00
29 Charging Bandits U :K: .25 .50
30 Charging Paladin U :W: .25 .50
31 Charging Rhino R :G: 2.00 4.00
32 Cloak of Feathers C :B: .15 .30
33 Cloud Dragon R :B: 7.50 15.00
34 Cloud Pirates C :B: .15 .30
35 Cloud Spirit U :B: .50 1.00
36 Command of Unsummoning U :B: .25 .50
37 Coral Eel C :B: .15 .30
38 Craven Giant C :R: .15 .30
39 Craven Knight C :K: .15 .30
40 Cruel Bargain R :K: 10.00 20.00
41 Cruel Fate R :B: 2.00 4.00
42 Cruel Tutor R :K: 9.00 18.00
43 Deep Wood U :G: .25 .50
44 Deep-Sea Serpent U :B: .25 .50
45 Defiant Stand U :W: .25 .50
46 Deja Vu C :B: .15 .30
47 Desert Drake U :R: .25 .50
48 Devastation R :R: 4.00 8.00
49 Devoted Hero C :W: .15 .30
50 Djinn of the Lamp R :B: 2.50 5.00
51 Dread Charge R :K: 2.00 4.00
52 Dread Reaper R :K: 2.00 4.00
53 Dry Spell U :K: .25 .50
54 Earthquake R :R: 4.00 8.00
55 Ebon Dragon R :K: 7.50 15.00
56 Elite Cat Warrior v1 C :G: .15 .30
57 Elite Cat Warrior v2 C :G: .15 .30
58 Elven Cache C :G: .15 .30
59 Elvish Ranger C :G: .15 .30
60 Endless Cockroaches R :K: 5.00 10.00
61 Exhaustion R :B: 2.50 5.00
62 False Peace C :W: .15 .30
63 Feral Shadow C :K: .15 .30
64 Final Strike R :K: 2.00 4.00
65 Fire Dragon R :R: 10.00 20.00
66 Fire Imp U :R: .25 .50
67 Fire Snake C :R: .15 .30
68 Fire Tempest R :R: 2.00 4.00
69 Flashfires U :R: .50 1.00
70 Fleet-Footed Monk C :W: .15 .30
71 Flux U :B: .50 1.00
72 Foot Soldiers C :W: .15 .30
73 Forest A C :L: .15 .30
74 Forest B C :L: .15 .30
75 Forest C C :L: .15 .30
76 Forest D C :L: .15 .30
77 Forked Lightning R :R: 2.50 5.00
78 Fruition C :G: .15 .30
79 Giant Octopus C :B: .15 .30
80 Giant Spider C :G: .15 .30
81 Gift of Estates R :W: 5.00 10.00
82 Goblin Bully C :R: .15 .30
83 Gorilla Warrior C :G: .15 .30
84 Gravedigger U :K: .25 .50
85 Grizzly Bears C :G: .15 .30
86 Hand of Death v1 C :K: .15 .30
87 Hand of Death v2 C :K: .15 .30
88 Harsh Justice R :W: 3.00 6.00
89 Highland Giant C :R: .15 .30
90 Hill Giant C :R: .15 .30
91 Horned Turtle C :B: .15 .30
92 Howling Fury C :K: .15 .30
93 Hulking Cyclops U :R: .50 1.00
94 Hulking Goblin C :R: .15 .30
95 Hurricane R :G: 2.00 4.00
96 Ingenious Thief U :B: .25 .50
97 Island A C :L: .15 .30
98 Island B C :L: .15 .30
99 Island C C :L: .15 .30
100 Island D C :L: .15 .30
101 Jungle Lion C :G: .15 .30
102 Keen-Eyed Archers C :W: .15 .30
103 King's Assassin R :K: 5.00 10.00
104 Knight Errant C :W: .15 .30
105 Last Chance R :R: 3.00 6.00
106 Lava Axe C :R: .15 .30
107 Lava Flow U :R: .25 .50
108 Lizard Warrior C :R: .15 .30
109 Man-o'-War U :B: .25 .50
110 Mercenary Knight R :K: 7.50 15.00
111 Merfolk of the Pearl Trident C :B: .15 .30
112 Mind Knives C :K: .15 .30
113 Mind Rot C :K: .15 .30
114 Minotaur Warrior C :R: .15 .30
115 Mobilize C :G: .15 .30
116 Monstrous Growth v1 C :G: .15 .30
117 Monstrous Growth v2 C :G: .15 .30
118 Moon Sprite U :G: .75 1.50
119 Mountain A C :L: .15 .30
120 Mountain B C :L: .15 .30
121 Mountain C C :L: .15 .30
122 Mountain D C :L: .15 .30
123 Mountain Goat U :R: .25 .50
124 Muck Rats C :K: .15 .30
125 Mystic Denial U :B: .50 1.00
126 Natural Order R :G: 3.00 6.00
127 Natural Spring U :G: .25 .50
128 Nature's Cloak R :G: 2.00 4.00
129 Nature's Lore C :G: .15 .30
130 Nature's Ruin U :K: .25 .50
131 Needle Storm U :G: .25 .50
132 Noxious Toad U :K: .25 .50
133 Omen C :B: .15 .30
134 Owl Familiar C :B: .15 .30
135 Panther Warriors C :G: .15 .30
136 Path of Peace C :W: .15 .30
137 Personal Tutor U :B: 5.00 10.00
138 Phantom Warrior R :B: 2.00 4.00
139 Pillaging Horde R :R: 3.00 6.00
140 Plains A C :L: .15 .30
141 Plains B C :L: .15 .30
142 Plains C C :L: .15 .30
143 Plains D C :L: .15 .30
144 Plant Elemental U :G: 1.50 3.00
145 Primeval Force R :G: 2.50 5.00
146 Prosperity R :B: 2.50 5.00
147 Pyroclasm R :R: 3.50 7.00
148 Python C :K: .15 .30
149 Raging Cougar C :R: .15 .30
150 Raging Goblin v1 C :R: .15 .30
151 Raging Goblin v2 C :R: .15 .30
152 Raging Minotaur C :R: .15 .30
153 Rain of Salt U :R: .50 1.00
154 Rain of Tears U :K: 1.00 2.00
155 Raise Dead C :K: .15 .30
156 Redwood Treefolk C :G: .15 .30
157 Regal Unicorn C :W: .15 .30
158 Renewing Dawn U :W: .25 .50
159 Rowan Treefolk C :G: .15 .30
160 Sacred Knight C :W: .15 .30
161 Sacred Nectar C :W: .15 .30
162 Scorching Spear C :R: .15 .30
163 Scorching Winds U :R: .25 .50
164 Seasoned Marshal U :W: .25 .50
165 Serpent Assassin R :K: 2.50 5.00
166 Serpent Warrior C :K: .15 .30
167 Skeletal Crocodile C :K: .15 .30
168 Skeletal Snake C :K: .15 .30
169 Snapping Drake C :B: .15 .30
170 Sorcerous Sight C :B: .15 .30
171 Soul Shred C :K: .15 .30
172 Spined Wurm C :G: .15 .30
173 Spiritual Guardian R :W: 2.00 4.00
174 Spitting Earth C :R: .15 .30
175 Spotted Griffin C :W: .15 .30
176 Stalking Tiger C :G: .15 .30
177 Starlight U :W: .25 .50
178 Starlit Angel U :W: 3.00 6.00
179 Steadfastness C :W: .15 .30
180 Stern Marshal R :W: 2.00 4.00
181 Stone Rain C :R: .15 .30
182 Storm Crow C :B: .15 .30
183 Summer Bloom R :G: 2.00 4.00
184 Swamp A C :L: .15 .30
185 Swamp B C :L: .15 .30
186 Swamp C C :L: .15 .30
187 Swamp D C :L: .75 1.50
188 Sylvan Tutor R :G: 4.00 8.00
189 Symbol of Unsummoning C :B: .15 .30
190 Taunt R :B: 2.00 4.00
191 Temporary Truce R :W: 2.00 4.00
192 Theft of Dreams U :B: .25 .50
193 Thing from the Deep R :B: 3.50 7.00
194 Thundering Wurm R :G: 2.00 4.00
195 Thundermare R :R: 3.00 6.00
196 Tidal Surge C :B: .15 .30
197 Time Ebb C :B: .15 .30
198 Touch of Brilliance C :G: .15 .30
199 Treetop Defense R :K: 1.00 2.00
200 Undying Beast C :G: .15 .30
201 Untamed Wilds U :G: .25 .50
202 Valorous Charge U :W: .25 .50
203 Vampiric Feast U :K: .50 1.00
204 Vampiric Touch C :K: .15 .30
205 Venerable Monk U :W: .25 .50
206 Vengeance U :W: .25 .50
207 Virtue's Ruin U :K: .50 1.00
208 Volcanic Dragon R :R: 4.00 8.00
209 Volcanic Hammer C :R: .15 .30
210 Wall of Granite U :R: .25 .50
211 Wall of Swords U :W: .50 1.00
212 Warrior's Charge v1 C :W: .15 .30
213 Warrior's Charge v2 C :W: .15 .30
214 Whiptail Wurm U :G: .25 .50
215 Wicked Pact R :K: 2.00 4.00
216 Willow Dryad C :G: .15 .30
217 Wind Drake C :B: .15 .30
218 Winds of Change R :R: 2.50 5.00
219 Winter's Grasp U :G: .50 1.00
220 Withering Gaze U :B: .50 1.00
221 Wood Elves R :G: 2.50 5.00
222 Wrath of God R :W: 12.00 25.00

1997 Magic The Gathering Vanguard

COMPLETE SET (32) 150.00 200.00
BOOSTER PACK 40.00 60.00
RELEASED IN SUMMER 1997
1 Ashnod R 3.00 5.00
2 Barrin R 3.00 5.00
3 Crovax R 3.00 5.00
4 Eladamri R 3.00 5.00
5 Ertai R 3.00 5.00
6 Gerrard R 3.00 5.00
7 Gix R 3.00 5.00
8 Greven il-Vec R 3.00 5.00
9 Hanna R 3.00 6.00
10 Karn R 3.00 5.00
11 Lyna R 3.00 5.00
12 Maraxus R 3.00 5.00
13 Mirri R 4.00 7.00
14 Mishra R 3.00 5.00
15 Multani R 4.00 7.00
16 Oracle R 3.00 5.00
17 Orim R 3.00 5.00
18 Rofellos R 3.00 5.00
19 Selenia R 3.00 5.00
20 Serra R 3.00 5.00
21 Sidar Kondo R 3.00 5.00
22 Sisay R 3.00 6.00
23 Sliver Queen, Brood Mother R 7.00 12.00
24 Squee R 3.00 5.00
25 Starke R 3.00 5.00
26 Tahngarth R 3.00 5.00
27 Takara R 3.00 6.00
28 Tawnos R 4.00 6.00
29 Titania R 3.00 6.00
30 Urza R 3.00 6.00
31 Volrath R 3.00 5.00
32 Xantcha R 3.00 5.00

1998 Magic The Gathering Portal Second Age

COMPLETE SET (165) 150.00 225.00
BOOSTER BOX (36 PACKS) 125.00 175.00
BOOSTER PACK (15 CARDS) 5.00 7.00
STARTER DECK BOX 70.00 110.00
STARTER DECK 8.00 11.00
RELEASED ON JUNE 1, 1998
1 Abyssal Nightstalker U :K: .50 1.00
2 Air Elemental U :B: .50 1.00
3 Alaborn Cavalier U :W: .50 1.00
4 Alaborn Grenadier C :W: .15 .30
5 Alaborn Musketeer C :W: .15 .30
6 Alaborn Trooper C :W: .15 .30
7 Alaborn Veteran R :W: 2.00 4.00
8 Alaborn Zealot U :W: .25 .50
9 Alluring Scent R :G: 2.00 4.00
10 Ancient Craving R :K: 3.00 6.00
11 Angel of Fury R :W: 6.00 12.00
12 Angel of Mercy U :W: 1.00 2.00
13 Angelic Blessing C :W: .15 .30
14 Angelic Wall C :W: .15 .30
15 Apprentice Sorcerer U :B: .50 1.00
16 Archangel R :W: 9.00 18.00
17 Armageddon R :W: 5.00 10.00
18 Armored Galleon U :B: 1.00 2.00
19 Armored Griffin U :W: .50 1.00
20 Barbtooth Wurm C :G: .15 .30
21 Bargain U :W: .75 1.50
22 Bear Cub C :G: .15 .30
23 Bee Sting U :G: .25 .50
24 Blaze U :R: 1.00 2.00
25 Bloodcurdling Scream U :K: .50 1.00
26 Breath of Life C :K: .15 .30
27 Brimstone Dragon R :R: 10.00 20.00
28 Brutal Nightstalker U :K: .50 1.00
29 Chorus of Woe C :K: .15 .30
30 Coastal Wizard R :B: 2.50 5.00
31 Coercion U :K: .50 1.00
32 Cruel Edict C :K: .15 .30
33 Cunning Giant R :R: 3.00 6.00
34 Dakmor Bat C :K: .15 .30
35 Dakmor Plague U :K: .50 1.00
36 Dakmor Scorpion C :K: .15 .30
37 Dakmor Sorceress R :K: 6.00 12.00
38 Dark Offering U :K: .50 1.00
39 Deathcoil Wurm R :G: 5.00 10.00
40 Deep Wood U :G: .25 .50
41 Deja Vu C :B: .15 .30
42 Denizen of the Deep R :B: 5.00 10.00
43 Earthquake R :R: 3.00 6.00
44 Exhaustion R :B: 2.00 4.00
45 Extinguish C :B: .15 .30
46 Eye Spy U :B: .50 1.00
47 False Summoning C :B: .15 .30
48 Festival of Trokin C :W: .15 .30
49 Forest C :L: .15 .30
50 Forest B C :L: .15 .30
51 Forest C C :L: .15 .30
52 Foul Spirit U :K: .50 1.00
53 Goblin Cavaliers C :R: .15 .30
54 Goblin Firestarter U :R: 1.00 2.00
55 Goblin General R :R: 5.00 10.00
56 Goblin Glider C :R: .15 .30
57 Goblin Lore U :R: 2.50 5.00
58 Goblin Matron U :R: 1.25 2.50
59 Goblin Mountaineer C :R: .15 .30
60 Goblin Piker C :R: .15 .30
61 Goblin Raider C :R: .15 .30
62 Goblin War Cry U :R: .50 1.00
63 Goblin War Strike C :R: .15 .30
64 Golden Bear C :G: .15 .30
65 Hand of Death C :K: .15 .30
66 Harmony of Nature U :G: 1.00 2.00
67 Hidden Horror R :K: 2.50 5.00
68 Hurricane R :G: 2.00 4.00
69 Ironhoof Ox U :G: .50 1.00
70 Island C :L: .15 .30
71 Island B C :L: .15 .30
72 Island C C :L: .15 .30
73 Jagged Lightning U :R: .25 .50
74 Just Fate R :W: 2.50 5.00
75 Kiss of Death U :K: .50 1.00
76 Lava Axe C :R: .15 .30
77 Lone Wolf U :G: .25 .50
78 Lurking Nightstalker C :K: .15 .30
79 Lynx C :G: .15 .30
80 Magma Giant R :R: 2.00 4.00
81 Mind Rot C :K: .15 .30
82 Moaning Spirit C :K: .15 .30
83 Monstrous Growth C :G: .15 .30
84 Mountain C :L: .15 .30
85 Mountain B C :L: .15 .30
86 Mountain C C :L: .15 .30
87 Muck Rats C :K: .15 .30
88 Mystic Denial U :B: .50 1.00
89 Natural Spring C :G: .15 .30
90 Nature's Lore C :G: .15 .30
91 Nightstalker Engine R :K: 2.50 5.00
92 Norwood Archers C :G: .15 .30
93 Norwood Priestess R :G: 12.00 25.00
94 Norwood Ranger C :G: .15 .30
95 Norwood Riders C :G: .15 .30
96 Norwood Warrior C :G: .15 .30
97 Obsidian Giant U :R: .50 1.00
98 Ogre Arsonist U :R: .50 1.00
99 Ogre Berserker C :R: .15 .30
100 Ogre Taskmaster U :R: .25 .50
101 Ogre Warrior C :R: .15 .30
102 Path of Peace C :W: .15 .30
103 Piracy R :B: 7.50 15.00
104 Plains C :L: .15 .30
105 Plains B C :L: .15 .30
106 Plains C C :L: .15 .30
107 Plated Wurm C :G: .15 .30
108 Predatory Nightstalker U :K: .50 1.00
109 Prowling Nightstalker C :K: .15 .30
110 Raging Goblin C :R: .15 .30
111 Raiding Nightstalker C :K: .15 .30
112 Rain of Daggers R :K: 5.00 10.00
113 Raise Dead C :K: .15 .30
114 Rally the Troops U :W: .50 1.00
115 Ravenous Rats C :K: .15 .30
116 Razorclaw Bear R :G: 4.00 8.00
117 Relentless Assault R :R: 2.00 4.00
118 Remove U :B: .25 .50
119 Renewing Touch U :G: .25 .50
120 Return of the Nightstalkers R :K: 4.00 8.00
121 Righteous Charge C :W: .15 .30
122 Righteous Fury R :W: 4.00 8.00
123 River Bear U :G: .50 1.00
124 Salvage C :G: .15 .30
125 Screeching Drake C :B: .15 .30
126 Sea Drake U :B: 15.00 30.00
127 Sleight of Hand C :B: .15 .30
128 Spitting Earth C :R: .15 .30
129 Steam Catapult R :W: 4.00 8.00
130 Steam Frigate C :B: .15 .30
131 Stone Rain C :R: .15 .30
132 Swamp C :L: .15 .30
133 Swamp B C :K: .15 .30
134 Swamp C C :G: .15 .30
135 Swarm of Rats C :G: .15 .30
136 Sylvan Basilisk R :B: 5.00 10.00
137 Sylvan Yeti R :B: 2.50 5.00
138 Talas Air Ship C :B: .15 .30
139 Talas Explorer C :B: .15 .30
140 Talas Merchant C :B: .15 .30
141 Talas Researcher R :B: 4.00 8.00
142 Talas Scout C :B: .15 .30
143 Talas Warrior R :B: 2.50 5.00
144 Temple Acolyte C :W: .15 .30
145 Temple Elder U :W: .50 1.00
146 Temporal Manipulation R :B: 30.00 60.00
147 Theft of Dreams U :B: .50 1.00
148 Tidal Surge C :B: .15 .30
149 Time Ebb C :B: .15 .30
150 Touch of Brilliance C :B: .15 .30
151 Town Sentry C :W: .15 .30
152 Tree Monkey C :G: .15 .30
153 Tremor C :R: .15 .30
154 Trokin High Guard C :W: .15 .30
155 Undo U :B: .25 .50
156 Untamed Wilds U :G: .50 1.00
157 Vampiric Spirit R :K: 4.00 8.00
158 Vengeance U :W: .25 .50
159 Volcanic Hammer C :R: .15 .30
160 Volunteer Militia C :W: .15 .30
161 Warrior's Stand U :W: .25 .50
162 Wild Griffin C :W: .15 .30
163 Wild Ox U :G: .25 .50
164 Wildfire R :R: 4.00 8.00
165 Wind Sail C :B: .15 .30

1998 Magic The Gathering Unglued

COMPLETE SET (93) 50.00 90.00
BOOSTER BOX (48 PACKS) 225.00 300.00
BOOSTER PACK (15 CARDS) 7.00 10.00
RELEASED ON AUGUST 11, 1998
69 Ashnod's Coupon R :A: 4.00 8.00
28 Big Furry Monster-L R :K: 6.00 12.00
29 Big Furry Monster-R R :K: 6.00 12.00
70 Blacker Lotus R :A: 3.50 7.00
71 Bronze Calendar U :A: .50 1.00
14 Bureaucracy R :B: 1.00 2.00
40 Burning Cinder Fury of Crimson Chaos Fire R :R:1.50 3.00
54 Cardboard Carapace R :G: 1.50 3.00
15 Censorship U :B: 1.00 2.00
72 Chaos Confetti C :A: .15 .30
1 Charm School U :W: .50 1.00
16 Checks and Balances U :B: .50 1.00
17 Chicken a la King R :B: 1.50 3.00
41 Chicken Egg C :R: .15 .30
18 Clam Session C :B: .15 .30
19 Clambassadors C :B: .15 .30
20 Clam-I-Am C :B: .15 .30
73 Clay Pigeon U :A: .50 1.00
21 Common Courtesy U :B: 1.00 2.00
30 Deadhead C :K: .15 .30
22 Denied! C :B: .15 .30
31 Double Cross C :K: .15 .30
42 Double Deal C :R: .15 .30
2 Double Dip C :W: .15 .30
55 Double Play C :G: .15 .30
23 Double Take C :B: .15 .30
56 Elvish Impersonators C :G: .15 .30
57 Flock of Rabid Sheep U :G: 1.00 2.00
88 Forest C :G: 1.50 3.00
24 Fowl Play C :B: .15 .30
25 Free-for-All R :B: 1.00 2.00
58 Free-Range Chicken C :G: .15 .30
59 Gerrymandering U :G: .50 1.00
3 Get a Life U :W: .50 1.00
60 Ghazban Ogress C :G: .15 .30
74 Giant Fan R :A: 1.00 2.00
43 Goblin Bookie C :R: .15 .30
44 Goblin Bowling Team C :R: .15 .30
45 Goblin Tutor U :R: 1.00 2.00
92 Goblin U :R: .50 1.00
61 Growth Spurt C :G: .15 .30
62 Gus C :G: .15 .30
32 Handcuffs U :K: .50 1.00
63 Hungry Hungry Heifer U :G: .50 1.00
46 Hurloon Wrangler C :R: .15 .30
4 I'm Rubber, You're Glue R :W: 2.00 4.00
64 Incoming! R :G: 2.00 4.00
33 Infernal Spawn of Evil R :K: 4.00 8.00
85 Island C :B: 1.50 3.00
75 Jack-in-the-Mox R :A: 1.50 3.00
47 Jalum Grifter R :R: 1.50 3.00
76 Jester's Sombrero R :A: 1.50 3.00
34 Jumbo Imp U :K: .50 1.00
5 Knight of the Hokey Pokey C :W: .15 .30
48 Krazy Kow C :R: .15 .30
49 Landfill R :R: 1.00 2.00
6 Lexivore U :W: .50 1.00
7 Look at Me, I'm the DCI R :W: 1.50 3.00
8 Mesa Chicken C :W: .15 .30
65 Mine, Mine, Mine! R :G: 2.50 5.00
77 Mirror Mirror R :A: 1.50 3.00
9 Miss Demeanor U :W: 1.00 2.00
87 Mountain C :R: 1.00 2.00
10 Once More with Feeling R :W: 1.50 3.00
35 Organ Harvest C :K: .15 .30
36 Ow R :K: 1.50 3.00
78 Paper Tiger C :A: .15 .30
89 Pegasus U :W: .50 1.00
84 Plains C :W: 1.00 2.00
37 Poultrygeist C :K: .15 .30
11 Prismatic Wardrobe C :W: .15 .30
26 Psychic Network R :B: 1.00 2.00
50 Ricochet U :R: .50 1.00
79 Rock Lobster C :A: .15 .30
80 Scissors Lizard C :A: .15 .30
12 Sex Appeal C :W: .15 .30
93 Sheep U :G: 1.00 2.00
90 Soldier U :W: .50 1.00
27 Sorry U :B: .50 1.00
51 Spark Fiend R :R: 1.50 3.00
81 Spatula of the Ages U :A: .50 1.00
66 Squirrel Farm R :G: 2.00 4.00
94 Squirrel U :G: 1.50 3.00
52 Strategy, Schmategy R :R: 2.00 4.00
86 Swamp C :K: 1.00 2.00
67 Team Spirit C :G: .15 .30
38 Temp of the Damned C :K: .15 .30
13 The Cheese Stands Alone R :W: 3.00 6.00
53 The Ultimate Nightmare U :B: 1.00 2.00
68 Timmy, Power Gamer R :G: 2.50 5.00
82 Urza's Contact Lenses U :A: .50 1.00
83 Urza's Science Fair Project U :A: .50 1.00
39 Volrath's Motion Sensor U :K: .50 1.00
91 Zombie U :K: .75 1.50

1999 Magic The Gathering Portal Three Kingdoms

COMPLETE SET (180) 600.00 850.00
BOOSTER BOX (36 PACKS) 1100.00 1250.00
BOOSTER PACK (15 CARDS) 15.00 25.00
STARTER DECK 10.00 30.00
RELEASED ON MAY 1, 1999
1 Alert Shu Infantry U :W: 2.00 4.00
67 Ambition's Cost R :K: 3.00 6.00
34 Balance of Power R :B: 5.00 10.00
4 Barbarian General U :R: 1.50 3.00
101 Barbarian Horde C :R: .50 1.00
102 Blaze U :R: 2.00 4.00
35 Borrowing 100,000 Arrows U :B: 2.50 5.00
133 Borrowing the East Wind R :G: 6.00 12.00
36 Brilliant Plan U :B: 2.00 4.00
37 Broken Dam C :B: .50 1.00
103 Burning Fields C :R: .50 1.00
104 Burning of Xinye R :R: 7.50 15.00
68 Cao Cao, Lord of Wei R :K: 7.50 15.00
69 Cao Ren, Wei Commander R :K: 4.00 8.00
38 Capture of Jingzhou R :B: 150.00 300.00
39 Champion's Victory U :B: 2.00 4.00
70 Coercion U :K: 2.00 4.00
105 Control of the Court U :R: 1.00 2.00
71 Corrupt Court Official U :K: 2.00 4.00
106 Corrupt Eunuchs U :R: 2.00 4.00
40 Council of Advisors U :B: 2.00 4.00
41 Counterintelligence U :B: 2.00 4.00
72 Cunning Advisor U :K: 2.00 4.00
73 Deception C :K: .50 1.00
107 Desert Sandstorm C :R: .50 1.00
74 Desperate Charge U :K: 1.00 2.00
108 Diaochan, Artful Beauty R :R: 6.00 12.00
109 Dong Zhou, the Tyrant R :R: 6.00 12.00
2 Eightfold Maze R :W: 6.00 12.00
3 Empty City Ruse U :W: 2.00 4.00
110 Eunuchs' Intrigues U :R: 2.00 4.00
42 Exhaustion R :B: 6.00 12.00

43 Extinguish C :B: .50 1.00
4 False Defeat C :W: .50 1.00
134 False Mourning U :G: 3.00 6.00
75 Famine U :K: 2.00 4.00
111 Fire Ambush C :R: .50 1.00
112 Fire Bowman U :R: 2.00 4.00
5 Flanking Troops U :W: 1.00 2.00
44 Forced Retreat C :B: .50 1.00
135 Forest Bear C :G: .50 1.00
178 Forest C :L: .50 1.00
179 Forest C :L: .50 1.00
180 Forest C :L: .50 1.00
76 Ghostly Visit C :K: .50 1.00
6 Guan Yu, Sainted Warrior R :W: 7.50 15.00
7 Guan Yu's 1,000-Li March R :W: 10.00 20.00
136 Heavy Fog U :G: 1.50 3.00
137 Hua Tuo, Honored Physician R :G: 5.00 10.00
8 Huang Zhong, Shu General R :W: 4.00 8.00
138 Hunting Cheetah U :G: 2.00 4.00
77 Imperial Edict C :K: .50 1.00
113 Imperial Recruiter U :R: 4.00 8.00
78 Imperial Seal R :K: 350.00 700.00
114 Independent Troops C :R: .50 1.00
169 Island (with beach) C :L: .50 1.00
170 Island (with river) C :L: .50 1.00
171 Island (no sky) C :L: .50 1.00
9 Kongming, Sleeping Dragon R :W: 10.00 20.00
10 Kongming's Contraptions R :W: 4.00 8.00
45 Lady Sun R :B: 6.00 12.00
139 Lady Zhurong, Warrior Queen R :G: 6.00 12.00
11 Liu Bei, Lord of Shu R :W: 6.00 12.00
140 Lone Wolf U :G: 1.50 3.00
12 Loyal Retainers U :W: 2.00 4.00
115 Lu Bu, Master-at-Arms R :R: 7.50 15.00
46 Lu Meng, Wu General R :B: 4.00 8.00
47 Lu Su, Wu Advisor R :B: 4.00 8.00
48 Lu Xun, Scholar General R :B: 3.00 6.00
116 Ma Chao, Western Warrior R :R: 4.00 8.00
141 Marshaling the Troops R :G: 5.00 10.00
142 Meng Huo, Barbarian King R :G: 15.00 30.00
143 Meng Huo's Horde C :G: .50 1.00
13 Misfortune's Gain C :W: .50 1.00
117 Mountain Bandit C :R: .50 1.00
175 Mountain C :L: .50 1.00
176 Mountain C :L: .50 1.00
177 Mountain C :L: .50 1.00
49 Mystic Denial U :B: 2.00 4.00
79 Overwhelming Forces R :K: 60.00 120.00
14 Pang Tong, Young Phoenix R :W: 4.00 8.00
15 Peach Garden Oath U :W: 2.00 4.00
166 Plains C :L: .50 1.00
167 Plains C :L: .50 1.00
168 Plains C :L: .50 1.00
80 Poison Arrow U :K: 2.00 4.00
50 Preemptive Strike C :B: .50 1.00
16 Rally the Troops U :W: 2.00 4.00
17 Ravages of War R :W: 100.00 200.00
118 Ravaging Horde U :R: 2.00 4.00
51 Red Cliffs Armada U :B: 2.00 4.00
119 Relentless Assault R :R: 4.00 8.00
120 Renegade Troops U :R: 2.00 4.00
81 Return to Battle C :K: .50 1.00
18 Riding Red Hare C :W: .50 1.00
144 Riding the Dilu Horse R :G: 4.00 8.00
121 Rockslide Ambush U :R: 2.00 4.00
122 Rolling Earthquake R :R: 60.00 120.00
52 Sage's Knowledge C :B: .50 1.00
19 Shu Cavalry C :W: .50 1.00
20 Shu Defender C :W: .50 1.00
21 Shu Elite Companions U :W: 2.00 4.00
22 Shu Elite Infantry C :W: .50 1.00
23 Shu Farmer C :W: .50 1.00
24 Shu Foot Soldiers C :W: .50 1.00
25 Shu General U :W: 2.00 4.00
26 Shu Grain Caravan C :W: .50 1.00
27 Shu Soldier-Farmers U :W: 2.00 4.00
82 Sima Yi, Wei Field Marshal R :K: 4.00 8.00
145 Slashing Tiger R :G: 4.00 8.00
146 Southern Elephant C :G: .50 1.00
147 Spoils of Victory U :G: 2.00 4.00
148 Spring of Eternal Peace C :G: .50 1.00
149 Stalking Tiger C :G: .50 1.00
83 Stolen Grain U :K: 2.00 4.00
84 Stone Catapult R :K: 5.00 10.00
123 Stone Rain C :R: .50 1.00
53 Strategic Planning U :B: 2.00 4.00
54 Straw Soldiers C :B: .50 1.00
55 Sun Ce, Young Conqueror R :B: 6.00 12.00
56 Sun Quan, Lord of Wu R :B: 6.00 12.00
172 Swamp (gray) C :L: .50 1.00
173 Swamp (green) C :L: .50 1.00
174 Swamp (orange) C :L: .50 1.00
150 Taoist Hermit U :G: 2.00 4.00
151 Taoist Mystic R :G: 3.00 6.00
152 Taunting Challenge R :G: 4.00 8.00
153 Three Visits C :G: .50 1.00
154 Trained Cheetah U :G: 2.00 4.00
155 Trained Jackal C :G: .50 1.00
156 Trip Wire U :G: 2.00 4.00
28 Vengeance U :W: 2.00 4.00
29 Virtuous Charge C :W: .50 1.00
30 Volunteer Militia C :W: .50 1.00
124 Warrior's Oath R :R: 4.00 8.00
31 Warrior's Stand U :W: 2.00 4.00
85 Wei Ambush Force C :K: .50 1.00
86 Wei Assassins U :K: 2.00 4.00
87 Wei Elite Companions U :K: 2.00 4.00
88 Wei Infantry C :K: .50 1.00
89 Wei Night Raiders U :K: 2.00 4.00
90 Wei Scout C :K: .50 1.00
91 Wei Strike Force C :K: .50 1.00
157 Wielding the Green Dragon C :G: .50 1.00
158 Wolf Pack R :G: 15.00 30.00
57 Wu Admiral U :B: 2.00 4.00
58 Wu Elite Cavalry C :B: .50 1.00
59 Wu Infantry C :B: .50 1.00
60 Wu Light Cavalry C :B: .50 1.00
61 Wu Longbowman U :B: 2.00 4.00
62 Wu Scout C :B: .50 1.00
63 Wu Spy U :B: 2.00 4.00
64 Wu Warship C :B: .50 1.00
92 Xiahou Dun, the One-Eyed R :K: 75.00 150.00
93 Xun Yu, Wei Advisor R :K: 4.00 8.00
125 Yellow Scarves Cavalry C :R: .50 1.00
126 Yellow Scarves General R :R: 4.00 8.00
127 Yellow Scarves Troops C :R: .50 1.00
94 Young Wei Recruit C :K: .50 1.00
129 Yuan Shao, the Indecisive R :R: 4.00 8.00
128 Yuan Shao's Infantry U :R: 2.00 4.00
32 Zhang Fei, Fierce Warrior R :W: 6.00 12.00
95 Zhang He, Wei General R :K: 5.00 10.00
96 Zhang Liao, Hero of Hefei R :K: 4.00 8.00
33 Zhao Zilong, Tiger General R :W: 5.00 10.00
65 Zhou Yu, Chief Commander R :B: 5.00 10.00
66 Zhuge Jin, Wu Strategist R :B: 5.00 10.00
130 Zodiac Dog C :R: .50 1.00
131 Zodiac Dragon R :R: 100.00 200.00
132 Zodiac Goat C :R: .50 1.00
159 Zodiac Horse U :G: 2.00 4.00
160 Zodiac Monkey C :G: .50 1.00
161 Zodiac Ox U :G: 2.00 4.00
97 Zodiac Pig U :K: 2.00 4.00
162 Zodiac Rabbit C :G: .50 1.00
98 Zodiac Rat C :K: .50 1.00
163 Zodiac Rooster C :G: .50 1.00
99 Zodiac Snake C :K: .50 1.00
164 Zodiac Tiger U :G: 2.00 4.00
165 Zuo Ci, the Mocking Sage R :G: 4.00 8.00

1999 Magic The Gathering Starter

COMPLETE SET (173) 250.00 300.00
BOOSTER BOX (36 PACKS) 175.00 250.00
BOOSTER PACK (15 CARDS) 5.00 8.00
STARTER DECK BOX (12 DECKS) 150.00 250.00
STARTER DECK 18.00 30.00
RELEASED ON APRIL 20, 1999
63 Abyssal Horror R :K: 1.00 2.00
32 Air Elemental U :B: .25 .50
124 Alluring Scent R :G: 1.00 2.00
64 Ancient Craving R :K: 1.50 3.00
1 Angel of Light U :W: .25 .50
2 Angel of Mercy U :W: .25 .50
3 Angelic Blessing C :W: .15 .30
4 Archangel R :W: 4.00 8.00
5 Ardent Militia U :W: .25 .50
6 Armageddon R :W: 2.50 5.00
125 Barbtooth Wurm C :G: .15 .30
7 Bargain U :W: .25 .50
8 Blinding Light R :W: 1.50 3.00
65 Bog Imp C :K: .15 .30
66 Bog Raiders C :K: .15 .30
67 Bog Wraith U :K: .50 1.00
9 Border Guard C :W: .15 .30
10 Breath of Life U :W: .25 .50
126 Bull Hippo U :G: .30 .75
11 Champion Lancer R :W: 2.00 4.00
12 Charging Paladin U :W: .25 .50
68 Chorus of Woe C :K: .15 .30
93 Cinder Storm U :R: .25 .50
69 Coercion U :K: .25 .50
33 Coral Eel C :B: .15 .30
34 Counterspell U :B: .25 .50
70 Dakmor Ghoul U :K: .25 .50
71 Dakmor Lancer R :K: 1.50 3.00
72 Dakmor Plague U :K: .25 .50
73 Dakmor Scorpion C :K: .15 .30
74 Dakmor Sorceress R :K: 5.00 10.00
75 Dark Offering U :K: .25 .50
35 Denizen of the Deep R :B: 2.50 5.00
94 Devastation R :R: 1.50 3.00
13 Devoted Hero C :W: .15 .30
14 Devout Monk C :W: .15 .30
76 Dread Reaper R :K: 1.50 3.00
127 Durkwood Boars C :G: .15 .30
15 Eager Cadet C* :W: .15 .30
95 Earth Elemental U :R: .25 .50
36 Exhaustion U :B: .25 .50
37 Extinguish C :B: .15 .30
38 Eye Spy U :B: .25 .50
16 False Peace U :W: .25 .50
77 Feral Shadow C :K: .15 .30
96 Fire Elemental U :R: .25 .50
97 Fire Tempest R :R: 1.00 2.00
17 Foot Soldiers C :W: .15 .30
172 Forest L :L: .15 .30
171 Forest L :L: .15 .30
170 Forest L :L: .15 .30
173 Forest L :L: .15 .30
18 Gerrard's Wisdom R :W: 1.50 3.00
39 Giant Octopus C :B: .15 .30
98 Goblin Cavaliers C :R: .15 .30
99 Goblin Chariot C :R: .15 .30
100 Goblin Commando U :R: .25 .50
101 Goblin General U :R: .25 .50
102 Goblin Glider U :R: .25 .50
103 Goblin Hero R* :R: 2.00 4.00
104 Goblin Lore U :R: .25 .50
105 Goblin Mountaineer C :R: .15 .30
106 Goblin Settler U :R: .25 .50
128 Gorilla Warrior C :G: .15 .30
78 Gravedigger U :K: .25 .50
79 Grim Tutor R :K: 125.00 200.00
129 Grizzly Bears C :G: .15 .30
80 Hand of Death C :K: .15 .30
81 Hollow Dogs C :K: .15 .30
82 Howling Fury U :K: .25 .50
107 Hulking Goblin C :R: .15 .30
108 Hulking Ogre U :R: .25 .50
40 Ingenious Thief C :B: .15 .30
160 Island L :L: .15 .30
159 Island L :L: .15 .30
158 Island L :L: .15 .30
161 Island L :L: .15 .30
109 Jagged Lightning U :R: .50 1.00
19 Knight Errant C :W: .15 .30
110 Last Chance R :R: 1.50 3.00
111 Lava Axe C :R: .15 .30
130 Lone Wolf C :G: .15 .30
20 Loyal Sentry R :W: 1.00 2.00
131 Lynx U :G: .25 .50
41 Man-o'-War U :B: .25 .50
42 Merfolk of the Pearl Trident C* :B: .25 .50
83 Mind Rot C :K: .15 .30
112 Mons's Goblin Raiders R* :R: 1.00 2.00
132 Monstrous Growth C :G: .15 .30
133 Moon Sprite U :G: .25 .50
166 Mountain L :L: .15 .30
167 Mountain L :L: .15 .30
168 Mountain L :L: .15 .30
169 Mountain L :L: .15 .30
84 Muck Rats C :K: .15 .30
134 Natural Spring U :G: .25 .50
135 Nature's Cloak R :G: 1.00 2.00
136 Nature's Lore C :G: .15 .30
137 Norwood Archers C :G: .15 .30
138 Norwood Ranger C :G: .15 .30
113 Ogre Warrior C :R: .15 .30
43 Owl Familiar U :B: .25 .50
21 Path of Peace C :W: .15 .30
44 Phantom Warrior R :B: 1.00 2.00
45 Piracy R :B: 5.00 10.00
154 Plains L :L: .15 .30
155 Plains L :L: .15 .30
156 Plains L :L: .15 .30
157 Plains L :L: .15 .30
139 Pride of Lions U :G: .25 .50
46 Psychic Transfer R :B: 1.50 3.00
114 Raging Goblin C :R: .15 .30
85 Raise Dead C :K: .15 .30
47 Ransack R :B: 1.00 2.00
86 Ravenous Rats U :K: .50 1.00
48 Relearn U :B: .25 .50
115 Relentless Assault R :R: 2.00 4.00
49 Remove Soul C :B: .15 .30
140 Renewing Touch U :G: .25 .50
22 Righteous Charge U :W: 2.50 5.00
23 Righteous Fury R :W: 1.00 2.00
24 Royal Falcon C* :W: .15 .30
25 Royal Trooper U :W: .25 .50
26 Sacred Nectar C :W: .15 .30
87 Scathe Zombies C* :K: .15 .30
116 Scorching Spear C :R: .15 .30
50 Sea Eagle C* :B: .15 .30
88 Serpent Warrior C :K: .15 .30
89 Shrieking Specter U :K: .25 .50
141 Silverback Ape U :G: .25 .50
51 Sleight of Hand C :B: .15 .30
52 Snapping Drake C :B: .15 .30
90 Soul Feast U :K: .25 .50
142 Southern Elephant C :G: .15 .30
117 Spitting Earth U :R: .25 .50
143 Squall C :G: .15 .30
27 Steadfastness C :W: .15 .30
118 Stone Rain C :R: .15 .30
53 Storm Crow C :B: .15 .30
91 Stream of Acid U :K: .25 .50
144 Summer Bloom R :G: 1.00 2.00
162 Swamp L :L: .15 .30
163 Swamp L :L: .15 .30
164 Swamp L :L: .15 .30
165 Swamp L :L: .15 .30
145 Sylvan Basilisk R :G: 1.50 3.00
146 Sylvan Yeti R :G: 1.00 2.00
147 Thorn Elemental R :G: 1.00 2.00
119 Thunder Dragon R :R: 20.00 35.00
54 Tidings U :B: .25 .50
55 Time Ebb C :B: .15 .30
56 Time Warp R :B: 3.00 6.00
57 Touch of Brilliance C :B: .15 .30
120 Trained Orgg R :R: 1.00 2.00
121 Tremor C :R: .15 .30
58 Undo U :B: .25 .50
148 Untamed Wilds U :G: .25 .50
28 Venerable Monk C :W: .15 .30
29 Vengeance U :W: .25 .50
30 Veteran Cavalier U :W: .25 .50
59 Vizzerdrix R :B: 1.00 2.00
122 Volcanic Dragon R :R: 2.00 4.00
123 Volcanic Hammer C :R: .15 .30
60 Water Elemental U :B: .25 .50
149 Whiptail Wurm U :G: .25 .50
150 Whirlwind R :G: .60 1.50
92 Wicked Pact R :K: 1.50 3.00
31 Wild Griffin C :W: .15 .30
151 Wild Ox U :G: .25 .50
152 Willow Elf C* :G: .15 .30
61 Wind Drake C :B: .15 .30
62 Wind Sail U :B: .25 .50
153 Wood Elves U :G: .25 .50

2000 Magic The Gathering Starter

COMPLETE SET (57) 15.00 40.00
RELEASED ON APRIL 24, 2000
1 Angelic Blessing C :W: .75 .75
2 Armored Pegasus C :W: .10 .25
3 Bog Imp C :K: .10 .25
4 Breath of Life U :W: .60 .60
5 Coercion C :K: .50 .50
6 Counterspell C :L: .75 .75
7 Disenchant C :W: 1.00 1.00
8 Drudge Skeletons C :K: .10 .25
9 Durkwood Boars C :G: .75 .75
10 Eager Cadet C :W: .60 .60
11 Flame Spirit C :R: .10 .25
12 Flight C :L: .10 .25
13 Forest L .10 .25
14 Forest L .10 .25
15 Giant Growth C :G: .10 .25
16 Giant Octopus C :L: .75 .75
17 Goblin Hero C :R: .10 .25
18 Hand of Death C :K: .75 .75
19 Hero's Resolve C :W: .10 .25
20 Inspiration C :L: .10 .25
21 Island L .10 .25
22 Island L .10 .25
23 Knight Errant C :W: .10 .25
24 Lava Axe C :R: .10 .25
25 Llanowar Elves C :G: 1.00 1.00
26 Merfolk of the Pearl Trident C :L: 20.00 20.00
27 Mons's Goblin Raiders C :R: .60 .60
28 Monstrous Growth C :G: .75 .75
29 Moon Sprite U :G: .60 .60
30 Mountain L .10 .25
31 Mountain L .10 .25
32 Obsianus Golem U 30.00 30.00
33 Ogre Warrior C :R: .50 .50
34 Orcish Oriflamme U :R: .50 .50
35 Plains L .10 .25
36 Plains L .10 .25
37 Prodigal Sorcerer C :L: .10 .25
38 Python C :K: .75 .75
39 Rod of Ruin U .50 .50
40 Royal Falcon C :W: .75 .75
41 Samite Healer C :W: .10 .25
42 Scathe Zombies C :K: .10 .25
43 Sea Eagle C :L: .10 .25
44 Shock C :R: .10 .25
45 Soul Net U .50 .50
46 Spined Wurm C :G: 3.00 3.00
47 Stone Rain C :R: .10 .25
48 Swamp L .10 .25
49 Swamp L .10 .25
50 Terror C :K: .10 .25
51 Time Ebb C :L: .10 .25
52 Trained Orgg R :R: 1.00 1.00
53 Venerable Monk C :W: .10 .25
54 Vizzerdrix R :L: 1.00 1.00
55 Wild Griffin C :W: .10 .25
56 Willow Elf C :G: .10 .25
57 Wind Drake C :L: .10 .25

2004 Magic The Gathering Unhinged

COMPLETE SET (141) 60.00 120.00
BOOSTER BOX (36 PACKS) 200.00 250.00
BOOSTER PACK (15 CARDS) 6.00 8.00
*FOIL: .75X TO 2X BASIC CARDS
RELEASED ON NOVEMBER 19, 2004
1 ___ U :B: .20 .50
2 Ach! Hans, Run! R :D: .30 .75
3 Aesthetic Consultation R :K: .30 .75
4 Ambiguity R :B: .30 .75
5 Artful Looter C :B: .10 .25
6 Ass Whuppin' R :D: .50 1.25
7 Assquatch R :R: .40 1.00
8 Atinlay Igpay U :W: .20 .50
9 Avatar of Me R :B: .60 1.50
10 AWOL C :W: .20 .50
11 Bad Ass C :K: .10 .25
12 B-I-N-G-O R :G: .40 1.00
13 Blast from the Past R :R: .50 1.25
14 Bloodletter C :K: .10 .25
15 Booster Tutor U :K: .20 .50
16 Bosom Buddy U :W: .20 .50
17 Brushstroke Paintermage C :B: .10 .25
18 Bursting Beebles C :B: .10 .25
19 Cardpecker C :W: .10 .25
20 Carnivorous Death-Parrot C :B: .10 .25
21 Cheap Ass C :W: .10 .25
22 Cheatyface U :B: .75 2.00
23 Circle of Protection: Art C :W: .10 .25
24 City of Ass R :L: 1.50 4.00
25 Collector Protector R :W: .30 .75
26 Creature Guy U :G: .20 .50
27 Curse of the Fire Penguin R :R: .30 .75
28 Deal Damage U :R: .20 .50
29 Double Header C :B: .10 .25
30 Drawn Together R :W: .30 .75
31 Duh C :K: .10 .25
32 Dumb Ass C :R: .10 .25
33 Elvish House Party U :G: .20 .50
34 Emcee U :W: .20 .50
35 Enter the Dungeon R :K: .40 1.00
36 Erase C :W: .10 .25
37 Eye to Eye U :K: .20 .50
38 Face to Face U :R: .20 .50
39 Farewell to Arms C :K: .10 .25
40 Fascist Art Director C :W: .10 .25
41 Fat Ass C :G: .10 .25
42 First Come, First Served U :W: .20 .50
43 Flaccify C :B: .10 .25
44 Forest L :L: 2.00 5.00
45 Form of the Squirrel R :G: .30 .75
46 Fraction Jackson R :G: .30 .75
47 Framed! C :B: .10 .25
48 Frankie Peanuts R :W: .30 .75
49 Frazzled Editor C :R: .10 .25
50 Gleemax R :A: .75 2.00
51 Gluetius Maximus U :G: .20 .50
52 Goblin Mime C :R: .10 .25
53 Goblin S.W.A.T. Team C :R: .10 .25
54 Goblin Secret Agent C :R: .10 .25
55 Granny's Payback U :G: .20 .50
56 Graphic Violence C :G: .10 .25
57 Greater Morphling R :B: .50 1.25
58 Head to Head U :W: .20 .50
59 Infernal Spawn of Infernal Spawn of Evil R :K: .75 2.00
60 Island L :L: 2.50 6.00
61 Johnny, Combo Player R :B: .75 2.00
62 Keeper of the Sacred Word C :G: .10 .25
63 Kill! Destroy! U :K: .20 .50
64 Ladies' Knight U :W: .20 .50
65 Land Aid '04 C :G: .10 .25
66 Laughing Hyena C :G: .10 .25
67 Letter Bomb R :A: .50 1.25
68 Little Girl C :W: .10 .25
69 Look at Me, I'm R&D R :W: .30 .75
70 Loose Lips C :B: .10 .25
71 Magical Hacker U :B: .20 .50
72 Man of Measure C :W: .10 .25
73 Mana Flair C :R: .10 .25
74 Mana Screw U :A: .20 .50
75 Market Research Long Card Name C :G: .10 .25
76 Meddling Kids R :D: .40 1.00
77 Mise U :B: .20 .50
78 Moniker Mage C :B: .10 .25
79 Monkey Monkey Monkey C :G: .10 .25
80 Mons's Goblin Waiters C :R: .10 .25
81 Mother of Goons C :K: .10 .25
82 Mountain L :L: 2.00 5.00
83 Mouth to Mouth U :B: .20 .50
84 Mox Lotus R :A: 4.00 10.00
85 My First Tome U :A: .20 .50
86 Name Dropping U :G: .20 .50
87 Necro-Impotence R :K: .30 .75
88 Now I Know My ABC's R :B: .30 .75
89 Number Crunch C :B: .10 .25
90 Old Fogey R :G: .30 .75
91 Orcish Paratroopers C :R: .10 .25
92 Persecute Artist U :K: .20 .50
93 Phyrexian Librarian U :K: .20 .50
94 Plains L :L: 2.00 5.00
95 Pointy Finger of Doom R :A: .40 1.00
96 Punctuate C :R: .10 .25
97 Pygmy Giant U :R: .20 .50
98 Question Elemental? U :B: .20 .50
99 R&D's Secret Lair R :L: .40 1.00
100 Rare-B-Gone R :D: .40 1.00
101 Red-Hot Hottie C :R: .10 .25
102 Remodel C :G: .10 .25
103 Richard Garfield, Ph.D. R :B: 1.00 2.50
104 Rocket-Powered Turbo Slug U :R: .40 1.00
105 Rod of Spanking U :A: .20 .50
106 S.N.O.T. C :G: .20 .50
107 Sauté C :R: .10 .25
108 Save Life U :W: .20 .50
109 Shoe Tree C :G: .10 .25
110 Side to Side U :G: .20 .50
111 Six-y Beast U :R: .20 .50
112 Smart Ass C :B: .10 .25
113 Spell Counter U :B: .20 .50
114 Standing Army C :W: .10 .25
115 Staying Power R :W: .30 .75
116 Stone-Cold Basilisk U :G: .20 .50
117 Stop That C :K: .10 .25
118 Supersize C :G: .10 .25
119 Swamp L :L: 2.50 6.00
120 Symbol Status U :G: .20 .50
121 Tainted Monkey C :K: .10 .25
122 The Fallen Apart C :K: .10 .25
123 Time Machine R :A: .30 .75
124 Togglodyte U :A: .20 .50
125 Topsy Turvy R :B: .30 .75
126 Touch and Go C :R: .10 .25
127 Toy Boat U :A: .20 .50
128 Uktabi Kong R :G: .40 1.00
129 Urza's Hot Tub U :A: .20 .50
130 Vile Bile C :K: .10 .25
131 Water Gun Balloon Game R :A: .30 .75
132 Wet Willie of the Damned C :K: .10 .25
133 When Fluffy Bunnies Attack C :K: .10 .25
134 Who/What/When/Where/Why R :D: .60 1.50
135 Wordmail C :W: .10 .25
136 Working Stiff U :K: .20 .50
137 World-Bottling Kit R :A: .30 .75
138 Yet Another Æther Vortex R :R: .30 .75
139 Zombie Fanboy U :K: .20 .50
140 Zzzyxas's Abyss R :K: .30 .75
141 Super Secret Tech R :A: 4.00 10.00

2009 Magic The Gathering Planechase

COMPLETE SET (211) 60.00 150.00
RELEASED ON SEPTEMBER 4, 2009
1 Akroma's Vengeance R :W: .40 1.00
2 Congregate C :W: .10 .25
3 Kor Sanctifiers C :W: .10 .25
4 Oblivion Ring C :W: .10 .25
5 Order U :W: .20 .50
6 Orim's Thunder C :W: .10 .25
7 Prison Term U :W: .20 .50
8 Soul Warden C :W: .10 .25
9 Ascendant Evincar R :K: .40 1.00
10 Beacon of Unrest R :K: 2.00 5.00
11 Beseech the Queen U :K: 1.50 4.00
12 Cadaverous Knight C :K: .10 .25
13 Consume Spirit U :K: .20 .50
14 Corpse Harvester U :K: .20 .50
15 Cruel Revival C :K: .10 .25
16 Dark Ritual C :K: .75 2.00
17 Death Baron R :K: 6.00 15.00
18 Dregscape Zombie C :K: .10 .25
19 Festering Goblin C :K: .10 .25
20 Grave Pact R :K: 4.00 10.00
21 Gravedigger C :K: .10 .25
22 Helldozer R :K: .40 1.00
23 Hideous End C :K: .10 .25
24 Incremental Blight U :K: .20 .50
25 Innocent Blood C :K: .10 .25
26 Nefashu R :K: .40 1.00
27 Noxious Ghoul U :K: .20 .50
28 Phyrexian Arena R :K: 4.00 10.00
29 Phyrexian Ghoul C :K: .10 .25
30 Profane Command R :K: .40 1.00
31 Rotting Rats C :K: .10 .25
32 Shepherd of Rot C :K: .10 .25
33 Soulless One U :K: .20 .50
34 Syphon Mind C :K: .10 .25
35 Syphon Soul C :K: .10 .25
36 Undead Warchief U :K: 2.00 5.00
37 Withered Wretch U :K: .20 .50
38 Arc Lightning C :R: .10 .25
39 Assault U :R: .20 .50
40 Blaze U :R: .20 .50
41 Bogardan Firefiend C :R: .10 .25
42 Bogardan Rager C :R: .10 .25
43 Browbeat U :R: .50 1.25
44 Chaos U :R: .20 .50
45 Cinder Elemental U :R: .20 .50
46 Cone of Flame U :R: .20 .50
47 Flamekin Harbinger U :R: .40 1.00
48 Flametongue Kavu U :R: .20 .50
49 Furnace of Rath R :R: .40 1.00
50 Goblin Offensive U :R: .40 1.00
51 Insurrection R :R: 1.50 4.00
52 Keldon Champion U :R: .20 .50
53 Menacing Ogre R :R: .40 1.00
54 Pyrotechnics U :R: .20 .50
55 Reckless Charge C :R: .10 .25
56 Relentless Assault R :R: .40 1.00
57 Rockslide Elemental U :R: .20 .50
58 Rolling Thunder C :R: .10 .25
59 Rorix Bladewing R :R: .40 1.00
60 Smokebraider C :R: .10 .25
61 Taurean Mauler R :R: .40 1.00
62 Battery U :G: .20 .50
63 Beast Hunt C :G: .10 .25
64 Briarhorn U :G: .20 .50
65 Explosive Vegetation U :G: .75 2.00
66 Fertile Ground C :G: .10 .25
67 Fertilid C :G: .10 .25
68 Forgotten Ancient R :G: 1.25 3.00
69 Ivy Elemental R :G: .40 1.00
70 Living Hive R :G: .40 1.00
71 Rampant Growth C :G: .10 .25
72 Search for Tomorrow C :G: .10 .25
73 Silverglade Elemental C :G: .10 .25
74 Tornado Elemental R :G: .40 1.00
75 Tribal Unity U :G: .20 .50
76 Verdant Force R :G: .40 1.00
77 Arsenal Thresher C :W/L/K: .10 .25

2009 Magic The Gathering Planechase

78 Balefire Liege R :W/R: 3.00 8.00
79 Battlegate Mimic C :W/R: .10 .25
80 Boros Guildmage U :W/R: .20 .50
81 Boros Swiftblade U :W/R: .20 .50
82 Branching Bolt C :R/G: .10 .25
83 Bull Cerodon U :W/R: .20 .50
84 Captain's Maneuver U :W/R: .20 .50
85 Cerodon Yearling C :W/R: .10 .25
86 Double Cleave C :W/R: .10 .25
87 Duergar Hedge-Mage U :W/R: .20 .50
88 Fires of Yavimaya U :R/G: .20 .50
89 Glory of Warfare R :W/R: .40 1.00
90 Hearthfire Hobgoblin U :W/R: .20 .50
91 Hull Breach C :R/G: .75 2.00
92 Lightning Helix U :W/R: 1.25 3.00
93 Mage Slayer U :R/G: .20 .50
94 Razia, Boros Archangel R :W/R: .75 2.00
95 Rumbling Slum R :R/G: .40 1.00
96 Savage Twister U :R/G: .20 .50
97 Sludge Strider U :W/L/K: .20 .50
98 Academy at Tolaria West C 1.25 3.00
99 Agyrem C 1.25 3.00
100 Ancient Den C .75 2.00
101 Arcbound Crusher U .40 1.00
102 Arcbound Slith U .20 .50
103 Bant C 1.25 3.00
104 Boros Garrison C .30 .75
105 Boros Signet C .10 .25
106 Bosh, Iron Golem R .40 1.00
107 Cabal Coffers U 5.00 12.00
108 Cliffside Market C 1.25 3.00
109 Copper Myr C .10 .25
110 Cranial Plating C 1.25 3.00
111 Darksteel Forge R 1.50 4.00
112 Door to Nothingness R .40 1.00
113 Eloren Wilds C .10 .25
114 Etched Oracle U .20 .50
115 Feeding Grounds C 1.25 3.00
116 Fields of Summer C 1.50 4.00
117 Glimmervoid Basin C .75 2.00
118 Gold Myr C .10 .25
119 Goldmeadow C .10 .25
120 Great Furnace C .40 1.00
121 Grixis C 1.25 3.00
122 Gruul Turf C .10 .25
123 Immersturm C .10 .25
124 Iron Myr C .10 .25
125 Isle of Vesuva C .10 .25
126 Izzet Steam Maze C .10 .25
127 Krosa C .10 .25
128 Leaden Myr C .10 .25
129 Leechridden Swamp U .50 1.25
130 Lethe Lake C 1.25 3.00
131 Llanowar C .10 .25
132 Lodestone Myr R .40 1.00
133 Loxodon Warhammer R .60 1.50
134 Mask of Memory U .20 .50
135 Minamo C .10 .25
136 Murasa C .10 .25
137 Myr Enforcer C .10 .25
138 Naar Isle C .10 .25
139 Naya C .10 .25
140 Nuisance Engine U .20 .50
141 Otaria C 1.50 4.00
142 Panopticon C .10 .25
143 Pentad Prism C .10 .25
144 Pentavus R .40 1.00
145 Pools of Becoming C .10 .25
146 Raven's Run C 1.25 3.00
147 Relic of Progenitus C .40 1.00
148 Sanctum of Serra C .10 .25
149 Sea of Sand C .10 .25
150 Seat of the Synod C .10 .25
151 Serum Tank U .20 .50
152 Shiv C .10 .25
153 Shivan Oasis U .20 .50
154 Silver Myr C .10 .25
155 Skeleton Shard U .20 .50
156 Skybreen C .10 .25
157 Sokenzan C .10 .25
158 Stronghold Furnace C .10 .25
159 Sunhome, Fortress of the Legion U .20 .50
160 Suntouched Myr C .10 .25
161 Tazeem C 10.00 25.00
162 Terramorphic Expanse C .10 .25
164 The Dark Barony C 1.25 3.00
165 The Eon Fog C 1.25 3.00
166 The Fourth Sphere C 1.25 3.00
167 The Great Forest C 1.25 3.00
168 The Hippodrome C 1.25 3.00
169 The Maelstrom C 1.25 3.00
170 Tree of Tales C .10 .25
171 Turri Island C .10 .25
172 Undercity Reaches C .10 .25
173 Vault of Whispers C .10 .25
174 Velis Vel C .10 .25
175 Wizard Replica C .10 .25
176 Broodstar R :L: .40 1.00
177 Fabricate U :L: .75 2.00
178 Forest L .10 .25
179 Forest L .10 .25
180 Forest L .10 .25
181 Forest L .10 .25
182 Forest L .10 .25
183 Island L .10 .25
184 Island L .10 .25
185 Island L .10 .25
186 Island L .10 .25
187 Keep Watch C :L: .10 .25
188 Master of Etherium R :L: 2.50 6.00
189 Mountain L .10 .25
190 Mountain L .10 .25
191 Mountain L .10 .25
192 Mountain L .10 .25
193 Mountain L .10 .25
194 Mountain L .10 .25
195 Mountain L .10 .25
196 Mountain L .10 .25
197 Mountain L .10 .25
198 Plains L .10 .25
199 Plains L .10 .25
200 Plains L .10 .25
201 Plains L .10 .25
202 Plains L .10 .25
203 Qumulox U :L: .20 .50
204 Sarcomite Myr C :L: .10 .25
205 Swamp L .10 .25
206 Swamp L .10 .25
207 Swamp L .10 .25
208 Swamp L .10 .25
209 Swamp L .10 .25
210 Thirst for Knowledge U :L: .20 .50
211 Vedalken Engineer C :L: .10 .25
212 Whiplash Trap C :L: .10 .25

2010 Magic The Gathering Archenemy

COMPLETE SET (150) 100.00 200.00
THEME DECK 25.00 40.00
RELEASED ON JUNE 18, 2010
1 Leonin Abunas R :W: .75 2.00
2 Metallurgeon U :W: .20 .50
3 Oblivion Ring C :W: .20 .50
4 Path to Exile U :W: 3.00 8.00
5 Sanctum Gargoyle C :W: .10 .25
6 March of the Machines R :B: .40 1.00
7 Master Transmuter R :B: 4.00 10.00
8 Spin into Myth U :B: .60 1.50
9 Avatar of Woe R :K: 1.50 4.00
10 Beacon of Unrest R :K: 1.50 4.00
11 Bog Witch C :K: .10 .25
12 Cemetery Reaper R :K: 1.00 2.50
13 Corpse Connoisseur U :K: .20 .50
14 Dregscape Zombie C :K: .10 .25
15 Extractor Demon R :K: 1.00 2.50
16 Festering Goblin C :K: .20 .50
17 Incremental Blight U :K: .20 .50
18 Infectious Horror C :K: .10 .25
19 Infest U :K: .20 .50
20 Makeshift Mannequin U :K: .20 .50
21 Reanimate U :K: 4.00 10.00
22 Reassembling Skeleton U :K: .20 .50
23 Scion of Darkness R :K: 1.00 2.50
24 Shriekmaw U :K: .75 2.00
25 Sign in Blood C :K: .20 .50
26 Twisted Abomination C :K: .10 .25
27 Urborg Syphon-Mage C :K: .10 .25
28 Zombie Infestation U :K: .40 1.00
29 Zombify U :K: .60 1.50
30 Battering Craghorn C :R: .10 .25
31 Breath of Darigaaz U :R: .20 .50
32 Chandra's Outrage C :R: .20 .50
33 Dragon Breath C :R: .10 .25
34 Dragon Fodder C :R: .40 1.00
35 Dragon Whelp U :R: .20 .50
36 Dragonspeaker Shaman U :R: 2.50 6.00
37 Fireball U :R: .20 .50
38 Flameblast Dragon R :R: .40 1.00
39 Furnace Whelp U :R: .20 .50
40 Gathan Raiders C :R: .10 .25
41 Hellkite Charger R :R: .40 1.00
42 Imperial Hellkite R :R: .40 1.00
43 Inferno Trap U :R: .20 .50
44 Kilnmouth Dragon R :R: .75 2.00
45 Ryusei, the Falling Star R :R: .60 1.50
46 Seething Song C :R: 1.00 2.50
47 Skirk Commando C :R: .10 .25
48 Skirk Marauder C :R: .10 .25
49 Taurean Mauler R :R: 1.50 4.00
50 Two-Headed Dragon R :R: .75 2.00
51 Volcanic Fallout U :R: .75 2.00
52 Chameleon Colossus R :G: 1.00 2.50
53 Feral Hydra R :G: 1.00 2.50
54 Fertilid C :G: .10 .25
55 Fierce Empath C :G: .60 1.50
56 Fog C :G: .10 .25
57 Forgotten Ancient R :G: 2.00 5.00
58 Gleeful Sabotage C :G: .20 .50
59 Harmonize U :G: 1.25 3.00
60 Hunting Moa U :G: .20 .50
61 Kamahl, Fist of Krosa R :G: 2.00 5.00
62 Krosan Tusker C :G: .20 .50
63 Leaf Gilder C :G: .10 .25
64 Molimo, Maro-Sorcerer R :G: .40 1.00
65 Plummet C :G: .10 .25
66 Primal Command R :G: 4.00 10.00
67 Rancor C :G: 1.25 3.00
68 Sakura-Tribe Elder C :G: 1.00 2.50
69 Shinen of Life's Roar C :G: .10 .25
70 Spider Umbra C :G: .40 1.00
71 Thelonite Hermit R :G: .40 1.00
72 Verdeloth the Ancient R :G: .40 1.00
73 Wall of Roots C :G: .75 2.00
74 Wickerbough Elder C :G: .40 1.00
75 Yavimaya Dryad U :G: .20 .50
76 Agony Warp C :B/:K: .10 .25
77 Architects of Will C :B/:K: .10 .25
78 Armadillo Cloak C :W/:G: .75 2.00
79 Avatar of Discord R :K/:R: .60 1.50
80 Batwing Brume U :W/:K: .60 1.50
81 Bituminous Blast U :K/:R: .20 .50
82 Branching Bolt C :R/:G: .10 .25
83 Colossal Might C :R/:G: .10 .25
84 Ethersworn Shieldmage C :W/:B: .10 .25
85 Fieldmist Borderpost C :W/:B: .10 .25
86 Fires of Yavimaya U :R/:G: .75 2.00
87 Heroes' Reunion U :W/:G: .40 1.00
88 Kaervek the Merciless R :K/:R: 1.25 3.00
89 Magister Sphinx R :W/:B/:K: .60 1.50
90 Mistvein Borderpost C :B/:K: .10 .25
91 Pale Recluse C :W/:G: .10 .25
92 Rakdos Guildmage U :K/:R: .20 .50
93 Savage Twister U :R/:G: .20 .50
94 Selesnya Guildmage U :W/:G: .20 .50
95 Terminate C :K/:R: .60 1.50
96 Torrent of Souls U :K/:R: .20 .50
97 Unbender Tine U :W/:B: .20 .50
98 Unmake C :W/:K: .75 2.00
99 Vampiric Dragon R :K/:R: 1.25 3.00
100 Watchwolf U :W/:G: .40 1.00
101 Wax/Wane U :G/:W: .20 .50
102 AEther Spellbomb C .10 .25
103 Azorius Signet C .40 1.00
104 Dimir Signet C .40 1.00
105 Dreamstone Hedron U .20 .50
106 Duplicant R 3.00 8.00
107 Everflowing Chalice U .75 2.00
108 Gruul Signet C .20 .50
109 Juggernaut U .20 .50
110 Lightning Greaves U 3.00 8.00
111 Lodestone Golem R .75 2.00
112 Memnarch R 3.00 8.00
113 Obelisk of Esper C .10 .25
114 Rakdos Signet C .20 .50
115 Skullcage U .20 .50
116 Sorcerer's Strongbox U .20 .50
117 Sun Droplet U .40 1.00
118 Sundering Titan R 2.00 5.00
119 Synod Centurion U .20 .50
120 Synod Sanctum U .20 .50
121 Thran Dynamo U 3.00 8.00
122 Thunderstaff U .20 .50
123 Artisan of Kozilek U .75 2.00
124 Barren Moor C .10 .25
125 Graypelt Refuge U .30 .75
126 Kazandu Refuge U .30 .75
127 Khalni Garden C .30 .75
128 Krosan Verge U .40 1.00
129 Llanowar Reborn U .40 1.00
130 Mosswort Bridge R 1.25 3.00
131 Nantuko Monastery U .30 .75
132 Rakdos Carnarium C .40 1.00
133 Secluded Steppe C .30 .75
134 Terramorphic Expanse C .10 .25
135 Tranquil Thicket C .40 1.00
136 Vitu-Ghazi, the City-Tree U .20 .50
137 Plains L .10 .25
138 Plains L .10 .25
139 Island L .10 .25
140 Island L .10 .25
141 Island L .10 .25
142 Swamp L .10 .25
143 Swamp L .10 .25
144 Swamp L .10 .25
145 Mountain L .10 .25
146 Mountain L .10 .25
147 Mountain L .10 .25
148 Forest L .10 .25
149 Forest L .10 .25
150 Forest L .10 .25

2010 Magic The Gathering Archenemy Oversized Schemes

COMPLETE SET (45) 25.00 60.00
RELEASED ON JUNE 18, 2010
1 All in Good Time 3.00 8.00
2 All Shall Smolder in My Wake .20 .50
3 Approach My Molten Realm .60 1.50
4 Behold the Power of Destruction 3.00 8.00
5 Choose Your Champion .20 .50
6 Dance, Pathetic Marionette 2.50 6.00
7 The Dead Shall Serve .20 .50
8 A Display of My Dark Power .60 1.50
9 Embrace My Diabolical Vision 1.25 3.00
10 Every Hope Shall Vanish .20 .50
11 Every Last Vestige Shall Rot .20 .50
12 Evil Comes to Fruition .60 1.50
13 The Fate of the Flammable .60 1.50
14 Feed the Machine .20 .50
15 I Bask in Your Silent Awe .20 .50
16 I Call on the Ancient Magics 1.25 3.00
17 I Delight in Your Convulsions .20 .50
18 I Know All, I See All .20 .50
19 Ignite the Cloneforge! .20 .50
20 Into the Earthen Maw 1.25 3.00
21 Introductions Are in Order .20 .50
22 The Iron Guardian Stirs .20 .50
23 Know Naught but Fire 1.25 3.00
24 Look Skyward and Despair .20 .50
25 May Civilization Collapse 1.00 2.50
26 Mortal Flesh Is Weak 2.00 5.00
27 My Crushing Masterstroke 3.00 8.00
28 My Genius Knows No Bounds 1.00 2.50
29 My Undead Horde Awakens 2.50 6.00
30 My Wish Is Your Command .20 .50
31 Nature Demands an Offering .20 .50
32 Nature Shields Its Own .20 .50
33 Nothing Can Stop Me Now .60 1.50
34 Only Blood Ends Your Nightmares .20 .50
35 The Pieces Are Coming Together .20 .50
36 Realms Befitting My Majesty .20 .50
37 Roots of All Evil .20 .50
38 Rotted Ones, Lay Siege .20 .50
39 Surrender Your Thoughts 1.25 3.00
40 Tooth, Claw, and Tail 3.00 8.00
41 The Very Soil Shall Shake 1.25 3.00
42 Which of You Burns Brightest .20 .50
43 Your Fate Is Thrice Sealed .20 .50
44 Your Puny Minds Cannot Fathom .20 .50
45 Your Will Is Not Your Own .20 .50

2011 Magic The Gathering Commander

COMPLETE SET (318) 75.00 200.00
BOOSTER BOX (36 PACKS)
BOOSTER PACK (15 CARDS)
RELEASED ON JUNE 17, 2011
1 Acidic Slime U :G: .20 .50
2 Acorn Catapult R .40 1.00
3 Aethersnipe C :B: .10 .25
4 Afterlife U :W: .20 .50
5 Akoum Refuge U .40 1.00
6 Akroma's Vengeance R :W: .60 1.50
7 Akroma, Angel of Fury R :R: 2.50 6.00
8 Alliance of Arms R :W: .40 1.00
9 Angel of Despair R 1.50 4.00
10 Angelic Arbiter R :W: .60 1.50
11 Anger U :R: .75 2.00
12 Animar, Soul of Elements M 6.00 15.00
13 Aquastrand Spider C :G: .10 .25
14 Arbiter of Knollridge R :W: .40 1.00
15 Archangel of Strife R :W: .75 2.00
16 Armillary Sphere C .10 .25
17 Artisan of Kozilek U .75 2.00
18 Attrition R :K: .60 1.50
19 Aura Shards U 2.50 6.00
20 Austere Command R :W: 3.00 8.00
21 Avatar of Fury R :R: .40 1.00
22 Avatar of Slaughter R :R: .40 1.00
23 Avatar of Woe R :K: 1.50 4.00
24 Awakening Zone R :G: 1.00 2.50
25 Azorius Chancery C .40 1.00
26 Azorius Guildmage U .20 .50
27 Baloth Woodcrasher U :G: .20 .50
28 Barren Moor C .10 .25
29 Basandra, Battle Seraph R 1.50 4.00
30 Bathe in Light U :W: .20 .50
31 Bestial Menace U :G: .20 .50
32 Bladewing the Risen R .75 2.00
33 Bojuka Bog C .40 1.00
34 Boros Garrison C .40 1.00
35 Boros Guildmage U .20 .50
36 Boros Signet C .10 .25
37 Brainstorm C :B: 1.50 4.00
38 Brawn U :G: .40 1.00
39 Breath of Darigaaz U :R: .20 .50
40 Brion Stoutarm R .40 1.00
41 Buried Alive U :K: .75 2.00
42 Butcher of Malakir R :K: .40 1.00
43 Call the Skybreaker R .40 1.00
44 Celestial Force R :W: .40 1.00
45 Chain Reaction R :R: .40 1.00
46 Champion's Helm R 2.00 5.00
47 Chaos Warp R :R: 5.00 12.00
48 Chartooth Cougar C :R: .10 .25
49 Chorus of the Conclave R .40 1.00
50 Chromeshell Crab R :B: .40 1.00
51 Cleansing Beam U :R: .20 .50
52 Cobra Trap U :G: .20 .50
53 Collective Voyage R :G: 1.50 4.00
54 Colossal Might C .10 .25
55 Comet Storm M :R: .60 1.50
56 Command Tower C 1.25 3.00
57 Congregate C :W: .20 .50
58 Conundrum Sphinx R :B: .40 1.00
59 Court Hussar U :B: .20 .50
60 Crescendo of War R :W: .40 1.00
61 Cultivate C :G: .60 1.50
62 Damia, Sage of Stone M 4.00 10.00
63 Dark Hatchling R :K: .40 1.00
64 Darksteel Ingot C .20 .50
65 Deadly Recluse C :G: .10 .25
66 Deadwood Treefolk U :G: .30 .75
67 Death by Dragons U :R: .20 .50
68 Death Mutation U .20 .50
69 Desecrator Hag C .10 .25
70 Diabolic Tutor U :K: .20 .50
71 Dimir Aqueduct C .40 1.00
72 Dimir Signet C .40 1.00
73 Disaster Radius R :R: .40 1.00
74 Dominus of Fealty R 1.25 3.00
75 Doom Blade C :K: .20 .50
76 Dragon Whelp U :R: .20 .50
77 Dread Cacodemon R :K: 1.00 2.50
78 Dreadship Reef U .40 1.00
79 Dreamborn Muse R :B: .40 1.00
80 Dreamstone Hedron U .20 .50
81 Duergar Hedge-Mage U .20 .50
82 Earthquake R :R: .40 1.00
83 Edric, Spymaster of Trest R 2.00 5.00
84 Electrolyze U 1.00 2.50
85 Elvish Aberration U :G: .20 .50
86 Eternal Witness U :G: 1.50 4.00
87 Evincar's Justice C :K: .20 .50
88 Evolving Wilds C .20 .50
89 Explosive Vegetation U :G: 1.25 3.00
90 Extractor Demon R :K: .40 1.00
91 Fact or Fiction U :B: 1.25 3.00
92 Fallen Angel R :K: .40 1.00
93 False Prophet R :W: .40 1.00
94 Faultgrinder C :R: .10 .25
95 Fellwar Stone U .40 1.00
96 Fertilid C :G: .10 .25
97 Fierce Empath C :G: .40 1.00
98 Fire // Ice U .40 1.00
99 Firespout U .60 1.50
100 Fists of Ironwood C :G: .20 .50
101 Flametongue Kavu U :R: .60 1.50
102 Fleshbag Marauder U :K: .40 1.00
103 Flusterstorm R :B: 12.00 30.00
104 Fog Bank U :B: .75 2.00
105 Footbottom Feast C :K: .10 .25
106 Forest (315) L .10 .25
107 Forest (316) L .10 .25
108 Forest (317) L .10 .25
109 Forest (318) L .10 .25
110 Forgotten Cave C .10 .25
111 Fungal Reaches U .30 .75
112 Furnace Whelp U :R: .20 .50
113 Garruk Wildspeaker M :G: 4.00 10.00
114 Ghave, Guru of Spores M 3.00 8.00
115 Ghostly Prison U :W: 3.00 8.00
116 Goblin Cadets U :R: .20 .50
117 Golgari Guildmage U .20 .50
118 Golgari Rot Farm C .10 .25
119 Golgari Signet C .10 .25
120 Gomazoa U :B: .50
121 Grave Pact R :K: 4.00 10.00
122 Gravedigger C :K: .10 .25
123 Gruul Signet C .10 .25
124 Gruul Turf C .25
125 Guard Gomazoa U :B: .20 .50
126 Gwyllion Hedge-Mage U .50
127 Harmonize U :G: 1.25 3.00
128 Hex R :K: .40 1.00
129 Homeward Path R 2.00 5.00
130 Hornet Queen R :G: 2.00
131 Hour of Reckoning R :W: .40 1.00
132 Howling Mine R 1.50
133 Hull Breach C .60 1.50
134 Hunting Pack U :G: .20 .50
135 Hydra Omnivore R :G: 1.50 4.00
136 Insurrection R :R: .75 2.00
137 Intet, the Dreamer R .40 1.00
138 Invigorate C :G: 1.25 3.00
139 Island (303) C .10 .25
140 Island (304) C .10 .25
141 Island (305) C .10 .25
142 Island (306) C .10 .25
143 Izzet Boilerworks C .40 1.00
144 Izzet Chronarch C .20 .50
145 Izzet Signet C .20 .50
146 Jotun Grunt U :W: .20 .50
147 Journey to Nowhere C :W: .30 .75
148 Jwar Isle Refuge U .40 1.00
149 Kaalia of the Vast M 12.00 30.00
150 Karador, Ghost Chieftain M 3.00 8.00
151 Kazandu Refuge U .20 .50
152 Kodama's Reach C :G: .40 1.00
153 Krosan Tusker C :G: .10 .25
154 Lash Out C :R: .10 .25
155 Lhurgoyf R :G: .40 1.00
156 Lightkeeper of Emeria U :W: .20 .50
157 Lightning Greaves U 2.50 6.00
158 Living Death R :K: 1.25 3.00
159 Lonely Sandbar C .20 .50
160 Magmatic Force R :R: .75 2.00
161 Magus of the Vineyard R :G: .40 1.00
162 Malfegor M .60 1.50
163 Mana-Charged Dragon R :R: 1.50 4.00
164 Martyr's Bond R :W: 1.00 2.50
165 Master Warcraft R .40 1.00
166 Memory Erosion R :B: .60 1.50
167 Minds Aglow R :B: 1.00 2.50
168 Molten Slagheap U .20 .50
169 Monk Realist C :W: .10 .25
170 Mortify U .60 1.50
171 Mortivore R :K: .40 1.00
172 Mother of Runes U :W: 3.00 8.00
173 Mountain (311) C .10 .25
174 Mountain (312) C .10 .25
175 Mountain (313) C .10 .25
176 Mountain (314) C .10 .25
177 Mulldrifter C :B: .40 1.00
178 Murmurs from Beyond C :B: .10 .25
179 Nantuko Husk C :K: .10 .25
180 Necrogenesis U .20 .50
181 Nemesis Trap U :K: .20 .50
182 Nezumi Graverobber U :K: .40 1.00
183 Nin, the Pain Artist R 1.50 4.00
184 Nucklavee U .20 .50
185 Numot, the Devastator R .40 1.00
186 Oblation R :W: .60 1.50
187 Oblivion Ring C :W: .20 .50
188 Oblivion Stone R 5.00 12.00
189 Oni of Wild Places U :R: .20 .50
190 Orim's Thunder C :W: .10 .25
191 Oros, the Avenger R .40 1.00
192 Orzhov Basilica C .40 1.00
193 Orzhov Guildmage U .20 .50
194 Orzhov Signet C .20 .50
195 Path to Exile U :W: 3.00 8.00
196 Patron of the Nezumi R :K: .40 1.00
197 Penumbra Spider C :G: .10 .25
198 Perilous Research U :B: .20 .50
199 Plains (299) C .10 .25
200 Plains (300) C .10 .25
201 Plains (301) C .10 .25
202 Plains (302) C .10 .25
203 Plumeveil U .20 .50
204 Pollen Lullaby U :W: .20 .50
205 Prison Term U :W: .60 1.50
206 Propaganda U :B: 1.50 4.00
207 Prophetic Bolt R .40 1.00
208 Prophetic Prism C .10 .25
209 Punishing Fire U :R: .60 1.50
210 Pyrohemia U :R: .30 .75
211 Rakdos Carnarium C .40 1.00
212 Rakdos Signet C .20 .50
213 Rapacious One U :R: .20 .50
214 Ray of Command C :B: .10 .25
215 Razorjaw Oni U :K: .20 .50
216 Reins of Power R :B: .40 1.00
217 Reiver Demon R :K: .60 1.50
218 Relic Crush C :G: .10 .25
219 Repulse C :B: .10 .25
220 Return to Dust U :W: .75 2.00
221 Riddlekeeper R :B: .60 1.50
222 Righteous Cause U :W: .20 .50
223 Riku of Two Reflections M 4.00 10.00
224 Rise from the Grave U :K: .20 .50
225 Ruhan of the Fomori M .60 1.50
226 Ruination R :R: .40 1.00
227 Rupture Spire C .20 .50
228 Sakura-Tribe Elder C :G: .75 2.00
229 Savage Twister U .20 .50
230 Scattering Stroke U :B: .20 .50
231 Scavenging Ooze R :G: 3.00 8.00
232 Scythe Specter R :K: .40 1.00
233 Secluded Steppe C .20 .50
234 Selesnya Evangel C .10 .25
235 Selesnya Guildmage U .20 .50
236 Selesnya Sanctuary C .40 1.00
237 Selesnya Signet C .20 .50
238 Serra Angel U :W: .20 .50
239 Sewer Nemesis R :K: 2.00 5.00
240 Shared Trauma R :K: .40 1.00
241 Shattered Angel U :W: .20 .50
242 Shriekmaw U :K: .60 1.50
243 Sigil Captain U .20 .50
244 Sign in Blood C :K: .20 .50
245 Simic Growth Chamber C .60 1.50
246 Simic Signet C .20 .50
247 Simic Sky Swallower R .75 2.00
248 Skullbriar, the Walking Grave R 2.50 6.00
249 Skullclamp U 3.00 8.00
250 Skyscribing U :B: .20 .50
251 Slipstream Eel C :B: .10 .25
252 Sol Ring U 2.00 5.00
253 Solemn Simulacrum R 2.50 6.00
254 Soul Snare U :W: .20 .50
255 Spawnwrithe R :G: .40 1.00
256 Spell Crumple U :B: 3.00 8.00
257 Spike Feeder U :G: .30 .75
258 Spitebellows U :R: .20 .50
259 Spurnmage Advocate U :W: .20 .50
260 Squallmonger U :G: .20 .50
261 Stitch Together U :K: .60 1.50
262 Storm Herd R :W: .40 1.00
263 Stranglehold R :R: 5.00 12.00
264 Sulfurous Blast U :R: .20 .50
265 Svogthos, the Restless Tomb U .50
266 Swamp (307) C .10 .25
267 Swamp (308) C .10 .25
268 Swamp (309) C .10 .25
269 Swamp (310) C .10 .25
270 Symbiotic Wurm R :G: .40 1.00
271 Syphon Flesh U :K: .30 .75
272 Syphon Mind C :K: .20 .50

273 Szadek, Lord of Secrets R .40 1.00
274 Tariel, Reckoner of Souls M 4.00 10.00
275 Temple of the False God U .30 .75
276 Teneb, the Harvester R .40 1.00
277 Terminate C .60 1.50
278 Terramorphic Expanse C .10 .25
279 The Mimeoplasm M 3.00 8.00
280 Trade Secrets R :B: .40 1.00
281 Tranquil Thicket C .20 .50
282 Trench Gorger R :B: .40 1.00
283 Tribute to the Wild U :G: .20 .50
284 Triskelavus R .40 1.00
285 Troll Ascetic R :G: .40 1.00
286 Unnerve C :K: .10 .25
287 Valley Rannet C .10 .25
288 Vampire Nighthawk U :K: .60 1.50
289 Vedalken Plotter U :B: .20 .50
290 Vengeful Rebirth U .20 .50
291 Veteran Explorer U :G: 1.50 4.00
292 Vish Kal, Blood Arbiter R .40 1.00
293 Vision Skeins C :B: .10 .25
294 Vivid Crag U .40 1.00
295 Vivid Creek U .40 1.00
296 Vivid Grove U .40 1.00
297 Vivid Marsh U .40 1.00
298 Vivid Meadow U .40 1.00
299 Voice of All U :W: .30 .75
300 Vorosh, the Hunter R .40 1.00
301 Vow of Duty U :W: .20 .50
302 Vow of Flight U :B: .20 .50
303 Vow of Lightning U :R: .20 .50
304 Vow of Malice U :K: .20 .50
305 Vow of Wildness U :G: .20 .50
306 Vulturous Zombie R .60 1.50
307 Wall of Denial U .60 1.50
308 Wall of Omens U :W: 1.00 2.50
309 Whirlpool Whelm C :B: .10 .25
310 Wild Ricochet R :R: .40 1.00
311 Windborn Muse R :W: .60 1.50
312 Windfall U :B: .40 1.00
313 Wonder U :B: .40 1.00
314 Wrecking Ball C .20 .50
315 Wrexial, the Risen Deep M .75 2.00
316 Yavimaya Elder C :G: .60 1.50
317 Zedruu the Greathearted M .75 2.00
318 Zoetic Cavern U .20 .50

2012 Magic the Gathering Planechase

COMPLETE SET (156) 50.00 120.00
CHAOS REIGNS DECK 25.00 50.00
NIGHT OF THE NINJA DECK 30.00 60.00
PRIMORDIAL HUNGER DECK 20.00 40.00
SAVAGE AURAS DECK 20.00 40.00
RELEASED ON SEPTEMBER 4, 2009
1 Armored Griffin U :W: .15 .40
2 Auramancer C :W: .10 .25
3 Auratouched Mage U :W: .15 .40
4 Cage of Hands C :W: .10 .25
5 Celestial Ancient R :W: .30 .75
6 Felidar Umbra U :W: 1.50 4.00
7 Ghostly Prison U :W: 2.50 6.00
8 Hyena Umbra C :W: .30 .75
9 Kor Spiritdancer R :W: 4.00 10.00
10 Mammoth Umbra U :W: .15 .40
11 Sigil of the Empty Throne R :W: .75 2.00
12 Spirit Mantle U :W: 1.00 2.50
13 Three Dreams R :W: .30 .75
14 Augury Owl C :B: .10 .25
15 Cancel C :B: .10 .25
16 Concentrate U :B: .15 .40
17 Guard Gomazoa U :B: .40 1.00
18 Higure, the Still Wind R :B: .40 1.00
19 Illusory Angel U :B: 1.25 3.00
20 Mistblade Shinobi C :B: .15 .40
21 Ninja of the Deep Hours C :B: .30 .75
22 Peregrine Drake U :B: .15 .40
23 Primal Plasma C :B: .10 .25
24 Sakashima's Student R :B: 4.00 10.00
25 See Beyond C :B: .10 .25
26 Sunken Hope R :B: .30 .75
27 Walker of Secret Ways U :B: .15 .40
28 Wall of Frost U :B: .15 .40
29 Whirlpool Warrior R :B: .30 .75
30 Assassinate C :K: .10 .25
31 Cadaver Imp C :K: .10 .25
32 Dark Hatchling R :K: .30 .75
33 Ink-Eyes, Servant of Oni R :K: 2.50 6.00
34 Liliana's Specter C :K: .10 .25
35 Okiba-Gang Shinobi C :K: .30 .75
36 Skullsnatcher C :K: .10 .25
37 Throat Slitter U :K: .40 1.00
38 Tormented Soul C :K: .10 .25
39 Arc Trail U :R: .15 .40
40 Beetleback Chief U :R: .75 2.00
41 Erratic Explosion C :R: .10 .25
42 Fiery Conclusion C :R: .10 .25
43 Fiery Fall C :R: .10 .25
44 Fling C :R: .10 .25
45 Hellion Eruption R :R: .30 .75
46 Hissing Iguanar C :R: .10 .25
47 Mark of Mutiny U :R: .15 .40
48 Mass Mutiny R :R: .40 1.00
49 Mudbutton Torchrunner C :R: .10 .25
50 Preyseizer Dragon R :R: 2.00 5.00
51 Rivals' Duel U :R: .15 .40
52 Thorn-Thrash Viashino C :R: .10 .25
53 Thunder-Thrash Elder U :R: .15 .40
54 Warstorm Surge R :R: .30 .75
55 Aura Gnarlid C :G: .10 .25
56 Awakening Zone R :G: .75 2.00
57 Beast Within U :G: .75 2.00
58 Boar Umbra U :G: .15 .40
59 Bramble Elemental C :G: .10 .25
60 Brindle Shoat U :G: .15 .40
61 Brutalizer Exarch U :G: .15 .40
62 Cultivate C :G: .75 2.00
63 Dowsing Shaman U :G: .15 .40
64 Dreampod Druid U :G: .15 .40
65 Gluttonous Slime U :G: .15 .40
66 Lumberknot U :G: .15 .40
67 Mitotic Slime R :G: .30 .75
68 Mycoloth R :G: 2.50 6.00
69 Nest Invader C :G: .10 .25
70 Nullmage Advocate C :G: .10 .25
71 Ondu Giant C :G: .10 .25
72 Overrun U :G: .15 .40
73 Penumbra Spider C :G: .10 .25
74 Predatory Urge R :G: .30 .75
75 Quiet Disrepair C :G: .10 .25
76 Rancor C :G: .75 2.00
77 Silhana Ledgewalker C :G: .75 2.00
78 Snake Umbra C :G: .10 .25
79 Tukatongue Thallid C :G: .10 .25
80 Viridian Emissary C :G: .10 .25
81 Wall of Blossoms U :G: 1.00 2.50
82 Baleful Strix U :B/K: 6.00 15.00
83 Bituminous Blast U :K/R: .15 .40
84 Bloodbraid Elf U :R/G: .75 2.00
85 Dimir Reality C :B/K: .10 .25
86 Dimir Infiltrator C :B/K: .10 .25
87 Dragonlair Spider R :R/G: 2.00 5.00
88 Elderwood Scion R :W/G: .75 2.00
89 Enigma Sphinx R :W/B/K: .30 .75
90 Enlisted Wurm U :W/G: .15 .40
91 Etherium-Horn Sorcerer R :B/R: .75 2.00
92 Fires of Yavimaya U :R/G: .40 1.00
93 Fusion Elemental U :W/B/K/R/G: .15 .40
94 Glen Elendra Liege R :B/K: .75 2.00
95 Hellkite Hatchling U :R/G: .15 .40
96 Indrik Umbra R :W/G: .75 2.00
97 Inkfathom Witch U :B/K: .15 .40
98 Kathari Remnant U :B/K: .15 .40
99 Krond the Dawn-Clad M :W/G: 2.50 6.00
100 Last Stand R :W/B/K/R/G: .30 .75
101 Maelstrom Wanderer M :B/R/G: 4.00 10.00
102 Noggle Ransacker U :B/R: .15 .40
103 Pollenbright Wings U :W/G: .15 .40
104 Shardless Agent U :B/G: 8.00 20.00
105 Silent-Blade Oni R :B/K: 3.00 8.00
106 Thromok the Insatiable M :R/G: 3.00 8.00
107 Vela the Night-Clad M :B/K: 2.00 5.00
108 Armillary Sphere C .10 .25
109 Farsight Mask U .15 .40
110 Flayer Husk C .10 .25
111 Fractured Powerstone C .10 .25
112 Quietus Spike R .75 2.00
113 Sai of the Shinobi U .15 .40
114 Thran Golem U .15 .40
115 Whispersilk Cloak U .40 1.00
116 Dimir Aqueduct C .60 1.50
117 Exotic Orchard R .60 1.50
118 Graypelt Refuge U .15 .40
119 Gruul Turf C .10 .25
120 Jwar Isle Refuge U .30 .75
121 Kazandu Refuge U .15 .40
122 Khalni Garden C .10 .25
123 Krosan Verge U .15 .40
124 Rupture Spire C .10 .25
125 Selesnya Sanctuary C .30 .75
126 Shimmering Grotto C .10 .25
127 Skarrg, the Rage Pits U .15 .40
128 Tainted Isle U .75 2.00
129 Terramorphic Expanse C .10 .25
130 Vitu-Ghazi, the City-Tree U .15 .40
131 Vivid Creek U .30 .75
132 Plains L .10 .25
133 Plains L .10 .25
134 Plains L .10 .25
135 Plains L .10 .25
136 Plains L .10 .25
137 Island L .10 .25
138 Island L .10 .25
139 Island L .10 .25
140 Island L .10 .25
141 Island L .10 .25
142 Swamp L .10 .25
143 Swamp L .10 .25
144 Swamp L .10 .25
145 Swamp L .10 .25
146 Swamp L .10 .25
147 Mountain L .10 .25
148 Mountain L .10 .25
149 Mountain L .10 .25
150 Mountain L .10 .25
151 Forest L .10 .25
152 Forest L .10 .25
153 Forest L .10 .25
154 Forest L .10 .25
155 Forest L .10 .25
156 Forest L .10 .25

2012 Magic The Gathering Commander's Arsenal

COMPLETE SET (18) 60.00 150.00
RELEASED ON NOVEMBER 2, 2012
1 Loyal Retainers U :W: 12.00 30.00
2 Desertion R :B: 4.00 10.00
3 Rhystic Study C :B: 5.00 12.00
4 Decree of Pain R :K: 5.00 12.00
5 Chaos Warp R :R: 8.00 20.00
6 Diaochan, Artful Beauty R :R: 2.00 5.00
7 Sylvan Library R :G: 20.00 50.00
8 Dragonlair Spider R :D: 3.00 8.00
9 Edric, Spymaster of Trest R :D: 2.50 6.00
10 Kaalia of the Vast M :D: 15.00 40.00
11 Maelstrom Wanderer M :D: 10.00 25.00
12 Mirari's Wake R :D: 8.00 20.00
13 The Mimeoplasm M :D: 5.00 12.00
14 Vela the Night-Clad M :D: 2.50 6.00
15 Command Tower C 6.00 15.00
16 Duplicant R 6.00 15.00
17 Mind's Eye R 4.00 10.00
18 Scroll Rack R 12.00 30.00

2013 Magic The Gathering Commander

COMPLETE SET (356) 100.00 200.00
RELEASED ON DECEMBER 20, 2013
1 Act of Authority R :W: .40 1.00
2 Aerie Mystics U :W: .20 .50
3 Ajani's Pridemate U :W: .60 1.50
4 Angel of Finality R :W: .60 1.50
5 Archangel U :W: .20 .50
6 Azorius Herald U :W: .20 .50
7 Cradle of Vitality R :W: .40 1.00
8 Curse of the Forsaken U :W: .20 .50
9 Darksteel Mutation U :W: .20 .50
10 Eternal Dragon R :W: .60 1.50
11 Fiend Hunter U :W: .20 .50
12 Flickerform R :W: .40 1.00
13 Flickerwisp U :W: .30 .75
14 Karmic Guide R :W: 1.50 4.00
15 Kirtar's Wrath R :W: .40 1.00
16 Kongming, "Sleeping Dragon" R :W: .40 1.00
17 Mirror Entity R :W: .75 2.00
18 Mystic Barrier R :W: .40 1.00
19 Razor Hippogriff U :W: .20 .50
20 Serene Master R :W: .40 1.00
21 Serra Avatar M :W: .60 1.50
22 Stonecloaker U :W: .20 .50
23 Survival Cache U :W: .20 .50
24 Tempt with Glory R :W: .40 1.00
25 Unexpectedly Absent R :W: 2.00 5.00
26 Wall of Reverence R :W: 1.00 2.50
27 Wrath of God R :W: 1.50 4.00
28 Arcane Denial C :B: .30 .75
29 Arcane Melee R :B: .40 1.00
30 Augur of Bolas U :B: .20 .50
31 Azami, Lady of Scrolls R :B: .40 1.00
32 Blue Sun's Zenith R :B: .60 1.50
33 Borrowing 100,000 Arrows U :B: .20 .50
34 Brilliant Plan U :B: .20 .50
35 Control Magic U :B: .30 .75
36 Curse of Inertia U :B: .20 .50
37 Deceiver Exarch U :B: .20 .50
38 Deep Analysis C :B: .20 .50
39 Dismiss U :B: .20 .50
40 Diviner Spirit U :B: .20 .50
41 Djinn of Infinite Deceits R :B: .40 1.00
42 Dungeon Geists R :B: .40 1.00
43 Echo Mage R :B: .40 1.00
44 Fog Bank U :B: .30 .75
45 Guard Gomazoa U :B: .20 .50
46 Hada Spy Patrol U :B: .20 .50
47 Illusionist's Gambit R :B: .40 1.00
48 Jace's Archivist R :B: .40 1.00
49 Lu Xun, Scholar General R :B: .40 1.00
50 Mnemonic Wall C :B: .10 .25
51 Opportunity U :B: .20 .50
52 Order of Succession R :B: 1.00
53 Propaganda U :B: .60 1.50
54 Prosperity U :B: .20 .50
55 Raven Familiar U :B: .20 .50
56 Sharding Sphinx R :B: 1.00
57 Skyscribing U :B: .20 .50
58 Stormscape Battlemage U :B: .20 .50
59 Strategic Planning U :B: .40 1.00
60 Tempt with Reflections R :B: .40 1.00
61 Thornwind Faeries C :B: .10 .25
62 Tidal Force R :B: 1.00
63 True-Name Nemesis R :B: 10.00 25.00
64 Uyo, Silent Prophet R :B: 1.00
65 Vision Skeins C :B: .10 .25
66 Wash Out U :B: .20 .50
67 Wonder U :B: .20 .50
68 Annihilate U :K: .20 .50
69 Army of the Damned M :K: .60 1.50
70 Baleful Force R :K: .30 .75
71 Curse of Shallow Graves U :K: .20 .50
72 Decree of Pain R :K: .60 1.50
73 Dirge of Dread C :K: .10 .25
74 Disciple of Griselbrand U :K: .20 .50
75 Endless Cockroaches R :K: .40 1.00
76 Endrek Sahr, Master Breeder R :K: .30 .75
77 Famine U :K: .20 .50
78 Fell Shepherd R :K: .40 1.00
79 Greed R :K: .40 1.00
80 Hooded Horror U :K: .20 .50
81 Infest U :K: .20 .50
82 Marrow Bats U :K: .20 .50
83 Nightscape Familiar C :K: .10 .25
84 Ophiomancer R :K: .60 1.50
85 Phthisis U :K: .20 .50
86 Phyrexian Delver R :K: 1.00
87 Phyrexian Gargantua U :K: .20 .50
88 Phyrexian Reclamation U :K: .20 .50
89 Price of Knowledge R :K: .40 1.00
90 Quagmire Druid C :K: .10 .25
91 Reckless Spite U :K: .20 .50
92 Sanguine Bond R :K: 3.00
93 Stronghold Assassin R :K: .40 1.00
94 Sudden Spoiling R :K: 1.00
95 Tempt with Immortality R :K: .40 1.00
96 Toxic Deluge R :K: 5.00 12.00
97 Vampire Nighthawk U :K: .60 1.50
98 Vile Requiem U :K: .20 .50
99 Viscera Seer C :K: .10 .25
100 Wight of Precinct Six U :K: .20 .50
101 Blood Rites U :R: .20 .50
102 Capricious Efreet R :R: .40 1.00
103 Charmbreaker Devils R :R: .40 1.00
104 Crater Hellion R :R: .40 1.00
105 Curse of Chaos U :R: .20 .50
106 Fireball U :R: .20 .50
107 Fissure Vent C :R: .10 .25
108 From the Ashes R :R: .40 1.00
109 Furnace Celebration U :R: .20 .50
110 Goblin Bombardment U :R: .50 1.25
111 Goblin Sharpshooter R :R: 1.00 2.50
112 Guttersnipe U :R: .30 .75
113 Incendiary Command R :R: .40 1.00
114 Inferno Titan M :R: .60 1.50
115 Magus of the Arena R :R: .40 1.00
116 Mass Mutiny R :R: .40 1.00
117 Molten Disaster R :R: .40 1.00
118 Rough/Tumble U :R: .20 .50
119 Slice and Dice U :R: .20 .50
120 Spitebellows U :R: .20 .50
121 Stalking Vengeance R :R: .40 1.00
122 Starstorm R :R: .40 1.00
123 Street Spasm U :R: .20 .50
124 Sudden Demise R :R: .75 2.00
125 Tempt with Vengeance R :R: .40 1.00
126 Terra Ravager U :R: .20 .50
127 Tooth and Claw R :R: .40 1.00
128 War Cadence U :R: .20 .50
129 Warstorm Surge R :R: .40 1.00
130 Where Ancients Tread R :R: .40 1.00
131 Widespread Panic R :R: .40 1.00
132 Wild Ricochet R :R: .40 1.00
133 Witch Hunt R :R: .40 1.00
134 Acidic Slime U :G: .20 .50
135 Avenger of Zendikar M :G: 2.50 6.00
136 Baloth Woodcrasher U :G: .20 .50
137 Bane of Progress R :G: .75 2.00
138 Brooding Saurian R :G: .40 1.00
139 Cultivate C :G: .30 .75
140 Curse of Predation U :G: .20 .50
141 Deadwood Treefolk U :G: .20 .50
142 Drumhunter U :G: .20 .50
143 Elvish Skysweeper C :G: .10 .25
144 Farhaven Elf C :G: .10 .25
145 Fecundity U :G: .20 .50
146 Foster R :G: .40 1.00
147 Grazing Gladehart C :G: .10 .25
148 Harmonize U :G: .60 1.50
149 Hua Tuo, Honored Physician R :G: .60 1.50
150 Hunted Troll R :G: .40 1.00
151 Jade Mage U :G: .20 .50
152 Kazandu Tuskcaller R :G: .40 1.00
153 Krosan Grip U :G: .30 .75
154 Krosan Tusker C :G: .10 .25
155 Krosan Warchief U :G: .20 .50
156 Mold Shambler C :G: .10 .25
157 Naya Soulbeast R :G: .40 1.00
158 Night Soil C :G: .10 .25
159 One Dozen Eyes U :G: .20 .50
160 Phantom Nantuko R :G: .40 1.00
161 Presence of Gond C :G: .10 .25
162 Primal Vigor R :G: 1.50 4.00
163 Rain of Thorns U :G: .20 .50
164 Rampaging Baloths M :G: .75 2.00
165 Ravenous Baloth R :G: .40 1.00
166 Reincarnation U :G: .20 .50
167 Restore U :G: .20 .50
168 Sakura-Tribe Elder C :G: .10 .25
169 Silklash Spider R :G: .40 1.00
170 Slice in Twain U :G: .20 .50
171 Spawning Grounds R :G: .40 1.00
172 Spoils of Victory U :G: .20 .50
173 Sprouting Vines C :G: .10 .25
174 Tempt with Discovery R :G: .75 2.00
175 Walker of the Grove U :G: .20 .50
176 AEthermage's Touch R :W:/:B: .40 1.00
177 Baleful Strix U :B:/:K: 2.00 5.00
178 Behemoth Sledge U :W:/:G: .20 .50
179 Boros Charm U :W:/:R: 1.25 3.00
180 Charnelhoard Wurm R :K:/:R:/:G: .40 1.00
181 Crosis's Charm U :B:/:K:/:R: .20 .50
182 Cruel Ultimatum R :B:/:K:/:R: .40 1.00
183 Death Grasp R :W:/:K: .40 1.00
184 Deathbringer Thoctar R :K:/:R: .40 1.00
185 Deepfire Elemental U :K:/:R: .20 .50
186 Derevi, Empyrial Tactician M :W:/:B:/:G: .60 1.50
OS FOIL
187 Dromar's Charm U :W:/:B:/:K: .20 .50
188 Fiery Justice R :W:/:R:/:G: .40 1.00
189 Filigree Angel R :W:/:B: .40 1.00
190 Fires of Yavimaya U :R:/:G: .20 .50
191 Gahiji, Honored One M :W:/:R:/:G: .60 1.50
OS FOIL
192 Grixis Charm U :B:/:K:/:R: .20 .50
193 Hull Breach C :R:/:G: .20 .50
194 Jeleva, Nephalia's Scourge M :B:/:K:/:R: .60 1.50
OS FOIL
195 Jund Charm U :K:/:R:/:G: .20 .50
196 Leafdrake Roost U :B:/:G: .20 .50
197 Lim-Dûl's Vault U :B:/:K: .60 1.50
198 Marath, Will of the Wild M :W:/:R:/:G: .60 1.50
OS FOIL
199 Mayael the Anima M :W:/:R:/:G: .60 1.50
OS FOIL
200 Naya Charm U :W:/:R:/:G: .20 .50
201 Nekusar, the Mindrazer M :B:/:K:/:R: .60 1.50
OS FOIL
202 Nivix Guildmage U :B:/:R: .20 .50
203 Oloro, Ageless Ascetic M :W:/:B:/:K: 1.00 2.50
OS FOIL
204 Prossh, Skyraider of Kher M :K:/:R:/:G: .75 2.00
OS FOIL
205 Rakeclaw Gargantuan C :W:/:R:/:G: .10 .25
206 Roon of the Hidden Realm M :W:/:B:/:G: .60 1.50
OS FOIL
207 Rubinia Soulsinger R :W:/:B:/:G: .40 1.00
OS FOIL
208 Savage Twister U :R:/:G: .20 .50
209 Scarland Thrinax U :K:/:R:/:G: .20 .50
210 Sek'Kuar, Deathkeeper R :K:/:R:/:G: .40 1.00
OS FOIL
211 Selesnya Charm U :W:/:G: .30 .75
212 Sharuum the Hegemon M :W:/:B:/:K: .60 1.50
OS FOIL
213 Shattergang Brothers M :K:/:R:/:G: .60 1.50
OS FOIL
214 Skyward Eye Prophets U :W:/:B:/:G: .20 .50
215 Soul Manipulation C :B:/:K: .10 .25
216 Spellbreaker Behemoth R :R:/:G: .40 1.00
217 Sphinx of the Steel Wind M :W:/:B:/:K: .60 1.50
218 Spinal Embrace R :B:/:K: .40 1.00
219 Sprouting Thrinax U :K:/:R:/:G: .20 .50
220 Sydri, Galvanic Genius M :W:/:B:/:K: .60 1.50
OS FOIL
221 Thraximundar M :B:/:K:/:R: .60 1.50
OS FOIL
222 Tidehollow Strix C :B:/:K: .10 .25
223 Tower Gargoyle U :W:/:B:/:K: .20 .50
224 Valley Rannet C :R:/:G: .10 .25
225 Vizkopa Guildmage U :W:/:K: .20 .50
226 Winged Coatl C :B:/:G: .10 .25
227 Augury Adept R :W:/:B: .40 1.00
228 Divinity of Pride R :W:/:K: 1.00 2.50
229 Golgari Guildmage U :K:/:G: .20 .50
230 Mistmeadow Witch U :W:/:B: .20 .50
231 Murkfiend Liege R :B:/:G: 1.00 2.50
232 Selesnya Guildmage U :W:/:G: .20 .50
233 Spiteful Visions R :K:/:R: 1.00
234 Thopter Foundry U :W:/:B:/:K: .20 .50
235 Armillary Sphere C .10 .25
236 Azorius Keyrune U .20 .50
237 Basalt Monolith U .40 1.00
238 Carnage Altar U .20 .50
239 Conjurer's Closet R .30 .75
240 Crawlspace R .40 1.00
241 Darksteel Ingot U .20 .50
242 Druidic Satchel R .30 .75
243 Eye of Doom R .30 .75
244 Jar of Eyeballs R .40 1.00
245 Leonin Bladetrap U .20 .50
246 Mirari R 1.50
247 Myr Battlesphere R .40 1.00
248 Nevinyrral's Disk R 1.50 4.00
249 Nihil Spellbomb C .10 .25
250 Obelisk of Esper C .10 .25
251 Obelisk of Grixis C .10 .25
252 Obelisk of Jund C .10 .25
253 Pilgrim's Eye C .10 .25
254 Plague Boiler R .40 1.00
255 Pristine Talisman C .10 .25
256 Seer's Sundial R .40 1.00
257 Selesnya Signet C .10 .25
258 Simic Signet C .10 .25
259 Sol Ring U 1.50 4.00
260 Spine of Ish Sah R .40 1.00
261 Sun Droplet U .20 .50
262 Surveyor's Scope R .40 1.00
263 Swiftfoot Boots U .20 .50
264 Sword of the Paruns R .40 1.00
265 Temple Bell R .40 1.00
266 Thousand-Year Elixir R .75 2.00
267 Thunderstaff U .20 .50
268 Tower of Fortunes R .40 1.00
269 Viseling U .20 .50
270 Wayfarer's Bauble C .10 .25
271 Well of Lost Dreams R .40 1.00
272 Akoum Refuge U .20 .50
273 Arcane Sanctum U .60 1.50
274 Azorius Chancery C .20 .50
275 Azorius Guildgate C .10 .25
276 Bant Panorama C .10 .25
277 Barren Moor C .10 .25
278 Bojuka Bog C .20 .50
279 Boros Garrison C .20 .50
280 Boros Guildgate C .20 .50
281 Command Tower C .60 1.50
282 Contested Cliffs R .40 1.00
283 Crumbling Necropolis U .30 .75
284 Dimir Guildgate C .20 .50
285 Drifting Meadow C .10 .25
286 Esper Panorama C .10 .25
287 Evolving Wilds C .10 .25
288 Faerie Conclave U .30 .75
289 Forgotten Cave C .10 .25
290 Golgari Guildgate C .20 .50
291 Golgari Rot Farm C .20 .50
292 Grim Backwoods R .40 1.00
293 Grixis Panorama C .10 .25
294 Gruul Guildgate C .20 .50
295 Homeward Path R 2.00 5.00
296 Izzet Boilerworks C .10 .25
297 Izzet Guildgate C .10 .25
298 Jund Panorama C .10 .25
299 Jungle Shrine U .20 .50
300 Jwar Isle Refuge U .20 .50
301 Kazandu Refuge U .20 .50
302 Khalni Garden C .10 .25
303 Kher Keep R 2.00
304 Llanowar Reborn U .20 .50
305 Lonely Sandbar C .10 .25
306 Molten Slagheap U .20 .50
307 Mosswort Bridge R .75 2.00
308 Naya Panorama C .10 .25
309 New Benalia U .20 .50
310 Opal Palace C .30 .75
311 Orzhov Basilica C .10 .25
312 Orzhov Guildgate C .20 .50
313 Rakdos Carnarium C .10 .25
314 Rakdos Guildgate C .10 .25
315 Rupture Spire C .10 .25
316 Saltcrusted Steppe U .20 .50
317 Savage Lands U .40 1.00
318 Seaside Citadel U .60 1.50
319 Secluded Steppe C .10 .25
320 Sejiri Refuge U .20 .50
321 Selesnya Guildgate C .20 .50
322 Selesnya Sanctuary C .20 .50
323 Simic Guildgate C .20 .50
324 Slippery Karst C .10 .25
325 Smoldering Crater C .10 .25
326 Springjack Pasture R .40 1.00
327 Temple of the False God U .20 .50
328 Terramorphic Expanse C .10 .25
329 Tranquil Thicket C .10 .25
330 Transguild Promenade C .10 .25
331 Urza's Factory U .20 .50
332 Vitu-Ghazi, the City-Tree U .20 .50
333 Vivid Crag U .20 .50
334 Vivid Creek U .20 .50
335 Vivid Grove U .20 .50
336 Vivid Marsh U .20 .50
337 Plains L .10 .25
338 Plains L .10 .25
339 Plains L .10 .25
340 Plains L .10 .25
341 Island L .10 .25
342 Island L .10 .25
343 Island L .10 .25
344 Island L .10 .25
345 Swamp L .10 .25
346 Swamp L .10 .25
347 Swamp L .10 .25
348 Swamp L .10 .25
349 Mountain L .10 .25
350 Mountain L .10 .25
351 Mountain L .10 .25
352 Mountain L .10 .25
353 Forest L .10 .25
354 Forest L .10 .25
355 Forest L .10 .25
356 Forest L .10 .25

2014 Magic The Gathering Conspiracy

COMPLETE SET (219) 50.00 120.00
*FOIL: 1X TO 2.5X BASIC CARDS
RELEASED ON JUNE 6, 2014
1 Advantageous Proclamation U .10 .30
2 Backup Plan R .40 1.00
3 Brago's Favor C .10 .25
4 Double Stroke U .10 .30
5 Immediate Action C .10 .25

Card	Low	High
6 Iterative Analysis U	.10	.30
7 Muzzio's Preparations C	.10	.25
8 Power Play U	.10	.30
9 Secret Summoning U	.10	.30
10 Secrets of Paradise C	.10	.25
11 Sentinel Dispatch C	.10	.25
12 Unexpected Potential U	.10	.30
14 Brago's Representative C :W:	.10	.25
15 Council Guardian U :W:	.10	.30
16 Council's Judgment R :W:	4.00	7.00
17 Custodi Soulbinders R :W:	.40	1.00
18 Custodi Squire C :W:	.10	.25
19 Rousing of Souls C :W:	.10	.25
20 Academy Elite R :B:	.40	1.00
21 Marchesa's Emissary C :B:	.10	.25
22 Marchesa's Infiltrator U :B:	.10	.30
23 Muzzio, Visionary Architect M :B:	1.25	2.50
24 Plea for Power R :B:	.40	1.00
25 Split Decision U :B:	.10	.30
26 Bite of the Black Rose U :K:	.10	.30
27 Drakestown Forgotten R :K:	.40	1.00
28 Grudge Keeper C :K:	.10	.25
29 Reign of the Pit R :K:	.40	1.00
30 Tyrant's Choice C :K:	.10	.25
31 Enraged Revolutionary C :R:	.10	.25
32 Grenzo's Cutthroat C :R:	.10	.25
33 Grenzo's Rebuttal R :R:	.40	1.00
34 Ignition Team R :R:	.40	1.00
35 Scourge of the Throne M :R:	5.00	8.00
36 Treasonous Ogre U :R:	.10	.30
37 Predator's Howl U :G:	.10	.30
38 Realm Seekers R :G:	.40	1.00
39 Selvala's Charge U :G:	.10	.30
40 Selvala's Enforcer C	.10	.25
41 Brago, King Eternal M :W: :B:	1.00	2.00
42 Dack Fayden M :B: :R:	15.00	25.00
43 Dack's Duplicate R :B: :R:	1.25	3.00
44 Deathreap Ritual U :K: :G:	.10	.30
45 Extract from Darkness U :G: :K:	.10	.30
46 Flamewright U :R: :W:	.10	.30
47 Grenzo, Dungeon Warden R :K: :R:	.75	2.00
48 Magister of Worth R :W: :K:	.40	1.00
49 Marchesa, the Black Rose M :D:	4.00	7.00
50 Marchesa's Smuggler U :B: :R:	.10	.30
51 Selvala, Explorer Returned R :G: :W:	.40	1.00
52 Woodvine Elemental U :G: :W:	.10	.30
53 Aether Searcher R	.40	1.00
54 Agent of Acquisitions U	.10	.30
55 Canal Dredger R	.40	1.00
56 Coercive Portal M	2.00	5.00
57 Cogwork Grinder R	.40	1.00
58 Cogwork Librarian C	.10	.25
59 Cogwork Spy C	.10	.25
60 Cogwork Tracker U	.10	.30
61 Deal Broker R	.40	1.00
62 Lore Seeker R	.40	1.00
63 Lurking Automaton C	.10	.25
64 Whispergear Sneak C	.10	.25
65 Paliano, the High City R	.40	1.00
66 Ajani's Sunstriker C :W:	.10	.25
67 Apex Hawks C :W:	.10	.25
68 Courier Hawk C :W:	.10	.25
69 Doomed Traveler C :W:	.10	.25
70 Glimmerpoint Stag U :W:	.10	.30
71 Guardian Zendikon C :W:	.10	.25
72 Intangible Virtue U :W:	.10	.30
73 Kor Chant C :W:	.10	.25
74 Moment of Heroism C :W:	.10	.25
75 Noble Templar C :W:	.10	.25
76 Pillarfield Ox C :W:	.10	.25
77 Pride Guardian C :W:	.10	.25
78 Pristine Angel M :W:	1.00	2.00
79 Reya Dawnbringer R :W:	.40	1.00
80 Rout R :W:	.40	1.00
81 Silverchase Fox C :W:	.10	.25
82 Soulcatcher U :W:	.10	.30
83 Stave Off C :W:	.10	.25
84 Swords to Plowshares U :W:	.10	.30
85 Unquestioned Authority U :W:	.10	.30
86 Valor Made Real C :W:	.10	.25
87 Vow of Duty U :W:	.10	.30
88 Wakestone Gargoyle U :W:	.10	.30
89 AEther Tradewinds C :B:	.10	.25
90 Air Servant U :B:	.10	.30
91 Brainstorm C :B:	.50	1.00
92 Breakthrough U :B:	.10	.30
93 Compulsive Research C :B:	.10	.25
94 Crookclaw Transmuter C :B:	.10	.25
95 Dream Fracture C :B:	.10	.25
96 Enclave Elite C :B:	.10	.25
97 Fact or Fiction U :B:	.10	.30
98 Favorable Winds U :B:	.10	.30
99 Grixis Illusionist C :B:	.10	.25
T1 Spirit Token :W:	.10	.30
T2 Demon Token :K:	.10	.30
T3 Zombie Token :K:	.10	.30
T4 Ogre Token :R:	.10	.30
T5 Elephant Token :G:	.10	.30
T6 Squirrel Token :G:	.50	1.00
T7 Wolf Token :G:	.10	.30
T8 Construct Token	.10	.30
T9 Emblem - Dack Fayden	1.00	2.00
100 Jetting Glasskite U :B:	.10	.30
101 Minamo Scrollkeeper C :B:	.10	.25
102 Misdirection R :B:	1.00	2.00
103 Plated Seastrider C :B:	.10	.25
104 Reckless Scholar C :B:	.10	.25
105 Screaming Seahawk C :B:	.10	.25
106 Shoreline Ranger C :B:	.10	.25
107 Stasis Cell C :B:	.10	.25
108 Stifle R :B:	3.00	5.00
109 Traveler's Cloak C :B:	.10	.25
110 Turn the Tide C :B:	.10	.25
111 Wind Dancer U :B:	.10	.30
112 Altar's Reap C :K:	.10	.25
113 Assassinate C :K:	.10	.25
114 Ill-Gotten Gains R :K:	.40	1.00
115 Infectious Horror C :K:	.10	.25
116 Liliana's Specter C :K:	.10	.25
117 Magus of the Mirror R :K:	.40	1.00
118 Morkrut Banshee U :K:	.10	.30
119 Necromantic Thirst C :K:	.10	.25
120 Phage the Untouchable M :K:	1.00	2.00
121 Plagued Rusalka U :K:	.10	.30
122 Quag Vampires C :K:	.10	.25
123 Reckless Spite U :K:	.10	.30
124 Skeletal Scrying U :K:	.10	.30
125 Smallpox U :K:	.10	.30
126 Stronghold Discipline C :K:	.10	.25
127 Syphon Soul C :K:	.10	.25
128 Tragic Slip C :K:	.10	.25
129 Twisted Abomination C :K:	.10	.25
130 Typhoid Rats C :K:	.10	.25
131 Unhallowed Pact C :K:	.10	.25
132 Vampire Hexmage U :K:	.10	.30
133 Victimize U :K:	.10	.30
134 Wakedancer C :K:	.10	.25
135 Zombie Goliath C :K:	.10	.25
136 Barbed Shocker U :R:	.10	.30
137 Boldwyr Intimidator U :R:	.10	.30
138 Brimstone Volley C :R:	.10	.25
139 Chartooth Cougar C :R:	.10	.25
140 Cinder Wall C :R:	.10	.25
141 Deathforge Shaman U :R:	.10	.30
142 Flaring Flame-Kin U :R:	.10	.30
143 Flowstone Blade C :R:	.10	.25
144 Heartless Hidetsugu R :R:	.40	1.00
145 Heckling Fiends U :R:	.10	.30
146 Lizard Warrior C :R:	.10	.25
147 Mana Geyser C :R:	.10	.25
148 Orcish Cannonade C :R:	.10	.25
149 Pitchburn Devils C :R:	.10	.25
150 Power of Fire C :R:	.10	.25
151 Skitter of Lizards C :R:	.10	.25
152 Sulfuric Vortex R :R:	.40	1.00
153 Torch Fiend C :R:	.10	.25
154 Trumpet Blast C :R:	.10	.25
155 Uncontrollable Anger U :R:	.10	.30
156 Vent Sentinel C :R:	.10	.25
157 Volcanic Fallout U :R:	.10	.30
158 Wrap in Flames C :R:	.10	.25
159 Charging Rhino C :G:	.10	.25
160 Copperhorn Scout C :G:	.10	.25
161 Echoing Courage C :G:	.10	.25
162 Elephant Guide U :G:	.10	.30
163 Elvish Aberration C :G:	.10	.25
164 Exploration R :G:	8.00	12.00
165 Gamekeeper U :G:	.10	.30
166 Gnarlid Pack C :G:	.10	.25
167 Howling Wolf C :G:	.10	.25
168 Hunger of the Howlpack C :G:	.10	.25
169 Hydra Omnivore M :G:	1.50	3.00
170 Lead the Stampede U :G:	.10	.30
171 Nature's Claim C :G:	.50	1.00
172 Pelakka Wurm U :G:	.10	.30
173 Plummet C :G:	.10	.25
174 Provoke C :G:	.10	.25
175 Relic Crush U :G:	.10	.30
176 Respite C :G:	.10	.25
177 Sakura-Tribe Elder C :G:	.15	.40
178 Scaled Wurm C :G:	.10	.25
179 Sporecap Spider C :G:	.10	.25
180 Squirrel Nest U :G:	.10	.30
181 Terastodon R :G:	.40	1.00
182 Wolfbriar Elemental R :G:	.40	1.00
183 Wrap in Vigor C :G:	.10	.25
184 Basandra, Battle Seraph R :R: :W:	.40	1.00
185 Decimate R	.50	1.25
186 Dimir Doppelganger R :B: :K:	.40	1.00
187 Edric, Spymaster of Trest R :G: :B:	.75	2.00
188 Fires of Yavimaya U :R: :G:	.10	.30
189 Mirari's Wake M :G: :W:	5.00	10.00
190 Mortify U :W: :K:	.10	.30
191 Pernicious Deed M :K: :G:	2.50	5.00
192 Sky Spirit U :W: :B:	.10	.30
193 Spiritmonger R :K: :G:	.40	1.00
194 Spontaneous Combustion U :K: :R:	.10	.30
195 Wood Sage U :G: :B:	.10	.30
196 Altar Of Dementia R	1.00	2.50
197 Deathrender R	2.00	3.00
198 Explorer's Scope U	.10	.30
199 Fireshrieker U	.10	.30
200 Galvanic Juggernaut U	.10	.30
201 Peace Strider U	.10	.30
202 Reito Lantern U	.10	.30
203 Runed Servitor U	.10	.30
204 Silent Arbiter R	.75	2.00
205 Spectral Searchlight U	.10	.30
206 Vedalken Orrery R	2.00	5.00
207 Warmonger's Chariot U	.10	.30
208 Mirrodin's Core U	.10	.30
209 Quicksand U :L:	.10	.30
210 Worldknit R	.40	1.00
210 Reflecting Pool R :L:	5.00	8.00

2016 Magic The Gathering Conspiracy Take The Crown

Card	Low	High
COMPLETE SET (221 CARDS)	325.00	425.00
BOOSTER BOX (36 PACKS)	90.00	100.00
BOOSTER PACK (15 CARDS)	3.00	4.50
RELEASED ON AUGUST 26, 2016		
1 Adrianas Valor C	.05	.15
2 Assemble the Rank and Vile C	.05	.15
3 Echoing Boon U	.05	.15
4 Emissarys Ploy R	.05	.15
5 Hired Heist C	.05	.15
6 Hold the Perimeter R	.05	.15
7 Hymn of the Wilds M	.30	.50
8 Incendiary Dissent C	.05	.15
9 Natuarl Unity C	.05	.15
10 Sovereigns Realm M	.30	.50
11 Summoners Bond U	.05	.15
12 Weight Advantage R	.05	.15
13 Ballot Broker C	.05	.15
14 Custodi Peacekeeper C	.05	.15
15 Custodi Soulcaller U	.05	.15
16 Lieutenants of the Guard C	.05	.15
17 Noble Banneret U	.05	.15
18 Palace Jailer U	.05	.15
19 Palace Sentinels C	.05	.15
20 Paliano Vanguard R	.10	.20
21 Protector of the Crown R	.15	.25
22 Recruiter of the Guard R	14.00	15.50
23 Sanctum Prelate M	15.00	18.00
24 Spectral Grasp U	.05	.15
25 Throne Warden C	.05	.15
26 Wings of the Guard C	.05	.15
27 Arcane Savant R	.10	.20
28 Canal Courier C	.05	.15
29 Coveted Peacock U	.05	.15
30 Expropriate M	3.25	3.75
31 Illusion of Choice U	.05	.15
32 Illusionary Informant C	.05	.15
33 Jeering Homunculus C	.05	.15
34 Keeper of Keys R	.10	.20
35 Messenger Jays C	.05	.15
36 Skittering Crustacean C	.05	.15
37 Spire Phantasm U	.05	.15
38 Stunt Double R	.75	1.15
39 Archdemon of Paliano R	.15	.25
40 Capital Punishment R	.30	.50
41 Custodi Lich R	.30	.50
42 Deadly Designs U	.05	.15
43 Garrulous Sycophant C	.05	.15
44 Marchesas Decree U	.05	.15
45 Regicide C	.05	.15
46 Sinuous Vermin C	.05	.15
47 Smuggler Captain U	.05	.15
48 Thorn of the Black Rose C	.05	.15
49 Besmirch U	.05	.15
50 Crown Hunter Hireling C	.05	.15
51 Deputized Protester C	.05	.15
52 Garbage Fire C	.05	.15
53 Goblin Racketeer C	.05	.15
54 Grenzo Havoc Raiser R	1.50	2.00
55 Grenzos Ruffians U	.05	.15
56 Pyretic Hunter U	.05	.15
57 Skyline Despot R	.30	.50
58 Subterranean Tremors M	2.00	2.50
59 Volatile Chimera R	.05	.15
60 Animus of Predation U	.05	.15
61 Borderland Explorer C	.05	.15
62 Caller of the Untamed R	.10	.20
63 Domesticated Hydra U	.05	.15
64 Entourage of Trest C	.05	.15
65 Fang of the Pack U	.05	.15
66 Leovolds Operative C	.05	.15
67 Menagerie Liberator C	.05	.15
68 Orchard Elemental C	.05	.15
69 Regal Behemoth R	.40	.60
70 Selvala Heart of the Wilds M	6.50	8.00
71 Selvalas Stampede R	1.75	2.00
72 Splitting Slime R	.20	.30
73 Adriana Captain of the Guard R	.30	.50
74 Daretti Ingenious Iconoclast M	10.00	12.00
75 Kaya Ghost Assassin M	10.00	12.00
76 Knights of the Black Rose U	.05	.15
77 Leovold Emissary of Trest M	10.00	12.00
78 Queen Marchesa M	3.75	4.75
79 Spy Kit U	.05	.15
80 Throne of the High City R	.40	.65
81 Affa Guard Hound U	.05	.15
82 Disenchant C	.05	.15
83 Doomed Traveler C	.05	.15
84 Faiths Reward R	.20	.35
85 Ghostly Possession C	.05	.15
86 Ghostly Prison U	3.00	3.25
87 Gleam of Resistance C	.05	.15
88 Gods Willing C	.05	.15
89 Guardian of the Gateless U	.05	.15
90 Hall of Arrows U	.05	.15
91 Hallowed Burial R	.50	.75
92 Hollowhenge Spirit U	.05	.15
93 Hundred Handed One R	.05	.15
94 Kill Shot C	.05	.15
95 Pariah R	.40	.60
96 Raise the Alarm C	.05	.15
97 Reviving Dose C	.05	.15
98 Spirit of the Hearth R	.10	.20
99 Wild Griffin C	.05	.15
100 Windborne Charge U	.05	.15
101 Zealous Strike C	.05	.15
102 Bonds of Quicksilver C	.05	.15
103 Caller of Gales C	.05	.15
104 Cloaked Siren C	.05	.15
105 Covenant of Minds R	.05	.15
106 Deceiver Exarch U	.15	.25
107 Desertion R	.75	1.25
108 Dismiss U	.05	.15
109 Divination C	.05	.15
110 Fleeting Distraction C	.05	.15
111 Followed Footsteps R	.50	.75
112 Into the Void U	.05	.15
113 Kami of the Crescent Moon R	.50	.75
114 Merfolk Looter U	.05	.15
115 Merfolk Skyscout U	.05	.15
116 Mnemonic Wall C	.05	.15
117 Negate C	.05	.15
118 Omenspeaker C	.05	.15
119 Repulse C	.05	.15
120 Serum Visions U	2.25	3.00
121 Show and Tell M	20.00	22.00
122 Sphinx of Magosi R	.05	.15
123 Traumatic Visions C	.05	.15
124 Vaporkin C	.05	.15
125 Vertigo Spawn U	.05	.15
126 Absorb Vis C	.05	.15
127 Altars Reap C	.05	.15
128 Avatar of Woe M	1.00	1.50
129 Blood Toll Harpy C	.05	.15
130 Child of Night C	.05	.15
131 Death Wind C	.05	.15
132 Diabolic Tutor U	.05	.15
133 Festergloom C	.05	.15
134 Driver of the Dead C	.05	.15
135 Farbog Boneflinger U	.05	.15
136 Fleshbag Marauder U	.05	.15
137 Guul Draz Specter R	.05	.15
138 Harvester of Souls R	.05	.15
139 Infest U	.05	.15
140 Inquisition of Kozilek R	7.50	9.50
141 Keepsake Gorgon U	.05	.15
142 Mausoleum Turnkey U	.05	.15
143 Murder C	.05	.15
144 Phyrexian Arena R	2.50	3.00
145 Public Execution U	.05	.15
146 Raise Dead C	.05	.15
147 Sangromancer R	.30	.50
148 Shambling Goblin C	.05	.15
149 Stormkirk Patrol C	.05	.15
150 Unnerve C	.05	.15
151 Burn Away U	.05	.15
152 Burning Wish R	1.25	2.00
153 Charmbreaker Devils R	.05	.15
154 Coordinated Assault U	.05	.15
155 Ember Beast C	.05	.15
156 Fiery Fall C	.05	.15
157 Flame Slash C	.05	.15
158 Gang of Devils U	.05	.15
159 Goblin Balloon Brigade C	.05	.15
160 Goblin Tunneler C	.05	.15
161 Gratuitous Violence R	.75	1.15
162 Guttersnipe U	.05	.15
163 Hamletback Goliath R	.05	.15
164 Havengul Vampire U	.05	.15
165 Hurly Burly C	.05	.15
166 Ill Tempered Cyclops C	.05	.15
167 Kilin Fiend C	.20	.30
168 Ogre Sentry C	.05	.15
169 Stoneshock Giant U	.05	.15
170 Sulfurous Blast U	.05	.15
171 Tormenting Voice C	.05	.15
172 Trumpet Blast C	.05	.15
173 Twing Bolt C	.05	.15
174 Beast Within U	1.25	1.75
175 Berserk M	20.00	25.00
176 Birds of Paradise R	4.00	5.00
177 Bushstrider U	.05	.15
178 Burgeoning R	4.25	5.00
179 Copperhorn Scout C	.05	.15
180 Explosive Vegetation U	.40	.60
181 Fade into Antiquity C	.05	.15
182 Forgotten Ancient R	.20	.30
183 Irresistible Prey U	.05	.15
184 Lace with Moonglove C	.05	.15
185 Lay of the Land C	.05	.15
186 Manaplasm U	.05	.15
187 Nessian Asp U	.05	.15
188 Netcaster Spider C	.05	.15
189 Overrun U	.05	.15
190 Plummet C	.05	.15
191 Prey Upon C	.05	.15
192 Ravenous Leucrocota C	.05	.15
193 Stength in Numbers C	.05	.15
194 Sylvan Bounty C	.05	.15
195 Voyaging Satyr C	.05	.15
196 Wild Pair R	.30	.50
197 Akroan Hoplite U	.05	.15
198 Ascended Lawmage U	.05	.15
199 Carnage Gladiator U	.05	.15
200 Coiling Oracle U	.05	.15
201 Dragonlair Spider R	.30	.50
202 Duskmantle Seer R	.10	.20
203 Gruul War Chant U	.05	.15
204 Juniper Order Ranger U	.20	.30
205 Pharikas Mender U	.05	.15
206 Shipwreck Singer U	.05	.15
207 Stormchaser Chimera U	.05	.15
208 Bronze Sable C	.05	.15
209 Hedron Matrix R	.10	.20
210 Hexplate Golem C	.05	.15
211 Horn of Greed R	1.00	1.50
212 Kitesail C	.05	.15
213 Opaline Unicorn C	.05	.15
214 Platinum Angel M	3.00	3.75
215 Psychosis Crawler R	.10	.20
216 Runed Servitor U	.05	.15
217 Dread Statuary U	.05	.15
218 Evolving Wilds C	.05	.15
219 Exotic Orchard R	.75	1.25
220 Rogues Passage U	.05	.15
221 Shimmering Grotto U	.05	.15
T1 The Monarch Token T	.05	.15
222 Kaya Ghost Assassin Alt Foil	160.00	200.00

2016 Magic The Gathering Conspiracy Take The Crown Foil

Card	Low	High
COMPLETE SET (223 CARDS)	1000.00	1300.00
BOOSTER BOX (36 PACKS)	90.00	120.00
BOOSTER PACK (15 CARDS)	3.00	5.00
RELEASED ON AUGUST 26, 2016		
1 Adrianas Valor C	.15	.30
2 Assemble the Rank and Vile C	.15	.30
3 Echoing Boon U	.20	.60
4 Emissarys Ploy R	1.75	2.50
5 Hired Heist C	.15	.30
6 Hold the Perimeter R	2.00	2.75
7 Hymn of the Wilds M	13.00	18.00
8 Incendiary Dissent C	.15	.30
9 Natuarl Unity C	.15	.30
10 Sovereigns Realm M	7.00	10.00
11 Summoners Bond U	1.25	1.75
12 Weight Advantage R	1.75	2.50
13 Ballot Broker C	.15	.30
14 Custodi Peacekeeper C	.15	.30
15 Custodi Soulcaller U	.20	.60
16 Lieutenants of the Guard C	.15	.30
17 Noble Banneret U	.20	.60
18 Palace Jailer U	1.75	2.25
19 Palace Sentinels C	.15	.30
20 Paliano Vanguard R	2.00	2.75
21 Protector of the Crown R	1.50	2.50
22 Recruiter of the Guard R	60.00	75.00
23 Sanctum Prelate M	75.00	90.00
24 Spectral Grasp U	.20	.60
25 Throne Warden C	.15	.30
26 Wings of the Guard C	.15	.30
27 Arcane Savant R	2.50	3.50
28 Canal Courier C	.15	.30
29 Coveted Peacock U	.20	.60
30 Expropriate M	25.00	35.00
31 Illusion of Choice U	1.75	2.25
32 Illusionary Informant C	.15	.30
33 Jeering Homunculus C	.15	.30
34 Keeper of Keys R	1.75	3.00
35 Messenger Jays C	.15	.30
36 Skittering Crustacean C	.15	.30
37 Spire Phantasm U	.20	.60
38 Stunt Double R	5.00	6.50
39 Archdemon of Paliano R	1.50	2.50
40 Capital Punishment R	1.75	3.00
41 Custodi Lich R	3.00	5.00
42 Deadly Designs U	.75	1.15
43 Garrulous Sycophant C	.15	.30
44 Marchesas Decree U	.75	1.25
45 Regicide C	.15	.30
46 Sinuous Vermin C	.15	.30
47 Smuggler Captain U	.20	.60
48 Thorn of the Black Rose C	.15	.30
49 Besmirch U	.50	.75
50 Crown Hunter Hireling C	.15	.30
51 Deputized Protester C	.15	.30
52 Garbage Fire C	.15	.30
53 Goblin Racketeer C	.15	.30
54 Grenzo Havoc Raiser R	12.00	16.00
55 Grenzos Ruffians U	1.75	2.15
56 Pyretic Hunter U	.20	.60
57 Skyline Despot R	2.00	3.00
58 Subterranean Tremors M	12.00	18.00
59 Volatile Chimera R	4.00	5.50
60 Animus of Predation U	.20	.60
61 Borderland Explorer C	.15	.30
62 Caller of the Untamed R	2.00	3.00
63 Domesticated Hydra U	1.25	1.75
64 Entourage of Trest C	.15	.30
65 Fang of the Pack U	.20	.60
66 Leovolds Operative C	.15	.30
67 Menagerie Liberator C	.15	.30
68 Orchard Elemental C	.15	.30
69 Regal Behemoth R	4.50	6.00
70 Selvala Heart of the Wilds M	35.00	50.00
71 Selvalas Stampede R	8.00	12.00
72 Splitting Slime R	2.00	3.00
73 Adriana Captain of the Guard R	5.50	7.00
74 Daretti Ingenious Iconoclast M	45.00	60.00
75 Kaya Ghost Assassin M	65.00	85.00
76 Knights of the Black Rose U	.75	1.15
77 Leovold Emissary of Trest M	60.00	75.00
78 Queen Marchesa M	60.00	75.00
79 Spy Kit U	2.00	2.50
80 Throne of the High City R	5.00	6.50
81 Affa Guard Hound U	.20	.60
82 Disenchant C	2.50	3.50
83 Doomed Traveler C	.15	.30
84 Faiths Reward R	1.25	2.00
85 Ghostly Possession C	.15	.30
86 Ghostly Prison U	8.00	12.00
87 Gleam of Resistance C	.15	.30
88 Gods Willing C	.15	.30
89 Guardian of the Gateless U	.75	1.15
90 Hall of Arrows U	.20	.60
91 Hallowed Burial R	4.50	6.00
92 Hollowhenge Spirit U	.20	.60
93 Hundred Handed One R	.40	.75
94 Kill Shot C	.15	.30
95 Pariah R	2.50	3.50
96 Raise the Alarm C	.15	.30
97 Reviving Dose C	.15	.30
98 Spirit of the Hearth R	1.50	2.50
99 Wild Griffin C	.15	.30
100 Windborne Charge U	.20	.60
101 Zealous Strike C	.15	.30
102 Bonds of Quicksilver C	.15	.30
103 Caller of Gales C	.15	.30
104 Cloaked Siren C	.15	.30
105 Covenant of Minds R	.75	1.50
106 Deceiver Exarch U	2.25	2.75
107 Desertion R	4.00	7.00
108 Dismiss U	.20	.60
109 Divination C	.15	.30
110 Fleeting Distraction C	.15	.30
111 Followed Footsteps R	3.50	5.00
112 Into the Void U	.20	.60
113 Kami of the Crescent Moon R	6.00	7.50
114 Merfolk Looter U	.20	.60
115 Merfolk Skyscout U	.20	.60
116 Mnemonic Wall C	.15	.30
117 Negate C	.15	.30
118 Omenspeaker C	.15	.30
119 Repulse C	.15	.30
120 Serum Visions U	7.00	8.50
121 Show and Tell M	50.00	60.00
122 Sphinx of Magosi R	.60	.80
123 Traumatic Visions C	.15	.30
124 Vaporkin C	.15	.30
125 Vertigo Spawn U	.20	.60
126 Absorb Vis C	.15	.30
127 Altars Reap C	.15	.30
128 Avatar of Woe M	3.50	5.00
129 Blood Toll Harpy C	.15	.30
130 Child of Night C	.15	.30
131 Death Wind C	.15	.30
132 Diabolic Tutor U	1.25	1.75
133 Festergloom C	.15	.30
134 Driver of the Dead C	.15	.30
135 Farbog Boneflinger U	.20	.60
136 Fleshbag Marauder U	2.00	2.50
137 Guul Draz Specter R	.50	.75
138 Harvester of Souls R	.75	1.25
139 Infest U	.20	.60
140 Inquisition of Kozilek R	35.00	50.00
141 Keepsake Gorgon U	.20	.60
142 Mausoleum Turnkey U	.20	.60
143 Murder C	1.25	1.50
144 Phyrexian Arena R	18.00	22.00
145 Public Execution U	.20	.60
146 Raise Dead C	.15	.30
147 Sangromancer R	2.50	3.50
148 Shambling Goblin C	.15	.30
149 Stormkirk Patrol C	.15	.30
150 Unnerve C	.15	.30
151 Burn Away U	.20	.60
152 Burning Wish R	7.00	10.00
153 Charmbreaker Devils R	.50	1.00

154 Coordinated Assault U .20 .60
155 Ember Beast C .15 .30
156 Fiery Fall C .15 .30
157 Flame Slash C .15 .30
158 Gang of Devils U .20 .60
159 Goblin Balloon Brigade C .15 .30
160 Goblin Tunneler C .15 .30
161 Gratuitous Violence R 7.00 10.00
162 Guttersnipe U .20 .60
163 Hamletback Goliath R .40 .75
164 Havengul Vampire U .20 .60
165 Hurly Burly C .15 .30
166 Ill Tempered Cyclops C .15 .30
167 Kilin Fiend C 2.50 3.50
168 Ogre Sentry C .15 .30
169 Stoneshock Giant U .20 .60
170 Sulfurous Blast U .20 .60
171 Tormenting Voice C .15 .30
172 Trumpet Blast C .15 .30
173 Twing Bolt C .15 .30
174 Beast Within U 8.00 12.00
175 Berserk M 65.00 80.00
176 Birds of Paradise R 8.00 12.00
177 Bushstrider U .20 .60
178 Burgeoning R 25.00 30.00
179 Copperhorn Scout C .15 .30
180 Explosive Vegetation U 1.50 2.25
181 Fade into Antiquity C .15 .30
182 Forgotten Ancient R 2.00 3.00
183 Irresistible Prey U .20 .60
184 Lace with Moonglove C .15 .30
185 Lay of the Land C .15 .30
186 Manaplasm U .20 .60
187 Nessian Asp U .20 .60
188 Netcaster Spider C .15 .30
189 Overrun U .20 .60
190 Plummet C .15 .30
191 Prey Upon C .15 .30
192 Ravenous Leucrocota C .15 .30
193 Stength in Numbers C .15 .30
194 Sylvan Bounty C .15 .30
195 Voyaging Satyr C .15 .30
196 Wild Pair R 1.50 2.50
197 Akroan Hoplite U .20 .60
198 Ascended Lawmage U .20 .60
199 Carnage Gladiator U .20 .60
200 Coiling Oracle U .20 .60
201 Dragonlair Spider R 2.50 3.50
202 Duskmantle Seer R 1.25 1.75
203 Gruul War Chant U .20 .60
204 Juniper Order Ranger U 1.50 2.00
205 Pharikas Mender U .20 .60
206 Shipwreck Singer U .20 .60
207 Stormchaser Chimera U .20 .60
208 Bronze Sable C .15 .30
209 Hedron Matrix R 1.00 1.50
210 Hexplate Golem C .15 .30
211 Horn of Greed R 10.00 15.00
212 Kitesail C .15 .30
213 Opaline Unicorn C .15 .30
214 Platinum Angel M 8.00 12.00
215 Psychosis Crawler R .75 1.25
216 Runed Servitor U .20 .60
217 Dread Statuary U .20 .60
218 Evolving Wilds C .15 .30
219 Exotic Orchard R 3.50 5.00
220 Rogues Passage U .20 .60
221 Shimmering Grotto U .20 .60
T1 The Monarch Token T .10 .25
222 Kaya Ghost Assassin Alt Foil M 150.00 200.00

2014 Magic The Gathering Commander

COMPLETE SET (366) 80.00 200.00
*FOIL: .75X TO 2X BASIC CARDS
RELEASED ON NOVEMBER 7, 2014
63 Adarkar Valkyrie R :W: .40 1.00
64 Afterlife U :W: .20 .50
1 Angel of the Dire Hour R :W: .40 1.00
2 Angelic Field Marshal R :W: .40 1.00
65 Armistice R :W: .40 1.00
3 Benevolent Offering R :W: .40 1.00
66 Brave the Elements U :W: .20 .50
67 Cathars' Crusade R :W: .40 1.00
68 Celestial Crusader U :W: .20 .50
4 Comeuppance R :W: .40 1.00
69 Condemn U :W: .20 .50
5 Containment Priest R :W: 8.00 20.00
70 Decree of Justice R :W: .40 1.00
6 Deploy to the Front R :W: .40 1.00
7 Fell the Mighty R :W: .40 1.00
71 Flickerwisp U :W: .20 .50
72 Geist-Honored Monk R :W: .40 1.00
73 Gift of Estates U :W: .20 .50
74 Grand Abolisher R :W: .75 2.00
8 Hallowed Spiritkeeper R :W: .40 1.00
9 Jazal Goldmane M :W: .60 1.50
75 Kemba, Kha Regent R :W: .40 1.00
76 Kor Sanctifiers C :W: .10 .25
77 Marshal's Anthem R :W: .40 1.00
78 Martial Coup R :W: .40 1.00
79 Mentor of the Meek R :W: .40 1.00
80 Midnight Haunting U :W: .20 .50
81 Mobilization R :W: .40 1.00
10A Nahiri, the Lithomancer M :W: 2.50 6.00
10B Nahiri, the Lithomancer (Oversized) M :W: .60 1.50
82 Nomads' Assembly R :W: .40 1.00
83 Oblation R :W: .40 1.00
84 Requiem Angel R :W: .40 1.00
85 Return to Dust U :W: .20 .50
86 Sacred Mesa R :W: .40 1.00
87 Serra Avatar M :W: .40 1.00
88 Silverblade Paladin R :W: .40 1.00
89 Skyhunter Skirmisher U :W: .20 .50
90 Spectral Procession U :W: .20 .50
91 Sun Titan M :W: .60 1.50
92 Sunblast Angel R :W: .40 1.00
93 True Conviction R :W: .40 1.00
94 Twilight Shepherd R :W: .40 1.00
95 White Sun's Zenith R :W: .40 1.00
96 Whitemane Lion C :W: .10 .25
97 Wing Shards U :W: .20 .50
11 AEther Gale R :B: .40 1.00
98 Azure Mage U :B: .20 .50
12 Breaching Leviathan R :B: .40 1.00
99 Brine Elemental U :B: .20 .50
100 Cackling Counterpart R :B: .40 1.00
101 Call to Mind U :B: .20 .50
102 Compulsive Research C :B: .10 .25
103 Concentrate U :B: .20 .50
104 Cyclonic Rift R :B: .40 1.00
105 Deep-Sea Kraken R :B: .40 1.00
106 Dismiss U :B: .20 .50
107 Distorting Wake R :B: .40 1.00
13 Domineering Will R :B: .40 1.00
14 Dulcet Sirens R :B: .40 1.00
108 Exclude C :B: .10 .25
109 Fathom Seer C :B: .10 .25
110 Fog Bank U :B: .20 .50
111 Fool's Demise U :B: .20 .50
112 Frost Titan M :B: .60 1.50
113 Hoverguard Sweepers R :B: .40 1.00
114 Infinite Reflection R :B: .40 1.00
15 Intellectual Offering R :B: .40 1.00
115 Into the Roil C :B: .10 .25
116 Ixidron R :B: .40 1.00
117 Lorthos, the Tidemaker M :B: .60 1.50
118 Mulldrifter C :B: .10 .25
119 Phyrexian Ingester R :B: .40 1.00
120 Pongify U :B: .20 .50
16 Reef Worm R :B: 1.50 4.00
121 Riptide Survivor U :B: .20 .50
122 Rite of Replication R :B: .50 1.25
123 Rush of Knowledge C :B: .10 .25
124 Sea Gate Oracle C :B: .10 .25
125 Shaper Parasite C :B: .10 .25
126 Sphinx of Jwar Isle R :B: .40 1.00
127 Sphinx of Magosi R :B: .40 1.00
128 Sphinx of Uthuun R :B: .40 1.00
17 Stitcher Geralf M :B: .60 1.50
18 Stormsurge Kraken R :B: .40 1.00
129 Stroke of Genius R :B: .40 1.00
19A Teferi, Temporal Archmage M :B: 2.50 6.00
19B Teferi, Temporal Archmage (Oversized) M :B: .60 1.50
130 Turn to Frog U :B: .20 .50
20 Well of Ideas R :B: .40 1.00
131 Willbender U :B: .20 .50
132 Abyssal Persecutor M :K: 1.25 3.00
133 AEther Snap R :K: .40 1.00
134 Annihilate U :K: .20 .50
135 Bad Moon R :K: .40 1.00
136 Black Sun's Zenith R :K: .40 1.00
137 Bloodgift Demon R :K: .40 1.00
138 Butcher of Malakir R :K: .40 1.00
139 Crypt Ghast R :K: .40 1.00
21 Demon of Wailing Agonies R :K: .40 1.00
140 Disciple of Bolas R :K: .40 1.00
141 Drana, Kalastria Bloodchief R :K: .40 1.00
142 Dread Return U :K: .20 .50
143 Dregs of Sorrow R :K: .40 1.00
144 Evernight Shade U :K: .20 .50
22 Flesh Carver R :K: .40 1.00
23 Ghoulcaller Gisa M :K: 1.00 2.50
145 Grave Titan M :K: 1.25 3.00
146 Gray Merchant of Asphodel C :K: .10 .25
24 Infernal Offering R :K: .40 1.00
147 Liliana's Reaver R :K: .40 1.00
148 Magus of the Coffers R :K: .40 1.00
25 Malicious Affliction R :K: 1.50 4.00
149 Morkrut Banshee U :K: .20 .50
150 Mutilate R :K: .40 1.00
151 Nantuko Shade R :K: .40 1.00
26 Necromantic Selection R :K: .40 1.00
152 Nekrataal U :K: .20 .50
27A Ob Nixilis of the Black Oath M :K: 2.50 6.00
27B Ob Nixilis of the Black Oath (Oversized) M :K: .60 1.50
28 Overseer of the Damned R :K: .40 1.00
153 Pestilence R :K: .40 1.00
154 Phyrexian Gargantua U :K: .20 .50
155 Pontiff of Blight R :K: .40 1.00
156 Profane Command R :K: .40 1.00
157 Promise of Power R :K: .40 1.00
29 Raving Dead R :K: .40 1.00
158 Read the Bones C :K: .10 .25
159 Reaper from the Abyss M :K: .60 1.50
160 Shriekmaw U :K: .20 .50
161 Sign in Blood C :K: .10 .25
162 Skeletal Scrying U :K: .20 .50
163 Skirsdag High Priest R :K: .40 1.00
30 Spoils of Blood R :K: .60 1.50
164 Sudden Spoiling R :K: .40 1.00
165 Syphon Mind C :K: .10 .25
166 Tendrils of Corruption C :K: .10 .25
167 Tragic Slip C :K: .10 .25
168 Vampire Hexmage U :K: .20 .50
169 Victimize U :K: .20 .50
31 Wake the Dead R :K: .75 2.00
170 Xathrid Demon M :K: .60 1.50
171 Beetleback Chief U :R: .20 .50
32 Bitter Feud R :R: .40 1.00
172 Blasphemous Act R :R: .40 1.00
173 Bogardan Hellkite M :R: .60 1.50
174 Chaos Warp R :R: 1.00 2.50
33A Daretti, Scrap Savant M :R: .60 1.50
33B Daretti, Scrap Savant (Oversized) M :R: .60 1.50
34 Dualcaster Mage R :R: 5.00 12.00
175 Faithless Looting C :R: .10 .25
35 Feldon of the Third Path M :R: 1.25 3.00
176 Flametongue Kavu U :R: .20 .50
177 Goblin Welder R :R: 1.00 2.50
178 Hoard-Smelter Dragon R :R: .40 1.00
36 Impact Resonance R :R: .40 1.00
37 Incite Rebellion R :R: .40 1.00
179 Ingot Chewer C :R: .10 .25
180 Magmaquake R :R: .40 1.00
38 Scrap Mastery R :R: .75 2.00
181 Spitebellows U :R: .20 .50
182 Starstorm R :R: .40 1.00
183 Tuktuk the Explorer R :R: .40 1.00
39 Tyrant's Familiar R :R: .40 1.00
40 Volcanic Offering R :R: .60 1.50
41 Warmonger Hellkite R :R: .60 1.50
184 Whipflare U :R: .20 .50
185 Word of Seizing R :R: .40 1.00
186 Beastmaster Ascension R :G: .40 1.00
187 Collective Unconscious R :G: .40 1.00
42 Creeperhulk R :G: .40 1.00
188 Desert Twister U :G: .20 .50
189 Drove of Elves U :G: .30 .75
190 Elvish Archdruid R :G: .40 1.00
191 Elvish Mystic C :G: .10 .25
192 Elvish Skysweeper C :G: .10 .25
193 Elvish Visionary C :G: .10 .25
194 Essence Warden C :G: .20 .50
195 Ezuri, Renegade Leader R :G: .40 1.00
196 Farhaven Elf C :G: .20 .50
197 Fresh Meat R :G: .40 1.00
43A Freyalise, Llanowar's Fury M :G: 3.00 8.00
43B Freyalise, Llanowar's Fury (Oversized) M :G: 1.00 2.50
44 Grave Sifter R :G: .40 1.00
198 Grim Flowering U :G: .20 .50
199 Harrow C :G: .20 .50
200 Hunting Triad U :G: .20 .50
201 Immaculate Magistrate R :G: .75 2.00
202 Imperious Perfect U :G: .75 2.00
203 Joraga Warcaller R :G: 1.25 3.00
45 Lifeblood Hydra C :G: .60 1.50
204 Llanowar Elves C :G: .10 .25
205 Lys Alana Huntmaster C :G: .10 .25
206 Masked Admirers R :G: .40 1.00
207 Overrun U :G: .20 .50
208 Overwhelming Stampede R :G: .40 1.00
209 Praetor's Counsel M :G: .60 1.50
210 Priest of Titania C :G: .75 2.00
211 Primordial Sage R :G: .40 1.00
212 Rampaging Baloths M :G: .60 1.50
213 Reclamation Sage U :G: .20 .50
46 Siege Behemoth R :G: .40 1.00
214 Silklash Spider R :G: .40 1.00
47 Song of the Dryads R :G: 1.50 4.00
215 Soul of the Harvest R :G: .40 1.00
48 Sylvan Offering R :G: .40 1.00
216 Sylvan Ranger C :G: .10 .25
217 Sylvan Safekeeper R :G: .40 1.00
218 Terastodon R :G: .40 1.00
219 Thornweald Archer C :G: .10 .25
49 Thunderfoot Baloth R :G: .75 2.00
220 Timberwatch Elf C :G: .10 .25
50 Titania, Protector of Argoth M :G: 2.00 5.00
221 Titania's Chosen U :G: .20 .50
222 Tornado Elemental R :G: .40 1.00
51 Wave of Vitriol R :G: .40 1.00
223 Wellwisher C :G: .20 .50
224 Whirlwind R :G: .40 1.00
225 Wolfbriar Elemental R :G: .40 1.00
52 Wolfcaller's Howl C :G: .10 .25
226 Wood Elves C :G: .10 .25
227 Wren's Run Packmaster R :G: .40 1.00
59 Arcane Lighthouse U :L: .60 1.50
284 Barren Moor C :L: .10 .25
286 Buried Ruin U :L: .20 .50
287 Coral Atoll U :L: .20 .50
288 Crypt of Agadeem R :L: .40 1.00
289 Crystal Vein U :L: .20 .50
290 Darksteel Citadel U :L: .20 .50
60 Flamekin Village R :L: .40 1.00
296 Forgotten Cave C :L: .10 .25
297 Gargoyle Castle R :L: .40 1.00
298 Ghost Quarter U :L: .20 .50
299 Great Furnace C :L: .10 .25
61 Myriad Landscape U :L: .30 .75
305 Oran-Rief, the Vastwood R :L: .40 1.00
307 Polluted Mire C :L: .10 .25
310 Secluded Steppe C :L: .10 .25
314 Temple of the False God U :L: .20 .50
315 Terramorphic Expanse C :L: .10 .25
316 Tranquil Thicket C :L: .10 .25
317 Zoetic Cavern U :L: .20 .50
228 Argentum Armor R :A: .40 1.00
229 Bonehoard R :A: .40 1.00
231 Bottle Gnomes U :A: .20 .50
232 Burnished Hart U :A: .20 .50
233 Caged Sun R :A: .40 1.00
234 Cathodion U :A: .20 .50
235 Charcoal Diamond U :A: .20 .50
236 Dreamstone Hedron U :A: .20 .50
237 Emerald Medallion R :A: .75 2.00
239 Everflowing Chalice U :A: .20 .50
240 Fire Diamond U :A: .20 .50
241 Ichor Wellspring C :A: .10 .25
242 Jalum Tome R :A: .40 1.00
244 Junk Diver R :A: .40 1.00
245 Lashwrithe R :A: .40 1.00
246 Liquimetal Coating U :A: .20 .50
248 Marble Diamond U :A: .20 .50
250 Mind Stone U :A: .20 .50
252 Moss Diamond U :A: .20 .50
256 Myr Sire C :A: .10 .25
258 Palladium Myr U :A: .20 .50
259 Panic Spellbomb C :A: .10 .25
260 Pearl Medallion R :A: .75 2.00
261 Pentavus R :A: .40 1.00
263 Predator, Flagship R :A: .40 1.00
265 Ruby Medallion R :A: 1.00 2.50
266 Sapphire Medallion R :A: 1.00 2.50
268 Skullclamp U :A: 1.25 3.00
269 Sky Diamond U :A: .20 .50
271 Solemn Simulacrum R :A: 1.50 4.00
273 Steel Hellkite R :A: .40 1.00
276 Sword of Vengeance R :A: .40 1.00
277 Thran Dynamo U :A: 1.00 2.50
280 Ur-Golem's Eye C :A: .10 .25
282 Worn Powerstone U :A: .20 .50
62 Artisan of Kozilek U .20 .50
53 Assault Suit U .20 .50
285 Bojuka Bog C .10 .25
230 Bosh, Iron Golem R .40 1.00
54 Commander's Sphere C .10 .25
55 Crown of Doom R .40 1.00
291 Dormant Volcano U .20 .50
292 Drifting Meadow C .10 .25
293 Emeria, the Sky Ruin R .40 1.00
238 Epochrasite U .20 .50
294 Everglades U .20 .50
295 Evolving Wilds C .10 .25
334 Forest (334) C .10 .25
335 Forest (335) C .10 .25
336 Forest (336) C .10 .25
337 Forest (337) C .10 .25
300 Haunted Fengraf C .10 .25
301 Havenwood Battleground U .20 .50
322 Island (322) C .10 .25
323 Island (323) C .10 .25
324 Island (324) C .10 .25
325 Island (325) C .10 .25
243 Jet Medallion R .75 2.00
302 Jungle Basin U .20 .50
303 Karoo U .20 .50
304 Lonely Sandbar C .10 .25
56 Loreseeker's Stone U .20 .50
247 Loxodon Warhammer R .40 1.00
249 Mask of Memory U .20 .50
57 Masterwork of Ingenuity R 1.50 4.00
251 Moonsilver Spear R .40 1.00
330 Mountain (330) C .10 .25
331 Mountain (331) C .10 .25
332 Mountain (332) C .10 .25
333 Mountain (333) C .10 .25
253 Mycosynth Wellspring C .10 .25
254 Myr Battlesphere R .40 1.00
255 Myr Retriever U .20 .50
257 Nevinyrral's Disk R .75 2.00
306 Phyrexia's Core U .20 .50
262 Pilgrim's Eye C .10 .25
318 Plains (318) C .10 .25
319 Plains (319) C .10 .25
320 Plains (320) C .10 .25
321 Plains (321) C .10 .25
264 Pristine Talisman C .10 .25
308 Reliquary Tower U .20 .50
309 Remote Isle C .10 .25
267 Seer's Sundial R .40 1.00
311 Slippery Karst C .10 .25
312 Smoldering Crater C .10 .25
270 Sol Ring U 1.25 3.00
272 Spine of Ish Sah R .40 1.00
274 Strata Scythe R .40 1.00
326 Swamp (326) C .10 .25
327 Swamp (327) C .10 .25
328 Swamp (328) C .10 .25
329 Swamp (329) C .10 .25
275 Swiftfoot Boots U .20 .50
313 Tectonic Edge U .75 2.00
278 Tormod's Crypt U .20 .50
279 Trading Post R .40 1.00
58 Unstable Obelisk U .20 .50
281 Wayfarer's Bauble C .10 .25
283 Wurmcoil Engine M 2.00 5.00
T1 Angel .10 .25
T2 Cat
T18 Ape .10 .25
T11 Zombie (Blue)
T36 Daretti Emblem .10 .25
T31 Tuktuk
T12 Demon (*/*) .10 .25
T16 Zombie (Black)
T13 Demon (5/5) .10 .25
T16 Zombie (Black)
T19 Elemental .10 .25
T21 Beast (3/3)
T22 Elephant .10 .25
T24 Elf Warrior
T23 Elf Druid .40 1.00
T20 Beast (4/4)
T8 Fish .10 .25
T11 Zombie (Blue)
T27 Gargoyle .10 .25
T24Elf Warrior
T14 Germ .10 .25
T16 Zombie (Black)
T17 Goblin .10 .25
T3 Goat
T15 Horror .10 .25
T16 Zombie (Black)
T4 Kor Soldier .10 .25
T5 Pegasus
T9 Kraken .10 .25
T11 Zombie (Blue)
T28 Myr .10 .25
T29 Pentavite
T35 Ob Nixilis Emblem .10 .25
Zombie
T6 Soldier .10 .25
T7 Spirit
T30 Stoneforged Blade .10 .25
T14 Germ
T34 Teferi Emblem .10 .25
T11 Zombie (Blue)
T25 Treefolk .10 .25
T26 Wolf
T10 Whale .10 .25
T11 Zombie (Blue)
T32 Wurm (Deathtouch) .10 .25
T3 Goat
T33 Wurm (Lifelink) .10 .25
T3 Goat

2013 Magic The Gathering Magic 2014 SDCC Black Variant

COMPLETE SET (5) 400.00 600.00
1 Ajani, Caller of the Pride M :W: 75.00 150.00
60 Jace, Memory Adept M :B: 75.00 150.00
102 Liliana of the Dark Realms M :K: 75.00 150.00
132 Chandra, Pyromaster M :R: 75.00 150.00
172 Garruk, Caller of Beasts M :G: 75.00 125.00

2014 Magic The Gathering Magic 2015 SDCC Black Variant

1 Ajani Steadfast 25.00 60.00
62 Jace, The Living Guildpact 20.00 50.00
103 Liliana Vess 25.00 60.00
134 Chandra Pyromaster 30.00 80.00
187 Nissa, Worldwaker 50.00 100.00
210 Garruk, Apex Predator 30.00 80.00
NNO Garruk's Axe NERF prop 15.00 40.00

1995 Magic The Gathering Chronicles

COMPLETE SET (125) 50.00 100.00
BOOSTER BOX (45 PACKS) 100.00 200.00
BOOSTER PACK (12 CARDS) 5.00 7.00
RELEASED ON JULY 1, 1995
1 Abu Ja'far U .50 1.00
2 Active Volcano C .15 .30
3 Akron Legionnaire U .50 10.50
4 Aladdin U .50 1.00
5 Angelic Voices U .50 1.00
6 Arcades Sabboth U 2.00 4.00
7 Arena of the Ancients U .50 1.00
8 Argothian Pixies C .15 .30
9 Ashnod's Altar C .15 .30
10 Ashnod's Transmogrant C .15 .30
11 Axelrod Gunnarson U .50 1.00
12 Ayesha Tanaka U .50 1.00
13 Azure Drake U .50 1.00
14 Banshee U .50 1.00
15 Barl's Cage U .50 1.00
16 Beasts of Bogardan U .50 1.00
17 Blood Moon U 2.00 4.00
18 Blood of the Martyr U .50 1.00
19 Bog Rats C .15 .30
20 Book of Rass U .50 1.00
21 Boomerang C .15 .30
22 Bronze Horse U .50 1.00
23 Cat Warriors C .15 .30
24 Chromium U 2.00 4.00
25 City of Brass U 4.00 8.00
26 Cocoon U .50 1.00
27 Concordant Crossroads U 2.50 5.00
28 Craw Giant U .50 1.00
29 Cuombajj Witches C .15 .30
30 Cyclone U .50 1.00
31 Dakkon Blackblade U 1.50 3.00
32 Dance of Many U .50 1.00
33 Dandân C .15 .30
34 D'Avenant Archer C .15 .30
35 Divine Offering C .15 .30
36 Emerald Dragonfly C .15 .30
37 Enchantment Alteration U .50 1.00
38 Erhnam Djinn U .50 1.00
39 Fallen Angel U .50 1.00
40 Fallen, The U .50 1.00
41 Feldon's Cane C .15 .30
42 Fire Drake U .50 1.00
43 Fishliver Oil C .15 .30
44 Flash Flood C .15 .30
45 Fountain of Youth C .15 .30
46 Gabriel Angelfire U 1.00 2.00
47 Gauntlets of Chaos U .50 1.00
48 Ghazbán Ogre C .15 .30
49 Giant Slug C .15 .30
50 Goblin Artisans U .50 1.00
51 Goblin Digging Team C .15 .30
52 Goblin Shrine C .15 .30
53 Goblins of the Flarg C .15 .30
54 Hasran Ogress C .15 .30
55 Hell's Caretaker U 2.50 5.00
56 Horn of Deafening U .50 1.00
57 Indestructible Aura C .15 .30
58 Ivory Guardians U .50 1.00
59 Jalum Tome U .50 1.00
60 Jeweled Bird U 1.00 2.00
61 Johan U .50 1.00
62 Juxtapose U .50 1.00
63 Keepers of the Faith C .15 .30
64 Kei Takahashi C .15 .30
65 Land's Edge U .50 1.00
66 Living Armor C .15 .30
67 Marhault Elsdragon C .15 .30
68 Metamorphosis C .15 .30
69 Mountain Yeti C .15 .30
70 Nebuchadnezzar U 1.00 2.00
71 Nicol Bolas U 2.00 4.00
72 Obelisk of Undoing U .50 1.00
73 Palladia-Mors U 2.00 4.00
74 Petra Sphinx U .50 1.00
75 Primordial Ooze U .15 .30
76 Puppet Master U .50 1.00
77 Rabid Wombat U .50 1.00
78 Rakalite U .50 1.00
79 Recall U .50 1.00
80 Remove Soul C .15 .30
81 Repentant Blacksmith C .15 .30
82 Revelation U .50 1.00
83 Rubinia Soulsinger U 1.00 2.00
84 Runesword C .15 .30
85 Safe Haven U 1.00 2.00
86 Scavenger Folk C .15 .30
87 Sentinel U .50 1.00
88 Serpent Generator U 1.00 2.00
89 Shield Wall U .50 1.00
90 Shimian Night Stalker U .50 1.00
91 Sivitri Scarzam C .15 .30
92 Sol'kanar the Swamp King U 1.50 3.00
93 Stangg U .50 1.00
94 Storm Seeker U .50 1.00
95 Takklemaggot U .50 1.00
96 Teleport U .50 1.00
97 Tobias Andrion C .15 .30
98 Tor Wauki C .15 .30
99 Tormod's Crypt C .30 .75
100 Transmutation C .15 .30
101 Triassic Egg U .50 1.00
102 Urza's Mine C .15 .30
103 Urza's Mine C .15 .30
104 Urza's Mine C .15 .30
105 Urza's Mine C .15 .30
106 Urza's Power Plant C .15 .30
107 Urza's Power Plant C .15 .30
108 Urza's Power Plant C .15 .30
109 Urza's Power Plant C .15 .30
110 Urza's Tower C .15 .30
111 Urza's Tower C .15 .30
112 Urza's Tower C .15 .30
113 Urza's Tower C .15 .30
114 Vaevictis Asmadi U 2.00 4.00
115 Voodoo Doll U .50 1.00
116 Wall of Heat C .15 .30
117 Wall of Opposition U .50 1.00
118 Wall of Shadows C .15 .30
119 Wall of Vapor C .15 .30
120 Wall of Wonder U .50 1.00
121 War Elephant C .15 .30
122 Witch Hunter U .50 1.00
123 Wretched, The U 1.50 3.00
124 Xira Arien U .50 1.00
125 Yawgmoth Demon U .50 1.00

2013 Magic The Gathering Modern Masters

Card	Low	High
COMPLETE SET (245)	150.00	400.00
*FOIL: .75X TO 2X BASIC CARDS		
RELEASED ON JUNE 7, 2013		
1 Adarkar Valkyrie R :W:	1.25	3.00
2 Amrou Scout C :W:	.12	.30
3 Amrou Seekers C :W:	.12	.30
4 Angel's Grace R :W:	.50	1.25
5 Auriok Salvagers R :W:	.40	1.00
6 Avian Changeling C :W:	.12	.30
7 Blinding Beam C :W:	.12	.30
8 Bound in Silence C :W:	.12	.30
9 Cenn's Enlistment C :W:	.12	.30
10 Cloudgoat Ranger U :W:	.25	.60
11 Court Homunculus C :W:	.12	.30
12 Dispeller's Capsule C :W:	.12	.30
13 Elspeth, Knight-Errant M :W:	10.00	25.00
14 Ethersworn Canonist R :W:	2.00	5.00
15 Feudkiller's Verdict U :W:	.25	.60
16 Flickerwisp U :W:	.30	.75
17 Gleam of Resistance C :W:	.12	.30
18 Hillcomber Giant C :W:	.12	.30
19 Ivory Giant C :W:	.12	.30
20 Kataki, War's Wage R :W:	1.25	3.00
21 Kithkin Greatheart C :W:	.12	.30
22 Meadowboon U :W:	.25	.60
23 Otherworldly Journey C :W:	.12	.30
24 Pallid Mycoderm C :W:	.12	.30
25 Path to Exile U :W:	2.50	6.00
26 Reveillark R :W:	1.50	4.00
27 Saltfield Recluse C :W:	.12	.30
28 Sanctum Gargoyle C :W:	.12	.30
29 Sandsower U :W:	.25	.60
30 Stir the Pride U :W:	.25	.60
31 Stonehewer Giant R :W:	1.25	3.00
32 Terashi's Grasp U :W:	.25	.60
33 Test of Faith C :W:	.12	.30
34 Veteran Armorer C :W:	.12	.30
35 Yosei, the Morning Star M :W:	2.00	5.00
36 AEthersnipe C :B:	.12	.30
37 Careful Consideration U :B:	.25	.60
38 Cryptic Command R :B:	10.00	25.00
39 Dampen Thought C :B:	.12	.30
40 Echoing Truth C :B:	.20	.50
41 Errant Ephemeron C :B:	.12	.30
42 Erratic Mutation C :B:	.12	.30
43 Esperzoa U :B:	.25	.60
44 Etherium Sculptor C :B:	.20	.50
45 Faerie Mechanist C :B:	.12	.30
46 Gifts Ungiven R :B:	2.00	5.00
47 Glen Elendra Archmage R :B:	2.00	5.00
48 Keiga, the Tide Star M :B:	1.50	4.00
49 Kira, Great Glass-Spinner R :B:	2.50	6.00
50 Latchkey Faerie C :B:	.12	.30
51 Logic Knot C :B:	.12	.30
52 Meloku the Clouded Mirror R :B:	.50	1.25
53 Mothdust Changeling C :B:	.12	.30
54 Mulldrifter U :B:	.25	.60
55 Narcomoeba U :B:	.40	1.00
56 Pact of Negation R :B:	2.50	6.00
57 Peer Through Depths C :B:	.20	.50
58 Perilous Research C :B:	.12	.30
59 Pestermite C :B:	.20	.50
60 Petals of Insight C :B:	.12	.30
61 Reach Through Mists C :B:	.12	.30
62 Riftwing Cloudskate U :B:	.25	.60
63 Scion of Oona R :B:	1.00	2.50
64 Spell Snare U :B:	1.50	4.00
65 Spellstutter Sprite C :B:	.20	.50
66 Take Possession U :B:	.25	.60
67 Thirst for Knowledge U :B:	.25	.60
68 Traumatic Visions C :B:	.12	.30
69 Vedalken Dismisser C :B:	.12	.30
70 Vendilion Clique M :B:	25.00	50.00
71 Absorb Vis C :K:	.12	.30
72 Auntie's Snitch U :K:	.25	.60
73 Blightspeaker C :K:	.12	.30
74 Bridge from Below R :K:	2.50	6.00
75 Dark Confidant M :K:	40.00	80.00
76 Death Cloud R :K:	.50	1.25
77 Death Denied C :K:	.20	.50
78 Death Rattle U :K:	.25	.60
79 Deepcavern Imp C :K:	.12	.30
80 Drag Down C :K:	.12	.30
81 Dreamspoiler Witches C :K:	.12	.30
82 Earwig Squad R :K:	.40	1.00
83 Executioner's Capsule U :K:	.25	.60
84 Extirpate R :K:	1.50	4.00
85 Facevaulter C :K:	.12	.30
86 Faerie Macabre C :K:	.20	.50
87 Festering Goblin C :K:	.12	.30
88 Horobi's Whisper U :K:	.25	.60
89 Kokusho, the Evening Star M :K:	4.00	10.00
90 Mad Auntie U :K:	.25	.60
91 Marsh Flitter U :K:	.25	.60
92 Peppersmoke C :K:	.12	.30
93 Phthisis U :K:	.25	.60
94 Rathi Trapper C :K:	.12	.30
95 Raven's Crime C :K:	.12	.30
96 Skeletal Vampire R :K:	.40	1.00
97 Slaughter Pact R :K:	.75	2.00
98 Stinkweed Imp C :K:	.12	.30
99 Street Wraith C :K:	.40	1.00
100 Syphon Life C :K:	.12	.30
101 Thieving Sprite C :K:	.12	.30
102 Tombstalker R :K:	1.00	2.50
103 Warren Pilferers C :K:	.12	.30
104 Warren Weirding C :K:	.20	.50
105 Blind-Spot Giant C :R:	.12	.30
106 Blood Moon R :R:	3.00	8.00
107 Brute Force C :R:	.12	.30
108 Countryside Crusher R :R:	.50	1.25
109 Crush Underfoot C :R:	.12	.30
110 Desperate Ritual U :R:	.25	.60
111 Dragonstorm R :R:	.50	1.25
112 Empty the Warrens C :R:	.20	.50
113 Fiery Fall C :R:	.12	.30
114 Fury Charm C :R:	.12	.30
115 Glacial Ray C :R:	.12	.30
116 Grapeshot C :R:	.20	.50
117 Greater Gargadon R :R:	.50	1.25
118 Grinning Ignus U :R:	.25	.60
119 Hammerheim Deadeye C :R:	.12	.30
120 Kiki-Jiki, Mirror Breaker M :R:	8.00	20.00
121 Lava Spike C :R:	.60	1.50
122 Mogg War Marshal C :R:	.20	.50
123 Molten Disaster R :R:	.40	1.00
124 Pardic Dragon U :R:	.25	.60
125 Pyromancer's Swath R :R:	.40	1.00
126 Rift Bolt C :R:	.50	1.25
127 Rift Elemental C :R:	.12	.30
128 Ryusei, the Falling Star M :R:	1.00	2.50
129 Shrapnel Blast U :R:	.30	.75
130 Squee, Goblin Nabob R :R:	.50	1.25
131 Stingscourger C :R:	.12	.30
132 Stinkdrinker Daredevil C :R:	.12	.30
133 Sudden Shock U :R:	.25	.60
134 Tar Pitcher U :R:	.25	.60
135 Thundercloud Shaman U :R:	.25	.60
136 Thundering Giant C :R:	.12	.30
137 Torrent of Stone C :R:	.12	.30
138 Tribal Flames U :R:	.25	.60
139 War-Spike Changeling C :R:	.12	.30
140 Citanul Woodreaders C :G:	.12	.30
141 Doubling Season R :G:	6.00	15.00
142 Durkwood Baloth C :G:	.12	.30
143 Echoing Courage C :G:	.12	.30
144 Eternal Witness U :G:	.60	1.50
145 Giant Dustwasp C :G:	.12	.30
146 Greater Mossdog C :G:	.12	.30
147 Hana Kami C :G:	.12	.30
148 Imperiosaur C :G:	.12	.30
149 Incremental Growth U :G:	.25	.60
150 Jugan, the Rising Star M :G:	1.00	2.50
151 Kodama's Reach C :G:	.20	.50
152 Krosan Grip U :G:	.40	1.00
153 Life from the Loam R :G:	1.25	3.00
154 Masked Admirers U :G:	.25	.60
155 Moldervine Cloak C :G:	.12	.30
156 Nantuko Shaman C :G:	.12	.30
157 Penumbra Spider C :G:	.12	.30
158 Reach of Branches U :G:	.25	.60
159 Riftsweeper U :G:	.25	.60
160 Rude Awakening R :G:	.40	1.00
161 Search for Tomorrow C :G:	.12	.30
162 Sporesower Thallid U :G:	.25	.60
163 Sporoloth Ancient C :G:	.12	.30
164 Summoner's Pact R :G:	2.00	5.00
165 Sylvan Bounty C :G:	.12	.30
166 Tarmogoyf M :G:	75.00	150.00
167 Thallid C :G:	.12	.30
168 Thallid Germinator C :G:	.12	.30
169 Thallid Shell-Dweller C :G:	.12	.30
170 Tooth and Nail R :G:	2.50	6.00
171 Tromp the Domains U :G:	.25	.60
172 Verdeloth the Ancient R :G:	.40	1.00
173 Walker of the Grove C :G:	.12	.30
174 Woodfall Primus R :G:	2.00	5.00
175 Electrolyze U :B/R:	.50	1.25
176 Grand Arbiter Augustin IV R :W/B:	1.50	4.00
177 Jhoira of the Ghitu R :B/R:	1.00	2.50
178 Knight of the Reliquary R :W/G:	2.50	6.00
179 Lightning Helix U :W/R:	1.50	4.00
180 Maelstrom Pulse R :K/G:	3.00	8.00
181 Mind Funeral U :B/K:	1.00	2.50
182 Progenitus M :W/B/K/R/G:	4.00	10.00
183 Sarkhan Vol M :R/G:	6.00	15.00
184 Tidehollow Sculler U :W/K:	.25	.60
185 Trygon Predator U :B/G:	.50	1.25
186 Cold-Eyed Selkie R :B/G:	.75	2.00
187 Demigod of Revenge R :K/R:	1.50	4.00
188 Divinity of Pride R :W/K:	2.00	5.00
189 Figure of Destiny R :W/R:	1.50	4.00
190 Kitchen Finks U :W/G:	2.00	5.00
191 Manamorphose U :R/G:	.75	2.00
192 Murderous Redcap U :K/R:	.30	.75
193 Oona, Queen of the Fae R :B/K:	1.00	2.50
194 Plumeveil U :W/B:	.25	.60
195 Worm Harvest U :K/G:	.25	.60
196 AEther Spellbomb C	.12	.30
197 AEther Vial R	6.00	15.00
198 Arcbound Ravager R	8.00	20.00
199 Arcbound Stinger C	.12	.30
200 Arcbound Wanderer C	.12	.30
201 Arcbound Worker C	.12	.30
202 Bonesplitter C	.20	.50
203 Chalice of the Void R	2.50	6.00
204 Engineered Explosives R	3.00	8.00
205 Epochrasite U	.25	.60
206 Etched Oracle U	.25	.60
207 Frogmite C	.20	.50
208 Lotus Bloom R	2.50	6.00
209 Myr Enforcer C	.20	.50
210 Myr Retriever U	.25	.60
211 Paradise Mantle U	.60	1.50
212 Pyrite Spellbomb C	.12	.30
213 Relic of Progenitus U	.50	1.25
214 Runed Stalactite C	.12	.30
215 Skyreach Manta C	.12	.30
216 Sword of Fire and Ice M	12.00	30.00
217 Sword of Light and Shadow M	10.00	25.00
218 Vedalken Shackles M	6.00	15.00
219 Academy Ruins R	2.00	5.00
220 Blinkmoth Nexus R	4.00	10.00
221 City of Brass R	2.00	5.00
222 Dakmor Salvage U	.25	.60
223 Glimmervoid R	4.00	10.00
224 Terramorphic Expanse C	.12	.30
225 Vivid Crag U	.25	.60
226 Vivid Creek U	.25	.60
227 Vivid Grove U	.25	.60
228 Vivid Marsh U	.25	.60
229 Vivid Meadow U	.25	.60
T1 Giant Warrior	.12	.30
T2 Kithkin Soldier	.12	.30
T3 Soldier	.60	1.50
T4 Illusion	.40	1.00
T5 Bat	.25	.60
T6 Goblin Rogue	.12	.30
T7 Spider	.12	.30
T8 Zombie	.12	.30
T9 Dragon	.40	1.00
T10 Goblin	.12	.30
T11 Elemental	.12	.30
T12 Saproling	.12	.30
T13 Treefolk Shaman	.12	.30
T14 Faerie Rogue	.12	.30
T15 Worm	.12	.30
T16 Emblem: Elspeth, Knight-Errant	3.00	8.00

2015 Magic The Gathering Modern Masters

Card	Low	High
COMPLETE SET (264)	600.00	800.00
BOOSTER BOX	240.00	250.00
BOOSTER PACK	13.00	16.00
*FOIL: .75X TO 2X BASIC CARDS		
RELEASED ON MAY 22, 2015		
1 All Is Dust R	7.00	10.00
2 Artisan of Kozilek U	.20	.35
3 Emrakul, the Aeons Torn M	30.00	35.00
4 Karn Liberated M	35.00	40.00
5 Kozilek, Butcher of Truth M	15.00	20.00
6 Ulamog, the Infinite Gyre M	12.00	15.00
7 Ulamog's Crusher C	.05	.15
8 Apostle's Blessing C :W:	.20	.35
9 Arrest C :W:	.05	.15
10 Battlegrace Angel R :W:	.40	.60
11 Celestial Purge U :W:	.15	.25
12 Conclave Phalanx C :W:	.05	.15
13 Court Homunculus C :W:	.05	.15
14 Daybreak Coronet R :W:	5.00	6.00
15 Dispatch U :W:	.40	.60
16 Elesh Norn, Grand Cenobite M :W:	15.00	18.00
17 Fortify C :W:	.05	.15
18 Hikari, Twilight Guardian U :W:	.15	.25
19 Indomitable Archangel R :W:	.40	.60
20 Iona, Shield of Emeria M :W:	6.00	7.50
21 Kami of Ancient Law C :W:	.05	.15
22 Kor Duelist U :W:	.15	.25
23 Leyline of Sanctity R :W:	10.00	13.00
24 Mighty Leap C :W:	.05	.15
25 Mirran Crusader R :W:	1.25	1.75
26 Mirror Entity R :W:	.75	1.25
27 Moonlit Strider C :W:	.05	.15
28 Myrsmith U :W:	.15	.25
29 Oblivion Ring U :W:	.30	.50
30 Otherworldly Journey C :W:	.05	.15
31 Raise the Alarm C :W:	.05	.15
32 Skyhunter Skirmisher C :W:	.05	.15
33 Spectral Procession U :W:	.25	.40
34 Sunlance C :W:	.05	.15
35 Sunspear Shikari C :W:	.05	.15
36 Taj-Nar Swordsmith U :W:	.15	.25
37 Terashi's Grasp C :W:	.05	.15
38 Waxmane Baku C :W:	.05	.15
39 Aethersnipe C :B:	.05	.15
40 Air Servant U :B:	.15	.25
41 Argent Sphinx R :B:	.15	.25
42 Cloud Elemental C :B:	.05	.15
43 Cryptic Command R :B:	18.00	21.00
44 Faerie Mechanist C :B:	.05	.15
45 Flashfreeze U :B:	.15	.25
46 Guile R :B:	.25	.40
47 Helium Squirter C :B:	.05	.15
48 Hurkyl's Recall R :B:	4.00	5.00
49 Inexorable Tide R :B:	.50	.75
50 Mana Leak C :B:	.30	.50
51 Mulldrifter U :B:	.40	.60
52 Narcolepsy C :B:	.05	.15
53 Novijen Sages U :B:	.15	.25
54 Qumulox U :B:	.15	.25
55 Remand U :B:	4.00	5.00
56 Repeal C :B:	.05	.15
57 Somber Hoverguard C :B:	.05	.15
58 Steady Progress C :B:	.05	.15
59 Stoic Rebuttal C :B:	.05	.15
60 Surrakar Spellblade R :B:	.15	.25
61 Telling Time C :B:	.05	.15
62 Tezzeret the Seeker M :B:	6.50	8.00
63 Tezzeret's Gambit U :B:	.40	.60
64 Thoughtcast C :B:	.20	.35
65 Thrummingbird C :B:	.05	.15
66 Vapor Snag C :B:	.30	.50
67 Vendilion Clique M :B:	20.00	25.00
68 Vigean Graftmage C :B:	.05	.15
69 Water Servant U :B:	.15	.25
70 Wings of Velis Vel C :B:	.05	.15
71 Bitterblossom M :K:	20.00	25.00
72 Bloodthrone Vampire C :K:	.05	.15
73 Bone Splinters C :K:	.05	.15
74 Daggerclaw Imp U :K:	.15	.25
75 Dark Confidant M :K:	33.00	38.00
76 Death Denied C :K:	.05	.15
77 Deathmark U :K:	.15	.25
78 Devouring Greed U :K:	.15	.25
79 Dismember U :K:	2.00	2.50
80 Dread Drone C :K:	.05	.15
81 Duskhunter Bat C :K:	.05	.15
82 Endrek Sahr, Master Breeder R :K:	.15	.25
83 Ghostly Changeling C :K:	.05	.15
84 Grim Affliction C :K:	.05	.15
85 Instill Infection C :K:	.05	.15
86 Midnight Banshee R :K:	.15	.25
87 Nameless Inversion C :K:	.05	.15
88 Necroskitter R :K:	.30	.50
89 Plagued Rusalka C :K:	.05	.15
90 Profane Command R :K:	.30	.50
91 Puppeteer Clique R :K:	.75	1.00
92 Reassembling Skeleton U :K:	.15	.25
93 Scavenger Drake U :K:	.15	.25
94 Scuttling Death C :K:	.05	.15
95 Shrivel C :K:	.05	.15
96 Sickle Ripper C :K:	.05	.15
97 Sign in Blood C :K:	.05	.15
98 Spread the Sickness U :K:	.15	.25
99 Surgical Extraction R :K:	5.00	6.50
100 Thief of Hope C :K:	.05	.15
101 Vampire Lacerator C :K:	.05	.15
102 Vampire Outcasts U :K:	.15	.25
103 Waking Nightmare C :K:	.05	.15
104 Banefire R :R:	.50	.75
105 Blades of Velis Vel C :R:	.05	.15
106 Blood Ogre C :R:	.05	.15
107 Bloodshot Trainee U :R:	.15	.25
108 Brute Force C :R:	.05	.15
109 Burst Lightning C :R:	.05	.15
110 Combust U :R:	.15	.25
111 Comet Storm M :R:	.60	1.00
112 Dragonsoul Knight C :R:	.05	.15
113 Goblin Fireslinger C :R:	.05	.15
114 Goblin War Paint C :R:	.05	.15
115 Gorehorn Minotaurs C :R:	.05	.15
116 Gut Shot C :R:	.20	.30
117 Hellkite Charger R :R:	.40	.60
118 Incandescent Soulstoke U :R:	.30	.50
119 Inner-Flame Igniter C :R:	.05	.15
120 Kiki-Jiki, Mirror Breaker M :R:	10.00	13.00
121 Lightning Bolt U :R:	3.00	4.00
122 Skarrgan Firebird U :R:	.15	.25
123 Smash to Smithereens C :R:	.05	.15
124 Smokebraider C :R:	.05	.15
125 Soulbright Flamekin C :R:	.05	.15
126 Spikeshot Elder R :R:	.15	.25
127 Spitebellows U :R:	.15	.25
128 Splinter Twin R :R:	2.50	3.00
129 Stormblood Berserker U :R:	.15	.25
130 Thunderblust R :R:	.30	.75
131 Tribal Flames C :R:	.05	.15
132 Viashino Slaughtermaster C :R:	.05	.15
133 Wildfire R :R:	.20	.30
134 Worldheart Phoenix U :R:	.15	.25
135 Wrap in Flames C :R:	.05	.15
136 Algae Gharial U :G:	.15	.25
137 All Suns' Dawn R :G:	.15	.25
138 Ant Queen R :G:	.30	.50
139 Aquastrand Spider C :G:	.05	.15
140 Bestial Menace U :G:	.15	.25
141 Commune with Nature C :G:	.05	.15
142 Cytoplast Root-Kin U :G:	.20	.30
143 Gnarlid Pack C :G:	.05	.15
144 Karplusan Strider U :G:	.15	.25
145 Kavu Primarch C :G:	.05	.15
146 Kozilek's Predator C :G:	.05	.15
147 Matca Rioters C :G:	.05	.15
148 Mutagenic Growth U :G:	1.00	1.50
149 Nest Invader C :G:	.05	.15
150 Noble Hierarch R :G:	58.00	65.00
151 Overwhelm U :G:	.15	.25
152 Overwhelming Stampede R :G:	.25	.40
153 Pelakka Wurm U :G:	.15	.25
154 Plummet C :G:	.05	.15
155 Primeval Titan M :G:	6.00	8.50
156 Rampant Growth C :G:	.05	.15
157 Root-Kin Ally U :G:	.15	.25
158 Scatter the Seeds C :G:	.05	.15
159 Scion of the Wild C :G:	.05	.15
160 Scute Mob R :G:	.40	.60
161 Simic Initiate C :G:	.05	.15
162 Sundering Vitae C :G:	.05	.15
163 Sylvan Bounty C :G:	.05	.15
164 Thrive C :G:	.05	.15
166 Tarmogoyf M :G:	120.00	130.00
167 Tukatongue Thallid C :G:	.05	.15
168 Vines of Vastwood C :G:	.75	1.25
169 Wolfbriar Elemental R :G:	4.00	10.00
170 Agony Warp U :M:	.15	.25
171 Apocalypse Hydra R :M:	.50	.75
172 Boros Swiftblade U :M:	.15	.25
173 Drooling Groodion U :M:	.15	.25
174 Electrolyze U :M:	.50	75.00
175 Ethercaste Knight U :M:	.15	.25
176 Ghost Council of Orzhova R :M:	.25	.40
177 Glassdust Hulk U :M:	.15	.25
178 Horde of Notions R :M:	.25	.40
179 Lorescale Coatl U :M:	.15	.25
180 Mystic Snake R :M:	.40	.60
181 Necrogenesis U :M:	.15	.25
182 Niv-Mizzet, the Firemind R :M:	1.00	1.50
183 Pillory of the Sleepless U :M:	.15	.25
184 Plaxcaster Frogling U :M:	.20	.35
185 Savage Twister U :M:	.15	.25
186 Shadowmage Infiltrator R :M:	.50	.75
187 Sigil Blessing U :M:	.15	.25
188 Vengeful Rebirth U :M:	.15	.25
189 Wrecking Ball U :M:	.15	.25
190 Ashenmoor Gouger U :M:	.15	.25
191 Creakwood Liege R :M:	2.25	3.00
192 Dimir Guildmage U :M:	.15	.25
193 Fulminator Mage R :M:	15.00	18.00
194 Hearthfire Hobgoblin U :M:	.15	.25
195 Nobilis of War R :M:	.15	.25
196 Restless Apparition U :M:	.15	.25
197 Selesnya Guildmage U :M:	.15	.25
198 Shrewd Hatchling U :M:	.15	.25
199 Swans of Bryn Argoll R :M:	.40	.60
200 Wilt-Leaf Liege R :M:	3.00	4.00
201 Alloy Myr C	.05	.15
202 Blinding Souleater C	.05	.15
203 Cathodion C	.05	.15
204 Chimeric Mass R	.15	.25
205 Copper Carapace C	.05	.15
206 Cranial Plating U	.60	1.00
207 Culling Dais U	.15	.25
208 Darksteel Axe U	.15	.25
209 Etched Champion R	2.75	3.25
210 Etched Monstrosity R	.15	.25
211 Etched Oracle U	.15	.25
212 Everflowing Chalice U	.25	.40
213 Expedition Map U	1.50	2.00
214 Flayer Husk C	.05	.15
215 Frogmite C	.05	.15
216 Glint Hawk Idol C	.05	.15
217 Gust-Skimmer C	.05	.15
218 Kitesail C	.05	.15
219 Lodestone Golem R	.40	.60
220 Lodestone Myr R	.15	.25
221 Long-Forgotten Gohei R	.15	.25
222 Mortarpod U	.15	.25
223 Mox Opal M	33.00	37.00
224 Myr Enforcer C	.05	.15
225 Precursor Golem R	.15	.25
226 Runed Servitor C	.05	.15
227 Rusted Relic C	.05	.15
228 Sickleslicer C	.05	.15
229 Skyreach Manta C	.05	.15
230 Spellskite R	20.00	23.00
231 Sphere of the Suns C	.05	.15
232 Sunforger R	.60	1.00
233 Tumble Magnet U	.15	.25
234 Wayfarer's Bauble C	.05	.15
235 Azorius Chancery U	.20	.35
236 Blinkmoth Nexus R	4.00	5.00
237 Boros Garrison U	.20	.30
238 Darksteel Citadel C	.40	.60
239 Dimir Aqueduct U	.60	1.00
240 Eldrazi Temple U	5.00	6.00
241 Evolving Wilds C	.05	.15
242 Eye of Ugin R	8.00	10.00
243 Golgari Rot Farm U	.15	.25
244 Gruul Turf U	.30	.50
245 Izzet Boilerworks U	.20	.30
246 Orzhov Basilica U	.25	.40
247 Rakdos Carnarium U	.20	.30
248 Selesnya Sanctuary U	.20	.30
249 Simic Growth Chamber U	.50	.75
T1 Eldrazi Spawn Token (Briclot)	.05	.15
T2 Eldrazi Spawn Token (Tedin)	.05	.15
T3 Eldrazi Spawn Token (Meignaud)	.05	.15
T4 Soldier Token :W:	.05	.15
T5 Spirit Token :W:	.05	.15
T6 Faerie Rogue Token :K:	.30	.50
T7 Germ Token :K:	.05	.15
T8 Thrull Token :K:	.05	.15
T9 Elephant Token :G:	.05	.15
T10 Insect Token :G:	.15	.25
T11 Saproling Token :G:	.05	.15
T12 Snake Token :G:	.05	.15
T13 Wolf Token :G:	.05	.15
T14 Worm Token :G:	.20	.30
T15 Golem Token	.05	.15
T16 Myr Token	.20	.35

2016 Magic The Gathering Eternal Masters

Card	Low	High
COMPLETE SET (249 CARDS)	600.00	700.00
BOOSTER BOX (24 PACKS)	260.00	300.00
BOOSTER PACK (15 CARDS)	10.00	15.00
*FOIL: 2X TO 2X BASIC CARDS		
RELEASED ON JUNE 10, 2016		
1 Aven Riftwatcher C	.05	.15
2 Balance MR	2.00	2.75
3 Ballynock Cohort C	.05	.15
4 Benevolent Bodyguard C	.05	.15
5 Calciderm U	.10	.20
6 Coalition Honor Guard C	.05	.15
7 Eight and a Half Tails R	1.25	1.75
8 Elite Vanguard C	.05	.15
9 Enlightened Tutor R	8.00	10.00
10 Faiths Fetters U	.10	.20
11 Field of Souls U	.10	.20
12 Glimmerpoint Stag U	.10	.20
13 Honden of Cleansing Fire U	.10	.20
14 Humble C	.05	.15
15 Intangible Virtue U	.20	.35
16 Jareth, Leonine Titan R	.30	.50
17 Karmic Guide R	1.75	2.25
18 Kor Hookmaster C	.05	.15
19 Mesa Enchantress U	.15	.25
20 Mistral Charger C	.05	.15
21 Monk Idealist C	.05	.15
22 Mother of Runes R	2.25	3.00
23 Pacifism C	.05	.15
24 Raise the Alarm C	.05	.15
25 Rally the Peasants C	.05	.15
26 Seal of Cleansing C	.05	.15
27 Second Thoughts C	.05	.15
28 Serra Angel U	.10	.20
29 Shelter C	.05	.15
30 Soulcatcher U	.10	.20
31 Squadron Hawk C	.20	.35
32 Swords to Plowshares U	2.00	2.25
33 Unexpectedly Absent R	.40	.75
34 Wall of Omens U	2.00	2.50
35 War Priest of Thune U	.10	.20
36 Welkin Guide C	.05	.15
37 Whitemane Lion C	.05	.15
38 Wrath of God R	4.00	4.50
39 Arcanis the Omnipotent R	1.00	1.50
40 Brainstorm U	.75	1.00
41 Cephalid Sage C	.05	.15
42 Control Magic R	.75	1.00
43 Counterspell C	1.25	1.75
44 Daze U	1.75	2.00
45 Deep Analysis C	.05	.15
46 Diminishing Returns R	.30	.50
47 Dream Twist C	.05	.15
48 Fact or Fiction U	.30	.50
49 Force of Will MR	80.00	95.00
50 Future Sight R	.40	.60
51 Gaseous Form C	.05	.15
52 Giant Tortoise C	.05	.15
53 Glacial Wall C	.05	.15
54 Honden of Seeing Winds U	.10	.20
55 Hydroblast U	.75	1.00
56 Inkwell Leviathan R	.40	.60
57 Jace, the Mind Sculptor MR	50.00	55.00
58 Jetting Glasskite U	.10	.20
59 Man O' War C	.05	.15
60 Memory Lapse C	.05	.15
61 Merfolk Looter U	.10	.20
62 Mystical Tutor R	5.25	6.00
63 Oonas Grace C	.05	.15
64 Peregrine Drake C	.50	.75
65 Phantom Master C	.05	.15
66 Phyrexian Ingester U	.10	.20
67 Prodigal Sorcerer U	.10	.20
68 Quiet Speculation U	.10	.20
69 Screeching Skaab C	.05	.15
70 Serendib Efreet R	.40	.60
71 Shoreline Ranger C	.05	.15
72 Silent Departure C	.05	.15

Card	Low	High
73 Sprite Noble U	.10	.20
74 Stupefying Touch C	.05	.15
75 Tidal Wave C	.05	.15
76 Warden of Evos Isle C	.05	.15
77 Wonder U	.15	.25
78 Animate Dead U	1.25	1.75
79 Annihilate U	.10	.20
80 Blightsoil Druid C	.05	.15
81 Blood Artist U	1.25	1.75
82 Braids, Cabal Minion R	.60	.80
83 Cabal Therapy U	3.00	3.75
84 Carrion Feeder C	.10	.20
85 Deadbridge Shaman C	.05	.15
86 Duress C	.10	.20
87 Entomb R	10.00	12.00
88 Eyeblights Ending C	.05	.15
89 Gravedigger C	.05	.15
90 Havoc Demon U	.10	.20
91 Honden of Nights Reach U	.10	.20
92 Hymn to Tourach U	1.00	1.50
93 Ichorid R	2.00	2.25
94 Innocent Blood C	.20	.30
95 Lys Alana Scarblade U	.10	.20
96 Malicious Affliction R	.75	1.00
97 Nausea C	.05	.15
98 Necropotence MR	6.00	8.00
99 Nekrataal U	.10	.20
100 Nights Whisper C	.40	.60
101 Phyrexian Gargantua U	.10	.20
102 Phyrexian Rager C	.05	.15
103 Plague Witch C	.05	.15
104 Prowling Pangolin C	.05	.15
105 Sengir Autocrat U	.10	.20
106 Sinkhole R	6.00	8.00
107 Skulking Ghost C	.05	.15
108 Toxic Deluge R	5.00	5.50
109 Tragic Slip C	.05	.15
110 Twisted Abomination C	.05	.15
111 Urborg Uprising C	.05	.15
112 Vampiric Tutor MR	25.00	30.00
113 Victimize U	.20	.35
114 Visara the Dreadful R	1.00	1.25
115 Wake of Vultures C	.05	.15
116 Wakedancer C	.05	.15
117 Avarax C	.05	.15
118 Battle Squadron U	.10	.20
119 Beetleback Chief U	.10	.20
120 Borderland Marauder C	.05	.15
121 Burning Vengeance U	.10	.20
122 Carbonize C	.05	.15
123 Chain Lightning U	3.25	4.00
124 Crater Hellion R	.15	.25
125 Desperate Ravings C	.05	.15
126 Dragon Egg C	.05	.15
127 Dualcaster Mage R	.60	.80
128 Faithless Looting C	.20	.35
129 Fervent Cathar C	.05	.15
130 Firebolt C	.10	.20
131 Flame Jab U	.10	.20
132 Gamble R	7.00	9.00
133 Ghitu Slinger U	.10	.20
134 Honden of Infinite Rage U	.10	.20
135 Keldon Champion U	.10	.20
136 Keldon Marauders C	.05	.15
137 Kird Ape C	.25	.40
138 Mogg Fanatic C	.05	.15
139 Mogg War Marshal C	.30	.50
140 Orcish Oriflamme C	.05	.15
141 Price of Progress U	1.75	2.15
142 Pyroblast U	1.75	2.00
143 Pyrokinesis R	.30	.50
144 Reckless Charge C	.05	.15
145 Rorix Bladewing R	.30	.50
146 Seismic Stomp C	.05	.15
147 Siege Gang Commander R	1.00	1.50
148 Sneak Attack MR	20.00	22.00
149 Stingscourger C	.05	.15
150 Sulfuric Vortex R	.40	.60
151 Tooth and Claw U	.10	.20
152 Undying Rage C	.05	.15
153 Wildfire Emissary C	.05	.15
154 Worldgorger Dragon MR	1.00	1.25
155 Young Pyromancer U	1.25	1.75
156 Abundant Growth C	.10	.20
157 Ancestral Mask U	.50	.75
158 Argothian Enchantress MR	5.00	6.00
159 Brawn U	.30	.50
160 Centaur Chieftain U	.10	.20
161 Civic Wayfinder C	.05	.15
162 Commune with the Gods C	.05	.15
163 Elephant Guide C	.05	.15
164 Elvish Vanguard C	.25	.40
165 Emperor Crocodile C	.05	.15
166 Flinthoof Boar U	.10	.20
167 Fog C	.05	.15
168 Gaes Blessing U	.20	.30
169 Green Suns Zenith R	5.00	5.75
170 Harmonize U	1.00	1.25
171 Heritage Druid R	5.25	6.00
172 Honden of Lifes Web U	.10	.20
173 Imperious Perfect R	1.50	2.00
174 Invigorate U	.50	.75
175 Llanowar Elves C	.10	.20
176 Lys Alana Huntmaster C	.05	.15
177 Natuarl Order MR	15.00	18.00
178 Natures Claim C	.30	.50
179 Nimble Mongoose C	.20	.35
180 Rancor U	2.00	2.25
181 Regal Force R	3.00	3.75
182 Roar of the Wurm U	.10	.20
183 Roots C	.05	.15
184 Seal of Strenght C	.05	.15
185 Sentinel Spider C	.05	.15
186 Silvos, Rogue Elemental R	.40	.60
187 Sylvan Library R	15.00	17.00
188 Sylvan Might C	.05	.15
189 Thornweald Archer C	.05	.15
190 Timberwatch Elf U	.25	.40
191 Werebear C	.05	.15
192 Wirewood Symbiote U	.75	1.00
193 Xantid Swarm R	.75	1.15
194 Yavimaya Enchantress C	.05	.15
195 Armadillo Cloak U	.40	.60
196 Baleful Strix R	4.00	4.50
197 Bloodbraid Elf U	2.25	2.75
198 Brago, King Eternal R	.75	1.00
199 Dack Fayden MR	15.00	18.00
200 Extract from Darkness U	.10	.20
201 Flame Kin Zealot U	.10	.20
202 Glare of Subdual R	.30	.50
203 Goblin Trenches R	.20	.30
204 Maelstrom Wanderer MR	8.00	10.00
205 Shaman of the Pack U	.15	.25
206 Shardless Agent R	5.00	6.00
207 Sphinx of the Steel Wind MR	1.00	1.25
208 Thunderclap Wyvern U	.10	.20
209 Trygon Predator U	.25	.40
210 Vindicate R	5.50	6.50
211 Void R	.30	.50
212 Wee Dragonauts U	.10	.20
213 Zealous Persecution U	.30	.50
214 Call the Skybreaker R	.15	.25
215 Deathrite Shaman R	4.00	4.50
216 Giant Solifuge R	.25	.35
217 Torrent of Souls U	.10	.20
218 Ashnods Altar U	1.75	2.15
219 Chrome Mox MR	12.00	15.00
220 Duplicant R	4.00	4.50
221 Emmessi Tome U	.10	.20
222 Goblin Charbelcher R	1.60	2.00
223 Isochron Scepter R	3.00	3.50
224 Juggernaut U	.10	.20
225 Mana Crypt MR	60.00	70.00
226 Millikin U	.10	.20
227 Mindless Automaton U	.10	.20
228 Nevinyrrals Disk R	1.00	1.50
229 Pilgrims Eye C	.05	.15
230 Prismatic Lens U	.15	.25
231 Relic of Progenitus U	1.50	2.00
232 Senseis Divining Top R	15.00	18.00
233 Ticking Gnomes U	.10	.20
234 Winter Orb R	3.50	4.50
235 Worn Powerstone U	.50	.75
236 Bloodfell Caves C	.05	.15
237 Blossoming Sands C	.05	.15
238 Dismal Backwater C	.05	.15
239 Jungle Hollow C	.05	.15
240 Karakas MR	50.00	55.00
241 Maze of Ith R	8.00	10.00
242 Mishras Factory U	.75	1.15
243 Rugged Highlands C	.05	.15
244 Scoured Barrens C	.05	.15
245 Swiftwater Cliffs C	.05	.15
246 Thornwood Falls C	.05	.15
247 Tranquil Cove C	.05	.15
248 Wasteland R	35.00	40.00
249 Wind Scarred Crag C	.05	.15

2016 Magic The Gathering Eternal Masters Foil

Card	Low	High
COMPLETE SET (249 CARDS)	2000.00	4000.00
BOOSTER BOX (24 PACKS)	240.00	300.00
BOOSTER PACK (15 CARDS)	6.00	15.00

*FOIL: X TO X BASIC CARDS
RELEASED ON JUNE 10, 2016

Card	Low	High
1 Aven Riftwatcher C	.30	.75
2 Balance MR	8.00	20.00
3 Ballynock Cohort C	.30	.75
4 Benevolent Bodyguard C	.30	.75
5 Calciderm U	.60	1.50
6 Coalition Honor Guard C	.30	.75
7 Eight and a Half Tails R	5.00	12.00
8 Elite Vanguard C	.30	.75
9 Enlightened Tutor R	30.00	60.00
10 Faiths Fetters U	.60	1.50
11 Field of Souls U	.60	1.50
12 Glimmerpoint Stag U	.60	1.50
13 Honden of Cleansing Fire U	.60	1.50
14 Humble C	.30	.75
15 Intangible Virtue U	1.25	3.00
16 Jareth, Leonine Titan R	3.00	8.00
17 Karmic Guide R	8.00	20.00
18 Kor Hookmaster C	.30	.75
19 Mesa Enchantress U	.60	1.50
20 Mistral Charger C	.30	.75
21 Monk Idealist C	.30	.75
22 Mother of Runes R	15.00	30.00
23 Pacifism C	.30	.75
24 Raise the Alarm C	.30	.75
25 Rally the Peasants C	.30	.75
26 Seal of Cleansing C	.30	.75
27 Second Thoughts C	.30	.75
28 Serra Angel U	.60	1.50
29 Shelter C	.30	.75
30 Soulcatcher U	.60	1.50
31 Squadron Hawk C	.30	.75
32 Swords to Plowshares U	4.00	10.00
33 Unexpectedly Absent R	10.00	25.00
34 Wall of Omens U	3.00	8.00
35 War Priest of Thune U	.60	1.50
36 Welkin Guide C	.30	.75
37 Whitemane Lion C	.30	.75
38 Wrath of God R	8.00	20.00
39 Arcanis the Omnipotent R	2.00	5.00
40 Brainstorm U	25.00	50.00
41 Cephalid Sage C	.30	.75
42 Control Magic R	8.00	20.00
43 Counterspell C	6.00	15.00
44 Daze U	20.00	40.00
45 Deep Analysis C	1.25	3.00
46 Diminishing Returns R	8.00	20.00
47 Dream Twist C	.30	.75
48 Fact or Fiction U	1.50	4.00
49 Force of Will MR	350.00	550.00
50 Future Sight R	4.00	10.00
51 Gaseous Form C	.30	.75
52 Giant Tortoise C	.30	.75
53 Glacial Wall C	.30	.75
54 Honden of Seeing Winds U	.60	1.50
55 Hydroblast U	8.00	20.00
56 Inkwell Leviathan R	2.00	5.00
57 Jace, the Mind Sculptor MR	150.00	250.00
58 Jetting Glasskite U	.60	1.50
59 Man O War C	1.50	4.00
60 Memory Lapse C	.30	.75
61 Merfolk Looter U	.60	1.50
62 Mystical Tutor R	20.00	40.00
63 Oonas Grace C	.30	.75
64 Peregrine Drake C	3.00	8.00
65 Phantom Master C	.30	.75
66 Phyrexian Ingester U	.60	1.50
67 Prodigal Sorcerer U	.60	1.50
68 Quiet Speculation U	.60	1.50
69 Screeching Skaab C	.30	.75
70 Serendib Efreet R	5.00	12.00
71 Shoreline Ranger C	.30	.75
72 Silent Departure C	.30	.75
73 Sprite Noble U	.60	1.50
74 Stupefying Touch C	.30	.75
75 Tidal Wave C	.30	.75
76 Warden of Evos Isle C	.30	.75
77 Wonder U	.60	1.50
78 Animate Dead U	3.00	8.00
79 Annihilate U	.60	1.50
80 Blightsoil Druid C	.30	.75
81 Blood Artist U	2.50	6.00
82 Braids, Cabal Minion R	6.00	15.00
83 Cabal Therapy U	5.00	12.00
84 Carrion Feeder C	1.25	3.00
85 Deadbridge Shaman C	.30	.75
86 Duress C	.30	.75
87 Entomb R	15.00	40.00
88 Eyeblights Ending C	.30	.75
89 Gravedigger C	.30	.75
90 Havoc Demon U	.60	1.50
91 Honden of Nights Reach U	.60	1.50
92 Hymn to Tourach U	5.00	12.00
93 Ichorid R	8.00	20.00
94 Innocent Blood C	2.50	6.00
95 Lys Alana Scarblade U	.60	1.50
96 Malicious Affliction R	6.00	15.00
97 Nausea C	.30	.75
98 Necropotence MR	8.00	20.00
99 Nekrataal U	.60	1.50
100 Nights Whisper C	2.50	6.00
101 Phyrexian Gargantua U	.60	1.50
102 Phyrexian Rager C	.30	.75
103 Plague Witch C	.30	.75
104 Prowling Pangolin C	.30	.75
105 Sengir Autocrat U	.60	1.50
106 Sinkhole R	20.00	40.00
107 Skulking Ghost C	.30	.75
108 Toxic Deluge R	30.00	60.00
109 Tragic Slip C	.30	.75
110 Twisted Abomination C	.30	.75
111 Urborg Uprising C	.30	.75
112 Vampiric Tutor MR	70.00	110.00
113 Victimize U	2.50	6.00
114 Visara the Dreadful R	2.00	5.00
115 Wake of Vultures C	.30	.75
116 Wakedancer C	.30	.75
117 Avarax C	.30	.75
118 Battle Squadron U	.60	1.50
119 Beetleback Chief U	2.50	6.00
120 Borderland Marauder C	.30	.75
121 Burning Vengeance U	.60	1.50
122 Carbonize C	.30	.75
123 Chain Lightning U	5.00	12.00
124 Crater Hellion R	.75	2.00
125 Desperate Ravings C	.30	.75
126 Dragon Egg C	.30	.75
127 Dualcaster Mage R	5.00	12.00
128 Faithless Looting C	.30	.75
129 Fervent Cathar C	.30	.75
130 Firebolt C	.30	.75
131 Flame Jab U	.60	1.50
132 Gamble R	40.00	80.00
133 Ghitu Slinger U	.60	1.50
134 Honden of Infinite Rage U	.60	1.50
135 Keldon Champion U	.60	1.50
136 Keldon Marauders C	.60	1.50
137 Kird Ape C	2.00	5.00
138 Mogg Fanatic C	.30	.75
139 Mogg War Marshal C	.30	.75
140 Orcish Oriflamme C	.30	.75
141 Price of Progress U	4.00	10.00
142 Pyroblast U	30.00	60.00
143 Pyrokinesis R	6.00	15.00
144 Reckless Charge C	.30	.75
145 Rorix Bladewing R	2.50	6.00
146 Seismic Stomp C	.30	.75
147 Siege Gang Commander R	2.50	6.00
148 Sneak Attack MR	30.00	60.00
149 Stingscourger C	.30	.75
150 Sulfuric Vortex R	3.00	8.00
151 Tooth and Claw U	.60	1.50
152 Undying Rage C	.30	.75
153 Wildfire Emissary C	.30	.75
154 Worldgorger Dragon MR	8.00	20.00
155 Young Pyromancer U	10.00	25.00
156 Abundant Growth C	.30	.75
157 Ancestral Mask U	2.50	6.00
158 Argothian Enchantress MR	20.00	40.00
159 Brawn U	1.50	4.00
160 Centaur Chieftain U	.60	1.50
161 Civic Wayfinder C	.30	.75
162 Commune with the Gods C	.30	.75
163 Elephant Guide C	.30	.75
164 Elvish Vanguard C	.75	2.00
165 Emperor Crocodile C	.50	1.25
166 Flinthoof Boar U	.60	1.50
167 Fog C	.30	.75
168 Gaes Blessing U	2.50	6.00
169 Green Suns Zenith R	6.00	15.00
170 Harmonize U	3.00	8.00
171 Heritage Druid R	8.00	20.00
172 Honden of Lifes Web U	.60	1.50
173 Imperious Perfect R	3.00	8.00
174 Invigorate U	4.00	10.00
175 Llanowar Elves C	.30	.75
176 Lys Alana Huntmaster C	.30	.75
177 Natuarl Order MR	50.00	80.00
178 Natures Claim C	1.50	4.00
179 Nimble Mongoose C	4.00	10.00
180 Rancor U	2.00	5.00
181 Regal Force R	8.00	20.00
182 Roar of the Wurm U	.60	1.50
183 Roots C	.30	.75
184 Seal of Strenght C	.30	.75
185 Sentinel Spider C	.30	.75
186 Silvos, Rogue Elemental R	2.50	6.00
187 Sylvan Library R	40.00	80.00
188 Sylvan Might C	.30	.75
189 Thornweald Archer C	.30	.75
190 Timberwatch Elf U	.60	1.50
191 Werebear C	.30	.75
192 Wirewood Symbiote U	4.00	10.00
193 Xantid Swarm R	4.00	10.00
194 Yavimaya Enchantress C	.30	.75
195 Armadillo Cloak U	1.50	4.00
196 Baleful Strix R	40.00	80.00
197 Bloodbraid Elf U	3.00	8.00
198 Brago, King Eternal R	4.00	10.00
199 Dack Fayden MR	100.00	150.00
200 Extract from Darkness U	.60	1.50
201 Flame Kin Zealot U	.60	1.50
202 Glare of Subdual R	1.50	4.00
203 Goblin Trenches R	2.50	6.00
204 Maelstrom Wanderer MR	20.00	40.00
205 Shaman of the Pack U	.60	1.50
206 Shardless Agent R	30.00	60.00
207 Sphinx of the Steel Wind MR	3.00	8.00
208 Thunderclap Wyvern U	.60	1.50
209 Trygon Predator U	.75	2.00
210 Vindicate R	8.00	20.00
211 Void R	7.50	4.00
212 Wee Dragonauts U	.60	1.50
213 Zealous Persecution U	2.00	5.00
214 Call the Skybreaker R	.75	2.00
215 Deathrite Shaman R	20.00	50.00
216 Giant Solifuge R	1.25	3.00
217 Torrent of Souls U	.60	1.50
218 Ashnods Altar U	10.00	25.00
219 Chrome Mox MR	30.00	60.00
220 Duplicant R	6.00	15.00
221 Emmessi Tome U	.60	1.50
222 Goblin Charbelcher R	6.00	15.00
223 Isochron Scepter R	4.00	10.00
224 Juggernaut U	.60	1.50
225 Mana Crypt MR	140.00	200.00
226 Millikin U	.60	1.50
227 Mindless Automaton U	.60	1.50
228 Nevinyrrals Disk R	3.00	8.00
229 Pilgrims Eye C	.30	.75
230 Prismatic Lens U	.60	1.50
231 Relic of Progenitus U	3.00	8.00
232 Senseis Divining Top R	50.00	80.00
233 Ticking Gnomes U	.60	1.50
234 Winter Orb R	20.00	45.00
235 Worn Powerstone U	8.00	20.00
236 Bloodfell Caves C	.30	.75
237 Blossoming Sands C	.30	.75
238 Dismal Backwater C	.30	.75
239 Jungle Hollow C	.30	.75
240 Karakas MR	115.00	150.00
241 Maze of Ith R	20.00	50.00
242 Mishras Factory U	8.00	20.00
243 Rugged Highlands C	.30	.75
244 Scoured Barrens C	.30	.75
245 Swiftwater Cliffs C	.30	.75
246 Thornwood Falls C	.30	.75
247 Tranquil Cove C	.30	.75
248 Wasteland R	70.00	110.00
249 Wind Scarred Crag C	.30	.75

2015 Magic The Gathering Origins

Card	Low	High
COMPLETE SET (293)	110.00	170.00
BOOSTER BOX (36 PACKS)	100.00	120.00
BOOSTER PACK (15 CARDS)	3.00	5.00

*FOIL: .75X TO 2X BASIC CARDS
RELEASED ON JULY 17, 2015

Card	Low	High
1 Akroan Jailer C :W:	.05	.15
2 Ampryn Tactician C :W:	.05	.15
3 Anointer of Champions U :W:	.05	.15
4 Archangel of Tithes M :W:	3.00	3.50
5 Auramancer C :W:	.05	.15
6 Aven Battle Priest C :W:	.05	.15
7 Blessed Spirits U :W:	.05	.15
8 Celestial Flare C :W:	.05	.15
9 Charging Griffin C :W:	.05	.15
10 Cleric of the Forward Order C :W:	.05	.15
11 Consul's Lieutenant U :W:	.05	.15
12 Enlightened Ascetic C :W:	.05	.15
13 Enshrouding Mist C :W:	.05	.15
15 Grasp of the Hieromancer C :W:	.05	.15
16 Hallowed Moonlight R :W:	.75	1.15
17 Healing Hands C :W:	.05	.15
18 Heavy Infantry C :W:	.05	.15
19 Hixus, Prison Warden R :W:	.05	.15
20 Knight of the Pilgrim's Road C :W:	.05	.15
21 Knight of the White Orchid R :W:	1.50	2.00
22 Knightly Valor U :W:	.05	.15
23 Kytheon, Hero of Akros M :W:	4.50	6.00
23 Gideon, Battle-Forged M	4.50	6.00
25 Kytheon's Irregulars R :W:	.05	.15
26 Mighty Leap C :W:	.05	.15
27 Murder Investigation U :W:	.05	.15
28 Patron of the Valiant U :W:	.05	.15
29 Relic Seeker R :W:	.15	.25
30 Sentinel of the Eternal Watch U :W:	.05	.15
31 Sigil of the Empty Throne R :W:	.20	.30
32 Stalwart Aven C :W:	.05	.15
33 Starfield of Nyx M :W:	1.75	2.25
34 Suppression Bonds C :W:	.05	.15
35 Swift Reckoning U :W:	.05	.15
36 Topan Freeblade C :W:	.05	.15
37 Totem-Guide Hartebeest U :W:	.05	.15
38 Tragic Arrogance R :W:	.50	.80
39 Valor in Akros U :W:	.05	.15
40 Vryn Wingmare R :W:	.20	.35
41 War Oracle U :W:	.05	.15
42 Yoked Ox C :W:	.05	.15
43 Alhammarret's Archive M	2.50	6.00
44 Anchor to the Æther U :B:	.05	.15
45 Artificer's Epiphany C :B:	.05	.15
46 Aspiring Aeronaut C :B:	.05	.15
47 Bone to Ash C :B:	.05	.15
48 Calculated Dismissal C :B:	.05	.15
49 Clash of Wills U :B:	.60	1.00
50 Claustrophobia C :B:	.05	.15
51 Day's Undoing M :B:	3.50	4.50
52 Deep-Sea Terror C :B:	.05	.15
53 Disciple of the Ring M :B:	.40	.60
54 Disperse C :B:	.05	.15
55 Displacement Wave R :B:	.15	.25
56 Dreadwaters C :B:	.05	.15
57 Faerie Miscreant C :B:	.05	.15
58 Harbinger of the Tides R :B:	.75	1.00
59 Hydrolash U :B:	.05	.15
61 Jace's Sanctum R :B:	.50	.75
62 Jhessian Thief U :B:	.05	.15
63 Maritime Guard C :B:	.05	.15
64 Mizzium Meddler R :B:	.05	.15
65 Negate C :B:	.05	.15
66 Nivix Barrier C :B:	.05	.15
67 Psychic Rebuttal U :B:	.05	.15
68 Ringwarden Owl C :B:	.05	.15
69 Scrapskin Drake C :B:	.05	.15
70 Screeching Skaab C :B:	.05	.15
71 Send to Sleep C :B:	.05	.15
72 Separatist Voidmage C :B:	.05	.15
73 Sigiled Starfish U :B:	.05	.15
74 Skaab Goliath U :B:	.05	.15
75 Soulblade Djinn R :B:	.05	.15
76 Sphinx's Tutelage U :B:	1.50	2.00
77 Stratus Walk C :B:	.05	.15
78 Talent of the Telepath R :B:	.30	.50
79 Thopter Spy Network R :B:	.40	.60
80 Tower Geist U :B:	.05	.15
81 Turn to Frog U :B:	.05	.15
82 Watercourser C :B:	.05	.15
83 Whirler Rogue U :B:	.25	.40
84 Willbreaker R :B:	.20	.30
85 Blightcaster U :K:	.05	.15
86 Catacomb Slug C :K:	.05	.15
87 Consecrated by Blood U :K:	.05	.15
88 Cruel Revival U :K:	.05	.15
89 Dark Dabbling C :K:	.05	.15
90 Dark Petition R :K:	1.25	1.75
91 Deadbridge Shaman C :K:	.05	.15
92 Demonic Pact M :K:	2.00	2.75
93 Despoiler of Souls R :K:	.05	.60
94 Erebos's Titan M :K:	.50	.75
95 Eyeblight Assassin C :K:	.05	.15
96 Eyeblight Massacre U :K:	.05	.15
97 Fetid Imp C :K:	.05	.15
98 Fleshbag Marauder U :K:	.20	.30
99 Gilt-Leaf Winnower R :K:	.15	.25
100 Gnarlroot Trapper U :K:	.05	.15
101 Graveblade Marauder R :K:	.15	.25
102 Infernal Scarring C :K:	.05	.15
103 Infinite Obliteration R :K:	.75	1.00
104 Kothophed, Soul Hoarder R :K:	.05	.15
105 Languish R :K:	2.00	3.50
106 Macabre Waltz C :K:	.05	.15
107 Malakir Cullblade U :K:	.05	.15
108 Nantuko Husk C :K:	.05	.15
109 Necromantic Summons U :K:	.05	.15
110 Necromantic Summons U :K:	.05	.15
111 Nightsnare C :K:	.05	.15
112 Priest of the Blood Rite R :K:	.10	.20
113 Rabid Bloodsucker C :K:	.05	.15
114 Read the Bones C :K:	.05	.15
115 Reave Soul C :K:	.05	.15
116 Returned Centaur C :K:	.05	.15
117 Revenant U :K:	.05	.15
118 Shadows of the Past U :K:	.05	.15
119 Shambling Ghoul C :K:	.05	.15
120 Tainted Remedy R :K:	.40	.60
121 Thornbow Archer C :K:	.05	.15
122 Tormented Thoughts U :K:	.05	.15
123 Touch of Moonglove C :K:	.05	.15
124 Undead Servant C :K:	.05	.15
125 Unholy Hunger C :K:	.05	.15
126 Weight of the Underworld C :K:	.05	.15
127 Abbot of Keral Keep R :R:	1.00	1.50
128 Acolyte of the Inferno U :R:	.05	.15
129 Act of Treason C :R:	.05	.15
130 Akroan Sergeant C :R:	.05	.15
131 Avaricious Dragon M :R:	.75	1.00
132 Bellows Lizard C :R:	.05	.15
133 Boggart Brute C :R:	.05	.15
134 Call of the Full Moon U :R:	.05	.15
136 Chandra's Fury C :R:	.05	.15
137 Chandra's Ignition R :R:	.20	.30
138 Cobblebrute C :R:	.05	.15
139 Demolish C :R:	.05	.15
140 Dragon Fodder C :R:	.05	.15
141 Embermaw Hellion R :R:	.05	.15
142 Enthralling Victor U :R:	.05	.15
143 Exquisite Firecraft R :R:	1.75	2.25
144 Fiery Conclusion U :R:	.05	.15
145 Fiery Impulse C :R:	.30	.50
146 Firefiend Elemental C :R:	.05	.15
147 Flameshadow Conjuring R :R:	.20	.30
148 Ghirapur Æther Grid U :R:	.05	.15
149 Ghirapur Gearcrafter C :R:	.05	.15
150 Goblin Glory Chaser U :R:	.05	.15
151 Goblin Piledriver R :R:	1.25	1.50
152 Infectious Bloodlust C :R:	.05	.15
153 Lightning Javelin C :R:	.05	.15
154 Mage-Ring Bully C :R:	.05	.15
155 Magmatic Insight U :R:	.50	.75
156 Molten Vortex R :R:	.15	.25
157 Pia and Kiran Nalaar R :R:	.75	1.00
158 Prickleboar C :R:	.05	.15
159 Ravaging Blaze U :R:	.05	.15
160 Scab-Clan Berserker R :R:	.20	.30
161 Seismic Elemental U :R:	.05	.15
162 Skyraker Giant U :R:	.05	.15
163 Smash to Smithereens C :R:	.05	.15
164 Subterranean Scout C :R:	.05	.15
165 Thopter Engineer U :R:	.20	.30
166 Titanic Growth C :G:	.05	.15
167 Volcanic Rambler C :R:	.05	.15
168 Aerial Volley C :G:	.05	.15
169 Animist's Awakening R :G:	.40	.60
170 Caustic Caterpillar C :G:	.05	.15
171 Conclave Naturalists U :G:	.05	.15
172 Dwynen's Elite U :G:	.30	.50
173 Dwynen, Gilt-Leaf Daen R :G:	.40	.60
174 Elemental Bond U :G:	.05	.15
175 Elvish Visionary C :G:	.05	.15
176 Evolutionary Leap R :G:	.60	1.00
177 Gaea's Revenge R :G:	.25	.40
178 Gather the Pack U :G:	.30	.50
179 The Great Aurora M :G:	.75	1.00
180 Herald of the Pantheon R :G:	.25	.40

181 Hitchclaw Recluse C :G:	.05	.15
182 Honored Hierarch R :G:	.15	.25
183 Joraga Invocation U :G:	.05	.15
184 Leaf Gilder C :G:	.05	.15
185 Llanowar Empath C :G:	.05	.15
186 Managorger Hydra R :G:	1.00	1.25
187 Mantle of Webs C :G:	.05	.15
188 Might of the Masses C :G:	.05	.15
190 Nissa, Sage Animist M :G:	7.50	11.00
191 Nissa, Vastwood Seer M :G:	7.50	11.00
192 Orchard Spirit C :G:	.05	.15
193 Outland Colossus R :G:	.05	.15
194 Pharika's Disciple C :G:	.05	.15
195 Reclaim C :G:	.05	.15
196 Rhox Maulers C :G:	.05	.15
197 Skysnare Spider U :G:	.05	.15
198 Somberwald Alpha U :G:	.05	.15
199 Sylvan Messenger U :G:	.05	.15
200 Timberpack Wolf C :G:	.05	.15
201 Titan's Strength C :R:	.05	.15
202 Undercity Troll U :G:	.05	.15
203 Valeron Wardens U :G:	.05	.15
204 Vastwood Gorger C :G:	.05	.15
205 Vine Snare C :G:	.05	.15
206 Wild Instincts C :G:	.05	.15
207 Woodland Bellower M :G:	.75	1.15
208 Yeva's Forcemage C :G:	.05	.15
209 Zendikar's Roil U :G:	.05	.15
210 Blazing Hellhound U :M:	.05	.15
211 Blood-Cursed Knight U :M:	.05	.15
212 Bounding Krasis U :M:	.05	.15
213 Citadel Castellan U :M:	.05	.15
214 Iroas's Champion U :M:	.05	.15
215 Possessed Skaab U :M:	.05	.15
216 Reclusive Artificer U :M:	.05	.15
217 Shaman of the Pack U :M:	.15	.25
218 Thunderclap Wyvern U :M:	.05	.15
219 Zendikar Incarnate U :M:	.05	.15
220 Alchemist's Vial C	.05	.15
221 Alhammarret, High Arbiter M :B:	2.50	3.50
222 Angel's Tomb U	.05	.15
223 Bonded Construct C	.05	.15
224 Brawler's Plate U	.05	.15
225 Chief of the Foundry U	.05	.15
226 Gold-Forged Sentinel U	.05	.15
227 Guardian Automaton C	.05	.15
228 Guardians of Meletis C	.05	.15
229 Hangarback Walker R	1.75	2.25
230 Helm of the Gods R	.20	.30
231 Jayemdae Tome U	.05	.15
232 Mage-Ring Responder R	.05	.15
233 Meteorite U	.05	.15
234 Orbs of Warding R	.25	.40
235 Prism Ring U	.05	.15
236 Pyromancer's Goggles M	2.00	2.75
237 Ramroller U	.05	.15
238 Runed Servitor U	.05	.15
239 Sigil of Valor U	.05	.15
23a Kytheon's Tactics C :W:	.05	.15
23b Gideon's Phalanx R :W:	.05	.15
240 Sword of the Animist R	1.25	2.00
241 Throwing Knife U	.05	.15
242 Veteran's Sidearm C	.05	.15
243 War Horn U	.05	.15
244 Battlefield Forge R	1.00	1.25
245 Caves of Koilos R	1.00	1.50
246 Evolving Wilds C	.05	.15
247 Foundry of the Consuls U	.15	.25
248 Llanowar Wastes R	1.25	1.75
249 Mage-Ring Network U	.60	1.00
250 Rogue's Passage U	.05	.15
251 Shivan Reef R	2.50	3.00
252 Yavimaya Coast R	1.50	2.00
253 Plains L :L:	.05	.15
254 Plains L :L:	.05	.15
255 Plains L :L:	.05	.15
256 Plains L :L:	.05	.15
257 Island L :L:	.05	.15
258 Island L :L:	.05	.15
259 Island L :L:	.05	.15
260 Island L :L:	.05	.15
261 Swamp L :L:	.05	.15
262 Swamp L :L:	.05	.15
263 Swamp L :L:	.05	.15
264 Swamp L :L:	.05	.15
265 Mountain L :L:	.05	.15
266 Mountain L :L:	.05	.15
267 Mountain L :L:	.05	.15
268 Mountain L :L:	.05	.15
269 Forest L :L:	.05	.15
270 Forest L :L:	.05	.15
271 Forest L :L:	.05	.15
272 Forest L :L:	.05	.15
273 Aegis Angel R :W:	.30	.50
274 Divine Verdict C :W:	.05	.15
275 Eagle of the Watch C :W:	.05	.15
276 Serra Angel U :W:	.30	.50
277 Into the Void U :B:	.20	.35
278 Mahamoti Djinn R :B:	.15	.25
279 Weave Fate C :B:	.20	.35
280 Flesh to Dust C :K:	.05	.15
281 Mind Rot C :K:	.40	.60
282 Nightmare R :K:	.15	.25
283 Sengir Vampire U :K:	.30	.50
284 Fiery Hellhound C :R:	.30	.50
285 Shivan Dragon R :R:	.25	.40
286 Plummet C :G:	.30	.50
287 Prized Unicorn U :G:	.20	.35
288 Terra Stomper R :G:	.30	.50
60a Jace, Vryn's Prodigy M :B:	23.00	26.00
60b Jace, Telepath Unbound M :B:	23.00	26.00
106a Liliana, Heretical Healer M :K:	7.00	8.00
106b Liliana, Defiant Necromancer M	7.00	8.00
135a Chandra, Fire of Kaladesh M :R:	3.00	3.50
135b Chandra, Roaring Flame M	3.00	3.50
189a Nissa's Revelation R :G:	.05	.15
189b Nissa's Pilgrimage C :G:	.05	.15

2007 Magic The Gathering Elves vs. Goblins

DUEL DECK	100.00	200.00
RELEASED ON NOVEMBER 16, 2007		
1 Akki Coalflinger U :R:	.20	.50
2 Boggart Shenanigans U :R:	.30	.50
3 Clickslither R :R:	.40	.75
4 Emberwilde Augur C :R:	.10	.25
5 Flamewave Invoker U :R:	.20	.50
6 Gempalm Incinerator U :R:	.60	1.50
7 Goblin Cohort C :R:	.10	.25
8 Goblin Matron U :R:	.75	2.00
9 Goblin Ringleader U :R:	1.25	3.00
10 Goblin Sledder C :R:	.10	.25
11 Goblin Warchief U :R:	1.50	4.00
12 Ib Halfheart, Goblin Tactician R :R:	.30	.75
13 Mogg Fanatic U :R:	.60	1.50
14 Mogg War Marshal C :R:	.40	1.00
15 Mudbutton Torchrunner C :R:	.10	.25
16 Raging Goblin C :R:	.10	.25
17 Reckless One U :R:	.30	.75
18 Siege-Gang Commander R :R:	1.25	3.00
19 Skirk Drill Sergeant U :R:	.20	.50
20 Skirk Fire Marshal R :R:	.40	1.00
21 Skirk Prospector C :R:	.20	.50
22 Skirk Shaman C :R:	.10	.25
23 Spitting Earth C :R:	.10	.25
24 Tar Pitcher U :R:	.20	.50
25 Tarfire C :R:	.10	.25
26 Allosaurus Rider R :G:	.40	1.00
27 Ambush Commander R :G:	1.50	4.00
28 Elvish Eulogist C :G:	.10	.25
29 Elvish Harbinger U :G:	1.25	3.00
30 Elvish Promenade U :G:	1.50	4.00
31 Elvish Warrior C :G:	.10	.25
32 Gempalm Strider U :G:	.20	.50
33 Giant Growth C :G:	.10	.25
34 Harmonize U :G:	.75	2.00
35 Heedless One U :G:	1.50	4.00
36 Imperious Perfect U :G:	2.50	6.00
37 Llanowar Elves C :G:	.30	.50
38 Lys Alana Huntmaster C :G:	.30	.75
39 Stonewood Invoker C :G:	.10	.25
40 Sylvan Messenger U :G:	.75	2.00
41 Timberwatch Elf C :G:	.60	1.50
42 Voice of the Woods R :G:	.60	1.50
43 Wellwisher C :G:	.75	2.00
44 Wildsize C :G:	.10	.25
45 Wirewood Herald C :G:	.20	.75
46 Wirewood Symbiote U :G:	1.25	3.00
47 Wood Elves C :G:	.20	.50
48 Wren's Run Vanquisher U :G:	.75	2.00
49 Forest L	.10	.40
50 Forest L	.10	.40
51 Forest L	.10	.40
52 Forest L	.10	.40
53 Mountain L	.10	.40
54 Mountain L	.10	.40
55 Mountain L	.10	.40
56 Mountain L	.10	.40
57 Forgotten Cave C	.10	.25
58 Goblin Burrows U	.20	.50
59 Moonglove Extract C	.10	.25
60 Slate of Ancestry R	.50	1.00
61 Tranquil Thicket C	.10	.25
62 Wirewood Lodge U	1.25	3.00
T1 Token: Elemental C	.40	.75
T2 Token: Elf Warrior C	.40	1.00
T3 Token: Goblin C	.40	1.00

2008 Magic The Gathering Jace vs. Chandra

COMPLETE SET (63)	15.00	40.00
DUEL DECK	50.00	100.00
RELEASED ON NOVEMBER 7, 2008		
1 AEthersnipe C :B:	.10	.25
2 Air Elemental U :B:	.20	.50
3 Ancestral Vision R :B:	2.00	5.00
4 Brine Elemental U :B:	.20	.50
5 Condescend C :B:	.20	.50
6 Counterspell C :B:	4.00	10.00
7 Daze C :B:	1.50	4.00
8 Errant Ephemeron C :B:	.20	.50
9 Fact or Fiction U :B:	1.50	4.00
10 Fathom Seer C :B:	.10	.25
11 Fledgling Mawcor U :B:	.20	.50
12 Guile R :B:	.50	1.25
13 Gush C :B:	.40	1.00
14 Jace Beleren M :B:	6.00	15.00
15 Man-o'-War C :B:	.30	.75
16 Martyr of Frost C :B:	.10	.25
17 Mulldrifter C :B:	.40	1.00
18 Ophidian C :B:	.10	.25
19 Quicksilver Dragon R :B:	.50	1.25
20 Repulse C :B:	.10	.25
21 Riftwing Cloudskate U :B:	.20	.50
22 Voidmage Apprentice C :B:	.20	.50
23 Wall of Deceit U :B:	.20	.50
24 Waterspout Djinn U :B:	.20	.50
25 Willbender U :B:	.25	.60
26 Chandra Nalaar M :R:	3.00	8.00
27 Chartooth Cougar C :R:	.10	.25
28 Cone of Flame U :R:	.20	.50
29 Demonfire R :R:	.50	1.25
30 Fireball U :R:	.20	.50
31 Fireblast C :R:	.75	2.00
32 Firebolt C :R:	.10	.25
33 Fireslinger C :R:	.10	.25
34 Flame Javelin U :R:	.60	1.50
35 Flamekin Brawler C :R:	.10	.25
36 Flametongue Kavu U :R:	.60	1.50
37 Flamewave Invoker U :R:	.20	.50
38 Furnace Whelp U :R:	.20	.50
39 Hostility R :R:	.40	1.00
40 Incinerate C :R:	.60	1.50
41 Ingot Chewer C :R:	.20	.50
42 Inner-Flame Acolyte C :R:	.10	.25
43 Magma Jet U :R:	2.00	5.00
44 Pyre Charger U :R:	.20	.50
45 Rakdos Pit Dragon R :R:	.75	2.00
46 Seal of Fire C :R:	.20	.50
47 Slith Firewalker U :R:	.20	.50
48 Soulbright Flamekin C :R:	.20	.50
49 Bottle Gnomes U	.20	.50
50 Elemental Shaman C	.20	.50
51 Keldon Megaliths U	.25	.60
52 Mind Stone U	.50	1.25
53 Oxidda Golem C	.10	.25
54 Spire Golem C	.10	.25
55 Terrain Generator U	.60	1.50
56 Island L	.10	.25
57 Island L	.10	.25
58 Island L	.10	.25
59 Island L	.10	.25
60 Mountain L	.10	.25
61 Mountain L	.10	.25
62 Mountain L	.10	.25
63 Mountain L	.10	.25

2009 Magic The Gathering Divine vs. Demonic

COMPLETE SET (62)	50.00	120.00
DUEL DECK	60.00	120.00
RELEASED ON APRIL 10, 2009		
1 Akroma, Angel of Wrath M :W:	12.00	30.00
2 Angel of Mercy U :W:	.20	.50
3 Angelic Benediction U :W:	.20	.50
4 Angelic Page C :W:	.20	.50
5 Angelic Protector U :W:	.20	.50
6 Angelsong C :W:	.10	.25
7 Charging Paladin C :W:	.10	.25
8 Faith's Fetters C :W:	.30	.75
9 Healing Salve C :W:	.10	.25
10 Icatian Priest U :W:	.20	.50
11 Luminous Angel R :W:	3.00	8.00
12 Otherworldly Journey U :W:	.20	.50
13 Pacifism C :W:	.10	.25
14 Reya Dawnbringer R :W:	3.00	8.00
15 Righteous Cause U :W:	.20	.50
16 Serra Advocate U :W:	.20	.50
17 Serra Angel R :W:	.30	.75
18 Serra's Boon U :W:	.20	.50
19 Serra's Embrace U :W:	.30	.75
20 Sustainer of the Realm U :W:	.20	.50
21 Twilight Shepherd R :W:	1.25	3.00
22 Venerable Monk C :W:	.10	.25
23 Abyssal Gatekeeper C :K:	.10	.25
24 Abyssal Specter U :K:	.20	.50
25 Barter in Blood U :K:	.40	1.00
26 Breeding Pit U :K:	.30	.75
27 Cackling Imp C :K:	.10	.25
28 Consume Spirit U :K:	.20	.50
29 Corrupt U :K:	.20	.50
30 Cruel Edict U :K:	.40	1.00
31 Daggerclaw Imp U :K:	.20	.50
32 Dark Banishing C :K:	.10	.25
33 Dark Ritual C :K:	1.25	3.00
34 Demonic Tutor U :K:	12.00	30.00
35 Demon's Jester C :K:	.10	.25
36 Duress C :K:	.40	1.00
37 Dusk Imp C :K:	.10	.25
38 Fallen Angel R :K:	.30	.75
39 Foul Imp C :K:	.10	.25
40 Kuro, Pitlord R :K:	.30	.75
41 Lord of the Pit M :K:	1.50	4.00
42 Oni Possession U :K:	.20	.50
43 Overeager Apprentice C :K:	.10	.25
44 Promise of Power R :K:	.40	1.00
45 Reiver Demon R :K:	.75	2.00
46 Soot Imp U :K:	.20	.50
47 Souldrinker U :K:	.20	.50
48 Stinkweed Imp C :K:	2.00	5.00
49 Unholy Strength C :K:	.10	.25
50 Angel's Feather U	.20	.50
51 Barren Moor C	.20	.50
52 Demon's Horn U	.20	.50
53 Marble Diamond U	.20	.50
54 Secluded Steppe C	.10	.25
55 Plains L	.20	.50
56 Plains L	.20	.50
57 Plains L	.20	.50
58 Plains L	.20	.50
59 Swamp L	.20	.50
60 Swamp L	.20	.50
61 Swamp L	.20	.50
62 Swamp L	.20	.50
T1 Demon - Token C	.40	1.00
T2 Spirit - Token C	.40	1.00
T3 Thrull - Token C	.60	1.50

2009 Magic The Gathering Garruk vs. Liliana

COMPLETE SET (66)	25.00	60.00
DUEL DECK	30.00	50.00
RELEASED ON OCTOBER 30, 2009		
1 Bad Moon R :K:	2.50	6.00
2 Corrupt U :K:	.20	.50
3 Deathgreeter C :K:	.10	.25
4 Drudge Skeletons C :K:	.10	.25
5 Enslave U :K:	.20	.50
6 Faerie Macabre C :K:	.10	.25
7 Fleshbag Marauder U :K:	.20	.50
8 Genju of the Fens U :K:	.20	.50
9 Ghost-Lit Stalker U :K:	.20	.50
10 Hideous End C :K:	.10	.25
11 Howling Banshee U :K:	.20	.50
12 Ichor Slick C :K:	.10	.25
13 Keening Banshee U :K:	.20	.50
14 Liliana Vess M :K:	6.00	15.00
15 Mutilate R :K:	2.50	6.00
16 Phyrexian Rager C :K:	.10	.25
17 Ravenous Rats C :K:	.10	.25
18 Rise from the Grave U :K:	.20	.50
19 Sign in Blood C :K:	.20	.50
20 Skeletal Vampire R :K:	1.25	3.00
21 Snuff Out C :K:	.10	.25
22 Tendrils of Corruption C :K:	.10	.25
23 Twisted Abomination C :K:	.10	.25
24 Urborg Syphon-Mage C :K:	.10	.25
25 Vampire Bats C :K:	.10	.25
26 Vicious Hunger C :K:	.10	.25
27 Wall of Bone U :K:	.20	.50
28 Albino Troll U :G:	.30	.75
29 Basking Rootwalla C :G:	.30	.75
30 Beast Attack U :G:	.20	.50
31 Blastoderm C :G:	.10	.25
32 Elephant Guide U :G:	.20	.50
33 Garruk Wildspeaker M :G:	6.00	15.00
34 Genju of the Cedars U :G:	.20	.50
35 Giant Growth C :G:	.10	.25
36 Harmonize U :G:	.20	.50
37 Indrik Stomphowler U :G:	.20	.50
38 Invigorate C :G:	.10	.25
39 Krosan Tusker C :G:	.10	.25
40 Lignify C :G:	.10	.25
41 Nature's Lore C :G:	.10	.25
42 Overrun U :G:	.20	.50
43 Plated Slagwurm R :G:	1.25	3.00
44 Rancor C :G:	.10	.25
45 Ravenous Baloth R :G:	1.50	4.00
46 Rude Awakening R :G:	.60	1.50
47 Stampeding Wildebeests U :G:	.20	.50
48 Vine Trellis C :G:	.10	.25
49 Wild Mongrel C :G:	.10	.25
50 Windstorm U :G:	.20	.50
51 Wirewood Savage C :G:	.10	.25
52 Polluted Mire C	.10	.25
53 Serrated Arrows C	.10	.25
54 Slippery Karst C	.10	.25
55 Treetop Village U	.20	.50
56 Forest L	.10	.25
57 Forest L	.10	.25
58 Forest L	.10	.25
59 Forest L	.10	.25
60 Swamp L	.10	.25
61 Swamp L	.10	.25
62 Swamp L	.10	.25
63 Swamp L	.10	.25
T1 Beast - Token C	.20	.50
T2 Beast - Token C	.20	.50
T3 Elephant - Token C	.40	1.00

2012 Magic The Gathering Phyrexia vs The Coalition

COMPLETE SET (73)	15.00	40.00
DUEL DECK	15.00	40.00
RELEASED ON MARCH 19, 2012		
1 Gerrard Capashen R :W:	.30	.75
2 Narrow Escape C :W:	.10	.25
3 Sunscape Battlemage U :W:	.20	.50
4 Allied Strategies U :B:	.20	.50
5 Evasive Action U :B:	.20	.50
6 Bone Shredder U :K:	.20	.50
7 Carrion Feeder C :K:	.20	.50
9 Dark Ritual C :K:	.75	2.00
10 Exotic Curse C :K:	.10	.25
11 Hideous End C :K:	.10	.25
12 Living Death R :K:	1.00	2.50
13 Order of Yawgmoth U :K:	.20	.50
14 Phyrexian Arena R :K:	1.25	3.00
15 Phyrexian Battleflies C :K:	.10	.25
16 Phyrexian Broodlings C :K:	.10	.25
17 Phyrexian Debaser C :K:	.10	.25
18 Phyrexian Defiler U :K:	.20	.50
19 Phyrexian Denouncer C :K:	.10	.25
20 Phyrexian Gargantua U :K:	.20	.50
21 Phyrexian Ghoul C :K:	.10	.25
22 Phyrexian Negator M :K:	1.25	3.00
23 Phyrexian Plaguelord R :K:	.30	.75
24 Priest of Gix U :K:	.20	.50
25 Sanguine Guard U :K:	.20	.50
26 Slay U :K:	.20	.50
27 Tendrils of Corruption C :K:	.10	.25
28 Thunderscape Battlemage U :R:	.20	.50
29 Tribal Flames C :R:	.20	.50
30 Urza's Rage M :R:	.60	1.50
31 Fertile Ground C :G:	.10	.25
32 Harrow C :G:	.20	.50
33 Nomadic Elf C :G:	.10	.25
34 Quirion Elves C :G:	.10	.25
35 Thornscape Apprentice C :G:	.10	.25
36 Thornscape Battlemage U :G:	.20	.50
37 Verduran Emissary U :G:	.20	.50
38 Yavimaya Elder C :G:	.40	1.00
39 Armadillo Cloak C :W: :G:	.40	1.00
40 Charging Troll U :W: :G:	.20	.50
41 Darigaaz, the Igniter R :K: :R: :G:	.60	1.50
42 Darigaaz's Charm U :K: :R: :G:	.10	.25
43 Gerrard's Command C :W: :G:	.10	.25
44 Rith, the Awakener R :W: :R: :G:	.75	2.00
45 Rith's Charm U :W: :R: :G:	.10	.25
46 Treva, the Renewer R :W: :L: :G:	.75	2.00
47 Treva's Charm U :W: :L: :G:	.10	.25
48 Coalition Relic R	1.50	4.00
49 Elfhame Palace U	.20	.50
50 Hornet Cannon U	.20	.50
51 Lightning Greaves U	1.00	2.50
52 Phyrexian Colossus R	.30	.75
53 Phyrexian Hulk U	.20	.50
54 Phyrexian Processor R	.75	2.00
55 Phyrexian Totem U	.20	.50
56 Phyrexian Vault U	.20	.50
57 Power Armor U	.20	.50
58 Puppet Strings U	.20	.50
59 Shivan Oasis U	.20	.50
60 Terramorphic Expanse C	.20	.50
61 Voltaic Key U	.40	1.00
62 Whispersilk Cloak U	.30	.75
63 Worn Powerstone U	.40	1.00
64 Forest L	.10	.25
65 Forest L	.10	.25
66 Island L	.10	.25
67 Mountain L	.10	.25
68 Plains L	.10	.25
69 Swamp L	.10	.25
70 Swamp L	.10	.25
71 Swamp L	.10	.25
72 Swamp L	.10	.25
73 Token: Hornet	.10	.25
74 Token: Minion	.10	.25

2010 Magic The Gathering Elspeth vs. Tezzeret

COMPLETE SET (79)	15.00	40.00
DUEL DECK	30.00	50.00
RELEASED ON SEPTEMBER 9, 2010		
1 Elspeth, Knight-Errant M :W:	8.00	20.00
2 Elite Vanguard U :W:	.20	.50
3 Goldmeadow Harrier C :W:	.10	.25
4 Infantry Veteran C :W:	.10	.25
5 Loyal Sentry R :W:	.30	.75
6 Mosquito Guard C :W:	.10	.25
7 Glory Seeker C :W:	.10	.25
8 Kor Skyfisher C :W:	.10	.25
9 Temple Acolyte C :W:	.10	.25
10 Kor Aeronaut U :W:	.20	.50
11 Burrenton Bombardier C :W:	.10	.25
12 Kor Hookmaster C :W:	.10	.25
13 Kemba's Skyguard C :W:	.10	.25
14 Celestial Crusader U :W:	.20	.50
15 Seasoned Marshal U :W:	.20	.50
16 Conclave Phalanx U :W:	.20	.50
17 Stormfront Riders U :W:	.20	.50
18 Catapult Master R :W:	.30	.75
19 Conclave Equenaut C :W:	.10	.25
20 Angel of Salvation R :W:	.30	.75
21 Sunlance C :W:	.10	.25
22 Swords to Plowshares U :W:	2.00	5.00
23 Journey to Nowhere C :W:	.30	.75
24 Mighty Leap C :W:	.10	.25
25 Raise the Alarm C :W:	.10	.25
26 Razor Barrier C :W:	.10	.25
27 Crusade R :W:	.60	1.50
28 Blinding Beam C :W:	.10	.25
29 Abolish U :W:	.20	.50
30 Saltblast U :W:	.20	.50
31 Swell of Courage U :W:	.20	.50
32 Daru Encampment U	.20	.50
33 Kabira Crossroads C	.10	.25
34 Rustic Clachan R	.30	.75
35 Plains L	.10	.25
36 Plains L	.10	.25
37 Plains L	.10	.25
38 Plains L	.10	.25
39 Tezzeret the Seeker M :B:	2.50	6.00
40 Arcbound Worker C	.20	.50
41 Steel Wall C	.10	.25
42 Runed Servitor U	.20	.50
43 Silver Myr C	.10	.25
44 Steel Overseer R	2.00	5.00
45 Assembly-Worker U	.20	.50
46 Serrated Biskelion U	.20	.50
47 Esperzoa U :B:	.20	.50
48 Master of Etherium R :B:	2.00	5.00
49 Trinket Mage C :B:	.20	.50
50 Clockwork Condor C	.10	.25
51 Frogmite C	.30	.75
52 Juggernaut U	.20	.50
53 Synod Centurion U	.20	.50
54 Faerie Mechanist C :B:	.10	.25
55 Clockwork Hydra U	.20	.50
56 Razormane Masticore R	.30	.75
57 Triskelion R	.30	.75
58 Pentavus R	.20	.50
59 Qumulox U :B:	.20	.50
60 Everflowing Chalice U	.75	2.00
61 AEther Spellbomb C	.10	.25
62 Elixir of Immortality U	.40	1.00
63 Contagion Clasp U	.40	1.00
64 Energy Chamber U	.75	2.00
65 Trip Noose U	.20	.50
66 Echoing Truth C :B:	.40	1.00
67 Moonglove Extract C	.10	.25
68 Thirst for Knowledge U :B:	.40	1.00
69 Argivian Restoration U :B:	.20	.50
70 Foil U :B:	.30	.75
71 Thoughtcast C :B:	.30	.75
72 Darksteel Citadel C	.75	2.00
73 Mishra's Factory U	2.00	5.00
74 Seat of the Synod C	.75	2.00
75 Stalking Stones U	.20	.50
76 Island L	.10	.25
77 Island L	.10	.25
78 Island L	.10	.25
79 Island L	.10	.25
T1 Token: Soldier	.10	.25

2011 Magic The Gathering Knights vs. Dragons

DUEL DECK	20.00	40.00
*FOIL: .75X TO 2X BASIC CARDS		
RELEASED ON APRIL 1, 2011		
1 Knight of the Reliquary M :W: :G:	4.00	10.00
2 Caravan Escort C :W:	.10	.25
3 Lionheart Maverick C :W:	.10	.25
4 Knight of Cliffhaven C :W:	.10	.25
5 Knight of Meadowgrain U :W:	1.25	3.00
6 Knight of the White Orchid R :W:	1.25	3.00
7 Leonin Skyhunter U :W:	.20	.50
8 Silver Knight U :W:	.75	2.00
9 White Knight U :W:	.30	.75
10 Knotvine Paladin R :W: :G:	.40	1.00
11 Steward of Valeron C :W: :G:	.10	.25
12 Benalish Lancer C :W:	.10	.25
13 Zhalfirin Commander U :W:	.20	.50
14 Knight Exemplar R :W:	1.50	4.00
15 Wilt-Leaf Cavaliers U :W: :G:	.75	2.00
16 Kabira Vindicator U :W:	.20	.50
17 Kinsbaile Cavalier R :W:	1.50	4.00
18 Alaborn Cavalier U :W:	.20	.50
19 Skyhunter Patrol C :W:	.10	.25
20 Plover Knights C :W:	.20	.50
21 Juniper Order Ranger U :W: :G:	.75	2.00
22 Paladin of Prahv U :W:	.20	.50
23 Harm's Way U :W:	.20	.50
24 Reciprocate U :W:	.30	.75
25 Edge of Autumn C :G:	.10	.25
26 Mighty Leap C :W:	.10	.25
27 Reprisal U :W:	.20	.50
28 Test of Faith U :W:	.20	.50
29 Heroes' Reunion U :W: :G:	.30	.75
30 Sigil Blessing C :W: :G:	.10	.25
31 Loxodon Warhammer R	1.00	2.50
32 Spidersilk Armor C :G:	.20	.50
33 Griffin Guide U :W:	.20	.50
34 Oblivion Ring C :W:	1.25	3.00
35 Grasslands U	.20	.50
36 Sejiri Steppe C	.10	.25
37 Selesnya Sanctuary C	.20	.50
38 Treetop Village U	1.25	3.00

Card	Low	High
39 Plains L	.10	.25
40 Plains L	.10	.25
41 Plains L	.10	.25
42 Plains L	.10	.25
43 Forest L	.10	.25
44 Forest L	.10	.25
45 Forest L	.10	.25
46 Forest L	.10	.25
47 Bogardan Hellkite M :R:	2.00	5.00
48 Cinder Wall C :R:	.10	.25
49 Skirk Prospector C :R:	.20	.50
50 Bloodmark Mentor U :R:	.40	1.00
51 Fire-Belly Changeling C :R:	.10	.25
52 Mudbutton Torchrunner C :R:	.20	.50
53 Dragonspeaker Shaman U :R:	1.25	3.00
54 Dragon Whelp U :R:	.20	.50
55 Henge Guardian U	.20	.50
56 Voracious Dragon R :R:	.40	1.00
57 Bogardan Rager C :R:	.10	.25
58 Mordant Dragon R :R:	.40	1.00
59 Kilnmouth Dragon R :R:	1.25	3.00
60 Shivan Hellkite R :R:	.40	1.00
61 Thunder Dragon R :R:	.75	2.00
62 Armillary Sphere C	.10	.25
63 Dragon's Claw U	.20	.50
64 Breath of Darigaaz U :R:	.20	.50
65 Dragon Fodder C :R:	.20	.50
66 Punishing Fire U :R:	.40	1.00
67 Spitting Earth C :R:	.10	.25
68 Captive Flame U :R:	.20	.50
69 Ghostfire C	.10	.25
70 Seething Song C :R:	1.25	3.00
71 Seismic Strike C :R:	.20	.50
72 Claws of Valakut C :R:	.10	.25
73 Temporary Insanity U :R:	.20	.50
74 Shiv's Embrace U :R:	.40	1.00
75 Cone of Flame U :R:	.20	.50
76 Fiery Fall C :R:	.10	.25
77 Jaws of Stone U :R:	.20	.50
78 Mountain L	.10	.25
79 Mountain L	.10	.25
80 Mountain L	.10	.25
81 Mountain L	.10	.25
T1 Token: Goblin	.10	.25

2011 Magic The Gathering Ajani vs. Nicol Bolas

Card	Low	High
DUEL DECK	15.00	30.00
*FOIL: .75X TO 2X BASIC CARDS		
RELEASED ON SEPTEMBER 2, 2011		
1 Ajani Vengeant M :W/R:	2.50	6.00
2 Kird Ape U :R:	.50	1.25
3 Essence Warden C :G:	.20	.50
4 Wild Nacatl C :G:	.20	.50
5 Loam Lion U :W:	.20	.50
6 Canyon Wildcat C :R:	.10	.25
7 Jade Mage U :G:	.20	.50
8 Sylvan Ranger C :G:	.10	.25
9 Ajani's Pridemate U :W:	.40	1.00
10 Qasali Pridemage C :W: :G:	.40	1.00
11 Grazing Gladehart C :G:	.10	.25
12 Fleetfoot Panther U :W: :G:	.20	.50
13 Woolly Thoctar U :W: :R: :G:	.30	.75
14 Briarhorn U :G:	.20	.50
15 Loxodon Hierarch R :W: :G:	.60	1.50
16 Spitemare U :W: :R:	.20	.50
17 Marisi's Twinclaws U :W: :R: :G:	.20	.50
18 Ageless Entity R :G:	.50	1.25
19 Pride of Lions U :G:	.20	.50
20 Nacatl Hunt-Pride U :W:	.20	.50
21 Firemane Angel R :W: :R:	.75	2.00
22 Ajani's Mantra C :W:	.10	.25
23 Lightning Helix U :W: :R:	2.00	4.00
24 Lead the Stampede U :G:	.20	.50
25 Griffin Guide U :W:	.20	.50
26 Recumbent Bliss C :W:	.10	.25
27 Searing Meditation R :W: :R:	.40	1.00
28 Behemoth Sledge U :W: :G:	.60	1.50
29 Naya Charm U :W: :R: :G:	.20	.50
30 Sylvan Bounty C :G:	.10	.25
31 Titanic Ultimatum R :W: :R: :G:	.40	1.00
32 Evolving Wilds C	.30	.75
33 Graypelt Refuge U	.30	.75
34 Jungle Shrine U	.75	2.00
35 Kazandu Refuge U	.30	.75
36 Sapseep Forest U	.20	.50
37 Vitu-Ghazi, the City-Tree U	.20	.50
38 Forest L	.10	.25
39 Forest L	.10	.25
40 Plains L	.10	.25
41 Mountain L	.10	.25
42 Nicol Bolas, Planeswalker M :B: :K: :R:	5.00	12.00
43 Surveilling Sprite C :B:	.10	.25
44 Nightscape Familiar C :K:	.20	.50
45 Slavering Nulls U :R:	.20	.50
46 Brackwater Elemental C :B:	.10	.25
47 Morgue Toad C :K:	.10	.25
48 Hellfire Mongrel U :R:	.20	.50
49 Dimir Cutpurse R :B: :K:	.60	1.50
50 Steamcore Weird C :B:	.10	.25
51 Moroii U :B: :K:	.20	.50
52 Blazing Specter R :K: :R:	.60	1.50
53 Fire-Field Ogre U :B: :K: :R:	.20	.50
54 Shriekmaw U :K:	.60	1.50
55 Ogre Savant C :R:	.10	.25
56 Jhessian Zombies C :B: :K:	.10	.25
57 Igneous Pouncer C :K: :R:	.10	.25
58 Vapor Snag C :B:	.50	1.25
59 Countersquall U :B: :K:	.60	1.50
60 Obelisk of Grixis C	.10	.25
61 Recoil C :B: :K:	.20	.50
62 Undermine R :B: :K:	1.25	3.00
63 Grixis Charm U :B: :K: :R:	.20	.50
64 Icy Manipulator U	.20	.50
65 Deep Analysis U :B:	.50	1.25
66 Agonizing Demise C :K:	.10	.25
67 Slave of Bolas U :B: :K: :R:	.20	.50
68 Elder Mastery U :B: :K: :R:	.20	.50
69 Cruel Ultimatum R :B: :K: :R:	.75	2.00
70 Profane Command R :K: :R:	.75	2.00
71 Spite: :Malice U :B: :K:	.20	.50
72 Pain: :Suffering U :K: :R:	.20	.50
73 Rise: :Fall U :K: :R:	.20	.50
74 Crumbling Necropolis U	.75	2.00
75 Rupture Spire C	.20	.50
76 Terramorphic Expanse C	.20	.50
77 Swamp L	.10	.25
78 Swamp L	.10	.25
79 Island L	.10	.25
80 Mountain L	.10	.25
T1 Token: Griffin	.10	.25
T2 Token: Saproling	.10	.25

2012 Magic The Gathering Venser vs. Koth

Card	Low	High
DUEL DECK	15.00	40.00
*FOIL: .75X TO 2X BASIC CARDS		
RELEASED ON MARCH 30, 2012		
1 Venser, the Sojourner M :W/B:	4.00	10.00
2 Whitemane Lion C :W:	.20	.50
3 Augury Owl C :B:	.10	.25
4 Coral Fighters U :B:	.20	.50
5 Minamo Sightbender U :B:	.20	.50
6 Mistmeadow Witch U :W/B:	.20	.50
7 Scroll Thief C :B:	.10	.25
8 Neurok Invisimancer C :B:	.10	.25
9 Slith Strider U :B:	.20	.50
10 Sky Spirit U :W/B:	.20	.50
11 Wall of Denial U :W/B:	.60	1.50
12 Galepowder Mage R :W:	.40	1.00
13 Kor Cartographer C :W:	.10	.25
14 Clone R :B:	.40	1.00
15 Cryptic Annelid U :B:	.20	.50
16 Primal Plasma C :B:	.10	.25
17 Sawtooth Loon U :W/B:	.20	.50
18 Cache Raiders U :B:	.20	.50
19 Windreaver R :W/B:	.40	1.00
20 Jedit's Dragoons C :W:	.10	.25
21 Sunblast Angel R :W:	.40	1.00
22 Sphinx of Uthuun R :B:	.40	1.00
23 Path to Exile U :W:	3.00	8.00
24 Preordain C :B:	.60	1.50
25 Sigil of Sleep C :B:	.20	.50
26 Revoke Existence C :W:	.10	.25
27 Angelic Shield U :W/B:	.20	.50
28 Oblivion Ring U :W:	.60	1.50
29 Safe Passage C :W:	.10	.25
30 Steel of the Godhead C :W/B:	.30	.75
31 Vanish into Memory U :W/B:	.20	.50
32 Overrule C :W/B:	.20	.50
33 Azorius Chancery C	.20	.50
34 Flood Plain U	.30	.75
35 New Benalia U	.20	.50
36 Sejiri Refuge U	.30	.75
37 Soaring Seacliff C	.10	.25
38 Plains L	.10	.25
39 Plains L	.10	.25
40 Plains L	.10	.25
41 Island L	.10	.25
42 Island L	.10	.25
43 Island L	.10	.25
44 Koth of the Hammer M :R:	4.00	10.00
45 Plated Geopede C :R:	.30	.75
46 Pygmy Pyrosaur C :R:	.10	.25
47 Pilgrim's Eye C	.20	.50
48 AEther Membrane U :R:	.20	.50
49 Fiery Hellhound C :R:	.10	.25
50 Vulshok Sorcerer C :R:	.10	.25
51 Anger U :R:	.60	1.50
52 Cosi's Ravager C :R:	.10	.25
53 Vulshok Berserker C :R:	.10	.25
54 Bloodfire Kavu U :R:	.20	.50
55 Stone Giant U :R:	.20	.50
56 Geyser Glider U :R:	.20	.50
57 Lithophage R :R:	.40	1.00
58 Torchling R :R:	.40	1.00
59 Chartooth Cougar C :R:	.30	.75
60 Earth Servant U :R:	.20	.50
61 Greater Stone Spirit U :R:	.20	.50
62 Bloodfire Colossus R :R:	.40	1.00
63 Wayfarer's Bauble C	.20	.50
64 Armillary Sphere C	.10	.25
65 Journeyer's Kite R	.75	2.00
66 Vulshok Morningstar U	.20	.50
67 Searing Blaze C :R:	.10	.25
68 Vulshok Battlegear U	.20	.50
69 Downhill Charge C :R:	.10	.25
70 Seismic Strike C :R:	.10	.25
71 Spire Barrage C :R:	.10	.25
72 Jaws of Stone U :R:	.20	.50
73 Volley of Boulders R :R:	.40	1.00
74 Mountain L	.10	.25
75 Mountain L	.10	.25
76 Mountain L	.10	.25
77 Mountain L	.10	.25

2012 Magic The Gathering Izzet vs. Golgari

Card	Low	High
DUAL DECK	8.00	20.00
RELEASED SEPTEMBER 9, 2012		
1 Brainstorm C :B:	2.00	5.00
2 Call to Heel C :B:	.10	.25
3 Dissipate U :B:	.30	.75
4 Force Spike C :B:	.20	.50
5 Overwhelming Intellect :B:	.20	.50
6 Reminisce U :B:	.20	.50
7 Steamcore Weird C :B:	.10	.25
8 Thunderheads U :B:	.20	.50
9 Train of Thought C :B:	.10	.25
10 Vacuumelt U :B:	.20	.50
11 Brain Weevil C :K:	.10	.25
12 Feast or Famine C :K:	.10	.25
13 Ghoul's Feast U :K:	.20	.50
14 Golgari Thug U :K:	.10	1.00
15 Nightmare Void U :K:	.20	.50
16 Plagued Rusalka U :K:	.20	.50
17 Ravenous Rats C :K:	.10	.25
18 Reassembling Skeleton U :K:	.20	.50
19 Sadistic Hypnotist U :K:	.20	.50
20 Stinkweed Imp C :K:	.10	.25
21 Twilight's Call R :K:	.30	.75
22 Vigor Mortis U :K:	.20	.50
23 Yoke of the Damned C :K:	.10	.25
24 Galvanoth R :R:	.30	.75
25 Kiln Fiend C :R:	.40	1.00
26 Magma Spray C :R:	.10	.25
27 Ogre Savant C :R:	.10	.25
28 Pyromatics C :R:	.10	.25
29 Street Spasm U :R:	.20	.50
30 Boneyard Wurm U :G:	.20	.50
31 Elves of Deep Shadow C :G:	.10	.25
32 Eternal Witness U :G:	1.25	3.00
33 Golgari Grave-Troll R :G:	.75	2.00
34 Greater Mossdog C :G:	.10	.25
35 Grim Flowering U :G:	.20	.50
36 Life from the Loam R :G:	1.25	3.00
37 Stingerfling Spider U :G:	.20	.50
38 Djinn Illuminatus R :B: :R:	.30	.75
39 Doomgape R :K: :G:	.30	.75
40 Dreg Mangler U :K: :G:	.20	.50
41 Fire/Ice U :R: :B:	.20	.50
42 Gelectrode U :B: :R:	.30	.75
43 Gleancrawler R :K: :G:	.30	.75
44 Goblin Electromancer C :B: :R:	.20	.50
45 Golgari Germination U :K: :G:	.20	.50
46 Golgari Rotwurm C :K: :G:	.10	.25
47 Invoke the Firemind R :B: :R:	.30	.75
48 Izzet Charm U :B: :R:	.30	.75
49 Izzet Chronarch C :B: :R:	.10	.25
50 Izzet Guildmage U :B: :R:	.20	.50
51 Jarad, Golgari Lich Lord M :K: :G:	.75	2.00
52 Korozda Guildmage U :K: :G:	.20	.50
53 Life/Death U :G: :K:	.20	.50
54 Niv-Mizzet, the Firemind :B: :R: M	1.50	4.00
55 Prophetic Bolt R :B: :R:	.30	.75
56 Putrefy U :K: :G:	.30	.75
57 Putrid Leech C :K: :G:	.10	.25
58 Quicksilver Dagger C :B: :R:	.10	.25
59 Shambling Shell C :K: :G:	.10	.25
60 Shrewd Hatchling U :B: :R:	.20	.50
61 Wee Dragonauts C :B: :R:	.10	.25
62 Barren Moor C	.10	.25
63 Dakmor Salvage U	.20	.50
64 Forgotten Cave C	.10	.25
65 Golgari Rot Farm C	.30	.75
66 Golgari Signet C	.10	.25
67 Isochron Scepter U	2.50	6.00
68 Izzet Boilerworks C	.10	.25
69 Izzet Signet C	.10	.25
70 Lonely Sandbar C	.10	.25
71 Nivix, Aerie of the Firemind U	.20	.50
72 Sphinx-Bone Wand R	.30	.75
73 Svogthos, the Restless Tomb U	.20	.50
74 Tranquil Thicket C	.10	.25
75 Forest L	.10	.25
76 Forest L	.10	.25
77 Forest L	.10	.25
78 Forest L	.10	.25
79 Island L	.10	.25
80 Island L	.10	.25
81 Island L	.10	.25
82 Island L	.10	.25
83 Mountain L	.10	.25
84 Mountain L	.10	.25
85 Mountain L	.10	.25
86 Mountain L	.10	.25
87 Swamp L	.10	.25
88 Swamp L	.10	.25
89 Swamp L	.10	.25
90 Swamp L	.10	.25
T1 Saproling	.20	.50

2013 Magic The Gathering Sorin vs. Tibalt

Card	Low	High
COMPLETE SET (81)		
*FOIL: .75X TO 2X BASIC CARDS		
RELEASED IN MARCH 2013		
1 Doomed Traveler C :W:	.10	.25
2 Field of Souls R :W:	.40	1.00
3 Twilight Drover R :W:	.40	1.00
4 Fiend Hunter U :W:	.20	.50
5 Mausoleum Guard U :W:	.20	.50
6 Phantom General U :W:	.20	.50
7 Spectral Procession U :W:	1.00	2.50
8 Wall of Omens U :W:	.75	2.00
9 Absorb Vis C :K:	.10	.25
10 Bloodrage Vampire C :K:	.10	.25
11 Bump in the Night C :K:	.10	.25
12 Child of Night C :K:	.10	.25
13 Duskhunter Bat C :K:	.10	.25
14 Mark of the Vampire C :K:	.10	.25
15 Mesmeric Fiend C :K:	.10	.25
16 Sorin's Thirst C :K:	.10	.25
17 Strangling Soot C :K:	.10	.25
18 Vampire Lacerator C :K:	.10	.25
19 Vampire's Bite C :K:	.10	.25
20 Ancient Craving R :K:	.40	1.00
21 Butcher of Malakir R :K:	.40	1.00
22 Corpse Connoisseur U :K:	.20	.50
23 Decompose U :K:	.20	.50
24 Gatekeeper of Malakir U :K:	.60	1.50
25 Lingering Souls U :K:	.30	.75
26 Reassembling Skeleton U :K:	.20	.50
27 Revenant Patriarch U :K:	.20	.50
28 Sengir Vampire U :K:	.20	.50
29 Urge to Feed U :K:	.20	.50
30 Vampire Nighthawk U :K:	.50	1.25
31 Vampire Outcasts U :K:	.20	.50
32 Ashmouth Hound C :R:	.10	.25
33 Blazing Salvo C :R:	.10	.25
34 Coal Stoker C :R:	.10	.25
35 Faithless Looting C :R:	.10	.25
36 Flame Slash C :R:	.20	.50
37 Geistflame C :R:	.10	.25
38 Goblin Arsonist C :R:	.10	.25
39 Mad Prophet C :R:	.10	.25
40 Vithian Stinger C :R:	.10	.25
41 Tibalt, the Fiend-Blooded M :R:	.60	1.50
42 Breaking Point R :R:	.40	1.00
43 Devil's Play R :R:	.40	1.00
44 Hellrider R :R:	.40	1.00
45 Lavaborn Muse R :R:	.40	1.00
46 Sulfuric Vortex R :R:	.30	.75
47 Browbeat U :R:	.50	1.25
48 Flame Javelin U :R:	.20	.50
49 Gang of Devils U :R:	.20	.50
50 Hellspark Elemental U :R:	.30	.75
51 Pyroclasm U :R:	.30	.75
52 Recoup U :R:	.20	.50
53 Scorched Rusalka U :R:	.20	.50
54 Scourge Devil U :R:	.20	.50
55 Skirsdag Cultist U :R:	.20	.50
56 Blightning C :D:	.30	.75
57 Terminate C :D:	.50	1.25
58 Unmake C :D:	.60	1.50
59 Sorin, Lord of Innistrad M :D:	2.00	5.00
60 Death Grasp R :D:	.40	1.00
61 Mortify U :D:	.50	1.25
62 Shambling Remains U :D:	.20	.50
63 Torrent of Souls U :D:	.20	.50
64 Zealous Persecution U :D:	.50	1.25
65 Spirit Token T	.30	.75
66 Evolving Wilds C	.20	.50
67 Rakdos Carnarium C	.20	.50
68 Mountain L	.10	.25
69 Mountain L	.10	.25
70 Mountain L	.10	.25
71 Plains L	.10	.25
72 Plains L	.10	.25
73 Plains L	.10	.25
74 Swamp (35) L	.10	.25
75 Swamp (36) L	.10	.25
76 Swamp (37) L	.10	.25
77 Swamp (78) L	.10	.25
78 Swamp (79) L	.10	.25
79 Swamp (80) L	.10	.25
80 Akoum Refuge U	.20	.50
81 Tainted Field U	.30	.75

2014 Magic The Gathering Jace vs. Vraska

Card	Low	High
DUEL DECK	25.00	60.00
RELEASED ON MARCH 14, 2014		
1 Acidic Slime U :G:	.30	.75
2 Aeon Chronicler R :B:	.60	1.50
3 Æther Adept C :B:	.20	.50
4 Æther Figment U :B:	.30	.75
5 Agoraphobia U :B:	.30	.75
6 Archaeomancer C :B:	.20	.50
7 Body Double R :B:	.75	2.00
8 Chronomaton U	1.00	2.50
9 Claustrophobia C :B:	.20	.50
10 Consume Strength C :K/G:	.20	.50
11 Control Magic U :B:	.50	1.25
12 Corpse Traders U :K:	.30	.75
13 Crosstown Courier C :B:	.30	.75
14 Death-Hood Cobra C :G:	.30	.75
15 Dread Statuary U	.30	.75
16 Dream Stalker C :B:	.20	.50
17 Drooling Groodion U :K/G:	.30	.75
18 Errant Ephemeron C :B:	.20	.50
19 Festerhide Boar C :G:	.20	.50
20 Forest L	.20	.50
21 Forest L	.20	.50
22 Forest L	.20	.50
23 Forest L	.20	.50
24 Forest L	.20	.50
25 Future Sight R :B:	2.00	5.00
26 Gatecreeper Vine C :G:	.20	.50
27 Golgari Guildgate C	.30	.75
28 Griptide C :B:	.20	.50
29 Grisly Spectacle C :K:	.20	.50
30 Halimar Depths C	.40	1.00
31 Highway Robber C :K:	.20	.50
32 Hypnotic Cloud C :K:	.20	.50
33 Into the Roil C :B:	.30	.75
34 Island L	.20	.50
35 Island L	.20	.50
36 Island L	.20	.50
37 Island L	.20	.50
38 Island L	.20	.50
39 Jace, Architect of Thought M :B:	4.00	10.00
40 Jace's Ingenuity U :B:	.30	.75
41 Jace's Mindseeker R :B:	.60	1.50
42 Jace's Phantasm U :B:	.75	2.00
43 Krovikan Mist C :B:	.40	1.00
44 Last Kiss C :K:	.30	.75
45 Leyline Phantom C :B:	.30	.75
46 Marsh Casualties U :K:	.30	.75
47 Memory Lapse C :B:	.30	.75
48 Merfolk Wayfinder U :B:	.30	.75
49 Mold Shambler C :G:	.20	.50
50 Nekrataal U :K:	.30	.75
51 Night's Whisper U :K:	.60	1.50
52 Ohran Viper R :G:	.75	2.00
53 Oran-Rief Recluse C :G:	.20	.50
54 Phantasmal Bear C :B:	.30	.75
55 Phantasmal Dragon U :B:	.30	.75
56 Prohibit C :B:	.30	.75
57 Pulse Tracker C :K:	.30	.75
58 Putrid Leech C :K/G:	.30	.75
59 Ray of Command C :B:	.20	.50
60 Reaper of the Wilds R :K/G:	.75	2.00
61 Remand U :B:	6.00	15.00
62 Riftwing Cloudskate U :B:	.30	.75
63 River Boa U :G:	.30	.75
64 Rogue's Passage U	.30	.75
65 Sadistic Augermage C :K:	.30	.75
66 Sea Gate Oracle C :B:	.20	.50
67 Shadow Alley Denizen C :K:	.20	.50
68 Slate Street Ruffian C :K:	.30	.75
69 Spawnwrithe R :G:	.60	1.50
70 Spelltwine R :B:	.60	1.50
71 Stab Wound C :K:	.20	.50
72 Stealer of Secrets C :B:	.30	.75
73 Stonefare Crocodile C :G:	.20	.50
74 Summoner's Bane U :B:	.30	.75
75 Swamp L	.20	.50
76 Swamp L	.20	.50
77 Swamp L	.20	.50
78 Swamp L	.20	.50
79 Swamp L	.20	.50
80 Tainted Wood U	.75	2.00
81 Tavern Swindler U :K:	.30	.75
82 Thought Scour C :B:	.30	.75
83 Tragic Slip C :K:	.40	1.00
84 Treasured Find U :K/G:	.30	.75
85 Underworld Connections R :K:	1.25	3.00
86 Vinelasher Kudzu R :G:	.60	1.50
87 Vraska the Unseen M :K/G:	2.00	5.00
88 Wight of Precinct Six U :K:	.40	1.00

2014 Magic The Gathering Speed vs. Cunning

Card	Low	High
DUEL DECK	12.00	30.00
RELEASED ON SEPTEMBER 5, 2014		
1 Arrow Volley Trap U :W:	.20	.50
2 Dauntless Onslaught U :W:	.20	.50
3 Hold the Line R :W:	.40	1.00
4 Infantry Veteran C :W:	.10	.25
5 Kor Hookmaster C :W:	.10	.25
6 Leonin Snarecaster C :W:	.10	.25
7 Lone Missionary C :W:	.10	.25
8 Master Decoy C :W:	.10	.25
9 Stave Off C :W:	.10	.25
10 Stonecloaker U :W:	.20	.50
11 Swift Justice C :W:	.10	.25
12 Aquamorph Entity C :B:	.10	.25
13 Arcanis the Omnipotent M :B:	2.50	6.00
14 Coral Trickster C :B:	.10	.25
15 Dregscape Zombie C :B:	.10	.25
16 Echo Tracer C :B:	.10	.25
17 Faerie Impostor U :B:	.20	.50
18 Faerie Invaders C :B:	.10	.25
19 Fathom Seer C :B:	.10	.25
20 Fleeting Distraction C :B:	.10	.25
21 Impulse C :B:	.10	.25
22 Jeskai Elder U :B:	.20	.50
23 Mana Leak C :B:	.20	.50
24 Repeal C :B:	.10	.25
25 Sphinx of Uthuun R :B:	.40	1.00
26 Thousand Winds R :B:	.40	1.00
27 Traumatic Visions C :B:	.10	.25
28 Whiplash Trap C :B:	.10	.25
29 Willbender U :B:	.20	.50
30 Bone Splinters C :K:	.10	.25
31 Fleshbag Marauder U :K:	.20	.50
32 Act of Treason C :R:	.10	.25
33 Arc Trail U :R:	.20	.50
34 Banefire R :R:	.40	1.00
35 Beetleback Chief U :R:	.20	.50
36 Fiery Fall C :R:	.10	.25
37 Frenzied Goblin U :R:	.20	.50
38 Fury of the Horde R :R:	.60	1.50
39 Ghitu Encampment U :R:	.20	.50
40 Goblin Bombardment U :R:	.20	.50
41 Goblin Warchief U :R:	.75	2.00
42 Hell's Thunder R :R:	.40	1.00
43 Hellraiser Goblin U :R:	.20	.50
44 Inferno Trap U :R:	.20	.50
45 Krenko's Command C :R:	.10	.25
46 Krenko, Mob Boss R :R:	1.50	4.00
47 Mardu Heart-Piercer U :R:	.20	.50
48 Ogre Battledriver R :R:	.40	1.00
49 Oni of Wild Places U :R:	.20	.50
50 Orcish Cannonade C :R:	.10	.25
51 Reckless Abandon C :R:	.10	.25
52 Scourge Devil U :R:	.20	.50
53 Shock C :R:	.10	.25
54 Sparkmage Apprentice C :R:	.10	.25
55 Lightning Angel R :D:	.40	1.00
56 Zurgo Helmsmasher M :D:	2.50	6.00
57 Flame-Kin Zealot U :R: :W:	.20	.50
58 Goblin Deathraiders C :K: :R:	.10	.25
59 Hussar Patrol C :W: :B:	.10	.25
60 Kathari Bomber C :K: :R:	.10	.25
61 Lightning Helix U :R: :W:	1.25	3.00
62 Shambling Remains U :K: :R:	.20	.50
63 Steam Augury R :G: :R:	.40	1.00
64 Evolving Wilds C :L:	.10	.25
65 Island L	.10	.25
66 Island L	.10	.25
67 Island L	.10	.25
68 Mountain L	.10	.25
69 Mountain L	.10	.25
70 Mountain L	.10	.25
71 Mountain L	.10	.25
72 Mystic Monastery U :L:	.30	.75
73 Nomad Outpost U :L:	.25	.60
74 Plains L	.10	.25
75 Plains L	.10	.25
76 Plains L	.10	.25
77 Plains L	.10	.25
78 Swamp L	.10	.25
79 Swamp L	.10	.25
80 Swamp L	.10	.25
81 Terramorphic Expanse C :L:	.10	.25
T1 Goblin Token	.20	.50

2015 Magic The Gathering Elspeth vs. Kiora

Card	Low	High
COMPLETE SET (65)	15.00	40.00
DUEL DECK	10.00	25.00
RELEASED ON FEBRUARY 27, 2015		
1 Banisher Priest U :W:	.20	.50
2 Captain of the Watch R :W:	.40	1.00
3 Celestial Flare C :W:	.10	.25
4 Court Street Denizen C :W:	.10	.25
5 Dauntless Onslaught U :W:	.20	.50
6 Decree of Justice R :W:	.40	1.00
7 Dictate of Heliod R :W:	.40	1.00
8 Elspeth, Sun's Champion M :W:	5.00	12.00
9 Gempalm Avenger C :W:	.10	.25
10 Gustcloak Harrier C :W:	.10	.25
11 Gustcloak Savior R :W:	.40	1.00
12 Gustcloak Sentinel U :W:	.20	.50
13 Gustcloak Skirmisher U :W:	.20	.50
14 Icatian Javelineers C :W:	.10	.25
15 Kinsbaile Skirmisher C :W:	.10	.25
16 Kor Skyfisher C :W:	.10	.25
17 Loxodon Partisan C :W:	.10	.25
18 Mighty Leap C :W:	.10	.25
19 Mortal's Ardor C :W:	.10	.25
20 Mother of Runes U :W:	1.25	3.00
21 Noble Templar C :W:	.10	.25
22 Precinct Captain R :W:	.40	1.00
23 Raise the Alarm C :W:	.10	.25
24 Soul Parry C :W:	.10	.25
25 Standing Troops C :W:	.10	.25
26 Sunlance C :W:	.10	.25
27 Veteran Armorsmith C :W:	.10	.25
28 Veteran Swordsmith C :W:	.10	.25
29 Accumulated Knowledge C :B:	.10	.25
30 AEtherize U :B:	.20	.50
31 Man-o'-War C :B:	.10	.25
32 Omenspeaker C :B:	.10	.25
33 Scourge of Fleets R :B:	.40	1.00
34 Sealock Monster U :B:	.20	.50
35 Surrakar Banisher C :B:	.10	.25
36 Whelming Wave R :B:	.40	1.00

2015 Magic The Gathering Elspeth vs. Kiora

Card	Low	High
37 Explore C :G:	.20	.50
38 Explosive Vegetation U :G:	.30	.75
39 Nessian Asp C :G:	.10	.25
40 Netcaster Spider C :G:	.10	.25
41 Time to Feed C :G:	.10	.25
42 Coiling Oracle C :M:	.10	.25
43 Kiora's Follower U :M:	.20	.50
44 Kiora, the Crashing Wave M :M:	4.00	10.00
45 Lorescale Coatl U :M:	.30	.75
46 Nimbus Swimmer U :M:	.20	.50
47 Peel from Reality C :M:	.10	.25
48 Plasm Capture R :M:	.40	1.00
49 Simic Sky Swallower R :M:	.40	1.00
50 Urban Evolution U :M:	.20	.50
51 Evolving Wilds C	.10	.25
52 Grazing Gladehart C	.10	.25
53 Inkwell Leviathan R	.75	2.00
54 Secluded Steppe C	.10	.25
55 Temple of the False God U	.20	.50
56 Forest (63) L	.10	.25
57 Forest (64) L	.10	.25
58 Forest (65) L	.10	.25
59 Island (60) L	.10	.25
60 Island (61) L	.10	.25
61 Island (62) L	.10	.25
62 Plains (30) L	.10	.25
63 Plains (31) L	.10	.25
64 Plains (32) L	.10	.25
65 Plains (33) L	.10	.25
T1 Kraken Token T	.20	.50
T2 Soldier Token T	.20	.50

2015 Magic The Gathering Duel Decks Anthology

Card	Low	High
COMPLETE SET (249)	60.00	120.00
RELEASED ON DECEMBER 5, 2014		
DD-1 Akroma, Angel of Wrath M :W:	6.00	15.00
DD-9 Angel of Mercy U :W:	.20	.50
DD-19 Angelic Benediction U :W:	.20	.50
DD-3 Angelic Page C :W:	.20	.50
DD-6 Angelic Protector U :W:	.20	.50
DD-15 Angelsong C :W:	.10	.25
DD-4 Charging Paladin C :W:	.10	.25
DD-20 Faith's Fetters C :W:	.10	.25
DD-14 Healing Salve C :W:	.10	.25
10 Icatian Priest U :W:	.20	.50
DD-12 Luminous Angel R :W:	1.50	4.00
DD-16 Otherworldly Journey U :W:	.20	.50
DD-17 Pacifism C :W:	.10	.25
DD-13 Reya Dawnbringer R :W:	.75	2.00
DD-22 Righteous Cause U :W:	.20	.50
DD-7 Serra Advocate U :W:	.20	.50
DD-10 Serra Angel U :W:	.20	.50
DD-18 Serra's Boon U :W:	.20	.50
DD-21 Serra's Embrace U :W:	.20	.50
DD-8 Sustainer of the Realm U :W:	.20	.50
DD-11 Twilight Shepherd R :W:	.40	1.00
DD-5 Venerable Monk C :W:	.10	.25
JC-17 Aethersnipe C :B:	.10	.25
JC-13 Air Elemental U :B:	.20	.50
JC-21 Ancestral Vision R :B:	3.00	8.00
JC-18 Brine Elemental U :B:	.20	.50
JC-28 Condescend C :B:	.10	.25
JC-24 Counterspell C :B:	1.50	4.00
JC-23 Daze C :B:	2.00	5.00
JC-20 Errant Ephemeron C :B:	.10	.25
JC-26 Fact or Fiction U :B:	.20	.50
JC-3 Fathom Seer C :B:	.10	.25
JC-10 Fledgling Mawcor U :B:	.20	.50
JC-14 Guile R :B:	.40	1.00
JC-27 Gush C :B:	.10	.25
JC-1 Jace Beleren M :B:	4.00	10.00
JC-8 Man-o'-War C :B:	.10	.25
JC-2 Martyr of Frost C :B:	.10	.25
JC-12 Mulldrifter C :B:	.10	.25
JC-9 Ophidian C :B:	.10	.25
JC-19 Quicksilver Dragon R :B:	.40	1.00
JC-25 Repulse C :B:	.10	.25
JC-15 Riftwing Cloudskate U :B:	.20	.50
JC-4 Voidmage Apprentice C :B:	.10	.25
JC-5 Wall of Deceit U :B:	.20	.50
JC-11 Waterspout Djinn U :B:	.20	.50
JC-6 Willbender U :B:	.20	.50
DD-31 Abyssal Gatekeeper C :K:	.10	.25
DD-40 Abyssal Specter U :K:	.20	.50
GL-48 Bad Moon R :K:	.75	2.00
DD-52 Barter in Blood U :K:	.20	.50
DD-53 Breeding Pit U :K:	.20	.50
DD-41 Cackling Imp C :K:	.10	.25
DD-56 Consume Spirit U :K:	.20	.50
DD-55 Corrupt U :K:	.20	.50
GL-57 Corrupt U :K:	.20	.50
DD-48 Cruel Edict U :K:	.20	.50
DD-33 Daggerclaw Imp U :K:	.20	.50
DD-50 Dark Banishing C :K:	.10	.25
DD-45 Dark Ritual C :K:	1.50	4.00
GL-33 Deathgreeter C :K:	.10	.25
DD-49 Demonic Tutor U :K:	8.00	20.00
DD-38 Demon's Jester C :K:	.10	.25
GL-36 Drudge Skeletons C :K:	.10	.25
DD-46 Duress C :K:	.10	.25
DD-34 Dusk Imp C :K:	.10	.25
GL-58 Enslave U :K:	.20	.50
GL-42 Faerie Macabre C :K:	.10	.25
DD-42 Fallen Angel U :K:	.20	.50
GL-38 Fleshbag Marauder U :K:	.20	.50
DD-32 Foul Imp C :K:	.10	.25
GL-47 Genju of the Fens U :K:	.20	.50
GL-34 Ghost-Lit Stalker U :K:	.20	.50
GL-52 Hideous End C :K:	.10	.25
GL-43 Howling Banshee U :K:	.20	.50
GL-51 Ichor Slick C :K:	.10	.25
GL-44 Keening Banshee U :K:	.20	.50
DD-44 Kuro, Pitlord R :K:	.40	1.00
GL-32 Liliana Vess M :K:	5.00	12.00
DD-30 Lord of the Pit M :K:	1.25	3.00
GL-55 Mutilate R :K:	.50	1.25
DD-51 Oni Possession U :K:	.20	.50
DD-35 Overeager Apprentice C :K:	.10	.25
GL-39 Phyrexian Rager C :K:	.10	.25
DD-54 Promise of Power R :K:	.40	1.00
GL-37 Ravenous Rats C :K:	.20	.50
DD-43 Reiver Demon R :K:	1.00	2.50
GL-56 Rise from the Grave U :K:	.20	.50
GL-49 Sign in Blood C :K:	.10	.25
GL-46 Skeletal Vampire R :K:	.40	1.00
GL-53 Snuff Out C :K:	1.00	2.50
DD-37 Soot Imp U :K:	.20	.50
DD-39 Souldrinker U :K:	.20	.50
DD-36 Stinkweed Imp C :K:	.10	.25
GL-54 Tendrils of Corruption C :K:	.10	.25
GL-45 Twisted Abomination C :K:	.10	.25
DD-47 Unholy Strength C :K:	.10	.25
GL-40 Urborg Syphon-Mage C :K:	.10	.25
GL-35 Vampire Bats C :K:	.10	.25
GL-50 Vicious Hunger C :K:	.10	.25
GL-41 Wall of Bone U :K:	.20	.50
EG-33 Akki Coalflinger U :R:	.20	.50
EG-54 Boggart Shenanigans U :R:	.20	.50
JC-34 Chandra Nalaar M :R:	2.00	5.00
JC-47 Chartooth Cougar C :R:	.10	.25
EG-34 Clickslither R :R:	.40	1.00
JC-54 Cone of Flame U :R:	.20	.50
JC-57 Demonfire R :R:	1.50	4.00
EG-35 Emberwilde Augur C :R:	.10	.25
JC-56 Fireball U :R:	.20	.50
JC-55 Fireblast C :R:	.50	1.25
JC-49 Firebolt C :R:	.10	.25
JC-36 Fireslinger C :R:	.10	.25
JC-53 Flame Javelin U :R:	.20	.50
JC-35 Flamekin Brawler C :R:	.10	.25
JC-42 Flametongue Kavu U :R:	.20	.50
EG-36 Flamewave Invoker U :R:	.20	.50
JC-40 Flamewave Invoker U :R:	.20	.50
JC-43 Furnace Whelp U :R:	.20	.50
EG-37 Gempalm Incinerator U :R:	.20	.50
EG-38 Goblin Cohort C :R:	.10	.25
EG-39 Goblin Matron U :R:	1.50	4.00
EG-40 Goblin Ringleader U :R:	3.00	8.00
EG-41 Goblin Sledder C :R:	.10	.25
EG-42 Goblin Warchief U :R:	1.50	4.00
JC-48 Hostility R :R:	.40	1.00
EG-43 Ib Halfheart, Goblin Tactician R :R:	.75	2.00
JC-51 Incinerate C :R:	.20	.50
JC-45 Ingot Chewer C :R:	.10	.25
JC-41 Inner-Flame Acolyte C :R:	.10	.25
JC-52 Magma Jet U :R:	.20	.50
EG-44 Mogg Fanatic U :R:	.40	1.00
EG-45 Mogg War Marshal C :R:	.10	.25
EG-46 Mudbutton Torchrunner C :R:	.10	.25
JC-38 Pyre Charger U :R:	.20	.50
EG-47 Raging Goblin C :R:	.10	.25
JC-44 Rakdos Pit Dragon R :R:	.40	1.00
EG-48 Reckless One U :R:	.20	.50
JC-50 Seal of Fire C :R:	.10	.25
EG-32 Siege-Gang Commander R :R:	.40	1.00
EG-49 Skirk Drill Sergeant U :R:	.20	.50
EG-50 Skirk Fire Marshal R :R:	.75	2.00
EG-51 Skirk Prospector C :R:	.10	.25
EG-52 Skirk Shaman C :R:	.10	.25
JC-39 Slith Firewalker U :R:	.20	.50
JC-37 Soulbright Flamekin C :R:	.10	.25
EG-55 Spitting Earth C :R:	.10	.25
EG-53 Tar Pitcher U :R:	.20	.50
EG-56 Tarfire C :R:	.10	.25
GL-3 Albino Troll U :G:	.20	.50
EG-2 Allosaurus Rider R :G:	.40	1.00
EG-1 Ambush Commander R :G:	.40	1.00
GL-2 Basking Rootwalla C :G:	.10	.25
GL-23 Beast Attack U :G:	.20	.50
GL-7 Blastoderm C :G:	.10	.25
GL-18 Elephant Guide U :G:	.20	.50
EG-3 Elvish Eulogist C :G:	.10	.25
EG-4 Elvish Harbinger U :G:	1.00	2.50
EG-20 Elvish Promenade U :G:	1.00	2.50
EG-5 Elvish Warrior C :G:	.10	.25
GL-1 Garruk Wildspeaker M :G:	4.00	10.00
EG-6 Gempalm Strider U :G:	.20	.50
GL-13 Genju of the Cedars U :G:	.20	.50
EG-21 Giant Growth C :G:	.10	.25
GL-14 Giant Growth C :G:	.10	.25
EG-22 Harmonize U :G:	.20	.50
GL-21 Harmonize U :G:	.60	1.50
EG-7 Heedless One U :G:	.75	2.00
EG-8 Imperious Perfect U :G:	1.00	2.50
GL-10 Indrik Stomphowler U :G:	.20	.50
GL-19 Invigorate C :G:	.75	2.00
GL-11 Krosan Tusker C :G:	.10	.25
GL-16 Lignify C :G:	.20	.50
EG-9 Llanowar Elves C :G:	.10	.25
EG-10 Lys Alana Huntmaster C :G:	.10	.25
GL-17 Nature's Lore C :G:	1.50	4.00
GL-24 Overrun U :G:	.20	.50
GL-12 Plated Slagwurm R :G:	.40	1.00
GL-15 Rancor C :G:	1.00	2.50
GL-8 Ravenous Baloth R :G:	.40	1.00
GL-22 Rude Awakening R :G:	.40	1.00
GL-9 Stampeding Wildebeests U :G:	.20	.50
EG-11 Stonewood Invoker C :G:	.10	.25
EG-12 Sylvan Messenger U :G:	.20	.50
EG-13 Timberwatch Elf C :G:	.10	.25
GL-4 Vine Trellis C :G:	.10	.25
EG-14 Voice of the Woods R :G:	.40	1.00
EG-15 Wellwisher C :G:	.60	1.50
GL-5 Wild Mongrel C :G:	.10	.25
EG-23 Wildsize C :G:	.10	.25
GL-25 Windstorm U :G:	.20	.50
EG-16 Wirewood Herald C :G:	.10	.25
GL-6 Wirewood Savage C :G:	.12	.30
EG-17 Wirewood Symbiote U :G:	.75	2.00
EG-18 Wood Elves C :G:	.12	.30
EG-19 Wren's Run Vanquisher U :G:	.40	1.00
DD-58 Barren Moor C :L:	.10	.25
EG-28 Forest L :L:	.10	.25
EG-29 Forest L :L:	.10	.25
EG-30 Forest L :L:	.10	.25
EG-31 Forest L :L:	.10	.25
GL-28 Forest L :L:	.10	.25
GL-29 Forest L :L:	.10	.25
GL-30 Forest L :L:	.10	.25
GL-31 Forest L :L:	.10	.25
EG-57 Forgotten Cave C :L:	.10	.25
EG-58 Goblin Burrows U :L:	.20	.50
JC-30 Island L :L:	.10	.25
JC-31 Island L :L:	.10	.25
JC-32 Island L :L:	.10	.25
JC-33 Island L :L:	.10	.25
JC-58 Keldon Megaliths U :L:	.20	.50
EG-59 Mountain L :L:	.10	.25
EG-60 Mountain L :L:	.10	.25
EG-61 Mountain L :L:	.10	.25
EG-62 Mountain L :L:	.10	.25
JC-59 Mountain L :L:	.10	.25
JC-60 Mountain L :L:	.10	.25
JC-61 Mountain L :L:	.10	.25
JC-62 Mountain L :L:	.10	.25
DD-26 Plains L :L:	.10	.25
DD-27 Plains L :L:	.10	.25
DD-28 Plains L :L:	.10	.25
DD-29 Plains L :L:	.10	.25
GL-59 Polluted Mire C :L:	.10	.25
DD-25 Secluded Steppe C :L:	.10	.25
GL-26 Slippery Karst C :L:	.10	.25
DD-59 Swamp L :L:	.10	.25
DD-60 Swamp L :L:	.10	.25
DD-61 Swamp L :L:	.10	.25
DD-62 Swamp L :L:	.25	.60
GL-60 Swamp L :L:	.10	.25
GL-61 Swamp L :L:	.10	.25
GL-62 Swamp L :L:	.10	.25
GL-63 Swamp L :L:	.10	.25
JC-29 Terrain Generator U :L:	1.25	3.00
EG-26 Tranquil Thicket C :L:	.10	.25
GL-27 Treetop Village U :L:	.20	.50
EG-27 Wirewood Lodge U :L:	1.00	2.50
DD-23 Angel's Feather U :A:	.20	.50
JC-7 Bottle Gnomes U :A:	.20	.50
DD-57 Demon's Horn U :A:	.20	.50
DD-24 Marble Diamond U :A:	.20	.50
JC-22 Mind Stone U :A:	.20	.50
EG-24 Moonglove Extract C :A:	.10	.25
JC-46 Oxidda Golem C :A:	.10	.25
GL-20 Serrated Arrows C :A:	.10	.25
EG-25 Slate of Ancestry R :A:	.75	2.00
JC-16 Spire Golem C :A:	.10	.25

2015 Magic The Gathering Zendikar vs. Eldrazi

Card	Low	High
COMPLETE SET (80)	20.00	35.00
RELEASED ON AUGUST 28, 2015		
1 Avenger of Zendikar M :G:	3.50	4.00
2 Affa Guard Hound U :W:	.05	.15
3 Caravan Escort C :W:	.05	.15
4 Kabira Vindicator U :W:	.05	.15
5 Knight of Cliffhaven C :W:	.05	.15
6 Makindi Griffin C :W:	.05	.15
7 Oust U :W:	.05	.15
8 Repel the Darkness C :W:	.05	.15
9 Sheer Drop C :W:	.05	.15
10 Beastbreaker of Bala Ged U :G:	.05	.15
11 Daggerback Basilisk C :G:	.05	.15
12 Frontier Guide U :G:	.05	.15
13 Graypelt Hunter C :G:	.05	.15
14 Grazing Gladehart C :G:	.05	.15
15 Groundswell C :G:	1.00	1.25
16 Harrow C :G:	.05	.15
17 Joraga Bard C :G:	.05	.15
18 Khalni Heart Expedition C :G:	.20	.30
19 Ondu Giant C :G:	.05	.15
20 Primal Command R :G:	1.00	1.50
21 Retreat to Kazandu U :G:	.05	.15
22 Scute Mob R :G:	.60	1.00
23 Tajuru Archer U :G:	.05	.15
24 Territorial Baloth C :G:	.05	.15
25 Turntimber Basilisk U :G:	.05	.15
26 Wildheart Invoker C :G:	.05	.15
27 Veteran Warleader R :M:	.20	.30
28 Explorer's Scope C :A:	.05	.15
29 Seer's Sundial R :A:	.15	.25
30 Stonework Puma C :A:	.05	.15
31 Evolving Wilds C :L:	.05	.15
32 Graypelt Refuge U :L:	.05	.15
33 Stirring Wildwood R :L:	1.00	1.25
34 Turntimber Grove C :L:	.05	.15
35 Plains L :L:	.05	.15
36 Plains L :L:	.05	.15
37 Plains L :L:	.05	.15
38 Forest L :L:	.05	.15
39 Forest L :L:	.05	.15
40 Forest L :L:	.05	.15
41 Oblivion Sower M	1.50	2.00
42 Artisan of Kozilek U	.30	.50
43 It That Betrays R	1.50	2.00
44 Ulamog's Crusher C	.05	.15
45 Bloodrite Invoker C :K:	.05	.15
46 Bloodthrone Vampire C :K:	.05	.15
47 Butcher of Malakir R :K:	.15	.25
48 Cadaver Imp C :K:	.05	.15
49 Consume the Meek R :K:	.15	.25
50 Corpsehatch U :K:	.05	.15
51 Dominator Drone C :K:	.05	.15
52 Heartstabber Mosquito C :K:	.05	.15
53 Induce Despair C :K:	.05	.15
54 Marsh Casualties U :K:	.05	.15
55 Pawn of Ulamog U :K:	.20	.30
56 Read the Bones C :K:	.05	.15
57 Smother U :K:	.05	.15
58 Vampire Nighthawk U :K:	.75	1.15
59 Emrakul's Hatcher C :R:	.05	.15
60 Forked Bolt C :R:	.40	.60
61 Hellion Eruption R :R:	.15	.25
62 Magmaw R :R:	.10	.20
63 Torch Slinger C :R:	.05	.15
64 Forerunner of Slaughter U :M:	.05	.15
65 Mind Stone U :A:	.15	.25
66 Runed Servitor U :A:	.05	.15
67 Akoum Refuge U :L:	.05	.15
68 Eldrazi Temple U :L:	6.00	7.50
69 Rocky Tar Pit U :L:	.05	.15
70 Swamp L :L:	.05	.15
71 Swamp L :L:	.05	.15
72 Swamp L :L:	.05	.15
73 Mountain L :L:	.05	.15
74 Mountain L :L:	.05	.15
75 Mountain L :L:	.05	.15
76 Eldrazi Spawn C :T:	.05	.15
77 Eldrazi Spawn C :T:	.05	.15
78 Eldrazi Spawn C :T:	.05	.15
79 Hellion C :T:	.05	.15
80 Plant C	.05	.15

2008 Magic The Gathering From the Vault Dragons

Card	Low	High
COMPLETE SET (15)	75.00	150.00
RELEASED ON AUGUST 28, 2008		
1 Ebon Dragon R :K:	3.00	8.00
2 Kokusho, the Evening Star R :K:	8.00	20.00
3 Bogarden Hellkite R :R:	2.50	6.00
4 Dragon Whelp R :R:	.75	2.00
5 Dragonstorm R :R:	5.00	12.00
6 Form of the Dragon R :R:	3.00	8.00
7 Shivan Dragon R :R:	1.50	4.00
8 Thunder Dragon R :R:	4.00	10.00
9 Two-Headed Dragon R :R:	2.00	5.00
10 Bladewing the Risen R :D:	3.00	8.00
11 Hellkite Overlord R :D:	3.00	8.00
12 Nicol Bolas R :D:	25.00	50.00
13 Niv-Mizzet, the Firemind R :D:	8.00	20.00
14 Rith, the Awakener R :D:	3.00	8.00
15 Draco R :A:	2.00	5.00

2009 Magic The Gathering From the Vault Exiled

Card	Low	High
COMPLETE SET (15)	75.00	125.00
RELEASED ON AUGUST 28, 2009		
1 Balance R :W:	2.50	6.00
2 Gifts Ungiven R :B:	3.00	8.00
3 Mystical Tutor R :B:	4.00	10.00
4 Serendib Efreet R :B:	2.50	6.00
5 Tinker R :B:	4.00	10.00
6 Necropotence R :K:	3.00	8.00
7 Goblin Lackey R :R:	6.00	15.00
8 Kird Ape R :R:	1.50	4.00
9 Berserk R :G:	20.00	50.00
10 Channel R :G:	2.00	5.00
11 Lotus Petal R :A:	4.00	10.00
12 Sensei's Divining Top R :A:	12.00	30.00
13 Skullclamp R :A:	2.50	6.00
14 Trinisphere R :A:	1.50	4.00
15 Strip Mine R :L:	6.00	15.00

2010 Magic The Gathering From the Vault Relics

Card	Low	High
COMPLETE SET (15)	75.00	125.00
RELEASED AUGUST 27, 2010		
1 Aether Vial M	10.00	25.00
2 Black Vise M	1.25	3.00
3 Isochron Scepter M	4.00	10.00
4 Ivory Tower M	1.50	4.00
5 Jester's Cap M	1.25	3.00
6 Karn, Silver Golem M	2.50	6.00
7 Masticore M	1.25	3.00
8 Memory Jar M	2.00	5.00
9 Mirari M	1.50	4.00
10 Mox Diamond M	12.00	30.00
11 Nevinyrral's Disk M	6.00	15.00
12 Sol Ring M	12.00	30.00
13 Sundering Titan M	1.50	4.00
14 Sword of Body and Mind M	5.00	12.00
15 Zuran Orb M	1.25	3.00

2011 Magic The Gathering From the Vault Legends

Card	Low	High
COMPLETE SET (15)	60.00	100.00
RELEASED ON AUGUST 8, 2011		
1 Mikaeus, the Lunarch M :W:	1.25	3.00
2 Sun Quan, Lord of Wu M :B:	1.50	4.00
3 Teferi, Mage of Zhalfir M :B:	4.00	10.00
4 Cao Cao, Lord of Wei M :K:	1.25	3.00
5 Visara the Dreadful M :K:	3.00	8.00
6 Kiki-Jiki, Mirror Breaker M :R:	10.00	25.00
7 Omnath, Locus of Mana M :G:	3.00	8.00
8 Captain Sisay M :W/G:	1.50	4.00
9 Doran, the Siege Tower M :W/B/G:	2.50	6.00
10 Kresh the Bloodbraided M :K/R/G:	1.50	4.00
11 Oona, Queen of the Fae M :B/K:	2.00	5.00
12 Progenitus M :W/B/K/R/G:	6.00	15.00
13 Rafiq of the Many M :W/B/G:	4.00	10.00
14 Sharuum the Hegemon M :W/B/K:	2.00	5.00
15 Ulamog, the Infinite Gyre M	20.00	40.00

2012 Magic The Gathering From the Vault Realms

Card	Low	High
COMPLETE SET (15)	75.00	150.00
RELEASED ON AUGUST 31, 2012		
1 Ancient Tomb M	10.00	25.00
2 Boseiju, Who Shelters All M	3.00	8.00
3 Cephalid Coliseum M	4.00	10.00
4 Desert M	1.50	4.00
5 Dryad Arbor M :G:	6.00	15.00
6 Forbidden Orchard M	3.00	8.00
7 Glacial Chasm M	2.50	6.00
8 Grove of the Burnwillows M	6.00	15.00
9 High Market M	2.50	6.00
10 Maze of Ith M	25.00	50.00
11 Murmuring Bosk M	2.50	6.00
12 Shivan Gorge M	2.00	5.00
13 Urborg, Tomb of Yawgmoth M	8.00	20.00
14 Vesuva M	6.00	15.00
15 Windbrisk Heights M	3.00	8.00

2013 Magic The Gathering From the Vault Twenty

Card	Low	High
COMPLETE SET (20)	75.00	150.00
RELEASED ON AUGUST 23, 2013		
1 Dark Ritual :K: M	2.50	6.00
2 Swords to Plowshares :W: M	5.00	12.00
3 Hymn to Tourach :K: M	4.00	10.00
4 Fyndhorn Elves :G: M	1.50	4.00
5 Impulse :B: M	1.00	2.50
6 Wall of Blossoms :G: M	1.25	3.00
7 Thran Dynamo M	2.50	6.00
8 Tangle Wire M	1.25	3.00
9 Fact or Fiction :B: M	1.25	3.00
10 Chainer's Edict :K: M	1.25	3.00
11 Akroma's Vengeance :W: M	1.25	3.00
12 Gilded Lotus M	4.00	10.00
13 Ink-Eyes, Servant of Oni :K: M	2.00	5.00
14 Char :R: M	1.00	2.50
15 Venser, Shaper Savant :B: M	6.00	15.00
16 Chameleon Colossus :G: M	1.00	2.50
17 Cruel Ultimatum :B::K::R: M	1.00	2.50
18 Jace, the Mind Sculptor :B: M	50.00	100.00
19 Green Sun's Zenith :G: M	3.00	8.00
20 Kessig Wolf Run M	1.25	3.00

2014 Magic The Gathering From the Vault Annihilation

Card	Low	High
COMPLETE SET (15)	12.00	30.00
RELEASED ON AUGUST 22, 2014		
1 Armageddon M :W:	2.00	5.00
2 Cataclysm M :W:	2.50	6.00
3 Martial Coup M :W:	1.00	2.50
4 Terminus M :W:	2.00	5.00
5 Wrath of God M :W:	2.50	6.00
6 Upheaval M :B:	.60	1.50
7 Fracturing Gust M :K:	1.25	3.00
8 Living Death M :K:	2.00	5.00
9 Virtue's Ruin M :K:	.50	1.25
10 Burning of Xinye M :R:	1.50	4.00
11 Decree of Annihilation M :R:	.40	1.00
12 Rolling Earthquake M :R:	3.00	8.00
13 Child of Alara M :D:	1.00	2.50
14 Firespout M :R: :G:	.60	1.50
15 Smokestack M :A:	2.00	5.00

2015 Magic The Gathering From the Vault Angels

COMPLETE SET (15)
RELEASED ON AUGUST 21, 2015
1 Akroma, Angel of Fury
2 Akroma, Angel of Wrath
3 Archangel of Strife
4 Aurelia, the Warleader
5 Avacyn, Angel of Hope
6 Baneslayer Angel
7 Entreat the Angels
8 Exalted Angel
9 Iona, Shield of Emeria
10 Iridescent Angel
11 Jenara, Asura of War
12 Lightning Angel
13 Platinum Angel
14 Serra Angel
15 Tariel, Reckoner of Souls

2016 Magic The Gathering From the Vault Lore

Card	Low	High
COMPLETE SET (16 CARDS)	70.00	585.00
FROM THE VAULT BOX	40.00	50.00
RELEASED ON AUGUST 19, 2016		
1 Beseech the Queen M	2.00	2.50
2 Cabal Ritual M	3.25	3.75
3 Conflux M	1.00	1.25
4 Dark Depths M	25.00	30.00
5 Glissa the Traitor M	1.00	1.50
6 Helvault M	.60	1.00
7 Memnarch M	4.00	4.75
8 Minds Desire M	1.25	1.75
9 Momir Vig Simic Visionary M	3.00	3.50
10 Near Dath Experience M	.60	1.00
11 Obliterate M	1.00	1.25
12 Phyrexian Processor M	1.00	1.25
13 Tolaria West M	3.75	4.25
14 Umezawas Jitte M	16.00	18.00
15 Unmask M	2.00	2.75
16 Marit Lage Token M	3.75	4.50

2009 Magic The Gathering Premium Deck Series Slivers

Card	Low	High
1 Acidic Sliver U :D:	.40	1.00
2 Amoeboid Changeline C :B:	.20	.50
3 Ancient Ziggurat U :L:	1.25	3.00
4 Aphetto Dredging C :K:	.20	.50
5 Armor Sliver U :W:	.30	.75
6 Barbed Sliver U :R:	.30	.75
7 Brood Sliver R :G:	1.50	4.00
8 Clot Sliver C :K:	.20	.50
9 Coat of Arms R :A:	2.00	5.00
10 Crystalline Sliver U :D:	2.00	5.00
11 Distant Melody C :B:	.20	.50
12 Forest C :L:	.20	.50
13 Frenzy Sliver C :K:	.20	.50
14 Fungus Sliver R :G:	.75	2.00
15 Fury Sliver U :R:	.40	1.00
16 Gemhide Sliver C :G:	.75	2.00
17 Heart Sliver C :R:	.75	2.00
18 Heartstone U :A:	.60	1.50
19 Hibernation Sliver U :D:	.30	.75
20 Homing Sliver C :R:	.30	.75
21 Island C :L:	.30	.75
22 Metallic Sliver C :A:	.30	.75
23 Might Sliver U :G:	.60	1.50
24 Mountain C :L:	.30	.75
25 Muscle Sliver C :G:	.75	2.00
26 Necrotic Sliver U :D:	1.25	3.00
27 Plains C :L:	.30	.75
28 Quick Sliver C :G:	.20	.50
29 Rootbound Crag R :L:	2.00	5.00
30 Rupture Spire C :L:	.30	.75
31 Sliver Overlord M :D:	2.00	5.00
32 Spectral Sliver U :K:	.30	.75
33 Spined Sliver U :D:	.30	.75
34 Swamp C :L:	.30	.75
35 Terramorphic Expanse C :L:	.30	.75
36 Victual Sliver U :D:	.30	.75
37 Virulent Sliver C :G:	.30	.75
38 Vivid Creek U :L:	.60	1.50
39 Vivid Grove U :L:	.60	1.50
40 Wild Pair R :G:	1.00	2.50
41 Winged Sliver C :B:	1.25	3.00

2010 Magic The Gathering Premium Deck Series Fire and Lightning

Card	Low	High
COMPLETE SET (34)	12.00	30.00
RELEASED ON NOVEMBER 19, 2010		
1 Ball Lightning R :R:	1.50	4.00
2 Browbeat U :R:	.60	1.50
3 Chain Lightning C :R:	6.00	15.00
4 Cinder Pyromancer C :R:	.10	.25
5 Fire Servant U :R:	.20	.50
6 Fireball U :R:	.20	.50
7 Fireblast C :R:	1.00	2.50
8 Flames of the Blood Hand U :R:	1.50	4.00
9 Grim Lavamancer R :R:	2.50	6.00
10 Hammer of Bogardan R :R:	.40	1.00
11 Hellspark Elemental U :R:	.75	2.00
12 Jackal Pup U :R:	.20	.50
13 Jaya Ballard, Task Mage R :R:	.20	.50
14 Keldon Champion U :R:	.20	.50

15 Keldon Marauders C :R:	.20	.50
16 Lightning Bolt C :R:	1.25	3.00
17 Mogg Fanatic U :R:	.20	.50
18 Mogg Flunkies C :R:	.10	.25
19 Pillage U :R:	.30	.75
20 Price of Progress U :R:	3.00	8.00
21 Reverberate R :R:	.40	1.00
22 Spark Elemental U :R:	.20	.50
23 Sudden Impact U :R:	.20	.50
24 Thunderbolt C :R:	.10	.25
25 Vulshok Sorcerer C :R:	.20	.50
26 Boggart Ram-Gang U :D:	.30	.75
27 Figure of Destiny R :D:	.75	2.00
28 Barbarian Ring U :L:	.20	.50
29 Ghitu Encampment U :L:	.20	.50
30 Mountain (31) L	.10	.25
31 Mountain (32) L	.10	.25
32 Mountain (33) L	.10	.25
33 Mountain (34) L	.10	.25
34 Teetering Peaks C :L:	.10	.25

2011 Magic The Gathering Premium Deck Series Graveborn

COMPLETE SET (30)	15.00	40.00
RELEASED ON NOVEMBER 18, 2011		
1 Blazing Archon R :W:	1.50	4.00
2 Animate Dead U :K:	1.25	3.00
3 Avatar of Woe R :K:	.40	1.00
4 Buried Alive U :K:	1.00	2.50
5 Cabal Therapy U :K:	5.00	12.00
6 Diabolic Servitude U :K:	.20	.50
7 Dread Return U :K:	1.00	2.50
8 Duress C :K:	.20	.50
9 Entomb R :K:	10.00	25.00
10 Exhume C :K:	.30	.75
11 Faceless Butcher C :K:	.20	.50
12 Hidden Horror U :K:	.20	.50
13 Last Rites C :K:	.20	.50
14 Putrid Imp C :K:	.30	.75
15 Reanimate U :K:	3.00	8.00
16 Sickening Dreams U :K:	.20	.50
17 Twisted Abomination C :K:	.20	.50
18 Zombie Infestation U :K:	.20	.50
19 Crosis, the Purger R :G:	2.00	5.00
20 Terastodon R :G:	.60	1.50
21 Verdant Force R :G:	.40	1.00
22 Inkwell Leviathan R	2.00	5.00
23 Sphinx of the Steel Wind M	.40	1.00
24 Crystal Vein L	.20	.50
25 Ebon Stronghold L	.20	.50
26 Polluted Mire L	.20	.50
27 Swamp (27) L	.10	.25
28 Swamp (28) L	.10	.25
29 Swamp (29) L	.10	.25
30 Swamp (30) L	.10	.25

1993-06 Magic The Gathering 6x9 Jumbos

1 Abeyance	8.00	15.00
3 Adarkar Wastes	4.00	6.00
5 All Hallow's Eve	10.00	20.00
17 Aswan Jaguar	8.00	12.00
19 Autumn Willow	6.00	8.00
112 Gem Bazaar	3.00	5.00
119 Goblin Polka Band	4.00	7.00
121 Greater Realm of Preservation		
122 Guardian Beast	15.00	22.00
126 Hurloon Minotaur	4.00	7.00
127 Hurricane	6.00	12.00
128 Hydroblast	6.00	15.00
129 Icy Manipulator	12.00	20.00
132 Incinerate	7.00	15.00
133 Incoming!	5.00	10.00
134 Infernal Contract	6.00	12.00
135 Infernal Spawn Of Evil	15.00	25.00
152 Island	2.00	3.00
153 Ivory Tower	8.00	15.00
155 Jester's Cap	3.00	7.00
156 Jokulhaups	5.00	8.00
157 Juzam Djinn	7.00	12.00
159 Karplusan Forest	1.00	2.00
163 Lhurgoyf	6.00	15.00
164 Library Of Alexandria	20.00	40.00
177 Meditate	7.00	12.00
180 Mirror Mirror	10.00	20.00
181 Mirror Universe	20.00	30.00
198 Mountain	3.00	5.00
201 Natural Balance	7.00	15.00
202 Necropolis of Azar	3.00	6.00
203 Necropotence	12.00	22.00
204 Nether Shadow	6.00	12.00
207 Orcish Catapult	3.00	6.00
208 Order of the White Shield	7.00	15.00
211 Pandora's Box	3.00	5.00
212 Personal Incarnation	7.00	15.00
227 Plains	2.00	4.00
230 Power Struggle	3.00	6.00
231 Pox	10.00	20.00
233 Prismatic Dragon	3.00	5.00
236 Prosperity	10.00	20.00
238 Pyroblast	6.00	12.00
239 Pyroclasm a	6.00	12.00
240 Pyroclasm b	10.00	20.00
244 Rainbow Knights	3.00	5.00
248 Recall	6.00	12.00
260 Serra Angel a	15.00	25.00
261 Serra Angel b	30.00	45.00
265 Shatterstorm	6.00	12.00
267 Shivan Dragon	10.00	20.00
269 Sibilant Spirit	7.00	15.00
277 Sol'kanar the Swamp King	4.00	7.00
283 Squandered Resources	10.00	20.00
284 Squirrel Farm	6.00	12.00
288 Stormbind	10.00	20.00
303 Swamp	2.00	4.00
306 Swords to Plowshares	15.00	25.00
316 Vampiric Tutor	20.00	30.00
317 Vesuvan Doppelganger	12.00	22.00
324 Wheel Of Fortune	20.00	30.00
325 Whimsy	3.00	5.00
331 Zuran Orb	10.00	20.00

1993-2010 Magic The Gathering Special Sets

All sets are complete.

1 Anthologies Set	40.00	60.00
3 Battle Royale Set	50.00	85.00
4 Beatdown Set	90.00	150.00
5 Beta Collector's Edition Set	800.00	1000.00
6 Deckmasters	35.00	45.00
78 Garfield/Finkel Deckmaster set	30.00	50.00
100 1997 World Champ Deck	25.00	35.00
110 1998 World Champ Deck	15.00	20.00
111 1998 World Champ Buehler Deck	20.00	30.00
120 1999 World Champ Deck	12.00	15.00
130 2000 World Champ Deck	20.00	25.00
140 2001 World Champ Deck	10.00	15.00
150 2002 World Champ Deck	12.00	18.00
151 2002 World Champ Kibler Deck	20.00	30.00
160 2003 World Champ Deck	10.00	12.00
170 2004 World Champ Deck	8.00	12.00

1993-14 Magic The Gathering Promos

1 Accumulated Knowledge (FNM) FOIL	10.00	15.00
2 Albino Troll (FNM) FOIL	4.00	8.00
3 APAC Land Set - a	12.00	18.00
4 APAC Land Set - b	12.00	18.00
5 APAC Land Set - c	12.00	18.00
6 Arc Lightning - FOIL	5.00	12.00
7 Archangel - Glossy Japanese	25.00	50.00
8 Arena	6.00	8.00
9 ARENA 2004 Land Set	8.00	11.00
10 Argothian Enchantress - FOIL	15.00	30.00
11 Armageddon - FOIL	35.00	50.00
12 Ashnod's Coupon - FOIL	5.00	10.00
13 Ass Whuppin' - FOIL	3.50	6.00
14 Aura of Silence (FNM) FOIL	3.00	6.00
15 Avalanche Riders (FNM) FOIL	5.00	10.00
16 Avatar of Hope - FOIL	6.00	12.00
17 Azorius Guildmage :M: FOIL		
18 Balance - Oversized 6X9	10.00	18.00
19 Balance (Judge Rew) FOIL	45.00	80.00
20 Balduvian Horde - Oversized 6X9	7.00	10.00
21 Balduvian Horde (Judge Rew) FOIL	7.00	15.00
22 Ball Lightning (Judge Rew) FOIL	18.00	30.00
23 Baron Sengir - Oversized 6X9	6.00	12.00
24 Beast of Burden - FOIL	3.00	6.00
25 Beast of Burden - FOIL Misprint	10.00	16.00
26 Black Knight - FOIL	8.00	11.00
27 Black Knight - Oversized 6X9	9.00	12.00
28 Black Lotus - Oversized 6X9	13.00	18.00
29 Blacker Lotus - Oversized 6X9	6.00	12.00
30 Blastoderm - FOIL	2.00	5.00
31 Blinking Spirit - Oversized 6X9	6.00	10.00
32 Bonesplitter - FOIL	3.00	7.00
33 Booster Tutor	4.00	7.00
34 Bottle Gnomes - FOIL	3.00	7.00
35 Brainstorm (FNM) FOIL	12.00	18.00
36 Brushland - Oversized 6X9	2.00	5.00
37 Budoka Pupil - FOIL	4.00	8.00
38 Cabal Therapy (FNM)	10.00	16.00
39 Cadaverous Bloom - Oversized 6X9	9.00	17.00
40 Call From the Grave - Oversized 6X9	6.00	12.00
41 Capsize (FNM) FOIL	4.00	8.00
42 Carnophage - FOIL	6.00	8.00
43 Carrion Feeder (FNM) FOIL	4.00	8.00
44 Chaos Orb - Oversized 6X9	6.00	8.00
45 Chill - FOIL	6.00	8.00
46 Circle of Protection: Art	5.00	8.00
47 City Of Brass - Oversized 6X9	12.00	22.00
48 City of Brass (JSS) FOIL	15.00	30.00
49 Colossal Whale P :B: FOIL		
50 Counterspell	10.00	15.00
51 Counterspell (Judge Rew) FOIL	10.00	20.00
52 Creeping Mold - FOIL	5.00	10.00
53 Crimson Hellkite - Oversized 6X9	6.00	12.00
54 Crusade (JSS) FOIL	9.00	15.00
55 Crystalline Sliver - FOIL	40.00	100.00
56 Cursed Scroll - Oversized 6X9	12.00	23.00
57 Dark Banishing - Oversized 6X9	10.00	16.00
58 Darksteel Ingot - FOIL	7.00	12.00
59 Dauthi Slayer - FOIL	6.00	10.00
60 Deflection - Oversized 6X9	6.00	10.00
61 Deranged Hermit (JUDGE) FOIL	8.00	15.00
62 Diabolic Edict - FOIL	12.00	18.00
63 Dimir Guildmage P FOIL		
64 Dirtcowl Wurm	7.00	10.00
65 Disenchant	7.00	10.00
66 Disenchant - Oversized 6X9	8.00	12.00
67 Disenchant (FNM) FOIL	8.00	15.00
68 Dismiss - FOIL	2.00	5.00
69 Dissipate - Oversized 6X9	5.00	8.00
70 Dissipate (FNM) FOIL	4.00	7.00
71 Drain Life - Oversized 6X9	10.00	15.00
72 Drain Life (FNM) FOIL	5.00	8.00
73 Duress - FOIL	8.00	15.00
74 Earthquake - Oversized 6X9	4.00	7.00
75 Elvish Aberration - FOIL	2.00	4.00
76 Elvish Lyrist (JSS) FOIL	2.00	4.00
77 Empyrial Armor - FOIL	3.00	6.00
78 Enduring Renewal - Oversized 6X9	10.00	15.00
79 Enlightened Tutor - FOIL	7.00	12.00
80 Erhnam Djinn - Oversized 6X9	8.00	12.00
81 Eternal Dragon (DCI) FOIL	25.00	50.00
82 Exalted Angel - FOIL	80.00	125.00
83 Faerie Dragon - Oversized 6X9	3.00	6.00
84 Fallen Angel - Oversized 6X9	10.00	17.00
85 False Prophet - FOIL	3.00	6.00
86 Feral Throwback - FOIL	2.00	4.00
87 Fireball	6.00	8.00
88 Fireball - Oversized 6X9	5.00	8.00
89 Fireball - Textless	4.00	7.00
90 Fireblast (FNM) FOIL	6.00	10.00
91 Fireslinger (FNM) FOIL	2.00	4.00
92 Flametongue Kavu (FNM) FOIL	7.00	10.00
93 Fling - FOIL	5.00	8.00
94 Forbid (FNM) FOIL	5.00	10.00
95 Force Of Nature - Oversized 6X9	6.00	12.00
96 Force of Nature P :G: FOIL		
97 Forest - 1996 Arena	5.00	8.00
98 Forest - 2003 Arena	2.00	4.00
99 Forest - 2004 Arena	2.00	4.00
100 Forest - APAC (Blue)	1.50	3.00
101 Forest - APAC (Clear)	2.00	4.00
102 Forest - APAC (Red)	2.00	4.00
103 Forest - EURO (Blue)	4.00	7.00
104 Forest - EURO (Purple)	4.00	7.00
105 Forest - EURO (Red)	4.00	7.00
106 Forest - FOIL Beta	3.00	6.00
107 Forest - FOIL Ice Age	2.00	4.00
108 Forest - FOIL Urza's Saga	3.00	5.00
109 Forest - GURU	15.00	30.00
110 Forest - Oversized 6X9	2.00	4.00
111 Fraternal Exaltation		
112 Fruitcake Elemental FOIL	25.00	50.00
113 Fungal Shambler - FOIL	2.00	4.00
114 Gaea's Blessing - FOIL	6.00	12.00
115 Gaea's Cradle - FOIL	35.00	60.00
116 Gemstone Mine (DCI) FOIL	50.00	70.00
117 Gemstone Mine (JUDGE)	50.00	85.00
118 Genju of Spires	8.00	12.00
119 Ghost–Lit Raider P :R: FOIL		
120 Giant Badger	4.00	7.00
121 Giant Badger (Spanish)		
122 Giant Growth - FOIL Beta	3.00	5.00
123 Giant Growth (FNM) FOIL	3.00	6.00
124 Gleancrawler FOIL	1.00	2.00
125 Glory - FOIL	4.00	6.00
126 Goblin Bombardment (FNM) FOIL	3.00	6.00
127 Goblin Mime	5.00	8.00
128 Granny's Payback	3.00	6.00
129 Grim Lavamancer (DCI) FOIL	45.00	80.00
130 Gruul Guildmage P FOIL		
131 Hammer of Bogardan - FOIL	10.00	15.00
132 Hedge Troll P :G: FOIL		
133 Helm of Kaldra - FOIL	2.00	5.00
134 Hermit Druid (Judge Rew) FOIL	15.00	25.00
135 Hypnotic Specter (Play.Rev)	15.00	20.00
136 Impulse - FOIL	6.00	10.00
137 Incinerate	4.00	7.00
138 Ink-Eyes, Servant of Oni - FOIL	6.00	8.00
139 Intuition (Judge Rew) FOIL	35.00	50.00
140 Island - 1996 Arena	3.00	6.00
141 Island - 2003 Arena FOIL	2.00	4.00
142 Island - 2004 Arena FOIL	2.00	3.00
143 Island - APAC (Blue)	3.00	6.00
144 Island - APAC (Clear)	3.00	6.00
145 Island - APAC (Red)	3.00	6.00
146 Island - EURO (Blue)	4.00	7.00
147 Island - EURO (Purple)	4.00	7.00
148 Island - EURO (Red)	4.00	7.00
149 Island - GURU	25.00	40.00
150 Island 1999 - FOIL Urza's Saga	3.00	6.00
151 Island 1999 - FOIL Urza's Saga No Symbol	10.00	18.00
152 Island 2001 - FOIL Ice Age	2.00	4.00
153 Island 2002- FOIL Beta	2.00	3.00
154 Jackal Pup (FNM) FOIL	4.00	8.00
155 Juggernaut (FNM) FOIL	8.00	10.00
156 Karn Silver Golem - FOIL	8.00	15.00
157 Krosan Tusker (FNM) FOIL	2.00	5.00
158 Krosan Warchief (FNM) FOIL	2.00	4.00
159 Laquatus's Champion - FOIL	3.00	5.00
160 Lightning Bolt (Judge Rew) FOIL	20.00	35.00
161 Lightning Dragon - FOIL	8.00	15.00
162 Lightning Helix FOIL	25.00	35.00
163 Lightning Hounds - FOIL	1.00	2.00
164 Lightning Rift (FNM) FOIL	2.00	3.00
165 Living Death (Judge Rew) FOIL	20.00	30.00
166 Llanowar Elves (FNM) FOIL	10.00	18.00
167 Longbow Archer (FNM) FOIL	3.00	5.00
168 Lord of Atlantis (JSS) FOIL	4.00	7.00
169 Lotus Bloom (DCI) FOIL	10.00	20.00
170 Lu Bu- Master-at-Arms (Singapore)	6.00	11.00
171 Magister of Worth P :M: FOIL		
172 Mana Crypt	30.00	50.00
173 Mana Leak - FOIL	7.00	11.00
174 Man-o'-War - FOIL	3.00	6.00
175 Marit Lage Token P		
176 Meddling Mage (DCI) FOIL	60.00	100.00
177 Memory Lapse (Judge Rew) FOIL	6.00	10.00
178 Mind Warp (FNM) FOIL	3.00	5.00
179 Mise	4.00	7.00
180 Mishra's Factory (DCI) FOIL	50.00	80.00
181 Mogg Fanatic (FNM) FOIL	6.00	10.00
182 Monstrous Hound	1.00	3.00
183 Mother of Runes (FNM) FOIL	5.00	10.00
184 Mountain - 1996 Arena	3.00	6.00
185 Mountain - 2003 Arena	2.00	3.00
186 Mountain - 2004 Arena	2.00	3.00
187 Mountain - APAC (Blue)	2.00	3.00
188 Mountain - APAC (Clear)	3.00	5.00
189 Mountain - APAC (Red)	3.00	5.00
190 Mountain - EURO (Blue)	4.00	7.00
191 Mountain - EURO (Purple)	4.00	7.00
192 Mountain - EURO (Red)	4.00	7.00
193 Mountain - FOIL Ice Age	2.00	3.00
194 Mountain - FOIL Urza's Saga	3.00	5.00
195 Mountain - GURU	20.00	35.00
196 Muscle Sliver (FNM) FOIL	5.00	10.00
197 Nalathni Dragon (Dragon Con 94)	2.00	4.00
198 Niv-Mizzet (DCI) FOIL	30.00	50.00
199 Oath of Druids (Judge Rew) FOIL	15.00	25.00
200 Ophidian (FNM) FOIL	4.00	7.00
201 Order Of The White Shield - Oversized 6X9	4.00	7.00
202 Overtaker - FOIL	1.00	2.00
203 Oxidize - Textless	4.00	7.00
204 Pernicious Deed (DCI) FOIL	40.00	80.00
205 Phyrexian Negator - FOIL	20.00	40.00
206 Pillage - FOIL	3.00	6.00
207 Plains - 1996 Arena	2.00	3.00
208 Plains - 2003 Arena	2.00	3.00
209 Plains - 2004 Arena	2.00	3.00
210 Plains - APAC (Blue)	3.00	5.00
211 Plains - APAC (Clear)	3.00	5.00
212 Plains - APAC (Red)	2.00	4.00
213 Plains - EURO (Blue)	4.00	7.00
214 Plains - EURO (Purple)	4.00	7.00
215 Plains - EURO (Red)	4.00	7.00
216 Plains - GURU	28.00	40.00
217 Plains 1999 - FOIL Urza's Saga	2.00	4.00
218 Plains 2001 - FOIL Ice Age	2.00	4.00
219 Plots that Spans Centuries P		
220 Pouncing Jaguar - FOIL	3.00	6.00
221 Powder Keg - FOIL	5.00	8.00
222 Priest of Titania (FNM) FOIL	5.00	11.00
223 Prodigal Sorcerer (FNM) FOIL	4.00	7.00
224 Proposal		
225 Psychatog - FOIL	7.00	12.00
226 Questing Pheldagrif - FOIL	1.00	2.00
227 Quirion Ranger (FNM) FOIL	3.00	6.00
228 Raging Kavu - FOIL	2.00	4.00
229 Rakdos Guildmage (DCI) FOIL	20.00	25.00
230 Rancor (FNM) FOIL	6.00	10.00
231 Rathi Assassin - FOIL	2.00	4.00
232 Reanimate (FNM) FOIL	6.00	10.00
233 Regrowth (DCI) FOIL	40.00	50.00
234 Revenant	5.00	8.00
235 Rewind - FOIL	6.00	11.00
236 Rhox - FOIL	2.00	4.00
237 River Boa (FNM) FOIL	6.00	10.00
238 Royal Assassin (JSS) FOIL	15.00	25.00
239 Rukh Egg - FOIL	2.00	4.00
240 Ryusei, the Falling Star - FOIL	4.00	7.00
241 Scent of Cinder	5.00	8.00
242 Scragnoth (FNM) FOIL	1.00	2.00
243 Seal of Cleansing - FOIL	5.00	8.00
244 Serra Angel - FOIL	40.00	70.00
245 Serra Avatar (JSS) FOIL	25.00	40.00
246 Serum Visions - FOIL	1.00	2.00
247 Sewers of Estark	1.00	3.00
248 Shard Phoenix (JSS) FOIL	10.00	18.00
249 Shield of Kaldra - FOIL	2.00	5.00
250 Shivan Dragon (Japanese Coro Coro)	5.00	10.00
251 Shock (FNM) FOIL	4.00	8.00
252 Shriekmaw T :K: FOIL		
253 Silent Specter - FOIL	3.00	5.00
254 Silver Knight (FNM) FOIL	3.00	5.00
255 Skirk Marauder - FOIL	1.00	2.00
256 Skittering Skirge - FOIL	2.00	4.00
257 Slice and Dice (FNM) FOIL	2.00	4.00
258 Slith Firewalker (JSS) FOIL	6.00	10.00
259 Smother (FNM) FOIL	3.00	6.00
260 Sol Ring (DCI) FOIL	30.00	60.00
261 Soldier Token (Red/White) P		
262 Soltari Priest (FNM) FOIL	5.00	8.00
263 Soul Collector - FOIL	3.00	6.00
264 Sparksmith (FNM) FOIL	3.00	6.00
265 Spike Feeder (FNM) FOIL	3.00	6.00
266 Spined Wurm (Top Deck)	5.00	10.00
267 Splendid Genesis	1000.00	2000.00
268 Staff of Nin P FOIL		
269 Staunch Defender (FNM) FOIL	1.00	3.00
270 Stone Rain (FNM) FOIL	5.00	8.00
271 Stone-Tongue Basilisk - FOIL	1.00	2.00
272 Storm Entity P :R: FOIL		
273 Stroke of Genius (Judge Rew) FOIL	18.00	30.00
274 Stupor - FOIL	2.00	4.00
275 Sudden Shock P :R: FOIL		
276 Swamp - 1996 Arena	2.00	4.00
277 Swamp - 2003 Arena	2.00	3.00
278 Swamp - 2004 Arena	2.00	3.00
279 Swamp - APAC (Blue)	2.00	4.00
280 Swamp - APAC (Clear)	2.00	5.00
281 Swamp - APAC (Red)	2.00	4.00
282 Swamp - EURO (Blue)	4.00	8.00
283 Swamp - EURO (Purple)	4.00	8.00
284 Swamp - EURO (Red)	4.00	8.00
285 Swamp - GURU	25.00	40.00
286 Swamp 1999 - FOIL Urza's Saga	3.00	5.00
287 Swamp 2001 - FOIL Ice Age	2.00	3.00
288 Sword of Kaldra - FOIL	3.00	5.00
289 Swords To Plowshares (FNM) FOIL	20.00	30.00
290 Terror - Textless	5.00	8.00
291 Terror (FNM) FOIL	6.00	12.00
292 Thorn Elemental (Japanese)	5.00	10.00
293 Thran Quarry (JSS) FOIL	6.00	11.00
294 Time Warp (Judge Rew) FOIL	25.00	40.00
295 Tradewind Rider (Judge Rew) FOIL	12.00	20.00
296 Treetop Village (FNM) FOIL	4.00	7.00
297 Tromokratis P :B: FOIL		
298 Two-Headed Dragon (JSS) FOIL	15.00	25.00
299 Uktabi Orangutan - FOIL	2.00	4.00
300 Underworld (DCI) FOIL	6.00	8.00
301 Underworld Dreams (2HG) FOIL	5.00	7.00
302 Vampiric Tutor - FOIL	20.00	40.00
303 Voidmage Prodigy - Alt Art	3.00	5.00
304 Voidslime (DCI) FOIL	40.00	60.00
305 Volcanic Geyser (FNM) FOIL	2.00	4.00
306 Volcanic Hammer (JSS) FOIL	2.00	4.00
307 Wall of Blossoms (FNM) FOIL	6.00	10.00
308 Warmonger - FOIL	1.00	2.00
309 Wasteland (DCI) FOIL	15.00	25.00
310 Whipcorder (FNM) FOIL	2.00	3.00
311 White Knight (FNM) FOIL	4.00	7.00
312 Willbender (FNM) FOIL	1.00	2.00
313 Windseeker Centaur	2.00	4.00
314 Withered Wretch (FNM) FOIL	2.00	5.00
315 Wrath of God (DCI) FOIL	20.00	40.00
316 Yawgmoth's Will (JUDGE) FOIL	25.00	50.00

2014 Magic The Gathering Khans of Tarkir Promos

160P Abzan Ascendancy		
163P Anafenza, the Foremost	4.00	10.00
164P Ankle Shanker	1.25	3.00
166P Avalanche Tusker	1.50	4.00
66P Bloodsoaked Champion	3.00	8.00
168P Butcher of the Horde	5.00	12.00
171P Crackling Doom	3.00	8.00
106P Crater's Claws	1.50	4.00
173P Deflecting Palm	2.50	6.00
36P Dig Through Time	12.00	30.00
108P Dragon-Style Twins	2.00	5.00
174P Duneblast	2.50	6.00
176P Flying Crane Technique	2.50	6.00
73P Grim Haruspex	1.50	4.00
133P Hardened Scales	1.50	4.00
12P Herald of Anafenza		
13P High Sentinels of Arashin		
42P Icy Blast		
179P Ivorytusk Fortress		
113P Jeering Instigator		
180P Jeskai Ascendancy	6.00	15.00
182P Kheru Lich Lord	1.50	4.00
185P Mardu Ascendancy	2.00	5.00
18P Master of Pearls		
190P Narset, Enlightened Master	5.00	12.00
82P Necropolis Fiend	2.00	5.00
193P Rakshasa Vizier		
144P Rattleclaw Mystic	2.50	6.00
195P Sage of the Inward Eye	1.25	3.00
199P Sidisi, Brood Tyrant	5.00	12.00
200P Siege Rhino	6.00	15.00
203P Sultai Ascendancy	1.25	3.00
206P Surrak Dragonclaw	5.00	12.00
207P Temur Ascendancy	2.50	6.00
58P Thousand Winds	2.50	6.00
154P Trail of Mystery	1.50	4.00
209P Trap Essence	2.50	6.00
210P Utter End	6.00	15.00
211P Villainous Wealth	3.00	8.00
214P Zurgo Helmsmasher	3.00	8.00

2015 Magic The Gathering Fate Reforged Promos

90P Alesha, Who Smiles at Death	6.00	15.00
91P Arcbond	4.00	10.00
62P Archfiend of Depravity	2.00	5.00
149P Atarka, World Render	6.00	15.00
64P Brutal Hordechief	8.00	20.00
9P Daghatar the Adamant	2.50	6.00
11P Dragonscale General	3.00	8.00
151P Dromoka, the Eternal	5.00	12.00
99P Flamerush Rider	1.50	4.00
100P Flamewake Phoenix	4.00	10.00
36P Jeskai Infiltrator	1.50	4.00
155P Kolaghan, the Storm's Fury	3.00	8.00
75P Mardu Strike Leader	4.00	10.00
19P Mastery of the Unseen	4.00	10.00
156P Ojutai, Soul of Winter	4.00	10.00
22P Rally the Ancestors	1.50	4.00
50P Sage-Eye Avengers		
137P Sandsteppe Mastodon	1.50	4.00
113P Shaman of the Great Hunt	5.00	12.00
138P Shamanic Revelation	2.00	5.00
52P Shu Yun, the Silent Tempest	3.00	8.00
157P Silumgar, the Drifting Death	4.00	10.00
27P Soulfire Grand Master	15.00	40.00
84P Soulflayer	1.50	4.00
54P Supplant Form	2.50	6.00
87P Tasigur, the Golden Fang	8.00	20.00
56P Torrent Elemental	4.00	10.00
143P Warden of the First Tree	6.00	15.00
146P Wildcall	2.00	5.00
148P Yasova Dragonclaw		

2015 Magic The Gathering Ugin's Fate Promos

COMPLETE SET (26)	80.00	150.00
RELEASED ON JANUARY 23, 2015		
96P Ainok Tracker (AA)	1.25	3.00
216P Altar of the Brood (AA)	4.00	10.00
123P Arashin War Beast (AA)	1.25	3.00
97P Arc Lightning (AA)	2.00	5.00
217P Briber's Purse (AA)	1.25	3.00
68P Debilitating Injury (AA)	1.25	3.00
131P Dragonscale Boon (AA)	1.50	4.00
98P Fierce Invocation (AA)	1.25	3.00
129P Formless Nurturing (AA)	1.50	4.00
220P Ghostfire Blade (AA)	3.00	8.00
73P Grim Haruspex (AA)	3.00	8.00
161P Hewed Stone Retainers (AA)	1.25	3.00
113P Jeering Instigator (AA)	3.00	8.00
36P Jeskai Infiltrator (AA)	4.00	10.00
19P Mastery of the Unseen (AA)	4.00	10.00
48P Mystic of the Hidden Way (AA)	1.25	3.00
46P Reality Shift (AA)	5.00	12.00
88P Ruthless Ripper (AA)	2.50	6.00
24P Smite the Monstrous (AA)	1.25	3.00
26P Soul Summons (AA)	2.00	5.00
85P Sultai Emissary (AA)	1.50	4.00
1P Ugin, the Spirit Dragon (AA)	60.00	120.00
164P Ugin's Construct (AA)	2.00	5.00
30P Watcher of the Roost (AA)	1.25	3.00
146P Wildcall (AA)	6.00	15.00
59P Write into Being (AA)	1.50	4.00

2015-16 Magic The Gathering Zendikar Expeditions

COMPLETE SET (25)	1100.00	2500.00
24 Arid Mesa M :L:	90.00	120.00
8 Blood Crypt M :L:	50.00	100.00
39 Forbidden Orchard M :L:		
18 Bloodstained Mire M :L:	80.00	120.00
15 Breeding Pool M :L:	50.00	80.00
5 Canopy Vista M :L:	20.00	40.00
4 Cinder Glade M :L:	20.00	40.00
16 Flooded Strand M :L:	150.00	180.00
11 Godless Shrine M :L:	60.00	90.00
6 Hallowed Fountain M :L:	50.00	80.00
21 Marsh Flats M :L:	80.00	110.00
25 Misty Rainforest M :L:	180.00	220.00
13 Overgrown Tomb M :L:	50.00	80.00
17 Polluted Delta M :L:	180.00	240.00
1 Prairie Stream M :L:	25.00	50.00
14 Sacred Foundry M :L:	50.00	80.00
22 Scalding Tarn M :L:	200.00	250.00
3 Smoldering Marsh M :L:	20.00	40.00
12 Steam Vents M :L:	80.00	110.00
9 Stomping Ground M :L:	60.00	90.00
2 Sunken Hollow M :L:	25.00	50.00
10 Temple Garden M :L:	50.00	80.00
23 Verdant Catacombs M :L:	130.00	180.00
7 Watery Grave M :L:	50.00	80.00
20 Windswept Heath M :L:	80.00	110.00
19 Wooded Foothills M :L:	100.00	140.00
26 Mystic Gate M :L:	25.00	50.00
27 Sunken Ruins M :L:	25.00	50.00
28 Graven Cairns M :L:	25.00	50.00
29 Fire-Lit Thicket M :L:	25.00	50.00
30 Wooded Bastion M :L:	25.00	50.00
31 Fetid Heath M :L:	25.00	50.00
32 Cascade Bluffs M :L:	30.00	60.00
33 Twilight Mire M :L:	40.00	70.00
34 Rugged Prairie M :L:	20.00	45.00
35 Flooded Grove M :L:	30.00	60.00
36 Ancient Tomb M :L:	50.00	80.00
37 Dust Bowl M :L:	20.00	45.00
38 Eye of Ugin M :L:	50.00	80.00
40 Horizon Canopy M :L:	80.00	110.00
41 Kor Haven M :L:	25.00	40.00
42 Mana Confluence M :L:	30.00	50.00
43 Strip Mine M :L:	50.00	70.00
44 Tectonic Edge M :L:	20.00	45.00
45 Wasteland M :L:	110.00	150.00

Pokemon

HOW TO USE

POKEMON

What's Listed
Products listed in the Price Guide typically: 1) are produced by licensed manufacturers, 2) are widely available and 3) have market activity on single items.

What the Columns Mean
The LO and HI columns reflect current retail selling ranges. The HI column on the right generally represents the full retail selling price. The LO column on the left generally represents the lowest price one would expect to find with extensive shopping.

Grading
All cards in the Price Guide are based on NrMint to Mint condition. Damaged cards are generally sold for 25 to 75 percent of Mint value. Toy prices are based on mint condition. Toys that are loose (out of package), are generally sold for 50 percent of the listed price.

Currency
This Price Guide is intended to reflect the entire North American market. All listed prices are in U.S. dollars.

Legend
C – Common

HOLO R – Holo rare

HOLO SR – Holo super rare

PR – Promo

R – Rare

U – Uncommon

UR – Ultra rare

Attention Dealers: If you would like to be a Price Guide Contributor for this almanac, please e-mail your name and phone number to: nonsports@beckett.com

1999 Pokemon Base 1st Edition

COMPLETE SET (102)	1500.00	3000.00
BOOSTER BOX (36 PACKS)	8000.00	11000.00
BOOSTER PACK (11 CARDS)	200.00	500.00
*SHADOWLESS BORDER: .75X TO 1.5X BASIC CARDS		
RELEASED ON JANUARY 9, 1999		
1 Alakazam HOLO R	80.00	120.00
2 Blastoise HOLO R	120.00	250.00
3 Chansey HOLO R	30.00	60.00
4 Charizard HOLO R	800.00	1100.00
5 Clefairy HOLO R	30.00	60.00
6 Gyarados HOLO R	50.00	100.00
7 Hitmonchan HOLO R	80.00	120.00
8 Machamp HOLO R	30.00	60.00
9 Magneton HOLO R	30.00	80.00
10 Mewtwo HOLO R	75.00	150.00
11 Nidoking HOLO R	30.00	60.00
12 Ninetales HOLO R	80.00	120.00
13 Poliwrath HOLO R	50.00	100.00
14 Raichu HOLO R	80.00	120.00
15 Venusaur HOLO R	250.00	400.00
16 Zapdos HOLO R	50.00	100.00
17 Beedrill R	15.00	30.00
18 Dragonair R	20.00	40.00
19 Dugtrio R	20.00	40.00
20 Electabuzz R	20.00	40.00
21 Electrode R	15.00	30.00
22 Pidgeotto R	15.00	30.00
23 Arcanine U	10.00	20.00
24 Charmeleon U	15.00	30.00
25 Dewgong U	3.00	8.00
26 Dratini U	4.00	10.00
27 Farfetch'd U	4.00	10.00
28 Growlithe U	4.00	10.00
29 Haunter U	4.00	10.00
30 Ivysaur U	15.00	30.00
31 Jynx U	3.00	8.00
32 Kadabra U	8.00	15.00
33 Kakuna (UER) U	3.00	8.00
34 Machoke U	5.00	12.00
35 Magikarp U	5.00	12.00
36 Magmar U	3.00	8.00
37 Nidorino U	3.00	8.00
38 Poliwhirl U	3.00	8.00
39 Porygon U	3.00	8.00
40 Raticate U	3.00	8.00
41 Seel U	3.00	8.00
42 Wartortle U	15.00	30.00
43 Abra C	2.00	5.00
44 Bulbasaur (UER) C	15.00	30.00
45 Caterpie (UER) C	6.00	15.00
46 Charmander C	15.00	30.00
47 Diglett C	3.00	8.00
48 Doduo C	3.00	8.00
49 Drowzee C	2.00	5.00
50 Gastly C	3.00	8.00
51 Koffing C	3.00	8.00
52 Machop C	3.00	8.00
53 Magnemite C	2.50	6.00
54 Metapod (UER) C	3.00	8.00
55 Nidoran-M C	2.50	6.00
56 Onix C	2.50	6.00
57 Pidgey C	2.50	6.00
58 Pikachu (Yellow cheeks Corr.) C	15.00	30.00
58 Pikachu (Red cheeks Error) C	15.00	30.00
59 Poliwag C	2.50	6.00
60 Ponyta C	2.50	6.00
61 Rattata C	2.50	6.00
62 Sandshrew C	2.50	6.00
63 Squirtle C	10.00	20.00
64 Starmie C	2.50	6.00
65 Staryu C	2.50	6.00
66 Tangela C	2.50	6.00
67 Voltorb (UER) C	2.50	6.00
68 Vulpix (UER) C	2.50	6.00
69 Weedle C	2.50	6.00
70 Clefairy Doll R	6.00	15.00
71 Computer Search R	12.00	25.00
72 Devolution Spray R	6.00	15.00
73 Impostor Professor Oak R	6.00	15.00
74 Item Finder R	10.00	20.00
75 Lass R	15.00	30.00
76 Pokemon Breeder R	15.00	30.00
77 Pokemon Trader R	6.00	15.00
78 Scoop Up R	6.00	15.00
79 Super Energy Removal R	8.00	15.00
80 Defender U	2.50	6.00
81 Energy Retrieval U	3.00	8.00
82 Full Heal U	1.50	4.00
83 Maintenance U	3.00	8.00
84 Plus Power U	3.00	8.00
85 Pokemon Center U	3.00	8.00
86 Pokemon Flute U	3.00	8.00
87 Pokédex U	3.00	8.00
88 Professor Oak U	3.00	8.00
89 Revive U	3.00	8.00
90 Super Potion U	3.00	8.00
91 Bill C	3.00	8.00
92 Energy Removal C	3.00	8.00
93 Gust of Wind C	3.00	8.00
94 Potion C	3.00	8.00
95 Switch C	3.00	8.00
96 Double Colorless Energy U	6.00	15.00
97 Fighting Energy	2.50	6.00
98 Fire Energy	2.50	6.00
99 Grass Energy	2.50	6.00
100 Lightning Energy	2.50	6.00
101 Psychic Energy	2.50	6.00
102 Water Energy	2.50	6.00

1999 Pokemon Base Unlimited

COMPLETE SET (102)	100.00	200.00
BOOSTER BOX (36 PACKS)	800.00	1300.00
BOOSTER PACK (11 CARDS)	20.00	40.00
STARTER SET (60 CARDS)	20.00	40.00
BLACKOUT DECK (60 CARDS)	40.00	80.00
BRUSHFIRE DECK (60 CARDS)	40.00	80.00
OVERGROWTH DECK (60 CARDS)	40.00	80.00
ZAP DECK (60 CARDS)	40.00	80.00
*SHADOWLESS BORDER: .75X TO 2X BASIC CARD		
CARD 8 MACHAMP ONLY IN STARTER DECKS		
RELEASED ON JANUARY 9, 1999		
1 Alakazam HOLO R	6.00	15.00
2 Blastoise HOLO R	15.00	30.00
3 Chansey HOLO R	3.00	8.00
4 Charizard HOLO R	30.00	60.00
5 Clefairy HOLO R	3.00	8.00
6 Gyarados HOLO R	3.00	8.00
7 Hitmonchan HOLO R	3.00	8.00
8 Machamp (holo) (R) 1st Ed. Only	3.00	8.00
9 Magneton HOLO R	3.00	8.00
10 Mewtwo HOLO R	5.00	12.00
11 Nidoking HOLO R	3.00	8.00
12 Ninetales HOLO R	3.00	8.00
13 Poliwrath HOLO R	3.00	8.00
14 Raichu HOLO R	3.00	8.00
15 Venusaur HOLO R	10.00	25.00
16 Zapdos HOLO R	3.00	8.00
17 Beedrill R	1.00	3.00
18 Dragonair R	1.00	3.00
19 Dugtrio R	1.00	3.00
20 Electabuzz R	1.00	3.00
21 Electrode R	1.00	3.00
22 Pidgeotto R	1.00	3.00
23 Arcanine U	1.25	4.00
24 Charmeleon U	1.00	3.00
25 Dewgong U	1.00	3.00
26 Dratini U	1.00	3.00
27 Farfetch'd U	1.00	3.00
28 Growlithe U	1.00	3.00
29 Haunter U	1.00	3.00
30 Ivysaur U	1.00	3.00
31 Jynx U	1.00	3.00
32 Kadabra U	1.00	3.00
33 Kakuna (Length/Length Error) U	1.00	3.00
33 Kakuna (Length/Weight Corr.) U	1.00	3.00
34 Machoke U	1.00	3.00
35 Magikarp U	1.00	3.00
36 Magmar U	1.00	3.00
37 Nidorino U	1.00	3.00
38 Poliwhirl U	1.00	3.00
39 Porygon U	1.00	3.00
40 Raticate U	1.00	3.00
41 Seel U	1.00	3.00
42 Wartortle U	1.00	3.00
43 Abra C	1.00	3.00
44 Bulbasaur (Length/Weight Corr.) C	1.00	3.00
44 Bulbasaur (Length/Length Error) C	1.00	3.00
45 Caterpie (HP 40 Error) C	1.00	3.00
45 Caterpie (40 HP Corr.) C	1.00	3.00
46 Charmander C	1.00	3.00
47 Diglett C	1.00	3.00
48 Doduo C	1.00	3.00
49 Drowzee C	1.00	3.00
50 Gastly C	1.00	3.00
51 Koffing C	1.00	3.00
52 Machop C	1.00	3.00
53 Magnemite C	1.00	3.00
54 Metapod (HP 70 Error) C	1.00	3.00
54 Metapod (70 HP Corr.) C	1.00	3.00
55 Nidoran C	1.00	3.00
56 Onix C	1.00	3.00
57 Pidgey C	1.00	3.00
58 Pikachu (Red cheeks Error) C	1.00	3.00
58 Pikachu (Yellow cheeks Corr.)C	1.00	3.00
59 Poliwag C	1.00	3.00
60 Ponyta C	1.00	3.00
61 Rattata C	1.00	3.00
62 Sandshrew C	1.00	3.00
63 Squirtle C	1.00	3.00
64 Starmie C	1.00	3.00
65 Staryu C	1.00	3.00
66 Tangela C	1.00	3.00
67 Voltorb (Monster Ball Error) C	1.00	3.00
67 Voltorb (Poké Ball Corr.) C	1.00	3.00
68 Vulpix (UER) C	1.00	3.00
69 Weedle C	1.00	3.00
70 Clefairy Doll R	1.00	3.00
71 Computer Search R	1.00	3.00
72 Devolution Spray R	1.00	3.00
73 Impostor Professor Oak R	1.00	3.00
74 Item Finder R	1.00	3.00
75 Lass R	1.00	3.00

76 Pokémon Breeder R	1.00	3.00
77 Pokémon Trader R	1.00	3.00
78 Scoop Up R	1.00	3.00
79 Super Energy Removal R	1.00	3.00
80 Defender U	1.00	3.00
81 Energy Retrieval U	1.00	3.00
82 Full Heal U	1.00	3.00
83 Maintenance U	1.00	3.00
84 Plus Power U	1.00	3.00
85 Pokémon Center U	1.00	3.00
86 Pokémon Flute U	1.00	3.00
87 Pokédex U	1.00	3.00
88 Professor Oak U	1.00	3.00
89 Revive U	1.00	3.00
90 Super Potion U	1.00	3.00
91 Bill C	1.00	3.00
92 Energy Removal C	1.00	3.00
93 Gust of Wind C	1.00	3.00
94 Potion C	1.00	3.00
95 Switch C	1.00	3.00
96 Double Colorless Energy U	1.00	3.00
97 Fighting Energy C	1.00	3.00
98 Fire Energy C	1.00	3.00
99 Grass Energy C	1.00	3.00
100 Lightning Energy C	1.00	3.00
101 Psychic Energy C	1.00	3.00
102 Water Energy C	1.00	3.00

1999 Pokemon Jungle 1st Edition

COMPLETE SET (64)	200.00	400.00
BOOSTER BOX (36 PACKS)	500.00	800.00
BOOSTER PACK (11 CARDS)	15.00	35.00
RELEASED ON JUNE 16, 1999		
1 Clefable HOLO R	6.00	15.00
2 Electrode HOLO R	5.00	12.00
3 Flareon HOLO R	10.00	25.00
4 Jolteon HOLO R	10.00	25.00
5 Kangaskhan HOLO R	6.00	15.00
6 Mr. Mime HOLO R	6.00	15.00
7 Nidoqueen HOLO R	12.00	30.00
8 Pidgeot HOLO R	6.00	15.00
9 Pinsir HOLO R	10.00	25.00
10 Scyther HOLO R	10.00	25.00
11 Snorlax HOLO R	15.00	30.00
12 Vaporeon HOLO R	10.00	25.00
13 Venomoth HOLO R	6.00	15.00
14 Victreebel HOLO R	10.00	25.00
15 Vileplume HOLO R	10.00	20.00
16 Wigglytuff HOLO R	6.00	15.00
17 Clefable R	3.00	6.00
18 Electrode (UER) R	5.00	12.00
19 Flareon R	3.00	8.00
20 Jolteon R	3.00	8.00
21 Kangaskhan R	2.00	5.00
22 Mr. Mime R	2.00	5.00
23 Nidoqueen R	2.00	5.00
24 Pidgeot R	2.00	5.00
25 Pinsir R	2.00	5.00
26 Scyther R	2.00	5.00
27 Snorlax R	2.00	5.00
28 Vaporeon R	2.00	5.00
29 Venomoth R	2.00	5.00
30 Victreebel R	2.00	5.00
31 Vileplume R	2.00	5.00
32 Wigglytuff R	2.00	5.00
33 Butterfree (1 Edition Corr.) U	2.00	5.00
33 Butterfree ("d" Edition Error) U	3.00	6.00
34 Dodrio U	1.00	3.00
35 Exeggutor U	1.00	3.00
36 Fearow U	1.00	3.00
37 Gloom U	1.00	3.00
38 Lickitung U	1.00	3.00
39 Marowak U	1.00	3.00
40 Nidorina U	1.00	3.00
41 Parasect U	1.00	3.00
42 Persian U	1.00	3.00
43 Primeape U	1.00	3.00
44 Rapidash U	1.00	3.00
45 Rhydon U	1.00	3.00
46 Seaking U	1.00	3.00
47 Tauros U	1.00	3.00
48 Weepinbell U	1.00	3.00
49 Bellsprout C	1.00	3.00
50 Cubone C	1.00	3.00
51 Eevee C	1.00	3.00
52 Exeggcute C	1.00	3.00
53 Goldeen C	1.00	3.00
54 Jigglypuff C	1.00	3.00
55 Mankey C	1.00	3.00
56 Meowth C	1.00	3.00
57 Nidoran-F C	1.00	3.00
58 Oddish C	1.00	3.00
59 Paras C	1.00	3.00
60 Pikachu C	2.00	5.00
61 Rhyhorn C	1.00	3.00
62 Spearow C	1.00	3.00
63 Venonat C	1.00	3.00
64 Trainer: Poké Ball C	1.00	3.00

1999 Pokemon Jungle Unlimited

COMPLETE SET (64)	50.00	100.00
BOOSTER BOX (36 PACKS)	300.00	400.00
BOOSTER PACK (11 CARDS)	8.00	20.00
POWER RESERVE DECK (60 CARDS)	15.00	25.00
WATER BLAST DECK (60 CARDS)	20.00	40.00
HOLO ERRORS ARE MISSING JUNGLE LOGO	8.00	15.00
RELEASED ON JUNE 16, 1999		
1A Clefable HOLO R	2.00	4.00
1 Clefable (holo) (R) (Error)	6.00	12.00
2A Electrode HOLO R	2.00	5.00
2B Electrode HOLO R (ERR)	6.00	12.00
3A Flareon HOLO R	2.00	5.00
3B Flareon HOLO R (ERR)	8.00	20.00
4A Jolteon HOLO R	2.00	5.00
4B Jolteon HOLO R (ERR)	8.00	20.00
5A Kangaskhan HOLO R	2.00	4.00
5B Kangaskhan HOLO R (ERR)	8.00	20.00
6A Mr. Mime HOLO R	2.00	4.00
6B Mr Mime HOLO R (ERR)	8.00	20.00
7A Nidoqueen HOLO R	2.00	5.00
7B Nidoqueen HOLO R (ERR)	8.00	20.00
8A Pidgeot HOLO R	2.00	4.00
8B Pidgeot HOLO R (ERR)	8.00	20.00
9A Pinsir HOLO R	2.00	4.00
9B Pinsir HOLO R (ERR)	8.00	20.00
10A Scyther HOLO R	2.00	4.00
10B Scyther HOLO R (ERR)	8.00	20.00
11A Snorlax HOLO R	2.00	5.00
11B Snorlax HOLO R (ERR)	8.00	20.00
12A Vaporeon HOLO R	2.00	4.00
12B Vaporeon HOLO R (ERR)	8.00	20.00
13A Venomoth HOLO R	2.00	5.00
13B Venomoth HOLO R (ERR)	8.00	20.00
14A Victreebel HOLO R	2.00	4.00
14B Victreebel HOLO R (ERR)	8.00	20.00
15A Vileplume HOLO R	2.00	4.00
15B Vileplume HOLO R (ERR)	8.00	20.00
16A Wigglytuff HOLO R	3.00	6.00
16B Wigglytuff HOLO R (ERR)	8.00	20.00
17 Clefable R	3.00	8.00
18 Electrode R	3.00	8.00
19 Flareon R	3.00	8.00
20 Jolteon R	3.00	8.00
21 Kangaskhan R	3.00	8.00
22 Mr. Mime R	3.00	8.00
23 Nidoqueen R	3.00	8.00
24 Pidgeot R	3.00	8.00
25 Pinsir R	3.00	8.00
26 Scyther R	3.00	8.00
27 Snorlax R	3.00	8.00
28 Vaporeon R	3.00	8.00
29 Venomoth R	3.00	8.00
30 Victreebel R	3.00	8.00
31 Vileplume R	3.00	8.00
32 Wigglytuff R	3.00	8.00
33 Butterfree U	1.00	2.50
34 Dodrio U	1.00	2.50
35 Exeggutor U	1.00	2.50
36 Fearow U	1.00	2.50
37 Gloom U	1.00	2.50
38 Lickitung U	1.00	2.50
39 Marowak U	1.00	2.50
40 Nidorina U	1.00	2.50
41 Parasect U	1.00	2.50
42 Persian U	1.00	2.50
43 Primeape U	1.00	2.50
44 Rapidash U	1.00	2.50
45 Rhydon U	1.00	2.50
46 Seaking U	1.00	2.50
47 Tauros U	1.00	2.50
48 Weepinbell U	1.00	2.50
49 Bellsprout C	1.00	2.50
50 Cubone C	1.00	2.50
51 Eevee C	1.00	2.50
52 Exeggcute C	1.00	2.50
53 Goldeen C	1.00	2.50
54 Jigglypuff C	1.00	2.50
55 Mankey C	1.00	2.50
56 Meowth C	1.00	2.50
57 Nidoran-F C	1.00	2.50
58 Oddish C	1.00	2.50
59 Paras C	1.00	2.50
60 Pikachu C	1.00	2.50
61 Rhyhorn C	1.00	2.50
62 Spearow C	1.00	2.50
63 Venonat C	1.00	2.50
64 Trainer: Poké Ball C	1.00	2.50

1999 Pokemon Fossil 1st Edition

COMPLETE SET (62)	200.00	400.00
BOOSTER BOX (36 PACKS)	400.00	700.00
BOOSTER PACK (11 CARDS)	8.00	20.00
RELEASED ON OCTOBER 10, 1999		
1 Aerodactyl HOLO R	4.00	10.00
2 Articuno HOLO R	10.00	25.00
3 Ditto HOLO R	8.00	20.00
4 Dragonite HOLO R	15.00	30.00
5 Gengar HOLO R	15.00	30.00
6 Haunter HOLO R	6.00	15.00
7 Hitmonlee HOLO R	10.00	25.00
8 Hypno HOLO R	6.00	15.00
9 Kabutops HOLO R	10.00	20.00
10 Lapras HOLO R	8.00	20.00
11 Magneton HOLO R	10.00	25.00
12 Moltres HOLO R	10.00	25.00
13 Muk HOLO R	6.00	15.00
14 Raichu HOLO R	8.00	20.00
15 Zapdos HOLO R	8.00	20.00
16 Aerodactyl R	3.00	8.00
17 Articuno R	5.00	12.00
18 Ditto R	4.00	10.00
19 Dragonite R	5.00	12.00
20 Gengar R	3.00	8.00
21 Haunter R	2.00	5.00
22 Hitmonlee R	3.00	8.00
23 Hypno R	1.50	4.00
24 Kabutops R	3.00	8.00
25 Lapras R	2.00	6.00
26 Magneton R	2.00	5.00
27 Moltres R	3.00	8.00
28 Muk R	3.00	8.00
29 Raichu R	3.00	8.00
30 Zapdos R	3.00	8.00
31 Arbok U	1.25	3.00
32 Cloyster U	1.25	3.00
33 Gastly U	1.25	3.00
34 Golbat U	1.25	3.00
35 Golduck U	1.25	3.00
36 Golem U	1.25	3.00
37 Graveler U	1.25	3.00
38 Kingler U	1.25	3.00
39 Magmar (U)	1.25	3.00
40 Omastar U	1.25	3.00
41 Sandslash U	1.25	3.00
42 Seadra U	1.25	3.00
43 Slowbro U	1.25	3.00
44 Tentacruel U	1.25	3.00
45 Weezing U	1.25	3.00
46 Ekans C	1.25	3.00
47 Geodude C	1.25	3.00
48 Grimer C	1.25	3.00
49 Horsea C	1.25	3.00
50 Kabuto C	1.25	3.00
51 Krabby C	1.25	3.00
52 Omanyte C	1.25	3.00
53 Psyduck C	1.25	3.00
54 Shellder C	1.25	3.00
55 Slowpoke C	1.25	3.00
56 Tentacool C	1.25	3.00
57 Zubat C	1.25	3.00
58 Old Man Fuji U	1.25	3.00
59 Energy Search C	1.25	3.00
60 Gambler C	1.25	3.00
61 Recycle C	1.25	3.00
62 Mysterious Fossil C	1.25	3.00

1999 Pokemon Fossil Unlimited

COMPLETE SET (62)	50.00	100.00
BOOSTER BOX (36 PACKS)	300.00	500.00
BOOSTER PACK (11 CARDS)	6.00	15.00
BODYGUARD DECK (60)	8.00	20.00
LOCK DOWN DECK (60)	15.00	30.00
RELEASED OCTOBER 10, 1999		
1 Aerodactyl HOLO R	2.00	6.00
2 Articuno HOLO R	4.00	10.00
3 Ditto HOLO R	3.00	8.00
4 Dragonite HOLO R	6.00	15.00
5 Gengar HOLO R	5.00	12.00
6 Haunter HOLO R	2.00	6.00
7 Hitmonlee HOLO R	3.00	8.00
8 Hypno HOLO R	3.00	8.00
9 Kabutops HOLO R	3.00	8.00
10 Lapras HOLO R	2.00	5.00
11 Magneton HOLO R	1.25	4.00
12 Moltres HOLO R	5.00	10.00
13 Muk HOLO R	1.50	4.00
14 Raichu HOLO R	2.00	7.00
15 Zapdos HOLO R	2.00	4.00
16 Aerodactyl R	1.00	2.00
17 Articuno R	2.00	4.00
18 Ditto R	1.00	3.00
19 Dragonite R	3.00	8.00
20 Gengar R	1.00	3.00
21 Haunter R	1.00	3.00
22 Hitmonlee R	2.00	5.00
23 Hypno R	1.00	3.00
24 Kabutops R	1.00	3.00
25 Lapras R	1.00	3.00
26 Magneton R	1.00	3.00
27 Moltres R	1.00	3.00
28 Muk R	1.00	3.00
29 Raichu R	1.00	3.00
30 Zapdos R	1.00	3.00
31 Arbok U	1.00	3.00
32 Cloyster U	1.00	3.00
33 Gastly U	1.00	3.00
34 Golbat U	1.00	3.00
35 Golduck U	1.00	3.00
36 Golem U	1.00	3.00
37 Graveler U	1.00	3.00
38 Kingler U	1.00	3.00
39 Magmar U	1.00	3.00
40 Omastar U	1.00	3.00
41 Sandslash U	1.00	3.00
42 Seadra U	1.00	3.00
43 Slowbro U	1.00	3.00
44 Tentacruel U	1.00	3.00
45 Weezing U	1.00	3.00
46 Ekans C	1.00	3.00
47 Geodude C	1.00	3.00
48 Grimer C	1.00	3.00
49 Horsea C	1.00	3.00
50 Kabuto C	1.00	3.00
51 Krabby C	1.00	3.00
52 Omanyte C	1.00	3.00
53 Psyduck C	1.00	3.00
54 Shellder C	1.00	3.00
55 Slowpoke C	1.00	3.00
56 Tentacool C	1.00	3.00
57 Zubat C	1.00	3.00
58 Old Man Fuji U	1.00	3.00
59 Energy Search C	1.00	3.00
60 Gambler C	1.00	3.00
61 Recycle C	1.00	3.00
62 Mysterious Fossil C	1.00	3.00

2000 Pokemon Base 2 Unlimited

COMPLETE SET (130)	120.00	200.00
BOOSTER BOX (36 CT)	400.00	500.00
BOOSTER PACK (11 CARDS)	10.00	15.00
GRASS CHOPPER DECK (60)	10.00	25.00
HOT WATER DECK (60)	10.00	25.00
LIGHTNING BUG DECK (60)	10.00	25.00
PSYCH OUT DECK (60)	10.00	25.00
RELEASED ON FEBRUARY 24, 2000		
1 Alakazam HOLO R	4.00	10.00
2 Blastoise HOLO R	10.00	25.00
3 Chansey HOLO R	2.00	5.00
4 Charizard HOLO R	25.00	50.00
5 Clefable HOLO R	2.00	6.00
6 Clefairy HOLO R	1.50	4.00
7 Gyarados HOLO R	3.00	8.00
8 Hitmonchan HOLO R	3.00	8.00
9 Magneton HOLO R	2.00	4.00
10 Mewtwo HOLO R	5.00	12.00
11 Nidoking HOLO R	4.00	10.00
12 Nidoqueen HOLO R	2.00	4.00
13 Ninetales HOLO R	2.50	6.00
14 Pidgeot HOLO R	2.50	6.00
15 Poliwrath HOLO R	2.50	6.00
16 Raichu HOLO R	3.00	8.00
17 Scyther HOLO R	3.00	8.00
18 Venusaur HOLO R	8.00	20.00
19 Wigglytuff HOLO R	2.50	7.00
20 Zapdos HOLO R	2.50	7.00
21 Beedrill R	1.25	3.00
22 Dragonair R	1.25	3.00
23 Dugtrio R	1.25	3.00
24 Electabuzz R	1.25	3.00
25 Electrode R	1.25	3.00
26 Kangaskhan R	1.25	3.00
27 Mr. Mime R	1.25	3.00
28 Pidgeotto R	1.25	3.00
29 Pinsir R	1.25	3.00
30 Snorlax R	1.25	3.00
31 Venomoth R	1.25	3.00
32 Victreebel R	1.25	3.00
33 Arcanine U	1.25	3.00
34 Butterfree U	1.25	3.00
35 Charmeleon U	1.25	3.00
36 Dewgong U	1.25	3.00
37 Dodrio U	1.25	3.00
38 Dratini U	1.25	3.00
39 Exeggutor U	1.25	3.00
40 Farfetch'd U	1.25	3.00
41 Fearow U	1.25	3.00
42 Growlithe U	1.25	3.00
43 Haunter U	1.25	3.00
44 Ivysaur (U)	1.25	3.00
45 Jynx U	1.25	3.00
46 Kadabra U	1.25	3.00
47 Kakuna U	1.25	3.00
48 Lickitung U	1.25	3.00
49 Machoke U	1.25	3.00
50 Magikarp U	1.25	3.00
51 Magmar U	1.25	3.00
52 Marowak U	1.25	3.00
53 Nidorina U	1.25	3.00
54 Nidorino U	1.25	3.00
55 Parasect U	1.25	3.00
56 Persian U	1.25	3.00
57 Poliwhirl U	1.25	3.00
58 Raticate U	1.25	3.00
59 Rhydon U	1.25	3.00
60 Seaking U	1.25	3.00
61 Seel U	1.25	3.00
62 Tauros U	1.25	3.00
63 Wartortle U	1.25	3.00
64 Weepinbell U	1.25	3.00
65 Abra C	.75	2.00
66 Bellsprout C	.75	2.00
67 Bulbasaur C	.75	2.00
68 Caterpie C	.75	2.00
69 Charmander C	.75	2.00
70 Cubone C	.75	2.00

71 Diglett C	.75	2.00
72 Doduo C	.75	2.00
73 Drowzee C	.75	2.00
74 Exeggcute C	.75	2.00
75 Gastly C	.75	2.00
76 Goldeen C	.75	2.00
77 Jigglypuff C	.75	2.00
78 Machop C	.75	2.00
79 Magnemite C	.75	2.00
80 Meowth C	.75	2.00
81 Metapod C	.75	2.00
82 Nidoran-F C	.75	2.00
83 Nidoran-M C	.75	2.00
84 Onix C	.75	2.00
85 Paras C	.75	2.00
86 Pidgey C	.75	2.00
87 Pikachu C	.75	2.00
88 Poliwag C	.75	2.00
89 Rattata C	.75	2.00
90 Rhyhorn C	.75	2.00
91 Sandshrew C	.75	2.00
92 Spearow C	.75	2.00
93 Squirtle C	.75	2.00
94 Starmie C	.75	2.00
95 Staryu C	.75	2.00
96 Tangela C	.75	2.00
97 Venonat C	.75	2.00
98 Voltorb C	.75	2.00
99 Vulpix C	.75	2.00
100 Weedle C	.75	2.00
101 Computer Search R	1.25	3.00
102 Imposter Professor Oak R	1.25	3.00
103 Item Finder R	1.25	3.00
104 Lass R	1.25	3.00
105 Pokémon Breeder R	1.25	3.00
106 Pokémon Trader R	1.25	3.00
107 Scoop Up R	1.25	3.00
108 Super Energy Removal R	1.25	3.00
109 Defender U	.75	2.00
110 Energy Retrieval U	.75	2.00
111 Full Heal U	.75	2.00
112 Maintenance U	.75	2.00
113 PlusPower U	.75	2.00
114 Pokémon Center U	.75	2.00
115 Pokédex U	.75	2.00
116 Professor Oak U	.75	2.00
117 Super Potion U	.75	2.00
118 Bill C	.75	2.00
119 Energy Removal C	.75	2.00
120 Gust of Wind C	.75	2.00
121 Poké Ball C	.75	2.00
122 Potion C	.75	2.00
123 Switch C	.75	2.00
124 Double Colorless Energy U	.75	2.00
125 Fighting Energy C	.50	1.50
126 Fire Energy C	.50	1.50
127 Grass Energy C	.50	1.50
128 Lightning Energy C	.50	1.50
129 Psychic Energy C	.50	1.50
130 Water Energy C	.50	1.50

2000 Pokemon Team Rocket 1st Edition

COMPLETE SET (82)	120.00	200.00
COMPLETE SET W/RAICHU (83)	120.00	200.00
BOOSTER BOX (36 PACKS)	400.00	500.00
BOOSTER PACK (11 CARDS)	12.00	15.00
RELEASED ON APRIL 24, 2000		
1 Dark Alakazam HOLO R	4.00	8.00
2 Dark Arbok HOLO R (ERR)	3.00	6.00
3 Dark Blastoise HOLO R	10.00	25.00
4 Dark Charizard HOLO R	20.00	45.00
5 Dark Dragonite HOLO R	10.00	20.00
6 Dark Dugtrio HOLO R	3.00	8.00
7 Dark Golbat HOLO R	3.00	8.00
8 Dark Gyarados HOLO R	5.00	12.00
9 Dark Hypno HOLO R	4.00	10.00
10 Dark Machamp HOLO R	5.00	12.00
11 Dark Magneton HOLO R	3.00	8.00
12 Dark Slowbro HOLO R	5.00	12.00
13 Dark Vileplume HOLO R	6.00	15.00
14 Dark Weezing HOLO R	3.00	8.00
15 Here Comes Team Rocket HOLO R	3.00	8.00
16 Rocket's Sneak Attack HOLO R	3.00	6.00
17 Rainbow Energy HOLO R	3.00	8.00
18 Dark Alakazam R	1.50	4.00
19 Dark Arbok R (ERR)	1.50	4.00
20 Dark Blastoise R	2.00	6.00
21 Dark Charizard R	10.00	20.00
22 Dark Dragonite R	1.50	4.00
23 Dark Dugtrio R	1.50	4.00
24 Dark Golbat R	1.25	3.00
25 Dark Gyarados R	1.50	4.00
26 Dark Hypno R	2.00	6.00
27 Dark Machamp R	1.25	3.00
28 Dark Magneton R	1.25	3.00
29 Dark Slowbro R	2.00	6.00
30 Dark Vileplume R	1.50	4.00
31 Dark Weezing R	1.00	2.50
32 Dark Charmeleon U	2.50	7.00
33 Dark Dragonair U	1.50	4.00
34 Dark Electrode U	1.50	4.00
35 Dark Flareon U	1.50	4.00
36 Dark Gloom U	1.50	4.00
37 Dark Golduck U	1.50	4.00
38 Dark Jolteon U	2.00	6.00
39 Dark Kadabra U	1.50	4.00
40 Dark Machoke U	1.50	4.00
41 Dark Muk U	1.50	4.00
42 Dark Persian U	1.50	4.00
43 Dark Primeape U	1.50	4.00
44 Dark Rapidash U (ERR)	1.50	4.00
45 Dark Vaporeon U	1.50	4.00
46 Dark Wartortle U	1.50	4.00
47 Magikarp U	1.00	3.00
48 Porygon U	1.00	3.00
49 Abra C	1.00	3.00
50 Charmander C	1.00	3.00
51 Dark Raticate C	1.00	3.00
52 Diglett C	1.00	3.00
53 Dratini C*	1.00	3.00
54 Drowzee C	1.00	3.00
55 Eevee C	1.00	3.00
56 Ekans C	1.00	3.00
57 Grimer C	1.00	3.00
58 Koffing C	1.00	3.00
59 Machop C	1.00	3.00
60 Magnemite C	1.00	3.00
61 Mankey C	1.00	3.00
62 Meowth C	1.00	3.00
63 Oddish C	1.00	3.00
64 Ponyta C	1.00	3.00
65 Psyduck C	1.00	3.00
66 Rattata C	1.00	3.00
67 Slowpoke C	1.00	3.00
68 Squirtle C	1.00	3.00
69 Voltorb C	1.00	3.00
70 Zubat C	1.00	3.00
71 Here Comes Team Rocket R	1.50	4.00
72 Rocket's Sneak Attack R	1.00	3.00
73 The Boss's Way U	1.00	3.00
74 Challenge U	1.00	3.00
75 Digger U	1.00	3.00
76 Imposter Oak's Revenge U	1.00	3.00
77 Nightly Garbage Run U	1.00	3.00
78 Gas Attack C	1.00	3.00
79 Sleep C	1.00	3.00
80 Rainbow Energy R	1.00	3.00
81 Full Heal Energy U	1.00	3.00
82 Potion Energy U	1.00	3.00
83 Dark Raichu HOLO R (ERR)	8.00	20.00

2000 Pokemon Team Rocket Unlimited

COMPLETE SET (82)	100.00	150.00
COMPLETE SET W/RAICHU (83)	100.00	150.00
BOOSTER BOX (36 PACKS)	325.00	450.00
BOOSTER PACK (11 CARDS)	8.00	20.00
THEME DECK (60 CARDS)	8.00	15.00
RELEASED ON APRIL 24, 2000		
1 Dark Alakazam HOLO R	1.50	4.00
2 Dark Arbok HOLO R (ERR)	1.50	4.00
3 Dark Blastoise HOLO R	4.00	10.00
4 Dark Charizard HOLO R	6.00	15.00
5 Dark Dragonite HOLO R	4.00	10.00
6 Dark Dugtrio HOLO R	1.50	4.00
7 Dark Golbat HOLO R	1.50	4.00
8 Dark Gyarados HOLO R	1.50	4.00
9 Dark Hypno HOLO R	1.50	4.00
10 Dark Machamp HOLO R	1.50	4.00
11 Dark Magneton HOLO R	1.50	4.00
12 Dark Slowbro HOLO R	1.50	4.00
13 Dark Vileplume HOLO R	1.50	4.00
14 Dark Weezing HOLO R	1.50	4.00
15 Here Comes Team Rocket HOLO R	1.50	4.00
16 Rocket's Sneak Attack HOLO R	1.50	4.00
17 Rainbow Energy HOLO R	1.50	4.00
18 Dark Alakazam R	1.50	4.00
19 Dark Arbok R (ERR)	1.50	4.00
20 Dark Blastoise R	4.00	10.00
21 Dark Charizard R	4.00	10.00
22 Dark Dragonite R	1.50	4.00
23 Dark Dugtrio R	1.50	4.00
24 Dark Golbat R	1.50	4.00
25 Dark Gyarados R	1.50	4.00
26 Dark Hypno R	1.50	4.00
27 Dark Machamp R	1.50	4.00
28 Dark Magneton R	1.50	4.00
29 Dark Slowbro R	1.50	4.00
30 Dark Vileplume R	1.50	4.00
31 Dark Weezing R	1.50	4.00
32 Dark Charmeleon U	.75	2.00
33 Dark Dragonair U	.75	2.00
34 Dark Electrode U	.75	2.00
35 Dark Flareon U	.75	2.00
36 Dark Gloom U	.75	2.00
37 Dark Golduck U	.75	2.00
38 Dark Jolteon U	1.25	3.00
39 Dark Kadabra U	.75	2.50
40 Dark Machoke U	.75	2.00
41 Dark Muk U	.75	2.00
42 Dark Persian U	.75	2.00
43 Dark Primeape U	.75	2.00
44 Dark Rapidash U (ERR)	.75	2.00
45 Dark Vaporeon U	.75	2.00
46 Dark Wartortle U	.75	2.00
47 Magikarp U	.75	2.00
48 Porygon U	.75	2.00
49 Abra C	.75	2.00
50 Charmander C	.75	2.00
51 Dark Raticate C	.75	2.00
52 Diglett C	.75	2.00
53 Dratini C	.75	2.00
54 Drowzee C	.75	2.00
55 Eevee C	.75	2.00
56 Ekans C	.75	2.00
57 Grimer C	.75	2.00
58 Koffing C	.75	2.00
59 Machop C	.75	2.00
60 Magnemite C	.75	2.00
61 Mankey C	.75	2.00
62 Meowth C	.75	2.00
63 Oddish C	.75	2.00
64 Ponyta C	.75	2.00
65 Psyduck C	.75	2.00
66 Rattata C	.75	2.00
67 Slowpoke C	.75	2.00
68 Squirtle C	.75	2.00
69 Voltorb C	.75	2.00
70 Zubat C	.75	2.00
71 Here Comes Team Rocket R	1.00	2.50
72 Rocket's Sneak Attack R	1.50	4.00
73 The Boss's Way U	.75	2.00
74 Challenge U	.75	2.00
75 Digger U	.75	2.00
76 Imposter Oak's Revenge U	.75	2.00
77 Nightly Garbage Run U	.75	2.00
78 Gas Attack C	.75	2.00
79 Sleep C	.75	2.00
80 Rainbow Energy R	1.50	4.00
81 Full Heal Energy U	.75	2.00
82 Potion Energy U	.75	2.00
83 Dark Raichu HOLO R (ERR)	3.00	8.00

2000 Pokemon Gym Heroes 1st Edition

COMPLETE SET (132)	160.00	300.00
UNOPENED BOX (36 PACKS)	450.00	650.00
UNOPENED PACK (11 CARDS)	10.00	25.00
RELEASED ON AUGUST 14, 2000		
1 Blaine's Moltres HOLO R	10.00	25.00
2 Brock's Rhydon HOLO R	6.00	15.00
3 Erika's Clefable HOLO R	6.00	15.00
4 Erika's Dragonair HOLO R	8.00	20.00
5 Erika's Vileplume HOLO R	5.00	12.00
6 Lt. Surge's Electabuzz HOLO R	10.00	25.00
7 Lt. Surge's Fearow HOLO R	6.00	15.00
8 Lt. Surge's Magneton HOLO R	5.00	12.00
9 Misty's Seadra (holo) (R)	4.00	10.00
10 Misty's Tentacruel HOLO R	4.00	10.00
11 Rocket's Hitmonchan HOLO R	6.00	15.00
12 Rocket's Moltres HOLO R	10.00	25.00
13 Rocket's Scyther HOLO R	10.00	25.00
14 Sabrina's Gengar HOLO R	15.00	30.00
15 Brock HOLO R	4.50	11.00
16 Erika HOLO R	15.00	30.00
17 Lt. Surge HOLO R	6.00	15.00
18 Misty HOLO R	4.50	11.00
19 The Rocket's Trap HOLO R	4.00	10.00
20 Brock's Golem R	1.50	4.00
21 Brock's Onix R	2.00	6.00
22 Brock's Rhyhorn R	1.50	4.00
23 Brock's Sandslash R	2.00	6.00
24 Brock's Zubat R	1.50	4.00
25 Erika's Clefairy R	1.50	4.00
26 Erika's Victreebel R	1.50	4.00
27 Lt. Surge's Electabuzz R	2.00	6.00
28 Lt. Surge's Raichu R	4.50	12.00
29 Misty's Cloyster R	2.00	6.00
30 Misty's Goldeen R	4.50	4.00
31 Misty's Poliwrath R	2.00	6.00
32 Misty's Tentacool R	2.00	6.00
33 Rocket's Snorlax R	4.00	10.00
34 Sabrina's Venomoth R	2.00	6.00
35 Blaine's Growlithe U	1.50	4.00
36 Blaine's Kangaskhan U	1.50	4.00
37 Blaine's Magmar U	1.50	4.00
38 Brock's Geodude U	.75	2.00
39 Brock's Golbat U	1.25	3.00
40 Brock's Graveler U	1.50	4.00
41 Brock's Lickitung U	1.50	4.00
42 Erika's Dratini U	.75	2.00
43 Erika's Exeggcute U	.75	2.00
44 Erika's Exeggutor U	.75	2.00
45 Erika's Gloom U	.75	2.00
46 Erika's Gloom U	.75	2.00
47 Erika's Oddish U	.75	2.00
48 Erika's Weepinbell U	.75	2.00
49 Erika's Weepinbell U	.75	2.00
50 Lt. Surge's Magnemite U	.75	2.00
51 Lt. Surge's Raticate U	.75	2.00
52 Lt. Surge's Spearow U	.75	2.00
53 Misty's Poliwhirl U	.75	2.00
54 Misty's Psyduck U	.75	2.00
55 Misty's Seaking U	.75	2.00
56 Misty's Starmie U	.75	2.00
57 Misty's Tentacool U	.75	2.00
58 Sabrina's Haunter U	.75	2.00
59 Sabrina's Jynx U	.75	2.00
60 Sabrina's Slowbro U	.75	2.00
61 Blaine's Charmander C	.75	2.00
62 Blaine's Growlithe C	.75	2.00
63 Blaine's Ponyta C	.75	2.00
64 Blaine's Tauros C	.75	2.00
65 Blaine's Vulpix C	.75	2.00
66 Brock's Geodude C	.75	2.00
67 Brock's Mankey C	.75	2.00
68 Brock's Mankey C	.75	2.00
69 Brock's Onix C	.75	2.00
70 Brock's Rhyhorn C	.75	2.00
71 Brock's Sandshrew C	.75	2.00
72 Brock's Sandshrew C	.75	2.00
73 Brock's Vulpix C	.75	2.00
74 Brock's Zubat C	.75	2.00
75 Erika's Bellsprout C	.75	2.00
76 Erika's Bellsprout C	.75	2.00
77 Erika's Exeggcute C	.75	2.00
78 Erika's Oddish C	.75	2.00
79 Erika's Tangela C	.75	2.00
80 Lt. Surge's Magnemite C	.75	2.00
81 Lt. Surge's Pikachu C	.75	2.00
82 Lt. Surge's Rattata C	.75	2.00
83 Lt. Surge's Spearow C	.75	2.00
84 Lt. Surge's Voltorb C	.75	2.00
85 Misty's Goldeen C	.75	2.00
86 Misty's Horsea C	.75	2.00
87 Misty's Poliwag C	.75	2.00
88 Misty's Seel C	.75	2.00
89 Misty's Shellder C	.75	2.00
90 Misty's Staryu C	.75	2.00
91 Sabrina's Abra C	.75	2.00
92 Sabrina's Drowzee C	.75	2.00
93 Sabrina's Gastly C	.75	2.00
94 Sabrina's Mr. Mime C	.75	2.00
95 Sabrina's Slowpoke C	.75	2.00
96 Sabrina's Venonat C	.75	2.00
97 Blaine's Quiz #1 R	2.00	6.00
98 Brock R	1.50	4.00
99 Charity R	1.50	4.00
100 Erika R	1.50	4.00
101 Lt. Surge R	1.50	4.00
102 Misty R	1.50	4.00
103 No Removal Gym R	3.00	8.00
104 The Rocket's Gym R	1.50	4.00
105 Blaine's Last Resort U	1.50	4.00
106 Brock's Training Method U	1.50	4.00
107 Celadon City Gym U	1.50	4.00
108 Cerulean City Gym U	1.50	4.00
109 Erika's Maids U	1.50	4.00
110 Erika's Perfume U	1.50	4.00
111 Good Manners U	1.50	4.00
112 Lt. Surge's Treaty U	1.50	4.00
113 Minion of Team Rocket U	1.50	4.00
114 Misty's Wrath U	1.50	4.00
115 Pewter City Gym U	1.50	4.00
116 Recall U	1.50	4.00
117 Sabrina's ESP U	1.50	4.00
118 Secret Mission U	1.50	4.00
119 Tickling Machine U	1.50	4.00
120 Vermillion City Gym U	1.50	4.00
121 Blaine's Gamble C	1.50	4.00
122 Energy Flow C	1.50	4.00
123 Misty's Duel C	1.50	4.00
124 Narrow Gym C	1.50	4.00
125 Sabrina's Gaze C	1.50	4.00
126 Trash Exchange C	1.50	4.00
127 Fighting Energy C	.75	2.00
128 Fire Energy C	.75	2.00
129 Grass Energy C	.75	2.00
130 Lightning Energy C	.75	2.00
131 Psychic Energy C	.75	2.00
132 Water Energy C	.75	2.00

2000 Pokemon Gym Heroes Unlimited

COMPLETE SET (132)	40.00	55.00
BOOSTER BOX (36 PACKS)	300.00	400.00
BOOSTER PACK (11 CARDS)	8.00	12.00
RELEASED ON AUGUST 14, 2000		
1 Blaine's Moltres HOLO R	3.00	6.00
2 Brock's Rhydon HOLO R	2.00	4.00
3 Erika's Clefable HOLO R	2.00	4.00
4 Erika's Dragonair HOLO R	1.00	3.00
5 Erika's Vileplume HOLO R	1.00	3.00
6 Lt. Surge's Electabuzz HOLO R	2.00	4.00
7 Lt. Surge's Fearow HOLO R	2.00	4.00
8 Lt. Surge's Magneton HOLO R	2.00	4.00
9 Misty's Seadra HOLO R	2.00	4.00
10 Misty's Tentacruel HOLO R	2.00	4.00
11 Rocket's Hitmonchan HOLO R	2.00	4.00
12 Rocket's Moltres HOLO R	2.00	4.00
13 Rocket's Scyther HOLO R	2.00	4.00
14 Sabrina's Gengar HOLO R	2.00	4.00
15 Brock HOLO R	2.00	4.00
16 Erika HOLO R	1.00	3.00
17 Lt. Surge HOLO R	2.00	4.00
18 Misty HOLO R	1.00	4.00
19 The Rocket's Trap HOLO R	2.00	4.00
20 Brock's Golem R	.50	1.00
21 Brock's Onix R	.50	1.00
22 Brock's Rhyhorn R	.50	1.00
23 Brock's Sandslash R	.50	1.00

24 Brock's Zubat R	.50	1.00
25 Erika's Clefairy R	.50	1.00
26 Erika's Victreebel R	.50	1.00
27 Lt. Surge's Electabuzz R	.50	1.00
28 Lt. Surge's Raichu R	.50	1.00
29 Misty's Cloyster R	.50	1.00
30 Misty's Goldeen R	.50	1.00
31 Misty's Poliwrath R	.50	1.00
32 Misty's Tentacool R	.50	1.00
33 Rocket's Snorlax R	.50	1.00
34 Sabrina's Venomoth R	.50	1.00
35 Blaine's Growlithe U	.20	.50
36 Blaine's Kangaskhan U	.20	.50
37 Blaine's Magmar U	.20	.50
38 Brock's Geodude U	.20	.50
39 Brock's Golbat U	.20	.50
40 Brock's Graveler U	.20	.50
41 Brock's Lickitung U	.20	.50
42 Erika's Dratini U	.20	.50
43 Erika's Exeggcute U	.20	.50
44 Erika's Exeggutor U	.20	.50
45 Erika's Gloom U	.20	.50
46 Erika's Gloom U	.20	.50
47 Erika's Oddish U	.20	.50
48 Erika's Weepinbell U	.20	.50
49 Erika's Weepinbell U	.20	.50
50 Lt. Surge's Magnemite U	.20	.50
51 Lt. Surge's Raticate U	.20	.50
52 Lt. Surge's Spearow U	.20	.50
53 Misty's Poliwhirl U	.20	.50
54 Misty's Psyduck U	.20	.50
55 Misty's Seaking U	.20	.50
56 Misty's Starmie U	.20	.50
57 Misty's Tentacool U	.20	.50
58 Sabrina's Haunter U	.20	.50
59 Sabrina's Jynx U	.20	.50
60 Sabrina's Slowbro U	.20	.50
61 Blaine's Charmander C	.10	.25
62 Blaine's Growlithe C	.10	.25
63 Blaine's Ponyta C	.10	.25
64 Blaine's Tauros C	.10	.25
65 Blaine's Vulpix C	.10	.25
66 Brock's Geodude C	.10	.25
67 Brock's Mankey C	.10	.25
68 Brock's Mankey C	.10	.25
69 Brock's Onix C	.10	.25
70 Brock's Rhyhorn C	.10	.25
71 Brock's Sandshrew C	.10	.25
72 Brock's Sandshrew C	.10	.25
73 Brock's Vulpix C	.10	.25
74 Brock's Zubat C	.10	.25
75 Erika's Bellsprout C	.10	.25
76 Erika's Bellsprout C	.10	.25
77 Erika's Exeggcute C	.10	.25
78 Erika's Oddish C	.10	.25
79 Erika's Tangela C	.10	.25
80 Lt. Surge's Magnemite C	.10	.25
81 Lt. Surge's Pikachu C	.25	.50
82 Lt. Surge's Rattata C	.10	.25
83 Lt. Surge's Spearow C	.10	.25
84 Lt. Surge's Voltorb C	.10	.25
85 Misty's Goldeen C	.10	.25
86 Misty's Horsea C	.10	.25
87 Misty's Poliwag C	.10	.25
88 Misty's Seel C	.10	.25
89 Misty's Shellder C	.10	.25
90 Misty's Staryu C	.10	.25
91 Sabrina's Abra C	.10	.25
92 Sabrina's Drowzee C	.10	.25
93 Sabrina's Gastly C	.10	.25
94 Sabrina's Mr. Mime C	.10	.25
95 Sabrina's Slowpoke C	.10	.25
96 Sabrina's Venonat C	.10	.25
97 Blaine's Quiz #1 R	.50	1.00
98 Brock R	.50	1.00
99 Charity R	.50	1.00
100 Erika R	.50	1.00
101 Lt. Surge R	.50	1.00
102 Misty R	.50	1.00
103 No Removal Gym R	.50	1.00
104 The Rocket's Gym R	.50	1.00
105 Blaine's Last Resort U	.20	.50
106 Brock's Training Method U	.20	.50
107 Celadon City Gym U	.20	.50
108 Cerulean City Gym U	.20	.50
109 Erika's Maids U	.20	.50
110 Erika's Perfume U	.20	.50
111 Good Manners U	.20	.50
112 Lt. Surge's Treaty U	.20	.50
113 Minion of Team Rocket U	.20	.50
114 Misty's Wrath U	.20	.50
115 Pewter City Gym U	.20	.50
116 Recall U	.20	.50
117 Sabrina's ESP U	.20	.50
118 Secret Mission U	.20	.50
119 Tickling Machine U	.20	.50
120 Vermillion City Gym U	.20	.50
121 Blaine's Gamble C	.10	.25
122 Energy Flow C	.10	.25
123 Misty's Duel C	.10	.25
124 Narrow Gym C	.10	.25
125 Sabrina's Gaze C	.10	.25
126 Trash Exchange C	.10	.25
127 Fighting Energy C	.10	.25
128 Fire Energy C	.10	.25
129 Grass Energy C	.10	.25
130 Lightning Energy C	.10	.25
131 Psychic Energy C	.10	.25
132 Water Energy C	.10	.25

2000 Pokemon Gym Challenge 1st Edition

COMPLETE SET (132)	140.00	250.00
BOOSTER BOX (36 PACKS)	600.00	800.00
BOOSTER PACK (11 CARDS)	10.00	25.00
RELEASED ON OCTOBER 16, 2000		
1 Blaine's Arcanine HOLO R	8.00	20.00
2 Blaine's Charizard HOLO R	25.00	60.00
3 Brock's Ninetales HOLO R	6.00	15.00
4 Erika's Venusaur HOLO R	8.00	20.00
5 Giovanni's Gyarados HOLO R	8.00	20.00
6 Giovanni's Machamp HOLO R	8.00	20.00
7 Giovanni's Nidoking HOLO R	6.00	15.00
8 Giovanni's Persian HOLO R	6.00	15.00
9 Koga's Beedrill HOLO R	4.00	10.00
10 Koga's Ditto HOLO R	5.00	12.00
11 Lt. Surge's Raichu HOLO R	6.00	15.00
12 Misty's Golduck HOLO R	6.00	15.00
13 Misty's Gyarados HOLO R	8.00	20.00
14 Rocket's Mewtwo HOLO R	15.00	30.00
15 Rocket's Zapdos HOLO R	8.00	20.00
16 Sabrina's Alakazam HOLO R	8.00	20.00
17 Blaine HOLO R	6.00	15.00
18 Giovanni HOLO R	3.00	8.00
19 Koga HOLO R	10.00	25.00
20 Sabrina HOLO R	6.00	15.00
21 Blaine's Ninetales R	2.00	6.00
22 Brock's Dugtrio R	1.50	4.00
23 Giovanni's Nidoqueen R	.75	2.00
24 Giovanni's Pinsir R	.75	2.00
25 Koga's Arbok R	.75	2.00
26 Koga's Muk R	.75	2.00
27 Koga's Pidgeotto R	.75	2.00
28 Lt. Surge's Jolteon R	3.00	8.00
29 Sabrina's Gengar R	6.00	15.00
30 Sabrina's Golduck R	1.50	4.00
31 Blaine's Charmeleon U	.75	2.00
32 Blaine's Dodrio U	.75	2.00
33 Blaine's Rapidash U	.75	2.00
34 Brock's Graveler U	.75	2.00
35 Brock's Primeape U	.75	2.00
36 Brock's Sandslash U	.75	2.00
37 Brock's Vulpix U	.75	2.00
38 Erika's Bellsprout U	.75	2.00
39 Erika's Bulbasaur U	.75	2.00
40 Erika's Clefairy U	.75	2.00
41 Erika's Ivysaur U	.75	2.00
42 Giovanni's Machoke U	.75	2.00
43 Giovanni's Meowth U	.75	2.00
44 Giovanni's Nidorina U	.75	2.00
45 Giovanni's Nidorino U	.75	2.00
46 Koga's Golbat U	.75	2.00
47 Koga's Kakuna U	.75	2.00
48 Koga's Koffing U	.75	2.00
49 Koga's Pidgey U	.75	2.00
50 Koga's Weezing U	.75	2.00
51 Lt. Surge's Eevee U	.75	2.00
52 Lt. Surge's Electrode U	.75	2.00
53 Lt. Surge's Raticate U	.75	2.00
54 Misty's Dewgong U	.75	2.00
55 Sabrina's Haunter U	.75	2.00
56 Sabrina's Hypno U	.75	2.00
57 Sabrina's Jynx U	.75	2.00
58 Sabrina's Kadabra U	.75	2.00
59 Sabrina's Mr. Mime U	.75	2.00
60 Blaine's Charmander C	.75	2.00
61 Blaine's Doduo C	.75	2.00
62 Blaine's Growlithe C	.75	2.00
63 Blaine's Mankey C	.75	2.00
64 Blaine's Ponyta C	.75	2.00
65 Blaine's Rhyhorn C	.75	2.00
66 Blaine's Vulpix C	.75	2.00
67 Brock's Diglett C	.75	2.00
68 Brock's Geodude C	.75	2.00
69 Erika's Jigglypuff C	.75	2.00
70 Erika's Oddish C	.75	2.00
71 Erika's Paras C	.75	2.00
72 Giovanni's Machop C	.75	2.00
73 Giovanni's Magikarp (C)	.75	2.00
74 Giovanni's Meowth C	.75	2.00
75 Giovanni's Nidoran (Fem) C	.75	2.00
76 Giovanni's Nidoran (Male) C	.75	2.00
77 Koga's Ekans C	.75	2.00
78 Koga's Grimer C	.75	2.00
79 Koga's Koffing C	.75	2.00
80 Koga's Pidgey C	.75	2.00
81 Koga's Tangela C	.75	2.00
82 Koga's Weedle C	.75	2.00
83 Koga's Zubat C	.75	2.00
84 Lt. Surge's Pikachu C	.75	2.00
85 Lt. Surge's Rattata C	.75	2.00
86 Lt. Surge's Voltorb C	.75	2.00
87 Misty's Horsea C	.75	2.00
88 Misty's Magikarp C	.75	2.00
89 Misty's Poliwag C	.75	2.00
90 Misty's Psyduck C	.75	2.00
91 Misty's Seel C	.75	2.00
92 Misty's Staryu C	.75	2.00
93 Sabrina's Abra C	.75	2.00
94 Sabrina's Abra C	.75	2.00
95 Sabrina's Drowzee C	.75	2.00
96 Sabrina's Gastly C	.75	2.00
97 Sabrina's Gastly C	.75	2.00
98 Sabrina's Porygon C	.75	2.00
99 Sabrina's Psyduck C	.75	2.00
100 Blaine R	1.50	4.00
101 Brock's Protection R	1.50	4.00
102 Chaos Gym R	1.50	4.00
103 Erika's Kindness R	1.50	4.00
104 Giovanni R	1.50	4.00
105 Giovanni's Last Resort R	1.50	4.00
106 Koga R	1.50	4.00
107 Lt. Surge's Secret Plan R	1.50	4.00
108 Misty's Wish R	2.00	6.00
109 Resistance Gym R	1.50	4.00
110 Sabrina R	1.50	4.00
111 Blaine's Quiz #2 U	.75	2.00
112 Blaine's Quiz #3 U	.75	2.00
113 Cinnabar City Gym U	.75	2.00
114 Fuchsia City Gym U	.75	2.00
115 Koga's Ninja Trick U	.75	2.00
116 Master Ball U	.75	2.00
117 Max Revive U	.75	2.00
118 Misty's Tears U	5.00	12.00
119 Rocket's Minefield Gym U	.75	2.00
120 Rocket's secret Experiment U	.75	2.00
121 Sabrina's Psychic Control U	.75	2.00
122 Saffron City Gym U	.75	2.00
123 Viridian City Gym U	.75	2.00
124 Fervor C	.75	2.00
125 Transparent Walls C	.75	2.00
126 Warp Point C	.75	2.00
127 Fighting Energy C	.50	1.50
128 Fire Energy C	.50	1.50
129 Grass Energy C	.50	1.50
130 Lightning Energy C	.50	1.50
131 Psychic Energy C	.50	1.50
132 Water Energy C	.50	1.50

2000 Pokemon Gym Challenge Unlimited

COMPLETE SET (132)	60.00	100.00
BOOSTER BOX (36 PACKS)	400.00	600.00
BOOSTER PACK (11 CARDS)	8.00	12.00
RELEASED ON OCTOBER 16, 2000		
1 Blaine's Arcanine HOLO R	4.50	11.00
2 Blaine's Charizard HOLO R	25.00	50.00
3 Brock's Ninetales HOLO R	3.00	8.00
4 Erika's Venusaur HOLO R	2.50	7.00
5 Giovanni's Gyarados HOLO R	3.00	8.00
6 Giovanni's Machamp HOLO R	3.00	8.00
7 Giovanni's Nidoking HOLO R	6.00	15.00
8 Giovanni's Persian HOLO R	2.00	6.00
9 Koga's Beedrill HOLO R	2.00	6.00
10 Koga's Ditto HOLO R	2.00	6.00
11 Lt. Surge's Raichu HOLO R	3.00	8.00
12 Misty's Golduck HOLO R	4.50	11.00
13 Misty's Gyarados HOLO R	5.00	12.00
14 Rocket's Mewtwo HOLO R	10.00	25.00
15 Rocket's Zapdos HOLO R	5.00	12.00
16 Sabrina's Alakazam HOLO R	3.00	8.00
17 Blaine's HOLO R	2.00	6.00
18 Giovanni HOLO R	2.00	6.00
19 Koga HOLO R	2.00	6.00
20 Sabrina HOLO R	2.00	6.00
21 Blaine's Ninetales R	1.50	4.00
22 Brock's Dugtrio R	1.50	4.00
23 Giovanni's Nidoqueen R	1.50	4.00
24 Giovanni's Pinsir R	1.50	4.00
25 Koga's Arbok R	1.50	4.00
26 Koga's Muk R	1.50	4.00
27 Koga's Pidgeotto R	1.50	4.00
28 Lt. Surge's Jolteon R	2.00	6.00
29 Sabrina's Gengar R	3.00	8.00
30 Sabrina's Golduck R	1.50	4.00
31 Blaine's Charmeleon U	.75	2.00
32 Blaine's Dodrio U	.75	2.00
33 Blaine's Rapidash U	.75	2.00
34 Brock's Graveler U	.75	2.00
35 Brock's Primeape U	.75	2.00
36 Brock's Sandslash U	.75	2.00
37 Brock's Vulpix U	.75	2.00
38 Erika's Bellsprout U	.75	2.00
39 Erika's Bulbasaur U	.75	2.00
40 Erika's Clefairy U	.75	2.00
41 Erika's Ivysaur U	.75	2.00
42 Giovanni's Machoke U	.75	2.00
43 Giovanni's Meowth U	.75	2.00
44 Giovanni's Nidorina U	.75	2.00
45 Giovanni's Nidorino U	.75	2.00
46 Koga's Golbat U	.75	2.00
47 Koga's Kakuna U	.75	2.00
48 Koga's Koffing U	.75	2.00
49 Koga's Pidgey U	.75	2.00
50 Koga's Weezing U	.75	2.00
51 Lt. Surge's Eevee U	.75	2.00
52 Lt. Surge's Electrode U	.75	2.00
53 Lt. Surge's Raticate U	.75	2.00
54 Misty's Dewgong U	.75	2.00
55 Sabrina's Haunter U	.75	2.00
56 Sabrina's Hypno U	.75	2.00
57 Sabrina's Jynx U	.75	2.00
58 Sabrina's Kadabra U	.75	2.00
59 Sabrina's Mr. Mime U	.75	2.00
60 Blaine's Charmander C	.75	2.00
61 Blaine's Doduo C	.75	2.00
62 Blaine's Growlithe C	.75	2.00
63 Blaine's Mankey C	.75	2.00
64 Blaine's Ponyta C	.75	2.00
65 Blaine's Rhyhorn C	.75	2.00
66 Blaine's Vulpix C	.75	2.00
67 Brock's Diglett C	.75	2.00
68 Brock's Geodude C	.75	2.00
69 Erika's Jigglypuff C	.75	2.00
70 Erika's Oddish C	.75	2.00
71 Erika's Paras C	.75	2.00
72 Giovanni's Machop C	.75	2.00
73 Giovanni's Magikarp C	.75	2.00
74 Giovanni's Meowth C	.75	2.00
75 Giovanni's Nidoran (Fem) C	.75	2.00
76 Giovanni's Nidoran (Male) C	.75	2.00
77 Koga's Ekans C	.75	2.00
78 Koga's Grimer C	.75	2.00
79 Koga's Koffing C	.75	2.00
80 Koga's Pidgey C	.75	2.00
81 Koga's Tangela C	.75	2.00
82 Koga's Weedle C	.75	2.00
83 Koga's Zubat C	.75	2.00
84 Lt. Surge's Pikachu C	.75	2.00
85 Lt. Surge's Rattata C	.75	2.00
86 Lt. Surge's Voltorb C	.75	2.00
87 Misty's Horsea C	.75	2.00
88 Misty's Magikarp C	.75	2.00
89 Misty's Poliwag C	.75	2.00
90 Misty's Psyduck C	.75	2.00
91 Misty's Seel C	.75	2.00
92 Misty's Staryu C	.75	2.00
93 Sabrina's Abra C	.75	2.00
94 Sabrina's Abra C	.75	2.00
95 Sabrina's Drowzee C	.75	2.00
96 Sabrina's Gastly C	.75	2.00
97 Sabrina's Gastly C	.75	2.00
98 Sabrina's Porygon C	.75	2.00
99 Sabrina's Psyduck C	.75	2.00
100 Blaine R	.75	2.00
101 Brock's Protection R	.75	2.00
102 Chaos Gym R	.75	2.00
103 Erika's Kindness R	.75	2.00
104 Giovanni R	.75	2.00
105 Giovanni's Last Resort R	.75	2.00
106 Koga R	.75	2.00
107 Lt. Surge's Secret Plan R	.75	2.00
108 Misty's Wish R	2.00	4.00
109 Resistance Gym R	.75	2.00
110 Sabrina R	.75	2.00
111 Blaine's Quiz #2 U	.75	2.00
112 Blaine's Quiz #3 U	.75	2.00
113 Cinnabar City Gym U	.75	2.00
114 Fuchsia City Gym U	.75	2.00
115 Koga's Ninja Trick U	.75	2.00
116 Master Ball U	.75	2.00
117 Max Revive U	.75	2.00
118 Misty's Tears U	.75	2.00
119 Rocket's Minefield Gym U	.75	2.00
120 Rocket's secret Experiment U	.75	2.00
121 Sabrina's Psychic Control U	.75	2.00
122 Saffron City Gym U	.75	2.00
123 Viridian City Gym U	.75	2.00
124 Fervor C	.75	2.00
125 Transparent Walls C	.75	2.00
126 Warp Point C	.75	2.00
127 Fighting Energy C	.75	2.00
128 Fire Energy C	.75	2.00
129 Grass Energy C	.75	2.00
130 Lightning Energy C	.75	2.00
131 Psychic Energy C	.75	2.00
132 Water Energy C	.75	2.00

2000 Pokemon Neo Genesis 1st Edition

COMPLETE SET (111)	120.00	200.00
BOOSTER BOX (36 PACKS)	700.00	900.00
BOOSTER PACK (11 CARDS)	20.00	25.00
RELEASED ON DECEMBER 16, 2000		
1 Ampharos HOLO R	5.00	12.00
2 Azumarill HOLO R	6.00	15.00
3 Bellossom HOLO R	5.00	12.00
4 Feraligatr Lv.56 HOLO R	10.00	25.00
5 Feraligatr Lv.69 HOLO R	10.00	25.00
6 Heracross HOLO R	4.50	11.00
7 Jumpluff HOLO R	3.00	8.00
8 Kingdra HOLO R	6.00	15.00
9 Lugia HOLO R	40.00	80.00
10 Meganium Lv.54 HOLO R	6.00	15.00
11 Meganium Lv.57 HOLO R	10.00	25.00
12 Pichu HOLO R	6.00	15.00
13 Skarmory HOLO R	6.00	15.00
14 Slowking HOLO R	8.00	20.00
15 Steelix HOLO R	5.00	12.00
16 Togetic HOLO R	8.00	20.00

17 Typhlosion Lv.55 HOLO R 20.00 40.00
18 Typhlosion Lv.57 HOLO R 20.00 40.00
19 Metal Energy HOLO R 3.00 8.00
20 Cleffa R 5.00 12.00
21 Donphan R 1.50 4.00
22 Elekid R 1.50 4.00
23 Magby R 1.50 4.00
24 Murkrow R 1.50 4.00
25 Sneasel R 1.50 4.00
26 Aipom U 1.00 3.00
27 Ariados U 1.00 3.00
28 Bayleef Lv.22 U 1.00 3.00
29 Bayleef Lv.39 U 1.00 3.00
30 Clefairy U 1.00 3.00
31 Croconaw Lv.34 U 1.00 3.00
32 Croconaw Lv.41 U 1.00 3.00
33 Electabuzz U 1.00 3.00
34 Flaaffy U 1.00 3.00
35 Furret U 1.00 3.00
36 Gloom U 1.00 3.00
37 Granbull U 1.00 3.00
38 Lanturn U 1.00 3.00
39 Ledian U 1.00 3.00
40 Magmar U 1.00 3.00
41 Miltank U 1.00 3.00
42 Noctowl U 1.00 3.00
43 Phanpy U 1.00 3.00
44 Piloswine U 1.00 3.00
45 Quagsire U 1.00 3.00
46 Quilava Lv.28 U 1.00 3.00
47 Quilava Lv.35 U 1.00 3.00
48 Seadra U 1.00 3.00
49 Skiploom U 1.00 3.00
50 Sunflora U 1.00 3.00
51 Togepi U 1.00 3.00
52 Xatu U 1.00 3.00
53 Chikorita Lv.12 C 1.00 3.00
54 Chikorita Lv.19 C 1.00 3.00
55 Chinchou C 1.00 3.00
56 Cyndaquil Lv.14 C 1.00 3.00
57 Cyndaquil Lv.21 C 1.00 3.00
58 Girafarig C 1.00 3.00
59 Gligar C 1.00 3.00
60 Hoothoot C 1.00 3.00
61 Hoppip C 1.00 3.00
62 Horsea C 1.00 3.00
63 Ledyba C 1.00 3.00
64 Mantine C 1.00 3.00
65 Mareep C 1.00 3.00
66 Marill C 1.00 3.00
67 Natu C 1.00 3.00
68 Oddish C 1.00 3.00
69 Onix C 1.00 3.00
70 Pikachu C 1.00 3.00
71 Sentret C 1.00 3.00
72 Shuckle C 1.00 3.00
73 Slowpoke C 1.00 3.00
74 Snubbull C 1.00 3.00
75 Spinarak C 1.00 3.00
76 Stantler C 1.00 3.00
77 Sudowoodo C 1.00 3.00
78 Sunkern C 1.00 3.00
79 Swinub C 1.00 3.00
80 Totodile Lv.13 C 1.00 3.00
81 Totodile Lv.20 C 1.00 3.00
82 Wooper C 1.00 3.00
83 Arcade Game R 1.00 3.00
84 Ecogym R 2.00 6.00
85 Energy Charge R 1.50 4.00
86 Focus Band R 2.00 6.00
87 Mary R 1.50 4.00
88 PokeGear R 1.00 3.00
89 Super Energy Retrieval R 1.00 3.00
90 Time Capsule R 1.00 3.00
91 Bill's Teleporter U 1.00 3.00
92 Card-Flip Game U 1.00 3.00
93 Gold Berry U 1.00 3.00
94 Miracle Berry U 1.00 3.00
95 New Pokedex U 1.00 3.00
96 Professor Elm U 1.00 3.00
97 Sprout Tower U 1.00 3.00
98 Super Scoop Up U 1.00 3.00
99 Berry C 1.00 3.00
100 Double Gust C 1.00 3.00
101 Moo-Moo Milk C 1.00 3.00
102 Pokemon March C 1.00 3.00
103 Super Rod C 1.00 3.00
104 Darkness Energy R 2.00 6.00
105 Recycle Energy R 2.00 6.00
106 Fighting Energy 1.00 3.00
107 Fire Energy 1.00 3.00
108 Grass Energy 1.00 3.00
109 Lightning Energy 1.00 3.00
110 Psychic Energy 1.00 3.00
111 Water Energy 1.00 3.00

2000 Pokemon Neo Genesis Unlimited

COMPLETE SET (111) 50.00 75.00
BOOSTER BOX (36 PACKS) 400.00 500.00
BOOSTER PACK (11 CARDS) 12.00 15.00
HOTFOOT DECK (60 CARDS) 4.00 10.00
COLD FUSION DECK (60 CARDS) 4.00 10.00
RELEASED DECEMBER 16, 2000
1 Ampharos HOLO R 2.00 4.00
2 Azumarill HOLO R 1.50 4.00
3 Bellossom HOLO R 2.00 4.00
4 Feraligatr Lv.56 HOLO R 5.00 12.00
5 Feraligatr Lv.69 HOLO R 5.00 12.00
6 Heracross HOLO R 4.00 10.00
7 Jumpluff HOLO R 2.00 4.00
8 Kingdra HOLO R 2.00 4.00
9 Lugia HOLO R 10.00 25.00
10 Meganium Lv.54 HOLO R 5.00 12.00
11 Meganium Lv.57 HOLO R 5.00 12.00
12 Pichu HOLO R 8.00 20.00
13 Skarmory HOLO R 2.00 6.00
14 Slowking HOLO R 2.00 6.00
15 Steelix HOLO R 2.00 6.00
16 Togetic HOLO R 3.00 8.00
17 Typhlosion Lv.55 HOLO R 8.00 20.00
18 Typhlosion Lv.57 HOLO R 8.00 20.00
19 Metal Energy HOLO R 2.00 6.00
20 Cleffa R 3.00 8.00
21 Donphan R 2.00 6.00
22 Elekid R 1.50 4.00
23 Magby R 1.50 4.00
24 Murkrow R 1.50 4.00
25 Sneasel R 1.50 4.00
26 Aipom U 1.25 3.00
27 Ariados U 1.25 3.00
28 Bayleef Lv.22 U 1.25 3.00
29 Bayleef Lv.39 U 1.25 3.00
30 Clefairy U 1.25 3.00
31 Croconaw Lv.34 U 1.25 3.00
32 Croconaw Lv.41 U 1.25 3.00
33 Electabuzz U 1.25 3.00
34 Flaaffy U 1.25 3.00
35 Furret U 1.25 3.00
36 Gloom U 1.25 3.00
37 Granbull U 1.25 3.00
38 Lanturn U 1.25 3.00
39 Ledian U 1.25 3.00
40 Magmar U 1.25 3.00
41 Miltank U 1.25 3.00
42 Noctowl U 1.25 3.00
43 Phanpy U 1.25 3.00
44 Piloswine U 1.25 3.00
45 Quagsire U 1.25 3.00
46 Quilava Lv.28 U 1.25 3.00
47 Quilava Lv.35 U 1.25 3.00
48 Seadra U 1.25 3.00
49 Skiploom U 1.25 3.00
50 Sunflora U 1.25 3.00
51 Togepi U 1.25 3.00
52 Xatu U 1.25 3.00
53 Chikorita Lv.12 C 1.25 3.00
54 Chikorita Lv.19 C 1.25 3.00
55 Chinchou C 1.25 3.00
56 Cyndaquil Lv.14 C 1.25 3.00
57 Cyndaquil Lv.21 C 1.25 3.00
58 Girafarig C 1.25 3.00
59 Gligar C 1.25 3.00
60 Hoothoot C 1.25 3.00
61 Hoppip C 1.25 3.00
62 Horsea C 1.25 3.00
63 Ledyba C 1.25 3.00
64 Mantine C 1.25 3.00
65 Mareep C 1.25 3.00
66 Marill C 1.25 3.00
67 Natu C 1.25 3.00
68 Oddish C 1.25 3.00
69 Onix C 1.25 3.00
70 Pikachu C 1.25 3.00
71 Sentret C 1.25 3.00
72 Shuckle C 1.25 3.00
73 Slowpoke C 1.25 3.00
74 Snubbull C 1.25 3.00
75 Spinarak C 1.25 3.00
76 Stantler C 1.25 3.00
77 Sudowoodo C 1.25 3.00
78 Sunkern C 1.25 3.00
79 Swinub C 1.25 3.00
80 Totodile Lv.13 C 1.25 3.00
81 Totodile Lv.20 C 1.25 3.00
82 Wooper C 1.25 3.00
83 Arcade Game R 1.25 3.00
84 Ecogym R 1.25 3.00
85 Energy Charge R 1.25 3.00
86 Focus Band R 1.25 3.00
87 Mary R 1.25 3.00
88 PokeGear R 1.25 3.00
89 Super Energy Retrieval R 1.25 3.00
90 Time Capsule R 1.25 3.00
91 Bill's Teleporter U 1.25 3.00
92 Card-Flip Game U 1.25 3.00
93 Gold Berry U 1.25 3.00
94 Miracle Berry U 1.25 3.00
95 New Pokedex U 1.25 3.00
96 Professor Elm U 1.25 3.00
97 Sprout Tower U 1.25 3.00
98 Super Scoop Up U 1.25 3.00
99 Berry C 1.25 3.00
100 Double Gust C 1.25 3.00
101 Moo-Moo Milk C 1.25 3.00
102 Pokemon March C 1.25 3.00
103 Super Rod C 1.25 3.00
104 Darkness Energy R 1.25 3.00
105 Recycle Energy R 1.25 3.00
106 Fighting Energy 1.25 3.00
107 Fire Energy 1.25 3.00
108 Grass Energy 1.25 3.00
109 Lightning Energy 1.25 3.00
110 Psychic Energy 1.25 3.00
111 Water Energy 1.25 3.00

2001 Pokemon Neo Discovery 1st Edition

COMPLETE SET (75) 150.00 300.00
BOOSTER BOX (36 PACKS) 800.00 1100.00
BOOSTER PACK (11 CARDS) 25.00 50.00
RELEASED ON JUNE 1, 2001
1 Espeon HOLO R 20.00 40.00
2 Forretress HOLO R 5.00 12.00
3 Hitmontop HOLO R 8.00 20.00
4 Houndoom HOLO R 8.00 20.00
5 Houndour HOLO R 6.00 15.00
6 Kabutops HOLO R 8.00 20.00
7 Magnemite HOLO R 6.00 15.00
8 Politoed HOLO R 6.00 15.00
9 Poliwrath HOLO R 6.00 15.00
10 Scizor HOLO R 8.00 20.00
11 Smeargle HOLO R 6.00 15.00
12 Tyranitar HOLO R 15.00 30.00
13 Umbreon HOLO R 30.00 60.00
14 Unown A HOLO R 5.00 12.00
15 Ursaring HOLO R 5.00 12.00
16 Wobbuffet HOLO R 5.00 12.00
17 Yanma HOLO R 5.00 12.00
18 Beedrill R 1.25 3.00
19 Butterfree R 2.00 6.00
20 Espeon R 4.00 10.00
21 Forretress R 1.25 3.00
22 Hitmontop R 2.00 6.00
23 Houndoom R 1.50 4.00
24 Houndour R 2.00 6.00
25 Kabutops R 1.50 4.00
26 Magnemite R 1.50 3.00
27 Politoed R 1.50 3.00
28 Poliwrath R 1.50 3.00
29 Scizor R 1.50 3.00
30 Smeargle R 1.50 3.00
31 Tyranitar R 4.00 10.00
32 Umbreon R 4.00 10.00
33 Unown A R 1.50 3.00
34 Ursaring R 1.50 3.00
35 Wobbuffet R 1.50 3.00
36 Yanma R 1.50 3.00
37 Corsola U .75 2.00
38 Eevee U .75 2.00
39 Houndour U 1.25 3.00
40 Igglybuff U 1.50 4.00
41 Kakuna U .75 2.00
42 Metapod U .75 2.00
43 Omastar U .75 2.00
44 Poliwhirl U .75 2.00
45 Pupitar U .75 2.00
46 Scyther U .75 2.00
47 Unown D U 1.50 3.00
48 Unown F U 1.50 3.00
49 Unown M U 1.50 3.00
50 Unown N U 1.50 3.00
51 Unown U U 1.50 3.00
52 Xatu U .75 2.00
53 Caterpie C .75 2.00
54 Dunsparce C .75 2.00
55 Hoppip C .75 2.00
56 Kabuto C .75 2.00
57 Larvitar C .75 2.00
58 Mareep C .75 2.00
59 Natu C .75 2.00
60 Omanyte C .75 2.00
61 Pineco C .75 2.00
62 Poliwag C .75 2.00
63 Sentret C .75 2.00
64 Spinarak C .75 2.00
65 Teddiursa C .75 2.00
66 Tyrogue C .75 2.00
67 Unown E C .75 2.00
68 Unown I C .75 2.00
69 Unown O C .75 2.00
70 Weedle C .75 2.00
71 Wooper C .75 2.00
72 Trainer: Fossil Egg U .75 2.00
73 Trainer: Hyper Devolution Spray U .75 2.00
74 Trainer: Ruin Wall U 1.25 3.00
75 Trainer: Energy Ark C 1.25 3.00

2001 Pokemon Neo Discovery Unlimited

COMPLETE SET (75) 80.00 200.00
BOOSTER BOX (36 PACKS) 500.00 650.00
BOOSTER PACK (11 CARDS) 10.00 25.00
BRAINWAVE DECK 10.00 25.00
WALLOP DECK 10.00 25.00
RELEASED ON JUNE 1, 2001
1 Espeon HOLO R 6.00 15.00
2 Forretress HOLO R 2.00 6.00
3 Hitmontop HOLO R 2.00 6.00
4 Houndoom HOLO R 2.00 6.00
5 Houndour HOLO R 2.00 6.00
6 Kabutops HOLO R 6.00 15.00
7 Magnemite HOLO R 2.00 6.00
8 Politoed HOLO R 2.00 6.00
9 Poliwrath HOLO R 1.50 4.00
10 Scizor HOLO R 5.00 12.00
11 Smeargle HOLO R 2.00 6.00
12 Tyranitar HOLO R 4.00 10.00
13 Umbreon HOLO R 8.00 20.00
14 Unown A HOLO R 1.50 4.00
15 Ursaring HOLO R 2.00 6.00
16 Wobbuffet HOLO R 1.75 5.00
17 Yanma HOLO R 1.75 5.00
18 Beedrill R 1.25 3.00
19 Butterfree R 1.25 3.00
20 Espeon R 2.00 6.00
21 Forretress R 1.25 3.00
22 Hitmontop R 1.25 3.00
23 Houndoom R 1.25 3.00
24 Houndour R 1.25 3.00
25 Kabutops R 1.25 3.00
26 Magnemite R 1.25 3.00
27 Politoed R 1.25 3.00
28 Poliwrath R 1.25 3.00
29 Scizor R 1.25 3.00
30 Smeargle R 1.25 3.00
31 Tyranitar R 1.50 4.00
32 Umbreon R 1.75 5.00
33 Unown A R 1.25 3.00
34 Ursaring R 1.25 3.00
35 Wobbuffet R 1.25 3.00
36 Yanma R 1.25 3.00
37 Corsola U .75 2.00
38 Eevee U .75 2.00
39 Houndour U .75 2.00
40 Igglybuff U .75 2.00
41 Kakuna U .75 2.00
42 Metapod U .75 2.00
43 Omastar U .75 2.00
44 Poliwhirl U .75 2.00
45 Pupitar U .75 2.00
46 Scyther U .75 2.00
47 Unown D U .75 2.00
48 Unown F U .75 2.00
49 Unown M U .75 2.00
50 Unown N U .75 2.00
51 Unown U U .75 2.00
52 Xatu U .75 2.00
53 Caterpie C .75 2.00
54 Dunsparce C .75 2.00
55 Hoppip C .75 2.00
56 Kabuto C .75 2.00
57 Larvitar C .75 2.00
58 Mareep C .75 2.00
59 Natu C .75 2.00
60 Omanyte C .75 2.00
61 Pineco C .75 2.00
62 Poliwag C .75 2.00
63 Sentret C .75 2.00
64 Spinarak C .75 2.00
65 Teddiursa C .75 2.00
66 Tyrogue C .75 2.00
67 Unown E C .75 2.00
68 Unown I C .75 2.00
69 Unown O C .75 2.00
70 Weedle C .75 2.00
71 Wooper C .75 2.00
72 Trainer: Fossil Egg U .75 2.00
73 Trainer: Hyper Devolution Spray U .75 2.00
74 Trainer: Ruin Wall U .75 2.00
75 Trainer: Energy Ark C .75 2.00

2001 Pokemon Neo Revelation 1st Edition

COMPLETE SET (66) 350.00 450.00
BOOSTER BOX (36 PACKS) 1200.00 1800.00
BOOSTER PACK (11 CARDS) 30.00 60.00
RELEASED ON SEPTEMBER 21, 2001
1 Ampharos HOLO R 6.00 15.00
2 Blissey HOLO R 6.00 15.00
3 Celebi HOLO R 15.00 30.00
4 Crobat HOLO R 6.00 15.00
5 Delibird HOLO R 4.00 10.00
6 Entei HOLO R 20.00 40.00
7 Ho-oh HOLO R 25.00 50.00
8 Houndoom HOLO R 15.00 30.00
9 Jumpluff HOLO R 4.00 10.00
10 Magneton HOLO R 4.00 10.00
11 Misdreavus HOLO R 8.00 20.00
12 Porygon2 HOLO R 8.00 20.00
13 Raikou HOLO R 20.00 40.00
14 Suicune HOLO R 20.00 40.00
15 Aerodactyl R 2.00 6.00
16 Celebi R 2.00 6.00
17 Entei R 2.00 6.00
18 Ho-oh R 6.00 15.00
19 Kingdra R 2.00 6.00
20 Lugia R 6.00 15.00
21 Raichu R 2.00 6.00
22 Raikou R 2.00 6.00
23 Skarmory R 2.00 6.00

24 Sneasel R 2.00 6.00
25 Starmie R 2.00 6.00
26 Sudowoodo R 2.00 6.00
27 Suicune R 2.00 6.00
28 Flaaffy U 1.25 3.00
29 Golbat U 1.25 3.00
30 Graveler U 1.25 3.00
31 Jynx U 1.25 3.00
32 Lanturn U 1.25 3.00
33 Magcargo U 1.25 3.00
34 Octillery U 1.25 3.00
35 Parasect U 1.25 3.00
36 Piloswine U 1.25 3.00
37 Seaking U 1.25 3.00
38 Stantler U 1.25 3.00
39 Unown B U 1.25 3.00
40 Unown Y U 1.25 3.00
41 Aipom C .75 2.00
42 Chinchou C .75 2.00
43 Farfetch'd C .75 2.00
44 Geodude C .75 2.00
45 Goldeen C .75 2.00
46 Murkrow C .75 2.00
47 Paras C .75 2.00
48 Quagsire C .75 2.00
49 Qwilfish C .75 2.00
50 Remoraid C .75 2.00
51 Shuckle C .75 2.00
52 Skiploom C .75 2.00
53 Slugma C .75 2.00
54 Smoochum C .75 2.00
55 Snubbull C .75 2.00
56 Staryu C .75 2.00
57 Swinub C .75 2.00
58 Unown K C .75 2.00
59 Zubat C .75 2.00
60 Balloon Berry U .75 2.00
61 Healing Field U .75 2.00
62 Pokemon Breeder Fields U .75 2.00
63 Rocket's Hideout U 1.50 4.00
64 Old Rod C .75 2.00
65 Shining Gyarados HOLO R 40.00 80.00
66 Shining Magikarp HOLO R 25.00 50.00

2001 Pokemon Neo Revelation Unlimited

COMPLETE SET (66) 250.00 350.00
BOOSTER BOX (36 PACKS) 700.00 900.00
BOOSTER PACK (11 CARDS) 15.00 30.00
*CARD VALUES ARE 50% OF 1ST EDITION PRICING.
RELEASED ON SEPTEMBER 21, 2001
1 Ampharos HOLO R 4.00 10.00
2 Blissey HOLO R 3.50 10.00
3 Celebi HOLO R 3.00 8.00
4 Crobat HOLO R 3.00 8.00
5 Delibird HOLO R 2.00 6.00
6 Entei HOLO R 6.00 15.00
7 Ho-oh HOLO R 15.00 30.00
8 Houndoom HOLO R 5.00 12.00
9 Jumpluff HOLO R 2.00 6.00
10 Magneton HOLO R 2.00 6.00
11 Misdreavus HOLO R 5.00 12.00
12 Porygon 2 HOLO R 3.00 8.00
13 Raikou HOLO R 6.00 15.00
14 Suicune HOLO R 6.00 15.00
15 Aerodactyl R 2.00 6.00
16 Celebi R 2.00 6.00
17 Entei R 2.00 6.00
18 Ho-oh R 2.00 6.00
19 Kingdra R 2.00 6.00
20 Lugia R 2.00 6.00
21 Raichu R 2.00 6.00
22 Raikou R 2.00 6.00
23 Skarmory R 2.00 6.00
24 Sneasel R 2.00 6.00
25 Starmie R 2.00 6.00
26 Sudowoodo R 2.00 6.00
27 Suicune R 2.00 6.00
28 Flaaffy U 1.25 3.00
29 Golbat U 1.25 3.00
30 Graveler U 1.25 3.00
31 Jynx U 1.25 3.00
32 Lanturn U 1.25 3.00
33 Magcargo U 1.25 3.00
34 Octillery U 1.25 3.00
35 Parasect U 1.25 3.00
36 Piloswine U 1.25 3.00
37 Seaking U 1.25 3.00
38 Stantler U 1.25 3.00
39 Unown B U 1.25 3.00
40 Unown Y U 1.25 3.00
41 Aipom C .75 2.00
42 Chinchou C .75 2.00
43 Farfetch'd C .75 2.00
44 Geodude C .75 2.00
45 Goldeen C .75 2.00
46 Murkrow C .75 2.00
47 Paras C .75 2.00
48 Quagsire C .75 2.00
49 Qwilfish C .75 2.00
50 Remoraid C .75 2.00
51 Shuckle C .75 2.00
52 Skiploom C .75 2.00
53 Slugma C .75 2.00
54 Smoochum C .75 2.00
55 Snubbull C .75 2.00
56 Staryu C .75 2.00
57 Swinub C .75 2.00
58 Unown K C .75 2.00
59 Zubat C .75 2.00
60 Balloon Berry U .75 2.00
61 Healing Field U .75 2.00
62 Pokemon Breeder Fields U .75 2.00
63 Rocket's Hideout U .75 2.00
64 Old Rod C .75 2.00
65 Shining Gyarados HOLO R 25.00 50.00
66 Shining Magikarp HOLO R 20.00 40.00

2002 Pokemon Neo Destiny 1st Edition

COMPLETE SET (113) 1000.00 1300.00
BOOSTER BOX (36 PACKS) 1800.00 2200.00
BOOSTER PACK (11 CARDS) 30.00 60.00
RELEASED ON FEBRUARY 28, 2001
1 Dark Ampharos HOLO R 8.00 20.00
2 Dark Crobat HOLO R 8.00 20.00
3 Dark Donphan HOLO R 8.00 20.00
4 Dark Espeon HOLO R 20.00 40.00
5 Dark Feraligatr HOLO R 10.00 25.00
6 Dark Gengar HOLO R 15.00 30.00
7 Dark Houndoom HOLO R 8.00 20.00
8 Dark Porygon2 HOLO R 8.00 20.00
9 Dark Scizor HOLO R 15.00 30.00
10 Dark Typhlosion HOLO R 15.00 30.00
11 Dark Tyranitar HOLO R 20.00 40.00
12 Light Arcanine HOLO R 20.00 40.00
13 Light Azumarill HOLO R 6.00 15.00
14 Light Dragonite HOLO R 20.00 45.00
15 Light Togetic HOLO R 8.00 20.00
16 Miracle Energy HOLO R 4.00 10.00
17 Dark Ariados R 1.25 3.00
18 Dark Magcargo R 1.25 3.00
19 Dark Omastar R 1.25 3.00
20 Dark Slowking R 2.00 6.00
21 Dark Ursaring R 1.25 3.00
22 Light Dragonair R 3.00 8.00
23 Light Lanturn R 1.25 3.00
24 Light Ledian R 1.25 3.00
25 Light Machamp R 1.25 3.00
26 Light Piloswine R 1.25 3.00
27 Unown G R 1.25 3.00
28 Unown H R 1.25 3.00
29 Unown W R 1.25 3.00
30 Unown X R 1.25 3.00
31 Chansey U 1.25 3.00
32 Dark Croconaw U 1.25 3.00
33 Dark Exeggutor U 1.25 3.00
34 Dark Flaaffy U 1.25 3.00
35 Dark Forretress U 1.25 3.00
36 Dark Haunter U 2.00 6.00
37 Dark Omanyte U 1.25 3.00
38 Dark Pupitar U 1.25 3.00
39 Dark Quilava U 1.25 3.00
40 Dark Wigglytuff U 1.25 3.00
41 Heracross U 1.25 3.00
42 Hitmonlee U 1.25 3.00
43 Houndour U 1.25 3.00
44 Jigglypuff U 1.25 3.00
45 Light Dewgong U 1.25 3.00
46 Light Flareon U 3.00 8.00
47 Light Golduck U 1.25 3.00
48 Light Jolteon U 3.00 8.00
49 Light Machoke U 1.25 3.00
50 Light Ninetales U 2.00 6.00
51 Light Slowbro U 1.25 3.00
52 Light Vaporeon U 2.00 6.00
53 Light Venomoth U 1.25 3.00
54 Light Wigglytuff U 1.25 3.00
55 Scyther U 1.25 3.00
56 Togepi U 1.25 3.00
57 Unown C U 1.25 3.00
58 Unown P U 1.25 3.00
59 Unown Q U 1.25 3.00
60 Unown Z U 1.25 3.00
61 Cyndaquil C 1.25 3.00
62 Dark Octillery C 1.25 3.00
63 Dratini C 1.25 3.00
64 Exeggcute C 1.25 3.00
65 Gastly C 1.25 3.00
66 Girafarig C 1.25 3.00
67 Gligar C 1.25 3.00
68 Growlithe C 1.25 3.00
69 Hitmonchan C 1.25 3.00
70 Larvitar C 1.25 3.00
71 Ledyba C 1.25 3.00
72 Light Sunflora C 1.25 3.00
73 Machop C 1.25 3.00
74 Mantine C 1.25 3.00
75 Mareep C 1.25 3.00
76 Phanpy C 1.25 3.00
77 Pineco C 1.25 3.00
78 Porygon C 1.25 3.00
79 Psyduck C 1.25 3.00
80 Remoraid C 1.25 3.00
81 Seel C 1.25 3.00
82 Slugma C 1.25 3.00
83 Sunkern C 1.25 3.00
84 Swinub C 1.25 3.00
85 Totodile C 1.25 3.00
86 Unown L C 1.25 3.00
87 Unown S C 1.25 3.00
88 Unown T C 1.25 3.00
89 Unown V C 1.25 3.00
90 Venonat C 1.25 3.00
91 Vulpix C 1.25 3.00
92 Broken Ground Gym R 2.00 6.00
93 EXP.ALL R 1.25 3.00
94 Impostor Professor Oak's Invention R 2.00 6.00
95 Radio Tower R 1.25 3.00
96 Thought Wave Machine R 1.25 3.00
97 Counterattack Claws U 1.25 3.00
98 Energy Amplifier U 1.25 3.00
99 Energy Stadium U 1.25 3.00
100 Lucky Stadium U 1.25 3.00
101 Pigmented Lens U 1.25 3.00
102 Pokemon Personality Test U 1.25 3.00
103 Team Rockets Evil Deeds U 1.25 3.00
104 Heal Powder C 1.25 3.00
105 Mail from Bill C 1.25 3.00
106 Shining Celebi HOLO R 60.00 100.00
107 Shining Charizard HOLO R 250.00 400.00
108 Shining Kabutops HOLO R 60.00 80.00
109 Shining Mewtwo HOLO R 80.00 120.00
110 Shining Noctowl HOLO R 35.00 65.00
111 Shining Raichu HOLO R 40.00 80.00
112 Shining Steelix HOLO R 70.00 110.00
113 Shining Tyranitar HOLO R 60.00 100.00

2002 Pokemon Neo Destiny Unlimited

COMPLETE SET (113) 600.00 800.00
BOOSTER BOX (36 PACKS) 800.00 1050.00
BOOSTER PACK (11 CARDS) 15.00 30.00
RELEASED FEBRUARY 8, 2001
1 Dark Ampharos HOLO R 3.00 8.00
2 Dark Crobat HOLO R 2.00 6.00
3 Dark Donphan HOLO R 2.00 6.00
4 Dark Espeon HOLO R 8.00 20.00
5 Dark Feraligatr HOLO R 4.00 10.00
6 Dark Gengar HOLO R 5.00 12.00
7 Dark Houndoom HOLO R 3.00 8.00
8 Dark Porygon2 HOLO R 4.00 10.00
9 Dark Scizor HOLO R 4.00 10.00
10 Dark Typhlosion HOLO R 3.00 8.00
11 Dark Tyranitar HOLO R 8.00 20.00
12 Light Arcanine HOLO R 6.00 15.00
13 Light Azumarill HOLO R 2.00 6.00
14 Light Dragonite HOLO R 8.00 20.00
15 Light Togetic HOLO R 3.50 9.00
16 Miracle Energy HOLO R 2.00 6.00
17 Dark Ariados R 1.50 4.00
18 Dark Magcargo R 1.50 4.00
19 Dark Omastar R 1.50 4.00
20 Dark Slowking R 1.50 4.00
21 Dark Ursaring R 1.50 4.00
22 Light Dragonair R 1.50 4.00
23 Light Lanturn R 1.50 4.00
24 Light Ledian R 1.50 4.00
25 Light Machamp R 1.50 4.00
26 Light Piloswine R 1.50 4.00
27 Unown G R 1.50 4.00
28 Unown H R 1.50 4.00
29 Unown W R 1.50 4.00
30 Unown X R 1.50 4.00
31 Chansey U 1.50 4.00
32 Dark Croconaw U 1.50 4.00
33 Dark Exeggutor U 1.50 4.00
34 Dark Flaaffy U 1.50 4.00
35 Dark Forretress U 1.50 4.00
36 Dark Haunter U 1.50 4.00
37 Dark Omanyte U 1.50 4.00
38 Dark Pupitar U 1.50 4.00
39 Dark Quilava U 1.50 4.00
40 Dark Wigglytuff U 1.50 4.00
41 Heracross U 1.50 4.00
42 Hitmonlee U 1.50 4.00
43 Houndour U 1.50 4.00
44 Jigglypuff U 1.50 4.00
45 Light Dewgong U 1.50 4.00
46 Light Flareon U 1.50 4.00
47 Light Golduck U 1.50 4.00
48 Light Jolteon U 1.50 4.00
49 Light Machoke U 1.50 4.00
50 Light Ninetales U 1.50 4.00
51 Light Slowbro U 1.50 4.00
52 Light Vaporeon U 1.50 4.00
53 Light Venomoth U 1.50 4.00
54 Light Wigglytuff U 1.50 4.00
55 Scyther U 1.50 4.00
56 Togepi U 1.50 4.00
57 Unown C U 1.50 4.00
58 Unown P U 1.50 4.00
59 Unown Q U 1.50 4.00
60 Unown Z U 1.50 4.00
61 Cyndaquil C .75 2.00
62 Dark Octillery C .75 2.00
63 Dratini C .75 2.00
64 Exeggcute C .75 2.00
65 Gastly C .75 2.00
66 Girafarig C .75 2.00
67 Gligar C .75 2.00
68 Growlithe C .75 2.00
69 Hitmonchan C .75 2.00
70 Larvitar C .75 2.00
71 Ledyba C .75 2.00
72 Light Sunflora C .75 2.00
73 Machop C .75 2.00
74 Mantine C .75 2.00
75 Mareep C .75 2.00
76 Phanpy C .75 2.00
77 Pineco C .75 2.00
78 Porygon C .75 2.00
79 Psyduck C .75 2.00
80 Remoraid C .75 2.00
81 Seel C .75 2.00
82 Slugma C .75 2.00
83 Sunkern C .75 2.00
84 Swinub C .75 2.00
85 Totodile C .75 2.00
86 Unown L C .75 2.00
87 Unown S C .75 2.00
88 Unown T C .75 2.00
89 Unown V C .75 2.00
90 Venonat C .75 2.00
91 Vulpix C .75 2.00
92 Broken Ground Gym R 1.50 4.00
93 EXP.ALL R 1.50 4.00
94 Impostor Prof.Oak's Invent.R 1.50 4.00
95 Radio Tower R 1.50 4.00
96 Thought Wave Machine R 1.50 3.00
97 Counterattack Claws U 1.25 3.00
98 Energy Amplifier U 1.25 3.00
99 Energy Stadium U 1.25 3.00
100 Lucky Stadium U 1.25 3.00
101 Pigmented Lens U 1.25 3.00
102 Pokemon Personality Test U 1.25 3.00
103 Team Rockets Evil Deeds U 1.25 3.00
104 Heal Powder C .75 2.00
105 Mail from Bill C .75 2.00
106 Shining Celebi HOLO R 25.00 50.00
107 Shining Charizard HOLO R 80.00 120.00
108 Shining Kabutops HOLO R 20.00 40.00
109 Shining Mewtwo HOLO R 30.00 60.00
110 Shining Noctowl HOLO R 20.00 35.00
111 Shining Raichu HOLO R 25.00 40.00
112 Shining Steelix HOLO R 25.00 50.00
113 Shining Tyranitar HOLO R 30.00 60.00

2002 Pokemon Legendary Collection

COMPLETE SET (110) 200.00 400.00
BOOSTER BOX (36 PACKS) 2200.00 2600.00
BOOSTER PACK (11 CARDS) 50.00 80.00
*BOX TOPPER 2X REGULAR VERSION
RELEASED ON MAY 24, 2002
1 Alakazam HOLO R 8.00 20.00
2 Articuno HOLO R 6.00 15.00
3 Charizard HOLO R 25.00 50.00
4 Dark Blastoise HOLO R 6.00 15.00
5 Dark Dragonite HOLO R 3.00 8.00
6 Dark Persian HOLO R 4.00 10.00
7 Dark Raichu HOLO R 3.00 89.00
8 Dark Slowbro HOLO R 2.00 6.00
9 Dark Vaporeon HOLO R 5.00 12.00
10 Flareon HOLO R 5.00 12.00
11 Gengar HOLO R 5.00 12.00
12 Gyarados HOLO R 2.00 6.00
13 Hitmonlee HOLO R 3.00 8.00
14 Jolteon HOLO R 4.00 10.00
15 Machamp HOLO R 3.00 8.00
16 Muk HOLO R 2.00 6.00
17 Ninetales HOLO R 3.00 8.00
18 Venusaur HOLO R 8.00 20.00
19 Zapdos HOLO R 4.00 10.00
20 Beedrill R 2.00 6.00
21 Butterfree R 2.00 6.00
22 Electrode R 2.00 6.00
23 Exeggutor R 2.00 6.00
24 Golem R 2.00 6.00
25 Hypno R 2.00 6.00
26 Jynx R 2.00 6.00
27 Kabutops R 2.00 6.00
28 Magneton R 2.00 6.00
29 Mewtwo R 3.00 8.00
30 Moltres R 2.00 6.00
31 Nidoking R 2.00 6.00
32 Nidoqueen R 2.00 6.00
33 Pidgeot R 2.00 6.00
34 Pidgeotto R 2.00 6.00
35 Rhydon R 2.00 6.00
36 Arcanine U 1.50 4.00
37 Charmeleon U 1.50 4.00
38 Dark Dragonair U 1.50 4.00
39 Dark Wartortle U 1.50 4.00
40 Dewgong U 1.50 4.00
41 Dodrio U 1.50 4.00
42 Fearow U 1.50 4.00
43 Golduck U 1.50 4.00
44 Graveler U 1.50 4.00
45 Growlithe U 1.50 4.00
46 Haunter U 1.50 4.00
47 Ivysaur U 1.50 4.00

Card	Low	High
48 Kabuto U	1.50	4.00
49 Kadabra U	1.50	4.00
50 Kakuna U	1.50	4.00
51 Machoke U	1.50	4.00
52 Magikarp U	1.50	4.00
53 Meowth U	1.50	4.00
54 Metapod U	1.50	4.00
55 Nidorina U	1.50	4.00
56 Nidorino U	1.50	4.00
57 Omanyte U	1.50	4.00
58 Omastar U	1.50	4.00
59 Primeape U	1.50	4.00
60 Rapidash U	1.50	4.00
61 Raticate U	1.50	4.00
62 Sandslash U	1.50	4.00
63 Seadra U	1.50	4.00
64 Snorlax U	1.50	4.00
65 Tauros U	1.50	4.00
66 Tentacruel U	1.50	4.00
67 Abra C	1.25	3.00
68 Bulbasaur C	1.25	3.00
69 Caterpie C	1.25	3.00
70 Charmander C	1.25	3.00
71 Doduo C	1.25	3.00
72 Dratini C	1.25	3.00
73 Drowzee C	1.25	3.00
74 Eevee C	1.25	3.00
75 Exeggcute C	1.25	3.00
76 Gastly C	1.25	3.00
77 Geodude C	1.25	3.00
78 Grimer C	1.25	3.00
79 Machop C	1.25	3.00
80 Magnemite C	1.25	3.00
81 Mankey C	1.25	3.00
82 Nidoran (F) C	1.25	3.00
83 Nidoran (M) C	1.25	3.00
84 Onix C	1.25	3.00
85 Pidgey C	1.25	3.00
86 Pikachu C	1.25	3.00
87 Ponyta C	1.25	3.00
88 Psyduck C	1.25	3.00
89 Rattata C	1.25	3.00
90 Rhyhorn C	1.25	3.00
91 Sandshrew C	1.25	3.00
92 Seel C	1.25	3.00
93 Slowpoke C	1.25	3.00
94 Spearow C	1.25	3.00
95 Squirtle C	1.25	3.00
96 Tentacool C	1.25	3.00
97 Voltorb C	1.25	3.00
98 Vulpix C	1.25	3.00
99 Weedle C	1.25	3.00
100 Full Heal Energy U	1.25	3.00
101 Potion Energy U	1.25	3.00
102 Pokemon Breeder R	3.00	8.00
103 Pokemon Trader R	1.25	3.00
104 Scoop Up R	2.00	6.00
105 Boss's Way U	1.25	3.00
106 Challenge! U	1.25	3.00
107 Energy Retrieval U	1.25	3.00
108 Bill C	1.25	3.00
109 Mysterious Fossil C	1.25	3.00
110 Potion C	1.25	3.00

2002 Pokemon Expedition

Card	Low	High
COMPLETE SET (165)	180.00	300.00
BOOSTER BOX (36 PACKS)	1150.00	1350.00
BOOSTER PACK (11 CARDS)	20.00	45.00
ELECTRIC GARDEN THEME DECK	10.00	25.00
*BOX TOPPER 1.5X REGULAR VERSION		
*REV.FOIL: .75X TO 2X BASIC CARDS		
RELEASED ON SEPTEMBER 15, 2002		
1 Alakazam HOLO R	6.00	15.00
2 Ampharos HOLO R	4.00	10.00
3 Arbok HOLO R	2.00	6.00
4 Blastoise HOLO R	8.00	20.00
5 Butterfree HOLO R	2.00	6.00
6 Charizard HOLO R	10.00	25.00
7 Clefable HOLO R	3.00	8.00
8 Cloyster HOLO R	2.00	6.00
9 Dragonite HOLO R	8.00	20.00
10 Dugtrio HOLO R	3.00	8.00
11 Fearow HOLO R	2.00	6.00
12 Feraligatr HOLO R	2.00	6.00
13 Gengar HOLO R	3.00	8.00
14 Golem HOLO R	3.00	8.00
15 Kingler HOLO R	2.00	6.00
16 Machamp HOLO R	2.00	6.00
17 Magby HOLO R	3.00	8.00
18 Meganium HOLO R	2.00	6.00
19 Mew HOLO R	15.00	30.00
20 Mewtwo HOLO R	8.00	20.00
21 Ninetales HOLO R	4.00	10.00
22 Pichu HOLO R	3.00	8.00
23 Pidgeot HOLO R	2.00	6.00
24 Poliwrath HOLO R	2.00	6.00
25 Raichu HOLO R	2.00	6.00
26 Rapidash HOLO R	3.00	8.00
27 Skarmory HOLO R	3.00	8.00
28 Typhlosion HOLO R	2.00	6.00
29 Tyranitar HOLO R	3.00	8.00
30 Venusaur HOLO R	3.00	8.00
31 Vileplume HOLO R	3.00	8.00
32 Weezing HOLO R	2.00	6.00
33 Alakazam R	1.50	4.00
34 Ampharos R	1.50	4.00
35 Arbok R	1.50	4.00
36 Blastoise R	1.50	4.00
37 Blastoise R	1.50	4.00
38 Butterfree R	1.50	4.00
39 Charizard R	3.00	8.00
40 Charizard R	3.00	8.00
41 Clefable R	1.50	4.00
42 Cloyster R	1.50	4.00
43 Dragonite R	1.50	4.00
44 Dugtrio R	1.50	4.00
45 Fearow R	1.50	4.00
46 Feraligatr R	1.50	4.00
47 Feraligatr R	1.50	4.00
48 Gengar R	1.50	4.00
49 Golem R	1.50	4.00
50 Kingler R	1.50	4.00
51 Machamp R	1.50	4.00
52 Magby R	1.50	4.00
53 Meganium R	1.50	4.00
54 Meganium R	1.50	4.00
55 Mew R	1.50	4.00
56 Mewtwo R	1.50	4.00
57 Ninetales R	1.50	4.00
58 Pichu R	1.50	4.00
59 Pidgeot R	1.50	4.00
60 Poliwrath R	1.50	4.00
61 Raichu R	1.50	4.00
62 Rapidash R	1.50	4.00
63 Skarmory R	1.50	4.00
64 Typhlosion R	1.50	4.00
65 Typhlosion R	1.50	4.00
66 Tyranitar R	1.50	4.00
67 Venusaur R	1.50	4.00
68 Venusaur R	1.50	4.00
69 Vileplume R	1.50	4.00
70 Weezing R	1.50	4.00
71 Bayleef U	.75	2.00
72 Chansey U	.75	2.00
73 Charmeleon U	.75	2.00
74 Croconaw U	.75	2.00
75 Dragonair U	.75	2.00
76 Electabuzz U	.75	2.00
77 Flaafy U	.75	2.00
78 Gloom U	.75	2.00
79 Graveler U	.75	2.00
80 Haunter U	.75	2.00
81 Hitmonlee U	.75	2.00
82 Ivysaur U	.75	2.00
83 Jynx U	.75	2.00
84 Kadabra U	.75	2.00
85 Machoke U	.75	2.00
86 Magmar U	.75	2.00
87 Metapod U	.75	2.00
88 Pidgeotto U	.75	2.00
89 Poliwhirl U	.75	2.00
90 Pupitar U	.75	2.00
91 Quilava U	.75	2.00
92 Wartortle U	.75	2.00
93 Abra C	.75	2.00
94 Bulbasaur C	.75	2.00
95 Bulbasaur C	.75	2.00
96 Caterpie C	.75	2.00
97 Charmander C	.75	2.00
98 Charmander C	.75	2.00
99 Chikorita C	.75	2.00
100 Chikorita C	.75	2.00
101 Clefairy C	.75	2.00
102 Corsola C	.75	2.00
103 Cubone C	.75	2.00
104 Cyndaquil C	.75	2.00
105 Cyndaquil C	.75	2.00
106 Diglett C	.75	2.00
107 Dratini C	.75	2.00
108 Ekans C	.75	2.00
109 Gastly C	.75	2.00
110 Geodude C	.75	2.00
111 Goldeen C	.75	2.00
112 Hoppip C	.75	2.00
113 Houndour C	.75	2.00
114 Koffing C	.75	2.00
115 Krabby C	.75	2.00
116 Larvitar C	.75	2.00
117 Machop C	.75	2.00
118 Magikarp C	.75	2.00
119 Mareep C	.75	2.00
120 Marill C	.75	2.00
121 Meowth C	.75	2.00
122 Oddish C	.75	2.00
123 Pidgey C	.75	2.00
124 Pikachu C	.75	2.00
125 Poliwag C	.75	2.00
126 Ponyta C	.75	2.00
127 Qwilfish C	.75	2.00
128 Rattata C	.75	2.00
129 Shellder C	.75	2.00
130 Spearow C	.75	2.00
131 Squirtle C	.75	2.00
132 Squirtle C	.75	2.00
133 Tauros C	.75	2.00
134 Totodile C	.75	2.00
135 Totodile C	.75	2.00
136 Vulpix C	.75	2.00
137 Bill's Maintenance C	.75	2.00
138 Copycat C	.75	2.00
139 Dual Ball C	.75	2.00
140 Energy Removal 2 U	.75	2.00
141 Energy Restore U	.75	2.00
142 Mary's Impulse U	.75	2.00
143 Master Ball U	.75	2.00
144 Multi Technical U	.75	2.00
145 Pokemon Nurse U	.75	2.00
146 Pokemon Reversal U	.75	2.00
147 Power Charge U	.75	2.00
148 Professor Elm's U	.75	2.00
149 Professor Oak's U	.75	2.00
150 Strength Charm U	.75	2.00
151 Super Scoop Up U	.75	2.00
152 Warp Point U	.75	2.00
153 Energy Search C	.75	2.00
154 Full Heal C	.75	2.00
155 Moo-moo Milk C	.75	2.00
156 Potion C	.75	2.00
157 Switch C	.75	2.00
158 Darkness Energy R	.75	2.00
159 Metal Energy R	.75	2.00
160 Fire Energy	.75	2.00
161 Rock Energy	.75	2.00
162 Grass Energy	.75	2.00
163 Lightning Energy	.75	2.00
164 Psychic Energy	.75	2.00
165 Water Energy	.75	2.00

2003 Pokemon Aquapolis

Card	Low	High
COMPLETE SET (186)	650.00	900.00
BOOSTER BOX (36 PACKS)	1600.00	2100.00
BOOSTER PACK (11 CARDS)	25.00	50.00
*REV.FOIL: .75X TO 2X BASIC CARDS		
THEME DECK	20.00	40.00
*BOX TOPPER: .75X TO 2X BASIC TOPPER		
RELEASED ON JANUARY 15, 2003		
1 Ampharos R	1.50	4.00
2 Arcanine R	5.00	12.00
3 Ariados R	1.50	4.00
4 Azumarill R	1.50	4.00
5 Bellossom R	1.50	4.00
6 Blissey R	1.50	4.00
7 Donphan R	1.50	4.00
8 Electrode R	1.50	4.00
9 Elekid R	1.50	4.00
10 Entei R	3.00	8.00
11 Espeon R	1.50	4.00
12 Exeggutor R	1.50	4.00
13 Exeggutor R	1.50	4.00
14 Houndoom R	1.50	4.00
15 Houndoom R	1.50	4.00
16 Hypno R	1.50	4.00
17 Jumpluff R	1.50	4.00
18 Jynx R	1.50	4.00
19 Kingdra R	1.50	4.00
20 Lanturn R	1.50	4.00
21 Lanturn R	1.50	4.00
22 Magneton R	1.50	4.00
23 Muk R	1.50	4.00
24 Nidoking R	1.50	4.00
25 Ninetales R	1.50	4.00
26 Octillery R	1.50	4.00
27 Parasect R	1.50	4.00
28 Porygon2 R	1.50	4.00
29 Primeape R	1.50	4.00
30 Quagsire R	1.50	4.00
31 Rapidash R	1.50	4.00
32 Scizor R	1.50	4.00
33 Slowbro R	1.50	4.00
34 Slowking R	1.50	4.00
35 Steelix R	1.50	4.00
36 Sudowoodo R	1.50	4.00
37 Suicune R	1.50	4.00
38 Tentacruel R	1.50	4.00
39 Togetic R	1.50	4.00
40 Tyranitar R	2.00	6.00
41 Umbreon R	1.50	4.00
42 Victreebel R	1.50	4.00
43 Vileplume R	1.50	4.00
44 Zapdos R	1.50	4.00
45 Bellsprout U	1.25	3.00
46 Dodrio U	1.25	3.00
47 Flaaffy U	1.25	3.00
48 Furret U	1.25	3.00
49 Gloom U	1.25	3.00
50A Golduck U	1.25	3.00
50B Golduck U	1.25	3.00
51 Growlithe U	1.25	3.00
52 Magnemite U	1.25	3.00
53 Marill U	1.25	3.00
54 Marowak U	1.25	3.00
55 Nidorino U	1.25	3.00
56 Pupitar U	1.25	3.00
57 Scyther U	1.25	3.00
58 Seadra U	1.25	3.00
59 Seaking U	1.25	3.00
60 Skiploom U	1.25	3.00
61 Smoochum U	1.25	3.00
62 Spinarak U	1.25	3.00
63 Tyrogue U	1.25	3.00
64 Voltorb U	1.25	3.00
65 Weepinbell U	1.25	3.00
66 Wooper U	1.25	3.00
67 Aipom C	.75	2.00
68 Bellsprout C	.75	2.00
69 Chansey C	.75	2.00
70 Chinchou C	.75	2.00
71 Chinchou C	.75	2.00
72 Cubone C	.75	2.00
73 Doduo C	.75	2.00
74A Drowzee C	.75	2.00
74B Drowzee C	.75	2.00
75 Eevee C	.75	2.00
76 Exeggcute C	.75	2.00
77 Exeggcute C	.75	2.00
78 Goldeen C	.75	2.00
79 Grimer C	.75	2.00
80 Growlithe C	.75	2.00
81 Hitmonchan C	.75	2.00
82 Hitmontop C	.75	2.00
83 Hoppip C	.75	2.00
84 Horsea C	.75	2.00
85 Horsea C	.75	2.00
86 Houndour C	.75	2.00
87 Houndour C	.75	2.00
88 Kangaskhan C	.75	2.00
89 Larvitar C	.75	2.00
90 Lickitung C	.75	2.00
91 Magnemite C	.75	2.00
92 Mankey C	.75	2.00
93 Mareep C	.75	2.00
94 Miltank C	.75	2.00
95A Mr. Mime C	.75	2.00
95B Mr. Mime C	.75	2.00
96 Nidoran C	.75	2.00
97 Oddish C	.75	2.00
98 Onix C	.75	2.00
99 Paras C	.75	2.00
100 Phanpy C	.75	2.00
101 Pinsir C	.75	2.00
102 Ponyta C	.75	2.00
103A Porygon C	.75	2.00
103B Porygon C	.75	2.00
104 Psyduck C	.75	2.00
105 Remoraid C	.75	2.00
106 Scyther C	.75	2.00
107 Sentret C	.75	2.00
108 Slowpoke C	.75	2.00
109 Smeargle C	.75	2.00
110 Sneasel C	.75	2.00
111 Spinarak C	.75	2.00
112 Tangela C	.75	2.00
113 Tentacool C	.75	2.00
114 Togepi C	.75	2.00
115 Voltorb C	.75	2.00
116 Vulpix C	.75	2.00
117 Wooper C	.75	2.00
118 Apricorn Forest R	.75	2.00
119 Darkness Cube U	.75	2.00
120 Energy Switch U	.75	2.00
121 Fighting Cube 01 U	.75	2.00
122 Fire Cube 01 U	.75	2.00
123 Forest Guardian U	.75	2.00
124 Grass Cube 01 U	.75	2.00
125 Healing Berry U	.75	2.00
126 Juggler U	.75	2.00
127 Lightning Cube 01 U	.75	2.00
128 Memory Berry U	.75	2.00
129 Metal Cube 01 U	.75	2.00
130 Pokémon Fan Club U	.75	2.00
131 Pokémon Park U	.75	2.00
132 Psychic Cube 01 U	.75	2.00
133 Seer U	.75	2.00
134 Super Energy Removal 2 U	.75	2.00
135 Time Shard U	.75	2.00
136 Town Volunteers U	.75	2.00
137 Traveling Salesman U	.75	2.00
138 Undersea Ruins U	.75	2.00
139 Power Plant U	.75	2.00
140 Water Cube 1 U	.75	2.00
141 Weakness Guard U	.75	2.00
142 Darkness Energy R	.75	2.00
143 Metal Energy R	.75	2.00
144 Rainbow Energy R	.75	2.00
145 Boost Energy U	.75	2.00
146 Crystal Energy U	.75	2.00
147 Warp Energy U	.75	2.00
148 Kingdra HOLO R	25.00	50.00
149 Lugia HOLO R	60.00	100.00
150 Nidoking HOLO R	25.00	50.00
H1 Ampharos HOLO R	6.00	15.00
H2 Arcanine HOLO R	15.00	30.00
H3 Ariados HOLO R	3.00	8.00
H4 Azumarill HOLO R	4.00	10.00
H5 Bellossom HOLO R	3.00	8.00
H6 Blissey HOLO R	3.00	8.00

H7 Electrode HOLO R	4.00	10.00
H8 Entei HOLO R	6.00	15.00
H9 Espeon HOLO R	15.00	30.00
H10 Exeggutor HOLO R	3.00	8.00
H11 Houndoom HOLO R	10.00	25.00
H12 Hypno HOLO R	4.00	10.00
H13 Jumpluff HOLO R	3.00	8.00
H14 Kingdra HOLO R	6.00	15.00
H15 Lanturn HOLO R	2.00	6.00
H16 Magneton HOLO R	3.00	8.00
H17 Muk HOLO R	5.00	12.00
H18 Nidoking HOLO R	6.00	15.00
H19 Ninetales HOLO R	6.00	15.00
H20 Octillery HOLO R	3.00	8.00
H21 Scizor HOLO R	5.00	12.00
H22 Slowking HOLO R	4.00	10.00
H23 Steelix HOLO R	4.00	10.00
H24 Sudowoodo HOLO R	6.00	15.00
H25 Suicune HOLO R	6.00	15.00
H26 Tentacruel HOLO R	3.00	8.00
H27 Togetic HOLO R	4.00	10.00
H28 Tyranitar HOLO R	8.00	20.00
H29 Umbreon HOLO R	10.00	25.00
H30 Victreebel HOLO R	3.00	8.00
H31 Vileplume HOLO R	4.00	10.00
H32 Zapdos HOLO R	8.00	20.00

2003 Pokemon Skyridge

REGULAR SET (150)	1000.00	1500.00
COMPLETE SET (182)	1800.00	2500.00
BOOSTER BOX (36 PACKS)	1800.00	2800.00
BOOSTER PACK (11 CARDS)	40.00	80.00
*REV.FOIL: .75X TO 2X BASIC CARDS	.10	.20
*JUMBO BOX TOPPERS: 6X TO 1.5X BASIC		
RELEASED MAY 12, 2003		
1 Aerodactyl R	2.00	6.00
2 Alakazam R	2.00	6.00
3 Arcanine R	2.00	6.00
4 Articuno R	2.00	6.00
5 Beedrill R	2.00	6.00
6 Crobat R	2.00	6.00
7 Dewgong R	2.00	6.00
8 Flareon R	2.00	6.00
9 Forretress R	2.00	6.00
10 Gengar R	2.00	6.00
11 Gyarados R	2.00	6.00
12 Houndoom R	2.00	6.00
13 Jolteon R	2.00	6.00
14 Kabutops R	2.00	6.00
15 Ledian R	2.00	6.00
16 Machamp R	2.00	6.00
17 Magcargo R	2.00	6.00
18 Magcargo R	2.00	6.00
19 Magneton R	2.00	6.00
20 Magneton R	2.00	6.00
21 Moltres R	2.00	6.00
22 Nidoqueen R	2.00	6.00
23 Omastar R	2.00	6.00
24 Piloswine R	2.00	6.00
25 Politoed R	2.00	6.00
26 Poliwrath R	2.00	6.00
27 Raichu R	2.00	6.00
28 Raikou R	2.00	6.00
29 Rhydon R	2.00	6.00
30 Starmie R	2.00	6.00
31 Steelix R	2.00	6.00
32 Umbreon R	2.00	6.00
33 Vaporeon R	2.00	6.00
34 Wigglytuff R	2.00	6.00
35 Xatu R	2.00	6.00
36 Electrode U	2.00	6.00
37 Kabuto U	2.00	6.00
38 Machoke U	2.00	6.00
39 Misdreavus U	2.00	6.00
40 Noctowl U	2.00	6.00
41 Omanyte U	2.00	6.00
42 Persian U	2.00	6.00
43 Piloswine U	2.00	6.00
44 Starmie U	2.00	6.00
45 Wobbuffet U	2.00	6.00
46 Abra C	1.75	5.00
47 Buried Fossil C	1.75	5.00
48 Cleffa C	1.75	5.00
49 Delibird C	1.75	5.00
50 Diglett C	1.75	5.00
51 Ditto C	1.75	5.00
52 Dugtrio C	1.75	5.00
53 Dunsparce C	1.75	5.00
54 Eevee C	1.75	5.00
55 Farfetch'd C	1.75	5.00
56 Forretress C	1.75	5.00
57 Gastly C	1.75	5.00
58 Girafarig C	1.75	5.00
59 Gligar C	1.75	5.00
60 Golbat C	1.75	5.00
61 Granbull C	1.75	5.00
62 Growlithe C	1.75	5.00
63 Haunter C	1.75	5.00
64 Heracross C	1.75	5.00
65 Hoothoot C	1.75	5.00
66 Houndour C	1.75	5.00
67 Igglybuff C	1.75	5.00
68 Jigglypuff C	1.75	5.00
69 Kadabra C	1.75	5.00
70 Kakuna C	1.75	5.00
71 Lapras C	1.75	5.00
72 Ledyba C	1.75	5.00
73 Ledyba C	1.75	5.00
74 Machop C	1.75	5.00
75 Magikarp C	1.75	5.00
76 Magnemite C	1.75	5.00
77 Mantine C	1.75	5.00
78 Meowth C	1.75	5.00
79 Murkrow C	1.75	5.00
80 Natu C	1.75	5.00
81 Nidoran F C	1.75	5.00
82 Nidoran F C	1.75	5.00
83 Nidorina C	1.75	5.00
84 Pikachu C	1.75	5.00
85 Pineco C	1.75	5.00
86 Pineco C	1.75	5.00
87 Poliwag C	1.75	5.00
88 Poliwhirl C	1.75	5.00
89 Raticate C	1.75	5.00
90 Rattata C	1.75	5.00
91 Rhyhorn C	1.75	5.00
92 Sandshrew C	1.75	5.00
93 Sandslash C	1.75	5.00
94 Seel C	1.75	5.00
95 Seel C	1.75	5.00
96 Shuckle C	1.75	5.00
97 Skarmory C	1.75	5.00
98 Slugma C	1.75	5.00
99 Slugma C	1.75	5.00
100 Snorlax C	1.75	5.00
101 Snubbull C	1.75	5.00
102 Stantler C	1.75	5.00
103 Staryu C	1.75	5.00
104 Staryu C	1.75	5.00
105 Sunflora C	1.75	5.00
106 Sunkern C	1.75	5.00
107 Swinub C	1.75	5.00
108 Swinub C	1.75	5.00
109 Teddiursa C	1.75	5.00
110 Ursaring C	1.75	5.00
111 Venomoth C	1.75	5.00
112 Venonat C	1.75	5.00
113 Voltorb C	1.75	5.00
114 Weedle C	1.75	5.00
115 Weedle C	1.75	5.00
116 Yanma C	1.75	5.00
117 Zubat C	1.75	5.00
118 Zubat C	1.75	5.00
119 Ancient Ruins U	1.75	5.00
120 Relic Hunter U	1.75	5.00
121 Apricorn U	1.75	5.00
122 Crystal Shard U	1.75	5.00
123 Desert Shaman U	1.75	5.00
124 Fast Ball U	1.75	5.00
125 Fisherman U	1.75	5.00
126 Friend Ball U	1.75	5.00
127 Hyper Potion U	1.75	5.00
128 Lure Ball U	1.75	5.00
129 Miracle Sphere (Alpha) U	1.75	5.00
130 Miracle Sphere (Beta) U	1.75	5.00
131 Miracle Sphere (Gamma)U	1.75	5.00
132 Mirage Stadium U	1.75	5.00
133 Mystery Plate (Alpha) U	1.75	5.00
134 Mystery Plate (Beta) U	1.75	5.00
135 Mystery Plate (Gamma) U	1.75	5.00
136 Mystery Plate (Delta) U	1.75	5.00
137 Mystery Zone U	1.75	5.00
138 Oracle U	1.75	5.00
139 Star Piece U	1.75	5.00
140 Underground Expedition U	1.75	5.00
141 Underground Lake U	1.75	5.00
142 Bounce Energy U	1.75	5.00
143 Cyclone Energy U	1.75	5.00
144 Retro Energy U	1.75	5.00
145 Celebi HOLO R	40.00	80.00
146 Charizard HOLO R	250.00	400.00
147 Crobat HOLO R	40.00	80.00
148 Golem HOLO R	40.00	80.00
149 Ho-oh HOLO R	60.00	100.00
150 Kabutops HOLO R	40.00	80.00
H1 Alakazam HOLO R	6.00	15.00
H2 Arcanine HOLO R	20.00	40.00
H3 Articuno HOLO R	15.00	30.00
H4 Beedrill HOLO R	8.00	20.00
H5 Crobat HOLO R	8.00	20.00
H6 Dewgong HOLO R	8.00	20.00
H7 Flareon HOLO R	10.00	25.00
H8 Forretress HOLO R	8.00	20.00
H9 Gengar HOLO R	20.00	40.00
H10 Gyarados HOLO R	10.00	25.00
H11 Houndoom HOLO R	8.00	20.00
H12 Jolteon HOLO R	10.00	25.00
H13 Kabutops HOLO R	8.00	20.00
H14 Ledian HOLO R	8.00	20.00
H15 Machamp HOLO R	8.00	20.00
H16 Magcargo HOLO R	8.00	20.00
H17 Magcargo HOLO R	8.00	20.00
H18 Magneton HOLO R	8.00	20.00
H19 Magneton HOLO R	8.00	20.00
H20 Moltres HOLO R	15.00	30.00
H21 Nidoqueen HOLO R	8.00	20.00
H22 Piloswine HOLO R	8.00	20.00
H23 Politoed HOLO R	8.00	20.00
H24 Poliwrath HOLO R	8.00	20.00
H25 Raichu HOLO R	8.00	20.00
H26 Raikou HOLO R	20.00	40.00
H27 Rhydon HOLO R	8.00	20.00
H28 Starmie HOLO R	8.00	20.00
H29 Steelix HOLO R	8.00	20.00
H30 Umbreon HOLO R	30.00	60.00
H31 Vaporeon HOLO R	20.00	40.00
H32 Xatu HOLO R	8.00	20.00

2003 Pokemon EX Ruby & Sapphire

COMPLETE SET (109)	100.00	150.00
BOOSTER BOX (36 PACKS)	350.00	450.00
BOOSTER PACK (9 CARDS)	7.00	18.00
*REV.FOIL: .75X TO 2X BASIC CARDS		
RUBY THEME DECK	8.00	20.00
SAPPHIRE THEME DECK	8.00	20.00
RELEASED ON JUNE 18, 2003		
1 Aggron HOLO R	2.00	4.00
2 Beautifly HOLO R	2.00	4.00
3 Blaziken HOLO R	2.00	4.00
4 Camerupt HOLO R	2.00	6.00
5 Delcatty HOLO R	2.00	6.00
6 Dustox HOLO R	2.00	4.00
7 Gardevoir HOLO R	2.00	4.00
8 Hariyama HOLO R	2.00	4.00
9 Manectric HOLO R	2.00	4.00
10 Mightyena HOLO R	2.00	4.00
11 Sceptile HOLO R	2.00	4.00
12 Slaking HOLO R	2.00	4.00
13 Swampert HOLO R	2.00	4.00
14 Wailord HOLO R	2.00	4.00
15 Blaziken R	.75	2.00
16 Breloom R	.75	2.00
17 Donphan R	.75	2.00
18 Nosepass R	.75	2.00
19 Pelipper R	.75	2.00
20 Sceptile R	.75	2.00
21 Seaking R	.75	2.00
22 Sharpedo R	.75	2.00
23 Swampert R	.75	2.00
24 Weezing R	.75	2.00
25 Aron U	.75	2.00
26 Cascoon U	.75	2.00
27 Combusken U	.75	2.00
28 Combusken U	.75	2.00
29 Delcatty U	.75	2.00
30 Electrike U	.75	2.00
31 Grovyle U	.75	2.00
32 Grovyle U	.75	2.00
33 Hariyama U	.75	2.00
34 Kirlia U	.75	2.00
35 Kirlia U	.75	2.00
36 Lairon (U)	.75	2.00
37 Lairon U	.75	2.00
38 Linoone U	.75	2.00
39 Manectric U	.75	2.00
40 Marshtomp U	.75	2.00
41 Marshtomp U	.75	2.00
42 Mightyena U	.75	2.00
43 Silcoon U	.75	2.00
44 Skitty U	.75	2.00
45 Slakoth U	.75	2.00
46 Swellow U	.75	2.00
47 Vigoroth U	.75	2.00
48 Wailmer U	.75	2.00
49 Aron C	.75	2.00
50 Aron C	.75	2.00
51 Carvanha C	.75	2.00
52 Electrike C	.75	2.00
53 Electrike C	.75	2.00
54 Koffing C	.75	2.00
55 Goldeen C	.75	2.00
56 Makuhita C	.75	2.00
57 Makuhita C	.75	2.00
58 Makuhita C	.75	2.00
59 Mudkip C	.75	2.00
60 Mudkip C	.75	2.00
61 Numel C	.75	2.00
62 Phanpy C	.75	2.00
63 Poochyena C	.75	2.00
64 Poochyena C	.75	2.00
65 Poochyena C	.75	2.00
66 Ralts C	.75	2.00
67 Ralts C	.75	2.00
68 Ralts C	.75	2.00
69 Shroomish C	.75	2.00
70 Skitty C	.75	2.00
71 Skitty C	.75	2.00
72 Taillow C	.75	2.00
73 Torchic C	.75	2.00
74 Torchic C	.75	2.00
75 Treecko C	.75	2.00
76 Treecko C	.75	2.00
77 Wingull C	.75	2.00
78 Wurmple C	.75	2.00
79 Zigzagoon C	.75	2.00
80 Trainer: Energy Removal 2 U	.75	2.00
81 Trainer: Energy Restore U	.75	2.00
82 Trainer: Energy Switch U	.75	2.00
83 Trainer: Lady Outing U	.75	2.00
84 Trainer: Lum Berry U	.75	2.00
85 Trainer: Oran Berry U	.75	2.00
86 Trainer: Poke Ball U	.75	2.00
87 Trainer: Pokemon Reversal U	.75	2.00
88 Trainer: PokeNav U	.75	2.00
89 Trainer: Professor Birch U	.75	2.00
90 Trainer: Energy Search C	.75	2.00
91 Trainer: Potion C	.75	2.00
92 Trainer: Switch C	.75	2.00
93 Darkness Energy R	.75	2.00
94 Metal Energy R	.75	2.00
95 Rainbow Energy R	.75	2.00
96 Chansey EX HOLO R	2.00	6.00
97 Electabuzz EX HOLO R	2.00	6.00
98 Hitmonchan EX HOLO R	2.00	6.00
99 Lapras EX HOLO R	2.00	6.00
100 Magmar EX HOLO R	2.00	6.00
101 Mewtwo EX HOLO R	3.00	8.00
102 Scyther EX HOLO R	2.00	6.00
103 Sneasel EX HOLO R	2.00	6.00
104 Grass Energy C	.75	2.00
105 Fighting Energy C	.75	2.00
106 Water Energy C	.75	2.00
107 Psychic Energy C	.75	2.00
108 Fire Energy C	.75	2.00
109 Lightning Energy C	.75	2.00

2003 Pokemon EX Sandstorm

COMPLETE SET (100)	90.00	150.00
REVERSE HOLOFOIL SET (100)	150.00	200.00
BOOSTER BOX (36 PACKS)	350.00	550.00
BOOSTER PACK (9 CARDS)	10.00	25.00
*REV.FOIL: .75X TO 2X REGULAR CARD		
RELEASED ON SEPTEMBER 17, 2003		
1 Armaldo HOLO R	2.00	4.00
2 Cacturne HOLO R	2.00	4.00
3 Cradily HOLO R	2.00	4.00
4 Dusclops HOLO R	2.00	4.00
5 Flareon HOLO R	2.00	6.00
6 Jolteon HOLO R	2.00	6.00
7 Ludicolo HOLO R	2.00	4.00
8 Lunatone HOLO R	2.00	4.00
9 Mawile HOLO R	2.00	4.00
10 Sableye HOLO R	2.00	4.00
11 Seviper HOLO R	2.00	4.00
12 Shiftry HOLO R	2.00	4.00
13 Solrock HOLO R	3.00	6.00
14 Zangoose HOLO R	2.00	4.00
15 Arcanine R	.75	2.00
16 Espeon R	.75	2.00
17 Golduck R	.75	2.00
18 Kecleon R	.75	2.00
19 Omastar R	.75	2.00
20 Pichu R	.75	2.00
21 Sandslash R	.75	2.00
22 Shiftry R	.75	2.00
23 Steelix R	.75	2.00
24 Umbreon R	.75	2.00
25 Vaporeon R	.75	2.00
26 Wobbuffet R	.75	2.00
27 Anorith U	.50	1.50
28 Anorith U	.50	1.50
29 Arbok U	.50	1.50
30 Azumarill U	.50	1.50
31 Azurill U	.50	1.50
32 Baltoy U	.50	1.50
33 Breloom U	.50	1.50
34 Delcatty U	.50	1.50
35 Electabuzz U	.50	1.50
36 Elekid U	.50	1.50
37 Fearow U	.50	1.50
38 Illumise U	.50	1.50
39 Kabuto U	.50	1.50
40 Kirlia U	.50	1.50
41 Lairon U	.50	1.50
42 Lileep U	.50	1.50
43 Lileep U	.50	1.50
44 Linoone U	.50	1.50
45 Lombre U	.50	1.50
46 Lombre U	.50	1.50
47 Murkrow U	.50	1.50
48 Nuzleaf U	.50	1.50
49 Nuzleaf U	.50	1.50
50 Pelipper U	.50	1.50
51 Quilava U	.50	1.50
52 Vigoroth U	.50	1.50
53 Volbeat U	.50	1.50
54 Wynaut U	.50	1.50
55 Xatu U	.50	1.50
56 Aron C	.50	1.50
57 Cacnea C	.50	1.50
58 Cacnea C	.50	1.50
59 Cyndaquil C	.50	1.50
60 Dunsparce C	.50	1.50
61 Duskull C	.50	1.50
62 Duskull C	.50	1.50
63 Eevee C	.50	1.50
64 Ekans C	.50	1.50

Card	Low	High
65 Growlithe C	.50	1.50
66 Lotad C	.50	1.50
67 Lotad C	.50	1.50
68 Marill C	.50	1.50
69 Natu C	.50	1.50
70 Omanyte C	.50	1.50
71 Onix C	.50	1.50
72 Pikachu C	.50	1.50
73 Psyduck C	.50	1.50
74 Ralts C	.50	1.50
75 Sandshrew C	.50	1.50
76 Seedot C	.50	1.50
77 Seedot C	.50	1.50
78 Shroomish C	.50	1.50
79 Skitty C	.50	1.50
80 Slakoth C	.50	1.50
81 Spearow C	.50	1.50
82 Trapinch C	.50	1.50
83 Wailmer C	.50	1.50
84 Wingull C	.50	1.50
85 Zigzagoon C	.50	1.50
86 Double Full Heal U	.50	1.50
87 Lanette's Net Search U	.50	1.50
88 Rare Candy U	.50	1.50
89 Wally's Training U	.50	1.50
90 Claw Fossil C	.50	1.50
91 Mysterious Fossil C	.50	1.50
92 Root Fossil C	.50	1.50
93 Multi Energy R	.50	1.50
94 Aerodactyl EX HOLO R	3.00	8.00
95 Aggron EX HOLO R	3.00	8.00
96 Gardevoir EX HOLO R	3.00	8.00
97 Kabutops EX HOLO R	3.00	8.00
98 Raichu EX HOLO R	5.00	12.00
99 Typhlosion EX HOLO R	3.00	8.00
100 Wailord EX HOLO R	3.00	8.00

2003 Pokemon EX Dragon

Card	Low	High
COMPLETE SET (100)	90.00	140.00
BOOSTER BOX (36 PACKS)	800.00	1000.00
BOOSTER PACK (9 CARDS)	10.00	25.00
*REV.FOIL: .75X TO 2X BASIC CARDS		
FIREFANG DECK	10.00	25.00
WINDBLAST DECK	10.00	25.00
RELEASED ON NOVEMBER 24, 2003		
1 Absol HOLO R	3.00	8.00
2 Altaria HOLO R	2.00	6.00
3 Crawdaunt HOLO R	2.00	6.00
4 Flygon HOLO R	3.00	8.00
5 Golem HOLO R	2.00	6.00
6 Grumpig HOLO R	2.00	6.00
7 Minun HOLO R	3.00	8.00
8 Plusle HOLO R	2.00	6.00
9 Roselia HOLO R	2.00	6.00
10 Salamence HOLO R	2.00	6.00
11 Shedinja HOLO R	2.00	6.00
12 Torkoal HOLO R	2.00	6.00
13 Crawdaunt R	1.25	3.00
14 Dragonair R	1.25	3.00
15 Flygon R	1.25	3.00
16 Girafarig R	1.25	3.00
17 Magneton R	1.25	3.00
18 Ninjask R	1.25	3.00
19 Salamence R	1.25	3.00
20 Shelgon R	1.25	3.00
21 Skarmory R	1.25	3.00
22 Vibrava R	1.25	3.00
23 Bagon U	.25	.75
24 Camerupt U	.25	.75
25 Combusken U	.25	.75
26 Dratini U	.25	.75
27 Flaaffy U	.25	.75
28 Forretress U	.25	.75
29 Graveler U	.25	.75
30 Graveler U	.25	.75
31 Grovyle U	.25	.75
32 Gyarados U	.25	.75
33 Horsea U	.25	.75
34 Houndoom U	.25	.75
35 Magneton U	.25	.75
36 Marshtomp U	.25	.75
37 Meditite U	.25	.75
38 Ninjask U	.25	.75
39 Seadra U	.25	.75
40 Seadra U	.25	.75
41 Shelgon U	.25	.75
42 Shelgon U	.25	.75
43 Shuppet U	.25	.75
44 Snorunt U	.25	.75
45 Swellow U	.25	.75
46 Vibrava U	.25	.75
47 Vibrava U	.25	.75
48 Whiscash U	.25	.75
49 Bagon C	.25	.75
50 Bagon C	.25	.75
51 Barboach C	.25	.75
52 Corphish C	.25	.75
53 Corphish C	.25	.75
54 Corphish C	.25	.75
55 Geodude C	.25	.75
56 Geodude C	.25	.75
57 Grimer C	.25	.75
58 Horsea U	.25	.75
59 Houndour C	.25	.75
60 Magikarp C	.25	.75
61 Magnemite C	.25	.75
62 Magnemite C	.25	.75
63 Magnemite C	.25	.75
64 Mareep C	.25	.75
65 Mudkip C	.25	.75
66 Nincada C	.25	.75
67 Nincada C	.25	.75
68 Nincada C	.25	.75
69 Numel C	.25	.75
70 Numel C	.25	.75
71 Pineco C	.25	.75
72 Slugma C	.25	.75
73 Spoink C	.25	.75
74 Spoink C	.25	.75
75 Swablu C	.25	.75
76 Taillow C	.25	.75
77 Torchic C	.25	.75
78 Trapinch C	.25	.75
79 Trapinch C	.25	.75
80 Treecko C	.25	.75
81 Wurmple C	.25	.75
82 Balloon Berry C	.25	.75
83 Buffer Piece C	.25	.75
84 Energy Recycle System C	.25	.75
85 High Pressure System C	.25	.75
86 Low Pressure System C	.25	.75
87 Mr. Briney's Compassion C	.25	.75
88 TV Reporter U	40.00	80.00
88R TV Reporter UR	.25	.75
89 Ampharos EX HOLO R	3.00	8.00
90 Dragonite EX HOLO R	6.00	15.00
91 Golem EX HOLO R	3.00	8.00
92 Kingdra EX HOLO R	2.00	6.00
93 Latias EX HOLO R	6.00	15.00
94 Latios EX HOLO R	6.00	15.00
95 Magcargo EX HOLO R	2.00	6.00
96 Muk EX HOLO R	3.00	8.00
97 Rayquaza EX HOLO R	3.00	8.00
98 Charmander HOLO R	6.00	15.00
99 Charmeleon HOLO R	4.00	10.00
100 Charizard HOLO R	40.00	80.00

2004 Pokemon EX Team Magma Vs Team Aqua

Card	Low	High
COMPLETE SET (97)	60.00	120.00
BOOSTER BOX (36 PACKS)	400.00	600.00
BOOSTER PACK (9 CARDS)	15.00	30.00
*REV.FOIL: .75X TO 2X REGULAR CARD		
RELEASED ON MARCH 15, 2004		
1 Team Aqua's Cacturne HOLO R	1.50	3.00
2 Team Aqua's Crawdaunt HOLO R	.75	2.00
3 Team Aqua's Kyogre HOLO R	2.00	5.00
4 Team Aqua's Manectric HOLO R	1.00	2.50
5 Team Aqua's Sharpedo HOLO R	2.50	6.00
6 Team Aqua's Walrein HOLO R	.75	2.00
7 Team Magma's Aggron HOLO R	1.00	2.50
8 Team Magma's Claydol HOLO R	.75	2.00
9 Team Magma's Groudon HOLO R	3.00	8.00
10 Team Magma's Houndoom HOLO R	2.00	5.00
11 Team Magma's Rhydon HOLO R	.75	2.00
12 Team Magma's Torkoal HOLO R	.75	2.00
13 Raichu R	.50	1.00
14 Team Aqua's Crawdaunt R	.50	1.00
15 Team Aqua's Mightyena R	.50	1.00
16 Team Aqua's Sealeo R	.50	1.00
17 Team Aqua's Seviper R	.50	1.00
18 Team Aqua's Sharpedo R	.50	1.00
19 Team Magma's Camerupt R	.50	1.00
20 Team Magma's Lairon R	.50	1.00
21 Team Magma's Mightyena R	.50	1.00
22 Team Magma's Rhydon R	.50	1.00
23 Team Magma's Zangoose R	.50	1.00
24 Team Aqua's Cacnea U	.20	.50
25 Team Aqua's Carvanha U	.20	.50
26 Team Aqua's Corphish U	.20	.50
27 Team Aqua's Electrike U	.20	.50
28 Team Aqua's Lanturn U	.20	.50
29 Team Aqua's Manectric U	.20	.50
30 Team Aqua's Mightyena U	.20	.50
31 Team Aqua's Sealeo U	.20	.50
32 Team Magma's Baltoy U	.20	.50
33 Team Magma's Claydol U	.20	.50
34 Team Magma's Houndoom U	.20	.50
35 Team Magma's Houndour U	.20	.50
36 Team Magma's Lairon U	.20	.50
37 Team Magma's Mightyena U	.20	.50
38 Team Magma's Rhyhorn U	.20	.50
39 Bulbasaur C	.10	.20
40 Cubone C	.10	.20
41 Jigglypuff C	.10	.20
42 Meowth C	.10	.20
43 Pikachu C	.10	.20
44 Psyduck C	.10	.20
45 Slowpoke C	.10	.20
46 Squirtle C	.10	.20
47 Team Aqua's Carvanha C	.10	.20
48 Team Aqua's Carvanha C	.10	.20
49 Team Aqua's Chinchou C	.10	.20
50 Team Aqua's Corphish C	.10	.20
51 Team Aqua's Corphish C	.10	.20
52 Team Aqua's Electrike C	.10	.20
53 Team Aqua's Electrike C	.10	.20
54 Team Aqua's Poochyena C	.10	.20
55 Team Aqua's Poochyena C	.10	.20
56 Team Aqua's Spheal C	.10	.20
57 Team Aqua's Spheal C	.10	.20
58 Team Magma's Aron C	.10	.20
59 Team Magma's Aron C	.10	.20
60 Team Magma's Baltoy C	.10	.20
61 Team Magma's Baltoy C	.10	.20
62 Team Magma's Houndour C	.10	.20
63 Team Magma's Houndour C	.10	.20
64 Team Magma's Numel C	.10	.20
65 Team Magma's Poochyena C	.10	.20
66 Team Magma's Poochyena C	.10	.20
67 Team Magma's Rhyhorn C	.10	.20
68 Team Magma's Rhyhorn C	.10	.20
69 Team Aqua Schemer U	.20	.50
70 Team Magma Schemer U	.20	.50
71 Archie U	.20	.50
72 Dual Ball U	.20	.50
73 Maxie U	.20	.50
74 Strength Charm U	.20	.50
75 Team Aqua Ball U	.20	.50
76 Team Aqua Belt U	.20	.50
77 Team Aqua Conspirator U	.20	.50
78 Team Aqua Hideout U	.20	.50
79 Team Aqua Technical Machine 01 U	.20	.50
80 Team Magma Ball U	.20	.50
81 Team Magma Belt U	.20	.50
82 Team Magma Conspirator U	.20	.50
83 Team Magma Hideout U	.20	.50
84 Team Magma Tech. Machine 01 U	.20	.50
85 Warp Point U	.20	.50
86 Aqua Energy U	.25	.75
87 Magma Energy U	.75	2.00
88 Double Rainbow Energy R	1.50	4.00
89 Blaziken EX HOLO R	8.00	20.00
90 Cradily EX HOLO R	6.00	15.00
91 Entei EX HOLO R	10.00	25.00
92 Raikou EX HOLO R	6.00	15.00
93 Sceptile EX HOLO R	8.00	20.00
94 Suicune EX HOLO R	8.00	20.00
95 Swampert EX HOLO R	8.00	20.00
96 Absol HOLO R	6.00	15.00
97 Jirachi HOLO R	4.00	10.00

2004 Pokemon EX Hidden Legends

Card	Low	High
COMPLETE SET (102)	150.00	250.00
BOOSTER BOX (36 PACKS)	700.00	800.00
BOOSTER PACK (9 CARDS)	8.00	20.00
*REV.FOIL: .75X TO 2X BASIC CARDS		
RELEASED ON JUNE 14, 2004		
1 Banette HOLO R	2.00	6.00
2 Claydol HOLO R	2.00	6.00
3 Crobat HOLO R	2.00	6.00
4 Dark Celebi HOLO R	2.00	6.00
5 Electrode HOLO R	2.00	6.00
6 Exploud HOLO R	2.00	6.00
7 Heracross HOLO R	2.00	6.00
8 Jirachi HOLO R	2.00	6.00
9 Machamp HOLO R	2.00	6.00
10 Medicham HOLO R	2.00	6.00
11 Metagross HOLO R	2.00	6.00
12 Milotic HOLO R	2.00	6.00
13 Pinsir HOLO R	2.00	6.00
14 Shiftry HOLO R	2.00	6.00
15 Walrein HOLO R	2.00	6.00
16 Bellossom R	.75	2.00
17 Chimecho R	.75	2.00
18 Gorebyss R	.75	2.00
19 Huntail R	.75	2.00
20 Masquerain R	.75	2.00
21 Metang R	.75	2.00
22 Ninetales R	.75	2.00
23 Rain Castform R	.75	2.00
24 Relicanth R	.75	2.00
25 Snow-cloud Castform R	.75	2.00
26 Sunny Castform R	.75	2.00
27 Tropius R	.75	2.00
28 Beldum U	.25	.75
29 Beldum U	.25	.75
30 Castform U	.25	.75
31 Claydol U	.25	.75
32 Corsola U	.25	.75
33 Dodrio U	.25	.75
34 Glalie U	.25	.75
35 Gloom U	.25	.75
36 Golbat U	.25	.75
37 Igglybuff U	.25	.75
38 Lanturn U	.25	.75
39 Loudred U	.25	.75
40 Luvdisc U	.25	.75
41 Machoke U	.25	.75
42 Medicham U	.25	.75
43 Metang U	.25	.75
44 Metang U	.25	.75
45 Nuzleaf U	.25	.75
46 Rhydon U	.25	.75
47 Sealeo U	.25	.75
48 Spinda U	.25	.75
49 Starmie U	.25	.75
50 Swalot U	.25	.75
51 Tentacruel U	.25	.75
52 Baltoy C	.25	.75
53 Baltoy C	.25	.75
54 Beldum C	.25	.75
55 Chikorita C	.25	.75
56 Chinchou C	.25	.75
57 Chinchou C	.25	.75
58 Clamperl C	.25	.75
59 Cyndaquil C	.25	.75
60 Doduo C	.25	.75
61 Feebas C	.25	.75
62 Gulpin C	.25	.75
63 Jigglypuff C	.25	.75
64 Machop C	.25	.75
65 Meditite C	.25	.75
66 Meditite C	.25	.75
67 Minun C	.25	.75
68 Oddish C	.25	.75
69 Plusle C	.25	.75
70 Rhyhorn C	.25	.75
71 Seedot C	.25	.75
72 Shuppet C	.25	.75
73 Snorunt C	.25	.75
74 Spheal C	.25	.75
75 Staryu C	.25	.75
76 Surskit C	.25	.75
77 Tentacool C	.25	.75
78 Togepi C	.25	.75
79 Totodile C	.25	.75
80 Voltorb C	.25	.75
81 Vulpix C	.25	.75
82 Whismur C	.25	.75
83 Zubat C	.25	.75
84 Ancient Technical Machine [Ice] U	.25	.75
85 Ancient Technical Machine [Rock] U	.25	.75
86 Ancient Technical Machine [Steel] U	.25	.75
87 Ancient Tomb U	.25	.75
88 Desert Ruins U	.25	.75
89 Island Cave U	.25	.75
90 Life Herb U	.25	.75
91 Magnetic Storm U	.25	.75
92 Steven's Advice U	.25	.75
93 Groudon EX HOLO R	4.00	10.00
94 Kyogre EX HOLO R	5.00	12.00
95 Metagross EX HOLO R	3.00	8.00
96 Ninetales EX HOLO R	6.00	15.00
97 Regice EX HOLO R	5.00	12.00
98 Regirock EX HOLO R	5.00	12.00
99 Registeel EX HOLO R	5.00	12.00
100 Vileplume EX HOLO R	3.00	8.00
101 Wigglytuff EX HOLO R	4.00	10.00
102 Groudon HOLO R	2.00	6.00

2004 Pokemon EX Fire Red Leaf Green

Card	Low	High
COMPLETE SET (116)	280.00	400.00
BOOSTER BOX (36 PACKS)	650.00	900.00
BOOSTER PACK (9 CARDS)	15.00	30.00
*REV.FOIL: .75X TO 2X BASIC CARDS		
RELEASED ON AUGUST 30, 2004		
1 Beedrill HOLO R	1.50	4.00
2 Butterfree HOLO R	2.00	6.00
3 Dewgong HOLO R	1.50	4.00
4 Ditto HOLO R	1.50	4.00
5 Exeggutor HOLO R	1.50	4.00
6 Kangaskhan HOLO R	1.50	4.00
7 Marowak HOLO R	1.50	4.00
8 Nidoking HOLO R	1.50	4.00
9 Nidoqueen HOLO R	1.50	4.00
10 Pidgeot HOLO R	1.50	4.00
11 Poliwrath HOLO R	1.50	4.00
12 Raichu HOLO R	4.00	10.00
13 Rapidash HOLO R	1.50	4.00
14 Slowbro HOLO R	1.50	4.00
15 Snorlax HOLO R	1.50	4.00
16 Tauros HOLO R	1.50	4.00
17 Victreebel HOLO R	1.50	4.00
18 Arcanine R	1.25	3.00
19 Chansey R	1.25	3.00
20 Cloyster R	1.25	3.00
21 Dodrio R	1.25	3.00
22 Dugtrio R	1.25	3.00
23 Farfetch'd R	1.25	3.00
24 Fearow R	1.25	3.00
25 Hypno R	1.25	3.00
26 Kingler R	1.25	3.00
27 Magneton R	1.25	3.00
28 Primeape R	1.25	3.00
29 Scyther R	1.25	3.00
30 Tangela R	1.25	3.00
31 Charmeleon U	.25	.75
32 Drowzee U	.25	.75
33 Exeggcute U	.25	.75
34 Haunter U	.25	.75
35 Ivysaur U	.25	.75
36 Kakuna U	.25	.75
37 Lickitung U	.25	.75
38 Mankey U	.25	.75
39 Metapod U	.25	.75
40 Nidorina U	.25	.75
41 Nidorino U	.25	.75
42 Onix U	.25	.75

43 Parasect U	.25	.75
44 Persian U	.25	.75
45 Pidgeotto U	.25	.75
46 Poliwhirl U	.25	.75
47 Porygon U	.25	.75
48 Raticate U	.25	.75
49 Venomoth U	.25	.75
50 Wartortle U	.25	.75
51 Weepinbell U	.25	.75
52 Wigglytuff U	.25	.75
53 Bellsprout C	.25	.75
54 Bulbasaur C	.25	.75
55 Bulbasaur C	.25	.75
56 Caterpie C	.25	.75
57 Charmander C	.25	.75
58 Charmander C	.25	.75
59 Clefairy C	.25	.75
60 Cubone C	.25	.75
61 Diglett C	.25	.75
62 Doduo C	.25	.75
63 Gastly C	.25	.75
64 Growlithe C	.25	.75
65 Jigglypuff C	.25	.75
66 Krabby C	.25	.75
67 Magikarp C	.25	.75
68 Magnemite C	.25	.75
69 Meowth C	.25	.75
70 Nidoran F C	.25	.75
71 Nidoran M C	.25	.75
72 Paras C	.25	.75
73 Pidgey C	.25	.75
74 Pikachu C	.25	.75
75 Poliwag C	.25	.75
76 Ponyta C	.25	.75
77 Rattata C	.25	.75
78 Seel C	.25	.75
79 Shellder C	.25	.75
80 Slowpoke C	.25	.75
81 Spearow C	.25	.75
82 Squirtle C	.25	.75
83 Squirtle C	.25	.75
84 Venonat C	.25	.75
85 Voltorb C	.25	.75
86 Weedle C	.25	.75
87 Bill's Maintenance U	.25	.75
88 Celio's Network U	.25	.75
89 Energy Removal 2 U	.25	.75
90 Energy Switch U	.25	.75
91 EXP.ALL U	.25	.75
92 Great Ball U	.25	.75
93 Life Herb U	.25	.75
94 Mt. Moon U	.25	.75
95 Poke Ball U	.25	.75
96 PokeDEX HANDY 909 U	.25	.75
97 Pokemon Reversal U	.25	.75
98 Professor Oak's Research U	.25	.75
99 Super Scoop Up U	.25	.75
100 VS Seeker U	6.00	15.00
101 Potion C	.25	.75
102 Switch C	.25	.75
103 Multi Energy HOLO R	.75	2.00
104 Blastoise EX HOLO R	15.00	30.00
105 Charizard EX HOLO R	60.00	100.00
106 Clefable EX HOLO R	3.00	8.00
107 Electrode EX HOLO R	3.00	8.00
108 Gengar EX HOLO R	8.00	20.00
109 Gyarados EX HOLO R	8.00	20.00
110 Mr. Mime EX HOLO R	3.00	8.00
111 Mr. Mime EX HOLO R	3.00	8.00
112 Venusaur EX HOLO R	15.00	30.00
113 Charmander HOLO R	4.00	10.00
114 Articuno EX HOLO R	5.00	12.00
115 Moltres EX HOLO R	5.00	12.00
116 Zapdos EX HOLO R	6.00	15.00

2004 Pokemon EX Team Rocket Returns

COMPLETE SET (111)	400.00	700.00
BOOSTER BOX (36 PACKS)	800.00	1100.00
BOOSTER PACK (9 CARDS)	15.00	30.00
*REV. FOIL: .75X TO 2X BASIC CARDS		
RELEASED ON NOVEMBER 4, 2004		
1 Azumarill HOLO R	2.00	6.00
2 Dark Ampharos HOLO R	2.00	6.00
3 Dark Crobat HOLO R	2.00	6.00
4 Dark Electrode HOLO R	2.00	6.00
5 Dark Houndoom HOLO R	2.00	6.00
6 Dark Hypno HOLO R	2.00	6.00
7 Dark Marowak HOLO R	2.00	6.00
8 Dark Octillery HOLO R	2.00	6.00
9 Dark Slowking HOLO R	2.00	6.00
10 Dark Steelix HOLO R	2.00	6.00
11 Jumpluff HOLO R	2.00	6.00
12 Kingdra HOLO R	2.00	6.00
13 Piloswine HOLO R	2.00	6.00
14 Togetic HOLO R	2.00	6.00
15 Dark Dragonite R	1.50	4.00
16 Dark Muk R	.75	2.00
17 Dark Raticate R	.75	2.00
18 Dark Sandslash R	.75	2.00
19 Dark Tyranitar R	.75	2.00
20 Dark Tyranitar R	.75	2.00
21 Delibird R	.75	2.00
22 Furret R	.75	2.00
23 Ledian R	.75	2.00
24 Magby R	.75	2.00
25 Misdreavus R	.75	2.00
26 Quagsire R	.75	2.00
27 Qwilfish R	.75	2.00
28 Yanma R	.75	2.00
29 Dark Arbok U	.75	2.00
30 Dark Ariados U	.75	2.00
31 Dark Dragonair U	1.50	4.00
32 Dark Dragonair U	1.50	4.00
33 Dark Flaaffy U	.75	2.00
34 Dark Golbat U	.75	2.00
35 Dark Golduck U	.75	2.00
36 Dark Gyarados U	1.50	4.00
37 Dark Houndoom U	.75	2.00
38 Dark Magcargo U	.75	2.00
39 Dark Magneton U	.75	2.00
40 Dark Pupitar U	.75	2.00
41 Dark Pupitar U	.75	2.00
42 Dark Weezing U	.75	2.00
43 Heracross U	.75	2.00
44 Magmar U	.75	2.00
45 Mantine U	.75	2.00
46 Rocket's Meowth U	.75	2.00
47 Rocket's Wobbuffet U	.75	2.00
48 Seadra U	.75	2.00
49 Skiploom U	.75	2.00
50 Togepi U	.75	2.00
51 Cubone C	.25	.75
52 Dratini C	.25	2.00
53 Dratini C	.25	2.00
54 Drowzee C	.25	2.00
55 Ekans C	.25	2.00
56 Grimer C	.25	2.00
57 Hoppip C	.25	2.00
58 Horsea C	.25	2.00
59 Houndour C	.25	2.00
60 Houndour C	.25	2.00
61 Koffing C	.25	2.00
62 Larvitar C	.25	2.00
63 Larvitar C	.25	2.00
64 Ledyba C	.25	2.00
65 Magikarp C	.25	2.00
66 Magnemite C	.25	2.00
67 Mareep C	.25	2.00
68 Marill C	.25	2.00
69 Onix C	.25	2.00
70 Psyduck C	.25	2.00
71 Rattata C	.25	2.00
72 Rattata C	.25	2.00
73 Remoraid C	.25	2.00
74 Sandshrew C	.25	2.00
75 Sentret C	.25	2.00
76 Slowpoke C	.25	2.00
77 Slugma C	.25	2.00
78 Spinarak C	.25	2.00
79 Swinub C	.25	2.00
80 Voltorb C	.25	2.00
81 Wooper C	.25	2.00
82 Zubat C	.25	2.00
83 Copycat U	.25	2.00
84 Pokemon Retriever U	.25	2.00
85 Pow! Hand Extension U	.25	2.00
86 Rocket's Admin. U	2.00	6.00
87 Rocket's Hideout U	.25	2.00
88 Rocket's Mission U	.25	2.00
89 Rocket's Poké Ball U	.25	2.00
90 Rocket's Tricky Gym U	.25	2.00
91 Surprise! Time Machine U	.25	2.00
92 Swoop! Teleporter U	.25	2.00
93 Venture Bomb U	.25	2.00
94 Dark Metal Energy U	.25	2.00
95 R Energy U	.25	2.00
96 Rocket's Articuno EX HOLO R	10.00	25.00
97 Rocket's Entei EX HOLO R	15.00	30.00
98 Rocket's Hitmonchan EX HOLO R	8.00	20.00
99 Rocket's Mewtwo EX HOLO R	20.00	40.00
100 Rocket's Moltres EX HOLO R	15.00	30.00
101 Rocket's Scizor EX HOLO R	8.00	20.00
102 Rocket's Scyther EX HOLO R	15.00	30.00
103 Rocket's Sneasel EX HOLO R	6.00	15.00
104 Rocket's Snorlax EX HOLO R	10.00	25.00
105 Rocket's Suicune EX HOLO R	10.00	25.00
106 Rocket's Zapdos EX HOLO R	15.00	30.00
107 Mudkip Gold Star HOLO R	50.00	100.00
108 Torchic Gold Star HOLO R	60.00	120.00
109 Treecko Gold Star HOLO R	50.00	100.00
110 Charmeleon SCT	3.00	8.00
111 Here Comes Team Rocket! SCT	10.00	25.00

2004 Pokemon EX Trainer Kit

COMPLETE SET (60)	7.00	12.00
RELEASED ON MARCH 15, 2005		
2 Latios HOLO R	2.00	5.00
4 Latias HOLO R	2.00	5.00

2005 Pokemon EX Deoxys

COMPLETE SET (108)	400.00	700.00
BOOSTER BOX (36 PACKS)	1000.00	1600.00
BOOSTER PACK (9 CARDS)	8.00	20.00
*REV.FOIL: .75X TO 2X BASIC CARDS		
RELEASED ON FEBRUARY 14, 2005		
1 Altaria HOLO R	2.00	6.00
2 Beautifly HOLO R	2.00	6.00
3 Breloom HOLO R	2.00	6.00
4 Camerupt HOLO R	2.00	6.00
5 Claydol HOLO R	2.00	6.00
6 Crawdaunt HOLO R	2.00	6.00
7 Dusclops HOLO R	2.00	6.00
8 Gyarados HOLO R	2.00	6.00
9 Jirachi HOLO R	2.00	6.00
10 Ludicolo HOLO R	2.00	6.00
11 Metagross HOLO R	2.00	6.00
12 Mightyena HOLO R	2.00	6.00
13 Ninjask HOLO R	2.00	6.00
14 Shedinja HOLO R	2.00	6.00
15 Slaking HOLO R	2.00	6.00
16 Deoxys (Normal) R	1.50	3.00
17 Deoxys (Attack) R	1.50	3.00
18 Deoxys (Defense) R	1.50	3.00
19 Ludicolo R	1.50	3.00
20 Magcargo R	1.50	3.00
21 Pelipper R	1.50	3.00
22 Rayquaza R	1.50	3.00
23 Sableye R	1.50	3.00
24 Seaking R	1.50	3.00
25 Shiftry R	1.50	3.00
26 Skarmory R	1.50	3.00
27 Tropius R	1.50	3.00
28 Whiscash R	1.50	3.00
29 Xatu R	1.50	3.00
30 Donphan U	.25	.75
31 Golbat U	.25	.75
32 Grumpig U	.25	.75
33 Lombre U	.25	.75
34 Lombre U	.25	.75
35 Lotad U	.25	.75
36 Lunatone U	.25	.75
37 Magcargo U	.25	.75
38 Manectric U	.25	.75
39 Masquerain U	.25	.75
40 Metang U	.25	.75
41 Minun U	.25	.75
42 Nosepass U	.25	.75
43 Nuzleaf U	.25	.75
44 Plusle U	.25	.75
45 Shelgon U	.25	.75
46 Silcoon U	.25	.75
47 Solrock U	.25	.75
48 Starmie U	.25	.75
49 Swellow U	.25	.75
50 Vigoroth U	.25	.75
51 Weezing U	.25	.75
52 Bagon C	.25	.75
53 Baltoy C	.25	.75
54 Barboach C	.25	.75
55 Beldum C	.25	.75
56 Carvanha C	.25	.75
57 Corphish C	.25	.75
58 Duskull C	.25	.75
59 Electrike C	.25	.75
60 Electrike C	.25	.75
61 Goldeen C	.25	.75
62 Koffing C	.25	.75
63 Lotad C	.25	.75
64 Magikarp C	.25	.75
65 Makuhita C	.25	.75
66 Natu C	.25	.75
67 Nincada C	.25	.75
68 Numel C	.25	.75
69 Phanpy C	.25	.75
70 Poochyena C	.25	.75
71 Seedot C	.25	.75
72 Shroomish C	.25	.75
73 Slakoth C	.25	.75
74 Slugma C	.25	.75
75 Slugma C	.25	.75
76 Spoink C	.25	.75
77 Staryu C	.25	.75
78 Surskit C	.25	.75
79 Swablu C	.25	.75
80 Taillow C	.25	.75
81 Wingull C	.25	.75
82 Wurmple C	.25	.75
83 Zubat C	.25	.75
84 Balloon Berry U	.25	.75
85 Crystal Shard U	.25	.75
86 Energy Charge U	.25	.75
87 Lady Outing U	.25	.75
88 Master Ball U	.25	.75
89 Meteor Falls U	.25	.75
90 Professor Cozmo's Discovery U	.25	.75
91 Space Center U	.25	.75
92 Strength Charm U	.25	.75
93 Boost Energy U	.25	.75
94 Healing Energy U	.25	.75
95 Scramble Energy U	.75	2.00
96 Crobat EX HOLO R	3.00	8.00
97 Deoxys EX (Normal) HOLO R	5.00	12.00
98 Deoxys EX (Attack) HOLO R	4.00	10.00
99 Deoxys EX (Defense) HOLO R	3.00	8.00
100 Hariyama EX HOLO R	3.00	8.00
101 Manectric EX HOLO R	3.00	8.00
102 Rayquaza EX HOLO R	3.00	8.00
103 Salamence EX HOLO R	8.00	20.00
104 Sharpedo EX HOLO R	5.00	12.00
105 Latias Gold Star HOLO R	80.00	140.00
106 Latios Gold Star HOLO R	80.00	140.00
107 Rayquaza Gold Star HOLO R	200.00	300.00
108 Rocket's Raikou EX HOLO R	6.00	15.00

2005 Pokemon EX Emerald

COMPLETE SET (107)	150.00	250.00
BOOSTER BOX (36 PACKS)	600.00	800.00
BOOSTER PACK (9 CARDS)	8.00	20.00
*REV.FOIL: .75X TO 2X BASIC CARDS		
RELEASED ON MAY 9, 2005		
1 Blaziken HOLO R	1.50	4.00
2 Deoxys HOLO R	1.50	4.00
3 Exploud HOLO R	1.50	4.00
4 Gardevoir HOLO R	1.50	4.00
5 Groudon HOLO R	1.50	4.00
6 Kyogre HOLO R	1.50	4.00
7 Manectric HOLO R	1.50	4.00
8 Milotic HOLO R	1.50	4.00
9 Rayquaza HOLO R	1.50	4.00
10 Sceptile HOLO R	1.50	4.00
11 Swampert HOLO R	1.50	4.00
12 Chimecho R	.75	2.00
13 Glalie R	.75	2.00
14 Groudon R	.75	2.00
15 Kyogre R	.75	2.00
16 Manectric R	.75	2.00
17 Nosepass R	.75	2.00
18 Relicanth R	.75	2.00
19 Rhydon R	.75	2.00
20 Seviper R	.75	2.00
21 Zangoose R	.75	2.00
22 Breloom U	.75	2.00
23 Camerupt U	.75	2.00
24 Claydol U	.75	2.00
25 Combusken U	.75	2.00
26 Dodrio U	.75	2.00
27 Electrode U	.75	2.00
28 Grovyle U	.75	2.00
29 Grumpig U	.75	2.00
30 Grumpig U	.75	2.00
31 Hariyama U	.75	2.00
32 Illumise U	.75	2.00
33 Kirlia U	.75	2.00
34 Linoone U	.75	2.00
35 Loudred U	.75	2.00
36 Marshtomp U	.75	2.00
37 Minun U	.75	2.00
38 Ninetales U	.75	2.00
39 Plusle U	.75	2.00
40 Swalot U	.75	2.00
41 Swellow U	.75	2.00
42 Volbeat U	.75	2.00
43 Baltoy C	.75	2.00
44 Cacnea C	.75	2.00
45 Doduo C	.75	2.00
46 Duskull C	.75	2.00
47 Electrike C	.75	2.00
48 Electrike C	.75	2.00
49 Feebas C	.75	2.00
50 Feebas C	.75	2.00
51 Gulpin C	.75	2.00
52 Larvitar C	.75	2.00
53 Luvdisc C	.75	2.00
54 Makuhita C	.75	2.00
55 Meditite C	.75	2.00
56 Mudkip C	.75	2.00
57 Numel C	.75	2.00
58 Numel C	.75	2.00
59 Pichu C	.75	2.00
60 Pikachu C	.75	2.00
61 Ralts C	.75	2.00
62 Rhyhorn C	.75	2.00
63 Shroomish C	.75	2.00
64 Snorunt C	.75	2.00
65 Spoink C	.75	2.00
66 Spoink C	.75	2.00
67 Swablu C	.75	2.00
68 Taillow C	.75	2.00
69 Torchic C	.75	2.00
70 Treecko C	.75	2.00
71 Voltorb C	.75	2.00
72 Vulpix C	.75	2.00
73 Whismur C	.75	2.00
74 Zigzagoon C	.75	2.00
75 Battle Frontier U	.75	2.00
76 Double Full Heal U	.75	2.00
77 Lanette's Net Search U	.75	2.00
78 Lum Berry U	.75	2.00
79 Mr. Stone's Project U	.75	2.00
80 Oran Berry U	.75	2.00
81 Pokenav U	.75	2.00
82 Professor Birch U	.75	2.00
83 Rare Candy U	.75	2.00
84 Scott U	.75	2.00
85 Wally's Training U	.75	2.00
86 Darkness Energy R	.75	2.00
87 Double Rainbow Energy R	.75	2.00

88 Metal Energy R .75 2.00
89 Mutli Energy R .75 2.00
90 Altaria EX HOLO R 5.00 12.00
91 Cacturne EX HOLO R 4.00 10.00
92 Camerupt EX HOLO R 3.00 8.00
93 Deoxys EX HOLO R 6.00 15.00
94 Dusclops EX HOLO R 6.00 15.00
95 Medicham EX HOLO R 6.00 15.00
96 Milotic EX HOLO R 10.00 25.00
97 Raichu EX HOLO R 10.00 25.00
98 Regice EX HOLO R 6.00 15.00
99 Regirock HOLO R 6.00 15.00
100 Registeel HOLO R 6.00 15.00
101 Grass Energy HOLO 3.00 8.00
102 Fire Energy HOLO 3.00 8.00
103 Water Energy HOLO 3.00 8.00
104 Lightning Energy HOLO 3.00 8.00
105 Psychic Energy HOLO 3.00 8.00
106 Fighting Energy HOLO 3.00 8.00
107 Farfetch'd Sct 3.00 8.00

2005 Pokemon EX Unseen Forces

COMPLETE SET (117) 400.00 600.00
BOOSTER BOX (36 PACKS) 500.00 650.00
BOOSTER PACK (9 CARDS) 10.00 25.00
*REV.FOIL: .75X TO 2X BASIC CARDS
RELEASED ON AUGUST 22, 2005
1 Ampharos HOLO R 2.00 6.00
2 Ariados HOLO R 2.00 6.00
3 Bellossom HOLO R 2.00 6.00
4 Feraligatr HOLO R 2.00 6.00
5 Flareon HOLO R 2.00 6.00
6 Forretress HOLO R 2.00 6.00
7 Houndoom HOLO R 2.00 6.00
8 Jolteon HOLO R 2.00 6.00
9 Meganium HOLO R 2.00 6.00
10 Octillery HOLO R 2.00 6.00
11 Poliwrath HOLO R 2.00 6.00
12 Porygon 2 HOLO R 2.00 6.00
13 Slowbro HOLO R 2.00 6.00
14 Slowking HOLO R 2.00 6.00
15 Sudowoodo HOLO R 2.00 6.00
16 Sunflora HOLO R 2.00 6.00
17 Typhlosion HOLO R 2.00 6.00
18 Ursaring HOLO R 2.00 6.00
19 Vaporeon HOLO R 2.00 6.00
20 Chansey R 1.25 3.00
21 Cleffa R 1.25 3.00
22 Electabuzz R 1.25 3.00
23 Elekid R 1.25 3.00
24 Hitmonchan R 1.25 3.00
25 Hitmonlee R 1.25 3.00
26 Hitmontop R 1.25 3.00
27 Ho-Oh R 1.25 3.00
28 Jynx R 1.25 3.00
29 Lugia R 1.25 3.00
30 Murkrow R 1.25 3.00
31 Smoochum R 1.25 3.00
32 Stantler R 1.25 3.00
33 Tyrogue R 1.25 3.00
34 Aipom U .25 .75
35 Bayleef U .25 .75
36 Clefable U .25 .75
37 Corsola U .25 .75
38 Croconaw U .25 .75
39 Granbull U .25 .75
40 Lanturn U .25 .75
41 Magcargo U .25 .75
42 Miltank U .25 .75
43 Noctowl U .25 .75
44 Quagsire U .25 .75
45 Quilava U .25 .75
46 Scyther U .25 .75
47 Shuckle U .25 .75
48 Smeargle U .25 .75
49 Xatu U .25 .75
50 Yanma U .25 .75
51 Chikorita C .25 .75
52 Chinchou C .25 .75
53 Cleffairy C .25 .75
54 Cyndaquil C .25 .75
55 Eevee C .25 .75
56 Flaafy C .25 .75
57 Gligar C .25 .75
58 Gloom C .25 .75
59 Hoothoot C .25 .75
60 Houndour C .25 .75
61 Larvitar C .25 .75
62 Mareep C .25 .75
63 Natu C .25 .75
64 Oddish C .25 .75
65 Onix C .25 .75
66 Pineco C .25 .75
67 Poliwag C .25 .75
68 Poliwhirl C .25 .75
69 Porygon C .25 .75
70 Pupitar C .25 .75
71 Remoraid C .25 .75
72 Slowpoke C .25 .75
73 Slugma C .25 .75
74 Snubbull C .25 .75
75 Spinarak C .25 .75
76 Sunkern C .25 .75
77 Teddiursa C .25 .75
78 Totodile C .25 .75
79 Wooper C .25 .75
80 Curse Powder U .25 .75
81 EnergyRecycle System U .25 .75
82 EnergyRemoval 2 U .25 .75
83 EnergyRoot U .25 .75
84 Energy Switch U .25 .75
85 Fluffy Berry U .25 .75
86 Mary'sRequest U .25 .75
87 Poke Ball U .25 .75
88 PokemonReversal U .25 .75
89 Professor Elm's Training Method U .25 .75
90 Protective Orb U .25 .75
91 Sitrus Berry U .25 .75
92 SolidRage U .25 .75
93 Warp Point U .25 .75
94 Energy Search C .25 .75
95 Potion C .25 .75
96 Darkness Energy R .75 2.00
97 Metal Energy R .75 .75
98 Boost Energy U .25 .75
99 Cyclone Energy U .25 .75
100 Warp Energy U .25 .75
101 Blissey EX UR HOLO 6.00 15.00
102 Espeon EX UR HOLO 8.00 20.00
103 Feraligatr EX UR HOLO 4.00 10.00
104 Ho-Oh EX UR HOLO 6.00 15.00
105 Lugia EX UR HOLO 25.00 50.00
106 Meganium EX UR HOLO 4.00 10.00
107 Politoed EX UR HOLO 5.00 12.00
108 Scizor EX UR HOLO 6.00 15.00
109 Steelix EX UR HOLO 4.00 10.00
110 Typhlosion EX UR HOLO 4.00 10.00
111 Tyranitar EX UR HOLO 8.00 20.00
112 Umbreon EX UR HOLO 8.00 20.00
113 Entei Gold Star HOLO R 25.00 50.00
114 Raikou Gold Star HOLO R 25.00 50.00
115 Suicune Gold Star HOLO R 25.00 50.00
116 Rocket's Persian EX HOLO R 3.00 8.00
117 Celebi EX SCT 20.00 40.00

2005 Pokemon EX Unseen Forces Unown

COMPLETE SET (28) 30.00 60.00
RELEASED ON AUGUST 22, 2005
A Unown 1.50 4.00
B Unown 1.50 4.00
C Unown 1.50 4.00
D Unown 1.50 4.00
E Unown 1.50 4.00
F Unown 1.50 4.00
G Unown 1.50 4.00
H Unown 1.50 4.00
I Unown 1.50 4.00
J Unown 1.50 4.00
K Unown 1.50 4.00
L Unown 1.50 4.00
M Unown 1.50 4.00
N Unown 1.50 4.00
O Unown 1.50 4.00
P Unown 1.50 4.00
Q Unown 1.50 4.00
R Unown 1.50 4.00
S Unown 1.50 4.00
T Unown 1.50 4.00
U Unown 1.50 4.00
V Unown 1.50 4.00
W Unown 1.50 4.00
X Unown 1.50 4.00
Y Unown 1.50 4.00
Z Unown 1.50 4.00
QM Unown 3.00 8.00
EP Unown 5.00 12.00

2005 Pokemon EX Delta Species

COMPLETE SET (113) 300.00 450.00
BOOSTER BOX (36 PACKS) 700.00 1000.00
BOOSTER PACK (9 CARDS) 15.00 30.00
*REV.FOIL: .75X TO 2X BASIC CARDS
RELEASED ON OCTOBER 31, 2005
1 Beedrill DS HOLO R 2.00 6.00
2 Crobat DS HOLO R 2.00 6.00
3 Dragonite DS HOLO R 2.00 6.00
4 Espeon DS HOLO R 2.00 6.00
5 Flareon DS HOLO R 2.00 6.00
6 Gardevoir DS HOLO R 2.00 6.00
7 Jolteon DS HOLO R 2.00 6.00
8 Latias DS HOLO R 2.00 6.00
9 Latios HOLO R 2.00 6.00
10 Marowak DS HOLO R 2.00 6.00
11 Metagross DS HOLO R 2.00 6.00
12 Mewtwo DS HOLO R 5.00 12.00
13 Rayquaza DS HOLO R 2.00 6.00
14 Salamence DS HOLO R 2.00 6.00
15 Starmie DS HOLO R 2.00 6.00
16 Tyranitar DS HOLO R 2.00 6.00
17 Umbreon DS HOLO R 2.00 6.00
18 Vaporeon DS HOLO R 2.00 6.00
19 Azumarill DS R .75 2.00
20 Azurill R .75 2.00
21 Holon's Electrode R .75 2.00
22 Holon's Magneton R .75 2.00
23 Hypno R .75 2.00
24 Mightyena DS R .75 2.00
25 Porygon2 R .75 2.00
26 Rain Castform R .75 2.00
27 Sandslash DS R .75 2.00
28 Slowking R .75 2.00
29 Snow-cloud Castform R .75 2.00
30 Starmie DS R .75 2.00
31 Sunny Castform R .75 2.00
32 Swellow R .75 2.00
33 Weezing R .75 2.00
34 Castform U .30 1.00
35 Ditto U .30 1.00
36 Ditto U .30 1.00
37 Ditto U .30 1.00
38 Ditto U .30 1.00
39 Ditto (U) .30 1.00
40 Ditto U .30 1.00
41 Dragonair DS U .30 1.00
42 Dragonair DS U .30 1.00
43 Golbat U .30 1.00
44 Hariyama U .30 1.00
45 Illumise U .30 1.00
46 Kakuna U .30 1.00
47 Kirlia U .30 1.00
48 Magneton U .30 1.00
49 Metang DS U .30 1.00
50 Persian U .30 1.00
51 Pupitar DS U .30 1.00
52 Rapidash U .30 1.00
53 Shelgon DS U .30 1.00
54 Shelgon DS U .30 1.00
55 Skarmory U .30 1.00
56 Volbeat U .30 1.00
57 Bagon DS C .30 1.00
58 Bagon DS C .30 1.00
59 Beldum DS C .30 1.00
60 Cubone C .30 1.00
61 Ditto C .30 1.00
62 Ditto C .30 1.00
63 Ditto C .30 1.00
64 Ditto C .30 1.00
65 Dratini DS C .30 1.00
66 Dratini DS C .30 1.00
67 Drowzee C .30 1.00
68 Eevee DS C .30 1.00
69 Eevee C .30 1.00
70 Holon's Magnemite C .30 1.00
71 Holon's Voltorb C .30 1.00
72 Koffing C .30 1.00
73 Larvitar DS C .30 1.00
74 Magnemite C .30 1.00
75 Makuhita C .30 1.00
76 Marill C .30 1.00
77 Meowth C .30 1.00
78 Ponyta C .30 1.00
79 Poochyena C .30 1.00
80 Porygon C .30 1.00
81 Ralts C .30 1.00
82 Sandshrew C .30 1.00
83 Slowpoke C .30 1.00
84 Staryu C .30 1.00
85 Staryu C .30 1.00
86 Taillow C .30 1.00
87 Weedle C .30 1.00
88 Zubat C .30 1.00
89 Dual Ball U .30 1.00
90 Great Ball U .30 1.00
91 Holon Farmer U .30 1.00
92 Holon Lass U .30 1.00
93 Holon Mentor U .30 1.00
94 Holon Research Tower U .30 1.00
95 Holon Researcher U .30 1.00
96 Holon Ruins U .30 1.00
97 Holon Scientist U .30 1.00
98 Holon Transceiver U .30 1.00
99 Master Ball U .30 1.00
100 Super Scoop Up U .30 1.00
101 Potion C .30 1.00
102 Switch C .30 1.00
103 Darkness Energy R .30 1.00
104 Holon Energy FF R .30 1.00
105 Holon Energy GL R .30 1.00
106 Holon Energy WP R .30 1.00
107 Metal Energy R .30 1.00
108 Flareon EX HOLO R 5.00 12.00
109 Jolteon EX HOLO R 5.00 12.00
110 Vaporeon EX HOLO R 5.00 12.00
111 Groudon Gold Star HOLO R 40.00 80.00
112 Kyogre Gold Star HOLO R 40.00 80.00
113 Metagross Gold Star HOLO R 35.00 70.00
114 Azumarill SCT 2.00 6.00

2006 Pokemon EX Legend Maker

COMPLETE SET (93) 300.00 500.00
BOOSTER BOX (36 PACKS) 700.00 900.00
BOOSTER PACK (9 CARDS) 15.00 30.00
*REV.FOIL: .75X TO 2X BASIC CARDS
RELEASED ON FEBRUARY 13, 2006
1 Aerodactyl HOLO R 2.00 6.00
2 Aggron HOLO R 2.00 6.00
3 Cradily HOLO R 2.00 6.00
4 Delcatty HOLO R 2.00 6.00
5 Gengar HOLO R 2.00 6.00
6 Golem HOLO R 2.00 6.00
7 Kabutops HOLO R 2.00 6.00
8 Lapras HOLO R 2.00 6.00
9 Machamp HOLO R 2.00 6.00
10 Mew HOLO R 2.00 6.00
11 Muk HOLO R 2.00 6.00
12 Shiftry HOLO R 2.00 6.00
13 Victreebel HOLO R 2.00 6.00
14 Wailord HOLO R 2.00 6.00
15 Absol R .75 2.00
16 Girafarig R .75 2.00
17 Gorebyss R .75 2.00
18 Huntail R .75 2.00
19 Lanturn R .75 2.00
20 Lunatone R .75 2.00
21 Magmar R .75 2.00
22 Magneton R .75 2.00
23 Omastar R .75 2.00
24 Pinsir R .75 2.00
25 Solrock R .75 2.00
26 Spinda R .75 2.00
27 Torkoal R .75 2.00
28 Wobbuffet R .75 2.00
29 Anorith U .20 .50
30 Cascoon U .20 2.00
31 Dunsparce U .20 2.00
32 Electrode U .20 2.00
33 Furret U .20 2.00
34 Graveler U .20 2.00
35 Haunter U .20 2.00
36 Kabuto U .20 2.00
37 Kecleon U .20 2.00
38 Lairon U .20 2.00
39 Machoke U .20 2.00
40 Misdreavus U .20 2.00
41 Nuzleaf U .20 2.00
42 Roselia U .20 2.00
43 Sealeo U .20 2.00
44 Tangela U .20 2.00
45 Tentacruel U .20 2.00
46 Vibrava U .20 2.00
47 Weepinbell U .20 2.00
48 Aron C .20 .50
49 Bellsprout C .20 .50
50 Chinchou C .20 .50
51 Clamperl C .20 .50
52 Gastly C .20 .50
53 Geodude C .20 .50
54 Grimer C .20 .50
55 Growlithe C .20 .50
56 Lileep C .20 .50
57 Machop C .20 .50
58 Magby C .20 .50
59 Magnemite C .20 .50
60 Omanyte C .20 .50
61 Seedot C .20 .50
62 Sentret C .20 .50
63 Shuppet C .20 .50
64 Skitty C .20 .50
65 Spheal C .20 .50
66 Tentacool C .20 .50
67 Trapinch C .20 .50
68 Voltorb C .20 .50
69 Wailmer C .20 .50
70 Wurmple C .20 .50
71 Wynaut C .20 .50
72 Cursed Stone U .20 .50
73 Fieldworker U .20 .50
74 Full Flame U .20 .50
75 Giant Stump U .20 .50
76 Power Tree U .20 .50
77 Strange Cave U .20 .50
78 Claw Fossil C .20 .50
79 Mysterious Fossil C .20 .50
80 Root Fossil C .20 .50
81 Rainbow Energy R .75 2.00
82 React Energy U .20 .50
83 Arcanine EX HOLO R 10.00 25.00
84 Armaldo EX HOLO R 6.00 15.00
85 Banette EX HOLO R 4.00 10.00
86 Dustox EX HOLO R 4.00 10.00
87 Flygon EX HOLO R 5.00 12.00
88 Mew EX HOLO R 10.00 25.00
89 Walrein EX HOLO R 3.00 8.00
90 Regice Gold Star HOLO R 30.00 60.00
91 Regirock Gold Star HOLO R 30.00 60.00
92 Registeel Gold Star HOLO R 30.00 60.00
93 Pikachu DS HOLO R 5.00 12.00

2006 Pokemon EX Holon Phantoms

COMPLETE SET (111) 100.00 150.00
BOOSTER BOX (36 PACKS) 400.00 500.00
BOOSTER PACK (9 CARDS) 10.00 15.00
THEME DECK 7.00 10.00
*REV.FOIL: .75X TO 2X BASIC CARDS
RELEASED ON MAY 3, 2006
1 Armaldo HOLO R 2.00 6.00
2 Cradily HOLO R 2.00 6.00
3 Deoxys (Attack) HOLO R 2.00 6.00

4 Deoxys (Defense) HOLO R	2.00	6.00
5 Deoxys (Normal) HOLO R	2.00	6.00
6 Deoxys (Speed) HOLO R	2.00	6.00
7 Flygon HOLO R	2.00	6.00
8 Gyarados HOLO R	2.00	6.00
9 Kabutops HOLO R	2.00	6.00
10 Kingdra HOLO R	2.00	6.00
11 Latias HOLO R	2.00	6.00
12 Latios HOLO R	2.00	6.00
13 Omastar HOLO R	2.00	6.00
14 Pidgeot HOLO R	2.00	6.00
15 Raichu HOLO R	2.00	6.00
16 Rayquaza HOLO R	2.00	6.00
17 Vileplume HOLO R	2.00	6.00
18 Absol R	.75	2.00
19 Bellossom R	.75	2.00
20 Blaziken R	.75	2.00
21 Latias R	.75	2.00
22 Latios R	.75	2.00
23 Mawile R	.75	2.00
24 Mewtwo R	2.00	6.00
25 Nosepass R	.75	2.00
26 Rayquaza R	.75	2.00
27 Regice R	.75	2.00
28 Regirock R	.75	2.00
29 Registeel R	.75	2.00
30 Relicanth R	.75	2.00
31 Sableye R	.75	2.00
32 Seviper R	.75	2.00
33 Torkoal R	.75	2.00
34 Zangoose R	.75	2.00
35 Aerodactyl U	.20	.50
36 Camerupt U	.20	.50
37 Chimecho U	.20	.50
38 Claydol U	.20	.50
39 Combusken U	.20	.50
40 Donphan U	.20	.50
41 EXeggutor U	.20	.50
42 Gloom U	.20	.50
43 Golduck U	.20	.50
44 Holon's Castform U	.50	1.50
45 Lairon U	.20	.50
46 Manectric U	.20	.50
47 Masquerain U	.20	.50
48 Persian U	.20	.50
49 Pidgeotto U	.20	.50
50 Primeape U	.20	.50
51 Raichu U	.20	.50
52 Seadra U	.20	.50
53 Sharpedo U	.20	.50
54 Vibrava U	.20	.50
55 Whiscash U	.20	.50
56 Wobbuffet U	.20	.50
57 Anorith C	.10	.20
58 Aron C	.10	.20
59 Baltoy C	.10	.20
60 Barboach C	.10	.20
61 Carvanha C	.10	.20
62 Corphish C	.10	.20
63 Corphish C	.10	.20
64 Electrike C	.10	.20
65 EXeggcute C	.10	.20
66 Horsea C	.10	.20
67 Kabuto C	.10	.20
68 Lileep C	.10	.20
69 Magikarp C	.10	.20
70 Mankey C	.10	.20
71 Meowth C	.10	.20
72 Numel C	.10	.20
73 Oddish C	.10	.20
74 Omanyte C	.10	.20
75 Phanpy C	.10	.20
76 Pichu C	.20	.50
77 Pidgey C	.10	.20
78 Pikachu C	.20	.50
79 Pikachu C	.20	.50
80 Poochyena C	.10	.20
81 Psyduck C	.10	.20
82 Surskit C	.10	.20
83 Torchic C	.10	.20
84 Trapinch C	.10	.20
85 Holon Adventurer U	.20	.50
86 Holon Fossil U	.20	.50
87 Holon Lake U	.20	.50
88 Mr. Stone's Project U	.20	.50
89 Professor Cozmo's Discovery U	.20	.50
90 Rare Candy U	3.00	5.00
91 Claw Fossil C	.10	.20
92 Mysterious Fossil C	.10	.20
93 Root Fossil C	.10	.20
94 Darkness Energy R	.50	1.00
95 Metal Energy R	.50	1.00
96 Multi Energy R	.50	1.00
97 d Rainbow Energy U	.20	.50
98 Dark Metal Energy U	.20	.50
99 Crawdaunt EX HOLO R	3.00	8.00
100 Mew EX HOLO R	8.00	20.00
101 Mightyena EX HOLO R	3.00	8.00
102 Gyarados Gold Star HOLO R	100.00	150.00
103 Mewtwo Gold Star HOLO R	60.00	100.00
104 Pikachu Gold Star HOLO R	60.00	100.00
105 Grass Energy HOLO R	2.00	6.00
106 Fire Energy HOLO R	2.00	6.00
107 Water Energy HOLO R	2.00	6.00
108 Lightning Energy HOLO R	2.00	6.00
109 Psychic Energy HOLO R	2.00	6.00
110 Fighting Energy HOLO R	2.00	6.00
111 Mew HOLO R	5.00	12.00

2006 Pokemon EX Crystal Guardians

COMPLETE SET (100)	200.00	300.00
BOOSTER BOX (36 PACKS)	800.00	1000.00
BOOSTER PACK (9 CARDS)	6.00	15.00
*REV.FOIL: .75X TO 2X BASIC CARDS		
1 Banette HOLO R	3.00	6.00
2 Blastoise DS HOLO R	2.00	6.00
3 Camerupt HOLO R	3.00	6.00
4 Charizard DS HOLO R	8.00	20.00
5 Dugtrio HOLO R	3.00	6.00
6 Ludicolo DS HOLO R	3.00	6.00
7 Luvdisc HOLO R	3.00	6.00
8 Manectric HOLO R	3.00	6.00
9 Mawile HOLO R	3.00	6.00
10 Sableye HOLO R	3.00	6.00
11 Swalot HOLO R	3.00	5.00
12 Tauros HOLO R	3.00	6.00
13 Wigglytuff HOLO R	3.00	6.00
14 Blastoise R	1.00	2.00
15 Cacturne DS R	.50	1.00
16 Combusken R	.50	1.00
17 Dusclops R	.50	1.00
18 Fearow DS R	.50	1.00
19 Grovyle DS R	.50	1.00
20 Grumpig R	.50	1.00
21 Igglybuff R	.50	1.00
22 Kingler DS R	.50	1.00
23 Loudred R	.50	1.00
24 Marshtomp R	.50	1.00
25 Medicham R	.50	1.00
26 Pelipper DS R	.50	1.00
27 Swampert R	.50	1.00
28 Venusaur R	.50	1.00
29 Charmeleon U	.20	.50
30 Charmeleon DS U	.20	.50
31 Combusken U	.20	.50
32 Grovyle U	.20	.50
33 Gulpin U	.20	.50
34 Ivysaur U	.20	.50
35 Ivysaur U	.20	.50
36 Lairon U	.20	.50
37 Lombre U	.20	.50
38 Marshtomp U	.20	.50
39 Nuzleaf U	.20	.50
40 Shuppet U	.20	.50
41 Skitty U	.20	.50
42 Wartortle U	.20	.50
43 Wartortle U	.20	.50
44 Aron C	.10	.20
45 Bulbasaur C	.10	.20
46 Bulbasaur C	.10	.20
47 Cacnea C	.10	.20
48 Charmander C	.10	.20
49 Charmander DS C	.10	.20
50 Diglett C	.10	.20
51 Duskull C	.10	.20
52 Electrike C	.10	.20
53 Jigglypuff C	.10	.20
54 Krabby C	.10	.20
55 Lotad C	.10	.20
56 Meditite C	.10	.20
57 Mudkip C	.10	.20
58 Mudkip C	.10	.20
59 Numel C	.10	.20
60 Seedot C	.10	.20
61 Spearow (C)	.10	.20
62 Spoink C	.10	.20
63 Squirtle C	.10	.20
64 Squirtle C	.10	.20
65 Torchic C	.10	.20
66 Torchic C	.10	.20
67 Treecko C	.10	.20
68 Treecko DS C	.10	.20
69 Whismur C	.10	.20
70 Wingull C	.10	.20
71 Bill's Maintenance U	.20	.50
72 Castaway U	.20	.50
73 Celio's Network U	.20	.50
74 Cessation Crystal U	.20	.50
75 Crystal Beach U	.20	.50
76 Crystal Shard U	.20	.50
77 Double Full Heal U	.20	.50
78 Dual Ball U	.20	.50
79 Holon Circle U	.20	.50
80 Memory Berry U	.20	.50
81 Mysterious Shard U	.20	.50
82 Poke Ball U	.20	.50
83 PokeNav U	.20	.50
84 Warp Point U	.20	.50
85 Windstorm U	.20	.50
86 Energy Search C	.10	.20
87 Potion C	.10	.20
88 Double Rainbow Energy R	3.00	5.00
89 Aggron EX HOLO R	4.00	10.00
90 Blaziken EX HOLO R	6.00	15.00
91 Delcatty EX HOLO R	3.00	8.00
92 Exploud EX HOLO R	2.00	6.00
93 Groudon EX HOLO R	5.00	12.00
94 Jirachi EX HOLO R	3.00	8.00
95 Kyogre EX HOLO R	3.00	8.00
96 Sceptile EX DS HOLO R	6.00	15.00
97 Shiftry EX HOLO R	2.00	6.00
98 Swampert EX HOLO R	6.00	15.00
99 Alakazam Gold Star HOLO R	30.00	60.00
100 Celebi Gold Star HOLO R	30.00	60.00

2006 Pokemon EX Dragon Frontiers

COMPLETE SET (101)	400.00	600.00
BOOSTER BOX (36 PACKS)	2000.00	2500.00
BOOSTER PACK (9 CARDS)	15.00	30.00
THEME DECK	10.00	25.00
*REV.FOIL: .75X TO 2X BASIC CARDS		
RELEASED ON NOVEMBER 8, 2006		
1 Ampharos DS HOLO R	1.50	4.00
2 Feraligatr DS HOLO R	1.50	4.00
3 Heracross DS HOLO R	1.50	4.00
4 Meganium DS HOLO R	1.50	4.00
5 Milotic DS HOLO R	1.50	4.00
6 Nidoking DS HOLO R	1.50	4.00
7 Nidoqueen DS HOLO R	1.50	4.00
8 Ninetales DS HOLO R	1.50	4.00
9 Pinsir DS HOLO R	1.50	4.00
10 Snorlax DS HOLO R	1.50	4.00
11 Togetic DS HOLO R	1.50	4.00
12 Typhlosion DS HOLO R	1.50	4.00
13 Arbok DS R	.50	1.00
14 Cloyster DS R	.50	1.00
15 Dewgong DS R	.50	1.00
16 Gligar DS R	.50	1.00
17 Jynx DS R	.50	1.00
18 Ledian DS R	.50	1.00
19 Lickitung DS R	.50	1.00
20 Mantine DS R	.50	1.00
21 Quagsire DS R	.50	1.00
22 Seadra DS R	.50	1.00
23 Tropius DS R	.50	1.00
24 Vibrava DS R	.50	1.00
25 Xatu DS R	.50	1.00
26 Bayleef DS U	.20	.50
27 Croconaw DS U	.20	.50
28 Dragonair DS U	.20	.50
29 Electabuzz DS U	.20	.75
30 Flaaffy DS U	.20	.50
31 Horsea DS U	.20	.50
32 Kirlia U	.20	.50
33 Kirlia DS U	.20	.50
34 Nidorina DS U	.20	.50
35 Nidorino DS U	.20	.50
36 Quilava DS U	.20	.50
37 Seadra DS U	.20	.50
38 Shelgon DS U	.20	.50
39 Smeargle DS U	.20	.50
40 Swellow DS U	.20	.50
41 Togepi DS U	.20	.50
42 Vibrava DS U	.20	.50
43 Bagon DS C	.10	.20
44 Chikorita DS C	.10	.20
45 Cyndaquil DS C	.10	.20
46 Dratini DS C	.10	.20
47 Ekans DS C	.10	.20
48 Elekid DS C	.10	.20
49 Feebas DS C	.10	.20
50 Horsea DS C	.10	.20
51 Larvitar C	.10	.20
52 Larvitar DS C	.10	.20
53 Ledyba DS C	.10	.20
54 Mareep DS C	.10	.20
55 Natu DS C	.10	.20
56 Nidoran DS C	.10	.20
57 Nidoran DS C	.10	.20
58 Pupitar C	.10	.20
59 Pupitar DS	.10	.20
60 Ralts C	.10	.20
61 Ralts DS C	.10	.20
62 Seel DS C	.10	.20
63 Shellder DS C	.10	.20
64 Smoochum DS C	.10	.20
65 Swablu DS C	.10	.20
66 Taillow DS C	.10	.20
67 Totodile DS C	.10	.20
68 Trapinch DS C	.10	.20
69 Trapinch DS C	.10	.20
70 Vulpix DS C	.10	.20
71 Wooper DS C	.10	.20
72 Buffer Piece U	.20	.50
73 Copycat U	.20	.50
74 Holon Legacy U	.20	.50
75 Holon Mentor U	.20	.50
76 Island Hermit U	.20	.50
77 Mr. Stone's Project U	.20	.50
78 Old Rod U	.20	.50
79 Professor Elm's Training Method U	.20	.50
80 Professor Oak's Research U	.20	.50
81 Strength Charm U	.20	.50
82 TV Reporter U	.20	.50
83 Switch C	.10	.20
84 Holon Energy FF R	.50	1.00
85 Holon Energy GL R	.50	1.00
86 Holon Energy WP R	.50	1.00
87 Boost Energy U	.20	.50
88 Rainbow Energy U	.20	.50
89 Scramble Energy U	.20	.50
90 Altaria EX DS HOLO R	4.00	10.00
91 Dragonite EX DS HOLO R	6.00	15.00
92 Flygon EX DS HOLO R	6.00	15.00
93 Gardevoir EX DS HOLO R	5.00	12.00
94 Kingdra EX DS HOLO R	4.00	10.00
95 Latias EX DS HOLO R	6.00	15.00
96 Latios EX DS HOLO R	6.00	15.00
97 Rayquaza EX DS HOLO R	6.00	15.00
98 Salamence EX DS HOLO R	6.00	15.00
99 Tyranitar EX DS HOLO R	8.00	20.00
100 Charizard Gold Star DS HOLO R	150.00	250.00
101 Mew Gold Star DS HOLO R	60.00	120.00

2007 Pokemon EX Power Keepers

COMPLETE SET (108)	300.00	500.00
BOOSTER BOX (36 PACKS)	400.00	600.00
BOOSTER PACK (9 CARDS)	6.00	15.00
*REV.FOIL: .75X TO 2X BASIC CARDS		
RELEASED ON FEBRUARY 14, 2007		
1 Aggron HOLO R	1.00	2.50
2 Altaria HOLO R	1.00	2.50
3 Armaldo HOLO R	1.00	2.50
4 Banette HOLO R	1.00	2.50
5 Blaziken HOLO R	1.00	2.50
6 Charizard HOLO R	6.00	15.00
7 Cradily HOLO R	1.00	2.50
8 Delcatty HOLO R	1.00	2.50
9 Gardevoir HOLO R	1.00	2.50
10 Kabutops HOLO R	1.00	2.50
11 Machamp HOLO R	1.00	2.50
12 Raichu HOLO R	1.00	2.50
13 Slaking HOLO R	1.00	2.50
14 Dusclops R	.60	1.50
15 Lanturn R	.60	1.50
16 Magneton R	.60	1.50
17 Mawile R	.60	1.50
18 Mightyena R	.60	1.50
19 Ninetales R	.60	1.50
20 Omastar R	.60	1.50
21 Pichu R	.60	1.50
22 Sableye R	.60	1.50
23 Seviper R	.60	1.50
24 Wobbuffet R	.60	1.50
25 Zangoose R	.60	1.50
26 Anorith U	.30	.75
27 Cacturne U	.30	.75
28 Charmeleon U	.30	.75
29 Combusken U	.30	.75
30 Glalie U	.30	.75
31 Kirlia U	.30	.75
32 Lairon U	.30	.75
33 Machoke U	.30	.75
34 Medicham U	.30	.75
35 Metang U	.30	.75
36 Nuzleaf U	.30	.75
37 Sealeo U	.30	.75
38 Sharpedo U	.30	.75
39 Shelgon U	.30	.75
40 Vibrava U	.30	.75
41 Vigoroth U	.30	.75
42 Aron C	.30	.75
43 Bagon C	.30	.75
44 Baltoy C	.30	.75
45 Beldum C	.30	.75
46 Cacnea C	.30	.75
47 Carvanha C	.30	.75
48 Charmander C	.30	.75
49 Chinchou C	.30	.75
50 Duskull C	.30	.75
51 Kabuto C	.30	.75
52 Lileep C	.30	.75
53 Machop C	.30	.75
54 Magnemite C	.30	.75
55 Meditite C	.30	.75
56 Omanyte C	.30	.75
57 Pikachu C	.30	.75
58 Poochyena C	.30	.75
59 Ralts C	.30	.75
60 Seedot C	.30	.75
61 Shuppet C	.30	.75
62 Skitty C	.30	.75
63 Slakoth C	.30	.75
64 Snorunt C	.30	.75
65 Spheal C	.30	.75
66 Swablu C	.30	.75
67 Torchic C	.30	.75
68 Trapinch C	.30	.75
69 Vulpix C	.30	.75
70 Wynaut C	.30	.75
71 Battle Frontier U	.30	.75
72 Drake's Stadium U	.30	.75
73 Energy Recycle System U	.30	.75
74 Energy Removal 2 U	.30	.75
75 Energy Switch U	.30	.75
76 Glacia's Stadium U	.50	1.25
77 Great Ball U	.30	.75

78 Master Ball U .30 .75
79 Phoebe's Stadium U .30 .75
80 Professor Birch U .30 .75
81 Scott U .30 .75
82 Sidney's Stadium U .30 .75
83 Steven's Advice U .50 1.25
84 Claw Fossil C .30 .75
85 Mysterious Fossil C .30 .75
86 Root Fossil C .30 .75
87 Darkness Energy R .30 .75
88 Metal Energy R .30 .75
89 Multi Energy R .30 .75
90 Cyclone Energy U .30 .75
91 Warp Energy U .30 .75
92 Absol EX HOLO R 3.00 8.00
93 Claydol EX HOLO R 3.00 8.00
94 Flygon EX HOLO R 2.00 6.00
95 Metagross EX HOLO R 2.00 6.00
96 Salamence EX HOLO R 5.00 12.00
97 Shiftry EX HOLO R 2.00 6.00
98 Skarmory EX HOLO R 2.00 6.00
99 Walrein EX HOLO R 3.00 8.00
100 Flareon Gold Star HOLO R 30.00 60.00
101 Jolteon Gold Star HOLO R 30.00 60.00
102 Vaporeon Gold Star HOLO R 30.00 60.00
103 Grass Energy HOLO R 1.50 4.00
104 Fire Energy HOLO R 1.50 4.00
105 Water Energy HOLO R 2.50 6.00
106 Lightning Energy HOLO R 1.50 4.00
107 Psychic Energy HOLO R 1.50 4.00
108 Fighting Energy HOLO R 1.50 4.00

2007 Pokemon Diamond and Pearl

COMPLETE SET (130) 50.00 100.00
BOOSTER BOX (36 PACKS) 150.00 300.00
BOOSTER PACK (9 CARDS) 2.00 6.00
*REV.FOIL: .75X TO 2X BASIC CARDS
COLLECTOR'S TIN 18.00 22.00
RELEASED ON MAY 23, 2007
1 Dialga HOLO R 1.25 3.00
2 Dusknoir HOLO R 1.25 3.00
3 Electivire HOLO R 1.25 3.00
4 Empoleon HOLO R 1.25 3.00
5 Infernape HOLO R 1.25 3.00
6 Lucario HOLO R 1.25 3.00
7 Luxray HOLO R 1.25 3.00
8 Magnezone HOLO R 1.25 3.00
9 Manaphy HOLO R 1.25 3.00
10 Mismagius HOLO R 1.25 3.00
11 Palkia HOLO R 1.25 3.00
12 Rhyperior HOLO R 1.25 3.00
13 Roserade HOLO R 1.25 3.00
14 Shiftry HOLO R 1.25 3.00
15 Skuntank HOLO R 1.25 3.00
16 Staraptor HOLO R 1.25 3.00
17 Torterra HOLO R 1.25 3.00
18 Azumarill R .60 1.50
19 Beautifly R .60 1.50
20 Bibarel R .60 1.50
21 Carnivine R .60 1.50
22 Clefable R .60 1.50
23 Drapion R .60 1.50
24 Drifblim R .60 1.50
25 Dustox R .60 1.50
26 Floatzel R .60 1.50
27 Gengar R .60 1.50
28 Heracross R .60 1.50
29 Hippowdon R .60 1.50
30 Lopunny R .60 1.50
31 Machamp R .60 1.50
32 Medicham R .60 1.50
33 Munchlax R .60 1.50
34 Noctowl R .60 1.50
35 Pachirisu R .60 1.50
36 Purugly R .60 1.50
37 Snorlax R .60 1.50
38 Steelix R .60 1.50
39 Vespiquen R .60 1.50
40 Weavile R .60 1.50
41 Wobbuffet R .60 1.50
42 Wynaut R .60 1.50
43 Budew U .25 .60
44 Cascoon U .25 .60
45 Cherrim U .25 .60
46 Drifloon U .25 .60
47 Dusclops U .25 .60
48 Elekid U .25 .60
49 Grotle U .25 .60
50 Haunter U .25 .60
51 Hippopotas U .25 .60
52 Luxio (U) .25 .60
53 Machoke U .25 .60
54 Magneton U .25 .60
55 Mantyke U 1.75 5.00
56 Monferno U .25 .60
57 Nuzleaf U .25 .60
58 Prinplup U .25 .60
59 Rapidash U .25 .60
60 Rhydon U .25 .60
61 Riolu U .25 .60
62 Seaking U .25 .60
63 Silcoon U .25 .60
64 Staravia U .25 .60
65 Unown A U .25 .60
66 Unown B U .25 .60
67 Unown C U .25 .60
68 Unown D U .25 .60
69 Azurill C .25 .60
70 Bidoof C .25 .60
71 Bonsly C .25 .60
72 Buizel C .25 .60
73 Buneary C .25 .60
74 Chatot C .25 .60
75 Cherubi C .25 .60
76 Chimchar C .25 .60
77 Clefairy C .25 .60
78 Cleffa C .25 .60
79 Combee C .25 .60
80 Duskull C .25 .60
81 Electabuzz C .25 .60
82 Gastly C .25 .60
83 Glameow C .25 .60
84 Goldeen C .25 .60
85 Hoothoot C .25 .60
86 Machop C .25 .60
87 Magnemite C .25 .60
88 Marill C .25 .60
89 Meditite C .25 .60
90 Mime Jr. C .25 .60
91 Misdreavus C .25 .60
92 Onix C .25 .60
93 Piplup C .25 .60
94 Ponyta C .25 .60
95 Rhyhorn C .25 .60
96 Roselia C .25 .60
97 Seedot C .25 .60
98 Shinx C .25 .60
99 Skorupi C .25 .60
100 Sneasel C .25 .60
101 Starly C .25 .60
102 Stunky C .25 .60
103 Turtwig C .25 .60
104 Wurmple C .25 .60
105 Double Full Heal U .25 .60
106 Energy Restore U .25 .60
107 Energy Switch U .25 .60
108 Night Pokemon Center U .25 .60
109 PlusPower U .25 .60
110 Poke Ball U .25 .60
111 Pokedex HANDY910s U .25 .60
112 Professor Rowan U .25 .60
113 Rival U .25 .60
114 Speed Stadium U .25 .60
115 Super Scoop Up U .25 .60
116 Warp Point U .25 .60
117 Energy Search C .25 .60
118 Potion C .25 .60
119 Switch C .25 .60
120 Empoleon Lv.X HOLO R 2.00 6.00
121 Infernape Lv.X HOLO R 3.00 8.00
122 Torterra Lv.X HOLO R 2.00 6.00
123 Grass Energy .50 1.25
124 Fire Energy .50 1.25
125 Water Energy .50 1.25
126 Lightning Energy .50 1.25
127 Fighting Energy .50 1.25
128 Psychic Energy .50 1.25
129 Darkness Energy .50 1.25
130 Metal Energy .50 1.25

2007 Pokemon DP Mysterious Treasures

COMPLETE SET (124) 80.00 120.00
BOOSTER BOX (36 PACKS) 150.00 200.00
BOOSTER PACK (10 CARDS) 3.00 7.00
*REV.FOIL: .75X TO 2X BASIC CARDS
RELEASED ON AUGUST 22, 2007
1 Aggron HOLO R 1.00 2.50
2 Alakazam HOLO R 1.00 2.50
3 Ambipom HOLO R 1.00 2.50
4 Azelf HOLO R 1.00 2.50
5 Blissey HOLO R 1.00 2.50
6 Bronzong HOLO R 1.00 2.50
7 Celebi HOLO R 1.00 2.50
8 Feraligatr HOLO R 1.00 2.50
9 Garchomp HOLO R 1.00 2.50
10 Honchkrow HOLO R 1.00 2.50
11 Lumineon HOLO R 1.00 2.50
12 Magmortar HOLO R 1.00 2.50
13 Meganium HOLO R 1.00 2.50
14 Mesprit HOLO R 1.00 2.50
15 Raichu HOLO R 1.00 2.50
16 Typhlosion HOLO R 1.00 2.50
17 Tyranitar HOLO R 1.00 2.50
18 Uxie HOLO R 1.00 2.50
19 Abomasnow R .40 1.00
20 Ariados R .40 1.00
21 Bastiodon R .40 1.00
22 Chimecho R .40 1.00
23 Crobat R .40 1.00
24 Exeggutor R .40 1.00
25 Glalie R .40 1.00
26 Gyarados R .40 1.00
27 Kricketune R .40 1.00
28 Manectric R .40 1.00
29 Mantine R .40 1.00
30 Mr. Mime R .40 1.00
31 Nidoqueen R .40 1.00
32 Ninetales R .40 1.00
33 Rampardos R .40 1.00
34 Slaking R .40 1.00
35 Sudowoodo R .40 1.00
36 Toxicroak R .40 1.00
37 Unown R .40 1.00
38 Ursaring R .40 1.00
39 Walrein R .40 1.00
40 Whiscash R .40 1.00
41 Bayleef U .25 .60
42 Chingling U .25 .60
43 Cranidos U .25 .60
44 Croconaw U .25 .60
45 Dewgong U .25 .60
46 Dodrio U .25 .60
47 Dunsparce U .25 .60
48 Gabite U .25 .60
49 Girafarig U .25 .60
50 Golbat U .25 .60
51 Graveler U .25 .60
52 Happiny U .25 .60
53 Lairon U .25 .60
54 Magmar U .25 .60
55 Masquerain U .25 .60
56 Nidorina U .25 .60
57 Octillery U .25 .60
58 Parasect U .25 .60
59 Pupitar U .25 .60
60 Quilava U .25 .60
61 Sandslash U .25 .60
62 Sealeo U .25 .60
63 Shieldon U .25 .60
64 Tropius U .25 .60
65 Unown E U .25 .60
66 Unown M U .25 .60
67 Unown T U .25 .60
68 Vigoroth U .25 .60
69 Abra C .25 .60
70 Aipom C .25 .60
71 Aron C .25 .60
72 Barboach C .25 .60
73 Bidoof C .25 .60
74 Bronzor C .25 .60
75 Buizel C .25 .60
76 Chansey C .25 .60
77 Chikorita C .25 .60
78 Croagunk C .25 .60
79 Cyndaquil C .25 .60
80 Doduo C .25 .60
81 Electrike C .25 .60
82 Exeggcute C .25 .60
83 Finneon C .25 .60
84 Geodude C .25 .60
85 Gible C .25 .60
86 Kricketot C .25 .60
87 Larvitar C .25 .60
88 Magby C .25 .60
89 Magikarp C .25 .60
90 Murkrow C .25 .60
91 Nidoran C .25 .60
92 Paras C .25 .60
93 Pichu C .25 .60
94 Pikachu C .25 .60
95 Remoraid C .25 .60
96 Sandshrew C .25 .60
97 Seel C .25 .60
98 Shinx C .25 .60
99 Slakoth C .25 .60
100 Snorunt C .25 .60
101 Snover C .25 .60
102 Spheal C .25 .60
103 Spinarak C .25 .60
104 Surskit C .25 .60
105 Teddiursa C .25 .60
106 Totodile C .25 .60
107 Vulpix C .25 .60
108 Zubat C .25 .60
109 Bebe's Search U .25 .60
110 Dusk Ball U .25 .60
111 Fossil Excavator U .25 .60
112 Lake Boundary U .25 .60
113 Night Maintenance U .25 .60
114 Quick Ball U .25 .60
115 Team Galactic's Wager U .25 .60
116 Armor Fossil C .25 .60
117 Skull Fossil C .25 .60
118 Multi Energy R .25 .60
119 Darkness Energy U .25 .60
120 Metal Energy U .25 .60
121 Electivire Lv.X HOLO R 2.00 6.00
122 Lucario Lv.X HOLO R 2.00 6.00
123 Magmortar Lv.X HOLO R 3.00 8.00
124 Time Space Distortion HOLO SCR 2.00 6.00

2007 Pokemon DP Secret Wonders

COMPLETE SET (132) 60.00 100.00
BOOSTER BOX (36 PACKS) 150.00 200.00
BOOSTER PACK (9 CARDS) 2.50 6.00
*REV.FOIL: .75X TO 2X BASIC CARDS
RELEASED ON NOVEMBER 7, 2007
1 Ampharos HOLO R 1.50 4.00
2 Blastoise HOLO R 1.50 4.00
3 Charizard HOLO R 4.00 10.00
4 Entei HOLO R 1.50 4.00
5 Flygon HOLO R 1.50 4.00
6 Gallade HOLO R 1.50 4.00
7 Gardevoir HOLO R 2.00 6.00
8 Gastrodon East Sea HOLO R 1.50 4.00
9 Gastrodon West Sea HOLO R 1.50 4.00
10 Ho-Oh HOLO R 1.50 4.00
11 Jumpluff HOLO R 1.50 4.00
12 Lickilicky HOLO R 1.50 4.00
13 Ludicolo HOLO R 1.50 4.00
14 Lugia HOLO R 4.00 10.00
15 Mew HOLO R 3.00 8.00
16 Raikou HOLO R 2.00 6.00
17 Roserade HOLO R 1.50 4.00
18 Salamence HOLO R 1.50 4.00
19 Suicune HOLO R 1.50 4.00
20 Venusaur HOLO R 1.50 4.00
21 Absol R .75 2.00
22 Arcanine R .75 2.00
23 Banette R .75 2.00
24 Dugtrio R .75 2.00
25 Electivire R .75 2.00
26 Electrode R .75 2.00
27 Furret R .75 2.00
28 Golduck R .75 2.00
29 Golem R .75 2.00
30 Jynx R .75 2.00
31 Magmortar R .75 2.00
32 Minun R .75 2.00
33 Mothim R .75 2.00
34 Nidoking R .75 2.00
35 Pidgeot R .75 2.00
36 Plusle R .75 2.00
37 Sharpedo R .75 2.00
38 Sunflora R .75 2.00
39 Unown S R .75 2.00
40 Weavile R .75 2.00
41 Wormadam Plant Cloak R .75 2.00
42 Wormadam Sandy Cloak R .75 2.00
43 Wormadam Trash Cloak R .75 2.00
44 Xatu R .75 2.00
45 Breloom U .25 .60
46 Charmeleon U .25 .60
47 Cloyster U .25 .60
48 Donphan U .25 .60
49 Farfetch'd U .25 .60
50 Flaaffy U .25 .60
51 Ivysaur U .25 .60
52 Kecleon U .25 .60
53 Kirlia U .25 .60
54 Lombre U .25 .60
55 Miltank U .25 .60
56 Muk U .25 .60
57 Nidorino U .25 .60
58 Pidgeotto U .25 .60
59 Pinsir U .25 .60
60 Quagsire U .25 .60
61 Raticate U .25 .60
62 Roselia U .25 .60
63 Sableye U .25 .60
64 Shelgon U .25 .60
65 Skiploom U .25 .60
66 Smeargle U .25 .60
67 Smoochum U .25 .60
68 Unown K U .25 .60
69 Unown N U .25 .60
70 Unown O U .25 .60
71 Unown X U .25 .60
72 Unown Z U .25 .60
73 Venomoth U .25 .60
74 Vibrava U .25 .60
75 Wartortle U .25 .60
76 Bagon C .25 .60
77 Bulbasaur C .25 .60
78 Burmy Plant Cloak C .25 .60
79 Burmy Sandy Cloak C .25 .60
80 Burmy Trash Cloak C .25 .60
81 Carvanha C .25 .60
82 Charmander C .25 .60
83 Clefairy C .25 .60
84 Corsola C .25 .60
85 Diglett C .25 .60
86 Duskull C .25 .60
87 Electabuzz C .25 .60
88 Grimer C .25 .60
89 Growlithe C .25 .60
90 Hoppip C .25 .60
91 Lickitung C .25 .60
92 Lotad C .25 .60
93 Magmar C .25 .60
94 Mareep C .25 .60
95 Murkrow C .25 .60
96 Natu C .25 .60
97 Nidoran C .25 .60
98 Phanpy C .25 .60
99 Pidgey C .25 .60
100 Psyduck C .25 .60

101 Qwilfish C .25 .60
102 Ralts C .25 .60
103 Rattata C .25 .60
104 Sentret C .25 .60
105 Shellder C .25 .60
106 Shellos East Sea C .25 .60
107 Shellos West Sea C .25 .60
108 Shroomish C .25 .60
109 Shuckle C .25 .60
110 Shuppet C .25 .60
111 Spinda C .25 .60
112 Squirtle C .25 .60
113 Stantler C .25 .60
114 Sunkern C .25 .60
115 Trapinch C .25 .60
116 Venonat C .25 .60
117 Voltorb C .25 .60
118 Wooper C .25 .60
119 Bebe's Search U .50 1.25
120 Night Maintenance U .25 .60
121 PlusPower U .25 .60
122 Professor Oak's Visit U .25 .60
123 Professor Rowan U .25 .60
124 Rival U .25 .60
125 Roseanne's Research U .75 2.00
126 Team Galactic's Mars U .25 .60
127 Potion C .25 .60
128 Switch C .25 .60
129 Darkness Energy U .25 .60
130 Metal Energy U .25 .60
131 Gardevoir LV.X HOLO R 2.50 6.00
132 Honchkrow LV.X HOLO R 2.50 6.00

2008 Pokemon DP Great Encounters

COMPLETE SET (106) 60.00 100.00
BOOSTER BOX (36 PACKS) 150.00 200.00
BOOSTER PACK (10 CARDS) 2.00 6.00
*REV.FOIL: .75X TO 2X BASIC CARDS
RELEASED FEBRUARY 13, 2008
1 Blaziken HOLO R 1.25 3.00
2 Cresselia HOLO R 1.25 3.00
3 Darkrai HOLO R 1.25 3.00
4 Darkrai HOLO R 1.25 3.00
5 Pachirisu HOLO R 1.25 3.00
6 Porygon-Z HOLO R 1.25 3.00
7 Rotom HOLO R 1.25 3.00
8 Sceptile HOLO R 1.50 4.00
9 Swampert HOLO R 1.25 3.00
10 Tangrowth HOLO R 1.25 3.00
11 Togekiss HOLO R 1.25 3.00
12 Altaria R 1.00 2.50
13 Beedrill R 1.00 2.50
14 Butterfree R 1.00 2.50
15 Claydol R 1.00 2.50
16 Dialga R 1.00 2.50
17 Exploud R 1.00 2.50
18 Houndoom R 1.00 2.50
19 Hypno R 1.00 2.50
20 Kingler R 1.00 2.50
21 Lapras R 1.00 2.50
22 Latias R 1.00 2.50
23 Latios R 1.00 2.50
24 Mawile R 1.00 2.50
25 Milotic R 1.00 2.50
26 Palkia R 1.00 2.50
27 Primeape R 1.00 2.50
28 Slowking R 1.00 2.50
29 Unown H R 1.00 2.50
30 Wailord R 1.00 2.50
31 Weezing R 1.00 2.50
32 Wigglytuff R 1.00 2.50
33 Arbok U .30 .75
34 Cacturne U .30 .75
35 Combusken U .30 .75
36 Delibird U .30 .75
37 Floatzel U .30 .75
38 Gorebyss U .30 .75
39 Granbull U .30 .75
40 Grovyle U .30 .75
41 Hariyama U .30 .75
42 Huntail U .30 .75
43 Linoone U .30 .75
44 Loudred U .30 .75
45 Magcargo U .30 .75
46 Marshtomp U .30 .75
47 Metapod U .30 .75
48 Pelipper U .30 .75
49 Porygon2 U .50 1.25
50 Purugly U .30 .75
51 Relicanth U .30 .75
52 Seviper U .30 .75
53 Skarmory U .30 .75
54 Slowbro U .30 .75
55 Togetic U .30 .75
56 Unown F U .30 .75
57 Unown G U .30 .75
58 Wailmer U .30 .75
59 Zangoose U .30 .75
60 Baltoy C .75 2.00
61 Buizel C .30 .75
62 Cacnea C .30 .75
63 Caterpie C .30 .75
64 Clamperl C .30 .75
65 Drowzee C .30 .75
66 Ekans C .30 .75
67 Feebas C .30 .75
68 Glameow C .30 .75
69 Houndour C .30 .75
70 Igglybuff C .30 .75
71 Illumise C .30 .75
72 Jigglypuff C .30 .75
73 Kakuna C .30 .75
74 Koffing C .30 .75
75 Krabby C .30 .75
76 Lunatone C .30 .75
77 Luvdisc C .30 .75
78 Makuhita C .30 .75
79 Mankey C .30 .75
80 Mudkip C .30 .75
81 Porygon C .30 .75
82 Slowpoke C .30 .75
83 Slugma C .30 .75
84 Snubbull C .30 .75
85 Solrock C .30 .75
86 Swablu C .30 .75
87 Tangela C .30 .75
88 Togepi C .30 .75
89 Torchic C .30 .75
90 Treecko C .30 .75
91 Unown L C .30 .75
92 Volbeat C .30 .75
93 Weedle C .30 .75
94 Whismur C .30 .75
95 Wingull C .30 .75
96 Zigzagoon C .30 .75
97 Amulet Coin U .30 .75
98 Felicity's Drawing U .30 .75
99 Leftovers U .30 .75
100 Moonlight Stadium U .75 2.00
101 Premier Ball U .30 .75
102 Rare Candy U 1.25 3.00
103 Cresselia LV.X HOLO R 2.00 6.00
104 Darkrai LV.X HOLO R 3.00 8.00
105 Dialga LV.X HOLO R 2.00 6.00
106 Palkia LV.X HOLO R 2.00 6.00

2008 Pokemon DP Majestic Dawn

COMPLETE SET (100) 85.00 150.00
BOOSTER BOX (36 PACKS) 200.00 300.00
BOOSTER PACK (10 CARDS) 2.50 6.00
*REV.FOIL: .75X TO 2X BASIC CARDS
RELEASED ON MAY 21, 2008
1 Articuno HOLO R 2.00 5.00
2 Cresselia HOLO R 2.00 5.00
3 Darkrai HOLO R 2.00 5.00
4 Dialga HOLO R 2.00 5.00
5 Glaceon HOLO R 3.00 8.00
6 Kabutops HOLO R 2.00 5.00
7 Leafeon HOLO R 2.50 6.00
8 Manaphy HOLO R 2.00 5.00
9 Mewtwo HOLO R 4.00 10.00
10 Moltres HOLO R 2.00 5.00
11 Palkia HOLO R 2.00 5.00
12 Phione HOLO R 2.00 5.00
13 Rotom HOLO R 2.00 5.00
14 Zapdos HOLO R 2.00 5.00
15 Aerodactyl R 1.25 3.00
16 Bronzong R 1.25 3.00
17 Empoleon R 1.25 3.00
18 Espeon R 1.25 3.00
19 Flareon R 1.25 3.00
20 Glaceon R 1.25 3.00
21 Hippowdon R 1.25 3.00
22 Infernape R 1.25 3.00
23 Jolteon R 1.25 3.00
24 Leafeon R 1.25 3.00
25 Minun R 1.25 3.00
26 Omastar R 1.25 3.00
27 Phione R 1.25 3.00
28 Plusle R 1.25 3.00
29 Scizor R 1.25 3.00
30 Torterra R 1.25 3.00
31 Toxicroak R 1.25 3.00
32 Umbreon R 2.00 6.00
33 Unown P R 1.25 3.00
34 Vaporeon R 1.25 3.00
35 Ambipom U .30 .75
36 Fearow U .30 .75
37 Grotle U .30 .75
38 Kangaskhan U .30 .75
39 Lickitung U .30 .75
40 Manectric U .30 .75
41 Monferno U .30 .75
42 Mothim U .30 .75
43 Pachirisu U .30 .75
44 Prinplup U .30 .75
45 Raichu U .30 .75
46 Scyther U .30 .75
47 Staravia U .30 .75
48 Sudowoodo U .30 .75
49 Unown Q U .30 .75
50 Aipom C .25 .60
51 Aipom C .25 .75
52 Bronzor C .25 .75
53 Buneary C .25 .75
54 Burmy Sand Cloak C .25 .75
55 Chatot C .25 .60
56 Chimchar C .25 .75
57 Chimchar C .25 .75
58 Chingling C .25 .75
59 Combee C .25 .75
60 Croagunk C .25 .75
61 Drifloon C .25 .75
62 Eevee C .25 .75
63 Eevee C .25 .75
64 Electrike C .25 .75
65 Glameow C .25 .75
66 Hippopotas C .25 .75
67 Kabuto C .25 .75
68 Munchlax C .25 .75
69 Omanyte C .25 .75
70 Pikachu C .25 .75
71 Piplup C .25 .75
72 Piplup C .25 .75
73 Shellos East Sea C .25 .75
74 Spearow C .25 .75
75 Starly C .25 .75
76 Stunky C .25 .75
77 Turtwig C .25 .75
78 Turtwig C .25 .75
79 Dawn Stadium U .25 .75
80 Dusk Ball U .25 .75
81 Energy Restore U .25 .75
82 Fossil Excavator U .25 .75
83 Mom's Kindness U .25 .75
84 Old Amber U .25 .75
85 Poke Ball U .25 .75
86 Quick Ball U .25 .75
87 Super Scoop Up U .25 .75
88 Warp Point C .25 .75
89 Dome Fossil C .25 .75
90 Energy Search C .25 .75
91 Helix Fossil C .25 .75
92 Call Energy U 2.00 6.00
93 Darkness Energy U .25 .75
94 Health Energy U .25 .75
95 Metal Energy U .25 .75
96 Recover Energy U .25 .75
97 Garchomp Lv X HOLO R 4.00 10.00
98 Glaceon Lv X HOLO R 8.00 20.00
99 Leafeon Lv X HOLO R 10.00 25.00
100 Porygon Z Lv X HOLO R 3.00 8.00

2008 Pokemon DP Legends Awakened

COMPLETE SET (146) 100.00 150.00
BOOSTER BOX (36 PACKS) 180.00 250.00
BOOSTER PACK (10 CARDS) 2.00 6.00
*REV.FOIL: .75X TO 2X BASIC CARDS
RELEASED ON AUGUST 20, 2008
1 Deoxys Normal Form HOLO R 1.50 4.00
2 Dragonite HOLO R 2.00 6.00
3 Froslass HOLO R 1.50 4.00
4 Giratina HOLO R 1.50 4.00
5 Gliscor HOLO R 1.50 4.00
6 Heatran HOLO R 1.50 4.00
7 Kingdra HOLO R 1.50 4.00
8 Luxray HOLO R 1.50 4.00
9 Mamoswine HOLO R 1.50 4.00
10 Metagross HOLO R 1.50 4.00
11 Mewtwo HOLO R 2.00 6.00
12 Politoed HOLO R 1.50 4.00
13 Probopass HOLO R 1.50 4.00
14 Rayquaza HOLO R 1.50 4.00
15 Regigigas HOLO R 1.50 4.00
16 Spiritomb HOLO R 1.50 4.00
17 Yanmega HOLO R 1.50 4.00
18 Armaldo R 1.50 4.00
19 Azelf R 2.00 5.00
20 Bellossom R 1.00 2.50
21 Cradily R 1.00 2.50
22 Crawdaunt R 1.00 2.50
23 Delcatty R 1.00 2.50
24 Deoxys Attack Form R 1.00 2.50
25 Deoxys Defense Form R 1.00 2.50
26 Deoxys Speed Form R 1.00 2.50
27 Ditto R 1.00 2.50
28 Forretress R 1.00 2.50
29 Groudon R 1.00 2.50
30 Heatran R 1.00 2.50
31 Jirachi R 1.00 2.50
32 Kyogre R 1.00 2.50
33 Lopunny R 1.00 2.50
34 Mesprit R 1.25 3.00
35 Poliwrath R 1.00 2.50
36 Regice R 1.00 2.50
37 Regigigas R 1.00 2.50
38 Regirock R 1.00 2.50
39 Registeel R 1.00 2.50
40 Shedinja R 1.00 2.50
41 Torkoal R 1.00 2.50
42 Unown ! R 1.00 2.50
43 Uxie R 2.00 5.00
44 Victreebel R 1.00 2.50
45 Vileplume R 1.00 2.50
46 Anorith U .30 .75
47 Camerupt U .30 .75
48 Castform U .30 .75
49 Castform Rain Form U .30 .75
50 Castform Snow-Cloud Form U .30 .75
51 Castform Sunny Form U .30 .75
52 Dragonair U .30 .75
53 Drifblim U .30 .75
54 Exeggutor U .30 .75
55 Gliscor U .30 .75
56 Grumpig U .30 .75
57 Houndoom U .30 .75
58 Lanturn U .30 .75
59 Lanturn U .30 .75
60 Ledian U .30 .75
61 Lucario U .30 .75
62 Luxio U .30 .75
63 Marowak U .30 .75
64 Metang U .30 .75
65 Metang U .30 .75
66 Mightyena U .30 .75
67 Ninjask U .30 .75
68 Persian U .30 .75
69 Piloswine U .30 .75
70 Seadra U .30 .75
71 Starmie U .30 .75
72 Swalot U .30 .75
73 Swellow U .30 .75
74 Tauros U .30 .75
75 Tentacruel U .30 .75
76 Unown J U .30 .75
77 Unown R U .30 .75
78 Unown U U .30 .75
79 Unown V U .30 .75
80 Unown W U .30 .75
81 Unown Y U .30 .75
82 Unown ? U .30 .75
83 Beldum C .25 .60
84 Beldum C .25 .60
85 Bellsprout C .25 .60
86 Buneary C .25 .60
87 Chinchou C .25 .60
88 Chinchou C .25 .60
89 Corphish C .25 .60
90 Cubone C .25 .60
91 Dratini C .25 .60
92 Drifloon C .25 .60
93 Exeggcute C .25 .60
94 Gligar C .25 .60
95 Gligar C .25 .60
96 Gloom C .25 .60
97 Gloom C .25 .60
98 Gulpin C .25 .60
99 Hitmonchan C .25 .60
100 Hitmonlee C .25 .60
101 Hitmontop C .25 .60
102 Horsea C .25 .60
103 Houndour C .25 .60
104 Ledyba C .25 .60
105 Lileep C .25 .60
106 Meowth C .25 .60
107 Misdreavus C .25 .60
108 Nincada C .25 .60
109 Nosepass C .25 .60
110 Numel C .25 .60
111 Oddish C .25 .60
112 Oddish C .25 .60
113 Pineco C .25 .60
114 Poliwag C .25 .60
115 Poliwhirl C .25 .60
116 Poochyena C .25 .60
117 Riolu C .25 .60
118 Shinx C .25 .60
119 Skitty C .25 .60
120 Sneasel C .25 .60
121 Spoink C .25 .60
122 Staryu C .25 .60
123 Swinub C .25 .60
124 Taillow C .25 .60
125 Tentacool C .25 .60
126 Tyrogue C .25 .60
127 Weepinbell C .25 .60
128 Yanma C .25 .60
129 Bubble Coat U .25 .60
130 Buck's Training U .25 .60
131 Cynthia's Feelings U .25 .60
132 Energy Pickup U .25 .60
133 Poké Radar U .25 .60
134 Snowpoint Temple U .25 .60
135 Stark Mountain U .25 .60
136 Technical Machine TS-1 U .25 .60
137 Technical Machine TS-2 U .25 .60
138 Claw Fossil C .25 .60
139 Root Fossil C .25 .60
140 Azelf LV.X HOLO R 4.00 10.00
141 Gliscor LV.X HOLO R 3.00 8.00
142 Magnezone LV.X HOLO R 3.00 8.00
143 Mesprit LV.X HOLO R 6.00 15.00
144 Mewtwo LV.X HOLO R .25 .60
145 Rhyperior LV.X HOLO R 2.50 6.00
146 Uxie LV.X HOLO R 8.00 20.00

2008 Pokemon DP Stormfront

COMPLETE SET (103)	100.00	150.00
BOOSTER BOX (36 PACKS)	200.00	300.00
BOOSTER PACK (10 CARDS)	6.00	8.00
*REV.FOIL: .75X TO 2X BASIC CARDS		
RELEASED NOVEMBER 5, 2008		
1 Dusknoir HOLO R	1.25	3.00
2 Empoleon HOLO R	1.25	3.00
3 Infernape HOLO R	1.25	3.00
4 Lumineon HOLO R	1.25	3.00
5 Magnezone HOLO R	1.25	3.00
6 Magnezone HOLO R	1.25	3.00
7 Mismagius HOLO R	1.25	3.00
8 Raichu HOLO R	1.25	3.00
9 Regigigas HOLO R	1.25	3.00
10 Sceptile HOLO R	1.25	3.00
11 Torterra HOLO R	1.25	3.00
12 Abomasnow R	1.25	3.00
13 Bronzong R	.60	1.50
14 Cherrim R	.60	1.50
15 Drapion R	.60	1.50
16 Drifblim R	.60	1.50
17 Dusknoir R	.60	1.50
18 Gengar R	3.00	8.00
19 Gyarados R	.60	1.50
20 Machamp R	1.25	3.00
21 Mamoswine R	.60	1.50
22 Rapidash R	.60	1.50
23 Roserade R	.60	1.50
24 Salamence R	.60	1.50
25 Scizor R	.60	1.50
26 Skuntank R	.60	1.50
27 Staraptor R	.60	1.50
28 Steelix R	3.00	8.00
29 Tangrowth R	.60	1.50
30 Tyranitar R	.60	1.50
31 Vespiquen R	.60	1.50
32 Bibarel U	.30	.75
33 Budew U	.30	.75
34 Dusclops U	.30	.75
35 Dusclops U	.30	.75
36 Electrode U	.30	.75
37 Electrode U	.30	.75
38 Farfetch'd U	.30	.75
39 Grovyle U	.30	.75
40 Haunter U	.30	.75
41 Machoke U	.30	.75
42 Magneton U	.30	.75
43 Magneton U	.30	.75
44 Miltank U	.30	.75
45 Pichu U	.30	.75
46 Piloswine U	.30	.75
47 Pupitar U	.30	.75
48 Sableye U	.30	.75
49 Scyther U	.30	.75
50 Shelgon U	.30	.75
51 Skarmory U	.30	.75
52 Staravia U	.30	.75
53 Bagon C	.30	.75
54 Bidoof C	.30	.75
55 Bronzor C	.30	.75
56 Cherubi C	.30	.75
57 Combee C	.30	.75
58 Drifloon C	.30	.75
59 Duskull C	.30	.75
60 Duskull C	.30	.75
61 Finneon C	.30	.75
62 Gastly C	.30	.75
63 Larvitar C	.30	.75
64 Machop C	.30	.75
65 Magikarp C	.30	.75
66 Magnemite C	.30	.75
67 Magnemite C	.30	.75
68 Misdreavus C	.30	.75
69 Onix C	.30	.75
70 Pikachu C	.30	.75
71 Ponyta C	.30	.75
72 Roselia C	.30	.75
73 Skorupi C	.30	.75
74 Snover C	.30	.75
75 Starly C	.30	.75
76 Stunky C	.30	.75
77 Swinub C	.30	.75
78 Tangela C	.30	.75
79 Treecko C	.30	.75
80 Voltorb C	.30	.75
81 Voltorb C	.30	.75
82 Conductive Quarry U	.30	.75
83 Energy Link U	.30	.75
84 Energy Switch U	.30	.75
85 Great Ball U	.30	.75
86 Luxury Ball U	.75	2.00
87 Marley's Request U	.30	.75
88 Poké Blower U	.30	.75
89 Poké Drawer U	.50	1.50
90 Poké Healer U	.30	.75
91 Premier Ball U	.30	.75
92 Potion C	.30	.75
93 Switch C	.30	.75
94 Cyclone Energy U	.30	.75
95 Warp Energy U	.30	.75
96 Dusknoir LV.X HOLO R	3.00	8.00
97 Heatran LV.X HOLO R	3.00	8.00
98 Machamp LV.X HOLO R	2.50	7.00
99 Raichu LV.X HOLO R	8.00	15.00
100 Regigigas LV.X HOLO R	3.00	8.00
101 Charmander HOLO R	6.00	15.00
102 Charmeleon HOLO R	5.00	12.00
103 Charizard HOLO R	15.00	30.00
SH1 Drifloon UR	3.00	8.00
SH2 Duskull UR	6.00	15.00
SH3 Voltorb	4.00	10.00

2009 Pokemon Platinum

COMPLETE SET (130)	50.00	100.00
BOOSTER BOX (36 PACKS)	150.00	200.00
BOOSTER PACK (10 CARDS)	5.00	8.00
*REV.FOIL: .75X TO 2X BASIC CARDS		
RELEASED FEBRUARY 11, 2009		
1 Ampharos HOLO R	1.50	4.00
2 Blastoise HOLO R	1.50	4.00
3 Blaziken HOLO R	1.50	4.00
4 Delcatty HOLO R	.75	2.00
5 Dialga HOLO R	.75	2.00
6 Dialga HOLO R	.75	2.00
7 Dialga G HOLO R	2.00	5.00
8 Gardevoir HOLO R	.75	2.00
9 Giratina HOLO R	.75	2.00
10 Giratina HOLO R	1.25	3.00
11 Manectric HOLO R	.75	2.00
12 Palkia G HOLO R	1.50	4.00
13 Rampardos HOLO R	1.25	3.00
14 Shaymin HOLO R	.75	2.00
15 Shaymin HOLO R	.75	2.00
16 Slaking HOLO R	.75	2.00
17 Weavile G HOLO R	1.25	3.00
18 Altaria R	.50	1.00
19 Banette R	.50	1.00
20 Bastiodon R	.50	1.00
21 Beautifly R	.50	1.00
22 Blissey R	.50	1.00
23 Dialga R	.50	1.00
24 Dugtrio R	.50	1.00
25 Dustox R	.50	1.00
26 Empoleon R	.50	1.00
27 Giratina R	.50	1.00
28 Giratina R	.50	1.00
29 Golduck R	.50	1.00
30 Gyarados G R	.50	1.00
31 Infernape R	.50	1.00
32 Kricketune R	.50	1.00
33 Lickilicky R	.50	1.00
34 Ludicolo R	.50	1.00
35 Luvdisc R	.50	1.00
36 Ninetales R	.50	1.00
37 Palkia R	.50	1.00
38 Shaymin R	.50	1.00
39 Torterra R	.50	1.00
40 Toxicroak G R	.50	1.00
41 Bronzong G U	.20	.50
42 Cacturne U	.20	.50
43 Carnivine U	.20	.50
44 Cascoon U	.20	.50
45 Combusken U	.20	.50
46 Cranidos U	.20	.50
47 Crobat G U	.20	.50
48 Flaaffy U	.20	.50
49 Grotle U	.20	.50
50 Houndoom G U	.20	.50
51 Kirlia U	.20	.50
52 Lombre U	.20	.50
53 Lucario U	.20	.50
54 Mightyena U	.20	.50
55 Mismagius U	.20	.50
56 Monferno U	.20	.50
57 Muk U	.20	.50
58 Octillery U	.20	.50
59 Prinplup U	.20	.50
60 Probopass U	.20	.50
61 Seviper U	.20	.50
62 Shieldon U	.20	.50
63 Silcoon (U)	.20	.50
64 Vigoroth U	.20	.50
65 Wartortle U	.20	.50
66 Zangoose U	.20	.50
67 Cacnea C	.10	.20
68 Carnivine C	.10	.20
69 Chansey C	.10	.20
70 Chimchar C	.10	.20
71 Combee C	.10	.20
72 Diglett C	.10	.20
73 Dunsparce C	.10	.20
74 Electrike C	.10	.20
75 Grimer C	.10	.20
76 Happiny C	.10	.20
77 Honchkrow G C	.10	.20
78 Kricketot C	.10	.20
79 Lapras C	.10	.20
80 Lickitung C	.10	.20
81 Lotad C	.10	.20
82 Mareep C	.10	.20
83 Misdreavus C	.10	.20
84 Nosepass C	.10	.20
85 Piplup C	.10	.20
86 Poochyena C	.10	.20
87 Psyduck C	.10	.20
88 Purugly G C	.10	.20
89 Ralts C	.10	.20
90 Remoraid C	.10	.20
91 Riolu C	.10	.20
92 Shuppet C	.10	.20
93 Skitty C	.10	.20
94 Skuntank G C	.10	.20
95 Slakoth C	.10	.20
96 Squirtle C	.10	.20
97 Swablu C	.10	.20
98 Tauros C	.10	.20
99 Torchic C	.10	.20
100 Torkoal C	.10	.20
101 Turtwig C	.10	.20
102 Vulpix C	.10	.20
103 Wurmple C	.10	.20
104 Broken Time-Space U	.20	.50
105 Cyrus's Conspiracy U	.20	.50
106 Galactic HQ U	.20	.50
107 Level Max U	.20	.50
108 Life Herb U	.20	.50
109 Looker's Investigation U	.20	.50
110 Memory Berry U	.20	.50
111 Miasma Valley U	.20	.50
112 Pluspower U	.20	.50
113 Poke Ball U	.20	.50
114 Pokedex Handy 910s U	.20	.50
115 Pokemon Rescue U	.20	.50
116 Energy Gain U	.20	.50
117 Power Spray U	.20	.50
118 Poke Turn U	.20	.50
119 Armor Fossil C	.10	.20
120 Skull Fossil C	.10	.20
121 Rainbow Energy U	.20	.50
122 Dialga G LV.X HOLO R	3.00	8.00
123 Drapion LV.X HOLO R	2.50	6.00
124 Giratina LV.X HOLO R	3.00	8.00
125 Palkia G LV.X HOLO R	2.00	5.00
126 Shaymin LV.X HOLO R	3.00	8.00
127 Shaymin LV.X HOLO R	3.00	8.00
128 Electabuzz HOLO R	.75	2.00
129 Hitmonchan HOLO R	.75	2.00
130 Scyther HOLO R	1.25	3.00
SH4 Lotad HOLO R	1.25	3.00
SH5 Swablu HOLO R	1.50	4.00
SH6 Vulpix HOLO R	4.00	10.00

2009 Pokemon Platinum Rising Rivals

COMPLETE SET (114)	150.00	200.00
BOOSTER BOX (36 PACKS)	250.00	350.00
BOOSTER PACK (10 CARDS)	3.00	8.00
*REV.FOIL: .75X TO 2X BASIC CARDS		
RELEASED ON MAY 20, 2009		
1 Arcanine HOLO R	1.25	3.00
2 Bastiodon GL HOLO R	1.25	3.00
3 Darkrai G HOLO R	1.25	3.00
4 Floatzel GL HOLO R	1.25	3.00
5 Flygon HOLO R	1.25	3.00
6 Froslass GL HOLO R	1.25	3.00
7 Jirachi HOLO R	1.25	3.00
8 Lucario GL HOLO R	1.25	3.00
9 Luxray GL HOLO R	1.25	3.00
10 Mismagius GL HOLO R	1.25	3.00
11 Rampardos GL HOLO R	1.25	3.00
12 Roserade GL HOLO R	1.25	3.00
13 Shiftry HOLO R	1.25	3.00
14 Aggron R	.50	1.00
15 Beedrill R	.50	1.00
16 Bronzong 4 R	.50	1.00
17 Drapion 4 R	.50	1.00
18 Espeon 4 R	.50	1.00
19 Flareon R	1.00	2.00
20 Gallade 4 R	.50	1.00
21 Gastrodon East Sea R	.50	1.00
22 Gastrodon West Sea R	.50	1.00
23 Golem 4 R	.50	1.00
24 Heracross 4 R	.50	1.00
25 Hippowdon R	.50	1.00
26 Jolteon R	1.00	2.00
27 Mamoswine GL R	.50	1.00
28 Mr. Mime 4 R	.50	1.00
29 Nidoking R	.50	1.00
30 Nidoqueen R	.50	1.00
31 Raichu GL R	.50	1.00
32 Rhyperior 4 R	.50	1.00
33 Snorlax R	.50	1.00
34 Vaporeon R	.50	1.00
35 Vespiquen 4 R	.50	1.00
36 Walrein R	.50	1.00
37 Yanmega 4 R	.50	1.00
38 Alakazam 4 U	.20	.50
39 Electrode G U	.20	.50
40 Gengar GL U	.20	.50
41 Glaceon U	.75	2.00
42 Hippowdon 4 U	.25	.75
43 Infernape 4 U	.20	.50
44 Lairon U	.20	.50
45 Leafeon U	.20	.50
46 Machamp GL U	.20	.50
47 Rapidash 4 U	.20	.50
48 Scizor 4 U	.20	.50
49 Sharpedo U	.20	.50
50 Starmie U	.20	.50
51 Steelix GL U	.20	.50
52 Tropius U	.20	.50
53 Vibrava U	.20	.50
54 Whiscash 4 U	.20	.50
55 Aerodactyl GL C	.10	.20
56 Ambipom G C	.10	.20
57 Aron C	.10	.20
58 Carvanha C	.10	.20
59 Eevee C	.75	2.00
60 Flareon 4 C	.10	.20
61 Forretress G C	.10	.20
62 Gliscor 4 C	.10	.20
63 Growlithe C	.10	.20
64 Hippopotas C	.10	.20
65 Houndoom 4 C	.10	.20
66 Kakuna C	.10	.20
67 Kecleon C	.10	.20
68 Koffing C	.10	.20
69 Munchlax C	.10	.20
70 Munchlax C	.10	.20
71 Nidoran F C	.10	.20
72 Nidoran M C	.10	.20
73 Nidorina C	.10	.20
74 Nidorino C	.10	.20
75 Nuzleaf C	.10	.20
76 Quagsire GL C	.10	.20
77 Sealeo C	.10	.20
78 Seedot C	.10	.20
79 Shellos East Sea C	.10	.20
80 Shellos West Sea C	.10	.20
81 Snorlax C	.10	.20
82 Spheal C	.10	.20
83 Staryu C	.10	.20
84 Trapinch C	.10	.20
85 Turtwig GL C	.10	.20
86 Weedle C	.10	.20
87 Weezing C	.10	.20
88 Aaron's Collection U	.20	.50
89 Bebe's Search U	.50	1.00
90 Bertha's Warmth U	.20	.50
91 Flint's Willpower U	.20	.50
92 Lucian's Assignment U	.20	.50
93 Pokemon Contest Hall U	.20	.50
94 Sunyshore City Gym U	.20	.50
95 Technical Machine G U	.20	.50
96 SP-Radar U	.20	.50
97 Underground Expedition U	.20	.50
98 Volkner's Philosophy U	2.00	4.00
99 Darkness Energy U	.20	.50
100 Metal Energy U	.20	.50
101 SP Energy U	.20	.50
102 Upper Energy U	.20	.50
103 Alakazam 4 LV.X HOLO R	3.00	8.00
104 Floatzel GL LV.X HOLO R	3.00	8.00
105 Flygon LV.X HOLO R	6.00	15.00
106 Gallade 4 LV.X HOLO R	4.00	10.00
107 Hippowdon LV.X HOLO R	3.00	8.00
108 Infernape 4 LV.X HOLO R	2.00	6.00
109 Luxray GL LV.X HOLO R	10.00	25.00
110 Mismagius GL LV.X HOLO R	2.00	6.00
111 Snorlax LV.X HOLO R	10.00	25.00
112 Pikachu HOLO R	6.00	15.00
113 Flying Pikachu HOLO R	6.00	15.00
114 Surfing Pikachu HOLO R	6.00	15.00
RT1 Fan Rotom HOLO R	2.00	6.00
RT2 Frost Rotom HOLO R	2.00	6.00
RT3 Heat Rotom HOLO R	2.00	6.00
RT4 Mow Rotom HOLO R	2.00	6.00
RT5 Wash Rotom HOLO R	2.00	6.00
RT6 Charons Choice HOLO R	1.50	4.00

2009 Pokemon Platinum Supreme Victors

COMPLETE SET (150)	175.00	250.00
BOOSTER BOX (36 PACKS)	200.00	250.00
BOOSTER PACK (10 CARDS)	6.00	8.00
*REV.FOIL: .75X TO 2X BASIC CARDS		
RELEASED ON AUGUST 19, 2009		
1 Absol G HOLO R	2.00	4.00
2 Blaziken FB HOLO R	2.00	4.00
3 Driftblim FB HOLO R	2.00	4.00
4 Electivire FB HOLO R	2.00	4.00
5 Garchomp HOLO R	2.00	5.00
6 Magmortar HOLO R	2.00	4.00
7 Metagross HOLO R	2.00	4.00
8 Rayquaza C HOLO R	3.00	5.00
9 Regigigas FB HOLO R	2.00	4.00
10 Rhyperior HOLO R	2.00	4.00
11 Staraptor FB HOLO R	2.00	4.00
12 Swampert HOLO R	2.00	4.00
13 Venusaur HOLO R	2.00	5.00
14 Yanmega HOLO R	2.00	4.00
15 Arcanine G R	.50	1.00
16 Articuno R	.50	1.00
17 Butterfree FB (R)	.50	1.00
18 Camerupt R	.50	1.00
19 Camerupt G R	.50	1.00
20 Charizard R	2.00	4.00
21 Chimecho R	.50	1.00

Card	Low	High
22 Claydol R	1.00	2.00
23 Crawdaunt R	.50	1.00
24 Dewgong R	.50	1.00
25 Dodrio R	.50	1.00
26 Dusknoir FB R	.50	1.00
27 Empoleon FB R	1.00	1.00
28 Exploud R	.50	1.50
29 Honchkrow R	.50	1.00
30 Lickilicky C R	.50	1.00
31 Lucario C R	1.00	2.00
32 Lunatone R	.50	1.00
33 Mawile R	.50	1.00
34 Medicham R	.50	1.00
35 Milotic C R	.50	1.00
36 Moltres R	1.00	2.00
37 Mr. Mime R	.50	1.00
38 Parasect R	.50	1.00
39 Primeape R	.50	1.00
40 Roserade C R	.50	1.00
41 Sableye R	.50	1.00
42 Sandslash R	.50	1.00
43 Seaking R	.50	1.00
44 Shedinja R	.50	1.00
45 Solrock R	.50	1.00
46 Spinda R	.50	1.00
47 Wailord R	2.00	4.00
48 Zapdos R	.50	1.00
49 Altaria C U	.20	.50
50 Arcanine U	.20	.50
51 Bibarel U	.20	.50
52 Breloom U	.20	.50
53 Carnivine U	.20	.50
54 Chatot G U	.20	.50
55 Cherrim U	.20	.50
56 Dragonite FB U	.20	.50
57 Drifblim U	.20	.50
58 Floatzel U	.20	.50
59 Gabite U	.20	.50
60 Garchomp C U	.50	1.00
61 Hippopotas U	.20	.50
62 Ivysaur U	.20	.50
63 Lopunny U	.20	.50
64 Loudred U	.20	.50
65 Magmar U	.20	.50
66 Manectric G U	.20	.50
67 Marshtomp U	.20	.50
68 Masquerain U	.20	.50
69 Metang U	.20	.50
70 Milotic U	.20	.50
71 Minun U	.20	.50
72 Murkrow U	.20	.50
73 Ninjask U	.20	.50
74 Numel U	.20	.50
75 Pinsir U	.20	.50
76 Plusle U	.20	.50
77 Raichu U	.50	1.00
78 Raticate U	.20	.50
79 Relicanth U	.20	.50
80 Rhydon U	.20	.50
81 Roserade U	.20	.50
82 Rotom U	.20	.50
83 Skarmory U	.20	.50
84 Spiritomb U	.20	.50
85 Staravia U	.20	.50
86 Togekiss C U	.20	.50
87 Wailmer U	.20	.50
88 Yanma U	.20	.50
89 Baltoy C	.10	.20
90 Beldum C	.10	.20
91 Bidoof C	.10	.20
92 Buizel C	.10	.20
93 Bulbasaur C	.10	.20
94 Buneary C	.10	.20
95 Chatot C	.10	.20
96 Cherubi C	.10	.20
97 Chimchar C	.10	.20
98 Chingling C	.10	.20
99 Combee C	.10	.20
100 Corphish C	.10	.20
101 Croagunk C	.10	.20
102 Doduo C	.10	.20
103 Drifloon C	.10	.20
104 Feebas C	.10	.20
105 Geodude C	.10	.20
106 Gible C	.10	.20
107 Goldeen C	.10	.20
108 Growlithe C	.10	.20
109 Kricketot C	.10	.20
110 Magikarp C	.10	.20
111 Magnemite C	.10	.20
112 Mankey C	.10	.20
113 Meditite C	.10	.20
114 Meowth C	.10	.20
115 Mime Jr C	.10	.20
116 Mudkip C	.10	.20
117 Nincada C	.10	.20
118 Pachirisu C	.10	.20
119 Paras C	.10	.20
120 Pikachu C	.20	.50
121 Piplup C	.10	.20
122 Rhyhorn C	.10	.20
123 Roselia C	.10	.20
124 Sandshrew C	.10	.20
125 Seel C	.10	.20
126 Shinx C	.10	.20
127 Shroomish C	.10	.20
128 Skorupi C	.10	.20
129 Starly C	.10	.20
130 Surskit C	.10	.20
131 Turtwig C	.10	.20
132 Whismur C	.10	.20
133 Zubat C	.10	.20
134 Battle Tower U	.20	.50
135 Champion Room U	.20	.50
136 Cynthia's Guidance U	.20	.50
137 Cyrus's Initiative U	.20	.50
138 Night Teleporter U	.20	.50
139 Palmer's Contribution U	.20	.50
140 VS. Seeker U	6.00	15.00
141 Absol G LV.X HOLO R	2.00	6.00
142 Blaziken FB LV.X HOLO R	2.50	6.00
143 Charizard G LV.X HOLO R	8.00	20.00
144 Electivire FB LV.X HOLO R	2.00	6.00
145 Garchomp C LV.X HOLO R	2.50	6.00
146 Rayquaza C LV.X HOLO R	6.00	15.00
147 Staraptor FB LV.X HOLO R	1.50	4.00
148 Articuno HOLO R	6.00	15.00
149 Moltres HOLO R	3.00	8.00
150 Zapdos HOLO R	4.00	10.00
SH7 Milotic HOLO R	6.00	15.00
SH8 Yanma HOLO R	3.00	8.00
SH9 Relicanth HOLO R	3.00	8.00

2009 Pokemon Platinum Arceus

Card	Low	High
COMPLETE SET (99)	100.00	150.00
BOOSTER BOX (36 PACKS)	200.00	300.00
BOOSTER PACK (10 CARDS)	6.00	8.00
*REV.FOIL: .75X TO 2X BASIC CARDS		
RELEASED ON NOVEMBER 4, 2009		
1 Charizard HOLO R	4.00	10.00
2 Froslass HOLO R	2.00	4.00
3 Heatran HOLO R	2.00	4.00
4 Kabutops HOLO R	2.00	4.00
5 Luxray HOLO R	2.00	4.00
6 Mothim HOLO R	2.00	4.00
7 Probopass HOLO R	2.00	4.00
8 Salamence HOLO R	2.00	4.00
9 Swalot HOLO R	2.00	4.00
10 Tangrowth HOLO R	2.00	4.00
11 Toxicroak HOLO R	2.00	4.00
12 Zapdos HOLO R	2.00	5.00
13 Aerodactyl R	.50	1.00
14 Bronzong R	.50	1.00
15 Cherrim R	.50	1.00
16 Gengar R	.75	2.00
17 Gengar R	1.50	4.00
18 Glalie R	.50	1.00
19 Golem R	.50	1.00
20 Hariyama R	.50	1.00
21 Lopunny R	.50	1.00
22 Manectric R	.50	1.00
23 Omastar R	.50	1.00
24 Pelipper R	.50	1.00
25 Pichu R	.50	1.00
26 Porygon Z R	.50	1.00
27 Raichu R	.50	1.00
28 Rapidash R	.50	1.00
29 Raticate R	.50	1.00
30 Sceptile R	.50	1.00
31 Sceptile R	.50	1.00
32 Spiritomb R	.50	1.00
33 Bronzong U	.20	.50
34 Bronzor U	.20	.50
35 Charmeleon U	.20	.50
36 Gastly U	.20	.50
37 Graveler U	.20	.50
38 Grovyle U	.20	.50
39 Grovyle U	.20	.50
40 Gulpin U	.20	.50
41 Haunter U	.20	.50
42 Haunter U	.20	.50
43 Luxio U	.20	.50
44 Manectric U	.20	.50
45 Pelipper U	.20	.50
46 Ponyta U	.20	.50
47 Rapidash U	.20	.50
48 Shelgon U	.20	.50
49 Wormadam U	.20	.50
50 Wormadam U	.20	.50
51 Wormadam U	.20	.50
52 Bagon C	.10	.20
53 Beedrill C	.10	.20
54 Bronzor C	.10	.20
55 Buneary C	.10	.20
56 Burmy C	.10	.20
57 Burmy C	.10	.20
58 Burmy C	.10	.20
59 Charmander C	.10	.20
60 Cherubi C	.10	.20
61 Croagunk C	.10	.20
62 Electrike C	.10	.20
63 Electrike C	.10	.20
64 Gastly C	.10	.20
65 Geodude C	.10	.20
66 Gulpin C	.10	.20
67 Kabuto C	.10	.20
68 Makuhita C	.10	.20
69 Nosepass C	.10	.20
70 Omanyte C	.10	.20
71 Pikachu C	.20	.50
72 Ponyta C	.10	.20
73 Rattata C	.10	.20
74 Shinx C	.10	.20
75 Snorunt (C)	.10	.20
76 Tangela C	.10	.20
77 Tangela C	.10	.20
78 Treecko C	.10	.20
79 Treecko C	.10	.20
80 Wingull C	.10	.20
81 Wingull C	.10	.20
82 Beginning Door U	.20	.50
83 Bench Shield U	.20	.50
84 Buffer Piece U	.20	.50
85 Department Store Girl U	.20	.50
86 Energy Restore U	.20	.50
87 Expert Belt U	.20	.50
88 Lucky Egg U	.20	.50
89 Old Amber U	.20	.50
90 Professor Oak's Visit U	.20	.50
91 Ultimate Zone U	.20	.50
92 Dome Fossil C	.10	.20
93 Helix Fossil C	.10	.20
94 Arceus LV X HOLO R	3.00	8.00
95 Arceus LV X HOLO R	5.00	12.00
96 Arceus LV X HOLO R	4.00	10.00
97 Gengar LV X HOLO R	4.00	10.00
98 Salamence LV X HOLO R	3.00	8.00
99 Tangrowth LV X HOLO R	2.00	6.00
SH10 Bagon (Rev H) R	4.00	10.00
SH11 Ponyta (Rev H) R	8.00	20.00
SH12 Shinx (Rev H) R	4.00	10.00
AR1 Arceus HOLO R	2.50	6.00
AR2 Arceus HOLO R	2.50	6.00
AR3 Arceus HOLO R	2.50	6.00
AR4 Arceus HOLO R	2.50	6.00
AR5 Arceus HOLO R	2.50	6.00
AR6 Arceus HOLO R	2.50	6.00
AR7 Arceus HOLO R	2.50	6.00
AR8 Arceus HOLO R	2.50	6.00
AR9 Arceus HOLO R	2.50	6.00

2010 Pokemon HeartGold SoulSilver

Card	Low	High
COMPLETE SET (123)	80.00	150.00
BOOSTER BOX (36 PACKS)	250.00	350.00
BOOSTER PACK (10 CARDS)	2.50	6.00
*REV.FOIL: .75X TO 2X BASIC CARDS		
RELEASED FEBRUARY 10, 2010		
1 Arcanine HOLO R	1.25	3.00
2 Azumarill HOLO R	1.25	3.00
3 Clefable HOLO R	1.25	3.00
4 Gyarados HOLO R	1.25	3.00
5 Hitmontop HOLO R	1.25	3.00
6 Jumpluff HOLO R	1.25	3.00
7 Ninetales HOLO R	1.25	3.00
8 Noctowl HOLO R	1.25	3.00
9 Quagsire HOLO R	1.25	3.00
10 Raichu HOLO R	1.25	3.00
11 Shuckle HOLO R	1.25	3.00
12 Slowking HOLO R	1.25	3.00
13 Wobbuffet HOLO R	1.25	3.00
14 Ampharos R	.50	1.00
15 Ariados R	.50	1.00
16 Butterfree R	.50	1.00
17 Cleffa R	.50	1.00
18 Exeggutor R	.50	1.00
19 Farfetch'd R	.50	1.00
20 Feraligatr R	.50	1.00
21 Furret R	.50	1.00
22 Granbull R	.50	1.00
23 Hypno R	.50	1.00
24 Lapras R	.50	1.00
25 Ledian R	.50	1.00
26 Meganium R	.50	1.00
27 Persian R	.50	1.00
28 Pichu R	.50	1.00
29 Sandslash R	.50	1.00
30 Smoochum R	.50	1.00
31 Sunflora R	.50	1.00
32 Typhlosion R	.50	1.00
33 Tyrogue R	.50	1.00
34 Weezing R	.50	1.00
35 Bayleef U	.20	.50
36 Blissey U	.20	.50
37 Corsola U	.20	.50
38 Croconaw U	.20	.50
39 Delibird U	.20	.50
40 Donphan U	.20	.50
41 Dunsparce U	.20	.50
42 Flaaffy U	.20	.50
43 Heracross U	.20	.50
44 Igglybuff U	.20	.50
45 Mantine U	.20	.50
46 Metapod U	.20	.50
47 Miltank U	.20	.50
48 Parasect U	.20	.50
49 Quilava U	.20	.50
50 Qwilfish U	.20	.50
51 Skiploom U	.20	.50
52 Slowbro U	.20	.50
53 Starmie U	.20	.50
54 Unown U	.20	.50
55 Unown U	.20	.50
56 Wigglytuff U	.20	.50
57 Caterpie (C)	.10	.25
58 Chansey C	.10	.25
59 Chikorita C	.10	.25
60 Clefairy C	.10	.25
61 Cyndaquil C	.10	.25
62 Drowzee C	.10	.25
63 Exeggcute C	.10	.25
64 Girafarig C	.10	.25
65 Growlithe C	.10	.25
66 Hoothoot C	.10	.25
67 Hoppip C	.10	.25
68 Jigglypuff C	.10	.25
69 Jynx C	.10	.25
70 Koffing C	.10	.25
71 Ledyba C	.10	.25
72 Magikarp C	.10	.25
73 Mareep C	.10	.25
74 Marill C	.10	.25
75 Meowth C	.10	.25
76 Paras C	.10	.25
77 Phanpy C	.10	.25
78 Pikachu C	.10	.25
79 Sandshrew C	.10	.25
80 Sentret C	.10	.25
81 Slowpoke C	.10	.25
82 Snubbull C	.10	.25
83 Spinarak C	.10	.25
84 Staryu C	.10	.25
85 Sunkern C	.10	.25
86 Totodile C	.10	.25
87 Vulpix C	.10	.25
88 Wooper C	.10	.25
89 Bill U	.20	.50
90 Copycat U	.20	.50
91 Energy Switch U	.20	.50
92 Fisherman U	.20	.50
93 Full Heal U	.20	.50
94 Moomoo Milk U	.20	.50
95 Poke Ball U	.20	.50
96 Pokegear 3.0 U	.20	.50
97 Pokemon Collector U	.75	2.00
98 Pokemon Communication U	.75	2.00
99 Pokemon Reversal U	.20	.50
100 Professor Elm's Training Method U	.20	.50
101 Professor Oak's New Theory U	.20	.50
102 Switch U	.20	.50
103 Double Colorless Energy U	2.00	5.00
104 Rainbow Energy U	1.00	2.00
105 Ampharos (Pr) (H) (R)	2.00	5.00
106 Blissey (Pr) (H) (R)	2.00	5.00
107 Donphan (Pr) (H) (R)	2.00	5.00
108 Feraligatr (Pr) (H) (R)	2.00	5.00
109 Meganium (Pr) (H) (R)	2.00	8.00
110 Typhlosion (Pr) (H) (R)	2.00	5.00
111 Ho-Oh LEG (Top) (H) (R)	6.00	15.00
112 Ho-Oh LEG (Bot) (H) (R)	6.00	15.00
113 Lugia LEG (Top) (H) (R)	6.00	15.00
114 Lugia LEG (Bot) (H) (R)	6.00	15.00
115 Grass Energy C	2.00	5.00
116 Fire Energy C	2.00	5.00
117 Water Energy C	2.00	5.00
118 Lightning Energy C	2.00	5.00
119 Psychic Energy C	2.00	5.00
120 Fighting Energy C	2.00	5.00
121 Darkness Energy C	2.00	5.00
122 Metal Energy C	2.00	5.00
123 Gyarados HOLO R	6.00	15.00
124 Alph Lithograph UR	2.50	6.00

2010 Pokemon HS Triumphant

Card	Low	High
COMPLETE SET (102)	75.00	125.00
BOOSTER BOX (36 PACKS)	150.00	200.00
BOOSTER PACK (10 CARDS)	2.50	6.00
*REV.FOIL: .75X TO 2X REGULAR CARD		
RELEASED ON NOVEMBER 3, 2010		
1 Aggron HOLO R	1.00	2.50
2 Altaria HOLO R	1.00	2.50
3 Celebi HOLO R	1.00	2.50
4 Drapion HOLO R	1.00	2.50
5 Mamoswine HOLO R	1.00	2.50
6 Nidoking HOLO R	1.00	2.50
7 Porygon-Z HOLO R	1.00	2.50
8 Rapidash HOLO R	1.00	2.50
9 Solrock HOLO R	1.00	2.50
10 Spiritomb HOLO R	1.00	2.50
11 Venomoth HOLO R	1.00	2.50
12 Victreebel HOLO R	1.00	2.50
13 Ambipom R	.40	1.00
14 Banette R	.40	1.00
15 Bronzong R	.40	1.00
16 Carnivine R	.40	1.00
17 Ditto R	.40	1.00
18 Dragonite R	.40	1.00
19 Dugtrio R	.40	1.00

Card	Low	High
20 Electivire R	.40	1.00
21 Elekid R	.40	1.00
22 Golduck R	.40	1.00
23 Grumpig R	.40	1.00
24 Kricketune R	.40	1.00
25 Lunatone R	.40	1.00
26 Machamp R	.40	1.00
27 Magmortar R	.40	1.00
28 Nidoqueen R	.40	1.00
29 Pidgeot R	.40	1.00
30 Sharpedo R	.40	1.00
31 Wailord R	.40	1.00
32 Dragonair U	.20	.50
33 Electabuzz U	.20	.50
34 Electrode U	.20	.50
35 Haunter U	.20	.50
36 Kangaskhan U	.20	.50
37 Lairon U	.20	.50
38 Lickilicky U	.20	.50
39 Luvdisc U	.20	.50
40 Machoke U	.20	.50
41 Magby U	.20	.50
42 Magmar U	.20	.50
43 Magneton U	.20	.50
44 Marowak U	.20	.50
45 Nidorina U	.20	.50
46 Nidorino U	.20	.50
47 Pidgeotto U	.20	.50
48 Piloswine U	.20	.50
49 Porygon2 U	.20	.50
50 Tentacruel U	.20	.50
51 Unown U	.20	.50
52 Wailmer U	.20	.50
53 Weepinbell U	.20	.50
54 Yanmega U	.20	.50
55 Aipom C	.10	.25
56 Aron C	.10	.25
57 Bellsprout C	.10	.25
58 Bronzor C	.10	.25
59 Carvanha C	.10	.25
60 Cubone C	.10	.25
61 Diglett C	.10	.25
62 Dratini C	.10	.25
63 Gastly C	.10	.25
64 Illumise C	.10	.25
65 Kricketot C	.10	.25
66 Lickitung C	.10	.25
67 Machop C	.10	.25
68 Magnemite C	.10	.25
69 Nidoran F C	.10	.25
70 Nidoran M C	.10	.25
71 Pidgey C	.10	.25
72 Ponyta C	.10	.25
73 Porygon C	.10	.25
74 Psyduck C	.10	.25
75 Shuppet C	.10	.25
76 Skorupi C	.10	.25
77 Spoink C	.10	.25
78 Swablu C	.10	.25
79 Swinub C	.10	.25
80 Tentacool C	.10	.25
81 Venonat C	.10	.25
82 Volbeat C	.10	.25
83 Voltorb C	.10	.25
84 Yanma C	.10	.25
85 Black Belt U	.20	.50
86 Indigo Plateau U	.20	.50
87 Junk Arm U	.75	2.00
88 Seeker U	.50	1.25
89 Twins U	.20	.50
90 Rescue Energy U	.20	.50
91 Absol Prime HOLO R	2.00	5.00
92 Celebi Prime HOLO R	2.00	5.00
93 Electrode Prime HOLO R	1.50	4.00
94 Gengar Prime HOLO R	6.00	15.00
95 Machamp Prime HOLO R	2.00	6.00
96 Magnezone Prime HOLO R	2.00	6.00
97 Mew Prime HOLO R	5.00	12.00
98 Yanmega Prime HOLO R	2.00	5.00
99 Darkrai & Cresselia LEG (R)	3.00	8.00
100 Darkrai & Cresselia LEG (R)	3.00	8.00
101 Palkia & Dialga LEGEND R	3.00	8.00
102 Palkia & Dialga LEGEND R	3.00	8.00
SP Alph Lithograph UR	2.00	5.00

2010 Pokemon HS Unleashed

Card	Low	High
COMPLETE SET (96)	80.00	120.00
BOOSTER BOX (36 PACKS)	200.00	250.00
BOOSTER PACK (10 CARDS)	6.00	8.00
*REV.FOIL: .75X TO 2X BASIC CARDS		
RELEASED ON MAY 12, 2010		
1 Jirachi HOLO R	1.25	3.00
2 Magmortar HOLO R	1.25	3.00
3 Manaphy HOLO R	1.25	3.00
4 Metagross HOLO R	1.25	3.00
5 Mismagius HOLO R	1.25	3.00
6 Octillery HOLO R	1.25	3.00
7 Politoed HOLO R	1.25	3.00
8 Shaymin HOLO R	1.25	3.00
9 Sudowoodo HOLO R	1.25	3.00
10 Torterra HOLO R	1.25	3.00
11 Xatu HOLO R	1.25	3.00
12 Beedrill R	.40	1.00
13 Blastoise R	.40	1.00
14 Crobat R	.40	1.00
15 Fearow R	.40	1.00
16 Floatzel R	.40	1.00
17 Kingdra R	.40	1.00
18 Lanturn R	.40	1.00
19 Lucario R	.40	1.00
20 Ninetales R	.40	1.00
21 Poliwrath R	.40	1.00
22 Primeape R	.40	1.00
23 Roserade R	.40	1.00
24 MetalSteelix R	.40	1.00
25 Torkoal R	.40	1.00
26 Tyranitar R	.40	1.00
27 Ursaring R	.40	1.00
28 Cherrim U	.20	.50
29 Dunsparce U	.20	.50
30 Golbat U	.20	.50
31 Grotle U	.20	.50
32 Kakuna U	.20	.50
33 Metang U	.20	.50
34 Minun U	.20	.50
35 Numel U	.20	.50
36 Plusle U	.20	.50
37 Poliwhirl U	.20	.50
38 Pupitar U	.20	.50
39 Pupitar U	.20	.50
40 Seadra U	.20	.50
41 Tauros U	.20	.50
42 Wartortle U	.20	.50
43 Aipom C	.10	.25
44 Beldum C	.10	.25
45 Buizel C	.10	.25
46 Carnivine C	.10	.25
47 Cherubi C	.10	.25
48 Chinchou C	.10	.25
49 Horsea C	.10	.25
50 Larvitar C	.10	.25
51 Larvitar C	.10	.25
52 Magmar C	.10	.25
53 Mankey C	.10	.25
54 Misdreavus C	.10	.25
55 Natu C	.10	.25
56 Onix C	.10	.25
57 Onix C	.10	.25
58 Poliwag C	.10	.25
59 Remoraid C	.10	.25
60 Riolu C	.10	.25
61 Roselia C	.10	.25
62 Spearow C	.10	.25
63 Squirtle C	.10	.25
64 Stantler C	.10	.25
65 Teddiursa C	.10	.25
66 Tropius C	.10	.25
67 Turtwig C	.10	.25
68 Vulpix C	.10	.25
69 Weedle C	.10	.25
70 Zubat C	.10	.25
71 Cheerleader's Cheer U	.20	.50
72 Dual Ball U	.20	.50
73 Emcee's Chatter U	.20	.50
74 Energy Returner U	.20	.50
75 Engineer's Adjustments U	.20	.50
76 Good Rod U	.20	.50
77 Interviewer's Questions U	.20	.50
78 Judge U	.75	2.00
79 Life Herb U	.20	.50
80 Plus Power U	.20	.50
81 Pokemon Circulator U	.20	.50
82 Rare Candy U	.75	2.00
83 Super Scoop Up U	.75	2.00
84 Crobat (Prime) HOLO R	2.50	6.00
85 Kingdra (Prime) HOLO R	2.50	6.00
86 Lanturn (Prime) HOLO R	2.00	5.00
87 Steelix (Prime) HOLO R	2.50	6.00
88 Tyranitar (Prime) HOLO R	3.00	8.00
89 Ursaring (Prime) HOLO R	2.50	6.00
90 Entei/Raikou LEG (H) (R)	5.00	12.00
91 Entei/Raikou LEG (H) (R)	5.00	12.00
92 Raikou/Suicune LEG (H) (R)	5.00	12.00
93 Raikou/Suicune LEG (H) (R)	5.00	12.00
94 Suicune/Entei LEG (H) (R)	5.00	12.00
95 Suicune/Entei LEG (H) (R)	5.00	12.00
96 Alph Lithograph R	2.50	6.00

2010 Pokemon HS Undaunted

Card	Low	High
COMPLETE SET (90)	75.00	125.00
BOOSTER BOX (36 PACKS)	200.00	250.00
BOOSTER PACK (10 CARDS)	6.00	8.00
*REV.FOIL: .75X TO 2X BASIC CARDS		
RELEASED ON AUGUST 18, 2010		
1 Bellossom HOLO R	1.50	3.00
2 Espeon HOLO R	1.50	3.00
3 Forretress HOLO R	1.50	3.00
4 Gliscor HOLO R	1.50	3.00
5 Houndoom HOLO R	1.50	3.00
6 Magcargo HOLO R	1.50	3.00
7 Scizor HOLO R	1.50	3.00
8 Smeargle HOLO R	1.50	3.00
9 Togekiss HOLO R	1.50	3.00
10 Umbreon HOLO R	1.50	3.00
11 Dodrio R	.40	1.00
12 Drifblim R	.40	1.00
13 Forretress R	.40	1.00
14 Hariyama R	.40	1.00
15 Honchkrow R	.40	1.00
16 Honchkrow R	.40	1.00
17 Leafeon R	.40	1.00
18 Metagross R	.40	1.00
19 Mismagius R	.40	1.00
20 Rotom R	.40	1.00
21 Skarmory R	.40	1.00
22 Tropius R	.40	1.00
23 Vespiquen R	.40	1.00
24 Vileplume R	.40	1.00
25 Weavile R	.40	1.00
26 Flareon U	.20	.50
27 Gloom U	.20	.50
28 Jolteon U	.20	.50
29 Lairon U	.20	.50
30 Metang U	.20	.50
31 Muk U	.20	.50
32 Pinsir U	.20	.50
33 Raichu U	.20	.50
34 Raticate U	.20	.50
35 Sableye U	.20	.50
36 Scyther U	.20	.50
37 Skuntank U	.20	.50
38 Slowbro U	.20	.50
39 Togetic U	.20	.50
40 Unown U	.20	.50
41 Vaporeon U	.20	.50
42 Aron C	.10	.25
43 Beldum C	.10	.25
44 Combee C	.10	.25
45 Doduo C	.10	.25
46 Drifloon C	.10	.25
47 Eevee C	.10	.25
48 Eevee C	.10	.25
49 Gligar C	.10	.25
50 Grimer C	.10	.25
51 Hitmonchan C	.10	.25
52 Hitmonlee C	.10	.25
53 Houndour C	.10	.25
54 Houndour C	.10	.25
55 Makuhita C	.10	.25
56 Mawile C	.10	.25
57 Misdreavus C	.10	.25
58 Murkrow C	.10	.25
59 Murkrow C	.10	.25
60 Oddish C	.10	.25
61 Pikachu C	.10	.25
62 Pineco C	.10	.25
63 Pineco C	.10	.25
64 Rattata C	.10	.25
65 Scyther C	.10	.25
66 Slowpoke C	.10	.25
67 Slugma C	.10	.25
68 Sneasel C	.10	.25
69 Stunky C	.10	.25
70 Togepi C	.10	.25
71 Burned Tower U	.20	.50
72 Defender U	.20	.50
73 Energy Exchanger U	.20	.50
74 Flower Shop Lady U	.20	.50
75 Legend Box U	.20	.50
76 Ruins of Alph U	.20	.50
77 Sage's Training U	.20	.50
78 Team Rocket's Trickery U	.20	.50
79 Darkness Energy U	.20	.50
80 Metal Energy U	.20	.50
81 Espeon Prime HOLO R	2.00	6.00
82 Houndoom Prime HOLO R	2.00	6.00
83 Raichu Prime HOLO R	4.00	10.00
84 Scizor Prime HOLO R	2.00	6.00
85 Slowking Prime HOLO R	2.00	6.00
86 Umbreon Prime HOLO R	5.00	12.00
87 Kyogre/Groudon LEG (H) (R)	8.00	20.00
88 Kyogre/Groudon LEG (H) (R)	8.00	20.00
89 Rayquaza/Deoxys LEG (H) (R)	8.00	20.00
90 Rayquaza/Deoxys LEG (H) (R)	8.00	20.00
SP Alph Lithograph UR	2.50	5.00

2011 Pokemon Black and White

Card	Low	High
COMPLETE SET (115)	50.00	100.00
BOOSTER BOX (36 PACKS)	100.00	120.00
BOOSTER PACK (10 CARDS)	3.00	5.00
*REV.FOIL: .75X TO 2X BASIC CARDS		
RELEASED ON APRIL 25, 2011		
1 Snivy C	.10	.25
2 Snivy C	.10	.25
3 Servine U	.20	.50
4 Servine U	.20	.50
5 Serperior HOLO R	.50	1.00
6 Serperior HOLO R	.50	1.00
7 Pansage C	.10	.25
8 Simisage U	.20	.50
9 Petilil C	.10	.25
10 Lilligant R	.40	1.00
11 Maractus U	.20	.50
12 Maractus R	.40	1.00
13 Deerling C	.10	.25
14 Sawsbuck R	.40	1.00
15 Tepig C	.10	.25
16 Tepig C	.10	.25
17 Pignite U	.20	.50
18 Pignite U	.20	.50
19 Emboar HOLO R	.50	1.00
20 Emboar HOLO R	.50	1.00
21 Pansear C	.10	.25
22 Simisear U	.20	.50
23 Darumaka C	.10	.25
24 Darumaka U	.20	.50
25 Darmanitan R	.40	1.00
26 Reshiram HOLO R	.50	1.00
27 Oshawott C	.10	.25
28 Oshawott C	.10	.25
29 Dewott U	.20	.50
30 Dewott U	.20	.50
31 Samurott HOLO R	.50	1.00
32 Samurott HOLO R	.50	1.00
33 Panpour C	.10	.25
34 Simipour U	.20	.50
35 Basculin U	.20	.50
36 Ducklett C	.10	.25
37 Swanna R	.40	1.00
38 Alomomola U	.20	.50
39 Alomomola R	.40	1.00
40 Blitzle C	.10	.25
41 Blitzle C	.10	.25
42 Zebstrika U	.20	.50
43 Zebstrika R	.40	1.00
44 Joltik C	.10	.25
45 Joltik C	.10	.25
46 Galvantula R	.40	1.00
47 Zekrom HOLO R	.50	1.50
48 Munna U	.20	.50
49 Musharna R	.40	1.00
50 Woobat C	.10	.25
51 Swoobat U	.20	.50
52 Venipede C	.10	.25
53 Whirlipede U	.20	.50
54 Scolipede R	.40	1.00
55 Solosis C	.10	.25
56 Duosion U	.20	.50
57 Reuniclus HOLO R	.50	1.50
58 Timburr C	.10	.25
59 Timburr C	.10	.25
60 Gurdurr U	.20	.50
61 Throh R	.40	1.00
62 Sawk R	.40	1.00
63 Sandile (C)	.10	.25
64 Krokorok U	.20	.50
65 Krookodile HOLO R	.50	1.50
66 Purrloin C	.10	.25
67 Liepard R	.40	1.00
68 Scraggy C	.10	.25
69 Scrafty R	.40	1.00
70 Zorua C	.10	.25
71 Zoroark HOLO R	1.00	2.00
72 Vullaby C	.10	.25
73 Mandibuzz R	.40	1.00
74 Klink C	.10	.25
75 Klang U	.20	.50
76 Klinklang HOLO R	.50	1.50
77 Patrat C	.10	.25
78 Patrat C	.10	.25
79 Watchog U	.20	.50
80 Lillipup C	.10	.25
81 Lillipup C	.10	.25
82 Herdier U	.20	.50
83 Stoutland R	.40	1.00
84 Pidove C	.10	.25
85 Tranquill U	.20	.50
86 Unfezant R	.40	1.00
87 Audino U	.20	.50
88 Minccino C	.10	.25
89 Cinccino R	.40	1.00
90 Bouffalant U	.20	.50
91 Bouffalant R	.40	1.00
92 Energy Retrieval U	.20	.50
93 Energy Search C	.10	.25
94 Energy Switch U	.20	.50
95 Full Heal U	.20	.50
96 PlusPower U	.20	.50
97 Poke Ball U	.20	.50
98 Pokedex U	.20	.50
99 Pokemon Communication U	.20	.50
100 Potion C	.10	.25
101 Professor Juniper U	.20	.50
102 Revive U	.20	.50
103 Super Scoop Up U	.20	.50
104 Switch U	.20	.50
105 Grass Energy C	.10	.25
106 Fire Energy C	.10	.25
107 Water Energy C	.10	.25
108 Lightning Energy C	.10	.25
109 Psychic Energy C	.10	.25
110 Fighting Energy C	.10	.25
111 Darkness Energy C	.10	.25
112 Metal Energy C	.10	.25
113 Reshiram HOLO SR	5.00	8.00
114 Zekrom HOLO SR	8.00	12.00
115 Pikachu UR	8.00	15.00

2011 Pokemon Black and White Emerging Powers

COMPLETE SET (98) 40.00 100.00
BOOSTER BOX (36 PACKS) 100.00 120.00
BOOSTER PACK (10 CARDS) 3.00 5.00
*REV.FOIL: .75X TO 2X BASIC CARDS
RELEASED ON AUGUST 31, 2011
1 Pansage C .10 .25
2 Simisage R .40 1.00
3 Sewaddle C .10 .25
4 Sewaddle C .10 .25
5 Swadloon U .20 .50
6 Swadloon U .20 .50
7 Leavanny R .75 2.00
8 Leavanny R .75 2.00
9 Cottonee C .10 .25
10 Cottonee C .10 .25
11 Whimsicott U .20 .50
12 Whimsicott R .40 1.00
13 Petilil C .10 .25
14 Lilligant U .20 .50
15 Deerling C .10 .25
16 Sawsbuck R .40 1.00
17 Virizion HOLO R 2.00 5.00
18 Pansear C .10 .25
19 Simisear R .40 1.00
20 Darumaka C .10 .25
21 Darmanitan R .60 1.50
22 Panpour C .10 .25
23 Simipour R .40 1.00
24 Basculin C .10 .25
25 Basculin U .20 .50
26 Ducklett C .10 .25
27 Swanna R .40 1.00
28 Cubchoo C .10 .25
29 Cubchoo C .10 .25
30 Beartic HOLO R .50 1.00
31 Beartic R .75 2.00
32 Emolga C .10 .25
33 Joltik C .10 .25
34 Galvantula U .20 .50
35 Thundurus HOLO R .50 1.00
36 Woobat C .10 .25
37 Swoobat R .40 1.00
38 Venipede C .10 .25
39 Whirlipede U .20 .50
40 Scolipede R .40 1.00
41 Sigilyph U .20 .50
42 Sigilyph U .20 .50
43 Gothita C .10 .25
44 Gothita C .10 .25
45 Gothorita U .20 .50
46 Gothorita U .20 .50
47 Gothitelle HOLO R .50 1.00
48 Gothitelle R .40 1.00
49 Roggenrola C .10 .25
50 Roggenrola C .10 .25
51 Boldore U .20 .50
52 Boldore U .20 .50
53 Gigalith R .40 1.00
54 Drilbur (U) .20 .50
55 Drilbur C .10 .25
56 Excadrill HOLO R .50 1.00
57 Excadrill R .50 1.00
58 Throh U .20 .50
59 Sawk U .20 .50
60 Sandile C .10 .25
61 Krokorok U .20 .50
62 Krookodile R .60 1.50
63 Terrakion HOLO R 1.00 2.50
64 Purrloin C .10 .25
65 Liepard R 1.50 4.00
66 Zorua U .20 .50
67 Zoroark HOLO R .50 1.00
68 Vullaby C .10 .25
69 Mandibuzz R .60 1.50
70 Ferroseed C .10 .25
71 Ferroseed C .10 .25
72 Ferrothorn R .40 1.00
73 Ferrothorn U .20 .50
74 Klink C .10 .25
75 Klang U .20 .50
76 Klinklang R .75 2.00
77 Cobalion HOLO R .50 1.00
78 Patrat C .10 .25
79 Watchog U .20 .50
80 Pidove C .10 .25
81 Tranquill U .20 .50
82 Unfezant R .60 1.50
83 Audino U .20 .50
84 Minccino C .10 .25
85 Cinccino U .20 .50
86 Rufflet C .10 .25
87 Rufflet C .10 .25
88 Braviary HOLO R .50 1.00
89 Tornadus HOLO R .50 1.00
90 Bianca U .50 1.25
91 Cheren U .20 .50
92 Crushing Hammer U .20 .50
93 Great Ball U .20 .50
94 Max Potion U .50 1.50
95 Pokemon Catcher U .50 1.50
96 Recycle U .20 .50
97 Thundurus Full Art UR 2.00 4.00
98 Tornadus Full Art UR 2.00 4.00

2011 Pokemon Black and White Noble Victories

COMPLETE SET (102) 75.00 125.00
BOOSTER BOX (36 PACKS) 100.00 120.00
BOOSTER PACK (10 CARDS) 3.00 5.00
*REV.FOIL: .75X TO 2X BASIC CARDS
RELEASED ON NOVEMBER 16, 2011
1 Sewaddle C .10 .25
2 Swadloon U .20 .50
3 Leavanny HOLO R .40 1.00
4 Petilil C .10 .25
5 Lilligant R .40 1.00
6 Dwebble C .10 .25
7 Crustle U .20 .50
8 Karrablast C .10 .25
9 Foongus C .10 .25
10 Amoonguss U .20 .50
11 Shelmet C .10 .25
12 Accelgor R 1.00 2.00
13 Virizion HOLO R 1.00 2.00
14 Victini HOLO R .50 12.00
15 Victini HOLO R .50 10.00
16 Pansear C .10 .25
17 Simisear U .20 .50
18 Heatmor U .20 .50
19 Larvesta C .10 .25
20 Larvesta C .10 .25
21 Volcarona R 1.00 2.00
22 Tympole C .10 .25
23 Palpitoad U .20 .50
24 Seismitoad R .60 1.50
25 Tirtouga U .20 .50
26 Carracosta R 1.00 2.00
27 Vanillite C .10 .25
28 Vanillish U .20 .50
29 Vanilluxe R 1.00 2.00
30 Frillish C .10 .25
31 Jellicent R .75 2.00
32 Cryogonal U .20 .50
33 Cryogonal R 1.00 2.00
34 Kyurem HOLO R 8.00 20.00
35 Blitzle C .10 .25
36 Zebstrika R .40 1.00
37 Emolga U .20 .50
38 Tynamo C 1.00 2.00
39 Tynamo C .10 .25
40 Eelektrik U 1.00 2.00
41 Eelektross HOLO R 1.00 4.00
42 Stunfisk C .10 .25
43 Victini R .50 8.00
44 Yamask C .10 .25
45 Yamask C .10 .25
46 Cofagrigus R .40 1.00
47 Cofagrigus R .40 1.00
48 Trubbish C .10 .25
49 Garbodor U .20 .50
50 Solosis C .10 .25
51 Duosion U .20 .50
52 Reuniclus R .40 1.00
53 Reuniclus R .40 1.00
54 Elgyem C .10 .25
55 Elgyem C .10 .25
56 Beheeyem R .40 1.00
57 Litwick C .10 .25
58 Litwick C .10 .25
59 Lampent U .20 .50
60 Chandelure R 1.00 8.00
61 Gigalith R .75 2.00
62 Timburr C .10 .25
63 Gurdurr U .20 .50
64 Conkeldurr HOLO R 1.00 4.00
65 Conkeldurr R .75 2.00
66 Archen U .20 .50
67 Archeops R 10.00 15.00
68 Stunfisk U .20 .50
69 Mienfoo C .10 .25
70 Mienshao U .20 .50
71 Golett C .10 .25
72 Golurk R .40 1.00
73 Terrakion HOLO R 2.00 5.00
74 Landorus HOLO R 1.00 10.00
75 Pawniard C .10 .25
76 Bisharp U .20 .50
77 Deino C .10 .25
78 Zweilous U .20 .50
79 Hydreigon HOLO R 5.00 12.00
80 Escavalier R .60 1.50
81 Pawniard C .10 .25
82 Bisharp HOLO R 2.00 5.00
83 Durant U .50 1.00
84 Cobalion HOLO R 1.50 2.50
85 Audino U .20 .50
86 Axew C .10 .25
87 Fraxure U .20 .50
88 Haxorus HOLO R 1.00 6.00
89 Druddigon R 1.00 4.00
90 Cover Fossil U .20 .50
91 Eviolite U .20 .50
92 N U 1.00 2.00
93 Plume Fossil U .20 .50
94 Rocky Helmet U .20 .50
95 Super Rod U .20 .50
96 Xtransceiver U .20 .50
97 Virizion Full Art UR 4.00 7.00
98 Victini Full Art UR 8.00 12.00
99 Terrakion Full Art UR 2.00 5.00
100 Cobalion Full Art UR 4.00 7.00
101 N Full Art UR 60.00 80.00
102 Meowth UR 3.00 6.00

2011 Pokemon Call of Legends

COMPLETE SET (95) 40.00 80.00
BOOSTER BOX (36 PACKS) 200.00 250.00
BOOSTER PACK (10 CARDS) 6.00 8.00
*REV.FOIL: .75X TO 2X BASIC CARDS
RELEASED ON FEBRUARY 9, 2011
1 Clefable HOLO R .40 1.00
2 Deoxys HOLO R .40 1.00
3 Dialga HOLO R .40 1.00
4 Espeon HOLO R .50 1.25
5 Forretress HOLO R .40 1.00
6 Groudon HOLO R 1.50 4.00
7 Gyarados HOLO R .40 1.00
8 Hitmontop HOLO R .40 1.00
9 Ho-Oh HOLO R 1.50 4.00
10 Houndoom HOLO R .40 1.00
11 Jirachi HOLO R .40 1.00
12 Kyogre HOLO R .60 1.50
13 Leafeon HOLO R .60 1.50
14 Lucario HOLO R .50 1.25
15 Lugia HOLO R 2.00 5.00
16 Magmortar HOLO R .40 1.00
17 Ninetales HOLO R .60 1.50
18 Pachirisu HOLO R .40 1.00
19 Palkia HOLO R .40 1.00
20 Rayquaza HOLO R 1.50 4.00
21 Smeargle HOLO R .60 1.50
22 Umbreon HOLO R .60 1.50
23 Ampharos R .30 .75
24 Cleffa R .40 1.00
25 Feraligatr R .30 .75
26 Granbull R .30 .75
27 Meganium R .30 .75
28 Mismagius R .30 .75
29 Mr. Mime R .30 .75
30 Pidgeot R .30 .75
31 Skarmory R .30 .75
32 Slowking R .30 .75
33 Snorlax R .30 .75
34 Tangrowth R .30 .75
35 Typhlosion R .30 .75
36 Tyrogue R .30 .75
37 Ursaring R .30 .75
38 Weezing R .30 .75
39 Zangoose R .30 .75
40 Bayleef U .20 .50
41 Croconaw U .20 .50
42 Donphan (U) .20 .50
43 Flaaffy U .20 .50
44 Flareon U .20 .50
45 Jolteon U .20 .50
46 Magby U .20 .50
47 Mime Jr. U .20 .50
48 Pidgeotto U .20 .50
49 Quilava U .20 .50
50 Riolu U .20 .50
51 Seviper U .20 .50
52 Vaporeon U .20 .50
53 Chikorita C .10 .25
54 Clefairy C .10 .25
55 Cyndaquil C .10 .25
56 Eevee C .10 .25
57 Hitmonchan C .10 .25
58 Hitmonlee C .10 .25
59 Houndour C .10 .25
60 Koffing C .10 .25
61 Magikarp C .10 .25
62 Magmar C .10 .25
63 Mareep C .10 .25
64 Mawile C .10 .25
65 Misdreavus C .10 .25
66 Phanpy C .10 .25
67 Pidgey C .10 .25
68 Pineco C .10 .25
69 Relicanth C .10 .25
70 Slowpoke C .10 .25
71 Snubbull C .10 .25
72 Tangela C .10 .25
73 Teddiursa C .10 .25
74 Totodile C .10 .25
75 Vulpix C .10 .25
76 Cheerleader's Cheer U .20 .50
77 Copycat U .20 .50
78 Dual Ball U .20 .50
79 Interviewer's Questions U .20 .50
80 Lost Remover U .20 .50
81 Lost World U .20 .50
82 Professor Elm's Training Method U .20 .50
83 Professor Oak's New Theory U .60 1.50
84 Research Record U .20 .50
85 Sage's Training U .20 .50
86 Darkness Energy U .20 .50
87 Metal Energy U .20 .50
88 Grass Energy C 6.00 10.00
89 Fire Energy C 6.00 10.00
90 Water Energy C 18.00 25.00
91 Lightning Energy C 10.00 15.00
92 Psychic Energy C 8.00 12.00
93 Fighting Energy C 8.00 12.00
94 Darkness Energy C 13.00 18.00
95 Metal Energy C 8.00 12.00

2011 Pokemon Call of Legends Recon Theme Deck Exclusives

16 Magmortar NONHOLO
17 Ninetales NONHOLO
34 Tangrowth (Cracked Ice Holo)

2011 Pokemon Call of Legends Retort Theme Deck Exclusives

6 Groudon NONHOLO
8 Hitmontop NONHOLO
14A Lucario NONHOLO
14B Lucario Cracked Ice HOLO

2011 Pokemon Call of Legends Shiny

COMPLETE SET (11) 40.00 80.00
SL1 Deoxys HOLO R 3.00 8.00
SL2 Dialga HOLO R 4.00 10.00
SL3 Entei HOLO R 3.00 8.00
SL4 Groudon HOLO R 4.00 10.00
SL5 Ho-Oh HOLO R 6.00 15.00
SL6 Kyogre HOLO R 4.00 10.00
SL7 Lugia HOLO R 5.00 12.00
SL8 Palkia HOLO R 3.00 8.00
SL9 Raikou HOLO R 3.00 8.00
SL10 Rayquaza HOLO R 6.00 15.00
SL11 Suicune HOLO R 4.00 10.00

2012 Pokemon Black and White Boundaries Crossed

COMPLETE SET (153) 100.00 250.00
BOOSTER BOX (36 PACKS) 120.00 150.00
BOOSTER PACK (10 CARDS) 4.00 6.00
*REV.FOIL: .75X TO 2X BASIC CARDS
RELEASED ON NOVEMBER 11, 2012
1 Oddish C .10 .25
2 Gloom U .20 .50
3 Vileplume HOLO R .75 2.00
4 Bellossom R .30 .75
5 Tangela C .10 .25
6 Tangrowth HOLO R .60 1.50
7 Scyther C .10 .25
8 Heracross U .20 .50
9 Celebi EX UR 4.00 8.00
10 Shaymin R .30 .75
11 Snivy C .10 .25
12 Servine U .20 .50
13 Serperior HOLO R .60 1.50
14 Cottonee C .10 .25
15 Whimsicott R .30 .75
16 Petilil U .20 .50
17 Lilligant R .30 .75
18 Charmander C .10 .25
19 Charmeleon U .20 .50
20 Charizard HOLO R 3.00 8.00
21 Numel C .10 .25
22 Camerupt R .30 .75
23 Victini R .40 1.00
24 Tepig C .10 .25
25 Pignite U .20 .50
26 Emboar HOLO R .60 1.50
27 Darumaka C .10 .25
28 Darmanitan U .20 .50
29 Squirtle C .10 .25
30 Wartortle U .20 .50
31 Blastoise HOLO R 3.00 5.00
32 Psyduck C .10 .25
33 Psyduck C .10 .25
34 Golduck U .20 .50
35 Golduck R .30 .75
36 Marill C .10 .25
37 Azumarill U .20 .50
38 Delibird U .20 .50
39 Oshawott C .10 .25
40 Dewott U .20 .50
41 Samurott HOLO R .60 1.50
42 Ducklett C .10 .25
43 Swanna U .20 .50
44 Frillish C .10 .25
45 Jellicent R .30 .75
46 Cryogonal U .20 .50
47 Keldeo HOLO R 1.00 2.50
48 Keldeo R .30 .75
49 Keldeo EX UR 4.00 8.00
50 Pikachu C .10 .25
51 Voltorb C .10 .25
52 Electrode U .20 .50
53 Electabuzz C .10 .25
54 Electivire HOLO R .60 1.50
55 Chinchou C .10 .25
56 Blitzle C .10 .25
57 Zebstrika HOLO R .60 1.50
58 Wobbuffet U .20 .50

59 Spoink C	.10	.25
60 Grumpig R	.30	.75
61 Duskull C	.10	.25
62 Dusclops U	.20	.50
63 Dusknoir HOLO R	2.00	5.00
64 Croagunk C	.10	.25
65 Croagunk U	.20	.50
66 Toxicroak R	.30	.75
67 Cresselia EX UR	3.00	5.00
68 Munna U	.20	.50
69 Musharna R	.30	.75
70 Woobat C	.10	.25
71 Swoobat R	.30	.75
72 Venipede C	.10	.25
73 Whirlipede U	.20	.50
74 Scolipede HOLO R	.60	1.50
75 Gothita C	.10	.25
76 Gothorita U	.20	.50
77 Meloetta (Holo) (R)	1.50	4.00
78 Sandshrew C	.10	.25
79 Sandslash U	.20	.50
80 Gligar C	.10	.25
81 Gliscor HOLO R	.60	1.50
82 Makuhita C	.10	.25
83 Trapinch C	.10	.25
84 Dwebble C	.10	.25
85 Crustle HOLO R	.60	1.50
86 Mienfoo C	.10	.25
87 Mienfoo U	.20	.50
88 Mienshao U	.20	.50
89 Landorus EX UR	8.00	12.00
90 Purrloin C	.10	.25
91 Liepard HOLO R	.60	1.50
92 Vullaby C	.10	.25
93 Mandibuzz U	.20	.50
94 Scizor HOLO R	.60	1.50
95 Skarmory U	.20	.50
96 Skarmory U	.20	.50
97 Klink U	.20	.50
98 Vibrava U	.20	.50
99 Flygon HOLO R	1.00	2.50
100 Black Kyurem R	.40	1.00
101 Black Kyurem EX UR	5.00	10.00
102 White Kyurem R	.40	1.00
103 White Kyurem EX UR	5.00	10.00
104 Rattata C	.10	.25
105 Raticate U	.20	.50
106 Meowth C	.10	.25
107 Farfetch'd U	.20	.50
108 Ditto HOLO R	2.00	5.00
109 Snorlax U	.20	.50
110 Togepi C	.10	.25
111 Dunsparce C	.10	.25
112 Taillow C	.10	.25
113 Skitty C	.10	.25
114 Delcatty U	.20	.50
115 Spinda C	.10	.25
116 Buneary C	.10	.25
117 Lopunny U	.20	.50
118 Patrat C	.10	.25
119 Watchog U	.20	.50
120 Lillipup C	.10	.25
121 Herdier U	.20	.50
122 Stoutland HOLO R	.60	1.50
123 Pidove C	.10	.25
124 Tranquill U	.20	.50
125 Unfezant R	.30	.75
126 Audino R	.30	.75
127 Aspertia City Gym U	.20	.50
128 Energy Search C	.10	.25
129 Great Ball U	.20	.50
130 Hugh U	.20	.50
131 Poke Ball C	.10	.25
132 Potion C	.10	.25
133 Rocky Helmet U	.20	.50
134 Skyla U	.75	3.00
135 Switch C	.10	.25
136 Town Map U	.20	.50
137 Computer Search UR	18.00	25.00
138 Crystal Edge HOLO R	.75	2.00
139 Crystal Wall HOLO R	.75	2.00
140 Gold Potion HOLO R	3.00	5.00
141 Celebi EX Full Art UR	10.00	15.00
142 Keldeo EX Full Art UR	20.00	25.00
143 Cresselia EX Full Art UR	5.00	10.00
144 Landorus EX Full Art UR	8.00	15.00
145 Black Kyurem EX Full Art UR	10.00	15.00
146 White Kyurem EX Full Art UR	15.00	20.00
147 Bianca Full Art UR	12.00	18.00
148 Cheren Full Art UR	5.00	10.00
149 Skyla Full Art UR	20.00	30.00
150 Golurk UR	5.00	10.00
151 Terrakion UR	6.00	12.00
152 Altaria UR	8.00	15.00
153 Rocky Helmet UR	4.00	8.00

2012 Pokemon Black and White Dark Explorers

COMPLETE SET (111)	120.00	300.00
BOOSTER BOX (36 PACKS)	300.00	400.00
BOOSTER PACK (10 CARDS)	8.00	10.00
*REV.FOIL: .75X TO 2X BASIC CARDS		
RELEASED ON MAY 9, 2012		
1 Bulbasaur C	.10	.25
2 Ivysaur U	.20	.50
3 Venusaur HOLO R	1.50	4.00
4 Scyther U	.20	.50
5 Carnivine R	.50	1.50
6 Leafeon R	1.00	2.50
7 Dwebble C	.10	.25
8 Crustle U	.20	.50
9 Karrablast C	.10	.25
10 Shelmet C	.10	.25
11 Accelgor R	.40	1.00
12 Flareon U	.20	.50
13 Entei EX HOLO R	10.00	15.00
14 Torchic C	.10	.25
15 Torchic C	.10	.25
16 Combusken U	.20	.50
17 Blaziken HOLO R	1.50	4.00
18 Torkoal U	.20	.50
19 Heatmor R	.40	1.00
20 Larvesta C	.10	.25
21 Larvesta C	.10	.25
22 Volcarona HOLO R	1.00	2.50
23 Slowpoke C	.10	.25
24 Slowbro U	.20	.50
25 Vaporeon U	.20	.50
26 Kyogre EX HOLO R	8.00	12.00
27 Piplup C	.10	.25
28 Prinplup U	.20	.50
29 Empoleon HOLO R	3.00	8.00
30 Glaceon R	.40	1.00
31 Tympole C	.10	.25
32 Palpitoad U	.20	.50
33 Vanillite C	.10	.25
34 Vanillish U	.20	.50
35 Ducklett (C)	.10	.25
36 Swanna R	.40	1.00
37 Jolteon U	.20	.50
38 Raikou EX HOLO R	6.00	12.00
39 Plusle C	.10	.25
40 Minun C	.10	.25
41 Joltik C	.10	.25
42 Joltik C	.10	.25
43 Galvantula R	.40	1.00
44 Tynamo C	.10	.25
45 Tynamo C	.10	.25
46 Eelektrik U	.20	.50
47 Eelektross HOLO R	1.50	4.00
48 Espeon R	.50	2.00
49 Slowking R	.40	1.00
50 Woobat C	.10	.25
51 Yamask U	.20	.50
52 Cofagrigus R	1.00	2.50
53 Aerodactyl R	1.00	2.50
54 Groudon EX HOLO R	8.00	12.00
55 Drilbur C	.10	.25
56 Excadrill R	.40	1.00
57 Excadrill R	.40	1.00
58 Timburr C	.10	.25
59 Gurdurr U	.20	.50
60 Umbreon U	1.00	2.00
61 Umbreon U	2.50	3.50
62 Sableye U	.20	.50
63 Darkrai EX HOLO R	3.00	6.00
64 Sandile C	.10	.25
65 Krokorok U	.20	.50
66 Krookodile HOLO R	2.00	5.00
67 Scraggy C	.10	.25
68 Scrafty R	1.00	2.50
69 Zorua C	.10	.25
70 Zorua C	.10	.25
71 Zoroark R	3.00	8.00
72 Bisharp R	.50	2.00
73 Vullaby U	.20	.50
74 Escavalier R	.40	1.00
75 Klink C	.10	.25
76 Klang U	.20	.50
77 Klinklang HOLO R	.50	2.00
78 Pawniard C	.10	.25
79 Bisharp R	.50	2.00
80 Chansey C	.10	.25
81 Chansey C	.10	.25
82 Blissey HOLO R	1.00	2.50
83 Eevee C	.10	.25
84 Eevee C	.10	.25
85 Chatot U	.20	.50
86 Lillipup C	.10	.25
87 Herdier U	.20	.50
88 Stoutland R	.50	2.00
89 Haxorus HOLO R	1.50	4.00
90 Tornadus EX HOLO R	3.00	6.00
91 Cheren U	.20	.50
92 Dark Claw U	.20	.50
93 Dark Patch U	3.00	4.00
94 Enhanced Hammer U	.20	.50
95 Hooligans Jim & Cas U	.20	.50
96 N U	1.00	2.00
97 Old Amber Aerodactyl U	.20	.50
98 Professor Juniper U	.20	.50
99 Random Receiver U	.20	.50
100 Rare Candy U	1.00	2.00
101 Twist Mountain U	.20	.50
102 Ultra Ball U	.20	.50
103 Entei EX HOLO SR	25.00	35.00
104 Kyogre EX HOLO SR	15.00	25.00
105 Raikou EX HOLO SR	15.00	25.00
106 Groudon EX HOLO SR	15.00	25.00
107 Darkrai EX HOLO SR	30.00	40.00
108 Tornadus EX HOLO SR	5.00	10.00
109 Gardevoir UR	20.00	30.00
110 Archeops UR	25.00	35.00
111 Pokemon Catcher UR	10.00	20.00

2012 Pokemon Black and White Dragons Exalted

COMPLETE SET (128)	80.00	200.00
BOOSTER BOX (36 PACKS)	100.00	120.00
BOOSTER PACK (10 CARDS)	3.00	5.00
*REV.FOIL: .75X TO 2X BASIC CARDS		
RELEASED ON AUGUST 15, 2012		
1 Hoppip C	.10	.25
2 Skiploom U	.20	.50
3 Jumpluff R	.30	.75
4 Yanma C	.10	.25
5 Yanmega R	.30	.75
6 Wurmple C	.10	.25
7 Silcoon U	.20	.50
8 Beautifly R	.30	.75
9 Cascoon U	.20	.50
10 Nincada C	.10	.25
11 Ninjask U	.20	.50
12 Roselia U	.20	.50
13 Roselia C	.10	.25
14 Roserade U	.20	.50
15 Roserade R	.30	.75
16 Maractus U	.20	.50
17 Foongus C	.10	.25
18 Vulpix C	.10	.25
19 Ninetales HOLO R	1.00	2.50
20 Magmar C	.10	.25
21 Magmortar R	.30	.75
22 Ho-Oh EX UR	8.00	12.00
23 Magikarp C	.10	.25
24 Gyarados R	.30	.75
25 Wailmer U	.20	.50
26 Wailord HOLO R	.60	1.50
27 Feebas C	.10	.25
28 Milotic HOLO R	.60	1.50
29 Spheal (C)	.10	.25
30 Sealeo U	.20	.50
31 Walrein R	.30	.75
32 Buizel C	.10	.25
33 Floatzel U	.20	.50
34 Tympole C	.10	.25
35 Palpitoad U	.20	.50
36 Seismitoad R	.30	.75
37 Alomomola R	.30	.75
38 Mareep C	.10	.25
39 Flaaffy U	.20	.50
40 Ampharos HOLO R	.60	1.50
41 Electrike C	.10	.25
42 Electrike C	.10	.25
43 Manectric R	.30	.75
44 Manectric R	.30	.75
45 Emolga U	.20	.50
46 Mew EX UR	13.00	18.00
47 Dustox R	.30	.75
48 Shedinja R	.30	.75
49 Drifloon C	.10	.25
50 Drifloon C	.10	.25
51 Drifblim R	.30	.75
52 Sigilyph HOLO R	3.00	8.00
53 Trubbish C	.10	.25
54 Garbodor HOLO R	1.00	2.00
55 Gothita C	.10	.25
56 Gothorita U	.20	.50
57 Gothitelle R	.30	.75
58 Golett C	.10	.25
59 Golurk HOLO R	.60	1.50
60 Cubone C	.10	.25
61 Marowak R	.30	.75
62 Nosepass C	.10	.25
63 Baltoy C	.10	.25
64 Claydol R	.30	.75
65 Roggenrola C	.10	.25
66 Boldore U	.20	.50
67 Gigalith HOLO R	.60	1.50
68 Throh U	.20	.50
69 Sawk U	.20	.50
70 Stunfisk U	.20	.50
71 Terrakion EX UR	4.00	7.00
72 Murkrow C	.10	.25
73 Honchkrow R	.30	.75
74 Houndour C	.10	.25
75 Houndoom R	.30	.75
76 Stunky C	.10	.25
77 Skuntank U	.20	.50
78 Aron C	.10	.25
79 Lairon U	.20	.50
80 Aggron HOLO R	.60	1.50
81 Registeel EX UR	4.00	7.00
82 Probopass R	.30	.75
83 Durant U	.20	.50
84 Altaria HOLO R	1.00	2.50
85 Rayquaza EX UR	3.00	6.00
86 Gible C	.10	.25
87 Gible C	.10	.25
88 Gabite U	.20	.50
89 Gabite U	.20	.50
90 Garchomp HOLO R	1.00	2.00
91 Garchomp R	.30	.75
92 Giratina EX UR	4.00	8.00
93 Deino C	.10	.25
94 Deino C	.10	.25
95 Zweilous U	.20	.50
96 Zweilous U	.20	.50
97 Hydreigon HOLO R	4.00	10.00
98 Hydreigon R	.30	.75
99 Aipom C	.10	.25
100 Ambipom R	.30	.75
101 Slakoth C	.10	.25
102 Vigoroth U	.20	.50
103 Slaking HOLO R	.60	1.50
104 Swablu U	.20	.50
105 Swablu C	.10	.25
106 Bidoof C	.10	.25
107 Bibarel U	.20	.50
108 Audino U	.20	.50
109 Minccino C	.10	.25
110 Bouffalant U	.20	.50
111 Rufflet C	.10	.25
112 Braviary R	.30	.75
113 Devolution Spray U	.20	.50
114 Giant Cape U	.20	.50
115 Rescue Scarf U	.20	.50
116 Tool Scrapper U	.20	.50
117 Blend Energy GFPD U	.60	1.50
118 Blend Energy WLFM U	.40	1.00
119 Ho-oh EX Full Art UR	20.00	30.00
120 Mew EX Full Art UR	35.00	45.00
121 Terrakion EX Full Art UR	5.00	10.00
122 Registeel EX Full Art UR	8.00	12.00
123 Rayquaza EX Full Art UR	15.00	25.00
124 Giratina EX Full Art UR	10.00	15.00
125 Serperior UR	8.00	15.00
126 Reuniclus UR	5.00	10.00
127 Krookodile UR	15.00	20.00
128 Rayquaza UR	15.00	25.00

2012 Pokemon Black and White Next Destinies

COMPLETE SET (105)	120.00	300.00
BOOSTER BOX (36 PACKS)	100.00	120.00
BOOSTER PACK (10 CARDS)	3.00	5.00
*REV.FOIL: .75X TO 2X BASIC CARDS		
RELEASED ON FEBRUARY 8, 2012		
1 Pinsir R	.40	1.00
2 Seedot C	.10	.25
3 Kricketot C	.10	.25
4 Kricketune U	.20	.50
5 Shaymin EX HOLO R	2.00	5.00
6 Pansage C	.10	.25
7 Simisage R	.40	1.00
8 Foongus (C)	.10	.25
9 Amoonguss R	.40	1.00
10 Growlithe C	.10	.25
11 Growlithe C	.10	.25
12A Arcanine R	.40	1.00
12B Arcanine STAFF	10.00	20.00
13 Arcanine U	.20	.50
14 Moltres HOLO R	.75	2.00
15 Pansear C	.10	.25
16 Simisear R	.40	1.00
17 Darumaka C	.10	.25
18 Litwick C	.10	.25
19 Lampent U	.20	.50
20 Chandelure HOLO R	2.50	6.00
21 Reshiram R	1.00	2.00
22 Reshiram EX HOLO R	3.00	6.00
23 Staryu C	.10	.25
24 Starmie U	.20	.50
25 Lapras R	.40	1.00
26 Lapras U	.20	.50
27 Articuno HOLO R	.75	2.00
28 Panpour C	.10	.25
29 Simipour R	.40	1.00
30 Basculin U	.20	.50
31 Vanillite C	.10	.25
32 Vanillish U	.20	.50
33 Vanilluxe HOLO R	2.50	6.00
34 Frillish U	.20	.50
35 Jellicent R	.40	1.00
36 Cubchoo C	.10	.25
37 Beartic R	.40	1.00
38 Kyurem EX HOLO R	3.00	6.00
39 Pikachu C	.10	.25
40 Raichu U	.20	.50
41 Zapdos HOLO R	1.50	4.00
42 Shinx C	.10	.25
43 Shinx C	.10	.25
44 Luxio U	.20	.50
45 Luxio U	.20	.50
46 Luxray HOLO R	1.00	2.00
47 Blitzle C	.10	.25
48 Zebstrika R	.40	1.00
49 Emolga U	.20	.50
50 Zekrom R	1.00	3.00
51 Zekrom EX HOLO R	4.00	8.00

52 Grimer C .10 .25
53 Muk R .40 1.00
54A Mewtwo EX HOLO R 3.00 6.00
54B Mewtwo EX HOLO JUMBO 4.00 10.00
55 Ralts C .10 .25
56 Kirlia U .20 .50
57 Gardevoir HOLO R 2.00 4.00
58 Munna C .10 .25
59 Musharna R .75 2.00
60 Darmanitan R 1.25 3.00
61 Elgyem C .10 .25
62 Beheeyem R .40 1.00
63 Riolu C .10 .25
64 Lucario HOLO R 2.00 5.00
65 Hippopotas C .10 .25
66 Hippowdon U .20 .50
67 Mienfoo C .10 .25
68 Mienshao U .20 .50
69 Sneasel C .10 .25
70 Weavile R 1.00 2.50
71 Nuzleaf U .20 .50
72 Shiftry R .75 2.00
73 Scraggy U .20 .50
74 Scrafty HOLO R .75 2.00
75 Bronzor C .10 .25
76 Bronzong R .40 1.00
77 Ferroseed C .10 .25
78 Jigglypuff U .20 .50
79 Wigglytuff R .40 1.00
80 Meowth C .10 .25
81 Persian R .40 1.00
82 Regigigas EX HOLO R 4.00 8.00
83 Pidove C .10 .25
84 Minccino U .20 .50
85 Cinccino HOLO R 1.00 2.50
86 Cilan U .20 .50
87 Exp. Share U .20 .50
88 Heavy Ball U .20 .50
89 Level Ball U .20 .50
90 Pokemon Center U .20 .50
91 Skyarrow Bridge U .20 .50
92 Double Colorless Energy U 1.00 2.00
93 Prism Energy U .20 .50
94 Shaymin EX HOLO SR 5.00 10.00
95 Reshiram EX HOLO SR 13.00 18.00
96 Kyurem EX HOLO SR 8.00 12.00
97 Zekrom EX HOLO SR 20.00 25.00
98 Mewtwo EX HOLO SR 35.00 45.00
99 Regigigas EX HOLO SR 20.00 30.00
100 Emboar UR 8.00 12.00
101 Chandelure UR 5.00 10.00
102 Zoroark UR 15.00 20.00
103 Hydreigon UR 10.00 15.00

2012 Pokemon Dragon Vault

COMPLETE SET (NO PROMOS) 20.00 40.00
PROMO CARDS ISSUED ONE PER BLISTER PACK
1 Dratini .15 .40
2 Dratini .15 .40
3 Dragonair .15 .40
4 Dragonair .15 .40
5 Dragonite .40 1.00
6 Bagon .15 .40
7 Shelgon .15 .40
8 Salamence .40 1.00
9a Latias .40 1.00
9b Latias PROMO .75 2.00
10a Latios .40 1.00
10b Latios PROMO .75 2.00
11a Rayquaza 3.00 8.00
11b Rayquaza PROMO 2.00 5.00
12 Axew .15 .40
13 Axew .15 .40
14 Fraxure .15 .40
15 Fraxure .15 .40
16b Haxorus .40 1.00
16a Haxorus PROMO .75 2.00
17b Druddigon .40 1.00
17a Druddigon PROMO .75 2.00
18 Exp. Share .15 .40
19 First Ticket 2.00 5.00
20 Super Rod .60 1.50
21 Kyurem 8.00 20.00
NNO Code Card 1.50 4.00

2013 Pokemon Black and White Legendary Treasures

COMPLETE SET (115) 50.00 120.00
BOOSTER BOX (36 PACKS) 100.00 120.00
BOOSTER PACK (10 CARDS) 3.00 5.00
*REV.FOIL: .75X TO 2X BASIC CARDS
RELEASED ON NOVEMBER 8, 2013
1 Tangela C .10 .25
2 Tangrowth R .25 .60
3 Shuckle U .15 .40
4 Cherubi U .15 .40
5 Carnivine U .15 .40
6 Snivy C .10 .25
7 Servine U .15 .40
8 Serperior HOLO R .40 1.00
9 Sewaddle C .10 .25
10 Sewaddle C .10 .25
11 Swadloon U .15 .40
12 Leavanny HOLO R .40 1.00
13 Dwebble C .10 .25
14 Crustle U .15 .40
15 Virizion HOLO R .40 1.00
16 Genesect HOLO R .50 1.25
17 Charmander C .10 .25
18 Charmeleon U .15 .40
19 Charizard (Holo) (R) 3.00 6.00
20 Vulpix C .10 .25
21 Ninetales R .25 .60
22 Moltres HOLO R .40 1.00
23 Victini HOLO R .40 1.00
24 Victini EX UR 3.00 6.00
25 Tepig C .10 .25
26 Pignite U .15 .40
27 Emboar HOLO R .75 2.00
28 Reshiram HOLO R .40 1.00
29 Reshiram EX UR 3.00 6.00
30 Magikarp C .10 .25
31 Gyarados R .25 .60
32 Articuno HOLO R .40 1.00
33 Piplup C .10 .25
34 Prinplup U .15 .40
35 Empoleon R .25 .60
36 Phione R .25 .60
37 Oshawott C .10 .25
38 Dewott U .15 .40
39 Samurott HOLO R .40 1.00
40 Tympole C .10 .25
41 Palpitoad U .15 .40
42 Seismitoad R .25 .60
43 Kyurem HOLO R .50 1.25
44 Kyurem EX UR 2.00 5.00
45 Keldeo EX UR 4.00 6.00
46 Zapdos HOLO R .40 1.00
47 Plusle U .15 .40
48 Minun U .15 .40
49 Emolga U .15 .40
50 Thundurus HOLO R .40 1.00
51 Zekrom HOLO R .40 1.00
52 Zekrom EX UR 4.00 7.00
53 Mewtwo HOLO R 2.00 4.00
54 Mewtwo EX UR 4.00 6.00
55 Natu C .10 .25
56 Xatu R .25 .60
57 Misdreavus C .10 .25
58 Mismagius R .25 .60
59 Ralts C .10 .25
60 Kirlia U .15 .40
61 Sableye U .15 .40
62 Croagunk C .10 .25
63 Toxicroak R .25 .60
64 Woobat C .10 .25
65 Swoobat U .15 .40
66 Sigilyph HOLO R .50 1.25
67 Trubbish C .10 .25
68 Garbodor HOLO R .75 2.00
69 Gothita C .10 .25
70 Gothita C .10 .25
71 Gothorita U .15 .40
72 Gothitelle HOLO R .40 1.00
73 Solosis C .10 .25
74 Solosis C .10 .25
75 Duosion U .15 .40
76 Reuniclus R .25 .60
77 Chandelure EX HOLO R 4.00 6.00
78 Meloetta HOLO R .40 1.00
79 Riolu U .15 .40
80 Lucario HOLO R .40 1.00
81 Gallade R .25 .60
82 Excadrill EX HOLO R 3.00 5.00
83 Stunfisk U .15 .40
84 Terrakion HOLO R .50 1.25
85 Landorus HOLO R .40 1.00
86 Meloetta R .25 .60
87 Spiritomb U .30 .75
88 Darkrai EX UR 3.00 5.00
89 Zorua C .10 .25
90 Zoroark HOLO R .40 1.00
91 Cobalion HOLO R .50 1.25
92 Altaria U .15 .40
93 Rayquaza HOLO R .50 1.25
94 Gible C .10 .25
95 Gabite U .15 .40
96 Garchomp HOLO R .60 1.50
97 Deino C .10 .25
98 Zweilous U .15 .40
99 Hydreigon HOLO R .60 1.50
100 Black Kyurem EX UR 5.00 10.00
101 White Kyurem EX UR 5.00 10.00
102 Lugia EX UR 2.00 5.00
103 Swablu C .10 .25
104 Minccino C .10 .25
105 Cinccino HOLO R .40 1.00
106 Druddigon U .15 .40
107 Bouffalant U .15 .40
108 Tornadus HOLO R .30 .75
109 Bianca U .15 .40
110 Cedric Juniper U .15 .40
111 Crushing Hammer U .15 .40
112 Energy Switch U .15 .40
113 Double Colorless Energy U .30 .75
114 Reshiram Full Art UR 25.00 35.00
115 Zekrom Full Art UR 25.00 35.00

2013 Pokemon Black and White Legendary Treasures Radiant Collection

COMPLETE SET (25) 8.00 20.00
RELEASED ON NOVEMBER 3, 2013
RC1 Snivy C .10 .25
RC2 Servine C .10 .25
RC3 Serperior U .15 .40
RC4 Growlithe U .15 .40
RC5 Torchic C .10 .25
RC6 Piplup U .15 .40
RC7 Pikachu U .25 .60
RC8 Ralts (C) .10 .25
RC9 Kirlia C .10 .25
RC10 Gardevoir U .15 .40
RC11 Meloetta EX UR 1.25 3.00
RC12 Stunfisk U .15 .40
RC13 Purrloin U .15 .40
RC14 Eevee U .15 .40
RC15 Teddiursa C .10 .25
RC16 Ursaring C .10 .25
RC17 Audino C .10 .25
RC18 Minccino C .10 .25
RC19 Cinccino U .15 .40
RC20 Elesa C .10 .25
RC21 Shaymin EX Full Art UR 1.50 4.00
RC22 Reshiram Full Art UR 2.00 5.00
RC23 Emolga Full Art UR 1.50 4.00
RC24 Mew EX Full Art UR 5.00 10.00
RC25 Meloetta EX Full Art UR11 2.00 5.00

2013 Pokemon Black and White Plasma Blast

COMPLETE SET (105) 80.00 200.00
BOOSTER BOX (36 PACKS) 100.00 120.00
BOOSTER PACK (10 CARDS) 3.00 5.00
*REV.FOIL: .75X TO 2X BASIC CARDS
RELEASED ON AUGUST 14, 2013
1 Surskit C .10 .25
2 Masquerain R .25 .60
3 Lileep U .15 .40
4 Cradily R .25 .60
5 Tropius U .15 .40
6 Karrablast C .10 .25
7 Shelmet C .10 .25
8 Accelgor R .25 .60
9 Virizion EX UR 5.00 10.00
10 Genesect R .25 .60
11 Genesect EX UR 5.00 10.00
12 Larvesta C .10 .25
13 Volcarona R .25 .60
14 Squirtle C .10 .25
15 Wartortle U .15 .40
16 Blastoise HOLO R 2.00 5.00
17 Lapras C .10 .25
18 Remoraid C .10 .25
19 Octillery U .15 .40
20 Suicune R .50 1.25
21 Snorunt C .10 .25
22 Glalie U .15 .40
23 Froslass R .25 .60
24 Relicanth U .15 .40
25 Snover C .10 .25
26 Abomasnow U .15 .40
27 Tirtouga U .15 .40
28 Carracosta R .25 .60
29 Ducklett C .10 .25
30 Kyurem EX HOLO R 2.50 5.00
31 Tynamo C .10 .25
32 Eelektrik U .15 .40
33 Eelektross HOLO R .25 .60
34 Drifloon C .10 .25
35 Drifblim R .25 .60
36 Uxie R .25 .60
37 Mesprit HOLO R .40 1.00
38 Azelf R .25 .60
39 Munna C .10 .25
40 Musharna U .15 .40
41 Sigilyph HOLO R 2.00 5.00
42 Solosis C .10 .25
43 Duosion U .15 .40
44 Reuniclus (R) .25 .60
45 Golett C .10 .25
46 Golurk HOLO R .25 .60
47 Machop C .10 .25
48 Machoke U .15 .40
49 Machamp HOLO R .25 .60
50 Machamp R .25 .60
51 Throh C .10 .25
52 Sawk C .10 .25
53 Archen U .15 .40
54 Archeops HOLO R .25 .60
55 Houndour C .10 .25
56 Houndoom HOLO R .25 .60
57 Aron C .10 .25
58 Lairon U .15 .40
59 Aggron R .25 .60
60 Jirachi EX UR 13.00 18.00
61 Escavalier R .25 .60
62 Bagon C .10 .25
63 Shelgon U .15 .40
64 Salamence HOLO R .60 1.50
65 Dialga EX UR 2.50 6.00
66 Palkia EX UR 3.00 6.00
67 Axew C .10 .25
68 Fraxure U .15 .40
69 Haxorus HOLO R .75 2.00
70 Druddigon C .10 .25
71 Kangaskhan C .10 .25
72 Porygon C .10 .25
73 Porygon2 U .15 .40
74 Porygon-Z HOLO R .25 .60
75 Teddiursa C .10 .25
76 Ursaring U .15 .40
77 Chatot U .15 .40
78 Caitlin U .15 .40
79 Cover Fossil U .15 .40
80 Energy Retrieval U .15 .40
81 Iris U .15 .40
82 Plume Fossil U .15 .40
83 Pokémon Catcher U .25 .75
84 Professor Juniper U .15 .40
85 Rare Candy U .75 2.00
86 Reversal Trigger U .15 .40
87 Root Fossil Lileep U .15 .40
88 Silver Bangle U .40 1.00
89 Silver Mirror U .25 .60
90 Ultra Ball U .75 .25
91 Plasma Energy U .15 .40
92 G Booster HOLO R 2.00 5.00
93 G Scope HOLO R 1.00 2.50
94 Master Ball HOLO R 2.00 5.00
95 Scoop Up Cyclone HOLO R 1.50 4.00
96 Virizion EX Full Art UR 10.00 15.00
97 Genesect EX Full Art UR 13.00 18.00
98 Jirachi EX Full Art UR 20.00 25.00
99 Dialga EX Full Art UR 10.00 15.00
100 Palkia EX Full Art UR 10.00 15.00
101 Iris Full Art UR 4.00 8.00
102 Exeggcute UR 15.00 25.00
103 Virizion UR 10.00 17.00
104 Dusknoir UR 6.00 12.00
105 Rare Candy UR 30.00 40.00

2013 Pokemon Black and White Plasma Freeze

COMPLETE SET (122) 120.00 300.00
BOOSTER BOX (36 PACKS) 150.00 200.00
BOOSTER PACK (10 CARDS) 4.00 6.00
*REV.FOIL: .75X TO 2X BASIC CARDS
RELEASED ON MAY 8, 2013
1 Weedle C .10 .25
2 Kakuna U .15 .40
3 Beedrill R .25 .60
4 Exeggcute U .15 .40
5 Exeggutor R .25 .60
6 Treecko C .10 .25
7 Grovyle U .15 .40
8 Sceptile HOLO R .40 1.00
9 Cacnea C .10 .25
10 Cacturne R .25 .60
11 Leafeon R .25 .60
12 Flareon U .15 .40
13 Heatran EX HOLO R 3.00 5.00
14 Litwick C .10 .25
15 Lampent U .15 .40
16 Chandelure HOLO R .60 1.50
17 Reshiram HOLO R .40 1.00
18 Horsea C .10 .25
19 Seadra U .15 .40
20 Vaporeon U .15 .40
21 Wooper C .10 .25
22 Quagsire R .25 .60
23 Glaceon R .25 .60
24 Tympole C .10 .25
25 Palpitoad U .15 .40
26 Seismitoad R .25 .60
27 Vanillite C .10 .25
28 Vanillish U .15 .40
29 Vanilluxe R .25 .60
30 Cryogonal U .15 .40
31 Kyurem HOLO R 4.00 10.00
32 Voltorb C .10 .25
33 Electrode HOLO R .40 1.00
34 Jolteon U .15 .40
35 Chinchou C .10 .25
36 Lanturn U .15 .40
37 Pachirisu C .10 .25
38 Thundurus EX HOLO R 3.00 6.00
39 Zekrom HOLO R .40 1.00
40 Nidoran F C .10 .25
41 Nidorina U .15 .40
42 Nidoqueen R .25 .60
43 Nidoran M C .10 .25
44 Nidorino U .15 .40
45 Grimer C .10 .25
46 Muk R .25 .60
47 Mr. Mime R .25 .60
48 Espeon U .15 .40
49 Sableye R .25 .60
50 Beldum C .10 .25
51 Metang U .15 .40

Card	Low	High
52 Metagross HOLO R	.30	.75
53 Deoxys EX HOLO R	2.50	5.00
54 Yamask C	.10	.25
55 Yamask C	.10	.25
56 Cofagrigus HOLO R	.30	.75
57 Cofagrigus R	.25	.60
58 Nidoking R	.25	.60
59 Mankey C	.10	.25
60 Primeape C	.10	.25
61 Onix U	.15	.40
62 Makuhita C	.10	.25
63 Hariyama R	.25	.60
64 Umbreon HOLO R	4.00	6.00
65 Sneasel (C)	.10	.25
66 Weavile R	.30	.75
67 Absol HOLO R	1.25	3.00
68 Sandile C	.10	.25
69 Krokorok U	.15	.40
70 Krookodile R	.25	.60
71 Pawniard C	.10	.25
72 Pawniard C	.10	.25
73 Bisharp R	.25	.60
74 Bisharp U	.15	.40
75 Deino C	.10	.25
76 Deino C	.10	.25
77 Zweilous U	.15	.40
78 Hydreigon HOLO R	.30	.75
79 Steelix R	.25	.60
80 Mawile U	.15	.40
81 Dratini C	.10	.25
82 Dragonair U	.15	.40
83 Dragonite HOLO R	.60	1.50
84 Kingdra HOLO R	.60	1.50
85 Latias EX HOLO R	4.00	7.00
86 Latios EX HOLO R	3.00	6.00
87 Rattata C	.10	.25
88 Raticate R	.25	.60
89 Eevee C	.10	.25
90 Eevee C	.10	.25
91 Hoothoot C	.10	.25
92 Noctowl U	.15	.40
93 Miltank U	.15	.40
94 Kecleon R	.25	.60
95 Starly C	.10	.25
96 Staravia U	.15	.40
97 Staraptor R	.25	.60
98 Tornadus EX HOLO R	3.00	6.00
99 Float Stone U	.30	.75
100 Frozen City U	.15	.40
101 Ghetsis HOLO R	1.50	4.00
102 Shadow Triad U	.15	.40
103 Superior Energy Retrieval U	.30	.75
104 Team Plasma Badge U	.15	.40
105 Team Plasma Ball U	.30	.75
106 Plasma Energy U	.15	.40
107 Life Dew HOLO R	4.00	6.00
108 Rock Guard HOLO R	3.50	6.00
109 Heatran EX HOLO SR	4.00	7.00
110 Thundurus EX HOLO SR	5.00	8.00
111 Deoxys EX HOLO SR	8.00	12.00
112 Latias EX HOLO SR	13.00	18.00
113 Latios EX HOLO SR	8.00	11.00
114 Tornadus EX HOLO SR	4.00	7.00
115 Ghetsis HOLO SR	8.00	12.00
116 Professor Juniper HOLO SR	18.00	25.00
117 Empoleon UR	25.00	35.00
118 Sigilyph UR	10.00	15.00
119 Garbodor UR	10.00	15.00
120 Garchomp UR	12.00	18.00
121 Max Potion UR	55.00	80.00
122 Ultra Ball UR	125.00	200.00

2013 Pokemon Black and White Plasma Storm

Card	Low	High
COMPLETE SET (138)	100.00	250.00
BOOSTER BOX (36 PACKS)	200.00	250.00
BOOSTER PACK (10 CARDS)	6.00	8.00
*REV.FOIL: .75X TO 2X BASIC CARDS		
RELEASED ON FEBRUARY 6, 2013		
1 Turtwig C	.10	.25
2 Grotle U	.20	.50
3 Torterra R	.30	.75
4 Combee C	.10	.25
5 Vespiquen R	.30	.75
6 Cherubi C	.10	.25
7 Cherrim R	.30	.75
8 Sewaddle C	.10	.25
9 Swadloon U	.20	.50
10 Leavanny R	.30	.75
11 Maractus U	.20	.50
12 Foongus C	.10	.25
13 Amoonguss U	.20	.50
14 Moltres EX UR	4.00	8.00
15 Chimchar C	.10	.25
16 Monferno U	.20	.50
17 Infernape HOLO R	.75	2.00
18 Victini EX UR	4.00	6.00
19 Pansear (C)	.10	.25
20 Simisear U	.20	.50
21 Litwick C	.10	.25
22 Lampent U	.20	.50
23 Heatmor U	.20	.50
24 Squirtle C	.10	.25
25 Articuno EX UR	6.00	10.00
26 Swinub C	.10	.25
27 Piloswine U	.20	.50
28 Mamoswine R	.30	.75
29 Lotad C	.10	.25
30 Lombre U	.20	.50
31 Ludicolo R	.30	.75
32 Carvanha C	.10	.25
33 Sharpedo R	.30	.75
34 Manaphy HOLO R	.60	1.50
35 Vanillite C	.10	.25
36 Vanillish U	.20	.50
37 Vanilluxe R	.30	.75
38 Frillish C	.10	.25
39 Jellicent R	.30	.75
40 Cubchoo C	.10	.25
41 Beartic R	.30	.75
42 Magnemite C	.10	.25
43 Magnemite C	.10	.25
44 Magneton U	.20	.50
45 Magneton U	.20	.50
46 Magnezone HOLO R	.50	1.50
47 Magnezone R	.30	.75
48 Zapdos EX UR	5.00	8.00
49 Rotom U	.20	.50
50 Joltik C	.10	.25
51 Galvantula U	.20	.50
52 Zubat C	.10	.25
53 Zubat C	.10	.25
54 Golbat U	.20	.50
55 Crobat HOLO R	.75	2.00
56 Koffing C	.10	.25
57 Koffing U	.20	.50
58 Weezing HOLO R	.60	1.50
59 Ralts C	.10	.25
60 Kirlia U	.20	.50
61 Gallade HOLO R	.60	1.50
62 Giratina R	.40	1.00
63 Trubbish U	.20	.50
64 Trubbish C	.10	.25
65 Trubbish C	.10	.25
66 Garbodor HOLO R	.40	1.00
67 Garbodor R	.30	.75
68 Elgyem C	.10	.25
69 Elgyem U	.20	.50
70 Beheeyem R	.30	.75
71 Phanpy C	.10	.25
72 Donphan U	.20	.50
73 Lunatone U	.20	.50
74 Solrock U	.20	.50
75 Riolu C	.10	.25
76 Riolu C	.10	.25
77 Lucario U	.20	.50
78 Lucario HOLO R	.60	1.50
79 Timburr C	.10	.25
80 Gurdurr U	.20	.50
81 Conkeldurr R	.30	.75
82 Purrloin C	.10	.25
83 Purrloin C	.10	.25
84 Liepard R	.30	.75
85 Scraggy C	.10	.25
86 Scrafty R	.30	.75
87 Skarmory R	.30	.75
88 Klink C	.10	.25
89 Klang U	.20	.50
90 Klinklang HOLO R	.50	1.50
91 Durant U	.20	.50
92 Durant U	.20	.50
93 Cobalion EX UR	2.00	5.00
94 Druddigon R	.30	.75
95 Black Kyurem EX HOLO R	14.00	20.00
96 White Kyurem EX UR	4.00	8.00
97 Clefairy C	.10	.25
98 Clefable R	.30	.75
99 Doduo C	.10	.25
100 Dodrio R	.30	.75
101 Snorlax R	.40	1.00
102 Togepi C	.10	.25
103 Togetic U	.20	.50
104 Togekiss HOLO R	.60	1.50
105 Whismur C	.10	.25
106 Loudred U	.20	.50
107 Exploud R	.30	.75
108 Lugia EX UR	3.00	6.00
109 Skitty C	.10	.25
110 Patrat C	.10	.25
111 Patrat C	.10	.25
112 Watchog U	.20	.50
113 Watchog R	.30	.75
114 Bouffalant R	.30	.75
115 Rufflet C	.10	.25
116 Braviary R	.30	.75
117 Bicycle U	.30	.75
118 Colress U	.75	2.00
119 Colress Machine U	.50	1.25
120 Escape Rope U	.30	.75
121 Ether U	.30	.75
122 Eviolite U	.40	1.00
123 Hypnotoxic Laser U	2.00	3.00
124 Plasma Frigate U	.20	.50
125 Team Plasma Grunt U	.20	.50
126 Virbank City Gym U	5.00	6.00
127 Plasma Energy U	.40	1.00
128 Dowsing Machine HOLO R	2.00	4.00
129 Scramble Switch HOLO R	2.00	5.00
130 Victory Piece HOLO R	.50	2.00
131 Victini EX Full Art UR	8.00	12.00
132 Articuno EX Full Art UR	10.00	15.00
133 Cobalion EX Full Art UR	5.00	10.00
134 Lugia EX Full Art UR	8.00	12.00
135 Colress Full Art UR	8.00	15.00
136 Charizard UR	60.00	80.00
137 Blastoise UR	35.00	45.00
138 Random Receiver UR	10.00	15.00

2014 Pokemon XY

Card	Low	High
COMPLETE SET (146)	80.00	200.00
BOOSTER BOX (36 PACKS)	100.00	120.00
BOOSTER PACK (10 CARDS)	3.00	5.00
*REV.FOIL: 1X TO 2X BASIC CARDS		
RELEASED ON FEBRUARY 5, 2014		
1 Venusaur EX UR	2.00	4.00
2 M Venusaur EX UR	10.00	15.00
3 Weedle C	.10	.25
4 Kakuna U	.15	.40
5 Beedrill R	.25	.60
6 Ledyba C	.10	.25
7 Ledian U	.15	.40
8 Volbeat U	.15	.40
9 Illumise U	.15	.40
10 Pansage C	.10	.25
11 Simisage R	.25	.60
12 Chespin C	.10	.25
13 Quilladin U	.15	.40
14 Chesnaught HOLO R	.50	1.25
15 Scatterbug C	.10	.25
16 Spewpa U	.15	.40
17 Vivillon HOLO R	.40	1.00
18 Skiddo C	.10	.25
19 Gogoat HOLO R	.40	1.00
20 Slugma C	.10	.25
21 Magcargo R	.25	.60
22 Pansear C	.10	.25
23 Simisear R	.25	.60
24 Fennekin C	.10	.25
25 Braixen U	.15	.40
26 Delphox HOLO R	1.00	4.00
27 Fletchinder U	.15	.40
28 Talonflame HOLO R	.40	1.00
29 Blastoise EX UR	3.00	7.00
30 M Blastoise EX UR	15.00	20.00
31 Shellder C	.10	.25
32 Cloyster R	.25	.60
33 Staryu C	.10	.25
34 Starmie R	.25	.60
35 Lapras HOLO R	.40	1.00
36 Corsola U	.15	.40
37 Panpour C	.10	.25
38 Simipour R	.25	.60
39 Froakie C	.10	.25
40 Frogadier U	.15	.40
41 Greninja HOLO R	5.00	8.00
42 Pikachu C	.10	.25
43 Raichu HOLO R	1.50	2.50
44 Voltorb C	.10	.25
45 Electrode U	.15	.40
46 Emolga EX UR	2.00	5.00
47 Ekans C	.10	.25
48 Arbok R	.25	.60
49 Spoink C	.10	.25
50 Grumpig R	.25	.60
51 Venipede C	.10	.25
52 Whirlipede (U)	.15	.40
53 Scolipede R	.25	.60
54 Phantump C	.10	.25
55 Trevenant HOLO R	8.00	13.00
56 Pumpkaboo C	.10	.25
57 Gourgeist HOLO R	1.00	2.50
58 Diglett C	.10	.25
59 Dugtrio R	.25	.60
60 Rhyhorn C	.10	.25
61 Rhydon R	.25	.60
62 Rhyperior HOLO R	.30	.75
63 Lunatone U	.15	.40
64 Solrock U	.15	.40
65 Timburr C	.10	.25
66 Gurdurr U	.15	.40
67 Conkeldurr R	.25	.60
68 Sableye U	.15	.40
69 Sandile C	.10	.25
70 Krokorok U	.15	.40
71 Krookodile R	.25	.60
72 Zorua C	.10	.25
73 Zoroark HOLO R	.30	.75
74 Inkay U	.15	.40
75 Inkay C	.10	.25
76 Malamar R	.25	.60
77 Malamar R	.25	.60
78 Yveltal R	1.25	3.00
79 Yveltal EX UR	4.00	8.00
80 Skarmory EX UR	2.00	5.00
81 Pawniard C	.10	.25
82 Bisharp R	.25	.60
83 Honedge C	.10	.25
84 Doublade U	.15	.40
85 Aegislash R	.25	.60
86 Aegislash HOLO R	.60	1.50
87 Jigglypuff C	.10	.25
88 Jigglypuff C	.10	.25
89 Wigglytuff R	.25	.60
90 Wigglytuff R	.25	.60
91 Mr. Mime U	.15	.40
92 Spritzee C	.10	.25
93 Aromatisse HOLO R	2.00	5.00
94 Swirlix C	.10	.25
95 Slurpuff HOLO R	.60	1.50
96 Xerneas R	1.00	2.50
97 Xerneas EX UR	3.00	6.00
98 Doduo C	.10	.25
99 Dodrio U	.15	.40
100 Tauros R	.25	.60
101 Dunsparce U	.15	.40
102 Taillow C	.10	.25
103 Swellow R	.25	.60
104 Skitty C	.10	.25
105 Delcatty U	.15	.40
106 Bidoof C	.10	.25
107 Bibarel R	.25	.60
108 Lillipup C	.10	.25
109 Herdier U	.15	.40
110 Stoutland R	.25	.60
111 Bunnelby C	.10	.25
112 Diggersby U	.15	.40
113 Fletchling C	.10	.25
114 Furfrou HOLO R	.40	1.00
115 Cassius U	.15	.40
116 Evosoda U	.40	1.00
117 Fairy Garden U	.15	.40
118 Great Ball U	.15	.40
119 Hard Charm U	.15	.40
120 Max Revive U	.15	.40
121 Muscle Band U	2.00	3.00
122 Professor Sycamore U	.40	1.00
123 Professor's Letter U	.30	.75
124 Red Card U	.75	2.00
125 Roller Skates U	.15	.40
126 Shadow Circle U	.15	.40
127 Shauna U	.40	1.00
128 Super Potion U	.15	.40
129 Team Flare Grunt U	.15	.40
130 Double Colorless Energy U	1.00	1.50
131 Rainbow Energy U	.40	1.00
132 Grass Energy C	.10	.25
133 Fire Energy C	.10	.25
134 Water Energy C	.10	.25
135 Lightning Energy C	.10	.25
136 Psychic Energy C	.10	.25
137 Fighting Energy C	.10	.25
138 Darkness Energy C	.25	.60
139 Metal Energy C	.25	.60
140 Fairy Energy C	.10	.25
141 Venusaur EX HOLO UR	8.00	15.00
142 Blastoise EX Full Art UR	10.00	20.00
143 Emolga EX HOLO UR	3.00	6.00
144 Yveltal EX HOLO UR	15.00	20.00
145 Skarmory EX HOLO UR	3.00	6.00
146 Xerneas EX HOLO UR	10.00	15.00

2014 Pokemon XY Flashfire

Card	Low	High
COMPLETE SET (109)	75.00	200.00
BOOSTER BOX (36 PACKS)	100.00	120.00
BOOSTER PACK (10 CARDS)	3.00	5.00
*REV.FOIL: 1X TO 2X BASIC CARDS		
RELEASED ON MAY 7, 2014		
1 Caterpie C	.10	.25
2 Metapod U	.15	.40
3 Butterfree R	.25	.60
4 Pineco C	.10	.25
5 Seedot C	.10	.25
6 Nuzleaf U	.15	.40
7 Shiftry HOLO R	.40	1.00
8 Roselia C	.10	.25
9 Roserade U	.15	.40
10 Maractus U	.15	.40
11 Charizard EX HOLO R	3.00	6.00
12 Charizard EX HOLO R	5.00	10.00
13 M Charizard EX HOLO R	35.00	45.00
14 Ponyta C	.10	.25
15 Rapidash U	.15	.40
16 Torkoal U	.15	.40
17 Fletchinder U	.15	.40
18 Litleo C	.10	.25
19 Litleo C	.10	.25
20 Pyroar HOLO R	1.50	2.50
21 Qwilfish R	.25	.60
22 Feebas C	.10	.25
23 Milotic HOLO R	.40	1.00
24 Spheal C	.10	.25
25 Sealeo U	.15	.40
26 Walrein R	.25	.60
27 Luvdisc U	.15	.40
28 Buizel C	.10	.25
29 Floatzel R	.25	.60
30 Bergmite C	.10	.25
31 Avalugg U	.15	.40

32 Shinx C .10 .25
33 Luxio U .15 .40
34 Luxray R .25 .60
35 Magnezone EX HOLO R 2.00 4.00
36 Helioptile C .10 .25
37 Heliolisk R .40 1.00
38 Duskull C .10 .25
39 Dusclops U .15 .40
40 Dusknoir HOLO R .40 1.00
41 Toxicroak EX HOLO R 2.00 5.00
42 Espurr C .10 .25
43 Meowstic R .75 1.50
44 Skrelp C .10 .25
45 Geodude C .10 .25
46 Graveler U .15 .40
47 Golem R .25 .60
48 Binacle C .10 .25
49 Barbaracle R .25 .60
50 Sneasel U .15 .40
51 Sneasel C .10 .25
52 Weavile (R) .40 1.00
53 Stunky C .10 .25
54 Stunky C .10 .25
55 Skuntank R .25 .60
56 Sandile C .10 .25
57 Krokorok U .15 .40
58 Scraggy C .10 .25
59 Scrafty R .40 1.00
60 Forretress R .25 .60
61 Durant R .25 .60
62 Flabébé C .10 .25
63 Flabébé C .10 .25
64 Floette R .25 .60
65 Floette U .15 .40
66 Florges HOLO R .75 1.50
67 Spritzee C .10 .25
68 Carbink HOLO R .75 1.50
69 M Charizard EX HOLO R 40.00 50.00
70 Druddigon HOLO R .75 1.50
71 Dragalge R .75 1.50
72 Goomy C .10 .25
73 Sliggoo U .15 .40
74 Goodra HOLO R .75 2.00
75 Pidgey C .10 .25
76 Pidgeotto U .15 .40
77 Pidgeot R .25 .60
78 Kangaskhan EX HOLO R 2.50 5.00
79 M Kangaskhan EX HOLO R 5.00 10.00
80 Snorlax R .25 .60
81 Sentret C .10 .25
82 Furret R .25 .60
83 Miltank U .15 .40
84 Buneary C .10 .25
85 Lopunny R .25 .60
86 Fletchling C .10 .25
87 Furfrou U .15 .40
88 Blacksmith U .75 1.50
89 Fiery Torch U .30 .75
90 Lysandre U .75 2.00
91 Magnetic Storm U .30 .75
92 Pal Pad U .40 1.00
93 Pokémon Center Lady U .30 .75
94 Pokémon Fan Club U .40 1.00
95 Protection Cube U .15 .40
96 Sacred Ash U .25 .60
97 Startling Megaphone U .40 1.00
98 Trick Shovel U .30 .75
99 Ultra Ball U .30 .75
100 Charizard EX Full Art UR 13.00 20.00
101 Magnezone EX HOLO UR 4.31 10.00
102 Toxicroak EX HOLO UR 3.00 6.00
103 Kangaskhan EX HOLO UR 3.00 7.00
104 Lysandre Full Art UR 18.00 25.00
105 Pokemon Center Lady Full Art UR 6.00 10.00
106 Pokemon Fan Club Full Art UR 4.00 7.00
107 M Charizard EX UR 40.00 50.00
108 M Charizard EX UR 50.00 60.00
109 M Kangaskhan UR 8.00 12.00

2014 Pokemon XY Furious Fists

COMPLETE SET (113) 80.00 200.00
BOOSTER BOX (36 PACKS) 100.00 120.00
BOOSTER PACK (10 CARDS) 3.00 5.00
*REV.FOIL: .75X TO 2X BASIC CARDS
RELEASED ON AUGUST 13, 2014
1 Bellsprout C .10 .25
2 Weepinbell U .15 .40
3 Victreebel HOLO R .20 .60
4 Heracross EX HOLO R 2.50 5.00
5 MegaHeracross EX HOLO R 5.00 10.00
6 Shroomish C .10 .25
7 Leafeon R .50 5.00
8 Shelmet C .10 .25
9 Accelgor U .15 .40
10 Magmar C .10 .25
11 Magmortar R .40 1.00
12 Torchic C .10 .25
13 Combusken U .15 .40
14 Blaziken HOLO R .75 2.00
15 Poliwag C .10 .25
16 Poliwhirl U .15 .40
17 Poliwrath HOLO R .75 2.00
18 Politoed R .75 2.00
19 Glaceon R .50 8.00
20 Seismitoad EX HOLO R 10.00 15.00
21 Cubchoo C .10 .25
22 Beartic R .50 1.25
23 Clauncher C .10 .25
24 Clawitzer HOLO R .50 3.00
25 Amaura U .40 1.00
26 Aurorus R .50 2.50
27 Pikachu C .10 .25
28 Raichu U .15 .40
29 Electabuzz C .10 .25
30 Electivire R .20 .60
31 Plusle C .10 .25
32 Minun (C) .10 .25
33 Thundurus R .20 .60
34 Dedenne U .15 .40
35 Drowzee C .10 .25
36 Hypno R .20 .60
37 Jynx R .20 .60
38 Skorupi C .10 .25
39 Gothita C .10 .25
40 Gothorita U .15 .40
41 Gothitelle R .20 .60
42 Golett C .10 .25
43 Golurk R .20 .60
44 Machop C .10 .25
45 Machoke U .15 .40
46 Machamp HOLO R .50 3.00
47 Hitmonlee U .15 .40
48 Hitmonchan U .15 .40
49 Hitmontop U .15 .40
50 Breloom R .20 .60
51 Makuhita C .10 .25
52 Hariyama R .20 .60
53 Trapinch C .10 .25
54 Lucario EX HOLO R 10.00 15.00
55 MegaLucario EX HOLO R 18.00 22.00
56 Mienfoo C .10 .25
57 Mienshao U .15 .40
58 Landorus HOLO R 3.00 4.00
59 Pancham U .15 .40
60 Pancham C .10 .25
61 Tyrunt U .60 1.50
62 Tyrantrum R .50 3.00
63 Hawlucha HOLO R 1.25 3.00
64 Hawlucha EX HOLO R 2.00 5.00
65 Drapion R .20 .60
66 Scraggy C .10 .25
67 Scrafty U .15 .40
68 Pangoro R .20 .60
69 Clefairy C .10 .25
70 Clefairy C .10 .25
71 Clefable U .15 .40
72 Sylveon R .50 3.00
73 Klefki U .15 .40
74 Dragonite EX HOLO R 3.00 6.00
75 Vibrava U .15 .40
76 Flygon R .50 8.00
77 Noivern HOLO R .50 1.25
78 Lickitung C .10 .25
79 Lickilicky U .15 .40
80 Eevee C .40 1.00
81 Slakoth C .10 .25
82 Vigoroth U .15 .40
83 Slaking HOLO R .60 1.50
84 Patrat C .10 .25
85 Watchog U .15 .40
86 Tornadus R .20 .60
87 Noibat C .10 .25
88 Battle Reporter U .15 .40
89 Energy Switch U .15 .40
90 Fighting Stadium U .40 1.00
91 Focus Sash U .40 1.00
92 Fossil Researcher U .40 1.00
93 Full Heal U .15 .40
94 Jaw Fossil U .40 1.00
95 Korrina U .40 1.00
96 Maintenance U .15 .40
97 Mountain Ring U .40 1.00
98 Sail Fossil U .40 1.00
99 Sparkling Robe U .40 1.00
100 Super Scoop Up U .15 .40
101 Tool Retriever U .15 .40
102 Training Center U .40 1.00
103 Herbal Energy U .40 1.00
104 Strong Energy U 2.00 3.00
105 Heracross HOLO SR 3.00 7.00
106 Seismitoad HOLO SR 15.00 20.00
107 Lucario HOLO SR 20.00 25.00
108 Dragonite HOLO SR 8.00 12.00
109 Battle Reporter HOLO SR 3.00 6.00
110 Fossil Researcher HOLO SR 3.00 5.00
111 Korrina HOLO SR 8.00 12.00
112 MegaHeracross UR 7.00 10.00
113 MegaLucario UR 18.00 23.00

2014 Pokemon XY Phantom Forces

COMPLETE SET (122) 100.00 250.00
BOOSTER BOX (36 PACKS) 100.00 120.00
BOOSTER PACK (10 CARDS) 3.00 5.00
*REV.FOIL: .75X TO 2X BASIC CARDS
RELEASED ON NOVEMBER 5, 2014
1 Venonat C .10 .25
2 Venomoth R .25 .60
3 Yanma C .10 .25
4 Yanmega R .25 .60
5 Sewaddle C .10 .25
6 Swadloon U .15 .40
7 Leavanny R .25 .60
8 Karrablast C .10 .25
9 Fletchinder U .15 .40
10 Talonflame R .25 .60
11 Litleo C .10 .25
12 Pyroar HOLO R .75 2.00
13 Krabby C .10 .25
14 Kingler U .15 .40
15 Totodile C .10 .25
16 Croconaw U .15 .40
17 Feraligatr HOLO R .25 .60
18 Finneon C .10 .25
19 Lumineon U .15 .40
20 Frillish C .10 .25
21 Jellicent R .25 .60
22 Alomomola C .10 .25
23 Manectric EX HOLO R 7.00 10.00
24 MegaManectric EX HOLO R 10.00 15.00
25 Pachirisu R .25 .60
26 Joltik C .10 .25
27 Galvantula R .25 .60
28 Helioptile C .10 .25
29 Helioptile C .10 .25
30 Heliolisk HOLO R .40 1.00
31 Zubat C .10 .25
32 Golbat U .15 .40
33 Crobat R 2.50 3.50
34 Gengar EX HOLO R 8.00 12.00
35 MegaGengar EX HOLO R 12.00 18.00
36 Wobbuffet U .15 .40
37 Gulpin C .10 .25
38 Swalot R .25 .60
39 Munna C .10 .25
40 Musharna R .25 .60
41 Litwick C .10 .25
42 Lampent U .15 .40
43 Chandelure HOLO R .25 .60
44 Pumpkaboo C .10 .25
45 Gourgeist HOLO R .25 .60
46 Gligar C .10 .25
47 Gliscor R .25 .60
48 Roggenrola C .10 .25
49 Boldore U .15 .40
50 Gigalith HOLO R .75 2.00
51 Murkrow C .10 .25
52 Honchkrow R .25 .60
53 Poochyena C .10 .25
54 Mightyena R .25 .60
55 Spiritomb R .25 .60
56 Purrloin C .10 .25
57 Liepard U .15 .40
58 Malamar EX HOLO R 2.50 6.00
59 Skarmory C .10 .25
60 Bronzor C .10 .25
61 Bronzong R .75 2.00
62 Dialga EX HOLO R 4.00 6.00
63 Heatran HOLO R .75 2.00
64 Escavalier R .25 .60
65 Aegislash EX HOLO R 4.00 6.00
66 Klefki U .15 .40
67 Florges EX HOLO R 2.00 4.00
68 Swirlix C .10 .25
69 Slurpuff HOLO R .40 1.00
70 Dedenne C .10 .25
71 Diancie HOLO R 1.00 2.50
72 Deino C .10 .25
73 Zweilous U .15 .40
74 Hydreigon HOLO R .60 1.50
75 Goomy C .10 .25
76 Sliggoo U .15 .40
77 Goodra HOLO R .75 2.00
78 Spearow C .10 .25
79 Fearow U .15 .40
80 Chansey C .10 .25
81 Blissey R .25 .60
82 Girafarig U .15 .40
83 Whismur C .10 .25
84 Loudred U .15 .40
85 Exploud R .25 .60
86 Regigigas HOLO R .75 2.00
87 Bunnelby C .10 .25
88 Diggersby R .25 .60
89 Fletchling C .10 .25
90 Furfrou U .15 .40
91 AZ U .15 .40
92 Battle Compressor U 5.00 6.00
93 Dimension Valley U .15 .40
94 Enhanced Hammer U .15 .40
95 Gengar Spirit Link U .15 .40
96 Hand Scope U .15 .40
97 Head Ringer HOLO R 5.00 10.00
98 Jamming Net HOLO R 1.00 2.00
99 Lysandre's Trump Card U .40 1.00
100 Manectric Spirit Link U .75 2.00
101 Professor Sycamore U .15 .40
102 Robo Substitute U .15 .40
103 Roller Skates U .15 .40
104 Shauna U .15 .40
105 Steel Shelter U .15 .40
106 Target Whistle U .15 .40
107 Tierno U .15 .40
108 Trick Coin U .15 .40
109 VS Seeker U 8.00 11.00
110 Xerosic U .15 .40
111 Double Colorless Energy U 1.00 2.00
112 Mystery Energy U .15 .40
113 Manectric EX UR 10.00 15.00
114 Gengar EX UR 10.00 15.00
115 Malamar EX UR 6.00 9.00
116 Florges EX UR 4.00 6.00
117 AZ UR 5.00 8.00
118 Lysandre's Trump Card UR 3.00 5.00
119 Xerosic UR 3.00 6.00
120 MegaManectric EX HOLO SR 15.00 20.00
121 MegaGengar EX HOLO SR 14.00 18.00
122 Dialga EX HOLO SR 25.00 35.00

2014 Pokemon XY Phantom Forces Exclusives

10P Talonflame (Theme Deck excl.)
12P Pyroar (Theme Deck excl.)
17P Feraligatr (Theme Deck excl.)
27P Galvantula (Theme Deck excl.)
30P Heliolisk (Theme Deck excl.)
95P Gengar Spirit Link (2-pack excl.)

2015 Pokemon XY Primal Clash

COMPLETE SET (164) 150.00 400.00
BOOSTER BOX (36 PACKS) 100.00 120.00
BOOSTER PACK (10 CARDS) 3.00 5.00
*REV.FOIL: .75X TO 2X BASIC CARDS
RELEASED ON FEBRUARY 4, 2015
1 Weedle C .10 .25
2 Kakuna U .15 .40
3 Beedrill R .25 .60
4 Tangela C .10 .25
5 Tangrowth R .25 .60
6 Treecko C .10 .25
7 Grovyle U .15 .40
8 Sceptile R .75 2.00
9 Sceptile HOLO R 2.00 5.00
10 Lotad C .15 .40
11 Lombre U .15 .40
12 Ludicolo HOLO R .50 1.00
13 Surskit C .10 .25
14 Masquerain U .15 .40
15 Shroomish C .10 .25
16 Breloom R .25 .60
17 Volbeat C .10 .25
18 Illumise C .10 .25
19 Trevenant EX HOLO R 3.00 5.00
20 Vulpix C .75 2.00
21 Ninetales R .60 1.50
22 Slugma C .10 .25
23 Magcargo U .15 .40
24 Magcargo R .75 2.00
25 Torchic C .20 .50
26 Torchic U .60 1.50
27 Combusken U .25 .60
28 Blaziken HOLO R 1.25 2.00
29 Camerupt EX HOLO R 2.50 4.00
30 Horsea C .25 .60
31 Seadra U .25 .60
32 Staryu C .10 .25
33 Mudkip C .15 .40
34 Marshtomp U .20 .50
35 Swampert R .40 1.00
36 Swampert HOLO R 2.00 3.00
37 Ludicolo R .50 1.00
38 Wailord EX HOLO R 7.00 10.00
39 Barboach C .10 .25
40 Whiscash U .15 .40
41 Whiscash R .50 1.00
42 Corphish C .10 .25
43 Feebas C .10 .25
44 Milotic HOLO R 3.00 4.00
45 Spheal C .10 .25
46 Spheal C .10 .25
47 Sealeo U .30 .75
48 Walrein R .25 .60
49 Clamperl C .15 .40
50 Huntail HOLO R 2.00 5.00
51 Gorebyss U .15 .40
52 Gorebyss R .50 1.00
53 Kyogre R .75 2.00
54 Kyogre EX HOLO R 3.00 5.00
55 Primal Kyogre EX HOLO R 10.00 15.00
56 Manaphy HOLO R 2.50 6.00
57 Chinchou C .10 .25
58 Lanturn U .15 .40
59 Electrike C .10 .25
60 Electrike U .60 1.50
61 Manectric HOLO R .75 2.00
62 Tynamo C .10 .25
63 Eelektrik U .15 .40
64 Eelektrik R 2.00 5.00
65 Eelektross HOLO R .50 1.00

66 Nidoran C	.10	.25
67 Nidorina U	.15	.40
68 Nidoqueen U	.20	.50
69 Nidoqueen R	.50	3.00
70 Tentacool C	.10	.25
71 Tentacool U	.40	1.00
72 Tentacruel R	.25	.60
73 Starmie R	.25	.60
74 Rhyhorn C	.10	.25
75 Rhydon U	.20	.50
76 Rhyperior R	.25	.60
77 Rhyperior HOLO R	.50	1.50
78 Nosepass C	.10	.25
79 Meditite C	.20	.50
80 Medicham HOLO R	.50	4.00
81 Medicham R	.75	2.00
82 Trapinch C	.10	.25
83 Solrock C	.60	1.50
84 Groudon R	.75	2.00
85 Groudon EX HOLO R	3.00	5.00
86 Primal Groudon EX HOLO R	13.00	17.00
87 Hippopotas C	.10	.25
88 Hippowdon HOLO R	.50	3.00
89 Drilbur C	.10	.25
90 Diggersby R	.40	1.00
91 Sharpedo EX HOLO R	2.00	4.00
92 Crawdaunt HOLO R	.50	1.00
93 Aggron EX HOLO R	3.00	5.00
94 MegaAggron EX HOLO R	7.00	10.00
95 Probopass R	.25	.60
96 Excadrill R	.75	2.00
97 Excadrill HOLO R	2.00	5.00
98 Honedge C	.20	.50
99 Doublade U	.20	.50
100 Aegislash HOLO R	.50	1.00
101 Mr. Mime U	.25	.75
102 Marill C	.10	.25
103 Azumarill R	.25	.60
104 Azumarill HOLO R	.50	1.00
105 Gardevoir EX HOLO R	3.00	6.00
106 MegaGardevoir EX HOLO R	6.00	20.00
107 Kingdra R	.60	1.50
108 Kingdra HOLO R	.50	1.50
109 Vibrava U	.15	.40
110 Flygon HOLO R	.60	1.50
111 Zigzagoon C	.10	.25
112 Linoone U	.15	.40
113 Skitty C	.10	.25
114 Delcatty R	.25	.60
115 Spinda C	.10	.25
116 Bidoof C	.50	1.25
117 Bidoof U	.75	2.00
118 Bibarel U	.15	.40
119 Bouffalant U	.20	.50
120 Bunnelby C	.10	.25
121 Bunnelby U	.75	2.00
122 Acro Bike U	1.25	2.00
123 Aggron Spirit Link U	.40	1.00
124 Archie's Ace in the Hole U	.40	1.00
125 Dive Ball U	1.50	2.50
126 Energy Retrieval U	.30	.75
127 Escape Rope U	.40	1.00
128 Exp. Share U	.75	2.00
129 Fresh Water Set U	.25	.60
130 Gardevoir Spirit Link U	.30	.75
131 Groudon Spirit Link U	.30	.75
132 Kyogre Spirit Link U	.25	.60
133 Maxie's Hidden Ball Trick U	.25	.60
134 Professor Birch's Observations U	3.00	4.00
135 Rare Candy U	.25	.60
136 Repeat Ball U	.40	1.00
137 Rough Seas U	1.50	2.50
138 Scorched Earth U	.60	1.50
139 Shrine of Memories U	.40	1.00
140 Silent Lab U	.40	1.00
141 Teammates U	.30	.75
142 Weakness Policy U	.40	1.00
143 Shield Energy U	.40	1.00
144 Wonder Energy U	.25	.60
145 Trevenant EX UR	4.00	7.00
146 Camerupt EX UR	5.00	12.00
147 Wailord EX UR	10.00	15.00
148 Kyogre EX UR	7.00	10.00
149 Primal Kyogre EX UR	14.00	18.00
150 Groudon EX UR	8.00	12.00
151 Primal Groudon EX UR	15.00	20.00
152 Sharpedo EX UR	4.00	7.00
153 Aggron EX UR	4.00	7.00
154 MegaAggron EX UR	10.00	15.00
155 Gardevoir EX UR	8.00	12.00
156 MegaGardevoir EX UR	7.00	11.00
157 Archie's Ace in the Hole UR	5.00	12.00
158 Maxie's Hidden Ball Trick UR	6.00	10.00
159 Professor Birch's Observations UR	13.00	17.00
160 Teammates UR	6.00	15.00
161 Dive Ball UR	15.00	20.00
162 Enhanced Hammer UR	8.00	12.00
163 Switch UR	12.00	18.00
164 Weakness Policy UR	6.00	15.00

2015 Pokemon XY Double Crisis

COMPLETE SET (34)	12.00	30.00
BOOSTER BOX (36 PACKS)	100.00	120.00
BOOSTER PACK (10 CARDS)	3.00	4.00
*REV.FOIL: .75X TO 2X BASIC CARDS		
RELEASED ON MARCH 25, 2015	3.00	5.00
1 Team Magma's Numel C	.20	.50
2 Team Magma's Camerupt HOLO R	2.50	4.00
3 Team Aqua's Spheal C	.20	.50
4 Team Aqua's Sealeo C	.20	.50
5 Team Aqua's Walrein HOLO R	.75	2.00
6 Team Aqua's Kyogre EX HOLO R	6.00	9.00
7 Team Aqua's Grimer C	.20	.50
8 Team Aqua's Muk HOLO R	.75	2.00
9 Team Aqua's Seviper C	.20	.50
10 Team Magma's Baltoy C	.20	.50
11 Team Magma's Claydol HOLO R	.75	2.00
12 Team Magma's Aron C	.20	.50
13 Team Magma's Lairon C	.20	.50
14 Team Magma's Aggron HOLO R	.50	1.00
15 Team Magma's Groudon EX HOLO R	5.00	8.00
16 Team Aqua's Poochyena C	.20	.50
17 Team Magma's Poochyena C	.20	.50
18 Team Aqua's Mightyena C	.20	.50
19 Team Magma's Mightyena C	.20	.50
20 Team Aqua's Carvanha C	.20	.50
21 Team Aqua's Sharpedo HOLO R	.50	1.00
22 Team Magma's Zangoose C	.20	.50
23 Aqua Diffuser U	.30	.75
24 Magma Pointer U	.30	.75
25 Team Aqua Admin U	.30	.75
26 Team Aqua Grunt U	.30	.75
27 Team Aqua's Great Ball U	.30	.75
28 Team Aqua's Secret Base U	1.50	2.00
29 Team Magma Admin U	.30	.75
30 Team Magma Grunt U	.30	.75
31 Team Magma's Great Ball U	.30	.75
32 Team Magma's Secret Base U	1.50	2.00
33 Double Aqua Energy U	.30	.75
34 Double Magma Energy U	.30	.75

2015 Pokemon XY Roaring Skies

COMPLETE SET (110)	120.00	250.00
BOOSTER BOX (36 PACKS)	100.00	120.00
BOOSTER PACK (10 CARDS)	3.00	5.00
*REV.FOIL: .75X TO 2X BASIC CARDS		
RELEASED ON MAY 6, 2015		
1 Exeggcute C	.10	.25
2 Exeggutor U	.15	.40
3 Wurmple C	.10	.25
4 Silcoon U	.15	.40
5 Beautifly HOLO R	.40	1.00
6 Cascoon C	.10	.25
7 Dustox U	.15	.40
8 Dustox R	.25	.60
9 Nincada C	.10	.25
10 Ninjask U	.15	.40
11 Shedinja R	.25	.60
12 Tropius U	.15	.40
13 Victini R	.40	1.00
14 Fletchinder U	.15	.40
15 Talonflame R	.25	.60
16 Articuno R	.40	1.00
17 Articuno R	.75	2.00
18 Wingull C	.10	.25
19 Pelipper U	.15	.40
20 Pikachu C	.10	.25
21 Voltorb C	.10	.25
22 Electrode U	.15	.40
23 Zapdos R	.25	.60
24 Electrike C	.10	.25
25 Manectric U	.15	.40
26 Thundurus EX HOLO R	3.00	5.00
27 Natu C	.10	.25
28 Natu C	.10	.25
29 Xatu R	.25	.60
30 Shuppet C	.40	1.00
31 Banette R	.25	.60
32 Banette R	.25	.60
33 Deoxys HOLO R	.75	1.50
34 Gallade EX HOLO R	2.00	4.00
35 MegaGallade EX HOLO R	3.00	7.00
36 Gligar C	.10	.25
37 Gliscor U	.15	.40
38 Binacle C	.10	.25
39 Hawlucha C	.10	.25
40 Absol HOLO R	.75	2.00
41 Inkay C	.10	.25
42 Jirachi HOLO R	.75	2.00
43 Togepi C	.10	.25
44 Togetic U	.15	.40
45 Togekiss R	.25	.60
46 Togekiss HOLO R	.75	2.00
47 Carbink R	.25	.60
48 Klefki R	.25	.60
49 Dratini C	2.00	5.00
50 Dragonair U	1.25	3.00
51 Dragonite R	.25	.60
52 Dragonite HOLO R	.75	1.50
53 Altaria U	.15	.40
54 Bagon C	.10	.25
55 Bagon C	.10	.25
56 Shelgon U	.15	.40
57 Salamence HOLO R	.50	1.50
58 Latios EX HOLO R	2.00	4.00
59 MegaLatios EX HOLO R	4.00	7.00
60 Rayquaza EX HOLO R	2.00	4.00
61 MegaRayquaza EX HOLO R	20.00	30.00
62 Hydreigon EX HOLO R	2.00	4.00
63 Reshiram HOLO R	.75	2.00
64 Zekrom HOLO R	.75	2.00
65 Spearow C	.10	.25
66 Fearow U	.15	.40
67 Meowth C	.10	.25
68 Dunsparce C	.10	.25
69 Skarmory R	.25	.60
70 Taillow C	.10	.25
71 Swellow R	.25	.60
72 Swellow HOLO R	.75	2.00
73 Swablu C	.10	.25
74 Altaria R	.25	.60
75 Rayquaza EX HOLO R	2.00	5.00
76 MegaRayquaza EX HOLO R	8.00	12.00
77 Shaymin EX HOLO R	40.00	50.00
78 Pidove C	.25	.50
79 Tranquill U	.15	.40
80 Unfezant U	.15	.40
81 Unfezant R	.25	.60
82 Fletchling C	.10	.25
83 Gallade Spirit Link U	.15	.40
84 Healing Scarf U	.15	.40
85 Latios Spirit Link U	10.00	25.00
86 Mega Turbo U	.30	.75
87 Rayquaza Spirit Link U	.15	.40
88 Revive U	3.00	8.00
89 Sky Field U	.40	1.00
90 Steven U	.40	1.00
91 Switch U	.25	.60
92 Trainers' Mail U	2.00	3.00
93 Ultra Ball U	.25	.60
94 Wally U	.40	1.00
95 Wide Lens U	.15	.40
96 Winona U	.40	1.00
97 Double Dragon Energy U	.60	1.50
98 Thundurus EX UR	3.00	5.00
99 Gallade EX UR	4.00	8.00
100 MegaGallade EX UR	4.00	6.00
101 Latios EX UR	6.00	15.00
102 MegaLatios EX UR	5.00	10.00
103 Hydreigon EX UR	3.00	4.00
104 Rayquaza EX UR	5.00	10.00
105 MegaRayquaza EX UR	10.00	15.00
106 Shaymin EX UR	50.00	60.00
107 Wally UR	4.00	7.00
108 Winona UR	3.00	6.00
109 Energy Switch UR	3.00	5.00
110 VS Seeker UR	25.00	35.00

2015 Pokemon XY Ancient Origins

COMPLETE SET (100)	120.00	250.00
BOOSTER BOX (36 PACKS)	100.00	120.00
BOOSTER PACK (10 CARDS)	3.00	5.00
*REV.FOIL: .75X TO 2X BASIC CARDS		
RELEASED ON AUGUST 12, 2015		
1 Oddish C	.10	.25
2 Gloom U	.20	.50
3 Vileplume R	.50	1.50
4 Bellossom U	.20	.50
5 Spinarak C	.10	.25
6 Ariados U	.20	.50
7 Sceptile EX HOLO R	4.00	7.00
8 MegaSceptile EX HOLO R	6.00	9.00
9 Combee C	.20	.50
10 Vespiquen (Intelligence Gathering) U	.25	.75
11 Vespiquen (Double) R	.40	1.00
12 Virizion HOLO R	1.25	3.00
13 Flareon U	.25	.75
14 Entei (Burning Roar) R	.40	1.00
15 Entei (Double) HOLO R	1.00	2.50
16 Larvesta C	.10	.25
17 Volcarona (Sun Birth) HOLO R	.50	1.50
18 Volcarona (Stop) R	.40	1.00
19 Magikarp C	.10	.25
20 Gyarados (Berserker Splash) R	.40	1.00
21 Gyarados (Double) HOLO R	.50	1.50
22 Vaporeon U	.20	.50
23 Relicanth C	.10	.25
24 Regice R	.50	1.25
25 Kyurem EX HOLO R	3.00	5.00
26 Jolteon HOLO R	.50	1.00
27 Ampharos EX HOLO R	2.50	4.00
28 MegaAmpharos EX HOLO R	5.00	7.00
29 Rotom U	.20	.50
30 Unown C	.10	.25
31 Baltoy (Spinning Attack) C	.10	.25
32 Baltoy (Stop) C	.10	.25
33 Claydol R	.40	1.00
34 Golett C	.10	.25
35 Golurk (Stop) R	.40	1.00
36 Hoopa EX HOLO R	5.00	7.50
37 Machamp EX HOLO R	2.00	4.00
38 Wooper C	.10	.25
39 Quagsire C	.10	.25
40 Regirock R	.50	1.25
41 Golurk (Dig Out) C	.10	.25
42 Tyranitar EX HOLO R	3.00	5.00
43 MegaTyranitar EX HOLO R	8.00	11.00
44 Sableye U	.20	.50
45 Inkay C	.10	.25
46 Malamar C	.10	.25
47 Beldum C	.10	.25
48 Metang U	.20	.50
49 Metagross (Magnetic Warp) R	.50	1.50
50 Metagross (Double) R	.40	1.00
51 Registeel R	.40	1.00
52 Ralts C	.10	.25
53 Kirlia U	.20	.50
54 Gardevoir HOLO R	1.25	3.00
55 Cottonee C	.10	.25
56 Whimsicott U	.20	.50
57 Giratina EX HOLO R	7.00	10.00
58 Goomy C	.10	.25
59 Sliggoo U	.20	.50
60 Goodra HOLO R	1.25	3.00
61 Meowth C	.10	.25
62 Persian C	.10	.25
63 Eevee C	.10	.25
64 Porygon C	.10	.25
65 Porygon2 U	.20	.50
66 Porygon-Z (Cyber Crush) R	.40	1.00
67 Porygon-Z (Stop) HOLO R	.50	1.00
68 Lugia EX HOLO R	5.00	8.00
69 Ace Trainer U	.20	.50
70 Ampharos Spirit Link U	.20	.50
71 Eco Arm U	.50	1.25
72 Energy Recycler U	.50	1.00
73 Faded Town U	5.00	12.00
74 Forest of Giant Plants U	.20	.50
75 Hex Maniac U	.50	1.00
76 Level Ball U	1.00	2.50
77 Lucky Helmet U	.20	.50
78 Lysandre U	.20	.50
79 Paint Roller U	1.50	4.00
80 Sceptile Spirit Link U	.20	.50
81 Tyranitar Spirit Link U	.20	.50
82 Dangerous Energy U	.20	.50
83 Flash Energy U	.20	.50
84 Sceptile EX UR	10.00	15.00
85 MegaSceptile EX UR	13.00	16.00
86 Kyurem EX UR	4.50	6.00
87 Ampharos EX UR	4.00	7.00
88 MegaAmpharos EX UR	8.00	12.00
89 Hoopa EX UR	14.00	18.00
90 Machamp EX UR	5.00	8.00
91 Tyranitar EX UR	5.00	8.00
92 MegaTyranitar EX UR	10.00	15.00
93 Giratina EX UR	10.00	15.00
94 Lugia EX UR	14.00	17.00
95 Steven UR	4.00	7.00
96 Primal Kyogre EX UR	15.00	20.00
97 Primal Groudon EX UR	15.00	20.00
98 MegaRayquaza EX UR	15.00	20.00
99 Energy Retrieval SCR	4.50	7.00
100 Trainers' Mail SCR	15.00	20.00

2016 Pokemon Generations

COMPLETE SET (83)	100.00	200.00
*REV.FOIL: .75X TO 2X BASIC CARDS		
RELEASE DATE FEBRUARY 22, 2016		
1 Venusaur EX HOLO R	2.50	6.00
2 MVenusaur EX HOLO R	2.00	5.00
3 Caterpie C	.10	.25
4 Metapod U	.20	.50
5 Butterfree HOLO R	.60	1.50
6 Paras C	.10	.25
7 Parasect R	.40	1.00
8 Tangela C	.10	.25
9 Pinsir R	.40	1.00
10 Leafeon EX HOLO R	4.00	10.00
11 Charizard EX HOLO R	5.00	12.00
12 MCharizard EX HOLO R	20.00	50.00
13 Ninetales EX HOLO R	2.00	5.00
14 Ponyta C	.10	.25
15 Rapidash R	.40	1.00
16 Magmar C	.10	.25
17 Blastoise EX HOLO R	2.50	6.00
18 MBlastoise EX HOLO R	6.00	15.00
19 Shellder C	.10	.25
20 Cloyster U	.20	.50
21 Krabby C	.10	.25
22 Magikarp C	.10	.25
23 Gyarados R	.40	1.00
24 Vaporeon EX HOLO R	2.00	5.00
25 Articuno HOLO R	4.00	10.00
26 Pikachu C	.30	.75
27 Raichu HOLO R	.75	2.00
28 Jolteon EX HOLO R	20.00	50.00
29 Zapdos HOLO R	4.00	10.00
30 Zubat C	.10	.25
31 Golbat U	.20	.50
32 Slowpoke C	.10	.25
33 Gastly C	.10	.25
34 Haunter U	.20	.50
35 Gengar HOLO R	1.00	2.50
36 Jynx R	.40	1.00

37 Meowstic EX HOLO R	2.00	5.00
38 Diglett C	.10	.25
39 Dugtrio R	.40	1.00
40 Machop C	.10	.25
41 Machoke U	.20	.50
42 Machamp HOLO R	.50	1.25
43 Geodude C	.10	.25
44 Graveler U	.20	.50
45 Golem HOLO R	.50	1.25
46 Golem EX HOLO R	1.50	4.00
47 Hitmonlee R	.40	1.00
48 Hitmonchan R	.40	1.00
49 Rhyhorn C	.10	.25
50 Clefairy C	.10	.25
51 Clefable U	.20	.50
52 Mr. Mime U	.20	.50
53 Meowth C	.10	.25
54 Persian U	.20	.50
55 Doduo C	.10	.25
56 Dodrio R	.40	1.00
57 Tauros R	.40	1.00
58 Snorlax R	.40	1.00
59 Clemont U	.30	.75
60 Crushing Hammer U	.20	.50
61 Energy Switch U	.20	.50
62 Evosoda U	.20	.50
63 Imakuni? U	.20	.50
64 Maintenance U	.30	.75
65 Max Revive U	.20	.50
66 Olympia U	.20	.50
67 Poke Ball U	.20	.50
68 Pokemon Center Lady U	.30	.75
69 Pokemon Fan Club U	.30	.75
70 Revitalizer U	.20	.50
71 Red Card U	.20	.50
72 Shauna U	.20	.50
73 Team Flare Grunt U	.40	1.00
74 Double Colorless Energy U	.40	1.00
75 Grass Energy C	.10	.25
76 Fire Energy C	.30	.75
77 Water Energy C	.30	.75
78 Lightning Energy C	.30	.75
79 Psychic Energy C	.30	.75
80 Fighting Energy C	.10	.25
81 Darkness Energy C	.10	.25
82 Metal Energy C	.30	.75
83 Fairy Energy C	.30	.75

2016 Pokemon XY Breakpoint

COMPLETE SET (123)	120.00	200.00
BOOSTER BOX (36 PACKS)	80.00	100.00
BOOSTER PACK (10 CARDS)	2.50	6.00
1 Chikorita C	.15	.25
2 Bayleef U	.20	.50
3 Mnium HOLO R	.50	1.25
4 Seedot C	.15	.25
5 Kricketot C	.15	.25
6 Kricketune U	.20	.50
7 Petilil C	.15	.25
8 Lilligant R	.40	1.00
9 Durant U	.20	.50
10 Growlithe C	.15	.25
11 Arcanine U	.20	.50
12 Numel C	.15	.25
13 Camerupt R	.40	1.00
14 Emboar EX HOLO R	2.00	3.00
15 Heatmor U	.20	.50
16 Psyduck C	.15	.25
17 Golduck R	.40	1.00
18 Golduck BREAK R	.75	1.50
19 Slowpoke C	.15	.25
20 Slowbro U	.20	.50
21 Slowking HOLO R	.50	1.25
22 Shellder	.15	.25
Razor Shell C		
23 Shellder	.15	.25
Clamp C		
24 Cloyster U	.20	.50
25 Staryu C	.15	.25
26 Gyarados EX HOLO R	2.50	3.50
27 MGyarados EX HOLO R	8.00	10.00
28 Lapras U	.20	.50
29 Corsola C	.15	.25
30 Suicune HOLO R	.50	1.25
31 Palkia EX HOLO R	3.50	4.50
32 Manaphy EX HOLO R	3.00	4.50
33 Tympole C	.15	.25
34 Palpitoad U	.20	.50
35 Seismitoad R	.40	1.00
36 Ducklett C	.15	.25
37 Swanna U	.20	.50
38 Froakie C	.15	.25
39 Frogadier U	.20	.50
40 Greninja R	.60	1.50
41 Greninja BREAK R	13.00	15.00
42 Electabuzz C	.15	.25
43 Electivire U	.20	.50
44 Shinx C	.15	.25
45 Luxio U	.20	.50
46 Luxray R	.40	1.00
47 Luxray BREAK R	1.75	2.50
48 Blitzle C	.15	.25
49 Zebstrika R	.40	1.00
50 Drowzee C	.15	.25
51 Hypno R	.40	1.00
52 Espeon EX HOLO R	3.00	4.00
53 Skorupi C	.15	.25
54 Drapion R	.40	1.00
55 Sigilyph U	.20	.50
56 Trubbish C	.15	.25
57 Garbodor HOLO R	1.00	1.50
58 Espurr C	.15	.25
59 Meowstic R	.40	1.00
60 Honedge C	.15	.25
61 Doublade U	.20	.50
62 Aegislash HOLO R	.50	1.25
63 Skrelp C	.15	.25
64 Phantump C	.15	.25
65 Trevenant R	.40	1.00
66 Trevenant BREAK R	4.00	5.50
67 Sudowoodo U	.20	.50
68 Gible C	.15	.25
69 Gabite U	.20	.50
70 Garchomp HOLO R	1.50	2.00
71 Pancham C	.15	.25
72 Nuzleaf U	.20	.50
73 Shiftry R	.40	1.00
74 Darkrai EX HOLO R	8.00	9.50
75 Pangoro R	.40	1.00
76 Scizor EX HOLO R	3.00	4.00
77 MScizor EX HOLO R	5.00	6.50
78 Mawile U	.20	.50
79 Ferroseed C	.15	.25
80 Ferrothorn R	.40	1.00
81 Clefairy C	.15	.25
82 Clefable R	.40	1.00
83 Togekiss EX HOLO R	2.00	2.50
84 Spritzee C	.15	.25
85 Aromatisse U	.20	.50
86 Dragalge HOLO R	.50	1.25
87 Rattata C	.15	.25
88 Raticate R	.40	1.00
89 Raticate BREAK R	1.50	2.50
90 Dunsparce U	.20	.50
91 Stantler U	.20	.50
92 Ho-Oh EX HOLO R	2.50	3.50
93 Glameow C	.15	.25
94 Purugly U	.20	.50
95 Furfrou C	.15	.25
96 All-Night Party U	.20	.50
97 Bursting Balloon U	.20	.50
98 Delinquent U	.50	1.25
99 Fighting Fury Belt U	2.50	4.00
100 Great Ball U	.20	.50
101 Gyarados Spirit Link U	.20	.50
102 Max Elixir U	4.50	5.50
103 Max Potion U	.40	1.00
104 Misty's Determination U	.20	.50
105 Pokemon Catcher U	.20	.50
106 Potion U	.20	.50
107 Professor Sycamore U	.60	.85
108 Psychic's Third Eye U	.20	.50
109 Puzzle of Time U	1.00	1.50
110 Reverse Valley U	.20	.50
111 Scizor Spirit Link U	.20	.50
112 Tierno U	.20	.50
113 Splash Energy U	.20	.50
114 Gyarados EX UR	4.00	5.50
115 MGyarados EX UR	9.00	11.00
116 Manaphy EX UR	4.50	6.00
117 Espeon EX UR	5.00	6.50
118 Darkrai EX UR	10.00	12.00
119 Scizor EX UR	4.00	5.50
120 MScizor EX UR	8.00	9.00
121 Ho-Oh EX UR	4.50	6.00
122 Skyla UR	11.50	13.00
123 Gyarados EX SCR	5.00	7.00

2016 Pokemon XY Fates Collide

COMPLETE SET (124)	120.00	180.00
*REV.FOIL: .75X TO 2X BASIC CARDS		
RELEASED ON MAY 2, 2016		
1 Shuckle U	.30	.75
2 Burmy C	.30	.75
3 Wormadam (Solar Ray) U	.30	.75
4 Mothim R	.30	.75
5 Snivy C	.30	.75
6 Servine U	.30	.75
7 Serperior R	.30	.75
8 Deerling C	.30	.75
9 Moltres R	.30	.75
10 Fennekin (Will-O-) C	.30	.75
11 Fennekin (Invite Out) C	.30	.75
12 Braixen U	.30	.75
13 Delphox HOLO R	1.00	2.00
14 Delphox BREAK R	3.00	6.00
15 Seel C	.30	.75
16 Dewgong U	.30	.75
17 Omanyte U	.30	.75
18 Omastar R	.30	.75
19 Omastar BREAK R	2.00	4.00
20 Glaceon EX HOLO R	4.00	8.00
21 White Kyurem HOLO R	.75	1.50
22 Binacle C	.30	.75
23 Barbaracle R	.30	.75
24 Rotom R	.30	.75
25 Alakazam EX HOLO R	4.00	8.00
26 MAlakazam EX HOLO R	7.50	15.00
27 Koffing C	.30	.75
28 Weezing U	.30	.75
29 Mew HOLO R	5.00	10.00
30 Spoink C	.30	.75
31 Grumpig R	.30	.75
32 Gothita C	.30	.75
33 Solosis C	.30	.75
34 Duosion U	.30	.75
35 Reuniclus R	.30	.75
36 Diglett C	.30	.75
37 Marowak R	.30	.75
38 Kabuto U	.30	.75
39 Kabutops R	.30	.75
40 Larvitar C	.30	.75
41 Larvitar C	.30	.75
42 Pupitar U	.30	.75
43 Regirock EX HOLO R	6.00	12.00
44 Wormadam (Sand Spray) U	.30	.75
45 Riolu C	.30	.75
46 Riolu C	.30	.75
47 Lucario (Beatdown) R	.30	.75
48 Hawlucha U	.30	.75
49 Carbink R	.50	1.00
50 Carbink (Safeguard) C	.30	.75
51 CarbinkBREAK R	4.00	8.00
52 Zygarde (Lookout) U	.30	.75
53 Zygarde (Rumble) R	.30	.75
54 Zygarde EX HOLO R	6.00	12.00
55 Umbreon EX HOLO R	4.00	8.00
56 Tyranitar HOLO R	.75	1.50
57 Vullaby C	.30	.75
58 Mandibuzz R	.30	.75
59 Wormadam (Return Attack) U	.30	.75
60 Bronzor C	.30	.75
61 Bronzong R	.30	.75
62 BronzongBREAK R	2.50	5.00
63 Lucario (Vacuum Wave) HOLO R	1.00	2.00
64 Genesect EX HOLO R	3.00	6.00
65 Jigglypuff C	.30	.75
66 Wigglytuff U	.30	.75
67 Mr. Mime R	.30	.75
68 Snubbull C	.30	.75
69 MAltaria EX HOLO R	4.00	8.00
70 Cottonee C	.30	.75
71 Whimsicott U	.30	.75
72 Diancie EX HOLO R	3.00	6.00
73 Kingdra EX HOLO R	3.00	6.00
74 Meowth C	.30	.75
75 Kangaskhan U	.30	.75
76 Aerodactyl R	.30	.75
77 Snorlax R	.30	.75
78 Lugia R	1.00	2.00
79 LugiaBREAK R	3.00	6.00
80 Whismur C	.30	.75
81 Loudred U	.30	.75
82 Exploud R	.30	.75
83 Altaria EX HOLO R	3.00	6.00
84 Audino EX HOLO R	3.00	6.00
85 MAudino EX HOLO R	4.00	8.00
86 Minccino (Cleaning Up) C	.30	.75
87 Minccino (Tail Smack) C	.30	.75
89 Cinccino (Sweeping Cure) U	.30	.75
90 Alakazam Spirit Link U	.30	.75
91 Altaria Spirit Link U	.30	.75
92 Audino Spirit Link U	.30	.75
93 Bent Spoon U	.30	.75
94 Chaos Tower U	.30	.75
95 Devolution Spray U	.30	.75
96 Dome Fossil Kabuto U	.30	.75
97 Energy Pouch U	.30	.75
98 Energy Reset U	.30	.75
99 Fairy Drop U	.30	.75
100 Fairy Garden U	.30	.75
101 Fossil Excavation Kit U	.30	.75
102 Helix Fossil Omanyte U	.30	.75
103 Lass's Special U	.30	.75
104 MCatcher U	.30	.75
105 N U	.50	1.00
106 Old Amber Aerodactyl U	.30	.75
107 Pokémon Fan Club U	.30	.75
108 Power Memory U	.30	.75
109 Random Receiver U	.30	.75
110 Scorched Earth U	.30	.75
111 Shauna U	.30	.75
112 Team Rocket's Handiwork U	.30	.75
113 Ultra Ball U	.30	.75
114 Double Colorless Energy U	.75	1.50
115 Strong Energy U	.75	1.50
116 Glaceon EX UR	7.50	15.00
117 Alakazam EX UR	6.00	12.00
118 MAlakazam EX UR	10.00	20.00
119 Umbreon EX UR	7.50	15.00
120 Genesect EX UR	6.00	12.00
121 MAltaria EX UR	4.00	8.00
122 Kingdra EX UR	4.00	8.00
123 Altaria EX UR	3.00	6.00
124 Team Rocket's Handiwork UR	4.00	8.00
125 Alakazam EX SR	10.00	20.00

2016 Pokemon XY Steam Siege

COMPLETE SET (116 CARDS)	150.00	250.00
RELEASED ON AUGUST 3, 2016		
1 Tangela C	.10	.30
2 Tangrowth U	.15	.45
3 Hoppip C	.10	.30
4 Skiploom U	.15	.45
5 Jumpluff R	.20	.60
6 Yanma C	.10	.30
7 Yanmega R	.75	2.00
8 YanmegaBREAK HOLO R	4.00	10.00
9 Seedot C	.10	.30
10 Nuzleaf U	.10	.30
11 Shiftry HOLO R	1.00	2.50
12 Foongus C	.10	.30
13 Amoonguss R	.20	.60
14 Larvesta C	.10	.30
15 Volcarona R	.20	.60
16 Ponyta C	.10	.30
17 Rapidash U	.15	.45
18 Chimchar C	.10	.30
19 Monferno U	.15	.45
20 Infernape HOLO R	1.25	3.00
21 TalonflameBREAK HOLO R	2.50	6.00
22 Litleo C	.10	.30
23 Pyroar R	.20	.60
24 PyroarBREAK HOLO R	2.50	6.00
25 Volcanion R	.60	1.50
26 VolcanionEX HOLO R	8.00	20.00
27 Mantine C	.10	.30
28 Shellos C	.10	.30
29 Gastrodon R	.20	.60
30 Oshawott C	.10	.30
31 Dewott U	.15	.45
32 Samurott R	.20	.60
33 Clauncher C	.10	.30
34 Clawitzer R	.20	.60
35 ClawitzerBREAK HOLO R	2.00	5.00
36 Bergmite C	.10	.30
37 Avalugg R	.20	.60
38 Mareep C	.10	.30
39 Flaaffy U	.15	.45
40 Ampharos HOLO R	.75	2.00
41 Joltik C	.10	.30
42 Galvantula R	.20	.60
43 Nidoran C	.10	.30
44 Nidorino U	.15	.45
45 Nidoking R	.20	.60
46 Drifloon C	.10	.30
47 Drifblim U	.15	.45
48 Litwick C	.10	.30
49 Lampent U	.15	.45
50 Chandelure HOLO R	1.00	2.50
51 Hoopa R	.60	1.50
52 Mankey C	.10	.30
53 Primeape R	.20	.60
54 Nosepass C	.10	.30
55 Probopass R	.20	.60
56 Anorith U	.15	.45
57 Armaldo R	.20	.60
58 Croagunk C	.10	.30
59 Toxicroak R	.20	.60
60 Sneasel C	.10	.30
61 Weavile R	.20	.60
62 Spiritomb R	.20	.60
63 Pawniard C	.10	.30
64 Bisharp HOLO R	1.25	3.00
65 Yveltal HOLO R	1.25	3.00
66 YveltalBREAK HOLO R	3.00	8.00
67 SteelixEX HOLO R	3.00	8.00
68 MegaSteelixEX HOLO R	5.00	12.00
69 Shieldon U	.15	.45
70 Bastiodon R	.20	.60
71 Klink C	.10	.30
72 Klang U	.15	.45
73 Klinklang HOLO R	1.00	2.50
74 Cobalion R	.20	.60
75 MagearnaEX HOLO R	2.50	6.00
76 Marill C	.10	.30
77 Azumarill U	.15	.45
78 GardevoirEX HOLO R	2.50	6.00
79 MegaGardevoirEX HOLO R	5.00	12.00
80 Klefki U	.15	.45
81 Xerneas HOLO R	1.25	3.00
82 XerneasBREAK HOLO R	6.00	15.00
83 Druddigon R	.20	.60
84 Deino C	.10	.30
85 Zweilous U	.15	.45
86 Hydreigon HOLO R	1.00	2.50
87 HydreigonBREAK HOLO R	2.00	5.00
88 Meowth C	.10	.30
89 Persian U	.15	.45
90 Aipom C	.10	.30
91 Ambipom U	.15	.45
92 Rufflet C	.10	.30
93 Braviary U	.15	.45
94 Fletchling C	.10	.30
95 Fletchinder U	.15	.45

Card	Low	High
96 Talonflame R	.75	2.00
97 Hawlucha U	.15	.45
98 Armor Fossil Shieldon U	.15	.45
99 Captivating Poke Puff U	.50	1.25
100 Claw Fossil Anorith U	.15	.45
101 Gardevoir Spirit Link U	.15	.45
102 Greedy Dice U	.15	.45
103 Ninja Boy U	.60	1.50
104 Pokemon Ranger U	.60	1.50
105 Special Charge U	.60	1.50
106 Steelix Spirit Link U	.15	.45
107 VolcanionEX UR Full Art	8.00	20.00
108 SteelixEX UR Full Art	4.00	10.00
109 MegaSteelixEX UR Full Art	8.00	20.00
110 MagearnaEX UR Full Art	5.00	12.00
111 GardevoirEX UR Full Art	4.00	10.00
112 MegaGardevoirEX UR Full Art	8.00	20.00
113 Pokemon Ranger UR Full Art	8.00	20.00
114 Professor Sycamore UR Full Art	30.00	45.00
115 VolcanionEX SCT	10.00	25.00
116 GardevoirEX SCT	6.00	15.00

2004 Pokemon Organized Play Series 1

Card	Low	High
COMPLETE SET (17)		
RELEASED IN SEPT. 2004	8.00	20.00
BOOSTER PACK (2 CARDS)	2.00	3.00
1 Blaziken R	.50	1.00
2 Metagross R	.50	1.00
3 Rayquaza R	.50	1.00
4 Sceptile R	.50	1.00
5 Swampert R	.50	1.00
6 Beautifly U	.20	.50
7 Masquerain U	.20	.50
8 Murkrow U	.20	.50
9 Pupitar U	.20	.50
10 Torkoal U	.20	.50
11 Larvitar C	.10	.20
12 Minun C	.20	.50
13 Plusle C	.20	.50
14 Surskit C	.10	.50
15 Swellow C	.10	.20
16 Armaldo EX R	4.00	10.00
17 Tyranitar EX R	5.00	10.00

2005 Pokemon Organized Play Series 2

Card	Low	High
BOOSTER PACK (2 CARDS)	2.00	3.00
RELEASED IN AUG. 2005		
1 Entei R	.50	1.00
2 Pidgeot R	.50	1.00
3 Raikou R	.50	1.00
4 Suicune R	1.00	2.00
5 Tauros R	.50	1.00
6 Venusaur R	2.00	2.00
7 Ivysaur U	.20	.50
8 Mr. Briney's Compassion U	.20	.50
9 Multi Technical Machine 01 U	.20	.50
10 Pokémon Park U	.20	.50
11 TV Reporter U	.20	.50
12 Bulbasaur C	.10	.20
13 Cacnea C	.10	.20
14 Luvdisc C	.10	.20
15 Phanpy C	.10	.20
16 Pikachu C	.20	.50
17 Celebi EX R	4.00	8.00

2006 Pokemon Organized Play Series 3

Card	Low	High
BOOSTER PACK (2 CARDS)	2.00	3.00
RELEASED IN APRIL 2006		
1B Blastoise HOLO R	10.00	20.00
1A Blastoise R	1.00	2.00
2B Flareon HOLO R	4.00	10.00
2A Flareon R	1.00	2.00
3A Jolteon R	.50	1.00
3B Jolteon HOLO R	4.00	10.00
4B Minun HOLO R	4.00	10.00
4A Minun R	1.00	2.00
5B Plusle HOLO R	4.00	10.00
5A Plusle R	1.00	2.00
6B Vaporeon HOLO R	4.00	10.00
6A Vaporeon R	1.00	2.00
7 Combusken U	.20	.50
8 Donphan U	.20	.50
9 Forretress U	.20	.50
10 High Pressure System U	.20	.50
11 Low Pressure System U	.20	.50
12 Ditto (Mr. Mime) C	.10	.20
13 Eevee C	.10	.20
14 Ivysaur C	.10	.20
15 Marshtomp C	.10	.20
16 Pichu Bros. C	2.00	4.00
17B Ho-oh EX HOLO R	5.00	12.00
17A Ho-oh EX R	1.00	2.00

2006 Pokemon Organized Play Series 4

Card	Low	High
BOOSTER PACK (2 CARDS)	2.00	3.00
RELEASED IN AUGUST 2006		
1 Chimecho R	1.00	2.00
2A Deoxys R	1.00	2.00
2B Deoxys HOLO R	4.00	10.00
3B Flygon HOLO R	3.00	6.00
3A Flygon R	1.00	2.00
4A Mew R	1.00	2.00
4B Mew HOLO R	4.00	10.00
5 Sceptile R	1.00	2.00
6B Combusken HOLO R	3.00	6.00
6A Combusken U	.20	.50
7 Grovyle U	.20	.50
8 Heal Energy U	.20	.50
9 Pokémon Fan Club U	.20	.50
10 Scramble Energy U	.20	.50
11B Mudkip HOLO R	3.00	7.00
11A Mudkip C	.10	.20
12 Pidgey C	.10	.20
13A Pikachu C	.50	1.00
13B Pikachu HOLO R	4.00	10.00
14 Squirtle C	.10	.20
15 Treecko C	.10	.20
16A Wobbuffet C	.10	.20
16B Wobbuffet HOLO R	3.00	6.00
17 Deoxys EX R	1.00	2.00

2007 Pokemon Organized Play Series 5

Card	Low	High
BOOSTER PACK (2 CARDS)	2.00	3.00
RELEASED IN MARCH 2007		
1A Ho-Oh R	1.00	2.00
1B Ho-Oh HOLO R	7.00	15.00
2A Lugia HOLO R	7.00	15.00
2B Lugia R	1.00	2.00
3B Mew R	1.00	2.00
3A Mew HOLO R	4.00	10.00
4 Double Rainbow Energy R	.50	1.00
5 Charmeleon U	.20	.50
6 Bill's Maintenance U	.20	.50
7 Rare Candy U	1.00	2.00
8 Boost Energy U	.20	.50
9 Delta Rainbow Energy U	.20	.50
10 Charmander C	.10	.20
11 Meowth C	.10	.20
12A Pikachu HOLO R	4.00	10.00
12B Pikachu C	.50	1.00
13 Pikachu C	.50	1.00
14A Pelipper HOLO R	3.00	6.00
14B Pelipper C	.10	.20
15B Zangoose C	.10	.20
15A Zangoose HOLO R	3.00	6.00
16 Espeon HOLO R	9.00	15.00
17 Umbreon R	4.00	8.00

2007 Pokemon Organized Play Series 6

Card	Low	High
BOOSTER PACK	2.00	3.00
RELEASED IN SEPT. 2007		
1 Bastiodon R	1.00	2.00
2 Lucario R	1.00	2.00
3A Manaphy R	.50	1.00
3B Manaphy HOLO R	3.00	6.00
4 Pachirisu R	1.00	2.00
5 Rampardos R	.50	1.00
6 Drifloon U	.20	.50
7A Gible U	.20	.50
7B Gible HOLO R	3.00	6.00
8B Riolu HOLO R	3.00	6.00
8A Riolu U	.20	.50
9A Pikachu U	.20	.50
9B Pikachu HOLO R	4.00	10.00
10 Staravia U	.20	.50
11 Bidoof C	.10	.20
12 Buneary C	.10	.20
13 Cherubi C	.10	.20
14B Chimchar HOLO R	4.00	8.00
14A Chimchar C	.10	.20
15B Piplup HOLO R	5.00	10.00
15A Piplup C	.10	.20
16 Starly C	.10	.20
17 Turtwig C	.10	.20

2008 Pokemon Organized Play Series 7

Card	Low	High
BOOSTER PACK (2 CARDS)	2.00	3.00
RELEASED IN FEB. 2008		
1 Ampharos R	2.00	5.00
2 Gallade R	4.00	8.00
3 Latias R	2.00	5.00
4 Latios R	2.00	4.00
5 Mothim R	2.00	4.00
6 Delibird U	.20	.50
7 Flaaffy U	.20	.50
8 Kirlia HOLO R	5.00	10.00
8 Kirlia U	.20	.50
9 Stantler U	.20	.50
10 Wormadam U	.20	.50
11 Burmy C	.20	.50
12 Burmy C	.10	.20
13 Corsola C	.10	.20
14 Mareep C	.20	.50
15 Ralts C	.20	.50
16 Sentret C	.20	.50
17 Spinda C	.20	.50

2008 Pokemon Organized Play Series 8

Card	Low	High
1 Heatran R	2.00	4.00
2 Lucario R	5.00	10.00
3 Luxray HOLO R	4.00	8.00
4 Probopass (Holo) (R)	4.00	8.00
5 Yanmega R	2.00	4.00
6 Cherrim U	.20	.50
7 Carnivine U	.20	.50
8 Luxio U	.20	.50
9 Night Maintenance U	.20	.50
10 Rare Candy U	2.00	4.00
11 Roseanne's Research U	2.00	4.00
12 Chimchar C	.10	.20
13 Croagunk C	.10	.20
14 Happiny C	.10	.20
15 Piplup C	.10	.20
16 Riolu C	.10	.20
17 Turtwig C	.10	.20

2009 Pokemon Organized Play Series 9

Card	Low	High
1 Garchomp	2.00	4.00
2 Manaphy	.20	.50
3 Raichu	.50	1.00
4 Regigigas	1.00	2.00
5 Rotom (Holo)	5.00	10.00
6 Buizel	.20	.50
7 Croagunk	.20	.50
8 Gabite	.20	.50
9 Lopunny	.20	.50
10 Pachirisu	.50	1.00
11 Pichu	.20	.50
12 Buneary	.20	.50
13 Chimchar	.20	.50
14 Gible	.20	.50
15 Pikachu	.50	1.00
16 Piplup	.20	.50
17 Turtwig	.20	.50

2008 Pokemon Burger King

Card	Low	High
CARD SET (12)	12.00	20.00
TOY SET (12)	10.00	20.00
INDIVIDUAL TOY	1.00	2.00
6 Lucario	1.00	2.00
9 Manaphy	1.00	3.00
35 Pachirisu	.50	1.00
49 Grotle	2.00	4.00
52 Happiny	.50	1.00
56 Monferno	.50	1.00
58 Prinplup	.50	1.00
76 Chimchar	.50	1.00
93 Piplup	.50	1.00
94 Pikachu	1.00	2.00
98 Shinx	.50	1.00
103 Turtwig	.50	1.00

2009 Pokemon Burger King Platinum

Card	Low	High
1 Chimchar	.25	.50
2 Dialga	1.00	2.00
3 Eevee	.25	.50
4 Giratina	1.00	2.00
5 Glaceon	.50	1.00
6 Leafeon	1.00	2.00
7 Meowth	.25	.50
8 Palkia	1.00	2.00
9 Pichu	.25	.50
10 Pikachu	.50	1.00
11 Piplup	.25	.50
12 Turtwig	.25	.50

1999-02 Pokemon Promo Star Wizards of the Coast

Card	Low	High
1 Pikachu 1st Edition (Jungle packs)	80.00	130.00
1A Pikachu (Pokemon League)	4.00	8.00
2 Electabuzz (First Movie)	2.00	4.00
3 Mewtwo (First Movie)	3.00	6.00
4 Pikachu (First Movie)	3.00	6.00
5 Dragonite (First Movie)	1.50	4.00
6 Arcanine (Pokemon League)	2.00	5.00
7 Jigglypuff (Cassette Mail-in)	2.00	4.00
8 Mew (Pokemon League)	.50	2.00
9 Mew HOLO (Pokemon League)	2.00	4.00
10 Meowth HOLO (TCG Game Boy)	2.00	5.00
11 Eevee (Pokemon League)	1.00	3.00
12 Mewtwo (Nintendo Magazine)	3.00	8.00
13 Venusaur (Strategy Guide)	8.00	20.00
14 Mewtwo (Movie Video)	3.00	8.00
15 Cool Porygon (Stadium Bundle)	3.00	8.00
16 Computer Error (Pokemon League)	1.00	3.00
17 Dark Persian (Nintendo Mag.)	3.00	8.00
17 Dark Persian (Nintendo Mag.)(Err)	80.00	120.00
18 TR's Meowth (Pokemon League)	1.00	3.00
19 Sabrina's Abra (Nintendo Mag.)	2.50	7.00
20 Psyduck (Pokemon League)	1.00	3.00
21 Moltres (Movie 2000)	1.00	3.00
22 Articuno (Movie 2000)	1.00	3.00
23 Zapdos (Movie 2000)	1.00	3.00
24 Birthday Pikachu HOLO (Pokemon League)	10.00	25.00
25 Flying Pikachu	3.00	8.00
26 Pikachu (Snap)	2.50	6.00
27 Pikachu (Movie 2000 Video)	1.25	3.00
28 Surfing Pikachu	1.50	4.00
29 Marill (Neo Genesis)	1.25	3.00
30 Togepi	3.00	7.00
31 Cleffa	1.00	2.00
32 Smeargle	1.00	3.00
33 Scizor	1.25	3.00
34 Entei HOLO (Movie 2001)	1.50	4.00
35 Pichu HOLO (Pokemon Lea.)	3.00	8.00
36 Igglybuff	1.00	3.00
37 Hitmontop	.75	2.00
38 Unown J	1.25	3.00
39 Misdreavus	1.00	2.00
40 Trainer: Pokemon Center	10.00	25.00
41 Trainer: Lucky Stadium	20.00	40.00
42 Trainer: Pokemon Tower	1.00	3.00
43 Machamp	1.50	4.00
44 Magmar	1.50	4.00
45 Scyther	1.50	4.00
46 Electabuzz	1.50	4.00
47 Mew (Lilypad)	5.00	12.00
48 Articuno	4.00	8.00
49 Snorlax	2.00	5.00
50 Celebi (movie promo)	1.25	3.00
51 Rapidash	2.00	5.00
52 Ho-oh	2.00	5.00
53 Suicune	2.00	5.00

1999-02 Pokemon American Promos - Wizards of the Coast

Card	Low	High
0 Aerodactyl (Fossil) (Pre-release)	5.00	10.00
0 Ancient Mew HOLO (Movie 2000)	4.00	10.00
0 Articuno,Moltres,Zapdos (Jumbo)	4.00	10.00
0 Brock's Vulpix W gold	2.00	4.00
0 Clefable (Jungle) (Green Logo Pre-release)	80.00	120.00
0 Dark Arbok W gold stamp	2.00	4.00
0 Dark Charmeleon W gold stamp	5.00	10.00
0 Dark Gyarados HOLO (Pre-rel.)	3.00	6.00
0 Exeggutor (Bilingual)	15.00	35.00
0 Hoppip (2002 E3)	5.00	12.00
0 Kabuto W gold stamped (TopDeck)	2.00	4.00
0 Meowth Gold Border Fruit by the Foot	8.00	15.00
0 Misty's Psyduck W gold stamped (TopDeck)	6.00	9.00
0 Misty's Seadra (Pre-release)	1.00	3.00
0 Pichu (2002 E3)	3.00	10.00
0 Pikachu E3 gold stamped	5.00	12.00
0 Pikachu E3 gold (Red Cheeks)	100.00	250.00
0 Pikachu Jumbo Size (TopDeck)	3.00	6.00
0 Pikachu PokeTour 1999 gold stamped	40.00	80.00
0 Pikachu W gold stamped (Duelist Mag. 41)	8.00	20.00
0 Professor Elm (Best of Game Gencon 2003)	1.25	3.00
0 Wartortle W gold (TopDeck Mag)	2.00	6.00
0 Gyarados (Pre-release)	3.00	6.00
0 Wartortle (Pre-release)	4.00	8.00
0 Psychic Energy Pokemon League 2002 P		
0 Fighting Energy Pokemon League 2002 P		
0 Grass Energy Pokemon League 2002 P		
0 Rainbow Energy Pokemon League 2002 P		
0 Lightning Energy Pokemon League 2002 P		
0 Fire Energy Pokemon League 2002 P		
0 Recycle Energy Pokemon League 2002 P		
0 Water Energy Pokemon League 2002 P		

2002-04 Pokemon USA Promo Cards

Card	Low	High
0 Bagon (Gencon)	10.00	20.00
0 Bagon (Inquest Magazine)	4.00	8.00
0 Bagon (Scrye Magazine)	4.00	8.00
0 Blastoise (Nat.Chmpship)	15.00	30.00
0 Chansey (ERR)	20.00	40.00
0 Gastly	30.00	60.00
0 Hoppip (2002 E3)	20.00	40.00
0 Pichu (2002 E3)	20.00	40.00
0 Shadow Lugia (jumbo)	10.00	20.00
1 Kyogre ex (Promo Star)	10.00	20.00
2 Groudon ex (Promo Star)	10.00	20.00
3 Treecko	4.00	10.00
4 Grovyle	4.00	8.00
5 Mudkip (H) (UK Promo)	5.00	10.00
6 Torchic (H) (UK Promo)	5.00	10.00
7 Treecko (H)	5.00	10.00
8 Torchic	4.00	9.00
9 Combusken	8.00	16.00
10 Mudkip (H)	4.00	10.00
11 Marshtomp	4.00	10.00
12 Pikachu (H) (Collector Tin)	8.00	12.00
13 Meowth (H) (Collector Tin)	2.00	5.00
14 Latias (Heroes Movie)	3.00	7.00
15 Latios (Heroes Movie)	3.00	7.00
16A Treecko (H) (EX Deck Tin)	1.00	2.00
16B Treecko (Target Stores)	1.00	2.00
17A Torchic (H) (EX Deck Tin)	1.00	2.00
17B Torchic (Target Stores)	1.00	2.00
18B Mudkip (H) (EX Deck Tin)	1.00	2.00
18A Mudkip (Target Stores)	1.00	2.00
19A Whismur (Target Stores)	1.00	2.00
19B Whismur (H) (EX Deck Tin)	1.00	2.00
20 Ludicolo (H) (EX Value Pack 1)	1.00	2.00
21 Jirachi (Jirachi: Wish Maker DVD)	1.00	2.00
22 Beldum (e-League June 2004)	1.00	2.00
23 Metang (Stadium Challenge 2004)	2.00	4.00
24 Chimecho (e-League July 2004)	30.00	60.00
25 Flygon (e-League August 2004)	10.00	20.00
26B Tropical Wind T (Worlds 2004)	1.00	2.00
26A Tropical Wind (2007)	200.00	300.00
27 Tropical Tidal Wave T (Worlds 2005)	1.00	2.00
28 Championship Arena T (Worlds 2005)	1.00	2.00
29 Celebi (H) (EX VP 2/EX Collector's Carry Tin)	1.00	2.00
30 Suicune (H) (EX VP 2/EX Collector's Carry Tin)	1.00	2.00
31 Moltres ex (H) (EX Collector's Tin 2)	1.00	2.00
32 Articuno ex (H) (EX Collector's Tin 2)	1.00	2.00
33 Zapdos ex (H) (EX Collector's Tin 2)	1.00	2.00
34 Typhlosion (H) (EX Value Pack 5)	1.00	2.00
35 Pikachu (H) (EX Value Pack 4)	1.00	2.00

36 Tropical Tidal Wave (Worlds)	1.00	2.00
37 Kyogre ex (H) (EX Collector's Tin 3)	1.00	2.00
38 Groudon ex (H) (EX Collector's Tin 3)	1.00	2.00
39 Rayquaza ex (H) (EX Collector's Tin 3)	1.00	2.00
40A Darkness Energy	10.00	20.00
40B Mew (H)	6.00	12.00

1999 Pokemon Best Winner Promos

COMPLETE SET (8)	20.00	30.00
1 Electabuzz HOLO	3.00	6.00
2 Hitmonchan HOLO	3.00	6.00
3 Professor Elm HOLO	3.00	6.00
4 Rocket's Sizor	1.00	2.00
5 Rocket's Sneasel	1.00	2.00
6 Dark Ivysaur	1.00	2.00
7 Dark Venusaur	1.00	2.00
8 Rocket's Mewtwo HOLO	3.00	6.00

2010-11 Pokemon HS Black Star Promos

COMPLETE SET (25)	50.00	100.00
HGSS1 Ho-Oh HGSS Poster Pack P	5.00	12.00
HGSS2 Lugia HGSS Poster Pack P	5.00	12.00
HGSS3 Pikachu HGSS Blister P	1.50	4.00
HGSS4 Wobbuffet HGSS Blister P	1.25	3.00
HGSS5 Hoothoot HGSS Blister P	1.50	4.00
HGSS6 Noctowl HGSS Blister P	1.50	4.00
HGSS7 Feraligatr Spring 2010 Collector's Tin P	1.50	4.00
HGSS8 Meganium Spring 2010 Collector's Tin P	1.50	4.00
HGSS9 Typhlosion Spring 2010 Collector's Tin P	1.50	4.00
HGSS10 Latias Cracked Ice Holo P	2.50	6.00
HGSS11 Latios Cracked Ice Holo P	2.50	6.00
HGSS12 Cleffa Unleashed Blister P	2.00	5.00
HGSS13 Smoochum Unleashed Blister P	1.25	3.00
HGSS14 Lapras Undaunted Blister P	1.25	3.00
HGSS15 Shcukle Undaunted Blister P	.75	2.00
HGSS16 Plusle Undaunted Blister P	.75	2.00
HGSS17 Minun Undaunted Blister P	.75	2.00
HGSS18 Tropical Tidal Wave 2010 World Championships P11	25.00	50.00
HGSS19 Raikou Fall 2010 Tin P	2.50	6.00
HGSS10CSM Latias Cosmos Holo P	1.25	3.00
HGSS20 Entei Fall 2010 Tin P	2.50	6.00
HGSS21 Suicune Fall 2010 Tin P	2.50	6.00
HGSS22 Porygon Triumphant Blister P	1.25	3.00
HGSS23 Porygon2 Triumphant Blister P	1.25	3.00
HGSS24 Hitmonchan Call of Legends Blister P	2.00	5.00
HGSS25 Hitmonlee Call of Legends Blister P	2.00	5.00
HGSS11CSM Latios Cosmos Holo P	1.25	3.00

2011 Pokemon McDonald's Promos

COMPLETE SET (12)	4.00	10.00

2012 Pokemon McDonald's Promos

COMPLETE SET (12)	10.00	25.00
1 Servine	1.25	3.00
2 Pansage	1.00	2.50
3 Dwebble	3.00	8.00
4 Pignite	2.50	6.00
5 Dewott	2.50	6.00
6 Emolga	1.50	4.00
7 Woobat	1.25	3.00
8 Drilbur	2.00	5.00
9 Purrloin	2.00	5.00
10 Scraggy	1.25	3.00
11 Klang	1.50	4.00
12 Axew	1.25	3.00

2010 Pokemon HeartGold SoulSilver Promos

1123 Arcanine (Non-Holo Ember Spark theme deck exclusive)
4123 Gyarados (Cracked Ice Holo Player's Collection exclusive)
7123 Ninetales (Cracked Ice Holo Stage 1 Blisters exclusive)
8123 Noctowl (Non-Holo Ember Spark theme deck exclusive)
10123 Raichu (Cracked Ice Holo Player's Pack exclusive)
20123 Feraligatr (Cosmos Holo Mind Flood theme deck exclusive)
26123 Meganium (Cosmos Holo Growth Clash theme deck exclusive)
28123 Pichu (HeartGold & SoulSilver stamp Prerelease)
32123 Typhlosion (Cosmos Holo Ember Spark theme deck exclusive)
39123 Delibird (Crosshatch Holo Pokemon League Snow Throw Season December 2010)
40123 Donphan (Crosshatch Holo Pokemon League Ring Drop Season September 2010)
78123 Pikachu (Pokemon Day 2010 stamped)
90123 Copycat (Crosshatch Holo Pokemon League Tepig Season June 2011)
97123 Pokemon Collector (Crosshatch Holo Player Rewards Program 2011-2012 Tier Two)
98123 Pokemon Communication (Crosshatch Holo Player Rewards Program 2010-2011 Tier Two)
100123 Professor Elm's Training Method (Crosshatch Holo Professor Program stamp March 2011)
101123 Professor Oak's New Theory (Crosshatch Holo Professor Program stamp March 2011)
103123 Double Colorless Energy (Crosshatch Holo Pokemon League Oshawott Season July 2011)
104123 Rainbow Energy (Crosshatch Holo Player Rewards Program 2011-2012 Tier Three)
20b123 Feraligatr (Cracked Ice Holo HeartGold & SoulSilver Series Collection exclusive)
26b123 Meganium (Cracked Ice Holo HeartGold & SoulSilver Series Collection exclusive)
28b123 Pichu (Staff HeartGold & SoulSilver stamp Prerelease)
32b123 Typhlosion (Cracked Ice Holo HeartGold & SoulSilver Series Collection exclusive)

2010 Pokemon HS Triumphant Promos

3102 Celebi (Non-Holo Zoroark: Master of Illusions DVD exclusive)
5102 Mamoswine (Cracked Ice Holo Verdant Frost theme deck exclusive)
6102 Nidoking (Cracked Ice Holo Royal Guard theme deck exclusive)
11102 Venomoth (Non-Holo Verdant Frost theme deck exclusive)
20102 Electivire (Triumphant stamp)
5b102 Mamoswine (Non-Holo Verdant Frost theme deck exclusive)
6b102 Nidoking (Non-Holo Royal Guard theme deck exclusive)
85102 Black Belt (Crosshatch Holo 2011 Player Rewards Tier 2)
87102 Junk Arm (Crosshatch Holo 2011 Player Rewards Tier 2)
88102 Seeker (Crosshatch Holo 2011 Player Rewards Tier 3)
20b102 Electivire (Staff Triumphant stamp)

2010 Pokemon HS Undaunted Promos

190 Bellossom (Non-Holo Daybreak theme deck exclusive)
290 Espeon (Cracked Ice Holo Daybreak theme deck exclusive)
490 Gliscor (Cracked Ice Holo Stage 1 Blisters exclusive)
590 Houndoom (Crosshatch Holo Pokemon League Disc Catch Season March 2011)
990 Togekiss (Non-Holo Daybreak theme deck exclusive)
1090 Umbreon (Cracked Ice Holo Nightfall theme deck exclusive)
1790 Leafeon (Undaunted stamp)
2b90 Espeon (Non-Holo Daybreak theme deck exclusive)
7990 Darkness Energy (Crosshatch Holo Pokemon League Disc Catch Season March 2011)
8090 Metal Energy (Crosshatch Holo Pokémon League Block Smash Season February 2011)
10b90 Umbreon (Non-Holo Nightfall theme deck exclusive)
17b90 Leafeon (Staff Undaunted stamp)

2010 Pokemon HS Unleashed Promos

295 Magmortar (Cracked Ice Holo Player's Collection exclusive)
495 Metagross (Cracked Ice Holo Player's Pack exclusive)
595 Mismagius (Non-Holo Chaos Control theme deck exclusive)
795 Politoed (Crosshatch Holo National Championships 2010-2011)
1095 Torterra (Cracked Ice Holo Pokemon Evolutions Box/Pokémon Evolutions Pack exclusive)
1195 Xatu (Cracked Ice Holo Stage 1 Blisters exclusive)
1395 Blastoise (Unleashed stamp)
1495 Crobat (Crosshatch Holo Pokemon League Hurdle Dash Season November 2010)
2195 Poliwrath (Crosshatch Holo Regional Championships 2010-2011)
2495 Steelix (Crosshatch Holo Pokemon League Block Smash Season February 2011)
2695 Tyranitar (Cosmos Holo Chaos Control theme deck exclusive)
3795 Poliwhirl (Crosshatch Holo State/Province/Territory Championships 2010-2011)
4395 Aipom (SDCC 2010 stamped)
5895 Poliwag (Crosshatch Holo City Championships 2010-2011)
7895 Judge (Crosshatch Holo Professor Program stamp January 2013)
7b95 Politoed (Staff Crosshatch Holo National Championships 2010-2011)
8295 Rare Candy (Crosshatch Holo Winter 2010-2011 Player Rewards Tier 2)
8395 Super Scoop Up (Crosshatch Holo Spring 2011 Player Rewards Tier 3)
13b95 Blastoise (Staff Unleashed stamp)
13c95 Blastoise (Cracked Ice Holo Pokemon Evolutions Box/Pokemon Evolutions Pack exclusive)
21b95 Poliwrath (Staff Crosshatch Holo Regional Championships 2010-2011)
24b95 Steelix (Cosmos Holo Steel Sentinel theme deck exclusive)
37b95 Poliwhirl (Staff Crosshatch Holo State/Province/Territory Championships 2010-2011)
58b95 Poliwag (Staff Crosshatch Holo City Championships 2010-2011)

2011 Pokemon Black and White Emerging Powers Promos

3098 Beartic (Cracked Ice Holo Next Destinies Stage 1 Blisters exclusive)
4098 Scolipede (Cracked Ice Holo Toxic Tricks theme deck exclusive)
4998 Roggenrola (Cracked Ice Holo Next Destinies Stage 2 Blisters exclusive)
5198 Boldore (Cracked Ice Holo Next Destinies Stage 2 Blisters exclusive)
5398 Gigalith (Emerging Powers stamp Prerelease)
5698 Excadrill (Cosmos Holo Dragons Exalted Stage 1 Blisters exclusive)
6298 Krookodile (Cracked Ice Holo Power Play theme deck exclusive)
8298 Unfezant (Crosshatch Holo Pokémon League Jet Season April 2012)
9598 Pokemon Catcher (Crosshatch Holo 2012 Player Rewards Tier 3)
30b98 Beartic (Cosmos Holo Water Gym Collector Pack exclusive)
53b98 Gigalith (Staff Emerging Powers stamp Prerelease)
53c98 Gigalith (Cracked Ice Holo Next Destinies Stage 2 Blisters exclusive)

2011 Pokemon Black and White Noble Victories Promos

3101 Leavanny (Non-Holo Fast Daze theme deck exclusive)
8101 Karrablast (Crosshatch Holo City Championships 2011-2012)
11101 Shelmet (Crosshatch Holo Regional Championships 2011-2012)
12101 Accelgor (Cracked Ice Holo Fast Daze theme deck exclusive)
13101 Virizion (Cosmos Holo Black & White Two Pack Blister exclusive)
32101 Cryogonal (Crosshatch Holo Pokemon League Freeze Season June 2012)
34101 Kyurem (Cosmos Holo Legendary Dragons of Unova Collection exclusive)
41101 Eelektross (Non-Holo Furious Knights theme deck exclusive)
43101 Victini (Noble Victories stamp Prerelease)
73101 Terrakion (Cosmos Holo Black & White Two Pack Blister exclusive)
80101 Escavalier (Cracked Ice Holo Furious Knights theme deck exclusive)
84101 Cobalion (Cosmos Holo Black & White Two Pack Blister exclusive)
87101 Fraxure (Crosshatch Holo Pokemon League Legend Season July 2012)
8b101 Karrablast (Staff Crosshatch Holo City Championships 2011-2012)
91101 Eviolite (Crosshatch Holo 2012 Player Rewards Tier 2)
11b101 Shelmet (Staff Crosshatch Holo Regional Championships 2011-2012)
12b101 Accelgor (Crosshatch Holo State/Province/Territory Championships 2011-2012)
12c101 Accelgor (Staff Crosshatch State/Province/Territory Championships 2011-2012)
43b101 Victini (Staff Noble Victories stamp Prerelease)
80b101 Escavalier (Crosshatch Holo National Championships 2011-2012)
80c101 Escavalier (Staff Crosshatch Holo National Championships 2011-2012)

2011 Pokemon Call of Legends Promos

695 Groudon (Non-Holo Retort theme deck exclusive)
895 Hitmontop (Non-Holo Retort theme deck exclusive)
1495 Lucario (Cracked Ice Holo Retort theme deck exclusive)
1695 Magmortar (Non-Holo Recon theme deck exclusive)
1795 Ninetales (Non-Holo Recon theme deck exclusive)
3395 Snorlax (Call of Legends stamp Prerelease)
3495 Tangrowth (Cracked Ice Holo Recon theme deck exclusive)
8895 Grass Energy (Crosshatch Holo 2011 Player Rewards Tier 1)
8995 Fire Energy (Crosshatch Holo 2011 Player Rewards Tier 1)
9095 Water Energy (Crosshatch Holo 2011 Player Rewards Tier 1)
9195 Lightning Energy (Crosshatch Holo 2011 Player Rewards Tier 1)
9295 Psychic Energy (Crosshatch Holo 2011 Player Rewards Tier 1)
9395 Fighting Energy (Crosshatch Holo 2011 Player Rewards Tier 1)
9495 Darkness Energy (Crosshatch Holo 2011 Player Rewards Tier 1)
9595 Metal Energy (Crosshatch Holo 2011 Player Rewards Tier 1)
14b95 Lucario (Non-Holo Retort theme deck exclusive)
33b95 Snorlax (Staff Call of Legends stamp Prerelease)

2012 Pokemon Black and White Boundaries Crossed Promos

13149 Serperior (Cosmos Holo Furious Fists Two Pack Blisters exclusive)
20149 Charizard (Cosmos Holo XY Two Pack Blisters/XY Knock Out Collection exclusive)
26149 Emboar (Cosmos Holo Furious Fists Two Pack Blisters exclusive)
31149 Blastoise (Non-Holo Ice Shock theme deck exclusive)
38149 Delibird (1st Place Crosshatch Holo Pokemon League Froakie/Xerneas Season League Challenge)
41149 Samurott (Cosmos Holo Furious Fists Two Pack Blisters exclusive)
54149 Electivire (Cosmos Holo Furious Fists Two Pack Blisters exclusive)
63149 Dusknoir (Cosmos Holo Psychic Gym Collector Pack/Furious Fists Two Pack Blisters exclusive)
94149 Scizor (Cosmos Holo Furious Fists Two Pack Blisters exclusive)
100149 Black Kyurem (Cracked Ice Holo Ice Shock theme deck exclusive)
102149 White Kyurem (Cracked Ice Holo Cold Fire theme deck exclusive)
134149 Skyla (Mirror Holo Pokémon League Chespin Season October 2013)
38b149 Delibird (2nd Place Crosshatch Holo Pokemon League Froakie/Xerneas Season League Challenge)
38c149 Delibird (3rd Place Crosshatch Holo Pokemon League Froakie/Xerneas Season League Challenge)
38d149 Delibird (4th Place Crosshatch Holo Pokemon League Froakie/Xerneas Season League Challenge)
41b149 Samurott (Non-Holo Cold Fire theme deck exclusive)
54b149 Electivire (Non-Holo Ice Shock theme deck exclusive)

2012 Pokemon Black and White Dark Explorers Promos

3108 Venusaur (Cosmos Holo XY Two Pack Blisters/XY Knock Out Collection exclusive)
12108 Flareon (Crosshatch Holo Winter Regional Championships 2012-2013)
17108 Blaziken (Cosmos Holo Plasma Blast Single Pack Blisters exclusive)
25108 Vaporeon (Crosshatch Holo European Spring Regional Championships 2012-2013)
29108 Empoleon (Non-Holo Shadows theme deck exclusive)
37108 Jolteon (Crosshatch Holo Autumn Regional Championships 2012-2013)
48108 Espeon (Crosshatch Holo National Championships 2012-2013)
4b108 Scyther (1st Place Crosshatch Holo Pokemon League Chespin/Fennekin Season League Challenge)
4c108 Scyther (2nd Place Crosshatch Holo Pokemon League Chespin/Fennekin Season League Challenge)
4d108 Scyther (3rd Place Crosshatch Holo Pokemon League Chespin/Fennekin Season League Challenge)
52108 Cofagrigus (Cracked Ice Holo Raiders theme deck exclusive)
60108 Umbreon (Crosshatch Holo Spring Regional Championships 2012-2013)
66108 Krookodile (Cosmos Holo Plasma Blast Single Pack Blisters exclusive)
67108 Scraggy (Mirror Reverse Holo Black & White Variety Blisters exclusive)
71108 Zoroark (Cracked Ice Holo Shadows theme deck exclusive)
84108 Eevee (Crosshatch Holo City Championships 2012-2013)
94108 Enhanced Hammer (Mirror Holo Pokemon League Xerneas Season February 2014)
98108 Professor Juniper (Crosshatch Holo Professor Program stamp January 2013)
12b108 Flareon (Staff Crosshatch Holo Winter Regional Championships 2012-2013)
25b108 Vaporeon (Staff Crosshatch Holo European Spring Regional Championships 2012-2013)
25c108 Vaporeon (Crosshatch Holo North American State Province Territory Championships 2012-2013)
25d108 Vaporeon (Staff Crosshatch Holo North American State Province Territory Championships 2012-2013)
37b108 Jolteon (Staff Crosshatch Holo Autumn Regional Championships 2012-2013)
48b108 Espeon (Staff Crosshatch Holo National Championships 2012-2013)
4E+108 Scyther (4th Place Crosshatch Holo Pokemon League Chespin/Fennekin Season League Challenge)
60b108 Umbreon (Staff Crosshatch Holo Spring Regional Championships 2012-2013)
66b108 Krookodile (Non-Holo Raiders theme deck exclusive)
84b108 Eevee (Staff Crosshatch Holo City Championships 2012-2013)

2012 Pokemon Black and White Dragons Exalted Promos

24124 Gyarados (Cosmos Holo XY Three Pack Blisters exclusive)
28124 Milotic (Cosmos Holo Water Gym Collector Pack exclusive)
40124 Ampharos (Cosmos Holo Legendary Treasures Single Pack Blisters exclusive)
52124 Sigilyph (Cosmos Holo Psychic Gym Collector Pack exclusive)
59124 Golurk (Non-Holo DragonSnarl theme deck exclusive)
80124 Aggron (Cosmos Holo Legendary Treasures Single Pack Blisters exclusive)
91124 Garchomp (Cracked Ice Holo DragonSpeed theme deck exclusive)
98124 Hydreigon (Cracked Ice Holo DragonSnarl theme deck exclusive)
117124 Blend Energy GFPD (Crosshatch Holo 2012 Player Rewards Tier 2)
118124 Blend Energy WLFM (Crosshatch Holo 2012 Player Rewards Tier 2)
28b124 Milotic (Non-Holo DragonSpeed theme deck exclusive)
91b124 Garchomp (Cosmos Holo XY Two Pack Blisters/XY Knock Out Collection exclusive)
98b124 Hydreigon (Cosmos Holo XY Two Pack Blisters/XY Knock Out Collection exclusive)

2012 Pokemon Black and White Next Destinies Promos

1299 Arcanine (Next Destinies stamp Prerelease)
1499 Moltres (Cosmos Holo Plasma Freeze Single Pack Blisters/Black & White Two Pack Blister exclusive)
2099 Chandelure (Cracked Ice Holo Dragons Exalted Three Pack Blisters exclusive)
2199 Reshiram (Tinsel Holo Explosive Edge theme deck exclusive)
2799 Articuno (Cosmos Holo Black & White Two Pack Blister exclusive)
4099 Raichu (Cosmos Holo Boundaries Crossed Stage 1 Blisters exclusive)
4199 Zapdos (Cosmos Holo Black & White Two Pack Blister exclusive)
4399 Shinx (Cracked Ice Holo Dark Explorers Stage 2 Blisters exclusive)
4699 Luxray (Cracked Ice Holo Dark Explorers Stage 2 Blisters exclusive)
5099 Zekrom (Tinsel Holo Voltage Vortex theme deck exclusive)
6299 Beheeyem (Cosmos Holo Boundaries Crossed Stage 1 Blisters exclusive)
6499 Lucario (Cosmos Holo Dark Explorers Stage 1 Blisters exclusive)
7499 Scrafty (Non-Holo Voltage Vortex theme deck exclusive)
7999 Wigglytuff (Cosmos Holo Plasma Storm Stage 1 Blisters exclusive)
8099 Meowth (Mirror Reverse Holo Black & White Variety Blisters exclusive)
8199 Persian (Cosmos Holo Dark Explorers Stage 1 Blisters exclusive)
12b99 Arcanine (Staff Next Destinies stamp Prerelease)
20b99 Chandelure (Non-Holo Explosive Edge theme deck exclusive)
46b99 Luxray (Cosmos Holo Lightning Gym Collector Pack exclusive)
46c99 Luxray (Non-Holo Voltage Vortex theme deck exclusive)

2013 Pokemon Black and White Legendary Treasures Promos

19113 Charizard (Cosmos Holo Mega Charizard Collection/Mega Charizard Box exclusive)
80113 Lucario (Cosmos Holo Mega Lucario Collection exclusive)
90113 Zoroark (Cosmos Holo Furious Fists Single Pack Blisters exclusive)
97113 Deino (1st Place Crosshatch Holo Pokemon League Yveltal/Chesnaught Season League Challenge)
109113 Bianca (Mirror Holo Pokémon League Froakie Season January 2014)
97b113 Deino (2nd Place Crosshatch Holo Pokemon League Yveltal/Chesnaught Season League Challenge)
97c113 Deino (3rd Place Crosshatch Holo Pokemon League Yveltal/Chesnaught Season League Challenge)
97d113 Deino (4th Place Crosshatch Holo Pokemon League Yveltal/Chesnaught Season League Challenge)

2013 Pokemon Black and White Plasma Blast Promos

5101 Tropius (Crosshatch Holo National Championships 2013-2014)
10101 Genesect (Cracked Ice Holo Mind Wipe theme deck exclusive)
13101 Volcarona (Cracked Ice Holo Solar Strike theme deck exclusive)
16101 Blastoise (Non-Holo Solar Strike theme deck exclusive)
46101 Golurk (Non-Holo Mind Wipe theme deck exclusive)
49101 Machamp (Cosmos Holo Flashfire Three Pack Blisters exclusive)
5b101 Tropius (Staff Crosshatch Holo National Championships 2013-2014)
69101 Haxorus (Cosmos Holo Flashfire Three Pack Blisters exclusive)
16b101 Blastoise (Error 2012 Cosmos Holo XY Two Pack Blisters exclusive)
16c101 Blastoise (Corrected 2013 Cosmos Holo XY Knock Out Collection exclusive)

2013 Pokemon Black and White Plasma Freeze Promos

11116 Leafeon (Cracked Ice Holo Psy Crusher theme deck exclusive)
17116 Reshiram (Cosmos Holo Legendary Dragons of Unova Collection exclusive)
23116 Glaceon (Cracked Ice Holo Frost Ray theme deck exclusive)
33116 Electrode (Non-Holo Frost Ray theme deck exclusive)
39116 Zekrom (Cosmos Holo Legendary Dragons of Unova Collection exclusive)
83116 Dragonite (Cosmos Holo XY Single Pack Blisters exclusive)
100116 Frozen City (Crosshatch Holo 2012-2013 Player Rewards Tier 3)
106116 Plasma Energy (Crosshatch Holo 2012-2013 Player Rewards Tier 3)
11b116 Leafeon (Crosshatch Holo European Spring Regional Championships 2013-2014)
11c116 Leafeon (Staff Crosshatch Holo European Spring Regional Championships 2013-2014)
11d116 Leafeon (Crosshatch Holo North American State/Province/Territory Championships 2013-2014)
23b116 Glaceon (Crosshatch Holo City Championships 2013-2014)
23c116 Glaceon (Staff Crosshatch Holo City Championships 2013-2014)
1.1E+115 Leafeon (Staff Crosshatch Holo North American State/Province/Territory Championships 2013-2014)

2013 Pokemon Black and White Plasma Storm Promos

17135 Infernape (Non-Holo Plasma Claw theme deck exclusive)
58135 Weezing (Non-Holo Plasma Shadow theme deck exclusive)
61135 Gallade (Cosmos Holo XY Three Pack Blisters exclusive)
62135 Giratina (Cracked Ice Holo Plasma Shadow theme deck exclusive)
94135 Druddigon (Cracked Ice Holo Plasma Claw theme deck exclusive)
118135 Colress (Crosshatch Holo 2012-2013 Player Rewards Tier 2)
120135 Escape Rope (Mirror Holo Pokémon League Yveltal Season April 2014)
123135 Hypnotoxic Laser (Crosshatch Holo 2012-2013 Player Rewards Tier 3)

2014 Pokemon XY Flashfire Promos

23106 Milotic (Non-Holo Mystic Typhoon Theme Deck exclusive)
31106 Avalugg (1st Place Crosshatch Holo Pokemon League Mauville/Lavaridge Season League Challenge)
37106 Heliolisk (Cracked Ice Holo Brilliant Thunder Theme Deck exclusive)
43106 Meowstic (Cracked Ice Holo Mystic Typhoon Theme Deck exclusive)
68106 Carbink (Non-Holo Battle Arena Decks Xerneas vs Yveltal exclusive)
88106 Blacksmith (Sheen Holo Pyroar Box exclusive)
89106 Fiery Torch (Sheen Holo Pyroar Box exclusive)
91106 Magnetic Storm (Crosshatch Holo Pokemon League Mauville Season February 2015)
94106 Pokémon Fan Club (Crosshatch Holo Pokemon League Petalburg Season May 2015)
31b106 Avalugg (2nd Place Crosshatch Holo Pokemon League Mauville/Lavaridge Season League Challenge)
31c106 Avalugg (3rd Place Crosshatch Holo Pokemon League Mauville/Lavaridge

Season League Challenge)
31d106 Avalugg (4th Place Crosshatch Holo Pokemon League Mauville/Lavaridge Season League Challenge)
89b106 Fiery Torch (Crosshatch Holo Pokemon League Lavaridge Season April 2015)

2014 Pokemon XY Furious Fists Promos

3111 Victreebel (Non-Holo Enchanted Echo Theme Deck exclusive)
8111 Shelmet (1st Place Crosshatch Holo Pokémon League Petalburg/Fortree Season League Challenge)
12111 Torchic (Crosshatch Holo City Championships 2014-2015)
13111 Combusken (Crosshatch Holo States 2014-2015 March 2015)
25111 Amaura (Cosmos Holo Ancient Power Box exclusive)
26111 Aurorus (Cosmos Holo Ancient Power Box exclusive)
46111 Machamp (Non-Holo Dark Hammer Theme Deck exclusive)
58111 Landorus (Non-Holo Dark Hammer Theme Deck exclusive)
61111 Tyrunt (Cosmos Holo Ancient Power Box exclusive)
62111 Tyrantrum (Cosmos Holo Ancient Power Box exclusive)
68111 Pangoro (Cracked Ice Holo Dark Hammer Theme Deck exclusive)
72111 Sylveon (Cracked Ice Holo Enchanted Echo Theme Deck exclusive)
8b111 Shelmet (2nd Place Crosshatch Holo Pokémon League Petalburg/Fortree Season League Challenge)
8c111 Shelmet (3rd Place Crosshatch Holo Pokémon League Petalburg/Fortree Season League Challenge)
8d111 Shelmet (4th Place Crosshatch Holo Pokémon League Petalburg/Fortree Season League Challenge)
92111 Fossil Researcher (Cosmos Holo Ancient Power Box exclusive)
12b111 Torchic (Staff Crosshatch Holo City Championships 2014-2015)
13b111 Combusken (Staff Crosshatch Holo States 2014-2015 March 2015)
13c111 Combusken (Crosshatch Holo Arena Cup 2014-2015 December 2014)
13d111 Combusken (Staff Crosshatch Holo Arena Cup 2014-2015 December 2014)

2014 Pokemon XY Phantom Forces Promos

10119 Talonflame (Cracked Ice Holo Burning Winds Theme Deck exclusive)
12119 Pyroar (Non-Holo Burning Winds Theme Deck exclusive)
17119 Feraligatr (Non-Holo Bolt Twister Theme Deck exclusive)
27119 Galvantula (Cracked Ice Holo Bolt Twister Theme Deck exclusive)
30119 Heliolisk (Non-Holo Bolt Twister Theme Deck exclusive)
77119 Goodra (Cosmos Holo Goodra Mini Album Blister Pack exclusive)
95119 Gengar Spirit Link (Sheen Holo Gengar Spirit Link 2-pack exclusive)

2015 Pokemon XY Primal Clash Promos

6160 Treecko (Sheen Holo Collector Chest exclusive)
25160 Torchic (Sheen Holo Collector Chest exclusive)
33160 Mudkip (Sheen Holo Collector Chest exclusive)
44160 Milotic (Non-Holo Ocean's Core Theme Deck exclusive)
53160 Kyogre (Cracked Ice Holo Ocean's Core Theme Deck exclusive)
61160 Manectric (Non-Holo Earth's Pulse Theme Deck exclusive)
84160 Groudon (Cracked Ice Holo Earth's Pulse Theme Deck exclusive)

2015 Pokemon XY Roaring Skies Promos

16108 Articuno (Cracked Ice Holo Aurora Blast Theme Deck exclusive)
23108 Zapdos (Cracked Ice Holo Storm Rider Theme Deck exclusive)
52108 Dragonite (Non-Holo Storm Rider Theme Deck exclusive)
57108 Salamence (Non-Holo Aurora Blast Theme Deck exclusive)
72108 Swellow (Non-Holo Aurora Blast Theme Deck exclusive)

1996 Pokemon Base Japanese

COMPLETE SET (102) 60.00 85.00
BOOSTER BOX (60 CT) 40.00 80.00
BOOSTER PACK (10 CARDS) 2.00 4.00
STARTER SET (60 CARDS) 15.00 20.00
1 Bulbasaur C .75 1.50
2 Ivysaur U 2.00 4.00
3 Venusaur HOLO R 8.00 15.00
4 Charmander C .50 1.00
5 Charmeleon U 3.00 5.00
6 Charizard HOLO R 25.00 35.00
7 Squirtle C 1.00 2.00
8 Wartortle U 1.50 3.00
9 Blastoise HOLO R 7.50 14.00
10 Caterpie C .50 1.00
11 Metapod C .50 1.00
13 Weedle C .50 1.00
14 Kakuna U .75 1.50
15 Beedrill R 3.00 5.00
16 Pidgey C .25 .50
17 Pidgeotto R 2.00 4.00
19 Rattata C .25 .50
20 Raticate U 1.00 2.00
25 Pikachu C 2.00 4.00
26 Raichu HOLO R 7.00 10.00
27 Sandshrew C .25 .50
32 Nidoran-M C .25 .50
33 Nidorino U .50 1.00
34 Nidoking HOLO R 3.00 6.00
35 Clefairy HOLO R 3.00 6.00
37 Vulpix C .25 .50
38 Ninetales HOLO R 10.00 15.00
50 Diglett C .25 .50
51 Dugtrio R 1.50 3.00
58 Growlithe U 1.00 2.00
59 Arcanine U 1.00 2.00
60 Poliwag C .25 .50
61 Poliwhirl U 2.00 3.00
62 Poliwrath HOLO R 3.00 6.00
63 Abra C .25 .75
64 Kadabra U .50 1.00
65 Alakazam HOLO R 5.00 8.00
66 Machop C .25 .50
67 Machoke U .50 1.00
68 Machamp HOLO R 4.00 7.00
77 Ponyta C .25 .50
81 Magnemite C .25 .50
82 Magneton HOLO R 3.00 6.00
83 Farfetch'd U .50 1.00
84 Doduo C .25 .50
86 Seel U 1.00 1.50
87 Dewgong U .50 1.00
92 Gastly C .25 .50
93 Haunter U 1.00 1.50
95 Onix C .25 .50
96 Drowzee C .25 .50
100 Voltorb C .25 .50
101 Electrode R 2.00 5.00
107 Hitmonchan HOLO R 4.00 8.00
109 Koffing C .25 .50
113 Chansey HOLO R 5.00 8.00
114 Tangela C .25 .50
120 Staryu C .25 .50
121 Starmie C .25 .50
124 Jynx U .50 1.00
125 Electabuzz R 3.00 5.00
126 Magmar U 1.00 2.00
129 Magikarp U .50 1.00
130 Gyarados HOLO R 4.00 8.00
137 Porygon U .50 1.00
145 Zapdos HOLO R 6.00 10.00
147 Dratini (U) .50 1.00
148 Dragonair R 3.00 5.00
150 Mewtwo HOLO R 10.00 15.00
NNO Trainer: Energy Retrieval C .25 .50
NNO Trainer: Pokédex U .50 1.00
NNO Trainer: Scoop Up R 1.00 3.00
NNO Trainer: Energy Removal C .25 .50
NNO Trainer: Plus Power U .50 1.00
NNO Trainer: Revive U .50 1.00
NNO Trainer: Devolution Spray R 1.00 3.00
NNO Trainer: Maintenance U .50 1.00
NNO Trainer: Professor Oak U 1.50 3.00
NNO Trainer: Bill C .25 .50
NNO Trainer: Gust of Wind C .25 .50
NNO Trainer: Pokémon Center U 1.00 2.00
NNO Trainer: Super Potion U .50 1.00
NNO Trainer: Defender U .50 1.00
NNO Trainer: Lass R 1.00 3.00
NNO Trainer: Potion C .25 .50
NNO Trainer: Computer Search R 1.00 3.00
NNO Trainer: Item Finder R 1.00 3.00
NNO Trainer: Pokémon Trader R 2.00 4.00
NNO Trainer: Clefairy Doll R 2.00 4.00
NNO Trainer: Imposter Prof. Oak R 1.00 3.00
NNO Trainer: Pokémon Flute U 1.00 2.00
NNO Trainer: Switch C .50 1.00
NNO Energy: Double Colorless U .50 1.00
NNO Trainer: Full Heal U .50 1.00
NNO Trainer: Pokémon Breeder R 1.00 3.00
NNO Trainer: Super Energy Removal R 1.00 3.00

1997 Pokemon Jungle Japanese

COMPLETE SET (48) 40.00 65.00
BOOSTER BOX (60 CT) 50.00 90.00
BOOSTER PACK (10 CARDS) 2.00 3.00
12 Butterfree U .50 1.00
18 Pidgeot HOLO R 4.00 7.00
21 Spearow C .25 .50
22 Fearow U .50 1.00
25 Pikachu C .75 1.50
29 Nidoran-F C .25 .50
30 Nidorina U .50 1.00
31 Nidoqueen HOLO R 2.00 4.00
36 Clefable HOLO R 2.00 4.00
39 Jigglypuff C .50 1.00
40 Wigglytuff HOLO R 2.00 4.00
43 Oddish C .25 .50
44 Gloom U .50 1.00
45 Vileplume HOLO R 2.00 4.00
46 Paras C .25 .50
47 Parasect U .50 1.00
48 Venonat C .25 .50
49 Venomoth HOLO R 2.00 4.00
52 Meowth C .25 .50
53 Persian U 1.00 2.00
56 Mankey C .25 .50
57 Primeape U .50 1.00
69 Bellsprout C .25 .50
70 Weepinbell U .75 1.50
71 Victreebel HOLO R 2.00 4.00
78 Rapidash U .75 1.50
85 Dodrio U .75 1.50
101 Electrode HOLO R 2.00 4.00
102 Exeggcute C .25 .50
103 Exeggutor U .75 1.50
104 Cubone C .25 .50
105 Marowak U .50 1.50
108 Lickitung U .75 1.50
111 Rhyhorn C .25 .50
112 Rhydon U .50 1.25
115 Kangaskhan HOLO R 2.00 4.00
118 Goldeen C .25 .50
119 Seaking U .50 1.25
122 Mr Mime HOLO R 2.00 4.00
123 Scyther HOLO R 2.00 5.00
127 Pinsir HOLO R 2.00 4.00
128 Tauros U .50 1.00
133 Eevee C .25 .75
134 Vaporeon HOLO R 2.00 4.00
135 Jolteon HOLO R 2.00 4.00
136 Flareon HOLO R 2.00 4.00
143 Snorlax HOLO R 2.00 4.00
NNO Trainer: Poké Ball C .25 .50

1997 Pokemon The Mystery of the Fossils Japanese

COMPLETE SET (48) 50.00 65.00
BOOSTER BOX (60 CT) 75.00 100.00
BOOSTER PACK (10 CARDS) 2.25 4.00
23 Ekans C .25 .75
24 Arbok U 1.00 2.00
26 Raichu HOLO R 2.00 5.00
28 Sandslash U .50 1.00
41 Zubat C .25 .50
42 Golbat U .50 1.50
54 Psyduck C .25 .50
55 Golduck U .50 1.00
72 Tentacool C .25 .50
73 Tentacruel U .50 1.00
74 Geodude C .25 .50
75 Graveler U .75 1.50
76 Golem U .75 1.50
79 Slowpoke C .25 .50
80 Slowbro U .50 1.00
82 Magneton HOLO R 2.00 4.00
88 Grimer C .25 .50
89 Muk HOLO R 2.00 4.00
90 Shellder C .25 .50
91 Cloyster U .50 1.00
92 Gastly U .50 1.25
93 Haunter HOLO R 2.00 4.00
94 Gengar HOLO R 5.00 10.00
97 Hypno HOLO R 3.00 6.00
98 Krabby C .25 .50
99 Kingler U .50 1.00
106 Hitmonlee HOLO R 3.00 6.00
110 Weezing U .50 1.25
116 Horsea C .25 .50
117 Seadra U 1.00 2.00
126 Magmar U 1.00 2.00
131 Lapras HOLO R 3.00 6.00
132 Ditto HOLO R 3.00 6.00
138 Omanyte (C) .25 .50
139 Omastar U .50 1.00
140 Kabuto C .25 .50
141 Kabutops HOLO R 2.00 4.00
142 Aerodactyl HOLO R 2.00 4.00
144 Articuno HOLO R 2.00 5.00
145 Zapdos HOLO R 2.00 4.00
146 Moltres HOLO R 3.00 6.00
149 Dragonite HOLO R 5.00 10.00
151 Mew HOLO R 7.00 15.00
NNO Trainer: Energy Transfer C .25 .50
NNO Trainer: Fuji Old Man U .50 1.00
NNO Trainer: Mysterious Fossil C .25 .50
NNO Trainer: Gambler (Dice) C .25 .50
NNO Trainer: Recycle C .25 .50

1997 Pokemon Rocket Gang Japanese

COMPLETE SET (65) 40.00 65.00
BOOSTER BOX (60 CT) 50.00 90.00
BOOSTER PACK (10 CARDS) 1.00 3.00
4 Charmander C .50 1.00
5 Dark Charmeleon U .50 1.00
6 Dark Charizard HOLO R 10.00 20.00
7 Squirtle C .50 1.00
8 Dark Wartortle U .50 1.00
9 Dark Blastoise HOLO R 5.00 8.00
19 Rattata C .25 .50
20 Dark Raticate C .25 .50
23 Ekans C .25 .50
24 Dark Arbok HOLO R 2.00 4.00
41 Zubat C .25 .50
42 Dark Golbat HOLO R 2.00 4.00
43 Oddish C .25 .50
44 Dark Gloom U .50 1.00
45 Dark Vileplume HOLO R 2.00 4.00
50 Diglett C .25 .50
51 Dark Dugtrio HOLO R 2.00 4.00
52 Meowth C .25 .75
53 Dark Persian C .25 .75
54 Psyduck C .25 .50
55 Dark Golduck U .50 1.00
56 Mankey C .25 .50
57 Dark Primeape U .50 1.50
63 Abra C .25 .50
64 Dark Kadabra U 1.00 2.00
65 Dark Alakazam HOLO R 2.00 4.00
66 Machop C .25 .50
67 Dark Machoke U .50 1.25
68 Dark Machamp HOLO R 2.00 4.00
77 Ponyta C .25 .50
78 Dark Rapidash C .25 .75
79 Slowpoke C .25 .50
80 Dark Slowbro HOLO R 2.00 4.00
81 Magnemite C .25 .50
82 Dark Magneton HOLO R 2.00 4.00
88 Grimer C .25 .50
89 Dark Muk U .50 1.00
96 Drowzee C .25 .50
97 Dark Hypno HOLO R 2.00 4.00
100 Voltorb C .25 .50
101 Dark Electrode U .50 1.00
109 Koffing C .25 .50
110 Dark Weezing HOLO R 2.00 4.00
129 Magikarp C .25 .50
130 Dark Gyarados HOLO R 4.00 5.00
133 Eevee C .25 .50
134 Dark Vaporeon U .50 1.00
135 Dark Jolteon U .50 1.00
136 Dark Flareon U .50 1.00
137 Porygon C .25 .50
147 Dratini C .25 .50
148 Dark Dragonair U 1.00 2.00
149 Dark Dragonite HOLO R 2.00 5.00
NNO Trainer: Challenge! U .75 1.50
NNO Energy: Potion C .25 .50
NNO Trainer: Sleep! C .25 .50
NNO Trainer: Nightly Garbage Run C .25 .50
NNO Trainer: Goop Gas Attack C .25 .50
NNO Trainer: Rocket's Sneak Attack HOLO R 3.00 6.00
NNO T. Here Comes Team Rocket HOLO R 10.00 15.00
NNO Energy: Full Heal C .25 .50
NNO Trainer: Impostor Oak's Revenge U 1.00 2.00
NNO Energy: Rainbow Energy HOLO R 2.00 4.00
NNO Trainer: Digger C .25 .50
NNO Trainer: The Boss's Way U .75 2.00

1998 Pokemon Gym Booster 1 Leaders Stadium Japanese

COMPLETE SET (96) 40.00 80.00
BOOSTER BOX (60 CT) 60.00 95.00
BOOSTER PACK (10 CARDS) 2.00 4.00
NIVI CITY GYM DECK #1 (BROCK) 10.00 20.00
HANADA GYM DECK #2 (MISTY) 8.00 16.00
KUCHIBA GYM DECK #3 (LT.SURGE) 10.00 20.00
TAMAMUSHI GYM DECK #4 (ERIKA) 10.00 20.00
YAMABUKI GYM DECK #5 (SABRINA) 8.00 16.00
GURNE GYM DECK #6 (BLAINE) 10.00 20.00
1 Erika's Bulbasaur U 1.00 2.00
19 Lt. Surge's Rattata C .25 .50
20 Lt. Surge's Raticate U .50 1.00
21 Lt. Surge's Spearow C .25 .50
22 Lt. Surge's Fearow HOLO R 2.00 4.00
25 Lt. Surge's Pikachu C .50 1.00
27 Brock's Sandshrew C .25 .50
28 Brock's Sandslash U .50 1.00
35 Erika's Clefairy U .75 2.00
36 Erika's Clefable HOLO R 2.00 4.00
37 Brock's Vulpix U .50 2.00
37 Brock's Vulpix C .25 .50
38 Brock's Ninetales HOLO R 2.00 4.00
39 Erika's Jigglypuff C .25 .50
41 Brock's Zubat C .25 .50
42 Brock's Golbat U .50 1.00
43 Erika's Oddish Lv 10 C .25 .50
43 Erika's Oddish Lv 15 C .25 .50
44 Erika's Gloom U .50 2.00
45 Erika's Vileplume HOLO R 2.00 4.00
46 Erika's Paras C .25 .50
50 Brock's Diglett C .25 .50
54 Misty's Psyduck C .25 .50
55 Misty's Golduck HOLO R 2.00 4.00
56 Brock's Mankey C .25 .50
57 Brock's Primeape U .50 1.00
60 Misty's Poliwag C .25 .50
61 Misty's Poliwhirl U 1.00 2.00
69 Erika's Bellsprout C .50 1.00
69 Erika's Bellsprout U .50 1.50
70 Erika's Weepingbell U .50 1.00
71 Erika's Victreebel R 1.00 2.00
72 Mist's Tentacool U .50 1.00
73 Misty's Tentacruel HOLO R 2.00 4.00
74 Brock's Geodude Lv. 15 C .25 .50
74 Brock's Geodude Lv. 13 C .25 .50
75 Brock's Graveler U 1.00 2.00
76 Brock's Golemn R 1.00 2.00
81 Lt. Surge's Magnemite C .25 .50
81 Lt. Surge's Magnemite U .50 1.00
82 Lt. Surge's Magneton HOLO R 2.00 4.00
86 Misty's Seel C .25 .50
87 Misty's Dwgong U .50 1.00
95 Brock's Onix C .25 .50
100 Lt. Surge's Voltorb C .25 .50
102 Erika's Exeggcute U .50 2.00
103 Erika's Exeggutor U 1.00 2.00
107 Rocket's Hitmonchan HOLO R 2.00 5.00
108 Brock's Lickitung U 1.00 2.00
111 Brock's Rhyhorn C .25 .50
112 Brock's Rhydon HOLO R 2.00 4.00
114 Erika's Tangela C .25 .50
116 Misty's Horsea Lv. 10 C .25 .50
116 Misty's Horsea Lv. 16 C .25 .50
117 Misty's Seadra HOLO R 2.00 4.00
118 Misty's Goldeen C .25 .50
120 Misty's Staryu C .25 .50
123 Rocket's Scyther HOLO R 3.00 6.00
125 Lt. Surge's Electabuzz HOLO R 2.00 4.00
129 Misty's Magikarp C .25 .50
130 Misty's Gyrados HOLO R 2.00 4.00
133 Lt. Surge's Eevee U 1.00 2.00
135 Lt. Surge's Jotleon R 1.00 2.00

146 Rocket's Moltres HOLO R	4.00	7.00
147 Erika's Dratini U	1.00	2.00
148 Erika's Dragonair HOLO R	2.00	5.00
NNO Trainer: Misty's Wrath U	1.00	2.00
NNO Trainer Vermilion City Gym U	.50	1.00
NNO Trainer Brock's Training Method	.50	1.00
NNO Trainer: Celadon City Gym U	.50	1.00
NNO Trainer: Pewter City Gym U	.50	1.00
NNO Trainer: Cerulean City Gym U	.50	1.00
NNO Trianer Lt. Surge's Treaty U	.50	1.00
NNO Trainer: Good Manners U	.50	1.00
NNO Trainer: Erika R	1.00	2.00
NNO Trainer: Erika's Kindness R	1.00	2.00
NNO Trainer: Misty R	1.00	2.00
NNO Trainer: Misty's Wish R	1.00	2.00
NNO Trainer Chaos Gym R	1.00	2.00
NNO Trainer: Secret Mission R	1.00	2.00
NNO Trainer: Brock R	1.00	2.00
NNO Trainer: Brock's Protection R	1.00	2.00
NNO Trainer: Resistance Gym R	1.00	2.00
NNO Trainer: Lt. Surge R	1.00	2.00
NNO Trainer: Lt. Surge's Secret Plan U	.50	1.00
NNO Trainer: No Removal Gym R	1.00	2.00
NNO Trainer: The Rocket's Traing Gym R	1.00	2.00
NNO Trainer: The Rocket's Trap HOLO R	3.00	4.00

1999 Pokemon Gym Booster 2 Challenge from the Darkness Japanese

COMPLETE SET (98)	40.00	60.00
BOOSTER BOX (60 CT)	55.00	85.00
BOOSTER PACK (10 CARDS)	2.00	3.00
2 Erika's Ivysaur U	1.00	2.00
3 Erika's Venusaur HOLO R	3.00	6.00
4 Blaine's Charmander C	.50	1.00
5 Blaine's Charmeleon U	1.00	2.00
6 Blaine's Charizard HOLO R	10.00	20.00
13 Koga's Weedle C	.25	.50
14 Koga's Kakuna U	1.00	2.00
15 Koga's Beedrill HOLO R	2.00	4.00
16 Koga's Pidgey Level 15 C	.25	.50
16 Koga's Pidgey Level 9 U	1.00	2.00
17 Koga's Pidgeotto R	1.00	2.00
23 Koga's Ekans C	.25	.50
24 Koga's Arbok R	1.00	2.00
26 Lt. Surge's Raichu HOLO R	2.00	5.00
29 Giovanni's Nidoran-F C	.25	.50
30 Giovanni's Nidorina (U)	.50	1.00
31 Giovanni's Nidoqueen R	1.00	2.00
32 Giovanni's Nidoran-M C	.25	.50
33 Giovanni's Nidorino U	.50	1.00
34 Giovanni's Nidoking HOLO R	2.00	4.00
37 Blaine's Vulpix C	.25	.50
38 Blaine's Ninetales R	1.00	2.00
41 Koga's Zubat C	.25	.50
42 Koga's Golbat U	.50	1.25
48 Sabrina's Venonat C	.25	.50
49 Sabrina's Venomoth R	1.00	2.00
51 Brock's Dugtrio R	1.00	2.00
52 Giovanni's Meowth Level 17 C	.25	.50
52 Giovanni's Meowth Level 12 U	1.00	2.00
53 Giovanni's Persian HOLO R	2.00	4.00
54 Sabrina's Psyduck C	.25	.50
55 Sabrina's Golduck R	1.00	2.00
56 Blaine's Mankey C	.25	.50
58 Blaine's Growlithe C	.25	.50
59 Blaine's Arcanine HOLO R	5.00	10.00
62 Misty's Poliwrath R	1.00	2.00
63 Sabrina's Abra C	.25	.50
64 Sabrina's Kadabra U	1.00	2.00
65 Sabrina's Alakazam HOLO R	2.00	4.00
66 Giovanni's Machop C	.25	.50
67 Giovanni's Machoke U	.50	1.00
68 Giovanni's Machamp HOLO R	2.00	4.00
77 Blaine's Ponyta C	.25	.50
78 Blaine's Rapidash U	.50	1.25
79 Sabrina's Slowpoke C	.25	.50
80 Sabrina's Slowbro U	.50	1.00
84 Blaine's Doduo Level 17 C	.25	.50
84 Imakuni's Doduo Level 15 R(White Star)	10.00	15.00
88 Koga's Grimer C	.25	.50
89 Koga's Muk R	2.00	4.00
92 Sabrina's Gastly U	.50	1.00
93 Sabrina's Haunter U	.50	1.00
94 Sabrina's Gengar HOLO R	2.00	4.00
96 Sabrina's Drowzee C	.25	.50
97 Sabrina's Hypno U	.50	1.00
109 Koga's Koffing Level 10 C	.25	.50
109 Koga's Koffing Level 15 U	.50	1.00
110 Koga's Weezing U	.50	1.00
111 Blaine's Rhyhorn C	.25	.50
113 Chansey U (White Diamond)	5.00	8.00
114 Koga's Tangela C	.25	.50
115 Blaine's Kangaskhan U	1.00	2.00
122 Sabrina's Mr. Mime C	.25	.75
124 Sabrina's Jynx U	.50	1.00
126 Blaine's Magmar U	1.00	2.00
127 Giovanni's Pinsir R	1.00	2.00
128 Blaine's Tauros C	.25	.50
129 Giovanni's Magikarp C	.25	.50
130 Giovanni's Gyarados HOLO R	2.00	4.00
132 Koga's Ditto HOLO R	2.00	4.00
137 Sabrina's Porygon C	.25	.75
143 Rocket's Snorlax R	2.00	4.00
145 Rocket's Zapdos HOLO R	3.00	6.00
146 Blaine's Moltres HOLO R	3.00	6.00
150 Rocket's Mewtwo HOLO R	4.00	8.00
NNO Trainer: Blaine's Gamble C	.50	1.00
NNO Trainer: Trash Exchange C	.50	1.00
NNO Trainer: Sabrina's Gaze C	5.00	10.00
NNO Trainer: Transparent Wallas C	.50	1.00
NNO Trainer: Warp Point C	.50	1.00
NNO Trainer: Blaine's Last Resort U	.50	1.00
NNO Trainer: Blaine's Quiz 3 U	.50	1.00
NNO Trainer: Koga's Ninja Trick U	5.00	10.00
NNO Trainer: Tickling Machine U	.50	1.00
NNO Trainer: Cinnabar City Gym U	.50	1.00
NNO Trainer: Fuchsia City Gym U	.50	1.00
NNO Trainer: Sabrina's ESP U	.50	1.00
NNO Trainer: Sabrina's Psychic Control U	.50	1.00
NNO Trainer: Minion of Team Rocket U	.50	1.00
NNO Trainer: Saffron City Gym U	.50	1.00
NNO Trainer: Rocket's Secret Experiment U	.50	1.00
NNO Trainer: Rocket's Minefield Gym U	.50	1.00
NNO Trainer: Blaine R	1.00	2.00
NNO Trainer: Koga R	1.00	2.00
NNO Trainer: Giovanni HOLO R	1.00	2.00
NNO Trainer: Giovanni's Last Resort R	1.00	2.00
NNO Trainer: Viridian City Gym R	1.00	2.00
NNO Trainer: Sabrina R	1.00	2.00

1999 Pokemon Gold, Silver, to a New World Japanese

COMPLETE SET (96)	60.00	100.00
BOOSTER BOX (60 CT)	50.00	75.00
BOOSTER PACK (10 CARDS)	3.00	4.00
STARTER SET (60)	20.00	25.00
25 Pikachu C	.50	1.25
35 Clefairy U	.50	1.00
43 Oddish C	.25	.50
44 Gloom U	.50	1.00
79 Slowpoke C	.25	.50
95 Onix C	.25	.50
116 Horsea C	.25	.50
117 Seadra U	.50	1.00
125 Electabuzz U	.50	1.50
126 Magmar U	.50	1.00
152 Chikorita C	.50	1.00
153 Bayleef U	.50	2.00
154 Meganium HOLO R	2.00	4.00
155 Cyndaquil C	.25	.50
156 Quilava U	.50	1.00
157 Typhlosion HOLO R	2.00	4.00
158 Totodile C	.50	1.00
159 Croconaw U	.75	2.00
160 Feraligatr HOLO R	3.00	6.00
161 Sentret C	.25	.50
162 Furret U	.50	1.00
163 Hoothoot C	.50	1.00
164 Noctowl U	.50	1.00
165 Ledyba C	.25	.75
166 Ledian U	.50	1.00
167 Spinarak C	.25	.50
168 Ariados U	.50	1.00
170 Chinchou C	.25	.50
171 Lanturn U	.50	1.00
172 Pichu HOLO R	4.00	8.00
173 Cleffa R	2.00	4.00
175 Togepi U	1.00	2.00
176 Togetic HOLO R	2.00	4.00
177 Natu C	.25	.50
178 Xatu U	.50	1.00
179 Mareep C	.25	.50
180 Flaaffy U	.50	1.00
181 Ampharos HOLO R	2.00	4.00
182 Bellossom HOLO R	2.00	4.00
183 Marill C	1.50	3.00
184 Azumarill HOLO R	2.00	4.00
185 Sudowoodo C	.25	.50
187 Hoppip C	.25	.50
188 Skiploom U	.50	1.25
189 Jumpluff HOLO R	2.00	4.00
190 Aipom U	.50	1.00
191 Sunkern C	.25	.50
192 Sunflora U	.50	1.00
194 Wooper C	.75	1.50
195 Quagsire U	.50	1.00
198 Murkrow R	2.00	4.00
199 Slowking HOLO R	2.00	4.00
203 Girafarig C	.25	.50
207 Gligar C	.25	.50
208 Steelix HOLO R	2.00	4.00
209 Snubbull C	1.00	1.50
210 Granbull U	.75	1.75
213 Shuckle C	.25	.50
214 Heracross HOLO R	2.00	4.00
215 Sneasel R	2.00	4.00
220 Swinub C	.25	.50
221 Piloswine U	.50	1.00
226 Mantine C	.25	.50
227 Skarmory HOLO R	2.00	4.00
230 Kingdra HOLO R	2.00	4.00
231 Phanpy U	.50	1.00
232 Donphan R	1.00	2.00
234 Stantler C	.25	.50
239 Elekid R	1.00	2.00
240 Magby R	1.00	2.00
241 Miltank U	.50	1.00
249 Lugia HOLO R	6.00	12.00
NNO Evil Energy R	1.00	2.00
NNO Recycle Energy R	1.00	2.00
NNO Steel Energy HOLO R	2.00	4.00
NNO Trainer: Acorn C	.25	.50
NNO Trainer: Bellsprout Tower U	.50	1.00
NNO T: Bill's Transfer Device U	.50	1.00
NNO Trainer: Card Machine U	.50	1.00
NNO Trainer: Ekoro Gym R	1.00	2.00
NNO Trainer: Energy Charge R	1.00	2.00
NNO T: Fighting Spirit Headband R	1.00	2.00
NNO Trainer: Golden Acorn U	.50	1.00
NNO Trainer: Kurumi (radio) R	1.00	2.00
NNO Trainer: Miracle Acorn U	.50	1.00
NNO Trainer: Moo Moo Milk C	.25	.50
NNO Trainer: New Pokédex U	.50	1.00
NNO Trainer: Poké Gear R	1.00	2.00
NNO Trainer: Pokémon Town C	.25	.50
NNO Trainer: Professor Utsugi U	.50	1.00
NNO T: Reverse Nomination C	.25	.50
NNO Trainer: Slot Machine R	1.00	2.00
NNO T: Super Energy Retrieval R	1.00	2.00
NNO Trainer: Super Rod C	.25	.50
NNO Trainer: Super Scoop Up U	.50	1.00
NNO Trainer: Time Capsule R	1.00	2.00

2000 Pokemon Crossing the Ruins Japanese

COMPLETE SET (57)	30.00	50.00
UNOPENED BOX (60 CT)	40.00	60.00
UNOPENED PACK (10 CARDS)	2.00	4.00
10 Caterpie C	.25	.50
11 Metapod U	.50	1.00
12 Butterfree HOLO R	2.00	4.00
13 Weedle C	.25	.50
14 Kakuna U	.50	1.00
15 Beedrill HOLO R	2.00	4.00
26 Dark Raichu HOLO R	3.00	6.00
60 Poliwag C	.25	.50
61 Poliwhirl U	.50	1.00
62 Poliwrath HOLO R	2.00	4.00
81 Magnemite HOLO R	2.00	4.00
123 Scyther U	.50	1.00
133 Eevee U	.50	1.00
138 Omanyte C	.25	.50
139 Omastar U	.50	1.00
140 Kabuto C	.25	.50
141 Kabutops HOLO R	2.00	4.00
161 Sentret C	.10	.25
167 Spinarak C	.25	.50
174 Igglybuff U	.50	1.00
177 Natu C	.25	.50
178 Xatu U	.50	1.00
179 Mareep C	.25	.50
186 Politoed HOLO R	2.00	4.00
187 Hoppip C	.25	.50
193 Yanma HOLO R	2.00	4.00
194 Wooper C	.25	.50
196 Espeon HOLO R	3.00	6.00
197 Umbreon HOLO R	2.00	4.00
201 Unown A HOLO R	2.00	4.00
201 Unown I C	.25	.75
201 Unown U U	2.00	3.00
201 Unown M U	.50	1.00
201 Unown F U	1.00	2.00
201 Unown D U	.75	1.50
202 Wobbuffet HOLO R	2.00	4.00
204 Pineco C	.25	.50
205 Forretress HOLO R	2.00	4.00
206 Dunsparce C	.25	.50
212 Scizor HOLO R	3.00	6.00
216 Teddiursa C	.25	.50
217 Ursaring HOLO R	2.00	4.00
222 Corsola U	.50	1.00
228 Houndour U	.50	1.25
228 Houndour HOLO R	3.00	6.00
229 Houndoom HOLO R	3.00	6.00
235 Smeargle HOLO R	2.00	4.00
236 Tyrogue C	.25	.50
237 Hitmontop HOLO R	2.00	4.00
246 Larvitar C	.25	.50
247 Pupitar U	.50	1.00
248 Tyranitar HOLO R	3.00	6.00
NNO Trainer: Egg U	.50	1.00
NNO Trainer: Energy Ark C	.50	1.00
NNO Trainer: Hyper Spray U	.50	1.00
NNO Trainer: Ruin Wall Pikachu U	1.00	2.00
NNO Trainer: Ruin Wall Raichu U	.75	1.50

2001 Pokemon Awakening Legends Japanese

COMPLETE SET (57)	35.00	60.00
UNOPENED BOX (60 CT)	40.00	60.00
UNOPENED PACK (10 CARDS)	1.00	2.00
26 Raichu U	.50	1.25
41 Zubat C	.25	.50
42 Golbat C	.25	.50
46 Paras C	.25	.50
47 Parasect U	.50	1.00
74 Geodude C	.25	.50
75 Graveler U	.50	1.00
82 Magneton HOLO R	2.00	4.00
83 Farfetch'd C	.25	.50
118 Goldeen C	.25	.50
119 Seaking U	.50	1.00
120 Staryu C	.25	.50
121 Starmie HOLO R	2.00	4.00
124 Jynx U	.50	1.00
129 Magikarp HOLO UR	6.00	12.00
130 Gyarados HOLO UR	6.00	12.00
142 Aerodactyl HOLO R	2.00	4.00
169 Crobat HOLO R	2.00	4.00
170 Chinchou C	.25	.50
171 Lanturn U	.50	1.00
180 Flaaffy U	.50	1.00
181 Ampharos HOLO R	2.00	4.00
188 Skiploom C	.25	.50
189 Jumpluff HOLO R	2.00	4.00
190 Aipom C	.25	.50
195 Quagsire C	.25	.50
198 Murkrow C	.25	.50
200 Misdreavus HOLO R	2.00	4.00
201 Unown K C	2.00	4.00
201 Unown Y U	1.50	3.00
201 Unown B U	1.50	3.00
209 Snubbull C	.25	.50
211 Qwilfish C	.25	.50
213 Shuckle U	.50	1.00
218 Slugma C	.25	.50
219 Magcargo U	.50	1.00
220 Swinub C	.25	.50
221 Piloswine U	.50	1.00
223 Remoraid C	.25	.50
224 Octillary U	.50	1.00
225 Delibird HOLO R	2.00	4.00
229 Houndoom HOLO R	3.00	4.00
230 Kingdra HOLO R	2.00	4.00
233 Porygon2 HOLO R	2.00	4.00
234 Stantler U	.50	1.00
238 Smoochum C	.25	.50
242 Blissey HOLO R	2.00	4.00
243 Raikou HOLO R	2.00	4.00
244 Entei HOLO R	2.00	4.00
245 Suicune HOLO R	3.00	5.00
250 Ho-oh HOLO R	3.00	5.00
251 Celebi HOLO R	3.00	5.00
NNO Trainer: Old Fishing Rod C	.25	.50
NNO Trainer: Rocket's Gengar R U	.50	1.00
NNO Trainer: Seed U	.50	1.00
NNO Trainer: Stadium U	.50	1.00
NNO Trainer: Dragonite U	.50	1.00

2001 Pokemon Darkness, and to Light Japanese

COMPLETE SET (113)	100.00	200.00
UNOPENED BOX (60 CT)	75.00	125.00
UNOPENED PACK (10 CARDS)	2.00	4.00
6 Charizard HOLO UR	10.00	20.00
26 Raichu HOLO UR	5.00	10.00
37 Vulpix C	.25	.50
38 Ninetales U	.50	1.00
39 Jigglypuff C	.25	.50
40 Wigglytuff Lv.33 U	.50	1.00
40 Wigglytuff Lv.24 U	.50	1.00
48 Venonat C	.25	.50
49 Venomoth U	.50	1.00
54 Psyduck C	.25	.50
55 Golduck U	.50	1.00
58 Growlithe C	.25	.50
59 Arcanine HOLO R	3.00	6.00
66 Machop C	.25	.50
67 Machoke U	.50	1.00
68 Machamp R	1.00	2.00
80 Slowbro U	.50	1.00
86 Seel C	.25	.50
87 Dewgong U	.50	1.00
92 Gastly C	.25	.50
93 Haunter U	.50	1.00
94 Gengar HOLO R	3.00	6.00
102 Exeggcute C	.25	.50
103 Exeggutor U	.25	.50
106 Hitmonlee U	.50	1.00
107 Hitmonchan C	.25	.50
113 Chansey U	.50	1.00
123 Scyther U	.50	1.00
134 Vaporeon U	.50	1.00
135 Jolteon U	.50	1.00
136 Flareon U	.50	1.00
137 Porygon C	.25	.50
138 Omanyte C	.25	.50
139 Omastar R	1.00	2.00
141 Kabutops HOLO UR	5.00	10.00
147 Dratini C	.25	.50
148 Dragonair R	1.00	2.00
149 Dragonite HOLO R	3.00	6.00
150 Mewtwo HOLO UR	8.00	12.00
155 Cyndaquil C	.25	.50
156 Quilava U	.50	1.00
157 Typhlosion HOLO R	3.00	5.00
158 Totodile C	.25	.50
159 Croconaw U	.25	.50
160 Feraligatr HOLO R	3.00	5.00
164 Noctowl HOLO R	8.00	12.00
165 Ledyba C	.25	.50

Card	Low	High
166 Ledian R	1.00	2.00
168 Ariados R	1.00	2.00
169 Crobat HOLO R	2.00	5.00
171 Lanturn R	.50	1.00
175 Togepi C	.25	.50
176 Togetic HOLO R	2.00	5.00
179 Mareep C	.25	.50
180 Flaffy U	.50	1.00
181 Ampharos HOLO R	2.00	5.00
184 Azumarill HOLO R	2.00	4.00
191 Sunkern C	.25	.50
192 Sunflora C	.25	.50
196 Espeon HOLO R	3.00	6.00
199 Slowking R	1.00	2.00
201 Unown T R	1.00	2.00
201 Unown S R	1.00	2.00
201 Unown H R	1.00	2.00
201 Unown X R	1.00	2.00
201 Unown Q U	2.00	4.00
201 Unown P U	2.00	4.00
201 Unown L C	1.00	3.00
201 Unown Z U	3.00	5.00
201 Unown G R	1.00	2.00
201 Unown W R	2.00	4.00
201 Unown C U	3.00	5.00
201 Unown V C	1.00	3.00
203 Girafarig C	.25	.50
204 Pineco C	.25	.50
205 Forretress U	.50	1.00
207 Gligar C	.25	.50
208 Steelix HOLO UR	3.00	6.00
212 Scizor HOLO R	3.00	7.00
214 Heracross U	.50	1.00
217 Ursaring R	1.00	2.00
218 Slugma C	.25	.50
219 Magcargo R	1.00	2.00
220 Swinub C	.25	.50
221 Piloswine R	1.00	2.00
223 Remoraid C	.25	.50
224 Octillery U	.50	1.00
226 Mantine C	.25	.50
228 Houndour C	.25	.50
229 Houndoom HOLO R	3.00	6.00
231 Phanpy C	.25	.50
232 Donphan HOLO R	3.00	6.00
233 Porygon2 HOLO R	3.00	6.00
246 Larvitar C	.25	.50
247 Pupitar U	.50	1.00
248 Tyranitar HOLO UR	6.00	10.00
248 Tyranitar HOLO R	4.00	8.00
251 Celebi HOLO UR	5.00	10.00
NNO Trainer: Counter Claw U	.50	1.00
NNO Trainer: Team Rocket's Secret Maneuvers U	.50	1.00
NNO Miracle Energy HOLO R	2.00	4.00
NNO Trainer: Energy Amplifier U	.50	1.00
NNO Trainer: Energy Stadium U	.50	1.00
NNO Trainer: Rocket's Secret Machine R	1.00	2.00
NNO Trainer: Radio Tower R	1.00	2.00
NNO Trainer: Determine Personality U	1.00	2.00
NNO Trainer: Bill's Mail C	.25	.50
NNO Trainer: Scope Lens U	.50	1.00
NNO Trainer: Lucky Stadium U	.50	1.00
NNO Trainer: Experience Share R	1.00	2.00
NNO Trainer: Impostor Oak's Invention R	1.00	2.00
NNO Trainer: Bumpy Gym R	1.00	2.00
NNO Trainer: All-Purpose Powder C	.25	.50

2001 Pokemon VS 1st Edition Japanese

Card	Low	High
COMPLETE SET (144)	250.00	500.00
FIRE/WATER BOOSTER BOX (10 PACKS)	600.00	800.00
GRASS/LIGHTNING BOOSTER BOX (10 PACKS)	600.00	800.00
PSYCHIC/FIGHTING BOOSTER BOX (10 PACKS)	600.00	800.00
FIRE/WATER PACK (30 CARDS)	40.00	80.00
GRASS/LIGHTNING PACK (30 CARDS)	40.00	80.00
PSYCHIC/FIGHTING PACK (30 CARDS)	40.00	80.00
1 Falkner's Pidgeot C	2.00	6.00
2 Falkner's Fearow C	1.25	3.00
3 Falkner's Farfetch'd C	1.50	4.00
4 Falkner's Dodrio C	2.00	6.00
5 Falkner's Togetic C	2.00	6.00
6 Falkner's Delibird C	2.00	6.00
7 Falkner's Skarmory HOLO R	8.00	20.00
8 Bugsy's Butterfree C	2.00	6.00
9 Bugsy's Beedrill C	2.00	6.00
10 Bugsy's Pinsir C	2.00	6.00
11 Bugsy's Ledian C	2.00	6.00
12 Bugsy's Yanma C	2.00	6.00
13 Bugsy's Scizor HOLO R	10.00	25.00
14 Whitney's Clefable C	2.00	6.00
15 Whitney's Wigglytuff C	2.00	6.00
16 Whitney's Persian C	2.00	6.00
17 Whitney's Lickitung C	2.00	6.00
18 Whitney's Furret C	2.00	6.00
19 Whitney's Miltank C	2.00	6.00
20 Morty's Ninetales C	2.00	6.00
21 Morty's Gengar C	5.00	6.00
22 Morty's Hypno C	2.00	6.00
23 Morty's Marowak C	2.00	6.00
24 Morty's Noctowl C	2.00	6.00
25 Morty's Murkrow HOLO R	6.00	15.00
26 Morty's Misdreavus C	2.00	6.00
27 Jasmine's Raichu C	2.00	6.00
28 Jasmine's Magneton C	2.00	6.00
29 Jasmine's Electabuzz C	2.00	6.00
30 Jasmine's Jolteon C	6.00	6.00
31 Jasmine's Ampharos C	2.00	6.00
32 Jasmine's Steelix HOLO R	10.00	25.00
33 Chuck's Primeape C	2.00	6.00
34 Chuck's Poliwrath C	2.00	6.00
35 Chuck's Rhydon C	2.00	6.00
36 Chuck's Tauros C	2.00	6.00
37 Chuck's Granbull C	2.00	6.00
38 Chuck's Donphan C	2.00	6.00
39 Pryce's Degong C	2.00	6.00
40 Pryce's Cloyster C	2.00	6.00
41 Pryce's Lapras C	2.00	6.00
42 Pryce's Articuno C	2.00	6.00
43 Pryce's Sneasel HOLO R	8.00	20.00
44 Pryce's Piloswine C	2.00	6.00
45 Pryce's Delibird C	2.00	6.00
46 Clair's Blastoise C	6.00	15.00
47 Clair's Jynx C	2.00	6.00
48 Clair's Gyarados C	2.00	6.00
49 Clair's Dragonite C	2.00	6.00
50 Clair's Politoed C	2.00	6.00
51 Clair's Mantine C	2.00	6.00
52 Clair's Kingdra C	2.00	6.00
53 Lt. Surge's Raichu C	2.00	6.00
54 Lt. Surge's Lanturn C	2.00	6.00
55 Sabrina's Xatu C	2.00	6.00
56 Sabrina's Espeon C	6.00	15.00
57 Misty's Lapras C	5.00	12.00
58 Misty's Quagsire C	2.00	6.00
59 Erika's Bellossom C	2.00	6.00
60 Erika's Jumpluff C	2.00	6.00
61 Janine's Beedrill C	2.00	6.00
62 Janine's Arbok C	2.00	6.00
63 Janine's Venomoth C	2.00	6.00
64 Janine's Weezing C	2.00	6.00
65 Janine's Ariados C	2.00	6.00
66 Janine's Crobat C	2.00	6.00
67 Janine's Shuckle C	2.00	6.00
68 Brock's Omastar C	2.00	6.00
69 Brock's Kabutops C	2.00	6.00
70 Blaine's Typhlosion C	3.00	6.00
71 Blaine's Magcargo C	2.00	6.00
72 Will's Slowbro C	2.00	6.00
73 Will's Exeggutor C	2.00	6.00
74 Will's Jynx C	2.00	6.00
75 Will's Xatu C	2.00	6.00
76 Will's Espeon C	6.00	6.00
77 Will's Slowking C	2.00	6.00
78 Will's Girafarig C	2.00	6.00
79 Koga's Crobat C	2.00	6.00
80 Koga's Forretress C	2.00	6.00
81 Bruno's Machamp C	2.00	6.00
82 Bruno's Hitmonlee C	2.00	6.00
83 Bruno's Hitmonchan C	2.00	6.00
84 Bruno's Steelix HOLO R	8.00	15.00
85 Bruno's Ursaring C	2.00	6.00
86 Bruno's Hitmontop C	2.00	6.00
87 Karen's Rapidash C	2.00	6.00
88 Karen's Magmar C	2.00	6.00
89 Karen's Flareon C	2.00	6.00
90 Karen's Tyranitar HOLO R	15.00	35.00
91 Karen's Umbreon HOLO R	20.00	40.00
92 Karen's Houndoom C	5.00	6.00
93 Rocket's Wobbuffet HOLO R	6.00	15.00
94 Rocket's Raikou HOLO R	8.00	20.00
95 Rocket's Entei HOLO R	8.00	20.00
96 Rocket's Suicune HOLO R	8.00	20.00
97 Lance's Charizard C	25.00	50.00
98 Lance's Gyarados C	2.00	6.00
99 Lance's Aerodactyl C	5.00	6.00
100 Lance's Dragonite C	6.00	15.00
101 Lance's Ampharos C	2.00	6.00
102 Lance's Kingdra C	2.00	6.00
103 Trainer: Falkner's TM 01 U	2.00	6.00
104 Trainer: Falkner's TM 02 U	2.00	6.00
105 Trainer: Bugsy's TM 01 U	2.00	6.00
106 Trainer: Bugsy's TM 02 U	2.00	6.00
107 Trainer: Whitney's TM 01 U	2.00	6.00
108 Trainer: Whitney's TM 02 U	2.00	6.00
109 Trainer: Morty's TM 01 U	2.00	6.00
110 Trainer: Morty's TM 02 U	2.00	6.00
111 Trainer: Jasmine's TM 01 U	2.00	6.00
112 Trainer: Jasmine's TM 02 U	2.00	6.00
113 Trainer: Chuck's TM 01 U	2.00	6.00
114 Trainer: Chuck's TM 02 U	2.00	6.00
115 Trainer: Pryce's TM 01 U	2.00	6.00
116 Trainer: Pryce's TM 02 U	2.00	6.00
117 Trainer: Clair's TM 01 U	2.00	6.00
118 Trainer: Clair's TM 02 U	2.00	6.00
119 Trainer: Janine's TM 01 U	2.00	6.00
120 Trainer: Janine's TM 02 U	2.00	6.00
121 Trainer: Will's TM 01 U	2.00	6.00
122 Trainer: Will's TM 02 U	2.00	6.00
123 Trainer: Bruno's TM 01 U	2.00	6.00
124 Trainer: Bruno's TM 02 U	2.00	6.00
125 Trainer: Karen's TM 01 U	2.00	6.00
126 Trainer: Karen's TM 02U	2.00	6.00
127 Trainer: Team Rocket's TM 01 U	2.00	6.00
128 Trainer: Lance's TM 01 U	2.00	6.00
129 Trainer: Lance's TM 02 U	2.00	6.00
130 Trainer: Potion C	1.50	4.00
131 Trainer: Moo-Moo Milk C	1.50	4.00
132 Trainer: Full Heal C	1.50	4.00
133 Trainer: Pokemon Reverse C	1.50	4.00
134 Trainer: Switch C	1.50	4.00
135 Trainer: Warp Point C	1.50	4.00
136 Trainer: Super Scoop Up C	1.50	4.00
137 Trainer: Energy Flow C	1.50	4.00
138 Trainer: Super Energy Retrieval C	1.50	4.00
139 Trainer: Energy Ark C	1.50	4.00
140 Trainer: Energy Revive C	1.50	4.00
141 Trainer: Master Ball C	1.50	4.00
142 Rocket's Tyranitar HOLO R	8.00	20.00
NNO Grass Energy NR	1.50	4.00
NNO Water Energy NR	1.50	4.00
NNO Fighting Energy NR	1.50	4.00
NNO Fire Energy NR	1.50	4.00
NNO Lightning Energy NR	1.50	4.00
NNO Psychic Energy NR	1.50	4.00
NNO Dark Energy HOLO	2.00	6.00
NNO Metal Energy HOLO	2.00	6.00
NNO Rainbow Energy HOLO	2.00	6.00

2001 Pokemon E Cards Series 1 Japanese

Card	Low	High
COMPLETE SET (128)	125.00	180.00
BOOSTER BOX (40 PACKS)	75.00	120.00
BOOSTER PACK (5 CARDS)	3.00	6.00
1 Koffing C	.25	.50
2 Hoppop C	.25	.50
3 Caterpie C	.25	.50
4 Ekans C	.25	.50
5 Oddish C	.25	.50
6 Vulpix C	.25	.50
7 Ponyta C	.25	.50
8 Poliwag C	.25	.50
9 Shellder C	.25	.50
10 Krabby C	.25	.50
11 Goldeen C	.25	.50
12 Magikarp C	.25	.50
13 Marill C	.25	.50
14 Quilfish C	.25	.50
15 Corsola C	.25	.50
16 Pikachu C	.50	1.00
17 Mareep C	.25	.50
18 Abra C	.25	.50
19 Gastly C	.25	.50
20 Diglett C	.25	.50
21 Machop C	.25	.50
22 Geodude C	.25	.50
23 Cubone C	.25	.50
24 Larvitar C	.25	.50
25 Pidgey C	.25	.50
26 Rattata C	.25	.50
27 Spearow C	.25	.50
28 Clefairy C	.25	.50
29 Meowth C	.25	.50
30 Tauros C	.25	.50
31 Dratini C	.25	.50
32 Houndour C	.25	.50
33 Metapod U	.50	1.00
34 Gloom U	.50	1.00
35 Magmar U	.50	1.00
36 Poliwhirl U	.50	1.00
37 Jynx U	.50	1.00
38 Electabuzz U	.50	1.00
39 Flaaffy U	.50	1.00
40 Kadabra U	.50	1.00
41 Haunter U	.50	1.00
42 Machoke U	.50	1.00
43 Graveler U	.50	1.00
44 Hitmonlee U	.75	1.25
45 Pupitar U	.50	1.00
46 Pidgeotto U	.50	1.00
47 Chansey U	.50	1.00
48 Dragonair U	.75	1.25
49 Trainer: Totodile U	.50	1.00
50 Trainer: Energy U	.50	1.00
51 Trainer: Super Energy Retrieval U	.50	1.00
52 Trainer: Marill U	.50	1.00
53 Trainer: U	.50	1.00
54 Trainer: Film Crew U	.50	1.00
55 Trainer: Super Scoop Up U	.50	1.00
56 Trainer: Necklace U	.50	1.00
57 Trainer: Pokeball U	.50	1.00
58 Trainer: Wooper U	.50	1.00
59 Trainer: Pokemon Reverse U	.50	1.00
60 Trainer: Electronics U	.50	1.00
61 Trainer: Master Ball U	.50	1.00
62 Trainer: U	.50	1.00
63 Trainer: (U)	.50	1.00
64 Trainer: Warp Point U	.50	1.00
65 Venusaur R	1.00	3.00
66 Butterfree R	1.00	2.00
67 Arbok R	1.00	2.00
68 Vileplume R	1.00	2.00
69 Weezing R	1.00	2.00
70 Meganium R	1.00	3.00
71 Charizard R	2.00	5.00
72 Ninetales R	1.00	2.00
73 Rapidash R	1.00	2.00
74 Typhlosion R	1.50	3.00
75 Magby R	1.00	2.00
76 Blastoise R	1.50	3.00
77 Poliwrath R	1.00	2.00
78 Cloyster R	1.00	2.00
79 Kingler R	1.00	2.00
80 Feraligatr R	1.50	3.00
81 Raichu R	1.50	3.00
82 Pichu R	1.50	4.00
83 Ampharos R	1.00	2.00
84 Alakazam R	1.00	2.00
85 Gengar R	1.00	2.00
86 Mewtwo R	1.50	3.00
87 Mew R	1.50	3.50
88 Dugtrio R	1.00	2.00
89 Machamp R	1.00	2.00
90 Golem R	1.00	2.00
91 Pidgeot R	1.00	2.00
92 Fearow R	1.00	2.00
93 Clefable R	1.00	2.00
94 Dragonite R	1.00	2.00
95 Tyranitar R	1.50	3.00
96 Skarmory R	1.00	2.00
97 Venusaur HOLO R	3.00	6.00
98 Butterfree HOLO R	2.00	4.00
99 Arbok HOLO R	2.00	4.00
100 Vileplume HOLO R	2.00	4.00
101 Weezing HOLO R	2.00	4.00
102 Meganium HOLO R	2.00	4.00
103 Charizard HOLO R	10.00	18.00
104 Ninetales HOLO R	2.00	4.00
105 Rapidash HOLO R	2.00	4.00
106 Typhlosion HOLO R	2.00	5.00
107 Magby HOLO R	2.00	4.00
108 Blastoise HOLO R	4.00	8.00
109 Poliwrath HOLO R	2.00	4.00
110 Cloyster HOLO R	2.00	4.00
111 Kingler HOLO R	2.00	4.00
112 Feraligatr HOLO R	2.00	5.00
113 Raichu HOLO R	2.00	4.00
114 Pichu HOLO R	3.00	6.00
115 Ampharos HOLO R	2.00	4.00
116 Alakazam HOLO R	2.00	4.00
117 Gengar HOLO R	2.00	4.00
118 Mewtwo HOLO R	4.00	8.00
119 Mew HOLO R	4.00	8.00
120 Dugtrio HOLO R	2.00	4.00
121 Machamp HOLO R	2.00	4.00
122 Golem HOLO R	2.00	4.00
123 Pidgeot HOLO R	2.00	4.00
124 Fearow HOLO R	2.00	4.00
125 Clefable HOLO R	2.00	4.00
126 Dragonite HOLO R	2.00	5.00
127 Tyranitar HOLO R	2.00	5.00
128 Skarmory HOLO R	2.00	4.00

1996-02 Pokemon Coro Coro Comics Japanese

Card	Low	High
0 Abra	3.00	5.00
0 Blastoise	15.00	25.00
0 Celebi (Jumbo VS)	20.00	30.00
0 Charizard (Jumbo size)	20.00	35.00
0 Cubone	5.00	10.00
0 Dratini	5.00	10.00
0 Entei (Jumbo)	10.00	20.00
0 Lt. Surge's Electabuzz	5.00	10.00
0 Farfetch'd	2.00	5.00
0 Blaine's Growlithe	5.00	10.00
0 Ho-oh	3.00	5.00
0 Jigglypuff	3.00	5.00
0 Lt. Surge's Jolteon	5.00	10.00
0 Legendary Birds (Jumbo Size)	8.00	15.00
0 Mankey	3.00	5.00
0 Marill	3.00	5.00
0 Meowth (Team Rocket)	3.00	5.00
0 Meowth GB	5.00	10.00
0 Mew on Lily Pad (Glossy)	8.00	15.00
0 Mew (Shiny)(holo)	8.00	16.00
0 Mewtwo	20.00	30.00
0 Mewtwo vs. Mew (Jumbo size)	25.00	35.00
0 Giovanni's Nidoking	5.00	10.00
0 Brock's Onix	3.00	5.00
0 Cleffa	2.00	4.00
0 Pichu, Pikachu (Jumbo)	10.00	20.00
0 Flying Pikachu	5.00	10.00
0 Ivy Pikachu	5.00	10.00
0 Pikachu, Jigglypuff, Clefairy (Jumbo)	15.00	25.00
0 Surfing Pikachu	5.00	10.00
0 Swimming Pikachu (Jumbo)	15.00	20.00
0 Scizor	5.00	10.00
0 Slowking	9.00	13.00
0 Misty's Staryu	5.00	10.00
0 Smoochum	5.00	10.00
0 Togepi	3.00	6.00
0 Unown R	5.00	10.00
0 Wooper	3.00	5.00
0 Trainer: Imakuni	7.00	10.00
0 Trainer: Koga's Ninja Trick Gym	3.00	6.00
0 Trainer: Girarudan Legendary Birds Movie	5.00	7.00
0 Trainer: Pikachu 2nd Anniversary (Jumbo)	5.00	10.00
0 Trainer: Pokemon Island	10.00	20.00

2001 Pokemon CD Promos Japanese

COMPLETE SET (10)	15.00	30.00
3 Venusaur HOLO (lightning bolt)	3.00	6.00
6 Charizard HOLO (lightning bolt)	6.00	12.00
9 Blastoise HOLO (lightning bolt)	4.00	8.00
59 Arcanine	1.00	2.00
137 Porygon HOLO	3.00	6.00
143 Snorlax HOLO	1.00	3.00
150 Mewtwo (glossy) (Poké Ball)	5.00	10.00
151 Mew (glossy) (Poké Ball)	4.00	8.00
NNO Trainer Card	.75	2.00
NNO Trainer Card with Onix	1.00	3.00

2000 Pokemon Neo Promos Japanese

COMPLETE SET (9)	10.00	15.00
152 Chikorita	1.00	2.00
153 Bayleef	1.00	2.00
154 Meganium HOLO	2.00	4.00
155 Cyndaquil	1.00	2.00
156 Quilava	1.00	2.00
157 Typhlosion HOLO	2.00	4.00
158 Totodile	1.00	2.00
159 Croconaw	1.00	2.00
160 Ferligatr (holo)	2.00	4.00

2000 Pokemon Neo 2 Promos Japanese

COMPLETE SET (9)	15.00	30.00
6 Charizard HOLO	8.00	15.00
133 Eevee	1.00	2.00
172 Pichu HOLO	3.00	6.00
196 Espeon	1.00	2.00
197 Umbreon	1.00	2.00
201 Unown E	.75	1.50
201 Unown O	.75	1.50
201 Unown N	.75	1.50
244 Entei (holo)	3.00	6.00

2001 Pokemon Neo 3 Promos Japanese

COMPLETE (9)	15.00	30.00
185 Sudowoodo	1.00	3.00
215 Sneasel	1.00	3.00
227 Skarmory	1.00	3.00
243 Raikou	3.00	6.00
244 Entei	3.00	6.00
245 Suicune	3.00	6.00
249 Lugia	6.00	10.00
250 Ho-oh	3.00	6.00
251 Celebi (holo)	6.00	12.00

2001 Pokemon VS Promos Japanese

0 Celebi (Fan Club Booklet)	8.00	16.00
0 Ho-oh (Coro Coro Comics)	8.00	15.00
0 Lapras (card game booklet)	10.00	15.00
0 Larvitar (ANA airlines promo)	12.00	20.00
0 Pikachu (ANA airlines promo)	12.00	20.00
0 Rapidash (Coro Coro Comics)	6.00	12.00
0 Scizor (fan club booklet)	6.00	12.00
0 Sneasel (Coro Coro promo)	10.00	20.00
0 Tyranitar (movie promo set)	15.00	30.00

2001-02 Pokemon E Card Promos Japanese

0 Celebi (Spaceworld 2001)	15.00	30.00
0 Kakureon (movie promo)	20.00	30.00
0 Latias,Latios (Jumbo Movie)	12.00	20.00
0 Pichu Brothers (movie promo)	20.00	30.00
0 Pikachu (McDonalds promo)	15.00	30.00
0 Suicune (Celebi DVD)	15.00	35.00
0 Tyrogue (McDonalds promo)	8.00	12.00
0 Umbreon (McDonalds promo)	20.00	40.00
0 Wooper (McDonalds promo)	5.00	10.00
0 Zapdos (McDonalds promo)	5.00	10.00
38P Pikachu (PokeFest 02)	20.00	40.00
39P Crystal Energy (PokeFest 02)	10.00	20.00
40P Boost Energy (PokeFest 02)	10.00	20.00
41P Warp Energy (PokeFest 02)	10.00	20.00
42P Pikachu (PokeFest 02)	5.00	10.00
43P Pichu (PokeFest 02)	5.00	10.00
44P Mewtwo (PokeFest 02)	5.00	10.00
45P Lugia (PokeFest 02)	5.00	10.00
46P Celebi (PokeFest 02)	6.00	12.00
47P Entei (Railroad promo)	6.00	12.00

1998 Pokemon Quick Starters Green Japanese

GREEN SET (27)	35.00	75.00
COMMON CARD	1.00	2.00
1 Bulbasaur	2.00	4.00
4 Charmander	2.00	4.00
10 Caterpie	3.00	5.00
11 Metapod	3.00	6.00
19 Rattata	3.00	6.00
29 Nidoran-F	3.00	6.00
32 Nidoran-M	3.00	6.00
35 Clefairy	2.00	4.00
37 Vulpix	3.00	6.00
58 Growlithe	3.00	6.00
63 Abra	3.00	6.00
64 Kadabra	6.00	10.00
77 Ponyta	3.00	6.00
78 Rapidash	3.00	6.00
92 Gastly	3.00	6.00
93 Haunter	3.00	6.00
113 Chansey	2.00	4.00
115 Kangaskhan	2.00	4.00
122 Mr Mime	2.00	4.00
123 Scyther HOLO	15.00	25.00
126 Magmar	3.00	6.00
127 Pinsir	3.00	6.00
137 Porygon	3.00	6.00
144 Articuno HOLO	30.00	40.00
150 Mewtwo	8.00	14.00
NNO Trainers or Energies	1.00	2.00
NNO Trainer: Master Ball HOLO	15.00	25.00

1998 Pokemon Quick Starters Red Japanese

RED SET (27)	60.00	100.00
COMMON CARD	2.00	4.00
7 Squirtle	2.00	4.00
25 Pikachu (Level13)	10.00	15.00
25 Pikachu (Level 5)	10.00	15.00
26 Raichu	2.00	5.00
27 Sandshrew	3.00	6.00
28 Sandslash	3.00	6.00
60 Poliwag	3.00	6.00
61 Poliwhirl	3.00	6.00
62 Poliwrath	3.00	6.00
66 Machop	3.00	6.00
67 Machoke	3.00	6.00
81 Magnemite	2.00	4.00
82 Magneton	3.00	6.00
84 Doduo	3.00	6.00
86 Seel	3.00	6.00
87 Dewgong	2.00	4.00
95 Onix	3.00	6.00
100 Voltorb	3.00	6.00
107 Hitmonlee	2.00	5.00
108 Lickitung	3.00	6.00
124 Jynx	3.00	6.00
131 Lapras	2.00	5.00
143 Snorlax	2.00	5.00
145 Zapdos HOLO	30.00	40.00
146 Moltres HOLO	30.00	45.00
NNO Trainers or Energies	1.00	2.00
NNO Trainer: Master Ball HOLO	15.00	25.00

1999 Pokemon Southern Islands Japanese

COMPLETE SET (18)	12.00	20.00
RAINBOW COLLECTION (9)	6.00	10.00
TROPICAL ISLAND COLLECTION (9)	6.00	10.00
2 Ivysaur (Rainbow)	2.00	4.00
8 Wartortle (Tropical)	2.00	4.00
12 Butterfree (Rainbow)	2.00	4.00
18 Pidgeot (Rainbow)	2.00	4.00
20 Raticate (Rainbow)	2.00	4.00
39 Jigglypuff (Rainbow)	2.00	4.00
45 Vileplume (holo) (Tropical)	3.00	6.00
57 Primeape (Tropical)	2.00	4.00
73 Tentacruel (Tropical)	2.00	4.00
95 Onix (Rainbow)	2.00	4.00
103 Exeggutor (Tropical)	2.00	4.00
108 Lickitung (Tropical)	1.00	3.00
131 Lapras (Tropical)	2.00	4.00
151 Mew (holo) (Rainbow)	3.00	6.00
NNO Marill (holo) (Tropical)	3.00	6.00
NNO Ledyba (holo) (Rainbow)	4.00	8.00
NNO Togepi (holo) (Rainbow)	3.00	6.00
NNO Slowking (holo) (Tropical)	3.00	6.00

1999 Pokemon Sweepstakes Japanese

COMPLETE SET 1 (3)	25.00	50.00
COMPLETE SET 2 (3)	25.00	50.00
0 Blastoise (set 1)	12.00	20.00
0 Charizard (set 1)	15.00	30.00
0 Venusaur (set 1)	5.00	10.00
0 Feraligatr (set 2)	10.00	20.00
0 Meganium (set 2)	10.00	20.00
0 Typhlosion (set 2)	10.00	20.00

2001 Pokemon Vending Series One Japanese

SERIES ONE SET (36)	40.00	60.00
VENDING SHEETS	5.00	15.00
1 Bulbasaur	5.00	8.00
4 Charmander	5.00	8.00
7 Squirtle	4.00	8.00
10 Caterpie	2.00	4.00
11 Metapod	3.00	4.00
13 Weedle	2.00	4.00
14 Kakuna	2.00	4.00
16 Pidgey	2.00	4.00
19 Rattata	2.00	4.00
25 Pikachu	8.00	16.00
29 Nidoran-F	2.00	4.00
32 Nidoran-M	2.00	4.00
35 Clefairy	5.00	8.00
40 Wigglytuff	3.00	5.00
41 Zubat	2.00	4.00
42 Golbat	2.00	4.00
46 Paras	2.00	4.00
47 Parasect	2.00	4.00
60 Poliwag	2.00	4.00
61 Poliwhirl	3.00	5.00
62 Poliwrath	3.00	5.00
63 Abra	3.00	5.00
74 Geodude	2.00	4.00
78 Rapidash	3.00	5.00
84 Doduo	2.00	4.00
85 Dodrio	2.00	4.00
108 Lickitung	2.00	4.00
113 Chansey	4.00	7.00
122 Mr Mime	4.00	7.00
127 Pinsir	2.00	4.00
133 Eevee	3.00	5.00
137 Porygon	2.00	4.00
143 Snorlax	3.00	5.00
150 Mewtwo	8.00	15.00
NNO Trainer: Glowing Moon	2.00	4.00
NNO Trainer: Mine Shaft	2.00	4.00

2001 Pokemon Vending Series Two Japanese

SERIES TWO SET (36)	35.00	60.00
VENDING SHEETS	10.00	20.00
21 Spearow	2.00	4.00
22 Fearow	2.00	4.00
26 Raichu	5.00	10.00
27 Sandshrew	2.00	4.00
49 Venomoth	3.00	5.00
66 Machop	2.00	4.00
67 Machoke	2.00	4.00
75 Graveller	2.00	4.00
81 Magnemite	2.00	4.00
82 Magneton	2.00	4.00
86 Seel	2.00	4.00
87 Dewgong	2.00	4.00
88 Grimer	2.00	4.00
90 Shellder	2.00	4.00
95 Onix	2.00	4.00
98 Krabby	2.00	4.00
100 Voltorb	3.00	5.00
105 Marowak	2.00	4.00
106 Hitmonlee	5.00	8.00
107 Hitmonchan	3.00	5.00
109 Koffing	2.00	4.00
114 Tangela	2.00	4.00
124 Jynx	2.00	4.00
125 Electabuzz	3.00	6.00
131 Lapras	3.00	5.00
132 Ditto	2.00	4.00
138 Omanyte	3.00	5.00
140 Kabuto	2.00	4.00
142 Aerodactyl	5.00	10.00
144 Articuno	5.00	10.00
145 Zapdos	5.00	10.00
146 Moltres	4.00	8.00
NNO Trainer: Floating Crystal	2.00	4.00
NNO Trainer: Glowing Poké Ball	2.00	4.00
NNO Trainer: Hitmonlee in crystal	3.00	5.00
NNO Trainer: Lots of Digletts	3.00	5.00

2001 Pokemon Vending Series Three Japanese

SERIES THREE SET (45)	30.00	60.00
VENDING SHEETS	5.00	15.00
17 Pidgeotto	2.00	4.00
24 Arbok	2.00	4.00
28 Sandslash	2.00	4.00
30 Nidorina	2.00	4.00
33 Nidorino	2.00	4.00
37 Vulpix	2.00	4.00
48 Venonat	2.00	4.00
55 Golduck	2.00	4.00
58 Growlithe	2.00	4.00
64 Kadabra (#1 & #2)	3.00	5.00
67 Machoke	3.00	4.00
69 Bellsprout	3.00	4.00
70 Weepinbell	3.00	5.00
75 Graveller	3.00	5.00
77 Ponyta	2.00	4.00
80 Slowbro	2.00	4.00
93 Haunter (#1 & #2)	3.00	5.00
97 Hypno	2.00	4.00
99 Kingler	2.00	4.00
104 Cubone	2.00	4.00
110 Weezing	2.00	4.00
112 Rhydon	2.00	4.00
115 Kangaskhan	3.00	6.00
116 Horsea	2.00	5.00
117 Seadra	2.00	4.00
120 Staryu	2.00	4.00
123 Scyther	4.00	8.00
126 Magmar	2.00	4.00
128 Tauros	2.00	4.00
138 Omanyte	2.00	4.00
150 Mewtwo	6.00	12.00
NNO Trainer: Mankey w/Poke Balls	2.00	4.00
NNO Trainer: Tower at Night	2.00	4.00
NNO WB Checklists	1.00	2.00
NNO WB Extra Rule: 6 Decks	3.00	6.00
NNO WB Extra Rule: 6 Players	4.00	8.00
NNO WB Extra Rule: Deck Swap	3.00	6.00
NNO WB Extra Rule: Girl & Boy	4.00	8.00
NNO WB Extra Rule: Meowth	4.00	7.00
NNO WB Pass Card	2.00	4.00
NNO WB Pikachu	10.00	15.00
NNO WB Pokemon Machine	2.00	4.00
NNO WB Red Guy in Hole	1.00	2.00
NNO WB Red Guy Rules	1.00	2.00
NNO WB Red Guy Trainer	1.00	2.00

2001 Pokemon Vending Series Three Mail-in Japanese

COMPLETE SET (5)	50.00	100.00
0 Alakazam HOLO	15.00	30.00
0 Gengar HOLO	15.00	30.00
0 Golem HOLO	15.00	30.00
0 Machamp HOLO	15.00	30.00
0 Omastar HOLO	15.00	30.00

2001 Pokemon Vending Series Double Zero Japanese

COMPLETE SET (3)	30.00	50.00
0 Mew (with bubbles)	10.00	20.00
0 Mewtwo	10.00	20.00
0 Pikachu (lightning bolt)	10.00	20.00

2001 Pokemon Video Starter Japanese

COMPLETE SET (82)	14.00	30.00
ENERGY CARDS (NOT LISTED)	.20	.50
0A Blastoise HOLO SD	8.00	12.00
0B Venusaur HOLO BD	8.00	12.00
1B Growlithe SD	1.00	2.00
1 Bulbasaur (BD)	1.50	3.00
2A Drowzee BD	1.00	2.00
2B Diglett SD	1.00	2.00
3A Raichu BD	1.50	3.00
3B Wartortle SD	1.00	2.00
9 Poliwag SD	1.00	2.00
10 Wartortle SD	1.00	2.00
13A Pikachu BD	2.00	5.00
13B Spearow SD	1.00	2.00
14 Jigglypuff SD	1.00	3.00
16B Squirtle SD	2.00	4.00
16A Meowth BD	1.00	2.00
18B Squirtle SD	2.00	4.00
18A Bulbasaur BD	1.50	3.00
22 Ivysaur BD	1.50	3.00
23 Double Colorless Energy BD	.50	1.00
25 Double Colorless Energy SD	.50	1.00
26A Electabuzz BD	1.00	2.00
26B Growlithe SD	1.00	2.00
29 Bulbasaur BD	1.50	3.00
30 Doduo BD	1.00	2.00
32A Ivysaur BD	1.50	3.00
32B Arcanine SD	2.00	4.00
35B Machop SD	1.00	2.00
35A Bulbasaur BD	1.50	3.00
37A Jynx BD	1.00	2.00
37B Squirtle SD	2.00	4.00
39A Koffing BD	1.00	2.00
39B Magmar SD	1.00	2.00
40A Pikachu BD	3.00	6.00
40B Squirtle SD	2.00	4.00

1998 Japanese Pokemon Web Set

COMPLETE SET (48)	40.00	75.00
SEALED PACK	3.00	7.00
1 Ivysaur C	4.00	7.00
2 Nidoran (M) C	4.00	8.00
3 Venonat C	3.00	5.00
4 Exeggcute C	3.00	5.00
5 Tangela C	7.00	10.00
6 Growlithe C	8.00	10.00
7 Charmeleon C	4.00	7.00
8 Vulpix C	8.00	10.00
9 Wartortle C	4.00	7.00
10 Marill C	3.00	6.00
11 Voltorb C	3.00	6.00
12 Slowpoke C	3.00	6.00
13 Diglett C	2.00	4.00
14 Hitmonlee C	3.00	6.00
15 Trainer: Bill's Teleporter C	8.00	14.00
16 Trainer: New Pokedex C	5.00	10.00
17 Dark Ivysaur U	4.00	7.00
18 Nidorino U	3.00	6.00
19 Venomoth U	3.00	6.00
20 Exeggutor U	3.00	6.00
21 Dark Weezing U	3.00	6.00
22 Dark Charmeleon U	4.00	7.00
23 Arcanine U	6.00	9.00
24 Dark Wartortle U	4.00	7.00
25 Pikachu U	5.00	8.00
26 Electrode U	3.00	6.00
27 Dark Kadabra U	3.00	6.00
28 Dark Slowbro U	8.00	12.00
29 Dugtrio U	3.00	6.00
30 Trainer: Max Revive U	5.00	8.00
31 Trainer: Hyper Devolution Spray U	5.00	8.00
32 Trainer: Pokemon Retransfer U	3.00	6.00
33 Nidoking R	3.00	6.00
34 Ninetails R	3.00	6.00
35 Magikarp R	3.00	6.00
36 Raichu R	3.00	6.00
37 Dark Alakazam R	3.00	6.00
38 Dragonite R	5.00	9.00
39 Meowth R	10.00	15.00
40 Trainer: Rocket's Sneak Attack R	7.00	10.00
41 Dark Venusaur HOLO R	15.00	25.00
42 Dark Charizard HOLO R	25.00	35.00
43 Moltres HOLO R	10.00	15.00
44 Dark Blastoise HOLO R	20.00	30.00
45 Articuno HOLO R	10.00	15.00
46 Zapdos HOLO R	10.00	15.00
47 Gengar HOLO R	40.00	60.00
48 Machamp HOLO R	15.00	25.00

YU-GI-OH!

HOW TO USE

What's Listed
Products listed in the Price Guide typically: 1) are produced by licensed manufacturers, 2) are widely available and 3) have market activity on single items.

What the Columns Mean
The LO and HI columns reflect current retail selling ranges. The HI column on the right generally represents the full retail selling price. The LO column on the left generally represents the lowest price one would expect to find with extensive shopping.

Grading
All cards in the Price Guide are based on NrMint to Mint condition. Damaged cards are generally sold for 25 to 75 percent of Mint value. Toy prices are based on mint condition. Toys that are loose (out of package), are generally sold for 50 percent of the listed price.

Currency
This Price Guide is intended to reflect the entire North American market. All listed prices are in U.S. dollars.

Legend
C – Common
GR – Ghost rare
GUR – Gold ultra rare
PR – Parallel rare
R – Rare
SCR – Secret rare
SFR – Starfoil rare
SR – Super rare
UR – Ultra rare
UTR – Ultimate rare

Attention Dealers: If you would like to be a Price Guide Contributor for this almanac, please e-mail your name and phone number to: nonsports@beckett.com

Beckett Yu-Gi-Oh! price guide sponsored by YugiohMint.com

2002 Yu-Gi-Oh Legend of Blue Eyes White Dragon 1st Edition

COMPLETE SET (126)	800.00	1000.00
BOOSTER BOX (24 PACKS)	1100.00	1300.00
BOOSTER PACK (9 CARDS)	40.00	80.00
*UNLIMITED: .4X TO .8X 1ST EDITION		
RELEASED ON MARCH 8, 2002		
LOB0 Tri-Horned Dragon SCR	40.00	80.00
LOB1 Blue-Eyes White Dragon UR	80.00	120.00
LOB2 Hitotsu-Me Giant C	.60	1.50
LOB3 Flame Swordsman SR	25.00	50.00
LOB4 Skull Servant C	.60	1.50
LOB5 Dark Magician UR	80.00	130.00
LOB6 Gaia The Fierce Knight UR	25.00	50.00
LOB7 Celtic Guardian SR	10.00	25.00
LOB8 Basic Insect C	.60	1.50
LOB9 Mammoth Graveyard C	.60	1.50
LOB10 Silver Fang C	.60	1.50
LOB11 Dark Gray C	.60	1.50
LOB12 Trial of Hell C	.60	1.50
LOB13 Nemuriko C	.60	1.50
LOB14 The 13th Grave C	.60	1.50
LOB15 Charubin Fire Knight R	1.50	4.00
LOB16 Flame Manipulator C	.60	1.50
LOB17 Monster Egg C	.60	1.50
LOB18 Firegrass C	.60	1.50
LOB19 Darkfire Dragon R	2.00	5.00
LOB20 Dark King of Abyss C	.60	1.50
LOB21 Fiend Reflection #2 C	.60	1.50
LOB22 Fusionist R	1.50	4.00
LOB23 Turtle Tiger C	.60	1.50
LOB24 Petit Dragon C	.60	1.50
LOB25 Petit Angel C	.60	1.50
LOB26 Hinotama Soul C	.60	1.50
LOB27 Aqua Madoor R	.75	2.00
LOB28 Kagemusha of Blue Flame C	.60	1.50
LOB29 Flame Ghost R	1.25	3.00
LOB30 Two-Mouth Darkruler C	.60	1.50
LOB31 Dissolverock C	.60	1.50
LOB32 Root Water C	.60	1.50
LOB33 The Furious Sea King C	.60	1.50
LOB34 Green Phantom King C	.60	1.50
LOB35 Ray & Temperature C	.60	1.50
LOB36 King Fog C	.60	1.50
LOB37 Mystical Sheep #2 C	.60	1.50
LOB38 Masaki Legendary Swordsman C	.60	1.50
LOB39 Kurama C	.60	1.50
LOB40 Legendary Sword SP	.60	1.50
LOB41 Beast Fangs SP	.60	1.50
LOB42 Violet Crystal SP	.60	1.50
LOB43 Book of Secret Arts SP	.60	1.50
LOB44 Power of Kaishin SP	.60	1.50
LOB45 Dragon Capture Jar R	1.50	4.00
LOB46 Forest C	.60	1.50
LOB47 Wasteland C	.60	1.50
LOB48 Mountain C	.60	1.50
LOB49 Sogen C	.60	1.50
LOB50 Umi C	.60	1.50
LOB51 Yami C	.60	1.50
LOB52 Dark Hole SR	10.00	25.00
LOB53 Raigeki SR	25.00	50.00
LOB54 Red Medicine C	.60	1.50
LOB55 Sparks C	.60	1.50
LOB56 Hinotama C	.60	1.50
LOB57 Fissure R	1.00	2.50
LOB58 Trap Hole SR	5.00	12.00
LOB59 Polymerization SR	10.00	25.00
LOB60 Remove Trap C	.60	1.50
LOB61 Two-Pronged Attack R	.75	2.00
LOB62 Mystical Elf SR	8.00	20.00
LOB63 Tyhone C	.60	1.50
LOB64 Beaver Warrior C	.60	1.50
LOB65 Gravedigger Ghoul R	.75	2.00
LOB66 Curse of Dragon SR	8.00	20.00
LOB67 Karbonala Warrior R	1.50	4.00
LOB68 Giant Soldier of Stone R	1.50	4.00
LOB69 Uraby C	.60	1.50
LOB70 Red Eyes B Dragon UR	180.00	220.00
LOB71 Reaper of the Cards R	1.00	2.50
LOB72 Witty Phantom C	.60	1.50
LOB73 Larvas C	.60	1.50
LOB74 Hard Armor C	.60	1.50
LOB75 Man Eater C	.60	1.50
LOB76 M-Warrior #1 C	.60	1.50
LOB77 M-Warrior #2 C	.60	1.50
LOB78 Spirit of the Harp R	.75	2.00
LOB79 Armaill C	.60	1.50
LOB80 Terra the Terrible C	.60	1.50
LOB81 Frenzied Panda C	.60	1.50
LOB82 Kumootoko C	.60	1.50
LOB83 Meda Bat C	.60	1.50
LOB84 Enchanting Mermaid C	.60	1.50
LOB85 Fireyarou C	.60	1.50
LOB86 Dragoness The Wicked R	1.25	3.00
LOB87 One-Eyed Shield Dragon C	.60	1.50
LOB88 Dark Energy SP	.60	1.50
LOB89 Laser Cannon Armor SP	.60	1.50
LOB90 Vile Germs SP	.60	1.50
LOB91 Silver Bow and Arrow SP	.60	1.50
LOB92 Dragon Treasure SP	.60	1.50
LOB93 Electro-Whip	.60	1.50
LOB94 Mystical Moon SP	.60	1.50
LOB95 Stop Defense R	.75	2.00
LOB96 Machine Convers. Factory SP	.60	1.50
LOB97 Raise Body Heat SP	.60	1.50
LOB98 Follow Wind SP	.60	1.50
LOB99 Goblin's Secret Remedy R	.75	2.00
LOB100 Final Flame R	1.25	3.00
LOB101 Swords of Rev. Light SR	4.00	10.00
LOB102 Metal Dragon R	1.25	3.00
LOB103 Spike Seadra C	.60	1.50
LOB104 Tripwire Beast C	.60	1.50
LOB105 Skull Red Bird C	.60	1.50
LOB106 Armed Ninja R	.75	2.00
LOB107 Flower Wolf R	.75	2.00
LOB108 Man-Eater Bug SR	8.00	20.00
LOB109 Sand Stone C	.60	1.50
LOB110 Hane-Hane R	.75	2.00
LOB111 Misairuzame C	.60	1.50
LOB112 Steel Ogre Grotto #1 C	.60	1.50
LOB113 Lesser Dragon C	.60	1.50
LOB114 Darkworld Thorns C	.60	1.50
LOB115 Drooling Lizard C	.60	1.50
LOB116 Armored Starfish C	.60	1.50
LOB117 Succubus Knight C	.60	1.50
LOB118 Monster Reborn UR	40.00	80.00
LOB119 Pot of Greed R	3.00	8.00
LOB120 Right Leg of Forbid.One UR	80.00	120.00
LOB121 Left Leg of Forbid.One UR	80.00	120.00
LOB122 Right Arm of Forbid.One UR	80.00	120.00
LOB123 Left Arm of Forbid.One UR	80.00	120.00
LOB124 Exodia the Forbidden One UR	150.00	200.00
LOB125 Gaia the Dragon Champion SCR	80.00	120.00

2002 Yu-Gi-Oh Metal Raiders 1st Edition

COMPLETE SET (144)	200.00	400.00
BOOSTER BOX (24 PACKS)	350.00	500.00
BOOSTER PACK (9 CARDS)	8.00	20.00
*UNLIMITED: .4X TO .8X 1ST EDITION		
RELEASED ON JUNE 26, 2002		
MRD0 Gate Guardian SCR	25.00	50.00
MRD1 Feral Imp SP	.75	2.00
MRD2 Winged Dragon C	.40	1.00
MRD3 Summoned Skull UR	30.00	60.00
MRD4 Rock Ogre Grotto 1 C	.30	.75
MRD5 Armored Lizard C	.30	.75
MRD6 Killer Needle C	.30	.75
MRD7 Larvae Moth C	.40	1.00
MRD8 Harpie Lady C	1.25	3.00
MRD9 Harpie Lady Sisters SR	8.00	20.00
MRD10 Kojikocy C	.30	.75
MRD11 Cocoon of Evolution SP	.60	1.50
MRD12 Crawling Dragon C	.30	.75
MRD13 Armored Zombie C	.30	.75
MRD14 Mask of Darkness R	1.00	2.50
MRD15 Doma the Angel of Silence C	.30	.75
MRD16 White Magical Hat R	.40	1.00
MRD17 Big Eye C	.30	.75
MRD18 B Skull Dragon UR	30.00	60.00
MRD19 Masked Sorcerer R	.40	1.00
MRD20 Roaring Ocean Snake C	.30	.75
MRD21 Water Omotics C	.30	.75
MRD22 Ground Attacker Bugroth C	.40	1.00
MRD23 Petit Moth C	.30	.75
MRD24 Elegant Egotist R	.75	2.00
MRD25 Sanga of Thunder SR	2.50	6.00
MRD26 Kazejin SR	4.00	10.00
MRD27 Suijin SR	4.00	10.00
MRD28 Mystic Lamp SP	.30	.75
MRD29 Steel Scorpion C	.30	.75
MRD30 Ocubeam C	.30	.75
MRD31 Leghul SP	.30	.75
MRD32 Ooguchi SP	.30	.75
MRD33 Leogun C	.30	.75
MRD34 Blast Juggler C	.30	.75
MRD35 Jinzo #7 SP	.60	1.50
MRD36 Magician of Faith R	1.50	4.00
MRD37 Ancient Elf C	.30	.75
MRD38 Deepsea Shark C	.30	.75
MRD39 Bottom Dweller C	.30	.75
MRD40 Destroyer Golem C	.40	1.00
MRD41 Kaminari Attack C	.40	1.00
MRD42 Rainbow Flower SP	.40	1.00
MRD43 Morinphen C	.30	.75
MRD44 Mega Thunderball C	.30	.75
MRD45 Tongyo C	.30	.75
MRD46 Empress Judge C	.30	.75
MRD47 Pale Beast C	.30	.75
MRD48 Electric Lizard C	.30	.75
MRD49 Hunter Spider C	.30	.75
MRD50 Ancient Lizard Warrior C	.30	.75
MRD51 Queen's Double SP	.75	2.00
MRD52 Trent C	.30	.75
MRD53 Disk Magician C	.30	.75
MRD54 Hyosube C	.30	.75
MRD55 Hibikime C	.40	1.00
MRD56 Fake Trap R	.60	1.50
MRD57 Tribute to the Doomed SR	1.50	4.00
MRD58 Soul Release C	.75	2.00
MRD59 Cheerful Coffin C	.40	1.00
MRD60 Change of Heart UR	15.00	30.00
MRD61 Baby Dragon SP	.40	1.00
MRD62 Blackland Fire Dragon C	.30	.75
MRD63 Swamp Battleguard C	.40	1.00
MRD64 Battle Steer C	.30	.75
MRD65 Time Wizard UR	35.00	70.00
MRD66 Saggi the Dark Clown C	.30	.75
MRD67 Dragon Piper C	.40	1.00
MRD68 Illusionist Faceless Mage C	.30	.75
MRD69 Sangan R	1.50	4.00
MRD70 Great Moth R	1.25	3.00
MRD71 Kuriboh SR	8.00	20.00
MRD72 Jellyfish C	.30	.75
MRD73 Castle of Dark Illusions C	1.25	3.00
MRD74 King of Yamimakai C	.30	.75
MRD75 Catapult Turtle SR	2.00	5.00
MRD76 Mystic Horseman C	.30	.75
MRD77 Rabid Horseman C	.40	1.00
MRD78 Crass Clown SP	.75	2.00
MRD79 Pumpking King of Ghosts C	.30	.75
MRD80 Dream Clown SP	.75	2.00
MRD81 Tainted Wisdom C	.30	.75
MRD82 Ancient Brain C	.40	1.00
MRD83 Guardian of Labyrinth C	.30	.75
MRD84 Prevent Rat C	.30	.75
MRD85 Little Swordsman of Aile C	.30	.75
MRD86 Princess of Tsurugi R	.50	1.25
MRD87 Protector of the Throne C	.30	.75
MRD88 Tremendous Fire C	.40	1.00
MRD89 Jirai Gumo C	.30	.75
MRD90 Shadow Ghoul R	.75	2.00
MRD91 Labyrinth Tank C	.30	.75
MRD92 Ryu-Kishin Powered C	.30	.75
MRD93 Bickuribox C	.30	.75
MRD94 Giltia the D Knight C	.60	1.50
MRD95 Launcher Spider C	.30	.75
MRD96 Giga-Tech Wolf C	.30	.75
MRD97 Thunder Dragon SP	2.00	5.00
MRD98 7 Colored Fish C	.30	.75
MRD99 Immortal of Thunder C	.30	.75
MRD100 Punished Eagle C	.30	.75
MRD101 Insect Soldiers of the Sky C	.30	.75
MRD102 Hoshiningen R	.40	1.00
MRD103 Musician King C	.40	1.00
MRD104 Yado Karu C	.30	.75
MRD105 Cyber Saurus C	1.50	4.00
MRD106 Cannon Soldier R	.40	1.00
MRD107 Muka Muka R	.40	1.00
MRD108 The Bistro Butcher C	.30	.75
MRD109 Star Boy R	.60	1.50
MRD110 Milus Radiant R	.40	1.00
MRD111 Flame Cerebus C	.30	.75
MRD112 Niwatori C	.30	.75
MRD113 Dark Elf R	.40	1.00
MRD114 Mushroom Man #2 C	.30	.75
MRD115 Lava Battleguard C	.30	.75
MRD116 Witch of Black Forest R	.75	2.00
MRD117 Little Chimera R	.40	1.00
MRD118 Bladefly R	.40	1.00
MRD119 Lady of Faith C	.30	.75
MRD120 Twin-Headed Thunder Dragon SR	1.00	3.00
MRD121 Witch's Apprentice R	.40	1.00
MRD122 Blue-Winged Crown C	.30	.75
MRD123 Skull Knight C	.30	.75
MRD124 Gazelle King of Myth Beasts SP	.40	1.00
MRD125 Garnecia Elefantis SR	.75	2.00
MRD126 Barrel Dragon UR	20.00	40.00
MRD127 Solemn Judgment UR	20.00	40.00
MRD128 Magic Jammer UR	5.00	12.00
MRD129 Seven Tools of the Bandit UR	5.00	12.00
MRD130 Horn of Heaven UR	10.00	25.00
MRD131 Shield and Sword R	.40	1.00
MRD132 Sword of Deep-Seated C	.30	.75
MRD133 Block Attack C	.30	.75
MRD134 The Unhappy Maiden SP	.40	1.00
MRD135 Robbin Goblin R	.40	1.00
MRD136 Germ Infection C	.30	.75
MRD137 Paralyzing Potion C	.30	.75
MRD138 Mirror Force UR	60.00	100.00
MRD139 Ring of Magnetism C	.40	1.00

Beckett Yu-Gi-Oh! price guide sponsored by YugiohMint.com

MRD140 Share the Pain C	.30	.75
MRD141 Stim-pack SP	.30	.75
MRD142 Heavy Storm SR	8.00	20.00
MRD143 Thousand Dragon SCR	8.00	20.00

2002 Yu-Gi-Oh Magic Ruler 1st Edition

COMPLETE SET (104)	100.00	175.00
HOBBY BOOSTER BOX (24 PACKS)	100.00	150.00
RETAIL BOOSTER BOX (36 PACKS)	100.00	150.00
BOOSTER PACK (9 CARDS)	3.00	8.00
*UNLIMITED: .4X TO .8X 1ST EDITION		
RELEASED ON SEPTEMBER 16, 2002		
MRL0 Blue Eyes Toon Dragon SCR	20.00	40.00
MRL1 Penguin Knight C	.30	.75
MRL2 Axe of Despair UR	4.00	10.00
MRL3 Black Pendant SR	.75	2.00
MRL4 Horn of Light C	.30	.75
MRL5 Malevolent Nuzzler C	.30	.75
MRL6 Spellbinding Circle UR	15.00	30.00
MRL8 Electric Snake C	.30	.75
MRL9 Queen Bird C	.30	.75
MRL-7 Metal Fish C	.30	.75
MRL10 Ameba R	.40	1.00
MRL11 Peacock C	.30	.75
MRL12 Maha Vailo SR	.75	2.00
MRL13 Guardian of Throne Room C	.30	.75
MRL14 Fire Kraken C	.30	.75
MRL15 Minar C	.30	.75
MRL16 Griggle C	.30	.75
MRL17 Tyhone #2 C	.60	1.50
MRL18 Ancient One of Deep Forest C	.30	.75
MRL19 Dark Witch C	.30	.75
MRL20 Weather Report C	.30	.75
MRL21 Mechanical Snail C	.30	.75
MRL22 Giant Turtle Feeds on Flames C	.30	.75
MRL23 Liquid Beast C	.30	.75
MRL24 Hiro's Shadow Scout R	.40	1.00
MRL25 High Tide Gyojin C	.30	.75
MRL26 Invader of the Throne SR	.75	2.00
MRL27 Whiptail Crow C	.30	.75
MRL28 Slot Machine C	.30	.75
MRL29 Relinquished UR	8.00	20.00
MRL30 Red Archery Girl C	.30	.75
MRL31 Gravekeeper's Servant C	1.50	4.00
MRL32 Curse of Fiend C	.40	1.00
MRL33 Upstart Goblin C	1.50	4.00
MRL34 Toll C	.30	.75
MRL35 Final Destiny C	.30	.75
MRL36 Snatch Steal UR	6.00	15.00
MRL37 Chorus of Sanctuary C	.30	.75
MRL38 Confiscation SR	6.00	15.00
MRL39 Delinquent Duo UR	8.00	20.00
MRL40 Darkness Approaches C	.30	.75
MRL41 Fairy's Hand Mirror C	.40	1.00
MRL42 Tailor of the Fickle C	.30	.75
MRL43 Rush Recklessly R	.40	1.00
MRL44 The Reliable Guardian C	.30	.75
MRL45 The Forceful Sentry UR	6.00	15.00
MRL46 Chain Energy C	.40	1.00
MRL47 Mystical Space Typhoon UR	30.00	60.00
MRL48 Giant Trunade SR	3.00	8.00
MRL49 Painful Choice SR	4.00	10.00
MRL50 Snake Fang C	.30	.75
MRL51 Black Illusion Ritual SR	2.50	6.00
MRL52 Octoberser C	.30	.75
MRL53 Psychic Kappa C	.30	.75
MRL54 Horn of the Unicorn R	.40	1.00
MRL55 Labyrinth Wall C	.30	.75
MRL56 Wall Shadow C	.30	.75
MRL57 Twin Long Rods #2 C	.30	.75
MRL58 Stone Ogre Grotto C	.30	.75
MRL59 Magical Labyrinth C	.30	.75
MRL60 Eternal Rest C	.30	.75
MRL61 Megamorph UR	3.00	8.00
MRL62 Commencement Dance C	.30	.75
MRL63 Hamburger Recipe C	.40	1.00
MRL64 House of Adhesive Tape C	.30	.75
MRL65 Eatgaboon C	.30	.75
MRL66 Turtle Oath C	.30	.75
MRL67 Performance of Sword C	.30	.75
MRL68 Hungry Burger C	.30	.75
MRL69 Crab Turtle C	.30	.75
MRL70 Ryu-Ran C	.30	.75
MRL71 Manga Ryu-Ran R	.40	1.00
MRL72 Toon Mermaid UR	5.00	12.00
MRL73 Toon Summoned Skull UR	8.00	20.00
MRL74 Jigen Bakudan C	.30	.75
MRL75 Hyozanryu R	.40	1.00
MRL76 Toon World SR	6.00	15.00
MRL77 Cyber Jar R	.75	2.00
MRL78 Banisher of the Light SR	.75	2.00
MRL79 Giant Rat R	.40	1.00
MRL80 Senju of Thousand Hands R	.40	1.00
MRL81 UFO Turtle R	.40	1.00
MRL82 Flash Assailant C	.30	.75
MRL83 Karate Man R	.30	.75
MRL84 Dark Zebra C	.30	.75
MRL85 Giant Germ R	.75	2.00
MRL86 Nimble Momonga R	.75	2.00
MRL87 Spear Cretin C	.30	.75
MRL88 Shining Angel R	.60	1.50
MRL89 Boar Soldier C	.30	.75
MRL90 Mother Grizzly R	.40	1.00
MRL91 Flying Kamakiri #1 R	.40	1.00
MRL92 Ceremonial Bell C	.30	.75
MRL93 Sonic Bird C	.30	.75
MRL94 Mystic Tomato R	.40	1.00
MRL95 Kotodama C	.30	.75
MRL96 Gaia Power C	.30	.75
MRL97 Umiiruka C	.40	1.00
MRL98 Molten Destruction C	.40	1.00
MRL99 Rising Air Current C	.40	1.00
MRL100 Luminous Spark C	.60	1.50
MRL101 Mystic Plasma Zone C	.60	1.50
MRL102 Messenger of Peace SR	3.00	8.00
MRL103 Serpent Night Dragon SCR	6.00	15.00

2002 Yu-Gi-Oh Pharaoh's Servant 1st Edition

COMPLETE SET (105)	100.00	150.00
HOBBY BOOSTER BOX (24 PACKS)	200.00	300.00
RETAIL BOOSTER BOX (36 PACKS)	550.00	700.00
BOOSTER PACK (9 CARDS)	3.00	8.00
*UNLIMITED: .4X TO .8X 1ST EDITION		
RELEASED OCTOBER 20, 2002		
PSV0 Jinzo SCR	45.00	80.00
PSV1 Steel Ogre Grotto #2 C	.30	.75
PSV2 Three-Headed Geedo C	.30	.75
PSV3 Parasite Paracide SR	.75	2.00
PSV4 7 Completed C	.30	.75
PSV5 Lightforce Sword R	.30	.75
PSV6 Chain Destruction UR	1.50	4.00
PSV7 Time Seal SP	.30	.75
PSV8 Graverobber SR	.75	2.00
PSV9 Gift of the Mystical Elf SP	.30	.75
PSV10 The Eye of Truth SP	.30	.75
PSV11 Dust Tornado SR	1.50	4.00
PSV12 Call of the Haunted UR	10.00	25.00
PSV13 Solomon's Lawbook C	.30	.75
PSV14 Earthshaker C	.30	.75
PSV15 Enchanted Javelin C	.30	.75
PSV16 Mirror Wall SR	.75	2.00
PSV17 Gust C	.30	.75
PSV18 Driving Snow C	.30	.75
PSV19 Armored Glass C	.30	.75
PSV20 World Suppression C	.30	.75
PSV21 Mystic Probe C	.30	.75
PSV22 Metal Detector C	.30	.75
PSV23 Numinous Healer SP	.30	.75
PSV24 Appropriate R	1.00	2.00
PSV25 Forced Requistion R	.75	2.00
PSV26 DNA Surgery SP	3.00	6.00
PSV27 The Regulation of Tribe C	.30	.75
PSV28 Backup Soldier SR	.75	2.00
PSV29 Major Riot SP	.30	.75
PSV30 Ceasefire UR	1.50	4.00
PSV31 Light of Intervention C	.30	.75
PSV32 Respect Play C	.30	.75
PSV33 Magical Hats SR	1.50	4.00
PSV34 Nobleman of Crossout SR	1.00	2.50
PSV35 Nobleman of Extermination R	.75	2.00
PSV36 The Shallow Grave R	.75	2.00
PSV37 Premature Burial UR	5.00	12.00
PSV38 Inspection SP	.40	1.00
PSV39 Prohibition R	1.00	2.50
PSV40 Morphing Jar #2 R	1.25	3.00
PSV41 Flame Champion C	.30	.75
PSV42 Twin-Headed Fire Dragon C	.30	.75
PSV43 Darkfire Soldier C	.30	.75
PSV44 Mr.Volcano C	.30	.75
PSV45 Darkfire Soldier #2 C	.30	.75
PSV46 Kiseitai SP	.30	.75
PSV47 Cyber Falcon C	.30	.75
PSV48 Flying Kamakiri #2 C	.30	.75
PSV49 Harpie's Brother C	.30	.75
PSV50 Buster Blader UR	20.00	40.00
PSV51 Michizure R	.40	1.00
PSV52 Minor Goblin Official SP	.30	.75
PSV53 Gamble C	.30	.75
PSV54 Attack and Receive C	.30	.75
PSV55 Solemn Wishes SP	1.50	4.00
PSV56 Skull Invitation R	.40	1.00
PSV57 Bubonic Vermin C	.30	.75
PSV58 Dark Bat C	.30	.75
PSV59 Oni Tank T-34 C	.30	.75
PSV60 Overdrive C	.30	.75
PSV61 Burning Land C	.30	.75
PSV62 Cold Wave C	.30	.75
PSV63 Fairy Meteor Crush SR	.75	2.00
PSV64 Limiter Removal SR	.75	2.00
PSV65 Rain of Mercy C	.30	.75
PSV66 Monster Recovery R	.40	1.00
PSV67 Shift R	.40	1.00
PSV68 Insect Imitation C	.60	1.50
PSV69 Dimensionhole R	.30	.75
PSV70 Ground Collapse C	.30	.75
PSV71 Magic Drain R	.60	1.50
PSV72 Infinite Dismissal C	.30	.75
PSV73 Gravity Bind R	1.25	3.00
PSV74 Type Zero Magic Crusher C	.30	.75
PSV75 Shadow of Eyes C	.30	.75
PSV76 The Legendary Fisherman UR	6.00	15.00
PSV77 Sword Hunter SP	.30	.75
PSV78 Drill Bug C	.30	.75
PSV79 Deepsea Warrior C	.30	.75
PSV80 Bite Shoes C	.30	.75
PSV81 Spikebot C	.30	.75
PSV82 Invitation to a Dark Sleep C	.30	.75
PSV83 Thousand-Eyes Idol SP	.40	1.00
PSV84 Thousand-Eyes Restrict UR	20.00	40.00
PSV85 Girochin Kuwagata C	.30	.75
PSV86 Hayabusa Knight R	.40	1.00
PSV87 Bombardment Beetle SP	.30	.75
PSV88 4-Starred Ladybug of Doom SP	.30	.75
PSV89 Gradius SP	.30	.75
PSV90 Red-Moon Baby R	.40	1.00
PSV91 Mad Sword Beast R	.30	.75
PSV92 Skull Mariner C	.30	.75
PSV93 The All-Seeing White Tiger C	.30	.75
PSV94 Goblin Attack Force UR	2.50	6.00
PSV95 Island Turtle SP	.30	.75
PSV96 Wingweaver C	.30	.75
PSV97 Science Soldier C	.30	.75
PSV98 Souls of the Forbidden C	.30	.75
PSV99 Dokuroyaiba C	.30	.75
PSV100 The Fiend Megacyber UR	2.00	5.00
PSV101 Gearfried the Iron Knight SR	.75	2.00
PSV102 Insect Barrier C	.30	.75
PSV103 Beast of Talwar UR	2.00	5.00
PSV104 Imperial Order SCR	8.00	20.00

2003 Yu-Gi-Oh Labyrinth of Nightmare 1st Edition

COMPLETE SET (105)	100.00	150.00
HOBBY BOOSTER BOX (24 PACKS)	200.00	300.00
RETAIL BOOSTER BOX (36 PACKS)	250.00	350.00
BOOSTER PACK (9 CARDS)	3.00	8.00
*UNLIMITED: .4X TO .8X 1ST EDITION		
RELEASED ON MARCH 1, 2003		
LON0 Gemini Elf SCR	10.00	25.00
LON1 The Masked Beast UR	3.00	8.00
LON2 Swordsman of Landstar C	.30	.75
LON3 Humanoid Slime SP	.40	1.00
LON4 Worm Drake C	.30	.75
LON5 Humanoid Worm Drake C	.30	.75
LON6 Revival Jam SR	2.00	5.00
LON7 Flying Fish C	.30	.75
LON8 Amphibian Beast R	.40	1.00
LON9 Shining Abyss C	.30	.75
LON10 Gadget Soldier C	.30	.75
LON11 Grand Tiki Elder C	.30	.75
LON12 Melchid the Four-Face Beast C	.30	.75
LON13 Nuvia the Wicked R	.40	1.00
LON14 Chosen One C	.30	.75
LON15 Mask of Weakness C	.30	.75
LON16 Curse of the Masked Beast C	.40	1.00
LON17 Mask of Dispel SR	.75	2.00
LON18 Mask of Restrict UR	10.00	25.00
LON19 Mask of the Accursed SR	1.00	2.50
LON20 Mask of Brutality R	.40	1.00
LON21 Return of the Doomed R	.30	.75
LON22 Lightning Blade C	.30	.75
LON23 Tornado Wall C	.40	1.00
LON24 Fairy Box C	.40	1.00
LON25 Torrential Tribute UR	6.00	15.00
LON26 Jam Breeding Machine R	.40	1.00
LON27 Infinite Cards R	.75	2.00
LON28 Jam Defender SP	.30	.75
LON29 Card of Safe Return UR	3.00	8.00
LON30 Lady Panther C	.30	.75
LON31 The Unfriendly Amazon C	.30	.75
LON32 Amazon Archer C	.30	.75
LON33 Crimson Sentry C	.30	.75
LON34 Fire Princess SR	.75	2.00
LON35 Lady Assailant of Flames C	.30	.75
LON36 Fire Sorcerer C	.30	.75
LON37 Spirit of the Breeze R	.40	1.00
LON38 Dancing Fairy C	.30	.75
LON39 Fairy Guardian C	.30	.75
LON40 Empress Mantis C	.30	.75
LON41 Cure Mermaid C	.30	.75
LON42 Hysteric Fairy C	.30	.75
LON43 Bio-Mage C	.30	.75
LON44 The Forgiving Maiden C	.30	.75
LON45 St. Joan C	.30	.75
LON46 Marie the Fallen One R	.40	1.00
LON47 Jar of Greed SR	1.25	3.00
LON48 Scroll of Bewitchment C	.30	.75
LON49 United We Stand UR	6.00	15.00
LON50 Mage Power UR	4.00	10.00
LON51 Offerings to the Doomed C	.30	.75
LON52 The Portrait's Secret C	.30	.75
LON53 The Gross Ghost of Fled Dreams C	.30	.75
LON54 Headless Knight C	.30	.75
LON55 Earthbound Spirit C	.30	.75
LON56 The Earl of Demise C	.30	.75
LON57 Boneheimer C	.30	.75
LON58 Flame Dancer C	.30	.75
LON59 Spherous Lady C	.30	.75
LON60 Lightning Conger C	.30	.75
LON61 Jowgen the Spiritualist R	1.50	4.00
LON62 Kycoo the Ghost Destroyer SR	1.50	4.00
LON63 Summoner of Illusions C	.30	.75
LON64 Bazoo the Soul-Eater SR	.75	2.00
LON65 Dark Necrofear UR	2.00	5.00
LON66 Soul of Purity and Light C	.30	.75
LON67 Spirit of Flames C	.30	.75
LON68 Aqua Spirit C	.30	.75
LON69 The Rock Spirit C	.30	.75
LON70 Garuda the Wind Spirit C	.30	.75
LON71 Gilasaurus R	.40	1.00
LON72 Tornado Bird R	.40	1.00
LON73 Dreamsprite C	.30	.75
LON74 Zombyra the Dark C	.40	1.00
LON75 Supply C	.30	.75
LON76 Maryokutai C	.30	.75
LON77 The Last Warrior (UR)	1.50	4.00
LON78 Collected Power C	.30	.75
LON79 Dark Spirit of the Silent SR	.60	1.50
LON80 Royal Command UR	.75	2.00
LON81 Riryoku Field SR	.75	2.00
LON82 Skull Lair C	.60	1.50
LON83 Graverobber's Retribution C	.30	.75
LON84 Deal of Phantom C	.40	1.00
LON85 Destruction Punch R	.40	1.00
LON86 Blind Destruction C	.30	.75
LON87 The Emperor's Holiday C	.30	.75
LON88 Destiny Board UR	6.00	15.00
LON89 Spirit Message I R	.40	1.00
LON90 Spirit Message N R	.40	1.00
LON91 Spirit Message A R	.40	1.00
LON92 Spirit Message L R	.40	1.00
LON93 The Dark Door C	.30	.75
LON94 Spiritualism R	.40	1.00
LON95 Cyclon Laser C	.30	.75
LON96 Bait Doll C	.30	.75
LON97 De-Fusion SR	.75	2.00
LON98 Fusion Gate C	3.00	8.00
LON99 Ekibyo Drakmord C	.30	.75
LON100 Miracle Dig C	.30	.75
LON101 Dragonic Attack C	.30	.75
LON102 Spirit Elimination C	.30	.75
LON103 Vengeful Bog Spirit SP	.40	1.00
LON104 Magic Cylinder SCR	5.00	12.00

2003 Yu-Gi-Oh Legacy of Darkness 1st Edition

COMPLETE SET (101)	100.00	150.00
HOBBY BOOSTER BOX (24 PACKS)	100.00	140.00
RETAIL BOOSTER BOX (36 PACKS)	140.00	180.00
BOOSTER PACK (9 CARDS)	3.00	8.00
*UNLIMITED: .4X TO .8X 1ST EDITION		
RELEASED ON JUNE 6, 2003		
LOD0 Yata-Garasu SCR	10.00	25.00
LOD2 Dark Balter the Terrible SR	1.50	4.00
LOD3 Lesser Fiend R	.40	1.00
LOD4 Possessed Dark Soul C	.30	.75
LOD5 Winged Minion C	.30	.75
LOD6 Skull Knight #2 C	.30	.75
LOD7 Ryu-Kishin Clown C	.30	.75
LOD8 Twin-Headed Wolf C	.30	.75
LOD9 Opticlops R	.40	1.00
LOD1 Dark Ruler Ha Des UR	2.00	5.00
LOD10 Bark of Dark Ruler C	.30	.75
LOD11 Fatal Abacus R	.40	1.00
LOD12 Life Absorbing Machine C	.30	.75
LOD13 The Puppet Magic of Dark Ruler C	.30	.75
LOD14 Soul Demolition C	.30	.75
LOD15 Double Snare C	.30	.75
LOD16 Freed the Matchless General UR	.75	2.00
LOD17 Throwstone Unit C	.30	.75
LOD18 Marauding Captain UR	2.50	6.00
LOD19 Ryu Senshi SR	.60	1.50
LOD20 Warrior Dai Grepher C	.30	.75
LOD21 Mysterious Guard C	.30	.75
LOD22 Frontier Wiseman C	.30	.75
LOD23 Exiled Force SR	.60	1.50
LOD24 The Hunter with 7 Weapons C	.30	.75
LOD25 Shadow Tamer R	.40	1.00
LOD26 Dragon Manipulator C	.30	.75
LOD27 The A Forces R	.75	2.00
LOD28 Reinforcements of the Army SR	2.50	6.00
LOD29 Array of Revealing Light R	.40	1.00
LOD30 The Warrior Returning Alive R	.60	1.50
LOD31 Ready for Intercepting C	.30	.75
LOD32 A Feint Plan C	.30	.75
LOD33 Emergency Provisions C	.40	1.00
LOD34 Tyrant Dragon UR	6.00	15.00
LOD35 Spear Dragon SR	1.50	4.00
LOD36 Spirit Ryu C	.30	.75
LOD37 The Dragon Dwelling in the Cave C	.30	.75
LOD38 Lizard Soldier C	.30	.75
LOD39 Fiend Skull Dragon SR	.75	2.00
LOD40 Cave Dragon SP	.60	1.50
LOD41 Gray Wing C	.30	.75
LOD42 Troop Dragon C	.30	.75
LOD43 The Dragon's Bead R	.40	1.00
LOD44 A Wingbeat of Giant Dragon C	.40	1.00
LOD45 Dragon's Gunfire C	.30	.75
LOD46 Stamping Destruction C	.30	.75
LOD47 Super Rejuvenation C	.50	1.00
LOD48 Dragon's Rage C	.50	1.00
LOD49 Burst Breath C	.30	.75
LOD50 Luster Dragon SR	.75	2.00
LOD51 Robotic Knight C	.30	.75
LOD52 Wolf Axwielder C	.30	.75
LOD53 The Illusory Gentleman C	.30	.75
LOD54 Robolady C	.30	.75
LOD55 Roboyarou C	.30	.75
LOD56 Fiber Jar UR	3.00	8.00
LOD57 Serpentine Princess C	.30	.75
LOD58 Patrician of Darkness C	.30	.75
LOD59 Thunder Nyan Nyan R	.40	1.00
LOD60 Gradius Option C	.30	.75
LOD61 Woodland Sprite C	.30	.75
LOD62 Airknight Parshath UR	2.00	5.00
LOD63 Twin-Headed Behemoth SR	.60	1.50
LOD64 Maharaghi SP	.30	.75
LOD65 Inaba White Rabbit SP	.60	1.50
LOD66 Susa Soldier R	.40	1.00
LOD67 Yamata Dragon UR	5.00	12.00
LOD68 Great Long Nose SP	.30	.75
LOD69 Otohime SP	.40	1.00
LOD70 Hino-Kagu-Tsuchi UR	4.00	10.00
LOD71 Asura Priest SR	1.25	3.00
LOD72 Fushi No Tori C	.30	.75
LOD73 Super Robolady C	.30	.75
LOD74 Super Roboyarou C	.30	.75
LOD75 Fengsheng Mirror C	.30	.75
LOD76 Spring of Rebirth C	.30	.75
LOD77 Heart of Clear Water C	.50	1.25
LOD78 A Legendary Ocean C	.30	.75
LOD79 Fusion Sword Murasame Blade R	.40	1.00
LOD80 Smoke Grenade of the Thief SP	.60	1.50
LOD81 Creature Swap UR	3.00	8.00
LOD82 Spiritual Energy Settle Machine C	.30	.75
LOD83 Second Coin Toss R	.60	1.50
LOD84 Convulsion of Nature C	.30	.75
LOD85 The Secret of the Bandit C	.30	.75
LOD86 After Genocide R	.40	1.00
LOD87 Magic Reflector R	.40	1.00
LOD88 Blast with Chain R	.40	1.00
LOD89 Disppear SP	.30	.75
LOD90 Bubble Crash C	.30	.75
LOD91 Royal Oppression R	.75	2.00
LOD92 Bottomless Trap Hole R	1.50	4.00
LOD93 Bad Reaction to Simochi C	.60	1.50
LOD94 Omnious Fortunetelling C	.30	.75
LOD95 Spirit's Invitation C	.30	.75
LOD96 Nutrient Z C	.40	1.00
LOD97 Drop Off SR	.75	2.00
LOD98 Fiend Comedian C	.30	.75
LOD99 Last Turn UR	2.50	6.00
LOD100 Injection Fairy Lily SCR	5.00	12.00

2003 Yu-Gi-Oh Pharaonic Guardian 1st Edition

COMPLETE SET (108)	60.00	150.00
HOBBY BOOSTER BOX (24 PACKS)	140.00	180.00
RETAIL BOOSTER BOX (36 PACKS)	150.00	200.00
BOOSTER PACK (9 CARDS)	3.00	8.00
*UNLIMITED: .4X TO .8X 1ST EDITION		
RELEASED ON JULY 18, 2003		
PGD0 Ring of Destruction SCR	3.00	8.00
PGD1 Molten Behemoth C	.30	.75
PGD2 Shapesnatch C	.30	.75
PGD3 Souleater C	.30	.75
PGD4 King Tiger Wanghu R	.60	1.50
PGD5 Birdface C	.30	.75
PGD6 Kryuel C	.30	.75
PGD7 Arsenal Bug C	.30	.75
PGD8 Maiden of the Aqua C	.40	1.00
PGD9 Jowl of Dark Demise R	.40	1.00
PGD10 Timeater C	.30	.75
PGD11 Mucus Yolk C	.30	.75
PGD12 Servant of Catabolism C	.30	.75
PGD13 Moisture Creature R	.40	1.00
PGD14 Gora Turtle R	.40	1.00
PGD15 Sasuke Samurai SR	.60	1.50
PGD16 Poison Mummy C	.30	.75
PGD17 Dark Dust Spirit C	.30	.75
PGD18 Royal Keeper C	.30	.75
PGD19 Wandering Mummy R	.40	1.00
PGD20 Great Dezard UR	.60	1.50
PGD21 Swarm of Scarabs C	.30	.75
PGD22 Swarm of Locusts C	.30	.75
PGD23 Giant Axe Mummy C	.30	.75
PGD24 8-Claws Scorpion C	.30	.75
PGD25 Guardian Sphinx UR	.60	1.50
PGD26 Pyramid Turtle R	.40	1.00
PGD27 Dice Jar C	.75	2.00
PGD28 Dark Scorpion Burglars C	.30	.75
PGD29 Don Zaloog UR	1.00	2.50
PGD30 Des Lacooda C	.30	.75
PGD31 Fushioh Richie UR	.60	1.50
PGD32 Cobraman Sakuzy C	.30	.75
PGD33 Book of Life SR	1.25	3.00
PGD34 Book of Taiyou C	.75	2.00
PGD35 Book of Moon R	1.25	3.00
PGD36 Mirage of Nightmare SR	.60	1.50
PGD37 Secret Pass to the Treasure C	.30	.75
PGD38 Call of the Mummy C	.30	.75
PGD39 Timidity C	.30	.75
PGD40 Pyramid Energy C	.30	.75
PGD41 Tutan Mask C	.30	.75
PGD42 Ordeal of a Traveler SP	.60	1.50
PGD43 Bottomless Shifting Sand C	.30	.75
PGD44 Curse of Royal R	.40	1.00
PGD45 Needle Ceiling C	.30	.75
PGD46 Statue of the Wicked SR	.60	1.50
PGD47 Dark Coffin C	.30	.75
PGD48 Needle Wall C	.30	.75
PGD49 Trap Dustshoot C	.40	1.00
PGD50 Pyro Clock of Destiny C	.30	.75
PGD51 Reckless Greed R	.60	1.50
PGD52 Pharaoh's Treasure R	.40	1.00
PGD53 Master Kyonshee C	.30	.75
PGD54 Kabazauls C	1.00	2.50
PGD55 Inpachi C	.30	.75
PGD56 Dark Jeroid R	.40	1.00
PGD57 Newdoria R	.40	1.00
PGD58 Helpoemer UR	4.00	10.00
PGD59 Gravekeeper's Spy C	.30	.75
PGD60 Gravekeeper's Curse C	.30	.75
PGD61 Gravekeeper's Guard C	.30	.75
PGD62 Gravekeepers's Spear Soldier C	.30	.75
PGD63 Gravekeeper's Vassal C	.60	1.50
PGD64 Gravekeeper's Watcher R	.40	1.00
PGD65 Gravekeeper's Chief SR	.60	1.50
PGD66 Gravekeeper's Cannonholder C	.30	.75
PGD67 Gravekeeper's Assailant C	.30	.75
PGD68 A Man with Wdjat C	.30	.75
PGD69 Mystical Knight of Jackal UR	1.50	4.00
PGD70 A Cat of Ill Omen C	.30	.75
PGD71 Yomi Ship C	.40	1.00
PGD72 Winged Sage Falcos R	.40	1.00
PGD73 An Owl of Luck C	.30	.75
PGD74 Charm of Shabti C	.30	.75
PGD75 Cobra Jar SP	.30	.75
PGD76 Spirit Reaper R	1.25	3.00
PGD77 Nightmare Horse SP	.40	1.00
PGD78 Reaper on the Nightmare SR	1.25	3.00
PGD79 Dark Designator R	.40	1.00
PGD80 Card Shuffle C	.30	.75
PGD81 Reasoning C	.30	.75
PGD82 Dark Room of Nightmare SR	.60	1.50
PGD83 Different Dimension Capsule C	.30	.75
PGD84 Necrovalley SR	.75	2.00
PGD85 Buster Rancher C	.30	.75
PGD86 Hieroglyph Lithograph C	.30	.75
PGD87 Dark Snake Syndrome C	.30	.75
PGD88 Terraforming C	.40	1.00
PGD89 Banner of Courage C	.30	.75
PGD90 Metamorphosis C	.30	.75
PGD91 Royal Tribute C	.60	1.50
PGD92 Reversal Quiz SP	.60	1.50
PGD93 Coffin Seller R	.40	1.00
PGD94 Curse of Aging C	.30	.75
PGD95 Barrel Behind the Door SR	.60	1.50
PGD96 Raigeki Break C	.40	1.00
PGD97 Narrow Pass C	.30	.75
PGD98 Disturbance Strategy C	.30	.75
PGD99 Trap of Board Eraser SR	.60	1.50
PGD100 Rite of Spirit C	.30	.75
PGD101 Non Aggression Area C	.30	.75

PGD102 D. Tribe C .30 .75
PGD103 Byser Shock UR .60 1.50
PGD104 Question UR 1.25 3.00
PGD105 Rope of Life UR .60 1.50
PGD106 Nightmare Wheel UR 2.00 5.00
PGD107 Lava Golem SCR 2.50 6.00

2003 Yu-Gi-Oh Magician's Force 1st Edition

COMPLETE SET (108) 225.00 350.00
BOOSTER BOX (24 PACKS) 500.00 800.00
BOOSTER PACK (9 CARDS) 7.00 10.00
*UNLIMITED: .4X TO .8X 1ST EDITION
RELEASED ON OCTOBER 10, 2003
MFC0 Dark Magician Girl SCR 80.00 120.00
MFC1 People Running About C .30 .75
MFC2 Oppressed People C .50 1.00
MFC3 United Resistance C .30 .75
MFC4 X-Head Cannon SR 2.00 5.00
MFC5 Y-Dragon Head SR 2.00 5.00
MFC6 Z-Metal Tank SR 2.00 5.00
MFC7 Dark Blade R .60 1.50
MFC8 Pitch-Dark Dragon C .30 .75
MFC9 Kiryu C .30 .75
MFC10 Decayed Commander C .30 .75
MFC11 Zombie Tiger C .30 .75
MFC12 Giant Orc C .30 .75
MFC13 Second Goblin C .30 .75
MFC14 Vampire Orchis C .30 .75
MFC15 Des Dendle C .30 .75
MFC16 Burning Beast C .30 .75
MFC17 Freezing Beast C .30 .75
MFC18 Union Rider C .30 .75
MFC19 D.D. Crazy Beast R .40 1.00
MFC20 Spell Canceller UR 4.00 10.00
MFC21 Neko Mane King C .50 1.00
MFC22 Helping Robo For Combat R .40 1.00
MFC23 Dimension Jar SP .30 .75
MFC24 Great Phantom Thief R .40 1.00
MFC25 Roulette Barrel C .30 .75
MFC26 Paladin of White Dragon UR 2.00 5.00
MFC27 White Dragon Ritual C .30 .75
MFC28 Frontline Base C .30 .75
MFC29 Demotion SP .30 .75
MFC30 Combination Attack R .40 1.00
MFC31 Kaiser Colosseum C .40 1.00
MFC32 Autonomous Action Unit C .30 .75
MFC33 Poison of the Old Man C .30 .75
MFC34 Ante R .40 1.00
MFC35 Dark Core R 1.00 2.00
MFC36 Raregold Armor C .40 1.00
MFC37 Metalsilver Armor C .30 .75
MFC38 Kishido Spirit C .30 .75
MFC39 Tribute Doll R .40 1.00
MFC40 Wave-Motion Cannon SP 4.00 8.00
MFC41 Huge Revolution C .30 .75
MFC42 Thunder of Ruler C .50 1.00
MFC43 Spell Shield Type-8 SR .75 2.00
MFC44 Meteorain C .30 .75
MFC45 Pineapple Blast C .30 .75
MFC46 Secret Barrel SP 1.25 3.00
MFC47 Physical Double C .30 .75
MFC48 Rivalry of Warlords C .40 1.00
MFC49 Formation Union C .30 .75
MFC50 Adhesion Trap Hole C .50 1.00
MFC51 XY-Dragon Cannon UR 8.00 20.00
MFC52 XYZ-Dragon Cannon UR 10.00 25.00
MFC53 XZ-Tank Cannon SR 5.00 12.00
MFC54 YZ-Tank Dragon SR 2.00 5.00
MFC55 Great Angus C .30 .75
MFC56 Aitsu C .30 .75
MFC57 Sonic Duck C .30 .75
MFC58 Luster Dragon UR 6.00 15.00
MFC59 Amazoness Paladin C .30 .75
MFC60 Amazoness Fighter SP .40 1.00
MFC61 Amazoness Swords Woman UR 3.00 8.00
MFC62 Amazoness Blowpiper C .30 .75
MFC63 Amazoness Tiger R .40 1.00
MFC64 Skilled White Magician SR 2.00 5.00
MFC65 Skilled Dark Magician SR 2.00 5.00
MFC66 Apprentice Magician R .50 1.25
MFC67 Old Vindictive Magician C .30 .75
MFC68 Chaos Command Magician UR 6.00 15.00
MFC69 Magical Marionette C .30 .75
MFC70 Pixie Knight C .30 .75
MFC71 Breaker the Magical Warrior UR 6.00 15.00
MFC72 Magical Plant Mandragola C .30 .75
MFC73 Magical Scientist C .30 .75
MFC74 Royal Magical Library C .30 .75
MFC75 Armor Exe R .40 1.00
MFC76 Tribe-Infecting Virus SR 1.50 4.00
MFC77 Des Koala R .60 1.50
MFC78 Cliff the Trap Remover SP .40 1.00
MFC79 Magical Merchant C .60 1.50
MFC80 Koitsu C .30 .75
MFC81 Cat's Ear Tribe R .40 1.00
MFC82 Ultimate Obedient Fiend SP .75 2.00
MFC83 Dark Cat with White Tail C .30 .75
MFC84 Amazoness Spellcaster C .30 .75
MFC85 Continuous Destruction Punch R .40 1.00
MFC86 Big Bang Shot R .40 1.00
MFC87 Gather Your Mind C .30 .75
MFC88 Mass Driver C .30 .75
MFC89 Senri Eye SP .30 .75
MFC90 Emblem of Dragon Destroyer C .50 1.00
MFC91 Jar Robber C .30 .75
MFC92 My Body as a Shield C .30 .75
MFC93 Pigeonholing Books of Spell SP .30 .75
MFC94 Mega Ton Magical Cannon R .40 1.00
MFC95 Pitch-Black Power Stone SP .40 1.00
MFC96 Amazoness Archers SR .75 2.00
MFC97 Dramatic Rescue R .40 1.00
MFC98 Exhausting Spell C .30 .75
MFC99 Hidden Book of Spell C .30 .75
MFC100 Miracle Restoring C .30 .75
MFC101 Remove Brainwashing C .50 1.00
MFC102 Disarmament C .30 .75
MFC103 Anti-Spell C .30 .75
MFC104 The Spell Absorbing Life C .30 .75
MFC105 Dark Paladin Correct Art UR 50.00 100.00
MFC105 Dark Paladin Misprint UR 40.00 80.00
MFC106 Double Spell UR 2.00 5.00
MFC107 Diffussion Wave-Motion SCR .60 1.50

2003 Yu-Gi-Oh Dark Crisis 1st Edition

COMPLETE SET (106) 125.00 175.00
HOBBY BOOSTER BOX (24 PACKS) 250.00 350.00
RETAIL BOOSTER BOX (36 PACKS) 350.00 450.00
BOOSTER PACK (9 CARDS) 3.00 8.00
*UNLIMITED: .4X TO .8X 1ST EDITION
RELEASED ON DECEMBER 1, 2003
DCR0 Vampire Lord SCR 6.00 15.00
DCR1 Battle Footballer C .30 .75
DCR2 Nin-Ken Dog C 1.00 2.50
DCR3 Acrobat Monkey C .30 .75
DCR4 Arsenal Summoner C .30 .75
DCR5 Guardian Elma C .30 .75
DCR6 Guardian Ceal UR .60 1.50
DCR7 Guardian Grarl UR 1.25 3.00
DCR8 Guardian Baou R .40 1.00
DCR9 Guardian Kay'est C .30 .75
DCR10 Guardian Tryce R .40 1.00
DCR11 Cyber Raider SP .30 .75
DCR12 Reflect Bounder UR 3.00 8.00
DCR13 Little-Winguard SP .30 .75
DCR14 Des Feral Imp R .40 1.00
DCR15 Different Dimension Dragon SR .60 1.50
DCR16 Shinato, King of a Higher Plane UR 2.50 6.00
DCR17 Dark Flare Knight SR 1.25 3.00
DCR18 Mirage Knight SR 1.25 3.00
DCR19 Berserk Dragon SR 1.50 4.00
DCR20 Exodia Necross UR 20.00 40.00
DCR21 Gyaku-Gire Panda SP .30 .75
DCR22 Blindly Loyal Goblin C .30 .75
DCR23 Despair from the Dark SP .30 .75
DCR24 Maju Garzett SP .30 .75
DCR25 Fear from the Dark R .40 1.00
DCR26 Dark Scorpion - Chick the Yellow C .30 .75
DCR27 D. D. Warrior Lady SR 1.00 2.50
DCR28 Thousand Needles C .30 .75
DCR29 Shinato's Ark SP .40 1.00
DCR30 A Deal with Dark Ruler SP .50 1.25
DCR31 Contract with Exodia SP .75 2.00
DCR32 Butterfly Dagger - Elma SR .60 1.50
DCR33 Shooting Star Bow - Ceal C .30 .75
DCR34 Gravity Axe - Grarl C .30 .75
DCR35 Wicked-Breaking Flamberge R .40 1.00
DCR36 Rod of Silence - Kay'est C .30 .75
DCR37 Twin Swords of Flashing Light C .30 .75
DCR38 Precious Cards from Beyond C .30 .75
DCR39 Rod of the Mind's Eye C .30 .75
DCR40 Fairy of the Spring C .30 .75
DCR41 Token Thanksgiving C .30 .75
DCR42 Morale Boost C .30 .75
DCR43 Non-Spellcasting Area C .30 .75
DCR44 Different Dimension Gate R .40 1.00
DCR45 Final Attack Orders C .30 .75
DCR46 Staunch Defender C .30 .75
DCR47 Ojama Trio SP 1.00 2.00
DCR48 Arsenal Robber C .30 .75
DCR49 Skill Drain R 2.00 5.00
DCR50 Really Eternal Rest C .30 .75
DCR51 Kaiser Glider UR 1.25 3.00
DCR52 Interdimensional Matter Trans. UR 1.25 3.00
DCR53 Cost Down UR 1.50 4.00
DCR54 Gagagigo C .30 .75
DCR55 D. D. Trainer C .30 .75
DCR56 Ojama Green C .30 .75
DCR57 Archfiend Soldier R 1.25 3.00
DCR58 Pandemonium Watchbear C .30 .75
DCR59 Sasuke Samurai #2 C .30 .75
DCR60 Dark Scorpion - Gorg C .30 .75
DCR61 Dark Scorpion - Meanae C .30 .75
DCR62 Outstanding Dog Marron SP .30 .75
DCR63 Great Maju Garzett R 1.50 4.00
DCR64 Iron Blacksmith Kotetsu C .30 .75
DCR65 Goblin of Greed C .30 .75
DCR66 Mefist the Infernal General R .40 1.00
DCR67 Vilepawn Archfiend C .30 .75
DCR68 Shadowknight Archfiend R .30 .75
DCR69 Darkbishop Archfiend R .40 1.00
DCR70 Desrook Archfiend C .30 .75
DCR71 Infernalqueen Archfiend R .40 1.00
DCR72 Terrorking Archfiend SR 1.50 4.00
DCR73 Skull Archfiend of Lightning UR 1.50 4.00
DCR74 Metallizing Parasite - Lunatite R .40 1.00
DCR75 Tsukuyomi R 1.50 4.00
DCR76 Mudora SR .40 1.00
DCR77 Keldo C .30 .75
DCR78 Kelbek C .30 .75
DCR79 Zolga C .30 .75
DCR80 Agido C .30 .75
DCR81 Legendary Flame Lord R .40 1.00
DCR82 Dark Master - Zorc SR .60 1.50
DCR83 Spell Reproduction C .30 .75
DCR84 Dragged Down into Grave C 1.25 3.00
DCR85 Incandescent Ordeal SP .30 .75
DCR86 Contract with the Abyss R .40 1.00
DCR87 Contract with the Dark Master SP .30 .75
DCR88 Falling Down SP .50 1.00
DCR89 Checkmate C .30 .75
DCR90 Cestus of Dagla C .30 .75
DCR91 Final Countdown SP .75 2.00
DCR92 Archfiend's Oath C .30 .75
DCR93 Mustering of Dark Scorpions C .30 .75
DCR94 Pandemonium SP .60 1.50
DCR95 Altar for Tribute C .30 .75
DCR96 Frozen Soul C .30 .75
DCR97 Battle-Scarred C .30 .75
DCR98 Dark Scorpion Combination R .40 1.00
DCR99 Archfiend's Roar C .75 2.00
DCR100 Dice Re-Roll SP .40 1.00
DCR101 Spell Vanishing SR .30 .75
DCR102 Sakuretsu Armor C .50 1.25
DCR103 Ray of Hope C .30 .75
DCR104 Blast Held by a Tribute UR 2.00 5.00
DCR105 Judgment of Anubis SCR 1.50 4.00

2004 Yu-Gi-Oh Invasion of Chaos 1st Edition

COMPLETE SET (112) 100.00 225.00
HOBBY BOOSTER BOX (24 PACKS) 1000.00 1500.00
RETAIL BOOSTER BOX (24 PACKS) 1000.00 1500.00
BOOSTER PACK (9 CARDS) 8.00 20.00
SPECIAL EDITION BOX (3 PACKS 1 VAR. CARD) 10.00 25.00
*UNLIMITED: .4X TO .8X 1ST EDITION
RELEASED ON MARCH 1, 2004
IOC0 Chaos Emperor Dragon - Envoy of the End SCT 25.00 50.00
IOC1 Ojama Yellow C .20 .50
IOC2 Ojama Black C .20 .50
IOC3 Soul Tiger C .20 .50
IOC4 Big Koala C .20 .50
IOC5 Des Kangaroo C .20 .50
IOC6 Crimson Ninja C .20 .50
IOC7 Strike Ninja UR 2.50 6.00
IOC8 Gale Lizard C .20 .50
IOC9 Spirit of the Pot of Greed SP .20 .50
IOC10 Chopman the Desperate Outlaw C .20 .50
IOC11 Sasuke Samurai #3 R .30 .75
IOC12 D.D. Scout Plane SR .60 1.50
IOC13 Beserk Gorilla R .40 1.00
IOC14 Freed the Brave Wanderer SR .40 1.00
IOC15 Coach Goblin C .20 .50
IOC16 Witch Doctor of Chaos SP .20 .50
IOC17 Chaos Necromancer SP .30 .75
IOC18 Chaosrider Gustaph SR .60 1.50
IOC19 Inferno C .20 .50
IOC20 Fenrir C .20 .50
IOC21 Gigantes C .20 .50
IOC22 Silpheed C .20 .50
IOC23 Chaos Sorcerer C .30 .75
IOC24 Gren Maju Da Eiza C .40 1.00
IOC25 Black Luster Soldier - Envoy of the Beginning UR 25.00 50.00
IOC26 Drillago R .30 .75
IOC27 Lekunga R .30 .75
IOC28 Lord Poison SP .40 1.00
IOC29 Bowganian SP .20 .50
IOC30 Granadora SP .20 .50
IOC31 Fuhma Shuriken R .30 .75
IOC32 Heart of the Underdog SP 1.50 4.00
IOC33 Wild Nature's Release SR .30 .75
IOC34 Ojama Delta Hurricane SP .30 .75
IOC35 Stumbling SP .60 1.50
IOC36 Chaos End C .20 .50
IOC37 Yellow Luster Shield C .20 .50
IOC38 Chaos Greed C .20 .50
IOC39 D.D. Designator SR .60 1.50
IOC40 D.D. Borderline C .20 .50
IOC41 Recycle C .20 .50
IOC42 Primal Seed C .20 .50
IOC43 Thunder Crash SP .20 .50
IOC44 Dimension Distortion SP .20 .50
IOC45 Reload SR .50 1.25
IOC46 Soul Absorption C .60 1.50
IOC47 Big Burn SR .40 1.00
IOC48 Blasting the Ruins C .20 .50
IOC49 Cursed Seal of Forbidden Spell C .75 2.00
IOC50 Tower of Babel C .20 .50
IOC51 Spatial Collapse C .20 .50
IOC52 Chain Disappearance R .75 2.00
IOC53 Zero Gravity C .20 .50
IOC54 Dark Mirror Force UR 2.00 5.00
IOC55 Energy Drain C .20 .50
IOC56 Giga Gagagigo SP 1.25 3.00
IOC57 Mad Dog of Darkness R .30 .75
IOC58 Neo Bug C .20 .50
IOC59 Sea Serpent Warrior of Darkness C .20 .50
IOC60 Terrorking Salmon C .20 .50
IOC61 Blazing Inpachi C .20 .50
IOC62 Burning Algae C .20 .50
IOC63 The Thing in the Crater C .20 .50
IOC64 Molten Zombie C .20 .50
IOC65 Dark Magician of Chaos UR 25.00 50.00
IOC66 Gora Turtle of Illusion C .20 .50
IOC67 Manticore of Darkness UR 1.25 3.00
IOC68 Stealth Bird SP .30 .75
IOC69 Sacred Crane C .40 1.00
IOC70 Enraged Battle Ox R .30 .75
IOC71 Don Turtle SP .20 .50
IOC72 Balloon Lizard C .20 .50
IOC73 Dark Dricreratops R .30 .75
IOC74 Hyper Hammerhead SP .20 .50
IOC75 Black Tyranno UR 1.00 2.50
IOC76 Anti-Aircraft Flower SP .20 .50
IOC77 Prickle Fairy C .20 .50
IOC78 Pinch Hopper SP 1.25 3.00
IOC79 Skull-Mark Ladybug SP .20 .50
IOC80 Insect Princess UR .60 1.50
IOC81 Amphibious Bugroth MK-3 C .20 .50
IOC82 Torpedo Fish SP .20 .50
IOC83 Levia-Dragon Daedalus UR 2.00 5.00
IOC84 Orca Mega-Fortress of Darkness SR .40 1.00
IOC85 Cannonball Spear Shellfish SP .30 .75
IOC86 Mataza the Zapper R .30 .75
IOC87 Guardian Angel Joan UR 1.50 4.00
IOC88 Manju of Ten Thousand Hands SP 1.25 3.00
IOC89 Getsu Fuhma R .30 .75
IOC90 Ryu Kokki C .20 .50
IOC91 Gryphon's Feather Duster C .20 .50
IOC92 Stray Lambs R .20 .50
IOC93 Smashing Ground SP .60 1.50
IOC94 Dimension Fusion UR 5.00 12.00
IOC95 Dedication through Light & Darkness SR 2.00 5.00
IOC96 Salvage C .50 1.25
IOC97 Ultra Evolution Pill R .30 .75
IOC98 Multiplication of Ants C .20 .50
IOC99 Earth Chant SP .20 .50
IOC100 Jade Insect Whistle C .20 .50
IOC101 Destruction Ring R .30 .75
IOC102 Fiend's Hand Mirror C .20 .50
IOC103 Compulsory Evacuation Device R 2.00 5.00
IOC104 A Hero Emerges C .20 .50
IOC105 Self-Destruct Button SP .50 1.25
IOC106 Curse of Darkness R 2.00 5.00
IOC107 Begone, Knave! C .20 .50
IOC108 DNA Transplant C .20 .50
IOC109 Robbin' Zombie R .30 .75
IOC110 Trap Jammer SR .75 2.00
IOC111 Invader of Darkness SCR 2.00 5.00

2004 Yu-Gi-Oh Ancient Sanctuary 1st Edition

COMPLETE SET (112) 60.00 140.00
BOOSTER BOX (24 PACKS) 90.00 110.00
BOOSTER PACK (9 CARDS) 3.00 6.00
*UNLIMITED: .4X TO .8X 1ST EDITION
RELEASED ON JUNE 1, 2004
AST0 The End of Anubis SCR 3.00 8.00
AST1 Gogiga Gagagigo C .20 .50
AST2 Warrior of Zera C .30 .75
AST3 Sealmaster Meisei R .30 .75
AST4 Mystical Shine Ball C .50 1.25
AST5 Metal Armored Bug C .20 .50
AST6 The Agent of Judment Saturn UR .75 2.00
AST7 The Agent of Wisdom Mercury R .30 .75
AST8 The Agent of Creation Venus R .75 2.00
AST9 The Agent of Force Mars SR .40 1.00
AST10 The Unhappy Girl C .20 .50
AST11 Soul-Absorbing Bone Tower R 1.00 2.50
AST12 The Kick Man C .20 .50
AST13 Vampire Lady C .20 .50
AST14 Stone Statue of the Aztecs SR .40 1.00
AST15 Rocket Jumper C .20 .50
AST16 Avatar of the Pot R .30 .75
AST17 Legendary Jujitsu Master C .30 .75
AST18 Gear Golem the Moving Fortress UR .75 2.00
AST19 KA-2 Des Scissors C .20 .50
AST20 Needle Burrower SR .30 .75
AST21 Sonic Jammer C .20 .50
AST22 Blowback Dragon UR 1.50 4.00
AST23 Zaborg the Thunder Monarch SR 1.50 4.00
AST24 Atomic Firefly C .20 .50
AST25 Mermaid Knight C .20 .50
AST26 Piranha Army C .20 .50
AST27 Two Thousand Needles C .20 .50
AST28 Disc Fighter C .20 .50
AST29 Arcane Archer of the Forest C .20 .50
AST30 Lady Ninja Yae C .60 1.50
AST31 Goblin King C .20 .50
AST32 Solar Flare Dragon C .20 .50
AST33 White Magician Pikeru C .20 .50
AST34 Archlord Zerato UR 2.00 5.00
AST35 Opti-Camouflage Armor C 1.50 4.00
AST36 Mystik Wok C .20 .50
AST37 Enemy Controller UR 3.00 8.00
AST38 Burst Stream of Destruction UR 8.00 20.00
AST39 Monster Gate C .20 .50
AST40 Amplifier SR 2.50 6.00
AST41 Weapon Change C .20 .50
AST42 The Sanctuary in the Sky SR 1.50 4.00
AST43 Earthquake C .20 .50
AST44 Talisman of Trap Sealing R .30 .75
AST45 Goblin Thief C .20 .50
AST46 Backfire C .20 .50
AST47 Micro Ray C .20 .50
AST48 Light of Judgment C .20 .50
AST49 Talisman of Spell Sealing R .30 .75
AST50 Wall of Revealing Light C .40 1.00
AST51 Solar Ray C .20 .50
AST52 Ninjitsu Art of Transformation C .50 1.25
AST53 Beckoning Light C .20 .50
AST54 Draining Shield R .75 2.00
AST55 Armor Break C .20 .50
AST56 Gigobyte C .20 .50
AST57 Mokey Mokey C 1.00 2.50
AST58 Kozaky C .20 .50
AST59 Fiend Scorpion C .20 .50
AST60 Pharaoh's Servant C .20 .50
AST61 Pharaonic Protector C .20 .50
AST62 Spirit of the Pharaoh UR .75 2.00
AST63 Theban Nightmare R .30 .75
AST64 Aswan Apparition C .20 .50
AST65 Protector of the Sanctuary C .20 .50
AST66 Nubian Guard C .20 .50
AST67 Legacy Hunter SR .40 1.00
AST68 Desertapir C .20 .50
AST69 Sand Gambler C .20 .50
AST70 3-Hump Lacooda C .20 .50
AST71 Ghost Knight of Jackal UR .50 1.25
AST72 Absorbing Kid from the Sky C .20 .50
AST73 Elephant Statue of Blessing C .20 .50
AST74 Elephant Statue of Disaster C .20 .50
AST75 Spirit Caller C .20 .50
AST76 Emissary of the Afterlife SR 1.00 2.50
AST77 Grave Protector R .30 .75
AST78 Double Coston R .30 .75
AST79 Regenerating Mummy C .20 .50
AST80 Night Assailant C .40 1.00
AST81 Man-Thro' Tho' C .20 .50
AST82 King of the Swamp R 4.00 10.00
AST83 Emissary of the Oasis C .20 .50
AST84 Special Hurricane R .30 .75
AST85 Order to Charge C .20 .50
AST86 Sword of the Soul-Eater C .20 .50
AST87 Dust Barrier C .20 .50
AST88 Soul Reversal C .20 .50
AST89 Spell Economics R .30 .75
AST90 Blessings of the Nile C .20 .50
AST91 7 C .20 .50
AST92 Level Limit - Area B SP 2.00 5.00
AST93 Enchanting Fitting Room C .20 .50
AST94 The Law of the Normal C .20 .50
AST95 Dark Magic Attack UR 15.00 30.00
AST96 Delta Attacker C .20 .50
AST97 Thousand Energy R .30 .75
AST98 Triangle Power R .30 .75
AST99 The Third Sarcophagus C .20 .50
AST100 The Second Sarcophagus C .20 .50
AST101 The First Sarcophagus SR .40 1.00
AST102 Dora of Fate C .20 .50
AST103 Judgment of the Desert C .20 .50
AST104 Human-Wave Tactics C .20 .50
AST105 Curse of Anubis UR .75 2.00
AST106 Desert Sunlight C .20 .50
AST107 Des Counterblow SR .30 .75
AST108 Labyrinth of Nightmare C .20 .50
AST109 Soul Resurrection R .30 .75
AST110 Order to Smash C .20 .50
AST111 Mazera Deville SCR 1.50 4.00

2004 Yu-Gi-Oh Soul of the Duelist 1st Edition

COMPLETE SET (60) 50.00 100.00
COMPLETE MASTER SET (85) 200.00 400.00
BOOSTER BOX (24 PACKS) 60.00 120.00
BOOSTER PACK (9 CARDS) 2.50 6.00
*UNLIMITED: .4X TO .8X 1ST EDITION
RELEASED ON OCTOBER 1, 2004
SODEN01 Charcoal Inpachi R .30 .75
SODEN01 Charcoal Inpachi UTR 1.25 3.00
SODEN02 Neo Aqua Madoor C .20 .50
SODEN03 Skull Dog Marron C .20 .50
SODEN04 Goblin Calligrapher C .20 .50
SODEN05 Ultimate Insect LV1 R .30 .75
SODEN05 Ultimate Insect LV1 UTR .75 2.00
SODEN06 Horus the Black Flame 1.50 4.00
Dragon LV4 R
SODEN06 Horus the Black Flame 3.00 8.00
SODEN07 Horus the Black Flame 3.00 8.00
Dragon LV6 SR
SODEN07 Horus the Black Flame 3.00 8.00
SODEN08 Horus the Black Flame 25.00 50.00
SODEN08 Horus the Black Flame 8.00 20.00
SODEN09 Dark Mimic LV1 C .20 .50
SODEN10 Dark Mimic LV3 R .30 .75
SODEN10 Dark Mimic LV3 (UTR) 2.00 5.00
SODEN11 Mystic Swordsman LV2 UTR 1.50 4.00
SODEN11 Mystic Swordsman LV2 R .30 .75
SODEN12 Mystic Swordsman LV4 UR .75 2.00
SODEN12 Mystic Swordsman LV4 UTR 2.50 6.00
SODEN13 Armed Dragon LV3 C .20 .50
SODEN14 Armed Dragon LV5 R .30 .75
SODEN14 Armed Dragon LV5 UTR 4.00 10.00
SODEN15 Armed Dragon LV7 UTR 10.00 25.00
SODEN15 Armed Dragon LV7 UR 4.00 10.00
SODEN16 Horus' Servant C .20 .50
SODEN17 Red-Eyes B. Chick C .30 .75
SODEN18 Malice Doll of Demise C .20 .50
SODEN19 Ninja Grandmaster Sasuke UTR 3.00 8.00
SODEN19 Ninja Grandmaster Sasuke R .40 1.00
SODEN20 Rafflesia Seduction R .30 .75
SODEN20 Rafflesia Seduction UTR .75 2.00
SODEN21 Ultimate Baseball Kid C .20 .50
SODEN22 Mobius the Frost Monarch SR .75 2.00
SODEN22 Mobius the Frost Monarch UTR 8.00 20.00
SODEN23 Element Dragon C .20 .50
SODEN24 Element Soldier C .20 .50
SODEN25 Howling Insect C .20 .50
SODEN26 Masked Dragon C .30 .75
SODEN27 Mind on Air R .30 .75
SODEN27 Mind on Air UTR 1.00 2.50
SODEN28 Unshaven Angler C .20 .50
SODEN29 The Trojan Horse C .20 .50
SODEN30 Nobleman-Eater Bug C .20 .50
SODEN31 Enraged Muka Muka C .20 .50
SODEN32 Hade-Hane C .20 .50
SODEN33 Penumbral Soldier Lady UTR .75 2.00
SODEN33 Penumbral Soldier Lady SR .40 1.00
SODEN34 Ojama King R .40 1.00
SODEN34 Ojama King UTR 2.00 5.00
SODEN35 Master of Oz UTR 6.00 15.00
SODEN35 Master of Oz R .30 .75
SODEN36 Sanwitch C .20 .50
SODEN37 Dark Factory of Mass Production C .60 1.50
SODEN38 Hammer Shot R .30 .75
SODEN38 Hammer Shot UTR 2.50 6.00
SODEN39 Mind Wipe C .20 .50
SODEN40 Abyssal Designator C .20 .50
SODEN41 Level Up! .30 .75
SODEN42 Inferno Fire Blast UR 3.00 8.00
SODEN42 Inferno Fire Blast UTR 10.00 25.00
SODEN43 Ectoplasmer SR .40 1.00
SODEN43 Ectoplasmer UTR .60 1.50
SODEN44 The Graveyard in .20 .50
the Fourth Dimension C
SODEN45 Two-Man Cell Battle C .20 .50
SODEN46 Big Wave Small Wave C .20 .50
SODEN47 Fusion Weapon C .20 .50
SODEN48 Ritual Weapon C .20 .50
SODEN49 Taunt C .20 .50
SODEN50 Absolute End C .20 .50
SODEN51 Spirit Barrier UTR 4.00 10.00
SODEN51 Spirit Barrier R 1.50 4.00
SODEN52 Ninjitsu Art of Decoy C .20 .50
SODEN53 Enervating Mist R .30 .75

Card	Low	High
SODEN53 Enervating Mist UTR	2.50	6.00
SODEN54 Heavy Slump C	.30	.75
SODEN55 Greed UTR	.60	1.50
SODEN55 Greed SR	.40	1.00
SODEN56 Mind Crush C	.60	1.50
SODEN57 Null and Void UTR	.60	1.50
SODEN57 Null and Void SR	.40	1.00
SODEN58 Gorgon's Eye C	.20	.50
SODEN59 Cemetary Bomb C	.20	.50
SODEN60 Hallowed Life Barrier UTR	.75	2.00
SODEN60 Hallowed Life Barrier SR	.40	1.00

2004 Yu-Gi-Oh Rise of Destiny 1st Edition

Card	Low	High
COMPLETE SET (60)	30.00	60.00
COMPLETE MASTER SET (85)	60.00	100.00
BOOSTER BOX (24 PACKS)	50.00	75.00
BOOSTER PACK (9 CARDS)	2.50	6.00
SE BOX (3 PACKS, 1 VARIANT)	6.00	15.00
*UNLIMITED: .4X TO .8X 1ST EDITION		
RELEASED ON NOVEMBER 24, 2004		
RDSEN01 Woodborg Inpachi	.20	.50
RDSEN02 Mighty Guard	.20	.50
RDSEN03 Bokoichi the Freightening Car	.20	.50
RDSEN04 Harpie Girl	.20	.50
RDSEN05 The Creator UR	1.25	3.00
RDSEN05 The Creator UTR	2.00	5.00
RDSEN06 The Creator Incarnate	.20	.50
RDSEN07 Ultimate Insect LV3 R	.30	.75
RDSEN07 Ultimate Insect LV3 UTR	.60	1.50
RDSEN08 Mystic Swordsman LV6 UR	2.50	6.00
RDSEN08 Mystic Swordsman LV6 UTR	3.00	8.00
RDSEN09 Silent Swordsman LV3 UR	1.50	4.00
RDSEN09 Silent Swordsman LV3 UTR	2.00	5.00
RDSEN10 Nightmare Penguin	.20	.50
RDSEN11 Heavy Mech Support Platform	.20	.50
RDSEN12 Perfect Machine King UR	2.50	6.00
RDSEN12 Perfect Machine King UTR	3.00	8.00
RDSEN13 Element Magician C	.20	.50
RDSEN14 Element Saurus C	.20	.50
RDSEN15 Roc from the Valley of Haze C	.20	.50
RDSEN16 Sasuke Samurai #4 R	.30	.75
RDSEN16 Sasuke Samurai #4 UTR	.60	1.50
RDSENT17 Harpie Lady 1 C	.40	1.00
RDSEN18 Harpie Lady 2 C	.20	.50
RDSEN19 Harpie Lady 3 C	.20	.50
RDSEN20 Raging Flame Sprite C	.20	.50
RDSEN21 Thestalos the Firestorm Monarch SR	.40	1.00
RDSEN21 Thestalos the Firestorm	5.00	12.00
RDSEN22 Eagle Eye C	.20	.50
RDSEN23 Tactical Espionage Expert C	.20	.50
RDSEN24 Invasion of Flames C	.20	.50
RDSEN25 Creeping Doom Manta C	.20	.50
RDSEN26 Pitch-Black Warwolf C	.20	.50
RDSEN27 Mirage Dragon C	.30	.75
RDSEN28 Gaia Soul (R)	.30	.75
RDSEN28 Gaia Soul (UTR)	.60	1.50
RDSEN29 Fox Fire C	.20	.50
RDSEN30 Big Core UTR	.60	1.50
RDSEN30 Big Core SR	.30	.75
RDSEN31 Fusilier Dragon (UTR)	1.25	3.00
RDSEN31 Fusilier Dragon (R)	.50	1.00
RDSEN32 Dekoichi (UTR)	1.50	4.00
RDSEN32 Dekoichi (R)	.30	.75
RDSEN33 A-Team: Trap Disposal Unit R	.30	.75
RDSEN33 A-Team: Trap Disposal Unit UTR	.60	1.50
RDSEN34 Homunculus the Alchemic Being C	.20	.50
RDSEN35 Dark Blade The Dragon Knight R	.30	.75
RDSEN35 Dark Blade The Dragon Knight UTR	1.00	2.50
RDSEN36 Mokey Mokey King C	.20	.50
RDSEN37 Serial Spell R	.30	.75
RDSEN37 Serial Spell UTR	.60	1.50
RDSEN38 Harpies' Hunting Ground C	.20	.50
RDSEN39 Triangle Ecstasy Spark UTR	2.00	5.00
RDSEN39 Triangle Ecstasy Spark UR	.40	1.00
RDSEN40 Necklace of Command R	.30	.75
RDSEN40 Necklace of Command UTR	.60	1.50
RDSEN41 Machine Duplication R	.30	.75
RDSEN41 Machine Duplication UTR	1.25	3.00
RDSEN42 Flint R	.30	.75
RDSEN42 Flint UTR	.60	1.50
RDSEN43 Mokey Mokey Smackdown C	.20	.50
RDSEN44 Back to Square One C	.20	.50
RDSEN45 Monster Reincarnation SR	.75	2.00
RDSEN45 Monster Reincarnation UTR	6.00	15.00
RDSEN46 Ballista of Rampart Smashing C	.20	.50
RDSEN47 Lighten the Load C	.20	.50
RDSEN48 Malice Dispersion C	.20	.50
RDSEN49 Tragedy SR	.30	.75
RDSEN49 Tragedy UTR	.60	1.50
RDSEN50 Divine Wrath UTR	3.00	8.00
RDSEN50 Divine Wrath SR	.60	1.50
RDSEN51 Xing Zhen Hu C	.20	.50
RDSEN52 Rare Metalmorph UTR	.60	1.50
RDSEN52 Rare Metalmorph R	.30	.75
RDSEN53 Fruits of Kozaky's Studies C	.30	.75
RDSEN54 Mind Haxorz C	.20	.50
RDSEN55 Fuh-Rin-Ka-Zan C	.20	.50
RDSEN56 Chain Burst UTR	.60	1.50
RDSEN56 Chain Burst R	.30	.75
RDSEN57 Pikeru's Circle of Enchantment SR	.30	.75
RDSEN57 Pikeru's Circle of Enchantment UTR	.75	2.00
RDSEN58 Spell Purification C	.20	.50
RDSEN59 Astral Barrier C	.20	.50
RDSEN60 Covering Fire UTR	.60	1.50
RDSEN60 Covering Fire R	.30	.75

2005 Yu-Gi-Oh Flaming Eternity 1st Edition

Card	Low	High
COMP.SET W/O UTR (60)	100.00	150.00
COMPLETE SET (85)	150.00	300.00
BOOSTER BOX (24 PACKS)	80.00	120.00
BOOSTER PACK (9 CARDS)	2.50	6.00
*UNLIMITED: .4X TO .8X 1ST EDITION		
RELEASED ON MARCH 3, 2005		
FETEN1 Space Mambo C	.10	.30
FETEN2 Divine Dragon Ragnarok C	.75	2.00
FETEN3 Chu-Ske The Mouse Fighter C	.10	.30
FETEN4 Insect Knight C	.10	.30
FETEN5 Sacred Phoenix of Nephthys UTR	4.00	10.00
FETEN5 Sacred Phoenix of Nephthys UR	1.50	4.00
FETEN6 Hand of Nephthys C	.10	.30
FETEN7 Ultimate Insect LV5 R	.40	1.00
FETEN7 Ultimate Insect LV5 UTR	3.00	8.00
FETEN8 Silent Swordsman LV5 UR	1.25	3.00
FETEN8 Silent Swordsman LV5 UTR	3.00	8.00
FETEN9 Granmarg the Rock Monarch SR	.75	2.00
FETEN9 Granmarg the Rock Monarch UTR	6.00	15.00
FETEN10 Element Valkyrie C	.10	.30
FETEN11 Element Doom C	.10	.30
FETEN12 Maji-Gire Panda C	.10	.30
FETEN13 Catnipped Kitty C	.10	.30
FETEN14 Behemoth the King of all Animals SR	.75	2.00
FETEN14 Behemoth the King of all Animals UTR	1.25	3.00
FETEN15 Big-Tusked Mammoth UTR	1.25	3.00
FETEN15 Big-Tusked Mammoth R	.40	1.00
FETEN16 Kangaroo Champ C	.10	.30
FETEN17 Hyena C	.10	.30
FETEN18 Blade Rabbit C	.10	.30
FETEN19 Mecha-Dog Marron C	.10	.30
FETEN20 Blast Magician UTR	2.00	6.00
FETEN20 Blast Magician SR	.75	2.00
FETEN21 Chiron the Mage UTR	1.50	4.00
FETEN21 Chiron the Mage R	.40	1.00
FETEN22 Gearfried the Swordsmaster UTR	4.00	10.00
FETEN22 Gearfried the Swordsmaster UR	2.00	5.00
FETEN23 Armed Samurai - Ben Kei C	.10	.30
FETEN24 Shadowslayer R	.40	1.00
FETEN24 Shadowslayer UTR	1.25	3.00
FETEN25 Golem Sentry C	.10	.30
FETEN26 Abare Ushioni C	.10	.30
FETEN27 The Light - Hex-Sealed Fusion C	.10	.30
FETEN28 The Dark - Hex-Sealed Fusion C	.10	.30
FETEN29 The Earth - Hex-Sealed Fusion C	.10	.30
FETEN30 Whirlwind Prodigy C	.10	.30
FETEN31 Flame Ruler C	.10	.30
FETEN32 Firebird C	.10	.30
FETEN33 Rescue Cat C	.10	.30
FETEN34 Brain Jacker R	.40	1.00
FETEN34 Brain Jacker UTR	1.25	3.00
FETEN35 Gatling Dragon UR	2.00	5.00
FETEN35 Gatling Dragon UTR	6.00	15.00
FETEN36 King Dragun SR	4.00	10.00
FETEN36 King Dragun UTR	8.00	20.00
FETEN37 A Feather of the Phoenix UTR	6.00	15.00
FETEN37 A Feather of the Phoenix SR	.75	2.00
FETEN38 Poison Fangs C	.10	.30
FETEN39 Spell Absorption R	1.25	3.00
FETEN39 Spell Absorption UTR	4.00	10.00
FETEN40 Lightning Vortex SR	1.50	4.00
FETEN40 Lightning Vortex UTR	10.00	25.00
FETEN41 Meteor of Destruction R	.40	1.00
FETEN41 Meteor of Destruction UTR	1.25	3.00
FETEN42 Swords of Concealing Light UTR	10.00	25.00
FETEN42 Swords of Concealing Light R	.50	1.25
FETEN43 Spiral Spear Strike UTR	3.00	8.00
FETEN43 Spiral Spear Strike R	.40	1.00
FETEN44 Release Restraint C	.10	.30
FETEN45 Centrifugal Field C	.10	.30
FETEN46 Fulfillment of the Contract C	.10	.30
FETEN47 Re-Fusion C	.75	2.00
FETEN48 The Big March of Animals C	.10	.30
FETEN49 Cross Counter UTR	1.25	3.00
FETEN49 Cross Counter R	.40	1.00
FETEN50 Pole Position C	.10	.30
FETEN51 Penalty Game! UTR	2.00	5.00
FETEN51 Penalty Game! R	.40	1.00
FETEN52 Threatening Roar C	.25	.75
FETEN53 Phoenix Wing Wind Blast UTR	15.00	30.00
FETEN53 Phoenix Wing Wind Blast R	.50	1.25
FETEN54 Good Goblin Housekeeping C	.10	.30
FETEN55 Beast Soul Swap C	.10	.30
FETEN56 Assault on GHQ R	.40	1.00
FETEN56 Assault on GHQ UTR	1.25	3.00
FETEN57 D.D. Dynamite C	.25	.75
FETEN58 Deck Devastation Virus UTR	20.00	40.00
FETEN58 Deck Devastation Virus SR	2.50	6.00
FETEN59 Elemental Burst C	.10	.30
FETEN60 Forced Ceasefire UTR	1.25	3.00
FETEN60 Forced Ceasefire R	.40	1.00

2005 Yu-Gi-Oh The Lost Millennium 1st Edition

Card	Low	High
COMPLETE SET (85)	115.00	225.00
BOOSTER BOX (24 PACKS)	60.00	100.00
BOOSTER PACK (9 CARDS)	2.50	6.00
SE PACK	8.00	20.00
*UNLIMITED: .4X TO .8X 1ST EDITION		
RELEASED ON JUNE 1, 2005		
SE1 Invader of Darkness UR	.75	2.00
SE2 Chaos Emperor Dragon UR	6.00	15.00
SE3 Mazera Deville UR	.75	2.00
SE4 End of Anubis UR	1.25	3.00
TLM1 Elemental Hero Avian C	.50	1.25
TLM2 Elemental Hero Burstinatrix C	.50	1.25
TLM3 Elemental Hero Clayman C	.50	1.25
TLM4 Elemental Hero Sparkman C	.50	1.25
TLM5 Winged Kuriboh SR	1.50	4.00
TLM6 Ancient Gear Golem UTR	10.00	25.00
TLM6 Ancient Gear Golem UR	3.00	8.00
TLM7 Ancient Gear Beast R	.40	1.00
TLM7 Ancient Gear Beast UTR	1.50	4.00
TLM8 Ancient Gear Soldier C	.20	.50
TLM9 Millennium Scorpion UTR	1.50	4.00
TLM9 Millennium Scorpion R	.40	1.00
TLM-5 Winged Kuriboh UTR	5.00	12.00
TLM10 Ultimate Insect LV7 SR	.75	2.00
TLM10 Ultimate Insect LV7 UTR	3.00	8.00
TLM11 Lost Guardian C	.20	.50
TLM12 Hieracosphinx SR	.75	2.00
TLM12 Hieracosphinx UTR	1.50	4.00
TLM13 Criosphinx UTR	1.50	4.00
TLM13 Criosphinx R	.40	1.00
TLM14 Moai Interceptor Cannons C	.20	.50
TLM15 Megarock Dragon SR	.75	2.00
TLM15 Megarock Dragon UTR	3.00	8.00
TLM16 Dummy Golem C	.20	.50
TLM17 Grave Ohja R	.40	1.00
TLM17 Grave Ohja UTR	1.50	4.00
TLM18 Mine Golem C	.20	.50
TLM19 Monk Fighter C	.20	.50
TLM20 Master Monk UTR	1.50	4.00
TLM20 Master Monk SR	.75	2.00
TLM21 Guardian Statue C	.20	.50
TLM22 Medusa Worm C	.20	.50
TLM23 D.D. Survivor R	.40	1.00
TLM23 D.D. Survivor UTR	3.00	8.00
TLM24 Mid Shield Gardna UTR	1.50	4.00
TLM24 Mid Shield Gardna R	.40	1.00
TLM25 White Ninja C	.20	.50
TLM26 Aussa the Earth Charmer C	.20	.50
TLM27 Eria the Water Charmer C	.20	.50
TLM28 Hiita the Fire Charmer C	.20	.50
TLM29 Wynn the Wind Charmer C	.20	.50
TLM30 Batteryman AA C	.20	.50
TLM31 Des Wombat C	.20	.50
TLM32 King of the Skull Servants C	.50	1.25
TLM33 Reshef the Dark Being UR	2.00	5.00
TLM33 Reshef the Dark Being UTR	5.00	12.00
TLM34 Elemental Mistress Doriado R	.40	1.00
TLM34 Elemental Mistress Doriado UTR	1.50	4.00
TLM35 Elemental Hero Flame Wingman UR	3.00	8.00
TLM35 Elemental Hero Flame Wingman UTR	5.00	12.00
TLM36 Elemental Hero Thunder Giant UR	2.50	6.00
TLM36 Elemental Hero Thunder Giant UTR	5.00	12.00
TLM37 Card of Sanctity SR	.75	2.00
TLM37 Card of Sanctity UTR	1.50	4.00
TLM38 Brain Control UTR	10.00	25.00
TLM38 Brain Control SR	.75	2.00
TLM39 Gift of the Martyr C	.20	.50
TLM40 Double Attack C	.20	.50
TLM41 Battery Charger C	.20	.50
TLM42 Kaminote Blow C	.20	.50
TLM43 Doriado's Blessing C	.20	.50
TLM44 Final Ritual of the Ancients C	.20	.50
TLM45 Legendary Black Belt UTR	1.50	4.00
TLM45 Legendary Black Belt R	.40	1.00
TLM46 Nitro Unit UTR	1.50	4.00
TLM46 Nitro Unit R	.40	1.00
TLM47 Shifting Shadows C	.20	.50
TLM48 Impenetrable Formation C	.20	.50
TLM49 Hero Signal R	.40	1.00
TLM49 Hero Signal UTR	1.50	4.00
TLM50 Pikeru's Second Sight C	.20	.50
TLM51 Minefield Eruption C	.20	.50
TLM52 Kozaky's Self-Destruct Button R	.40	1.00
TLM52 Kozaky's Self-Destruct Button UTR	1.50	4.00
TLM53 Mispolymerization C	.20	.50
TLM54 Level Conversion Lab C	.20	.50
TLM55 Rock Bombardment C	.20	.50
TLM56 Grave Lure C	.20	.50
TLM57 Token Feastevil R	.40	1.00
TLM57 Token Feastevil UTR	1.50	4.00
TLM58 Spell-Stopping Statute R	.40	1.00
TLM58 Spell-Stopping Statute UTR	1.50	4.00
TLM59 Royal Surrender UTR	1.50	4.00
TLM59 Royal Surrender R	.40	1.00
TLM60 Lone Wolf C	.20	.50

2005 Yu-Gi-Oh Cybernetic Revolution 1st Edition

Card	Low	High
COMPLETE SET (60)	180.00	350.00
BOOSTER BOX (24 PACKS)	90.00	110.00
BOOSTER PACK (9 CARDS)	2.50	6.00
*UNLIMITED: .4X TO .8X 1ST EDITION		
RELEASED ON AUGUST 6, 2005		
CRV1 Cycloid C	.10	.30
CRV2 Soitsu C	.10	.30
CRV3 Mad Lobster C	.10	.30
CRV4 Jelly Beans Man C	.10	.30
CRV5 Winged Kuriboh LV 10 UR	3.00	8.00
CRV5 Winged Kuriboh LV 10 UTR	10.00	25.00
CRV6 Patroid C	.10	.30
CRV7 Gyroid C	.10	.30
CRV8 Steamroid C	.10	.30
CRV9 Drillroid C	.10	.30
CRV11 Jetroid C	.10	.30
CRV17 Cybernetic Cyclops C	.10	.30
CRV18 Mechanical Hound C	.10	.30
CRV19 Cyber Archfiend C	.10	.30
CRV22 Giant Kozaky C	.10	.30
CRV23 Indomitable Fighter Lei Lei C	.10	.30
CRV24 Protective Soul Ailin C	.10	.30
CRV25 Doitsu C	.10	.30
CRV26 Des Frog C	.10	.30
CRV27 T.A.D.P.O.L.E. C	.10	.30
CRV28 Poison Draw Frog C	.10	.30
CRV29 Tyranno Infinity C	.10	.30
CRV30 Batteryman C	.10	.30
CRV31 Ebon Magician Curran C	.10	.30
CRV33 Steam Gyroid C	.10	.30
CRV38 Fusion Recovery C	.10	.30
CRV40 Dragon's Mirror C	.10	.30
CRV42 Des Croaking C	.10	.30
CRV43 Pot of Generosity C	.10	.30
CRV44 Shien's Spy C	.10	.30
CRV50 Spiritual Earth Art - Kurogane C	.10	.30
CRV51 Spiritual Water Art - Aoi C	.10	.30
CRV52 Spiritual Fire Art - Kurenai C	.10	.30
CRV53 Spiritual Wind Art - Miyabi C	.10	.30
CRV54 A Rival Appears! C	.10	.30
CRV55 Magical Explosion R	.40	1.00
CRV55 Magicial Explosion UTR	3.00	8.00
CRV58 Conscription C	.10	.30
CRV60 Prepare to Strike Back C	.10	.30
CRV10A UFOroid SR	.75	2.00
CRV10B UFOroid UTR	.75	2.00
CRV12A Wroughtweiler R	.40	1.00
CRV12B Wroughtweiler UTR	1.50	4.00
CRV13B Dark Catapulter UTR	.40	1.00
CRV13B Dark Catapulter UTR	.75	2.00
CRV14A Elemental Hero Bubbleman R	.40	3.00
CRV14B Elemental Hero Bubbleman UTR	15.00	30.00
CRV15A Cyber Dragon SR	3.00	8.00
CRV15B Cyber Dragon UTR	30.00	60.00
CRV16A Cybernetic Magician SR	.75	2.00
CRV16B Cybernetic Magician UTR	.75	2.00
CRV20A Goblin Elite Attack Force SR	.75	2.00
CRV20B Goblin Elite Attack Force UTR	1.50	4.00
CRV21A B.E.S. Crystal Core SR	.75	2.00
CRV21B B.E.S. Crystal Core UTR	1.00	2.50
CRV32A D.D.M. Different Dimension (R)	.40	1.00
CRV32B D.D.M. Different Dimension UTR	1.00	2.50
CRV34A UFOroid Fighter UR	1.00	2.50
CRV34B UFOroid Fighter UTR	2.50	6.00
CRV35A Cyber Twin Dragon SR	2.50	6.00
CRV35B Cyber Twin Dragon UTR	10.00	25.00
CRV36A Cyber End Dragon UR	6.00	15.00
CRV36B Cyber End Dragon UTR	25.00	50.00
CRV37A Power Bond UR	3.00	8.00
CRV37B Power Bond UTR	15.00	30.00
CRV39A Miracle Fusion R	.40	1.00
CRV39B Miracle Fusion UTR	8.00	20.00
CRV41A System Down R	.40	1.00
CRV41B System Down UTR	10.00	25.00
CRV45A Transcendant Wings R	.40	1.00
CRV45B Transcendent Wings UTR	3.00	8.00
CRV46A Bubble Shuffle R	.40	1.00
CRV46B Bubble Shuffle UTR	.75	2.00
CRV47A Spark Blaster R	.40	1.00
CRV47B Spark Blaster UTR	.75	2.00
CRV48A Skyscraper SR	1.00	2.50
CRV48B Skyscraper UTR	3.00	8.00
CRV49A Fire Darts R	.40	1.00
CRV49B Fire Darts UTR	.75	2.00
CRV56A Rising Energy R	.40	1.00
CRV56B Rising Energy UTR	1.00	2.50
CRV57A D.D. Trap Hole R	.40	1.00
CRV57B D.D. Trap Hole UTR	.75	2.00
CRV59A Dimension Wall R	.40	1.00
CRV59B Dimension Wall UTR	2.50	6.00

2005 Yu-Gi-Oh Elemental Energy 1st Edition

Card	Low	High
COMPLETE SET (60)	200.00	400.00
BOOSTER BOX (24 PACKS)	80.00	120.00
BOOSTER PACK (9 CARDS)	2.50	6.00
*UNLIMITED: .4X TO .8X 1ST EDITION		
RELEASED ON NOVEMBER 30, 2005		
EEN1 Zure, Knight of Dark World C	.20	.50
EEN2 V-Tiger Jet C	.20	.50
EEN3 Blade Skater C	.20	.50
EEN4 Queen's Knight R	.40	1.00
EEN4 Queen's Knight UTR	3.00	8.00
EEN5 Jack's Knight UTR	15.00	30.00
EEN5 Jack's Knight R	.40	1.00
EEN6 King's Knight UTR	3.00	8.00
EEN6 King's Knight R	.40	1.00
EEN7 Elemental Hero Bladedge UTR	4.00	10.00
EEN7 Elemental Hero Bladedge SR	.75	2.00
EEN8 Elemental Hero Wildheart C	.20	.50
EEN9 Reborn Zombie C	.20	.50
EEN10 Chthonian Soldier UTR	.75	2.00
EEN10 Chthonian Soldier R	.40	1.00
EEN11 W-Wing Catapult C	.20	.50
EEN12 Infernal Incinerator C	.20	.50
EEN13 Hydrogeddon C	.20	.50
EEN14 Oxygeddon C	.20	.50
EEN15 Water Dragon UTR	2.50	6.00
EEN15 Water Dragon SR	.75	2.00
EEN16 Etoile Cyber C	.20	.50
EEN17 B.E.S. Tetran UTR	.75	2.00
EEN17 B.E.S. Tetran SR	.75	2.00
EEN18 Nanobreaker C	.20	.50
EEN19 Rapid-Fire Magician UTR	.75	2.00
EEN19 Rapid-Fire Magician R	.40	1.00
EEN20 Beiige, Vanguard of Dark World C	.20	.50
EEN21 Broww, Huntsman of Dark World UTR	5.00	12.00
EEN21 Broww, Huntsman of Dark World R	.40	1.00
EEN22 Brron, Mad King of Dark World UTR	.75	2.00
EEN22 Brron, Mad King of Dark World R	.40	1.00
EEN23 Sillva, Warlord of Dark World UTR	2.50	6.00
EEN23 Sillva, Warlord of Dark World R	.40	1.00
EEN24 Goldd, Wu-Lord of Dark World UTR	2.50	6.00
EEN24 Goldd, Wu-Lord of Dark World SR	.75	2.00
EEN25 Scarr, Scout of Dark World C	.20	.50
EEN26 Familiar-Possessed - Aussa C	.20	.50
EEN27 Familiar-Possessed - Eria C	.20	.50
EEN28 Familiar-Possessed - Hiita C	.20	.50
EEN29 Familiar-Possessed - Wynn C	.20	.50
EEN30 VW-Tiger Catapult C	.20	.50
EEN31 VWXYZ-Dragon Catapult Cannon UTR	3.00	8.00
EEN31 VWXYZ-Dragon Catapult Cannon SR	.75	2.00
EEN32 Cyber Blader UTR	1.50	4.00
EEN32 Cyber Blader SR	.75	2.00
EEN33 Elem.Hero Rampart Blast. UTR	8.00	20.00
EEN33 Elemental Hero Rampart Blaster UR	2.00	5.00
EEN34 Elemental Hero Tempest UTR	20.00	40.00
EEN34 Elemental Hero Tempest UR	2.50	6.00
EEN35 Elemental Hero Wildedge UTR	40.00	80.00
EEN35 Elemental Hero Wildedge UR	2.50	6.00
EEN36 Elem. Hero Shining Flare UTR	60.00	100.00
EEN36 Elem. Hero Shining Flare UR	6.00	15.00
EEN37 Pot of Avarice UTR	15.00	30.00
EEN37 Pot of Avarice SR	.75	2.00
EEN38 Dark World Lightning C	.20	.50
EEN39 Level Modulation C	.20	.50
EEN40 Ojamagic C	.20	.50
EEN41 Ojamuscle C	.20	.50
EEN42 Feather Shot UTR	.75	2.00
EEN42 Feather Shot R	.40	1.00
EEN43 Bonding - H2O C	.20	.50
EEN44 Chthonian Alliance UTR	.75	2.00
EEN44 Chthonian Alliance R	.40	1.00
EEN45 Armed Changer UTR	.75	2.00
EEN45 Armed Changer R	.40	1.00
EEN46 Branch! C	.20	.50
EEN47 Boss Rush C	.20	.50
EEN48 Gateway to Dark World C	.20	.50
EEN49 Hero Barrier UTR	.75	2.00
EEN49 Hero Barrier R	.40	1.00
EEN50 Chthonian Blast UTR	.75	2.00
EEN50 Chthonian Blast R	.40	1.00
EEN51 The Forces of Darkness C	.20	.50
EEN52 Dark Deal C	.20	.50
EEN53 Simultaneous Loss C	.20	.50
EEN54 Weed Out C	.20	.50
EEN55 The League of Uniform Nomenclature C	.20	.50
EEN56 Roll Out! C	.20	.50
EEN57 Chthonian Polymer C	.20	.50
EEN58 Feather Wind C	.20	.50
EEN59 Non-Fusion Area C	.20	.50
EEN60 Level Limit - Area A UTR	.75	2.00
EEN60 Level Limit - Area A R	.40	1.00

2006 Yu-Gi-Oh Shadow of Infinity 1st Edition

Card	Low	High
COMPLETE SET (60)	200.00	400.00
BOOSTER BOX (24 PACKS)	80.00	110.00
BOOSTER PACK (9 CARDS)	2.50	6.00
*UNLIMITED: .4X TO .8X 1ST EDITION		
RELEASED ON FEBRUARY 18, 2006		
SOI1 Uria, Lord of Searing Flames UR	3.00	8.00
SOI1 Uria, Lord of Searing Flames UTR	70.00	100.00
SOI2 Hamon, Lord of Striking Thunder UTR	40.00	70.00
SOI2 Hamon, Lord of Striking Thunder UR	3.00	8.00
SOI3 Raviel, Lord of Phantasms UTR	30.00	60.00
SOI3 Raviel, Lord of Phantasms UR	3.00	8.00
SOI4 Elemental Hero Neo Bubbleman C	.10	.30
SOI5 Hero Kid C	.10	.30
SOI6 Cyber Barrier Dragon SR	.60	1.50
SOI6 Cyber Barrier Dragon UTR	2.50	6.00
SOI7 Cyber Laser Dragon UR	3.00	8.00
SOI7 Cyber Laser Dragon UTR	8.00	20.00
SOI8 Ancient Gear C	.10	.30
SOI9 Ancient Gear Cannon C	.10	.30
SOI10 Proto-Cyber Dragon R	.40	1.00
SOI10 Proto-Cyber Dragon UTR	3.00	8.00
SOI11 Adhesive Explosive R	.40	1.00
SOI11 Adhesive Explosive UTR	1.00	2.50
SOI12 Machine King Prototype C	.10	.30
SOI13 B.E.S. Covered Core SR	.60	1.50
SOI13 B.E.S. Covered Core UTR	1.25	3.00
SOI14 D.D. Guide C	.10	.30
SOI15 Chain Thrasher C	.10	.30
SOI16 Disciple of the Forbidden Spell C	.10	.30
SOI17 Tenkabito Shien C	.10	.30
SOI18 Parasitic Ticky C	.10	.30
SOI19 Gokipon C	.10	.30
SOI20 Silent Insect C	.10	.30
SOI21 Chainsaw Insect UTR	2.50	6.00
SOI21 Chainsaw Insect R	.40	1.00
SOI22 Anteatereatingant C	.10	.30
SOI23 Saber Beetle C	.10	.30
SOI24 Doom Dozer R	.60	1.50
SOI24 Doom Dozer UTR	3.00	8.00
SOI25 Treeborn Frog UTR	8.00	20.00
SOI25 Treeborn Frog R	.60	1.50
SOI26 Beelze Frog C	.10	.30
SOI27 Princess Pikeru UTR	2.50	6.00
SOI27 Princess Pikeru R	.40	1.00
SOI28 Princess Curran R	.40	1.00
SOI28 Princess Curran UTR	2.50	6.00
SOI29 Memory Crusher R	.40	1.00
SOI29 Memory Crusher UTR	.75	2.00
SOI30 Malice Ascendant C	.10	.30
SOI31 Grass Phantom C	.10	.30
SOI32 Sand Moth C	.10	.30
SOI33 Divine Dragon-Excelion UTR	1.00	2.50
SOI33 Divine Dragon - Excelion SR	.60	1.50
SOI34 Ruin, Queen of Oblivion SR	.60	1.50
SOI34 Ruin, Queen of Oblivion UTR	3.00	8.00
SOI35 Demise, King of Armageddon UTR	4.00	10.00
SOI35 Demise, King of Armageddon SR	3.00	8.00
SOI36 D.3.S. Frog C	.10	.30
SOI37 Hero Heart C	.10	.30
SOI38 Magnet Circle LV2 C	.10	.30
SOI39 Ancient Gear Factory C	.10	.30
SOI40 Ancient Gear Drill C	.10	.30
SOI41 Phantasmal Martyrs R	.40	1.00
SOI41 Phantasmal Martyrs UTR	1.00	2.50
SOI42 Cyclone Bommerang UTR	1.00	2.50
SOI42 Cyclone Boomerang R	.40	1.00
SOI43 Symbol of Heritage C	.10	.30
SOI44 Trial of the Princesses C	.10	.30
SOI45 Photon Generator Unit C	.10	.30
SOI46 End of the World C	.10	.30
SOI47 Ancient Gear Castle SR	.60	1.50
SOI47 Ancient Gear Castle UTR	1.00	2.50
SOI48 Samsara C	.10	.30
SOI49 Super Junior Confrontation C	.10	.30
SOI50 Miracle Kids C	.10	.30
SOI51 Attack Reflector Unit C	.10	.30
SOI52 Damage Condenser UTR	2.00	5.00
SOI52 Damage Condenser SR	.60	1.50

SOI53 Karma Cut R	.75	2.00
SOI53 Karma Cut UTR	6.00	15.00
SOI54 Next to be Lost C	.10	.30
SOI55 Generation Shift C	.10	.30
SOI56 Full Salvo C	.10	.30
SOI57 Success Probability 0% C	.10	.30
SOI58 Option Hunter UTR	1.00	2.50
SOI58 Option Hunter R	.40	1.00
SOI59 Goblin Out of the Frying Pan R	.40	1.00
SOI59 Goblin Out of the Frying Pan UTR	1.00	2.50
SOI60 Malfunction UTR	1.00	2.50
SOI60 Malfunction R	.40	1.00

2006 Yu-Gi-Oh Enemy of Justice 1st Edition

COMPLETE SET (60)	100.00	175.00
BOOSTER BOX (24 PACKS)	60.00	80.00
BOOSTER PACK (9 CARDS)	2.50	6.00
*UNLIMITED: .4X TO .8X 1ST EDITION		
RELEASED ON MAY 17, 2006		
EOJ1 Destiny Hero - Doom Lord C	.10	.30
EOJ2 Destiny Hero - Captain Tenacious C	.10	.30
EOJ3A Destiny Hero - Diamond Dude R	.40	1.00
EOJ3B Destiny Hero - Diamond Dude UTR	8.00	20.00
EOJ4A Destiny Hero - Dreadmaster UR	1.00	2.50
EOJ4B Destiny Hero - Dreadmaster UTR	5.00	12.00
EOJ5 Cyber Tutu C	.10	.30
EOJ6 Cyber Gymnast C	.10	.30
EOJ7A Cyber Prima SR	.60	1.50
EOJ7B Cyber Prima UTR	1.00	2.50
EOJ8 Cyber Kirin C	.10	.30
EOJ9A Cyber Phoenix SR	.75	2.00
EOJ9B Cyber Phoenix UTR	3.00	8.00
EOJ10 Searchlightman C	.10	.30
EOJ11A Victory Viper XX03 SR	.60	1.50
EOJ11B Victory Viper XX03 UTR	1.25	3.00
EOJ12 Swift Birdman Joe C	.10	.30
EOJ13A Harpie's Pet Baby Dragon R	.50	1.25
EOJ13B Harpie's Pet Baby Dragon UTR	4.00	10.00
EOJ14 Majestic Mech - Senku C	.10	.30
EOJ15A Majestic Mech - Ohka R	.40	1.00
EOJ15B Majestic Mech - Ohka UTR	1.00	2.50
EOJ16A Majestic Mech - Goryu SR	.60	1.50
EOJ16B Majestic Mech - Goryu UTR	1.00	2.50
EOJ17 Royal Knight C	.10	.30
EOJ18A Herald of Green Light R	.40	1.00
EOJ18B Herald of Green Light UTR	1.50	4.00
EOJ19A Herald of Purple Light R	.40	1.00
EOJ19B Herald of Purple Light UTR	1.50	4.00
EOJ20 Bountiful Artemis C	.10	.30
EOJ21 Layard the Liberator C	.10	.30
EOJ22A Banisher of the Radiance R	.60	1.50
EOJ22B Banisher of Radiance UTR	4.00	10.00
EOJ23A Voltanis the Adjudicator UR	1.50	4.00
EOJ23B Voltanis the Adjudicator UTR	2.50	6.00
EOJ24 Guard Dog C	.10	.30
EOJ25 Whirlwind Weasel C	.10	.30
EOJ26 Avalanching Aussa C	.10	.30
EOJ27 Raging Eria C	.10	.30
EOJ28 Blazing Hiita C	.10	.30
EOJ29 Storming Wynn C	.10	.30
EOJ30 Batteryman D C	.10	.30
EOJ31A Super-Electromagnetic SR	.60	1.50
EOJ31B Super-Electromagnetic UTR	1.25	3.00
EOJ32A Elem. Hero Phoenix UR	2.00	5.00
EOJ32B Elem. Hero Phoenix UTR	20.00	40.00
EOJ33A Elem. Hero Shining Phoenix UR	2.00	5.00
EOJ33B Elem. Hero Shining Phoenix UTR	20.00	40.00
EOJ34 Elemental Hero Mariner C	.10	.30
EOJ35A Elemental Hero Wild Wingman SR	.60	1.50
EOJ35B Elemental Hero Wild Wingman UTR	1.50	4.00
EOJ36 Elemental Hero Necroid Shaman C	.10	.30
EOJ37 Misfortune C	.10	.30
EOJ38 H - Heated Heart C	.10	.30
EOJ39 E - Emergency Call C	.10	.30
EOJ40 R - Righteous Justice C	.10	.30
EOJ41 O - Oversoul C	.10	.30
EOJ42A HERO Flash!! R	.40	1.00
EOJ42B HERO Flash!! UTR	1.00	2.50
EOJ43 Power Capsule C	.10	.30
EOJ44 Celestial Transformation C	.10	.30
EOJ45A Guard Penalty R	.40	1.00
EOJ45B Guard Penalty UTR	1.00	2.50
EOJ46 Grand Convergence C	.10	.30
EOJ47 Dimensional Fissure C	.10	.30
EOJ48A Clock Tower Prison SR	.60	1.50
EOJ48B Clock Tower Prison UTR	1.50	4.00
EOJ49A Life Equalizer R	.75	2.00
EOJ49B Life Equalizer UTR	4.00	10.00
EOJ50 Elemental Recharge C	.10	.30
EOJ51A Destruction of Destiny R	.40	1.00
EOJ51B Destruction of Destiny UTR	1.00	2.50
EOJ52 Destiny Signal C	.10	.30
EOJ53A D - Time R	.40	1.00
EOJ53B D - Time UTR	1.00	2.50
EOJ54 D - Shield C	.10	.30
EOJ55 Icarus Attack C	.50	1.25
EOJ56A Elemental Absorber R	.40	1.00
EOJ56B Elemental Absorber UTR	1.00	2.50
EOJ57 Macro Cosmos C	.40	1.00
EOJ58A Miraculous Descent R	.40	1.00
EOJ58B Miraculous Descent UTR	1.25	3.00
EOJ59 Shattered Axe C	.10	.30
EOJ60A Forced Back R	1.50	4.00
EOJ60B Forced Back UTR	4.00	10.00

2006 Yu-Gi-Oh Power of the Duelist 1st Edition

COMPLETE SET (60)	80.00	150.00
BOOSTER BOX (24 PACKS)	50.00	80.00
BOOSTER PACK (9 CARDS)	2.50	6.00
*UNLIMITED: .4X TO .8X 1ST EDITION		
RELEASED ON AUGUST 16, 2006		
POTD1 Elemental Hero Neos C	.10	.30
POTD2 Sabersaurus C	.10	.30
POTD3 Neo-Spacian Aqua Dolphin SR	2.50	6.00
POTD3 Neo-Spacian Aqua Dolphin UTR	1.50	4.00
POTD4 Neo-Spacian Flare Scarab UTR	2.50	6.00
POTD4 Neo-Spacian Flare Scarab SR	.60	1.50
POTD5 Neo-Spacian Dark Panther UTR	3.00	8.00
POTD5 Neo-Spacian Dark Panther SR	.60	1.50
POTD6 Chrysalis Dolphin C	.10	.30
POTD7 Rallis The Star Bird C	.10	.30
POTD8 Submarineroid R	.40	1.00
POTD8 Submarineroid UTR	1.50	4.00
POTD9 Ambulanceroid C	.10	.30
POTD10 Decoyroid C	.10	.30
POTD11 Rescueroid C	.10	.30
POTD12 Destiny Hero-Double Dude UTR	1.50	4.00
POTD12 Destiny Hero-Double Dude SR	.60	1.50
POTD13 Destiny Hero-Defender C	.10	.30
POTD14 Destiny Hero-Dogma UTR	4.00	10.00
POTD14 Destiny Hero-Dogma SR	.60	1.50
POTD15 Destiny Hero-Blade Master C	.10	.30
POTD16 Destiny Hero-Fear Monger C	.10	.30
POTD17 Destiny Hero-Dasher R	.40	1.00
POTD17 Destiny Hero Dasher UTR	1.50	4.00
POTD18 Black Ptera C	.10	.30
POTD19 Black Stego C	.10	.30
POTD20 Ultimate Tyranno UTR	2.00	5.00
POTD20 Ultimate Tyranno SR	.60	1.50
POTD21 Miracle Jurassic Egg C	.10	.30
POTD22 Babycerasaurus C	.10	.30
POTD23 Bitelon C	.10	.30
POTD24 Alien Grey C	.10	.30
POTD25 Alien Skull C	.10	.30
POTD26 Alien Hunter C	.10	.30
POTD27 Alien Warrior R	.40	1.00
POTD27 Alien Warrior UTR	2.00	5.00
POTD28 Alien Mother UTR	1.50	4.00
POTD28 Alien Mother R	.40	1.00
POTD29 Cosmic Horror Gangi'el UTR	1.50	4.00
POTD29 Cosmic Horror Gangi'el R	.40	1.00
POTD30 Flying Saucer Muusik'I C	.10	.30
POTD31 Elemental Hero Aqua Neos UTR	1.50	4.00
POTD31 Elemental Hero Aqua Neos UR	1.50	4.00
POTD32 Elemental Hero Flare Neos UR	1.50	4.00
POTD32 Elemental Hero Flare Neos UTR	4.00	10.00
POTD33 Elemental Hero Dark Neos UR	1.50	4.00
POTD33 Elemental Hero Dark Neos UTR	5.00	12.00
POTD34 Chimeratech Overdragon UR	1.50	4.00
POTD34 Chimeratech Overdragon UTR	8.00	20.00
POTD35 Ambulance Rescueroid C	.10	.30
POTD36 Super Vehicroid Jumbo Drill UTR	1.50	4.00
POTD36 Super Vehicroid Jumbo Drill SR	.60	1.50
POTD37 Contact C	.10	.30
POTD38 Fake Hero C	.10	.30
POTD39 Spell Calling UTR	1.50	4.00
POTD39 Spell Calling R	.40	1.00
POTD40 Vehicroid Connection Zone C	.10	.30
POTD41 D-Spirit C	.10	.30
POTD42 Overload Fusion UTR	5.00	12.00
POTD42 Overload Fusion R	.60	1.50
POTD43 Cyclone Blade UTR	1.50	4.00
POTD43 Cyclone Blade R	.40	1.00
POTD44 Future Fusion UTR	5.00	12.00
POTD44 Future Fusion R	.75	2.00
POTD45 Common Soul C	.10	.30
POTD46 Neo Space UTR	3.00	8.00
POTD46 Neo Space R	.40	1.00
POTD47 Mausoleum of the Emperor C	.10	.30
POTD48 Dark City R	.40	1.00
POTD48 Dark City UTR	1.50	4.00
POTD49 Destiny Mirage C	.10	.30
POTD50 D-Chain R	.40	1.00
POTD50 D-Chain UTR	1.50	4.00
POTD51 Crop Circles C	.10	.30
POTD52 The Paths of Destiny C	.50	1.25
POTD53 Orbital Bombardment C	.10	.30
POTD54 Royal Writ of Taxation C	.10	.30
POTD55 Wonder Garage C	.10	.30
POTD56 Supercharge R	.40	1.00
POTD56 Supercharge UTR	1.50	4.00
POTD57 Cyber Summon Blaster R	.40	1.00
POTD57 Cyber Summon Blaster UTR	1.50	4.00
POTD58 Fossil Excavation C	.10	.30
POTD59 Synthetic Seraphim C	.10	.30
POTD60 Brainwashing Beam C	.10	.30

2006 Yu-Gi-Oh Cyberdark Impact 1st Edition

COMPLETE SET (60)	100.00	200.00
BOOSTER BOX (24 PACKS)	50.00	80.00
BOOSTER PACK (9 CARDS)	2.50	6.00
*UNLIMITED: .4X TO .8X 1ST EDITION		
RELEASED ON NOVEMBER 15, 2006		
CDIP1A Cyberdark Horn SR	1.25	3.00
CDIP1B Cyberdark Horn ULT	2.50	6.00
CDIP2A Cyberdark Edge SR	1.50	4.00
CDIP2B Cyberdark Edge ULT	4.00	10.00
CDIP3A Cyberdark Keel SR	1.25	3.00
CDIP3B Cyberdark Keel ULT	2.00	5.00
CDIP4 Cyber Ogre C	.10	.30
CDIP5A Cyber Esper SR	1.00	2.50
CDIP5B Cyber Esper ULT	1.00	2.50
CDIP6 Allure Queen LV3 C	.10	.30
CDIP7A Allure Queen LV5 R	.40	1.00
CDIP7B Allure Queen LV5 ULT	2.00	5.00
CDIP8A Allure Queen LV7 UR	2.00	5.00
CDIP8B Allure Queen LV7 ULT	6.00	15.00
CDIP9 Dark Lucius LV4 C	.10	.30
CDIP10A Dark Lucius LV6 R	.40	1.00
CDIP10B Dark Lucius LV6 ULT	1.00	2.50
CDIP11A Dark Lucius LV8 UR	1.00	2.50
CDIP11B Dark Lucius LV8 ULT	2.50	6.00
CDIP12 Stray Asmodian C	.10	.30
CDIP13 Abaki C	.10	.30
CDIP14 Flame Ogre C	.10	.30
CDIP15 Snipe Hunter C	.40	1.00
CDIP16 Blast Asmodian C	.10	.30
CDIP17 Vanity's Fiend ULT	25.00	50.00
CDIP17 Vanity's Fiend R	.40	1.00
CDIP18 Barrier Statue of the Abyss C	.10	.30
CDIP19 Barrier Statue of the Torrent C	.10	.30
CDIP20 Barrier Statue of the Inferno C	.10	.30
CDIP21 Barrier Statue of the Stormwinds C	.10	.30
CDIP22 Barrier Statue of the Drought C	.10	.30
CDIP23 Barrier Statue of the Heavens C	.10	.30
CDIP24A Vanity's Ruler R	3.00	8.00
CDIP24B Vanity's Ruler ULT	6.00	15.00
CDIP25A Iris, the Earth Mother R	.40	1.00
CDIP25B Iris, the Earth Mother ULT	1.00	2.50
CDIP26A Lightning Punisher R	.40	1.00
CDIP26B Lightning Punisher ULT	1.00	2.50
CDIP27 Queen's Bodyguard C	.10	.30
CDIP28 Combo Fighter C	.10	.30
CDIP29A Combo Master R	.40	1.00
CDIP29B Combo Master ULT	1.00	2.50
CDIP30 Man Beast of Ares C	.10	.30
CDIP31A Rampaging Rhynos R	.40	1.00
CDIP31B Rampaging Rhynos ULT	1.00	2.50
CDIP32A Storm Shooter SR	.60	1.50
CDIP32B Storm Shooter ULT	1.00	2.50
CDIP33 Alien Infiltrator C	.10	.30
CDIP34 Alien Mars C	.10	.30
CDIP35A Cyberdark Dragon UR	2.00	5.00
CDIP35B Cyberdark Dragon ULT	15.00	30.00
CDIP36A Cyber Ogre 2 UR	1.25	3.00
CDIP36B Cyber Ogre 2 ULT	3.00	8.00
CDIP37 Corruption Cell A C	.10	.30
CDIP38A Flash of the Forbidden Spell R	.40	1.00
CDIP38B Flash of the Forbidden Spell ULT	1.00	2.50
CDIP39 Ritual Foregone C	.10	.30
CDIP40 Instant Fusion C	2.50	6.00
CDIP41 Counter Cleaner C	.10	.30
CDIP42 Linear Accelerator Cannon C	.10	.30
CDIP43 Chain Strike C	.10	.30
CDIP44A Miraculous Rebirth R	.40	1.00
CDIP44B Miraculous Rebirth ULT	1.00	2.50
CDIP45 Mystical Wind Typhoon C	.10	.30
CDIP46 Level Down!? C	.10	.30
CDIP47A Degenerate Circuit R	.40	1.00
CDIP47B Degenerate Circuit ULT	1.00	2.50
CDIP48 Senet Switch C	.10	.30
CDIP49A Blasting Fuse R	.40	1.00
CDIP49B Blasting Fuse ULT	1.00	2.50
CDIP50 Straight Flush C	.10	.30
CDIP51 Justi-Break C	.10	.30
CDIP52A Dimensional Inversion R	.40	1.00
CDIP52B Dimensional Inversion ULT	1.00	2.50
CDIP53 Chain Healing C	.10	.30
CDIP54 Chain Detonation C	.10	.30
CDIP55 Byroad Sacrifice C	.10	.30
CDIP56A Trojan Blast SR	.60	1.50
CDIP56B Trojan Blast ULT	1.00	2.50
CDIP57 Accumulated Fortune C	.10	.30
CDIP58A Cyber Shadow Gardna SR	1.00	2.50
CDIP58B Cyber Shadow Gardna ULT	3.00	8.00
CDIP59 Vanity's Call C	.10	.30
CDIP60A Black Horn of Heaven R	.50	1.25
CDIP60B Black Horn of Heaven ULT	5.00	12.00

2007 Yu-Gi-Oh Strike of Neos 1st Edition

COMPLETE SET (94)	150.00	300.00
BOOSTER BOX (24 PACKS)	80.00	120.00
BOOSTER PACK (9 CARDS)	2.50	6.00
*UNLIMITED: .4X TO .8X 1ST EDITION		
RELEASED ON FEBRUARY 28, 2007		
STON1A Gene-Warped Warwolf SR	.75	2.00
STON1B Gene-Warped Warwolf UTR	1.50	4.00
STON2A Frostosaurus R	.40	1.00
STON2B Frostosaurus UTR	2.00	5.00
STON3A Spiral Serpent R	.40	1.00
STON3B Spiral Serpent UTR	1.00	2.50
STON4A Neo-Spacian Air Hummingbird SR	.75	2.00
STON4B Neo-Spacian Air Hummingbird UTR	2.50	6.00
STON5A Neo-Spacian Grand Mole R	.75	2.00
STON5B Neo-Spacian Grand Mole UTR	6.00	15.00
STON6 Neo-Spacian Glow Moss C	.10	.30
STON7 The Six Samurai - Yaichi C	.10	.30
STON8 The Six Samurai - Kamon C	.10	.30
STON9 The Six Samurai - Yariza C	.10	.30
STON10 The Six Samurai - Nisashi C	.10	.30
STON11 The Six Samurai - Zanji C	.10	.30
STON12 The Six Samurai - Irou C	.10	.30
STON13A Great Shogun Shien SR	.60	1.50
STON13B Great Shogun Shien UTR	3.00	8.00
STON14 Shien's Footsoldier C	.10	.30
STON15A Sage of Silence R	.40	1.00
STON15B Sage of Silence UTR	1.25	3.00
STON16 Sage of Stillness C	.10	.30
STON17A Reign-Beaux, Overlord of Dark World UR	1.00	2.50
STON17B Reign-Beaux, Overlord of Dark World UTR	2.00	5.00
STON18 Kahkki, Guerilla of Dark World C	.10	.30
STON19 Gren, Tactician of Dark World C	.10	.30
STON20A Fusion Devourer R	.40	1.00
STON20B Fusion Devourer UTR	1.00	2.50
STON21 Electric Virus C	.10	.30
STON22 Puppet Plant C	.10	.30
STON23 Marionette Mite C	.10	.30
STON24A D.D. Crow R	.40	1.00
STON24B D.D. Crow UTR	6.00	15.00
STON25 Silent Abyss C	.10	.30
STON26 Firestorm Prominence C	.10	.30
STON27 Raging Earth C	.10	.30
STON28 Destruction Cyclone C	.10	.30
STON29 Radiant Spirit C	.10	.30
STON30 Umbral Soul C	.10	.30
STON31 Alien Psychic C	.10	.30
STON32 Lycanthrope C	.10	.30
STON33 Cú Chulainn the Awakened C	.10	.30
STON34A Elemental Hero Air Neos UR	8.00	20.00
STON34B Elemental Hero Air Neos UTR	15.00	30.00
STON35A Elemental Hero Grand Neos UR	1.00	2.50
STON35B Elemental Hero Grand Neos UTR	5.00	12.00
STON36A Elemental Hero Glow Neos UR	1.50	4.00
STON36B Elemental Hero Glow Neos UTR	3.00	8.00
STON37A Ancient Rules R	2.00	5.00
STON37B Ancient Rules UTR	6.00	15.00
STON38A Dark World Dealings SR	2.00	5.00
STON38B Dark World Dealings UTR	8.00	20.00
STON39A Neos Force R	.40	1.00
STON39B Neos Force UTR	1.00	2.50
STON40 Legendary Ebon Steed C	.10	.30
STON41 A Cell Scatter Burst C	.10	.30
STON42A Twister R	.40	1.00
STON42B Twister UTR	2.50	6.00
STON43 Synthesis Spell C	.10	.30
STON44 Emblem of the Awakening C	.10	.30
STON45 Advanced Ritual Art C	.10	.30
STON46A Card Trader SR	.60	1.50
STON46B Card Trader UTR	1.25	3.00
STON47 Shien's Castle of Mist C	.10	.30
STON48A Skyscraper 2 - Hero City SR	1.25	3.00
STON48B Skyscraper 2 - Hero City UTR	2.00	5.00
STON49 Change of Hero - Reflector Ray C	.10	.30
STON50A Hero Medal R	.40	1.00
STON50B Hero Medal UTR	1.00	2.50
STON51 Return of the Six Samurai C	.10	.30
STON52A Eliminating the League R	.40	1.00
STON52B Eliminating the League UTR	1.00	2.50
STON53 Flashbang C	.10	.30
STON54A The Transmigration Prophecy R	.40	1.00
STON54B The Transmigration Prophecy UTR	2.00	5.00
STON55 Anti-Fusion Device C	.10	.30
STON56 Ritual Sealing C	.10	.30
STON57A Birthright SR	.60	1.50
STON57B Birthright UTR	1.00	2.50
STON58 Swift Samurai Storm!	.10	.30
STON59A Cloak and Dagger R	.40	1.00
STON59B Cloak and Dagger UTR	1.50	4.00
STON60A Pulling the Rug R	.40	1.00
STON60B Pulling the Rug UTR	2.00	5.00
STON61 Neo-Parshath, Sky Paladin SCR	2.00	5.00
STON62 Meltiel, Sage of the Sky SCR	4.00	10.00
STON63 Harvest Angel of Wisdom SCR	2.00	5.00
STON64 Freya, Spirit of Victory SCR	6.00	15.00
STON65 Nova Summoner SCR	2.50	6.00
STON66 Radiant Jeral SCR	1.50	4.00
STON67 Gellenduo SCR	5.00	12.00
STON68 Aegis of Gaia SCR	1.25	3.00
STONO Grandmaster of Six Samurai SCR	8.00	20.00

2007 Yu-Gi-Oh Force of the Breaker 1st Edition

COMPLETE SET (94)	150.00	400.00
BOOSTER BOX (24 PACKS)	140.00	200.00
BOOSTER PACK (9 CARDS)	2.50	6.00
*UNLIMITED: .4X TO .8X 1ST EDITION		
RELEASED ON MAY 16, 2007		
FOTB00 Volcanic Rocket SCR	15.00	30.00
FOTB01 Crystal Beast Ruby Carbuncle C	.20	.50
FOTB02 Crystal Beast Amethyst Cat C	.20	.50
FOTB03 Crystal Beast Emerald Tortoise C	.20	.50
FOTB04 Crystal Beast Topaz Tiger R	.60	1.50
FOTB04 Crystal Beast Topaz Tiger UTR	8.00	20.00
FOTB05 Crystal Beast Amber Mammoth C	.20	.50
FOTB06 Crystal Beast Cobalt Eagle C	.20	.50
FOTB07 Crystal Beast Sapphire Pegasus UR	2.00	5.00
FOTB07 Crystal Beast Sapphire Pegasus UTR	15.00	30.00
FOTB08 Volcanic Doomfire UTR	2.50	6.00
FOTB08 Volcanic Doomfire UR	1.25	3.00
FOTB09 Volcanic Shell UTR	5.00	12.00
FOTB09 Volcanic Shell R	1.50	4.00
FOTB10 Volcanic Scattershot C	.20	.50
FOTB11 Volcanic Blaster C	.20	.50
FOTB12 Volcanic Slicer UTR	2.50	6.00
FOTB12 Volcanic Slicer R	.60	1.50
FOTB13 Volcanic Hammerer C	.20	.50
FOTB14 Elemental Hero Captain Gold UTR	2.00	5.00
FOTB14 Elemental Hero Captain Gold UR	.75	2.00
FOTB15 Gravekeeper's Commandant R	.75	2.00
FOTB15 Gravekeeper's Commandant UTR	3.00	8.00
FOTB16 Warrior of Atlantis R	.40	1.00
FOTB16 Warrior of Atlantis UTR	1.25	3.00
FOTB17 Destroyersaurus R	.60	1.50
FOTB17 Destroyersaurus UTR	.75	2.00
FOTB18 Zeradias, Herald of Heaven R	.60	1.50
FOTB18 Zeradias, Herald of Heaven UTR	5.00	12.00
FOTB19 Archfiend General UTR	1.50	4.00
FOTB19 Archfiend General R	.75	2.00
FOTB20 Harpie Queen UTR	20.00	40.00
FOTB20 Harpie Queen R	1.50	4.00
FOTB21 Sky Scourge Enrise UTR	1.00	2.50
FOTB21 Sky Scourge Enrise SR	.60	1.50
FOTB22 Sky Scourge Norleras UTR	8.00	20.00
FOTB22 Sky Scourge Norleras SR	.60	1.50
FOTB23 Sky Scourge Invicil SR	.60	1.50
FOTB23 Sky Scourge Invicil UTR	1.25	3.00
FOTB24 Goe Goe the Gallant Ninja R	.40	1.00
FOTB24 Goe Goe the Gallant Ninja UTR	.75	2.00
FOTB25 Mei-Kou, Master of Barriers C	.20	.50
FOTB26 Raiza the Storm Monarch SR	1.25	3.00
FOTB26 Raiza the Storm Monarch UTR	6.00	15.00
FOTB27 Seismic Crasher C	.20	.50
FOTB28 Dweller in the Depths C	.20	.50
FOTB29 Magna-Slash Dragon C	.20	.50
FOTB30 Gravi-Crush Dragon C	.20	.50
FOTB31 Soul of Fire SR	.60	1.50
FOTB31 Soul of Fire UTR	.75	2.00
FOTB32 Crystal Beacon C	.20	.50
FOTB33 Rare Value UR	.75	2.00
FOTB33 Rare Value UTR	3.00	8.00
FOTB34 Crystal Blessing C	.20	.50
FOTB35 Crystal Abundance C	.20	.50
FOTB36 Crystal Promise C	.20	.50
FOTB37 Lucky Iron Axe UTR	1.00	2.50
FOTB37 Lucky Iron Axe R	.40	1.00
FOTB38 Tornado C	.20	.50
FOTB39 Wild Fire C	.20	.50
FOTB40 Blaze Accelerator C	.20	.50
FOTB41 Tri-Blaze Accelerator SR	1.00	2.50
FOTB41 Tri-Blaze Accelerator UTR	2.00	5.00
FOTB42 Field Barrier C	.20	.50
FOTB43 A Cell Breeding Device C	.20	.50
FOTB44 Otherworld - The A Zone C	.20	.50
FOTB45 Ancient City - Rainbow Ruins R	.40	1.00
FOTB45 Ancient City - Rainbow Ruins UTR	8.00	20.00
FOTB46 Triggered Summon R	.40	1.00
FOTB46 Triggered Summon UTR	1.00	2.50
FOTB47 Last Resort C	.20	.50
FOTB48 Crystal Raigeki C	.20	.50
FOTB49 Volcanic Recharge C	.20	.50
FOTB50 Terrible Deal C	.20	.50
FOTB51 Breakthrough! C	.20	.50
FOTB52 Backs to the Wall C	.20	.50
FOTB53 Introduction to Gallantry C	.20	.50
FOTB54 Secrets of the Gallant C	.20	.50
FOTB55 Radiant Mirror Force SR	.75	2.00
FOTB55 Radiant Mirror Force UTR	3.00	8.00
FOTB56 Hard-sellin' Goblin C	.20	.50
FOTB57 Hard-sellin' Zombie C	.20	.50
FOTB58 Mass Hypnosis C	.20	.50
FOTB59 Gem Flash Energy C	.20	.50
FOTB60 Firewall UTR	1.00	2.50
FOTB60 Firewall R	.40	1.00
FOTB61 Diabolos, King of the Abyss SCR	3.00	8.00
FOTB62 Lich Lord, King SCR	1.25	3.00
FOTB63 Prometheus, King of the Shadows SCR	1.50	4.00
FOTB64 Mist Archfield SCR	2.00	5.00
FOTB65 Plague Wolf SCR	1.00	2.50
FOTB66 Recurring Nightmare SCR	5.00	12.00
FOTB67 Sword of Dark Rites SCR	1.25	3.00
FOTB68 Eradicator Epidemic SCR	8.00	20.00

2007 Yu-Gi-Oh Tactical Evolution 1st Edition

COMPLETE SET (103)	150.00	300.00
BOOSTER BOX (24 PACKS)	80.00	120.00
BOOSTER PACK (9 CARDS)	2.50	6.00
*UNLIMITED: .4X TO .8X 1ST EDITION		
RELEASED ON AUGUST 15, 2007		
TAEV01 Alien Shocktrooper C	.10	.30
TAEV02 Volcanic Rat C	.10	.30
TAEV03 Renge Gatekeeper Dark World C	.10	.30
TAEV04 Hunter Dragon R	.40	1.00
TAEV05 Venom Cobra C	.10	.30
TAEV06 Rainbow Dragon SCR	6.00	15.00
TAEV06 Rainbow Dragon GR	40.00	80.00
TAEV07 Chrysalis Pantail C	.10	.30
TAEV08 Chrysalis Chicky C	.10	.30
TAEV09 Chrysalis Pinny C	.10	.30
TAEV10 Chrysalis Larva C	.10	.30
TAEV11 Chrysalis Mole C	.10	.30
TAEV12 Necro Gardna SR	.75	2.00
TAEV12 Necro Gardna UTR	2.50	6.00
TAEV13 Vennominaga Deity of Pois.Snakes SCR	30.00	60.00
TAEV14 Vennominon King of Pois.Snakes UR	.75	2.00
TAEV14 Vennominon King of Pois. Snakes UTR	2.00	5.00
TAEV15 Venom Snake C	.10	.30
TAEV16 Venom Boa C	.10	.30
TAEV17 Venom Serpent C	.10	.30
TAEV18 Elemental Hero Neos Alius UTR	4.00	10.00
TAEV18 Elemental Hero Neos Alius SR	1.00	2.50
TAEV19 Chthonian Emperor Dragon UR	1.25	3.00
TAEV19 Chthonian Emperor Dragon UTR	1.50	4.00
TAEV20 Aquarian Alessa SR	.60	1.50
TAEV20 Aquarian Alessa UTR	1.00	2.50
TAEV21 Lucky Pied Piper SR	1.50	4.00
TAEV21 Lucky Pied Piper UTR	1.00	2.50
TAEV22 Grasschopper R	.40	1.00
TAEV23 Goggle Golem C	.10	.30
TAEV24 Dawnbreak Gardna C	.10	.30
TAEV25 Doom Shaman UTR	1.00	2.50
TAEV25 Doom Shaman SR	.60	1.50
TAEV26 King Pyron C	.10	.30
TAEV27 Shadow Delver C	.10	.30
TAEV28 Flint Lock C	.10	.30
TAEV29 Gravitic Orb C	.10	.30
TAEV30 Phantom Cricket C	.10	.30
TAEV31 Crystal Seer UTR	.75	2.00
TAEV31 Crystal Seer UR	.75	2.00
TAEV32 Neo Space Pathfinder R	.60	1.50
TAEV33 Frost and Flame Dragon SCR	2.00	5.00
TAEV34 Desert Twister UTR	.75	2.00
TAEV34 Desert Twister UR	.75	2.00
TAEV35 Ritual Raven C	.10	.30
TAEV36 Razor Lizard C	.10	.30
TAEV37 Light Effigy C	.10	.30
TAEV38 Dark Effigy C	.10	.30
TAEV39 Zombie Master UTR	15.00	30.00
TAEV39 Zombie Master SR	1.25	3.00
TAEV40 Neo-Spacian Marine Dolphin C	.10	.30
TAEV41 Elemental Hero Marine Neos R	.40	1.00
TAEV42 Elemental Hero Darkbright UTR	4.00	10.00
TAEV42 Elemental Hero Darkbright UR	1.25	3.00
TAEV43 Elemental Hero Magma Neos SCR	8.00	20.00
TAEV44 Ojama Knight C	.10	.30
TAEV45 Fifth Hope UTR	1.50	4.00
TAEV45 Fifth Hope SR	.75	2.00
TAEV46 Reverse of Neos C	.10	.30
TAEV47 Convert Contract C	.10	.30
TAEV48 Cocoon Party C	.10	.30
TAEV49 NEX C	.10	.30
TAEV50 Cocoon Rebirth C	.10	.30
TAEV52 Snake Rain R	.75	2.00
TAEV53 Venom Shot C	.10	.30

Card	Low	High
TAEV54 Cyberdark Impact! SCR	15.00	30.00
TAEV55 Flint Missile C	.10	.30
TAEV56 Double Summon R	1.25	3.00
TAEV57 Summoner's Art R	.40	1.00
TAEV58 Creature Seizure C	.10	.30
TAEV59 Phalanx Pike R	1.25	3.00
TAEV60 Symbols of Duty R	.40	1.00
TAEV61 Amulet of Ambition C	.10	.30
TAEV62 Broken Bamboo Sword C	1.25	3.00
TAEV63 Mirror Gate UTR	1.00	2.50
TAEV63 Mirror Gate SR	.60	1.50
TAEV64 Hero Counterattack C	.10	.30
TAEV65 Cocoon Veil C	.10	.30
TAEV66 Snake Whistle C	.10	.30
TAEV67 Damage = Reptile R	.40	1.00
TAEV68 Snake Deity's Command R	.40	1.00
TAEV69 Rise of the Snake Deity C	.10	.30
TAEV70 Ambush Fangs C	.10	.30
TAEV71 Venom Burn C	.10	.30
TAEV72 Common Charity R	.40	1.00
TAEV73 Destructive Draw C	.10	.30
TAEV74 Shield Spear C	.10	.30
TAEV75 Strike Slash C	.10	.30
TAEV76 Spell Reclamation R	.40	1.00
TAEV77 Trap Reclamation R	.40	1.00
TAEV78 Gift Card C	1.50	4.00
TAEV79 The Gift of Greed C	.10	.30
TAEV80 Counter Counter C	.10	.30
TAEV81 Ocean's Keeper R	.40	1.00
TAEV82 Thousand-Eyes Jellyfish R	.40	1.00
TAEV83 Cranium Fish SCR	1.50	4.00
TAEV84 Abyssal Kingshark SCR	1.25	3.00
TAEV85 Mormolith SCR	.75	2.00
TAEV86 Fossil Tusker R	.40	1.00
TAEV87 Phantom Dragonray Bronto R	.40	1.00
TAEV88 Il Blud SCR	4.00	10.00
TAEV89 Blazewing Butterfly SR	.60	1.50
TAEV89 Blazewing Butterfly UTR	1.00	2.50
TAEV000 Gemini Summoner SCR	1.25	3.00
TAEV000 Gemini Summoner SR	2.00	5.00

2007 Yu-Gi-Oh Gladiator's Assault 1st Edition

Card	Low	High
COMPLETE SET (110)	300.00	600.00
BOOSTER BOX (24 PACKS)	125.00	200.00
BOOSTER PACK (9 CARDS)	2.50	6.00
*UNLIMITED: .4X TO .8X 1ST EDITION		
RELEASED ON NOVEMBER 14, 2007		
GLAS0 Gladiator Beast Octavius SCR	1.50	4.00
GLAS1 Chamberlain of Six Samurai C	.20	.50
GLAS2 Cloudian Smoke Ball C	.20	.50
GLAS3 Evil Hero Malicious Edge UTR	2.00	5.00
GLAS3 Evil Hero Malicious Edge SR	.60	1.50
GLAS4 Evil Hero Infernal Gainer R	.40	1.00
GLAS5 Cloudian Eye of Typhoon SR	.60	1.50
GLAS5 Cloudian Eye of Typhoon UTR	1.00	2.50
GLAS6 Cloudian Ghost Fog C	.20	.50
GLAS7 Cloudian Nimbusman C	.20	.50
GLAS8 Cloudian Sheep Cloud SR	.60	1.50
GLAS8 Cloudian Sheep Cloud UTR	1.00	2.50
GLAS9 Cloudian Poison Cloud C	.20	.50
GLAS10 Cloudian Acid Cloud R	.40	1.00
GLAS11 Cloudian Cirrostratus R	.75	2.00
GLAS12 Cloudian Altus R	.40	1.00
GLAS13 Cloudian Turbulence C	.20	.50
GLAS14 Truckroid C	.20	.50
GLAS15 Stealthroid C	.20	.50
GLAS16 Expressroid R	.40	1.00
GLAS17 Gladiator Beast Alexander SR	.60	1.50
GLAS17 Gladiator Beast Alexander UTR	1.00	2.50
GLAS18 Gladiator Beast Spartacus R	.40	1.00
GLAS19 Gladiator Beast Murmillo R	.40	1.00
GLAS20 Gladiator Beast Bestiari C	.20	.50
GLAS21 Gladiator Beast Laquari R	.60	1.50
GLAS22 Gladiator Beast Hoplomus C	.20	.50
GLAS23 Gladiator Beast Dimacari C	.20	.50
GLAS24 Gladiator Beast Secutor C	.20	.50
GLAS25 Test Ape C	.20	.50
GLAS26 Witch Doctor of Sparta C	.20	.50
GLAS27 Infinity Dark C	.20	.50
GLAS28 Magical Reflect Slime C	.20	.50
GLAS29 Ancient Gear Knight C	.20	.50
GLAS30 Goblin Black Ops R	.40	1.00
GLAS31 Gambler of Legend C	.20	.50
GLAS32 Enishi, Shiens Chancellor UR	.75	2.00
GLAS32 Enishi, Shiens Chancellor UTR	1.50	4.00
GLAS33 Spirit of the Six Samurai C	.20	.50
GLAS34 Alien Telepath R	.40	1.00
GLAS35 Alien Hypno C	.20	.50
GLAS36 Elemental Hero Chaos Neos GR	8.00	20.00
GLAS36 Elemental Hero Chaos Neos SCR	2.00	5.00
GLAS36 Elemental Hero Chaos Neos (Rainbow Dragon Err) GR	100.00	150.00
GLAS37 Elemental Hero Plasma Vice SCR	2.50	6.00
GLAS38 Evil Hero Inferno Wing UR	.75	2.00
GLAS38 Evil Hero Inferno Wing UTR	2.00	5.00
GLAS39 Evil Hero Lightning Golem UR	.75	2.00
GLAS39 Evil Hero Lightning Golem UTR	1.25	3.00
GLAS40 Evil Hero Dark Gaia R	.40	1.00
GLAS41 Super Vehicroid Stealth Union SCR	4.00	10.00
GLAS42 Superalloy Beast Raptinus C	.20	.50
GLAS43 Gladiator Beast Gaiodiaz R	.20	.50
GLAS44 Gladiator Beast Heraklinos SCR	4.00	10.00
GLAS45 Contact Out C	.20	.50
GLAS46 Swing of Memories C	.20	.50
GLAS47 Dark Fusion R	1.50	4.00
GLAS48 Diamond-Dust Cyclone R	.40	1.00
GLAS49 Summon Cloud C	.20	.50
GLAS50 Lucky Cloud C	.20	.50
GLAS51 Fog Control C	.20	.50
GLAS52 Cloudian Squall C	.20	.50
GLAS53 Super Double Summon C	.20	.50
GLAS54 Colosseum Cage Gladiatr Beasts R	1.25	3.00
GLAS55 Glad Beasts Bttle Halberd C	.20	.50
GLAS56 Glad. Beasts Battle Gladius C	.20	.50
GLAS57 Glad.Beasts Battle Manica R	.40	1.00
GLAS58 Gladiator Beasts Respite R	.40	1.00
GLAS59 Gladiators Return C	.20	.50
GLAS60 Soul Devouring Bamboo Sword C	.20	.50
GLAS61 Cunning of the Six Samurai UTR	1.50	4.00
GLAS61 Cunning of the Six Samurai SR	.60	1.50
GLAS62 A Cell Incubator C	.20	.50
GLAS63 Over Limit C	.20	.50
GLAS64 No Entry!! C	.20	.50
GLAS65 Natural Disaster C	.20	.50
GLAS66 Rain Storm C	.20	.50
GLAS67 Updraft UTR	1.00	2.50
GLAS67 Updraft SR	.60	1.50
GLAS68 Release from Stone C	.20	.50
GLAS69 Light-Imprisoning Mirror C	.60	1.50
GLAS70 Shadow-Imprisoning Mirror C	.60	1.50
GLAS71 Disarm C	.20	.50
GLAS72 Parry C	.20	.50
GLAS73 Swiftstrike Armor C	.20	.50
GLAS74 DoubleEdged Sword Tech C	.20	.50
GLAS75 Energy-Absorbing Monolith UTR	1.00	2.50
GLAS75 Energy-Absorbing Monolith SR	.60	1.50
GLAS76 Cell Explosion Virus R	.40	1.00
GLAS77 Detonator Circle A C	.20	.50
GLAS78 Interdimensional Warp C	.20	.50
GLAS79 Foolish Revival C	.20	.50
GLAS80 An Unfortunate Report C	.20	.50
GLAS81 Gladiator Beast Torax UTR	1.00	2.50
GLAS81 Gladiator Beast Torax SR	.60	1.50
GLAS82 Test Tiger UR	.75	2.00
GLAS82 Test Tiger UTR	4.00	10.00
GLAS83 Defensive Tactics SR	.60	1.50
GLAS83 Defensive Tactics UTR	1.00	2.50
GLAS84 Dragon Ice SCR	4.00	10.00
GLAS85 Tongue Twister SCR	4.00	10.00
GLAS86 Skreech SCR	1.50	4.00
GLAS87 Royal Firestorm Guards SCR	15.00	30.00
GLAS88 Veil of Darkness SCR	2.00	5.00
GLAS89 Security Orb UTR	25.00	50.00
GLAS89 Security Orb UR	.75	2.00
GLAS90 Necroface SCR	40.00	80.00
GLAS91 Gil Garth SCR	8.00	20.00
GLAS92 Soul Taker SCR	20.00	40.00
GLAS93 Magic Formula SCR	40.00	80.00
GLAS94 Silent Doom SCR	15.00	30.00

2008 Yu-Gi-Oh Phantom Darkness 1st Edition

Card	Low	High
COMPLETE SET (109)	200.00	400.00
BOOSTER BOX (24 PACKS)	300.00	500.00
BOOSTER PACK (9 CARDS)	3.00	8.00
*UNLIMITED: .4X TO .8X 1ST EDITION		
RELEASED ON FEBRUARY 13, 2008		
PTDN0 Dark Grepher SCR	6.00	15.00
PTDN2 Atlantean Pikeman C	.10	.30
PTDN3 Rainbow Dark Dragon SCR	5.00	12.00
PTDN4 Samsara Lotus C	.10	.30
PTDN5 Regenerating Rose C	.10	.30
PTDN6 Yubel SR	1.00	2.50
PTDN7 Yubel - Terror Incarnate UTR	1.25	3.00
PTDN7 Yubel - Terror Incarnate UR	1.00	2.50
PTDN8 Yubel - The Ultimate Nightmare SCR	4.00	10.00
PTDN9 Armored Cybern C	.10	.30
PTDN10 Cyber Valley SR	1.00	2.50
PTDN11 Cyber Ouroboros C	.10	.30
PTDN12 Volcanic Counter SR	.60	1.50
PTDN13 Fire Trooper C	.10	.30
PTDN14 Destiny Hero - Dunker C	.10	.30
PTDN15 Destiny Hero - Departed C	.10	.30
PTDN16 Dark Horus UR	1.00	2.50
PTDN16 Dark Horus UTR	1.25	3.00
PTDN17 The Dark Creator SCR	3.00	8.00
PTDN18 Dark Nephthys UR	.75	2.00
PTDN18 Dark Nephthys UTR	1.00	2.50
PTDN19 Dark Armed Dragon SCR	25.00	50.00
PTDN20 Dark Crusader C	.10	.30
PTDN21 Armageddon Knight SR	1.50	4.00
PTDN22 Doomsday Horror SR	.60	1.50
PTDN23 Obsidian Dragon C	.10	.30
PTDN24 Shadowpriestess of Ohm R	.40	1.00
PTDN25 Gemini Lancer C	.10	.30
PTDN26 Gigaplant R	2.00	5.00
PTDN27 Future Samurai R	.40	1.00
PTDN28 Vengeful Shinobi C	.10	.30
PTDN29 The Immortal Bushi C	.10	.30
PTDN30 Field-Commander Rahz SR	.60	1.50
PTDN31 Gladiator Beast Darius C	.10	.30
PTDN32 Imprisoned Queen Archfiend C	.10	.30
PTDN33 Black Veloci C	.10	.30
PTDN34 Superancient Deepsea King Coelacanth UR	.75	2.00
PTDN34 Superancient Deepsea King Coelacanth UTR	1.25	3.00
PTDN35 Cannon Soldier MK-2 C	.10	.30
PTDN36 The Calculator C	.10	.30
PTDN37 Sea Koala C	.10	.30
PTDN38 Blue Thunder T-45 C	.10	.30
PTDN39 Magnetic Mosquito C	.10	.30
PTDN40 Earth Effigy C	.10	.30
PTDN41 Wind Effigy C	.10	.30
PTDN42 Neo-Spacian Twinkle Moss C	.10	.30
PTDN43 Elemental Hero Storm Neos SR	.75	2.00
PTDN44 Rainbow Neos GR	10.00	25.00
PTDN44 Rainbow Neos SCR	3.00	8.00
PTDN45 Rainbow Veil C	.10	.30
PTDN46 Super Polymerization R	.75	2.00
PTDN47 Vicious Claw C	.10	.30
PTDN48 Instant Neo Space C	.10	.30
PTDN49 Mirage Tube C	.10	.30
PTDN50 Spell Chronicle C	.10	.30
PTDN51 Dimension Explosion C	.10	.30
PTDN52 Cybernetic Zone C	.10	.30
PTDN53 The Beginning of the End UR	.75	2.00
PTDN53 The Beginning of the End UTR	2.50	6.00
PTDN54 Dark Eruption SR	.75	2.00
PTDN55 Fires of Doomsday R	1.25	3.00
PTDN56 Unleash Your Power! C	.10	.30
PTDN57 Chain Summoning C	.10	.30
PTDN58 Acidic Downpour C	.10	.30
PTDN59 Six Samurai United R	.75	2.00
PTDN60 Gladiator Beast's Battle Archi.Shield C	.10	.30
PTDN61 Gladiator Proving Ground C	.10	.30
PTDN62 Dark World Grimoire C	.10	.30
PTDN63 Rainbow Path C	.10	.30
PTDN64 Rainbow Life R	.75	2.00
PTDN65 Sinister Seeds C	.10	.30
PTDN66 Hate Buster R	.40	1.00
PTDN67 Chain Material C	.10	.30
PTDN68 Alchemy Cycle C	.10	.30
PTDN69 Cybernetic Hidden Technology C	.10	.30
PTDN70 Dark Spirit Art - Greed R	.40	1.00
PTDN71 Dark Illusion R	1.00	2.50
PTDN72 Escape from Dark Dimension SR	1.50	4.00
PTDN73 Gemini Trap Hole C	.10	.30
PTDN74 Drastic Drop Off UTR	6.00	15.00
PTDN74 Drastic Drop Off UR	1.25	3.00
PTDN75 All-Out Attacks C	.10	.30
PTDN76 Double Tag Team C	.10	.30
PTDN77 Offering to the Snake Deity R	.40	1.00
PTDN78 Cry Havoc! R	.40	1.00
PTDN79 Transmigration Break C	.10	.30
PTDN80 Fine C	.10	.30
PTDN81 Darklord Zerato SCR	2.00	5.00
PTDN82 Darknight Parshath UTR	1.00	2.50
PTDN82 Darknight Parshath UR	.75	2.00
PTDN83 Deepsea Macrotrema R	.40	1.00
PTDN84 Allure of Darkness UR	8.00	20.00
PTDN84 Allure of Darkness UTR	30.00	60.00
PTDN85 Metabo Globster R	.40	1.00
PTDN86 Golden Flying Fish SR	.60	1.50
PTDN87 Prime Material Dragon SR	1.00	2.50
PTDN88 Lonefire Blossom R	1.50	4.00
PTDN89 Aztekipede, the Worm Warrior R	.40	1.00
PTDN90 Vampire's Curse UTR	1.00	2.50
PTDN90 Vampire's Curse UR	1.00	2.50
PTDN91 Castle Gate R	.40	1.00
PTDN92 Dark-Eyes Illusionist R	.40	1.00
PTDN93 Legendary Fiend R	.40	1.00
PTDN94 Metal Reflect Slime UTR	2.50	6.00
PTDN94 Metal Reflect Slime UR	2.00	5.00
PTDN95 Zoma the Spirit SR	.75	2.00
PTDN96 Call of the Earthbound R	.40	1.00
PTDN97 Dark Red Enchanter SCR	3.00	8.00
PTDN98 Goblin Zombie SCR	8.00	20.00
PTDN99 Belial Marquis of Darkness SCR	1.50	4.00

2008 Yu-Gi-Oh Light of Destruction 1st Edition

Card	Low	High
COMPLETE SET (100)	150.00	400.00
BOOSTER BOX (24 PACKS)	200.00	400.00
BOOSTER PACK (9 CARDS)	3.00	8.00
*UNLIMITED: .4X TO .8X 1ST EDITION		
RELEASED ON MAY 13, 2008		
LODT1 Honest SCR	10.00	25.00
LODT1 Honest GR	30.00	60.00
LODT2 Cross Porter C	.10	.30
LODT3 Miracle Flipper C	.10	.30
LODT4 Destiny Hero - Dread Servant C	.10	.30
LODT5 Volcanic Queen C	.75	2.00
LODT6 Jinzo - Returner R	1.50	4.00
LODT7 Jinzo - Lord SR	1.50	4.00
LODT8 Arcana Force 0 - The Fool C	.10	.30
LODT9 Arcana Force I - The Magician C	.10	.30
LODT00 Guardian of Order SCR	4.00	10.00
LODT10 Arcana Force III - The Empress C	.10	.30
LODT11 Arcana Force IV - The Emperor C	.10	.30
LODT12 Arcana Force VI - The Lovers C	.10	.30
LODT13 Arcana Force VII - The Chariot C	.10	.30
LODT14 Arcana Force XIV - Temperance R	.40	1.00
LODT15 Arcana Force XVIII - The Moon C	.10	.30
LODT16 Arcana Force XXI - The World UR	1.50	4.00
LODT16 Arcana Force XXI - The World UTR	2.50	6.00
LODT17 Arcana Force EX - The Dark Ruler SCR	2.00	5.00
LODT19 Lyla, Lightsworn Sorceress UTR	8.00	20.00
LODT19 Lyla, Lightsworn Sorceress UR	3.00	8.00
LODT20 Garoth, Lightsworn Warrior C	.10	.30
LODT21 Lumina, Lightsworn Summoner R	.40	1.00
LODT22 Ryko, Lightsworn Hunter SR	.40	1.00
LODT23 Wulf, Lightsworn Beast SR	.40	1.00
LODT24 Celestia, Lightsworn Angel UR	.75	2.00
LODT24 Celestia, Lightsworn Angel UTR	1.50	4.00
LODT25 Gragonith, Lightsworn Dragon C	.10	.30
LODT26 Judgment Dragon SCR	15.00	30.00
LODT27 Dark Valkyria R	.40	1.00
LODT28 Substitoad R	.30	.75
LODT29 Unifrog C	.10	.30
LODT30 Batteryman Charger C	.10	.30
LODT31 Batteryman Industrial Strength R	.50	1.25
LODT32 Batteryman Micro-Cell C	.10	.30
LODT33 Goblin Recon Squad C	.10	.30
LODT34 Interplanetary Invader A C	.10	.30
LODT35 Diskblade Rider R	.40	1.00
LODT36 Golden Ladybug R	1.25	3.00
LODT37 DUCKER Mobile Cannon SR	.75	2.00
LODT38 The Lady in Wight C	.10	.30
LODT39 Simorgh, Bird of Ancestry R	.40	1.00
LODT40 Cloudian - Storm Dragon C	.10	.30
LODT41 Phantom Dragon UTR	.40	1.00
LODT41 Phantom Dragon UR	.40	1.00
LODT42 Destiny End Dragoon UR	1.25	3.00
LODT42 Destiny End Dragoon UTR	2.50	6.00
LODT43 Ultimate Ancient Gear Golem UTR	5.00	12.00
LODT43 Ultimate Ancient Gear Golem UR	5.00	12.00
LODT44 Gladiator Beast Gyzarus SR	.40	1.00
LODT45 Hero Mask C	.10	.30
LODT46 Space Gift C	.10	.30
LODT47 Demise of the Land C	.60	1.50
LODT48 D - Formation C	.10	.30
LODT49 Spell Gear C	.10	.30
LODT50 Cup of Ace C	.40	1.00
LODT51 Light Barrier R	.20	.30
LODT52 Solar Recharge UTR	8.00	20.00
LODT52 Solar Recharge UR	2.00	5.00
LODT53 Realm of Light C	.10	.30
LODT54 Wetlands C	.75	2.00
LODT55 Quick Charger C	.10	.30
LODT56 Short Circuit C	.10	.30
LODT57 Light of Redemption SR	.40	1.00
LODT58 Mystical Cards of Light C	.20	.30
LODT59 Level Tuning C	.20	.30
LODT60 Deck Lockdown R	.75	2.00
LODT61 Ribbon of Rebirth R	.20	.50
LODT62 Golden Bamboo Sword C	1.50	4.00
LODT63 Limit Reverse C	.10	.30
LODT64 Hero Blast R	.20	.50
LODT65 Rainbow Gravity C	.10	.30
LODT66 D - Fortune C	.10	.30
LODT67 Reversal of Fate C	.10	.30
LODT68 Tour of Doom C	.20	.30
LODT69 Arcana Call C	.10	.30
LODT70 Light Spiral C	.50	1.25
LODT71 Glorious Illusion R	.20	.50
LODT72 Destruction Jammer R	1.25	3.00
LODT73 Froggy Forcefield R	.20	.50
LODT74 Portable Battery Pack C	.10	.30
LODT75 Gladiator Lash C	.10	.30
LODT76 Raging Cloudian C	.10	.30
LODT77 Sanguine Swamp C	.10	.30
LODT78 Lucky Chance C	.10	.30
LODT79 Summon Limit C	.10	.30
LODT80 Dice Try! C	.10	.30
LODT81 Aurkus, Lightsworn Druid SR	.75	2.00
LODT82 Ehren, Lightsworn Monk SCR	4.00	10.00
LODT83 Dark General Freed SCR	1.25	3.00
LODT84 Magical Exemplar SR	1.25	3.00
LODT85 Maniacal Servant R	.20	.50
LODT86 Nimble Musasabi R	.20	.50
LODT87 Flame Spirit Ignis R	.20	.50
LODT88 Super-Ancient Dinobeast UTR	1.25	3.00
LODT88 Super-Ancient Dinobeast UR	1.25	3.00
LODT89 Vanquishing Light SR	.60	1.50
LODT90 Tualatin SCR	2.00	5.00
LODT91 Divine Knight Ishzark SR	.40	1.00
LODT92 Angel 07 SCR	2.00	5.00
LODT93 Union Attack SR	.60	1.50
LODT94 Owner's Seal R	4.00	10.00
LODT95 Helios Trice Megistus SR	.60	1.50
LODT96 Dangerous Machine Type-6 UTR	.40	1.00
LODT96 Dangerous Machine Type-6 UR	.40	1.00
LODT97 Maximum Six UTR	.40	1.00
LODT97 Maximum Six UR	.40	1.00
LODT98 Fog King SCR	10.00	25.00
LODT99 Fossil Dyna Pachycephalo SCR	6.00	15.00

2008 Yu-Gi-Oh The Duelist Genesis 1st Edition

Card	Low	High
COMPLETE SET (100)	200.00	400.00
BOOSTER BOX (24 PACKS)	70.00	100.00
BOOSTER PACK (9 CARDS)	3.00	8.00
*UNLIMITED: .4X TO .8X 1ST EDITION		
RELEASED ON SEPTEMBER 2, 2008		
TDGS000 Avenging Knight Parshath SCR	1.50	4.00
TDGS001 Turbo Booster C	.10	.30
TDGS002 Nitro Synchron SR	.40	1.00
TDGS003 Quillbolt Hedgehog C	.10	.30
TDGS004 Ghost Gardna C	.10	.30
TDGS005 Shield Warrior R	.40	1.00
TDGS006 Small Piece Golem C	.10	.30
TDGS007 Medium Piece Golem C	.10	.30
TDGS008 Big Piece Golem R	.40	1.00
TDGS009 Sinister Sprocket SR	.30	.75
TDGS010 Dark Resonator R	.40	1.00
TDGS011 Twin-Shield Defender C	.10	.30
TDGS012 Jutte Fighter C	.10	.30
TDGS013 Handcuffs Dragon R	.40	1.00
TDGS014 Montage Dragon UR	1.50	4.00
TDGS014 Montage Dragon UTR	2.50	6.00
TDGS015 Gonogo C	.10	.30
TDGS016 Mind Master R	.40	1.00
TDGS017 Doctor Cranium C	.10	.30
TDGS018 Krebons C	.10	.30
TDGS019 Mind Protector C	.10	.30
TDGS020 Psychic Commander C	.50	1.25
TDGS021 Psychic Snail C	.10	.30
TDGS022 Telekinetic Shocker C	.10	.30
TDGS023 Destructotron C	.10	.30
TDGS024 Gladiator Beast Equeste C	.10	.30
TDGS025 Jenis, Lightsworn Mender C	.50	1.25
TDGS026 Dharc the Dark Charmer C	.10	.30
TDGS027 Mecha Bunny C	.10	.30
TDGS028 Oyster Meister C	.10	.30
TDGS029 Twin-Barrel Dragon SR	.30	.75
TDGS030 Izanagi SR	.30	.75
TDGS031 Kunoichi C	.10	.30
TDGS032 Beast of the Pharaoh C	.10	.30
TDGS033 Dark Hunter UTR	.75	2.00
TDGS033 Dark Hunter UR	.40	1.00
TDGS034 Kinka-byo SR	2.50	6.00
TDGS035 Yamato-no-Kami R	.40	1.00
TDGS036 Silent Strider C	.10	.30
TDGS037 Noisy Gnat C	.10	.30
TDGS038 Multiple Piece Golem UR	.40	1.00
TDGS038 Multiple Piece Golem UTR	.75	2.00
TDGS039 Nitro Warrior UR	.50	1.25
TDGS039 Nitro Warrior UTR	1.00	2.50
TDGS040 Stardust Dragon GR	70.00	100.00
TDGS040 Stardust Dragon UR	3.00	8.00
TDGS040 Stardust Dragon UTR	15.00	30.00
TDGS041 Red Dragon Archfiend UR	3.00	8.00
TDGS041 Red Dragon Archfiend UTR	4.00	10.00
TDGS042 Goyo Guardian UTR	6.00	15.00
TDGS042 Goyo Guardian UR	2.50	6.00
TDGS043 Magical Android SR	1.25	3.00
TDGS044 Thought Ruler Archfiend UR	2.00	5.00
TDGS044 Thought Ruler Archfiend UTR	4.00	10.00
TDGS045 Fighting Spirit R	.40	1.00
TDGS046 Domino Effect C	.10	.30
TDGS047 Junk Barrage C	.10	.30
TDGS048 Battle Tuned C	.10	.30
TDGS049 De-Synchro R	.40	1.00
TDGS050 Lightwave Tuning C	.10	.30
TDGS051 Psi-Station C	.10	.30
TDGS052 Psi-Impulse C	.10	.30
TDGS053 Emergency Teleport UR	5.00	12.00
TDGS053 Emergency Teleport UTR	20.00	40.00
TDGS054 Sword of Kusanagi C	.10	.30
TDGS055 Orb of Yasaka C	.40	1.00
TDGS056 Mirror of Yata C	.10	.30
TDGS057 Geartown C	.10	.30
TDGS058 Power Filter SR	.50	1.25
TDGS059 Lightsworn Sabre SR	1.00	2.50
TDGS060 Unstable Evolution SR	.30	.75
TDGS061 Recycling Batteries	.40	1.00
TDGS062 Book of Eclipse C	.40	1.00
TDGS063 Equip Shot C	.10	.30
TDGS064 Graceful Revival R	.40	1.00
TDGS065 Defense Draw R	.40	1.00
TDGS066 Remote Revenge C	.10	.30
TDGS067 Spacegate C	.10	.30
TDGS068 Synchro Deflector C	.10	.30
TDGS069 Broken Blocker SR	.30	.75
TDGS070 Psychic Overload UTR	1.50	4.00
TDGS070 Psychic Overload UR	.40	1.00
TDGS071 Psychic Rejuvenation C	.10	.30
TDGS072 Telepathic Power C	.10	.30
TDGS073 Mind Over Matter R	.40	1.00
TDGS074 Gladiator Beast War Chariot SR	.75	2.00
TDGS075 Lightsworn Barrier C	.10	.30
TDGS076 Intercept SR	2.50	6.00
TDGS077 Judgment of Thunder C	.10	.30
TDGS078 Fish Depth Charge C	.10	.30
TDGS079 Needlebug Nest C	.60	1.50
TDGS080 Overworked C	.10	.30
TDGS081 Counselor Lily SR	.40	1.00
TDGS082 Herald of Orange Light R	.40	1.00
TDGS083 Izanami R	.40	1.00
TDGS084 Maiden of Macabre R	.40	1.00
TDGS085 Hand of the Six Samurai SCR	1.25	3.00
TDGS086 Cyber Shark SCR	1.25	3.00
TDGS087 Grapple Blocker R	.40	1.00
TDGS088 Telekinetic Charging Cell R	.40	1.00
TDGS089 Charge of the Light Brigade SCR	20.00	40.00
TDGS090 The Tricky R	.40	1.00
TDGS091 Tricky Spell 4 C	.10	.30
TDGS092 Trap of Darkness R	.40	1.00
TDGS093 The Selection R	.40	1.00
TDGS094 Splendid Venus SCR	1.25	3.00
TDGS095 Fiendish Engine W SCR	.50	1.25
TDGS096 Cold Enchanter R	.40	1.00
TDGS097 Ice Master SCR	1.50	4.00
TDGS098 Kunai with Chain SR	.40	1.00
TDGS099 Toy Magician SCR	1.50	4.00
TDGSSE2 Gladiator Beast Heraklinos SR	.30	.75
TDGSSP1 Avenging Knight Parshath SR	2.00	5.00

2008 Yu-Gi-Oh Crossroads of Chaos 1st Edition

Card	Low	High
COMPLETE SET (111)	200.00	400.00
BOOSTER BOX (24 PACKS)	80.00	120.00
BOOSTER PACK (9 CARDS)	2.50	6.00
*UNLIMITED: .4X TO .8X 1ST EDITION	.40	1.00
RELEASED ON NOVEMBER 18, 2009		
CSOC0 Rose, Warrior of Revenge UR	2.00	5.00
CSOC0 Rose, Warrior of Revenge UTR	2.50	6.00
CSOC1 Healing Wave Generator C	.10	.30
CSOC2 Turbo Synchron R	1.00	2.50
CSOC3 Mad Archfiend R	.75	2.00
CSOC4 Wall of Ivy C	.10	.30
CSOC5 Copy Plant C	.10	.30
CSOC6 Morphtronic Celfon C	.10	.30
CSOC7 Morphtronic Magnen C	.10	.30
CSOC8 Morphtronic Datatron C	.10	.30
CSOC9 Morphtronic Boomboxen R	.60	1.50
CSOC10 Morphtronic Cameran C	.10	.30
CSOC11 Morphtronic Radion R	.75	2.00
CSOC12 Morphtronic Clocken C	.10	.30
CSOC13 Gadget Hauler C	.10	.30
CSOC14 Gadget Driver C	.10	.30
CSOC15 Search Striker R	.75	2.00
CSOC16 Pursuit Chaser C	.10	.30
CSOC17 Iron Chain Repairman R	.60	1.50
CSOC18 Iron Chain Snake C	.10	.30
CSOC19 Iron Chain Blaster C	.10	.30
CSOC20 Iron Chain Coil C	.10	.30
CSOC21 Power Injector C	.10	.30
CSOC22 Storm Caller R	.75	2.00
CSOC23 Psychic Jumper C	.10	.30
CSOC24 Nettles C	.10	.30
CSOC25 Gigantic Cephalotus C	.10	.30
CSOC26 Horseytail C	.10	.30
CSOC27 Botanical Girl C	.10	.30
CSOC28 Cursed Fig C	.10	.30
CSOC29 Tytannial, Princess of Camellias UTR	1.50	4.00
CSOC29 Tytannial, Princess of Camellias UR	4.00	10.00
CSOC30 Zombie Mammoth C	.10	.30
CSOC31 Plaguespreader Zombie UR	2.00	5.00
CSOC31 Plaguespreader Zombie UTR	10.00	25.00
CSOC32 Goblin Decoy Squad C	.10	.30
CSOC33 Comrade Swordsman of Landstar C	.10	.30
CSOC34 Hanewata SR	1.25	3.00
CSOC35 The White Stone of Legend C	.50	1.25
CSOC36 Tiger Dragon R	1.25	3.00
CSOC37 Jade Knight C	.10	.30
CSOC38 Turbo Warrior UR	3.00	8.00

CSOC38 Turbo Warrior UTR 1.00 2.50
CSOC39 Black Rose Dragon GR 70.00 110.00
CSOC39 Black Rose Dragon UR 4.00 10.00
CSOC39 Black Rose Dragon UTR 15.00 30.00
CSOC40 Iron Chain Dragon R 1.50 4.00
CSOC41 Psychic Lifetrancer R 1.50 4.00
CSOC42 Queen of Thorns SR 2.00 5.00
CSOC43 Doomkaiser Dragon UR 1.50 4.00
CSOC43 Doomkaiser Dragon UTR 2.50 6.00
CSOC44 Revived King Ha Des UR 2.00 5.00
CSOC44 Revived King Ha Des UTR 3.00 8.00
CSOC45 Card Rotator C .10 .30
CSOC46 Seed of Deception C .10 .30
CSOC47 Mark of the Rose UR 1.50 4.00
CSOC47 Mark of the Rose UTR 1.50 4.00
CSOC48 Black Garden SR 1.25 3.00
CSOC49 Factory of 100 Machines C .10 .30
CSOC50 Morphtronic Accelerator R .60 1.50
CSOC51 Morphtronic Cord C .10 .30
CSOC52 Morphtronic Engine C .10 .30
CSOC53 Poison Chain C .10 .30
CSOC54 Paralyzing Chain R .60 1.50
CSOC55 Teleport C .10 .30
CSOC56 Psychokinesis UR 1.50 4.00
CSOC56 Psychokinesis UTR 1.00 2.50
CSOC57 Miracle Fertilizer R .75 2.00
CSOC58 Fragrance Storm C .10 .30
CSOC59 The World Tree R .75 2.00
CSOC60 Everliving Underworld Cannon C .10 .30
CSOC61 Secret Village of the Spellcasters SR 10.00 25.00
CSOC62 Omega Goggles C .10 .30
CSOC63 Battle Mania SR .75 2.00
CSOC64 Confusion Chaff C .10 .30
CSOC65 Urgent Tuning SR 1.25 3.00
CSOC66 Synchro Strike C .10 .30
CSOC67 Prideful Roar R .75 2.00
CSOC68 Revival Gift C .10 .30
CSOC69 Lineage of Destruction C .10 .30
CSOC70 Doppelganger C .10 .30
CSOC71 Morphtransition C .10 .30
CSOC72 Morphtronic Monitron C .10 .30
CSOC73 Psychic Trigger SR 1.00 2.50
CSOC74 Pollinosis R .40 1.00
CSOC75 Bamboo Scrap C .10 .30
CSOC76 Plant Food Chain C .10 .30
CSOC77 Trap of the Imperial Tomb R .40 1.00
CSOC78 DNA Checkup C .10 .30
CSOC79 Gozen Match C .50 1.25
CSOC80 Giant Trap Hole C .10 .30
CSOC81 Seed of Flame UR 1.50 4.00
CSOC81 Seed of Flame UTR 3.00 8.00
CSOC82 Cactus Fighter R .60 1.50
CSOC83 Overdrive Teleporter SCR 10.00 25.00
CSOC84 Rai-Jin SR .75 2.00
CSOC85 Rai-Mei SR 2.00 5.00
CSOC86 Gladiator Beast Retiari SCR 2.50 6.00
CSOC87 Night's End Sorcerer SR 2.50 6.00
CSOC88 Tempest Magician SCR 3.00 8.00
CSOC89 Treacherous Trap Hole SCR 10.00 25.00
CSOC90 Puppet Master SR .75 2.00
CSOC91 Time Machine SCR 1.50 4.00
CSOC92 Virus Cannon R .60 1.50
CSOC93 Machine Lord Ur SCR 1.50 4.00
CSOC94 Mosaic Manticore R .40 1.00
CSOC95 Goka, the Pyre of Malice SR .75 2.00
CSOC96 Red Ogre SR .75 .30
CSOC97 Neos Wiseman SCR 2.50 6.00
CSOC98 Elem. Hero Divine SCR 2.00 5.00
CSOC99 Botanical Lion SR 3.00 8.00

2009 Yu-Gi-Oh Crimson Crisis 1st Edition

COMPLETE SET (100) 75.00 150.00
BOOSTER BOX (24 PACKS) 40.00 80.00
BOOSTER PACK (9 CARDS) 2.50 6.00
*UNLIMITED: .4X TO .8X 1ST EDITION
RELEASED ON MARCH 3, 2009
CRMS0 Colossal Fighter/Assault Mode SCR 1.25 3.00
CRMS1 Turret Warrior SR .75 2.00
CRMS2 Debris Dragon R .40 1.00
CRMS3 Hyper Synchron R .40 1.00
CRMS4 Red Dragon Archfiend UTR 3.00 8.00
CRMS4 Red Dragon Archfiend GR 6.00 15.00
CRMS4 Red Dragon Archfiend UR 2.50 6.00
CRMS5 Trap Eater C .60 1.50
CRMS6 Twin-Sword Marauder C .10 .30
CRMS7 Dark Tinker C .10 .30
CRMS8 Blackwing - Gale the Whirlwind R .40 1.00
CRMS9 Blackwing - Bora the Spear C .50 1.25
CRMS10 Blackwing - Sirocco the Dawn C .10 .30
CRMS11 Twilight Rose Knight SR 1.00 2.50
CRMS12 Summon Reactor SK C .10 .30
CRMS13 Trap Reactor-Y FI C .10 .30
CRMS14 Spell Reactor-RE C .10 .30
CRMS15 Black Salvo SR .75 2.00
CRMS16 Flying Fortress SKY FIRE R .40 1.00
CRMS17 Morphtronic Boarden C .10 .30
CRMS18 Morphtronic Slingen C .10 .30
CRMS19 Doomkaiser Dragon UR .75 2.00
CRMS19 Doomkaiser Dragon UTR .75 2.00
CRMS20 Hyper Psychic Blaster UR .75 2.00
CRMS20 Hyper Psychic Blaster UTR 1.00 2.50
CRMS21 Arcanite Magician UR 2.00 5.00
CRMS21 Arcanite Magician UTR 2.00 5.00
CRMS22 Arcane Apprentice R .40 1.00
CRMS23 Assault Mercenary C .10 .30
CRMS24 Assault Beast R .60 1.50
CRMS25 Night Wing Sorceress C .10 .30
CRMS26 Lifeforce Harmonizer UR .75 2.00
CRMS26 Lifeforce Harmonizer UTR .75 2.00
CRMS27 Gladiator Beast Samnite R .40 1.00
CRMS28 Dupe Frog C .10 .30
CRMS29 Flip Flop Frog C .10 .30
CRMS30 B.E.S. Big Core MK-2 R .40 1.00
CRMS31 Inmato R .40 1.00
CRMS32 Scanner SR .75 2.00
CRMS33 Dimension Fortress Weapon SR .75 2.00
CRMS34 Desert Protector C .10 .30
CRMS35 Cross-Sword Beetle C .10 .30
CRMS36 Bee List Soldier C .10 .30
CRMS37 Hydra Viper C .10 .30
CRMS38 Alien Overlord R .40 1.00
CRMS39 Alien Ammonite R .40 1.00
CRMS40 Dark Strike Fighter SR .75 2.00
CRMS41 Blackwing Armor Master UR 1.00 2.50
CRMS41 Blackwing Armor Master UTR 2.50 6.00
CRMS42 Hyper Psychic Blaster UR 2.50 6.00
CRMS42 Hyper Psychic Blaster UTR 1.50 4.00
CRMS43 Arcanite Magician SR .75 2.00
CRMS44 Cosmic Fortress Gol'gar UR 3.00 8.00
CRMS44 Cosmic Fortress Gol'gar UTR 4.00 10.00
CRMS45 Prevention Star C .10 .30
CRMS46 Vengeful Servant C .10 .30
CRMS47 Star Blast R .40 1.00
CRMS48 Raptor Wing Strike C .10 .30
CRMS49 Morphtronic Rusty Engine C .10 .30
CRMS50 Morphtronic Map C .10 .30
CRMS51 Assault Overload C .10 .30
CRMS52 Assault Teleport C .10 .30
CRMS53 Assault Revival C .10 .30
CRMS54 Psychic Sword C .10 .30
CRMS55 Telekinetic Power Well C 1.50 4.00
CRMS56 Indomitable Gladiator Beast C .75 2.00
CRMS57 Seed Cannon C .10 .30
CRMS58 Super Solar Nutrient C .10 .30
CRMS59 Six Scrolls of the Samurai C .10 .30
CRMS60 Verdant Sanctuary C .10 .30
CRMS61 Arcane Barrier R .40 1.00
CRMS62 Mysterious Triangle C .10 .30
CRMS63 Assault Mode Activate C .10 .30
CRMS64 Spirit Force SR .75 2.00
CRMS65 Descending Lost Star C .10 .30
CRMS66 Shining Silver Force R .40 1.00
CRMS67 Half or Nothing C .10 .30
CRMS68 Nightmare Archfiends C 1.25 3.00
CRMS69 Ebon Arrow C .10 .30
CRMS70 Ivy Shackles C .10 .30
CRMS71 Fake Explosion C .10 .30
CRMS72 Morphtronic Forcefield C .10 .30
CRMS73 Morphtronic Mix-up C .10 .30
CRMS74 Assault Slash C .10 .30
CRMS75 Assault Counter C .10 .30
CRMS76 Psychic Tuning R .40 1.00
CRMS77 Metaphysical Regeneration C .10 .30
CRMS78 Trojan Gladiator Beast C .10 .30
CRMS79 Wall of Thorns R .50 1.25
CRMS80 Planet Pollutant Virus R .40 1.00
CRMS81 Dark Voltanis SCR 3.00 8.00
CRMS82 Prime Material Falcon SCR .40 1.00
CRMS83 Bone Crusher UTR .75 2.00
CRMS83 Bone Crusher UR .75 2.00
CRMS84 Alien Kid SR .75 2.00
CRMS85 Totem Dragon SR 2.00 5.00
CRMS86 Royal Swamp Eel SR .75 2.00
CRMS87 Submarine Frog C .10 .30
CRMS88 Code A Ancient Ruins SR 1.25 3.00
CRMS89 Synchro Change R .40 1.00
CRMS90 Multiply SR 1.50 4.00
CRMS91 Makiu, the Magical Mist R .40 1.00
CRMS92 Assault Armor R .40 1.00
CRMS93 Puppet King SCR .40 1.00
CRMS94 Zeta Reticulant SCR .40 1.00
CRMS95 Tethys, Goddess of Light SCR 2.00 5.00
CRMS96 Ido the Supreme Magical Force SCR .40 1.00
CRMS97 Violet Witch UTR .50 1.25
CRMS97 Violet Witch UR .75 2.00
CRMS98 Greed Quasar SCR 1.25 3.00
CRMS99 Armoroid SR .75 2.00

2009 Yu-Gi-Oh Raging Battle 1st Edition

COMPLETE SET (100) 150.00 250.00
BOOSTER BOX (24 PACKS) 40.00 80.00
BOOSTER PACK (9 CARDS) 2.00 5.00
*UNLIMITED: .4X TO .8X 1ST EDITION
RELEASED ON MAY 12, 2009
RGBT00 Battlestorm SCR 1.50 4.00
RGBT01 Rockstone Warrior SR .75 2.00
RGBT02 Level Warrior SR 1.00 2.50
RGBT03 Strong Wind Dragon UTR 2.00 5.00
RGBT03 Strong Wind Dragon UR 2.00 5.00
RGBT04 Dark Verger R .40 1.00
RGBT05 Phoenixian Seed C .10 .30
RGBT06 Phoenixian Cluster Amaryllis SR .50 1.25
RGBT07 Rose Tentacles C .10 .30
RGBT08 Hedge Guard C .10 .30
RGBT09 Evil Thorn C .10 .30
RGBT10 Blackwing - Blizzard the Far North R .75 2.00
RGBT11 Blackwing - Shura the Blue Flame C .10 .30
RGBT12 Blackwing - Kalut the Moon Shadow C .40 1.00
RGBT13 Blackwing - Elphin the Raven UTR .75 2.00
RGBT13 Blackwing - Elphin the Raven UR .40 1.00
RGBT14 Morphtronic Remoten R 1.00 2.50
RGBT15 Morphtronic Videon C .10 .30
RGBT16 Morphtronic Scopen C .40 1.00
RGBT17 Gadget Arms C .10 .30
RGBT18 Torapart R .40 1.00
RGBT19 Earthbound Immortal Aslla Piscu UR 1.50 4.00
RGBT19 Earthbound Immortal Aslla Piscu UTR 1.50 4.00
RGBT20 Earthbound Immortal Ccapac UR 6.00 15.00
RGBT20 Earthbound Immortal Ccapac UTR 3.00 8.00
RGBT21 Koa'ki Meiru Valafar SR .75 2.00
RGBT22 Koa'ki Meiru Powerhand SR .40 1.00
RGBT23 Koa'ki Meiru Guardian C .10 .30
RGBT24 Koa'ki Meiru Drago UTR 20.00 40.00
RGBT24 Koa'ki Meiru Drago UR 8.00 20.00
RGBT25 Koa'ki Meiru Ice R .40 1.00
RGBT26 Koa'ki Meiru Doom C .10 .30
RGBT27 Brain Golem R .40 1.00
RGBT28 Minoan Centaur C .10 .30
RGBT29 Reinforced Human Psychic Borg SR .75 2.00
RGBT30 Master Gig C .10 .30
RGBT31 Emissary from Pandemonium C .10 .30
RGBT32 Gigastone Omega C .10 .30
RGBT33 Alien Dog C .10 .30
RGBT34 Spined Gillman C .10 .30
RGBT35 Deep Sea Diva R .40 1.00
RGBT36 Mermaid Archer C .10 .30
RGBT37 Lava Dragon C .10 .30
RGBT38 Vanguard of the Dragon C .10 .30
RGBT39 G.B. Hunter C .10 .30
RGBT40 Exploder Dragonwing UR 2.00 5.00
RGBT40 Exploder Dragonwing UTR 2.00 5.00
RGBT41 Blackwing Armed Wing SR .50 1.25
RGBT42 Power Tool Dragon GR 6.00 15.00
RGBT42 Power Tool Dragon UTR 2.50 6.00
RGBT42 Power Tool Dragon UR 2.00 5.00
RGBT43 Trident Dragion UR 1.25 3.00
RGBT43 Trident Dragion UTR 2.00 5.00
RGBT44 Sea Dragon Lord Gishilnodon SR 1.25 3.00
RGBT45 One for One R .75 2.00
RGBT46 Mind Trust C .10 .30
RGBT47 Thorn of Malice C .10 .30
RGBT48 Magic Planter SR 4.00 10.00
RGBT49 Wonder Clover C .10 .30
RGBT50 Against the Wind R .40 1.00
RGBT51 Black Whirlwind C 1.25 3.00
RGBT52 Junk Box C .10 .30
RGBT53 Double Tool C&D C .10 .30
RGBT54 Morphtronic Repair Unit C .10 .30
RGBT55 Iron Core of Koa'ki Meiru R .40 1.00
RGBT56 Iron Core Immediate Disposal C .10 .30
RGBT57 Urgent Synthesis C .10 .30
RGBT58 Psychic Path C .75 2.00
RGBT59 Natural Tune C .10 .30
RGBT60 Supremacy Berry C .10 .30
RGBT61 Forbidden Chalice UTR 10.00 25.00
RGBT61 Forbidden Chalice UR 3.00 8.00
RGBT62 Calming Magic R .40 1.00
RGBT63 Miracle Locus C .10 .30
RGBT64 Crimson Fire C .10 .30
RGBT65 Tuner Capture C .10 .30
RGBT66 Overdoom Line C .10 .30
RGBT67 Wicked Rebirth C .10 .30
RGBT68 Delta Crow - Anti Reverse SR 1.25 3.00
RGBT69 Level Retuner C .10 .30
RGBT70 Fake Feather C .10 .30
RGBT71 Trap Stun C .50 1.25
RGBT72 Morphtronic Bind C .10 .30
RGBT73 Reckoned Power C .10 .30
RGBT74 Automatic Laser C .10 .30
RGBT75 Attack of the Cornered Rat C .10 .30
RGBT76 Proof of Powerlessness C .10 .30
RGBT77 Bone Temple Block C .10 .30
RGBT78 Grave of the Super UTR 6.00 15.00
RGBT78 Grave of the Super UR 6.00 15.00
RGBT79 Swallow Flip SR .40 1.00
RGBT80 Mirror of Oaths C .10 .30
RGBT81 Koa'ki Meiru War Arms SR .75 2.00
RGBT82 Immortal Ruler SCR 4.00 10.00
RGBT83 Hardened Armed Dragon SCR 3.00 8.00
RGBT84 Moja R .40 1.00
RGBT85 Beast Striker SR .40 1.00
RGBT86 King of the Beasts SCR 1.50 4.00
RGBT87 Swallow's Nest SR 5.00 12.00
RGBT88 Overwhelm SCR 3.00 8.00
RGBT89 Berserking R .40 1.00
RGBT90 Spell of Pain R .40 1.00
RGBT91 Light End Dragon SCR 1.50 4.00
RGBT92 Chaos-End Master SCR 4.00 10.00
RGBT93 Sphere of Chaos SCR 8.00 20.00
RGBT94 Snowman Eater R .40 1.00
RGBT95 Tree Otter R .40 1.00
RGBT96 Ojama Red R 1.00 2.50
RGBT97 Ojama Blue R 1.50 4.00
RGBT98 Ojama Country R 1.50 4.00
RGBT99 Emperor Sem R .40 1.00

2009 Yu-Gi-Oh Ancient Prophecy 1st Edition

COMPLETE SET (100) 115.00 200.00
BOOSTER BOX (24 PACKS) 50.00 90.00
BOOSTER PACK (9 CARDS) 2.50 6.00
RELEASED ON SEPTEMBER 1, 2009
ANPR0 XX-Saber Gardestrike SCR 1.50 4.00
ANPR1 Kuribon R .40 1.00
ANPR2 Sunny Pixie C .10 .30
ANPR3 Sunlight Unicorn C .10 .30
ANPR4 Blackwing - Mistral the Silver Shield C .10 .30
ANPR5 Blackwing - Vayu UR .75 2.00
ANPR5 Blackwing - Vayu UTR 1.50 4.00
ANPR6 Blackwing - Fane the Steel Chain C .10 .30
ANPR7 Morphtronic Magnen Bar C .10 .30
ANPR8 Jester Lord R .40 1.00
ANPR9 Jester Confit SR 1.50 4.00
ANPR10 Fortune Lady Light R .50 1.25
ANPR11 Fortune Lady Fire R .40 1.00
ANPR12 Infernity Beast C .10 .30
ANPR13 Darksea Rescue R .40 1.00
ANPR14 Darksea Float C .10 .30
ANPR15 Turbo Rocket R .40 1.00
ANPR16 Earthbound Immortal Cusillu UR 1.00 2.50
ANPR16 Earthbound Immortal Cusillu UTR 1.50 4.00
ANPR17 Earthboudn Immortal Chacu UTR 3.00 8.00
ANPR17 Earthbound Immortal Chacu UR 1.50 4.00
ANPR18 Koa'ki Meiru Boulder C .10 .30
ANPR19 Koa'ki Meiru Crusader SR 1.00 2.50
ANPR20 Koa'ki Meiru Speeder R .40 1.00
ANPR21 Koa'ki Meiru Tornado R .40 1.00
ANPR22 Koa'ki Meiru Hydro Barrier C .10 .30
ANPR23 Scary Moth C .10 .30
ANPR24 Shiny Black C C .10 .30
ANPR25 Armed Sea Hunter C .10 .30
ANPR26 Divine Dragon Aquabizarre C .10 .30
ANPR27 Fishborg Blaster C .10 .30
ANPR28 Shark Cruiser C .10 .30
ANPR29 Armored Axon Kicker C .10 .30
ANPR30 Genetic Woman C .10 .30
ANPR31 Magicat R .40 1.00
ANPR32 Cyborg Doctor C .10 .30
ANPR33 White Potan C .10 .30
ANPR34 Minefieldriller SR .60 1.50
ANPR35 XX-Saber Faultroll SR 1.50 4.00
ANPR36 XX-Saber Ragigura C .10 .30
ANPR37 Flamvell Firedog R .40 1.00
ANPR38 Ancient Crimson Ape C .10 .30
ANPR39 Falchion R .40 1.00
ANPR40 Ancient Fairy Dragon GR 15.00 30.00
ANPR40 Ancient Fairy Dragon UTR 6.00 15.00
ANPR40 Ancient Fairy Dragon UR 2.00 5.00
ANPR41 Turbo Cannon SR .75 2.00
ANPR42 Archfiend Zombie-Skull SR 8.00 20.00
ANPR43 Ancient Sacred Wyvern UTR 6.00 15.00
ANPR43 Ancient Sacred Wyvern UR 3.00 8.00
ANPR44 XX-Saber Gottoms UR .75 2.00
ANPR44 XX-Saber Gottoms UTR 1.50 4.00
ANPR45 Release Restraint Wave C .10 .30
ANPR46 Silver Wing C .10 .30
ANPR47 Advance Draw C .10 .30
ANPR48 Ancient Forest SR .75 2.00
ANPR49 Emergency Assistance C .10 .30
ANPR50 Spirit Burner C .10 .30
ANPR51 Future Visions SR 3.00 8.00
ANPR52 Core Compression SR 1.00 2.50
ANPR53 Core Blaster C .10 .30
ANPR54 Solidarity R 1.25 3.00
ANPR55 Hydro Pressure Cannon C .10 .30
ANPR56 Water Hazard C .10 .30
ANPR57 Brain Research Lab C .20 .75
ANPR58 Saber Slash SR .75 2.00
ANPR59 Sword of Sparkles C .10 .30
ANPR60 Rekindling C .10 .30
ANPR61 Ancient Leaf C .50 1.25
ANPR62 Fossil Dig C .40 1.00
ANPR63 Skill Successoı SR .75 2.00
ANPR64 Reinforce Truth R .40 1.00
ANPR65 Pixie Ring C .10 .30
ANPR66 Fairy Wind C .10 .30
ANPR67 Imperial Custom C .60 1.50
ANPR68 Discord SR .40 1.00
ANPR69 Slip of Fortune C .10 .30
ANPR70 Depth Amulet C .10 .30
ANPR71 Damage Translation C .10 .30
ANPR72 Battle Teleportation C .10 .30
ANPR73 Core Reinforcement R .40 1.00
ANPR74 Iron Core Luster C .10 .30
ANPR75 Battle of the Elements C .10 .30
ANPR76 Aegis of the Ocean Dragon Lord C .10 .30
ANPR77 Psychic Soul C .10 .30
ANPR78 Flamvell Counter C .10 .30
ANPR79 At One With the Sword C .10 .30
ANPR80 A Major Upset C .10 .30
ANPR81 XX-Saber Fulhelmknight R .40 1.00
ANPR82 Koa'ki Meiru Ghoulungulate UTR .50 1.25
ANPR82 Koa'ki Meiru Ghoulungulate UR .75 2.00
ANPR83 Koa'ki Meiru Gravirose UTR .75 2.00
ANPR83 Koa'ki Meiru Gravirose UR .75 2.00
ANPR84 Psychic Emperor R .40 1.00
ANPR85 Card Guard SCR 4.00 10.00
ANPR86 Flamvell Commando UTR .75 2.00
ANPR86 Flamvell Commando UR .75 2.00
ANPR87 Pseudo Space R 3.00 8.00
ANPR88 Greed Grado SCR 1.50 4.00
ANPR89 Revival of the Immortals SR .60 1.50
ANPR90 Arcana Knight Joker R 1.50 4.00
ANPR91 Armityle the Chaos Phantom SCR 10.00 25.00
ANPR92 White Night Dragon SCR 3.00 8.00
ANPR93 Card Blocker SCR .50 1.25
ANPR94 Gaia Plate the Earth Giant UR 1.50 4.00
ANPR94 Gaia Plate the Earth Giant UTR 3.00 8.00
ANPR95 Sauropod Brachion R .40 1.00
ANPR96 Gaap the Divine Soldier R .40 1.00
ANPR97 Beast Machine King Barbaros Ur SR .75 2.00
ANPR98 Kasha SCR 1.00 2.50
ANPR99 Elemental Hero Gaia SCR 4.00 10.00

2009 Yu-Gi-Oh Stardust Overdrive 1st Edition

COMPLETE SET (100) 175.00 300.00
BOOSTER BOX (24 PACKS) 80.00 120.00
BOOSTER PACK (9 CARDS) 2.50 6.00
*UNLIMITED: .4X TO .8X 1ST EDITION
RELEASED ON NOVEMBER 17, 2009
SOVR0 Koa'ki Meiru Beetle SR .75 2.00
SOVR1 Majestic Dragon SR 1.25 3.00
SOVR2 Stardust Xiaolong R .60 1.50
SOVR3 Max Warrior SR .75 2.00
SOVR4 Quickdraw Synchron C .10 .30
SOVR5 Level Eater C .10 .30
SOVR6 Zero Gardna R .60 1.50
SOVR7 Regulus C .10 .30
SOVR8 Infernity Necromancer C .10 .30
SOVR9 Fortune Lady Wind R .75 2.00
SOVR10 Fortune Lady Water R .75 2.00
SOVR11 Fortune Lady Dark R 1.00 2.50
SOVR12 Fortune Lady Earth R .75 2.00
SOVR13 Solitaire Magician C .10 .30
SOVR14 Catoblepas and the Witch of Fate R .40 1.00
SOVR15 Dark Spider C .10 .30
SOVR16 Ground Spider C .10 .30
SOVR17 Relinquished Spider C .10 .30
SOVR18 Spyder Spider C .10 .30
SOVR19 Mother Spider R .40 1.00
SOVR20 Reptilianne Gorgon C .10 .30
SOVR21 Reptilianne Medusa C .10 .30
SOVR22 Reptilianne Scylla C .10 .30
SOVR23 Reptilianne Viper C .10 .30
SOVR24 Earthbound Immortal Ccarayhua UR 1.50 4.00
SOVR24 Earthbound Immortal Ccarayhua UTR 3.00 8.00
SOVR25 Earthbound Immortal Uru UR 2.50 6.00
SOVR25 Earthbound Immortal Uru UTR 3.00 8.00
SOVR26 Earth. Immortal Wiraqocha UTR 1.25 3.00
SOVR26 Earth. Immortal Wiraqocha UR 1.50 4.00
SOVR27 Koa'ki Meiru Sea Panther C .10 .30
SOVR28 Koa'ki Meiru Rooklord SR .75 2.00
SOVR29 Tuned Magician C .10 .30
SOVR30 Crusader of Endymion UTR 6.00 15.00
SOVR30 Crusader of Endymion UR 1.50 4.00
SOVR31 Woodland Archer C .10 .30
SOVR32 Knight of the Red Lotus SR 2.50 6.00
SOVR33 Energy Bravery C .10 .30
SOVR34 Swap Frog C .10 .30
SOVR35 Lord British Space Fighter R .60 1.50
SOVR36 Oshaleon C .10 .30
SOVR37 Djinn Releaser of Rituals R .60 1.50
SOVR38 Djinn Presider of Rituals R .40 1.00
SOVR39 Divine Grace - Northwemko UTR 2.00 5.00
SOVR39 Divine Grace - Northwemko UR 1.50 4.00
SOVR40 Majestic Star Dragon UTR 2.00 5.00
SOVR40 Majestic Star Dragon UR 1.50 4.00
SOVR40 Majestic Star Dragon GR 8.00 20.00
SOVR41 Blackwing - Silverwind UR 1.50 4.00
SOVR41 Blackwing - Silverwind UTR 1.25 3.00
SOVR42 Reptilianne Hydra SR .75 2.00
SOVR43 Black Brutdrago SR .75 2.00
SOVR44 Explosive Magician UTR 3.00 8.00
SOVR44 Explosive Magician UR 2.00 5.00
SOVR45 Spider Web C .10 .30
SOVR46 Earthbound Whirlwind SR .60 1.50
SOVR47 Savage Colosseum C .10 .30
SOVR48 Attack Pheromones C .10 .30
SOVR49 Molting Escape C .10 .30
SOVR50 Reptilianne Spawn C .10 .30
SOVR51 Fortune's Future SR 2.00 5.00
SOVR52 Time Passage C .10 .30
SOVR53 Iron Core Armor C .10 .30
SOVR54 Herculean Power C .10 .30
SOVR55 Gemini Spark C .10 .30
SOVR56 Ritual of Grace C .10 .30
SOVR57 Preparation of Rites SR 1.25 3.00
SOVR58 Moray of Greed C .50 1.25
SOVR59 Spiritual Forest C .10 .30
SOVR60 Raging Mad Plants R .40 1.00
SOVR61 Insect Neglect C .10 .30
SOVR62 Faustian Bargain C .75 2.00
SOVR63 Slip Summon C .10 .30
SOVR64 Synchro Barrier C .10 .30
SOVR65 Enlightenment C .10 .30
SOVR66 Bending Destiny C .10 .30
SOVR67 Inherited Fortune R .40 1.00
SOVR68 Spider Egg C .10 .30
SOVR69 Wolf in Sheep's Clothing C .10 .30
SOVR70 Earthbound Wave C .10 .30
SOVR71 Roar of the Earthbound C .10 .30
SOVR72 Limit Impulse C .10 .30
SOVR73 Infernity Force C .10 .30
SOVR74 Nega-Ton Corepanel R .40 1.00
SOVR75 Gemini Counter C .10 .30
SOVR76 Gemini Booster C .10 .30
SOVR77 Ritual Buster C .10 .30
SOVR78 Stygian Dirge C 2.00 5.00
SOVR79 Seal of Wickedness SR .75 2.00
SOVR80 Appointer of the Red Lotus C .10 .30
SOVR81 Koa'ki Meiru Maximus UTR 1.25 3.00
SOVR81 Koa'ki Meiru Maximus UR 1.50 4.00
SOVR82 Shire, Lightsworn Spirit SR .75 2.00
SOVR83 Rinyan, Lightsworn Rogue R .60 1.50
SOVR84 Yellow Baboon, Archer UTR 1.25 3.00
SOVR84 Yellow Baboon, Archer UR 1.50 4.00
SOVR85 Gemini Scorpion R .40 1.00
SOVR86 Metabo-Shark SR .75 2.00
SOVR87 Earthbound Revival R .40 1.00
SOVR88 Reptilianne Poison R .40 1.00
SOVR89 Gateway of the Six SR 2.50 6.00
SOVR90 Dark Rabbit R .40 1.00
SOVR91 Shine Palace R .60 1.50
SOVR92 Dark Simorgh SCR 15.00 30.00
SOVR93 Victoria SCR 10.00 25.00
SOVR94 Ice Queen SCR 1.50 4.00
SOVR95 Shutendoji SCR 4.00 10.00
SOVR96 Archlord Kristya SCR 20.00 40.00
SOVR97 Guardian Eatos SCR 50.00 100.00
SOVR98 Clear Vice Dragon SCR 1.50 4.00
SOVR99 Clear World SCR 1.00 2.50

2010 Yu-Gi-Oh Absolute Powerforce 1st Edition

COMPLETE SET (100) 100.00 200.00
BOOSTER BOX (24 PACKS) 40.00 80.00
BOOSTER PACK (9 CARDS) 2.00 5.00
*UNLIMITED CARDS: .4X TO .8X 1ST EDITION
RELEASED ON FEBRUARY 16, 2010
ABPF0 Grvkpr's Prstss SR .75 2.00
ABPF1 Unicycular C .10 .30
ABPF2 Bicular C .10 .30
ABPF3 Tricular C .10 .30
ABPF4 Drill Synchron R .40 1.00
ABPF5 Ogre Scarlet Sorrow SR .75 2.00
ABPF6 Battle Fader UR 2.00 5.00
ABPF6 Battle Fader UTR 8.00 20.00
ABPF7 Power Supplier C .10 .30
ABPF8 Magic Hole Golem C .10 .30
ABPF9 Power Invader C .10 .30
ABPF10 Dark Bug R .40 1.00
ABPF11 Sword Master .10 .30
ABPF12 Witch Black Rose UTR 2.00 5.00

Card	Low	High
ABPF12 Witch Black Rose UR	1.50	4.00
ABPF13 Rose Fairy C	.10	.30
ABPF14 Dragon Queen SR	.75	2.00
ABPF15 Reptilianne Servant C	.10	.30
ABPF16 Reptilianne Gardna C	.10	.30
ABPF17 Reptilianne Naga C	.10	.30
ABPF18 Reptilianne Vaskii R	.40	1.00
ABPF19 Oracle of the Sun SR	.75	2.00
ABPF20 Fire Ant Ascator C	.10	.30
ABPF21 Weeping Idol C	.10	.30
ABPF22 Apocatequil C	.10	.30
ABPF23 Supay C	.10	.30
ABPF24 Informer Spider C	.10	.30
ABPF25 Koa Mei Urnight UR	1.50	4.00
ABPF25 Koa Mei Urnight UTR	1.50	4.00
ABPF26 XX-Saber Garsem R	.40	1.00
ABPF27 Grvkpr's Visionary SR	.75	2.00
ABPF28 Grvkpr's Dscndnt R	.40	1.00
ABPF29 Black Potan C	.10	.30
ABPF30 Shreddder C	.10	.30
ABPF31 Pandaborg C	.10	.30
ABPF32 Codarus C	.10	.30
ABPF33 Consecrated Light C	.10	.30
ABPF34 Gundari C	.10	.30
ABPF35 Cyber Dragon Zwei R	.40	1.00
ABPF36 Oilman C	.10	.30
ABPF37 Djinn Cursenchanter R	.40	1.00
ABPF38 Djinn Prognosticator R	.40	1.00
ABPF39 Garlandolf, King UTR	1.50	4.00
ABPF39 Garlandolf, King UR	1.50	4.00
ABPF40 Maj Red Dragon GR	5.00	12.00
ABPF40 Maj Red Dragon UR	1.50	4.00
ABPF40 Maj Red Dragon UTR	1.50	4.00
ABPF41 Drill Warrior UR	1.50	4.00
ABPF41 Drill Warrior UTR	1.50	4.00
ABPF42 Sun Dragon Inti UR	1.50	4.00
ABPF42 Sun Dragon Inti UTR	1.50	4.00
ABPF43 Moon Dragon UR	1.50	4.00
ABPF43 Moon Dragon UTR	1.50	4.00
ABPF44 XX-Saber Hyunlei UTR	3.00	8.00
ABPF44 XX-Saber Hyunlei UR	2.50	6.00
ABPF45 Cards Consonance SR	2.50	6.00
ABPF46 Variety Comes Out C	.10	.30
ABPF47 Reptilianne Rage C	.10	.30
ABPF48 Advance Force C	.10	.30
ABPF49 Viper's Rebirth C	.10	.30
ABPF50 Temple of the Sun C	.10	.30
ABPF51 Rocket Pilder C	.10	.30
ABPF52 Break! Draw! C	.10	.30
ABPF53 Power Pickaxe R	.40	1.00
ABPF54 Spider's Lair C	.10	.30
ABPF55 Iron Core SR	.75	2.00
ABPF56 Gravekeeper's Stele C	.10	.30
ABPF57 Machine Assembly Line C	.10	.30
ABPF58 Ritual of Destruction C	.10	.30
ABPF59 Ascending Soul R	.40	1.00
ABPF60 Ritual Cage R	.40	1.00
ABPF61 Pot of Benevolence C	.60	1.50
ABPF62 Synchro Control SR	.75	2.00
ABPF63 Changing Destiny C	.10	.30
ABPF64 Fiendish Chain SR	3.00	8.00
ABPF65 Nature's Reflection C	.10	.30
ABPF66 Serpent Suppression C	.10	.30
ABPF67 Meteor Flare C	.10	.30
ABPF68 Offering Immortals R	.40	1.00
ABPF69 Destruct Potion C	.10	.30
ABPF70 Call of the Reaper C	.10	.30
ABPF71 Lair Wire C	.10	.30
ABPF72 Core Blast R	.40	1.00
ABPF73 Saber Hole SR	1.50	4.00
ABPF74 Machine King - 3000 B.C. C	.10	.30
ABPF75 Alien Brain C	.10	.30
ABPF76 Forgotten Temple of the Deep C	.10	.30
ABPF77 Tuner's Scheme SR	.75	2.00
ABPF78 Psi-Curse C	.10	.30
ABPF79 Widespread Dud C	.10	.30
ABPF80 Inverse Universe C	.10	.30
ABPF81 XX-Saber Emrsblde SCR	2.00	5.00
ABPF82 Alchemist Blk Spils UR	1.50	4.00
ABPF82 Alchemist Blk Spils UTR	2.00	5.00
ABPF83 Super-Nimble Mega SR	.75	2.00
ABPF84 Cactus Bouncer SCR	8.00	20.00
ABPF85 Dragonic Guard SR	.75	2.00
ABPF86 The Dragon Dwllng SR	.75	2.00
ABPF87 Djinn Disserere SCR	1.50	4.00
ABPF88 Earthbound Linewalker SCR	2.00	5.00
ABPF89 Core Transport SCR	1.50	4.00
ABPF90 Gale Dogra R	.40	1.00
ABPF91 Berfomet R	.40	1.00
ABPF92 Chimera Flying R	.40	1.00
ABPF93 Viser Des R	.40	1.00
ABPF94 Evil Blast R	.40	1.00
ABPF95 Shield Wing SCR	1.50	4.00
ABPF96 Undrgrnd Archnd SCR	1.50	4.00
ABPF97 Zeman the Ape SCR	1.50	4.00
ABPF98 Skull Conductor R	.40	1.00
ABPF99 Shield Worm R	.40	1.00

2010 Yu-Gi-Oh The Shining Darkness 1st Edition

Card	Low	High
COMPLETE SET (111)	100.00	200.00
BOOSTER BOX (24 PACKS)	60.00	90.00
BOOSTER PACK (9 CARDS)	3.00	4.00
RELEASED ON MAY 11, 2010		
TSHD0 XX-Saber Boggart SR	.75	2.00
TSHD1 Blackwing - Ghibli the Searing Wind	.10	.30
TSHD2 Blackwing Gust R	.40	1.00
TSHD3 Blackwing Breeze UR	1.50	4.00
TSHD3 Blackwing Breeze UR	1.00	2.50
TSHD4 Changer Synchron	.10	.30
TSHD5 Card Breaker	.10	.30
TSHD6 Second Booster	.10	.30
TSHD7 Archfiend Interceptor	.10	.30
TSHD8 Dread Dragon R	.50	1.25
TSHD9 Trust Guardian SR	.40	1.00
TSHD10 Flare Resonator	.10	.30
TSHD11 Synchro Magnet	.10	.30
TSHD12 Infernity Mirage SR	1.25	3.00
TSHD13 Infernity Randomizer	.10	.30
TSHD14 Infernity Beetle R	.75	2.00
TSHD15 Infernity Avenger (R)	.40	1.00
TSHD16 Revival Rose R	.40	1.00
TSHD17 Morphtronic Vacuumen	.10	.30
TSHD18 Bird of Roses SR	.75	2.00
TSHD19 Spore	.10	.30
TSHD20 Fairy Archer	.10	.30
TSHD21 Biofalcon	.10	.30
TSHD22 Cherry Inmato R	.40	1.00
TSHD23 Magidog R	.40	1.00
TSHD24 Lyna the Light Charmer	.10	.30
TSHD25 Wattgiraffe SR	4.00	10.00
TSHD26 Wattfox	.10	.30
TSHD27 Wattwoodpecker	.10	.30
TSHD28 Koa'ki Meiru Sandman	.10	.30
TSHD29 Memory Crush King	.10	.30
TSHD30 Delta Tri R	.40	1.00
TSHD31 Trigon	.10	.30
TSHD32 Testudo Erat SP	1.00	2.50
TSHD33 Ronintoadin	.20	.60
TSHD34 Batteryman AAA	.10	.30
TSHD35 Batteryman Fuel Cell R	1.25	3.00
TSHD36 Key Mouse	.10	.30
TSHD37 Core Destroyer R	.40	1.00
TSHD38 Hunter of Black SP	.20	.50
TSHD39 Herald Perfect UTR	5.00	12.00
TSHD39 Herald Perfect UR	.75	2.00
TSHD40 Black-Winged GR	6.00	15.00
TSHD40 Black-Winged UTR	1.00	2.50
TSHD40 Black-Winged UR	1.00	2.50
TSHD41 Chaos King UTR	1.00	2.50
TSHD41 Chaos King UR	1.25	3.00
TSHD42 Infernity Doom UTR	2.00	5.00
TSHD42 Infernity Doom UR	1.50	4.00
TSHD43 Splendid Rose UR	.50	1.25
TSHD43 Splendid Rose UTR	.75	2.00
TSHD44 Chaos Goddess SCR	3.00	8.00
TSHD45 Black-Winged Strafe	.10	.30
TSHD46 Cards for Black UTR	.75	2.00
TSHD46 Cards for Black UR	1.00	2.50
TSHD47 ZERO-MAX SR	.40	1.00
TSHD48 Infernity Launcher SR	1.00	2.50
TSHD49 Into The Void UR	20.00	35.00
TSHD49 Into The Void UTR	25.00	40.00
TSHD50 Intercept Wave UTR	.40	1.00
TSHD50 Intercept Wave UR	.75	2.00
TSHD51 Pyramid of Wonders R	.40	1.00
TSHD52 The Fountain R	.40	1.00
TSHD53 Dragon Laser	.10	.30
TSHD54 Wattcube	.10	.30
TSHD55 Electromagnetic R	.40	1.00
TSHD56 Worm Call	.10	.30
TSHD57 Magic Triangle of the Ice Barrier	.10	.30
TSHD58 Koa'ki Meiru Initialize	.10	.30
TSHD59 Dawn of the Herald	.10	.30
TSHD60 Forbidden Graveyard	.10	.30
TSHD61 Leeching the Light	.10	.30
TSHD62 Corridor of Agony SP	.20	.50
TSHD63 Power Frame SR	.40	1.00
TSHD64 Blackwing Bcklsh R	.40	1.50
TSHD65 Blackwing - Bombardment	.10	.30
TSHD66 Black Thunder	.10	.30
TSHD67 Guard Mines R	.40	1.00
TSHD68 Infernity Reflector	.10	.30
TSHD69 Infernity Break	.10	.30
TSHD70 Damage Gate SR	.40	1.00
TSHD71 Infernity Inferno R	.40	1.00
TSHD72 Phantom Hand	.10	.30
TSHD73 Assault Spirits	.10	.30
TSHD74 Blossom Bombardment	.10	.30
TSHD75 Morphtronics, Scramble!	.10	.30
TSHD76 Power Break	.10	.30
TSHD77 Koa'ki Meiru Shield R	.40	1.00
TSHD78 Crevice into the Different Dimension	.10	.30
TSHD79 Synchro Ejection SR	.40	1.00
TSHD80 Chaos Trap Hole SP	4.00	10.00
TSHD81 XX-Saber Drksl UR	.50	1.25
TSHD81 XX-Saber Drksl UTR	2.50	6.00
TSHD82 Koa Mei Prttype R	.40	1.00
TSHD83 Snyffus SCR	.40	1.00
TSHD84 Nimble Sunfish SR	.50	1.25
TSHD85 Akz, the Pumer R	.40	1.00
TSHD86 Saber Vault SCR	.40	1.00
TSHD87 Core Overclock SR	.40	1.00
TSHD88 Wave-Motion SCR	.40	1.00
TSHD89 Infernity Barrier SCR	2.50	6.00
TSHD90 Genex Controller	.20	.60
TSHD91 Genex Undine	.10	.30
TSHD92 Genex Searcher R	.40	1.00
TSHD93 X-Saber Palomuro	.50	1.25
TSHD94 X-Saber Pashuul	.10	.30
TSHD95 Hydro Genex SR	.40	1.00
TSHD96 Light Gazer SR	.40	1.00
TSHD97 Genex Neutron SCR	.40	1.00
TSHD98 Infernity Dstryr SCR	.40	1.00
TSHD99 Koa Mei Bergzak SCR	1.50	4.00

2010 Yu-Gi-Oh Duelist Revolution 1st Edition

Card	Low	High
COMPLETE SET (110)	175.00	300.00
BOOSTER BOX (24 PACKS)	150.00	300.00
BOOSTER PACK (9 CARDS)	3.00	8.00
RELEASED ON AUGUST 17, 2010		
DREV0 Scrap Archfiend SR	1.25	3.00
DREV1 Earthquake Giant	.10	.30
DREV2 Effect Veiler UTR	50.00	80.00
DREV2 Effect Veiler UR	8.00	20.00
DREV3 Dash Warrior	.10	.30
DREV4 Damage Eater	.10	.30
DREV5 A/D Changer	.10	.30
DREV6 Stronghold Guardian	.10	.30
DREV7 Playful Possum R	.40	1.00
DREV8 Egotistical Ape R	.40	1.00
DREV9 Uni-Horned Familiar	.10	.30
DREV10 Monoceros	.10	.30
DREV11 D.D. Unicorn Knight R	.40	1.00
DREV12 Unibird SR	.40	1.00
DREV13 Bicorn Re'em	.10	.30
DREV14 Mine Mole	.10	.30
DREV15 Trident Warrior SR	.40	1.00
DREV16 Delta Flyer R	2.00	5.00
DREV17 Rhinotaurus	.10	.30
DREV18 Hypnocorn R	.40	1.00
DREV19 Scrap Chimera SR	.50	1.25
DREV20 Scrap Goblin	.10	.30
DREV21 Scrap Beast R	.40	1.00
DREV22 Scrap Hunter R	.40	1.00
DREV23 Scrap Golem R	.40	1.00
DREV24 Wattbetta	.10	.30
DREV25 Wattlemur	.10	.30
DREV26 Wattpheasant	.10	.30
DREV27 Naturia Mosquito	.10	.30
DREV28 Naturia Beans	.10	.30
DREV29 Naturia Bamboo (UTR)	2.50	6.00
DREV29 Naturia Bamboo (UR)	2.00	5.00
DREV30 Amazoness Sage	.10	.30
DREV31 Amazoness Trainee	.10	.30
DREV32 Amazoness Queen SR	3.00	8.00
DREV33 Lock Cat	.10	.30
DREV34 Elephun	.10	.30
DREV35 Synchro Fusionist R	.40	1.00
DREV36 Ambitious Goler R	.40	1.00
DREV37 Final Psychic Ogre	.10	.30
DREV38 Dragon Knight (UR)	.75	2.00
DREV38 Dragon Knight (UTR)	.50	1.25
DREV38 Dragon Knight Draco-Equiste GR	2.50	6.00
DREV39 Ultimate Axon Kick (SR)	1.25	3.00
DREV40 Thunder Unicorn UR	.50	1.25
DREV40 Thunder Unicorn UTR	.75	2.00
DREV41 Voltic Bicorn UTR	.75	2.00
DREV41 Voltic Bicorn UR	.50	1.25
DREV42 Lightning Tricorn UR	.50	1.25
DREV42 Lightning Tricorn UTR	.75	2.00
DREV43 Scrap Dragon UR	2.00	5.00
DREV43 Scrap Dragon UTR	5.00	12.00
DREV44 Wattchimera UR	.50	1.25
DREV44 Wattchimera UTR	.75	2.00
DREV45 Blind Spot Strike	.10	.30
DREV46 Double Cyclone	.10	.30
DREV47 Scrapyard SR	.40	1.00
DREV48 Scrapstorm SR	.40	1.00
DREV49 Scrap Sheen	.10	.30
DREV50 Wattcine	.10	.30
DREV51 Naturia Forest	.10	.30
DREV52 Landoise's Luminous (R)	.40	1.00
DREV53 Amazoness Village R	.40	1.00
DREV54 Amazoness Fighting	.10	.30
DREV55 Unicorn Beacon SR	.40	1.00
DREV56 Beast Rage	.10	.30
DREV57 Miracle Synchro Fusion	.20	.75
DREV58 Pestilence	.10	.30
DREV59 Cursed Armaments	.10	.30
DREV60 Wiseman's Chalice SR	.40	1.00
DREV61 Summoning Curse	.75	2.00
DREV62 Pot of Duality SCR	8.00	20.00
DREV63 Desperate Tag	.10	.30
DREV64 Battle Instinct	.10	.30
DREV65 Howl of the Wild	.10	.30
DREV66 Parallel Selection R	.40	1.00
DREV67 Reanimation Wave R	.40	1.00
DREV68 Barrier Wave	.10	.30
DREV69 Chain Whirlwind	.10	.30
DREV70 Scrap Rage	.10	.30
DREV71 Wattcannon	.10	.30
DREV72 Amazoness Wllpwr (R)	.40	1.00
DREV73 Queen's Pawn	.10	.30
DREV74 Beast Rising	.10	.30
DREV75 Horn of Phantom (R)	.40	1.00
DREV76 Paradox Fusion SR	1.00	2.50
DREV77 Solemn Warning UTR	40.00	60.00
DREV77 Solemn Warning UR	6.00	15.00
DREV78 Anti-Magic Prism	.10	.30
DREV79 Chivalry UTR	2.00	5.00
DREV79 Chivalry UR	1.00	2.50
DREV80 Light of Destruction	.10	.30
DREV81 Amazoness Scouts R	.40	1.00
DREV82 Naturia Pnpple (SCR)	.75	2.00
DREV83 D.D. Destroyer R	.40	1.00
DREV84 Dark Desertapir R	.40	1.00
DREV85 Psychic Nghtmre (SCR)	1.50	4.00
DREV86 Guts of Steel R	.40	1.00
DREV87 Amznss Hrlm (SR)	1.00	2.50
DREV88 Amznss Shmnsm (SR)	.40	1.00
DREV89 Super Rush (SR)	.40	1.00
DREV90 Mystical Refpanel SCR	8.00	20.00
DREV91 Fabled Raven SCR	2.50	6.00
DREV92 Cyclone Creator (SCR)	.75	2.00
DREV93 Miracle's Wake SCR	.75	2.00
DREV94 Flamvell Poun	.10	.30
DREV95 Flamvell Archer	.10	.30
DREV96 Flamvell Fiend	.10	.30
DREV97 Genex Worker	.10	.30
DREV98 Genex Power Planner	.10	.30
DREV99 Stygian Street (SCR)	2.00	5.00

2010 Yu-Gi-Oh Starstrike Blast 1st Edition

Card	Low	High
COMPLETE SET (100)	200.00	275.00
BOOSTER BOX (24 PACKS)	75.00	125.00
BOOSTER PACK (9 CARDS)	3.50	6.00
RELEASED ON NOVEMBER 16, 2010		
STBLEN000 Archfiend Empress SR	.75	2.00
STBLEN001 Swift Scarecrow	.40	1.00
STBLEN002 Mirror Ladybug	.10	.30
STBLEN003 Reed Butterfly	.10	.30
STBLEN004 Needle Soldier	.10	.30
STBLEN005 Necro Linker	.10	.30
STBLEN006 Rescue Warrior	.10	.30
STBLEN007 Power Giant UTR	1.50	4.00
STBLEN007 Power Giant UR	.75	2.00
STBLEN008 Vice Berserker	.10	.30
STBLEN009 Lancer Archfiend R	.40	1.00
STBLEN010 Power Breaker SR	1.00	2.50
STBLEN011 Extra Veiler	.10	.30
STBLEN012 Synchro Soldier	.10	.30
STBLEN013 Creation Resonator R	.40	1.00
STBLEN014 Attack Gainer	.10	.30
STBLEN015 Blackwing - Etesian of Two Swords	.10	.30
STBLEN016 Blackwing - Aurora the Northern Lights R	.40	1.00
STBLEN017 Blackwing - Abrolhos the Megaquake R	.40	1.00
STBLEN018 Glow-Up Bulb UTR	10.00	25.00
STBLEN018 Glow Up Bulb UR	3.00	8.00
STBLEN019 Karakuri Soldier mdl 236 Nisamu	.10	.30
STBLEN020 Karakuri Merchant mdl 177 Inashichi R	.40	1.00
STBLEN021 Karakuri Strategist mdl 248 Nishipachi	.40	1.00
STBLEN022 Karakuri Ninja mdl 339 Sazank SR	.50	1.25
STBLEN023 Karakuri Bushi mdl 6318 Muzanichiha R	.40	1.00
STBLEN024 Scrap Soldier R	.40	1.00
STBLEN025 Scrap Searcher	.10	.30
STBLEN026 Wattkiwi	.10	.30
STBLEN027 Watthopper	.10	.30
STBLEN028 Wattdragonfly	.10	.30
STBLEN029 Wattsquirrel R	.40	1.00
STBLEN030 Naturia Cherries SR	5.00	12.00
STBLEN031 Naturia Pumpkin	.10	.30
STBLEN032 Naturia Stag Beetle	.10	.30
STBLEN033 Dance Princess of the Ice Barrier SR	3.00	8.00
STBLEN034 Chain Dog R	.40	1.00
STBLEN035 Wightmare	2.50	6.00
STBLEN036 Anarchist Monk Ranshin SR	1.00	2.50
STBLEN037 Delg the Dark Monarch SR	3.00	8.00
STBLEN038 Supreme Arcanite Magician UTR	3.00	8.00
STBLEN038 Supreme Arcanite Magician UR	3.00	8.00
STBLEN039 Gaia Drake, the Universal Force UTR	6.00	15.00
STBLEN039 Gaia Drake the Universal Force UR	5.00	12.00
STBLEN040 Shooting Star Dragon GR	10.00	25.00
STBLEN040 Shooting Star Dragon UR	3.00	8.00
STBLEN040 Shooting Star Dragon UTR	4.00	10.00
STBLEN041 Formula Synchron R	2.00	5.00
STBLEN042 Red Nova Dragon UTR	3.00	8.00
STBLEN042 Red Nova Dragon UR	1.50	4.00
STBLEN043 Karakuri Shogun mdl 00 Burei UR	.75	2.00
STBLEN043 Karakuri Shogun mdl 00 Burei UTR	2.00	5.00
STBLEN044 Scrap Twin Dragon UTR	2.00	5.00
STBLEN044 Scrap Twin Dragon UR	1.50	4.00
STBLEN045 Tuning UTR	5.00	12.00
STBLEN045 Tuning UR	2.00	5.00
STBLEN046 Karakuri Showdown Castle R	.40	1.00
STBLEN047 Golden Gearbox	.10	.30
STBLEN048 Karakuri Anatomy	.10	.30
STBLEN049 Scrap Lube	.10	.30
STBLEN050 Wattcastle R	.40	1.00
STBLEN051 Wattjustment	.10	.30
STBLEN052 Barkion's Bark	.10	.30
STBLEN053 Leodrake's Mane	.10	.30
STBLEN054 Medallion of the Ice Barrier	.10	.30
STBLEN055 Mirror of the Ice Barrier	.10	.30
STBLEN056 Koa'ki Ring	.10	.30
STBLEN057 Darkworld Shackles	.10	.30
STBLEN058 Axe of Fools	.10	.30
STBLEN059 Cursed Bill	.10	.30
STBLEN060 Tokkosho of Ghost Destroying R	.40	1.00
STBLEN061 Heat Wave R	.40	1.00
STBLEN062 White Elephant's Gift	.10	.30
STBLEN063 D2 Shield SR	.75	2.00
STBLEN064 Red Screen	.10	.30
STBLEN065 Blackback SR	.75	2.00
STBLEN066 Defenders Intersect	.10	.30
STBLEN067 Gravity Collapse R	.40	1.00
STBLEN068 Blackwing - Boobytrap	.10	.30
STBLEN069 Star Siphon	.10	.30
STBLEN070 Half Counter	.10	.30
STBLEN071 Karakuri Trick House	.10	.30
STBLEN072 Karakuri Klock SR	.50	1.25
STBLEN073 Scrap Crash	.10	.30
STBLEN074 Wattkeeper	.10	.30
STBLEN075 Exterio's Fang	.10	.30
STBLEN076 Vanity's Emptiness	1.25	3.00
STBLEN077 Different Dimension Ground SR	1.25	3.00
STBLEN078 Powersink Stone	.60	1.50
STBLEN079 Tyrant's Temper SR	1.50	4.00
STBLEN080 Dark Trap Hole	1.25	3.00
STBLEN081 Skull Meister SCR	8.00	20.00
STBLEN082 Droll & Lock Bird R	1.00	2.50
STBLEN083 Spellstone Sorcerer Karood SCR	1.00	2.50
STBLEN084 Scrap Mind Reader SCR	.50	1.25
STBLEN085 Gravekeeper's Recruiter R	2.50	6.00
STBLEN086 Psi-Blocker SCR	2.50	6.00
STBLEN087 Koa'ki Meiru Wall R	.40	1.00
STBLEN088 Karakuri Barrel mdl 96 Shinkuro R	.40	1.00
STBLEN089 Mischief of the Yokai UTR	1.50	4.00
STBLEN089 Mischief of the Yokai UR	1.00	2.50
STBLEN090 Karakuri Spider	.10	.30
STBLEN091 Royal Knight of the Ice Barrier SR	.75	2.00
STBLEN092 Ally Salvo R	.40	1.00
STBLEN093 Ally of Justice Thousand Arms	.10	.30
STBLEN094 Ally of Justice Unknown Crusher	.10	.30
STBLEN095 Genex Ally Duradark SCR	.75	2.00
STBLEN096 The Fabled Rubyruda SCR	1.00	2.50
STBLEN097 Dragunity Knight - Vajrayana SR	2.00	5.00
STBLEN098 Dragunity Knight - Gae Dearg SCR	25.00	50.00
STBLEN099 Genex Ally Axel SCR	1.00	2.50

2011 Yu-Gi-Oh Storm of Ragnarok 1st Edition

Card	Low	High
COMPLETE SET (111)	100.00	200.00
BOOSTER BOX (24 PACKS)	60.00	90.00
BOOSTER PACK (9 CARDS)	2.50	4.00
RELEASED ON FEBRUARY 8, 2011		
STOR000 Vortex Whrlwnd SR	.20	.60
STOR001 Cosmic Compass C	.10	.30
STOR002 Doppelwarrior R	.20	.60
STOR003 Stardust Phantom R	.20	.60
STOR004 D.D. Sprite SR	.20	.60
STOR005 Top Runner C	.10	.30
STOR006 Barrier Resonator C	.10	.30
STOR007 Blackwing Boreas R	.20	.60
STOR008 Blackwing Brisote	.10	.30
STOR009 Blackwing Calima	.10	.30
STOR010 Tanngrisnir SR	.20	.60
STOR011 Guldfaxe R	.20	.60
STOR012 Garmr	.10	.30
STOR013 Tanngnjostr R	.20	.60
STOR014 Ljosalf	.10	.30
STOR015 Svartalf SR	.20	.60
STOR016 Dverg R	.20	.60
STOR017 Valkyrie of Nordic SR	.75	2.00
STOR018 Mimir of Nordic	.10	.30
STOR019 Tyr Nordic Chmpns R	.20	.60
STOR020 LSS Kizan SR	2.50	6.00
STOR021 LSS Enishi UR	.50	1.25
STOR021 LSS Enishi UTR	2.00	5.00
STOR022 LSS Kageki R	.20	.60
STOR023 LSS Shinai	.10	.30
STOR024 LSS Mizuho	.10	.30
STOR025 Kagemusha	.75	2.00
STOR026 Shien's Squire C	.10	.30
STOR027 Karakuri Watchdog	.40	1.00
STOR028 Karakuri Ninja	.10	.30
STOR029 Scrap Worm R	.20	.60
STOR030 Scrap Shark C	.10	.30
STOR031 Wattberyx R	.20	.60
STOR032 Wattmole C	.10	.30
STOR033 SW Basses SR	.20	.60
STOR034 SW Drumss SR	.20	.60
STOR035 SW Piaano R	.20	.60
STOR036 Majioshaleon C	.10	.30
STOR037 Yaksha C	.10	.30
STOR038 Thor, Lord Aesir UR	1.00	2.50
STOR038 Thor, Lord Aesir UTR	2.00	5.00
STOR039 Loki, Lord Aesir UTR	1.25	3.00
STOR039 Loki, Lord Aesir UR	1.00	2.50
STOR040 Odin, Father Aesir UR	1.00	2.50
STOR040 Odin, Father Aesir UTR	1.00	2.50
STOR040 Odin, Father Aesir GR	3.00	8.00
STOR041 LSS Shi En UTR	8.00	20.00
STOR041 LSS Shi En UR	4.00	10.00
STOR042 Karakuri Steel UR	.75	2.00
STOR042 Karakuri Steel UTR	2.00	5.00
STOR043 Atomic Scrap UTR	.50	1.25
STOR043 Atomic Scrap UR	.50	1.25
STOR044 Watthydra SR	.20	.60
STOR045 Nordic Relic Draupnir C	.10	.30
STOR046 Gotterdammerung C	.10	.30
STOR047 March Towards R	.20	.60
STOR048 Shien's Smoke R	.20	.60
STOR049 Six Strike Triple	.20	.60
STOR050 Asceticism of SS R	2.50	6.00
STOR051 Temple of the Six SR	.20	.60
STOR052 Karakuri Cash Cache C	.10	.30
STOR053 Karakuri Gold Dust C	.10	.30
STOR054 Wattkey C	.10	.30
STOR055 Strdst Shmmer (SR)	1.50	4.00
STOR056 Resonator Engine C	.10	.30
STOR057 Token Sundae C	.10	.30
STOR058 Foolish Return R	.20	.60
STOR059 Divine Wind	.10	.30
STOR060 Vylon Matter C	.10	.30
STOR061 Forbidden Lance SR	1.50	4.00
STOR062 Terminal World C	.10	.30
STOR063 Hope for Escape R	.60	1.50
STOR064 Zero Force C	.10	.30
STOR065 Blackboost C	.10	.30
STOR066 Divine Relic Mjollnir C	.10	.30
STOR067 Solemn Authority C	.10	.30
STOR068 NR Brisingamen	.10	.30
STOR069 NR Laevateinn	.10	.30
STOR070 NR Gungnir R	.20	.60
STOR071 Golden Apples SCR	.75	2.00
STOR072 Odin's Eye C	.10	.30
STOR073 Gleipnir, Fetters UR	.75	2.00
STOR073 Gleipnir, Fetters UTR	1.25	3.00
STOR074 Muskni Magtma R	.20	.60
STOR075 Shien's Scheme C	.10	.30
STOR076 Token Stampede C	.10	.30
STOR077 Xing Zhen Hu Replica C	.10	.30
STOR078 Tyrant's Tirade C	.10	.30
STOR079 Tiki Curse C	.10	.30
STOR080 Tiki Soul C	.10	.30
STOR081 Vanadis of NA SCR	3.00	8.00
STOR082 Shien's Daredevil R	.20	.60
STOR083 Karakuri Muso UR	.50	1.25
STOR083 Karakuri Muso UTR	.50	1.25
STOR084 Scrap Breaker SCR	.50	1.25
STOR085 Chaos Hunter SCR	5.00	12.00
STOR086 Maxx C SCR	20.00	40.00
STOR087 Nordic Lights UR	.50	1.25
STOR087 Nordic Lights UTR	.50	1.25
STOR088 NR Megingiord SCR	.50	1.25
STOR089 Six Strike Thunder SCR	.50	1.25
STOR090 Cyber Shield C	.10	.30
STOR091 Hourglass of Courage C	.10	.30
STOR092 Needle Ball C	.10	.30
STOR093 Blood Sucker C	.10	.30
STOR094 Overpowering Eye R	.20	.60

STOR095 Worm Illidan C .10 .30
STOR096 Worm Jetelikpse C .10 .30
STOR097 Worm King SR .20 .60
STOR098 EH Ice Edge SR .75 2.00
STOR099 Vylon Delta SCR 1.50 4.00

2011 Yu-Gi-Oh Extreme Victory 1st Edition

COMPLETE SET (110) 125.00 250.00
BOOSTER BOX (24 PACKS) 50.00 75.00
BOOSTER PACK (9 CARDS) 2.50 4.00
RELEASED ON MAY 10, 2011
EXVC000 Reborn Tengu SR 1.00 2.50
EXVC001 Junk Servant R .50 1.25
EXVC002 Unknown Synchron .10 .30
EXVC003 Salvage Warrior R .30 .75
EXVC004 Necro Defender R .30 .75
EXVC005 Mystic Piper SCR 8.00 20.00
EXVC006 Force Resonator .10 .30
EXVC007 Clock Resonator .10 .30
EXVC008 Hillen Tengu SR .40 1.00
EXVC009 Kogarashi UTR 1.50 4.00
EXVC009 Kogarashi UR .75 2.00
EXVC010 Morphtronic Lantron .10 .30
EXVC011 Morphtronic Staplen .10 .30
EXVC012 Meklord Army of Wisel .10 .30
EXVC013 Meklord Army of Skiel .10 .30
EXVC014 Meklord Army Granel R .30 .75
EXVC015 Dragon Asterisk SR .40 1.00
EXVC016 Cyber Magician SR .40 1.00
EXVC017 T.G. Striker R .50 1.25
EXVC018 T.G. Jet Falcon .10 .30
EXVC019 T.G. Catapult Dragon .10 .30
EXVC020 T.G. Warwolf .10 .30
EXVC021 T.G. Rush Rhino R .40 1.00
EXVC022 Buster Blaster R .50 1.25
EXVC023 Esper Girl .10 .30
EXVC024 Mental Seeker .10 .30
EXVC025 Silent Psych Wiz SR .40 1.00
EXVC026 Serene Psychic Witch .10 .30
EXVC027 Hushed Psych Cleric R .75 2.00
EXVC028 Elder of Six Samurai .10 .30
EXVC029 Shien's Advisor SR .40 1.00
EXVC030 Karakuri Komachi .10 .30
EXVC031 Karakuri Ninja .10 .30
EXVC032 Scrap Kong .10 .30
EXVC033 Tradetoad R .30 .75
EXVC034 Gladiator Tygerius .10 .30
EXVC035 Jar Turtle .10 .30
EXVC036 Aurora Paragon .10 .30
EXVC037 Junk Berserker UTR 2.00 5.00
EXVC037 Junk Berserker GR 2.50 6.00
EXVC037 Junk Berserker UR 1.00 2.50
EXVC038 Life Strm Dragon UR 1.50 4.00
EXVC038 Life Strm Dragon UTR 2.00 5.00
EXVC039 Recipro Dragonfly R .75 2.00
EXVC040 Wonder Magician UTR 1.25 3.00
EXVC040 Wonder Magician UR .75 2.00
EXVC041 Power Gladiator SR .40 1.00
EXVC042 Blade Blaster UR .75 2.00
EXVC042 Blade Blaster UTR 1.00 2.50
EXVC043 Halberd Cannon UR .75 2.00
EXVC043 Halberd Cannon UTR 1.00 2.50
EXVC044 Ovrmnd Archfnd UTR 1.25 3.00
EXVC044 Ovrmnd Archfnd UR 1.50 4.00
EXVC045 Scarlet Security .10 .30
EXVC046 Red Dragon Vase .10 .30
EXVC047 Resonator Call R .60 1.50
EXVC048 Resonant Destruction .10 .30
EXVC049 Fortissimo the Mobile .10 .30
EXVC050 Boon of the Meklord .10 .30
EXVC051 Resolute Meklord Army .10 .30
EXVC052 Reboot .10 .30
EXVC053 TGX1-HL .10 .30
EXVC054 TGX300 .10 .30
EXVCE55 ESP Amplifier .10 .30
EXVC056 Psychic Feel Zone R 1.25 3.00
EXVC057 Shien's Dojo SR .40 1.00
EXVC058 Runaway Karakuri .10 .30
EXVC059 Contact Aquamirror .10 .30
EXVC060 Soundproofed R .30 .75
EXVC061 Out of the Blue .10 .30
EXVC062 Self-Mummification .10 .30
EXVC063 Red Carpet .10 .30
EXVC064 Power-Up Adapter .10 .30
EXVC065 Chaos Infinity R .50 1.25
EXVC066 Mektimed Blast .10 .30
EXVC067 Meklord Factory .10 .30
EXVC068 TGX3-DX2 R .50 1.25
EXVC069 TG-SX1 .10 .30
EXVC070 TG1-EM1 .10 .30
EXVC071 Psychic Reactor .10 .30
EXVC072 Brain Hazard R .50 1.25
EXVC073 Six Style - Dual Wield .10 .30
EXVC074 Karakuri Cash SR .40 1.00
EXVC075 Tyrant's Tantrum .10 .30
EXVC076 Debunk SR 1.00 2.50
EXVC077 Sealing Ceremony .10 .30
EXVC078 Safe Zone SR 1.50 4.00
EXVC079 Localized Tornado .40 1.00
EXVC080 W Nebula Meteorite .10 .30
EXVC081 Vampire Dragon SCR 1.25 3.00
EXVC082 Dodger Dragon SR 1.50 4.00
EXVC083 Mara Alfar UR .75 2.00
EXVC083 Mara Alfar UTR 1.25 3.00
EXVC084 Tour Guide Undrwrld SCR 8.00 20.00
EXVC085 Psi-Beast R .60 1.50
EXVC086 Gladiator Beast UR 1.25 3.00
EXVC086 Gladiator Beast UTR 1.50 4.00
EXVC087 Gladiator Taming SCR .40 1.00
EXVC088 Full House R .50 1.25
EXVC089 Psych Shckwve SCR 3.00 8.00
EXVC090 Axe Dragonute .10 .30
EXVC091 Lancer Dragonute SR .40 1.00
EXVC092 Lancer Lindwurm .10 .30
EXVC093 EH Neos Knight UR 3.00 8.00
EXVC093 EH Neos Knight UTR 3.00 8.00
EXVC094 Meklord Emperor SCR 1.50 4.00
EXVC095 Meklord Fortress R .30 .75
EXVC096 Blackwing Rain Shadow R .60 1.50
EXVC097 Scrap Orthros SCR 1.25 3.00
EXVC098 Naturia Eggplant SR .40 1.00
EXVC099 Blue Rose SCR 1.50 4.00

2011 Yu-Gi-Oh Generation Force 1st Edition

COMPLETE SET (111) 100.00 200.00
BOOSTER BOX (24 PACKS) 60.00 90.00
BOOSTER PACK (9 CARDS) 2.50 4.00
RELEASED ON AUGUST 16, 2011
GENFEN000 Xyz Veil SR .25 .75
GENFEN001 Gagaga Magician SR .20 .60
GENFEN002 Gogogo Golem .10 .30
GENFEN003 Achacha Archer .10 .30
GENFEN004 Goblindbergh .25 .75
GENFEN005 Big Jaws R .20 .60
GENFEN006 Skull Kraken .10 .30
GENFEN007 Drill Barnacle .10 .30
GENFEN008 Jawsman R .20 .60
GENFEN009 Crashbug X .10 .30
GENFEN010 Crashbug Y .10 .30
GENFEN011 Crashbug Z .10 .30
GENFEN012 Super Crashbug SR .20 .60
GENFEN013 Wind-Up Soldier .10 .30
GENFEN014 Wind-Up Magician R .20 .60
GENFEN015 Wind-Up Juggler SR .20 .60
GENFEN016 Wind-Up Dog .10 .30
GENFEN017 Wind-Up Snail R .20 .60
GENFEN018 Spearfish Soldier .10 .30
GENFEN019 Flyfang .10 .30
GENFEN020 Skystarray R .20 .60
GENFEN021 Airorca R .20 .60
GENFEN022 Wingtortoise R .20 .60
GENFEN023 Space-Time Police UR .20 .60
GENFEN023 Space-Time Police UTR .40 1.00
GENFEN024 Time Escaper SR .20 .60
GENFEN025 Gem-Elephant .10 .30
GENFEN026 Laval Magma Cannoneer .10 .30
GENFEN027 Gishki Diviner R .20 .60
GENFEN028 Gusto Codor .10 .30
GENFEN029 Saambell the Summoner .10 .30
GENFEN030 Gearglano .10 .30
GENFEN031 Poki Draco .10 .30
GENFEN032 Master of the Flaming Dragonswords .10 .30
GENFEN033 Perditious Puppeteer .10 .30
GENFEN034 Blue-Blooded Oni SR .25 .75
GENFEN035 Ghost Ship R .20 .60
GENFEN036 Absolute Crusader SR .20 .60
GENFEN037 Big Emperor Penguin .10 .30
GENFEN038 Milla the Temporal Magician .10 .30
GENFEN039 17: Leviathan Dragon GR 3.00 8.00
GENFEN039 17: Leviathan Dragon UTR .75 2.00
GENFEN039 17: Leviathan Dragon UR .50 1.25
GENFEN040 Submersible Carrier SR .20 .60
GENFEN041 Number 34: Terror-Byte UTR .40 1.00
GENFEN041 Number 34: Terror-Byte UR .20 .60
GENFEN042 Wind-Up Zenmaister UTR .50 1.25
GENFEN042 Wind-Up Zenmaister UR .20 .60
GENFEN043 Leviair the Sea Dragon UTR 15.00 30.00
GENFEN043 Leviair the Sea Dragon UR 6.00 15.00
GENFEN044 Tiras, Keeper of Genesis SCR 4.00 10.00
GENFEN045 Wonder Wand UTR 4.00 10.00
GENFEN045 Wonder Wand UR 2.50 6.00
GENFEN046 Double Up Chance .10 .30
GENFEN047 Thunder Short .10 .30
GENFEN048 Aqua Jet .10 .30
GENFEN049 Surface SR 1.25 3.00
GENFEN050 Crashbug Road .10 .30
GENFEN051 Infected Mail SR .20 .60
GENFEN052 Cracking .10 .30
GENFEN053 Legendary Wind-Up .10 .30
GENFEN054 Wind-Up Factory SR 1.00 2.50
GENFEN055 Fish and Kicks .10 .30
GENFEN056 Future Glow .10 .30
GENFEN057 Vylon Filament .10 .30
GENFEN058 Quill Pen of Gulldos SR 1.25 3.00
GENFEN059 Star Changer R .20 .60
GENFEN060 Oni-Gami Combo .10 .30
GENFEN061 Resonance Device R .20 .60
GENFEN062 Peeking Goblin .10 .30
GENFEN063 Asleep at the Switch .10 .30
GENFEN064 Poseidon Waves .10 .30
GENFEN065 Explosive Urchin .10 .30
GENFEN066 Damage Vaccine MAX .10 .30
GENFEN067 Overwind .10 .30
GENFEN068 Underworld Egg Clutch .10 .30
GENFEN069 Oh F!sh! R .20 .60
GENFEN070 Bright Future R .20 .60
GENFEN071 Past Image .10 .30
GENFEN072 Burgeoning Whirlflame .10 .30
GENFEN073 Treaty on Uniform Nomenclature .10 .30
GENFEN074 Utopian Aura .10 .30
GENFEN075 United Front R .20 .60
GENFEN076 Curse of the Circle R .20 .60
GENFEN077 Tyrant's Tummyache .10 .30
GENFEN078 Attention! R .20 .60
GENFEN079 Raigeki Bottle UTR .40 1.00
GENFEN079 Raigeki Bottle UR .20 .60
GENFEN080 Gravelstorm .10 .30
GENFEN081 Sea Lancer R .20 .60
GENFEN082 Piercing Moray UR .20 .60
GENFEN082 Piercing Moray UTR .40 1.00
GENFEN083 Lost Blue Breaker SCR .40 1.00
GENFEN084 Pain Painter SCR 3.00 8.00
GENFEN085 Orient Dragon SCR .75 2.00
GENFEN086 Adreus, Keeper SCR 15.00 30.00
GENFEN087 Fish and Swaps R .20 .60
GENFEN088 Painful Return R .20 .60
GENFEN089 Smashing Horn SCR 1.50 4.00
GENFEN090 Elemental HERO Flash .10 .30
GENFEN091 Vision HERO Trinity SR 2.50 6.00
GENFEN092 Phantom Magician .10 .30
GENFEN093 Elemental HERO Nova UTR 8.00 20.00
GENFEN093 Elemental HERO Nova UR 8.00 20.00
GENFEN094 Masked HERO Goka R 1.00 2.50
GENFEN095 Masked HERO Vapor SR 3.00 8.00
GENFEN096 Vision HERO Adoration SCR 8.00 20.00
GENFEN097 Mask Change .40 1.00
GENFEN098 A Hero Lives UTR 8.00 20.00
GENFEN098 A Hero Lives UR 3.00 8.00
GENFEN099 Steelswarm Roach SCR 2.50 6.00

2011 Yu-Gi-Oh Photon Shockwave 1st Edition

COMPLETE SET (111) 100.00 200.00
BOOSTER BOX (24 PACKS) 50.00 80.00
BOOSTER PACK (9 CARDS) 2.50 4.00
RELEASED ON NOVEMBER 15, 2011
PHSW000 Alexandrite Dragon SR .75 2.00
PHSW001 Bunilla .10 .30
PHSW002 Rabidragon .10 .30
PHSW003 Rai Rider .10 .30
PHSW004 Stinging Swordsman .10 .30
PHSW005 Kagetokage R .25 .60
PHSW006 Acorno .10 .30
PHSW007 Pinecono .10 .30
PHSW008 Friller Rabca SR .20 .60
PHSW009 Shark Stickers .10 .30
PHSW010 Needle Sunfish .10 .30
PHSW011 Galaxy-Eyes Dragon UTR 3.00 8.00
PHSW011 Galaxy-Eyes Dragon GR 8.00 20.00
PHSW011 Galaxy-Eyes Dragon UR 2.50 6.00
PHSW012 Daybreaker R .25 .60
PHSW013 Lightserpent SR .20 .60
PHSW014 Plasma Ball .10 .30
PHSW015 Photon Cerberus R .25 .60
PHSW016 Evoltile Gephyro .10 .30
PHSW017 Evoltile Westlo SR .75 2.00
PHSW018 Evoltile Odonto .10 .30
PHSW019 Evolsaur Vulcano R .25 .60
PHSW020 Evolsaur Cerato UTR 1.00 2.50
PHSW020 Evolsaur Cerato UR .60 1.50
PHSW021 Evolsaur Diplo R .25 .60
PHSW022 Wind-Up Warrior .10 .30
PHSW023 Wind-Up Knight R .25 .60
PHSW024 Wind-Up Hunter SR .20 .60
PHSW025 Wind-Up Bat .10 .30
PHSW026 Wind-Up Kitten (UR) 1.25 3.00
PHSW026 Wind-Up Kitten UTR 1.50 4.00
PHSW027 D.D. Telepon R .25 .60
PHSW028 Wattcobra .10 .30
PHSW029 Naturia Marron .10 .30
PHSW030 Prior of the Ice Barrier .10 .30
PHSW031 Senior Silver Ninja .10 .30
PHSW032 Rodenut .10 .30
PHSW033 Fenghuang SR .20 .60
PHSW034 Tribe-Shocking Virus R .25 .60
PHSW035 Goblin Pothole Squad .10 .30
PHSW036 Creepy Coney .10 .30
PHSW037 Rescue Rabbit SCR 6.00 15.00
PHSW038 Baby Tiragon R .40 1.00
PHSW039 83: Galaxy Queen SR .40 1.00
PHSW040 Black Ray Lancer SR .20 .60
PHSW041 10: Illumiknight UR .40 1.00
PHSW041 10: Illumiknight UTR .60 1.50
PHSW042 20: Giga-Brilliant SR .20 .60
PHSW043 Evolzar Laggia UTR 1.50 4.00
PHSW043 Evolzar Laggia UR .50 1.25
PHSW044 Thunder End Dragon UR 4.00 10.00
PHSW044 Thunder End Dragon UTR 5.00 12.00
PHSW045 Attraffic Control .10 .30
PHSW046 Ego Boost .10 .30
PHSW047 Monster Slots .10 .30
PHSW048 Cross Attack .10 .30
PHSW049 Xyz Gift UTR .40 1.00
PHSW049 Xyz Gift UR .20 .60
PHSW050 Photon Veil UR .50 1.25
PHSW050 Photon Veil UTR 1.50 4.00
PHSW051 Photon Lead .40 1.00
PHSW052 Photon Booster R .25 .60
PHSW053 Evo-Karma .10 .30
PHSW054 Evo-Miracle .10 .30
PHSW055 Zenmailfunction .10 .30
PHSW056 Extra Gate SR .20 .60
PHSW057 Shard of Greed SCR .75 2.00
PHSW058 Murmur of the Forest R .25 .60
PHSW059 Tri-Wight .50 1.25
PHSW060 One Day of Peace .75 2.00
PHSW061 Space Cyclone .10 .30
PHSW062 Poisonous Winds .40 1.00
PHSW063 Heartfelt Appeal .10 .30
PHSW064 Fiery Fervor .10 .30
PHSW065 Damage Diet .10 .30
PHSW066 Copy Knight R .25 .60
PHSW067 Mirror Mail .10 .30
PHSW068 Fish Rain .10 .30
PHSW069 Icy Crevasse .10 .30
PHSW070 Lumenize .20 .60
PHSW071 Evolutionary Bridge .10 .30
PHSW072 Zenmairch .10 .30
PHSW073 Wattcancel .10 .30
PHSW074 Champion's Vigilance .10 .30
PHSW075 Darklight SR .20 .60
PHSW076 Tyrant's Throes R .75 2.00
PHSW077 Sound the Retreat! .10 .30
PHSW078 Deep Dark Trap Hole R .40 1.00
PHSW079 Eisbahn R .40 1.00
PHSW080 Sealing Ceremony of Suiton .10 .30
PHSW081 Photon Sabre Tiger SR .40 1.00
PHSW082 Evolsaur Pelta R .25 .60
PHSW083 Wind-Up Rabbit SCR .75 2.00
PHSW084 D-Boyz SCR .75 2.00
PHSW085 Latinum, Exarch UR .20 .60
PHSW085 Latinum, Exarch UTR .60 1.50
PHSW086 Evolzar Dolkka SCR .75 2.00
PHSW087 Wind-Up Zenmaines SCR .75 2.00
PHSW088 Xyz Territory R .25 .60
PHSW089 Dark Smog SCR .75 2.00
PHSW090 Sergeant Electro UTR .40 1.00
PHSW090 Sergeant Electro UR .20 .60
PHSW091 Vylon Ohm .10 .30
PHSW092 Laval Dual Slasher .10 .30
PHSW093 Gem-Turtle SR .40 1.00
PHSW094 Laval Lancelord .10 .30
PHSW095 Gishki Beast R .25 .60
PHSW096 Gem-Knight Emerald R .25 .60
PHSW097 Junk Defender R .25 .60
PHSW098 Metaion, Timelord SCR .75 2.00
PHSW099 Infernity Knight SR .20 .60

2012 Yu-Gi-Oh Order of Chaos 1st Edition

COMPLETE SET (113) 250.00 350.00
BOOSTER BOX (24 PACKS) 50.00 80.00
BOOSTER PACK (9 CARDS) 2.50 4.00
RELEASED ON JANUARY 24, 2012
ORCS000 Axe - Zektahawk UR .50 1.25
ORCS000 Axe - Zektahawk SR .25 .75
ORCS001 Kurivolt .10 .30
ORCS002 Darklon .10 .30
ORCS003 Gagaga Girl SCR 2.00 5.00
ORCS004 Gogogo Giant R .10 .30
ORCS005 ZW - Unicorn Spear R .10 .30
ORCS006 Shocktopus .10 .30
ORCS007 Photon Lizard R .10 .30
ORCS008 Photon Thrasher R .50 1.25
ORCS009 Photon Crusher .10 .30
ORCS010 Photon Leo .10 .30
ORCS011 Photon Circle .10 .30
ORCS012 Reverse Buster R .10 .30
ORCS013 Flame Armor Ninja .10 .30
ORCS014 Air Armor Ninja .10 .30
ORCS015 Aqua Armor Ninja .10 .30
ORCS016 Earth Armor Ninja .10 .30
ORCS017 Inzektor Hornet SR 1.50 4.00
ORCS018 Inzektor Ant .10 .30
ORCS019 Inzektor Centipede .10 .30
ORCS020 Inzektor Dragonfly R .10 .30
ORCS021 Inzekt Giga-Mantis UTR .50 1.25
ORCS021 Inzekt Giga-Mantis UR .50 1.25
ORCS022 Inzektor Giga-Weevil .10 .30
ORCS023 Wind-Up Rat SR .50 1.25
ORCS024 Wind-Up Honeybee .10 .30
ORCS025 Evoltile Pleuro .10 .30
ORCS026 Evoltile Casinerio R .10 .30
ORCS027 Evolsaur Elias .10 .30
ORCS028 Evolsaur Terias .10 .30
ORCS029 Grandmaster Hanzo UR .50 1.25
ORCS029 Grandmaster Hanzo UTR 1.50 4.00
ORCS030 Masked Ninja Ebisu .10 .30
ORCS031 Upstart Golden Ninja .10 .30
ORCS032 Chow Len the Prophet .10 .30
ORCS033 Familiar-Possessed - Dharc .10 .30
ORCS034 Dark Blade the Captain R .10 .30
ORCS035 Trance Archfiend SP .10 .30
ORCS036 Divine Dragon Apocralyph .10 .30
ORCS037 Darkstorm Dragon SR .25 .75
ORCS038 Numen erat Testudo .10 .30
ORCS039 Twin Photon Lizard UR .50 1.25
ORCS039 Twin Photon Lizard UTR .50 1.25
ORCS040 C39: Utopia Ray UTR .75 2.00
ORCS040 C39: Utopia Ray UR .50 1.25
ORCS040 C39: Utopia Ray GR 2.50 6.00
ORCS041 Blade Armor Ninja SR .75 2.00
ORCS042 12: Crimson Shadow UTR .50 1.25
ORCS042 12: Crimson Shadow UR .50 1.25
ORCS043 96: Dark Mist UR .75 2.00
ORCS043 96: Dark Mist UTR .75 2.00
ORCS044 Wind-Up Carrier UTR 2.50 6.00
ORCS044 Wind-Up Carrier UR 2.50 6.00
ORCS045 Evolzar Solda UTR .50 1.25
ORCS045 Evolzar Solda UR 1.25 3.00
ORCS046 Inzektor Exa-Beetle SCR 1.50 4.00
ORCS047 Full-Force Strike .10 .30
ORCS048 Gagagabolt R .10 .30
ORCS049 Double Defender .10 .30
ORCS050 Galaxy Storm .10 .30
ORCS051 Ninjitsu Alchemy SR .25 .75
ORCS052 Star Light, Star Bright .10 .30
ORCS053 Armor Blast SR .25 .75
ORCS054 Sword - Zektkaliber UTR .50 1.25
ORCS054 Sword - Zektkaliber UR 1.00 2.50
ORCS055 Weights & Zenmaisures R .10 .30
ORCS056 Primordial Soup .10 .30
ORCS057 Evo-Force SR .25 .75
ORCS058 Dark Mambele .10 .30
ORCS059 Creeping Darkness SR .25 .75
ORCS060 Shrine of Mist Valley R .10 .30
ORCS061 Xyz Burst .10 .30
ORCS062 Galaxy Wave .10 .30
ORCS063 Dicephoon .10 .30
ORCS064 Counterforce .10 .30
ORCS065 Gagagaguard R .10 .30
ORCS066 Xyz Reflect UTR .50 1.25
ORCS066 Xyz Reflect UR .50 1.25
ORCS067 Splash Capture .10 .30
ORCS068 Armor Ninjitsu Freezing .10 .30
ORCS069 Armor Ninjitsu Freezing .25 .75
ORCS070 Inzektor Orb R .10 .30
ORCS071 Variable Form .10 .30
ORCS072 Zenmailstrom .10 .30
ORCS073 Degen-Force .10 .30
ORCS074 Evo-Branch .10 .30
ORCS075 Ninjitsu Super-Trans SR 1.00 2.50
ORCS076 Xyz Reborn SCR 2.50 6.00
ORCS077 Over Capacity R .10 .30
ORCS078 The Huge Revolution is Over 1.00 2.50
ORCS079 Royal Prison R .10 .30
ORCS080 Sealing Ceremony of Katon .10 .30
ORCS081 Inzektor Hopper R .10 .30
ORCS082 Wind-Up Shark SR .25 .75
ORCS083 Evoltile Najasho SR .25 .75
ORCS084 White Dragon Ninja SCR 3.00 8.00
ORCS085 Interplanet. Dragon .10 .30
ORCS086 Tour Bus Undrwrld SCR 1.25 3.00
ORCS087 Photon Trident .10 .30
ORCS088 Evo-Instant R .10 .30
ORCS089 Ninjitsu Duplication R .10 .30
ORCS090 White Night Queen R .10 .30
ORCS091 Danipon .10 .30
ORCS092 Sweet Corn .10 .30
ORCS093 Vampire Koala .10 .30
ORCS094 Koalo-Koala .10 .30
ORCS095 Dark Diviner SR .25 .75
ORCS096 Dark Flattop R .10 .30
ORCS097 Driven Daredevil SCR .60 1.50
ORCS098 Arsenal Zenmaioh SCR 10.00 25.00
ORCS099 M-X-Saber Invoker SCR 5.00 12.00
ORCSSP1 Axe - Zektahawk PROMO .10 .30

2012 Yu-Gi-Oh Order of Chaos Special Edition

COMPLETE SET (2) 5.00 10.00
ONE PER SPECIAL EDITION BOX
ORCSSE1 Effect Veiler SR 2.50 6.00
ORCSSE2 Winged Dragon (SR) 2.00 5.00

2012 Yu-Gi-Oh Galactic Overlord 1st Edition

COMPLETE SET (111) 250.00 350.00
BOOSTER BOX (24 PACKS) 60.00 90.00
BOOSTER PACK (9 CARDS) 3.00 4.00
RELEASED ON MAY 8, 2012
GAOV000 Noble Knight SR .20 .60
GAOV001 Wattaildragon .10 .30
GAOV002 Hieratic Seal of the Sun Dragon Overlord .10 .30
GAOV003 Overlay Owl .10 .30
GAOV004 Tasuke Knight SR .20 .60
GAOV005 Gagaga Gardna R .25 .75
GAOV006 Cardcar D SCR 2.50 6.00
GAOV007 Overlay Eater .10 .30
GAOV008 Hammer Shark R .25 .75
GAOV009 Hammer Bounzer SR .20 .60
GAOV010 Blade Bounzer .10 .30
GAOV011 Phantom Bounzer .10 .30
GAOV012 Morpho Butterspy .10 .30
GAOV013 Swallowtail Butterspy .10 .30
GAOV014 Moonlit Papillon .10 .30
GAOV015 Jumbo Drill SR .20 .60
GAOV016 Rocket Arrow Express R .25 .75
GAOV017 Cameraclops .10 .30
GAOV018 Hieratic Dragon of Nuit .10 .30
GAOV019 Dragon of Gebeb SR 1.00 2.50
GAOV020 Hieratic Dragon of Eset .10 .30
GAOV021 Hieratic Dragon of Nebthet .20 .75
GAOV022 Dragon of Tefnuit R .25 .75
GAOV023 Hieratic Dragon of Su .10 .30
GAOV024 Hieratic Dragon of Asar R .25 .75
GAOV025 Dragon of Sutekh UR .60 1.50
GAOV025 Dragon of Sutekh UTR .60 1.50
GAOV026 Evoltile Lagosucho .10 .30
GAOV027 Evolsaur Darwino .10 .30
GAOV028 Inzektor Firefly .10 .30
GAOV029 Inzektor Ladybug .10 .30
GAOV030 Inzektor Earwig .10 .30
GAOV031 Inzektor Giga-Cricket R .25 .75
GAOV032 Lightray Sorcerer R .25 .75
GAOV033 Lightray Daedalus .10 .30
GAOV034 Lightray Gearfried R .25 .75
GAOV035 Lightray Diabolos R .25 .75
GAOV036 Lady of D. .40 1.00
GAOV037 Absorbing Jar R .25 .75
GAOV038 Red-Headed Oni .10 .30
GAOV039 Flame Tiger .10 .30
GAOV040 Nomadic Force .10 .30
GAOV041 Neo Galaxy-Eyes UR 5.00 12.00
GAOV041 Neo Galaxy-Eyes (GR) 8.00 20.00
GAOV041 Neo Galaxy-Eyes UTR 5.00 12.00
GAOV042 Shark Drake UTR .60 1.50
GAOV042 Shark Drake UR 1.00 2.50
GAOV043 Photon Strike SCR 1.50 4.00
GAOV044 Photon Papilloperative R .25 .75
GAOV045 Force Focus UR .60 1.50
GAOV045 Force Focus UTR .60 1.50
GAOV046 Gaia Dragon SR 8.00 20.00
GAOV047 Dragon King of Atum SR 3.00 8.00
GAOV048 Dragon Overlord SCR 4.00 10.00
GAOV049 Dragun Djinn SR 5.00 12.00
GAOV050 Inzektor Exa-Stag UTR .60 1.50
GAOV050 Inzektor Exa-Stag UR .60 1.50
GAOV051 Bound Wand (SR) .75 2.00
GAOV052 Mini-Guts .10 .30
GAOV053 Falling Current .10 .30
GAOV054 Berserk Scales .10 .30
GAOV055 Night Beam UR 1.25 3.00
GAOV055 Night Beam UTR 2.00 5.00
GAOV056 Seal of Convocation R 1.00 2.50
GAOV057 Hieratic Seal of Supremacy .10 .30
GAOV058 Evo-Diversity R .25 .75
GAOV059 Evo-Price R .25 .75
GAOV060 Final Inzektion R .25 .75
GAOV061 Crossbow - Zektarrow R .25 .75
GAOV062 Xyz Unit UR .60 1.50
GAOV062 Xyz Unit UTR .60 1.50
GAOV063 That Wacky Magic .10 .30
GAOV064 Constellar Belt .10 .30
GAOV065 Storm .10 .30
GAOV066 Nitwit Outwit .10 .30

Card	Low	High
GAOV067 Gamushara	.10	.30
GAOV068 Commander of Swords	.10	.30
GAOV069 Bounzer Guard	.10	.30
GAOV070 Butterflyoke	.10	.30
GAOV071 Hieratic Seal of Banishment	.10	.30
GAOV072 Seal of Reflection SR	.40	1.00
GAOV073 Zekt Conversion UR	.60	1.50
GAOV073 Zekt Conversion UTR	.60	1.50
GAOV074 Inzektor Gauntlet	.10	.30
GAOV075 Return	.10	.30
GAOV076 Dimension Slice R	.25	.75
GAOV077 Light Art - Hijiri SR	.20	.60
GAOV078 Sealing Ceremony of Raiton	.10	.30
GAOV079 Aquamirror Cycle	.10	.30
GAOV080 Double Payback	.10	.30
GAOV081 Ancient Dragon R	.25	.75
GAOV082 Hieratic Seal of the Dragon King	.10	.30
GAOV083 Evoltile Elginero SR	.20	.60
GAOV084 Lightray Grepher R	.25	.75
GAOV085 Tardy Orc SCR	.40	1.00
GAOV086 Draconnection UTR	5.00	12.00
GAOV086 Draconnection UR	3.00	8.00
GAOV087 Trial and Tribulation SCR	1.50	4.00
GAOV088 Seal From Ashes SCR	1.50	4.00
GAOV089 Xyz Wrath	.10	.30
GAOV090 Big Eye SCR	5.00	12.00
GAOV091 Lucky Straight SCR	1.50	4.00
GAOV092 Beetron UTR	.60	1.50
GAOV092 Beetron UR	.60	1.50
GAOV093 Influence Dragon	.10	.30
GAOV094 Bright Star Dragon	.75	2.00
GAOV095 Bufen	.10	.30
GAOV096 Doom Donuts	.10	.30
GAOV097 Nimble Manta	.10	.30
GAOV098 Shining Elf SR	.20	.60
GAOV099 Flelf SR	.20	.60

2012 Yu-Gi-Oh Return of the Duelist 1st Edition

Card	Low	High
COMPLETE SET (111)	250.00	350.00
BOOSTER BOX (24 PACKS)	70.00	100.00
BOOSTER PACK (9 CARDS)	3.00	5.00
RELEASED ON AUGUST 28, 2012		
REDU000 Noble Knight Gawayn SR	.25	.75
REDU001 Trance the Magic Swordsman C	.10	.30
REDU002 Damage Mage C	.10	.30
REDU003 ZW - Phoenix Bow R	.15	.40
REDU004 Photon Caesar C	.10	.30
REDU005 Heroic Challenger - Spartan C	.10	.30
REDU006 Heroic Challenger - War Hammer C	.10	.30
REDU007 Heroic Challenger - Swordshield C	.10	.30
REDU008 Heroic Challenger	.15	.40
REDU009 Chronomaly Mayan Machine C	.10	.30
REDU010 Chronomaly Colossal Head R	.15	.40
REDU011 Chronomaly Golden Jet C	.20	.60
REDU012 Chronomaly Crystal Bones R	.15	.40
REDU013 Chronomaly Crystal Skull R	.15	.40
REDU014 Chronomaly Moai C	.10	.30
REDU015 Spellbook Magician UTR	5.00	12.00
REDU015 Spellbook Magician UR	4.00	10.00
REDU016 Amores of Prophecy C	.10	.30
REDU017 Temperance of	1.50	4.00
REDU018 Strength of Prophecy C	.10	.30
REDU019 Charioteer of Prophecy C	.10	.30
REDU020 High Priestess SCR	6.00	15.00
REDU021 Madolche Mewfeuille C	.40	1.00
REDU022 Madolche Baaple C	.10	.30
REDU023 Madolche Chouxvalier R	.15	.40
REDU024 Madolche Magileine SR	6.00	15.00
REDU025 Madolche Butlerusk C	.10	.30
REDU026 Madolche Puddingcess UTR	2.50	6.00
REDU026 Madolche Puddingcess UR	2.00	5.00
REDU027 Geargiano Mk-II R	.15	.40
REDU028 Geargiaccelerator C	.10	.30
REDU029 Geargiarsenal R	.15	.40
REDU030 Geargiarmor SR	.60	1.50
REDU031 Uniflora, Mystical Beast of the Forest C	.10	.30
REDU032 Little Trooper C	.10	.30
REDU033 Silver Sentinel UTR	.40	1.00
REDU033 Silver Sentinel UR	.20	.60
REDU034 Dust Knight R	.15	.40
REDU035 Block Golem C	.10	.30
REDU036 Atlantean Attack Squad C	.10	.30
REDU037 Illusory Snatcher SR	.25	.75
REDU038 Grandsoil the	1.25	3.00
REDU039 Three Thousand Needles SP	.15	.40
REDU040 Goblin Marauding Squad SP	.15	.40
REDU041 Heroic Champ. Excal. UTR	1.50	4.00
REDU041 Heroic Champ. Excal. GR	3.00	8.00
REDU041 Heroic Champ. Excal. UR	1.25	3.00
REDU042 Chronomaly Crystal SR	.75	2.00
REDU043 No. 33: Chronomaly UR	2.00	5.00
REDU043 No. 33: Chronomaly UTR	2.00	5.00
REDU044 Super. Robot UR	.75	2.00
REDU044 Super. Robot UTR	.60	1.50
REDU045 Hierophant of Prophecy UTR	.60	1.50
REDU045 Hierophant of Prophecy UR	.60	1.50
REDU046 Gear Gigant X SCR	3.00	8.00
REDU047 Alchemic Magician SR	1.25	3.00
REDU048 Soul of Silvermountain SR	.25	.75
REDU049 Fairy King Albverdich R	.15	.40
REDU050 Sword Breaker SR	.25	.75
REDU051 Gagagarevenge SR	.50	1.25
REDU052 Overlay Regen C	.10	.30
REDU053 Heroic Chance C	.10	.30
REDU054 Chronomaly Technology C	.10	.30
REDU055 Chronomaly Pyramid Eye Tablet C	.10	.30
REDU056 Galaxy Queen's Light C	.10	.30
REDU057 Spellbook of Secrets UTR	6.00	15.00
REDU057 Spellbook of Secrets UR	5.00	12.00
REDU058 Spellbook of Power C	.20	.60
REDU059 Spellbook of Life SR	1.25	3.00
REDU060 Spellbook of Wisdom R	.15	.40
REDU061 Madolche Chateau C	.10	.30
REDU062 Where Art Thou? C	1.00	2.50
REDU063 Generation Force C	.10	.30
REDU064 Catapult Zone C	.10	.30
REDU065 Cold Feet SP	.15	.40
REDU066 Impenetrable Attack C	.10	.30
REDU067 Gagagarush C	.10	.30
REDU068 Heroic Retribution Sword C	.10	.30
REDU069 Stonehenge Methods C	.10	.30
REDU070 Madolche Lesson C	.10	.30
REDU071 Madolche Waltz C	.10	.30
REDU072 Madolche Tea Break R	.15	.40
REDU073 Xyz Soul C	.10	.30
REDU074 Compulsory Escape Device C	.10	.30
REDU075 Turnabout C	.10	.30
REDU076 Void Trap Hole SR	1.25	3.00
REDU077 Three of a Kind C	.10	.30
REDU078 Soul Drain R	.15	.40
REDU079 Rebound SR	.25	.75
REDU080 Lucky Punch SP	.15	.40
REDU081 Prophecy Destroyer UR	.20	.60
REDU081 Prophecy Destroyer UTR	.40	1.00
REDU082 Lightray Madoor C	.10	.30
REDU083 Blue Dragon Ninja SR	.25	.75
REDU084 Imairuka R	.15	.40
REDU085 Revival Golem R	.15	.40
REDU086 Noble Arms - Gallatin C	.10	.30
REDU087 Spellbook Library R	.15	.40
REDU088 Advance Zone SCR	1.00	2.50
REDU089 Ninjitsu Art of Shadow Sealing C	.10	.30
REDU090 Chewbone C	.10	.30
REDU091 Eco, Mystical Spirit of the Forest R	.15	.40
REDU092 No. 6: Chronomaly SCR	.75	2.00
REDU093 Miracle Contact SCR	6.00	15.00
REDU094 Advanced Dark SCR	1.50	4.00
REDU095 Pahunder R	.15	.40
REDU096 Mahunder R	.15	.40
REDU097 Sishunder R	.15	.40
REDU098 No. 91: Thunder Spark UTR	1.25	3.00
REDU098 No. 91: Thunder Spark UR	1.25	3.00
REDU099 Spirit Converter SCR	.40	1.00

2012 Yu-Gi-Oh Return of the Duelist Special Edition

Card	Low	High
COMPLETE SET (2)	2.00	5.00
ONE PER SPECIAL EDITION BOX		
REDUSE1 T.G. Hyper Librarian SR	1.50	4.00
REDUSE2 Acid Golem of Destruction SR	1.00	2.50

2012 Yu-Gi-Oh Abyss Rising 1st Edition

Card	Low	High
COMPLETE SET (111)	300.00	500.00
BOOSTER BOX (24 PACKS)	50.00	80.00
BOOSTER PACK (9 CARDS)	3.00	4.50
RELEASED ON NOVEMBER 9, 2012		
ABYR000 Ignoble Knight SR	.25	.75
ABYR001 Gagaga Caesar R	.25	.60
ABYR002 Bull Blader C	.10	.30
ABYR003 Achacha Chanbara C	.10	.30
ABYR004 Mogmole C	.10	.30
ABYR005 Grandram C	.10	.30
ABYR006 Tripod Fish C	.10	.30
ABYR007 Deep Sweeper C	.10	.30
ABYR008 Heroic Challenger - Extra Sword C	.10	.30
ABYR009 Heroic Challenger - Night Watchman C	.10	.30
ABYR010 Planet Pathfinder C	.10	.30
ABYR011 Solar Wind Jammer C	.10	.30
ABYR012 Heraldic Beast Aberconway C	.10	.30
ABYR013 Heraldic Beast Berners Falcon C	.10	.30
ABYR014 Mermail Abysslinde UTR	2.50	6.00
ABYR014 Mermail Abysslinde UR	2.50	6.00
ABYR015 Mermail Abyssgunde R	.25	.60
ABYR016 Mermail Abyssfilde C	.10	.30
ABYR017 Mermail Abyssturge R	.25	.60
ABYR018 Mermail Abysspike R	.40	1.00
ABYR019 Mermail Abysslung C	.10	.30
ABYR020 Mermail Abyssmegalo SCR	6.00	15.00
ABYR021 Stoic of Prophecy C	.10	.30
ABYR022 Hermit of Prophecy C	.10	.30
ABYR023 Justice of Prophecy R	.60	1.50
ABYR024 Emperor of Prophecy R	.25	.60
ABYR025 Madolche Croiwanssant C	.10	.30
ABYR026 Madolche Marmalmaid C	.10	.30
ABYR027 Madolche Messengelato R	1.00	2.50
ABYR028 Abyss Warrior C	.10	.30
ABYR029 Snowman Creator C	.10	.30
ABYR030 Fishborg Planter C	.10	.30
ABYR031 Nimble Angler C	.10	.30
ABYR032 Shore Knight R	.25	.60
ABYR033 Mecha Sea Dragon Plesion C	.10	.30
ABYR034 Metallizing Parasite - Soltite C	.10	.30
ABYR035 Moulinglacia SCR	5.00	12.00
ABYR036 House Duston C	.10	.30
ABYR037 Puny Penguin SP	.10	.30
ABYR038 Missing Force SP	.10	.30
ABYR039 No.32 Shark Drake GR	2.00	5.00
ABYR039 No.32 Shark Drake UTR	1.00	2.50
ABYR039 No.32 Shark Drake UR	.75	2.00
ABYR040 One-Eyed Skill Gainer SR	.40	1.00
ABYR041 Gagaga Cowboy SR	.75	2.00
ABYR042 Heroic Champion - Gandiva UR	1.00	2.50
ABYR042 Heroic Champion - Gandiva UTR	1.50	4.00
ABYR043 Heroic Champion - Kusanagi SR	1.25	3.00
ABYR044 Number 9: Dyson Sphere UR	1.50	4.00
ABYR044 Number 9: Dyson Sphere UTR	1.50	4.00
ABYR045 No.8 Heraldic King SR	.60	1.50
ABYR046 Mermail Abyssgaios UR	1.00	2.50
ABYR046 Mermail Abyssgaios UTR	1.50	4.00
ABYR047 Empress of Prophecy UR	.25	.75
ABYR047 Empress of Prophecy UTR	.40	1.00
ABYR048 Madolche Queen Tiaramisu UR	1.00	2.50
ABYR048 Madolche Queen Tiaramisu UTR	2.50	6.00
ABYR049 Snowdust Giant R	.25	.60
ABYR050 Gagagigo the Risen R	.25	.60
ABYR051 One-Shot Wand C	.10	.30
ABYR052 Different Dimension Deepsea Trench C	.10	.30
ABYR053 Tannhauser Gate SR	.25	.75
ABYR054 Gravity Blaster C	.10	.30
ABYR055 Advanced Heraldry Art R	.25	.60
ABYR056 Abyss-scale of the Kraken C	.10	.30
ABYR057 Lemuria, the Forgotten City C	.10	.30
ABYR058 Spellbook of Eternity R	.25	.60
ABYR059 Spellbook of Fate UR	2.00	5.00
ABYR059 Spellbook of Fate UTR	2.50	6.00
ABYR060 The Grand Spellbook Tower SCR	2.00	5.00
ABYR061 Madolche Ticket C	.10	.30
ABYR062 Forbidden Dress SR	.25	.75
ABYR063 Final Gesture C	.10	.30
ABYR064 Mind Pollutant R	.25	.60
ABYR065 The Humble Sentry SP	.10	.30
ABYR066 Battle Break C	.10	.30
ABYR067 Bubble Bringer SR	.25	.75
ABYR068 Heroic Gift C	.10	.30
ABYR069 Heroic Advance C	.10	.30
ABYR070 Xyz Xtreme !! C	.10	.30
ABYR071 Abyss-squall SR	.25	.75
ABYR072 Abyss-sphere UR	2.00	5.00
ABYR072 Abyss-sphere UTR	2.00	5.00
ABYR073 Abyss-strom R	.25	.60
ABYR074 Madolchepalooza SR	1.00	2.50
ABYR075 Memory of an Adversary SR	.25	.75
ABYR076 Magic Deflector C	1.00	2.50
ABYR077 That Wacky Alchemy! UR	.15	.40
ABYR077 That Wacky Alchemy! UTR	.25	.75
ABYR078 Cash Back SR	.75	2.00
ABYR079 Unification C	.10	.30
ABYR080 Retort SCR	1.25	3.00
ABYR081 Mermail Abyssmander R	.25	.60
ABYR082 Red Dragon Ninja SR	.25	.75
ABYR083 Slushy R	.25	.60
ABYR084 Abyss Dweller SR	1.00	2.50
ABYR085 Giant Soldier of Steel SCR	.40	1.00
ABYR086 Noble Arms - Arfeudutyr R	.25	.60
ABYR087 Spellbook Library SCR	.50	1.25
ABYR088 Spellbook Star Hall R	.25	.60
ABYR089 Attack the Moon! SR	.25	.75
ABYR090 Electromagnetic Bagworm C	.10	.30
ABYR091 Rage of the Deep Sea C	.10	.30
ABYR092 Ape Magician C	.10	.30
ABYR093 Snowdust Dragon C	.10	.30
ABYR094 Snow Dragon C	.10	.30
ABYR095 Uminotaurus R	.25	.60
ABYR096 Fishborg Launcher C	.10	.30
ABYR097 Papa-Corn R	.25	.60
ABYR098 Thunder Sea Horse SCR	1.00	2.50
ABYR099 Bahamut Shark SCR	2.00	5.00

2012 Yu-Gi-Oh Abyss Rising Special Edition

Card	Low	High
ONE PER SPECIAL EDITION BOX		
ABYRSE1 Gagaga Girl SR	1.00	2.50
ABYRSE2 Dark Smog SR	1.00	2.50

2013 Yu-Gi-Oh Cosmo Blazer 1st Edition

Card	Low	High
COMPLETE SET (111)	350.00	500.00
BOOSTER BOX (24 PACKS)	80.00	100.00
BOOSTER PACK (9 CARDS)	3.00	4.00
RELEASED ON JANUARY 25, 2013		
CBLZ000 Noble Arms - Caliburn SR	.25	.75
CBLZ001 Dododo Bot C	.10	.30
CBLZ002 Gogogo Ghost C	.10	.30
CBLZ003 Bacon Saver C	.10	.30
CBLZ004 Amarylease C	.10	.30
CBLZ005 ZW - Lightning Blade R	.15	.40
CBLZ006 ZW - Tornado Bringer R	.15	.40
CBLZ007 ZW - Ultimate Shield C	.10	.30
CBLZ008 Gagaga Clerk SR	1.00	2.50
CBLZ009 Spear Shark C	.10	.30
CBLZ010 Double Shark C	.10	.30
CBLZ011 Xyz Remora C	.10	.30
CBLZ012 Hyper-Ancient Shark Megalodon R	.15	.40
CBLZ013 Heraldic Beast Basilisk C	.10	.30
CBLZ014 Heraldic Beast Eale C	.10	.30
CBLZ015 Heraldic Beast Twin-Headed Eagle R	.15	.40
CBLZ016 Heraldic Beast Unicorn C	.10	.30
CBLZ017 Heraldic Beast Leo R	.15	.40
CBLZ018 Garbage Ogre C	.10	.30
CBLZ019 Garbage Lord C	.10	.30
CBLZ020 Orbital 7 SR	.25	.75
CBLZ021 Brotherhood of the Fire Fist - Hawk C	.10	.30
CBLZ022 Brotherhood of the Fire Fist - Raven C	.10	.30
CBLZ023 Brotherhood of the Fire Fist - Gorilla R	.15	.40
CBLZ024 Brotherhood of the Fire Fist - Bear UTR	1.50	4.00
CBLZ024 Brotherhood of the Fire Fist - Bear UR	.60	1.50
CBLZ025 Brotherhood of the Fire Fist - Dragon SR	1.00	2.50
CBLZ026 Brotherhood of the Fire Fist - Snake SR	.25	.75
CBLZ027 Brotherhood of the Fire Fist - Swallow SR	.25	.75
CBLZ028 Hazy Flame Cerbereus C	.10	.30
CBLZ029 Hazy Flame Griffin C	.10	.30
CBLZ030 Hazy Flame Sphynx C	.10	.30
CBLZ031 Hazy Flame Peryton R	.15	.40
CBLZ032 Mermail Abyssdine SR	.25	.75
CBLZ033 Mermail Abyssnose C	.10	.30
CBLZ034 Mermail Abyssleed SCR	2.50	6.00
CBLZ035 Fool of Prophecy SR	.25	.75
CBLZ036 Reaper of Prophecy SR	.25	.75
CBLZ037 Brushfire Knight R	.15	.40
CBLZ038 Inari Fire C	.10	.30
CBLZ039 Valkyrian Knight SR	1.00	2.50
CBLZ040 Pyrorex the Elemental SCR	.50	1.25
CBLZ041 Pyrotech Mech - Shiryu C	.10	.30
CBLZ042 Leotaur C	.10	.30
CBLZ043 Star Drawing SP	.40	1.00
CBLZ044 Red Duston SP	.10	.30
CBLZ045 Heart-eartH Dragon GR	2.50	6.00
CBLZ045 Heart-eartH Dragon UTR	1.50	4.00
CBLZ045 Heart-eartH Dragon UR	1.25	3.00
CBLZ046 No. 53: Heart-eartH UR	.60	1.50
CBLZ046 No. 53: Heart-eartH UTR	1.00	2.50
CBLZ047 ZW - Leo Arms UTR	.60	1.50
CBLZ047 ZW - Leo Arms UR	.60	1.50
CBLZ048 Brohood - Tiger King UTR	1.25	3.00
CBLZ048 Brohood - Tiger King UR	.60	1.50
CBLZ049 Hazy Flame Basiltrice R	.15	.40
CBLZ050 Mermail Abysstrite SR	.60	1.50
CBLZ051 Diamond Dire Wolf SCR	4.00	10.00
CBLZ052 Lightning Chidori UTR	4.00	10.00
CBLZ052 Lightning Chidori UR	2.50	6.00
CBLZ053 Slacker Magician R	.40	1.00
CBLZ054 Zerozerock C	.10	.30
CBLZ055 Gagagadraw SR	.25	.75
CBLZ056 Xyz Double Back C	.10	.30
CBLZ057 Heraldry Reborn R	.15	.40
CBLZ058 Fire Formation - Tensu C	.10	.30
CBLZ059 Fire Formation - Tenki C	.25	.75
CBLZ060 Hazy Pillar C	.10	.30
CBLZ061 Abyss-scale of Cetus C	.10	.30
CBLZ062 Spellbook of Master SCR	1.50	4.00
CBLZ063 The Big Cattle Drive C	.10	.30
CBLZ064 March of the Monarchs C	.25	.75
CBLZ065 Quick Booster UTR	.60	1.50
CBLZ065 Quick Booster UR	.60	1.50
CBLZ066 After the Storm C	.10	.30
CBLZ067 Goblin Circus SP	.10	.30
CBLZ068 Dimension Gate C	.10	.30
CBLZ069 Xyz Dimension Splash C	.10	.30
CBLZ070 Heraldry Change C	.10	.30
CBLZ071 Fire Formation - Tensen C	.10	.30
CBLZ072 Fire Formation - Tenken C	.10	.30
CBLZ073 Ultimate Fire Formation - Seito R	.15	.40
CBLZ074 Hazy Glory C	.10	.30
CBLZ075 Abyss-scorn C	.10	.30
CBLZ076 Spikeshield with Chain C	.10	.30
CBLZ077 Xyz Tribalrivals C	.10	.30
CBLZ078 Breakthrough Skill UTR	8.00	20.00
CBLZ078 Breakthrough Skill UR	2.50	6.00
CBLZ079 Jurrac Impact C	.10	.30
CBLZ080 Dice-nied SP	.10	.30
CBLZ081 Knight Medraut SCR	3.00	8.00
CBLZ082 Hazy Flame Mantikor R	.15	.40
CBLZ083 Mermail Abyssteus UR	8.00	20.00
CBLZ083 Mermail Abyssteus UTR	15.00	30.00
CBLZ084 Bonfire Colossus SCR	.20	.60
CBLZ085 Fairy Elfuria SCR	1.25	3.00
CBLZ086 Artorigus, King UTR	.60	1.50
CBLZ086 Artorigus, King UR	.60	1.50
CBLZ087 Infernal Flame Vixen R	.15	.40
CBLZ088 Spell Wall C	.10	.30
CBLZ089 Kickfire SCR	.75	2.00
CBLZ090 Crimson Sunbird C	.10	.30
CBLZ091 Ignition Beast Volcannon C	.10	.30
CBLZ092 Noble Knight Joan R	.15	.40
CBLZ093 Crimson Blader R	.60	1.50
CBLZ094 Infernity Archer R	.25	.75
CBLZ095 Blackwing - Gladius the Midnight Sun R	.15	.40
CBLZ096 Blackwing - Damascus the Polar Night R	.15	.40
CBLZ097 Brohood - Horse Prince SR	1.25	3.00
CBLZ098 Brohood - Spirit R	.15	.40
CBLZ099 Brohood - Lion Emperor SR	.75	2.00

2013 Yu-Gi-Oh Cosmo Blazer Special Edition

Card	Low	High
ONE PER SPECIAL EDITION BOX		
CBLZSE1 Wind-Up Shark SR	.75	2.00
CBLZSE2 Blade Armor Ninja SR	1.50	4.00

2013 Yu-Gi-Oh Lord of the Tachyon Galaxy 1st Edition

Card	Low	High
COMPLETE SET (111)	100.00	250.00
BOOSTER BOX (24 PACKS)	80.00	100.00
BOOSTER PACK (9 CARDS)	4.00	5.00
RELEASED ON MAY 17, 2013		
LTGY000 MPB Turtleracer SR	.20	.60
LTGY001 Bachibachibachi C	.10	.30
LTGY002 Gogogo Gigas R	.15	.40
LTGY003 Mimimic C	.10	.30
LTGY004 Dotedotengu C	.10	.30
LTGY005 Tatakawa Knight C	.10	.30
LTGY006 Little Fairy C	.10	.30
LTGY007 Sharkraken C	.10	.30
LTGY008 Big Whale R	.15	.40
LTGY009 Starfish C	.10	.30
LTGY010 Panther Shark C	.10	.30
LTGY011 Eagle Shark C	.10	.30
LTGY012 Blizzard Falcon C	.10	.30
LTGY013 Aurora Wing C	.10	.30
LTGY014 Radius, the Half-Moon Dragon C	.10	.30
LTGY015 Parsec, the Interstellar Dragon C	.10	.30
LTGY016 Battlin' Boxer Headgeared C	.10	.30
LTGY017 Battlin' Boxer Glassjaw C	.10	.30
LTGY018 Battlin' Boxer Sparrer C	.10	.30
LTGY019 Battlin' Boxer Switchitter C	.10	.30
LTGY020 Battlin' Boxer Counterpunch C	.10	.30
LTGY021 MPB Megaraptor SR	.20	.60
LTGY022 MPB Tetherwolf R	.15	.40
LTGY023 MPB Blackfalcon	.10	.30
LTGY024 MPB Stealthray	.10	.30
LTGY025 MPB Hamstrat UTR	.60	1.50
LTGY025 MPB Hamstrat UR	.20	.75
LTGY026 BFF - Wolf	.10	.30
LTGY027 BFF - Leopard	.10	.30
LTGY028 BFF - Rhino R	.15	.40
LTGY029 BFF - Buffalo R	.15	.40
LTGY030 Mermail Abyssocea C	.10	.30
LTGY031 Wheel of Prophecy R	.15	.40
LTGY032 Madolche Hootcake SR	.75	2.00
LTGY033 Legendary Atlantean Tridon C	.10	.30
LTGY034 Fire King Avatar Garunix C	.20	.60
LTGY035 Harpie Channeler UTR	2.50	6.00
LTGY035 Harpie Channeler UR	2.00	5.00
LTGY036 Altitude Knight R	.15	.40
LTGY037 Windrose the Elemental SCR	.40	1.00
LTGY038 Redox, Dragon Ruler R	.25	.75
LTGY039 Tidal, Dragon Rule R	.25	.75
LTGY040 Blaster, Dragon Ruler R	.40	1.00
LTGY041 Tempest, Dragon Rule R	.25	.75
LTGY042 Risebell the Star Adjuster SP	.10	1.00
LTGY043 Green Duston SP	.10	.30
LTGY044 No.107: Galaxy-Eyes GR	20.00	40.00
LTGY044 No.107: Galaxy-Eyes UTR	15.00	30.00
LTGY044 No.107: Galaxy-Eyes UR	8.00	20.00
LTGY045 Gauntlet Launcher UTR	.60	1.50
LTGY045 Gauntlet Launcher UR	.20	.75
LTGY046 Fairy Cheer Girl R	.15	.40
LTGY047 CXyz Dark Fairy Cheer Girl R	.15	.40
LTGY048 Shark Fortress C	.10	.30
LTGY049 Ice Beast Zerofyne R	1.25	3.00
LTGY050 Battlin' Boxer Lead Yoke R	.15	.40
LTGY051 No.105: Star Cestus SR	.60	1.50
LTGY052 No.105: Comet Cestus UTR	.60	1.50
LTGY052 No.105: Comet Cestus UR	.20	.75
LTGY053 MPB Dracossack SCR	5.00	12.00
LTGY054 BFF - Cardinal SCR	.40	1.00
LTGY055 Harpie's Pet Phantasmal Dragon R	.20	.60
LTGY056 King of the Feral Imps C	.10	.30
LTGY057 Gagagawind C	.10	.30
LTGY058 Magnum Shield C	.10	.30
LTGY059 Xyz Revenge R	.15	.40
LTGY060 RUM Barian's Force UTR	.60	1.50
LTGY060 RUM Barian's Force UR	.20	.75
LTGY061 Scramble!! Scramble!! UTR	.60	1.50
LTGY061 Scramble!! Scramble!! UR	.20	.75
LTGY062 Fire Formation - Gyokkou SR	.50	1.25
LTGY063 Spellbook of Judgment SCR	1.25	3.00
LTGY064 Abyss-scale of the Mizuchi C	.10	.30
LTGY065 Hysteric Sign SR	1.50	4.00
LTGY066 Sacred Sword SR	.75	2.00
LTGY067 Jewels of the Valiant C	.10	.30
LTGY068 Summon Breaker SP	.10	.30
LTGY069 Pinpoint Guard SCR	1.00	2.50
LTGY070 Memory Loss C	.10	.30
LTGY071 Torrential Reborn SCR	.40	1.00
LTGY072 Xyz Block C	.10	.30
LTGY073 Aerial Recharge C	.10	.30
LTGY074 Do a Barrel Roll R	.15	.40
LTGY075 Fire Formation - Kaiyo C	.10	.30
LTGY076 Madolche Nights SR	.20	.60
LTGY077 Geargiagear SR	.20	.60
LTGY078 High Tide on Fire Island C	.10	.30
LTGY079 Mind Drain C	.10	.30
LTGY080 Dragoncarnation SP	.20	.60
LTGY081 Noble Knight Gwalchavad UTR	.60	1.50
LTGY081 Noble Knight Gwalchavad UR	.20	.75
LTGY082 BFF - Coyote SCR	.40	1.00
LTGY083 Mermail Abyssbalaen UR	.20	.75
LTGY083 Mermail Abyssbalaen UTR	.60	1.50
LTGY084 Trifortressops R	.15	.40
LTGY085 Ghost Fairy Elfobia SR	.20	.60
LTGY086 Totem Bird SCR	.75	2.00
LTGY087 Noble Arms of Destiny SR	.20	.60
LTGY088 Spellbook of Miracles C	.10	.30
LTGY089 Five Brothers Explosion C	.10	.30
LTGY090 Sonic Warrior C	.10	.30
LTGY091 Constellar Omega UTR	.60	1.50
LTGY091 Constellar Omega UR	.50	1.25
LTGY092 Number 69: Heraldry Crest R	.15	.40
LTGY093 Constellar Sombre SR	.20	.60
LTGY094 Evilswarm Kerykeion SR	.75	2.00
LTGY095 Reactan, Dragon Ruler of Pebbles C	.10	.30
LTGY096 Stream, Dragon Ruler of Droplets C	.10	.30
LTGY097 Burner, Dragon Ruler of Sparks C	.10	.30
LTGY098 Lightning, Dragon Ruler of Drafts C	.10	.30
LTGY099 Duck Fighter SR	.20	.60

2013 Yu-Gi-Oh Judgment of the Light 1st Edition

Card	Low	High
COMPLETE SET (106)	100.00	250.00
BOOSTER BOX (24 PACKS)	60.00	80.00
BOOSTER PACK (9 CARDS)	3.00	4.00
RELEASED ON AUGUST 9, 2013		
JOTL000 Galaxy Serpent SR	.50	1.25
JOTL001 DZW - Chimera Clad R	.10	.30
JOTL002 V Salamander R	.10	.30
JOTL003 Interceptomato C	.10	.30
JOTL004 Spell Recycler C	.10	.30
JOTL005 Xyz Agent C	.10	.30
JOTL006 Super Defense Robot Lio C	.10	.30
JOTL007 Super Defense Robot Elephan C	.10	.30
JOTL008 Super Defense Robot Monki C	.10	.30
JOTL009 Star Seraph Scout C	.10	.30
JOTL010 Star Seraph Sage C	.10	.30
JOTL011 Star Seraph Sword C	.10	.30
JOTL012 Umbral Horror Ghoul C	.10	.30
JOTL013 Umbral Horror Unform C	.10	.30
JOTL014 Umbral Horror Will o' the Wisp C	.10	.30
JOTL015 Schwarzschild Limit Dragon C	.10	.30
JOTL016 Bujin Yamato UR	.60	1.50
JOTL017 Bujingi Quilin SR	.25	.75
JOTL018 Bujingi Turtle C	.10	.30
JOTL019 Bujingi Wolf C	.10	.30
JOTL020 Bujingi Crane R	.10	.30
JOTL021 Bujingi Ophidian C	.10	.30
JOTL022 Mecha Phantom Beast Warbluran R	.10	.30
JOTL023 Mecha Phantom Beast Blue Impala UR	.25	.75
JOTL024 Mecha Phantom Beast Coltwing C	.10	.30
JOTL025 Mecha Phantom Beast Harrliard C	.10	.30
JOTL026 Brotherhood of the Fire Fist - Boar R	.10	.30
JOTL027 Brotherhood of the Fire Fist - Caribou C	.10	.30
JOTL028 World of Prophecy SCR	.40	1.00
JOTL029 Archfiend Heiress R	.10	.30
JOTL030 Archfiend Cavalry R	.10	.30
JOTL031 Archfiend Emperor, the First Lord of Horror R	.10	.30
JOTL032 Traptrix Atrax R	.10	.30
JOTL033 Traptrix Myrmeleo R	.50	1.25
JOTL034 Traptrix Nepenthes C	.10	.30
JOTL035 The Calibrator C	.10	.30

JOTL036 Talaya, Princess of Cherry Blossoms SR .40 1.00
JOTL037 Cheepcheepcheep C .10 .30
JOTL038 Masked Chameleon UR 1.50 4.00
JOTL039 Flying C SP .40 1.00
JOTL040 Yellow Duston SP .10 .30
JOTL041 Mecha Phantom Beast Concoruda SR .25 .75
JOTL042 Brotherhood of the Fire Fist - Kirin R .10 .30
JOTL043 Mist Bird Clausolas SR .75 2.00
JOTL044 Underworld Fighter Balmung R .10 .30
JOTL045 Armades, Keeper of Boundaries SCR 2.00 5.00
JOTL046 HTS Psyhemuth SR .25 .75
JOTL047 Star Eater UTR 4.00 10.00
JOTL047 Star Eater SCR 4.00 10.00
JOTL047 Star Eater GR 8.00 20.00
JOTL048 Number C39: Utopia Ray Victory UTR 2.50 6.00
JOTL048 Number C39: Utopia Ray Victory SR 2.50 6.00
JOTL049 Shark Caesar C .10 .30
JOTL050 Starliege Lord Galaxion SR .25 .75
JOTL051 Googly-Eyes Drum Dragon C .10 .30
JOTL052 Ice Princess Zereort C .10 .30
JOTL053 Number 102: Star Seraph Sentry R .10 .30
JOTL054 Number 66: Master Key Beetle SR .75 2.00
JOTL055 Number 104: Masquerade R .50 1.25
JOTL056 Number C104: Umbral Horror UTR .75 2.00
JOTL056 Number C104: Umbral Horror SR .40 1.00
JOTL057 Bujintei Susanowo UR .25 .75
JOTL057 Bujintei Susanowo UTR .75 2.00
JOTL058 Herald of Pure Light SR 2.50 6.00
JOTL059 Rank-Up-Magic Numeron Force UR .25 .75
JOTL059 Rank-Up-Magic Numeron Force UTR .40 1.00
JOTL060 Xyz Reception C .10 .30
JOTL061 Sargasso the D.D. Battlefield C .10 .30
JOTL062 Sargasso Lighthouse C .10 .30
JOTL063 Bujincarnation R .10 .30
JOTL064 Vertical Landing C .10 .30
JOTL065 Fire Formation - Yoko SR .25 .75
JOTL066 Archfiend Palabyrinth R .10 .30
JOTL067 Transmodify SCR 10.00 25.00
JOTL068 Black and White Wave C .10 .30
JOTL069 Single Purchase SP .10 .30
JOTL070 Reverse Glasses C .10 .30
JOTL071 Xyz Revenge Shuffle C .10 .30
JOTL072 Corrupted Keys R .10 .30
JOTL073 Vain Betrayer C .10 .30
JOTL074 Bujin Regalia - The Sword C .10 .30
JOTL075 Bujinfidel C .10 .30
JOTL076 Sonic Boom C .10 .30
JOTL077 Traptrix Trap Hole Nightmare SR .60 1.50
JOTL078 Xyz Reversal C .10 .30
JOTL079 Shapesister UR .25 .75
JOTL080 Armageddon Designator SP .10 .30
JOTL081 Bujingi Warg C .10 .30
JOTL082 Mecha Phantom Beast Aerosguin UR .25 .75
JOTL083 Cockadoodledoo UR 2.50 6.00
JOTL084 Noble Knight Drystan SCR .40 1.00
JOTL085 Tour Bus To Forbidden Realms R .10 .30
JOTL086 Confronting the C R .10 .30
JOTL087 Angel of Zera SCR .50 1.25
JOTL088 Xyz Encore UR .60 1.50
JOTL089 Moon Dance Ritual R .10 .30
JOTL090 The Atmosphere C .10 .30
JOTL091 Junk Blader C .10 .30
JOTL092 Coach Captain Bearman UR .25 .75
JOTL093 Coach Soldier Wolfbark SCR 2.00 5.00
JOTL094 Brotherhood Fire Fist - Rooster SCR 1.00 2.50
JOTL095 Fire King Avatar Yaksha SR 1.50 4.00
JOTL096 Fishborg Archer C .10 .30
JOTL097 Fencing Fire Ferret C .10 .30
JOTL098 Kujakujaku C .10 .30
JOTL099 Madolche Chickolates C .10 .30

2013 Yu-Gi-Oh Judgment of the Light Deluxe Edition

JOTLDE1 Archfiend Emperor, the First Lord of Horror UR 1.25 3.00
JOTLDE2 Flying C UR .75 2.00
JOTLDE3 Dragon Shield J SR 1.00 2.50
JOTLDE4 Vampire Kingdom SR 1.25 3.00

2013 Yu-Gi-Oh Shadow Specters

COMPLETE SET (107) 75.00 200.00
BOOSTER BOX (24 PACKS) 60.00 80.00
BOOSTER PACK (9 CARDS) 3.00 4.00
RELEASED ON NOVEMBER 8, 2013
SHSP000 Ghostrick Ghoul SR .20 .60
SHSP001 Labradorite Dragon SR 2.50 6.00
SHSP002 Chow Chow Chan C .10 .30
SHSP003 Malicevorous Spoon C .10 .30
SHSP004 Malicevorous Fork C .10 .30
SHSP005 Malicevorous Knife C .10 .30
SHSP006 Battlin' Boxer Rib Gardna C .10 .30
SHSP007 Battlin' Boxer Rabbit Puncher C .10 .30
SHSP008 Secret Sect Druid Wid C .10 .30
SHSP009 Secret Sect Druid Dru C .10 .30
SHSP010 Mythic Tree Dragon C .10 .30
SHSP011 Mythic Water Dragon C .10 .30
SHSP012 Armed Protector Dragon C .10 .30
SHSP013 Soul Drain Dragon C .10 .30
SHSP014 Baby Raccoon Ponpoko C .10 .30
SHSP015 Baby Raccoon Tantan C .10 .30
SHSP016 Ghostrick Lantern SR 2.50 6.00
SHSP017 Ghostrick Specter C .10 .30
SHSP018 Ghostrick Witch C .10 .30
SHSP019 Ghostrick Yuki-onna C .10 .30
SHSP020 Ghostrick Jiangshi C .10 .30
SHSP021 Ghostrick Stein C .10 .30
SHSP022 Bujin Mikazuchi UR 1.00 2.50
SHSP023 Bujingi Crow R .10 .30
SHSP024 Bujingi Ibis C .10 .30
SHSP025 Bujingi Boar C .10 .30
SHSP026 Bujingi Centipede C .10 .30
SHSP027 Mecha Phantom Beast Sabre Hawk C .10 .30
SHSP028 Mecha Phantom Beast Kalgriffin R .10 .30
SHSP029 Vampire Sorcerer UR 2.00 5.00
SHSP030 Shadow Vampire SCR .50 1.25
SHSP031 Vampire Grace C .10 .30
SHSP032 Pumprincess the Princess of Ghosts C .10 .30
SHSP033 Yellow-Bellied Oni C .10 .30
SHSP034 Vampire Hunter SR .20 .60
SHSP035 Aratama R .10 .30
SHSP036 Rasetsu C .10 .30
SHSP037 Skelesaurus C .10 .30
SHSP038 Knight Day Grepher C .10 .30
SHSP039 Genomix Fighter UR .15 .40
SHSP040 Marina, Princess of Sunflowers SR .20 .60
SHSP041 Granmarg the Mega Monarch SCR .50 1.25
SHSP042 Swarm of Crows R .10 .30
SHSP043 Terrene Toothed Tsuchinoko C .10 .30
SHSP044 Risebell the Star Psycher SP .10 .30
SHSP045 Blue Duston SP .10 .30
SHSP046 Number C96: Dark Storm UTR .40 1.00
SHSP046 Number C96: Dark Storm SR .20 .60
SHSP047 Number 65: Djinn Buster R .10 .30
SHSP048 Number C65: King Overfiend R .10 .30
SHSP049 Battlin' Boxer Cheat Commissioner R .10 .30
SHSP050 Number 46: Dragluon UTR 5.00 12.00
SHSP050 Number 46: Dragluon SR 2.50 6.00
SHSP051 Number 64: Ronin Raccoon Sandayu R .40 1.00
SHSP052 Ghostrick Alucard UTR 2.50 6.00
SHSP052 Ghostrick Alucard UR 1.50 4.00
SHSP053 Bujintei Kagutsuchi UR .60 1.50
SHSP053 Bujintei Kagutsuchi UTR .75 2.00
SHSP054 Crimson Knight Vampire Bram UR 1.25 3.00
SHSP055 Meliae of the Trees SCR .50 1.25
SHSP056 Divine Dragon Knight Felgrand SCR 6.00 15.00
SHSP056 Divine Dragon Knight Felgrand GR 8.00 20.00
SHSP056 Divine Dragon Knight Felgrand UTR 6.00 15.00
SHSP057 Puralis, the Purple Pyrotile R .10 .30
SHSP058 Giganticastle R .10 .30
SHSP059 Gagagatag C .10 .30
SHSP060 Battlin' Boxing Spirits SR .60 1.50
SHSP061 Dragon Shield C .10 .30
SHSP062 Ghostrick Mansion C .10 .30
SHSP063 Bujin Regalia - The Mirror R .10 .30
SHSP064 Vampire Kingdom C .10 .30
SHSP065 Pot of Dichotomy SCR 1.00 2.50
SHSP066 Swords at Dawn R .10 .30
SHSP067 Return of the Monarchs UR 2.50 6.00
SHSP068 Sacred Serpent's Wake C .10 .30
SHSP069 Magicalized Duston Mop SP .10 .30
SHSP070 Burst Rebirth R .10 .30
SHSP071 Numbers Overlay Boost C .10 .30
SHSP072 Intrigue Shield C .10 .30
SHSP073 Ghostrick Vanish C .10 .30
SHSP074 Ghostrick Scare C .10 .30
SHSP075 Vampire Takeover SR .20 .60
SHSP076 Mistake SCR 1.00 2.50
SHSP077 Chain Ignition C .10 .30
SHSP078 Grisaille Prison R .50 1.25
SHSP079 Survival of the Fittest C .10 .30
SHSP080 BIG Win!! SP .10 .30
SHSP081 Bujingi Raven R .10 .30
SHSP082 Vampire Duke R .10 .30
SHSP083 Archfiend Giant R .10 .30
SHSP084 Lady of the Lake SCR .50 1.25
SHSP085 Noble Knight Borz SR .20 .60
SHSP086 Ignoble Knight of High Laundsallyn SCR .50 1.25
SHSP087 Sacred Noble Knight of King Artorigus UR .75 2.00
SHSP088 Noble Arms - Excaliburn SR .20 .60
SHSP089 Sinister Yorishiro UR .60 1.50
SHSP090 Celestial Wolf Lord, Blue Sirius UR .60 1.50
SHSP091 Mira the Star-Bearer C .10 .30
SHSP092 Dragard SR .60 1.50
SHSP093 White Dragon Wyverburster C .10 .30
SHSP094 Kidmodo Dragon SR 1.50 4.00
SHSP095 Secret Sanctuary of the Spellcasters R .10 .30
SHSP096 Black Dragon Collapserpent C .10 .30
SHSP097 Armored Kappa SR .20 .60
SHSP098 Oh Tokenbaum! R .10 .30
SHSP099 Vivid Knight R .10 .30
SHSPSP1 Ghostrick Ghoul UR .60 1.50

2013 Yu-Gi-Oh Shadow Specters Special Edition

ONE PER SPECIAL EDITION BOX
SHSPSE1 Stardust Dragon SR 1.50 4.00
SHSPSE2 Tuning SR .50 1.25

2014 Yu-Gi-Oh Legacy of the Valiant 1st Edition

COMPLETE SET (107) 95.00 140.00
BOOSTER BOX (24 PACKS) 80.00 100.00
BOOSTER PACK (9 CARDS) 4.00 5.00
RELEASED ON JANUARY 24, 2014
LVAL000 Sylvan Bladefender SR .15 .25
LVAL001 White Duston SP .10 .20
LVAL002 ZW - Asura Strike R .10 .20
LVAL003 Gillagillancer C .05 .15
LVAL004 Rainbow Kuriboh SCR 1.25 1.75
LVAL005 Overlay Sentinel C .05 .15
LVAL006 Overlay Booster C .05 .15
LVAL007 Photon Chargeman C .05 .15
LVAL008 Chronomaly Moai Carrier C .05 .15
LVAL009 Chronomaly Winged Sphinx C .05 .15
LVAL010 Deep-Space Cruiser IX C .05 .15
LVAL011 Gorgonic Golem C .05 .15
LVAL012 Gorgonic Gargoyle C .05 .15
LVAL013 Gorgonic Ghoul C .05 .15
LVAL014 Gorgonic Cerberus C .05 .15
LVAL015 Sylvan Peaskeeper R .10 .20
LVAL016 Sylvan Komushroomo R .20 .35
LVAL017 Sylvan Marshalleaf UR .50 .75
LVAL018 Sylvan Flowerknight SR .25 .40
LVAL019 Sylvan Guardioak C .05 .15
LVAL020 Sylvan Hermitree UR 1.25 2.00
LVAL021 Ghostrick Jackfrost C .05 .15
LVAL022 Ghostrick Mary SR 3.50 4.00
LVAL023 Ghostrick Nekomusume C .05 .15
LVAL024 Ghostrick Skeleton C .05 .15
LVAL025 Ghostrick Mummy C .05 .15
LVAL026 Bujin Arasuda UR .50 .75
LVAL027 Bujingi Peacock R .10 .20
LVAL028 Bujingi Swallow C .05 .15
LVAL029 Bujingi Fox R .10 .20
LVAL030 Bujingi Hare SR 1.00 1.50
LVAL031 Gravekeeper's Nobleman UR 2.25 3.00
LVAL032 Gravekeeper's Ambusher C .05 .15
LVAL033 Gravekeeper's Shaman SR .50 .75
LVAL034 Gravekeeper's Oracle UR 1.00 1.25
LVAL035 Mystic Macrocarpa Seed C .05 .15
LVAL036 Kalantosa, Mystical Beast of the Forest C .05 .15
LVAL037 Nikitama R .20 .35
LVAL038 Black Brachios C .05 .15
LVAL039 Chirubimé, Princess of Autumn Leaves SR .30 .50
LVAL040 Mobius the Mega Monarch GR 3.50 5.00
LVAL040 Mobius the Mega Monarch SCR 1.25 2.00
LVAL041 Sirenorca C .05 .15
LVAL042 Xyz Avenger C .05 .15
LVAL043 Tackle Crusader C .05 .15
LVAL044 Majosheldon SP .10 .20
LVAL045 Paladin of Photon Dragon R .10 .20
LVAL046 Number C101: Silent Honor DARK UTR 2.00 3.00
LVAL046 Number C101: Silent Honor DARK UR 2.00 3.00
LVAL047 Number 101: Silent Honor ARK UTR 7.00 9.00
LVAL047 Number 101: Silent Honor ARK UR 2.50 4.00
LVAL048 Number 39: Utopia Roots R .50 .75
LVAL048 Number 39: Utopia Roots UTR 2.50 3.50
LVAL049 Number C69: Heraldry Crest of Horror R .30 .50
LVAL050 Number C92: Heart-eartH Chaos Dragon R .10 .20
LVAL051 Gorgonic Guardian C .05 .15
LVAL052 Alsei, the Sylvan High Protector UR 3.50 5.00
LVAL053 Ghostrick Dullahan R 2.50 3.00
LVAL054 Bujintei Tsukuyomi UR 8.00 10.00
LVAL054 Bujintei Tsukuyomi UTR 20.00 25.00
LVAL055 Fairy Knight Ingunar SR .30 .50
LVAL056 Evilswarm Exciton Knight SCR 9.00 12.00
LVAL057 Downerd Magician SCR 1.25 2.00
LVAL058 Leo, the Keeper of the Sacred Tree R .75 1.25
LVAL059 Rank-Up-Magic Astral Force UR .75 1.25
LVAL059 Rank-Up-Magic Astral Force UTR 4.00 5.00
LVAL060 Rank-Down-Magic Numeron Fall R .10 .20
LVAL061 Xyz Shift C .05 .15
LVAL062 Luminous Dragon Ritual C .05 .15
LVAL063 Mount Sylvania SR .30 .50
LVAL064 Ghostrick Museum C .05 .15
LVAL065 Bujinunity R .10 .20
LVAL066 Hidden Temples of Necrovalley R .10 .20
LVAL067 Onomatopaira R .60 1.00
LVAL068 Xyz Override C .05 .15
LVAL069 Stand-Off SP .10 .20
LVAL070 Shared Ride SCR .60 1.00
LVAL071 Release, Reverse, Burst C .05 .15
LVAL072 Purge Ray C .05 .15
LVAL073 Sylvan Blessing C .05 .15
LVAL074 Ghostrick-Go-Round R .75 1.25
LVAL075 Bujin Regalia - The Jewel C .05 .15
LVAL076 Imperial Tombs of Necrovalley SCR 2.00 2.50
LVAL077 The Monarchs Awaken C .05 .15
LVAL078 Skill Prisoner SR .30 .50
LVAL079 Oath of Companionship R .10 .20
LVAL080 Duston Roller SP .10 .20
LVAL081 Sylvan Mikorange R .10 .20
LVAL082 Ghostrick Yeti C .05 .15
LVAL083 Bujingi Pavo SR .20 .30
LVAL084 Gravekeeper's Heretic R .20 .30
LVAL085 Noble Knight Peredur SR .20 .30
LVAL086 Gwenhwyfar, Queen of Noble Arms SCR 1.00 1.50
LVAL087 Powered Inzektron SR .40 .75
LVAL088 Obedience Schooled SR .60 1.00
LVAL089 The First Monarch SCR .60 1.00
LVAL090 Dark Artist C .05 .15
LVAL091 Swordsman from a Distant Land C .05 .15
LVAL092 Queen Angel of Roses SR .20 .30
LVAL093 Rose Witch C .05 .15
LVAL094 Snapdragon C .05 .15
LVAL095 Alpacaribou, Mystical Beast of the Forest C .05 .15
LVAL096 Mighty Warrior C .05 .15
LVAL097 Dododo Buster C .05 .15
LVAL098 Interplanetarypurplythorny Beast C .05 .15
LVAL099 Starship Spy Plane C .05 .15
LVALSP1 Sylvan Bladefender UR .60 1.50

2014 Yu-Gi-Oh Legacy of the Valiant Deluxe Edition

COMPLETE SET (4) 5.00 10.00
ONE SET PER DELUXE EDITION BOX
LVALDE1 Sylvan Peaskeeper UR .15 .40
LVALDE2 Ghostric Jackfrost UR .50 1.25
LVALDE3 Sylvan Cherubsprout SR .40 1.00
LVALDE4 Bujintervention SR .15 .40

2014 Yu-Gi-Oh Primal Origin 1st Edition

COMPLETE SET (111) 60.00 150.00
BOOSTER BOX (24 PACKS) 60.00 80.00
BOOSTER PACK (9 CARDS) 3.00 4.00
RELEASED ON MAY 16, 2014
PRIOEN000A Artifact Scythe SR .40 1.00
PRIOEN000B Artifact Scythe UR 1.25 3.00
PRIOEN001 ZS - Vanish Sage C .10 .30
PRIOEN002 Galaxy Mirror Sage C .10 .30
PRIOEN003 Galaxy Tyranno R .15 .40
PRIOEN004 Heliosphere Dragon C .10 .30
PRIOEN005 Mermaid Shark R .15 .40
PRIOEN006 Gazer Shark C .10 .30
PRIOEN007 Blizzard Thunderbird C .10 .30
PRIOEN008 Battlin' Boxer Big Bandage C .10 .30
PRIOEN009 Battlin' Boxer Veil C .10 .30
PRIOEN010 Umbral Horror Ghost C .10 .30
PRIOEN011 Artifact Moralltach SR .75 2.00
PRIOEN012 Artifact Beagalltach C .10 .30
PRIOEN013 Artifact Failnaught C .10 .30
PRIOEN014 Artifact Aegis C .10 .30
PRIOEN015 Artifact Achilleshield C .10 .30
PRIOEN016 Artifact Labrys C .10 .30
PRIOEN017 Artifact Caduceus R .15 .40
PRIOEN018 Sylvan Cherubsprout C .10 .30
PRIOEN019A Sylvan Snapdrassinagon R .15 .40
PRIOEN019B Sylvan Snapdrassinagon UR .20 .75
PRIOEN020 Sylvan Lotuswain C .10 .30
PRIOEN021 Sylvan Sagequoia UR .50 1.25
PRIOEN022 Ghostrick Doll C .10 .30
PRIOEN023 Ghostrick Warwolf C .10 .30
PRIOEN024 Bujin Hirume UR 1.00 2.50
PRIOEN025 Traptrix Dionaea R .15 .40
PRIOEN026 Mecha Phantom Beast O-Lion R .15 .40
PRIOEN027 Hazy Flame Hydra C .10 .30
PRIOEN028 Madolche Anjelly UR 3.00 8.00
PRIOEN029 Pilica, Descendant of Gusto SR 1.50 4.00
PRIOEN030 Gladiator Beast Augustus R .15 .40
PRIOEN031 Lucent, Netherlord of Dark World SR 2.00 5.00
PRIOEN032 Ancient Gear Box C .10 .30
PRIOEN033 Dawn Knight R .15 .40
PRIOEN034 Majesty's Fiend SCR 5.00 12.00
PRIOEN035 Thestalos the Mega Monarch SCR 5.00 12.00
PRIOEN036 Beautunaful Princess R .15 .40
PRIOEN037 Nopenguin C .10 .30
PRIOEN038 Condemned Maiden C .10 .30
PRIOEN039 Starduston C .10 .30
PRIOEN040A Number 62: Galaxy-Eyes Prime Photon Dragon UR 5.00 12.00
PRIOEN040B Number 62: Galaxy-Eyes Prime Photon Dragon UTR8.00 20.00
PRIOEN041 Number C107: Neo Galaxy-Eyes Tachyon Dragon UTR1.25 3.00
PRIOEN041 Number C107: Neo Galaxy-Eyes Tachyon Dragon SR .75 2.00
PRIOEN042 Number 103: Ragnazero R .75 2.00
PRIOEN043 Number C103: Ragnafinity R .15 .40
PRIOEN044A Number C102: Archfiend Seraph SR .40 1.00
PRIOEN044B Number C102: Archfiend Seraph UTR .40 1.00
PRIOEN045 Number 80: Rhapsody in Berserk R .40 1.00
PRIOEN046 Number C80: Requiem in Berserk R .15 .40
PRIOEN047 Number 43: Manipulator of Souls C .10 .30
PRIOEN048 Number C43: High Manipulator of Chaos R .15 .40
PRIOEN049 Artifact Durendal UTR 3.00 8.00
PRIOEN049 Artifact Durendal UR 2.00 5.00
PRIOEN050 Orea, the Sylvan High Arbiter SCR .75 2.00
PRIOEN051 Ghostrick Socuteboss R .60 1.50
PRIOEN052A Bujinki Amaterasu SCR .75 2.00
PRIOEN052B Bujinki Amaterasu GR 2.00 5.00
PRIOEN052C Bujinki Amaterasu UTR 1.00 2.50
PRIOEN053 Phantom Fortress Enterblathnir R .15 .40
PRIOEN054 Cairngorgon, Antiluminescent Knight SR .40 1.00
PRIOEN055 Phonon Pulse Dragon R .15 .40
PRIOEN056 Reverse Breaker C .10 .30
PRIOEN057 Galactic Charity C .10 .30
PRIOEN058 Rank-Up-Magic - The Seventh One SCR .75 2.00
PRIOEN059 Don Thousand's Throne R .15 .40
PRIOEN060 Artifact Ignition UR 2.00 5.00
PRIOEN061 Artifacts Unleashed C .10 .30
PRIOEN062 Sylvan Charity UR .20 .75
PRIOEN063 Ghostrick Parade C .10 .30
PRIOEN064 Bujintervention C .10 .30
PRIOEN065 Diamond Core of Koa'ki Meiru C .10 .30
PRIOEN066 Scrap Factory C .10 .30
PRIOEN067 Forbidden Scripture SCR .75 2.00
PRIOEN068 Jackpot 7 C .10 .30
PRIOEN069 Double Dragon Descent C .10 .30
PRIOEN070 Tachyon Chaos Hole SR .40 1.00
PRIOEN071 Last Counter UR .20 .75
PRIOEN072 Artifact Sanctum UR 3.00 8.00
PRIOEN073 Sylvan Waterslide C .10 .30
PRIOEN074 Ghostrick Night C .50 1.25
PRIOEN075 Bujincident C .10 .30
PRIOEN076 The Monarchs Erupt SR .40 1.00
PRIOEN077 Evo-Singularity C .10 .30
PRIOEN078 Xyz Universe R .50 1.25
PRIOEN079A And the Band Played On C .10 .30
PRIOEN079B And the Band Played On UR .20 .75
PRIOEN080 Tri-and-Guess C .10 .30
PRIOEN081 Noble Knight Brothers SCR 2.00 5.00
PRIOEN082 Noble Knight Eachtar SR .40 1.00
PRIOEN083 Sylvan Princessprout SR .40 1.00
PRIOEN084 Bujingi Sinyou UR .20 .75
PRIOEN085 Vampire Vamp SR .75 2.00
PRIOEN086 Gladiator Beast Nerokius SCR 1.25 3.00
PRIOEN087 Noble Knights of the Round Table UR .20 .75
PRIOEN088 Avalon SR .40 1.00
PRIOEN089 Escalation of the Monarchs SR .60 1.50
PRIOEN090 Bolt Penguin C .10 .30
PRIOEN091 Phantom King Hydride C .10 .30
PRIOEN092 Number 42: Galaxy Tomahawk C .10 .30
PRIOEN093 Rose Archer R .15 .40
PRIOEN094 Shogi Knight C .10 .30
PRIOEN095 Gimmick Puppet Des Troy C .10 .30
PRIOEN096 ZW - Sleipnir Mail C .10 .30
PRIOEN097 Number 48: Shadow Lich C .10 .30
PRIOEN098 Galaxy Dragon C .10 .30
PRIOEN099 Hundred-Footed Horror C .10 .30
PRIOENDE3 Agent of Entropy - Uranus R .50 1.25
PRIOENDE4 Re-Cover R .15 .40

2014 Yu-Gi-Oh Duelist Alliance 1st Edition

COMPLETE SET (105) 140.00 200.00
BOOSTER BOX (24 PACKS) 100.00 120.00
BOOSTER PACK (9 CARDS) 5.00
RELEASED ON AUGUST 15, 2014
DUEAEN000 Dragon Horn Hunter SR .75 1.25
DUEAEN001 Flash Knight R .15 .25
DUEAEN002 Foucault's Cannon SR .50 .75
DUEAEN003 Metaphys Armed Dragon C .05 .15
DUEAEN004 Odd-Eyes Pendulum Dragon SCR 4.00 6.00
DUEAEN004u Odd-Eyes Pendulum Dragon UTR 7.00 9.00
DUEAEN005 Performapal Skeeter Skimmer C .05 .15
DUEAEN006 Performapal Whip Snake R .15 .25
DUEAEN007 Performapal Sword Fish C .05 .15
DUEAEN008 Performapal Hip Hippo C .05 .15
DUEAEN009 Performapal Kaleidoscorp R .15 .25
DUEAEN010 Performapal Turn Toad R .15 .25
DUEAEN011 Superheavy Samurai Blue Brawler C .05 .15
DUEAEN012 Superheavy Samurai Swordsman C .05 .15
DUEAEN013 Superheavy Samurai Big Benkei R .15 .25
DUEAEN014 Aria the Melodious Diva C .05 .15
DUEAEN015 Sonata the Melodious Diva C .05 .15
DUEAEN016 Mozarta the Melodious Maestra R .15 .25
DUEAEN017 Battleguard King C .05 .15
DUEAEN018 Satellarknight Deneb UR 7.00 8.50
DUEAEN019 Satellarknight Altair R .50 .80
DUEAEN020 Satellarknight Vega C .05 .15
DUEAEN021 Satellarknight Alsahm SR 1.25 2.00
DUEAEN022 Satellarknight Unukalhai C .05 .15
DUEAEN023 Shaddoll Falco R .75 1.25
DUEAEN024 Shaddoll Hedgehog C .05 .15
DUEAEN025 Shaddoll Squamata C .05 .15
DUEAEN026 Shaddoll Dragon R 1.25 1.75
DUEAEN027 Shaddoll Beast R .40 .75
DUEAEN028 Suanni, Fire of the Yang Zing SR 2.25 3.00
DUEAEN029 Bi'an, Earth of the Yang Zing SR 1.00 1.50
DUEAEN030 Bixi, Water of the Yang Zing SR 1.50 2.00
DUEAEN031 Pulao, Wind of the Yang Zing SR .20 .30
DUEAEN032 Chiwen, Light of the Yang Zing UR 2.50 6.00
DUEAEN033 Artifact Chakram C .05 .15
DUEAEN034 Artifact Lancea C .05 .15
DUEAEN035 Nefarious Archfiend Eater of Nefariousness C .05 .15
DUEAEN036 The Agent of Entropy - Uranus C .05 .15
DUEAEN037 Djinn Demolisher of Rituals C .05 .15
DUEAEN038 Batteryman 9-Volt C .05 .15
DUEAEN039 Resonance Insect C .05 .15
DUEAEN040 Breaker the Dark Magical Warrior C .05 .15
DUEAEN041 Raiza the Mega Monarch SCR 1.25 1.75
DUEAEN042 Dogu C .05 .15
DUEAEN043 Hypnosister SR .30 .50
DUEAEN044 Re-Cover C .05 .15
DUEAEN045 Deskbot 001 C .05 .15
DUEAEN046 Spy-C-Spy C .05 .15
DUEAEN047 Wightprince C .05 .15
DUEAEN048 El Shaddoll Winda UR 6.00 8.00
DUEAEN049 El Shaddoll Construct UR 2.75 4.00
DUEAEN049u El Shaddoll Construct UTR 7.00 10.00
DUEAEN050 Saffira, Queen of Dragons UR 6.00 7.50
DUEAEN050 Saffira, Queen of Dragons UTR 10.00 13.00
DUEAEN051 Baxia, Brightness of the Yang Zing SCR 4.00 5.00
DUEAEN051u Baxia, Brightness of the Yang Zing UTR 7.50 9.00
DUEAEN052 Samsara, Dragon of Rebirth SR 1.00 1.50
DUEAEN053 Stellarknight Delteros SCR 1.25 1.75
DUEAEN053g Stellarknight Delteros GR 3.50 5.00
DUEAEN053u Stellarknight Delteros UTR 1.50 2.50
DUEAEN054 Castel, the Skyblaster Musketeer SR 2.50 3.50
DUEAEN055 Hippo Carnival C .05 .15
DUEAEN056 Feast of the Wild LV5 C .05 .15
DUEAEN057 Stellarknight Alpha C .05 .15
DUEAEN058 Satellarknight Skybridge R .15 .25
DUEAEN059 Shaddoll Fusion SR 12.00 15.00
DUEAEN060 Curse of the Shadow Prison C .05 .15
DUEAEN061 Yang Zing Path SCR 6.00 8.00
DUEAEN062 Yang Zing Prana C .05 .15
DUEAEN063 Hymn of Light C .05 .15
DUEAEN064 Diacocension C .05 .15
DUEAEN065 Magical Spring SCR 3.50 5.00
DUEAEN066 The Monarchs Stormforth C .25 .40
DUEAEN067 Pop-Up C .05 .15
DUEAEN068 Battleguard Rage C .05 .15
DUEAEN069 Battleguard Howling C .05 .15
DUEAEN070 Stellarnova Wave C .05 .15
DUEAEN071 Stellarnova Alpha UR 4.00 5.00
DUEAEN072 Sinister Shadow Games UR 1.00 1.50
DUEAEN073 Shaddoll Core SR .60 1.00
DUEAEN074 Yang Zing Creation UR 2.00 3.00
DUEAEN075 Yang Zing Unleashed C .05 .15
DUEAEN076 Chain Dispel C .05 .15
DUEAEN077 Face-Off R .15 .25
DUEAEN078 Pendulum Back SR .30 .50
DUEAEN079 Time-Space Trap Hole SCR 1.75 3.00
DUEAEN080 That Six C .05 .15
DUEAEN081 Doomstar Magician UR .40 .75
DUEAEN082 Scarm, Malebranche of the Burning Abyss R .60 1.00
DUEAEN083 Graff, Malebranche of the Burning Abyss R .15 .25
DUEAEN084 Cir, Malebranche of the Burning Abyss R .30 .50
DUEAEN085 Dante, Traveler of the Burning Abyss SCR 9.00 11.00
DUEAEN086 The Traveler and the Burning Abyss SR .60 1.00
DUEAEN087 U.A. Mighty Slugger R .25 .40
DUEAEN088 U.A. Perfect Ace R .50 .75
DUEAEN089 U.A. Stadium C .05 .15
DUEAEN090 Gaia, the Polar Knight C .05 .15
DUEAEN091 Gaia, the Mid-Knight Sun C .05 .15
DUEAEN092 Chaos Seed C .05 .15
DUEAEN093 Exchange of Night and Day C .05 .15
DUEAEN094 Number 58: Burner Visor C .05 .15
DUEAEN095 Felis, Lightsworn Archer UR 7.00 10.00
DUEAEN096 Fishborg Doctor C .05 .15
DUEAEN097 Panzer Dragon R .60 1.00
DUEAEN098 Cloudcastle C .05 .15
DUEAEN099 Pilgrim Reaper C .05 .15

2014 Yu-Gi-Oh The New Challengers 1st Edition

COMPLETE SET (119) 120.00 250.00
BOOSTER BOX (24 PACKS) 60.00 70.00
BOOSTER PACK (9 CARDS) 3.00 4.00
RELEASED ON NOVEMBER 7, 2014
NECHEN000 Lancephorhynchus SR .15 .40
NECHEN001 Performapal Cheermole R .10 .30
NECHEN002 Performapal Trampolynx R .10 .30
NECHEN003 Block Spider C .10 .30
NECHEN004 Canon the Melodious Diva C .10 .30
NECHEN005 Serenade the Melodious Diva C .10 .30
NECHEN006 Elegy the Melodious Diva C .10 .30
NECHEN007 Shopina the Melodious Maestra R .10 .30
NECHEN008 Superheavy Samurai Kabuto C .10 .30
NECHEN009 Superheavy Samurai Scales R .10 .30
NECHEN010 Superheavy Samurai Soulfire Suit C .10 .30

NECHEN011 Superheavy Samurai Soulshield Wall C .10 .50
NECHEN012 Superheavy Samurai Soulbreaker Armor C .10 .30
NECHEN013 Superheavy Samurai Soulbang Cannon C .10 .30
NECHEN014 Edge Imp Sabres SR 2.00 5.00
NECHEN015 Fluffal Leo C .10 .30
NECHEN016 Fluffal Bear C .10 .30
NECHEN017 Fluffal Dog R .50 1.25
NECHEN018 Fluffal Owl R .40 1.00
NECHEN019 Fluffal Cat C .10 .30
NECHEN020 Fluffal Rabbit C .10 .30
NECHEN021 Qliphort Scout UR .50 1.25
NECHEN022 Qliphort Carrier SR .50 1.25
NECHEN023 Qliphort Helix SR 1.25 3.00
NECHEN024 Qliphort Disk SCR .75 2.00
NECHEN025 Qliphort Shell R .10 .30
NECHEN026 Apoqliphort Towers R .10 .30
NECHEN027 Satellarknight Sirius R .10 .30
NECHEN028 Satellarknight Procyon C .10 .30
NECHEN029 Satellarknight Betelgeuse C .10 .30
NECHEN030 Shaddoll Hound C .10 .30
NECHEN031 Taotie, Shadow of the Yang Zing SR .15 .40
NECHEN032 Jiaotu, Darkness of the Yang Zing UR 6.00 15.00
NECHEN033 Lindbloom C .10 .30
NECHEN034 Night Dragolich UR .60 1.50
NECHEN035 Unmasked Dragon R .10 .30
NECHEN036 Machina Megaform SR .15 .40
NECHEN037 Zaborg the Mega Monarch UR 1.00 2.50
NECHEN038 Valerifawn, Mystical Beast of the Forest C .10 .30
NECHEN039 Rescue Hamster SR 1.50 4.00
NECHEN040 Watch Dog C .10 .30
NECHEN041 Denko Sekka UR 3.00 8.00
NECHEN042 Deskbot 002 C .10 .30
NECHEN043 Ms. Judge NR .10 .30
NECHEN044 Scrounging Goblin NR .10 .30
NECHEN045 Herald of Ultimateness UR .40 1.00
NECHEN046 Frightfur Bear R .10 .30
NECHEN046u Frightfur Bear UTR .75 2.00
NECHEN047 Frightfur Wolf R .50 1.25
NECHEN048 El Shaddoll Grysta SCR .75 2.00
NECHEN049 El Shaddoll Shekhinaga SCR .75 2.00
NECHEN049u El Shaddoll Shekhinaga UTR 2.00 5.00
NECHEN050 First of the Dragons SR 1.00 2.50
NECHEN051 Yazi, Evil of the Yang Zing SCR .75 2.00
NECHEN051u Yazi, Evil of the Yang Zing UTR 1.50 4.00
NECHEN052 Herald of the Arc Light SR .75 2.00
NECHEN053 Dark Rebellion Xyz Dragon SCR 2.00 5.00
NECHEN053u Dark Rebellion Xyz Dragon UTR 3.00 8.00
NECHEN054 Stellarknight Triverr UR .15 .40
NECHEN054u Stellarknight Triverr UTR .60 1.50
NECHEN055 Wonder Balloons C .10 .30
NECHEN056 Mimiclay C .10 .30
NECHEN057 Draw Muscle R .10 .30
NECHEN058 Magical Star Illusion C .10 .30
NECHEN059 1st Movement Solo SR .60 1.50
NECHEN060 Toy Vendor C .10 .30
NECHEN061 Sagliffice UR .20 .60
NECHEN062 Laser Qlip C .10 .30
NECHEN063 Hexatellarknight C .10 .30
NECHEN064 El Shaddoll Fusion SR .40 1.00
NECHEN065 Celestia C .10 .30
NECHEN066 Oracle of the Herald C .10 .30
NECHEN067 Strike of the Monarchs C .10 .30
NECHEN068 Cursed Bamboo Sword C .10 .30
NECHEN069 Command Performance C .10 .30
NECHEN070 Performapal Revival C .10 .30
NECHEN071 Punch-in-the-Box C .10 .60
NECHEN072 The Phantom Knights of Shadow Veil C .10 .30
NECHEN073 Qlimate Change C .10 .30
NECHEN074 Qlipper Launch C .10 .30
NECHEN075 Yang Zing Brutality C .10 .30
NECHEN076 Naturia Sacred Tree R .10 .30
NECHEN077 Oasis of Dragon Souls R .75 2.00
NECHEN078 Fusion Reserve UR 2.50 6.00
NECHEN079 Solemn Scolding SCR 3.00 8.00
NECHEN080 Different Dimension Encounter C .10 .30
NECHEN081 Fusion Substitute C .20 .60
NECHEN082 Rubic, Malebranche of the Burning Abyss UR 1.25 3.00
NECHEN083 Alich, Malebranche of the Burning Abyss R .10 .30
NECHEN084 Calcab, Malebranche of the Burning Abyss R .10 .30
NECHEN085 Virgil, Rock Star of the Burning Abyss SCR .75 2.00
NECHEN086 Fire Lake of the Burning Abyss SR .40 1.00
NECHEN087 U.A. Midfielder R .50 1.25
NECHEN088 U.A. Goalkeeper R .10 .30
NECHEN089 U.A. Powered Jersey C .10 .30
NECHEN090 Ruffian Railcar C .10 .30
NECHEN091 SZW - Fenrir Sword C .10 .30
NECHEN092 Gogogo Goram C .10 .30
NECHEN093 Dododo Driver C .10 .30
NECHEN094 Xyz Change Tactics R .10 .30
NECHEN095 Number 39: Utopia Beyond SR 1.25 3.00
NECHEN096 CXyz Barian Hope SR .15 .40
NECHEN097 Shogi Lance C .10 .30
NECHEN098 Guiding Light C .10 .30
NECHEN099 Number 99: Utopic Dragon SCR 2.00 5.00
NECHENS01 Lancephorhynchus SR .15 .40
NECHENS02 Edge Imp Sabres SR 2.00 5.00
NECHENS03 Qliphort Carrier SR .50 1.25
NECHENS04 Qliphort Helix SR 1.25 3.00
NECHENS05 Taotie, Shadow of the Yang Zing SR .15 .40
NECHENS06 Machina Megaform SR .15 .40
NECHENS07 Rescue Hamster SR 1.50 4.00
NECHENS08 First of the Dragons SR .75 2.00
NECHENS09 Herald of the Arc Light SR .75 2.00
NECHENS10 1st Movement Solo SR .50 1.25
NECHENS11 El Shaddoll Fusion SR .40 1.00
NECHENS12 Fire Lake of the Burning Abyss SR .40 1.00
NECHENS13 Number 39: Utopia Beyond SR 1.25 3.00
NECHENS14 CXyz Barian Hope SR .15 .40

2015 Yu-Gi-Oh Secrets of Eternity 1st Edition

COMPLETE SET (105) 95.00 125.00
BOOSTER BOX (24 PACKS) 50.00 60.00
BOOSTER PACK (9 CARDS) 3.00 4.00
UNLISTED C .10 .30
UNLISTED R .30 .50
RELEASED ON JANUARY 16, 2015
SECEEN000 Dragoons of Draconia R .20 .30
SECEEN001 Performapal Fire Mufflerlion C .05 .15
SECEEN002 Performapal Partnaga C .05 .15
SECEEN003 Performapal Friendonkey C .05 .15
SECEEN004 Performapal Spikeagle C .05 .15
SECEEN005 Performapal Slamp Turtle C .05 .15
SECEEN006 Performapal Trump Witch R .10 .20
SECEEN007 Superheavy Samurai Flutist SR 1.75 2.25
SECEEN008 Superheavy Samurai Trumpeter SR .60 1.00
SECEEN009 Superheavy Samurai Soulpiercer C .05 .15
SECEEN010 Superheavy Samurai Soulbeads C .05 .15
SECEEN011 Raidraptor - Vanishing Lanius C .05 .15
SECEEN012 Gem-Knight Lapis C .05 .15
SECEEN013 Infernoid Antra SR .50 .75
SECEEN014 Infernoid Harmadik UR 2.00 3.00
SECEEN015 Infernoid Patrulea R .30 .45
SECEEN016 Infernoid Piaty C .05 .15
SECEEN017 Infernoid Seitsemas C .05 .15
SECEEN018 Infernoid Attondel C .05 .15
SECEEN019 Infernoid Onuncu SCR .60 1.00
SECEEN019u Infernoid Onuncu UTR 1.50 2.00
SECEEN020 Qliphort Monolith SCR 25.00 28.00
SECEEN021 Qliphort Cephalopod SR .75 1.25
SECEEN022 Qliphort Stealth UR 1.75 2.25
SECEEN023 Apoqliphort Skybase UR .40 .60
SECEEN024 Satellarknight Capella C .05 .15
SECEEN025 Satellarknight Rigel SR .40 .60
SECEEN026 Yosenju Magat C .05 .15
SECEEN027 Yosenju Tsujik C .05 .15
SECEEN028 Dance Princess of the Nekroz R .05 .15
SECEEN029 Spiritual Beast Rampengu C .10 .20
SECEEN030 Morphtronic Smartfon C .05 .15
SECEEN031 Jinzo - Jector SR .50 .75
SECEEN032 Skilled Blue Magician SR .40 .60
SECEEN033 Koa'ki Meiru Overload R .20 .30
SECEEN034 Jigabyte C .05 .15
SECEEN035 Caius the Mega Monarch UR 7.00 8.50
SECEEN036 Thunderclap Skywolf SR .05 .15
SECEEN037 Lightning Rod Lord SR .20 .35
SECEEN038 Dragon Dowser R .05 .15
SECEEN039 Frontline Observer R .05 .15
SECEEN040 Uni-Zombie C .80 1.15
SECEEN041 Deskbot 003 C .80 1.15
SECEEN042 Legendary Maju Garzett C .20 .30
SECEEN043 Marmiting Captain C .05 .15
SECEEN044 Nekroz of Gungnir SCR .75 1.25
SECEEN044u Nekroz of Gungnir UTR 1.75 2.00
SECEEN045 Rune-Eyes Pendulum Dragon UR .75 1.25
SECEEN046 Gem-Knight Lady Lapis Lazuli R .05 .15
SECEEN047 El Shaddoll Wendigo SR .30 .50
SECEEN048 Superheavy Samurai Warlord Susanowo SR 1.75 2.15
SECEEN048u Superheavy Samurai Warlord Susanowo UTR 2.50 3.00
SECEEN049 Metaphys Horus UR 1.75 2.25
SECEEN049u Metaphys Horus UTR 3.50 4.50
SECEEN050 Raidraptor - Rise Falcon C .05 .15
SECEEN051 Stellarknight Constellar Diamond UR 1.25 1.75
SECEEN051u Stellarknight Constellar Diamond UTR 4.00 5.00
SECEEN052 Sky Cavalry Centaurea UR 5.00 6.50
SECEEN053 Illusion Balloons C .05 .15
SECEEN054 Raidraptor - Nest R .10 .20
SECEEN055 Constellar Twinkle C .05 .15
SECEEN056 Gottoms' Second Call R .05 .15
SECEEN057 Void Seer SR .60 1.00
SECEEN058 Void Expansion R .05 .15
SECEEN059 Nephe Shaddoll Fusion SCR .75 1.00
SECEEN060 Nekroz Cycle R .25 .40
SECEEN061 Tenacity of the Monarchs R .50 .75
SECEEN062 Dragunity Divine Lance C .05 .15
SECEEN063 Pot of Riches SCR 2.00 2.50
SECEEN064 A Wild Monster Appears! SCR .60 1.00
SECEEN065 Pendulum Shift C .05 .15
SECEEN066 Extra Net C .05 .15
SECEEN067 Performapal Call C .05 .15
SECEEN068 Wall of Disruption C .05 .15
SECEEN069 Last Minute Cancel C .05 .15
SECEEN070 Raidraptor - Readiness C .05 .15
SECEEN071 Eye of the Void UR .25 .40
SECEEN072 Void Launch SR .10 .20
SECEEN073 Re-qliate C .05 .15
SECEEN074 Ritual Beast Ambush C .30 .40
SECEEN075 Zenmaiday C .05 .15
SECEEN076 Unpossessed C .05 .15
SECEEN077 Blaze Accelerator Reload C .05 .15
SECEEN078 Soul Transition SCR 4.75 5.50
SECEEN079 Echo Oscillation C .05 .15
SECEEN080 Double Trap Hole C .05 .15
SECEEN081 Mischief of the Gnomes C .20 .30
SECEEN082 Farfa, Malebranche of the Burning Abyss R .80 1.00
SECEEN083 Libic, Malebranche of the Burning Abyss R .15 .25
SECEEN084 Cagna, Malebranche of the Burning Abyss R .20 .30
SECEEN085 Malacoda, Netherlord of the Burning Abyss SCR 4.00 4.50
SECEEN085 Malacoda, Netherlord of the Burning Abyss GR 5.50 6.50
SECEEN086 Good & Evil in the Burning Abyss SR .75 1.00
SECEEN087 U.A. Playmaker R .05 .15
SECEEN088 U.A. Blockbacker R .15 .25
SECEEN089 U.A. Turnover Tactics R .10 .20
SECEEN090 Gogogo Golem - Golden Form C .05 .15
SECEEN091 Dododo Witch C .05 .15
SECEEN092 Dododo Swordsman C .05 .15
SECEEN093 Toy Knight C .05 .15
SECEEN094 Explossum C .05 .15
SECEEN095 Swordsman of Revealing Light UR 1.75 2.25
SECEEN096 Doggy Diver R .05 .15
SECEEN097 Level Lifter C .05 .15
SECEEN098 Gogogo Talisman C .05 .15
SECEEN099 Soul Strike C .05 .15

2015 Yu-Gi-Oh Secrets of Eternity Unlimited

COMPLETE SET (106 CARDS) 95.00 125.00
BOOSTER BOX (24 PACKS) 50.00 60.00
BOOSTER PACK (9 CARDS) 3.00 4.00
UNLISTED C .10 .30
UNLISTED R .30 .50
RELEASED ON JANUARY 16, 2015
SECEEN000 Dragoons of Draconia R .20 .30
SECEEN001 Performapal Fire Mufflerlion C .05 .15
SECEEN002 Performapal Partnaga C .10 .30
SECEEN003 Performapal Friendonkey C .10 .30
SECEEN004 Performapal Spikeagle C .10 .30
SECEEN005 Performapal Slamp Turtle C .10 .30
SECEEN006 Performapal Trump Witch R .10 .20
SECEEN007 Superheavy Samurai Flutist SR 1.75 2.25
SECEEN008 Superheavy Samurai Trumpeter SR .60 1.00
SECEEN009 Superheavy Samurai Soulpiercer C .10 .30
SECEEN010 Superheavy Samurai Soulbeads C .10 .30
SECEEN011 Raidraptor - Vanishing Lanius C .10 .30
SECEEN012 Gem-Knight Lapis C .10 .30
SECEEN013 Infernoid Antra SR .50 .75
SECEEN014 Infernoid Harmadik UR 2.00 3.00
SECEEN015 Infernoid Patrulea R .30 .45
SECEEN016 Infernoid Piaty C .10 .30
SECEEN017 Infernoid Seitsemas C .10 .30
SECEEN018 Infernoid Attondel C .10 .30
SECEEN019 Infernoid Onuncu SCR .60 1.00
SECEEN019u Infernoid Onuncu UTR 1.50 2.00
SECEEN020 Qliphort Monolith SCR 25.00 28.00
SECEEN021 Qliphort Cephalopod SR .75 1.25
SECEEN022 Qliphort Stealth UR 1.75 2.25
SECEEN023 Apoqliphort Skybase UR .40 .60
SECEEN024 Satellarknight Capella C .10 .30
SECEEN025 Satellarknight Rigel SR .40 .60
SECEEN026 Yosenju Magat C .10 .30
SECEEN027 Yosenju Tsujik C .10 .30
SECEEN028 Dance Princess of the Nekroz R .05 .15
SECEEN029 Spiritual Beast Rampengu C .10 .20
SECEEN030 Morphtronic Smartfon C .05 .15
SECEEN031 Jinzo - Jector SR .50 .75
SECEEN032 Skilled Blue Magician SR .40 .60
SECEEN033 Koa'ki Meiru Overload R .20 .30
SECEEN034 Jigabyte C .10 .30
SECEEN035 Caius the Mega Monarch UR 7.00 8.50
SECEEN036 Thunderclap Skywolf SR .05 .15
SECEEN037 Lightning Rod Lord SR .20 .35
SECEEN038 Dragon Dowser R .05 .15
SECEEN039 Frontline Observer R .05 .15
SECEEN040 Uni-Zombie C .05 .15
SECEEN041 Deskbot 003 C .80 1.15
SECEEN042 Legendary Maju Garzett C .05 .15
SECEEN043 Marmiting Captain C .10 .30
SECEEN044 Nekroz of Gungnir SCR .75 1.25
SECEEN044u Nekroz of Gungnir UTR 1.75 2.00
SECEEN045 Rune-Eyes Pendulum Dragon UR .75 1.25
SECEEN046 Gem-Knight Lady Lapis Lazuli R .05 .15
SECEEN047 El Shaddoll Wendigo SR .30 .50
SECEEN048 Superheavy Samurai Warlord Susanowo SR 1.75 2.15
SECEEN048u Superheavy Samurai Warlord Susanowo UTR 2.50 3.00
SECEEN049 Metaphys Horus UR 1.75 2.25
SECEEN049u Metaphys Horus UTR 3.50 4.50
SECEEN050 Raidraptor - Rise Falcon C .10 .30
SECEEN051 Stellarknight Constellar Diamond UR 1.25 1.75
SECEEN051u Stellarknight Constellar Diamond UTR 4.00 5.00
SECEEN052 Sky Cavalry Centaurea UR 5.00 6.50
SECEEN053 Illusion Balloons C .10 .30
SECEEN054 Raidraptor - Nest R .10 .20
SECEEN055 Constellar Twinkle C .10 .30
SECEEN056 Gottoms' Second Call R .05 .15
SECEEN057 Void Seer SR .60 1.00
SECEEN058 Void Expansion R .05 .15
SECEEN059 Nephe Shaddoll Fusion SCR .75 1.00
SECEEN060 Nekroz Cycle R .25 .40
SECEEN061 Tenacity of the Monarchs R .50 .75
SECEEN062 Dragunity Divine Lance C .10 .30
SECEEN063 Pot of Riches SCR 2.00 2.50
SECEEN064 A Wild Monster Appears! SCR .60 1.00
SECEEN065 Pendulum Shift C .10 .30
SECEEN066 Extra Net C .10 .30
SECEEN067 Performapal Call C .10 .30
SECEEN068 Wall of Disruption C .10 .30
SECEEN069 Last Minute Cancel C .10 .30
SECEEN070 Raidraptor - Readiness C .10 .30
SECEEN071 Eye of the Void UR .25 .40
SECEEN072 Void Launch SR .10 .20
SECEEN073 Re-qliate C .10 .30
SECEEN074 Ritual Beast Ambush C .25 .40
SECEEN075 Zenmaiday C .05 .15
SECEEN076 Unpossessed C .05 .15
SECEEN077 Blaze Accelerator Reload C .05 .15
SECEEN078 Soul Transition SCR 4.75 5.50
SECEEN079 Echo Oscillation C .05 .15
SECEEN080 Double Trap Hole C .05 .15
SECEEN081 Mischief of the Gnomes C .20 .15
SECEEN082 Farfa, Malebranche of the Burning Abyss R .80 1.00
SECEEN083 Libic, Malebranche of the Burning Abyss R .15 .25
SECEEN084 Cagna, Malebranche of the Burning Abyss R .20 .30
SECEEN085 Malacoda Netherlord of the Burning Abyss GR 5.50 6.50
SECEEN085 Malacoda, Netherlord of the Burning Abyss SCR 4.00 4.50
SECEEN086 Good & Evil in the Burning Abyss SR .75 1.00
SECEEN087 U.A. Playmaker R .05 .15
SECEEN088 U.A. Blockbacker R .15 .25
SECEEN089 U.A. Turnover Tactics R .10 .20
SECEEN090 Gogogo Golem - Golden Form C .05 .15
SECEEN091 Dododo Witch C .05 .15
SECEEN092 Dododo Swordsman C .05 .15
SECEEN093 Toy Knight C .05 .15
SECEEN094 Explossum C .05 .15
SECEEN095 Swordsman of Revealing Light UR 1.75 2.25
SECEEN096 Doggy Diver R .05 .15
SECEEN097 Level Lifter C .05 .15
SECEEN098 Gogogo Talisman C .10 .30
SECEEN099 Soul Strike C .10 .30

2015 Yu-Gi-Oh Crossed Souls 1st Edition

COMPLETE SET (105) 180.00 230.00
BOOSTER BOX (24 PACKS) 50.00 75.00
BOOSTER PACK (9 CARDS) 2.00 5.00
RELEASED ON MAY 15, 2015
CROSEN000 Sea Dragoons of Draconia R .05 .15
CROSEN001 Phantom Gryphon C .05 .15
CROSEN002 Performapal Elephammer R .10 .20
CROSEN003 Performapal Bowhopper C .05 .15
CROSEN004 Performapal Lizardraw C .15 .25
CROSEN005 Performapal Springoose C .05 .15
CROSEN006 Superheavy Samurai Big Waraji C .05 .15
CROSEN007 Superheavy Samurai Gigagloves C .05 .15
CROSEN008 Superheavy Samurai Battleball SR 2.25 3.00
CROSEN009 Superheavy Samurai Soulbuster Gauntlet C .05 .15
CROSEN010 Soprano the Melodious Songstress C .05 .15
CROSEN011 Fluffal Sheep C .05 .15
CROSEN012 Edge Imp Saw C .05 .15
CROSEN013 Edge Imp Chain C .05 .15
CROSEN014 Edge Imp Tomahawk R .10 .20
CROSEN015 Edge Imp Frightfuloid C .05 .15
CROSEN016 Raidraptor - Sharp Lanius C .05 .15
CROSEN017 Raidraptor - Mimicry Lanius C .05 .15
CROSEN018 Yosenju Kodam C .05 .15
CROSEN019 Yosenju Oyam R .05 .15
CROSEN020 Satellarknight Zefrathuban UR .75 1.15
CROSEN021 Stellarknight Zefraxciton R .10 .20
CROSEN022 Shaddoll Zefranaga C .05 .15
CROSEN023 Shaddoll Zefracore C .05 .15
CROSEN024 Zefraxi, Treasure of the Yang Zing UR 8.75 10.00
CROSEN025 Zefraniu, Secret of the Yang Zing R 1.00 1.75
CROSEN026 Zefrasaber, Swordmaster of the Nekroz C .05 .15
CROSEN027 Zefraxa, Flame Beast of the Nekroz C .05 .15
CROSEN028 Ritual Beast Tamer Zeframpilica C .05 .15
CROSEN029 Ritual Beast Tamer Zefrawendi R .05 .15
CROSEN030 Infernoid Pirmais UR 1.50 2.00
CROSEN031 Infernoid Sjette C .05 .15
CROSEN032 Infernoid Devyaty UR 4.00 4.75
CROSEN033 Ghost Ogre & Snow Rabbit SCR 20.00 23.00
CROSEN034 Magma Dragon C .05 .15
CROSEN035 Deskbot 004 C .20 .30
CROSEN036 Doomdog Octhros C .05 .15
CROSEN037 Putrid Pudding Body Buddies C .10 .30
CROSEN038 Nekroz of Sophia SCR 1.00 1.50
CROSEN038u Nekroz of Sophia UTR 1.25 1.75
CROSEN039 Schuberta the Melodious Maestra R .15 .25
CROSEN040 Bloom Diva the Melodious Choir UR 5.00 6.00
CROSEN041 Frightfur Leo SR 1.50 2.00
CROSEN042 Frightfur Sheep SR 4.00 4.75
CROSEN043 Frightfur Chimera R .05 .15
CROSEN043u Frightfur Chimera UTR 1.00 1.50
CROSEN044 El Shaddoll Anoyatyllis SCR 7.00 9.00
CROSEN045 Ritual Beast Ulti-Gaiapelio UR 3.50 4.25
CROSEN045u Ritual Beast Ulti-Gaiapelio UTR 4.00 6.00
CROSEN046 Clear Wing Synchro Dragon GR 23.00 26.00
CROSEN046 Clear Wing Synchro Dragon SCR 15.00 18.00
CROSEN046u Clear Wing Synchro Dragon UTR 16.00 20.00
CROSEN047 Chaofeng, Phantom of the Yang Zing SR 2.00 2.75
CROSEN048 Raidraptor - Blaze Falcon R .10 .20
CROSEN049 Raidraptor - Revolution Falcon R .10 .20
CROSEN050 Tellarknight Ptolemaeus UR 2.00 2.50
CROSEN050u Tellarknight Ptolemaeus UTR 2.25 3.00
CROSEN051 Madolche Puddingcess Chocolat-a-la-Mode UR 2.00 2.50
CROSEN052 Performapal Recasting C .05 .15
CROSEN053 Fusion Conscription R .40 .60
CROSEN054 Frightfur Factory C .05 .15
CROSEN055 Suture Rebirth R .05 .15
CROSEN056 Frightfur Fusion R .40 .60
CROSEN057 Rank-Up-Magic Revolution Force R .15 .25
CROSEN058 Yosen Whirlwind C .05 .15
CROSEN059 Zefra Path C .05 .15
CROSEN060 Oracle of Zefra SCR 4.75 5.75
CROSEN061 Void Vanishment SR .25 .40
CROSEN062 Galaxy Cyclone SCR 5.00 6.50
CROSEN063 Harmonic Oscillation C .05 .15
CROSEN064 Pendulum Rising C .05 .15
CROSEN065 Unexpected Dai SR 2.75 3.50
CROSEN066 Performapal Pinch Helper C .05 .15
CROSEN067 Melodious Illusion R .15 .25
CROSEN068 Fluffal Crane C .05 .15
CROSEN069 Designer Frightfur C .05 .15
CROSEN070 Dizzying Winds of Yosen Village C .05 .15
CROSEN071 Chosen of Zefra C .05 .15
CROSEN072 Zefra Divine Strike SR 1.25 2.00
CROSEN073 Void Purification R .05 .15
CROSEN074 Jar of Avarice SCR 6.75 7.75
CROSEN075 Lose 1 Turn UR 3.75 4.50
CROSEN076 Fiend Griefing C .05 .15
CROSEN077 Abyss Stungray C .05 .15
CROSEN078 Statue of Anguish Pattern C .05 .15
CROSEN079 Monster Rebone SR .20 .30
CROSEN080 Diceversity C .10 .30
CROSEN081 Moon Mirror Shield R .30 .50
CROSEN082 Draghig, Malebranche of the Burning Abyss SR .20 .30
CROSEN083 Barbar, Malebranche of the Burning Abyss R .10 .20
CROSEN084 Dante, Pilgrim of the Burning Abyss SCR 2.25 2.75
CROSEN085 The Terminus of the Burning Abyss UR .30 .50
CROSEN086 U.A. Dreadnought Dunker C .05 .15
CROSEN087 U.A. Rival Rebounder C .05 .15
CROSEN088 U.A. Signing Deal C .05 .15
CROSEN089 U.A. Penalty Box C .05 .15
CROSEN090 Half Unbreak C .05 .15
CROSEN091 The Melody of Awakening Dragon SR 9.00 11.00
CROSEN092 Cybernetic Fusion Support C .05 .15
CROSEN093 Powerful Rebirth SR .50 .75
CROSEN094 Number S39: Utopia Prime SR 2.75 3.25
CROSEN095 Galaxy-Eyes Full Armor Photon Dragon SR 7.00 8.00
CROSEN096 Performapal Thunderhino C .05 .15
CROSEN097 Primitive Butterfly C .05 .15
CROSEN098 Junk Anchor R .05 .15
CROSEN099 Harpie Harpist SR 1.00 1.75

2015 Yu-Gi-Oh Crossed Souls Unlimited

COMPLETE SET (106 CARDS) 180.00 230.00
BOOSTER BOX (24 PACKS) 50.00 75.00
BOOSTER PACK (9 CARDS) 3.00 5.00
UNLISTED C .10 .30
UNLISTED R .30 .50
RELEASED ON MAY 15, 2016
CROSEN000 Sea Dragoons of Draconia R .05 .15
CROSEN001 Phantom Gryphon C .05 .15
CROSEN002 Performapal Elephammer R .10 .20
CROSEN003 Performapal Bowhopper C .05 .15
CROSEN004 Performapal Lizardraw C .15 .25
CROSEN005 Performapal Springoose C .05 .15
CROSEN006 Superheavy Samurai Big Waraji C .05 .15
CROSEN007 Superheavy Samurai Gigagloves C .05 .15
CROSEN008 Superheavy Samurai Battleball SR 2.25 3.00
CROSEN009 Superheavy Samurai Soulbuster Gauntlet C .05 .15
CROSEN010 Soprano the Melodious Songstress C .05 .15
CROSEN011 Fluffal Sheep C .05 .15
CROSEN012 Edge Imp Saw C .05 .15
CROSEN013 Edge Imp Chain C .05 .15
CROSEN014 Edge Imp Tomahawk R .10 .20
CROSEN015 Edge Imp Frightfuloid C .05 .15
CROSEN016 Raidraptor - Sharp Lanius C .05 .15
CROSEN017 Raidraptor - Mimicry Lanius C .05 .15
CROSEN018 Yosenju Kodam C .05 .15
CROSEN019 Yosenju Oyam R .05 .15
CROSEN020 Satellarknight Zefrathuban UR .75 1.15
CROSEN021 Stellarknight Zefraxciton R .10 .20
CROSEN022 Shaddoll Zefranaga C .05 .15
CROSEN023 Shaddoll Zefracore C .05 .15
CROSEN024 Zefraxi, Treasure of the Yang Zing UR 8.75 10.00
CROSEN025 Zefraniu, Secret of the Yang Zing R 1.00 1.75
CROSEN026 Zefrasaber, Swordmaster of the Nekroz C .05 .15
CROSEN027 Zefraxa, Flame Beast of the Nekroz C .05 .15
CROSEN028 Ritual Beast Tamer Zeframpilica C .05 .15
CROSEN029 Ritual Beast Tamer Zefrawendi R .05 .15
CROSEN030 Infernoid Pirmais UR 1.50 2.00
CROSEN031 Infernoid Sjette C .05 .15
CROSEN032 Infernoid Devyaty UR 4.00 4.75
CROSEN033 Ghost Ogre & Snow Rabbit SCR 15.00 18.00
CROSEN034 Magma Dragon C .05 .15
CROSEN035 Deskbot 004 C .20 .30
CROSEN036 Doomdog Octhros C .05 .15
CROSEN037 Putrid Pudding Body Buddies C .10 .30
CROSEN038 Nekroz of Sophia SCR 1.00 1.50
CROSEN039 Nekroz of Sophia UTR 1.25 1.75
CROSEN040 Schuberta the Melodious Maestra R .15 .25
CROSEN041 Bloom Diva the Melodious Choir UR 5.00 6.00
CROSEN042 Frightfur Leo SR 1.50 2.00
CROSEN043 Frightfur Sheep SR 4.00 4.75
CROSEN044 Frightfur Chimera R .05 .15
CROSEN045 Frightfur Chimera UTR 1.00 1.50
CROSEN046 El Shaddoll Anoyatyllis SCR 7.00 9.00
CROSEN047 Ritual Beast Ulti-Gaiapelio UR 3.50 4.25
CROSEN048 Ritual Beast Ulti-Gaiapelio UTR 4.00 6.00
CROSEN049 Clear Wing Synchro Dragon SCR 15.00 18.00
CROSEN050 Clear Wing Synchro Dragon GR 23.00 26.00
CROSEN051 Clear Wing Synchro Dragon UTR 16.00 20.00
CROSEN052 Chaofeng, Phantom of the Yang Zing SR 2.00 2.75
CROSEN053 Raidraptor - Blaze Falcon R .10 .20
CROSEN054 Raidraptor - Revolution Falcon R .10 .20
CROSEN055 Tellarknight Ptolemaeus UR 2.00 2.50
CROSEN056 Tellarknight Ptolemaeus UTR 2.25 3.00
CROSEN057 Madolche Puddingcess Chocolat-a-la-Mode UR 2.00 2.50
CROSEN058 Performapal Recasting C .10 .30
CROSEN059 Fusion Conscription R .40 .60
CROSEN060 Frightfur Factory C .10 .30
CROSEN061 Suture Rebirth R .05 .15
CROSEN062 Frightfur Fusion R .40 .60
CROSEN063 Rank-Up-Magic Revolution Force R .15 .25
CROSEN064 Yosen Whirlwind C .10 .30
CROSEN065 Zefra Path C .10 .30
CROSEN066 Oracle of Zefra SCR 4.75 5.75
CROSEN067 Void Vanishment SR .25 .40
CROSEN068 Galaxy Cyclone SCR 5.00 6.50
CROSEN069 Harmonic Oscillation C .10 .30
CROSEN070 Pendulum Rising C .10 .30
CROSEN071 Unexpected Dai SR 2.75 3.50
CROSEN072 Performapal Pinch Helper C .10 .30
CROSEN073 Melodious Illusion R .15 .25
CROSEN074 Fluffal Crane C .10 .30
CROSEN075 Designer Frightfur C .10 .30
CROSEN076 Dizzying Winds of Yosen Village C .10 .30
CROSEN077 Chosen of Zefra C .10 .30
CROSEN078 Zefra Divine Strike SR 1.25 2.00
CROSEN079 Void Purification R .05 .15
CROSEN080 Jar of Avarice SCR 6.75 2.75
CROSEN081 Lose 1 Turn UR 3.75 4.50
CROSEN082 Fiend Griefing C .10 .30
CROSEN083 Abyss Stungray C .10 .30
CROSEN084 Statue of Anguish Pattern C .10 .30
CROSEN085 Monster Rebone SR .20 .30
CROSEN086 Diceversity C .10 .30
CROSEN087 Moon Mirror Shield R .30 .50
CROSEN088 Draghig, Malebranche of the Burning Abyss SR .20 .30
CROSEN089 Barbar, Malebranche of the Burning Abyss R .10 .20
CROSEN090 Dante, Pilgrim of the Burning Abyss SCR 2.25 2.75
CROSEN091 The Terminus of the Burning Abyss UR .30 .50
CROSEN092 U.A. Dreadnought Dunker C .10 .30
CROSEN093 U.A. Rival Rebounder C .10 .30
CROSEN094 U.A. Signing Deal C .10 .30
CROSEN095 U.A. Penalty Box C .10 .30
CROSEN096 Half Unbreak C .05 .15
CROSEN097 The Melody of Awakening Dragon SR 9.00 11.00
CROSEN098 Cybernetic Fusion Support C .05 .15
CROSEN099 Powerful Rebirth SR .50 .75
CROSEN038u Number S39: Utopia Prime SR 2.75 3.25
CROSEN043u Galaxy-Eyes Full Armor Photon Dragon SR 7.00 8.00
CROSEN045u Performapal Thunderhino C .10 .30
CROSEN046u Primitive Butterfly C .10 .30

Card	Low	High
CROSEN050u Junk Anchor R	.05	.15
CROSEN046 Harpie Harpist SR	1.00	1.75

2015 Yu-Gi-Oh Clash of Rebellions 1st Edition

Card	Low	High
COMPLETE SET (105)	180.00	230.00
BOOSTER BOX (24 PACKS)	60.00	80.00
BOOSTER PACK (9 CARDS)	3.00	4.00
UNLISTED C	.15	.40
UNLISTED R	.25	.60
RELEASED ON AUGUST 7, 2015		
COREEN000 Sky Dragoons of Draconia R	.05	.15
COREEN001 Mystery Shell Dragon C	.05	.15
COREEN002 Risebell the Summoner C	.05	.15
COREEN003 Xiangke Magician SR	4.00	5.00
COREEN004 Xiangsheng Magician SR	1.50	1.75
COREEN005 Performapal Camelump C	.05	.15
COREEN006 Performapal Drummerilla C	.05	.15
COREEN007 Superheavy Samurai Blowtorch C	.05	.15
COREEN008 Opera the Melodious Diva C	.05	.15
COREEN009 Tamtam the Melodious Diva C	.05	.15
COREEN010 Fluffal Mouse SR	2.75	3.50
COREEN011 D/D Pandora C	.05	.15
COREEN012 Crystal Rose R	.10	.20
COREEN013 Raidraptor - Fuzzy Lanius C	.05	.15
COREEN014 Raidraptor - Singing Lanius C	.05	.15
COREEN015 Performage Damage Juggler C	.15	.25
COREEN016 Performage Flame Eater C	.05	.15
COREEN017 Performage Hat Tricker C	.05	.15
COREEN018 Performage Trick Clown C	.10	.20
COREEN019 Performage Stilts Launcher C	.05	.15
COREEN020 Red-Eyes Black Flare Dragon SR	7.50	8.50
COREEN021 The Black Stone of Legend SCR	33.00	37.00
COREEN022 Black Metal Dragon C	.20	.30
COREEN023 Red-Eyes Archfiend of Lightning SR	1.50	1.75
COREEN024 Keeper of the Shrine C	.25	.35
COREEN025 Luster Pendulum, the Dracoslayer SR	.75	1.25
COREEN026 Igknight Squire C	.05	.15
COREEN027 Igknight Crusader SR	1.00	1.25
COREEN028 Igknight Templar UR	5.25	6.00
COREEN029 Igknight Paladin C	.05	.15
COREEN030 Igknight Margrave C	.05	.15
COREEN031 Igknight Gallant C	.05	.15
COREEN032 Igknight Lancer R	.05	.15
COREEN033 Igknight Champion R	.05	.15
COREEN034 Aromage Jasmine SCR	8.75	9.50
COREEN035 Aromage Cananga C	.05	.15
COREEN036 Aromage Rosemary UR	2.00	2.50
COREEN037 Aromage Bergamot R	.05	.15
COREEN038 Aroma Jar C	.05	.15
COREEN039 Infernoid Decatron SR	.75	1.00
COREEN040 Bird of Paradise Lost C	.05	.15
COREEN041 Magical Abductor R	1.00	1.25
COREEN042 Archfiend Eccentrick SCR	10.00	11.50
COREEN043 Toon Cyber Dragon R	1.00	1.15
COREEN044 Deskbot 005 C	.20	.30
COREEN045 Retaliating C NR	.10	.30
COREEN046 D/D/D Oracle King d'Arc R	.60	.80
COREEN047 Gem-Knight Lady Brilliant Diamond UR	.40	.60
COREEN048 Archfiend Black Skull Dragon UR	5.00	6.50
COREEN048u Archfiend Black Skull Dragon UTR	4.25	5.50
COREEN049 Infernoid Tierra UR	.30	.50
COREEN049u Infernoid Tierra UTR	.75	1.25
COREEN050 Ignister Prominence, the Blasting Dracoslayer UR	1.00	1.50
COREEN050u Ignister Prominence, the Blasting Dracoslayer UTR	3.00	4.25
COREEN051 Odd-Eyes Rebellion Dragon SCR	10.00	12.00
COREEN051u Odd-Eyes Rebellion Dragon UTR	11.00	13.00
COREEN052 D/D/D Marksman King Tell R	.10	.20
COREEN053 Performage Trapeze Magician R	.20	.30
COREEN054 Red-Eyes Flare Metal Dragon SCR	5.00	6.00
COREEN054 Red-Eyes Flare Metal Draogn GR	10.00	13.00
COREEN054u Red-Eyes Flare Metal Dragon UTR	5.50	7.00
COREEN055 Pianissimo C	.05	.15
COREEN056 Brilliant Fusion SR	7.00	9.00
COREEN057 Rank-Up-Magic Raptor's Force C	.05	.15
COREEN058 Bubble Barrier C	.05	.15
COREEN059 Red-Eyes Fusion SR	3.25	3.75
COREEN060 Cards of the Red Stone UR	5.00	6.00
COREEN061 Ignition Phoenix C	.05	.15
COREEN062 Aroma Garden C	.05	.15
COREEN063 Void Imagination SR	.30	.50
COREEN064 Back-Up Rider C	.05	.15
COREEN065 Mistaken Arrest SCR	.60	1.00
COREEN066 Wavering Eyes C	.15	.25
COREEN067 Chicken Game C	.75	1.25
COREEN068 Brilliant Spark C	.05	.15
COREEN069 Raidraptor - Return C	.05	.15
COREEN070 Raptor's Gust C	.15	.25
COREEN071 Trick Box C	.05	.15
COREEN072 Return of the Red-Eyes C	.05	.15
COREEN073 Igknight Burst R	.05	.15
COREEN074 Humid Winds C	.05	.15
COREEN075 Dried Winds SR	.25	.35
COREEN076 Storming Mirror Force SCR	6.50	8.50
COREEN077 Ferret Flames C	.05	.15
COREEN078 Balance of Judgment C	.05	.15
COREEN079 Extra Buck R	.05	.15
COREEN080 Side Effects? NR	.10	.30
COREEN081 Extinction on Schedule C	.05	.15
COREEN082 Kozmo Farmgirl UR	2.00	2.50
COREEN083 Kozmo Goodwitch SR	.50	.75
COREEN084 Kozmo Slipride R	.20	.30
COREEN085 Kozmo Forerunner R	.10	.20
COREEN086 Kozmotown R	.05	.15
COREEN087 Dogoran, the Mad Flame Kaiju R	.60	1.00
COREEN088 Kumongous, the Sticky String Kaiju R	.50	.75
COREEN089 Kyoutou Waterfront C	.05	.15
COREEN090 Performapal Silver Claw C	.05	.15
COREEN091 Escher the Frost Vassal C	.05	.15
COREEN092 Absorb Fusion UR	.75	1.25
COREEN093 Performapal Salutiger C	.05	.15
COREEN094 Superheavy Samurai Ogre Shutendoji SR	2.00	2.50
COREEN095 Hi-Speedroid Kendama UR	.25	.40
COREEN096 Dragonig R	.05	.15
COREEN097 Mandragon R	.05	.15
COREEN098 Tatsunoko SCR	9.00	10.00
COREEN099 Secret Blast C	.05	.15
COREENSE1 Ultimaya Tzolkin SR	2.75	3.25
COREENSE2 Frightfur Tiger SR	.30	.50
COREENSE3 Engraver of the Mark SR	.05	.15
COREENSE4 Destruction Sword Flash SR	.05	.15

2015 Yu-Gi-Oh Clash of Rebellions Unlimited

Card	Low	High
COMPLETE SET (110 CARDS)	180.00	230.00
BOOSTER BOX (24 PACKS)	60.00	80.00
BOOSTER PACK (9 CARDS)	3.00	5.00
UNLISTED C	.10	.25
UNLISTED R	.30	.50
RELEASED ON AUGUST 7, 2015		
COREEN000 Sky Dragoons of Draconia UR	.05	.15
COREEN001 Mystery Shell Dragon C	.05	.15
COREEN002 Risebell the Summoner C	.05	.15
COREEN003 Xiangke Magician SR	4.00	5.00
COREEN004 Xiangsheng Magician SR	1.50	1.75
COREEN005 Performapal Camelump C	.05	.15
COREEN006 Performapal Drummerilla C	.05	.15
COREEN007 Superheavy Samurai Blowtorch C	.05	.15
COREEN008 Opera the Melodious Diva C	.05	.15
COREEN009 Tamtam the Melodious Diva C	.05	.15
COREEN010 Fluffal Mouse SR	2.75	3.50
COREEN011 D/D Pandora C	.05	.15
COREEN012 Crystal Rose R	.10	.20
COREEN013 Raidraptor - Fuzzy Lanius C	.05	.15
COREEN014 Raidraptor - Singing Lanius C	.05	.15
COREEN015 Performage Damage Juggler C	.15	.25
COREEN016 Performage Flame Eater C	.05	.15
COREEN017 Performage Hat Tricker C	.05	.15
COREEN018 Performage Trick Clown C	.10	.20
COREEN019 Performage Stilts Launcher C	.05	.15
COREEN020 Red-Eyes Black Flare Dragon SR	7.50	8.50
COREEN021 The Black Stone of Legend SCR	33.00	37.00
COREEN022 Black Metal Dragon C	.20	.30
COREEN023 Red-Eyes Archfiend of Lightning SR	1.50	1.75
COREEN024 Keeper of the Shrine C	.05	.15
COREEN025 Luster Pendulum, the Dracoslayer SR	.75	1.25
COREEN026 Igknight Squire C	.05	.15
COREEN027 Igknight Crusader SR	1.00	1.25
COREEN028 Igknight Templar UR	5.25	6.00
COREEN029 Igknight Paladin C	.05	.15
COREEN030 Igknight Margrave C	.05	.15
COREEN031 Igknight Gallant C	.05	.15
COREEN032 Igknight Lancer R	.05	.15
COREEN033 Igknight Champion R	.05	.15
COREEN034 Aromage Jasmine SCR	8.75	9.50
COREEN035 Aromage Cananga C	.05	.15
COREEN036 Aromage Rosemary UR	2.00	2.50
COREEN037 Aromage Bergamot R	.05	.15
COREEN038 Aroma Jar C	.05	.15
COREEN039 Infernoid Decatron SR	.75	1.00
COREEN040 Bird of Paradise Lost C	.05	.15
COREEN041 Magical Abductor R	1.00	1.25
COREEN042 Archfiend Eccentrick SCR	10.00	11.50
COREEN043 Toon Cyber Dragon R	1.00	1.15
COREEN044 Deskbot 005 C	.20	.30
COREEN045 Retaliating C NR	.10	.30
COREEN046 D/D/D Oracle King d'Arc R	.60	.80
COREEN047 Gem-Knight Lady Brilliant Diamond UR	.40	.60
COREEN048 Archfiend Black Skull Dragon UR	5.00	6.50
COREEN048u Archfiend Black Skull Dragon UTR	4.25	5.50
COREEN049 Infernoid Tierra UR	.30	.50
COREEN049u Infernoid Tierra UTR	.75	1.25
COREEN050 Ignister Prominence, the Blasting Dracoslayer UR	1.00	1.50
COREEN050u Ignister Prominence, the Blasting Dracoslayer UTR	3.00	4.25
COREEN051 Odd-Eyes Rebellion Dragon SCR	10.00	12.00
COREEN051u Odd-Eyes Rebellion Dragon UTR	11.00	13.00
COREEN052 D/D/D Marksman King Tell R	.10	.20
COREEN053 Performage Trapeze Magician R	.20	.30
COREEN054 Red-Eyes Flare Metal Dragon SCR	5.00	6.00
COREEN054 Red-Eyes Flare Metal Draogn GR	10.00	13.00
COREEN054u Red-Eyes Flare Metal Dragon UTR	5.50	7.00
COREEN055 Pianissimo C	.05	.15
COREEN056 Brilliant Fusion SR	7.00	9.00
COREEN057 Rank-Up-Magic Raptor's Force C	.05	.15
COREEN058 Bubble Barrier C	.05	.15
COREEN059 Red-Eyes Fusion SR	3.25	3.75
COREEN060 Cards of the Red Stone UR	5.00	6.00
COREEN061 Ignition Phoenix C	.05	.15
COREEN062 Aroma Garden C	.05	.15
COREEN063 Void Imagination SR	.30	.50
COREEN064 Back-Up Rider C	.05	.15
COREEN065 Mistaken Arrest SCR	.60	1.00
COREEN066 Wavering Eyes C	.15	.25
COREEN067 Chicken Game C	.75	1.25
COREEN068 Brilliant Spark C	.05	.15
COREEN069 Raidraptor - Return C	.05	.15
COREEN070 Raptor's Gust C	.15	.25
COREEN071 Trick Box C	.05	.15
COREEN072 Return of the Red-Eyes C	.05	.15
COREEN073 Igknight Burst R	.05	.15
COREEN074 Humid Winds C	.05	.15
COREEN075 Dried Winds SR	.25	.35
COREEN076 Storming Mirror Force SCR	6.50	8.50
COREEN077 Ferret Flames C	.05	.15
COREEN078 Balance of Judgment C	.05	.15
COREEN079 Extra Buck R	.05	.15
COREEN080 Side Effects? NR	.10	.30
COREEN081 Extinction on Schedule C	.05	.15
COREEN082 Kozmo Farmgirl UR	2.00	2.50
COREEN083 Kozmo Goodwitch SR	.50	.75
COREEN084 Kozmo Slipride R	.20	.30
COREEN085 Kozmo Forerunner R	.10	.20
COREEN086 Kozmotown R	.20	.30
COREEN087 Dogoran, the Mad Flame Kaiju R	.60	1.00
COREEN088 Kumongous, the Sticky String Kaiju R	.50	.75
COREEN089 Kyoutou Waterfront C	.20	.30
COREEN090 Performapal Silver Claw C	.05	.15
COREEN091 Escher the Frost Vassal C	.05	.15
COREEN092 Kozmotown R	.75	1.25
COREEN093 Performapal Salutiger C	.05	.15
COREEN094 Superheavy Samurai Ogre Shutendoji SR	2.00	2.50
COREEN095 Hi-Speedroid Kendama UR	.25	.40
COREEN096 Dragonig R	.05	.15
COREEN097 Mandragon R	.05	.15
COREEN098 Tatsunoko SCR	9.00	10.00
COREEN099 Secret Blast C	.05	.15
COREENSE1 Ultimaya Tzolkin SR	2.75	3.25
COREENSE2 Frightfur Tiger SR	.30	.50
COREENSE3 Engraver of the Mark SR	.05	.15
COREENSE4 Destruction Sword Flash SR	.05	.15

2015 Yu-Gi-Oh Dimension of Chaos

Card	Low	High
COMPLETE SET (106)	250.00	300.00
BOOSTER BOX (24 PACKS)	100.00	120.00
BOOSTER PACK (9 CARDS)	5.00	8.00
UNLISTED C	.10	.25
UNLISTED R	.30	.50
RELEASED ON NOVEMBER 6, 2015		
DOCSEN000 Samurai Cavalry of Reptier R	.20	.30
DOCSEN001 Performapal Secondonkey R	.40	.60
DOCSEN002 Performapal Splashmammoth R	.20	.30
DOCSEN003 Performapal Helpprincess R	.20	.30
DOCSEN004 Superheavy Samurai Thief C	.05	.15
DOCSEN005 Superheavy Samurai Transporter C	.05	.15
DOCSEN006 Superheavy Samurai Drum C	.05	.15
DOCSEN007 Superheavy Samurai Soulhorns C	.05	.15
DOCSEN008 Gameciel, the Sea Turtle Kaiju R	4.00	4.50
DOCSEN009 Superheavy Samurai Soulclaw C	.05	.15
DOCSEN010 Fluffal Wings C	.05	.15
DOCSEN010 D/D Berfomet R	.60	1.00
DOCSEN011 D/D Swirl Slime C	.15	.25
DOCSEN012 D/D Necro Slime C	.20	.30
DOCSEN013 Raidraptor - Wild Vulture C	.05	.15
DOCSEN014 Raidraptor - Skull Eagle C	.05	.15
DOCSEN015 Performage Mirror Conductor C	.05	.15
DOCSEN016 Performage Plushfire C	.05	.15
DOCSEN017 The Legendary Fisherman III SR	.40	.75
DOCSEN018 Assault Blackwing - Kunai the Drizzle R	.15	.25
DOCSEN019 Charging Gaia the Fierce Knight UR	4.75	5.25
DOCSEN020 Sphere Kuriboh R	.25	.35
DOCSEN021 Super Soldier Soul C	.05	.15
DOCSEN022 Beginning Knight SR	1.00	1.75
DOCSEN023 Evening Twilight Knight SR	2.50	3.50
DOCSEN024 Vector Pendulum, the Dracoverlord SR	1.50	2.00
DOCSEN025 Majespecter Cat - Nekomata SR	1.25	2.00
DOCSEN026 Majespecter Raccoon - Bunbuku UR	15.00	18.00
DOCSEN027 Majespecter Crow - Yata C	.05	.15
DOCSEN028 Majespecter Fox - Kyubi C	.05	.15
DOCSEN029 Majespecter Unicorn - Kirin R	2.00	2.75
DOCSEN030 Igknight Cavalier C	.15	.25
DOCSEN031 Igknight Veteran C	.05	.15
DOCSEN032 Graydle Slime R	.30	.50
DOCSEN033 Graydle Alligator C	.05	.15
DOCSEN034 Graydle Cobra C	.05	.15
DOCSEN035 Graydle Eagle C	.05	.15
DOCSEN036 Skilled Red Magician R	.10	.20
DOCSEN037 Giant Pairfish R	.10	.20
DOCSEN038 Toon Barrel Dragon R	.25	.35
DOCSEN039 Deskbot 006 C	.25	.50
DOCSEN040 Pot of The Forbidden SP	1.25	2.00
DOCSEN041 Dr. Frankenderp SP	.05	.15
DOCSEN042 Black Luster Soldier - Super Soldier UR	6.50	7.25
DOCSEN042 Black Luster Soldier - Super Soldier UTR	8.00	9.00
DOCSEN043 Frightfur Sabre-Tooth UR	10.00	12.00
DOCSEN044 D/D/D Wave Oblivion King Caesar Ragnarok SR	4.00	6.00
DOCSEN045 Odd-Eyes Vortex Dragon SCR	10.00	13.00
DOCSEN045 Odd-Eyes Vortex Dragon UTR	15.00	16.50
DOCSEN046 Scarlight Red Dragon Archfiend SCR	18.00	20.00
DOCSEN046 Scarlight Red Dragon Archfiend UTR	20.00	23.00
DOCSEN046 Scarlight Red Dragon Archfiend GR	23.00	25.00
DOCSEN047 Assault Blackwing - Raikiri the Rain Shower UTR	8.00	9.00
DOCSEN047 Assault Blackwing - Raikiri the Rain Shower UR	7.00	8.00
DOCSEN048 Graydle Dragon SR	2.75	3.50
DOCSEN049 Deskbot Jet C	.15	.25
DOCSEN050 D/D/D Duo-Dawn King Kali Yuga SR	2.25	3.00
DOCSEN051 Raidraptor - Fiend Eagle R	.15	.25
DOCSEN052 Majester Paladin, the Ascending Dracoslayer UR	1.25	1.75
DOCSEN052 Majester Paladin, the Ascending Dracoslayer UTR	2.75	3.50
DOCSEN053 Shuffle Reborn C	.05	.15
DOCSEN054 Rank-Up-Magic Raid Force R	.25	.35
DOCSEN055 Raptor's Ultimate Mace C	.05	.15
DOCSEN056 Super Soldier Ritual R	.30	.50
DOCSEN057 Gateway to Chaos SR	2.00	2.50
DOCSEN058 Majesty's Pegasus SR	.75	1.00
DOCSEN059 Majespecter Storm C	.05	.15
DOCSEN060 Majespecter Cyclone SR	.50	.75
DOCSEN061 Igknight Reload UR	5.50	7.00
DOCSEN062 Graydle Impact C	.05	.15
DOCSEN063 Odd-Eyes Fusion SCR	15.00	18.00
DOCSEN064 Psychic Blade C	.05	.15
DOCSEN065 Painful Decision SCR	12.00	15.00
DOCSEN066 Super Rush Headlong SP	.05	.15
DOCSEN067 Frightfur March C	.05	.15
DOCSEN068 D/D/D Contract Change C	.05	.15
DOCSEN069 Dark Contract with Errors C	.05	.15
DOCSEN070 Super Soldier Rebirth C	.05	.15
DOCSEN071 Super Soldier Shield UR	1.25	2.00
DOCSEN072 Majespecter Tornado UR	2.50	3.25
DOCSEN073 Majespecter Tempest C	.15	.25
DOCSEN074 Graydle Parasite SR	1.25	1.75
DOCSEN075 Graydle Split C	.05	.15
DOCSEN076 Blazing Mirror Force SCR	2.00	2.50
DOCSEN077 Pendulum Area R	.05	.15
DOCSEN078 Urgent Ritual Art SCR	1.25	1.75
DOCSEN079 Grand Horn of Heaven C	.30	.50
DOCSEN080 First-Aid Squad SP	.05	.15
DOCSEN081 Painful Escape SCR	1.25	1.75
DOCSEN082 Kozmo Strawman UR	2.25	3.00
DOCSEN083 Kozmoll Wickedwitch C	.05	.15
DOCSEN084 Kozmo DOG Fighter SR	.30	.50
DOCSEN085 Kozmo Dark Destroyer SCR	8.00	10.00
DOCSEN086 Kozmo Lightsword C	.05	.15
DOCSEN087 Radian, the Multidimensional Kaiju R	1.25	1.75
DOCSEN089 Kaiju Capture Mission C	.20	.30
DOCSEN090 D/D/D Wave King Caesar R	.30	.50
DOCSEN091 D/D Savant Galilei C	.05	.15
DOCSEN092 D/D Savant Kepler C	.20	.30
DOCSEN093 Dark Contract with the Gate C	.20	.30
DOCSEN094 Dark Contract with the Swamp King C	.20	.30
DOCSEN095 Dark Contract with the Witch C	.05	.15
DOCSEN096 Contract Laundering C	.05	.15
DOCSEN097 D/D/D Human Resources C	.05	.15
DOCSEN098 D/D/D Rebel King Leonidas SR	5.00	6.50
DOCSEN099 D/D/D Oblivion King Abyss Ragnarok R	3.25	4.25

2016 Yu-Gi-Oh Breakers of Shadow 1st Edition

Card	Low	High
COMPLETE SET (100)	115.00	160.00
BOOSTER BOX	70.00	90.00
BOOSTER PACK	2.50	6.00
UNLISTED C	.15	.40
UNLISTED R	.40	1.00
RELEASED ON JANUARY 15, 2016		
BOSHEN000 Steel Cavalry of Dinon R	.10	.30
BOSHEN001 Tuning Magician SR	.10	.20
BOSHEN002 Timebreaker Magician R	.10	.30
BOSHEN003 Performapal Monkeyboard C	.05	.15
BOSHEN004 Performapal Guitartle R	.10	.30
BOSHEN005 Performapal Bit Bite Turtle C	.05	.15
BOSHEN006 Performapal Rain Goat C	.05	.15
BOSHEN007 Performapal Trump Girl C	.05	.15
BOSHEN008 Superheavy Samurai Magnet C	.05	.15
BOSHEN009 Superheavy Samurai Prepped Defense C	.05	.15
BOSHEN010 Superheavy Samurai General Jade C	.05	.15
BOSHEN011 Superheavy Samurai General Coral C	.05	.15
BOSHEN012 Solo the Melodious Songstress C	.05	.15
BOSHEN013 Score the Melodious Diva C	.05	.15
BOSHEN014 Blackwing - Harmattan the Dust C	.05	.15
BOSHEN015 Twilight Ninja Shingetsu C	.05	.15
BOSHEN016 Twilight Ninja Nichirin, the Chunin C	.05	.15
BOSHEN017 Twilight Ninja Getsuga, the Shogun R	.10	.30
BOSHEN018 Buster Blader, the Destruction Swordmaster UR	1.25	2.00
BOSHEN019 Buster Whelp of the Destruction Swordsman SR	.20	.30
BOSHEN020 Dragon Buster Destruction Sword C	.05	.15
BOSHEN021 Wizard Buster Destruction Sword C	.05	.15
BOSHEN022 Robot Buster Destruction Sword C	.05	.15
BOSHEN023 Master Pendulum, the Dracoslayer SR	.60	1.00
BOSHEN024 Dinomist Stegosaur C	.05	.15
BOSHEN025 Dinomist Plesios C	.05	.15
BOSHEN026 Dinomist Pteran R	.10	.30
BOSHEN027 Dinomist Brachion C	.05	.15
BOSHEN028 Dinomist Ceratops C	.05	.15
BOSHEN029 Dinomist Rex SR	.20	.35
BOSHEN030 Majespecter Toad - Ogama SR	.05	.15
BOSHEN031 Shiranui Spectralsword UR	1.00	1.50
BOSHEN032 Shiranui Smith C	.05	.15
BOSHEN033 Shiranui Spiritmaster R	.10	.30
BOSHEN034 Shiranui Samurai C	.05	.15
BOSHEN035 Dark Doriado C	.05	.15
BOSHEN036 Guiding Ariadne SR	.15	.25
BOSHEN037 Al-Lumi'raj C	.05	.15
BOSHEN038 Toon Buster Blader R	.10	.30
BOSHEN039 Deskbot 007 C	.05	.15
BOSHEN040 Deskbot 008 C	.05	.15
BOSHEN041 Engraver of the Mark SP	.05	.15
BOSHEN042 Zany Zebra SP	.05	.15
BOSHEN043 Odd-Eyes Gravity Dragon UR	.75	1.00
BOSHEN044 Goyo Emperor R	.10	.30
BOSHEN045 Buster Blader, the Dragon Destroyer Swordsman SCR	5.00	7.00
BOSHEN045 Buster Blader, the Dragon Destroyer Swordsman SCR	.10	.30
BOSHEN046 Dinoster Power, the Mighty Dracoslayer R	.30	.50
BOSHEN047 Enlightenment Paladin UR	.60	1.15
BOSHEN048 Superheavy Samurai Beast Kyubi R	.10	.30
BOSHEN049 Hi-Speedroid Hagoita R	.10	.30
BOSHEN050 Goyo Defender R	.10	.30
BOSHEN051 Goyo King R	.10	.30
BOSHEN052 Buster Dragon UR	2.75	4.00
BOSHEN053 Shiranui Samuraisaga C	.05	.15
BOSHEN054 Shiranui Shogunsaga UR	.60	1.00
BOSHEN055 Aegaion the Sea Castrum C	.05	.15
BOSHEN056 Performance Hurricane C	.05	.15
BOSHEN057 Pendulum Storm SR	.10	.20
BOSHEN058 Hi-Speed Re-Level C	.05	.15
BOSHEN059 Destruction Swordsman Fusion C	.05	.15
BOSHEN060 Karma of the Destruction Swordsman C	.05	.15
BOSHEN061 Draco Face-Off C	.05	.15
BOSHEN062 Dinomic Powerload C	.05	.15
BOSHEN063 Dinomist Charge C	.05	.15
BOSHEN064 Majespecter Sonics C	.05	.15
BOSHEN065 Shiranui Style Synthesis C	.05	.15
BOSHEN066 Odd-Eyes Advent R	.10	.30
BOSHEN067 Twin Twisters SR	10.00	12.00
BOSHEN068 Mistaken Accusation SP	.05	.15
BOSHEN069 Dragon's Bind C	.05	.15
BOSHEN070 Follow Wing C	.05	.15
BOSHEN071 Reject Reborn R	.10	.30
BOSHEN072 Destruction Sword Flash C	.05	.15
BOSHEN073 Dinomist Rush C	.05	.15
BOSHEN074 Majespecter Supercell SR	.05	.15
BOSHEN075 Shiranui Style Swallow's Slash C	.05	.15
BOSHEN076 Quaking Mirror Force UR	10.00	13.00
BOSHEN077 Pendulum Reborn R	.10	.30
BOSHEN078 Forbidden Apocrypha C	.05	.15
BOSHEN079 Solemn Strike SCR	28.00	33.00
BOSHEN080 Bad Luck Blast SP	.05	.15
BOSHEN081 Ultimate Providence SCR	2.00	3.00
BOSHEN082 Kozmo Tincan UR	5.00	6.50
BOSHEN083 Kozmo Soartroopers SR	.20	.30
BOSHEN084 Kozmo Delta Shuttle C	.05	.15
BOSHEN085 Kozmo Dark Eclipser SCR	2.75	3.50
BOSHEN086 Kozmojo SCR	10.00	12.00
BOSHEN087 Gadarla, the Mystery Dust Kaiju R	.10	.30
BOSHEN088 Jizukiru, the Star Destroying Kaiju R	1.00	1.75
BOSHEN089 Interrupted Kaiju Slumber SR	.60	1.00
BOSHEN090 Performapal Pendulum Sorcerer SCR	6.75	8.00
BOSHEN091 Fiendish Rhino Warrior R	.40	.60
BOSHEN092 Neptabyss, the Atlantean Prince UR	1.00	1.50
BOSHEN093 Chimeratech Rampage Dragon SR	.20	.35
BOSHEN094 Cyber Dragon Infinity SCR	14.00	17.00
BOSHEN095 Red-Eyes Retro Dragon SR	.20	.35
BOSHEN096 Dharma-Eye Magician SR	.05	.15
BOSHEN097 Black Luster Soldier - Sacred Soldier UR	.75	1.15
BOSHEN098 Arisen Gaia the Fierce Knight R	.10	.30
BOSHEN099 Traptrix Rafflesia SCR	4.75	6.00
BOSHENSE1 Beast-Eyes Pendulum Dragon SR	.10	.30
BOSHENSE2 Number 23: Lancelot Dark Knight of the Underworld SR	.10	.30
BOSHENSE3 Beacon of White SR	.10	.30
BOSHENSE4 Forge of the True Dracos SR	.10	.30

2016 Yu-Gi-Oh Breakers of Shadow Unlimited

Card	Low	High
BOSHEN000 Steel Cavalry of Dinon R	.10	.30
BOSHEN001 Tuning Magician SR	.10	.30
BOSHEN002 Timebreaker Magician R	.10	.30
BOSHEN003 Performapal Monkeyboard C	.10	.30
BOSHEN004 Performapal Guitartle R	.10	.30
BOSHEN005 Performapal Bit Bite Turtle C	.10	.30
BOSHEN006 Performapal Rain Goat C	.10	.30
BOSHEN007 Performapal Trump Girl C	.10	.30
BOSHEN008 Superheavy Samurai Magnet C	.10	.30
BOSHEN009 Superheavy Samurai Prepped Defense C	.10	.30
BOSHEN010 Superheavy Samurai General Jade C	.10	.30
BOSHEN011 Superheavy Samurai General Coral C	.10	.30
BOSHEN012 Solo the Melodious Songstress C	.10	.30
BOSHEN013 Score the Melodious Diva C	.10	.30
BOSHEN014 Blackwing Harmattan the Dust C	.10	.30
BOSHEN015 Twilight Ninja Shingetsu C	.10	.30
BOSHEN016 Twilight Ninja Nichirin, the Chunin C	.10	.30
BOSHEN017 Twilight Ninja Getsuga, the Shogun R	.10	.30
BOSHEN018 Buster Blader, the Destruction Swordmaster UR	2.50	6.00
BOSHEN019 Buster Whelp of the Destruction Swordsman SR	.10	.30
BOSHEN020 Dragon Buster Destruction Sword C	.10	.30
BOSHEN021 Wizard Buster Destruction Sword C	.10	.30
BOSHEN022 Robot Buster Destruction Sword C	.10	.30
BOSHEN023 Master Pendulum, the Dracoslayer SR	.10	.30
BOSHEN024 Dinomist Stegosaur C	.10	.30
BOSHEN025 Dinomist Plesios C	.10	.30
BOSHEN026 Dinomist Pteran R	.10	.30
BOSHEN027 Dinomist Brachion C	.10	.30
BOSHEN028 Dinomist Ceratops C	.10	.30
BOSHEN029 Dinomist Rex SR	.40	1.00
BOSHEN030 Majespecter Toad Ogama SR	.10	.30
BOSHEN031 Shiranui Spectralsword UR	.75	2.00
BOSHEN032 Shiranui Smith C	.10	.30
BOSHEN033 Shiranui Spiritmaster R	.10	.30
BOSHEN034 Shiranui Samurai C	.10	.30
BOSHEN035 Dark Doriado C	.10	.30
BOSHEN036 Guiding Ariadne SR	.10	.30
BOSHEN037 AlLumiraj C	.10	.30
BOSHEN038 Toon Buster Blader R	.10	.30
BOSHEN039 Deskbot 007 C	.10	.30
BOSHEN040 Deskbot 008 C	.10	.30
BOSHEN041 Engraver of the Mark SP	.10	.30
BOSHEN042 Zany Zebra SP	.10	.30
BOSHEN043 OddEyes Gravity Dragon UR	.50	1.25
BOSHEN044 Goyo Emperor R	.10	.30
BOSHEN045 Buster Blader, the Dragon Destroyer Swordsman SCT	.10	.30
BOSHEN045 Buster Blader, the Dragon Destroyer Swordsman SCR	2.50	6.00
BOSHEN046 Dinoster Power, the Mighty Dracoslayer R	.10	.30
BOSHEN047 Enlightenment Paladin UR	.50	1.25
BOSHEN048 Superheavy Samurai Beast Kyubi R	.10	.30
BOSHEN049 HiSpeedroid Hagoita R	.10	.30
BOSHEN050 Goyo Defender R	.10	.30
BOSHEN051 Goyo King R	.10	.30
BOSHEN052 Buster Dragon UR	.50	1.25
BOSHEN053 Shiranui Samuraisaga C	.10	.30
BOSHEN054 Shiranui Shogunsaga UR	.75	2.00
BOSHEN055 Aegaion the Sea Castrum C	.10	.30
BOSHEN056 Performance Hurricane C	.10	.30
BOSHEN057 Pendulum Storm SR	.10	.30
BOSHEN058 HiSpeed ReLevel C	.10	.30
BOSHEN059 Destruction Swordsman Fusion C	.10	.30
BOSHEN060 Karma of the Destruction Swordsman C	.10	.30
BOSHEN061 Draco FaceOff C	.10	.30
BOSHEN062 Dinomic Powerload C	.10	.30
BOSHEN063 Dinomist Charge C	.10	.30
BOSHEN064 Majespecter Sonics C	.10	.30
BOSHEN065 Shiranui Style Synthesis C	.10	.30
BOSHEN066 OddEyes Advent R	.10	.30
BOSHEN067 Twin Twisters SR	5.00	12.00
BOSHEN068 Mistaken Accusation SP	.10	.30
BOSHEN069 Dragons Bind C	.10	.30
BOSHEN070 Follow Wing C	.10	.30
BOSHEN071 Reject Reborn R	.10	.30
BOSHEN072 Destruction Sword Flash C	.10	.30
BOSHEN073 Dinomist Rush C	.10	.30
BOSHEN074 Majespecter Supercell SR	.10	.30
BOSHEN075 Shiranui Style Swallows Slash C	.10	.30
BOSHEN076 Quaking Mirror Force UR	.40	1.00
BOSHEN077 Pendulum Reborn R	.10	.30
BOSHEN078 Forbidden Apocrypha C	.10	.30
BOSHEN079 Solemn Strike SCT	30.00	45.00
BOSHEN080 Bad Luck Blast SP	.10	.30
BOSHEN081 Ultimate Providence SCT	1.50	4.00
BOSHEN082 Kozmo Tincan UR	5.00	12.00
BOSHEN083 Kozmo Soartroopers SR	.10	.30
BOSHEN084 Kozmo Delta Shuttle C	.10	.30
BOSHEN085 Kozmo Dark Eclipser SCT	1.25	3.00
BOSHEN086 Kozmojo SCT	8.00	20.00
BOSHEN087 Gadarla, the Mystery Dust Kaiju R	.10	.30
BOSHEN088 Jizukiru, the Star Destroying Kaiju R	.40	1.00
BOSHEN089 Interrupted Kaiju Slumber SR	.40	1.00
BOSHEN090 Performapal Pendulum Sorcerer SCT	8.00	20.00
BOSHEN091 Fiendish Rhino Warrior R	.40	1.00
BOSHEN092 Neptabyss, the Atlantean Prince UR	.60	1.50

BOSHEN093 Chimeratech Rampage Dragon SR	.10	.30
BOSHEN094 Cyber Dragon Infinity SCT	20.00	35.00
BOSHEN095 RedEyes Retro Dragon SR	.10	.30
BOSHEN096 DharmaEye Magician SR	.10	.30
BOSHEN097 Black Luster Soldier Sacred Soldier UR	.40	1.00
BOSHEN098 Arisen Gaia the Fierce Knight R	.10	.30
BOSHEN099 Traptrix Rafflesia SCT	3.00	8.00
BOSHENSE1 Beast-Eyes Pendulum Dragon SR	.10	.30
BOSHENSE2 Number 23: Lancelot Dark Knight of the Underworld SR	.10	.30
BOSHENSE3 Beacon of White SR	.10	.30
BOSHENSE4 Forge of the True Dracos SR	.10	.30

2016 Yu-Gi-Oh Shining Victories 1st Edition

COMPLETE SET (100)	175.00	225.00
BOOSTER BOX (24 PACKS)	65.00	90.00
BOOSTER PACK (9 CARDS)	2.00	5.00
UNLISTED C	.10	.25
UNLISTED R	.10	.25
Released on May 6th, 2016		
SHVIEN000 Magical Cavalry of Cxulub R	.10	.25
SHVIEN001 Angel Trumpeter C	.05	.15
SHVIEN002 Performapal Sellshell Crab C	.05	.15
SHVIEN003 Performapal Odd-Eyes Light Phoenix R	.20	.50
SHVIEN004 Performapal Odd-Eyes Unicorn R	.25	.75
SHVIEN005 Performapal Fireflux C	.05	.15
SHVIEN006 Speedroid Den-Den Daiko Duke R	.10	.25
SHVIEN007 Speedroid Pachingo-Kart R	.10	.25
SHVIEN008 Lunalight Blue Cat R	.20	.50
SHVIEN009 Lunalight Purple Butterfly C	.05	.15
SHVIEN010 Lunalight White Rabbit C	.05	.15
SHVIEN011 Lunalight Black Sheep C	.05	.15
SHVIEN012 Lunalight Wolf C	.05	.15
SHVIEN013 Lunalight Tiger C	.05	.15
SHVIEN014 Raidraptor - Avenge Vulture C	.05	.15
SHVIEN015 Raidraptor - Pain Lanius C	.05	.15
SHVIEN016 Raidraptor - Booster Strix C	.05	.15
SHVIEN017 Blackwing - Decay the Ill Wind C	.05	.15
SHVIEN018 Dragon Spirit of White UR	10.00	13.00
SHVIEN019 Protector with Eyes of Blue C	.05	.15
SHVIEN020 Sage with Eyes of Blue UR	20.00	22.00
SHVIEN021 Master with Eyes of Blue C	.05	.15
SHVIEN022 The White Stone of Ancients UR	20.00	23.00
SHVIEN023 Lector Pendulum, the Dracoverlord UR	1.00	1.50
SHVIEN024 Amorphage Gluttony R	.10	.25
SHVIEN025 Amorphage Lechery UR	.60	1.00
SHVIEN026 Amorphage Greed R	.10	.25
SHVIEN027 Amorphage Envy R	.10	.25
SHVIEN028 Amorphage Wrath C	.05	.15
SHVIEN029 Amorphage Pride C	.05	.15
SHVIEN030 Amorphage Sloth SCT	4.50	5.50
SHVIEN031 Amorphage Goliath SR	.10	.30
SHVIEN032 Dinomist Spinos C	.05	.15
SHVIEN033 Digital Bug Cocoondenser C	.05	.15
SHVIEN034 Digital Bug Centibit C	.05	.15
SHVIEN035 Digital Bug Websolder C	.05	.15
SHVIEN036 Red-Eyes Toon Dragon SR	.10	.30
SHVIEN037 Ryu Okami C	.05	.15
SHVIEN038 Tenmataitei R	.10	.25
SHVIEN039 Spirit of the Fall Wind R	.05	.15
SHVIEN040 Ghost Reaper & Winter Cherries SCT	25.00	30.00
SHVIEN041 Gendo the Ascetic Monk C	.05	.15
SHVIEN042 Deskbot 009 C	.05	.15
SHVIEN043 Dicelops C	.05	.15
SHVIEN044 Amorphactor Pain, the Imagination Dracoverlord SR	.10	.30
SHVIEN045 Bloom Prima the Melodious Choir R	.05	.15
SHVIEN046 Lunalight Cat Dancer R	.50	1.25
SHVIEN047 Lunalight Panther Dancer UR	2.00	3.00
SHVIEN048 Lunalight Leo Dancer SR	.10	.30
SHVIEN049 Crystal Wing Synchro Dragon SCT	35.00	40.00
SHVIEN050 Hi-Speedroid Puzzle R	.10	.25
SHVIEN051 Assault Blackwing - Chidori the Rain Sprinkling SR	.10	.30
SHVIEN052 Blue-Eyes Spirit Dragon SCT	14.00	16.00
SHVIEN053 Raidraptor - Ultimate Falcon SR	.10	.30
SHVIEN054 Digital Bug Scaradiator C	.05	.15
SHVIEN055 Digital Bug Corebage C	.05	.15
SHVIEN056 Digital Bug Rhinosebus SR	.10	.30
SHVIEN057 Fortissimo C	.05	.15
SHVIEN058 Rank-Up-Magic Skip Force R	.20	.50
SHVIEN059 Mausoleum of White R	.30	.45
SHVIEN060 Beacon of White C	.05	.15
SHVIEN061 Forge of the True Dracos C	.05	.15
SHVIEN062 Amorphous Persona UR	.40	.75
SHVIEN063 Amorphage Infection SR	.10	.30
SHVIEN064 Bug Matrix C	.05	.15
SHVIEN065 Pre-Preparation of Rites SR	2.50	3.25
SHVIEN066 Fusion Tag R	.20	.50
SHVIEN067 Tuner's High SR	.10	.30
SHVIEN068 Deskbot Base C	.05	.15
SHVIEN069 Finite Cards C	.05	.15
SHVIEN070 Re-dyce-cle C	.05	.15
SHVIEN071 Lunalight Reincarnation Dance C	.05	.15
SHVIEN072 Amorphage Lysis R	.10	.25
SHVIEN073 Dinomist Eruption C	.05	.15
SHVIEN074 Bug Emergency C	.05	.15
SHVIEN075 Drowning Mirror Force SCT	12.00	15.00
SHVIEN076 Wonder Xyz C	.05	.15
SHVIEN077 Rise to Full Height C	.05	.15
SHVIEN078 Bad Aim C	.05	.15
SHVIEN079 Unwavering Bond UR	1.25	1.75
SHVIEN080 Graceful Tear C	.05	.15
SHVIEN081 Cattle Call SR	.10	.30
SHVIEN082 Kozmo Scaredy Lion SR	.10	.30
SHVIEN083 Kozmoll Dark Lady SCT	7.00	9.00
SHVIEN084 Kozmo Landwalker SR	.10	.30
SHVIEN085 Kozmo Dark Planet SCT	4.00	4.75
SHVIEN086 Kozmourning C	.05	.15
SHVIEN087 Thunder King, the Lightningstrike Kaiju R	.25	.75
SHVIEN088 Super Anti-Kaiju War Machine Mecha-Dogoran R	.25	.75
SHVIEN089 The Kaiju Files C	.05	.15
SHVIEN090 Cuben C	.05	.15
SHVIEN091 World Carrotweight Champion C	.05	.15
SHVIEN092 Fire King Island C	.05	.15
SHVIEN093 Dwarf Star Dragon Planeter C	.05	.15
SHVIEN094 Geargianchor C	.05	.15
SHVIEN095 Geargia Change C	.05	.15
SHVIEN096 Stardust Sifr Divine Dragon UR	1.00	1.50
SHVIEN097 Hot Red Dragon Archfiend King Calamity UR	.40	.60
SHVIEN098 Priestess with Eyes of Blue SR	.10	.30
SHVIEN099 Blue-Eyes Twin Burst Dragon SCT	10.00	12.00
SHVIENSE1 Ebon Illusion Magician SR	.10	.30
SHVIENSE2 Elemental HERO Core SR	.10	.30
SHVIENSE3 Magician's Rob SR	.10	.30
SHVIENSE4 Scapeghost SR	.10	.30

2016 Yu-Gi-Oh The Dark Side of Dimensions Movie Pack First Edition

COMPLETE SET (57 CARDS)	40.00	60.00
BOOSTER BOX (24 CARDS)	60.00	80.00
BOOSTER PACK (5 CARDS)	2.00	5.00
RELEASED ON JULY 21, 2016		
MVP1EN001 Neo Blue Eyes Ultimate Dragon UR	1.50	2.00
MVP1EN002 Kaiser Vorse Raider UR	.10	.30
MVP1EN003 Assault Wyvern UR	.10	.30
MVP1EN004 Blue Eyes Chaos MAX Dragon UR	2.00	3.00
MVP1EN005 Deep Eyes White Dragon UR	.30	.50
MVP1EN006 Pandemic Dragon UR	.10	.30
MVP1EN007 Dragons Fighting Spirit UR	.10	.30
MVP1EN008 Chaos Form UR	3.50	5.00
MVP1EN009 Induced Explosion UR	.10	.30
MVP1EN010 Counter Gate UR	.10	.30
MVP1EN011 Krystal Avatar UR	.10	.30
MVP1EN012 Sentry Soldier of Stone UR	.10	.30
MVP1EN013 Marshmacaron UR	.10	.30
MVP1EN014 Berry Magician Girl UR	.60	1.00
MVP1EN015 Apple Magician Girl UR	.35	.50
MVP1EN016 Kiwi Magician Girl UR	.60	1.00
MVP1EN017 Silver Gadget UR	2.50	3.50
MVP1EN018 Gold Gadget UR	2.50	3.50
MVP1EN019 Dark Magic Veil UR	3.50	4.50
MVP1EN020 Magical Contract Door UR	.10	.30
MVP1EN021 Dimension Reflector UR	.10	.30
MVP1EN022 Dig of Destiny UR	.10	.30
MVP1EN023 Dimension Sphinx UR	.10	.30
MVP1EN024 Dimension Guardian UR	.10	.30
MVP1EN025 Dimension Mirage UR	.10	.30
MVP1EN026 Dark Horizon UR	.10	.30
MVP1EN027 Metamorphortress UR	.10	.30
MVP1EN028 Magicians Defense UR	.40	.60
MVP1EN029 Final Geas UR	.10	.30
MVP1EN030 Metalhold the Moving Blockade UR	.10	.30
MVP1EN031 Spiritual Swords of Revealing Light UR	.10	.30
MVP1EN032 Vijam the Cubic Seed UR	.10	.30
MVP1EN033 Dark Garnex the Cubic Beast UR	.10	.30
MVP1EN034 Blade Garoodia the Cubic Beast UR	.10	.30
MVP1EN035 Buster Gundil the Cubic Behemoth UR	.10	.30
MVP1EN036 Geira Guile the Cubic King UR	.10	.30
MVP1EN037 Vulcan Dragni the Cubic King UR	.10	.30
MVP1EN038 Indiora Doom Volt the Cubic Emperor UR	.10	.30
MVP1EN039 Crimson Nova the Dark Cubic Lord UR	.10	.30
MVP1EN040 Crimson Nova Trinity the Dark Cubic Lord UR	.10	.30
MVP1EN041 Cubic Karma UR	.10	.30
MVP1EN042 Cubic Wave UR	.10	.30
MVP1EN043 Cubic Rebirth UR	.10	.30
MVP1EN044 Cubic Mandala UR	.10	.30
MVP1EN045 Unification of the Cubic Lords UR	.10	.30
MVP1EN046 Blue Eyes Alternative White Dragon UR	10.00	12.00
MVP1EN047 Clear Kuriboh UR	.10	.30
MVP1EN048 Celtic Guard of Noble Arms UR	.10	.30
MVP1EN049 GandoraX the Dragon of Demolition UR	.10	.30
MVP1EN050 Lord Gaia the Fierce Knight UR	.10	.30
MVP1EN051 Lemon Magician Girl UR	.60	1.50
MVP1EN052 Chocolate Magician Girl UR	5.50	7.00
MVP1EN053 Palladium Oracle Mahad UR	1.25	1.75
MVP1EN054 Dark Magician UR	1.25	1.75
MVP1EN055 BlueEyes White Dragon UR	2.25	3.00
MVP1EN056 Dark Magician Girl UR	1.25	2.00
MVP1EN057 Slifer the Sky Dragon UR	1.50	2.00

2016 Yu-Gi-Oh The Dark Illusion First Edition

COMPLETE SET (100 CARDS)	210.00	275.00
BOOSTER BOX (24 PACKS)	65.00	85.00
BOOSTER PACK (9 CARDS)	2.50	6.00
UNLISTED C	.10	.30
UNLISTED R	.15	.40
RELEASED ON AUGUST 5TH, 2016		
TDILEN000 Magical Something R	.10	.30
TDILEN001 Performapal BotEyes Lizard C	.10	.25
TDILEN002 Performapal Gongato C	.10	.25
TDILEN003 Performapal Extra Slinger C	.10	.25
TDILEN004 Performapal Inflater Tapir C	.10	.25
TDILEN005 Performapal Gumgumouton R	.10	.30
TDILEN006 Performapal Bubblebowwow C	.10	.25
TDILEN007 Performapal Radish Horse C	.10	.25
TDILEN008 Performapal Life Swordsman C	.10	.25
TDILEN009 Acrobatic Magician R	.10	.30
TDILEN010 DD Savant Thomas R	.10	.30
TDILEN011 DD Savant Nikola C	.10	.25
TDILEN012 Blackwing Tornado the Reverse Wind C	.10	.25
TDILEN013 Blackwing Gofu the Vague Shadow C	.10	.25
TDILEN014 Red Warg C	.10	.25
TDILEN015 Red Gardna C	.10	.25
TDILEN016 Red Mirror C	.10	.25
TDILEN017 Magician of Dark Illusion SR	1.25	1.75
TDILEN018 Magicians Robe C	.10	.25
TDILEN019 Magicians Rod SR	.75	1.25
TDILEN020 Master Peace the True Dracoslayer UR	.30	.50
TDILEN021 Metalfoes Steelen C	.10	.25
TDILEN022 Metalfoes Silverd C	.10	.25
TDILEN023 Metalfoes Goldriver R	2.00	3.00
TDILEN024 Metalfoes Volflame R	2.00	3.00
TDILEN025 True King Agnimazud the Vanisher UR	.50	.75
TDILEN026 Dinomist Ankylos C	.10	.25
TDILEN027 Triamid monster C	.10	.25
TDILEN028 Triamid Hunter R	.10	.30
TDILEN029 Triamid Master R	.10	.30
TDILEN030 Triamid Sphinx SR	.20	.35
TDILEN031 Shiranui Solitaire UR	6.00	8.00
TDILEN032 Toon Dark Magician SR	.40	.60
TDILEN033 Scapeghost C	.10	.25
TDILEN034 Block Dragon UR	.40	.60
TDILEN035 Amaterasu SR	.15	.30
TDILEN036 Dragon Ninja monster C	.10	.25
TDILEN037 Spell Strider SR	.15	.30
TDILEN038 Zap Mustung C	.10	.25
TDILEN039 Totem Five C	.10	.25
TDILEN040 Tuning Gum R	.10	.30
TDILEN041 Wrecker Panda SR	.10	.25
TDILEN042 Fairy Tail Snow SP	.75	1.00
TDILEN043 Metalfoes Adamante R	.25	.40
TDILEN044 Metalfoes Orichalc C	.10	.25
TDILEN045 Metalfoes Crimsonite R	.25	.40
TDILEN046 Nirvana High Paladin SCR	8.00	10.00
TDILEN047 Assault Blackwing Sayo the Rain Hider R	.10	.30
TDILEN048 Assault Blackwing Sohaya the Rain Storm C	.10	.25
TDILEN049 Assault Blackwing Onimaru the Divine Thunder SR	.20	.60
TDILEN050 Tyrant Red Dragon Archfiend UR	1.50	2.25
TDILEN051 Coral Dragon SCR	12.00	14.00
TDILEN052 Ebon High Magician SR	.40	.60
TDILEN053 Super Hippo Carnival C	.10	.25
TDILEN054 Luna Light Perfume SR	.20	.35
TDILEN055 Frightfur Sanctuary C	.10	.25
TDILEN056 Forbidden Dark Contract with the Swamp King C	.10	.25
TDILEN057 Dark Magical Circle SCR	30.00	35.00
TDILEN058 Illusion Magic R	.30	.50
TDILEN059 Dark Magic Expanded C	.10	.25
TDILEN060 Metamorformation SR	.20	.35
TDILEN061 Metalfoes Fusion SR	.40	.75
TDILEN062 Triamid Fortress C	.10	.25
TDILEN063 Triamid Cruiser R	.10	.30
TDILEN064 Triamid Kingolem R	.10	.30
TDILEN065 Cosmic Cyclone SCR	12.00	15.00
TDILEN066 Pot of Desires SCR	70.00	80.00
TDILEN067 Magical MidBreaker Field C	.10	.25
TDILEN068 Card of the Soul SP	.10	.25
TDILEN069 Fusion Fright Waltz C	.10	.25
TDILEN070 King Scarlet C	.10	.25
TDILEN071 Magician Navigation SCR	20.00	22.00
TDILEN072 Metalfoes Counter C	.10	.25
TDILEN073 Metalfoes Combination SR	.40	.75
TDILEN074 Triamid Pulse R	.10	.30
TDILEN075 Destruction Sword Memories C	.10	.25
TDILEN076 Floodgate Trap Hole UR	5.50	7.00
TDILEN077 Premature Return UR	.50	.75
TDILEN078 Unified Front C	.10	.25
TDILEN079 Pendulum Hole C	.10	.25
TDILEN080 The Forceful Checkpoint SCR	2.50	3.50
TDILEN081 Ninjitsu Art Notebook C	.10	.25
TDILEN082 Subterror Nemesis Warrior R	.10	.30
TDILEN083 Subterror Behemoth Umastryx UR	3.50	4.50
TDILEN084 Subterror Behemoth Stalagmo UR	3.50	5.00
TDILEN085 The Hidden City SCR	12.00	15.00
TDILEN086 SPYRAL Super Agent UR	8.00	12.00
TDILEN087 SPYRAL QuikFix R	.10	.30
TDILEN088 SPYRAL GEAR Drone R	.10	.30
TDILEN089 SPYRAL GEAR Big Red R	.10	.30
TDILEN090 Heavy Freight Train Derricrane C	.10	.25
TDILEN091 Number 81 Superdreadnought Rail Cannon Super Dora SR	.40	.75
TDILEN092 Revolving Switchyard C	.10	.25
TDILEN093 Dragodies the Empowered Warrior C	.10	.25
TDILEN094 Empowerment C	.10	.25
TDILEN095 Paleozoic Olenoides C	.10	.25
TDILEN096 Paleozoic Hallucigenia C	.10	.25
TDILEN097 Paleozoic Canadia C	.10	.25
TDILEN098 Paleozoic Pikaia C	.10	.25
TDILEN099 Paleozoic Anomalocaris SR	.20	.35

2009 Yu-Gi-Oh Hidden Arsenal Limited Edition

COMPLETE SET (30)	8.00	20.00
BOOSTER BOX (24 PACKS)	80.00	100.00
BOOSTER PACK (5 CARDS)	2.50	6.00
RELEASED ON NOVEMBER 10, 2009		
HA011 Blizzed, Defender of the Ice Barrier SCR	.10	.30
HA012 Blizzard Warrior SR	.10	.30
HA013 Cryomancer of the Ice Barrier SCR	.20	.75
HA014 Mist Valley Thunderbird SCR	.10	.30
HA015 Mist Valley Shaman SCR	.10	1.50
HA016 Mist Valley Soldier SCR	.40	1.00
HA017 Flamvell Dragnov SR	.10	1.50
HA018 Flamvell Magician SR	.10	1.50
HA019 Flamvell Guard SR	.20	.75
HA0110 X-Saber Axel SR	.10	.30
HA0111 X-Saber Airbellum SCR	.10	.30
HA0112 X-Saber Uruz SR	.10	.30
HA0113 Commander Gottoms SCR	.10	1.50
HA0114 Ally of Justice Clausolas SR	.10	.30
HA0115 Ally of Justice Garadholg SR	.10	.30
HA0116 Ally of Justice Rudra SR	.10	1.00
HA0117 Worm Apocalypse SR	.10	1.00
HA0118 Worm Barses SR	.10	1.00
HA0119 Worm Cartaros SR	.10	1.00
HA0120 Worm Dimikles SR	.10	1.00
HA0121 Worm Erokin SCR	.10	1.00
HA0122 Brionac, Dragon SCR	2.00	5.00
HA0123 Mist Wurm SCR	2.00	5.00
HA0124 Flamvell Uruquizas SCR	.40	1.00
HA0125 X-Saber Urbellum SCR	.10	.30
HA0126 Ally of Justice Catastor SCR	1.25	3.00
HA0127 Wrath of Neos SCR	.20	.75
HA0128 Detonate SR	.10	.30
HA0129 Berserker Crush SR	.10	1.00
HA0130 Evolution Burst SCR	.20	.75

2010 Yu-Gi-Oh Hidden Arsenal 2 1st Edition

COMPLETE SET (60)	40.00	80.00
BOOSTER BOX (24 PACKS)	30.00	40.00
BOOSTER PACK (5 CARDS)	2.00	3.00
RELEASED ON JULY 20, 2010		
HA021 Naturia Beetle SR	.40	1.00
HA022 Naturia Rock SR	.40	1.00
HA023 Naturia Guardian SCR	.60	1.50
HA024 Naturia Vein SR	.40	1.00
HA025 Genex Furnace SR	.40	1.00
HA026 Genex Gaia SR	.40	1.00
HA027 Genex Spare SR	.40	1.00
HA028 Genex Turbine SR	.40	1.00
HA029 Genex Doctor SR	.40	1.00
HA0210 Genex Solar SCR	.60	1.50
HA0211 Dai-sojo of the Ice Barrier SCR	.60	1.50
HA0212 Medium of the Ice Barrier SR	.60	1.50
HA0213 Mist Valley Baby Roc SR	.40	1.00
HA0214 Mist Valley Executor SR	.40	1.00
HA0215 Flamvell Grunika SR	.40	1.00
HA0216 Flamvell Baby SR	.40	1.00
HA0217 Ally Mind SR	.40	1.00
HA0218 Ally of Justice Nullfier SR	.40	1.00
HA0219 Ally of Justice Searcher SR	.40	1.00
HA0220 Ally of Justice Enemy Catcher SR	.40	1.00
HA0221 Ally of Justice Thunder Armor SR	.40	1.00
HA0222 Ally of Justice Cosmic SCR	.60	1.50
HA0223 Worm Linx SR	.40	1.00
HA0224 Worm Millidith SR	.40	1.00
HA0225 Worm Noble SR	.40	1.00
HA0226 Naturia Beast SCR	3.00	8.00
HA0227 Dewloren, Tiger King SCR	3.00	8.00
HA0228 Thermal Genex SCR	.60	1.50
HA0229 Geo Genex SCR	.60	1.50
HA0230 Ally of Justice Field Marshal SCR	.75	2.00
HA0231 Fabled Lurrie SR	.40	1.00
HA0232 Fabled Grimro SCR	.40	1.00
HA0233 Fabled Gallabas SCR	.60	1.50
HA0234 Fabled Kushano SR	.60	1.50
HA0235 Jurrac Protops SR	.40	1.00
HA0236 Jurrac Velo SR	1.00	2.50
HA0237 Jurrac Monoloph SR	.40	1.00
HA0238 Jurrac Tyrannus SCR	.75	2.00
HA0239 Naturia Antjaw SR	.40	1.00
HA0240 Naturia Spiderfang SR	.40	1.00
HA0241 Naturia Rosewhip SR	.60	1.50
HA0242 Naturia Cosmobeet SR	.40	1.00
HA0243 Genex Blastfan SR	.40	1.00
HA0244 Genex Recycled SR	.40	1.00
HA0245 Genex Army SCR	.60	1.50
HA0246 Pilgrim of the Ice Barrier SR	.40	1.00
HA0247 Geomancer of the Ice Barrier SR	.40	1.00
HA0248 Mist Valley Falcon SR	.60	1.50
HA0249 Mist Valley Apex Avian SCR	5.00	12.00
HA0250 Ally of Justice Reverse Break SR	.40	1.00
HA0251 Ally of Justice Unlimiter SR	.40	1.00
HA0252 Worm Opera SR	.40	1.00
HA0253 Worm Prince SR	.40	1.00
HA0254 Worm Queen SCR	.60	1.50
HA0255 Worm Rakuyeh SR	.40	1.00
HA0256 Fabled Valkyrus SCR	2.00	5.00
HA0257 Jurrac Giganoto SCR	1.50	4.00
HA0258 Naturia Leodrake SCR	.60	1.50
HA0259 Windmill Genex SCR	.60	1.50
HA0260 Mist Valley Thunder Lord SCR	.60	1.50

2010 Yu-Gi-Oh Hidden Arsenal 3 1st Edition

COMPLETE SET (60)	40.00	80.00
BOOSTER BOX (24 PACKS)	40.00	50.00
BOOSTER PACK (5 CARDS)	2.00	3.00
RELEASED ON DECEMBER 7, 2010		
HA03EN001 Fabled Urustos SR	.25	.60
HA03EN002 Fabled Krus SCR	2.00	5.00
HA03EN003 Fabled Topi SR	.25	.60
HA03EN004 Fabled Soulkius SCR	.50	1.25
HA03EN005 Fabled Miztoji SR	.25	.60
HA03EN006 Jurrac Ptera SR	.25	.60
HA03EN007 Jurrac Iguanon SR	.25	.60
HA03EN008 Jurrac Brachis SR	.25	.60
HA03EN009 Jurrac Spinos SR	.25	.60
HA03EN010 Naturia Dragonfly SR	.25	.60
HA03EN011 Naturia Sunflower SR	.25	.60
HA03EN012 Naturia Cliff SCR	1.50	4.00
HA03EN013 Naturia Tulip SR	.25	.60
HA03EN014 R-Genex Turbo SR	.25	.60
HA03EN015 R-Genex Overseer SR	.25	.60
HA03EN016 R-Genex Crusher SR	.25	.60
HA03EN017 R-Genex Magma SR	.25	.60
HA03EN018 Shock Troops SR	.30	.75
HA03EN019 Samurai of the Ice Barrier SR	.25	.60
HA03EN020 Dewdark of the Ice Barrier SR	.50	1.25
HA03EN021 Caravan of the Ice Barrier SR	.25	.60
HA03EN022 Worm Solid SR	.25	.60
HA03EN023 Worm Tentacles SR	.25	.60
HA03EN024 Worm Ugly SR	.25	.60
HA03EN025 Worm Victory SCR	.50	1.25
HA03EN026 Fabled Leviathan SCR	.60	1.50
HA03EN027 Jurrac Velphito SCR	1.00	2.50
HA03EN028 Naturia Barkion SCR	10.00	25.00
HA03EN029 Locomotion R-Genex SCR	.50	1.25
HA03EN030 Gungnir, Dragon of the Ice Barrier SCR	6.00	15.00
HA03EN031 Dragunity Dux SCR	1.00	2.50
HA03EN032 Dragunity Legionnaire SR	.25	.60
HA03EN033 Dragunity Tribus SR	.25	.60
HA03EN034 Dragunity Darkspear SR	.30	.75
HA03EN035 Dragunity Phalanx SCR	5.00	12.00
HA03EN036 Fabled Dyf SR	.25	.60
HA03EN037 Fabled Ashenveil SCR	.60	1.50
HA03EN038 Fabled Oltro SR	.25	.60
HA03EN039 Jurrac Titano SCR	.50	1.25
HA03EN040 Jurrac Guaiba SR	.25	.60
HA03EN041 Jurrac Stauriko SR	.25	.60
HA03EN042 Naturia Horneedle SR	.25	.60
HA03EN043 Naturia Fruitfly SR	.25	.60
HA03EN044 Naturia Hydrangea SR	.25	.60
HA03EN045 R-Genex Accelerator SR	.25	.60
HA03EN046 R-Genex Oracle SR	.25	.60
HA03EN047 R-Genex Ultimum SR	.25	.60
HA03EN048 Spellbreaker of the Ice Barrier SR	.25	.60
HA03EN049 General Grunard SCR	1.25	3.00
HA03EN050 Ally of Justice Omni-Weapon SCR	.50	1.25
HA03EN051 Ally of Justice Quarantine SR	.25	.60
HA03EN052 Ally of Justice Cycle Reader SR	.25	.60
HA03EN053 Worm Warlord SR	.25	.60
HA03EN054 Worm Xex SR	.25	.60
HA03EN055 Worm Yagan SR	.25	.60
HA03EN056 Worm Zero SCR	.60	1.50
HA03EN057 Dragunity Knight - Gae Bulg SCR	1.00	2.50
HA03EN058 Fabled Ragin SCR	1.50	4.00
HA03EN059 Vindikite R-Genex SCR	.50	1.25
HA03EN060 Ally of Justice Decisive SCR	4.00	10.00

2011 Yu-Gi-Oh Hidden Arsenal 4 1st Edition

COMPLETE SET (60)	25.00	50.00
BOOSTER BOX (24 PACKS)	60.00	80.00
BOOSTER PACK (5 CARDS)	3.00	4.00
RELEASED ON APRIL 19, 2011		
HA04EN001 Genex Ally Remote SR	.15	.40
HA04EN002 Genex Ally Powercell SCR	.25	.75
HA04EN003 Genex Ally Changer SR	.15	.40
HA04EN004 Genex Ally Volcannon SR	.15	.40
HA04EN005 Genex Ally Solid SR	.15	.40
HA04EN006 The Fabled Chawa SR	.15	.40
HA04EN007 The Fabled Catsith SR	.50	1.25
HA04EN008 The Fabled Cerburrel SCR	.25	.75
HA04EN009 The Fabled Ganashia SR	.15	.40
HA04EN010 The Fabled Nozoochee SR	.15	.40
HA04EN011 Dragunity Militum SR	.15	.40
HA04EN012 Dragunity Primus Pilus SCR	.25	.75
HA04EN013 Dragunity Brandistock SR	.15	.40
HA04EN014 Dragunity Javelin SR	.15	.40
HA04EN015 Jurrac Dino SR	.15	.40
HA04EN016 Jurrac Gallim SR	.15	.40
HA04EN017 Jurrac Aeolo SR	.15	.40
HA04EN018 Jurrac Herra SR	.25	.75
HA04EN019 Naturia Butterfly SR	.15	.40
HA04EN020 Naturia Ladybug SR	.15	.40
HA04EN021 Naturia Strawberry SR	.15	.40
HA04EN022 Defender of the Ice Barrier SR	.25	.75
HA04EN023 Warlock of the Ice Barrier SR	.15	.40
HA04EN024 Sacred Spirit SR	.15	.40
HA04EN025 General Raiho SCR	.25	.75
HA04EN026 Genex Ally Triarm SCR	.25	.75
HA04EN027 The Fabled Unicore SCR	.50	1.25
HA04EN028 Dragunity Knight - Trident SCR	.75	2.00
HA04EN029 Jurrac Meteor SCR	.25	.75
HA04EN030 Naturia Landoise SCR	.25	.75
HA04EN031 Neo Flamvell Origin SR	.15	.40
HA04EN032 Neo Flamvell Hedgehog SR	.15	.40
HA04EN033 Neo Flamvell Shaman SR	.15	.40
HA04EN034 Neo Flamvell Garuda SR	.15	.40
HA04EN035 Neo Flamvell Sabre SCR	.25	.75
HA04EN036 Genex Ally Chemistrer SR	.15	.40
HA04EN037 Genex Ally Birdman SR	.40	1.00
HA04EN038 Genex Ally Bellflame SR	.15	.40
HA04EN039 Genex Ally Crusher SR	.15	.40
HA04EN040 Genex Ally Reliever SCR	.25	.75
HA04EN041 The Fabled Peggulsus SR	.15	.40
HA04EN042 The Fabled Kokkator SR	.15	.40
HA04EN043 Fabled Dianaira SCR	.25	.75
HA04EN044 Dragunity Corsesca SR	.15	.40
HA04EN045 Dragunity Partisan SR	.15	.40
HA04EN046 Dragunity Pilum SR	.15	.40
HA04EN047 Dragunity Angusticlavii SR	.15	.40
HA04EN048 Naturia Stinkbug SR	.15	.40
HA04EN049 Naturia Mantis SR	.15	.40
HA04EN050 Naturia Ragweed SR	.15	.40
HA04EN051 Naturia White Oak SCR	.25	.75
HA04EN052 Strategist of the Ice Barrier SR	.15	.40
HA04EN053 Secret Guards SR	.15	.40
HA04EN054 General Gantala SCR	.25	.75
HA04EN055 Naturia Exterio SCR	.25	.75
HA04EN056 Ancient Flamvell Deity SCR	.25	.75
HA04EN057 Genex Ally Triforce SCR	.25	.75
HA04EN058 The Fabled Kudabbi SCR	.25	.75
HA04EN059 Dragunity Knight - Barcha SCR	.75	2.00
HA04EN060 Trishula, Dragon SCR	15.00	30.00

2011 Yu-Gi-Oh Hidden Arsenal 5 1st Edition

COMPLETE SET (60)	100.00	200.00
BOOSTER BOX (24 PACKS)	30.00	40.00
BOOSTER PACK (5 CARDS)	2.00	3.00
RELEASED ON DECEMBER 6, 2011		
HA05001 Gem Garnet SR	2.00	5.00
HA05002 Gem Sapphire SR	.40	1.00
HA05003 Gem Tourmaline SR	.40	1.00
HA05004 Gem Alexandrite SCR	.75	2.00
HA05005 Gem-Armadillo SCR	2.00	5.00
HA05006 Gem-Merchant SR	.10	.30
HA05007 Laval Miller SR	.10	.30
HA05008 Soaring Eagle Above the Searing Land SR	.10	.30
HA05009 Laval Warrior SR	.10	.30
HA05010 Prominence, Molt SR	.10	.30
HA05011 Laval Forest Sprite SR	.10	.30
HA05012 Kayenn, the Master SR	.10	.30
HA05013 Laval Burner SR	.10	.30
HA05014 Laval Judgment (SCR)	.25	.75
HA05015 Vylon Cube SR	.50	1.25
HA05016 Vylon Vanguard SR	.10	.30
HA05017 Vylon Charger SR	.10	.30
HA05018 Vylon Soldier SR	.10	.30
HA05019 Gem-Knight Ruby SCR	.75	2.00
HA05020 Gem Aquamarine SCR	.25	.75
HA05021 Gem-Knight Topaz SCR	.40	1.00
HA05022 Lavalval Dragon SCR	.25	.75
HA05023 Laval the Greater SCR	.25	.75
HA05024 Vylon Sigma SCR	.25	.75
HA05025 Vylon Epsilon SCR	1.50	4.00
HA05026 Gem-Knight Fusion SR	.40	1.00
HA05027 Searing Fire Wall SR	.10	.30
HA05028 Vylon Material SR	.10	.30

HA05029 Gem-Enhancement SR	.10	.30
HA05030 Molten Whirlwind Wall SR	.10	.30
HA05031 Gishki Abyss SR	1.00	2.50
HA05032 Gishki Vanity SR	.10	.30
HA05033 Gishki Marker SR	.10	.30
HA05034 Gishki Chain SCR	.25	.75
HA05035 Gishki Ariel SR	.25	.75
HA05036 Gishki Shadow SR	.40	1.00
HA05037 Gusto Gulldo SR	.50	1.25
HA05038 Gusto Egul SR	.40	1.00
HA05039 Gusto Thunbolt SR	.10	.30
HA05040 Winda, Priestess SR	.50	1.25
HA05041 Caam, Serenity SCR	2.50	6.00
HA05042 Windaar, Sage SR	.10	.30
HA05043 Steelswarm Cell SR	.10	.30
HA05044 Steelswarm Scout SR	.10	.30
HA05045 Steelswarm Gatekeeper SR	.10	.30
HA05046 Steelswarm Caller SR	.10	.30
HA05047 Steels Mantis SCR	.25	.75
HA05048 Steels Moth SR	.10	.30
HA05049 Steels Girastag SCR	.25	.75
HA05050 Steels Caucastag SCR	.50	1.25
HA05051 Evigishki Mind SCR	.25	.75
HA05052 Evigishki Soul SCR	.50	1.25
HA05053 Daigusto Gulldos SCR	.40	1.00
HA05054 Daigusto Eguls SCR	.25	.75
HA05055 Gishki Aquamirror SR	1.50	4.00
HA05056 Contact Gusto SCR	.60	1.50
HA05057 First Step SR	.10	.30
HA05058 Aquamirror Meditation SR	.10	.30
HA05059 Blessings for Gusto SR	.10	.30
HA05060 Infestation Wave SR	.10	.30

2012 Yu-Gi-Oh Hidden Arsenal 6 1st Edition

COMPLETE SET (60)	50.00	100.00
BOOSTER BOX (24 PACKS)	40.00	50.00
BOOSTER PACK (5 CARDS)	3.00	4.00
RELEASED ON JULY 24, 2012		
HA06001 Gem-Knight Crystal SR	.20	.60
HA06002 Laval Volcano Handmaiden SR	.10	.30
HA06003 Laval Cannon SCR	.25	.75
HA06004 Vylon Sphere SR	.10	.30
HA06005 Vylon Tetra SR	.10	.30
HA06006 Vylon Stella SR	.10	.30
HA06007 Vylon Prism SR	.15	.40
HA06008 Vylon Hept SR	.10	.30
HA06009 Gishki Reliever SR	.10	.30
HA06010 Gishki Noellia SR	.10	.30
HA06011 Gusto Squirro SR	.10	.30
HA06012 Reeze, Whirlwind of Gusto SR	.10	.30
HA06013 Steelswarm Genome SR	.10	.30
HA06014 Steelswarm Sentinel SR	.10	.30
HA06015 Steelswarm Sting SR	.10	.30
HA06016 Steelswarm Longhorn SCR	.25	.75
HA06017 Steelswarm Hercules SCR	.25	.75
HA06018 Evigishki Tetrogre SCR	.25	.75
HA06019 Gem-Knight Citrine SCR	.75	2.00
HA06020 Gem-Knight Prismaura SCR	.75	2.00
HA06021 Laval Stennon SCR	.25	.75
HA06022 Vylon Alpha SCR	.25	.75
HA06023 Vylon Omega SCR	.25	.75
HA06024 Daigusto Sphreez SCR	.75	2.00
HA06025 Vylon Component SR	.10	.30
HA06026 Vylon Element SR	.10	.30
HA06027 Forbidden Arts of the Gishki SR	.10	.30
HA06028 Pyroxene Fusion SR	.10	.30
HA06029 Infestation Ripples SR	.10	.30
HA06030 Infestation Tool SR	.10	.30
HA06031 Gem-Knight Obsidian SR	.40	1.00
HA06032 Gem-Knight Iolite SR	.20	.50
HA06033 Gem-Knight Amber SR	.20	.60
HA06034 Laval Lakeside Lady SCR	.40	1.00
HA06035 Laval Coatl SR	.10	.30
HA06036 Laval Blaster SR	.10	.30
HA06037 Vylon Pentachloro SR	.10	.30
HA06038 Vylon Tesseract SR	.10	.30
HA06039 Vylon Stigma SR	.10	.30
HA06040 Gishki Vision SR	.25	.75
HA06041 Gishki Emilia SR	.25	.75
HA06042 Gishki Mollusk SR	.10	.30
HA06043 Gusto Falco SR	.10	.30
HA06044 Kamui, Hope of Gusto SR	.20	.60
HA06045 Musto, Oracle of Gusto SR	.10	.30
HA06046 Evigishki Gustkraken SCR	.25	.75
HA06047 Gem-Knight Amethyst SCR	.40	1.00
HA06048 Lavalval Dragun SCR	.25	.75
HA06049 Daigusto Falcos SCR	.25	.75
HA06050 Gem-Knight Pearl SCR	.50	1.25
HA06051 Lavalval Ignis SCR	.25	.75
HA06052 Vylon Disigma SCR	1.50	4.00
HA06053 Evigishki Merrowgeist SCR	.25	.75
HA06054 Daigusto Phoenix SCR	2.00	5.00
HA06055 Particle Fusion SR	.10	.30
HA06056 Vylon Polytope SR	.10	.30
HA06057 Vylon Segment SR	.10	.30
HA06058 Dustflame Blast SR	.10	.30
HA06059 Aquamirror Illusion SR	.10	.30
HA06060 Whirlwind of Gusto SR	.10	.30

2013 Yu-Gi-Oh Hidden Arsenal 7 1st Edition

COMPLETE SET (70)	80.00	120.00
BOOSTER BOX (24 PACKS)	100.00	120.00
BOOSTER PACK (5 CARDS)	4.00	5.00
RELEASED ON APRIL 25, 2013		
HA07001 Gem-Knight Sardonyx SR	.25	.40
HA07002 Laval Phlogis SR	.15	.25
HA07003 Gishki Avance SR	.15	.25
HA07004 Gusto Griffin SR	.15	.25
HA07005 Constellar Sheratan SR	.15	.25
HA07006 Constellar Aldebaran SR	.15	.25
HA07007 Constellar Algiedi SR	.30	.50
HA07008 Constellar Pollux SR	.30	.50
HA07009 Constellar Zubeneschamali SR	.40	.75
HA07010 Constellar Virgo SR	.15	.25
HA07011 Evilswarm Heliotrope SR	.25	.40
HA07012 Evilswarm Zahak SR	.15	.25
HA07013 Evilswarm Ketos SR	.15	.25
HA07014 Evilswarm O'lantern SR	.15	.25
HA07015 Evilswarm Mandragora SR	.30	.50
HA07016 Evilswarm Hraesvelg SR	.15	.25
HA07017 Evigishki Levianima SCR	.20	.30
HA07018 Gem-Knight Zirconia SR	.75	1.00
HA07019 Lavalval Chain SCR	4.50	6.00
HA07020 Daigusto Emeral SCR	15.00	20.00
HA07021 Constellar Hyades SCR	.40	.75
HA07022 Constellar Pleiades SCR	.60	1.00
HA07023 Evilswarm Nightmare SR	.50	.75
HA07024 Evilswarm Bahamut SCR	.60	1.00
HA07025 Molten Conduction Field SCR	.20	.30
HA07026 Gishki Photomirror SR	.15	.25
HA07027 Constellar Star Chart SCR	.15	.25
HA07028 Fragment Fusion SR	.15	.25
HA07029 Dust Storm of Gusto SR	.15	.25
HA07030 Infestation Infection SCR	.30	.50
HA07031 D.D. Esper Star Sparrow SCR	.30	.50
HA07032 Beast-Warrior Puma SR	.15	.25
HA07033 Phoenix Beast Gairuda SR	.15	.25
HA07034 Ironhammer the Giant SR	.15	.25
HA07035 D.D. Jet Iron SR	.15	.25
HA07036 Aye-Iron SR	.15	.25
HA07037 Tin Goldfish SR	8.00	10.00
HA07038 Gearspring Spirit SR	.50	.75
HA07039 Gem-Knight Lazuli SR	1.50	2.50
HA07040 Gishki Natalia SR	.15	.25
HA07041 Constellar Sial SR	.15	.25
HA07042 Constellar Rasalhague SR	.15	.25
HA07043 Constellar Leonis SR	.15	.25
HA07044 Constellar Acubens SR	.15	.25
HA07045 Constellar Kaus SCR	.25	.75
HA07046 Constellar Alrescha SR	.15	.25
HA07047 Constellar Antares SR	.15	.25
HA07048 Evilswarm Castor SR	1.00	1.50
HA07049 Evilswarm Obliviwisp SR	.15	.25
HA07050 Evilswarm Azzathoth SR	.15	.25
HA07051 Evilswarm Thunderbird SCR	.60	1.00
HA07052 Evilswarm Salamandra SR	.15	.25
HA07053 Evilswarm Golem SR	.15	.25
HA07054 Evilswarm Coppelia SR	.15	.25
HA07055 Sophia, Goddess of Rebirth SCR	1.00	1.50
HA07056 Gishki Psychelone SR	.15	.25
HA07057 Gishki Zielgigas SCR	1.50	2.50
HA07058 Gem-Knight Seraphinite SR	15.00	20.00
HA07059 Gem-Knight Master Diamond SCR	.50	.60
HA07060 Tin Archduke SCR	.20	.30
HA07061 Constellar Praesepe SCR	.60	1.00
HA07062 Constellar Ptolemy M7 SCR	3.50	5.00
HA07063 Evilswarm Thanatos SCR	.60	1.00
HA07064 Evilswarm Ophion SCR	7.00	10.00
HA07065 Evilswarm Ouroboros SCR	3.50	5.00
HA07066 Iron Call SCR	2.50	4.00
HA07067 Constellar Star Cradle SR	.15	.25
HA07068 Infestation Pandemic SCR	2.00	3.00
HA07069 Constellar Meteor SR	.15	.25
HA07070 Infestation Terminus SR	.15	.25

2013 Yu-Gi-Oh Number Hunters 1st Edition

COMPLETE SET (60)	40.00	80.00
BOOSTER BOX (24 PACKS)	40.00	50.00
BOOSTER PACK (5 CARDS)	3.00	4.00
RELEASED ON JULY 12, 2013		
NUMH001 Chronomaly Aztec Mask Golem SR	.10	.30
NUMH002 Chronomaly Cabrera Trebuchet SR	.10	.30
NUMH003 Chronomaly Mud Golem SR	.10	.30
NUMH004 Chronomaly Sol Monolith SR	.10	.30
NUMH005 Gimmick Puppet Egg Head SR	.50	1.25
NUMH006 Gimmick Puppet Gear Changer SR	.20	.60
NUMH007 Gimmick Puppet Twilight Joker SR	.10	.30
NUMH008 Gimmick Puppet Scissor Arms SR	.20	.60
NUMH009 Gimmick Puppet Nightmare SR	.10	.30
NUMH010 Heroic Challenger - Ambush Soldier SCR	.20	.60
NUMH011 Heroic Challenger - Clasp Sword SR	.10	.30
NUMH012 Blue Mountain Butterspy SR	.40	1.00
NUMH013 Box of Friends SCR	1.25	3.00
NUMH014 Zombowwow SR	.10	.30
NUMH015 Gash the Dust Lord SR	.10	.30
NUMH016 Zubaba Knight SR	.10	.30
NUMH017 Gogogo Golem SR	.10	.30
NUMH018 Kagetokage SR	.25	.75
NUMH019 Kurivolt SR	.10	.30
NUMH020 Gogogo Giant SR	.10	.30
NUMH021 Gagaga Gardna SR	.10	.30
NUMH022 Photon Cerberus SR	.10	.30
NUMH023 Photon Lizard SR	.10	.30
NUMH024 Rocket Arrow Express SR	.10	.30
NUMH025 Battle Warrior SR	.10	.30
NUMH026 Number 54: Lion Heart SCR	1.50	4.00
NUMH027 Number 15: Gimmick Puppet Giant Grinder SCR	2.50	6.00
NUMH028 Number 44: Sky Pegasus SCR	1.00	2.50
NUMH029 Number 49: Fortune Tune SCR	1.50	4.00
NUMH030 Number 57: Tri-Head Dust Dragon SCR	.60	1.50
NUMH031 Number 63: Shamoji Soldier SR	.10	.30
NUMH032 Number 74: Master of Blades SCR	1.50	4.00
NUMH033 Number 85: Crazy Box SR	.40	1.00
NUMH034 Number 87: Queen of the Night SR	.60	1.50
NUMH035 Mechquipped Angineer SR	.40	1.00
NUMH036 CXyz Mechquipped Djinn Angeneral SR	.10	.30
NUMH037 Coach King Giantrainer SCR	.20	.60
NUMH038 CXyz Coach Lord Ultimatrainer SCR	1.50	4.00
NUMH039 Norito the Moral Leader SCR	1.50	4.00
NUMH040 CXyz Simon the Great Moral Leader SCR	.20	.60
NUMH041 Comics Hero King Arthur SCR	1.50	4.00
NUMH042 CXyz Comics Hero Legend Arthur SCR	.20	.60
NUMH043 Battlecruiser Dianthus SR	.10	.30
NUMH044 CXyz Battleship Cherry Blossom SCR	.20	.60
NUMH045 Skypalace Gangaridai SCR	.50	1.25
NUMH046 CXyz Skypalace Babylon SCR	.20	.60
NUMH047 Photon Alexandra Queen SCR	.20	.60
NUMH048 Night Papilloperative SR	.10	.30
NUMH049 Uniformed Void SR	.10	.30
NUMH050 Princess Cologne SCR	.20	.60
NUMH051 Baby Tiragon SR	.10	.30
NUMH052 Chakra SR	.10	.30
NUMH053 Resurrection of Chakra SR	.10	.30
NUMH054 Gimmick Puppet Ritual SR	.10	.30
NUMH055 Stoic Challenge SR	.10	.30
NUMH056 Overlay Capture SR	.10	.30
NUMH057 Insect Armor with Laser Cannon SR	.10	.30
NUMH058 Number Wall SCR	.60	1.50
NUMH059 Heraldry Record SR	.10	.30
NUMH060 Butterspy Protection SR	.10	.30

2014 Yu-Gi-Oh Dragons of Legend 1st Edition

COMPLETE SET (51)	115.00	150.00
BOOSTER BOX (24 PACKS)	200.00	350.00
BOOSTER PACK (9 CARDS)	3.00	8.00
RELEASED ON APRIL 25, 2014		
DRLGEN001 Legendary Knight Timaeus SCR	5.00	8.00
DRLGEN002 Kuribandit SCR	2.50	3.50
DRLGEN003 Amulet Dragon SCR	15.00	20.00
DRLGEN004 Dark Magician Girl the Dragon Knight SCR	25.00	30.00
DRLGEN005 The Eye of Timaeus SCR	30.00	35.00
DRLGEN006 Legend of Heart SCR	6.00	8.00
DRLGEN007 Berserker Soul SCR	.20	.35
DRLGEN008 Relay Soul SR	.15	.25
DRLGEN009 Guardian Eatos SR	.15	.25
DRLGEN010 Guardian Dreadscythe SCR	2.00	2.75
DRLGEN011 Celestial Sword Eatos SR	.15	.25
DRLGEN012 Reaper Scythe Dreadscythe SR	.20	.35
DRLGEN013 Guarded Treasure SCR	2.00	2.50
DRLGEN014 Soul Charge SR	2.50	3.50
DRLGEN015 Sabatiel The Philosopher's Stone SR	.15	.25
DRLGEN016 Flash Fusion SR	.15	.25
DRLGEN017 Battle Fusion SR	.40	.75
DRLGEN018 Final Fusion SR	.15	.25
DRLGEN019 Pair Cycroid SR	.15	.25
DRLGEN020 Ayers Rock Sunrise SR	.15	.25
DRLGEN021 Doble Passe SCR	.60	1.00
DRLGEN022 Carboneddon SR	.40	.60
DRLGEN023 Mathematician SCR	1.00	1.50
DRLGEN024 Ra's Disciple SCR	5.50	7.00
DRLGEN025 Mound of the Bound Creator SCR	4.00	5.00
DRLGEN026 Shooting Star SCR	.20	.30
DRLGEN027 Blackwing Oroshi the Squall SR	.75	1.25
DRLGEN028 Blackwing Steam the Cloak SR	.15	.25
DRLGEN029 Blackwing Hurricane the Tornado SR	.15	.25
DRLGEN030 Black Sonic SCR	4.00	5.00
DRLGEN031 Black Wing Revenge SR	.15	.25
DRLGEN032 Shadow Impulse SR	.15	.25
DRLGEN033 Assault Dog SR	.15	.25
DRLGEN034 Gate Blocker SCR	.20	.30
DRLGEN035 Wiretap SR	.50	.80
DRLGEN036 Lionhearted Locomotive SR	.15	.25
DRLGEN037 Express Train Trolley Olley SCR	.20	.30
DRLGEN038 Construction Train Signal Red SR	.15	.25
DRLGEN039 Train Connection SR	.15	.25
DRLGEN040 Abyss Splash SR	.40	.60
DRLGEN041 Abyss Supra Splash SR	.15	.25
DRLGEN042 Rank Up Magic Quick Chaos SCR	1.00	2.00
DRLGEN043 Chaos Chimera Dragon SR	.15	.25
DRLGEN044 Rank Up Magic Admiration of the Thousands SCR	.20	.35
DRLGEN045 Magic Hand SR	.15	.25
DRLGEN046 Fire Hand SCR	1.00	1.50
DRLGEN047 Ice Hand SCR	1.00	1.50
DRLGEN048 Prominence Hand SR	.15	.25
DRLGEN049 Giant Red Hand SR	.15	.25
DRLGEN050 Lillybot SR	.15	.25
DRLGEN051 Rising Sun Slash SR	.15	.25

2015 Yu-Gi-Oh The Secret Forces 1st Edition

COMPLETE SET (60)	80.00	100.00
BOOSTER BOX (24 PACKS)	80.00	100.00
BOOSTER PACK (9 CARDS)	4.00	5.00
UNLISTED SR	.40	1.00
UNLISTED R		
RELEASED ON FEBRUARY 13, 2015		
THSFEN001 Mayosenju Daibak SCR	3.50	4.15
THSFEN002 Yosenju Misak SCR	.15	.25
THSFEN003 Yosenju Kama 1 SCR	.75	1.00
THSFEN004 Yosenju Kama 2 SCR	.80	1.00
THSFEN005 Yosenju Kama 3 SCR	.75	1.15
THSFEN006 Yosenju Shinchu L SR	.10	.20
THSFEN007 Yosenju Shinchu R SR	.15	.25
THSFEN008 Yosen Training Grounds SR	.05	.15
THSFEN009 Yosenjus' Secret Move SR	.15	.25
THSFEN010 Shurit, Strategist of the Nekroz SR	.15	.25
THSFEN011 Great Sorcerer of the Nekroz SR	.05	.15
THSFEN012 Exa, Enforcer of the Nekroz SR	.05	.15
THSFEN013 Nekroz of Clausolas SCR	.50	.75
THSFEN014 Nekroz of Brionac SCR	10.00	12.00
THSFEN015 Nekroz of Trishula SCR	14.00	16.00
THSFEN016 Nekroz of Unicore SCR	.50	.75
THSFEN017 Nekroz of Valkyrus SCR	25.00	28.00
THSFEN018 Nekroz of Catastor SCR	.20	.30
THSFEN019 Nekroz of Decisive Armor SCR	.20	.30
THSFEN020 Nekroz Mirror SCR	.30	.50
THSFEN021 Nekroz Kaleidoscope SCR	1.00	1.50
THSFEN022 Ritual Beast Tamer Lara SCR	.40	.60
THSFEN023 Ritual Beast Tamer Elder SCR	1.25	1.75
THSFEN024 Ritual Beast Tamer Wen SCR	.30	.50
THSFEN025 Spiritual Beast Apelio SR	.60	1.00
THSFEN026 Spiritual Beast Pettlephin SR	.05	.15
THSFEN027 Spiritual Beast Cannahawk SR	.20	.30
THSFEN028 Ritual Beast Ulti-Apelio SCR	1.75	2.15
THSFEN029 Ritual Beast Ulti-Pettlephin SCR	.75	1.15
THSFEN030 Ritual Beast Ulti-Cannahawk SCR	.30	.50
THSFEN031 Ritual Beast's Bond SR	.05	.15
THSFEN032 Ritual Beast Steeds SR	.25	.40
THSFEN033 Manju of the Ten Thousand Hands SR	5.00	5.75
THSFEN034 Necro Gardna SR	.05	.15
THSFEN035 Armageddon Knight SR	.60	1.00
THSFEN036 Djinn Releaser of Rituals SR	.05	.15
THSFEN037 Djinn Presider of Rituals SR	.05	.15
THSFEN038 Djinn Cursenchanter of Rituals SR	.05	.15
THSFEN039 Djinn Prognosticator of Rituals SR	.05	.15
THSFEN040 Djinn Disserere of Rituals SR	.15	.25
THSFEN041 Gishki Chain SR	.05	.15
THSFEN042 Gishki Shadow SR	.05	.15
THSFEN043 Gishki Noellia SR	.05	.15
THSFEN044 Cardcar D SR	.20	.30
THSFEN045 Gishki Vision SR	.05	.15
THSFEN046 Altitude Knight SR	.05	.15
THSFEN047 Abyss Dweller SR	1.00	1.50
THSFEN048 Soul Release SR	.20	.30
THSFEN049 Soul Absorption SR	.10	.20
THSFEN050 Ritual Weapon SR	.05	.15
THSFEN051 Burial from a Different Dimension SR	.75	1.25
THSFEN052 Advanced Ritual Art SR	.60	1.00
THSFEN053 Preparation of Rites SR	.20	.30
THSFEN054 Ascending Soul SR	.05	.15
THSFEN055 Ritual Cage SR	.05	.15
THSFEN056 Divine Wind of Mist Valley SR	.05	.15
THSFEN057 Fire Formation - Tenki SR	1.25	1.75
THSFEN058 Royal Decree SR	1.00	1.50
THSFEN059 Vanity's Emptiness SR	2.00	2.75
THSFEN060 Aquamirror Cycle SR	.05	.15

2015 Yu-Gi-Oh World Superstars

COMPLETE SET (52)	55.00	70.00
BOOSTER BOX (24 PACKS)	40.00	60.00
BOOSTER PACK (9 CARDS)	3.00	4.00
RELEASED ON APRIL 17, 2015		
WSUPEN001 Chronomaly Nebra Disk SCR	.40	.60
WSUPEN002 Number 36: Chronomaly Chateau Huyuk SR	.05	.15
WSUPEN003 Heraldic Beast Amphisbaena SR	.10	.20
WSUPEN004 Number 18: Heraldry Patriarch SR	.15	.25
WSUPEN005 Augmented Heraldry SR	.05	.15
WSUPEN006 Gagaga Sister SCR	.60	1.00
WSUPEN007 Number 55: Gogogo Goliath SR	.15	.25
WSUPEN008 Dodododraw SR	.05	.15
WSUPEN009 Galaxy-Eyes Cloudragon SR	.30	.50
WSUPEN010 Galaxy Soldier SCR	23.00	28.00
WSUPEN011 Photon Stream of Destruction SR	.05	.15
WSUPEN012 Tachyon Transmigration SCR	.75	1.00
WSUPEN013 Battlin' Boxer Shadow SR	.05	.15
WSUPEN014 Number 79: Battlin' Boxer Nova Kaiser SR	.20	.30
WSUPEN015 Jolt Counter SR	.05	.15
WSUPEN016 Heroic Challenger - Assault Halberd SR	.30	.50
WSUPEN017 Heroic Challenger - Thousand Blades SR	.40	.60
WSUPEN018 Star Seraph Scepter SCR	1.25	1.75
WSUPEN019 Star Seraph Scale SR	.05	.15
WSUPEN020 Star Seraph Sovereignty SCR	10.00	12.00
WSUPEN021 Numeral Hunter SCR	.15	.25
WSUPEN022 Number 86: Heroic Champion - Rhongomyniad SCR	.75	1.00
WSUPEN023 Humhumming the Key Djinn SR	.05	.15
WSUPEN024 Onomatopia SCR	.10	.20
WSUPEN025 Marshalling Field SCR	.10	.20
WSUPEN026 Number F0: Utopic Future SCR	3.00	3.50
WSUPEN027 Gagaga Samurai SR	.25	.40
WSUPEN028 Gagaga Mancer SR	.05	.15
WSUPEN029 Guard Go! SR	.05	.15
WSUPEN030 Hi-Five the Sky SCR	.15	.25
WSUPEN031 The Door of Destiny SCR	.10	.20
WSUPEN032 Elemental HERO Blazeman SCR	3.00	3.50
WSUPEN033 Naturia Gaiastrio SR	.05	.15
WSUPEN034 Mecha Phantom Beast Jaculuslan SR	.05	.15
WSUPEN035 Ghostrick Angel of Mischief SR	.60	1.00
WSUPEN036 Flowerbot SR	.05	.15
WSUPEN037 Humpty Grumpty SR	.05	.15
WSUPEN038 Dragoroar SR	.05	.15
WSUPEN039 Planckton SR	.05	.15
WSUPEN040 Guerilla Kite SR	.05	.15
WSUPEN041 Wattsychic Fighter SR	.05	.15
WSUPEN042 Earthshattering Event SCR	.10	.20
WSUPEN043 Ghostrick Break SR	.05	.15
WSUPEN044 P.M. Captor SR	.05	.15
WSUPEN045 Spiritual Whisper SR	.05	.15
WSUPEN046 Xyz-Raypierce SR	.05	.15
WSUPEN047 Heavy Knight of the Flame SR	.05	.15
WSUPEN048 BOXer SR	.05	.15
WSUPEN049 Kabuki Dragon SR	.05	.15
WSUPEN050 Pendulum Impenetrable SCR	.30	.50
WSUPEN051 Legendary Dragon of White SCR	4.50	5.50
WSUPEN052 Legendary Magician of Dark SCR	4.25	5.25

2015 Yu-Gi-Oh Dragons of Legend 2 First Edition

COMPLETE SET (45)	80.00	100.00
BOOSTER BOX (24 PACKS)	60.00	80.00
BOOSTER PACK (9 CARDS)	3.00	4.00
RELEASED ON JULY 17, 2015		
DRL2EN001 Timaeus the Knight of Destiny SCR	.20	.30
DRL2EN002 Legendary Knight Critias SCR	.20	.30
DRL2EN003 Doom Virus Dragon SCR	8.50	10.00
DRL2EN004 Tyrant Burst Dragon SCR	.40	.60
DRL2EN005 Mirror Force Dragon SCR	13.00	15.00
DRL2EN006 The Fang of Critias SCR	3.50	5.00
DRL2EN007 Tyrant Wing SR	.15	.25
DRL2EN008 Legendary Knight Hermos SCR	.15	.25
DRL2EN009 Time Magic Hammer SCR	.15	.25
DRL2EN010 Rocket Hermos Cannon SCR	.15	.25
DRL2EN011 Goddess Bow SCR	.15	.25
DRL2EN012 Red-Eyes Black Dragon Sword SCR	.60	1.00
DRL2EN013 The Claw of Hermos SCR	5.50	6.50
DRL2EN014 Roulette Spider SR	.05	.15
DRL2EN015 Double Magical Arm Bind SR	.05	.15
DRL2EN016 Lord of the Red SCR	1.25	1.75
DRL2EN017 Red-Eyes Transmigration SR	.15	.25
DRL2EN018 Paladin of Dark Dragon SCR	.75	1.00
DRL2EN019 Dark Dragon Ritual SR	.20	.30
DRL2EN020 Red-Eyes Spirit SR	1.00	1.25
DRL2EN021 Red-Eyes Burn SR	.20	.30
DRL2EN022 Toon Ancient Gear Golem SR	.60	1.00
DRL2EN023 Toon Kingdom SCR	24.00	26.00
DRL2EN024 Toon Rollback SR	.20	.30
DRL2EN025 Shadow Toon SR	.40	.60
DRL2EN026 Comic Hand SCR	1.50	2.00
DRL2EN027 Mimicat SCR	15.00	17.00
DRL2EN028 Toon Mask SCR	1.00	1.25
DRL2EN029 Toon Briefcase SR	.40	.60
DRL2EN030 Prediction Princess Coinorma SR	.15	.25
DRL2EN031 Prediction Princess Petalelf SR	.05	.15
DRL2EN032 Prediction Princess Astromorrigan SR	.05	.15
DRL2EN033 Prediction Princess Arrowsylph SR	.05	.15
DRL2EN034 Prediction Princess Crystaldine SR	.05	.15
DRL2EN035 Prediction Princess Tarotrei SCR	3.00	3.75
DRL2EN036 Prediction Ritual SR	.25	.40
DRL2EN037 Black Cat-astrophe SR	.05	.15
DRL2EN038 Reverse Reuse SR	.05	.15
DRL2EN039 Aquaactress Tetra SR	.05	.15
DRL2EN040 Aquaactress Guppy SR	.05	.15
DRL2EN041 Aquaactress Arowana SR	.05	.15
DRL2EN042 Aquarium Stage SR	.05	.15
DRL2EN043 Aquarium Set SR	.05	.15
DRL2EN044 Aquarium Lighting SR	.05	.15
DRL2EN045 Aqua Story - Urashima SR	.05	.15

2016 Yu-Gi-Oh Wing Raiders 1st Edition

COMPLETE SET (60)	110.00	140.00
BOOSTER BOX	50.00	75.00
BOOSTER PACK	2.00	5.00
UNLISTED C	.10	.25
UNLISTED R	.10	.30
RELEASED ON FEBRUARY 12, 2016		
WIRAEN001 The Phantom Knights of Ancient Cloak UR	7.00	10.00
WIRAEN002 The Phantom Knights of Silent Boots SR	.50	.80
WIRAEN003 The Phantom Knights of Ragged Gloves C	.10	.25
WIRAEN004 The Phantom Knights of Cloven Helm R	.10	.30
WIRAEN005 The Phantom Knights of Fragile Armor SR	.10	.20
WIRAEN006 The Phantom Knights of Break Sword SCR	40.00	45.00
WIRAEN007 Dark Rebellion Xyz Dragon R	1.00	1.50
WIRAEN008 Phantom Knights' Spear R	.10	.30
WIRAEN009 Phantom Knights' Fog Blade UR	10.00	15.00
WIRAEN010 Phantom Knights' Sword R	.10	.30
WIRAEN011 Phantom Knights' Wing C	.10	.25
WIRAEN012 The Phantom Knights of Shadow Veil C	.10	.25
WIRAEN013 Booby Trap E SR	.20	.35
WIRAEN014 Raidraptor - Necro Vulture SR	.10	.20
WIRAEN015 Raidraptor - Last Strix C	.10	.25
WIRAEN016 Raidraptor - Vanishing Lanius C	.10	.25
WIRAEN017 Raidraptor - Fuzzy Lanius C	.10	.25
WIRAEN018 Raidraptor - Singing Lanius C	.10	.25
WIRAEN019 Raidraptor - Sharp Lanius C	.10	.25
WIRAEN020 Raidraptor - Mimicry Lanius C	.10	.25
WIRAEN021 Raidraptor - Tribute Lanius UR	3.00	4.00
WIRAEN022 Raidraptor - Force Strix SCR	14.00	17.00
WIRAEN023 Raidraptor - Revolution Falcon C	.10	.25
WIRAEN024 Raidraptor - Satellite Cannon Falcon SCR	8.00	10.00
WIRAEN025 Raidraptor - Call UR	1.00	1.50
WIRAEN026 Raidraptor - Nest C	.10	.25
WIRAEN027 Rank-Up-Magic Doom Double Force R	.10	.30
WIRAEN028 Rank-Up-Magic Soul Shave Force SR	.20	.35
WIRAEN029 Raidraptor - Readiness C	.10	.25
WIRAEN030 Super Quantum Red Layer UR	7.00	8.50
WIRAEN031 Super Quantum Green Layer SR	.20	.35
WIRAEN032 Super Quantum Blue Layer R	.30	.50
WIRAEN033 Super Quantal Fairy Alphan C	.10	.25
WIRAEN034 Super Quantal Mech Beast Grampulse R	.60	1.00
WIRAEN035 Super Quantal Mech Beast Aeroboros SR	.20	.30
WIRAEN036 Super Quantal Mech Beast Magnaliger UR	1.00	1.50
WIRAEN037 Super Quantal Mech King Great Magnus SCR	1.75	2.25
WIRAEN038 Super Quantal Mech Ship Magnacarrier R	.10	.30
WIRAEN039 Super Quantal Mech Sword - Magnaslayer C	.10	.25
WIRAEN040 Crane Crane C	.10	.25
WIRAEN041 Harpie Harpist R	.10	.30
WIRAEN042 Gem-Knight Pearl C	.10	.25
WIRAEN043 Gagaga Cowboy R	.30	.50
WIRAEN044 Zubaba General C	.10	.25
WIRAEN045 Number 66: Master Key Beetle C	.10	.25
WIRAEN046 Ghostrick Alucard R	.30	.50
WIRAEN047 Number 101: Silent Honor ARK SR	1.75	2.15
WIRAEN048 Bujinki Amaterasu C	.10	.25
WIRAEN049 Cairngorgon, Antiluminescent Knight C	.10	.25
WIRAEN050 Number 52: Diamond Crab King SCR	1.75	2.25
WIRAEN051 Mystical Space Typhoon C	.30	.50
WIRAEN052 Reinforcement of the Army C	.10	.25
WIRAEN053 Forbidden Chalice C	.10	.25
WIRAEN054 Swallow's Nest R	.10	.30
WIRAEN055 Rank-Up-Magic Astral Force C	.10	.25
WIRAEN056 Bottomless Trap Hole C	.40	.60
WIRAEN057 Call of the Haunted C	.10	.25
WIRAEN058 Icarus Attack SR	.20	.35
WIRAEN059 Needlebug Nest C	.10	.25
WIRAEN060 Xyz Reborn SR	.40	.60

2016 Yu-Gi-Oh Millennium Pack 1st Edition

COMPLETE SET (48)	30.00	40.00
BOOSTER BOX (36 PACKS)	40.00	50.00
BOOSTER PACK (5 CARDS)	1.00	1.50
RELEASED ON APRIL 15, 2016		
MIL1EN001 The Winged Dragon of Ra - Immortal Phoenix UR	3.00	3.50
MIL1EN002 Curse of Dragonfire UR	.25	.40
MIL1EN003 Holding Arms SR	.25	.40
MIL1EN004 Holding Legs SR	.75	1.00
MIL1EN005 Gandora the Dragon of Destruction C	.10	.15
MIL1EN006 Gilford the Lightning C	.10	.15
MIL1EN007 Exodius the Ultimate Forbidden Lord C	.10	.15
MIL1EN008 Relinquished C	.10	.15
MIL1EN009 Dark Master - Zorc C	.10	.15
MIL1EN010 Sky Galloping Gaia the Dragon Champion SR	.25	.40
MIL1EN011 B. Skull Dragon C	.10	.15
MIL1EN012 Five-Headed Dragon C	.20	.30
MIL1EN013 Rebellion UR	.30	.50
MIL1EN014 Card of Demise UR	20.00	23.00
MIL1EN015 Left Arm Offering SR	2.00	2.50
MIL1EN016 The True Name SR	.40	.75
MIL1EN017 Symbol of Friendship R	.10	.15

Card	Low	High
MIL1EN018 Shrink C	.10	.15
MIL1EN019 Scapegoat C	.10	.15
MIL1EN020 Black Illusion Ritual C	.10	.15
MIL1EN021 Contract with the Dark Master C	.10	.15
MIL1EN022 Trap Hole of Spikes SR	.60	1.00
MIL1EN023 Ring of Destruction C	.20	.30
MIL1EN024 Nightmare Wheel C	.10	.15
MIL1EN025 Celtic Guardian R	.10	.15
MIL1EN026 Gaia The Fierce Knight R	.10	.15
MIL1EN027 Red-Eyes B. Dragon C	.20	.30
MIL1EN028 Summoned Skull C	.10	.15
MIL1EN029 La Jinn the Mystical Genie of the Lamp C	.10	.15
MIL1EN030 Launcher Spider C	.10	.15
MIL1EN031 Tiger Axe C	.10	.15
MIL1EN032 Vorse Raider C	.10	.15
MIL1EN033 Pendulum Machine C	.10	.15
MIL1EN034 Kuriboh C	.10	.15
MIL1EN035 Red-Eyes Black Metal Dragon C	.10	.15
MIL1EN036 Panther Warrior R	.10	.15
MIL1EN037 Viser Des C	.10	.15
MIL1EN038 Flame Swordsman R	.10	.15
MIL1EN039 Thousand Dragon R	.10	.15
MIL1EN040 XYZ-Dragon Cannon R	.10	.15
MIL1EN041 Dark Paladin C	.30	.50
MIL1EN042 Toon World C	.10	.15
MIL1EN043 Spiral Spear Strike C	.10	.15
MIL1EN044 Acid Trap Hole R	.10	.15
MIL1EN045 Metalmorph C	.10	.15
MIL1EN046 Widespread Ruin R	.10	.15
MIL1EN047 Crush Card Virus C	.20	.30
MIL1EN048 Kunai with Chain R	.10	.15

2015 Yu-Gi-Oh High-Speed Riders

Card	Low	High
COMPLETE SET (60)	140.00	165.00
BOOSTER BOX (24 PACKS)	55.00	75.00
BOOSTER PACK	3.00	5.00
RELEASED ON OCTOBER 2, 2015		
HSRDEN001 Speedroid Terrortop SR	12.00	15.00
HSRDEN002 Speedroid Tri-Eyed Dice C	.05	.15
HSRDEN003 Speedroid Double Yoyo C	.05	.15
HSRDEN004 Speedroid Razorang R	.05	.15
HSRDEN005 Speedroid Menko C	.40	.60
HSRDEN006 Speedroid Taketomborg SR	.75	1.25
HSRDEN007 Speedroid Ohajikid R	.15	.25
HSRDEN008 Speedroid Red-Eyed Dice SR	.25	.40
HSRDEN009 Hi-Speedroid Kendama R	.10	.20
HSRDEN010 Hi-Speedroid Chanbara SCR	6.00	7.00
HSRDEN011 Speed Recovery SR	.20	.35
HSRDEN012 Shock Surprise R	.10	.20
HSRDEN013 Synchro Cracker C	.05	.15
HSRDEN014 Dice Roll Battle R	.05	.15
HSRDEN015 Red Sprinter SR	.20	.35
HSRDEN016 Red Resonator C	.75	1.00
HSRDEN017 Synkron Resonator C	.15	.25
HSRDEN018 Chain Resonator C	.05	.15
HSRDEN019 Mirror Resonator SR	.10	.20
HSRDEN020 Dark Resonator C	.05	.15
HSRDEN021 Vice Dragon C	.05	.15
HSRDEN022 Red Wyvern SCR	4.50	5.50
HSRDEN023 Red Dragon Archfiend C	.15	.25
HSRDEN024 Red Nova Dragon R	.30	.50
HSRDEN025 Resonator Call C	.05	.15
HSRDEN026 Red Cocoon C	.05	.15
HSRDEN027 Red Carpet R	.05	.15
HSRDEN028 PSY-Frame Driver R	.20	.30
HSRDEN029 PSY-Framegear Alpha C	.05	.15
HSRDEN030 PSY-Framegear Beta UR	3.25	4.00
HSRDEN031 PSY-Framegear Gamma UR	3.00	3.75
HSRDEN032 PSY-Framegear Delta R	.25	.35
HSRDEN033 PSY-Framegear Epsilon C	.05	.15
HSRDEN034 PSY-Framelord Zeta SR	.20	.30
HSRDEN035 PSY-Framelord Omega SCR	53.00	56.00
HSRDEN036 PSY-Frame Circuit R	.25	.35
HSRDEN037 PSY-Frame Overload R	.20	.30
HSRDEN038 Goyo Chaser UR	.20	.30
HSRDEN039 Goyo Predator UR	.20	.30
HSRDEN040 Hot Red Dragon Archfiend SR	1.00	1.25
HSRDEN041 Hot Red Dragon Archfiend Abyss UR	8.00	10.00
HSRDEN042 Hot Red Dragon Archfiend Bane SCR	7.75	9.00
HSRDEN043 Stardust Spark Dragon SR	3.00	3.75
HSRDEN044 Black Rose Moonlight Dragon SR	5.00	6.00
HSRDEN045 Expressroid C	.05	.15
HSRDEN046 Krebons C	.05	.15
HSRDEN047 Armoroid C	.05	.15
HSRDEN048 Silent Psychic Wizard C	.05	.15
HSRDEN049 Serene Psychic Witch C	.05	.15
HSRDEN050 Hushed Psychic Cleric C	.05	.15
HSRDEN051 Cardcar D C	.20	.30
HSRDEN052 Trishula, Dragon of the Ice Barrier SCR	24.00	28.00
HSRDEN053 Mystical Space Typhoon C	.50	.75
HSRDEN054 Emergency Teleport UR	1.50	2.00
HSRDEN055 Psychokinesis C	.05	.15
HSRDEN056 Pot of Duality R	1.25	1.75
HSRDEN057 Future Glow C	.05	.15
HSRDEN058 Compulsory Evacuation Device C	.20	.30
HSRDEN059 Supercharge C	.05	.15
HSRDEN060 Psychic Overload C	.05	.15

2016 Yu-Gi-Oh Dragons of Legend Unleashed First Edition

Card	Low	High
COMPLETE SET (73 CARDS)	60.00	90.00
BOOSTER BOX (24 PACKS)	60.00	75.00
BOOSTER PACK (5 CARDS)	2.50	5.00
RELEASED ON AUGUST 19, 2016		
DRL3EN001 OddEyes Mirage Dragon SCR	1.75	2.25
DRL3EN002 Performapal Uni UR	.10	.30
DRL3EN003 Performapal Corn UR	.10	.30
DRL3EN004 Raidraptor Napalm Dragonius UR	.10	.30
DRL3EN005 Raidraptor Blade Burner Falcon UR	.10	.30
DRL3EN006 The Tripper Mercury SCR	.20	.35
DRL3EN007 The Blazing Mars SCR	.20	.35
DRL3EN008 The Grand Jupiter SCR	.20	.35
DRL3EN009 The Despair Uranus SCR	.20	.35
DRL3EN010 The Suppression Pluto SCR	.20	.35
DRL3EN011 Cyber Petit Angel UR	.40	.75
DRL3EN012 Cyber Angel Benten SCR	7.50	8.50
DRL3EN013 Cyber Angel Idaten SCR	2.25	3.25
DRL3EN014 Cyber Angel Dakini SCR	1.00	1.50
DRL3EN015 Machine Angel Ritual UR	.40	.60
DRL3EN016 Ritual Sanctuary SCR	12.00	15.00
DRL3EN017 Red Nova SCR	.25	.40
DRL3EN018 Zushin the Sleeping Giant UR	.10	.30
DRL3EN019 HandHolding Genie UR	.10	.30
DRL3EN020 Scrum Force UR	.10	.30
DRL3EN021 Number 100 Numeron Dragon SCR	.75	1.25
DRL3EN022 Number 24 Dragulas the Vampiric Dragon SCR	.75	1.25
DRL3EN023 Number 45 Crumble Logos the Prophet of Demolition SCR	1.00	1.50
DRL3EN024 Number 51 Finisher the Strong Arm SCR	.20	.35
DRL3EN025 Number 59 Crooked Cook UR	.30	.50
DRL3EN026 Number 78 Number Archive UR	.10	.30
DRL3EN027 Number 98 Antitopian SCR	.60	1.00
DRL3EN028 Cipher Wing UR	.10	.30
DRL3EN029 GalaxyEyes Cipher Dragon SCR	7.50	9.00
DRL3EN030 Galaxy Stealth Dragon SCR	.60	1.00
DRL3EN031 Flower Cardian Pine SCR	.40	.60
DRL3EN032 Flower Cardian Zebra Grass UR	.10	.30
DRL3EN033 Flower Cardian Willow UR	.10	.30
DRL3EN034 Flower Cardian Paulownia UR	.10	.30
DRL3EN035 Flower Cardian Pine with Crane UR	.10	.30
DRL3EN036 Flower Cardian Zebra Grass with Moon UR	.10	.30
DRL3EN037 Flower Cardian Willow with Calligrapher UR	.10	.30
DRL3EN038 Flower Cardian Paulownia with Phoenix UR	.10	.30
DRL3EN039 Flower Cardian Lightshower SCR	.40	.75
DRL3EN040 Flower Gathering UR	.10	.30
DRL3EN041 Legendary Knight Timaeus UR	.35	.50
DRL3EN042 Kuribandit UR	.40	.75
DRL3EN043 Amulet Dragon UR	1.25	1.75
DRL3EN044 Dark Magician Girl the Dragon Knight UR	2.75	3.50
DRL3EN045 The Eye of Timaeus UR	4.25	5.50
DRL3EN046 Legend of Heart UR	.40	.60
DRL3EN047 Berserker Soul UR	.10	.30
DRL3EN048 Relay Soul UR	.10	.30
DRL3EN049 Guardian Dreadscythe UR	.10	.30
DRL3EN050 Reaper Scythe Dreadscythe UR	.10	.30
DRL3EN051 Soul Charge UR	1.50	2.25
DRL3EN052 Ras Disciple UR	.60	1.00
DRL3EN053 Mound of the Bound Creator UR	.10	.30
DRL3EN054 Wiretap UR	.10	.30
DRL3EN055 Timaeus the Knight of Destiny UR	.30	.50
DRL3EN056 Legendary Knight Critias UR	.10	.30
DRL3EN057 Doom Virus Dragon UR	.60	1.00
DRL3EN058 Tyrant Burst Dragon UR	2.00	3.00
DRL3EN059 Mirror Force Dragon UR	.75	1.25
DRL3EN060 The Fang of Critias UR	.75	1.25
DRL3EN061 Tyrant Wing UR	.10	.30
DRL3EN062 Legendary Knight Hermos UR	.10	.30
DRL3EN063 Time Magic Hammer UR	.10	.30
DRL3EN064 Rocket Hermos Cannon UR	.10	.30
DRL3EN065 Goddess Bow UR	.10	.30
DRL3EN066 RedEyes Black Dragon Sword UR	.10	.30
DRL3EN067 The Claw of Hermos UR	.50	.75
DRL3EN068 Lord of the Red UR	.10	.30
DRL3EN069 RedEyes Transmigration UR	.10	.30
DRL3EN070 The Seal of Orichalcos UR	.25	.40
DRL3EN071 Snow Plow Hustle Rustle UR	.10	.30
DRL3EN072 Night Express Knight UR	2.25	3.25
DRL3EN073 Special Schedule UR	.50	.80

2004 Yu-Gi-Oh Dark Beginnings 1

Card	Low	High
COMPLETE SET (250)	150.00	300.00
BOOSTER BOX (24 PACKS)	150.00	300.00
BOOSTER PACK (13 CARDS)	2.50	6.00
RELEASED ON OCTOBER 27, 2004		
DB1EN001 Penguin Knight	.10	.25
DB1EN002 Axe of Despair R	.40	1.00
DB1EN003 Black Pendant R	.25	.60
DB1EN004 Horn of Light	.10	.25
DB1EN005 Malevolent Nuzzler	.10	.25
DB1EN006 Spellbinding Circle R	.25	.60
DB1EN007 Electric Snake	.10	.25
DB1EN008 Ameba	.10	.25
DB1EN009 Maha Vailo	.10	.25
DB1EN010 Minar	.10	.25
DB1EN011 Griggle	.10	.25
DB1EN012 Hiro's Shadow Scout	.10	.25
DB1EN013 Invader of the Throne	.10	.25
DB1EN014 Slot Machine	.10	.25
DB1EN015 Relinquished SR	.40	1.00
DB1EN016 Red Archery Girl	.10	.25
DB1EN017 Gravekeeper's Servant	.75	1.50
DB1EN018 Upstart Goblin	2.50	6.00
DB1EN019 Toll	.10	.25
DB1EN020 Final Destiny	.10	.25
DB1EN021 Snatch Steal UR	2.50	4.00
DB1EN022 Chorus of Sanctuary	.10	.25
DB1EN023 Confiscation	.10	.25
DB1EN024 Delinquent Duo SR	5.00	12.00
DB1EN025 Fairy's Hand Mirror	.10	.25
DB1EN026 Tailor of the Fickle	.10	.25
DB1EN027 Rush Recklessly	.10	.25
DB1EN028 The Reliable Guardian	.10	.25
DB1EN029 The Forceful Sentry R	.25	.60
DB1EN030 Chain Energy	.10	.25
DB1EN031 Mystical Space Typhoon SR	3.00	8.00
DB1EN032 Giant Trunade R	.25	.60
DB1EN033 Painful Choice	.10	.25
DB1EN034 Horn of the Unicorn	.10	.25
DB1EN035 Labyrinth Wall	.10	.25
DB1EN036 Eternal Rest	.10	.25
DB1EN037 Megamorph SR	.75	2.00
DB1EN038 Manga Ryu-Ran	.10	.25
DB1EN039 Toon Mermaid	1.50	4.00
DB1EN040 Toon Summoned Skull R	.50	1.00
DB1EN041 Hyozanryu	.10	.25
DB1EN042 Toon World	.10	.25
DB1EN043 Cyber Jar R	.40	1.00
DB1EN044 Banisher of the Light	.25	.60
DB1EN045 Giant Rat R	.25	.60
DB1EN046 Senju of the Thousand Hands	.25	.60
DB1EN047 UFO Turtle	.10	.25
DB1EN048 Flash Assailant	.10	.25
DB1EN049 Karate Man	.10	.25
DB1EN050 Giant Germ	.40	1.00
DB1EN051 Nimble Momonga R	.40	1.00
DB1EN052 Shining Angel	.10	.25
DB1EN053 Mother Grizzly	.10	.25
DB1EN054 Flying Kamakiri #1	.10	.25
DB1EN055 Ceremonial Bell	.10	.25
DB1EN056 Sonic Bird	.10	.25
DB1EN057 Mystic Tomato R	.40	1.00
DB1EN058 Kotodama	.10	.25
DB1EN059 Gaia Power	.10	.25
DB1EN060 Umiiruka	.10	.25
DB1EN061 Molten Destruction	.10	.25
DB1EN062 Rising Air Current	.20	.50
DB1EN063 Luminous Spark	.25	.60
DB1EN064 Mystic Plasma Zone	.10	.25
DB1EN065 Messenger of Peace	.75	2.00
DB1EN066 Blue-Eyes Toon Dragon SR	2.00	5.00
DB1EN067 Jinzo UR	3.00	8.00
DB1EN068 Parasite Paracide	.10	.25
DB1EN069 Lightforce Sword	.10	.25
DB1EN070 Chain Destruction	.40	1.00
DB1EN071 Time Seal	.10	.25
DB1EN072 Graverobber	.10	.25
DB1EN073 Gift of the Mystical Elf	.10	.25
DB1EN074 The Eye of Truth	.10	.25
DB1EN075 Dust Tornado R	.25	.60
DB1EN076 Call Of The Haunted SR	1.25	3.00
DB1EN077 Enchanted Javelin	.10	.25
DB1EN078 Mirror Wall	.10	.30
DB1EN079 Numinous Healer	.10	.25
DB1EN080 Forced Requisition	.25	.60
DB1EN081 DNA Surgery	1.25	3.00
DB1EN082 Backup Soldier	.10	.25
DB1EN083 Ceasefire SR	.25	.60
DB1EN084 Light of Intervention	.10	.25
DB1EN085 Respect Play	.10	.25
DB1EN086 Imperial Order UR	.60	1.50
DB1EN087 Magical Hats R	.50	1.25
DB1EN088 Nobleman of Crossout SR	.75	2.00
DB1EN089 Nobleman of Extermination	.10	.25
DB1EN090 The Shallow Grave	.40	1.00
DB1EN091 Premature Burial SR	2.50	1.00
DB1EN092 Morphing Jar #2 R	.40	2.00
DB1EN093 Kiseitai	.10	.25
DB1EN094 Harpie's Brother	.10	.25
DB1EN095 Buster Blader SR	1.25	3.00
DB1EN096 Dark Sage UR	3.00	10.00
DB1EN097 Big Shield Guardna UR	1.25	3.00
DB1EN098 Blue-Eyes White Dragon UR	1.50	4.00
DB1EN099 Hitotsu-Me Giant	.10	.25
DB1EN100 Flame Swordsman R	.25	.60
DB1EN101 Skull Servant	.40	1.00
DB1EN102 Dark Magician UR	1.00	2.50
DB1EN103 Gaia The Fierce Knight R	.25	.60
DB1EN104 Celtic Guardian	.10	.25
DB1EN105 Mammoth Graveyard	.10	.25
DB1EN106 Silver Fang	.10	.25
DB1EN107 Flame Manipulator	.10	.25
DB1EN108 Dark King of the Abyss	.10	.25
DB1EN109 Aqua Madoor	.10	.25
DB1EN110 Masaki the Legendary Swordsman	.10	.25
DB1EN111 Dragon Capture Jar	.10	.25
DB1EN112 Umi	.10	.25
DB1EN113 Dark Hole SR	1.25	3.00
DB1EN114 Raigeki UR	20.00	40.00
DB1EN115 Red Medicine	.10	.25
DB1EN116 Hinotama	.10	.25
DB1EN117 Fissure R	.25	.60
DB1EN118 Trap Hole R	.25	.60
DB1EN119 Polymerization	.40	6.00
DB1EN120 Mystical Elf	.10	.25
DB1EN121 Beaver Warrior	.10	.25
DB1EN122 Gaia the Dragon Champion R	.40	1.00
DB1EN123 Curse of Dragon	.10	.25
DB1EN124 Giant Soldier of Stone	.10	.25
DB1EN125 Uraby	.10	.25
DB1EN126 Red-Eyes B. Dragon SR	.75	2.00
DB1EN127 Reaper of the Cards	.10	.25
DB1EN128 Stop Defense	.10	.25
DB1EN129 Swords of Revealing Light SR	1.25	3.00
DB1EN130 Armed Ninja	.10	.25
DB1EN131 Man-Eater Bug R	.40	1.00
DB1EN132 Hane-Hane	.10	.25
DB1EN133 Monster Reborn UR	2.00	15.00
DB1EN134 Pot of Greed SR	3.00	8.00
DB1EN135 Right Leg of the Forbidden One	2.50	6.00
DB1EN136 Left Leg of the Forbidden One	2.00	5.00
DB1EN137 Right Arm of the Forbidden One	2.00	5.00
DB1EN138 Left Arm of the Forbidden One	2.00	5.00
DB1EN139 Exodia the Forbidden One UR	3.00	8.00
DB1EN140 Feral Imp	.10	.25
DB1EN141 Winged Dragon	.10	.25
DB1EN142 Summoned Skull SR	.75	2.00
DB1EN143 Armored Lizard	.10	.25
DB1EN144 Larvae Moth	.10	.25
DB1EN145 Harpie Lady	.10	.25
DB1EN146 Harpie Lady Sisters	.10	.25
DB1EN147 Kojikocy	.10	.25
DB1EN148 Cocoon of Evolution	.25	.60
DB1EN149 Armored Zombie	.10	.25
DB1EN150 Mask of Darkness	.10	.25
DB1EN151 White Magical Hat	.10	.25
DB1EN152 Big Eye	.10	.25
DB1EN153 B. Skull Dragon SR	2.00	10.00
DB1EN154 Masked Sorcerer	.10	.25
DB1EN155 Petit Moth	.10	.25
DB1EN156 Elegant Egotist	.40	1.00
DB1EN157 Sanga of the Thunder	.75	2.00
DB1EN158 Kazejin	.10	.25
DB1EN159 Suijin	.25	.60
DB1EN160 Mystic Lamp	.10	.25
DB1EN161 Blast Juggler	.10	.25
DB1EN162 Jinzo #7	.10	.25
DB1EN163 Magician of Faith R	.40	1.00
DB1EN164 Fake Trap	.10	.25
DB1EN165 Tribute to The Doomed R	.25	.60
DB1EN166 Soul Release	.25	.60
DB1EN167 The Cheerful Coffin	.40	1.00
DB1EN168 Change of Heart UR	2.00	4.00
DB1EN169 Makyura the Destructor SR	1.25	3.00
DB1EN170 Exchange SR	.75	2.00
DB1EN171 Minor Goblin Official	.10	.25
DB1EN172 Gamble	.10	.25
DB1EN173 Attack and Receive	.10	.25
DB1EN174 Solemn Wishes	2.00	5.00
DB1EN175 Skull Invitation	.10	.25
DB1EN176 Bubonic Vermin	.10	.25
DB1EN177 Burning Land	.10	.25
DB1EN178 Fairy Meteor Crush R	.25	.60
DB1EN179 Limiter Removal R	.25	.60
DB1EN180 Rain of Mercy	.10	.25
DB1EN181 Monster Recovery	.10	.25
DB1EN182 Shift	.10	.25
DB1EN183 Dimensionhole	.10	.25
DB1EN184 Ground Collapse	.10	.25
DB1EN185 Magic Drain R	.25	.60
DB1EN186 Infinite Dismissal	.10	.25
DB1EN187 Gravity Bind	.10	.25
DB1EN188 Type Zero Magic Crusher	.10	.25
DB1EN189 Shadow of Eyes R	.25	.60
DB1EN190 The Legendary Fisherman R	.40	4.00
DB1EN191 Sword Hunter	.10	.25
DB1EN192 Drill Bug	.10	.25
DB1EN193 Deepsea Warrior	.10	.25
DB1EN194 Thousand-Eyes Idol	.10	.25
DB1EN195 Thousand-Eyes Restrict UR	6.00	15.00
DB1EN196 Hayabusa Knight R	.25	.60
DB1EN197 Bombardment Beetle	.10	.25
DB1EN198 4-Starred Ladybug of Doom	.10	.25
DB1EN199 Gradius	.10	.25
DB1EN200 Red-Moon Baby	.10	.25
DB1EN201 Mad Sword Beast R	.25	.60
DB1EN202 Goblin Attack Force SR	.40	1.00
DB1EN203 The Fiend Megacyber R	.40	2.00
DB1EN204 Gearfried the Iron Knight R	.25	.60
DB1EN205 Insect Barrier	.10	.25
DB1EN206 Swordsman of Landstar	.10	.25
DB1EN207 Humanoid Slime	.10	.25
DB1EN208 Worm Drake	.10	.25
DB1EN209 Humanoid Worm Drake	.10	.25
DB1EN210 Revival Jam	.75	2.00
DB1EN211 Amphibian Beast	.10	.25
DB1EN212 Shining Abyss	.10	.25
DB1EN213 Grand Tiki Elder	.10	.25
DB1EN214 The Masked Beast SR	.40	1.00
DB1EN215 Melchid the Four-Face Beast	.10	.25
DB1EN216 Nuvia the Wicked	.10	.25
DB1EN217 Chosen One	.10	.25
DB1EN218 Mask of Weakness	.10	.25
DB1EN219 Curse of the Masked Beast	.10	.25
DB1EN220 Mask of Dispel	.10	.25
DB1EN221 Mask of Restrict	8.00	1.25
DB1EN222 Mask of the Accursed	.10	.25
DB1EN223 Mask of Brutality	.10	.25
DB1EN224 Return of the Doomed	.10	.25
DB1EN225 Lightning Blade	.10	.25
DB1EN226 Tornado Wall	.10	.25
DB1EN227 Fairy Box	.10	.25
DB1EN228 Torrential Tribute UR	2.00	5.00
DB1EN229 Jam Breeding Machine	.10	.25
DB1EN230 Infinite Cards	1.25	3.00
DB1EN231 Jam Defender	.10	.25
DB1EN232 Card of Safe Return	.25	.60
DB1EN233 Amazoness Archer	.10	.25
DB1EN234 Fire Princess	.10	.25
DB1EN235 Spirit of the Breeze	.10	.25
DB1EN236 Dancing Fairy	.10	.25
DB1EN237 Cure Mermaid	.10	.25
DB1EN238 Hysteric Fairy	.10	.25
DB1EN239 The Forgiving Maiden	.10	.25
DB1EN240 St. Joan	.10	.25
DB1EN241 Marie the Fallen One	.10	.25
DB1EN242 Jar of Greed R	.60	1.50
DB1EN243 Scroll of Bewitchment	.25	.60
DB1EN244 United We Stand UR	2.50	6.00
DB1EN245 Mage Power UR	2.00	5.00
DB1EN246 The Portrait's Secret	.10	.25
DB1EN247 The Gross Ghost of Fled Dreams	.10	.25
DB1EN248 Headless Knight	.10	.25
DB1EN249 Earthbound Spirit	.10	.25
DB1EN250 The Earl of Demise	.10	.25

2005 Yu-Gi-Oh Dark Revelation 1

Card	Low	High
COMPLETE SET (267)	150.00	250.00
BOOSTER BOX (24 PACKS)	70.00	100.00
BOOSTER PACK (13 CARDS)	2.50	6.00
RELEASED ON MARCH 19, 2005		
DR1001 Master Kyonshee C	.20	.75
DR1002 Kabazauls C	.20	.75
DR1003 Inpachi C	.20	.75
DR1004 Dark Jeroid R	.40	1.00
DR1005 Newdoria R	.40	1.00
DR1006 Helpoemer SR	.75	2.00
DR1007 Gravekeeper's Spy C	.20	.75
DR1008 Gravekeeper's Curse C	.20	.75
DR1009 Gravekeeper's Guard C	.20	.75
DR1010 Gravekeeper's Spear Soldier C	.20	.75
DR1011 Gravekeeper's Vassal C	.20	.75
DR1012 Gravekeeper's Watcher C	.20	.75
DR1013 Gravekeeper's Chief R	.40	1.00
DR1014 Gravekeeper's Cannonholder C	.20	.75
DR1015 Gravekeeper's Assailant C	.20	.75
DR1016 A Man with Wdjat C	.20	.75
DR1017 Mystical Knight of Jackal SR	.75	2.00
DR1018 A Cat of Ill Omen C	1.50	4.00
DR1019 Yomi Ship C	.20	.75
DR1020 Winged Sage Falcos C	.20	.75
DR1021 An Owl of Luck C	.20	.75
DR1022 Charm of Shabti C	.20	.75
DR1023 Cobra Jar C	.20	.75
DR1024 Spirit Reaper R	.40	1.00
DR1025 Nightmare Horse C	.20	.75
DR1026 Reaper on the Nightmare R	1.00	2.50
DR1027 Dark Designator C	.20	.75
DR1028 Card Shuffle C	.20	.75
DR1029 Reasoning C	.75	2.00
DR1030 Dark Room of Nightmare C	.20	.75
DR1031 Different Dimension Capsule C	.20	.75
DR1032 Necrovalley SR	.75	2.00
DR1033 Buster Rancher C	.20	.75
DR1034 Hieroglyph Lithograph C	.20	.75
DR1035 Dark Snake Syndrome C	.20	.75
DR1036 Terraforming C	.75	2.00
DR1037 Banner of Courage C	.20	.75
DR1038 Metamorphosis C	.75	2.00
DR1039 Roayl Tribute C	.20	.75
DR1040 Reversal Quiz C	.20	.75
DR1041 Coffin Seller SR	.75	2.00
DR1042 Curse of Aging C	.20	.75
DR1043 Barrel Behind the Door R	.40	1.00
DR1044 Raigeki Break C	.20	.75
DR1045 Narrow Pass C	.20	.75
DR1046 Disturbance Strategy C	.20	.75
DR1047 Trap of Board C	.20	.75
DR1048 Rite of Spirit C	.20	.75
DR1049 Non Aggression Area C	.20	.75
DR1050 D. Tribe C	.20	.75
DR1051 Lava Golem UR	1.50	4.00
DR1052 Byser Shock UR	.75	2.00
DR1053 Question SR	.75	2.00
DR1054 Rope of Life R	.40	1.00
DR1055 Nightmare Wheel UR	1.25	3.00
DR1056 People Running About C	.20	.75
DR1057 Oppressed People C	.20	.75
DR1058 United Resistance C	.20	.75
DR1059 X-Head Cannon R	.40	1.00
DR1060 Y-Dragon Head R	.40	1.00
DR1061 Z-Metal Tank R	.40	1.00
DR1062 Dark Blade C	.20	.75
DR1063 Pitch-Dark Dragon C	.20	.75
DR1064 Kiryu C	.20	.75
DR1065 Decayed Commander C	.20	.75
DR1066 Zombie Tiger C	.20	.75
DR1067 Giant Orc C	.20	.75
DR1068 Second Goblin C	.20	.75
DR1069 Vampire Orchis C	.20	.75
DR1070 Des Dendle C	.20	.75
DR1071 Burning Beast C	.20	.75
DR1072 Freezing Beast C	.20	.75
DR1073 Union Rider C	.20	.75
DR1074 D.D. Crazy Beast C	.20	.75
DR1075 Spell Canceller UR	4.00	10.00
DR1076 Neko Mane King C	.20	.75
DR1077 Helping Robo For Combat C	.20	.75
DR1078 Dimension Jar C	.20	.75
DR1079 Great Phantom Thief C	.20	.75
DR1080 Roulette Barrel C	.20	.75
DR1081 Paladin of White Dragon SR	.75	2.00
DR1082 White Dragon Ritual C	.20	.75
DR1083 Frontline Base C	.20	.75
DR1084 Demotion C	.20	.75
DR1085 Combination Attack C	.20	.75
DR1086 Kaiser Colosseum C	2.50	6.00
DR1087 Autonomous Action Unit C	.20	.75
DR1088 Poison of the Old Man C	.20	.75
DR1089 Ante C	.20	.75
DR1090 Dark Core C	.20	.75
DR1091 Raregold Armor C	.20	.75
DR1092 Metalsilver C	.20	.75
DR1093 Kishido Spirit C	.20	.75
DR1094 Tribute Doll C	.20	.75
DR1095 Wave-Motion Cannon C	2.50	6.00
DR1096 Huge Revolution C	.20	.75
DR1097 Thunder of Ruler C	.20	.75
DR1098 Spell Shield Type-8 SR	.75	2.00
DR1099 Meteorain C	.20	.75
DR1100 Pineapple Blast C	.20	.75
DR1101 Secret Barrel C	.20	.75
DR1102 Physical Double C	.20	.75
DR1103 Rivalry of Warlords C	.50	1.25
DR1104 Formation Union C	.20	.75
DR1105 Adhesion Trap Hole C	.20	.75
DR1106 XY-Dragon Cannon R	2.50	6.00
DR1107 XYZ-Dragon Cannon UR	.75	2.00
DR1108 XZ-Tank Cannon R	1.50	4.00
DR1109 YZ-Tank Cannon R	1.00	2.50
DR1110 Great Angus C	.20	.75
DR1111 Aitsu C	.20	.75
DR1112 Sonic Duck C	.20	.75
DR1113 Luster Dragon C	.20	.75
DR1114 Amazoness Paladin C	.20	.75
DR1115 Amazoness Fighter C	.20	.75
DR1116 Amazoness Swords Woman SR	1.25	3.00
DR1117 Amazoness Blowpiper C	.20	.75
DR1118 Amazoness Tiger C	.20	.75
DR1119 Skilled White Magician R	.40	1.00
DR1120 Skilled Dark Magician R	1.00	2.50
DR1121 Apprentice Magician C	.20	.75

DR1122 Old Vindictive Magician C	.20	.75
DR1123 Chaos Command Magician SR	2.00	5.00
DR1124 Magical Marionette C	.20	.75
DR1125 Pixie Knight C	.20	.75
DR1126 Breaker the Magical Warrior UR	1.25	3.00
DR1127 Magical Plant Mandragola C	.20	.75
DR1128 Magical Scientist R	.40	1.00
DR1129 Royal Magical Library C	.75	2.00
DR1130 Armor Exe C	.20	.75
DR1131 Tribe-Infecting Virus R	1.25	3.00
DR1132 Des Koala R	.75	2.00
DR1133 Cliff the Trap Remover C	.20	.75
DR1134 Magical Merchant C	.20	.75
DR1135 Koitsu C	.20	.75
DR1136 Cat's Ear Tribe C	.20	.75
DR1137 Ultimate Obedient Fiend C	.20	.75
DR1138 Dark Cat with White Tail C	.20	.75
DR1139 Amazoness Spellcaster C	.20	.75
DR1140 Continuous Destruction Punch C	.20	.75
DR1141 Big Bang Shot R	.40	1.00
DR1142 Gather Your Mind C	.20	.75
DR1143 Mass Driver C	.20	.75
DR1144 Senri Eye C	.20	.75
DR1145 Emblem of Dragon Destroyer C	2.00	5.00
DR1146 Jar Robber C	.20	.75
DR1147 My Body as a Shield C	.20	.75
DR1148 Pigeonholing Books of Spell C	.20	.75
DR1149 Mega Ton Magical Cannon C	.20	.75
DR1150 Pitch-Black Power Stone C	.20	.75
DR1151 Amazoness Archers SR	.75	2.00
DR1152 Dramatic Rescue R	.40	1.00
DR1153 Exhausting Spell C	.20	.75
DR1154 Hidden Book of Spell C	.20	.75
DR1155 Miracle Restoring C	.20	.75
DR1156 Remove Brainwashing C	2.50	6.00
DR1157 Disarmament C	.20	.75
DR1158 Anti-Spell C	.20	.75
DR1159 The Spell Absorbing Life C	.20	.75
DR1160 Dark Paladin UR	8.00	20.00
DR1161 Double Spell UR	1.25	3.00
DR1162 Diffusion Wave-Motion C	.20	.75
DR1163 Battle Footballer C	.20	.75
DR1164 Nin-Ken Dog C	.20	.75
DR1165 Acrobat Monkey C	.20	.75
DR1166 Arsenal Summoner C	.20	.75
DR1167 Guardian Elma C	.20	.75
DR1168 Guardian Ceal R	.40	1.00
DR1169 Guardian Grarl R	.50	1.25
DR1170 Guardian Baou C	.20	.75
DR1171 Guardian Kay'est C	.20	.75
DR1172 Guardian Tryce C	.20	.75
DR1173 Cyber Raider C	.20	.75
DR1174 Reflect Bounder SR	.75	2.00
DR1175 Little-Winguard C	.20	.75
DR1176 Des Feral Imp C	.20	.75
DR1177 Different Dimension Dragon SR	.75	2.00
DR1178 Shinato, King of a Higher Plane SR	2.00	5.00
DR1179 Dark Flare Knight SR	.75	2.00
DR1180 Mirage Knight SR	.75	2.00
DR1181 Berserk Dragon SR	.75	2.00
DR1182 Exodia Necross SR	10.00	25.00
DR1183 Gyaku-Gire Panda C	.20	.75
DR1184 Blindly Loyal Goblin C	.20	.75
DR1185 Despair from the Dark C	.20	.75
DR1186 Maju Garzett C	.20	.75
DR1187 Fear from the Dark R	.40	1.00
DR1188 Dark Scorpion Chick the Yellow C	.20	.75
DR1189 D.D. Warrior Lady SR	1.25	3.00
DR1190 Thousand Needles C	.20	.75
DR1191 Shinato's Ark C	.20	.75
DR1192 A Deal with Dark Ruler C	.20	.75
DR1193 Contract with Exodia C	1.50	4.00
DR1194 Butterfly Dagger - Elma R	.40	1.00
DR1195 Shooting Star Bow - Ceal C	.20	.75
DR1196 Gravity Axe - Grarl C	.20	.75
DR1197 Wicked-Breaking Flamberge Baou C	.20	.75
DR1198 Rod of Silence - Kay'est C	.20	.75
DR1199 Twin Swords of Flashing Light - Tryce C	.20	.75
DR1200 Precious Cards from Beyond C	1.25	3.00
DR1201 Rod of the Mind's Eye C	.20	.75
DR1202 Fairy of the Spring C	.20	.75
DR1203 Token Thanksgiving C	.20	.75
DR1204 Morale Boost C	.20	.75
DR1205 Non-Spellcasting Area C	.20	.75
DR1206 Different Dimension Gate R	.40	1.00
DR1207 Final Attack Orders C	.20	.75
DR1208 Staunch Defender C	.20	.75
DR1209 Ojama Trio C	.75	2.00
DR1210 Arsenal Robber C	.20	.75
DR1211 Skill Drain R	1.50	4.00
DR1212 Really Eternal Rest C	.20	.75
DR1213 Kaiser Glider UR	.75	2.00
DR1214 Interdimensional Matter UR	.75	2.00
DR1215 Cost Down UR	1.50	4.00
DR1216 Gagagigo C	.20	.75
DR1217 D.D. Trainer C	.20	.75
DR1218 Ojama Green C	.20	.75
DR1219 Archfiend Soldier C	.20	.75
DR1220 Pandemonium Watchbear C	.20	.75
DR1221 Sasuke Samurai #2 C	.20	.75
DR1222 Dark Scorpion Gorg the Strong C	.20	.75
DR1223 Dark Scorpion Meanae the Thorn C	.20	.75
DR1224 Outstanding Dog Marron C	.75	2.00
DR1225 Great Maju Garzett C	1.50	4.00
DR1226 Iron Blacksmith Kotetsu C	.20	.75
DR1227 Goblin of Greed C	.20	.75
DR1228 Mefist the Infernal General C	.20	.75
DR1229 Vilepawn Archfiend C	.20	.75
DR1230 Shadowknight Archfiend C	.20	.75
DR1231 Darkbishop Archfiend C	.20	.75
DR1232 Desrook Archfiend C	.20	.75
DR1233 Infernalqueen Archfiend C	.20	.75
DR1234 Terrorking Archfiend SR	1.25	3.00
DR1235 Skull Archfiend of Lightning UR	.75	2.00
DR1236 Metallizing Parasite Lunatite C	.20	.75
DR1237 Tsukuyomi C	.75	2.00
DR1238 Mudora R	.40	1.00
DR1239 Keldo C	.20	.75
DR1240 Kelbek C	.20	.75
DR1241 Zolga C	.20	.75
DR1242 Agido C	.20	.75
DR1243 Legendary Flame Lord R	.40	1.00
DR1244 Dark Master Zorc SR	.75	2.00
DR1245 Spell Reproduction C	.20	.75
DR1246 Dragged Down into the Grave C	.75	2.00
DR1247 Incandescent Ordeal C	.20	.75
DR1248 Contract with the Abyss C	.20	.75
DR1249 Contract with the Dark Master C	.20	.75
DR1250 Falling Down C	.20	.75
DR1251 Checkmate C	.20	.75
DR1252 Cestus of Dagla C	.20	.75
DR1253 Final Countdown C	.75	2.00
DR1254 Archfiend's Oath C	.20	.75
DR1255 Mustering of the Dark Scorpions C	.20	.75
DR1256 Pandemonium R	.40	1.00
DR1257 Altar for Tribute C	.20	.75
DR1258 Frozen Soul C	.20	.75
DR1259 Battle-Scarred C	.20	.75
DR1260 Dark Scorpion Combination C	.20	.75
DR1261 Archfiend's Roar C	.20	.75
DR1262 Dice Re-Roll C	.20	.75
DR1263 Spell Vanishing R	.40	1.00
DR1264 Sakuretsu Armor C	.20	.75
DR1265 Ray of Hope C	.20	.75
DR1266 Blast Held by a Tribute UR	.75	2.00
DR1267 Judgment of Anubis UR	1.25	3.00

2005 Yu-Gi-Oh Dark Beginnings 2

COMPLETE SET (250)	100.00	200.00
BOOSTER BOX (24 PACKS)	90.00	140.00
BOOSTER PACK (13 CARDS)	2.50	6.00
RELEASED ON JULY 27, 2005		
DB2001 Jowgen the Spiritualist R	.40	1.00
DB2002 Kycoo the Ghost Destroyer R	.40	1.00
DB2003 Bazoo the Soul-Eater R	.40	1.00
DB2004 Dark Necrofear UR	.75	2.00
DB2005 Soul of Purity and Light C	.10	.30
DB2006 Aqua Spirit C	.75	2.00
DB2007 The Rock Spirit C	.10	.30
DB2008 Gilasaurus C	.10	.30
DB2009 Tornado Bird C	.10	.30
DB2010 Zombyra the Dark C	.10	.30
DB2011 Maryokutai C	.10	.30
DB2012 The Last Warrior SR	1.00	2.50
DB2013 Dark Spirit of the Silent C	.10	.30
DB2014 Royal Command R	.40	1.00
DB2015 Riryoku Field R	.40	1.00
DB2016 Skull Lair C	.10	.30
DB2017 Graverobber's Retribution C	.10	.30
DB2018 Destruction Punch C	.10	.30
DB2019 Blind Destruction C	.10	.30
DB2020 The Emperor's Holiday C	.10	.30
DB2021 Destiny Board C	1.25	3.00
DB2022 Spirit Message 'I' C	.10	.30
DB2023 Spirit Message 'N' C	.10	.30
DB2024 Spirit Message 'A' C	.10	.30
DB2025 Spirit Message 'L' C	.10	.30
DB2026 The Dark Door C	.10	.30
DB2027 Spiritualism R	.40	1.00
DB2028 Cyclon Laser C	.10	.30
DB2029 De-Fusion C	.75	2.00
DB2030 Fusion Gate R	2.00	5.00
DB2031 Ekibyo Drakmord C	.10	.30
DB2032 Miracle Dig C	1.25	3.00
DB2033 Vengeful Bog Spirit C	.10	.30
DB2034 Blade Knight UR	1.00	2.50
DB2035 Baby Dragon C	.10	.30
DB2036 Blackland Fire Dragon C	.10	.30
DB2037 Battle Steer C	.10	.30
DB2038 Time Wizard SR	3.00	8.00
DB2039 Saggi the Dark Clown C	.10	.30
DB2040 Dragon Piper C	.10	.30
DB2041 Illusionist Faceless Mage C	.10	.30
DB2042 Sangan R	.40	1.00
DB2043 Great Moth C	.10	.30
DB2044 Kuriboh R	.40	1.00
DB2045 Thousand Dragon C	.10	.30
DB2046 King of Yamimakai C	.10	.30
DB2047 Catapult Turtle SR	.75	2.00
DB2048 Mystic Horseman C	.10	.30
DB2049 Rabid Horseman C	.10	.30
DB2050 Crass Clown C	.10	.30
DB2051 Dream Clown C	.10	.30
DB2052 Princess of Tsurugi C	.10	.30
DB2053 Tremendous Fire C	.10	.30
DB2054 Jirai Gumo C	.10	.30
DB2055 Shadow Ghoul C	.10	.30
DB2056 Ryu-Kishin Powered C	.10	.30
DB2057 Launcher Spider C	.20	.50
DB2058 Thunder Dragon C	1.25	3.00
DB2059 The Immortal of Thunder C	.10	.30
DB2060 Hoshiningen C	.10	.30
DB2061 Cannon Soldier SR	.75	2.00
DB2062 Muka Muka C	.10	.30
DB2063 The Bistro Butcher C	.10	.30
DB2064 Star Boy C	.10	.30
DB2065 Milus Radiant C	.10	.30
DB2066 Witch of the Black Forest R	.40	1.00
DB2067 Little Chimera C	.10	.30
DB2068 Bladefly C	.10	.30
DB2069 Twin-Headed Thunder Dragon C	.20	.50
DB2070 Witch's Apprentice C	.10	.30
DB2071 Gazelle the King of Mythical Beasts C	.10	.30
DB2072 Barrel Dragon UR	1.00	2.50
DB2073 Solemn Judgment SR	1.25	3.00
DB2074 Magic Jammer SR	1.00	2.50
DB2075 Seven Tools of the Bandit SR	.75	2.00
DB2076 Horn of Heaven R	1.25	3.00
DB2077 Shield & Sword C	.10	.30
DB2078 Block Attack C	.10	.30
DB2079 The Unhappy Maiden C	.10	.30
DB2080 Robbin' Goblin C	.10	.30
DB2081 Mirror Force SR	3.00	8.00
DB2082 Ring of Magnetism R	.40	1.00
DB2083 Share the Pain C	.10	.30
DB2084 Heavy Storm SR	1.00	2.50
DB2085 Oscillo Hero #2 C	.10	.30
DB2086 Soul of the Pure C	.10	.30
DB2087 Dark-Piercing Light C	.10	.30
DB2088 The Statue of Easter Island C	.10	.30
DB2089 Shining Friendship C	.10	.30
DB2090 The Wicked Worm Beast C	.10	.30
DB2091 Tiger Axe C	.10	.30
DB2092 Axe Raider C	.10	.30
DB2093 Mechanicalchaser C	.10	.30
DB2094 Gemini Elf C	.10	.30
DB2095 Graceful Charity R	.40	1.00
DB2096 Two-Headed King Rex C	.10	.30
DB2097 Goddess with the Third Eye C	.10	.30
DB2098 Lord of the Lamp C	.10	.30
DB2099 Machine King C	.10	.30
DB2100 Cyber-Stein R	6.00	15.00
DB2101 Dragon Seeker C	.10	.30
DB2102 Needle Worm C	1.25	3.00
DB2103 Greenkappa C	.10	.30
DB2104 Morphing Jar R	1.25	3.00
DB2105 Penguin Soldier C	.10	.30
DB2106 Royal Decree SR	2.50	6.00
DB2107 Magical Thorn C	.40	1.00
DB2108 Restructer Revolution C	.10	.30
DB2109 Fusion Sage C	1.25	3.00
DB2110 Total Defense Shogun SR	1.00	2.50
DB2111 Swift Gaia the Fierce Knight UR	.75	2.00
DB2112 Obnoxious Celtic Guard UR	1.00	2.50
DB2113 Luminous Soldier C	.10	.30
DB2114 Command Knight SR	1.00	2.50
DB2115 Kaiser Sea Horse C	.10	.30
DB2116 Vampire Lord UR	1.50	4.00
DB2117 Toon Goblin Attack Force C	1.50	4.00
DB2118 Toon Cannon Soldier C	.10	.30
DB2119 Toon Gemini Elf C	1.50	4.00
DB2120 Toon Masked Sorcerer C	1.50	4.00
DB2121 Toon Table of Contents C	1.25	3.00
DB2122 Toon Defense C	.75	2.00
DB2123 Insect Queen UR	1.50	4.00
DB2124 Dark Ruler Ha Des UR	.75	2.00
DB2125 Dark Balter the Terrible R	.40	1.00
DB2126 Lesser Fiend C	.10	.30
DB2127 Possessed Dark Soul C	.10	.30
DB2128 Winged Minion C	.10	.30
DB2129 Skull Knight #2 C	.10	.30
DB2130 Twin-Headed Wolf C	.10	.30
DB2131 Opticlops C	.10	.30
DB2132 Bark of Dark Ruler C	.10	.30
DB2133 Fatal Abacus C	.10	.30
DB2134 The Puppet Magic of Dark Ruler C	.20	.50
DB2135 Soul Demolition C	.10	.30
DB2136 Double Snare C	.10	.30
DB2137 Freed the Matchless General UR	1.00	2.50
DB2138 Marauding Captain R	.40	1.00
DB2139 Ryu Senshi R	.40	1.00
DB2140 Warrior Dai Grepher C	.10	.30
DB2141 Mysterious Guard C	.10	.30
DB2142 Frontier Wiseman C	.10	.30
DB2143 Exiled Force C	.10	.30
DB2144 Shadow Tamer C	.10	.30
DB2145 Dragon Manipulator C	.10	.30
DB2146 The A. Forces C	.10	.30
DB2147 Reinforcement of the Army R	.60	1.50
DB2148 Array of Revealing Light C	.10	.30
DB2149 The Warrior Returning Alive C	.10	.30
DB2150 Emergency Provisions R	.40	1.00
DB2151 Tyrant Dragon UR	2.50	6.00
DB2152 Spear Dragon SR	.75	2.00
DB2153 Spirit Ryu C	.10	.30
DB2154 Fiend Skull Dragon R	.40	1.00
DB2155 Cave Dragon C	.10	.30
DB2156 Gray Wing C	.10	.30
DB2157 Troop Dragon C	.20	.50
DB2158 The Dragon's Bead C	.10	.30
DB2159 A Wingbeat of Giant Dragon C	.10	.30
DB2160 Dragon's Gunfire C	.10	.30
DB2161 Stamping Destruction C	.10	.30
DB2162 Super Rejuvenation C	.10	.30
DB2163 Dragon's Rage C	.10	.30
DB2164 Burst Breath C	.10	.30
DB2165 Luster Dragon #2 C	.10	.30
DB2166 Fiber Jar R	1.50	4.00
DB2167 Serpentine Princess C	.10	.30
DB2168 Patrician of Darkness C	.10	.30
DB2169 Thunder Nyan Nyan R	.40	1.00
DB2170 Gradius' Option C	.10	.30
DB2171 Injection Fairy Lily UR	2.50	6.00
DB2172 Woodland Sprite C	.10	.30
DB2173 Airknight Parshath SR	1.25	3.00
DB2174 Twin-Headed Behemoth C	.20	.50
DB2175 Maharaghi C	.10	.30
DB2176 Inaba White Rabbit C	.10	.30
DB2177 Yata-Garasu C	.50	1.25
DB2178 Susa Soldier SR	.75	2.00
DB2179 Yamata Dragon SR	2.00	5.00
DB2180 Great Long Nose C	.10	.30
DB2181 Otohime C	.10	.30
DB2182 Hino-Kagu-Tsuchi UR	1.25	3.00
DB2183 Asura Priest C	.10	.30
DB2184 Fushi No Tori C	.10	.30
DB2185 Spring of Rebirth C	.10	.30
DB2186 Heart of Clear Water C	.10	.30
DB2187 A Legendary Ocean C	.10	.30
DB2188 Fusion Sword Murasame Blade C	.10	.30
DB2189 Smoke Grenade of the Thief C	.10	.30
DB2190 Creature Swap SR	.75	2.00
DB2191 Spiritual Energy Settle Machine C	.10	.30
DB2192 Second Coin Toss C	.10	.30
DB2193 Convulsion of Nature C	.10	.30
DB2194 The Secret of the Bandit C	.10	.30
DB2195 After the Struggle C	.10	.30
DB2196 Magic Reflector C	1.25	3.00
DB2197 Blast with Chain R	.40	1.00
DB2198 Disappear C	.10	.30
DB2199 Bubble Crash C	.10	.30
DB2200 Royal Oppression R	.40	1.00
DB2201 Bottomless Trap Hole C	1.25	3.00
DB2202 Bad Reaction to Simochi C	1.25	3.00
DB2203 Ominous Fortunetelling C	.10	.30
DB2204 Spirit's Invitation C	.10	.30
DB2205 Drop Off C	.10	.30
DB2206 Last Turn R	.60	1.50
DB2207 King Tiger Wanghu C	.10	.30
DB2208 Birdface C	.10	.30
DB2209 Kryuel C	.10	.30
DB2210 Arsenal Bug C	.10	.30
DB2211 Maiden of the Aqua C	.10	.30
DB2212 Jowls of Dark Demise C	.10	.30
DB2213 Mucus Yolk C	.10	.30
DB2214 Moisture Creature C	.10	.30
DB2215 Gora Turtle C	.10	.30
DB2216 Sasuke Samurai R	.40	1.00
DB2217 Dark Dust Spirit C	.10	.30
DB2218 Royal Keeper C	.10	.30
DB2219 Wandering Mummy C	.10	.30
DB2220 Great Dezard SR	.75	2.00
DB2221 Swarm of Scarabs C	.10	.30
DB2222 Swarm of Locusts C	.10	.30
DB2223 Giant Axe Mummy C	.10	.30
DB2224 Guardian Sphinx UR	.75	2.00
DB2225 Pyramid Turtle R	.40	1.00
DB2226 Dice Jar C	.10	.30
DB2227 Dark Scorpion Burglars C	.10	.30
DB2228 Don Zaloog SR	1.00	2.50
DB2229 Fushioh Richie UR	1.00	2.50
DB2230 Book of Life SR	1.50	4.00
DB2231 Book of Taiyou C	.10	.30
DB2232 Book of Moon C	.10	.30
DB2233 Mirage of Nightmare C	.10	.30
DB2234 Secret Pass to the Treasures C	.10	.30
DB2235 Call of the Mummy C	.10	.30
DB2236 Timidity C	.10	.30
DB2237 Pyramid Energy C	.10	.30
DB2238 Tutan Mask C	.10	.30
DB2239 Ordeal of a Traveler C	.10	.30
DB2240 Bottomless Shifting Sand C	.10	.30
DB2241 Curse of Royal C	.10	.30
DB2242 Needle Ceiling C	.10	.30
DB2243 Statue of the Wicked R	.40	1.00
DB2244 Dark Coffin C	.10	.30
DB2245 Needle Wall C	.10	.30
DB2246 Trap Dustshoot C	.10	.30
DB2247 Reckless Greed C	.10	.30
DB2248 Pharaoh's Treasure C	.10	.30
DB2249 Perfectly Ultimate Great Moth UR	2.00	5.00
DB2250 Black Illusion Ritual C	.10	.30

2005 Yu-Gi-Oh Dark Revelation 2

COMPLETE SET (224)	150.00	300.00
BOOSTER BOX (24 PACKS)	180.00	300.00
BOOSTER PACK (13 CARDS)	3.00	8.00
RELEASED ON OCTOBER 20, 2005		
DR2001 Ojama Yellow C	.25	.75
DR2002 Ojama Black C	.25	.75
DR2003 Soul Tiger C	.25	.75
DR2004 Big Koala C	.25	.75
DR2005 Des Kangaroo C	.25	.75
DR2006 Crimson Ninja C	.25	.75
DR2007 Strike Ninja UR	2.50	6.00
DR2008 Gale Lizard C	.25	.75
DR2009 Spirit of the Pot of Greed C	.25	.75
DR2010 Chopman the Desperate Outlaw C	.25	.75
DR2011 Sasuke Samurai #3 C	.25	.75
DR2012 D.D. Scout Plane R	.40	1.00
DR2013 Berserk Gorilla R	.40	1.00
DR2014 Freed the Brave Wanderer SR	.75	2.00
DR2015 Coach Goblin C	.25	.75
DR2016 Witch Doctor of Chaos C	.25	.75
DR2017 Chaos Necromancer C	.25	.75
DR2018 Chaosrider Gustaph SR	.75	2.00
DR2019 Inferno C	.25	.75
DR2020 Fenrir R	.25	.75
DR2021 Gigantes C	.25	.75
DR2022 Silpheed C	.25	.75
DR2023 Chaos Sorcerer C	.25	.75
DR2024 Gren Maju Da Eiza C	.25	.75
DR2025 Black Luster Soldier - EOB UR	20.00	40.00
DR2026 Drillago R	.40	1.00
DR2027 Lekunga R	.40	1.00
DR2028 Lord Poison C	.25	.75
DR2029 Bowganian C	.25	.75
DR2030 Granadora C	.25	.75
DR2031 Fuhma Shuriken C	.25	.75
DR2032 Heart of the Underdog C	2.50	6.00
DR2033 Wild Nature's Release R	.40	1.00
DR2034 Ojama Delta Hurricane!! C	.25	.75
DR2035 Stumbling C	.25	.75
DR2036 Chaos End C	.25	.75
DR2037 Yellow Luster Shield C	.25	.75
DR2038 Chaos Greed C	.25	.75
DR2039 D.D. Designator SR	.75	2.00
DR2040 D.D. Borderline C	.25	.75
DR2041 Recycle C	.25	.75
DR2042 Primal Seed C	.25	.75
DR2043 Thunder Crash C	.25	.75
DR2044 Dimension Distortion C	.25	.75
DR2045 Reload SR	.25	.75
DR2046 Soul Absorption C	.25	.75
DR2047 Big Burn SR	1.25	3.00
DR2048 Blasting the Ruins C	.25	.75
DR2049 Cursed Seal of the Forbidden Spell C	.25	.75
DR2050 Tower of Babel C	.25	.75
DR2051 Spatial Collapse C	.25	.75
DR2052 Chain Disappearance R	.40	1.00
DR2053 Zero Gravity C	.25	.75
DR2054 Dark Mirror Force SR	2.50	6.00
DR2055 Energy Drain C	.25	.75
DR2056 Chaos Emperor Dragon - EOE UR	20.00	40.00
DR2057 Giga Gagagigo C	.25	.75
DR2058 Mad Dog of Darkness C	.25	.75
DR2059 Neo Bug C	.25	.75
DR2060 Sea Serpent Warrior of Darkness C	.25	.75
DR2061 Terrorking Salmon C	.25	.75
DR2062 Blazing Inpachi C	.25	.75
DR2063 Burning Algae C	.25	.75
DR2064 The Thing in the Crater C	.25	.75
DR2065 Molten Zombie C	.25	.75
DR2066 Dark Magician of Chaos UR	20.00	40.00
DR2067 Gora Turtle of Illusion C	.25	.75
DR2068 Manticore of Darkness SR	.75	2.00
DR2069 Stealth Bird R	.40	1.00
DR2070 Sacred Crane C	.25	.75
DR2071 Enraged Battle Ox C	.25	.75
DR2072 Don Turtle C	.25	.75
DR2073 Balloon Lizard C	.25	.75
DR2074 Dark Driceratops C	.25	.75
DR2075 Hyper Hammerhead C	.25	.75
DR2076 Black Tyranno UR	1.25	3.00
DR2077 Anti-Aircraft Flower C	.25	.75
DR2078 Prickle Fairy C	.25	.75
DR2079 Pinch Hopper C	.25	.75
DR2080 Skull-Mark Ladybug C	.25	.75
DR2081 Insect Princess UR	.25	.75
DR2082 Amphibious Bugroth MK-3 R	.40	1.00
DR2083 Torpedo Fish C	.25	.75
DR2084 Levia-Dragon - Daedalus UR	2.00	5.00
DR2085 Orca Mega-Fortress of Drknss R	.40	1.00
DR2086 Cannonball Spear Shellfish C	.25	.75
DR2087 Mataza the Zapper R	.40	1.00
DR2088 Guardian Angel Joan SR	.75	2.00
DR2089 Manju of the Ten Thousand Hands C	.25	.75
DR2090 Getsu Fuhma C	.25	.75
DR2091 Ryu Kokki SR	1.50	4.00
DR2092 Gryphon's Feather Duster C	.25	.75
DR2093 Stray Lambs R	.40	1.00
DR2094 Smashing Ground C	.25	.75
DR2095 Dimension Fusion SR	4.00	10.00
DR2096 Dedication Light and Darkness SR	2.00	5.00
DR2097 Salvage C	.25	.75
DR2098 Ultra Evolution Pill C	.25	.75
DR2099 Multiplication of Ants C	.25	.75
DR2100 Earth Chant C	.25	.75
DR2101 Jade Insect Whistle C	.25	.75
DR2102 Destruction Ring C	.25	.75
DR2103 Fiend's Hand Mirror C	.25	.75
DR2104 Compulsory Evacuation Device R	1.50	4.00
DR2105 A Hero Emerges C	.25	.75
DR2106 Self-Destruct Button C	.25	.75
DR2107 Curse of Darkness R	.40	1.00
DR2108 Begone, Knave! C	.25	.75
DR2109 DNA Transplant C	.25	.75
DR2110 Robbin' Zombie R	.40	1.00
DR2111 Trap Jammer R	.40	1.00
DR2112 Invader of Darkness UR	.75	2.00
DR2113 Gogiga Gagagigo C	.25	.75
DR2114 Warrior of Zera C	.25	.75
DR2115 Sealmaster Meisei C	.25	.75
DR2116 Mystic Shine Ball C	.25	.75
DR2117 Metal Armored Bug C	.25	.75
DR2118 The Agent of Judgment - Saturn SR	.75	2.00
DR2119 The Agent of Wisdom - Mercury C	.25	.75
DR2120 The Agent of Creation - Venus C	.25	.75
DR2121 The Agent of Force - Mars C	.25	.75
DR2122 The Unhappy Girl C	.25	.75
DR2123 Soul-Absorbing Bone Tower C	.25	.75
DR2124 The Kick Man C	.25	.75
DR2125 Vampire Lady C	.25	.75
DR2126 Stone Statue of the Aztecs R	.40	1.00
DR2127 Rocket Jumper C	.25	.75
DR2128 Avatar of the Pot C	.25	.75
DR2129 Legendary Jujitsu Master C	.25	.75
DR2130 Gear Golem the Moving Fortress SR	.75	2.00
DR2131 KA-2 Des Scissors C	.25	.75
DR2132 Needle Burrower R	.40	1.00
DR2133 Sonic Jammer C	.25	.75
DR2134 Blowback Dragon UR	1.50	4.00
DR2135 Zaborg the Thunder Monarch SR	1.25	3.00
DR2136 Atomic Firefly C	.25	.75
DR2137 Mermaid Knight R	.40	1.00
DR2138 Piranha Army C	.25	.75
DR2139 Two Thousand Needles C	.25	.75
DR2140 Disc Fighter C	.25	.75
DR2141 Arcane Archer of the Forest C	.25	.75
DR2142 Lady Ninja Yae C	.25	.75
DR2143 Goblin King C	.25	.75
DR2144 Solar Flare Dragon C	.25	.75
DR2145 White Magician Pikeru C	.25	.75
DR2146 Archlord Zerato UR	2.00	5.00
DR2147 Opti-Camouflage Armor C	2.00	5.00
DR2148 Mystik Wok C	.25	.75
DR2149 Enemy Controller SR	2.00	5.00
DR2150 Burst Stream of Destruction SR	6.00	15.00
DR2151 Monster Gate C	.25	.75
DR2152 Amplifier R	2.00	5.00

DR2153 Weapon Change C .25 .75
DR2154 The Sanctuary in the Sky C .25 .75
DR2155 Earthquake C .25 .75
DR2156 Talisman of Trap Sealing C .25 .75
DR2157 Goblin Thief C .25 .75
DR2158 Backfire C .25 .75
DR2159 Micro Ray C .25 .75
DR2160 Light of Judgment C .25 .75
DR2161 Talisman of Spell Sealing C .25 .75
DR2162 Wall of Revealing Light C .25 .75
DR2163 Solar Ray C .25 .75
DR2164 Ninjitsu Art of Transformation C .25 .75
DR2165 Beckoning Light C .25 .75
DR2166 Draining Shield R .40 1.00
DR2167 Armor Break C .25 .75
DR2168 Mazera DeVille UR .75 2.00
DR2169 Gigobyte C .25 .75
DR2170 Mokey Mokey C .25 .75
DR2171 Kozaky C .25 .75
DR2172 Fiend Scorpion C .25 .75
DR2173 Pharaoh's Servant C .25 .75
DR2174 Pharaonic Protector C .25 .75
DR2175 Spirit of the Pharaoh UR 1.25 3.00
DR2176 Theban Nightmare R .40 1.00
DR2177 Aswan Apparition C .25 .75
DR2178 Protector of the Sanctuary R .40 1.00
DR2179 Nubian Guard C .25 .75
DR2180 Legacy Hunter SR .75 2.00
DR2181 Desertapir C .25 .75
DR2182 Sand Gambler C .25 .75
DR2183 3-Hump Lacooda C .25 .75
DR2184 Ghost Knight of Jackal UR .75 2.00
DR2185 Absorbing Kid from the Sky C .25 .75
DR2186 Elephant Statue of Blessing C .25 .75
DR2187 Elephant Statue of Disaster C .25 .75
DR2188 Spirit Caller C .25 .75
DR2189 Emissary of the Afterlife SR 1.25 3.00
DR2190 Grave Protector C .25 .75
DR2191 Double Coston R .40 1.00
DR2192 Regenerating Mummy C .25 .75
DR2193 Night Assailant R 1.50 4.00
DR2194 Man-Thro' Tro' C .25 .75
DR2195 King of the Swamp C 6.00 15.00
DR2196 Emissary of the Oasis C .25 .75
DR2197 Special Hurricane R .40 1.00
DR2198 Order to Charge C .25 .75
DR2199 Sword of the Soul-Eater C .25 .75
DR2200 Dust Barrier C .25 .75
DR2201 Soul Reversal C .25 .75
DR2202 Spell Economics R .40 1.00
DR2203 Blessings of the Nile C .25 .75
DR2204 7 C .25 .75
DR2205 Level Limit - Area B R 1.25 3.00
DR2206 Enchanting Fitting Room C .25 .75
DR2207 The Law of the Normal C .25 .75
DR2208 Dark Magic Attack UR 3.00 8.00
DR2209 Delta Attacker C .25 .75
DR2210 Thousand Energy C .25 .75
DR2211 Triangle Power C .25 .75
DR2212 The Third Sarcophagus C .25 .75
DR2213 The Second Sarcophagus C .25 .75
DR2214 The First Sarcophagus SR .75 2.00
DR2215 Dora of Fate C .25 .75
DR2216 Judgment of the Desert C .25 .75
DR2217 Human-Wave Tactics C .25 .75
DR2218 Curse of Anubis SR .75 2.00
DR2219 Desert Sunlight C .25 .75
DR2220 Des Counterblow R .40 1.00
DR2221 Labyrinth of Nightmare C .25 .75
DR2222 Soul Resurrection R .40 1.00
DR2223 Order to Smash C .25 .75
DR2224 The End of Anubis UR 1.50 4.00

2006 Yu-Gi-Oh Dark Revelation 3

COMPLETE SET (240) 150.00 300.00
BOOSTER BOX (24 PACKS) 100.00 140.00
BOOSTER PACK (12 CARDS) 2.50 6.00
RELEASED ON NOVEMBER 25, 2006
DR3001 Charcoal Inpachi R .40 1.00
DR3002 Neo Aqua Madoor C .10 .30
DR3003 Skull Dog Marron C .10 .30
DR3004 Goblin Calligrapher C .10 .30
DR3005 Ultimate Insect LV1 R .40 1.00
DR3006 Horus the Black Flame Dragon LV4 R 1.25 3.00
DR3007 Horus the Black Flame Dragon LV6 SR 2.50 6.00
DR3008 Horus the Black Flame Dragon LV8 UR 4.00 10.00
DR3009 Dark Mimic LV1 C .10 .30
DR3010 Dark Mimic LV3 R .40 1.00
DR3011 Mystic Swordsman LV2 R 1.50 4.00
DR3012 Mystic Swordsman LV4 UR 2.00 5.00
DR3013 Armed Dragon LV3 C .10 .30
DR3014 Armed Dragon LV5 R .40 1.00
DR3015 Armed Dragon LV7 UR 4.00 10.00
DR3016 Horus' Servant C .10 .30
DR3017 Red-Eyes B. Chick C .75 2.00
DR3018 Malice Doll of Demise C .10 .30
DR3019 Ninja Grandmaster Sasuke R 1.25 3.00
DR3020 Rafflesia Seduction R .40 1.00
DR3021 Ultimate Baseball Kid .10 .30
DR3022 Mobius the Frost Monarch SR 5.00 12.00
DR3023 Element Dragon C .10 .30
DR3024 Element Soldier C .10 .30
DR3025 Howling Insect C .10 .30
DR3026 Masked Dragon C .10 .30
DR3027 Mind on Air R .40 1.00
DR3028 Unshaven Angler C .10 .30
DR3029 The Trojan Horse C .10 .30
DR3030 Nobleman-Eater Bug C .10 .30
DR3031 Enraged Muka Muka C .10 .30
DR3032 Hade-Hane C .10 .30
DR3033 Penumbral Soldier Lady SR 1.00 2.50
DR3034 Ojama King R .40 1.00
DR3035 Master of OZ R 1.25 3.00
DR3036 Sanwitch C .10 .30
DR3037 Dark Factory of Mass Production C .75 2.00
DR3038 Hammer Shot R .40 1.00
DR3039 Mind Wipe C .10 .30
DR3040 Abyssal Designator C .10 .30
DR3041 Level Up! C .75 2.00
DR3042 Inferno Fire Blast UR 4.00 10.00
DR3043 Ectoplasmer SR 1.00 2.50
DR3044 The Graveyard in the Fourth Dimension C .10 .30
DR3045 Two-Man Cell Battle C .10 .30
DR3046 Big Wave Small Wave C .10 .30
DR3047 Fusion Weapon C .10 .30
DR3048 Ritual Weapon C .10 .30
DR3049 Taunt C .10 .30
DR3050 Absolute End C .10 .30
DR3051 Spirit Barrier R 1.25 3.00
DR3052 Ninjitsu Art of Decoy C .10 .30
DR3053 Enervating Mist R .40 1.00
DR3054 Heavy Slump C .10 .30
DR3055 Greed SR 1.00 2.50
DR3056 Mind Crush C 1.25 3.00
DR3057 Null and Void SR 1.00 2.50
DR3058 Gorgon's Eye C .10 .30
DR3059 Cemetery Bomb C .10 .30
DR3060 Hallowed Life Barrier SR 1.00 2.50
DR3061 Woodborg Inpachi C .10 .30
DR3062 Mighty Guard C .10 .30
DR3063 Bokoichi the Freightening Car C .10 .30
DR3064 Harpie Girl C .10 .30
DR3065 The Creator UR 2.50 6.00
DR3066 The Creator Incarnate C .10 .30
DR3067 Ultimate Insect LV3 R .40 1.00
DR3068 Mystic Swordsman LV6 UR 4.00 10.00
DR3069 Silent Swordsman LV3 UR 1.00 2.50
DR3070 Nightmare Penguin C .10 .30
DR3071 Heavy Mech Support Platform C .10 .30
DR3072 Perfect Machine King UR 4.00 10.00
DR3073 Element Magician C .10 .30
DR3074 Element Saurus C .10 .30
DR3075 Roc from the Valley of Haze C .10 .30
DR3076 Sasuke Samurai #4 R .40 1.00
DR3077 Harpie Lady 1 C .10 .30
DR3078 Harpie Lady 2 C .10 .30
DR3079 Harpie Lady 3 C .10 .30
DR3080 Raging Flame Sprite C .10 .30
DR3081 Thestalos the Firestorm Monarch SR 2.00 5.00
DR3082 Eagle Eye C .10 .30
DR3083 Tactical Espionage Expert C .10 .30
DR3084 Invasion of Flames C .10 .30
DR3085 Creeping Doom Manta C .10 .30
DR3086 Pitch-Black Warwolf C .10 .30
DR3087 Mirage Dragon C .10 .30
DR3088 Gaia Soul the Combustible Collective R .40 1.00
DR3089 Fox Fire C .10 .30
DR3090 Big Core SR 1.00 2.50
DR3091 Fusilier Dragon, the Dual-Mode Beast R 1.25 3.00
DR3092 Dekoichi the Battlechanted Locomotive R .40 1.00
DR3093 A-Team: Trap Disposal Unit R .40 1.00
DR3094 Homunculus the Alchemic Being C .10 .30
DR3095 Dark Blade the Dragon Knight R 1.25 3.00
DR3096 Mokey Mokey King C .10 .30
DR3097 Serial Spell R .40 1.00
DR3098 Harpies' Hunting Ground C .10 .30
DR3099 Triangle Ecstasy Spark SR 1.00 2.50
DR3100 Necklace of Command R .40 1.00
DR3101 Machine Duplication R 2.50 6.00
DR3102 Flint R .40 1.00
DR3103 Mokey Mokey Smackdown C .10 .30
DR3104 Back to Square One C .10 .30
DR3105 Monster Reincarnation SR 3.00 8.00
DR3106 Ballista of Rampart Smashing C .10 .30
DR3107 Lighten the Load C .10 .30
DR3108 Malice Dispersion C .10 .30
DR3109 Tragedy SR 1.00 2.50
DR3110 Divine Wrath SR 2.50 6.00
DR3111 Xing Zhen Hu C .10 .30
DR3112 Rare Metalmorph R .40 1.00
DR3113 Fruits of Kozaky's Studies C .10 .30
DR3114 Mind Haxorz C .10 .30
DR3115 Fuh-Rin-Ka-Zan C .10 .30
DR3116 Chain Burst R .40 1.00
DR3117 Pikeru's Circle of Enchantment SR 1.00 2.50
DR3118 Spell Purification C .10 .30
DR3119 Astral Barrier C .10 .30
DR3120 Covering Fire R .40 1.00
DR3121 Space Mambo C .10 .30
DR3122 Divine Dragon Ragnarok C 1.25 3.00
DR3123 Chu-Ske the Mouse Fighter C .10 .30
DR3124 Insect Knight C .10 .30
DR3125 Sacred Phoenix of Nephthys UR 2.00 5.00
DR3126 Hand of Nephthys C .10 .30
DR3127 Ultimate Insect LV5 R .40 1.00
DR3128 Silent Swordsman LV5 UR 2.00 5.00
DR3129 Granmarg the Rock Monarch SR 3.00 8.00
DR3130 Element Valkyrie C .10 .30
DR3131 Element Doom C .10 .30
DR3132 Maji-Gire Panda C .10 .30
DR3133 Catnipped Kitty C .10 .30
DR3134 Behemoth the King of All Animals SR 1.00 2.50
DR3135 Big-Tusked Mammoth R .40 1.00
DR3136 Kangaroo Champ C .10 .30
DR3137 Hyena C .10 .30
DR3138 Blade Rabbit C .10 .30
DR3139 Mecha-Dog Marron C .10 .30
DR3140 Blast Magician SR 1.00 2.50
DR3141 Chiron the Mage R .40 1.00
DR3142 Gearfried the Swordmaster UR 2.50 6.00
DR3143 Armed Samurai - Ben Kei C .10 .30
DR3144 Shadowslayer R .40 1.00
DR3145 Golem Sentry C .10 .30
DR3146 Abare Ushioni C .10 .30
DR3147 The Light - Hex-Sealed Fusion C .10 .30
DR3148 The Dark - Hex-Sealed Fusion C .10 .30
DR3149 The Earth - Hex-Sealed Fusion C .10 .30
DR3150 Whirlwind Prodigy C .10 .30
DR3151 Flame Ruler C .10 .30
DR3152 Firebird C .10 .30
DR3153 Rescue Cat C .10 .30
DR3154 Brain Jacker R .40 1.00
DR3155 Gatling Dragon UR 2.50 6.00
DR3156 King Dragun SR 5.00 12.00
DR3157 A Feather of the Phoenix SR 2.00 5.00
DR3158 Poison Fangs C .10 .30
DR3159 Spell Absorption R 4.00 10.00
DR3160 Lightning Vortex SR 2.50 6.00
DR3161 Meteor of Destruction R .40 1.00
DR3162 Swords of Concealing Light R 1.50 4.00
DR3163 Spiral Spear Strike R .40 1.00
DR3164 Release Restraint C .10 .30
DR3165 Centrifugal Field C .10 .30
DR3166 Fulfillment of the Contract C .10 .30
DR3167 Re-Fusion C 1.25 3.00
DR3168 The Big March of Animals C .10 .30
DR3169 Cross Counter R .40 1.00
DR3170 Pole Position C .10 .30
DR3171 Penalty Game! R .40 1.00
DR3172 Threatening Roar C .75 2.00
DR3173 Phoenix Wing Wind Blast R 1.25 3.00
DR3174 Good Goblin Housekeeping C .10 .30
DR3175 Beast Soul Swap C .10 .30
DR3176 Assault on GHQ R .40 1.00
DR3177 D.D. Dynamite C .10 .30
DR3178 Deck Devastation Virus SR 4.00 10.00
DR3179 Elemental Burst C .10 .30
DR3180 Forced Ceasefire R .40 1.00
DR3181 Elemental Hero Avian C .10 .30
DR3182 Elemental Hero Burstinatrix C .10 .30
DR3183 Elemental Hero Clayman C .10 .30
DR3184 Elemental Hero Sparkman C .10 .30
DR3185 Winged Kuriboh SR 2.50 6.00
DR3186 Ancient Gear Golem UR 3.00 8.00
DR3187 Ancient Gear Beast R .40 1.00
DR3188 Ancient Gear Soldier C .10 .30
DR3189 Millennium Scorpion R .40 1.00
DR3190 Ultimate Insect LV7 SR 2.50 6.00
DR3191 Lost Guardian C .10 .30
DR3192 Hieracosphinx SR 1.00 2.50
DR3193 Criosphinx R .40 1.00
DR3194 Moai Interceptor Cannons C .10 .30
DR3195 Megarock Dragon SR 1.00 2.50
DR3196 Dummy Golem C .10 .30
DR3197 Grave Ohja R .40 1.00
DR3198 Mine Golem C .10 .30
DR3199 Monk Fighter C .10 .30
DR3200 Master Monk SR 1.00 2.50
DR3201 Guardian Statue C .10 .30
DR3202 Medusa Worm C .10 .30
DR3203 D.D. Survivor R .40 1.00
DR3204 Mid Shield Gardna R .40 1.00
DR3205 White Ninja C .10 .30
DR3206 Aussa the Earth Charmer C .10 .30
DR3207 Eria the Water Charmer C .10 .30
DR3208 Hiita the Fire Charmer C .10 .30
DR3209 Wynn the Wind Charmer C .10 .30
DR3210 Batteryman AA C .75 2.00
DR3211 Des Wombat C .10 .30
DR3212 King of the Skull Servants C .10 .30
DR3213 Reshef the Dark Being UR 2.50 6.00
DR3214 Elemental Mistress Doriado R .40 1.00
DR3215 Elemental Hero Flame Wingman UR 3.00 8.00
DR3216 Elemental Hero Thunder Giant UR 2.50 6.00
DR3217 Card of Sanctity SR 1.00 2.50
DR3218 Brain Control SR 2.50 6.00
DR3219 Gift of the Martyr C .10 .30
DR3220 Double Attack C .10 .30
DR3221 Battery Charger C .75 2.00
DR3222 Kaminote Blow C .10 .30
DR3223 Doriado's Blessing C .10 .30
DR3224 Final Ritual of the Ancients C .10 .30
DR3225 Legendary Black Bel R .40 1.00
DR3226 Nitro Unit R .40 1.00
DR3227 Shifting Shadows C .10 .30
DR3228 Impenetrable Formation C .10 .30
DR3229 Hero Signal R .40 1.00
DR3230 Pikeru's Second Sight C .10 .30
DR3231 Minefield Eruption C .10 .30
DR3232 Kozaky's Self-Destruct Button R .40 1.00
DR3233 Mispolymerization C .10 .30
DR3234 Level Conversion Lab .10 .30
DR3235 Rock Bombardment C .10 .30
DR3236 Grave Lure C .10 .30
DR3237 Token Feastevil R .40 1.00
DR3238 Spell-Stopping StatuteRare R .40 1.00
DR3239 Royal Surrender R .40 1.00
DR3240 Lone Wolf C .10 .30

2007 Yu-Gi-Oh Dark Revelation 4

COMPLETE SET (245) 400.00 800.00
BOOSTER BOX (24 PACKS) 200.00 400.00
BOOSTER PACK (12 CARDS) 10.00 20.00
RELEASED ON NOVEMBER 14, 2007
DR041 Cycroid C .20 .50
DR042 Soitsu C .20 .50
DR043 Mad Lobster C .20 .50
DR044 Jerry Beans Man C .20 .50
DR045 Winged Kuriboh LV10 UR 2.50 6.00
DR046 Patroid C .20 .50
DR047 Gyroid R .20 .50
DR048 Steamroid R .40 1.00
DR049 Drillroid SR 1.25 3.00
DR0410 UFOroid C .40 1.00
DR0411 Jetroid C .20 .50
DR0412 Wroughtweiler C .20 .50
DR0413 Dark Catapulter C .20 .50
DR0414 Elemental Hero Bubbleman C .75 2.00
DR0415 Cyber Dragon UR 8.00 20.00
DR0416 Cybernetic Magician R .40 1.00
DR0417 Cybernetic Cyclopean C .20 .50
DR0418 Mechanical Hound C 2.50 6.00
DR0419 Cyber Archfiend C .20 .50
DR0420 Goblin Elite Attack Force SR 1.25 3.00
DR0421 B.E.S. Crystal Core SR 1.25 3.00
DR0422 Giant Kozaky C .20 .50
DR0423 Indomitable Fighter Lei Lei C .20 .50
DR0424 Protective Soul Ailin C .20 .50
DR0425 Doitsu C .20 .50
DR0426 Des Frog C .40 1.00
DR0427 T.A.D.P.O.L.E. C .20 .50
DR0428 Poison Draw Frog C .20 .50
DR0429 Tyranno Infinity R .40 1.00
DR0430 Batteryman C C .20 .50
DR0431 Ebon Magician Curran C .20 .50
DR0432 D.D.M. Different Dimension R 2.00 5.00
DR0433 Steam Gyroid C .20 .50
DR0434 UFOroid Fighter R 1.25 3.00
DR0435 Cyber Twin Dragon UR 2.50 6.00
DR0436 Cyber End Dragon UR 4.00 10.00
DR0437 Power Bond SR 2.50 6.00
DR0438 Fusion Recovery C .20 .50
DR0439 Miracle Fusion SR 4.00 10.00
DR0440 Dragon's Mirror SR 25.00 50.00
DR0441 System Down R 2.00 5.00
DR0442 Des Croaking C .20 .50
DR0443 Pot of Generosity C .20 .50
DR0444 Shien's Spy C .20 .50
DR0445 Transcendent Wings C .50 1.25
DR0446 Bubble Shuffle C .20 .50
DR0447 Spark Blaster C .20 .50
DR0448 Skyscraper R .40 1.00
DR0449 Fire Darts C .20 .50
DR0450 Spiritual Earth Art - Kurogane C .20 .50
DR0451 Spiritual Water Art - Aoi C .20 .50
DR0452 Spiritual Fire Art - Kurenai C .20 .50
DR0453 Spiritual Wind Art - Miyabi C .20 .50
DR0454 A Rival Appears! C .20 .50
DR0455 Magical Explosion C .20 .50
DR0456 Rising Energy R .40 1.00
DR0457 D.D. Trap Hole C .20 .50
DR0458 Conscription C .20 .50
DR0459 Dimension Wall R 2.50 6.00
DR0460 Prepare to Strike Back C .20 .50
DR0461 Zure, Knight of Dark World C .20 .50
DR0462 V-Tiger Jet C .20 .50
DR0463 Blade Skater C .20 .50
DR0464 Queen's Knight R 2.00 5.00
DR0465 Jack's Knight R 2.00 5.00
DR0466 King's Knight R 2.00 5.00
DR0467 Elemental Hero Bladedge SR 1.25 3.00
DR0468 Elemental Hero Wildheart SR 2.50 6.00
DR0469 Reborn Zombie C .20 .50
DR0470 Chthonian Soldier C .20 .50
DR0471 W-Wing Catapult C .20 .50
DR0472 Internal Incinerator C .20 .50
DR0473 Hydrogeddon SR 1.25 3.00
DR0474 Oxygeddon C .20 .50
DR0475 Water Dragon R 1.25 3.00
DR0476 Etoile Cyber C .20 .50
DR0477 B.E.S. Tetran SR 1.25 3.00
DR0478 Nanobreaker C .20 .50
DR0479 Rapid-Fire Magician R 1.25 3.00
DR0480 Beiige, Vanguard of Dark World C .20 .50
DR0481 Broww, Huntsman of Dark World R 1.25 3.00
DR0482 Brron, Mad King of Dark World R 2.00 5.00
DR0483 Sillva, Warlord of Dark World UR 2.50 6.00
DR0484 Goldd, Wu-Lord of Dark World UR 2.50 6.00
DR0485 Scarr, Scout of Dark World C .20 .50
DR0486 Familiar-Possessed - Aussa C .20 .50
DR0487 Familiar-Possessed - Eria C .20 .50
DR0488 Familiar-Possessed - Hiita C .20 .50
DR0489 Familiar-Possessed - Wynn C .20 .50
DR0490 VW-Tiger Catapult C .20 .50
DR0491 VWXYZ-Dragon Catapult Cannon R .40 1.00
DR0492 Cyber Blader R .75 2.00
DR0493 Elemental Hero Rampart Blaster R 4.00 10.00
DR0494 Elemental Hero Tempest SR 1.25 3.00
DR0495 Elemental Hero Wildedge R .40 1.00
DR0496 Elem. Hero Shining Flare UR 5.00 12.00
DR0497 Pot of Avarice UR 6.00 15.00
DR0498 Dark World Lightning R .40 1.00
DR0499 Level Modulation C .20 .50
DR04100 Ojamagic R .40 1.00
DR04101 Ojamuscle C .20 .50
DR04102 Feather Shot C .20 .50
DR04103 Bonding - H2O C .20 .50
DR04104 Chthonian Alliance C .20 .50
DR04105 Armed Changer C .20 .50
DR04106 Branch! C .20 .50
DR04107 Boss Rush C .20 .50
DR04108 Gateway to Dark World C .20 .50
DR04109 Hero Barrier C .20 .50
DR04110 Chthonian Blast C .20 .50
DR04111 The Forces of Darkness C .20 .50
DR04112 Dark Deal R 1.25 3.00
DR04113 Simultaneous Loss C .20 .50
DR04114 Weed Out C .20 .50
DR04115 The League of Uniform Nomenclature C .20 .50
DR04116 Roll Out! C .20 .50
DR04117 Chthonian Polymer C .20 .50
DR04118 Feather Wind C .20 .50
DR04119 Non-Fusion Area C .75 2.00
DR04120 Level Limit - Area A R .40 1.00
DR04121 Uria, Lord of Searing Flames UR 3.00 8.00
DR04122 Hamon, Lord of Striking Thunder UR 3.00 8.00
DR04123 Raviel, Lord of Phantasms UR 3.00 8.00
DR04124 Elemental Hero Neo Bubbleman C .20 .50
DR04125 Hero Kid R .40 1.00
DR04126 Cyber Barrier Dragon R .40 1.00
DR04127 Cyber Laser Dragon R .40 1.00
DR04128 Ancient Gear C .20 .50
DR04129 Ancient Gear Cannon C .20 .50
DR04130 Proto-Cyber Dragon SR 1.25 3.00
DR04131 Adhesive Explosive C .20 .50
DR04132 Machine King Prototype C .20 .50
DR04133 B.E.S. Covered Core SR 1.25 3.00
DR04134 D.D. Guide C .20 .50
DR04135 Chain Thrasher C .20 .50
DR04136 Disciple of the Forbidden Spell C .20 .50
DR04137 Tenkabito Shien R 2.00 5.00
DR04138 Parasitic Ticky C .20 .50
DR04139 Gokipon C .20 .50
DR04140 Silent Insect C .20 .50
DR04141 Chainsaw Insect R .40 1.00
DR04142 Anteatereatingant R .40 1.00
DR04143 Saber Beetle R .40 1.00
DR04144 Doom Dozer R 3.00 8.00
DR04145 Treeborn Frog UR 8.00 20.00
DR04146 Beelze Frog C .20 .50
DR04147 Princess Pikeru R 1.25 3.00
DR04148 Princess Curran R .40 1.00
DR04149 Memory Crusher C .20 .50
DR04150 Malice Ascendant C .20 .50
DR04151 Grass Phantom C .20 .50
DR04152 Sand Moth R .40 1.00
DR04153 Divine Dragon - Excelion SR 1.25 3.00
DR04154 Ruin, Queen of Oblivion SR 1.25 3.00
DR04155 Demise, King of Armageddon SR 2.00 5.00
DR04156 D.3.S. Frog C .20 .50
DR04157 Hero Heart C .20 .50
DR04158 Magnet Circle LV2 C .20 .50
DR04159 Ancient Gear Factory C .20 .50
DR04160 Ancient Gear Drill R .40 1.00
DR04161 Phantasmal Martyrs C .20 .50
DR04162 Cyclone Boomerang C .20 .50
DR04163 Symbol of Heritage C .20 .50
DR04164 Trial of the Princesses C .20 .50
DR04165 Photon Generator Unit C .20 .50
DR04166 End of the World C .75 2.00
DR04167 Ancient Gear Castle SR 1.25 3.00
DR04168 Samsara C .20 .50
DR04169 Super Junior Confrontation C .20 .50
DR04170 Miracle Kids C .20 .50
DR04171 Attack Reflector Unit C .20 .50
DR04172 Damage Condenser SR 1.25 3.00
DR04173 Karma Cut SR 6.00 15.00
DR04174 Next to be Lost C .20 .50
DR04175 Generation Shift C .75 2.00
DR04176 Full Salvo C .20 .50
DR04177 Success Probability 0 C .20 .50
DR04178 Option Hunter C .20 .50
DR04179 Goblin Out of the Frying Pan R .40 1.00
DR04180 Malfunction R .40 1.00
DR04181 Destiny Hero - Doom Lord R 6.00 15.00
DR04182 Destiny Hero - Captain Tenacious C .20 .50
DR04183 Destiny Hero - Diamond Dude SR 3.00 8.00
DR04184 Destiny Hero - Dreadmaster R .75 2.00
DR04185 Cyber Tutu C .40 1.00
DR04186 Cyber Gymnast R .40 1.00
DR04187 Cyber Prima R 1.25 3.00
DR04188 Cyber Kirin C .20 .50
DR04189 Cyber Phoenix UR 2.50 6.00
DR04190 Searchlightman C .20 .50
DR04191 Victory Viper XX03 SR 1.25 3.00
DR04192 Swift Birdman Joe C .20 .50
DR04193 Harpie's Pet Baby Dragon R 1.25 3.00
DR04194 Majestic Mech - Senku C .20 .50
DR04195 Majestic Mech - Ohka SR 1.25 3.00
DR04196 Majestic Mech - Goryu SR 1.25 3.00
DR04197 Royal Knight C .20 .50
DR04198 Herald of Green Light R 1.25 3.00
DR04199 Herald of Purple Light R 1.25 3.00
DR04200 Bountiful Artemis SR 80.00 110.00
DR04201 Layard the Liberator C .20 .50
DR04202 Banisher of the Radiance SR 4.00 10.00
DR04203 Voltanis the Adjudicator UR 2.50 6.00
DR04204 Guard Dog C .20 .50
DR04205 Whirlwind Weasel C .20 .50
DR04206 Avalanching Aussa C .20 .50
DR04207 Raging Eria C .20 .50
DR04208 Blazing Hiita C .20 .50
DR04209 Storming Wynn C .20 .50
DR04210 Batteryman D C .20 .50
DR04211 Super-Electromagnetic UR 2.50 6.00
DR04212 Elemental Hero Phoenix Enforcer R .40 1.00
DR04213 Elem. Hero Shining Phoenix UR 2.50 6.00
DR04214 Elemental Hero Mariner C .20 .50
DR04215 Elemental Hero Wild Wingman R 2.50 6.00
DR04216 Elemental Hero Necroid Shaman C .20 .50
DR04217 Misfortune C .20 .50
DR04218 H - Heated Heart C .20 .50
DR04219 E - Emergency Call C .50 1.25
DR04220 R - Righteous Justice C .20 .50
DR04221 O - Oversoul C .20 .50
DR04222 HERO Flash!! C .20 .50
DR04223 Power Capsule C .20 .50
DR04224 Celestial Transformation R .40 1.00
DR04225 Guard Penalty R .40 1.00
DR04226 Grand Convergence R .40 1.00
DR04227 Dimensional Fissure R 2.00 5.00
DR04228 Clock Tower Prison R .40 1.00
DR04229 Life Equalizer R 1.25 3.00
DR04230 Elemental Recharge C .20 .50
DR04231 Destruction of Destiny C .20 .50
DR04232 Destiny Signal R .40 1.00
DR04233 D - Time C .20 .50
DR04234 D - Shield C .20 .50
DR04235 Icarus Attack SR 20.00 40.00
DR04236 Elemental Absorber C .20 .50

DR04237 Macro Cosmos SR 15.00 30.00
DR04238 Miraculous Descent SR 1.25 3.00
DR04239 Shattered Axe C .20 .50
DR04240 Forced Back R 2.50 6.00
DR04241 Satellite Cannon SCR 8.00 20.00
DR04242 Gilford the Lightning SCR 4.00 10.00
DR04243 Exarion Universe SCR 25.00 50.00
DR04244 D.D. Assailant SCR 8.00 20.00
DR04245 Kaibaman SCR 15.00 30.00

2008 Yu-Gi-Oh Retro Pack 1

COMPLETE SET (100) 400.00 500.00
BOOSTER BOX (8 SETS) 150.00 200.00
SET (3 PACKS) 25.00 30.00
BOOSTER PACK (9 CARDS) 5.00 6.00
RELEASED ON JULY 8, 2008
RP010 Blue-Eyes Ultimate Dragon SCR 15.00 30.00
RP011 Blue-Eyes White Dragon UR 30.00 60.00
RP013 Dark Magician UR 15.00 30.00
RP015 Raigeki UR 115.00 140.00
RP016 Fissure R 1.50 4.00
RP0111 Red-Eyes B. Dragon UR 8.00 20.00
RP0112 Swords of Revealing Light SR 2.50 6.00
RP0116 Monster Reborn SR 6.00 15.00
RP0117 Right Leg of the Forbidden One R 5.00 12.00
RP0118 Left Leg of the Forbidden One R 5.00 12.00
RP0119 Right Arm of the Forbidden One R 5.00 12.00
RP0120 Left Arm of the Forbidden One R 5.00 12.00
RP0121 Exodia the Forbidden One UR 10.00 25.00
RP0122 Gaia the Dragon Champion SR 2.00 5.00
RP0123 Gate Guardian UR 10.00 25.00
RP0124 Summoned Skull SR 2.50 6.00
RP0126 Harpie Lady Sisters R 1.00 2.50
RP0128 B. Skull Dragon R 5.00 12.00
RP0130 Sanga of the Thunder R 2.00 5.00
RP0131 Kazejin R 1.50 4.00
RP0132 Suijin R 1.50 4.00
RP0133 Magician of Faith R 1.50 4.00
RP0135 Time Wizard SR 5.00 12.00
RP0136 Sangan SR 8.00 20.00
RP0137 Kuriboh SR 2.00 5.00
RP0138 Catapult Turtle SR 2.00 5.00
RP0144 Barrel Dragon R 2.50 6.00
RP0145 Solemn Judgment SR 8.00 20.00
RP0148 Heavy Storm R 1.25 3.00
RP0150 Blue-Eyes Toon Dragon R 4.00 10.00
RP0151 Axe of Despair R 1.25 3.00
RP0154 Relinquished UR 3.00 8.00
RP0159 Painful Choice R 4.00 10.00
RP0161 Megamorph R 1.00 2.50
RP0182 Messenger of Peace R 2.00 5.00
RP0184 Card Destruction R 2.50 6.00
RP0185 La Jinn the Mystical Genie of the Lamp SR 20.00 35.00
RP0186 Lord of D. R 1.00 2.50
RP0187 The Flute of Summoning Dragon R 1.50 4.00
RP0188 Graceful Charity R 2.00 5.00
RP0190 Scapegoat UR 40.00 70.00
RP0191 Blast Sphere SCR 20.00 40.00
RP0192 Copycat SCR 50.00 80.00
RP0193 Relieve Monster SCR 10.00 25.00
RP0194 Cloning SCR 15.00 30.00
RP0195 Kaibaman SCR 20.00 40.00
RP0196 Cyber Harpie Lady SCR 150.00 250.00
RP0197 Amazoness Chain Master SCR 35.00 70.00
RP0198 Embodiment of Apophis SCR 20.00 40.00
RP0199 Exchange of the Spirit SCR 50.00 80.00
RP01100 Ancient Lamp SCR 25.00 50.00

2009 Yu-Gi-Oh Retro Pack 2

COMPLETE SET (101) 300.00 500.00
BOOSTER BOX (8 SETS) 150.00 300.00
SET (3 PACKS) 10.00 25.00
BOOSTER PACK (9 CARDS) 5.00 12.00
RELEASED ON JULY 28, 2009
RP020 Gorz the Emissary of Darkness SCR 1.25 3.00
RP021 Jinzo UR 2.50 6.00
RP024 Chain Destruction R .75 2.00
RP027 Mirror Wall UR 1.25 3.00
RP029 Ceasefire R .75 2.00
RP0210 Magical Hats R 1.25 3.00
RP0213 Buster Blader SR 1.25 3.00
RP0215 Limiter Removal SR 1.50 4.00
RP0219 The Legendary Fisherman R .60 1.50
RP0221 Thousand-Eyes Restrict UR 8.00 20.00
RP0225 Gearfried the Iron Knight R .60 1.50
RP0227 The Masked Beast SR .40 1.00
RP0228 Revival Jam R 1.00 2.50
RP0235 Infinite Cards R 2.00 5.00
RP0236 Jam Defender SR .60 1.50
RP0238 United We Stand UR 2.50 6.00
RP0239 Mage Power R .75 2.00
RP0242 Dark Necrofear SR .40 1.00
RP0245 Destiny Board SR 2.00 5.00
RP0250 Magic Cylinder R .60 1.50
RP0252 Dark Ruler Ha Des UR .75 2.00
RP0254 Freed the Matchless General R .60 1.50
RP0256 Tyrant Dragon SR 1.00 2.50
RP0258 Airknight Parshath R 1.25 3.00
RP0259 Yamata Dragon R .40 1.00
RP0260 Hino-Kagu-Tsuchi SR 2.50 6.00
RP0265 Injection Fairy Lily UR 1.25 3.00
RP0266 Ring of Destruction SCR 6.00 15.00
RP0268 Don Zaloog R 1.25 3.00
RP0272 Dark Jeroid R .40 1.00
RP0273 Newdoria R .60 1.50
RP0274 Helpoemer UR 1.25 3.00
RP0279 Necrovalley R 1.50 4.00
RP0281 Nightmare Wheel R 1.50 4.00
RP0282 Lava Golem SR .75 2.00
RP0283 Morphing Jar R 2.50 6.00
RP0284 Royal Decree R 1.25 3.00
RP0285 Swift Gaia the Fierce Knight UR 1.00 2.50
RP0286 Obnoxious Celtic Guardian R .40 1.00
RP0287 Kaiser Sea Horse R .40 1.00
RP0288 Insect Queen SR .60 1.50
RP0289 Alpha The Magnet Warrior R .60 1.50
RP0290 Beta The Magnet Warrior R .60 1.50
RP0291 Gamma The Magnet Warrior R .60 1.50
RP0292 Valkyrion the Magna Warrior SCR 10.00 25.00
RP0293 Harpie's Pet Dragon SCR 20.00 40.00
RP0294 Archfiend of Gilfer SCR 3.00 8.00
RP0295 Light and Darkness Dragon SCR 20.00 45.00
RP0296 Blue-Eyes Shining Dragon SCR 150.00 225.00
RP0297 Dragon Master Knight SCR 50.00 90.00
RP0298 Victory Dragon SCR 8.00 20.00
RP0299 Green Baboon, Defender of the Forest SCR 4.00 10.00
RP02100 Dreadscythe Harvester SCR 1.00 2.50

2008 Yu-Gi-Oh Gold

COMPLETE SET (45) 60.00 120.00
BOOSTER BOX (5 PACKS) 250.00 400.00
BOOSTER PACK (25 CARDS) 40.00 80.00
RELEASED ON APRIL 2, 2008
GLD101 7 Colored Fish C .10 .30
GLD102 Sonic Bird C .10 .30
GLD103 Jinzo GUR 1.50 4.00
GLD104 Summoner Of Illusions C .10 .30
GLD105 Fire Princess C .10 .30
GLD106 Needle Worm C 1.25 3.00
GLD107 8-Claws Scorpion C .10 .30
GLD108 Swarm Of Scarabs C .20 .60
GLD109 Swarm Of Locusts C .10 .30
GLD110 Des Lacooda C .20 .60
GLD111 Newdoria C .10 .30
GLD112 Don Zaloog GUR .40 1.00
GLD113 Old Vindictive Magician C .10 .30
GLD114 Breaker the Magical Warrior GUR 1.00 2.50
GLD115 D.D. Warrior Lady GUR 1.00 2.50
GLD116 Dark Magician of Chaos GUR 8.00 20.00
GLD117 Stealth Bird C .60 1.50
GLD118 Regenerating Mummy C .10 .30
GLD119 Solar Flare Dragon C .10 .30
GLD120 Rare Metal Dragon C .10 .30
GLD121 Nightmare Penguin C .10 .30
GLD122 Cyber Dragon GUR 1.25 3.00
GLD123 Sillva, Warlord Of Dark World C .40 1.00
GLD124 Goldd, Wu-Lord Of Dark World GUR .40 1.00
GLD125 Doom Dozer C .10 .30
GLD126 Grandmaster of the Six Samurai GUR 1.25 3.00
GLD127 Prometheus, King Of Shadows GUR .40 1.00
GLD128 Blue-Eyes Ultimate Dragon GUR 10.00 25.00
GLD129 Chimeratech Overdragon GUR .75 2.00
GLD130 Swords of Revealing Light GUR 1.00 2.50
GLD131 Heavy Storm GUR .75 2.00
GLD132 Reinforcement of the Army GUR 1.25 3.00
GLD133 Brain Control GUR .75 2.00
GLD134 Offerings To The Doomed C .10 .30
GLD135 Non-Spellcasting Area C .10 .30
GLD136 Mist Body C .75 2.00
GLD137 Pandemonium C .40 1.00
GLD138 Crush Card Virus GUR 8.00 20.00
GLD139 Mirror Force GUR 4.00 10.00
GLD140 Torrential Tribute GUR 1.25 3.00
GLD141 Needle Ceiling C .40 1.00
GLD142 Royal Command C .10 .30
GLD143 Rivalry Of Warlords C 1.00 2.50
GLD144 Skill Drain C 1.50 4.00
GLD145 Spell Shield Type-8 C .10 .30

2009 Yu-Gi-Oh Gold Series 2

COMPLETE SET (100) 30.00 60.00
BOOSTER BOX (5 CARDS) 60.00 100.00
BOOSTER PACK (25 CARDS) 15.00 30.00
RELEASED ON MAY 27, 2009
GLD21 Sangan GUR .75 2.00
GLD22 Des Volstgalph GUR .75 2.00
GLD23 Lekunga C .20 .50
GLD24 Lord Poison C .20 .50
GLD25 Rigorous Reaver C .20 .50
GLD26 Zaborg the Thunder Monarch C .20 .50
GLD27 Mobius the Frost Monarch C .20 .50
GLD28 Thestalos the Firestorm Monarch C .20 .50
GLD29 Granmarg the Rock Monarch C .20 .50
GLD210 Treeborn Frog C .20 .50
GLD211 Phantom Beast Cross-Wing C .20 .50
GLD212 Phantom Beast Wild-Horn C .20 .50
GLD213 Phantom Beast Thunder-Pegasus C .20 .50
GLD214 Phantom Beast Rock-Lizard C .20 .50
GLD215 Winged Rhynos C .20 .50
GLD216 Snipe Hunter C .20 .50
GLD217 The Six Samurai - Yaichi C .20 .50
GLD218 The Six Samurai - Kamon C .20 .50
GLD219 The Six Samurai - Yariza C .20 .50
GLD220 The Six Samurai - Nisashi C .20 .50
GLD221 The Six Samurai - Zanji C .20 .50
GLD222 The Six Samurai - Irou C .20 .50
GLD223 Volcanic Rocket GUR 1.00 2.50
GLD224 Volcanic Shell C 1.25 3.00
GLD225 Elemental Hero Captain Gold GUR 1.00 2.50
GLD226 Raiza the Storm Monarch GUR 1.00 2.50
GLD227 Necro Gardna GUR .75 2.00
GLD228 Elemental Hero Neos Alius C .20 .50
GLD229 Test Tiger GUR 1.00 2.50
GLD230 Royal Firestorm Guards GUR 1.00 2.50
GLD231 Dark Armed Dragon GUR 2.00 5.00
GLD232 Prime Material Dragon GUR .75 2.00
GLD233 Caius the Shadow Monarch GUR 1.25 3.00
GLD234 Exile of the Wicked C .20 .50
GLD235 Warrior Elimination C .20 .50
GLD236 Giant Trunade C .20 .50
GLD237 Mind Control GUR 1.00 2.50
GLD238 Skyscraper C 1.25 3.00
GLD239 Future Fusion GUR 1.00 2.50
GLD240 Gold Sarcophagus GUR 1.50 4.00
GLD241 Shien's Castle of Mist C .20 .50
GLD242 Six Samurai United C .20 .50
GLD243 Veil of Darkness GUR .75 2.00
GLD244 Solemn Judgment GUR 1.00 2.50
GLD245 Bottomless Trap Hole GUR 1.25 3.00
GLD246 Compulsory Evacuation Device C .20 .50
GLD247 Begone, Knave! C .20 .50
GLD248 Phoenix Wing Wind Blast GUR 1.00 2.50
GLD249 Return of the Six Samurai C .20 .50
GLD250 Double-Edged Sword Technique C .20 .50

2010 Yu-Gi-Oh Gold Series 3

COMPLETE SET (50) 30.00 75.00
BOOSTER BOX (5 PACKS) 80.00 120.00
BOOSTER PACK (25 CARDS) 15.00 30.00
RELEASED ON JUNE 23, 2010
GLD31 Mist Valley Watcher C .10 .25
GLD33 Amazoness Archer C .10 .25
GLD34 Amazoness Paladin C .10 .25
GLD35 Amazoness Fighter C .10 .25
GLD36 Amazoness Swords Woman C .20 .50
GLD37 Amazoness Blowpiper C .10 .25
GLD38 Amazoness Tiger C .10 .25
GLD39 Destiny Hero - Malicious 1.25 3.00
GLD3-2 Vice Dragon GUR 1.00 2.50
GLD310 Freya, Spirit of Victory C .20 .50
GLD311 Nova Summoner C .20 .50
GLD312 Exploder Dragon GUR 1.00 2.50
GLD313 Goblin Zombie C .75 2.00
GLD314 Elemental Hero Prisma GUR 2.50 6.00
GLD315 Dimensional Alchemist GUR 1.00 2.50
GLD316 Judgment Dragon GUR 1.50 4.00
GLD317 Amazoness Chain Master C .10 .25
GLD318 Mezuki GUR 1.00 2.50
GLD319 Plaguespreader Zombie GUR 1.00 2.50
GLD320 Thunder King Rai-Oh GUR 1.25 3.00
GLD321 Blackwing - Gale GUR 1.00 2.50
GLD322 Blackwing - Bora the Spear C .50 1.25
GLD323 Blackwing - Sirocco the Dawn C .50 1.25
GLD324 Blackwing - Blizzard the Far North C .50 1.25
GLD325 Blackwing - Shura the Blue Flame C .50 1.25
GLD326 Blackwing - Kalut .50 1.25
GLD327 Infernity Archfiend GUR 1.00 2.50
GLD328 Infernity Dwarf C .10 .25
GLD329 Infernity Guardian C .10 .25
GLD330 Reese the Ice Mistress C .20 .50
GLD331 Numbing Grub in the Ice Barrier C .10 .25
GLD332 Mist Condor C .10 .25
GLD333 Mist Valley Windmaster C .10 .25
GLD334 Worm Falco C .10 .25
GLD335 Worm Gulse C .10 .25
GLD336 Worm Hope C .10 .25
GLD337 Stardust Dragon GUR 2.50 6.00
GLD338 Blackwing Armor Master GUR 1.00 2.50
GLD339 Blackwing Armed Wing GUR 1.00 2.50
GLD340 Mystical Space Typhoon GUR 1.50 4.00
GLD341 My Body as a Shield GUR 1.00 2.50
GLD342 Smashing Ground GUR 1.00 2.50
GLD343 Enemy Controller GUR 1.00 2.50
GLD344 Destiny Draw C .30 .75
GLD345 Black Whirlwind C 1.25 3.00
GLD346 Amazoness Archers C .10 .25
GLD347 Dramatic Rescue C .10 .25
GLD348 Magical Arm Shield C .10 .25
GLD349 Icarus Attack GUR 1.00 2.50
GLD350 Aegis of Gaia C .10 .25

2011 Yu-Gi-Oh Gold Series 4

COMPLETE SET (50) 100.00 150.00
BOOSTER BOX (5 PACKS) 60.00 120.00
BOOSTER PACK (25 CARDS) 15.00 30.00
RELEASED ON JULY 1, 2011
GLD4001 Millennium Shield .25 .75
GLD4002 Pendulum Machine .25 .75
GLD4003 The Wicked Worm Beast .25 .75
GLD4004 Goddess with the Third Eye .25 .75
GLD4005 Beastking of the Swamps .25 .75
GLD4006 Versago the Destroyer .25 .75
GLD4007 Morphing Jar GUR .50 1.25
GLD4008 Goddess of Whim .25 .75
GLD4009 Injection Fairy Lily .25 .75
GLD4010 Gravekeeper's Spy GUR .40 1.00
GLD4011 Spirit Reaper GUR .50 1.25
GLD4012 Chaos Sorcerer GUR 1.25 3.00
GLD4013 Black Luster Soldier GUR 4.00 10.00
GLD4014 White-Horned Dragon .25 .75
GLD4015 Toon Dark Magician Girl .50 1.25
GLD4016 Meltiel, Sage of the Sky .25 .75
GLD4017 Radiant Jeral .25 .75
GLD4018 Diabolos, King of the Abyss .25 .75
GLD4019 Lich Lord, King of the Underworld .25 .75
GLD4020 Prometheus, King of the Shadows .25 .75
GLD4021 Mormolith .25 .75
GLD4022 Darklord Zerato GUR .25 .75
GLD4023 Doomcaliber Knight GUR .50 1.25
GLD4024 Ryko, Lightsworn Hunter GUR .50 1.25
GLD4025 Celestia, Lightsworn Angel GUR .25 .75
GLD4026 Tytannial, Princess GUR .25 .75
GLD4027 Summoner Monk GUR 1.25 3.00
GLD4028 Genesis Dragon 1.00 2.50
GLD4029 Orichalcos Shunoros .25 .75
GLD4030 Obelisk the Tormentor GUR 6.00 15.00
GLD4031 Five-Headed Dragon GUR 1.25 3.00
GLD4032 Gladiator Beast Gyzarus GUR .50 1.25
GLD4033 Eternal Drought .25 .75
GLD4034 Eradicating Aerosol .25 .75
GLD4035 Soul Exchange .25 .75
GLD4036 Toon World .25 .75
GLD4037 Graceful Dice .25 .75
GLD4038 Sage's Stone 1.25 3.00
GLD4039 Toon Table of Contents GUR 2.50 6.00
GLD4040 Pot of Avarice GUR .50 1.25
GLD4041 Recurring Nightmare 1.00 2.50
GLD4042 Sword of Dark Rites .25 .75
GLD4043 Trade-In 1.25 3.00
GLD4044 Magic Formula .25 .75
GLD4045 Robbin' Goblin .25 .75
GLD4046 Skull Dice .25 .75
GLD4047 Royal Oppression GUR .50 1.25
GLD4048 Xing Zhen Hu .25 .75
GLD4049 Deck Devastation Virus 1.00 2.50
GLD4050 Trap Stun GUR 1.25 3.00

2012 Yu-Gi-Oh Gold Series Haunted Mine

COMPLETE SET (55) 50.00 100.00
BOOSTER BOX (5 PACKS) 60.00 80.00
BOOSTER PACK (25 CARDS) 20.00 30.00
RELEASED ON JUNE 12, 2012
GLD5001 Blue-Eyes White GGR 8.00 20.00
GLD5002 Patrician of Darkness C .10 .30
GLD5003 Pyramid Turtle C .10 .30
GLD5004 Dark Scorpion Burglars C .10 .30
GLD5005 Don Zaloog C .20 .60
GLD5006 Helpoemer C .10 .30
GLD5007 Dark Scorpion - Cliff the Trap Remover C .10 .30
GLD5008 Despair from the Dark C .10 .30
GLD5009 Fear from the Dark C .10 .30
GLD5010 Dark Scorpion - Chick the Yellow C .10 .30
GLD5011 Dark Scorpion - Gorg the Strong C .10 .30
GLD5012 Dark Scorpion - Meanae the Thorn C .10 .30
GLD5013 Ryu Kokki C .10 .30
GLD5014 Vampire Lady C .10 .30
GLD5015 Double Coston C .10 .30
GLD5016 Regenerating Mummy C .10 .30
GLD5017 Dark Mimic LV1 C .10 .30
GLD5018 Dark Mimic LV3 C .10 .30
GLD5019 Zombie Master C .40 1.00
GLD5020 Gernia C .10 .30
GLD5021 Goblin Zombie C .75 2.00
GLD5022 The Lady in Wight C .40 1.00
GLD5023 Red Ogre C .10 .30
GLD5024 Gorz the Emissary of Darkness GGR 2.50 6.00
GLD5025 Bone Crusher C .10 .30
GLD5026 Fabled Grimro GLD .50 1.25
GLD5027 Master Hyperion GLD .50 1.25
GLD5028 Grapha, Dragon Lord GR .50 1.25
GLD5029 Sephylon, the Ultimate GR .50 1.25
GLD5030 Herald of Perfection GGR 2.50 6.00
GLD5031 Brionac, Dragon GR 2.50 6.00
GLD5032 Naturia Beast GLD 1.50 4.00
GLD5033 Naturia Barkion GGR 2.00 5.00
GLD5034 Formula Synchron GLD 2.00 5.00
GLD5035 Karakuri Steel Shogun GR .75 2.00
GLD5036 Number 39: Utopia GLD 1.50 4.00
GLD5037 Dark Hole GLD 1.25 3.00
GLD5038 Mystical Space GGR 4.00 10.00
GLD5039 Book of Life C .25 .75
GLD5040 Call of the Mummy C .10 .30
GLD5041 Spellbook Organization C .20 .60
GLD5042 Mustering of the Dark Scorpions C .10 .30
GLD5043 Pyramid of Wonders C .10 .30
GLD5044 Dawn of the Herald C .20 .60
GLD5045 Solemn Judgment GGR 2.00 5.00
GLD5046 Call of the Haunted GLD 1.25 3.00
GLD5047 Physical Double C .10 .30
GLD5048 Hidden Spellbook C .10 .30
GLD5049 Zoma the Spirit C .40 1.00
GLD5050 Embodiment of Apophis C .10 .30
GLD5051 Machine King - 3000 B.C. C .10 .30
GLD5052 Starlight Road GLD .50 1.25
GLD5053 Tiki Curse C .10 .30
GLD5054 Tiki Soul C .10 .30
GLD5055 Copy Knight C .10 .30

2014 Yu-Gi-Oh Premium Gold 1st Edition

COMPLETE SET (90) 60.00 150.00
BOOSTER BOX (5 PACKS) 80.00 100.00
BOOSTER PACK (15 CARDS) 20.00 30.00
RELEASED ON MARCH 28, 2014
PGLD001 Gimmick Puppet Dreary Doll SCR .60 1.50
PGLD002 Gimmick Puppet Magnet Doll SCR .40 1.00
PGLD003 Chronomaly Tula Guardian SCR .20 .60
PGLD004 Big Belly Knight SCR .20 .60
PGLD005 Power Tool Mecha Dragon SCR .20 .60
PGLD006 Ancient Pixie Dragon SCR .75 2.00
PGLD007 Junk Puppet SCR .20 .60
PGLD008 Chronomaly City Babylon SCR .20 .60
PGLD009 Utopia Buster SCR .20 .60
PGLD010 Chronomaly Gordian Knot SCR .20 .60
PGLD011 Gimmick Puppet Humpty Dumpty SCR .20 .60
PGLD012 Gimmick Puppet Shadow Feeler SCR .20 .60
PGLD013 Silent Wobby SCR .20 .60
PGLD014 Dynatherium SCR .20 .60
PGLD015 Dragonecro Nethersoul Dragon SCR 1.00 2.50
PGLD016 Beelze of the Diabolic Dragons SCR 8.00 20.00
PGLD017 Blackfeather Darkrage Dragon SCR .75 2.00
PGLD018 Number C6: Chronomaly Chaos Atlandis SCR .20 .60
PGLD019 Number C15: Gimmick Puppet Giant Hunter SCR .20 .60
PGLD020 Number C40: Gimmick Puppet of Dark Strings SCR .40 1.00
PGLD021 Number C88: Gimmick Puppet Disaster Leo SCR .40 1.00
PGLD022 Number C9: Chaos Dyson Sphere SCR .20 .60
PGLD023 Number 13: Embodiment of Crime SCR .20 .60
PGLD024 Number 31: Embodiment of Punishment SCR .20 .60
PGLD025 Number 82: Heartlandraco SCR 2.50 6.00
PGLD026 Tri-Edge Levia SCR .50 1.25
PGLD027 Rank-Up-Magic Argent Chaos Force SCR 1.25 3.00
PGLD028 Gagaga Academy Emergency Network SCR 1.00 2.50
PGLD029 Ghost of a Grudge SCR 1.00 2.50
PGLD030 Obelisk the Tormentor SCR 8.00 20.00
PGLD031 The Winged Dragon of Ra SCR 8.00 20.00
PGLD032 Slifer the Sky Dragon SCR 8.00 20.00
PGLD033 Dark Magician Girl GR 2.00 5.00
PGLD034 Lonefire Blossom GR 1.50 4.00
PGLD035 Honest GR 1.00 2.50
PGLD036 Effect Veiler GR 3.00 8.00
PGLD037 Gagaga Magician GR .50 1.25
PGLD038 Galaxy-Eyes Photon Dragon GR 2.00 5.00
PGLD039 Lightpulsar Dragon GR .75 2.00
PGLD040 Darkflare Dragon GR .50 1.25
PGLD041 Eclipse Wyvern GR .50 1.25
PGLD042 Crane Crane GR .50 1.25
PGLD043 Colossal Fighter GR .20 .60
PGLD044 Number 32: Shark Drake GR .50 1.25
PGLD045 Brotherhood of the Fire Fist - Tiger King GR .50 1.25
PGLD046 Solar Recharge GR .50 1.25
PGLD047 Forbidden Chalice GR 1.00 2.50
PGLD048 Forbidden Lance GR 1.00 2.50
PGLD049 Forbidden Dress GR .50 1.25
PGLD050 Fire Formation - Tenki GR .50 1.25
PGLD051 Jinzo GR 1.00 2.50
PGLD052 Breaker the Magical Warrior GR .50 1.25
PGLD053 Cyber Dragon GR 1.00 2.50
PGLD054 Goldd, Wu-Lord of Dark World GR .15 .40
PGLD055 Blue-Eyes Ultimate Dragon GR 8.00 20.00
PGLD056 Chimeratech Overdragon GR .75 2.00
PGLD057 Swords of Revealing Light GR .50 1.25
PGLD058 Reinforcement of the Army GR .50 1.25
PGLD059 Mirror Force GR 1.25 3.00
PGLD060 Torrential Tribute GR 1.00 2.50
PGLD061 Des Volstgalph GR .50 1.25
PGLD062 Raiza the Storm Monarch GR .50 1.25
PGLD063 Necro Gardna GR .15 .40
PGLD064 Dark Armed Dragon GR 1.50 4.00
PGLD065 Prime Material Dragon GR .50 1.25
PGLD066 Caius the Shadow Monarch GR .50 1.25
PGLD067 Mind Control GR .50 1.25
PGLD068 Gold Sarcophagus GR 1.00 2.50
PGLD069 Bottomless Trap Hole GR 1.00 2.50
PGLD070 Phoenix Wing Wind Blast GR .50 1.25
PGLD071 Exploder Dragon GR .50 1.25
PGLD072 Judgment Dragon GR 1.50 4.00
PGLD073 Mezuki GR .75 2.00
PGLD074 Plaguespreader Zombie GR .75 2.00
PGLD075 Thunder King Rai-Oh GR 1.00 2.50
PGLD076 Stardust Dragon GR 2.00 5.00
PGLD077 Blackwing Armor Master GR .50 1.25
PGLD078 Blackwing Armed Wing GR .15 .40
PGLD079 Mystical Space Typhoon GR 1.25 3.00
PGLD080 Icarus Attack GR .75 2.00
PGLD081 Morphing Jar GR .50 1.25
PGLD082 Gravekeeper's Spy GR .15 .40
PGLD083 Spirit Reaper GR .50 1.25
PGLD084 Chaos Sorcerer GR .75 2.00
PGLD085 Black Luster Soldier - Envoy of the Beginning GR 3.00 8.00
PGLD086 Ryko, Lightsworn Hunter GR .20 .60
PGLD087 Celestia, Lightsworn Angel GR .15 .40
PGLD088 Tytannial, Princess of Camellias GR .15 .40
PGLD089 Summoner Monk GR 1.25 3.00
PGLD090 Trap Stun GR .75 2.00

2015 Yu-Gi-Oh Premium Gold Return of the Bling 1st Edition

COMPLETE SET (91 CARDS) 115.00 150.00
BOOSTER BOX (5 PACKS) 60.00 80.00
BOOSTER PACK 15.00 20.00
RELEASED ON MARCH 20, 2015
PGL2EN001 Junk Giant GSR .10 .20
PGL2EN002 Absolute King Back Jack GSR .30 .40
PGL2EN003 Rose Lover GSR .30 .50
PGL2EN004 Rose Paladin GSR .20 .35
PGL2EN005 Ghost Charon, the Underworld Boatman GSR .15 .25
PGL2EN006 Blackwing - Kris the Crack of Dawn GSR 3.00 4.50
PGL2EN007 Blackwing - Pinaki the Waxing Moon GSR 1.25 2.00
PGL2EN008 Peropero Cerperus GSR .30 .50
PGL2EN009 Tristan, Knight of the Underworld GSR .50 .75
PGL2EN010 Isolde, Belle of the Underworld GSR .25 .40
PGL2EN011 Masked HERO Anki GSR .60 1.00
PGL2EN012 Blackwing Tamer - Obsidian Hawk Joe GSR .40 .60
PGL2EN013 Blackwing - Nothung the Starlight GSR 1.75 2.00
PGL2EN014 Dragocytos Corrupted Nethersoul Dragon GSR .60 1.00
PGL2EN015 Number 95: Galaxy-Eyes Dark Matter Dragon GSR 3.25 4.00
PGL2EN016 Cat Shark GSR .60 1.00
PGL2EN017 Number 14: Greedy Sarameya GSR .20 .35
PGL2EN018 Number 21: Frozen Lady Justice GSR .30 .50
PGL2EN019 Parallel Twister GSR .20 .35
PGL2EN020 Stardust Re-Spark GSR .20 .35
PGL2EN021 Santa Claws GSR .80 1.15
PGL2EN022 Right Leg of the Forbidden One GDR 2.00 2.50
PGL2EN023 Left Leg of the Forbidden One GDR 2.00 2.50
PGL2EN024 Right Arm of the Forbidden One GDR 2.00 2.50
PGL2EN025 Left Arm of the Forbidden One GDR 2.00 2.50
PGL2EN026 Exodia the Forbidden One GDR 3.00 3.50
PGL2EN027 Sinister Serpent GDR .20 .35
PGL2EN028 Card Trooper GDR .20 .35
PGL2EN029 Elemental HERO Neos Alius GDR .20 .35
PGL2EN030 Dandylion GDR .40 .60
PGL2EN031 Debris Dragon GDR .60 1.00
PGL2EN032 Mystical Beast of Serket GDR .20 .35
PGL2EN033 Glow-Up Bulb GDR 7.00 8.00
PGL2EN034 Metaion, the Timelord GDR .20 .35
PGL2EN035 Bujin Yamato GDR .50 .75
PGL2EN036 Traptrix Atrax GDR .20 .35
PGL2EN037 Traptrix Myrmeleo GDR 1.00 1.25
PGL2EN038 Traptrix Nepenthes GDR .20 .35
PGL2EN039 Mathematician GDR .75 1.15
PGL2EN040 Sylvan Sagequoia GDR .20 .35
PGL2EN041 Traptrix Dionaea GDR .60 1.00
PGL2EN042 Goyo Guardian GDR 2.50 3.00
PGL2EN043 Armades, Keeper of Boundaries GDR 2.00 2.50
PGL2EN044 Lavalval Chain GDR 1.75 2.25
PGL2EN045 Madolche Queen Tiaramisu GDR .60 1.00
PGL2EN046 Number 101: Silent Honor ARK GDR 2.25 3.00
PGL2EN047 Downerd Magician GDR 1.75 2.25
PGL2EN048 Raigeki GDR 17.00 20.00
PGL2EN049 Book of Moon GDR .60 1.00
PGL2EN050 Advanced Ritual Art GDR 3.00 3.50
PGL2EN051 Foolish Burial GDR 1.50 2.00
PGL2EN052 Charge of the Light Brigade GDR .50 .75
PGL2EN053 Rekindling GDR .20 .35

PGL2EN054 Preparation of Rites GDR .20 .35
PGL2EN055 Pot of Duality GDR 2.00 3.00
PGL2EN056 Temple of the Kings GDR .20 .35
PGL2EN057 The Grand Spellbook Tower GDR .40 .60
PGL2EN058 Rank-Up-Magic Barian's Force GDR .20 .35
PGL2EN059 Rank-Up-Magic Numeron Force GDR .20 .35
PGL2EN060 Rank-Up-Magic Astral Force GDR .25 .40
PGL2EN061 Sylvan Charity GDR .20 .35
PGL2EN062 Ceasefire GDR .20 .35
PGL2EN063 Ring of Destruction GDR .40 .75
PGL2EN064 Chain Disappearance GDR 1.00 1.25
PGL2EN065 Compulsory Evacuation Device GDR .50 .75
PGL2EN066 Exchange of the Spirit GDR .20 .35
PGL2EN067 Karma Cut GDR 1.00 1.25
PGL2EN068 Solemn Warning GDR 3.50 4.00
PGL2EN069 Traptrix Trap Hole Nightmare GDR .60 1.00
PGL2EN070 Crush Card Virus GDR 1.50 2.00
PGL2EN071 Veil of Darkness GDR .20 .35
PGL2EN072 Elemental HERO Prisma GDR 5.50 7.00
PGL2EN073 Blackwing - Gale the Whirlwind GDR 1.00 1.50
PGL2EN074 My Body as a Shield GDR .20 .35
PGL2EN075 Smashing Ground GDR .20 .35
PGL2EN076 Enemy Controller GDR .20 .35
PGL2EN077 Doomcaliber Knight GDR .20 .35
PGL2EN078 Five-Headed Dragon GDR .80 1.15
PGL2EN079 Gladiator Beast Gyzarus GDR .20 .35
PGL2EN080 Blue-Eyes White Dragon GDR 2.00 2.50
PGL2EN081 Gorz the Emissary of Darkness GDR 1.00 1.50
PGL2EN082 Master Hyperion GDR .20 .35
PGL2EN083 Grapha, Dragon Lord of Dark World GDR .40 .60
PGL2EN084 Sephylon, the Ultimate Timelord GDR .20 .35
PGL2EN085 Herald of Perfection GDR 7.50 8.25
PGL2EN086 Naturia Beast GDR 2.00 2.50
PGL2EN087 Naturia Barkion GDR .75 1.00
PGL2EN088 Formula Synchron GDR 4.50 5.00
PGL2EN089 Dark Hole GDR 1.00 1.25
PGL2EN090 Call of the Haunted GDR 1.00 1.50
PGL2EN091 Starlight Road GDR .40 .60

2016 Yu-Gi-Oh Infinite Gold

COMPLETE SET (100) 120.00 160.00
RELEASED ON MARCH 18, 2016
PGL3EN001 Angmarl the Fiendish Monarch GSCR .25 .40
PGL3EN002 Junk Changer GSCR .10 .15
PGL3EN003 Junkuriboh GSCR .10 .20
PGL3EN004 Magical King Moonstar GSCR .10 .20
PGL3EN005 Stardust Charge Warrior GSCR 1.75 2.25
PGL3EN006 Phantasmal Lord Ultimitl Bishbaalkin GSCR .20 .35
PGL3EN007 Number 37: Hope Woven Dragon Spider Shark GSCR 1.00 1.50
PGL3EN008 Number 38: Hope Harbinger Dragon Titanic Galaxy GSCR 8.00 10.00
PGL3EN009 Number 35: Ravenous Tarantula GSCR .40 .60
PGL3EN010 Number 84: Pain Gainer GSCR .75 1.15
PGL3EN011 Number 77: The Seven Sins GSCR 8.00 10.00
PGL3EN012 Frost Blast of the Monarchs GSCR .30 .50
PGL3EN013 Tsukumo Slash GSCR .10 .20
PGL3EN014 Shining Hope Road GSCR .10 .20
PGL3EN015 The Phantom Knights of Shade Brigandine GSCR .10 .20
PGL3EN016 The Phantom Knights of Dark Gauntlets GSCR .10 .25
PGL3EN017 The Phantom Knights of Tomb Shield GSCR .10 .20
PGL3EN018 Dark Advance GSCR .10 .15
PGL3EN019 King's Consonance GSCR .20 .35
PGL3EN020 Red Supremacy GSCR .10 .20
PGL3EN021 Beatrice, Lady of the Eternal GSCR 3.75 4.50
PGL3EN022 Fire Hand GSCR .60 1.00
PGL3EN023 Ice Hand GSCR .60 1.00
PGL3EN024 Kozmo Farmgirl GSCR 1.25 1.75
PGL3EN025 Kozmo Goodwitch GSCR .20 .35
PGL3EN026 Kozmo Sliprider GSCR .60 1.00
PGL3EN027 Kozmo Forerunner GSCR .40 .60
PGL3EN028 Kozmo Strawman GSCR 1.25 1.75
PGL3EN029 Kozmoll Wickedwitch GSCR .40 .75
PGL3EN030 Kozmo DOG Fighter GSCR .20 .30
PGL3EN031 Kozmo Dark Destroyer GSCR 2.25 2.75
PGL3EN032 Kozmotown GSCR .40 .60
PGL3EN033 Kozmo Lightsword GSCR .10 .20
PGL3EN034 Horn of Heaven GSCR .40 .60
PGL3EN035 Black Horn of Heaven GSCR .40 .60
PGL3EN036 Treacherous Trap Hole GSCR .20 .35
PGL3EN037 Deep Dark Trap Hole GSCR .15 .25
PGL3EN038 Void Trap Hole GSCR .20 .35
PGL3EN039 Time-Space Trap Hole GSCR .75 1.15
PGL3EN040 Grand Horn of Heaven GSCR .50 .75
PGL3EN041 Vector Pendulum, the Dracoverlord GLDR .75 1.25
PGL3EN042 Maxx "C" GLDR 10.00 12.50
PGL3EN043 Scarm, Malebranche of the Burning Abyss GLDR .75 1.15
PGL3EN044 Graff, Malebranche of the Burning Abyss GLDR .20 .35
PGL3EN045 Cir, Malebranche of the Burning Abyss GLDR .30 .50
PGL3EN046 Rubic, Malebranche of the Burning Abyss GLDR .20 .35
PGL3EN047 Alich, Malebranche of the Burning Abyss GLDR .20 .35
PGL3EN048 Calcab, Malebranche of the Burning Abyss GLDR .20 .35
PGL3EN049 Farfa, Malebranche of the Burning Abyss GLDR 1.00 1.50
PGL3EN050 Libic, Malebranche of the Burning Abyss GLDR .20 .35
PGL3EN051 Cagna, Malebranche of the Burning Abyss GLDR .20 .35
PGL3EN052 Ghost Ogre & Snow Rabbit GLDR 8.50 9.50
PGL3EN053 Draghig, Malebranche of the Burning Abyss GLDR .30 .75
PGL3EN054 Barbar, Malebranche of the Burning Abyss GLDR .30 .75
PGL3EN055 Luster Pendulum, the Dracoslayer GLDR .60 1.00
PGL3EN056 Archfiend Eccentrick GLDR 4.75 5.50
PGL3EN057 Chimeratech Fortress Dragon GLDR 1.25 1.75
PGL3EN058 Dante, Pilgrim of the Burning Abyss GLDR .30 .45
PGL3EN059 Black Rose Dragon GLDR .75 1.25
PGL3EN060 Arcanite Magician GLDR .35 .60
PGL3EN061 Virgil, Rock Star of the Burning Abyss GLDR .15 .25
PGL3EN062 Ignister Prominence, the Blasting Dracoslayer GLDR .50 .75
PGL3EN063 Number 11: Big Eye GLDR 3.75 4.25
PGL3EN064 Digvorzhak, King of Heavy Industry GLDR .75 1.00
PGL3EN065 Daigusto Emeral GLDR 10.00 13.00
PGL3EN066 Constellar Pleiades GLDR .75 1.15
PGL3EN067 Gagaga Cowboy GLDR .60 1.00
PGL3EN068 Abyss Dweller GLDR .75 1.25
PGL3EN069 Bahamut Shark GLDR 1.25 2.00
PGL3EN070 Lightning Chidori GLDR .40 .75
PGL3EN071 Constellar Ptolemy M7 GLDR .60 1.00
PGL3EN072 Evilswarm Ouroboros GLDR .30 .45
PGL3EN073 Number 61: Volcasaurus GLDR .75 1.25
PGL3EN074 Norito the Moral Leader GLDR .20 .35
PGL3EN075 Number 106: Giant Hand GLDR 7.00 8.00
PGL3EN076 Castel, the Skyblaster Musketeer GLDR 2.25 2.75
PGL3EN077 Dante, Traveler of the Burning Abyss GLDR 3.50 4.25
PGL3EN078 Red-Eyes Flare Metal Dragon GLDR 3.25 3.75
PGL3EN079 Majester Paladin, the Ascending Dracoslayer GLDR .50 .75
PGL3EN080 Reasoning GLDR .30 .50
PGL3EN081 Emergency Teleport GLDR 1.25 1.75
PGL3EN082 Spell Shattering Arrow GLDR .25 .50
PGL3EN083 Mask Change GLDR .30 .45
PGL3EN084 Shared Ride GLDR .15 .25
PGL3EN085 The Monarchs Stormforth GLDR .60 1.00
PGL3EN086 Mask Change II GLDR .60 1.00
PGL3EN087 Galaxy Cyclone GLDR 4.25 5.00
PGL3EN088 The Terminus of the Burning Abyss GLDR .10 .15
PGL3EN089 Mistaken Arrest GLDR .15 .25
PGL3EN090 Draco Face-Off GLDR .25 .40
PGL3EN091 Remove Brainwashing GLDR .20 .35
PGL3EN092 Dark Mirror Force GLDR .20 .35
PGL3EN093 Radiant Mirror Force GLDR .20 .35
PGL3EN094 Fairy Wind GLDR .20 .35
PGL3EN095 Breakthrough Skill GLDR 1.00 1.50
PGL3EN096 Mistake GLDR .50 .75
PGL3EN097 The Traveler and the Burning Abyss GLDR .20 .35
PGL3EN098 Fire Lake of the Burning Abyss GLDR .20 .35
PGL3EN099 Storming Mirror Force GLDR 4.50 5.25
PGL3EN100 Blazing Mirror Force GLDR .60 1.00

2011 Yu-Gi-Oh Legendary Collection 2

COMPLETE SET (279) 450.00 600.00
BOOSTER BOX (5 PACKS) 50.00 70.00
BOOSTER PACK (25 CARDS) 10.00 15.00
RELEASED ON OCTOBER 4, 2011
LC02001 Uria, Searing Flames UR 1.25 3.00
LC02002 Hamon, Striking UR 2.00 5.00
LC02003 Raviel, Phantasms UR 1.00 2.50
LC02004 Darklord Asmodeus UR .50 1.25
LC02005 Darklord Superbia UR .50 1.25
LC02006 Darklord Edeh Arae UR .50 1.25
LC02007 Cyber Larva UR .50 1.25
LC02008 Lion Alligator UR .50 1.25
LC02009 Spawn Alligator UR .50 1.25
LC02010 HERO Great Tornado UR .50 1.25
LC02011 Parallel World Fusion UR .50 1.25
LC02012 Dragonic Tactics UR .50 1.25
LC02013 Court of Justice UR .50 1.25
LCGX001 Elemental HERO Avian .20 .50
LCGX002 HERO Avian (alt) SCR 1.50 4.00
LCGX003 Elemental HERO Burstinatrix .50 1.25
LCGX004 HERO Burstin (alt) SCR 1.25 3.00
LCGX005 Elemental HERO Clayman 1.25 3.00
LCGX006 Elemental HERO Sparkman .20 .50
LCGX007 HERO Spark (alt) SCR 1.25 3.00
LCGX008 Elemental HERO Neos 1.00 2.50
LCGX009 Winged Kuriboh .75 2.00
LCGX010 Winged Kuriboh LV10 1.50 4.00
LCGX011 Wroughtweiler .20 .50
LCGX012 Elemental HERO Bubbleman .40 1.00
LCGX013 Elemental HERO Bladedge .20 .50
LCGX014 Elemental HERO Wildheart .20 .50
LCGX015 HERO Necroshade R .40 1.00
LCGX016 Hero Kid .20 .50
LCGX017 Neo-Spacian Aqua Dolphin 1.00 2.50
LCGX018 Neo-Spacian Flare Scarab .50 1.25
LCGX019 Neo-Spacian Dark Panther .20 .50
LCGX020 Card Trooper .20 .50
LCGX021 Neo-Spacian Air Hummingbird .60 1.50
LCGX022 Neo-Spacian Grand Mole .20 .50
LCGX023 Neo-Spacian Glow Moss .20 .50
LCGX024 Elemental HERO Stratos .75 2.00
LCGX025 Elemental HERO Ocean R .50 1.25
LCGX026 Elemental HERO Captain Gold .75 2.00
LCGX027 Necro Gardna SCR .75 2.00
LCGX028 HERO Neos Alius SCR .75 2.00
LCGX029 HERO Malicious SCR .75 2.00
LCGX030 Evil HERO Infernal Gainer .20 .50
LCGX031 HERO Infernal Prodigy R .50 1.25
LCGX032 Card Ejector SR .75 2.00
LCGX033 Elemental Hero Prisma 2.50 6.00
LCGX034 HERO Woodsman SR .75 2.00
LCGX035 Elemental HERO Knospe R .50 1.25
LCGX036 Elemental HERO Poison Rose R .75 2.00
LCGX037 Elemental HERO Heat .50 1.25
LCGX038 HERO Lady Heat .75 2.00
LCGX039 Elemental HERO Voltic .20 .50
LCGX040 Neos Wiseman UR 1.00 2.50
LCGX041 Gallis Star Beast SCR .75 2.00
LCGX042 Dandylion SCR .75 2.00
LCGX043 Winged Kuriboh LV9 SCR .75 2.00
LCGX044 Card Blocker UR .50 1.25
LCGX045 HERO Flame SCR 2.50 6.00
LCGX046 HERO Thunder Giant 1.25 3.00
LCGX047 HERO Rampart Blaster SR .75 2.00
LCGX048 HERO Tempest SR 2.50 6.00
LCGX049 HERO Wildedge 1.50 4.00
LCGX050 HERO Shining SCR 4.00 10.00
LCGX051 HERO Steam Healer R 1.50 4.00
LCGX052 HERO Electrum UR .75 2.00
LCGX053 HERO Mudballman SR .75 2.00
LCGX054 Elemental HERO Mariner .20 .50
LCGX055 HERO Wild Wingman .20 .50
LCGX056 HERO Necroid Shaman .20 .50
LCGX057 HERO Aqua Neos SR .75 2.00
LCGX058 HERO Flare Neos .20 .50
LCGX059 HERO Dark Neos SCR .75 2.00
LCGX060 HERO Grand Neos SR .75 2.00
LCGX061 HERO Glow Neos R 1.25 3.00
LCGX062 HERO Marine Neos .20 .50
LCGX063 HERO Darkbright SR .75 2.00
LCGX064 HERO Magma Neos SR 2.50 6.00
LCGX065 HERO Chaos Neos UR 1.25 3.00
LCGX066 HERO Plasma Vice 2.00 5.00
LCGX067 HERO Inferno Wing SR .75 2.00
LCGX068 HERO Lightning SR .75 2.00
LCGX069 HERO Dark Gaia SR .75 2.00
LCGX070 HERO Wild Cyclone SR .75 2.00
LCGX071 HERO Infernal Sniper UR .50 1.25
LCGX072 HERO Malicious Fiend SR .75 2.00
LCGX073 HERO Storm Neos .60 1.50
LCGX074 Rainbow Neos SR .75 2.00
LCGX075 HERO Terra Firma SR .75 2.00
LCGX076 HERO Inferno SR .50 1.25
LCGX077 HERO Divine Neos UR .75 2.00
LCGX078 Miracle Fusion UR .40 1.00
LCGX079 Transcendent Wings .20 .50
LCGX080 Bubble Shuffle R .20 .50
LCGX081 Spark Blaster .20 .50
LCGX082 Skyscraper 1.50 4.00
LCGX083 Feather Shot R .20 .50
LCGX084 Burst Return R .20 .50
LCGX085 Hero Heart .20 .50
LCGX086 Cyclone Boomerang .20 .50
LCGX087 Flute of Summoning UR .50 1.25
LCGX088 H - Heated Heart .20 .50
LCGX089 E - Emergency Call .20 .50
LCGX090 R - Righteous Justice .20 .50
LCGX091 O - Oversoul .20 .50
LCGX092 Hero Flash!! R .20 .50
LCGX093 Fake Hero R .20 .50
LCGX094 Neo Space R .20 .50
LCGX095 Instant Fusion UR 5.00 12.00
LCGX096 Neos Force .20 .50
LCGX097 Skyscraper 2 SCR 1.25 3.00
LCGX098 Fifth Hope SCR 1.25 3.00
LCGX099 Dark Fusion UR 2.50 6.00
LCGX100 Dark Calling R .75 2.00
LCGX101 Super Polymer. SCR .75 2.00
LCGX102 Instant Neo Space .20 .50
LCGX103 Hero Mask .20 .50
LCGX104 Space Gift .20 .50
LCGX105 Rose Bud R .20 .50
LCGX106 HERO's Bond .20 .50
LCGX107 Hero Signal .20 .50
LCGX108 Hero Barrier .20 .50
LCGX109 Feather Wind .20 .50
LCGX110 Hero Ring SR .75 2.00
LCGX111 Clay Charge .20 .50
LCGX112 Miracle Kids .20 .50
LCGX113 Edge Hammer .20 .50
LCGX114 Kid Guard UR .50 1.25
LCGX115 Elemental Recharge .20 .50
LCGX116 Change of Hero - Reflector Ray .20 .50
LCGX117 Hero Spirit .20 .50
LCGX118 Hero Counterattack .20 .50
LCGX119 Mirror Gate UR .50 1.25
LCGX120 Hero Blast .20 .50
LCGX121 Terra Firma Gravity R .20 .50
LCGX122 HERO - Doom Lord .20 .50
LCGX123 HERO - Captain Tenacious .20 .50
LCGX124 HERO - Diamond SR .75 2.00
LCGX125 HERO - Dreadmaster SR .75 2.00
LCGX126 HERO - Double Dude .20 .50
LCGX127 HERO - Defender R .60 1.50
LCGX128 HERO - Dogma SR .75 2.00
LCGX129 HERO - Blade Master .20 .50
LCGX130 HERO - Fear Monger .20 .50
LCGX131 HERO - Dasher .20 .50
LCGX132 HERO - Malicious 1.50 4.00
LCGX133 HERO - Disk SCR .75 2.00
LCGX134 HERO - Plasma SR .75 2.00
LCGX135 HERO - Dunker .20 .50
LCGX136 HERO - Departed .20 .50
LCGX137 HERO - Dread Servant .20 .50
LCGX138 HERO Phoenix SR .75 2.00
LCGX139 HERO Shining SCR 1.25 3.00
LCGX140 Destiny End Dragoon SR 1.50 4.00
LCGX141 Clock Tower Prison .20 .50
LCGX142 D - Spirit .20 .50
LCGX143 Cyclone Blade .20 .50
LCGX144 Dark City .20 .50
LCGX145 Destiny Draw SCR .75 2.00
LCGX146 Over Destiny R .40 1.00
LCGX147 D - Formation .20 .50
LCGX148 Destiny Signal .20 .50
LCGX149 D-Time R .20 .50
LCGX150 D - Shield .20 .50
LCGX151 Destiny Mirage R .20 .50
LCGX152 D - Chain .20 .50
LCGX153 D - Counter .20 .50
LCGX154 D - Fortune .20 .50
LCGX155 Crystal Beast Ruby Carbuncle .20 .50
LCGX156 Crystal Beast Amethyst Cat .20 .50
LCGX157 Crystal Beast Emerald Tortoise .20 .50
LCGX158 Crystal Beast Topaz Tiger .20 .50
LCGX159 Crystal Beast Amber Mammoth .50 1.25
LCGX160 Crystal Beast Cobalt Eagle .20 .50
LCGX161 Crystal Beast Saph SR 2.00 5.00
LCGX162 Rainbow Dragon UR 2.50 6.00
LCGX163 Crystal Beacon R .20 .50
LCGX164 Rare Value SR .75 2.00
LCGX165 Crystal Blessing R .20 .50
LCGX166 Crystal Abundance R .20 .50
LCGX167 Crystal Promise R .20 .50
LCGX168 Ancient City - Rainbow .20 .50
LCGX169 Crystal Release UR .75 2.00
LCGX170 Crystal Tree UR 1.25 3.00
LCGX171 Crystal Raigeki .20 .50
LCGX172 Crystal Pair .75 2.00
LCGX173 Rainbow Path .20 .50
LCGX174 Rainbow Gravity .20 .50
LCGX175 Cyber Dragon UR 1.00 2.50
LCGX176 Cyber Dragon (alt) SCR 2.00 5.00
LCGX177 Proto-Cyber Dragon UR .50 1.25
LCGX178 Cyber Phoenix UR .50 1.25
LCGX179 Cyber Valley UR 1.00 2.50
LCGX180 Cyber Twin Dragon SCR .75 2.00
LCGX181 Cyber End Dragon SCR 3.00 8.00
LCGX182 Cyber Dragon (alt) SCR 3.00 8.00
LCGX183 Chimera Over SCR 1.25 3.00
LCGX184 Power Bond SCR 4.00 10.00
LCGX185 Overload Fusion R .60 1.50
LCGX186 Future Fusion UR 1.00 2.50
LCGX187 Magical Mallet UR 2.00 5.00
LCGX188 Dark End Dragon SCR .75 2.00
LCGX189 Light End Dragon UR .50 1.25
LCGX190 Hydrogeddon UR .50 1.25
LCGX191 Vennominaga Deity UR .50 1.25
LCGX192 Vennominon the King SR .75 2.00
LCGX193 Phantom of Chaos SCR 2.00 5.00
LCGX194 Phantom Skyblaster SCR .75 2.00
LCGX195 Grave Squirmer .20 .50
LCGX196 Grinder Golem 1.00 2.50
LCGX197 Yubel SCR 2.00 5.00
LCGX198 Yubel - Terror Inc SCR .75 2.00
LCGX199 Yubel - The Ultimate SCR 2.00 5.00
LCGX200 Mezuki .50 1.25
LCGX201 Cold Enchanter .20 .50
LCGX202 Ice Master .20 .50
LCGX203 Thunder King Rai-Oh 1.00 2.50
LCGX204 Darkness Destroy SCR .75 2.00
LCGX205 White Night Dragon UR .50 1.25
LCGX206 Kasha UR .50 1.25
LCGX207 Ice Queen UR .50 1.25
LCGX208 Shutendoji UR .50 1.25
LCGX209 Clear Vice Dragon SR .75 2.00
LCGX210 Darklord Desire SR .75 2.00
LCGX211 Armityle the Chaos UR 8.00 20.00
LCGX212 Fusion Recovery 2.50 6.00
LCGX213 System Down 2.00 5.00
LCGX214 Grand Convergence R .20 .50
LCGX215 Dim Fissure SCR 1.25 3.00
LCGX216 Venom Swamp .20 .50
LCGX217 Clear World SR .75 2.00
LCGX218 Macro Cosmos UR 1.25 3.00
LCGX219 Rise of the Snake Deity .20 .50
LCGX220 Dim Prison UR 1.25 3.00
LCGX221 Offering to the Snake .20 .50
LCGX222 Chamberlain of the Six .20 .50
LCGX223 Gladiator Beast Andal .20 .50
LCGX224 D.D. Survivor .20 .50
LCGX225 Banisher of Radiance SCR .75 2.00
LCGX226 Grandmaster of Samurai .20 .50
LCGX227 Six Samurai - Yaichi .20 .50
LCGX228 Six Samurai - Kamon .20 .50
LCGX229 Six Samurai - Yariza .20 .50
LCGX230 Six Samurai - Nisashi .20 .50
LCGX231 Six Samurai - Zanji .20 .50
LCGX232 Six Samurai - Irou .20 .50
LCGX233 Great Shogun Shien SCR 1.25 3.00
LCGX234 D.D. Crow SR .75 2.00
LCGX235 Beast Octavius UR .50 1.25
LCGX236 Beast Murmillo SCR .75 2.00
LCGX237 Beast Bestiari SCR 2.00 5.00
LCGX238 Beast Laquari SCR .75 2.00
LCGX239 Beast Hoplomus SCR .75 2.00
LCGX240 Beast Secutor SCR .75 2.00
LCGX241 Enishi, Chancellor SR .75 2.00
LCGX242 Test Tiger SCR .75 2.00
LCGX243 Rainbow Dark Dragon UR 1.25 3.00
LCGX244 Beast Darius SCR 1.25 3.00
LCGX245 Jain, Paladin UR .50 1.25
LCGX246 Garoth, Warrior UR 1.00 2.50
LCGX247 Lumina, Summoner UR 1.25 3.00
LCGX248 Wulf, Beast UR .50 1.25
LCGX249 Judgment Dragon .20 .50
LCGX250 Aurkus, Druid UR .50 1.25
LCGX251 Beast Equeste SCR 1.00 2.50
LCGX252 Beast Lanista UR .50 1.25
LCGX253 Beast Heraklinos SR .75 2.00
LCGX254 Beast's Respite R .20 .50
LCGX255 Gladiator's Return R .20 .50
LCGX256 Cunning of the Six Samurai .20 .50
LCGX257 Gladiator Ground R .20 .50
LCGX258 Light of Redemption .20 .50
LCGX259 Gateway of the Six .20 .50
LCGX260 Non-Fusion Area .60 1.50
LCGX261 Success Probability 0 .20 .50
LCGX262 Return of the Six Samurai .20 .50
LCGX263 Swiftstrike Armor R .20 .50
LCGX264 Double-Edged Sword .20 .50
LCGX265 Defensive Tactics UR .50 1.25
LCGX266 Beast War Chariot SCR 1.25 3.00

2012 Yu-Gi-Oh Ra Yellow Mega Pack 1st Edition

COMPLETE SET (113) 60.00 120.00
BOOSTER BOX (24 PACKS) 150.00 200.00
BOOSTER PACK (11 CARDS) 5.00 6.00
RELEASED ON FEBRUARY 21, 2012
RYMP001 Elemental HERO Avian ALT .20 .60
RYMP002 Elemental HERO Burstinatrix ALT .40 1.00
RYMP003 Elemental HERO Sparkman ALT .25 .75
RYMP004 Elemental HERO Neos .20 .60
RYMP005 Elemental HERO Necroshade .20 .60
RYMP006 Card Trooper .15 .40
RYMP007 Neo-Spacian Grand SR .25 .75
RYMP008 Elemental HERO Stratos .60 1.50
RYMP009 Necro Gardna SCR .25 .75
RYMP010 Elem HERO Neos SCR .40 1.00
RYMP011 Card Ejector .15 .40
RYMP012 Elemental HERO Prisma 1.50 4.00
RYMP013 Gallis the Star Beast .15 .40
RYMP014 Winged Kuriboh LV9 R .25 .60
RYMP015 Card Blocker .15 .40
RYMP016 Elemental HERO Flame Wingman R 1.25 3.00
RYMP017 Elemental HERO Electrum .50 1.25
RYMP018 Elemental HERO Mudballman .50 1.25
RYMP019 Rainbow Neos .20 .60
RYMP020 Elemental HERO Divine Neos .25 .75
RYMP021 Miracle Fusion (UR) .60 1.50
RYMP022 The Flute of Summoning Kuriboh .20 .60
RYMP023 H - Heated Heart SCR .25 .75
RYMP024 E - Emergency Call SCR 1.25 3.00
RYMP025 R - Right Justice SCR .25 .75
RYMP026 O - Oversoul SCR .25 .75
RYMP027 Hero Flash!! SCR .25 .75
RYMP028 Instant Fusion UR 4.00 10.00
RYMP029 Super Polymer SCR .75 2.00
RYMP030 Hero Mask .15 .40
RYMP031 Hero Signal SR .25 .75
RYMP032 Hero Blast SR .25 .75
RYMP033 Destiny HERO - Diamond Dude .20 .60
RYMP034 HERO - Malicious SCR 2.50 6.00
RYMP035 Destiny HERO - Disk Commander R .25 .60
RYMP036 Destiny HERO - Plasma .75 2.00
RYMP037 Destiny Draw SCR 1.25 3.00
RYMP038 Destiny Signal SR .25 .75
RYMP039 Destiny Mirage .15 .40
RYMP040 Crystal Beast Ruby SR .40 1.00
RYMP041 Crystal Beast Ameth SR .25 .75
RYMP042 Crystal Beast Emerald SR .25 .75
RYMP043 Crystal Beast Topaz SR .60 1.50
RYMP044 Crystal Beast Amber SR .50 1.25
RYMP045 Crystal Beast Cobalt SR .50 1.25
RYMP046 Crystal Beast Sapphire Pegasus 1.50 4.00
RYMP047 Rainbow Dragon 1.50 4.00
RYMP048 Crystal Beacon SCR .25 .75
RYMP049 Rare Value .40 1.00
RYMP050 Crystal Blessing SCR .25 .75
RYMP051 Crystal Abundance SCR .25 .75
RYMP052 Crystal Promise SCR .25 .75
RYMP053 Ancient City - Rainbow Ruins .15 .40
RYMP054 Crystal Release .40 1.00
RYMP055 Crystal Raigeki SR .25 .75
RYMP056 Rainbow Path .15 .40
RYMP057 Rainbow Gravity .15 .40
RYMP058 Cyber Dragon 1.25 3.00
RYMP059 Cyber Dragon ALT SCR 1.50 4.00
RYMP060 Cyber End Dragon ALT R 1.25 3.00
RYMP061 Chimeratech Over R .40 1.00
RYMP062 Power Bond .40 1.00
RYMP063 Overload Fusion .75 2.00
RYMP064 Future Fusion UR .75 2.00
RYMP065 Magical Mallet .75 2.00
RYMP066 Dark End Dragon SR .25 .75
RYMP067 Light End Dragon SR .25 .75
RYMP068 Vennominaga the Deity of Poisonous Snakes R .25 .60
RYMP069 Vennominon the King of Poisonous Snakes .15 .40
RYMP070 Yubel R 1.25 3.00
RYMP071 Yubel - Terror Incarnate R .60 1.50
RYMP072 Ultimate Nightmare R .75 2.00
RYMP073 Mezuki .60 1.50
RYMP074 Thunder King Rai-Oh .75 2.00
RYMP075 Kasha .15 .40
RYMP076 Shutendoji .15 .40
RYMP077 Darklord Desire .15 .40
RYMP078 Fusion Recovery 2.50 6.00
RYMP079 System Down 1.50 4.00
RYMP080 Grand Convergence .15 .40
RYMP081 Dimensional Fissure SCR .60 1.50
RYMP082 Macro Cosmos UR .75 2.00
RYMP083 Rise of the Snake Deity .15 .40
RYMP084 Dimensional Prison UR .75 2.00
RYMP085 Offering to the Snake Deity .15 .40
RYMP086 D.D. Survivor .15 .40
RYMP087 Grandmaster of the Six Samurai .15 .40
RYMP088 The Six - Yaichi UR .25 .75
RYMP089 The Six - Kamon UR .25 .75
RYMP090 The Six - Yariza UR .25 .75
RYMP091 The Six - Nisashi UR .25 .75
RYMP092 The Six - Zanji UR .25 .75
RYMP093 The Six - Irou UR .25 .75
RYMP094 Great Shogun Shien .15 .40
RYMP095 D.D. Crow SR .25 .75
RYMP096 Gladiator Beast SCR .25 .75
RYMP097 Enishi, Shien's Chancellor .15 .40
RYMP098 Test Tiger .25 .75
RYMP099 Rainbow Dark Dragon .40 1.00
RYMP100 Jain, Paladin UR .25 .75
RYMP101 Garoth, Warrior R .25 .60
RYMP102 Lumina, Summoner UR .75 2.00
RYMP103 Wulf, Beast UR .50 1.25
RYMP104 Judgement Dragon .15 .40
RYMP105 Aurkus, Lightsworn Druid .15 .40
RYMP106 Gladiator Beast Lanista .15 .40
RYMP107 Gladiator Beast's Respite .15 .40
RYMP108 Gladiator's Return .15 .40
RYMP109 Cunning of the Six Samurai .15 .40
RYMP110 Gladiator Proving UR .25 .75
RYMP111 Gateway of the Six .15 .40
RYMP112 Double-Edged Sword UR .40 1.00
RYMP113 Gladiator Beast Chariot R .40 1.00

2012 Yu-Gi-Oh Legendary Collection 3 Yugi's World

COMPLETE SET (306) 150.00 300.00
BOOSTER BOX (5 PACKS) 30.00 50.00
BOOSTER PACK (25 CARDS) 4.00 5.00
RELEASED ON OCTOBER 2, 2012
LCYW001 Dark Magician SCR 1.25 3.00
LCYW002 Gaia The Fierce Knight SR .60 1.50
LCYW003 Celtic Guardian SR .60 1.50
LCYW004 Silver Fang UR .40 1.00
LCYW005 Mystical Elf C .15 .40
LCYW006 Curse of Dragon R .25 .75
LCYW007 Giant Soldier of Stone C .15 .40

Card	Low	High
LCYW008 Feral Imp C	.15	.40
LCYW009 Winged Dragon, Guardian of the Fortress #1 UR	.40	1.00
LCYW010 Summoned Skull SR	1.00	2.50
LCYW011 Gazelle the King of Mythical Beasts UR	.75	2.00
LCYW012 Alpha the Magnet Warrior C	.15	.40
LCYW013 Beta the Magnet Warrior C	.20	.60
LCYW014 Gamma the Magnet Warrior C	.15	.40
LCYW015 Queen's Knight UR	1.00	2.50
LCYW016 Jack's Knight UR	1.25	3.00
LCYW017 King's Knight UR	.75	2.00
LCYW018 Kuriboh SR	.60	1.50
LCYW019 Catapult Turtle R	.25	.75
LCYW020 Buster Blader SCR	2.50	6.00
LCYW021 Valkyrion the Magna Warrior SR	.60	1.50
LCYW022 Dark Magician Girl SCR	4.00	10.00
LCYW023 Breaker the Magical Warrior UR	.75	2.00
LCYW024 Mirage Knight C	.15	.40
LCYW025 Black Luster Soldier - Envoy of the Beginning SCR	4.00	10.00
LCYW026 Dark Magician of Chaos SCR	5.00	12.00
LCYW027 Dark Sage C	1.25	3.00
LCYW028 Dark Magician Knight C	1.50	4.00
LCYW029 Sorcerer of Dark Magic C	1.50	4.00
LCYW030 Watapon C	.15	.40
LCYW031 Swift Gaia the Fierce Knight C	.15	.40
LCYW032 Big Shield Gardna SCR	1.25	3.00
LCYW033 Silent Swordsman LV3 C	.15	.40
LCYW034 Silent Swordsman LV5 C	.15	.40
LCYW035 Silent Swordsman LV7 C	.50	1.25
LCYW036 Obnoxious Celtic Guard C	.15	.40
LCYW037 Silent Magician LV4 C	.50	1.25
LCYW038 Silent Magician LV8 C	.50	1.25
LCYW039 Green Gadget UR	.40	1.00
LCYW040 Red Gadget UR	.40	1.00
LCYW041 Yellow Gadget UR	.40	1.00
LCYW042 Archfiend of Gilfer R	.25	.75
LCYW043 The Tricky C	.15	.40
LCYW044 Gorz the Emissary of Darkness UR	1.00	2.50
LCYW045 Berfomet SR	.60	1.50
LCYW046 Black Luster Soldier C	.40	1.00
LCYW047 Magician of Black Chaos C	1.50	4.00
LCYW048 Dark Paladin SCR	8.00	20.00
LCYW049 Dark Flare Knight C	.40	1.00
LCYW050 Dragon Master Knight SR	2.50	6.00
LCYW051 Arcana Knight Joker SCR	2.50	6.00
LCYW052 Chimera the Flying Mythical Beast SR	.60	1.50
LCYW053 Dark Hole SCR	1.00	2.50
LCYW054 Raigeki SCR	10.00	25.00
LCYW055 Fissure SR	.60	1.50
LCYW056 Polymerization SR	1.25	3.00
LCYW057 Swords of Revealing Light UR	.40	1.00
LCYW058 Monster Reborn UR	1.00	2.50
LCYW059 Pot of Greed SCR	1.50	4.00
LCYW060 Card Destruction SCR	.60	1.50
LCYW061 Heavy Storm UR	.40	1.00
LCYW062 Mystical Space Typhoon SCR	1.50	4.00
LCYW063 De-Fusion C	.40	1.00
LCYW064 Graceful Charity SCR	2.00	5.00
LCYW065 Double Spell SR	.60	1.50
LCYW066 Diffusion Wave-Motion SR	.60	1.50
LCYW067 Thousand Knives C	.15	.40
LCYW068 Heart of the Underdog C	.15	.40
LCYW069 Dedication through Light and Darkness SCR	3.00	8.00
LCYW070 Black Luster Ritual C	1.50	4.00
LCYW071 Dark Magic Attack C	.40	1.00
LCYW072 Knight's Title C	.15	.40
LCYW073 Sage's Stone R	1.50	4.00
LCYW074 Brain Control SCR	.75	2.00
LCYW075 Magical Dimension C	.15	.40
LCYW076 Mystic Box C	.15	.40
LCYW077 Magicians Unite C	.15	.40
LCYW078 Black Magic Ritual C	1.00	2.50
LCYW079 Dark Magic Curtain R	1.00	2.50
LCYW080 Gold Sarcophagus C	1.00	2.50
LCYW081 Soul Taker C	.15	.40
LCYW082 Magic Formula C	.40	1.00
LCYW083 Union Attack C	.15	.40
LCYW084 Tricky Spell 4 C	.15	.40
LCYW085 Spell Shattering Arrow C	.50	1.25
LCYW086 Multiply R	.75	2.00
LCYW087 Makiu, the Magical Mist C	.15	.40
LCYW088 Detonate C	.15	.40
LCYW089 Seven Tools of the Bandit SCR	.60	1.50
LCYW090 Horn of Heaven SCR	.60	1.50
LCYW091 Mirror Force SCR	1.25	3.00
LCYW092 Spellbinding Circle C	.15	.40
LCYW093 Lightforce Sword SR	.60	1.50
LCYW094 Chain Destruction C	.15	.40
LCYW095 Dust Tornado UR	.40	1.00
LCYW096 Magical Hats C	.50	1.25
LCYW097 Shift SR	.60	1.50
LCYW098 Collected Power C	.15	.40
LCYW099 Magic Cylinder SR	.60	1.50
LCYW100 Magician's Circle SR	1.00	2.50
LCYW101 Stronghold the Moving Fortress UR	.40	1.00
LCYW102 Soul Rope C	.15	.40
LCYW103 Blue-Eyes Toon Dragon R	.75	2.00
LCYW104 Manga Ryu-Ran R	.25	.75
LCYW105 Toon Mermaid R	1.25	3.00
LCYW106 Toon Summoned Skull R	.25	.75
LCYW107 Toon Gemini Elf R	.25	.75
LCYW108 Toon Goblin Attack Force R	2.00	5.00
LCYW109 Toon Cannon Soldier R	2.00	5.00
LCYW110 Toon Masked Sorcerer R	2.00	5.00
LCYW111 Toon Dark Magician Girl R	.75	2.00
LCYW112 Dark-Eyes Illusionist R	.25	.75
LCYW113 Relinquished R	.40	1.00
LCYW114 Black Illusion Ritual R	.25	.75
LCYW115 Toon World R	.50	1.25
LCYW116 Toon Table of Contents R	1.25	3.00
LCYW117 Dragon Capture Jar R	.25	.75
LCYW118 Toon Defense R	.75	2.00
LCYW119 Man-Eater Bug C	.15	.40
LCYW120 Sangan SCR	1.50	4.00
LCYW121 Morphing Jar UR	.40	1.00
LCYW122 Puppet Master C	.15	.40
LCYW123 Dark Master - Zorc C	.15	.40
LCYW124 Change of Heart SCR	2.00	5.00
LCYW125 Exchange SCR	.60	1.50
LCYW126 The Dark Door R	.25	.75
LCYW127 Spiritualism C	.15	.40
LCYW128 Contract with the Dark Master C	.15	.40
LCYW129 Guardian Elma C	.15	.40
LCYW130 Guardian Ceal C	.15	.40
LCYW131 Guardian Grarl C	.40	1.00
LCYW132 Guardian Baou C	.15	.40
LCYW133 Guardian Kay'est C	.15	.40
LCYW134 Guardian Tryce C	.15	.40
LCYW135 My Body as a Shield C	.15	.40
LCYW136 Butterfly Dagger - Elma C	.50	1.25
LCYW137 Shooting Star Bow - Ceal C	.50	1.25
LCYW138 Gravity Axe - Grarl C	.15	.40
LCYW139 Wicked-Breaking Flamberge - Baou C	.15	.40
LCYW140 Rod of Silence - Kay'est C	.15	.40
LCYW141 Twin Swords of Flashing Light - Tryce C	.75	2.00
LCYW142 Monster Reincarnation R	.25	.75
LCYW143 Gil Garth UR	.40	1.00
LCYW144 Bowganian SR	.60	1.50
LCYW145 Machine Duplication SR	1.50	4.00
LCYW146 Hidden Soldiers R	.25	.75
LCYW147 Rope of Life SCR	.60	1.50
LCYW148 Malevolent Catastrophe SR	.60	1.50
LCYW149 Harpie's Feather Duster SCR	4.00	10.00
LCYW150 Gravity Bind SR	.60	1.50
LCYW151 Mechanicalchaser UR	.40	1.00
LCYW152 Solemn Judgment SCR	.60	1.50
LCYW153 Magic Jammer SCR	.75	2.00
LCYW154 Sinister Serpent SCR	.60	1.50
LCYW155 Mirage of Nightmare SCR	.60	1.50
LCYW156 Ordeal of a Traveler C	.40	1.00
LCYW157 Tri-Horned Dragon SR	.60	1.50
LCYW158 Two-Headed King Rex SCR	.75	2.00
LCYW159 Millennium Shield SR	.60	1.50
LCYW160 Cosmo Queen UR	.75	2.00
LCYW161 Fire Princess UR	.40	1.00
LCYW162 Command Knight C	.40	1.00
LCYW163 Malice Doll of Demise R	.25	.75
LCYW164 White-Horned Dragon SR	.60	1.50
LCYW165 Green Baboon, Defender of the Forest C	.15	.40
LCYW166 Summoner Monk UR	1.50	4.00
LCYW167 Commander Covington SCR	.60	1.50
LCYW168 Machina Soldier SCR	.60	1.50
LCYW169 Machina Sniper SCR	.60	1.50
LCYW170 Machina Defender SCR	.60	1.50
LCYW171 Machina Force SCR	.60	1.50
LCYW172 Limiter Removal UR	.75	2.00
LCYW173 Reinforcement of the Army SR	.60	1.50
LCYW174 Dragged Down into the Grave SR	1.00	2.50
LCYW175 Ectoplasmer R	.25	.75
LCYW176 Mind Control UR	.40	1.00
LCYW177 Trap Hole UR	.40	1.00
LCYW178 Imperial Order SCR	.75	2.00
LCYW179 Mask of Restrict C	6.00	15.00
LCYW180 Torrential Tribute SCR	1.00	2.50
LCYW181 Bottomless Trap Hole UR	1.00	2.50
LCYW182 Royal Decree UR	1.00	2.50
LCYW183 Gravekeeper's Spy UR	.40	1.00
LCYW184 Gravekeeper's Guard UR	.40	1.00
LCYW185 Gravekeeper's Spear Soldier UR	.40	1.00
LCYW186 Gravekeeper's Watcher C	.15	.40
LCYW187 Gravekeeper's Chief UR	.40	1.00
LCYW188 Gravekeeper's Cannonholder UR	.40	1.00
LCYW189 Gravekeeper's Assailant UR	.50	1.25
LCYW190 Charm of Shabti C	.15	.40
LCYW191 Gravekeeper's Commandant UR	1.25	3.00
LCYW192 Gravekeeper's Descendant UR	1.00	2.50
LCYW193 Gravekeeper's Recruiter UR	3.00	8.00
LCYW194 Necrovalley UR	1.50	4.00
LCYW195 Royal Tribute UR	.75	2.00
LCYW196 Rite of Spirit C	.50	1.25
LCYW197 Horus the Black Flame Dragon LV4 C	.15	.40
LCYW198 Horus the Black Flame Dragon LV6 C	.25	.75
LCYW199 Horus the Black Flame Dragon LV8 C	1.50	4.00
LCYW200 Mystic Swordsman LV2 C	.15	.40
LCYW201 Mystic Swordsman LV4 C	.15	.40
LCYW202 Mystic Swordsman LV6 C	.40	1.00
LCYW203 Armed Dragon LV3 C	.15	.40
LCYW204 Armed Dragon LV5 C	.15	.40
LCYW205 Armed Dragon LV7 C	1.50	4.00
LCYW206 Horus' Servant C	.15	.40
LCYW207 Level Up! C	.60	1.50
LCYW208 Dark Grepher C	1.50	4.00
LCYW209 Dark Horus C	.15	.40
LCYW210 The Dark Creator C	.15	.40
LCYW211 Dark Nephthys C	.15	.40
LCYW212 Darklord Zerato C	.15	.40
LCYW213 Darknight Parshath C	.15	.40
LCYW214 Dark General Freed C	.15	.40
LCYW215 D.D. Warrior Lady R	.25	.75
LCYW216 D.D. Scout Plane R	.25	.75
LCYW217 D.D. Assailant R	.25	.75
LCYW218 D.D. Warrior R	.25	.75
LCYW219 Skull Servant UR	2.00	5.00
LCYW220 Dark King of the Abyss SCR	.60	1.50
LCYW221 Aqua Madoor SCR	.60	1.50
LCYW222 Yaranzo SR	.60	1.50
LCYW223 Takriminos SR	.60	1.50
LCYW224 Megasonic Eye SR	.60	1.50
LCYW225 Yamadron SR	.60	1.50
LCYW226 Three-Legged Zombie SR	.60	1.50
LCYW227 Fairy's Gift SR	.60	1.50
LCYW228 Kanan the Swordmistress UR	.40	1.00
LCYW229 Mystical Shine Ball SR	.60	1.50
LCYW230 Big Eye R	.25	.75
LCYW231 Banisher of the Light C	.15	.40
LCYW232 Giant Rat SCR	.60	1.50
LCYW233 UFO Turtle SCR	.60	1.50
LCYW234 Giant Germ C	.40	1.00
LCYW235 Nimble Momonga C	.75	2.00
LCYW236 Shining Angel SCR	.60	1.50
LCYW237 Mother Grizzly SCR	.60	1.50
LCYW238 Flying Kamakiri #1 SCR	.60	1.50
LCYW239 Mystic Tomato SCR	.60	1.50
LCYW240 Morphing Jar #2 SR	.60	1.50
LCYW241 Goddess of Whim C	.15	.40
LCYW242 Kycoo the Ghost Destroyer SCR	.75	2.00
LCYW243 Summoner of Illusions C	.15	.40
LCYW244 Needle Worm UR	1.25	3.00
LCYW245 Pyramid Turtle SCR	.60	1.50
LCYW246 Spirit Reaper UR	.40	1.00
LCYW247 Arsenal Summoner C	.15	.40
LCYW248 Chaos Sorcerer SR	.60	1.50
LCYW249 Levia-Dragon - Daedalus SCR	.60	1.50
LCYW250 Manju of the Ten Thousand Hands C	1.25	3.00
LCYW251 Invader of Darkness C	.15	.40
LCYW252 The Agent of Wisdom - Mercury SR	.60	1.50
LCYW253 The Agent of Creation - Venus SR	.60	1.50
LCYW254 Solar Flare Dragon SR	.60	1.50
LCYW255 Emissary of the Afterlife C	.40	1.00
LCYW256 King of the Swamp C	4.00	10.00
LCYW257 The Creator C	.25	.75
LCYW258 The Creator Incarnate C	.15	.40
LCYW259 Sacred Phoenix of Nephthys SR	.60	1.50
LCYW260 Hand of Nephthys R	.25	.75
LCYW261 Armed Samurai - Ben Kei C	.15	.40
LCYW262 The Light - Hex-Sealed Fusion C	.15	.40
LCYW263 The Dark - Hex-Sealed Fusion C	.15	.40
LCYW264 The Earth - Hex-Sealed Fusion C	.15	.40
LCYW265 Upstart Goblin UR	4.00	10.00
LCYW266 Messenger of Peace C	1.00	2.50
LCYW267 Prohibition SCR	.20	.50
LCYW268 Fusion Gate SR	1.50	4.00
LCYW269 Creature Swap UR	.40	1.00
LCYW270 Book of Moon SCR	.60	1.50
LCYW271 Dark Snake Syndrome R	.25	.75
LCYW272 Non-Spellcasting Area C	.15	.40
LCYW273 Contract with the Abyss C	.15	.40
LCYW274 Stray Lambs C	.15	.40
LCYW275 Smashing Ground UR	.40	1.00
LCYW276 Salvage SR	1.00	2.50
LCYW277 Earth Chant C	.15	.40
LCYW278 Spell Economics C	.15	.40
LCYW279 Level Limit - Area B C	.75	2.00
LCYW280 A Feather of the Phoenix SCR	.60	1.50
LCYW281 Swords of Concealing Light UR	4.00	10.00
LCYW282 Centrifugal Field C	.15	.40
LCYW283 Acid Trap Hole R	.25	.75
LCYW284 DNA Surgery C	1.25	3.00
LCYW285 Reckless Greed SR	1.25	3.00
LCYW286 Raigeki Break SR	.60	1.50
LCYW287 Goblin Fan C	.15	.40
LCYW288 Sakuretsu Armor SR	1.00	2.50
LCYW289 Chain Disappearance C	.40	1.00
LCYW290 Dark Mirror Force R	1.00	2.50
LCYW291 Compulsory Evacuation Device SCR	.60	1.50
LCYW292 DNA Transplant C	.15	.40
LCYW293 Beckoning Light UR	.40	1.00
LCYW294 Draining Shield C	.50	1.25
LCYW295 Mind Crush UR	1.00	2.50
LCYW296 Penalty Game! C	.15	.40
LCYW297 Threatening Roar SCR	.75	2.00
LCYW298 Phoenix Wing Wind Blast SCR	.60	1.50
LCYW299 Level Limit - Area A C	.15	.40
LCYW300 Black Horn of Heaven SCR	.60	1.50
LCYW301 Solemn Warning C	1.50	4.00
LCYW302 Right Leg of the Forbidden One SCR	2.50	6.00
LCYW303 Left Leg of the Forbidden One SCR	2.50	6.00
LCYW304 Right Arm of the Forbidden One SCR	2.50	6.00
LCYW305 Left Arm of the Forbidden One SCR	2.50	6.00
LCYW306 Exodia the Forbidden One SCR	2.50	6.00

2012 Yu-Gi-Oh Legendary Collection 3 Yugi's World Box Bonus

Card	Low	High
COMPLETE SET (7)	4.00	8.00
ONE SET PER LEGENDARY COLLECTION 3 BOX		
LC03001 The Seal of Orichalcos UR	.60	1.50
LC03002 Dark Necrofear UR	.40	1.00
LC03003 Guardian Eatos UR	.40	1.00
LC03004 Five-Headed Dragon UR	.40	1.00
LC03005 Emissary of Darkness Token UR	.40	1.00
LC03006 Pink Kuriboh Token UR	.40	1.00
LC03007 Orange Kuriboh Token UR	.40	1.00

2013 Yu-Gi-Oh Legendary Collection 4 Joey's World

Card	Low	High
COMPLETE SET (298)	120.00	300.00
BOOSTER BOX (5 PACKS)	20.00	40.00
BOOSTER PACK (9 CARDS)	4.00	5.00
RELEASED ON OCTOBER 11, 2013		
LCJW001 Flame Manipulator C	.20	.60
LCJW002 Masaki the Legendary Swordsman C	.20	.60
LCJW003 Red-Eyes B. Dragon UR	.60	1.50
LCJW004 Rude Kaiser C	.20	.60
LCJW005 Rock Ogre Grotto 1 C	.20	.60
LCJW006 Baby Dragon SR	.15	.50
LCJW007 Axe Raider C	.20	.60
LCJW008 Tiger Axe C	.20	.60
LCJW009 Garoozis C	.20	.60
LCJW010 Swordsman of Landstar C	.20	.60
LCJW011 Cyber-Tech Alligator C	.20	.60
LCJW012 Alligator's Sword C	.60	1.50
LCJW013 Meotoko C	.20	.60
LCJW014 Kageningen C	.20	.60
LCJW015 Stone Armadiller C	.20	.60
LCJW016 Anthrosaurus C	.20	.60
LCJW017 Skull Stalker C	.20	.60
LCJW018 Wolf C	.20	.60
LCJW019 Hero of the East C	.20	.60
LCJW020 Swamp Battleguard C	.20	.60
LCJW021 Time Wizard C	.50	1.25
LCJW022 Lava Battleguard C	.20	.60
LCJW023 Jinzo R	.40	1.00
LCJW024 The Legendary Fisherman C	.20	.60
LCJW025 Sword Hunter C	.20	.60
LCJW026 Hayabusa Knight C	.20	.60
LCJW027 Mad Sword Beast C	.20	.60
LCJW028 Goblin Attack Force C	.20	.60
LCJW029 The Fiend Megacyber C	.20	.60
LCJW030 Gearfried the Iron Knight C	.20	.60
LCJW031 Red-Eyes Black Metal Dragon C	.75	2.00
LCJW032 Marauding Captain C	.20	.60
LCJW033 Fiber Jar C	.75	2.00
LCJW034 Sasuke Samurai C	.20	.60
LCJW035 Neko Mane King C	.20	.60
LCJW036 Little-Winguard C	.20	.60
LCJW037 Insect Queen C	.20	.60
LCJW038 Red-Eyes B. Chick SR	.50	1.25
LCJW039 Red-Eyes Darkness Dragon C	2.00	5.00
LCJW040 Gearfried the Swordmaster C	.20	.60
LCJW041 Gilford the Lightning C	.20	.60
LCJW042 Rocket Warrior C	.40	1.00
LCJW043 Panther Warrior C	.20	.60
LCJW044 Gilford the Legend C	.20	.60
LCJW045 Copycat C	.75	2.00
LCJW046 Divine Knight Ishzark C	.20	.60
LCJW047 Maximum Six C	.20	.60
LCJW048 Comrade Swordsman of Landstar C	.20	.60
LCJW049 Red-Eyes Wyvern C	2.50	6.00
LCJW050 Red-Eyes Darkness Metal Dragon SCR	6.00	15.00
LCJW051 Phoenix Gearfried C	.20	.60
LCJW052 Lightray Gearfried C	.20	.60
LCJW053 Flame Swordsman C	.20	.60
LCJW054 B. Skull Dragon R	.75	2.00
LCJW055 Thousand Dragon C	.20	.60
LCJW056 Alligator's Sword Dragon C	.20	.60
LCJW057 Raigeki SCR	10.00	25.00
LCJW058 Hinotama C	.20	.60
LCJW059 Polymerization SR	1.25	3.00
LCJW060 Monster Reborn UR	1.00	2.50
LCJW061 Pot of Greed SCR	1.00	2.50
LCJW062 Salamandra C	.20	.60
LCJW063 Giant Trunade C	.20	.60
LCJW064 Premature Burial C	.20	.60
LCJW065 Graceful Dice C	.20	.60
LCJW066 Scapegoat SCR	.60	1.50
LCJW067 The Warrior Returning Alive C	.20	.60
LCJW068 Meteor of Destruction C	.20	.60
LCJW069 Release Restraint C	.20	.60
LCJW070 Foolish Burial SCR	2.50	6.00
LCJW071 Silent Doom SR	.15	.50
LCJW072 Dangerous Machine Type-6 C	.20	.60
LCJW073 Trap Hole C	.20	.60
LCJW074 Skull Dice C	.20	.60
LCJW075 Metalmorph C	.20	.60
LCJW076 Fairy Box C	.20	.60
LCJW077 Collected Power C	.20	.60
LCJW078 Bottomless Trap Hole SCR	1.50	4.00
LCJW079 Drop Off C	.20	.60
LCJW080 Magical Arm Shield C	.20	.60
LCJW081 Kunai with Chain C	.20	.60
LCJW082 Harpie Lady SR	.15	.50
LCJW083 Harpie Girl C	.20	.60
LCJW084 Dunames Dark Witch UR	.15	.40
LCJW085 Harpie Lady Sisters C	.20	.60
LCJW086 Harpie's Pet Dragon UR	2.00	5.00
LCJW087 Amazoness Paladin SR	.15	.50
LCJW088 Amazoness Fighter C	.20	.60
LCJW089 Amazoness Tiger UR	.10	.30
LCJW090 Harpie Lady 1 SR	.40	1.00
LCJW091 Harpie Lady 2 SR	.15	.50
LCJW092 Harpie Lady 3 SR	.15	.50
LCJW093 Harpie's Pet Baby Dragon C	.75	2.00
LCJW094 Harpie Queen UR	1.50	4.00
LCJW095 Amazoness Scouts C	.20	.60
LCJW096 Cyber Harpie Lady C	2.00	5.00
LCJW097 Harpie Dancer UR	3.00	8.00
LCJW098 Elegant Egotist SR	.15	.50
LCJW099 Harpie's Feather Duster SCR	3.00	8.00
LCJW100 Amazoness Spellcaster C	.20	.60
LCJW101 Spell Reproduction C	.20	.60
LCJW102 Harpies' Hunting Ground SR	.15	.50
LCJW103 Triangle Ecstasy Spark C	.20	.60
LCJW104 Amazoness Village C	.20	.60
LCJW105 Cyber Shield C	.20	.60
LCJW106 Fairy's Hand Mirror C	.20	.60
LCJW107 Mirror Wall C	.20	.60
LCJW108 Gravity Bind C	.20	.60
LCJW109 Shadow of Eyes C	.20	.60
LCJW110 Gryphon Wing C	.20	.60
LCJW111 Trap Jammer SCR	.75	2.00
LCJW112 Hysteric Party SR	.40	1.00
LCJW113 Revival Jam C	.20	.60
LCJW114 Dark Jeroid C	.20	.60
LCJW115 Newdoria C	.20	.60
LCJW116 Helpoemer C	.20	.60
LCJW117 Lava Golem R	.10	.30
LCJW118 Drillago C	.20	.60
LCJW119 Lekunga C	.20	.60
LCJW120 Lord Poison C	.20	.60
LCJW121 Makyura the Destructor C	.20	.60
LCJW122 Legendary Fiend C	.20	.60
LCJW123 Black Pendant C	.20	.60
LCJW124 Jam Breeding Machine C	.20	.60
LCJW125 Vengeful Bog Spirit C	.20	.60
LCJW126 Card of Sanctity C	.20	.60
LCJW127 Magical Stone Excavation C	.20	.60
LCJW128 Spell of Pain C	.20	.60
LCJW129 Magic Jammer C	.20	.60
LCJW130 Mirror Force SCR	1.00	2.50
LCJW131 Jam Defender C	.75	2.00
LCJW132 Coffin Seller C	.20	.60
LCJW133 Rope of Life C	.20	.60
LCJW134 Nightmare Wheel C	.20	.60
LCJW135 Judgment of Anubis C	.75	2.00
LCJW136 Malevolent Catastrophe C	.20	.60
LCJW137 Relieve Monster C	.20	.60
LCJW138 Metal Reflect Slime C	.50	1.25
LCJW139 Serpent Night Dragon C	.20	.60
LCJW140 Two-Headed King Rex C	.20	.60
LCJW141 Crawling Dragon C	.20	.60
LCJW142 Kabazauls SCR	.25	.75
LCJW143 Sabersaurus SCR	.25	.75
LCJW144 Tomozaurus C	.20	.60
LCJW145 Little D C	.20	.60
LCJW146 Sword Arm of Dragon C	.20	.60
LCJW147 Megazowler C	.20	.60
LCJW148 Gilasaurus C	.20	.60
LCJW149 Tyrant Dragon C	.20	.60
LCJW150 Dark Driceratops C	.20	.60
LCJW151 Hyper Hammerhead C	.20	.60
LCJW152 Black Tyranno C	.20	.60
LCJW153 Tyranno Infinity C	.20	.60
LCJW154 Black Ptera C	.20	.60
LCJW155 Black Stego C	.20	.60
LCJW156 Miracle Jurassic Egg C	.20	.60
LCJW157 Babycerasaurus C	.20	.60
LCJW158 Destroyersaurus SCR	.25	.75
LCJW159 Bracchio-Raidus C	.20	.60
LCJW160 Ultra Evolution Pill C	.20	.60
LCJW161 Big Evolution Pill C	.20	.60
LCJW162 Tail Swipe C	.20	.60
LCJW163 Jurassic World C	.60	1.50
LCJW164 Fossil Dig C	.60	1.50
LCJW165 Fossil Excavation C	.20	.60
LCJW166 Hunting Instinct C	.20	.60
LCJW167 Survival Instinct C	.20	.60
LCJW168 Volcanic Eruption C	.20	.60
LCJW169 Seismic Shockwave C	.20	.60
LCJW170 Seiyaryu C	.20	.60
LCJW171 Launcher Spider C	.20	.60
LCJW172 Slot Machine C	.20	.60
LCJW173 Zoa C	.20	.60
LCJW174 Ancient Tool C	.20	.60
LCJW175 Giganto C	.20	.60
LCJW176 Sword Slasher C	.20	.60
LCJW177 Barrel Dragon C	.20	.60
LCJW178 Metalzoa C	.20	.60
LCJW179 Machine King C	.20	.60
LCJW180 Blast Sphere C	.20	.60
LCJW181 Fiendish Engine Ω C	.20	.60
LCJW182 Solemn Judgment SCR	.60	1.50
LCJW183 Dragon Zombie C	.20	.60
LCJW184 Armored Zombie C	.60	1.50
LCJW185 The Snake Hair C	.20	.60
LCJW186 Vampire Baby C	.20	.60
LCJW187 Patrician of Darkness C	.20	.60
LCJW188 Dark Dust Spirit C	.20	.60
LCJW189 Pyramid Turtle SR	.15	.50
LCJW190 Spirit Reaper UR	.60	1.50
LCJW191 Vampire Lord C	.20	.60
LCJW192 Despair from the Dark C	.20	.60
LCJW193 Fear from the Dark C	.20	.60
LCJW194 Ryu Kokki C	.20	.60
LCJW195 Soul-Absorbing Bone Tower C	.20	.60
LCJW196 Vampire Lady C	.20	.60
LCJW197 Regenerating Mummy C	.20	.60
LCJW198 Vampire Genesis C	.20	.60
LCJW199 Reborn Zombie C	.20	.60
LCJW200 Plague Wolf C	.20	.60
LCJW201 Return Zombie C	.20	.60
LCJW202 Zombie Master C	.20	.60
LCJW203 Il Blud C	.20	.60
LCJW204 Vampire's Curse C	.60	1.50
LCJW205 Goblin Zombie C	1.25	3.00
LCJW206 Red-Eyes Zombie Dragon R	.10	.30
LCJW207 Malevolent Mech - Goku En C	.20	.60
LCJW208 Paladin of the Cursed Dragon C	.20	.60
LCJW209 Skull Conductor C	.20	.60
LCJW210 Great Mammoth of Goldfine C	.20	.60
LCJW211 Book of Life UR	.60	1.50
LCJW212 Call of the Mummy SR	.15	.50
LCJW213 Zombie World UR	1.25	3.00
LCJW214 Everliving Underworld Cannon C	.20	.60
LCJW215 Pyramid of Wonders C	.20	.60
LCJW216 Overpowering Eye C	.20	.60
LCJW217 Call of the Haunted SR	1.00	2.50
LCJW218 Tutan Mask C	.20	.60
LCJW219 Trap of the Imperial Tomb C	.20	.60
LCJW220 Labyrinth Wall C	.20	.60
LCJW221 Dungeon Worm C	.20	.60
LCJW222 Monster Tamer C	.20	.60
LCJW223 Gate Guardian C	2.00	5.00
LCJW224 Sanga of the Thunder C	.40	1.00
LCJW225 Kazejin C	.40	1.00
LCJW226 Suijin C	.50	1.25
LCJW227 Jirai Gumo C	.20	.60
LCJW228 Shadow Ghoul C	.20	.60
LCJW229 Wall Shadow C	.20	.60
LCJW230 Labyrinth Tank C	.20	.60
LCJW231 Magical Labyrinth C	.20	.60
LCJW232 Fairy Meteor Crush C	.20	.60
LCJW233 Tribute Doll C	.20	.60
LCJW234 Riryoku C	.20	.60
LCJW235 Summoned Skull R	.40	1.00
LCJW236 Beast of Talwar R	.10	.30
LCJW237 Toon Summoned Skull R	.10	.30
LCJW238 Lesser Fiend R	.10	.30
LCJW239 Shadow Tamer R	.10	.30
LCJW240 Fiend Skull Dragon R	.10	.30
LCJW241 A Deal with Dark Ruler R	.10	.30
LCJW242 Beiige, Vanguard of Dark World UR	.60	1.50

LCJW243 Broww, Huntsman of Dark World SCR	.75	2.00
LCJW244 Brron, Mad King of Dark World UR	.10	.30
LCJW245 Sillva, Warlord of Dark World SCR	.25	.75
LCJW246 Goldd, Wu-Lord of Dark World SCR	.25	.75
LCJW247 Scarr, Scout of Dark World C	.20	.60
LCJW248 Snoww, Unlight of Dark World SCR	.50	1.25
LCJW249 Dark World Lightning SCR	.25	.75
LCJW250 Gateway to Dark World SCR	.25	.75
LCJW251 Dark World Dealings SR	1.25	3.00
LCJW252 Dark World Grimoire C	.20	.60
LCJW253 The Gates of Dark World UR	.60	1.50
LCJW254 The Forces of Darkness C	.20	.60
LCJW255 Gravekeeper's Spy SCR	.25	.75
LCJW256 Gravekeeper's Curse C	.20	.60
LCJW257 Gravekeeper's Vassal C	.20	.60
LCJW258 Gravekeeper's Priestess R	.10	.30
LCJW259 Gravekeeper's Visionary R	.10	.30
LCJW260 Necrovalley C	.50	1.25
LCJW261 Gravekeeper's Stele UR	.60	1.50
LCJW262 Dice Jar C	.20	.60
LCJW263 Roulette Barrel C	.20	.60
LCJW264 Blowback Dragon C	.20	.60
LCJW265 Snipe Hunter C	.20	.60
LCJW266 Twin-Barrel Dragon C	.20	.60
LCJW267 Gatling Dragon C	.20	.60
LCJW268 Second Coin Toss C	.20	.60
LCJW269 Blind Destruction C	.20	.60
LCJW270 Needle Wall C	.20	.60
LCJW271 Dice Re-Roll C	.20	.60
LCJW272 Dice Try C	.20	.60
LCJW273 Sixth Sense C	.75	2.00
LCJW274 Adhesion Trap Hole C	.20	.60
LCJW275 D.D. Trap Hole C	.20	.60
LCJW276 Giant Trap Hole C	.20	.60
LCJW277 Treacherous Trap Hole C	.75	2.00
LCJW278 Chaos Trap Hole C	5.00	12.00
LCJW279 Cave Dragon C	.20	.60
LCJW280 Injection Fairy Lily C	.20	.60
LCJW281 Berserk Dragon C	.20	.60
LCJW282 Strike Ninja C	.20	.60
LCJW283 Dark Hole SCR	.75	2.00
LCJW284 Heavy Storm UR	.60	1.50
LCJW285 Mystical Space Typhoon SCR	1.50	4.00
LCJW286 Reinforcement of the Army UR	.60	1.50
LCJW287 Super Rejuvenation SR	.15	.50
LCJW288 Book of Moon SCR	.75	2.00
LCJW289 Stray Lambs UR	.10	.30
LCJW290 Pot of Avarice SCR	.50	1.25
LCJW291 Trade-In UR	4.00	10.00
LCJW292 Horn of Heaven UR	.60	1.50
LCJW293 Chain Destruction R	.10	.30
LCJW294 Torrential Tribute SCR	1.25	3.00
LCJW295 Compulsory Evacuation Device SCR	.50	1.25
LCJW296 Spirit Barrier C	.75	2.00
LCJW297 Black Horn of Heaven UR	.60	1.50
LCJW298 Imperial Iron Wall UR	1.00	2.50

2013 Yu-Gi-Oh Legendary Collection 4 Joey's World Box Bonus

COMPLETE SET (9)	2.00	5.00
ONE SET PER LEGENDARY COLLECTION 4 BOX		
LC04001 Blue Flame Swordsman UR	.10	.30
LC04002 Harpie Lady Phoenix Formation UR	.10	.30
LC04003 Card of Last Will UR	.10	.30
LC04004 Blue Sheep Token UR	.10	.30
LC04005 Orange Sheep Token UR	.10	.30
LC04006 Pink Sheep Token UR	.10	.30
LC04007 Yellow Sheep Token UR	.10	.30
LC04008 White Lamb Token UR	.10	.30
LC04009 Pink Lamb Token UR	.10	.30

2002 Yu-Gi-Oh Collector Tins

Complete Set Sealed (6)	150.00	175.00
Black Skull Dragon Sealed Box	30.00	45.00
Black Skull Dragon Tin Only	8.00	15.00
Blue Eyes White Dragon Sealed Box	25.00	35.00
Blue Eyes White Dragon Tin Only	8.00	12.00
Dark Magician Sealed Box	25.00	30.00
Dark Magician Tin Only	5.00	8.00
Lord of D Sealed Box	20.00	28.00
Lord of D Tin Only	4.00	7.00
Red Eyes B Dragon Sealed Box	30.00	35.00
Red Eyes B Dragon Tin Only	6.00	10.00
Summoned Skull Sealed Box	22.00	30.00
Summoned Skull Tin Only	4.00	8.00
BPT001 Dark Magician SCR	3.00	8.00
BPT002 Summoned Skull SCR	2.50	6.00
BPT003 Blue Eyes White Dragon SCR	2.00	5.00
BPT004 Lord of D SCR	1.00	2.50
BPT005 Red Eyes B Dragon SCR	1.50	4.00
BPT006 B. Skull Dragon SCR	2.50	6.00

2003 Yu-Gi-Oh Collector Tins

Complete Tin Set sealed (6)	140.00	200.00
Blue-Eyes White Dragon Sealed Box	25.00	35.00
Blue-Eyes White Dragon Tin Only	5.00	10.00
Buster Blader Sealed Box	20.00	30.00
Buster Blader Tin Only	4.00	7.00
Dark Magician Sealed Box	22.00	30.00
Dark Magician Tin Only	5.00	8.00
Gearfried the Iron Knight Sealed Box	15.00	20.00
Gearfried the Iron Knight Tin Only	3.00	5.00
Jinzo Sealed Box	30.00	45.00
Jinzo Tin Only	7.00	15.00
XYZ-Dragon Cannon Sealed Box	20.00	28.00
XYZ-Dragon Cannon Tin Only	5.00	10.00
BPT007 Dark Magician	2.00	5.00
BPT008 Buster Blader	3.00	8.00
BPT009 Blue-Eyes White Dragon	5.00	12.00
BPT010 XYZ-Dragon Cannon	1.00	2.50
BPT011 Jinzo	2.50	6.00
BPT012 Gearfried the Iron Knight	.75	2.00

2004 Yu-Gi-Oh Collector Tins

Complete Tin Set sealed (6)	5.00	15.00
Blade Knight Sealed Tin	20.00	40.00
Command Knight Sealed Tin	20.00	40.00
Insect Queen Sealed Tin	20.00	40.00
Obnoxious Celtic Guardian Sealed Tin	20.00	40.00
Swift Knight Gaia Sealed Tin	20.00	40.00
Total Defense Shogun Sealed Tin	20.00	40.00
CT1001 Total Defense Shogun SCT	1.25	3.00
CT1002 Blade Knight SCT	1.25	3.00
CT1003 Command Knight SCT	1.25	3.00
CT1004 Swift Gaia The Fierce Knight SCT	1.25	3.00
CT1005 Insect Queen SCT	1.25	3.00
CT1006 Obnoxious Celtic Guardian SCT	1.00	2.50

2005 Yu-Gi-Oh Collector Tins

Complete Tin Set Sealed (6)	200.00	400.00
Collector Tins (empty)	3.00	8.00
Gilford the Lightning Sealed Tin	30.00	60.00
Exarion Sealed Tin	20.00	40.00
Vorse Raider Sealed Tin	40.00	80.00
Dark Magician Girl Sealed Tin	50.00	110.00
Rocket Warrior Sealed Tin	20.00	40.00
Panther Warrior Sealed Tin	40.00	80.00
CT2001 Gilford the Lightning P	1.00	2.50
CT2002 Exarion Universe P	2.50	6.00
CT2003 Vorse Raider P	5.00	12.00
CT2004 Dark Magician Girl P	6.00	15.00
CT2005 Rockety Warrior P	4.00	10.00
CT2006 Panther Warrior P	3.00	8.00

2006 Yu-Gi-Oh Collector Tins

CT03001 Elemental HERO Neos SCR	2.00	5.00
CT03002 Cyber Dragon SCR	2.50	6.00
CT03003 Raviel, Lord of Phantasms SCR	1.50	4.00
CT03004 Elemental HERO Shining Flare Wingman SCR	2.50	6.00
CT03005 Uria, Lord of Searing Flames SCR	2.50	6.00
CT03006 Hamon, Lord of Striking Thunder SCR	2.00	5.00

2007 Yu-Gi-Oh Collector Tins

CT04001 Elemental HERO Grand Neos SCR	.75	2.00
CT04002 Crystal Beast Sapphire Pegasus SCR	2.00	5.00
CT04003 Destiny HERO - Plasma SCR	1.25	3.00
CT04004 Volcanic Doomfire SCR	1.25	3.00
CT04005 Rainbow Dragon SCR	2.50	6.00
CT04006 Elemental HERO Plasma Vice SCR	2.00	5.00

2008 Yu-Gi-Oh Collector Tins

Stardust Dragon Tin	30.00	40.00
Red Dragon Archfiend Tin	30.00	40.00
Black Rose Dragon Tin	30.00	40.00
Turbo Warrior Tin	25.00	35.00
Yusei Fudo Tin	30.00	40.00
CT05001 Stardust Dragon SCR	1.50	4.00
CT05002 Red Dragon Archfiend SCR	1.25	3.00
CT05003 Black Rose Dragon SCR	1.50	4.00
CT05004 Turbo Warrior SCR	.75	2.00
CT05S01 Montage Dragon SR	1.25	3.00
CT05S02 Nitro Warrior SR	.40	1.00
CT05S03 Goyo Guardian SR	2.00	5.00

2009 Yu-Gi-Oh Collector Tins

Ancient Fairy Dragon Tin	15.00	25.00
Power Tool Dragon Tin	15.00	25.00
Majestic Star Dragon Tin	15.00	25.00
Earthbound Immortal Wiraquocha Rasca Tin	15.00	25.00
CT06001 Power Tool Dragon SCR	.75	2.00
CT06002 Ancient Fairy Dragon SCR	1.25	3.00
CT06003 Majestic Star Dragon SCR	.50	1.25
CT06004 Earthbound Immortal Wiraqocha Rasca SCR	.40	1.00
CT06S01 Blackwing - Elphin the Raven SCR	.40	1.00
CT06S02 Earthbound Immortal Aslla piscu SCR	.40	1.00
CT06S03 Earthbound Immortal Chacu Challhua SCR	.40	1.00
CT06S04 XX-Saber Gottoms SCR	.40	1.00
DP09001 Stardust Dragon/Assault Mode UR	.40	1.00
RGBTPP1 Iron Core of Koa'ki Meiru UR	.40	1.00
RGBTPP2 Blackwing - Shura the Blue Flame SR	.40	1.00
RGBTPP3 Koa'ki Meiru Guardian SR	.40	1.00
RGBTPP4 Moja UR	.40	1.00
RGBTPP5 Master Gig SR	.40	1.00
RGBTPP6 Level Retuner SR	.40	1.00

2010 Yu-Gi-Oh Collector Tins

CT07001 Majestic Red Dragon SCR	.75	2.00
CT07002 Black-Winged Dragon SCR	.75	2.00
CT07003 Dragon Knight Draco-Equiste SCR	.75	2.00
CT07004 Shooting Star Dragon SCR	2.50	2.00
CT07005 Red Nova Dragon SCR	2.00	5.00
CT07006 Elemental HERO Stratos SR	.75	2.00
CT07007 Van'Dalgyon the Dark Dragon Lord SR	.75	2.00
CT07008 Cyber Dinosaur SR	.75	2.00
CT07009 Battle Fader SR	.75	2.00
CT07010 Green Baboon, Defender of the Forest SR	.75	2.00
CT07011 The Wicked Eraser SR	.75	2.00
CT07012 Blackwing - Vayu the Emblem of Honor SR	.75	2.00
CT07013 Chimeratech Fortress Dragon SR	4.00	10.00
CT07014 Archfiend of Gilfer SR	.75	2.00
CT07015 The Wicked Dreadroot SR	.75	2.00
CT07016 Dark Armed Dragon SR	.75	2.00
CT07017 Dragonic Knight SR	.75	2.00
CT07018 Elemental HERO Ocean SR	.75	2.00
CT07019 Dreadscythe Harvester SR	.75	2.00
CT07020 Gandora the Dragon of Destruction SR	.75	2.00
CT07021 Stardust Dragon SR	1.50	4.00
CT07022 Magician's Valkyria SR	2.50	6.00
CT07023 The Wicked Avatar SR	1.50	4.00
CT07024 Exodius the Ultimate Forbidden Lord SR	.75	2.00
CT07025 Red Dragon Archfiend SR	.75	2.00

2010 Yu-Gi-Oh Duelist Pack Collection Tins

Red Tin	15.00	25.00
Yellow Tin	15.00	25.00
Purple Tin	15.00	25.00
Three Cards per tin		
One Starlight Road per tin		
DPCT004 Starlight Road SCR	4.00	10.00
DPCTY01 Junk Synchron UR	3.00	8.00
DPCTY02 Quillbolt Hedgehog SR	1.50	4.00
DPCTY03 Synchro Blast Wave SR	1.50	4.00
DPCTY04 Drill Synchron UR	2.50	6.00
DPCTY05 Speed Warrior SR	1.25	3.00
DPCTY06 Advance Draw SR	1.25	3.00
DPCTY07 Scrap-Iron Scarecrow UR	2.50	6.00
DPCTY08 Level Eater SR	1.25	3.00
DPCTY09 One for One SR	1.25	3.00

2011 Yu-Gi-Oh Collector Tins

CT08001 Number 17: Leviathan Dragon SCR	.40	1.00
CT08002 Wind-Up Zenmaister SCR	.40	1.00
CT08003 Galaxy-Eyes Photon Dragon SCR	1.50	4.00
CT08004 Number 10: Illumiknight SCR	.40	1.00
CT08005 Beast King Barbaros SR	.40	1.00
CT08006 Dark Simorgh SR	.40	1.00
CT08007 Stygian Street Patrol SR	.40	1.00
CT08008 Pot of Duality SR	.75	2.00
CT08009 Neo-Parshath, the Sky Paladin SR	.40	1.00
CT08010 Archlord Kristya SR	1.00	2.50
CT08011 Elemental HERO Gaia SR	.40	1.00
CT08012 Fossil Dyna Pachycephalo SR	.40	1.00
CT08013 Guardian Eatos SR	.40	1.00
CT08014 Malefic Stardust Dragon SR	.40	1.00
CT08015 Solemn Warning SR	1.25	3.00
CT08016 Ehren, Lightsworn Monk SR	.40	1.00
CT08017 XX-Saber Darksoul SR	.40	1.00
CT08018 The Tyrant Neptune SR	.40	1.00

2012 Yu-Gi-Oh Collector Tins

CT09001 Evolzar Dolkka SCR	.25	.75
CT09002 Heroic Champion - Excalibur SCR	1.25	3.00
CT09003 Ninja Grandmaster Hanzo SCR	.25	.75
CT09004 Hieratic Sun Dragon Overlord of Heliopolis SCR	2.00	5.00
CT09005 Genex Neutron SR	.25	.75
CT09006 Scrap Dragon SR	.75	2.00
CT09007 Dark Highlander SR	.25	.75
CT09008 Wind-Up Zenmaines SR	.25	.75
CT09009 Blizzard Princess SR	.25	.75
CT09010 Wind-Up Rabbit SR	.25	.75
CT09011 Evolzar Laggia SR	.25	.75
CT09012 Maxx C SR	5.00	12.00
CT09013 Tour Guide From the Underworld SR	1.50	4.00
CT09014 Number 16: Shock Master SR	.75	2.00
CT09015 Rescue Rabbit SR	.40	1.00
CT09016 Malefic Truth Dragon SR	.25	.75
CT09017 X-Saber Souza SR	.25	.75
CT09018 Leviair the Sea Dragon SR	3.00	8.00
CT09019 Prophecy Destroyer SCR	.25	.75
CT09020 Endless Decay SR	.25	.75
CT09021 Steelswarm Roach SR	1.00	2.50
CT09022 Photon Strike Bounzer SR	.50	1.25
CT09023 Infernity Barrier SR	.25	.75

2013 Yu-Gi-Oh Collector Tins

CT10001 Tidal, Dragon Ruler of Waterfalls SCR	.40	1.00
CT10002 Blaster, Dragon Ruler of Infernos SCR	.75	2.00
CT10003 Redox, Dragon Ruler of Boulders SCR	.40	1.00
CT10004 Tempest, Dragon Ruler of Storms SCR	.40	1.00
CT10005 Black Luster Soldier - Envoy of the Beginning SR	2.00	5.00
CT10006 Ally of Justice Catastor SR	1.00	2.50
CT10007 Superdreadnought Rail Cannon Gustav Max SR	.25	.75
CT10008 Brotherhood of the Fire Fist - Bear SR	.25	.75
CT10009 Karakuri Shogun mdl 00 Burei SR	.25	.75
CT10010 Gagaga Cowboy SR	.75	2.00
CT10011 Number 40: Gimmick Puppet of Strings SR	.25	.75
CT10012 Diamond Dire Wolf SR	1.25	3.00
CT10013 Number 88: Gimmick Puppet of Leo SR	.25	.75
CT10014 Spellbook of the Master SR	.25	.75
CT10015 Rank-Up-Magic Barian's Force SR	.25	.75
CT10016 Thunder Sea Horse SR	.25	.75
CT10017 Gear Gigant X SR	.50	1.25
CT10018 Number 50: Blackship of Corn SR	1.00	2.50

2013 Yu-Gi-Oh Zexal Collection Tin

COMPLETE SET (24)	8.00	20.00
ZTIN001 Dododo Warrior SR	.10	.30
ZTIN002 No. 61: Volcasaurus UR	1.25	3.00
ZTIN003 Number 19: Freezadon UR	.10	.30
ZTIN004 Gagagaback SR	.10	.30
ZTIN005 Gagagashield UR	.40	1.00
ZTIN006 Photon Pirate SR	.10	.30
ZTIN007 Photon Satellite SR	.10	.30
ZTIN008 Photon Slasher SR	.10	.30
ZTIN009 Kuriphoton UR	.10	.30
ZTIN010 Dimension Wanderer SR	.10	.30
ZTIN011 Galaxy Wizard UR	2.00	5.00
ZTIN012 Galaxy Knight UR	2.00	5.00
ZTIN013 Number 56: Gold Rat SR	.10	.30
ZTIN014 Starliege Paladynamo UR	1.00	2.50
ZTIN015 Message in a Bottle SR	.10	.30
ZTIN016 Accellight UR	.20	.60
ZTIN017 Galaxy Expedition UR	1.50	4.00
ZTIN018 Galaxy Zero SR	.20	.60
ZTIN019 Triple Star Trion SR	.10	.30
ZTIN020 Zubaba Buster SR	.10	.30
ZTIN021 Chachaka Archer SR	.10	.30
ZTINV01 Gagaga Magician UTR	.10	.30
ZTINV02 No. 20: Giga-Brilliant UTR	.20	.60
ZTINV03 Gagagabolt UTR	.10	.30

2014 Yu-Gi-Oh Mega Tin Mega Pack

CT11EN001 Brotherhood of the Fire Fist - Tiger King UR		
CT11EN002 Bujintei Susanowo UR		
CT11EN003 Brotherhood of the Fire Fist - Gorilla SR		
CT11EN004 Number 47: Nightmare Shark SR		
CT11EN005 Bujingi Crane SR		
CT11EN006 Archfiend Commander SR		
MP14EN001 Mecha Phantom Beast Turtletracer SR		
MP14EN002 Battlin' Boxer Headgeared C	.15	.25
MP14EN003 Battlin' Boxer Glassjaw C	.15	.25
MP14EN004 Battlin' Boxer Sparrer C	.15	.25
MP14EN005 Battlin' Boxer Switchitter C	.15	.25
MP14EN006 Battlin' Boxer Counterpunch C	.15	.25
MP14EN007 Mecha Phantom Beast Megaraptor SR		
MP14EN008 Mecha Phantom Beast Tetherwolf R		
MP14EN009 Mecha Phantom Beast Blackfalcon C	.15	.25
MP14EN010 Mecha Phantom Beast Stealthray C	.15	.25
MP14EN011 Mecha Phantom Beast Hamstrat UR		
MP14EN012 Brotherhood of the Fire Fist - Wolf C	.15	.25
MP14EN013 Brotherhood of the Fire Fist - Leopard C	.15	.25
MP14EN014 Brotherhood of the Fire Fist - Rhino R		
MP14EN015 Brotherhood of the Fire Fist - Buffalo R		
MP14EN016 Mermail Abyssocea C	.15	.25
MP14EN017 Wheel of Prophecy R		
MP14EN018 Madolche Hootcake SR		
MP14EN019 Legendary Atlantean Tridon C	.15	.25
MP14EN020 Fire King Avatar Garunix C	.50	.75
MP14EN021 Harpie Channeler UR		
MP14EN022 Windrose the Elemental Lord SCR		
MP14EN023 Risebell the Star Adjuster C	.15	.25
MP14EN024 Number 107: Galaxy-Eyes Tachyon Dragon UR		
MP14EN025 Gauntlet Launcher UR		
MP14EN026 Shark Fortress C	.40	.60
MP14EN027 Battlin' Boxer Lead Yoke R		
MP14EN028 Number 105: Battlin' Boxer Star Cestus SR		
MP14EN029 Number C105: Battlin' Boxer Comet Cestus UR		
MP14EN030 Mecha Phantom Beast Dracossack SCR		
MP14EN031 Brotherhood of the Fire Fist - Cardinal SCR		
MP14EN032 Harpie's Pet Phantasmal Dragon R		
MP14EN033 King of the Feral Imps C	.30	.50
MP14EN034 Gagagawind C	.15	.25
MP14EN035 Magnum Shield C	.15	.25
MP14EN036 Rank-Up-Magic Barian's Force UR		
MP14EN037 Scramble!! Scramble!! UR		
MP14EN038 Fire Formation - Gyokkou SR		
MP14EN039 Spellbook of Judgment SCR		
MP14EN040 Abyss-scale of the Mizuchi C	.15	.25
MP14EN041 Hysteric Sign SR		
MP14EN042 Sacred Sword of Seven Stars SR		
MP14EN043 Summon Breaker C	.15	.25
MP14EN044 Pinpoint Guard SCR		
MP14EN045 Memory Loss C	.15	.25
MP14EN046 Torrential Reborn SCR		
MP14EN047 Xyz Block C	.15	.25
MP14EN048 Aerial Recharge C	.15	.25
MP14EN049 Do a Barrel Roll R		
MP14EN050 Fire Formation - Kaiyo C	.15	.25
MP14EN051 Madolche Nights SR		
MP14EN052 Geargiagear SR		
MP14EN053 Mind Drain C	.15	.25
MP14EN054 Brotherhood of the Fire Fist - Coyote SCR		
MP14EN055 Mermail Abyssbalaen UR		
MP14EN056 Totem Bird SCR		
MP14EN057 Spellbook of Miracles C	.15	.25
MP14EN058 Five Brothers Explosion C	.15	.25
MP14EN059 Constellar Omega UR		
MP14EN060 Constellar Sombre SR		
MP14EN061 Evilswarm Kerykeion SR		
MP14EN062 Interceptomato C	.15	.25
MP14EN063 Super Defense Robot Lio C	.15	.25
MP14EN064 Super Defense Robot Elephan C	.15	.25
MP14EN065 Super Defense Robot Monki C	.15	.25
MP14EN066 Umbral Horror Ghoul C	.15	.25
MP14EN067 Umbral Horror Unform C	.15	.25
MP14EN068 Umbral Horror Will o' the Wisp C	.15	.25
MP14EN069 Bujin Yamato UR		
MP14EN070 Bujingi Quilin SR		
MP14EN071 Bujingi Turtle C	.15	.25
MP14EN072 Bujingi Wolf C	.15	.25
MP14EN073 Bujingi Crane R		
MP14EN074 Bujingi Ophidian C	.15	.25
MP14EN075 Mecha Phantom Beast Warbluran R		
MP14EN076 Mecha Phantom Beast Blue Impala UR		
MP14EN077 Mecha Phantom Beast Coltwing C	.15	.25
MP14EN078 Mecha Phantom Beast Harrliard C	.15	.25
MP14EN079 Brotherhood of the Fire Fist - Boar R		
MP14EN080 Brotherhood of the Fire Fist - Caribou C	.15	.25
MP14EN081 World of Prophecy SCR		
MP14EN082 Archfiend Heiress R		
MP14EN083 Archfiend Cavalry R		
MP14EN084 Archfiend Emperor, the First Lord of Horror R		
MP14EN085 Traptrix Atrax R		
MP14EN086 Traptrix Myrmeleo R		
MP14EN087 Traptrix Nepenthes C	.15	.25
MP14EN088 The Calibrator C	.15	.25
MP14EN089 Talaya, Princess of Cherry Blossoms SR		
MP14EN090 Cheepcheepcheep C	.15	.25
MP14EN091 Masked Chameleon UR		
MP14EN092 Flying "C" C	.50	.75
MP14EN093 Mecha Phantom Beast Concoruda SR		
MP14EN094 Brotherhood of the Fire Fist - Kirin R		
MP14EN095 Armades, Keeper of Boundaries SCR		
MP14EN096 Star Eater SCR		
MP14EN097 Starliege Lord Galaxion SR		
MP14EN098 Googly-Eyes Drum Dragon C	.15	.25
MP14EN099 Number 66: Master Key Beetle SR		
MP14EN100 Bujintei Susanowo UR		
MP14EN101 Rank-Up-Magic Numeron Force UR		
MP14EN102 Bujincarnation R		
MP14EN103 Vertical Landing C	.15	.25
MP14EN104 Fire Formation - Yoko SR		
MP14EN105 Archfiend Palabyrinth R		
MP14EN106 Transmodify SCR		
MP14EN107 Bujin Regalia - The Sword C	.15	.25
MP14EN108 Bujinfidel C	.15	.25
MP14EN109 Sonic Boom C	.15	.25
MP14EN110 Traptrix Trap Hole Nightmare SR		
MP14EN111 Shapesister UR		
MP14EN112 Armageddon Designator C	.15	.25
MP14EN113 Bujingi Warg C	.15	.25
MP14EN114 Mecha Phantom Beast Aerosguin UR		
MP14EN115 Cockadoodledoo UR		
MP14EN116 Angel of Zera SCR		
MP14EN117 Xyz Encore UR		
MP14EN118 Coach Captain Bearman UR		
MP14EN119 Coach Soldier Wolfbark SCR		
MP14EN120 Brotherhood of the Fire Fist - Rooster SCR		
MP14EN121 Fire King Avatar Yaksha SR		
MP14EN122 Fishborg Archer C	.15	.25
MP14EN123 Fencing Fire Ferret C	.15	.25
MP14EN124 Kujakujaku C	.15	.25
MP14EN125 Madolche Chickolates C	.15	.25
MP14EN126 Ghostrick Ghoul SR		
MP14EN127 Malicevorous Spoon C	.15	.25
MP14EN128 Malicevorous Fork C	.15	.25
MP14EN129 Malicevorous Knife C	.15	.25
MP14EN130 Battlin' Boxer Rib Gardna C	.15	.25
MP14EN131 Battlin' Boxer Rabbit Puncher C	.15	.25
MP14EN132 Secret Sect Druid Wid C	.15	.25
MP14EN133 Secret Sect Druid Dru C	.15	.25
MP14EN134 Mythic Tree Dragon C	.15	.25
MP14EN135 Mythic Water Dragon C	.15	.25
MP14EN136 Baby Raccoon Ponpoko C	.15	.25
MP14EN137 Baby Raccoon Tantan C	.15	.25
MP14EN138 Ghostrick Lantern SR		
MP14EN139 Ghostrick Specter C	.15	.25
MP14EN140 Ghostrick Witch C	.15	.25
MP14EN141 Ghostrick Yuki-onna C	.15	.25
MP14EN142 Ghostrick Jiangshi C	.15	.25
MP14EN143 Ghostrick Stein C	.15	.25
MP14EN144 Bujin Mikazuchi UR		
MP14EN145 Bujingi Crow R		
MP14EN146 Bujingi Ibis C	.15	.25
MP14EN147 Bujingi Boar C	.15	.25
MP14EN148 Bujingi Centipede C	.15	.25
MP14EN149 Mecha Phantom Beast Sabre Hawk C	.15	.25
MP14EN150 Mecha Phantom Beast Kalgriffin R		
MP14EN151 Vampire Sorcerer UR		
MP14EN152 Shadow Vampire SCR		
MP14EN153 Vampire Grace C	.15	.25
MP14EN154 Pumprincess the Princess of Ghosts C	.15	.25
MP14EN155 Vampire Hunter SR		
MP14EN156 Genomix Fighter UR		
MP14EN157 Mariña, Princess of Sunflowers SR		
MP14EN158 Granmarg the Mega Monarch SCR		
MP14EN159 Risebell the Star Psycher C	.15	.25
MP14EN160 Battlin' Boxer Cheat Commissioner R		
MP14EN161 Number 64: Ronin Raccoon Sandayu R		
MP14EN162 Ghostrick Alucard UR		
MP14EN163 Bujintei Kagutsuchi UR		
MP14EN164 Crimson Knight Vampire Bram UR		
MP14EN165 Meliae of the Trees SCR		
MP14EN166 Divine Dragon Knight Felgrand SCR		
MP14EN167 Gagagatag C	.15	.25
MP14EN168 Battlin' Boxing Spirits SR		
MP14EN169 Ghostrick Mansion C	.15	.25
MP14EN170 Bujin Regalia - The Mirror R		
MP14EN171 Vampire Kingdom C	.15	.25
MP14EN172 Pot of Dichotomy SCR		
MP14EN173 Return of the Monarchs UR		
MP14EN174 Ghostrick Vanish C	.15	.25
MP14EN175 Ghostrick Scare C	.15	.25
MP14EN176 Vampire Takeover SR		
MP14EN177 Mistake SCR		
MP14EN178 Survival of the Fittest C	.15	.25
MP14EN179 Bujingi Raven R		
MP14EN180 Vampire Duke R		
MP14EN181 Archfiend Giant R		
MP14EN182 Sinister Yorishiro UR		
MP14EN183 Celestial Wolf Lord, Blue Sirius UR		
MP14EN184 White Dragon Wyverburster C	.15	.25
MP14EN185 Black Dragon Collapserpent C	.15	.25
MP14EN186 Sylvan Bladefender SR		
MP14EN187 Gilfagillancer C	.15	.25
MP14EN188 Rainbow Kuriboh SCR		
MP14EN189 Photon Chargeman C	.15	.25
MP14EN190 Chronomaly Moai Carrier C	.15	.25
MP14EN191 Chronomaly Winged Sphinx C	.15	.25
MP14EN192 Gorgonic Golem C	.15	.25
MP14EN193 Gorgonic Gargoyle C	.15	.25
MP14EN194 Gorgonic Ghoul C	.15	.25
MP14EN195 Gorgonic Cerberus C	.15	.25
MP14EN196 Sylvan Peaskeeper R		
MP14EN197 Sylvan Komushroomo R		
MP14EN198 Sylvan Marshalleaf UR		
MP14EN199 Sylvan Flowerknight SR		
MP14EN200 Sylvan Guardioak C	.15	.25
MP14EN201 Sylvan Hermitree UR		
MP14EN202 Ghostrick Jackfrost C	.15	.25
MP14EN203 Ghostrick Mary SR		
MP14EN204 Ghostrick Nekomusume C	.15	.25
MP14EN205 Ghostrick Skeleton C	.15	.25
MP14EN206 Ghostrick Mummy C	.15	.25
MP14EN207 Bujin Arasuda UR		
MP14EN208 Bujingi Peacock R		
MP14EN209 Bujingi Swallow C	.15	.25
MP14EN210 Bujingi Fox R		
MP14EN211 Bujingi Hare SR		
MP14EN212 Gravekeeper's Nobleman UR		
MP14EN213 Gravekeeper's Ambusher C	.15	.25
MP14EN214 Gravekeeper's Shaman SR		
MP14EN215 Gravekeeper's Oracle UR		
MP14EN216 Chirubimé, Princess of Autumn Leaves SR		
MP14EN217 Mobius the Mega Monarch SCR		
MP14EN218 Number C101: Silent Honor DARK UR		
MP14EN219 Number 101: Silent Honor ARK UR		
MP14EN220 Gorgonic Guardian C	.15	.25
MP14EN221 Alsei, the Sylvan High Protector UR		
MP14EN222 Ghostrick Dullahan R		
MP14EN223 Bujintei Tsukuyomi UR		
MP14EN224 Evilswarm Exciton Knight SCR		
MP14EN225 Downerd Magician SCR		
MP14EN226 Rank-Up-Magic Astral Force UR		
MP14EN227 Mount Sylvania SR		
MP14EN228 Ghostrick Museum C	.15	.25
MP14EN229 Bujinunity R		
MP14EN230 Hidden Temples of Necrovalley R		
MP14EN231 Shared Ride SCR		

MP14EN232 Sylvan Blessing C .15 .25
MP14EN233 Ghostrick-Go-Round R
MP14EN234 Bujin Regalia - The Jewel C .15 .25
MP14EN235 Imperial Tombs of Necrovalley SCR
MP14EN236 The Monarchs Awaken C .15 .25
MP14EN237 Skill Prisoner SR
MP14EN238 Sylvan Mikorange R
MP14EN239 Ghostrick Yeti C .15 .25
MP14EN240 Bujingi Pavo SR
MP14EN241 Gravekeeper's Heretic R
MP14EN242 Obedience Schooled SR
MP14EN243 The First Monarch SCR
MP14EN244 Alpacaribou, Mystical Beast of the Forest C .15 .25
MP14EN245 Dododo Buster C .15 .25
MP14EN246 Interplanetarypurplythorny Beast C .15 .25
MP14EN247 Starship Spy Plane C .15 .25

2014 Yu-Gi-Oh Legendary Collection 5D's

COMPLETE SET (265) 120.00 250.00
BOOSTER BOX (5 PACKS) 20.00 30.00
BOOSTER PACK (9 PACKS) 3.00 4.00
RELEASED ON OCTOBER 24, 2014
LC05EN001 Jormungardr the Nordic Serpent UR .40 1.00
LC05EN002 Fenrir the Nordic Wolf UR .75 2.00
LC05EN003 Stardust Flash UR 1.50 4.00
LC05EN004 Black Rose Dragon UR 1.50 4.00
LC05EN005 Shooting Quasar Dragon UR 1.50 4.00
LC5DEN001 Sonic Chick C .10 .20
LC5DEN002 Junk Synchron SCR 1.25 3.00
LC5DEN003 Speed Warrior C .10 .20
LC5DEN004 Nitro Synchron C .10 .20
LC5DEN005 Quillbolt Hedgehog SCR .75 2.00
LC5DEN006 Turbo Synchron C .10 .20
LC5DEN007 Tuningware SCR 2.00 5.00
LC5DEN008 Turret Warrior R .25 .60
LC5DEN009 Debris Dragon SCR 2.50 6.00
LC5DEN010 Hyper Synchron C .10 .20
LC5DEN011 Road Synchron C .10 .20
LC5DEN012 Majestic Dragon C 2.00 3.00
LC5DEN013 Quickdraw Synchron UR 1.50 4.00
LC5DEN014 Level Eater R .25 .60
LC5DEN015 Drill Synchron SR .40 1.00
LC5DEN016 Shield Wing R .25 .60
LC5DEN017 Synchron Explorer UR 1.25 3.00
LC5DEN018 Effect Veiler C 4.50 5.00
LC5DEN019 Bri Synchron C .10 .20
LC5DEN020 Doppelwarrior SR 1.50 4.00
LC5DEN021 Junk Servant C .10 .20
LC5DEN022 Unknown Synchron SCR 1.25 3.00
LC5DEN023 Junk Defender C .10 .20
LC5DEN024 Junk Forward C .10 .20
LC5DEN025 Junk Blader C .10 .20
LC5DEN026 Mono Synchron R 1.25 3.00
LC5DEN027 Steam Synchron R 1.25 3.00
LC5DEN028 Dragon Knight Draco-Equiste R .25 .60
LC5DEN029 Junk Warrior SR .40 1.00
LC5DEN030 Colossal Fighter SCR .40 1.00
LC5DEN031 Stardust Dragon C 3.00 3.50
LC5DEN031u Stardust Dragon UR 1.25 3.00
LC5DEN032 Nitro Warrior C .10 .20
LC5DEN033 Turbo Warrior C .10 .20
LC5DEN034 Armory Arm SCR 3.00 8.00
LC5DEN035 Road Warrior C 1.25 1.75
LC5DEN036 Majestic Star Dragon SR .25 .60
LC5DEN037 Junk Archer SR .75 2.00
LC5DEN038 Drill Warrior SCR .40 1.00
LC5DEN039 Junk Destroyer SR .40 1.00
LC5DEN040 Shooting Star Dragon SR 2.50 6.00
LC5DEN041 Formula Synchron SCR 3.00 8.00
LC5DEN042 Lightning Warrior UR .60 1.50
LC5DEN043 Junk Berserker SR .50 1.25
LC5DEN044 Junk Barrage C .10 .20
LC5DEN045 One for One UR .60 1.50
LC5DEN046 Silver Wing C .10 .20
LC5DEN047 Advance Draw UR 1.25 3.00
LC5DEN048 Cards of Consonance UR .60 1.50
LC5DEN049 Tuning C .10 .20
LC5DEN050 Battle Waltz C .10 .20
LC5DEN051 Scrap-Iron Scarecrow UR 2.00 5.00
LC5DEN052 Graceful Revival C .10 .20
LC5DEN053 Urgent Tuning C .10 .20
LC5DEN054 Spirit Force C .10 .20
LC5DEN055 Descending Lost Star C .10 .20
LC5DEN056 Starlight Road UR .75 2.00
LC5DEN057 Dark Resonator C .10 .20
LC5DEN058 Trap Eater UR .40 1.00
LC5DEN059 Vice Dragon C .10 .20
LC5DEN060 Strong Wind Dragon R .75 2.00
LC5DEN061 Battle Fader SCR 1.50 4.00
LC5DEN062 Flare Resonator C .10 .20
LC5DEN063 Power Breaker R .25 .60
LC5DEN064 Extra Veiler C .10 .20
LC5DEN065 Creation Resonator C 1.75 2.50
LC5DEN066 Barrier Resonator C .10 .20
LC5DEN067 Force Resonator C .10 .20
LC5DEN068 Clock Resonator C .10 .20
LC5DEN069 Red Dragon Archfiend C .10 .20
LC5DEN069u Red Dragon Archfiend UR 2.00 5.00
LC5DEN070 Exploder Dragonwing R .40 1.00
LC5DEN071 Majestic Red Dragon SR .40 1.00
LC5DEN072 Chaos King Archfiend SR .40 1.00
LC5DEN073 Red Nova Dragon SR 1.25 3.00
LC5DEN074 Crimson Blader SCR 2.00 5.00
LC5DEN075 Resonator Engine C .10 .20
LC5DEN076 Scarlet Security SR .50 1.25
LC5DEN077 Red Dragon Vase R .25 .60
LC5DEN078 Resonator Call C .10 .20
LC5DEN079 Resonant Destruction C .10 .20
LC5DEN080 Crimson Fire R .25 .60
LC5DEN081 Changing Destiny C .10 .20
LC5DEN082 Fiendish Chain SCR 5.00 12.00
LC5DEN083 Red Screen C .10 .20
LC5DEN084 Red Carpet C .10 .20
LC5DEN085 Twilight Rose Knight C 1.00 1.50
LC5DEN086 Violet Witch R .25 .60
LC5DEN087 Dark Verger C .10 .20
LC5DEN088 Rose Tentacles R .25 .60
LC5DEN089 Hedge Guard UR .75 2.00
LC5DEN090 Evil Thorn C .10 .20
LC5DEN091 Rose Fairy C .10 .20
LC5DEN092 Glow-Up Bulb SCR 5.00 12.00
LC5DEN093 Blue Rose Dragon SR .50 1.25
LC5DEN094 Fallen Angel of Roses UR .60 1.50
LC5DEN095 Rosaria, the Stately Fallen Angel UR .60 1.50
LC5DEN096 Queen Angel of Roses UR .60 1.50
LC5DEN097 Rose Witch C .10 .20
LC5DEN098 Rose Archer SR .40 1.00
LC5DEN099 Black Rose Dragon C 1.00 1.50
LC5DEN100 Splendid Rose R .25 .60
LC5DEN101 Black Garden SCR .75 2.00
LC5DEN102 Fragrance Storm UR .40 1.00
LC5DEN103 Thorn of Malice C .10 .20
LC5DEN104 Magic Planter UR 4.00 10.00
LC5DEN105 Ivy Shackles C .10 .20
LC5DEN106 Overdoom Line C .10 .20
LC5DEN107 Wicked Rebirth C .10 .20
LC5DEN108 Blossom Bombardment C .10 .20
LC5DEN109 Star Siphon C .10 .20
LC5DEN110 Blackwing - Gale the Whirlwind UR .40 1.00
LC5DEN111 Blackwing - Bora the Spear UR 1.25 3.00
LC5DEN112 Blackwing - Sirocco the Dawn UR .40 1.00
LC5DEN113 Blackwing - Blizzard the Far North UR .75 2.00
LC5DEN114 Blackwing - Shura the Blue Flame UR .40 1.00
LC5DEN115 Blackwing - Kalut the Moon Shadow UR .40 1.00
LC5DEN116 Blackwing - Elphin the Raven C .10 .20
LC5DEN117 Blackwing - Mistral the Silver Shield C .10 .20
LC5DEN118 Blackwing - Vayu the Emblem of Honor SCR .40 1.00
LC5DEN119 Blackwing - Fane the Steel Chain C .10 .20
LC5DEN120 Blackwing - Ghibli the Searing Wind C .10 .20
LC5DEN121 Blackwing - Gust the Backblast C .10 .20
LC5DEN122 Blackwing - Breeze the Zephyr C .10 .20
LC5DEN123 Blackwing - Etesian of Two Swords C .10 .20
LC5DEN124 Blackwing - Aurora the Northern Lights C .10 .20
LC5DEN125 Blackwing - Abrolhos the Megaquake C .10 .20
LC5DEN126 Blackwing - Boreas the Sharp C .10 .20
LC5DEN127 Blackwing - Brisote the Tailwind C .10 .20
LC5DEN128 Blackwing - Calima the Haze C .10 .20
LC5DEN129 Blackwing - Kogarashi the Wanderer C .10 .20
LC5DEN130 Blackwing - Kochi the Daybreak C .10 .20
LC5DEN131 Blackwing - Gladius the Midnight Sun UR .75 2.00
LC5DEN132 Blackwing Armor Master SCR .40 1.00
LC5DEN133 Blackwing Armed Wing UR .40 1.00
LC5DEN134 Blackwing - Silverwind the Ascendant SR .40 1.00
LC5DEN135 Black-Winged Dragon C 2.00 3.00
LC5DEN135u Black-Winged Dragon UR .50 1.25
LC5DEN136 De-Synchro SR 1.25 3.00
LC5DEN137 Raptor Wing Strike C .10 .20
LC5DEN138 Black Whirlwind UR 2.50 6.00
LC5DEN139 Cards for Black Feathers R .25 .60
LC5DEN140 Delta Crow - Anti Reverse SCR 1.50 4.00
LC5DEN141 Trap Stun SCR 2.50 6.00
LC5DEN142 Blackwing - Backlash C .10 .20
LC5DEN143 Blackback C .10 .20
LC5DEN144 Blackboost C .10 .20
LC5DEN145 Black Return C .10 .20
LC5DEN146 Earthbound Immortal Aslla Piscu SR .40 1.00
LC5DEN147 Earthbound Immortal Ccapac Apu SR .50 1.25
LC5DEN148 Earthbound Immortal Cusillu SR .40 1.00
LC5DEN149 Earthbound Immortal Chacu Challhua SR .40 1.00
LC5DEN150 Earthbound Immortal Wiraqocha Rasca SR .40 1.00
LC5DEN151 Earthbound Immortal Ccarayhua SR .40 1.00
LC5DEN152 Earthbound Immortal Uru SR .40 1.00
LC5DEN153 Earthbound Linewalker SR .40 1.00
LC5DEN154 Hundred Eyes Dragon SR .40 1.00
LC5DEN155 Earthbound Whirlwind R .25 .60
LC5DEN156 Earthbound Revival C .10 .20
LC5DEN157 Revival of the Immortals C .10 .20
LC5DEN158 Earthbound Wave R .25 .60
LC5DEN159 Roar of the Earthbound C .10 .20
LC5DEN160 Offering to the Immortals C .10 .20
LC5DEN161 Meklord Astro Mekanikle SCR .75 2.00
LC5DEN162 Meklord Emperor Granel SR .40 1.00
LC5DEN163 Meklord Army of Wisel R .25 .60
LC5DEN164 Meklord Army of Skiel R .25 .60
LC5DEN165 Meklord Army of Granel C .10 .20
LC5DEN166 Meklord Astro Dragon Asterisk SCR .50 1.25
LC5DEN167 Meklord Emperor Skiel SR 2.00 5.00
LC5DEN168 Meklord Emperor Wisel SR .40 1.00
LC5DEN169 Fortissimo the Mobile Fortress C .10 .20
LC5DEN170 Boon of the Meklord Emperor C .10 .20
LC5DEN171 The Resolute Meklord Army C .10 .20
LC5DEN172 Reboot C .10 .20
LC5DEN173 Meklord Fortress SR .40 1.00
LC5DEN174 Chaos Infinity SR .60 1.50
LC5DEN175 Mektimed Blast C .10 .20
LC5DEN176 Meklord Factory SR .40 1.00
LC5DEN177 Tanngrisnir of the Nordic Beasts SCR .40 1.00
LC5DEN178 Guldfaxe of the Nordic Beasts SCR .40 1.00
LC5DEN179 Garmr of the Nordic Beasts C .10 .20
LC5DEN180 Tanngnjostr of the Nordic Beasts SCR 1.50 4.00
LC5DEN181 Ljosalf of the Nordic Alfar C .10 .20
LC5DEN182 Svartalf of the Nordic Alfar UR 3.00 8.00
LC5DEN183 Dverg of the Nordic Alfar SCR .40 1.00
LC5DEN184 Valkyrie of the Nordic Ascendant SCR .75 2.00
LC5DEN185 Mimir of the Nordic Ascendant C .10 .20
LC5DEN186 Tyr of the Nordic Champions C .10 .20
LC5DEN187 Vanadis of the Nordic Ascendant UR 1.25 3.00
LC5DEN188 Mara of the Nordic Alfar C .10 .20
LC5DEN189 Thor, Lord of the Aesir SCR .75 2.00
LC5DEN190 Loki, Lord of the Aesir SCR .40 1.00
LC5DEN191 Odin, Father of the Aesir SCR .40 1.00
LC5DEN192 Nordic Relic Draupnir R .25 .60
LC5DEN193 Gotterdammerung C .10 .20
LC5DEN194 March Towards Ragnarok C .10 .20
LC5DEN195 The Nordic Lights C .10 .20
LC5DEN196 Divine Relic Mjollnir R .25 .60
LC5DEN197 Solemn Authority C .10 .20
LC5DEN198 Nordic Relic Brisingamen R .25 .60
LC5DEN199 Nordic Relic Laevateinn R .25 .60
LC5DEN200 Nordic Relic Gungnir UR .50 1.25
LC5DEN201 The Golden Apples R .25 .60
LC5DEN202 Odin's Eye C .10 .20
LC5DEN203 Gleipnir, the Fetters of Fenrir SCR .75 2.00
LC5DEN204 Nordic Relic Megingjord R .25 .60
LC5DEN205 T.G. Cyber Magician SCR 2.00 5.00
LC5DEN206 T.G. Striker UR 1.25 3.00
LC5DEN207 T.G. Jet Falcon C .10 .20
LC5DEN208 T.G. Catapult Dragon C .10 .20
LC5DEN209 T.G. Warwolf SCR 1.25 3.00
LC5DEN210 T.G. Rush Rhino UR .40 1.00
LC5DEN211 T.G. Hyper Librarian SCR .40 1.00
LC5DEN212 T.G. Recipro Dragonfly C .10 .20
LC5DEN213 T.G. Wonder Magician SCR 5.00 12.00
LC5DEN214 T.G. Power Gladiator C .10 .20
LC5DEN215 T.G. Blade Blaster SR .40 1.00
LC5DEN216 T.G. Halberd Cannon SR .40 1.00
LC5DEN217 TGX1-HL UR .75 2.00
LC5DEN218 TGX300 C .10 .20
LC5DEN219 TGX3-DX2 UR .50 1.25
LC5DEN220 TG-SX1 C .10 .20
LC5DEN221 TG1-EM1 SCR .75 2.00
LC5DEN222 Black Salvo C .10 .20
LC5DEN223 Oracle of the Sun C .10 .20
LC5DEN224 Fire Ant Ascator R .25 .60
LC5DEN225 Supay R .25 .60
LC5DEN226 Super-Nimble Mega Hamster SCR .75 2.00
LC5DEN227 Maxx "C" UR 3.00 8.00
LC5DEN228 Metaion, the Timelord SR .75 2.00
LC5DEN229 Sephylon, the Ultimate Timelord SR .40 1.00
LC5DEN230 Avenging Knight Parshath C .10 .20
LC5DEN231 Goyo Guardian SR 4.00 10.00
LC5DEN232 Magical Android UR .75 2.00
LC5DEN233 Thought Ruler Archfiend SCR 1.00 2.50
LC5DEN234 Dark Strike Fighter C .10 .20
LC5DEN235 Hyper Psychic Blaster R .25 .60
LC5DEN236 Power Tool Dragon C .60 1.00
LC5DEN237 Trident Dragion SCR 1.25 3.00
LC5DEN238 Ancient Fairy Dragon C .10 .20
LC5DEN238u Ancient Fairy Dragon UR 1.25 3.00
LC5DEN239 Ancient Sacred Wyvern SCR 2.00 5.00
LC5DEN240 Mist Wurm UR 2.00 5.00
LC5DEN241 Sun Dragon Inti C .10 .20
LC5DEN242 Moon Dragon Quilla C .10 .20
LC5DEN243 Stygian Sergeants SCR .40 1.00
LC5DEN244 Naturia Beast UR 2.00 5.00
LC5DEN245 Naturia Barkion UR 2.50 6.00
LC5DEN246 Life Stream Dragon C .40 .60
LC5DEN247 Orient Dragon UR .60 1.50
LC5DEN248 Driven Daredevil R .25 .60
LC5DEN249 Vulcan the Divine SCR 3.00 8.00
LC5DEN250 Synchro Blast Wave C .10 .20
LC5DEN251 Emergency Teleport SCR 10.00 25.00
LC5DEN252 Savage Colosseum C .10 .20
LC5DEN253 Vanity's Emptiness SCR 15.00 40.00
LC5DEN254 Roaring Earth C .10 .20
LC5DEN255 Debunk SCR 2.50 6.00
LC5DEN256 Full House SCR .75 2.00

2014 Yu-Gi-Oh Noble Knights of the Round Table Boxed Set

NKRTEN001 Merlin PR
NKRTEN002 Noble Knight Bedwyr PR
NKRTEN003 Noble Knight Artorigus PR
NKRTEN004 Noble Knight Gawayn PR
NKRTEN005 Ignoble Knight of Black Laundsallyn PR
NKRTEN006 Noble Knight Medraut PR
NKRTEN007 Noble Knight Gwalchavad PR
NKRTEN008 Noble Knight Drystan PR
NKRTEN009 Noble Knight Borz PR
NKRTEN010 Noble Knight Peredur PR
NKRTEN011 Noble Knight Eachtar PR
NKRTEN012 Gwenhwyfar, Queen of Noble Arms PR
NKRTEN013 Lady of the Lake PR
NKRTEN014 Honest PR
NKRTEN015 Knight Day Grepher PR
NKRTEN016 Dawn Knight PR
NKRTEN017 Last Chapter of the Noble Knights PR
NKRTEN018 Noble Knights of the Round Table PR
NKRTEN019 Noble Arms - Gallatin PR
NKRTEN020 Noble Arms - Arfeudutyr PR
NKRTEN021 Noble Arms - Caliburn PR
NKRTEN022 Noble Arms of Destiny PR
NKRTEN023 Noble Arms - Excaliburn PR
NKRTEN024 Dark Hole PR
NKRTEN025 Swords of Revealing Light PR
NKRTEN026 Reinforcement of the Army PR
NKRTEN027 Book of Moon PR
NKRTEN028 Foolish Burial PR
NKRTEN029 Release Restraint Wave PR
NKRTEN030 Swords at Dawn PR
NKRTEN031 Avalon PR
NKRTEN032 Call of the Haunted PR
NKRTEN033 Malevolent Catastrophe PR
NKRTEN034 Dimensional Prison PR
NKRTEN035 Solemn Warning PR
NKRTEN036 Ignoble Knight of High Laundsallyn PR
NKRTEN037 Artorigus, King of the Noble Knights PR
NKRTEN038 Sacred Noble Knight of King Artorigus PR
NKRTEN039 Effect Veiler PR
NKRTEN040 Mystical Space Typhoon PR
NKRTEN041 Gold Sarcophagus PR
NKRTEN042 Forbidden Lance PR
NKRTEN043 Torrential Tribute PR
NKRTEN044 Compulsory Evacuation Device PR

2015 Yu-Gi-Oh Yugi's Legendary Decks

COMPLETE SET (133 CARDS) 80.00 110.00
RELEASED ON DECEMBER 11, 2015
YGLDENA00 Electromagnetic Turtle SCR 1.00 1.50
YGLDENA01 Black Lusfer Soldier C .20 .30
YGLDENA02 Black Luster Soldier - Envoy of the Beginning C 2.25 2.75
YGLDENA03 Dark Magician C 3.75 5.00
YGLDENA04 Dark Magician Girl C .60 1.00
YGLDENA05 Gaia The Fierce Knight C .05 .15
YGLDENA06 Summoned Skull C .05 .15
YGLDENA07 Curse of Dragon C .05 .15
YGLDENA08 Catapult Turtle C .05 .15
YGLDENA09 Celtic Guardian C .05 .15
YGLDENA10 Winged Dragon, Guardian of the Fortress #1 C .05 .15
YGLDENA11 Feral Imp C .05 .15
YGLDENA12 Beaver Warrior C .05 .15
YGLDENA13 Griffore C .05 .15
YGLDENA14 Mystical Elf C .05 .15
YGLDENA15 Giant Soldier of Stone C .05 .15
YGLDENA16 Mammoth Graveyard C .05 .15
YGLDENA17 Exodia the Forbidden One UR 2.50 3.00
YGLDENA18 Right Leg of the Forbidden One UR 1.50 2.00
YGLDENA19 Left Leg of the Forbidden One UR 1.50 2.00
YGLDENA20 Right Arm of the Forbidden One UR 1.50 2.00
YGLDENA21 Left Arm of the Forbidden One UR 1.50 2.00
YGLDENA22 Kuriboh C .05 .15
YGLDENA23 Monster Reborn C .40 .60
YGLDENA24 Swords of Revealing Light C .05 .15
YGLDENA25 Mystic Box C .10 .20
YGLDENA26 Brain Control C .05 .15
YGLDENA27 Monster Recovery C .05 .15
YGLDENA28 Spell Shattering Arrow C .40 .60
YGLDENA29 Horn of the Unicorn C .05 .15
YGLDENA30 Mystical Moon C .05 .15
YGLDENA31 Burning Land C .05 .15
YGLDENA32 Multiply C .15 .25
YGLDENA33 Detonate C .05 .15
YGLDENA34 Makiu, the Magical Mist C .05 .15
YGLDENA35 Polymerization C 1.25 2.00
YGLDENA36 Black Luster Ritual C .05 .15
YGLDENA37 Mirror Force C 1.25 1.75
YGLDENA38 Magical Hats C .30 .40
YGLDENA39 The Eye of Truth C .05 .15
YGLDENA40 Shift C .05 .15
YGLDENA41 Gaia the Dragon Champion C .05 .15
YGLDENB00 Dark Renewal SCR 9.00 10.50
YGLDENB01 Valkyrion the Magna Warrior UR .30 .50
YGLDENB02 Dark Magician UR 3.00 3.50
YGLDENB03 Dark Magician Girl UR 2.25 3.00
YGLDENB04 Buster Blader C .30 .50
YGLDENB05 Archfiend of Gilfer C .05 .15
YGLDENB06 Jack's Knight C .05 .15
YGLDENB07 Queen's Knight C .05 .15
YGLDENB08 King's Knight C .05 .15
YGLDENB09 Berfomet C .05 .15
YGLDENB10 Gazelle the King of Mythical Beasts C .05 .15
YGLDENB11 Alpha The Magnet Warrior C .15 .25
YGLDENB12 Beta The Magnet Warrior C .15 .25
YGLDENB13 Gamma The Magnet Warrior C .15 .25
YGLDENB14 Big Shield Gardna C .05 .15
YGLDENB15 Kuriboh C .05 .15
YGLDENB16 Monster Reborn C .40 .60
YGLDENB17 Swords of Revealing Light UR .20 .30
YGLDENB18 Dark Magic Curtain C .60 1.00
YGLDENB19 Thousand Knives C .30 .50
YGLDENB20 Magic Formula C .25 .40
YGLDENB21 Magical Dimension C .60 1.00
YGLDENB22 Diffusion Wave-Motion C .05 .15
YGLDENB23 Double Spell C .05 .15
YGLDENB24 Ectoplasmer C .05 .15
YGLDENB25 Soul Taker C .05 .15
YGLDENB26 Pot of Greed C 1.25 1.75
YGLDENB27 Card Destruction C .05 .15
YGLDENB28 Exchange C .05 .15
YGLDENB29 Monster Recovery C .05 .15
YGLDENB30 Polymerization C 1.50 2.00
YGLDENB31 De-Fusion C .25 .45
YGLDENB32 Multiply C .15 .25
YGLDENB33 Mirror Force UR 1.75 2.15
YGLDENB34 Magical Hats C .20 .35
YGLDENB35 Magic Cylinder C .60 1.00
YGLDENB36 Spellbinding Circle C .05 .15
YGLDENB37 Lightforce Sword C .05 .15
YGLDENB38 Chain Destruction C .05 .15
YGLDENB39 Soul Rope C .05 .15
YGLDENB40 Tragedy C .05 .15
YGLDENB41 Chimera the Flying Mythical Beast C .05 .15
YGLDENC00 Black Illusion SCR 1.25 1.75
YGLDENC01 Magician of Black Chaos UR .75 1.15
YGLDENC02 Dark Magician of Chaos UR 3.00 3.50
YGLDENC03 Gandora the Dragon of Destruction C .05 .15
YGLDENC04 Silent Magician LV8 UR .40 .60
YGLDENC05 Silent Magician LV4 C .50 .75
YGLDENC06 Silent Swordsman LV7 C .25 .40
YGLDENC07 Silent Swordsman LV5 C .05 .15
YGLDENC08 Silent Swordsman LV3 C .05 .15
YGLDENC09 Dark Magician UR .75 1.25
YGLDENC10 Dark Magician Girl C .60 1.00
YGLDENC11 Buster Blader C .05 .15
YGLDENC12 The Tricky C .05 .15
YGLDENC13 Jack's Knight C .05 .15
YGLDENC14 Queen's Knight C .05 .15
YGLDENC15 King's Knight C .05 .15
YGLDENC16 Green Gadget C .05 .15
YGLDENC17 Red Gadget C .05 .15
YGLDENC18 Yellow Gadget C .05 .15
YGLDENC19 Skilled Dark Magician C .50 .75
YGLDENC20 Skilled White Magician C .05 .15
YGLDENC21 Blockman C .05 .15
YGLDENC22 Marshmallon C 2.00 2.50
YGLDENC23 Kuriboh C .05 .15
YGLDENC24 Monster Reborn C .40 .60
YGLDENC25 Swords of Revealing Light C .05 .15
YGLDENC26 Gold Sarcophagus UR 4.00 4.75
YGLDENC27 Card of Sanctity C .05 .15
YGLDENC28 Polymerization C 1.00 1.75
YGLDENC29 Dark Magic Attack C 1.00 1.50
YGLDENC30 Magicians Unite C .05 .15
YGLDENC31 Dedication through Light and Darkness C 2.00 2.25
YGLDENC32 Black Magic Ritual C .05 .15
YGLDENC33 Tricky Spell 4 C .05 .15
YGLDENC34 Emblem of Dragon Destroyer C 1.00 1.25
YGLDENC35 Marshmallon Glasses C .05 .15
YGLDENC36 Mirror Force C 2.00 2.25
YGLDENC37 Magician's Circle C 1.00 1.50
YGLDENC38 Shattered Axe C .05 .15
YGLDENC39 Stronghold the Moving Fortress C .05 .15
YGLDENC40 Miracle Restoring C .05 .15
YGLDENC41 Dark Paladin C 2.00 2.50
YGLDENG01 Slifer the Sky Dragon UR 2.25 3.00
YGLDENG02 Obelisk the Tormentor UR 2.75 3.25
YGLDENG03 The Winged Dragon of Ra UR 2.25 3.00
YGLDENTKN Token UR .50 .75
NN01 Duelist Kingdom UR .30 .50
NN02 Glory of the King's Hand UR .30 .50
NN03 Set Sail for the Kingdom UR .25 .40

2006 Yu-Gi-Oh Duelist Pack Jaden Yuki 1st Edition

COMPLETE SET (30) 20.00 50.00
BOOSTER BOX (5 PACKS) 125.00 200.00
BOOSTER PACK (25 CARDS) 2.50 6.00
RELEASED ON FEBRUARY 8, 2006
DP1EN001 Elemental HERO Avian C .25 .75
DP1EN002 Elemental HERO Burstinatrix C .25 .75
DP1EN003 Elemental HERO Clayman C .25 .75
DP1EN004 Elemental HERO Sparkman C .25 .75
DP1EN005 Winged Kuriboh R .75 2.00
DP1EN006 Winged Kuriboh LV10 R 1.25 3.00
DP1EN007 Wroughtweiler C .25 .75
DP1EN008 Dark Catapulter C .25 .75
DP1EN009 Elemental HERO Bubbleman C .25 .75
DP1EN010 Elemental HERO Flame Wingman SR 2.00 5.00
DP1EN011 Elemental HERO Thunder Giant R .75 2.00
DP1EN012 Elemental HERO Rampart Blaster R .75 2.00
DP1EN013 Elemental HERO Steam Healer UR 3.00 8.00
DP1EN014 Polymerization C .75 2.00
DP1EN015 Fusion Sage C .75 2.00
DP1EN016 The Warrior Returning Alive C .25 .75
DP1EN017 Feather Shot C .25 .75
DP1EN018 Transcendent Wings C .25 .75
DP1EN019 Bubble Shuffle C .25 .75
DP1EN020 Spark Blaster C .25 .75
DP1EN021 Skyscraper R 1.50 4.00
DP1EN022 Burst Return SR .25 .75
DP1EN023 Bubble Blaster SR .25 .75
DP1EN024 Bubble Illusion UR 1.50 4.00
DP1EN025 A Hero Emerges C .25 .75
DP1EN026 Draining Shield C .25 .75
DP1EN027 Negate Attack R .25 .75
DP1EN028 Hero Signal C .25 .75
DP1EN029 Feather Wind R .25 .75
DP1EN030 Clacy Charge SR .25 .75

2006 Yu-Gi-Oh Duelist Pack Chazz Princeton 1st Edition

COMPLETE SET (30) 40.00 80.00
BOOSTER BOX (30 PACKS) 125.00 200.00
BOOSTER PACK (6 CARDS) 2.50 6.00
RELEASED ON FEBRUARY 8, 2006
DP2EN001 V-Tiger Jet C .25 .75
DP2EN002 Ojama Green C .25 .75
DP2EN003 Ojama Yellow C .25 .75
DP2EN004 Ojama Black C .25 .75
DP2EN005 X-Head Cannon C .25 .75
DP2EN006 Y-Dragon Head C .25 .75
DP2EN007 Z-Metal Tank C .25 .75
DP2EN008 W-Wing Catapult C .25 .75
DP2EN009 Infernal Incinerator R .25 .75
DP2EN010 Armed Dragon LV3 C .25 .75
DP2EN011 Armed Dragon LV5 C .25 .75
DP2EN012 Armed Dragon LV7 SR 2.50 6.00
DP2EN013 Armed Dragon LV10 UR 15.00 30.00
DP2EN014 XYZ-Dragon Cannon R .25 .75
DP2EN015 Ojama King C .25 .75
DP2EN016 VW-Tiger Catapult R .25 .75
DP2EN017 VWXYZ-Dragon Catapult Cannon R .25 .75
DP2EN018 Ojama Delta Hurricane!! C .25 .75
DP2EN019 Level Modulation R .25 .75
DP2EN020 Ojamagic R .25 .75
DP2EN021 Ojamuscle R .25 .75
DP2EN022 Chthonian Alliance C .25 .75
DP2EN023 Armed Changer C .25 .75
DP2EN024 Magical Mallet SR 1.25 3.00
DP2EN025 Inferno Reckless Summon SR 3.00 8.00
DP2EN026 Ring of Defense UR 3.00 8.00
DP2EN027 Ojama Trio C .40 1.00
DP2EN028 Chtonian Blast C .25 .75
DP2EN029 Chthonian Polymer C .25 .75
DP2EN030 The Grave of Enkindling SR .25 .75

2007 Yu-Gi-Oh Duelist Pack Jaden Yuki 2 1st Edition

COMPLETE SET (30) 15.00 40.00
BOOSTER BOX (30 PACKS) 100.00 150.00
BOOSTER PACK (6 CARDS) 2.50 6.00
RELEASED ON FEBRUARY 7, 2007
DP03EN018 R - Righteous Justice C .25 .75
DP03EN019 O - Oversoul C .25 .75
DP03EN020 Hero Flash!! C .25 .75
DP03EN021 Contact C .25 .75
DP03EN022 Fake Hero C .25 .75
DP03EN023 Common Soul C .25 .75
DP03EN024 Neo Space C .25 .75
DP03EN025 Light Laser SR .25 .75
DP03EN026 Burial from a Different Dimension UR 3.00 8.00
DP03EN027 Hero Barrier C .25 .75

DP03EN028 Miracle Kids C	.25	.75
DP03EN029 Edge Hammer SR	.25	.75
DP03EN030 Kid Guard SR	.25	.75

2007 Yu-Gi-Oh Duelist Pack Zane Truesdale 1st Edition

COMPLETE SET (30)	20.00	50.00
BOOSTER BOX (30 PACKS)	125.00	200.00
BOOSTER PACK (6 CARDS)	2.50	6.00
RELEASED ON APRIL 17, 2007		
DP04EN001 Cyber Dragon R	1.25	3.00
DP04EN002 Cyber Barrier Dragon R	.25	.75
DP04EN003 Cyber Laser Dragon R	1.25	3.00
DP04EN004 Prot-Cyber Dragon C	.25	.75
DP04EN005 Cyber Kirin C	.25	.75
DP04EN006 Cyber Phoenix C	.25	.75
DP04EN007 Cyberdark Horn C	1.25	3.00
DP04EN008 Cyberdark Edge C	.75	2.00
DP04EN009 Cyberdark Keel C	.75	2.00
DP04EN010 Infernal Dragon UR	2.50	6.00
DP04EN011 Cyber Twin Dragon R	.25	.75
DP04EN012 Cyber End Dragon R	2.00	5.00
DP04EN013 Chimeratech Overdragon R	.60	1.50
DP04EN014 Cyberdark Dragon SR	.75	2.00
DP04EN015 Mystical Space Typhoon C	.40	1.00
DP04EN016 Limiter Removal C	.25	.75
DP04EN017 De-Fusion C	.75	2.00
DP04EN018 Creature Swap C	.25	.75
DP04EN019 Different Dimension Capsule C	.50	1.25
DP04EN020 Power Bond R	.25	.75
DP04EN021 Photon Generator Unit C	.25	.75
DP04EN022 Overload Fusion C	.25	.75
DP04EN023 Future Fusion C	.60	1.50
DP04EN024 Ruthless Denial SR	.25	.75
DP04EN025 Call of the Haunted C	.25	.75
DP04EN026 Trap Jammer C	.40	1.00
DP04EN027 Attack Reflector Unit C	.25	.75
DP04EN028 Return Soul SR	.25	.75
DP04EN029 Damage Polarizer UR	1.25	3.00
DP04EN030 Fusion Guard SR	.25	.75

2007 Yu-Gi-Oh Duelist Pack Aster Phoenix 1st Edition

COMPLETE SET (30)	15.00	40.00
BOOSTER BOX (30 PACKS)	125.00	200.00
BOOSTER PACK (6 CARDS)	2.50	6.00
RELEASED ON APRIL 17, 2007		
DP05EN019 Dark City C	.25	.75
DP05EN020 Destiny Draw UR	4.00	10.00
DP05EN021 Over Destiny SR	.25	.75
DP05EN022 Elemental Recharge C	.25	.75
DP05EN023 Destruction of Destiny C	.25	.75
DP05EN024 Destiny Signal C	.25	.75
DP05EN025 D - Time C	.25	.75
DP05EN026 D - Shield C	.25	.75
DP05EN027 Destiny Mirage C	.25	.75
DP05EN028 D - Chain C	.25	.75
DP05EN029 D - Counter SR	.25	.75
DP05EN030 Eternal Dread SR	.25	.75

2008 Yu-Gi-Oh Duelist Pack Jaden Yuki 3

COMPLETE SET (30)	10.00	30.00
BOOSTER BOX (30 PACKS)	80.00	120.00
BOOSTER PACK (6 CARDS)	2.50	6.00
RELEASED ON JANUARY 22, 2008		
DP61 Neo-Spacian Air Hummingbird C	.50	1.25
DP62 Neo-Spacian Grand Mole R	.40	1.00
DP63 Neo-Spacian Glow Moss C	.10	.30
DP64 Elemental Hero Captain Gold R	.50	1.25
DP65 Elemental Hero Neos Alius C	.10	.30
DP66 Evil Hero Malicious Edge SR	1.50	4.00
DP67 Evil Hero Infernal Gainer C	.10	.30
DP68 Evil Hero Infernal Prodigy SR	.75	2.00
DP69 Armor Breaker R	.40	1.00
DP610 Evil Hero Dark Gaia C	.10	.30
DP611 Evil Hero Wild Cyclone UR	.75	2.00
DP612 Evil Hero Infernal Sniper SR	.25	.75
DP613 Evil Hero Malicious Fiend UR	2.00	5.00
DP614 Skyscraper 2 - Hero City SR	1.50	4.00
DP615 Reverse of Neos C	.10	.30
DP616 Convert Contact C	.10	.30
DP617 Swing of Memories C	.40	1.00
DP618 Dark Fusion C	.75	2.00
DP619 Dark Calling R	.75	2.00
DP620 Revoke Fusion R	.60	1.50
DP621 Hero Medal C	.10	.30
DP622 Mirror Gate C	.10	.30
DP623 Hero Counterattack C	.10	.30
DP623 Over Limit C	.10	.30
DP625 Hero's Rule 2 R	.20	.75

2008 Yu-Gi-Oh Duelist Pack Jesse Anderson

COMPLETE SET (30)	10.00	30.00
BOOSTER BOX (30 PACKS)	80.00	120.00
BOOSTER PACK (6 CARDS)	.25	6.00
RELEASED ON JANUARY 22, 2008		
DP71 Crystal Beast Ruby Carbuncle C	.10	.30
DP72 Crystal Beast Amethyst Cat R	.40	1.00
DP73 Crystal Beast Emerald Tortoise C	.10	.30
DP74 Crystal Beast Topaz Tiger R	.40	1.00
DP75 Crystal Beast Amber Mammoth C	.10	.30
DP76 Crystal Beast Cobalt Eagle C	.10	.30
DP77 Phantom Skyblaster UR	.40	1.00
DP78 Grave Squirmer SR	.60	1.50
DP79 Grinder Golem SR	2.00	5.00
DP710 Magna-Slash Dragon C	.10	.30
DP711 Gravi-Crush Dragon C	.10	.30
DP712 Twister C	.20	.75
DP713 Crystal Beacon C	.10	.30
DP714 Crystal Blessing C	.10	.30
DP715 Crystal Abundance R	.40	1.00
DP716 Crystal Promise C	.10	.30
DP717 Ancient City - Rainbow Ruins R	.40	1.00
DP718 Hand Destruction R	1.25	3.00
DP719 Crystal Release SR	.60	1.50
DP720 Crystal Tree SR	1.25	3.00
DP721 Triggered Summon C	.10	.30
DP722 Last Resort C	.10	.30
DP723 Crystal Raigeki C	.10	.30
DP724 Crystal Counter UR	2.50	6.00
DP725 Crystal Pair R	.50	1.25

2009 Yu-Gi-Oh Duelist Pack Yusei Fudo 1

COMPLETE SET (30)	10.00	25.00
BOOSTER BOX (30 PACKS)	50.00	80.00
BOOSTER PACK (6 CARDS)	2.00	5.00
RELEASED ON FEBRUARY 24, 2009		
DP81 Junk Synchron C	.10	.30
DP82 Speed Warrior C	.10	.30
DP83 Turbo Booster C	.10	.30
DP84 Nitro Synchron R	.40	1.00
DP85 Quillbolt Hedgehog C	.10	.30
DP86 Ghost Gardna C	.10	.30
DP87 Shield Warrior C	.10	.30
DP88 Healing Wave Generator C	.10	.30
DP89 Turbo Synchron R	.40	1.00
DP810 Fortress Warrior SR	.25	.50
DP811 Tuningware UR	1.00	2.50
DP812 Junk Warrior R	.40	1.00
DP813 Nitro Warrior R	.40	1.00
DP814 Stardust Dragon SR	2.00	5.00
DP815 Turbo Warrior R	.40	1.00
DP816 Armory Arm UR	2.00	5.00
DP817 Fighting SPirit C	.10	.30
DP818 Domino Effect C	.10	.30
DP819 Junk Barrage C	.10	.30
DP820 Card Rotator C	.10	.30
DP821 Equip Shot C	.10	.30
DP822 Graceful Revival C	.10	.30
DP823 Defense Draw C	.25	.50
DP824 Remote Revenge C	.10	.30
DP825 Battle Mania R	.40	1.00
DP826 Confusion Chaff C	.10	.30
DP827 Urgent Tuning R	.40	1.00
DP828 Synchro Strike C	.10	.30
DP829 Give and Take SR	.25	.50
DP830 Limiter Overload SR	.25	.50

2010 Yu-Gi-Oh Duelist Pack Yusei Fudo 2

COMPLETE SET (30)	80.00	120.00
BOOSTER BOX (30 PACKS)	60.00	80.00
BOOSTER PACK (6 CARDS)	3.00	4.00
RELEASED ON JANUARY 26, 2010		
DP0901 Power Up the Warriors STRAT	.10	.30
DP0902 Super Synchro Summon STRAT	.10	.20
DP0903 Substitute Synchron STRAT	.10	.20
DP0904 Combo Chain STRAT	.10	.20
DP0905 Protect Your Tuner and Gain the Edge STRAT	.10	.20
DP0906 Bring Assault Mode Activate to Your Hand STRAT	.10	.20
DP0907 Match the Level and Draw STRAT	.10	.20
DP0908 Deploy Monsters from the Deck STRAT	.10	.20
DP0909 Emissary Eater STRAT	.10	.20
DP0910 Checklist STRAT	.10	.20
DP09001 Stardust Dragon/Assault Mode SR	.40	1.00
DP09002 Road Synchron R	.25	1.50
DP09003 Turret Warrior R	.25	1.00
DP09004 Debris Dragon	.10	.30
DP09005 Hyper Synchron	.10	.30
DP09006 Rockstone Warrior R	.25	.30
DP09007 Level Warrior	.10	.30
DP09008 Majestic Dragon	.75	2.00
DP09009 Max Warrior R	.25	.30
DP09010 Quickdraw Synchron	.10	.30
DP09011 Level Eater	.10	.30
DP09012 Zero Gardna	.10	.30
DP09013 Gauntlet Warrior UR	.40	1.00
DP09014 Eccentric Boy SR	.40	1.00
DP09015 Road Warrior R	.75	2.00
DP09016 Junk Archer UR	2.50	6.00
DP09017 Prevention Star	.10	.30
DP09018 One for One R	.25	.30
DP09019 Release Restraint Wave	.10	.30
DP09020 Silver Wing	.10	.30
DP09021 Advance Draw	.10	.30
DP09022 Assault Mode Activate	.10	.30
DP09023 Spirit Force	.10	.30
DP09024 Descending Lost Star	.10	.30
DP09025 Miracle Locus	.10	.30
DP09026 Skill Successor R	.25	.30
DP09027 Reinforce Truth	.10	.30
DP09028 Slip Summon	.10	.30
DP09029 Scrubbed Raid SR	.40	1.00
DP09030 Tuner's Barrier SR	.40	1.00

2011 Yu-Gi-Oh Duelist Pack Yusei Fudo 3

COMPLETE SET (30)		
BOOSTER BOX (36 PACKS)	50.00	60.00
BOOSTER PACK (6 CARDS)	3.00	4.00
RELEASED ON JANUARY 21, 2011		
DP10EN001 Sonic Chick	.10	.30
DP10EN002 Shield Wing	.10	.30
DP10EN003 Stardust Xiaolong	.10	.30
DP10EN004 Drill Synchron	.10	.30
DP10EN005 Card Breaker	.10	.30
DP10EN006 Second Booster	.10	.30
DP10EN007 Effect Veiler R	2.50	6.00
DP10EN008 Dash Warrior	.10	.30
DP10EN009 Damage Eater	.10	.30
DP10EN010 A/D Changer	.10	.30
DP10EN011 Stronghold Guardian	.10	.30
DP10EN012 Boost Warrior SR	.60	1.50
DP10EN013 Justice Bringer UR	.40	1.00
DP10EN014 Bri Synchron UR	.40	1.00
DP10EN015 Big One Warrior SR	.40	1.00
DP10EN016 Dragon Knight Draco-Equiste SR	.40	1.00
DP10EN017 Majestic Star Dragon R	.40	1.00
DP10EN018 Drill Warrior R	.40	1.00
DP10EN019 Cards of Consonance	.50	1.25
DP10EN020 Variety Comes Out	.10	.30
DP10EN021 Blind Spot Strike	.10	.30
DP10EN022 Double Cyclone	.10	.30
DP10EN023 Battle Waltz R	.40	1.00
DP10EN024 Synchro Gift R	.40	1.00
DP10EN025 Starlight Road R	.40	1.00
DP10EN026 Synchro Barrier	.10	.30
DP10EN027 Power Frame	.10	.30
DP10EN028 Desperate Tag	.10	.30
DP10EN029 Card of Sacrifice R	.40	1.00
DP10EN030 Synchro Material SR	.40	1.00

2011 Yu-Gi-Oh Duelist Pack Crow

COMPLETE SET (30)		
BOOSTER BOX (36 PACKS)	50.00	60.00
BOOSTER PACK (5 CARDS)	3.00	4.00
UNLISTED C	.15	.40
RELEASED ON MAY 31, 2011		
DP11EN001 Blackwing - Gale the Whirlwind R	.60	1.50
DP11EN002 Blackwing - Bora the Spear R	.50	1.25
DP11EN003 Blackwing - Blizzard the Far North	.60	1.50
DP11EN004 Blackwing - Shura the Blue Flame R	.40	1.00
DP11EN005 Blackwing - Elphin the Raven R	.40	1.00
DP11EN006 Blackwing - Mistral the Silver Shield	.10	.30
DP11EN007 Blackwing - Fane the Steel Chain	.10	.30
DP11EN008 Blackwing - Ghibli the Searing Wind	.10	.30
DP11EN009 Blackwing - Gust the Backblast	.10	.30
DP11EN010 Blackwing - Kochi the Daybreak R	.40	1.00
DP11EN011 Blackwing - Jetstream the Blue Sky UR	.75	2.00
DP11EN012 Blackwing - Zephyros the Elite UR	4.00	10.00
DP11EN013 Blackwing Armor Master SR	.50	1.25
DP11EN014 Blackwing Armed Wing R	.40	1.00
DP11EN015 Blackwing - Silverwind the Ascendant R	.40	1.00
DP11EN016 Black-Winged Dragon SR	.50	1.25
DP11EN017 Raptor Wing Strike	.10	.30
DP11EN018 Against the Wind	.10	.30
DP11EN019 Black-Winged Strafe	.10	.30
DP11EN020 Cards for Black Feathers	.10	.30
DP11EN021 Ebon Arrow	.10	.30
DP11EN022 Delta Crow - Anti Reverse	.75	2.00
DP11EN023 Level Retuner	.10	.30
DP11EN024 Fake Feather	.10	.30
DP11EN025 Blackwing - Backlash	.10	.30
DP11EN026 Blackwing - Bombardment	.10	.30
DP11EN027 Black Thunder	.10	.30
DP11EN028 Guard Mines	.10	.30
DP11EN029 Black Feather Beacon SR	.40	1.00
DP11EN030 Black Return SR	.40	1.00

2009 Yu-Gi-Oh Duelist Pack Yugi

COMPLETE SET (30)	40.00	80.00
BOOSTER BOX (30 PACKS)	150.00	250.00
BOOSTER PACK (6 CARDS)	3.00	8.00
RELEASED ON JULY 7, 2009		
DPYG1 Dark Magician R	.40	1.00
DPYG2 Summoned Skull SR	2.00	5.00
DPYG3 Queen's Knight C	.25	
DPYG4 Jack's Knight C	.25	
DPYG5 Kuriboh C	.25	
DPYG6 Catapult Turtle C	.25	
DPYG7 Buster Blader C	.25	
DPYG8 Dark Magician Girl SR	2.50	6.00
DPYG9 Big Shield Gardna C	.25	
DPYG10 Sorcerer of Dark Magic SR	3.00	8.00
DPYG11 King's Knight C	.25	
DPYG12 Green Gadget C	.25	.75
DPYG13 Red Gadget C	.25	.75
DPYG14 Yellow Gadget C	.25	.75
DPYG15 Marshmallon R	1.25	3.00
DPYG16 Dark Paladin UR	8.00	20.00
DPYG17 Black Luster Soldier R	.40	1.00
DPYG18 Swords of Revealing Light C	.25	.75
DPYG19 Monster Reborn R	.40	1.00
DPYG20 Polymerization SR	8.00	20.00
DPYG21 Exchange R	.40	1.00
DPYG22 Black Luster Ritual C	.25	.75
DPYG23 Diffusion Wave-Motion C	.25	.75
DPYG24 Brain Control C	.25	.75
DPYG25 Card of Sanctity R	.40	1.00
DPYG26 Spellbinding Circle C	.25	.75
DPYG27 Mirror Force UR	2.00	5.00
DPYG28 Magical Hats R	.75	2.00
DPYG29 Lightforce Sword C	.25	.75
DPYG30 Stronghold the Moving Fortress C	.25	.75

2010 Yu-Gi-Oh Duelist Pack Kaiba

COMPLETE SET (40)		
BOOSTER BOX (36 PACKS)	200.00	350.00
BOOSTER PACK (5 CARDS)	6.00	15.00
RELEASED ON APRIL 20, 2010		
DPKB01 BlueEyes White Dragon SR	15.00	30.00
DPKB02 HitotsuMe Giant C	.30	.75
DPKB03 Judge Man C	.30	.75
DPKB04 Swordstalker C	.30	.75
DPKB05 La Jinn the Mystical Genie of the Lamp C	.50	1.25
DPKB06 Saggi the Dark Clown C	.30	.75
DPKB07 XHead Cannon C	.40	1.00
DPKB08 Vorse Raider C	.50	1.25
DPKB09 Lord of D. C	.40	1.00
DPKB10 Cyber Jar UTR	4.00	10.00
DPKB11 YDragon Head C	.40	1.00
DPKB12 ZMetal Tank C	.40	1.00
DPKB13 Vampire Lord R	.60	1.50
DPKB14 Different Dimension Dragon R	.60	1.50
DPKB15 Kaiser Glider R	.50	1.25
DPKB16 Chaos Emperor Dragon Envoy of the End UTR	25.00	50.00
DPKB17 Kaiser Sea Horse R	.40	1.00
DPKB18 Enraged Battle Ox C	.30	.75
DPKB19 Peten the Dark Clown R	.50	1.25
DPKB20 Familiar Knight C	.30	.75
DPKB21 Ancient Lamp C	.30	.75
DPKB22 The White Stone of Legend SR	8.00	20.00
DPKB23 Malefic BlueEyes White Dragon UR	1.25	3.00
DPKB24 Paladin of White Dragon R	.50	1.25
DPKB25 XYZDragon Cannon SR	.75	2.00
DPKB26 BlueEyes Ultimate Dragon UR	8.00	20.00
DPKB27 Dragon Master Knight UR	4.00	10.00
DPKB28 Polymerization C	.75	2.00
DPKB29 Pot of Greed UTR	8.00	20.00
DPKB30 The Flute of Summoning Dragon C	.30	.75
DPKB31 Magic Reflector C	1.25	3.00
DPKB32 White Dragon Ritual C	.40	1.00
DPKB33 Cost Down R	1.25	3.00
DPKB34 Ring of Defense C	.40	1.00
DPKB35 Fiend's Sanctuary SR	.75	2.00
DPKB36 Ring of Destruction UTR	5.00	12.00
DPKB37 Interdimensional Matter Transporter C	.40	1.00
DPKB38 Return from the Different Dimension SR	.75	2.00
DPKB39 Crush Card Virus UTR	20.00	40.00
DPKB40 Cloning C	.30	.75

2015 Yu-Gi-Oh Duelist Pack Battle City

COMPLETE SET (47 CARDS)	45.00	60.00
BOOSTER BOX (36 PACKS)	40.00	60.00
BOOSTER PACK (5 CARDS)	2.00	4.00
UNLISTED C	.10	.30
UNLISTED R	.20	.40
RELEASED ON JUNE 19, 2016		
DPBCEN001 The Winged Dragon of Ra - Sphere Mode UR	15.00	18.00
DPBCEN002 Juragedo SR	4.00	5.25
DPBCEN003 Legion the Fiend Jester SR	2.00	5.00
DPBCEN004 Anti-Magic Arrows UR	2.25	2.75
DPBCEN005 Multiple Destruction UR	.20	.35
DPBCEN006 Black Luster Soldier SR	2.50	3.15
DPBCEN007 Black Luster Ritual C	.05	.15
DPBCEN008 Dark Magician SR	1.00	1.25
DPBCEN009 Dark Magician Girl SR	4.50	6.00
DPBCEN010 Buster Blader R	.50	.75
DPBCEN011 Archfiend of Gilfer C	.05	.15
DPBCEN012 Jack's Knight C	.05	.15
DPBCEN013 Queen's Knight C	.05	.15
DPBCEN014 King's Knight C	.05	.15
DPBCEN015 Kuriboh C	.05	.15
DPBCEN016 Blue-Eyes White Dragon UR	4.50	5.50
DPBCEN017 Lord of D. C	.05	.15
DPBCEN018 The Flute of Summoning Dragon C	.05	.15
DPBCEN019 Enemy Controller C	.05	.15
DPBCEN020 Crush Card Virus R	.75	1.15
DPBCEN021 Red-Eyes B. Dragon SR	1.25	1.75
DPBCEN022 Gearfried the Iron Knight C	.05	.15
DPBCEN023 Rocket Warrior C	.05	.15
DPBCEN024 Time Wizard C	.20	.30
DPBCEN025 Foolish Burial R	.60	1.00
DPBCEN026 Insect Queen C	.05	.15
DPBCEN027 Jinzo R	.60	1.00
DPBCEN028 The Legendary Fisherman C	.05	.15
DPBCEN029 Dragged Down into the Grave C	.10	.20
DPBCEN030 Embodiment of Apophis R	.05	.15
DPBCEN031 The Masked Beast R	.05	.15
DPBCEN032 Curse of the Masked Beast C	.05	.15
DPBCEN033 Dark Necrofear R	.05	.15
DPBCEN034 Lava Golem R	.20	.30
DPBCEN035 Magical Stone Excavation C	.05	.15
DPBCEN036 Malevolent Catastrophe C	.05	.15
DPBCEN037 Harpie Lady C	.05	.15
DPBCEN038 Harpie Lady Sisters C	.05	.15
DPBCEN039 Elegant Egotist C	.05	.15
DPBCEN040 Hysteric Party C	.05	.15
DPBCEN041 Barrel Dragon R	.05	.15
DPBCEN042 Blast Sphere C	.05	.15
DPBCEN043 Blue-Eyes Toon Dragon C	.25	.40
DPBCEN044 Toon Dark Magician Girl C	.40	.60
DPBCEN045 Toon Gemini Elf C	.15	.25
DPBCEN046 Toon World C	.25	.40
DPBCEN047 Toon Table of Contents R	2.00	2.75

2013 Yu-Gi-Oh Star Pack 2013

COMPLETE SET (50)		
BOOSTER BOX (50 PACKS)	80.00	100.00
BOOSTER PACK (3 CARDS)	3.00	4.00
*STARFOIL: .6X TO 1.5X BASIC CARDS		
SP13001 Zubaba Knight C	.25	.75
SP13002 Gagaga Magician C	.25	.75
SP13003 Gogogo Golem C	.25	.75
SP13004 Achacha Archer C	.25	.75
SP13005 Goblindbergh C	.60	1.50
SP13006 Big Jaws C	.25	.75
SP13007 Skull Kraken C	.25	.75
SP13008 Galaxy-Eyes Photon Dragon C	1.50	4.00
SP13009 Kagetokage C	1.25	3.00
SP13010 Friller Rabca C	.75	2.00
SP13011 Needle Sunfish C	.25	.75
SP13012 Photon Cerberus C	.25	.75
SP13013 Kurivolt C	.25	.75
SP13014 Darklon C	.25	.75
SP13015 Flame Armor Ninja C	.25	.75
SP13016 Air Armor Ninja C	.25	.75
SP13017 Aqua Armor Ninja C	.25	.75
SP13018 Earth Armor Ninja C	.25	.75
SP13019 Flelf C	.40	1.00
SP13020 Chewbone C	.50	1.25
SP13021 Number 39: Utopia C	.50	1.25
SP13022 Grenosaurus C	.25	.75
SP13023 No. 17: Leviathan Dragon	.50	1.25
SP13024 Submersible Aero Shark	.25	.75
SP13025 Number 34: Terror-Byte C	.75	2.00
SP13026 Number 10: Illumiknight C	.75	2.00
SP13027 Baby Tiragon C	.25	.75
SP13028 Number 83: Galaxy Queen C	.50	1.25
SP13029 Black Ray Lancer C	.60	1.50
SP13030 Number 12: Crimson Shadow Armor Ninja C	.25	.75
SP13031 Number 96: Dark Mist C	.75	2.00
SP13032 Wonder Wand C	.40	1.00
SP13033 Infected Mail C	.25	.75
SP13034 Ego Boost C	.25	.75
SP13035 Monster Slots C	.25	.75
SP13036 Heartfelt Appeal C	.25	.75
SP13037 Icy Crevasse C	.25	.75
SP13038 Nitwit Outwit C	.25	.75
SP13039 Faith Bird C	.25	.75
SP13040 Gilford the Lightning C	.25	.75
SP13041 Gandora the Dragon	.25	.75
SP13042 Metalmorph C	.25	.75
SP13043 Arcana - Dark Ruler	.25	.75
SP13044 Arcana - Light Ruler	.60	1.50
SP13045 Barbaroid, Battle Machine	6.00	15.00
SP13046 Elemental HERO Escuridao C	2.00	5.00
SP13047 Meklord Emperor Wisel C	.25	.75
SP13048 Seven Swords Warrior C	.25	.75
SP13049 Catapult Warrior C	.75	2.00
SP13050 One for One C	.25	.75

2014 Yu-Gi-Oh Star Pack 2014

COMPLETE SET (50)		
BOOSTER BOX (50 PACKS)	30.00	40.00
BOOSTER PACK (3 CARDS)	2.00	3.00
*STARFOIL: .5X TO 1.2X BASIC CARDS		
RELEASED ON FEBRUARY 21, 2014		
SP14001 Gogogo Golem C	.10	.30
SP14002 Daybreaker C	.10	.30
SP14003 Gogogo Giant C	.10	.30
SP14004 ZW - Unicorn Spear C	.10	.30
SP14005 Shocktopus C	.10	.30
SP14006 Photon Lizard C	.10	.30
SP14007 Photon Thrasher C	.75	2.00
SP14008 Photon Crusher C	.10	.30
SP14009 Reverse Breaker C	.10	.30
SP14010 Tasuke Knight C	.10	.30
SP14011 Gagaga Gardna C	.10	.30
SP14012 Cardcar D C	.40	1.00
SP14013 Hammer Shark C	.10	.30
SP14014 Jumbo Drill C	.10	.30
SP14015 Rocket Arrow Express C	.10	.30
SP14016 Aye-Iron C	.10	.30
SP14017 Tin Goldfish C	1.25	3.00
SP14018 Dododo Warrior C	.10	.30
SP14019 Zubaba Buster C	.10	.30
SP14020 Twin Photon Lizard C	.10	.30
SP14021 Thunder End Dragon C	2.00	5.00
SP14022 Number C39: Utopia Ray C	.10	.30
SP14023 Number 32: Shark Drake C	.50	1.25
SP14024 Photon Strike Bounzer C	.75	2.00
SP14025 Photon Papilloperative C	.40	1.00
SP14026 Number 25: Force Focus C	.40	1.00
SP14027 Number 7: Lucky Straight C	.50	1.25
SP14028 Muzurhythm the String Djinn C	.10	.30
SP14029 Temtempo the Percussion Djinn C	.10	.30
SP14030 Melomelody the Brass Djinn C	.10	.30
SP14031 Maestroke the Symphony Djinn C	.50	1.25
SP14032 Cross Attack C	.10	.30
SP14033 Gagagabolt C	.10	.30
SP14034 Star Light, Star Bright C	.10	.30
SP14035 Bound Wand C	.10	.30
SP14036 Mini-Guts C	.10	.30
SP14037 Xyz Effect C	.10	.30
SP14038 Xyz Reflect C	.20	.60
SP14039 Morphing Jar #2 C	.10	.30
SP14040 Magical Merchant C	.50	1.25
SP14041 Reasoning C	1.00	2.50
SP14042 Ma'at C	.10	.30
SP14043 Chimeratech Overdragon C	.10	.30
SP14044 Malefic Truth Dragon C	.10	.30
SP14045 Guldfaxe of the Nordic Beasts C	.50	1.25
SP14046 Svartalf of the Nordic Alfar C	.10	.30
SP14047 Valkyrie of the Nordic Ascendant C	1.00	2.50
SP14048 Thor, Lord of the Aesir C	.60	1.50
SP14049 Loki, Lord of the Aesir C	.10	.30
SP14050 Odin, Father of the Aesir C	.50	1.25

2015 Yu-Gi-Oh Star Pack ARC-V

COMPLETE SET (50 CARDS)	25.00	35.00
BOOSTER BOX	30.00	40.00
BOOSTER PACK (3 CARDS)	1.00	2.50
RELEASED ON JUNE 12, 2015		
SP15EN001 Gem-Knight Tourmaline C	.60	1.00
SP15EN002 Swamp Battleguard C	.10	.20
SP15EN003 Lava Battleguard C	.10	.20
SP15EN004 Mobius the Frost Monarch C	.20	.35
SP15EN005 XX-Saber Fulhelmknight C	.10	.20
SP15EN006 XX-Saber Boggart Knight C	.40	.60
SP15EN007 Constellar Algiedi C	.10	.20
SP15EN008 Constellar Kaus C	.20	.35
SP15EN009 Mobius the Mega Monarch C	1.75	2.15
SP15EN010 Stargazer Magician C	.25	.40
SP15EN011 Timegazer Magician C	.40	.60
SP15EN012 Odd-Eyes Pendulum Dragon C	.10	.20
SP15EN013 Performapal Whip Snake C	.10	.20
SP15EN014 Performapal Sword Fish C	.10	.20
SP15EN015 Performapal Hip Hippo C	.10	.20
SP15EN016 Performapal Kaleidoscorp C	.10	.20
SP15EN017 Superheavy Samurai Big Benkei C	.75	1.15
SP15EN018 Aria the Melodious Diva C	.10	.20
SP15EN019 Mozarta the Melodious Maestra C	.20	.30
SP15EN020 Battleguard King C	.10	.20
SP15EN021 Performapal Trampolynx C	.10	.20
SP15EN022 Edge Imp Sabres C	4.00	4.50
SP15EN023 Fluffal Bear C	.10	.20
SP15EN024 Performapal Fire Mufflerlion C	.10	.20
SP15EN025 Performapal Partnaga C	.10	.20
SP15EN026 Performapal Friendonkey C	.10	.20
SP15EN027 Performapal Trump Witch C	.10	.20
SP15EN028 Superheavy Samurai Trumpeter C	.75	1.15
SP15EN029 Raidraptor - Vanishing Lanius C	.50	.75
SP15EN030 Gem-Knight Master Diamond C	.20	.30
SP15EN031 Frightfur Bear C	.10	.20
SP15EN032 Rune-Eyes Pendulum Dragon C	.50	.75
SP15EN033 X-Saber Souza C	.10	.20
SP15EN034 Superheavy Samurai Warlord Susanowo C	2.75	3.50
SP15EN035 Constellar Pleiades C	.75	1.15

SP15EN036 Dark Rebellion Xyz Dragon C 2.00 5.00
SP15EN037 Raidraptor - Rise Falcon C .10 .20
SP15EN038 Polymerization C 3.50 4.50
SP15EN039 Gem-Knight Fusion C .75 1.15
SP15EN040 Hippo Carnival C .10 .20
SP15EN041 Feast of the Wild LV5 C .10 .20
SP15EN042 Wonder Balloons C .10 .20
SP15EN043 Toy Vendor C .50 .75
SP15EN044 Illusion Balloons C .10 .20
SP15EN045 Raidraptor - Nest C .25 .40
SP15EN046 Command Performance C .10 .20
SP15EN047 Performapal Revival C .10 .20
SP15EN048 The Phantom Knights of Shadow Veil C .10 .20
SP15EN049 Wall of Disruption C .10 .20
SP15EN050 Raidraptor - Readiness C .10 .20

2015 Yu-Gi-Oh Star Pack ARC-V Shatterfoil

COMPLETE SET (50 CARDS) 45.00 60.00
BOOSTER BOX 30.00 40.00
BOOSTER PACK (3 CARDS) 1.00 2.50
UNLISTED C .20 .50
RELEASED ON JUNE 12, 2015
SP15EN001s Gem-Knight Tourmaline .30 .50
SP15EN002s Swamp Battleguard .20 .30
SP15EN003s Lava Battleguard .20 .30
SP15EN004s Mobius the Frost Monarch .30 .50
SP15EN005s XX-Saber Fulhelmknight .30 .50
SP15EN006s XX-Saber Boggart Knight .50 .75
SP15EN007s Constellar Algiedi .20 .35
SP15EN008s Constellar Kaus .50 .75
SP15EN009s Mobius the Mega Monarch 1.50 2.00
SP15EN010s Stargazer Magician .30 .50
SP15EN011s Timegazer Magician .30 .50
SP15EN012s Odd-Eyes Pendulum Dragon 3.00 3.75
SP15EN013s Performapal Whip Snake .20 .30
SP15EN014s Performapal Sword Fish .20 .30
SP15EN015s Performapal Hip Hippo .20 .30
SP15EN016s Performapal Kaleidoscorp .20 .30
SP15EN017s Superheavy Samurai Big Benkei .40 .75
SP15EN018s Aria the Melodious Diva .60 1.00
SP15EN019s Mozarta the Melodious Maestra .60 1.00
SP15EN020s Battleguard King .20 .60
SP15EN021s Performapal Trampolynx .25 .40
SP15EN022s Edge Imp Sabres 3.25 4.00
SP15EN023s Fluffal Bear 4.00 5.00
SP15EN024s Performapal Fire Mufflerlion .20 .30
SP15EN025s Performapal Partnaga .60 1.00
SP15EN026s Performapal Friendonkey .20 .30
SP15EN027s Performapal Trump Witch .20 .30
SP15EN028s Superheavy Samurai Trumpeter 1.00 1.25
SP15EN029s Raidraptor - Vanishing Lanius 3.00 4.00
SP15EN030s Gem-Knight Master Diamond .20 .30
SP15EN031s Frightfur Bear .30 .50
SP15EN032s Rune-Eyes Pendulum Dragon .60 1.00
SP15EN033s X-Saber Souza .20 .30
SP15EN034s Superheavy Samurai Warlord Susanowo 3.00 3.75
SP15EN035s Constellar Pleiades 1.00 1.75
SP15EN036s Dark Rebellion Xyz Dragon 3.75 4.15
SP15EN037s Raidraptor - Rise Falcon 3.75 4.15
SP15EN038s Polymerization 2.00 3.00
SP15EN039s Gem-Knight Fusion .75 1.00
SP15EN040s Hippo Carnival .20 .30
SP15EN041s Feast of the Wild LV5 .60 1.00
SP15EN042s Wonder Balloons .20 .60
SP15EN043s Toy Vendor 2.50 3.15
SP15EN044s Illusion Balloons .25 .40
SP15EN045s Raidraptor - Nest 2.25 3.00
SP15EN046s Command Performance .20 .30
SP15EN047s Performapal Revival .20 .30
SP15EN048s The Phantom Knights of Shadow Veil .30 .50
SP15EN049s Wall of Disruption .20 .30
SP15EN050s Raidraptor - Readiness .40 .75

2002 Yu-Gi-Oh Tournament Series 1

COMPLETE SET (30) 85.00 150.00
BOOSTER BOX (20 PACKS) 400.00 500.00
BOOSTER PACK (3 CARDS) 10.00 20.00
RELEASED ON SEPTEMBER 21, 2002
TP1001 Mechanical Chaser UR 30.00 60.00
TP1002 Axe Raider SR 10.00 25.00
TP1003 Kwagar Hercules SR 4.00 10.00
TP1004 Patrol Robo SR 4.00 10.00
TP1005 White Hole SR 15.00 30.00
TP1006 Elf's Light R 8.00 20.00
TP1007 Steel Shell R 5.00 12.00
TP1008 Blue Medicine R 2.50 6.00
TP1009 Raimei R 3.00 8.00
TP1010 Burning Spear R 3.00 8.00
TP1011 Gust Fan R 4.00 10.00
TP1012 Tiger Axe R 3.00 6.00
TP1013 Goddess with Third Eye R 3.00 8.00
TP1014 Beastking of Swamps R 3.00 8.00
TP1015 Versago the Destroyer R 8.00 20.00
TP1016 Oscillo Hero #2 C 1.50 4.00
TP1017 Giant Flea C 1.50 4.00
TP1018 Bean Soldier C 1.50 4.00
TP1019 The Statue of Easter Island C 1.50 4.00
TP1020 Corroding Shark C 1.50 4.00
TP1021 WOW Warrior C 1.50 4.00
TP1022 Winged Dragon C 1.50 4.00
TP1023 Oscillo Hero C 1.50 4.00
TP1024 Shining Friendship C 1.50 4.00
TP1025 Hercules Beetle C 1.50 4.00
TP1026 Judgement Hand C 1.50 4.00
TP1027 Wodan The Resident C 1.50 4.00
TP1028 Cyber Soldier C 1.50 4.00
TP1029 Cockroach Knight C 2.50 6.00
TP1030 Kuwagata Alpha C 1.50 4.00

2002 Yu-Gi-Oh Tournament Series 2

COMPLETE SET (30) 250.00 300.00
BOOSTER BOX (20 PACKS) 400.00 500.00
BOOSTER PACK (3 CARDS) 4.00 20.00
RELEASED ON DECEMBER 21, 2002
TP2001 Morphing Jar UR 180.00 220.00
TP2002 Dragon Seeker SR 8.00 20.00
TP2003 Giant Red Seasnake SR 6.00 15.00
TP2004 Exile of the Wicked SR 2.50 6.00
TP2005 Call of the Grave SR 2.50 6.00
TP2006 Mikazukinoyaiba R 15.00 30.00
TP2007 Skull Guardian R 20.00 40.00
TP2008 Novox's Prayer R 3.00 8.00
TP2009 Dokurorider R 6.00 15.00
TP2010 Revival of Dokurorider R 2.50 6.00
TP2011 Beautiful Headhuntress R 3.00 8.00
TP2012 Sonic Maid R 5.00 12.00
TP2013 Mystical Sheep #1 R 2.00 5.00
TP2014 Warrior of Tradition R 6.00 15.00
TP2015 Soul of the Pure R 2.00 5.00
TP2016 Dancing Elf C 1.00 2.50
TP2017 Turu-Purun C 1.00 2.50
TP2018 Dharma Cannon C 1.00 2.50
TP2019 Stuffed Animal C 1.00 2.50
TP2020 Spirit of the Books C 1.00 2.50
TP2021 Faith Bird C 1.00 2.50
TP2022 Takuhee C 1.00 2.50
TP2023 Maiden of the Moonlight C 1.50 4.00
TP2024 Queen of Autumn Leaves C 1.00 2.50
TP2025 Two-Headed King Rex C 1.00 2.50
TP2026 Garoozis C 1.50 4.00
TP2027 Crawling Dragon C 1.00 2.50
TP2028 Parrot Dragon C 1.00 2.50
TP2029 Sky Dragon C 1.00 2.50
TP2030 Water Magician C 1.00 2.50

2003 Yu-Gi-Oh Tournament Series 3

COMPLETE SET (20) 100.00 200.00
BOOSTER BOX (20 PACKS) 400.00 500.00
BOOSTER PACK (3 CARDS) 10.00 20.00
RELEASED ON MARCH 29, 2003
TP3001 Needle Worm UR 30.00 50.00
TP3002 Anti Raigeki SR 20.00 40.00
TP3003 Mechanicalchaser SR 3.00 8.00
TP3004 B.Skull Dragon SR 15.00 30.00
TP3005 Horn of Heaven SR 15.00 30.00
TP3006 Axe Raider R 2.00 5.00
TP3007 Kwagar Hercules R 2.00 4.00
TP3008 Patrol Robo R 1.50 4.00
TP3009 White Hole R 2.00 5.00
TP3010 Dragon Capture Jar C .75 2.00
TP3011 Goblin's Secret Remedy C .75 2.00
TP3012 Final Flame C .75 2.00
TP3013 Spirit of the Harp C .75 2.00
TP3014 Pot of Greed C .75 2.00
TP3015 Karbonala Warrior C .75 2.00
TP3016 Darkfire Dragon C .75 2.00
TP3017 Elegant Egotist C .75 2.00
TP3018 Dark Elf C .75 2.00
TP3019 Little Chimera C .75 2.00
TP3020 Bladefly C .75 2.00

2003 Yu-Gi-Oh Tournament Series 4

Complete Set (20) 100.00 150.00
Booster Box (20 packs) 400.00 500.00
Booster Pack (3 cards) 10.00 20.00
RELEASED ON NOVEMBER 15, 2003
TP4001 Royal Decree UR 40.00 80.00
TP4002 Morphing Jar SR 10.00 25.00
TP4003 Megamorph SR 2.00 5.00
TP4004 Chain Destruction SR 2.00 5.00
TP4005 The Fiend Megacyber SR 1.50 4.00
TP4006 Dragon Seeker R 1.25 3.00
TP4007 Giant Red Seasnake R 1.25 3.00
TP4008 Exile of the Wicked R 1.25 3.00
TP4009 Call of the Grave R 2.00 5.00
TP4010 Rush Recklessly C .75 2.00
TP4011 Giant Rat C .75 2.00
TP4012 Senju of Thousand Hands C .75 2.00
TP4013 Karate Man C .75 2.00
TP4014 Nimble Momonga C .75 2.00
TP4015 Mystic Tomato C .75 2.00
TP4016 Nobleman of Extermination C .75 2.00
TP4017 Magic Drain C .75 2.00
TP4018 Gravity Bind C .75 2.00
TP4019 Hayabusa Knight C .75 2.00
TP4020 Mad Sword Beast C .75 2.00

2004 Yu-Gi-Oh Tournament Series 5

COMPLETE SET (20) 25.00 50.00
BOOSTER BOX (20 PACKS) 400.00 500.00
BOOSTER PACK (3 CARDS) 2.50 6.00
RELEASED ON OCTOBER 15, 2004
TP5001 Luminous Soldier UR 2.50 6.00
TP5002 Big Shield Gardna SR 2.00 5.00
TP5003 Magical Thorn SR 2.00 5.00
TP5004 Luster Dragon SR 2.50 6.00
TP5005 Needle Worm SR 6.00 15.00
TP5006 Kycoo the Ghost Destroyer R 1.00 2.50
TP5007 Bazoo the Soul-Eater R 1.00 2.50
TP5008 Book of Life R 1.00 2.50
TP5009 Trap Board Eraser R 1.00 2.50
TP5010 Goddess with the Third Eye C 1.00 2.50
TP5011 Jowgen the Spiritualist C .25 .75
TP5012 Tornado Bird C .25 .75
TP5013 Destruction Punch C .25 .75
TP5014 Beastking of the Swamps C .25 .75
TP5015 Versago the Destroyer C .25 .75
TP5016 Mysticak Sheep #1 C .25 .75
TP5017 Pyramid Turtle C .25 .75
TP5018 Curse of Royal C .25 .75
TP5019 Winged Sage Falcos C .25 .75
TP5020 Dark Designator C .25 .75

2005 Yu-Gi-Oh Tournament Series 6

Complete Set (20) 50.00 80.00
Booster Box (20 packs) 400.00 500.00
Booster Pack (3 cards) 10.00 20.00
RELEASED ON JUNE 1, 2005
TP6001 Toon Cannon Soldier UR 15.00 30.00
TP6002 Toon Table of Contents SR 10.00 25.00
TP6003 Fusion Sage SR 3.00 8.00
TP6004 Royal Decree SR 3.00 8.00
TP6005 Restructer Revolution SR 1.00 2.50
TP6006 Spear Dragon R .75 2.00
TP6007 Airknight Parshath R .75 2.00
TP6008 Susa Soldier R .75 2.00
TP6009 Yamata Dragon R .75 2.00
TP6010 Dark Balter the Terrible C .60 1.50
TP6011 Ryu Senshi C .60 1.50
TP6012 Emergency Provisions C .60 1.50
TP6013 Fiend Skull Dragon C .60 1.50
TP6014 Thunder Nyan Nyan C .60 1.50
TP6015 Last Turn C .60 1.50
TP6016 Archfiend Marmot of Nefariousness C .60 1.50
TP6017 Sleeping Lion C .60 1.50
TP6018 Nekogal #1 C .60 1.50
TP6019 Burglar C .60 1.50
TP6020 Clown Zombie C .60 1.50

2006 Yu-Gi-Oh Tournament Series 7

COMPLETE SET (20) 60.00 140.00
BOOSTER BOX (20 PACKS) 400.00 500.00
BOOSTER PACK (3 CARDS) 10.00 20.00
RELEASED ON NOVEMBER 10, 2005
TP71 D.D. Warrior UR 6.00 15.00
TP72 Warrior Eliminator SR 3.00 8.00
TP73 Fortress Whale SR 40.00 80.00
TP74 Luminous Soldier SR 2.00 5.00
TP75 Breaker the Magical Warrior SR 10.00 25.00
TP76 Goblin Attack Force R 1.00 3.00
TP77 Amazoness Swords Woman R 2.00 5.00
TP78 Chaos Command Magician R 2.00 5.00
TP79 Scapegoat R .75 2.00
TP710 Soul Exchange C .75 2.00
TP711 Fortress Whale's Oath C .75 2.00
TP712 Skilled Dark Magician C .75 2.00
TP713 Skilled White Magician C .75 2.00
TP714 Wall of Illusion C .75 2.00
TP715 Last Will C .75 2.00
TP716 Haniwa C .75 2.00
TP717 Prisman C .75 2.00
TP718 Millennium Golem C .75 2.00
TP719 Dig Break C .75 2.00
TP720 Nekogal #2 C .75 2.00

2006 Yu-Gi-Oh Tournament Series 8

COMPLETE SET (7) 180.00 250.00
BOOSTER BOX (20 PACKS) 400.00 500.00
BOOSTER PACK (3 CARDS) 10.00 20.00
RELEASED ON APRIL 28, 2006
TP81 Magical Arm Shield UR 10.00 25.00
TP82 Harpies Feather Duster SR 100.00 130.00
TP83 Slate Warrior SR 25.00 6.00
TP84 Dunames Dark Witch SR 10.00 25.00
TP85 Garma Sword SR 25.00 50.00
TP86 Zaborg the Thunder Monarch R .75 2.00
TP87 Granmarg the Rock Monarch R .75 2.00
TP88 Mobius Frost Monarch R .75 2.00
TP89 Thestalos the Firestorm Monarch R .75 2.00
TP810 Garma Sword Oath C .75 2.00
TP811 Berserk Gorilla C .75 2.00
TP812 Ultimate Offering C .75 2.00
TP813 Gatekeeper C .75 2.00
TP814 Behegon C .75 2.00
TP815 Violent Rain C .75 2.00
TP816 Temple of Skulls C .75 2.00
TP817 Blocker C .75 2.00
TP818 Wretched Ghost of the Attic C .75 2.00
TP819 Sectarian of Secrets C .75 2.00
TP820 Necrolancer the Timelord C .75 2.00

2006 Yu-Gi-Oh Champion Pack One

COMPLETE SET (20) 200.00 300.00
BOOSTER BOX (20 PACKS) 400.00 500.00
BOOSTER PACK (3 CARDS) 10.00 20.00
RELEASED ON NOVEMBER 11, 2006
CP11 Satellite Cannon UR 15.00 30.00
CP12 Book of Moon SR 120.00 160.00
CP13 Metamorphosis SR 40.00 80.00
CP14 Sakuretsu Armor SR 10.00 25.00
CP15 Night Assailant SR 10.00 25.00
CP16 Big Shield Gardna R .75 2.00
CP17 Limiter Removal R .75 2.00
CP18 Solemn Judgment R .75 2.00
CP19 Reflect Bounder R .75 2.00
CP110 Enemy Controller R .75 2.00
CP111 Pot of Avarice R .75 2.00
CP112 Thunder Kid C .60 1.50
CP113 Mysterious Guard C .60 1.50
CP114 King Tiger Wanghu C .60 1.50
CP115 My Body as a Shield C .60 1.50
CP116 Final Countdown C .60 1.50
CP117 Mudora C .60 1.50
CP118 Stealth Bird C .60 1.50
CP119 Emissary of the Afterlife C .60 1.50
CP120 Threatening Roar C .60 1.50

2006 Yu-Gi-Oh Champion Pack Two

COMPLETE SET (20) 60.00 120.00
BOOSTER BOX (20 PACKS) 400.00 500.00
BOOSTER PACK (3 CARDS) 10.00 20.00
RELEASED ON FEBRUARY 6, 2007
CP21 Magical Stone Excavation UR 10.00 25.00
CP22 Nimble Momonga SR 5.00 12.00
CP23 Magician of Faith SR 25.00 50.00
CP24 Pyramid Turtle SR 3.00 8.00
CP25 Smashing Ground SR 5.00 12.00
CP26 Kuriboh R 2.00 4.00
CP27 Abyss Solider R 1.00 2.00
CP28 Ring of Destruction R 2.00 5.00
CP29 Morphing Jar R 4.00 7.00
CP210 Dark Master - Zorc R 1.00 2.00
CP211 Magicial Dimension R 1.00 2.50
CP212 Happy Lover C 3.00 8.00
CP213 Rush Recklessly C .20 .50
CP214 Ceasefire C .75 2.00
CP215 Thunder Dragon C .75 2.00
CP216 Twin-Headed Behemoth C .75 2.00
CP217 Book of Taiyou C .75 2.00
CP218 Terraforming C .75 2.00
CP219 Big Bang Shot C .20 .50
CP220 Stray Lambs C .20 .50

2007 Yu-Gi-Oh Champion Pack Game Three

COMPLETE SET (7) 45.00 90.00
BOOSTER BOX (20 PACKS) 400.00 500.00
BOOSTER PACK (3 CARDS) 10.00 20.00
RELEASED ON MAY 15, 2007
CP03EN001 Magicians Unite UR 4.00 10.00
CP03EN002 Spirit Reaper SR 8.00 20.00
CP03EN003 Gravekeeper's Spy SR 15.00 30.00
CP03EN004 Sniper Hunter SR 5.00 12.00
CP03EN005 Dark World Lightning SR 2.50 6.00
CP03EN006 D.D. Assailant R .50 1.25
CP03EN007 Goldd Wu-Lord of Dark World R .50 1.25
CP03EN008 Manticore of Darkness R .50 1.25
CP03EN009 The Agent of Judgment - Saturn R .50 1.25
CP03EN010 Pikeru's Circle of Enchantment R .50 1.25
CP03EN011 Widespread Ruin R .50 1.25
CP03EN012 Fairy Dragon C .50 1.25
CP03EN013 Chiron the Mage C .50 1.25
CP03EN014 Kaibaman C .50 1.25
CP03EN015 B.E.S. Crystal Core C .50 1.25
CP03EN016 Gravekeeper's Chief C .50 1.25
CP03EN017 Wild Nature's Release C .50 1.25
CP03EN018 A Feather of the Phoenix C .50 1.25
CP03EN019 Contract with the Abyss C .50 1.25
CP03EN020 Necrovalley C .50 1.25

2007 Yu-Gi-Oh Champion Pack Game Four

COMPLETE SET (5) 25.00 60.00
BOOSTER BOX (20 PACKS) 400.00 500.00
BOOSTER PACK (3 CARDS) 10.00 20.00
RELEASED ON MAY 15, 2007
CP04EN001 Germa UR 4.00 10.00
CP04EN002 Ultimate Offering SR 8.00 20.00
CP04EN003 Bottomless Trap Hole SR 90.00 120.00
CP04EN004 Apprentice Magician SR 4.00 10.00
CP04EN005 Hydrogeddon SR 2.50 6.00
CP04EN006 Confiscation R .75 2.00
CP04EN007 Freed the Brave Wanderer R .75 2.00
CP04EN008 Divine Sword - Phoenix Blade R .75 2.00
CP04EN009 Return from the Different Dimension R .75 2.00
CP04EN010 Kinetic Soldier R .75 2.00
CP04EN011 Magician's Circle R .75 2.00
CP04EN012 Soul Exchange C .50 1.25
CP04EN013 Mother Grizzly C .50 1.25
CP04EN014 Grand Tlki Elder C .50 1.25
CP04EN015 Gigantes C .50 1.25
CP04EN016 Robbin' Goblin C .50 1.25
CP04EN017 Manju of the Ten Thousand Hands C .50 1.25
CP04EN018 Hand of Nephtyhys C .50 1.25
CP04EN019 D.D. Survivor C .50 1.25
CP04EN020 Treeborn Frog C .50 1.25

2008 Yu-Gi-Oh Champion Pack Game Five

COMPLETE SET (20 CARDS) 60.00 120.00
BOOSTER BOX (20 PACKS) 400.00 500.00
BOOSTER PACK (3 CARDS) 10.00 20.00
RELEASED ON JANUARY 8, 2008
CP51 Fiend's Sanctuary UR 10.00 25.00
CP52 Giant Germ SR 4.00 10.00
CP53 Magical Merchant SR 6.00 15.00
CP54 Wave Motion Cannon SR 8.00 20.00
CP55 Trap Dustshoot SR 8.00 20.00

2008 Yu-Gi-Oh Champion Pack Game Six

COMPLETE SET (20) 40.00 100.00
BOOSTER BOX (20 CARDS) 400.00 500.00
Booster Pack (3 CARDS) 10.00 20.00
RELEASED ON MAY 12, 2008
CP61 Rigorous Reaver UR 1.50 4.00
CP62 Destiny Hero - Fear Monger SR 4.00 10.00
CP63 Old Vindictive Magician SR 4.00 10.00
CP64 Phoenix Wing Wind Blast SR 10.00 25.00
CP65 Blaze Accelerator SR 4.00 10.00
CP66 Call of Darkness R .75 2.00
CP67 Blade Knight R .75 2.00
CP68 Super-Electromagnetic Voltech Dragon R .75 2.00
CP69 Elemental Hero Stratos R 1.25 3.00
CP610 Helios Duo Megistus R .75 2.00
CP611 Mage Power R 2.00 5.00
CP612 Sentinel of the Seas C .75 2.00
CP613 Batteryman AA C .75 2.00
CP614 Theban Nightmare C .75 2.00
CP615 Majestic Mech - Ohka C .75 2.00
CP616 Soul of Purity and Light C .75 2.00
CP617 Amplifier C 2.00 5.00
CP618 Cold Wave C .75 2.00
CP619 Magical Hats C .75 2.00
CP620 Dimension Wall C 2.00 5.00

2008 Yu-Gi-Oh Champion Pack Game Seven

COMPLETE SET (20) 80.00 150.00
BOOSTER BOX (20 PACKS) 400.00 500.00
BOOSTER PACK (3 CARDS) 10.00 20.00
RELEASED ON SEPTEMBER 13, 2008
CP71 Voltic Kong UR 1.50 4.00
CP72 Legendary Jujitsu Master SR 1.50 4.00
CP73 Threatening Roar SR 5.00 12.00
CP74 Gladiator Beast Bestiari SR 6.00 15.00
CP75 Lonefire Blossom SR 30.00 60.00
CP76 Elemental Hero Ocean R 4.00 10.00
CP77 Fairy King Truesdale R 1.50 4.00
CP78 Spell Striker R 1.25 3.00
CP79 Vanity's Fiend R 6.00 15.00
CP710 Dark World Dealings R 1.50 4.00
CP711 Doom Shaman R 1.25 3.00
CP712 Shovel Crusher C .75 2.00
CP713 Life Absorbing Machine C .75 2.00
CP714 Fusilier Dragon, the DualMode Beast C .75 2.00
CP715 Homunculus the Alchemic Being C .75 2.00
CP716 Memory Crusher C .75 2.00
CP717 Instant Fusion C 3.00 8.00
CP718 Dimensional Inversion C .75 2.00
CP719 Ancient Rules C 4.00 10.00
CP720 Counter Counter C .75 2.00

2009 Yu-Gi-Oh Champion Pack Game Eight

COMPLETE SET (20) 75.00 150.00
BOOSTER BOX (20 PACKS) 400.00 500.00
BOOSTER PACK (3 CARDS) 10.00 20.00
RELEASED ON MAY 29, 2012
CP81 Gravity Behemoth UR 1.50 4.00
CP82 Prohibition SR 4.00 10.00
CP83 Mind Crush SR 20.00 40.00
CP84 Dimensional Fissure SR 6.00 15.00
CP85 Lumina, Lightsworn Summoner SR 30.00 60.00
CP86 Magician's Valkyria R 4.00 10.00
CP87 Silent Magician LV4 R 2.00 5.00
CP88 Great Shogun Shien R .50 1.25
CP89 Herald of Creation R .40 1.00
CP810 Burial from a Different Dimension R 1.25 3.00
CP811 Necro Gardna R .40 1.00
CP812 Mushroom Man C .75 2.00
CP813 Royal Oppression C 3.00 8.00
CP814 Beckoning Light C .30 1.00
CP815 Neo-Spacian Dark Panther C .30 1.00
CP816 Alien Warrior C .30 1.00
CP817 Alien Mother C .30 1.00
CP818 Vanity's Ruler C .75 2.00
CP819 Miraculous Rebirth C .30 1.00
CP820 Cell Explosion Virus C .30 1.00

2009 Yu-Gi-Oh Turbo Pack 1

COMPLETE SET (21) 40.00 100.00
BOOSTER BOX (100 PACKS) 300.00 400.00
BOOSTER PACK (3 CARDS) 3.00 8.00
RELEASED ON AUGUST 15, 2009
TU10 Judgment Dragon UTR 20.00 40.00
TU11 Doomcaliber Knight UR 2.50 6.00
TU12 Garoth, Lightsworn Warrior SR 1.25 3.00
TU13 Krebons SR 2.50 6.00
TU14 Gladiator Beast Samnite SR .75 2.00
TU15 Black Whirlwind SR 5.00 12.00
TU16 Crush Card Virus R 1.25 3.00
TU17 Satellite Cannon R .60 1.50
TU18 Rescue Cat R .60 1.50
TU19 Grandmaster of the Six Samurai R .60 1.50
TU110 TradeIn R 1.50 4.00
TU111 Armageddon Knight R .75 2.00
TU112 Book of Moon C .40 1.00
TU113 Terraforming C .75 2.00
TU114 Hand Destruction C 1.00 2.50
TU115 Gladiator Beast Murmillo C .40 1.00
TU116 Gladiator Beast Bestiari C .40 1.00
TU117 Gladiator Beast Laquari C .40 1.00
TU118 Golden Flying Fish C .40 1.00
TU119 Ryko, Lightsworn Hunter C .40 1.00
TU120 D.D.R. Different Dimension Reincarnation C .40 1.00

2010 Yu-Gi-Oh Turbo Pack 2

COMPLETE SET (21) 60.00 140.00
BOOSTER BOX (100 PACKS) 300.00 400.00
BOOSTER PACK (3 CARDS) 10.00 20.00
RELEASED ON JANUARY 9, 2010
TU20 Gladiator Beast Heraklinos UTR 2.00 5.00
TU21 Chaos Sorcerer UR 8.00 20.00
TU22 Gravekeeper's Assailant SR 1.25 3.00
TU23 Magical Dimension SR 20.00 35.00
TU24 Foolish Burial SR 20.00 40.00
TU25 Beckoning Light SR 1.25 3.00
TU26 Gravekeeper's Spear Soldier R .75 2.00
TU27 My Body as a Shield R .50 1.25
TU28 Magical Stone Excavation R .60 1.50
TU29 Mist Archfiend R .60 1.50
TU210 Light-Imprisoning Mirror R 1.00 2.50
TU211 Shadow-Imprisoning Mirror R 1.00 2.50
TU212 Anti-Spell Fragrance C .40 1.00
TU213 Gravekeeper's Cannonholder C .40 1.00
TU214 Necrovalley C .40 1.00
TU215 Autonomous Action Unit C .40 1.00
TU216 Anti-Spell Fragrance C 6.00 15.00
TU217 Reflect Bounder C .40 1.00
TU218 Mausoleum of the Emperor C .40 1.00
TU219 Gravekeeper's Commandant C .75 2.00
TU220 Iron Core of Koa'ki Meiru C .40 1.00

2010 Yu-Gi-Oh Turbo Pack 3

COMPLETE SET (21 CARDS)
BOOSTER BOX
BOOSTER PACK
RELEASED ON JULY 12, 2010
TU03EN000 Caius the Shadow Monarch UTR 15.00 30.00
TU03EN001 Dark Grepher UR 3.00 8.00
TU03EN002 Rescue Cat SR 8.00 20.00
TU03EN003 Morphtronic Celfon SR 2.50 6.00
TU03EN004 Rekindling SR 3.00 8.00
TU03EN005 Treacherous Trap Hole SR 6.00 15.00
TU03EN006 Gladiator Beast Retiari R 1.25 3.00
TU03EN007 XX-Saber Faultroll R .40 1.00
TU03EN008 XX-Saber Ragigura R .40 1.00
TU03EN009 Magical Android R .40 1.00
TU03EN010 Dark Eruption R .40 1.00
TU03EN011 Saber Slash R .40 1.00
TU03EN012 Destiny Hero - Diamond Dude C .10 .30
TU03EN013 D.D. Crow C .20 .75
TU03EN014 Superancient Deepsea King Coelacanth C .10 .30
TU03EN015 Koa'ki Meiru Drago C 1.50 4.00
TU03EN016 Kycoo the Ghost Destroyer C .10 .30

TU03EN017 Nobleman of Crossout C .10 .30
TU03EN018 Cloak and Dagger C .10 .30
TU03EN019 Gladiator Beast War Chariot C .40 1.00
TU03EN020 Pollinosis C .10 .30

2010 Yu-Gi-Oh Turbo Pack 4

COMPLETE SET 50.00 100.00
BOOSTER BOX
BOOSTER PACK
RELEASED ON November 19, 2010
TU04-EN000 Tragoedia UTR 15.00 30.00
TU04-EN001 Goftoms' Emergency Call UR 3.00 8.00
TU04-EN002 Debris Dragon SR 2.50 6.00
TU04-EN003 Blackwing - Sirocco the Dawn SR 1.50 4.00
TU04-EN004 Deep Sea Diva SR 15.00 30.00
TU04-EN005 Compulsory Evacuation Device SR 8.00 20.00
TU04-EN006 Dunames Dark Witch R .40 1.00
TU04-EN007 The End of Anubis R .60 1.50
TU04-EN008 Psychic Commander R .75 2.00
TU04-EN009 Advanced Ritual Art R .40 1.00
TU04-EN010 Bark of Dark Ruler R .40 1.00
TU04-EN011 Swallow Flip R .40 1.00
TU04-EN012 Wattkid C .25 .75
TU04-EN013 Oscillo Hero C .25 .75
TU04-EN014 Mokey Mokey C .25 .75
TU04-EN015 Key Mace C .25 .75
TU04-EN016 King of the Skull Servants C .50 1.25
TU04-EN017 Dark Hole C .40 1.00
TU04-EN018 Amazoness Spellcaster C .25 .75
TU04-EN019 Gladiator Proving Ground C .25 .75
TU04-EN020 White Hole C .60 1.50

2011 Yu-Gi-Oh Turbo Pack 5

TU05-EN000 Colossal Fighter UTR 4.00 10.00
TU05-EN001 Dark Hole UR 2.50 6.00
TU05-EN002 Gladiator Beast Laquari SR 1.00 2.50
TU05-EN003 Snowman Eater SR 1.50 4.00
TU05-EN004 Six Samurai United SR 15.00 30.00
TU05-EN005 Spell Shattering Arrow SR 2.50 6.00
TU05-EN006 Puppet Plant R .40 1.00
TU05-EN007 Wulf, Lightsworn Beast R .25 .75
TU05-EN008 Cyber Eltanin R .20 .60
TU05-EN009 Torrential Tribute R .75 2.00
TU05-EN010 Escape from the Dark Dimension R .75 2.00
TU05-EN011 Zoma the Spirit R .50 1.25
TU05-EN012 Manju of the Ten Thousand Hands C 1.25 3.00
TU05-EN013 Abyssal Kingshark C .15 .40
TU05-EN014 Spirit of the Six Samurai C .15 .40
TU05-EN015 Black Salvo C .15 .40
TU05-EN016 Darkness Neosphere C 1.25 3.00
TU05-EN017 Miracle Fusion C .75 2.00
TU05-EN018 Shield Crush C .15 .40
TU05-EN019 Seven Tools of the Bandit C .15 .40
TU05-EN020 Royal Command C .15 .40

2011 Yu-Gi-Oh Turbo Pack 6

TU06-EN000 Dark Armed Dragon UTR 25.00 50.00
TU06-EN001 Sangan UR 5.00 12.00
TU06-EN002 Chain Disappearance SR 5.00 12.00
TU06-EN003 Masked Dragon SR 3.00 8.00
TU06-EN004 Fishborg Blaster SR 2.00 5.00
TU06-EN005 Quickdraw Synchron SR 10.00 25.00
TU06-EN006 Zombie Master R .50 1.25
TU06-EN007 Stardust Dragon R 2.00 5.00
TU06-EN008 Red Dragon Archfiend R 1.00 2.50
TU06-EN009 Black Garden R .50 1.25
TU06-EN010 Armory Arm R 1.25 3.00
TU06-EN011 Alector, Sovereign of Birds C .15 .40
TU06-EN012 Fusion Gate C 1.25 3.00
TU06-EN013 Kinetic Soldier C .10 .30
TU06-EN014 Greenkappa C .10 .30
TU06-EN015 Creature Swap C .15 .40
TU06-EN016 Magical Dimension C .20 .60
TU06-EN017 Bountiful Artemis C .50 1.25
TU06-EN018 Gemini Spark C .20 .60
TU06-EN019 Golem Dragon C .75 2.00
TU06-EN020 Transforming Sphere C .10 .30

2012 Yu-Gi-Oh Turbo Pack 7

TU07-EN000 Ally of Justice Catastor UTR 4.00 10.00
TU07-EN001 Book of Moon UR 5.00 12.00
TU07-EN002 Ninja Grandmaster Sasuke SR .40 1.00
TU07-EN003 Yellow Gadget SR 2.00 5.00
TU07-EN004 X-Saber Pashuul SR 2.00 5.00
TU07-EN005 Horn of the Phantom Beast SR 2.50 6.00
TU07-EN006 Dark Horus R .20 .60
TU07-EN007 Lightning Warrior R .60 1.50
TU07-EN008 Primal Seed R .25 .75
TU07-EN009 Big Evolution Pill R .25 .75
TU07-EN010 Tail Swipe R .25 .75
TU07-EN011 Geartown R .40 1.00
TU07-EN012 Seiyaryu C .25 .75
TU07-EN013 Serpent Night Dragon C .25 .75
TU07-EN014 Kotodama C .10 .30
TU07-EN015 Gokipon C .25 .75
TU07-EN016 Goe Goe the Gallant Ninja C .25 .75
TU07-EN017 Herald of Orange Light C .25 .75
TU07-EN018 Blackwing - Sirocco the Dawn C .25 .75
TU07-EN019 Ninjitsu Art of Transformation C .25 .75
TU07-EN020 Ninjitsu Art of Decoy C .25 .75

2012 Yu-Gi-Oh Turbo Pack 8

TU08-EN000 Thunder King Rai-Oh UTR 15.00 30.00
TU08-EN001 Skill Drain UR 15.00 30.00
TU08-EN002 Green Gadget SR 2.00 5.00
TU08-EN003 Red Gadget SR 2.00 5.00
TU08-EN004 Upstart Goblin SR 15.00 30.00
TU08-EN005 Mirror of Oaths SR 1.00 2.50
TU08-EN006 Alligator's Sword R .50 1.25
TU08-EN007 Lost Guardian R .10 .30
TU08-EN008 Alligator's Sword Dragon R .20 .60
TU08-EN009 Magicians Unite R .10 .30
TU08-EN010 Ready for Intercepting R .10 .30
TU08-EN011 Gozen Match R 1.50 4.00
TU08-EN012 Elephant Statue of Blessing C .10 .30
TU08-EN013 Elephant Statue of Disaster C .10 .30
TU08-EN014 Gemini Imps C .10 .30
TU08-EN015 Flamvell Firedog C .10 .30
TU08-EN016 Wind-Up Factory C .50 1.25
TU08-EN017 The Emperor's Holiday C .10 .30
TU08-EN018 Really Eternal Rest C .10 .30
TU08-EN019 Rock Bombardment C .10 .30
TU08-EN020 Magician's Circle C .75 2.00

2012 Yu-Gi-Oh Astral Pack One

AP01EN001 Tsukuyomi UTR 8.00 20.00
AP01EN002 Debris Dragon UTR 8.00 20.00
AP01EN003 Photon Thrasher UTR 8.00 20.00
AP01EN004 Flamvell Firedog SR .40 1.00
AP01EN005 Genex Undine SR .75 2.00
AP01EN006 Kagemusha of the Six Samurai SR 3.00 8.00
AP01EN007 Inzektor Centipede SR .75 2.00
AP01EN008 Hieratic Dragon of Tefnuit SR 2.00 5.00
AP01EN009 Terraforming SR 8.00 20.00
AP01EN010 Moray of Greed SR 1.50 4.00
AP01EN011 Mask Change SR 1.50 4.00
AP01EN012 Hidden Armory SR 1.25 3.00
AP01EN013 The Gates of Dark World SR .40 1.00
AP01EN014 Hyena C
AP01EN015 Dragon Ice C
AP01EN016 Cyber Shark C .75 2.00
AP01EN017 Swift Scarecrow C .50 1.25
AP01EN018 Elemental HERO Ice Edge C .75 2.00
AP01EN019 Mystical Sand C 1.50 4.00
AP01EN020 Spiritual Forest C .15 .40
AP01EN021 Closed Forest C .20 .60
AP01EN022 Shrine of Mist Valley C .15 .40
AP01EN023 Thunder of Ruler C .15 .40
AP01EN024 Fuh-Rin-Ka-Zan C .15 .40
AP01EN025 Astral Barrier C .15 .40

2013 Yu-Gi-Oh Astral Pack Two

AP02EN001 Atlantean Dragoons UTR 30.00 60.00
AP02EN002 Photon Papilloperative UTR 4.00 10.00
AP02EN003 Spellbook of Power UTR 25.00 50.00
AP02EN004 Interplanetarypurplythorny Dragon SR .40 1.00
AP02EN005 Geargiaccelerator SR 1.00 2.50
AP02EN006 Atlantean Heavy Infantry SR 2.50 6.00
AP02EN007 Slushy SR .20 .60
AP02EN008 Brotherhood of the Fire Fist - Hawk SR .20 .60
AP02EN009 Brotherhood of the Fire Fist - Raven SR .20 .60
AP02EN010 Harpies' Hunting Ground SR .40 1.00
AP02EN011 Gemini Spark SR 3.00 8.00
AP02EN012 Spiritual Water Art - Aoi SR .50 1.25
AP02EN013 Trap Stun SR .75 2.00
AP02EN014 Sky Scout C .20 .60
AP02EN015 Cyber Phoenix C .20 .60
AP02EN016 Light and Darkness Dragon C .75 2.00
AP02EN017 Justice of Prophecy C .40 1.00
AP02EN018 Barox C 1.25 3.00
AP02EN019 Pot of Avarice C .40 1.00
AP02EN020 Instant Fusion C 3.00 8.00
AP02EN021 Recycling Batteries C .20 .60
AP02EN022 Machina Armored Unit C .20 .60
AP02EN023 Photon Veil C .75 2.00
AP02EN024 Hysteric Party C .40 1.00
AP02EN025 Token Stampede C .20 .60

2013 Yu-Gi-Oh Astral Pack Three

AP03EN001 Atlantean Marksman UTR 20.00 35.00
AP03EN002 Maestroke the Symphony Djinn UTR 3.00 8.00
AP03EN003 Fire Formation - Tenki UTR 20.00 35.00
AP03EN004 Serene Psychic Witch SR .25 .75
AP03EN005 Mermail Abyssgunde SR 1.50 4.00
AP03EN006 Falling Down SR .25 .75
AP03EN007 Miracle Fertilizer SR 1.00 2.50
AP03EN008 Noble Arms - Gallatin SR .25 .75
AP03EN009 Spellbook Library of the Crescent SR 1.00 2.50
AP03EN010 Noble Arms - Arfeudutyr SR .25 .75
AP03EN011 Spellbook Star Hall SR .50 1.25
AP03EN012 Pollinosis SR .25 .75
AP03EN013 Wall of Thorns SR .25 .75
AP03EN014 Curtain of the Dark Ones C 1.00 2.50
AP03EN015 Jowgen the Spiritualist C .50 1.25
AP03EN016 Swarm of Scarabs C .25 .75
AP03EN017 Swarm of Locusts C .25 .75
AP03EN018 Des Lacooda C .25 .75
AP03EN019 Imprisoned Queen Archfiend C .25 .75
AP03EN020 Vampire Dragon C .50 1.25
AP03EN021 Kamionwizard C 2.50 6.00
AP03EN022 Gladiator Beast's Battle Archfiend Shield C .25 .75
AP03EN023 Deck Lockdown C .50 1.25
AP03EN024 Super Solar Nutrient C .25 .75
AP03EN025 Archfiend's Roar C .25 .75
AP03EN026 Heavy Slump C .25 .75

2014 Yu-Gi-Oh Astral Pack Four

COMPLETE SET (26 CARDS) 130.00 150.00
BOOSTER PACK 2.00 5.00
UNLISTED C .10 .30
RELEASED ON FEBRUARY 27, 2014
AP04EN001 Dandylion UTR 7.50 8.50
AP04EN002 Maxx "C" UTR 75.00 80.00
AP04EN003 Necrovalley UTR 18.00 22.00
AP04EN004 Blackwing - Gale the Whirlwind SR 1.00 1.50
AP04EN005 Blackwing - Kalut the Moon Shadow SR 2.75 3.50
AP04EN006 Consecrated Light SR .30 .50
AP04EN007 Swift Scarecrow SR 1.75 2.25
AP04EN008 Crimson Blader SR 1.75 2.15
AP04EN009 Break! Draw! SR .20 .30
AP04EN010 Spellbook of Wisdom SR 2.50 3.00
AP04EN011 Spellbook of Eternity SR .80 1.15
AP04EN012 Fire Formation - Tensu SR 1.75 2.15
AP04EN013 Soul Drain SR 1.25 2.00
AP04EN014 Wings of Wicked Flame C .50 .75
AP04EN015 Morphing Jar #2 C .20 .30
AP04EN016 Magical Merchant C .40 .60
AP04EN017 Lonefire Blossom C 2.00 2.50
AP04EN018 Fossil Dyna Pachycephalo C 1.00 1.50
AP04EN019 Tytannial, Princess of Camellias C .15 .25
AP04EN020 Scrap Beast C .30 .50
AP04EN021 Ma'at C .10 .20
AP04EN022 Mavelus C 10.00 13.00
AP04EN023 Reasoning C .50 .80
AP04EN024 Archfiend's Oath C .20 .30
AP04EN025 Black Garden C .75 1.00
AP04EN026 Scrapstorm C .20 .35

2014 Yu-Gi-Oh Astral Pack Five

COMPLETE SET (26) 60.00 75.00
BOOSTER BOX (100 PACKS) 350.00 400.00
BOOSTER PACK (3 CARDS) 2.00 3.00
RELEASED ON JULY 25, 2014
AP05EN001 Bujin Yamato UTR 6.50 7.50
AP05EN002 Gagaga Cowboy UTR 15.00 17.00
AP05EN003 Pot of Duality UTR 33.00 36.00
AP05EN004 Card Trooper SR .15 .25
AP05EN005 Jenis, Lightsworn Mender SR .50 .75
AP05EN006 Geargiarsenal SR .25 .40
AP05EN007 Mermail Abysspike SR .75 1.00
AP05EN008 Star Drawing SR 1.50 2.00
AP05EN009 Bujingi Turtle SR .50 .75
AP05EN010 Advanced Ritual Art SR .75 1.00
AP05EN011 Charge of the Light Brigade SR .50 .75
AP05EN012 Overworked SR .20 .30
AP05EN013 Full House SR .75 1.00
AP05EN014 Blackland Fire Dragon C .30 .50
AP05EN015 Copy Plant C .20 .35
AP05EN016 Hanewata C .10 .20
AP05EN017 Rinyan, Lightsworn Rogue C .10 .20
AP05EN018 Skelgon C .10 .20
AP05EN019 Queen of Thorns C .75 1.00
AP05EN020 Empress of Prophecy C .15 .25
AP05EN021 Soul Exchange C .10 .20
AP05EN022 Book of Moon C .30 .50
AP05EN023 Lightsworn Sabre C .30 .50
AP05EN024 Spiritual Forest C .10 .20
AP05EN025 Spellbook Library of the Heliosphere C .30 .50
AP05EN026 Jurrac Impact C .10 .20

2014 Yu-Gi-Oh Astral Pack Six

COMPLETE SET (28) 70.00 85.00
BOOSTER BOX (100 PACKS) 350.00 400.00
BOOSTER PACK (3 CARDS) 2.00 3.00
RELEASED ON DECEMBER 12, 2014
AP06EN001 Tour Guide From the Underworld UTR 24.00 26.00
AP06EN002 Number 11: Big Eye UTR 17.00 20.00
AP06EN003 Traptrix Trap Hole Nightmare UTR 6.50 8.00
AP06EN004 Traptrix Myrmeleo SR .75 1.15
AP06EN005 White Dragon Wyverburster SR .75 1.00
AP06EN006 Black Dragon Collapserpent SR .75 1.15
AP06EN007 Superheavy Samurai Big Benkei SR .50 .80
AP06EN008 Shaddoll Beast SR 2.00 2.25
AP06EN009 Underworld Fighter Balmung SR .30 .50
AP06EN010 Number 80: Rhapsody in Berserk SR 1.50 2.00
AP06EN011 Summoner's Art SR 5.00 6.00
AP06EN012 Bujincarnation SR .75 1.15
AP06EN013 Infernity Break SR .40 .60
AP06EN014 Sea Kamen C .30 .80
AP06EN015 Gruesome Goo C .60 .75
AP06EN016 Amazon of the Seas C .50 .75
AP06EN017 King of the Skull Servants C .50 .75
AP06EN018 Vanity's Fiend C 2.75 3.15
AP06EN019 Van'Dalgyon the Dark Dragon Lord C .20 .30
AP06EN020 Machina Fortress C 1.00 1.25
AP06EN021 Man-eating Black Shark C 1.00 1.75
AP06EN022 Madolche Queen Tiaramisu C .40 .75
AP06EN023 Nobleman of Crossout C .20 .30
AP06EN024 Thunder Crash C .20 .30
AP06EN025 The Monarchs Stormforth C .25 .40
AP06EN026 Ceasefire C .20 .30
AP06EN027 Royal Command C .20 .30
AP06EN028 Cursed Seal of the Forbidden Spell C .75 1.00

2015 Yu-Gi-Oh Astral Pack Seven

COMPLETE SET (27 CARDS) 95.00 115.00
BOOSTER PACK 3.00 5.00
UNLISTED C .20 .60
RELEASED ON JUNE 5 2015
AP07EN001 Gaia Dragon, the Thunder Charger UR 23.00 26.00
AP07EN002 Castel, the Skyblaster Musketeer UR 35.00 40.00
AP07EN003 Spell Shattering Arrow UR 7.00 9.00
AP07EN004 Satellarknight Altair SR 3.75 5.00
AP07EN005 Satellarknight Unukalhai SR 3.00 3.75
AP07EN006 Djinn Demolisher of Rituals SR .60 1.00
AP07EN007 Scarm, Malebranche of the Burning Abyss SR 1.75 2.25
AP07EN008 Leo, the Keeper of the Sacred Tree SR 2.25 2.75
AP07EN009 Number 103: Ragnazero SR 2.00 2.25
AP07EN010 Level Limit - Area B SR 1.50 2.00
AP07EN011 Twister SR .30 .50
AP07EN012 Dragon Ravine SR 3.75 4.25
AP07EN013 Level Limit - Area A SR .30 .50
AP07EN014 Invader from Another Dimension C .60 1.00
AP07EN015 Lord of the Lamp C .50 .75
AP07EN016 Senju of the Thousand Hands C 1.00 1.75
AP07EN017 Voltanis Scattershot C .30 .50
AP07EN018 Gladiator Beast Bestiari C .25 .35
AP07EN019 Madolche Puddingcess C 1.50 2.00
AP07EN020 Brotherhood of the Fire Fist - Spirit C .50 .75
AP07EN021 Soul Hunter C .60 1.00
AP07EN022 Dawn of the Herald C 2.00 2.75
AP07EN023 Storm C .40 .60
AP07EN024 Spiritual Wind Art - Miyabi C .40 .60
AP07EN025 Light-Imprisoning Mirror C 1.50 2.25
AP07EN026 Shadow-Imprisoning Mirror C 1.25 1.75
AP07EN027 Fairy Wind C .30 .50

2015 Yu-Gi-Oh Astral Pack Eight

COMPLETE SET (27 CARDS) 100.00 120.00
BOOSTER PACK (3 CARDS) 3.00 5.00
RELEASED ON DECEMBER 12 2014
AP08EN001 Trishula, Dragon of the Ice Barrier UTR 35.00 40.00
AP08EN002 Mystical Space Typhoon UTR 24.00 27.00
AP08EN003 Fiendish Chain UTR 15.00 18.00
AP08EN004 Igknight Margrave SR .60 1.00
AP08EN005 Igknight Gallant SR .50 .75
AP08EN006 Toon Masked Sorcerer SR 2.75 3.25
AP08EN007 Graff, Malebranche of the Burning Abyss SR .40 .60
AP08EN008 Black Luster Soldier - Envoy of the Evening Twilight SR .60 1.00
AP08EN009 Spiritual Beast Rampengu SR 2.25 3.00
AP08EN010 Instant Fusion SR 5.00 6.50
AP08EN011 Kozmotown SR 1.00 1.25
AP08EN012 Book of Eclipse SR 3.25 4.00
AP08EN013 Lose 1 Turn SR 3.25 4.00
AP08EN014 Rhaimundos of the Red Sword C .75 1.00
AP08EN015 Fireyarou C .50 .75
AP08EN016 Twin-Headed Behemoth C .20 .30
AP08EN017 Swift Gaia the Fierce Knight C .20 .30
AP08EN018 Kinka-byo C 1.25 1.75
AP08EN019 Red-Eyes Wyvern C 1.00 1.50
AP08EN020 Gem-Knight Obsidian C .30 .50
AP08EN021 Vermillion Sparrow C .60 1.00
AP08EN022 Masked HERO Koga C .15 .25
AP08EN023 Machine Duplication C 2.00 3.00
AP08EN024 U.A. Stadium C .15 .25
AP08EN025 Black Horn of Heaven C .25 .35
AP08EN026 Safe Zone C 1.00 1.50
AP08EN027 Unpossessed C .20 .30

2016 Yu-Gi-Oh OTS Tournament Pack 1

COMPLETE SET (27 CARDS) 100.00 120.00
BOOSTER BOX (100 PACKS) 350.00 500.00
BOOSTER PACK (3 CARDS) 2.50 6.00
UNLISTED C .25 .75
UNLISTED SR .75 2.00
Released of March 18th, 2016
OP01EN001 Bountiful Artemis UTR 8.00 10.00
OP01EN002 Vanity's Fiend UTR 20.00 25.00
OP01EN003 Masked HERO Dark Law UTR 30.00 35.00
OP01EN004 Droll & Lock Bird SR 1.00 1.50
OP01EN005 Infernoid Patrulea SR .60 1.00
OP01EN006 Performapal Lizardraw SR 2.00 2.75
OP01EN007 Performapal Skullcrobat Joker SR 1.75 2.25
OP01EN008 Performapal Monkeyboard SR .60 1.00
OP01EN009 Performapal Guitartle SR 1.00 1.50
OP01EN010 Dinoster Power, the Mighty Dracoslayer SR 1.50 2.00
OP01EN011 Anti-Spell Fragrance SR 13.00 17.00
OP01EN012 Imperial Iron Wall SR 1.25 2.00
OP01EN013 Typhoon SR 2.25 3.25
OP01EN014 Skull Servant C .75 1.25
OP01EN015 Battle Warrior C .40 .75
OP01EN016 Mezuki C 1.00 1.50
OP01EN017 The White Stone of Legend C .75 1.15
OP01EN018 Flying "C" C .75 1.00
OP01EN019 Zombie Warrior C 2.00 3.00
OP01EN020 Michael, the Arch-Lightsworn C .75 1.25
OP01EN021 Cyber Dragon Nova C 1.50 2.00
OP01EN022 Mage Power C .20 .75
OP01EN023 Offerings to the Doomed C .10 .20
OP01EN024 Monster Gate C .25 .40
OP01EN025 Allure of Darkness C 9.00 11.00
OP01EN026 Summoning Curse C .30 .50
OP01EN027 Advance Zone C+D2 .40 .60

2016 Yu-Gi-Oh OTS Tournament Pack 2

COMPLETE SET (27 CARDS) 110.00 135.00
BOOSTER BOX (100 PACKS) 350.00 500.00
BOOSTER PACK (3 CARDS) 2.50 6.00
RELEASED ON JULY 22, 2016
OP02EN001 Fog King UTR 7.00 10.00
OP02EN002 Kuraz the Light Monarch UTR 12.00 16.00
OP02EN003 Raigeki UTR 45.00 50.00
OP02EN004 Gameciel the Sea Turtle Kaiju SR 8.00 11.00
OP02EN005 Fiendish Rhino Warrior SR 2.50 3.00
OP02EN006 Mithra the Thunder Vassal SR 1.50 1.75
OP02EN007 The Phantom Knights of Ragged Gloves SR 3.75 4.25
OP02EN008 Super Quantum Blue Layer SR 1.25 1.75
OP02EN009 System Down SR 5.00 7.00
OP02EN010 Mask of Restrict SR 4.00 5.00
OP02EN011 Ninjitsu Art of Transformation SR 1.25 1.75
OP02EN012 Armor Ninjitsu Art of Freezing SR .60 1.00
OP02EN013 The Prime Monarch SR 2.00 3.00
OP02EN014 Takuhee C 1.75 2.25
OP02EN015 Temple of Skulls C 1.75 2.15
OP02EN016 Dark Eradicator Warlock C .40 .60
OP02EN017 Infernity Archfiend C .50 .75
OP02EN018 Cyber Dragon Core C .60 1.00
OP02EN019 Galaxy Dragon C .30 .50
OP02EN020 Prediction Princess Coinorma C .50 .75
OP02EN021 Prediction Princess Tarotrei C .60 1.00
OP02EN022 Skullbird C 2.00 2.50
OP02EN023 United We Stand C .60 1.00
OP02EN024 The Melody of Awakening Dragon C 4.00 5.50
OP02EN025 Prediction Ritual C .30 .50
OP02EN026 Ninjitsu Art of SuperTransformation C .40 .75
OP02EN027 Wiretap C .60 1.00

2012 Yu-Gi-Oh Battle Pack Epic Dawn

COMPLETE SET (220) 75.00 150.00
BOOSTER BOX (36 PACKS) 60.00 80.00
BOOSTER PACK (5 CARDS) 3.00 4.00
*STARFOIL: .6X TO 1.5X BASIC CARDS
RELEASED ON MAY 28, 2012
BP01001 Witch of the Black R .25 .75
BP01002 Cyber Jar R .25 .75
BP01003 Jinzo R .50 1.25
BP01004 Injection Fairy Lily R .25 .75
BP01005 Dark Dust Spirit R .25 .75
BP01006 Skull Archfiend R .25 .75
BP01007 Dark Magician R .75 2.00
BP01008 Blowback Dragon R .25 .75
BP01009 Mobius the Frost R .25 .75
BP01010 Fox Fire R .25 .75
BP01011 Ancient Gear Golem R .25 .75
BP01012 Treeborn Frog R .25 .75
BP01013 Super Conductor R .25 .75
BP01014 Gold the Emissary R .75 2.00
BP01015 Raiza the Storm R .25 .75
BP01016 White Night Dragon R .25 .75
BP01017 Deep Diver R .25 .75
BP01018 Caius the Shadow R .50 1.25
BP01019 Krebons R .25 .75
BP01020 Tragoedia R .50 1.25
BP01021 Obelisk the Tormentor R 5.00 12.00
BP01022 Machina Fortress R .75 2.00
BP01023 Tour Guide R 1.25 3.00
BP01024 Number 39: Utopia R .50 1.25
BP01025 Gachi Gachi Gantetsu R .25 .75
BP01026 Grenosaurus R .25 .75
BP01027 Num. 17: Leviathan R .25 .75
BP01028 Wind-Up Zenmaister R .25 .75
BP01029 Tiras, Keeper R 2.00 5.00
BP01030 Adreus, Keeper R 2.50 6.00
BP01031 Gem-Knight Pearl R .25 .75
BP01032 Raigeki R 10.00 25.00
BP01033 Swords of Revealing R .25 .75
BP01034 Pot of Greed R .60 1.50
BP01035 Harpie's Feather R 2.50 6.00
BP01036 Graceful Charity R .25 .75
BP01037 Change of Heart (R) .75 2.00
BP01038 Heavy Storm R .25 .75
BP01039 Snatch Steal R .25 .75
BP01040 Premature Burial R .25 .75
BP01041 Soul Exchange R .25 .75
BP01042 Scapegoat R .25 .75
BP01043 United We Stand R 1.50 4.00
BP01044 Creature Swap R .25 .75
BP01045 Burden of Mighty R .25 .75
BP01046 Pot of Duality R .60 1.50
BP01047 Solemn Judgment R .25 .75
BP01048 Mirror Force R 1.00 2.50
BP01049 Call of the Haunted R .25 .75
BP01050 Ring of Destruction R .75 2.00
BP01051 Torrential Tribute R .75 2.00
BP01052 Metal Reflect Slime R .40 1.00
BP01053 Skill Drain R 2.00 5.00
BP01054 Divine Wrath R .25 .75
BP01055 Dark Bribe R .75 2.00
BP01056 Greenkappa .10 .30
BP01057 Penguin Soldier .10 .30
BP01058 Mysterious Guard .10 .30
BP01059 Exiled Force .10 .30
BP01060 Old Vindictive Magician .10 .30
BP01061 Breaker of the Magical .10 .30
BP01062 Grave Squirmer .10 .30
BP01063 Ryko, Lightsworn Hunter .10 .30
BP01064 Snowman Eater .10 .30
BP01065 Fissure .10 .30
BP01066 Tribute to the Doomed .10 .30
BP01067 Axe of Despair .10 .30
BP01068 Mystical Space Typhoon .50 1.25
BP01069 Horn of the Unicorn .10 .30
BP01070 Offerings to the Doomed .10 .30
BP01071 Bait Doll .10 .30
BP01072 Book of Moon .10 .30
BP01073 Autonomous Action Unit .10 .30
BP01074 Ante .10 .30
BP01075 Big Bang Shot .10 .30
BP01076 Fiend's Sanctuary .10 .30
BP01077 Different Dimension Gate .10 .30
BP01078 Enemy Controller .10 .30
BP01079 Monster Gate .10 .30
BP01080 Shield Crush .10 .30
BP01081 Fighting Spirit .10 .30
BP01082 Forbidden Chalice .10 .30
BP01083 Darkworld Shackles .10 .30
BP01084 Forbidden Lance .75 2.00
BP01085 Infected Mail .10 .30
BP01086 Ego Boost .10 .30
BP01087 Kunai with Chain .10 .30
BP01088 Dust Tornado .10 .30
BP01089 Windstorm of Etaqua .10 .30
BP01090 Magic Drain .10 .30
BP01091 Magic Cylinder .10 .30
BP01092 Shadow Spell .10 .30
BP01093 Blast with Chain .10 .30
BP01094 Needle Ceiling .10 .30
BP01095 Reckless Greed .40 1.00
BP01096 Nightmare Wheel .10 .30
BP01097 Spell Shield Type-8 .10 .30
BP01098 Interdimensional Matter Transporter .10 .30
BP01099 Compulsory Evacuation .10 .30
BP01100 Prideful Roar .10 .30
BP01101 Half or Nothing .10 .30
BP01102 Skill Successor .10 .30
BP01103 Pixie Ring .10 .30
BP01104 Changing Destiny .10 .30
BP01105 Fiendish Chain 1.00 2.50
BP01106 Inverse Universe .10 .30
BP01107 Miracle's Wake .10 .30
BP01108 Power Frame .10 .30
BP01109 Damage Gate .10 .30
BP01110 Liberty at Last! .10 .30
BP01111 Luster Dragon .10 .30
BP01112 Archfiend Soldier .10 .30
BP01113 Mad Dog of Darkness .10 .30
BP01114 Charcoal Inpachi .10 .30
BP01115 Insect Knight .10 .30
BP01116 Gene-Warped Warwolf .10 .30
BP01117 Buster Blader .10 .30
BP01118 Goblin Attack Force .10 .30
BP01119 Bazoo the Soul-Eater .10 .30
BP01120 Zombyra the Dark .10 .30
BP01121 Slate Warrior .10 .30
BP01122 Dark Ruler Ha Des .10 .30
BP01123 Freed the Matchless General .10 .30
BP01124 Airknight Parshath .10 .30
BP01125 Asura Priest .10 .30

BP01126 Exarion Universe .10 .30
BP01127 Vampire Lord .10 .30
BP01128 Toon Gemini Elf .10 .30
BP01129 King Tiger Wanghu .10 .30
BP01130 Guardian Sphinx .10 .30
BP01131 Skilled White Magician .10 .30
BP01132 Zaborg the Thunder Monarch .10 .30
BP01133 D.D. Assailant .10 .30
BP01134 Theban Nightmare .10 .30
BP01135 The Tricky .10 .30
BP01136 Raging Flame Sprite .10 .30
BP01137 Chiron the Mage .10 .30
BP01138 Cyber Dragon .10 .30
BP01139 Cybernetic Magician .10 .30
BP01140 Goblin Elite Attack Force .10 .30
BP01141 Doomcaliber Knight .10 .30
BP01142 Chainsaw Insect .10 .30
BP01143 Card Trooper .10 .30
BP01144 Voltic Kong .10 .30
BP01145 Botanical Lion .10 .30
BP01146 Ancient Gear Knight .10 .30
BP01147 Blizzard Dragon .40 1.00
BP01148 Beast King Barbaros .10 .30
BP01149 The Calculator .10 .30
BP01150 Gaap the Divine Soldier .10 .30
BP01151 Arcana Force XIV - Temperance .10 .30
BP01152 Dark Valkyria .10 .30
BP01153 Alector, Sovereign of Birds .10 .30
BP01154 Twin-Barrel Dragon .10 .30
BP01155 Abyssal Kingshark .10 .30
BP01156 Jurrac Protops .10 .30
BP01157 Hedge Guard .10 .30
BP01158 Fabled Ashenveil .10 .30
BP01159 Backup Warrior .10 .30
BP01160 Ambitious Gofer .10 .30
BP01161 Power Giant .10 .30
BP01162 Card Guard .10 .30
BP01163 Yaksha .10 .30
BP01164 Gogogo Golem .10 .30
BP01165 Big Jaws .10 .30
BP01166 Wind-Up Soldier .10 .30
BP01167 Wind-Up Dog .10 .30
BP01168 Milla the Temporal Magician .10 .30
BP01169 Ape Fighter .10 .30
BP01170 Wind-Up Warrior .10 .30
BP01171 Giant Soldier of Stone .10 .30
BP01172 Mask of Darkness .10 .30
BP01173 Morphing Jar .10 .30
BP01174 Muka Muka .10 .30
BP01175 Blast Sphere .10 .30
BP01176 Big Shield Gardna .10 .30
BP01177 Gilasaurus .10 .30
BP01178 Possessed Dark Soul .10 .30
BP01179 Twin-Headed Behemoth .10 .30
BP01180 Makyura the Destructor .10 .30
BP01181 Helping Robo for Combat .10 .30
BP01182 Zolga .10 .30
BP01183 Chaos Necromancer .10 .30
BP01184 Stealth Bird .40 1.00
BP01185 Hyper Hammerhead .10 .30
BP01186 Grave Protector .10 .30
BP01187 Night Assailant .10 .30
BP01188 Pitch-Black Warwolf .10 .30
BP01189 Dekoichi .10 .30
BP01190 Gyroid .10 .30
BP01191 Drillroid .10 .30
BP01192 Gravitic Orb .10 .30
BP01193 Cloudian - Poison Cloud .10 .30
BP01194 Des Mosquito .10 .30
BP01195 Mad Reloader .10 .30
BP01196 Phantom of Chaos .50 1.25
BP01197 Cyber Valley .10 .30
BP01198 Blue Thunder T-45 .10 .30
BP01199 Vortex Trooper .10 .30
BP01200 DUCKER Mobile Cannon .10 .30
BP01201 Worm Barses .10 .30
BP01202 Shield Warrior .10 .30
BP01203 Dark Resonator .10 .30
BP01204 Noisy Gnat .10 .30
BP01205 Fabled Raven .10 .30
BP01206 Fortress Warrior .10 .30
BP01207 Twin-Sword Marauder .10 .30
BP01208 Level Warrior .10 .30
BP01209 Level Eater .10 .30
BP01210 Naturia Strawberry .10 .30
BP01211 Battle Fader .50 1.25
BP01212 Amazoness Sage .10 .30
BP01213 Amazoness Trainee .10 .30
BP01214 Hardened Armed Dragon 1.00 2.50
BP01215 Blackwing - Zephyros .10 .30
BP01216 Tanngrisnir of the Nordic Beasts .10 .30
BP01217 Shine Knight .10 .30
BP01218 Gagaga Magician .10 .30
BP01219 Goblindbergh .10 .30
BP01220 Psi-Blocker .40 1.00

2013 Yu-Gi-Oh Battle Pack 2 War of the Giants

COMPLETE SET (212) 30.00 80.00
BOOSTER BOX (36 PACKS) 40.00 60.00
BOOSTER PACK (5 CARDS) 2.00 3.00
*MOSAIC: .6X TO 1.5X BASIC CARDS
RELEASED ON JUNE 28, 2013
BP02001 Luster Dragon C .25 .75
BP02002 Gene-Warped Warwolf C .10 .30
BP02003 Frostosaurus R .25 .75
BP02004 Alexandrite Dragon C .20 .60
BP02005 Magician of Faith R .50 1.25
BP02006 Maha Vailo C .10 .30
BP02007 Cyber Jar R .25 .75
BP02008 Goblin Attack Force C .10 .30
BP02009 The Fiend Megacyber R .25 .75
BP02010 Revival Jam C .10 .30
BP02011 Kycoo the Ghost Destroyer C .10 .30
BP02012 Bazoo the Soul-Eater C .10 .30
BP02013 Gilasaurus C .10 .30
BP02014 Zombyra the Dark C .10 .30
BP02015 Sinister Serpent C .20 .60
BP02016 Airknight Parshath R .25 .75
BP02017 Twin-Headed Behemoth C .10 .30
BP02018 Injection Fairy Lily R .25 .75
BP02019 Helping Robo for Combat C .10 .30
BP02020 Little-Winguard C .10 .30
BP02021 D.D. Warrior Lady R .25 .75
BP02022 Zolga C .10 .30
BP02023 Dark Magician of Chaos R .75 2.00
BP02024 Hyper Hammerhead C .10 .30
BP02025 Mataza the Zapper C .10 .30
BP02026 Guardian Angel Joan R .25 .75
BP02027 Slate Warrior R .25 .75
BP02028 D.D. Assailant R .25 .75
BP02029 Ninja Grandmaster Sasuke C .10 .30
BP02030 Pitch-Black Warwolf C .10 .30
BP02031 Mirage Dragon C .10 .30
BP02032 Big Shield Gardna C .10 .30
BP02033 Toon Gemini Elf C .10 .30
BP02034 Chiron the Mage C .10 .30
BP02035 Ancient Gear Golem R .25 .75
BP02036 Gyroid C .10 .30
BP02037 Steamroid C .10 .30
BP02038 Drillroid C .10 .30
BP02039 Cyber Dragon C .25 .75
BP02040 Goblin Elite Attack Force C .10 .30
BP02041 Exarion Universe C .10 .30
BP02042 Mythical Beast Cerberus C .10 .30
BP02043 Treeborn Frog C .20 .60
BP02044 Submarineroid C .10 .30
BP02045 Ultimate Tyranno R .25 .75
BP02046 Super Conductor Tyranno R .25 .75
BP02047 Brain Crusher R .25 .75
BP02048 Card Trooper C .10 .30
BP02049 Blockman C .10 .30
BP02050 Spell Striker C .50 1.25
BP02051 Winged Rhynos C .10 .30
BP02052 Necro Gardna C .10 .30
BP02053 Herald of Creation C .10 .30
BP02054 Evil HERO Malicious Edge R .25 .75
BP02055 Truckroid R .25 .75
BP02056 Ancient Gear Knight C .10 .30
BP02057 Dragon Ice C .10 .30
BP02058 Copycat C .50 1.25
BP02059 Cyber Valley R .25 .75
BP02060 Darklord Zerato R .25 .75
BP02061 Belial - Marquis of Darkness R .25 .75
BP02062 Doomcaliber Knight C .10 .30
BP02063 Exodius the Ultimate Forbidden Lord C .25 .75
BP02064 Dark Valkyria R .25 .75
BP02065 Phantom Dragon R .25 .75
BP02066 Shield Warrior C .10 .30
BP02067 Dark Resonator C .10 .30
BP02068 Krebons R .25 .75
BP02069 The Tricky C .10 .30
BP02070 Splendid Venus R .25 .75
BP02071 Plaguespreader Zombie C .50 1.25
BP02072 Machine Lord Ur C .10 .30
BP02073 Mosaic Manticore R .25 .75
BP02074 Botanical Lion C .10 .30
BP02075 Blizzard Dragon C .20 .60
BP02076 Des Mosquito C .10 .30
BP02077 Dandylion C .25 .75
BP02078 Fortress Warrior C .10 .30
BP02079 Twin-Sword Marauder C .10 .30
BP02080 Beast King Barbaros R .25 .75
BP02081 Hedge Guard C .10 .30
BP02082 Card Guard C .10 .30
BP02083 White Night Dragon R .25 .75
BP02084 Beast Machine King Barbaros Ür R .25 .75
BP02085 Evocator Chevalier C .10 .30
BP02086 Battle Fader C .60 1.50
BP02087 Oracle of the Sun C .10 .30
BP02088 Samurai of the Ice Barrier C .10 .30
BP02089 Jurrac Titano R .25 .75
BP02090 Darklord Desire R .25 .75
BP02091 Power Giant C .10 .30
BP02092 Anarchist Monk Ranshin C .10 .30
BP02093 Ape Fighter C .10 .30
BP02094 Tanngrisnir of the Nordic Beasts C .10 .30
BP02095 Chaos Hunter R .25 .75
BP02096 Axe Dragonute C .10 .30
BP02097 Vylon Soldier C .10 .30
BP02098 Blackwing - Zephyros the Elite C .20 .60
BP02099 Zubaba Knight C .10 .30
BP02100 Gogogo Golem C .10 .30
BP02101 Needle Sunfish C .10 .30
BP02102 Shocktopus C .10 .30
BP02103 Photon Thrasher C .60 1.50
BP02104 Interplanetarypurplythorny Dragon C .10 .30
BP02105 Tour Bus From the Underworld C .10 .30
BP02106 Vylon Tetra C .10 .30
BP02107 Vylon Stella C .10 .30
BP02108 Vylon Prism C .10 .30
BP02109 Photon Wyvern R .25 .75
BP02110 Tasuke Knight C .10 .30
BP02111 Gagaga Gardna C .10 .30
BP02112 Cardcar D R .25 .75
BP02113 Flame Tiger C .10 .30
BP02114 Tardy Orc C .10 .30
BP02115 Bull Blader R .25 .75
BP02116 Solar Wind Jammer C .10 .30
BP02117 Mermail Abyssmegalo R 3.00 8.00
BP02118 Dododo Bot C .10 .30
BP02119 Bacon Saver C .10 .30
BP02120 Amaryllease C .10 .30
BP02121 Hyper-Ancient Shark Megalodon R .25 .75
BP02122 Pyrotech Mech - Shiryu R .25 .75
BP02123 Aye-Iron C .10 .30
BP02124 Mecha Phantom Beast Hamstrat C .10 .30
BP02125 Obelisk the Tormentor R 6.00 15.00
BP02126 The Winged Dragon of Ra R 5.00 12.00
BP02127 Slifer the Sky Dragon R 8.00 20.00
BP02128 Monster Reborn R .50 1.25
BP02129 Pot of Greed R .75 2.00
BP02130 Shield & Sword C .10 .30
BP02131 Axe of Despair C .10 .30
BP02132 Malevolent Nuzzler C .10 .30
BP02133 Rush Recklessly C .10 .30
BP02134 Horn of the Unicorn C .10 .30
BP02135 Premature Burial R .25 .75
BP02136 Scapegoat C .20 .60
BP02137 Graceful Charity R .25 .75
BP02138 Book of Moon C .25 .75
BP02139 Reasoning C .75 2.00
BP02140 Autonomous Action Unit C .10 .30
BP02141 Big Bang Shot C .10 .30
BP02142 Riryoku C .10 .30
BP02143 Gravity Axe - Grarl C .10 .30
BP02144 Enemy Controller C .10 .30
BP02145 Earthquake C .10 .30
BP02146 Shrink C .10 .30
BP02147 Swords of Concealing Light C 1.00 2.50
BP02148 Nightmare's Steelcage C .10 .30
BP02149 Mausoleum of the Emperor C .10 .30
BP02150 Card Trader R .25 .75
BP02151 Fiend's Sanctuary C .10 .30
BP02152 Union Attack C .10 .30
BP02153 Fighting Spirit C .10 .30
BP02154 Star Blast C .10 .30
BP02155 Forbidden Chalice C .10 .30
BP02156 Reptilianne Rage C .10 .30
BP02157 Rocket Pilder C .10 .30
BP02158 Half Shut C .10 .30
BP02159 Cursed Armaments C .10 .30
BP02160 Pot of Duality R .75 2.00
BP02161 Axe of Fools C .10 .30
BP02162 Forbidden Lance C .75 2.00
BP02163 Blustering Winds C .10 .30
BP02164 Ego Boost C .10 .30
BP02165 Shard of Greed R .25 .75
BP02166 Full-Force Strike R .25 .75
BP02167 Photon Sanctuary C .40 1.00
BP02168 Forbidden Dress C .10 .30
BP02169 Reverse Trap C .10 .30
BP02170 Waboku C .20 .60
BP02171 Call of the Haunted R .40 1.00
BP02172 Mirror Wall C .10 .30
BP02173 Metalmorph C .10 .30
BP02174 Mask of Weakness C .10 .30
BP02175 Reckless Greed R .25 .75
BP02176 Rope of Life C .10 .30
BP02177 Windstorm of Etaqua C .10 .30
BP02178 Zero Gravity C .10 .30
BP02179 A Hero Emerges C .10 .30
BP02180 Embodiment of Apophis C .10 .30
BP02181 Draining Shield C .40 1.00
BP02182 Curse of Anubis C .10 .30
BP02183 Labyrinth of Nightmare C .10 .30
BP02184 Threatening Roar C .25 .75
BP02185 Rising Energy C .10 .30
BP02186 Magical Arm Shield C .10 .30
BP02187 Shattered Axe C .10 .30
BP02188 Stronghold the Moving Fortress C .10 .30
BP02189 Strike Slash C .10 .30
BP02190 No Entry!! C .10 .30
BP02191 Cloning C .10 .30
BP02192 Sinister Seeds C .10 .30
BP02193 Metal Reflect Slime C .50 1.25
BP02194 Zoma the Spirit C .10 .30
BP02195 Miniaturize C .10 .30
BP02196 Spacegate C .10 .30
BP02197 Overworked C .10 .30
BP02198 Kunai with Chain C .10 .30
BP02199 Prideful Roar C .10 .30
BP02200 Time Machine C .25 .75
BP02201 Half or Nothing C .10 .30
BP02202 Miracle Locus C .10 .30
BP02203 Skill Successor C .10 .30
BP02204 Power Frame C .10 .30
BP02205 Damage Gate C .10 .30
BP02206 Miracle's Wake C .10 .30
BP02207 Half Counter C .10 .30
BP02208 The Golden Apples R .25 .75
BP02209 Tiki Curse C .10 .30
BP02210 Tiki Soul C .10 .30
BP02211 Impenetrable Attack C .10 .30
BP02212 Memory of an Adversary R .25 .75
BP02213 Dimension Gate C .10 .30
BP02214 Spikeshield with Chain R .25 .75
BP02215 Breakthrough Skill C .75 2.00

2013 Yu-Gi-Oh Battle Pack 2 War of the Giants Mosaic Rare

*MOSAIC RARE: .6X TO 1.5X BASIC CARDS
STATED ODDS 1:1
BP02125 Obelisk the Tormentor R 6.00 15.00
BP02126 The Winged Dragon of Ra R 6.00 15.00
BP02127 Slifer the Sky Dragon R 12.00 30.00

2014 Yu-Gi-Oh Battle Pack 2 War of the Giants Round 2

COMPLETE SET (103) 20.00 60.00
BOOSTER BOX (6 PACKS) 80.00 100.00
BOOSTER PACK (5 CARDS) 15.00 20.00
RELEASED ON JANUARY 17, 2014
BPR2001 Evilswarm Heliotrope C .10 .30
BPR2002 Wall of Illusion SR .25 .75
BPR2003 Big Eye C .10 .30
BPR2004 Kazejin SR .25 .75
BPR2005 Otohime C .10 .30
BPR2006 Yomi Ship SR .25 .75
BPR2007 Winged Sage Falcos C .10 .30
BPR2008 Cyber Raider C .10 .30
BPR2009 Berserk Gorilla C .10 .30
BPR2010 Invader of Darkness C .10 .30
BPR2011 Legendary Jujitsu Master SR .25 .75
BPR2012 Blade Knight C .10 .30
BPR2013 Big-Tusked Mammoth SR .25 .75
BPR2014 Golem Sentry SR .25 .75
BPR2015 Adhesive Explosive SR .25 .75
BPR2016 Cyber Gymnast SR .25 .75
BPR2017 Cyber Prima (SR) .25 .75
BPR2018 Majestic Mech - Goryu C .10 .30
BPR2019 Destiny HERO - Defender C .40 1.00
BPR2020 Archfiend of Gilfer SR .25 .75
BPR2021 Legendary Fiend SR .25 .75
BPR2022 Lyla, Lightsworn Sorceress SR 1.00 2.50
BPR2023 Montage Dragon C .75 2.00
BPR2024 Cursed Fig SR .25 .75
BPR2025 Red Ogre SR .25 .75
BPR2026 Blackwing - Elphin the Raven SR .25 .75
BPR2027 Sauropod Brachion C .10 .30
BPR2028 Worm Apocalypse C .10 .30
BPR2029 Worm Jetelikpse C .10 .30
BPR2030 Infernity Destroyer SR .25 .75
BPR2031 Medium of the Ice Barrier C .10 .30
BPR2032 A/D Changer C .10 .30
BPR2033 Playful Possum C .10 .30
BPR2034 Hypnocorn SR .25 .75
BPR2035 Wattlemur C .10 .30
BPR2036 Fabled Soulkius SR .25 .75
BPR2037 Power Breaker C .10 .30
BPR2038 Jurrac Gallim C .10 .30
BPR2039 General Raiho of the Ice Barrier SR .25 .75
BPR2040 Meklord Army of Granel SR .25 .75
BPR2041 Skull Kraken C .10 .30
BPR2042 Skystarray C .10 .30
BPR2043 Sergeant Electro SR .25 .75
BPR2044 Chow Len the Prophet SR .25 .75
BPR2045 White Night Queen C .10 .30
BPR2046 Junk Forward C .10 .30
BPR2047 Swallowtail Butterspy C .10 .30
BPR2048 Cameraclops SR .25 .75
BPR2049 Madolche Baaple SR .25 .75
BPR2050 Evilswarm Ketos SR .25 .75
BPR2051 Evilswarm Mandragora C .20 .60
BPR2052 Mogmole C .10 .30
BPR2053 Deep Sweeper C .10 .30
BPR2054 Heroic Challenger - Night Watchman C .10 .30
BPR2055 Garbage Lord C .10 .30
BPR2056 D.D. Esper Star Sparrow C .10 .30
BPR2057 Evilswarm Obliviwisp C .10 .30
BPR2058 Evilswarm Salamandra C .10 .30
BPR2059 Dododo Warrior SR .25 .75
BPR2060 Mecha Phantom Beast Tetherwolf C .10 .30
BPR2061 Mecha Phantom Beast Blackfalcon C .10 .30
BPR2062 Mecha Phantom Beast Stealthray SR .25 .75
BPR2063 Gentlemander C .10 .30
BPR2064 Schwarzschild Limit Dragon C .10 .30
BPR2065 Tribute to The Doomed SR .25 .75
BPR2066 Share the Pain SR .25 .75
BPR2067 Slim-Pack C .10 .30
BPR2068 Black Pendant C .10 .30
BPR2069 Megamorph SR .25 .75
BPR2070 Dark Core SR .50 1.25
BPR2071 Different Dimension Gate SR .25 .75
BPR2072 Back to Square One SR .25 .75
BPR2073 Mystic Box SR .25 .75
BPR2074 Lucky Iron Axe C .10 .30
BPR2075 Double Summon C 1.00 2.50
BPR2076 Ribbon of Rebirth C .10 .30
BPR2077 Release Restraint Wave SR .25 .75
BPR2078 Berserk Scales C .10 .30
BPR2079 Shift SR .25 .75
BPR2080 Riryoku Field C .10 .30
BPR2081 Needle Ceiling C .25 .75
BPR2082 Pineapple Blast C .10 .30
BPR2083 Adhesion Trap Hole SR .25 .75
BPR2084 Covering Fire C .10 .30
BPR2085 Conscription C .10 .30
BPR2086 Chthonian Blast C .10 .30
BPR2087 Dark Bribe SR 1.25 3.00
BPR2088 Nordic Relic Laevateinn SR .25 .75
BPR2089 Nordic Relic Brisingamen SR .25 .75
BPR2090 Attention! C .10 .30
BPR2091 Raigeki Bottle SR .25 .75
BPR2092 Nitwit Outwit C .10 .30
BPR2093 Butterflyoke SR .25 .75
BPR2094 Dimension Slice C .20 .60
BPR2095 Magical Explosion SR .25 .75
BPR2096 Memory Loss C .10 .30
BPR2097 Butterspy Protection C .10 .30
BPR2098 Reverse Glasses C .10 .30
BPR2099 Fog King UR 6.00 15.00
BPR2100 High Priestess of Prophecy UR 2.50 6.00
BPR2101 Dragunity Knight - Vajrayana UR 2.00 5.00
BPR2102 Number 11: Big Eye UR 2.50 6.00
BPR2103 Safe Zone UR 1.25 3.00

2014 Yu-Gi-Oh Battle Pack 3 Monster League

COMPLETE SET (220 CARDS) 40.00 75.00
BOOSTER BOX (36 PACKS) 25.00 40.00
BOOSTER PACK 2.00 4.50
RELEASED ON AUGUST 1, 2014
BP03EN001 Jerry Beans Man C .15 .25
BP03EN002 Bazoo the Soul-Eater C .15 .25
BP03EN003 Frontier Wiseman C .15 .25
BP03EN004 Arsenal Bug R .15 .40
BP03EN005 Breaker the Magical Warrior R .20 .60
BP03EN006 Mudora R .15 .40
BP03EN007 Gale Lizard C .15 .25
BP03EN008 Berserk Gorilla R .15 .40
BP03EN009 Lord Poison C .15 .25
BP03EN010 Sacred Crane C .15 .25
BP03EN011 Enraged Battle Ox C .15 .25
BP03EN012 Hyper Hammerhead C .15 .25
BP03EN013 Slate Warrior R .15 .40
BP03EN014 Toon Gemini Elf R .15 .40
BP03EN015 Chiron the Mage R .15 .40
BP03EN016 Gyroid C .15 .25
BP03EN017 Goblin Elite Attack Force R .15 .40
BP03EN018 Mythical Beast Cerberus C .15 .25
BP03EN019 Machine King Prototype R .15 .40
BP03EN020 Cyber Phoenix C .15 .25
BP03EN021 Victory Viper XX03 C .15 .25
BP03EN022 Herald of Green Light C .15 .25
BP03EN023 Herald of Purple Light C .15 .25
BP03EN024 Submarineroid C .15 .25
BP03EN025 Black Stego C .15 .25
BP03EN026 Card Trooper R .15 .40
BP03EN027 Freya, Spirit of Victory C .15 .25
BP03EN028 Exploder Dragon C .30 .50
BP03EN029 Dweller in the Depths C .15 .25
BP03EN030 Winged Rhynos R .15 .40
BP03EN031 Blizzard Dragon R .20 .60
BP03EN032 Evil HERO Infernal Gainer C .15 .25
BP03EN033 Ancient Gear Knight R .15 .40
BP03EN034 Royal Firestorm Guards R .25 .75
BP03EN035 Dark Crusader C .15 .25
BP03EN036 The Immortal Bushi C .15 .25
BP03EN037 Black Veloci R .15 .40
BP03EN038 Sea Koala C .15 .25
BP03EN039 Blue Thunder T-45 R .15 .40
BP03EN040 Golden Flying Fish R .15 .40
BP03EN041 Aztekipede, the Worm Warrior R .15 .40
BP03EN042 Jain, Lightsworn Paladin R .15 .40
BP03EN043 Diskblade Rider R .15 .40
BP03EN044 Magical Exemplar R .20 .60
BP03EN045 Rigorous Reaver C .15 .25
BP03EN046 Mezuki R .60 1.50
BP03EN047 Gonogo C .15 .25
BP03EN048 Telekinetic Shocker R .15 .40
BP03EN049 Destructotron C .15 .25
BP03EN050 Herald of Orange Light R .40 1.00
BP03EN051 Psychic Jumper C .15 .25
BP03EN052 Seed of Flame C .15 .25
BP03EN053 Cross-Sword Beetle R .60 1.00
BP03EN054 Defender, the Magical Knight C .15 .25
BP03EN055 Battlestorm R .15 .40
BP03EN056 Koa'ki Meiru Guardian R .15 .40
BP03EN057 Koa'ki Meiru Drago R .75 2.00
BP03EN058 Koa'ki Meiru Doom R .15 .40
BP03EN059 Spined Gillman R .15 .40
BP03EN060 Vanguard of the Dragon R .15 .40
BP03EN061 Koa'ki Meiru War Arms C .15 .25
BP03EN062 Tree Otter C .25 .40
BP03EN063 X-Saber Airbellum C .15 .25
BP03EN064 Sunlight Unicorn R .15 .40
BP03EN065 Card Guard R .15 .40
BP03EN066 Koa'ki Meiru Beetle R .15 .40
BP03EN067 Reptilianne Gorgon C .15 .25
BP03EN068 Metabo-Shark R .15 .40
BP03EN069 Shutendoji C .30 .50
BP03EN070 Gauntlet Warrior C .15 .25
BP03EN071 Shreddder C .15 .25
BP03EN072 Koa'ki Meiru Sandman R .15 .40
BP03EN073 Jurrac Protops C .15 .25
BP03EN074 Mist Valley Falcon R .15 .40
BP03EN075 Trident Warrior R .15 .40
BP03EN076 Rhinotaurus R .15 .40
BP03EN077 Hypnocorn C .15 .25
BP03EN078 Stygian Street Patrol C .40 .60
BP03EN079 Fabled Ashenveil C .15 .25
BP03EN080 Chain Dog C .15 .25
BP03EN081 Koa'ki Meiru Wall R .15 .40
BP03EN082 Genex Ally Bellflame R .15 .40
BP03EN083 Meklord Army of Granel C .15 .25
BP03EN084 Silent Psychic Wizard R .15 .40
BP03EN085 Dodger Dragon R .50 1.25
BP03EN086 Wind-Up Juggler R .15 .40
BP03EN087 Airorca C .15 .25
BP03EN088 Time Escaper C .15 .25
BP03EN089 Lion Alligator R .15 .40
BP03EN090 Friller Rabca C .15 .25
BP03EN091 Vylon Ohm C .15 .25
BP03EN092 Shocktopus C .15 .25
BP03EN093 Chow Len the Prophet R .15 .40
BP03EN094 Vampire Koala R .15 .40
BP03EN095 Flame Tiger R .15 .40
BP03EN096 Tardy Orc R .15 .40
BP03EN097 Madolche Baaple C .15 .25
BP03EN098 Evilswarm Ketos R .15 .40
BP03EN099 Evilswarm O'lantern C .15 .25
BP03EN100 Electromagnetic Bagworm C .15 .25
BP03EN101 Uminotaurus C .15 .25
BP03EN102 Leotaur R .15 .40
BP03EN103 Aye-Iron R .15 .40
BP03EN104 Evilswarm Thunderbird C .30 .50
BP03EN105 Magical Undertaker C .15 .25
BP03EN106 Gentlemander C .15 .25
BP03EN107 Fencing Fire Ferret R .15 .40
BP03EN108 Skelesaurus R .15 .40
BP03EN109 Knight Day Grepher R .15 .40
BP03EN110 Gorgonic Golem C .15 .25
BP03EN111 Ghostrick Jackfrost C .15 .25
BP03EN112 Black Brachios R .15 .40
BP03EN113 Tackle Crusader C .15 .25
BP03EN114 Stegocyber C .15 .25
BP03EN115 Master Craftsman Gamil C .15 .25
BP03EN133 Swords of Revealing Light C .15 .25
BP03EN134 Rush Recklessly C .15 .25
BP03EN135 7 Completed C .15 .25
BP03EN136 Premature Burial C .15 .25

Card	Low	High
BP03EN137 Mask of Brutality C	.15	.25
BP03EN138 Offerings to the Doomed C	.15	.25
BP03EN139 Scapegoat C	.30	.50
BP03EN140 The Warrior Returning Alive C	.15	.25
BP03EN141 Dragon's Gunfire C	.15	.25
BP03EN142 Stamping Destruction C	.15	.25
BP03EN143 Fusion Sword Murasame Blade C	.15	.25
BP03EN144 Creature Swap C	.15	.25
BP03EN145 Book of Life C	.25	.40
BP03EN146 Call of the Mummy C	.15	.25
BP03EN147 Banner of Courage C	.15	.25
BP03EN148 Cestus of Dagla C	.15	.25
BP03EN149 Enemy Controller C	.15	.25
BP03EN150 Earthquake C	.15	.25
BP03EN151 Swords of Concealing Light C	3.75	5.00
BP03EN152 Magicians Unite C	.15	.25
BP03EN153 Ribbon of Rebirth C	.15	.25
BP03EN154 Valhalla, Hall of the Fallen C	1.75	2.25
BP03EN155 Fighting Spirit C	.15	.25
BP03EN156 Psi-Station C	.15	.25
BP03EN157 Unstable Evolution C	.15	.25
BP03EN158 Recycling Batteries C	.20	.30
BP03EN159 Book of Eclipse C	.60	1.00
BP03EN160 Mark of the Rose C	.30	.50
BP03EN161 Psychokinesis C	.15	.25
BP03EN162 Miracle Fertilizer C	.75	1.00
BP03EN163 Psychic Sword C	.15	.25
BP03EN164 Forbidden Chalice C	.30	.50
BP03EN165 Raging Mad Plants C	.15	.25
BP03EN166 Reptilianne Rage C	.15	.25
BP03EN167 Machine Assembly Line C	.15	.25
BP03EN168 Pyramid of Wonders C	.15	.25
BP03EN169 Cursed Armaments C	.15	.25
BP03EN170 Wattjustment C	.15	.25
BP03EN171 Closed Forest C	.15	.25
BP03EN172 Forbidden Lance C	1.00	1.50
BP03EN173 Wonder Wand C	.30	.50
BP03EN174 Murmur of the Forest C	.15	.25
BP03EN175 Bound Wand C	.15	.25
BP03EN176 Night Beam C	.30	.50
BP03EN177 Spellbook of Wisdom C	.50	.75
BP03EN178 Call of the Atlanteans C	.15	.25
BP03EN179 One-Shot Wand C	.15	.25
BP03EN180 Forbidden Dress C	.15	.25
BP03EN181 Noble Arms - Arfeudutyr C	.15	.25
BP03EN182 Noble Arms - Caliburn C	.15	.25
BP03EN183 Ayers Rock Sunrise C	.15	.25
BP03EN184 Forbidden Scripture C	.15	.25
BP03EN185 Card Advance C	5.00	6.00
BP03EN186 Bashing Shield C	.20	.35
BP03EN187 Call of the Haunted C	.15	.25
BP03EN188 Mirror Wall C	.15	.25
BP03EN189 Metalmorph C	.15	.25
BP03EN190 Mask of Weakness C	.15	.25
BP03EN191 Bark of Dark Ruler C	.15	.25
BP03EN192 Ready for Intercepting C	.15	.25
BP03EN193 Burst Breath C	.15	.25
BP03EN194 Blast with Chain C	.15	.25
BP03EN195 Tutan Mask C	.15	.25
BP03EN196 Windstorm of Etaqua C	.15	.25
BP03EN197 Zero Gravity C	.15	.25
BP03EN198 Shadow Spell C	.15	.25
BP03EN199 Curse of Anubis C	.15	.25
BP03EN200 Rare Metalmorph C	.15	.25
BP03EN201 Magical Arm Shield C	.15	.25
BP03EN202 Dark Bribe C	1.00	1.50
BP03EN203 Chaos Burst C	.15	.25
BP03EN204 No Entry!! C	.15	.25
BP03EN205 Hate Buster C	.15	.25
BP03EN206 Miniaturize C	.15	.25
BP03EN207 Psychic Overload C	.15	.25
BP03EN208 Telepathic Power C	.15	.25
BP03EN209 Mind Over Matter C	.20	.30
BP03EN210 Kunai with Chain C	.15	.25
BP03EN211 Pollinosis C	.15	.25
BP03EN212 Plant Food Chain C	.15	.25
BP03EN213 Miracle Locus C	.15	.25
BP03EN214 Skill Successor C	.15	.25
BP03EN215 Alien Brain C	.15	.25
BP03EN216 Forgotten Temple of the Deep C	.15	.25
BP03EN217 Psi-Curse C	.15	.25
BP03EN218 Damage Gate C	.15	.25
BP03EN219 Super Rush Recklessly C	.15	.25
BP03EN220 Miracle's Wake C	.15	.25
BP03EN221 Nordic Relic Laevateinn C	.15	.25
BP03EN222 Psychic Reactor C	.15	.25
BP03EN223 Poseidon Wave C	.15	.25
BP03EN224 Raigeki Bottle C	.15	.25
BP03EN225 Butterflyoke C	.15	.25
BP03EN226 Dimension Gate C	.15	.25
BP03EN227 Breakthrough Skill C	1.00	1.50
BP03EN228 Pinpoint Guard C	.25	.40
BP03EN229 Memory Loss C	.15	.25
BP03EN230 Butterspy Protection C	.15	.25
BP03EN231 Intrigue Shield C	.15	.25
BP03EN232 Inspiration C	.15	.25
BP03EN233 Ghosts From the Past C	.15	.25
BP03EN234 Unbreakable Spirit C	.15	.25
BP03EN235 Typhoon C	.75	1.25
BP03EN236 Swamp Mirrorer C	.25	.40
BP03EN237 Quantum Cat C	.40	.60

2015 Yu-Gi-Oh War of the Giants Reinforcements

Card	Low	High
COMPLETE SET (104 CARDS)	40.00	60.00
RELEASED ON		
WGRTEN001 Evilswarm Heliotrope C	.30	.50
WGRTEN002 Wall of Illusion SR	.30	.50
WGRTEN003 Big Eye C	.20	.30
WGRTEN004 Kazejin SR	.25	.40
WGRTEN005 Otohime C	.10	.20
WGRTEN006 Yomi Ship SR	.15	.25
WGRTEN007 Winged Sage Falcos C	.10	.20
WGRTEN008 Cyber Raider C	.10	.20
WGRTEN009 Berserk Gorilla C	.15	.25
WGRTEN010 Invader of Darkness C	.10	.20
WGRTEN011 Legendary Jujitsu Master SR	.15	.25
WGRTEN012 Blade Knight C	.10	.20
WGRTEN013 Big-Tusked Mammoth SR	.15	.25
WGRTEN014 Golem Sentry SR	.20	.35
WGRTEN015 Adhesive Explosive SR	.15	.25
WGRTEN016 Cyber Gymnast SR	.15	.25
WGRTEN017 Cyber Prima SR	.20	.30
WGRTEN018 Majestic Mech - Goryu C	.10	.20
WGRTEN019 Destiny HERO - Defender C	.60	1.00
WGRTEN020 Archfiend of Gilfer SR	.20	.30
WGRTEN021 Legendary Fiend SR	.30	.50
WGRTEN022 Lyla, Lightsworn Sorceress SR	2.00	2.50
WGRTEN023 Montage Dragon C	1.50	1.75
WGRTEN024 Cursed Fig SR	.15	.25
WGRTEN025 Red Ogre SR	.15	.25
WGRTEN026 Blackwing - Elphin the Raven SR	.15	.25
WGRTEN027 Sauropod Brachion C	.20	.30
WGRTEN028 Worm Apocalypse C	.10	.20
WGRTEN029 Worm Jetelikpse C	.10	.20
WGRTEN030 Infernity Destroyer SR	.25	.40
WGRTEN031 Medium of the Ice Barrier C	.20	.30
WGRTEN032 A/D Changer C	.10	.20
WGRTEN033 Playful Possum C	.10	.20
WGRTEN034 Hypnocorn SR	.15	.25
WGRTEN035 Wattlemur C	.15	.25
WGRTEN036 Fabled Soulkius SR	.20	.35
WGRTEN037 Power Breaker C	.10	.20
WGRTEN038 Jurrac Gallim C	.15	.25
WGRTEN039 General Raiho of the Ice Barrier SR	.15	.25
WGRTEN040 Meklord Army of Granel SR	.15	.25
WGRTEN041 Skull Kraken C	.10	.20
WGRTEN042 Skystarray C	.10	.20
WGRTEN043 Sergeant Electro SR	.15	.25
WGRTEN044 Chow Len the Prophet SR	.15	.25
WGRTEN045 White Night Queen C	.10	.20
WGRTEN046 Junk Forward C	.40	.60
WGRTEN047 Swallowtail Butterspy C	.10	.20
WGRTEN048 Cameraclops SR	.15	.25
WGRTEN049 Madolche Baaple SR	.30	.50
WGRTEN050 Evilswarm Ketos SR	.15	.25
WGRTEN051 Evilswarm Mandragora C	.40	.60
WGRTEN052 Mogmole C	.10	.20
WGRTEN053 Deep Sweeper C	.10	.20
WGRTEN054 Heroic Challenger - Night Watchman C	.15	.25
WGRTEN055 Garbage Lord C	.20	.30
WGRTEN056 D.D. Esper Star Sparrow C	.10	.20
WGRTEN057 Evilswarm Obliviwisp C	.10	.20
WGRTEN058 Evilswarm Salamandra C	.30	.50
WGRTEN059 Dododo Warrior SR	.20	.35
WGRTEN060 Mecha Phantom Beast Tetherwolf C	.10	.20
WGRTEN061 Mecha Phantom Beast Blacktalcon C	.15	.25
WGRTEN062 Mecha Phantom Beast Stealthray SR	.15	.25
WGRTEN063 Gentlemander C	.15	.25
WGRTEN064 Schwarzschild Limit Dragon C	.50	.75
WGRTEN065 Tribute to The Doomed SR	.15	.25
WGRTEN066 Share the Pain SR	.30	.50
WGRTEN067 Stim-Pack C	.10	.20
WGRTEN068 Black Pendant C	.10	.20
WGRTEN069 Megamorph SR	.75	1.00
WGRTEN070 Dark Core SR	.75	1.15
WGRTEN071 Different Dimension Gate SR	.20	.35
WGRTEN072 Back to Square One SR	.40	.60
WGRTEN073 Mystic Box SR	.60	1.00
WGRTEN074 Lucky Iron Axe C	.10	.20
WGRTEN075 Double Summon C	2.00	2.25
WGRTEN076 Ribbon of Rebirth C	.10	.20
WGRTEN077 Release Restraint Wave SR	.50	.80
WGRTEN078 Berserk Scales C	.10	.20
WGRTEN079 Shift SR	.20	.30
WGRTEN080 Riryoku Field C	.10	.20
WGRTEN081 Needle Ceiling C	.50	.75
WGRTEN082 Pineapple Blast C	.10	.20
WGRTEN083 Adhesion Trap Hole SR	.30	.50
WGRTEN084 Covering Fire C	.10	.20
WGRTEN085 Conscription C	.10	.20
WGRTEN086 Chthonian Blast C	.10	.20
WGRTEN087 Dark Bribe SR	3.00	3.50
WGRTEN088 Nordic Relic Brisingamen SR	.15	.25
WGRTEN089 Nordic Relic Laevateinn SR	.25	.40
WGRTEN090 Attention! C	.10	.20
WGRTEN091 Raigeki Bottle SR	.15	.25
WGRTEN092 Nitwit Outwit C	.10	.20
WGRTEN093 Butterflyoke SR	.15	.25
WGRTEN094 Dimension Slice C	.40	.60
WGRTEN095 That Wacky Alchemy! C	.10	.20
WGRTEN096 Memory Loss C	.20	.35
WGRTEN097 Butterspy Protection C	.15	.25
WGRTEN098 Reverse Glasses C	.10	.20
WGRTEN099 Fog King UR	.15	.25
WGRTEN100 High Priestess of Prophecy UR	5.00	5.50
WGRTEN101 Dragunity Knight - Vajrayana UR	4.00	5.00
WGRTEN102 Number 11: Big Eye UR	5.00	6.00
WGRTEN103 Safe Zone UR	2.50	3.25
WGRTEN104 Zubaba General UR	.15	.25

2002 Yu-Gi-Oh Kaiba Starter Deck 1st Edition

Card	Low	High
Complete Set (50)	80.00	120.00
SDK1 Blue Eyes White Dragon UR	50.00	100.00
SDK2 Hitotsu-Me Giant C	.20	.50
SDK3 Ryu-Kishin C	.20	.50
SDK4 Wicked Worm Beast C	.20	.50
SDK5 Battle Ox C	.20	.50
SDK6 Koumori Dragon C	.20	.50
SDK7 Judge Man C	.20	.50
SDK8 Rogue Doll C	.20	.50
SDK9 Kojikocy C	.20	.50
SDK10 Uraby C	.20	.50
SDK11 Gyakutenno Megami C	.20	.50
SDK12 Mystic Horseman C	.20	.50
SDK13 Terra the Terrible C	.20	.50
SDK14 Dark Titan of Terror C	.20	.50
SDK15 Dark Assassin C	.50	1.00
SDK16 Master and Expert C	.20	.50
SDK17 Unknown Warrior of Fiend C	.20	.50
SDK18 Mystic Clown C	.20	.50
SDK19 Ogre of Black Shadow C	.20	.50
SDK20 Dark Energy C	.20	.50
SDK21 Invigoration C	.20	.50
SDK22 Dark Hole C	.50	1.00
SDK23 Ookazi C	.20	.50
SDK24 Ryu-Kishin Powered C	.20	.50
SDK25 Swordstalker C	.20	.50
SDK26 La Jinn the Mystical Genie C	1.00	2.00
SDK27 Rude Kaiser C	.50	1.00
SDK28 Destroyer Golem C	.20	.50
SDK29 Skull Red Bird C	.20	.50
SDK30 D. Human C	.20	.50
SDK31 Pale Beast C	.20	.50
SDK32 Fissure C	.50	1.00
SDK33 Trap Hole C	.20	.50
SDK34 Two-Pronged Attack C	.20	.50
SDK35 De-Spell C	.20	.50
SDK36 Monster Reborn C	2.00	4.00
SDK37 Inexperienced Spy C	.20	.50
SDK38 Reinforcements C	.20	.50
SDK39 Ancient Telescope C	.20	.50
SDK40 Just Desserts C	.20	.50
SDK41 Lord of D. SR	1.25	3.00
SDK42 Flute of Summoning Dragon SR	1.25	3.00
SDK43 Mysterious Puppeteer C	.20	.50
SDK44 Trap Master C	.10	.30
SDK45 Sogen C	.20	.50
SDK46 Hane-Hane C	.20	.50
SDK47 Reverse Trap C	.20	.50
SDK48 Reverse Trap C	.20	.50
SDK49 Castle Walls C	.20	.50
SDK50 Ultimate Offering C	.20	.50

2002 Yu-Gi-Oh Yugi Starter Deck 1st Edition

Card	Low	High
Complete Set (50)	100.00	150.00
SDY1 Mystical Elf C	.75	2.00
SDY2 Feral Imp C	.75	2.00
SDY3 Winged Dragon Guardian C	.75	2.00
SDY4 Summoned Skull C	.75	2.00
SDY5 Beaver Warrior C	.75	2.00
SDY6 Dark Magician UR	60.00	100.00
SDY7 Gaia The Fierce Knight C	.75	2.00
SDY8 Curse of Dragon C	.75	2.00
SDY9 Celtic Guardian C	.75	2.00
SDY10 Mammoth Graveyard C	.75	2.00
SDY11 Great White C	.75	2.00
SDY12 Silver Fang C	.75	2.00
SDY13 Giant Soldier of Stone C	.75	2.00
SDY14 Dragon Zombie C	.75	2.00
SDY15 Doma Angel of Silence C	.75	2.00
SDY16 Ansatsu C	.75	2.00
SDY17 Witty Phantom C	.75	2.00
SDY18 Claw Reacher C	.75	2.00
SDY19 Mystic Clown C	.75	2.00
SDY20 Sword of Dark Destruction C	.75	2.00
SDY21 Book of Secret Arts C	.75	2.00
SDY22 Dark Hole C	.75	2.00
SDY23 Dian Keto the Cure Master C	.75	2.00
SDY24 Ancient Elf C	.75	2.00
SDY25 Magical Ghost C	.75	2.00
SDY26 Fissure C	.75	2.00
SDY27 Trap Hole C	.75	2.00
SDY28 Two-Pronged Attack C	.75	2.00
SDY29 De-Spell C	.75	2.00
SDY30 Monster Reborn C	.75	2.00
SDY31 Reinforcements C	.75	2.00
SDY32 Change of Heart C	.75	2.00
SDY33 The Stern Mystic C	.75	2.00
SDY34 Wall of Illusion C	.75	2.00
SDY35 Neo the Magic Swordsman C	.75	2.00
SDY36 Baron of Fiend Sword C	.75	2.00
SDY37 Man-Eating Treasure Chest C	.75	2.00
SDY38 Sorcerer of the Doomed C	.75	2.00
SDY39 Last Will C	.75	2.00
SDY40 Waboku C	.75	2.00
SDY41 Soul Exchange SR	2.50	6.00
SDY42 Card Destruction SR	.75	2.00
SDY43 Trap Master C	.75	2.00
SDY44 Dragon Capture Jar C	.75	2.00
SDY45 Yami C	.75	2.00
SDY46 Man-Eater Bug C	.75	2.00
SDY47 Reverse Trap C	.75	2.00
SDY48 Remove Trap C	.75	2.00
SDY49 Castle Walls C	.75	2.00
SDY50 Ultimate Offering C	.75	2.00

2003 Yu-Gi-Oh Joey Starter Deck 1st Edition

Card	Low	High
Complete Set (50)	30.00	50.00
SDJ1 Red-Eyes B. Dragon UR	8.00	20.00
SDJ2 Swordsman of Landstar C	.60	1.50
SDJ3 Baby Dragon C	.60	1.50
SDJ4 Spirit of the Harp C	.60	1.50
SDJ5 Island Turtle C	.60	1.50
SDJ6 Flame Manipulator C	.60	1.50
SDJ7 Masaki The Legendary Swordsman C	.60	1.50
SDJ8 7 Colored Fish C	.60	1.50
SDJ9 Armored Lizard C	.60	1.50
SDJ10 Darkfire Soldier #1 C	.60	1.50
SDJ11 Harpie's Brother C	.60	1.50
SDJ12 Gearfried the Iron Knight C	.60	1.50
SDJ13 Karate Man C	.60	1.50
SDJ14 Milus Radiant C	.60	1.50
SDJ15 Time Wizard C	.60	1.50
SDJ16 Maha Vailo C	.60	1.50
SDJ17 Magician of Faith C	.60	1.50
SDJ18 Big Eye C	.60	1.50
SDJ19 Sangan C	.60	1.50
SDJ20 Princess of Tsurugi C	.60	1.50
SDJ21 White Magical Hat C	.60	1.50
SDJ22 Penguin Soldier SR	.60	1.50
SDJ23 Thousand Dragon C	.60	1.50
SDJ24 Flame Swordsman C	.60	1.50
SDJ25 Malevolent Nuzzler C	.60	1.50
SDJ26 Dark Hole C	.60	1.50
SDJ27 Dian Keto C	.60	1.50
SDJ28 Fissure C	.60	1.50
SDJ29 De-Spell C	.60	1.50
SDJ30 Change of Heart C	.60	1.50
SDJ31 Block Attack C	.60	1.50
SDJ32 Giant Trunade C	.60	1.50
SDJ33 The Reliable Guardian C	.60	1.50
SDJ34 Remove Trap C	.60	1.50
SDJ35 Monster Reborn C	.60	1.50
SDJ36 Polymerization C	.60	1.50
SDJ37 Mountain C	.60	1.50
SDJ38 Dragon Treasure C	.60	1.50
SDJ39 Eternal Rest C	.60	1.50
SDJ40 Shield & Sword C	.60	1.50
SDJ41 Scapegoat SR	.60	1.50
SDJ42 Just Desserts C	.60	1.50
SDJ43 Trap Hole C	.60	1.50
SDJ44 Reinforcements C	.60	1.50
SDJ45 Castle Walls C	.60	1.50
SDJ46 Waboku C	.60	1.50
SDJ47 Ultimate Offering C	.60	1.50
SDJ48 Seven Tools of the Bandit C	.60	1.50
SDJ49 Fake Trap C	.60	1.50
SDJ50 Reverse Trap C	.60	1.50

2003 Yu-Gi-Oh Pegasus Starter Deck 1st Edition

Card	Low	High
Complete Set (50)	20.00	40.00
SDP1 Relinquished UR	3.00	8.00
SDP2 Red Archery Girl C	.20	.50
SDP3 Ryu-Ran C	.20	.50
SDP4 Illusionist Faceless Mage C	.20	.50
SDP5 Rogue Doll C	.20	.50
SDP6 Uraby C	.20	.50
SDP7 Giant Soldier of Stone C	.20	.50
SDP8 Aqua Madoor C	.20	.50
SDP9 Toon Alligator C	.75	2.00
SDP10 Hane-Hane C	.20	.50
SDP11 Sonic Bird C	.20	.50
SDP12 Jigen Bakudan C	.20	.50
SDP13 Mask of Darkness C	.20	.50
SDP14 Witch of the Black Forest C	.20	.50
SDP15 Man-Eater Bug C	.20	.50
SDP16 Muka Muka C	.20	.50
SDP17 Dream Clown C	.20	.50
SDP18 Armed Ninja C	.20	.50
SDP19 Hiro's Shadow C	.20	.50
SDP20 Blue-Eyes Toon Dragon C	.50	1.00
SDP21 Toon Summoned Skull C	.20	.50
SDP22 Manga Ryu-Ran C	.20	.50
SDP23 Toon Mermaid C	.50	1.00
SDP24 Toon World C	1.00	2.00
SDP25 Black Pendant C	.20	.50
SDP26 Dark Hole C	.50	1.00
SDP27 Dian Keto The Cure Master C	.20	.50
SDP28 Fissure C	.20	.50
SDP29 De-Spell C	.20	.50
SDP30 Change of Heart C	.20	.50
SDP31 Stop Defense C	.20	.50
SDP32 Mystical Space Typhoon C	.20	.50
SDP33 Rush Recklessly C	.20	.50
SDP34 Remove Trap C	.20	.50
SDP35 Monster Reborn C	.50	1.00
SDP36 Soul Release C	.20	.50
SDP37 Yami C	.20	.50
SDP38 Black Illusion Ritual C	.20	.50
SDP39 Ring of Magnetism C	.20	.50
SDP40 Graceful Charity SR	1.50	4.00
SDP41 Trap Hole C	.20	.50
SDP42 Reinforcements C	.20	.50
SDP43 Castle Walls C	.20	.50
SDP44 Waboku C	.20	.50
SDP45 Seven Tools of the Bandit C	.20	.50
SDP46 Ultimate Offering C	.20	.50
SDP47 Robbin Goblin C	.20	.50
SDP48 Magic Jammer C	.20	.50
SDP49 Enchanted Javelin C	.20	.50
SDP50 Gryphon Wing SR	.50	1.00

2004 Yu-Gi-Oh Kaiba Evolution Starter Deck 1st Edition

Card	Low	High
Complete Set (50)	3.00	6.00
SKE-1 Blue-Eyes White Dragon (UR)	5.00	10.00

2004 Yu-Gi-Oh Yugi Evolution Starter Deck 1st Edition

Card	Low	High
Complete Set (50)	12.00	20.00
SYE1 Dark Magician UR	3.00	6.00
SYE24 Black Luster Soldier	2.00	5.00

2005 Yu-Gi-Oh Dragon's Roar 1st Edition

Card	Low	High
Complete Set (28)	8.00	20.00
SD1E1 Red-Eyes Darkness Dragon UR	2.00	5.00
SD1E2 Red-Eyes B. Dragon C	.50	1.00
SD1E3 Luster Dragon C	.20	.50
SD1E4 Twin-Headed Behemoth C	.20	.50
SD1E5 Armed Dragon LV3 C	.20	.50
SD1E6 Armed Dragon LV5 C	.20	.50
SD1E7 Red-Eyes B. Chick C	.20	.50
SD1E8 Element Dragon C	.20	.50
SD1E9 Masked Dragon C	.20	.50
SD1E10 Snatch Steal C	.20	.50
SD1E11 Mystical Space Typhoon C	.50	1.25
SD1E12 Nobleman of Crossout C	.20	.50
SD1E13 Premature Burial C	.20	.50
SD1E14 Swords of Revealing Light C	.20	.50
SD1E15 Pot of Greed C	.50	1.25
SD1E16 Heavy Storm C	.20	.50
SD1E17 Stamping Destruction C	.20	.50
SD1E18 Creature Swap C	.20	.50
SD1E19 Reload C	.20	.50
SD1E20 The Graveyard in the Fourth Dimension C	.20	.50
SD1E21 Call of the Haunted C	.20	.50
SD1E22 Ceasefire C	.20	.50
SD1E23 The Dragon's Bead C	.20	.50
SD1E24 Dragon's Rage C	.20	.50
SD1E25 Reckless Greed C	.40	1.00
SD1E26 Interdimensional Matter C	.20	.50
SD1E27 Trap Jammer C	.20	.50
SD1E28 Curse of Anubis C	.20	.50

2005 Yu-Gi-Oh Zombie Madness 1st Edition

Card	Low	High
Complete Set (28)	6.00	15.00
SD2E1 Vampire Genesis UR	1.50	4.00
SD2E2 Master Kyonshee C	.20	.50
SD2E3 Vampire Lord C	.20	.50
SD2E4 Dark Dust Spirit C	.20	.50
SD2E5 Pyramid Turtle C	.20	.50
SD2E6 Spirit Reaper C	.20	.50
SD2E7 Despair From The Dark C	.20	.50
SD2E8 Ryu Kokki C	.20	.50
SD2E9 Soul-Absorbing Bone Tower C	.20	.50
SD2E10 Vampire Lady C	.20	.50
SD2E11 Double Coston C	.20	.50
SD2E12 Regenerating Mummy C	.20	.50
SD2E13 Snatch Steal C	.40	1.00
SD2E14 Mystical Space Typhoon C	.75	2.00
SD2E15 Giant Trunade C	.20	.50
SD2E16 Nobleman of Crossout C	.20	.50
SD2E17 Pot of Greed C	.50	1.25
SD2E18 Card of Safe Return C	.20	.50
SD2E19 Heavy Storm C	.20	.50
SD2E20 Creature Swap C	.20	.50
SD2E21 Book of Life C	.20	.50
SD2E22 Call of the Mummy C	.20	.50
SD2E23 Reload C	.20	.50
SD2E24 Dust Tornado C	.20	.50
SD2E25 Torrential Tribute C	.75	2.00
SD2E26 Magic Jammer C	.20	.50
SD2E27 Reckless Greed C	.50	1.25
SD2E28 Compulsory Evacuation Device C	.20	.50

2005 Yu-Gi-Oh Blaze of Destruction

Card	Low	High
Complete Set (31)	6.00	15.00
Structure Deck	8.00	20.00
SD3001 Infernal Flame Emperor UR	.50	1.50
SD3002 Great Angus C	.25	.75
SD3003 Blazing Inpachi C	.25	.75
SD3004 UFO Turtle C	.25	.75
SD3005 Little Chimera C	.25	.75
SD3006 Inferno C	.25	.75
SD3007 Molten Zombie C	.25	.75
SD3008 Solar Flare Dragon C	.25	.75
SD3009 Ultimate Baseball Kid C	.25	.75
SD3010 Raging Flame Sprite C	.25	.75
SD3011 Thestalos the Firestorm Monarch C	.25	.75
SD3012 Gaia Soul the Combustible Collective C	.25	.75
SD3013 Fox Fire C	.25	.75
SD3014 Snatch Steal C	.25	.75
SD3015 Mystical Space Typhoon C	.25	.75
SD3016 Molten Destruction C	.25	.75
SD3017 Nobleman of Crossout C	.25	.75
SD3018 Premature Burial C	.25	.75
SD3019 Pot of Greed C	.25	.75
SD3020 Tribute to the Doomed C	.25	.75
SD3021 Heavy Storm C	.25	.75
SD3022 Dark Room of Nightmare C	.25	.75
SD3023 Reload C	.25	.75
SD3024 Level Limit - Area B C	.25	.75
SD3025 Necklace of Command C	.25	.75
SD3026 Meteor of Destruction C	.25	.75
SD3027 Dust Tornado C	.25	.75
SD3028 Call of the Haunted C	.25	.75
SD3029 Jar of Greed C	.25	.75
SD3030 Spell Shield Type-8 C	.25	.75
SD3031 Backfire C	.25	.75

2005 Yu-Gi-Oh Fury from the Deep

Card	Low	High
Complete Set (32)	8.00	20.00
Structure Deck	12.00	30.00
SD4001 Ocean Dragon Lord - Neo- Daedalus UR	.75	2.00
SD4002 7 Colored Fish C	.20	.50
SD4003 Sea Serpent Warrior of Darkness C	.20	.50
SD4004 Space Mambo C	.20	.50
SD4005 Mother Grizzly C	.20	.50
SD4006 Star Boy C	.20	.50
SD4007 Tribe-Infecting Virus C	.75	2.00
SD4008 Fenrir C	.20	.50
SD4009 Amphibious Bugroth MK-3 C	.20	.50
SD4010 Levia-Dragon - Daedalus C	.50	1.25
SD4011 Mermaid Knight C	.20	.50
SD4012 Mobius the Frost Monarch C	.20	.50
SD4013 Unshaven Angler C	.20	.50
SD4014 Creeping Doom Manta C	.20	.50
SD4015 Snatch Steal C	.20	.50
SD4016 Mystical Space Typhoon C	.50	1.25
SD4017 Premature Burial C	.20	.50
SD4018 Pot of Greed C	.50	1.25
SD4019 Heavy Storm C	.20	.50
SD4020 A Legendary Ocean C	.20	.50
SD4021 Creature Swap C	.20	.50
SD4022 Reload C	.20	.50
SD4023 Salvage C	.25	.75
SD4024 Hammer Shot C	.20	.50
SD4025 Big Wave Small Wave C	.20	.50
SD4026 Dust Tornado C	.20	.50
SD4027 Call of the Haunted C	.20	.50
SD4028 Gravity Bind C	.20	.50
SD4029 Tornado Wall C	.20	.50
SD4030 Torrential Tribute C	.60	1.50
SD4031 Spell Shield Type-8 C	.20	.50
SD4032 Xing Zhen Hu C	.20	.50

2006 Yu-Gi-Oh Warrior's Triumph

Complete Set (36)	10.00	25.00
Structure Deck	12.00	30.00
SD5001 Gilford the Legend UR	.75	2.00
SD5002 Warrior Lady of the Wasteland C	.25	.75
SD5003 Dark Blade C	.25	.75
SD5004 Goblin Attack Force C	.25	.75
SD5005 Gearfried the Iron Knight C	.25	.75
SD5006 Swift Gaia the Fierce Knight C	.25	.75
SD5007 Obnoxious Celtic Guard C	.25	.75
SD5008 Command Knight C	.40	1.00
SD5009 Marauding Captain C	.25	.75
SD5010 Exiled Force C	.25	.75
SD5011 D.D. Warrior Lady C	.25	.75
SD5012 Mataza the Zapper C	.25	.75
SD5013 Mystic Swordsman LV2 C	.25	.75
SD5014 Mystic Swordsman LV4 C	.25	.75
SD5015 Ninja Grandmaster Sasuke C	.25	.75
SD5016 Gearfried the Swordmaster C	.25	.75
SD5017 Armed Samurai - Ben Kei C	.25	.75
SD5018 Divine Sword - Phoenix Blade C	.25	.75
SD5019 Snatch Steal C	.25	.75
SD5020 Mystical Space Typhoon C	.50	1.25
SD5021 Giant Trunade C	.25	.75
SD5022 Lightning Blade C	.25	.75
SD5023 Heavy Storm C	.25	.75
SD5024 Reinforcement of the Army C	.25	.75
SD5025 The Warrior Returning Alive C	.25	.75
SD5026 Fusion Sword Murasame Blade C	.25	.75
SD5027 Wicked-Breaking Flamberge - Baou C	.25	.75
SD5028 Fairy of the Spring C	.25	.75
SD5029 Reload C	.25	.75
SD5030 Lightning Vortex C	.25	.75
SD5031 Swords of Concealing Light C	.75	2.00
SD5032 Release Restraint C	.25	.75
SD5033 Call of the Haunted C	.25	.75
SD5034 Magic Jammer C	.25	.75
SD5035 Royal Decree C	1.25	3.00
SD5036 Blast with Chain C	.25	.75

2006 Yu-Gi-Oh Spellcaster's Judgment

Complete Set (36)	10.00	25.00
Structure Deck	20.00	40.00
SD6001 Dark Eradicator Warlock UR	2.00	5.00
SD6002 Mythical Beast Cerberus C	.25	.75
SD6003 Dark Magician C	.25	.75
SD6004 Gemini Elf C	.25	.75
SD6005 Magician of Faith C	.25	.75
SD6006 Skilled Dark Magician C	.25	.75
SD6007 Apprentice Magician C	.25	.75
SD6008 Chaos Command Magician C	1.25	3.00
SD6009 Breaker the Magical Warrior C	.25	.75
SD6010 Royal Magical Library C	.60	1.50
SD6011 Tsukuyomi C	.60	1.50
SD6012 Chaos Sorcerer C	.25	.75
SD6013 White Magician Pikeru C	.25	.75
SD6014 Blast Magician C	.25	.75
SD6015 Ebon Magician Curran C	.25	.75
SD6016 Rapid-Fire Magician C	.25	.75
SD6017 Magical Blast C	.25	.75
SD6018 Mystical Space Typhoon C	.60	1.50
SD6019 Nobleman of Crossout C	.25	.75
SD6020 Premature Burial C	.25	.75
SD6021 Swords of Revealing Light C	.25	.75
SD6022 Mage Power C	.25	.75
SD6023 Heavy Storm C	.25	.75
SD6024 Diffusion Wave-Motion C	.25	.75
SD6025 Reload C	.25	.75
SD6026 Dark Magic Attack C	.25	.75
SD6027 Spell Absorption C	.75	2.00
SD6028 Lightning Vortex C	.25	.75
SD6029 Magical Dimension C	.25	.75
SD6030 Mystic Box C	.40	1.00
SD6031 Nightmare's Steelcage C	.25	.75
SD6032 Call of the Haunted C	.25	.75
SD6033 Spell Shield Type-8 C	.25	.75
SD6034 Pitch-Black Power Stone C	.25	.75
SD6035 Divine Wrath C	.25	.75
SD6036 Magic Cylinder C	.40	1.00

2006 Yu-Gi-Oh Invincible Fortress 1st Edition

Complete Set (32)	8.00	20.00
Structure Deck	15.00	30.00
SD7001 Exxod, Master of the Guard UR	.60	1.50
SD7002 Great Spirit C	.20	.50
SD7003 Giant Rat C	.20	.50
SD7004 Maharaghi C	.20	.50
SD7005 Guardian Sphinx C	.20	.50
SD7006 Gigantes C	.20	.50
SD7007 Stone Statue of the Aztecs C	.25	.75
SD7008 Golem Sentry C	.20	.50
SD7009 Hieracosphinx C	.20	.50
SD7010 Criosphinx C	.20	.50
SD7011 Moai Interceptor Cannons C	.20	.50
SD7012 Megarock Dragon C	.20	.50
SD7013 Guardian Statue C	.20	.50
SD7014 Medusa Worm C	.20	.50
SD7015 Sand Moth C	.20	.50
SD7016 Canyon C	.40	1.00
SD7017 Mystical Space Typhoon C	.60	1.50
SD7018 Premature Burial C	.20	.50
SD7019 Swords of Revealing Light C	.20	.50
SD7020 Shield & Sword C	.20	.50
SD7021 Magical Mallet C	.75	2.00
SD7022 Hammer Shot C	.20	.50
SD7023 Ectoplasmer C	.20	.50
SD7024 Brain Control C	.20	.50
SD7025 Shifting Shadows C	.20	.50
SD7026 Waboku C	.20	.50
SD7027 Ultimate Offering C	.20	.50
SD7028 Magic Drain C	.20	.50
SD7029 Robbin' Goblin C	.20	.50
SD7030 Ordeal of a Traveler C	.25	.75
SD7031 Reckless Greed C	.40	1.00
SD7032 Compulsory Evacuation Device C	.20	.50

2006 Yu-Gi-Oh Lord of the Storm

Complete Set (36)	8.00	20.00
Structure Deck	8.00	20.00
SD8001 Simorgh, Bird of Divinity UR	.20	.50
SD8002 Sonic Shooter C	.20	.50
SD8003 Sonic Duck C	.20	.50
SD8004 Harpie Girl C	.20	.50
SD8005 Slate Warrior C	.20	.50
SD8006 Flying Kamakiri #1 C	.20	.50
SD8007 Harpie Lady Sisters C	.20	.50
SD8008 Bladefly C	.20	.50
SD8009 Birdface C	.20	.50
SD8010 Silpheed C	.20	.50
SD8011 Lady Ninja Yae C	.40	1.00
SD8012 Roc from the Valley of Haze C	.20	.50
SD8013 Harpie Lady 1 C	.20	.50
SD8014 Harpie Lady 2 C	.20	.50
SD8015 Harpie Lady 3 C	.20	.50
SD8016 Swift Birdman Joe C	.20	.50
SD8017 Harpie's Pet Baby Dragon C	.50	1.25
SD8018 Card Destruction C	.20	.50
SD8019 Mystical Space Typhoon C	.50	1.25
SD8020 Nobleman of Crossout C	.20	.50
SD8021 Elegant Egotist C	.20	.50
SD8022 Heavy Storm C	.20	.50
SD8023 Reload C	.20	.50
SD8024 Harpies' Hunting Ground C	.20	.50
SD8025 Triangle Ecstasy Spark C	.20	.50
SD8026 Lightning Vortex C	.20	.50
SD8027 Hysteric Party C	.40	1.00
SD8028 Aqua Chorus C	.20	.50
SD8029 Dust Tornado C	.20	.50
SD8030 Call of the Haunted C	.20	.50
SD8031 Magic Jammer C	.20	.50
SD8032 Dark Coffin C	.20	.50
SD8033 Reckless Greed C	.40	1.00
SD8034 Sakuretsu Armor C	.20	.50
SD8035 Ninjitsu Art of Transformation C	.40	1.00
SD8036 Icarus Attack C	.60	1.50

2006 Yu-Gi-Oh Dinosaur's Rage

Complete Set	6.00	15.00
Structure Deck	10.00	25.00
Special Edition Deck w/5-Headed Dragon	10.00	20.00
Five-Headed Dragon is a Wal-Mart Exclusive		
SD9001 Super Conductor Tyranno UR	.60	1.50
SD9002 Kabazauls C	.20	.50
SD9003 Sabersaurus C	.20	.50
SD9004 Mad Sword Beast C	.20	.50
SD9005 Gilasaurus C	.20	.50
SD9006 Dark Driceratops C	.20	.50
SD9007 Hyper Hammerhead C	.20	.50
SD9008 Black Tyranno C	.20	.50
SD9009 Tyranno Infinity C	.20	.50
SD9010 Hydrogeddon C	.20	.50
SD9011 Oxygeddon C	.20	.50
SD9012 Black Ptera C	.20	.50
SD9013 Black Stego C	.20	.50
SD9014 Ultimate Tyranno C	.20	.50
SD9015 Miracle Jurassic Egg C	.20	.50
SD9016 Babycerasaurus C	.20	.50
SD9017 Big Evolution Pill C	.20	.50
SD9018 Tail Swipe C	.20	.50
SD9019 Jurassic World C	.20	.50
SD9020 Sebek's Blessing C	.20	.50
SD9021 Riryoku C	.20	.50
SD9022 Mesmeric Control C	.20	.50
SD9023 Mystical Space Typhoon C	.60	1.50
SD9024 Megamorph C	.20	.50
SD9025 Heavy Storm C	.20	.50
SD9026 Lightning Vortex C	.20	.50
SD9027 Magical Mallet C	.75	2.00
SD9028 Hunting Instinct C	.20	.50
SD9029 Survival Instinct C	.20	.50
SD9030 Volcanic Eruption C	.20	.50
SD9031 Seismic Shockwave C	.20	.50
SD9032 Magical Arm Shield C	.20	.50
SD9033 Negate Attack C	.20	.50
SD9034 Goblin Out of the Frying Pan C	.20	.50
SD9035 Malfunction C	.20	.50
SD9036 Fossil Excavation C	.20	.50
SD9SS1 Five-Headed Dragon UR	.75	2.00

2007 Yu-Gi-Oh Machine Re-Volt

Complete Set (37)	8.00	20.00
Structure Deck	10.00	25.00
SD10001 Ancient Gear Dragon Gadjiltron UR	.40	1.00
SD10002 Ancient Gear Gadjiltron Chimera C	.25	.75
SD10003 Ancient Gear Engineer C	.60	1.50
SD10004 Boot-Up Soldier - Dread Dynamo C	.25	.75
SD10005 Mechanicalchaser C	.25	.75
SD10006 Green Gadget C	.25	.75
SD10007 Red Gadget C	.25	.75
SD10008 Yellow Gadget C	.25	.75
SD10009 Cannon Soldier C	.25	.75
SD10010 Gear Golem the Moving Fortress C	.25	.75
SD10011 Heavy Mech Support Platform C	.25	.75
SD10012 Ancient Gear Golem C	.25	.75
SD10013 Ancient Gear Beast C	.25	.75
SD10014 Ancient Gear Soldier C	.25	.75
SD10015 Ancient Gear C	.25	.75
SD10016 Ancient Gear Cannon C	.25	.75
SD10017 Ancient Gear Workshop C	.40	1.00
SD10018 Ancient Gear Tank C	.25	.75
SD10019 Ancient Gear Explosive C	.25	.75
SD10020 Ancient Gear Fist C	.25	.75
SD10021 Ancient Gear Factory C	.25	.75
SD10022 Ancient Gear Drill C	.25	.75
SD10023 Ancient Gear Castle C	.25	.75
SD10024 Mystical Space Typhoon C	.50	1.25
SD10025 Limiter Removal C	.25	.75
SD10026 Heavy Storm C	.25	.75
SD10027 Enemy Controller C	.25	.75
SD10028 Weapon Change C	.25	.75
SD10029 Machine Duplication C	1.25	3.00
SD10030 Pot of Avarice C	.25	.75
SD10031 Stronghold the Moving Fortress C	.25	.75
SD10032 Ultimate Offering C	.25	.75
SD10033 Sakuretsu Armor C	.25	.75
SD10034 Micro Ray C	.25	.75
SD10035 Rare Metalmorph C	.25	.75
SD10036 Covering Fire C	.25	.75
SD10037 Roll Out! C	.25	.75

2008 Yu-Gi-Oh Zombie World

Structure Deck Zombie World	8.00	20.00
SDZW1 Red-Eyes Zombie Dragon UR	.75	2.00
SDZW2 Malevolent Mech - Goku En C	.25	.75
SDZW3 Paladin of the Cursed Dragon C	.25	.75
SDZW4 Gernia C	.25	.75
SDZW5 Patrician of Darkness C	.25	.75
SDZW6 Royal Keeper C	.25	.75
SDZW7 Pyramid Turtle C	.25	.75
SDZW8 Master Kyonshee C	.25	.75
SDZW9 Spirit Reaper C	.25	.75
SDZW10 Getsu Fuhma C	.25	.75
SDZW11 Ryu Kokki C	.25	.75
SDZW12 Regenerating Mummy C	.25	.75
SDZW13 Des Lacooda C	.25	.75
SDZW14 Marionette Mite C	.25	.75
SDZW15 Plague Wolf C	.25	.75
SDZW16 Zombie Master C	.25	.75
SDZW17 Zombie World C	1.00	2.50
SDZW18 Spell Shattering Arrow C	.50	1.25
SDZW19 Cold Wave C	.25	.75
SDZW20 Magical Stone Excavation C	.25	.75
SDZW21 Card of Safe Return C	.25	.75
SDZW22 Creature Swap C	.25	.75
SDZW23 Book of Life C	.25	.75
SDZW24 Call of the Mummy C	.25	.75
SDZW25 Terraforming C	.60	1.50
SDZW26 Pot of Avarice C	.25	.75
SDZW27 Shrink C	.25	.75
SDZW28 Field Barrier C	.25	.75
SDZW29 Soul Taker C	.25	.75
SDZW30 Ribbon of Rebirth C	.25	.75
SDZW31 Card Destruction C	.25	.75
SDZW32 Imperial Iron Wall C	.75	2.00
SDZW33 Dust Tornado C	.25	.75
SDZW34 Bottomless Trap Hole C	1.00	2.50
SDZW35 Tutan Mask C	.25	.75
SDZW36 Waboku C	.25	.75
SDZW37 Magical Arm Shield C	.25	.75

2009 Yu-Gi-Oh Spellcaster's Command Structure Deck

Structure Deck Spellcaster's Command	10.00	25.00
SDSC1 Endymion, the Master Magician UR	1.25	3.00
SDSC2 Disenchanter	.20	.75
SDSC3 Defender, the Magical Knight	.40	1.00
SDSC4 Hannibal Necromancer	.20	.75
SDSC5 Summoner Monk	.75	2.00
SDSC6 Dark Red Enchanter	.20	.75
SDSC7 Skilled Dark Magician	.20	.75
SDSC8 Apprentice Magician	.20	.75
SDSC9 Old Vindictive Magician	.20	.75
SDSC10 Magical Marionette	.20	.75
SDSC11 Breaker the Magical Warrior	.20	.75
SDSC12 Magical Plant Mandragola	.20	.75
SDSC13 Royal Magical Library	.60	1.50
SDSC14 Blast Magician	.20	.75
SDSC15 Mythical Beast Cerberus	.20	.75
SDSC16 Mei-Kou, Master of Barriers	.20	.75
SDSC17 Crystal Seer	.20	.75
SDSC18 Magical Exemplar	.20	.75
SDSC19 Magical Citadel of Endymion	1.25	3.00
SDSC20 Spell Power Grasp	.75	2.00
SDSC21 Magicians Unite	.20	.75
SDSC22 Mist Body	.40	1.00
SDSC23 Malevolent Nuzzler	.20	.75
SDSC24 Giant Trunade	.20	.75
SDSC25 Fissure	.20	.75
SDSC26 Swords of Revealing Light	.20	.75
SDSC27 Mage Power	.20	.75
SDSC28 Terraforming	.50	1.25
SDSC29 Enemy Controller	.20	.75
SDSC30 Book of Moon	.20	.75
SDSC31 Magical Blast	.20	.75
SDSC32 Magical Dimension	.20	.75
SDSC33 Twister	.20	.75
SDSC34 Field Barrier	.20	.75
SDSC35 Magician's Circle	.40	1.00
SDSC36 Pitch-Black Power Stone	.20	.75
SDSC37 Tower of Babel	.20	.75
SDSC38 Magic Cylinder	.20	.75

2009 Yu-Gi-Oh Warrior's Strike

Structure Deck Warrior's Strike	8.00	12.00
SDWS1 Phoenix Gearfried UR	.40	1.00
SDWS2 Evocator Chevalier SR	.10	.25
SDWS3 Featherizer SR	.10	.25
SDWS4 Gemini Soldier C	.10	.25
SDWS5 Spell Striker C	.40	1.00
SDWS6 Freed the Matchless General C	.10	.25
SDWS7 Marauding Captain C	.10	.25
SDWS8 Exiled Force C	.10	.25
SDWS9 D.D. Warrior Lady C	.60	1.50
SDWS10 Card Trooper C	.10	.25
SDWS11 Gemini Summoner C	.10	.25
SDWS12 Blazewing Butterfly C	.10	.25
SDWS13 D.D. Warrior C	.10	.25
SDWS14 Future Samurai C	.10	.25
SDWS15 Field-Commander Rahz C	.10	.25
SDWS16 Dark Valkyria C	.10	.25
SDWS17 Supervise C	.50	1.25
SDWS18 Mind Control C	.10	.25
SDWS19 Burden of the Mighty C	.75	2.00
SDWS20 Silent Doom C	.10	.25
SDWS21 Hidden Armory C	.60	1.50
SDWS22 Nightmare's Steelcage C	.10	.25
SDWS23 Mystical Space Typhoon C	.10	.25
SDWS24 Ekibyo Drakmord C	.10	.25
SDWS25 Reinforcement of the Army C	.10	.25
SDWS26 Big Bang Shot C	.10	.25
SDWS27 Divine Sword - Phoenix Blade C	.10	.25
SDWS28 Double Summon C	1.25	3.00
SDWS29 Symbols of Duty C	.10	.25
SDWS30 Swing of Memories C	.10	.25
SDWS31 Unleash Your Power! C	.10	.25
SDWS32 Dark Bribe C	.75	2.00
SDWS33 Kunai with Chain C	.10	.25
SDWS34 Sakuretsu Armor C	.60	1.50
SDWS35 Soul Resurrection C	.10	.25
SDWS36 Justi-Break C	.10	.25
SDWS37 Birthright C	.10	.25
SDWS38 Gemini Trap Hole C	.10	.25

2010 Yu-Gi-Oh Machina Mayhem

Structure Deck Machina Mayhem	8.00	20.00
SDMM1 Machina Fortress UR	.75	2.00
SDMM2 Machina Gearframe SR	.60	1.50
SDMM3 Machina Peacekeeper SR	.60	1.50
SDMM4 Scrap Recycler	.10	.25
SDMM5 Commander Covington	.10	.25
SDMM6 Machina Soldier	.40	1.00
SDMM7 Machina Sniper	.10	.25
SDMM8 Machina Defender	.10	.25
SDMM9 Machina Force	.10	.25
SDMM10 Kinetic Soldier	.10	.25
SDMM11 Blast Sphere	.10	.25
SDMM12 Heavy Mech Support Platform	.10	.25
SDMM13 Cyber Dragon	.10	.25
SDMM14 Proto-Cyber Dragon	.10	.25
SDMM15 Green Gadget	.10	.25
SDMM16 Red Gadget	.10	.25
SDMM17 Yellow Gadget	.10	.25
SDMM18 Armored Cybern	.10	.25
SDMM19 Cyber Valley	1.25	3.00
SDMM20 The Big Saturn	.10	.25
SDMM21 Machina Armored Unit	.10	.25
SDMM22 Prohibition	.10	.25
SDMM23 Swords of Revealing Light	.10	.25
SDMM24 Shrink	.10	.25
SDMM25 Frontline Base	.10	.25
SDMM26 Machine Duplication	.10	.25
SDMM27 Inferno Reckless Summon	.10	.25
SDMM28 Hand Destruction	.75	2.00
SDMM29 Card Trader	.10	.25
SDMM30 Solidarity	.40	1.00
SDMM31 Time Machine	.10	.25
SDMM32 Dimensional Prison	2.50	6.00
SDMM33 Metalmorph	.10	.25
SDMM34 Rare Metalmorph	.10	.25
SDMM35 Ceasefire	.10	.25
SDMM36 Compulsory Evacuation Device	.10	.25
SDMM37 Roll Out!	.10	.25

2010 Yu-Gi-Oh Marik

Complete Set (38)	8.00	20.00
SDMA01 Gil Garth	.15	.40
SDMA02 Mystic Tomato	.15	.40
SDMA03 Viser Des	.15	.40
SDMA04 Legendary Fiend	.15	.40
SDMA05 Dark Jeroid	.15	.40
SDMA06 Newdoria	.15	.40
SDMA07 Gravekeeper's Spy	.75	2.00
SDMA08 Gravekeeper's Curse	.15	.40
SDMA09 Gravekeeper's Guard	.75	2.00
SDMA10 Gravekeeper's Spear Soldier	.25	.60
SDMA11 Gravekeeper's Chief	.25	.60
SDMA12 Gravekeeper's Cannonholder	.25	.60
SDMA13 Gravekeeper's Assailant	.25	.60
SDMA14 Lava Golem UR	.75	2.00
SDMA15 Drillago	.15	.40
SDMA16 Bowganian	.15	.40
SDMA17 Gravekeeper's Commandant	.25	.60
SDMA18 Gravekeeper's Visionary	.25	.60
SDMA19 Gravekeeper's Descendant	.25	.60
SDMA20 Mystical Space Typhoon	.75	2.00
SDMA21 Nightmare's Steelcage	.25	.60
SDMA22 Creature Swap	.25	.60
SDMA23 Book of Moon	2.00	5.00
SDMA24 Dark Room of Nightmare	.15	.40
SDMA25 Necrovalley	.40	1.00
SDMA26 Foolish Burial	.40	1.00
SDMA27 Magical Stone Excavation	.25	.60
SDMA28 Allure of Darkness	1.50	4.00
SDMA29 Acid Trap Hole	.15	.40
SDMA30 Mirror Force	2.50	6.00
SDMA31 Skull Invitation	.15	.40
SDMA32 Coffin Seller	.15	.40
SDMA33 Nightmare Wheel	.30	.75
SDMA34 Metal Reflect Slime	.30	.75
SDMA35 Malevolent Catastrophe	.25	.60
SDMA36 Dark Illusion	.25	.60
SDMA37 Mystical Beast of Serket UR	.40	1.00
SDMA38 Temple of the Kings UR	.40	1.00

2011 Yu-Gi-Oh Dragunity Legion

Complete Set (39)	8.00	20.00
SDDL01 Dragunity Arma Leyvaten UTR	.40	1.00
SDDL02 Dragunity Arma Mystletainn SR	.40	1.00
SDDL03 Dragunity Aklys SR	.40	1.00
SDDL04 Dragunity Dux	.25	.60
SDDL05 Dragunity Legionnaire	.15	.40
SDDL06 Dragunity Tribus	.15	.40
SDDL07 Dragunity Darkspear	.15	.40
SDDL08 Dragunity Militum	.15	.40
SDDL09 Dragunity Primus Pilus	.15	.40
SDDL10 Dragunity Brandistock	.15	.40
SDDL11 Dragunity Javelin	.15	.40
SDDL12 Mist Valley Falcon	.15	.40
SDDL13 Hunter Owl	.15	.40
SDDL14 Garuda the Wind Spirit	.15	.40
SDDL15 Flying Kamakiri #1	.15	.40
SDDL16 Spear Dragon	.15	.40
SDDL17 Twin-Headed Behemoth	.15	.40
SDDL18 Armed Dragon LV3	.15	.40
SDDL19 Armed Dragon LV5	.15	.40
SDDL20 Masked Dragon	.25	.60
SDDL21 Dragon Ravine	.75	2.00
SDDL22 Dragon Mastery	.25	.60
SDDL23 United We Stand	1.25	3.00
SDDL24 Mage Power	.40	1.00
SDDL25 Dragon's Gunfire	.15	.40
SDDL26 Stamping Destruction	.15	.40
SDDL27 Creature Swap	.25	.60
SDDL28 Monster Reincarnation	.25	.60
SDDL29 Foolish Burial	.40	1.00
SDDL30 Card Destruction	.15	.40
SDDL31 Windstorm of Etaqua	.15	.40
SDDL32 Relieve Monster	.25	.60
SDDL33 Legacy of Yata-Garasu	.15	.40
SDDL34 Final Attack Orders	.15	.40
SDDL35 Mirror Force	.75	2.00
SDDL36 Dragon's Rage	.15	.40
SDDL37 Bottomless Trap Hole	.75	2.00
SDDL38 Spiritual Wind Art - Miyabi	.15	.40
SDDL39 Icarus Attack	.75	2.00

2011 Yu-Gi-Oh Lost Sanctuary

Complete Set (38)	8.00	20.00
SDLS01 Master Hyperion UR	2.00	5.00
SDLS02 The Agent of Mystery - Earth SR	1.00	2.50
SDLS03 The Agent of Miracles - Jupiter SR	.75	2.00
SDLS04 The Agent of Judgment - Saturn	.30	.75
SDLS05 The Agent of Wisdom - Mercury	.30	.75
SDLS06 The Agent of Creation - Venus	.30	.75
SDLS07 The Agent of Force - Mars	.30	.75
SDLS08 Mystical Shine Ball	.30	.75
SDLS09 Splendid Venus	.50	1.25
SDLS10 Tethys, Goddess of Light	.75	2.00
SDLS11 Victoria	.60	1.50
SDLS12 Athena	.40	1.00
SDLS13 Marshmallon	1.00	2.50
SDLS14 Hecatrice	.40	1.00
SDLS15 Shining Angel	.60	1.50
SDLS16 Soul of Purity and Light	.60	1.50
SDLS17 Airknight Parshath	.30	.75
SDLS18 Nova Summoner	.60	1.50
SDLS19 Zeradias, Herald of Heaven	.30	.75
SDLS20 Honest	.75	2.00
SDLS21 Hanewata	.30	.75
SDLS22 Consecrated Light	.60	1.50
SDLS23 Cards from the Sky	1.00	2.50
SDLS24 Valhalla, Hall of the Fallen	.50	1.25
SDLS25 Terraforming	.60	1.50
SDLS26 Smashing Ground	1.00	2.50
SDLS27 The Sanctuary in the Sky	.75	2.00
SDLS28 Celestial Transformation	.30	.75
SDLS29 Burial from a Different Dimension	1.50	4.00
SDLS30 Mausoleum of the Emperor	.60	1.50
SDLS31 Solidarity	1.50	4.00
SDLS32 The Fountain in the Sky	.30	.75
SDLS33 Divine Punishment	.60	1.50
SDLS34 Return from the Different Dimension	.60	1.50
SDLS35 Torrential Tribute	1.50	4.00
SDLS36 Beckoning Light	.40	1.00
SDLS37 Miraculous Descent	.30	.75
SDLS38 Solemn Judgment	4.00	10.00

2012 Yu-Gi-Oh Samurai Warlords Structure Deck

COMPLETE SET (41)	6.00	12.00
STRUCTURE DECK	7.50	15.00
SDWA001 Chamberlain of the Six Samurai	.10	.30
SDWA002 Grandmaster of the Six Samurai	.10	.30
SDWA003 The Six Samurai - Yariza	.10	.30
SDWA004 The Six Samurai - Zanji	.10	.30
SDWA005 The Six Samurai - Nisashi	.10	.30
SDWA006 The Six Samurai - Yaichi	.10	.30
SDWA007 The Six Samurai - Kamon	.10	.30
SDWA008 The Six Samurai - Irou	.10	.30
SDWA009 Great Shogun Shien	.10	.30
SDWA010 Shien's Footsoldier	.10	.30
SDWA011 Enishi, Shien's Chancellor	.10	.30
SDWA012 Spirit of the Six Samurai	.10	.30
SDWA013 Future Samurai	.10	.30
SDWA014 The Immortal Bushi	.10	.30
SDWA015 Hand of the Six Samurai	.10	.30
SDWA016 Legendary Six Samurai - Kizan	1.25	3.00
SDWA017 Legendary Six Samurai - Enishi	15.00	.40
SDWA018 Legendary Six Samurai - Kageki SR	.20	.60
SDWA019 Shien's Squire	.10	.30
SDWA020 Shien's Daredevil	.10	.30
SDWA021 Elder of the Six Samurai	.10	.30
SDWA022 Shien's Advisor	.10	.30
SDWA023 Dark Hole	.50	1.25
SDWA024 The A. Forces	.10	.30
SDWA025 Reinforcement of the Army	.20	.60
SDWA026 The Warrior Returning Alive	.10	.30
SDWA027 Cunning of the Six Samurai	.10	.30
SDWA028 Six Samurai United	.40	1.00
SDWA029 Gateway of the Six	.10	.30
SDWA030 Shien's Smoke Signal SR	.25	.75
SDWA031 Temple of the Six	.10	.30
SDWA032 Shien's Dojo	.20	.60
SDWA033 Rivalry of Warlords	1.25	3.00
SDWA034 Return of the Six Samurai	.10	.30
SDWA035 Double-Edged Sword Technique	.10	.30

SDWA036 Fiendish Chain 1.25 3.00
SDWA037 Musakani Magatama .15 .40
SDWA038 Shien's Scheme .10 .30
SDWA039 Six Strike - Thunder Blast .10 .30
SDWA040 Six Style - Dual Wield .10 .30
SDWA041 Shadow of the Six Samurai - Shien (UR) .10 .30

2012 Yu-Gi-Oh Realm of the Sea Emperor

COMPLETE SET (39) 5.00 10.00
STRUCTURE DECK 5.00 10.00
SDRE001 Poseidra, the Atlantean UR .10 .30
SDRE002 Atlantean Dragoons SR .40 1.00
SDRE003 Atlantean Marksman .75 2.00
SDRE004 Atlantean Heavy Infantry .75 2.00
SDRE005 Atlantean Pikeman .10 .30
SDRE006 Atlantean Attack Squad .10 .30
SDRE007 Lost Blue Breaker .10 .30
SDRE008 Armed Sea Hunter .10 .30
SDRE009 Spined Gillman .10 .30
SDRE010 Deep Sea Diva .02 .60
SDRE011 Mermaid Archer .10 .30
SDRE012 Codarus .10 .30
SDRE013 Warrior of Atlantis .10 .30
SDRE014 Abyss Soldier .20 .60
SDRE015 Skreech .10 .30
SDRE016 Snowman Eater .10 .30
SDRE017 Nightmare Penguin .10 .30
SDRE018 Penguin Soldier .10 .30
SDRE019 Deep Diver .10 .30
SDRE020 Reese the Ice Mistress .10 .30
SDRE021 Mother Grizzly .10 .30
SDRE022 Friller Rabca .10 .30
SDRE023 Call of the Atlanteans SR .10 .30
SDRE024 A Legendary Ocean .10 .30
SDRE025 Terraforming .60 1.50
SDRE026 Water Hazard .10 .30
SDRE027 Aqua Jet .10 .30
SDRE028 Surface .75 2.00
SDRE029 Moray of Greed .60 1.50
SDRE030 Salvage .40 1.00
SDRE031 Dark Hole .40 1.00
SDRE032 Big Wave Small Wave .10 .30
SDRE033 Aegis of the Ocean Dragon Lord .10 .30
SDRE034 Forgotten Temple of the Deep .10 .30
SDRE035 Tornado Wall .10 .30
SDRE036 Torrential Tribute .60 1.50
SDRE037 Spiritual Water Art - Aoi .10 .30
SDRE038 Gravity Bind .40 1.00
SDRE039 Poseidon Wave .10 .30

2013 Yu-Gi-Oh Onslaught of the Fire Kings

COMPLETE SET (39) 6.00 12.00
STRUCTURE DECK 7.50 15.00
SDOK001 Fire King High Avatar Garunix UR .75 2.00
SDOK002 Fire King Avatar Barong C 1.00 2.50
SDOK003 Fire King Avatar Kirin C .10 .30
SDOK004 Sacred Phoenix of Nephthys C .10 .30
SDOK005 Manticore of Darkness C .10 .30
SDOK006 Goka, the Pyre of Malice C .10 .30
SDOK007 Hazy Flame Hyppogrif C .10 .30
SDOK008 Laval Lancelord C .10 .30
SDOK009 Flamvell Firedog C .10 .30
SDOK010 Flamvell Poun C .10 .30
SDOK011 Neo Flamvell Sabre C .10 .30
SDOK012 Royal Firestorm Guards C .10 .30
SDOK013 Volcanic Rocket C .50 1.25
SDOK014 Volcanic Counter C .10 .30
SDOK015 Molten Zombie C .10 .30
SDOK016 Spirit of Flames C .10 .30
SDOK017 Raging Flame Sprite C .10 .30
SDOK018 Fox Fire C .10 .30
SDOK019 Flame Tiger C .10 .30
SDOK020 Little Chimera C .10 .30
SDOK021 UFO Turtle C .10 .30
SDOK022 Onslaught of the Fire Kings SR 1.00 2.50
SDOK023 Circle of the Fire Kings SR .60 1.50
SDOK024 Rekindling C .10 .30
SDOK025 Blaze Accelerator C .10 .30
SDOK026 Wild Nature's Release C .10 .30
SDOK027 Pot of Duality C .75 2.00
SDOK028 Hand Destruction C 1.00 2.50
SDOK029 Creature Swap C .10 .30
SDOK030 Burden of the Mighty C .10 .30
SDOK031 Backfire C .10 .30
SDOK032 Flamvell Counter C .10 .30
SDOK033 Phoenix Wing Wind Blast C .50 1.25
SDOK034 Horn of the Phantom Beast C .50 1.25
SDOK035 Blast with Chain C .10 .30
SDOK036 Spiritual Fire Art - Kurenai C .10 .30
SDOK037 Regretful Rebirth C .10 .30
SDOK038 Nightmare Wheel C .10 .30
SDOK039 Call of the Haunted C .10 .30

2013 Yu-Gi-Oh Saga of Blue-Eyes White Dragon

COMPLETE SET (40) 7.50 15.00
Structure Deck 7.50 15.00
SDBE001 Blue-Eyes White Dragon UR 1.25 3.00
SDBE002 Rabidragon C .15 .40
SDBE003 Alexandrite Dragon C .30 .75
SDBE004 Luster Dragon C .15 .40
SDBE005 Flamvell Guard C .15 .40
SDBE006 Maiden with Eyes of Blue SR 2.00 5.00
SDBE007 Rider of the Storm Winds C .15 .40
SDBE008 Darkstorm Dragon C .15 .40
SDBE009 Kaiser Glider C .15 .40
SDBE010 Hieratic Dragon of Tefnuit C .15 .40
SDBE011 Mirage Dragon C .15 .40
SDBE012 Divine Dragon Apocralyph C .15 .40
SDBE013 The White Stone of Legend C .50 1.25
SDBE014 Kaibaman C .15 .40
SDBE015 Herald of Creation C .15 .40
SDBE016 Kaiser Sea Horse C .15 .40
SDBE017 Honest C .15 .40
SDBE018 Shining Angel C .15 .40
SDBE019 Dragon Shrine SR 1.25 3.00
SDBE020 Silver's Cry C 2.00 5.00
SDBE021 Burst Stream of Destruction C .15 .40
SDBE022 Stamping Destruction C .15 .40
SDBE023 A Wingbeat of Giant Dragon C .15 .40
SDBE024 Trade-In C 1.25 3.00
SDBE025 Cards of Consonance C .40 1.00
SDBE026 White Elephant's Gift C .15 .40
SDBE027 One for One C .15 .40
SDBE028 Monster Reborn C .40 1.00
SDBE029 Dragonic Tactics C .15 .40
SDBE030 Soul Exchange C .15 .40
SDBE031 Swords of Revealing Light C .15 .40
SDBE032 Enemy Controller C .15 .40
SDBE033 Castle of Dragon Souls C .15 .40
SDBE034 Fiendish Chain C 1.00 2.50
SDBE035 Kunai with Chain C .15 .40
SDBE036 Damage Condenser C .15 .40
SDBE037 Call of the Haunted C .15 .40
SDBE038 Compulsory Evacuation Device C .30 .75
SDBE039 Champion's Vigilance C .15 .40
SDBE040 Azure-Eyes Silver Dragon UR 1.25 3.00

2013 Yu-Gi-Oh Kaiba Reloaded Starter Deck

STARTER DECK 4.00 10.00
YSKR001 Blue-Eyes White Dragon UTR 2.50 6.00
YSKR001 Blue-Eyes White Dragon C 1.50 4.00
YSKR002 Aqua Madoor C .10 .30
YSKR003 La Jinn the Mystical Genie of the Lamp C .10 .30
YSKR004 Battle Ox C .10 .30
YSKR005 Opticlops C .10 .30
YSKR006 The Dragon Dwelling in the Cave C .10 .30
YSKR007 Luster Dragon C .10 .30
YSKR008 X-Head Cannon C .10 .30
YSKR009 Mad Dog of Darkness C .10 .30
YSKR010 Vorse Raider C .10 .30
YSKR011 Alexandrite Dragon C .10 .30
YSKR012 Wattaildragon C .10 .30
YSKR013 Twin-Headed Behemoth C .10 .30
YSKR014 Yomi Ship C .10 .30
YSKR015 Des Feral Imp C .10 .30
YSKR016 Kaiser Sea Horse C .10 .30
YSKR017 Chaos Necromancer C .10 .30
YSKR018 Blade Knight C .10 .30
YSKR019 Horus the Black Flame Dragon LV4 C .25 .75
YSKR020 Horus the Black Flame Dragon LV6 C .10 .30
YSKR021 Cybernetic Cyclopean C .10 .30
YSKR022 Puppet Plant C .10 .30
YSKR023 Des Mosquito C .10 .30
YSKR024 Tiger Dragon C .10 .30
YSKR025 Vanguard of the Dragon C .10 .30
YSKR026 Divine Dragon Apocralyph C .10 .30
YSKR027 Interplanetarypurplythorny Dragon C .10 .30
YSKR028 Dark Hole C .50 1.25
YSKR029 Soul Exchange C .10 .30
YSKR030 Tribute to The Doomed C .10 .30
YSKR031 Rush Recklessly C .10 .30
YSKR032 Mystical Space Typhoon C .50 1.25
YSKR033 Offerings to the Doomed C .10 .30
YSKR034 Stamping Destruction C .10 .30
YSKR035 Enemy Controller C .10 .30
YSKR036 Burst Stream of Destruction C .10 .30
YSKR037 Shrink C .10 .30
YSKR038 Shield Crush C .10 .30
YSKR039 Silent Doom C .10 .30
YSKR040 Dragonic Tactics C .10 .30
YSKR041 Spellbinding Circle C .10 .30
YSKR042 Trap Hole C .10 .30
YSKR043 Sakuretsu Armor C .10 .30
YSKR044 Shadow Spell C .10 .30
YSKR045 Widespread Ruin C .10 .30
YSKR046 Threatening Roar C .20 .60
YSKR047 Birthright C .10 .30
YSKR048 Damage Gate C .10 .30

2013 Yu-Gi-Oh Yugi Reloaded Starter Deck

STARTER DECK 4.00 10.00
YSYR001 Dark Magician C .20 .60
YSYR001 Dark Magician UTR 1.00 2.50
YSYR002 Mystical Elf C .10 .30
YSYR003 Giant Soldier of Stone C .10 .30
YSYR004 Summoned Skull C .20 .60
YSYR005 Neo the Magic Swordsman C .10 .30
YSYR006 Gemini Elf C .10 .30
YSYR007 Dark Blade C .10 .30
YSYR008 Kuriboh C .10 .30
YSYR009 Buster Blader C .20 .60
YSYR010 4-Starred Ladybug of Doom C .10 .30
YSYR011 Dark Magician Girl C 1.00 2.50
YSYR012 Skilled White Magician C .10 .30
YSYR013 Skilled Dark Magician C .10 .30
YSYR014 Old Vindictive Magician C .10 .30
YSYR015 Breaker the Magical Warrior C .10 .30
YSYR016 Double Coston C .10 .30
YSYR017 Silent Swordsman LV3 C .10 .30
YSYR018 Silent Swordsman LV5 C .10 .30
YSYR019 Green Gadget C .10 .30
YSYR020 Red Gadget C .10 .30
YSYR021 Yellow Gadget C .10 .30
YSYR022 Electric Virus C .10 .30
YSYR023 Magician's Valkyria C 2.00 5.00
YSYR024 The Tricky C .10 .30
YSYR025 Dark Hole C .50 1.25
YSYR026 Swords of Revealing Light C .10 .30
YSYR027 Black Pendant C .10 .30
YSYR028 Mystical Space Typhoon C .50 1.25
YSYR029 Mage Power C .40 1.00
YSYR030 Book of Moon C .20 .60
YSYR031 Thousand Knives C .10 .30
YSYR032 Dark Magic Attack C .50 1.25
YSYR033 Magical Dimension C .20 .60
YSYR034 Ancient Rules C 2.50 6.00
YSYR035 Magicians Unite C .10 .30
YSYR036 Soul Taker C .10 .30
YSYR037 Shard of Greed C .10 .30
YSYR038 Trap Hole C .10 .30
YSYR039 Waboku C .10 .30
YSYR040 Mirror Force C 1.25 3.00
YSYR041 Spellbinding Circle C .10 .30
YSYR042 Call of the Haunted C .10 .30
YSYR043 Magic Cylinder C .40 1.00
YSYR044 Miracle Restoring C .10 .30
YSYR045 Zero Gravity C .10 .30
YSYR046 Rising Energy C .10 .30

2014 Yu-Gi-Oh Cyber Dragon Revolution

COMPLETE SET (39) 20.00 35.00
STRUCTURE DECK 5.00 10.00
SDCR001 Cyber Dragon Core SR 1.75 2.25
SDCR002 Cyber Dragon Drei SR 2.25 3.00
SDCR004 Cyber Dragon Zwei .15 .25
SDCR005 Proto-Cyber Dragon .15 .25
SDCR006 Cyber Valley .15 .25
SDCR007 Cyber Larva .15 .25
SDCR008 Cyber Phoenix .15 .25
SDCR009 Cyber Dinosaur .15 .25
SDCR010 Cyber Eltanin .15 .25
SDCR011 Armored Cybern .15 .25
SDCR012 Satellite Cannon .15 .25
SDCR013 Solar Wind Jammer .15 .25
SDCR014 Jade Knight .15 .25
SDCR015 FalchionB .15 .25
SDCR016 Reflect Bounder .15 .25
SDCR017 The Light - Hex-Sealed Fusion .15 .25
SDCR018 Shining Angel .15 .25
SDCR019 Cyber Repair Plant 3.50 5.00
SDCR020 Evolution Burst .15 .25
SDCR021 Super Polymerization 1.00 2.00
SDCR022 Power Bond .40 .75
SDCR023 Limiter Removal .20 .35
SDCR024 Megamorph .15 .25
SDCR025 D.D.R. - Different Dimension Reincarnation .30 .50
SDCR026 Mystical Space Typhoon .60 1.00
SDCR027 Light of Redemption .15 .25
SDCR028 Machina Armored Unit .15 .25
SDCR029 Cyber Network .25 .45
SDCR030 Cybernetic Hidden Technology .15 .25
SDCR031 Three of a Kind .15 .25
SDCR032 Trap Stun 1.00 1.25
SDCR033 Dimensional Prison 1.00 1.50
SDCR034 Malevolent Catastrophe .15 .25
SDCR035 Waboku .30 .50
SDCR036 Call of the Haunted .15 .25
SDCR037 Cyber Twin Dragon UR .30 .50
SDCR038 Cyber Dragon Nova UR 2.75 3.25
SDCR003a Cyber Dragon (black) .20 .35
SDCR003b Cyber Dragon (white) .40 .75

2014 Yu-Gi-Oh Realm of Light

COMPLETE SET (36) 10.00 25.00
BOOSTER BOX
BOOSTER PACK
RELEASED ON JUNE 27, 2014
SDLIEN001 Alexandrite Dragon C .10 .30
SDLIEN002 Minerva, Lightsworn Maiden SR .50 1.25
SDLIEN003 Raiden, Hand of the Lightsworn SR 1.50 4.00
SDLIEN004 Judgment Dragon C .20 .60
SDLIEN005 Gragonith, Lightsworn Dragon C .10 .30
SDLIEN006 Celestia, Lightsworn Angel C .10 .30
SDLIEN007 Jain, Lightsworn Paladin C .10 .30
SDLIEN008 Lyla, Lightsworn Sorceress C .10 .30
SDLIEN009 Garoth, Lightsworn Warrior C .10 .30
SDLIEN010 Wulf, Lightsworn Beast C .10 .30
SDLIEN011 Ehren, Lightsworn Monk C .10 .30
SDLIEN012 Lumina, Lightsworn Summoner C .10 .30
SDLIEN013 Aurkus, Lightsworn Druid C .10 .30
SDLIEN014 Shire, Lightsworn Spirit C .10 .30
SDLIEN015 Ryko, Lightsworn Hunter C .10 .30
SDLIEN016 Honest C .20 .60
SDLIEN017 Lightray Diabolos C .10 .30
SDLIEN018 Lightray Daedalus C .10 .30
SDLIEN019 Vylon Prism C .10 .30
SDLIEN020 Fabled Raven C .10 .30
SDLIEN021 The Fabled Cerburrel C .10 .30
SDLIEN022 Blackwing - Zephyros the Elite C .10 .30
SDLIEN023 Necro Gardna C .10 .30
SDLIEN024 Lightsworn Sanctuary UR .40 1.00
SDLIEN025 Realm of Light C .10 .30
SDLIEN026 Solar Recharge C .20 .60
SDLIEN027 Charge of the Light Brigade C .10 .30
SDLIEN028 Monster Reincarnation C .10 .30
SDLIEN029 Foolish Burial C .25 .75
SDLIEN030 Glorious Illusion C .10 .30
SDLIEN031 Lightsworn Barrier C .10 .30
SDLIEN032 Vanquishing Light C .10 .30
SDLIEN033 Beckoning Light C .10 .30
SDLIEN034 Skill Successor C .10 .30
SDLIEN035 Breakthrough Skill C .60 1.50
SDLIEN036 Michael, the Arch-Lightsworn UR .40 1.00

2015 Yu-Gi-Oh HERO Strike

COMPLETE SET (45) 20.00 30.00
STRUCTURE DECK 10.00 15.00
UNLISTED C .15 .40
RELEASED ON JANUARY 30, 2015
SDHSEN001 Elemental HERO Shadow Mist SR 3.75 5.00
SDHSEN002 Elemental HERO Ocean C .20 .30
SDHSEN003 Elemental HERO Woodsman C .20 .30
SDHSEN004 Elemental HERO Voltic C .05 .15
SDHSEN005 Elemental HERO Heat C .05 .15
SDHSEN006 Elemental HERO Avian C .05 .15
SDHSEN007 Elemental HERO Neos C .20 .30
SDHSEN008 Elemental HERO Neos Alius C .15 .25
SDHSEN009 Elemental HERO Bladedge C .05 .15
SDHSEN010 Elemental HERO Necroshade C .15 .25
SDHSEN011 Elemental HERO Wildheart C .20 .30
SDHSEN012 Elemental HERO Bubbleman C .60 1.00
SDHSEN013 Neo-Spacian Grand Mole C .20 .30
SDHSEN014 Honest C .40 .60
SDHSEN015 Card Trooper C .05 .15
SDHSEN016 Winged Kuriboh C .30 .50
SDHSEN017 Summoner Monk C 1.25 1.75
SDHSEN018 Homunculus the Alchemic Being C .05 .15
SDHSEN019 Mask Change II C .40 .60
SDHSEN020 Form Change C .25 .40
SDHSEN021 Mask Charge C 1.00 1.30
SDHSEN022 Mask Change C .25 .35
SDHSEN023 Polymerization C 1.25 2.00
SDHSEN024 Miracle Fusion C .60 1.00
SDHSEN025 Parallel World Fusion C .05 .15
SDHSEN026 A Hero Lives C 3.00 4.00
SDHSEN027 Hero Mask C .05 .15
SDHSEN028 H - Heated Heart C .05 .15
SDHSEN029 E - Emergency Call C .05 .15
SDHSEN030 R - Righteous Justice C .05 .15
SDHSEN031 O - Oversoul C .05 .15
SDHSEN032 Reinforcement of the Army C .20 .30
SDHSEN033 The Warrior Returning Alive C .05 .15
SDHSEN034 Pot of Duality C 1.75 2.15
SDHSEN035 Hero Signal C .05 .15
SDHSEN036 Hero Blast C .05 .15
SDHSEN037 Call of the Haunted C .15 .25
SDHSEN038 Bottomless Trap Hole C .50 .75
SDHSEN039 Compulsory Evacuation Device C .25 .35
SDHSEN040 Battleguard Howling C .05 .15
SDHSEN041 Contrast HERO Chaos UR .15 .25
SDHSEN042 Masked HERO Koga SR .20 .30
SDHSEN043 Masked HERO Divine Wind SR .20 .30
SDHSEN044 Masked HERO Dark Law SR 3.00 3.50
SDHSEN045 Elemental HERO Great Tornado C .05 .15

2015 Yu-Gi-Oh Master of Pendulum

COMPLETE SET (43 CARDS) 14.00 20.00
STRUCTURE DECK 10.00 15.00
RELEASED ON DECEMBER 4, 2015
SDMPEN001 Dragonpulse Magician C .50 .75
SDMPEN009 Odd-Eyes Pendulum Dragon C .05 .15
SDMPEN017 Fencing Fire Ferret C .05 .15
SDMPEN025 Sky Iris C 1.75 2.25
SDMPEN033 Forbidden Dress C .05 .15
SDMPEN041 Odd-Eyes Meteorburst Dragon UR .75 1.00
SDMPEN002 Dragonpit Magician C 2.00 2.25
SDMPEN003 Nobledragon Magician SR .15 .25
SDMPEN004 Oafdragon Magician SR .40 .60
SDMPEN005 Wisdom-Eye Magician SR .25 .40
SDMPEN006 Performapal Skullcrobat Joker C .25 .35
SDMPEN007 Stargazer Magician C .05 .15
SDMPEN008 Timegazer Magician C .05 .15
SDMPEN010 Performapal Silver Claw C .05 .15
SDMPEN011 Performapal Salutiger C .05 .15
SDMPEN012 Performapal Trump Witch C .05 .15
SDMPEN013 Metaphys Armed Dragon C .05 .15
SDMPEN014 Chaos Hunter C .20 .30
SDMPEN015 Fusilier Dragon, the Dual-Mode Beast C .05 .15
SDMPEN016 Lyla, Lightsworn Sorceress C .10 .20
SDMPEN018 Inari Fire C .05 .15
SDMPEN019 Nefarious Archfiend Eater of Nefariousness C .05 .15
SDMPEN020 Jigabyte C .05 .15
SDMPEN021 Goblindbergh C .30 .50
SDMPEN022 X-Saber Airbellum C .05 .15
SDMPEN023 Magna Drago C .05 .15
SDMPEN024 Re-Cover C .05 .15
SDMPEN026 Pendulum Call C 1.00 1.50
SDMPEN027 Pendulum Shift C .05 .15
SDMPEN028 Pendulum Rising C .05 .15
SDMPEN029 Sacred Sword of Seven Stars C .20 .30
SDMPEN030 Summoner's Art C 1.25 2.00
SDMPEN031 Mystical Space Typhoon C .50 .75
SDMPEN032 Scapegoat C .05 .15
SDMPEN034 Polymerization C 1.25 1.75
SDMPEN035 Terraforming C .75 1.00
SDMPEN036 Pendulum Back C .05 .15
SDMPEN037 Powerful Rebirth C .15 .25
SDMPEN038 Traptrix Trap Hole Nightmare C .30 .50
SDMPEN039 Torrential Tribute C .50 .75
SDMPEN040 Eradicator Epidemic Virus C .05 .15
SDMPEN042 Odd-Eyes Absolute Dragon UR .40 .60
SDMPEN043 Rune-Eyes Pendulum Dragon C .05 .15

2016 Yu-Gi-Oh Emperor of Darkness 1st Edition

COMPLETE SET (42) 10.00 15.00
RELEASED ON JANUARY 29, 2016
SR01EN000 Ehther the Heavenly Monarch UR .40 .70
SR01EN001 Erebus the Underworld Monarch UR .40 .70
SR01EN002 Eidos the Underworld Squire SR .50 .75
SR01EN003 Edea the Heavenly Squire SR .50 .75
SR01EN004 Caius the Shadow Monarch C .20 .30
SR01EN005 Zaborg the Thunder Monarch C .10 .25
SR01EN006 Granmarg the Rock Monarch C .10 .25
SR01EN007 Mobius the Frost Monarch C .10 .25
SR01EN008 Thestalos the Firestorm Monarch C .10 .25
SR01EN009 Raiza the Storm Monarch C .10 .25
SR01EN010 Lucius the Shadow Vassal C .10 .25
SR01EN011 Mithra the Thunder Vassal C .10 .25
SR01EN012 Landrobe the Rock Vassal C .10 .25
SR01EN013 Escher the Frost Vassal C .10 .25
SR01EN014 Berlineth the Firestorm Vassal C .10 .25
SR01EN015 Garum the Storm Vassal C .10 .25
SR01EN016 Illusory Snatcher C .10 .25
SR01EN017 Tragoedia C .15 .25
SR01EN018 Dandylion C .10 .25
SR01EN019 Mathematician C .20 .30
SR01EN020 Level Eater C .10 .25
SR01EN021 Battle Fader C .20 .30
SR01EN022 Rainbow Kuriboh C .10 .25
SR01EN023 Pantheism of the Monarchs SR .60 1.00
SR01EN024 Domain of the True Monarchs C .75 1.15
SR01EN025 March of the Monarchs C .10 .25
SR01EN026 Return of the Monarchs C .20 .30
SR01EN027 The Monarchs Stormforth C .20 .35
SR01EN028 Strike of the Monarchs C .10 .25
SR01EN029 Tenacity of the Monarchs C .10 .25
SR01EN030 Soul Exchange C .10 .25
SR01EN031 Enemy Controller C .10 .25
SR01EN032 Dicephoon C .10 .25
SR01EN033 Soul Charge C 1.75 2.15
SR01EN034 The Prime Monarch C .60 .80
SR01EN035 The First Monarch C .10 .25
SR01EN036 Escalation of the Monarchs C .10 .25
SR01EN037 The Monarchs Awaken C .10 .25
SR01EN038 The Monarchs Erupt C .10 .25
SR01EN039 By Order of the Emperor C .10 .25
SR01EN040 Pinpoint Guard C .10 .25
SR01ENTKN Token C .20 .30

2016 Yu-Gi-Oh Starter Deck Yuya 1st Edition

COMPLETE SET 10.00 20.00
STARTER DECK 8.00 12.00
UNLISTED C .10 .30
RELEASED ON MAY 27, 2016
YS16EN001 Performapal Sleight Hand Magician UR .30 .50
YS16EN002 Performapal King Bear UR .30 .50
YS16EN003 Performapal Swincobra C .10 .30
YS16EN004 Performapal Momoncarpet SR .20 .30
YS16EN005 Performapal Parrotrio SR .30 .45
YS16EN006 Performapal Longphone Bull SR .20 .30
YS16EN007 Performapal Teeter Totter Hopper C .10 .30
YS16EN008 Odd-Eyes Pendulum Dragon C .10 .30
YS16EN009 Stargazer Magician C .10 .30
YS16EN010 Timegazer Magician C .10 .30
YS16EN011 Performapal Drummerilla C .10 .30
YS16EN012 Performapal Secondonkey C .10 .30
YS16EN013 Performapal Hip Hippo C .10 .30
YS16EN014 Foucault's Cannon C .10 .30
YS16EN015 Archfiend Eccentrick C 3.00 4.50
YS16EN016 Gene-Warped Warwolf C .10 .30
YS16EN017 Beast King Barbaros C .10 .30
YS16EN018 Pitch-Black Warwolf C .10 .30
YS16EN019 Dragon Dowser C .10 .30
YS16EN020 Giant Rat C .10 .30
YS16EN021 Performapal Dramatic Theater C .10 .30
YS16EN022 Smile World C .10 .30
YS16EN023 Hippo Carnival C .10 .30
YS16EN024 Draw Muscle C .10 .30
YS16EN025 Mystical Space Typhoon C .50 .75
YS16EN026 Lightning Vortex C .10 .30
YS16EN027 Book of Moon C .10 .30
YS16EN028 Lucky Iron Axe C .10 .30
YS16EN029 Burden of the Mighty C .10 .30
YS16EN030 Back-Up Rider C .10 .30
YS16EN031 Performapal Show Down C .10 .30
YS16EN032 Performapal Pinch Helper C .10 .30
YS16EN033 Wall of Disruption C .10 .30
YS16EN034 Ceasefire C .10 .30
YS16EN035 Raigeki Break C .10 .30
YS16EN036 Draining Shield C .10 .30
YS16EN037 Threatening Roar C .10 .30
YS16EN038 Dark Bribe C 1.25 1.75
YS16EN039 Chaos Burst C .10 .30
YS16EN040 Pendulum Reborn C .10 .30
YS16ENT01 Hippo Token Orange T .10 .30
YS16ENT02 Hippo Token Yellow T .10 .30
YS16ENT03 Hippo Token Blue T .10 .30

2016 YuGiOh Rise of the True Dragons Structure Deck First Edition

COMPLETE SET (42 CARDS) 13.00 20.00
STRUCTURE DECK 10.00 15.00
RELEASED ON JULY 8, 2016
SR02EN000 Arkbrave Dragon UR .25 .40
SR02EN001 Divine Dragon Lord Felgrand UR .25 .40
SR02EN002 Dragon Knight of Creation SR .20 .30
SR02EN003 Paladin of Felgrand C .10 .25
SR02EN004 Guardian of Felgrand C .10 .25
SR02EN005 Felgrand Dragon C .10 .25
SR02EN006 Darkblaze Dragon C .10 .25
SR02EN007 Herald of Creation C .10 .25
SR02EN008 Decoy Dragon C .10 .25
SR02EN009 Red-Eyes Darkness Metal Dragon C .40 .60
SR02EN010 Red-Eyes Wyvern C .10 .25
SR02EN011 White Night Dragon C .10 .25
SR02EN012 Darkstorm Dragon C .10 .25
SR02EN013 Armed Protector Dragon C .10 .25
SR02EN014 Evilswarm Zahak C .10 .25
SR02EN015 Eclipse Wyvern C .10 .25
SR02EN016 White Dragon Wyverburster C .10 .25
SR02EN017 Black Dragon Collapserpent C .10 .25
SR02EN018 Keeper of the Shrine C .10 .25
SR02EN019 Kidmodo Dragon C .10 .25
SR02EN020 Jain, Lightsworn Paladin C .10 .25
SR02EN021 Ehren, Lightsworn Monk C .10 .25
SR02EN022 Raiden, Hand of the Lightsworn C .30 .45
SR02EN023 Card Trooper C .10 .25
SR02EN024 Ruins of the Divine Dragon Lords SR .10 .20
SR02EN025 Return of the Dragon Lords SR 6.50 9.00
SR02EN026 Dragon Ravine C .10 .25
SR02EN027 A Wingbeat of Giant Dragon C .10 .25
SR02EN028 Trade-In C .75 1.00
SR02EN029 Foolish Burial C .10 .25
SR02EN030 Hand Destruction C .10 .25
SR02EN031 Reinforcement of the Army C .10 .25
SR02EN032 The Warrior Returning Alive C .10 .25
SR02EN033 Charge of the Light Brigade C .10 .25
SR02EN034 Terraforming C .75 1.25
SR02EN035 Dragon's Rebirth C .10 .25
SR02EN036 Burst Breath C .10 .25
SR02EN037 Needlebug Nest C .10 .25
SR02EN038 Breakthrough Skill C .30 .45
SR02EN039 Call of the Haunted C .10 .25
SR02EN040 Oasis of Dragon Souls C .10 .25
SR02ENTKN Dragon Lord Token C .10 .25

Bushiroad

HOW TO USE

What's Listed

Products listed in the Price Guide typically: 1) are produced by licensed manufacturers, 2) are widely available and 3) have market activity on single items.

What the Columns Mean

The LO and HI columns reflect current retail selling ranges. The HI column on the right generally represents the full retail selling price. The LO column on the left generally represents the lowest price one would expect to find with extensive shopping.

Grading

All cards in the Price Guide are based on NrMint to Mint condition. Damaged cards are generally sold for 25 to 75 percent of Mint value. Toy prices are based on mint condition. Toys that are loose (out of package), are generally sold for 50 percent of the listed price.

Currency

This Price Guide is intended to reflect the entire North American market. All listed prices are in U.S. dollars.

Legend

BR – Buddy rare. Exclusive to Future Card Buddyfight.
C – Common
CC – Climax common
CR – Climax rare. One of each card per Weiss Schwarz booster box.
PR – Promo card. These cards are available at special events and conventions.
R – Rare
RR – Double rare
RRR – Triple rare
SP – Special. These are either holofoil or signature cards. Usually come one per booster box.
SR – Super rare
SSP – Super special
U – Uncommon

Attention Dealers: If you would like to be a Price Guide Contributor for this almanac, please e-mail your name and phone number to: nonsports@beckett.com

2011 Cardfight Vanguard Descent of the King of Knights

COMPLETE SET (92)	150.00	300.00
BOOSTER BOX (36 PACKS)	60.00	80.00
BOOSTER PACK (5 CARDS)	3.00	4.00
RELEASED ON DECEMBER 10, 2011		
BT01001 Alfred RRR	6.00	15.00
BT01002 Blaster Blade RRR	6.00	15.00
BT01003 Barcgal RRR	2.00	5.00
BT01004 Dragonic Overlord RRR	4.00	10.00
BT01005 Aleph RRR	1.50	4.00
BT01006 CEO Amaterasu RRR	4.00	10.00
BT01007 Cocoa RRR	2.00	5.00
BT01008 Asura Kaiser RRR	4.00	10.00
BT01009 Lohengrin RR	.75	2.00
BT01010 Gancelot RR	.75	2.00
BT01011 Iseult RR	8.00	20.00
BT01012 Llew RR	2.00	5.00
BT01013 Vortex Dragon RR	.75	2.00
BT01014 Aleph RR	.75	2.00
BT01015 Barri RR	8.00	20.00
BT01016 Conroe RR	2.50	6.00
BT01017 Maiden of Libra RR	.75	2.00
BT01018 Mocha RR	2.00	5.00
BT01019 Chocolat RR	6.00	15.00
BT01020 Juggernaut Maximum RR	3.00	8.00
BT01021 Gallatin R	.20	.50
BT01022 Nehalem R	.20	.50
BT01023 Tejas R	.20	.50
BT01024 Tahr R	.75	2.00
BT01025 Apollon R	.75	2.00
BT01026 Wiseman R	.75	2.00
BT01027 Lozenge Magus R	.75	2.00
BT01028 Mr. Invincible R	.40	1.00
BT01029 Brutal Jack R	.75	2.00
BT01030 King of Sword R	.40	1.00
BT01031 Queen of Heart R	.40	1.00
BT01032 Battleraizer R	.60	1.50
BT01033 Deathrex R	.20	.50
BT01034 Blightops R	.20	.50
BT01035 Voidmaster R	.20	.50
BT01036 Demon Eater R	.20	.50
BT01037 Monster Frank R	.20	.50
BT01038 Commodore Blueblood R	.60	1.50
BT01039 Hell Spider R	.20	.50
BT01040 Bloody Hercules R	.20	.50
BT01041 Randolf C	.10	.25
BT01042 Marron C	.10	.25
BT01043 Lien C	.10	.25
BT01044 Wingal C	.10	.25
BT01045 Govannon C	.10	.25
BT01046 Flogal C	.10	.25
BT01047 Elaine C	.10	.25
BT01048 Bahr C	.10	.25
BT01049 Gojo C	.10	.25
BT01050 Jarran C	.10	.25
BT01051 Monica C	.10	.25
BT01052 Ganlu C	.10	.25
BT01053 Genjo C	.10	.25
BT01054 Gemini C	.10	.25
BT01055 Milk C	.10	.25
BT01056 Nike C	.10	.25
BT01057 Dream Eater C	.10	.25
BT01058 Miracle Kid C	.10	.25
BT01059 Hungry Dumpty C	.10	.25
BT01060 Tough Boy C	.10	.25
BT01061 Shout C	.10	.25
BT01062 Clay-doll Mechanic C	.10	.25
BT01063 Shining Lady C	.10	.25
BT01064 Lucky Girl C	.10	.25
BT01065 Clara C	.10	.25
BT01066 Sonic Noa C	.10	.25
BT01067 Shieldon C	.10	.25
BT01068 Chigasumi C	.10	.25
BT01069 Dreadmaster C	.10	.25
BT01070 Hagakure C	.10	.25
BT01071 Blue Dust C	.10	.25
BT01072 Nightmare Baby C	.10	.25
BT01073 Rock the Wall C	.10	.25
BT01074 Brakki C	.10	.25
BT01075 Wonder Boy	.10	.25
BT01076 Milly C	.10	.25
BT01077 Romario C	.10	.25
BT01078 Guiding Zombie C	.10	.25
BT01079 Karma Queen C	.10	.25
BT01080 Madame Mirage C	.10	.25
BT01S01 King of Knights, Alfred SP	15.00	40.00
BT01S02 Blaster Blade SP	20.00	50.00
BT01S03 Barcgal SP	6.00	15.00
BT01S04 Dragonic Overlord SP	12.00	30.00
BT01S05 CEO Amaterasu SP	15.00	40.00
BT01S06 Battle Sister, Cocoa SP	12.00	30.00
BT01S07 Asura Kaiser SP	12.00	30.00
BT01S08 Solitary Knight, Gancelot SP	6.00	15.00
BT01S09 Vortex Dragon SP	4.00	10.00
BT01S10 Maiden of Libra SP	4.00	10.00
BT01S11 Lozenge Magus SP	20.00	50.00
BT01S12 Battleraizer SP	10.00	25.00

2012 Cardfight Vanguard Breaker of Limits

COMPLETE SET (125)	200.00	350.00
BOOSTER BOX (36 PACKS)	60.00	80.00
BOOSTER PACK (5 CARDS)	3.00	4.00
RELEASED ON MAY 19, 2012		
BT06001 Kiriel RRR	2.50	6.00
BT06002 Nociel RRR	4.00	10.00
BT06003 Cocytus RRR	4.00	10.00
BT06004 Blond Ezel RRR	12.00	30.00
BT06005 Viviane RRR	3.00	8.00
BT06006 Vermillion RRR	12.00	30.00
BT06007 Shiden RRR	1.50	4.00
BT06008 Azure Dragon RRR	3.00	8.00
BT06009 Ergodiel RR	1.50	4.00
BT06010 Armaros RR	1.00	2.50
BT06011 Nociel RR	2.50	6.00
BT06012 Requiel RR	5.00	12.00
BT06013 Deadly Swordmaster RR	.75	2.00
BT06014 Thanatos RR	.75	2.00
BT06015 Agravain RR	.75	2.00
BT06016 Sleygal Dagger RR	2.00	5.00
BT06017 Mark RR	8.00	20.00
BT06018 Indra RR	2.00	5.00
BT06019 Dragonic Deathscythe RR	3.00	8.00
BT06020 Guld RR	5.00	12.00
BT06021 Feather Palace R	.60	1.50
BT06022 Geniel R	.60	1.50
BT06023 Calamity Flame R	.60	1.50
BT06024 Barbiel R	.75	2.00
BT06025 Ergodiel R	.60	1.50
BT06026 Miracle Feather Nurse R	.60	1.50
BT06027 Nightstorm R	.40	1.00
BT06028 Skeleton Demon World Knight R	.40	1.00
BT06029 Deadly Spirit R	.60	1.50
BT06030 Pietro R	.60	1.50
BT06031 Deadly Nightmare R	.60	1.50
BT06032 Beaumains R	.60	1.50
BT06033 Tripp R	.60	1.50
BT06034 Nimue R	.75	2.00
BT06035 Kyrph R	.60	1.50
BT06036 Gyras R	.60	1.50
BT06037 Thunderstorm Dragoon R	.40	1.00
BT06038 Garuda R	.60	1.50
BT06039 Raien R	.60	1.50
BT06040 Photon Bomber Wyvern R	.60	1.50
BT06041 Saishin R	.60	1.50
BT06042 White Tiger R	.60	1.50
BT06043 Adriel C	.10	.25
BT06044 Million Ray Pegasus C	.10	.25
BT06045 Mastima C	.10	.25
BT06046 Penem C	.10	.25
BT06047 Besnel C	.10	.25
BT06048 Thousand Ray Pegasus C	.10	.25
BT06049 Heavenly Injector C	.10	.25
BT06050 Lancet Shooter C	.10	.25
BT06051 Bringer of the Water of Life C	.10	.25
BT06052 Clutch Rifle Angel C	.10	.25
BT06053 Lightning Charger C	.10	.25
BT06054 Thermometer Angel C	.10	.25
BT06055 Rocket Dash Unicorn C	.10	.25
BT06056 Bouquet Toss Messenger C	.10	.25
BT06057 Aurora Ribbon Pidgeon C	.10	.25
BT06058 Critical Hit Angel C	.10	.25
BT06059 Nociel C	.10	.25
BT06060 Sunny Smile Angel C	.10	.25
BT06061 Zombie Shark C	.10	.25
BT06062 Ghost Ship C	.10	.25
BT06063 Ghost Pirate of the Freezing Night C	.10	.25
BT06064 Silver C	.10	.25
BT06065 Skeleton Gargoyle C	.10	.25
BT06066 Child Frank C	.10	.25
BT06067 John the Ghost C	.10	.25
BT06068 Ripple's Banshee C	.10	.25
BT06069 Dragon Spirit C	.10	.25
BT06070 Ghost Pirate of the Cursed Gun C	.10	.25
BT06071 Captain Night Kid C	.10	.25
BT06072 Skeleton Captain Cut C	.10	.25
BT06073 Demon Cannonball C	.10	.25
BT06074 Hook Arm Zombie C	.10	.25
BT06075 Doctor Rouge C	.10	.25
BT06076 Underworld's Helmsman C	.10	.25
BT06077 Greed Shade C	.10	.25
BT06078 Gigantech Crusher C	.10	.25
BT06079 Manaidan C	.10	.25
BT06080 Gigantech Commander C	.10	.25
BT06081 Elephas C	.10	.25
BT06082 Providence Strategist C	.10	.25
BT06083 Gareth C	.10	.25
BT06084 Waving Owl C	.10	.25
BT06085 Tron C	.10	.25
BT06086 Cron C	.10	.25
BT06087 Greeting Drummer C	.10	.25
BT06088 Flames of Victory C	.10	.25
BT06089 Coongal C	.10	.25
BT06090 Laudine C	.10	.25
BT06091 Satellitefall Dragon C	.10	.25
BT06092 Breakthrough Dragon C	.10	.25
BT06093 Curse Gun Wyvern C	.10	.25
BT06094 Ensei C	.10	.25
BT06095 Red River Dragoon C	.10	.25
BT06096 Stealth Fighter C	.10	.25
BT06097 Youtsu C	.10	.25
BT06098 Spark Kid Dragoon C	.10	.25
BT06099 Katarina C	.10	.25
BT06100 Malevolent Djinn C	.10	.25
BT06101 DreadCharge Dragon C	.10	.25
BT06102 Brightlance Dragon C	.10	.25
BT06103 Rising Phoenix C	.10	.25
BT06104 Moai the Great C	.10	.25
BT06105 Black Tortoise C	.10	.25
BT06106 Marvelous Honey C	.10	.25
BT06107 Almighty Reporter C	.10	.25
BT06108 Scarlet Bird C	.10	.25
BT06109 Red Card Dealer C	.10	.25
BT06110 Turboraizer C	.10	.25
BT06111 Muscle Hercules C	.10	.25
BT06112 Bolta C	.10	.25
BT06113 Cup Bowler C	.10	.25
BT06S01 Circular Saw, Kiriel SP	10.00	25.00
BT06S02 Battle Cupid, Nociel SP	6.00	15.00
BT06S03 Ice Prison Necromancer, Cocytus SP	8.00	20.00
BT06S04 Incandescent Lion, Blond Ezel SP	25.00	60.00
BT06S05 Player of the Holy Bow, Viviane SP	12.00	30.00
BT06S06 Dragonic Kaiser, Vermillion SP	20.00	50.00
BT06S07 Desert Gunner, Shiden SP	6.00	15.00
BT06S08 Beast Deity, Azure Dragon SP	8.00	20.00
BT06S09 Cosmo Healer, Ergodiel SP	6.00	15.00
BT06S10 Death Seeker, Thanatos SP	6.00	15.00
BT06S11 Knight of Fury, Agravain SP	4.00	10.00
BT06S12 Vajra Emperor, Indra SP	4.00	10.00

2012 Cardfight Vanguard Cavalry of Black Steel

COMPLETE SET (53)	100.00	200.00
BOOSTER BOX (15 PACKS)	30.00	40.00
BOOSTER PACK (5 CARDS)	2.00	3.00
RELEASED ON JULY 7, 2012		
EB03001 Demonic Lord RRR	5.00	12.00
EB03002 Spec. Duke Dragon RRR	10.00	25.00
EB03003 Reckless Express RR	2.50	6.00
EB03004 Martail Arts Mutant RR	2.50	6.00
EB03005 White Dragon Knight RR	2.50	6.00
EB03006 Origin Mage, Ildona RR	2.50	6.00
EB03007 Dragonic Lawkeeper RR	4.00	10.00
EB03008 Jelly Beans R	.60	1.50
EB03009 Dudley Daisy R	.60	1.50
EB03010 Bewitching Officer R	.75	2.00
EB03011 Toxic Trooper R	.60	1.50
EB03012 Toxic Soldier R	.75	2.00
EB03013 Gigantech Destroyer R	1.00	2.50
EB03014 Blk Dragon Knight R	1.25	3.00
EB03015 Blk Dragon Whelp R	.75	2.00
EB03016 Twin Shine Swordsman R	1.00	2.50
EB03017 Dragonic Executioner R	1.00	2.50
EB03018 Dudley Douglas C	.10	.25
EB03019 Fierce Leader, Zachary C	.10	.25
EB03020 Field Driller C	.10	.25
EB03021 Medical Manager C	.10	.25
EB03022 Smart Leader, Dark Bringer C	.10	.25
EB03023 Kungfu Kicker C	.10	.25
EB03024 Gyro Slinger C	.10	.25
EB03025 Commander, Garry Gannon C	.10	.25
EB03026 Iron Fist Mutant, Roly Poly C	.10	.25
EB03027 Transmutated Thief, Steal Spider C	.10	.25
EB03028 Machining Mosquito C	.10	.25
EB03029 Pest Professor, Mad Fly C	.10	.25
EB03030 Megacolony Battler C C	.10	.25
EB03031 Awaking Dragonfly C	.10	.25
EB03032 Flash Edge Valkyrie C	.10	.25
EB03033 Scout of Darkness C	.30	.75
EB03034 Blade Feather Valkyrie C	.10	.25
EB03035 War-horse C	.20	.50
EB03036 Falcon Knight C	.20	.50
EB03037 Knight of Determination C	.20	.50
EB03038 Eagle Knight of the Skies C	.10	.25
EB03039 Miru Biru C	.10	.25
EB03040 Knight of Fighting Spirit, Dordona C	.10	.25
EB03041 Cross Shot, Garp C	.10	.25
EB03042 Dragon Armored Knight C	.10	.25
EB03043 Grapeshot Wyvern C	.10	.25

EB03044 Omniscience Madonna C .10 .25
EB03045 Onmyoji of the Moonlit Night C .10 .25
EB03046 Blue Scale Deer C .10 .25
EB03047 Petal Fairy C .10 .25
EB03S01 Demonic Lord, Dudley Emperor SP 20.00 50.00
EB03S02 Spectral Duke Dragon SP 30.00 80.00
EB03S03 Martial Arts Mutant, Master Beetle SP 15.00 40.00
EB03S04 White Dragon Knight, Pendragon SP 10.00 25.00
EB03S05 Origin Mage, Ildona SP 10.00 25.00
EB03S06 Dragonic Lawkeeper SP 15.00 40.00

2012 Cardfight Vanguard Demonic Lord Invasion

COMPLETE SET (94) 300.00 450.00
BOOSTER BOX (30 PACKS) 80.00 100.00
BOOSTER PACK (5 CARDS) 4.00 5.00
RELEASED ON AUGUST 11, 2012
BT03001 Stil Vampir RRR 2.00 5.00
BT03002 Demon World Marquis RRR 8.00 20.00
BT03003 Nightmare Doll, Alice RRR 8.00 20.00
BT03004 Ravenous Dragon RRR 2.00 5.00
BT03005 Swordsman of Explosive RRR 12.00 30.00
BT03006 Goddess of Full Moon RRR 10.00 25.00
BT03007 Goddess of Half Moon RRR 12.00 30.00
BT03008 Ultimate Lifeform RRR 1.00 2.50
BT03009 Edel Rose RR 1.50 4.00
BT03010 Gwynn the Ripper RR 1.25 3.00
BT03011 March Rabbit RR 6.00 15.00
BT03012 Doreen the Thruster RR 2.50 6.00
BT03013 Dusk Illusionist, Robert RR 1.25 3.00
BT03014 Crimson Beast Tamer RR 6.00 15.00
BT03015 Mirror Demon RR 1.25 3.00
BT03016 Hades Hypnotist RR 8.00 20.00
BT03017 Archbird RR 5.00 12.00
BT03018 Knight of Godly RR 3.00 8.00
BT03019 Dual Axe Archdragon RR 2.50 6.00
BT03020 Super Dimensional RR 4.00 10.00
BT03021 Imprisoned Fallen R .40 1.00
BT03022 Werwolf Sieger R .50 1.25
BT03023 Demon of Aspiration, Amon R .40 1.00
BT03024 Alluring Succubus R 1.25 3.00
BT03025 Vermillion Gatekeeper R .40 1.00
BT03026 Bloody Calf R .40 1.00
BT03027 Barking Manticore R .50 1.25
BT03028 Barking Cerberus R .40 1.00
BT03029 Skull Juggler R .40 1.00
BT03030 Midnight Bunny R 1.00 2.50
BT03031 Turquoise Beast Tamer R .50 1.25
BT03032 Hades Ringmaster R .40 1.00
BT03033 Raging Dragon, Blastsaurus R .60 1.50
BT03034 Ravenous Dragon, Megarex R 1.00 2.50
BT03035 Savage Warrior R .40 1.00
BT03036 Toypugal R .75 2.00
BT03037 Drangal R .50 1.25
BT03038 Oracle Guardian, Blue Eye R .40 1.00
BT03039 Godhawk, Ichibyoshi R .40 1.00
BT03040 Circle Magus R .50 1.25
BT03041 Death Army Lady R .75 2.00
BT03042 Death Army Guy R 1.00 2.50
BT03043 Decadent Succubus C .10 .25
BT03044 Prisoner Beast C .10 .25
BT03045 Poet of Darkness, Amon C .10 .25
BT03046 Blitzritter C .10 .25
BT03047 Hades Puppet Master C .10 .25
BT03048 Cursed Doctor C .10 .25
BT03049 Dark Queen of Nightmareland C .10 .25
BT03050 Elephant Juggler C .10 .25
BT03051 Hungry Clown C .10 .25
BT03052 Dark Metal Bicorn C .10 .25
BT03053 Dynamite Juggler C .10 .25
BT03054 Spiral Master C .10 .25
BT03055 Candy Clown C .10 .25
BT03056 Rainbow Magician C .10 .25
BT03057 Vacuum Mammoth C .10 .25
BT03058 Savage Destroyer C .10 .25
BT03059 Raging Dragon, Sparksaurus C .10 .25
BT03060 Herbivorous Dragon, Brutosaurus C .10 .25
BT03061 Pack Dragon, Tinyrex C .10 .25
BT03062 Savage Shaman C .10 .25
BT03063 Black Cannon Tiger C .10 .25
BT03064 Knight of Tribulations, Galahad C .10 .25
BT03065 Gigantech Dozer C .10 .25
BT03066 Swordsman of the Blaze, Palamedes C .10 .25
BT03067 Knight of Quests, Galahad C .10 .25
BT03068 Borgal C .10 .25
BT03069 Alabaster Owl C .10 .25
BT03070 Secretary Angel C .10 .25
BT03071 Oracle Guardian, Red Eye C .10 .25
BT03072 Faithful Angel C .10 .25
BT03073 Goddess of the Crescent Moon, Tsukuyomi C .10 .25
BT03074 Battle Sister, Vanilla C .10 .25
BT03075 Victory Maker C .10 .25
BT03076 Flame Edge Dragon C .10 .25
BT03077 Dragon Dancer, Lourdes C .10 .25
BT03078 Blue Ray Dracokid C .10 .25
BT03079 Cannon Ball C .10 .25
BT03080 Masked Police, Grander C .10 .25
BT03081 Karenroid, Daisy C .10 .25
BT03082 Workerpod, Saturday C .10 .25
BT03S02 Demon World Marquis, Amon SP 12.00 30.00
BT03S03 Nightmare Doll, Alice SP 12.00 30.00
BT03S04 Ravenous Dragon, Gigarex SP 6.00 15.00
BT03S05 Swordsman of the Explosive Flames, Palamedes SP 20.00 50.00
BT03S06 Goddess of the Full Moon, Tsukuyomi SP25.00 60.00
BT03S08 Ultimate Lifeform, Cosmo Lord SP 6.00 15.00
BT03S10 Gwynn the Ripper SP 8.00 20.00
BT03S14 Crimson Beast Tamer SP 15.00 40.00
BT03S18 Knight of Godly Speed, Galahad SP 6.00 15.00
BT03S19 Dual Axe Archdragon SP 8.00 20.00
BT03S20 Super Dimensional Robo, Daiyusha SP15.00 40.00
BT03S30 Turquoise Beast Tamer SP 20.00 50.00

2012 Cardfight Vanguard Eclipse of Illusionary Shadows

COMPLETE SET (94) 400.00 550.00
BOOSTER BOX (36 PACKS) 60.00 80.00
BOOSTER PACK (5 CARDS) 3.00 4.00
RELEASED ON DECEMBER 14, 2012
BT04001 Phantom Blaster Dragon RRR 15.00 40.00
BT04002 Darkness Maiden, Macha RRR 6.00 15.00
BT04003 Skull Witch, Nemain RRR 8.00 20.00
BT04004 Enigman Storm RRR 3.00 8.00
BT04005 Evil Armor General, Giraffa RRR 5.00 12.00
BT04006 Amber Dragon, Eclipse RRR 5.00 12.00
BT04007 Heatnail Salamander RRR 4.00 10.00
BT04008 Stern Blaukluger RRR 6.00 15.00
BT04009 Dark Metal Dragon RR 3.00 8.00
BT04010 Gururubau RR 3.00 8.00
BT04011 Dark Shield, Mac Lir RR 10.00 25.00
BT04012 Enigman Wave RR 2.50 6.00
BT04013 Cosmo Break RR 3.00 8.00
BT04014 Diamond Ace RR 5.00 12.00
BT04015 Commander Laurel RR 2.50 6.00
BT04016 Elite Mutant, Giraffa RR 3.00 8.00
BT04017 Paralize Madonna RR 4.00 10.00
BT04018 Amber Dragon, Dusk RR 3.00 8.00
BT04019 Blaukluger RR 5.00 12.00
BT04020 Fang of Light, Garmore RR 4.00 10.00
BT04021 Silver Spear Demon, Gusion R .40 1.00
BT04022 Dark Mage, Badhabh Caar R .75 2.00
BT04023 Knight of Darkness, Rugos R .75 2.00
BT04024 Blaster Dark R 5.00 12.00
BT04025 Cursed Lancer R .75 2.00
BT04026 Fullbau R .40 1.00
BT04027 Enigman Rain R .40 1.00
BT04028 Twin Order R .40 1.00
BT04029 Platinum Ace R .40 1.00
BT04030 Cosmo Roar R .75 2.00
BT04031 Enigman Flow R .40 1.00
BT04032 Death Warden Ant Lion R .75 2.00
BT04033 Violent Vesper R .40 1.00
BT04034 Water Gang R .40 1.00
BT04035 Gloom Flyman R .40 1.00
BT04036 Megacolony Battler B R .75 2.00
BT04037 Larva Mutant, Giraffa R .40 1.00
BT04038 Lizard Soldier, Raopia R .40 1.00
BT04039 Amber Dragon, Dawn R .75 2.00
BT04040 Armored Fairy, Shubiela R .40 1.00
BT04041 Blaujunger R .40 1.00
BT04042 Beast Knight, Garmore R .40 1.00
BT04043 Demon World Castle, Donnerschlag C .10 .25
BT04044 Demon World Castle, Fatalita C .10 .25
BT04045 Black Sage, Charon C .10 .25
BT04046 Witch of Nostrum, Arianrhod C .10 .25
BT04047 Doranbau C .10 .25
BT04048 Blaster Javelin C .10 .25
BT04049 Zappbau C .10 .25
BT04050 Grim Reaper C .10 .25
BT04051 Abyss Freezer C .10 .25
BT04052 Darkside Trumpeter C .10 .25
BT04053 Abyss Healer C .10 .25
BT04054 Enigman Shine C .10 .25
BT04055 Enigroid Comrade C .10 .25
BT04056 Enigman Ripple C .10 .25
BT04057 Glory Maker C .10 .25
BT04058 Justice Cobalt C .10 .25
BT04059 Army Penguin C .10 .25
BT04060 Cosmo Fang C .10 .25
BT04061 Justice Rose C .10 .25
BT04062 Ironcutter Beetle C .10 .25
BT04063 Tail Joe C .10 .25
BT04064 Pupa Mutant, Giraffa C .10 .25
BT04065 Stealth Millepede C .10 .25
BT04066 Sharp Nail Scorpio C .10 .25
BT04067 Raider Mantis C .10 .25
BT04068 Sonic Cicada C .10 .25
BT04069 Medical Battler, Ranpli C .10 .25
BT04070 Garnet Dragon, Flash C .10 .25
BT04071 Lava Arm Dragon C .10 .25
BT04072 Amber Dragon, Daylight C .10 .25
BT04073 Red Gem Carbuncle C .10 .25
BT04074 Flame Seed Salamander C .10 .25
BT04075 Eisenkugel C .10 .25
BT04076 Dancing Wolf C .10 .25
BT04077 Blaupanzer C .10 .25
BT04078 Toolkit Boy C .10 .25
BT04079 Fighting Battleship, Prometheus C .10 .25
BT04080 Grapple Mania C .10 .25
BT04081 Snogal C .10 .25
BT04082 Brugal C .10 .25
BT04S01 Phantom Blaster Dragon SP 50.00 100.00
BT04S02 Darkness Maiden, Macha SP 20.00 50.00
BT04S03 Skull Witch, Nemain SP 15.00 40.00
BT04S04 Enigman Storm SP 10.00 25.00
BT04S05 Evil Armor General, Giraffa SP 10.00 25.00
BT04S06 Amber Dragon, Eclipse SP 12.00 30.00
BT04S07 Stern Blaukluger SP 15.00 40.00
BT04S08 Dark Metal Dragon SP 10.00 25.00
BT04S09 Amber Dragon, Dusk SP 12.00 30.00
BT04S10 Blaukluger SP 8.00 20.00
BT04S11 Fang of Light, Garmore SP 10.00 25.00
BT04S12 Blaster Dark SP 60.00 120.00

2012 Cardfight Vanguard Onslaught of Dragon Souls

COMPLETE SET (92) 250.00 400.00
BOOSTER BOX (36 PACKS) 30.00 40.00
BOOSTER PACK (5 CARDS) 2.00 3.00
RELEASE DATE MARCH 10, 2012
BT02001 Sky Diver RRR 6.00 15.00
BT02002 Spirit Exceed RRR 2.50 6.00
BT02003 Ruin Shade RRR 8.00 20.00
BT02004 Soul Savior RRR 15.00 30.00
BT02005 Blazing Flare RRR 6.00 15.00
BT02006 Blockade RRR 4.00 10.00
BT02007 Coco RRR 2.00 5.00
BT02008 Lion Heat RRR 3.00 8.00
BT02009 General Seifried RR 2.00 5.00
BT02010 Marilyn RR 6.00 15.00
BT02011 Basskirk RR 3.00 8.00
BT02012 Negromarl RR 1.25 3.00
BT02013 Captain Nightmist RR 3.00 8.00
BT02014 Gust Jinn RR 6.00 15.00
BT02015 Young Pegasus RR 2.50 6.00
BT02016 Chain-attack RR 1.00 2.50
BT02017 Silent Tom RR 8.00 20.00
BT02018 Magician Girl Kirara RR 1.50 4.00
BT02019 Twin Blader RR 8.00 20.00
BT02020 Flores RR 1.00 2.50
BT02021 Unite Attacker R .20 .50
BT02022 Black Panther R .20 .50
BT02023 Dudley Dan R .30 .75
BT02024 Mecha Trainer R .20 .50
BT02025 Dancing Cutlass R .20 .50
BT02026 Chappie the Ghostie R .30 .75
BT02027 Gigantech Charger R .30 .75
BT02028 Barron R .20 .50
BT02029 Akane R .40 1.00
BT02030 Pongal R 1.00 2.50
BT02031 Blazing Core Dragon R 1.25 3.00
BT02032 Kimnara R 1.25 3.00
BT02033 Luck Bird R .20 .50
BT02034 Skyptero R .20 .50
BT02035 Dragon Egg R .20 .50
BT02036 Aqua R .20 .50
BT02037 Caravel R .20 .50
BT02038 Master Fraude R .20 .50
BT02039 Scientist Monkey Rue R .20 .50
BT02040 Geograph Giant R .20 .50
BT02041 Panzer Gale C .10 .25
BT02042 Devil Summoner C .10 .25
BT02043 Cyclone Blitz C .10 .25
BT02044 Spike Brothers Assault Squad C .10 .25
BT02045 Sonic Breaker C .10 .25
BT02046 Cheerful Lynx C .10 .25
BT02047 Tiara C .10 .25
BT02048 Silence Joker C .10 .25
BT02049 Skeleton Swordsman C .10 .25
BT02050 Samurai Spirit C .10 .25
BT02051 Evil Shade C .10 .25
BT02052 Knight Spirit C .10 .25
BT02053 Skeleton Lookout C .10 .25
BT02054 Rick the Ghostie C .10 .25
BT02055 Rough Seas Banshee C .10 .25
BT02056 Gordon C .40 1.00
BT02057 Soul Guiding Elf C .10 .25
BT02058 Pixy Fife and Drum C .10 .25
BT02059 Margal C .10 .25
BT02060 Berger C .10 .25
BT02061 Iron Tail Dragon C .10 .25
BT02062 Reas C .10 .25
BT02063 Nafd C .10 .25
BT02064 Gattling Claw Dragon C .30 .75
BT02065 Security Guardian C .10 .25
BT02066 One Who Gazes at the Truth C .10 .25
BT02067 Emergency Alarmer C .10 .25
BT02068 Psychic Bird C .10 .25
BT02069 Dinochaos C .10 .25
BT02070 Cannon Gear C .10 .25
BT02071 NGM Prototype C .10 .25
BT02072 Cray Soldier C .10 .25
BT02073 Three Minutes C .10 .25
BT02074 Red Lightning C .10 .25
BT02075 Blazer Idols C .10 .25
BT02076 Lady Bomb C .10 .25
BT02077 Phantom Black C .10 .25
BT02078 Megacolony Battler A C .10 .25
BT02079 Silver Wolf C .10 .25
BT02080 Intelli-Mouse C .10 .25
BT02S01 Sky Diver SP 10.00 25.00
BT02S02 Spirit Exceed SP 8.00 20.00
BT02S03 Ruin Shade SP 12.00 30.00
BT02S04 Soul Savior Dragon SP 25.00 60.00
BT02S05 Blazing Flare Dragon SP 12.00 30.00
BT02S06 Seal Dragon, Blockade SP 8.00 20.00
BT02S07 Scarlet Witch, Coco SP 10.00 25.00
BT02S08 Lion Heat SP 12.00 30.00
BT02S09 General Seifried SP 8.00 20.00
BT02S10 Witch Doctor of the Abyss, Negromarl SP4.00 10.00
BT02S11 Top Idol, Flores SP 15.00 40.00
BT02S12 Top Idol, Aqua SP 12.00 30.00

2013 Cardfight Vanguard Awakening of Twin Blades

COMPLETE SET (92) 250.00 400.00
BOOSTER BOX (36 PACKS) 60.00 80.00
BOOSTER PACK (5 CARDS) 3.00 4.00
RELEASED ON FEBRUARY 22, 2013
BT05001 Covert Demonic Dragon, Mandala Lord RRR 5.00 12.00
BT05002 Majesty Lord Blaster RRR 12.00 30.00
BT05003 Star Call Trumpeter RRR 6.00 15.00
BT05004 Phantom Blaster Overlord RRR 12.00 30.00
BT05005 Dragonic Overlord The End RRR 25.00 50.00
BT05006 Miracle Beauty RRR 4.00 10.00
BT05007 King of Diptera, Beelzebub RRR 2.00 5.00
BT05008 Mistress Hurricane RRR 1.50 4.00
BT05009 Maiden of Trailing Rose RR 4.00 10.00
BT05010 Glass Beads Dragon RR 2.00 5.00
BT05011 Maiden of Blossom Rain RR 5.00 12.00
BT05012 Stealth Fiend, Midnight Crow RR 1.25 3.00
BT05013 Stealth Beast, Leaves Mirage RR 5.00 12.00
BT05014 Knight of Loyalty, Bedivere RR 4.00 10.00
BT05015 Knight of Friendship, Kay RR 3.00 8.00
BT05016 Wingal Brave RR 3.00 8.00
BT05017 Moonlight Witch, Vaha RR 1.50 4.00
BT05018 Knight of Nullity, Masquerade RR 5.00 12.00
BT05019 Evil-eye Princess, Euryale RR 1.50 4.00
BT05020 Street Bouncer RR 1.25 3.00
BT05021 Frontline Valkyrie, Laurel R 1.00 2.50
BT05022 Knight of Harvest, Gene R .60 1.50
BT05023 Avatar of the Plains, Behemoth R .60 1.50
BT05024 Iris Knight R .60 1.50
BT05025 Hey Yo Pineapple R .60 1.50
BT05026 Shield Seed Squire R .60 1.50
BT05027 Stealth Fiend, Kurama Lord R .60 1.50
BT05028 Stealth Dragon, Voidgelga R .75 2.00
BT05029 Stealth Beast, Bloody Mist R .60 1.50
BT05030 Caped Stealth Rogue, Shanaou R .60 1.50
BT05031 Stealth Dragon, Cursed Breath R .75 2.00
BT05032 Stealth Dragon, Turbulent Edge R .75 2.00
BT05033 Stealth Beast, Million Rat R .75 2.00
BT05034 Stealth Beast, Evil Ferret R .60 1.50
BT05035 Conjurer of Mithril R .75 2.00
BT05036 Knight of Purgatory, Skull Face R .75 2.00
BT05037 Apocalypse Bat R .75 2.00
BT05038 Burning Horn Dragon R 1.25 3.00
BT05039 Flame of Promise, Aermo R .75 2.00
BT05040 Demonic Dragon Mage, Mahoraga R .60 1.50
BT05041 Magical Police Quilt R .75 2.00
BT05042 Devil Child R .75 2.00
BT05043 Knight of Verdure, Gene C .10 .25
BT05044 Colossal Wings, Simurgh C .10 .25
BT05045 Spiritual Tree Sage, Irminsul C .10 .25
BT05046 Corolla Dragon C .10 .25
BT05047 Caramel Popcorn C .10 .25
BT05048 Lady of the Sunlight Forest C .10 .25
BT05049 Blade Seed Squire C .10 .25
BT05050 Lily Knight of the Valley C .10 .25
BT05051 Pea Knight C .10 .25
BT05052 Chestnut Bullet C .10 .25
BT05053 Dancing Sunflower C .10 .25
BT05054 Sweet Honey C .10 .25
BT05055 Watering Elf C .10 .25
BT05056 Stealth Beast, White Mane C .10 .25
BT05057 Stealth Rogue of Silence, Shijimamaru C.10 .25
BT05058 Stealth Beast, Leaf Raccoon C .10 .25
BT05059 Stealth Beast, Moon Edge C .10 .25
BT05060 Stealth Beast, Cat Rouge C .10 .25
BT05061 Stealth Fiend, Yukihime C .10 .25
BT05062 Stealth Fiend, Dart Spider C .10 .25
BT05063 Powerful Sage, Bairon C .10 .25
BT05064 Dream Painter C .10 .25
BT05065 Silent Sage, Sharon C .10 .25
BT05066 Nightmare Painter C .10 .25
BT05067 Phantom Bringer Demon C .10 .25
BT05068 Death Feather Eagle C .10 .25
BT05069 Battle Maiden, Tagitsuhime C .10 .25
BT05070 White Rabbit of Inaba C .10 .25
BT05071 Battle Sister, Ginger C .10 .25
BT05072 Doom Bringer Griffin C .10 .25
BT05073 Top Gun C .10 .25
BT05074 Anthrodroid C .10 .25
BT05075 The Gong C .10 .25
BT05076 Super Dimensional Robo, Dailady C .10 .25
BT05077 Guide Dolphin C .10 .25
BT05078 Dark Soul Conductor C .10 .25
BT05079 Hysteric Shirley C .10 .25
BT05080 Big League Bear C .10 .25
BT05081 Madcap Marionette C .10 .25
BT05082 Sky High Walker C .10 .25
BT05S01 Covert Demonic Dragon, Mandala Lord SP15.00 40.00
BT05S02 Majesty Lord Blaster SP 25.00 60.00
BT05S03 Star Call Trumpeter SP 8.00 20.00
BT05S04 Phantom Blaster Overlord SP 20.00 50.00
BT05S05 Dragonic Overlord the End SP 25.00 60.00
BT05S06 Miracle Beauty SP 8.00 20.00
BT05S07 King of Diptera, Beelzebub SP 8.00 20.00
BT05S08 Mistress Hurricane SP 6.00 15.00
BT05S09 Maiden of Trailing Rose SP 8.00 20.00
BT05S10 Stealth Fiend, Midnight Crow SP 6.00 15.00

2013 Cardfight Vanguard Blue Storm Armada

COMPLETE SET (114) 200.00 350.00
BOOSTER BOX (36 PACKS) 60.00 80.00
BOOSTER PACK (5 CARDS) 3.00 4.00
RELEASED ON SEPTEMBER 22, 2013
BT08001 Ultimate Dimensional Robo, Great Daiyusha RRR 6.00 15.00
BT08002 Galactic Beast, Zeal RRR 3.00 8.00
BT08003 Arboros Dragon, Sephirot RRR 4.00 10.00
BT08004 White Lily Musketeer, Cecilia RRR 5.00 12.00
BT08005 Blue Storm Dragon, Maelstrom RRR 10.00 25.00
BT08006 Hydro Hurricane Dragon RRR 2.00 5.00
BT08007 Storm Rider, Basil RRR 8.00 20.00
BT08008 Sealed Demon Dragon, Dungaree RRR 2.00 5.00
BT08009 Operator Girl, Mika RR .60 1.50
BT08010 Dimensional Robo, Daidragon RR 2.50 6.00
BT08011 Cherry Blossom Musketeer, Augusto RR 1.50 4.00
BT08012 Lily of the Valley Musketeer, Kaivant RR .75 2.00
BT08013 Maiden of Rainbow Wood RR .75 2.00
BT08014 Water Lily Musketeer, Ruth RR 1.25 3.00
BT08015 Lily of the Valley Musketeer, Rebecca RR 1.50 4.00
BT08016 Military Dragon, Raptor Colonel RR 5.00 12.00
BT08017 Destruction Dragon, Dark Rex RR 2.00 5.00
BT08018 Tear Knight, Valeria RR 2.00 5.00
BT08019 Emerald Shield, Paschal RR 10.00 25.00
BT08020 Armed Instructor, Bison RR .60 1.50
BT08021 Enigman Cyclone R .25 .60
BT08022 Lady Justice R .25 .60
BT08023 Subterranean Beast, Magma Lord R .25 .60
BT08024 Devourer of Planets, Zeal R .25 .60
BT08025 Dimensional Robo, Dailander R .40 1.00
BT08026 Dimensional Robo, Goyusha R .25 .60
BT08027 Larva Beast, Zeal R .25 .60
BT08028 Arboros Dragon, Timber R .40 1.00
BT08029 Arboros Dragon, Ratoon R .25 .60
BT08030 Military Dragon, Raptor Captain R .40 1.00
BT08031 Winged Dragon, Slashptero R .25 .60
BT08032 Assault Dragon, Pachyphalos R .25 .60
BT08033 Winged Dragon, Beamptero R .25 .60
BT08034 Military Dragon, Raptor Soldier R .25 .60
BT08035 Storm Rider, Diamantes R .40 1.00
BT08036 Tear Knight, Lazarus R .25 .60
BT08037 Storm Rider, Eugen R .25 .60
BT08038 Torpedo Rush Dragon R .25 .60
BT08039 Aqua Breath Dracokid R .25 .60
BT08040 Thunder Spear Wielding Exorcist Knight R .25 .60
BT08041 Compass Lion R .25 .60
BT08042 Coiling Duckbill R .25 .60
BT08043 Interdimensional Ninja, Tsukikage C .10 .25
BT08044 Cosmic Mothership C .10 .25
BT08045 Cosmic Rider C .10 .25
BT08046 Assault Monster, Gunrock C .10 .25
BT08047 Eye of Destruction, Zeal C .10 .25
BT08048 Dimensional Robo, Daimariner C .10 .25
BT08049 Mysterious Navy Admiral, Gogoth C .10 .25
BT08050 Psychic Grey C .10 .25
BT08051 Speedster C .10 .25
BT08052 Fighting Saucer C .10 .25
BT08053 Warrior of Destiny, Dai C .10 .25
BT08054 Gem Monster, Jewelmine C .10 .25
BT08055 Noise Monster, Decibelon C .10 .25
BT08056 Dissection Monster, Kaizon C .10 .25
BT08057 Dimensional Robo, Daibattles C .10 .25
BT08058 Black Lily Musketeer, Hermann C .10 .25
BT08059 World Snake, Ouroboros C .10 .25
BT08060 Exploding Tomato C .10 .25
BT08061 World Bearing Turtle, Ahkbara C .10 .25
BT08062 Tulip Musketeer, Almira C .10 .25
BT08063 Poison Mushroom C .10 .25
BT08064 Arboros Dragon, Branch C .10 .25
BT08065 Tulip Musketeer, Mina C .10 .25
BT08066 Boon Bana-na C .10 .25
BT08067 Fruits Basket Elf C .10 .25
BT08068 Broccolini Musketeer, Kirah C .10 .25
BT08069 Night Queen Musketeer, Daniel C .10 .25
BT08070 Four Leaf Fairy C .10 .25
BT08071 Maiden of Morning Glory C .10 .25
BT08072 Hibiscus Musketeer, Hanah C .10 .25
BT08073 Savage War Chief C .10 .25
BT08074 Citadel Dragon, Brachiocastle C .10 .25
BT08075 Savage Warlock C .10 .25
BT08076 Carrier Dragon, Brachiocarrier C .10 .25
BT08077 Military Dragon, Raptor Sergeant C .10 .25
BT08078 Savage Magus C .10 .25
BT08079 Fortress Ammonite C .10 .25
BT08080 Transport Dragon, Brachioporter C .10 .25
BT08081 Baby Ptero C .10 .25
BT08082 Dragon Bird, Firepteryx C .10 .25
BT08083 Carry Trilobite C .10 .25
BT08084 Matriarch's Bombardment Beast C .10 .25
BT08085 Ironclad Dragon, Steelsaurus C .10 .25
BT08086 Titan of the Pyroxene Mine C .10 .25
BT08087 Distant Sea Advisor, Vassilis C .10 .25
BT08088 Veteran Strategic Commander C .10 .25
BT08089 Whale Supply Fleet, Kairin Maru C .10 .25
BT08090 Tear Knight, Theo C .10 .25
BT08091 Stream Trooper C .10 .25
BT08092 Reliable Strategic Commander C .10 .25
BT08093 Officer Cadet, Erikk C .10 .25
BT08094 Mothership Intelligence C .10 .25
BT08095 Enemy Seeking Seagull Soldier C .10 .25
BT08096 Black Celestial Maiden, Kali C .10 .25
BT08097 Dragon Monk, Kinkaku C .10 .25
BT08098 Lightning Sword Wielding Exorcist Knight C .10 .25
BT08099 Dragon Monk, Ginkaku C .10 .25
BT08100 Exorcist Mage, Koh Koh C .10 .25
BT08101 Mischievous Girl, Kyon-she C .10 .25
BT08102 Blackboard Parrot C .10 .25
BT08S01 Ultimate Dimensional Robo, Great Daiyusha SP 10.00 25.00
BT08S02 Galactic Beast, Zeal SP 8.00 20.00
BT08S03 Arboros Dragon, Sephirot SP 8.00 20.00
BT08S04 White Lily Musketeer, Cecilia SP 10.00 25.00
BT08S05 Blue Storm Dragon, Maelstrom SP 25.00 60.00
BT08S06 Hydro Hurricane Dragon SP 5.00 12.00
BT08S07 Storm Rider, Basil SP 15.00 40.00
BT08S08 Sealed Demon Dragon, Dungaree SP 8.00 20.00
BT08S09 Operator Girl, Mika SP 12.00 30.00
BT08S10 Maiden of Rainbow Wood SP 12.00 30.00
BT08S11 Military Dragon, Raptor Colonel SP 6.00 15.00
BT08S12 Destruction Dragon, Dark Rex SP 8.00 20.00

2013 Cardfight Vanguard Clash of the Knights and Dragons

COMPLETE SET (114) 350.00 500.00
BOOSTER BOX (36 PACKS) 40.00 60.00
BOOSTER PACK (5 CARDS) 2.00 3.00
RELEASED ON JUNE 28, 2013
BT09001 Covert Demonic Dragon, Magatsu Storm RRR 3.00 8.00
BT09002 Blue Storm Supreme Dragon, Glory Maelstrom RRR 8.00 20.00
BT09003 Goddess of the Sun, Amaterasu RRR 4.00 10.00
BT09004 Ultra Beast Deity, Illuminal Dragon RRR 4.00 10.00
BT09005 Crimson Impact, Metatron RRR 5.00 12.00
BT09006 Blazing Lion, Platina Ezel RRR 12.00 30.00
BT09007 Conviction Dragon, Chromejailer Dragon RRR 6.00 15.00
BT09008 Dragonic Kaiser Vermillion THE BLOOD RRR 15.00 40.00
BT09009 Fantasy Petal Storm, Shirayuki RR 2.50 6.00
BT09010 Platinum Blond Fox Spirit, Tamamo RR 2.00 5.00
BT09011 Tri-Stinger DragonRR .40 1.00

BT09012 Battle Sister, Cookie RR 2.00 5.00
BT09013 Battler of the Twin Brush, Polaris RR 1.25 3.00
BT09014 Halo Shield, Mark RR 5.00 12.00
BT09015 Lord of the Demonic Winds, Vayu RR .40 1.00
BT09016 Wyvern Guard, Guld RR 3.00 8.00
BT09017 Starlight Melody Tamer, Farah RR 1.25 3.00
BT09018 Nightmare Summoner, Raqiel RR 1.00 2.50
BT09019 Blaster Blade Spirit RR 2.50 6.00
BT09020 Blaster Dark Spirit RR 1.50 4.00
BT09021 Stealth Dragon, Magatsu Gale R .40 1.00
BT09022 Stealth Fiend, Oboro Cart R .25 .60
BT09023 Stealth Dragon, Magatsu Wind R .25 .60
BT09024 Storm Rider, Lysander R .25 .60
BT09025 Storm Rider, Damon R .25 .60
BT09026 Battle Siren, Theresa R .25 .60
BT09027 Storm Rider, Nicolas R .25 .60
BT09028 Tri-holl DracokidR .25 .60
BT09029 Battle Deity, Susanoo R .25 .60
BT09030 Battle Maiden, Sayorihime R .25 .60
BT09031 Beast Deity, Yamatano Drake R .25 .60
BT09032 Hollow Nomad R .25 .60
BT09033 Beast Deity, Golden Anglet R .40 1.00
BT09034 Beast Deity, Blank Marsh R .30 .75
BT09035 Mobile Hospital, Elysium R .25 .60
BT09036 Knight of Passion, Bagdemagus R .40 1.00
BT09037 Advance of the Black Chains, Kahedin R .25 .60
BT09038 Dreaming Sage, Corron R .25 .60
BT09039 Dusty Plasma Dragon R 1.00 2.50
BT09040 Exorcist Demonic Dragon, Indigo R .25 .60
BT09041 Barking Wyvern R .25 .60
BT09042 Fire Juggler R .25 .60
BT09043 Spiked Club Stealth Rogue, Arahabaki C .10 .25
BT09044 Stealth Beast, Gigantoad C .10 .25
BT09045 Stealth Dragon, Royale Nova C .10 .25
BT09046 Stealth Beast, Spell Hound C .10 .25
BT09047 Stealth Rogue of Summoning, Jiraiya C .10 .25
BT09048 Stealth Dragon, Magatsu Breath C .10 .25
BT09049 Stealth Beast, Night Panther C .10 .25
BT09050 Stealth Beast, Flame Fox C .10 .25
BT09051 Stealth Rogue of Body Replacement, Kokuenmaru C .10 .25
BT09052 Fox Tamer, Izuna C .20 .50
BT09053 Stealth Fiend, Monster Lantern C .10 .25
BT09054 Stealth Fiend, Rokuro Lady C .10 .25
BT09055 Stealth Fiend, Karakasa Spirit C .10 .25
BT09056 Stealth Fiend, River Child C .10 .25
BT09057 Stealth Beast, Cat Devil C .10 .25
BT09058 Deck Sweeper C .10 .25
BT09059 Light Signals Penguin Soldier C .10 .25
BT09060 Officer Cadet, Astraea C .10 .25
BT09061 Pyroxene Beam Blue Dragon Soldier C .10 .25
BT09062 Supersonic Sailor C .10 .25
BT09063 Gentle Jimm C .10 .25
BT09064 Oracle Guardian, Sphinx C .10 .25
BT09065 Rock Witch, GaGa C .10 .25
BT09066 Battle Sister, Cream C .10 .25
BT09067 Machine-gun Talk RyanC .10 .25
BT09068 Solar Maiden, Uzume C .10 .25
BT09069 Supple Bamboo Princess, Kaguya C .10 .25
BT09070 Heroic Hani C .10 .25
BT09071 Transraizer C .10 .25
BT09072 Burstraizer C .10 .25
BT09073 Stoic Hani C .10 .25
BT09074 Transmigrating Evolution, Miraioh C .10 .25
BT09075 Lionet Heat C .10 .25
BT09076 Crimson Drive, Aphrodite C .20 .50
BT09077 Examine Angel C .10 .25
BT09078 Crimson Mind, Baruch C .20 .50
BT09079 Emergency Vehicle C .10 .25
BT09080 Candlelight Angel C .10 .25
BT09081 Crimson Heart, Nahas C .10 .25
BT09082 Rampage Cart Angel C .10 .25
BT09083 Fever Therapy Nurse C .20 .50
BT09084 Vocal Chicken C .10 .25
BT09085 Melodica Cat C .10 .25
BT09086 Parabolic Moose C .10 .25
BT09087 Barcode Zebra C .10 .25
BT09088 Recorder Dog C .10 .25
BT09089 Sharpener Beaver C .10 .25
BT09090 Protractor Peacock C .10 .25
BT09091 Gardening Mole C .10 .25
BT09092 Castanet Donkey C .10 .25
BT09093 Holy Mage of the Gale C .10 .25
BT09094 Stronghold of the Black Chains, Hoel C .10 .25
BT09095 Dantegal C .10 .25
BT09096 Runebau C .10 .25
BT09097 Exorcist Mage, Roh Roh C .10 .25
BT09098 Deity Sealing Kid, Soh Koh C .10 .25
BT09099 Spark Edge Dracokid C .20 .50
BT09100 Exorcist Mage, Lin Lin C .10 .25
BT09101 Magical Partner C .10 .25
BT09102 Smiling Presenter C .10 .25
BT09S01 Covert Demonic Dragon, Magatsu Storm SP 8.00 20.00
BT09S02 Blue Storm Supreme Dragon, Glory Maelstrom SP 15.00 40.00
BT09S03 Goddess of the Sun, Amaterasu SP 15.00 40.00
BT09S04 Ultra Beast Deity, Illuminal Dragon SP 10.00 25.00
BT09S05 Crimson Impact, Metatron SP 12.00 30.00
BT09S06 Blazing Lion, Platina Ezel SP 25.00 60.00
BT09S07 Conviction Dragon, Chromejailer Dragon SP 12.00 30.00
BT09S08 Dragonic Kaiser Vermillion THE BLOOD SP 25.00 60.00
BT09S09 Battle Sister, Cookie SP 12.00 30.00
BT09S10 Starlight Melody Tamer, Farah SP 8.00 20.00
BT09S11 Blaster Blade Spirit SP 10.00 25.00
BT09S12 Blaster Dark Spirit SP 12.00 30.00

2013 Cardfight Vanguard Rampage of the Beast

COMPLETE SET (114) 200.00 350.00
BOOSTER BOX (36 PACKS) 60.00 80.00
BOOSTER PACK (5 CARDS) 3.00 4.00
RELEASED ON SEPTEMBER 29, 2012
BT07001 School Hunter, Leo-paid RRR 5.00 12.00
BT07002 Guardian of Truth, Lox RRR 2.00 5.00
BT07003 Binoculus Tiger RRR 6.00 15.00
BT07004 Silver Thorn Dragon Tamer, Luquier RRR 10.00 25.00
BT07005 Dark Lord of Abyss RRR 2.50 6.00
BT07006 Emerald Witch, LaLa RRR 2.00 5.00
BT07007 White Hare in the Moon's Shadow, Pellinore RRR 5.00 12.00
BT07008 Chief Nurse, Shamsiel RRR 8.00 20.00
BT07009 School Dominator, Apt RR 1.00 2.50
BT07010 Lamp Camel RR 1.00 2.50
BT07011 Monoculus Tiger RR 1.25 3.00
BT07012 Cable Sheep RR 5.00 12.00
BT07013 Sword Magician, Sarah RR 2.50 6.00
BT07014 Fire Breeze, Carrie RR 1.00 2.50
BT07015 Peek-a-boo RR 1.00 2.50
BT07016 Magician of Quantum Mechanics RR 1.00 2.50
BT07017 Blade Wing Reijy RR 5.00 12.00
BT07018 Emblem Master RR 3.00 8.00
BT07019 Yellow Bolt RR 3.00 8.00
BT07020 Listener of Truth, Dindrane RR 5.00 12.00
BT07021 Pencil Hero, Hammsuke R .25 .60
BT07022 Dumbbell Kangaroo R .25 .60
BT07023 Magnet Crocodile R .40 1.00
BT07024 Law Official, Lox R .25 .60
BT07025 Pencil Squire, Hammsuke R .75 2.00
BT07026 Thermometer Giraffe R .25 .60
BT07027 Tank Mouse R .25 .60
BT07028 Flask Marmoset R .25 .60
BT07029 Midnight Invader R .40 1.00
BT07030 Dancing Princess of the Night Sky R .40 1.00
BT07031 Bull's Eye, Mia R .25 .60
BT07032 Purple Trapezist R 1.50 4.00
BT07033 Evil Eye Basilisk R .25 .60
BT07034 Hades Carriage of the Witching Hour R .25 .60
BT07035 Free Traveler R .25 .60
BT07036 Courting Succubus R 1.25 3.00
BT07037 Sky Witch, NaNa R .25 .60
BT07038 Battle Sister, Glace R .75 2.00
BT07039 Little Witch, LuLu R .25 .60
BT07040 Photon Archer, Griflet R .40 1.00
BT07041 Lop Ear Shooter R 2.00 5.00
BT07042 Spring Breeze Messenger R .25 .60
BT07043 Calculator Hippo C .10 .25
BT07044 Schoolbag Sea Lion C .10 .25
BT07045 Red Pencil Rhino C .10 .25
BT07046 Pencil Knight, Hammsuke C .10 .25
BT07047 Globe Armadillo C .10 .25
BT07048 Explosion Scientist, Bunta C .10 .25
BT07049 Multimeter Giraffe C .10 .25
BT07050 Canvas Koala C .10 .25
BT07051 Thumbtack Fighter, Resanori C .10 .25
BT07052 Tick Tock Flamingo C .10 .25
BT07053 Bringer of Knowledge, Lox C .10 .25
BT07054 Element Glider C .10 .25
BT07055 Failure Scientist, Ponkichi C .10 .25
BT07056 Feather Penguin C .10 .25
BT07057 Hula Hoop Capybara C .10 .25
BT07058 Acorn Master C .10 .25
BT07059 Schoolyard Prodigy, Lox C .10 .25
BT07060 Triangle Cobra C .20 .50
BT07061 Fortune-bringing Cat C .20 .50
BT07062 Alarm Chicken C .10 .25
BT07063 Eraser Alpaca C .10 .25
BT07064 Dictionary Goat C .40 1.00
BT07065 Ruler Chameleon C .20 .50
BT07066 Nightmare Doll, Amy C .10 .25
BT07067 Dreamy Fortress C .10 .25
BT07068 See-saw Game Loser C .10 .25
BT07069 Drawing Dread C .10 .25
BT07070 Jumping Glenn C .10 .25
BT07071 Dreamy Ammonite C .10 .25
BT07072 See-saw Game Winner C .10 .25
BT07073 Pinky Piggy C .10 .25
BT07074 Girl Who Crossed the Gap C .10 .25
BT07075 Innocent Magician C .10 .25
BT07076 Flyer Flyer C .10 .25
BT07077 Cracker Musician C .10 .25
BT07078 Popcorn Boy C .20 .50
BT07079 Poison Juggler C .40 1.00
BT07080 Demon Chariot of the Witching Hour C .10 .25
BT07081 Beast in Hand C .10 .25
BT07082 Cyber Beast C .10 .25
BT07083 Demon Bike of the Witching Hour C .20 .50
BT07084 Beautiful Harpuia C .10 .25
BT07085 Mirage Maker C .10 .25
BT07086 Rune Weaver C .10 .25
BT07087 Greedy Hand C .10 .25
BT07088 Devil in Shadow C .10 .25
BT07089 Mad Hatter of Nightmareland C .10 .25
BT07090 Hungry Egg of Nightmareland C .10 .25
BT07091 Cheshire Cat of Nightmareland C .20 .50
BT07092 Dark Knight of Nightmareland C .40 1.00
BT07093 Battle Sister, Souffle C .10 .25
BT07094 Oracle Guardian, Shisa C .10 .25
BT07095 Moonsault Swallow C .10 .25
BT07096 Battle Sister, Eclair C .10 .25
BT07097 Master of Pain C .10 .25
BT07098 Disciple of Pain C .10 .25
BT07099 Speeder Hound C .20 .50
BT07100 Doctroid Megalos C .10 .25
BT07101 Doctroid Micros C .10 .25
BT07102 Hope Child, Turiel C .10 .25
BT07S01 School Hunter, Leo-paid SP 8.00 20.00
BT07S02 Guardian of Truth, Lox SP 4.00 10.00
BT07S03 Binoculus Tiger SP 6.00 15.00
BT07S04 Silver Thorn Dragon Tamer, Luquier SP 15.00 40.00
BT07S05 Dark Lord of Abyss SP 6.00 15.00
BT07S06 Emerald Witch, LaLa SP 5.00 12.00
BT07S07 White Hare in the Moon's Shadow, Pellinore SP 10.00 25.00
BT07S08 Chief Nurse, Shamsiel SP 15.00 40.00
BT07S09 School Dominator, Apt SP 4.00 10.00
BT07S10 Monoculus Tiger SP 4.00 10.00
BT07S11 Sword Magician, Sarah SP 10.00 25.00
BT07S12 Blade Wing Reijy SP 12.00 30.00

2013 Cardfight Vanguard Seal Dragons Unleashed

COMPLETE SET (114) 250.00 400.00
BOOSTER BOX (36 PACKS) 50.00 60.00
BOOSTER PACK (5 CARDS) 2.00 3.00
RELEASED ON OCTOBER 25, 2013
BT11001 Prophecy Celestial, Ramiel RRR 8.00 20.00
BT11002 Solidify Celestial, Zerachiel RRR 6.00 15.00
BT11003 Goddess of Good Luck, Fortuna RRR 4.00 10.00
BT11004 Hellfire Seal Dragon, Blockade Inferno RRR 4.00 10.00
BT11005 Dauntless Drive Dragon RRR 15.00 40.00
BT11006 Eradicator, Sweep Command Dragon RRR 3.00 8.00
BT11007 Blue Flight Dragon, Trans-core Dragon RRR 12.00 30.00
BT11008 Last Card, Revonn RRR 3.00 8.00
BT11009 Adamantine Celestial, Aniel RR 4.00 10.00
BT11010 Seal Dragon, Blockade RR .60 1.50
BT11011 Seal Dragon, Rinocross RR 5.00 12.00
BT11012 Ancient Dragon, Spinodriver RR 5.00 12.00
BT11013 Ancient Dragon, Tyrannolegend RR 1.50 4.00
BT11014 Ravenous Dragon, Battlerex RR .20 .50
BT11015 Ancient Dragon, Paraswall RR 2.50 6.00
BT11016 Armor Break Dragon RR .60 1.50
BT11017 Fiendish Sword Eradicator, Cho-Ou RR 5.00 12.00
BT11018 Thundering Ripple, Genovious RR 1.50 4.00
BT11019 Tear Knight, Lucas RR .60 1.50
BT11020 Emerald Shield, Paschal RR 4.00 10.00
BT11021 Mobile Hospital, Assault Hospice R .20 .50
BT11022 Reverse Aura Phoenix R .20 .50
BT11023 Essence Celestial, Becca R .20 .50
BT11024 Wild Shot Celestial, Raguel R .40 1.00
BT11025 Candle Celestial, Sariel R .60 1.50
BT11026 Underlay Celestial, Hesediel R .40 1.00
BT11027 Myth Guard, La Superba R .20 .50
BT11028 Witch of Ravens, Chamomile R .75 2.00
BT11029 Witch of Frogs, Melissa R .75 2.00
BT11030 Demonic Dragon Berserker, Gandharva R .20 .50
BT11031 Seal Dragon, Hunger Hell Dragon R .60 1.50
BT11032 Seal Dragon, Jacquard R .40 1.00
BT11033 Seal Dragon, Chambray R .20 .50
BT11034 Savage Hunter R .20 .50
BT11035 Ancient Dragon, Criollofall R .40 1.00
BT11036 Ancient Dragon, Beamankylo R .40 1.00
BT11037 Ancient Dragon, Iguanogorg R .40 1.00
BT11038 Demonic Sword Eradicator, Raioh R .20 .50
BT11039 Steel-blooded Eradicator, Shuki R 1.25 3.00
BT11040 Titan of the Beam Cannon Tower R .20 .50
BT11041 Rising Ripple, Pavroth R .40 1.00
BT11042 Starting Ripple, Alecs R .20 .50
BT11043 Booting Celestial, Sandalphon C .10 .25
BT11044 Capsule Gift Nurse C .10 .25
BT11045 Doctroid Argus C .10 .25
BT11046 Marking Celestial, Arabhaki C .20 .50
BT11047 Order Celestial, Yeqon C .10 .25
BT11048 Drugstore Nurse C .20 .50
BT11049 First Aid Celestial, Peniel C .10 .25
BT11050 Cure Drop Angel C .10 .25
BT11051 Hot Shot Celestial, Samyaza C .20 .50
BT11052 Celestial, Landing Pegasus C .10 .25
BT11053 Encourage Celestial, Tamiel C .10 .25
BT11054 Recovery Celestial, Ramuel C .20 .50
BT11055 Crimson Witch, Radish C .10 .25
BT11056 Pineapple Law C .10 .25
BT11057 Witch of Prohibited Books, Cinnamon C .10 .25
BT11058 Vivid Rabbit C .10 .25
BT11059 Seal Dragon, Spike Hell Dragon C .10 .25
BT11060 Seal Dragon, Corduroy C .20 .50
BT11061 Breath of Demise, Vulcanis C .10 .25
BT11062 Dragon Knight, Lotf C .10 .25
BT11063 Demonic Dragon Berserker, Kubanda C .20 .50
BT11064 Seal Dragon, Flannel C .20 .50
BT11065 Seal Dragon, Kersey C .20 .50
BT11066 Breath of Origin, Rolamandri C .10 .25
BT11067 Demonic Dragon Mage, Shagara C .10 .25
BT11068 Seal Dragon, Terrycloth C .20 .50
BT11069 Demonic Dragon Mage, Diva C .10 .25
BT11070 Red Pulse Dracokid C .10 .25
BT11071 Seal Dragon, Biella C .20 .50
BT11072 Seal Dragon, Dobby C .10 .25
BT11073 Seal Dragon, Shirting C .20 .50
BT11074 Seal Dragon, Artpique C .40 1.00
BT11075 Ancient Dragon, Stegobuster C .10 .25
BT11076 Ancient Dragon, Dinocrowd C .10 .25
BT11077 Launcher Mammoth C .10 .25
BT11078 Savage Archer C .10 .25
BT11079 Ancient Dragon, Triplasma C .10 .25
BT11080 Ancient Dragon, Gattlingaro C .10 .25
BT11081 Savage Illuminator C .10 .25
BT11082 Ancient Dragon, Baby Rex C .10 .25
BT11083 Savage Patriarch C .10 .25
BT11084 Ancient Dragon, Dinodile C .10 .25
BT11085 Ancient Dragon, Titanocargo C .10 .25
BT11086 Ancient Dragon, Caudinoise C .10 .25
BT11087 Ancient Dragon, Ornithhealer C .10 .25
BT11088 Dragon Dancer, Julia C .10 .25
BT11089 Lizard Soldier, Ryoshin C .10 .25
BT11090 Eradicator, First Thunder Dracokid C .10 .25
BT11091 Flag of Raijin, Corposant C .10 .25
BT11092 Mobile Battleship, Archelon C .10 .25
BT11093 Twin Strike Brave Shooter C .20 .50
BT11094 Titan of the Beam Rifle C .10 .25
BT11095 Silent Ripple, Sotirio C .10 .25
BT11096 Mercenary Brave Shooter C .20 .50
BT11097 Battle Siren, Euphenia C .10 .25
BT11098 Advance Party Brave Shooter C .10 .25
BT11099 Battle Siren, Cagli C .10 .25
BT11100 Jet-ski Rider C .10 .25
BT11101 Ice Floe Angel C .10 .25
BT11102 Mass Production Sailor C .20 .50
BT11S01 Prophecy Celestial, Ramiel SP 12.00 30.00
BT11S02 Solidify Celestial, Zerachiel SP 12.00 30.00
BT11S03 Goddess of Good Luck, Fortuna SP 12.00 30.00
BT11S04 Hellfire Seal Dragon, Blockade Inferno SP 6.00 15.00
BT11S05 Dauntless Drive Dragon SP 25.00 60.00
BT11S06 Eradicator, Sweep Command Dragon SP 8.00 20.00
BT11S07 Blue Flight Dragon, Trans-core Dragon SP 15.00 40.00
BT11S08 Last Card, Revonn SP 8.00 20.00
BT11S09 Ancient Dragon, Spinodriver SP 10.00 25.00
BT11S10 Ancient Dragon, Tyrannolegend SP 6.00 15.00
BT11S11 Armor Break Dragon SP 2.00 5.00
BT11S12 Thundering Ripple, Genovious SP 8.00 20.00

2013 Cardfight Vanguard Triumphant Return of the King of Knights

COMPLETE SET (114) 250.00 400.00
BOOSTER BOX (36 PACKS) 50.00 60.00
BOOSTER PACK (5 CARDS) 2.00 3.00
RELEASED ON DECEMBER 14, 2013
BT10001 Pure Heart Jewel Knight, Ashlei RRR 8.00 20.00
BT10002 Leading Jewel Knight, Salome RRR 3.00 8.00
BT10003 Liberator of the Round Table, Alfred RRR 10.00 25.00
BT10004 Oracle Queen, Himiko RRR 8.00 20.00
BT10005 Eternal Goddess, Iwanagahime RRR 2.50 6.00
BT10006 Eradicator, Dragonic Descendant RRR 8.00 20.00
BT10007 Eradicator, Gauntlet Buster Dragon RRR 6.00 15.00
BT10008 Beast Deity, Ethics Buster RRR 6.00 15.00
BT10009 Dogmatize Jewel Knight, Sybill RR 1.25 3.00
BT10010 Flashing Jewel Knight, Iseult RR 6.00 15.00
BT10011 Halo Liberator, Mark RR 8.00 20.00
BT10012 Liberator of the Flute, Escrad RR 4.00 10.00
BT10013 Battle Deity of the Night, Artemis RR 1.25 3.00
BT10014 Broom Witch, Callaway RR .40 1.00
BT10015 Goddess of Self-sacrifice, Kushinada RR 8.00 20.00
BT10016 Supreme Army Eradicator, Zuitan RR 2.50 6.00
BT10017 Eradicator Wyvern Guard, Guld RR 8.00 20.00
BT10018 Grateful Catapult RR .40 1.00
BT10019 Bad End Dragger RR 1.50 4.00
BT10020 Cheer Girl, Marilyn RR 1.50 4.00
BT10021 Dignified Silver Dragon R .20 .50
BT10022 Fellowship Jewel Knight, Tracie R .40 1.00
BT10023 Jewel Knight, Prizmy R .20 .50
BT10024 Dreaming Jewel Knight, Tiffany R .20 .50
BT10025 Fast Chase Liberator, Josephus R .40 1.00
BT10026 Wingal Liberator R .20 .50
BT10027 Witch of Wolves, Saffron R .20 .50
BT10028 Battle Maiden, Izunahime R .20 .50
BT10029 Battle Maiden, Sahohime R .75 2.00
BT10030 Twilight Hunter, Artemis R .40 1.00
BT10031 Battle Maiden, Tatsutahime R .20 .50
BT10032 Battle Maiden, Tamayorihime R .20 .50
BT10033 Aiming for the Stars, Artemis R .20 .50
BT10034 Martial Arts General, Daimu R .20 .50
BT10035 Double Gun Eradicator, Hakusho R .20 .50
BT10036 Eradicator, Saucer Cannon Wyvern R .20 .50
BT10037 Ceremonial Bonfire Eradicator, Castor R .20 .50
BT10038 Ambush Dragon Eradicator, Linchu R .20 .50
BT10039 Armored Heavy Gunner R .20 .50
BT10040 Beast Deity, Hatred Chaos R .75 2.00
BT10041 Rabbit House R .20 .50
BT10042 Dudley Mason R .40 1.00
BT10043 Knight of the Explosive Axe, Gornement C .10 .25
BT10044 Uncompromising Knight, Ideale C .10 .25
BT10045 Knight of Details, Claudin C .10 .25
BT10046 Stinging Jewel Knight, Shellie C .10 .25
BT10047 Rushhgal C .10 .25
BT10048 Jewel Knight, Glitmy C .10 .25
BT10049 Blazing Jewel Knight, Rachelle C .20 .50
BT10050 Primgal C .10 .25
BT10051 Devoting Jewel Knight, Tabitha C .10 .25
BT10052 Ardent Jewel Knight, Polli C .10 .25
BT10053 Muungal C .10 .25
BT10054 Knight of Far Arrows, Saphir C .20 .50
BT10055 Boulder Smashing Knight, Segwarides C .10 .25
BT10056 Guiding Falcony C .10 .25
BT10057 Liberator, Flare Mane Stallion C .10 .25
BT10058 Holy Squire, Enide C .10 .25
BT10059 Liberator of Hope, Epona C .20 .50
BT10060 Flogal Liberator C .20 .50
BT10061 Scheduler Angel C .10 .25
BT10062 Myth Guard, Antares C .10 .25
BT10063 Clever Jake C .10 .25
BT10064 Witch of Owls, Paprika C .10 .25
BT10065 Myth Guard, Orion C .10 .25
BT10066 Battle Maiden, Mihikarihime C .10 .25
BT10067 Bowstring of Heaven and Earth, Artemis C .10 .25
BT10068 Witch of Cats, Cumin C .10 .25
BT10069 Snipe Snake C .20 .50
BT10070 Myth Guard, Sirius C .10 .25
BT10071 Cluster Hamster C .20 .50
BT10072 Cyber Tiger C .10 .25
BT10073 Battle Maiden, Kukurihime C .20 .50
BT10074 Bandit Danny C .10 .25
BT10075 Fancy Monkey C .10 .25
BT10076 Spark Cockerel C .10 .25
BT10077 Patrol Guardian C .10 .25
BT10078 Witch of Big Pots, Laurier C .10 .25
BT10079 Demonic Dragon Berserker, Sandila C .20 .50
BT10080 Blood Axe Dragoon C .10 .25
BT10081 Demonic Dragon Mage, Majila C .10 .25
BT10082 Sword Dance Eradicator, Hisen C .20 .50
BT10083 Dragon Dancer, Agnes C .10 .25
BT10084 Lightning Fist Eradicator, Dui C .10 .25
BT10085 Eradicator, Strike-dagger Dragon C .10 .25
BT10086 Djinn of the Thunder Break C .10 .25
BT10087 Sacred Spear Eradicator, Pollux C .20 .50
BT10088 Eradicator, Spy-eye Wyvern C .10 .25
BT10089 Bloody Reign C .10 .25
BT10090 Beast Deity, Hilarity Destroyer C .10 .25
BT10091 Machinery Angel C .20 .50
BT10092 Beast Deity, Riot Horn C .10 .25
BT10093 Battle Arm Leprechaun C .20 .50
BT10094 Anti-battleroid Gunner C .10 .25
BT10095 Blow Kiss Olivia C .10 .25
BT10096 Go For Broke C .10 .25
BT10097 Charging Bill Collector C .10 .25
BT10098 UFO (Unlucky Flying Object) C .10 .25
BT10099 Tyrant Receiver C .20 .50
BT10100 Dudley Phantom C .20 .50
BT10101 Reign of Terror, Thermidor C .10 .25
BT10102 Baby Face Izaac C .20 .50
BT10S01 Pure Heart Jewel Knight, Ashlei SP 15.00 40.00
BT10S02 Leading Jewel Knight, Salome SP 12.00 30.00
BT10S03 Liberator of the Round Table, Alfred SP 12.00 30.00
BT10S04 Oracle Queen, Himiko SP 10.00 25.00
BT10S05 Eternal Goddess, Iwanagahime SP 6.00 15.00
BT10S06 Eradicator, Dragonic Descendant SP 20.00 50.00
BT10S07 Eradicator, Gauntlet Buster Dragon SP 12.00 30.00
BT10S08 Beast Deity, Ethics Buster SP 12.00 30.00
BT10S09 Dogmatize Jewel Knight, Sybill SP 8.00 20.00
BT10S10 Battle Deity of the Night, Artemis SP 8.00 20.00
BT10S11 Wingal Liberator SP 6.00 15.00
BT10S12 Blaster Blade Liberator SP 25.00 60.00

2014 Cardfight Vanguard Binding Force of the Black Rings

COMPLETE SET (114) 400.00 550.00
BOOSTER BOX (36 PACKS) 50.00 60.00
BOOSTER PACK (5 CARDS) 2.00 3.00
RELEASED ON FEBRUARY 21, 2014
BT12001 Revenger, Raging Form Dragon RRR 20.00 50.00
BT12002 Wolf Fang Liberator, Garmore RRR 5.00 12.00
BT12003 Eradicator, Vowing Saber Dragon Reverse RRR 4.00 10.00
BT12004 Demon Conquering Dragon, Dungaree Unlimited RRR 1.25 3.00
BT12005 Star-vader, Nebula Lord Dragon RRR 10.00 25.00
BT12006 Schwarzschild Dragon RRR 3.00 8.00
BT12007 Demon Marquis, Amon Reverse RRR 6.00 15.00
BT12008 Silver Thorn Dragon Queen, Luquier Reverse RRR 10.00 25.00
BT12009 Witch of Cursed Talisman, Etain RR 1.25 3.00
BT12010 Dark Cloak Revenger, Tartu RR 6.00 15.00
BT12011 Dark Revenger, Mac Lir RR 10.00 25.00
BT12012 Barcgal Liberator RR 1.25 3.00
BT12013 Iron Fan Eradicator, Nirrti RR .60 1.50
BT12014 Barrier Star-vader, Promethium RR 10.00 25.00
BT12015 King of Masks, Dantarian RR 2.00 5.00
BT12016 Master of Fifth Element RR 1.25 3.00
BT12017 Amon's Follower, Vlad Specula RR 2.50 6.00
BT12018 Miracle Pop, Eva RR 4.00 10.00
BT12019 Nightmare Doll, Chelsea RR 1.50 4.00
BT12020 Silver Thorn Hypnos, Lydia RR 5.00 12.00
BT12021 Barrier Troop Revenger, Dorint R 1.00 2.50
BT12022 Revenger, Dark Bond Trumpeter R .40 1.00
BT12023 Frontline Revenger, Claudas R .40 1.00
BT12024 Liberator, Bagpipe Angel R .60 1.50
BT12025 Whirlwind Axe Wielding Exorcist Knight R .40 1.00
BT12026 Homing Eradicator, Rochishin R .40 1.00
BT12027 Rising Phoenix R .40 1.00
BT12028 Resonance Hammer Wielding Exorcist Knight R .40 1.00
BT12029 Exorcist Mage, Dan Dan R .40 1.00
BT12030 Schrodinger's Lion R .40 1.00
BT12031 Gravity Collapse Dragon R .60 1.50
BT12032 Opener of Dark Gates R .40 1.00
BT12033 Star-vader, Dust Tail Unicorn R .40 1.00
BT12034 Micro-hole Dracokid R .20 .50
BT12035 Werbear Soldner R .20 .50
BT12036 Amon's Follower, Psycho Grave R .40 1.00
BT12037 Amon's Follower, Ron Geenlin R .40 1.00
BT12038 Amon's Follower, Fool's Palm R .40 1.00
BT12039 Fire Ring Griffin R .20 .50
BT12040 Silver Thorn Marionette, Lillian R 1.25 3.00
BT12041 Silver Thorn Beast Tamer, Maricica R 1.00 2.50
BT12042 Silver Thorn, Rising Dragon R 1.00 2.50
BT12043 Demon World Castle, Zerschlagen C .20 .50
BT12044 Jacbau Revenger C .20 .50
BT12045 Demon World Castle, Zweispeer C .10 .25
BT12046 Malice Revenger, Dylan C .20 .50
BT12047 Sonbau C .10 .25
BT12048 Spinbau Revenger C .10 .25
BT12049 Revenger, Air Raid Dragon C .40 1.00
BT12050 Revenger, Waking Angel C .20 .50
BT12051 Gigantech Pillar Fighter C .10 .25
BT12052 Overcast Liberator, Geraint C .10 .25
BT12053 Pikgal C .10 .25
BT12054 May Rain Liberator, Bruno C .10 .25
BT12055 Sunrise Unicorn C .10 .25
BT12056 Liberator, Cheer Up Trumpeter C .10 .25
BT12057 Daybreak Liberator, Muron C .10 .25
BT12058 Conquering Eradicator, Dokkasei C .20 .50
BT12059 Eradicator, Blade Hang Dracokid C .20 .50
BT12060 Eradicator, Blue Gem Carbuncle C .40 1.00
BT12061 Catastrophstinger C .10 .25
BT12062 Innocent Blade, Heartless C .10 .25
BT12063 Furious Claw Star-vader, Niobium C .10 .25
BT12064 Gamma Burst, Fenrir C .10 .25
BT12065 Singularity Sniper C .20 .50
BT12066 Le Maul C .20 .50
BT12067 Gravity Ball Dragon C .20 .50
BT12068 Demon Claw Star-vader, Lanthanum C .40 1.00
BT12069 Strafing Star-vader, Ruthenium C .20 .50
BT12070 Paradox Nail, Fenrir C .20 .50
BT12071 White Night, Fenrir C .20 .50
BT12072 Star-vader, Weiss Soldat C .40 1.00
BT12073 Star-vader, Scounting Ferris C .10 .25
BT12074 Star-vader, Moon Commander C .20 .50
BT12075 Number of Terror C .10 .25

BT12076 Amon's Follower, Hell's Draw C .20 .50
BT12077 Werleopard Soldat C .20 .50
BT12078 Frog Knight C .20 .50
BT12079 Amon's Follower, Hell's Deal C .10 .25
BT12080 Amon's Follower, Phu Geenlin C .10 .25
BT12081 Dimension Creeper C .10 .25
BT12082 Werhase Bandito C .20 .50
BT12083 Amon's Follower, Fate Collector C .20 .50
BT12084 Werfuchs Hexa C .10 .25
BT12085 Amon's Follower, Cruel Hand C .20 .50
BT12086 Amon's Follower, Psychic Waitress C .20 .50
BT12087 Amon's Follower, Meteor Cracker C .10 .25
BT12088 Amon's Follower, Hell's Trick C .20 .50
BT12089 Master of Giant Flying Knives C .20 .50
BT12090 Tightrope Holder C .10 .25
BT12091 Flying Hippogriff C .10 .25
BT12092 Silver Thorn Assistant, Irina C .20 .50
BT12093 Silver Thorn Beast Tamer, Ana C .20 .50
BT12094 Silver Thorn, Breathing Dragon C .40 1.00
BT12095 Tightrope Tumbler C .20 .50
BT12096 Elegant Elephant C .10 .25
BT12097 Silver Thorn Assistant, Ionela C .20 .50
BT12098 Tone of a Journey, Willi C .10 .25
BT12099 Silver Thorn Barking, Dragon C .40 1.00
BT12100 Silver Thorn Marionette, Natasha C .20 .50
BT12101 Silver Thorn Beast Tamer, Serge C .20 .50
BT12102 Silver Thorn Juggler, Nadia C .10 .25
BT12S01 Revenger, Raging Form Dragon SP 30.00 80.00
BT12S02 Wolf Fang Liberator, Garmore SP 15.00 40.00
BT12S03 Eradicator, Vowing Saber Dragon Reverse SP 12.00 30.00
BT12S04 Demon Conquering Dragon, Dungaree Unlimited SP 6.00 15.00
BT12S05 Star-vader, Nebula Lord Dragon SP 20.00 50.00
BT12S06 Schwarzschild Dragon SP 8.00 20.00
BT12S07 Demon Marquis, Amon Reverse SP 12.00 30.00
BT12S08 Silver Thorn Dragon Queen, Luquier Reverse SP 30.00 80.00
BT12S09 King of Masks, Dantarian SP 8.00 20.00
BT12S10 Miracle Pop, Eva SP 10.00 25.00
BT12S11 Demon World Marquis, Amon SP 12.00 30.00
BT12S12 Blaster Dark Revenger SP 30.00 80.00

2014 Cardfight Vanguard Brilliant Strike

COMPLETE SET (114) 150.00 300.00
BOOSTER BOX (36 PACKS) 50.00 60.00
BOOSTER PACK (5 CARDS) 3.00 4.00
RELEASED ON JULY 18, 2014
BT14001 Broken Heart Jewel Knight, Ashlei Reverse RRR 8.00 20.00
BT14002 Liberator of Bonds, Gancelot Zenith RRR12.00 30.00
BT14003 Salvation Lion, Grand Ezel Scissors RRR10.00 25.00
BT14004 Sunlight Goddess, Yatagarasu RRR 5.00 12.00
BT14005 Omniscience Regalia, Minerva RRR 10.00 25.00
BT14006 Dauntless Dominate Dragon "Reverse" RRR6.00 15.00
BT14007 Eradicator, Ignition Dragon RRR 8.00 20.00
BT14008 Eradicator, Tempest Bolt Dragon RRR 2.50 6.00
BT14009 Sanctuary of Light, Planetal Dragon RR 2.00 5.00
BT14010 Banding Jewel Knight, Miranda RR 2.00 5.00
BT14011 Summoning Jewel Knight, Gloria RR 3.00 8.00
BT14012 Sword Formation Liberator, Igraine RR 2.50 6.00
BT14013 Goddess of the Shield, Aegis RR 2.50 6.00
BT14014 Covert Demonic Dragon, Kagurabloom RR3.00 8.00
BT14015 Covert Demonic Dragon, Hyakki Vogue "Reverse" RR 2.50 6.00
BT14016 Silver Collar Snowstorm, Sasame RR 1.50 4.00
BT14017 Eradicator, Lorentz Force Dragon RR 1.25 3.00
BT14018 Maiden of Venus Trap "Reverse" RR 1.50 4.00
BT14019 Lord of the Deep Forests, Master Wisteria RR 2.00 5.00
BT14020 Red Rose Musketeer, Antonio RR 3.00 8.00
BT14021 Sanctuary of Light, Determinator R .40 1.00
BT14022 Linking Jewel Knight, Tilda R .40 1.00
BT14023 Sanctuary of Light, Planet Lancer R .40 1.00
BT14024 Treasure Liberator, Calogrenant R .40 1.00
BT14025 Blue Sky Liberator, Hengist R .40 1.00
BT14026 Knight of Scorching Scales, Eliwood R .40 1.00
BT14027 Battle Maiden, Mizuha R .40 1.00
BT14028 Goddess of Trees, Jupiter R .40 1.00
BT14029 Battle Maiden, Amenohoakari R .40 1.00
BT14030 Vorpal Cannon Dragon R .40 1.00
BT14031 Fire God, Agni R .40 1.00
BT14032 Dominate Drive Dragon R .40 1.00
BT14033 Dragon Knight, Akram R .40 1.00
BT14034 Dragon Knight, Sadig R .40 1.00
BT14035 Investigating Stealth Rogue, Amakusa R .40 1.00
BT14036 Stealth Rogue of DemoniCHair, Gurenjishi R .40 1.00
BT14037 Stealth Rogue of Umbrella, Sukerokku R .40 1.00
BT14038 Certain Kill Eradicator, Ouei R .40 1.00
BT14039 Spiritual Sphere Eradicator, Nata R .40 1.00
BT14040 White Rose Musketeer, Alberto R .40 1.00
BT14041 Maiden of Cherry Bloom R .40 1.00
BT14042 Maiden of Cherry Stone R .40 1.00
BT14043 Knight of Courage, Ector C .10 .25
BT14044 Mystical Hermit C .10 .25
BT14045 Jewel Knight, Treanme C .10 .25
BT14046 Sanctuary of Light, Little Storm C .10 .25
BT14047 Jewel Knight, Melme C .10 .25
BT14048 Security Jewel Knight, Arwen C .10 .25
BT14049 Desire Jewel Knight, Heloise C .10 .25
BT14050 Jewel Knight, Noble Stinger C .10 .25
BT14051 Jewel Knight, Sacred Unicorn C .10 .25
BT14052 Jewel Knight, Opt Harpist C .10 .25
BT14053 Jewel Knight, Hilmy C .10 .25
BT14054 Sacred Guardian Beast, Ceryneian C .10 .25
BT14055 Liberator, Burning Blow C .10 .25
BT14056 Dorgal Liberator C .10 .25
BT14057 Twin Holy Beast, Black Lion C .10 .25
BT14058 Green Axe Knight, Taliesyn C .10 .25
BT14059 Knight of Passion, Tor C .10 .25
BT14060 Twin Holy Beast, White Lion C .10 .25
BT14061 Flying Sword Liberator, Gorlois C .10 .25
BT14062 Throw Blade Knight, Maleagant C .10 .25
BT14063 Scarlet Lion Cub, Caria C .10 .25
BT14064 Liberator, Grand Crack C .10 .25
BT14065 Nappgal Liberator C .10 .25
BT14066 Angelic Wiseman C .10 .25
BT14067 Myth Guard, Fomalhaut C .10 .25
BT14068 Grape Witch, Grappa C .10 .25
BT14069 Myth Guard, Denebola C .10 .25
BT14070 Battle Maiden, Kayanarumi C .10 .25
BT14071 Orange Witch, Valencia C .10 .25
BT14072 Myth Guard, Achernar C .10 .25
BT14073 Goddess of Union, Juno C .10 .25
BT14074 Ordain Owl C .10 .25
BT14075 Spectral Sheep C .10 .25
BT14076 Dragon Knight, Jalal C .10 .25
BT14077 Flame Star Seal Dragon Knight C .10 .25
BT14078 Dragon Knight, Lezar C .10 .25
BT14079 Demonic Dragon Mage, Taksaka C .10 .25
BT14080 Diable Drive Dragon C .10 .25
BT14081 Explosive Claw Seal Dragon Knight C .10 .25
BT14082 Calamity Tower Wyvern C .10 .25
BT14083 Prison Egg Seal Dragon Knight C .10 .25
BT14084 Lizard Soldier, Goraha C .10 .25
BT14085 Fire of Repose, Gira C .10 .25
BT14086 Wyvern Strike, Free C .10 .25
BT14087 Dragon Dancer, Barbara C .10 .25
BT14088 Stealth Beast, Chain Geek C .10 .25
BT14089 Stealth Beast, Deathly Dagger C .10 .25
BT14090 Stealth Rogue of Kite, Goemon C .10 .25
BT14091 Stealth Rogue of Dagger, Yaiba C .10 .25
BT14092 Stealth Rogue of Dark Night, Krog C .10 .25
BT14093 Roaring Thunder Bow, Zafura C .10 .25
BT14094 Plasma Scimitar Dragoon C .10 .25
BT14095 Dragon Dancer, Agatha C .10 .25
BT14096 Wyvern Strike, Zaroos C .10 .25
BT14097 Wishing Djinn C .10 .25
BT14098 Jackin' Pumpkin C .10 .25
BT14099 Lotus Druid C .10 .25
BT14100 Maiden of Physalis C .10 .25
BT14101 Maiden of Egg Plant C .10 .25
BT14102 Blue Rose Musketeer, Ernest C .10 .25
BT14S01 Broken Heart Jewel Knight, Ashlei "Reverse" SP 8.00 20.00
BT14S02 Liberator of Bonds, Gancelot Zenith SP12.00 30.00
BT14S03 Salvation Lion, Grand Ezel Scissors SP10.00 25.00
BT14S04 Sunlight Goddess, Yatagarasu SP 6.00 15.00
BT14S05 Omniscience Regalia, Minerva SP 25.00 60.00
BT14S06 Dauntless Dominate Dragon "Reverse" SP8.00 20.00
BT14S07 Eradicator, Ignition Dragon SP 15.00 40.00
BT14S08 Eradicator, Tempest Bolt Dragon SP 6.00 15.00
BT14S09 Sanctuary of Light, Planetal Dragon SP8.00 20.00
BT14S10 Banding Jewel Knight, Miranda SP 12.00 30.00
BT14S15 Covert DemoniCDragon, Hyakki Vogue "Reverse" SP 5.00 12.00
BT14S18 Maiden of Venus Trap "Reverse" SP 6.00 15.00

2014 Cardfight Vanguard Catastrophic Outbreak

COMPLETE SET (114) 500.00 650.00
BOOSTER BOX (36 CARDS) 50.00 60.00
BOOSTER PACK (5 PACKS) 2.00 3.00
RELEASED ON MAY 2, 2014
BT13001 Cleanup Celestial, Ramiel Reverse RRR12.00 30.00
BT13002 Shura Stealth Dragon, Kujikiricongo RRR10.00 25.00
BT13003 Strongest Beast Deity, Ethics Buster Extreme RRR 15.00 40.00
BT13004 Deadliest Beast Deity, Ethics Buster Reverse RRR 12.00 30.00
BT13005 Dark Dimensional Robo, Reverse Daiyusha RRR 12.00 30.00
BT13006 Original Saver, Zero RRR 6.00 15.00
BT13007 Star-vader, Chaos Breaker Dragon RRR30.00 80.00
BT13008 Blue Wave Dragon, Tetra-drive Dragon RRR15.00 40.00
BT13009 Emergency Celestial, Danielle RR .10 .25
BT13010 Shura Stealth Dragon, Kabukicongo RR5.00 12.00
BT13011 Stealth Beast, Mijingakure RR 4.00 10.00
BT13012 Beast Deity, Brainy Papio RR 2.50 6.00
BT13013 Beast Deity, Solar Falcon RR 4.00 10.00
BT13014 Dimensional Robo, Daishield RR 6.00 15.00
BT13015 Star-vader, Colony Maker RR 6.00 15.00
BT13016 Lord of the Seven Seas, Nightmist RR 8.00 20.00
BT13017 Ice Prison Hades Emperor, Cocytus Reverse RR 10.00 25.00
BT13018 Cobalt Wave Dragon RR 12.00 30.00
BT13019 School Punisher, Leo-pald Reverse RR 6.00 15.00
BT13020 Honorary Professor, Chatnoir SP
BT13020 Honorary Professor, Chatnoir RR 8.00 20.00
BT13021 Operation Celestial, Armen R 1.25 3.00
BT13022 Nursing Celestial, Narelle R 1.25 3.00
BT13023 Stealth Fiend, Daidarahoushi R 1.25 3.00
BT13024 Stealth Beast, Tamahagane R .75 2.00
BT13025 Stealth Beast, Kuroko R 1.25 3.00
BT13026 Beast Deity, Max Beat R 1.25 3.00
BT13027 Energy Charger R 1.25 3.00
BT13028 Space Leviathan, Dogrumadra R .40 1.00
BT13029 Dimensional Robo, Daiheart R .30 .75
BT13030 Dimensional Robo, Daidriller R 1.25 3.00
BT13031 Dimensional Robo, Gocannon R 1.50 4.00
BT13032 Dimensional Robo, Daimagnum R 1.50 4.00
BT13033 Knight of Entropy R 8.00 20.00
BT13034 Paradise Elk R 1.25 3.00
BT13035 Earnest Star-vader, Selenium R 1.25 3.00
BT13036 Rotten Sea Necromancer, Barbaros R .30 .75
BT13037 Sea Strolling Banshee R 1.25 3.00
BT13038 Tidal Assault R .75 2.00
BT13039 Wheel Assault R 2.00 5.00
BT13040 Bubble Edge Dracokid R 1.25 3.00
BT13041 Abacus Bear R 2.00 5.00
BT13042 Wash Up Racoon R .30 .75
BT13043 Dressing Barrage, Sathariel C .10 .25
BT13044 Surgical Celestial, Batariel C .10 .25
BT13045 Twinkle Knife Angel C .10 .25
BT13046 Anesthesia Celestial, Rumael C .10 .25
BT13047 Tender Pigeon C .10 .25
BT13048 Puncture Celestial, Gadriel C .10 .25
BT13049 Oborozakura C .20 .50
BT13050 Stealth Dragon, Kokujyo C .10 .25
BT13051 Stealth Fiend, Gozouu C .10 .25
BT13052 Stealth Rogue of the Night, Sakurafubuki C.20 .50
BT13053 Tempest Stealth Rogue, Fuuki C .10 .25
BT13054 Stealth Dragon, Kodachi Fubuki C .10 .25
BT13055 Stealth Fiend, Mezuou C .10 .25
BT13056 Banquet Stealth Rogue, Shutenmaru C .10 .25
BT13057 Stealth Dragon, Kurogane C .30 .75
BT13058 Stealth Fiend, Ohtsuzura C .10 .25
BT13059 Stealth Fiend, Zashikihime C .10 .25
BT13060 Stealth Fiend, Mashiromomen C .10 .25
BT13061 Death Army Commander C .10 .25
BT13062 Beast Deity, Damned Leo C .40 1.00
BT13063 Gatlingraizer C .10 .25
BT13064 Beast Deity, Desert Gator C .10 .25
BT13065 Beast Deity, Night Jackal C .10 .25
BT13066 Beast Deity, Death Stinger C .10 .25
BT13067 Beast Deity, Van Paurus C .10 .25
BT13068 Beast Deity, Bright Cobra C .40 1.00
BT13069 Beast Deity, Rescue Bunny C .10 .25
BT13070 Fusion Monster, Bugreed C .10 .25
BT13071 Shock Monster, Vipple C .30 .75
BT13072 Heat Ray Monster, Gigabolt C .10 .25
BT13073 Beam Monster, Raidrum C .10 .25
BT13074 Hypnotism Monster, Nechoroly C .10 .25
BT13075 Demon-eye Monster, Gorgon C .10 .25
BT13076 Dimensional Robo, Daicrane C .10 .25
BT13077 Dimensional Robo, Goflight C .10 .25
BT13078 Dimensional Robo, Gorescue C .10 .25
BT13079 Supergiant Lady Gunner C .10 .25
BT13080 Devastation Star-vader, Tungsten C .10 .25
BT13081 Prison Gate Star-vader, Palladium C .10 .25
BT13082 Asteroid Belt Lady Gunner C .10 .25
BT13083 Star-vader, Chaos Beat Dragon C .10 .25
BT13084 Black Ring Chain, Pleiades C .10 .25
BT13085 Dragon Corrode, Corrupt Dragon C .10 .25
BT13086 Peter the Ghostie C .10 .25
BT13087 Gunshot of Sorrow, Nightflare C .10 .25
BT13088 Keen Eye Sky Trooper C .10 .25
BT13089 Marine General of the Furious Tides, Myrtus C .10 .25
BT13090 Battle Siren, Calista C .10 .25
BT13091 Abyssal Sniper C .25
BT13092 Deuterium Gun Dragon C .10 .25
BT13093 Tidal Rescue Sea Turtle Soldier C .10 .25
BT13094 Shallows Sweeper C .10 .25
BT13095 Heavy Rush Dragon C .10 .25
BT13096 Swimming Patrol Seal Soldier C .10 .25
BT13097 Apprentice Gunner, Solon C .10 .25
BT13098 Battle Siren, Mallika C .30 .75
BT13099 Cosmic Cheetah C .10 .25
BT13100 Whistle Hyena C .10 .25
BT13101 Telescope Rabbit C .10 .25
BT13102 Holder Hedgehog C .10 .25
BT13S001 Cleanup Celestial, Ramiel Reverse SP12.00 30.00
BT13S002 Shura Stealth Dragon, Kujikiricongo SP10.00 25.00
BT13S003 Strongest Beast Deity, Ethics Buster Extreme SP 15.00 40.00
BT13S004 Deadliest Beast Deity, Ethics Buster Reverse SP 12.00 30.00
BT13S005 Dark Dimensional Robo, Reverse Daiyusha SP 12.00 30.00
BT13S006 Original Saver, Zero SP 6.00 15.00
BT13S007 Star-vader, Chaos Breaker Dragon SP30.00 80.00
BT13S008 Blue Wave Dragon, Tetra-drive Dragon SP15.00 40.00
BT13S016 Lord of the Seven Seas, Nightmist SP 8.00 20.00
BT13S017 Ice Prison Hades Emperor, Cocytus Reverse SP 6.00 15.00
BT13S019 School Punisher, Leo-pald Reverse SP8.00 20.00

2014 Cardfight Vanguard Champions of the Cosmos

COMPLETE SET (39) 80.00 120.00
BOOSTER BOX (15 PACKS) 30.00 40.00
BOOSTER PACK (5 CARDS) 2.00 3.00
RELEASED ON JUNE 6, 2014
EB08001 Immortal, Asura Kaiser RRR 1.50 4.00
EB08002 Galaxy Blaukluger RRR 6.00 15.00
EB08003 Mond Blaukluger RRR 8.00 20.00
EB08004 Asura Kaiser RR 2.00 5.00
EB08005 Stern Blaukluger RR 4.00 10.00
EB08006 Mars Blaukluger RR 2.00 5.00
EB08007 Flower Ray Leprechaun RR .40 1.00
EB08008 Blau Dunkelheit RR 1.50 4.00
EB08009 Armored Heavy Gunner R .75 2.00
EB08010 Brutal Jack R .40 1.00
EB08011 Jupiter Blaukluger R .75 2.00
EB08012 Grosse Baer R .50 1.25
EB08013 Daredevil Samurai R .40 1.00
EB08014 Blaukluger R .50 1.25
EB08015 Polar Stern R .60 1.50
EB08016 Morgenrot R .60 1.50
EB08017 Pluto Blaukluger C .30 .75
EB08018 Muscle Hercules C .30 .75
EB08019 Eisenkugel C .30 .75
EB08020 Hungry Dumpty C .30 .75
EB08021 Tough Boy C .30 .75
EB08022 Oasis Girl C .30 .75
EB08023 Clay-doll Mechanic C .30 .75
EB08024 Bear Down Samurai C 1.50 4.00
EB08025 Almighty Reporter C .30 .75
EB08026 Blaupanzer C .30 .75
EB08027 Blade Arm Leprechaun C .30 .75
EB08028 Blaujunger C .30 .75
EB08029 Schones Wetter C .50 1.25
EB08030 Shining Lady C .30 .75
EB08031 Schnee Regen C .30 .75
EB08032 The Gong C .30 .75
EB08033 Regenbogen C .40 1.00
EB08034 Starker Wind C .30 .75
EB08035 Battleraizer C .30 .75
EB08S01 Immortal, Asura Kaiser SP 6.00 15.00
EB08S02 Galaxy Blaukluger SP 15.00 40.00
EB08S03 Mond Blaukluger SP 12.00 30.00
EB08S08 Blau Dunkelheit SP 15.00 40.00

2014 Cardfight Vanguard Dimensional Brave Kaiser

TD12001 Super Dimensional Robo, Daikaiser 5.00 12.00
TD12002 Super Dimensional Robo, Daiyusha 1.50 4.00
TD12003 Electro-star Combination, Cosmogreat .30 .75
TD12004 Dimensional Robo, Daifighter .30 .75
TD12005 Dimensional Robo, Daidragon 1.50 4.00
TD12006 Dimensional Robo, Kaizard 3.00 8.00
TD12007 Super Dimensional Robo, Dailady .30 .75
TD12008 Dimensional Robo, Daidriller .30 .75
TD12009 Karenroid, Daisy .30 .75
TD12010 Dimensional Robo, Daitiger .30 .75
TD12011 Dimensional Robo, Daimariner .30 .75
TD12012 Dimensional Robo, Daibrave 1.25 3.00
TD12013 Dimensional Robo, Goyusha .30 .75
TD12014 Dimensional Robo, Daibattles .30 .75
TD12015 Dimensional Robo, Daicrane .30 .75
TD12016 Dimensional Robo, Goflight .30 .75
TD12017 Dimensional Robo, Gorescue .30 .75

2014 Cardfight Vanguard Diva's Duet

COMPLETE SET (43) 250.00 400.00
BOOSTER BOX (15 PACKS) 40.00 60.00
BOOSTER PACK (5 CARDS) 3.00 4.00
RELEASED ON AUGUST 15, 2014
EB10001 Duo Stage Storm, Iori RRR 8.00 20.00
EB10002 Duo Temptation, Reit RRR 30.00 80.00
EB10003 Duo True Sister, Meer RRR 25.00 60.00
EB10004 Duo Flower Girl, Lily RR 5.00 12.00
EB10005 Duo Mini Heart, Rhone RR 2.50 6.00
EB10006 PRISM-Duo, Yarmuk C .20 .50
EB10007 Duo Promise Day, Colima RR 5.00 12.00
EB10008 PRISM-Duo, Slaney RR 6.00 15.00
EB10009 Duo Sweet Rhythm, Vilaine R 1.25 3.00
EB10010 Duo Kelpie Jockey, Syr Darya R .30 .75
EB10011 Duo Dream Idol, Sana R 1.25 3.00
EB10012 Duo Magical Mic, Sharlene R .25 .60
EB10013 Duo Far Marine Chateau, Thames R .75 2.00
EB10014 Duo Petit Etoile, Peace R .75 2.00
EB10015 Duo Pretty Horn, Ural R .40 1.00
EB10016 PRISM-Duo, Avon C .40 1.00
EB10017 Duo Lady Canotier, Salinas C .30 .75
EB10018 Duo Toybox, Menam C .30 .75
EB10019 Duo White Crystal, Ricca C .30 .75
EB10020 PRISM-Duo, Aria RR 12.00 30.00
EB10021 Duo Afternoon Tea, Parana C .30 .75
EB10022 Duo Shiny Tone, Chicora C .20 .50
EB10023 Duo Dream Idol, Myne C .30 .75
EB10024 Duo Beast Ear, Loulou C .50 1.25
EB10025 PRISM-Duo, Tisa R .40 1.00
EB10026 Duo Clear Parasol, Kura C .30 .75
EB10027 Duo Lovers' Singer, Darling C .30 .75
EB10028 Duo Treasure Hunter, Swany C .20 .50
EB10029 Duo Pride Crown, Madeira C .40 1.00
EB10030 Duo Gran Pasturn, Syanon C .20 .50
EB10031 Duo Morning Charm, Liffey C .30 .75
EB10032 Duo Lamplight Melody, Tigris C .30 .75
EB10033 Duo Soulful Melody, Selenga C .30 .75
EB10034 Duo Tropical Healer, Mejelda C .40 1.00
EB10035 Duo Night Wing, Dungrilo C .40 1.00
EB10S01 Duo Stage Storm, Iori SP 20.00 50.00
EB10S02 Duo Temptation, Reit SP 80.00 150.00
EB10S03 Duo True Sister, Meer SP 50.00 100.00
EB10S04 Duo Flower Girl, Lily SP 8.00 20.00
EB10S05 Duo Mini Heart, Rhone SP 8.00 20.00
EB10S06 PRISM-Duo, Slaney SP 8.00 20.00
EB10S07 Duo Promise Day, Colima SP 6.00 15.00
EB10S08 PRISM-Duo, Aria SP 15.00 40.00

2014 Cardfight Vanguard Divine Dragon Progression

COMPLETE SET (35) 50.00 100.00
BOOSTER BOX (15 PACKS) 30.00 40.00
BOOSTER PACK (5 CARDS) 2.00 3.00
RELEASED ON JUNE 6, 2014
EB09001 Transcendence Dragon, Dragonic Nouvelle Vague RRR 12.00 30.00
EB09002 Cruel Dragon RRR 5.00 12.00
EB09003 Blast Bulk Dragon RRR 3.00 8.00
EB09004 Dragonic Overlord RR 2.00 5.00
EB09005 Dragonic Lawkeeper RR 2.00 5.00
EB09006 Nouvellecritic Dragon RR 3.00 8.00
EB09007 Dragonic Gaias RR 5.00 12.00
EB09008 Dragon Dancer, Maria RR 3.00 8.00
EB09009 Dragon Monk, Goku R .50 1.25
EB09010 Dragon Knight, Neshat R .50 1.25
EB09011 Berserk Dragon R .75 2.00
EB09012 Bellicosity Dragon R 2.00 5.00
EB09013 Dragon Knight, Ashgar R .75 2.00
EB09014 Nouvelleroman Dragon R 1.25 3.00
EB09015 Lizard Soldier, Raopia R .50 1.25
EB09016 Lizard Soldier, Conroe R .50 1.25
EB09017 Dragon Knight, Morteza C .30 .75
EB09018 Beikin Grim Dragon C .60 1.50
EB09019 Genie Soldat C .20 .50
EB09020 Prowling Dragon, Striken C .30 .75
EB09021 Dragon Knight, Nehalem C .30 .75
EB09022 Demonic Dragon Mage, Kongara C .30 .75
EB09023 Embodiment of Armor, Bahr C .30 .75
EB09024 Guard Griffin C .30 .75
EB09025 Flame of Hope, Aermo C .30 .75
EB09026 Demonic Dragon Madonna, Joka C .30 .75
EB09027 Scale Dragon of the Magma Cave C .30 .75
EB09028 Red Pulse Dracokid C .30 .75
EB09029 Blue Ray Dracokid C .20 .50
EB09030 Embodiment of Spear, Tahr C .50 1.25
EB09031 Dragon Dancer, Monica C .30 .75
EB09032 Lizard Soldier, Ganlu C .30 .75
EB09033 Dragon Monk, Genjo C .40 1.00
EB09034 Gattling Claw Dragon C .20 .50
EB09035 Flame Seed Salamander C .30 .75

2014 Cardfight Vanguard Fighter Collection 2014

COMPLETE SET (37) 60.00 120.00
FIGHTER'S COLLECTION BOX (10 PACKS)
FIGHTER'S COLLECTION PACK (3 CARDS)
RELEASED ON NOVEMBER 7, 2014
FC02001 Splitting Seeker, Brutus RRR 4.00 10.00
FC02002 Brawler, Shotgun Blow Dragon RRR 4.00 10.00
FC02003 Ultimate Dimensional Robo, Great Daikaiser RRR 10.00 25.00
FC02004 Sprout Jewel Knight, Camille RRR .40 1.00
FC02005 Floral Magus RRR .40 1.00
FC02006 Halberd Revenger, Peredur RRR .75 2.00
FC02007 Twin Blade Liberator, Margaux RRR .40 1.00
FC02008 Spiral Celestial, Hellm RRR 1.25 3.00
FC02009 Goddess of Four Seasons, Persephone RRR.40 1.00
FC02010 Hellfire Seal Dragon, Weathercloth RRR1.00 2.50
FC02011 Ancient Dragon, Volcatops RRR 1.25 3.00
FC02012 Shura Stealth Dragon, Yozakuracongo RRR.40 1.00
FC02013 Covert Demonic Dragon, Kasumi Rouge RRR .40 1.00
FC02014 Eradicator, Twin Thunder Dragon RRR .40 1.00
FC02015 Merkur Blaukluger RRR .40 1.00
FC02016 Super Dimensional Robo, Shadowkaiser RRR .40 1.00
FC02017 Super Dimensional Robo, Daiyard RRR 1.25 3.00
FC02018 Edicting Star-vader, Halcium RRR .60 1.50
FC02019 Echo of Nemesis RRR .75 2.00
FC02020 Demonic Lord, Dudley Lucifer RRR .40 1.00
FC02021 Bunny Queen Beast Tamer RRR .40 1.00
FC02022 Drift Ice Swordsman, Nightsnow RRR 1.50 4.00
FC02023 Duo Delicious Girl, Chao RRR .40 1.00
FC02024 Blue Storm Marine General, Demetrius RRR2.50 6.00
FC02025 Machining Warsickle RRR 1.00 2.50
FC02026 Sage's Egg, Minette RRR .75 2.00
FC02027 Holly Musketeer, Elvira RRR 1.00 2.50
FC02028 Combined Strength Seeker, Locrinus RRR.40 1.00
FC02029 Military Brawler, Lisei RRR 2.50 6.00
FC02S01 Majesty Lord Blaster SP 5.00 12.00
FC02S02 Goddess of the Full Moon, Tsukuyomi SP5.00 12.00
FC02S03 Phantom Blaster Overlord SP 3.00 8.00
FC02S04 Dragonic Overlord the End SP 20.00 50.00
FC02S05 Eradicator, Vowing Sword Dragon SP 2.50 6.00
FC02S06 Perfect Raizer SP 2.00 5.00
FC02S07 Top Idol, Pacifica SP 2.50 6.00

2014 Cardfight Vanguard Infinite Rebirth

COMPLETE SET (115) 150.00 300.00
BOOSTER BOX (36 PACKS) 40.00 60.00
BOOSTER PACK (5 CARDS) 2.00 3.00
RELEASED ON SEPTEMBER 19, 2014
BT15000 Star-vader, "Omega" Glendios R-RRR 3.00 8.00
BT15001 Revenger, Desperate Dragon RRR 2.00 5.00
BT15002 Revenger, Dragruler Phantom RRR 4.00 10.00
BT15003 Liberator, Monarch Sanctuary Alfred RRR 3.00 8.00
BT15004 Dragonic Overlord RRR 8.00 20.00
BT15005 Dragonic Overlord "The Re-birth" RRR 4.00 10.00
BT15006 Star-vader, "Reverse" Cradle RRR 2.00 5.00
BT15007 Silver Thorn Dragon Empress, Venus Luquier RRR 6.00 15.00
BT15008 Blue Storm Karma Dragon, Maelstrom "Reverse" RRR 3.00 8.00
BT15009 Revenger, Bloodmaster RR 1.25 3.00
BT15010 Hellrage Revenger, Quesal RR 2.00 5.00
BT15011 Black-winged Swordbreaker RR 1.25 3.00
BT15013 Liberator, Star Rain Trumpeter RR 2.00 5.00
BT15014 Dragonic Burnout RR 6.00 15.00
BT15015 Dragon Knight, Gimel RR 2.50 6.00
BT15016 Star-vader, Freezeray Dragon RR 2.00 5.00
BT15017 Blue Storm Guardian Dragon, Icefall Dragon RR 2.00 5.00
BT15018 Machining Spark Hercules RR 3.00 8.00
BT15019 Unrivaled Blade Rogue, Cyclomatooth RR 5.00 12.00
BT15020 Machining Ladybug RR 2.00 5.00
BT15021 Sharp Fang Witch, Fodla R .40 1.00
BT15022 Cursed Lancer R .40 1.00
BT15023 Wily Revenger, Mana R .40 1.00
BT15024 Judgebau Revenger R .40 1.00
BT15025 Red Rainbow Liberator, Balin R .40 1.00
BT15026 White Rainbow Liberator, Balan R .40 1.00
BT15027 Starry Skies Liberator, Guinevere R .40 1.00
BT15028 Yearning Liberator, Arum R .40 1.00
BT15029 Lizard Soldier, Fargo R .40 1.00
BT15030 Star-vader, Magnet Hollow R .40 1.00
BT15031 Star-vader, Cold Death Dragon R .40 1.00
BT15032 Taboo Star-vader, Rubidium R .40 1.00
BT15033 Star-vader, Ruin Magician R .40 1.00
BT15034 Star-vader, Worldline Dragon R .40 1.00
BT15035 Nightmare Doll, Carroll R .40 1.00
BT15036 Silver Thorn Assistant, Zelma R .40 1.00
BT15037 Marinetail Dragon R .40 1.00
BT15038 Blue Storm Marine General, Gregorios R .40 1.00
BT15039 Blue Storm Battle Princess, Crysta Elizabeth R .40 1.00
BT15040 Blue Storm Cadet, Marios R .40 1.00
BT15041 Machining Red Soldier R .40 1.00
BT15042 Machining Locust R .40 1.00
BT15043 Gigantech Keeper C .10 .25
BT15044 Overcoming Revenger, Rukea C .10 .25
BT15045 Demon World Castle, Sturmangriff C .10 .25
BT15046 Sharp Point Revenger, Shadow Lancer C .10 .25
BT15047 Self-control Revenger, Rakia C .10 .25
BT15048 Eloquence Revenger, Glonn C .10 .25

BT15049 Wing Edge Panther C .10 .25
BT15050 Gautgal C .10 .25
BT15051 History Liberator, Merron C .10 .25
BT15052 Mastigal C .10 .25
BT15053 Sharp Point Liberator, Gold Lancer C .10 .25
BT15054 Physical Force Liberator, Zorron C .10 .25
BT15055 Lucky Sign Rabbit C .10 .25
BT15056 Flower Gardener C .10 .25
BT15057 Demonic Dragon Berserker, Houkenyasha C .10 .25
BT15058 Dragon Knight, Dalette C .10 .25
BT15059 Wyvern Strike, Jiet C .10 .25
BT15060 Eternal Bringer Griffin C .10 .25
BT15061 Violence Horn Dragon C .10 .25
BT15062 Dragon Knight, Razer C .10 .25
BT15063 Lizard Soldier, Grom C .10 .25
BT15064 Demonic Dragon Mage, Apalala C .10 .25
BT15065 Treasure Hunt Dracokid C .10 .25
BT15066 Fire of Determination, Puralis C .10 .25
BT15067 Dragon Dancer, Therese C .10 .25
BT15068 Soundless Archer, Conductance C .10 .25
BT15069 Negligible Hydra C .10 .25
BT15070 Planet Collapse Star-vader, Erbium C .10 .25
BT15071 Imaginary Orthos C .10 .25
BT15072 Engraving Star-vader, Praseodymium C .10 .25
BT15073 Origin Fist, Big Bang C .10 .25
BT15074 Star-vader, Sparkdoll C .10 .25
BT15075 Star-vader, Jeiratail C .10 .25
BT15076 Star-vader, Brushcloud C .10 .25
BT15077 Recollection Star-vader, Tellurium C .10 .25
BT15078 Silver Thorn, Upright Lion C .10 .25
BT15079 Miss Direction C .10 .25
BT15080 Brassie Bunny C .10 .25
BT15081 Silver Thorn Beast Tamer, Emile C .10 .25
BT15082 Titan of the Capturing Arm C .10 .25
BT15083 Blue Storm Marine General, Lysandros C .10 .25
BT15084 Blue Storm Soldier, Tempest Assault C .10 .25
BT15085 Blue Storm Marine General, Spyros C .10 .25
BT15086 Mobile Battleship, Cetus C .10 .25
BT15087 Blue Storm Marine General, Hermes C .10 .25
BT15088 Blue Storm Soldier, Tempest Blader C .10 .25
BT15089 Swim Patrol Jellyfish Soldier C .10 .25
BT15090 Battle Siren, Ketty C 3.00 8.00
BT15091 Blue Storm Soldier, Missile Trooper C .10 .25
BT15092 Blue Storm Battle Princess, Doria C .10 .25
BT15093 Angler Soldier of the Blue Storm Fleet C .10 .25
BT15094 Blue Storm Soldier, Kitchen Sailor C .10 .25
BT15095 Machining Tarantula C .10 .25
BT15096 Machining Papilio C .10 .25
BT15097 Machining Black Soldier C .10 .25
BT15098 Machining Caucasus C .10 .25
BT15099 Machining Little Bee C .10 .25
BT15100 Machining Scorpion C .10 .25
BT15101 Machining Bombyx C .10 .25
BT15102 Machining Cicada C .10 .25
BT15S01 Revenger, Desperate Dragon SP 2.00 5.00
BT15S02 Revenger, Dragruler Phantom SP 10.00 25.00
BT15S03 Liberator, Monarch Sanctuary Alfred SP 10.00 25.00
BT15S04 Dragonic Overlord SP 15.00 40.00
BT15S05 Dragonic Overlord "The Re-birth" SP 8.00 20.00
BT15S06 Star-vader, "Reverse" Cradle SP 6.00 15.00
BT15S07 Silver Thorn Dragon Empress, Venus Luquier SP 12.00 30.00
BT15S08 Blue Storm Karma Dragon, Maelstrom "Reverse" SP 6.00 15.00
BT15S09 Liberator, Star Rain Trumpeter SP 2.00 5.00
BT15S10 Dragonic Burnout SP 8.00 20.00
BT15S11 Machiningark Hercules SP 4.00 10.00
BT15S12 Unrivaled Blade Rogue, Cyclomatooth SP 4.00 10.00
BT15012 Liberator, Holy Shine Dragon RR 4.00 10.00

2014 Cardfight Vanguard Legion of Dragons and Blades

COMPLETE SET (116) 300.00 450.00
BOOSTER BOX (36 PACKS) 60.00 80.00
BOOSTER PACK (5 CARDS) 3.00 4.00
RELEASED ON DECEMBER 19, 2014
BT16001 Seeker, Sing Saver Dragon RRR 6.00 15.00
BT16002 Honest Seeker, Egbert RRR 2.00 5.00
BT16003 Brawler, Bigbang Knuckle Dragon RRR 6.00 15.00
BT16004 Brawler, Wild Rush Dragon RRR 4.00 10.00
BT16005 Ultimate Raizer Mega Flare RRR 8.00 20.00
BT16006 Metalborg, Sin Buster RRR 5.00 12.00
BT16007 Emerald Blaze RRR 2.00 5.00
BT16008 Peony Musketeer, Martina RRR 5.00 12.00
BT16009 Blaster Blade Seeker RR 5.00 12.00
BT16010 Guardian Law Seeker, Shiron RR 4.00 10.00
BT16011 Brawler, Bigbang Slash Dragon RR 2.00 5.00
BT16012 Hardship Brawler, Toshu RR 2.00 5.00
BT16013 Phoenix Raizer Drill Wing RR 2.00 5.00
BT16014 Shieldraizer RR 2.00 5.00
BT16015 Metalborg, Dryon RR 5.00 12.00
BT16016 Metalborg, Bri Knuckle RR 2.00 5.00
BT16017 Bloody Ogre RR 2.00 5.00
BT16018 Baron Amadeus RR 2.00 5.00
BT16019 Licorice Musketeer, Vera RR 12.00 30.00
BT16020 Moth Orchid Musketeer, Christie RR 2.50 6.00
BT16021 Crossbow Seeker, Gildas R .40 1.00
BT16022 Flail Seeker, Hasbasado R .40 1.00
BT16023 Glynngal Seeker R .40 1.00
BT16025 Brawler Youjin R .40 1.00
BT16026 Threatening Brawler, Koumei R .40 1.00
BT16027 Tonfa Wielding Brawler, Aak R .40 1.00
BT16028 Brawler, Fighting Dracokid R .40 1.00
BT16029 Ultimate Raizer Dual Flare R .40 1.00
BT16030 Phoenix Raizer Flame Wing R .40 1.00
BT16031 Tankraizer R .40 1.00
BT16032 Energyraizer R .40 1.00
BT16033 Metalborg, Ur Buster R .40 1.00
BT16034 Metalborg, Lionetter R .40 1.00
BT16035 Metalborg, Iunbot R .40 1.00
BT16036 Metalborg, Black Boy R .40 1.00
BT16037 Silver Blaze R .40 1.00
BT16038 Frozen Ogre R .40 1.00
BT16039 Machine Gun Gloria R .40 1.00
BT16040 Peony Musketeer, Thule R .40 1.00
BT16041 Licorice Musketeer, Saul R .40 1.00
BT16042 Camellia Musketeer, Tamara R .40 1.00
BT16043 Seeker, Gigantech Driver C .10 .25
BT16044 Sky Bow Seeker, Morvi C .10 .25
BT16045 Shibelgal Seeker C .10 .25
BT16046 Sky Arrow Seeker, Lunete C .10 .25
BT16047 Seeker, Tranquil Unicorn C .10 .25
BT16048 Seeker, Hartmy C .10 .25
BT16049 Seeker, Harold Breath Dragon C .10 .25
BT16050 Seeker, Bucephalus C .10 .25
BT16051 Brawler, Headband of Grid C .10 .25
BT16052 Wild Brawler, Shugi C .10 .25
BT16053 Demonic Dragon Brawler, Kadloo C .10 .25
BT16054 Brawler, Igo C .10 .25
BT16055 Brawler, Dropkick Wyvern C .10 .25
BT16056 Fledging Phoenix Brawler, Koutenshou C .10 .25
BT16057 Brawler of Heavens, Youzen C .10 .25
BT16058 Brawler of Battles, Haoka C .10 .25
BT16059 Nobody From Orimecha C .10 .25
BT16060 Marine Raizer Anchor Arm C .10 .25
BT16061 Marine Raizer High Torpedo C .10 .25
BT16062 Wingraizer C .10 .25
BT16063 Rapidraizer C .10 .25
BT16064 Cannonraizer C .10 .25
BT16065 Carvingraizer C .10 .25
BT16066 Reserveraizer C .10 .25
BT16067 Space Pit C .10 .25
BT16068 Raizer Pilot, Huey C .10 .25
BT16069 Meteoraizer C .10 .25
BT16070 Raizer Crew C .10 .25
BT16071 Raizer Girl, Kate C .10 .25
BT16072 Subliminal Gray C .10 .25
BT16073 Metalborg, Sandstorm C .10 .25
BT16074 Metalborg, Cezalion C .10 .25
BT16075 Metalborg, Digarion C .10 .25
BT16076 Metalborg, Russell Blizzard C .10 .25
BT16077 Metalborg, Bull Dump C .10 .25
BT16078 Metalborg, Express C .10 .25
BT16079 Metalborg, Mist Ghost C .10 .25
BT16080 Metalborg, Black Doctor C .10 .25
BT16081 Metalborg, Death Blade C .10 .25
BT16082 Metalborg, Mech Rogue C .10 .25
BT16083 Metalborg, Battle Roller C .10 .25
BT16084 Metalborg, Black Nurse C .10 .25
BT16085 Metalborg, Devil Loader C .10 .25
BT16086 Metalborg, Operator Kirika C .10 .25
BT16087 Dudley Moses C .10 .25
BT16088 Dudley Monti C .10 .25
BT16089 Jumbo the Stungun C .10 .25
BT16090 Treasured, Mirage Panther C .10 .25
BT16091 Oasis Boy C .10 .25
BT16092 Cyclone Johnny C .10 .25
BT16093 Cheer Girl, Pauline C .10 .25
BT16094 Cheer Girl, Adared C .10 .25
BT16095 Carnation Musketeer, Richard C .10 .25
BT16096 Carnation Musketeer, Berutti C .10 .25
BT16097 Bellflower Musketeer, Ewelina C .10 .25
BT16098 Narcissus Musketeer, Joachim C .10 .25
BT16099 Hydrangea Musketeer, Ivar C .10 .25
BT16100 Anemone Musketeer, Susanna C .10 .25
BT16101 Baby's Breath Musketeer, Laisa C .10 .25
BT16102 Lotus Musketeer, Liana C .10 .25
BT16L01 Seeker, Sing Saver Dragon LR 12.00 30.00
BT16L02 Blaster Blade Seeker LR 12.00 30.00
BT16S01 Seeker, Sing Saver Dragon SP 30.00 80.00
BT16S02 Brawler, Bigbang Knuckle Dragon SP 10.00 25.00
BT16S03 Ultimate Raizer Mega Flare SP 25.00 60.00
BT16S04 Metalborg, Sin Buster SP 8.00 20.00
BT16S05 Emerald Blaze SP 5.00 12.00
BT16S06 Peony Musketeer, Martina SP 12.00 30.00
BT16S07 Blaster Blade Seeker SP 6.00 15.00
BT16S08 Brawler, Bigbang Slash Dragon SP 20.00 50.00
BT16S09 Ultimate Raizer Dual Flare SP 12.00 30.00
BT16S10 Metalborg, Ur Buster SP 8.00 20.00
BT16S11 Silver Blaze SP 15.00 40.00
BT16S12 Peony Musketeer, Thule SP 12.00 30.00
BT16-024 Advance Party Seeker, File R 1.25 3.00

2014 Cardfight Vanguard Mystical Magus

COMPLETE SET (35) 50.00 100.00
BOOSTER BOX (36 PACKS) 30.00 40.00
BOOSTER PACK (5 CARDS) 2.00 3.00
RELEASED ON APRIL 11, 2014
EB07001 Hexagonal Magus RRR 15.00 40.00
EB07002 Battle Sister, Parfait RRR 8.00 20.00
EB07003 Battle Sister, Monaka RR 10.00 25.00
EB07004 Stellar Magus RR 3.00 8.00
EB07005 Battle Sister, Cocotte RR 4.00 10.00
EB07006 Briolette Magus RR 2.00 5.00
EB07007 Tetra Magus RR 5.00 12.00
EB07008 Imperial Daughter R 1.00 2.50
EB07009 Evil-eye Princess, Euryale R 1.25 3.00
EB07010 Oracle Agent, Roys R .30 .75
EB07011 Cuore Magus R 1.50 4.00
EB07012 Promise Daughter R .40 1.00
EB07013 Battle Sister, Macaron R 1.50 4.00
EB07014 Crescent Magus R 2.00 5.00
EB07015 Little Witch, LuLu R .60 1.50
EB07016 Sailand Magus C .10 .25
EB07017 Battle Sister, Tart C .10 .25
EB07018 Battle Sister, Caramel C .10 .25
EB07019 Blue Scale Deer C .60 1.50
EB07020 Onmyoji of the Moonlit Night C .20 .50
EB07021 Oracle Guardian, Gemini C .10 .25
EB07022 Circle Magus C .10 .25
EB07023 Battle Sister, Omelet C .30 .75
EB07024 Ripis Magus C .10 .25
EB07025 Battle Sister, Maple C .10 .25
EB07026 Petal Fairy C .10 .25
EB07027 Battle Sister, Lemonade C .10 .25
EB07028 Luck Bird C .10 .25
EB07029 Battle Sister, Ginger C .10 .25
EB07030 Miracle Kid C .10 .25
EB07031 Battle Sister, Tiramisa C .10 .25
EB07032 Battle Sister, Assam C .10 .25
EB07033 Battle Sister, Chai C .10 .25
EB07034 Psychic Bird C .20 .50
EB07035 Lozenge Magus C .10 .25

2014 Cardfight Vanguard Purgatory Revenger

TD10001 Illusionary Revenger, Mordred Phantom 4.00 10.00
TD10002 Venomous Breath Dragon .30 .75
TD10003 Labyrinth Revenger, Arawn .20 .50
TD10004 Darkness Revenger, Rugos .25 .60
TD10005 Nullity Revenger, Masquerade 1.50 4.00
TD10006 Blaster Dark Revenger 2.00 5.00
TD10007 Koilbau Revenger .25 .60
TD10008 Revenger Fortress, Fatalita .25 .60
TD10009 Black Sage, Charon .20 .50
TD10010 Sacrilege Revenger, Baal-berith .25 .60
TD10011 Transient Revenger, Masquerade .20 .50
TD10012 Branbau Revenger .25 .60
TD10013 Crisis Revenger, Fritz .20 .50
TD10014 Grim Revenger .30 .75
TD10015 Freezing Revenger .40 1.00
TD10016 Awaking Revenger .25 .60
TD10017 Healing Revenger .20 .50

2014 Cardfight Vanguard Requiem at Dusk

EB11001 Witch of Enchantment, Fianna RRR 15.00 40.00
EB11002 Revenger, Phantom Blaster Abyss RRR 20.00 50.00
EB11003 Blaster Dark Revenger Abyss RRR 8.00 20.00
EB11004 Cultus Witch, Rias RR 3.00 8.00
EB11005 Ambitious Spirit Revenger, Cormac RR 4.00 10.00
EB11006 Inspection Witch, Deirdre RR 5.00 12.00
EB11007 Battle Spirit Revenger, Mackart RR 5.00 12.00
EB11008 Barrier Witch, Grainne RR 8.00 20.00
EB11009 Witch of Cursed Talisman, Etain R .40 1.00
EB11010 Demon World Castle, ToteZiegel R .75 2.00
EB11011 Witch of Reality, Femme R 8.00 20.00
EB11012 Moonlight Witch, Vaha R 3.00 8.00
EB11013 Skull Witch, Nemain R .50 1.25
EB11014 Witch of Precious Stones, Dana R 4.00 10.00
EB11015 Witch of Choice, Eriu R .10 .25
EB11016 Witch of Banquets, Lir R .40 1.00
EB11017 Meteor Witch, Manisa C .10 .25
EB11018 Dark Mage, Badhabh Caar C .10 .25
EB11019 Comet Witch, Serva C .10 .25
EB11020 Witch of Godly Speed, Amel C .10 .25
EB11021 Demon World Castle, Fatalita C .10 .25
EB11022 Redmew Revenger C .10 .25
EB11023 Ruin Witch, Scathach C .10 .25
EB11024 Fighting Spirit Revenger, Lyfechure C .10 .25
EB11025 Witch of Nostrum, Arianrhod C .10 .25
EB11026 Witch of Pursuit, Sekuana C .75 2.00
EB11027 Howlbau Revenger C .10 .25
EB11028 Creeping Dark Goat C .10 .25
EB11029 Revenger, Air Raid Dragon C .10 .25
EB11030 Black Crow Witch, Eine C .10 .25
EB11031 Lizard Witch, Aife C .10 .25
EB11032 Freezing Revenger C .75 2.00
EB11033 Revenger, Waking Angel C .10 .25
EB11034 Black Cat Witch, Milkre C .10 .25
EB11035 Witch of Goats, Medb C .10 .25
EB11L01 Revenger, Phantom Blaster Abyss LR 25.00 60.00
EB11L02 Blaster Dark Revenger Abyss LR 25.00 60.00
EB11S01 Witch of Enchantment, Fianna SP 15.00 40.00
EB11S02 Revenger, Phantom Blaster Abyss SP 15.00 40.00
EB11S03 Blaster Dark Revenger Abyss SP 30.00 80.00
EB11S04 Barrier Witch, Grainne SP 8.00 20.00
EB11S05 Witch of Reality, Femme SP 8.00 20.00
EB11S06 Illusionary Revenger, Mordred Phantom SP 20.00 50.00

2014 Cardfight Vanguard Seeker of Hope

TD14001 Seeker, Sacred Wingal 2.00 5.00
TD14002 Secret Sword Seeker, Vortigern .25 .60
TD14003 Blue Flame Seeker, Taranis .30 .75
TD14004 Natural Talent Seeker, Valrod .30 .75
TD14005 Blaster Blade Seeker 5.00 12.00
TD14006 Full Bloom Seeker, Cerdic 2.50 6.00
TD14007 Provocation Seeker, Blumenthal .20 .50
TD14008 Vladgal Seeker .30 .75
TD14009 Seeker, Youthful Mage .40 1.00
TD14010 Good Faith Seeker, Cynric .30 .75
TD14011 Seeker of the Right Path, Gangalen .40 1.00
TD14012 Seeker, Rune Eagle .30 .75
TD14013 Heroic Spirit Seeker, Mark .30 .75
TD14014 Certain Kill Seeker, Modron .20 .50
TD14015 Messegal Seeker .30 .75
TD14016 Warning Seeker, Maris .20 .50
TD14017 Seeker, Loving Healer .40 1.00

2014 Cardfight Vanguard Star-Vader Invasion

TD11001 Star-vader, Infinite Zero Dragon 2.00 5.00
TD11002 Raid Star-vader, Francium .25 .60
TD11003 Twilight Baron .30 .75
TD11004 Soaring Star-vader, Krypton .20 .50
TD11005 Star-vader, Mobius Breath Dragon 1.00 2.50
TD11006 Unrivaled Star-vader, Radon 2.50 6.00
TD11007 Star-vader, Pulsar Bear .25 .60
TD11008 Swift Star-vader, Strontium .25 .60
TD11009 Hollow Twin Blades, Binary Star .25 .60
TD11010 Pursuit Star-vader, Fermium .20 .50
TD11011 Demonic Bullet Star-vader, Neon .20 .50
TD11012 Star-vader, Aurora Eagle .25 .60
TD11013 Nova Star-vader, Actinium .25 .60
TD11014 Star-vader, Meteor Liger .20 .50
TD11015 Star-vader, Nebula Captor .25 .60
TD11016 Keyboard Star-vader, Bismuth .25 .60
TD11017 Star-vader, Stellar Garage .20 .50

2014 Cardfight Vanguard Successor of the Sacred Regalia

TD13001 Regalia of Wisdom, Angelica 4.00 10.00
TD13002 Battle Maiden, Mizuha .30 .75
TD13003 Witch of Wolves, Saffron .20 .50
TD13004 Battle Maiden, Izunahime .20 .50
TD13005 Battle Maiden, Sahohime .25 .60
TD13006 Goddess of Trees, Jupiter .75 2.00
TD13007 Battle Maiden, Shitaterahime .20 .50
TD13008 Battle Maiden, Mihikarihime .20 .50
TD13009 Battle Maiden, Tatsutahime .20 .50
TD13010 Existence Angel .75 2.00
TD13011 Witch of Cats, Cumin .20 .50
TD13012 Apple Witch, Cider .25 .60
TD13013 Reflector Angel .25 .60
TD13014 Lemon Witch, Limonccino .20 .50
TD13015 Bandit Danny .20 .50
TD13016 Patrol Guardian .20 .50
TD13017 Witch of Big Pots, Laurier .20 .50

2014 Cardfight Vanguard Waltz of the Goddess

COMPLETE SET (43) 200.00 350.00
BOOSTER BOX (15 PACKS) 60.00 80.00
BOOSTER PACK (5 CARDS) 4.00 5.00
RELEASED ON NOVEMBER 21, 2014
EB12001 Cosmic Regalia, CEO Yggdrasill RRR 12.00 30.00
EB12002 White Snake Witch, Mint RRR 8.00 20.00
EB12003 Regalia of Wisdom and Courage, Brynhildr RRR 3.00 8.00
EB12004 Witch of Sea Eagles, Fennel RR .75 2.00
EB12005 Regalia of Midnight, Nyx RR .40 1.00
EB12006 Regalia of Midday, Hemera RR 3.00 8.00
EB12007 Witch of Strawberries, Framboise RR 4.00 10.00
EB12008 Regalia of Frozen Breath, Svalin RR 1.50 4.00
EB12009 Wisdom Keeper, Metis R .30 .75
EB12010 Myth Guard, Procyon R .75 2.00
EB12011 Witch of Golden Eagles, Jasmine R .30 .75
EB12012 Regalia of Fate, Norn R 10.00 25.00
EB12013 Black Snake Witch, Chicory R .40 1.00
EB12014 Goddess of Trees, Jupiter R .40 1.00
EB12015 Regalia of Abundance, Freya R .75 2.00
EB12016 Regalia of Prayer, Pray Angel R .25 .60
EB12017 Regalia of Love, Cypris C .20 .50
EB12018 Regalia of Beauty, Venus C .30 .75
EB12019 Witch of Ravens, Chamomile C .20 .50
EB12020 Myth Guard, Orion C .40 1.00
EB12021 Witch of Frogs, Melissa C .20 .50
EB12022 Regalia of Purity, Pure Angel C .20 .50
EB12023 Exorcism Regalia, Shiny Angel C .40 1.00
EB12024 Goddess of Union, Juno C .20 .50
EB12025 Witch of Peaches, Bellini C .20 .50
EB12026 Regalia of Congratulations, Bleach Angel C .20 .50
EB12027 Myth Guard, Sirius C .30 .75
EB12028 Witch of House Mouse, Koroha C .20 .50
EB12029 Far Sight Regalia, Clear Angel C .25 .60
EB12030 Fancy Monkey C .20 .50
EB12031 Spark Cockerel C .20 .50
EB12032 Regalia of Benevolence, Eir C .20 .50
EB12033 Battle Maiden, Kukurihime C .20 .50
EB12034 Regalia of Foredoom, Lot Angel C .20 .50
EB12035 Mirror Regalia, Achlis C .20 .50
EB12L01 Cosmic Regalia, CEO Yggdrasill LR 30.00 80.00
EB12L02 Regalia of Fate, Norn LR 25.00 60.00
EB12S01 Cosmic Regalia, CEO Yggdrasill SP 50.00 100.00
EB12S02 White Snake Witch, Mint SP 15.00 40.00
EB12S03 Regalia of Wisdom and Courage, Brynhildr SP 6.00 15.00
EB12S04 Regalia of Fate, Norn SP 12.00 30.00
EB12S05 Black Snake Witch, Chicory SP 8.00 20.00
EB12S06 Regalia of Wisdom, Angelica SP 15.00 40.00

2014 Cardfight Vanguard Will of the Locked Dragon

TD17001 Star-vader, Garnet Star Dragon 4.00 10.00
TD17002 Star-vader, Graviton .25 .60
TD17003 Heavy Bomber Star-vader, Berkelium .25 .60
TD17004 Bombing Star-vader, Magnesium .20 .50
TD17005 Companion Star Star-vader, Photon 6.00 15.00
TD17006 Unrivaled Star-vader, Radon .75 2.00
TD17007 Star-vader, Sinister Eagle .25 .60
TD17008 Star-vader, Stronghold .25 .60
TD17009 Star-vader, Satellite Mirage .25 .60
TD17010 Throwing Star-vader, Thorium .20 .50
TD17011 Mana Shot Star-vader, Neon .20 .50
TD17012 Star-vader, Crumble Mare .25 .60
TD17013 Vacant Space Star-vader, Quantum .40 1.00
TD17014 Star-vader, Apollo Nail Dragon .40 1.00
TD17015 Vortex Star-vader, Molybdenum .25 .60
TD17016 Star-vader, Gamma Dile .25 .60
TD17017 Star-vader, Pixie Powder .30 .80

2015 Cardfight Vanguard Blue Cavalry of the Divine Marine Spirits Japanese

GTD04001 Marine General of the Heavenly Scale, Tidal-bore Dragon
GTD04002 Transcendent of Storms, Savas
GTD04003 Titan of Beam Fist Fight
GTD04004 Battery Boom Dragon
GTD04005 Kelpie Rider, Dennis
GTD04006 Battle Siren, Rhode
GTD04007 Magnum Assault
GTD04008 Hydro Hammer Sailor
GTD04009 Kelpie Rider, Polo
GTD04010 Railgun Assault
GTD04011 Gun Diver Dracokid
GTD04012 Battle Siren, Phaedra
GTD04013 Mine Star Trooper
GTD04014 Officer Cadet, Andrei
GTD04015 Bubble Bazooka Dracokid
GTD04016 Rainbow Sniper
GTD04017 Keen Eye Sea Horse Soldier
GTD04018 Battle Siren, Carolina
GTD04019 Officer Cadet, Alexpose

2015 Cardfight Vanguard Flower Maiden of Purity Japanese

GTD03001 Flower Princess of Spring Color, Arborea
GTD03002 Flower Maiden of Ranunculus, Ayesha
GTD03003 Jungle Lord Dragon
GTD03004 Full Bloom Dragon
GTD03005 Blooming Maiden, Kera
GTD03006 Grace Knight
GTD03007 Maiden of Gladiolus
GTD03008 Kakokawa Kiwi
GTD03009 Sprout Maiden, Dian
GTD03010 Coral Berry Squire
GTD03011 Gardener Elf
GTD03012 100 Orange
GTD03013 Maiden of Safflower
GTD03014 Spring Waiting Maiden, Oz
GTD03015 Maiden of Dimorphous
GTD03016 Plenty Turnip
GTD03017 Lavender Knight
GTD03018 Fairy Light Dragon
GTD03019 Maiden of Daybreak

2015 Cardfight Vanguard Academy of Divas

COMPLETE SET (53) 400.00 600.00
RELEASED ON AUGUST 25, 2015
GCB01001 School Etoile, Olyvia GR 1.00 2.50
GCB01002 PR?ISM-Promise, Princess Labrador RRR 25.00 60.00
GCB01003 Duo Eternal Sister, Meer RRR 10.00 25.00
GCB01004 Miracle Voice, Lauris RRR .75 2.00
GCB01005 Ideal Walking Weather, Emilia RRR 15.00 40.00
GCB01006 Sincere Girl, Liddy RR 25.00 60.00
GCB01007 Admired Sparkle, Spica RR 2.00 5.00
GCB01008 Duo Fantasia, Lamry RR 2.50 6.00
GCB01009 Unbelievagirl, Potpourri RR 12.00 30.00
GCB01010 Superb New Student, Shizuku RR 1.00 2.50
GCB01011 Image Master, Kukuri RR .75 2.00
GCB01012 Cherished Phrase, Reina RR 2.50 6.00
GCB01013 Fluffy Ribbon, Somni R 1.00
GCB01014 Duo Lovely Angel, Nemuel R .60 1.50
GCB01015 Duo Lovely Devil, Vepar R .75 2.00
GCB01016 Duo Beloved Child of the Sea Palace, Minamo R 2.00 5.00
GCB01017 PR?ISM-Promise, Princess Celtic R .75 2.00
GCB01018 Talent of Perseverance, Shandee R 1.50 4.00
GCB01019 Duo Gorgeous Lady, Kazuha R .75 2.00
GCB01020 PR?ISM-Promise, Princess Leyte R .75 2.00
GCB01021 Secret Smile, Puumo R .75 2.00
GCB01022 First Lesson, Akari R .50 1.25
GCB01023A Duo Love Joker, Chulym R .40 1.00
GCB01023B Duo Love Joker, Chulym (B) R 1.25 3.00
GCB01024 Dreamer Dreamer! Krk R .40 1.00
GCB01025 Little Princess, Himari C 2.00 5.00
GCB01026 Afternoon Tea Party, Couver C .10 .25
GCB01027 Top Gear Idol, Sanya C .10 .25
GCB01028 Mystery Solving Time, Ithil C .10 .25
GCB01029 Victory Appeal, Filier C .10 .25
GCB01030 Reticent Diva, Isuca C .10 .25
GCB01031 PR?ISM-Duo, Loretta (B) C .10 .25
GCB01032 Full Throttle Idol, Lurrie C .10 .25
GCB01033 Sweet Paradise, Manya C .10 .25
GCB01034 Beware of Surprises, Almin C .10 .25
GCB01035 One Blow Fight, Hinata C .10 .25
GCB01036 Finger Magic, Mako C .10 .25
GCB01037 Morning Impact, Lips C .10 .25
GCB01038 Southern Harmony, Melvi C .10 .25
GCB01039 Cold Eye, Sara C .10 .25
GCB01040 Lover of Hearts, Penelotta C .10 .25
GCB0131W PR?ISM-Duo, Loretta (W) C .10 .25
GCB01S01 School Etoile, Olivia SP 120.00 200.00
GCB01S02 Duo Eternal Sister, Meer SP 30.00 80.00
GCB01S03 Miracle Voice, Lauris SP 30.00 80.00
GCB01S04 Strolling Weather, Emilia SP 60.00 120.00
GCB01S05 Sincere Girl, Liddy SP
GCB01S06 Admired Sparkle, Spica SP
GCB01S07 Duo Fantasia, Ramli SP
GCB01S08 Unbelievagirl, Potpourri SP 20.00 50.00
GCB01S09 Superb New Student, Shizuku SP 25.00 60.00
GCB01S10 Image Master, Kukuri SP
GCB01S11 Important Phrase, Reina SP 50.00 100.00

2015 Cardfight Vanguard Blazing Perdition

COMPLETE SET (164) 150.00 300.00
BOOSTER BOX (36 PACKS) 50.00 60.00
BOOSTER PACK (5 CARDS) 3.00 4.00
RELEASED ON JANUARY 23, 2015
BT17001 Bluish Flame Liberator, Prominence Core RRR 6.00 15.00
BT17002 Murasame Liberator, Coil RRR .75 2.00
BT17003 Perdition Dragon, Pain Laser Dragon RRR 3.00 8.00
BT17004 Perdition Dragon, Vortex Dragonewt RRR 6.00 15.00
BT17005 Brawler, Big Bang Knuckle Buster RRR 8.00 20.00
BT17006 Star-vader, Imaginary Plane Dragon RRR 1.25 3.00
BT17007 Star-vader, Dark Zodiac RRR 1.50 4.00
BT17008 Blue Storm Wave Dragon, Tetra-burst Dragon RRR 5.00 12.00
BT17009 Seeker, Purgation Breath Dragon RR 3.00 8.00
BT17010 Locus Liberator, Asclepius RR 6.00 15.00
BT17011 Light Formation Liberator, Erdre RR 5.00 12.00
BT17012 Perdition Dragon, Menace Laser Dragon RR 1.25 3.00
BT17013 Perdition Dragon, Rampart Dragon RR .40 1.00
BT17014 Ancient Dragon, Tyrannoquake RR 1.50 4.00
BT17015 Ancient Dragon, Rockmine RR 2.50 6.00
BT17016 Ionization Star-vader, Hafnium RR .40 1.00
BT17017 Star-vader, Rejection Dragon RR .75 2.00

BT17018 Young Pirate Noble, Pinot Noir RR .40 1.00
BT17019 Reef Banshee RR .40 1.00
BT17020 Blue Storm Battle Princess, Electra RR .75 2.00
BT17021 Brave Stride Seeker, Cherin R .40 1.00
BT17022 Shower Liberator, Trahern R .40 1.00
BT17023 Liberator, Lawful Trumpeter R 1.00 2.50
BT17024 Twin Axe Liberator, Bassia R .40 1.00
BT17025 Koronagal Liberator R 1.25 3.00
BT17026 Perdition Dragon, Heat Wing Dragon R .40 1.00
BT17027 Perdition Dragon, Whirlwind Dragon R .40 1.00
BT17028 Perdition Dragon, Tinder Spear Dracokid R .40 1.00
BT17029 Ancient Dragon, Magmaarmor R .40 1.00
BT17030 Ancient Dragon, Tyrannobite R 1.25 3.00
BT17031 Ancient Dragon, Night Armor R .40 1.00
BT17032 Brawler, Big Bang Slash Buster R .40 1.00
BT17033 Star-vader, Astro Reaper R .40 1.00
BT17034 Flash Gun Star-vader, Osmium R .75 2.00
BT17035 Star-vader, Volt Line R .40 1.00
BT17036 Star-vader, Robin Knight R .40 1.00
BT17037 Witch Doctor of the Dead Sea, Negrobolt R .40 1.00
BT17038 Pirate Belle, Pinot Blanc R .40 1.00
BT17039 Dragon Undead, Ghoul Dragon R .40 1.00
BT17040 Blue Storm Marine General, Zaharias R .40 1.00
BT17041 Blue Storm Marine General, Ianis R .40 1.00
BT17042 Blue Storm Marine General, Starless R .40 1.00
BT17043 Seeker, Sebrumy C .10 .25
BT17044 Jewel Knight, Sabremy C 2.00 5.00
BT17045 Lake Maiden, Lien C .25 .60
BT17046 Composed Seeker, Lucius C .75 2.00
BT17047 Seeker, Platina Rider C .10 .25
BT17048 Spear-line Liberator, Marius C .10 .25
BT17049 Liberator, Feather Lion C .10 .25
BT17050 Liberator, Holy Wizard C .10 .25
BT17051 Natural Liberator C .15 .40
BT17052 Liberator, Bright Bicorn C .60
BT17053 Liberator, Holy Acolyte C .20 .50
BT17054 Liberator, Blessing Arrow Angel C .20 .50
BT17055 Steel Blade Liberator, Alwilla C .20 .50
BT17056 Ketchgal Liberator C .10 .25
BT17057 Perdition Berserker, Jaratkaru C .10 .25
BT17058 Perdition Dragon Knight, Jamileh C .10 .25
BT17059 Perdition Mage, Asticah C .10 .25
BT17060 Perdition Dragon Knight, Sabha C .10 .25
BT17061 Perdition Wyvern, Boom C .10 .25
BT17062 Perdition Battler, Maleikoh C .10 .25
BT17063 Perdition Battler, Maleisei C .10 .25
BT17064 Seal Dragon Sprite, Mulciber C .10 .25
BT17065 Perdition Dragon Knight, Gia C .10 .25
BT17066 Perdition Wyvern, Grue C .10 .25
BT17067 Perdition Dragon Knight, Sahar C .10 .25
BT17068 Perdition Dragon, Buster Rain Dragon C .10 .25
BT17069 Perdition Sprite, Flarelooper C .10 .25
BT17070 Perdition Dancer, Agafia C .10 .25
BT17071 Perdition Cleric, Hakkai C .10 .25
BT17072 Ancient Dragon Twin Axe Warrior C .10 .25
BT17073 Ancient Dragon, Tyrannoblaze C .10 .25
BT17074 Ancient Dragon, Crestrunner C .10 .25
BT17075 Ancient Dragon, Babysaurus C .10 .25
BT17076 Ancient Dragon Flame Maiden C .10 .25
BT17077 Ancient Dragon, Chaoticbird C .10 .25
BT17078 Spirited Brawler, Kohkin C .10 .25
BT17079 Eradicator, Egghelm Dracokid C .10 .25
BT17080 Sturdy Feet Brawler, Tohkon C .10 .25
BT17081 Brawler, Volt Knuckle Dracokid C .10 .25
BT17082 Brawler, Heavy Trailer Dragon C .10 .25
BT17083 Star-vader, Metal Griffin C .10 .25
BT17084 Emission Line Star-vader, Antimony C .10 .25
BT17085 Ray Star-vader, Samarium C .10 .25
BT17086 Eclipse Star-vader, Charcoal C .10 .25
BT17087 Deception Star-vader, Nickel C .10 .25
BT17088 Star-vader, Atom Router C .10 .25
BT17089 Star-vader, Butterfly Effect C .10 .25
BT17090 Star-vader, Null Chameleon C .10 .25
BT17091 Shockwave Star-vader, Dysprosium C .10 .25
BT17092 Boatswain, Arman C .10 .25
BT17093 Brutal Shade C .10 .25
BT17094 Cleaving Shade C .10 .25
BT17095 Fledgling Pirate, Pinot Gris C .10 .25
BT17096 Jimmy the Ghostie C .10 .25
BT17097 Hungry Mimick C .10 .25
BT17098 Performing Zombie C .10 .25
BT17099 Mako Shark Soldier of the Blue Storm Fleet C .10 .25
BT17100 Blue Storm Soldier, Tempest Boarder C .10 .25
BT17101 Mola Mola Soldier of the Blue Storm Fleet C .10 .25
BT17102 Blue Storm Cadet, Anos C .10 .25
BT17L01 Bluish Flame Liberator, Prominence Core LR 10.00 25.00
BT17L02 Oath Liberator, Aglovale LR 12.00 30.00
BT17L03 Perdition Dragon, Vortex Dragonewt LR 5.00 12.00
BT17L13 Perdition Dragon, Whirlwind Dragon LR 12.00 30.00
BT17S01 Bluish Flame Liberator, Prominence Core SP 12.00 30.00
BT17S02 Murasame Liberator, Coil SP 3.00 8.00
BT17S03 Perdition Dragon, Pain Laser Dragon SP 6.00 15.00
BT17S04 Perdition Dragon, Vortex Dragonewt SP 2.50 6.00
BT17S05 Brawler, Big Bang Knuckle Buster SP 6.00 15.00
BT17S06 Star-vader, Imaginary Plane Dragon SP 10.00 25.00
BT17S07 Star-vader, Dark Zodiac SP 8.00 20.00
BT17S08 Blue Storm Wave Dragon, Tetra-burst Dragon SP 15.00 40.00
BT17S09 Seeker, Purgation Breath Dragon SP 4.00 10.00
BT17S10 Perdition Dragon, Menace Laser Dragon SP 4.00 10.00
BT17S11 Ancient Dragon, Tyrannoquake SP 12.00 30.00
BT17S12 Young Pirate Noble, Pinot Noir SP 6.00 15.00

2015 Cardfight Vanguard Cosmic Roar

COMPLETE SET (35) 20.00 50.00
BOOSTER BOX (15 PACKS) 30.00 40.00
BOOSTER PACK (5 CARDS) 2.00 3.00
RELEASED ON APRIL 17, 2015
GEB01001 99th-gen Dimensional Robo Commander, Great Daiearth RRR 6.00 15.00
GEB01002 Super Cosmic Hero, X-tiger RRR 10.00 25.00
GEB01003 Great Cosmic Hero, Grandgallop RRR 6.00 15.00
GEB01004 Dark Superhuman, Omega RR .75 2.00
GEB01005 Super Cosmic Hero, X-falcon RR 1.00 2.50
GEB01006 Cosmic Hero, Grandfire RR 1.00 2.50
GEB01007 Cosmic Hero, Grandguard RR 5.00 12.00
GEB01008 Cosmic Hero, Grandbeat RR .60 1.50
GEB01009 Enigman Tornado R .40 1.00
GEB01010 New Era Beast, Zeal R .40 1.00
GEB01011 Metalborg, Barrengrader R .40 1.00
GEB01012 Cosmic Hero, Grandsub R .40 1.00
GEB01013 Dimensional Robo, Daijet R .40 1.00
GEB01014 Cosmic Hero, Grandrope R .40 1.00
GEB01015 Cosmic Hero, Grandwagon R .40 1.00
GEB01016 Metalborg, Grasscutter R .40 1.00
GEB01017 Great Cosmic Hero, Grandbazooka C .10 .25
GEB01018 Enigman Night Sky C .10 .25
GEB01019 Cosmic Hero, Grandkungfu C .10 .25
GEB01020 Ionization Monster, Plazm C .10 .25
GEB01021 Metalborg, Magmafork C .10 .25
GEB01022 Cosmic Hero, Grandpolice C .10 .25
GEB01023 Enigman Cloud C .10 .25
GEB01024 Cosmic Hero, Grandchopper C .10 .25
GEB01025 Dimensional Robo, Dailion C .10 .25
GEB01026 Evolution Monster, Davain C .10 .25
GEB01027 Metalborg, Hammerhel C .10 .25
GEB01028 Cosmic Hero, Grandseed C .10 .25
GEB01029 Dimensional Robo, Daishoot C .10 .25
GEB01030 Metalborg, Locobattler C .10 .25
GEB01031 Dimensional Robo, Daiwolf C .10 .25
GEB01032 Masked Police, Guunjoe C .10 .25
GEB01033 Cosmic Hero, Grandrescue C .10 .25
GEB01034 Enigman Sunset C .10 .25
GEB01035 Operator Girl, Reika C .10 .25

2015 Cardfight Vanguard Divine Swordsmen of the Shiny Star

COMPLETE SET (19)
RELEASED ON FEBRUARY 27, 2015
GTD02001 Shrouded Divine Knight, Gablade 1.50 4.00
GTD02002 Blue Sky Knight, Altmile 5.00 12.00
GTD02003 Aura Shooter Dragon .10 .25
GTD02004 Profound Sage, Kunron .10 .25
GTD02005 Absolute Blade Knight, Livarot .10 .25
GTD02006 Knight of Twin Sword 4.00 10.00
GTD02007 Transmigration Knight, Brede .75 2.00
GTD02008 Mithrilguard Lion .10 .25
GTD02009 Lunar Crescent Knight, Felax .10 .25
GTD02010 Archer of Heaven's Tower .10 .25
GTD02011 Knight of Steel Wing .10 .25
GTD02012 Milky Way Unicorn .10 .25
GTD02013 Rainbow Guardian .30 .75
GTD02014 Shining Knight, Millius .12 .30
GTD02015 Burning Mane Lion .10 .25
GTD02016 Pixy Assault Captain .10 .25
GTD02017 Knight of Festival .10 .25
GTD02018 Healing Pegasus .10 .25
GTD02019 Margal .40 1.00

2015 Cardfight Vanguard Fighter's Collection

COMPLETE SET (50) 60.00 100.00
RELEASED ON JUNE 19, 2015
GFC01001 Holy Dragon, Religious Soul Saver GR 3.00 8.00
GFC01002 Moon Deity Who Governs Night, Tsukuyomi GR 2.00 5.00
GFC01003 Absolution Lion King, Mithril Ezel GR 3.00 8.00
GFC01004 Supreme Heavenly Emperor Dragon, Dragonic Overlord the Ace GR 8.00 20.00
GFC01005 True Brawler, Big Bang Knuckle Turbo GR 5.00 12.00
GFC01006 Death Star-vader, Omega Loop Glendios GR 2.50 6.00
GFC01007 Blue Storm Marshal Dragon, Admiral Maelstrom GR 2.50 6.00
GFC01008 Interdimensional Dragon, Epoch-maker Dragon GR 1.25 3.00
GFC01009 Holy Celestial, Mikhael RRR 1.25 3.00
GFC01010 True Revenger, Dragruler Revenant RRR 1.25 3.00
GFC01011 Sacred Flame Ultimate Regalia, Demeter RRR 1.50 4.00
GFC01012 Rikudo Stealth Dragon, Jorurirakan RRR 1.25 3.00
GFC01013 Super Ancient Dragon, Pearly Titan RRR 2.00 5.00
GFC01014 Cosmetic Snowfall, Shirayuki RRR .40 1.00
GFC01015 War Deity, Asura Kaiser RRR .50 1.25
GFC01016 Hyper Metalborg, Heavyduke RRR 1.25 3.00
GFC01017 Great Warrior, Dudley Geronimo RRR .40 1.00
GFC01018 Amon's Talon, Marchocias RRR .75 2.00
GFC01019 Silver Thorn Dragon Master, Mystique Luquier RRR 3.00 8.00
GFC01020 Ice Prison Hades Deity, Cocytus Negative RRR .75 2.00
GFC01021 Legendary PR?ISM-Duo, Nectaria RRR 3.00 8.00
GFC01022 Carapace Mutant Deity, Machining Destroyer RRR 4.00 10.00
GFC01023 School Special Investigator, Leo-pald Chaser RRR .20 .50
GFC01024 White Lily Musketeer Captain, Cecilia RRR .40 1.00
GFC01025 Holy Dragon, Sanctuary Guard Regalie RR .40 1.00
GFC01026 Raincloud-calling Nine-headed Dragon King RR .30 .75
GFC01027 Holy Seraph, Uriel RR .75 2.00
GFC01028 Dark Knight, Efnysien RR .50 1.25
GFC01029 Golden Dragon, Scourge Point Dragon RR 1.50 4.00
GFC01030 Great Angel, Doom Brace RR 1.25 3.00
GFC01031 Divine Dragon Knight, Zahm RR .20 .50
GFC01032 Rikudo Stealth Dragon, Gedatsurakan RR .20 .50
GFC01033 Destruction Tyrant, Archraider RR .20 .50
GFC01034 Ambush Demon Stealth Rogue, Kagamijishi RR 1.25 3.00
GFC01035 Avatar of Heroic Spirits, Vishnu RR .20 .50
GFC01036 Meteokaiser, Tribrut RR .25 .60
GFC01037 Dark Superhuman, Pretty Cat RR .20 .50
GFC01038 Nebula Dragon, Maximum Seal Dragon RR .75 2.00
GFC01039 Godly-speed, Flash Bruce RR .20 .50
GFC01040 Great Demon, Soulless Demagogue RR .40 1.00
GFC01041 Miracle of Luna Square, Clifford RR .25 .60
GFC01042 Interdimensional Beast, Upheaval Pegasus RR 1.00 2.50
GFC01043 Pirate King of the Abyss, Blueheart RR .40 1.00
GFC01044 Legend of the Glass Shoe, Amoric RR 1.00 2.50
GFC01045 Marine General of Heavenly Silk, Sokrates RR .25 .60
GFC01046 Deforestation Mutant Deity, Jaggydevil RR .20 .50
GFC01047 Omniscience Dragon, Wisdom Teller Dragon RR .20 .50
GFC01048 Sacred Tree Dragon, Multivitamin Dragon RR .20 .50
GFC01049 Rain Element, Madew RR 2.00 5.00
GFC01050 Light Elemental, Peaker RR .20 .50

2015 Cardfight Vanguard Flower Maiden of Purity

COMPLETE SET (19)
RELEASED ON FEBRUARY 27, 2015
GTD03001 Flower Princess of Spring, Arborea .75 2.00
GTD03002 Ranunculus Flower Maiden, Ahsha 2.50 6.00
GTD03003 Jungle Lord Dragon .10 .25
GTD03004 Full Bloom Dragon .10 .25
GTD03005 Blossoming Maiden, Cela .10 .25
GTD03006 Grace Knight .12 .30
GTD03007 Maiden of Gladiolus .60 1.50
GTD03008 Qool Qute Qiwi .10 .25
GTD03009 Budding Maiden, Diane .10 .25
GTD03010 Coral Berry Squire .10 .25
GTD03011 Gardener Elf .10 .25
GTD03012 100 Orange .20 .50
GTD03013 Maiden of Safflower .10 .25
GTD03014 Spring-Heralding Maiden, Ozu .10 .25
GTD03015 Maiden of Dimorphotheca .10 .25
GTD03016 Heave-ho Turnip .10 .25
GTD03017 Lavender Knight .10 .25
GTD03018 Fairy Light Dragon .10 .25
GTD03019 Maiden of Daybreak .60 1.50

2015 Cardfight Vanguard Generation Stride

COMPLETE SET
BOOSTER BOX (36 PACKS)
BOOSTER PACK (5 CARDS)
RELEASED ON MARCH 13, 2015
GBT01001 Interdimensional Dragon, Chronoscommand Dragon GR
GBT01002 Holy Dragon, Saint Blow Dragon RRR
GBT01003 Sword Deity of the Thunder Break, Takemikazuchi RRR
GBT01004 Supreme Heavenly Battle Deity, Susanoo RRR
GBT01005 Flame Emperor Dragon King, Root Flare Dragon RRR
GBT01006 Dragonic Overlord The X RRR
GBT01007 Meteorkaiser, Viktoplasma RRR
GBT01008 Exxtreme Battler, Victor RRR
GBT01009 Interdimensional Dragon, Ragnaclock Dragon RRR
GBT01010 Knight of Fragment RR
GBT01011 Holy Knight Guardian RR
GBT01012 Diviner, Kuroikazuchi RR 1.00
GBT01013 Arbitrator, Amenosagiri RR 4.00
GBT01014 Dragonic Blademaster RR 5.00
GBT01015 Twilight Arrow Dragon RR
GBT01016 Protect Orb Dragon RR
GBT01017 Cool Hank RR 4.00
GBT01018 Lady Cyclone RR
GBT01019 Fatewheel Dragon RR
GBT01020 Relic Master Dragon RR
GBT01021 Steam Maiden, Arlim RR
GBT01022 Knight of Great Spear R
GBT01023 Starlight Violinist R
GBT01024 Laurel Knight, Sicilus R
GBT01025 Soaring Auspicious Beast, Qilin R
GBT01026 Obligate Robin R
GBT01027 Tankman Mode Morning Star R
GBT01028 Divine Sword, Ame-no-Murakumo R 1.00
GBT01029 Imperial Shrine Guard, Hahiki R
GBT01030 Divine Dragon Knight, Mahmud R 1.00
GBT01031 Flame of Strength, Aetniki R
GBT01032 Lava Flow Dragon R
GBT01033 Dragon Monk Gyokuryu R 1.00
GBT01034 Wyvernkid Ragla R
GBT01035 Meteorkaiser, Vikt Ten R
GBT01036 Muscle Shriek R
GBT01037 Masuraoraizer R
GBT01038 Extreme Battler, Arashid R
GBT01039 Ruin Disposal Dragon R
GBT01040 Steam Knight, Puzur Ili R
GBT01041 Steam Breath Dragon R
GBT01042 Steam Scalar, Gigi R
GBT01043 Miracle Element, Atmos R
GBT01044 Knight of Militarism, Marianus C
GBT01045 Seeker, Proud Roar Lion C
GBT01046 Gigantech Shot-Putter C
GBT01047 Knight of Shield Bash C
GBT01048 Bravogal Seeker C .25
GBT01049 Knight of Drawn Sword C
GBT01050 Knight of Flash C
GBT01051 Encourage Angel C
GBT01052 Battle Sister, Mille-feuille C .25
GBT01053 Imperial Shrine Guard, Asuha C
GBT01054 Diviner, Shinatsuhiko C 5.00
GBT01055 Tankman Mode Beam Cannon C
GBT01056 Battle Sister, Marshmallow C .25
GBT01057 Imperial Shrine Guard, Tsunagai C
GBT01058 Diviner, Kuebiko C .25
GBT01059 Battle Sister, Lollipop C .25
GBT01060 Able Neil C .25
GBT01061 Assault Dive Eagle C .25
GBT01062 Huge Harvest Daikokuten C
GBT01063 Diviner, Sukunahikona C .25
GBT01064 Paisley Magus C
GBT01065 Nebula Witch, NoNo C
GBT01066 Double Perish Dragon C .25
GBT01067 Wyvern Strike, Doha C
GBT01068 Dragon Knight, Jabad C .25
GBT01069 Hulk Roar Dragon C
GBT01070 Perdition Berserker, Heileita C
GBT01071 Dragon Knight, Tanaz C .25
GBT01072 Wyvern Strike, Garan C
GBT01073 Dragon Knight, Monireh C .25
GBT01074 Perdition Dancer, Anna C
GBT01075 Dragon Knight, Rashid C .25
GBT01076 Magnum Shot Dracokid C
GBT01077 Dragon Dancer, Ekaterina C .25
GBT01078 Mother Orb Dragon C
GBT01079 Lizard Soldier, Beira C
GBT01080 Super Extreme Leader, Mu Sashi C
GBT01081 Extreme Battler, Kenbeam C
GBT01082 Extreme Battler, Gunzork C
GBT01083 Extreme Battler, Sazanda C
GBT01084 Starlight Hedgehog C
GBT01085 Extreme Battler, Kendhol C
GBT01086 Aura Baller C .25
GBT01087 Katanaraizer C
GBT01088 Beast Deity, Frog Master C .25
GBT01089 Final Wrench C
GBT01090 Extreme Battler, Runbhol C
GBT01091 Extreme Battler, Hajimaru C
GBT01092 Extreme Battler, Zanbara C
GBT01093 Drone Baron C
GBT01094 Shadow Clone, Gesoraz C
GBT01095 Ring Girl, Ai C
GBT01096 Energy Girl C
GBT01097 Steam Maiden, Elul C
GBT01098 Mechanized Gear Tiger C
GBT01099 Summit Crest Gear Wolf C
GBT01100 Steam Rider, Dizcal C
GBT01101 Timepiece Dracokid C
GBT01102 Steam Battler, Meshda C
GBT01103 Wakey Wakey Worker C

2015 Cardfight Vanguard Soaring Ascent of Gale and Blossom

COMPLETE SET (115) 150.00 300.00
BOOSTER BOX (36 PACKS) 50.00 60.00
BOOSTER PACK (5 CARDS) 3.00 4.00
RELEASED ON MAY 22, 2015
GBT02001 Flower Princess of Spring's Beginning, Primavera GR 2.00 5.00
GBT02002 Divine Knight of Flashing Flame, Samuel RRR 3.00 8.00
GBT02003 Conquering Supreme Dragon, Conquest Dragon RRR 10.00 25.00
GBT02004 Dragonic Vanquisher RRR 1.25 3.00
GBT02005 Interdimensional Dragon, Faterider Dragon RRR 3.00 8.00
GBT02006 Marine General of Heavenly Silk, Lambros RRR 15.00 40.00
GBT02007 Omniscience Dragon, Managarmr RRR 4.00 10.00
GBT02008 Famous Professor, Bigbelly RRR 2.50 6.00
GBT02009 Sacred Tree Dragon, Jingle Flower Dragon RRR 8.00 20.00
GBT02010 Knight of Refinement, Benizel RR 3.00 8.00
GBT02011 Bringer of Dreams, Belenus RR 2.50 6.00
GBT02012 Dragonic Kaiser Crimson RR 1.25 3.00
GBT02013 Voltage Horn Dragon RR 2.00 5.00
GBT02014 Dragon Dancer, Anastasia RR 5.00 12.00
GBT02015 Glimmer Breath Dragon RR 12.00
GBT02016 Heart Thump Worker RR 6.00 15.00
GBT02017 Blue Storm Marine General, Michael RR .50 1.25
GBT02018 Ocean Keeper, Plato RR 1.25 3.00
GBT02019 Crayon Tiger RR 2.50 6.00
GBT02020 Contradictory Instructor, Shell Master RR 2.00 5.00
GBT02021 Maiden of Passionflower RR 1.50 4.00
GBT02022 Hidden Sage, Miron R .40 1.00
GBT02023 Lightning Dragon Knight, Zorras R .75 2.00
GBT02024 Mighty Bolt Dragoon R .40 1.00
GBT02025 Harbringer Dracokid R .40 1.00
GBT02026 Nixie Number Dragon R .40 1.00
GBT02027 Steam Knight, Xang R .40 1.00
GBT02028 Steam Mage, En-narda R .40 1.00
GBT02029 Marine General of the Wave Sword Slash, Max R .40 1.00
GBT02030 Blue Storm Marine General, Milos R .40 1.00
GBT02031 Kelpie Rider, Nikki R .75 2.00
GBT02032 Battle Siren, Orthia R .40 1.00
GBT02033 Immortality fessor, Phoeniciax R .40 1.00
GBT02034 Hot-blooded Professor, Guru Tiger R .40 1.00
GBT02035 Capable Assistant, Guru Wolf R .40 1.00
GBT02036 Set Square Penguin R .40 1.00
GBT02037 Diligent Assistant, Minibelly R .40 1.00
GBT02038 Balloon Raccoon R .40 1.00
GBT02039 Maiden of Frilldrod R .40 1.00
GBT02040 Knight of Transience, Maredream R .40 1.00
GBT02041 Valkyrie of Reclamation, Padmini R .40 1.00
GBT02042 Knight of Transience, Marehope R .40 1.00
GBT02043 Snow Element, Blizza R 1.25 3.00
GBT02044 Pure Wind Jewel Knight, Kymbelinus C .10 .25
GBT02045 Heat Wind Jewel Knight, Cymbeline C .10 .25
GBT02046 Jaggy Shot Dragoon C .10 .25
GBT02047 Roar of Chaos Deity, Rudra C .10 .25
GBT02048 Wyvern Strike, Bargs C .10 .25
GBT02049 Heat Blade Dragoon C .10 .25
GBT02050 Two-sword Eradicator, Koenshak C .10 .25
GBT02051 Undying Eradicator, Schub C .10 .25
GBT02052 Demonic Dragon Berserker, Chatura C .10 .25
GBT02053 Thunder Shout Dragoon C .10 .25
GBT02054 Assault Eradicator, Saikei C .10 .25
GBT02055 Wyvern Strike, Pyglma C .25
GBT02056 Plasma Dance Dragoon C .10 .25
GBT02057 Djinn of Paranoia C .10 .25
GBT02058 Deity of Love, Kama C .10 .25
GBT02059 Ionization Eradicator, Capnis C .10 .25
GBT02060 Dragon Dancer, Vianne C .10 .25
GBT02061 Dimension Expulsion Colossus C .10 .25
GBT02062 Steam Maiden, Ishin C .10 .25
GBT02063 Distance-running Gear Horse C .10 .25
GBT02064 Iron-fanged Gear Hound C .10 .25
GBT02065 Steam Maiden, Ul-nin C .10 .25
GBT02066 Mist Geyser Dragon C .10 .25
GBT02067 Brass-winged Gear Hawk C .10 .25
GBT02068 Steam Maiden, Jushil C .10 .25
GBT02069 Vainglory-dream Gear Cat C .10 .25
GBT02070 Strikehead Dragon C .10 .25
GBT02071 Blue Storm Soldier, Rascal Sweeper C .10 .25
GBT02072 High Tide Sniper C .10 .25
GBT02073 Sabre Flow Sailor C .10 .25
GBT02074 Assassinate Sailor C .10 .25
GBT02075 Tactics Sailor C .10 .25
GBT02076 Whirlwind Brave Shooter C .10 .25
GBT02077 Battle Siren, Stacia C .10 .25
GBT02078 Officer Cadet, Cyril C .10 .25
GBT02079 Surge Breath Dragon C .10 .25
GBT02080 Blue Storm Marine General, Despina C .10 .25
GBT02081 Contradiction Instructor, Tusk Master C .10 .25
GBT02082 Hardworking Scientist, Nyanshiro C .10 .25
GBT02083 Sleepy Tapir C .10 .25
GBT02084 Malicious Sabre C .10 .25
GBT02085 Deposition Scientist, Nyankuro C .10 .25
GBT02086 Paint Otter C .10 .25
GBT02087 Mohawk Hyena C .10 .25
GBT02088 Pencil Koala C .10 .25
GBT02089 Cutter Falcon C .10 .25
GBT02090 Cafeteria Sea Otter C .10 .25
GBT02091 Broadcast Rabbit C .10 .25
GBT02092 Protractor Utan C .10 .25
GBT02093 Vegetable Avatar Dragon C .10 .25
GBT02094 Barrage Warrior, Watermelon C .10 .25
GBT02095 Wheel Wind Dragon C .10 .25
GBT02096 Maiden of Lost Memory C .10 .25
GBT02097 Snowdrop Musketeer, Pirkko C .10 .25
GBT02098 Maiden of Canna C .10 .25
GBT02099 Melancholy Warrior, Onion C .10 .25
GBT02100 Maiden of Sprouts, Ho C .10 .25
GBT02101 Magnolia Knight C .10 .25
GBT02102 Gardenia Musketeer, Alan C .10 .25
GBT02103 Rain Elemental, Tear C .10 .25
GBT02S01 Flash Flame Divine Knight, Samuil SP 20.00
GBT02S02 Supreme Conquering Dragon, Conquest Dragon SP 10.00 25.00
GBT02S03 Dragonic Vanquisher SP 3.00 8.00
GBT02S04 Interdimensional Dragon, Fate Rider Dragon SP 5.00 12.00
GBT02S05 Marine General of the Sky and Earth, Lambros SP 20.00 50.00
GBT02S06 Omniscience Dragon, Managarmr SP 8.00 20.00
GBT02S07 Famous Professor, Bigbelly SP 6.00 15.00
GBT02S08 Sacred Tree Dragon, Jingle Flower Dragon SP 10.00 25.00
GBT02S09 Dream Bringer, Belenus SP 8.00 20.00
GBT02S10 Dragonic Kaiser Crimson SP 6.00 15.00
GBT02S11 Voltage Horn Dragon SP 5.00 12.00
GBT02S12 Heart Thump Worker SP 8.00 20.00

2015 Cardfight Vanguard Sovereign Star Dragon

COMPLETE SET (116) 200.00 350.00
BOOSTER BOX (36 PACKS) 60.00 80.00
BOOSTER PACK (5 CARDS) 4.00 5.00
RELEASED ON JULY 10, 2015
GBT03001 Phantom Blaster Dragon GR 15.00 40.00
GBT03002 Genesis Dragon, Amnesty Messiah GR 20.00 50.00
GBT03003 Supremacy Black Dragon, Aurageyser Dragon RRR 10.00 25.00
GBT03004 Supremacy Dragon, Claret Sword Dragon RRR 4.00 10.00
GBT03005 Golden Dragon, Spearcross Dragon RRR 5.00 12.00
GBT03006 Sunrise Ray Knight, Gurguit RRR 3.00 8.00
GBT03007 Divine Dragon Knight, Mustafa RRR 2.50 6.00
GBT03008 Ambush Demon Stealth Dragon, Homura Raider RRR 2.00 5.00
GBT03009 Nebula Dragon, Big Crunch Dragon RRR 8.00 20.00
GBT03010 Abominable One, Gilles de Rais RRR 6.00 15.00
GBT03011 Karma Collector RR 3.00 8.00
GBT03012 Holy Mage, Pwyll RR 1.50 4.00
GBT03013 Holy Mage, Bryderi RR 1.50 4.00
GBT03014 Dragon Knight, Jannat RR 1.00
GBT03015 Covert Demonic Dragon, Magatsu Typhoon RR .40 1.00
GBT03016 Stealth Rogue of Revelation, Yasuie RR 3.00
GBT03017 Stealth Beast, White Heron RR 1.25 3.00
GBT03018 Mixed Deletor, Keios RR .40 1.00
GBT03019 Flowers in Vacuum, Cosmo Wreath RR 8.00 20.00
GBT03020 Scharhrot Vampir RR 1.50 4.00
GBT03021 Squallmaker Vampir RR .50 1.25
GBT03022 Flag Breaker RR .75 2.00
GBT03023 Adroit Revenger, Teymon R .40 1.00
GBT03024 Scornful Knight, Gyva R .40 1.00
GBT03025 Cherishing Knight, Branwen R .40 1.00
GBT03026 Fast Chase Golden Knight, Cambell R 1.00 2.50
GBT03027 Taciturn Liberator, Brennius R .40 1.00
GBT03028 Dawning Knight, Gorboduc R .40 1.00
GBT03029 Ascendant Liberator, Barbtruc R .40 1.00
GBT03030 Heroic Saga Dragon R .40 1.00
GBT03031 Dragon Knight, Imahd R .40 1.00
GBT03032 Ambush Demon Stealth Fiend, Ushimitsu Train R .40 1.00
GBT03033 Stealth Dragon, Runestar R .40 1.00
GBT03034 Stealth Rogue of the Flowered Hat, Fujino R .40 1.00
GBT03035 Gateway Stealth Rogue, Ataka R .40 1.00
GBT03036 Cradle of the Stars, Stellar Maker R 1.00 2.50
GBT03037 Lady Battler of the Gravity Well R .40 1.00
GBT03038 Destiny Dealer R .40 1.00

GBT03039 Love Tempest, Kisskill Lira R .40 1.00
GBT03040 Psychic of Storm, Rigil R .40 1.00
GBT03041 Sweet Predator R .40 1.00
GBT03042 Flirtatious Succubus R .40 1.00
GBT03043 Succubus of Pure Love R .40 1.00
GBT03044 Earth Elemental, Pokkur R .40 1.00
GBT03045 Demon World Castle, Totwachter C .10 .25
GBT03046 Fair Knight, Gwawl C .10 .25
GBT03047 Knight of Diligence, Mazorlf C .10 .25
GBT03048 Tempting Revenger, Finegas C .10 .25
GBT03049 Night Sky Eagle C .10 .25
GBT03050 Blitz Knight, Bolfri C .10 .25
GBT03051 Demon World Castle, Streitenturm C .10 .25
GBT03052 Promising Knight, David C .10 .25
GBT03053 Witch of Black Doves, Goewin C .10 .25
GBT03054 Cursed Eye Raven C .10 .25
GBT03055 Veteran Knight, Danvallo C .10 .25
GBT03056 Lofty Head Lion C .10 .25
GBT03057 Knight of Dawnlight, Jago C .10 .25
GBT03058 Law-abiding Knight, Cloten C .10 .25
GBT03059 Braygal C .10 .25
GBT03060 Knight of Morning Shadow, Kimarcus C .10 .25
GBT03061 Butterfly Liberator, Kordeira C .10 .25
GBT03062 After-glow Liberator, Belinus C .10 .25
GBT03063 Sleimy C .10 .25
GBT03064 Rising Lionet C .10 .25
GBT03065 Air Raid Lion C .10 .25
GBT03066 Peeping Rabbit C .10 .25
GBT03067 Pharmacy Witch C .10 .25
GBT03068 Gigantech Ringer C .10 .25
GBT03069 Dragon Knight, Soheil C .10 .25
GBT03070 Demonic Dragon Berserker, Putana C .10 .25
GBT03071 Dragon Knight, Mahmit C .10 .25
GBT03072 Seal Dragon, Gariserge C .10 .25
GBT03073 Dragon Knight, Maldi C .10 .25
GBT03074 Volcano Gale Dragon C .10 .25
GBT03075 Seal Dragon, Tarpaulin Dracokid C .10 .25
GBT03076 Tenjiku Stealth Rogue, Dokube C .10 .25
GBT03077 Stealth Beast, Emissary Crow C .10 .25
GBT03078 Stealth Fiend, Yunayuki C .10 .25
GBT03079 Stealth Beast, Charcoal Fox C .10 .25
GBT03080 Chain Sickle Stealth Rogue, Onifundo C .10 .25
GBT03081 Stealth Dragon, Hiden Scroll C .10 .25
GBT03082 Lady Gunner of the Neutron Star C .10 .25
GBT03083 Heavymaterial Dragon C .10 .25
GBT03084 Chain-battle Star-vader, Technetium C .10 .25
GBT03085 Deriding Deletor, Aieda C .10 .25
GBT03086 Sword Draw Star-vader, Vorium C .10 .25
GBT03087 Spawn of the Spiral Nebula C .10 .25
GBT03088 Asteroid Wolf C .10 .25
GBT03089 Cramping Deletor, Edy C .10 .25
GBT03090 Werwolf Jaeger C .10 .25
GBT03091 Amon's Follower, Hell's Nail C .10 .25
GBT03092 Knife Conductor C .10 .25
GBT03093 Krise Vampir C .10 .25
GBT03094 Amon's Follower, Mad Eye C .10 .25
GBT03095 Killing Dollmaster C .10 .25
GBT03096 Lunatic Masquerade C .10 .25
GBT03097 Amon's Follower, Barmaid Grace C .10 .25
GBT03098 Werfleder Ordonnaz C .10 .25
GBT03099 Amon's Follower, Grausam C .10 .25
GBT03100 Wertigre Fanatica C .10 .25
GBT03101 Endless Boozer C .10 .25
GBT03102 Monochrome of Nightmareland C .10 .25
GBT03103 Alice of Nightmareland C .10 .25
GBT03104 Air Elemental, Fwarlun C .10 .25
GBT03S01 Sovereign Black Dragon, Aurageyser Dragon SP 20.00 50.00
GBT03S02 Sovereign Dragon, Claret Sword Dragon SP 12.00 30.00
GBT03S03 Golden Dragon, Spear Cross Dragon SP 8.00 20.00
GBT03S04 Knight of Rising Sunshine, Gurguit SP 3.00 8.00
GBT03S05 Divine Dragon Knight, Mustafa SP 2.00 5.00
GBT03S06 Ambush Demonic Stealth Dragon, Homura Raider SP 6.00 15.00
GBT03S07 Nebula Dragon, Big Crunch Dragon SP 12.00 30.00
GBT03S08 One Who is Abhorrent, Gilles de Rais SP 10.00 25.00
GBT03S09 Karma Collector SP 15.00 40.00
GBT03S10 Covert Demonic Dragon, Magatsu Typhoon SP 4.00 10.00
GBT03S11 Stealth Fiend, White Heron SP 4.00 10.00
GBT03S12 Flower Blooming in the Vacuum, Cosmolis SP 25.00

2015 Cardfight Vanguard The Dark Ren Suzugamori

COMPLETE SET (15)
RELEASED ON JUNE 19, 2015
GLD01001 Dark Dragon, Phantom Blaster Diablo .50 1.25
GLD01002 Dark Great Mage, Badhabh Caar .10 .25
GLD01003 Blaster Dark Diablo .20 .50
GLD01004 Bloodstained Battle Knight, Dorint .10 .25
GLD01005 Dark Night Maiden, Macha .25 .60
GLD01006 Unorthodox Shield, Mac Lir .10 .25
GLD01007 Dark Heart Trumpeter .40 1.00
GLD01008 Pitch Black Sage, Charon .12 .30
GLD01009 Arduous Battle Knight, Claudas .12 .30
GLD01010 Little Skull Witch, Nemain .40 1.00
GLD01011 Fullbau Brave 5.00 12.00
GLD01012 Revenger, Undead Angel .10 .25
GLD01013 Leaping Knight, Ligan Lumna .10 .25
GLD01014 Flatbau .10 .25
GLD01015 Howl Owl .12 .30

2015 Cardfight Vanguard G-CB02 Commander of the Incessant Waves

COMPLETE SET (46 CARDS) 200.00 300.00
BOOSTER BOX (12 PACKS) 50.00 75.00
BOOSTER PACK (7 CARDS) 2.50 6.00
UNLISTED C .10 .30
UNLISTED R .10 .30
RELEASED ON DECEMBER 11, 2015
GCB02001 Storm Dominator Commander Thavas GR 50.00 80.00
GCB02002 Blue Wave Marshal Dragon Tetraboil Dragon SP 20.00 35.00
GCB02002 Blue Wave Marshal Dragon Tetraboil Dragon RRR 4.00 10.00
GCB02003 Blue Wave Dragon Angerboil Dragon RRR 5.00 12.00
GCB02003 Blue Wave Dragon Angerboil Dragon SP 25.00 40.00
GCB02004 Blue Storm Dragon Maelstrom SP 20.00 35.00
GCB02004 Blue Storm Dragon Maelstrom RRR 2.50 6.00
GCB02005 Jockey of the Great Sea Skyros SP 8.00 20.00
GCB02005 Jockey of the Great Sea Skyros RRR 2.00 5.00
GCB02006 Surging Ripple Prodromos RR 1.00 2.50
GCB02007 Blue Wave Marine General Folvos RR 1.50 4.00
GCB02008 Battle Siren Adelaide RR 1.25 3.00
GCB02009 Blue Wave Soldier Bright Shooter RR .40 1.00
GCB02010 Blue Storm Battle Princess Theta RR .20 .60
GCB02011 Blue Storm Shield Homerus SP 4.00 10.00
GCB02011 Blue Storm Shield Homerus RR .60 1.50
GCB02012 Kelpie Rider Petros RR 2.00 5.00
GCB02013 Rolling Ripple Miltiadis R .20 .60
GCB02014 Titan of the Trench Patrol R .10 .30
GCB02015 Wavehunt Sailor R .10 .30
GCB02016 Marine General of the Sonic Speed Nektarios R .10 .30
GCB02017 Couple Dagger Sailor R .10 .30
GCB02018 Blue Storm Battle Princess Lynpia R .10 .30
GCB02019 Penguin Soldier of the Blue Storm Fleet R .10 .30
GCB02020 Battle Siren Melania R .10 .30
GCB02021 Flash Ripple Odysseus R .10 .30
GCB02022 Battle Siren Cloris R .10 .30
GCB02023 Blue Wave Dragon Dagger Master Dracokid R .10 .30
GCB02024 Blue Wave Soldier Brutal Trooper R .10 .30
GCB02025 Cobalt Neon Dragon C .10 .30
GCB02026 Blue Storm Marine General Sebastian C .10 .30
GCB02027 Unruly Ripple Lapis C .10 .30
GCB02028 Tear Knight Timos C .10 .30
GCB02029 Battle Siren Nicoletta C .10 .30
GCB02030 Reconinforce Orca Soldier C .10 .30
GCB02031 Dispatch Mission Seagull Soldier C .10 .30
GCB02032 Violent Shooter C .10 .30
GCB02033 Mindeye Sailor C .10 .30
GCB02034 Flashroll Commando C .10 .30
GCB02035 Kelpie Rider Mitros C .10 .30
GCB02036 Blue Storm Battleship Wadatsumi C .10 .30
GCB02037 Sea Otter Soldier of the Blue Storm Fleet C .10 .30
GCB02038 Medical Officer of the Blue Storm Fleet C .10 .30
GCB02039 Ripple of Demise Orest C .10 .30
GCB02040 Blue Storm Battle Princess Doris C .10 .30
GCB02S06 One Who Surpasses the Storm Thavas SP 50.00 80.00

2015 Cardfight Vanguard Soul Strike Against the Supreme

COMPLETE SET (122)
BOOSTER BOX (36 PACKS) 60.00 80.00
BOOSTER PACK (5 CARDS) 4.00 5.00
RELEASED ON OCTOBER 2, 2015
GBT04SR01 Interdimensional Dragon, Chronoscommand Dragon SCR
GBT04SR05 Supremacy Black Dragon, Aurageyser Doomed SCR
GBT04001 Supremacy Black Dragon, Aurageyser Doomed GR
GBT04002 Chronodragon Nextage GR
GBT04003 Soaring Divine Knight, Altmile RRR
GBT04004 Holy Seraph, Raphael RRR
GBT04005 Black Shiver, Gabriel RRR
GBT04006 Mythical Destroyer Beast, Vanargandr RRR
GBT04007 Mythic Beast, Fenrir RRR
GBT04008 Raging Spear Mutant Deity, Stun Beetle RRR
GBT04009 Intimidating Mutant, Darkface RRR
GBT04010 Dream-spinning Ranunculus, Ahsha RRR
GBT04011 Knight of Reform, Pir RR
GBT04012 Crimson Lore, Metatron RR
GBT04013 Black Slice, Harut RR
GBT04014 Black Record, Israfil RR
GBT04015 Taboo Demonic Mage, Kafir RR
GBT04016 Unappeasable Biter, Gleipnir RR
GBT04017 Goddess of Decline, Hel RR
GBT04018 Upstream Dragon RR
GBT04019 Rebel Mutant, Starshield RR
GBT04020 Maiden of Rambling Rose RR
GBT04021 Flower Cluster Maiden, Salianna RR
GBT04022 Flower Garden Maiden, Mailis RR
GBT04023 Techgal R
GBT04024 Holy Seraph, Raziel R
GBT04025 Accident Celestial, Batarel R
GBT04026 Control Celestial, He-el R
GBT04027 Black Call, Nakir R
GBT04028 Solid Celestial, Adnarel R
GBT04029 Knight of Inflation, Gilvers R
GBT04030 Darkpride Dragon R
GBT04031 Dark Quartz Dragon R
GBT04032 Goddess of the Skies, Dione R
GBT04033 Mythic Serpent, Jormungand R
GBT04034 Mythic Beast, Skoll R
GBT04035 Steam Fighter, Balif R
GBT04036 Steam Fighter, Ul-nigin R
GBT04037 Poisonous Spear Mutant Deity, Paraspear R
GBT04038 Machining Scorpion mk II R
GBT04039 Machining Mosquito mk II R
GBT04040 Fascinated Mutant, Sweet Cocktail R
GBT04041 Nova Mutant, Little Dorcas R
GBT04042 Maiden of Flower Screen R
GBT04043 Early Flowering Maiden, Pia R
GBT04044 Heat Elemental, Bwah R
GBT04045 Archer of Sanctuary C
GBT04046 Knight of Dexterity, Jed C
GBT04047 Battle Song Angel C
GBT04048 Jumpgal C
GBT04049 Straight Jewel Knight, Bartram C
GBT04050 Mobile Hospital, Healing Palace C
GBT04051 Nurse of Broken Heart C
GBT04052 Dream Light Unicorn C
GBT04053 Black Pain, Marut C
GBT04054 Confidence Celestial, Lumiel C
GBT04055 Doctoroid Premas C
GBT04056 Nurse Cap Dalmatian C
GBT04057 Black Candle, Azrael C
GBT04058 Nurse of Danger Heart C
GBT04059 MRI Angel C
GBT04060 Nurse of Sweet Heart C
GBT04061 Invert Celestial, Asbeel C
GBT04062 Doctoroid Lifros C
GBT04063 Sturdy Knight, Grosne C
GBT04064 Witch of Treasured Books, Adra C
GBT04065 Cleverness Knight, Convalle C
GBT04066 Witch's Familiar, Kuroma C
GBT04067 Meditation Knight, Mac Nessa C
GBT04068 Goddess of Hearths, Hestia C
GBT04069 God of Dreams, Oneiroi C
GBT04070 Witch of White Hares, Cardamom C
GBT04071 Flying Kelly C
GBT04072 String Warning, Dromi C
GBT04073 Reflecting Regalia, Mirror Angel C
GBT04074 Mythic Beast, Hati C
GBT04075 Witch of Melons, Thyme C
GBT04076 Cramer Harry C
GBT04077 Feter of Leather, Leyding C
GBT04078 Bumping Buffalo C
GBT04079 Witch of Cherries, Poppy C
GBT04080 Goddess of Youth, Hebe C
GBT04081 Witch's Familiar, Shiroma C
GBT04082 Dreaming Dragon C
GBT04083 Steam Knight, Kalium C
GBT04084 Forethought Gear Fox C
GBT04085 Steam Worker, Kuda C
GBT04086 Steam Fighter, Rugal-Banda C
GBT04087 Long Horn Hunter C
GBT04088 Buster Mantis C
GBT04089 Abyss Diver C
GBT04090 Megacolony Battler D C
GBT04091 Scissor Finger C
GBT04092 Machining Yellow Jacket C
GBT04093 Machining Slater C
GBT04094 Young Executive, Crimebug C
GBT04095 Bad Trip C
GBT04096 Machining Scarab C
GBT04097 Cocoon Healer C
GBT04098 Machining Firefly C
GBT04099 Earth Dreamer C
GBT04100 Crystalwing Dragon C
GBT04101 Wisteria Knight C
GBT04102 Hollyhock Knight C
GBT04103 3 Apple Sisters C
GBT04104 Dark Elemental, Dokuzurk C
GBT04S01 Soaring Divine Knight, Altmile SP
GBT04S02 Holy Seraph, Raphael SP
GBT04S03 Black Shiver, Gabriel SP
GBT04S04 Mythical Destroyer Beast, Vanargandr SP
GBT04S05 Mythic Beast, Fenrir SP
GBT04S06 Raging Spear Mutant Deity, Stun Beetle SP
GBT04S07 Intimidating Mutant, Darkface SP
GBT04S08 Dream-spinning Ranunculus, Ahsha SP
GBT04S09 Black Record, Israfil SP
GBT04S10 Goddess of Decline, Hel SP
GBT04S11 Rebellion Mutant, Star Shield SP
GBT04S12 Maiden of Rambling Rose SP
GBT04SR02 Flower Princess of Spring's Beginning, Primavera SCR
GBT04SR03 Phantom Blaster Dragon SCR
GBT04SR04 Genesis Dragon, Amnesty Messiah SCR
GBT04SR06 Chronodragon Nextage SCR

2016 Cardfight Vanguard G Booster Set 5 Moonlit Dragonfang

COMPLETE SET (121 CARDS) 300.00 500.00
BOOSTER BOX (30 PACKS) 50.00 80.00
BOOSTER PACK (5 CARDS) 2.50 6.00
UNLISTED C .10 .30
UNLISTED R .10 .30
RELEASED ON JANUARY 29, 2016
GBT05001 Genesis Dragon Excelics Messiah GR 15.00 30.00
GBT05002 Dragon Masquerade Harri GR 15.00 30.00
GBT05003 Dragon Destroyer Battle Deity Kamususanoo RRR 3.00 8.00
GBT05003 Dragon Destroyer Battle Deity Kamususanoo SP 10.00 25.00
GBT05004 One Who Views the Planet Globe Magus SP 8.00 20.00
GBT05004 One Who Views the Planet Globe Magus RRR 2.00 5.00
GBT05005 Conquering Supreme Dragon Dragonic Vanquisher VOLTAGE RRR 3.00 8.00
GBT05005 Conquering Supreme Dragon Dragonic Vanquisher VOLTAGE SP 8.00 20.00
GBT05006 True Eradicator Finish Blow Dragon SP 3.00 8.00
GBT05006 True Eradicator Finish Blow Dragon RRR 1.25 3.00
GBT05007 Death Starvader Chaos Universe RRR 5.00 12.00
GBT05007 Death Starvader Chaos Universe SP 35.00 50.00
GBT05008 Jester Demonic Dragon Lunatec Dragon SP 15.00 30.00
GBT05008 Jester Demonic Dragon Lunatec Dragon RRR 5.00 12.00
GBT05009 Nightmare Doll Catherine RRR 1.00 2.50
GBT05009 Nightmare Doll Catherine SP 8.00 20.00
GBT05010 Clockfencer Dragon SP 5.00 12.00
GBT05010 Clockfencer Dragon RRR 1.50 4.00
GBT05011 Imperial Shrine Guard Akagi RR .20 .60
GBT05011 Imperial Shrine Guard Akagi SP 3.00 8.00
GBT05012 Divine Sword Kusanagi RR 1.00 2.50
GBT05013 Eradicator Angercharge Dragon RR .20 .60
GBT05014 Rockclimb Dragoon RR .20 .60
GBT05014 Rockclimb Dragoon SP 4.00 10.00
GBT05015 Lightning of Triumphant Return Reseph RR .50 1.25
GBT05016 Arrester Messiah RR 4.00 10.00
GBT05016 Arrester Messiah SP 20.00 35.00
GBT05017 Lady Battler of the White Dwarf RR .20 .60
GBT05018 Blink Messiah RR 3.00 8.00
GBT05019 Darkside Princess RR 4.00 10.00
GBT05020 Darkside Mirror Master RR 4.00 10.00
GBT05020 Darkside Mirror Master SP 20.00 35.00
GBT05021 Darkside Sword Master RR 3.00 8.00
GBT05022 Steam Maiden Melem RR 8.00 20.00
GBT05023 Rigid Crane R .10 .30
GBT05024 Imperial Shrine Guard Sumiyoshi R .10 .30
GBT05025 Virtuoso Housekeeper R .10 .30
GBT05026 Battle Sister Taffy R .10 .30
GBT05027 Great Composure Dragon R .10 .30
GBT05028 Detonix Stinger Dragoon R .10 .30
GBT05029 One Strike Two Hits Djinn R .10 .30
GBT05030 Cloudmaster Dragon R .10 .30
GBT05031 Recklessness Dragon R .10 .30
GBT05032 Chainbolt Dragoon R .10 .30
GBT05033 Starvader Chaosbringer R .20 .60
GBT05034 Meteor Monk of the Force Foot R .10 .30
GBT05035 Sacrifice Messiah R .40 1.00
GBT05036 Burstlaugh Dragon R .10 .30
GBT05037 Flying Peryton R .50 1.25
GBT05038 Masquerade Bunny R 1.50 4.00
GBT05039 Silver Thorn Matador Maddock R .10 .30
GBT05040 Fiery March Colossus R .40 1.00
GBT05041 Steam Battler KugBau R .10 .30
GBT05042 Twicetalented Gear Hound R .10 .30
GBT05043 Cornerstone Gear Turtle R .10 .30
GBT05044 Earth Elemental Dogetts R .10 .30
GBT05045 Flip Croony C .10 .30
GBT05046 Ring Magus C .10 .30
GBT05047 Shrewd Concierge C .10 .30
GBT05048 Rhombus Magus C .10 .30
GBT05049 Tankman Mode Interrupt C .10 .30
GBT05050 Octagon Magus C .10 .30
GBT05051 Cone Magus C .10 .30
GBT05052 Beamshower Turtle C .10 .30
GBT05053 Semilunar Magus C .10 .30
GBT05054 Magical Calico C .10 .30
GBT05055 Triangle Magus C .10 .30
GBT05056 Battle Sister Muffin C .10 .30
GBT05057 Blitzspear Dragoon C .10 .30
GBT05058 Foot Brawler Teiroc C .10 .30
GBT05059 Hammerknuckle Dragon C .10 .30
GBT05060 Fiendish Sword Eradicator Chojun C .10 .30
GBT05061 Desert Gunner Kojin C .10 .30
GBT05062 Machinegun Eradicator Kantou C .10 .30
GBT05063 Secret Fist Brawler Kokon C .10 .30
GBT05064 Dragon Dancer Bernadette C .10 .30
GBT05065 Eradicator Raretalent Dracokid C .10 .30
GBT05066 Wildrun Dragoon C .10 .30
GBT05067 Brawler Streetfight Dragon C .10 .30
GBT05068 Lady Battler of the Accretion Disc C .10 .30
GBT05069 Mirrorworld Lion C .10 .30
GBT05070 Disorder Starvader Iron C .10 .30
GBT05071 Starholder Dragon C .10 .30
GBT05072 Turmoil Starvader Zinc C .10 .30
GBT05073 Divide Monk of the Shattering Fist C .10 .30
GBT05074 Providential Child of Gravitational Collapse C .10 .30
GBT05075 Involution Starvader Carbon C .10 .30
GBT05076 Starvader Paradigm Shift Dragon C .10 .30
GBT05077 Beauteous Beast Tamer Alexis C .10 .30
GBT05078 Fullsmile Wyvern C .10 .30
GBT05079 Intensely Spicy Clown C .10 .30
GBT05080 Silver Thorn Magician Clemens C .10 .30
GBT05081 Nightmare Doll Ginny C .10 .30
GBT05082 Hellsgate Magician C .10 .30
GBT05083 Intensely Sweet Clown C .10 .30
GBT05084 Silver Thorn Puppet Master Euphemia C .10 .30
GBT05085 Silver Thorn Magician Colette C .10 .30
GBT05086 Nightmare Doll Leslie C .10 .30
GBT05087 Fire Ring Wyvern C .10 .30
GBT05088 Dreaming Bicorn C .10 .30
GBT05089 Nightmare Doll Mirabel C .10 .30
GBT05090 Prankster Girl of Mirrorland C .10 .30
GBT05091 Breastflare Dragon C .10 .30
GBT05092 Metalglider Dragon C .10 .30
GBT05093 Heavy Ironhammer Colossus C .10 .30
GBT05094 Steam Knight Lugal C .10 .30
GBT05095 Lost City Dragon C .10 .30
GBT05096 Steam Maiden Balulu C .10 .30
GBT05097 Steam Fighter UrZaba C .10 .30
GBT05098 Steam Worker Etana C .10 .30
GBT05099 Gear Bat of Recasting C .10 .30
GBT05100 Steam Scara Merkar C .10 .30
GBT05101 Tick Tock Worker C .10 .30
GBT05102 Paradoxcannon Dracokid C .10 .30
GBT05103 Steam Battler UrWatar C .10 .30
GBT05104 Heat Elemental Juge C .10 .30
GBT05SR01EN Supreme Heavenly Battle Deity Susanoo SCR 15.00 30.00
GBT05SR02EN Pentagonal Magus SCR 8.00 20.00
GBT05SR03EN Eradicator Gauntlet Buster Dragon SCR 10.00 25.00
GBT05SR04EN Starvader Chaos Breaker Dragon SCR 70.00 100.00
GBT05SR05EN Nightmare Doll Alice SCR 50.00 80.00

2016 Cardfight Vanguard G Booster Set 6 Transcension of Blade and Blossom

COMPLETE SET (121 CARDS) 500.00 800.00
BOOSTER BOX (30 PACKS) 50.00 80.00
BOOSTER PACK (5 CARDS) 2.50 6.00
UNLISTED C .10 .30
UNLISTED R .10 .30
RELEASED ON MARCH 25, 2016
GBT06001 Transcending the Heavens Altmile GR 8.00 20.00
GBT06002 Ranunculus in Glorious Bloom Ahsha GR 15.00 30.00
GBT06003 Counteroffensive Knight Suleiman RRR 1.25 3.00
GBT06003 Counteroffensive Knight Suleiman SP 6.00 15.00
GBT06004 Dark Dragon Spectral Blaster Diablo SP 20.00 40.00
GBT06004 Dark Dragon Spectral Blaster Diablo RRR 8.00 20.00
GBT06005 Whirlwind of Darkness Vortimer Diablo SP 20.00 35.00
GBT06005 Whirlwind of Darkness Vortimer Diablo RRR 3.00 8.00
GBT06006 Meteokaiser Victor RRR 3.00 8.00
GBT06006 Meteokaiser Victor SP 15.00 30.00
GBT06007 Exxtreme Battler Danshark RRR .50 1.25
GBT06007 Exxtreme Battler Danshark SP 3.00 8.00
GBT06008 Mist Phantasm Pirate King Nightrose SP 50.00 70.00
GBT06008 Mist Phantasm Pirate King Nightrose RRR 15.00 30.00
GBT06009 Ghoul Dragon Gast Dragon SP 5.00 12.00
GBT06009 Ghoul Dragon Gast Dragon RRR 1.25 3.00
GBT06010 Cornflower Flower Maiden Ines RRR 2.00 5.00
GBT06010 Cornflower Flower Maiden Ines SP 6.00 15.00
GBT06011 Model Knight Orhan RR .20 .60
GBT06012 Hope Keeper RR .75 2.00
GBT06012 Hope Keeper SP 5.00 12.00
GBT06013 Black Chain Flame Dance Formation Hoel RR 3.00 8.00
GBT06014 Extreme Battler Headstrongbattle RR .40 1.00
GBT06015 Extreme Battler Breakpass RR .75 2.00
GBT06016 Curtain Call Announcer Mephisto RR 2.00 5.00
GBT06017 Crescent Moon Juggler RR .75 2.00
GBT06018 Hoop Master RR 1.25 3.00
GBT06018 Hoop Master SP 5.00 12.00
GBT06019 Witch Doctor of Languor Negrolazy RR 3.00 8.00
GBT06020 Waterspout Djinn SP 20.00 35.00
GBT06020 Waterspout Djinn RR 5.00 12.00
GBT06021 Ideal Maiden Thuria RR 1.00 2.50
GBT06022 Cherry Blossom Blizzard Maiden Lilga RR .75 2.00
GBT06022 Cherry Blossom Blizzard Maiden Lilga SP 6.00 15.00
GBT06023 Knight of Light Order R .10 .30
GBT06024 Favored Pupil of Light and Dark Llew R .40 1.00
GBT06025 Headwind Knight Selim R .10 .30
GBT06026 Resurgent Knight Stius R .10 .30
GBT06027 Black Chain Spirit Dance Formation Kahedin R .40 1.00
GBT06028 Bassinet Knight Oscar R .10 .30
GBT06029 Ultimate Raizer Gloryhand R .10 .30
GBT06030 Ultimate Raizer Speedstar R .10 .30
GBT06031 Extreme Battler Arbarail R .10 .30
GBT06032 Extreme Battler Malyaki R .10 .30
GBT06033 Extreme Battler Kabutron R .10 .30
GBT06034 Flying Manticore R .10 .30
GBT06035 Cutie Paratrooper R .20 .60
GBT06036 Cat Knight in High Boots R .10 .30
GBT06037 Ghostie Great King Obadiah R .20 .60
GBT06038 Ruin Shade R .10 .30
GBT06039 Tommy the Ghostie Brothers R 1.25 3.00
GBT06040 Witch Doctor of the Powdered Bone Negrobone R .40 1.00
GBT06041 Forbidden Space Banshee R .10 .30
GBT06042 Redleaf Dragon R .10 .30
GBT06043 Pure Maiden Katrina R .10 .30
GBT06044 Peach Orchard Maiden Elmy R .10 .30
GBT06045 Shyngal C .10 .30
GBT06046 Hopesong Angel C .10 .30
GBT06047 Scouting Owl C .10 .30
GBT06048 Blasterfriend Barcgal C .10 .30
GBT06049 Knight of Powercharge C .10 .30
GBT06050 Sarugal C .10 .30
GBT06051 Floral Paladin Flogal C .10 .30
GBT06052 Deathspray Dragon C .10 .30
GBT06053 Blaster Axe C .10 .30
GBT06054 Greymyu C .10 .30
GBT06055 Dark Saga Painter C .10 .30
GBT06056 Blaster Rapier C .10 .30
GBT06057 Revenger Darkless Angel C .10 .30
GBT06058 Abyss Summoner C .10 .30
GBT06059 Revenger of Vigor Maur C .10 .30
GBT06060 Blaster Dagger C .10 .30
GBT06061 Fullbau Diablo C .10 .30
GBT06062 Grave Horn Unicorn C .10 .30
GBT06063 Tactician of Godlycalculations Orphe C .10 .30
GBT06064 Illegal Alchemist C .10 .30
GBT06065 Mage of the Rogue Eye Arsur C .10 .30
GBT06066 Envoy of Righteousness Crystaldevil C .10 .30
GBT06067 Beast Deity Jackalord C .10 .30
GBT06068 Babyface Narcissus C .10 .30
GBT06069 Master Kungfu C .10 .30
GBT06070 Kumar the Destroyer C .10 .30
GBT06071 Shinobiraizer C .10 .30
GBT06072 Beast Deity Horned Hulk C .10 .30
GBT06073 Rajadamnern Kid C .10 .30
GBT06074 Turboraizer Custom C .10 .30
GBT06075 Totem Brothers C .10 .30
GBT06076 Training Therapist C .10 .30
GBT06077 Beast Deity Great Eater C .10 .30
GBT06078 Perfect Referee 299 C .10 .30
GBT06079 Artilleryman C .10 .30
GBT06080 Dreaming Pegasus C .10 .30
GBT06081 Signal Snake Tamer C .10 .30
GBT06082 Silver Thorn Assistant Dixie C .10 .30
GBT06083 Mighty Rogue Nightstorm C .10 .30
GBT06084 Seven Seas Dragon Undead Prisoner Dragon C .10 .30
GBT06085 Sleepless Skipper Blackgick C .10 .30
GBT06086 Seven Seas Master Swordsman Slash Shade C .10 .30
GBT06087 Skeleton Cannoneer C .10 .30
GBT06088 Witch Doctor of the Seven Seas Raisruler C .10 .30
GBT06089 Seven Seas Helmsman Nightcrow C .10 .30
GBT06090 Headstart Zombie C .10 .30
GBT06091 Seven Seas Apprentice Nightrunner C .10 .30
GBT06092 Assault Command Carignan C .10 .30
GBT06093 Looting Cutlass C .10 .30

GBT06094 Mick the Ghostie and Family C .10 .30
GBT06095 Greenshot Elf C .10 .30
GBT06096 Maiden of Damask Rose C .10 .30
GBT06097 Cropmaker Dragon C .10 .30
GBT06098 Af Roccoli C .10 .30
GBT06099 Tomboy Elf C .10 .30
GBT06100 Maiden of Rambler C .10 .30
GBT06101 Maiden of Noisette C .10 .30
GBT06102 Tsukken Don C .10 .30
GBT06103 Cosmos Pixy Lizbeth C .10 .30
GBT06104 Air Elemental Twitterun C .10 .30
GBT06SCR01 Blue Sky Knight Altmile SCR 60.00 85.00
GBT06SCR02 Ranunculus 100.00 120.00
Flower Maiden Ahsha SCR
GBT06SCR03 Exxtreme Battler Victor SCR 60.00 85.00
GBT06SCR04 Revenger Phantom Blaster Abyss SCR20.00 35.00
GBT06SCR05 Blaster Dark Revenger Abyss SCR20.00 35.00

2016 Cardfight Vanguard G Booster Set 7 Glorious Bravery of Radiant Sword

COMPLETE SET (141 CARDS) 600.00 1000.00
BOOSTER BOX (30 PACKS) 50.00 80.00
BOOSTER PACK (5 CARDS) 2.50 6.00
UNLISTED C .10 .30
UNLISTED R .10 .30
RELEASED ON JUNE 17, 2016
GBT07001 Sunrise Ray Radiant Sword Gurguit GR25.00 40.00
GBT07001 Sunrise Ray Radiant Sword Gurguit SGR35.00 50.00
GBT07002 Supreme Heavenly Emperor 8.00 20.00
Dragon Defeat Flare Dragon SGR
GBT07002 Supreme Heavenly Emperor 8.00 20.00
Dragon Defeat Flare Dragon GR
GBT07003 Black Seraph Gavrail RRR 6.00 15.00
GBT07003 Black Seraph Gavrail SP 25.00 40.00
GBT07004 Knight of Springs Light Perimore SP 8.00 20.00
GBT07004 Knight of Springs Light Perimore RRR3.00 8.00
GBT07005 Supreme Heavenly Emperor 8.00 20.00
Dragon Dragonic Blademaster Taiten RRR
GBT07005 Supreme Heavenly Emperor 25.00 40.00
Dragon Dragonic Blademaster Taiten SP
GBT07006 Super Cosmic Hero Xgallop SP 5.00 12.00
GBT07006 Super Cosmic Hero Xgallop RRR 2.00 5.00
GBT07007 Cosmic Hero Grandvolver RRR 1.00 2.50
GBT07007 Cosmic Hero Grandvolver SP 20.00 35.00
GBT07008 Wings of Recurrence Blade Wing Reijy SP6.00 15.00
GBT07008 Wings of Recurrence .60 1.50
Blade Wing Reijy RRR
GBT07009 Interdimensional 4.00 10.00
Dragon Bind Time Dragon RRR
GBT07009 Interdimensional 8.00 20.00
Dragon Bind Time Dragon SP
GBT07010 Chronofang Tiger SP 18.00 30.00
GBT07010 Chronofang Tiger RRR 3.00 8.00
GBT07011 Holy Seraph Suriel RR .60 1.50
GBT07012 Doctroid Remnon RR 1.25 3.00
GBT07012 Doctroid Remnon SP 8.00 20.00
GBT07013 Black Spark Munkar RR 1.25 3.00
GBT07014 Golden Beast Sleimy Flare RR .75 2.00
GBT07015 Scarface Lion RR 2.00 5.00
GBT07016 Flame Wing Steel Beast Denial Griffin RR2.00 5.00
GBT07017 Escort Dragon Attendant Reas RR .50 1.25
GBT07017 Escort Dragon Attendant Reas SP 5.00 12.00
GBT07018 Super Cosmic Hero Xcarivou RR .40 1.00
GBT07019 Cosmic Hero Grandleaf SP 6.00 15.00
GBT07019 Cosmic Hero Grandleaf RR .20 .60
GBT07020 Nighttime Gentleman SaintGermain RR .50 1.25
GBT07021 Oneeyed Succubus RR .50 1.25
GBT07022 Highbrow Steam Raphanna SP 3.00 8.00
GBT07022 Highbrow Steam Raphanna RR .60 1.50
GBT07023 Retractor Sarakiel R .10 .30
GBT07024 Black Dream Zabaniya R .10 .30
GBT07025 Black Bomber Maalik R .10 .30
GBT07026 Nurse of Smash Heart R .10 .30
GBT07027 Dawnngal R .10 .30
GBT07028 Flame Wind Lion Wonder Ezel R .10 .30
GBT07029 Sunshine Knight Jeffrey R .40 1.00
GBT07030 Holy Mage Irena R .10 .30
GBT07031 Spherical Lord Dragon R .10 .30
GBT07032 Dragon Fang Chainshots Sutherland R .10 .30
GBT07033 Radiant Dragon R .20 .60
GBT07034 Dragon Knight Roia R .10 .30
GBT07035 Super Giant of Light Enigman Crossray R.10 .30
GBT07036 Great Cosmic Hero Grandmantle R .10 .30
GBT07037 Cosmic Hero Grandrifter R .10 .30
GBT07038 Mask of Demonic Frenzy Ericrius R .20 .60
GBT07039 Ninebreak Hustler R .10 .30
GBT07040 Doppel Vampir R .40 1.00
GBT07041 Doreen the Thruster R .40 1.00
GBT07042 Blade Wing Tyrwhitt R .10 .30
GBT07043 Interdimensional Beast .10 .30
Floatgear Hippogriff R
GBT07044 Steam Scalar Emellanna R .10 .30
GBT07045 Requiem Pegasus C .10 .30
GBT07046 Treatment Nurse C .10 .30
GBT07047 Frontal Celestial Melejal C .10 .30
GBT07048 Laser Clutcher Keel C .10 .30
GBT07049 Rear Impetus Celestial Armaiti C .10 .30
GBT07050 Celestial Emergency Pegasus C .10 .30
GBT07051 Drill Motor Nurse C .10 .30
GBT07052 Black Report Ridwan C .10 .30
GBT07053 Surgery Angel C .10 .30
GBT07054 Knight of Compassionate Light Bradott C.10 .30
GBT07055 Bullrgal C .10 .30
GBT07056 Knight of the Faint Sun Marcia C .10 .30
GBT07057 Crimson Lion Beast Howell C .10 .30
GBT07058 Holy Mage Connor C .10 .30
GBT07059 Aquamarine Lion Shyte C .10 .30
GBT07060 Bashhgal C .10 .30
GBT07061 Player of the Holy Pipe Gerrie C .10 .30
GBT07062 Dragon Knight Basuit C .10 .30
GBT07063 Wyvern Strike Galgi C .10 .30
GBT07064 Dragon Knight Nadim C .10 .30
GBT07065 Seal Dragon Barathea C .10 .30
GBT07066 Apex Dragon Mage Kinnara C .10 .30
GBT07067 Dragon Dancer Marcel C .10 .30
GBT07068 Dragon Knight Nadel C .10 .30
GBT07069 Seal Dragon Doskin C .10 .30
GBT07070 Serrated Dracokid C .10 .30
GBT07071 Spiritburn Dragon C .10 .30
GBT07072 Inspire Yell Dragon C .10 .30
GBT07073 Cosmic Hero Grandgardy C .10 .30
GBT07074 Elegance Feather C .10 .30
GBT07075 Enigman Crescent C .10 .30
GBT07076 Menacing Monster Golmenas C .10 .30
GBT07077 Enigman Squall C .10 .30
GBT07078 Cosmic Hero Grandvicle C .10 .30
GBT07079 Foxy Charmy C .10 .30
GBT07080 Magical Inspector Tolbe C .10 .30
GBT07081 Cosmic Hero Grandhop C .10 .30
GBT07082 Justice Gold C .10 .30
GBT07083 Enigman Warm C .10 .30
GBT07084 Operator Girl Erika C .10 .30
GBT07085 Cosmic Hero Grandscold C .10 .30
GBT07086 Frosty Steeple C .10 .30
GBT07087 Tragic Claw C .10 .30
GBT07088 Blade Wing Sykes C .10 .30
GBT07089 Threein the Dark C .10 .30
GBT07090 Combust Vampir C .10 .30
GBT07091 Serpent Charmer C .10 .30
GBT07092 Blade Wing Rodbiss C .10 .30
GBT07093 Enigmatic Assassin C .10 .30
GBT07094 Werbrummbar Soldat C .10 .30
GBT07095 Squareone Dragon C .10 .30
GBT07096 Steam Knight Mudar C .10 .30
GBT07097 Drainvalve Dragon C .10 .30
GBT07098 Quiet Sleepcalling Gear Tapir C .10 .30
GBT07099 Steam Fighter Attab C .10 .30
GBT07100 Parallel Barrel Dragon C .10 .30
GBT07101 Steam Fighter Nanneya C .10 .30
GBT07102 Toothedge Dracokid C .10 .30
GBT07103 Steam Scalar Lange C .10 .30
GBT07104 Snow Elemental Hyakko C .10 .30
GBT07S13 Golden Beast Sleimy Flare SP 4.00 10.00
GBT07S14 Sunrise Ray Knight Gurguit SP 20.00 35.00
GBT07S15 Dawning Knight Gorboduc SP 8.00 20.00
GBT07S16 Scarface Lion SP 6.00 15.00
GBT07S17 Holy Seraph Suriel SP 10.00 25.00
GBT07S18 Black Shiver Gavrail SP 25.00 40.00
GBT07S19 Black Call Nakir SP 20.00 35.00
GBT07S20 Black Spark Munkar SP 10.00 25.00
GBT07S21 Flame Wing Steel Beast Denial Griffin SP20.00 35.00
GBT07S22 Dragonic Blademaster SP 10.00 25.00
GBT07S23 Lava Flow Dragon SP 30.00 55.00
GBT07S24 Dragon Knight Jannat SP 15.00 30.00
GBT07S25 Super Cosmic Hero Xcarivou SP 5.00 12.00
GBT07S26 Great Cosmic Hero Grandgallop SP 30.00 45.00
GBT07S27 Cosmic Hero Grandrope SP 8.00 20.00
GBT07S28 Cosmic Hero Grandbeat SP 8.00 20.00
GBT07S29 Abominable One Gilles de Rais SP 20.00 35.00
GBT07S30 Nighttime Gentleman SaintGermain SP4.00 10.00
GBT07S31 Scharhrot Vampir SP 20.00 35.00
GBT07S32 Succubus of Pure Love SP 25.00 40.00
GBT07S33 Oneeyed Succubus SP 20.00 35.00
GBT07S34 Steam Scalar Emellanna SP 6.00 15.00
GBT07S35 Steam Maiden Arlim SP 40.00 55.00

2016 Cardfight Vanguard G-CB03 Blessing of Divas

COMPLETE SET (73 CARDS) 2000.00 3000.00
BOOSTER BOX (12 PACKS) 25.00 45.00
BOOSTER PACK (7 CARDS) 2.50 6.00
UNLISTED C .10 .30
UNLISTED R .10 .30
RELEASED ON JULY 29, 2016
GCB03001 Celebrate Voice Lauris GR 8.00 20.00
GCB03001 Celebrate Voice Lauris SGR 15.00 30.00
GCB03001 Celebrate Voice Lauris SP 65.00 85.00
GCB03001 Celebrate Voice Lauris WSP 200.00 300.00
GCB03002 PRISMImage Sunshine Vert SP 120.00 160.00
GCB03002 PRISMImage Sunshine Vert WSP 300.00 400.00
GCB03002 PRISMImage Sunshine Vert RRR 5.00 12.00
GCB03003 Frontier Star Coral SP 65.00 85.00
GCB03003 Frontier Star Coral WSP 180.00 220.00
GCB03003 Frontier Star Coral RRR 2.50 6.00
GCB03004 Peaceful Voice Raindear RRR 2.50 6.00
GCB03004 Peaceful Voice Raindear SP 60.00 85.00
GCB03004 Peaceful Voice Raindear WSP 150.00 200.00
GCB03005 Sparkle in Her Heart Spica RRR 1.00 2.50
GCB03005 Sparkle in Her Heart Spica WSP 90.00 110.00
GCB03005 Sparkle in Her Heart Spica SP 35.00 50.00
GCB03006 Prestige Cetia RRR 1.00 2.50
GCB03006 Prestige Cetia SP 25.00 40.00
GCB03006 Prestige Cetia WSP 80.00 100.00
GCB03007 Hand in Hand Leona WSP 120.00 160.00
GCB03007 Hand in Hand Leona RR .50 1.25
GCB03007 Hand in Hand Leona SP 45.00 60.00
GCB03008 Great Ascent Liddy WSP 65.00 85.00
GCB03008 Great Ascent Liddy SP 30.00 45.00
GCB03008 Great Ascent Liddy RR .40 1.00
GCB03009 BrandNewPRISM Garnet RR .40 1.00
GCB03009 BrandNewPRISM Garnet SP 35.00 50.00
GCB03009 BrandNewPRISM Garnet WSP 120.00 160.00
GCB03010 Magical Charge Vita SP 35.00 50.00
GCB03010 Magical Charge Vita WSP 80.00 120.00
GCB03010 Magical Charge Vita RR .40 1.00
GCB03011 Brilliant Ocean Elly SP 35.00 50.00
GCB03011 Brilliant Ocean Elly WSP 60.00 80.00
GCB03011 Brilliant Ocean Elly RR .20 .60
GCB03012 Garland Blossom Ayna RR .20 .60
GCB03012 Garland Blossom Ayna WSP 80.00 120.00
GCB03012 Garland Blossom Ayna SP 30.00 45.00
GCB03013 Miracle Twintail Wyz RR .75 2.00
GCB03013 Miracle Twintail Wyz SP 25.00 40.00
GCB03013 Miracle Twintail Wyz WSP 45.00 60.00
GCB03014 Flying Mermaid Frederica R .10 .30
GCB03015 Whitely Noble Fantine R .10 .30
GCB03016 Active Pink Lalana R .10 .30
GCB03017 Inspect Sisters Robel R .10 .30
GCB03018 PRISMImage Sunshine Rosa R .10 .30
GCB03019 Artless Charmy Wakana R .10 .30
GCB03020 Admire Successor Lyrica R .10 .30
GCB03021 Monotone Innocence Yuka R .10 .30
GCB03022 Dash Sisters Rabel R .10 .30
GCB03023 BrandNewPRISM Emeral R .10 .30
GCB03024 Duo Create Quill Ilya R .10 .30
GCB03025 Wholehearted Dream Meruru R .10 .30
GCB03026 PRISMImage Sunshine Clear R .10 .30
GCB03027 Jump to the Water Surface Amelie R .10 .30
GCB03028 Skillful Performer Minori C .10 .30
GCB03029 Splash Daughter Rachel C .10 .30
GCB03030 Shyness Laguna Lapla C .10 .30
GCB03031 Duo Creamy Caramel Cornet C .10 .30
GCB03032 Onestroke Art Carla C .10 .30
GCB03033 Intellect Polish Seyna C .10 .30
GCB03034 Duo Caprice Cats Marjona C .10 .30
GCB03035 Piping Hot Suifa C .10 .30
GCB03036 Tidal Art Marie C .10 .30
GCB03037 New Song Announcement Alti C .10 .30
GCB03038 Colorful Smiling Fratte C .10 .30
GCB03039 Duo Cotton Sleeper Ichika C .10 .30
GCB03040 BrandNewPRISM Sapphire C .10 .30
GCB03041 Tiny Precious May C .10 .30
GCB03042 Impact Punch Michiru C .10 .30
GCB03043 Voice of Fate Kasumi C .10 .30
GCB03044 Sweet Temptation Riko C .10 .30
GCB03045 Heartful Ale Fundy C .10 .30
GCB03Re01 School Etoile Olyvia R 8.00 20.00

2014 Future Card Buddyfight Brave's Explosion

TRIAL DECK 8.00 12.00
RELEASED ON JULY 4, 2014
TD040001 Silver Warrior, Quenzwei C .10 .25
TD040002 Legendary Warrior, Gao C .30 .75
TD040002r Legendary Warrior, Gao RR 2.50 6.00
TD040003 Monk of Bread Deity, Prios C .15 .40
TD040004 Craftsman, Baku C .15 .40
TD040005 Dachs, Cobalt C .10 .25
TD040006 Master Thief, Strohl Bird C .10 .25
TD040007 Fledgling Warrior, Ocker Glaser C .15 .40
TD040008 Sage, Kuguru C .30 .75
TD040009 Mameshiba, Cobalt C .75 2.00
TD040010 Rolling Stone C
TD040011 Oracle of Tubal C
TD040012 Pillar of Fire C 1.25 3.00
TD040013 Dungeon Pit C .10 .25
TD040014 Divine Protection of Shalsana C .20 .50
TD040015 Mission Card "Form a Party!" C .10 .25
TD040015r Mission Card "Form a Party!" RR
TD040016 Mission Card "Defeat the Monsters!" C .10 .25
TD040017 Conquering Blade, .15 .40
Dungeon Domination C
TD040018 Origin Blade, Enemy Breaker C .10 .25
TD040019 Dead End Crush! C .15 .40
TD040019r Dead End Crush! RR .50 1.25
TD040020 Dungeon World C .40 1.00

2014 Future Card Buddyfight Burning Valor

COMPLETE SET (51)
RELEASED ON MARCH 14, 2014
CP010001 Purgatory Knights, Death Sickle Dragon RRR
CP010002 Dragon Knight, Geronimo RRR
CP010003 Jackknife Aggressor RRR 8.00 20.00
CP010004 Thunder Knights, Halberd Dragon RRR
CP010005 Dragon Knight, Nobunaga RRR
CP010006 Dragon Fist Mystery, Dragonic Kaiser Nova RRR
CP010007 Inferno Armor Dragon RR 4.00 10.00
CP010008 Super Armordragon, Aura Sword Dragon RR
CP010009 Dragon Knight, Kamitsumiyaou RR
CP010010 Jackknife Thunder Storm RR 3.00 8.00
CP010011 Dragon Knight, Iwamoto RR 1.50 4.00
CP010012 Dragon Knight, El Quixote RR 6.00 12.00
CP010013 Twin Dragonblades, Dragoanthem RR
CP010014 Dragon Knight Mystery, Ultimate Smash RR
CP010015 Dragon Knight, Hammurabi the Great R.40 1.00
CP010016 Jackknife Dragon R 3.00 8.00
CP010017 Drum Bunker Dragon R 2.00 5.00
CP010018 Dragon Knight, Rudel R .40 1.00
CP010019 Dragon Knight, Wyatt Earp R .40 1.00
CP010020 Dragon Knight, Red Baron R .40 1.00
CP010021 Dragonic Formation R .40 1.00
CP010022 Dragon Crush R .60 1.50
CP010023 Green Dragon Shield R .75 2.00
CP010024 Cavalry Academy R .40 1.00
CP010025 Damascus Armor Dragon C .10 .25
CP010026 Firerod Dragon C .10 .25
CP010027 Hammer Mace Dragon C .10 .25
CP010028 Katzvalker Drake C .10 .25
CP010029 Double Sword Dragon C .10 .25
CP010030 Dragon Knight, Liechtenauer C .10 .25
CP010031 Dragon Knight, Jeanne d'Arc C .10 .25
CP010032 Dragon Knight, Masamune C .10 .25
CP010033 Blade Wing Dragon C .10 .25
CP010034 Bronze Shield Dragon C .10 .25
CP010035 Death Rattle Dragon C .10 .25
CP010036 Super Slash, Dragothrasher C .10 .25
CP010037 Dragonic Thunder C .10 .25
CP010038 Dragon Breath C .10 .25
CP010039 Astral Force C .10 .25
CP010040 Wrath of Dragon C .10 .25
CP010041 Dragoenergy C .10 .25
CP010042 Red Dragon Knights .10 .25
Burning Devastation Song C
CP010043 Blue Dragon Knights Proud Soul Song C.10 .25
CP010044 Dragonblade, Dragofearless C 2.50 6.00
CP010045 Jackknife Diaspash BR
CPS010001 Purgatory Knights, 3.00 8.00
Death Sickle Dragon SP
CPS010002 Dragon Knight, Geronimo SP 1.50 4.00
CPS010003 Jackknife Aggressor SP 6.00 12.00
CPS010004 Thunder Knights, Halberd Dragon SP10.00 25.00
CPS010006 Dragon Fist Mystery, 2.00 5.00
Dragonic Kaiser Nova SP
CPS010012 Dragon Knight, El Quixote SP

2014 Future Card Buddyfight Cyber Ninja Squad

RELEASED ON APRIL 5, 2014
BT020001 Super Armordragon, Galvanic Feather Dragon RRR
BT020002 Center of the World, Mary Sue RRR
BT020003 Great Spell, My Grandfather Clock RRR3.00 8.00
BT020004 Emperor Dragon, Gael Khan RRR 3.00 8.00
BT020005 Superior Strength Ninja, Kotaro Fuma RRR
BT020006 Nanomachine Ninja, Tsukikage RRR 10.00 25.00
BT020007 Evil in Heart, Yamigitsune RRR 12.00 30.00
BT020008 Secret Sword, Star Crusher RRR
BT020009 Dragon Knight, Vlad Dracula RR
BT020010 Emigurette Dragon RR
BT020011 Witch of Destruction, 1.50 4.00
Hearty the Devastator RR
BT020012 Great Duke, Astaroth RR 2.00 5.00
BT020013 Twin Horn Dragon, Ark Giraffa RR
BT020014 Nightflight Dragon, Rahal RR
BT020015 Extermination Ninja, Slashing Asura RR
BT020016 Tempest, Garo-oh RR 2.00 5.00
BT020017 Electron Ninja, Shiden RR 5.00 12.00
BT020018 Art of Explosive Hades Fall RR 5.00 12.00
BT020019 Demon Way, Karakurenai RR 1.50 4.00
BT020020 Secret Sword, Lethal Formation RR
BT020021 Psychic Knife Dragon R 4.00 10.00
BT020022 Dragonic Paratrooper R 1.25 3.00
BT020023 Victory Slash! R 1.00 2.50
BT020024 Magic Knight of Darkness, Dunkelheit R.40 1.00
BT020025 Magic Knight of Light, Licht R .40 1.00
BT020026 Kosher R .40 1.00
BT020027 Key of Solomon, First Volume R .40 1.00
BT020028 Key of Solomon, Second Volume R 1.50 4.00
BT020029 Armorknight Ifrit R .40 1.00
BT020030 Armorknight Tiger R .40 1.00
BT020031 Exorcist Stomp R .40 1.00
BT020032 Armorknight Formation R .40 1.00
BT020033 Sky Rush, Garyu-oh R .40 1.00
BT020034 Flash Strike, Yamaihebi R .40 1.00
BT020035 Cyber Onmyoji, Seimei R .40 1.00
BT020036 Phantom Ninja, Kashinkoji R .40 1.00
BT020037 Clear Serenity R .40 1.00
BT020038 Shinobi Scrolls R .40 1.00
BT020039 Return to the Underworld R 1.25 3.00
BT020040 Elite Sword, Mikazuki Munechika R .40 1.00
BT020041 Secret Sword, Moon Fang R .40 1.00
BT020042 Secret Sword, Shooting Star R .40 1.00
BT020043 Actor Knights the World R 1.50 4.00
BT020044 Ultimate Buddy! R 2.00 5.00
BT020045 Blaze Gauntlet Dragon U .15 .40
BT020046 Dragon Knight, Ryoma U .15 .40
BT020047 White Dragon Shield U 2.50 6.00
BT020048 Dragonblade, Dragobreach U .15 .40
BT020049 Dandy Guy, Sitri U .15 .40
BT020050 Cloud-riding Hop Hob U .15 .40
BT020051 Demon Realm Computer, Vassago U .15 .40
BT020052 De Guaita Crush Knuckle! U 1.25 3.00
BT020053 Holy Moly! U .15 .40
BT020054 Chillax! U .15 .40
BT020055 Bastin Caps U .15 .40
BT020056 Armorknight Trent U .15 .40
BT020057 Strong Horn Dragon, Diatlus U .15 .40
BT020058 Armorknight Wall Lizard U 1.25 3.00
BT020059 Wandering Ninja, Tobikato U .15 .40
BT020060 Blood Knife, Kimensai U .15 .40
BT020061 Accelerate Ninja, Hayate U .15 .40
BT020062 Art of Item Blasting U .15 .40
BT020063 Art of Body Replacement U .15 .40
BT020064 Ninja Arts, Steel Ball U .15 .40
BT020065 Shooting Cross Knives, Right-hand U .15 .40
BT020066 Spinning Windmill Knives, Back-hand U.15 .40
BT020067 Demon Way, Geppakugiri U .15 .40
BT020068 Demon Way, Shienrekka U .15 .40
BT020069 Actor Knights Chariot U .15 .40
BT020070 Actor Knights High Priestess U .15 .40
BT020071 Actor Knights the Magician U .15 .40
BT020072 Fool Aims for the Wilderness U .15 .40
BT020073 Fool's Journey U .15 .40
BT020074 Burning Bow U 1.50 4.00
BT020075 Thousand Rapier Dragon C .40 1.00
BT020076 Raid Claw Dragon C .10 .25
BT020077 Dragon Knight, Shingen C .10 .25
BT020078 Force Return C .10 .25
BT020079 Dragobond C .10 .25
BT020080 Eastern Demon Sword Emperor, Baal C .10 .25
BT020081 Protector of Friendship, Barbados C .10 .25
BT020082 Black Demon Swordsman, Jace Aldis C.10 .25
BT020083 Finisher Bow, Leraje C .10 .25
BT020084 Gunrod, Martil C .40 1.00
BT020085 Violent Dragon, Boralios C .10 .25
BT020086 Fire Manipulating Dragon, Volgaraid C .10 .25
BT020087 Mantis Dragon, Drantis C .10 .25
BT020088 Armorknight Chimera C .10 .25
BT020089 Armorknight Polar Bear C .10 .25
BT020090 Blade Tiger, Gurenenbu C .10 .25
BT020091 Mobile Ninja, Jiraiya C .10 .25
BT020092 Armed Priest Soldier, Benkei C .10 .25
BT020093 Sea-splitting Irukamaru C .10 .25
BT020094 Steel Wall, Beheading Crab C .10 .25
BT020095 Stealth Ninja, Kirikakure Saizo C .10 .25
BT020096 Steel Head, Helmet Bear C .10 .25
BT020097 Demon Way, Sakurafubuki C .10 .25
BT020098 Demon Way, Noroihikagami C .10 .25
BT020099 Ninja Blade, Kurogachi C .10 .25
BT020100 Actor Knights Hermit C .25
BT020101 Actor Knights the Fool C .10 .25
BT020102 Actor Knights Lovers C .10 .25
BT020103 Gambit C .10 .25
BT020104 Castling C .10 .25
BT020105 Martial Arts Dragon Emperor, 15.00 40.00
Duel Siegar BR
BTS020001 Super Armordragon, 6.00 15.00
Galvanic Feather Dragon SP
BTS020002 Center of the World, Mary Sue SP
BTS020004 Emperor Dragon, Gael Khan SP
BTS020005 Superior Strength Ninja, Kotaro Fuma SP
BTS020006 Nanomachine Ninja, Tsukikage SP 15.00 40.00
BTS020007 Evil in Heart, Yamigitsune SP
BTS020009 Dragon Knight, Vlad Dracula SP
BTS020011 Witch of Destruction, Hearty the Devastator SP
BTS020012 Great Duke, Astaroth SP
BTS020016 Tempest, Garo-oh SP
BTS020017 Electron Ninja, Shiden SP
BTS020020 Secret Sword, Lethal Formation SP

2014 Future Card Buddyfight Dark Pulse

TD060007 Black Dragon, Death Gracia
TD060008 Black Dragon, Decipience
TD060003 Black Dragon, Dividers
TD060005 Black Dragon, Tarandus
TD060014 Black Revenger
TD060017 Black Sword, Heartbreaker
TD060020 Darkness Dragon World
TD060016 Death Claw, Grim Reaper
TD060011 Death Damage
TD060004 Death Ruler, Abriel
TD060010 Death Ruler, Alea
TD060018 Demonic Strike Arts, Death Requim
TD060015 Midnight Shadow
TD060009 Purgatory Knights, Black Knife Dragon
TD060006 Purgatory Knights, Giant Scissor Dragon
TD060001 Purgatory Knights, Satan Force Dragon
TD060012 Sudden DEATH!
TD060002 There is Only Death, Dalleon
TD060013 Vampire Fang

2014 Future Card Buddyfight Darkness Fable

RELEASED ON OCTOBER 10, 2014
BT040001 Super Armordragon, 3.00 8.00
Gargantua Blade Dragon RRR
BT040001s Super Armordragon, Gargantua Blade Dragon SP
BT040002 Jackknife "Gold Ritter" RRR 6.00 15.00
BT040002s Jackknife "Gold Ritter" SP
BT040003 Demon Wolf, Fenrir RRR 5.00 12.00
BT040004 Great Magician, Merlin RRR 5.00 12.00
BT040005 Sword of the King, Excalibur RRR 2.50 6.00
BT040006 Black Dragon, Maveltaker RRR .60 1.50
BT040006s Black Dragon, Maveltaker SP
BT040007 Devil Stigma RRR 5.00 12.00
BT040008 Slow Pain Fall RRR
BT040008s Slow Pain Fall SP 2.50 6.00
BT040009 Dragon Knight, Napoleon RR 1.50 4.00
BT040010 Jackknife "Berserker" RR
BT040011 Jackknife "Burn Energy" RR
BT040012 Gorgon Three Sisters, Euryale RR 2.00 5.00
BT040013 Knights of the Round Table, 3.00 8.00
King Arthur RR
BT040013s Knights of the Round Table, 6.00 15.00
King Arthur SP
BT040014 Lord of the Forest, Zlatorog RR 4.00 10.00
BT040015 Wind Fairy, Sylph RR 2.50 6.00
BT040016 Symbel Gard RR 5.00 12.00
BT040017 Death Ruler, Curse RR
BT040018 Death Wizard Dragon RR
BT040019 Judgment Day RR
BT040020 Nightmare Despair RR
BT040021 Jackknife "Jaeger" R .40 1.00
BT040022 Twin Horned King of .40 1.00
Knights, Alexander R
BT040023 Gargantua Blade, Black Smasher R .60 1.50
BT040024 Roaring Slash!! Gargantua Punisher!! R .40 1.00
BT040024s Roaring Slash!! Gargantua Punisher!! SP
BT040025 Colossal Sea Monster, Cetus R .40 1.00
BT040026 Demonic Beast, Grendel R .40 1.00
BT040027 Armored Dragon, Cuelebre R .40 1.00
BT040028 Golden Blade, Chrysaor R .40 1.00
BT040029 Gorgon Three Sisters, Medusa R .40 1.00
BT040030 Spring Healed Jack R .40 1.00
BT040031 Ice Blade, Joker R 2.50 6.00
BT040031s Ice Blade, Joker SP
BT040032 Great Spell, Ragnarok R .40 1.00
BT040032s Great Spell, Ragnarok SP
BT040033 Great Spell, Thunder of Zeus R 3.00 8.00
BT040034 Decree of Dullahan R .75 2.00
BT040035 Breathen Gard R .40 1.00
BT040036 Immortal Sword, Durandal R .40 1.00
BT040036s Immortal Sword, Durandal SP
BT040037 Divine Protection, Prydwen R 1.50 4.00
BT040038 Bloody Moon Dragon R 1.25 3.00
BT040039 Death Dragon, Deathgaze Dragon R 1.50 4.00
BT040039s Death Dragon, Deathgaze Dragon SP10.00 25.00
BT040040 Death Ruler, Gallows R 2.00 5.00
BT040040s Death Ruler, Gallows SP
BT040041 Death Grip R 3.00 8.00
BT040041s Death Grip SP
BT040042 Abyss Symphony R 2.00 5.00
BT040043 Evil Death Scythe R .40 1.00
BT040044 Arcana Flash R .40 1.00
BT040045 Destroy Hammer Dragon U .15 .40
BT040046 Spike Shoulder "Blazing" U .15 .40
BT040047 Dragonic Counter U .15 .40
BT040048 Jackknife Gift U .15 .40
BT040049 Dragonic Force Field U .15 .40
BT040050 Corpse Swallower, Hraesvelgr U .15 .40

BT040051 Wawel Drache U .15 .40
BT040052 Frost Giant, Hrimthurs U .15 .40
BT040053 Knights of the Round Table, Gawain U .15 .40
BT040054 Furious Unicorn U .15 .40
BT040055 Knights of the Round Table, Galahad U .15 .40
BT040056 Dragon Vanquishing Emperor, Beowulf U .15 .40
BT040057 Knights of the Round Table, Gareth U .75 2.00
BT040058 Ainsel's Damage Rebound U .15 .40
BT040059 Great Spell, Fimbulwinter U 1.50 4.00
BT040060 Elixir of Aesculapius U 1.50 4.00
BT040061 Shield of Achilles U .15 .40
BT040062 Dragon Vanquishing Sword, Balmung U .15 .40
BT040063 Rune Staff U 2.00 5.00
BT040064 Death Ruler, Pain U .15 .40
BT040065 Death Ruler, Executei U .15 .40
BT040066 Black Dragon, Fundula U .15 .40
BT040067 Death Ruler, Cremation U .15 .40
BT040068 Black Dragon, Cold Blade U .15 .40
BT040069 Death Ruler, Burial U 1.25 3.00
BT040070 Death Shield U .15 .40
BT040071 Guillotine Cutter U .15 .40
BT040072 Lunatic U .15 .40
BT040073 Dark Energy U 1.25 3.00
BT040074 Actor Knights Fortune U .15 .40
BT040075 Forbidden Edge Dragon C .10 .25
BT040076 Thunder Knights, Pallasch Sword Dragon C .10 .25
BT040077 Dragon Knight, Musashi C .10 .25
BT040078 Left Sword Dragon C .10 .25
BT040079 Right Sword Dragon C .10 .25
BT040080 Center Sword Dragon C .10 .25
BT040081 Viking Sword Dragon C .10 .25
BT040082 Enchant Wand Dragon C .10 .25
BT040083 Iron Dragon, Tarasque C .10 .25
BT040084 Knights of the Round Table, Percival C .10 .25
BT040085 Getters Cursed Dragon C .10 .25
BT040086 Gorgon Three Sisters, Stheno C .10 .25
BT040087 Divine Stallion, Pegasus C .10 .25
BT040088 Power of Mythology C .10 .25
BT040089 Heroic Spirit C .10 .25
BT040090 The Wydar Sarkal C 1.25 3.00
BT040091 Berserk Gard C .10 .25
BT040092 Gleipnir C .10 .25
BT040093 Holy Grail C .10 .25
BT040094 Divine Armor, Aegis C .10 .25
BT040095 Famous Sword, Hrunting C 3.00 8.00
BT040096 Death Ruler, Soulbreaker C .10 .25
BT040097 Black Dragon, Death Hang C .10 .25
BT040098 Death Ruler, Atihima C .10 .25
BT040099 Dark Stalker Dragon C .10 .25
BT040100 Black Dragon, Needle Fang C .10 .25
BT040101 Black Dragon Shield C 1.50 4.00
BT040102 Demonic Talon, Vampire Claw C .10 .25
BT040103 Actor Knights Devil C .10 .25
BT040104 Fortune-shield C .10 .25
BT040105 Purgatory Knights Leader, Demios Sword Dragon BR 12.00 30.00

2014 Future Card Buddyfight Dominant Dragons

TD01001EN Gigant Sword Dragon C
TD01002EN Jamadhar Dragon C
TD01003EN Rising Flare Dragon C
TD01004EN Extreme Sword Dragon C
TD01005EN Thousand Rapier Dragon C
TD01006EN Bear-Trap Fang Dragon C
TD01007EN Systemic Dagger Dragon C
TD01008EN Bronze Shield Dragon C
TD01009EN Dragonic Grimoire C
TD01011EN Dragoenergy C
TD01012EN Green Dragon Shield C
TD01013EN Dragonblade, Dragobrave C
TD01014EN Dragonblade, Dragofearless C
TD01015EN Gargantua Punisher!! C
TD01016EN My Buddy! (Drum Bunker Dragon) C
TD01017EN Dragon World C
TD01003ENr Rising Flare Dragon RR
TD01015ENr Gargantua Punisher!! RR
TD01010EN Dragon Breath C

2014 Future Card Buddyfight Dragon Chief

RELEASED ON JANUARY 31, 2014
BT010001 Super Armordragon, Buster Cannon Dragon RRR
BT010001s Super Armordragon, Buster Cannon Dragon SP
BT010002 Drum Bunker Dragon, "Barrier Breaker" RRR
BT010002s Drum Bunker Dragon, "Barrier Breaker" SP
BT010003 Pile Bunker Dragon RRR 15.00 40.00
BT010004 Rebel, Belial RRR
BT010004s Rebel, Belial SP
BT010005 Herb Magician, Soichiro Tenjiku RRR
BT010006 Demon Lord, Asmodai RRR
BT010006s Demon Lord, Asmodai SP
BT010007 Devil Advantage RRR
BT010008 Armorknight Demon RRR
BT010008s Armorknight Demon SP 1.50 4.00
BT010009 Dragon Knight, Maximilian RR
BT010010 Day of the Dragon RR 12.00 30.00
BT010011 Steel Fist, Dragoknuckle RR 6.00 15.00
BT010011s Steel Fist, Dragoknuckle SP
BT010012 Gargantua Punisher!! RR 6.00 15.00
BT010012s Gargantua Punisher!! SP
BT010013 Demon Realm Negotiator, Gusion RR .75 2.00
BT010014 Magician of Glass, Will Glassart RR 1.50 4.00
BT010015 Magical Goodbye RR 5.00 12.00
BT010016 Diabolical Hardcore! RR 1.25 3.00
BT010016s Diabolical Hardcore! SP
BT010017 Armorknight Medusa RR
BT010018 Fighting Dragon, Demongodol RR 5.00 12.00
BT010018s Fighting Dragon, Demongodol SP 2.50 6.00
BT010019 Thunder Devastation RR 3.00 8.00
BT010020 Lord Aura Meditation RR
BT010021 Drum Bunker Dragon R
BT010021s Drum Bunker Dragon SP
BT010022 Dragonic Destroy R 2.50 6.00
BT010023 Knightenergy R 1.50 4.00
BT010024 Blue Dragon Shield R 1.50 4.00
BT010025 Dragon's Seal R 6.00 15.00
BT010026 Demon Programmer, Marbas R .40 1.00
BT010027 Liar, Fullfool R 1.50 4.00
BT010028 Barriermaster, Shadowflash R .40 1.00
BT010029 Demon Doctor, Buer R .40 1.00
BT010030 Begone!! R .40 1.00
BT010031 Nice one! R .40 1.00
BT010032 The Ark R .40 1.00
BT010033 Great Spell, Saturday Night Devil Fever R .40 1.00
BT010034 Gunrod, Bechstein R .40 1.00
BT010035 Axe Dragon, Dorcas R .40 1.00
BT010036 Armorknight Golem R .40 1.00
BT010037 Armorknight Cerberus R .40 1.00
BT010037s Armorknight Cerberus SP .40 1.00
BT010038 Saberclaw Dragon, Valken R .40 1.00
BT010039 Armorknight Succubus R 2.00 5.00
BT010040 Double Guillotine R .40 1.00
BT010041 Hysteric Spear R .40 1.00
BT010042 Drill Bunker!! R 2.00 5.00
BT010042s Drill Bunker!! SP
BT010043 King the Dominator R .40 1.00
BT010044 Buddy Help R 1.50 4.00
BT010045 Dragon Knight, Masakado UC .15 .40
BT010046 Dragon Knight, Hannibal UC .15 .40
BT010047 Dragon Knight, Jeanne d'Arc UC .15 .40
BT010048 Spike Shoulder Dragon UC .15 .40
BT010049 Dragonic Heal UC 1.50 4.00
BT010050 The Skies in your Hand UC .15 .40
BT010051 Twin Attack Tactics UC .15 .40
BT010052 Fallen Angel of Rage, Beleth UC .15 .40
BT010053 Fire Starter, Ganzack UC .15 .40
BT010054 Demon Realm Death Metal, Valefar UC .15 .40
BT010055 Mage Disciple, Rody UC .15 .40
BT010056 Preacher of Beauty, Gremory UC .15 .40
BT010057 Trans-flame UC .15 .40
BT010058 Quick Summon UC .15 .40
BT010059 Abra Cadabra! UC 1.50 4.00
BT010060 Noisy Danceroom UC .15 .40
BT010061 Gunrod, Stradivarius UC .15 .40
BT010062 Grassland Dragon, Grassrunner UC .15 .40
BT010063 Clash Dragon, Gaelcorga UC .15 .40
BT010064 Armor Reuse UC .15 .40
BT010065 Battle Spirit Unite UC 2.00 5.00
BT010066 Duel Law UC .25 .60
BT010067 Night in the Wild UC .15 .40
BT010068 Control Unit, Suppression Queen UC .15 .40
BT010069 Combat Unit, Guardian Rook UC .15 .40
BT010070 Skewer UC .15 .40
BT010071 Buddy Charge UC 1.25 3.00
BT010072 Chessenergy UC .15 .40
BT010073 Battlefield Military Band UC .15 .40
BT010074 Checkmate UC .15 .40
BT010075 Dragon Knight, Alexander C .10 .25
BT010076 Steel Gauntlet Dragon C .10 .25
BT010077 Latale Shield Dragon C .10 .25
BT010078 Dragon Knight, Leonidas C .10 .25
BT010079 Dragonic Shoot C .10 .25
BT010080 Dragonblade, Dragobrave C .10 .25
BT010081 Dance Magician, Albrecht C .10 .25
BT010082 Fallen Angel, Paimon C .10 .25
BT010083 Kenjy of the Explosive Fists C .10 .25
BT010084 Demon Maestro, Bathin C .10 .25
BT010085 Demon Knight, Aibolos C .10 .25
BT010086 Demon Realm Warrior, Zepar C .10 .25
BT010087 Oops! C .10 .25
BT010088 Solomon's Shield C .10 .25
BT010089 Raging Dragon, Zargus C .10 .25
BT010090 Soaring Dragon, Sylphide C .10 .25
BT010091 Bloodwind Dragon, Elyrseagar C .10 .25
BT010092 Armorknight Gargoyle C .10 .25
BT010093 Bluechase Dragon, Garg C .10 .25
BT010094 Earth-shattering Slash C .10 .25
BT010095 Boulder Piercing Spear C .10 .25
BT010096 Attack Unit, Flying Bishop C .10 .25
BT010097 Mobile Unit, Soldier Pawn C .10 .25
BT010098 Battle Unit, Knight Fighter C .10 .25
BT010099 Royal Fork C .10 .25
BT010100 Destruction (card) C .10 .25
BT010101 Neutralize C .10 .25
BT010102 Pawn Storm C .10 .25
BT010103 Burning Sword C .10 .25
BT010104 Burning Dagger C .10 .25
BT010105 Jackknife Dragon BR 12.00 30.00
PR0003EN Magic World C

2014 Future Card Buddyfight Dragon World

IS010005EN Bear-Trap Fang Dragon
IS010009EN Dragon Breath
IS010015EN Dragon World
IS010012EN Dragonblade, Dragobrave
IS010013EN Dragonblade, Dragofearless
IS010008EN Dragonic Heal
IS010010EN Dragonic Shoot
IS010002EN Extreme Sword Dragon
IS010001EN Gigant Sword Dragon
IS010011EN Green Dragon Shield
IS010007EN Latale Shield Dragon
IS010014EN Reckless Angerrrr!!
IS010003EN Steel Gauntlet Dragon
IS010006EN Systemic Dagger Dragon
IS010004EN Thousand Rapier Dragon

2014 Future Card Buddyfight Dragonic Force

TD030002r Jackknife "Dispersal" RR
TD030004r Jackknife Dragon RR
TD030018r Dragonic Punisher RR
TD030001 Jackknife "Thunder Storm" C
TD030002 Jackknife "Dispersal" C
TD030003 Gust Charging Dragon C
TD030004 Jackknife Dragon C
TD030005 Hammer Mace Dragon C
TD030006 Zantetsunodachi Dragon C
TD030007 Grave Horn Dragon C
TD030008 Slashknife Dragon C
TD030009 Latale Shield Dragon C
TD030010 Bronze Shield Dragon C
TD030011 Jackknife Braveheart C
TD030012 Dragon Flame C
TD030013 Dragoenergy C
TD030014 Dragonic Charge C
TD030015 Green Dragon Shield C
TD030016 Dragonblade, Dragobrave C
TD030017 Dragonblade, Dragofearless C
TD030018 Dragonic Punisher C
TD030019 Dragon World C

2014 Future Card Buddyfight Drum's Adventures

RELEASED ON JULY 4, 2014
BT030001 Jackknife "Beistand" RRR
BT030001s Jackknife "Beistand" SP
BT030002 Thunder Knights Leader, Kommandeur Fahne RRR
BT030002s Thunder Knights Leader, Kommandeur Fahne SP
BT030003 Dragon Knight, Kondou RRR 2.50 6.00
BT030003s Dragon Knight, Kondou SP 1.25 3.00
BT030004 Dragowizard, Qinus Axia RRR 6.00 15.00
BT030005 Wanderer, the Gold RRR 2.50 6.00
BT030006 Demon Lord, Gagnar RRR
BT030007 Legendary Brave, Tasuku RRR 2.00 5.00
BT030007s Legendary Brave, Tasuku SP
BT030008 Dragonblade Wielding Sheila Vanna RRR 1.50 4.00
BT030009 Super Armordragon, Vulverize Dragon RR 3.00 8.00
BT030010 Thunder Knights, Bastard-sword Dragon RR 5.00 12.00
BT030011 Dragon Knight, Soushi RR
BT030012 Barbarish Anger-! RR 2.50 6.00
BT030012s Barbarish Anger-! SP
BT030013 Magical Secretary, Genjuro Saki RR .75 2.00
BT030014 Mana Booster, Melergim RR
BT030015 Undefeatable, Setsujishi RR
BT030016 Sky Ninja, Yamigarasu RR
BT030016s Sky Ninja, Yamigarasu SP
BT030017 Bladewing Phoenix RR
BT030018 Dancing Magician, Tetsuya RR 6.00 15.00
BT030019 Dungeon Explosion RR 10.00 25.00
BT030020 Brave Equipment, Glory Seeker RR
BT030020s Brave Equipment, Glory Seeker SP 5.00 12.00
BT030021 Super Armordragon, Daring Armor Dragon R .40 1.00
BT030022 Million Rapier Dragon R .75 2.00
BT030023 Thunder Knights, Battle Axe Dragon R .40 1.00
BT030024 Thunder Knights, Drum Bunker Dragon R 3.00 8.00
BT030025 Awl Pike Dragon R .40 1.00
BT030026 Thunder Knights, Dragoarcher R .40 1.00
BT030027 Dragon Barrier R 1.50 4.00
BT030028 Thunder Formation! R 1.50 4.00
BT030029 Thunder Blade, Dragobreaker R .40 1.00
BT030030 Dragowizard, Magician Drum R .40 1.00
BT030030s Dragowizard, Magician Drum SP
BT030031 Great Spell, Deus Ex Machina R .40 1.00
BT030032 Power Ray Maximum R .40 1.00
BT030033 Gotcha! R .40 1.00
BT030034 Elite Sword, Onimaru R 1.50 4.00
BT030035 Guardian Dragon of Ruins, Meteor Rain R 2.00 5.00
BT030036 Brave, Drum R 4.00 10.00
BT030036s Brave, Drum SP
BT030037 Magical Fortress, Orser Kleinz R 5.00 12.00
BT030038 Mimic with Surprise R .40 1.00
BT030039 Missile Wizard, Adrick R 1.25 3.00
BT030040 Evil-Break R 5.00 12.00
BT030041 Continue! R .40 1.00
BT030042 Mission Card "Rest at Nozaro Hot Springs!" R .40 1.00
BT030043 Brave's Sword, Sommer Sword R .40 1.00
BT030044 Actor Knights Emperor R .40 1.00
BT030045 Tail Sword Dragon U .15 .40
BT030046 Thunder Knights, Sword Shield Dragon U .15 .40
BT030047 Tuck Sword Dragon U .60 1.50
BT030048 Dragon Knight, Hijikata U .15 .40
BT030049 Wolf of Mibu U .40 1.00
BT030050 Dragonblade, Dragoseele U 2.00 5.00
BT030052 Flame Master, Ganzack "Dva" U .75 2.00
BT030053 Dragowizard, Tempest Wing U .15 .40
BT030054 Dragowizard, Burning Wand U 1.25 3.00
BT030055 You The Man! U 1.25 3.00
BT030056 Magic Arm, Burning Fist U 2.50 6.00
BT030057 Sniping Ninja, Yoichi U 1.25 3.00
BT030058 Secret Arts, Dance of the Guardian Swords U .15 .40
BT030059 Ninja Arts, Serpent Glare U .15 .40
BT030060 Dark Ninja Technique, Poisonous Swamp Formation U 1.25 3.00
BT030061 Blood Bath on Gojo Great Bridge U .25 .60
BT030062 Tosa Dog, Kobold U .25 .60
BT030063 Thunder Spaltis U 4.00 10.00
BT030064 One-Eyed Demon Lord, Keith One-Eyed U .15 .40
BT030065 Big Surprise Pandora U 1.25 3.00
BT030066 Magic Release of Sicilia U .15 .40
BT030067 Dangerous Fuse U .15 .40
BT030068 Divine Protection of Shalsana U .15 .40
BT030069 Demon Lord's Dungeon U .15 .40
BT030070 Dragon Vanquishing Sword, Dragon Slayer U .15 .40
BT030071 Dominion Rod U 1.00 2.50
BT030072 Actor Knights High Priest U .15 .40
BT030073 Actor Knights Hanged Man U 1.25 3.00
BT030074 Justice Hammer U .15 .40
BT030075 Bardiche Drake C .30 .75
BT030076 Shadow Shamshir Dragon C .30 .75
BT030077 Dragon Knight, Kagekiyo C .10 .25
BT030078 Alloy Lance Dragon C .10 .25
BT030079 Blade Chakram Dragon C .30 .75
BT030080 Thunder Knights, Broad Sword Dragon C .10 .25
BT030081 Dragon Knight, Saito C .30 .75
BT030082 Thunder Knights, Main Gauche Dragon C .10 .25
BT030083 Thunder Knights, Iron Fist Dragon C .10 .25
BT030084 Bucket Arm Dragon C .10 .25
BT030085 Dragon Knight, Nagakura C .30 .75
BT030086 Thunder Knights, Brass Shield Dragon C .10 .25
BT030087 Leather Buckler Dragon C .10 .25
BT030088 Dragogenius C 2.00 5.00
BT030089 Magical Fighter, Seijuro Mado C .30 .75
BT030090 Dragowizard, Rainbow Horn C .30 .75
BT030091 Toudou the Unseen Hand C .30 .75
BT030092 Bye Bye Later! C .30 .75
BT030093 Aftermath, Gagaku C .10 .25
BT030094 Flame Art Ninja, Gokuen C .30 .75
BT030095 Jumping Ninja, Sarutobi C .10 .25
BT030096 Skull Golem, Mazubaha C 1.00 2.50
BT030097 Doberman, Kobold C .10 .25
BT030098 Gummy Slime C .10 .25
BT030099 Scout, Kiwa the Straight Man C .10 .25
BT030100 Fate Skeleton C .10 .25
BT030101 Monster Master's Staff, Arelta C .75 2.00
BT030102 Actor Knights Justice C .30 .75
BT030103 Actor Knights Empress C .10 .25
BT030104 Emperor Shield C .10 .25
BT030105 Armorknight Cerberus "A" BR 15.00 40.00

2014 Future Card Buddyfight Immortal Entities

EB010001s Sun Fist, Sunshine Impact SP
EB010002s Duel Sieger "Tempest Enforcer" SP
EB010003s Dragon Knight, Richard SP
EB010004s Dimensional Demonic Dragon, Ladis the Tyrant SP
EB010006s Evil Crusher, Steel Dragon Barrage! SP
EB010014s Space Dragon Emperor, Galiazond SP
EB010001 Sun Fist, Sunshine Impact RRR
EB010002 Duel Sieger "Tempest Enforcer" RRR
EB010003 Dragon Knight, Richard RR
EB010004 Dimensional Demonic Dragon, Ladis the Tyrant RR
EB010005 Fortune Dragon, Forbolka RR
EB010006 Evil Crusher, Steel Dragon Barrage! RR
EB010007 Divine Dragon Creation RR
EB010008 Systemic Dagger "Onca" R
EB010009 Dragobulk Stormschlag R
EB010010 Evil Sins, Shumokuzame R
EB010011 Bandit Ninja, Goemon R
EB010012 Duel Sieger "Spartand" R
EB010013 Martial Arts Dragon Emperor, Duel Sieger R
EB010014 Space Dragon Emperor, Galiazond R
EB010015 Flame Dragon Emperor, Magmanova R
EB010016 Dragon Emperor Legend R
EB010017 Dragon Flame Cascade R
EB010018 Blow-hammer Dragon U
EB010019 Ironchain Dragon U
EB010020 Hundred Face Ninja, Muraku U
EB010021 Silver Dragon, Adelaide U
EB010022 Storm Dragon Emperor, Thundertornado U
EB010023 Rock Dragon Emperor, Vragos U
EB010024 Blue Dragon, Thunder Horn U
EB010025 Dragonverse U
EB010026 Dragonlution U
EB010027 Rise & Fall of Dragons U
EB010028 Dragon Knight, Gilles de Rais C
EB010029 Dirge Drill Dragon C
EB010030 Dragon Knight, Socrates C
EB010031 Dragonic Dash C
EB010032 Dragospeed C
EB010033 Sword Skill Bare Hand Intercept C
EB010034 Ninja Arts, Half-kill C
EB010035 Gold Dragon, Abend C
EB010036 Ice Dragon, Knoke-isle C
EB010037 Vitesse, Purple Diamond Dragon C
EB010038 Ice Dragon Emperor, Glacies C
EB010039 Flame Fairy Dragon, Tialvette C
EB010040 Wind Fairy Dragon, Sufa C
EB010041 Ice Fairy Dragon, Garbolette C
EB010042 Feather Dragon, Talwar C
EB010043 Dies, Azurite Dragon C
EB010044 Dragon Outlaw C
EB010045 Bold Dragon C
EB010046 Dragon Dreams C
EB010047 Dragon Thunder C
EB010048 Thunder Knights, Drum Bunker Dragon BR

2014 Future Card Buddyfight Ninja Onslaught

TD050001r Noble Ninja, Momochitanba RR
TD050005r Tsukikage, Blademaster Mode RR
TD050001 Noble Ninja, Momochitanba C
TD050002 Lethal Sword Ninja, Zantetsu C
TD050003 Wandering Ninja, Tobikato C
TD050004 Agent Ninja, Rinzo C
TD050005 Tsukikage, Blademaster Mode C
TD050006 Electro Ninja, Electric Teru C
TD050007 Stealth Ninja, Kirikakure Saizo C
TD050008 Accelerate Ninja, Hayate C
TD050009 Demon Way, Geppakugiri C
TD050010 Demon Way, Noroihikagami C
TD050011 Shooting Cross Knives, Right-hand C
TD050012 Ninja Arts, Steel Ball C
TD050013 Clear Serenity C
TD050014 Art of Item Blasting C
TD050015 Art of Body Replacement C
TD050016 Ninja Blade, Kurogachi C
TD050017 Secret Sword, Lethal Formation RR
TD050018 Secret Sword, Shooting Star C
TD050019 Secret Sword, Moon Fang C
TD050020 Katana World (card) C

2014 Future Card Buddyfight Savage Steel

TD020003r Armorknight Cerberus RR
TD020015r Drill Bunker!! RR
TD020001 Armorknight Black Drake C
TD020002 Armorknight Griffin C
TD020003 Armorknight Cerberus C
TD020004 Armorknight Minotaur C
TD020005 Armorknight Ogre C
TD020006 Armorknight Hellhound C
TD020007 Armorknight Wizard C
TD020008 Armorknight Eagle C
TD020009 Crimson Slash C
TD020010 Survival Chance C
TD020011 Battle Aura Circle C
TD020012 Invigorating Breath C
TD020013 Hysteric Spear C
TD020014 Boulder Piercing Spear C
TD020015 Drill Bunker!! C
TD020016 My Buddy! (Armorknight Cerberus) C
TD020017 Danger World C

2014 Future Card Buddyfight Super Strong Buddy Rare

SS010005 Bear-Trap Fang Dragon C
SS010007 Blade Wing Dragon C
SS010018 Blaster Tornado, Red Dragon Roaring Supreme RR
SS010018c Blaster Tornado, Red Dragon Roaring Supreme C
SS010015 Blue Dragon Shield RR
SS010008 Boomerang Dragon C
SS010013 Dragon Return System C
SS010019 Dragon World C
SS010017 Dragonblade, Dragobreach C
SS010016 Dragonblade, Drum Sword C
SS010010 Dragonic Assault C
SS010012 Dragonic Charge C
SS010014 Dragonic Grimoire C
SS010003 Drum Bunker Dragon C
SS010001 Drum Bunker Dragon, "Dual Wield" BR
SS010001r Drum Bunker Dragon, "Dual Wield" RR
SS010004 Fang Slade Drum C
SS010023 Fire Giant, Surtr C
SS010029 Fog Wall, Navalbonds C
SS010033 Gleipnir C
SS010037 Great Spell Finisher, Heroic Fire Blade Laevateinn! RR
SS010037c Great Spell Finisher, Heroic Fire Blade Laevateinn! C
SS010031 Great Spell, Fimbulwinter C
SS010030 Great Spell, Ragnarok C
SS010035 Holy Grail C
SS010032 Horn of Demise, Gjallarhorn C
SS010026 Horse of the King of Gods, Sleipnir C
SS010020 Ice Blade "Astralux" BR
SS010020r Ice Blade "Astralux" RR
SS010027 Ice Blade, Joker RR
SS010027c Ice Blade, Joker C
SS010022 Ice Emperor, Thrudgelmir C
SS010038 Legend World C
SS010028 Loki the Ehrgeiz C
SS010021 Moon Wolf, Managarmr RR
SS010021c Moon Wolf, Managarmr C
SS010006 Raid Claw Dragon C
SS010009 Red Dragon Shield C
SS010036 Rune Staff C
SS010024 Shadow Soldiers of the King of Gods, Wotanshadow C
SS010034 Shield of Achilles C
SS010002 Super Armordragon, Vajra Blaster Dragon RR
SS010002c Super Armordragon, Vajra Blaster Dragon C
SS010025 Wicked Dragon, Nidhogg C
SS010011 Wrath of Dragon C

2014 Future Card Buddyfight Tomorrow Asmodai

TD070001 Champion Wrestler Asmodai
TD070002 Dance! Asmodai
TD070003 Fallen Angel of Rage, Beleth
TD070004 Demon Realm Death Metal, Valefar
TD070005 Let's Play! Asmodai
TD070006 Fallen Angel, Paimon
TD070007 Demon Realm Warrior, Zepar
TD070008 Event Producer Aym
TD070009 Oops!
TD070010 Key of Solomon, First Volume
TD070011 Speed Summon
TD070012 Nice one!
TD070013 Solomon's Shield
TD070014 Chillax!
TD070015 I'm Wicked!
TD070016 Gunrod, Bechstein
TD070017 Asmodai Eternal Rolling Back-drop!
TD070018 Magic World

2015 Future Card Buddyfight Break to the Future

BT050001 Super Armordragon, General Boldness RRR
BT050001s Super Armordragon, General Boldness SP
BT050002 Super Armordragon, Drum Breaker Dragon RRR
BT050002s Super Armordragon, Drum Breaker Dragon SP
BT050003 Venom Harpe Dragon RRR
BT050004 Cavalry Dragon, Hyperion RRR 10.00
BT050004s Cavalry Dragon, Hyperion SP
BT050005 Artificial Angel, Virginie Casta RRR 8.00
BT050005s Artificial Angel, Virginie Casta SP
BT050006 Super Lethal Formation RRR
BT050006s Super Lethal Formation SP
BT050007 Death Ruler, Thirteen RRR 4.00
BT050007s Death Ruler, Thirteen SP 20.00
BT050008 Black Dragon of Demise, Death Tallica RRR 1.50
BT050008s Black Dragon of Demise, Death Tallica SP 20.00
BT050009 Great Evil Dragon, Samael Apocalypse RRR 4.00

BT050009s Great Evil Dragon, Samael Apocalypse SP 12.00
BT050010 Purgatory Knights, Gairahm Lance Dragon RRR
BT050011 Dragon Knight, Spartax RR 5.00
BT050012 Dragon Knight, Tomoe RR 8.00
BT050013 Gauntlet Sword Dragon RR
BT050014 Tomahawk Dragon RR
BT050015 Street Racer, Eligos RR
BT050016 Great Spell, Devil's Rock and Roll RR 2.50
BT050016s Great Spell, Devil's Rock and Roll SP 6.00
BT050017 White Dragon Hermit, Nanase RR
BT050017s White Dragon Hermit, Nanase SP
BT050018 Cat Shadow, Aoihime RR 5.00
BT050019 Electric Speed Ninja, Inazuma RR 5.00
BT050020 Treachery, Jakikarasu RR
BT050021 Death Ruler, Gruen RR 4.00
BT050022 Black Dragon, Spinechiller RR 2.00
BT050023 Purgatory Knights, Sword Breaker Dragon RR
BT050024 Purgatory Knights, Crossbow Dragon RR
BT050025 Purgatory Knights, Forever RR
BT050026 Zweihander Dragon R
BT050027 Dragon Knight, Motonari R 1.00
BT050028 Dragon Knight, Mitsuhide R 1.00
BT050029 Missile Bunker Dragon R 1.00
BT050030 Dragon Trust R 1.00
BT050031 Demon Sommelier, Zagan R 1.00
BT050032 Magic Artist, Andy R 1.00
BT050033 No Pain No Gain R 1.00
BT050034 Overstand! R 1.00
BT050035 Check It Out! R 1.00
BT050036 Solomon's Great Barrier R
BT050037 Magic School, Sephirot R 1.00
BT050038 Gunrod, Del Gesu R 1.00
BT050039 Martial Arts, Oosumi R 1.00
BT050040 Lock Ninja, Setsui R 1.00
BT050041 Diversion Troublemaker, Bakemujina R 1.00
BT050042 Secret Sword, Comet R
BT050043 Secret Sword, Morning Star R
BT050044 Divine Demon Slayer, Amenoohahari R 1.00
BT050045 Lamenting Black Steel, Balomdahl R 1.00
BT050046 Purgatory Knights Leader, Demios Sword Dragon R
BT050046s Purgatory Knights Leader, Demios Sword Dragon SP
BT050047 Death Ruler, Mastermind R 1.00
BT050048 Death Ruler, Averia R 1.00
BT050049 Purgatory Knights, Knuckleduster Dragon R
BT050050 Death Astray R 1.00
BT050051 Nightmare Revive R 1.00
BT050052 Crush that Body, and Sustain Mine R 1.00
BT050053 Distortion Punisher!! R 2.50
BT050053s Distortion Punisher!! SP
BT050054 Brutal Disaster! R 1.00
BT050055 Actor Knights Judgement R 1.00
BT050056 Ultimate Sword Dragon U
BT050057 Great Labrys Dragon U .50
BT050058 Dragon Knight, Bokuden U .50
BT050059 Twin Brudes Dragon U
BT050060 One to One U .50
BT050061 Dragon Cavalry Arts, The Glorious Legacy U .50
BT050062 57th Generation Great Magician Merlin, Unryu Togetsu U .50
BT050063 Demon Realm Architect, Gamigin U .50
BT050064 Warrior, Halphas U
BT050065 Gentleman, Malphas U .50
BT050066 Epic Fail! U .50
BT050067 Disperser of Conflagration, Shiromizuchi U .50
BT050068 Arts of Heat Haze U .50
BT050069 Water Technique, Minawagakushi U
BT050070 Elite Sword, Juzumaru U .50
BT050071 Secret Sword, Glittering Star U
BT050072 Purgatory Knights, Mad Halberd Dragon U
BT050073 Black Knight, Goldred U .50
BT050074 Purgatory Knights, Cruel Command U
BT050075 Shooter of Magic Bullets, Gaspard U
BT050076 Purgatory Flame that Resides Within that Body U
BT050077 Dead Scream U .50
BT050078 Death Game U .50
BT050079 Death Counter U .50
BT050080 Accel End U .50
BT050081 Redupsion Blood U
BT050082 Life Dwells in the Flames of Hades Too U .50
BT050083 Pain Field U .50
BT050084 Black Agenda U .50
BT050085 Purgatory Sword, Fatal U
BT050086 Actor Knights Death U .50
BT050087 Celtic Cross Spread U .50
BT050088 One Oracle U .50
BT050089 Blade of Athame U .50
BT050090 Behemoth Claymore Dragon C .25
BT050091 Dragon Knight, Hartman C .25
BT050092 Dragon Knight, Crazy Horse C .25
BT050093 Blue Sky Knights, Bonblade Dragon C .25
BT050094 Diamond Shield Dragon C .25
BT050095 Separate Whip Dragon C
BT050096 Knight Counter C .25
BT050097 Dragonic Survey C .25
BT050098 Golden Dragon Shield C .25
BT050099 Dragon Arms, Dragokeeper C .25
BT050100 Sky Poet, Amon C
BT050101 Dragowizard, Gan Alkimia C .25
BT050102 Dragowizard, Mitschuler C .25
BT050103 Demon Realm Scientist, Purson C .25
BT050104 Bestie! C .25
BT050105 Fang Style Ninja, Kibashachi C .25
BT050106 Perfect Beauty, Hyoshi Shirasagi C
BT050107 Runaway Female Ninja, Yukishiro C
BT050108 Loud Laugh Ninja, Fugumaru C .25
BT050109 Striking with the Back of My Sword! C
BT050110 Demon Way, Kiribusuma C .25
BT050111 Water Technique, Shinotsukuame C
BT050112 Demon Swordsman, Deathstorm C .25
BT050113 Death Ruler, Skull C .25
BT050114 Demonic Dark Emperor, Grobius C .25
BT050115 Obsidian Mane, Grieva C .25
BT050116 Purgatory Knights, Blood Axe Dragon C
BT050117 Black Knight, Hell Rapier C .25
BT050118 Purgatory Knights, Silver Staff Dragon C
BT050119 Hand of Muramasa, Katsukiyo C .25
BT050120 Thirsting Creature, Zanzara C
BT050121 Purgatory Knights, Iron Gerd Dragon C
BT050122 Unfulfilled Desire, Greedy Beak C
BT050123 Death Ruler, Deathcusion C .25
BT050124 Hades Knight, Goldba C .25
BT050125 Death Ruler, Asphyxia C .25
BT050126 Death Ruler, Gespenst C .25
BT050127 Bloody Dance C .25
BT050128 Black Armor C .25
BT050129 Crisis Field C .25
BT050130 Purgatory Hyme, The Cursed Being of the Faraway Homeland C
BT050131 Actor Knights Strength C .25
BT050132 Actor Knights Tower C .25
BT050133 Actor Knights Temperance C .25
BT050134 Burn Ship Soul C .25
BT050135 Card Burn BR 25.00

2015 Future Card Buddyfight Crimson Fist

HSD010001 First Crimson Chieftain, Greatest General C
HSD010002 Crimson Battler, Extreme Blow Dragon C
HSD010003 Crimson Battler, Boosted Dragon C
HSD010004 Crimson Battler, Grand Kick Dragon C
HSD010005 Crimson Battler, Spin Nail Dragon C
HSD010006 Crimson Battler, Hammer Ball Dragon C
HSD010007 Crimson Battler, Starting Dragon C
HSD010008 Crimson Battler, Maintenance Kid C
HSD010009 Dragonic Gate Breaker C
HSD010010 Dragonic Directive C
HSD010011 Primeval Dragon Shield C
HSD010012 Dragonic Aura C
HSD010013 Green Dragon Shield C
HSD010014 Assail Sword, Dragoraptor C
HSD010015 Battle Spirit Fist, Dragosoul C
HSD010016 Crimson Soul Grenade!! C
HSD010017 Dragon World C

2015 Future Card Buddyfight Dragonic Star

HTD010005 Child Star, Astrojet C
HTD010006 Dragonarms, Cavalier C
HTD010008 The Crater, Basin C
HTD010009 Dragonarms, Divisigator C
HTD010010 Star Blast C
HTD010013 Shining Rain C
HTD010014 Proto Barrier C
HTD010015 Star Saber, Reflection C
HTD010016 Photon Saber, Meteor C
HTD010017 Photon Edge Universe! C
HTD010001r Cosmo Strada, Galaxias RR
HTD010001 Cosmo Strada, Galaxias C
HTD010002 Demonblaze, Maxwell C
HTD010003 Stardust, Globule C
HTD010004 Rainbow Vision, Shadowscare C
HTD010006r Dragonarms, Cavalier RR
HTD010007 Dragonarms, Vogel C
HTD010011 Planet Memory C
HTD010012 Speculight Ring C
HTD010017r Photon Edge Universe! RR
HTD010018 Star Dragon World C

2015 Future Card Buddyfight Galaxy Burst

HBT020004 Fairy King, Oberon RRR
HBT020006 Cosmic Storm, Greisen ZK RRR
HBT020007 Sixth Omni Storm Lord, Variable Cord RRR
HBT020008 Star Guardian, Jackknife RRR
HBT020011 Yumi Ninja, Suiha RR
HBT020015 Odd Bird, Harpy RR
HBT020017 Dragonic Armored Ship, Marshal Fortress RR
HBT020018 Dragonarms Factory RR
HBT020021 Super Armordragon, Gran Railgun Dragon R
HBT020023 Crimson Battler, Double Katar Dragon R
HBT020024 Crimson Battler, Power Stamp Dragon R
HBT020025 Dragon Knight, Lincoln R
HBT020026 Trap Master Dragon R
HBT020027 Dragon Knight, Cromwell R
HBT020030 4000 Festival! R
HBT020031 Ring of Crimson R
HBT020032 Demonic Descend Ninja, Zeon R
HBT020034 Hidden Sword Ninja, Sekitetsu R
HBT020040 Purplish Green Dragon, Peluda R
HBT020041 Cait Sith in Boots R
HBT020042 Vert Deus, Matrix R
HBT020043 Dragonarms, Elgar Cannon R
HBT020045 Earth Barrier R
HBT020048 Cut Whip Dragon U
HBT020050 Thunder Knights, Slide Wing Dragon U
HBT020052 Dragonic Loop U
HBT020054 Outlander, Bokunryu U
HBT020055 One-Eyed Ninja, Refu U
HBT020056 Demon Kid, Hiunmaru U
HBT020057 Rampage, Chizomegumo U
HBT020059 Reinforced Formation of Hundred Demons U
HBT020061 Demon Way, Oborogenbu U
HBT020064 Loyal Unicorn U
HBT020065 Night Witch, Clear U
HBT020066 Death Summoning Tears of the Banshee U
HBT020068 Annoying Ways of the Troll U
HBT020069 The Godjenesis! U
HBT020070 Photon Crown, Geocorona U
HBT020071 Brun Deus, Akision U
HBT020073 Star Saber, Asteroid U
HBT020075 Battle Deity Robo, Azul Dragon U
HBT020078 Thunder Knights, Sword Bunker Dragon C
HBT020079 Kris Knife Dragon C
HBT020081 Systemic Dagger, Black Edge C
HBT020086 Japanese Blade Ninja, Hachimonji C
HBT020088 Ceremony of Exorcism C
HBT020091 White Dragon, Gwiber C
HBT020096 Algis Gard C
HBT020097 Giant Star, Leitning C
HBT020098 Mother Space, Oortcloud C
HBT020099 Azul, Tesslamagna C
HBT020103 Battle Deity Robo, Spear Kart C
HBT020104 Battle Deity Robo, Missile Dog C
HBT020105 End of War C
HBT020106 Fall Back C
HBT020107 Disturb C
HBT020110 Great Fiend, Yamigedo Secret
HBT020111 Soaring Flame, Lindwurm Secret
HBT020113 Thunder Claw, Narukami Secret
HBT020002s First Omni Beast Lord, Ziun SP
HBT020005s Seventh Omni Earth Lord, Count Dawn SP
HBT020119EN Firestone Dragon C
HBT020121EN Flame Giant, Surtr C
HBT020001 Armordeity, Dynamis RRR
HBT020002 First Omni Beast Lord, Ziun RRR
HBT020003 Nanomachine Ninja, Byakuya RRR
HBT020005 Seventh Omni Earth Lord, Count Dawn RRR
HBT020007s Sixth Omni Storm Lord, Variable Cord SP
HBT020009 Jackknife Anzestor RR
HBT020010 Ghoul Deity, Gojinmaru RR
HBT020012 Lightning Speed, Tsukiusagi RR
HBT020013 Water Slash Sword, Murasame RR
HBT020014 Deity of the Death and Sun, Bloody King RR
HBT020016 Divine Spear, Gungnir RR
HBT020019 Sudden Wormhole RR
HBT020020 Thunder Claw, Narukami RR
HBT020022 Fatal Arms Dragon R
HBT020028 Dragon Knight, Lenus R
HBT020029 Thunder Knights, Silverchain Dragon R
HBT020033 Kalavinka, Uguisukomachi R
HBT020035 Demonic Way of Hundred Demons, Akishoki R
HBT020036 Odd Ritual, Skull Festival R
HBT020037 Absolute Sword, Azure Cascade Formation R
HBT020038 Wolfman, Gutz R
HBT020039 Valkyrie, Brilliant Brynhildr R
HBT020044 Barracal Barret R
HBT020046 Radiant Punisher!! R
HBT020047 Battle Deity Robo, GIZAI Emperor R
HBT020049 Thunder Knights, Spike Shoulder Dragon U
HBT020051 Fist of the Red Battler U
HBT020053 Thunderclap, Goraiko U
HBT020058 Sword Skill, Sen-no-Sen U
HBT020060 Ninja Arts, Mat Flipping Technique U
HBT020062 Dashing in the Moonlight, Red Cap U
HBT020063 Fairy Knight, Daoine Shee U
HBT020067 Book of Illusions, Mabinogion U
HBT020072 Dragonarms, Artiliger U
HBT020074 Photon Saber, Filament U
HBT020076 Battle Deity Robo, Search Whale U
HBT020077 Operation Restraint U
HBT020080 Crimson Battler, Burn Guts Dragon C
HBT020082 Dragon Knight, Ranmaru C
HBT020083 Dragonic Teamwork C
HBT020084 Martial Bones Fist, Dragosquare C
HBT020085 Almighty, Dokakusai C
HBT020087 Composed, Kageitachi C
HBT020089 Demon Way, Fool's Festival C
HBT020090 Elite Sword, Dojigiri C
HBT020092 Carved Stallion of Dreams, Dalahast C
HBT020093 Red Dragon, Welsh C
HBT020094 Demonic Beast of Gem, Vouivre C
HBT020095 Great Spell, Weiterstadt C
HBT020100 Shooting Star, Balmeteor C
HBT020101 Star Cruiser, Orbital C
HBT020102 Dragonarms, Winchisker C
HBT020108 Star Guardian, Jackknife BR
HBT020109 Great Fiend, Yamigedo RRR
HBT020112 Reinforced Formation of Hundred Demons Secret
HBT020114 Parade of Hundred Demons RR
HBT020115EN Crimson Battler, Rock Bunker Dragon R
HBT020116EN Crimson Battler, Heavy-impact Dragon R
HBT020117EN Dragonic Assault U
HBT020118EN Tempest Sword, Makiarashi U
HBT020120EN Buddy Buddy BAAAAAN!! C
HBT020122EN Evil Dragon, Nidhogg C

2015 Future Card Buddyfight Golden Buddy Pack Ver. E

PP010060EN Boomerang Dragon RR
PP010061EN Ice Blade Astralkus RR
PP010001 Skyblue Dragon, Crystal Saber RR
PP010002 Drop Arms Dragon RR
PP010003 Colichemarde Dragon RR
PP010004 Dragon Knight, Sanosuke RR
PP010005 Dragon Knight, Selim RR
PP010006 Disturb Hand Dragon RR
PP010007 Heavy-Armor Dragon RR
PP010008 Dragon Knight, Slayman RR
PP010009 Armorknight Lethal Drake RR
PP010010 Wasp Blast Dragon, Gigabeera RR
PP010011 Skeleton Armored Dragon, Medrogirus RR
PP010012 Armorknight Eagle A RR
PP010013 Demon Realm Knights Leader, Sabnac RR
PP010014 Chain Magic Master, Link RR
PP010015 Reminiscing the Homeland Marcosius RR
PP010016 Magic Power Researcher, Ren Kogasaki RR
PP010017 Breakthrough Ninja, Rasenmaru RR
PP010018 Defiant, Sabifukuro RR
PP010019 Agent Ninja, Mamiya RR
PP010020 Moss Wall, Fudogame RR
PP010021 Ghoul Dragon Emperor, Adil Diablos RR
PP010022 Emerald Dragon Emperor, Jedaflight RR
PP010023 Seek Dragon Emperor, Azludea RR
PP010024 Sky Dragon, Japerrot RR
PP010025 Guardian Dragon of Demon Lord Castle, Deukruzar RR
PP010026 Wandering Salaryman Buddyfighter, Amigo?Takata RR
PP010027 Young Pope, Alex RR
PP010028 One Gauge Demon RR
PP010029 First Tribulation, Gold Lion of Nemea RR
PP010030 Glacier Dragon, Zilant RR
PP010031 Panther Robed Knight, Tariel RR
PP010032 Valkyrie, Omniscience Alvidol RR
PP010033 Graveyard of Demonic Swords, Graybard RR
PP010034 Eternal Silence, Orbit RR
PP010035 Extreme Prison, Zwinger RR
PP010036 Infectious Malevolence, Yuberium RR
PP010037 Death Ruler, Manifile RR
PP010038 Death Ruler, Galkheight RR
PP010039 Purgatory Knights, Eval Grebe Dragon RR
PP010040 Purgatory Knights, Lunacy Wand Dragon RR
PP010041 Jackknife Aggressor BR
PP010042 Drum Bunker Dragon BR
PP010043 Dragon Knight, El Quixote BR
PP010044 Armorknight Demon BR
PP010045 Fighting Dragon, Demongodol BR
PP010046 Center of the World, Mary Sue BR
PP010047 Demon Lord, Asmodai BR
PP010048 Nanomachine Ninja, Tsukikage BR
PP010049 Evil in Heart, Yamigitsune BR
PP010050 Duel Sieger Tempest Enforcer BR
PP010051 Duel Sieger Spartand BR
PP010052 Bladewing Phoenix BR
PP010053 Legendary Brave, Tasuku BR
PP010054 Immortal Sword, Durandal BR
PP010055 Wind Fairy, Sylph BR
PP010056 Demonic Demise Dragon, Azi Dahaka BR
PP010057 Death Ruler, Gallows BR
PP010058 Captain Answer BR
PP010059EN Drum Bunker Dragon, Dual Wield RR
PP010062EN Stallion of the Divine King, Sleipnir RR

2015 Future Card Buddyfight Malicious Demons

HTD020002 Dark Dragon, Demochill C
HTD020005 Thunder Summoner, Reiki C
HTD020007 Living Mad Gazer C
HTD020009 Hundred Demons Sorcery, Tennomimakari C
HTD020011 Hundred Demons' Tome of Judgement C
HTD020012 Starved Yamigedo C
HTD020015 Fiendish Blade, Urahonekui C
HTD020016 Beast Mode, Hungry Claw War! C
HTD020017 Parade of Hundred Demons C
HTD020001r Hundred Demons General, Gokumengaiou RR
HTD020001 Hundred Demons General, Gokumengaiou C
HTD020003 Evil Dragon, Gataraoroch C
HTD020004 Poisonous Water Dragon, Zazamera C
HTD020006 Corpse Spirit, Draogul C
HTD020008 Ogre Size Dragon C
HTD020010 Hundred Demons Sorcery, Ryubokushihai C
HTD020012r Starved Yamigedo RR
HTD020013 Hundred Demons Sorcery, Yamitagae C
HTD020014 Hungry Claw, Raiga C

2015 Future Card Buddyfight Miracle Impack

HEB010004 Emergency Launch! Decker Drum RRR
HEB010005 Super Combidragon, Brainbaltes RR
HEB010006 Armorknight Iblis RR
HEB010010 Mech Army Demon Lord, Agos Marh RR
HEB010011 King's Wave, Caliburn Grief RR
HEB010015 Battle Dragon Slaying Crush R
HEB010024 Dragon Tooth Warrior R
HEB010027 Adventurer's Staff, Alcsbane R
HEB010028 Phoenix Radiation! R
HEB010035 Armorknight Salamander U
HEB010036 Sibling Dragon, Foonbaltes U
HEB010040 Infinite Demon Slay Slash U
HEB010044 Demon Way, Ukishizumi Ikusabune U
HEB010048 Trouble Ghost, Shuffler X U
HEB010053 Quiescence of Cassiade U
HEB010055 Fortune Select! U
HEB010057 White Valor, Lord Takuto U
HEB010063 Danger World Secret
HEB010001 Armorknight Archangel RRR
HEB010002 Blue Knight, Noboru RRR
HEB010003 Legendary Messiah, Tasuku RRR
HEB010003s Legendary Messiah, Tasuku SP
HEB010006s Armorknight Iblis SP
HEB010007 Infinite Armament, Dangerous Cradle RR
HEB010008 Death Master, Lelag Monarch RR
HEB010009 Province Baron, Shido RR
HEB010012 Red Warrior, Road Blader RR
HEB010013 Dragon Secret Arts, Dragonic Resurrection R
HEB010014 Battle Aura Dragon, Extreme-Aura R
HEB010016 Unyielding Spirit R
HEB010017 Battle Dragon Bursting Charge! R
HEB010018 Shredding Battle Wall R
HEB010019 Judge Asmodai's Super Impartial 3 Rounds, Rock! Paper! Scissors! R
HEB010020 New-Era Great Spell, The Creation R
HEB010021 Ninja Arts, Art of Bursting Machine Gun R
HEB010022 Dragon's Life and Death, Future and Past! R
HEB010023 Hades Dragon Chief, Red Arrogant R
HEB010025 Bronze Golem, Jalsh R
HEB010026 Hidden Crossbow R
HEB010028s Phoenix Radiation! SP
HEB010029 Asgard Saga R
HEB010030 Violence Familiar! R
HEB010031 Unmovable Steel Mech, Ganzallar R
HEB010032 Prepped and OK to Launch! R
HEB010033 Determination of the Fist Fighter, Grapple Soul U
HEB010034 Armorknight Centaur U
HEB010037 Armorknight Ogre A U
HEB010038 Armorknight Jetfighter U
HEB010039 Sibling Dragon, Kibaltes U
HEB010041 Training of Skill and Life U
HEB010042 Spear of Will, Agito U
HEB010043 Demon Arms Door, ArMoreD Gate! U
HEB010045 Charge of Virtuous Blood! U
HEB010046 Diamond Golem, Fluud U
HEB010047 Steel Golem, Futoff U
HEB010049 Iron Golem, Nasr U
HEB010050 Swordsman of the East, Zanya U
HEB010051 Apprentice Ninja, Akatsuki U
HEB010052 Entangle Roper U
HEB010054 Mission Card THE Teamwork U
HEB010056 Dark Interment, Over the Grudge U
HEB010058 That is an Afterimage U
HEB010059 Rock Splitter Sword, Gaia Crush! U
HEB010060 Emergency Trans! U
HEB010061 Emergency Launch! Decker Drum BR
HEB010062 Dragon World Secret
HEB010064 Magic World Secret
HEB010065 Katana World Secret
HEB010066 Dungeon World Secret

2015 Future Card Buddyfight Radiant Force

HSD020001 Adventure Continent, Gunvellz C
HSD020002 Rescue Dragon, Crossbuster C
HSD020003 Eco-Hero Solarpanelman C
HSD020004 Heavy Trooper, Iron Saver C
HSD020007 Cyber Police Hyper Rescue C
HSD020009 There, I See It! C
HSD020011 It's About Time I Got Serious! C
HSD020013 Launch! Buddy Police C
HSD020014 I'm Still Alive! C
HSD020005 Radio Controlled Machine, Maxstorm C
HSD020006 Stray Warrior, Vier C
HSD020008 Draw Away the Lackeys! C
HSD020010 Justice Will Prevail! C
HSD020012 I've Seen Through Your Moves! C
HSD020015 Army Rifle, Line Thunder C
HSD020016 Equation of Victory, Winning Formula! C
HSD020017 Hero World (card) C

2015 Future Card Buddyfight Shadow vs. Hero

HEB020001 Great Sword Deity, Kaizerion RRR
HEB020003 Shadow Hero, Schwarz RRR
HEB020006 Rescue Dragon, Forcearms RR
HEB020009 Gaigrander 01 RR
HEB020010 Darkness Fist, Gwen RR
HEB020011 Evil Esthetics RR
HEB020014 Grand Calibur, Zeldline R
HEB020016 Rescue Dragon, Dragschoebel R
HEB020019 Rescue Dragon, Projet Gunner R
HEB020022 Bird Deity, Sabird R
HEB020023 Combatant, Nebatt R
HEB020027 I'm Finished with You R
HEB020028 First Darkhero Hideout R
HEB020031 But He is of the Lowest Rank R
HEB020032 Infinity Death Crest! R
HEB020033 Brave Energy Full Drive! R
HEB020034 Steel Beast Battle Robo, Gaidenor U
HEB020035 Corrupted One, Erational U
HEB020038 Gaigrander, Analyze Form U
HEB020039 Sacrifice, Iron Moon Slash U
HEB020041 Radio Controlled Machine, Bodhum Breaker U
HEB020044 Cyber Police, Heroic Blader U
HEB020049 Thief Cat U
HEB020050 Rescue Dragon, Nightstalker U
HEB020051 Ocean Deity, Slashark U
HEB020052 Be Glad That You Can be of Use to Me U
HEB020054 I Leave...the Rest to You U
HEB020055 It's Here, the NEW Suit! U
HEB020057 Long-Range Cannon U
HEB020061 Shadow Requiem U
HEB020062 Superior Justice Driver! U
HEB020004s Rescue Dragon, Justice Drum SP
HEB020005s Rescue Dragon Leader, Immortal Spirit SP
HEB020008s Fiery Inspector, Prominence Burst SP
HEB020002 Captain Answer Final Mode RRR
HEB020003s Shadow Hero, Schwarz SP
HEB020004 Rescue Dragon, Justice Drum RRR
HEB020005 Rescue Dragon Leader, Immortal Spirit RR
HEB020007 Gaigrander 02 RR
HEB020008 Fiery Inspector, Prominence Burst RR
HEB020012 Sneak Judgement RR
HEB020013 Combitrooper, Dziem R
HEB020015 Violet Valor, Lord Crow R
HEB020017 Rescue Dragon, Transmission R
HEB020018 Rescue Dragon, Northern Bird R
HEB020020 Cyber Police, Commander Gale R
HEB020021 Grand RuLer, Silbarrier R
HEB020024 Momentary Flash R
HEB020025 Body of Steel R
HEB020026 Fighting for the Sake of Others R
HEB020029 Super Headquarters, Brave Fort R
HEB020030 I've Come Back to Take You Down! R
HEB020036 Buster Bone Armor U
HEB020037 Gaigrander, Finish Form U
HEB020040 Cyber Police, Stealth Hunter U
HEB020042 The Scar U
HEB020043 Beast Deity, Tigerthrust U
HEB020045 Rescue Dragon, Erase Flare U
HEB020046 Judgement, Hollow Strydom U
HEB020047 Rescue Dragon, Doctor Aid U
HEB020048 Radio Control Machine, Makishi Rider U
HEB020053 I Have No Business with the Likes of You! U
HEB020056 Arduous Training U
HEB020058 I Won't Let that Happen! U
HEB020059 For Such an Attack to... U
HEB020060 It Doesn't Work!! U
HEB020063 Dead or Alive! U
HEB020064 Rescue Dragon, Justice Drum BR

2016 Luck and Logic Growth and Genesis

COMPLETE SET (137 CARDS) 200.00 400.00

BOOSTER BOX (20 PACKS) 55.00 85.00
BOOSTER PACK (7 CARDS) 2.00 5.00
UNLISTED C .10 .30
UNLISTED U .20 .75
RELEASED ON JUNE 24TH, 2016
BT01001EN Power of Bonds Tamaki RR 10.00 25.00
BT01001EN Power of Bonds Tamaki SP 80.00 120.00
BT01001EN Power of Bonds Tamaki SR 20.00 40.00
BT01002EN Six Fists Sena RR 1.50 4.00
BT01002EN Six Fists Sena SR 3.00 8.00
BT01003EN Yellow Dragon of Rage Tamaki RR 5.00 12.00
BT01003EN Yellow Dragon of Rage Tamaki SR 8.00 20.00
BT01004EN Full Force Strike Sena R .75 2.00
BT01005EN Carange Leg, Sena R 1.25 3.00
BT01006EN Achieving Her Goal Sena R .75 2.00
BT01007EN In a Rush Tamaki R 1.50 4.00
BT01008EN Girl that Likes Sweets Xiaolin R 2.50 6.00
BT01009EN Smile of Satisfaction, Tamaki U .20 .75
BT01010EN Beyond the Battle Sena U .20 .75
BT01011EN Summoned by the Ocean Tamaki U .60 1.25
BT01012EN Counter Current Shock Tamaki U .60 1.50
BT01013EN Permeating Willpower Sena U .20 .75
BT01014EN Skilled Writing Tamaki U .40 1.00
BT01015EN Personification of Battle Asura U .20 .75
BT01016EN Incomplete Talent Xiaolin U .50 1.25
BT01017EN Repelling Dragon Scale Tamaki C .10 .30
BT01018EN Musical Performance Training Tamaki C .10 .30
BT01019EN Establishing the Target Tamaki C .10 .30
BT01020EN Monitoring Tamaki C .10 .30
BT01021EN The Decision to Protect Sena C .10 .30
BT01022EN In a Hurry Sena C .10 .30
BT01023EN A Little Relaxation Tamaki C .10 .30
BT01024EN Working Hard Asura C .10 .30
BT01025EN Successor Divine Music Otohime C .10 .30
BT01026EN Speak with My Fists U .50 1.25
BT01027EN Defense Tactics Lecture C .10 .30
BT01028EN Dragon Cradle PxR 2.50 6.00
BT01029EN Blood Bath Coliseum PxC .10 .30
BT01030EN Artistic Aquarium PxC .10 .30
BT01031EN Forbidden Overtrance Yoshichika RR 2.00 5.00
BT01031EN Forbidden Overtrance Yoshichika SR 3.00 8.00
BT01032EN Crushing Evil, Yoshichika SR 3.00 8.00
BT01032EN Crushing Evil, Yoshichika SP 8.00 20.00
BT01032EN Crushing Evil, Yoshichika RR 2.00 5.00
BT01033EN Going to Hades Mejiko SR 5.00 12.00
BT01033EN Going to Hades Mejiko RR 4.00 10.00
BT01034EN Full of Conviction Yoshichika R .75 2.00
BT01035EN Leaving Behind Her Grudge Mejiko R .75 2.00
BT01036EN Belief in the Occult Mejiko R 1.25 3.00
BT01037EN Ready to Go Yoshichika R .75 2.00
BT01038EN Fierce God Rasetsu R .75 2.00
BT01039EN Rapid Fall Mejiko U .20 .75
BT01040EN Brief Victory Yoshichika U .20 .75
BT01041EN Flash of Demon Yoshichika U .20 .75
BT01042EN One Sided Trance Mejiko U .20 .75
BT01043EN First Trance Yoshichika U .20 .75
BT01044EN Errands in the Early Afternoon Yoshichika U .40 1.00
BT01045EN Genius Monk of Great Envy Huang Huang U .20 .75
BT01046EN Fondly Remembering Rasetsu U .20 .75
BT01047EN Dispelling Secret Technique Yoshichika C .10 .30
BT01048EN Invisible Sword Stroke Yoshichika C .10 .30
BT01049EN Rosary of Sorrow Mejiko C .10 .30
BT01050EN Swordswoman Yoshichika C .10 .30
BT01051EN Twin Fine Blades Yoshichika C .10 .30
BT01052EN Girl that Senses the Supernatuarl Mejiko C .10 .30
BT01053EN Intracerebral Simulation Yoshichika C .10 .30
BT01054EN Enjoying Life Huang Huang C .10 .30
BT01055EN Beautiful Master Fencer Hibana C .10 .30
BT01056EN Unforeseen Summoning U .20 .30
BT01057EN Fighting Trance C .10 .30
BT01058EN Age of Civil Wars PxR 1.25 3.00
BT01059EN Mega Heavy Hard Luck PxC .10 .30
BT01060EN Sword to Sword PxC .10 .30
BT01061EN Super Tiger Claw Chloe SR 8.00 20.00
BT01061EN Super Tiger Claw Chloe SP 25.00 50.00
BT01061EN Super Tiger Claw Chloe RR 8.00 20.00
BT01062EN Reserved Fighting Ashley SR 2.00 5.00
BT01062EN Reserved Fighting Ashley RR 1.00 2.50
BT01063EN White Tiger Fist Chloe SR 5.00 12.00
BT01063EN White Tiger Fist Chloe RR 3.00 8.00
BT01064EN Stirring Up Trouble Chloe R .75 2.00
BT01065EN Driving Them Away Ashley R .75 2.00
BT01066EN Indulging in Reading Ashley R .75 2.00
BT01067EN Counterattack Commence Chloe R 1.50 4.00
BT01068EN Free Spirited Daiga R 1.50 4.00
BT01069EN Complete Devotion Ashley U .20 .75
BT01070EN Solid Armor Ashley U .20 .75
BT01071EN Concentration of Mind Chloe U .20 .75
BT01072EN Attack from the Trees Chloe U .60 1.50
BT01073EN Differing Ideals Ashley U .20 .75
BT01074EN Full Speed Patrol Chloe U .50 1.25
BT01075EN Strength to Smash Boulders Daiga U .20 .75
BT01076EN Jade of the Cliffs U .20 .75
BT01077EN Meal Before Battle Chloe C .10 .30
BT01078EN Trident Wielder Chloe C .10 .30
BT01079EN Cautious and Careful Ashley C .10 .30
BT01080EN Seaside Guard Chloe C .10 .30
BT01081EN Sprinting Chloe C .10 .30
BT01082EN Daydreaming Maiden Ashley C .10 .30
BT01083EN Returning to Supreme Bliss Chloe C .10 .30
BT01084EN Midday Drink Jade C .10 .30
BT01085EN Calm Time Fyrill C .10 .30
BT01086EN Barrier of Shadows U .20 .30
BT01087EN Goddess of the Waterfront C .10 .30
BT01088EN Golden Exercise PxR 1.50 4.00
BT01089EN Last Survivor PxC .10 .30
BT01090EN Slow Wave PxC .10 .30
BT01091EN Longbow in the Moonlight Aoi SR 20.00 40.00
BT01091EN Longbow in the Moonlight Aoi RR 10.00 25.00
BT01092EN Going at Dusk Sieghard RR 1.25 3.00
BT01092EN Going at Dusk Sieghard SR 2.00 5.00
BT01093EN Extreme Destruction of Boxes Aoi RR 2.50 6.00
BT01093EN Extreme Destruction of Boxes Aoi SR 3.00 8.00
BT01094EN Mastery of the Air Leap Aoi R .75 2.00
BT01095EN Soaring in Blue Skies Sieghard R .75 2.00
BT01096EN Youth of Sincerity Sieghard R .75 2.00
BT01097EN Full Bodied Sweets Aoi R 1.25 3.00
BT01098EN Lotta of the Sativa R 1.00 2.50
BT01099EN Breakthrough at the Speed of Sound Sieghard U .20 .75
BT01100EN Continuation of Combat Aoi U .20 .75
BT01101EN Eyes of the Skies Sieghard U .20 .75
BT01102EN Wings to the Future Sieghard U .20 .75
BT01103EN Taut Bow Aoi U .20 .75
BT01104EN Busy Morning Aoi U .50 1.25
BT01105EN Lucia of the Swallowblacks U .20 .75
BT01106EN Body Guard Lotta U .75 2.00
BT01107EN Three Steps Ahead Aoi C .10 .30
BT01108EN Tempest of Destruction Aoi C .10 .30
BT01109EN First Flight Sieghard C .10 .30
BT01110EN Buffalo Form Aoi C .10 .30
BT01111EN Bunny Style Aoi C .10 .30
BT01112EN Dress Up Doll Sieghard C .10 .30
BT01113EN Archery Uniform Aoi C .10 .30
BT01114EN Smiling in the Spirit World Lucia C .10 .30
BT01115EN Melchi of Spring Anticipation C .10 .30
BT01116EN Non Standard U .20 .30
BT01117EN Vow to Pass Over Dimensions C .10 .30
BT01118EN Lunatic Burst PxR 3.00 8.00
BT01119EN Tornado Disco PxC .10 .30
BT01120EN Milky Paradise PxC .10 .30
BT01G001EN Chloe Maxwell SCR 30.00 60.00
BT01G002EN Tamaki Yurine SCR 80.00 120.00

2016 Luck and Logic Growth and Genesis Foil

BT01009EN Smile of Satisfaction, Tamaki U .75 2.00
BT01010EN Beyond the Battle Sena U .75 2.00
BT01011EN Summoned by the Ocean Tamaki U 1.00 2.50
BT01012EN Counter Current Shock Tamaki U 1.00 2.50
BT01013EN Permeating Willpower Sena U .75 2.00
BT01014EN Skilled Writing Tamaki U .75 2.00
BT01015EN Personification of Battle Asura U .75 2.00
BT01016EN Incomplete Talent Xiaolin U .75 2.00
BT01017EN Repelling Dragon Scale Tamaki C .40 1.00
BT01018EN Musical Performance Training Tamaki C .40 1.00
BT01019EN Establishing the Target Tamaki C .40 1.00
BT01020EN Monitoring Tamaki C .40 1.00
BT01021EN The Decision to Protect Sena C .40 1.00
BT01022EN In a Hurry Sena C .40 1.00
BT01023EN A Little Relaxation Tamaki C .40 1.00
BT01024EN Working Hard Asura C .40 1.00
BT01025EN Successor Divine Music Otohime C .40 1.00
BT01026EN Speak with My Fists U .75 2.00
BT01027EN Defense Tactics Lecture C .75 2.00
BT01028EN Dragon Cradle PxR 4.00 10.00
BT01029EN Blood Bath Coliseum PxC .40 1.00
BT01030EN Artistic Aquarium PxC .40 1.00
BT01039EN Rapid Fall Mejiko U .75 2.00
BT01040EN Brief Victory Yoshichika U .75 2.00
BT01041EN Flash of Demon Yoshichika U .75 2.00
BT01042EN One Sided Trance Mejiko U .75 2.00
BT01043EN First Trance Yoshichika U .75 2.00
BT01044EN Errands in the Early Afternoon Yoshichika U .75 2.00
BT01045EN Genius Monk of Great Envy Huang Huang U .75 2.00
BT01046EN Fondly Remembering Rasetsu U .75 2.00
BT01047EN Dispelling Secret Technique Yoshichika C .40 1.00
BT01048EN Invisible Sword Stroke Yoshichika C .40 1.00
BT01049EN Rosary of Sorrow Mejiko C .40 1.00
BT01050EN Swordswoman Yoshichika C .40 1.00
BT01051EN Twin Fine Blades Yoshichika C .40 1.00
BT01052EN Girl that Senses the Supernatuarl Mejiko C .40 1.00
BT01053EN Intracerebral Simulation Yoshichika C .40 1.00
BT01054EN Enjoying Life Huang Huang C .40 1.00
BT01055EN Beautiful Master Fencer Hibana C .40 1.00
BT01056EN Unforeseen Summoning U .75 2.00
BT01057EN Fighting Trance C .40 1.00
BT01058EN Age of Civil Wars PxR 2.00 5.00
BT01059EN Mega Heavy Hard Luck PxC .40 1.00
BT01060EN Sword to Sword PxC .40 1.00
BT01069EN Complete Devotion Ashley U .75 2.00
BT01070EN Solid Armor Ashley U .75 2.00
BT01071EN Concentration of Mind Chloe U .75 2.00
BT01072EN Attack from the Trees Chloe U 1.50 4.00
BT01073EN Differing Ideals Ashley U .75 2.00
BT01074EN Full Speed Patrol Chloe U .75 2.00
BT01075EN Strength to Smash Boulders Daiga U .75 2.00
BT01076EN Jade of the Cliffs U .75 2.00
BT01077EN Meal Before Battle Chloe C .40 1.00
BT01078EN Trident Wielder Chloe C .40 1.00
BT01079EN Cautious and Careful Ashley C .40 1.00
BT01080EN Seaside Guard Chloe C .40 1.00
BT01081EN Sprinting Chloe C .40 1.00
BT01082EN Daydreaming Maiden Ashley C .40 1.00
BT01083EN Returning to Supreme Bliss Chloe C .40 1.00
BT01084EN Midday Drink Jade C .40 1.00
BT01085EN Calm Time Fyrill C .75 2.00
BT01086EN Barrier of Shadows U .75 2.00
BT01087EN Goddess of the Waterfront C .40 1.00
BT01088EN Golden Exercise PxR 2.00 5.00
BT01089EN Last Survivor PxC .40 1.00
BT01090EN Slow Wave PxC .40 1.00
BT01099EN Breakthrough at the Speed of Sound Sieghard U .75 2.00
BT01100EN Continuation of Combat Aoi U .75 2.00
BT01101EN Eyes of the Skies Sieghard U .75 2.00
BT01102EN Wings to the Future Sieghard U .75 2.00
BT01103EN Taut Bow Aoi U .75 2.00
BT01104EN Busy Morning Aoi U .75 2.00
BT01105EN Lucia of the Swallowblacks U .75 2.00
BT01106EN Body Guard Lotta U 2.00 5.00
BT01107EN Three Steps Ahead Aoi C .40 1.00
BT01108EN Tempest of Destruction Aoi C .40 1.00
BT01109EN First Flight Sieghard C .40 1.00
BT01110EN Buffalo Form Aoi C .40 1.00
BT01111EN Bunny Style Aoi C .40 1.00
BT01112EN Dress Up Doll Sieghard C .40 1.00
BT01113EN Archery Uniform Aoi C .40 1.00
BT01114EN Smiling in the Spirit World Lucia C .40 1.00
BT01115EN Melchi of Spring Anticipation C .40 1.00
BT01116EN Non Standard U .75 2.00
BT01117EN Vow to Pass Over Dimensions C .40 1.00
BT01118EN Lunatic Burst PxR 4.00 10.00
BT01119EN Tornado Disco PxC .40 1.00
BT01120EN Milky Paradise PxC .40 1.00
BT01G001EN Chloe Maxwell SCR 30.00 60.00
BT01G002EN Tamaki Yurine SCR 80.00 120.00

2016 Luck and Logic Believe and Betray

COMPLETE SET (149 CARDS) 350.00 600.00
BOOSTER BOX (20 PACKS) 60.00 80.00
BOOSTER PACK (7 CARDS) 3.00 5.00
UNLISTED C .15 .25
UNLISTED U .25 .40
UNLISTED R 1.00 2.00
RELEASED ON AUGUST 26TH, 2016
BT02001EN Overtrance of Holy Light Yoshichika RR 2.00 3.00
BT02001EN SP Overtrance of Holy Light Yoshichika SP 10.00 20.00
BT02001EN SR Overtrance of Holy Light Yoshichika SR 3.00 5.00
BT02002EN Pain Pain Go Away Tamaki RR 1.50 3.50
BT02002EN SP Pain Pain Go Away Tamaki SP 20.00 30.00
BT02002EN SR Pain Pain Go Away Tamaki SR 5.00 8.00
BT02003EN Sublime Vow Athena RR 2.00 3.00
BT02003EN SP Sublime Vow Athena SP' 20.00 40.00
BT02003EN SR Sublime Vow Athena SR 5.00 8.00
BT02004EN Fluttering Whip of Love Tamaki R 1.00 2.00
BT02005EN A Hero Once Again Yoshichika R 1.00 2.00
BT02006EN Combination Play Yoshichika R 1.00 2.00
BT02007EN Shield of Fortitude Yoshichika R 1.00 2.00
BT02008EN Built Up Trust Tamaki R 1.00 2.00
BT02009EN Lost Logic Yoshichika R 1.00 2.00
BT02010EN Persuade with Love Venus R 1.00 2.00
BT02011EN Victory Together Tamaki U .20 .35
BT02012EN Repelling Evil Tamaki U .20 2.00
BT02013EN Shield Smash Yoshichika U .20 2.00
BT02014EN Scarlet Whip Coming Apart Tamaki U .20 2.00
BT02015EN Lovely Dress Tamaki U .20 2.00
BT02016EN Proficient Command Yoshichika U .20 2.00
BT02017EN Intervention Obligation Yoshichika U .20 2.00
BT02018EN Rescue Prayer Tamaki U .20 2.00
BT02019EN Talents of a Logicalist Yoshichika U .20 2.00
BT02020EN Under the Cherry Blossoms Athena U .20 2.00
BT02021EN Goddess of Love and Beauty Venus U .20 2.00
BT02022EN Tenacious Fortification Yoshichika C .15 .25
BT02023EN Whos the Next Opponent Tamaki C .15 .25
BT02024EN Mission of a Logicalist Tamaki C .15 .25
BT02025EN Desire to Grow Stronger Yoshichika C .15 .25
BT02026EN Peaceful Day Off Tamaki C .15 .25
BT02027EN Trance Talent Yoshichika C .15 .25
BT02028EN Philanthropism Venus C .15 .25
BT02029EN Power Taken In Athena C .15 .25
BT02030EN Goddess of Wisdom and Strategy Athena C .15 .25
BT02031EN Tears of Joy Athena C .15 .25
BT02032EN Keeper and Center Back U .20 2.00
BT02033EN Reflection C .15 .25
BT02034EN Shioris Welcome C .15 .25
BT02035EN Honey Embrace R 1.00 2.00
BT02036EN Patriot Smash C .15 .25
BT02037EN Quiet Square C .15 .25
BT02038EN Gigantomachia C .15 .25
BT02039EN Binding Snake Venom Yukari RR 1.00 2.00
BT02039EN SP Binding Snake Venom Yukari SP 20.00 30.00
BT02039EN SR Binding Snake Venom Yukari SR 2.00 3.00
BT02040EN Explosive Leader Veronica R 1.00 2.00
BT02040EN SP Explosive Leader Veronica SP 15.00 20.00
BT02041EN Snake That Glares at Frogs Yukari R 1.00 2.00
BT02042EN Heat Detection Yukari R 1.00 2.00
BT02043EN Fueled by Revenge Veronica R 1.00 2.00
BT02044EN Diligent Manager Yukari R 1.00 2.00
BT02045EN Covenant Decree Quetzie R 1.00 2.00
BT02046EN Observing Septpia Nemesis R 1.00 2.00
BT02047EN Opportunity in a Pinch Yukari U .20 2.00
BT02048EN Lure to Minefield Veronica U .20 2.00
BT02049EN Air Transportation Yukari U .20 2.00
BT02050EN Total Elimination Veronica U .20 2.00
BT02051EN Shrine Maiden of the Gods Yukari U .20 2.00
BT02052EN Many Bombs Veronica U .20 2.00
BT02053EN Handmade Choclate Yukari U .20 2.00
BT02054EN Frontline Commander Veronica U .20 2.00
BT02055EN Try Hard Yukari U .20 2.00
BT02056EN Wounded Headstrong Veronica C .15 .25
BT02057EN Burning Sentiments Veronica C .15 .25
BT02058EN You Wont Get Away Yukari C .15 .25
BT02059EN It's a Fight Yukari C .15 .25
BT02060EN Seasoned Warrior Clown Veronica C .15 .25
BT02061EN Precise Support Yukari C .15 .25
BT02062EN Ladylike Day Off Veronica C .15 .25
BT02063EN Director Mobilize Veronica C .15 .25
BT02064EN Thanking for Hard Work Yukari C .15 .25
BT02065EN On a Chopping Board Quetzie C .15 .25
BT02066EN Teaching Nemesis C .15 .25
BT02067EN Snake God Quetzie C .15 .25
BT02068EN Goddess of Anger and Punishment Nemesis C .15 .25
BT02069EN Electric Shock Order U .20 2.00
BT02070EN Three Day Feast C .15 .25
BT02071EN End of Guilty R 1.00 2.00
BT02072EN First Impact C .15 .25
BT02073EN Trick and Torment C .15 .25
BT02074EN Venomous Amphitheater C .15 .25
BT02075EN Arrogant Olga RR 1.00 2.00
BT02075EN SR Arrogant Olga SR 3.00 5.00
BT02076EN A Match for a Thousand Chloe RR 1.00 2.00
BT02076EN SP A Match for a Thousand Chloe SP 8.00 15.00
BT02076EN SR A Match for a Thousand Chloe SR 5.00 8.00
BT02077EN Overtrance of Despair Olga R 1.00 2.00
BT02078EN Eroding Darkness Olga R 1.00 2.00
BT02079EN Going All Out Olga R 1.00 2.00
BT02080EN Saber Dance Chloe R 1.00 2.00
BT02081EN Merry Alliance Olga R 1.00 2.00
BT02082EN Fallen Angel Allure Olga R 1.00 2.00
BT02083EN Race to the Scene Chloe R 1.00 2.00
BT02084EN Paradise Together Lucifer R 1.00 2.00
BT02085EN Despair or Destruction Olga U .20 2.00
BT02086EN Finishing Blow Chloe U .20 2.00
BT02087EN Celebration of Coexistence Olga U .20 2.00
BT02088EN Piercing Faith Chloe U .20 2.00
BT02089EN ALCAS Number One Aggressor Chloe U .20 2.00
BT02090EN Friendship Chocolate Chloe U .20 2.00
BT02091EN Straight Line Chloe U .20 2.00
BT02092EN Infer and Go Valkyrie U .20 2.00
BT02093EN Goddess of War Valkyrie U .20 2.00
BT02094EN Opening the Gates to Other Worlds Lucifer U .20 2.00
BT02095EN Serious Effort Olga C .15 .25
BT02096EN The Battle is Just Beginning Chloe C .15 .25
BT02097EN Overwhelming Strength Olga C .15 .25
BT02098EN Easy as Pie Chloe C .15 .25
BT02099EN Waiting for Her Cue Chloe C .15 .25
BT02100EN Looking for a Covenanter Olga C .15 .25
BT02101EN Checking Out New Stuff Chloe C .15 .25
BT02102EN Independent Training Chloe C .15 .25
BT02103EN Transcendent Field Vision Olga C .15 .25
BT02104EN Ruler of Sept Heaven Lucifer C .15 .25
BT02105EN Close Encounters of the Third Kind Valkyrie C .15 .25
BT02106EN Scornful Sneer Lucifer C .15 .25
BT02107EN Chloes Surprise Plan Filled with Holes U .20 2.00
BT02108EN Gravity Star U .15 .25
BT02109EN Decider Battle R 1.00 2.00
BT02110EN Satans Birthday C .15 .25
BT02111EN Successive Duel C .15 .25
BT02112EN Madness Jail C .15 .25
BT02113EN Released from the Curse Mana RR 3.00 5.00
BT02113EN SR Released from the Curse Mana SR 6.00 10.00
BT02114EN Good Job Mana RR 3.00 5.00
BT02114EN SP Good Job Mana SP 40.00 60.00
BT02114EN SR Good Job Mana SR 8.00 15.00
BT02115EN Paving a Way to the Future Mana R 1.00 2.00
BT02116EN Breaking Out of Her Shell Mana R 1.00 2.00
BT02117EN Dietary Guidance Artemis R 1.00 2.00
BT02118EN Rapid Fire Mana U .20 2.00
BT02119EN Patient Gun Point Mana U .20 2.00
BT02120EN Covenant from the Heart Mana U .20 2.00
BT02121EN Sleeping Smile Artemis U .20 2.00
BT02122EN Bullet from High Altitude Mana C .15 .25
BT02123EN Capable Sniper Mana C .15 .25
BT02124EN Secret Sign Mana C .15 .25
BT02125EN Target in Sight Mana C .15 .25
BT02126EN Staying Smile Mana C .15 .25
BT02127EN Sword of Ice Mana C .15 .25
BT02128EN Supporting Mana Artemis C .15 .25
BT02129EN Ambush Bullet U .20 2.00
BT02130EN Mission Success U .20 2.00
BT02131EN Stardust Archery R 1.00 2.00
BT02132EN Moddy Poetry C .15 .25
BT02G001EN Athena SCR 60.00 100.00
BT02G002EN Yoshichika Tsurugi SCR 60.00 100.00

2016 Luck and Logic Believe and Betray Foil

COMPLETE SET (149 CARDS) 350.00 600.00
BOOSTER BOX (20 PACKS) 60.00 80.00
BOOSTER PACK (7 CARDS) 3.00 5.00
UNLISTED C .30 .50
UNLISTED U .40 .75
UNLISTED R 1.00 2.00
RELEASED ON AUGUST 26TH, 2016
BT02001EN Overtrance of Holy Light Yoshichika RR 2.00 3.00
BT02001EN SP Overtrance of Holy Light Yoshichika SP 10.00 20.00
BT02001EN SR Overtrance of Holy Light Yoshichika SR 3.00 5.00
BT02002EN Pain Pain Go Away Tamaki RR 1.50 2.50
BT02002EN SP Pain Pain Go Away Tamaki SP 20.00 30.00
BT02002EN SR Pain Pain Go Away Tamaki SR 5.00 8.00
BT02003EN Sublime Vow Athena RR 2.00 3.00
BT02003EN SP Sublime Vow Athena SP' 20.00 40.00
BT02003EN SR Sublime Vow Athena SR 5.00 8.00
BT02004EN Fluttering Whip of Love Tamaki R 1.00 2.00
BT02005EN A Hero Once Again Yoshichika R 1.00 2.00
BT02006EN Combination Play Yoshichika R 1.00 2.00
BT02007EN Shield of Fortitude Yoshichika R 1.00 2.00
BT02008EN Built Up Trust Tamaki R 1.00 2.00
BT02009EN Lost Logic Yoshichika R 1.00 2.00
BT02010EN Persuade with Love Venus R 1.00 2.00
BT02011EN Victory Together Tamaki U .40 .75
BT02012EN Repelling Evil Tamaki U .40 .75
BT02013EN Shield Smash Yoshichika U .40 .75
BT02014EN Scarlet Whip Coming Apart Tamaki U .40 .75
BT02015EN Lovely Dress Tamaki U .40 .75
BT02016EN Proficient Command Yoshichika U .40 .75
BT02017EN Intervention Obligation Yoshichika U .40 .75
BT02018EN Rescue Prayer Tamaki U .40 .75
BT02019EN Talents of a Logicalist Yoshichika U .40 .75
BT02020EN Under the Cherry Blossoms Athena U .40 .75
BT02021EN Goddess of Love and Beauty Venus U .40 .75
BT02022EN Tenacious Fortification Yoshichika C .30 .50
BT02023EN Whos the Next Opponent Tamaki C .30 .50
BT02024EN Mission of a Logicalist Tamaki C .30 .50
BT02025EN Desire to Grow Stronger Yoshichika C .30 .50
BT02026EN Peaceful Day Off Tamaki C .30 .50
BT02027EN Trance Talent Yoshichika C .30 .50
BT02028EN Philanthropism Venus C .30 .50
BT02029EN Power Taken In Athena C .30 .50
BT02030EN Goddess of Wisdom and Strategy Athena C .30 .50
BT02031EN Tears of Joy Athena C .30 .50
BT02032EN Keeper and Center Back U .40 .75
BT02033EN Reflection C .30 .50
BT02034EN Shioris Welcome C .30 .50
BT02035EN Honey Embrace R 1.00 2.00
BT02036EN Patriot Smash C .30 .50
BT02037EN Quiet Square C .30 .50
BT02038EN Gigantomachia C .30 .50
BT02039EN Binding Snake Venom Yukari RR 1.00 2.00
BT02039EN SP Binding Snake Venom Yukari SP 20.00 30.00
BT02039EN SR Binding Snake Venom Yukari SR 2.00 3.00
BT02040EN Explosive Leader Veronica R 1.00 2.00
BT02040EN SP Explosive Leader Veronica SP 15.00 20.00
BT02041EN Snake That Glares at Frogs Yukari R 1.00 2.00
BT02042EN Heat Detection Yukari R 1.00 2.00
BT02043EN Fueled by Revenge Veronica R 1.00 2.00
BT02044EN Diligent Manager Yukari R 1.00 2.00
BT02045EN Covenant Decree Quetzie R 1.00 2.00
BT02046EN Observing Septpia Nemesis R 1.00 2.00
BT02047EN Opportunity in a Pinch Yukari U .40 .75
BT02048EN Lure to Minefield Veronica U .40 .75
BT02049EN Air Transportation Yukari U .40 .75
BT02050EN Total Elimination Veronica U .40 .75
BT02051EN Shrine Maiden of the Gods Yukari U .40 .75
BT02052EN Many Bombs Veronica U .40 .75
BT02053EN Handmade Choclate Yukari U .40 .75
BT02054EN Frontline Commander Veronica U .40 .75
BT02055EN Try Hard Yukari U .40 .75
BT02056EN Wounded Headstrong Veronica C .30 .50
BT02057EN Burning Sentiments Veronica C .30 .50
BT02058EN You Wont Get Away Yukari C .30 .50
BT02059EN It's a Fight Yukari C .30 .50
BT02060EN Seasoned Warrior Clown Veronica C .30 .50
BT02061EN Precise Support Yukari C .30 .50
BT02062EN Ladylike Day Off Veronica C .30 .50
BT02063EN Director Mobilize Veronica C .30 .50
BT02064EN Thanking for Hard Work Yukari C .30 .50
BT02065EN On a Chopping Board Quetzie C .30 .50
BT02066EN Teaching Nemesis C .30 .50
BT02067EN Snake God Quetzie C .30 .50
BT02068EN Goddess of Anger and Punishment Nemesis C .30 .50
BT02069EN Electric Shock Order U .40 .75
BT02070EN Three Day Feast C .30 .50
BT02071EN End of Guilty R 1.00 2.00
BT02072EN First Impact C .30 .50
BT02073EN Trick and Torment C .30 .50
BT02074EN Venomous Amphitheater C .30 .50
BT02075EN Arrogant Olga RR 1.00 1.50
BT02075EN SR Arrogant Olga SR 3.00 5.00
BT02076EN A Match for a Thousand Chloe RR 1.00 2.00
BT02076EN SP A Match for a Thousand Chloe SP 10.00 15.00
BT02076EN SR A Match for a Thousand Chloe SR 5.00 8.00
BT02077EN Overtrance of Despair Olga R 1.00 2.00
BT02078EN Eroding Darkness Olga R 1.00 2.00
BT02079EN Going All Out Olga R 1.00 2.00
BT02080EN Saber Dance Chloe R 1.00 2.00
BT02081EN Merry Alliance Olga R 1.00 2.00
BT02082EN Fallen Angel Allure Olga R 1.00 2.00
BT02083EN Race to the Scene Chloe R 1.00 2.00
BT02084EN Paradise Together Lucifer R 1.00 2.00
BT02085EN Despair or Destruction Olga U .40 .75
BT02086EN Finishing Blow Chloe U .40 .75
BT02087EN Celebration of Coexistence Olga U .40 .75
BT02088EN Piercing Faith Chloe U .40 .75
BT02089EN ALCAS Number One Aggressor Chloe U .40 .75
BT02090EN Friendship Chocolate Chloe U .40 .75
BT02091EN Straight Line Chloe U .40 .75
BT02092EN Infer and Go Valkyrie U .40 .75
BT02093EN Goddess of War Valkyrie U .40 .75
BT02094EN Opening the Gates to Other Worlds Lucifer U .40 .75
BT02095EN Serious Effort Olga C .30 .50
BT02096EN The Battle is Just Beginning Chloe C .30 .50
BT02097EN Overwhelming Strength Olga C .30 .50
BT02098EN Easy as Pie Chloe C .30 .50
BT02099EN Waiting for Her Cue Chloe C .30 .50
BT02100EN Looking for a Covenanter Olga C .30 .50
BT02101EN Checking Out New Stuff Chloe C .30 .50
BT02102EN Independent Training Chloe C .30 .50
BT02103EN Transcendent Field Vision Olga C .30 .50
BT02104EN Ruler of Sept Heaven Lucifer C .30 .50
BT02105EN Close Encounters of the Third Kind Valkyrie C .30 .50
BT02106EN Scornful Sneer Lucifer C .30 .50
BT02107EN Chloes Surprise Plan Filled with Holes U .40 .75
BT02108EN Gravity Star U .30 .50
BT02109EN Decider Battle R 1.00 2.00
BT02110EN Satans Birthday C .30 .50
BT02111EN Successive Duel C .30 .50
BT02112EN Madness Jail C .30 .50
BT02113EN Released from the Curse Mana RR 3.00 5.00
BT02113EN SR Released from the Curse Mana SR 6.00 10.00
BT02114EN Good Job Mana RR 3.00 5.00
BT02114EN SP Good Job Mana SP 40.00 60.00
BT02114EN SR Good Job Mana SR 8.00 15.00
BT02115EN Paving a Way to the Future Mana R 1.00 2.00
BT02116EN Breaking Out of Her Shell Mana R 1.00 2.00
BT02117EN Dietary Guidance Artemis R 1.00 2.00
BT02118EN Rapid Fire Mana U .40 .75
BT02119EN Patient Gun Point Mana U .40 .75

BT02120EN Covenant from the Heart Mana U .40 .75
BT02121EN Sleeping Smile Artemis U .40 .75
BT02122EN Bullet from High Altitude Mana C .30 .50
BT02123EN Capable Sniper Mana C .30 .50
BT02124EN Secret Sign Mana C .30 .50
BT02125EN Target in Sight Mana C .30 .50
BT02126EN Staying Smile Mana C .30 .50
BT02127EN Sword of Ice Mana C .30 .50
BT02128EN Supporting Mana Artemis C .30 .50
BT02129EN Ambush Bullet U .40 .75
BT02130EN Mission Success U .40 .75
BT02131EN Stardust Archery R 1.00 2.00
BT02132EN Moddy Poetry C .30 .50
BT02G001EN Athena SCR 60.00 100.00
BT02G002EN Yoshichika Tsurugi SCR 60.00 100.00

2008 Weiss Schwarz Da Capo TD

DCW0104T Akane Hanasaki C
DCW0112T Irreplaceable Allies U
DCW0105T Koko and Nanaka C
DCW0102T Kotori in Casual Clothing U
DCW0109T Koyomi Shirakawa U
DCW0111T Miharu and Nemu U
DCW0119T Miharu's Music Box U
DCW0113T Minatsu, HM-A06 Type C
DCW0103T Miss Kazami Academy Contest U
DCW0118T Nanako and Goat C
DCW0108T Nanako Saitama U
DCW0107T Nanako, Manga Artist R
DCW0114T Nemu in Yukata C
DCW0110T Robot Miharu U
DCW0101T Tamaki Konomiya R
DCW0106T Wedding Ceremony Songstress U
DCW0120T Welcome Back C
DCW0115T Yume in Gymnastics Outfit C
DCW0117T Yume in Pajamas C
DCW0116T Yuzu and Jin C

2008 Weiss Schwarz Da Capo-Da Capo II

DCW01070 A Counter Well Done U
DCW01038 Akana Hanasaki C
DCW01029 Akane in Pajama R
DCW01087 Alice Tsukishiro C
DCW01080 Alice, Holding Philos R
DCW01098 Alice's Wish CR
DCW01045 Allies and Important Person U
DCW01091 Anzu in Swimsuits C
DCW01079 Anzu Yukimura R
DCW01004 Asumi Kiryuu R
DCW01072 Banana Parfait C
DCW01020 Cat-Eared Maid U
DCW01022 Cooking of Asakura Sisters C
DCW01023 Day of Nullified Existence CR
DCW01094 Doll Play U
DCW01073 Dream of a Lost Child CR
DCW01024 Dreams of Magicians CC
DCW01043 Ear Cleaning R
DCW01018 Erase Memory R
DCW01050 For My Important One CC
DCW01096 Group Picture C
DCW01013 Harimao C
DCW01093 Horrible at Horror R
DCW01025 I Must Go CC
DCW01099 I Shall Not Forget CC
DCW01069 Irreplaceable Allies U
DCW01014 Izumiko Murasaki C
DCW01008 Izumiko, Easy Suits U
DCW01035 Junichi Asakura U
DCW01032 Kanae Kudou U
DCW01016 Kasumi Kiryuu C
DCW01041 Koko and Nanaka C
DCW01027 Koko in New Year Outfit RR
DCW01030 Koko Tsukishima R
DCW01030R Koko Tsukishima RRR
DCW01036 Kotori in Casual Outfit U
DCW01031 Kotori, School Idol R
DCW01058 Koyomi Shirakawa U
DCW01039 Kudou in School Uniform C
DCW01061 Maika Mizukoshi U
DCW01089 Mako and Moe C
DCW01077 Mako Mizukoshi RR
DCW01088 Mako, Music Club C
DCW01085 Maya Sawai U
DCW01078 Mayuki Kousaka R
DCW01053 Miharu Amakase R
DCW01060 Miharu and Nemu U
DCW01074 Miharu's Music Box CC
DCW01033 Mii-Kun and Tomo-Chan U
DCW01086 Minatsu and Anzu and Koko U
DCW01081 Minatsu and Maya R
DCW01081R Minatsu and Maya RRR
DCW01068 Minatsu Awakens R
DCW01063 Minatsu, HM-A06 Type C
DCW01054 Minatu in Y-Shirt R
DCW01007 Misaki Sagisawa U
DCW01044 Miss Kazami Academy Contest U
DCW01076 Moe Mizukoshi RR
DCW01062 Myu C
DCW01026 Nanaka in New Year Outfit RR
DCW01034 Nanaka in Ski Wear U
DCW01071 Nanako and Goat C
DCW01057 Nanako Saitama U
DCW01055 Nanako, Manga Artist R
DCW01003 Nemu and Sakura R
DCW01052 Nemu and Yume, Homemade Bento Boxes RR
DCW01056 Nemu Asakura R
DCW01056R Nemu Asakura RRR
DCW01064 Nemu in Yukata C
DCW01046 Nemu's Bento Box C
DCW01082 Officer Bridge Yagi U
DCW01002 Otome Asakura RR
DCW01010 Otome in Miko Outfit U
DCW01017 Otome, Talented and Pretty Student Council President C
DCW01048 Passing Warmth CR
DCW01097 Private Lesson C
DCW01100 Quality of Memories CC
DCW01019 Resolution U
DCW01059 Robot Miharu U
DCW01011 Sakura in Swimsuits U
DCW01015 Sakura Yoshino C
DCW01001 Sakura, School President RR
DCW01083 Seba U
DCW01092 Sleepy Moe C
DCW01084 Suginami U
DCW01090 Suginami, Unofficial News Club C
DCW01028 Tamaki Konomiya R
DCW01042 Tamaki, Ideal Japanese Woman C
DCW01021 The Person inside the Mascot C
DCW01047 Transfer Student C
DCW01040 Trio Girls Known as "Snow, Moon and Flower" C
DCW01012 Utamaru C
DCW01037 Wataru Itabashi C
DCW01049 Wedding Ceremony Songstress CC
DCW01075 Welcome Back CC
DCW01095 Xylophone Fortune Reading U
DCW01005 Yoriko Sagisawa R
DCW01009 Yoshiyuki Sakurai U
DCW01006 Yume and Otome R
DCW01006R Yume and Otome RRR
DCW01051 Yume in Good Spirits RR
DCW01065 Yume in Gymnastic Clothing C
DCW01067 Yume in Pajama C
DCW01066 Yuzu and Shin C
DCW01023S Day of Nullified Existence SP
DCW01048S Passing Warmth SP
DCW01073S Dream of a Lost Child SP
DCW01099S I Shall Not Forget SP

2008 Weiss Schwarz Da Capo-Da Capo II Extra

DCW01E16 Alice in Swimsuits R
DCW01E15 Anzu, Little Devil R
DCW01E14 Bath with Cat C
DCW01E04 Izumiko in Swimsuits C
DCW01E07 Koko in Swimsuits C
DCW01E06 Kotori in Swimsuits R
DCW01E17 Maya in Swimsuits C
DCW01E12 Miharu in Swimsuits C
DCW01E08 Nanaka & Yume in Swimsuits C
DCW01E05 Nanaka in Swimsuits R
DCW01E02 Nemu & Sakura in Swimsuits C
DCW01E11 Nemu in Swimsuits R
DCW01E01 Otome in Swimsuits R
DCW01E18 Playing in the Creek! C
DCW01E09 Tamaki in Swimsuits C
DCW01E10 Watermelon Smashing C
DCW01E03 Yume & Sakura in Swimsuits C
DCW01E13 Yume in Swimsuits C

2008 Weiss Schwarz Disgaea

DGS02075 A Passing-by Overlord CC
DGS02039 Adele and Rosalind C
DGS02078 Almaz von Almadin Adamant R
DGS02025 And Then, Legend CC
DGS02032 Angel Trainee Flonne U
DGS02050 Assassin from Celestia CC
DGS02033 Average Cleric U
DGS02013 Bad Student Raspberyl C
DGS02017 Battle Otaku Adele C
DGS02022 Battle Tournament Commences C
DGS02060 Beauty Baron Mid-Boss U
DGS02023 Believe in Me CR
DGS02066 Captain Gordon, Defender of Earth C
DGS02095 Cellphone U
DGS02004 Childhood Friend Raspberyl R
DGS02004S Childhood Friend Raspberyl SR
DGS02003 Crane-Folding Asuka R
DGS02071 Dark Assembly U
DGS02097 Dark Hero C
DGS02091 Dark Hero Octalley C
DGS02086 Daughter of the Overlord Roselind U
DGS02019 Defeat Overlord God R
DGS02068 Demon Girl Etna, the Ultimate Beauty C
DGS02005 Devil Buster Adele R
DGS02005S Devil Buster Adele SR
DGS02069 Dissection Experiment R
DGS02041 Distinguished Samurai C
DGS02064 Elite Red Mage C
DGS02035 Etna and Flonne U
DGS02062 Etna, the Overlord Assassin C
DGS02049 Even A Demon Needs Love CC
DGS02044 Everything is Mine R
DGS02009 Excellent Salvatore U
DGS02057 Fake Laharl U
DGS02002 Fallen Angel Flonne RR
DGS02093 Family Studies Teacher Mr Champloo C
DGS02054 Former Angel Flonne R
DGS02054S Former Angel Flonne SR
DGS02039 Genius Rune Knight C
DGS02042 Good-for-Nothing Archer C
DGS02090 Hero Almaz C
DGS02021 Important Allies? U
DGS02065 Invincible Robot Thursday C
DGS02067 Jennifer, Assistant to the Defender of Earth C
DGS02016 Jiiya C
DGS02081 Killing Machine Sapphire R
DGS02074 King of the Earth CC
DGS02084 Kunoichi Yukimaru U
DGS02056 Kurtis, Defender of Earth R
DGS02030 Laharl and Etna R
DGS02030S Laharl and Etna SR
DGS02037 Laharl and Flonne C
DGS02051 Laharl and Maoh RR
DGS02051R Laharl and Maoh RRR
DGS02010 Legendary Graduating Raspberyl U
DGS02024 Let's Modify CC
DGS02008 Lilian's Crazy Kid U
DGS02036 Love Maniac Flonne U
DGS02015 Majin Etna C
DGS02072 Make up C
DGS02012 Maoh and Raspberyl C
DGS02029 Matron Prinny R
DGS02070 Mecha-Jennifer U
DGS02053 Mr Big Star R
DGS02007 Netherworld's Top Student Maoh U
DGS02098 Newlywed Queen CR
DGS02100 Overlord Almaz CC
DGS02011 Overlord Laharl U
DGS02006 Overlord Maoh R
DGS02099 Overlord Summoning CC
DGS02073 Overlord Zenon Defeated CR
DGS02055 Overlord's Vassal Etna R
DGS02055S Overlord's Vassal Etna SR
DGS02034 Petty Thief U
DGS02094 Pile of Pudding R
DGS02046 Plot of the Education Council U
DGS02059 Prince Laharl of the Netherworld U
DGS02038 Prinny Squad C
DGS02079 Push-and-Dash Octalley R
DGS02001 Raspberyl and Flonne RR
DGS02001R Raspberyl and Flonne RRR
DGS02076 Raspberyl and Sapphire RR
DGS02076S Raspberyl and Sapphire SR
DGS02047 Revival of the Bow C
DGS02085R Roselind and Sapphire RRR
DGS02085 Roselind and Sapphire U
DGS02089 Roselind's Vassal Taro C
DGS02077 Sapphire Rhodonite RR
DGS02077S Sapphire Rhodonite SR
DGS02043 Seraph Lamington C
DGS02014 Sexy Demon Wannabe Hanako C
DGS02088 Sheltered Miss Roselind C
DGS02082 Stealthy Teacher Mr Champloo U
DGS02080 Strange Frog Tink R
DGS02063 Strongest in the Word Etna C
DGS02083 Stubborn Rosalind U
DGS02092 Super Hero Ouram C
DGS02031 Super Overlord Baal R
DGS02048 Super Overlord Bishoujo CR
DGS02061 Supreme Overlord Laharl U
DGS02096 Technical Difficulties U
DGS02020 The Strongest Overlord U
DGS02027 Tyrant Etna RR
DGS02027R Tyrant Etna RRR
DGS02026 Unemployed Etna RR
DGS02026S Unemployed Etna SR
DGS02040 Universe Police Justice Flonne C
DGS02087 Un-ladylike Princess Sapphire C
DGS02058 Vyers, the Dark Adonis Mid-Boss U
DGS02045 Winged Slayer U
DGS02052 Worst Overlord Laharl RR
DGS02028 Young Etna R
DGS0225SP And Then, Legend SP
DGS0248SP Super Overlord Bishoujo SP
DGS0275SP A Passing-by Overlord SP
DGS0296SP Newlywed Queen SP

2008 Weiss Schwarz Disgaea TD

DGS02T09 Assassin from Celestia
DGS02T03 Average Cleric
DGS02T16 Beauty Baron Mid-Boss
DGS02T14 Captain Gordon, Defender of Earth
DGS02T15 Demon Girl Etna, the Ultimate Beauty
DGS02T07 Etna and Flonne
DGS02T10 Etna, the Overlord Assassin
DGS02T04 Genius Rune Knight
DGS02T06 Good-for-Nothing Archer
DGS02T18 King of the Earth
DGS02T01 Laharl and Flonne
DGS02103 Overlord Laharl and his Vassal Etna
DGS02T13 Prince Laharl of the Netherworld
DGS02T02 Prinny Squad
DGS02104 Raspberyl and Sapphire All Ready for Gym
DGS02T08 Revival of the Bow
DGS02T12 Super Robot Thursday
DGS02T17 Supreme Overlord Laharl
DGS02T05 Universe Police Justice Flonne
DGS02T11 Vyers, the Dark Adonis Mid-Boss

2008 Weiss Schwarz Fate/stay Night

FSS03005 Ally of Justice Shirou R
FSS03005S Ally of Justice Shirou SR
FSS03054 Archer, Clumsy Yet Loyal R
FSS03059 Archer, Iron-Wrought Spirit U
FSS03064 Archer, Red Knight C
FSS03007 Ayako Mitsuzuri U
FSS03042 Azure Wind Lancer C
FSS03049 Bellerophon CC
FSS03090 Caster, Sorceress of Betrayal C
FSS03083 Caster, Sorceress of the Ages U
FSS03098 Caster's Wish CR
FSS03080 Cruel Tiny One Illya R
FSS03080S Cruel Tiny One Illya SR
FSS03052 Darkened Holy Sword Saber RR
FSS03024 Excalibur CC
FSS03056 Faker Archer R
FSS03099 Forest of Winter CC
FSS03021 Funny Lion U
FSS03047 Gae Bolg C
FSS03093 Ganryuu, Nameless Koujirou C
FSS03019 Gate of Babylon R
FSS03072 Gem MAgic C
FSS03071 Gem Sword Zelretch U
FSS03010 Gilgamesh, Golden Hero King U
FSS03004 Gilgamesh, Oldest King R
FSS03004S Gilgamesh, Oldest King SR
FSS03023 Golden Farewell CR
FSS03094 Good Friends Trio R
FSS03084 Hassan-i-Sabah U
FSS03050 Heaven's Feel CC
FSS03044 Hug of Sisters R
FSS03008 Hungry Ones U
FSS03086 Illya and Berserker U
FSS03016 Illya and Shirou C
FSS03095 Illya, Dancing in the Snow U
FSS03077 Illya, Tiny Holy Grail RR
FSS03078 Illyasviel von Einzbern R
FSS03078R Illyasviel von Einzbern RRR
FSS03025 Infinite Sword Creation/Unlimited Blade Works CC
FSS03017 Instructor Fuji C
FSS03014 Issei Ryuudou C
FSS03100 Justeaze, Saint of Winter CC
FSS03088 Kaede Makidera C
FSS03089 Kane Himuro C
FSS03085 Kirei and Gilgamesh U
FSS03082 Kirei Kotomine, Executer U
FSS03076 Kirei, Game Master RR
FSS03011 Kiritsugu Emiya U
FSS03091 Koujirou Sasaki C
FSS03036 Lancer, Lethal Crimson Lance U
FSS03027 Legendary Hero Berserker RR
FSS03040 Leysritt C
FSS03034 Luviagelita Edelfelt U
FSS03097 Mapo Tofu C
FSS03026 Master Sakura RR
FSS03075 Mischievous Smile CC
FSS03045 Mystic Eye: Cybele U
FSS03087 No 1 Pupil C
FSS03038 Peaceful Days Rider C
FSS03096 Rain of Light Shots U
FSS03069 Rho Aias R
FSS03057 Rider and Shinji U
FSS03029 Rider, Battle Ready R
FSS03029S Rider, Battle Ready SR
FSS03033 Rider, Swift Cavalry U
FSS03043 Rider, Youngest Daughter of Gorgon C
FSS03061 Rin and Archer U
FSS03067 Rin and Saber C
FSS03058 Rin and Shirou U
FSS03053 Rin in Pajama R
FSS03053S Rin in Pajama SR
FSS03063 Rin Tohsaka C
FSS03060 Rin, Average One U
FSS03065 Rin, Bloodline of Gem Magic C
FSS03055 Rin, Gandr Shooter R
FSS03055R Rin, Gandr Shooter RRR
FSS03062 Rin, Red Devil C
FSS03066 Saber Alter C
FSS03018 Saber, Bearer of Holy Sword C
FSS03015 Saber, Best Heroic Spirit C
FSS03012 Saber, Fresh out of the Bath C
FSS03009 Saber, Invisible Sword U
FSS03002 Saber, King of Knights RR
FSS03002R Saber, King of Knights RRR
FSS03003 Saber, Monster Instructor R
FSS03037 Sakura and Rider C
FSS03051 Sakura in Black RR
FSS03051S Sakura in Black SR
FSS03028 Sakura Matou R
FSS03028R Sakura Matou RRR
FSS03068 Sakura, Black Holy Grail C
FSS03048 Sakura, Happy? CR
FSS03041 Sakura, Laudable Girl C
FSS03031 Sakura, Opened Heart R
FSS03031S Sakura, Opened Heart SR
FSS03032 Sakuram, Successor of Matou U
FSS03046 Sakura's Care U
FSS03035 Sella and Leys U
FSS03039 Sella C
FSS03006 Shirou and Saber R
FSS03001 Shirou Emiya RR
FSS03022 Shirou VS Gilgamesh C
FSS03081 Souichirou and Caster R
FSS03081S Souichirou and Caster SR
FSS03092 Souichirou Kuzuki C
FSS03020 Summon Saber U
FSS03013 Taiga Fujimura C
FSS03073 Unlimited Blade Works CR
FSS03070 Violent Summon U
FSS03074 Words of Warewell CC
FSS03030 Worst Enemy Berserker R
FSS03079 Yukika Saegusa R
FSS0323SP Golden Farewell SP
FSS0346SP Sakura, Happy? SP
FSS0375SP Mischievous Smile SP
FSS0398SP Caster's Wish SP

2008 Weiss Schwarz Fate/stay Night TD

FSS03T15 Archer, Iron-Wrought Spirit
FSS03T11 Archer, Red Knight
FSS03T16 Blackened Holy Grail Sakura
FSS03103 Freeloaders of the Emiya Household
FSS03T09 Funny Lion
FSS03T05 Gilgamesh, Golden Hero King
FSS03T14 Jewel-Magic Bloodline Rin
FSS03T06 Master Fuji
FSS03T18 Mischievous Smile
FSS03T02 Mitsuzuri Ayako
FSS03T12 Rin, Red Devil
FSS03T03 Ryuudou Issei
FSS03T01 Saber After a Bath
FSS03102 Saber and Sakura in Swimsuits
FSS03T07 Saber, Bearer of the Sacred Sword
FSS03T04 Saber, Most Skilled Spirit
FSS03T08 Summon Saber
FSS03T10 The Sword of Promised Victory
FSS03T13 Tohsaka Rin
FSS03T17 Words of Farewell

2008 Weiss Schwarz Little Busters

LBW02087 3 Sisters Kud C
LBW02071 A Crimson Red Wristband C
LBW02048 A Singular Merit CR
LBW02093 American Pasttime R
LBW02041 Apron Haruka C
LBW02046 Black White C
LBW02096 Bright Panties C
LBW02006 Bunny Girl Yuiko R
LBW02027 Costumed Mascot Kud RR
LBW02098 Critical Point CR
LBW02023 Days Together with Rin CR
LBW02064 Detective Yuiko C
LBW02092 Dressed Up Komari C
LBW02072 Ear Cleaning C
LBW02076 Fairy Tale Girl Komari RR
LBW02074 For Some Point in the Future CC
LBW02017 Godly Poor Control Rin C
LBW02095 Hands Full of Books U
LBW02061 Haruka and Kanata U
LBW02063 Haruka and Mio C
LBW02059 Haruka in Summer Outfit U
LBW02031 Haruka Saigusa R
LBW02049 Humming of the Breeze CC
LBW02050 Hypocrite Acting Like the Top Student CC
LBW02020 I'll Wash Your Back- U
LBW02019 Into the Dream U
LBW02052 Investigator Haruka RR
LBW02021 It's A Gold Game C
LBW02058 Kanata Futaki U
LBW02080 Kengo Miyazawa R
LBW02033 Kojirou Kamikita U
LBW02012 Komari Kamikita C
LBW02038 Kud and Kanata C
LBW02083 Kud and Komari U
LBW02030 Kud and Sasami R
LBW02040 Kud and Strelka C
LBW02088 Kud in Wonderland C
LBW02086 Kudryavka Anatolyevna Strugatskaya U
LBW02037 Kudryavka Noumi C
LBW02016 Kyousuke and Rin C
LBW02084 Kyousuke Natsume U
LBW02004 Leader Kyousuke R
LBW02067 Literature Girl Mio C
LBW02073 Little Busters CR
LBW02081 Little Devil Girl Midori R
LBW02045 Loves Cleaning U
LBW02091 Manager Mio C
LBW02035 Masato and Kengo U
LBW02013 Masato Inohara C
LBW02029 Mascot Kud R
LBW02085 Mask the Saitou U
LBW02060 Midori Nishizono U
LBW02089 Mio and Midori C
LBW02053 Mio Nishizono R
LBW02053R Mio Nishizono RRR
LBW02068 Mirror mirror R
LBW02078 Miyuki Kokishi R
LBW02034 Moral Guard Kanata U
LBW02065 Muscle Idiot Masato C
LBW02082 Mysteric Blue Mio U
LBW02054 Natsume and Naoe R
LBW02077 Natural Material Mio RR
LBW02043 New Challenger R
LBW02003 Noble Kitten Rin R
LBW02003R Noble Kitten Rin RRR
LBW02062 Noisy Maiden Haruka C
LBW02039 Normal Young Man Riki C
LBW02005 Nurse Outfit Komari R
LBW02025 Observation with Just the Two of Us CC
LBW02079 Pleasantly Cute Komari R
LBW02079R Pleasantly Cute Komari RRR
LBW02036 Pony Girl Rin U
LBW02097 Proof of Friendship C
LBW02040 Queen Cat Sasami C
LBW02015 Queen of Heart in Tender Care Yuiko C
LBW02057 Red Riding Hood Mio U
LBW02024 Return of the Leader CC
LBW02055 Riki Naoe R
LBW02014 Rin and Komari C
LBW02002 Rin and Riki RR
LBW02010 Rin and Sasami U
LBW02028 Rin Natsume R
LBW02028R Rin Natsume RRR
LBW02099 Ritual in the Middle of the Night CC
LBW02094 Royal Princess Parfait U
LBW02001 Sasami Sasasegawa RR
LBW02018 Secret Weapon of the Cat Trainer R
LBW02022 Sharing An Umbrella C
LBW02056 Sisterly Yuiko R
LBW02069 Sleep by Sunburn U
LBW02011 Snack Loving Komari U
LBW02008 Softball Club Trio U
LBW02051 Splendid Sword Saint Yuiko RR
LBW02044 State of Emergency U
LBW02042 Strongest Kid Kengo C
LBW02047 Study Group C
LBW02026 Surrounded by Cats Rin RR
LBW02075 Things Entrusted CC
LBW02032 Trouble Maker Haruka U
LBW02100 Two Long Shadows CC
LBW02070 Unreal Situation U
LBW02009 Wedding Dress Rin U
LBW02066 Yuiko and Haruko C
LBW02007 Yuiko Kurugaya U
LBW02025S Observation with Just the Two of Us SP
LBW02048S A Singular Merit SP
LBW02074S For Some Point in the Future SP
LBW02099S Ritual in the Middle of the Night SP

2008 Weiss Schwarz Little Busters Ecstasy

LBW06090 A-chan Senpai C
LBW06001 Ace Batting 4th Sasami RR
LBW06001R Ace Batting 4th Sasami RRR
LBW06057 Advisor Riki U
LBW06091 Away from this Life Mio C
LBW06012 Beautiful Handling Yuiko C
LBW06009 Best Friends Rin and Komari U
LBW06023 Best Place CR
LBW06050 Best Shot CC
LBW06062 Big Sister Kanata C
LBW06071 Busy Kanata U
LBW06008 Cat Dash Rin U
LBW06035 Cheerfully Noisy Haruka U
LBW06059 Cool and Playful Yuiko U
LBW06003 Costumed Mascot Sasami R
LBW06058 Cyber? Mio U
LBW06034 Dog Lover Sasami U
LBW06043 Eager and Impatient Kud C
LBW06067 Eager Muscle Masato C
LBW06056 Ecstasy Mode Saya R
LBW06044 Empty Dinner R
LBW06045 End of Tears U
LBW06074 Escape CC
LBW06072 Everything Is within A Dream C
LBW06053 Excellent Spy? Saya R
LBW06048 Farewell CR
LBW06037 Favorite Things Rin C
LBW06022 Fish Observation C
LBW06075 Fleeting Existence CC
LBW06064 Good Sisters Haruka and Kanata C
LBW06086 Happy Spiral Komari U
LBW06073 Hard-Working Chairman CR
LBW06028 Haruka in Casual Clothing R
LBW06051 Haruka, Water Shot RR
LBW06051S Haruka, Water Shot SR
LBW06069 Important Thing R
LBW06095 Incredible Deja Vu U
LBW06033 International Kud U
LBW06099 It'll Be Okay CC
LBW06004 Jun Tokikaze R
LBW06038 Kanata in Yukata C
LBW06052 Kanata, Dispelled RR
LBW06052R Kanata, Dispelled RRR
LBW06036 Kanata, Holding Hands U
LBW06054 Kanata, Untrue to Herself R
LBW06039 Kengo in Uniform C
LBW06083 Kengo, Wounded Huge Rookie U
LBW06006 Komari in Casual Clothing R
LBW06076 Komari, Thoughts Entrusting RR
LBW06076S Komari, Thoughts Entrusting SR
LBW06046 Kuro's Wish U
LBW06030 Lonely Sasami R
LBW06030R Lonely Sasami RRR
LBW06029 Love-Hate Kanata R
LBW06029S Love-Hate Kanata SR
LBW06007 Masato Inohara U
LBW06077 Mio and Midori in Swimsuits RR
LBW06077R Mio and Midori in Swimsuits RRR
LBW06081 Mio in Maid Uniform R
LBW06068 Mio in the Sunlight C
LBW06055 Mio, Resting in the Tree Shades R
LBW06055S Mio, Resting in the Tree Shades SR
LBW06041 Miss Working Hard Kud C
LBW06092 Miyuki of the Archery Club C
LBW06016 Mood-Maker Komari C
LBW06047 Moving C
LBW06013 Operation Meeting Kyousuke C
LBW06084 Perfect Invincible Girl Saya U
LBW06025 Piano that Kepy Playing CC
LBW06094 Promise by the Lake R
LBW06019 Protected Place R
LBW06085 Quarter Girl Kud U
LBW06096 Rest U
LBW06078 Returning Child Kud R
LBW06078S Returning Child Kud SR
LBW06079 Riki and Kyousuke, Saddened by Farewell R
LBW06017 Riki and Masato, Roommates C
LBW06049 Riki, I'm Home CC
LBW06031 Rin and Dorj R
LBW06015 Rin with Resolution C
LBW06002 Rin, Doing Her Best RR
LBW06002S Rin, Doing Her Best SR
LBW06026 Rin, Threatening RR
LBW06026S Rin, Threatening SR
LBW06089 Rising Stock Komari C
LBW06040 Sasami, Prodeful C
LBW06070 Saya, Caught U
LBW06087 Saya, Clumsy Spy C
LBW06080 Saya, Standing Ready R
LBW06088 Secret Orders Kyousuke C
LBW06018 Self-Righteous Sasami C
LBW06063 Sexy Role Yuiko C
LBW06082 Shadowless Girl Midori U
LBW06005 Sister Yuiko R
LBW06005S Sister Yuiko SR
LBW06042 Sisters Being Compared Haruka and Kanata C
LBW06065 Skillful Spy Saya C
LBW06021 Slowly Breaking Heart U
LBW06010 Strongest Rivals Rin and Sasami U
LBW06061 Strongest Woman Yuiko U
LBW06060 Talkative Haruka U
LBW06097 The Answer Finally Reached C
LBW06020 The One Waited on Is Yet to Come U
LBW06100 Trap on the Rooftop CC
LBW06024 Trial from Older Brother CC
LBW06066 Troublesome Girl Haruka C
LBW06098 We Are Little Busters CR
LBW06093 Western-Eastern Compromise Kud C
LBW06014 Wishing Star Komari C
LBW06032 Women's Uniform Riki U
LBW06027 Worrisome Haruka RR
LBW06011 Yuiko in Maid Uniform U
LBW0605SP Sister Yuiko SP
LBW0623SP Best Place SP
LBW0653SP Excellent Spy? Saya SP
LBW0656SP Ecstasy Mode Saya SP

2008 Weiss Schwarz Little Busters TD

LBW02T20 2 Long Shadows C
LBW02T17 3 Sisters Kud C
LBW02T12 American Pastime R
LBW02T08 Apron Haruka C
LBW02T19 Dress Up Komari C
LBW02T10 Humming of the Breeze U
LBW02T11 Hypocrite Acting Like the Top Student C
LBW02T02 Kojirou Kamikita U
LBW02T14 Kud and Komari U
LBW02T05 Kudryavka Noumi C
LBW02T15 Kyousuke Natsume U
LBW02T01 Mascot Kud R
LBW02T18 Mio and Midori C
LBW02T13 Mysteric Blue Mio U
LBW02T06 Normal Young Man Riki C
LBW02T03 Pony Girl Rin U
LBW02T07 Queen Cat Sasami C
LBW02T16 Royal Princess Parfait U
LBW02T04 State of Emergency U
LBW02T09 Strongest Kid Kengo C

2008 Weiss Schwarz Nanoha StrikerS

NSW04021 A Little Improvement U
NSW04075 A Promise with Mama CC
NSW04052 Ace of Aces Nanoha RR
NSW04052R Ace of Aces Nanoha RRR
NSW04058 Agito, Sword Spirit of Fire U
NSW04083 Alto and Lucino, Communications U
NSW04012 Amy, Mother of Two C
NSW04007 Arf, Familiar U
NSW04076 Blessed Wing Reinforce II RR
NSW04076S Blessed Wing Reinforce II SR
NSW04094 Can You Help Me? R
NSW04079 Carim Gracia R
NSW04005 Caro and Friedrich R
NSW04011 Caro and Voltaire U
NSW04001 Caro Ru Lushe RR
NSW04001S Caro Ru Lushe SR
NSW04004 Caro, Dragon Summoner R
NSW04016 Chrono, Captain of Claudia C
NSW04033 Cinque, Bomber of Dancing Blades U
NSW04039 Dieci, Sniping Bomber C
NSW04049 Divine Buster CC
NSW04045 Doing Whatever I Want? U
NSW04024 Dragon Knight Summoning CC
NSW04062 Due, Fake Appearance Secret Agent C
NSW04019 Early Morning Training R
NSW04018 Erio and Caro C
NSW04008 Erio Mondial U
NSW04003 Erio, Lance Knight Initiate R
NSW04022 Failed Landing C
NSW04013 Fate and Arf C
NSW04009 Fate, Golden Flash U
NSW04025 Fire Dragon Flash CC
NSW04020 F's Legacy U
NSW04032 Genya Nakajima U
NSW04074 Getting Out- CC
NSW04031 Ginga Nakajima R
NSW04089 Griffith Lowran C
NSW04080 Guardian Knight Shamal and Guardian Beast Zafira R
NSW04077 Hayate and Rein RR
NSW04077S Hayate and Rein SR
NSW04088 Hayate Yagami C
NSW04081 Hayate, Lord of the Last Dark Sky R
NSW04081R Hayate, Lord of the Last Dark Sky RRR
NSW04023 Hesitate No Longer CR
NSW04098 Hraesvelgr CR
NSW04044 I Don't Want to Be Alone R
NSW04050 I Have Come to Help CC
NSW04091 Inspector Verossa C
NSW04047 Just Like Practice C
NSW04087 Laguna Granscenic C
NSW04048 Last Simulation Battle CR
NSW04100 Limit Release CC
NSW04015 Lindy, Officer of General Affairs C
NSW04029 Lutecia Alpine R
NSW04042 Lutecia and Hakutenou C
NSW04072 Mama, Good Child C
NSW04037 Mariel, Mechanic Maester C
NSW04006 Nanoha and Fate R
NSW04006R Nanoha and Fate RRR
NSW04035 Nanoha and Subaru U
NSW04067 Nanoha and Vita C
NSW04066 Nanoha and Vivio C
NSW04060 Nanoha Takamachi U
NSW04064 Nanoha, Battle Techniques Instructor C
NSW04043 Nove and Wendi C
NSW04040 Otto and Deed C
NSW04095 Pledge of Alto U
NSW04097 Prophetinschriften C
NSW04054 Quattro, Illusionist R
NSW04084 Reinforce II U
NSW04055 Scaglietti, Dimensional Criminal R
NSW04092 Schach Nouera C
NSW04063 Sein, Deep Cover Spy C
NSW04078 Shamal, Hand of the Healing Wind R
NSW04082 Shario, Mechanic Designer U
NSW04017 Signum and Rein C
NSW04010 Signum, Flame General U
NSW04014 Signum, Vice Captain C
NSW04070 Silver Curtain U
NSW04093 Sister Schach C
NSW04090 Sniper Vice C
NSW04096 Something to Protect U
NSW04073 Starlight Breaker CR
NSW04041 Subaru and Ginga, Calibers C
NSW04036R Subaru and Teana RRR
NSW04036 Subaru and Teana U
NSW04028 Subaru Nakajima R
NSW04027 Subaru, Front Attacker RR
NSW04027S Subaru, Front Attacker SR
NSW04038 Teana Lanster C
NSW04026 Teana, Center Guard RR
NSW04026S Teana, Center Guard SR
NSW04065 Tre and Sette C
NSW04002 True Sonic Form Fate RR
NSW04002S True Sonic Form Fate SR
NSW04099 Unbreakable Things CC
NSW04071 Unisoning U
NSW04030 Uno, Scaglietti's Secretary R
NSW04086 Verossa and Schach U
NSW04057 Vita, Battle Instructor U
NSW04056 Vita, Knight of the Iron Hammer R
NSW04056S Vita, Knight of the Iron Hammer SR
NSW04051 Vivio RR
NSW04051S Vivio SR
NSW04053 Vivio Takamachi R
NSW04061 Vivio, Saint King U
NSW04069 Wide Area Search R
NSW04046 Wing Road U
NSW04034 Yuuno, Chief Librarian of Infinite Library U
NSW04085 Zafira, Fiierce Guardian Beast U
NSW04068 Zest Grangaitz C
NSW04059 Zest, Wandering Knight U
NSW0424SP Dragon Knight Summoning SP
NSW0449SP Divine Buster SP
NSW0473SP Starlight Breaker SP
NSW0498SP Hraesvelgr SP

2008 Weiss Schwarz Nanoha StrikerS TD

NSW04T18 A Promise with Mama
NSW04T11 Agito, Sword Spirit of Fire
NSW04T01 Arf, Familiar
NSW04T06 Erio & Caro
NSW04T04 Erio Mondial
NSW04T08 Failed Landing
NSW04T02 Fate & Arf
NSW04T05 Fate, Golden Flash
NSW04T09 Fire Dragon Flash
NSW04T17 Mama, Good Child
NSW04T102 Mother of Two
NSW04T101 Nanoha & Fate & Hayate
NSW04T15 Nanoha & Vita
NSW04T13 Nanoha & Vivio
NSW04T12 Nanoha, Battle Techniques Instructor
NSW04T07 Signum, Flame General
NSW04T03 Signum, Vice Captain
NSW04T10 Vita, Battle Instructor
NSW04T16 Zest Grangaitz
NSW04T14 Zest, Wandering Knight

2008 Weiss Schwarz Persona 3

P3S01036 Aigis and Athena U
P3S01035 Aigis in Dress U
P3S01029 Aigis R
P3S01027 Aigisand Palladion RR
P3S01056 Akihiko and Caesar R
P3S01056R Akihiko and Caesar RRR
P3S01067 Akihiko and Polydeuces C
P3S01052 Akihiko Sanada RR
P3S01014 Akinari Kamiki C
P3S01005 Amada and Kala-Nemi R
P3S01016 Amada and Nemisis C
P3S01044 Analyze U
P3S01070 Armageddon U
P3S01013 Bebe C
P3S01096 Blue-Beard Pharmacy C
P3S01037 Bunkichi and Mitsuko C
P3S01065 Chidori and Medea C
P3S01051 Chidori RR
P3S01087 Chihiro Fushimi C
P3S01019 Dark Hour U
P3S01069 DEATH U
P3S01047 Dreams of Aigis C
P3S01082 Eiichirou Takeba U
P3S01077 Elizabeth RR
P3S01024 End of Revenge CC
P3S01095 Execution U
P3S01100 Father's Last Wishes CC
P3S01020 Featherman R, Phoenix Sentai U
P3S01030 Fuuka and Juno R
P3S01033 Fuuka and Lucia U
P3S01026 Fuuka in Swimsuit RR
P3S01038 Fuuka Yamagishi C
P3S01043 Group Attack Chance R
P3S01089 Hidetoshi Odagiri C
P3S01080 Igor R
P3S01045 Infirmary U
P3S01094 Jack Brothers U
P3S01060 Jin and Moros U
P3S01066 Jin C
P3S01028 Jun Kanzato R
P3S01059 Junpei and Hermes U
P3S01055 Junpei and Trismegistus R
P3S01064 Junpei Iori C
P3S01039 Kazushi Miyamoto C
P3S01088 Keisuke Hiraga C
P3S01001 Ken Amada RR
P3S01007 Kinji Tomochika U
P3S01009 Koromaru and Cerberus U
P3S01012 Koromaru C
P3S01046 Level Up C
P3S01050 Living Being CC
P3S01015 Maiko C
P3S01042 Mamoru Hayasema C
P3S01022 Mayoidou C
P3S01048 Mechanical Maiden CR
P3S01054 Megumi Kayano R
P3S01031 Metis and Psyche R
P3S01031R Metis and Psyche RRR
P3S01034 Metis U
P3S01021 Midsummer Night's Dream C
P3S01092 Mitsuru and Artemisia C
P3S01078 Mitsuru and Penthesilea R
P3S01076 Mitsuru in Swimsuit RR
P3S01084 Mitsuru Kirijo U
P3S01058 Mutatsu U
P3S01032 Natsuki Moriyama U
P3S01063 Nozomi Suemitsu C
P3S01074 Nyx Avatar CC
P3S01099 Oath-Matching Promise CC
P3S01023 Outdoor Bath CR
P3S01003 Pharos R
P3S01010 President Tanaka U
P3S01075 Promise to Friends CC
P3S01006 Protagonist and Messiah R
P3S01002 Protagonist and Orpheus RR
P3S01017 Protagonist and Thanatos C
P3S01008 Protagonist U
P3S01072 Reaper C
P3S01086 Ryo Kanzato U
P3S01004 Ryoji Mochizuki R
P3S01004R Ryoji Mochizuki RRR
P3S01011 Shin Kanzato U
P3S01053 Shinjiro and Castor R
P3S01057 Shinjiro Aragaki U
P3S01097 Shuffle Time C
P3S01083 Shuuji Ikutsuki U
P3S01098 Strongest One CR
P3S01071 Symbolic C
P3S01061 Takaya and Hypnos U
P3S01062 Takaya C
P3S01090 Takeharu Kirijo C
P3S01018 Tartarus R
P3S01068 Tatsumi East Police Box R
P3S01041 Teacher Toriumi C
P3S01073 Thank You CR
P3S01025 The Last Choice CC
P3S01049 Unbreakable Bond CC
P3S01093 Velvet Room R
P3S01085 Yukari and Io U
P3S01081 Yukari and Isis R
P3S01081R Yukari and Isis RRR
P3S01079 Yukari in Swimsuit R
P3S01091 Yukari Takeba C
P3S01040 Yuuko Nishwaki C
P3S01023S Outdoor Bath SP
P3S01049S Unbreakable Bond SP
P3S01073S Thank You SP
P3S01098S Strongest One SP

2008 Weiss Schwarz Persona 3 TD

P3S0101T Amada and Kala-Nemi R
P3S0110T Amada and Nemesis C
P3S0108T Bebe C
P3S0114T Final Selection C
P3S0116T Fushimi Chihiro C
P3S0121T Kanzato Shin PR
P3S0105T Kanzeto Shin U
P3S0118T Kirijou Takeharu C
P3S0103T Koromaru and Cerberus U
P3S0107T Koromaru C
P3S0109T Maiko C
P3S0112T Mayoi Dou C
P3S0119T Mitsuro and Artemisia C
P3S0115T Mitsuru and Penthesilea R
P3S0120T Oath of Commitment U
P3S0117T Odagiri Hidetoshi C
P3S0104T President Tanaka U
P3S0111T Protagonist and Thanatos C
P3S0106T Shadow Time U
P3S0113T The End of Vengeance U
P3S0102T Tomochika Kenji U

2008 Weiss Schwarz The Familiar of Zero

ZMW03025 A Match CC
ZMW03089 Agnes Chevalier de Milan C
ZMW03082 Agnes, Captain of the Musketeers U
ZMW03092 Agnes, Chasing Suspect C
ZMW03048 Animal Choir CR
ZMW03049 Bath of Two CC
ZMW03071 Betrayal of Wardes C
ZMW03100 Blade of Revenge CC
ZMW03027 Cattleya Yvette La Baume Le Blanc de La Fontaine RR
ZMW03029 Cattleya, Second Daughter R
ZMW03029S Cattleya, Second Daughter SR
ZMW03009 Charlotte Helene Orleans U
ZMW03045 Charming Fairy Bustier U
ZMW03066 Colbery of Flame Snake C
ZMW03003 Commoner Familiar Saito R
ZMW03023 Contract CR
ZMW03059 Derflinger, Legendary Sword U
ZMW03018 Dispel Magic R
ZMW03008 Duchess Valliere U
ZMW03091 Eleonore Albertine Le Blanc De La Blois De La Valliere C
ZMW03031 Eleonore and Cattleya R
ZMW03031R Eleonore and Cattleya RRR
ZMW03076 Eleonore, First Daughter RR
ZMW03080 Eleonore, Special Teacher R
ZMW03080S Eleonore, Special Teacher SR
ZMW03021 Familiar Fair C
ZMW03012 Familiar of Zero Saito C
ZMW03095 Flower of Eclair D'amour U
ZMW03042 Fouquet, the Crumbling Dirt C
ZMW03052 Gandalfr Saito RR
ZMW03050 Golem CC
ZMW03040 Guiche the Bronze C
ZMW03085 Henrietta and Wales U
ZMW03086 Henrietta de Tristain U
ZMW03079 Henrietta, Princess of Tristain R
ZMW03022 Hexagon Magic C
ZMW03038 Jessica C
ZMW03004 Julio Chesare R
ZMW03058 Katie the Ember U
ZMW03055 Kirche and Tabitha R
ZMW03055S Kirche and Tabitha SR
ZMW03057 Kirche Augusta Frederica von Anhalt Zerbst U
ZMW03051 Kirche of Fever RR
ZMW03067 Kirche, Multiple Lover C
ZMW03073 Legendary Familiar CR
ZMW03033 Little Nee-Sama Cattleya U
ZMW03098 Looking for Seal CR
ZMW03035 Louise and Cattleya U
ZMW03078 Louise and Eleonore R
ZMW03077 Louise and Henrietta RR
ZMW03077R Louise and Henrietta RRR
ZMW03056 Louise and Kirche, Bad Company R
ZMW03060 Louise and Saito U
ZMW03005 Louise and Siesta R
ZMW03005R Louise and Siesta RRR
ZMW03005S Louise and Siesta SR
ZMW03039 Louise and Tiffania C
ZMW03002 Louise in Maid Outfit RR
ZMW03002S Louise in Maid Outfit SR
ZMW03064 Louise in Sailor Uniform C
ZMW03061 Louise in Swimsuit U
ZMW03065 Louise in Wedding Dress C
ZMW03010 Louise of the Black Cat U
ZMW03053 Louise of Void R
ZMW03053S Louise of Void SR
ZMW03013 Louise the Zero C
ZMW03043 Louise's Part-time Job R
ZMW03072 Massacre of D'Angleterre C
ZMW03046 Medusa's Glasses C
ZMW03041 Michelle C
ZMW03019 Military Training U
ZMW03087 Montmorency of the Perfume C
ZMW03099 Oath of Wind and Water CC
ZMW03034 Old Osmond U
ZMW03090 Oliver Cromwell C
ZMW03070 Operation Hostage Rescue U
ZMW03097 Pinching Tiny Louise C
ZMW03093 Power of Charm Potion R
ZMW03068 Power of Void R
ZMW03088 Princess Henrietta, Childhood Friend C
ZMW03069 Proof of Re-Contract U
ZMW03044 Punishment U
ZMW03014 Quiet Tabitha C
ZMW03074 Reward CC
ZMW03020 Robe of Dragons U
ZMW03096 Royalty Spanning Rainbow C
ZMW03054 Saito and Derflinger R
ZMW03006 Saito and Siesta R
ZMW03062 Saito Hiraga C
ZMW03063 Saito in Virgin Mode C
ZMW03047 Saito's Disposition C
ZMW03028 Scarron R
ZMW03084 Sheffield U
ZMW03083 Siesta in Sailor Uniform U
ZMW03030 Siesta in Swimsuit R
ZMW03030S Siesta in Swimsuit SR
ZMW03036 Siesta U
ZMW03081 Siesta, Bunny Girl R
ZMW03081S Siesta, Bunny Girl SR
ZMW03007 Sylphid U
ZMW03015 Tabitha and Illococoo C
ZMW03001 Tabitha of the Yukikaze RR
ZMW03011 Tabitha, Dragon User U
ZMW03024 Tabitha's Secret CC
ZMW03075 Temptation of Fever CC
ZMW03032 Tiffania Westwood U
ZMW03026 Tiffania, Half-Elf RR
ZMW03026R Tiffania, Half-Elf RRR
ZMW03037 Verdandi C
ZMW03016 Wales Tudor C
ZMW03017 Wardes the Lightning C
ZMW03094 Water Spirit U
ZMW0301SP Tabitha of the Yukikaze SP
ZMW0351SP Kirche of Fever SP
ZMW0353SP Louise of Void SP
ZMW0379SP Henrietta, Princess of Tristain SP

2008 Weiss Schwarz The Familiar of Zero TD

ZMW03T09 A Match
ZMW03T07 Charlotte Helene Orleans
ZMW03T12 Chii Nee-sama Cattleya
ZMW03T01 Familiar of Zero Saito
ZMW03T15 Fouquet, the Crumbling Dirt
ZMW03T103 Golden Fairy Tiffania
ZMW03T18 Golem
ZMW03T10 Jessica
ZMW03T16 Louise and Cattleya
ZMW03T102 Louise Francoise Le Blanc de La Valliere
ZMW03T03 Louise the Zero
ZMW03T13 Michelle
ZMW03T14 Old Osmond
ZMW03T04 Quiet Tabitha
ZMW03T17 Saito's Disposition
ZMW03T02 Sylphid
ZMW03T05 Tabitha and Illococoo
ZMW03T08 Tabitha's Secret
ZMW03T11 Tiffania Westwood
ZMW03T06 Wardes the Lightning

2009 Weiss Schwarz CANAAN Extra

CNSE0224 Alphard & Liang Qi C
CNSE0223 Alphard, Head of Snake C
CNSE0216 Alphard, Loser Who Lost Her Past R
CNSE0218 Alphard, Terrorist R
CNSE0226 Being with Name of Canaan C

CNSE0222 Canaan & Alphard, Sister Pupils C
CNSE0212 Canaan & Maria, Important Friends C
CNSE0209 Canaan, Destruction Worker C
CNSE0211 Canaan, Substitute of Iron Battle C
CNSE0208 Canaan, Synesthete C
CNSE0203 Canaan, Victim Whose Past Was Stolen R
CNSE0225 Cummings, President of Daedara Company C
CNSE0214 Dearest Friends C
CNSE0215 Hakko, Flower Blooming in Heart R
CNSE0217 Liang Qi, Secretary to the President R
CNSE0201 Maria & Minorikawa, Journalists R
CNSE0207 Maria Oosawa C
CNSE0204 Maria, Driven Cameraman R
CNSE0206 Maria, Item of Memories C
CNSE0210 Natsume, Lookout C
CNSE0219 Nene, New Idol C
CNSE0205 Place of Hope Canaan R
CNSE0213 Predator of Snake C
CNSE0227 Snake i nthe Sky C
CNSE0202 Treasure Cannan & Maria R
CNSE0220 Yunyun, Natural Girl C
CNSE0221 Yunyun, Poor Part-Timer C

2009 Weiss Schwarz CLANNAD Vol. 1 Extra

CLWE0120 Akio Furukawa C
CLWE0107 Do You Like This School? C
CLWE0113 Fuuko and Kouko C
CLWE0111 Fuuko, Ghost Girl C
CLWE0108 Fuuko, Legendary Starfish User R
CLWE0124 Girl of the Fantasy World C
CLWE0125 Kotomi Ichinose C
CLWE0123 Kotomi, Destructor of Rhythm C
CLWE0122 Kotomi, Honorary Book Committee Member R
CLWE0126 Kyou and Ryou C
CLWE0118 Kyou, Berserking Girl C
CLWE0115 Kyou, Loves Caring R
CLWE0117 Kyou, Thinking of Younger Sister C
CLWE0121 Nagisa and Kotomi R
CLWE0116 Nagisa and Kyou, Bakery C
CLWE0104 Nagisa Furukawa C
CLWE0105 Nagisa, Caretaker C
CLWE0101 Nagisa, Drama Club President R
CLWE0103 Nagisa, Girl Who Stood Still R
CLWE0127 Present to My Daughter C
CLWE0119 Sanae Furukawa C
CLWE0102 Tomoya Okazaki R
CLWE0110 Tomoyo, All-Around in Sports C
CLWE0109 Tomoyo, Family Feel R
CLWE0112 Tomoyo, Legendary Girl C
CLWE0114 Until the End of the Dream C
CLWE0106 Youhei Sunohara C

2009 Weiss Schwarz CLANNAD Vol. 2 Extra

CLWE0407 Fuuko Ibuki C
CLWE0408 Fuuko in Pajamas C
CLWE0416 Kotomi, At Her Own Pace C
CLWE0415 Kotomi, Genius Girl R
CLWE0410 Kyou and Tomoyo R
CLWE0411 Kyou Fujibaya R
CLWE0413 Kyou, Chairman C
CLWE0414 Love Triangle C
CLWE0403 Mei, Love Cupid C
CLWE0412 Nagisa and Kyou C
CLWE0401 Nagisa and Ushio R
CLWE0402 Nagisa Okazaki C
CLWE0417 Ryou, Fortune Telling Lover C
CLWE0404 Tomoya, Optimistic C
CLWE0405 Tomoyo Sakagami R
CLWE0406 Tomoyo, Student Council President R
CLWE0409 Tomoyo's Vow C
CLWE0418 Yuusuke Yoshino C

2009 Weiss Schwarz Fate/hollow ataraxia Extra

FHSE03003 All the Evil in the World Avenger R
FHSE03031 Archer, Priest of the Tohsaka Shrine R
FHSE03004 Avenger, Anti-Hero C
FHSE03016 Bazett & Lancer, Past Memories C
FHSE03018 Bazett Fraga McRemitz R
FHSE03021 Bazett, Battle Situation C
FHSE03011 Bazett, Endless Holy Grail War C
FHSE03014 Bazett, Reluctant Farewell R
FHSE03039 Caren Ortensia R
FHSE03041 Caren, Demon Possessed C
FHSE03040 Caren, Magdala's Holy Shroud C
FHSE03035 Caren, Mysterious Girl C
FHSE03009 Clash! Dead Bridge R
FHSE03027 Edelfelt Sisters C
FHSE03010 Enuma Elish R
FHSE03023 Escort C
FHSE03026 Favorite Space C
FHSE03025 Fragarach C
FHSE03002 Gilgamesh, Children's Idol C
FHSE03045 Hammer of the Sorceress R
FHSE03042 Illya & Berserker, Battering Ram C
FHSE03038 Illya in Swimsuit C
FHSE03036 Illya, Full of Energy C
FHSE03024 Important Place R
FHSE03015 Lancer on an Off-Day C
FHSE03028 Magical Girl Kaleido Ruby R
FHSE03037 Medea Kuzuki R
FHSE03034 Mimic Tohsaka R
FHSE03005 Otoko Hotaruzuka C
FHSE03043 Restful Night C
FHSE03019 Rider in Swimsuit C
FHSE03033 Rin & Archer, Crimson under Moonlight C
FHSE03032 Rin in Swimsuit C
FHSE03030 Rin, Maiden of the Tohsaka Shrine C
FHSE03006 Saber in Miko Outfit C
FHSE03008 Saber, King by the Lake C
FHSE03007 Saber, Peaceful Days C
FHSE03001 Saber, the Guardian C
FHSE03013 Sakura & Rider, Shared Fate R
FHSE03020 Sakura in Dress R
FHSE03017 Sakura in Swimsuit C
FHSE03022 Sella & Leys in Swimsuits C
FHSE03044 Spiral Ladder C
FHSE03012 Stheno & Euryale C
FHSE03029 Tyrant Saber Alter R
FHSE031SP Saber, the Guardian SP
FHSE032SP Gilgamesh, Children's Idol SP
FHSE033SP All the Evil in the World Avenger SP
FHSE034SP Avenger, Anti-Hero SP
FHSE035SP Otoko Hotaruzuka SP
FHSE036SP Saber in Miko Outfit SP
FHSE037SP Saber, Peaceful Days SP
FHSE038SP Saber, King by the Lake SP
FHSE039SP Clash! Dead Bridge SP
FHSE0310SP Enuma Elish SP
FHSE0311SP Bazett, Endless Holy Grail War SP
FHSE0312SP Stheno & Euryale SP
FHSE0313SP Sakura & Rider, Shared Fate SP
FHSE0314SP Bazett, Reluctant Farewell SP
FHSE0315SP Lancer on an Off-Day SP
FHSE0316SP Bazett & Lancer, Past Memories SP
FHSE0317SP Sakura in Swimsuit SP
FHSE0318SP Bazett Fraga McRemitz SP
FHSE0319SP Rider in Swimsuit SP
FHSE0320SP Sakura in Dress SP
FHSE0321SP Bazett, Battle Situation SP
FHSE0322SP Sella & Leys in Swimsuits SP
FHSE0323SP Escort SP
FHSE0324SP Important Place SP
FHSE0325SP Fragarach SP
FHSE0326SP Favorite Space SP
FHSE0327SP Edelfelt Sisters SP
FHSE0328SP Magical Girl Kaleido Ruby SP
FHSE0329SP Tyrant Saber Alter SP
FHSE0330SP Rin, Maiden of the Tohsaka Shrine SP
FHSE0331SP Archer, Priest of the Tohsaka Shrine SP
FHSE0332SP Rin in Swimsuit SP
FHSE0333SP Rin & Archer, Crimson under Moonlight SP
FHSE0334SP Mimic Tohsaka SP
FHSE0335SP Caren, Mysterious Girl SP
FHSE0336SP Illya, Full of Energy SP
FHSE0337SP Medea Kuzuki SP
FHSE0338SP Illya in Swimsuit SP
FHSE0339SP Caren Ortensia SP
FHSE0340SP Caren, Magdala's Holy Shroud SP
FHSE0341SP Caren, Demon Possessed SP
FHSE0342SP Illya & Berserker, Battering Ram SP
FHSE0343SP Restful Night SP
FHSE0344SP Spiral Ladder SP
FHSE0345SP Hammer of the Sorceress SP

2009 Weiss Schwarz Haruhi

SYW08050 Already Making Big Profit CC
SYW08018 Arakawa, Dandy Butler C
SYW08047 Baseball Tournament C
SYW08074 Birth of SOS Brigade CC
SYW08020 Camping Night U
SYW08067 Cat-Eared Haruhi C
SYW08037 Cat-Eared Mikuru U
SYW08092 Cat-Eared Nagato C
SYW08034 Cat-Eared Tsuruya-san U
SYW08025 Closed Space CC
SYW08096 Don't Leave Me U
SYW08048 Everyday Life of Haruhi Suzumiya CR
SYW08022 Fumoffu C
SYW08023 Good News from Haruhi Suzumiya CR
SYW08073 Happy Valentine CR
SYW08051 Haruhi and Kyon, Christmas Party RR
SYW08005 Haruhi and Kyon, Observable Trust R
SYW08032 Haruhi and Mikuru in Swimsuits R
SYW08032S Haruhi and Mikuru in Swimsuits SR
SYW08061 Haruhi and Mikuru in Yukatas U
SYW08041 Haruhi and Nagato and Mikuru, Bunny Girls C
SYW08083 Haruhi and Nagato in Swimsuits U
SYW08055 Haruhi and Tiny Haruhi, Center of the World R
SYW08055S Haruhi and Tiny Haruhi, Center of the World SR
SYW08054 Haruhi in the Hot Spring R
SYW08053 Haruhi in Yukata R
SYW08053S Haruhi in Yukata SR
SYW08064 Haruhi Suzumiya C
SYW08057 Haruhi, Beach Volleyball R
SYW08068 Haruhi, Cracker C
SYW08060 Haruhi, Disliked Boredom U
SYW08059 Haruhi, Dressed Up U
SYW08063 Haruhi, Hands Full of Bouquet C
SYW08062 Haruhi, Happy Valentine U
SYW08052 Haruhi, SOS Brigade Chief RR
SYW08058 Haruhi, Super Editor-in-Chief U
SYW08065 Haruhi, Vocalist C
SYW08072 I Am Not Interested in Normal Humans C
SYW08098 I Will Tell You about Myself CR
SYW08011 Itsuki Koizumi U
SYW08093 Kimidori, Client No 1 C
SYW08015 Koizumi in Apron C
SYW08004 Koizumi, Mysterious Transfer Student R
SYW08004R Koizumi, Mysterious Transfer Student RRR
SYW08013 Kunikida, Classmate C
SYW08014 Kyon in Apron C
SYW08010 Kyon in Club Office U
SYW08007 Kyon in Yukata R
SYW08007S Kyon in Yukata SR
SYW08001 Kyon RR
SYW08001R Kyon RRR
SYW08019 Kyon's Little Sister and Asakura C
SYW08009 Kyon's Little Sister in Swimsuits U
SYW08003 Kyon's Little Sister, Christmas Party R
SYW08003S Kyon's Little Sister, Christmas Party SR
SYW08095 Message on the Bookmark U
SYW08017 Mikuru and Kyon, Overworked C
SYW08026 Mikuru and Mikuru (Big), Time Travelers RR
SYW08026R Mikuru and Mikuru (Big), Time Travelers RRR
SYW08035 Mikuru and Tsuruya-san, Beach Volelyball U
SYW08029 Mikuru Asahina R
SYW08038 Mikuru at the Signing Event C
SYW08045 Mikuru Beam U
SYW08042 Mikuru from the Future C
SYW08027 Mikuru, Blunderer RR
SYW08033 Mikuru, Dressed Up U
SYW08031 Mikuru, Girl Who Leapt Through Time R
SYW08031R Mikuru, Girl Who Leapt Through Time RRR
SYW08039 Mikuru, Mascot of SOS Brigade C
SYW08044 Mikuru, Miracle Girl C
SYW08040 Mikuru, Waitress C
SYW08076 Nagato and Asakura and Kimidori, Aliens RR
SYW08076R Nagato and Asakura and Kimidori, Aliens RRR
SYW08012 Nagato and Koizumi in Club Office U
SYW08089 Nagato and Kyon's Little Sister in Yukatas C
SYW08084 Nagato and Mikuru in the Hot Spring U
SYW08090 Nagato in Apron C
SYW08082 Nagato in China Dress R
SYW08082S Nagato in China Dress SR
SYW08085 Nagato, Beach Volleyball U
SYW08088 Nagato, Christmas Party C
SYW08094 Nagato, Cool Girl C
SYW08077 Nagato, Dressed Up RR
SYW08077R Nagato, Dressed Up RRR
SYW08091 Nagato, Eating Watermelon C
SYW08079 Nagato, Girl with Glasses R
SYW08079S Nagato, Girl with Glasses SR
SYW08086 Nagato, Guitarist U
SYW08081 Nagato, Quiet Character R
SYW08087 Nagato, Terminal of Data Integration Thought Entity U
SYW08056 Normal Haruhi R
SYW08006 Normal Kyon R
SYW08080 Ryoko Asakura R
SYW08002 Santa Girl Haruhi and Kyon RR
SYW08070 Searching Tour in the City U
SYW08024 sleeping beauty_ CC
SYW08075 Someday in the Rain CC
SYW08008 Sonou Mori U
SYW08099 Struggle in the Information Controlled Space CC
SYW08016 Taniguchi, Classmate C
SYW08049 That's Classified CC
SYW08021 The Path Home on A Rainy Day U
SYW08069 Trouble Girl Haruhi C
SYW08043 Tsuruya-san and Mikuru, Christmas Party C
SYW08030 Tsuruya-san in the Hot Spring R
SYW08028 Tsuruya-san, Dressed Up R
SYW08028S Tsuruya-san, Dressed up SR
SYW08036 Tsuruya-san, Waitress U
SYW08100 Um, That's Impossible CC
SYW08097 Unlinking Information C
SYW08066 Victory Declaration Haruhi C
SYW08046 Voluntarily Accompanying? U
SYW08071 World with Faded Colors U
SYW08078 Yuki Nagato R
SYW0852SP Haruhi, SOS Brigade Chief SP
SYW0856SP Normal Haruhi SP

2009 Weiss Schwarz Haruhi TD

SYW08T09 Birth of the SOS Brigade
SYW08T05 Cat-Eared Haruhi
SYW08T12 Cat-Eared Nagato
SYW08T03 Haruhi and Mikuru in Yukata
SYW08T14 Haruhi and Nagato in Swimsuits
SYW08T01 Haruhi Suzumiya
SYW08T07 Haruhi, Cracker
SYW08T02 Haruhi, Hands Full of Bouquet
SYW08T04 Haruhi, Vocalist
SYW08T17 I Will Tell You about Myself
SYW08T15 Nagato and Mikuru in the Hot Spring
SYW08T11 Nagato, Christmas Party
SYW08T13 Nagato, Eating Watermelon
SYW08101 Normal Haruhi and Mikuru
SYW08102 Normal Nagato
SYW08T10 Someday in the Rain
SYW08T08 Trouble Girl Haruhi
SYW08T16 Unlink Information
SYW08T06 Victory Declaration Haruhi

2009 Weiss Schwarz Idolmaster

IMS07095 A Certain Day's Scenery U
IMS07020 Acting Lesson U
IMS07003 Ami and Mami, Energetic Is Important R
IMS07012 Ami and Mami, Troublemakers U
IMS07015 Ami and Mami, Twin Beasts C
IMS07011 Ami and Mami, Uncontrollable? U
IMS07005 Ami Futami R
IMS07005S Ami Futami SR
IMS07078 Azuka, Healing Character R
IMS07080 Azusa Miura R
IMS07080S Azusa Miura SR
IMS07090 Azusa, Easily Lost C
IMS07087 Azusa, My Pace U
IMS07081 Azusa, Sisterly R
IMS07085 Azusa, Unhurried and Leisurely U
IMS07076 Chihaya Kisaragi RR
IMS07076S Chihaya Kisaragi SR
IMS07089 Chihaya, Cool and Stoic C
IMS07092 Chihaya, Genius Singer C
IMS07082 Chihaya, Goddess of Songs R
IMS07086 Chihaya, Serious U
IMS07091 Chihaya, Vocalist C
IMS07021 Clothing Change U
IMS07047 Daily Spectacle C
IMS07097 Dance Lesson C
IMS07045 Expression Lesson U
IMS07050 Flower Girl CC
IMS07048 Furufuru Future CR
IMS07046 Going Out of Your Way U
IMS07055 Haruka Amami R
IMS07055S Haruka Amami SR
IMS07060 Haruka, Ditzy Girl U
IMS07051 Haruka, Gentle and Positive RR
IMS07062 Haruka, Natural Talent U
IMS07069 Haruka, Passionate for Songs C
IMS07064 Haruka, Regular Girl C
IMS07029 Hibiki Ganaha R
IMS07029S Hibiki Ganaha SR
IMS07043 Hibiki, Ally of Justice C
IMS07032 Hibiki, Animal Lover R
IMS07035 Hibiki, Natural Colors U
IMS07038 Hibiki, Sunny Girl C
IMS07074 I Want CC
IMS07007 Iori Minase R
IMS07007S Iori Minase SR
IMS07014 Iori, Full of Self-confidence C
IMS07009 Iori, Hates Losing U
IMS07001 Iori, Prideful Queen RR
IMS07017 Iori, Proof of Appreciation C
IMS07019 Iori, Shrew-Like Lady C
IMS07073 Kirame Kirari CR
IMS07024 Kosmos, Cosmos CC
IMS07027 Kotori Otonashi RR
IMS07027S Kotori Otonashi SR
IMS07056 Kotori, Birth of an Idol? R
IMS07008 Kotori, Morning Greetings U
IMS07088 Kotori, Supporting Role C
IMS07098 Lots and Lots CR
IMS07096 Lyrics Lesson U
IMS07054 Makoto Kikuchi R
IMS07054S Makoto Kikuchi SR
IMS07061 Makoto, Gallant and Fearlessly Determined U
IMS07057 Makoto, High Motivation R
IMS07068 Makoto, Powerful Girl C
IMS07065 Makoto, Prince-sama C
IMS07059 Makoto, Sports Lover U
IMS07006 Mami Futami R
IMS07006S Mami Futami SR
IMS07075 Meisou Mind CC
IMS07025 Memories of Two CC
IMS07028 Miki Hoshii R
IMS07028S Miki Hoshii SR
IMS07037 Miki, Being Fancy U
IMS07036 Miki, Completed Visual Queen U
IMS07041 Miki, Hopeful New Star C
IMS07034 Miki, Seduction Expert U
IMS07026 Miki, Troubled and Falling RR
IMS07070 Morning Greetings U
IMS07049 Next Life CC
IMS07022 Pose Lesson C
IMS07071 Present U
IMS07040 President Kuroi C
IMS07042 President Takagi C
IMS07077 Ritsuko Akizuki RR
IMS07077S Ritsuko Akizuki SR
IMS07094 Ritsuko, Almighty C
IMS07079 Ritsuko, Eager to Research R
IMS07084 Ritsuko, Panicking U
IMS07083 Ritsuko, Smart And Bright U
IMS07093 Ritsuko, Toeing the Line C
IMS07023 Star to Star CR
IMS07100 Stay By Me CC
IMS07030 Takane Shijou R
IMS07030S Takane Shijou SR
IMS07033 Takane, Away from Common Life U
IMS07039 Takane, Presence of a Princess C
IMS07031 Takane, Princess R
IMS07044 Takane, Under the Moonlight C
IMS07099 The Moment Our Eyes Met CC
IMS07072 Voice Lesson C
IMS07053 Yayoi Takatsuki R
IMS07053S Yayoi Takatsuki SR
IMS07066 Yayoi, 200 Cheerful C
IMS07063 Yayoi, Bright Smile C
IMS07052 Yayoi, Full Power RR
IMS07067 Yayoi, High-Five C
IMS07058 Yayoi, Working Hard U
IMS07004 Yukiho Hagiwara R
IMS07004S Yukiho Hagiwara SR
IMS07013 Yukiho, Digging a Hole C
IMS07002 Yukiho, Enthusiast RR
IMS07016 Yukiho, Shy Thoughts C
IMS07010 Yukiho, Tea Power U
IMS07018 Yukiho, Working Hard C
IMS0723SP Star to Star SP
IMS0748SP Furufuru Future SP
IMS0774SP I Want SP
IMS0799SP The Moment Our Eyes Met SP

2009 Weiss Schwarz Idolmaster TD

IMS07T14 Azusa, Unhurried and Leisurely
IMS07T12 Chihaya, Cool and Stoic
IMS07102 Chihaya, Hard Worker
IMS07T13 Chihaya, Vocalist
IMS07T08 Haruka, Passionate for Songs
IMS07T01 Haruka, Regular Girl
IMS07101 Haruka, Song Lover
IMS07T10 I Want
IMS07T11 Kotori, Supporting Role
IMS07T03 Makoto, Gallant and Fearlessly Determined
IMS07T07 Makoto, Powerful Girl
IMS07T04 Makoto, Prince-sama
IMS07T02 Makoto, Sports Lover
IMS07T09 Present
IMS07T15 Ritsuko, Almighty
IMS07T16 The Moment Our Eyes Meet
IMS07T05 Yayoi, 200 Cheerful
IMS07T06 Yayoi, High-Five

2009 Weiss Schwarz King of Fighters

KFS05072 104 Shiki: Aragami C
KFS05017 Adelheid C
KFS05053 Andy Bogard R
KFS05096 Art of Fighting Team U
KFS05032 Ash, Plunderer R
KFS05032R Ash, Plunderer RRR
KFS05041 Ash, Sneering Crimson Shadow C
KFS05083 Athena Asamiya U
KFS05077 Athena in Sailor Uniform RR
KFS05077S Athena in Sailor Uniform SR
KFS05011 Benimaru Nikaidou U
KFS05039 Billy Kane C
KFS05030 Billy, Faithful Shadow of Geese R
KFS05015 Blue Mary C
KFS05075 Buster Wolf CC
KFS05003 Chang and Choi R
KFS05052 Chris RR
KFS05052S Chris SR
KFS05029 Clark Steel R
KFS05043 Clark, Quiet Mercenary C
KFS05097 Continue C
KFS05033 Daimon, Judo Practictioner U
KFS05100 Diamond Edge CC
KFS05094 Dragon Ki Kensou C
KFS05064 Duolon C
KFS05063 Eiji Kisaragi C
KFS05038 Elizabeth Blanctorche C
KFS05071 Fatal Fury Team U
KFS05024 Fate of 660 Years Ago CC
KFS05034 Geese Howard U
KFS05027 Geese, Bad Charisma RR
KFS05027S Geese, Bad Charisma SR
KFS05088 Gentsai Chin C
KFS05049 Germinal CC
KFS05012 Goenitz of the Wild Winds U
KFS05037 Goro Daimon U
KFS05074 Hana Arashi CC
KFS05026 Hiedern, Cold Assassin RR
KFS05099 Illegitimate Child of Baddies CC
KFS05016 Iori Yagami C
KFS05007 Iori, Berserking R
KFS05007S Iori, Berserking SR
KFS05004 Iori, Sealed One R
KFS05004R Iori, Sealed One RRR
KFS05070 Japan Team U
KFS05059 Joe Higashi U
KFS05085 K' U
KFS05014 Kasumi Toudou C
KFS05086 Kensou Sei U
KFS05005 Kim, Educator of Justice R
KFS05018 Kim, Treasure of the Tae Kwon Do World C
KFS05022 Kin 1211 Style: Ya Otome C
KFS05001 King RR
KFS05019 King, Beauty of Kicks C
KFS05081 Kula Diamond R
KFS05076 Kula, Ice Beauty RR
KFS05076R Kula, Ice Beauty RRR
KFS05091 Kula, Icicle Doll C
KFS05065 KUSANAGI C
KFS05002 Kyo and Iori RR
KFS05051 Kyo Kusanagi RR
KFS05051R Kyo Kusanagi RRR
KFS05006 Kyo, Prince of Flames R
KFS05006S Kyo, Prince of Flames SR
KFS05062 Kyo, Successor of Powerful Flames U
KFS05008 Kyo, Sweeper U
KFS05036 Leona Hiedern U
KFS05028 Leona, Silent Soldier R
KFS05028S Leona, Silent Soldier SR
KFS05067 Magaki C
KFS05068 Mai Shiranui C
KFS05054 Mai, Gorgeous Female Ninja R
KFS05054S Mai, Gorgeous Female Ninja SR
KFS05009 Mary, Free Agent U
KFS05010 Mature and Vice U
KFS05093 Maxima C
KFS05046 Member Select U
KFS05047 Mission And Pride C
KFS05042 Nameless C
KFS05057 Omega Rugal R
KFS05082 One Who Exceeds K R
KFS05025 Perfect Victory CC
KFS05045 Provoke U
KFS05095 Psycho Soldier Team U
KFS05020 Purple Flame and Green Flame U
KFS05040 Raiden C
KFS05035 Ralf Jones U
KFS05089 Ramon C
KFS05048 Rashoumon CR
KFS05090 Robert Garcia C
KFS05080 Ryo Sakazaki R
KFS05061 Ryuji Yamazaki U
KFS05031 Shen Woo R
KFS05058 Shermie U
KFS05060 Shermie, Provoking U
KFS05013 Shingo Yabuki C
KFS05098 Super Phoenix Infinity CR
KFS05092 Takuma Sakazaki C
KFS05056 Terry Bogard R
KFS05066 Terry, Wild Wolf C
KFS05021 The Sun and the Moon U
KFS05023 Trinity Two CR
KFS05055 Trry and Andy R
KFS05050 Truth Seeker CC
KFS05073 Ura 108 Shiki: Orochi nagi CR
KFS05087 Whip U
KFS05078 Whip, Rookie of Ikari Team R
KFS05069 Yashiro Nanakase C
KFS05084 Yuri Sakazaki U
KFS05079 Yuri, Tomboy Girl R
KFS05079S Yuri, Tomboy Girl SR
KFS05044 Zheprime Nameless C
KFS05100S Diamond Edge SP
KFS0523SP Trinity Two SP
KFS0548SP Rashoumon SP
KFS0574SP Hana Arashi SP

2009 Weiss Schwarz King of Fighters TD

KFS05T03 Blue Mary
KFS05T09 Eiji Kisaragi
KFS05T16 Hana Arashi
KFS05T01 Iori Yagami
KFS05101 Iori, Purple Flame of Revenge
KFS05T04 Kim, Treasure of the Tae Kwan Do World
KFS05102 Kyo, Running Red Lotus
KFS05T02 Kyo, Sweeper
KFS05T11 Magaki
KFS05T12 Mai Shiranui
KFS05T06 Perfect Victory
KFS05T05 Purple Flame and Green Flame
KFS05T13 Ryuji Yamazaki
KFS05T08 Shermie
KFS05T10 Shermie, Provoking
KFS05T07 Terry, Wild Wolf
KFS05T15 Ura 108 Shiki: Orochi Nagi
KFS05T14 Yashiro Nanakase

2009 Weiss Schwarz Little Busters Ecstasy TD

1 Female Spy Saya
2 Friends Rin and Komari
3 Happy Spiral Komari
4 Incredible Deja Vu
5 It'll Be Okay
6 Kud from Wonderland
7 Looking Down at the Evening City, Rin and Komari
8 Mood-Maker Komari
9 Quarter Girl Kud
10 Rin and Komari
11 Rising Stock Komari
12 Sayaka in Yukata
13 Self-Righteous Sasami
14 The Piano that Kept Playing
15 Trial from Older Brother
16 Western-Eastern Compromise Kud
17 Wishing Star Komari
18 Yuiko in Maid Uniform

2009 Weiss Schwarz Lucky Star

LSW05095 100 Mega Shock U
LSW05027 Akira Kogami RR
LSW05035 Ayano Minegishi U
LSW05034 Ayano, Accommodating U
LSW05042 Ayano, Different Culture C
LSW05020 Battle Mode U
LSW05096 Boooo C
LSW05074 Chocolate Cornet CC
LSW05070 Diet U
LSW05072 Doggie And Minami C
LSW05022 Dream-Like Life C
LSW05023 End of Summer Vacation CR
LSW05041 Fuyuki Amahara C
LSW05049 Goldfish Scooping CC
LSW05025 Good Idea CC
LSW05024 Graduation Ceremony CC
LSW05066 Hiiragi Sisters in Pajamas C
LSW05031 Hikaru Sakuraba R
LSW05099 Hiyori Starting CC
LSW05094 Hiyori Tamura C
LSW05003 Hiyori, Hobbyist R
LSW05003S Hiyori, Hobbyist SR
LSW05018 Hiyori, Outlaw C
LSW05086 Hiyori, Thinking That Way U
LSW05038 Kagami and Tsukasa C
LSW05032 Kagami Hiiragi R
LSW05036 Kagami, 100 Times Cuter U
LSW05030 Kagami, Older Sister of the Twins R
LSW05030S Kagami, Older Sister of the Twins SR
LSW05059 Kagami, Patissiere U
LSW05052 Kagami, Tsundere Express RR
LSW05052R Kagami, Tsundere Express RRR
LSW05037 Kagami-sama U
LSW05083 Kanata Izumi U
LSW05089 Konata and Hiyori and Patty C
LSW05026 Konata and Kagami and Tsukasa RR
LSW05069 Konata and Kagami C
LSW05065 Konata and Yutaka C
LSW05053 Konata Izumi R
LSW05055 Konata, At Her Own Pace R
LSW05076 Konata, Battlefield RR
LSW05076R Konata, Battlefield RRR
LSW05057 Konata, Embarrassed R
LSW05057S Konata, Embarrassed SR
LSW05077 Konata, Fast Girl RR
LSW05090 Konata, Getting Out of Bath C
LSW05084 Konata, Meganekko Geki LOVE U
LSW05013 Kou Yasaka C
LSW05005 Kou, Anime Resarch Club President R
LSW05054 Kuroi-Sensei R
LSW05050 Lucky Channel CC
LSW05056 Minami Iwasaki R
LSW05008 Minami, Cool And Good-Looking U
LSW05068 Minami, Easily Misunderstood C
LSW05011 Minami, Infirmary Officer U
LSW05058 Minami, Petting U
LSW05029 Misao Kusakabe R
LSW05029S Misao Kusakabe SR
LSW05033 Misao, 3-Second Rule U
LSW05043 Misao, Genki Girl C
LSW05009 Miyuki and Minami U
LSW05016 Miyuki as Child C
LSW05017 Miyuki Takara C
LSW05088 Miyuki, Chairman Character C
LSW05002 Miyuki, Completionist General RR
LSW05002R Miyuki, Completionist General RRR
LSW05087 Miyuki, High Spec U
LSW05006 Miyuki, Renowned Detective R
LSW05082 Miyuki, Strongest Character R
LSW05091 Miyuki, Teeth Hurting C
LSW05093 Nanako Kuroi C
LSW05085 Nanako, Online Gamer U
LSW05073 Nonchalant Happiness CR
LSW05071 One for Safekeeping And One for Promoting C
LSW05080 Patricia in A Hot Country R
LSW05080S Patricia in A Hot Country SR
LSW05078 Patricia Martin R
LSW05046 Pigtails C
LSW05021 Regrettable Strike C
LSW05098 Small Breast Is A Status And Rare CR
LSW05081 Soujirou and Kanata R
LSW05081S Soujirou and Kanata SR
LSW05079 Soujirou Izumi R
LSW05048 Summer Festival CR
LSW05045 The Most Natural Thing U
LSW05100 The Place Where I Feel Most Safe CC
LSW05047 The Usual C
LSW05001 Tsukasa Hiiragi RR
LSW05039 Tsukasa Who Tried Her Best C
LSW05040 Tsukasa, Ambushing C
LSW05014 Tsukasa, Dreaming Maiden C
LSW05028 Tsukasa, Dressed Up R
LSW05028R Tsukasa, Dressed Up RRR
LSW05044 Tsukasa, Loves Snacks C
LSW05007 Tsukasa, Natural R
LSW05007S Tsukasa, Natural SR
LSW05012 Tsukasa, Pampered Child U
LSW05075 Valentine CC
LSW05064 Yui Narumi C
LSW05067 Yui-chan, Loop Shooter C
LSW05092 Yukari Takara C
LSW05019 Yutaka and Minami and Hiyori C
LSW05004 Yutaka and Minami R
LSW05051 Yutaka and Yui RR
LSW05051S Yutaka and Yui SR
LSW05015 Yutaka Kobayakawa C
LSW05063 Yutaka, Buying Charms C
LSW05062 Yutaka, Fairy Tale-Like U
LSW05010 Yutaka, Finally Said Her Name U
LSW05061 Yutaka, Great Material U
LSW05060 Yutaka, Walking Charming Points U
LSW05097 Zero Hour on New Year's Eve C
LSW05100S The Place Where I Feel Most Safe SP
LSW0524SP Graduation Ceremony SP
LSW0548SP Summer Festival SP
LSW0573SP Nonchalant Happiness SP

2009 Weiss Schwarz Lucky Star TD

LSW05T02 Ayano, Accommodating
LSW05T04 Fuyuki Amahara
LSW05T08 Goldfish Scooping
LSW05T11 Hiiragi Sisters in Pajamas
LSW05T01 Kagami and Tsukasa
LSW05T06 Kagami-sama
LSW05T15 Konata and Kagami
LSW05102 Konata and Yui
LSW05T10 Konata and Yutaka
LSW05T09 Lucky Channel
LSW05T14 Minami, Easily Misunderstood
LSW05T12 Minami, Petting
LSW05T05 Misao, Genki Girl
LSW05T07 Pigtails
LSW05101 Scared Tsukasa
LSW05T03 Tsukasa Who Tried Her Best
LSW05T16 Valentine
LSW05T13 Yui-chan, Loop Shooter

2009 Weiss Schwarz Persona 4

COMPLETE SET (116)		
BOOSTER BOX (20 PACKS)	80.00	100.00
BOOSTER PACK (8 CARDS)	4.00	5.00

RELEASED ON OCTOBER 24, 2014
P4S08056 Adachi, Game Feeling R
P4S08063 Adachi, Skipping Out on Junes C
P4S08067 Adachi, Top Brain of the Station C
P4S08088 Ai Ebihara, Manager C
P4S08083 Assertion of Youth Teddie U
P4S08013 Ayane Matsunaga, Brass Band Club C
P4S08025 Brave Blade CC
P4S08025S Brave Blade SR
P4S08032 Chie and Suzuka Gongen R
P4S08043 Chie and Yukiko, Important Friends C
P4S08034 Chie in Swimsuit U
P4S08040 Chie in Yukata C
P4S08035 Chie, Golden Right Foot U
P4S08038 Chie, Reliable Prince C
P4S08027 Chie, Self-claimed Kung Fu Research Club RR
P4S08049 Chie's Pursuit CC
P4S08080 Chihiro Fushimi, Student Council President R
P4S08064 Clerk of Gasoline Stand C
P4S08070 Curry That Should Not Be Had U
P4S08042 Daisuke Nagase, Soccer Club C
P4S08018 Doujima, Oath of Father C
P4S08003 Doujima, Proof of Family R
P4S08033 Eri Minami, Caretaker of Schoolchildren U
P4S08047 Fishing Master of the River C
P4S08036 Fox of Tatsuhime Shrine U
P4S08050 Full Analysis CC
P4S08050R Full Analysis RRR
P4S08048 Godhand CR
P4S08048S Godhand SR
P4S08028 Hisano Kuroda, Shinigami R
P4S08021 Junes U
P4S08051 Kanji and Rokuten-Maou RR
P4S08065 Kanji in Yukata C
P4S08061 Kanji, Man of Legend U
P4S08069 Kanji, Plushie Master C
P4S08053 Kanji, True Strength R
P4S08068 Kanji-chan, Overly Horrible C
P4S08046 King Game U
P4S08030 Kou Ichijo, Basketball Club R
P4S08092 Kumada-chan C
P4S08099 Mabufudyne CC
P4S08099S Mabufudyne SR
P4S08096 Maggie's Tarot Reading U
P4S08077 Margaret, Attendant During Travels RR
P4S08077S Margaret, Attendant During Travels SR
P4S08087 Margaret, Controller of Power U
P4S08020 Mayonaga TV U
P4S08100 Megidolaon CC
P4S08071 Mid-term Test U
P4S08074 Mighty Swing CC
P4S08074S Mighty Swing SR
P4S08098 My Christmas Eve CR
P4S08098R My Christmas Eve RRR
P4S08023 Myriad Truths CR
P4S08023R Myriad Truths RRR
P4S08010 Nanako in Yukata U
P4S08006 Nanako, Junes Lover R
P4S08006S Nanako, Junes Lover SR
P4S08014 Nanako, Marriage Declaration C
P4S08059 Naoki Konishi, Little Brother of the Victim U
P4S08085 Naoto and Sukuna Hikona U
P4S08081 Naoto and Yamato Takeru R
P4S08094 Naoto in Sailor Uniform C
P4S08084 Naoto, Detective Prince U
P4S08089 Naoto, Famous Detective C
P4S08078 Naoto, Full Strength Following R
P4S08091 Naoto, Infinite Possibilities C
P4S08024 Never More CC
P4S08072 One Hit C
P4S08095 Poem of Souls of All Humans U
P4S08002 Protagonist and Izanagi RR
P4S08007 Protagonist and Nanako, Close Brother And Sister R
P4S08011 Protagonist, Leader U
P4S08004 Protagonist, Power of WILD R
P4S08015 Protagonist-chan, Miss Contest? C
P4S08031 Rise and Himiko R
P4S08037 Rise and Kanzeon U
P4S08041 Rise in Yukata C
P4S08029 Rise, Entertainer R
P4S08029S Rise, Entertainer SR
P4S08039 Rise, Healing Wave C
P4S08026 Rise, True Self RR
P4S08044 Rise-chi in Swimsuit C
P4S08005 Saki Konishi, Daughter of Wine Shope R
P4S08073 Salvation CR
P4S08073R Salvation RRR
P4S08066 Sayoko Uehara, Nurse C
P4S08045 Self-Proclaimed Special Search Unit U
P4S08090 Shuu Nakajima, Student C
P4S08082 teddie and Kaumi R
P4S08079 Teddie and Kintoki Douji R
P4S08097 Teddie Arrives C
P4S08076 Teddie in Yukata RR
P4S08093 Teddie Spec 2 C
P4S08086 Teddie, Idol of Junes U
P4S08022 Warm Embrace C
P4S08075 Will of the World CC
P4S08019 Yousuke and Susano-o C
P4S08001 Yousuke in Yukata RR
P4S08017 Yousuke, Bandaid to Friendship C
P4S08016 Yousuke, Protagonist's Sidekick C
P4S08012 Yousuke, Son of the Shop Manager U
P4S08008 Yousuke-chan, Prince of Disappointment U
P4S08062 Yukiko and Amaterasu U
P4S08054 Yukiko in Swimsuit R
P4S08052 Yukiko in Yukata RR
P4S08055 Yukiko, Funny Switch R
P4S08055S Yukiko, Funny Switch SR
P4S08060 Yukiko, One Hit to Win U
P4S08058 Yukiko, Reliable Princess U
P4S08057 Yukiko, Young Proprietress R
P4S08009 Yumi Ozawa, Drama Club U
P4S0802SP Protagonist and Izanagi SP
P4S0831SP Rise and Himiko SP
P4S0832SP Chie and Suzuka Gongen SP
P4S0881SP Naoto and Yamato Takeru SP

2009 Weiss Schwarz Persona 4 TD

P4S08T01 Ayane Matsunaga, Wind Instrument Club
P4S08T10 Brave Server
P4S08T12 Declaration of Youth Kuma
P4S08T06 Doujima, Promise of Father
P4S08101 Key of the Contract Protagonist
P4S08T14 Kumada-chan
P4S08T16 Mahabufudain
P4S08T11 Manager Ai Ebihara
P4S08T02 Miss Complex? Protagonist-chan
P4S08T04 Nanako in Yukata
P4S08T13 Naoto, Famoust Detective
P4S08T09 Never More
P4S08102 Perapera Bear
P4S08T07 Protagonist, Leader
P4S08T15 The Poem of Souls of All Humans
P4S08T08 Yousuke and Susanoo
P4S08T05 Yousuke, Bandage to Friendship
P4S08T03 Yousuke, Protagonist's Sidekick

2009 Weiss Schwarz Phantom TD

PTW07T17 Anger
PTW07T10 Best Work Ein
PTW07T03 Cal Devens
PTW07T04 Cal, Dressing Up
PTW07T07 Cal, Practicing
PTW07102 Cleaning Cal
PTW07T16 Conclusion
PTW07T13 Drei, Berserking
PTW07T14 Drei, Flourishing Gunplay
PTW07T12 Drei, New Phantom
PTW07T05 Ein in Swimsuits
PTW07T11 Ein, No1 Girl
PTW07101 Elen and Reiji, Peaceful Life
PTW07T06 Elen in Sailor Suit
PTW07T15 Elen VS Drei
PTW07T02 Elen, Reiji's Kid Sister
PTW07T01 Hungry Cal
PTW07T09 Memories of Wind
PTW07T08 Training

2009 Weiss Schwarz Sengoku Basara

SBS06023 Ambition of Unification CR
SBS06031 Avatar of Toushou Ieyasu Tokugawa R
SBS06041 Azure Crusher Hanbei Takenaka C
SBS06071 Battle of Kawanakashima U
SBS06090 Beautiful Sword Kasuka C
SBS06049 Beauty Dies Young CC
SBS06034 Best Cuisine Matsu U
SBS06073 Best of Japanese Troops CR
SBS06021 Bloodline of Demon U
SBS06061 Blue and Red Masamune & Yukimura U
SBS06040 Bluffing Yoshimoto Imagawa C
SBS06027 Brilliantly Strong Keiji Maeda RR
SBS06027R Brilliantly Strong Keiji Maeda RRR
SBS06028 Broad-Minded Toshiie Maeda R
SBS06067 Chant of Battle Spirit Yukimura Sanada C
SBS06043 Cold-Blooded Strategist Motonari Mouri C
SBS06059 Cold-hearted Sasuke Sarutobi U
SBS06006 Coldly Looking Down Mitsuhide Akechi R
SBS06048 Conflict CR
SBS06055 Conqueror God of War Shingen Takeda' R
SBS06035 Conqueror Hdeyoshi Toyotomi U
SBS06016 Crush Mitsuhide Akechi C
SBS06017 Demon King of the Sixth Domain Nobunaga Oda C
SBS06015 Dispelling Evil Ranmaru Mori C
SBS06095 Dragon And Right Eye U
SBS06047 Dreamy C
SBS06054 Expert of Utsusemi Sasuke Sarutobi R
SBS06054S Expert of Utsusemi Sasuke Sarutobi SR
SBS06050 Fissure CC
SBS06062 Flawless Motochika Chosokabe U
SBS06025 Flowery Oath CC
SBS06044 Flowery Path of Koi Keiji Maeda C
SBS06046 Food Couple U
SBS06070 From the Same Birthplace U
SBS06058 Furinkazan Shingen Takeda U
SBS06094 Gale Flight Kotaro Fuuma C
SBS06093 Genius of Battle Kenshin Uesugi C
SBS06026 Genius Strategist Hanbei Takenaka RR
SBS06083 God of War Kenshi Uesugi U
SBS06013 Greedy Emperor Kennyo Honganji C
SBS06066 Groundshaking Musashi Miyamoto C
SBS06078 Hero of Oshu Masamune Date R
SBS06065 Hero of Sengoku Period Motochika Chosokabe C
SBS06080 Humanity's Chivalry Koujurou Katakura R
SBS06080S Humanity's Chivalry Koujurou Katakura SR
SBS06072 Kabukimono C
SBS06098 King of Date Troops CR
SBS06092 Kunoichi Kasuga C
SBS06012 Lamenting Soul Nobunaga Oda U
SBS06057 Last Fortress of Takeda Shingen R
SBS06097 Legendary Ninja C
SBS06045 Legendary Stage U
SBS06077 Lightning Speed Holy General Kenshin Uesugi RR
SBS06024 Love Battle!? CC
SBS06011 Love Battle!? Itsuki & Xavi U
SBS06014 Mamushi's Daughter Nouhime C
SBS06051 Man of Sea Motochika Chosokabe RR
SBS06051S Man of Sea Motochika Chosokabe SR
SBS06086 Masamune's Confidant Koujurou Katakura U
SBS06001 Naive And Romantic Itsuki RR
SBS06001S Naive And Romantic Itsuki SR
SBS06005 Natural Child Itsuki R
SBS06069 One Cut Kill Yoshihiro Shimazu C
SBS06088 One-Eyed Dragon Masamune Date C
SBS06075 Oni of Onigashima CC
SBS06053 Oni of the West Sea Motochika Chosokabe R
SBS06091 Overflowing Love Xavi C
SBS06063 Passionate Yukimura Sanada C
SBS06018 Poisoned Teeth Mitsuhide Akechi C
SBS06081 Precocious And Resolute Ujimasa Houjou R
SBS06096 Press On...! U
SBS06082 Refined Guy Masamune Date' R
SBS06082R Refined Guy Masamune Date' RRR
SBS06068 Reliable Brother Motochika Chosokabe C
SBS06036 Remained Time Hanbei Takenaka U
SBS06079 Right Eye of the Dragon Koujurou Katakura R
SBS06009 Rumor Gossiper Oichi U
SBS06064 Sanada Ninja Squad Leader Sasuke Sarutobi C
SBS06020 Silent Killed U
SBS06019 Singular Hidehisa Matsunaga C
SBS06003 Sky Conquering Demong King Nobunaga Oda R
SBS06003R Sky Conquering Demong King Nobunaga Oda RRR
SBS06056 Sky Conquering Lance Yukimura Sanada R
SBS06056R Sky Conquering Lance Yukimura Sanada RRR
SBS06004 Son of Demon King Ranmaru Mori R
SBS06084 Southern Barbaric Ways Xavi U
SBS06099 Speedy Like the Wind And Lightning CC
SBS06052 Speedy Under the Blue Sky Sasuke Sarutobi RR
SBS06042 Storm of Koi Keiji Maeda C
SBS06033 Strong Troops, Rich Country Hideyoshi Toyotomi U
SBS06037 Strongest of Sengoku Tadakatsu Honda U
SBS06039 Surface of Ice Motonari Mouri C
SBS06030 Talented And Beautiful Matsu R
SBS06030S Talented And Beautiful Matsu SR
SBS06022 Treason C
SBS06029 Trickery General Motonari Mouri R
SBS06074 Two Ninjas CC
SBS06076 Under the Moonlight, For You Kasuga RR
SBS06076S Under the Moonlight, For You Kasuga SR
SBS06085 Unlimited Six-Claw Style Masamune Date U
SBS06087 Unrivaled in World Masamune Date U
SBS06002 Unrivaled Profusion Nouhime RR
SBS06002S Unrivaled Profusion Nouhime SR
SBS06008 Unwavering Faith Nagamasa Asai U
SBS06038 Vagabond Keiji Maeda C
SBS06089 Vice General Koujurou Katakura C
SBS06032 Warrior Emperor Hideyoshi Toyotomi R
SBS06032S Warrior Emperor Hideyoshi Toyotomi SR
SBS06100 Warrior of Love CC
SBS06010 Wife of Demon King Nouhime U
SBS06060 Young Fighter of Takeda Yukimura Sanada U
SBS06007 Younger Sister of Demon King Oichi R
SBS0623SP Ambition of Unification SP
SBS0648SP Conflict SP
SBS0673SP Best of Japanese Troops SP
SBS0698SP King of Date Troops SP

2009 Weiss Schwarz Sengoku Basara TD

SBS06T06 Blue and Red Masamune and Yukimura
SBS06T11 Chant of Battle Spirit Yukimura Sanada
SBS06T05 Fissure
SBS06T13 Flawless Motochika Chosokabe
SBS06T04 Flowery Path of Koi Keiji Maeda
SBS06T09 Furinkazan Shingen Takeda
SBS06T07 Hero of Sengoku Period Motochika Chosokabe
SBS06T15 Japanese No1 Troops
SBS06T14 Kabukimono
SBS06101 Koi Tactics Keiji Maeda
SBS06T16 Oni of Onigashima
SBS06T08 Passionate Yukimura Sanada
SBS06T12 Reliable Brother Motochika Chosokabe
SBS06T10 Sanada Ninja Squad Leader Sasuke Sarutobi
SBS06T03 Storm of Koi Keiji Maeda
SBS06T02 Strong Troops, Rich Country Hideyoshi Toyotomi
SBS06102 Sworn Enemies Masamune and Yukimura
SBS06T01 Vagabond Keiji Maeda

2009 Weiss Schwarz Shining Force EXA

SES04035 Amitaliri and Faulklin U
SES04053 Amitaliri, Acting According to Her Feelings R
SES04040 Amitaliri, Bomber Girl C
SES04028 Amitaliri, Demonic Girl R
SES04028S Amitaliri, Demonic Girl SR
SES04056 Amitaliri, Phoenix Trainer R
SES04052 Amitaliri, Pretty Girl Heroine RR
SES04052S Amitaliri, Pretty Girl Heroine SR
SES04036 Amitaliri, Self-Proclaimed Genius Witch Girl U
SES04062 Amitaliri, Surprised U
SES04054 Amitaliri, Witch R
SES04017 Avalon, Golden Knight C
SES04011 Avalon, Legendary Hero U
SES04096 Awakening of Geo-Fortress U
SES04097 Battle Again C
SES04099 Blade of Fate CC
SES04039 Catheana, Only One Who Understands the Emperor C
SES04072 Crimson Palace C
SES04019 Curse of the Holy Sword Toma and Cyrille C
SES04063 Cyrille and Amitaliri in Swimsuits C
SES04008 Cyrille and Zhirra U
SES04010 Cyrille and Zhirra, Friendly U
SES04082 Cyrille and Zhirra, Understanding Destiny R
SES04092 Cyrille in Swimsuits C
SES04006 Cyrille in Witch Hat R
SES04013 Cyrille, Angry C
SES04091 Cyrille, Angry While Blushing C
SES04077 Cyrille, Cat-Eared RR
SES04077R Cyrille, Cat-Eared RRR
SES04080 Cyrille, Changing R
SES04079 Cyrille, Chef R
SES04001 Cyrille, Girl with Many Mysteries RR
SES04001S Cyrille, Girl with Many Mysteries SR
SES04093 Cyrille, Good Student C
SES04014 Cyrille, Laughing C
SES04076 Cyrille, Master of the Holy Sword RR
SES04076S Cyrille, Master of the Holy Sword SR
SES04025 Cyrille's Feelings CC
SES04100 Cyrille's Truth CC
SES04047 Dignity of the King C
SES04095 Discouraged U
SES04034 Duga, Prideful Werewolf U
SES04044 Duga, Wild Beast C
SES04050 Elven Warrior CC
SES04065 Faulklin, Afraid C
SES04055 Faulklin, Attendent to Amitaliri R
SES04027 Faulklin, Gotten Lost RR
SES04027R Faulklin, Gotten Lost RRR
SES04067 Faulklin, Likes to Cry C
SES04059 Faulklin, Loyal Hound U
SES04031 Faulklin, Young Boy of Beastman Tribes R
SES04049 Faulklin's Self-Introduction CC
SES04038 Fluffy Tail Faulklin C
SES04005 Gadfort, Kentauros Knight R
SES04018 Gadfort, Kind Knight C
SES04033 Gantetsu, Master Craftsman U
SES04085 Garyu, Ancient Dragon U
SES04015 Gilnay and Hikanay C
SES04048 Goal La Vaes CR
SES04020 Guardian of the Geo-Fortress U
SES04024 Holy Sword, Shining Force CC
SES04074 I'll Become La Vaes Someday CC
SES04066 Lurnazael, Second-in-Command to the Queen C
SES04042 Maebelle, Archer C
SES04032 Maebelle, Denizen of the Forest R
SES04026 Maebelle, Gluttonous RR
SES04046 Magical Fortress U
SES04087 Master Cyrille U
SES04012 Master Toma U
SES04088 Money Over Life Bornay C
SES04089 Phillip, Commander C
SES04098 Power of the Holy Sword CR
SES04045 Pursuer U
SES04029 Quintol Faulklin R
SES04029S Quintol Faulklin SR
SES04043 Ragnadaam III C
SES04037 Ragnadaam, Emperor Aiming for the Sky U
SES04030 Ragnadaam, Young Lion Emperor R
SES04051 Riemsianne La Vaes RR

SES04051R Riemsianne La Vaes RRR
SES04060 Riemsianne, Hellfire of Purgatory U
SES04068 Riemsianne, Leader of the Demon Tribe C
SES04057 Riemsianne, Queen of Fyrlandt R
SES04057S Riemsianne, Queen of Fyrlandt SR
SES04061 Riemsianne, Seducing U
SES04064 Riemsianne, Successor to the Name "La Vaes" C
SES04069 Rival Cyrille and Amitaliri C
SES04073 Seduction of La Vaes CR
SES04094 Single-Horned Garyu C
SES04058 Strongest Ball Defense Theory Adam U
SES04075 That Is Mine CC
SES04021 The Other Holy Sword U
SES04016 Toma and Cyrille C
SES04002 Toma and Zenus RR
SES04007 Toma, Chosen One R
SES04007R Toma, Chosen One RRR
SES04083 Toma, Hot-blooded U
SES04090 Toma, Lord of Geo-Fortress C
SES04078 Toma, Master of the Holy Sword R
SES04078S Toma, Master of the Holy Sword SR
SES04003 Toma, Outlaw R
SES04081 Toma, Overfilled with Sense of Justice R
SES04004 Toma, Wild Child R
SES04004S Toma, Wild Child SR
SES04041 Too Much Over-Confidence Amitaliri C
SES04086 Two Holy Swords Toma and Cyrille U
SES04070 Unleashed Skyship U
SES04023 VS Boar CR
SES04009 Way of the Chivalry Gadfort U
SES04022 Will of Toma C
SES04071 Young Lion Emperor VS La Vaes U
SES04084 Zenus and Zhirra U
SES0424SP Holy Sword, Shining Force SP
SES0448SP Goal La Vaes SP
SES0473SP Seduction of La Vaes SP
SES0499SP Blade of Fate SP

2009 Weiss Schwarz Shining Force EXA TD

SE04T16 2 Books of the Sacred Sword Toma and Cyrille
SE04T05 Avalon, Golden Knight
SE04T18 Blade of Destiny
SE04T03 Chivalry Gadfort
SE04T07 Curse of the Sacred Sword Toma and Cyrille
SE04T02 Cyrille and Zhirra
SE04T17 Cyrille's Truth
SE04T12 Embarrased Angry Cyrille
SE04101 Energetic Toma
SE04T06 Good Friends Cyrille and Zhirra
SE04T14 Honor-roll Student Cyrille
SE04102 Knowledgeable Cyrille
SE04T08 Master Toma
SE04T01 Outraged Cyrille
SE04T10 Sacred Sword Shining Force
SE04T15 Slicing Angle Garyu
SE04T13 Swimsuit Cyrille
SE04T04 Toma and Cyrille
SE04T09 Toma's Pride
SE04T11 Zenus and Zhirra

2010 Weiss Schwarz Angel Beats and Kud Wafter

ABW11025 A Lady's Greatest Happiness CC
ABW11004 A Solitary Angel R
KWW11085 A-Chan Senpai, Evil Schemes U
KWW11086 A-Chan Senpai, Family Studies Club President U
KWW11090 A-Chan Senpai, Kud's Ally C
KWW11078 A-Chan Senpai, Superficial Knowledge of Sex R
KWW11078S A-Chan Senpai, Superficial Knowledge of Sex SR
ABW11073 Afterlife Battlefront CR
ABW11024 Angel Alight CC
ABW11017 Angel, Enemy of the Front C
ABW11021 Angel's Mapo Tofu U
KWW11048 Astronomical Observation CR
ABW11072 Call Me Christ C
KWW11100 Encounter by the Poolside CC
KWW11099 Exotic Pledge CC
KWW11050 Explosion Accident CC
ABW11064 Fujimaki and Ooyama C
KWW11095 Gruesome News U
KWW11094 Hermit A-Chan Senpai C
KWW11081 Himuro, Kud's Childhood Friend R
KWW11091 Himuro, Out of Bath C
KWW11087 Himuro, Rocket Launch Experiment U
KWW11088 Himuro, Science Club President C
KWW11084 Himuro, Big Fan of Pheasant's Eyes U
ABW11066 Hinata, Getting Going C
ABW11060 Hinata, Responding to Thoughts U
ABW11015 Hisako, Sisterly C
ABW11022 Hypnotism C
KWW11096 Icarus U
KWW11047 Image Change C
ABW11014 Iwasawa, Charismatic Vocal C
ABW11012 Iwasawa, Leader of GirlDeMo U
ABW11053 Kanade and Yuri, Allied Front R
ABW11005 Kanade in Straw Hats R
ABW11018 Kanade, Clumsy Opposition C
ABW11002 Kanade, Heart of Yuzuru RR
ABW11002S Kanade, Heart of Yuzuru SR
ABW11010 Kanade, Reason for Fighting U
ABW11001 Kanade, Sending Everyone Off RR
ABW11007 Kanade, Standing Still R
ABW11007S Kanade, Standing Still SR
ABW11008 Kanade, Student Council President U
KWW11041 Kanata, Ally of Kid Sisters C
KWW11043 Kanata, Dorm Advisor C
KWW11040 Kanata, Innocence C
KWW11031 Kanata, Punctual R
KWW11031S Kanata, Punctual SR
KWW11082 Kud in Swimsuits R
KWW11089 Kud in Yukata C
KWW11076 Kud, Admiring the Universe RR
KWW11083 Kud, CRamming U
KWW11037 Kud, Cute Girlfriend U
KWW11026 Kud, Daily Homemade Cooking RR
KWW11035 Kud, Enjoying the Date U
KWW11080 Kud, Gear of "Like" R
KWW11080S Kud, Gear of "Like" SR
KWW11028 Kud, Lap Pillow Under the Tree Shades R
KWW11079 Kud, Light of Balloons R
KWW11093 Kud, Shopping C
KWW11034 Kud, Sniffing U
KWW11032 Kud, Step Towards Unbounded Heights R
KWW11032S Kud, Step Towards Unbounded Heights SR
ABW11069 Matsushita 5-dan C
ABW11076 Memory While Alive CC
ABW11009 Naoi, Self-Proclaimed God U
KWW11097 NO SIGNAL C
ABW11067 Noda, Opposition C
ABW11071 Operation Tornado U
ABW11058 Otonashi, Conflicting U
ABW11056 Otonashi, Seeking the Past R
ABW11013 Otonashi, Understanding Kanade C
ABW11019 Otonashi, Who Has No Memories of His Life C
ABW11023 Power to Protect CR
ABW11075 Returned Feeling CC
KWW11036 Riki and Kud, Just the Two of Them U
KWW11030 Riki and Kud, Things Believed R
KWW11033 Riki, Kud's Boyfriend U
KWW11049 Road to Mile High CC
KWW11046 Running U
KWW11045 Sharing Room at One Point U
KWW11029 Shiina Arizuki R
KWW11027 Shiina, Dream Chaser Girl RR
KWW11027R Shiina, Dream Chaser Girl RRR
KWW11042 Shiina, Feelings Towards Nanohana C
KWW11038 Shiina, Insisting on Materials C
ABW11054 Shiina, Skill of 100 People R
ABW11054S Shiina, Skill of 100 People SR
ABW11055 SSS Yuri R
KWW11077 Stardust Himuro RR
KWW11077R Stardust Himuro RRR
ABW11065 Takamatsu, Looks Thinner in Clothing C
ABW11020 The Song They Wanted to Sing U
ABW11070 Thrust Engine U
ABW11068 TK, Real Identity Unknown C
KWW11044 Ui Arizuki C
KWW11039 Ui, Waitress C
KWW11098 Wish of Grounded Albina CR
ABW11003 Yui, Assistant of GirlDeMo R
ABW11016 Yui, Iwasawa's Successor C
ABW11011 Yui, Mounting Position U
ABW11006 Yui, Wanting to Do A Lot R
ABW11006R Yui, Wanting to Do A Lot RRR
KWW11092 Yuki Himuro C
ABW11061 Yuri, Commander U
ABW11063 Yuri, Executing Operation C
ABW11062 Yuri, Graduating from this World U
ABW11057 Yuri, Resisting the Absurd Destiny R
ABW11057S Yuri, Resisting the Absurd Destiny SR
ABW11052 Yuri, Sister Role RR
ABW11052R Yuri, Sister Role RRR
ABW11051 Yuri, Strategic Provokes RR
ABW11059 Yusa, Operator U
ABW1101SP Kanade, Sending Everyone Off SP
ABW1151SP Yuri, Strategic Provokes SP
KWW1126SP Kud, Daily Homemade Cooking SP
KWW1176SP Kud, Admiring the Universe SP

2010 Weiss Schwarz Angel Beats and Kud Wafter TD

ABW11T07 A Lady's Greatest Happiness
KWW11T09 A-Chan Senpai, Family Studies Club President
ABW11T04 Angel, Enemy of the Battlefront
KWW11T13 Encounter by the Poolside
KWW11T14 Exotic Pledge
KWW11105 Frankly- Kud
ABW11103 Girl Who Fights Destiny
KWW11T10 Himuro, Out of Bath
KWW11T08 Himuro, Science Club President
ABW11T02 Hisako, Sisterly
ABW11T01 Iwasawa, Charismatic Vocal
ABW11T05 Iwasawa, Leader of GirlDeMo
ABW11101 Kanade, the Girl Called "Angel"
KWW11T11 Kud, Shopping
KWW11102 Kud, the Girl with Wings
ABW11T06 Otonashi, Who Has No Memories of His Life
KWW11T12 Resting A-Chan Senpai
ABW11104 Yui, Big Fan of GirlDeMo
ABW11T03 Yui, Iwasawa's Successor

2010 Weiss Schwarz CLANNAD Vol. 3 Extra

CLWE0747 Akio Furukawa RE
CLWE0721 Big Sister Kyou C
CLWE0734 Do You Like This School? RE
CLWE0713 Encounter And FArewell C
CLWE0714 Family's Bond C
CLWE0740 Fuuko and Kouko RE
CLWE0761 Fuuko Ibuki RE
CLWE0762 Fuuko in Pajamas RE
CLWE0738 Fuuko, Ghost Girl RE
CLWE0735 Fuuko, Legendary Starfish User RE
CLWE0717 Fuuko, Ushio's Friend C
CLWE0724 Girl of the Doomed World C
CLWE0751 Girl of the Fantasy World RE
CLWE0726 Kotomi and Tomoyo C
CLWE0752 Kotomi Ichinose RE
CLWE0770 Kotomi, At Her Own Pace RE
CLWE0750 Kotomi, Destructor of Rhythm RE
CLWE0769 Kotomi, Genius Girl RE
CLWE0749 Kotomi, Honorary Book Committee Member RE
CLWE0723 Kotomi, Natural Girl R
CLWE0753 Kyou and Ryou RE
CLWE0764 Kyou and Tomoyo RE
CLWE0765 Kyou Fujibaya RE
CLWE0745 Kyou, Berserking Girl RE
CLWE0767 Kyou, Chairman RE
CLWE0742 Kyou, Loves Caring RE
CLWE0744 Kyou, Thinking of Younger Sister RE
CLWE0720 Kyou, Ushio's Homeroom Teacher R
CLWE0768 Love Triangle RE
CLWE0712 Lovers Nagisa and Tomoya C
CLWE0757 Mei, Love Cupid RE
CLWE0718 Misae Sagara C
CLWE0748 Nagisa and Kotomi RE
CLWE0722 Nagisa and Kyou and Ryou C
CLWE0727 Nagisa and Kyou and Ryou, Waitresses C
CLWE0766 Nagisa and Kyou RE
CLWE0743 Nagisa and Kyou, Bakery RE
CLWE0709 Nagisa and Mei C
CLWE0710 Nagisa and Sanae, Friendly Mother And Daughter C
CLWE0711 Nagisa and Tomoya and Akio, Warm Family C
CLWE0755 Nagisa and Ushio RE
CLWE0731 Nagisa Furukawa RE
CLWE0756 Nagisa Okazaki RE
CLWE0732 Nagisa, Caretaker RE
CLWE0728 Nagisa, Drama Club President RE
CLWE0730 Nagisa, Girl Who Stood Still RE
CLWE0706 Nagisa, Loves Dumplings R
CLWE0708 Nagisa, Loves This Town C
CLWE0703 Nagisa, Sickly Girl R
CLWE0701 Nagisa, Student of Hikarizaka High School R
CLWE0705 Nagisa, Tomoya's Lover R
CLWE0754 Present to My Daughter RE
CLWE0771 Ryou, Fortune Telling Lover RE
CLWE0746 Sanae Furukawa RE
CLWE0716 Tomoya in Pajama C
CLWE0729 Tomoya Okazaki RE
CLWE0702 Tomoya, Invitation to Date R
CLWE0758 Tomoya, Optimistic RE
CLWE0759 Tomoyo Sakagami RE
CLWE0737 Tomoyo, All-Around in Sports RE
CLWE0736 Tomoyo, Family Feel RE
CLWE0739 Tomoyo, Legendary Girl RE
CLWE0719 Tomoyo, Strongest Woman C
CLWE0760 Tomoyo, Student Council President RE
CLWE0715 Tomoyo, Transfer Student R
CLWE0763 Tomoyo's Vow RE
CLWE0741 Until the End of the Dream RE
CLWE0707 Ushio Okazaki C
CLWE0704 Ushio, Daughter of Nagisa R
CLWE0733 Youhei Sunohara RE
CLWE0725 Yukine Miyazawa C
CLWE0772 Yuusuke Yoshino RE

2010 Weiss Schwarz Da Capo II Plus Communication Extra

DCWE02001 Aisia in Santa Suit R
DCWE02006 Akane, Going on a Trip R
DCWE02014 Anzu, Wishing upon a Star R
DCWE02018 Chairman's Miko Outfit C
DCWE02010 Erica in Swimsuits R
DCWE02013 Erica, Sleepwalking C
DCWE02008 Koko, Halloween C
DCWE02009 Let's Eat Together C
DCWE02004 Luxurious Worry C
DCWE02003 Mahiru, Sending Souls C
DCWE02015 Maya, Volunteer Miko C
DCWE02016 Mayuki in the Hydrangea Field R
DCWE02011 Minatsu, Tossing Beans C
DCWE02007 Nanaka, Songstress C
DCWE02002 Otome, Doll R
DCWE02005 Selfish Aisia C
DCWE02017 Sorry. And, thank you C
DCWE02012 Yume, Moon Watching C

2010 Weiss Schwarz Da Capo Plus Communication TD

DCW09T07 Aisia in Maid Uniform
DCW09103 Confessing, Sakura
DCW09105 Hypocritical Yume
DCW09T09 Kotori and Nemu and Sakura
DCW09T06 Mahiru in Gymnastics Outfit
DCW09T11 Myu, Truthful And Holding On
DCW09T12 Nemu, Disciplinary Committee
DCW09102 Nemu, Dumplings Over Flowers
DCW09T14 Only One Wish
DCW09T02 Otome, Age of Sophistication
DCW09101 Otome, Caretaker
DCW09T05 Otome, Uniform of Attached School
DCW09T03 Sakura in Maid Uniform
DCW09T04 Sakura, Cute and Energetic
DCW09T08 Season of Cherry Blooming
DCW09104 Unwithering Cherry Blossom
DCW09T13 White Christmas
DCW09T10 Yume and Otome and Erica
DCW09T01 Yuuhi Takanashi

2010 Weiss Schwarz Da Capo-Da Capo II Plus Communication

DCW09078 3 Baka Suginami and Yoshiyuki and Wataru R
DCW09050 Act of Conveying CC
DCW09030 Ai Hanasaki R
DCW09030S Ai Hanasaki SR
DCW09019 Aisia in Maid Uniform C
DCW09001 Aisia, Magician of Toys RR
DCW09001S Aisia, Magician of Toys SR
DCW09009 Aisia, Special Supplement Lessons U
DCW09034 Akane in Miko Outfit U
DCW09039 Akane, Cooking C
DCW09036 Akane, New Scenery U
DCW09090 Alice, Poker Face C
DCW09088 Anzu in Pajama C
DCW09084 Anzu, Choosing Ski Wear U
DCW09092 Anzu, Cooking C
DCW09077 Anzu, New Student Council President RR
DCW09095 Bento with Maya U
DCW09046 C- Confess? C
DCW09094 Erica Murasaki R
DCW09054S Erica Murasaki SR
DCW09062 Erica, Going on a Trip U
DCW09066 Erica's Decision C
DCW09097 Faces of Family CR
DCW09097R Faces of Family RRR
DCW09100 Friends CC
DCW09004 Girl Carrying Cherry Branches R
DCW09004S Girl Carrying Cherry Branches SR
DCW09072 Image Seen in Someday's Dream CR
DCW09072R Image Seen in Someday's Dream RRR
DCW09099 Invitation to the Rooftop CC
DCW09012 Justice Magician Otome U
DCW09031 Koko, Cooking R
DCW09029 Koko, Date on Temple Festival R
DCW09037 Koko, Holding Hands U
DCW09027 Koko, Unchanged Birthplace RR
DCW09064 Kotori and Nemu and Sakura C
DCW09042 Kotori in Pajama C
DCW09033 Kotori Shirakawa U
DCW09026 Kotori, Shopping RR
DCW09043 Kumiko Takamatsu C
DCW09024 Last Amount of Time CC
DCW09098 Last Chance CR
DCW09022 Last Inquiry CR
DCW09018 Mahiru in Gymnastics Outfit C
DCW09008 Mahiru Takanashi U
DCW09007 Mahiru, An Important Meeting R
DCW09040 Maki, Gallant C
DCW09087 Mako, Lively and Hates Losing U
DCW09086 Maya, Cooking U
DCW09093 Maya, Dating C
DCW09079 Maya, White Clothing R
DCW09080 Mayuki in Ski Wear R
DCW09091 Mayuki, Ace of Track and Field Club C
DCW09082 Mayuki, Hates Losing So Works Hard R
DCW09082S Mayuki, Hates Losing So Works Hard SR
DCW09085 Megumi Imai U
DCW09067 Miharu, Unforgettable Memory C
DCW09044 Miki Asahina C
DCW09028 Miki in Gymnastics Outfit R
DCW09055 Minatsu Amakase R
DCW09069 Minatsu, Banana-min C
DCW09058 Minatsu, Dog Loving U
DCW09074 Minatsu's Wish CC
DCW09076 Moe and Mako, Nabe Party RR
DCW09076S Moe and Mako, Nabe Party SR
DCW09083 Moe, Extremely Her Own Way U
DCW09094 Moe, Mysterious Xylophone Girl C
DCW09063 Myu, Cleaning C
DCW09057 Myu, Successful Cooking R
DCW09059 Myu, Truthful And Holding On U
DCW09038 Nanaka and Koko, Light Music Band C
DCW09041 Nanaka in Gymnastics Outfit C
DCW09035 Nanaka Shirakawa U
DCW09032 Nanaka, Holding Hands R
DCW09032S Nanaka, Holding Hands SR
DCW09068 Nemu, Accommodating C
DCW09051 Nemu, Energetic RR
DCW09051S Nemu, Energetic SR
DCW09061 Nemu, Judgment U
DCW09075 Only One Wish CC
DCW09014 Otome, Age of Sophistication C
DCW09002 Otome, Awkward Days RR
DCW09017 Otome, Uniform of Attached School C
DCW09020 Otome's Bento U
DCW09025 Please Be Happy CC
DCW09071 Present for Sakuya C
DCW09015 Sakura in Maid Uniform C
DCW09016 Sakura, Cute and Energetic C
DCW09011 Sakura, Magician U
DCW09006 Sakura, Returned Childhood Friend R
DCW09045 Scene Seen in Dreams U
DCW09023 Season of Cherry Blooming CR
DCW09023R Season of Cherry Blooming RRR
DCW09056 Senpai Miharu R
DCW09021 Service Battle C
DCW09081 Snow-Moon-Flower Koko and Anzu and Akane R
DCW09047 Song of Kotori CR
DCW09047R Song of Kotori RRR
DCW09089 Suzume Isowashi C
DCW09048 The Last Date CR
DCW09096 Tomorrow's Wake-Up Forecast C
DCW09049 Trustworthy CC
DCW09073 Truth CR
DCW09070 White Christmas U
DCW09005 Yoriko, Working Hard R
DCW09010 Yuki Asakura U
DCW09003 Yuki, Mother of the Asakura Household R
DCW09065 Yume and Otome and Erica C
DCW09060 Yume Asakura U
DCW09052 Yume, Image Seen in that Dream RR
DCW09053 Yume, Obedient Yet Spoiled Child R
DCW09013 Yuuhi Takanashi C
DCW0902SP Otome, Awkward Days SP
DCW0927SP Koko, Unchanged Birthplace SP
DCW0952SP Yume, Image Seen in that Dream SP
DCW0977SP Anzu, New Student Council President SP

2010 Weiss Schwarz Evangelion Rebuild

EVS12087 10th Angel U
EVS12035 3rd Angel U
EVS12034 4th Angel U
EVS12039 5th Angel C
EVS12092 6th Angel C
EVS12064 7th Angel C
EVS12066 8th Angel C
EVS12070 9th Angel C
EVS12062 Ace of the Euro Air Force Asuka U
EVS12050 Adults' Convenience And Own Goal CC
EVS12021 Angel's Assault U
EVS12057 Asuka in Test Plugsuit R
EVS12057S Asuka in Test Plugsuit SR
EVS12054 Asuka in the Elevator R
EVS12068 Asuka in the Purification Test Facility C
EVS12051 Asuka Langley Shikinami RR
EVS12051R Asuka Langley Shikinami RRR
EVS12061 Asuka, Cooking!? U
EVS12052 Asuka, Finishing Blow RR
EVS12067 Asuka, Monopolizing? C
EVS12055 Asuka, Moving R
EVS12055S Asuka, Moving SR
EVS12058 Asuka, Pointing Out Mistakes U
EVS12065 Asuka, Ready for Deployment C
EVS12056 Asuka, Unaccepting R
EVS12093 Ayanami in Her Apartment C
EVS12090 Ayanami, Bandaged C
EVS12078 Ayanami, Classmate R
EVS12078S Ayanami, Classmate SR
EVS12076 Ayanami, Emergency Conscription RR
EVS12076R Ayanami, Emergency Conscription RRR
EVS12077 Ayanami, EVA-00 Pilot RR
EVS12095 Ayanami, Greeting C
EVS12082 Ayanami, Pledge to Protect Shinji R
EVS12082S Ayanami, Pledge to Protect Shinji SR
EVS12081 Ayanami, Tasked with Defense R
EVS12099 Ayanami's Smile CC
EVS12027 Beast Mari RR
EVS12027S Beast Mari SR
EVS12100 Can You Back Off? CC
EVS12098 Desperation Attack CR
EVS12072 Disinfection U
EVS12096 Dummy System U
EVS12048 Encounter on the Rooftop CR
EVS12079 EVA-00, Test Model (Revised) R
EVS12091 EVA-00, Test Model C
EVS12002 EVA-01 (Awaken State 1) RR
EVS12012 EVA-01 Pilot Shinji U
EVS12019 EVA-01, G-Type Equipment C
EVS12023 EVA-01's First Battle CR
EVS12060 EVA-02, Air-thrust S-Type Equipment U
EVS12031 EVA-02, Beast State 2 R
EVS12031S EVA-02, Beast State 2 SR
EVS12069 EVA-02, Regular Practical Type C
EVS12042 Evangelion Locally Specified EVA-05 C
EVS12016 Evangelion Test EVA-01 C
EVS12074 Finishing Blow CC
EVS12001 First Battle Shinji RR
EVS12001R First Battle Shinji RRR
EVS12025 Future Entrusted CC
EVS12088 Gendo Ikari C
EVS12080 Gendo, Giving Orders R
EVS12046 Hidden Code "The Beast" U
EVS12053 Hikari Horaki R
EVS12047 Invitation to a Date U
EVS12037 Kaji, Escaped U
EVS12009 Kaworu Nagisa U
EVS12006 Kaworu on the Lunar Surface R
EVS12006S Kaworu on the Lunar Surface SR
EVS12063 Kensuke Aida C
EVS12089 Kozo Fuyutsuki C
EVS12043 Makoto Hyuga C
EVS12026 Mari Illustrious Makinami RR
EVS12026R Mari Illustrious Makinami RRR
EVS12045 Mari in Cockpit of EVA-05 C
EVS12038 Mari, Deploying C
EVS12036 Mari, Determined U
EVS12032 Mari, Hard Fighting R
EVS12028 Mari, Looking at the Sky R
EVS12040 Mari, New Plugsuits C
EVS12029 Mari, Secret Entry R
EVS12033 Mari, the Other EVA-02 Pilot U
EVS12030 Maya Ibuki R
EVS12010 Misato in the Living Room U
EVS12013 Misato in the Picture C
EVS12005 Misato Katsuragi R
EVS12018 Misato, Driver C
EVS12017 Misato, Emergency Situation C
EVS12007 Misato, Entrusting the Future R
EVS12007S Misato, Entrusting the Future SR
EVS12097 Mysterious Facility U
EVS12024 Operation Yashima CC
EVS12008 PenPen U
EVS12004 Pre-Mission Shinji R
EVS12085 Rei Ayanami U
EVS12094 Ritsuki, Meeting Again C
EVS12083 Ritsuko Akagi U
EVS12044 Ryoji Kaji C
EVS12071 Sealed EVA-02 U
EVS12022 Second Impact U
EVS12041 Shigeru Aoba C
EVS12020 Shinji Ikari C
EVS12014 Shinji on the Rooftop C
EVS12003 Shinji, Bento Duty R
EVS12011 Shinji, Fired!? U
EVS12015 Shinji, Meeting C
EVS12084 Smiling Ayanami U
EVS12049 The Last Card CC
EVS12075 Three People Needed CC
EVS12059 Toji Suzuhara U
EVS12073 Worst Possible Situation CR
EVS12086 Yelling EVA-00 (Revised) U
EVS1202SP EVA-01 (Awaken State 1) SP
EVS1229SP Mari, Secret Entry SP
EVS1252SP Asuka, Finishing Blow SP
EVS1277SP Ayanami, EVA-00 Pilot SP

2010 Weiss Schwarz Evangelion Rebuild TD

EVS12T11 6th Angel
EVS12T08 Angel's Assault
EVS12103 Ayanami & Gendou

EVS12102 Ayanami by the Window
EVS12T12 Ayanami in Her Room
EVS12T10 Ayanami, Bandaged
EVS12104 Ayanami, Entry Plug
EVS12T13 Ayanami's Smile
EVS12T14 Can You Back Off?
EVS12T07 EVA-01, G-Type Equipment
EVS12T04 Evangelion Test EVA-01
EVS12T06 Misato, Driver
EVS12T05 Misato, Emergency Situation
EVS12101 Misato, Operation Chief
EVS12T09 Operation Yashima
EVS12T02 Picture of Misato
EVS12T01 Shinji on the Rooftop
EVS12T03 Shinji, Meeting
EVS12105 Shinji, Transfer Student

2010 Weiss Schwarz Fairy Tail

COMPLETE SET (116)
BOOSTER BOX (20 PACKS) 60.00 80.00
BOOSTER PACK (8 CARDS) 3.00 4.00
RELEASED ON
FTS09034 Aquarius, Aquarius U
FTS09009 Aria of the Sky U
FTS09097 Banquet of Demons U
FTS09039 Beast Arm Elfman C
FTS09004 Black Wing Armor Erza R
FTS09004R Black Wing Armor Erza RRR
FTS09023 Blumenblatt CR
FTS09073 Brilliant Flames of the Fire Dragon CR
FTS09091 Cana Alberona C
FTS09093 Cana, Magical Cards C
FTS09048 Celestial Power CR
FTS09047 Changeling U
FTS09025 Circle Sword CC
FTS09049 DEAR KABY CC
FTS09021 Destroying the Moon? U
FTS09072 Dragon Egg U
FTS09054 Erza Scarlet R
FTS09003 Erza, Extremely Close Type R
FTS09003S Erza, Extremely Close Type SR
FTS09010 Erza, Large Luggage U
FTS09001 Erza, Magical Swordsman RR
FTS09008 Erza, S-Level Magician U
FTS09002 Erza, Titania RR
FTS09002S Erza, Titania SR
FTS09017 Erza, Top Female Magician of Fairy Tail C
FTS09022 Fairy Law U
FTS09024 Fairy Tail CC
FTS09005 Flame Empress Armor Erza R
FTS09050 Force Gate Closure CC
FTS09055 Gajeel of Iron Dragon R
FTS09058 Gajeel Redfox U
FTS09070 Gajeel, Iron Dragon Slayer Mage C
FTS09057 Gajeel, Strongest Man of Phantom Lord R
FTS09077 Gray Fullbuster RR
FTS09077R Gray Fullbuster RRR
FTS09086 Gray, Determined U
FTS09082 Gray, Fairy Tail Magician R
FTS09082R Gray, Fairy Tail Magician RRR
FTS09092 Gray, Ice Magic C
FTS09088 Gray, Lyon's Junior C
FTS09085 Gray, Natsu's Quarrel Partner U
FTS09081 Gray, Stripping Habit R
FTS09078 Gray, Ur's Apprentice R
FTS09078S Gray, Ur's Apprentice SR
FTS09064 Happy C
FTS09066 Happy, Natsu's Partner C
FTS09006 Heaven's Wheel Armor Erza R
FTS09006R Heaven's Wheel Armor Erza RRR
FTS09099 Ice Cannon CC
FTS09098 Ice Geyser CR
FTS09076 Juvia Lockser RR
FTS09076S Juvia Lockser SR
FTS09083 Juvia of the Great Sea U
FTS09084 Juvia, Maiden in Love U
FTS09095 Juvia, Phantom Magician C
FTS09046 Key to the Gate U
FTS09007 Laxus, Grandson of Makarov R
FTS09015 Laxus, S-Level Magician C
FTS09014 Levy McGarden C
FTS09033 Lisanna U
FTS09036 Loke, Ring Magic U
FTS09044 Lucy and Happy C
FTS09040 Lucy Heartfilia C
FTS09042 Lucy in Maid Outfit C
FTS09037 Lucy, Celestial Magician U
FTS09031 Lucy, Daughter of Heartfilia Household R
FTS09027 Lucy, Fairy Tail Magician RR
FTS09032 Lucy, Holder Type Magician R
FTS09028 Lucy, Lady of Heartfilia Zaibatsu R
FTS09028R Lucy, Lady of Heartfilia Zaibatsu RRR
FTS09029 Lucy, Literature Girl R
FTS09026 Lucy, Rookie Magician RR
FTS09026S Lucy, Rookie Magician SR
FTS09030 Lucy, Still A Rookie R
FTS09030S Lucy, Still A Rookie SR
FTS09089 Lyon, Sub-Zero Emperor C
FTS09018 Makarov, Ten Wizard Saints C
FTS09012 Master Jose, Phantom Lord U
FTS09013 Master Makarov, Fairy Tail C
FTS09038 Mirajane, Fairy Tail Mascot C
FTS09035 Mirajane, Former S-Level Magician U
FTS09096 Moon Drip U
FTS09019 Mystogan, S-Level Magician C
FTS09053 Natsu and Happy R
FTS09053S Natsu and Happy SR
FTS09061 Natsu and Happy, Childhood U
FTS09065 Natsu Dragneel C
FTS09063 Natsu, Always Full Strength C
FTS09060 Natsu, Child Raised as Dragon U
FTS09052 Natsu, Fairy Tail Magician RR
FTS09062 Natsu, Flame Dragon Slayer Mage U
FTS09051 Natsu, Living by Instinct RR
FTS09051S Natsu, Living by Instinct SR
FTS09056 Natsu, Power of Dragon R
FTS09056R Natsu, Power of Dragon RRR
FTS09068 Natsu, Surprisingly Calm C
FTS09059 Natsu, Trouble Child U
FTS09067 Natsu, Young Dragon C
FTS09090 New Target Gray C
FTS09020 No Longer Lost Erza C
FTS09011 Porlyusica, Healing Magician U
FTS09074 Roar of the Fire Dragon CC
FTS09075 Roar of the Iron Dragon CC
FTS09016 Shinigami Erigor C
FTS09094 Siegrain, Young Council Member C
FTS09071 S-Level Quest U
FTS09041 Sol of the Land C
FTS09043 Speaks with Fists Elfman C
FTS09069 Totomaru of the Conflagration C
FTS09080 Ur, Gray's Master R
FTS09079 Ur's Teaching Gray R
FTS09087 Ur's Tear Ultear U
FTS09045 Virgo the Virgo C
FTS09100 Water Lock CC
FTS0927SP Lucy, Fairy Tail Magician SP
FTS0952SP Natsu, Fairy Tail Magician SP

2010 Weiss Schwarz Fairy Tail TD

FTS09T07 DEAR KABY
FTS09102 Erza, Armor Mage
FTS09T11 Gajeel, Iron Dragon Slayer Mage
FTS09105 Gray, Ice Shaper Mage
FTS09T08 Happy
FTS09T05 Lucy and Happy
FTS09T02 Lucy Heartfilia
FTS09T03 Lucy in Maid Outfit
FTS09101 Lucy, Cute Celestial Spirit Summoner
FTS09T01 Mirajane, Fairy Tail Mascot
FTS09T09 Natsu Dragneel
FTS09T12 Natsu, Fire Dragon Slayer Mage
FTS09103 Natsu, Flame Mage
FTS09T10 Natsu, Young Dragon
FTS09T14 Roar of the Fire Dragon
FTS09T13 S-Level Quest
FTS09T04 Speaks with Fists Elfman
FTS09104 The Day that Happy Was Born
FTS09T06 Virgo the Virgo

2010 Weiss Schwarz Index and Railgun

RGW10050 A Teacher's Obsession CC
RGW10073 Ability and Power CR
IDW10012 Accelerator U
IDW10010 Accelerator, Strongest of the Academy City U
RGW10067 Aggressive Kuroko C
RGW10047 AIM Burst U
IDW10094 Aisa Himegami C
RGW10038 Anti-Skill Tessou C
IDW10095 Aureolus Izzard, Forbidden Magician C
RGW10041 Awatsuki, Swimming Club C
RGW10049 Best Friends CC
RGW10072 Chaser– U
IDW10078 Deep Blood Himegami R
IDW10004 Delta Force Touma R
IDW10021 Dragon Strike U
RGW10040 Dummy Check Jyuuhuku C
IDW10002 Esper Accelerator RR
IDW10002R Esper Accelerator RRR
RGW10039 Harumi Kiyama C
IDW10097 Healing Magic U
IDW10084 Heaven Canceller U
IDW10080 Hyouka and Index R
IDW10006 Imagine Breaker Touma R
IDW10088 Index, Beast Girl C
IDW10086 Index, Controller of Index Librorum Prohibitorum U
IDW10092 Index, Hungry Sister C
IDW10079 Index, Magic Book Library R
IDW10079S Index, Magic Book Library SR
IDW10076 Index, Mysterious Pure White Girl RR
IDW10087 Index, Perfect Memory U
IDW10077 Index-Librorum-Prohibitorum RR
IDW10077R Index-Librorum-Prohibitorum RRR
IDW10098 Index's Specialty CR
RGW10053 Judgment Kuroko R
RGW10053S Judgment Kuroko SR
RGW10037 Judgment Uiharu U
RGW10056 Judgment? Mikoto R
RGW10048 Judgment's Resolution CR
IDW10090 Kaori Kanzaki C
RGW10028 Kazari Uiharu R
RGW10028R Kazari Uiharu RRR
RGW10042 Kiyama, Developer of Level Upper C
IDW10005 Komoe Tsukuyomi R
IDW10018 Komoe, Perfectly Child-Like Adult Teacher C
RGW10030 Konori in Swimsuits R
RGW10059 Kuroko Shirai U
RGW10058 Kuroko, Believe in Justice U
RGW10070 Kuroko, Mikoto's Partner C
IDW10013 Kuroko, Mikoto's Roommate C
IDW10007 Last Order, Administrator of Misaka Network R
IDW10007S Last Order, Administrator of Misaka Network SR
IDW10017 Last Order, Serial Number 20001 C
RGW10029 Level 0 Saten R
RGW10029S Level 0 Saten SR
IDW10008 Level 0 Touma U
RGW10060 Level 4 Kuroko U
RGW10057 Level 5 Mikoto R
IDW10100 Magician of Necessarius CC
IDW10015 Maika Tsuchimikado C
IDW10022 Meeting U
RGW10044 Mii Konori C
RGW10061 Mikoto and Kuroko in Swimsuits U
RGW10055 Mikoto and Kuroko, Senpai and Kouhai R
RGW10055R Mikoto and Kuroko, Senpai and Kouhai RRR
RGW10054 Mikoto Misaka R
RGW10054S Mikoto Misaka SR
IDW10016 Mikoto, "Bzzt" Middle School Student C
RGW10063 Mikoto, Ace of Tokiwadai C
RGW10065 Mikoto, Electro Master C
IDW10001 Mikoto, Memories from Childhood RR
RGW10066 Mikoto, No 3 of Academy City C
RGW10062 Mikoto, Strongest and Invincible Electric Princess U
IDW10023 Misaka Network CR
IDW10020 Misaka, Clone No 10032 C
IDW10003 Misaka's Little Sister R
IDW10003S Misaka's Little Sister SR
RGW10064 Mitsuko Kongou C
IDW10019 Motoharu Tsuchimikado C
RGW10031 Multiskill Kiyama R
IDW10009 Original Mikoto U
RGW10071 Pool Cleaning U
IDW10024 Power to Negate All CC
IDW10085 Priestess Kanzaki U
RGW10074 Railgun CC
RGW10051 Railgun Mikoto RR
RGW10033 Ruiko Saten U
IDW10082 Saint Kanzaki R
IDW10082S Saint Kanzaki SR
IDW10089 Sasha Kruezhev C
RGW10045 Saten, "Level Upper" user C
RGW10036 Saten, Uiharu's Dear Friend U
IDW10091 Sherry Cromwell C
IDW10083 Sister Index U
IDW10014 Sisters C
RGW10068 Skinship Mikoto and Kuroko C
RGW10046 Skirt Lifting U
IDW10096 Spell Intercept U
IDW10099 St George's Sanctuary CC
IDW10093 Stiyl Magnus C
IDW10081 Stiyl, Genius Magician R
IDW10025 Strongest Enemy in Academy City CC
RGW10052 Teleporter Kuroko RR
IDW10011 Touma Kamijou U
RGW10069 Touma, Ability to Counter All Abilities C
RGW10032 Uiharu and Saten R
RGW10032S Uiharu and Saten SR
RGW10027 Uiharu in Swimsuits RR
RGW10034 Uiharu with Flower Accessories U
RGW10026 Uiharu, Elite Operator RR
RGW10035 Uiharu, Kuroko's Partner U
RGW10043 Wannai, Swimming Club C
RGW10075 Work of Judgment CC
IDW1006SP Imagine Breaker Touma SP
IDW10076S Index, Mysterious Pure White Girl SP
RGW1051SP Railgun Mikoto SP
RGW1052SP Teleporter Kuroko SP

2010 Weiss Schwarz Melty Blood

MBS10039 27 Dead Apostle Ancestors Night of Wallachia C
MBS10066 Akiha in Pajama C
MBS10069 Akiha in Uniform C
MBS10051 Akiha Tohno RR
MBS10058 Akiha, Head of the Tohno Household U
MBS10056 Akiha, Student of Asagami Private Girls Academy R
MBS10087 Aoko, Destruction Specialized Magician U
MBS10090 Aoko, Magician C
MBS10079 Aoko, Successor of Fifth Magic R
MBS10079S Aoko, Successor of Fifth Magic SR
MBS10010 Arcueid Brunestud U
MBS10009 Arcueid, Blood-lusting U
MBS10012 Arcueid, Princess of True Ancestors U
MBS10002 Arcueid, Royalty of True Ancestors RR
MBS10002R Arcueid, Royalty of True Ancestors RRR
MBS10018 Arcueid, True-Ancestor-Killer True Ancestor C
MBS10004 Arcueid, Tyrant R
MBS10015 Arcueid, Vampire C
MBS10085 Back-Alley Alliance Satsuki U
MBS10030 Back-Alley Alliance Sion R
MBS10049 Barrel Replica CC
MBS10097 Beast of 666 U
MBS10005 Berserking Arcueid, Fallen True Ancestor R
MBS10019 Berserking Arcuied C
MBS10075 Bond of Sisters CC
MBS10047 By Your Hand U
MBS10021 Cat of the Universe U
MBS10080 Chaos Nrvnqsr Chaos R
MBS10081 Ciel Acting Executioner R
MBS10082 Ciel R
MBS10082R Ciel RRR
MBS10086 Ciel, Big Curry Lover U
MBS10091 Ciel, Holy Scripture Holder C
MBS10078 Ciel, No7 of the Burial Agency R
MBS10083 Ciel, Shiki's Senpai U
MBS10076 Ciel, User of Black Keys RR
MBS10074 Crimson Lord Ubiquitous Rebirth: Scarlet Flame Hammer CC
MBS10073 Crimson Lord: Origami CR
MBS10073S Crimson Lord: Origami SR
MBS10068 Crimson Red Vermillion Akiha C
MBS10060 Doctor Amber Kohaku U
MBS10025 Dreams of Bubbles CC
MBS10025S Dreams of Bubbles SR
MBS10072 End of Dreams U
MBS10100 Extermination of Dead Apostles CC
MBS10050 For My Friend CC
MBS10062 G Akiha U
MBS10089 Heretic Hunter Ciel C
MBS10065 Hisui and Kohaku, Good Sisters C
MBS10063 Hisui C
MBS10057 Hisui, Maid of the Tohno Household R
MBS10057S Hisui, Maid of the Tohno Household SR
MBS10052 Hisui, Maid who Loves Cleanliness RR
MBS10067 Hisui, Shiki's Attendant C
MBS10059 Hisui, Thinking of Big Sister U
MBS10071 Humanities Master Plan U
MBS10064 Kohaku and Hisui in China Dress C
MBS10055 Kohaku, Cheerful Housekeeper R
MBS10053 Kohaku, Japanese Apron Devil R
MBS10061 Kohaku, Maid of the Tohno Household U
MBS10070 Kouma Kishima C
MBS10023 Marble Phantasm CR
MBS10033 Mecha-Hisui U
MBS10026 Memory Partition Sion RR
MBS10092 Michael Roa Valdamjong C
MBS10094 Miss Blue Aoko C
MBS10054 Mixed Blood Akiha R
MBS10054R Mixed Blood Akiha RRR
MBS10040 Miyako Arima C
MBS10036 Miyako, Eight Extremities Fists U
MBS10031 Miyako, Oldest Daughter of Arima Household R
MBS10031S Miyako, Oldest Daughter of Arima Household SR
MBS10006 Mystic Eyes of Death Perception Shiki R
MBS10093 Neko-Arc Chaos C
MBS10034 Neko-Arc U
MBS10046 New Tatari U
MBS10035 Night of Wallachia U
MBS10095 Nrvnqsr Chaos C
MBS10022 Pride of the Nanayas U
MBS10098 Reality Marble: Depletion Garden CR
MBS10098S Reality MArble: Depletion Garden SR
MBS10017 Ren C
MBS10003 Ren on a Certain Day R
MBS10014 Ren, Black Cat C
MBS10011 Ren, Dream Demon U
MBS10041 Riesbyfe Stridberg C
MBS10029 Riesbyfe, Maiden of Holy Shield R
MBS10027 Riesbyfe, Paladin RR
MBS10043 Riesbyfe, Sion's Friend C
MBS10045 Sand of Osiris C
MBS10084 Satsuki Yumizuka U
MBS10088 Satsuki, Newborn Unfortunate Vampire C
MBS10077 Satsuki, Vampire for Justice RR
MBS10024 Seventeen Cuts CC
MBS10099 Seventh Holy Scripture CC
MBS10020 Shiki Nanaya C
MBS10016 Shiki Tohno C
MBS10007 Shiki, Adopted Son of Tohno Household R
MBS10013 Shiki, Hating Rumors C
MBS10028 Sion Eltnam Atlasia R
MBS10042 Sion, Atlas Academy Resident C
MBS10038 Sion, Riesbyfe's Friend C
MBS10032 Sion, Spiritual Hacker R
MBS10032R Sion, Spiritual Hacker RRR
MBS10044 Sion, Vampire C
MBS10096 TATARI Returns U
MBS10048 True Apocrypha Gamaliel CR
MBS10048S True Apocrypha Gamaliel SR
MBS10037 Vampire Sion, Successor to TATARI U
MBS10008 White Ren U
MBS10001 White Ren, Fairy of the Snow Plains RR
MBS10001S White Ren, Fairy of the Snow Plains SR
MBS1004SP Arcueid, Tyrant SP
MBS1028SP Sion Eltnam Atlasia SP
MBS1056SP Akiha, Student of Asagami Private Girls Academy SP
MBS1076SP Ciel, User of Black Keys SP

2010 Weiss Schwarz Melty Blood TD

MBS10T05 Arcueid, Princess of Shinso
MBS10101 Arcueid, Pure Heart
MBS10T01 Arcueid, Vampire
MBS10T04 Arcuied Brunestud
MBS10T13 Barrel Replica
MBS10T07 Miyako Arima
MBS10T11 Miyako, Eight Extremities Fists
MBS10T03 Ren
MBS10102 Ren, Familiar
MBS10T08 Riesbyfe Stridberg
MBS10T06 Seventeen Cuts
MBS10103 Shall We Play Around for a While?
MBS10T02 Shiki Tohno
MBS10104 Sion, Alchemist
MBS10T09 Sion, Atlas Academy Resident
MBS10T10 Sion, Vampire
MBS10T12 Vampire Sion, Successor to TATARI
MBS10105 White Ren, Familiar

2010 Weiss Schwarz Milky Holmes

MKS11024 A Date with Just the Two of Us CC
MKS11020 Almighty Toys? U
MKS11012 Always Smiling Sheryl U
MKS11001 Apron Nero RR
MKS11088 Arsene's Butler Yutaka C
MKS11100 Black Cat Bookmark CC
MKS11081 Black Tea Loving Cordelia R
MKS11026 Book-Loving Elly RR
MKS11026S Book-Loving Elly SR
MKS11062 Brave yet Single Minded Sheryl U
MKS11041 Casual Cloth Elly C
MKS11007 Cat-Ear Nero R
MKS11097 Cat-eared Magnifying Glass C
MKS11083 Chief Admiring Elly U
MKS11008 Chief Chef Mr Ishinagare U
MKS11018 Classmate Nezu-kun C
MKS11040 Close Combat Hirano C
MKS11052 Clumsy Detective Sheryl RR
MKS11014 Controlling Nero C
MKS11089 Cordelia and Elly C
MKS11096 Cordelia's Garden U
MKS11099 Cordelia's Proposal CC
MKS11090 Cordelica Glauca C
MKS11071 Critical Chop U
MKS11082 Deep Sigh Cordelia R
MKS11075 Direct Hack CC
MKS11029 Elly and Nero R
MKS11027 Embarassed Elly RR
MKS11058 Energetic Nero U
MKS11034 Enjoy Cleaning Cordelia U
MKS11025 First Encounter with Opera CC
MKS11093 Former Great Detective Kobayashi C
MKS11093S Former Great Detective Kobayashi SR
MKS11063 Fortune Cookie Tsugiko C
MKS11067 G4's Leader Kokoro C
MKS11022 Gathering Foodstuffs C
MKS11069 Gluttonous Nero C
MKS11032 Halloween Night Elly R
MKS11078 Halloween Night Henriette R
MKS11078S Halloween Night Henriette SR
MKS11031 Hercule Barton R
MKS11030 Hirano and Saku R
MKS11037S Hirano Hasegawa SR
MKS11037 Hirano Hasegawa U
MKS11098 Hyper-Sensitive CR
MKS11045 Ideal Room U
MKS11044 Information Gatherer Saku C
MKS11070 Inhale U
MKS11053 IQ1300? Kokoro R
MKS11064 Joint Investigation Kokoro and Sheryl C
MKS11028 Jumping the Gun Cordelia R
MKS11060S Kobayashi's Rival Kamitsu SR
MKS11060 Kobayashi's Rival Kamitsu U
MKS11057 Kokoro Akechi R
MKS11057S Kokoro Akechi SR
MKS11084 Leader of the Phantom Thief Empire Arsene U
MKS11091 Lost in Thought Elly C
MKS11050 Merry-Go-Round CC
MKS11039 My Pace Saku C
MKS11010 Narcisscist Nijyuri Sensei U
MKS11055 Natural Girl Sheryl R
MKS11017 Nero and Sheryl C
MKS11005 Nero Yuzurizaki R
MKS11005S Nero Yuzurizaki SR
MKS11036 No-Good Cordelia U
MKS11003 Opera Kobayashi R
MKS11079 Panicking Cordelia R
MKS11072 PDA C
MKS11085 Perfect Butler Tachi U
MKS11092 Phantom Thief Arsene C
MKS11049 Plushie And Hercule CC
MKS11066 Problem Child Nero C
MKS11073 Psychokinesis CR
MKS11059 Recording Sheryl U
MKS11033 Rei Kamitsu U
MKS11087S Reliable Sister Cordelia SR
MKS11087 Reliable Sister Cordelia U
MKS11095 Repay Kindness with Hatred U
MKS11035S Saku Tooyama SR
MKS11035 Saku Tooyama U
MKS11051 Sherlock Shellingford RR
MKS11051S Sherlock Shellingford SR
MKS11074 Sherlock's Lap Pillow CC
MKS11065 Sheryl Amongst Cherry Blossoms C
MKS11013 Sheryl and Kamaboko C
MKS11094 Shy Girl Elly C
MKS11061 Sister Role Tsugiko U
MKS11054 Snack-offering Nero R
MKS11021 Snacky Detective U
MKS11004 Sports Festival Nero and Elly R
MKS11023 Stealth And Toys CR
MKS11047 Stubbornly Opened Door C
MKS11086 Student Council President Henriette U
MKS11046 Sudden Dazzle U
MKS11011 Sugar Rush Nero U
MKS11077 Team Unifier Cordelia RR
MKS11043 Tenacious Cordelia C
MKS11009S Three-Card Rat SR
MKS11009 Three-Card Rat U
MKS11019 Three-Card Stone River C
MKS11019S Three-Card Stone River SR
MKS11015 Three-Card Twenty C
MKS11015S Three-Card Twenty SR
MKS11080 Timid Elly R
MKS11068 Toys Activated Sheryl C
MKS11048 Tri-Ascend CR
MKS11056 Tsugiko Zenigata R
MKS11056S Tsugiko Zenigata SR
MKS11076 Uniform Cordelia RR
MKS11042 Uniform Elly C
MKS11002 Uniform Nero RR
MKS11038 Yukata Elly C
MKS11016 Yukata Nero C
MKS11006 Yukata Sheryl R
MKS1107SP Cat-Ear Nero SP
MKS1132SP Halloween Night Elly SP
MKS1152SP Clumsy Detective Sheryl SP
MKS1176SP Uniform Cordelia SP

2010 Weiss Schwarz Milky Holmes TD

MKS11T07 Brave yet Single Minded Sheryl
MKS11T15 Cat-eared Magnifying Glass
MKS11T10 Cordelica Glauca
MKS11T08 Direct Hack
MKS11T01 Energetic Nero
MKS11T13 Former Great Detective Kobayashi
MKS11T05 G4's Leader Kokoro
MKS11T06 Gluttonous Nero
MKS11T02 Joint Investigation Kokoro and Sheryl
MKS11T11 Lost in Thought Elly
MKS11104 Milky Holmes Assemble
MKS11102 Milky Holmes Cordelia
MKS11103 Milky Holmes Elly
MKS11105 Milky Holmes Nero
MKS11101 Milky Holmes Sheryl
MKS11T12 Phantom Thief Arsene
MKS11T04 Problem Child Nero
MKS11T09 Psychokinesis
MKS11T03 Sheryl Amongst Cherry Blossoms
MKS11T14 Shy Girl Elly

2010 Weiss Schwarz Nanoha A's

NAW12029 Alisa and Little Arf R
NAW12029S Alisa and Little Arf SR

NAW12042 Alisa and Suzuka C
NAW12039 Alisa and Suzuka, 9th Graders C
NAW12034 Alisa, Divider U
NAW12038 Amy Limietta C
NAW12026 Amy, Asura's No 3 RR
NAW12048 Arc-en-ciel CR
NAW12048S Arc-en-ciel SR
NAW12014 Arf, Extremely Rough C
NAW12091 Aria Liese and Rotte Liese C
NAW12087 Assisting Strong Ones Reinforce U
NAW12040 Big Brother Chrono C
NAW12001 Big Sister Alicia RR
NAW12047 Budding Friendship C
NAW12036 Buddy Quartet U
NAW12027 Chrono and Amy, Notable Partners RR
NAW12031 Chrono, Commissioned Officer R
NAW12037 Chrono, Power to Change the Future U
NAW12015 Confused Fate C
NAW12095 Curse of the Book of the Darkness U
NAW12049 Eternal Coffin CC
NAW12073 Exelion Buster CR
NAW12073S Exelion Buster SR
NAW12072 Extreme Range Artillery Fire C
NAW12024 Farewell to the Ideal CC
NAW12013 Fate T Liete Lotte C
NAW12016 Fate Vs Signum C
NAW12007 Fate with Bardiche Assault R
NAW12009 Fate, 9th Grader U
NAW12033 Fate, First Time at the School U
NAW12100 For My Beloved CC
NAW12032 Friends Alisa R
NAW12010 Friends Fate U
NAW12030 Friends Suzuka R
NAW12050 Get Well Soon CC
NAW12088 Gil Graham, Battle-hardened Fighter C
NAW12028 Hayate and Suzuka R
NAW12078 Hayate in Infirmary R
NAW12092 Hayate of the Yagami Household C
NAW12086 Hayate, 9th Grader U
NAW12081 Hayate, King of the Night Sky R
NAW12077 Hayate, Master RR
NAW12098 Healing Power CR
NAW12075 Heaven Roaring Smash CC
NAW12045 Home Visit U
NAW12074 I can be shot CC
NAW12020 Introducing CVK792 U
NAW12079 Leti Lowran R
NAW12002 Lightning Fate RR
NAW12023 Lightning Flash CR
NAW12023S Lightning Flash SR
NAW12041 Lindy, Kind Mother C
NAW12043 Lindy, Unrivaled Sweet Tooth C
NAW12070 Magic Training U
NAW12035 Mariel Atenza U
NAW12094 Masked Warrior C
NAW12076 Master Program Will of the Book of the Darkness RR
NAW12076S Master Program Will of the Book of the Darkness SR
NAW12046 Memories of a Day Far Away U
NAW12096 Mirror of Travels U
NAW12063 Nanoha and Yuuno C
NAW12066 Nanoha Takamachi Aria Liese C
NAW12058 Nanoha Vs Vita U
NAW12057 Nanoha with Raising Heart Exelion R
NAW12053 Nanoha, 9th Grader R
NAW12067 Nanoha, Blessing C
NAW12055 Nanoha, Injured R
NAW12069 Nanoha, No Holds Barred C
NAW12012 Piercing Arf U
NAW12017 Playing Fate and Arf C
NAW12018 Precia, Kind Mother C
NAW12071 Present from Hayate U
NAW12097 Program of Knights of Protection C
NAW12089 Reinforce, the World's Most Fortunate Magic Book C
NAW12054 Reunion Nanoha and Fate R
NAW12004 Rinis, Familiar R
NAW12090 Shamal of the Yagami Household C
NAW12080 Shamal, Knight of the Lake R
NAW12019 Signum of the Yagami Household C
NAW12008 Signum, Knight of Sword U
NAW12006 Signum, Warrior R
NAW12011 Sonic Form Fate U
NAW12005 Strong Enemy Signum R
NAW12025 Sturm Falken CC
NAW12044 Suzuka, Loves Readin C
NAW12022 Swarm of Questions C
NAW12021 Thoughts to the Lord U
NAW12099 Time of Awakening CC
NAW12099S Time of Awakening SR
NAW12052 Unwavering Will Nanoha RR
NAW12052S Unwavering Will Nanoha SR
NAW12059 Vita and Zafira U
NAW12062 Vita of the Yagami Household U
NAW12051 Vita, Crimson Iron Rider RR
NAW12056 Vita, Knight of the Bok of Darkness R
NAW12065 Vita, Petite C
NAW12082 Wolkenritter Shamal R
NAW12003 Wolkenritter Signum R
NAW12003S Wolkenritter Signum SR
NAW12064 Wolkenritter Vita C
NAW12084 Wolkenritter Zafira U
NAW12083 Yukie Ishida, Physician in Charge for Hayate U
NAW12060 Yuuno Scrya U
NAW12068 Yuuno, Archaeologist C
NAW12061 Yuuno, Rear Support U
NAW12093 Zafira of the Yagami Household C
NAW12085 Zafira, Shield Guardian Beast U
NAW1202SP Lightning Fate SP
NAW1206SP Signum, Warrior SP
NAW1230SP Friends Suzuka SP
NAW1231SP Chrono, Commissioned Officer SP
NAW1251SP Vita, Crimson Iron Rider SP
NAW1257SP Nanoha with Raising Heart Exelion SP
NAW1277SP Hayate, Master SP
NAW1280SP Shamal, Knight of the Lake SP

2010 Weiss Schwarz Nanoha A's TD

NAW12101 Brother and Sister on the Battlefield
NAW12T01 Confused Fate
NAW12T14 Curse of the Book of Darkness
NAW12T03 Fate Vs Signum
NAW12T15 For My Beloved
NAW12T11 Gil Graham, Battle-hardened Fighter
NAW12102 Hayate and Signum
NAW12T12 Hayate of Yagami Household
NAW12103 Irreplacable Friendship Nanoha and Fate
NAW12104 Nanoha and Fate and Hayate in Battle Outfit
NAW12T05 Playing Fate and Arf
NAW12T04 Precia, Kind Mother
NAW12T09 Reinforce, the World's Most Fortunate Magic Book
NAW12T10 Shamal of Yagami Household
NAW12T06 Signum of Yagami Household
NAW12T02 Signum, Knight of Sword
NAW12T07 Sonic Form Fate
NAW12105 Standby Ready
NAW12T08 Sturm Falken
NAW12T13 Zafira of Yagami Household

2010 Weiss Schwarz Railgun S TD

RGW26T06 Escape from Dark Alleys
RGW26085 Kuroko, Friendly 4-Man Group
RGW26T10 Kuroko, Full of Justice
RGW26T07 Kuroko, Working
RGW26T05 Location Triangulation
RGW26T12 Mikoto at the Hospital
RGW26T08 Mikoto at the Library
RGW26083 Mikoto, Friendly 4-Man Group
RGW26T11 Mikoto, On the Way to School
RGW26084 Mikoto, Works Hard
RGW26T09 Queen Misaki Shokuhou
RGW26T14 Railgun
RGW26T04 Saten at the Hospital
RGW26082 Saten, Friendly 4-Man Group
RGW26T03 Saten, Seeking help
RGW26T02 Strawberry Oden Uiharu
RGW26081 Uiharu, Friendly 4-Man Group
RGW26T01 Uiharu, Worrying
RGW26T13 When the Cat's Away

2010 Weiss Schwarz Railgun TD

RGW10T09 Aggressive Kuroko
RGW10T02 Awatsuki, Swimming Club
RGW10T06 Best Friends
RGW10T03 Kiyama, Developer of Level Upper
RGW10T07 Kuroko Shirai
RGW10T11 Kuroko, Mikoto's Partner
RGW10105 Kuroko, Student of Tokiwadai Middle School
RGW10T05 Mii Konori
RGW10T08 Mikoto, Electro Master
RGW10T12 Mikoto, Strongest and Invincible Electric Princess
RGW10102 Mikoto, Student of Tokiwadai Middle School
RGW10T13 Pool Cleaning
RGW10104 Promise of Two
RGW10T14 Railgun
RGW10103 Saten, Student of Sakugawa Middle School
RGW10T10 Skinship Mikoto and Kuroko
RGW10T01 Uiharu with Flower Accessories
RGW10T04 Uiharu, Kuroko's Partner
RGW10101 Uiharu, Student of Sakugawa Middle School

2010 Weiss Schwarz Sengoku Basara Anime Extra

SBSE0531 Attack the Odawara Castle! C
SBSE0540 Avatar of Vaisravana Kenshin Uesugi C
SBSE0536 Azure Lightning Masamune Date R
SBSE0545 Azure Oni C
SBSE0526 Blazing Soul Yukimura Sanada C
SBSE0504 Broken Bond Nagamasa & Oichi C
SBSE0534 Calm And Composed Kojuro Katakura R
SBSE0511 Center Pillar Toshiie Maeda C
SBSE0507 Cold-Blooded General Motonari Mouri R
SBSE0510 Commander-in-Chief of Toyotomi Army Hideyoshi R
SBSE0542 Confidant of One-Eyed Dragon Kojuro Katakura C
SBSE0501 Crazed Aura Mitsuhide Akechi R
SBSE0524 Crimson Flame Yukimura Sanada R
SBSE0522 Custom of Pirates Motochika Chousokabe R
SBSE0502 Demon King of the Sengoku Nobunaga Oda R
SBSE0538 Dragon's Claw Masamune Date C
SBSE0517 Driving the Sengoku Keiji Maeda C
SBSE0503 Dual Firearms Nouhime C
SBSE0532 Duel to the Death C
SBSE0515 First of Conqueror Hideyoshi Toyotomi C
SBSE0543 God of War Kenshin & Sword Kasuga C
SBSE0509 Good Mother And Wife Matsu R
SBSE0505 Grand Order of Samurai Dictatorship C
SBSE0514 Invade in Stealth Hanbei Takenaka C
SBSE0512 Kabuki Keiji Maeda C
SBSE0525 Lord of Shikoku Motochika Chousokabe C
SBSE0519 Matsu's Cooking C
SBSE0529 Movile Fortress Fugaku Motochika Chosokabe C
SBSE0527 Naive Personality Yukimura Sanada C
SBSE0539 One-Eyed Dragon of Ou Masamune Date C
SBSE0513 Rare Strategist Motonari Mouri C
SBSE0520 Return to Chaos! C
SBSE0530 Secrecy Running on the Battlefield Sasuke Sarutobi C
SBSE0528 Six-Claw Masamune & Twin Lance Yukimura C
SBSE0535 Strategist of the Date Troops Kojuro Katakura R
SBSE0508 Strategist of Toyotomi Hanbei Takenaka R
SBSE0518 Stubborn Will Motonari Mouri C
SBSE0516 Supreme King of Sengoku Hideyoshi Toyotomi C
SBSE0506 The One Who Cuts A Path Keiji Maeda R
SBSE0523 Tiger of Kai Shingen Takeda R
SBSE0544 Twin Dragons Masamune & Kojuro C
SBSE0541 Uesugi Army Kasuga C
SBSE0533 Unrivaled Bravery Masamune Date R
SBSE0537 Young And Charismatic Masamune Date C
SBSE0521 Young Fierce General Yukimura Sanada R

2011 Weiss Schwarz Angel Beats Extra

ABWE1036 Battle Against Shadow C
ABWE1026 Godfather Yuri R
ABWE1029 Handle Name Takeyama C
ABWE1028 Hinata, Baseball Boy C
ABWE1027 Hinata, Thinking of Allies C
ABWE1017 Hisako, Prideful Guitarist C
ABWE1002 Iwasawa and Hisako, Understanding of Expectations R
ABWE1013 Iwasawa, Guitar Performer C
ABWE1010 Kanade in Swimsuit C
ABWE1006 Kanade, Farewell Words R
ABWE1012 Kanade, Former Strong Enemy C
ABWE1018 Kanade, Normal Girl C
ABWE1003 Kanate, End of Opposition R
ABWE1005 Maradona Yui R
ABWE1004 Messenger of God Tenshi R
ABWE1019 Naoi, Two-Faced C
ABWE1021 Operation Tornado feat Yui C
ABWE1009 Otonashi, Beating Memories C
ABWE1025 Otonashi, Irregularity of the World R
ABWE1008 Sekine and Irie, Good Pair C
ABWE1032 Shiina, Arrogant Kunoichi C
ABWE1023 Shiyusa, Talented Controller R
ABWE1020 Somewhere, Some Other Time C
ABWE1033 Takamatsu, Unleashed Self C
ABWE1035 TK, Sunny Dancer C
ABWE1015 Yui and Hinata, Like Couples C
ABWE1014 Yui, Always Energetic C
ABWE1011 Yui, Lowbrow Yet Hard-Working C
ABWE1007 Yui, Passionate Girl R
ABWE1001 Yui, Romantic Role R
ABWE1016 Yui, Second Generation Vocalist C
ABWE1030 Yuri, Antagonist C
ABWE1034 Yuri, Can't Forgive God C
ABWE1031 Yuri, Kanade's Friend C
ABWE1022 Yuri, Opposition Cleared R
ABWE1024 Yuri, Time to Depart R

2011 Weiss Schwarz Bakemonogatari

COMPLETE SET (117)
BOOSTER BOX (20 PACKS) 80.00 100.00
BOOSTER PACK (8 CARDS) 4.00 5.00
RELEASED ON FEBRUARY 14, 2014
BMS15025 A Girl Cursed CC
BMS15021 Actually Fighting U
BMS15081 Black Hanekawa R
BMS15081S Black Hanekawa SR
BMS15092 Cat-Eared Tsubasa Hanekawa C
BMS15013 Didn't Mean to Mayoi Hachikuji C
BMS15097 Don't Tell Anyone U
BMS15096 Energy Drain Black Hanekawa C
BMS15022 Fast Talking U
BMS15074 Girl That Bites CC
BMS15049 Girl Without Weight CC
BMS15073 Hitagi Club CR
BMS15067 Hitagi Senjougahara in Casual Clothing C
BMS15061 Hitagi Senjougahara, Battle Situation U
BMS15057 Hitagi Senjougahara, Completely Armored R
BMS15057S Hitagi Senjougahara, Completely Armored SR
BMS15035 Hitagi Senjougahara, Dating U
BMS15037 Hitagi Senjougahara, Forceful U
BMS15042 Hitagi Senjougahara, Good with Voice Impersonation C
BMS15055 Hitagi Senjougahara, Hollow Girl R
BMS15055R Hitagi Senjougahara, Hollow Girl RRR
BMS15031 Hitagi Senjougahara, Koyomi's Lover R
BMS15031R Hitagi Senjougahara, Koyomi's Lover RRR
BMS15030 Hitagi Senjougahara, Malicious Talker R
BMS15029 Hitagi Senjougahara, Off Day R
BMS15029S Hitagi Senjougahara, Off Day SR
BMS15059 Hitagi Senjougahara, True Feelings U
BMS15066 Hitagi Senjougahara, Weightless Girl C
BMS15052 Hitagi, Girl Who Encountered a Crab RR
BMS15063 Karen Araragi and Tsukihi Araragi C
BMS15062 Karen Araragi U
BMS15080 Koyomi Araragi and Hitagi Senjougahara, Lovers R
BMS15080R Koyomi Araragi and Hitagi Senjougahara, Lovers RRR
BMS15003 Koyomi Araragi on Mother's Day R
BMS15069 Koyomi Araragi, Answer to Proposal C
BMS15036 Koyomi Araragi, Hates Mornings U
BMS15041 Koyomi Araragi, Protagonist Who Helps Everyone C
BMS15089 Koyomi Araragi, Running Around C
BMS15053 Koyomi Araragi, Tsukkomi R
BMS15016 Koyomi Araragi, Vampire-Like Human C
BMS15024 Mayoi All the Time CC
BMS15002 Mayoi Hachikuji RR
BMS15068 Mayoi Hachikuji, Elementary School Student C
BMS15012 Mayoi Hachikuji, Floating Spirit U
BMS15004 Mayoi Hachikuji, Girl Who Keeps Wandering R
BMS15004S Mayoi Hachikuji, Girl Who Keeps Wandering SR
BMS15019 Mayoi Hachikuji, Hungry C
BMS15011 Mayoi Hachikuji, Looking Down at Koyomi U
BMS15005 Mayoi Hachikuji, Lost Cow R
BMS15005R Mayoi Hachikuji, Lost Cow RRR
BMS15006 Mayoi Hachikuji, Lost Snail Girl R
BMS15065 Mayoi Hachikuji, Well-Acquainted C
BMS15054 Mayoi Kachikuji, Large Knapsack R
BMS15051 Mayoi, Girl with Pigtails RR
BMS15051S Mayoi, Girl with Pigtails SR
BMS15023 Means to Remain Existing CR
BMS15084 Meme Oshino U
BMS15086 Meme Oshino, Authority on Monster Changing U
BMS15095 Meme Oshino, Man Who Sees Through Everything C
BMS15099 My Everything CC
BMS15083 Nadeko Sengoku U
BMS15088 Nadeko Sengoku, Ambushing U
BMS15090 Nadeko Sengoku, Curse Removal Ritual C
BMS15087 Nadeko Sengoku, Cursed Girl U
BMS15001 Nadeko Sengoku, Easily Embarassed RR
BMS15001S Nadeko Sengoku, Easily Embarassed SR
BMS15093 Nadeko Sengoku, Girl of Age C
BMS15008 Nadeko Sengoku, Maniac Girl U
BMS15015 Nadeko Sengoku, One-Way Crush C
BMS15082 Nadeko Sengoku, Rewards for Curse Removal R
BMS15010 Nadeko Sengoku, Shy Girl U
BMS15077 Nadeko Sengoku, Snake-Coiled Girl RR
BMS15078 Nadeko Sengoku, Tsukihi-Chan's Classmate R
BMS15078S Nadeko Sengoku, Tsukihi-Chan's Classmate SR
BMS15098 Nadeko Snake CR
BMS15047 Rainy Devil U
BMS15071 Ritual of Waking up U
BMS15050 Secret Rewards CC
BMS15017 Shinobu Oshino C
BMS15020 Shinobu Oshino, Claims to be 500 Years Old C
BMS15018 Shinobu Oshino, Donuts Lover C
BMS15009 Shinobu Oshino, End of A Vampire U
BMS15014 Shinobu Oshino, Human-Like Vampire C
BMS15007 Shinobu Oshino, Vampire R
BMS15046 Stalking U
BMS15033 Suruga Hanbaru, Monkey Hands? U
BMS15032 Suruga Kanbaru R
BMS15032S Suruga Kanbaru SR
BMS15070 Suruga Kanbaru, BL-Lover C
BMS15056 Suruga Kanbaru, Devil's Left Hand R
BMS15043 Suruga Kanbaru, Extremely Truthful C
BMS15039 Suruga Kanbaru, Former Ace of the Basketball Club C
BMS15027 Suruga Kanbaru, Girl Wished upon a Monkey RR
BMS15040 Suruga Kanbaru, Good with Girls C
BMS15028 Suruga Kanbaru, Just Broke Through R
BMS15060 Suruga Kanbaru, Sports Girl U
BMS15034 Suruga Kanbaru, True to Self U
BMS15048 Suruga Monkey CR
BMS15064 Suruka Kanbaru in Casual Clothing C
BMS15100 Tsubasa Cat CC
BMS15094 Tsubasa Hanekawa C
BMS15085 Tsubasa Hanekawa in Pajamas U
BMS15076 Tsubasa Hanekawa, Cat-Enchanted Girl RR
BMS15045 Tsubasa Hanekawa, Chairman Amongst Chairmans C
BMS15026 Tsubasa Hanekawa, Family Issues RR
BMS15079 Tsubasa Hanekawa, Inner Feelings R
BMS15091 Tsubasa Hanekawa, Knowing Everything C
BMS15038 Tsubasa Hanekawa, Knowledgeable C
BMS15044 Tsubasa Hanekawa, Well Conducted C
BMS15058 Tsukihi Araragi U
BMS15072 Tsundere? U
BMS15075 While the Devil Is Gone CC
BMS1506SP Mayoi Hachikuji, Lost Snail Girl SP
BMS1527SP Suruga Kanbaru, Girl Wished upon a Monkey SP
BMS1552SP Hitagi, Girl Who Encountered a Crab SP
BMS1576SP Tsubasa Hanekawa, Cat-Enchanted Girl SP
BMS1577SP Nadeko Sengoku, Snake-Coiled Girl SP

2011 Weiss Schwarz Bakemonogatari TD

BMS15104 Big Crab
BMS15T12 Cat-Eared Tsubasa Hanekawa
BMS15T09 Hitagi Club
BMS15T06 Hitagi Senjougahara in Casual Clothing
BMS15T03 Hitagi Senjougahara, Battle Situation
BMS15102 Hitagi Senjougahara, Extremely Suspicious
BMS15103 Hitagi Senjougahara, Tender-Cared Daughter
BMS15T05 Hitagi Senjougahara, Weightless Girl
BMS15T01 Karen Araragi and Tsukihi Araragi
BMS15101 Koyomi Araragi, Unmoving Taciturnity
BMS15T07 Mayoi Hachikuji, Elementary School Student
BMS15T04 Mayoi Hachikuji, Well-Acquainted
BMS15T14 My Everything
BMS15T10 Nadeko Sengoku, Curse Removal Ritual
BMS15T13 Nadeko Sengoku, Girl of Age
BMS15T08 Suruga Kanbaru, BL-Lover
BMS15T02 Suruka Kanbaru in Casual Clothing
BMS15T11 Tsubasa Hanekawa in Pajamas
BMS15105 Tsubasa Hanekawa, Ultimate Perfect Student

2011 Weiss Schwarz Black Rock Shooter Extra

BRSE0627 Black Blade Black Rock Shooter C
BRSE0606 Black Gold Saw C
BRSE0604 Black Gold Saw, Blade of Darkness C
BRSE0631 Black Rock Shooter, Blue Fiery Eyes C
BRSE0624 Black Rock Shooter, Blue Shock R
BRSE0625 Black Rock Shooter, Darkness Rider R
BRSE0622 Black Rock Shooter, Girl from an Alien World R
BRSE0626 Black Rock Shooter, Standing Still C
BRSE0608 Cold Smile Dead Master R
BRSE0634 Comet Black Rock Shooter C
BRSE0618 Dead Master, Black Throne C
BRSE0617 Dead Master, Dancing in Darkness C
BRSE0609 Dead Master, Emerald Eyes R
BRSE0612 Dead Master, Girl from an Alien World C
BRSE0613 Dead Master, Hollow C
BRSE0611 Dead Master, Lord of Eternal Darkness R
BRSE0610 Dead Scythe Dead Master R
BRSE0633 Encounter Black Rock Shooter and Dead Master C
BRSE0623 Mato and Yomi, Contrasting Girls R
BRSE0629 Mato Kuroi C
BRSE0628 Mato, First-Year Ace Hopeful C
BRSE0621 Mato, Naive and Romantic R
BRSE0632 Mato, Thinking of Friends C
BRSE0630 Rock Cannon Black Rock Shooter C
BRSE0635 Rock Cannon C
BRSE0620 Shadow Floating in Darkness C
BRSE0619 Star-Shaped Strap C
BRSE0602 Strength R
BRSE0636 Who Are You? C
BRSE0615 Yomi Takanashi C
BRSE0614 Yomi, Hope of the Volleyball Club C
BRSE0616 Yomi, Mature Bishoujo C
BRSE0607 Yomi, Returned from Overseas R
BRSE0605 Yuu C
BRSE0601 Yuu, Classmate R
BRSE0603 Yuu, Elite Manager C

2011 Weiss Schwarz Disgaea 4 Extra

DGSE0821 Altina, Illegal Immigrant from Heaven C
DGSE0817 Altina, Nurse C
DGSE0814 Altina, Phantom Thief Angel R
DGSE0816 Altina, Ubiquitous R
DGSE0819 Angel of Greed Vulcano C
DGSE0841 Arctaare C
DGSE0842 Arctaare, Hellmaster C
DGSE0823 Bond between Angel and Demon C
DGSE0838 Desco, Fancy Dreaming R
DGSE0843 Desco, Last Boss Training C
DGSE0837 Desco, Maiden Aiming for Last Boss R
DGSE0840 Desco, Master of Special Section C
DGSE0806 Emizel, Impertinent Kid C
DGSE0807 Emizel, Leader of Special Killing Operation Squad C
DGSE0810 Emizel, Netherworld President Junior C
DGSE0803 Emizel, Reaper R
DGSE0831 Fenrich, Absolute Allegiance C
DGSE0830 Fenrich, Butler of Werewolves C
DGSE0824 Fenrich, Caretaker of Prinnies R
DGSE0828 Fenrich, Strategist of Val-sama R
DGSE0845 Final Weapon Appears C
DGSE0839 Final Weapon DESCO R
DGSE0815 Flonne, Archangel R
DGSE0804 Fuuka Kazamatsuri R
DGSE0808 Fuuka, Girl with a Prinny Cap C
DGSE0801 Fuuka, Leader of Prinny Eliminator Squad R
DGSE0809 Fuuka, Middle School Student Who Fell into Hell C
DGSE0822 Great Flonneger X, Super Alloy Robot C
DGSE0818 Nemo, Convictor C
DGSE0820 Nice Body Etna C
DGSE0805 Onee-Sama Fuuka C
DGSE0832 Overlord Laharl, President C
DGSE0844 Perfect Version Deszet C
DGSE0813 Phoenix's Promise C
DGSE0836 Pledge by Moon C
DGSE0835 Power of "Bond" C
DGSE0812 Prinny Wars C
DGSE0811 Raspberyl, President C
DGSE0825 Sardine Power Valvatorez R
DGSE0802 Thoughts of a Maiden Fuuka R
DGSE0826 Valvatorez, Asthetics of Evil R
DGSE0833 Valvatorez, Demon with Pride C
DGSE0829 Valvatorez, Educator of Prinnies C
DGSE0834 Valvatorez, Traitor to Gods C
DGSE0827 Valvatorez, Tyrant R

2011 Weiss Schwarz Fairy Tail Extra

FTSE1014 And Always Be Kind C
FTSE1015 Angel, Celestial Spirit Magician R
FTSE1043 Charle, Caretaker of Wendy C
FTSE1010 Dark Ecriture Freed C
FTSE1002 Erza, Alongside Beloved Friends R
FTSE1011 Erza, Occasional Cloth Change C
FTSE1003 Erza, Youth Days R
FTSE1033 Flame Lotus: Phoenix Sword C
FTSE1030 Gajeel, Unexpected Alliance C
FTSE1041 Grey, Ice Fortress C
FTSE1025 Happy, Nekomander R
FTSE1037 Healing Magic Wendy R
FTSE1032 Igneel, Flame Dragon C
FTSE1024 It's Not A Sin! C
FTSE1001 Jellal, Youth Days R
FTSE1013 Jerral, Ruler of the Tower of Heaven C
FTSE1036 Juvia, Fairy Tail Magician R
FTSE1004 Laxus Dreyar R
FTSE1012 Laxus' Grandpa Makarov C
FTSE1009 Levy, Tiny Fairy C
FTSE1023 LOVE & LUCKY C
FTSE1018 Lucy, Alongside Dear Friends C
FTSE1016 Lucy, Beautiful Bond R
FTSE1019 Lucy, Your Decision C
FTSE1046 Maiden of the Sky Wendy PR
FTSE1021 Mirajane, Kind Smiles C
FTSE1034 Natsu vs. Zero C
FTSE1026 Natsu, Dragon Force R
FTSE1027 Natsu, Place Where We Return To R
FTSE1028 Natsu, Power of Friends R
FTSE1029Ang Oracion Seis C
FTSE1029Bra Oracion Seis C
FTSE1029Cob Oracion Seis C
FTSE1029Hot Oracion Seis C
FTSE1029Mid Oracion Seis C
FTSE1029Rac Oracion Seis C
FTSE1008 Perfume Magic Ichiya C
FTSE1022 Prayers of the Six Demons (Oracion Seis) C
FTSE1005 Robe of Yuuen Erza R
FTSE1040 Roubaul, Master of Cait Shelter C
FTSE1006 Seith Magic [Human Possession] Bickslow C
FTSE1045 Sky Dragon's Roar C
FTSE1007 Stone Eyes Evergreen C
FTSE1044 Unison Raid Juvia C
FTSE1017 Unison Raid Lucy C
FTSE1035 Wendy Marvell R
FTSE1042 Wendy, Honest And Laudable C
FTSE1038 Wendy, Sky Dragon Slayer R
FTSE1039 Wendy, Youth Days C
FTSE1031 Zero, Master of Oracion Seis C
FTSE1020Ari Zodiacal Celestial Spirit C
FTSE1020Gem Zodiacal Celestial Spirit C
FTSE1020Leo Zodiacal Celestial Spirit C
FTSE1020Sgr Zodiacal Celestial Spirit C
FTSE1020Tau Zodiacal Celestial Spirit C
FTSE1020Vir Zodiacal Celestial Spirit C

2011 Weiss Schwarz Fate/zero TD

FZS17T07 Assistant Machine, Maiya
FZS17T13 Clock Tower Elite, Kayneth
FZS17T09 Einzbern Castle
FZS17T08 First Time Out Irisviel von Einzbern
FZS17T15 Gae Dearg
FZS17T14 Gordius Wheel
FZS17104 Hill of Camlann

FZS17T12 Imposing and Majestic, Rider
FZS17T05 Invisible Air Saber
FZS17T02 Irisviel von Einzbern
FZS17T11 Loyal and Brave, Lancer
FZS17T06 Mage-Killer Kiritsugu
FZS17T03 Maiya Hisau
FZS17T10 Proof of Entry, Waver
FZS17101 Proxy Master, Irisviel
FZS17T04 Riding Skill, Saber
FZS17102 Saber in a Dark Suit
FZS17105 Shallow Blooded Magus, Waver
FZS17T01 Summoned Heroine, Saber
FZS17103 Top Class, Saber

2011 Weiss Schwarz Guilty Crown TD

GCS16T08 Awakened Power of Kings
GCS16T11 Daryl Yan
GCS16T09 Funell
GCS16T03 Gai, Command Tower of the Mortuary
GCS16103 Gai, For the Future Wished For
GCS16T04 Gai, Young Leader
GCS16T12 Inori, Pure Emotions
GCS16101 Inori, the Meaning of Being Here
GCS16T13 Inori, Web Artist
GCS16102 Shu, Decision Time
GCS16T05 Shu, Hidden Potential
GCS16T10 Shu, Normal High School Student
GCS16104 Songstress Inori
GCS16T15 Trial of Courage
GCS16T14 Truth of Void Genome
GCS16T02 Undertaker Algo
GCS16T07 Undertaker Gai
GCS16T06 Undertaker Oogumo
GCS16T01 Undertaker Shibungi
GCS16105 Warped Accomplice

2011 Weiss Schwarz Idolmaster 2

IMS14047 9:02pm CR
IMS14033 Ami, Charming Venus U
IMS14039 Ami, Futami Sister's Cutie C
IMS14037 Ami, Invincible Sisters U
IMS14030 Ami, Ryuuguu Komachi R
IMS14030S Ami, Ryuuguu Komachi SR
IMS14040 Azusa, Charming Venus C
IMS14031 Azusa, Ryuuguu Komachi R
IMS14031S Azusa, Ryuuguu Komachi SR
IMS14044 Azusa, Singing of Love C
IMS14036 Azusa, Supporing Role U
IMS14097 Battling Jupiter U
IMS14071 BK MANIAC U
IMS14099 Bluebird CC
IMS14022 Burst Appeal U
IMS14048 Cast a Spell CR
IMS14092 Chihaya in Casual Clothing C
IMS14091 Chihaya, Charming Venus C
IMS14078 Chihaya, Giving It All on Songs R
IMS14078S Chihaya, Giving It All on Songs SR
IMS14094 Chihaya, Lesson Today Too C
IMS14087 Chihaya, Phoenix Songstress U
IMS14076 Chihaya, Pink Diamond 765 RR
IMS14024 Do-Dai CC
IMS14046 Dotop TV U
IMS14025 First Stage CC
IMS14074 GO MY WAY CC
IMS14023 Good Morning Breakfast CR
IMS14068 Haruka in Casual Clothing C
IMS14059 Haruka, Charming Venus U
IMS14060 Haruka, Heart Mark U
IMS14070 Haruka, Pink Diamond 765 C
IMS14054 Haruka, Proactive and Cheerful R
IMS14054S Haruka, Proactive and Cheerful SR
IMS14052 Haruka, Straight-ahead Idol RR
IMS14096 Hell Training of 765 Productions U
IMS14049 Here we go CR
IMS14067 Hibiki in Casual Clothing C
IMS14065 Hibiki, Charming Venus C
IMS14062 Hibiki, Loves Everyone U
IMS14063 Hibiki, Pet Search C
IMS14057 Hibiki, Pink Diamond 765 R
IMS14055 Hibiki, Southern Girl R
IMS14055S Hibiki, Southern Girl SR
IMS14051 Hibiki, Victory Sign RR
IMS14042 Iori, Charming Venus C
IMS14045 Iori, First Rival C
IMS14027 Iori, I'm the Idol RR
IMS14028 Iori, Leader of Ryuuguu Komachi R
IMS14028S Iori, Leader of Ryuuguu Komachi SR
IMS14035 Junjirou Takagi U
IMS14043 Jupiter, Assassins from 961 Production C
IMS14090 Kotori-san, Always Able to Support C
IMS14032 Kotori-san, Encore R
IMS14032S Kotori-san, Encore SR
IMS14058 Kotori-san, Queen of Daydreaming? U
IMS14016 Kotori-san, Ubiquitous C
IMS14010 Kotori-san, Workplace's Idol U
IMS14021 LUCKY RABBIT U
IMS14083 Makoto in Casual Clothing U
IMS14088 Makoto, Charming Venus C
IMS14080 Makoto, Girl As Brilliant As the Blue Sky R
IMS14080S Makoto, Girl As Brilliant As the Blue Sky SR
IMS14085 Makoto, Image Change U
IMS14095 Makoto, Pink Diamond 765 C
IMS14082 Makoto, Super Lady R
IMS14008 Mami in Casual Clothing U
IMS14014 Mami, Charming Venus C
IMS14003 Mami, Futami Sisters' Healer R
IMS14003S Mami, Futami Sisters' Healer SR
IMS14018 Mami, Pink Diamond 765 C
IMS14001 Mami, Solo Debut RR
IMS14012 Mami, Top Sisters U
IMS14064 Miki in Casual Clothing C
IMS14053 Miki, Carnivorous Little Devil R
IMS14053S Miki, Carnivorous Little Devil SR
IMS14066 Miki, Charming Venus C
IMS14061 Miki, Good Style U
IMS14069 Miki, Love Attack C
IMS14056 Miki, Pink Diamond 765 R
IMS14100 My Best Friend CC
IMS14050 Positive CC
IMS14038 President Kuroi, Active in the Shadows C
IMS14072 Quintet Live U
IMS14073 relations CR
IMS14034 Ritsuko, Charming Venus U
IMS14041 Ritsuko, Jack-of-All-Trades Idol C
IMS14029 Ritsuko, Producer of Ryuuguu Komachi R
IMS14029S Ritsuko, Producer of Ryuuguu Komachi SR
IMS14026 Ritsuko, Shadow Ruler RR
IMS14075 shiny smile CC
IMS14079 Takane in Casual Clothing R
IMS14077 Takane, Aiming for the Top RR
IMS14089 Takane, Always Prepared C
IMS14084 Takane, Charming Venus U
IMS14081 Takane, Graceful Princess R
IMS14081S Takane, Graceful Princess SR
IMS14086 Takane, Pink Diamond 765 U
IMS14093 Takane, Princess' Off-Day C
IMS14098 The Agent Departs at Night CR
IMS14019 Yayoi as Berochoro C
IMS14015 Yayoi in Casual Clothing C
IMS14017 Yayoi, Charming Venus C
IMS14002 Yayoi, Everyone's Sister RR
IMS14005 Yayoi, Life-Sized Idol R
IMS14005S Yayoi, Life-Sized Idol SR
IMS14009 Yayoi, Pink Diamond 765 U
IMS14013 Yukiho in Casual Clothing C
IMS14004 Yukiho, Always Trembling R
IMS14004S Yukiho, Always Trembling SR
IMS14020 Yukiho, Charming Venus C
IMS14007 Yukiho, Day of Promise R
IMS14011 Yukiho, Pink Diamond 765 U
IMS14006 Yukiho, Portrait R
IMS1402SP Yayoi, Everyone's Sister SP
IMS1427SP Iori, I'm the Idol SP
IMS1452SP Haruka, Straight-ahead Idol SP
IMS1487SP Chihaya, Phoenix Songstress SP

2011 Weiss Schwarz Idolmaster 2 TD

IMS14105 A Certain Day's 765 Production
IMS14T14 BK MANIAC
IMS14T07 Do-Dai
IMS14T15 GO MY WAY
IMS14T11 Haruka in Casual Clothing
IMS14T08 Haruka, Charming Venus
IMS14104 Haruka, Orthodox Idol
IMS14T13 Haruka, Pink Diamond 765
IMS14T09 Hibiki, Charming Venus
IMS14T04 Kotori-san, Ubiquitous
IMS14T02 Mami, Charming Venus
IMS14T10 Miki, Charming Venus
IMS14T12 Miki, Love Attack
IMS14102 Miki, Unit Member
IMS14T05 Yayoi as Berochoro
IMS14T03 Yayoi in Casual Clothing
IMS14103 Yayoi, Unit Member
IMS14T01 Yukiho in Casual Clothing
IMS14T06 Yukiho, Charming Venus
IMS14101 Yukiho, Unit Member

2011 Weiss Schwarz Index II and Railgun

IDW13001 Accelerator in the Underworld RR
IDW13015 Accelerator Strongest Esper C
IDW13010 Accelerator, Change in Routine U
RGW13060 Aero Hand Kongou U
IDW13094 Agnese Sanctis U
IDW13085 Agnese, Wielder of Lotus Wand U
IDW13019 Awaki Musujime C
RGW13073 Battle on the Highway CR
RGW13047 Big Spider U
IDW13025 Borrowed Goods Race CC
RGW13031 Clairvoyance Konori R
IDW13076 Dedicatus545 Index RR
RGW13068 Dorm Supervisor C
IDW13013 Electrode Release Accelerator U
RGW13029 Erii Haruue R
IDW13089 Fortis931 Styl C
RGW13039 Haruue in Yukata C
RGW13071 Hint U
IDW13023 Imagine Breaker CR
IDW13078 Index in Cheerleading Outfit R
IDW13091 Index in Swimsuits C
IDW13082 Index, Incredible Sister R
IDW13090 Index, Parasite of the Touma Household C
IDW13083 Index, Walking Church U
IDW13093 Itsuwa of Formerly Amakusa Catholics C
IDW13087 Kanzaki, Former Amakusa Catholics U
RGW13040 Kiyama, Brain Biologist C
RGW13037 Kiyama, Teacher of Children U
IDW13003 Komoe in Cheerleading Outfit R
RGW13045 Konori, Leather Jacket Full of Memories C
RGW13064 Kuroko by the Water C
RGW13070 Kuroko in Yukata C
RGW13061 Kuroko, 177th Branch U
RGW13059 Kuroko, Admiration for Onee-Sama U
IDW13021 Kuroko, Dutiful 7th Grader C
RGW13057 Kuroko, Modern Girl R
IDW13004 Kuroko, Onee-Sama's Herald R
RGW13065 Kuroko, Recorder C
RGW13056 Kuroko, Tokiwadai's Lady R
IDW13009 Last Order, Mischievous Child U
IDW13018 Last Order, Sisters' Controller C
IDW13092 Laura Stuart C
RGW13034 Level 2 Haruue U
RGW13067 Maid of Maids Kongou C
IDW13008 Maika, Maid Candidate U
IDW13097 Meaning of Cross U
RGW13052 Mikoto and Kuroko, Under One Roof RR
RGW13066 Mikoto in Dress C
RGW13062 Mikoto in Pajamas U
RGW13063 Mikoto in Yukata C
RGW13054 Mikoto, Embodiment of Justice R
RGW13055 Mikoto, Girl Who Doesn't Like to Lose R
RGW13053 Mikoto, School Life R
RGW13051 Mikoto, Self-Confidence with Support RR
RGW13058 Mikoto, Tokiwadai's Lady U
IDW13011 Mikoto, Unwilling to Lose U
IDW13005 Misaka, Mikoto's Kid Sister R
IDW13014 Misuzu Misaka C
IDW13012 Multi-Spy Tsuchimikado U
IDW13098 Not a Big Deal? CR
RGW13072 Obsession U
IDW13002 Onee-Sama Mikoto RR
IDW13079 Orsola Aquinas R
IDW13088 Orsola, Missionary to A Heretic State C
IDW13095 Ouma Yamisaka C
RGW13074 Railgun CC
IDW13022 Realistic Narrative Shock U
IDW13080 Route Disturbe Orsola Aquinas R
IDW13086 Saiji Tatemiya U
RGW13027 Saten by the Water RR
RGW13038 Saten in Yukata C
RGW13035 Saten, Normal Girl U
RGW13042 Saten, Surprise and Lowbrows C
RGW13032 Saten, Uiharu's Classmate R
RGW13049 Seeing Erii Again CC
IDW13016 Seiri Fukiyose C
IDW13099 Sheol Fear CC
RGW13046 Someone's Watching U
IDW13094 Styl, Rune Magician C
IDW13024 Strongest Man in the Academy City CC
RGW13026 Telepathy Haruue RR
IDW13096 Temptation on the Stall U
IDW13100 The Girl Who Eats A Lot CC
IDW13077 The Sister with Silver Hair and Blue Eyes RR
RGW13069 Therestina Kihara Lifeline C
RGW13036 Thermal Hand Uiharu U
IDW13081 Touma and Index, Always Merriful R
IDW13020 Touma, High School Student in Academy City C
IDW13006 Touma, Index' Protector R
IDW13007 Touma, Man with A Special Right Hand R
RGW13041 Tsuzuri Tessou C
RGW13044 Uiharu and Saten, Good Classmates C
RGW13030 Uiharu by the Water R
RGW13033 Uiharu in Yukata U
RGW13043 Uiharu, Backup Role C
RGW13028 Uiharu, Saten's Classmate R
RGW13075 Unexpected Alliance CC
IDW13017 Unlucky Touma C
RGW13048 Welcome CR
RGW13050 What I Can Do CC

2011 Weiss Schwarz Index II and Railgun TD

IDW13103 Accelerator, No1 of the Academy City
IDW13T01 Accelerator, Strongest Esper
IDW13T04 Awaki Musujime
IDW13T09 Fortis931 Styl
IDW13T07 Imagine Breaker
IDW13101 Index, Living in the Academy City
IDW13T10 Index, Parasite of the Touma Household
IDW13102 Index, Winter Present
IDW13T12 Kanzaki, Former Amakusa Catholics
IDW13T06 Kuroko, Dutiful 7th Grader
IDW13T03 Last Order, Sisters' Controller
IDW13T11 Laura Stuart
IDW13105 Mikoto, Untrue to Heart
IDW13T05 Multi-Spy Tsuchimikado
IDW13T13 Ouma Yamisaka
IDW13104 Science and Magic Touma and Index
IDW13T08 Strongest Man in the Academy City
IDW13T14 The Girl Who Eats a Lot
IDW13T02 Unlucky Touma

2011 Weiss Schwarz Katanagatari Extra TD

KGSE07T06 Akutou Shichimi
KGSE0706 Capable Subordinate of Princess Hitei Emonzaemon Souda
KGSE0742 Cheerio
KGSE0745 End of Travels
KGSE07T03 Hakuhei Sabi, Fallen Swordsman
KGSE07T02 Head of Sanzu Shrine Meisai Tsuruga
KGSE0710 Meisai Tsuruga, Sentouryuu
KGSE07T04 Nanami and Shichika, Youth
KGSE07T07 One Japanese Katana Shichika Yasuri
KGSE0714 Princess Hitei's Tricks
KGSE0707 Shinou Isshouryuu Zanki Kiguchi
KGSE07T05 Togame and Shichika, Travels of Two
KGSE07T01 Togame and Shichika, Under the Cherry Blossom Storm
KGSE0736 Togame, Ingenious Strategist
KGSE0741 Togame, Smart Strategies and Knacks

2011 Weiss Schwarz Macross Frontier

MFS13048 After Class Overflow CR
MFS13039 Ai-kun C
MFS13049 Aimo CC
MFS13100 Alcatraz Visit Live CC
MFS13053 Alto and Ranka, Closer R
MFS13054 Alto and Sheryl, Running from Vajra R
MFS13064 Alto on Mayan Island C
MFS13063 Alto Saotome C
MFS13065 Alto, Apple Valkyrie C
MFS13062 Alto, End of Triangular U
MFS13058 Alto, Gothic Lolita U
MFS13052 Alto, Mission to Reach out with Songs RR
MFS13067 Alto, Played by Sheryl C
MFS13068 Alto, Playing Young Female C
MFS13055 Alto, Pride of the Pilot R
MFS13051 Alto, Seeking Real Sky RR
MFS13051R Alto, Seeking Real Sky RRR
MFS13057r Alto, Triangular R
MFS13057s Alto, Triangular R
MFS13001 Black Bunny Sheryl RR
MFS13069 Bobby Margot C
MFS13015 Brera Sterne C
MFS13020 Brera, Ranka's Real Brother C
MFS13059 Canaria Berstein U
MFS13088 Catherine Glass C
MFS13085 Clan on the Mayan Island U
MFS13080 Clan, Ending Sorrow R
MFS13082 Clan, Everyday's Smile R
MFS13094 Clan, Idol Unit of SMS? C
MFS13078 Clan, Kindly Watching Over R
MFS13076 Clan, LOVELY BOMBER RR
MFS13076S Clan, LOVELY BOMBER SR
MFS13077 Clan, Microned RR
MFS13077R Clan, Microned RRR
MFS13084 Clan, Stealing Roasted Pork U
MFS13012 Diamond Crevasse Sheryl U
MFS13021 Extinguished Life U
MFS13008 Grace O'Connor U
MFS13003 Grace, Dying Wish R
MFS13098 Guitar Snipe CR
MFS13042 Interstellar Flight Ranka C
MFS13060 Jeffrey Wilder U
MFS13092 Leon Mishima C
MFS13075 Lion CC
MFS13028 Love is Dog Fight Ranka R
MFS13028R Love is Dog Fight RRR
MFS13079 Luca Angelloni R
MFS13087 Luca in the Cockpit U
MFS13091 Luca, Nyan Nya Ramen Delivery C
MFS13074 Macross Attack CC
MFS13056 Macross Quarter Storm Attack Mode R
MFS13056S Macross Quarter Storm Attack Mode SR
MFS13093 Michel, LOVELY BOMBER C
MFS13083 Mihail Blanc U
MFS13099 Miraculously Alive CC
MFS13097 Mishima's Conspiracy U
MFS13066 Monica, Falling for Someone C
MFS13047 Mysterious Scout U
MFS13033 Nanase Matsuura U
MFS13024 Northern Cross CC
MFS13096 Nyan Nyan Ramen U
MFS13025 Obelisk CC
MFS13089 Ozma Lee C
MFS13090 Ozma, Ranka's step-brother C
MFS13081 Ozma, Something to Risk Life to Protect R
MFS13004 Pinky Nurse Sheryl R
MFS13004R Pinky Nurse Sheryl RRR
MFS13071 Prison Break from Alcatraz U
MFS13050 Rainbow-colored Bear CC
MFS13030 Ranka and Alto, Praying for Safety R
MFS13029 Ranka and Sheryl, Love Rivals R
MFS13029S Ranka and Sheryl, Love Rivals SR
MFS13044 Ranka Lee, Super Dimension Cinderella C
MFS13038 Ranka on Mayan Island C
MFS13045 Ranka, Alone C
MFS13043 Ranka, First CM Song C
MFS13032 Ranka, Innocent in Sailor Uniform R
MFS13032S Ranka, Innocent in Sailor Uniform SR
MFS13026 Ranka, Naive and Blooming RR
MFS13031 Ranka, Pushing on Alto's Back R
MFS13037 Ranka, Reclamation Heavy Machinery U
MFS13046 Ranka, Rescued U
MFS13041 Ranka, Starlight Natto C
MFS13035 Ranka, Yearning to Become Songstress U
MFS13018 Rival's Instinct Sheryl C
MFS13017 Sheryl and Alto, Gyro Bike Date C
MFS13009 Sheryl and Ranka, Summer Beach U
MFS13022 SHERYL ARREST U
MFS13016 Sheryl by the Lake C
MFS13011 Sheryl Nome, Galactic Fairy U
MFS13006 Sheryl, Beautiful Little Devil R
MFS13006S Sheryl, Beautiful Little Devil SR
MFS13002 Sheryl, Decision in Her Youth Days RR
MFS13019 Sheryl, Loveslinger C
MFS13013 Sheryl, Mission Code "Galactic Fairy" C
MFS13014 Sheryl, Visited by Alto C
MFS13007 Singing Is Life Sheryl" R
MFS13007S Singing Is Life Sheryl" SR
MFS13027 Songs are Magic Ranka RR
MFS13027S Songs are Magic Ranka SR
MFS13072 Symbiotic with Vajra U
MFS13023 Universal Bunny CR
MFS13034 Vajra (Large) U
MFS13040 Vajra (Small) C
MFS13036 Vajra Queen U
MFS13061 VB-6 Koenig Monster (Canaria) U
MFS13086 VF-25G Messiah (Mihail) U
MFS13095 VF-25S Messiah (Ozma) C
MFS13010 VF-27 Lucifer (Brera) U
MFS13005 White Bunny Sheryl R
MFS13005S White Bunny Sheryl SR
MFS13073 Wings of Farewell CR
MFS13070 YF-29 Durandal (Alto) C
MFS1301SP Black Bunny Sheryl SP
MFS1326SP Ranka, Naive and Blooming SP
MFS1355SP Alto, Pride of the Pilot SP
MFS1382SP Clan, Everyday's Smile SP

2011 Weiss Schwarz Macross Frontier TD

MFS13T14 Aimo
MFS13T06 Diamond Crevasse Sheryl
MFS13T04 Loveslinger Sheryl
MFS13T07 Obelisk
MFS13T11 Ranka Lee, Super Dimension Cinderella
MFS13101 Ranka on That Day
MFS13T10 Ranka, First CM Song
MFS13T12 Ranka, Lonely
MFS13105 Ranka, Mascot
MFS13T13 Ranka, Rescued
MFS13T09 Ranka, Starlight Natto
MFS13T03 Rival's Instinct Sheryl
MFS13T02 Sheryl by the Lake
MFS13T05 Sheryl Nome, Galactic Fairy
MFS13103 Sheryl, Date in Disguise
MFS13104 Sheryl, False Songstress
MFS13T01 Sheryl, Mission Code "Galactic Fairy"
MFS13102 Sheryl, Nagging Bunny
MFS13T08 Universal Bunny

2011 Weiss Schwarz Milky Holmes Phantom Thief ESB

MKSE0923 Arsene, Bewitching Gaze C
MKSE0919 Arsene, Charming Phantom Thief R
MKSE0921 Arsene, Provoking Gaze C
MKSE0917 Arsene, Seeking Good Rivals R
MKSE0927 Bewitching Toys C
MKSE0920 Cordelia, Cute Swimsuit C
MKSE0918 Cordelia, Tragic Heroine? R
MKSE0926 Decisive Battle! Phantom Thief VS Detective C
MKSE0912 Elly, Embarrassing Swimsuit C
MKSE0911 Elly, Trembling R
MKSE0901 Flame Toys Rat R
MKSE0910 Flying Nero C
MKSE0915 Henriette in Yukata R
MKSE0916 Henriette, Carelessly Overslept R
MKSE0922 Henriette, Poyoyon's Girl C
MKSE0925 I Did It C
MKSE0903 Mary & Kate C
MKSE0924 Mysterious Shadow C
MKSE0902 Nero, Doing Great with Toys R
MKSE0908 Nero, Tanned Skin C
MKSE0907 Oxidized Silver Stone River C
MKSE0905 Rat, Rebelling C
MKSE0909 Self-Loving Twenty C
MKSE0913 Sheryl in June R
MKSE0914 Sheryl, Petit Body C
MKSE0904 Stone River, Treasure Robber C
MKSE0906 Twenty & Twenty C

2011 Weiss Schwarz Rewrite

RWW15022 Akane in Casual Clothing C
RWW15018 Akane in Uniform C
RWW15002 Akane Senri RR
RWW15064 Akane, Rebelling Against the Order C
RWW15041 Arata Imamiya C
RWW15065 Assassin Midow C
RWW15068 Atonement CR
RWW15068R Atonement RRR
RWW15059 Awaken Spell Chihaya U
RWW15066 Birth of Monster U
RWW15033 Chairman of Earth Lucia R
RWW15033S Chairman of Earth Lucia SR
RWW15019 Chibu-Mosu C
RWW15024 Chihaya in Casual Clothing C
RWW15053 Chihaya in Swimsuit R
RWW15053S Chihaya in Swimsuit SR
RWW15021 Chihaya in Uniform C
RWW15052 Chihaya Ohtori RR
RWW15013 Chihaya's Butler Sakuya U
RWW15004 Clumsy Girl Chihaya R
RWW15067 Confront C
RWW15046 Curse of the Sun and Wind U
RWW15025 Cycling with Sunbeam through the Leaves U
RWW15062 Discovered Aurora Kotarou C
RWW15014 Dream And Truth Akane U
RWW15096 End of World U
RWW15020 Eternal Rival Haruhiko C
RWW15079 Fate of Scattered Cherry Blossom Sakuya U
RWW15061 Female Saint's Servant Shimako C
RWW15032 First Date Lucia RR
RWW15083 For Whom Shizuru U
RWW15085 Forest Girl Kotori U
RWW15080 Fumbling in the Dark Kagari U
RWW15011 Gil and Bani U
RWW15017 Green Movement Association Kotori C
RWW15099 Heart of Kotori CC
RWW15044 Iron Fist Punishment Lucia C
RWW15077 Kagari, Standing Still in the Moonlit Night R
RWW15012 Kazako's Outlaw Yoshino U
RWW15081 Key Girl Kagari U
RWW15071 Kind Words Kagari RR
RWW15071S Kind Words Kagari SR
RWW15005 Kotarou's Rival Inoue R
RWW15023 Kotori in Casual Clothing C
RWW15016 Kotori in Uniform C
RWW15072 Kotori Kanbe RR
RWW15082 Kotori, Deep in Sleep U
RWW15001 Little Forest Kotori RR
RWW15001S Little Forest Kotori SR
RWW15042 Living God of the Extra-Spicy World Lucia C
RWW15100 Lost Memories CC
RWW15030 Lost Transfer Student CC
RWW15094 Lucia in Casual Clothing C
RWW15087 Lucia in Maid Outfit C
RWW15040 Lucia in the Sunflower Field U
RWW15091 Lucia in Uniform C
RWW15036 Lucia Konohana R
RWW15047 Lucia VS Shizuru C
RWW15026 Mach Knuckle: Point Zero U
RWW15027 Magical Girl of the Academy C
RWW15058 Martel's Important Person Akane U
RWW15098 Meeting CR
RWW15098R Meeting RRR
RWW15009 Mischievous Big Eater Girl Chihaya U
RWW15076 Mistletoe's Contractor Kotori R
RWW15056 Never-ending Transcription Akane R
RWW15063 Ohtori Virus Chihaya C
RWW15007 Old Friend Kotori R
RWW15084 Only One Kagari U

RWW15003 President of the Occult Research Club Akane R
RWW15008 Protection Bandage Chihaya R
RWW15097 Really Short Goodbye C
RWW15049 Receiving Power CC
RWW15070 Retaliation CC
RWW15039 Rewriter Kotarou U
RWW15015 Sakuya Ohtori U
RWW15069 Sakuya VS Kotarou CC
RWW15035 Saury Lover Shizuru R
RWW15043 Shizuru in Battle Outfit C
RWW15093 Shizuru in Casual Clothing C
RWW15031 Shizuru in Maid Outfit RR
RWW15088 Shizuru in Uniform C
RWW15078 Shizuru Nakatsu R
RWW15034 Shizuru, Intercepting R
RWW15038 Shizuru, Upward Glances U
RWW15086 Similar People Kotori C
RWW15050 Small Happiness CC
RWW15050S Small Happiness SR
RWW15028 Smile And Tears CR
RWW15028R Smile And Tears RRR
RWW15055 Song of Destruction Akane R
RWW15055S Song of Destruction Akane SR
RWW15045 Sougen Esaka C
RWW15010 Speed Fight Kotarou U
RWW15054 Strongest Monster Sakuya R
RWW15095 System Tree of Possibilities U
RWW15092 The Being Known as "Sakuya" C
RWW15089 The Role of the Night Kotarou C
RWW15029 The Usual Fun CC
RWW15029S The Usual Fun SR
RWW15090 Theory of Life Kagari C
RWW15073 To Save the Planet Lucia R
RWW15037 Touka Nishikujou U
RWW15006 Treasured Material Kotori R
RWW15075 Two People Together Shizuru R
RWW15075S Two People Together Shizuru SR
RWW15048 Two's World CR
RWW15048R Two's World RRR
RWW15074 Under the Bright Moonlight Kotarou and Kagari R
RWW15051 Unsociable Girl Akane RR
RWW15057 Young Lady of Ohtori Household Chihaya U
RWW15060 Your Path And My Path Midow U
RWW1502SP Akane Senri SP
RWW1536SP Lucia Konohana SP
RWW1552SP Chihaya Ohtori SP
RWW1572SP Kotori Kanbe SP
RWW1578SP Shizuru Nakatsu SP

2011 Weiss Schwarz Rewrite TD

RWW15T07 Akane in Casual Clothing
RWW15T04 Akane in Uniform
RWW15T09 Chihaya in Casual Clothing
RWW15T06 Chihaya in Uniform
RWW15T05 Chihaya's Butler Sakuya
RWW15105 Everyone's Gardening
RWW15104 Happy Dessert Time Lucia
RWW15102 Height Comparing Shizuru
RWW15T03 Kazako's Outlaw Yoshino
RWW15103 Kotarou Tennouji
RWW15T08 Kotori in Casual Clothing
RWW15T01 Kotori in Uniform
RWW15101 Kotori, Resting in the Tree Shades
RWW15T16 Lost Memories
RWW15T11 Lost Transfer Student
RWW15T15 Lucia in Casual Clothing
RWW15T13 Lucia in Uniform
RWW15T14 Shizuru in Casual Clothing
RWW15T12 Shizuru in Uniform
RWW15T02 Speed Fight Kotarou
RWW15T10 Witch of the Academy

2011 Weiss Schwarz Shana

SSW14026 Alast Tooru U
SSW14068 Anything Is Possible CC
SSW14066 Battle at the Tendoukyuu CR
SSW14028 Battle Declaration in the School CR
SSW14081 Beautiful Whim Pheles U
SSW14099 Birth of Denizens in This World CC
SSW14065 Challenge of Homemade Cooking U
SSW14041 Chanter of Elegies Margery Daw R
SSW14018 Chigusa Sakai C
SSW14005 Clumsy Shana R
SSW14074 Corpse Retriever Lamis R
SSW14071 Crimson-Colored Struggle CC
SSW14075 Destructive Blade Sabrac R
SSW14097 Devouring City U
SSW14098 Direct Confrontation CR
SSW14025 Eita Tanaka C
SSW14047 Flame Haze Margery U
SSW14039 Flame Haze Wilhelmina R
SSW14039S Flame Haze Wilhelmina SR
SSW14084 Friagne and Marianne U
SSW14076 Friagne, Flame Haze Murderer R
SSW14013 Fumina Konoe U
SSW14030 Go to Midnight Lost Child CC
SSW14019 Hayato Ike C
SSW14089 He who Loves Himself Sorath and Engulfed in Love for Others Tiriel C
SSW14067 Heaven-and-Earth Sundering CR
SSW14090 Hecate in Yukata C
SSW14082 Hecate, Empty Existence U
SSW14078 Hecate, Great Priestess R
SSW14073 Hecate, Maiden of Oracle RR
SSW14073R Hecate, Maiden of Oracle RRR
SSW14077 Hecate, Moment of Confrontation R
SSW14077S Hecate, Moment of Confrontation SR
SSW14085 Hecate, Opened Vessel U
SSW14087 Hunter Friagne C
SSW14058 Improvisational Poem of Slaughter Margery C
SSW14083 Judge of Paradoxes Bel Peol U
SSW14016 Kazumi as Juliet C
SSW14002 Kazumi in A Dress RR
SSW14021 Kazumi in Maid Outfit C
SSW14007 Kazumi Yoshida R
SSW14004 Kazumi, A Step Forward R
SSW14023 Kazumi, Student of Misaki High SChool C
SSW14009 Keisaku Satou U
SSW14003 Konoe in Maid Outfit R
SSW14024 Konoe, Transfer Student with Suspicions C
SSW14038 Lovely Goblet Margery R
SSW14038S Lovely Goblet Margery SR
SSW14057 Manipulator of Objects Wilhelmina Carmel C
SSW14049 Margery and Marchosias U
SSW14052 Margery Daw C
SSW14055 Margery in Swimsuits C
SSW14072 Master Throne Hecate RR
SSW14022 Matake Oagata C
SSW14044 Mathilde Saint-Omer U
SSW14061 Mobilizer of Ceremonial Equipment Khamsin Nbh'w C
SSW14092 Pheles, Wheeler of Wind C
SSW14070 Power of Will CC
SSW14086 Rainbow Wings Merihim C
SSW14100 Retrival of Vessels CC
SSW14063 Seal U
SSW14088 Seeking Researcher Dantalion C
SSW14069 Seized Lead CC
SSW14031 Shana and Alastor RR
SSW14031S Shana and Alastor SR
SSW14050 Shana and Alastor, Go to Yuji C
SSW14042 Shana and Yuji R
SSW14042R Shana and Yuji RRR
SSW14048 Shana as Dorothy U
SSW14012 Shana in Swimsuits U
SSW14011 Shana who Loves Melon Bread U
SSW14035 Shana, Apostle of Extermination R
SSW14035R Shana, Apostle of Extermination RRR
SSW14020 Shana, Confused C
SSW14045 Shana, Contractor of Alastor U
SSW14001 Shana, Development of the Town RR
SSW14008 Shana, First Time Feeling This R
SSW14008S Shana, First Time Feeling This SR
SSW14040 Shana, Flame Sword Shana U
SSW14054 Shana, Flame-Haired Blazing-Eyed Hunter C
SSW14034 Shana, Great Vessel RR
SSW14037 Shana, Moment of Confrontation R
SSW14037S Shana, Moment of Confrontation SR
SSW14033 Shana, Prideful RR
SSW14033R Shana, Prideful RRR
SSW14056 Shana, Something to Protect C
SSW14059 Shana, Staring into the Futre C
SSW14046 Shana, Wings of Crimson U
SSW14053 Shana, Wish And Mission C
SSW14064 Silver Flame U
SSW14027 Start of Seishuu Festival U
SSW14096 Statue of Pride U
SSW14095 Tenmoku Ikko C
SSW14029 The Feeling that Nothing Can Be Done CC
SSW14079 Thousand Changes Sydonay R
SSW14080 Three-Eyed Female Monster Bel Peol U
SSW14062 Torch And Flame Haze U
SSW14094 Trinity Hecate C
SSW14093 Trinity Sydonay C
SSW14091 Village of Jestful Slumber Mea C
SSW14060 Wilhelmina and Tiamat C
SSW14051 Wilhelmina Carmel C
SSW14043 Wilhelmina, 3 Minute Cooking U
SSW14032 Wilhelmina, Beautiful Princess of "Unrivaled Battle Techniques" RR
SSW14036 Wilhelmina, Contractor to Tiamat R
SSW14017 Yuji as Romeo C
SSW14014 Yuji Sakai U
SSW14006 Yuji, Changed "Torch" R
SSW14015 Yuji, Mysteries of Midnight Lost Child U
SSW14010 Yukari Hirai U
SSW1401SP Shana, Development of the Town SP
SSW1402SP Kazumi in A Dress SP
SSW1432SP Wilhelmina, Beautiful Princess of "Unrivaled Battle Techniques" SP
SSW1434SP Shana, Great Vessel SP
SSW1441SP Chanter of Elegies Margery Daw SP
SSW1472SP Master Throne Hecate SP

2011 Weiss Schwarz Shana TD

SSW14T14 Anything is Possible
SSW14102 Educator Wilhelmina
SSW14105 Flame Haze Shana
SSW14T07 Improvisational Poem of Slaughter Margery
SSW14T09 Manipulator of Objects Wilhelmina Carmel
SSW14T05 Margery Daw
SSW14T11 Mobilizer of Ceremonial Equipment Khamsin Nbh'w
SSW14T13 Power of Will
SSW14T02 Puzzled Shana
SSW14T01 Shana who Loves Melon Bread
SSW14101 Shana, Bearer of the Vairocana of the Offering Room
SSW14T10 Shana, Contractor of Alastor
SSW14T06 Shana, Flame-Haired Blazing-Eyed Hunter
SSW14104 Shana, Fluttered and Black-clothed
SSW14T08 Shana, Something to Protect
SSW14103 Shana, Student of the Misaki High School
SSW14T03 The Feeling That Nothing Can Be Done
SSW14T12 Torch and Flame Haze
SSW14T04 Wilhelmina Carmel

2012 Weiss Schwarz Accel World

AWS18073 5th Chrome Disaster C
AWS18096 Aqua Current, Quiet Pretty Lady C
AWS18040 Ash Roller U
AWS18047 Ash Roller, Chivalry Skull Mask C
AWS18050 Ash Roller, Good Rival C
AWS18003 Beautiful Girl Kuroyukihime R
AWS18003S Beautiful Girl Kuroyukihime SR
AWS18025 Betrayal U
AWS18012 Black King Black Lotus U
AWS18009 Black Lotus R
AWS18009R Black Lotus RRR
AWS18010 Black Lotus, Encountering Nearby Duels U
AWS18018 Black Lotus, Return of the King C
AWS18079 Black Waves CC
AWS18071 Bloody Storm Scarlet Rain C
AWS18092 Bouncer Aqua Current C
AWS18037 Chiyuri Kurashima R
AWS18049 Chiyuri, Beloved Charisma C
AWS18046 Chiyuri, Bright And Energetic C
AWS18033 Chiyuri, Carefree Talk R
AWS18033S Chiyuri, Carefree Talk SR
AWS18036 Chiyuri, Caring for Friends R
AWS18034 Chiyuri, Ice Cream for Apology R
AWS18031 Chiyuri, Sea of Cushions RR
AWS18031R Chiyuri, Sea of Cushions RRR
AWS18045 Chiyuri, Silver Cat C
AWS18048 Chiyuri, Sunny Smile C
AWS18044 Chiyuri, Surprised Look C
AWS18043 Chiyuri, Youth C
AWS18053 Chiyuri's Tears CR
AWS18052 Chori Chime U
AWS18054 Citron Call CC
AWS18067 Crikin, Strongest Name U
AWS18068 Crimson Kingbolt C
AWS18084 Cyan Pile R
AWS18087 Cyan Pile, Trustworthy Partner U
AWS18095 Cyan Pile, Unlimited Neutral Field C
AWS18029 Death by Piercing CC
AWS18055 Demonic Commandeer CC
AWS18077 Disaster Armor U
AWS18041 Dusk Taker U
AWS18028 Emotion First Felt Since Birth CC
AWS18098 Forced Revolution U
AWS18085 Fuuko Kurasaki R
AWS18083 Fuuko, Gentle Smile R
AWS18083S Fuuko, Gentle Smile SR
AWS18088 Fuuko, Neet And Pretty U
AWS18026 Gale Thruster U
AWS18078 Hailstorm Domination CR
AWS18020 Haruyuki, Bullied Kid C
AWS18017 Haruyuki, Pink Piggy C
AWS18021 Haruyuki, Scatterbrain C
AWS18024 Haruyuki, the Wall in the Way C
AWS18015 Haruyuki, To the Height Where Mankind Hasn't Reached U
AWS18016 Haruyuki, Young Man Hoping for Wings C
AWS18032 Healer Lime Bell RR
AWS18027 Heart Wishing for the Sky CR
AWS18051 Hydro Dealer U
AWS18061 Immobile Fortress Scarlet Rain R
AWS18076 Invincible U
AWS18080 Judgment Blow CC
AWS18030 Knight of 'Black King' CC
AWS18023 Kuroyukihime in Ponytail C
AWS18002 Kuroyukihime RR
AWS18004 Kuroyukihime, Intimate Relations R
AWS18004S Kuroyukihime, Intimate Relations SR
AWS18019 Kuroyukihime, Madonna of the Academy C
AWS18006 Kuroyukihime, Maiden in Love R
AWS18006R Kuroyukihime, Maiden in Love RRR
AWS18013 Kuroyukihime, Promise at Dusk U
AWS18008 Kuroyukihime, Pure Possessiveness R
AWS18008S Kuroyukihime, Pure Possessiveness SR
AWS18014 Kuroyukihime, Real Strength U
AWS18005 Kuroyukihime, The Goal Chased After R
AWS18005S Kuroyukihime, The Goal Chased After SR
AWS18100 Lightning Cyan Spike CC
AWS18038 Lime Bell U
AWS18042 Lime Bell, Betrayer U
AWS18035 Lime Bell, Optimistic R
AWS18090 Mana Itosu C
AWS18070 Megumi Wakamiya C
AWS18074 Niko and Pard, Best of 'Prominence' C
AWS18065 Niko, Angel Mode U
AWS18059 Niko, Cute Second Cousin? R
AWS18059R Niko, Cute Second Cousin? RRR
AWS18056 Niko, Good at Cooking RR
AWS18056S Niko, Good at Cooking SR
AWS18064 Niko, Heart Thumping in Bath U
AWS18075 Niko, Sassiness C
AWS18063 Niko, Slaying Over U
AWS18069 Pard, Nerima's Maid C
AWS18097 Piledriver U
AWS18099 Power of Spirit CR
AWS18060 Rain and Leopard R
AWS18062 Red King Scarlet Rain R
AWS18093 Ruka Asato C
AWS18072 Scarlet Rain, Berseking of Dear Friend C
AWS18058 Scarlet Rain, Passionate R
AWS18039 Seiji Noumi U
AWS18001 Silver Crow in A Predicament RR
AWS18001S Silver Crow in A Predicament SR
AWS18007 Silver Crow, Challenging Strong Enemies R
AWS18066 Silver Crow, Darkness of Heart U
AWS18011 Silver Crow, Rookie Burst Linker U
AWS18022 Silver Crow, Silvery Wings C
AWS18089 Sky Raker, Ash's Master U
AWS18086 Sky Raker, Former Ally U
AWS18081 Sky Raker, Living as Hermit RR
AWS18094 Takumu, Glass-Guy Character C
AWS18082 Takumu, Kendo Club RR
AWS18091 Takumu, New Ally C
AWS18057 Yuniko Kouzuki RR
AWS1802SP Kuroyukihime SP
AWS1837SP Chiyuri Kurashima SP
AWS1857SP Yuniko Kouzuki SP
AWS1885SP Fuuko Kurasaki SP

2012 Weiss Schwarz Accel World TD

AWS18T03 Black Lotus, Return of the King
AWS18T12 Chiyuri, Bright And Cheerful
AWS18101 Chiyuri, Childhood Friend Caretaker
AWS18T13 Chiyuri, Loving Charm
AWS18T11 Chiyuri, Silver Cat
AWS18T14 Citron Call
AWS18T09 Emotion First Felt Since Birth
AWS18T05 Haruyuki, Bullied Kid
AWS18T01 Haruyuki, Pink Piggy
AWS18T08 Haruyuki, the Wall in the Way
AWS18T10 Knight of <Black King>
AWS18105 Kuroyukihime in Bed Clothing
AWS18T04 Kuroyukihime, Madonna of the Academy
AWS18102 Kuroyukihime, Miraculous Survival
AWS18103 Kuroyukihime, Pitch Black Swallowtail
AWS18T06 Kuroyukihime, Promise at Dusk
AWS18104 Silver Crow
AWS18T02 Silver Crow, Rookie Burst Linker
AWS18T07 Silver Crow, Silvery Wings

2012 Weiss Schwarz Da Capo III

DC3W18072 Aoi, A Future We Are Heading Towards RR
DC3W18090 Aoi, Energetic C
DC3W18071 Aoi, Flowers Is Busy RR
DC3W1871S Aoi, Flowers Is Busy SR
DC3W18092 Aoi, Getting Out of Bath C
DC3W18081 Aoi, Important Time U
DC3W18075 Aoi, Midnight Date R
DC3W18080 Aoi, Pacing U
DC3W18076 Aoi, Pampered Mode R
DC3W1876S Aoi, Pampered Mode SR
DC3W18093 Aoi, Sickly Dog-like Girl C
DC3W18086 Aoi, Sunny Girl C
DC3W18078 Aoi, True Feeligns R
DC3W18083 Aoi, Under Starlit Sky U
DC3W18094 Aoi, Working Girl C
DC3W18017 Category 5 U
DC3W18067 Cattleya of Pride CR
DC3W1867R Cattleya of Pride RRR
DC3W18063 Charles in Gymnastics Clothes C
DC3W18051 Charles, After the First Date U
DC3W18011 Charles, At Ease C
DC3W18001 Charles, Causing Commotion RR
DC3W1801S Charles, Causing Commotion SR
DC3W18015 Charles, Heart-Thumping Bath Cleaning C
DC3W18052 Charles, Irremovable Past U
DC3W18057 Charles, Light Pranks C
DC3W18058 Charles, Morning Accident C
DC3W18041 Charles, On Top of Lap Pillow RR
DC3W1841S Charles, On Top of Lap Pillow SR
DC3W18048 Charles, Smiles to Protect R
DC3W18005 Charles, Student Council President of Kazemidori R
DC3W18016 Elizabeth, Academy President of Kazamidori C
DC3W18009 Eto's Wish Charles U
DC3W18068 Farewell Present CC
DC3W18098 Fir~st Lesson CC
DC3W18020 Flwers that Keep Blooming CC
DC3W1820R Flwers that Keep Blooming RRR
DC3W18037 For My Beloved Lover U
DC3W18055 Himeno, Bad-Tempered C
DC3W18026 Himeno, Brother-And-Sister-Only Gathering U
DC3W18043 Himeno, Feelings Inside R
DC3W18030 Himeno, Feelings to Be Told U
DC3W18029 Himeno, Going Out with Nii-San U
DC3W18062 Himeno, Her First Uniform C
DC3W18061 Himeno, Just Like Before C
DC3W18042 Himeno, Overslept RR
DC3W1842S Himeno, Overslept SR
DC3W18032 Himeno, Pitiful Art Skills C
DC3W18031 Himeno, Smiles to Protect C
DC3W18045 Himeno, Stiff R
DC3W18022 Himeno, Two's Happiness RR
DC3W18012 Ian and Rurica, Clumsy People C
DC3W18035 Kiyotaka and Himeno, Mutual Understanding C
DC3W18049 Kiyotaka, Words to Be Told U
DC3W18034 Kousuke and Himeno, Interesting People C
DC3W18099 Lots of Dreams CC
DC3W18019 Magic of Happiness CR
DC3W1819R Magic of Happiness RRR
DC3W18040 Magic to Connect Hearts CC
DC3W1840R Magic to Connect Hearts RRR
DC3W18100 Magical Mist CC
DC3W18100R Magical Mist RRR
DC3W18024 Magician of Justice Himeno R
DC3W1824S Magician of Justice Himeno SR
DC3W18027 Mary and Edward, Childhood Friends U
DC3W18007 Master Ricca U
DC3W18064 Mikoto, Club Member Number One C
DC3W18053 Minatsu, Robot President U
DC3W18096 Miracle of the Unwilting Cherry Blossom U
DC3W18066 New Year's Kiss U
DC3W18065 Nice to Meet You, Lulu-nee U
DC3W18070 Normal Newspaper Club CC
DC3W18038 Place of Heart U
DC3W18018 Present on Holy N?ight U
DC3W18097 Proof of Friendship CR
DC3W1897R Proof of Friendship RRR
DC3W18039 Proof of Love CR
DC3W1839R Proof of Love RRR
DC3W18060 Ricca in Around-the-House Wear C
DC3W18003 Ricca, Buoying Date R
DC3W18047 Ricca, Confession on Holy Night R
DC3W18010 Ricca, Everyone's Power U
DC3W18050 Ricca, Feelings of "Love" U
DC3W18054 Ricca, Genius Pretty Magician Girl U
DC3W18002 Ricca, Irreplaceable Magic RR
DC3W18046 Ricca, Official Newspaper Club President R
DC3W1846S Ricca, Official Newspaper Club President SR
DC3W18044 Ricca, Overspilling Feelings R
DC3W18013 Ricca, Seal to Exclude the Mist C
DC3W18056 Ricca, Surprisingly Childlike C
DC3W18004 Ricca, To the Future Seen in Dreams R
DC3W1804S Ricca, To the Future Seen in Dreams SR
DC3W18073 Sakura, Important things R
DC3W1873S Sakura, Important things SR
DC3W18014 Sakura, Innocent C
DC3W18077 Sakura, Miracle Returned R
DC3W1877S Sakura, Miracle Returned SR
DC3W18006 Santa's First Love Charles R
DC3W18082 Sara in Gymnastics Cloths U
DC3W18088 Sara, A Little Spoiled C
DC3W18036 Sara, Always By the Side C
DC3W18084 Sara, Big Crisis U
DC3W18025 Sara, Commemoration of Two R
DC3W18085 Sara, Echoed Thumping C
DC3W18074 Sara, Enjoyable Off-Day R
DC3W1874S Sara, Enjoyable Off-Day SR
DC3W18079 Sara, Eternal Promise R
DC3W18033 Sara, Flailing C
DC3W18028 Sara, Practicing U
DC3W18023 Sara, Relaxing Date R
DC3W18021 Sara, Special Smile RR
DC3W1821S Sara, Special Smile SR
DC3W18091 Sara, Younger Classmate C
DC3W18089 Suginami, Natural Troublemaker C
DC3W18087 Suginami, Ubiquitous Trickster C
DC3W18069 Talking by the Seaside CC
DC3W18095 Tiny Body U
DC3W18008 Tomoe, Academy's Seasonal Greetings U
DC3W18059 Yuzu and Yuuhi, Carefree Assistants C
DC3W1822S Himeno, Two's Happiness SP
DC3W182SP Ricca, Irreplaceable Magic SP
DC3W1848S Charles, Smiles to Protect SP
DC3W1872S Aoi, A Future We Are Heading Towards SP
DC3W1879S Sara, Eternal Promise SP

2012 Weiss Schwarz Da Capo III TD

DC3W18T14 Aoi, Energetic
DC3W18T16 Aoi, Sickly Dog-like Girl
DC3W18102 Aoi, Substance Over Style
DC3W18T11 Aoi, Sunny Girl
DC3W18T07 Charles in Gymnastics Clothes
DC3W18T03 Charles, Light Pranks
DC3W18T04 Charles, Morning Accident
DC3W18101 Charles, Welcome to Christmas Party
DC3W18T17 Fir~st Lesson
DC3W18105 Himenu in Yukata
DC3W18T01 Himeno, Bad-Tempered
DC3W18T06 Himeno, Her First Uniform
DC3W18T08 Nice to Meet You, Lulu-nee
DC3W18T09 Normal Newspaper Club
DC3W18T05 Ricca in Around-the-House Wear
DC3W18103 Ricca, Girl in Love
DC3W18T02 Ricca, Surprisingly Childlike
DC3W18104 Sara in Ski Wear
DC3W18T13 Sara, A Little Spoiled
DC3W18T15 Sara, Younger Classmate
DC3W18T12 Suginami, Ubiquitous Trickster
DC3W18T10 Talking by the Seaside

2012 Weiss Schwarz Dog Days Extra

DDWE1233 Cinque Izumi C
DDWE1230 Cinque, Summon Hero C
DDWE1218 Dalkian, Freedom Knight R
DDWE1221 Eclair Martinozzi R
DDWE1225 Ecle, Captain of Lop-Eared squad C
DDWE1231 Ecle, Praetorian Guard Captain C
DDWE1209 Gaul Galette des Rois C
DDWE1202 Gaul, Prince of Galette R
DDWE1207 Genoise Jaune C
DDWE1208 Genoise Vert C
DDWE1213 Grandvert, Magic Battleaxe C
DDWE1216 Hero Express Cinque R
DDWE1235 Hero's Arrival! C
DDWE1203 Leo, Fair and Square R
DDWE1210 Leo, Silent Determination C
DDWE1206 Leo, Solitary Charge C
DDWE1212 Leo, Sudden Declaration of War C
DDWE1204 Leo, Unrivaled Battle R
DDWE1201 Leonmitchelli Galette des Rois R
DDWE1214 Lion King Explosion C
DDWE1205 Lion King Leo R
DDWE1215 Magic God Optical Flash C
DDWE1232 Millhi, Encounter at the Bath! C
DDWE1228 Millhi, Looking on C
DDWE1223 Millhi, Lord of Biscotti C
DDWE1219 Millhi, Lord's Determination R
DDWE1227 Millhi, Proxy Operation C
DDWE1217 Millhi, Summon Lord R
DDWE1222 Millhiore Firianno Biscotti R
DDWE1234 Monster Ball C
DDWE1229 Rico, Chief Researcher C
DDWE1226 Rico, Loves Machine! C
DDWE1236 Rico's Support C
DDWE1220 Ricotta Elmar R
DDWE1211 Violet, Personal Attendant C
DDWE1224 Yukikaze, Head of Secret Squad R

2012 Weiss Schwarz Dog Days Extra TD

DDWE12T05 Amelita, Secretary to the Princess TD
DDWE12T07 Cinque, Millhi's Hero TD
DDWE1230 Cinque, Summon Hero C
DDWE12T09 Definitely In Love TD
DDWE1231 Ecle, Praetorian Guard Captain C
DDWE1207 Genoise Jaune C
DDWE12T02 Genoise Noir TD
DDWE12T08 Holy Sabre TD
DDWE12T04 Leo, Knight of King of Beasts TD
DDWE1210 Leo, Silent Determination C
DDWE12T01 Leo, Talented with Weapons TD
DDWE1228 Millhi, Looking on C
DDWE1223 Millhi, Lord of Biscotti C
DDWE1234 Monster Ball C
DDWE12T06 Rizel, Head of Maids TD
DDWE12T03 Rouge, Guard Maid TD
DDWE1211 Violet, Personal Attendant C

2012 Weiss Schwarz Fate/zero

COMPLETE SET (110)
BOOSTER BOX (20 PACKS) 150.00 200.00

BOOSTER PACK (8 CARDS) 6.00 8.00
RELEASED ON
FZS17099 8th Pact CR
FZS17060 Archer, Best Wine R
FZS17060S Archer, Best Wine SR
FZS17091 Archer, Current World After Reincarnation U
FZS17061 Archer, Golden King R
FZS17074 Archer, I'm the Best C
FZS17065 Archer, King Amongst Kings U
FZS17057 Archer, King of All RR
FZS17071 Archer, Oldest Human King C
FZS17058 Archer, Pride of Nobility R
FZS17058R Archer, Pride of Nobility RRR
FZS17079 Archer, Solitude Way of the King C
FZS17082 Arondite C
FZS17093 Assassin, One of Many C
FZS17059 Berserker, Beast Hungering for Blood R
FZS17070 Berserker, Dark Killing Intent U
FZS17062 Berserker, Materialized Curse R
FZS17056 Berserker, Warrior of Madness RR
FZS17056S Berserker, Warrior of Madness SR
FZS17053 Bond of King And Servant CC
FZS17090 Caster, Beauty of Death U
FZS17088 Caster, Sadistic Artst R
FZS17050 Command Mantra U
FZS17026 Demolition U
FZS17085 Ea, Sword of Rupture CC
FZS17027 Einzbern Castle C
FZS17030 Excalibur CC
FZS17084 Farewell with Rin CC
FZS17024 First Time Outside Irisviel C
FZS17097 Flame of Hell U
FZS17055 Gae Dearg CC
FZS17054 Gordius Wheel CC
FZS17075 His Highness Archer C
FZS17016 Illya, Innocent Girl C
FZS17020 Invisible Air Saber C
FZS17052 Ionioi Hetairoi CR
FZS17014 Irisviel and Illya, Mother and Daughter U
FZS17017 Irisviel von Einzbern C
FZS17001 Irisviel, Doll of Einzbern RR
FZS17010 Irisviel, Girl Living as Human U
FZS17008 Irisviel, Vessel of Grail R
FZS17008S Irisviel, Vessel of Grail SR
FZS17072 Kariya Matou C
FZS17078 Kariya, Man Who Ran Away from Destiny C
FZS17068 Kariya, Payment of Life U
FZS17033 Kayneth El-Melloi Archibald R
FZS17049 Kayneth, Elite of the Clock Tower C
FZS17047 Kayneth, Genius Magus C
FZS17089 Kirei Kotomine R
FZS17094 Kirei, Apprentice C
FZS17087 Kirei, Movement of Soul R
FZS17096 Kirei, Protector of Religion C
FZS17086 Kirei, Void Within RR
FZS17086S Kirei, Void Within SR
FZS17004 Kiritsugu, Heretic Style R
FZS17003 Kiritsugu, Justice to Believe in RR
FZS17003R Kiritsugu, Justice to Believe in RRR
FZS17012 Kiritsugu, the Ideal Chased After U
FZS17021 Kiritsugu, Time to Hunt C
FZS17046 Lancer, Bravery And Justice C
FZS17041 Lancer, Charming Looks U
FZS17037 Lancer, Dispelling Crimson Lance R
FZS17039 Lancer, Way of the Knight U
FZS17035 Left Hand of Saber Lancer R
FZS17035S Left Hand of Saber Lancer SR
FZS17022 Magus Killer Kiritsugu C
FZS17019 Maiya Hisau C
FZS17023 Maiya, Assistance Machinery C
FZS17005 Maiya, Quiet Assistant R
FZS17013 Maiya, Spare Parts for Kiritsugu U
FZS17029 Origin Bullet CC
FZS17007 Prana Release Saber R
FZS17007R Prana Release Saber RRR
FZS17051 Precious Sword And Magical Lance U
FZS17083 Real Form of the Fallen Knight CR
FZS17045 Rider, Bold Disposition C
FZS17034 Rider, Conceited R
FZS17034R Rider, Conceited RRR
FZS17036 Rider, Conqueror of Macedonia R
FZS17032 Rider, King of Military Might RR
FZS17040 Rider, Magnificent Lord U
FZS17042 Rider, Majestic U
FZS17069 Rin, Young Successor U
FZS17092 Risei, Observer C
FZS17095 Ryuunosuke, Homocidal Sadist C
FZS17006 Saber, Elegant King of Knights R
FZS17006S Saber, Elegant King of Knights SR
FZS17009 Saber, End of Rule R
FZS17009S Saber, End of Rule SR
FZS17002 Saber, Ideal King RR
FZS17015 Saber, Noble Phantasm Unleashed U
FZS17018 Saber, Skill of "Riding" C
FZS17073 Sakura and Aoi and Rin, Memory of a Day in Distant Past C
FZS17067 Sakura, Affected Heart U
FZS17098 Sea Monster U
FZS17025 Searching for Winterbud U
FZS17011 Shirou, Hope of the Future U
FZS17043 Sola-Ui Nuada-Re Sophia-Ri C
FZS17080 Sword of Azoth U
FZS17028 Symbl of Determination CR
FZS17077 Tokiomi, Gem Magic C
FZS17063 Tokiomi, Head of the Tohsa Household R
FZS17064 Tokiomi, Proper Magus U
FZS17076 Tokiomi, Strategy to Victory C
FZS17100 Trickery of Destiny CC
FZS17081 Vimana U
FZS17048 Waver "McKenzie" C
FZS17031 Waver Velvet RR
FZS17031S Waver Velvet SR
FZS17038 Waver, Apprentice Magus U
FZS17044 Waver, Proof of Participation in War C
FZS17066 Zougen, Obsession of Matou U
FZS1702SP Saber, Ideal King SP
FZS1732SP Rider, King of Military Might SP
FZS1737SP Lancer, Dispelling Crimson Lance SP
FZS1757SP Archer, King of All SP

2012 Weiss Schwarz Fate/zero Extra

FZSE1323 Artist Ryunosuke C
FZSE1322 Caster, Teacher of Ryunosuke C
FZSE1319 Gae Buidhe C
FZSE1318 Holy Grail Dialogue C
FZSE1307 Irisviel, Precious Gem C
FZSE1301 Irisviel, Pure And Innocent R
FZSE1314 Kayneth, Royalty at Birth C
FZSE1320 Kirei, Father with Questions R
FZSE1321 Kirei, Truth Seeker of the Holy Church R
FZSE1308 Kiritsugu, Cold-Blooded Hound C
FZSE1305 Kiritsugu, Trump of Einzbern C
FZSE1311 Lancer, Cursed Yellow Lance R
FZSE1310 Lancer, Two Magical Lances R
FZSE1304 Maiya, Female Soldier R
FZSE1303 Protector of Vessel Irisviel R
FZSE1313 Rider, Ambition to Conquer the World C
FZSE1312 Rider, Legendary Conqueror King R
FZSE1317 Rider, My Path of Kingship C
FZSE1325 Risei Kotomine C
FZSE1327 Ryunosuke Uryu C
FZSE1306 Saber, Girl of Heroic Spirit C
FZSE1302 Saber, Metallic Gale R
FZSE1309 Strike Air C
FZSE1315 Volumen Hydragyrum Kayneth C
FZSE1316 Waver, Self-Proclaimed Genius Magician C
FZSE1324 Zabaniya Assassin C
FZSE1326 Zabaniya Assassin C

2012 Weiss Schwarz Idolmaster Anime

IMS21071 765 Production, Everyone Gather U
IMS21078a A Certain Day's Scenery U
IMS21078b A Certain Day's Scenery U
IMS21107 Ai and Mai, Lively Parent And Child RE
IMS21054 Ai, Brilliance of Next Generation C
IMS21108 Ai, Straightforward Wherever RE
IMS21114 Ai, Talent As Idol RE
IMS21115 ALIVE RE
IMS21001 Ami and Mami, Trickery Boss RR
IMS21001R Ami and Mami, Trickery Boss RRR
IMS21036 Ami, Beautiful Sisters Detectives C
IMS21032 Ami, Exclusive Interview C
IMS21031 Ami, Idol Full Power U
IMS21030 Ami, Twin Drive U
IMS21017 Ami-Mami-chan Mami C
IMS21025 Azusa, OFF Time R
IMS21025R Azusa, OFF Time RRR
IMS21026 Azusa, Run Bride R
IMS21021 Azusa, Seaside RR
IMS21027 Azusa, Short Hair U
IMS21121 Azusa, Thinking of Dreams RE
IMS21112 Challenging the Limits Ai RE
IMS21080 CHANGE CC
IMS21125 Chihaya, Advice of Songs RE
IMS21072 Chihaya, Frog Kitchen C
IMS21076 Chihaya, Live? On Sundays C
IMS21061 Chihaya, New Promise RR
IMS21064 Chihaya, OFF Time R
IMS21064R Chihaya, OFF Time RRR
IMS21122 CINERIA, Net Idol RE
IMS21018a Clothing Change U
IMS21018b Clothing Change U
IMS21110 Dashing Mini-Tank Ai RE
IMS21104 Dazzling World RE
IMS21123 Eri Mizutani RE
IMS21073 Eri, Brilliance of Next Generation C
IMS21118 Eri, Group Lesson RE
IMS21124 Eri, Inherited Dream RE
IMS21120 Eri, Multi-Artist RE
IMS21119 Eri, Quite Incredulous RE
IMS21047 Hamzo, Hibiki's Partner U
IMS21049 Haruka, Can't Let It Be U
IMS21046 Haruka, Center of 765 Production R
IMS21050 Haruka, Live? On Sundays U
IMS21052 Haruka, Rookie Idol C
IMS21111 Haruka, Special Judge RE
IMS21045 Haruka, To the Next Stage R
IMS21045R Haruka, To the Next Stage RRR
IMS21048 Hibiki, Business Trip Event U
IMS21041 Hibiki, Got It RR
IMS21051R Hibiki, Together With Everyone RRR
IMS21051 Hibiki, Together With Everyone U
IMS21053 Hibiki, Tricycle Dash C
IMS21097 Hibiki, Tropical Girl RE
IMS21014 Hikari, Shinkan Shoujo C
IMS21033 Iori During Sports Festival C
IMS21093 Iori, Idol Favorite RE
IMS21035 Iori, Kira Kira Cute C
IMS21028R Iori, OFF Time RRR
IMS21028 Iori, OFF Time U
IMS21024 Iori, Super Beautiful Girl Idol R
IMS21015 Kotori, Padded Kimono C
IMS21012 Kotori, Person of Interest C
IMS21011 Kotori, Secret Songstress U
IMS21003 Kotori-san, Support Anywhere R
IMS21019 Little Match Girl CC
IMS21113 Mai, Legendary Idol RE
IMS21069 Makoto, Action Star U
IMS21077 Makoto, Makko-Makorin C
IMS21066 Makoto, Makoto's Prince R
IMS21063 Makoto, OFF Time R
IMS21063R Makoto, OFF Time RRR
IMS21105 Makoto, Special Coach RE
IMS21007 Mami, ALLSTAR Live U
IMS21009 Mami, Full Power Idol U
IMS21106 Manami, Supporting Role RE
IMS21059 Marionette's Heart CC
IMS21042 Miki, Awakened Genius RR
IMS21044 Miki, Hidden Talent? R
IMS21044R Miki, Hidden Talent? RRR
IMS21055 Miki, Return to Stage C
IMS21101 Miki, Self-Confidence Towards Songs RE
IMS21056 Miki, Sexy Santa C
IMS21126 Precog RE
IMS21058a Present U
IMS21058b Present U
IMS21094 President Ishikawa RE
IMS21068 President Kuroi, Jupiter's Wire Puller U
IMS21057 President Takagi, Mysterious Person? C
IMS21117 Producer Ozaki RE
IMS21067 Producer, First Job U
IMS21043 Producer, Reliable? R
IMS21079 Promise CC
IMS21060 READY CC
IMS21020 Rest@rt Myself CC
IMS21029 Ritsuko and Ryuuguu Komachi U
IMS21023 Ritsuko, OFF Time R
IMS21023R Ritsuko, OFF Time RRR
IMS21116 Ritsuko, Premonition of Incident RE
IMS21022 Ritsuko, Return to Idoldom RR
IMS21037 Ritsuko, Wavering Devil Sergeant C
IMS21098 Ryou and Yumeko, Uneven Pair RE
IMS21096 Ryou, A Step Towards Dreams RE
IMS21100 Ryou, Big Secret RE
IMS21034 Ryou, Brilliance of Next Generation C
IMS21095 Ryou, Idol's Cousin RE
IMS21103 Ryou, Not Giving Up Dreams RE
IMS21039 Seven-Colored Button CC
IMS21038a Sidetracked U
IMS21038b Sidetracked U
IMS21038c Sidetracked U
IMS21040 SMOKY THRILL CC
IMS21062 Takane of Ancient Capital RR
IMS21099 Takane, Beautiful Girl RE
IMS21065 Takane, OFF Time R
IMS21065R Takane, OFF Time RRR
IMS21075 Takane, One-Day Police Chief C
IMS21074 Takane, Ramen Hunter C
IMS21070 Touma, Jupiter's Farewell U
IMS21091 Twin High Five Ami and Mami RE
IMS21013 Yayoi, Bean Sprouts Festival C
IMS21006 Yayoi, Cooking Sa-Shi-Su-Se-So R
IMS21109 Yayoi, Everyone's Idol RE
IMS21005 Yayoi, REST@RT R
IMS21005R Yayoi, REST@RT RRR
IMS21008 Yayoi, Someday I Want to Eat Steak U
IMS21010 Yukiho Backstage U
IMS21004 Yukiho, Courage for a Step R
IMS21004R Yukiho, Courage for a Step RRR
IMS21092 Yukiho, Kind Senpai RE
IMS21016 Yukiho, Modification Plan C
IMS21002 Yukiho, Passionate Snow White RR
IMS21102 Yumeko Sakurai RE
IMS2102SP Yukiho, Passionate Snow White SP
IMS2103SP Kotori-san, Support Anywhere SP
IMS2106SP Yayoi, Cooking Sa-Shi-Su-Se-So SP
IMS2109SP Mami, Full Power Idol SP
IMS2122SP Ritsuko, Return to Idoldom SP
IMS2124SP Iori, Super Beautiful Girl Idol SP
IMS2126SP Azusa, Run Bride SP
IMS2131SP Ami, Idol Full Power SP
IMS2141SP Hibiki, Got It SP
IMS2142SP Miki, Awakened Genius SP
IMS2146SP Haruka, Center of 765 Production SP
IMS2161SP Chihaya, New Promise SP
IMS2162SP Takane of Ancient Capital SP
IMS2166SP Makoto, Makoto's Prince SP

2012 Weiss Schwarz Idolmaster Anime TD

IMS21T12 A Certain Day's Scenery
IMS21T02 Ai, Brillance of Next Generation
IMS21T14 CHANGE
IMS21T06 Chihaya, Frog Kitchen
IMS21T10 Chihaya, Is This Really Live? Sunday
IMS21084 Chihaya, Unleashed
IMS21T07 Eri, Brilliance of Next Generation
IMS21083 Haruka, Hoping for Bond
IMS21T01 Haruka, Rookie Idol
IMS21085 Hibiki, Hibiki Challenge
IMS21T09 Makoto, Action Star
IMS21082 Makoto, ALLSTAR LIVE
IMS21T11 Makoto, Makko-Makorin
IMS21081 Miki, Admiration for Ryuuguu Komachi
IMS21T03 Miki, Return to Stage
IMS21T04 Miki, Sexy Santa
IMS21T13 Promise
IMS21T05 READY
IMS21T08 Takane, Ramen Hunter

2012 Weiss Schwarz Madoka Magica

COMPLETE SET (120)
BOOSTER BOX (20 PACKS) 100.00 120.00
BOOSTER PACK (8 CARDS) 4.00 5.00
RELEASED ON May 31, 2013
MMW17078 A Magical Girl Appears U
MMW17080 Being on Your Own is Lonely CC
MMW17100 Both Miracles And Magic Exist CC
MMW17036 Continue to Fight Homura U
MMW17007 Dessert Witch Charlotte U
MMW17059 Don't Tell Anyone in Class CC
MMW17017 Grief Seed U
MMW17044 Hitomi Shizuki C
MMW17038 Homura Akemi U
MMW17023 Homura, Beautiful Looks R
MMW17023S Homura, Beautiful Looks SR
MMW17045 Homura, Black-haired Girl C
MMW17034 Homura, Determined U
MMW17025 Homura, Hidden Feelings R
MMW17025S Homura, Hidden Feelings SR
MMW17040 Homura, Holding onto Bonds C
MMW17050 Homura, Lonely Battle C
MMW17028 Homura, Magical Girl of Time R
MMW17028R Homura, Magical Girl of Time RRR
MMW17041 Homura, Thinking of Madoka C
MMW17035 Homura, Time-Travelling Backwards U
MMW17021 Homura, Tragic Determination RR
MMW17039 Homura, Transfer Student C
MMW17024 Homura, Watching Over R
MMW17097 Incubator U
MMW17099 I've Been Such A Fool CR
MMW17049 Junko Kaname C
MMW17070 Kyoko in the Back Alley U
MMW17062 Kyoko Sakura RR
MMW17074 Kyoko who Finally Arrived C
MMW17061 Kyoko, Battle-loving RR
MMW17061R Kyoko, Battle-loving RRR
MMW17068 Kyoko, Confession of the Past U
MMW17072 Kyoko, Farewell on the Subway Platform C
MMW17076 Kyoko, Magical Girl of the Spear C
MMW17064 Kyoko, Multi-Section Spear R
MMW17073 Kyoko, New Magical Girl C
MMW17071 Kyoko, Red Soul Gem C
MMW17065 Kyoko, Selfish One R
MMW17065S Kyoko, Selfish One SR
MMW17063 Kyoko, Sharing Apples R
MMW17066 Kyoko, Shouting R
MMW17066S Kyoko, Shouting SR
MMW17069 Kyoko, Wishing for a Miracle U
MMW17077 Kyoko's Determination U
MMW17092 Kyousuke Kamijou C
MMW17075 Kyubey, Extra-terrestial Lifeform C
MMW17003 Kyubey, Making Contract R
MMW17067 Kyubey, Supporting Role U
MMW17053 Law of Cycles U
MMW17047 Madoka and Homura, Best Friends C
MMW17037 Madoka Kaname U
MMW17048 Madoka of the Blue Sky C
MMW17031 Madoka, Bond with Homura U
MMW17032 Madoka, Confronting Walpurgis Night U
MMW17029 Madoka, Fate's Final Destination R
MMW17029S Madoka, Fate's Final Destination SR
MMW17052 Madoka, Feather-like Skirt C
MMW17043 Madoka, Infirmary Officer C
MMW17026 Madoka, Magical Girl of the Bow R
MMW17026S Madoka, Magical Girl of the Bow SR
MMW17033 Madoka, Protecting Hope U
MMW17046 Madoka, Second-year Student of Mitakihara Middle School C
MMW17030 Madoka, Ultimate R
MMW17030R Madoka, Ultimate RRR
MMW17027 Madoka, Wavering Feelings R
MMW17055 Madoka's Wish CR
MMW17005 Mami in Pajamas R
MMW17002 Mami Tomoe RR
MMW17010 Mami, Binding Magic U
MMW17011 Mami, Enjoying Tea C
MMW17014 Mami, Entrusting the Future C
MMW17012 Mami, Giving Advice C
MMW17016 Mami, Graceful C
MMW17015 Mami, Kindly Watching Over C
MMW17004 Mami, Senior Magical Girl R
MMW17004S Mami, Senior Magical Girl SR
MMW17006 Mami, Shouldering Fate R
MMW17006R Mami, Shouldering Fate RRR
MMW17001 Mami, Silver Magical Gun RR
MMW17001S Mami, Silver Magical Gun SR
MMW17013 Mami, Veteran Magical Girl C
MMW17009 Mami, Wish for Survival U
MMW17054 Meaningless Chain U
MMW17090 Mermaid Witch U
MMW17058 My Best Friend CC
MMW17008 No Longer Alone Mami U
MMW17056 No Longer Relying on Others CC
MMW17019 Nothing Scares Me Anymore CR
MMW17082 Sayaka Miki RR
MMW17079 Sayaka VS Kyoko CR
MMW17084 Sayaka, Admiration for Mami R
MMW17089 Sayaka, Ally of Justice U
MMW17096 Sayaka, Battling While Hurting C
MMW17093 Sayaka, Childhood Friend of Kamijou-kun C
MMW17087 Sayaka, Classmate U
MMW17091 Sayaka, Confrontation C
MMW17083 Sayaka, Fighting for People R
MMW17088 Sayaka, Found Her Wish U
MMW17085 Sayaka, Healing Prayer R
MMW17085S Sayaka, Healing Prayer SR
MMW17086 Sayaka, Hollow Eyes R
MMW17086S Sayaka, Hollow Eyes SR
MMW17095 Sayaka, Magical Girl of the Sword C
MMW17081 Sayaka, Rookie Magical Girl RR
MMW17081R Sayaka, Rookie Magical Girl RRR
MMW17094 Sayaka, Second-year Student of Mitakihara Middle School C
MMW17098 Sayaka's Wish U
MMW17022 Secrecy Madoka RR
MMW17051 Stage Device's Witch Walpurgis Night C
MMW17018 Sudden Happening U
MMW17060 The Girl From the Dream CC
MMW17057 Time Manipulation CC
MMW17020 Tiro Finale CC
MMW17042 To Protect Everyone Madoka C
MMW1702SP Mami Tomoe SP
MMW1721SP Homura, Tragic Determination SP
MMW1722SP Secrecy Madoka SP
MMW1762SP Kyoko Sakura SP
MMW1782SP Sayaka Miki SP

2012 Weiss Schwarz Madoka Magica TD

COMPLETE SET (50)
BOOSTER BOX (6)
BOOSTER PACK ()
RELEASED ON
MMW17103 A Lonely Fight, Homura
MMW17T13 Ally of Justice, Sayaka
MMW17101 Battle with Walpurgisnacht, Homura
MMW17T10 Childhood Friend of Kamijo, Sayaka
MMW17102 Common Wishes, Sayaka and Kyoko
MMW17T01 Dark-haired Girl, Homura
MMW17T05 Homura Akemi
MMW17T07 I won't rely on anyone anymore
MMW17T09 Kyousuke Kamijou
MMW17T06 Law of the Cycle
MMW17T04 Madoka Kaname
MMW17T03 Madoka of the Blue Skies
MMW17T12 Magical Girl of Swords, Sayaka
MMW17T14 Miracles and magic are real
MMW17T02 Nurse's Aide, Madoka
MMW17105 Ordinary Girl, Madoka
MMW17T11 Second-year of Mitakihara Middle School, Sayaka
MMW17104 Smiling Sayaka
MMW17T08 The Girl from the Dream

2012 Weiss Schwarz Milky Holmes 2

MK2S19089 Arsene, Crime Committed on New Year's Eve C
MK2S19090 Arsene, Pretty Royal Heart C
MK2S19081 Arsene, Pride of Phantom Thief R
MK2S1981S Arsene, Pride of Phantom Thief SR
MK2S19092 Cagliostro, Phantom Thief C
MK2S19087 Colon-chan, Girl Detective U
MK2S19028 Cordelia in Gymnastic Cloth R
MK2S19084 Cordelia in Japanese Clothing U
MK2S19076 Cordelia in Summer Outfit RR
MK2S1976S Cordelia in Summer Outfit SR
MK2S19044 Cordelia, Agricultural Girl C
MK2S19091 Cordelia, Full of Self-Confidence C
MK2S19093 Cordelia, Girl of the Detective City C
MK2S19082 Cordelia, Great Big Sister R
MK2S19085 Cordelia, Stunning Swimsuit Look U
MK2S19033 Cordelia, Taking An Occasional Break U
MK2S19077 Cordelia, Talking to Someone RR
MK2S19100 Cordelia's Plan CC
MK2S19049 Demonstration CC
MK2S19099 Desperation Oolong Tea CC
MK2S1912S Ellery Himeyuri SR
MK2S19012 Ellery Himeyuri U
MK2S19026 Elly in Cheerleading Outfit RR
MK2S19078 Elly in Japanese Clothing R
MK2S19030 Elly in Summer Outfit R
MK2S1930S Elly in Summer Outfit SR
MK2S19041 Elly, Agricultural Girl C
MK2S19079 Elly, Bunny-Eared R
MK2S19095 Elly, Common Sense Type C
MK2S19032 Elly, Full of Knowledge R
MK2S19035 Elly, G5 U
MK2S19029 Elly, Girl of the Detective City R
MK2S19036 Elly, Wild Chrysanthemum-like Pervert U
MK2S19048 Elly's Part-Time Job CR
MK2S19098 Escape From Reality CR
MK2S19074 First Dance CC
MK2S19050 G3's Day Off CC
MK2S19046 God of Lard U
MK2S1986S Henriette in Dress SR
MK2S19086 Henriette in Dress U
MK2S19094 Henriette, Dance Teacher C
MK2S19080 Henriette, Graceful Ordinary Day R
MK2S19043 Himeyuri, Caring about Kobayashi C
MK2S19009 Himeyuri, Stunning Swimsuit Look U
MK2S19034 Hirano in Casual Clothing U
MK2S19045 Hirano, Ancient Martial Artists C
MK2S1937S Hirano, Phantom Thief Incident Investigation Team SR
MK2S19037 Hirano, Phantom Thief Incident Investigation Team U
MK2S19038 Indecisive Himeyuri C
MK2S1983S Josephine Mystere SR
MK2S19083 Josephine Mystere U
MK2S19008 Kamaboko U
MK2S19042 Kamitsu, In Charge of G4 C
MK2S19020 Kobayashi, Temporary Return to Home Country C
MK2S19060 Kokoro, Debut in the Break Room U
MK2S19056 Kokoro, Himeyuri's Senpai R
MK2S1961S Kokoro, Phantom Thief Incident Investigation Team SR
MK2S19061 Kokoro, Phantom Thief Incident Investigation Team U
MK2S19064 Kokoro, Self-Proclaimed Genius Beautiful Girl C
MK2S19067 Kokoro, Tulip Class C
MK2S19070 Kokoro, World Exposition Mascot C
MK2S19071 Kokoro-chan Goods U
MK2S19096 Mecha-Cordelia U
MK2S19021 Mold U
MK2S19055 Nero in Japanese Clothing R
MK2S19001 Nero in Summer Outfit RR
MK2S1901S Nero in Summer Outfit SR
MK2S19066 Nero, Agricultural Girl C
MK2S19017 Nero, Animals Are Friends C
MK2S19004 Nero, Bunny-Eared R
MK2S19007 Nero, Frank at Heart R
MK2S19002 Nero, Girl of the Detective City RR
MK2S19006 Nero, Glasses Girl R
MK2S19013 Nero, New Semester C
MK2S19059 Nero, Route Searching U
MK2S19014 Nezu, Broken-Hearted C
MK2S19063 Poporo Mark 2 C
MK2S19018 Rat, Loyal Servant C
MK2S19072 Real Baritsu U
MK2S19097 Return of Arsene U
MK2S19073 Revival of Toys CR
MK2S19025 Ruined Farm CC
MK2S19027 Saku & Hirano & Tsugiko, Phantom Thief Incident Investigation Team RR

MK2S19039 Saku, Glasses Girl C
MK2S19031 Saku, Phantom Thief Incident Investigation Team R
MK2S1931S Saku, Phantom Thief Incident Investigation Team SR
MK2S19040 Saku, Recalculating C
MK2S19022 See You Again on the Dining Table U
MK2S19047 Shaggy Book U
MK2S19054 Sheryl in Japanese Clothing R
MK2S19057 Sheryl in Summer Outfit R
MK2S1957S Sheryl in Summer Outfit SR
MK2S19053 Sheryl on Stage R
MK2S19068 Sheryl, Agricultural Girl C
MK2S19052 Sheryl, Energetic as Merit RR
MK2S19003 Sheryl, Floating with Water Wings R
MK2S19062 Sheryl, Getting Close to the Phantom Thief Empire U
MK2S19016 Sheryl, Girl of the Detective City C
MK2S19011 Sheryl, New Semester U
MK2S19051 Sheryl, Time of Confrontation RR
MK2S19010 Stone River, Loyal Servant U
MK2S19015 Stone River, Sultry Man C
MK2S19024 Sudden Transfer Order CC
MK2S19023 Ten Million Yen CR
MK2S19019 TKB Nijuuri C
MK2S19058 Tsugiko, G4's Big Sister U
MK2S19069 Tsugiko, Phantom Thief Incident Investigation Team C
MK2S1969S Tsugiko, Phantom Thief Incident Investigation Team SR
MK2S19065 Tsugiko, Professional Skills C
MK2S19005 Twenty, Loyal Servant R
MK2S19075 Yo-Yo Police CC
MK2S19088 Yutaka, Kind Young Man C
MK2S1975P Nero, Frank at Heart SP
MK2S1932SP Elly, Full of Knowledge SP
MK2S1952SP Sheryl, Energetic as Merit SP
MK2S1982SP Cordelia, Great Big Sister SP

2012 Weiss Schwarz Milky Holmes 2 TD

MK2S19T05 Cordelia, Agriculture Girl
MK2S19105 Cordelia, Resume Investigation!
MK2S19T07 Demonstration
MK2S19T03 Elly, Agriculture Girl
MK2S19101 Elly, Resume Investigating!
MK2S19T14 First Dance
MK2S19T04 Himeyuri, Caring about Kobayashi
MK2S19103 Himeyuri, New Commander
MK2S19T06 Hirano, Ancient Martial Artist
MK2S19T01 Indecisive Himeyuri
MK2S19T11 Kokoro, Tulip Class
MK2S19T10 Nero, Agriculture Girl
MK2S19102 Nero, Resume Investigating!
MK2S19T13 Real Baritsu
MK2S19T08 Rest Day of G3
MK2S19T02 Saku, Glasses Girl
MK2S19T12 Sheryl, Agriculture Girl
MK2S19104 Sheryl, Resume Investigation!
MK2S19T09 Tsugiko, Pro-like Skills

2012 Weiss Schwarz Rewrite Harvest Festa

RWW20006 A Cup to Wake Up Sakuya U
RWW20017 Akane in Swimsuits C
RWW20041 Akane, After A Bath RR
RWW20041S Akane, After A Bath SR
RWW20040 Akari's Determination CC
RWW20040R Akari's Determination RRR
RWW20043 All Her Strength Akane R
RWW20055 Altar of Dragon God CC
RWW20055R Altar of Dragon God RRR
RWW20038 Amidst Miracle And Warmth U
RWW20072 Amidst the Silvery Wold Lucia C
RWW20045 Beloved Quaesitor Akane R
RWW20045S Beloved Quaesitor Akane SR
RWW20042 Beloved Quaesitor Chihaya RR
RWW20042S Beloved Quaesitor Chihaya SR
RWW20058 Beloved Quaesitor Kagari R
RWW20058S Beloved Quaesitor Kagari SR
RWW20001 Beloved Quaesitor Kotori RR
RWW20001S Beloved Quaesitor Kotori SR
RWW20027 Beloved Quaesitor Lucia RR
RWW20027S Beloved Quaesitor Lucia SR
RWW20026 Beloved Quaesitor Shizuru RR
RWW20026S Beloved Quaesitor Shizuru SR
RWW20057 Best Memories Kagari RR
RWW20030 Blitz Attack Shizuru R
RWW20022 Caught Werefish Yoshino U
RWW20004 Charismatic Witch-Sama Akane R
RWW20059 Corolla of Blessing Kotori R
RWW20050 Courage to Face It Akane C
RWW20046 Crimson-lit Night Akane U
RWW20025 Crossed Feelings CC
RWW20025R Crossed Feelings RRR
RWW20028 Day of Departure Lucia R
RWW20028S Day of Departure Lucia SR
RWW20060 Destiny Rewritten Kagari R
RWW20060S Destiny Rewritten Kagari SR
RWW20063 Destiny Rewritten Kotori R
RWW20063S Destiny Rewritten Kotori SR
RWW20019 Everyone Gather Chihaya C
RWW20069 Expressing Emotions Kagari U
RWW20061 Extremely Spicy Reconcilation Lucia R
RWW20015 Future of Two Chihaya C
RWW20014 Future of Two Kotarou C
RWW20076 Gennaji's Menra Shizuru C
RWW20011 Heart of NEET Akane U
RWW20005 Highest Blessing Kotori R
RWW20009 Honest Feelings Kotori U
RWW20039 Honored Promise CR
RWW20039R Honored Promise RRR
RWW20075 Hope of the World Kagari C
RWW20021 Human-made Miracle Kotarou C
RWW20051 I'm Not An Idiot? Chihaya C
RWW20007 Inoue in Swimsuits U
RWW20065 Kagari Mirakuru U
RWW20031 Kill Enemies on Sight Shizuru U
RWW20048 Knight of Blossoms Sakuya U
RWW20016 Kotori in Swimsuits C
RWW20036 Leave the Past for the Future Nishikujou C
RWW20062 Let's Quest Shizuru R
RWW20062S Let's Quest Shizuru SR
RWW20032 Lucia in Swimsuits U
RWW20033 Lucia's Proxy Kotarou U
RWW20056 Magical Third Planetary Fairy Creamy Kagarin RR
RWW20073 Miracle Girl Kagari C
RWW20002 Mischievous Kiss Chihaya RR
RWW20002S Mischievous Kiss Chihaya SR
RWW20079 Momentary Dream CR
RWW20079R Momentary Dream RRR
RWW20020 Number One Reason Kotori C
RWW20071 Occult Research Club Gather Lucia C
RWW20003 Official Couple Chihaya R
RWW20023 On This Beautiful Day, With Out Whole Hearts C
RWW20078 One Who Lit the Watchfire C
RWW20044 Path to Walk Together Chihaya R
RWW20074 Peaceful Time Lucia C
RWW20053 Platinum Ticket U
RWW20024 Playing Water With Everyone CR
RWW20080 Possibility Remained CC
RWW20029 Seat of Strongest Shizuru R
RWW20070 Seeking Good Memories Kagari U
RWW20037 Shizuru in Swimsuits C
RWW20035 Shizuru, Holding Hands C
RWW20064 Single Goal Lucia R
RWW20018 Small Happiness Kotori C
RWW20054 Someone to Protect CR
RWW20054R Someone to Protect RRR
RWW20068 Sometime, Somewhere Kagari U
RWW20052 Student Council President Suzy Middle C
RWW20067 Student Who Understands the Differences Kagari U
RWW20077 System Tree of Possibilities U
RWW20008 Talented High School Student Reporter Inoway U
RWW20034 The Other Lucia Akari C
RWW20047 Under the Brilliant Blue Sky Chihaya U
RWW20013 Unexpected Blunder Chihaya and Sakuya U
RWW20010 Vacation Mood Kotori U
RWW20066 Vacation Mood Shizuru U
RWW20049 Very Interested Shimako C
RWW20012 Yoshino's Ideal Super Yoshino U
RWW2004SP Charismatic Witch-Sama Akane SP
RWW2030SP Blitz Attack Shizuru SP
RWW2044SP Path to Walk Together Chihaya SP
RWW2056SP Magical Third Planetary Fairy Creamy Kagarin SP
RWW2057SP Best Memories Kagari SP
RWW2059SP Corolla of Blessing Kotori SP
RWW2064SP Single Goal Lucia SP

2012 Weiss Schwarz Robotics Notes

RNW16050 A Summer Adventure CC
RNW16077 Airi RR
RNW16077R Airi RRR
RNW16087 Airi Yukifune U
RNW16093 Airi, Full of Energy C
RNW16016 Airi, Hollow Pretty Girl C
RNW16085 Airi, Mode Change U
RNW16080 Airi, Summer Festival R
RNW16080S Airi, Summer Festival SR
RNW16003 Airi, Taking A Walk R
RNW16018 Airi, Under the Blue Sky C
RNW16018S Airi, Under the Blue Sky SR
RNW16002 Akiho Senomiya RR
RNW16091 Akiho, Cat-Ear Maid C
RNW16017 Akiho, Charging Recklessly C
RNW16020 Akiho, During Maintenance C
RNW16082 Akiho, Favorite Food Refreshments R
RNW16082S Akiho, Favorite Food Refreshments SR
RNW16008 Akiho, New Club Member Welcoming Party U
RNW16014 Akiho, President of Robotics Club C
RNW16079 Akiho, Robot Otaku R
RNW16001 Akiho, Tokyo World Exposition RR
RNW16005 Akiho, You're My Life Savior R
RNW16096 Anemone Group Unconsciousness Incident U
RNW16071 By the Two of Them in Closed Space U
RNW16025 Circle of Determination CC
RNW16098 Cold Sleep CR
RNW16075 Conflict with Father CC
RNW16013R Expansion Place Akiho RRR
RNW16013 Expansion Place Akiho U
RNW16049 Extended Hand CC
RNW16033R Frau and Junna, Incredible Relationship RRR
RNW16033 Frau and Junna, Incredible Relationship U
RNW16027 Frau in Swimsuits RR
RNW16027R Frau in Swimsuits RRR
RNW16056 Frau in Yukata R
RNW16052 Frau Koujiro RR
RNW16052S Frau Koujiro SR
RNW16029 Frau, Failed Suicide Attempt? R
RNW16038 Frau, Forbidden Delusion C
RNW16069 Frau, Genius Programmer C
RNW16058 Frau, HP 0 U
RNW16054 Frau, Kill-Ballad Battle R
RNW16054S Frau, Kill-Ballad Battle SR
RNW16043 Frau, Real Feelings C
RNW16062 Frau, Sharing Secrets U
RNW16081 Geji-nee R
RNW16088 Geji-nee, Airi's Other Half C
RNW16094 Geji-nee, Mode Change C
RNW16072 Genki and Rosetta U
RNW16022 Gunvarrel, Icon of Justice C
RNW16060 Hiromu Hidaka U
RNW16100 Irreplacable Memory CC
RNW16097 Iru-O U
RNW16032 Junna Daitoku R
RNW16041 Junna in Yukata C
RNW16041S Junna in Yukata SR
RNW16037 Junna, Age of Worry U
RNW16031 Junna, Dispersed Feelings R
RNW16057 Junna, Family Side R
RNW16068 Junna, Motion Actress C
RNW16026 Junna, Past Trauma RR
RNW16051 Junna, Petit But Strong RR
RNW16051S Junna, Petit But Strong SR
RNW16064 Junna, Timid Karate Girl C
RNW16053 Junna, Uneasy Eyes R
RNW16036 Junna, Yoira-Iki Festival U
RNW16009S Kaito and Akiho, Reliable Allies SR
RNW16009 Kaito and Akiho, Reliable Allies U
RNW16011 Kaito, A Certain Summer Day U
RNW16010 Kaito, After Class U
RNW16019 Kaito, Battle Gamer C
RNW16006 Kaito, Battle Spirit Lit R
RNW16012 Kaito, Kill-Ballad Battle U
RNW16007 Kaito, Last Battle R
RNW16004 Kaito, New Club Member Welcoming Party R
RNW16045 Kaoruko Usui C
RNW16035 Kenichirou Senomiya U
RNW16074 Kind Big Sister of Children CC
RNW16089 Kou Kimijima C
RNW16086 Kou Kimijima, Mastermind of the Conspiracy U
RNW16046 Lightning Strike U
RNW16063 M45 C
RNW16095 misaki Senomiya C
RNW16078 Misaki, High School Period R
RNW16084 Misaki, Released From the Bind U
RNW16059 Mister Pleiades U
RNW16039 Mitsuhiko Nagafukada C
RNW16092 Mizuka Irei C
RNW16083 Mizuka, Berserking of HUG U
RNW16028 Nae Tennouji R
RNW16030 Nae, First Battle R
RNW16040 Nae, Yoira-Iki Festival C
RNW16076 Relative Chart Under the Blue Sky Airi RR
RNW16023 Robot Will Save the World CR
RNW16055 Subaru, Abandoned Dream R
RNW16065 Subaru, Arrogant Stance C
RNW16070 Subaru, Everyone Gather at Hangar C
RNW16066 Subaru, New Club Member Welcoming Party C
RNW16061 Subaru, Visitor to the Ruins U
RNW16067 Subaru, Yoira-Iki Festival C
RNW16042 Sumio Nagafukada C
RNW16021 Super Gan-tsuku 1 U
RNW16047 Super Rinpei U
RNW16048 Taking the Step CR
RNW16015 Tanegashi Machine 3 Kai C
RNW16034 Tetsuharu Fujita U
RNW16024 The Dream Being Chased Constantly CC
RNW16073 To Make Gunvarrel Shine CR
RNW16090 Toshiyuki Sawada C
RNW16099 White Christmas Eve CC
RNW16044 Yoshirou-kun C
RNW1602SP Akiho Senomiya SP
RNW1656SP Frau in Yukata SP
RNW1657SP Junna, Family Side SP
RNW1676SP Relative Chart Under the Blue Sky Airi SP

2012 Weiss Schwarz Robotics Notes TD

RNW16T01 Airi, Hollow Pretty Girl
RNW16103 Airi, Rumored Ghost?
RNW16T03 Akiho, Charging Recklessly
RNW16T05 Akiho, During Maintenance
RNW16102 Akiho, Eagerly Waited Operation Test
RNW16T02 Akiho, President of Robotics Club
RNW16T13 By the Two of Them in Closed Space
RNW16105 Childhood Friends Akiho and Kaito
RNW16T06 Circle of Determination
RNW16T12 Frau, Genius Programmer
RNW16101 Frau, Girl Appearing on Tanegashima
RNW16T09 Frau, HP 0
RNW16T11 Junna, Motion Actress
RNW16104 Junna, Reliable One of the Family
RNW16T08 Junna, Timid Karate Girl
RNW16T04 Kaito, Battle Gamer
RNW16T14 Kind Big Sister of Children
RNW16T10 Subaru, Arrogant Stance
RNW16T07 The Dream Being Chased Constantly

2012 Weiss Schwarz Shana Final Extra

SSWE1521 Archer of Aurora Chiara Toscana C
SSWE1533 Bel Peol, Out of the World Strategies C
SSWE1523 Braider of Trembling Might Sophie Sawallisch C
SSWE1525 Clashed Feelings C
SSWE1535 General Sydonay C
SSWE1528 God of Creation The Snake of the Festival R
SSWE1529 Hecate, Divine Summoning R
SSWE1534 Hecate, Result of Thousands of Wishes C
SSWE1503 Kazumi, Cat-Eared C
SSWE1505 Kazumi, Courage to Not Run Away C
SSWE1504 Kazumi, Wavering Feelings C
SSWE1507 Margery, Top-Tier Power of Unrestraint R
SSWE1509 Margery, Final Battle R
SSWE1520 Mobilizer of Ceremonial Equipment Khamsin Nbh'w C
SSWE1510 Persona Equipped, Wilhelmina R
SSWE1526 Priestess Hecate R
SSWE1515 Puppeteer of Devilish Skills Sale Habichtsburg C
SSWE1517 Scatterer of Sparkling Light Rebecca Reed C
SSWE1502 Shana in Distress C
SSWE1518 Shana, All Or Nothing C
SSWE1506 Shana, Key of Growth R
SSWE1511 Shana, Love Is All R
SSWE1501 Shana, On the Day which Yuji Disappeared R
SSWE1512 Shana, Path to Walk with Yuji R
SSWE1522 Shana, Reason And Feelings C
SSWE1519 Shana, Spiral of Struggles C
SSWE1513 Shana, Strongest Powers of Unrestraint C
SSWE1508 Shana, Trust in the Blade R
SSWE1516 Shana, Unwavering Heart C
SSWE1527 Strategist Bel Peol R
SSWE1530 Sydonay, Sadness of Farewell C
SSWE1524 To the New World C
SSWE1536 Until the Next Time Wishes Come to Fruitation C
SSWE1514 Wilhelmina, For the Mission C
SSWE1531 Yuji, Real Existence C
SSWE1532 Yuji, Reason And Feeling C

2012 Weiss Schwarz Symphogear

SGW19096 Ame-no-Habakiri U
SGW19107 BILLION MAIDEN PR
SGW19048 Chris' Dream CR
SGW19033 Chris in Her Youth U
SGW19027 Chris Yukine RR
SGW19042 Chris, Aggressive C
SGW19041 Chris, Armored Girl C
SGW19030 Chris, Bearer of Symphogear R
SGW19032 Chris, Burning Fighting Spirit R
SGW19032S Chris, Burning Fighting Spirit SR
SGW19029 Chris, Calming Place R
SGW19029S Chris, Calming Place SR
SGW19026 Chris, Gathered Power RR
SGW19031 Chris, Hidden Kindness R
SGW19028 Chris, Lone Wolf R
SGW19028R Chris, Lone Wolf RRR
SGW19039 Chris, Mysterious Girl C
SGW19035 Chris, Overwhelming Battle Strength U
SGW19043 Chris, Time of Confrontation C
SGW19037 Chris, Untrue to Herself U
SGW19034 Chris, Warrior Wielding Ichii-Bal U
SGW19023 Do Not Give Up Living CR
SGW19020 Durandal Awakening U
SGW19097 Enveloping Kindness C
SGW19106 FIRST LOVE SONG PR
SGW19098 FLIGHT FEATHERS CR
SGW19022 Fusion with Relic C
SGW19059 Genjuro Kazanari U
SGW19068 Genjuro, Trustworthy Commander C
SGW19021 Gungnir U
SGW19002 Hibiki Tachibana RR
SGW19011 Hibiki, Beats of Awakening U
SGW19007 Hibiki, Determination of the Heart R
SGW19007R Hibiki, Determination of the Heart RRR
SGW19017 Hibiki, Doing Her Best C
SGW19019 Hibiki, Easily Ignored C
SGW19004 Hibiki, Energetic as Merit R
SGW19004S Hibiki, Energetic as Merit SR
SGW19015 Hibiki, First Live Concert C
SGW19001 Hibiki, Full Power Punch RR
SGW19012 Hibiki, Hands Holding Everyone Together U
SGW19014 Hibiki, Important Person of Interest C
SGW19010 Hibiki, Kind Warrior U
SGW19013 Hibiki, Normal World C
SGW19003 Hibiki, Pain in Her Chest R
SGW19009 Hibiki, Power of Music U
SGW19008 Hibiki, Promise to Dear Friend U
SGW19006 Hibiki, Reason to Fight R
SGW19006S Hibiki, Reason to Fight SR
SGW19005 Hibiki, Source of Power R
SGW19018 Hibiki, Strengthening Training C
SGW19016 Hibiki, Transforming C
SGW19024 I Have Something to Protect CC
SGW19046 Ichii-Bal U
SGW19053 Kanade Amou R
SGW19053S Kanade Amou SR
SGW19063 Kanade on That Day C
SGW19062 Kanade, Bearer of Symphogear U
SGW19067 Kanade, Bearing Justice C
SGW19066 Kanade, Moodmaker C
SGW19052 Kanade, Power to Win RR
SGW19051 Kanade, Tsubasa's Partner RR
SGW19051R Kanade, Tsubasa's Partner RRR
SGW19069 Kanade, Wild And Free C
SGW19055 Kanade, ZweiWing R
SGW19108 Last 'Infinity' METEOR PR
SGW19071 Last Stage U
SGW19049 MEGA DETH QUARTET CC
SGW19057 Miku Kohinata R
SGW19065 Miku, Bond of Friendship C
SGW19056 Miku, Hibiki's Best Friend R
SGW19056S Miku, Hibiki's Best Friend SR
SGW19054 Miku, Strong-Willed R
SGW19058 Miku, Substitute Guardian U
SGW19045 Nehushtan Armor U
SGW19036 Noise (Episode 1) U
SGW19038 Noise (Episode 4) C
SGW19040 Phine, Lady with Noble Feel C
SGW19044 Phine, Priestess C
SGW19070 Ridian Private Music Academy U
SGW19060 Ryoko Sakurai U
SGW19061 Ryoko, At Her Own Pace U
SGW19064 Ryoko, Talented Researcher C
SGW19075 School Song of Ridian Private Music Academy CC
SGW19109 Shadowbind PR
SGW19047 Staff of Solomon C
SGW19073 STARDUST 'Infinity' FOTON CR
SGW19025 Symphogear CC
SGW19100 The Blue Flash CC
SGW19072 Tower of Babel C
SGW19082 Tsubasa Kazanari R
SGW19086 Tsubasa on that Day U
SGW19078 Tsubasa, Changing R
SGW19078S Tsubasa, Changing SR
SGW19089 Tsubasa, Cold Personality C
SGW19079 Tsubasa, Desperate Battle R
SGW19092 Tsubasa, Facing Noise C
SGW19085 Tsubasa, First Date U
SGW19090 Tsubasa, Hospitalized C
SGW19081 Tsubasa, Joy of Singing R
SGW19081R Tsubasa, Joy of Singing RRR
SGW19093 Tsubasa, Nonchalant Life C
SGW19076 Tsubasa, Sadness of Lost RR
SGW19080 Tsubasa, Standing Dignifiedly R
SGW19084 Tsubasa, Steeled like the Sword U
SGW19091 Tsubasa, Thinking of Kanade C
SGW19077 Tsubasa, Time of Determination RR
SGW19077S Tsubasa, Time of Determination SR
SGW19083 Tsubasa, Trust Towards Allies U
SGW19088 Tsubasa, Unresonating Sound C
SGW19087 Tsubasa, Way of the Sentinel U
SGW19050 Warmth Forgotten CC
SGW19099 We Were Two Back Then CC
SGW19074 Wing of Backlight CC
SGW19095 Zessho U
SGW19094 ZweiWing Kanade and Tsubasa C
SGW1902SP Hibiki Tachibana SP
SGW1927SP Chris Yukine SP
SGW1957SP Miku Kohinata SP
SGW1982SP Tsubasa Kazanari SP

2012 Weiss Schwarz Symphogear TD

SGW19103 Hibiki, Bearer of Symphogear
SGW19T04 Hibiki, Beats of Awakening
SGW19T05 Hibiki, Doing Her Best
SGW19T06 Hibiki, Easily Ignored
SGW19T03 Hibiki, First Live Concert
SGW19T02 Hibiki, Important Person of Interest
SGW19101 Hibiki, Miku's Best Friend
SGW19T01 Hibiki, Normal World
SGW19T07 I Have Something to Protect
SGW19T14 The Blue Flash
SGW19104 Tsubasa, Bearer of Symphogear
SGW19T08 Tsubasa, Cold Personality
SGW19T10 Tsubasa, Facing Noise
SGW19102 Tsubasa, Putting Self into Fights
SGW19T09 Tsubasa, Thinking of Kanade
SGW19105 Tsubasa, Top Artist
SGW19T11 Tsubasa, Way of the Sentinel
SGW19T13 We Were Two Back Then
SGW19T12 ZweiWing Kanade and Tsubasa

2013 Weiss Schwarz Da Capo 10th Anniversary

DCW23012 Aisia, Hopeful Puppy Eyes U
DCW23006 Aisia, Last Moments R
DCW23006S Aisia, Last Moments SR
DCW23019 Aisia, Time of Happiness C
DCW23033 Akane & Midori, At Their Own Pace U
DCW23032 Akane, Feeling the Warmth R
DCW23032S Akane, Feeling the Warmth SR
DCW23092 Alice, Best Heart-Thumping C
DCW23098 Always Together, Always Smiling. U
DCW23087 Anzu, From Hypothesis to Reality U
DCW23094 Anzu, Malicious Language Maid C
DCW23076 Anzu, Small Mystery RR
DCW23076R Anzu, Small Mystery RRR
DCW23084 Anzu, Victory Sign U
DC3W23077 Aoi, Dream-Like Night RR
DC3W23082 Aoi, Happy Smiles R
DC3W2382S Aoi, Happy Smiles SR
DC3W23091 Aoi, Playing Water by the Shore C
DC3W23004 Charles, Kind Warmth R
DC3W23004R Charles, Kind Warmth RRR
DC3W23020 Charles, Someday's Memory C
DC3W23010 Elizabeth, Playful Urchin U
DCW23057 Erica, Dignified Style R
DCW23057S Erica, Dignified Style SR
DCW23058 Erica, Private Lesson U
DCW23090 Fall in Love Royal Straight Flush Shiiren C
DCW23024 Foresight of Happiness CR
DCW23024R Foresight of Happiness RRR
DC3W23042 Himeno, Relaxing at the Beach C
DC3W23027 Himeno, Ticklish Future RR
DC3W23048 Himeno's Determination U
DC3W23049 Irreplaceable Family CR
DC3W2349R Irreplaceable Family RRR
DCW23016 Izumiko, With Marvelous Boyfriend C
DCW23009 Justice Magician Yuki U
DCW23039 Kanae, Awkward Separation C
DCW23093 Kasumi, Life of Sisters C
DCW23074 Kiss of Oath CR
DCW23074R Kiss of Oath RRR
DCW23043 Koko, Dancing with Yukata at Bon Festival C
DCW23034 Koko, Everyone's Session! U
DCW23030 Koko, Has Not Changed R
DCW23030S Koko, Has Not Changed SR
DCW23038 Kotori, Cherry-Colored Miracle U
DCW23029 Kotori, Date of Only Two R
DCW23029S Kotori, Date of Only Two SR
DCW23028 Kotori, Favorite Song R
DCW23028R Kotori, Favorite Song RRR
DCW23045 Kotori, Turning Feelings into Words C
DCW23017 Mahiru, Big Ruckus! C
DCW23007 Mahiru, Everyone's Happiness R
DCW23007S Mahiru, Everyone's Happiness SR
DCW23059 Maika, Treasure So-called Friends U
DCW23086 Mako, Her Home Cooking U
DCW23079 Mako, Silvery Melody R
DCW23079S Mako, Silvery Melody SR
DCW23089 Maya, Returned SSP C
DCW23081 Maya, Smiling Robot R
DCW23081S Maya, Smiling Robot SR
DCW23080 Mayuki, Beloved Senpai R
DCW23080S Mayuki, Beloved Senpai SR
DCW23083 Mayuki, Hiding Her Embarassment U
DCW23096 Mayuki, To Even Higher Places C
DCW23055 Miharu, Lovers' Proof R
DCW23055S Miharu, Lovers' Proof SR
DCW23085 Miharu, Senpai And Banana C
DCW23075 Miharu's Feelings CC
DCW23044 Miki, Mahiru's Family C
DCW23040 Mikkun, Heart-Thumping C
DC3W23069 Mikoto, Normal Outfit Is Bunny!? C
DCW23053 Minatsu, Going on a New Trip R
DCW23053S Minatsu, Going on a New Trip SR
DCW23062 Minatsu, Returned Smile U
DCW23066 Minatsu, Time for Only Two C
DCW23014 Misaki, Night of White Miracle C
DCW23088 Moe, New Future U
DCW23078 Moe, Searing Couple R

DCW23078S Moe, Searing Couple SR
DCW23095 Moe, To the Dream World C
DCW23070 Myu-san, Enjoyable Shopping C
DCW23047 Nanaka, Each's Own Feelings C
DCW23035 Nanaka, Everyone's Session! U
DCW23026 Nanaka, My Feelings RR
DCW23026R Nanaka, My Feelings RRR
DCW23067 Nanako, Battle of Aiyue C
DCW23063 Nemu, Caretaking Nurse U
DCW23068 Nemu, Happy Times C
DCW23054 Nemu, Old Memories R
DCW23054S Nemu, Old Memories SR
DCW23052 Nemu, Overspilling Feelings RR
DCW23073 One of Thousand U
DCW23021 Otome, Always Together C
DCW23001 Otome, Gentle Smiles RR
DCW23011 Otome, Just Like Childhood Days U
DCW23003 Otome, Sweet Moment R
DCW23003S Otome, Sweet Moment SR
DCW23064 Phantom Thief Princess Erica C
DCW23100 Precious Flute CC
DC3W23008 Ricca, Familiar Feeling U
DCW23005 Ricca, New Magic R
DC3W2305R Ricca, New Magic RRR
DCW23085 Rino, Time at Ease U
DCW23072 Rio & Flora & Kamie C
DCW23002 Sakura, Evidence of Becoming an Adult RR
DCW23002R Sakura, Evidence of Becoming an Adult RRR
DCW23018 Sakura, Happiness of Family C
DCW23015 Sakura, Princess of the Royal Capital C
DC3W23031 Sara, Practicing Love! R
DC3W2331R Sara, Practicing Love! RRR
DC3W23037 Sara, Truly Single-Minded U
DCW23023 Secret of Two U
DCW23061 Shinobu, Yearning! U
DCW23013 Shinya & Asa & Yuuhi, Album of Memories U
DCW23097 Suginami & Suginami, Danger When Mixed! C
DCW23046 Tamaki, Future of Two C
DC3W23099 To Onii-chan CR
DC3W2399R To Onii-chan RRR
DCW23041 Tomo-chan, Admiration for the Band C
DC3W23022 Tomoe, Hotly Debating C
DCW23025 Uncontrollable Feelings CC
DCW23036 Wataru, Everyone's Sesison! U
DCW23050 Will We Meet Again CC
DCW23071 Yume, Cat-Eared C
DCW23056 Yume, Gentle Kiss R
DCW23056S Yume, Gentle Kiss SR
DCW23060 Yume, Hand-Made Hydrangea U
DCW23051 Yume, Time of Two RR
DCW23051R Yume, Time of Two RRR
DC3W2327S Himeno, Ticklish Future SP
DCW2377S Aoi, Dream-Like Night SP
DCW2301SP Otome, Gentle Smiles SP
DCW2352SP Nemu, Overspilling Feelings SP

2013 Weiss Schwarz Da Capo 10th Anniversary Mix TD

DCW23T08 Aisia, Hopeful Puppy Eyes
DC3W23T06 Charles, Someday's Memory
DC3W23T05 Elizabeth, Playful Urchin
DCW23T11 Erica, Personal Lesson
DCW23104 Everyday is Embarassing
DCW23T02 Izumiko, With Marvelous Boyfriend
DC3W23T03 Mahiru, Big Ruckus
DCW23105 Memory with Onii-san
DCW23T12 Miharu, Senpai and Banana
DCW23T15 Miharu's Feelings
DCW23T14 Myu-san, Enjoyable Shopping
DCW23T13 Nemu, Happy Time
DCW23T07 Otome, Always Together
DCW23101 Otome, Home Tutor Onee-chan
DC3W23T04 Ricca, Familiar Feeling
DC3W23102 Ricca, the Bond Called Fate
DCW23T01 Sakura, Princess of the Royal Capital
DC3W23T09 Tomoe, Hotly Debating
DCW23T10 Uncontrollable Feelings
DCW23103 Yume, Second Button Charm

2013 Weiss Schwarz Da Capo III Anime Extra

DC3WE1634 Aoi, Battle Outfit!? C
DC3WE1632 Aoi, Battle Preparation? C
DC3WE1624 Aoi, Like A Younger Sister R
DC3WE1626 Aoi, Power Recharged! R
DC3WE1636 Being Spoiled C
DC3WE1602 Charles, Full of Love R
DC3WE1619 Charles, Straightforward Invitation C
DC3WE1607 Charles, Together Is Happiness R
DC3WE1616 Charles, Working Hard C
DC3WE1613 Eri, Student Council President of Kazami Academy C
DC3WE1604 Himeno, From Now on Always R
DC3WE1610 Himeno, Good at Cooking C
DC3WE1614 Himeno, The Path Home with the Two of Us C
DC3WE1606 Himeno, Unchanged Time R
DC3WE1609 Kiyotaka, Considerate Feelings C
DC3WE1617 Mikoto, Single-Minded about Love C
DC3WE1608 Minatsu, An Adult Brain? C
DC3WE1601 Ricca, Confident Proposal R
DC3WE1612 Ricca, Full of Motivation! C
DC3WE1603 Ricca, Red Thread of Fate R
DC3WE1621 Ricca, Special Existence C
DC3WE1605 Ricca, Suddenly Closing in! R
DC3WE1633 Sakura, at the Promised Place C
DC3WE1625 Sakura, to the Place We Belong R
DC3WE1627 Sara, An Incredible Dream R
DC3WE1629 Sara, Heart-Racing Delusions? C
DC3WE1631 Sara, Practice Together C
DC3WE1628 Sara, the Promise After School R
DC3WE1615 Shiki, Sharp-Tongued C
DC3WE1630 Suginami, Good Rival C
DC3WE1623 The Place I Want to Always Be at C
DC3WE1618 Tomoe, Battle Type C
DC3WE1635 Under the Cherry Blossom Tree C
DC3WE1622 Warm Place C
DC3WE1611 Yuuhi, Assistant to the Heard of Agency C
DC3WE1620 Yuzu, Assistant to the Heard of Agency C

2013 Weiss Schwarz Da Capo III Anime Extra Promos

DC3WPR010 Aoi, Always Smiling
DC3WPR005 Aoi, Always the Same Question
DC3WPRP24 Aoi, Full of Girl Skills?
DC3WPRP15 Aoi, Orange Bikini
DC3WE16P02 Aoi, Surprised!
DC3WPR007 Charles, Kind And Sweet Big Sister
DC3WPRP25 Charles, Lightly Red Imagery
DC3WPR002 Charles, Sighing
DC3WPRP12 Charles, White Bikini
DC3WPR003 Himeno, Blooming Love Talk
DC3WPR008 Himeno, Childhood Friend Untrue to Her Feelings
DC3WPRP22 Himeno, Normal Path to School
DC3WPRP13 Himeno, Pink Frilly Swimsuit
DC3WPRP11 Ricca, Black Bikini
DC3WPR021 Ricca, Full of Self-Confidence
DC3WPR006 Ricca, Idol of the Academy
DC3WPR001 Ricca, Magician in the Last Life?
DC3WPRP26 Sakura, One Promise
DC3WPR004 Sara, Blooming Love Talk
DC3WPRP14 Sara, School Swimsuit
DC3WPR009 Sara, Serious And Working Hard
DC3WPRP23 Sara, Studying with Senpai
DC3WE16P01 Sara, Warning to Senpai!

2013 Weiss Schwarz Day Break Illusion

GTW29019 Akari & Ginka, Deepened Friendship C
GTW29038 Akari & Luna, Suddenly Closing in! C
GTW29057 Akari in Swimsuits R
GTW29057S Akari in Swimsuits SR
GTW29056 Akari, Girl of Destiny R
GTW29056R Akari, Girl of Destiny RRR
GTW29052 Akari, Power of the Sun RR
GTW29052S Akari, Power of the Sun SR
GTW29051 Akari, Rookie Member RR
GTW29054 Akari, Shining in the Morning Sun R
GTW29039 Ariel Valtiel Westcott C
GTW29030 Ariel, Wielder of The Judgement R
GTW29048 Beautiful Vacation CR
GTW29024 Biggest Horror of the Summer CC
GTW29023 Bloodstained Future CR
GTW29016 Daemonia of the Star C
GTW29034 Etia Visconti U
GTW29029 Etia, Wielder of The World R
GTW29010 Ginka in Combat U
GTW29005 Ginka, Calculated R
GTW29017 Ginka, Deploy Order C
GTW29020 Ginka, Depressed C
GTW29012 Ginka, Father's Child U
GTW29001 Ginka, Girl of Destiny RR
GTW29001R Ginka, Girl of Destiny RRR
GTW29007 Ginka, Golden Colored Light R
GTW29007S Ginka, Golden Colored Light SR
GTW29004 Ginka, Happy Time R
GTW29003 Ginka, Loves Takoyaki R
GTW29003S Ginka, Loves Takoyaki SR
GTW29008 Ginka, Open-Hearted Girl from Kansai U
GTW29002 Ginka, Power of the Temperance RR
GTW29006 Ginka, Rookie Member R
GTW29015 Ginka, Shining in the Morning Light C
GTW29013 Ginka, Warm Consideration C
GTW29022 Ginka's Room U
GTW29055 Hinata Taiyo R
GTW29053 Itsuki, Tendo Trio Sisters R
GTW29009 Laplace, Mysterious Existence U
GTW29026 Luna in Combat RR
GTW29028 Luna in Swimsuits R
GTW29028S Luna in Swimsuits SR
GTW29033 Luna on An Anxious Night U
GTW29035 Luna, Flushed Cheeks U
GTW29031 Luna, Girl of Destiny R
GTW29031R Luna, Girl of Destiny RRR
GTW29045 Luna, Half-Crying C
GTW29040 Luna, Happy Time C
GTW29041 Luna, Kind Smile C
GTW29037 Luna, Power of the Moon U
GTW29027 Luna, Rookie Member RR
GTW29043 Luna, Shining in the Morning Light C
GTW29036 Luna, Tearing Vain U
GTW29042 Luna, Unexpectedly Enthralled C
GTW29032 Luna, Wolf Girl R
GTW29032S Luna, Wolf Girl SR
GTW29050 Lunar Eclipse CC
GTW29025 Million Dollar Gold Coins CC
GTW29018 Mutsumi, Tendo Trio Sisters C
GTW29044 Nanase, Tendo Trio Sisters C
GTW29047 Power of Healing U
GTW29021 Return from the Battle U
GTW29011 Schrödinger, Mysterious Existence U
GTW29049 Shine from the Amaryllis Flower CC
GTW29046 Wheel of Fate U
GTW29014 Yatarou Shirokane C
GTW2902SP Ginka, Power of the Temperance SP
GTW2927SP Luna, Rookie Member SP
GTW2929SP Etia, Wielder of The World SP
GTW2930SP Ariel, Wielder of The Judgement SP
GTW2951SP Akari, Rookie Member SP

2013 Weiss Schwarz Devil Survivor 2 Anime Extra

DS2SE1603 Airi, Active Girl R
DS2SE1638 Alcor, Incredible Existence C
DS2SE1630 Anguished One Alcor R
DS2SE1628 Byakko Summoning C
DS2SE1606 Daichi & Evil Frost R
DS2SE1627 Dead Face Video C
DS2SE1644 Demon Fusion C
DS2SE1608 Devil Summoner Airi R
DS2SE1612 Devil Summoner Daichi C
DS2SE1632 Devil Summoner Fumi R
DS2SE1602 Devil Summoner Hibiki R
DS2SE1623 Devil Summoner Hinako C
DS2SE1601 Devil Summoner Io R
DS2SE1625 Devil Summoner Joe C
DS2SE1611 Devil Summoner Jungo C
DS2SE1604 Devil Summoner Keita R
DS2SE1641 Devil Summoner Makoto C
DS2SE1640 Devil Summoner Otome C
DS2SE1617 Devil Summoner Ronaldo C
DS2SE1633 Devil Summoner Yamato R
DS2SE1643 Dragon Stream C
DS2SE1636 Fumi, No Care for Daily Chores C
DS2SE1620 Hibiki & Byakko C
DS2SE1605 Hibiki, Rare Quality R
DS2SE1621 Hibiki, Will to Fight C
DS2SE1616 Hibiki, Will to Survive C
DS2SE1619 Hinako, Big Sister Like C
DS2SE1629 I, Want to Live C
DS2SE1622 Io & Lugh C
DS2SE1607 Io, 7-Day Battle R
DS2SE1610 Io, Knows Everyone R
DS2SE1615 Io, Thinking of Family C
DS2SE1618 Joe, Not Serious C
DS2SE1624 Jungo, Kind Cook C
DS2SE1613 Keita, Lone Wolf C
DS2SE1626 Lucifer C
DS2SE1631 Makoto, Gallant Beauty R
DS2SE1637 Otome, JP's Exclusive Doctor C
DS2SE1614 Ronaldo, Ex-Ploice C
DS2SE1609 Shining One Hibiki R
DS2SE1639 Yamato & Cerberus C
DS2SE1645 Yamato VS Alcor C
DS2SE1635 Yamato, Power of Dragon Stream C
DS2SE1642 Yamato, Severing Fate C
DS2SE1634 Yamato, the Last Battle R

2013 Weiss Schwarz Disgaea D2 Extra

DGSE1734 Barbara, Demon Waiting instructions C
DGSE1707 Birth of New Overlord C
DGSE1720 Conversation Between Big Brother and Little Sister C
DGSE1729 Dignity of Overlord Laharl C
DGSE1716 Emergency Revival Pure Flonne C
DGSE1736 Eternal Idol C
DGSE1709 Etna, Cute Little Demon R
DGSE1718 Etna, Dumbfounded C
DGSE1717 Etna, Meanie Demon C
DGSE1713 Etna, Player 2 Character C
DGSE1723 Etna, Sharp Tsukkomi R
DGSE1714 Flonne, Fallen Angel of Love C
DGSE1725 Flonne, Loves Tokusatsu R
DGSE1708 Flonne, Preacher of Love R
DGSE1722 Laharl, Egocentric Overlord R
DGSE1724 Laharl, Leader of the Netherworld R
DGSE1732 Laharl, New Overlord C
DGSE1726 Laharl, Son of the Last Overlord R
DGSE1731 Laharl-chan C
DGSE1733 Laharl-chan, Idol Overlord C
DGSE1701 Little Sister Aura Sicily R
DGSE1711 Majin of Aloofness Etna R
DGSE1721 Netherworld Enveloped by Love C
DGSE1735 Next Episode Preview C
DGSE1706 Overlord Sicily C
DGSE1712 Prinnigar X R
DGSE1710 Pure Flonne, Awakened Angel R
DGSE1719 Rampaging Treasure Xenolith C
DGSE1727 Reborn Krichevskoy C
DGSE1730 Sadistic Etna C
DGSE1704 Seat of Overlord Sicily C
DGSE1703 Sicily, Field Trip Feel C
DGSE1702 Sicily, Mysterious Angel R
DGSE1705 Sicily, Present from Celestia C
DGSE1728 Voluptuous Laharl-chan C
DGSE1715 Xenolith, Mysterious Demon C
DGSE1702S Sicily, Mysterious Angel SP
DGSE1710S Pure Flonne, Awakened Angel SP
DGSE1711S Majin of Aloofness Etna SP
DGSE1722S Laharl, Egocentric Overlord SP

2013 Weiss Schwarz Dog Days Dash Extra

DDWE1704 Adel, Hero Mask R
DDWE1716 Brave Connect C
DDWE1743 Change My Heart C
DDWE1737 Cinque, Hero Crystal C
DDWE1705 Couvert Eschenbach Pastillage R
DDWE1701 Couvert, Admiration Kept Inside R
DDWE1709 Couvert, Apprentice Lord C
DDWE1712 Couvert, Heavenly Spear Coumars C
DDWE1707 Couvert, Lord of Pastillage C
DDWE1713 Couvert, Mage Type C
DDWE1703 Couvert, Welcoming R
DDWE1742 Dalkian, Strongest in the Continent C
DDWE1738 Ecle, Awkward Feelings C
DDWE1739 Ecle, Battle of the Sealed Cave C
DDWE1718 Garnet Spark C
DDWE1720 Gaul, Hero Crystal R
DDWE1744 Heart Relation R
DDWE1729 Hero Time C
DDWE1735 Isuka Makishima C
DDWE1726 Jaune and Vert C
DDWE1723 Leo, Acting Lord of Galette C
DDWE1727 Leo, Lion King Samurai C
DDWE1721 Leo, Millhi's Childhood Friend R
DDWE1740 Millhi, Looking Up C
DDWE1736 Millhi, Summer Reunion C
DDWE1734 Millhi, World Idol R
DDWE1725 Nanami Takatsuki C
DDWE1724 Nanami, Master And Rival C
DDWE1722 Nanami, One Summer Adventure C
DDWE1728 Nanami, Wave-Riding Hero C
DDWE1730 Nanami's Hair-Grooming C
DDWE1719 Noir, Summer Camp R
DDWE1711 Rebecca Anderson C
DDWE1714 Rebecca, Demon Crystal C
DDWE1702 Rebecca, Divine Sword Mercurius R
DDWE1708 Rebecca, Flying-Type Hero C
DDWE1710 Rebecca, Putting Her Hair Down C
DDWE1706 Rebecca, Speeding Through the Sky C
DDWE1732 Riko, Inventist R
DDWE1745 Shiny Heart Shiny Smile C
DDWE1715 Valerio Calvados C
DDWE1731 Wave Rider C
DDWE1717 Witch Cannon, Supreme Demon King Mode C
DDWE1733 Yukikaze, Battle of the Sealed Cave R
DDWE1741 Yukikaze, Summer Camp C

2013 Weiss Schwarz Fate/kaleid Liner Prisma Illya Extra

PISE1827 Believing Miyu C
PISE1833 Birth Magical Girl CC
PISE1835 Class Card Lancer CC
PISE1836 Class Card Saber CC
PISE1834 Class Card, Archer CC
PISE1802 Five Storm Shots Rin R
PISE1802S Five Storm Shots Rin SR
PISE1832 Friends Illya and Miyu C
PISE1829 Illya in Pajamas C
PISE1813 Illya, Dreaming Girl R
PISE1815 Illya, End of the Night R
PISE1828 Illya, Guided Fate C
PISE1810 Illya, Kaleid Magical Girl R
PISE1809 Illya, Normal Girl R
PISE1819 Illya, Practicing Magic C
PISE1817 Kaleidoscope Illya R
PISE1817S Kaleidoscope Illya SR
PISE1818 Kaleidoscope Miyu R
PISE1818S Kaleidoscope Miyu SR
PISE1805 Luvia, Former Master C
PISE1807 Luvia, Kaleid Sapphire C
PISE1806 Luvia, Overbearing Lady C
PISE1826 Magical Ruby C
PISE1820 Magical Sapphire C
PISE1825 Miyu in Casual Clothing C
PISE1812 Miyu in Maid Uniform R
PISE1816 Miyu the Realist R
PISE1821 Miyu, Kaleid Magical Girl C
PISE1830 Miyu, Moonstruck C
PISE1811 Miyu, Perfect Supergirl? R
PISE1824 Miyu, Sudden Transfer Student C
PISE1831 Miyu, the Other Magical Girl C
PISE1814 Mother Irisviel R
PISE1823 Promise Illya C
PISE1804 Rin, Former Master C
PISE1803 Rin, Kaleid Ruby C
PISE1808 Rin, Top Candidate for Clock Tower C
PISE1822 Sella and Leys, Einzbern Household C
PISE1801 Seven Blazing Shots Luvia R
PISE1801S Seven Blazing Shots Luvia SR

2013 Weiss Schwarz Gargantia

GGS23070 Amy in Swimsuit C
GGS23053 Amy, Bright Smiles R
GGS23053R Amy, Bright Smiles RRR
GGS23057 Amy, Dancer R
GGS23057S Amy, Dancer SR
GGS23055 Amy, Full of Interest R
GGS23060 Amy, Impressed U
GGS23056 Amy, Life on the Ship R
GGS23051 Amy, Messenger RR
GGS23051R Amy, Messenger RRR
GGS23052 Amy, Realized Feelings RR
GGS23059 Amy, Running Up U
GGS23061S Amy, Smiling SR
GGS23061 Amy, Smiling U
GGS23054 Amy, Surprising Meeting R
GGS23054S Amy, Surprising Meeting SR
GGS23058 Bebel, Admiration for the Universe U
GGS23007 Bellows, Carnival R
GGS23016 Bellows, Disappointed C
GGS23006 Bellows, Offering Advice R
GGS23011 Bellows, One Request U
GGS23009 Bellows, Puzzled Eyes U
GGS23002 Bellows, Salvager RR
GGS23004 Bellows, Surprised Look R
GGS23074 Ceremony of Friendship CC
GGS23039 Chamber in Battle U
GGS23037 Chamber, Calm Day U
GGS23030 Chamber, Carrying Luggage R
GGS23029 Chamber, Fishing R
GGS23034 Chamber, Gathering Fresh Water U
GGS23043 Chamber, Gravity Waver C
GGS23038S Chamber, Hunting Whalesquid SR
GGS23038 Chamber, Hunting Whalesquid U
GGS23027 Chamber, Machine Caliber RR
GGS23084 Chamber, Mission to Fulfill U
GGS23026 Chamber, Own Conclusion RR
GGS23036S Chamber, Responding SR
GGS23036 Chamber, Responding U
GGS23031 Chamber, Tinplate General R
GGS23031R Chamber, Tinplate General RRR
GGS23099 Confronting Pirates CC
GGS23048 Deflector Beam CR
GGS23071 Dried Foods U
GGS23072 Escape C
GGS23008 Fairlock, Fleet Commander U
GGS23073 Gargantia on the Verdurous Planet CR
GGS23065 Grace, Following Amy C
GGS23064 Happy Amy C
GGS23096 Hidden Truth C
GGS23095 Hideauze C
GGS23094 Hideauze, Process of Evolution C
GGS23014 Joe, Working C
GGS23093 Kugel, Fake Reunion C
GGS23086 Kugel, Superior U
GGS23033 Ledo and Chamber, Falling from the sky U
GGS23078 Ledo and Chamber, Under the Sky R
GGS23091 Ledo in the Cockpit C
GGS23089 Ledo, Adventurer U
GGS23082 Ledo, Collapse of Will R
GGS23077 Ledo, Farewell to Galactic Alliance of Humankind RR
GGS23081 Ledo, Farewell to the Favorite Ride R
GGS23083 Ledo, Life on the Ship U
GGS23079 Ledo, Meditating R
GGS23079S Ledo, Meditating SR
GGS23092 Ledo, Pondering C
GGS23088 Ledo, Strong Glare U
GGS23090 Ledo, Trial-And-Error Smile C
GGS23080 Ledo, Unfamiliar Land R
GGS23080S Ledo, Unfamiliar Land SR
GGS23076 Ledo, Young Man from the Sky RR
GGS23076R Ledo, Young Man From the Sky RRR
GGS23097 Ledo's Flute C
GGS23035 Lukkage Yunboro U
GGS23040 Lukkage, Great Pirate C
GGS23044 Lukkage, Rebellion C
GGS23032 Lukkage, Wave Riding R
GGS23047 Maximize Neuro-plus-powered C
GGS23069 Melty in Swimsuit C
GGS23062 Melty, Making a Joke U
GGS23066 Melty, Mischievous Kid C
GGS23015 Myta, Looking at the Sea of Fog C
GGS23024 New Alliance Leader CC
GGS23019 Oldham, Doctor C
GGS23042 Paraem, Lukkage's Attendent C
GGS23041 Parinuri, Lukkage's Attendent C
GGS23010 Pinion, Barbeque Party U
GGS23012 Pinion, Escaped U
GGS23013 Pinion, Frivolous One U
GGS23017 Pinion, Memory of Older Brother C
GGS23001 Ridget in Mourning RR
GGS23005 Ridget in Swimsuit R
GGS23018 Ridget, New Alliance Leader C
GGS23020 Ridget, Questioning C
GGS23003 Ridget, Vice Representative of the Fleet R
GGS23003S Ridget, Vice Representative of the Fleet SR
GGS23067 Saaya in Swimsuit C
GGS23068 Saaya, Composed Girl C
GGS23063 Saaya, Relaxing U
GGS23021 Salvage U
GGS23049 Shove It, Tinplate Bastard CC
GGS23022 Sky Ladder C
GGS23046 Steelplate Chamber C
GGS23028 Striker, Battle Stance R
GGS23045 Striker, Calling Itself God C
GGS23098 The Last Supporting Enlightenment CR
GGS23075 Thus, Come Back CC
GGS23025 Treasure Island Seen in the Dream CC
GGS23050 Wave-Riding Lobster CC
GGS23087 Whalesquid U
GGS23023 Whomever Catches Fish Gets Fresh Water CR
GGS23085 Young Hideauze Lifeform U
GGS23100 Young Man from the Sky CC
GGS2327SP Chamber, Machine Caliber SP
GGS2352SP Amy, Realized Feelings SP
GGS2377SP Ledo, Farewell to Galactic Alliance of Humankind SP
GGS2378SP Ledo and Chamber, Under the Sky SP

2013 Weiss Schwarz Hatsune Miku Project Diva F

COMPLETE SET (150)		
BOOSTER BOX (20 PACKS)	60.00	80.00
BOOSTER PACK (8 CARDS)	3.00	4.00
RELEASED ON		

PDS22039 39 GET Hatsune Miku U
PDS22098a ACUTE CR
PDS22098b ACUTE CR
PDS22098R ACUTE RRR
PDS22013 Akita Neru Original U
PDS22096 Ashes to Ashes C
PDS22035 atsune Miku Cat Cape U
PDS22095 Close, but SAFE C
PDS22050 Continuation of Dream CC
PDS22036 Continuation of Dream Hatsune Miku U
PDS22020 Continuation of Dream Kagamine Len C
PDS22019 Continuation of Dream Kagamine Rin C
PDS22066 Continuation of Dream Megurine Luka C
PDS22050S Continuation of Dream SR
PDS22072 DYE CR
PDS22072R DYE RRR
PDS22026 Electronic Songstress Hatsune Miku RR
PDS22026X Electronic Songstress Hatsune Miku XR
PDS22079 Endless Singing Hatsune Miku R
PDS22079X Endless Singing Hatsune Miku XR
PDS22023 Fire Flower CR
PDS22023R Fire Flower RRR
PDS22097 FREELY TOMORROW CR
PDS22097R FREELY TOMORROW RRR
PDS22044 Full Power Mikku Miku Hatsune Miku C
PDS22038 Hatsune Miku Append U
PDS22080 Hatsune Miku Agitation R
PDS22080S Hatsune Miku Agitation SR
PDS22067 Hatsune Miku Dark Angel C
PDS22041 Hatsune Miku Deep Sky C
PDS22051 Hatsune Miku Emerald RR
PDS22051R Hatsune Miku Emerald RRR
PDS22037 Hatsune Miku FOnewear Style U
PDS22045 Hatsune Miku Hello, Good night C
PDS22033 Hatsune Miku Holy Goddess U
PDS22043 Hatsune Miku Honey Whip C
PDS22030 Hatsune Miku Ichi no Sakura: Cherry Blossom R
PDS22030R Hatsune Miku Ichi no Sakura: Cherry Blossom RRR
PDS22089 Hatsune Miku Innocent U
PDS22028 Hatsune Miku Linkage R
PDS22028S Hatsune Miku Linkage SR

PDS22083 Hatsune Miku Memoria U
PDS22040 Hatsune Miku Pansy C
PDS22034 Hatsune Miku Pierretta U
PDS22094 Hatsune Miku Purple Swallowtail C
PDS22058 Hatsune Miku Rin-chan Love Squad No1 U
PDS22068 Hatsune Miku Science Girl C
PDS22090 Hatsune Miku Solitude C
PDS22088 Hatsune Miku Star Voice U
PDS22027 Hatsune Miku Stubborn Factory Chief RR
PDS22027R Hatsune Miku Stubborn Factory Chief RRR
PDS22029 Hatsune Miku Summer Memory R
PDS22029S Hatsune Miku Summer Memory SR
PDS22042 Hatsune Miku SW School Swimwear C
PDS22082 Hatsune Miku SW Water Balloon Bikini R
PDS22082S Hatsune Miku SW Water Balloon Bikini SR
PDS22099 Kagamine Hachi Hachi Flower Wars CC
PDS22099S Kagamine Hachi Hachi Flower Wars SR
PDS22016 Kagamine Len Append C
PDS22084a Kagamine Len Bad Boy U
PDS22084b Kagamine Len Bad Boy U
PDS22015 Kagamine Len Crane C
PDS22003S Kagamine Len Ni no Sakura: Butterfly SR
PDS22010 Kagamine Len Ni no Sakura: Fan Dance U
PDS22003 Kagamine Len Ni no Sakura: Ko R
PDS22002 Kagamine Len Original RR
PDS22002R Kagamine Len Original RRR
PDS22081 Kagamine Len Phoenix Moon R
PDS22081S Kagamine Len Phoenix Moon SR
PDS22011 Kagamine Len Receiver U
PDS22005 Kagamine Len Star Mine R
PDS22005S Kagamine Len Star Mine SR
PDS22009 Kagamine Len SW Boxer U
PDS22017 Kagamine Len Tricker C
PDS22014 Kagamine Rin Append U
PDS22006 Kagamine Rin Cherry Moon R
PDS22006S Kagamine Rin Cherry Moon SR
PDS22018 Kagamine Rin Future Style C
PDS22008 Kagamine Rin Melancholy U
PDS22007 Kagamine Rin Original R
PDS22007R Kagamine Rin Original RRR
PDS22076 Kagamine Rin Rain RR
PDS22076S Kagamine Rin Rain SR
PDS22001 Kagamine Rin Scissors RR
PDS22001S Kagamine Rin Scissors SR
PDS22087 Kagamine Rin SW School U
PDS22004 Kagamine Rin SW Striped Bikini R
PDS22004S Kagamine Rin SW Striped Bikini SR
PDS22012 Kagamine Rin Transmitter U
PDS22078 KAITO General R
PDS22078S KAITO General SR
PDS22086 KAITO Guilty U
PDS22093 KAITO Rei no Sakura: Blue Snow C
PDS22091 KAITO Requiem C
PDS22092 KAITO SW Half Spats C
PDS22077 KAITO and MEIKO Original RR
PDS22077R KAITO and MEIKO Original RRR
PDS22061 Kasane Teto Original U
PDS22071 MEGANE C
PDS22064 Megurine Luka Amour U
PDS22054 Megurine Luka Eternal White R
PDS22054S Megurine Luka Eternal White SR
PDS22057 Megurine Luka Original R
PDS22057R Megurine Luka Original RRR
PDS22059 Megurine Luka Rin-chan Love Squad No2 U
PDS22052 Megurine Luka Ruby RR
PDS22052R Megurine Luka Ruby RRR
PDS22069 Megurine Luka San no Sakura: Maple Scent C
PDS22063 Megurine Luka Soft Light Coordination U
PDS22060 Megurine Luka SW Competition Type U
PDS22053 Megurine Luka SW Resort Bikini R
PDS2253SS Megurine Luka SW Resort Bikini SR
PDS22056 MEIKO Blue Crystal R
PDS22056S MEIKO Blue Crystal SR
PDS22062 MEIKO Noel Rouge U
PDS22070 MEIKO Rei no Sakura: Red Pillar C
PDS22055 MEIKO SW Long Pareo R
PDS22055S MEIKO SW Long Pareo SR
PDS22065 MEIKO SW Water Polo C
PDS22021 Melancholic C
PDS22073 Nostalogic CR
PDS22073R Nostalogic RRR
PDS22025 Remote Control CC
PDS22025S Remote Control SR
PDS22075a Rin-chan Now CC
PDS22075b Rin-chan Now CC
PDS22075S Rin-chan Now SR
PDS22048 SadisticMusic Factory CR
PDS22048R SadisticMusic Factory RRR
PDS22047a Senbonzakura CR
PDS22047b Senbonzakura CR
PDS22047c Senbonzakura CR
PDS22047R Senbonzakura RRR
PDS22032 Songs for You Hatsune Miku R
PDS22032X Songs for You Hatsune Miku XR
PDS22022 Tengaku CR
PDS22022R Tengaku RRR
PDS22049 Time Machine CC
PDS22049S Time Machine SR
PDS22024 Tokyo Teddy Bear CC
PDS22024S Tokyo Teddy Bear SR
PDS22100 Unhappy Refrain CC
PDS22100S Unhappy Refrain SR
PDS22046 Weekender Girl C
PDS22031 With You, Two of Us Hatsune Miku R
PDS22031X With You, Two of Us Hatsune Miku XR
PDS22074a World's End Dance Hall CC
PDS22074b World's End Dance Hall CC
PDS22074S World's End Dance Hall SR
PDS22085 Yowane Haku Original U

2013 Weiss Schwarz Hatsune Miku Project Diva F TD

PDS22106R Black Rock Shooter RRR
PDS22106 Blackand#9733;Rock Shooter
PDS22103 Blackand#9733;Rock Shooter Hatsune Miku
PDS22T05 Continuation of Dream Kagamine Len
PDS22T04 Continuation of Dream Kagamine Rin
PDS22T12 Full Power Mikku Miku Hatsune Miku
PDS22T09 Hatsune Miku "Deep Sky"
PDS22T11 Hatsune Miku "FOnewear Style"
PDS22104a Hatsune Miku "Heartbeat"
PDS22104b Hatsune Miku "Heartbeat"
PDS22T10 Hatsune Miku "Honey Whip"
PDS22105 Hatsune Miku "Original"
PDS22105S Hatsune Miku "Original" SR
PDS22T08 Hatsune Miku "Pansy"
PDS22T01 Kagamine Len "Append"
PDS22T02 Kagamine Len "Tricker"
PDS22T03 Kagamine Rin "Future Style"
PDS22T06 Melancholic
PDS22101 Next to You Hatsune Miku
PDS22107 ODDS and ENDS
PDS22107R ODDS and ENDS RRR
PDS22T07 Tengaku
PDS22102 To the Best Stage Hatsune Miku
PDS22102X To the Best Stage Hatsune Miku XR

2013 Weiss Schwarz Little Busters Anime

LBW21040 Awkward Friendship CC
LBW21040S Awkweard Friendship SR
LBW21052 Bath with Big Sis Haruka C
LBW21043 Big Sister, Thinking of Little Sis Kanata R
LBW21008 Candidate for Next Captain Sasami U
LBW21036 Cause And Effect Haruka C
LBW21025 Cute is Justice Kud R
LBW21025S Cute is Justice Kud SR
LBW21073 Dream And Reality Mio & Midori C
LBW21062 Dream of Going to the Universe Kud RR
LBW21078 Farewell Yukichi!! U
LBW21030a Fitting Clothing Riki U
LBW21030b Fitting Clothing Riki U
LBW21057 Fly You to the Classroom! U
LBW21061 Fun Time Komari RR
LBW21042 Gaze of Curiosity Yuiko R
LBW21042R Gaze of Curiosity Yuiko RRR
LBW21032 Good Friends Komari & Rin C
LBW21038 Hah, It Was Great U
LBW21031 Holding Hands Haruka & Kanata U
LBW21002 Ideal Miyazawa-sama Sasami R
LBW21002R Ideal Miyazawa-sama Sasami RRR
LBW21024 Important things Haruka R
LBW21020 Invincible Kurugaya CC
LBW21020S Invincible Kurugaya SR
LBW21067 Kind Resident Assistant A-chan Senpai U
LBW21076 Komari & Kud Wearing Aprons C
LBW21072 Kud's Mother Chernushka C
LBW21035 Kud's Roommate Kanata C
LBW21080 Let's go Live CC
LBW21080S Let's go Live SR
LBW21044 Little Busters Haruka R
LBW21044S Little Busters Haruka SR
LBW21006 Little Busters Kengo & Masato R
LBW21006S Little Busters Kengo & Masato SR
LBW21003 Little Busters Komari R
LBW21003S Little Busters Komari SR
LBW21023 Little Busters Kud R
LBW21023S Little Busters Kud SR
LBW21066 Little Busters Kyousuke R
LBW21066S Little Busters Kyousuke SR
LBW21064 Little Busters Mio R
LBW21064S Little Busters Mio SR
LBW21065 Little Busters Riki R
LBW21005 Little Busters Rin R
LBW21005S Little Busters Rin SR
LBW21046 Little Busters Yuiko R
LBW21046S Little Busters Yuiko SR
LBW21059 Little Busters! CR
LBW21059R Little Busters! RRR
LBW21075 Living Like How I Wanted Kengo C
LBW21017 Looking Up at the Night Sky U
LBW21029 Maiden in Love Sasami U
LBW21016 Marvelous Things Komari C
LBW21027 Masato's Rival Kengo U
LBW21026 Moral Committee President Katana R
LBW21026R Moral Committee President Katana RRR
LBW21050 Moving Time, Riki U
LBW21014 Muscle in Danger Masato C
LBW21051 Muscle Sensation Masato C
LBW21018 My Best Puppet Show CR
LBW21018R My Best Puppet Show RRR
LBW21007 Natsume -slash- Naoe U
LBW21063 New Bond Komari R
LBW21009 New Bond Rin U
LBW21019 New Story CR
LBW21019R New Story RRR
LBW21033 No.1 Pretty Girl within School Sasami C
LBW21021 Normal Smile Haruka RR
LBW21010a One Cut, Two Pieces Yuiko U
LBW21010b One Cut, Two Pieces Yuiko U
LBW21070 Place Closest to Sky Komari U
LBW21011 Prime Suspect Yuiko C
LBW21071 Rainy With A Chance of Sun Mio Nishizono U
LBW21037 Rampaging Weapons Rin C
LBW21039 Regained Bond CR
LBW21039R Regained Bond RRR
LBW21028 Save the Cafeteria! Rin U
LBW21004 Searching for Secret, Rin R
LBW21048 Secret of Two Mio U
LBW21056 Spartan Committee Chairman Kanata C
LBW21001 Step to Courage Rin RR
LBW21068 Strike Box Kud U
LBW21047 Tearful Confession Kanata U
LBW21077 Tentacles Kud C
LBW21055 The Other Mio Nishizono, Midori C
LBW21060 The Promise Made Back Then CC
LBW21060S The Promise Made Back Then SR
LBW21069 The Wish of Two Komari U
LBW21015 Things That Are Lost Komari C
LBW21012 Time of Beginning Kyousuke C
LBW21079 To the 50-Nautical-Mile-High Sky CR
LBW21079R To the 50-Nautical-Mile-High Sky RRR
LBW21034 Transfer Female Student Kud C
LBW21022 Troubled Thoughts Rin R
LBW21022S Troubled Thoughts Rin SR
LBW21045 True Wish Midori R
LBW21049 Trust from Deep Inside Haruka U
LBW21041 Two as One Mio RR
LBW21058a Warmth of Family U
LBW21058b Warmth of Family U
LBW21074 Watching Over the Future Koshiki C
LBW21053 Widening World Mio C
LBW21013 Yui-chan Yuiko C
LBW21054 Yuiko Wearing An Apron C
LBW2101SP Step to Courage Rin SP
LBW2121SP Normal Smile Haruka SP
LBW2141SP Two as One Mio SP
LBW2161SP Fun Time Komari SP
LBW2162SP Dream of Going to the Universe Kud SP
LBW2165SP Little Busters Riki SP

2013 Weiss Schwarz Little Busters Anime TD

LBW21T06 A Wonderful Thing Komari
LBW21T02 Candidate for Next Captaincy Sasami
LBW21T10 Friends Komari & Rin
LBW21102 Helping Together Kud
LBW21T09 Invincible Kurugaya
LBW21105 Lillte Busters!
LBW21105R Lillte Busters! RRR
LBW21T07 Look Up at the Night Sky
LBW21T11 Masato's Rival Kengo
LBW21T04 Muscle Close Call Masato
LBW21T08 New Story
LBW21104 Our Story Riki
LBW21T13 Rampant Weaponry Rin
LBW21T14 Retributive Justice Haruka
LBW21101 Spiral Theory of Happiness Komari
LBW21103 Strength of Being Straightforward Rin
LBW21103S Strength of Being Straightforward Rin SP
LBW21T01 Time of Beginning Kyousuke
LBW21T12 Transfer Student Girl Kud
LBW21T05 What Have I Lost Komari
LBW21T03 Yui-chan Yuiko

2013 Weiss Schwarz Love Live

COMPLETE SET (151)		
BOOSTER BOX (20 PACKS)	60.00	80.00
BOOSTER PACK (8 CARDS)	3.00	4.00
RELEASED ON MAY 23, 2014		

LLW24088 Alpaca C
LLW24038 Arisa Ayase C
LLW24045 Bliss U
LLW24099 Club Entry Declaration CC
LLW24095 Doing Push-Ups While Smiling U
LLW24096 Dream Since Childhood U
LLW24016 Eri Ayase C
LLW24042 Eri in Maid Uniform C
LLW24040 Eri in Swimsuit C
LLW24044 Eri, Quarter Russian C
LLW24026 Eri, Student Council President RR
LLW24026R Eri, Student Council President RRR
LLW24031 Eri, Third-Year Student at Otonokizaka Academy R
LLW24031S Eri, Third-Year Student at Otonokizaka Academy SR
LLW24046 Everyone Taking A Bathe in the Sea U
LLW24071 Everyone Tree Climbing U
LLW24074 Favorite Place CC
LLW24073 First Feelings CR
LLW24100 Girl in the Music Room CC
LLW24090 Hanayo in Maid Uniform C
LLW24084 Hanayo in Swimsuit U
LLW24018 Hanayo Koizumi C
LLW24091 Hanayo, First-Year Student at Otonokizaka Academy C
LLW24077 Hanayo, Loves Idols RR
LLW24077R Hanayo, Loves Idols RRR
LLW24094 Hanayo, New Self C
LLW24078 Hanayo, Rin's Childhood Friend R
LLW24078S Hanayo, Rin's Childhood Friend SR
LLW24058 Honoka in Maid Uniform U
LLW24068 Honoka in Swimsuit C
LLW24022 Honoka Kousaka C
LLW24063 Honoka, Daughter of a Japanese Candy Store C
LLW24054 Honoka, Energetic as Merit R
LLW24054R Honoka, Energetic as Merit RRR
LLW24069 Honoka, Second-Year Student at Otonokizaka Academy C
LLW24055 Honoka, Traction of Myu's R
LLW24055S Honoka, Traction of Myu's SR
LLW24060 Koroti, True Feelings U
LLW24011 Kotori Minami U
LLW24066 Kotori, Daughter of the Trustee Chairperson C
LLW24051 Kotori, Second-Year Student at Otonokizaka Academy RR
LLW24051S Kotori, Second-Year Student at Otonokizaka Academy SR
LLW24053 Kotori, Vice-Leader Type R
LLW24053R Kotori, Vice-Leader Type RRR
LLW24072 Lack-of-Style Steps U
LLW24070 Makeshift Disguise U
LLW24021 Maki Nishikino C
LLW24092 Maki, Confident C
LLW24081 Maki, First-Year Student at Otonokizaka Academy R
LLW24081S Maki, First-Year Student at Otonokizaka Academy SR
LLW24085 Maki, Giving the Last Push U
LLW24079 Maki, Good at Singing R
LLW24079R Maki, Good at Singing RRR
LLW24082 Maki, Prideful U
LLW24061 Meanie Kotori U
LLW24047 Memory of That Day U
LLW24025 Mermaid festa vol1 CC
LLW24064 Minalinsky Kotori C
LLW24098 Myu's Friends CR
LLW24015a New Start Myu's C
LLW24015b New Start Myu's C
LLW24015c New Start Myu's C
LLW24015d New Start Myu's C
LLW24015e New Start Myu's C
LLW24015f New Start Myu's C
LLW24015g New Start Myu's C
LLW24015h New Start Myu's C
LLW24015i New Start Myu's C
LLW24034 Niko in Maid Uniform U
LLW24017 Niko Yazawa C
LLW24032 Niko, Club President U
LLW24027 Niko, Idol Otaku RR
LLW24027S Niko, Idol Otaku SR
LLW24035 Niko, Loves Mischiefs U
LLW24041 Niko, Secretly Plotting C
LLW24029 Niko, Third-Year Student at Otonokizaka Academy R
LLW24029R Niko, Third-Year Student at Otonokizaka Academy RRR
LLW24097 Normal Practice Routine? U
LLW24043 Nozomi in Maid Uniform C
LLW24033 Nozomi in Swimsuit U
LLW24020 Nozomi Toujou C
LLW24028 Nozomi, Spiritual Power R
LLW24028S Nozomi, Spiritual Power SR
LLW24037 Nozomi, Thinking of Friends C
LLW24030 Nozomi, Third-Year Student at Otonokizaka Academy R
LLW24030R Nozomi, Third-Year Student at Otonokizaka Academy RRR
LLW24024 Our LIVE is LIFE with You CC
LLW24005 Our LIVE is LIFE with You Eri Ayase R
LLW24010 Our LIVE is LIFE with You Hanayo Koizumi R
LLW24002 Our LIVE is LIFE with You Honoka Kousaka RR
LLW24007 Our LIVE is LIFE with You Kotori Minami R
LLW24001 Our LIVE is LIFE with You Maki Nishikino RR
LLW24009 Our LIVE is LIFE with You Niko Yazawa R
LLW24003 Our LIVE is LIFE with You Nozomi Toujou RR
LLW24008 Our LIVE is LIFE with You Rin Hoshizora R
LLW24004 Our LIVE is LIFE with You Umi Sonoda R
LLW24039 Pretty Eri C
LLW24019 Rin Hoshizora C
LLW24086 Rin in Maid Uniform U
LLW24089 Rin in Swimsuit C
LLW24087 Rin, Athletic Type C
LLW24076 Rin, First-Year Student at Otonokizaka Academy RR
LLW24076R Rin, First-Year Student at Otonokizaka Academy RRR
LLW24093 Rin, Gathering Material C
LLW24080 Rin, Hanayo's Childhood Friend R
LLW24080S Rin, Hanayo's Childhood Friend SR
LLW24083 Secret Talk Maki U
LLW24036 Secret Talk Nozomi U
LLW24006a Summer-color Smile is 1, 2, Jump Myu's R
LLW24006b Summer-color Smile is 1, 2, Jump Myu's R
LLW24006c Summer-color Smile is 1, 2, Jump Myu's R
LLW24006d Summer-color Smile is 1, 2, Jump Myu's R
LLW24006e Summer-color Smile is 1, 2, Jump Myu's R
LLW24006f Summer-color Smile is 1, 2, Jump Myu's R
LLW24006g Summer-color Smile is 1, 2, Jump Myu's R
LLW24006h Summer-color Smile is 1, 2, Jump Myu's R
LLW24006i Summer-color Smile is 1, 2, Jump Myu's R
LLW24050 Tarot Reading CC
LLW24049 Things Truly Wanted to Be Done CC
LLW24012a Tight 'love' Approaching Myu's U
LLW24012b Tight 'love' Approaching Myu's U
LLW24012c Tight 'love' Approaching Myu's U
LLW24012d Tight 'love' Approaching Myu's U
LLW24012e Tight 'love' Approaching Myu's U
LLW24012f Tight 'love' Approaching Myu's U
LLW24012g Tight 'love' Approaching Myu's U
LLW24012h Tight 'love' Approaching Myu's U
LLW24012i Tight 'love' Approaching Myu's U
LLW24057 Umi in Maid Uniform U
LLW24013 Umi Sonoda U
LLW24059 Umi, Archery Club U
LLW24062 Umi, Explosion of Fantasizing C
LLW24056 Umi, Japanese Lady R
LLW24056R Umi, Japanese Lady RRR
LLW24052 Umi, Second-Year Student at Otonokizaka Academy RR
LLW24052S Umi, Second-Year Student at Otonokizaka Academy SR
LLW24067 Umi, Youth Days C
LLW24014 Us in the Moment Myu's U
LLW24048 Work to Bring Smiles CR
LLW24075 You Are the Worst CC
LLW24023 Youth Can Surely Be Heard CR
LLW24065 Yukiho Kousaka C
LLW2401SP Our LIVE is LIFE with You Maki Nishikino SP
LLW2402SP Our LIVE is LIFE with You Honoka Kousaka SP
LLW2403SP Our LIVE is LIFE with You Nozomi Toujou SP
LLW2404SP Our LIVE is LIFE with You Umi Sonoda SP
LLW2405SP Our LIVE is LIFE with You Eri Ayase SP
LLW2407SP Our LIVE is LIFE with You Kotori Minami SP
LLW2408SP Our LIVE is LIFE with You Rin Hoshizora SP
LLW2409SP Our LIVE is LIFE with You Niko Yazawa SP
LLW2410SP Our LIVE is LIFE with You Hanayo Koizumi SP

2013 Weiss Schwarz Love Live TD

LLW24T07 Everyone Tree Climbing
LLW24T08 First Feelings
LLW24T02 Honoka, Daughter of a Japanese Candy Store
LLW24T05 Honoka, Second-Year Student at Otonokizaka Academy
LLW24T03 Kotori, Daughter of the Trustee Chairperson
LLW24T06 Meanie Kotori
LLW24110 Oh,LoveandPeace Myu's
LLW24T04 Umi, Archery Club
LLW24T01 Umi, Explosion of Fantasizing
LLW24112a Us in the Moment
LLW24112b Us in the Moment
LLW24112c Us in the Moment
LLW24111 Wonderful Rush
LLW24103 Wonderful Rush Eri Ayase
LLW24106 Wonderful Rush Hanayo Koizumi
LLW24109 Wonderful Rush Honoka Kousaka
LLW24108 Wonderful Rush Kotori Minami
LLW24104 Wonderful Rush Maki Nishikino
LLW24101 Wonderful Rush Niko Yazawa
LLW24105 Wonderful Rush Nozomi Toujou
LLW24107 Wonderful Rush Rin Hoshizora
LLW24102 Wonderful Rush Umi Sonoda

2013 Weiss Schwarz Nanoha The Movie 2nd A's

N2W25017 Alicia, Pestering C
N2W25030 Alisa and Suzuka, Christmas Party C
N2W25013 Arf, Feeling of Gratitude U
N2W25078 Awakening of the Book of Darkness U
N2W25029 Chrono, Memories about the "Book of Darkness" Incident C
N2W25023 End of the Dreams CR
N2W25055 Exelion Buster ACS CC
N2W25028 Extremely Large Freezing Magic Chrono U
N2W25003 Fate, Afterwards R
N2W25003S Fate, Afterwards SR
N2W25015 Fate, Feeling Nice C
N2W25014 Fate, Final Battle U
N2W25004 Fate, For Her Friends R
N2W25004R Fate, For Her Friends RRR
N2W25008 Fate, Ideal Family R
N2W25008S Fate, Ideal Family SR
N2W25019 Fate, New Power C
N2W25007 Fate, Place to Which She Belongs R
N2W25007S Fate, Place to Which She Belongs SR
N2W25001 Fate, Return of Lightning RR
N2W25001R Fate, Return of Lightning RRR
N2W25009 Fate, Reunited After A Long Time U
N2W25006 Fate, Sonic Drive R
N2W25006S Fate, Sonic Drive SR
N2W25005 Fate, Victory Declaration R
N2W25053 For Hayate CR
N2W25057 Hayate and Reinforce as One RR
N2W25057R Hayate and Reinforce as One RRR
N2W25072 Hayate, Free from Curse C
N2W25060 Hayate, Happy Phone Time R
N2W25060R Hayate, Happy Phone Time RRR
N2W25070 Hayate, Looking for Something C
N2W25059 Hayate, Making Breakfast R
N2W25059S Hayate, Making Breakfast SR
N2W25064 Hayate, Master of "Yagami Household" U
N2W25067 Hayate, Moment of Farewell U
N2W25074 Hayate, Punishing Misbehaving Kids C
N2W25056 Hayate, Unison in RR
N2W25026 Lindy, Battle Stance R
N2W25026S Lindy, Battle Stance SR
N2W25027 Lindy, Memory of the Past U
N2W25079 Morning at the Yagami Household CR
N2W25054 Morning of Promise CC
N2W25047 Nanoha and Fate, Oath Between Two C
N2W25036 Nanoha, Accel Mode R
N2W25043 Nanoha, Accel Shooter U
N2W25035 Nanoha, Cartridge System R
N2W25035R Nanoha, Cartridge System RRR
N2W25033 Nanoha, Cheerful R
N2W25033S Nanoha, Cheerful SR
N2W25031 Nanoha, Determined Look RR
N2W25031R Nanoha, Determined Look RRR
N2W25038 Nanoha, Exelion Mode R
N2W25038S Nanoha, Exelion Mode SR
N2W25041 Nanoha, New Power U
N2W25048 Nanoha, Reunited After A Long Time C
N2W25039 Nanoha, Sudden Attack U
N2W25045 Nanoha, Truth to be Told U
N2W25080 Petrifying Lance, Mistilteinn CC
N2W25020 Precia and Rinis, Ideal Family C
N2W25069 Reinforce II, Spring Winds C
N2W25062 Reinforce, Moment of Farewell R
N2W25062S Reinforce, Moment of Farewell SR
N2W25065 Reinforce, Nap Time U
N2W25061 Reinforce, Overspilling Passion R
N2W25061S Reinforce, Overspilling Passion SR
N2W25068 Reinforce, Wishing Upon Friends U
N2W25071 Reminiscence Reinforce C
N2W25076 Shamal, Bureau Worker C
N2W25075 Shamal, Captured Core C
N2W25073 Shamal, Expert of Supporting Magic C
N2W25063 Shamal, Overslept U
N2W25058 Shamal, Support Role R
N2W25058S Shamal, Support Role SR
N2W25021 Signum, Bureau Worker C
N2W25012 Signum, Declaration of a General U
N2W25011 Signum, Encounter on the Rooftop U
N2W25010 Signum, Mysterious Swordsman U
N2W25016 Signum, SchlangebeiBen C
N2W25002 Signum, Something to Protect RR
N2W25002R Signum, Something to Protect RRR
N2W25018 Signum, Waking Up C
N2W25024 Strike of Lightning God CC
N2W25025 Strong Enemy in the Way CC
N2W25052 To Not Hurt Anyone U
N2W25032 Vita, Angry Look RR
N2W25032R Vita, Angry Look RRR
N2W25051 Vita, Bureau Worker C
N2W25034 Vita, Eating R
N2W25042 Vita, Encounter on the Rooftop U
N2W25044 Vita, First Time Fighting Together U
N2W25049 Vita, Happy Days C
N2W25037 Vita, Heroic Determination R
N2W25037S Vita, Heroic Determination SR
N2W25046 Vita, Present from Hayate C
N2W25040 Vita, Schwalbefliegen U

N2W25022 Walking Together Nicely U
N2W25050 Yuuno, Advisor C
N2W25077 Zafira, Full Speed Sprint C
N2W25066 Zafira, Piercing U
N2W255SSP Fate, Victory Declaration SSP
N2W2534S Vita, Eating SSP
N2W2536S Nanoha, Accel Mode SSP
N2W2556S Hayate, Unison in SSP

2013 Weiss Schwarz Nisemonogatari

NMS24049 Bird of the Afterworld Tsukihi Araragi R
NMS24049R Bird of the Afterworld Tsukihi Araragi RRR
NMS24068 Bitten! CC
NMS24018 Ceremony that is One More Step Up U
NMS24019 Encounter at the Ruins CR
NMS24066 Expected Happenings U
NMS24027 Fire Fence Bee Karen Araragi R
NMS24021 Fire Sisters Karen Araragi RR
NMS24021S Fire Sisters Karen Araragi SR
NMS24056 Fire Sisters Tsukihi Araragi U
NMS24029 Forgery Deishu Kaiki U
NMS24044 Girl Who Knows Everything CC
NMS24020 Greeting at the Door CC
NMS24065 Hentai Suruga Kanbaru C
NMS24022 Hitagi Senjougahara as Lover RR
NMS24022S Hitagi Senjougahara as Lover SR
NMS24030 Hitagi Senjougahara, Sharp Instinct U
NMS24026 Hitagi Senjougahara, Someone to Protect R
NMS24026R Hitagi Senjougahara, Someone to Protect RRR
NMS24063 Hitagi Senjougahara, Unexpected Words C
NMS24048 Hitagi Senjougahari, Farewell to the Past R
NMS24039 Karen Araragi, Bond of Family C
NMS24031 Karen Araragi, Brushing Teeth U
NMS24037 Karen Araragi, Famous at Tsuganoki 2nd Junior High C

NMS24025 Karen Araragi, Girl Given by Bee R
NMS24025R Karen Araragi, Girl Given by Bee RRR
NMS24023 Karen Araragi, In Charge of Battle R
NMS24032 Karen Araragi, Light Feeling U
NMS24034 Karen Araragi, Morning Sight U
NMS24028 Karen Araragi, the Larger Kid Sister U
NMS24045 Karen Bee CC
NMS24071 Koyomi Araragi, Heading to Battle RR
NMS24036 Koyomi Araragi, Pride of Big Brother C
NMS24012 Koyomi Araragi, Sudden Attack C
NMS24055 Koyomi Araragi, Things about Little Sisters U
NMS24017 Mayoi Hachikuji, Being Shy C
NMS24053 Mayoi Hachikuji, Exchanged Promise U
NMS24052 Mayoi Hachikuji, Normal Goodbye R
NMS24052S Mayoi Hachikuji, Normal Goodbye SR
NMS24064 Mayoi Hachikuji, Secrets C
NMS24005 Mayoi Hachikuji, Word Called Courage R
NMS24080 Meaning of Family CC
NMS24008 Nadeko Sengoku, Dressed Up U
NMS24014 Nadeko Sengoku, First Guest C
NMS24072 Nadeko Sengoku, Headband R
NMS24001 Nadeko Sengoku, Spell RR
NMS24001S Nadeko Sengoku, Spell SR
NMS24077 Nadeko Sengoku, Two's Play C
NMS24070 Platinum-Grade Anger CC
NMS24011 Shinobu Oshino in the Flower Fields U
NMS24013 Shinobu Oshino in the Shadows C
NMS24004 Shinobu Oshino, Blessing of the Moon R
NMS24004R Shinobu Oshino, Blessing of the Moon RRR
NMS24016 Shinobu Oshino, Blonde With Gold Eyes C
NMS24009 Shinobu Oshino, Dignified Amongst Vampires U
NMS24007 Shinobu Oshino, For the Help U
NMS24015 Shinobu Oshino, in Good Mood C
NMS24010 Shinobu Oshino, Living in the Shadow U
NMS24002 Shinobu Oshino, Master and Servant Relationship RR
NMS24002S Shinobu Oshino, Master and Servant Relationship SR
NMS24006 Shinobu Oshino, Serious Mode R
NMS24003 Shinobu Oshino, Return Path R
NMS24079 Strength of Loser U
NMS24054 Suruga Kanbaru, Acceleration Device U
NMS24050 Suruga Kanbaru, Feeling of Openness R
NMS24050S Suruga Kanbaru, Feeling of Openness SR
NMS24033 Suruga Kanbaru, Playing Hanaluda U
NMS24040 Suruga Kanbaru, Pure And Innocent C
NMS24042 Teeth Brushing Time CR
NMS24069 Treatment of Memory CC
NMS24024 Tsubasa Hanekawa, Advice as Benefactor R
NMS24024S Tsubasa Hanekawa, Advice as Benefactor SR
NMS24073 Tsubasa Hanekawa, Helper of the Little Sisters U
NMS24035 Tsubasa Hanekawa, Home Tutor C
NMS24041 Tsubasa Hanekawa, Mischievous Heart C
NMS24076 Tsubasa Hanekawa, Path Home C
NMS24046 Tsukihi Araragi, Cuckoo Girl RR
NMS24051 Tsukihi Araragi, Famous at Tsuganoki 2nd Junior High R
NMS24051S Tsukihi Araragi, Famous at Tsuganoki 2nd Junior High SR
NMS24058 Tsukihi Araragi, Impulsive Personality U
NMS24057 Tsukihi Araragi, In Charge of Strategy U
NMS24059 Tsukihi Araragi, Loves Kimono C
NMS24062 Tsukihi Araragi, Morning Sight C
NMS24061 Tsukihi Araragi, Tea Club C
NMS24060 Tsukihi Araragi, the Smaller Little Sister C
NMS24047 Tsukihi Araragi, Undying Strange RR
NMS24067 Tsukihi Phoenix CR
NMS24043 Two at the Beach CC
NMS24075 Unlimited Rulebook Yotsugi Ononoki C
NMS24038 What is Justice Karen Araragi C
NMS24074 Yotsugi Ononoki, Tsukumogami U
NMS24078 Yozuru Kagenui, Onmyouji C
NMS2423SP Karen Araragi, In Charge of Battle SP
NMS2427SP Fire Fence Bee Karen Araragi SP
NMS2446SP Tsukihi Araragi, Cuckoo Girl SP
NMS2447SP Tsukihi Araragi, Undying Strange SP

2013 Weiss Schwarz Persona 4 Ultimate Extra

P4SE1515 Aigis, Reunited Sisters C
P4SE1522 Akihiko, Fist to Protect C
P4SE1517 Anger of Labrys C
P4SE1518 Asterius Appears C
P4SE1531 Beast of Libido Teddie C
P4SE1512 Body Number 024 C
P4SE1536 Breaking Into the Broadcasting Room! C
P4SE1510 Bullish President of Massacre Shadow Labrys R
P4SE1504 Captain Resentment Yousuke Hanamura C
P4SE1523 Career-Risking Battle Kanji C
P4SE1514 Chie, Future Woman Police C
P4SE1533 Elizabeth, In the Midst of Eternal Journey C
P4SE1527 Genko And Bond C
P4SE1521 Hard to Conquer Snow 'Black' Yukiko Amagi R
P4SE1507 Heartless Angel Full of Armaments Aigis R
P4SE1526 Horror of Object X C
P4SE1530 Killjoy Detective With IQ 2000 Naoto Shirogane R
P4SE1516 Labrys, Fateful Encounter C
P4SE1509 Male-Rivalling Dragon of Footwork Chie Satonaka R
P4SE1534 Mitsuru, Captain of Shadow Walker C
P4SE1503 Nanako, Helping Out C
P4SE1535 Naoto, Undercover Investigation C
P4SE1506 P-1 Grand Prix Commencing! C
P4SE1511 President Teddie, Organizer of P-1 Grand Prix! C
P4SE1524 Protein Junkie of Steel Fist! Akihiko Sanada C
P4SE1513 Rise, P-1 Grand Prix Exclusive Live C
P4SE1529 Solitude Execution Queen! Mitsuru Kirijou R
P4SE1502 Steel Sister Complex Leader Yu Narukami R
P4SE1508 Steel Student Council President of Eighth High School Labrys R
P4SE1528 Teddie, Self-Proclaimed Special Investigation Squad R
P4SE1520 Thrilling Hard-Muscled Emperor Kanji Tatsumi R
P4SE1525 Warrior Training C
P4SE1532 Worst Elevator Girl in the History Elizabeth C
P4SE1501 Yousuke, Self-Proclaimed Special Investigation Squad R

P4SE1505 Yu, Self-Proclaimed Special Investigation Squad C
P4SE1519 Yukiko, Promise with Friends R

2013 Weiss Schwarz Psycho-Pass Extra

PPSE1401 A Beast to Hunt a Beast Kougami R
PPSE1404 Akane Tsunemori R
PPSE1415 Akane, Talent for Inspector C
PPSE1425 Che Guzon R
PPSE1420 Chosen Existence R
PPSE1435 Confronted Two R
PPSE1426 Criminally Asymptomatic Makishima R
PPSE1421 Fateful Encounter C
PPSE1411 Hound three Kougami C
PPSE1412 Kougami During Training C
PPSE1416 Kougami, Back When He Was Inspector C
PPSE1419 Kougami, Bouquet of Roses C
PPSE1414 Kougami, Determination Towards Investigation C
PPSE1410 Kougami, Enforcer C
PPSE1418 Kougami, Seeing the Depth C
PPSE1402 Kougami, Target to Seek R
PPSE1403 Latent Criminal Kougami R
PPSE1407 Lemonade Candy Akane C
PPSE1431 Makishima, A Rose C
PPSE1423 Makishima, Cold Glare R
PPSE1433 Makishima, Deep Foresight C
PPSE1429 Makishima, Mysterious Man C
PPSE1428 Makishima, Refined Intelligence C
PPSE1430 Makishima, Resistance Towards the Controlling Society C
PPSE1432 Makishima, Undercover as Art Teacher C
PPSE1406 Nobuchika Ginoza C
PPSE1405 Shinya Kougami R
PPSE1409 Shion Karanomori C
PPSE1427 Shuugo Makishima R
PPSE1413 Shuusei Kagari C
PPSE1434 Sibyl System C
PPSE1424 Smile of Saint Makishima R
PPSE1417 Tomomi Masaoka C
PPSE1422 Unit One of the Public Safety Bureau's Criminal Investigation Division C
PPSE1436 Unpunishable Crime C
PPSE1408 Yayoi Kunizuka C

2013 Weiss Schwarz Railgun S

RGW26058 Academy City Kuroko RR
RGW26070 Academy City Mikoto U
RGW26029 Academy City Misaka's Little Sister C
RGW26036 Academy City Saten RR
RGW26036S Academy City Saten SR
RGW26040 Academy City Uiharu R
RGW26040S Academy City Uiharu SR
RGW26013 Accelerator, Experiment Candidate U
RGW26011 Accelerator, First Experiment U
RGW26002 Accelerator, Level 6 Shift Project RR
RGW26002S Accelerator, Level 6 Shift Project SR
RGW26017 Accelerator, No-Mercy Personality U
RGW26006 Accelerator, Overwhelming Power R
RGW26026 Accelerator, Path to Invincibility C
RGW26035 Bomb User CC
RGW26030 Doll Bomb U
RGW26054 Escape from Dark Alleys CR
RGW26078 Eyewitness CR
RGW26016 Frenda Seivelun U
RGW26028 Frenda, Bomb User C
RGW26004 Frenda, Inteference Acts R
RGW26050 Haruue, Munching C
RGW26010 ITEM Frenda R
RGW26010R ITEM Frenda RRR
RGW26007 ITEM Kinuhata R
RGW26003 ITEM Mugino RR
RGW26003R ITEM Mugino RRR
RGW26014 ITEM Takitsubo U
RGW26066 Kuroko, Full of Justice U
RGW26060 Kuroko, One Who Protects Peace R
RGW26060S Kuroko, One Who Protects Peace SR
RGW26067 Kuroko, Serious about Work U
RGW26071 Kuroko, Working C
RGW26041 Level 1 Uiharu U
RGW26009 Level 5 Mugino R
RGW26055 Location Triangulation CC
RGW26018 Meltdowner Mugino U
RGW26033 Meltdowner CR
RGW26061 Mental Out Shokuhou R
RGW26069 Mikoto at the Hospital U
RGW26072 Mikoto at the Library C
RGW26062 Mikoto, A Certain Day Off R
RGW26062R Mikoto, A Certain Day Off RRR
RGW26073 Mikoto, Admired Being C
RGW26068 Mikoto, Determination on the Bridge U
RGW26064 Mikoto, Good Grade U
RGW26065 Mikoto, Good Sport Reflexes U
RGW26076 Mikoto, On the Way to School C
RGW26057 Mikoto, Taking a Walk RR
RGW26057R Mikoto, Taking a Walk RRR
RGW26056 Mikoto, Where the Coin Goes RR
RGW26015 Misaka, No 9982 of the Mass Production U
RGW26001 Misaka's Little Sister, Clone RR
RGW26001S Misaka's Little Sister, Clone SR
RGW26022 Misaka's Little Sister, Loves Annimals C
RGW26008 Misaka's Little Sister, Radio Noise Project R
RGW26021 Mugino, Fourth of the Academy City C
RGW26024 Mugino, Leader of the Dark Organization C
RGW26048 Musashino Milk Konori C
RGW26005 Nunotaba, Genius Scientist R
RGW26005S Nunotaba, Genius Scientist SR
RGW26020 Nunotaba, Student of the Nagatenjouki Academy C
RGW26037 Passion Green Saten R
RGW26059 Passion Orange Mikoto R
RGW26059S Passion Orange Mikoto SR
RGW26038 Passion Pink Uiharu R
RGW26063 Passion Purple Kuroko R
RGW26063S Passion Purple Kuroko SR
RGW26075 Pigtails Kuroko C
RGW26074 Queen Misaki Shokuhou C
RGW26027 Radio Noise Misaka's Little Sister C
RGW26079 Railgun CC
RGW26042 Saten and Uiharu, Good Friend U
RGW26052 Saten at the Hospital C
RGW26044 Saten in Living Room Wear U
RGW26045 Saten, Gossiping U
RGW26051 Saten, Seeking help C
RGW26046 Saten, Sharp-Nosed C
RGW26053 Searching for Stored Value Card U
RGW26032 Siblings CR
RGW26023 Sisters C
RGW26049 Strawberry Oden Uiharu C
RGW26034 Strongest And Weakest CC
RGW26031 Testament U
RGW26019 Touma Kamijou Touma U
RGW26025 Touma, A Certain High School's Student C
RGW26012 Touma, Incredible Power U
RGW26043 Uiharu, Daydreaming U
RGW26039 Uiharu, in Charge of Gathering Information R
RGW26047 Uiharu, Worrying C
RGW26080 Unchangable Past CC
RGW26077 When the Cat's Away C
RGW2608SP Misaka's Little Sister, Radio Noise Project SP
RGW2656SP Mikoto, Where the Coin Goes SP
RGW2658SP Academy City Kuroko SP
RGW2661SP Mental Out Shokuhou SP

2013 Weiss Schwarz Sword Art Online

COMPLETE SET (121)
BOOSTER BOX (20 PACKS) 120.00 150.00
BOOSTER PACK (8 CARDS) 5.00 6.00
RELEASED ON JULY 19, 2013
SAOS20023 A Sworn Promise CR
SAOS20095 Agil, Axe Warrior C
SAOS20017 Asuna - Start of the Battle C
SAOS20005 Asuna Changes Clothes R
SAOS20006 Asuna Dozed Off R
SAOS20001 Asuna Invites to Party RR
SAOS20015 Asuna Jumps to Conclusions C
SAOS20003 Asuna Lays on the Sofa R
SAOS20012 Asuna Replies to a Proposal U
SAOS20011 Asuna Takes Shelter U
SAOS20007R Asuna, Dignified Strength RRR
SAOS2006R Asuna, Dozing Off RRR
SAOS20001S Asuna, Invitation to Party SR
SAOS20003S Asuna, Lays on the Sofa SR
SAOS20007 Asuna's Commanding Strength R
SAOS20008 Asuna's Married Life U
SAOS20014 Asuna's Strong Bond C
SAOS20009 Asuna's True Expression U
SAOS20020 Asuna's Veteran Cooking Skill C
SAOS20062 Beast Tamer Silica C
SAOS20077 Black Swordsman Kirito RR
SAOS20077R Black Swordsman Kirito RRR
SAOS20066 Cornered Silica C
SAOS20059 Cute Mischief, Silica U
SAOS20058 Dagger User, Silica U
SAOS20025 Duel in the Arena CC
SAOS20067 Encouraging Lisbeth C
SAOS20099 End of the World CC
SAOS20041 Fairy King, Oberon C
SAOS20054 Familiar, Pina U
SAOS20073 First Adventure CC
SAOS20033 Gentle Ally, Recon U
SAOS20013 Guild Commander, Heathcliff U
SAOS20068 Happening Silica C
SAOS20042 Healing Magic U
SAOS20019 Heathcliff's Hidden Identity C
SAOS20004 Imprisoned Queen, Asuna R
SAOS20034 Kendo Girl, Suguha U
SAOS20086 Kirito, Appraising U
SAOS20094 Kirito, Becoming Member of Knights of the Blood C
SAOS20090 Kirito, Beginning of Battle C
SAOS20087 Kirito, Casual Kindness U
SAOS20082 Kirito, Discovery of Unique Skill R
SAOS20080 Kirito, For People Important to Him R
SAOS20080S Kirito, For People Important to Him SR
SAOS20079 Kirito, Putting Self on the Battlefield R
SAOS20079R Kirito, Putting Self on the Battlefield RRR
SAOS20093 Kirito, Snow Mountain on Floor 55 C
SAOS20083 Kirito, Solo Player U
SAOS20089 Kirito, Stable Everyday Life C
SAOS20085 Kirito, Strong Bond U
SAOS20078 Klein, Katana Wielder R
SAOS20018 Laughing Coffin C
SAOS20036 Leafa Gets Her Hand Bit U
SAOS2026R Leafa, Magic Swordsman RRR
SAOS2027R Leafa, Pure Wish RRR
SAOS2030S Leafa, Sylph Girl SR
SAOS20035 Leafa's Bashful Expression U
SAOS20039 Leafa's in a Panic C
SAOS20027 Leafa's Pure Wish RR
SAOS20037 Leafa's Sharp Observation C
SAOS20002 Lightning Flash Asuna RR
SAOS20047 Like a Younger Sister, Silica RR
SAOS20063 Like an Idol, Silica C
SAOS20052 Lisbeth Changes Clothes R
SAOS20061 Lisbeth the Blacksmith C
SAOS20048 Lisbeth's Blessings R
SAOS20053 Lisbeth's Determined Confession R
SAOS20060 Lisbeth's Positive Smile U
SAOS20050 Lisbeth's Professional Pride R
SAOS2052S Lizbeth, Changing SR
SAOS20056 Mace User, Lisbeth U
SAOS20026 Magic Swordsman, Leafa RR
SAOS20016 Observer, Kuradeel C
SAOS20065 Pina's Heart C
SAOS20074 Pina's Resurrection CC
SAOS20070 Pneuma Flower U
SAOS20096 Proposal U
SAOS20075 Realization of True Feelings CC
SAOS20043 Recon's Courage C
SAOS20028 Reliable Guide, Leafa R
SAOS20045 Repressed Feelings CC
SAOS20021 Returning to the Front Lines U
SAOS20084 Sachi, Black Cats of the Full Moon U
SAOS20091 Sachi, Blooming Attachment C
SAOS20046 Searching Lisbeth RR
SAOS20072 Seeking Warmth CR
SAOS20022 Self-sacrifice C
SAOS20055 Silica - Like a Date U
SAOS20057 Silica - Start of the Adventure U
SAOS2049S Silica in "Flower Garden" SR
SAOS20049 Silica in the «Flower Garden» R
SAOS20064 Silica Leaves the Party C
SAOS2059R Silica, Cute Mischief RRR
SAOS2047R Silica, Little Sister-like Being RRR
SAOS20069 Silica's Gratitude C
SAOS20051 Silica's Unyielding Trust R
SAOS20044 Spell Chanting CR
SAOS20024 Star Splash CC
SAOS20100 Sudden Farewell CC
SAOS20031 Suguha in Uniform R
SAOS20038 Suguha Out of the Bath C
SAOS20032 Suguha Persuading Herself U
SAOS2029S Suguha, Wavering Feelings SR
SAOS20040 Suguha's Mixed Emotions C
SAOS20029 Suguha's Shaken Feelings R
SAOS20030 Sylph Girl, Leafa R
SAOS20097 Thank You, Goodbye U
SAOS20098 User of "Dual Wield" CR
SAOS20010 Vice Commander, Asuna U
SAOS20071 White Dragon's Lair C
SAOS20081 Yui, Artificial Intelligence R
SAOS20088 Yui, Child of the Two C
SAOS20092 Yui, Lovely Child C
SAOS20076 Yui, Mysterious Girl RR
SAOS2076S Yui, Mysterious Girl SR
SAOS202SP Flash Asuna SP
SAOS2028SP Leafa, Trustworthy Guide SP
SAOS2051SP Silica, Straightforward Trust SP
SAOS2053SP Lizbeth, Determined to Propose SP
SAOS2081SP Yui, Artificial Intelligence SP

2013 Weiss Schwarz Sword Art Online TD Deck

SAOS20T02 Asuna - Start of the Battle
SAOS20105 Asuna Enters the Underground Dungeon
SAOS20T01 Asuna Jumps to Conclusions
SAOS20T04 Asuna Replies to a Proposal
SAOS20T05 Asuna's Veteran Cooking Skill
SAOS20T11 Axe Warrior, Agil
SAOS20103 Beater Kirito
SAOS20T14 Dual-wielding User
SAOS20T13 End of the World
SAOS20T03 Heathcliff's Hidden Identity
SAOS20T12 Kirito - Snow Mountain on Floor 55
SAOS20T07 Kirito - Start of the Battle
SAOS20104 Kirito and Asuna
SAOS20T10 Kirito Joins the Knights of the Blood Oath
SAOS20101 Lead Group Asuna
SAOS20102 Lead Group Kirito
SAOS20T09 Lovely Girl, Yui
SAOS20T06 Star Splash
SAOS20T08 Their Child, Yui

2013 Weiss Schwarz Symphogear G

SGW27020 Always Helping Others Hibiki C
SGW27096 Ame-no-Habakiri R
SGW27090 Aoi Tomosato C
SGW27047 Awakening of Fine U
SGW27010 Berserk Hibiki U
SGW27076 Black Gungnir C
SGW27051 Burst Spear: Gungnir Maria RR
SGW27051S Burst Spear: Gungnir Maria SR
SGW27066 Chris in Gymnastics Cloth C
SGW27052 Chris in Swimsuits RR
SGW27062 Chris, Being Kiddish U
SGW27072 Chris, Being True to Herself C
SGW27068 Chris, Chasing After C
SGW27064 Chris, Loves Songs U
SGW27060 Chris, Overwhelming Firepower R
SGW27060S Chris, Overwhelming Firepower SR
SGW27055 Chris, Own Role R
SGW27055R Chris, Own Role RRR
SGW27059 Chris, Shouldered Burden R
SGW27078 Declaration of War CC
SGW27037 Dr. Ver U
SGW27050 Final Omega Form: Dystopia CC
SGW27049 Final Oppression: Neverland CR
SGW27054 Fine Reincarnate Maria RR
SGW27100 Flash of the Cavalry Blade CC
SGW27021 Fusion Case No. 1 Hibiki C
SGW27085 Genjurou, Hibiki's Master U
SGW27024 Gungnir R
SGW27016 Hibiki at the Fall Cherry Blossom Festival C
SGW27003 Hibiki in Swimsuits R
SGW27003S Hibiki in Swimsuits SR
SGW27005 Hibiki, Entrusted Song R
SGW27001 Hibiki, Gathered Power RR
SGW27001R Hibiki, Gathered Power RRR
SGW27014 Hibiki, Looking Straight U
SGW27077 HORIZON SPEAR CR
SGW27074 Ichii-Bal U
SGW27079 Key of Babylonia CC
SGW27039 Kirika & Shiraba, Friendly Two U
SGW27031 Kirika Akatsuki R
SGW27031S Kirika Akatsuki SR
SGW27038 Kirika, Bright And Energetic U
SGW27036 Kirika, Jumping in U
SGW27018 Kuriyo Andou C
SGW27028 Liuxing CC
SGW27053 Long Range Wide Area Attack Chris RR
SGW27056 Maria Cadenzavna Eve R
SGW27073 Maria, Afte the Battle C
SGW27071 Maria, Determination to Follow Through C
SGW27069 Maria, Kind Girl C
SGW27061 Maria, Songstress of the World U
SGW27065 Maria, the Other Gungnir U
SGW27063 Maria, True Wish U
SGW27019 Miku Released C
SGW27011 Miku, Bearer of Consumables U
SGW27017 Miku, Date After A Long While C
SGW27015 Miku, For the Warm World U
SGW27004 Miku, Imprisoned R
SGW27023 Miku, Power of Purging Misfortune C
SGW27006 Miku, Student at Lydian R
SGW27006S Miku, Student at Lydian SR
SGW27009 Miku, Will to Live U
SGW27013 Miku, Worrying U
SGW27030 Miku's Wish CC
SGW27046 Nephilim Nova C
SGW27043 Noise C
SGW27002 Offensive Spear: Gungnir Hibiki RR
SGW27042 Professor Nastassja C
SGW27057 QUEENS of MUSIC Maria R
SGW27057R QUEENS of MUSIC Maria RRR
SGW27084 QUEENS of MUSIC Tsubasa R
SGW27084R QUEENS of MUSIC Tsubasa RRR
SGW27034 Receptor Children Kirika R
SGW27035 Receptor Children Shirabe R
SGW27080 RED HOT BLAZE CC
SGW27091 Sakuya Fujitaka C
SGW27067 Serena Cadenzavna Eve C
SGW27026 Shen Shou Jing C
SGW27093 Shinji Ogawa C
SGW27008 Shiori Terashima U
SGW27032 Shirabe Tsukuyomi R
SGW27032S Shirabe Tsukuyomi SR
SGW27041 Shirabe, Disguise With Glasses C
SGW27040 Shirabe, Jumping in C
SGW27045 Shirabe, Quiet Girl C
SGW27025 Shooting Star for the Two U
SGW27048 Solomon's Cane U
SGW27097 Stories of Heroes U
SGW27027 Superb Song Combination Arts CR
SGW27007 Superb Song Hibiki R
SGW27075 Thing Truly Wanted to be Done U
SGW27099 Thousand Falling Tears CR
SGW27095 Tsubasa in Gymnastics Cloth C
SGW27083 Tsubasa, Battle-Hardened R
SGW27083S Tsubasa, Battle-Hardened SR
SGW27087 Tsubasa, Blade to Continue U
SGW27086 Tsubasa, Confronting Chris U
SGW27082 Tsubasa, Drawn Blade RR
SGW27088 Tsubasa, Feelings Not Wasted U
SGW27092 Tsubasa, Preparation for the School Festival C
SGW27089S Tsubasa, Singing on the Battlefield SR
SGW27089 Tsubasa, Singing on the Battlefield U
SGW27081 Tsubasa, Strength Training RR
SGW27094 Tsubasa, Student at Lydian C
SGW27029 Vitalization CC
SGW27098 Words Kanade Left Behind C
SGW27070 X-Drive Mode Chris C
SGW27012 X-Drive Mode Hibiki U
SGW27033 X-Drive Mode Kirika R
SGW27058 X-Drive Mode Maria R
SGW27044 X-Drive Mode Shirabe C
SGW27022 Yumi Itaba C
SGW2702SP Offensive Spear: Gungnir Hibiki SP
SGW2715SP Miku, For the Warm World SP
SGW2734SP Receptor Children Kirika SP
SGW2735SP Receptor Children Shirabe SP
SGW2753SP Long Range Wide Area Attack Chris SP
SGW2754SP Fine Reincarnate Maria SP
SGW2782SP Tsubasa, Drawn Blade SP

2013 Weiss Schwarz Vividred Operation

VRW22066 Akane and Momo, Friendly Sisters C
VRW22042 Akane Isshiki RR
VRW22047 Akane, Always Positive R
VRW22047R Akane, Always Positive RRR
VRW22041 Akane, Bright And Straight RR
VRW22051 Akane, Center of Everyone U
VRW22085 Akane, Docking with Aoi R
VRW22004 Akane, Docking with Himawari R
VRW22028 Akane, Docking with Wakaba U
VRW22056 Akane, Looking Straight U
VRW22044 Akane, Mayo Ramen R
VRW22045 Akane, Naive And Romantic R
VRW22045S Akane, Naive And Romantic SR
VRW22069 Akane, Near-Miss Hearts C
VRW22065 Akane, Newspaper Delivery C
VRW22072 Akane, Pallet Suits Equipped C
VRW22048 Akane, Tent Type R
VRW22067 Alone, Catastrophe for Mankind C
VRW22058 Alone, Mysterious Being U
VRW22082 Aoi Futaba RR
VRW22093 Aoi in Casula Clothing C
VRW22084 Aoi in Swimsuits R
VRW22089 Aoi, Bento on the Rooftops U
VRW22088 Aoi, Confession of Truth U
VRW22090R Aoi, Especially Energetic RRR
VRW22090 Aoi, Especially Energetic U
VRW22095 Aoi, First Battle C
VRW22083 Aoi, Graceful Girl R
VRW22083S Aoi, Graceful Girl SR
VRW22087 Aoi, Morning Special Training U
VRW22096 Aoi, Pallet Suits Equipped C
VRW22094 Aoi, Snack Time C
VRW22073 Connected Hearts U
VRW22053 Crow, "Their" Herald U
VRW22074 Feather-Shaped Birthmark C
VRW22040 Fun Competition CC
VRW22016 Himawari (Sunflower) And Himawari C
VRW22009 Himawari in Swimsuits U
VRW22002 Himawari Shinomiya RR
VRW22011S Himawari, Full of Curiosity SR
VRW22011 Himawari, Full of Curiosity U
VRW22007 Himawari, Genius Hacker U
VRW22013 Himawari, Invitation to Study Gathering C
VRW22005 Himawari, Loves Factory R
VRW22001 Himawari, Opening up Her Heart RR
VRW22001R Himawari, Opening up Her Heart RRR
VRW22014 Himawari, Pallet Suits Equipped C
VRW22003 Himawari, Physical Ed Period R
VRW22008 Himawari, Reader Model U
VRW22012 Himawari, Shut-in Girl C
VRW22037 Himawari's Bodyguard U
VRW22017 Himawari's Camera U
VRW22080 I Won't Say Goodbye CC
VRW22064 Kenjirou, Great Scientist C
VRW22062 Mashiro Isshiki C
VRW22033 Mizuha Amagi C
VRW22060 Momo, Hard Working C
VRW22099 Naked Impact CR
VRW22078 Naked Rang CC
VRW22018 Nakid Collider C
VRW22019 New Friends CR
VRW22097 Operation Cocoon Break U
VRW22100 Operation Key Appears CC
VRW22024 Operation Vivid Green R
VRW22046 Operation Vivid Red R
VRW22015 Operation Vivid Yellow C
VRW22086 Operation Vivid Blue R
VRW22075 Power to Save the World CR
VRW22054 Rei in Swimsuits U
VRW22059 Rei Kuroki RR
VRW22052 Rei, Alone U
VRW22043 Rei, Blunt Replies R
VRW22043R Rei, Blunt Replies RRR
VRW22049 Rei, Destructor R
VRW22055 Rei, Docking with Akane U
VRW22070 Rei, Girl of Parallel World C
VRW22063 Rei, Granted Power C
VRW22068 Rei, Mysterious Girl C
VRW22057 Rei, Near-Miss Hearts U
VRW22061 Rei, Physical Ed Period C
VRW22071 Rei, Proof That I Am Myself C
VRW22076 Rei's Mission CC
VRW22038 Special Training Method of Tengen Rishin-ryu C
VRW22098 Surprisingly Powerful C
VRW22091 Texture on Aoi U
VRW22010 Texture on Himawari U
VRW22022 Texture on Wakaba RR
VRW22039 Vivid Blade CR
VRW22081 Vivid Blue RR
VRW22081S Vivid Blue SR
VRW22020 Vivid Collider CC
VRW22025 Vivid Green R
VRW22025S Vivid Green SR
VRW22079 Vivid Momo, Operation CC
VRW22077 Vivid Punch CC
VRW22050 Vivid Red R
VRW22050S Vivid Red SR
VRW22006 Vivid Yellow R
VRW22006S Vivid Yellow SR
VRW22032 Wakaba in Casual Clothing C
VRW22030 Wakaba in Swimsuits U
VRW22026 Wakaba Saegusa R
VRW22035 Wakaba, Attendant to Himawari C
VRW22021 Wakaba, Girl Who Hates Losing RR
VRW22021R Wakaba, Girl Who Hates Losing RRR
VRW22031 Wakaba, Good with Books And Martial Arts U
VRW22027 Wakaba, Loves Cute Things U
VRW22023 Wakaba, Mastery R
VRW22023S Wakaba, Mastery SR
VRW22034 Wakaba, Pallet Suits Equipped C
VRW22029 Wakaba, Physical Ed Period U
VRW22036 Wakaba, True Strength C
VRW22092 Yuuri Shijou C
VRW2202SP Himawari Shinomiya SP
VRW2226SP Wakaba Saegusa SP
VRW2242SP Akane Isshiki SP
VRW2259SP Rei Kuroki SP
VRW2282SP Aoi Futaba SP

2013 Weiss Schwarz Vividred Operation TD

VRW22T10 Casual Clothes, Aoi
VRW22T09 Confession of Truth, Aoi
VRW22T07 Connected Hearts
VRW22T06 Equip Pallete Suit Akane
VRW22T13 Equip Pallete Suit Aoi
VRW22T12 First Battle, Aoi
VRW22103 First Time Docking, Akane
VRW22102 Going to School, Momo
VRW22T02 Great Professor, Kenjirou
VRW22T05 Hearts Missing One Another, Akane
VRW22T04 Mysterious Girl, Rei
22T15 Naked Impact
VRW22T08 Naked Rang
VRW22T03 Newspaper Delivery, Akane
22T14 Operation Appears
VRW22105 Power to Protect, Aoi
VRW22T01 Responsible One, Momo
VRW22101 Snack Time, Akane
VRW22T11 Snack Time, Aoi
VRW22104 The Two Who Became One, Vivid Blue

2014 Weiss Schwarz Angel Beats Re-Edit

COMPLETE SET (153)		
BOOSTER BOX (20 PACKS)	80.00	100.00
BOOSTER PACK (8 CARDS)	4.00	5.00
RELEASED ON JULY 25, 2014		

ABW31054 A Lady's Greatest Happiness CC
ABW31018 A Solitary Angel U
ABW31101 After the Battle CR
ABW31103 Afterlife Battlefront CC
ABW31055 Angel Alight CC
ABW31040 Angel, Enemy of the Battlefront C
ABW31052 Another Time, Another Place CC
ABW31112 Another Time, Another Place CR
ABW31100 Call Me Christ C
ABW31117 Core of the World CR
ABW31110 Crow Song Iwasawa C
ABW31068 Godfather Yuri R
ABW31068R Godfather Yuri RRR
ABW31090 Handle Name Takeyama C
ABW31096 Hinata and Otonashi, Known Partners of the Battlefront C
ABW31088 Hinata, Getting Going C
ABW31092 Hinata, Responding to Feelings C
ABW31087 Hinata, Thinking of Allies C
ABW31044 Hisako, Prideful Guitarist C
ABW31109 Hisako, Sub-Leader C
ABW31109R Hisako, Sub-Leader RRR
ABW31049 Hypnotism C
ABW31042 Irie and Hisako C
ABW31108 Irie, Powerful Performance C
ABW31108R Irie, Powerful Performance RRR
ABW31007 Iwasawa and Hisako, Understanding of Expectations R
ABW31007R Iwasawa and Hisako, Understanding of Expectations RRR
ABW31009 Iwasawa, Cool Beauty R
ABW31009R Iwasawa, Cool Beauty RRR
ABW31037 Iwasawa, Guitar Performer C
ABW31038 Kanade and Otonashi C
ABW31063 Kanade and Yuri, Allied Front R
ABW31063R Kanade and Yuri, Allied Front RRR
ABW31025 Kanade in Straw Hats U
ABW31033 Kanade in Swimsuit C
ABW31106 Kanade Tachibana RR
ABW31005 Kanade, Angel Wings R
ABW31005R Kanade, Angel Wings RRR
ABW31026 Kanade, Being Nonchalant U
ABW31045 Kanade, Clumsy Opposition C
ABW31013 Kanade, Farewell Words R
ABW31013R Kanade, Farewell Words RRR
ABW31012 Kanade, Heart of Yuzuru R
ABW31012R Kanade, Heart of Yuzuru RRR
ABW31019 Kanade, Innocent Eyes U
ABW31027 Kanade, Normal Girl U
ABW31003 Kanade, Operation Meeting R
ABW31003R Kanade, Operation Meeting RRR
ABW31043 Kanade, Pink Cape C
ABW31036 Kanade, Quiet Sight C
ABW31021 Kanade, Reason for Fighting U
ABW31001 Kanade, Sending Everyone Off RR
ABW31001R Kanade, Sending Everyone Off RRR
ABW31010 Kanade, Standing Still R
ABW31010R Kanade, Standing Still RRR
ABW31016 Kanade, Student Council President U
ABW31029 Kanade, Under the Blue Sky U
ABW31111 Kanade, Waking up C
ABW31111R Kanade, Waking up RRR
ABW31008 Kanade, Worrying R
ABW31008R Kanade, Worrying RRR
ABW31006 Kanate, End of Opposition R
ABW31006R Kanate, End of Opposition RRR
ABW31105 Little Braver Yui RR
ABW31105R Little Braver Yui RRR
ABW31097 Matsushita 5-dan C
ABW31050 Memories of GirlDeMo CR
ABW31102 Memories of Previous Life CC
ABW31002 Messenger of God Angel RR
ABW31002R Messenger of God Angel RRR
ABW31020 Naoi, Hypnotist U
ABW31035 Naoi, Self-Proclaimed God C
ABW31047 Naoi, Two-Faced C
ABW31084 Noda and Ooyama C
ABW31089 Noda, Opposition C
ABW31098 Operation Tornado U
ABW31031 Otonashi, Beating Memories C
ABW31070 Otonashi, Conflicting U
ABW31067 Otonashi, Irregularity of the World R
ABW31067R Otonashi, Irregularity of the World RRR
ABW31081 Otonashi, Seeking the Past U
ABW31115 Otonashi, Student Council President C
ABW31030 Otonashi, Understanding Kanade C
ABW31046 Otonashi, Who Has No Memories of His Previous Life C
ABW31053 Power to Protect CC
ABW31104 Returned Feelings CC
ABW31032 Sekine and Irie, Always Together C
ABW31107 Sekine, Loves Mischief C
ABW31107R Sekine, Loves Mischief RRR
ABW31093 Shiina, Arrogant Kunoichi C
ABW31064 Shiina, Martial Art Elite R
ABW31064R Shiina, Martial Art Elite RRR
ABW31066 Shiina, Skill of 100 People R
ABW31066R Shiina, Skill of 100 People RRR
ABW31114 Shiina, Tension MAX C
ABW31080 SSS Yuri U
ABW31094 Takamatsu, Haven't Stripped Enough C
ABW31086 Takeyama, Genius Hacker C
ABW31048 The Song They Wanted to Sing U
ABW31099 Thrust Engine U
ABW31051 Time of Farewell CC
ABW31083 TK, Horrible at English C
ABW31095 TK, Real Identity Unknown C
ABW31017 Yui and Hinata U
ABW31024 Yui and Hinata, Like Couples U
ABW31022 Yui, Always Energetic U
ABW31015 Yui, Assistant of GirlDeMo U
ABW31041 Yui, Baseball Girl C
ABW31039 Yui, Iwasawa's Successor C
ABW31034 Yui, Lowbrow Yet Hard-Working C
ABW31023 Yui, Mounting Position U
ABW31014 Yui, Passionate Girl R
ABW31014R Yui, Passionate Girl RRR
ABW31011 Yui, Realization of Dreams R
ABW31011R Yui, Realization of Dreams RRR
ABW31004 Yui, Romantic Role R
ABW31004R Yui, Romantic Role RRR
ABW31028 Yui, Wanting to Do A Lot U
ABW31074 Yuri in Swimsuit U
ABW31113 Yuri Nakamura RR
ABW31059 Yuri on a Winter Day R
ABW31059R Yuri on a Winter Day RRR
ABW31072 Yuri, Antagonist U
ABW31077 Yuri, Commander U
ABW31062 Yuri, Daunting Gaze R
ABW31062R Yuri, Daunting Gaze RRR
ABW31116 Yuri, Demon-like Commander C
ABW31082 Yuri, Executing Operation C
ABW31078 Yuri, Graduating from this World U
ABW31060 Yuri, Invitation to the Battlefront R
ABW31060R Yuri, Invitation to the Battlefront RRR
ABW31091 Yuri, Kanade's Friend C
ABW31057 Yuri, Opposition Cleared RR
ABW31057R Yuri, Opposition Cleared RRR
ABW31079 Yuri, Path of Each's Own U
ABW31085 Yuri, Pillar for Everyone C
ABW31069 Yuri, Resisting the Absurd Destiny R
ABW31069R Yuri, Resisting the Absurd Destiny RRR
ABW31061 Yuri, Role of Big Sister R
ABW31061R Yuri, Role of Big Sister RRR
ABW31058 Yuri, Solo Activities RR
ABW31058R Yuri, Solo Activities RRR
ABW31056 Yuri, Strategic Provokes RR
ABW31056R Yuri, Strategic Provokes RRR
ABW31075 Yuri, Time to Depart U
ABW31076 Yuri, Unresonable Request U
ABW31065 Yusa, Messenger R
ABW31065R Yusa, Messenger RRR
ABW31073 Yusa, Operator U
ABW31071 Yusa, Talented Radio Operator U
ABW31106S Kanade Tachibana SP
ABW31110S Crow Song Iwasawa SP
ABW31113S Yuri Nakamura SP

2014 Weiss Schwarz Angel Beats Re-Edit TD

ABW31T01 Sekine and Irie, Good Pair
ABW31T02 Yui, Big Fan of GirlDeMo
ABW31T03 Iwasawa, Charismatic Vocal
ABW31T04 Kanade, Former Strong Enemy
ABW31T05 Hisako, Sisterly
ABW31T06 Kanade, the Girl Called Angel
ABW31T07 Yui, Second Generation Vocalist
ABW31T08 Girl Who Fights Destiny
ABW31T09 Iwasawa, Leader of GirlDeMo
ABW31T10 Maradona Yui
ABW31T11 Angel's Mapo Tofu
ABW31T12 Operation Tornado feat Yui
ABW31T13 Fujimaki and Ooyama
ABW31T14 Takamatsu, Looks Thinner in Clothing
ABW31T15 Hinata, Baseball Boy
ABW31T16 Fujimaki, Biting Dog
ABW31T17 Takamatsu, Unleashed Self
ABW31T18 Yuri, Can't Forgive God
ABW31T19 TK, Sunny Dancer
ABW31T20 Kanade and Yuri, Almost Like Sisters
ABW31T21 Battle Against Shadow
ABW31T22 Kanade, Model Student
ABW31T23 Yuri, Luck of the Draw?
ABW31T24 Otonashi and Kanade on a Winter Day

2014 Weiss Schwarz Crayon Shin-chan

CSS28032 Action Mask R
CSS28065 Ageo and Matsuzaka and Yoshinaga C
CSS28028 Ai Suotome R
CSS28049 All-Star CC
CSS28020 Angry Shiro C
CSS28039 Bo-chan in Swimsuit C
CSS28059 Bo-chan, Divider U
CSS28037 Bo-chan, Secretly Skilled U
CSS28090 Boushichi, Ancestor C
CSS28008 Buriburizaemon U
CSS28098 Extended Time CR
CSS28074 Familiar Scent CC
CSS28021 Family Portrait U
CSS28073 Floating Happiness CC
CSS28024 Handkerchief of Important Memories CC
CSS28058 Himawari, Greeting Everyone U
CSS28010 Himawari, Loves Shiny Stuff U
CSS28019 Himawari, Mischievous Child C
CSS28005 Himawari, Strongest 0-Year-Old R
CSS28088 Himawari, Watching over C
CSS28068 Himawari, World's Fair Defense Squad C
CSS28094 Hiroshi Thinking of Child C
CSS28051 Hiroshi, as "Hiroshi SUN" RR
CSS28051S Hiroshi, as "Hiroshi SUN" SR
CSS28077 Hiroshi, Battle Preparation RR
CSS28077S Hiroshi, Battle Preparation SR
CSS28002 Hiroshi, Father of the House RR
CSS28014 Hiroshi, Joy of Family C
CSS28060 Hiroshi, Joy of Having Family U
CSS28078 Hiroshi, Looking up at the Blue Sky R
CSS28081 Hiroshi, Positioning Weapon R
CSS28016 Hiroshi, Section Chief C
CSS28067 Hiroshi, World's Fair Defense Squad C
CSS28071 Hiroshi's Boots U
CSS28075 I Will Protect the Future CR
CSS28075R I Will Protect the Future RRR
CSS28018 Kantam Robo C
CSS28027 Kasukabe Defense Organization RR
CSS28027S Kasukabe Defense Organization SR
CSS28045 Kazama-kun in Swimsuit C
CSS28031 Kazama-kun, Elite Kindergartener R
CSS28054 Kazama-kun, Unease Stare R
CSS28084 Kazuma, Ancestor U
CSS28062 Ken and Chako U
CSS28033 Kindergarten Chief, Scary-Looking U
CSS28096 Letter from Myself U
CSS28038 Masao-kun in Swimsuit C
CSS28070 Masao-kun, Berserking C
CSS28043 Masao-kun, Timid Personality C
CSS28080 Matabei, Blue Sky Samurai R
CSS28086 Matabei, Strict Ijiri U
CSS28034 Micchi and Yoshirin U
CSS28042 Mimiko Sakura C
CSS28055 Misae, as "Magical Girl Misarin" R
CSS28055S Misae, as "Magical Girl Misarin" SR
CSS28083 Misae, Battle Preparation U
CSS28009 Misae, Joy of Family U
CSS28006 Misae, Mother's Love R
CSS28015 Misae, Special Noogie Attack C
CSS28066 Misae, World's Fair Defense Squad C
CSS28023 My House is Gone CR
CSS28035 Nanako, Female College Student Love Interest U
CSS28095 Nene, Ancestor C
CSS28036 Nene, Precocious Girl U
CSS28044 Nene-chan in Swimsuit C
CSS28064 Nene-chan, Crane's Roar C
CSS28025 New Family CC
CSS28025R New Family RRR
CSS28012 Nohara Household, Happy Family U
CSS28004 Normal Shinnosuke R
CSS28004S Normal Shinnosuke SR
CSS28097 Oath of Warrior U
CSS28100 One Drop CC
CSS28100R One Drop RRR
CSS28089 Oomasa, Ancestor C
CSS28046 Plushie BunnyOchan U
CSS28085 Ren, Princess of Kasuga Castle U
CSS28040 Saitama Crimson Scorpions C
CSS28022 Scent of Jasmine U
CSS28050 Shin-chan's Love CC
CSS28029 Shinnosuke, Anger Spilling Over R
CSS28026 Shinnosuke, Being Silly RR
CSS28026S Shinnosuke, Being Silly SR
CSS28053 Shinnosuke, Big Brother Taking Care of Little Sister R
CSS28079 Shinnosuke, Big-But R
CSS28069 Shinnosuke, Carrying out the Mission C
CSS28056 Shinnosuke, Driver R
CSS28093 Shinnosuke, Escort Role C
CSS28007 Shinnosuke, Fateful Mischief R
CSS28092 Shinnosuke, Feelings to the Sky C
CSS28052 Shinnosuke, for the Future RR
CSS28001 Shinnosuke, Frivolous RR
CSS28057 Shinnosuke, Greeting Everyone R
CSS28013 Shinnosuke, Kindergartener Who Can't Summon a Gust C
CSS28082 Shinnosuke, Not Afraid of Anything R
CSS28087 Shinnosuke, Oath of a Man U
CSS28030 Shinnosuke, Runaway Youth R
CSS28076 Shinnosuke, Silly Samurai RR
CSS28076S Shinnosuke, Silly Samurai SR
CSS28041 Shinnosuke, Talented C
CSS28011 Shinnosuke, the Brassiere Mask Returns U
CSS28063 Shinnosuke, World's Fair Defense Squad C
CSS28091 Shiro, Dig Here Woof Woof C
CSS28061 Shiro, Driver? U
CSS28003 Shiro, Part of the Family R
CSS28003S Shiro, Part of the Family SR
CSS28017 Shiro, Taking a Walk C
CSS28048 Singing Time CR
CSS28048R Singing Time RRR
CSS28072 Snack, Cascabian U
CSS28099 Uncontainable Feelings CC
CSS28047 World of Dreams U
CSS2801SP Shinnosuke, Frivolous SP
CSS2802SP Hiroshi, Father of the House SP
CSS2805SP Himawari, Strongest 0-Year-Old SP
CSS2806SP Misae, Mother's Love SP

2014 Weiss Schwarz Crayon Shin-chan TD

1 Always Together
2 Butt Alien
3 Family is Nice to Have
4 Himawari, Adorable Little Sister
5 Himawari, Child's Puppy-Eye Attack
6 Himawari, Child's Puppy-Eye Attack RRR
7 Himawari, Full of Energy
8 Hiroshi, No 1 Japanese Salaryman
9 Misae, Strong Mother
10 Nohara Household Go-
11 Shinnosuke in Pajama
12 Shinnosuke Nohara
13 Shinnosuke, Friendly Siblings
14 Shinnosuke, Full of Energy
15 Shinnosuke, Kindergartener Who Summons the Storm
16 Shinnosuke, Kindergartener Who Summons the Storm SR
17 Shinnosuke, Snack Time
18 Shinnosuke, Wannabe Hero
19 Shiro, Cotton Candy Dog
20 Shiro, Perplexed

2014 Weiss Schwarz Da Capo Sakura Saku Extra

DCWE2004 Aisia, Magic to Fall in Love R
DCWE2014 Alone Aisia C
DCWE2030 Anzu, Words Forgot to Say C
DC3WE2026 Aoi, Girl of Many Mysteries C
DC3WE2020 Charles, Autumn of Appetite C
DCWE2017 Dreamlike Scenery C
DCWE2012 End of the Dream Story Sakura C
DCWE2024 Erica, the Usual Disturbance C
DC3WE2008 Himeno, Summer Memories R
DCWE2016 I Will Not Forget. C
DCWE2005 Koko, Dressed Up R
DCWE2018 Kotori, By Your Side C
DC3WE2002 Magician of Justice Girl R
DCWE2013 Mahiru, Christmas Memory C
DCWE2025 Miharu, Important Wish C
DC3WE2023 Mikoto in Swimsuits C
DCWE2021 Minatsu in Swimsuits C
DCWE2019 Nanaka, Overslept C
DCWE2007 Nemu, Always Together R
DCWE2001 Otome, Cherry-Colored Confession R
DC3WE2009 Ricca, Welcoming New Students! R
DC3WE2027 Sakura, Pleasant Big Sister C
DCWE2011 Sakura, Returned Head of the Academy C
DCWE2003 Sakura, World of Reunion R
DC3WE2010 Sara, New Club Member R
DC3WE2022 Shiki in Swimsuits C
DC3WE2029 Sumomo, For the Smile C
DCWE2015 Unwithering Cherry Blossom C
DC3WE2028 Youko, Cute Club President C
DCWE2006 Yume, Honest Feelings R
DC3WE2008S Himeno, Summer Memories SP
DC3WE2009S Ricca, Welcoming New Students! SP
DC3WE2010S Sara, New Club Member SP

2014 Weiss Schwarz Gigant Shooter Tsukasa Extra

GSTSE2225 Ataru, Blessed Child of the Fertile Land C
GSTSE2215 Ataru, Burnt out R
GSTSE2218 Ataru, Pinpoint Tsukkomi R
GSTSE2221 Ataru, Silent Fighting Will C
GSTSE2212 Crunching Water Cutter C
GSTSE2222 Delinquent Elementary School Student C
GSTSE2211 Galactica Dragon C
GSTSE2230 Great Bison Impact C
GSTSE2224 Kirito, Dark Magician of the Abyss C
GSTSE2223 Kirito, Hidden Message in Speech C
GSTSE2214 Kirito, Part of the Power R
GSTSE2219 Kirito, Secretly Skilled R
GSTSE2213 Manabu, Admiration for Tsukasa R
GSTSE2228 Manabu, Moved to Tears C
GSTSE2216 Manabu, Ready for Battle R
GSTSE2227 Manabu, Refreshing Breeze Blowing Through C
GSTSE2205 Miruko, Goddess of the Clear Water R
GSTSE2202 Miruko, Hates to Lose R
GSTSE2203 Miruko, Tsundere Beauty R
GSTSE2207 Miruko, Victory for the Dream C
GSTSE2220 Ruri, Adorable Beauty C
GSTSE2217 Ruri, Ataru's Little Sister R
GSTSE2226 Ruri, the Tiny Strength C
GSTSE2229 Shining Grasshopper C
GSTSE2210 Tsukasa, Illegitimate Child of the Burning Flames C
GSTSE2204 Tsukasa, Loves Gigant R
GSTSE2209 Tsukasa, Searching for King Manger C
GSTSE2201 Tsukasa, Stable Gigant Brain R
GSTSE2208 Tsukasa's Father, Missing C
GSTSE2206 Tsukasa's Mother, Surprisingly Skilled C
GSTSE223SP Miruko, Tsundere Beauty SP
GSTSE224SP Tsukasa, Loves Gigant SP
GSTSE2213SP Manabu, Admiration for Tsukasa SP
GSTSE2218SP Ataru, Pinpoint Tsukkomi SP

2014 Weiss Schwarz Girl Friend Beta TD

GFW33T08 Chihaya Something
GFW33T20 Chloe Lemaire, Everyone's Place
GFW33T03 Chloe Lemaire, Japanese Culture
GFW33T01 Elena Mochizuki, Amusement
GFW33T18 Elena Mochizuki, Fierce Shots on the Battlefield
GFW33T19 Fumio Murakami, A Book to You
GFW33T16 Fumio Murakami, Looking Up at the Starry Sky
GFW33T05 Ichigo, Teaching you
GFW33T12 Isuzu Shiranui, Nervous Visit
GFW33T17 Kokomi Shiina, After Class
GFW33T13 Kokomi Shiina, Sports Camp
GFW33T07 Mimatsuri Kaga, Reading

GFW33T06 Momoko Asahina, Fluffy Keyboard
GFW33T04 Nae Yuuki, Stagehand as a Main Role
GFW33T15 Nice Shoot
GFW33T02 Nonoka Sasahara, Wishing to Get Better
GFW33T14 Return Gift of White Day
GFW33T10 Rui Kamijou, Childhood Friend's Bento Box
GFW33T11 Saya Kagurazaka, Reverse Interviewing
GFW33T09 Strike!
GFW33T19S Fumio Murakami, A Book to You SP
GFW33T16SP Fumio Murakami, Looking Up at the Starry Sky SP
GFW33T17SP Kokomi Shiina, After Class SP
GFW33T18SP Elena Mochizuki, Fierce Shots on the Battlefield SP
GFW33T20SP Chloe Lemaire, Everyone's Place SP

2014 Weiss Schwarz Haruhi Extra

SYWE0915 Bamboo Leaf Rhapsody Haruhi R
SYWE0921 End of Summer C
SYWE0919a Endless Eight C
SYWE0919b Endless Eight C
SYWE0919c Endless Eight C
SYWE0919d Endless Eight C
SYWE0919e Endless Eight C
SYWE0919f Endless Eight C
SYWE0919g Endless Eight C
SYWE0919h Endless Eight C
SYWE0919i Endless Eight C
SYWE0912 Guiding Role C
SYWE0917 Haruhi in Swimsuits C
SYWE0914 Haruhi, Flower Viewing R
SYWE0916 Haruhi, Girl Who Changes the World C
SYWE0918 Haruhi, Summer Festival C
SYWE0920 I Am Here C
SYWE0902 Koizumi, Talking about Stars C
SYWE0901 Kyon & Koizumi C
SYWE0906 Kyon & Mikuru, Time Travel R
SYWE0903 Kyon, Looking Up at the Sky C
SYWE0904 Kyon's Little Sister, 5th Grader C
SYWE0923 Magician Nagato & Shamisen R
SYWE0907 Mikuru (Big), Meeting Mikuru R
SYWE0911 Mikuru, Cicada Catching Competition C
SYWE0910 Mikuru, Flower Viewing C
SYWE0909 Mikuru, Part-Time Job C
SYWE0905 Mikuru, Wishing upon the Stars R
SYWE0926 Nagato, Flower Viewing C
SYWE0922 Nagato, Observer R
SYWE0925 Nagato, Standby Mode C
SYWE0924 Nagato, Summer Festival R
SYWE0927 Nights of Remaining Two Weeks C
SYWE0913 Super Director Haruhi R
SYWE0908 Tsuruya-san, Energetic Senpai C

2014 Weiss Schwarz Hatsune Miku Project Diva F 2nd

COMPLETE SET (164)
BOOSTER BOX (20 PACKS) 60.00 80.00
BOOSTER PACK (8 CARDS) 3.00 4.00
RELEASED ON FEBRUARY 6, 2015
PDS29115 A Thousand Year Solo (DIVA edit) CC
PDS29115S A Thousand Year Solo (DIVA edit) SR
PDS29087a Akatsuki Arrival CC
PDS29087b Akatsuki Arrival CC
4 Megurine Luka Original (F 2nd) SP
PDS29087S Akatsuki Arrival SR
PDS29027 Always Ringing Hatsune Miku RR+
PDS29027R Always Ringing Hatsune Miku RRR
PDS29082 Blackjack U
PDS29113 Cantarella ~grace edition~ CR
PDS29113S Cantarella ~grace edition~ SR
PDS29020a Colorful x Melody U
PDS29020b Colorful x Melody U
PDS29055 DECORATOR CC
PDS29055S DECORATOR SR
PDS29085 Destroy, Destroy CR
PDS29085S Destroy, Destroy SR
PDS29084 Double Lariat CR
PDS29084S Double Lariat SR
PDS29053 Double-Sided Lovers CR
PDS29053S Double-Sided Lovers SR
PDS29021 Envy Catwalk C
PDS29116 erase or zero CC
PDS29116S erase or zero SR
PDS29056 Glory 3usi9 CC
PDS29056S Glory 3usi9 SR
PDS29090a Hatsuen Miku Rosa Bianca R
PDS29090b Hatsuen Miku Rosa Bianca R
PDS29080 Hatsune Miku Avant-Garde C
PDS29061 Hatsune Miku Bless You R
PDS29061R Hatsune Miku Bless You RRR
PDS29073 Hatsune Miku Butterfly C
PDS29040 Hatsune Miku Cat Girl C
PDS29013a Hatsune Miku Chat Noir C
PDS29013b Hatsune Miku Chat Noir C
PDS29019 Hatsune Miku Colorful Drop C
PDS29046 Hatsune Miku Conflict C
PDS29042 Hatsune Miku Dimension C
PDS29036 Hatsune Miku Flouncy Pastel U
PDS29104 Hatsune Miku Flower Carriage C
PDS29103 Hatsune Miku Flower Language C
PDS29043 Hatsune Miku Gothic C
PDS29045 Hatsune Miku Heart Hunter C
PDS29037 Hatsune Miku Infinity U
PDS29011 Hatsune Miku Liar U
PDS29028 Hatsune Miku Magician RR
PDS29028R Hatsune Miku Magician RRR
PDS29106a Hatsune Miku Marionette C
PDS29106b Hatsune Miku Marionette C
PDS29038R Hatsune Miku Meteorite RRR
PDS29038 Hatsune Miku Meteorite U
PDS29075 Hatsune Miku Miku Hood C
PDS29107 Hatsune Miku Moonlight Swallowtail C
PDS29044 Hatsune Miku Natural C
PDS29048 Hatsune Miku no Gekishou R
PDS29041 Hatsune Miku Noble C
PDS29032 Hatsune Miku Orange Blossom R
PDS29032R Hatsune Miku Orange Blossom RRR
PDS29033 Hatsune Miku Orbit R
PDS29101 Hatsune Miku Rasetsu And Mukuro U
PDS29105 Hatsune Miku Regret C
PDS29031 Hatsune Miku School R
PDS29035 Hatsune Miku Seven-Colored Line R
PDS29035R Hatsune Miku Seven-Colored Line RRR
PDS29034 Hatsune Miku Siren R
PDS29034R Hatsune Miku Siren RRR
PDS29015 Hatsune Miku Street Pop C
PDS29047 Hatsune Miku Stroll Style C
PDS29068 Hatsune Miku Supreme U
PDS29029 Hatsune Miku V3 RR
PDS29029R Hatsune Miku V3 RRR
PDS29097 Hatsune Miku VintageDress U
PDS29030 Hatsune Miku White Dress R
PDS29026 Hatsune Miku, Resonating DIVA RR+
PDS29026X Hatsune Miku, Resonating DIVA XR
PDS29096b Kagamine Len Aitetsu Fox Spirit U
PDS29096a Kagamine Len Aitetsu U
PDS29109 Kagamine Len Ayasaki C
PDS29017 Kagamine Len Ciel C
PDS29099 Kagamine Len Eraser U
PDS29003 Kagamine Len Original (F 2nd) R
PDS29003X Kagamine Len Original (F 2nd) XR
PDS29005 Kagamine Len Punkish R
PDS29014 Kagamine Len School Jersey C
PDS29006 Kagamine Len Strange Dark R
PDS29008 Kagamine Len White Bear in Love U
PDS29012 Kagamine Len White Edge U
PDS29018 Kagamine Rin Cheerful Candy C
PDS29007 Kagamine Rin Dreaming Panda R
PDS29009 Kagamine Rin Fairy Dress U
PDS29010 Kagamine Rin Faker U
PDS29004 Kagamine Rin Kagerou R
PDS29001 Kagamine Rin Original (F 2nd) RR+
PDS29001X Kagamine Rin Original (F 2nd) XR
PDS29002 Kagamine Rin Reactor RR
PDS29016 Kagamine Rin Soleil C
PDS29108 Kagamine Rin Sunflower C
PDS29095b Kagamine Rin Suou Fox Spirit U
PDS29095a Kagamine Rin Suou U
PDS29093 KAITO Autumn Shower R
PDS29110 KAITO Cyber Cat C
PDS29094 KAITO Holiday U
PDS29092 KAITO Original (F 2nd) R
PDS29092R KAITO Original (F 2nd) RRR
PDS29098 KAITO Originator U
PDS29091a KAITO Rosa Blue R
PDS29091b KAITO Rosa Blue R
PDS29089 KAITO V3 RR
PDS29089R KAITO V3 RRR
PDS29100 KAITO Violet U
PDS29102 KAITO White Blazer C
PDS29112 Knife C
PDS29022 Kokoro CR
PDS29022S Kokoro SR
PDS29086 Luka Luka Night Fever CC
PDS29086S Luka Luka Night Fever SR
PDS29058 Megurine Luka Cybernation RR
PDS29058R Megurine Luka Cybernation RRR
PDS29065 Megurine Luka Floral U
PDS29074 Megurine Luka Flower C
PDS29066 Megurine Luka Fraulein U
PDS29071 Megurine Luka Hard Rock U
PDS29057 Megurine Luka Original (F 2nd) RR+
PDS29057X Megurine Luka Original (F 2nd) XR
PDS29078 Megurine Luka Recruitor C
PDS29081 Megurine Luka Successor C
PDS29064a Megurine Luka Temptation R
PDS29064b Megurine Luka Temptation R
PDS29064R Megurine Luka Temptation RRR
PDS29077 Megurine Luka VF Suit C
PDS29060 Megurine Luka Witch Girl Style R
PDS29070 MEIKO Blazing U
PDS29063 MEIKO Crimson Leaves R
PDS29076 MEIKO Fluffy Coat C
PDS29079 MEIKO Lorelei C
PDS29072 MEIKO Marine Ribbon C
PDS29059 MEIKO Original (F 2nd) RR
PDS29059R MEIKO Original (F 2nd) RRR
PDS29067 MEIKO Scarlet U
PDS29069 MEIKO Taisei Romance U
PDS29050 Melt C
PDS29024 Meltdown CC
PDS29024S Meltdown SR
PDS29039 Miku Miku ni Shite Ageru~ (Shite Yanyo) U
PDS29051 Miracle Paint C
PDS29052 Packaged CR
PDS29052S Packaged SR
PDS29111 Pair of Wintry Winds U
PDS29025 Paradichlorobenzene CC
PDS29025S Paradichlorobenzene SR
PDS29088 Reaching Everywhere Hatsune Miku RR
PDS29088R Reaching Everywhere Hatsune Miku RRR
PDS29114 Romeo And Cinderella CR
PDS29114S Romeo And Cinderella SR
PDS29062 Sakune Meiko Original R
PDS29023 soundless voice CR
PDS29023S soundless voice SR
PDS29054 SPiCa - 39's Giving Day Edition- CC
PDS29054S SPiCa - 39's Giving Day Edition- SR
PDS29049 Two Dimension Dream Fever U
PDS29083 World is Mine C
PDS2901SP Kagamine Rin Original (F 2nd) SP
PDS2903SP Kagamine Len Original (F 2nd) SP
PDS2926SP Hatsune Miku, Resonating DIVA SP

2014 Weiss Schwarz Idolmaster Dearly Stars Extra

IMSE0420 Ai & Mai, Lively Parent And Child C
IMSE0416 Ai, Straightforward Wherever R
IMSE0424 Ai, Talent As Idol C
IMSE0425 ALIVE C
IMSE0433 Azusa, Thinking of Dreams C
IMSE0417 Challenging the Limits Ai R
IMSE0429 Chihaya, Advice of Songs R
IMSE0434 CINERIA, Net Idol C
IMSE0422 Dashing Mini-Tank Ai C
IMSE0414 Dazzling World C
IMSE0428 Eri Mizutani R
IMSE0431 Eri, Group Lesson C
IMSE0435 Eri, Inherited Dream C
IMSE0432 Eri, Multi-Artist C
IMSE0427 Eri, Quite Incredulous R
IMSE0423 Haruka, Special Judge C
IMSE0405 Hibiki, Tropical Girl R
IMSE0403 Iori, Idol Favorite C
IMSE0418 Mai, Legendary Idol R
IMSE0415 Makoto, Special Coach R
IMSE0419 Manami, Supporting Role C
IMSE0412 Miki, Self-Confidence Towards Songs C
IMSE0436 Precog C
IMSE0408 President Ishikawa C
IMSE0430 Producer Ozaki C
IMSE0426 Ritsuko, Premonition of Incident R
IMSE0410 Ryou & Yumeko, Uneven Pair C
IMSE0404 Ryou, A Step Towards Dreams R
IMSE0406 Ryou, Big Secret R
IMSE0409 Ryou, Idol's Cousin C
IMSE0407 Ryou, Not Giving Up Dreams R
IMSE0411 Takane, Beautiful Girl C
IMSE0401 Twin High Five! Ami & Mami C
IMSE0421 Yayoi, Everyone's Idol C
IMSE0402 Yukiho, Kind Senpai C
IMSE0413 Yumeko Sakurai C

2014 Weiss Schwarz Idolmaster Movie

IMS30086a 765 Productions, Across the Sea of Light! U
IMS30086b 765 Productions, Across the Sea of Light! U
IMS30086c 765 Productions, Across the Sea of Light! U
IMS30037a 765 Productions, Bursting! U
IMS30037b 765 Productions, Bursting! U
IMS30037c 765 Productions, Bursting! U
IMS30062a 765 Productions, Coming Together! U
IMS30062b 765 Productions, Coming Together! U
IMS30062c 765 Productions, Coming Together! U
IMS30073 765 Productions, Fight-!! CR
IMS30036a 765 Productions, Goal is Top Idol! U
IMS30036b 765 Productions, Goal is Top Idol! U
IMS30036c 765 Productions, Goal is Top Idol! U
IMS30078 765 Productions, Seven-Colored Story R
IMS30012a 765 Productions, To the Stage With Everyone! U
IMS30012b 765 Productions, To the Stage With Everyone! U
IMS30012c 765 Productions, To the Stage With Everyone! U
IMS30029 Ami, Beyond the Brilliant Future R
IMS30029S Ami, Beyond the Brilliant Future SR
IMS30041 Ami, Determination to Appear on Stage C
IMS30047 Ami, Knowing the Time of Separation C
IMS30028 Azusa, Beyond the Brilliant Future! R
IMS30028S Azusa, Beyond the Brilliant Future! SR
IMS30043 Azusa, Determination to Appear on Stage C
IMS30034 Azusa, Lost as Usual U
IMS30046 Azusa, Thinking of Everyone C
IMS30089 Chihaya, Advancing Forward C
IMS30077 Chihaya, Beyond the Brilliant Future! RR
IMS30077S Chihaya, Beyond the Brilliant Future! SR
IMS30092 Chihaya, Determination to Appear on Stage C
IMS30083 Chihaya, Heading for an Overseas Recording Session U
IMS30096 Chihaya's Camera U
IMS30075 Fate of the World CC
IMS30021 Glowsticks U
IMS30048 GO MY WAY!! CR
IMS30065 Hamzo, Loves Sunflower Seeds! C
IMS30054 Haruka as the Leader R
IMS30051 Haruka, Beyond the Brilliant Future! RR
IMS30051S Haruka, Beyond the Brilliant Future! SR
IMS30063 Haruka, Nominated as Leader C
IMS30058 Haruka, Start of the Training Camp! U
IMS30053 Hibiki, Beyond the Brilliant Future R
IMS30053S Hibiki, Beyond the Brilliant Future SR
IMS30067 Hibiki, Determination to Appear on Stage C
IMS30059 Hibiki, Holding Back Tears U
IMS30060 Hibiki, Popular With Kids! U
IMS30027 Iori, Beyond the Brilliant Future! RR
IMS30027S Iori, Beyond the Brilliant Future! SR
IMS30045 Iori, Daily Life Slowing Changing C
IMS30042 Iori, Determination to Appear on Stage C
IMS30033 Iori, Fully Drenched U
IMS30009 Kotori, Thinking About the Rain U
IMS30022 Kotori-san Daydreaming U
IMS30023 Kotori-san Running Through CR
IMS30017 Kotori-san, Worked Hard Today Too C
IMS30097 Kotori-san's Rain Doll U
IMS30061 Like True Self Miki U
IMS30032 Live in the Moment Ami R
IMS30030 Live in the Moment Azusa R
IMS30082 Live in the Moment Chihaya R
IMS30056 Live in the Moment Haruka R
IMS30055 Live in the Moment Hibiki R
IMS30031 Live in the Moment Iori R
IMS30002 Live in the Moment Kotori-san RR
IMS30081 Live in the Moment Makoto R
IMS30057 Live in the Moment Miki R
IMS30005 Live in the Moment R
IMS30039 Live in the Moment Ritsuko R
IMS30079 Live in the Moment Takane R
IMS30003 Live in the Moment Yayoi R
IMS30004 Live in the Moment Yukiho R
IMS30071 Macthing Practice Outfit U
IMS30080 Makoto, Beyond the Brilliant Future! R
IMS30080S Makoto, Beyond the Brilliant Future! SR
IMS30090 Makoto, Determination to Appear on Stage C
IMS30087 Makoto, Fierce Battle in the Rain! U
IMS30088 Makoto, Swimming After Practice C
IMS30016 Mami, Ancient Legend Story C
IMS30035 Mami, Ancient Legend Story U
IMS30011 Mami, Being Worried U
IMS30006 Mami, Beyond the Brilliant Future! R
IMS30006S Mami, Beyond the Brilliant Future! SR
IMS30013 Mami, Determination to Appear on Stage C
IMS30024 MASTERPIECE CC
IMS30049 MASTERPIECE CC
IMS30074 MASTERPIECE CC
IMS30099 MASTERPIECE CC
IMS30025 Meeting After Dinner! CC
IMS30052 Miki, Beyond the Brilliant Future RR
IMS30052S Miki, Beyond the Brilliant Future SR
IMS30066 Miki, Determination to Appear on Stage C
IMS30064 Miki, Hollywood Debut! C
IMS30098 Movie Sleeping Beauty CR
IMS30069 Old Friend and President Takagi C
IMS30070 President Takagi, Looking to Tomorrow C
IMS30068 Producer, Day of Departure C
IMS30091 Producer, to Advance Himself C
IMS30019 Producer, Watching the Growth C
IMS30100 Rainbow-Colored Miracle CC
IMS30050a Ramune-Colored Youth CC
IMS30050b Ramune-Colored Youth CC
IMS30050c Ramune-Colored Youth CC
IMS30026 Ritsuko, Beyond the Brilliant Future! RR
IMS30026S Ritsuko, Beyond the Brilliant Future! SR
IMS30044 Ritsuko, Female Teacher C
IMS30038 Ritsuko, One Thought U
IMS30040 Ritsuko, Sparta-Style Lecturing C
IMS30085 Takane, Appearing at Dinner! U
IMS30076 Takane, Beyond the Brilliant Future! RR
IMS30076S Takane, Beyond the Brilliant Future! SR
IMS30094 Takane, Determination to Appear on Stage C
IMS30084 Takane, Telling A Legend U
IMS30104 To the Highest Stage! PR
IMS30095 Touma, Unexpected Reunion C
IMS30072 Weekly Entertainment Rush U
IMS30008 Yayoi, Acting in a Commercial U
IMS30007S Yayoi, Beyond the Brilliant Future! SR
IMS30007 Yayoi, Beyond the Brilliant Future! R
IMS30015 Yayoi, Determination to Appear on Stage C
IMS30018 Yayoi, Exciting Training Camp! C
IMS30093 Yoshizawa, Reporter C
IMS30020 Yukiho, Appearing on the Stage C
IMS30010 Yukiho, As a Veteran U
IMS30001 Yukiho, Beyond the Brilliant Future! RR
IMS30001S Yukiho, Beyond the Brilliant Future! SR
IMS30014 Yukiho, Determination to Appear on Stage C
IMS3002SP Live in the Moment Kotori-san SP
IMS3003SP Live in the Moment Yayoi SP
IMS3004SP Live in the Moment Yukiho SP
IMS3005SP Live in the Moment SP
IMS3030SP Live in the Moment Azusa SP
IMS3031SP Live in the Moment Iori SP
IMS3032SP Live in the Moment Ami SP
IMS3039SP Live in the Moment Ritsuko SP
IMS3055SP Live in the Moment Hibiki SP
IMS3056SP Live in the Moment Haruka SP
IMS3057SP Live in the Moment Miki SP
IMS3079SP Live in the Moment Takane SP
IMS3081SP Live in the Moment Makoto SP
IMS3082SP Live in the Moment Chihaya SP

2014 Weiss Schwarz Idolmaster Movie Promos

IMS30103 Everyone's Breath
IMS30P03 Haruka, Moving On to the Future with Everyone
IMS30101 New Stage Costumes
IMS30P01 Rivals!? Haruka & Miki
IMS30P02 The Sleeping Beauty Haruka & Miki & Chihaya
IMS30102 Typical 765 Productions

2014 Weiss Schwarz Kantai Collection

KCS25115 Abukuma, 6th Nagara-class Light Cruiser C
KCS25017 Agano, 1st Agano-class Light Cruiser U
KCS25035 Akagi Kai, Akagi-class Aircraft Carrier RR+
KCS25075 Akagi of the First Carrier Division, Deploying CR
KCS25075R Akagi of the First Carrier Division, Deploying RRR
KCS25046S Akatsuki, 1st Akatsuki-class Destroyer SR
KCS25046 Akatsuki, 1st Akatsuki-class Destroyer U
KCS25055 Akebono, 8th Ayanami-class Destroyer C
KCS25013 Akigumo, 19th Kagero-class Destroyer U
KCS25033 All Airplane Squadron, Begin Launching CR
KCS25033R All Airplane Squadron, Begin Launching RRR
KCS25127 Anti-Submarine Squadron, Charge CC
KCS25127R Anti-Submarine Squadron, Charge RRR
KCS25050 Aoba, 1st Aoba-class Heavy Cruiser U
KCS25148 Arare, 9th Asashio-class Destroyer C
KCS25152 Arashio, 4th Asashio-class Destroyer C
KCS25141 Asashio, 1st Asashio-class Destroyer U
KCS25158 Ashigara, 3rd Myoukou-class Heavy Cruiser C
KCS25054 Atago, 2nd Takao-class Heavy Cruiser U
KCS25077 Aviation Battleship, Deploy CC
KCS25077R Aviation Battleship, Deploy RRR
KCS25044 Ayanami, 1st Ayanami-class Destroyer U
KCS25076 Ban-ba-ka-ban CR
KCS25076R Ban-ba-ka-ban RRR
KCS25027 Chikuma, 2nd Tone-class Heavy Cruiser C
KCS25040 Chitose Carrier Kai-Ni, 1st Chitose-class Light Aircraft Carrier R
KCS25069 Chitose, 1st Chitose-class Seaplane Tender C
KCS25069S Chitose, 1st Chitose-class Seaplane Tender SR
KCS25041 Chiyoda Carrier Kai-Ni, 2nd Chitose-class Light Aircraft Carrier R
KCS25070 Chiyoda, 2nd Chitose-class Seaplane Tender C
KCS25070S Chiyoda, 2nd Chitose-class Seaplane Tender SR
KCS25071 Choukai, 4th Takao-class Heavy Cruiser C
KCS25031 Compass C
KCS25078 Definitely Night Battle CC
KCS25078R Definitely Night Battle RRR
KCS25161 Don't Underestimate the Power of Big 7 CR
KCS25161R Don't Underestimate the Power of Big 7 RRR
KCS25160 Food Supply Ship Mamiya C
KCS25091 Fubuki, 1st Fubuki-class Destroyer U
KCS25102 Fumitsuki, 7th Mutsuki-class Destroyer C
KCS25047 Furutaka, 1st Furutaka-class Heavy Cruiser U
KCS25121 Fusou Kai, 1st Fusou-class Aviation Battleship C
KCS25098 Fusou, 1st Fusou-class Battleship U
KCS25157 Haguro, 4th Myoukou-class Heavy Cruiser C
KCS25084 Haruna, 3rd Kongou-class Battleship RR
KCS25045 Hatsuharu, 1st Hatsuharu-class Destroyer U
KCS25006 Hatsukaze, 7th Kagero-class Destroyer R
KCS25062 Hatsushimo, 4th Hatsuharu-class Destroyer C
KCS25110 Hatsuyuki, 3rd Fubuki-class Destroyer C
KCS25056 Hibiki, 2nd Akatsuki-class Destroyer C
KCS25081 Hiei Kai-Ni, 2nd Kongou-class Battleship RR+
KCS25081S Hiei Kai-Ni, 2nd Kongou-class Battleship SR
KCS25083 Hiei, 2nd Kongou-class Battleship RR
KCS25083S Hiei, 2nd Kongou-class Battleship SR
KCS25138 Hiryuu, Hiryuu-class Aircraft Carrier R
KCS25018 Hiyou, 1st Hiyou-class Light Aircraft Carrier U
KCS25099 Houshou, Houshou-class Light Aircraft Carrier U
KCS25043 Hyuuga Kai, 2nd Ise-class Aviation Battleship R
KCS25052 Hyuuga, 2nd Ise-class Battleship U
KCS25124 I Expected So, Raise the Anchor CR
KCS25124R I Expected So, Raise the Anchor RRR
KCS25024 I-168, 1st Kaidai VIa Submarine C
KCS25021 I-19 Kai, 3rd Junsen-class Type B Submarine U
KCS25026 I-19, 3rd Junsen-class Type B Submarine C
KCS25030 I-401, 2nd I-400 class Submarine C
KCS25029 I-58 Kai, 3rd Junsen-class Type B Kai II Submarine C
KCS25016 I-58, 3rd Junsen-class Type B Kai II Submarine U
KCS25019 I-8 Kai, 2nd Junsen-class Type J-3 Submarine U
KCS25009 I-8, 2nd Junsen-class Type J-3 Submarine R
KCS25057 Ikazuchi, Works Hard C
KCS25125 I'll Clean It Up CC
KCS25125R I'll Clean It Up RRR
KCS25061 Inazuma, Blunderer C
KCS25042 Ise Kai, 1st Ise-class Aviation Battleship R
KCS25051 Ise, 1st Ise-class Battleship U
KCS25106 Isonami, 9th Fubuki-class Destroyer C
KCS25090 Isuzu Kai-Ni, Leave the Flagship to Me R
KCS25114 Isuzu, 2nd Nagara-class Light Cruiser C
KCS25122 Item Shop Girl C
KCS25079 It's Akatsuki's Turn, Watch Closely CC
KCS25079R It's Akatsuki's Turn, Watch Closely RRR
KCS25066 Jintsuu, 2nd Sendai-class Light Destroyer C
KCS25028 Junyou, 2nd Hiyou-class Light Aircraft Carrier C
KCS25036 Kaga, Kaga-class Aircraft Carrier RR
KCS25036S Kaga, Kaga-class Aircraft Carrier SR
KCS25011 Kagero, 1st Kagero-class Destroyer U
KCS25068 Kako, 2nd Furutaka-class Heavy Cruiser C
KCS25155 Kasumi, 10th Asashio-class Destroyer C
KCS25103 Kikuzuki, 9th Mutsuki-class Destroyer C
KCS25113 Kinu, 5th Nagara-class Light Cruiser C
KCS25039 Kinugasa Kai-Ni, 2nd Aoba-class Heavy Cruiser R
KCS25039S Kinugasa Kai-Ni, 2nd Aoba-class Heavy Cruiser SR
KCS25067 Kinugasa, 2nd Aoba-class Heavy Cruiser C
KCS25085 Kirishima, 4th Kongou-class Battleship RR
KCS25085S Kirishima, 4th Kongou-class Battleship SR
KCS25111 Kisaragi, 2nd Mutsuki-class Destroyer C
KCS25089 Kiso Kai-Ni, 5th Kuma-class Torpedo Cruiser R
KCS25117 Kiso, 5th Kuma-class Light Cruiser C
KCS25087 Kitakami Kai-Ni, 3rd Kuma-class Torpedo Cruiser R
KCS25094 Kitakami, 3rd Kuma-class Light Cruiser U
KCS25080 Kongou Kai-Ni, 1st Kongou-class Battleship RR+
KCS25082 Kongou, 1st Kongou-class Battleship RR
KCS25096 Kuma, 1st Kuma-class Light Cruiser U
KCS25139 Kumano Kai, 4th Mogami-class Aviation Cruiser R
KCS25130 Kumano, 4th Mogami-class Heavy Cruiser RR
KCS25130S Kumano, 4th Mogami-class Heavy Cruiser SR
KCS25023 Kuroshio, 3rd Kagero-class Destroyer C
KCS25162 Leave It to Suzuya- CR
KCS25162R Leave It to Suzuya- RRR
KCS25164 Let's Have a Wonderful Party CC
KCS25164R Let's Have a Wonderful Party RRR
KCS25007 Maikaze, 18th Kagero-class Destroyer R
KCS25015 Makigumo, 2nd Yuugumo-class Destroyer U
KCS25072 Maya, 3rd Takao-class Heavy Cruiser C
KCS25150 Michishio, 3rd Asashio-class Destroyer C
KCS25153 Midare, 6th Shiratsuyu-class Destroyer C
KCS25107 Mikazuki, 10th Mutsuki-class Destroyer C
KCS25136 Mikuma Kai, 2nd Mogami-class Aviation Cruiser R
KCS25144S Mikuma, 2nd Mogami-class Heavy Destroyer SR
KCS25144 Mikuma, 2nd Mogami-class Heavy Destroyer U
KCS25074 Mission Girl C
KCS25112 Miyuki, 4th Fubuki-class Destroyer C
KCS25108 Mochizuki, 11th Mutsuki-class Destroyer C
KCS25147 Mogami Kai, 1st Mogami-class Aviation Cruiser U
KCS25143 Mogami, 1st Mogami-class Heavy Cruiser U
KCS25101 Murakumo, 5th Fubuki-class Destroyer C
KCS25149 Murasame, 3rd Shiratsuyu-class Destroyer C
KCS25002 Musashi, 2nd Yamato-class Battleship RR+
KCS25002S Musashi, 2nd Yamato-class Battleship SR
KCS25131 Mutsu, 2nd Nagato-class Battleship RR
KCS25131S Mutsu, 2nd Nagato-class Battleship SR
KCS25092 Mutsuki, 1st Mutsuki-class Destroyer U
KCS25145 Myoukou, 1st Myoukou-class Heavy Cruiser U
KCS25159 Nachi, 2nd Myoukou-class Heavy Cruiser C
KCS25012 Naganami, 4th Yuugumo-class Destroyer U
KCS25097 Nagara, 1st Nagara-class Light Cruiser U
KCS25128 Nagato, 1st Nagato-class Battleship RR+
KCS25109 Nagatsuki, 8th Mutsuki-class Destroyer C
KCS25048 Naka, 3rd Sendai-class Light Cruiser U
KCS25118 Natori, 3rd Nagara-class Light Cruiser C
KCS25058 Nenohi, 2nd Hatsuharu-class Destroyer C
KCS25025 Noshiro, 2nd Agano-class Light Cruiser C
KCS25063 Oboro, 7th Ayanami-class Destroyer C
KCS25088 Ooi Kai-Ni, 4th Kuma-class Torpedo Cruiser R
KCS25095 Ooi, 4th Kuma-class Light Cruiser U
KCS25154 Ooshio, 2nd Asashio-class Destroyer C
KCS25123 Ready Fire CR
KCS25123R Ready Fire RRR

KCS25032 Ready for Shelling and Torpedo Launching CR
KCS25032R Ready for Shelling and Torpedo Launching RRR
KCS25053 Ryuujou, Ryuujou-class Light Aircraft Carrier U
KCS25104 Satsuki, 5th Mutsuki-class Destroyer C
KCS25060 Sazanami, 9th Ayanami-class Destroyer C
KCS25163 Second Carrier Division, Deploy CC
KCS25163R Second Carrier Division, Deploy RRR
KCS25049 Sendai, 1st Sendai-class Light Cruiser U
KCS25133 Shigure Kai-Ni, Lucky Destroyer R
KCS25133S Shigure Kai-Ni, Lucky Destroyer SR
KCS25151 Shigure, 2nd Shiratsuyu-class Destroyer C
KCS25059 Shikinami, 2nd Ayanami-class Destroyer C
KCS25003 Shimakaze, Shimakaze-class Destroyer RR
KCS25003S Shimakaze, Shimakaze-class Destroyer SR
KCS25022 Shiranui, 2nd Kagero-class Destroyer C
KCS25142 Shiratsuyu, 1st Shiratsuyu-class Destroyer U
KCS25105 Shirayuki, 2nd Fubuki-class Destroyer C
KCS25146 Shouhou, 1st Shouhou-class Light Aircraft Carrier U
KCS25005 Shoukaku, 1st Shoukaku-class Aircraft Carrier RR
KCS25005S Shoukaku, 1st Shoukaku-class Aircraft Carrier SR
KCS25135 Souryuu, Souryuu-class Aircraft Carrier R
KCS25156 Suzukaze, 10th Shiratsuyu-class Destroyer C
KCS25137 Suzuya Kai, 3rd Mogami-class Aviation Cruiser R
KCS25129 Suzuya, 3rd Mogami-class Heavy Cruiser RR
KCS25129S Suzuya, 3rd Mogami-class Heavy Cruiser SR
KCS25034 Swift as the Island Wind CC
KCS25034R Swift as the Island Wind RRR
KCS25073 Takao, 1st Takao-class Heavy Cruiser C
KCS25119 Tama, 2nd Kuma-class Light Cruiser C
KCS25093 Tatsuta, 2nd Tenryuu-class Light Cruiser U
KCS25086 Tenryuu Kai, 1st Tenryuu-class Light Cruiser R
KCS25020 Tone, 1st Tone-class Heavy Cruiser U
KCS25126 Torpedo Cruiser, Deploy CC
KCS25126R Torpedo Cruiser, Deploy RRR
KCS25064 Ushio, 10th Ayanami-class Destroyer C
KCS25038 Verniy, "Trustworthy" Destroyer R
KCS25038S Verniy, "Trustworthy" Destroyer SR
KCS25065 Wakaba, 3rd Hatsuharu-class Destroyer C
KCS25010 Yahagi, 3rd Agano-class Light Cruiser R
KCS25100 Yamashiro Kai, 2nd Fusou-class Aviation Battleship U
KCS25120 Yamashiro, 2nd Fusou-class Battleship C
KCS25001 Yamato, 1st Yamato-class Battleship RR+
KCS25008 Yukikaze, Miracle Destroyer R
KCS25116 Yura, 4th Nagara-class Light Cruiser C
KCS25037 Yuubari, Yuubari-class Light Cruiser R
KCS25132 Yuudachi Kai-Ni, 4th Shiratsuyu-class Destroyer R
KCS25132S Yuudachi Kai-Ni, 4th Shiratsuyu-class Destroyer SR
KCS25140 Yuudachi, 4th Shiratsuyu-class Destroyer U
KCS25014 Yuugumo, 1st Yuugumo-class Destroyer U
KCS25134 Zuihou, 2nd Shouhou-class Light Aircraft Carrier R
KCS25004 Zuikaku, 2nd Shoukaku-class Aircraft Carrier RR
KCS2501SP Yamato, 1st Yamato-class Battleship SP
KCS2503SP Shimakaze, Shimakaze-class Destroyer SP
KCS2504SP Zuikaku, 2nd Shoukaku-class Aircraft Carrier SP
KCS2508SP Yukikaze, Miracle Destroyer SP
KCS251SSP Yamato, 1st Yamato-class Battleship SSP
KCS2535SP Akagi Kai, Akagi-class Aircraft Carrier SP
KCS2536SP Kaga, Kaga-class Aircraft Carrier SP
KCS2537SP Yuubari, Yuubari-class Light Cruiser SP
KCS253SSP Shimakaze, Shimakaze-class Destroyer SSP
KCS2554SP Atago, 2nd Takao-class Heavy Cruiser SP
KCS2557SP Ikazuchi, Works Hard SP
KCS2561SP Inazuma, Blunderer SP
KCS2580SP Kongou Kai-Ni, 1st Kongou-class Battleship SP
KCS2584SP Haruna, 3rd Kongou-class Battleship SP
KCS2586SP Tenryuu Kai, 1st Tenryuu-class Light Cruiser SP
KCS2587SP Kitakami Kai-Ni, 3rd Kuma-class Torpedo Cruiser SP
KCS2591SP Fubuki, 1st Fubuki-class Destroyer SP
KCS25128SP Nagato, 1st Nagato-class Battleship SP
KCS2582SSP Kongou, 1st Kongou-class Battleship SSP
KCS25128SSP Nagato, 1st Nagato-class Battleship SSP

2014 Weiss Schwarz Kantai Collection TD

KCS25T07 Akagi of the First Carrier Division, Deploying
KCS25T21 Akagi, Akagi-class Aircraft Carrier
KCS25T18 Anti-Submarine Squadron, Charge
KCS25T20 Choukai, Fully Prepared
KCS25T08 Definitely Night Battle
KCS25T17 Fusou Kai, 1st Fusou-class Aviation Battleship
KCS25T14 Fusou, 1st Fusou-class Battleship
KCS25T02 Hatsushimo, 4th Hatsuharu-class Destroyer
KCS25T15 Houshou, Houshou-class Light Aircraft Carrier
KCS25T23 Ikazuchi, 3rd Akatsuki-class Destroyer
KCS25T01 Inazuma, Blunderer
KCS25T16 Isuzu Kai-Ni, Leave the Flagship to Me
KCS25T12 Isuzu, 2nd Nagara-class Light Cruiser
KCS25T05 Kako, 2nd Furutaka-class Heavy Cruiser
KCS25T09 Kikuzuki, 9th Mutsuki-class Destroyer
KCS25T19 Maya, Full of Confidence
KCS25T11 Mutsuki, 1st Mutsuki-class Destroyer
KCS25T10 Nagatsuki, 8th Mutsuki-class Destroyer
KCS25T04 Naka, 3rd Sendai-class Light Cruiser
KCS25T03 Oboro, 7th Ayanami-class Destroyer
KCS25T06 Ryuujou, Ryuujou-class Light Aircraft Carrier
KCS25T13 Tama, 2nd Kuma-class Light Cruiser
KCS25T22 Tenryuu, 1st Tenryuu-class Light Cruiser

2014 Weiss Schwarz Katanagatari Extra

KGSE0737 7th Master of Kyoutouryuu Shichika Yasuri C
KGSE0706 Capable Subordinate of Princess Hitei Emonzaemon Souda C
KGSE0716 Chainbound Kuizame R
KGSE0742 Cheerio-! C
KGSE0744 Clash: Nanami versus Shichika C
KGSE0704 Emonzaemon, Masked Man R
KGSE0745 End of Travels C
KGSE0713 Family That Becomes Sheath Konayuki Itezora C
KGSE0730 First Move 'Suzuran' Shichika Yasuri R
KGSE0702 Ginkaku Uneri, Lord of the Geku Castle R
KGSE0724 God Houou C
KGSE0715 Hades Koumori R
KGSE0718 Houou, Maniwa R
KGSE0711 Hyorigou, Mechanic Doll C
KGSE0708 Immortal Rinne Higaki C
KGSE0723 Infect Kyouken C
KGSE0703 Japan's Strongest Swordsman Hakuhei Sabi R
KGSE0705 Kanara Azekura, Captain of the Armored Pirates C
KGSE0732 Kyouto Yasuri R
KGSE0720 Longevity Umigame C
KGSE0735 Lord of the Yasuri Household Nanami C
KGSE0721 Maniwa Bug Group, Maniwa Ninja Troops C
KGSE0710 Meisai Tsuruga, Sentouryuu C
KGSE0733 Nanami Yasuri R
KGSE0738 Nanami Yasuri, Weak yet Genius C
KGSE0726 Ninjutsu: Danzaien C
KGSE0701 Princess Hitei, Supervisor of the Inspection Station R
KGSE0709 Princess Hitei, Togame's Rival C
KGSE0714 Princess Hitei's Tricks C
KGSE0728 Princess Yousha R
KGSE0722 Propagate Penguin C
KGSE0719 Read Kawauso C
KGSE0717 Reverse-Talk Shirasagi R
KGSE0725 Rewind Oshidori C
KGSE0743 Shichika Hachiretsu (Kai) C
KGSE0707 Shinou Isshouryuu Zanki Kiguchi C
KGSE0712 Strength of Decline Princess Hitei C
KGSE0731 Togame & Shichika, Travel of Trials R
KGSE0734 Togame, Brain Work Specialist C
KGSE0727 Togame, Encounter with Shichika R
KGSE0740 Togame, Focused C
KGSE0736 Togame, Ingenious Strategist C
KGSE0729 Togame, Last Directive R
KGSE0741 Togame, Smart Strategies and Knacks C
KGSE0739 Togame's Blade Shichika Yasuri C

2014 Weiss Schwarz Katanagatari Extra Promos

KGSE0748 Power of Acknowledgment Togame
KGSE0747 Togame & Shichika, Beginning the Trip
KGSE0746 Togame & Shicika, Trip to Gather Katanas

2014 Weiss Schwarz Kill La Kill

COMPLETE SET (120)		
BOOSTER BOX (20 PACKS)	60.00	80.00
BOOSTER PACK (8 CARDS)	4.00	5.00

RELEASED ON SEPTEMBER 26, 2014
KLKS27089 Absolute Terror, Satsuki C
KLKS27071 Ambitious, Satsuki RR
KLKS27014 Anachronostic Brat, Matarou C
KLKS27086 At the Top of the Tower, Satsuki C
KLKS27016 Barazou, Town's Illegitimate Doctor C
KLKS27073 Before the Final Battle, Satsuki R
KLKS27047 Berserk Ryuuko R
KLKS27036 Boxing Club Leader, Fukuroda C
KLKS27026 CEO of REVOCS, Ragyo R
KLKS27006 Class 2-A, Ryuuko R
KLKS27018 Classic Trap U
KLKS27064 Connected By Blood, Ryuuko C
KLKS27093 Data Master, Inumata C
KLKS27048 Declaration of War Ryuuko R
KLKS27043 Deepening Bonds, Ryuuko R
KLKS27033 Disciplinary Committee Trap Developer, Oogure C
KLKS27083 Discovering a Path to Victory, Satsuki U
KLKS27038 Disguise U
KLKS27010 Eating Croquettes, Mako U
KLKS27081 Family Konjac Business, Sanageyama U
KLKS27069 Fated Battle CC
KLKS27054 Feelings of Togetherness Mako U
KLKS27076 Fierce Spirit, Satsuki R
KLKS27007 Fight Club Member, Ryuuko R
KLKS27004 Fight Club President, Mako R
KLKS27053 Finding a Voice, Senketsu U
KLKS27046 First Encounter with Senketsu, Ryuuko R
KLKS27074 First Step Towards Ambition, Satsuki R
KLKS27012 Following Along, Guts C
KLKS27015 Freeloading off the Mankanshoku Family, Ryuuko C
KLKS27075 Genius Hacker, Inumata R
KLKS27068 Graduating From a Sailor Uniform CR
KLKS2768R Graduating from Sailor Uniform RRR
KLKS27027 Grand Couturier, Nui U
KLKS27035 Hakodate, Tennis Club PResident C
KLKS27028 Head Butler of the Kiryuin Family, Cloide U
KLKS27077 High Aspirations, Satsuki R
KLKS27100 Honnouji Academy Elite Four, Ultimate Battle Regalia CC
KLKS27019 I Said It's My Turn Now CR
KLKS2719R I Said, It's My Turn RRR
KLKS27020 Itadakima-su CC
KLKS27088 Jakuzure, Elite Four of the Student Council C
KLKS2766S Junketsu SR
KLKS2795S Junketsu SR
KLKS27066 Junketsu U
KLKS27095 Junketsu U
KLKS27080 Keeping Order, Gamagoori U
KLKS27099 Life Fiber Override, Kamui Junketsu CC
KLKS27070 Life Fiber Synchronize, Kamui Senketsu CC
KLKS27056 Looking for a "Girl With a Scissors Blade", Ryuuko C
KLKS27013 Mako with Glasses C
KLKS2701S Mako, Not-so-great Daughter of Illegitimate Doctor SR
KLKS2703R Mako, Worrying RRR
KLKS27029 Mental Refitting" Ragyo U
KLKS27065 Mikisugi, Mysterious Man C
KLKS27042 My Final Decision Is to Wear It Ryuuko RR
KLKS27063 Naked Nudist, Mikisugi C
KLKS27060 Naniwa Kinman High School, Takarada C
KLKS27057 Neighbouring Seat, Mako C
KLKS27001 Not-So-Great Daughter of a Sketchy Doctor, Mako RR
KLKS27052 Nudist Beach Member, Kinagase U
KLKS27037 Nui, Mysterious Girl C
KLKS2724R Nui, Owner of Scissors RRR
KLKS2725S Nui, Passing by SR
KLKS27025 Passing By, Nui R
KLKS27021 Preparing for the Birth of the Cocoon Planet, Ragyo RR
KLKS27023 Pulling Threads, Nui R
KLKS27031 Ragyo's Secretary, Hououmaru U
KLKS27030 Ready-Made, Nui U
KLKS27067 Red Gauntlet U
KLKS27044 Rescuing Senketsu Ryuuko R
KLKS2706S Ryuko of 2-A SR
KLKS2746S Ryuko, First Encounter with Senketsu SR
KLKS2741R Ryuko, to a New Self RRR
KLKS27058 Ryuko, Transfer Student C
KLKS27008 Ryuuko In Pajamas U
KLKS27049 Ryuuko's Father, Isshin U
KLKS27045 Ryuuko's Only Outfit, Senketsu R
KLKS27091 Sanageyama, Elite Four of the Student Council C
KLKS2773S Satsuki, Before the Final Battle SR
KLKS2771R Satsuki, Being Ambitious RRR
KLKS27062 Satsuki, Looking up at the Sky C
KLKS27094 Satsuki, Smiling C
KLKS27085 Satsuki's Butler, Soroi C
KLKS27078 Satsuki's Childhood Friend, Jakuzure R
KLKS27034 Satsuki's Mother, Ragyo C
KLKS27024 Scissors Owner, Nui R
KLKS2745S Senketsu, Ryuko's Outfit SR
KLKS27061 Senketsu's Power, Ryuuko C
KLKS27079 Sewing Club President, Iori U
KLKS27084 Shingantsu Stronger than Tengantsu, Sanageyama U
KLKS27040 Shinra Koketsu, Absolute Domination CC
KLKS27005 Sightseeing in Osaka, Mako R
KLKS27096 Soroi's Black Tea U
KLKS27092 Student Council Elite Four, Gamagoori C
KLKS27087 Student Council Elite Four, Inumuta C
KLKS27011 Super Self-Paced Mom, Sukuyo C
KLKS27017 Suspicious Croquettes U
KLKS27059 Talking Sailor Uniform, Senketsu C
KLKS27022 The Wheel of Fate, Nui RR
KLKS27098 There Is Nothing Wrong With My Actions CC
KLKS27041 To a New Self, Ryuuko RR
KLKS27097 To Honnouji Academy CR
KLKS2797R To Honnouji Academy RRR
KLKS27082 To the Beginning of the Song, Jakuzure U
KLKS27050 Together with Senketsu, Satsuki U
KLKS27090 Transforming With Each Perversion, Gamagoori C
KLKS27039 Unexpected Confession CR
KLKS2739R Unexpected Confession RRR
KLKS27009 Unmoving, Mako U
KLKS27002 Unstoppable, Mako RR
KLKS27072 Wanting to Protect the World, Satsuki RR
KLKS27051 Wearing Junketsu, Ryuuko U
KLKS27055 Wearing Senketsu, Satsuki U
KLKS27032 Whimsical, Nui C
KLKS27003 Worrying, Mako R
KLKS2702S Mako, Can't Be Stopped SP
KLKS2722S Nui, Threaded Gears of Fate SP
KLKS2742S Ryuko, Decided to Wear and Finish the Fight SP
KLKS2772S Satsuki, For the World Wishing to Protect SP

2014 Weiss Schwarz Kill La Kill TD

KLKS27T19 Best Friends Ryuko and Mako
KLKS27T19R Best Friends Ryuko and Mako RRR
KLKS27T19S Best Friends Ryuko and Mako SP
KLKS27T13 Gamagoori, Elite Four of the Student Council
KLKS27T09 Inumuta, Elite Four of the Student Council
KLKS27T10 Jakuzure, Elite Four of the Student Council
KLKS27T15 Life Fiber Override, Kamui Junketsu
KLKS27T08 Life Fiber Synchronize, Kamui Senketsu
KLKS27T18 Mako, "Super" Extremely Natural Girl
KLKS27T18R Mako, "Super" Extremely Natural Girl RRR
KLKS27T01 Mako, Next Seat Over
KLKS27T06 Mikisugi, Mysterious Man
KLKS27T07 Red Gauntlet
KLKS27T04 Ryuko, Power with Senketsu
KLKS27T05 Ryuko, Related by Blood
KLKS27T02 Ryuko, Transfer Student
KLKS27T16 Ryuko, Wandering Female High School Student
KLKS27T12 Sanageyama, Elite Four of the Student Council
KLKS27T11 Satsuki, Absolute Terror
KLKS27T17 Satsuki, Bearer of the Other Kamui
KLKS27T20 Satsuki, Controlling Student Council President
KLKS27T03 Senketsu, Talking Sailor Uniform
KLKS27T14 There Are No Gaps in My Actions

2014 Weiss Schwarz Little Busters Card Mission Extra

LBWE2116 Dream of the Mother And Daughter C
LBWE2110 Haruka, Making a Stall Loop R
LBWE2120 Haruka, Shield of Aegis!? C
LBWE2109 I'm Not Excited! C
LBWE2121 Kanata, Date Lovers C
LBWE2111 Kanata, Shrine Maiden Kagura R
LBWE2125 Kengo, Laughing Heartily R
LBWE2102 Komari, Happily Playing Catch R
LBWE2104 Komari, Heart-thumping Donuts C
LBWE2129 Komari, Stellar Observation C
LBWE2127 Kud, Happy Halloween! C
LBWE2115 Kud, Let's Play Baseball! C
LBWE2113 Kud, Playing Catch With Pillows C
LBWE2126 Kyousuke, Devil Coach of Fire C
LBWE2103 Kyousuke, Stage On! R
LBWE2119 Masato, Large Pork Cutlet Over Rice! R
LBWE2123 Mio, Talented Producer C
LBWE2124 Mio, Unchanged Song, Unchanged Sky R
LBWE2118 Riki, Daydream Wedding R
LBWE2107 Riki, Searching Mystery C
LBWE2112 Rin, Large Bloom in the Night Sky C
LBWE2106 Rin, Little Cheergirl C
LBWE2101 Rin, Shape of Feelings R
LBWE2108 Sasami, Because I'm With You C
LBWE2114 Sasami, Secret Self-Training C
LBWE2128 Saya, Ace Sniper C
LBWE2117 Saya, Calling a Home Run R
LBWE2130 twinkle starlights C
LBWE2122 Yuiko, Males Not Allowed C
LBWE2105 Yuiko, Snow Queen C
LBWE211SP Rin, Shape of Feelings SP
LBWE212SP Komari, Happily Playing Catch SP
LBWE213SP Kyousuke, Stage On! SP
LBWE2117SP Saya, Calling a Home Run SP
LBWE2118SP Riki, Daydream Wedding SP
LBWE2119SP Masato, Large Pork Cutlet Over Rice! SP
LBWE2125SP Kengo, Laughing Heartily SP

2014 Weiss Schwarz Little Busters EX Extra

LBW02E08 Ace of the Softball Club Sasami C
LBW02E04 Big Brother Kyousuke C
LBW02E12 Brave Yuiko C
LBW02E01 Caretaker Sasami R
LBW02E14 Crane Game C
LBW02E09 Double Shift Chairman Kanata C
LBW02E15 Exotic Kud R
LBW02E11 Expressionless and Unsociable Kanata R
LBW02E17 Loves Reading Mio C
LBW02E13 Muscle Revolutionary Masato C
LBW02E02 New Leader Riki R
LBW02E03 Optimisticg Magic Komari C
LBW02E06 Precision Machine on the Mound Rin C
LBW02E05 Sasami's Homemade Cooking C
LBW02E10 Saya Tokido R
LBW02E07 Silly Girl Haruka C
LBW02E18 Simple and Stupid Kengo C
LBW02E16 Woman Spy Saya C

2014 Weiss Schwarz Little Busters Refrain Anime Extra

LBWE1811 A Page of Juvenile Life Riki C
LBWE1846 Battle Veteran Saya U
LBWE1834 Berserking Strongest Masato U
LBWE1849 Break Time U
LBWE1839 Chiffon Cake for Two U
LBWE1829 Continuation of Dream Yuiko RR
LBWE1836 Empty Feelings Yuiko C
LBWE1832 Everlasting Dream Yuiko R
LBWE1827 Everyone Together Rin C
LBWE1850 Final Battle C
LBWE1822 Fireworks Show of Love Riki U
LBWE1840 Forget-me-not C
LBWE1847 Frivolous A-chan Senpai C
LBWE1819 Fun Life Kud R
LBWE1818 Fun Life Rin R
LBWE1809 Hotcake Party Komari C
LBWE1837 Hotcake Party Mio C
LBWE1807 Hotcake Party Rin U
LBWE1833 Hotcake Party Yuiko U
LBWE1814 I Want to Meet You All. C
LBWE1838 Important Dear Friend Masato C
LBWE1801 Irreplaceable Time Rin RR
LBWE1841 Kind World Saya RR
LBWE1842 Last Moments Saya RR
LBWE1808 Last Scenery Komari U
LBWE1817 Loves Big Sister Haruka R
LBWE1810 Painful Decision Kyousuke C
LBWE1844 Partners on the Battlefield Riki & Saya R
LBWE1830 Peaceful Days Kanata RR
LBWE1845 President of Dark Executives Tokikaze U
LBWE1843 Repeated Scenery Saya R
LBWE1806 Returned Leader Kyousuke U
LBWE1812 Rin, Working Hard C
LBWE1848 Saya, Taking a Bath C
LBWE1824 Scrupulous Sasami C
LBWE1813 Secret of the World U
LBWE1835 Serious Kanata C
LBWE1825 Something to Protect Kengo C
LBWE1803 Sunset-colored Feelings Rin R
LBWE1804 The End And the Beginning Kyousuke R
LBWE1828 To Find What Was Lost. C
LBWE1826 To Outside This World Haruka C
LBWE1805 To Outside This World Komari R
LBWE1823 To Outside This World Kud C
LBWE1831 To Outside This World Mio R
LBWE1821 Undying Friendship Kengo U
LBWE1815 We Should Date C
LBWE1802 What I Can Do Now Riki R
LBWE1820 What I Can Do Now Rin R
LBWE1816 Words of Reunion Sasami RR

2014 Weiss Schwarz Log Horizon Extra

LHSE2002 Akatsuki, Assassin RR
LHSE2009 Akatsuki, Maiden's Heart R
LHSE2003 Akatsuki, Master's Ninja RR
LHSE2006 Akatsuki, Not Good at Dressing Herself? R
LHSE2014 Akatsuki, Quiet Worker U
LHSE2011 Akatsuki, Two's Waltz U
LHSE2023 Akatsuki-chan Changed Clothes C
LHSE2025 Crescent Moon Alliance C
LHSE2039 Crusty U
LHSE2012 Henrietta U
LHSE2013 Henrietta, Reliable Accountant U
LHSE2047 Isaac C
LHSE2005 Isuzu R
LHSE2022 Isuzu, Bard C
LHSE2010 Isuzu, Rudy's Owner? U
LHSE2036 Lenessia U
LHSE2049 Log Horizon C
LHSE2021 Marielle, Cleric C
LHSE2001 Marielle, Nagisa's Angel RR
LHSE2018 Marielle, Owner of Crescent Moon C
LHSE2048 Mind Shock C
LHSE2040 Minori U
LHSE2027 Minori, Field Monitor RR
LHSE2041 Minori, Maiden's Heart C
LHSE2034 Naotsugu, Guardian R
LHSE2033 Naotsugu, Reliable Partner R
LHSE2026 Nyanta RR
LHSE2038 Nyanta, Everyone's Chief U
LHSE2031 Nyanta, Log Horizon R
LHSE2020 Puchi Akatsuki C
LHSE2042 Puchi Naotsugu C
LHSE2045 Puchi Shiroe C
LHSE2016 Rundelhaus C
LHSE2007 Rundelhaus, Adventurer R
LHSE2015 Rundelhaus, Sorcerer U
LHSE2008 Serara R
LHSE2004 Serara, Crescent Moon Alliance R
LHSE2017 Serara, Loves Nyanta-san C
LHSE2032 Shiroe, Determination to Change the World R
LHSE2029 Shiroe, Full Control Encount R
LHSE2035 Shiroe, Guildmaster U
LHSE2028 Shiroe, Log Horizon Representative RR
LHSE2046 Shiroe, Scribe C
LHSE2030 Shiroe, Two's Waltz R
LHSE2019 Shouryu C
LHSE2050 Simplified Full Control Encount C
LHSE2037 Soujirou U
LHSE2044 Touya C
LHSE2043 Touya, Samurai C
LHSE2024 Two's Waltz C
LHSE2001S Marielle, Nagisa's Angel SP
LHSE2003S Akatsuki, Master's Ninja SP
LHSE2028S Shiroe, Log Horizon Representative SP

2014 Weiss Schwarz Log Horizon TD

LHSE20T02 Akatsuki
LHSE20T08 Akatsuki Angered
LHSE20T2R Akatsuki RRR
LHSE20T2S Akatsuki SP
LHSE20T04 Akatsuki, Actually A Pretty Girl
LHSE20T05 Akatsuki, Blushing
LHSE20T09 Assassinate
LHSE20T19 Delicate Combination
LHSE20T18 Enchanter's Support
LHSE20T20 First Loot
LHSE20T06 Henrietta, Treasurer of Crescent Moon Alliance
LHSE20T03 Marielle Using Telepathy
LHSE20T07 Marielle, Representative of Crescent Moon Alliance
LHSE20T16 Naotsugu
LHSE20T13 Naotsugu, First Actual Battle
LHSE20T10 Nyanta the Cook
LHSE20T12 Nyanta, Swashbuckler
LHSE20T01 Serara, Druid
LHSE20T15 Shiroe
LHSE20T15R Shiroe RRR
LHSE20T14 Shiroe, Confident Look
LHSE20T17 Shiroe, Enchanter
LHSE20T17S Shiroe, Enchanter SR
LHSE20T11 Shiroe, Riding a Griffon

2014 Weiss Schwarz Love Live Extra

LLWE1916 Always, No Matter What C
LLWE1911 Anju Yuuki C
LLWE1917 Door of Dreams C
LLWE1910 Erina Toudou C
LLWE1922 Good Idea Eri C
LLWE1925 Hanayo, Discovered Idol C
LLWE1919 Honoka, Student Council President C
LLWE1904 It Is a Miracle (Japanese text) R
LLWE1920 Kotori, Designer C
LLWE1926 Maki, Creating Melody C
LLWE1924 Niko, Proud of Lyrics C
LLWE1923 Nozomi, Thinking of Underclassmen C
LLWE1927 Rin, Crying Hard C
LLWE1918 Shocking Party C
LLWE1914 Slump C
LLWE1915 That Is Our Miracle C
LLWE1909 That Is Our Miracle Eri Ayase R
LLWE1907 That Is Our Miracle Hanayo Koizumi R
LLWE1903 That Is Our Miracle Honoka Kousaka R
LLWE1902 That Is Our Miracle Kotori Minami R
LLWE1901 That Is Our Miracle Niko Yazawa R
LLWE1905 That Is Our Miracle Nozomi Toujou R
LLWE1906 That Is Our Miracle Umi Sonoda R
LLWE1913 Towards the Dream Myu's C
LLWE1912 Tsubasa Kira C
LLWE1921 Umi, Attack on Summit C
LLWE1901S That Is Our Miracle Niko Yazawa SP
LLWE1902S That Is Our Miracle Kotori Minami SP
LLWE1903S That Is Our Miracle Honoka Kousaka SP
LLWE1904S It Is a Miracle (Japanese text) SP
LLWE1905S That Is Our Miracle Nozomi Toujou SP
LLWE1906S That Is Our Miracle Umi Sonoda SP
LLWE1907S That Is Our Miracle Hanayo Koizumi SP
LLWE1909S That Is Our Miracle Eri Ayase SP

2014 Weiss Schwarz Love Live School Idol Festival

LLW28007 After School Songstress Maki R
LLW28007R After School Songstress Maki RRR
LLW28072 Alpaca U
LLW28016 Card of Destiny Nozomi U
LLW28030 Concentration Umi C
LLW28024 Cooked Rice- Hanayo U
LLW28028 Cute- Eri C
LLW28039 Eri in Casual Clothing R
LLW28039S Eri in Casual Clothing SR
LLW28041 Eri in Lesson Outfit U
LLW28049 Eri in Pajama C
LLW28032 Eri's Confession Booth Eri C
LLW28002 Fox's Wedding Eri RR
LLW28002R Fox's Wedding Eri RRR
LLW28029 Full Smiles Honoko C
LLW28023 Goddess of Healing Kotori U
LLW28069 Going Out Together Hanayo R
LLW28069S Going Out Together Hanayo SR
LLW28045 Going Out Together- Eri C
LLW28064 Going Out Together- Honoka R
LLW28054S Going Out Together- Honoka SR
LLW28057 Going Out Together- Kotori U
LLW28067 Going Out Together- Maki RR
LLW28067S Going Out Together- Maki SR
LLW28048 Going Out Together- Niko C

LLW28042S Going Out Together– Nozomi SR
LLW28042 Going Out Together– Nozomi U
LLW28071 Going out Together– Rin U
LLW28062 Going Out Together– Umi C
LLW28015 Gonna Eat You? Honoka R
LLW28015R Gonna Eat You? Honoka RRR
LLW28077 Hanayo in Casual Clothing C
LLW28079 Hanayo in Lesson Outfit C
LLW28070 Hanayo in Pajama U
LLW28018 Heart of Flame Honoka U
LLW28026 Here Is What You Ordered– Hanayo C
LLW28061 Honoka in Casual Clothing C
LLW28064 Honoka in Lesson Outfit C
LLW28059 Honoka in Pajama U
LLW28031 I'll Teach You– Niko C
LLW28006 Incredible Sympathy Hanayo RR
LLW28006R Incredible Sympathy Hanayo RRR
LLW28058 Kotori in Casual Clothing U
LLW28056 Kotori in Lesson Outfit R
LLW28056S Kotori in Lesson Outfit SR
LLW28060 Kotori in Pajama U
LLW28017 Lovebind Umi U
LLW28075 Maki in Casual Clothing C
LLW28076 Maki in Pajama C
LLW28074 Makin in Lesson Outfit U
LLW28033 Marvelous Sweats Kotori C
LLW28034 Myu's Symbol of Energy Rin C
LLW28047 Niko in Casual Clothing C
LLW28047S Niko in Casual Clothing SR
LLW28038 Niko in Lesson Outfit RR
LLW28038R Niko in Lesson Outfit RRR
LLW28043 Niko in Pajama U
LLW28022 Niko Is Popular Niko U
LLW28014 No brand girls Eri R
LLW28014X No brand girls Eri XR
LLW28013 No brand girls Hanayo R
LLW28013X No brand girls Hanayo XR
LLW28001 No brand girls Honoka RR
LLW28001X No brand girls Honoka XR
LLW28009 No brand girls Kotori R
LLW28009X No brand girls Kotori XR
LLW28012 No brand girls Maki R
LLW28012X No brand girls Maki XR
LLW28008 No brand girls Niko R
LLW28008X No brand girls Niko XR
LLW28005 No brand girls Nozomi RR
LLW28005X No brand girls Nozomi XR
LLW28011 No brand girls Rin R
LLW28011X No brand girls Rin XR
LLW28010 No brand girls Umi R
LLW28010X No brand girls Umi XR
LLW28046 Nozomi in Casual Clothing C
LLW28040 Nozomi in Lesson Outfit R
LLW28040R Nozomi in Lesson Outfit RRR
LLW28044 Nozomi in Pajama U
LLW28019 Please Watch Rin meow– Rin U
LLW28025 Raccoon Sleep– Nozomi U
LLW28068 Rin in Casual Outfit R
LLW28068S Rin in Casual Outfit SR
LLW28078 Rin in Lesson Outfit C
LLW28073 Rin in Pajama U
LLW28051 School Idol Festival Honoka RR
LLW28063 School Idol Festival Jotori C
LLW28053 School Idol Festival Umi R
LLW28053R School Idol Festival Umi RRR
LLW28020 Secret Examination Room Maki U
LLW28003 Sheep's Feeling Kotori RR
LLW28003R Sheep's Feeling Kotori RRR
LLW28027 Smile And Smile Niko C
LLW28037 Snow halation CC
LLW28021 Spiritual Power Nozomi U
LLW28050 Summer-color Smile is 1, 2, Jump CC
LLW28080 Tight "love" Approaching CC
LLW28052 Umi in Casual Clothing RR
LLW28052S Umi in Casual Clothing SR
LLW28065 Umi in Lesson Outfit C
LLW28055 Umi in Pajama R
LLW28004 Whimsical Cat Rin RR
LLW28004R Whimsical Cat Rin RRR
LLW28035 White Rabbit of Luck Umi C
LLW28066 Wonderful Rush CC
LLW28036 You're the Next Target Maki C

2014 Weiss Schwarz Nisekoi

COMPLETE SET (117)

BOOSTER BOX (20 PACKS)	60.00	80.00
BOOSTER PACK (8 CARDS)	3.00	4.00

RELEASED ON JANUARY 23, 2015
NKW30074 Ad Lib CC
NKW30068 Chitoge as Ghost C
NKW30055 Chitoge as Juliet R
NKW30055S Chitoge as Juliet SR
NKW30011 Chitoge in Swimsuits U
NKW30014 Chitoge in Youth Days C
NKW30009 Chitoge in Yukata U
NKW30007 Chitoge, After A Bath R
NKW30007S Chitoge, After A Bath SR
NKW30051 Chitoge, Deepened Friendship RR
NKW30051R Chitoge, Deepened Friendship RRR
NKW30017 Chitoge, First Date C
NKW30058 Chitoge, First Love U
NKW30012 Chitoge, Good at Every Sport U
NKW30003 Chitoge, Horrible at Love R
NKW30020 Chitoge, Lovers!? C
NKW30002 Chitoge, Maiden's Heart RR
NKW30069 Chitoge, Not Understanding What Happened C
NKW30053 Chitoge, Surprising Side R
NKW30016 Chitoge, Transfer Student C
NKW30005 Chitoge, Weekend Date R
NKW30060 Chitoge, Words of Promise U
NKW30021 Claude C
NKW30049 Closed Space CC
NKW30023 Diary CR
NKW30100 Exchanged Promise CC
NKW30073 Feelings of 10 Years CR
NKW30024 Fictitious Love CC
NKW30072 For You... U
NKW30025 Hairpin CC
NKW30018 Heroines in Love C
NKW30098 I...... Lied...... CR
NKW30075 Juliet in Love CC
NKW30050 Juliet Just for You CC
NKW30030 Kosaki in Swimsuits R
NKW30030S Kosaki in Swimsuits SR
NKW30040 Kosaki in Yukata C
NKW30027 Kosaki, After School Date RR
NKW30027R Kosaki, After School Date RRR
NKW30081 Kosaki, Angel in White Clothing R
NKW30081S Kosaki, Angel in White Clothing SR
NKW30091 Kosaki, At the Secret Place C
NKW30092 Kosaki, Denying C
NKW30045 Kosaki, Emotion Overloading C
NKW30031 Kosaki, Exceptional Smile R
NKW30035 Kosaki, Fateful Draw of Lots U
NKW30088 Kosaki, Fictitious Love!? U
NKW30080 Kosaki, First Visit R
NKW30043 Kosaki, Gentle Smile C
NKW30089 Kosaki, Kind Look From the Side C
NKW30076 Kosaki, Maiden's Heart RR
NKW30095 Kosaki, Mild Personality C
NKW30086 Kosaki, Progression of the Two U
NKW30033 Kosaki, Store's Mascot Girl U
NKW30087 Kosaki, Tilting Head U
NKW30048 Large Back CR
NKW30078 Marika in Swimsuits R
NKW30078S Marika in Swimsuits SR
NKW30063 Marika in Yukata C
NKW30096 Marika Tachibana C
NKW30054 Marika, Active Girl R
NKW30057 Marika, Daughter of the Police Chief R
NKW30077 Marika, Fierce Attack RR
NKW30077R Marika, Fierce Attack RRR
NKW30065 Marika, Long-Awaited Reunion C
NKW30061 Marika, Lovely Lady U
NKW30056 Marika, Loving Carnage R
NKW30056S Marika, Loving Carnage SR
NKW30052 Marika, Maiden's Heart RR
NKW30085 Marika, Mischievous Kiss U
NKW30062 Marika, Promise of Date U
NKW30070 Marika, Raku's Fiancee C
NKW30079 Marika, Straightforward Feelings R
NKW30064 Marika, Throwing A Tantrum C
NKW30059 Marika, Tilting Her Head U
NKW30067 Marika, Transfer Student C
NKW30022 Pendant of Promise U
NKW30046 Pendant of Promise U
NKW30071 Pendant of Promise U
NKW30097 Pendant of Promise U
NKW30047 Poker Face!? U
NKW30099 Promise of a Day Long Gone CC
NKW30084 Raku Being Similar U
NKW30008 Raku Ichijou U
NKW30066 Raku, Acting Like Lover C
NKW30042 Raku, Kind And Thoughtful C
NKW30093 Raku, Love Triangle? C
NKW30013 Raku, Wonderful Darling!? U
NKW30094 Ruri in Swimsuits C
NKW30082 Ruri, Girl With Glasses R
NKW30082R Ruri, Girl With Glasses RRR
NKW30083 Ruri, Kosaki's Dear Friend U
NKW30006 Seishirou in Swimsuits R
NKW30039 Seishirou in Youth Days C
NKW30041 Seishirou in Yukata C
NKW30019 Seishirou Tsugumi C
NKW30015 Seishirou, Change of Heart C
NKW30032 Seishirou, Date Feeling R
NKW30004 Seishirou, Dramatically Changed Looks!? R
NKW30004S Seishirou, Dramatically Changed Looks!? SR
NKW30001 Seishirou, First Time Feeling RR
NKW30001R Seishirou, First Time Feeling RRR
NKW30029 Seishirou, Girls' Uniform R
NKW30029S Seishirou, Girls' Uniform SR
NKW30010 Seishirou, Heart-Thumping U
NKW30037 Seishirou, Lovesick U
NKW30026 Seishirou, Maiden's Heart RR
NKW30038 Seishirou, Not Being True to Self C
NKW30044 Seishirou, Shocking Truth C
NKW30028 Seishirou, Studying about Love R
NKW30036 Seishirou, Talented Hitman U
NKW30034 Seishirou, Transfer Student U
NKW30090 Shuu, Frivolous C
NKW3002SP Chitoge, Maiden's Heart SP
NKW3026SP Seishirou, Maiden's Heart SP
NKW3052SP Marika, Maiden's Heart SP
NKW3076SP Kosaki, Maiden's Heart SP

2014 Weiss Schwarz Nisekoi Promos

NKW30101 Chibi Chitoge
NKW30105 Chibi Kosaki
NKW30104 Chibi Marika
NKW30102 Chibi Raku
NKW30106 Chibi Ruri
NKW30103 Chibi Seishirou
NKW30P02 Chitoge, Lovey-Dovey Couple!?
NKW30P01 Chitoge, Summer Clothes
NKW30P04 Chitoge, To the Highest Stage
NKW30P03 Kosaki, Along with Raku!?
NKW30P05 Kosaki, To the Highest Stage

2014 Weiss Schwarz Nisekoi TD

NKW30T07 Chitoge Kirisaki
NKW30T07R Chitoge Kirisaki RRR
NKW30T07S Chitoge Kirisaki SP
NKW30T7SR Chitoge Kirisaki SR
NKW30T03 Chitoge, First Date
NKW30T06 Chitoge, Love Triangle?
NKW30T05 Chitoge, Lovers?
NKW30T02 Chitoge, Transfer Student
NKW30T09 Fictitious Love
NKW30T12 Kosaki in Denail
NKW30T16 Kosaki Onodera
NKW30T16R Kosaki Onodera RRR
NKW30T10 Kosaki, Kind Look From the Side
NKW30T13 Kosaki, Love Triangle?
NKW30T15 Kosaki, Tilting Head
NKW30T17 Marika Tachibana
NKW30T19 No Way It
NKW30T08 Pendant of Promise
NKW30T18 Promise of a Day Long Gone
NKW30T01 Raku Ichijou
NKW30T14 Raku, Love Triangle?
NKW30T11 Ruri Miyamoto
NKW30T04 Seishirou Tsugumi

2014 Weiss Schwarz Persona 4 Extra

P4SE0107 Chie & Tomoe R
P4SE0109 Chie Satonaka C
P4SE0110 Current Pretty Girl Idol C
P4SE0106 Izanagi Awakens C
P4SE0112 Kanji & Take-Mikazuchi C
P4SE0114 Kanji Tatsumi C
P4SE0115 My Turn! C
P4SE0105 Nanako Dojima C
P4SE0117 Naoto Shirogane R
P4SE0116 Operation Charge And Reverse Pick-Up C
P4SE0101 Protagonist (P4) R
P4SE0108 Rise Kujikawa R
P4SE0103 Ryotaro Dojima C
P4SE0118 Teddie C
P4SE0102 Yousuke & Jiraiya R
P4SE0104 Yousuke Hanamura C
P4SE0111 Yukiko & Konohana Sakuya R
P4SE0113 Yukiko Amagi C

2014 Weiss Schwarz Persona Q Extra

PQSE2120 Gekkou High Group Akihiko C
PQSE2103 Gekkou High Group Amada C
PQSE2109 Gekkou High Group Fuuka R
PQSE2118 Gekkou High Group Junpei R
PQSE2106 Gekkou High Group Koromaru C
PQSE2127 Gekkou High Group Mitsuru C
PQSE2102 Gekkou High Group P3 Protagonist R
PQSE2121 Gekkou High Group Shinjiro C
PQSE2125 Gekkou High Group Yukari C
PQSE2104 Morning Nanako C
PQSE2130 Noisy Dining C
PQSE2111 Rei & Zen, Mysterious Couple R
PQSE2124 Resident of the Velvet Room Elizabeth R
PQSE2129 Resident of the Velvet Room Margaret C
PQSE2128 Resident of the Velvet Room Marie C
PQSE2126 Resident of the Velvet Room Theodore C
PQSE2107 Shadow of the Labyrinth C
PQSE2116 Someone to Protect C
PQSE2108 Those Who Challenge the Mystery C
PQSE2115 Time to Rest C
PQSE2113 Yaso High Group Aigis C
PQSE2112 Yaso High Group Chie C
PQSE2117 Yaso High Group Kanji R
PQSE2123 Yaso High Group Naoto R
PQSE2101 Yaso High Group P4 Protagonist R
PQSE2114 Yaso High Group Rise C
PQSE2122 Yaso High Group Teddie R
PQSE2105 Yaso High Group Yousuke C
PQSE2119 Yaso High Group Yukiko C
PQSE2110 Zen & Rei, Lost Memories R
PQSE2110S Zen & Rei, Lost Memories SP
PQSE2111S Rei & Zen, Mysterious Couple SP

2014 Weiss Schwarz Sword Art Online 2 Extra

COMPLETE SET (38)

BOOSTER BOX (6 PACKS)	40.00	50.00
BOOSTER PACK (8 CARDS)	5.00	6.00

RELEASED ON APRIL 10, 2015
SAOSE2336 A Tiny Step C
1 Kirito, Fateful End SP
SAOSE2304 Asuna, An Autumn Walk C
2 Sinon, the Last Strike SP
SAOSE2301 Asuna, Moment of Tranquility R
SAOSE2303 Asuna, Normal ALO Life C
SAOSE2302 Asuna, Painful Memories C
SAOSE2315 Bullet to Cause Death Death Gun C
SAOSE2332 Check Six Sinon C
SAOSE2317 Estoc Wielder of Fate C
SAOSE2312 Grim Reaper Appears Death Gun C
SAOSE2327 Kazuto, An Autumn Walk C
SAOSE2330 Kirito, Beautiful Avatar C
SAOSE2329 Kirito, Choosing to Fight C
SAOSE2333 Kirito, Confronting Death Gun C
SAOSE2323 Kirito, Fateful End R
SAOSE2326 Kirito, Swimming Submerged C
SAOSE2320 Kirito, Temporal Alliance R
SAOSE2313 Kyouji, Overly Attached C
SAOSE2306 Leafa, Gathering Materials C
SAOSE2314 Lizbeth, Hunting Mobs With Everyone C
SAOSE2310 Lizbeth, Watching the Battle With Everyone C
SAOSE2316 Normal Silica C
SAOSE2334 Old Name C
SAOSE2335 Phantom Bullet C
SAOSE2311 Red Player Death Gun C
SAOSE2328 Shino, Want to Become Stronger C
SAOSE2308 Shouichi Shinkawa R
SAOSE2307 Silica, Gathering Materials R
SAOSE2319 Sinon in the Midst of Sunlight Through the Leaves R
SAOSE2331 Sinon, Angered C
SAOSE2325 Sinon, Basic Knowledge of Guns C
SAOSE2318 Sinon, Ideal Self R
SAOSE2322 Sinon, Strong Being R
SAOSE2321 Sinon, Temporal Alliance R
SAOSE2324 Sinon, the Last Strike R
SAOSE2309 Sterben Death Gun R
SAOSE2305 Suguha, Moment of Sibling Time R

2014 Weiss Schwarz Sword Art Online 2 Extra Promos

SAOSE23P04 Kazuto and Asuna in Uniform
SAOSE23P02 Kirito, Challenging Death Gun
SAOSE23P03 Sinon and Kirito, Triumphant Team
SAOSE23P01 Sinon, Mission at Dusk

2014 Weiss Schwarz Sword Art Online 2 Trial

SAOSE23T10 Asuna, Place to Return
SAOSE23T18 Belated Self-Introduction
SAOSE23T06 Death Gun, True Power
SAOSE23T07 Death Gun, Unexpected Encounter
SAOSE23T04 Death Gun, Unidentified
SAOSE23T16 Kirito, Determination to Shoot
SAOSE23T09 Kirito, Just Like a Girl
SAOSE23T11 Kirito, M9000-type Avatar
SAOSE23T11R Kirito, M9000-type Avatar RRR
SAOSE23T02 Kyouji, Protecting Shino
SAOSE23T01 Kyouji, Relaxed Talk
SAOSE23T03 Lisbeth, Gathering Materials
SAOSE23T15 Machine of Ice Sinon
SAOSE23T15R Machine of Ice Sinon RRR
SAOSE23T20 Partner Hecate II
SAOSE23T08 Power of Death Gun
SAOSE23T13 Shino, Another Self
SAOSE23T05 Silica, Full of Confidence
SAOSE23T17 Sinon, Excellent Sniper
SAOSE23T17R Sinon, Excellent Sniper RRR
SAOSE23T12 Sinon, Kind Guide
SAOSE23T14 Swordsman in the World of Guns Kirito
SAOSE23T14S Swordsman in the World of Guns Kirito SR
SAOSE23T19 Wielder of Photon Sword
SAOSE23T14SP Swordsman in the World of Guns Kirito SP
SAOSE23T15SP Machine of Ice Sinon SP

2014 Weiss Schwarz Sword Art Online Vol. 2

COMPLETE SET (98)

BOOSTER BOX (20 PACKS)	80.00	100.00
BOOSTER PACK (8 CARDS)	3.00	4.00

RELEASED ON APRIL 25, 2014
SAOS26059 Accident in Battle CR
SAOS26075 Agil, Broker C
SAOS26014 Akihiko Kayaba C
SAOS26017 Alicia Rue, Lord of "Cait Sith" C
SAOS26013 Asuna, "Conquering Team"'s Off Day C
SAOS26006 Asuna Yuuki R
SAOS26006S Asuna Yuuki SR
SAOS26012 Asuna, "Undine" Girl C
SAOS26007 Asuna, Bride of the Fairy King U
SAOS26004 Asuna, Debuting Home Cooking R
SAOS26004S Asuna, Debuting Home Cooking SR
SAOS26009 Asuna, Family Side U
SAOS26005 Asuna, Inside the Bird Cage R
SAOS26010 Asuna, Kind Appearance U
SAOS26002 Asuna, Light of Hope RR
SAOS26001 Asuna, Optimistic Feeling RR
SAOS2601R Asuna, Optimistic Feeling RRR
SAOS26003 Asuna, Precious Time R
SAOS26016 Asuna, Putting Self in the Frontline C
SAOS26011 Asuna, Shy Smile U
SAOS26015 Asuna, Ways to Enjoy Vacation C
SAOS26018 Asuna's Present U
SAOS26079 Confronting the Strongest Player CR
SAOS26058 Demonic Sword Gram U
SAOS26057 Eugene, Commander C
SAOS26039 Fairy Dance CR
SAOS26064 Kazuto, Challenging "ALO" R
SAOS2664R Kazuto, Challenging "ALO" RRR
SAOS26070 Kazuto, Encounter with MMO U
SAOS26050 Keiko Ayano U
SAOS26052 Keiko in Uniform C
SAOS26049 Keiko, Cease-Fire Agreement U
SAOS26073 Kirito in "Flower Garden" C
SAOS26062 Kirito, "Dual Wield" Demon RR
SAOS26065 Kirito, "Spriggan" Youth R
SAOS2665S Kirito, "Spriggan" Youth SR
SAOS26076 Kirito, Battle in the Frontlines C
SAOS26067 Kirito, Newlywed Life U
SAOS26069 Kirito, Two Worlds U
SAOS26066 Kirito, Unwavering Determination R
SAOS26063 Kirito, Waiting Out Rain R
SAOS26077 Klein, Frank Man C
SAOS26022 Leafa and Suguha, Virtual And Reality RR
SAOS26021 Leafa, "Sylph" Expert RR
SAOS26025 Leafa, Girl of Virtual World R
SAOS2625S Leafa, Girl of Virtual World SR
SAOS26033 Leafa, Taking Off From Territory C
SAOS26030 Leafa, Troubled Maiden U
SAOS26023 Leafa, Unyielding Girl R
SAOS26044 Lisbeth, "Leprechaun" Girl R
SAOS2644S Lisbeth, "Leprechaun" Girl SR
SAOS26053 Lisbeth, Adventure to Gather Materials C
SAOS26046 Lisbeth, Brilliant Smile R
SAOS26056 Lisbeth, Kind Warmth C
SAOS26055 Lisbeth, Making a Decision C
SAOS26048 Lisbeth, Realization of Affection U
SAOS26008 Living Legend Heathcliff U
SAOS26040 Memory of Last Night CC
SAOS2671S Navigation Pixie Yui SR
SAOS26071 Navigation Pixie Yui U
SAOS26074 Oberon, Game Master C
SAOS26019 On Top of "Yggdrasil" CR
SAOS26032 Recon, Caring about Something C
SAOS26080 Reunion with Yui CC
SAOS26020 Revelation of "the Wife" CC
SAOS26047 Rika Shinozaki U
SAOS2651R Rika, Cease-Fire Agreement RRR
SAOS26051 Rika, Cease-Fire Agreement U
SAOS26037 Sakuya, Lord of "Sylph" C
SAOS26041 Silica, "Cait Sith" Girl RR
SAOS26045 Silica, Embarrassed Look R
SAOS2645S Silica, Embarrassed Look SR
SAOS26043 Silica, Looking Up at the Sky R
SAOS26054 Silica, On Guard to Kindness C
SAOS26042 Silica, Relieved Smile RR
SAOS26027 Speedholic Leafa U
SAOS26026 Suguha, Changing R
SAOS2626S Suguha, Changing SR
SAOS26034 Suguha, Cooking C
SAOS26029 Suguha, Kirito's Little Sister U
SAOS26024 Suguha, Supporting Big Brother R
SAOS2624R Suguha, Supporting Big Brother RRR
SAOS26031 Suguha, Tutor U
SAOS26036 Suguha, Youth Days C
SAOS26038 Swilvane Specialty U
SAOS26078 The Seed U
SAOS26060 Until the Smile Returns CC
SAOS26028 Veteran Player Leafa U
SAOS26072 Yui in Summer Dress C
SAOS26061 Yui, Adventure to Find Mama RR
SAOS26068 Yui, Memories Regained U
SAOS26074 Yui, Simple Answer C
SAOS2622S Leafa and Suguha, Virtual And Reality SP
SAOS262SP Asuna, Beacon of Hope SP
SAOS2641S Silica, "Cait Sith" Girl SP
SAOS2646S Lisbeth, Brilliant Smile SP
SAOS2661S Yui, Adventure to Find Mama SP
SAOS2662S Kirito, "Dual Wield" Demon SP

2014 Weiss Schwarz Terra Formars Trial

TFS32T09 Bombardier Beetle God Lee
TFS32T08 Carrying Out Mission Shoukichi Komachi
TFS32T11 Carrying Out Mission Thien
TFS32T12 Crew of Bugs 2 Chang Ming-Ming
TFS32T06 Crew of Bugs 2 Nanao Akita
TFS32T10 Crew of Bugs 2 Shoukichi Komachi
TFS32T10S Crew of Bugs 2 Shoukichi Komachi SR
TFS32T14 Crew of Bugs 2 Thien
TFS32T14R Crew of Bugs 2 Thien RRR
TFS32T07 Desert Locust Thien
TFS32T01 Emerald Cockroach Wasp Victoria Wood
TFS32T18 Encountering Known Beings
TFS32T05 Encountering Enemies
TFS32T17 Giant Hornet Shoukichi Komachi
TFS32T13 Human Transformation Shoukichi Komachi
TFS32T02a King of Harmful Bugs Terraformar
TFS32T02b King of Harmful Bugs Terraformar
TFS32T02R King of Harmful Bugs Terraformar
TFS32T16 Paraponera Clavata Donatello K. Davis
TFS32T15 Rainbow Stag Beetle Maria Viren
TFS32T03 Sleeping Chironomid Ichiro Hiruma
TFS32T04 Species' Sudden Evolvement
TFS32T19 Those Who Lost

2015 Weiss Schwarz Attack on Titan Booster

COMPLETE SET (129)

BOOSTER BOX (20 PACKS)	60.00	80.00
BOOSTER PACK (8 CARDS)	3.00	4.00

RELEASED ON JULY 31, 2015
AOTS35E001 Beyond the Walls Eren RRR
AOTS35E002 Resisting Fate Armin RR
AOTS35E003 Resisting Fate Eren RR
AOTS35E004 Entrance Ceremony Annie R
AOTS35E005 Paving a Way for the Future Eren R
AOTS35E006 Paving a Way for the Future Armin R
AOTS35E007 Readiness Eren R
AOTS35E008 Firm Will Eren Titan R
AOTS35E009 Guiding Force to the Truth Armin U
AOTS35E010 Recurring Tragedy Eren U
AOTS35E011 Gentle Ally Conny U
AOTS35E012 Humanity's Rage Eren Titan U
AOTS35E013 Key to Humanity's Counterattack Eren U
AOTS35E014 Call From the Heart Armin U
AOTS35E015 104th Cadet Corps Class Annie U
AOTS35E016 Confused Feelings Armin C
AOTS35E017 104th Cadet Corps Class Eren C
AOTS35E018 104th Cadet Corps Class Conny C
AOTS35E019 Garrison Regiment Hannes C
AOTS35E020 Rite of Passage Armin C
AOTS35E021 Memories of the Past Eren C
AOTS35E022 Garrison Regiment Commander Pyxis C
AOTS35E023 Brave Warrior Eren C
AOTS35E024 Confusion Armin C
AOTS35E025 Titan Ability Eren Titan C
AOTS35E027 Titan's Power U
AOTS35E028 Since That Day RRR
AOTS35E030 Crushing Blow CC
AOTS35E031 Beyond the Walls Levi RRR
AOTS35E032 Resisting Fate Levi RR
AOTS35E033 Violent Ripples Levi R
AOTS35E034 Gentle Smile Petra R
AOTS35E035 Overfastidious Personality Levi R
AOTS35E036 Humanity's Strongest Soldier Levi R
AOTS35E037 Frank Disposition Hange R
AOTS35E038 No.1 Oddball Hange U
AOTS35E039 Member of Levi Squad Petra U
AOTS35E040 Cool Personality Levi U
AOTS35E041 Cold Stare Levi U
AOTS35E042 Scout Regiment Commanding Officer Erwin U
AOTS35E043 Member of Levi Squad Eld U
AOTS35E044 Member of Levi Squad Gunther U
AOTS35E045 Scout Regiment Captain Levi C
AOTS35E046 Uplifting Moment Hange C
AOTS35E047 Member of Levi Squad Oruo C
AOTS35E048 Scout Regiment Section Commander Hange C
AOTS35E049 Proud Soldier Levi C
AOTS35E050 Outer Wall Research Erwin C

AOTS35E051 Biological Research U
AOTS35E052 Lesson U
AOTS35E053 The Wings of Freedom RRR
AOTS35E054 Special Operations Squad CC
AOTS35E055 Truth CC
AOTS35E056 104th Cadet Corps Class Christa RR
AOTS35E057 Resisting Fate Mikasa RR
AOTS35E058 Beyond the Walls Mikasa RRR
AOTS35E059 Battle Stance Jean R
AOTS35E060 Paving a Way for the Future Mikasa R
AOTS35E061 Awkward Affection Mikasa R
AOTS35E062 104th Cadet Corps Class Sasha R
AOTS35E063 Direct Sword Mikasa R
AOTS35E064 Calm and Collected Mikasa U
AOTS35E065 Strong Bloodlust Mikasa U
AOTS35E066 Healing Goddess Christa U
AOTS35E067 104th Cadet Corps Class Mikasa U
AOTS35E068 104th Cadet Corps Class Jean U
AOTS35E069 Bold Crime Sasha U
AOTS35E070 104th Cadet Corps Class Reiner U
AOTS35E071 Strong Spirit Reiner C
AOTS35E072 104th Cadet Corps Class Marco C
AOTS35E073 104th Cadet Corps Class Ymir C
AOTS35E074 Strong Appetite Sasha C
AOTS35E075 Disheartened Mikasa C
AOTS35E076 104th Cadet Corps Class Bertholdt C
AOTS35E077 Battle Stance Mikasa C
AOTS35E078 Sore Loser Personality Jean C
AOTS35E079 Tolerant Personality Marco C
AOTS35E080 Sharp Tongue Ymir C
AOTS35E081 Hand of Salvation U
AOTS35E083 The World the Girl Saw RRR
AOTS35E084 I Can Hear His Heartbeat CC
AOTS35E085 Same Class CC
AOTS35E086 Towering Threat Titan R
AOTS35E087 Captured Titan Sawney R
AOTS35E088 High Intellect Female Titan R
AOTS35E089 Plan of Capture Female Titan R
AOTS35E090 Enormous Stature Colossal Titan R
AOTS35E091 Hard Exterior Armored Titan U
AOTS35E092 Threat to Humanity Colossal Titan U
AOTS35E093 Broken Wall Colossal Titan U
AOTS35E096 Overwhelming Power Female Titan C
AOTS35E097 Cruel Smile Titan C
AOTS35E098 Forest of Giant Trees U
AOTS35E099 And, in 850....... RRR
AOTS35E100 Subjugation CC
AOTS35E101 Chimi Armin PR
AOTS35E102 Chimi Conny PR
AOTS35E103 Chimi Eren PR
AOTS35E104 Chimi Annie PR
AOTS35E105 Chimi Hange PR
AOTS35E106 Chimi Levi PR
AOTS35E107 Chimi Sasha PR
AOTS35E108 Chimi Christa PR
AOTS35E109 Chimi Mikasa PR
AOTS35E110 Chimi Jean PR
AOTS35E111 Chimi Reiner PR
AOTS35E112 Chimi Colossal Titan PR
AOTS35E002S Resisting Fate Armin SR
AOTS35E006S Paving a Way for the Future Eren SR
AOTS35E026a Anti-Titan Device Omni-Directional Mobility Gear U
AOTS35E026b Anti-Titan Device Omni-Directional Mobility Gear U
AOTS35E026c Anti-Titan Device Omni-Directional Mobility Gear U
AOTS35E029a What We should Focus On CC
AOTS35E029b What We should Focus On CC
AOTS35E033S Violent Ripples Levi SR
AOTS35E037S Frank Disposition Hange R
AOTS35E056S 104th Cadet Corps Class Christa SR
AOTS35E060S Paving a Way for the Future Mikasa SR
AOTS35E082a Anti-Titan Device Snap Blade U
AOTS35E082b Anti-Titan Device Snap Blade U
AOTS35E082c Anti-Titan Device Snap Blade U
AOTS35E089S Plan of Capture Female Titan SR
AOTS35E094a Predation Titan C
AOTS35E094b Predation Titan C
AOTS35E094c Predation Titan C
AOTS35E100S Subjugation SR
AOTS35E003SP Resisting Fate Eren SP
AOTS35E032SP Resisting Fate Levi SP
AOTS35E057SP Resisting Fate Mikasa SP

2015 Weiss Schwarz Attack on Titan Trial

AOTS35TE01 Armin Arlelt
AOTS35TE02 Honor on the Battlefield Eren
AOTS35TE03 A Chain of Tragedies Armin
AOTS35TE04 A Chain of Tragedies Eren
AOTS35TE05 Activated Power Eren
AOTS35TE06 Hope in the Darkness of Despair Armin
AOTS35TE07 Hope in the Darkness of Despair Eren Titan
AOTS35TE08 Sudden Reinforcement Eren Titan
AOTS35TE09 Conny Springer
AOTS35TE10 Eren Jaeger
AOTS35TE11 The Emblem on Their Backs
AOTS35TE12 One Step Forward
AOTS35TE13 First Battle
AOTS35TE14 A Chain of Tragedies Mikasa
AOTS35TE15 Sasha Braus
AOTS35TE16 Honor on the Battlefield Mikasa
AOTS35TE17 Hope in the Darkness of Despair Mikasa
AOTS35TE18 Mikasa Ackermann
AOTS35TE19 Jean Kirschtein
AOTS35TE20 Day of Resolution
AOTS35TE01R Armin Arlelt RRR
AOTS35TE10S Eren Jaeger SR
AOTS35TE18R Mikasa Ackermann RRR
AOTS35TE10SP Eren Jaeger SP

2015 Weiss Schwarz Fate/stay night Unlimited Blade Works Booster

COMPLETE SET (116)
BOOSTER BOX (20 PACKS) 60.00 80.00
BOOSTER PACK (8 CARDS) 3.00 4.00
RELEASED ON AUGUST 21, 2015
FSS34001P Saber, Knight's Personality SP
FSS34002R Saber's Master Shirou RRR
FSS34003P Saber, Knight's Oath SP
FSS34004S Shirou, Steeled to Fight Alongside SR
FSS34005S Heroic Spirit Saber SR
FSS34006S Saber, Prepared to Fight Together SR
FSS34036R Heroic Spirit Rider RRR
FSS34037S Sakura, Symbol of Normalcy SR
FSS34051P Rin, For Victory SP
FSS34052P Rin, Day of Date SP
FSS34053R Heroic Spirit Archer RRR
FSS34054S Rin, Smile of A Little Devil SR
FSS34055S Rin, as a Magician SR
FSS34056S Archer, Rin's Servant SR
FSS34076R Heroic Spirit Caster RRR
FSS34078S Illya, Silver Thread Alchemy - Wings of Desire SR
FSS34001 Style of a Knight, Saber RR
FSS34002 Saber's Master Shirou RR
FSS34003 A Knight's Oath, Saber RR
FSS34004 Resolution to Fight Together, Shirou R
FSS34005 Heroic Spirit Saber R
FSS34006 Resolution to Fight Together, Saber R
FSS34007 Resolution Not to Fight, Shirou R
FSS34008 Battle with Soichiro, Saber R
FSS34009 Shirou in the Morning Glow R
FSS34010 Battle in the Field Saber R
FSS34011 Battle After School Shirou U
FSS34012 Past Hero, Saber U
FSS34013 Confronting a Servant, Shirou U
FSS34014 Heading for the Rescue, Saber U
FSS34015 Mischievous Smile, Taiga U
FSS34016 Servant Gilgamesh U
FSS34017 Kind Soul, Shirou U
FSS34018 Archery Club Captain, Mitsuzuri U
FSS34019 Commanding Aura, Saber C
FSS34020 At the School Cafeteria, Mitsuzuri C
FSS34021 Shirou's Close Friend Issei C
FSS34022 Tinkering With Machines Shirou C
FSS34023 During Morning Practice, Mitsuzuri C
FSS34024 Usual Morning, Shirou C
FSS34025 Student Council President, Issei C
FSS34026 Usual Morning, Taiga C
FSS34027 Activating a Command Seal, Shirou C
FSS34028 Servant with Blond Hair C
FSS34029 Hidden Weapon, Saber C
FSS34030 Temporary Rest U
FSS34031 Self-Training C
FSS34032 Armor Release CR
FSS34033 A Fateful Night CC
FSS34034 Anger Towards Evil CC
FSS34035 Summoning Saber CC
FSS34036 Heroic Spirit Rider RR
FSS34037 Daily Symbol, Sakura R
FSS34038 Bewitching Beauty, Rider R
FSS34039 Heroic Spirit Lancer R
FSS34040 Morning Greeting, Sakura U
FSS34041 Archery Club Member, Sakura U
FSS34042 Bystander Lancer U
FSS34043 Self-concious, Shinji C
FSS34044 Archery Club Vice-captain, Shinji C
FSS34045 Moving Like a Beast, Lancer C
FSS34046 Usual Morning, Sakura C
FSS34047 Shinji's Servant, Rider C
FSS34048 Noble Phantasm Unleashed U
FSS34049 Dancing After School CR
FSS34050 Bounded Field CC
FSS34051 For Victory, Rin RR
FSS34052 Great Day for a Date, Rin RR
FSS34053 Heroic Spirit Archer RR
FSS34054 Devilish Smile, Rin R
FSS34055 As a Mage, Rin R
FSS34056 Rin's Servant, Archer R
FSS34057 Latecomer, Archer R
FSS34058 Cursed Magic Bullet, Rin R
FSS34059 A Master's Mental State, Ri R
FSS34060 A Bowman's True Value, Archer R
FSS34061 Proof of Contract, Rin U
FSS34062 Fashionable Glasses, Rin U
FSS34063 Proof of Contract, Archer U
FSS34064 Archer, Surprise Attack U
FSS34065 A Bowman's Speciality, Archer U
FSS34066 Cynic, Archer C
FSS34067 Rough Summoning, Archer C
FSS34068 Dual-wielding Bowman, Archer C
FSS34069 A Different Morning, Rin C
FSS34070 Summon Rites, Rin C
FSS34071 Father's Keepsake U
FSS34072 Tohsaka's Magic Crest CR
FSS34073 Summoning Ritual CC
FSS34074 Precision Piercing CC
FSS34075 A Bowman's Speciality CC
FSS34076 Heroic Spirit Caster RR
FSS34077 Mages' Fighting Style, Caster R
FSS34078 Silver Thread Alchemy Elgen Lied, Illya R
FSS34079 Heroic Spirit Assassin R
FSS34080 Caster's Master Soichiro Kuzuki U
FSS34081 Rin's Classmate, Kane Himuro U
FSS34082 Overwhelming Violence, Berserker U
FSS34083 Lady, Illya U
FSS34084 Hypocritical Courtesy, Kirei U
FSS34085 Finishing Move, Assassin U
FSS34086 Tactician, Caster U
FSS34087 Warning Before the Battle, Illya C
FSS34088 Modern Power, Kirei C
FSS34089 Heroic Spirit Berserker C
FSS34090 Rin's Classmate, Yukika Saegusa C
FSS34091 Berseker's Master Illya C
FSS34092 Rin's Classmate, Kaede Makidera C
FSS34093 Rule-breaking Noble Phantasm, Caster C
FSS34094 Overseer of the Holy Grail War, Kirei C
FSS34095 Reticent Teacher, Soichiro Kuzuki C
FSS34096 Illusion Magic U
FSS34097 Taken U
FSS34098 Immense Power C
FSS34099 Illya's Magic, Storch Ritter CR
FSS34100 Rule-breaking Noble Phantasm CC

2015 Weiss Schwarz Fate/stay night Unlimited Blade Works Trial

FSS34T16P Saber, participation Saber to Joining the Holy Grail War SP
FSS34T16R Saber, participation Saber to Joining the Holy Grail War RRR
FSS34T18S Rin & Archer, and phosphorus for For Victory SR
FSS34T19P Rin, Gem Magician SP
FSS34T19R Rin, Gem Magician RRR
FSS34T01 Saber, Dignified Air
FSS34T02 Shirou, Tinkering With Machines
FSS34T03 Shirou, A Normal Morning
FSS34T04 Saber, Heroes From the Past
FSS34T05 Shirou, Friendly to Others
FSS34T06 Saber, Concealed Weapon
FSS34T07 Self-Training
FSS34T08 Fateful Night
FSS34T09 Rin, Proof of Pact
FSS34T10 Archer, Rough Summoning
FSS34T11 Archer, Bowman Wielding Two Blades
FSS34T12 A Different Than Normal Morning
FSS34T13 Rin, Summoning Ritual
FSS34T14 Ritual of Summoning Ritual
FSS34T15 Skills of a Bowman
FSS34T16 Saber, participation Saber to Joining the Holy Grail War
FSS34T17 Archer, Archer work of the Job of a Familiar
FSS34T18 Rin & Archer, and phosphorus for For Victory
FSS34T19 Rin, Gem Magician
FSS34T20 Shirou, Enhancing Magic

2016 Weiss Schwarz Extra Booster NISEKOI False Love

COMPLETE SET (39 CARDS) 250.00 300.00
BOOSTER BOX (6 PACKS) 40.00 50.00
BOOSTER PACK (6 CARDS) 3.00 5.00
RELEASED ON AUGUST 19, 2016
NKWE22E01 Unrivaled Beauty Chitoge R 1.00 2.00
NKWE22E02 Pajama Party Chitoge R 1.50 2.50
NKWE22E02SP Pajama Party Chitoge SP 65.00 75.00
NKWE22E03 Magical Gorilla Chitoge C .30 .50
NKWE22E04 To and From School Raku C .30 .50
NKWE22E05 New Life Chitoge C .30 .50
NKWE22E06 Great Style Chitoge C .30 .50
NKWE22E07 But Its All About You C .30 .50
NKWE22E08 Neighbor Haru R 5.00 8.00
NKWE22E09 New Life Haru R 2.50 3.50
NKWE22E10 Tsugumyaa R 1.00 2.00
NKWE22E11 Swimsuit Haru R 1.00 2.00
NKWE22E12 Pajama Party Haru R 3.50 5.00
NKWE22E12SP Pajama Party Haru SP 70.00 85.00
NKWE22E13 New Life Seishiro C .30 .50
NKWE22E14 Harus Friend Fuu C .30 .50
NKWE22E15 Clue Haru C .30 .50
NKWE22E16 Paula McCoy C .30 .50
NKWE22E17 From Here On Seishiro C .30 .50
NKWE22E18 Haru Onodera C .30 .50
NKWE22E19 Beehives White Fang Paula C .30 .50
NKWE22E20 Someday My Prince Will C 1.00 2.00
NKWE22E21 Magical Police Marika R 1.00 2.00
NKWE22E22 Marikas Dress Look C .30 .50
NKWE22E23 New Life Marika C .30 .50
NKWE22E24 Draw of the Shop Haru R 2.00 3.00
NKWE22E25 Freshman Haru R 2.00 3.00
NKWE22E26 Magical Patissiere Kosaki R 1.00 2.00
NKWE22E27 Pajama Party Kosaki R 4.00 6.00
NKWE22E27SP Pajama Party Kosaki SP 75.00 90.00
NKWE22E28 Sisters Taking a Bath Kosaki C .30 .50
NKWE22E29 Rurin C .30 .50
NKWE22E30 Fuus Prank Haru C .30 .50
NKWE22E31 Sisters Taking a Bath Haru C .30 .50
NKWE22E32 110000 Miracle Kosaki C .75 1.25
NKWE22E33 New Life Kosaki C .30 .50
NKWE22E34 Head Tilt Haru C .30 .50
NKWE22E35 New Life Ruri C .30 .50
NKWE22E36 Contract Concluded C 1.00 2.00

2016 Weiss Schwarz Love Live DX Vol 2

COMPLETE SET (230 CARDS) 1500.00 2250.00
BOOSTER BOX (20 PACKS) 60.00 80.00
BOOSTER PACK (8 CARDS) 3.00 5.00
UNLISTED C .10 .30
UNLISTED U .30 .50
UNLISTED R .50 1.00
RELEASED ON AUGUST 26, 2016
LLENW02E001 Maid Outfit us R 30.00 40.00
LLENW02E001auR Maid Outfit us R 25.00 35.00
LLENW02E001buR Maid Outfit us R 20.00 30.00
LLENW02E001cuR Maid Outfit us R 15.00 25.00
LLENW02E001duR Maid Outfit us R 15.00 25.00
LLENW02E001euR Maid Outfit us R 10.00 20.00
LLENW02E001fuR Maid Outfit us R 10.00 20.00
LLENW02E001guR Maid Outfit us R 10.00 20.00
LLENW02E001huR Maid Outfit us R .50 1.00
LLENW02E001iuR Maid Outfit us R .50 1.00
LLENW02E002 Tea Time Kotori Hanayo U .20 .50
LLENW02E003 Leader of us Honoka C .10 .30
LLENW02E004 Summer Festival Date Eli Ayase RR8.00 15.00
LLENW02E004SP Summer Festival Date Eli Ayase SP 75.00 100.00
LLENW02E005 Angelic Angel Nozomi Tojo RR 3.00 8.00
LLENW02E006 Summer Festival Date Nico Yazawa RR 3.00 8.00
LLENW02E006SP Summer Festival Date Nico Yazawa SP 80.00 100.00
LLENW02E007 Angelic Angel Eli Ayase RR 1.00 2.00
LLENW02E008 Summer Festival Date Nozomi Tojo RR 3.00 8.00
LLENW02E008SP Summer Festival Date Nozomi Tojo SP 70.00 90.00
LLENW02E009 We Are A Single Light Nico Yazawa RR 15.00 25.00
LLENW02E010 Dressed Up Nozomi Tojo R .50 1.00
LLENW02E010R Dressed Up Nozomi Tojo RRR 5.00 10.00
LLENW02E011 Angelic Angel Nico Yazawa R 2.50 4.00
LLENW02E012 Sweets Fairy Nozomi Tojo R .50 1.00
LLENW02E012S Sweets Fairy Nozomi Tojo SR 3.00 8.00
LLENW02E013 Sweets Fairy Nico Yazawa R .50 1.00
LLENW02E013S Sweets Fairy Nico Yazawa SR 3.00 8.00
LLENW02E014 Dressed Up Eli Ayase R 1.00 2.00
LLENW02E014R Dressed Up Eli Ayase RRR 8.00 15.00
LLENW02E015 Heartbeat Eli Ayase R .50 1.00
LLENW02E016 Heartbeat Nozomi Tojo R .50 1.00
LLENW02E017 Sweets Fairy Eli Ayase R .50 1.00
LLENW02E017S Sweets Fairy Eli Ayase SR 3.00 8.00
LLENW02E018 Dressed Up Nico Yazawa R 2.50 4.00
LLENW02E018R Dressed Up Nico Yazawa RRR 10.00 20.00
LLENW02E019 Taking Care of Nails Nico U .20 .50
LLENW02E020 Apple Candy and You Eli Ayase U .20 .50
LLENW02E021 Great Summer Break Nico Yazawa U.20 .50
LLENW02E022 Someday from Here On Maki Nico Rin U .20 .50
LLENW02E023 Snack Time Nozomi Nico U .20 .50
LLENW02E024 Christmas Date Nico Yazawa U .20 .50
LLENW02E025 Festival Girl Nozomi Tojo U .20 .50
LLENW02E026 Christmas Date Nozomi Tojo U .20 .50
LLENW02E027 A Present for You Eli Ayase U .20 .50
LLENW02E028 Secret Gift U .20 .50
LLENW02E029 Happiest Girl U .20 .50
LLENW02E030 Lucky New Year U .20 .50
LLENW02E031 Your Special Santa Nozomi Tojo C .10 .30
LLENW02E032 New Years Treat Nico Yazawa C .10 .30
LLENW02E033 Autumn With Books Eli Ayase C .10 .30
LLENW02E034 Chinese Vampire Nozomi Tojo C .10 .30
LLENW02E035 Marching Girl Eli Ayase C .10 .30
LLENW02E036 Western Girl Nico Yazawa C .10 .30
LLENW02E037 Doll Festival Nico Yazawa C .10 .30
LLENW02E038 Student of Otonokizaka High Alisa C.10 .30
LLENW02E039 Sunny Day Song Eli Ayase C .10 .30
LLENW02E040 Light••Umbrella Eli Ayase C .10 .30
LLENW02E041 Shrine Maiden Outfit Nozomi Tojo C.10 .30
LLENW02E042 Sunny Day Song Alisa Ayase C .10 .30
LLENW02E043 Good Girl Christmas Nico Yazawa C.10 .30
LLENW02E044 School Matters Eli C .10 .30
LLENW02E045 Special Stew Eli Ayase C .10 .30
LLENW02E046 Homely Idol Nico Yazawa C .10 .30
LLENW02E047 Christmas Date Eli Ayase C .10 .30
LLENW02E048 Full Course of Luck Nozomi Tojo C.10 .30
LLENW02E049 Sunny Day Song Nico Yazawa C .10 .30
LLENW02E050 Sunny Day Song Nozomi Tojo C .10 .30
LLENW02E051 Hug Attack Nozomi Tojo C .10 .30
LLENW02E052 A Piece of Chocolate R .50 1.00
LLENW02E053 Special Chocolate R .50 1.00
LLENW02E054a We Are A Single Light R 35.00 55.00
LLENW02E054aSP We Are A Single Light SP 35.00 55.00
LLENW02E054b We Are A Single Light R 20.00 40.00
LLENW02E054bSP We Are A Single Light SP 30.00 50.00
LLENW02E054c We Are A Single Light R 40.00 60.00
LLENW02E054cSP We Are A Single Light SP 40.00 60.00
LLENW02E055 Happy Valentine C .10 .30
LLENW02E056 Heartbeat C .10 .30
LLENW02E057 Angelic Angel C .10 .30
LLENW02E058 We Are A Single Light Kotori Minami RR 3.00 8.00
LLENW02E059 Angelic Angel Umi Sonoda RR 3.00 8.00
LLENW02E060 Summer Festival Date Kotori Minami RR 1.00 2.50
LLENW02E060SP Summer Festival Date Kotori Minami SP 50.00 70.00
LLENW02E061 Summer Festival Date Honoka Kosaka RR 3.00 8.00
LLENW02E061SP Summer Festival Date Honoka Kosaka SP 50.00 70.00
LLENW02E062 Summer Festival Date Umi Sonoda RR 3.00 8.00
LLENW02E062SP Summer Festival Date Umi Sonoda SP 80.00 100.00
LLENW02E063 Sunny Day Song Honoka Kosaka RR3.00 8.00
LLENW02E064 Dressed Up Honoka Kosaka R 2.50 4.00
LLENW02E064R Dressed Up Honoka Kosaka RRR10.00 20.00
LLENW02E065 Sweets Fairy Kotori Minami R .50 1.00
LLENW02E065S Sweets Fairy Kotori Minami SR 3.00 8.00
LLENW02E066 Dressed Up Kotori Minami R 1.00 6.00
LLENW02E066R Dressed Up Kotori Minami RRR 8.00 12.00
LLENW02E067 Dressed Up Umi Sonoda R .50 1.00
LLENW02E067R Dressed Up Umi Sonoda RRR 5.00 10.00
LLENW02E068 Sweets Fairy Umi Sonoda R .50 1.00
LLENW02E068S Sweets Fairy Umi Sonoda SR 3.00 8.00
LLENW02E069 Sweets Fairy Honoka Kosaka R .50 1.00
LLENW02E069S Sweets Fairy Honoka Kosaka SR3.00 8.00
LLENW02E070 Sunny Day Song Umi Sonoda R 1.00 2.50
LLENW02E071 Angelic Angel Honoka Kosaka R .50 1.00
LLENW02E072 Angelic Angel Kotori Minami R 2.50 4.00
LLENW02E073 The First Step Honoka U .20 .50
LLENW02E074 Everyones Festival Honoka Kosaka U.20 .50
LLENW02E075 Christmas Date Kotori Minami U .20 .50
LLENW02E076 Pure Night Umi Sonoda U .20 .50
LLENW02E077 Lets go slowly Honoka Kosaka U .20 .50
LLENW02E078 Cool Evening Breeze Kotori Minami U.20 .50
LLENW02E079 Christmas Date Umi Sonoda U .20 .50
LLENW02E080 Christmas Date Honoka Kosaka U .20 .50
LLENW02E081 Happy New Year? U .20 .50
LLENW02E082 New Years Dream U .20 .50
LLENW02E083 Yearly Greetings U .20 .50
LLENW02E084 Maid Outfit Umi C .10 .30
LLENW02E085 Snow Lady Umi Sonoda C .10 .30
LLENW02E086 White Christmas Kotori Minami C .10 .30
LLENW02E087 Taisho Era Girl Honoka Kosaka C .10 .30
LLENW02E088 Snowy Night Umi Sonoda C .10 .30
LLENW02E089 Cotton Kimono Umi Sonoda C .10 .30
LLENW02E090 In Practice Umi Sonoda C .10 .30
LLENW02E091 Sunny Day Song Kotori Minami C .10 .30
LLENW02E092 Sunny Day Song Yukiho Kosaka C .10 .30
LLENW02E093 Student of Otonokizaka High Yukiho C .10 .30
LLENW02E094 Sunny Day Song Tsubasa Kira C .10 .30
LLENW02E095 Sunny Day Song Erena Todo C .10 .30
LLENW02E096 Sunny Day Song Anju Yuki C .10 .30
LLENW02E097 Future Style Honoka Kosaka C .10 .30
LLENW02E098 Angel Nurse Kotori Minami C .10 .30
LLENW02E099 Blissful Snacks Honoka Kosaka C .10 .30
LLENW02E100 Candle Night Honoka Kosaka C .10 .30
LLENW02E101 Angel Nurse Kotori Minami C .10 .30
LLENW02E102 Bird Watching Kotori Minami C .10 .30
LLENW02E103 Future Style Umi Sonoda C .10 .30
LLENW02E104 Homuras Star Honoka Kosaka C .10 .30
LLENW02E105 Hiking Honoka Kosaka C .10 .30
LLENW02E106 Female Singer C .10 .30
LLENW02E107 Swimsuit Kotori C .10 .30
LLENW02E108 Thankful Feast Umi Sonoda C .10 .30
LLENW02E109 Open Wide Kotori Minami C .10 .30
LLENW02E110 Find Your Answer C .10 .30
LLENW02E111 Secret Desire R .50 1.00
LLENW02E112a We Are A Single Light R 25.00 45.00
LLENW02E112aSP We Are A Single Light SP 25.00 45.00
LLENW02E112b We Are A Single Light R 30.00 50.00
LLENW02E112bSP We Are A Single Light SP 30.00 50.00
LLENW02E112c We Are A Single Light R 35.00 55.00
LLENW02E112cSP We Are A Single Light SP 35.00 55.00
LLENW02E113 Lots o Animals C .10 .30
LLENW02E114 Sweet and Smooth C .10 .30
LLENW02E115 Future Style C .10 .30
LLENW02E116 Sunny Day Song C .10 .30
LLENW02E117 Summer Festival Date Maki Nishikino RR 10.00 20.00
LLENW02E117SP Summer Festival Date Maki Nishikino SP 80.00 120.00
LLENW02E118 Hello Count the Stars Rin Hoshizora RR 3.00 8.00
LLENW02E119 We Are A Single Light Maki Nishikino RR 15.00 25.00
LLENW02E120 Summer Festival Date Rin Hoshizora RR 1.00 2.00
LLENW02E120SP Summer Festival Date Rin Hoshizora SP 35.00 55.00
LLENW02E121 Summer Festival Date Hanayo Koizumi RR 3.00 8.00
LLENW02E121SP Summer Festival Date Hanayo Koizumi SP 40.00 60.00
LLENW02E122 Angelic Angel Hanayo Koizumi RR1.00 2.50
LLENW02E123 Sweets Fairy Hanayo Koizumi R .50 1.00
LLENW02E123R Sweets Fairy Hanayo Koizumi SR3.00 8.00
LLENW02E124 Sweets Fairy Rin Hoshizora R .50 1.00
LLENW02E124R Sweets Fairy Rin Hoshizora SR 3.00 8.00
LLENW02E125 Sunny Day Song Hanayo Koizumi R.50 1.00
LLENW02E126 Dressed Up Rin Hoshizora R .50 1.00
LLENW02E126R Dressed Up Rin Hoshizora RRR 4.00 8.00
LLENW02E127 Angelic Angel Maki Nishikino R 2.50 4.00
LLENW02E128 Dressed Up Hanayo Koizumi R .50 1.00
LLENW02E128R Dressed Up Hanayo Koizumi RRR4.00 8.00
LLENW02E129 Sweets Fairy Maki Nishikino R .50 1.00
LLENW02E129S Sweets Fairy Maki Nishikino SR3.00 8.00
LLENW02E130 Angelic Angel Rin Hoshizora R .50 1.00
LLENW02E131 Dressed Up Maki Nishikino R 2.00 3.50
LLENW02E131R Dressed Up Maki Nishikino RRR15.00 25.00
LLENW02E132 Secret Expression Maki U .20 .50
LLENW02E133 Melody Played Maki U .20 .50
LLENW02E134 In the Middle of Recording Rin Hanayo U .20 .50
LLENW02E135 Christmas Date Hanayo Koizumi U .20 .50
LLENW02E136 Bon Dance Rin Hoshizora U .20 .50
LLENW02E137 Goldfish Scooper Maki Nishikino U.20 .50
LLENW02E138 Christmas Date Rin Hoshizora U .20 .50
LLENW02E139 Night StallHopping Hanayo Koizumi U .20 .50
LLENW02E140 Christmas Date Maki Nishikino U .20 .50
LLENW02E141 Alpaca U .20 .50
LLENW02E142 Finest Once a Year U .20 .50
LLENW02E143 Mochi is Rice Too U .20 .50
LLENW02E144 365 Happy Days U .20 .50
LLENW02E145 Gothic Girl Maki Nishikino C .10 .30
LLENW02E146 Princess Kaguya Rin Hoshizora C .10 .30
LLENW02E147 Elven Ties Hanayo Koizumi C .10 .30
LLENW02E148 Lets Skate Together Hanayo Koizumi C .10 .30
LLENW02E149 Christmas Carol Maki Nishikino C .10 .30
LLENW02E150 Scattering Beans Maki Nishikino C.10 .30
LLENW02E151 Sunny Day Song Rin Hoshizora C .10 .30
LLENW02E152 A Service for You Maki Nishikino C.10 .30
LLENW02E153 Christmas Bells Rin Hoshizora C .10 .30
LLENW02E154 Secret Recipes Maki Nishikino C .10 .30
LLENW02E155 My Christmas Treat Hanayo Koizumi C .10 .30
LLENW02E156 Fluffy Alpaca C .10 .30
LLENW02E157 Homemade Ramen Rin Hoshizora C.10 .30
LLENW02E158 Snow Sprite Rin Hoshizora C .10 .30
LLENW02E159 Sunny Day Song Maki Nishikino C.10 .30
LLENW02E160 View the Full Moon Rin Hoshizora C.10 .30
LLENW02E161 Healing Menu Hanayo Koizumi C .10 .30
LLENW02E162 Clam Hunting Hanayo Koizumi C .10 .30
LLENW02E163 Hello Count the Stars Hanayo Koizumi R .50 1.00
LLENW02E164 Romantic Valentine R .50 1.00
LLENW02E165a We Are A Single Light R 25.00 45.00
LLENW02E165aSP We Are A Single Light SP 25.00 45.00
LLENW02E165b We Are A Single Light R 50.00 70.00
LLENW02E165bSP We Are A Single Light SP 50.00 70.00
LLENW02E165c We Are A Single Light R 20.00 30.00
LLENW02E165cSP We Are A Single Light SP 20.00 40.00
LLENW02E166 Rins Secret C .10 .30
LLENW02E167 Makis Secret C .10 .30
LLENW02E168 Hello Count the Stars C .10 .30
LLENW02E169 Time for Home Economics C .10 .30

Dragon Ball Z

HOW TO USE

What's Listed

Products listed in the Price Guide typically: 1) are produced by licensed manufacturers, 2) are widely available and 3) have market activity on single items.

What the Columns Mean

The LO and HI columns reflect current retail selling ranges. The HI column on the right generally represents the full retail selling price. The LO column on the left generally represents the lowest price one would expect to find with extensive shopping.

Grading

All cards in the Price Guide are based on NrMint to Mint condition. Damaged cards are generally sold for 25 to 75 percent of Mint value. Toy prices are based on mint condition. Toys that are loose (out of package), are generally sold for 50 percent of the listed price.

Currency

This Price Guide is intended to reflect the entire North American market. All listed prices are in U.S. dollars.

Legend

C – Common

PR - Promo

R – Rare

U – Uncommon

UR – Ultra rare

Attention Dealers: If you would like to be a Price Guide Contributor for this almanac, please e-mail your name and phone number to: nonsports@beckett.com

1995 Dragon Ball Z Ani-Mayhem

Item	LO	HI
COMPLETE SET (232)	125.00	175.00
BOOSTER BOX (60 PACKS)	120.00	200.00
BOOSTER PACKS (9 CARDS)	5.00	9.00
STARTER DECK	15.00	30.00
1 Adult Gohan R	4.00	8.00
2 Atlia U	.50	1.00
3 Baba R	2.00	4.00
4 Baby Gohan C	1.00	2.00
5 Bubbles R	3.00	6.00
6 Bulma C	2.00	4.00
7 Chi-Chi C	1.00	2.00
8 Chiao-Tzu R	1.00	3.00
9 Farmer with shotgun C	.10	.25
10 Future Trunks UR	8.00	16.00
11 Gohan the Barbarian U	.50	1.00
12 Goku C	2.00	4.00
13 Goku (different)R	6.00	12.00
14 Goten R	4.00	8.00
15 Gregory R	1.00	3.00
16 Kami R	3.00	6.00
17 Krillin C	1.00	2.00
18 Lunch U	1.00	2.00
19 Master Roshi U	1.00	2.00
20 Nail U	2.00	4.00
21 Oolong U	1.00	2.00
22 Ox-King U	1.00	2.00
23 Piccolo R	4.00	8.00
24 Super Saiyan Goku UR	10.00	20.00
25 Super Saiyan Goten UR	8.00	16.00
26 Super Saiyan Trunks UR	8.00	16.00
27 Tien (Tenshinhan)C	1.00	2.00
28 Trunks C	1.00	3.00
29 Yajirobe C	1.00	2.00
30 Yamcha C	.10	.25
31 Young Gohan U	2.00	4.00
32 Bump on the Head R	1.50	3.00
33 Good Deed U	.25	.50
34 Heavy Gravity Training R	2.00	4.00
35 Leap of Faith U	.25	.50
36 M.V.P. C	.10	.25
37 Speed II C	.10	.25
38 Spirit C	.10	.25
39 Spirit Fighting C	.10	.25
40 Survey R	1.00	3.00
41 Survival Training U	.25	.50
42 Weighted Clothing U	.25	.50
43 Algebra R	1.00	3.00
44 Airbus U	.25	.50
45 Blasters C	.10	.25
46 Dragon Radar R	1.00	3.00
47 Dream Mirror R	1.00	3.00
48 Floating Car C	.10	.25
49 Giant's Toy Biplane U	.25	.50
50 Goz' Flying Machine R	1.00	3.00
51 Gravity Ship R	1.00	3.00
52 Hand Gun U	.25	.50
53 Kai's Dimensional Sedan R	1.00	3.00
54 Light R	1.00	3.00
55 Namek Ship R	1.00	3.00
56 Razor Balls C	.10	.25
57 Rocket Launcher U	.25	.50
58 Saiyan Space Pod C	.10	.25
59 Scouter C	.50	1.00
60 Change Direction C	.10	.25
61 Destructo Disc R	1.00	3.00
62 Divert Attack R	3.00	6.00
63 Dodonpa C	.10	.25
64 Fake Item R	1.00	3.00
65 False Moon R	2.00	4.00
66 Genki-Dama (Spirit Ball)R	3.00	6.00
67 Gohan is Angry C	.25	.50
68 Haste U	.25	.50
69 Hey, You're not Dead C	.10	.25
70 High Ground C	.10	.25
71 Jan-ken-Po C	.10	.25
72 Just a Scratch R	1.00	3.00
73 Kamehameha U	1.00	3.00
74 Keen Observation R	1.00	3.00
75 Know When to Run U	.25	.50
76 Laser Eyes C	.10	.25
77 Makkankoupousou R	2.00	4.00
78 Meltdown R	1.00	3.00
79 Mindtrap R	2.00	4.00
80 Moon Destruction C	.10	.25
81 Mother Instinct U	.25	.50
82 Out of the Frying Pan U	.25	.50
83 Regeneration U	.25	.50
84 Rescue R	1.00	3.00
85 Shen Lon UR	6.00	12.00
86 Shield R	1.00	3.00
87 Spilt Form C	.10	.25
88 Sunshine Daydream U	.25	.50
89 Telekinese R	2.00	4.00
90 Time Out! C	.10	.25
91 Ultimate Sacrifice R	1.00	3.00
92 Who Sows the Wind C	.10	.25
93 Equipment Retrieval U	1.50	3.00
94 Frothy Mugs of Water C	.10	.25
95 Great King Yemma R	1.00	3.00
96 Guardian of the Earth R	1.00	3.00
97 Guru R	1.00	3.00
98 Hiding Out U	.25	.50
99 King Kai C	.25	.50
100 Medical Regenerator U	.25	.50
101 Power Sense U	.25	.50
102 Power Up U	1.00	3.00
103 Refuge R	1.00	3.00
104 Slow Moving Traffic C	.10	.25
105 Training with Kami U	.25	.50
106 Gohan's Cave C	.10	.25
107 King Kai's Bungalow U	1.00	2.00
108 Lunch's House C	.10	.25
109 Roshi's Veranda C	1.00	3.00
110 Otherworld Lounge U	.25	.50
111 West Side City Hospital U	.25	.50
112 Dragon Ball C	.10	.25
113 2 Dragon Balls U	3.00	6.00
114 3 Dragon Balls R	4.00	8.00
115 Baby Dragon U	.25	.50
116 Capsule Army Knife C	.10	.25
117 Firewood C	.10	.25
118 Flying Nimbus R	2.00	4.00
119 Gohan's Supplies C	.10	.25
120 King Yemma's Fruit U	.25	.50
121 Lemlia C	.10	.25
122 Mighty Fridge C	.10	.25
123 Presents U	.25	.50
124 Samurai Gohan R	2.00	4.00
125 Senzu Beans R	2.00	4.00
126 Ships Auto-Toilet R	1.00	3.00
127 Sleepy Grass C	.10	.25
128 Tail Steak C	.10	.25
129 Technological Artifact C	.10	.25
130 Tortoise R	1.00	3.00
131 Alien Jungle C	.10	.25
132 Alien Landing Site C	.10	.25
133 Arena C	.10	.25
134 Baseball Stadium C	.25	.50
135 Beware: Bathroom! C	.50	1.00
136 Café C	.10	.25
137 Campground U	.25	.50
138 Capsule Corporation U	.25	.50
139 Desert Battleground C	.10	.25
140 Dr. Weelo's Fortress R	1.00	3.00
141 Forest Glade U	.25	.50
142 Freeza's Ship R	2.00	4.00
143 Frozen Wastes C	.10	.25
144 Garlic Jr.'s Palace U	.25	.50
145 Goku and Chi-Chi's House U	.50	1.00
146 Hong Kong U	.25	.50
147 Illusionary Castle C	.10	.25
148 Kami's Floating Palace U	.25	.50
149 King Kai's Planetoid R	1.00	3.00
150 King Yemma's Palace C	.50	1.00
151 Pendulum Training Room R	1.00	3.00
152 Planet Arlia C	.10	.25
153 Planet Freeza C	1.00	2.00
154 Planet Namek R	1.00	3.00
155 Planet Vegeta R	2.00	4.00
156 Princess Snake's Palace R	1.00	3.00
157 Snake Way U	.25	.50
158 Dodria C	.75	1.50
159 Freeza (1st form)R	4.00	8.00
160 Garlic Jr. U	1.00	3.00
161 Ginger C	.10	.25
162 Ginyu U	.75	1.50
163 Kidnapped C	.10	.25
164 Nappa C	1.00	2.00
165 Princess Snake U	.25	.50
166 Raditz C	.25	.50
167 Raiichi and Zaakro C	.10	.25
168 Recoom C	.75	1.50
169 Sabre-Toothed Tiger C	.10	.25
170 Tares R	2.00	4.00
171 The Dead Zone U	.25	.50
172 Vegeta U	4.00	8.00
173 Acid Head U	.25	.50
174 Asteroid Field U	.25	.50
175 Baby Saiyan R	3.00	6.00
176 Catch Bubbles R	1.00	3.00
177 Demon Hordes U	.25	.50
178 Don't Be A Dummy C	.10	.25
179 Dr. Weelo R	1.00	3.00
180 Dr. Weelo's Bio Men U	1.00	2.00
181 Ebi-Furiya U	.25	.50
182 Excessive Gravity U	.25	.50
183 Full Moon U	1.00	2.00
184 Goz C	.10	.25
185 Guldo C	.10	.25
186 Homework C	.10	.25
187 Hungry Dinasaur C	.10	.25
188 Ibuprofen and Quickly! U	.25	.50
189 Impending Doom U	.25	.50
190 Kishiime C	.10	.25
191 Loner U	.25	.50
192 Mez C	.10	.25
193 Miso-Cutsun U	.25	.50
194 Mystery Foe R	2.00	4.00
195 No Help! U	.25	.50
196 Overload C	.10	.25
197 Property Damage U	.25	.50
198 Pterodactyl C	.10	.25
199 Saibamen U	.25	.50
200 Shinseiju Tree R	2.00	4.00
201 Squeeeeeeeeeze! U	.25	.50
202 The Pit C	.10	.25
203 Watch That 1st Step U	.25	.50
204 Willpower U	.25	.50
205 Zarbon R	1.00	3.00
206 Back Kick U	.25	.50
207 Be with you C	.10	.25
208 Bench Brawl U	.25	.50
209 Berserk U	.25	.50
210 Crushing Left U	.25	.50
211 Devestating Attack C	.10	.25
212 Double Blow C	.25	.50
213 Drop Kick C	.10	.25
214 Films About Gladiators U	.25	.50
215 Flying Kick C	.10	.25
216 Fried C	.10	.25
217 Grace C	.10	.25
218 Gut Punch C	.10	.25
219 Head Butt C	.10	.25
220 In My Sights C	.10	.25
221 Incoming C	.10	.25
222 Just a Trim C	.10	.25
223 Leg Sweep C	.10	.25
224 Lunch Break U	.25	.50
225 Oooh! It Got Me! U	.25	.50
226 Pinned C	.10	.25
227 Pummel C	.10	.25
228 Screwed U	.25	.50
229 Shock C	.10	.25
230 To Much Sun C	.10	.25
231 Wild Swing C	.10	.25
232 Yipes C	.10	.25

2000 Dragon Ball Z Saiyan Saga Limited

Item	LO	HI
COMPLETE SET (250)	200.00	400.00
UNOPENED BOX (36 PACKS)	75.00	150.00
UNOPENED PACK (9 CARDS)	2.00	5.00
1 Orange Standing Fist Punch C	.10	.30
2 Orange One Knuckle Punch C	.10	.30
3 Orange Two Knuckle Punch C	.10	.30
4 Orange Leg Sweep C	.10	.30
5 Orange Arm Bar C	.10	.30
6 Red Lunge Punch C	.10	.30
7 Red Reverse Punch C	.10	.30
8 Red Knife Hand C	.10	.30
9 Red Palm Heel Strike C	.10	.30
10 Red Elbow StrikeC	.10	.30
11 Blue Forward Foot Sweep C	.10	.30
12 Blue Hip Spring Throw C	.10	.30
13 Blue Round Throw C	.10	.30
14 Blue Shoulder Wheel C	.10	.30
15 Earth Dragon Ball 1 C	.10	.30
16 Earth Dragon Ball 2 C	.10	.30
17 Hidden Power Level C	.10	.30

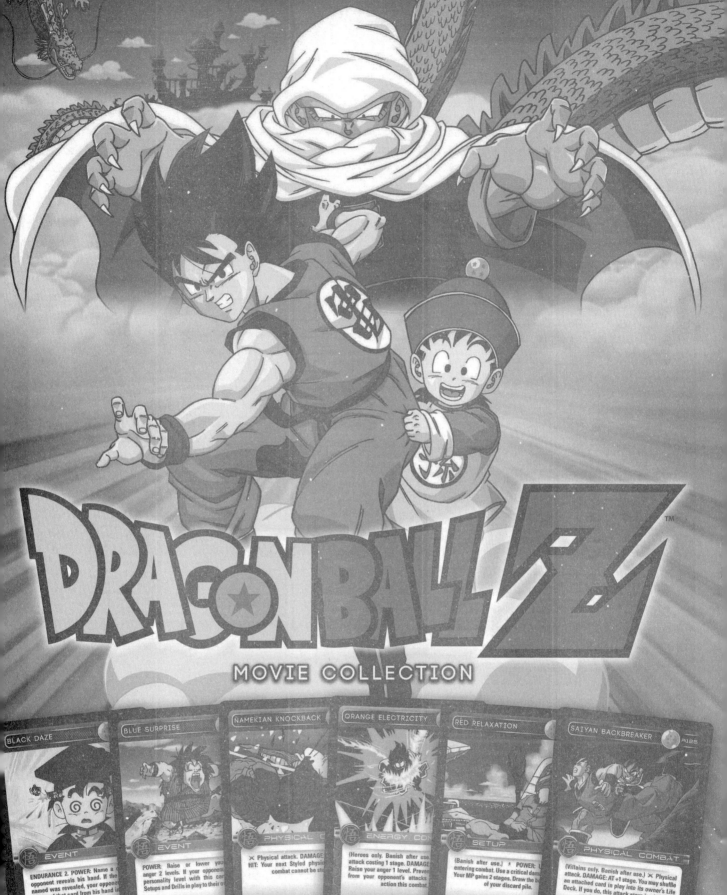

18 Saiyan Arm Throw C .10 .30
19 Saiyan Full Spin Kick C .10 .30
20 Saiyan Pressure Punch C .10 .30
21 Saiyan Neck Hold C .10 .30
22 Power Up C .10 .30
23 Burning Rage C .10 .30
24 Goku's Surprise Attack C .10 .30
25 Goku's Physical Attack C .10 .30
26 Gohan's Physical Attack C .10 .30
27 Tien's Physical Attack C .10 .30
28 Vegeta's Physical Stance C .10 .30
29 Yajirobe's Physical Attack C .10 .30
30 Fall 7 times, get up 8 times C .10 .30
31 Fortify Your Spirit C .10 .30
32 The Untroubled Mind is Focused C .10 .30
33 It's the Little Things That Matter C .10 .30
34 Straining Off-Balancing Move C .10 .30
35 Straining, Penetrating Attack Move C .10 .30
36 Straining Fake Left Move C .10 .30
37 Straining Tripping Move C .10 .30
38 Straining Arm Drag Move C .10 .30
39 Straining Ankle Smash Move C .10 .30
40 Straining Energy Defense Move C .10 .30
41 Straining Head Lock Move C .10 .30
42 Straining Rolling Escape Move C .10 .30
43 Senzu Bean C .10 .30
44 Goku Body Throw C .10 .30
45 Saiyan City Destruction C .10 .30
46 Goku Anger Attack C .10 .30
47 Raditz Total Defense C .10 .30
48 Goku's Touch C .10 .30
49 Orange Wrist Flex Takedown C .10 .30
50 Orange Shoulder Throw C .10 .30
51 Orange Hip Throw C .10 .30
52 Orange Neck Restraints C .10 .30
53 Orange Holding After Takedown C .10 .30
54 Red Knee Strike C .10 .30
55 Red Front Kick C .10 .30
56 Red Side Kick C .10 .30
57 Red Round Kick C .10 .30
58 Red Back Kick C .10 .30
59 Blue Big Outside Drop C .10 .30
60 Blue One Arm Shoulder Throw C .10 .30
61 Blue Body Drop Throw U .10 .30
62 Blue Inner Leg Throw U .10 .30
63 Blue Big Whirl Throw U .10 .30
64 Blue Ground Holding U .10 .30
65 Black Fore Fist Punch U .10 .30
66 Black Knife Hand Strike U .10 .30
67 Black Elbow Strike U .10 .30
68 Black Front Kick U .10 .30
69 Black Side Kick U .10 .30
70 Black Turning Kick U .10 .30
71 Black Back Kick U .10 .30
72 Black Axe Heel Kick U .10 .30
73 Black Rear Spin Kick U .10 .30
74 Black Jump Turn Kick U .10 .30
75 Earth Dragon Ball 3 U .10 .30
76 Earth Dragon Ball 4 U .10 .30
77 Earth Dragon Ball 5 U .10 .30
78 Roshi Training U .10 .30
79 King Kai Training U .10 .30
80 Saiyan Training U .10 .30
81 Saiyan Armor U .10 .30
82 Tien U .10 .30
83 Tien U .10 .30
84 Yamcha U .10 .30
85 Yamcha U .10 .30
86 Chi-Chi U .10 .30
87 Bulma U .10 .30
88 King Kai Uniform U .10 .30
89 Dream Chamber Training U .10 .30
90 Mother's Touch U .10 .30
91 Saiyan Energy Throw U .10 .30
92 Saiyan Energy Defense U .10 .30
93 Saiyan Mental Energy Attack U .10 .30
94 Saiyan Energy Blast U .10 .30
95 Saiyan Energy Aura U .10 .30
96 Saiyan Sweeping Defense U .10 .30
97 Power Up More U .10 .30
98 Power Up the Most U .10 .30
99 Blazing Anger U .10 .30
100 Vegeta's Surprise Defense U .10 .30
101 Goku Honor Duel U .10 .30
102 Raditz Honor Duel U .10 .30
103 Piccolo Honor Duel U .10 .30
104 Chiaotzu U .10 .30
105 Chiaotzu U .10 .30
106 Yajirobe U .10 .30
107 Yajirobe U .10 .30
108 Goku's Energy Defense U .10 .30
109 Piccolo's Energy Attack U .10 .30
110 Piccolo's Physical Defense U .10 .30
111 Gohan's Energy Defense U .10 .30
112 Krillin's Physical Defense U .10 .30
113 Krillin's Energy Attack U .10 .30
114 Tien's Energy Defense U .10 .30
115 Yamcha's Energy Attack U .10 .30
116 Yamcha's Physical Defense U .10 .30
117 Raditz Energy Wall U .10 .30
118 Raditz Physical Defense U .10 .30
119 Vegeta's Energy Blast U .10 .30
120 Nappa's Energy Aura U .10 .30
121 Nappa's Physical Resistance U .10 .30
122 Yajirobe's Energy Attack U .10 .30
123 Chaiotzu's Energy Manipulation U .10 .30
124 Red Penetrating Defense Drill U .10 .30
125 Blue Off-Balancing Opponent Drill U .10 .30
126 Orange Lifting Drill U .10 .30
127 Black Takedown Drill U .10 .30
128 Red Knee Pick Drill U .10 .30
129 Blue Deceiving Drill U .10 .30
130 Orange Tripping Drill U .10 .30
131 Black Bear Hug Drill U .10 .30
132 Red Rolling Drill U .10 .30
133 Blue Reversal Drill U .10 .30
134 Orange Off-Balancing Drill U .10 .30
135 Black Arm Bar Drill U .10 .30
136 Black Free-Style Drill U .10 .30
137 Orange Spontaneous Drill U .10 .30
138 Blue Cradle Drill U .10 .30
139 Red Wrist Control Drill U .10 .30
140 Red Reading Drill U .10 .30
141 Blue Enemies Drill U .10 .30
142 Orange Energy Drill U .10 .30
143 Black Physical Drill U .10 .30
144 Red Coordination Drill U .10 .30
145 Blue Breakfall Drill U .10 .30
146 Orange Body Shifting Drill U .10 .30
147 Black Striking Drill U .10 .30
148 Red Pressure- Point Drill U .10 .30
149 Meditation Drill U .10 .30
150 Blue Neck Restraint Drill U .10 .30
151 Orange Joint Restraint Drill U .10 .30
152 Black Defender Drill U .10 .30
153 Goku Energy Blast U .10 .30
154 Piccolo Sidestep U .10 .30
155 Piccolo Defense Drill U .10 .30
156 Ally's Sacrifice U .10 .30
157 Eyes of the Dragon U .10 .30
158 Goku (Level 1) P 2.00 5.00
159 Goku (Level 2) P 2.00 5.00
160 Goku (Level 3) P 2.00 5.00
161 Piccolo (Level 1) P 2.00 5.00
162 Piccolo (Level 2) P 2.00 5.00
163 Piccolo (Level 3) P 2.00 5.00
164 Gohan (Level 1) P 2.00 5.00
165 Gohan (Level 2) P 2.00 5.00
166 Gohan (Level 3) P 2.00 5.00
167 Krillin (Level 1) P 2.00 5.00
168 Krillin (Level 2) P 2.00 5.00
169 Krillin (Level 3) P 2.00 5.00
170 Raditz (Level 1) P 2.00 5.00
171 Raditz (Level 2) P 2.00 5.00
172 Raditz (Level 3) P 2.00 5.00
173 Vegeta (Level 1) P 2.00 5.00
174 Vegeta (Level 2) P 2.00 5.00
175 Vegeta (Level 3) P 2.00 5.00
176 Nappa (Level 1) P 2.00 5.00
177 Nappa (Level 2) P 2.00 5.00
178 Nappa (Level 3) P 2.00 5.00
179 Goku (Level 1) P 2.00 5.00
180 Piccolo (Level 1) P 2.00 5.00
181 Gohan (Level 1) P 2.00 5.00
182 Krillin (Level 1) P 2.00 5.00
183 Raditz (Level 1) P 2.00 5.00
184 Vegeta (Level 1) P 2.00 5.00
185 Nappa (Level 1) P 2.00 5.00
186 Earth Dragon Ball 6 R 1.00 2.50
187 Earth Dragon Ball 7 R 1.00 2.50
188 Earth Dragon Ball Capture R .40 1.00
189 Earth Dragon Ball Combat R .40 1.00
190 Enraged R .40 1.00
191 A Beginner's Heart is Dedicated R .40 1.00
192 Teaching the Unteachable Observation R .40 1.00
193 Respect the Spirit R .40 1.00
194 Unselfish Behavior is the Best R .40 1.00
195 Hero Advantage R .40 1.00
196 Saiyan Honor Quest R .40 1.00
197 Saiyan Battle Terms R .40 1.00
198 Saiyan Appraisal Maneuver R .40 1.00
199 Dream Fighting R .40 1.00
200 Cutting the Tail R .40 1.00
201 The Tail Grows Back R .40 1.00
202 Goku's Lucky Break R .40 1.00
203 Saiyan Truce Card R .40 1.00
204 Battle Pausing R .40 1.00
205 Grabbing the Tail R .40 1.00
206 Nappa's Blinding Stare R .40 1.00
207 Power Gifting R .40 1.00
208 Terrible Wounds R .40 1.00
209 Broken Scouter R .40 1.00
210 Raditz Flying Kick R .40 1.00
211 Tien Mind Reading Trick R .40 1.00
212 Piccolo's Flight R .40 1.00
213 Plant Two Saibaimen R .40 1.00
214 Gohan's Father Save R .40 1.00
215 Krillin's Drill R .40 1.00
216 Krillins's Energy Disk R .40 1.00
217 Ribs Broken R .40 1.00
218 Unexpected Allies R .40 1.00
219 Raditz Energy Burst R .40 1.00
220 Vegeta's Stance R .40 1.00
221 Vegeta's Quickness Drill R 2.50 6.00
222 Bulma Finds a Dragon Ball R .40 1.00
223 Bulma Finds a Drill R .40 1.00
224 Baba Witch Viewing Drill R .40 1.00
225 Baba Energy Blast R .40 1.00
226 T-Rex Defense R .40 1.00
227 T-Rex Offense R .40 1.00
228 Vegeta's Plans R .40 1.00
229 Ally Wins R .40 1.00
230 Chiaotzu's Drill R .40 1.00
231 Goku's Mixing Drill R .40 1.00
232 Red Life Attack Drill R .40 1.00
233 Blue Life Defense Drill R .40 1.00
234 Orange Focusing Drill R .40 1.00
235 Black Shadow Drill R .40 1.00
236 Saiyan Power Drill R .40 1.00
237 Goku's Capturing Drill R .40 1.00
238 Kings Kai's Calming R .40 1.00
239 Roshi's Calming R .40 1.00
240 Vegeta's Trick R .40 1.00
241 Vegeta's Dragon Ball Capture R .40 1.00
242 Dream Machine Battle R .40 1.00
243 Saibaimen R .40 1.00
244 Saibaimen R .40 1.00
245 Saibaimen R .40 1.00
246 Saibaimen R .40 1.00
247 Goku's Truce UR 20.00 40.00
248 Goku's Plan UR 20.00 40.00
249 Medic Kit UR 40.00 80.00
250 Chiaotzu's Physical Defense UR 30.00 45.00

2000 Dragon Ball Z Frieza Preview Limited

COMPLETE SET (6) 6.00 12.00
INSERTS IN FRIEZA SAGA BOOSTER PACKS
PV1 The Talking Ends Here! C .20 .60
PV2 Just Kidding C .20 .60
PV3 No, Really Drill? U .20 .60
PV4 Good Advice U .20 .60
PV5 The Luck of Trunks R 2.00 5.00
PV6 Trunks Makes Himself Clear R 2.00 5.00

2000 Dragon Ball Z Frieza Saga Limited

COMPLETE SET (125) 200.00 450.00
BOOSTER BOX (36 PACKS) 250.00 400.00
BOOSTER PACK (11 CARDS) 3.00 8.00
*FOIL: 1X TO 2X BASIC CARDS
1 Orange Planet Destruction C .10 .30
2 Orange Kamehemeha Attack C .10 .30
3 Orange Taunting Attack C .10 .30
4 Red Energy Suspension C .10 .30
5 Red Energy Disk C .10 .30
6 Red Energy Disk Blasting C .10 .30
7 Blue Energy Flight C .10 .30
8 Recoome Boom C .10 .30
9 Saiyan Rapture C .10 .30
10 Saiyan Concussion Punch C .10 .30
11 Saiyan Rapid Deflection C .10 .30
12 Saiyan Energy Focus C .10 .30
13 Empowerment C .10 .30
14 Goku's Righteous Force C .10 .30
15 Gohan's Temper C .10 .30
16 Tien's Jolting Aura C .10 .30
17 Vegeta's Jolting Slash C .10 .30
18 Saiyan Concentration C .10 .30
19 Powerful Followers C .10 .30
20 Straining, Floating Attack Move C .10 .30
21 Straining Blasting Move C .10 .30
22 Straining Energy Move C .10 .30
23 Straining Defense Move C .10 .30
24 Straining Blocking Move C .10 .30
25 Straining Focusing Move C .10 .30
26 A Hospital Stay C .10 .30
27 Orange Thumbs Up C .10 .30
28 Orange Fist Detonation C .10 .30
29 Goku's Sudden Outburst C .10 .30
30 Time's a Warrior Tool C .40 1.00
31 Dodoria Energy Attack C .10 .30
32 Dodoria Flames of Fury C .10 .30
33 Jeice Flash Attack C .10 .30
34 Saiyan Planet Explosion C .10 .30
35 Saiyan Focusing Power C .10 .30
36 Alien Anger C .10 .30
37 Jeice (level 1) U .10 .30
38 Dodoria (level 1) U .10 .30
39 Tien (level 3) U .10 .30
40 Yamcha (level 3) U .10 .30
41 Chi-Chi (level 2) U .10 .30
42 Bulma (level 2) U .10 .30
43 Chiaotzu (level 3) U .10 .30
44 Yajirobe the Hero (level 3) U .10 .30
45 Guldo (level 1) U .10 .30
46 Guldo (level 2) U .10 .30
47 Guldo (level 3) U .10 .30
48 Dende the unlikely Hero (level 1) U .10 .30
49 Frieza Smiles U .10 .30
50 Captain Ginyu Realization U .10 .30
51 Jeice Shouts U .10 .30
52 Jeice Comet Attack U .10 .30
53 Dodoria Boom U .10 .30
54 Goku's Energy Absorbtion U .10 .30
55 Guldo's Time Feeze Drill U .10 .30
56 Gohan's Anger Blast U .10 .30
57 Krillin's Anger Blast U .10 .30
58 Tien's Power Burst U .10 .30
59 Yamcha's Skillful Defense U .10 .30
60 Vegeta's Gallic Gun U .10 .30
61 Vegeta's Powering Up U .10 .30
62 Captain Ginyu's Visionary Attack U .10 .30
63 Yajirobe's Gifting Drill U .10 .30
64 Chiaotzu's Glaring Power U .10 .30
65 Red Energy Defense Drill U .10 .30
66 Blue Mental Drill U .10 .30
67 Orange Destruction Drill U .10 .30
68 Black Zarbon Transformation Drill U .10 .30
69 Red Phasing Drill U .10 .30
70 Blue Allies Drill U .10 .30
71 Orange Leg Drill U .10 .30
72 Black Energy Stamina Drill U .10 .30
73 Red Implosion Drill U .10 .30
74 Captain Ginyu Reversal Drill U .10 .30
75 Jeice's Style Drill U .10 .30
76 Vegeta Getting Bashed Drill U .10 .30
77 Dende Healing Drill U .10 .30
78 Gohan Anger Drill U .10 .30
79 Frieza's Influencing Drill U .10 .30
80 Black Erasing Drill U .10 .30
81 Krillin's Power Block U .10 .30
82 Black Standing Position U .10 .30
83 Black Right Cross U .10 .30
84 Black Driving Leg Throw U .10 .30
85 Straining Outburst Move U .10 .30
86 Straining Neck Move U .10 .30
87 Krillin's Concentration U .10 .30
88 Hero Enraged U .10 .30
89 Vegeta On Namek (level 4) R 3.00 8.00
90 Krillin On Namek (level 4) R 2.00 5.00
91 Nappa Restored (level 4) R 2.00 5.00
92 Raditz Restored (level 4) R 2.00 5.00
93 Goku On Namek (level 4) R 3.00 8.00
94 Piccolo (level 4) R 2.00 5.00
95 Gohan (level 4) R 2.00 5.00
96 Nail The Namekian (level 1) R 2.00 5.00
97 Straining Force Positioning Move R 1.00 3.00
98 Blue Stance R 1.00 3.00
99 Blue Energy Outburst R 1.00 3.00
100 Kami as Your Ally R 1.00 3.00
101 Hero Teamwork Drill R 1.00 3.00
102 Villain's TeamworkDrill R 1.00 3.00
103 Human Technology R 1.00 3.00
104 Power R 1.00 3.00
105 Dende's Help R 1.00 3.00
106 Goku's Super Saiyan Blast R 1.00 3.00
107 Piccolo's Wisdom R 1.00 3.00
108 Yamcha's Good Wishes R 1.00 3.00
109 Captain Ginyu's Sacrifice R 1.00 3.00
110 Nail the Namekian Hero (level 3) R 1.00 3.00
111 Krillin's Power Tap R 1.00 3.00
112 Black Swift Elbow Strike R 1.00 3.00
113 Kami Fades R 1.00 3.00
114 Gohan's Stomp R 1.00 3.00
115 Piccolo's Stomp R 1.00 3.00
116 Goku's Quickness R 1.00 3.00
117 Nail Inspired (level 2) R 1.00 3.00
118 The Plan R 1.00 3.00
119 Mommy's Coming Dear R 1.00 3.00
120 Bulma's Scouter R 1.00 3.00
121 This Too Shall Past R 1.00 3.00
122 Focusing Is Everything R 1.00 3.00
123 Red Foot Jolt R 1.00 3.00
124 Frieza the Master UR 30.00 50.00
125 Super Saiyan Goku (level 4) UR 150.00 250.00

2001 Dragon Ball Z Trunks Preview

COMPLETE SET (6 CARDS) 5.00 10.00
INSERTS IN TRUNKS SAGA BOOSTER PACKS
PV1 Android 20 Absorbing Drill C .50 1.00
PV2 Android 20 Powers Up C .50 1.00
PV3 Android Effect U 1.00 2.00
PV4 Super Saiyan Effect U 1.00 2.00
PV5 Too Late R 2.00 4.00
PV6 Trunks Finds the Answer R 2.00 4.00

2001 Dragon Ball Z Trunks Saga

COMPLETE SET (200) 175.00 250.00
UNOPENED BOX (36 PACKS) 125.00 200.00
UNOPENED PACK (11 CARDS) 4.00 6.00
STARTER DECK 12.00 20.00
*FOIL: .75X TO 1.5X BASIC CARDS
1 Orange Energy Blast C .25 .50
2 Red Kienzan Discs C .25 .50
3 Namek Dragon Ball 2 C .25 .50
4 Captain Ginyu Frog C .25 .50
5 Krillin's Kamehameha Outburst C .25 .50
6 Straining Outburst Move C .25 .50
7 Namekian Glare Attack C .25 .50
8 Namekian Braced Attack C .25 .50
9 Namekian Thrust C .25 .50
10 Namekian Blocking Defense C .25 .50
11 Red Implosion Lunge C .25 .50
12 Blue Stomach Eruption C .25 .50
13 Orange Power Shifting Drill C .25 .50
14 Orange Surprise Blast C .25 .50
15 Orange Dashing Gut Punch C .25 .50
16 Orange Straight Jab C .25 .50
17 Black Defensive Aura C .25 .50
18 Black Flying Kick C .25 .50
19 Black Finger Block C .25 .50
20 Black Defensive Burst C .25 .50
21 Black Overpowering Attack C .50 1.00
22 Red Blazing Aura C .25 .50
23 Red Gravity Drill C .25 .50
24 Red Energy Shield C .25 .50
25 Namek Dragon Ball 1 C .50 .75
26 Spice and his friends C .25 .50
27 Spice Prepares an Energy Blast C .25 .50
28 Vinegar has Plans C .25 .50
29 Vinegar's Revenge C .25 .50
30 Black Water Confusion Drill C .25 .50
31 Garlic Jr's Kyokaika Technique C .25 .50
32 Garlic Jr's Energy Blast C .25 .50
33 Garlic Jr's Black Water Mist C .25 .50
34 Krillin Lashes Out C .25 .50
35 Krillin takes a Shot C .25 .50
36 Frieza's Finger Tip Energy Blast C .75 1.50
37 King Cold Smiles C .25 .50
38 King Cold's End C .25 .50
39 Goku's Ready C .50 1.00
40 Tien's Ready C .25 .50
41 Blue Driving Face Off U .50 1.00
42 Breakthrough Drill U .50 1.00
43 Blue Thrusting Fist Strike U .50 1.00
44 Chiaotzu's Psychic Halt U .50 1.00
45 Black Head Strike U .50 1.00
46 Black Hug Maneuver U .50 1.00
47 Black Driving Palm Strike U .50 1.00
48 Dodoria's Waiting Game U .50 1.00
49 Frieza's Aura Shot U .50 1.00
50 Saiyan Knee Strike U .50 1.00
51 Frieza's Powering Rage U .50 1.00
52 Namekian Fighting U .50 1.00
53 Captain Ginyu Moves to Attack U .50 1.00
54 Captain Ginyu's Energy Attack U .50 1.00
55 Namekian Attack Drill U .50 1.00
56 Frieza's Tail Hold U .50 1.00
57 Frieza's Imitation Grows U .50 1.00
58 Scoring Aura Shot U .50 1.00
59 Frieza is Ready U .50 1.00
60 Namekian Physical Drill U .50 1.00
61 Namekian Energy Drill U .50 1.00
62 Burter's Power Stance U .50 1.00
63 Red Shattering Leap U .50 1.00
64 Gohan's Quest U .50 1.00
65 Krillin's Quest U .50 1.00
66 Namekian's Head Strike U .50 1.00
67 Red Knee Eruption U .50 1.00
68 Red Face Upheaval U .50 1.00
69 Orange Special Beam Cannon U .50 1.00
70 Orange Resistance U .50 1.00
71 Orange Special Beam Cannon Drill U .50 1.00
72 Black Energy Web U .50 1.00
73 Black Energy Blast U 1.00 2.00
74 Black Energy Deflection Drill U 1.00 2.00
75 Red Power Rush U .50 1.00
76 Red Lightning Slash U .50 1.00
77 Red Energy Blast U 1.00 2.00
78 Red Eye Laser Assault U .50 1.00
79 Namek Dragon Ball 3 U 1.00 2.00
80 Namek Dragon Ball 4 U 1.00 2.00
81 Trunks Slash U 1.00 3.00
82 Trunks High Strike U 1.00 3.00
83 Trunks Cuts Down U 1.00 3.00
84 Trunks Energy Sphere U 5.00 10.00
85 Trunks Effortless Drill U 1.00 3.00
86 Trunks Planning Drill U 1.00 3.00
87 Trunks Sword Position 1 U 2.00 4.00
88 Trunks Sword Position 2 U 2.00 4.00
89 Trunks Sword Position 3 U 2.00 4.00
90 Trunks Sword Position 4 U 2.00 4.00
91 Expectant Trunks U 1.00 3.00
92 Trunks Draws Steel U 1.00 3.00
93 Trunks Stands Ready U 1.00 3.00
94 Double Saiyans U 1.00 3.00
95 Blue Softening Stance U .50 1.00
96 Blue Awakening U .50 1.00
97 Blue Leaving U .50 1.00
98 Trunks Strikes U 1.00 3.00
99 Trunks Swiftly Moving U 1.00 3.00
100 Frieza, the Revived (level 4) U 3.00 6.00
101 Garlic Jr. the Void Master (level 4) U 1.00 3.00
102 Spice, the Punisher (level 4) U 1.00 2.00
103 Vinegar, the Attacker (level 4) U 2.00 4.00
104 Jeice, With Style (level 2) U 1.00 3.00
105 Jeice Attacks (level 3) U .50 1.00
106 Captain Ginyu (level 1) U .50 1.00
107 Captain Ginyu the Leader (level 2) U .50 1.00
108 Captain Ginyu Changes (level 3) U .50 1.00
109 Dodoria (level 1) U 1.00 3.00
110 Dodoria, in Flight (level 2) U 1.00 2.00
111 Dodoria the Mocking (level 3) U 1.00 2.00
112 Guru as your ally R 1.00 3.00
113 Namek Dragon Ball 6 R 2.00 4.00
114 Namek Dragon Ball 7 R 2.00 4.00
115 Namekian Dragon Ball Combat R 1.00 3.00
116 Guru Fades R 1.00 3.00
117 Frieza's Featherlight Touch R 1.00 3.00
118 What Was I Thinking R 1.00 3.00
119 Hero's Lucky Break R 1.00 3.00
120 Thought Comes Before Action R 1.00 3.00
121 A Hero's Heart Is Strong R 1.00 3.00
122 An Amusing Trick R 1.00 3.00
123 Drills Are For The Weak R 1.00 3.00
124 Hero's Way R 1.00 3.00
125 Don't You Just Hate That R 1.00 3.00
126 Vegeta Scans the City R 2.00 4.00
127 Goku's Battle Ready R 2.00 4.00
128 Gohan Spots the Imposter Drill R 2.00 4.00
129 Piccolo and Heroes Gather R 1.00 3.00

130 Krillin's Heat Seaking Blast R	3.00	6.00
131 Chi-Chi Searches R	.75	2.50
132 Nail Takes Extra Effort R	1.00	3.00
133 Roshi's Thoughts R	1.00	3.00
134 King Kai's Thoughts R	1.00	3.00
135 Namek Dragon Ball Wish R	2.00	4.00
136 Namek Dragon Ball 5 R	3.00	6.00
137 Nail Combat Drill R	1.00	3.00
138 Orange Energy Dan Drill R	2.00	3.00
139 Orange Junction Energy Blast R	1.00	3.00
140 Black Smoothness Drill R	4.00	8.00
141 Black Physical Focus R	2.00	4.00
142 Red Evasion Drill R	1.00	3.00
143 Red King Cold Observation R	3.00	6.00
144 Red Style Mastery R	6.00	10.00
145 Black Style Mastery R	8.00	12.00
146 Orange Style Mastery R	5.00	10.00
147 Namekian Style Mastery R	5.00	8.00
148 Saiyan Style Mastery R	8.00	12.00
149 Blue Style Mastery R	8.00	12.00
150 Trunks the Hero (level 4) R	6.00	10.00
151 Vegeta, Saiyan Prince (level 4) R	4.00	8.00
152 Gohan Empowered (level 4) R	5.00	10.00
153 Piccolo Enraged (level 4) R	4.00	8.00
154 Krillin (level 1) R	4.00	8.00
155 Krillin Enraged (level 2) R	6.00	10.00
156 Krillin, the Warrior (level 3) R	4.00	8.00
157 Where There's Life There's Hope UR	40.00	80.00
158 Villain's True Power UR	20.00	40.00
159 Goku, the Unbeatable UR	30.00	50.00
160 King Cold, the All Powerful UR	20.00	40.00
161 Frieza the Monster (level 1) P	3.00	6.00
162 Frieza the Conqueror (level 2) P	3.00	6.00
163 Frieza the Cyborg (level 3) P	3.00	6.00
164 Goku, the Leader (level 1) P	2.00	4.00
165 Goku, the Defender (level 2) P	2.00	4.00
166 Goku, the Protector (level 3) P	2.00	4.00
167 Piccolo, the Avenger (level 1) P	2.00	4.00
168 Piccolo, Revived (level 2) P	2.00	4.00
169 Piccolo, the Hero (level 3) P	3.00	7.00
170 Gohan, the Furious (level 1) P	2.00	4.00
171 Gohan, the Fighter (level 2) P	2.00	4.00
172 Gohan, the Warrior (level 3) P	2.00	4.00
173 Vegeta, the Determined (level 1) P	2.00	4.00
174 Vegeta, the Powerful (level 2) P	3.00	6.00
175 Vegeta, in Training (level 3) P	3.00	6.00
176 Garlic Jr. (level 1) P	2.00	4.00
177 Garlic Jr. the Master (level 2) P	2.00	4.00
178 Garlic Jr. the Monster (level 3) P	2.00	4.00
179 Spice (level 1) P	2.00	4.00
180 Spice, the Leader (level 2) P	2.00	4.00
181 Spice, the Warrior (level 3) P	2.00	4.00
182 Vinegar (level 1) P	2.00	4.00
183 Vinegar, the Fighter (level 2) P	1.00	3.00
184 Vinegar, the Henchman (level 3) P	1.00	3.00
185 Trunks (level 1) P	3.00	6.00
186 Trunks, the Swordsman (level 2) P	3.00	6.00
187 Super Saiyan Trunks (level 3) P	3.00	6.00
188 King Cold (level 1) P	3.00	6.00
189 King Cold, the Destroyer (level 2) P	2.00	4.00
190 King Cold, the Ruler (level 3) P	2.00	4.00
191 Frieza the Master (level 2) HT	3.00	6.00
192 Goku (level 2) HT	4.00	8.00
193 Piccolo (level 2) HT	4.00	8.00
194 Gohan (level 2) HT	3.00	6.00
195 Vegeta (level 2) HT	4.00	8.00
196 Garlic Jr., the Merciless (level 2) HT	2.00	4.00
197 Spice, the Enchanter (level 2) HT	3.00	6.00
198 Vinegar, the Battler (level 2) HT	3.00	6.00
199 Trunks, the Saiyan (level 2) HT	6.00	12.00
200 King Cold, Galactic Ruler (level 2) HT	4.00	8.00

2001 Dragon Ball Z Android Saga Limited

COMPLETE SET (125)	150.00	250.00
UNOPENED BOX (36 PACKS)	200.00	400.00
UNOPENED PACK (12 CARDS)	3.00	8.00
*FOIL: .75X TO 1.5X BASIC CARDS		
1 Android 17's Neck Hold C	.10	.30
2 Android 18's Low Blow C	.10	.30
3 Android 19's Body Slam C	.10	.30
4 Android 19's Energy Burst C	.10	.30
5 Android 20 Is Caught Off Guard C	.10	.30
6 Android 20's Energy Burst C	.10	.30
7 Blasted Land C	.10	.30
8 Gravity Chamber C	.10	.30
9 Black Confusion Drill C	.10	.30
10 Black Draining Aura C	.10	.30
11 Black Jump Kick C	.10	.30
12 Black Taunting Attack C	.10	.30
13 Blue Defensive Flight C	.10	.30
14 Blue Foot Smash C	.10	.30
15 Blue Glare Attack C	.10	.30
16 Blue Idea C	.10	.30
17 Blue Sidestep C	.10	.30
18 Gohan's Ready C	.10	.30
19 Goku's Conquering Stance C	.10	.30
20 Goku's Right Knee Smash C	.10	.30
21 Namekian Blocking Stance C	.10	.30
22 Namekian Defensive Stance C	.10	.30
23 Namekian Determination C	.10	.30
24 Namekian Dodging Technique C	.10	.30
25 Namekian Energy Absorption C	.10	.30
26 Namekian Wrist Grab C	.10	.30
27 Orange Fist Catch C	.10	.30
28 Orange Palm Blast C	.10	.30
29 Piccolo's Stance C	.10	.30
30 Red Burning Stance C	.10	.30
31 Red Energy Charge C	.10	.30
32 Red Power Drain C	.10	.30
33 Red Power Lift C	.10	.30
34 Blue Battle Readiness C	.10	.30
35 Saiyan Glare C	.10	.30
36 Saiyan Inspection C	.10	.30
37 Android 17's Back Bash U	.10	.30
38 Android 17's Haymaker U	.10	.30
39 Android 20's Energy Drive U	.10	.30
40 Android 20's Enraged U	.10	.30
41 Android 20's Search Pattern U	.10	.30
42 Android Attack Drill U	.10	.30
43 Hyperbolic Time Chamber U	.10	.30
44 Master Roshi's Island U	.10	.30
45 Black Anger Stance U	.10	.30
46 Black Energy Assault U	.10	.30
47 Black Gut Wrench U	.10	.30
48 Black Off-Balancing Punch U	.10	.30
49 Gohan's Peaceful Stance U	.10	.30
50 Black Power Up U	.10	.30
51 Black Searching Technique U	.10	.30
52 Black Side Thrust U	.10	.30
53 Black Studying Drill U	.10	.30
54 Blue Betrayal U	.10	.30
55 Blue Holding Drill U	.10	.30
56 Blue Right Cross U	.10	.30
57 Blue Rush U	.10	.30
58 Blue Smirk U	.10	.30
59 Bulma's Looking Good U	.10	.30
60 Goku's Training U	.10	.30
61 Namekian Elbow Smash U	.10	.30
62 Namekian Finishing Effort U	.10	.30
63 Namekian Focusing Effort U	.10	.30
64 Namekian Forearm Smash U	.10	.30
65 Orange Aura Drill U	.10	.30
66 Orange Energy Glare U	.10	.30
67 Orange Energy Phasing Drill U	.10	.30
68 Orange Power Ball U	.10	.30
69 Orange Power Beam U	.10	.30
70 Orange Stare Down U	.10	.30
71 Orange Sword Slash U	.10	.30
72 Orange Uppercut U	.10	.30
73 Red Dueling Drill U	.10	.30
74 Red Hunting Drill U	.10	.30
75 Red Knee Bash U	.10	.30
76 Saiyan Flying Tackle U	.10	.30
77 Saiyan Focus U	.10	.30
78 Saiyan Heads Up U	.10	.30
79 Saiyan Left Kick U	.10	.30
80 Saiyan Wrist Block U	.10	.30
81 Saiyan Destiny U	.10	.30
82 Senzu Effect U	.10	.30
83 Straining Energy Blast Move U	.10	.30
84 Straining Jump Kick Move U	.10	.30
85 Red Lifting KickU	.10	.30
86 Tien's Mental Conditioning U	.10	.30
87 Tien's Solar Flare U	.10	.30
88 Unexpected Company U	.10	.30
89 Android 17 Smirks R	1.00	2.50
90 Android 18's Stare Down R	2.00	5.00
91 Android 19's Distress R	1.00	2.50
92 City in Turmoil R	1.00	2.50
93 Winter Countryside R	1.00	2.50
94 Kami's Floating Island R	1.00	2.50
95 Defenseless Beach R	1.00	2.50
96 Dying Planet R	1.00	2.50
97 Black Mischievous Drill R	1.00	2.50
98 Black Scout Maneuver R	2.00	5.00
99 Blue Terror R	1.00	2.50
100 Goku's Heart Disease R	1.00	2.50
101 Knockout Drill R	1.00	2.50
102 Namekian Friendship R	1.00	2.50
103 Namekian Teamwork R	1.00	2.50
104 Orange Eye Beam R	1.00	2.50
105 Orange Rage R	1.00	2.50
106 Orange Searching Maneuver R	1.00	2.50
107 Rebellion R	1.00	2.50
108 Red Counterstrike R	1.00	2.50
109 Red Tactical Drill R	1.00	2.50
110 Saiyan Face Stomp R	1.00	2.50
111 Saiyan Lightning Dodge R	1.00	2.50
112 Severe Bruises R	1.00	2.50
113 Tien's Flight R	1.00	2.50
114 Android 16 (level 1) R	1.50	4.00
115 Android 17 (level 1) R	2.00	5.00
116 Android 18 Standing (level 1) R	2.00	5.00
116 Android 18 Running (level 1) R	3.00	8.00
117 Android 19 (level 1) R	1.50	4.00
118 Android 20 (level 1) R	1.50	4.00
119 Piccolo, The Trained (level 1) R	2.00	5.00
120 Tien, The Watcher (level 4) R	1.50	4.00
121 Vegeta, The Ready (level 1) R	6.00	15.00
122 Yajirobe, The Unstoppable (level 4) R	2.00	5.00
123 Yamcha Is There (level 4) R	2.00	5.00
124 The Hero Is Down UR	30.00	60.00
125 Trunks Guardian Drill UR	60.00	100.00

2001 Dragon Ball Z Android Preview Limited

COMPLETE SET	6.00	12.00
INSERTS IN ANDROID SAGA BOOSTER PACKS		
C1 Cell Smiles	1.00	3.00
C2 Cell's Dark Attack	2.00	4.00
C3 Cell's Energy Blast	1.00	3.00
C4 Cell's Defense	2.00	4.00
C5 Awful Abrasions	2.00	4.00
C6 Cell's Threatening Position	2.00	4.00

2001 Dragon Ball Z Cell Saga Limited

COMPLETE SET (200)	175.00	200.00
BOOSTER BOX (36 PACKS)	45.00	80.00
BOOSTER PACK (12 CARDS)	3.00	4.00
STARTER DECK	15.00	20.00
LIMITED EDITION CARDS ADD 10% TO VALUE.		
1 Blue Sliding Dodge C	.25	.50
2 Red Side Step C	.25	.50
3 Blue Fist Strike C	.25	.50
4 Orange Focused Blast C	.25	.50
5 Orange Blast C	.25	.50
6 Saiyan Right Cross C	.25	.50
7 Namekian Energy Ray C	.25	.50
8 Black Fatality C	.25	.50
9 Blue Fight C	.25	.50
10 Saiyan Defensive Stance C	.25	.50
11 Namekian Backflip C	.25	.50
12 Namekian Physical Stance C	.25	.50
13 Namekian Destruction Blast C	.25	.50
14 Saiyan Energy Orb C	.50	.75
15 Saiyan Counterstrike C	.25	.50
16 Saiyan Energy Attack C	.25	.50
17 Blue Backflip C	.25	.50
18 Saiyan Left Hook C	.25	.50
19 Black Power Punch C	.25	.50
20 Black Quick Blast C	.25	.50
21 Orange Sidestep C	.25	.50
22 Namekian Headbutt C	.25	.50
23 Black Twin Blast C	.25	.50
24 Saiyan Palm Blast C	.50	1.00
25 Blue Swift Dodge C	.25	.50
26 Black Forearm Block C	.25	.50
27 Red Flight C	.25	.50
28 Red Defensive Jump C	.25	.50
29 Orange Strike C	.25	.50
30 Black Strike C	.25	.50
31 Orange Energy Deflection C	.25	.50
32 Red Power Strike C	.25	.50
33 Red Face Strike C	.25	.50
34 Namekian Power Kick C	.25	.50
35 Orange Left Kick C	.25	.50
36 Red Driving Jab C	.25	.50
37 Red Crush C	.25	.50
38 Black Neck Break C	.25	.50
39 Dende Dragon Ball 1 C	.50	1.00
40 Dende Dragon Ball 2 C	.50	1.00
41 Saiyan Tripple Kick U	.50	1.00
42 Namekian Fist Block U	.50	1.00
43 Namekian Special Beam Cannon U	.50	1.00
44 Namekian Bash U	.50	1.00
45 Namekian Energy Catch U	.50	1.00
46 Red Offensive Stance U	.50	1.00
47 Blue Evasion U	.50	1.00
48 Orange Energy Focus U	1.00	2.00
49 Namekian Upward Dash U	.50	1.00
50 Saiyan Left Punch U	1.00	2.00
51 Black Dodge U	.50	1.00
52 Orange Energy Discharge U	.50	1.00
53 Saiyan Power Kick U	.50	1.00
54 Saiyan Strike U	1.00	2.00
55 Orange Power Blast U	.50	1.00
56 Blue Palm Shot U	.50	1.00
57 Red Jump U	.50	1.00
58 Namekian Rock Crush U	1.00	2.00
59 Saiyan High Jump Kick U	.50	1.00
60 Saiyan Flying Kick U	.50	1.00
61 Orange Solar Flare U	1.00	2.00
62 Red Dodge U	.50	1.00
63 Orange Sideshot U	1.00	2.00
64 Black Side Block U	.50	1.00
65 Blue Blackflip U	.50	1.00
66 Blue Wrist Block U	.50	1.00
67 Orange Ally Drill U	.50	1.00
68 Heroes Discovery U	.50	1.00
69 Piccolo's Determination U	.50	1.00
70 The Car U	.50	1.00
71 Krillin's Thoughts U	.50	1.00
72 Capsule Corp. Ship U	.50	1.00
73 Dende Dragon Ball 3 U	2.00	4.00
74 Dende Dragon Ball 4 U	2.00	4.00
75 Dende Dragon Ball 5 U	2.00	4.00
76 Exuastion U	.50	1.00
77 Trunks Prepares U	.50	1.00
78 Smokescreen U	.50	1.00
79 Time Chamber Training U	.50	1.00
80 Gohan's Stance U	1.00	2.00
81 Grappling Stance U	.50	1.00
82 Cell's Android Absorbtion U	1.00	2.00
83 Ally Rescue U	.50	1.00
84 Yamcha, the Friend (Level 1) U	.50	1.00
85 Yamcha, the Battler (Level 2) U	.50	1.00
86 Tien, the Swift (Level 1) U	.50	1.00
87 Tien, the Leader (Level 3) U	1.00	2.00
88 Yamcha, the Powerful (Level 3) U	.50	1.00
89 Krillin, the Friend (Level 1) U	.50	1.00
90 Android 19 (Level 1) U	2.00	4.00
91 Tien's Tri-Beam U	.50	1.00
92 Orange Deflection U	.50	1.00
93 Krillin's Solar Flare U	1.00	2.00
94 Namekian Side Kick U	.50	1.00
95 Android 19, Recalled (Level 2) U	2.00	4.00
96 Namekian Energy Deflection U	1.00	2.00
97 Krillin, the Champion (Level 3) U	1.00	2.00
98 Android 19, Recharged (Level 3) U	1.00	2.00
99 Krillin, the Hero (Level 2) U	1.00	2.00
100 Speaking With The King Drill U	1.00	2.00
101 Orange Goku's Kamehameha U	1.00	2.00
102 Straining Hand Blast Move U	1.00	2.00
103 Tien, the Quick (Level 2) U	.50	1.00
104 Blue Straight Jab U	.50	1.00
105 Namekian Power Up U	1.00	2.00
106 Android 16 Detects U	.50	1.00
107 Orange Gaze U	1.00	2.00
108 Namekian Energy Beam U	.50	1.00
109 Bulma, the Expert (Level 3) U	1.00	3.00
110 Krillin Asks For Help U	.50	1.00
111 Namekian Regeneration U	1.00	2.00
112 Namekian Dash Attack R	2.00	4.00
113 Madness! R	2.00	4.00
114 Chi-Chi, the Wife (Level 3) R	2.00	4.00
115 Focusing R	2.00	4.00
116 Stunned R	2.00	4.00
117 Blue Assistance Drill R	2.00	4.00
118 Mr. Popo's Calming R	2.00	4.00
119 Namekian Preparation Drill R	2.00	4.00
120 Krillin Unleashed R	2.00	4.00
121 Dende Dragon Ball 6 R	3.00	6.00
122 Dende Dragon Ball 7 R	3.00	6.00
123 Cell's Power Drain R	2.00	4.00
124 Saiyan Power Blast R	3.00	6.00
125 Run Away R	2.00	4.00
126 Blue Style Mastery R	2.00	4.00
127 Trunks, the Powerful (Level 4) R	3.00	6.00
128 Blueprints R	2.00	4.00
129 Black Style Mastery R	4.00	8.00
130 Saiyan Style Mastery R	4.00	8.00
131 Red Style Mastery R	4.00	8.00
132 Piccolo, the Namek (Level 4) R	3.00	6.00
133 Android 18 (Level 4)	4.00	8.00
134 Gohan, the Winner (Level 5) R	5.00	8.00
135 Goku (Level 4) R	5.00	10.00
136 Cell, the Master (Level 5) R	4.00	8.00
137 Cell, the Destroyer (Level 4) R	4.00	8.00
138 Gohan, Ascendant (Level 4) R	5.00	8.00
139 Krillin, the Mighty (Level 4) R	3.00	6.00
140 Orange Style Mastery R	4.00	8.00
141 Namekian Style Mastery R	3.00	6.00
142 Red Feint R	2.00	4.00
143 Blue Elbow Drop R	1.00	3.00
144 Blue Driving Punch Drill R	2.00	4.00
145 Blue Left Cross Punch R	1.00	3.00
146 Orange City Destruction R	2.00	4.00
147 Orange Halting Drill R	3.00	6.00
148 Saiyan Offensive Rush R	3.00	6.00
149 Namekian Fusion R	2.00	4.00
150 Android 16's Battle Charge R	2.00	4.00
151 Namekian Fist Smash R	2.00	4.00
152 Android 16's Rage R	2.00	4.00
153 Namekian Energy Focus R	2.00	4.00
154 Vegeta, Ascendant (Level 4) R	6.00	12.00
155 Saiyan Rapid Fire R	3.00	6.00
156 Blue Head Charge R	2.00	4.00
157 Z Warriors Gather UR	25.00	50.00
158 Cell's Presence UR	25.00	50.00
159 Vegeta, the Revitalized (lvl 5) UR	40.00	75.00
160 Goku, the All Powerful (lvl 5) UR	40.00	75.00
161 Goku, the Hero (Level 1) P	3.00	6.00
162 Goku, the Saiyan (Level 2 P	3.00	6.00
163 Goku, the Perfect Warrior (Level 3) P	4.00	8.00
164 Gohan, the Champion (Level 1) P	3.00	6.00
165 Gohan, the Swift (Level 2) P	3.00	6.00
166 Gohan, the Mighty (Level 3) P	3.00	6.00
167 Vegeta, the Powerful (Level 1) P	3.00	6.00
168 Vegeta, the All Powerful (Level 2) P	3.00	6.00
169 Vegeta, the Prince (Level 3) P	4.00	8.00
170 Piccolo, the Warrior (Level 1) P	3.00	6.00
171 Piccolo, the Champion (Level 2) P	3.00	6.00
172 Piccolo, the Destroyer (Level 3) P	4.00	8.00
173 Trunks, the Swift (Level 1) P	3.00	6.00
174 Trunks, the Quick (Level 2) P	3.00	6.00
175 Trunks, the Mighty (Level 3) P	4.00	8.00
176 Android 16 (Level 1) P	2.00	4.00
177 Android 16, the Machine (Level 2) P	3.00	6.00
178 Android 16, the Battler (Level 3) P	2.00	4.00
179 Android 17 (Level 1) P	3.00	6.00
180 Android 17, the Leader (Level 2) P	4.00	8.00
181 Android 17, the Fighter (Level 3) P	3.00	6.00
182 Android 18 (Level 1) P	3.00	6.00
183 Android 18, the Model (Level 2) P	4.00	6.00
184 Android 18, the Machine (Level 3) P	3.00	6.00
185 Android 20 (Level 1) P	3.00	6.00
186 Android 20, the Doctor (Level 2) P	3.00	6.00
187 Android 20, Schemer (Level 3) P	3.00	6.00
188 Cell, Stage One (Level 1) P	3.00	6.00
189 Cell, Stage Two (Level 2) P	3.00	6.00
190 Cell, Perfect (Level 3) P	4.00	6.00
191 Goku, Earth's Hero (Level 3) HT	4.00	8.00
192 Gohan, Super Saiyan (Level 3) HT	4.00	8.00
193 Vegeta, the Last Prince (Level 3) HT	4.00	8.00
194 Piccolo, Earth's Protector (lvl 3) HT	3.00	6.00
195 Trunks, Time's Hero (Level 3) HT	4.00	8.00
196 Android 16, the Fighter (Level 3) HT	5.00	8.00
197 Android 17, the Destroyer (lvl 3) HT	3.00	6.00
198 Android 18, the Smart One (lvl 3) HT	5.00	8.00
199 Android 20, the Destructor (lvl 3) HT	4.00	8.00
200 Cell, the Perfect Warrior (Level 3) HT	7.00	14.00

2001 Dragon Ball Z Cell Preview Limited

COMPLETE SET (6)	5.00	10.00
INSERTS IN ANDROID SAGA BOOSTER PACKS.		
1 Cell's Draining C	.40	1.00
2 Cell's Arena C	.40	1.00
3 Cell's Last Strike U	.40	1.00
4 They're All There U	.40	1.00
5 Heroes Battleground R	2.00	5.00
6 Cell's Style R	2.00	5.00

2002 Dragon Ball Z Cell Games Saga Limited

COMPLETE SET (125)	150.00	200.00
UNOPENED BOX (36 PACKS)	50.00	70.00
UNOPENED PACK (12 CARDS)	3.00	4.00
*FOIL: .75X TO 1.5X BASIC CARDS		
1 Black Explosion C	.25	.50
2 Black Fist Lock C	.25	.50
3 Black Preparation C	.25	.50
4 Blue Forced Punch C	.25	.50
5 Blue Thrusted Blast C	.25	.50
6 Deadly Attack C	.25	.50
7 Flashback C	.25	.50
8 Gohan's Kick C	.50	1.00
9 Gohan's Strike C	.50	1.00
10 Namekian Crushing Hold C	.25	.50
11 Namekian Fist Dodge C	.25	.50
12 Namekian Flying Kick C	.25	.50
13 Namekian Foot Lunge C	.25	.50
14 Orange Dragon Aid C	.25	.50
15 Orange Uniting Strike C	.25	.50
16 Power Boost C	.25	.50
17 Red Anger Rising C	.50	1.00
18 Red Drop Kick C	1.00	2.00
19 Red Duck C	.25	.50
20 Red Fist Lunge C	.25	.50
21 Red Flying Attack C	.50	1.00
22 Red Shifty Maneuver C	.25	.50
23 Saiyan Ally Strike C	1.00	2.00
24 Saiyan Blocking Technique C	.25	.50
25 Saiyan Energy Surprise C	.25	.50
26 Saiyan Fist Attack C	.50	1.00
27 Saiyan Knee Block C	.25	.50
28 Saiyan Power Rush C	.25	.50
29 Saiyan Triple Blast C	.25	.50
30 Strength Training C	.25	.50
31 Time to Party C	.50	1.00
32 Black Anticipation Drill U	.50	1.00
33 Black Blasting Beam U	.50	1.00
34 Double Black Attack Drill U	.50	1.00
35 Black Hand Energy Blast U	1.00	2.00
36 Black Face Slap U	.50	1.00
37 Black Recovery U	.50	1.00
38 Black Saving Drill U	.50	1.00
39 Black Shifting Drill U	1.00	2.00
40 Black Wrist Block U	.50	1.00
41 Blue Arm Blast U	.50	1.00
42 Blue Defensive Effect U	.50	1.00
43 Blue Energy Arrow U	.50	1.00
44 Blue Energy Blast U	.50	1.00
45 Blue Prepared Drill U	.50	1.00
46 Blue Recovery Drill U	.50	1.00
47 Blue Pivot Kick U	.50	1.00
48 Blue Stamina Drill U	.50	1.00
49 Blue Total Resistance U	.50	1.00
50 Bracing for Impact U	.50	1.00
51 Caught in the Act U	.50	1.00
52 Cell's Power Burst U	2.00	4.00
53 Cell's Instant Transmission U	1.00	2.00
54 Cell's Swift Strike U	1.00	2.00
55 Energy Rush U	.50	1.00
56 Everyone is Attacked! U	.50	1.00
57 Fighting in Cover U	.50	1.00
58 Cell's Backslap U	1.00	2.00
59 Namekian Restoration U	.50	1.00
60 Namekian Dragon Blast U	.50	1.00
61 Namekian Energy Spike U	.50	1.00
62 Namekian Face Smack U	.50	1.00
63 Namekian Piercing Beam U	.50	1.00
64 Namekian Power Stance Drill U	1.00	2.00
65 Namekian Quick Blast U	.50	1.00
66 Namekian Ready Drill U	.50	1.00
67 Namekian Right Cross U	.50	1.00
68 Namekian Scouting U	.50	1.00
69 Orange Beatdown U	1.00	2.00
70 Orange Burning Aura Drill U	1.00	2.00
71 Orange Energy Concentration U	2.00	4.00
72 Orange Energy Setup U	.50	1.00
73 Orange Energy Shot U	.50	1.00
74 Orange Fateful Attack U	.50	1.00
75 Orange Aggressive Technique U	1.00	2.00
76 Orange Steady Drill U	1.00	2.00
77 Piccolo's Fury U	.50	1.00
78 Prepared Dodge U	.50	1.00

79 Protective Shelter U .50 1.00
80 Quick Combat Drill U 1.00 2.00
81 Red Energy Drill U 1.00 2.00
82 Red Energy Surprise U 1.00 2.00
83 Red Forward Stance Drill U 1.00 2.00
84 Red Overhand Slash U 1.00 2.00
85 Red Power Punch U 2.00 4.00
86 Red Shielded Strike U 1.00 2.00
87 Saiyan Energy Drill U .50 1.00
88 Saiyan Protectant Drill U .50 1.00
89 Saiyan Pride U .50 1.00
90 Senzu Drill U 1.00 2.00
91 Something Dangerous is Coming! U .50 1.00
92 Tien's Block U .50 1.00
93 Blue Windup Blast R 2.00 4.00
94 Cell Jr. 1 (Level 1) R 3.00 6.00
95 Injured R 1.00 3.00
96 Saiyan Face Smash R 1.00 3.00
97 Surprise Hit R 1.00 3.00
98 Cell Jr. 2 (Level 1) R 3.00 6.00
99 Goku's Farewell R 4.00 8.00
100 Korin's Tower R 1.00 3.00
101 The Power of the Dragon R 3.00 5.00
102 Megaton Bull Crusher R 2.00 4.00
103 Orange Energy Smash R 2.00 4.00
104 Blue Fist Smash R 1.00 3.00
105 Double Teaming R 1.00 3.00
106 Straining Rebirth Move R 1.00 3.00
107 Android 18's Effect R 2.00 4.00
108 Aura Clash R 3.00 6.00
109 Group Attack R 3.00 6.00
110 Orange Focused Attack R 1.00 3.00
111 Caught Off Guard Drill R 3.00 6.00
112 Vegeta's Anger Drill R 2.00 4.00
113 Who's da Man! R 3.00 6.00
114 Dende (Level 2) R 2.00 4.00
115 Cell Jr. 1 (Level 2) R 3.00 6.00
116 Goku's Dragon Ball Quest R 2.00 4.00
117 Chazke Village R 1.00 3.00
118 Vegeta's Surprised R 2.00 4.00
119 Gohan's Elbow Block R 2.00 4.00
120 Straining Redirection Move R 2.00 4.00
121 Cosmic Backlash R 3.00 6.00
122 Chiaotzu (Level 2) R 3.00 6.00
123 Dragon's Victory R 2.00 4.00
124 Trunks, the Battler UR 50.00 80.00
125 Piccolo, the Defender (Level 5) UR 40.00 75.00

2002 Dragon Ball Z Cell Games Saga - Tuff Enuff

COMPLETE SET (22) 20.00 40.00
INSERTS IN CELL GAMES SAGA BOOSTERS
TF1 Black Smackdown 2.00 4.00
TF2 Blue Smackdown 2.00 4.00
TF3 Namekian Smackdown 1.00 2.00
TF4 Orange Smackdown 2.00 4.00
TF5 Red Smackdown 2.00 4.00
TF6 Saiyan Smackdown 2.00 4.00
TF7 Garlic Jr.'s Palm Blast 1.00 3.00
TF8 Loser With Style Drill 2.00 4.00
TF9 Krillin's Coolness Drill 2.00 4.00
TF10 Are You Tuff Enough??? 2.00 4.00
TF11 Bubbles Drill 1.50 3.00
TF12 Namekain Side Swipe 1.00 3.00
TF13 Orange Energy Stance 2.00 4.00
TF14 Namekian Charging Stance 1.00 3.00
TF15 Blue Show Off 1.00 3.00
TF16 Straining Double Strike Move 2.00 4.00
TF17 Saiyan Anger Strike 2.00 4.00
TF18 Black Energy Stance 2.00 4.00
TF19 Blue Goku's Power Kick 2.00 4.00
TF20 Blue Frustration Drill 2.00 4.00
TF21 Black Transformation (CC Pwr Pk) 3.00 5.00
TF22 Tien and Yamcha Strike (CC Pwr Pk) 3.00 5.00

2002 Dragon Ball Z Cell Games Preview Limited

COMPLETE SET (7) 10.00 20.00
INSERTS IN CELL GAMES SAGA BOOSTER PACKS
1 Celestial Games Begin C 1.00 3.00
2 Goku Helping Drill C 1.00 3.00
3 Gohan Meditates U 2.00 4.00
4 Gathering of Warriors U 1.50 2.50
5 Brothers in Training R 2.00 4.00
6 Chi-Chi on Attack! R 2.00 4.00
7 Learning the Moves (CC Pwr Pk) 3.00 6.00

2002 Dragon Ball Z World Games Saga Limited

COMPLETE SET (201) 200.00 300.00
BOOSTER BOX (36 PACKS) 45.00 70.00
BOOSTER PACK (12 CARDS) 3.00 3.75
CELESTIAL FIGHTER STARTER DECK 10.00 15.00
*FOIL: .75X TO 1.5X BASIC CARDS
1 Black Back Power Hit C .25 .50
2 Black Defensive Stance C .25 .50
3 Black Elbow Counter C .25 .50
4 Black Light Jab C .25 .50
5 Black Quick Strike C .25 .50
6 Black Reversal Strike C .25 .50
7 Blue Defensive Stance C .25 .50
8 Blue Fire Kick C .25 .50
9 Blue Flying Kick C .25 .50
10 Blue Forearm Block C .25 .50
11 Blue Right Power Strike C .25 .50
12 Blue Sneak Attack C .25 .50
13 Blue Thunder Flash C .25 .50
14 Goten's Focused Blast C .25 .50
15 Earth Dragon Ball 3 C .50 1.00
16 Namekian Battle Stance C .25 .50
17 Namekian Elbow Strike C .25 .50
18 Namekian Halting Stance C .25 .50
19 Namekian Light Jab C .25 .50
20 Namekian Surprise Attack C .25 .50
21 Namekian Throw C .25 .50
22 Orange Flying Drop Kick C .25 .50
23 Orange Gut Wrench C .25 .50
24 Orange Knockout C .25 .50
25 Orange Palm Block C .25 .50
26 Red Creative Block C .25 .50
27 Red Energy Defensive Stance C .25 .50
28 Red Flying Kick C .25 .50
29 Red Goku's Energy Blast C .25 .50
30 Red Kid Trunks' Blast C .25 .50
31 Saiyan Abduction C .25 .50
32 Saiyan Defensive Sphere C .25 .50
33 Saiyan Energy Ball C .25 .50
34 Saiyan Readied Attack C .25 .50
35 Straining Cry Baby Move C .25 .50
36 Straining Diving Punch Move C .25 .50
37 Straining Reversal Move C .25 .50
38 The Middle of Nowhere C .25 .50
39 Kid Trunks' Palm Blast C .25 .50
40 Black Back Breaker U .50 1.00
41 Black Driving Elbow Strike U .50 1.00
42 Black Duck U .50 1.00
43 Black Fist Catch U .50 1.00
44 Black Majin Blast U .50 1.00
45 Black Point Blank Kamehameha U 1.00 2.00
46 Black Super Kick U .50 1.00
47 Black Triple Team U .50 1.00
48 Black Videl's Power Kick U .50 1.00
49 Blue Back Kick U .50 1.00
50 Blue Energy Transformation U .50 1.00
51 Blue Heat Seeking Blast U .50 1.00
52 Blue Lightning Block U .50 1.00
53 Blue Quick Blast U .50 1.00
54 Blue Rebound U .50 1.00
55 Blue Videl's Knee Bash U .75 1.50
56 Chapuchai's Multiform U .50 1.00
57 Goku"s Quickness Drill U 1.00 2.00
58 Hercule's Drop Kick U .50 1.00
59 Hero's Drill U .50 1.00
60 Jackie Chun's Energy Attack U 1.00 2.00
61 Like Father, Like Son U .50 1.00
62 Majin Fist Block U .50 1.00
63 Majin Display of Power U 1.00 2.00
64 Majin Knee Strike U .50 1.00
65 Majin Overwhelming Attack U .50 1.00
66 Namekian Combo U .50 1.00
67 Namekian Double Blast U .50 1.00
68 Namekian Ducking Technique U .50 1.00
69 Namekian Eye Beam U .50 1.00
70 Namekian Final Flash U .50 1.00
71 Namekian Flight U .50 1.00
72 Namekian Focused Blast U .50 1.00
73 Namekian Focused Jab U 1.00 2.00
74 Namekian Focused Kick U 1.00 2.00
75 Namekian Heat Seeking Blast U .50 1.00
76 Namekian Knee Strike U .50 1.00
77 Namekian Offense U .50 1.00
78 Namekian Pikkon's Defense U .50 1.00
79 Namekian Swift Strike U .50 1.00
80 Namekian Tornado Attack U .50 1.00
81 Orange Close Call U 1.00 2.00
82 Orange Direct Strike U .50 1.00
83 Orange Diving Attack U 1.00 2.00
84 Orange Friendship U .50 1.00
85 Orange Light Jab U .50 1.00
86 Orange Overpowering Attack U 1.00 2.00
87 Orange Power Grip U .50 1.00
88 Orange Power Kick U 1.00 2.00
89 Orange Power Stance U .50 1.00
90 Orange Right Cross U .50 1.00
91 Arqua's Arena U .50 1.00
92 Orange Videl's Jump Kick U .75 1.50
93 Pikkon's Truce U .50 1.00
94 Red Aggression U .50 1.00
95 Red Double Strike U .50 1.00
96 Red Energy Drill U .50 1.00
97 Red Energy Focus U 1.00 2.00
98 Red Heat Seeking Blast U .50 1.00
99 Krillin, the Father U 1.00 2.00
100 Red Light Jab U .50 1.00
101 Red Lightning Strike U .50 1.00
102 Red Solar Flare U .50 1.00
103 Red Trap U .50 1.00
104 Red Videl's Elbow Smash U .50 1.00
105 Saiyan Discharge U .50 1.00
106 Saiyan Finger Block U .50 1.00
107 Saiyan Flight U 1.00 2.00
108 Saiyan Focused Block U .50 1.00
109 Saiyan Heritage Drill U .50 1.00
110 Saiyan Jump Shot U .50 1.00
111 Saiyan Kamehameha U .50 1.00
112 Saiyan Light Jab U .50 1.00
113 Saiyan Side Step U .50 1.00
114 Saiyan Swift Kick U .50 1.00
115 Saiyan Uppercut U .50 1.00
116 Straining Counterstrike Move U .50 1.00
117 Straining Focused Move U .50 1.00
118 The Truck U 1.00 2.00
119 Black Style Mastery R 5.00 10.00
120 Blue Style Mastery R 5.00 10.00
121 Capsule Corp. R 1.00 3.00
122 Chapuchai R 2.00 4.00
123 Chapuchai, the Tiny R 2.00 4.00
124 Chapuchai, the Tenacious R 2.00 4.00
125 East Kai Sensei R 5.00 8.00
126 Freestyle Mastery R 6.00 10.00
127 Froug R 2.00 4.00
128 Froug, the Underdog R 2.00 4.00
129 Froug, the Huge R 2.00 4.00
130 Gohan, the Energized R 4.00 8.00
131 Goku, the King's Pupil R 4.00 8.00
132 Grand Kai R 5.00 8.00
133 Red Jump Kick R 4.00 8.00
134 Krillin, the Husband R 2.00 4.00
135 Krillin, the Great R 2.00 4.00
136 Majin Spopovich R 3.00 6.00
137 Majin Spopovich, the Empowered R 3.00 6.00
138 Majin Spopovich, the Revitalized R 3.00 6.00
139 Namekian Style Mastery R 3.00 6.00
140 North Kai Sensei R 4.00 8.00
141 Olibu, the Honorable R 3.00 6.00
142 Orange Style Mastery R 3.00 6.00
143 Torbie, the Silent R 2.00 4.00
144 Torbie, the Prepared R 2.00 4.00
145 Torbie, Unleashed R 2.00 4.00
146 Pikkon, the Hero R 4.00 6.00
147 Red Style Mastery R 3.00 6.00
148 Saiyan Style Mastery R 4.00 8.00
149 South Kai Sensei R 4.00 8.00
150 Tapkar R 3.00 6.00
151 Tapkar, the Speedy R 3.00 6.00
152 Tapkar, the Fastest R 3.00 6.00
153 Arqua, the Water Champion R 2.00 4.00
154 Arqua, the Agile R 2.00 4.00
155 Arqua, Unleashed R 2.00 4.00
156 West Kai Sensei R 4.00 8.00
157 World Tournament R 4.00 8.00
158 Evil Presence Drill UR 15.00 30.00
159 Goku, the Galaxy's Hero UR 30.00 60.00
160 Goku's Blinding Strike UR 25.00 50.00
161 Pikkon, the Prized Fighter UR 25.00 50.00
162 Vegeta, the Proud (Level 1) P 3.00 6.00
163 Vegeta, the Mighty (Level 2) P 3.00 6.00
164 Vegeta, the Dark Hero (Level 3) P 3.00 6.00
165 Vegeta (Level 1) HT 4.00 8.00
166 Gohan, the Great Saiyaman (Level 1) P 1.00 3.00
167 Gohan, the Protector (Level 2) P 1.00 3.00
168 Gohan, the Righteous (Level 3) P 1.00 3.00
169 Gohan (Level 1) HT 3.00 6.00
170 Goku, the Warrior (Level 1) P 3.00 6.00
171 Goku, the Competitor (Level 2) P 3.00 6.00
172 Goku, the Proud (Level 3) P 3.00 6.00
173 Goku (Level 1) HT 6.00 12.00
174 Goten, the Playful (Level 1) P 3.00 6.00
175 Goten, the Brother (Level 2) P 3.00 6.00
176 Goten, the Young Saiyan (Level 3) P 3.00 6.00
177 Goten (Level 1) HT 4.00 8.00
178 Kid Trunks, the Junior Champion (Level 1) P 2.00 4.00
179 Kid Trunks, the Boastful (Level 2) P 2.00 4.00
180 Kid Trunks, the Young Saiyan (Level 3) P 2.00 4.00
181 Kid Trunks (Level 1) HT 3.00 6.00
182 Maraikoh, the Vicious (Level 1) P 2.00 4.00
183 Maraikoh, the Strong (Level 2) P 2.00 4.00
184 Maraikoh, the Mighty (Level 3) P 2.00 4.00
185 Maraikoh (Level 1) HT 2.00 4.00
186 Olibu, the Magical Hero (Level 1) P 2.00 4.00
187 Olibu, the Courageous (Level 2) P 2.00 4.00
188 Olibu, the Powerful (Level 3) P 2.00 4.00
189 Olibu (Level 1) HT 2.00 4.00
190 Pikkon, the Silent (Level 1) P 1.00 3.00
191 Pikkon, the Serious (Level 2) P 1.00 3.00
192 Pikkon, the Powerful (Level 3) P 1.00 3.00
193 Pikkon (Level 1) HT 2.00 4.00
194 Piccolo, the Majunior (Level 1) P 3.00 5.00
195 Piccolo, the Mentor (Level 2) P 3.00 5.00
196 Piccolo, the Former Guardian (Level 3) P 3.00 5.00
197 Piccolo (Level 1) HT 5.00 8.00
198 Videl, the Student (Level 1) P 3.00 4.00
199 Videl, the Protector (Level 2) P 3.00 4.00
200 Videl, the Determined (Level 3) P 3.00 4.00
201 Videl (Level 1) HT 4.00 6.00

2002 Dragon Ball Z Babidi Saga Preview Cards

INSERTS IN WORLD GAMES SAGA BOOSTER PACKS
1 Face Off (C) 1.00 3.00
2 Righteous Strike (C) 1.00 3.00
3 Evil's True Face (U) 2.00 4.00
4 Energy Drain (U) 2.00 4.00
5 Supreme Kai's Power Hold (R) 5.00 10.00
6 Supreme Kai (R) 7.00 14.00
7 Majin Vegeta, the Dark Prince (R) 8.00 15.00

2003 Dragon Ball Z Babidi Saga Limited

COMPLETE SET (123) 150.00 225.00
BOOSTER BOX (36 PACKS) 45.00 80.00
BOOSTER PACK (12 CARDS) 3.00 4.00
*FOIL: .75X TO 1.5X BASIC CARDS
1 Android 18's Iron Defense C .25 .50
2 Black Chained Strike C .75 1.50
3 Black Palm Reversal C .25 .50
4 Black Personal Smack C .50 1.00
5 Black Power Catch C .25 .50
6 Black Quick Kick C .25 .50
7 Blue Cape Swing C .25 .50
8 Blue Reflexes C .25 .50
9 Blue Shifting Maneuver C .25 .50
10 Blue Speediness C .25 .50
11 Combo C .50 1.00
12 Entering the Arena C .25 .50
13 Hercule's Power Stance C .25 .50
14 Heroic Shoulder Slam C .25 .50
15 Majin Death Focus C .25 .50
16 Orange Crushing Kick C .25 .50
17 Orange Dodge C .25 .50
18 Orange Elbow Smash C .25 .50
19 Orange Firebreath C .25 .50
20 Orange Right Punch C .25 .50
21 Red Forearm Block C .25 .50
22 Red Resistance C .25 .50
23 Red Slide C .25 .50
24 Red Thrusting Beam C .25 .50
25 Red Uppercut C .25 .50
26 Saiyan Duck C .25 .50
27 Saiyan Energy Rapture C .25 .50
28 Saiyan Might C .25 .50
29 Saiyan Power Block C .25 .50
30 Saiyan Prepared Smash C .25 .50
31 Straining Counter Punch U .25 .50
32 Android 18's Kneeing Drill U .25 .50
33 Android 18's Pressure Routine U .25 .50
34 Android 18's Throwing Drill U .25 .50
35 Majin Babidi's Ship U .25 .50
36 Black Backstab U .25 .50
37 Black Conservation Drill U .25 .50
38 Black Face Crush U .25 .50
39 Black Pummeling Strike U .25 .50
40 Black Reverse Kick U .25 .50
41 Black Surprise Maneuver U .25 .50
42 Blue Destruction Beam U .25 .50
43 Blue Leverage U .25 .50
44 Blue Palm Sphere U .25 .50
45 Blue Prevention Drill U .25 .50
46 Blue Torso Strike U .25 .50
47 Majin Vegeta U 3.00 6.00
48 Chi-Chi's Cheering Drill U .50 1.00
49 Majin Dabura's Offensive Leverage U .50 1.00
50 Majin Dabura's Petrifying Spit U .50 1.00
51 Energy Empowerment Drill U .50 1.00
52 Energy Storage Drill U .50 1.00
53 Goku's Berserk U .50 1.00
54 Goku's Shifted Balance Drill U .50 1.00
55 Goten's Flying Drill U .50 1.00
56 Hercule, the World Champion U .50 1.00
57 Majin Vegeta, the Evil U 2.00 4.00
58 In the Grove U .50 1.00
59 Majin Buu's Egg Drill U .50 1.00
60 Majin Defense Drill U .50 1.00
61 Majin Lightning Hit U .50 1.00
62 Majin Power Deflection U .50 1.00
63 Majin Power Drill U .50 1.00
64 Majin Power Shift U .50 1.00
65 Majin Pui Pui U .50 1.00
66 Majin Pui Pui, the Henchman U .50 1.00
67 Majin Babidi U 3.00 6.00
68 Majin Vegeta's Frantic Attack U .50 1.00
69 Majin Vegeta's Powerful Drill U .50 1.00
70 Majin Yakon U 1.00 3.00
71 Majin Yakon, the Monster U 1.00 3.00
72 Majin Babidi, the Wizard U 1.00 3.00
73 Majin Dabura U .50 1.00
74 Orange Critical Hit U .50 1.00
75 Orange High Block U .50 1.00
76 Orange Body Kick U .50 1.00
77 Orange Surprise Reaction U 1.00 2.00
78 Orange Temple Strike U .50 1.00
79 Paper, Rock, Sissors U .50 1.00
80 Red Energy Outburst U .50 1.00
81 Majin Dabura, King of Fighting U .50 1.00
82 Red Air Kick U .50 1.00
83 Red Physical Drill U .50 1.00
84 Splash Damage Drill U .50 1.00
85 Surprising Strength Drill U .50 1.00
86 Red Tilted Punch U .50 1.00
87 Saiyan Chin Kick U .50 1.00
88 Saiyan Movement U .50 1.00
89 Saiyan Aura Blast U .50 1.00
90 Saiyan Suspended Blast U .50 1.00
91 Majin Vegeta's Rage U 3.00 6.00
92 Videl, Tournament Ready U 1.00 3.00
93 Android 18, the Mom R 2.00 4.00
94 Majin Babidi's Power Extension R 2.00 4.00
95 Black Pivot Kick R 1.00 3.00
96 Blue Energy Dive R 2.00 4.00
97 Daughter's Joy R 2.00 4.00
98 Gohan, Energized R 3.00 6.00
99 Goku, the Legendary R 5.00 10.00
100 Hercule's Close Save U 2.00 4.00
101 Heroic Force R 2.00 4.00
102 Initiative R 2.00 4.00
103 M R 1.00 3.00
104 Majin Pui Pui, the Flashy R 2.00 4.00
105 Majin Yakon, the Absorber R 1.00 3.00
106 Majin Babidi, the Evil Genius R 3.00 5.00
107 Orange Backstab R 1.00 3.00
108 Red Face Slap R 1.00 3.00
109 Majin Dabura, Meditated R 3.00 6.00
110 Majin Quickness R 4.00 8.00
111 Blue Trapped Strike R 2.00 4.00
112 Heroic Sword Catch R 2.00 4.00
113 Majin Vegeta, Uncontrollable R 4.00 8.00
114 Majin Vegeta, the Malicious R 4.00 8.00
115 Orange Rapid Attack R 3.00 6.00
116 Red Energy Rings R 1.00 3.00
117 Red Meditation Drill R 2.00 4.00
118 Red Sniping Shot R 3.00 6.00
119 Risky Maneuver R 3.00 6.00
120 Saiyan Headshot R 1.00 3.00
121 Supreme Kai, the Mentor R 2.00 4.00
122 Majin Vegeta UR 30.00 60.00
123 Majin Vegeta, the Malevolent UR 50.00 80.00

2003 Dragon Ball Z Babidi Saga Android Movie

INSERTED IN THE BABIDI SAGA CARD PACKS
M1 Android 13 5.00 10.00
M2 Android 13 5.00 10.00
M3 Super Android 13 6.00 12.00
M4 Android 15 4.00 8.00
M5 Android 15 4.00 8.00
M6 Android 15 5.00 8.00
M7 Android 14 8.00 12.00
M8 Super Android 13's Destruction Bomb 5.00 10.00
M9 Super Android 13's Ridge Hand 2.00 4.00
M10 Android 13's Prepared Stance 6.00 12.00
M11 Goku's Defense Drill 3.00 6.00
M12 Blue Android 15's Energy Ball 2.00 4.00
M13 Gohan's Braced Energy Beam 3.00 6.00
M14 Android 14's Power Kick 4.00 8.00
M15 Gohan 5.00 10.00
M16 Super Saiyan Goku 5.00 10.00
M17 Saiyan Power Stance 2.00 4.00
M18 Goku's Quick Save 2.00 4.00
M19 Straining Spirit Bomb 2.00 4.00
M20 Super Android 13's Physical Resistance 2.00 4.00
M21 Red Android 13's Rapid Blast 3.00 6.00
M22 Heroic Final Strike 2.00 4.00
M23 Super Saiyan Trunks 6.00 10.00
M24 Trunks Swordplay Drill 10.00 15.00
M25 Android 18's Drop Kick 3.00 6.00
M26 Android 16's Grapple 2.00 4.00
M27 Breakfall 2.00 4.00
M28 Android 17's Left Blast 2.00 4.00
M29 Android Tag Team 3.00 6.00
M30 Android 18's Palm Blast 3.00 6.00
M31 Android 19's Dodge 2.00 4.00
M32 Android 18's Left Hook 2.00 4.00
M33 Betrayal 2.00 4.00
M34 Injured Circuits 3.00 6.00

2003 Dragon Ball Z Buu Saga Limited

COMPLETE SET (200) 225.00 275.00
BOOSTER BOX (36 PACKS) 50.00 75.00
BOOSTER PACK (12 CARDS) 3.00 4.00
*FOIL: .75X TO 1.5X BASIC CARDS
1 Alt. Dende Dragon Ball 1 C .50 1.00
2 Alt. Dende Dragon Ball 2 C .50 1.00
3 Black Arm Stretch C .25 .50
4 Black Head Crush C .25 .50
5 Black Floating Popo Defense C .25 .50
6 Black Diving Energy Drop C .25 .50
7 Blue Healing Ray C .25 .50
8 Blue High Block C .25 .50
9 Blue Slam C .25 .50
10 Carpet Attack Technique C .25 .50
11 Energy Gathering C .25 .50
12 Focused Sword Strike C .25 .50
13 Gohan's Sword Slash C .50 1.00
14 Gohan's Sword Sweep C .50 1.00
15 Gohan's Sword Thrust C .50 1.00
16 Goku's Power Attack C .25 .50
17 Heroic Quick Kick C .25 .50
18 Horrified C .25 .50
19 Krillin's Flight C .25 .50
20 Majin Demise C .25 .50
21 Majin Hand Clap C .25 .50
22 Orange Chin Break C .25 .50
23 Orange Energy Catch C .25 .50
24 Orange Energy Guard C .25 .50
25 Orange Spy Drill C .25 .50
26 Red Ball Throw C .25 .50
27 Red Fast Ball C .25 .50
28 Red Fist Catch C .25 .50
29 Red Passive Block C .25 .50
30 Red Power Block C .25 .50
31 Red Vigor Orb C .25 .50
32 Saiyan Energy Deflection C .25 .50
33 Saiyan Hand Swipe C .25 .50
34 Saiyan Snap Kick C .25 .50
35 Saiyan Direct Strike C .25 .50
36 Underwater Kick C .25 .50
37 West City U .50 1.00
38 Alt. Dende Dragon Ball 3 U .75 1.50
39 Alt. Dende Dragon Ball 4 U .75 1.50
40 Alt. Dende Dragon Ball 5 U .75 1.50
41 Bee U .75 1.50
42 Black Face Smash U .50 1.00
43 Black Gambit U .50 1.00

Card	Low	High
44 Black Gravity Drop U	.50	1.00
45 Black Heroic Side Kick U	.50	1.00
46 Black Overhead Smack U	.50	1.00
47 Black Secret U	.50	1.00
48 Black Snap Kick U	.50	1.00
49 Black Weakness Drill U	.50	1.00
50 Blue Devastation U	.50	1.00
51 Blue Belly Kick U	.50	1.00
52 Blue Draining Blast U	.50	1.00
53 Blue Energy Cannon U	.50	1.00
54 Blue Eye Gouge U	.50	1.00
55 Blue Friendship U	.50	1.00
56 Blue Gambit U	.50	1.00
57 Blue Head Kick U	.50	1.00
58 Blue Protective Bubble U	1.00	2.00
59 Blue Stomach Smash U	.50	1.00
60 Blue Upward Block U	.50	1.00
61 City Ablaze U	.50	1.00
62 Cookie! U	.75	1.50
63 Energy Ricochet U	.50	1.00
64 Flight Training U	1.00	2.00
65 Gohan's Swordplay Drill U	.50	1.00
66 Goku Swiftly Moving U	.50	1.00
67 Goku's Escape U	.50	1.00
68 Healing Magic U	.50	1.00
69 Hercule's Underground Training Area U	.50	1.00
70 Heroic Head Kick U	.50	1.00
71 Heroic Kamehameha U	.50	1.00
72 Krillin, Z Warrior U	.50	1.00
73 Majin Buu's House U	1.00	2.00
74 Majin Buu's Invincibility U	1.00	2.00
75 Majin Buu's Magical Ray U	.50	1.00
76 Majin Buu's Stomach Throw U	.50	1.00
77 Majin Head Blow U	1.00	2.00
78 Namekian Gambit U	.50	1.00
79 Namekian Shield Destruction U	.75	1.50
80 Namekian Shuto U	.50	1.00
81 Orange Car Push U	.50	1.00
82 Orange Face Breaker U	.50	1.00
83 Orange Face Crunch U	.50	1.00
84 Orange Flight U	.50	1.00
85 Orange Gambit U	.50	1.00
86 Orange Hiding Drill U	.50	1.00
87 Orange Mouth Shot U	.50	1.00
88 Orange Right Hook U	.50	1.00
89 Orange Sneak Attack U	.50	1.00
90 Orange Trick Shot U	.50	1.00
91 Physical Defense Drill U	.50	1.00
92 Red Arm Swioe U	.50	1.00
93 Red Force Punch U	.50	1.00
94 Red Front Jab U	.50	1.00
95 Red Gambit U	.50	1.00
96 Red Joker Drill U	.50	1.00
97 Red Overhead Crush U	.50	1.00
98 Red Pressure Technique U	.50	1.00
99 Red Spiked Blast U	.50	1.00
100 Saiyan Assault U	.50	1.00
101 Saiyan Energy Bomb U	.50	1.00
102 Saiyan Concentrated Blast U	.50	1.00
103 Saiyan Gambit U	.50	1.00
104 Saiyan Hurricane Kick U	.50	1.00
105 Saiyan Ki Ball U	1.00	2.00
106 Saiyan Onslaught U	.50	1.00
107 Saiyan Overwhelming Drill U	.50	1.00
108 Saiyan Power Beam U	.50	1.00
109 Saiyan Strength Blast U	.50	1.00
110 The Other World U	.50	1.00
111 Vegeta's Sacrifice U	1.00	2.00
112 Whiplash U	.50	1.50
113 Z Sword Plateau U	.50	1.00
114 Majin Buu U	1.00	2.00
115 Korin R	1.00	3.00
116 Goku, Super Saiyan Ascended R	2.00	4.00
117 Kid Trunks R	1.00	2.00
118 Goten R	2.00	4.00
119 Majin Dabura D.O.A. R	2.00	4.00
120 Majin Babidi R	1.00	2.00
121 Alt. Dende Dragon Ball 6 R	1.00	2.00
122 Alt. Dende Dragon Ball 7 R	1.00	2.00
123 Black Front Punch R	1.00	3.00
124 Black Right Kick R	1.00	3.00
125 Black Royal Flush Drill R	1.00	3.00
126 Black Style Mastery R	3.00	5.00
127 Blue Electrical Gunk R	1.00	3.00
128 Blue Style Mastery R	3.00	5.00
129 Deaf! R	1.00	3.00
130 Dende R	1.00	3.00
131 Freestyle Mastery R	2.00	4.00
132 Gotenks' Flight R	1.00	3.00
133 Hercule R	1.00	3.00
134 Losing Battle R	1.00	2.00
135 Majin Buu's Body Slam R	1.00	2.00
136 Majin Buu's Charged Attack R	1.00	2.00
137 Majin Buu's Flight R	3.00	5.00
138 Elder Kai Sensei R	4.00	6.00
139 Namekian Style Mastery R	2.00	4.00
140 Oolong R	1.00	3.00
141 Orange Destruction Ball R	1.00	2.00
142 Orange Style Mastery R	2.00	4.00
143 Red Cross Punch R	1.00	3.00
144 Red Style Mastery R	2.00	4.00
145 Saiyan Pressure Technique R	1.00	3.00
146 Saiyan Style Mastery R	5.00	10.00
147 Supreme Kai's Help R	2.00	4.00
148 Supreme Kai's Kid Push R	2.00	4.00
149 The Fusion Dance R	3.00	6.00
150 The Eternal Dragon Quest UR	25.00	50.00
151 Majin Buu UR	30.00	60.00
152 Goku, Super Saiyan 3 UR	50.00	80.00
153 Master Roshi Sensei UR	30.00	60.00
154 Gotenks (PC) HT	15.00	20.00
155 Gotenks, Super Saiyan (PC) HT	20.00	35.00
156 Goku	3.00	5.00
157 Goku, Super Saiyan	3.00	5.00
158 Goku, Super Saiyan 2	3.00	5.00
159 Goku HT	4.00	8.00
160 Goku GF	4.00	8.00
161 Gohan	3.00	5.00
162 Gohan	3.00	5.00
163 Gohan, Mystic Training	4.00	8.00
164 Gohan HT	4.00	8.00
165 Gohan GF	4.00	8.00
166 Kid Trunks	2.00	4.00
167 Kid Trunks	2.00	4.00
168 Kid Trunks	2.00	4.00
169 Kid Trunks HT	3.00	6.00
170 Kid Trunks GF	2.00	4.00
171 Goten	2.00	4.00
172 Goten	2.00	4.00
173 Goten	2.00	4.00
174 Goten HT	3.00	5.00
175 Goten GF	3.00	5.00
176 Piccolo	2.00	4.00
177 Piccolo	2.00	4.00
178 Piccolo	2.00	4.00
179 Piccolo HT	3.00	5.00
180 Majin Dabura	1.00	3.00
181 Majin Dabura	1.00	3.00
182 Majin Dabura	1.00	3.00
183 Majin Dabura HT	2.00	4.00
184 Majin Babidi	1.00	3.00
185 Majin Babidi	1.00	3.00
186 Majin Babidi	1.00	3.00
187 Majin Babidi HT	2.00	4.00
188 Majin Babidi GF	2.00	4.00
189 Majin Vegeta	3.00	5.00
190 Majin Vegeta	3.00	5.00
191 Majin Vegeta	3.00	5.00
192 Majin Vegeta HT	4.00	8.00
193 Majin Vegeta GF	4.00	8.00
194 Majin Buu	2.00	4.00
195 Majin Buu, the Rotund	2.00	4.00
196 Majin Buu, Pink People Eater	2.00	4.00
197 Majin Buu HT	4.00	8.00
198 Majin Buu GF	4.00	8.00
199 Majin Buu HT	4.00	8.00
200 Majin Buu GF	4.00	8.00

2003 Dragon Ball Z Buu Saga Broly Movie

INSERTED IN THE BUU SAGA CARD PACKS

Card	Low	High
1 Broly	12.00	20.00
2 Broly, the Enraged Saiyan	12.00	20.00
3 Broly, Super Saiyan	12.00	20.00
4 Broly, the Legendary Saiyan	20.00	30.00
5 Broly, the Unstoppable	8.00	15.00
6 Broly's Energy Burst	6.00	12.00
7 Broly's Evil Drill	4.00	8.00
8 Broly's Might	4.00	8.00
9 Broly's Overwhelming Attacks	4.00	8.00
10 Broly's Supreme Power	4.00	8.00
11 Saiyan Broly Smash	5.00	8.00
12 Saiyan Charge	3.00	6.00
13 Saiyan Cliff Slam	3.00	5.00
14 Saiyan Clothesline	2.00	4.00
15 Saiyan Enraged	3.00	6.00
16 Saiyan Setup	3.00	6.00
17 Saiyan Surprise	4.00	8.00
18 Battle of the Saiyans	2.00	4.00
19 Common Techniques	1.00	3.00
20 Goku's Instant Teleportation	2.00	4.00
21 Goku's Running Defense	3.00	6.00
22 Heroic Drill	3.00	6.00
23 Power Smack	1.00	3.00
24 Pure Defense	2.00	4.00
25 Krillin's Quick Kicks	2.00	4.00
26 Efficient Medicine	.50	1.00
27 Master Roshi	2.00	4.00
28 Comet Kumolre	1.00	2.00
29 Mind Control Device	2.00	4.00
30 New Vegeta	3.00	6.00
31 Paragus	1.00	2.00
32 Heroic Double Team	2.00	4.00
33 Namekian Precise Aim Drill	2.00	4.00
34 Power Transfer	.50	1.00
35 Saiyan Energy Toss	1.00	2.00
36 Vegeta's Energy Blast	3.00	6.00

2003 Dragon Ball Z Fusion Saga Preview Limited

Card	Low	High
COMPLETE SET (6)	8.00	15.00
INSERTS IN BABIDI SAGA BOOSTER PACKS		
1 Gokus Flight	.50	1.00
2 Majin Buus Choke Hold	1.00	2.00
3 Majin Bibidi the Mastermind	1.00	2.00
4 Peaceful Times U	1.00	2.00
5 The Power of Porunga R	3.00	6.00
6 Devastation Drill R	5.00	10.00

2003 Dragon Ball Z Fusion Saga

Card	Low	High
COMPLETE SET (125)	150.00	200.00
BOOSTER BOX (36 PACKS)	55.00	75.00
BOOSTER PACK (12 CARDS)	3.00	4.00
*FOIL: .75X TO 1.5X BASIC CARDS		
1 Black High Kick C	.25	.50
2 Black Jaw Hammer C	.25	.50
3 Black Shift Kick C	.25	.50
4 Blue Knockdown C	.25	.50
5 Determination Drill C	.25	.50
6 Dimension Scream C	.25	.50
7 Hercule's Assault Drill C	.25	.50
8 Hercule's Immunity C	.25	.50
9 Heroic Effort C	.25	.50
10 Majin Buu, Evil Buu (Level 1) C	.50	1.00
11 Majin Buu's Heel Kick C	.50	1.00
12 Majin Buu's Taunt C	.25	.50
13 Nooooooooooooooo! C	.25	.50
14 Orange Splitting Headache C	.25	.50
15 Orange Strength C	.25	.50
16 Paused Pose C	.25	.50
17 Red Holding Drill C	.25	.50
18 Red Striking Drill C	.25	.50
19 Release C	.25	.50
20 Saiyan Neutralization C	.25	.50
21 Saiyan Power C	.25	.50
22 Saiyan Spindletop Punch C	.25	.50
23 Taking Cover C	.25	.50
24 Tien's Surprise Technique C	.25	.50
25 Underdog Drill C	.25	.50
26 Underdog Drop Kick C	.25	.50
27 Up Close and Personal C	.25	.50
28 Vegito's Charged Blast C	.25	.50
29 Vegito's Drop Kick C	.25	.50
30 Vegito's Leg Catch C	.25	.50
31 Vegito's Uppercut C	.25	.50
32 Advanced Basics C	.25	.50
33 Apocalyptic Battle U	.30	.75
34 Black Big Bang U	.30	.75
35 Black Dark Energy U	.30	.75
36 Black Jawbreaker U	.30	.75
37 Black Karmic Strike U	.30	.75
38 Black Protection Orb U	.30	.75
39 Black Restraint U	.30	.75
40 Black Spin Kick U	.30	.75
41 Blue Beatdown U	.30	.75
42 Blue Energy Guard U	.30	.75
43 Blue Forceful Explosion U	.30	.75
44 Blue Gut Implosion U	.30	.75
45 Blue Longshot U	.30	.75
46 Blue Multi-Jab U	.30	.75
47 Blue Stopping Technique U	.30	.75
48 Blue Weaving U	.30	.75
49 Boomstick U	.30	.75
50 Devious Moves U	.30	.75
51 Elder Kai's Sacrifice U	.30	.75
52 Gohan's Forearm Block U	.30	.75
53 Gohan's Left Energy Release U	.30	.75
54 Heroic Charge U	.30	.75
55 Intensity Drill U	.30	.75
56 Krillin's Sacrifice U	.50	1.00
57 Majin Buu, Piccolo Absorbed (Level 3) U	1.00	2.00
58 Majin Buu, Super Buu (Level 2) U	1.00	2.00
59 Majin Buu's Bicycle Kick U	.30	.75
60 Majin Buu's Goo U	.30	.75
61 Majin Buu's Stomach U	.30	.75
62 Majin Static Orb U	.30	.75
63 Namekian Finger Blast U	.30	.75
64 Narrow Escape U	.30	.75
65 Orange Energy Break U	.30	.75
66 Orange Headshot U	.30	.75
67 Orange Laser Drill U	.30	.75
68 Orange Protection Drill U	.30	.75
69 Orange Rush U	.30	.75
70 Overcharge U	.30	.75
71 Ready for Action U	.30	.75
72 Red Cross Slash U	.30	.75
73 Red Energy Slap U	.30	.75
74 Red Physical Fortification U	.30	.75
75 Red Rapid Deflection U	.30	.75
76 Red Rapid Energy U	.30	.75
77 Red Repeated Flares U	.30	.75
78 Red Static Shot U	.30	.75
79 Redeemed U	.30	.75
80 Saiyan Blitz U	.30	.75
81 Saiyan Elusion U	.30	.75
82 Saiyan Explosion U	.30	.75
83 Saiyan Gut Kick U	.30	.75
84 Saiyan Neckbreaker U	.30	.75
85 Saiyan Perfect Defense U	.30	.75
86 Saiyan Push U	.30	.75
87 Saiyan Two Gun Woo U	.30	.75
88 Sneaky Tricks U	.30	.75
89 Unlocked Potential U	.30	.75
90 Vegeta, the Celestial (Level 1) U	.75	1.50
91 Vegeta's Blurred Kick U	.30	.75
92 Yamcha, the Amazing (Level 1) U	.30	.75
93 Black Energy Swirl R	1.00	2.00
94 Black Uppercut R	2.00	4.00
95 Blue Backhand R	1.00	3.00
96 Blue Leapfrog Drill R	1.00	3.00
97 Blue Lunge R	2.00	4.00
98 Dazed R	1.00	3.00
99 Den-Goku (Level 1) R	3.00	5.00
100 Gohan, Earth's Protector (Level 5) R	3.00	6.00
101 Gohan, Mystic Empowered (Level 4) R	2.00	4.00
102 Gotenks' Kamikaze Ghost R	3.00	6.00
103 Hercule-Goku (Level 1) R	3.00	6.00
104 Last Ditch Effort R	1.00	3.00
105 Majin Buu, Gohan Absorbed (Level 5) R	3.00	6.00
106 Majin Buu, Gotenks Absorbed (Level 4) R	3.00	6.00
107 Majin Buu's Energy Spray R	1.00	3.00
108 Majin Buu's Kamikaze Ghost (Level 1) R	2.00	4.00
109 Majin Buu's New House R	1.00	3.00
110 Majin Planet Destruction Blast R	1.00	3.00
111 Majin Thrust R	2.00	4.00
112 Namekian Door Explosion R	1.00	3.00
113 Orange Reflex R	1.00	3.00
114 Potara Earrings R	4.00	8.00
115 Red Drop R	1.00	3.00
116 Red Leverage Blast R	1.00	3.00
117 Red Mouth Cannon R	1.00	3.00
118 Red Whiplash R	2.00	4.00
119 Saiyan Overcharged Blast R	1.00	3.00
120 Straining Power Move R	1.00	3.00
121 Transformation R	2.00	4.00
122 Vegeta's Fury R	1.00	3.00
123 Vegito (Level 1) R	6.00	12.00
124 Gotenks, Super Saiyan 3 (Level 3) UR	50.00	75.00
125 Vegito, Super Saiyan (Level 2) UR	50.00	75.00

2003 Dragon Ball Z Fusion Saga Cosmic Anthology

INSERTED IN THE FUSION SAGA CARD PACKS

Card	Low	High
CA1 Supreme West Kai (Level 1)	8.00	16.00
CA2 Supreme West Kai (Level 2)	6.00	10.00
CA3 Supreme West Kai (Level 3)	5.00	10.00
CA4 Dr. Willow (Level 1)	3.00	6.00
CA5 Dr. Willow (Level 2)	3.00	6.00
CA6 Dr. Willow (Level 3)	3.00	6.00
CA7 Zarbon (Level 1)	2.00	4.00
CA8 Zarbon, Transformed (Level 2)	2.00	4.00
CA9 Zarbon, Fanatical (Level 3)	2.00	4.00
CA10 Turles, the Mysterious (Level 1)	4.00	8.00
CA11 Turles, the Proud (level 2)	2.00	4.00
CA12 Turles, the Saiyan Warrior (level 3)	2.00	4.00
CA13 Caterpy (Level 1)	3.00	6.00
CA14 Caterpy, the Grappler (Level 2)	2.00	4.00
CA15 Caterpy, the Tenacious (Level 3)	.10	.25
CA16 Gohan's Immense Power	2.00	4.00
CA17 Goku's Power Pole	4.00	8.00
CA18 Energetic Fruit	2.00	4.00
CA19 Icarus	3.00	6.00
CA20 Tree of Might	3.00	6.00
CA21 Goku's Super Saiyan Catch	4.00	8.00
CA22 Knowledge Transfer	3.00	6.00
CA23 Piccolo's Power Blast	5.00	10.00
CA24 Cooler's Surprise Attack	3.00	6.00
CA25 Returning the Favor	1.00	3.00
CA26 Ingrain in the Membrane	1.00	3.00
CA27 Alt. Earth Dragon Ball 3	3.00	6.00
CA28 Goku's Quick Dodge	5.00	10.00
CA29 Energy Pouch	4.00	6.00
CA30 Master Roshi's Back Kick	3.00	6.00
CA31 Gohan's Energy Deflection	2.00	4.00
CA32 Makyo Star	3.00	6.00
CA33 Piccolo's Destruction Attack	2.00	4.00
CA34 Blue Style Mastery	3.00	6.00
CA35 A Hero's Heart is Strong	2.00	4.00
CA36 Black Scout Maneuver	3.00	6.00

2003 Dragon Ball Z Kid Buu Saga Preview Limited

INSERTS IN THE FUSION SAGA PACKS

Card	Low	High
1 Trunks Aerial Kick C	.25	.50
2 Pans Right Blast C	.25	.50
3 Uubs Energy Drill U	.30	.75
4 Goku Young Again R	.30	.75
5 The Power of Porunga R	1.00	3.00
6 The Might of Shenron R	1.00	2.50

2003 Dragon Ball Z Kid Buu Saga Limited

Card	Low	High
COMPLETE SET (125)	120.00	200.00
BOOSTER BOX (36 PACKS)	45.00	65.00
BOOSTER PACK (12 CARDS)	2.50	3.50
*FOIL: 1X TO 2X BASIC CARDS		
1 Alt. Namek Dragon Ball 1 C	.25	.50
2 Alt. Namek Dragon Ball 2 C	.25	.50
3 Alt. Namek Dragon Ball 3 C	.25	.50
4 Black Exertion C	.25	.50
5 Black Groveling Drill C	.25	.50
6 Black Magic C	.25	.50
7 Black Parry C	.25	.50
8 Blue Biting Drill C	.25	.50
9 Blue Double Blast C	.25	.50
10 Blue Ki Build Up C	.25	.50
11 Blue Sledgehammer C	.25	.50
12 Blue Stretch Kick C	.25	.50
13 Fierce Left Kick C	.25	.50
14 Hercule's Realization C	.25	.50
15 Heroic Power Detonation C	.25	.50
16 Ki Catalyst C	.25	.50
17 Majin Hair Pull C	.25	.50
18 Namekian Remedy Drill C	.25	.50
19 Orange Arm Break C	.25	.50
20 Orange Discharge Drill C	.25	.50
21 Orange Hand-clasp Drill C	.25	.50
22 Overwhelmed C	.25	.50
23 Pan's High Slap C	.25	.50
24 Red Bullrush Drill C	.25	.50
25 Red Kaio-Ken Drill C	.25	.50
26 Red Puppy Slap C	.25	.50
27 Saiyan Aggression Drill C	.25	.50
28 Saiyan Dashing Kick C	.25	.50
29 Saiyan Stop C	.25	.50
30 Stupendous Strike C	.25	.50
31 The Help of Earth C	.25	.50
32 Alt. Namek Dragon Ball 4 U	1.00	3.00
33 Alt. Namek Dragon Ball 5 U	1.00	3.00
34 Android 18, the Mom (Level 1) U	1.00	3.00
35 Black Bicycle Kick U	.30	.75
36 Black Buffer Block U	.30	.75
37 Black Impressive Slap U	.30	.75
38 Black Swivel Attack U	.30	.75
39 Blue Alliance U	.30	.75
40 Blue Deviation Drill U	.30	.75
41 Blue Dikaio Blast U	.30	.75
42 Blue Face Crunch U	.30	.75
43 Blue Impulse U	.30	.75
44 Blue Villains Drill U	.30	.75
45 Bulma, the Wife (Level 1) U	1.00	3.00
46 CHARGE! U	.30	.75
47 Chi-chi, the Grandmother (Level 1) U	1.00	3.00
48 Earth's Demise U	.30	.75
49 Energy Lob U	.30	.75
50 Goku's Setup Strike U	1.00	3.00
51 Goku's Supreme Kamehameha U	1.00	3.00
52 Hercule, the Everlasting World Champ (Level 1) U	2.00	4.00
53 Kid Trunks, Teenager (Level 1) U	3.00	6.00
54 Krillin's Destructo Disk U	1.00	3.00
55 Majin Buu, Kid Buu (Level 2) U	2.00	5.00
56 Majin Buu, Kid Buu (Level 3) U	2.00	5.00
57 Majin Buu's Backstabbing Kick U	1.00	3.00
58 Majin Dabura, the Redeemed (Level 1) U	.30	.75
59 Billions of Mini Majin Buus U	2.00	5.00
60 Masterful Moves U	.30	.75
61 Orange Carnage U	2.00	5.00
62 Orange Gutter Swipe U	.30	.75
63 Orange Might U	.30	.75
64 Orange Obliteration U	.30	.75
65 Orange Vegeta's Assault U	1.00	3.00
66 Pan, Granddaughter of Goku (Level 1) U	1.00	3.00
67 Poof! U	.30	.75
68 Power Headbutt U	.30	.75
69 Provoke Drill U	.30	.75
70 Quick Teleportation Drill U	2.00	5.00
71 Recoome's Vogue Drill U	.30	.75
72 Red Aerial Force U	.30	.75
73 Red Annihilation U	.30	.75
74 Red Clap U	.30	.75
75 Red Elbow Drop U	.30	.75
76 Red Power Slam U	.30	.75
77 Red Sword Cleave U	.30	.75
78 Red Thunder Clap U	.30	.75
79 Saiyan Brace U	.30	.75
80 Saiyan Desperation U	.30	.75
81 Saiyan Energy Bullet U	.30	.75
82 Saiyan Jeering Drill U	.30	.75
83 Saiyan Youth Bruise U	.30	.75
84 Ultimate Defense U	.30	.75
85 Ultra Uppercut U	2.00	5.00
86 Uub (Level 1) U	1.00	3.00
87 Uub, the Quick Learner (Level 2) U	1.00	3.00
88 Vegeta's Ill Temper U	.30	.75
89 Videl, the Heroic (Level 1) U	1.00	3.00
90 Welcome Home Drill U	.30	.75
91 Yajirobe, Retired (Level 1) U	1.00	3.00
92 Yamcha, the Single (Level 2) U	1.00	3.00
93 Alt. Namek Dragon Ball 6 R	3.00	5.00
94 Alt. Namek Dragon Ball 7 R	3.00	5.00
95 Black Chaos Detonation R	1.00	3.00
96 Black Disarray Drill R	1.00	3.00
97 Black Drop Kick R	1.00	3.00
98 Black Swerve R	1.00	3.00
99 Blue Reverse R	1.00	3.00
100 Fond Memories R	1.00	3.00
101 Gohan, the Bookworm (Level 1) R	3.00	6.00
102 Goku Sensei R	4.00	8.00
103 Hercule's "Dream Sequence" R	1.00	3.00
104 King Kai, Earth's Mentor (Level 1) R	1.00	3.00
105 Majin Buu, Kid Buu (Level 4) R	3.00	6.00
106 Majin Buu, Kid Buu (Level 5) R	4.00	8.00
107 Majin Buu's Prepped Crash R	1.00	3.00
108 Orange Head Mash R	1.00	3.00
109 Orange Intense Power R	1.00	3.00
110 Orange Ki Assailment R	1.00	3.00
111 Orange Massacre R	1.00	3.00
112 Red Axe Heel Kick R	1.00	3.00
113 Red Hunger Drill R	1.00	3.00
114 Red Left Bolt R	1.00	3.00
115 Red Voltage Missle R	1.00	3.00
116 Saiyan Acute Rapid Slam R	1.00	3.00
117 Saiyan Beef R	2.00	4.00
118 Saiyan Handstand R	1.00	3.00
119 Saiyan Lurch R	1.00	3.00
120 Intense Observation Drill R	2.00	4.00
121 Uub, Enraged (Level 3) R	2.00	4.00
122 Vegeta, Settled Down (Level 2) R	2.00	4.00
123 Vile Energy R	1.00	3.00
124 Earth's Spirit Bomb UR	25.00	40.00
125 Piccolo Sensei UR	25.00	40.00

2003 Dragon Ball Z Kid Buu Saga Bojack Unbound

INSERTED IN THE KID BUU SAGA PACKS

Card	Low	High
1 Ohhhhhhhhhhh YEAH!	3.00	6.00
2 Krillin's Smoothness Drill	2.00	4.00
3 Trunks, the Weaponmaster (Level 1)	8.00	12.00
4 Kogu (Level 1)	3.00	6.00
5 Zangya (Level 1)	5.00	10.00
6 Bujin (Level 1)	4.00	8.00
7 Bido (Level 1)	5.00	10.00
8 Bojack (Level 1)	8.00	16.00
9 Bojack, the Villianous (Level 2)	4.00	10.00
10 Bojack, the Notorious (Level 3)	8.00	16.00
11 The Sword of Trunks	6.00	10.00
12 Snake Way	1.00	3.00
13 Saiyan Outburst	1.00	3.00
14 Vegeta's Elbow Slam	5.00	10.00
15 Orange Brick Breaker	1.00	3.00
16 Red Plasma Catapult	2.00	4.00
17 Black Eradication	1.00	3.00
18 Master Roshi's Gawking Drill	2.00	4.00
19 Bulma and Chi-chi's Stare Off	1.00	3.00
20 Tien's Focused Beam	2.00	4.00
21 Trunks' Back Bash	2.00	4.00
22 Zangya's Leaping Rush Down	1.00	3.00
23 Kogu's Dual Strike	2.00	4.00
24 Trunks' Deadly Impact	2.00	4.00
25 Heroic Power Shot	1.00	3.00
26 Triple Torpedo	6.00	10.00
27 Bojack's Overhead Toss	3.00	6.00
28 Bojack's Left Palm Charge	3.00	6.00
29 Bojack's Defensive Shield	3.00	6.00
30 Zangya's Entrapping Strings	1.00	3.00
31 Gohan's Obliteration	2.00	4.00
32 Power Overwhelming	1.00	3.00
33 Bojack's Extreme Assailment	3.00	6.00
34 Bido's Charge	3.00	6.00
35 Bojack's Double-Palmed Blitz	.50	1.00
36 Empowered Kamehameha	2.00	4.00

2003 Dragon Ball GT Baby Saga Preview Limited

Card	Low	High
COMPLETE SET (6)	10.00	20.00
INSERTED IN KIDD BUU SAGA PACKS		
1 Piccolos Knowledge Drill C	1.00	3.00
2 Android 18s Power Beam C	1.00	2.00
3 Nefarious Pact U	2.00	4.00
4 Black Clash U	2.00	4.00
5 Black Smoke Dragon R	4.00	6.00
6 Vegeta Super Saiyan R	5.00	10.00

2004 Dragon Ball GT Baby Saga Limited

Card	Low	High
COMPLETE SET (301)	175.00	225.00
BOOSTER BOX (24 PACKS)	45.00	70.00
BOOSTER PACK (12 CARDS)	3.00	3.75
*FOIL: 1X TO 2X BASIC CARDS		
1 Metal Mending ST	.20	.50
2 Goku's Finger Throw ST	.50	1.00
3 Saiyan Lift ST	.20	.50
4 Orange Double Shot ST	.20	.50
5 Saiyan Soaring Swerve ST	.20	.50
6 Red Close Call ST	.10	.25
7 Red Ducking Coverage ST	.10	.25
8 Blue Concentrated Blast ST	.20	.50
9 Orange Close Guard ST	.10	.25
10 Baby Vegeta's Immobile Defense C	.10	.25
11 Baby Vegeta's Viciousness C	.10	.25
12 Baby's Surprise Grapple C	.10	.25
13 Black Agile Reaction C	.10	.25
14 Black Buffer C	.10	.25
15 Black Combat Defense C	.10	.25
16 Black Energy Dodge C	.10	.25
17 Black Firebreath C	.10	.25
18 Black Flight C	.10	.25
19 Black Full Force Impact C	.10	.25
20 Black Laser Beams C	.10	.25
21 Black Laser Dodge C	.10	.25
22 Black Precise Aim C	.10	.25
23 Black Robot Wallop C	.10	.25
24 Black Star Dragon Ball 1 C	.10	.25
25 Black Star Dragon Ball 2 C	.10	.25
26 Black Thwack C	.10	.25
27 Black Torso Shift C	.10	.25
28 Blue Aversion C	.10	.25
29 Blue Distorted Knee C	.10	.25
30 Blue Double Barrel C	.10	.25
31 Blue Fallback C	.10	.25
32 Blue Forced Impact C	.10	.25
33 Blue Full Defense C	.10	.25
34 Blue Gliding Shirk C	.10	.25
35 Blue Hand Clasp C	.10	.25
36 Blue Ki Burst C	.10	.25
37 Blue Lofty Finesse C	.10	.25
38 Blue Power Absorption C	.10	.25
39 Blue Resistance C	.10	.25
40 Elevation C	.10	.25
41 Energy Overload Drill C	.10	.25
42 Fiesta Pan C	.10	.25
43 Flying Blades C	.10	.25
44 General Rilldo's Rocket Punch C	.10	.25
45 Goku to the Rescue C	.10	.25
46 Goku's Chin Break C	.10	.25
47 Goku's Energy Spray C	.10	.25
48 Hidden Power Level C	.10	.25
49 Inner Strength Drill C	.10	.25
50 Lookin' Pimp-like C	.10	.25
51 Orange Blurred Movement C	.10	.25
52 Orange Distortion C	.10	.25
53 Orange Dogfight C	.10	.25
54 Orange Drift C	.10	.25
55 Orange Ducking Resistance C	.10	.25
56 Orange Hand Lock C	.10	.25
57 Orange Revealing Attack C	.10	.25
58 Orange Revenge Death Ball C	.10	.25
59 Orange Scolding C	.10	.25
60 Orange Soaring Evasion C	.10	.25
61 Orange Stomach Slam C	.10	.25
62 Orange Warm-up Drill C	.10	.25
63 Orange Wrist Interception C	.10	.25
64 Pan's Anger Strike C	.10	.25
65 Pan's Spirit Attack C	.10	.25
66 Red Aerial Glide C	.10	.25
67 Red Blindside C	.10	.25
68 Red Crash C	.10	.25
69 Red Crippler C	.10	.25
70 Red Earth Shatter C	.10	.25
71 Red Erratic Flutter C	.10	.25
72 Red Headbutt C	.10	.25
73 Red Hypersonic Knockout C	.10	.25
74 Red Mix Up C	.10	.25
75 Red Perfection C	.10	.25
76 Red Stout Restraint C	.10	.25
77 Red Strength Squeeze C	.10	.25
78 Red Surprise Launch C	.10	.25
79 Saiyan Anchored Clamp C	.10	.25
80 Saiyan Arrogant Snare C	.10	.25
81 Saiyan Braced Resistance C	.10	.25
82 Saiyan Choke Hold C	.10	.25
83 Saiyan Cross Punch C	.10	.25
84 Saiyan Elbow Slam C	.10	.25
85 Saiyan Flawless Snatch C	.10	.25
86 Saiyan Fly Swat C	.10	.25
87 Saiyan Headbutt C	.10	.25
88 Saiyan Love C	.10	.25
89 Saiyan Sole Stop C	.10	.25
90 Saiyan Space Nova C	.10	.25
91 Saiyan Stomp C	.10	.25
92 Saiyan Weighted Lunge C	.10	.25
93 Strengthened Ki Drill C	.10	.25
94 Super Saiyans Unite C	.10	.25
95 Trunks' Flying Uppercut C	.10	.25
96 Trunks' Horizontal Encounter C	.10	.25
97 Uub's Blitz C	.10	.25
98 Uub's Finger Blast C	.10	.25
99 Uub's Majin Focus C	.10	.25
100 Wink Wink, Nudge Nudge C	.10	.25
101 Baby Gohan (Level 1) U	.30	.75
102 Baby Goten (Level 1) U	.30	.75
103 Baby Vegeta's Flaming Death Ball U	.50	1.00
104 Baby's Breakout U	.50	1.00
105 Baby's Liquidity U	.50	1.00
106 Black Butterfingers U	.30	.75
107 Black Covert Operations Drill U	.30	.75
108 Black Elbow Block U	.30	.75
109 Black Opposition U	.30	.75
110 Black Power Strike U	.30	.75
111 Black Rising Knee U	.30	.75
112 Black Star Dragon Ball 3 U	.50	1.00
113 Black Star Dragon Ball 4 U	.50	1.00
114 Black Uber Blast U	.30	.75
115 Blue Announcer Drill U	.30	.75
116 Blue Body Manipulation U	.30	.75
117 Blue Data Download U	.30	.75
118 Blue Draining Kamehameha U	.50	1.00
119 Blue Imminent Destruction U	.30	.75
120 Blue Plea U	.30	.75
121 Blue Power Boost U	.30	.75
122 Blue Prepped Attack U	.30	.75
123 Blue Seizure U	.30	.75
124 Bulla (Level 1) U	.30	.75
125 Bulma, the Mom (Level 1) U	.30	.75
126 Dr. Myuu's Destiny U	.30	.75
127 Dr. Myuu's Horror U	.30	.75
128 Elder Kai (Level 1) U	.30	.75
129 Emperor Pilaf (Level 1) U	.30	.75
130 General Rilldo's Metalization U	.30	.75
131 Giru (Level 1) U	.30	.75
132 Giru, the Helper (Level 2) U	.30	.75
133 Gohan (Level 1) U	.50	1.00
134 Goten (Level 1) U	.50	1.00
135 Hercule (Level 1) U	.30	.75
136 Hercule, the Great (Level 2) U	.30	.75
137 Kabito Kai (Level 1) U	.30	.75
138 Mai (Level 1) U	.30	.75
139 Majin Buu (Level 1) U	.50	1.00
140 Majin Buu, the Cherub (Level 2) U	.50	1.00
141 Mutant Robot (Level 1) U	.30	.75
142 Orange Effective Illusion U	.30	.75
143 Orange Fierce Discharge U	.30	.75
144 Orange Ki Assault U	.30	.75
145 Orange Menacing Attack U	.30	.75
146 Orange Proximity Blasts U	.30	.75
147 Orange Reverse Elbow U	.30	.75
148 Orange Safety Drill U	.30	.75
149 Orange Slide U	.30	.75
150 Power Up the Most U	.30	.75
151 Red Anticipation U	.30	.75
152 Red Dice Chucker U	.30	.75
153 Red Double Guard U	.30	.75
154 Red Hasty Release U	.30	.75
155 Red Scissors U	.30	.75
156 Red Snappy Reflexes U	.30	.75
157 Red Torso Pound U	.30	.75
158 Red Traverse Punch U	.30	.75
159 Road Rage U	.30	.75
160 Saiyan Agile Swerve U	.30	.75
161 Saiyan Charged Kamehameha U	.30	.75
162 Saiyan Destiny U	.30	.75
163 Saiyan Exertive Attack U	.30	.75
164 Saiyan Planet Explosion U	.30	.75
165 Saiyan Power Deflection U	.30	.75
166 Saiyan Spirit Shock U	.30	.75
167 Saiyan Strength Drill U	.50	1.00
168 Shu (Level 1) U	.30	.75
169 Shusugoro (Level 1) U	.30	.75
170 Sigma Force (Level 1) U	.30	.75
171 Sugoro (Level 1) U	.30	.75
172 Sugoro, Shapeshifter (Level 2) U	.30	.75
173 Trunks Searching U	.50	1.00
174 Vegeta (Level 1) U	1.00	2.00
175 Videl (Level 1) U	.30	.75
176 Baby (Level 4) R	1.00	2.00
177 Baby Vegeta (Level 4) R	3.00	6.00
178 Black Concealed Weaponry Drill R	1.00	2.00
179 Black Coolness Drill R	1.00	2.00
180 Black Geezer Patrol R	1.00	2.00
181 Black Interruption R	1.00	2.00
182 Black Leadership Drill R	1.00	2.00
183 Black Parental Guidance R	1.00	2.00
184 Black Star Dragon Ball 5 R	2.00	4.00
185 Black Star Dragon Ball 6 R	3.00	6.00
186 Black Star Dragon Ball 7 R	2.00	4.00
187 Black Style Mastery R	3.00	8.00
188 Black Style Mastery R	3.00	8.00
189 Black Throwdown R	1.00	2.00
190 Blue Ball Control Drill R	1.00	2.00
191 Blue Ball Gathering R	1.00	2.00
192 Blue Clobber R	1.00	2.00
193 Blue Kamehameha R	1.00	3.00
194 Blue Might Drill R	1.00	2.00
195 Blue Slipup R	1.00	2.00
196 Blue Style Mastery R	3.00	6.00
197 Blue Style Mastery R	3.00	6.00
198 Blue Trap Drill R	1.00	2.00
199 Champions of Earth R	1.00	2.00
200 Chi-chi, the Grandmother (Level 1) R	1.00	2.00
201 Dr. Myuu (Level 4) R	1.00	2.00
202 Epic Battle of Saiyans R	2.00	4.00
203 Fistful of Pain R	1.00	2.00
204 General Rilldo's Force Field R	2.00	4.00
205 General Rilldo's Invulnerability R	1.00	2.00
206 Goku, Golden Oozaru (Level 4) R	4.00	8.00
207 Goku's Brawling R	1.00	3.00
208 Goku's Mixing Drill R	1.00	3.00
209 Hercule, the Colossal (Level 3) R	1.00	2.00
210 Majin Buu, the Benevolent (Level 3) R	2.00	4.00
211 Masterful Defense R	1.00	2.00
212 Meanacing Evil R	1.00	2.00
213 Orange Absorbing Drill R	1.00	2.00
214 Orange Augmenting Drill R	1.00	2.00
215 Orange Escaping Drill R	1.00	2.00
216 Orange Family R	1.00	2.00
217 Orange Focusing Drill R	1.00	2.00
218 Orange Gameshow Drill R	1.00	2.00
219 Orange Removal System R	1.00	2.00
220 Orange Style Mastery R	3.00	6.00
221 Orange Style Mastery R	3.00	6.00
222 Pan, the Spirited (Level 4) R	1.00	2.00
223 Red Blowback R	1.00	2.00
224 Red Bolstered Defense R	1.00	2.00
225 Red Fingertip Blast R	1.00	2.00
226 Red Jumping Smash R	1.00	2.00
227 Red Personal Vendetta R	1.00	2.00
228 Red Shaving Drill R	1.00	2.00
229 Red Style Mastery R	5.00	8.00
230 Red Style Mastery R	5.00	8.00
231 Red Tail Pull R	1.00	2.00
232 Saiyan Firm Stance R	1.00	2.00
233 Saiyan Jump Kick R	1.00	2.00
234 Saiyan Outrage R	1.00	2.00
235 Saiyan Power Punch R	1.00	2.00
236 Saiyan Quest R	1.00	2.00
237 Saiyan Rage Drill R	1.00	2.00
238 Saiyan Style Mastery R	1.00	2.00
239 Saiyan Supreme Mastery R	5.00	9.00
240 Saiyan Trickery Drill R	1.00	2.00
241 Super Gallic Gun R	1.00	2.00
242 The Dragon Awaits R	1.00	3.00
243 Trunks, the Brilliant (Level 4) R	1.00	3.00
244 Majuub (Level 4) R	1.00	3.00
245 Vegeta's Quickness Drill R	1.00	2.00
246 Baby Vegeta, Golden Oozaru (Level 5) UR	20.00	30.00
247 Black Crosscheck UR	10.00	18.00
248 Blue Narrow Escape UR	10.00	18.00
249 Goku, Super Saiyan 4 (Level 5) UR	35.00	50.00
250 It's the Inside That Counts UR	8.00	18.00
251 Orange Fishing Drill UR	8.00	18.00
252 Red Toe Pierce UR	15.00	25.00
253 Saiyan Ground Slide UR	8.00	18.00
254 Baby (Level 2) ST	2.00	5.00
255 Baby (Level 3) ST	2.00	5.00
256 Baby (Level 1) ST	2.00	5.00
257 Baby Vegeta (Level 3) ST	2.00	5.00
258 Baby Vegeta (Level 1) ST	2.00	5.00
259 Baby Vegeta (Level 2) ST	2.00	5.00
260 Dr. Myuu (Level 1) ST	1.00	3.00
261 Dr. Myuu (Level 2) ST	1.00	3.00
262 Dr. Myuu (Level 3) ST	1.00	3.00
263 General Rilldo (Level 3) ST	1.00	3.00
264 General Rilldo (Level 1) ST	1.00	3.00
265 General Rilldo (Level 2) ST	1.00	3.00
266 Goku (Level 1) ST	2.00	4.00
267 Goku, Super Saiyan (Level 2) ST	2.00	4.00
268 Goku, Super Saiyan 3 (Level 3) ST	2.00	4.00
269 Pan (Level 1) ST	1.00	3.00
270 Pan, the Young Saiyan (Level 3) ST	1.00	3.00
271 Pan, the Youthful (Level 2) ST	1.00	3.00
272 Trunks (Level 1) ST	1.00	3.00
273 Trunks, Super Saiyan (Level 3) ST	1.00	3.00
274 Trunks, the Scientific (Level 2) ST	1.00	3.00
275 Uub (Level 1) ST	1.00	2.00
276 Majuub (Level 3) ST	1.00	2.00
277 Majuub (Level 2) ST	1.00	2.00
278 Baby (Level 1) (HT) ST	1.00	3.00
279 Baby (Level 2) (HT) ST	1.00	3.00
280 Baby (Level 3) (HT) ST	1.00	3.00
281 Baby Vegeta (Level 2) (HT) ST	2.00	4.00
282 Baby Vegeta (Level 3) (HT) ST	2.00	4.00
283 Baby Vegeta (Level 1) (HT) ST	2.00	4.00
284 Dr. Myuu (Level 3) (HT) ST	1.00	2.00
285 Dr. Myuu (Level 3) (HT) ST	1.00	2.00
286 Dr. Myuu (Level 2) (HT) ST	1.00	2.00
287 General Rilldo (Level 3) (HT) ST	1.00	2.00
288 General Rilldo (Level 1) (HT) ST	1.00	2.00
289 General Rilldo (Level 2) (HT) ST	1.00	2.00
290 Goku (Level 1) (HT) ST	2.00	4.00
291 Goku, Earth's Protector (Level 3) (HT) ST	2.00	4.00
292 Goku, Energized (Level 2) (HT) ST	2.00	4.00
293 Pan (Level 1) (HT) ST	1.00	2.50
294 Pan, the Agile (Level 2) (HT) ST	1.00	2.50
295 Pan, the Vivacious (Level 3) (HT) ST	1.00	2.50
296 Trunks (Level 1) (HT) ST	1.00	2.00
297 Trunks (Level 3) (HT) ST	1.00	2.00
298 Trunks, Teen Saiyan (Level 2) (HT) ST	1.00	2.00
299 Majuub (Level 3) (HT) ST	1.50	3.50
300 Uub (Level 1) (HT) ST	1.50	3.50
301 Majuub (Level 2) (HT) ST	1.50	3.50

2004 Dragon Ball GT Lost Episodes Limited

Card	Low	High
COMPLETE SET (154)	150.00	225.00
BOOSTER BOX (24 PACKS)	35.00	60.00
BOOSTER PACK (10 CARDS)	3.00	3.75
*FOIL: 1.5X TO 3X BASIC CARDS		
1 A Meeting of the Minds C	.10	.25
2 Artistic Fright Drill C	.10	.25
3 Black Bear Hug C	.10	.25
4 Black Bracing Drill C	.10	.25
5 Black Capture C	.10	.25
6 Black Foul Weather C	.10	.25
7 Black Idol Discharge C	.10	.25
8 Black Overwhelming Surprise C	.10	.25
9 Black Triple Kick C	.10	.25
10 Blue Charged Energy Blast C	.10	.25
11 Blue Cower C	.10	.25
12 Blue Goku's Kamehameha C	.10	.25
13 Blue Lifting Drill C	.10	.25
14 Blue Overhead Block C	.10	.25
15 Blue Overhead Toss C	.10	.25
16 Bon Para Para C	.10	.25
17 Buried! C	.10	.25
18 Dazzle the Public C	.10	.25
19 Electrocuted C	.10	.25
20 Exploration Drill C	.10	.25
21 Glare of the Dragon C	.10	.25
22 Goku's Childish Taunt C	.10	.25
23 Goku's Left Evade C	.10	.25
24 Goku's Ride C	.10	.25
25 I've Got What You Want! C	.10	.25
26 Luud C	.10	.25
27 Mutchy C	.10	.25
28 Orange Disorientation C	.10	.25
29 Orange Emperor Pilaf's Command C	.10	.25
30 Orange Expectant Dodge C	.10	.25
31 Orange Groveling Drill C	.10	.25
32 Orange Peace Drill C	.10	.25
33 Orange Right Ki Explosion C	.10	.25
34 Orange Right Thrust C	.10	.25
35 Pan's Extreme Assailment C	.10	.25
36 Pan's Tea Time Drill C	.10	.25
37 Red Aggravated Bite C	.10	.25
38 Red Combined Blast C	.10	.25
39 Red Discovered Crouch C	.10	.25
40 Red Elusive Drill C	.10	.25
41 Red Energy Dismissal C	.10	.25
42 Red Harried Crawl C	.10	.25
43 Red Internal Ki Blast C	.10	.25
44 Red Swift Dodge C	.10	.25
45 Saiyan Amazement C	.10	.25
46 Saiyan Egged C	.10	.25
47 Saiyan Crushing Elbow C	.10	.25
48 Saiyan Pan's Foot Capture C	.10	.25
49 Saiyan Pan's Left Salvo C	.10	.25
50 Saiyan Trunks' Enraged Glare C	.10	.25
51 Saiyan Youth Aggression C	.10	.25
52 Zoonama C	.10	.25
53 Black Back Whip U	.30	.75
54 Blue Betrayal U	.30	.75
55 Black Energy Drain U	.30	.75
56 Black Excitement U	.30	.75
57 Black Pan's Energy Beam U	.30	.75
58 Black Right Energy Release U	.30	.75
59 Black Sand Blast U	.30	.75
60 Black Webbed Restraint U	.30	.75
61 Blue Doll Dress Up U	.30	.75
62 Blue Empowered Blast U	.30	.75
63 Blue Energy Thrust U	.30	.75
64 Blue Roller Coaster U	.30	.75
65 Bon Para Para, the DJ U	.30	.75
66 Cardinal Mutchy Mutchy U	.30	.75
67 Dolltaki U	.30	.75
68 Dr. Myuu U	.30	.75
69 Emperor Pilaf, the Greedy U	.30	.75
70 Extensive Eating Drill U	.30	.75
71 General Rilldo U	.30	.75
72 Orange Uppercut U	.30	.75
73 Goku's Elbow Guard U	.30	.75
74 Goku's Entrapped Drill U	.30	.75
75 Goku's Sword Catch U	.30	.75
76 Ledgic, the Fighter U	.30	.75
77 Ledgic the Weapon Maste U	.30	.75
78 Luud, the Stoic U	.30	.75
79 Luud, the Feral U	.30	.75
80 Made Over U	.30	.75
81 Mai, the Startled U	.30	.75
82 Orange Chasing Drill U	.30	.75
83 Orange Desperation Beam U	.30	.75
84 Orange Electrified Charge U	.30	.75
85 Orange Gnawing Drill U	.30	.75
86 Orange Marriage U	.30	.75
87 Orange Prepared Brace U	.30	.75
88 Preparing for Impact U	.30	.75
89 Red Criminal Intent U	.30	.75
90 Red Entranced Drill U	.30	.75
91 Red Evasive Maneuver U	.30	.75
92 Red Molar Lift U	.30	.75
93 Red Reentry U	.30	.75
94 Saiyan Restraint U	.30	.75
95 Saiyan Right Block U	.30	.75
96 Saiyan Silent Drill U	.30	.75
97 Saiyan Spying Drill U	.30	.75
98 Saiyan Taunt U	.30	.75
99 Son Para Para U	.30	.75
100 Goku U	.30	.75
101 Wanted Poster: Goku U	.30	.75
102 Wanted Poster: Pan U	.30	.75
103 Wanted Poster: Trunks U	.30	.75
104 Zoonama, the Autocrat U	.30	.75
105 The Power of the Dragon R	1.00	3.50
106 Black Blinding Beams R	1.00	3.00
107 Black Ground Hugging Drill R	1.00	2.00
108 Black Maniacal Laughter R	1.00	2.00
109 Black Reflection R	1.00	2.00
110 Black Sparring Block R	1.00	2.00
111 Blue Ball Fascination R	1.00	2.00
112 Blue Energy Deflection R	1.00	2.00
113 Blue Hostage Drill R	1.00	2.00
114 Blue Moment of Peace R	1.00	2.00
115 Blue Present R	1.00	2.00
116 Blue Trunks' Energy Discharge R	1.00	2.00
117 Bon Para Para, the Joyous R	1.00	2.00
118 Don Para Para R	1.00	2.00
119 Dragon Ball Everlasting R	1.00	3.00
120 Emperor Pilaf, the Appalled R	1.00	2.00
121 Foreshadowing R	1.00	2.00
122 Giru, the Rescuer R	1.00	2.00
123 Giru, the Fearful R	1.00	2.00
124 Goku, the Determined R	2.00	4.00
125 Gust of Wind R	1.00	3.00
126 Impressive Entrance R	1.00	2.00
127 King Kai Sensei R	1.00	2.00
128 Ledgic R	1.00	2.00
129 Mai, the Bold R	1.00	2.00
130 Orange Burst R	1.00	2.00
131 Orange Goku's Energy Volley R	1.00	3.00
132 Orange Left Ki Blast R	1.00	2.00
133 Orange Volcano R	1.00	2.00
134 Pan R	1.00	2.00
135 Pan R	1.00	2.00
136 Red Angered Search R	1.00	2.00
137 Red Debt R	1.00	2.00
138 Red Losing Battle R	1.00	3.00
139 Red Tooth Removal R	1.00	3.00
140 Red Unsuspecting Trip R	1.00	2.00
141 Saiyan Catch R	1.00	3.00
142 Saiyan Charged Attack R	1.00	2.00
143 Saiyan Chase R	2.00	4.00
144 Saiyan Goodbye R	1.00	2.00
145 Saiyan Lunge R	1.00	2.00
146 Showdown R	1.00	2.00
147 Trunks R	1.00	3.00
148 Trunks' Left Elbow Smash R	1.50	3.00
149 Trunks' Thoughts R	1.50	3.00
150 Zoonama, Discombobulated R	1.00	2.00
151 Bulma Sensei UR	15.00	30.00
152 Captured! UR	20.00	40.00
153 Trunks, Super Saiyan UR	25.00	50.00
154 Pan, the Persistent UR	20.00	40.00

2002 Dragon Ball Z Capsule Corp. Power Pack

COMPLETE SET (33 CARDS)	.25	.50
30 Time Is A Warrior's Tool	1.00	2.00
CP1 King Kai	2.00	4.00
CP2 King Kai	2.00	4.00
CP3 King Kai	2.00	4.00
CP4 Lord Slug	1.00	2.00
CP5 Lord Slug	1.00	2.00
CP6 Lord Slug	1.00	2.00
CP7 Master Roshi	1.00	2.00
CP8 Master Roshi	1.00	2.00
CP9 Master Roshi	1.00	2.00
CP10 Future Gohan	2.00	4.00
CP11 Future Gohan	2.00	4.00
CP12 Future Gohan	2.00	4.00
CP13 Ginyu Force	1.00	2.00
CP14 Ginyu Force	1.00	2.00
CP15 Ginyu Force	1.00	2.00
GB2 Blue Happiness	.50	1.00
GB3 Orange Scatter Shot	.50	1.00
GB4 Namekian Dash	.50	1.00
GB5 Saiyan Cross Punch	1.00	2.00
GB6 Black Body Destruction	1.00	2.00
GB7 Gathering of Heroes	2.00	4.00
GB8 Warriors Clash	2.00	4.00
GB9 Taunting Drill	1.00	2.00

2003 Dragon Ball Z Limited Edition Collector's Tin

PICCOLO TIN	20.00	25.00
SUPER SAIYAN GOHAN TIN	20.00	25.00
SUPER SAIYAN VEGETA TIN	25.00	30.00
SUPER SAIYAN 3 GOKU TIN	25.00	30.00

EACH TIN INCLUDES THE FOLLOWING:
9 EXCLUSIVE COLLECTOR'S CLUB CARDS
2 BABIDI SAGA BOOSTERS PACKS
2 BUU SAGA BOOSTERS PACKS
2 FUSION SAGA BOOSSTER PACKS

1 Majin Buu's Loogie	1.00	3.00
2 A New Addition	1.00	3.00
3 Jawbreaker Hailstorm	2.00	4.00
4 Pan's Victory	2.00	4.00

1994 Dragon Ball Z Carddass GT3

Complete Set (94-135)	15.00	30.00

Manufactured by Bandai

2001 Dragon Ball Z Promos

K1 King Cold, the Mighty	12.00	20.00
M1 Cooler (Video Promo)	3.00	6.00
M2 Cooler, th Mighty (Video Promo)	3.00	6.00
M3 Cooler, the Shredder (Video Promo)	3.00	6.00
CC1 Namekian Strike	15.00	30.00
IR1 Super Saiyan Goku	10.00	20.00
IR2 Super Saiyan Gohan	10.00	20.00
SZ1 Black Lunge (SZ Championship)	10.00	20.00
SZ2 Victorious	20.00	40.00
SZ3 Champion Drill	50.00	100.00

2002 Dragon Ball Z Promos

J1 Fatherly Advice (Judge card)	55.00	75.00
K1 King Kai	35.00	55.00
K2 King Kai	30.00	50.00
K3 King Kai	35.00	55.00
L1 Warriors Preperation	40.00	80.00
L2 Line Up	15.00	30.00
L3 Team Work Kamehameha	40.00	80.00
IR3 Play Fighting (Toy insert)	5.00	10.00
IR4 Videls's Head Kick (Toy insert)	4.00	8.00
IR5 Huge Drill (Toy insert)	8.00	16.00
IR6 Saiyan Training (Toy insert)	5.00	10.00
IR7 Goku's Reunion (Toy insert)	6.00	12.00
IR8 Blue Saving Catch Drill (Toy insert)	4.00	8.00
IR9 Excitement (Toy insert)	6.00	12.00
IR10 Strike a Pose (Toy insert)	6.00	12.00
IR11 Babidi's Evil Plans (Toy insert)	5.00	10.00
IR12 Red Blowing Steam Drill (Toy insert)	8.00	15.00
IR13 Saiyan Straight Shot (Toy insert)	4.00	8.00
IR14 Stop Fighting (Toy insert)	6.00	12.00
IR15 Z Warriors Band Together (Toy insert)	4.00	8.00
IR16 Saiyan Knee Block (Toy insert)	6.00	10.00
IR17 Make a Wish (Toy insert)	10.00	15.00
IR18 Goku's Head Pull (Toy insert)	5.00	10.00
IR19 Pose With Style (Toy insert)	6.00	12.00
IR20 Releasing the Sword (Toy insert)	10.00	20.00
IR21 Long Journey (Toy Insert)	8.00	12.00
IR22 Black Upward Dodge (Toy Insert)	10.00	20.00
IR23 Saiyan Face Jab	3.00	6.00
IR24 Gotenks' Head Butt	5.00	10.00
IR25 Tien's Power Stance	6.00	12.00
IR26 Vegito's Gut Punch	8.00	15.00
IR27 Super Buu's Absorbtion	6.00	12.00
IR28 Catch Drill (Toy Insert)	5.00	10.00
IR29 Orange Prepared Stance (Toy Insert)	8.00	12.00
IR30 I Did'nt Want This (Toy Insert)	.10	.25
IR31 Pikkon's Leg Catch (Toy Insert)	12.00	20.00
IR32 Super Buu's Choke Hold (Toy Insert)	8.00	16.00
IR33 Gohan's Nimbus Cloud (Toy Insert)	12.00	20.00
IR34 Emotional Baggage (Toy Insert)	8.00	15.00
IR35 Gohan's Jump Kick	8.00	16.00
IR36 Ring Out (Toy Insert)	7.00	14.00
IR37 Black Sweeping Strike (Toy Insert)	7.00	14.00
IR38 The Parings (Toy Insert)	6.00	10.00
MP1 Cell's Final Battle	5.00	10.00
SZ4 Champion Belt (GENCON)	10.00	20.00
SZ5 Victorious Drill	35.00	75.00
SZ6 Champion's Aura	300.00	500.00
INF1 Red Overbearing Attack	12.00	20.00
INF2 Confrontation	6.00	12.00

2003 Dragon Ball Z Promos

F1 Grand Kai's Palace (DBGT Video)	8.00	12.00
F1 Grand Kai's Palace (DBGT Video) Gold	12.00	20.00
F2 Half Nelson (DBGT Video)	8.00	12.00
F2 Half Nelson (DBGT Video) Gold	12.00	20.00
F3 Orange Conversion Drill (DBGT Video)	5.00	10.00
F4 Black Stomach Breaker	5.00	10.00
J1 Fatherly Advice	25.00	45.00
J2 Blue Backbreaker	30.00	60.00
K4 Gohan's Power Hit	20.00	30.00
X1 Frieza's Anger Blast	10.00	20.00
X2 Vegeta's Energy Focus	10.00	20.00
X3 Motherly Rage	8.00	15.00
X4 Body Slam	8.00	15.00
X5 Piccolo's Power Ball	10.00	20.00
BR1 Broly, the Calm	2.00	4.00
BR2 Broly, Super Saiyan	2.00	4.00
BR3 Broly, Empowered	3.00	6.00
CB1 Power of Cookies!	10.00	15.00
CC2 Aerial Maneuver	12.00	25.00
CC3 Homework Time...	8.00	16.00
CC4 Impressive Power	8.00	16.00
CC5 Piccolo's Multiform	8.00	16.00
CC6 Majin Funny Face	8.00	16.00
CC7 Unbelievable Strength	3.00	5.00
CC8 Namekian Sky Beam	6.00	12.00
GS1 Startled	3.00	6.00
SJ1 Goku, the Mighty	4.00	8.00
SZ7 Let the Games Begin	8.00	15.00
TR1 Krillin's Overhead Smack	3.00	6.00
TR2 Vegeta's Energy Thrust	7.00	12.00
TR3 Trunks Sword Slice	15.00	30.00
GKI1 You're Invited	110.00	185.00
UR15 Vegeta, the Revitalized		
UR16 Goku, the All Powerful		
UR20 Goku, the Galaxy's Hero		

2004 Dragon Ball Z Promos

HT1 Goku, the Victorious	20.00	40.00
HT2 Baby Vegeta	10.00	22.00
HT3 Super Android 17	10.00	22.00
OP5 Orange Two Palm Woo	6.00	12.00
OP10 Valese	3.00	8.00
OP22 Frieza's Vengence	10.00	20.00
OP30 Super Android 17's Ki Focus	140.00	200.00
OP34 Super Android 17's Ki Intensity	150.00	235.00

2000 Dragon Ball Z Burger King Promos

* Without figures

BK1 Goku's Attack	.20	.60
BK2 Gohan's Anger	.20	.60
BK3 Krillin's Trick	.20	.60
BK4 Piccolo's Revenge	.20	.60
BK5 Frieza's Spirit	.20	.60
BK6 Super Saiyan Goku's Power	.20	.60
BK7 Vegeta's Smirk	.20	.60

2000 Saiyan Saga Promo Cards

Gold foils were randomly inserted in DBZ videos.
Non-foils were inserts from Magazines.

P1 Goku (Gold Foil) (DBZ Video)	5.00	10.00
P2 Piccolo (Gold Foil) (DBZ Video)	3.00	6.00
P3 Vegeta (Gold Foil) (DBZ Video)	5.00	10.00
P4 Raditz (Gold Foil) (DBZ Video)	4.00	8.00
P4 Goku (Magazine Promo)	5.00	8.00
P5 Gohan (Gold Foil) (DBZ Video)	4.00	8.00
P6 Krillin (Gold Foil) (DBZ Video)	3.00	6.00
P7 Nappa (Gold Foil) (DBZ Video)	3.00	6.00
P115 Nappa (Magazine Promo)	4.00	8.00

2000 Dragon Ball Z Frieza Saga Promos

P1 It's Just Not Worth It!	5.00	10.00
P2 Captain Ginyu Transformed	5.00	10.00
P3 Calming Sanctuary	4.00	8.00
P4 Dragons Glare	5.00	10.00
P5 Frieza's Force Buble	6.00	12.00
P6 The Last Wish	4.00	8.00
P7 Friends Help Friends	8.00	16.00
P8 Goku's Good Swift Kick	10.00	15.00
P9 Red Blocking Hand	8.00	15.00
P10 Orange Forceful Kick	6.00	12.00
P11 Vegeta's Lunge	12.00	20.00
P12 Frieza (Hi-Tech) (Redemption)	6.00	12.00
P13 Garlic Jr. (Hi-Tech) (Redemption)	6.00	10.00
P14 Trunks (Hi-Tech) (Redemption)	30.00	50.00
P15 Captain Ginyu (Hi-Tech) (Redemption)	12.00	20.00
P16 Spice (Hi-Tech) (Redemption)	10.00	15.00
P17 Vinegar (Hi-Tech) (Redemption)	10.00	20.00

2001 Dragon Ball Z Trunks Saga Promos

Manufactured by Score

? Android 18 (Trunks Saga Insert)	6.00	12.00
P1 Trunks Defensive Crouch	5.00	10.00
P2 Confrontation	5.00	10.00
P3 Concentration Drill	6.00	10.00
P4 Blue Battle Drill	4.00	8.00
P5 Tien Stands Ready	5.00	10.00
P6 King Cold's Sword Trick	4.00	8.00
P7 Garlic Jr.'s Revenge	6.00	12.00
P8 Trunks Power Strike	8.00	12.00
P9 Surprise!	10.00	20.00
P10 Showdown	6.00	12.00

2001 Android Saga Promo Cards

Manufactured by Score

P1 The Eyes Have It	8.00	15.00
P2 Foreboding Evidence (DBZ Cardgame.Com)	2.00	4.00
P3 A Burst of Energy (Scrye)	4.00	8.00
P4 Krillin's Search (Beckett DBZ Collector)	4.00	8.00
P5 Android 19 Is Stoic	6.00	12.00
P6 Krillin Is Ready (Irwin)	5.00	10.00
P7 Android 16 Smiles (Retailer Exclusive/ Newsletter)	6.00	12.00
P8 Yamcha's Right Cross (Inquest)	4.00	8.00
P9 Goku's Hesitation (Z Warrior Newsletter)	8.00	16.00
P10 Planet Vegeta	8.00	16.00
P11 Goku's Dashing Punch (GENCON)	8.00	16.00

2002 Cell Saga Promo Cards

Manufactured by Score

P1 Cell's Self Destruct	4.00	8.00
P2 Cell's Domination	5.00	10.00
P3 Kami's Idea (Volunteer Program)	12.00	30.00
P4 He's Safe (Magazine Promo)	6.00	12.00
P5 Just Thinking (Web offer)	.25	.50
P6 Land in Pain	2.00	4.00
P7 It's all about time (Capsule Corp Set)		
P8 Trunks Thinking	4.00	8.00
P9 Looking Good (Inquest)	4.00	8.00
P10 Piccolo's Fist Block (Mall Tour)	4.00	8.00

2002 World Games Saga Promo Cards

P1 Celestial Battleground	6.00	12.00
P2 Chi-Chi	3.00	6.00
P3 Heroic Block	2.00	4.00
P4 Huh???	6.00	10.00
P5 Majin's Perfect Defense	4.00	8.00
P6 Quick Recovery Drill	3.00	6.00
P7 Red Pressured Attack	4.00	8.00
P8 Saiyan Crush	4.00	8.00
P9 Tapkar on the Move	6.00	10.00
P10 Videl's Battle Ready	3.00	6.00

2003 Babidi Saga Promo Cards

Manufactured by Score

P1 Babidi's Magic	4.00	8.00
P3 Goku's Energy Clash	4.00	8.00
P4 Goku's Energy Explosion	5.00	10.00
P5 Jewel	3.00	6.00
P6 Majin Strength Maneuver	4.00	8.00
P7 Master Roshi's Makeshift Background	6.00	10.00
P8 Outer Space	4.00	8.00
P9 A Raditz Memory	5.00	10.00
P10 Total Defense Drill	3.00	6.00

2003 Buu Saga Promo Cards

Manufactured by Score

P1 Outburst Drill	3.00	6.00
P2 Goku's Power Strike	2.00	4.00
P3 Majin Buu's Furry	2.00	4.00
P4 Deceptive Moves	3.00	6.00
P5 Kid Trunks, the Fighter	4.00	8.00
P6 Red Mouth Shot	2.00	5.00
P7 Black Misguiding Punch	2.00	4.00
P8 Goku's Face Break	.10	.25
P9 Releasing Untapped Potential	2.00	4.00
P10 Majin Buu's Smooch	4.00	8.00

2003 Fusion Saga Promo Cards

Manufactured by Score

P1 Gotenks' Fast Action	2.00	4.00
P2 Hercule Draws Steel	1.00	3.00
P3 Heroic Head Throw	2.00	4.00
P4 Human Extinction Attack	2.00	4.00
P5 Locked On	2.00	4.00
P6 Orange Blitzkrieg	4.00	8.00
P7 Vegeta, the Celestial	8.00	16.00
P8 Orange Palm Technique	3.00	6.00
P9 Orange Power Point	3.00	6.00
P10 Taking a Break	2.00	4.00
??? Kid Buu	4.00	8.00
??? Ubb	4.00	8.00

2003 Dragon Ball Z Kraft Cheese Promos

Complete Set (10)	12.00	25.00

Found in Kraft Chese single packs.

K1 Gohan's Kamehameha	1.00	3.00
K2 It's Empty?	1.00	3.00
K3 Supreme Kai Sensei	4.00	8.00
K4 Majin Rapid Fire	3.00	6.00
K5 Stop!	3.00	6.00
K6 Majin Buu Childish Taunt	3.00	6.00
K7 Multi-Purpose Strike	1.00	3.00
K8 Racing Drill	1.00	3.00
K9 Overhead Squeal	1.00	3.00
K10 Gohan, Released Level 3	4.00	8.00

2002 Dragon Ball Z Score Wrapper Redemption Promos

Cards are redeemed by mail

R1 Android 15 (Lvl 1) (HT)	3.00	6.00
R2 Android 15 (Lvl 2) (HT)	3.00	6.00
R3 Android 16 (Lvl 1) (HT)	6.00	10.00
R4 Android 16 (Lvl 2) (HT)	6.00	10.00
R5 Android 17 (Lvl 1) (HT)	6.00	12.00
R6 Android 17 (Lvl 2) (HT)	6.00	12.00
R7 Android 18 (Lvl 1) (HT)	8.00	16.00
R8 Android 18 (Lvl 2) (HT)	8.00	12.00
R9 Cell Stage One (HT)	25.00	35.00
R10 Cell (Level 2) (HT)	20.00	25.00
R11 Super Saiyan Vegeta (Level 1)	6.00	10.00
R12 King Kai's New Home	6.00	10.00
R13 Goku's House	6.00	10.00
R14 Android 16, the Warrior	10.00	15.00
R15 Android 17, the Energized	10.00	15.00
R16 Android 18, the Survivor	12.00	16.00
R17 Android 19, Refreshed	8.00	12.00
R18 Android 20, the Mastermind	6.00	10.00
CR1 Interesting Information	2.00	4.00
CR2 Remote Control	3.00	6.00
CR3 Cell's Choke Hold	4.00	8.00
CR4 Peekaboo!	3.00	6.00
CGR1 Cell's Charge	5.00	8.00
CGR2 Flashy Move	3.00	6.00
CGR3 Big Man on Campus	4.00	8.00
CGR4 Gohan's Heroic Uppercut	.25	.50

2003 Dragon Ball Z Score Wrapper Redemption Promos

CR1 Mr. Popo	3.00	6.00
CR2 Mr. Popo	3.00	6.00
CR3 Mr. Popo	4.00	8.00
CR4 Rescuing Drill	3.00	6.00
CR5 Feverish	3.00	6.00
CR6 Frieza's Daunting Bombardment	2.00	4.00
CR7 Interview with the Green Guy	4.00	8.00
CR8 DELETED!	4.00	8.00
CR9 Gotenks' Potential	4.00	8.00
CR10 Nagging Drill	3.00	6.00
CR11 Goku's High Kick	4.00	8.00

2002 Dragon Ball Z Gohan Season

Complete Set (12)	15.00	30.00

These promo cards are given out for tournament play.
Manufactured by Score

L1 Warriors Preperation (foil)	6.00	10.00
L1 Warriors Preparation	2.00	4.00
L1-0 Gohan Season	6.00	10.00
L1-1 Showing off your Power	1.00	3.00
L1-2 Multi-form Training	1.00	3.00
L1-3 Garlic Jr's Double Blast	2.00	4.00
L1-4 Blast from the Passt	2.00	4.00
L1-5 Energy Explosion	2.00	4.00
L1-6 Pain Hurts	2.00	4.00
L1-7 Gohan's Defense Drill	3.00	6.00
L1-8 I'm a PoPo in a Bottle	2.00	4.00
L1-9 Gohan Season	2.00	4.00

2003 Dragon Ball Z Krillin Season

Complete Set (11)	10.00	20.00

These cards were given out for participating in tournament play.

L2 Line Up	5.00	10.00
L2-0 Krillin Season	3.00	6.00
L2-1 Krillin's Help	2.00	4.00
L2-2 Below the Belt	2.00	4.00
L2-3 Krillin's Face Slap	1.00	3.00
L2-4 Clash of the Titans	4.00	8.00
L2-5 Feeding Frenzy	3.00	6.00
L2-6 Taunt	1.00	3.00
L2-7 I Want You!	3.00	6.00
L2-8 That Tickles!	3.00	6.00
L2-9 Krillin Season (Redemption Card)	10.00	20.00

2003 Dragon Ball Z Yamcha Season

Complete Set (12)	12.00	20.00

These cards were given out for participating in tournament play.

L3 Team Work Kamehameha	1.00	2.00
L3 Team Work Kamehameha (Foil)	1.00	2.00
L3-0 Yamcha Season	1.00	2.00
L3-1 Defepsive Stance	1.00	2.00
L3-2 Super Arm Cannon of Super Stuff!	1.00	2.00
L3-3 Huge Strength Maneuver	1.00	2.00
L3-4 Yamcha Practice Drill	1.00	2.00
L3-5 A Pair of Goodness	1.00	2.00
L3-6 Yamcha Vigor	1.00	2.00
L3-7 Out for a Walk	1.00	2.00
L3-8 Mean Squeeze	1.00	2.00
L3-9 Yamcha season you Win	1.00	2.00

2003 Goku Season

Complete Set (11)	10.00	20.00

2005 Dragon Ball Z Arrival

COMPLETE SET (254)	200.00	250.00
BOOSTER BOX (12 PACKS)	10.00	20.00
BOOSTER PACK (10 CARDS)	2.00	3.00
1 Black Arrogant Block C	.10	.20
2 Black Back Lift C	.10	.20
3 Black Chest Beam C	.10	.20
4 Black Chin Punch C	.10	.20
5 Black Dash C	.10	.20
6 Black Encouragement C	.10	.20
7 Black Face Strike C	.10	.20
8 Black Jump Kick C	.10	.20
9 Black Left Blast C	.10	.20
10 Black Moon Energy C	.10	.20
11 Black Preparation C	.10	.20
12 Black Stance C	.10	.20
13 Blue Forceful Burst C	.10	.20
14 Blue Leaping Knee C	.10	.20
15 Blue Left Blast C	.10	.20
16 Blue Left Dodge C	.10	.20
17 Blue Overhead Pound C	.10	.20
18 Blue Rage C	.10	.20
19 Blue Shielding C	.10	.20
20 Blue Shoot 'em Up C	.10	.20
21 Blue Showdown C	.10	.20
22 Blue Spit C	.10	.20
23 Blue Stalemate C	.10	.20
24 Blue Uppercut C	.10	.20
25 Chiaotzu - Energy Charged C	.10	.20
26 Chiaotzu - Silently Strong C	.10	.20
27 Earth Dragon Ball 1 C	.10	.20
28 Earth Dragon Ball 2 C	.10	.20
29 Earth Dragon Ball 3 C	.10	.20
30 Gohan - Confident Youth C	.10	.20
31 Gohan - Resolute Ally C	.10	.20
32 Gohan's Dream C	.10	.20
33 Krillin - Smiling Warrior C	.10	.20
34 Krillin's Determination C	.10	.20
35 Namekian Capture C	.10	.20
36 Namekian Charged Attack C	.10	.20
37 Namekian Concentration C	.10	.20
38 Namekian Cross Block C	.10	.20
39 Namekian Face Blast C	.10	.20
40 Namekian Finger Defense C	.10	.20
41 Namekian Focusing C	.10	.20
42 Namekian Ground Slam C	.10	.20
43 Namekian Intense Beam C	.10	.20
44 Namekian Pound C	.10	.20
45 Namekian Rear Kick C	.10	.20
46 Namekian Wrist Grab C	.10	.20
47 Nappa - Ready Saiyan C	.10	.20
48 Nappa's Protective Aura C	.10	.20
49 Orange Bite C	.10	.20
50 Orange Dinosaur Chase C	.10	.20
51 Orange Energy Clash C	.10	.20
52 Orange Energy Flare C	.10	.20
53 Orange Evade C	.10	.20
54 Orange Laughter C	.10	.20
55 Orange Mouth Beam C	.10	.20
56 Orange Power Up C	.10	.20
57 Orange Right Kick C	.10	.20
58 Orange Stomach Thrust C	.10	.20
59 Orange Shock C	.10	.20
60 Orange Surprise C	.10	.20
61 Raditz - Saiyan Invader C	.10	.20
62 Raditz - Deadly Herald C	.10	.20
63 Raditz's Triumph C	.10	.20
64 Red Cover Up C	.10	.20
65 Red Energy Dive C	.10	.20
66 Red Fingertip Shot C	.10	.20
67 Red Forceful Blast C	.10	.20
68 Red Glare C	.10	.20
69 Red Leaping Kick C	.10	.20
70 Red Leaping Thrust C	.10	.20
71 Red Left Punch C	.10	.20
72 Red Recharge C	.10	.20
73 Red Right Cross C	.10	.20
74 Red Right Kick C	.10	.20
75 Red Youth Bite C	.10	.20
76 Saibaimen - Alien Henchman C	.10	.20
77 Saibaimen - Vicious Combatant C	.10	.20
78 Saibaimen's Seeds C	.10	.20
79 Saiyan Destructive Thrust C	.10	.20
80 Saiyan Dive C	.10	.20
81 Saiyan Evasion C	.10	.20
82 Saiyan Fingertip Blast C	.10	.20
83 Saiyan Flying Kick C	.10	.20
84 Saiyan Head Crush C	.10	.20
85 Saiyan Intense Ki Ball C	.10	.20
86 Saiyan Monkey Beam C	.10	.20
87 Saiyan Shadowing C	.10	.20
88 Saiyan Sinister Smirks C	.10	.20
89 Saiyan Skull Grab C	.10	.20
90 Saiyan Unbalanced Dodge C	.10	.20
91 Tien - Prepared Z Warrior C	.10	.20
92 Tien's Help C	.10	.20
93 Vegeta's Aura C	.10	.20
94 Yamcha - Aloof Fighter C	.10	.20
95 Yamcha - Baseball Extraordinaire C	.10	.20
96 Yamcha's Stance C	.10	.20
97 Black Crying U	.20	.50
98 Black Diving Elbow U	.20	.50
99 Black Electric Tendrils U	.20	.50
100 Black Fastball U	.20	.50
101 Black Finale U	.20	.50
102 Black Power Up U	.20	.50
103 Black Quick Shot U	.20	.50
104 Black Right Block U	.20	.50
105 Black Throw U	.20	.50
106 Black Water Pound U	.20	.50
107 Blue Breakaway U	.20	.50
108 Blue Breakout U	.20	.50
109 Blue Bubble Breath U	.20	.50
110 Blue Cheer U	.20	.50
111 Blue Earth Pound U	.20	.50
112 Blue Forearm Block U	.20	.50
113 Blue Lunge U	.20	.50
114 Blue Snacks U	.20	.50
115 Blue Utility Beam U	.20	.50

116 Blue Wing Destruction U	.20	.50
117 Chaiotzu's Self Destruct U	.20	.50
118 Chiaotzu's Help U	.20	.50
119 Earth Dragon Ball 4 U	.20	.50
120 Earth Dragon Ball 5 U	.20	.50
121 Gohan's Masenko Blast U	.20	.50
122 Goku - Battle Ready U	.20	.50
123 Goku - Enraged U	.20	.50
124 Goku's Taunt U	.20	.50
125 Krillin - Serious Battler U	.20	.50
126 Krillin - Energy Blastin' U	.20	.50
127 Namekian Blinding Ray U	.20	.50
128 Namekian Braced Beam U	.20	.50
129 Namekian Confidence U	.20	.50
130 Namekian Elbow U	.20	.50
131 Namekian Evasion U	.20	.50
132 Namekian Eye Lasers U	.20	.50
133 Namekian Ki Burst U	.20	.50
134 Namekian Left Cross U	.20	.50
135 Namekian Support U	.20	.50
136 Namekian Surprise U	.20	.50
137 Nappa - Faithful Cohort U	.20	.50
138 Nappa - Ki Charged U	.20	.50
139 Orange Catch U	.20	.50
140 Orange Dance U	.20	.50
141 Orange Finger Detonation U	.20	.50
142 Orange High Knee U	.20	.50
143 Orange Lockup U	.20	.50
144 Orange Lunge U	.20	.50
145 Orange Palm Blast U	.20	.50
146 Orange Relaxation U	.20	.50
147 Orange Sacrificial Block U	.20	.50
148 Orange Sword Slice U	.20	.50
149 Piccolo - Suited For Battle U	.20	.50
150 Piccolo - Angered Namek U	.20	.50
151 Piccolo - Surprised Namek U	.20	.50
152 Piccolo's Regeneration U	.20	.50
153 Raditz - Villainous Vanguard U	.20	.50
154 Raditz - Swift to Fight U	.20	.50
155 Red Braced Attack U	.20	.50
156 Red Breakout U	.20	.50
157 Red Charged Burst U	.20	.50
158 Red Dashing Attack U	.20	.50
159 Red Electrified Attack U	.20	.50
160 Red Knee Strike U	.20	.50
161 Red Overhead Block U	.20	.50
162 Red Peace U	.20	.50
163 Red Right Hook U	.20	.50
164 Red Sword Slash U	.20	.50
165 Saibaimen's Self Destruct U	.20	.50
166 Saiyan Dashing Kick U	.20	.50
167 Saiyan Energy Gathering U	.20	.50
168 Saiyan Escaping Kick U	.20	.50
169 Saiyan Happiness U	.20	.50
170 Saiyan Ki Flare U	.20	.50
171 Saiyan Left Hit U	.20	.50
172 Saiyan Math U	.20	.50
173 Saiyan Playtime U	.20	.50
174 Saiyan Thrust U	.20	.50
175 Saiyan Triangle Burst U	.20	.50
176 Tien - Ready For Action U	.20	.50
177 Tien's Tri-Beam U	.20	.50
178 Vegeta - Rage Empowered U	.20	.50
179 Vegeta - Arrogant Prince U	.20	.50
180 Yamcha's Controlled Ki Ball U	.20	.50
181 Black Charged Ball R	1.00	2.00
182 Black Dragon Support R	1.00	2.00
183 Black Head Slam R	1.00	2.00
184 Black Huge Burst R	1.00	2.00
185 Black Overpowering Mastery R	1.00	2.00
186 Black Upward Kick R	1.00	2.00
187 Black Z Warriors' Support R	1.00	2.00
188 Blue Energy Beam R	1.00	2.00
189 Blue Forceful Mastery R	1.00	2.00
190 Blue Knee R	1.00	2.00
191 Blue Lockup R	1.00	2.00
192 Blue Lunch R	1.00	2.00
193 Blue Shout R	1.00	2.00
194 Blue Strength R	1.00	2.00
195 Blue Tail Grab R	1.00	2.00
196 Dragon Ball Radar R	1.00	2.00
197 Earth Dragon Ball 6 R	1.00	2.00
198 Earth Dragon Ball 7 R	1.00	2.00
199 Goku - Heroic Friend R	2.00	3.00
200 Goku - Desperate Savior R	2.00	3.00
201 Goku's Kamehameha R	2.00	3.00
202 Krillin - Peaceful Z Warrior R	1.00	2.00
203 Krillin's Destructo Disk R	1.00	2.00
204 Namekian Blocking Hand R	1.00	2.00
205 Namekian Conservation Mastery R	1.00	2.00
206 Namekian Defensive Stance R	1.00	2.00
207 Namekian Force Push R	1.00	2.00
208 Namekian Finger Charge R	1.00	2.00
209 Namekian Intimidation R	1.00	2.00
210 Namekian Right Jab R	1.00	2.00
211 Namekian Secret R	1.00	2.00
212 Nappa - Energy Enhanced R	1.00	2.00
213 Nappa's Bull Rush R	1.00	2.00
214 Orange Destructive Beam R	1.00	2.00
215 Orange Dinner R	1.00	2.00
216 Orange Finger Ball R	1.00	2.00
217 Orange Lookout R	2.00	3.00
218 Orange Lunging Jab R	1.00	2.00
219 Orange Rapture R	1.00	2.00
220 Orange Skillful Mastery R	1.00	2.00
221 Paid Off R	1.00	2.00
222 Piccolo - Fearless Combatant R	1.00	2.00
223 Piccolo's Special Beam Cannon R	1.00	2.00
224 Raditz's Tail Whip R	1.00	2.00
225 Red Destructive Blast R	1.00	2.00
226 Red Double Kick R	1.00	2.00
227 Red Ki Aura R	1.00	2.00
228 Red Left Kick R	1.00	2.00
229 Red Mouth Cannon R	1.00	2.00
230 Red Reversal Mastery R	1.00	2.00
231 Red Shout R	1.00	2.00
232 Refill R	1.00	2.00
233 Saiyan Aggressive Mastery R	1.00	2.00
234 Saiyan Jump R	1.00	2.00
235 Saiyan Ki Charge R	1.00	2.00
236 Saiyan Personal Ki Ball R	1.00	2.00
237 Saiyan Rest R	1.00	2.00
238 Saiyan Right Punch R	2.00	3.00
239 Saiyan Battle Armor R	1.00	2.00
240 Vegeta - Prince of All Saiyans R	2.00	3.00
241 Vegeta - Saiyan Warrior R	2.00	3.00
242 Vegeta's Gallic Gun R	2.00	3.00
243 Goku - Desperate Savior ST	1.00	2.00
244 Krillin - Peaceful Z Warrior ST	1.00	2.00
245 Nappa - Energy Enhanced ST	1.00	2.00
246 Piccolo - Fearless Combatant ST	1.00	2.00
247 Raditz - Villainous Vanguard ST	1.00	2.00
248 Vegeta - Prince of All Saiyans ST	1.00	2.00
249 Scouter Goku ST	1.00	2.00
250 Scouter Krillin ST	1.00	2.00
251 Scouter Nappa ST	1.00	2.00
252 Scouter Piccolo ST	1.00	2.00
253 Scouter Raditz ST	1.00	2.00
F1 Broly - Bio-Broly P	2.50	5.00

2008 Dragon Ball Destructive Fury

COMPLETE SET (108)	30.00	60.00
BOOSTER BOX (24 PACKS)	40.00	80.00
BOOSTER PACK (10 CARDS)	2.50	5.00
*FOIL: 1X TO 2X BASIC CARDS		
EV043 Shallow Idea C	.10	.25
EV044 Return from Other World U	.20	.50
EV045 New Adventure C	.10	.25
EV046 Antagonism C	.10	.25
EV047 Mustle Tower R	1.00	2.00
EV048 Cell Game U	.20	.50
EV049 The Only Aim C	.10	.25
EV050 Android Project C	.10	.25
EV051 Ginyu Force Gathered! R	1.00	2.00
EV052 New Scanner R	1.00	2.00
EV053 The Next World Martial Arts Championship U	.20	.50
EV054 Saiyan's Pride C	.10	.25
EV055 Appearance of a Hero U	.20	.50
EV056 The Saviour? U	.20	.50
EV057 Marriage C	.10	.25
EV058 Comfortable Place U	.20	.50
EV059 Growing Good Will C	.10	.25
EV060 The Ball of Seal U	.20	.50
EV061 Surprise C	.10	.25
EV062 Resistance of the Majin C	.10	.25
EV063 Exposure ST	.50	1.00
EV064 Special Fighting Pose ST	.50	1.00
TE073 Power Pole R	1.00	2.00
TE074 Teleportation U	.20	.50
TE075 Comrade's Assistance C	.10	.25
TE076 Tri-Beam R	1.00	2.00
TE077 Breaking Through the Limit R	1.00	2.00
TE078 Masenko R	1.00	2.00
TE079 Super Kamehameha SR	3.00	6.00
TE080 Clone Jutsu U	.20	.50
TE081 Powered Gun U	.20	.50
TE082 Rocket Punch U	.20	.50
TE083 Unexpected Counter C	.10	.25
TE084 Birth of the Perfect Form R	1.00	2.00
TE085 Hell Flash SR	3.00	8.00
TE086 Irregular Attack C	.10	.25
TE087 Battle Suit C	.10	.25
TE088 Bindining Technique U	.20	.50
TE089 Recoome Kick R	1.00	2.00
TE090 Energy Cannon R	1.00	2.00
TE091 Body Change U	.20	.50
TE092 Overflowing Aura U	.20	.50
TE093 Big Bang Attack SR	1.50	3.00
TE094 Disguise Suit C	.10	.25
TE095 Huge Difference in Power U	.20	.50
TE096 Super Gravity Room U	.20	.50
TE097 Emergency Stop Switch C	.10	.25
TE098 Making a Deal Behind the Scenes C	.10	.25
TE099 A Girl's Heart R	1.00	2.00
TE100 Beginning of the Training C	.10	.25
TE101 Expanding Vibration R	1.00	2.00
TE102 Peculiar Space C	.10	.25
TE103 Sorcery U	.20	.50
TE104 Petrification U	.20	.50
TE105 Pure Impulse C	.10	.25
TE106 Thunder Flash R	1.00	2.00
TE107 Counter Against Evil Containment Wave R	1.00	2.00
TE108 Dynamic Mess Em Up Punch ST	.50	1.00
TE109 Enormous Fighting Aura ST	.50	1.00
WA095 Trunks C	.10	.25
WA096 Goten C	.10	.25
WA097 Krillin U	.20	.50
WA098 Tien U	.20	.50
WA099 Goku (GT) R	1.00	2.00
WA100 Gohan C	.10	.25
WA101 Piccolo R	1.00	2.00
WA102 Trunks (Super Saiyan) SR	1.50	3.00
WA103 Goku (Super Saiyan 3) SR	3.00	6.00
WA104 Ninja Murasaki C	.10	.25
WA105 General White C	.10	.25
WA106 Colonel Violet U	.20	.50
WA107 Staff Officer Black C	.10	.25
WA108 Major Metallitron U	.20	.50
WA109 Buyon C	.10	.25
WA110 Cell Jr. R	1.00	2.00
WA111 Android 16 R	1.00	2.00
WA112 Cell (Perfect Form) SR	1.50	3.00
WA113 West Kai U	.20	.50
WA114 South Kai U	.20	.50
WA115 East Kai U	.20	.50
WA116 Guldo U	.20	.50
WA117 Recoome C	.10	.25
WA118 Burter U	.20	.50
WA119 Jeice C	.10	.25
WA120 Captain Ginyu R	1.00	2.00
WA121 Vegeta (Brain Washed) SR	1.50	3.00
WA122 Announcer C	.10	.25
WA123 Launch C	.10	.25
WA124 Android 8 U	.20	.50
WA125 Chi-Chi C	.10	.25
WA126 Videl U	.20	.50
WA127 Pan R	1.00	2.00
WA128 Olibu C	.10	.25
WA129 Android 18 R	1.00	2.00
WA130 Great Saiyaman SR	1.50	3.00
WA131 Babidi C	.10	.25
WA132 Bibidi C	.10	.25
WA133 Piccolo Jr. U	.20	.50
WA134 Pui Pui C	.10	.25
WA135 Yakon C	.10	.25
WA136 Pikkon R	1.00	2.00
WA137 Dabura R	1.00	2.00
WA138 Super Garlic Jr. R	1.00	2.00
WA139 Majin Buu SR	2.00	4.00
WA140 Gohan ST	.50	1.00
WA141 Great Saiyaman ST	.50	1.00
WA142 Vegeta ST	.50	1.00
WA143 Mecha Frieza ST	.50	1.00

2008 Dragon Ball The Awakening

COMPLETE SET (100)	30.00	60.00
BOOSTER BOX (24 PACKS)	30.00	60.00
BOOSTER PACK (10 CARDS)	2.50	4.00
*FOIL: 1X TO 2X BASIC CARDS		
EV023 Reunion C	.10	.25
EV024 Outcome of the Training C	.10	.25
EV025 To Planet Namek U	.20	.50
EV026 Mysterious Boy from the Future R	1.00	2.00
EV027 Red Ribbon Army C	.10	.25
EV028 Trap in the Pilaf's Castle U	.20	.50
EV029 Unleashed Threat C	.10	.25
EV030 Premonition of Desperation C	.10	.25
EV031 Emission of the Aura C	.10	.25
EV032 Throwing the Elite Unit into the Front Line U	.20	.50
EV033 All Kais Gathered! C	.10	.25
EV034 Never Ending Nightmare R	1.00	2.00
EV035 Love at First Sight U	.20	.50
EV036 Lone Wolf C	.10	.25
EV037 Prophecy of Fortuneteller Baba R	1.00	2.00
EV038 Master Roshi's Full Power C	.10	.25
EV039 Union of the Warriors C	.10	.25
EV040 Unleashed Hidden Power C	.10	.25
EV041 Avenger C	.10	.25
EV042 Exhausted C	.10	.25
TE038 Hermit Style Uniform C	.10	.25
TE039 Wolf Fang Fist C	.10	.25
TE040 Nimbus Cloud R	1.00	2.00
TE041 Rapid Sword Drawing U	.20	.50
TE042 Destructo Disk R	1.00	2.00
TE043 Awakened by the Anger SR	1.50	3.00
TE044 Spirit Bomb R	1.00	2.00
TE045 Supernatural Power C	.10	.25
TE046 Four Witches Technique U	.20	.50
TE047 Hostage U	.20	.50
TE048 Flying on a Pole C	.10	.25
TE049 Absorption of Energy U	.20	.50
TE050 Copied Skill R	1.00	2.00
TE051 Barrier R	1.00	2.00
TE052 Saibamen Capsule U	.20	.50
TE053 Ruthless Blow C	.10	.25
TE054 Medical Machine C	.10	.25
TE055 Countdown to the Destruction U	.20	.50
TE056 Gallic Gun SR	1.50	3.00
TE057 Pride of Elite R	1.00	2.00
TE058 Psylock Smasher R	1.00	2.00
TE059 Temptation C	.10	.25
TE060 Time Machine U	.20	.50
TE061 Sleepy-Boy Technique C	.10	.25
TE062 Momentary Battle U	.20	.50
TE063 Microminiaturizer U	.20	.50
TE064 Double Knock Out R	1.00	2.00
TE065 Medicine from the Future R	1.00	2.00
TE066 Evil Cannon C	.10	.25
TE067 Healing Power C	.10	.25
TE068 Black Water Mist C	.10	.25
TE069 Evil Containment Wave U	.20	.50
TE070 Hyperbolic Time Chamber U	.20	.50
TE071 The Last Gamble SR	1.00	2.00
TE072 Revival of The Shenron R	1.00	2.00
WA050 Bulma U	.20	.50
WA051 Dr. Brief C	.10	.25
WA052 Yamcha C	.10	.25
WA053 Gohan R	1.00	2.00
WA054 Krillin C	.10	.25
WA055 Goku U	.20	.50
WA056 Trunks SR	2.00	4.00
WA057 Piccolo U	.20	.50
WA058 Gohan (Super Saiyan) SR	4.00	8.00
WA059 Monster Carrot C	.10	.25
WA060 Supreme Commander Red R	1.00	2.00
WA061 Chiaotzu C	.10	.25
WA062 Colonel Silver C	.10	.25
WA063 General Blue U	.20	.50
WA064 Tien U	.20	.50
WA065 Android 19 R	1.00	2.00
WA066 Android 20 R	1.00	2.00
WA067 Cell (The 2nd Form) SR	5.00	10.00
WA068 Saibamen C	.10	.25
WA069 Bubles C	.10	.25
WA070 Gregory C	.10	.25
WA071 Dodoria U	.20	.50
WA072 Zarbon U	.20	.50
WA073 Zarbon (Transformed) R	1.00	2.00
WA074 Bardock R	1.00	2.00
WA075 Vegeta (Super Saiyan) SR	6.00	12.00
WA076 Frieza (Full Power Form) SR	1.50	3.00
WA077 Launch U	.20	.50
WA078 Chi-Chi R	1.00	2.00
WA079 Hercule C	.10	.25
WA080 Korin U	.20	.50
WA081 King Chapa C	.10	.25
WA082 Ox-King C	.10	.25
WA083 Mr. Popo C	.10	.25
WA084 Mysterious Martial Artist R	1.00	2.00
WA085 Shien SR	1.50	3.00
WA086 Dende U	.20	.50
WA087 Guru U	.20	.50
WA088 Salt C	.10	.25
WA089 Mustard C	.10	.25
WA090 Vineger C	.10	.25
WA091 Spice C	.10	.25
WA092 Garlic Jr. R	1.00	2.00
WA093 Nail R	1.00	2.00
WA094 Lord Slug SR	3.00	6.00

2008 Dragon Ball The Warriors Return

COMPLETE SET (113)	25.00	50.00
BOOSTER BOX (24 PACKS)	20.00	50.00
BOOSTER PACK (9 CARDS)	1.25	3.00
*FOIL: 1X TO 2X BASIC CARDS		
EV001 Training in the Korin Tower C	.10	.25
EV002 Lesson by Master Roshi U	.20	.50
EV003 Rapid Movement U	.20	.50
EV004 Full Moon C	.10	.25
EV005 Powerful Backup U	.20	.50
EV006 Emperor Pilaf's Plot C	.10	.25
EV007 No Mercy C	.10	.25
EV008 Ambition of Dr. Gero U	.20	.50
EV009 Crumbled Pride C	.10	.25
EV010 Legendary Tribe Saiyan C	.10	.25
EV011 Invasion of the Planet C	.10	.25
EV012 Absolute Fear R	.75	1.50
EV013 Pafu Pafu C	.10	.25
EV014 Journey of Adventure C	.10	.25
EV015 World Martial Arts Championship U	.20	.50
EV016 Capsule Corporation C	.10	.25
EV017 Threat of the Evil Tribe C	.10	.25
EV018 Terrifying Plan C	.10	.25
EV019 Selection of the Race R	.75	1.50
EV020 Reviving Power C	.10	.25
EV021 Combination ST	.50	1.00
EV022 Captured ST	.50	1.00
TE001 Janken-Goo U	.20	.50
TE002 Spirit Ball C	.10	.25
TE003 Solar Flare C	.10	.25
TE004 Afterimage U	.20	.50
TE005 Kamehameha R	.75	1.50
TE006 One Last Attack R	.75	1.50
TE007 Kaio-Ken R	.75	1.50
TE008 Reversal U	.20	.50
TE009 Overwhelming Power C	.10	.25
TE010 Dodonpa R	.75	1.50
TE011 Hyper Evolution C	.10	.25
TE012 Reinforced Body C	.10	.25
TE013 Merciless Attack R	.75	1.50
TE014 Awakening of the Evil U	.20	.50
TE015 Scanner C	.10	.25
TE016 Resisting Power U	.20	.50
TE017 Appearance of the Unknown Enemy C	.10	.25
TE018 Stomping R	.75	1.50
TE019 True Power R	.75	1.50
TE020 Roar R	.75	1.50
TE021 Death Ball R	.75	1.50
TE022 Searching for Dragon Ball C	.10	.25
TE023 Super Holy Water U	.20	.50
TE024 Cross Arm Dive C	.10	.25
TE025 Bankoku Bikkuri Sho C	.10	.25
TE026 Senzu Beans U	.20	.50
TE027 Hoipoi-Capsule R	.75	1.50
TE028 Accident U	.20	.50
TE029 Evil Wave Explosion U	.20	.50
TE030 Giant Body Just C	.10	.25
TE031 Summoning the Hidden Power U	.20	.50
TE032 Absorbed Power C	.10	.25
TE033 Special Beam R	.75	1.50
TE034 Evil Force Organized! U	.20	.50
TE035 Kami's Shrine C	.10	.25
TE036 Power of the Instinct ST	.50	1.00
TE037 Frieza's henchmen ST	.50	1.00
WA001 Goku C	.10	.25
WA002 Yamcha C	.10	.25
WA003 Krillin U	.20	.50
WA004 Master Roshi R	.75	1.50
WA005 Tien U	.20	.50
WA006 Chiaotzu C	.10	.25
WA007 Gohan SR	1.50	3.00
WA008 Goku (Super Saiyan) SR	2.00	4.00
WA009 Giant Ape R	.75	1.50
WA010 Emperor Pilaf U	.20	.50
WA011 Shu C	.10	.25
WA012 Mai C	.10	.25
WA013 Emperor Pilaf Machine U	.20	.50
WA014 Master Shen C	.10	.25
WA015 Mercenary Tao R	.75	1.50
WA016 Android #17 R	.75	1.50
WA017 Android #18 R	.75	1.50
WA018 Cell R	.75	1.50
WA019 Raditz C	.10	.25
WA020 Nappa C	.10	.25
WA021 Vegeta SR	2.00	4.00
WA022 Raspberry C	.10	.25
WA023 Kyui C	.10	.25
WA024 Frieza SR	1.50	3.00
WA025 Frieza (The 2nd Form) R	.75	1.50
WA026 Frieza (The Final Form) SR	1.50	3.00
WA027 Kaio U	.20	.50
WA028 Bulma U	.20	.50
WA029 Oolong U	.20	.50
WA030 Puar U	.20	.50
WA031 Fortuneteller Baba R	.75	1.50
WA032 Giran C	.10	.25
WA033 Ranfan R	.75	1.50
WA034 Nam U	.20	.50
WA035 Jackie Chun R	.75	1.50
WA036 Yajirobe C	.10	.25
WA037 King Piccolo SR	2.50	5.00
WA038 Piano U	.20	.50
WA039 Tambourine U	.20	.50
WA040 Cymbal C	.10	.25
WA041 Piccolo Jr. U	.20	.50
WA042 Kami R	.75	1.50
WA043 Piccolo SR	1.00	2.00
WA044 Yamu C	.10	.25
WA045 Spopovich U	.20	.50
WA046 Goku ST SR	.50	1.00
WA047 Krillin ST	.30	.75
WA048 Frieza ST SR	.50	1.00
WA049 Frieza (The 3rd Form) ST	.30	.75
WI001 Emperor Pilaf's Wish ST SR	1.00	2.00
WI002 Oolong's Wish ST SR	1.00	2.00
WI003 Upa's Wish ST SR	2.00	4.00
WI004 Frieza's Last Wish ST SR	1.00	2.00
WI005 Dende's Wish SR	1.00	2.00

2009 Dragon Ball Clash of Sagas

COMPLETE SET (108)	40.00	80.00
BOOSTER BOX (24 PACKS)	40.00	80.00
BOOSTER PACK (10 CARDS)	2.50	5.00
*FOIL: 1X TO 2X BASIC CARDS		
EV085 Ascending to a new level R	.75	1.50
EV086 Strength from loss U	.20	.50
EV087 A Hero's Arrival U	.20	.50
EV088 Weighted training C	.10	.25
EV089 Backup has arrived C	.10	.25
EV090 Roll Call U	.20	.50
EV091 Base of Operations R	.75	1.50
EV092 Fading Riches C	.10	.25
EV093 Cold Legacy R	.75	1.50
EV094 Pain and Power U	.20	.50
EV095 UFO landing U	.20	.50
EV096 Power Struggle R	.75	1.50
EV097 Preparation for Battle U	.20	.50
EV098 Unexpected Strength C	.10	.25
EV099 Alternate Future SR	2.50	5.00
EV100 Mystery Pots C	.10	.25
EV101 Awakening of Power U	.20	.50
EV102 Threat multiplied R	.75	1.50
EV103 Namekian Fusion R	.75	1.50
EV104 Conflict Averted C	.10	.25
TE145 Super Dragon Fist SR	4.00	8.00
TE146 Kamehameha R	.75	1.50
TE147 Destructo Disk U	.20	.50
TE148 Burning Attack C	.10	.25
TE149 Spirit Bomb U	.20	.50
TE150 Energy Shield R	.75	1.50
TE151 Electric Attack C	.10	.25
TE152 Greed is Good C	.10	.25
TE153 Exploiting the weak C	.10	.25
TE154 Dirty Trick C	.10	.25
TE155 Power Surge R	.75	1.50
TE156 Syphon of energy C	.10	.25
TE157 Betrayal of Alliegence U	.20	.50
TE158 Powerful Heritage U	.20	.50
TE159 Energy Sword U	.20	.50
TE160 Shock Wave C	.10	.25

TE161 Ultimate Transformation SR 1.50 3.00
TE162 Ultimate Sacrifice R .75 1.50
TE163 Tri-Beam R .75 1.50
TE164 Will of the People C .10 .25
TE165 Katana Slice C .10 .25
TE166 Sparring Match U .20 .50
TE167 Shouts of Support C .10 .25
TE168 Strategy session U .20 .50
TE169 Special Beam Cannon C .10 .25
TE170 Mouth Beam C .10 .25
TE171 Arm Stretch C .10 .25
TE172 Laser Shot R .75 1.50
TE173 Hyper Tornado U .20 .50
TE174 Regeneration of lost limbs C .10 .25
WA190 Gohan (Super Saiyan) U .20 .50
WA191 Goku SR 1.50 3.00
WA192 Future Trunks (Super Saiyan) U .20 .50
WA193 Piccolo R .75 1.50
WA194 Tien U .20 .50
WA195 Trunks C .10 .25
WA196 Goten C .10 .25
WA197 Chiatzu C .10 .25
WA198 Yamcha C .10 .25
WA199 Krillin C .10 .25
WA200 Gogeta SR 6.00 12.00
WA201 Dr. Gero C .10 .25
WA202 Emperor Pilaf C .10 .25
WA203 Janemba R .75 1.50
WA204 Kogu C .10 .25
WA205 Bido U .20 .50
WA206 Bujin C .10 .25
WA207 Zangya C .10 .25
WA208 Bojack SR 3.00 6.00
WA209 Dr. Wheelo C .10 .25
WA210 Super 17 SR 3.00 6.00
WA211 Vegeta (Super Saiyan) R .75 1.50
WA212 Nappa C .10 .25
WA213 Daizu C .10 .25
WA214 Turles R .75 1.50
WA215 Grand Kai C .10 .25
WA216 Old Kai C .10 .25
WA217 Broly SR 7.50 15.00
WA218 Kibito Kai U .20 .50
WA219 Cooler (The 3rd Form) R .75 1.50
WA220 King Cold C .10 .25
WA221 Arale C .10 .25
WA222 Dr. Brief C .10 .25
WA223 Master Roshi C .10 .25
WA224 Videl U .20 .50
WA225 Yajirobe U .20 .50
WA226 Mr. Popo U .20 .50
WA227 18 R .75 1.50
WA228 Hercule C .10 .25
WA229 Papaya Man R .75 1.50
WA230 Pan U .20 .50
WA231 Gokule R .75 1.50
WA232 Drum C .10 .25
WA233 Dr. Myu C .10 .25
WA234 Baby C .10 .25
WA235 Kami C .10 .25
WA236 Rhildo U .20 .50
WA237 Rhildo (Mecha) R .75 1.50
WA238 Kid Buu SR 2.00 4.00
WA239 Pikkon U .20 .50
WA240 Buu U .20 .50
WA241 King Piccolo R .75 1.50

2009 Dragon Ball Fusion

COMPLETE SET (113) 30.00 60.00
BOOSTER BOX (24 PACKS) 30.00 60.00
BOOSTER PACK (10 CARDS) 2.50 5.00
*FOIL: 1X TO 2X BASIC CARDS
EV063 Exposure ST .50 1.00
EV064 Special Fighting Pose ST .50 1.00
EV065 Flexible Way of Thinking U .20 .50
EV066 Education-Conscious Mother R .75 1.50
EV067 Training in the Other World C .10 .25
EV068 Pose Practice C .10 .25
EV069 Unreasonable Fee R .75 1.50
EV070 Invisible Opponent U .20 .50
EV071 Mysterious Android U .20 .50
EV072 Lost Pride C .10 .25
EV073 Appointment to the Force C .10 .25
EV074 Rule by the Evil U .20 .50
EV075 Quick wit of Kibito Kai R .75 1.50
EV076 Proud Clan U .20 .50
EV077 Succeeded Knowledge C .10 .25
EV078 New Pupil R .75 1.50
EV079 Wedding Dress in Flames C .10 .25
EV080 Orange Star High School C .10 .25
EV081 New Majin U .20 .50
EV082 Lottery C .10 .25
EV083 Lost Dragon Ball C .10 .25
EV084 Fear by Majin R .75 1.50
TE108 Dynamic Mess Em Up Punch ST .50 1.00
TE109 Enormous Fighting Aura ST .50 1.00
TE110 Continuous Die Die Missile R .75 1.50
TE111 Cosmic Halo U .20 .50
TE112 Unstoppable Evolution C .10 .25
TE113 Kaio-Ken X 20 R .75 1.50
TE114 Fusion R .75 1.50
TE115 Super Ghost Kamikaze Attack R .75 1.50
TE116 Potara Fusion SR 1.00 2.00
TE117 Sneaking Footsteps C .10 .25
TE118 Sucking Blood U .20 .50
TE119 Hidden Weapon C .10 .25
TE120 Devilmite Beam R .75 1.50
TE121 Attack of the Androids U .20 .50
TE122 Self Explosion R .75 1.50
TE123 Super Dodonpa U .20 .50
TE124 Exceptional Power U .20 .50
TE125 Z Sword C .10 .25
TE126 Salza Blade U .20 .50
TE127 Unexpected Outcome C .10 .25
TE128 Dignity of the Conqueror R .75 1.50
TE129 Power Ball C .10 .25
TE130 Final Flash SR 1.50 3.00
TE131 Clever Play C .10 .25
TE132 Sudden Change C .10 .25
TE133 Cheer From the Goddesses U .20 .50
TE134 Succeeded Talent R .75 1.50
TE135 Eight Hand Technique R .75 1.50
TE136 Bashosen U .20 .50
TE137 Buried Legacy C .10 .25
TE138 Rage R .75 1.50
TE139 Malice U .20 .50
TE140 Transformation Beam C .10 .25
TE141 Charging the Energy U .20 .50
TE142 Wipe Out Attack SR 1.00 2.00
TE143 Wave Cannon C .10 .25
TE144 Super Evil Wave Explosion U .20 .50
WA140 Gohan ST .50 1.00
WA141 Great Saiyaman ST SR .75 1.50
WA142 Vegeta ST .50 1.00
WA143 Mecha Frieza ST SR .75 1.50
WA144 Ox-King C .10 .25
WA145 Dende U .20 .50
WA146 Chi-Chi C .10 .25
WA147 Goten (Super Saiyan) R .75 1.50
WA148 Trunks (Super Saiyan) R .75 1.50
WA149 Gotenks R 1.00 2.00
WA150 Goku (GT Super Saiyan) R .75 1.50
WA151 Ultimate Gohan SR 1.50 3.00
WA152 Vegito SR 3.00 6.00
WA153 Dracula Man C .10 .25
WA154 Guard Robot U .20 .50
WA155 Mummy Man C .10 .25
WA156 Akuman R .75 1.50
WA157 Mecha Mercenary Tao U .20 .50
WA158 Android 14 R .75 1.50
WA159 Android 15 C .10 .25
WA160 Android 13 R .75 1.50
WA161 Android 13 (United) SR 2.00 4.00
WA162 King Yemma U .20 .50
WA163 Captain Ginyu C .10 .25
WA164 Kibito C .10 .25
WA165 Neiz C .10 .25
WA166 Doore C .10 .25
WA167 Captain Salza R .75 1.50
WA168 Supreme Kai U .20 .50
WA169 Giant Ape (Battle Suit) R .75 1.50
WA170 Cooler (The 4th form) SR 4.00 8.00
WA171 Giru C .10 .25
WA172 Upa C .10 .25
WA173 Bora R .75 1.50
WA174 Annin C .10 .25
WA175 Videl U .20 .50
WA176 Mutaito R .75 1.50
WA177 Trunks R .75 1.50
WA178 Uub SR 1.00 2.00
WA179 Mighty Mask SR 1.50 3.00
WA180 Lord Don Kee C .10 .25
WA181 Zoonama C .10 .25
WA182 Sansho C .10 .25
WA183 Nicky C .10 .25
WA184 Ginger C .10 .25
WA185 Ledgic U .20 .50
WA186 King Piccolo ST SR .75 1.50
WA187 Evil Majin Buu R .75 1.50
WA188 Majin Buu (Fused) SR 2.00 4.00
WA189 Goku ST SR .75 1.50
WI006 Regaining the Power ST .50 1.00
WI007 Existence of Hero ST .50 1.00
WI008 Porunga of the Planet Namek ST .50 1.00
WI009 Revival of the Earth ST .50 1.00

2014 Dragon Ball Z

COMPLETE SET (314) 200.00 400.00
BOOSTER BOX (24 PACKS) 60.00 80.00
BOOSTER PACK (12 CARDS) 2.50 6.00
STARTER DECK (69 CARDS) 12.00 15.00
*FOIL: 1.2X TO 3X BASIC CARDS
COMPLETE RAINBOW SET (30) 30.00 80.00
RELEASED ON OCTOBER 17, 2014
C1 Namek Dragon Ball 1 C .10 .25
C2 Namek Dragon Ball 2 C .10 .25
C3 Namek Dragon Ball 3 C .10 .25
C4 Trunks – Inquisitive C .10 .25
C5 Trunks – Resolved C .10 .25
C6 Captain Ginyu – Leader C .10 .25
C7 Captain Ginyu – Energized C .10 .25
C8 Chaozu – Resurrected C .10 .25
C9 Tenshinhan – Returned C .10 .25
C10 Guldo – Ginyu Force C .10 .25
C11 Recoome – Ginyu Force C .10 .25
C12 Nappa – Space Traveler C .10 .25
C13 Black Erasing Drill C .10 .25
C14 Black Concussive Blast C .10 .25
C15 Black Corruption C .10 .25
C16 Black Hug Maneuver C .10 .25
C17 Black Knee Catch C .10 .25
C18 Black Lunge C .10 .25
C19 Black Punishment C .10 .25
C20 Blue Battle Readiness C .10 .25
C21 Blue Trick C .10 .25
C22 Blue Battle Drill C .10 .25
C23 Blue Biting Drill C .10 .25
C24 Blue Defensive Effect C .10 .25
C25 Blue Defensive Flight C .10 .25
C26 Blue Draining Blast C .10 .25
C27 Blue Head Knock C .10 .25
C28 Blue Reverse C .10 .25
C29 Namekian Chop C .10 .25
C30 Namekian Double Strike C .10 .25
C31 Namekian Dragon Blast C .10 .25
C32 Namekian Energy Toss C .10 .25
C33 Namekian Maximum Will C .10 .25
C34 Namekian Onslaught C .10 .25
C35 Namekian Right Throw C .10 .25
C36 Orange Aura Drill C .10 .25
C37 Orange Joint Restraint Drill C .10 .25
C38 Orange Defensive Blast C .10 .25
C39 Orange Distracting Beam C .10 .25
C40 Orange Energy Absorption C .10 .25
C41 Orange Precise Shot C .10 .25
C42 Orange Refocus C .10 .25
C43 Orange Revenge C .10 .25
C44 Red Hunting Drill C .10 .25
C45 Red Back Kick C .10 .25
C46 Red Double Strike C .10 .25
C47 Red Duck C .10 .25
C48 Red Flares C .10 .25
C49 Red Shattering Leap C .10 .25
C50 Red Shoulder Grab C .10 .25
C51 Saiyan Cheap Shot C .10 .25
C52 Saiyan Energy Focus C .10 .25
C53 Saiyan Clothesline C .10 .25
C54 Saiyan Energy Toss C .10 .25
C55 Saiyan Foot Stomp C .10 .25
C56 Saiyan Pinpoint Blast C .10 .25
C57 Saiyan Scouting C .10 .25
C58 Saiyan Supreme Block C .10 .25
C59 Saiyan Uppercut C .10 .25
C60 It's Over 9,000! C .10 .25
U61 Namek Dragon Ball 4 U .20 .50
U62 Namek Dragon Ball 5 U .20 .50
U63 Namek Dragon Ball 6 U .20 .50
U64 Trunks – Energy Charged U .20 .50
U65 Trunks – Young Super Saiyan U .20 .50
U66 Captain Ginyu – Body Change U .20 .50
U67 Captain Ginyu – Frog U .20 .50
U68 Bulma – Genius U .20 .50
U69 ChiChi – Armed and Dangerous U .20 .50
U70 Yamcha – Action Ready U .20 .50
U71 Burter – Ginyu Force U .20 .50
U72 Jiece – Ginyu Force U .20 .50
U73 Black Searching Technique U .20 .50
U74 Black Adaptation U .20 .50
U75 Black Barrage U .20 .50
U76 Black Delay U .20 .50
U77 Black Swerve U .20 .50
U78 Black Swirl U .20 .50
U79 Blue Blockade U .20 .50
U80 Blue Betrayal U .20 .50
U81 Blue Farewell U .20 .50
U82 Blue Lunar Ray U .20 .50
U83 Blue Shifting Maneuver U .20 .50
U84 Namekian Wish U .20 .50
U85 Namekian Finger Lasers U .20 .50
U86 Namekian Flinch U .20 .50
U87 Namekian Hybrid Defense U .20 .50
U88 Namekian Targeted Strike U .20 .50
U89 Namekian Zone Pressure U .20 .50
U90 Orange Empowered Drill U .20 .50
U91 Orange Energy Phasing Drill U .20 .50
U92 Orange Escape U .20 .50
U93 Orange Inspection U .20 .50
U94 Orange Offensive Strike U .20 .50
U95 Orange Overhead Smash U .20 .50
U96 Red Despair Drill U .20 .50
U97 Red Escape U .20 .50
U98 Red Jump Kick U .20 .50
U99 Red Lightning Slash U .20 .50
U100 Red Power Punch U .20 .50
U101 Red Shielded Strike U .20 .50
U102 Saiyan Domination U .20 .50
U103 Saiyan Gut Kick U .20 .50
U104 Saiyan Multi-blast U .20 .50
U105 Saiyan Surprise U .20 .50
U106 Saiyan Wrist Block U .20 .50
U107 Visiting The Past U .20 .50
U108 Battle Pausing U .20 .50
U109 Blinding Energy Move U .20 .50
U110 Devastating Blow U .20 .50
U111 Empowered Flying Kick U .20 .50
U112 Enraged Blast U .20 .50
U113 Overpowering Attack U .20 .50
U114 Quickness Drill U .20 .50
U115 Frieza's Captive Strike U .20 .50
U116 Gohan's Power Punch U .20 .50
U117 Goku's Kaio-Ken U .20 .50
U118 Krillin's Solar Flare U .20 .50
U119 Piccolo's Weighted Clothing U .20 .50
U120 Vegeta's Anger U .20 .50
R121 Namek Dragon Ball 7 R 2.00 5.00
R122 Black Devious Mastery R .75 2.00
R123 Black Mischievous Drill R .75 2.00
R124 Black Disorienting Blow R .75 2.00
R125 Black Reflection R .75 2.00
R126 Black Scout Maneuver R .75 2.00
R127 Blue Protective Mastery R .75 2.00
R128 Blue Lunge R 1.00 2.50
R129 Blue Terror R .75 2.00
R130 Blue Trapped Strike R .75 2.00
R131 Namekian Knowledge Mastery R .75 2.00
R132 Namekian Dragon Clan R .75 2.00
R133 Namekian Overtime R .75 2.00
R134 Namekian Palm Shots R .75 2.00
R135 Namekian Planned Attack R .75 2.00
R136 Orange Adaptive Mastery R .75 2.00
R137 Orange Focusing Drill R .75 2.00
R138 Orange Searching Maneuver R .75 2.00
R139 Orange Uppercut R .75 2.00
R140 Red Enraged Mastery R .75 2.00
R141 Red Forward Stance Drill R 1.00 2.50
R142 Red Heel Kick R .75 2.00
R143 Red Left Bolt R .75 2.00
R144 Red Observation R .75 2.00
R145 Saiyan Empowered Mastery R .75 2.00
R146 Saiyan Acute Rapid Slam R .75 2.00
R147 Saiyan Elbow Drop R .75 2.00
R148 Saiyan Power Up R .75 2.00
R149 Dragon Radar R .75 2.00
R150 Confrontation R 2.00 5.00
R151 Stare Down R 2.00 5.00
R152 Time Is A Warrior's Tool R 3.00 8.00
R153 Captain Ginyu's Body Switch R 1.50 4.00
R154 Frieza's Supernova R 1.50 4.00
R155 Gohan's Masenko R .75 2.00
R156 Goku's Kamehameha R 1.50 4.00
R157 Krillin's Destructo Disk R 1.50 4.00
R158 Piccolo's Special Beam Cannon R .75 2.00
R159 Trunks' Sword Slash R .75 2.00
R160 Vegeta's Galick Gun R .75 2.00
UR161 Heroic Plan UR 20.00 40.00
UR162 Villainous Visage UR 40.00 70.00
UR163 Heroic Energy Sphere UR 100.00 120.00
UR164 Villainous Energy Sphere UR 100.00 120.00
S1 Vegeta – Prince of Saiyans .60 1.50
S2 Vegeta – Villainous .60 1.50
S3 Vegeta – Empowered .60 1.50
S4 Vegeta – Renewed .60 1.50
S5 Goku – Protector of Earth .60 1.50
S6 Goku – Kaio-Ken Enhanced .60 1.50
S7 Goku – Energy Gatherer .60 1.50
S8 Goku – Super Saiyan .60 1.50
S9 Gohan – Resilient Child .60 1.50
S10 Gohan – Young Warrior .60 1.50
S11 Gohan – Determined .60 1.50
S12 Gohan – Armored .60 1.50
S13 Krillin – Ready .60 1.50
S14 Krillin – Energetic .60 1.50
S15 Krillin – Ready For Battle .60 1.50
S16 Krillin – Enraged .60 1.50
S17 Frieza – Tyrant .60 1.50
S18 Frieza – Transformed .60 1.50
S19 Frieza – Galactic Conquerer .60 1.50
S20 Frieza – Revived .60 1.50
S21 Piccolo – Stoic .60 1.50
S22 Piccolo – Combat Stance .60 1.50
S23 Piccolo – Unleashed .60 1.50
S24 Piccolo – Fused .60 1.50
S25 Saiyan Empowered Mastery .75 2.00
S26 Orange Adaptive Mastery .60 1.50
S27 Red Enraged Mastery .60 1.50
S28 Black Devious Mastery .60 1.50
S29 Blue Protective Mastery .60 1.50
S30 Namekian Knowledge Mastery .60 1.50
S31 Black Power Up .60 1.50
S32 Blue Stretch Kick .60 1.50
S33 Namekian Concentration .60 1.50
S34 Orange Energy Gathering .60 1.50
S35 Red Burning Rage .60 1.50
S36 Saiyan Offensive Rush .60 1.50
S37 Black Targeting Drill .60 1.50
S38 Blue Mental Drill .60 1.50
S39 Namekian Combat Drill .60 1.50
S40 Orange Devouring Drill .60 1.50
S41 Orange Energy Dan Drill .60 1.50
S42 Orange Steady Drill .60 1.50
S43 Red Tactical Drill .60 1.50
S44 Saiyan Retaliation Drill .60 1.50
S45 Black Command .60 1.50
S46 Blue Reprimand .60 1.50
S47 Namekian Silencing .60 1.50
S48 Orange Excavation .60 1.50
S49 Red Blazing Aura .60 1.50
S50 Saiyan Prelude .60 1.50
S51 Black Lightning Storm .60 1.50
S52 Black Capture .60 1.50
S53 Blue Arm Blast .60 1.50
S54 Blue Energy Overload .60 1.50
S55 Namekian Overhead Blast .60 1.50
S56 Namekian Focused Beams .60 1.50
S57 Orange Palm Blasts .60 1.50
S58 Orange Rage .60 1.50
S59 Red Heating Beams .60 1.50
S60 Red Energy Blast .60 1.50
S61 Red Energy Outburst .60 1.50
S62 Saiyan Triangle Beams .60 1.50
S63 Saiyan Energy Rupture .60 1.50
S64 Black Swipe .60 1.50
S65 Blue Guard .60 1.50
S66 Blue Avoidance .60 1.50
S67 Namekian Crossed Guard .60 1.50
S68 Orange Energy Evasion .60 1.50
S69 Red Energy Defensive Stance .60 1.50
S70 Saiyan Focus .60 1.50
S71 Black Defensive Burst .60 1.50
S72 Black Entanglement .60 1.50
S73 Black Side Thrust .60 1.50
S74 Blue Torpedo .60 1.50
S75 Blue Round Throw .60 1.50
S76 Namekian Crushing Slam .60 1.50
S77 Namekian Elbow Strike .60 1.50
S78 Orange Truck Lift .60 1.50
S79 Red Lifting Kick .60 1.50
S80 Red Power Lift .60 1.50
S81 Saiyan Direct Strike .60 1.50
S82 Saiyan Flying Tackle .60 1.50
S83 Saiyan Left Kick .60 1.50
S84 Saiyan Sabotage .60 1.50
S85 Black Finger Block .60 1.50
S86 Blue Fist Catch .60 1.50
S87 Blue Wrist Block .60 1.50
S88 Namekian Knee Block .60 1.50
S89 Namekian Narrow Escape .60 1.50
S90 Red Catch .60 1.50
S91 Blue Ki Build Up .60 1.50
S92 Namekian Fusion .60 1.50
S93 Orange Celebration .60 1.50
S94 Red Blaze .60 1.50
S95 Saiyan Enraged .60 1.50
S96 Black Smoothness Drill .60 1.50
S97 Blue Positioning Drill .60 1.50
S98 Namekian Heritage Drill .60 1.50
S99 Orange Burning Aura Drill .60 1.50
S100 Orange Guardian Drill .60 1.50
S101 Orange Hiding Drill .60 1.50
S102 Red Intimidation Drill .60 1.50
S103 Saiyan Analysis Drill .60 1.50
S104 Black Taunt .60 1.50
S105 Blue Rest .60 1.50
S106 Namekian Regeneration .60 1.50
S107 Orange Destruction .60 1.50
S108 Red Burning Stance .60 1.50
S109 Saiyan Preparation .60 1.50
S110 Black Energy Toss .60 1.50
S111 Black Interceptor Barrage .60 1.50
S112 Black Energy Web .60 1.50
S113 Blue Neck Beam .60 1.50
S114 Namekian Double Palm Burst .60 1.50
S115 Namekian Sudden Blast .60 1.50
S116 Orange Power Point .60 1.50
S117 Orange Stare Down .60 1.50
S118 Red Frenzied Blasts .60 1.50
S119 Red Surrounded Beams .60 1.50
S120 Red Static Shot .60 1.50
S121 Saiyan Diving Burst .60 1.50
S122 Saiyan Straight Shot .60 1.50
S123 Black Speedy Dodge .60 1.50
S124 Blue Defensive Stance .60 1.50
S125 Blue Narrow Escape .60 1.50
S126 Namekian Stance .60 1.50
S127 Namekian Energy Guard .60 1.50
S128 Orange Energy Catch .60 1.50
S129 Red Energy Shield .60 1.50
S130 Saiyan Energy Deflection .60 1.50
S131 Black Flying Kick .60 1.50
S132 Black Left Kick .60 1.50
S133 Black Jab .60 1.50
S134 Black Strike .60 1.50
S135 Blue Fist Smash .60 1.50
S136 Namekian Pound .60 1.50
S137 Namekian Side Kick .60 1.50
S138 Orange Launcher .60 1.50
S139 Red Right Cross .60 1.50
S140 Red Power Rush .60 1.50
S141 Saiyan Face Stomp .60 1.50
S142 Saiyan Light Jab .60 1.50
S143 Blue Crouch .60 1.50
S144 Blue Swift Block .60 1.50
S145 Namekian Forceful Block .60 1.50
S146 Orange Cover Up .60 1.50
S147 Orange Quick Dodge .60 1.50
S148 Red Blocking Hand .60 1.50
S149 Saiyan Arm Catch .60 1.50
S150 Saiyan Lightning Dodge .60 1.50

2014 Dragon Ball Z Rainbow

COMPLETE SET (30) 30.00 80.00
S1 Vegeta – Prince of Saiyans 1.25 3.00
S2 Vegeta – Villainous 1.25 3.00
S3 Vegeta – Empowered 4.00 10.00
S4 Vegeta – Renewed 5.00 12.00
S5 Goku – Protector of Earth 3.00 8.00
S6 Goku – Kaio-Ken Enhanced 1.25 3.00

S7 Goku – Energy Gatherer 1.25 3.00
S8 Goku – Super Saiyan 6.00 15.00
S9 Gohan – Resilient Child 2.50 6.00
S10 Gohan – Young Warrior 2.50 6.00
S11 Gohan – Determined 2.50 6.00
S12 Gohan – Armored 1.25 3.00
S13 Krillin – Ready 3.00 8.00
S14 Krillin – Energetic 1.25 3.00
S15 Krillin – Ready For Battle 1.25 3.00
S16 Krillin – Enraged 1.25 3.00
S17 Frieza – Tyrant 1.25 3.00
S18 Frieza – Transformed 1.25 3.00
S19 Frieza – Galactic Conquerer 5.00 12.00
S20 Frieza – Revived 1.25 3.00
S21 Piccolo – Stoic 4.00 10.00
S22 Piccolo – Combat Stance 2.50 6.00
S23 Piccolo – Unleashed 3.00 8.00
S24 Piccolo – Fused 4.00 10.00
S25 Saiyan Empowered Mastery 1.25 3.00
S26 Orange Adaptive Mastery 1.25 3.00
S27 Red Enraged Mastery 1.25 3.00
S28 Black Devious Mastery 1.25 3.00
S29 Blue Protective Mastery 1.25 3.00
S30 Namekian Knowledge Mastery 1.25 3.00

2014 Dragon Ball Z Promos

P6 Piccolo - Stoic 8.00 20.00
P7 Goku's Kamehameha 1.00 2.50
P8 Time Is A Warrior's Tool 6.00 15.00
P9 Vegeta's Galick Gun 1.25 3.00
P10 Confrontation 4.00 10.00
P11 Trunks' Sword Slash 1.25 3.00
P12 Stare Down 8.00 20.00
P13 Frieza - Tyrant 8.00 20.00
P14 Gohan's Masenko 2.00 5.00
P15 Frieza's Supernova 1.50 4.00
P16 Black Scout Maneuver 5.00 12.00
P17 Piccolo's Special Beam Cannon .75 2.00
P18 Blue Terror 3.00 8.00
P19 Captain Ginyu's Body Switch 1.50 4.00
P20 Saiyan Power Up 4.00 10.00
P21 Krillin's Destructo Disk 3.00 8.00

2014 Dragon Ball Z SDCC Promos

EXCLUSIVE TO SAN DIEGO COMIC CON
P1 Vegeta Prince Of Saiyans 2.00 5.00
P2 Goku Protector Of Earth 2.00 5.00
P3 Gohan Resilient Child 2.00 5.00
P4 Krillin Ready 8.00 20.00
P5 Goku Super Saiyan God 60.00 100.00

2015 Dragon Ball Z Heroes and Villains

COMPLETE SET (142) 60.00 120.00
BOOSTER BOX (24 PACKS) 60.00 80.00
BOOSTER PACK (12 CARDS) 2.00 3.00
*FOIL: 1.2X TO 3X BASIC CARDS
RELEASED ON MARCH 6, 2015
C1 Nail - Watchful C .10 .25
C2 Nail - Protector C .10 .25
C3 Nappa - Rested C .10 .25
C4 Nappa - Smirking C .10 .25
C5 Raditz - True Saiyan C .10 .25
C6 Raditz - Confident C .10 .25
C7 Tenshinhan - Patient C .10 .25
C8 Tenshinhan - Stubborn C .10 .25
C9 Captain Ginyu - Aggressive C .10 .25
C10 Dodoria - Lackey C .10 .25
C11 Frieza - Mastermind C .10 .25
C12 Gohan - Trained C .10 .25
C13 Krillin - Supportive C .10 .25
C14 Zarbon - Loyal Servant C .10 .25
C15 Black Radiating Drill C .10 .25
C16 Black Barrier Destruction C .10 .25
C17 Black Evasion C .10 .25
C18 Black Fist Lock C .10 .25
C19 Black Overpowering Attack C .10 .25
C20 Black Chomp C .10 .25
C21 Black Refusal C .10 .25
C22 Black Hair Trap C .10 .25
C23 Blue Lifting Drill C .10 .25
C24 Blue Cover Up C .10 .25
C25 Blue Fear C .10 .25
C26 Blue Bat Attack C .10 .25
C27 Blue Determined Attack C .10 .25
C28 Blue Hand Blast C .10 .25
C29 Blue Glare C .10 .25
C30 Namekian Self-training C .10 .25
C31 Namekian Forearm Block C .10 .25
C32 Namekian Chin Grab C .10 .25
C33 Namekian Lift C .10 .25
C34 Namekian Short Kick C .10 .25
C35 Namekian Energy Beams C .10 .25
C36 Namekian Quick Shot C .10 .25
C37 Orange Driving Drill C .10 .25
C38 Orange Torching Drill C .10 .25
C39 Orange Calming Drill C .25 .25
C40 Orange Crashing Drill C .25 .25
C41 Orange Energy Bubble C .25 .25
C42 Orange Nudge C .25 .25
C43 Orange Double Palm Beam C .25 .25
C44 Red Destiny C .25 .25
C45 Red Emergency C .25 .25
C46 Red Containment C .25 .25
C47 Red Sacrifice C .25 .25
C48 Red Restraint C .25 .25
C49 Red Knee Lift C .25 .25
C50 Red Leap C .25 .25
C51 Saiyan Protection Drill C .25 .25
C52 Saiyan Strength Test C .25 .25
C53 Saiyan Drive By C .25 .25
C54 Saiyan Blocking Technique C .25 .25
C55 Saiyan Hand Swipe C .25 .25
C56 Saiyan Driving Punch C .25 .25
C57 Saiyan Charged Fist C .25 .25
C58 Captain Ginyu's Pain C .25 .25
C59 Energetic Left Blast C .25 .25
C60 Combination Drill C .25 .25
U61 Nail - Unflinching U .20 .50
U62 Nail - Combat Ready U .20 .50
U63 Nappa - Overconfident U .20 .50
U64 Nappa - Enraged U .20 .50
U65 Raditz - Angered U .20 .50
U66 Raditz - Triumphant U .20 .50
U67 Tenshinhan - Prepared U .20 .50
U68 Tenshinhan - Smug U .20 .50
U69 Goku - Thoughtful U .20 .50
U70 Piccolo - Waiting U .20 .50
U71 Trunks - Bashful U .20 .50
U72 Vegeta - Impatient U .20 .50
U73 Black Viewing Drill U .20 .50
U74 Black Foreshadowing U .20 .50
U75 Black Upward Dodge U .20 .50
U76 Black Overhead Burst U .20 .50
U77 Blue Joy Ride U .20 .50
U78 Blue Flinch U .20 .50
U79 Blue Leverage U .20 .50
U80 Blue Face Crunch U .20 .50
U81 Namekian Shocking Drill U .20 .50
U82 Namekian Hurried Quest U .20 .50
U83 Namekian Patient Block U .20 .50
U84 Namekian Jump Kick U .20 .50
U85 Orange Catch U .20 .50
U86 Orange Charged Kick U .20 .50
U87 Orange Saving Kick U .20 .50
U88 Orange Elbow U .20 .50
U89 Red City Destruction U .20 .50
U90 Red Palm Strike U .20 .50
U91 Red Stomach Dive U .20 .50
U92 Red Club U .20 .50
U93 Saiyan Unleashing Drill U .20 .50
U94 Saiyan Rescue U .20 .50
U95 Saiyan Spin Kick U .20 .50
U96 Saiyan Right Blast U .20 .50
U97 Raditz's Dirty Tactics U .20 .50
U98 Nail's Heritage U .20 .50
U99 Nappa's Confidence U .20 .50
U100 Tenshinhan's Preparation U .20 .50
R101 Black Declaration R .75 2.00
R102 Black Head Charge R .75 2.00
R103 Black Enraged Assault R 1.00 2.50
R104 Focused Assault R 1.25 3.00
R105 Black Counter Ball R .75 2.00
R106 Blue Taming Technique R .75 2.00
R107 Blue Overpowering Drill R .75 2.00
R108 Blue Leaping Kick R .75 2.00
R109 Blue Crush R .75 2.00
R110 Blue Back Break R .75 2.00
R111 Namekian Cut Off R .75 2.00
R112 Namekian Backhand R 1.25 3.00
R113 Namekian Clash R .75 2.00
R114 Namekian High Knee R .75 2.00
R115 Namekian Confident Burst R 1.25 3.00
R116 Orange Possession Drill R .75 2.00
R117 Orange Chasing Drill R .75 2.00
R118 Orange Dodge R .75 2.00
R119 Orange Hand Cannon R .75 2.00
R120 Orange Mini Ball R .75 2.00
R121 Red Embarrassing Drill R .75 2.00
R122 Red Stop R .75 2.00
R123 Red Controlled Attack R .75 2.00
R124 Red Overpower R .75 2.00
R125 Red Combined Blast R .75 2.00
R126 Saiyan Intimidation R .75 2.00
R127 Saiyan Outrage R .75 2.00
R128 Saiyan Grab R .75 2.00
R129 Saiyan Body Blow R .75 2.00
R130 Saiyan Prepped Ball R .75 2.00
R131 Isolation R .75 2.00
R132 Withering Fire R 1.50 4.00
R133 Crushing Beam R 4.00 10.00
R134 Face Smash R .75 2.00
R135 Wall Breaker R 5.00 12.00
R136 Nail's Dashing Attack R .75 2.00
R137 Nappa's Energized Charge R .75 2.00
R138 Raditz's Offensive Guard R .75 2.00
R139 Tenshinhan's Draining Blast R .75 2.00
R140 Trunks' Sword Stance R .75 2.00
UR141 Heroic Assistance UR 8.00 20.00
UR142 Villainous Empowerment UR 8.00 20.00

2015 Dragon Ball Z Heroes and Villains Promos

P1 Saiyan Intimidation 1.25 3.00
P2 Isolation 4.00 10.00
P3 Orange Dodge 2.00 5.00
P4 Wall Breaker 8.00 20.00
P5 Red Overpower 1.25 3.00
P6 Withering Fire 6.00 15.00
P7 Blue Crush 1.25 3.00
P8 Black Enraged Assault 4.00 10.00
P9 Namekian Clash 4.00 10.00
P10 Saiyan Outrage 8.00 20.00
P11 Red Controlled Attack 4.00 10.00
P12 Orange Possession Drill 3.00 8.00
P13 Black Declaration 2.00 5.00
P14 Blue Overpowering Drill 3.00 8.00
P15 Saiyan Body Blow 1.50 4.00
P16 Red Stop 6.00 15.00
P17 Orange Hand Cannon 3.00 8.00

2015 Dragon Ball Z The Movie Collection

COMPLETE SET (142) 60.00 120.00
BOOSTER BOX (24 PACKS) 60.00 80.00
BOOSTER PACK (12 CARDS) 2.00 3.00
*FOIL: 1.2X TO 3X BASIC CARDS
RELEASED ON JUNE 26, 2015
C1 Kami – Guardian C .10 .25
C2 Master Roshi – Scouted C .10 .25
C3 Oolong – Concerned C .10 .25
C4 Yajirobe – Bundled C .10 .25
C5 Dr. Wheelo – Intelligent C .10 .25
C6 Garlic Jr. – Confrontational C .10 .25
C7 Lord Slug – Amazed C .10 .25
C8 Turles – Fighter C .10 .25
C9 Black Amusement Drill C .10 .25
C10 Black Chopping Drill C .10 .25
C11 Black Blinding Burst C .10 .25
C12 Black Dense Ball C .10 .25
C13 Black Dismissal C .10 .25
C14 Black Flying Knee C .10 .25
C15 Black Resistance C .10 .25
C16 Black Stop C .10 .25
C17 Blue Minions C .10 .25
C18 Blue Escaping Drill C .10 .25
C19 Blue Barrier C .10 .25
C20 Blue Encircled Strike C .10 .25
C21 Blue Floating Beam C .10 .25
C22 Blue Rejection C .10 .25
C23 Blue Safeguard C .10 .25
C24 Blue Slash C .10 .25
C25 Namekian Reinforced Drill C .10 .25
C26 Namekian Choke C .10 .25
C27 Namekian Clench C .10 .25
C28 Namekian Mouth Beam C .10 .25
C29 Namekian Reinforced Block C .10 .25
C30 Namekian Reinforced Defense C .10 .25
C31 Namekian Reinforced Charge C .10 .25
C32 Namekian Reinforced Jab C .10 .25
C33 Namekian Right Burst C .10 .25
C34 Orange Disaster Drill C .10 .25
C35 Orange Confidence C .10 .25
C36 Orange Desperation C .10 .25
C37 Orange Eruption C .10 .25
C38 Orange Extension C .10 .25
C39 Orange Flee C .10 .25
C40 Orange Gathering C .10 .25
C41 Orange Reactive Strike C .10 .25
C42 Orange Smash C .10 .25
C43 Red Maneuvering Drill C .10 .25
C44 Red Saving Drill C .10 .25
C45 Red Face Break C .10 .25
C46 Red Hop C .10 .25
C47 Red Resourceful Block C .10 .25
C48 Red Right Punch C .10 .25
C49 Red Slide C .10 .25
C50 Red Vaulted Kick C .10 .25
C51 Saiyan Hanging Out Drill C .10 .25
C52 Saiyan Charge C .10 .25
C53 Saiyan Counter Kick C .10 .25
C54 Saiyan Enjoyment C .10 .25
C55 Saiyan Evasion C .10 .25
C56 Saiyan Headbutt C .10 .25
C57 Saiyan Leaping Burst C .10 .25
C58 Saiyan Overpowering Blast C .10 .25
C59 Saiyan Swat C .10 .25
C60 Lookout Drill C .10 .25
U61 Dr. Wheelo – Big Brain U .20 .50
U62 Dr. Wheelo – Scheming U .20 .50
U63 Dr. Wheelo – Confined U .20 .50
U64 Dr. Wheelo – Robotic U .20 .50
U65 Garlic Jr. – Commanding U .20 .50
U66 Garlic Jr. – Crazed U .20 .50
U67 Garlic Jr. – Observant U .20 .50
U68 Garlic Jr. – Transformed U .20 .50
U69 Lord Slug – Aged U .20 .50
U70 Lord Slug – Successful U .20 .50
U71 Lord Slug – Renewed U .20 .50
U72 Lord Slug – Huge U .20 .50
U73 Turles – Shadowy U .20 .50
U74 Turles – Watchful U .20 .50
U75 Turles – Triumphant U .20 .50
U76 Turles – Conquering U .20 .50
U77 Black Chaos U .20 .50
U78 Black Entrance U .20 .50
U79 Black Back Strike U .20 .50
U80 Black Teamwork U .20 .50
U81 Black Tracing Beam U .20 .50
U82 Blue Dominance U .20 .50
U83 Blue Double Blast U .20 .50
U84 Blue Intervention U .20 .50
U85 Blue Surround U .20 .50
U86 Blue Upward Barrage U .20 .50
U87 Namekian Disturbance U .20 .50
U88 Namekian Erasing Blast U .20 .50
U89 Namekian Gut Punch U .20 .50
U90 Orange Captivity Drill U .20 .50
U91 Orange Commanding Drill U .20 .50
U92 Orange Distracting Drill U .20 .50
U93 Red Dazing Drill U .20 .50
U94 Red Freezing Beam U .20 .50
U95 Red Tandem Attack U .20 .50
U96 Red Trailing Blast U .20 .50
U97 Saiyan Freedom U .20 .50
U98 Saiyan Aerial Attack U .20 .50
U99 Saiyan Lunge U .20 .50
U100 Saiyan Upward Kick U .20 .50
R101 Black Chin Kick R 2.00 5.00
R102 Black Combo R 1.50 4.00
R103 Black Dash R 1.50 4.00
R104 Black Daze R 1.00 2.50
R105 Blue Observation Drill R .75 2.00
R106 Blue Precarious Defense R 1.25 3.00
R107 Blue Surprise R .75 2.00
R108 Blue Takedown R 1.50 4.00
R109 Namekian Growth R 1.25 3.00
R110 Namekian Knockback R 1.00 2.50
R111 Namekian Overwatch R 1.50 4.00
R112 Namekian Right Kick R .75 2.00
R113 Namekian Surprise Attack R .75 2.00
R114 Orange Spotlight R 1.25 3.00
R115 Orange Electricity R 1.25 3.00
R116 Orange Empowered Kick R 1.25 3.00
R117 Orange Uncontrolled Blast R 1.00 2.50
R118 Red Relaxation R 2.00 5.00
R119 Red Threatening Drill R .75 2.00
R120 Red Mule Kick R 1.50 4.00
R121 Red Restriction R 1.25 3.00
R122 Red Retreat R 1.00 2.50
R123 Saiyan Arrival R .75 2.00
R124 Saiyan Menace R 1.00 2.50
R125 Saiyan Backbreaker R .75 3.00
R126 Saiyan Studying R .75 2.00
R127 Dr. Wheelo's Revival R 1.00 2.50
R128 Dr. Wheelo's History R 1.25 3.00
R129 Garlic Jr.'s Dead Zone R 1.25 3.00
R130 Garlic Jr.'s Counter Blast R 1.25 3.00
R131 Lord Slug's Fist Slam R 1.00 2.50
R132 Lord Slug's Regeneration R 1.25 3.00
R133 Turles' Fruit R 1.25 3.00
R134 Turles' Energy Ring R 1.50 4.00
R135 Information Gathering R 1.00 2.50
R136 Tree of Might R 1.50 4.00
R137 Ensnared R .75 2.00
R138 Flip Toss R .75 2.00
R139 Pulverize R 3.00 8.00
R140 Sagacious Strike R 2.50 6.00
UR141 I'll Dig Your Grave! UR 90.00 125.00
UR142 True Power UR 8.00 20.00

2015 Dragon Ball Z Evolution

COMPLETE SET (174) 150.00 300.00
RELEASED ON OCTOBER 30, 2015
C1 Black Pop-up C .10 .25
C2 Black Inactivity Drill C .10 .25
C3 Black Remembrance Drill C .10 .25
C4 Black Explosion C .10 .25
C5 Black Headbutt C .10 .25
C6 Black Impediment C .10 .25
C7 Black Protection C .10 .25
C8 Black Request C .10 .25
C9 Black Travelling Punch C .10 .25
C10 Blue Cleanse C .10 .25
C11 Blue Counter C .10 .25
C12 Blue Energy Focus C .10 .25
C13 Blue Eye Lasers C .10 .25
C14 Blue Flight C .10 .25
C15 Blue Knee C .10 .25
C16 Blue Shopping C .10 .25
C17 Blue Vehicle Destruction C .10 .25
C18 Namekian Reinforced Catch C .10 .25
C19 Namekian Assistance Drill C .10 .25
C20 Namekian Cleansing Drill C .10 .25
C21 Namekian Catch C .10 .25
C22 Namekian Deflection C .10 .25
C23 Namekian Door Destruction C .10 .25
C24 Namekian Elbow Drop C .10 .25
C25 Namekian Intervention C .10 .25
C26 Namekian Wrist Strike C .10 .25
C27 Orange Audience C .10 .25
C28 Orange Intense Training Drill C .10 .25
C29 Orange Investigation Drill C .10 .25
C30 Orange Retrieval Drill C .10 .25
C31 Orange Concealment C .10 .25
C32 Orange Duck C .10 .25
C33 Orange Fracture C .10 .25
C34 Orange Ki Blast C .10 .25
C35 Orange Left Punch C .10 .25
C36 Orange Outburst C .10 .25
C37 Orange Sideswipe C .10 .25
C38 Orange Upward Strike C .10 .25
C39 Red Examination Drill C .10 .25
C40 Red Chop C .10 .25
C41 Red Cross Block C .10 .25
C42 Red Quick Jab C .10 .25
C43 Red Right Knee C .10 .25
C44 Red Robotic Blast C .10 .25
C45 Red Smash C .10 .25
C46 Red Vault C .10 .25
C47 Saiyan Flight C .10 .25
C48 Saiyan Inspection Drill C .40 1.00
C49 Saiyan Blockade C .10 .25
C50 Saiyan Concussive Blast C .10 .25
C51 Saiyan Discovery C .10 .25
C52 Saiyan Empowered Smash C .10 .25
C53 Saiyan Energy Outburst C .60 1.50
C54 Saiyan Lifting Kick C .10 .25
C55 Saiyan Overhead Kick C .10 .25
C56 Saiyan Palm Block C .10 .25
C57 Saiyan Smack C .10 .25
C58 Acquisition Drill C .10 .25
C59 Android Superiority C .10 .25
C60 Shoulder Slam C .10 .25
U61 Black Signal U .20 .50
U62 Black Empowered Elbow U .20 .50
U63 Black Energy Discharge U .20 .50
U64 Black Shoulder Charge U .20 .50
U65 Black Tunneling Ball U .20 .50
U66 Black Wilt U .20 .50
U67 Blue Hush U .20 .50
U68 Blue Awakening Drill U .20 .50
U69 Blue Face Grab U .20 .50
U70 Blue Palm Shot U .20 .50
U71 Namekian Aerial Knee U .20 .50
U72 Namekian Downward Blast U .20 .50
U73 Namekian Energy Assault U .20 .50
U74 Namekian Leaping Kick U 1.00 2.50
U75 Orange Scorn U .20 .50
U76 Red Premonition U .20 .50
U77 Red Chest Beam U .20 .50
U78 Red Collision U 1.00 2.50
U79 Red Forceful Strike U .20 .50
U80 Red Intense Blast U .20 .50
U81 Saiyan Empowered Slide U 1.00 2.50
U82 Saiyan Fierce Kick U .20 .50
U83 Saiyan Interruption U .20 .50
U84 Saiyan Sword Strike U .20 .50
U85 Android 19 - Stoic U .20 .50
U86 Android 19 - Pondering U .20 .50
U87 Android 19 - Unimpressed U .20 .50
U88 Android 19 - Patient U .20 .50
U89 Android 20 - Focused U .20 .50
U90 Android 20 - Unfazed U .20 .50
U91 Android 20 - Surprised U .20 .50
U92 Android 20 - Master Planner U .20 .50
U93 Vegeta - Unrelenting U .20 .50
U94 Korin - Watching From Afar U .20 .50
U95 Maron - Popular U .20 .50
U96 Turtle - Protective U .20 .50
U97 Android 17 - Beckoning U .20 .50
U98 Android 18 - Smirking U .20 .50
U99 Android 19 - Injured U .20 .50
U99b Android 20 - Mastermind U .20 .50
R101 Black Learning Drill R .75 2.00
R102 Black Empowered Sword Slash R 1.00 2.50
R103 Blue Kiss R .75 2.00
R104 Blue Entertaining Drill R .75 2.00
R105 Blue Transportation Drill R .75 2.00
R106 Blue Belly Bash R .75 2.00
R107 Blue Wash R .75 2.00
R108 Namekian Waiting R .75 2.00
R109 Namekian Enhancement R .75 2.00
R110 Namekian Overcharge R .75 2.00
R111 Orange Freezing Drill R .75 2.00
R112 Orange Reading Drill R .75 2.00
R113 Orange Accumulated Burst R .75 2.00
R114 Orange Drain R .75 2.00
R115 Red Analysis R .75 2.00
R116 Red Antidote R .75 2.00
R117 Red Eye Beams R .75 2.00
R118 Red Rage R .75 2.00
R119 Saiyan Peace R .75 2.00
R120 Saiyan Dash R .75 2.00
R121 Saiyan Destructive Blast R .75 2.00
R122 Saiyan Tracking Blast R .75 2.00
R123 Android 17's Van R 1.25 3.00
R124 Android 17's Back Smash R 1.00 2.50
R125 Android 18's Arm Breaker R .75 2.00
R126 Android 18's Toss R 1.25 3.00
R127 Android 19's Energy Absorption R 1.25 3.00
R128 Android 19's Choke R .75 2.00
R129 Android 20's Scouting Drill R 1.00 2.50
R130 Android 20's Domination R 2.50 6.00
R131 Vegeta's Destruction Blast R .75 2.00
R132 Elimination R .75 2.00
R133 Android Attack Drill R 1.50 4.00
R134 Moment of Peace R .75 2.00
R135 Android Presence R .75 2.00
R136 Energized Strike R 2.50 6.00
R137 Enhanced Reflexes R 3.00 8.00
R138 Optic Blast R 3.00 8.00

Card	Low	High
R139 Sinister Choke R	8.00	20.00
R140 Tug of War R	1.25	3.00
UR141 Defiant Challenge UR	40.00	80.00
UR142 Hidden Power Drill UR	25.00	50.00
UR143 Goku - Dashing UR	8.00	20.00
UR144 Vegeta - Elite UR	8.00	20.00
S1 Trunks - Returned	1.50	4.00
S2 Trunks - Swordmaster	3.00	8.00
S3 Trunks - Defiant	3.00	8.00
S4 Trunks - Overpowering	4.00	10.00
S5 Saiyan Rampaging Mastery	2.50	6.00
S6 Goku - Relaxed	2.00	5.00
S7 Goku - Motivated	6.00	15.00
S8 Goku - Calm	4.00	10.00
S9 Goku - Dashing	5.00	12.00
S10 Blue Tag Team Mastery	1.50	4.00
S11 Piccolo - Composed	1.50	4.00
S12 Piccolo - Anticipating	3.00	8.00
S13 Piccolo - Ferocious	1.50	4.00
S14 Piccolo - Revitalized	1.25	3.00
S15 Namekian Restored Mastery	1.25	3.00
S16 Vegeta - Calculating	4.00	10.00
S17 Vegeta - On The Move	2.50	6.00
S18 Vegeta - Super Saiyan	3.00	8.00
S19 Vegeta - Elite	5.00	12.00
S20 Orange Adept Mastery	2.50	6.00
S21 Android 17 - Judgmental	1.25	3.00
S22 Android 17 - Imposing	4.00	10.00
S23 Android 17 - Battle Ready	1.25	3.00
S24 Android 17 - In Action	2.50	6.00
S25 Red Ruthless Mastery	3.00	8.00
S26 Android 18 - Directing	1.25	3.00
S27 Android 18 - Threatening	1.25	3.00
S28 Android 18 - Effective	1.50	4.00
S29 Android 18 - Determined	4.00	10.00
S30 Black Perceptive Mastery	2.50	6.00

2016 Dragon Ball Z Perfection

Card	Low	High
COMPLETE SET (142)	100.00	150.00
COMPLETE SET W/DR (147)	150.00	250.00
COMPLETE SET W/DR AND HI-TECH (152)	200.00	300.00
COMPLETE SET W/DR, HI-TECH, AND RAINBOW (157)	300.00	450.00
BOOSTER BOX		
BOOSTER PACK		
RELEASED ON FEBRUARY 26, 2016		
C1 Android Headbutt C	.10	.25
C2 Debilitating Volley C	.10	.25
C3 Vicious Strike C	.10	.25
C4 Villainous Energy Beam C	.10	.25
C5 Black Analysis C	.10	.25
C6 Black Obstructing Drill C	.10	.25
C7 Black Destructive Beam C	.10	.25
C8 Black Easy Block C	.10	.25
C9 Black Energy Bubble C	.10	.25
C10 Black Enraged Outburst C	.10	.25
C11 Black Haunting C	.10	.25
C12 Black Nightmare C	.10	.25
C13 Black Sidestep C	.10	.25
C14 Black Unstable Punch C	.10	.25
C15 Blue Vision C	.10	.25
C16 Blue Guarding Drill C	.10	.25
C17 Blue Clash C	.10	.25
C18 Blue Concentrated Blast C	.10	.25
C19 Blue Energy Shield C	.10	.25
C20 Blue Head Kick C	.10	.25
C21 Blue Outbreak C	.10	.25
C22 Blue Overcharge C	.10	.25
C23 Blue Slide C	.10	.25
C24 Blue Sword Rage C	.10	.25
C25 Namekian Flight C	.10	.25
C26 Namekian Risk C	.10	.25
C27 Namekian Back Kick C	.10	.25
C28 Namekian Backflip C	.10	.25
C29 Namekian Chest Explosion C	.10	.25
C30 Namekian Counter Blast C	.10	.25
C31 Namekian Heel Kick C	.10	.25
C32 Namekian Resistance C	.10	.25
C33 Namekian Right Elbow C	.10	.25
C34 Orange Charging Drill C	.10	.25
C35 Orange Examination Drill C	.10	.25
C36 Orange Observing Drill C	.10	.25
C37 Orange Thumbs Up Drill C	.10	.25
C38 Orange Energy Deflection C	.10	.25
C39 Orange Enraged Bash C	.10	.25
C40 Orange Fixation C	.10	.25
C41 Orange Planned Block C	.10	.25
C42 Orange Tank Barrage C	.10	.25
C43 Red Bribe C	.10	.25
C44 Red Cover Drill C	.10	.25
C45 Red Cannon C	.10	.25
C46 Red Capture C	.10	.25
C47 Red Chest Pierce C	.10	.25
C48 Red Inferno C	.10	.25
C49 Red Interference C	.10	.25
C50 Red Sword Stab C	.10	.25
C51 Red Tandem Blast C	.10	.25
C52 Saiyan Demolishing Beam C	.10	.25
C53 Saiyan Emergence C	.10	.25
C54 Saiyan Energy Aura C	.10	.25
C55 Saiyan Face Strike C	.10	.25
C56 Saiyan Flip C	.10	.25
C57 Saiyan Leaping Strike C	.10	.25
C58 Saiyan Obstruction C	.10	.25
C59 Saiyan Rapid Fire C	.10	.25
C60 Saiyan Skull Jab C	.10	.25
U61 Master Roshi - Expectant U	.20	.50
U62 Master Roshi - Overwhelmed U	.20	.50
U63 Master Roshi - Catcher U	.20	.50
U64 Master Roshi - Barricade U	.20	.50
U65 Yamcha - Sleeping U	.20	.50
U66 Yamcha - On The Move U	.20	.50
U67 Yamcha - Surprised U	.20	.50
U68 Yamcha - Happy U	.20	.50
U69 Android 16 - Awoken U	.20	.50
U70 Android 16 - Distracted U	.20	.50
U71 Android 16 - Enraged U	.20	.50
U72 Android 16 - Injured U	.20	.50
U73 Dr. Brief - Analyzing U	.20	.50
U74 Mr. Popo - Guide U	.20	.50
U75 Android 16 - Unmoving U	.20	.50
U76 Cell - Larval U	.20	.50
U77 Android Defensive Blast U	.20	.50
U78 Pesky Barrage U	.20	.50
U79 Playful Punch U	.20	.50
U80 Black Confident Shot U	.20	.50
U81 Black Grounding Bash U	.20	.50
U82 Black Sharp Kick U	.20	.50
U83 Blue Eating Drill U	.20	.50
U84 Blue Challenging Strike U	.20	.50
U85 Blue Dispersing Beam U	.20	.50
U86 Namekian Searching Drill U	.20	.50
U87 Namekian Focused Ball U	.20	.50
U88 Namekian Hand Burst U	.20	.50
U89 Namekian Preparation U	.20	.50
U90 Orange Dressing Room U	.20	.50
U91 Orange Charge U	.20	.50
U92 Orange Clearing Blast U	.20	.50
U93 Orange Stab U	.20	.50
U94 Red Glare U	.20	.50
U95 Red Infuriated Attack U	.20	.50
U96 Red Right Blast U	.20	.50
U97 Saiyan Transformation Drill U	.20	.50
U98 Saiyan Back Crash U	.20	.50
U99 Saiyan Crunch U	.20	.50
U100 Saiyan Sword Skill U	.20	.50
R101 Master Roshi's Slumber R	1.50	4.00
R102 Master Roshi's Back Strike R	3.00	8.00
R103 Yamcha's Expert Assistance R	1.00	2.50
R104 Yamcha's Rescue R	2.00	5.00
R105 Android 16's Tranquility R	.75	2.00
R106 Android 16's Rocket Punch R	1.00	2.50
R107 Cell's Draining Attack R	1.25	3.00
R108 Cell's Style R	1.50	4.00
R109 Tenshinhan's Tri-Beam R	1.00	2.50
R110 Trunks' Slam R	1.50	4.00
R111 Aggressive Sword Drill R	.75	2.00
R112 Clash of Wills R	.75	2.00
R113 Dashing Sword Attack R	1.50	4.00
R114 Heroic Jab R	.75	2.00
R115 Overwhelming Power R	2.50	6.00
R116 Black Discovery R	.75	2.00
R117 Black Choke R	.75	2.00
R118 Black Double Team R	.75	2.00
R119 Black Extreme Blast R	.75	2.00
R120 Blue Training R	.75	2.00
R121 Blue Head Charge R	.75	2.00
R122 Blue Restraint R	.75	2.00
R123 Blue Toss R	.75	2.00
R124 Namekian Back Smash R	.75	2.00
R125 Namekian Energized Bash R	.75	2.00
R126 Namekian Face Crush R	.75	2.00
R127 Namekian Resilience R	.75	2.00
R128 Orange Hoping Drill R	.75	2.00
R129 Orange Ki Ball R	.75	2.00
R130 Orange Overflowing Burst R	.75	2.00
R131 Orange Right Beam R	.75	2.00
R132 Red Channel Surfing Drill R	.75	2.00
R133 Red Aerial Assault R	.75	2.00
R134 Red Back Bash R	.75	2.00
R135 Red Downward Burst R	.75	2.00
R136 Red Powerful Strike R	.75	2.00
R137 Saiyan Extreme Training R	.75	2.00
R138 Saiyan Charged Kick R	.75	2.00
R139 Saiyan Ki Burst R	.75	2.00
R140 Saiyan Overhead Flare R	.75	2.00
UR141 Power Mimic UR	15.00	30.00
UR142 Heroic Dashing Punch UR	25.00	50.00
DR1A Cell - Imperfect DR	15.00	30.00
DR1 Cell - Imperfect DR	6.00	15.00
DR2 Cell - Semi-Perfect DR	10.00	20.00
DR3 Cell - Perfect DR	15.00	30.00
DR4 Cell - Unstoppable DR	15.00	30.00
DR1AHT Cell - Imperfect DR Hi-Tech	8.00	20.00
DR1BHT Cell - Imperfect DR Hi-Tech	6.00	15.00
DR2HT Cell - Semi-Perfect DR Hi-Tech	6.00	15.00
DR3HT Cell - Perfect DR Hi-Tech	6.00	15.00
DR4HT Cell - Unstoppable DR Hi-Tech	8.00	20.00
DR1ARB Cell - Imperfect DR Rainbow	15.00	40.00
DR1BRB Cell - Imperfect DR Rainbow	10.00	25.00
DR2RB Cell - Semi-Perfect DR Rainbow	10.00	25.00
DR3RB Cell - Perfect DR Rainbow	12.00	30.00
DR4RB Cell - Unstoppable DR Rainbow	15.00	30.00

2016 Dragonball Z Vengeance

Card	Low	High
COMPLETE SET (143 CARDS)	200.00	450.00
BOOSTER BOX 24 PACKS	50.00	85.00
BOOSTER PACK 12 CARDS	2.50	6.00
UNLISTED C	.10	.30
UNLISTED U	.10	.30
UNLISTED R	2.00	5.00
RELEASED ON JULY 1ST, 2016		
C1 Black Android Programming C	.10	.30
C2 Black Astonishing Drill C	.10	.30
C3 Black Recollection Drill C	.10	.30
C4 Black Downward Beam C	.10	.30
C5 Black Face Kick C	.10	.30
C6 Black Fist Catch C	.10	.30
C7 Black Impact C	.10	.30
C8 Black Overload C	.10	.30
C9 Black Running Guard C	.10	.30
C10 Black Sword Attack C	.10	.30
C11 Black Vaulted Strike C	.10	.30
C12 Blue Intimidation C	.10	.30
C13 Blue Reinforcements C	.10	.30
C14 Blue Save C	.10	.30
C15 Blue Seizing Drill C	.10	.30
C16 Blue Waiting Drill C	.10	.30
C17 Blue Android Headbutt C	.10	.30
C18 Blue Brush Aside C	.10	.30
C19 Blue Flying Kick C	.10	.30
C20 Blue Rehabilitation C	.10	.30
C21 Blue Swat C	.10	.30
C22 Namekian Impending Doom C	.10	.30
C23 Namekian Vanishing Drill C	.10	.30
C24 Namekian Airborne Attack C	.10	.30
C25 Namekian Arm Shield C	.10	.30
C26 Namekian Concern C	.10	.30
C27 Namekian MultiOpponent Combat C	.10	.30
C28 Namekian Protective Posture C	.10	.30
C29 Namekian Robotic Destruction C	.10	.30
C30 Namekian Team Up C	.10	.30
C31 Orange Bravado C	.10	.30
C32 Orange Eviction C	.10	.30
C33 Orange Shopping Drill C	.10	.30
C34 Orange Welcoming Drill C	.10	.30
C35 Orange Combined Burst C	.10	.30
C36 Orange Earthquake C	.10	.30
C37 Orange Fierce Attack C	.10	.30
C38 Orange Frenzied Assault C	.10	.30
C39 Orange Interference C	.10	.30
C40 Orange Withdrawal C	.10	.30
C41 Red Reconnaissance Drill C	.10	.30
C42 Red Android Palm Blast C	.10	.30
C43 Red Body Block C	.10	.30
C44 Red Departing Shot C	.10	.30
C45 Red Disregard C	.10	.30
C46 Red Ejection C	.10	.30
C47 Red High Kick C	.10	.30
C48 Red Lasers C	.10	.30
C49 Red Training Burst C	.10	.30
C50 Red Wallop C	.10	.30
C51 Saiyan Targeting C	.10	.30
C52 Saiyan Assistance C	.10	.30
C53 Saiyan Clash C	.10	.30
C54 Saiyan Club C	.10	.30
C55 Saiyan Ferocious Blast C	.10	.30
C56 Saiyan Severing Punch C	.10	.30
C57 Saiyan Sword Dodge C	.10	.30
C58 Saiyan Tantrum C	.10	.30
C59 Android Arm Breaker C	.50	1.25
C60 Quick Blast C	.10	.30
U61 Android 13 Redneck Robot U	.10	.30
U62 Android 13 Amused U	.10	.30
U63 Android 13 Dark Villain U	.10	.30
U64 Android 13 Surging Strength U	.10	.30
U65 Broly Survivor U	.10	.30
U66 Broly Determined U	.10	.30
U67 Broly Legendary U	.10	.30
U68 Broly Relentless U	.10	.30
U69 Cooler Familiar Face U	.10	.30
U70 Cooler Transformed U	.10	.30
U71 Cooler Menace U	.10	.30
U72 Cooler Overlord U	.10	.30
U73 Gohan To The Rescue U	.10	.30
U74 Krillin Quick U	.10	.30
U75 Master Roshi Restrained U	.10	.30
U76 Trunks Protective U	.10	.30
U77 Icarus Supportive U	.10	.30
U78 Android 13 Powerful U	.10	.30
U79 Android 14 Stoic U	.10	.30
U80 Android 15 Relaxed U	.10	.30
U81 Broly Undaunted U	.10	.30
U82 Cooler Angered U	.10	.30
U83 Paragus Desperate Father U	.10	.30
U84 Salza Henchman U	.10	.30
U85 Black Invitation U	.10	.30
U86 Black Liberation U	.10	.30
U87 Blue Hunt U	.10	.30
U88 Blue Skid U	.10	.30
U89 Namekian Empowered Charge U	.10	.30
U90 Namekian Face Off U	.10	.30
U91 Namekian Salvo U	.10	.30
U92 Orange Snoozing Drill U	.10	.30
U93 Orange Android Rising Punch U	.10	.30
U94 Red Integration U	.10	.30
U95 Red Double Blast U	.10	.30
U96 Red Furious Lunge U	.10	.30
U97 Saiyan Recovery U	.10	.30
U98 Saiyan Terrifying Strike U	.10	.30
U99 PointBlank Volley U	.50	1.25
U100 Villainous Power Ball U	.40	1.00
R101 Black Impatience R	2.00	5.00
R102 Black Dispersion R	2.00	5.00
R103 Black Dive R	2.00	5.00
R104 Black Drain R	2.00	5.00
R105 Blue Blanketing Blasts R	2.00	5.00
R106 Blue Decapitation R	2.00	5.00
R107 Blue Discharge R	2.00	5.00
R108 Blue Ki Ball R	2.00	5.00
R109 Blue Return Fire R	2.00	5.00
R110 Namekian Pep Talk R	2.00	5.00
R111 Namekian Harvesting Drill R	2.00	5.00
R112 Namekian Electrifying Grab R	2.00	5.00
R113 Namekian Dash R	2.00	5.00
R114 Namekian Ending R	2.00	5.00
R115 Orange Intimidating Drill R	2.00	5.00
R116 Orange Counter Ball R	2.00	5.00
R117 Orange Hug R	2.00	5.00
R118 Orange Immense Blast R	2.00	5.00
R119 Orange Sword Chop R	2.00	5.00
R120 Red Sword Slicing Drill R	2.00	5.00
R121 Red Fantasy R	2.00	5.00
R122 Red Motivational Kick R	2.00	5.00
R123 Red Stylish Entrance R	2.00	5.00
R124 Saiyan Overpowering Aura Drill R	2.00	5.00
R125 Saiyan Denial R	2.00	5.00
R126 Saiyan Extinguishing Blast R	2.00	5.00
R127 Saiyan Lob R	2.00	5.00
R128 Saiyan Thrust R	2.00	5.00
R129 Saiyan Trample R	2.00	5.00
R130 Saiyan Trap R	2.00	5.00
R131 Singing Drill R	2.00	5.00
R132 Android Insubordination R	2.50	6.00
R133 Sobering Hammer R	3.00	8.00
R134 Stomach Crusher R	4.00	10.00
R135 Android 13s SS Deadly Bomber R	3.00	8.00
R136 Android 13s Impenetrable Defense R	2.50	6.00
R137 Brolys Eraser Cannon R	3.00	8.00
R138 Brolys Face Crusher R	4.00	10.00
R139 Coolers Rebirth R	3.00	8.00
R140 Coolers Supernova R	4.00	10.00
UR141 Surprise Attack UR	30.00	60.00
UR142 Unleashed UR	45.00	80.00
DR1 Instant Transmission DR	30.00	50.00
NONUM Broly Active Player T	3.00	8.00
NONUM Goku Active Player T	3.00	8.00

2016 Dragonball Z Vengeance Foil

Card	Low	High
COMPLETE SET (143 CARDS)	650.00	1500.00
BOOSTER BOX 24 PACKS	50.00	85.00
BOOSTER PACK 12 CARDS	2.50	6.00
UNLISTED C	1.50	4.00
UNLISTED U	1.50	4.00
UNLISTED R	5.00	12.00
RELEASED ON JULY 1ST, 2016		
C1 Black Android Programming C	1.50	4.00
C2 Black Astonishing Drill C	1.50	4.00
C3 Black Recollection Drill C	1.50	4.00
C4 Black Downward Beam C	1.50	4.00
C5 Black Face Kick C	1.50	4.00
C6 Black Fist Catch C	1.50	4.00
C7 Black Impact C	1.50	4.00
C8 Black Overload C	1.50	4.00
C9 Black Running Guard C	1.50	4.00
C10 Black Sword Attack C	1.50	4.00
C11 Black Vaulted Strike C	1.50	4.00
C12 Blue Intimidation C	1.50	4.00
C13 Blue Reinforcements C	1.50	4.00
C14 Blue Save C	1.50	4.00
C15 Blue Seizing Drill C	1.50	4.00
C16 Blue Waiting Drill C	2.50	6.00
C17 Blue Android Headbutt C	1.50	4.00
C18 Blue Brush Aside C	1.50	4.00
C19 Blue Flying Kick C	1.50	4.00
C20 Blue Rehabilitation C	1.50	4.00
C21 Blue Swat C	1.50	4.00
C22 Namekian Impending Doom C	1.50	4.00
C23 Namekian Vanishing Drill C	1.50	4.00
C24 Namekian Airborne Attack C	1.50	4.00
C25 Namekian Arm Shield C	1.50	4.00
C26 Namekian Concern C	1.50	4.00
C27 Namekian MultiOpponent Combat C	1.50	4.00
C28 Namekian Protective Posture C	1.50	4.00
C29 Namekian Robotic Destruction C	1.50	4.00
C30 Namekian Team Up C	1.50	4.00
C31 Orange Bravado C	1.50	4.00
C32 Orange Eviction C	1.50	4.00
C33 Orange Shopping Drill C	1.50	4.00
C34 Orange Welcoming Drill C	1.50	4.00
C35 Orange Combined Burst C	1.50	4.00
C36 Orange Earthquake C	1.50	4.00
C37 Orange Fierce Attack C	1.50	4.00
C38 Orange Frenzied Assault C	1.50	4.00
C39 Orange Interference C	1.50	4.00
C40 Orange Withdrawal C	1.50	4.00
C41 Red Reconnaissance Drill C	1.50	4.00
C42 Red Android Palm Blast C	1.50	4.00
C43 Red Body Block C	1.50	4.00
C44 Red Departing Shot C	1.50	4.00
C45 Red Disregard C	1.50	4.00
C46 Red Ejection C	1.50	4.00
C47 Red High Kick C	1.50	4.00
C48 Red Lasers C	1.50	4.00
C49 Red Training Burst C	1.50	4.00
C50 Red Wallop C	1.50	4.00
C51 Saiyan Targeting C	1.50	4.00
C52 Saiyan Assistance C	1.50	4.00
C53 Saiyan Clash C	1.50	4.00
C54 Saiyan Club C	1.50	4.00
C55 Saiyan Ferocious Blast C	1.50	4.00
C56 Saiyan Severing Punch C	1.50	4.00
C57 Saiyan Sword Dodge C	1.50	4.00
C58 Saiyan Tantrum C	2.50	6.00
C59 Android Arm Breaker C	8.00	20.00
C60 Quick Blast C	6.00	15.00
U61 Android 13 Redneck Robot U	6.00	15.00
U62 Android 13 Amused U	6.00	15.00
U63 Android 13 Dark Villain U	6.00	15.00
U64 Android 13 Surging Strength U	6.00	15.00
U65 Broly Survivor U	8.00	20.00
U66 Broly Determined U	8.00	20.00
U67 Broly Legendary U	8.00	20.00
U68 Broly Relentless U	8.00	20.00
U69 Cooler Familiar Face U	8.00	20.00
U70 Cooler Transformed U	8.00	20.00
U71 Cooler Menace U	8.00	20.00
U72 Cooler Overlord U	8.00	20.00
U73 Gohan To The Rescue U	5.00	12.00
U74 Krillin Quick U	3.00	8.00
U75 Master Roshi Restrained U	5.00	12.00
U76 Trunks Protective U	8.00	20.00
U77 Icarus Supportive U	5.00	12.00
U78 Android 13 Powerful U	3.00	8.00
U79 Android 14 Stoic U	3.00	8.00
U80 Android 15 Relaxed U	3.00	8.00
U81 Broly Undaunted U	3.00	8.00
U82 Cooler Angered U	3.00	8.00
U83 Paragus Desperate Father U	3.00	8.00
U84 Salza Henchman U	3.00	8.00
U85 Black Invitation U	5.00	12.00
U86 Black Liberation U	1.50	4.00
U87 Blue Hunt U	1.50	4.00
U88 Blue Skid U	1.50	4.00
U89 Namekian Empowered Charge U	1.50	4.00
U90 Namekian Face Off U	1.50	4.00
U91 Namekian Salvo U	1.50	4.00
U92 Orange Snoozing Drill U	1.50	4.00
U93 Orange Android Rising Punch U	1.50	4.00
U94 Red Integration U	1.50	4.00
U95 Red Double Blast U	1.50	4.00
U96 Red Furious Lunge U	1.50	4.00
U97 Saiyan Recovery U	1.50	4.00
U98 Saiyan Terrifying Strike U	1.50	4.00
U99 PointBlank Volley U	15.00	30.00
U100 Villainous Power Ball U	10.00	25.00
R101 Black Impatience R	5.00	12.00
R102 Black Dispersion R	5.00	12.00
R103 Black Dive R	5.00	12.00
R104 Black Drain R	5.00	12.00
R105 Blue Blanketing Blasts R	5.00	12.00
R106 Blue Decapitation R	5.00	12.00
R107 Blue Discharge R	5.00	12.00
R108 Blue Ki Ball R	5.00	12.00
R109 Blue Return Fire R	5.00	12.00
R110 Namekian Pep Talk R	5.00	12.00
R111 Namekian Harvesting Drill R	5.00	12.00
R112 Namekian Electrifying Grab R	5.00	12.00
R113 Namekian Dash R	5.00	12.00
R114 Namekian Ending R	5.00	12.00
R115 Orange Intimidating Drill R	5.00	12.00
R116 Orange Counter Ball R	5.00	12.00
R117 Orange Hug R	5.00	12.00
R118 Orange Immense Blast R	5.00	12.00
R119 Orange Sword Chop R	5.00	12.00
R120 Red Sword Slicing Drill R	5.00	12.00
R121 Red Fantasy R	5.00	12.00
R122 Red Motivational Kick R	5.00	12.00
R123 Red Stylish Entrance R	5.00	12.00
R124 Saiyan Overpowering Aura Drill R	5.00	12.00
R125 Saiyan Denial R	5.00	12.00
R126 Saiyan Extinguishing Blast R	5.00	12.00
R127 Saiyan Lob R	5.00	12.00
R128 Saiyan Thrust R	5.00	12.00
R129 Saiyan Trample R	5.00	12.00
R130 Saiyan Trap R	5.00	12.00
R131 Singing Drill R	5.00	12.00
R132 Android Insubordination R	6.00	15.00
R133 Sobering Hammer R	10.00	25.00
R134 Stomach Crusher R	25.00	50.00
R135 Android 13s SS Deadly Bomber R	8.00	20.00
R136 Android 13s Impenetrable Defense R	8.00	20.00
R137 Brolys Eraser Cannon R	10.00	25.00
R138 Brolys Face Crusher R	20.00	40.00
R139 Coolers Rebirth R	10.00	25.00
R140 Coolers Supernova R	10.00	25.00
UR141 Surprise Attack UR	30.00	60.00
NONUM Broly Active Player T	3.00	8.00
NONUM Goku Active Player T	3.00	8.00

GAMING

HOW TO USE

What's Listed
Products listed in the Price Guide typically: 1) are produced by licensed manufacturers, 2) are widely available and 3) have market activity on single items.

What the Columns Mean
The LO and HI columns reflect current retail selling ranges. The HI column on the right generally represents the full retail selling price. The LO column on the left generally represents the lowest price one would expect to find with extensive shopping.

Grading
All cards in the Price Guide are based on NrMint to Mint condition. Damaged cards are generally sold for 25 to 75 percent of Mint value. Toy prices are based on mint condition. Toys that are loose (out of package), are generally sold for 50 percent of the listed price.

Currency
This Price Guide is intended to reflect the entire North American market. All listed prices are in U.S. dollars.

Legend

C – Common

CR – Colossal rare (Dinosaur King)

F- Fixed rarity

G – Gold stamp (Digimon)

GR – Gold rare (Dinosaur King)

HOLO – Holofoil

HR – Hidden rare (InuYashu)

MR – Master/Mythic rare

NR – No rarity

PR – Promo/Proxy

R – Rare

SE – Starter exclusive

SP – Short printed/Special

SR – Super rare

U- Uncommon

VR – Very rare (Duel Masters)

XR – Xtra rare

Attention Dealers: If you would like to be a Price Guide Contributor for this almanac, please e-mail your name and phone number to: nonsports@beckett.com.

1999 7th Sea Broad Sides

	LO	HI
COMPLETE SET (318)		
BOOSTER BOX (36 PACKS)	40.00	50.00
BOOSTER PACK (15 CARDS)	1.00	1.50

1 12-Pound Cannon Volley C
2 16-Pound Cannon Volley U
3 20-Pound Cannon Volley R
4 A Better Offer C
5 A Hero's Courage R
6 A Sailor's Quarrel C
7 Again, Boys R
8 Ambush Boarding R
9 Artifact Leg R
10 Away Boarders! R
11 Bad Maps C
12 Bad Powder C
13 Betrayal R
14 Black Heart U
15 Calm Before the Storm C
16 Carousing C
17 Castillian Gunpowder U
18 Chain Shot R
19 Cheap Barrels U
20 Courtly Manner U
21 Crescent Fire U
22 Crossing the T R
23 Cut the Ropes C
24 Dark Temptations R
25 Dead Men Tell No Tales R
26 Death From Above! R
27 Decks Awash R
28 Decks Running Red R
29 Derwyddon's Schemes R
30 Direct Hit! C
31 Disarmed! R
32 Divvying the Plunder R
33 Evasive Course R
34 Eyepatch U
35 Fire the Chase Guns! R
36 Flogging U
37 From Stem to Gudgeon C
38 Gambling House R
39 Gold Only Buys Obedience C
40 Good Shot! C
41 Grape Shot R
42 Grappling Hooks C
43 Handsome Scar U
44 Hiding in the Reefs C
45 High Seas Boarding C
46 Hired Swordsman R
47 Hole in the Hull U
48 Hook U
49 I Fights Better Drunk C
50 I Told You Not To Trust Him R
51 Into the Fray R
52 It's Who You Know C
53 Last Second Cannon Volley R
54 Leviathan Bone R
55 Mermaids U
56 Mind Your P's and Q's R
57 Misfire C
58 Monkey's Fist U
59 Mutiny! R
60 Narrow Escape U
61 Near Miss C
62 Nice Try! R
63 No Escape! R
64 Off Course U
65 One With the Sails U
66 Out of Rum U
67 Panache U
68 Peg Leg U
69 Piles of Skulls R
70 Point Blank Cannon Volley C
71 Prepare for Boarding C
72 Press Gang C
73 Queen of the Sea R
74 Quick Reload U
75 Quick Sailing U
76 Quick Tack C
77 Ramming Speed R
78 Red Skies at Morning R
79 Red Skies at Night C
80 Rough Voyage U
81 Sabotaged Sails U
82 Sailing Under the Jolly Roger U
83 Scarlet Hook of Madness R
84 Scurvy U
85 Slip of the Tongue C
86 Sniper U
87 Son of a Gun R
88 Southern Trade Winds R
89 Speed Isn't Everything C
90 St. Roger's Day C
91 Steal Their Wind U
92 Steering Clear C
93 Stirring Speech R
94 Syrneth Crystal Eye R
95 Tagging C
96 Target Their Powder Rooms! R
97 The Better Part of Valor C
98 The Great Grey U
99 The Living Storm U
100 The Sailor's Curse U
101 Too Close for Comfort C
102 Unexpected Turn of Events U
103 Vodanken R
104 Wenching C
105 When All Else Fails C
106 Who Can You Trust? R
107 You Won't Be Needin' This! R
108 Aimon RichÈ du Purisse C
109 Alesio R
110 Andrei Levovich C
111 Angus McCloud U
112 Antonio Aldonez U
113 Archaeologists C
114 Arturo Rodriguez R
115 Babette U
116 Blacktooth Bill C
117 Bloody Bonnie McGee R
118 Brennan U
119 Brutes C
120 Buccaneers C
121 Bully Boys C
122 Burke R
123 Carlos Altenar C
124 Celedoine R
125 Cosette R
126 Denny La Bree C
127 Domingo U
128 Domingo Marten de Avila U
129 Don Deanna U
130 Donna R
131 Dorf Klinderhoff R
132 Fancy Dans C
133 Felipe Jose de Granjero R
134 Fierbas Desaix du Paix U
135 Foul Weather Jack C
136 Fyodor Zastienchivy U
137 Gerald Hohne U
138 Gerard Rois et Reines R
139 Gilles Allais du Crieux U
140 Grimey Stubbs R
141 Grousin' George R
142 Invar Andersson U
143 Isabeau Dubois du Arrent C
144 Jack Tars C
145 Jack Trades R
146 Jacob Faust U
147 Javier de Bejarano R
148 Jemy C
149 Jens Bjorn U
150 Jillison Brown C
151 Jimmy Bass U
152 Joern Keitelsson R
153 Julius Caligari U
154 Korintine Nicolovich R
155 Leonard Pinkerton U
156 Li'l Jim U
157 Lord Windamshire U
158 Louis Sices du Sices C
159 Lucky Lou U
160 Lucrezia U
161 Luis de Rioja C
162 Lyin' John Fox C
163 Mad Mario U
164 Maggie Malone C
165 Manuel Dejavez U
166 Margaretta Orduno R
167 Mark Scars R
168 Marketeers C
169 Maureen Leveque U
170 Michael Fitzhugh U
171 Michel Rois et Reines U
172 Mountainous Mike U
173 Mr. Smythe U
174 Needle Nose Nye C
175 Otiro U
176 Padre Alfonso R
177 Padre Esteban C
178 Paule du Paix U
179 Pepin R
180 Phelan Cole U
181 Phineas Flynn U
182 Powder Monkeys C
183 Rafael de St. Theresa C
184 Red Scarves C
185 Reggie Wilcox R
186 Riant Gaucher R
187 Riggers C
188 Roger Gaffrin U
189 Rosa Maria de Barcino U
190 Rosamonde du Montaigne C
191 Samuel Sanderson C
192 Samuel Smitts C
193 Sandoval's Guard C
194 Scott Jay R
195 Sean McCorley U
196 Shellbacks C
197 Sidney U
198 Slippery Sal U
199 Solomon Sails U
200 The Calloways U
201 Thom Brunner C
202 Thomas Metzger U
203 Timothy le Beau R
204 Tom Toblin U
205 Two-Toe Terrence C
206 Velik U
207 Vincent Rochester C
208 Warren Abbotsford U
209 Wee Willy R
210 Wilhelm Dunst R
211 William Fodd U
212 William Toss C
213 Across the Mirror C
214 Ancient Maps R
215 Avalon Noble C
216 Barrels of Beer C
217 Bjornsson's Horn R
218 Bolts of Fine Cloth C
219 Casks of Fine Wine C
220 Castillian Merchant Ship C
221 Castillian Swordmaster U
222 Crashing Seas C
223 Cutlass of Command U
224 Eisen Cannons C
225 Forbidden Delicacies C
226 Franzini's Lost Notebooks C
227 From the Depths R
228 Ivory Spyglass R
229 Keel of Rowan Wood R
230 Lady Katerina C
231 Mordekai's Casket U
232 Passionate Duel U
233 Raze the Village C
234 Rose & Cross Apprentice C
235 Sails of Wind R
236 Save the Princess C
237 Scraping the Bottom U
238 Sidhe Sails U
239 Sinking of the Swan C
240 Stolen Guns U
241 Storms Make Sailors C
242 The Ocean's Teeth R
243 Ussuran Pelts C
244 Vodacce Valuables U
245 We Need Us an Ussuran Gunner U
246 Wind at Your Back C
247 Winds of Fate C
248 Wreckers R
249 Asprey C
250 Augusto Rodriguez C
251 Avoid Fate R
252 Billy Bones U
253 Broken Compass Inn C
254 Captain's Quarters R
255 Cat O' Nine Tails U
256 Confusion R
257 Cutlass C
258 Fate's Blessing R
259 Fine Galley C
260 Flashing Swords Inn U
261 Galleon of the Treasure Fleet C
262 Glamour Knowledge R
263 Glimpse of the Skein R
264 Good King Sandoval R
265 Grappling Gun R
266 Hammocks R
267 Here There Be Monsters U
268 Hidden Knife U
269 Lumiére de l'Empereur F
270 Mad Jack O'Bannon R
271 Master Gunner C
272 Master of the Tops C
273 Montaigne Puzzle Sword U
274 Montaigne Valet C
275 Mr. Briggs R
276 Musketeers C
277 Only Two Came Out U
278 Peek at the Future R
279 Persuasion R
280 Port Master R
281 Porte Knowledge R
282 Porte Ward R
283 Queen Elaine R
284 Queen of the Sidhe R
285 Rats! U
286 Reclusive Backers C

287 Red C
288 Romantic Captive R
289 Rough Waters U
290 Seven League Striders U
291 St. Roger's Blessing! R
292 Swiveling Cannon U
293 Take No Prisoners! U
294 The Gallows F
295 The Inquisition U
296 The Marquis d'Arrent R
297 The Queen's Reward F
298 The Reaper F
299 The Shield Man F
300 The Spear of Theus F
301 Through the Portal R
302 Treasure Hold U
303 Vincenzo Caligari R
304 Waylaid C
305 Who Shot the Albatross? U
306 Willowed Ropes U
307 Corazon del Castille F
308 Grenouille du Gr'ce F
309 The Black Dawn F
310 The Crimson Roger F
311 The Discovery F
312 The Hanged Man F
313 Allende F
314 Berek F
315 Enrique Orduno F
316 Guy McCormick F
317 Reis F
318 The General F

1999 7th Sea No Quarter

COMPLETE SET (318)		
BOOSTER BOX (36 PACKS)	60.00	80.00
BOOSTER PACK (15 CARDS)	2.00	2.50

1 Target Their Powder Rooms! R
2 You Won't Be Needin' This! R
3 12-Pound Cannon Volley C
4 16-Pound Cannon Volley U
5 20-Pound Cannon Volley R
6 A Better Offer C
7 A Hero's Courage R
8 A Sailor's Quarrel C
9 Again, Boys R
10 Ambush Boarding R
11 Artifact Leg R
12 Away Boarders! R
13 Bad Maps C
14 Bad Powder C
15 Betrayal R
16 Black Heart U
17 Calm Before the Storm C
18 Carousing C
19 Castillian Gunpowder U
20 Chain Shot R
21 Cheap Barrels U
22 Courtly Manner U
23 Crescent Fire U
24 Crossing the T R
25 Cut the Ropes C
26 Dark Temptations R
27 Dead Men Tell No Tales R
28 Death From Above! R
29 Decks Awash R
30 Decks Running Red R
31 Derwyddon's Schemes R
32 Direct Hit! C
33 Disarmed! R
34 Divvying the Plunder R
35 Evasive Course R
36 Eyepatch U
37 Fire the Chase Guns! R
38 Flogging U
39 From Stem to Gudgeon C
40 Gambling House R
41 Gold Only Buys Obedience C
42 Good Shot! C
43 Grape Shot R
44 Grappling Hooks C
45 Handsome Scar U
46 Hiding In the Reefs C
47 High Seas Boarding C
48 Hired Swordsman R
49 Hole in the Hull U
50 Hook U
51 I Fights Better Drunk C
52 I Told You Not To Trust Him R
53 Into the Fray R
54 It's Who You Know C
55 Last Second Cannon Volley R
56 Leviathan Bone R
57 Mermaids U
58 Mind Your P's and Q's R
59 Misfire C
60 Monkey's Fist U
61 Mutiny! R
62 Narrow Escape U
63 Near Miss C
64 Nice Try! R
65 No Escape! R
66 Off Course U
67 One With the Sails U
68 Out of Rum U
69 Panache U
70 Peg Leg U
71 Piles of Skulls R
72 Point Blank Cannon Volley C
73 Prepare for Boarding C
74 Press Gang C
75 Queen of the Sea R
76 Quick Reload U
77 Quick Sailing U
78 Quick Tack C
79 Ramming Speed R
80 Red Skies at Morning R
81 Red Skies at Night C
82 Rough Voyage U
83 Sabotaged Sails U
84 Sailing Under the Jolly Roger U
85 Scarlet Hook of Madness R
86 Scurvy U
87 Slip of the Tongue C
88 Sniper U
89 Son of a Gun R
90 Southern Trade Winds R
91 Speed Isn't Everything C
92 St. Roger's Day C
93 Steal Their Wind U
94 Steering Clear C
95 Stirring Speech R
96 Syrneth Crystal Eye R
97 Tagging C
98 The Better Part of Valor C
99 The Great Grey U
100 The Living Storm U
101 The Sailor's Curse U
102 Too Close for Comfort C
103 Unexpected Turn of Events U
104 Vodanken R
105 Wenching C
106 When All Else Fails C
107 Who Can You Trust? R
108 Lyin' John Fox C
109 Aimon RichE du Purisse C
110 Alesio R
111 Andrei Levovich C
112 Angus McCloud U
113 Antonio Aldonez U
114 Archaeologists C
115 Arturo Rodriguez R
116 Babette U
117 Blacktooth Bill C
118 Bloody Bonnie McGee R
119 Brennan U
120 Brutes C
121 Buccaneers C
122 Bully Boys C
123 Burke R
124 Carlos Altenar C
125 Celedoine R
126 Cosette R
127 Denny La Bree C
128 Domingo U
129 Domingo Marten de Avila U
130 Don Deanna U
131 Donna R
132 Dorf Klinderhoff R
133 Fancy Dans C
134 Felipe Jose de Granjero R
135 Fierbas Desaix du Paix U
136 Foul Weather Jack C
137 Fyodor Zastienchivy U
138 Gerald Hohne U
139 Gerard Rois et Reines R
140 Gilles Allais du Crieux U
141 Grimey Stubbs R
142 Grousin' George R
143 Invar Andersson U
144 Isabeau Dubois du Arrent C
145 Jack Tars C
146 Jack Trades R
147 Jacob Faust U
148 Javier de Bejarano R
149 Jemy C
150 Jens Bjorn U
151 Jillison Brown C
152 Jimmy Bass U
153 Joern Keitelsson R
154 Julius Caligari U
155 Korintine Nicolovich R
156 Leonard Pinkerton U
157 Li'l Jim U
158 Lord Windamshire U
159 Louis Sices du Sices C
160 Lucky Lou U
161 Lucrezia U
162 Luis de Rioja C
163 Mad Mario U
164 Maggie Malone C
165 Manuel Dejavez U
166 Margaretta Orduno R
167 Mark Scars R
168 Marketeers C
169 Maureen Leveque U
170 Michael Fitzhugh U
171 Michel Rois et Reines U
172 Mountainous Mike U
173 Mr. Smythe U
174 Needle Nose Nye C
175 Otiro U
176 Padre Alfonso R
177 Padre Esteban C
178 Paule du Paix U
179 Pepin R
180 Phelan Cole U
181 Phineas Flynn U
182 Powder Monkeys C
183 Rafael de St. Theresa C
184 Red Scarves C
185 Reggie Wilcox R
186 Riant Gaucher R
187 Riggers C
188 Roger Gaffrin U
189 Rosa Maria de Barcino U
190 Rosamonde du Montaigne C
191 Samuel Sanderson C
192 Samuel Smitts C
193 Sandoval's Guard C
194 Scott Jay R
195 Sean McCorley U
196 Shellbacks C
197 Sidney U
198 Slippery Sal U
199 Solomon Sails U
200 The Calloways U
201 Thom Brunner C
202 Thomas Metzger U
203 Timothy le Beau R
204 Tom Toblin U
205 Two-Toe Terrence C
206 Velik U
207 Vincent Rochester C
208 Warren Abbotsford U
209 Wee Willy R
210 Wilhelm Dunst R
211 William Fodd U
212 William Toss C
213 Across the Mirror C
214 Ancient Maps R
215 Avalon Noble C
216 Barrels of Beer C
217 Bjornsson's Horn R
218 Bolts of Fine Cloth C
219 Casks of Fine Wine C
220 Castillian Merchant Ship C
221 Castillian Swordmaster U
222 Crashing Seas C
223 Cutlass of Command U
224 Eisen Cannons C
225 Forbidden Delicacies C
226 Franzini's Lost Notebooks C
227 From the Depths R
228 Ivory Spyglass R
229 Keel of Rowan Wood R
230 Lady Katerina C
231 Mordekai's Casket U
232 Passionate Duel U
233 Raze the Village C
234 Rose & Cross Apprentice C
235 Sails of Wind R
236 Save the Princess C
237 Scraping the Bottom U
238 Sidhe Sails U
239 Sinking of the Swan C
240 Stolen Guns U
241 Storms Make Sailors C
242 The Ocean's Teeth R
243 Ussuran Pelts C
244 Vodacce Valuables U
245 We Need Us an Ussuran Gunner U
246 Wind at Your Back C
247 Winds of Fate C
248 Wreckers R
249 Take No Prisoners! U
250 Asprey C
251 Augusto Rodriguez C
252 Avoid Fate R
253 Billy Bones U
254 Broken Compass Inn C
255 Captain's Quarters R
256 Cat O' Nine Tails U
257 Charter F
258 Confusion R
259 Constitution F
260 Cutlass C
261 Fate's Blessing R
262 Fine Galley C
263 Flashing Swords Inn U
264 Galleon of the Treasure Fleet C
265 Glamour Knowledge R
266 Glimpse of the Skein R
267 Good King Sandoval R
268 Grappling Gun R
269 Hammocks R
270 Here There Be Monsters U
271 Hidden Knife U
272 Letter of Marque F
273 Mad Jack O'Bannon R
274 Master Gunner C
275 Master of the Tops C
276 Montaigne Puzzle Sword U
277 Montaigne Valet C
278 Mr. Briggs R
279 Musketeers C
280 Naval Sanction F
281 Only Two Came Out U
282 Peek at the Future R
283 Persuasion R
284 Port Master R
285 Porte Knowledge R
286 Porte Ward R
287 Queen Elaine R
288 Queen of the Sidhe R
289 Rats! U
290 Reclusive Backers C
291 Red C
292 Romantic Captive R
293 Rough Waters U
294 Seal of the Sun King F
295 Seven League Striders U
296 St. Roger's Blessing! R
297 Swiveling Cannon U
298 The Inquisition U
299 The Marquis d'Arrent R
300 The Pact of the Crimson Rogers F
301 Through the Portal R
302 Treasure Hold U
303 Vincenzo Caligari R
304 Waylaid C
305 Who Shot the Albatross? U
306 Willowed Ropes U
307 Corazon del Castille F
308 Grenouille du Gr'ce F
309 The Black Dawn F
310 The Crimson Roger F
311 The Discovery F
312 The Hanged Man F
313 Allende F
314 Berek F
315 Enrique Orduno F
316 Guy McCormick F
317 Reis F
318 The General F

1999 7th Sea Shifting Tides

COMPLETE SET(155)		
BOOSTER BOX (36 PACKS)	20.00	30.00
BOOSTER PACK (15 CARDS)	.75	1.00

1 ...No Barter... U
2 ...No Quarter! R
3 Allow Me... U
4 Beat You To It! R
5 Don't Mess With Me, Boy! R
6 Listen! U
7 No Banter... C
8 Please, Take Your Time! U
9 Repel Boarders! C
10 That Hurts! U
11 Barnacles U
12 Blows Up In Your Face U
13 Boarded By Skeletons R
14 Burn Their Sails R
15 Challenge to a Duel C
16 Close Range Cannon Volley C
17 Desperate Move R
18 Errant Match C
19 Fire and Steel R
20 Haunted by the Past R
21 Headed Out U
22 Heroic Stand U
23 Into the Fog C
24 Lady's Kiss C
25 Last Second Escape! C
26 Lightening the Load U
27 Major Hull Damage R
28 Minor Hull Damage C
29 Obscured by Smoke U
30 Poor Jack C
31 Reporting Drunk C
32 Sharp Shooter U
33 Shot Across the Bow R
34 Tar, Tar, and More Tar R
35 To Fight Another Day R
36 Vesten Pride R
37 Victory for the Bold U
38 Vodanken's Breath R
39 Would Be Traders C
40 Wounded R
41 Brother Mattias Brewer U
42 Long Tall Harry R
43 Lucky Vandrad Hallvardson C
44 Alister McGurk C
45 Ambroise Praisse du Richetoisse U
46 Arnlaug Rijs Bragison C
47 Augusto de Augustin R
48 Billy "Bilge Rat" Bones R
49 Botas Rojas C
50 Brawny Rowers C
51 Connor Lynch R
52 Cutthroats C
53 Delaina Darling C
54 Egil Bergljot Larrson U
55 Felix "l'Aigle" C
56 Fid Blue-Eye R
57 Gino Napoli U
58 Graham Hapworth C
59 Gris Hallisdottir U
60 Gustolph Hirsch U
61 Gytha Ives C
62 Hoskuld Hardrada R
63 Jaques Renault R
64 Jorund Guttormson U
65 Kedish the Crescent R
66 Kirsten Blumfeld U
67 Leila U
68 Lowly Captives C
69 Marcel Entour C
70 Michel Rois et Reines U
71 Musette Falisci R
72 Oar Team C
73 Orm Greybeard U
74 Peter Silver U
75 Red the Adventurer U
76 Red Thorfild R
77 Rognvald Brandson R
78 Rosamonde du Montaigne R
79 Santino Medrano U
80 Scurvy Dogs C
81 Sigvaldi Sveinson R
82 Tarsis the Mad R
83 The Gullet U
84 The Kire R
85 Thordis Bjerregaard U
86 Timothy le Beau F
87 Ulf Karlseen R
88 Valkyries C
89 Vivianna Etalon du Toille C
90 Willie Wilcox U
91 Aether Compass R
92 Barcino Fortress U
93 Fine Rope and Tackle C
94 Fresh Powder C
95 Montaigne Exports U
96 Navigational Tools C
97 Offensive Maneuvers C
98 Ring of Honor R
99 Ring of Villany R
100 Runed Ship's Wheel R
101 Sighted Pistol C
102 Slashing Across the Decks R
103 Spit in Death's Eye C
104 Stolen Documents C
105 Stolen Sword U
106 The Second Switch R
107 Captain R
108 Pack 'em In! U
109 Advanced Swordsmanship R
110 Adventuring Gally U
111 Allied Warship U
112 Armed Brig U
113 Armed Frigate U
114 Basic Swordsmanship C
115 Castillian Navy U
116 Cheap Cutlass C
117 Cheap Sails C
118 Cheap Tools C
119 Coastal Patrols U
120 Corsairs Figurehead R
121 Crescent Treasures U
122 Dirk C
123 El Vago R
124 Fine Boots C
125 Good Use of Space C
126 Gosse Figurehead R
127 Herje (Ruin) R
128 Kjott (Flesh) F
129 Main Gauche C
130 Nod (Intensity) U
131 Northern Allies U
132 Panzerhand C
133 Pocket Money C
134 Powder Keg Tavern R
135 Pulling Through R
136 Ruby Earring C
137 Scarlet Launch R
138 Scary Tattoo C
139 Secret of the Winds R
140 Silver Earring C
141 Small Fortress U
142 Speedy Courier U
143 Stans (Calm) U
144 Sterk (Wholeness) U
145 Styrke (Strength) U
146 The Ogre U
147 The River R
148 Tugging the Strands R
149 Unexpected Hero C
150 Vesten Figurehead R
151 Villskap (Fury) U
152 Le PrÈdateur des Mers F
153 The Revensj F
154 Amiral Alazais Valoix-Praisse III F
155 Yngvild Olafssdottir F

1999 7th Sea Strange Vistas

COMPLETE SET(156)		
BOOSTER BOX (36 PACKS)	30.00	40.00
BOOSTER PACK (15 CARDS)	1.00	1.50

1 I'll Be Taking That... U
2 Man the Bilge Pumps! C
3 Stroke, Stroke... U
4 Take it Like a Man! U
5 There's More Where They Came From U
6 Throw Me the Whip! C
7 Walk the Plank! U
8 Warship to Port! C
9 X Almost Marks the Spot R
10 All For One! U
11 Becalmed C
12 Berek's Already Done That U
13 Brotherhood Pride R
14 Cannister Shot C
15 Castille Pride R
16 Corsair Pride R
17 Crimson Roger Pride R
18 Customs Check U
19 Danger on the High Seas C
20 Dispatching The Scum R
21 Disregard R
22 Drop a Boarding Net C
23 Experience is the Best Teacher R
24 Explorer Pride R
25 Fancy Swordplay C
26 First Mate's Watch R
27 Ghouls Sneak on Board U
28 Gosse Pride R
29 Gunnery at its Finest C
30 Helpful Advice U
31 Infection U
32 Lemons C
33 Long Range Cannon Volley C
34 Low on Shot R
35 McCormick's Quest R
36 Montaigne Pride R
37 Parting Shot C
38 Plague of Boca C
39 Prayer U
40 Purple Heaves R
41 Riposte C
42 Run 'im Through! C
43 Sea Dog Pride R
44 Secrets of the Tops C
45 Sharp Maneuvering C
46 Taking the Hit C
47 The Captain's Word R
48 The General's Tactics R
49 The Three Fate Witches U
50 The Wrath of Reis R
51 ThÈah Eats the Weak C
52 Turning Enemies Into Friends U
53 Uprising! U
54 Wake of Estallio C
55 Wild Party! R
56 Al-Katim C
57 Andre Braudel R
58 Andres Donovich C

59 Bjorn Brind U
60 Dalia U
61 Daniel U
62 Dunti U
63 Dupre & Hans C
64 Edahgo R
65 Entertainers C
66 Espera C
67 Galafre Flaubert du Dore U
68 Galley Captives C
69 Gaspar R
70 Hamish R
71 Henderson C
72 Hernando Ochoa C
73 Iken of Venderheim R
74 Imshi R
75 Inil U
76 Joseph Dunn C
77 Julia C
78 Mabela U
79 Martin Tytus C
80 Melinda Gosse R
81 Miguel Cortez U
82 Mike Fitzpatrick U
83 Sergei Nyasvy U
84 Seven-Color Sam C
85 Shala R
86 Thomas Gosse U
87 Torvo Espada R
88 Tyree the Worthless R
89 Volta R
90 A Gallant Stand C
91 Ancient Training Techniques U
92 Artifact Cannon R
93 Back Alley Rum U
94 Boatload of Jennys U
95 Braving the Nor'wester R
96 Crossfire R
97 Dangerous Cargo U
98 Dredging the Trade River U
99 Escorting the MacDuff C
100 Fancy Footwork U
101 Fine Rigging U
102 Making of a Hero R
103 Palace Raid C
104 Sidhe Storm R
105 Staying Ahead of Trouble R
106 Strength isn't Everything C
107 Syrneth Tiller C
108 The Finest Cannons... C
109 The First Switch R
110 Their Captain's Will C
111 Trinkets and Baubles U
112 Ussuran Intrigue U
113 We're Doomed! U
114 A Sailor's First Skill C
115 Aldana School U
116 Ambrogia School U
117 Belaying Pin C
118 Belit R
119 Cargo Hook C
120 Common Pier C
121 Cool Castillian Blood U
122 Cross of Virtue R
123 Donovan School U
124 Eisenfaust School U
125 Giovanni Villanova R
126 Gold Earring C
127 Grappling Cannon C
128 Harpoon C
129 Jack-of-All-Trades R
130 Jean-Marie Rois-et-Reines U
131 Jenny House C
132 Kalem the Believer R
133 Kheired-Din's Secret R
134 Leegstra School U
135 Long Hand U
136 Musket C
137 Old Flame R
138 Pistol C
139 Posh Quarters R
140 Ramming Spike U
141 Retired Smuggler C
142 Rigged for Speed R
143 Roger School U
144 Safe Path U
145 Shore Knowledge U
146 Special Gift U
147 The Code F
148 The Unwritten Rules F
149 Valroux School U
150 Warship R
151 Well Equipped Sick Bay R
152 Well Stocked Armory R
153 Strange Skies F
154 Uncharted Course F
155 Kheired-Din F
156 Philip Gosse F

2000 7th Sea Black Sails

COMPLETE SET(54)
STARTER DECK (50 CARDS) 10.00 20.00
1 Innocent Bystander
2 Kiss of Death
3 Log of the Black Freighter
4 Marooned
5 Moaning Song of the Dead
6 Never Knew Him
7 Power of Purity
8 Run'em Down, Boys!
9 Skull Shot
10 To the Death!
11 Would-Be Gunners
12 Rigger Morris
13 Dalia
14 Denny La Bree
15 Don Deanna
16 Gilles Allais du Crieux
17 Iken of Venderheim
18 Lord Windamshire
19 Mark Scars
20 Moldy Morris
21 No-Leg William
22 Pete "Gang" Green
23 Reinheart the Ripper
24 Samuel Smitts
25 Skeletal Brutes
26 Skeletal Cannon Crew
27 Skeletal Dans
28 Skeletal Deck Hands
29 Skeletal Saboteurs
30 Skeletal Sail Crew
31 Skeletal Shore Gang
32 Skeletal Thugs
33 Stench
34 The Bloat
35 Thomas Gosse
36 Ulrich the Unholy
37 Victor of Luthon
38 William Toss
39 Cursed Cutlass
40 Feed the Hunger
41 Gold Coins
42 High Morale
43 Scarlet Gem of Death
44 Well of Purity
45 Armed Sloop
46 Black Heart of the Sea
47 Black Siren
48 Plague Ship
49 Savage Storm
50 The Curse
51 The Traitor's Scream
52 Vile Temple
53 The Black Freighter
54 Captain Necros

2000 7th Sea Fate's Debt

COMPLETE SET(156)
BOOSTER BOX (36 PACKS) 20.00 30.00
BOOSTER PACK (15 CARDS) .75 1.00
1 Cut a Path! U
2 Fire as She Passes! C
3 Heave To! U
4 My Last Bit of Luck U
5 She Canna Take It! R
6 She'll Hold Together C
7 A Hero at Last C
8 A Pirate's Reputation U
9 A Single Shot R
10 A Thousand Fires Alight R
11 Awaiting the Signal C
12 Better off Chum U
13 Blasted Bulkhead U
14 Bloody Fight U
15 Broken Mast C
16 But, not in Vain C
17 Call to Arms C
18 Captured! U
19 Crackers on Demand R
20 Crossbow Bolt C
21 Dockside Raid U
22 Dust to Dust U
23 Entwining Kelp C
24 False Colors C
25 Foolish Bet C
26 Free Men Can Do Anything C
27 Fresh Fruit C
28 Fresh Water C
29 Frozen Sails C
30 Hard Tack C
31 Headhunters C
32 Hidden Crew C
33 Hidden Rum C
34 Holy Vision U
35 Honorable Surrender U
36 Ice Storm U
37 Ivory Totem U
38 Launching the Falcon's Roost U
39 Lice R
40 Loot and Pillage U
41 Mad Martin's Tattoos C
42 Nasty Bit 'o Luck C
43 Next of Kin U
44 No Fun to be a Captive C
45 No Space For Luxuries U
46 Not Quite Dead C
47 Orduno's Honor C
48 Powering Through R
49 Quaranteened Port C
50 Sails Don't Bleed C
51 Second Chance C
52 Shining Example R
53 Steady Leak R
54 The Betrayal of Allende C
55 The Destruction of the Spear U
56 The Fury of the Rogers C
57 The Futility of It All U
58 The Next Chapter C
59 The Nibelungen's Price R
60 The Sinking of the Hanged Man U
61 The Spear of the West Wind U
62 The Stake U
63 Too Strong to Die U
64 Undead Ambush C
65 Vengence of the Damned R
66 Whites of Their Eyes C
67 Worthless Trinket U
68 Would-Be Adventurers U
69 Lyin' John Fox R
70 Niklaas Wynkoop C
71 Ahmed Khalid U
72 Alec Mercer C
73 Alix Brower C
74 Benny Gimble U
75 Delaina Darling U
76 Donna U
77 Dunti F
78 Edahgo R
79 Emily de Gallegos U
80 Fierbas Desaix du Paix R
81 Frieda Kesler U
82 Fyodor Zastienchivy R
83 Hamish U
84 Hauptmann von Lichen C
85 Hull Rot Bill C
86 Imshi U
87 Joseph Gallegos de Avila C
88 Julius Caligari R
89 Kirsten Blumfeld U
90 Kurt Weinberg C
91 Lieutenant Novak C
92 Lt. Juan Rodriguez de Soldano C
93 Luis de Rioja R
94 Mabela R
95 Maximillian C
96 Mike Fitzpatrick C
97 Moldy Morris R
98 Montaigne Marines C
99 Petro Angelina C
100 Piotr the Badger C
101 Red Thorfild R
102 Reggie Wilcox F
103 Reynaldo Pasado U
104 Roger Gaffrin R
105 Rosamaria Falisci U
106 Scott Preston U
107 Shala R
108 Skeletal Dregs U
109 The Calloways R
110 Uriah the Dribbler U
111 Ursula von Stahl R
112 Velik U
113 Whalers U
114 William Highport U
115 Yr Hagin Bronsson U
116 Foul Weather Jack's Map, Part I R
117 Foul Weather Jack's Map, Part II R
118 Foul Weather Jack's Map, Part III R
119 Foul Weather Jack's Map, Part IV R
120 Nibelungen Forge R
121 The Fourth Switch R
122 The Lure of Gold R
123 Have at um' Boys! C
124 I've Seen Worse U
125 Alesio's Fate U
126 Arisent R
127 Bad Surgeon R
128 Caligari's Island R
129 Carleon R
130 Demon Eyes R
131 Eyes of Reason U
132 Fool's Errand C
133 le Beau's Compass R
134 Overstocked U
135 Preparing for a Long Voyage U
136 Reis' Brides R
137 Responsive Helm R
138 Salted Meat C
139 San Cristobal R
140 Scatter Pistol U
141 Senor Ladron R
142 Sousdal R
143 St. Roger's Spyglass R
144 Stealing the Falcon's Roost R
145 Swivel Gun C
146 The Guiding Gem of Hierro R
147 The Setine Key R
148 The Witches' Shears R
149 Val Mokk R
150 Die Seevogel R
151 Freedom's Key F
152 The Dolphin R
153 The Falcon's Roost F
154 The Invictus R
155 Ernesto Castillus F
156 Jeremiah Berek F

2000 7th Sea Horizon's Edge

COMPLETE SET (106)
BOOSTER BOX (48 PACKS) 50.00 60.00
BOOSTER PACK (11 CARDS) 1.00 1.50
1 A Little Broadside Help U
2 A Little On-Shore Help U
3 Allende 's Rescue C
4 Death Stare R
5 Destiny and Loyalty C
6 First Mate's Duel U
7 Hit to the Deck U
8 Inquisition Witch Hunt U
9 Iron Mask C
10 Lyin' John's Fate U
11 Northern Trade Route C
12 Predators of the Sea R
13 Pushing the Limits R
14 Southern Trade Route C
15 Swelling Tides C
16 The Discovery Attacks C
17 The Path to San Cristobal C
18 Andare de Castillo C
19 Andre Braudel F
20 Benny Gimble R
21 Captive Thugs C
22 Cathwulf Vogt R
23 Connor Lynch R
24 Daring Fools U
25 Foul Weather Jack R
26 Franco Vesefe R
27 Gerard Rois et Reines R
28 Grendel Thorton C
29 Grutch R
30 Gullbait Friedrich R
31 Hector Beuchamp du Charouse U
32 Heinrich Logan U
33 Ian O'Toole U
34 Ilya "Gadalka" Letinovich C
35 J.P. Wardbraddon R
36 Jacques Renault R
37 James Stiller R
38 Josephina Culpepper C
39 Juliet Jones C
40 Korintine Nicolovich F
41 Louis Fontaine R
42 Miguel Bascalle R
43 Montaigne Musketeers C
44 Naughty Dan U
45 No-Leg William R
46 Percival du Lac R
47 Peter Silver R
48 Roald Andreasson C
49 Roberta Estrada R
50 Rosa Maria de Barcino R
51 Singing Sal C
52 Soren "Painless" Halstead C
53 Sylvia Étalon du Toille U
54 Talia del Emelia R
55 Ten Barrels Bob U
56 Two Dagger Dirk C
57 Ulfgar Jor Brønsen C
58 Undead Boarders C
59 Valgard Skaardalneir R
60 Vinchenzo de Tonelli U
61 Volta R
62 "Magpie" Muscov R
63 Blink Attack U
64 Faerie Path U
65 Grandmother Ussura U
66 Hidden Fate Heritage C
67 Hidden Glamour Heritage C
68 Hidden Lærdom Heritage C
69 Hidden Porté Heritage C
70 Hidden Pyeryem Heritage C
71 Lucrezia's Prophecy U
72 Mark of the Grumfather U
73 Taking El Toro Rojo U
74 The Porté Escape U
75 The Rise of Cabora C
76 The Sixth Switch R
77 A Blooded Coin U
78 Alesio's Sacrifice U
79 Berserker School U
80 Bones of Our Ancestors R
81 Get To It! R
82 Local Assistance R
83 Reis' Fury C
84 Robin Goodfellow U
85 San Cristobal Under Siege R
86 Sparrow Hawk U
87 Spectral Aura U
88 Syrneth Navigator U
89 The Eternal Grave R
90 Trickster's Grin C
91 Tungsinn ("Gloom") R
92 We'll Get Him Back! U
93 Into the Tower U
94 One Shot — Make it Count C
95 Rewrite the Rules C
96 Sorcerer's Lament U
97 Surprise Rescue U
98 The Coming Tempest C
99 Through the 7th Sea U
100 What Does Not Kill Us C
101 Eisen Dreizack R
102 El Toro Rojo F
103 The Redeemer F
104 Captain Cosette F
105 Captain Melinda Gosse F
106 Der Kire R

2000 7th Sea Reaper's Fee

COMPLETE SET (156)
BOOSTER BOX (36 PACKS) 80.00 100.00
BOOSTER PACK (15 CARDS) 2.00 3.00
RELEASED ON
1 All Hands on Deck! U
2 Arm Yourselves! U
3 Brace Yourselves! U
4 Look Lively, Men! U
5 Man the Tops! U
6 Prepare for the Worst! U
7 To the Cannons! U
8 A Killer Revealed R
9 Allende's Folly U
10 At the Ready R
11 Back It Up C
12 Called Away C
13 Claw of Thalusai C
14 Dark Past R
15 Fair Skies R
16 Fate's Revenge R
17 For the Greater Good R
18 Foul Weather Ahead R
19 Gosse's Folly U
20 Hired Saboteurs C
21 Hit to the Captain's Quarters R
22 Hit to the Galley R
23 Hit to the Main Mast R
24 Hit to the Powder Room R
25 Hold Your Ground C
26 It Doesn't Matter C
27 Javier's Mistake R
28 Line and Winch C
29 Orduno's Folly U
30 Prosperous Ventures R
31 Tear their Sails R
32 The Black Freighter's Folly U
33 The Corsair's Folly U
34 The Explorer's Folly U
35 The General's Plan R
36 The Kire's Pen R
37 The Rogers' Folly U
38 The Sea Dog's Folly U
39 The Unrelenting Depths C
40 The Vestenmannavnjar's Folly U
41 The Witches Return C
42 Valoix's Folly U
43 Butcher Pinchot R
44 Cat's Claw Fornier U
45 Long Tall Harry R
46 Pincushion Paolo C
47 Scorchmark Van Hoffman C
48 Aleen Van Ostrand C
49 Andrei Levovich U
50 Bardo Murillo C
51 Berserkers C
52 Bethesda Quinn C
53 Carlos Altenar R
54 Catwulf Vogt U
55 Deck Hands C
56 Dorf Klinderhoff R
57 Dupre and Hans R
58 Eisen Mercs C
59 Elena Agnelli C
60 Erich Carlberg U
61 Felipe Jose de Granjero R
62 Fyddych O'Bannon C
63 Gina "the Jackal" U
64 Grigorii Popvich U
65 Gris Hallisdottir R
66 Gustolph Hirsch R
67 Henry the Clockmaker C
68 Inquisitor Bascalle F
69 Isabeau Dubois du Arrent R
70 Jacob Faust R
71 Jaime Espejo U
72 Jamie Sices du Sices U
73 Jelena C
74 Joris Hartig C
75 Josette Quadros C
76 Ketty Tappan C
77 Kitka Maritova C
78 Lucrezia R
79 Master Allen Trel R
80 Miguel Sandoval de Castillo U
81 Morgause Mercuri C
82 Nodar the Falcon U
83 Orf Helfir F
84 Padre Alfonso R
85 Pepin R
86 Percis d'Cassell C
87 Pounder C
88 Renfeld Throckmorton U
89 Riant Gaucher R
90 Roberta Estrada R
91 Rupella Lagrippe U
92 Sergeant Benitez U
93 Svein Hegge Hjermstad U
94 Torvo Espada R
95 Ulfied Jansson C
96 Wenching Jim U
97 Wilhelm Dunst R
98 Willie Wilcox R
99 Zoya the Serpent U
100 A Hearty Individual U
101 Message from Margaretta C
102 One Fell Swoop C
103 The Fifth Switch R
104 The General's Armor C
105 The Seal of the Thalusai R
106 The Shattered Spear R
107 The Siren's Jaw R
108 The Undiscovered Port U
109 Anointed by Theus C
110 Braiding the Strands R
111 Crystal Earring C
112 Dashing Blade R
113 Eye of Sky and Sea R
114 Fair Warning R
115 Gespucci Bernoulli C
116 Grenade C
117 Kodiak Bear U
118 Matushka's Blessing U
119 Owl U
120 Rabbit R
121 Red Fox U
122 Reise (Journey) R
123 Sharing a Cot R
124 Sight 'Em Up C
125 Snow Leopard U
126 Starke C
127 Steel Earring C
128 The Word of the Vagabond R
129 Throwing Knives C
130 The Lightbringer is Ours! U
131 Cossette's Mutiny U
132 Eternal Desire C
133 First Tide C
134 Hidden Talents C
135 High King Asbjornsson C
136 Imprisonment in El Morro C
137 Jacques and the Kire U
138 Lyin' John Flees U
139 Message From the Grave U
140 Neither Asked Nor Given C
141 The Island C
142 The Rage of the Vesten C
143 The Revenge of the Damned U
144 The Trail of the Dead C
145 The Trial of Orduno U

146 The Vision Spreads C
147 Vendel Sorcery U
148 Visions of the Isle U
149 Yngvild's Plan U
150 El Fuego Negro F
151 The Santa Cecilia R
152 The Sea Lion F
153 The Wayward Route R
154 Captain Jorund Guttormson F
155 Captain Margaretta Orduno F
156 Sebastiano Scogna R

2000 7th Sea Scarlet Seas

COMPLETE SET (156)		
BOOSTER BOX (36 PACKS)	30.00	40.00
BOOSTER PACK (15 CARDS)	.75	1.25

1 ...and He Makes Witty Repartee R
2 ...and One for All C
3 ...He Rides Well... R
4 7th Sea Eddy R
5 A Coward Among Us U
6 Backs to the Wall C
7 Bad Luck R
8 Barracuda R
9 Below the Waterline C
10 Best Served Cold... U
11 Big Target R
12 Call to Duty C
13 Cheap Gunpowder C
14 Clear Skies R
15 Clear the Decks C
16 Confusion on Deck C
17 Dark Dreams C
18 Dashing Duel U
19 Desperate Wages U
20 Destiny's Touch C
21 Disguised Ship C
22 Don't Make Me Ask Again R
23 Double the Rum Ration R
24 Down to the Nub U
25 Extra Watch C
26 Friendly Winds U
27 Guns Blazing C
28 Harsh Light of Reality R
29 He Fights Well... R
30 I'm Not Left-Handed R
31 It's a Trap U
32 Jorund's Betrayal R
33 King Before Captain U
34 Land Lubber R
35 Lightning Flash C
36 Livestock C
37 Locked in Death R
38 Moment of Glory U
39 Night of Horror U
40 No Survivors! C
41 Out of Action U
42 Pulled From the Sea C
43 Sea Chantey U
44 She's Coming Apart! U
45 Slow Tack C
46 Succubus R
47 Swimming with Sharks C
48 Swing from the Rigging C
49 Syrneth Guardians R
50 The Few, theProud... U
51 Therein Lies the Tale U
52 Tools of the Trade C
53 Top Dog R
54 Underwater Cave U
55 Unreliable U
56 Vestenmannavnjar Funeral R
57 Vile Duel U
58 Will Do You No Good! C
59 Without a Trace U
60 Adeeb Al-Amid C
61 Andrew Littlejohn C
62 Angus McCloud R
63 Annie Rush C
64 Babette R
65 Barnacle Pete U
66 Butcher Pinchot U
67 Celedoine F
68 Cornelius Van Brock C
69 Faisal U
70 Francois Gaulle dul Motte C
71 Gaspar R
72 Geno U
73 Gerald Hohne R
74 Gillian the Razor C
75 Hoskuld Hardrada R
76 Inil R
77 Inquisitor Bascalle R
78 Javier de Bejarano R
79 Jemy U
80 Joern Keitlsson F
81 Li'l Jim R
82 Marc Pierre U
83 Maria Forlani U
84 Max Discher C
85 Mumblety Peg R
86 Natalia Ivanonva C
87 Nicole Cowbey U
88 Ort Helfir U
89 Pertruccio Garibaldi U
90 Phelan Cole R
91 Ricardo Ramos U
92 Rita del Zepeda C
93 Sabine Montjoy C
94 Sean McCorley R
95 Skeletal Boarding Gang U
96 Velda Conklin C
97 Vestenmannavnjar Archers C
98 Battle of San Felipe C
99 Duel with a Castillian U
100 Eisen Cannon Balls C
101 Eisen Steel U
102 Eye of the Storm R
103 Favor for a Noble C
104 Gem of Warning R
105 Syrneth Powder R
106 The Third Switch C
107 Through the Magic Mirror U
108 Ussuran Brawl U
109 Blockade C
110 Brenden Stafford R
111 By the Gods... R
112 Cafe of Broken Dreams C
113 Cannons of La Bucca U
114 Cheap Cannons C
115 Defense of the Motherland R
116 Diplomatic Envoy R
117 Dry Docks R
118 Fate's Web U
119 Fear and Fire U
120 Hand of the Sirens U
121 High Seas Cannoning C
122 Host (Harvest) R
123 Hostile Harbor C
124 Howls of Vengence C
125 La Bucca Defenses R
126 Marker Barrel U
127 Master of Wind and Tide U
128 Merchant Quarter C
129 Merchant Ship C
130 Montaigne Ship of the Line R
131 Mother in Law U
132 Phantom Topman R
133 Queen Eleanor R
134 Rabbit's Foot C
135 Rats in the Hold R
136 Rum Runners C
137 Rune Knowledge U
138 Secret Stash C
139 Ship's Boat R
140 Ship's Brig U
141 Show of Force U
142 Speak Softly... U
143 Swift Vengeance U
144 Tempting the Portal R
145 The Crow's Nest U
146 The Grey Queen's Price R
147 The Right Place R
148 Tight-Knit Crew R
149 Topaz Pendant C
150 Vendel Smugglers C
151 Vengeful Serpent U
152 Vodacce Pirates U
153 The Hurricane F
154 The Scarlet Roger F
155 Captain Bonnie Maggie F
156 Captain Reis F

2001 7th Sea Iron Shadow

COMPLETE SET (618)		
BOOSTER BOX (48 PACKS)	120.00	200.00
BOOSTER PACK (11 CARDS)	3.00	5.00

1 12-Pound Cannon Volley C
2 16-Pound Cannon Volley C
3 20-Pound Cannon Volley U
4 A Better Offer C
5 A Final Test C
6 A Little Broadside Help F
7 A Little Financial Help U
8 A Little Sailing Help U
9 Almost Missed R
10 Ambush Boarding R
11 Another Betrayal R
12 Away Boarders U
13 Becalmed F
14 Below the Waterline F
15 Betrayal R
16 Better Off Churn F
17 Black Heart F
18 Blocked Passages R
19 Bum Rush R
20 Burn Their Sails U
21 Canister Shot F
22 Carousing C
23 Charge U
24 Cheap Barrels U
25 Close Range Cannon Volley C
26 Cluttered Ship U
27 Courtly Manner F
28 Crossing Swords C
29 Crossing the T R
30 Dead Men Tell No Tales U
31 Derwyddon's Schemes U
32 Desperate Wages U
33 Direct Hit! F
34 Divvying the Plunder U
35 Errant Match C
36 Experience Has Its Rewards R
37 Extra Watch F
38 Eyepatch F
39 False Colors F
40 Fancy Swordplay C
41 Fateful Block R
42 Fire and Steel U
43 Fire Ships U
44 Flogging F
45 Gold Only Buys Obedience C
46 Guns Blazing F
47 Haunted by the Past U
48 Headhunters C
49 He's Mine C
50 Hiding in the Reefs F
51 Hired Swordsman U
52 Holy Vision F
53 Into the Fog F
54 Kiss of Death F
55 Know Your Opponent U
56 Land Lubber U
57 Last Ditch Cannon Attack R
58 Last Second Escape! F
59 Lemons F
60 Lice U
61 Life Raft C
62 Line and Winch F
63 Log of the Black Freighter F
64 Look The Devil in the Eye R
65 Major Hull Damage R
66 Mermaids C
67 Mind Your P's and Q's U
68 Minor Hull Damage F
69 Monkey's Fist U
70 Much Needed Repairs R
71 Nasty Bit o' Luck F
72 No Fun to Be a Captive F
73 No Space for Luxuries U
74 Piles of Skulls U
75 Pistol Hand C
76 Poor Jack F
77 Prayer F
78 Press Gang C
79 Purple Heaves R
80 Queen of the Sea U
81 Reporting Drunk C
82 Retribution C
83 Riposte F
84 Sabotaged Sails F
85 Sailing Under the Jolly Roger F
86 Scurvy C
87 Set Adrift R
88 Skull Shot C
89 Southern Trade Winds U
90 St. Roger's Day C
91 Stand Together C
92 Steal Their Wind F
93 Stirring Speech R
94 Syrneth Guardians U
95 Tar, Tar and More Tar U
96 The Better Part of Valor C
97 The Figurehead Released R
98 The Fury of the Rogers C
99 The General's Plan U
100 The General's Tactics F
101 The Island's Heart R
102 The Next Chapter C
103 The Nibelungen's Price U
104 The Price of Impatience U
105 The Sacrifice U
106 The Sailor's Curse U
107 The Sole Presence R
108 The Wellspring U
109 Théah Eats the Weak C
110 Top Dog U
111 Unreliable U
112 Up and Ready C
113 Very Minor Damage U
114 Vestenmannavnjar Funeral F
115 Vodanken U
116 Wenching F
117 Whatever the Cost R
118 Who Can You Trust? U
119 Wild Party! U
120 Would-Be Adventurers U
121 Would-Be Gunners U
122 Would-Be Traders C
123 Your Word is Your Bond R
124 "Beat You To It!" U
125 "Fire as She Passes!" F
126 "Fire the Chase Guns!" F
127 "It's A Trap." F
128 "Prepare for Boarding!" C
129 "Ramming Speed!" F
130 "Repel Boarders!" C
131 "Take It Like a Man!" F
132 "There's More Where They Came From" F
133 "Will Do You No Good!" C
134 "X" Almost Marks the Spot U
135 Adeeb Al-Amid C
136 Ahmed Khalid F
137 Aimon Riché du Pourisse C
138 Alec Mercer C
139 Aleen Van Ostrand F
140 Allister McGurk C
141 Andre Braudel R
142 Andrei Levovich C
143 Andres Donovich F
144 Andrew Littlejohn F
145 Angus McCloud U
146 Annie Rush C
147 Antonio Aldonez R
148 Augusto de Augustin R
149 Benny Gimble U
150 Benoit "The Buccaneer" Racine U
151 Berserkers C
152 Billy "Bilge Rat" Bones R
153 Brawny Rowers F
154 Brennan U
155 Brutes C
156 Buccaneers F
157 Captive Thugs F
158 Carlos Altenar F
159 Cathwulf Vogt F
160 Celedoine R
161 Cornelius van Brock F
162 Cutthroats F
163 Daniel F
164 Delaina Darling F
165 Delaina Darling F
166 Denny La Bree F
167 Denny La Bree F
168 Domingo Marten de Avila F
169 Dorf Klinderhoff F
170 Dorf Klinderhoff R
171 Dr. Carel Voorhees U
172 Dupre & Hans F
173 Dupre & Hans F
174 Edahgo R
175 Edahgo F
176 Edouard du Chevalier R
177 Egil Bergljot Larrson F
178 Ellena Hawksflight U
179 Entertainers F
180 Fancy Dans C
181 Feeny Bonegnawer U
182 Felipe Jose de Granjero F
183 Fierbas Desaix du Paix U
184 Figaro "Lightfinger" Falisci U
185 Fortunado U
186 François Gaulle du Motte C
187 Frieda Kesler U
188 Galafré Flaubert du Doré U
189 Galley Captives F
190 Gaspar R
191 Gaspar F
192 Gearalt Gilbertine R
193 Geno F
194 Gerard Rois et Reines R
195 Gilles Allais du Crieux F
196 Gillian the Razor F
197 Grendel Thorton F
198 Gris Hallisdottir R
199 Gus Heimfather U
200 Gustolph Hirsch U
201 Gwendolyn Buckminster C
202 Hauptmann von Lichen C
203 Hector Beauchamp du Charouse F
204 Henderson R
205 Henderson F
206 Hernando Ochoa C
207 Ian O'Toole F
208 Inil F
209 Inquisitor Carlino U
210 Isabeau Dubois du Arrent F
211 Jack Tars F
212 Jacob Faust F
213 Jacques Renault R
214 Jaimé Espejo U
215 Jason the Troubadour U
216 Jelena F
217 Jemy C
218 Jensson Cloudmaster R
219 Jibril Al-Khadeem C
220 Jillison Brown F
221 Jimmy Bass R
222 Joern Keitelsson R
223 Johnny Terwilliger C
224 Joseph Gallegos de Avila F
225 Josette Quadros C
226 Juliet Jones C
227 Julius Caligari F
228 Julius Caligari F
229 Kerry Delancy C
230 Ketty Tappan C
231 Kirstov Throat-Mangler U
232 Kitka Moritova C
233 Korintine Nicolovich R
234 Kurt Weinberg F
235 Li'l Jim F
236 Lord Windamshire F
237 Louis Sices du Sices F
238 Lowly Captives C
239 Lt. Juan Rodriguez de Soldano C
240 Lucrezia F
241 Lucrezia R
242 Mabela F
243 Maggie Malone R
244 Maggie Malone C
245 Manuel Dejavez U
246 Marcel Entour F
247 Maria Forlani U
248 Marianna the Cleaner C
249 Marketeers C
250 Master Allen Trel R
251 Maureen Leveque U
252 Michél Rois et Reines F
253 Mohdest Mercanto U
254 Moldy Morris F
255 Montaigne Marines F
256 Morgause Mercuri C
257 Mumblety Peg R
258 Natalia Ivanova F
259 Naughty Dan U
260 Needle Nose Nye F
261 No-Leg William U
262 Noah the Toady King R
263 Nodar the Falcon F
264 Orm Greybeard F
265 Padre Alfonso F
266 Padre Esteban F
267 Pepin R
268 Percis d'Cassell F
269 Pertruccio Garibaldi U
270 Pete "Gang" Greene F
271 Peter Silver F
272 Petro Angelina F
273 Phelan Cole R
274 Phelan Cole F
275 Phineas Flynn F
276 Piotr the Badger C
277 Ramford Riddick U
278 Red Thorfild F
279 Reinheart the Ripper F
280 Reynaldo Pasado F
281 Riant Gaucher R
282 Riggers C
283 Rita Del Zepeda F
284 Rosa Maria de Barcino F
285 Rosamonde du Montaigne F
286 Samuel Sanderson F
287 Samuel Smitts F
288 Samuel Smitts F
289 Santos de los Puentes U
290 Scurvy Dogs F
291 Sean McCorley F
292 Sergeant Benitez U
293 Sergei Nyasvy U
294 Shellbacks C
295 Sidney F
296 Skeletal Brutes F
297 Skeletal Cannon Crew F
298 Skeletal Dans F
299 Skeletal Saboteurs F
300 Skeletal Sail Crew F
301 Solomon Sails U
302 Stench F
303 Svein Hegge Hjermstad U
304 Tarsis the Mad R
305 Ten Barrels Bob F
306 The Bloat C
307 The Navigator U
308 The Raven R
309 Thom Brunner F
310 Thordis Bjerregaard U
311 Timothy le Beau F
312 Torvo Espada R
313 Ulf Karlssen R
314 Ulfgar Jor Bransen C
315 Ulfied Jansson C
316 Ulrich the Unholy F
317 Undead Adventurers C
318 Undead Boarders F
319 Velda Conklin F
320 Velik F
321 Victor of Luthon R
322 Vincenzo de Tonelli U
323 Vivianne Étalon du Toille F
324 Volta R
325 Whalers F
326 William Fodd U
327 William Highport U
328 William Toss F
329 Willie Wilcox R
330 Yr Hägin Brønsson F
331 Zoya the Serpent U
332 "Brother" Mattias Brewer F
333 "Butcher" Pinchot U
334 "Lucky" Vandrad Hallvardson C
335 "Lyin" John Fox F
336 "Magpie" Muscov F
337 "Pincushion" Paolo C
338 "Rigger" Mortis F
339 Across the Mirror F
340 Ancient Training Techniques F
341 Artifact Cannon F
342 Avalon Noble F
343 Back Alley Rum F
344 Battle of San Felipe C
345 Bjørnsson's Horn R
346 Boatload of Jennys F
347 Castillian Merchant Ship F
348 Castillian Swordmaster U
349 Dangerous Cargo F
350 Dead Man's Cave R
351 Doing Time U
352 Eisen Cannons F
353 Escorting the MacDuff C
354 Eye of the Storm F
355 Faerie Path F
356 Fine Rigging F
357 Fine Rope and Tackle F
358 Foul Weather Jack's Map, Part I R
359 Foul Weather Jack's Map, Part II R
360 Foul Weather Jack's Map, Part III R
361 Foul Weather Jack's Map, Part IV R
362 Franzini's Lost Notebooks F
363 Fresh Powder F
364 From The Depths! R
365 Gold Coins F
366 Lady Katerina C
367 Learning the Controls U
368 Lucrezia 's Prophecy F
369 Mark of the Grumfather F
370 Navigational Tools C
371 Passionate Duel F
372 Rose & Cross Apprentice C
373 Save the Princess F
374 Scarlet Gem of Death F
375 Seizing La Boca R
376 Seizing the Forbidden Sea R
377 Seizing the Frothing Sea R
378 Seizing the Mirror R
379 Seizing the Trade Sea R
380 Sidhe Sails F
381 Sinking of the Swan F
382 Stolen Guns U
383 Strength of Destiny C
384 Syrneth Barometer R
385 Syrneth Powder F
386 Syrneth Tiller F
387 Taking El Toro Rojo U
388 The Battle of San Cristobal U
389 The Finest Cannons... F
390 The Firebird R
391 The General's Armor F
392 The Last Shot R
393 The Lost Swordsman Knack R
394 The Ocean's Teeth R
395 The Porté Escape F
396 The Siren's Jaw F
397 Their Captain's Will F
398 Trinkets and Baubles F
399 True Faith U
400 Valor's Cove C

401 Vodacce Valuables F
402 We Needs Us An Ussuran Gunner F
403 Winds of Fate F
404 Wreckers R
405 A Blooded Coin F
406 A Sailor's First Skill C
407 Advanced Gunnery R
408 Advanced Swordsmanship R
409 Advanced Topmanship R
410 Adventuring Galley U
411 Arisent R
412 Armed Brig F
413 Armed Frigate F
414 Armed Sloop F
415 Asprey F
416 Avoid Fate F
417 Belaying Pin C
418 Belit F
419 Berek's Pistols F
420 Berserker School F
421 Between Heaven and Earth R
422 Bite the Bullet U
423 Black Heart of the Sea F
424 Black Siren F
425 Blockade F
426 Bonnie's Knives F
427 Braiding the Strands F
428 Brenden Stafford F
429 Broken Compass Inn C
430 Caligari's Island R
431 Cargo Hook C
432 Cat O' Nine Tails F
433 Cheap Sails F
434 Cleaners R
435 Cross of Virtue U
436 Crystal Earring C
437 Deck Cannons U
438 Defense of the Motherland R
439 Demon Eyes F
440 Drusilla Gallegos de Aldana C
441 El Vago F
442 Ernesto's Power R
443 Fate's Binding R
444 Fate's Blessing R
445 Fear and Fire U
446 Fine Boots C
447 Fine Galley F
448 Flashing Swords Inn C
449 Galleon of the Treasure Fleet C
450 Gold Earring C
451 Good King Sandoval F
452 Good Use of Space F
453 Gosse's Rapier F
454 Grappling Cannon F
455 Grappling Gun R
456 Hammocks R
457 Harpoon C
458 Here There Be Monsters C
459 Hidden Powder Stash U
460 High Seas Cannoning C
461 Hostile Harbor F
462 Jack-of-All-Trades U
463 Jenny House C
464 Kheired-Din's Scimitar F
465 Kheired-Din's Secret F
466 Kodiak Bear F
467 Leegstra School F
468 Long Hand U
469 Loyal Castillian R
470 Loyal Port R
471 Main Gauche C
472 Master Gunner C
473 Master of the Tops C
474 McCormick's Compass F
475 Merchant Ship F
476 Montaigne Ship of the Line R
477 Montaigne Valet C
478 Musket F
479 Musketeers C
480 Native Waters R
481 Necros' Sword F
482 Nød (Intensity) F
483 Only Two Came Out F
484 Orduño's Cutlass F
485 Overstocked C
486 Owl F
487 Persuasion F
488 Phantom Topman R
489 Pistol F
490 Pocket Money F
491 Posh Quarters R
492 Powder Keg Tavern U
493 Reaper's Grip R
494 Reclusive Backers C
495 Red C
496 Red Fox F
497 Reis' Scythe F
498 Respect of your Men R
499 Responsive Helm R
500 Romantic Captive U
501 Ruby Earring C
502 Rum Runners C
503 Safe Path F
504 Scary Tattoo C
505 Secret of the Winds R
506 Señor Ladrón F
507 Seven League Striders F
508 Show of Force C
509 Silver Earring C
510 Small Fortress F
511 Snarling Face R
512 Snow Leopard F
513 Soldano Swordsman School U
514 Speak Softly... U
515 Special Gift F
516 Spectral Aura F
517 Speedy Courier F
518 Stans (Calm) U
519 Steel Earring C
520 Sterk (Wholeness) U
521 Styrke (Strength) F
522 Swivel Gun F
523 Swiveling Cannon F
524 The Burning of the Capital R
525 The Gateway R
526 The General's Fist F
527 The Guiding Gem of Hierro F
528 The Inquisition U
529 The Setine Key F
530 The Sorcerer's Duty R
531 Throwing Knives F
532 Tiger Claws U
533 Treasure Hold F
534 Trickster 's Grin F
535 Two Hands Are Better Than One R
536 Vendel Smugglers F
537 Vengeful Serpent U
538 Villskap (Fury) F
539 Vincenzo Caligari F
540 Ward of the Albatross R
541 Well-Equipped Sick Bay F
542 Willowed Ropes F
543 Yngvild's Axe F
544 "Captain" F
545 "Pack 'em In!" F
546 "Take No Prisoners!" F
547 "We're Doomed!" F
548 Bad Weather C
549 Blood Enemies U
550 Broken Shackles R
551 Caligari's Doom C
552 Crucible of Faith U
553 Eternal Desire F
554 Guilders Say More Than Words C
555 Imprisonment in El Morro C
556 Jacques and the Kire U
557 Lyin' John Flees U
558 Message From the Grave F
559 Packed Gunpowder C
560 Pitching Deck C
561 Surprise Rescue F
562 Taking from the Rich C
563 The Coming Tempest C
564 The Rage of the Vesten F
565 The Trail of Dead F
566 The Value of the Hunt U
567 The Vision Spreads F
568 To the Last Man U
569 Vendel Sorcery F
570 Yngvild's Plan F
571 Corazón del Castille F
572 Eisen Driezack R
573 El Fuego Negro F
574 El Toro Rojo F
575 Freedom's Key F
576 Grenouille du Grâce F
577 Le Prédateur des Mers F
578 Strange Skies F
579 Syrneth Ship R
580 The Black Dawn F
581 The Black Freighter F
582 The Crimson Roger F
583 The Discovery F
584 The Dolphin R
585 The Falcon's Roost F
586 The Freighter F
587 The Hanged Man F
588 The Hurricane F
589 The Leviathan R
590 The Massacre R
591 The Redeemer F
592 The Revensj F
593 The Scarlet Roger F
594 The Sea Lion F
595 The Wayward Soldier R
596 Uncharted Course F
597 Aaron Blackstone R
598 Allende F
599 Amiral Alazais Valoix-Praisse III F
600 Berek F
601 Captain Bonnie McGee F
602 Captain Cosette F
603 Captain Jorund Guttormson F
604 Captain Margaretta Orduño F
605 Captain Melinda Gosse F
606 Captain Necros F
607 Captain Reis F
608 Comte Robert Méchant F
609 Der Kire R
610 Enrique Orduño F
611 Ernesto Castillus F
612 Guy McCormick F
613 Jeremiah Berek F
614 Kheired-Din F
615 Philip Gosse F
616 Reis F
617 The General F
618 Yngvild Olafssdottir F

2001 7th Sea Syrenth Secret

COMPLETE SET (161)		
BOOSTER BOX (36 PACKS)	30.00	40.00
BOOSTER PACK (15 CARDS)	.75	1.25

1 Caltrops C
2 Dalia and Ernesto C
3 El Esoque Occulto C
4 Endings and Beginnings C
5 Expeditous Retreat C
6 Fateful Duel C
7 Flee Your Enemies C
8 Fugitives C
9 Guerilla Tactics C
10 In the Nick of Time C
11 Leaping From Rooftops C
12 Nightblade C
13 Poisoned Wine C
14 Pursue Your Enemies C
15 Regrouping C
16 Seduction C
17 Seize the Reins C
18 Syrneth Lock C
19 The Freighter's Ashes C
20 The Trap Is Sprung C
21 The Witch C
22 Unexpected Reunion C
23 Ussuran Madhouse C
24 Voices of the Dead C
25 Aindriu McKenna C
26 Aldaron the Dark C
27 Alicia Soldano de Granjero C
28 Alison Fairlight C
29 Belinda Thackuray R
30 Carmilla Bernoulli C
31 Cristophé du Fae C
32 Dieter Von Glowen, Shield Man C
33 Dimitri "the Bear" Romanovski F
34 Doña Arantxa Grijalva C
35 Doña Lucia del Torres C
36 Dryope Vestini R
37 EJ Tojo C
38 Erik the Bold C
39 Feathertuft R
40 Felix Guy-Daniel R
41 Graham MacLennan C
42 Halverd Solness R
43 Herrmann Stumpf F
44 Hildegun C
45 Inga Danziger C
46 Ingeborg Davinsson R
47 Kristin Abjornsdottir C
48 Lakov R
49 Lazare Tourville R
50 Listing Peter C
51 Longcoat Lucy C
52 Mad Darius McIntrick C
53 Maria-Soledad Rivera y Aldana R
54 Meraldo Avalos C
55 Noam C
56 Paul Norton R
57 Pedro Alameda C
58 Professora Jacinta Navarro del Garci C
59 Rachel Milligan R
60 Renzo Raymondi R
61 Reynaldo Lucani C
62 Richter Hoffmann C
63 Rose Thornne C
64 Sabira Mallah C
65 Senor Ladron, Second Mate R
66 Skeletal Marketeers C
67 Soner Iqbal C
68 Steel Tooth Bob C
69 The Ooze C
70 Tom "Grave" Stone C
71 Two Pistol Penny C
72 Valery Allamand C
73 Black Stone Veteran C
74 Choose Your Battles C
75 Damsel in Distress C
76 Die Kreuzritter Acolyte C
77 Down with l'Empereur! R
78 Freeing Felipe R
79 MacEachern Blade R
80 Rope Descending Device C
81 Settling the Matter C
82 The Black Glove C
83 The Heroine of San Cristobal C
84 The Horror of the Hook C
85 The Syrneth Rings R
86 Wearing the Black Ring C
87 Ambush From the Shadows C
88 Arciniega's Cordial C
89 Brilliant Disguise C
90 Daylen's Cordial C
91 Die Kruezritter Membership R
92 Dietrich Sword C
93 Diving Apparatus C
94 Don Julio del Bejarano de Castillo R
95 Dust of Irritation C
96 Dust of Petrification C
97 El Puñal Occulto School R
98 Encoding Device C
99 Evangeline Rois et Reines du Rogne R
100 Garrotte C
101 Hidden Compartment C
102 Into the Shadows C
103 Invisible College Membership R
104 Karolan's Drum R
105 Los Vagos Henchman C
106 Los Vagos Membership F
107 Magebane Cordial C
108 Miles Valroux du Martise R
109 Mortis Swordsman School R
110 Multiple Barrel Artillery Piece C
111 Necare Swordsman School R
112 Oil of Sloth C
113 Petrigal's Cordial C
114 Philter of Champions C
115 Rilasciare Membership R
116 Rose and Cross Membership R
117 Rosenkreuz's Secret C
118 Rum Flask C
119 Safe Harbor C
120 Scrying Bowl R
121 Sophia's Daughters Membership F
122 Stronghold of La Bucca R
123 Syrneth Dagger C
124 The Bonita Swordsman School R
125 The Flash Rifle C
126 The Holy Flag of the Creseant Empire R
127 The Jolly Roger of the Black Freighter R
128 The Jolly Roger of the Brotherhood of the Coast F
129 The Jolly Roger of the Crimson Rogers R
130 The Jolly Roger of the Sea Dogs R
131 The Mask of El Vago C
132 The Noble Emblem of the Montaigne Navy F
133 The Noble Flag of the Castillian Armada R
134 The Prized Emblem of the Explorer's Society R
135 The Proud Banner of the Vestenmannavnjar R
136 The Syrneth Secret R
137 The Vow C
138 Uppmann's Coat C
139 Vipera ex Morsi Swordsman School R
140 Gentlemen's Club C
141 Jorund's Warning C
142 Matushka's Gate C
143 Reis' Legacy C
144 The Montaigne Revolution C
145 The Sinking of the Hurricane C
146 Things to Come C
147 Valoix's Crime C
148 La Venganza F
149 The Ram R
150 The Stalward Raider R
151 The Wayward Swan F
152 Reis R
153 Captain Flanagan R
154 Captain Upham R
155 Inquisitor Figueroa R
156 Joaquin Orduño F
157 Kheired-Din, the Reborn R
158 Maria Aloise F
159 Scar R
160 Tyler Jones R
161 Ysabette du Montaigne F

2012 Android Netrunner Core Set '12

1 Noise: Hacker Extraordinaire 1
2 Deja Vu 2
3 Demolition Run 3
4 Stimhack 3
5 Cyberfeeder 3
6 Grimoire 1
7 Corroder 2
8 Datasucker 2
9 Djinn 2
10 Medium 2
11 Mimic 2
12 Parasite 3
13 Wyrm 2
14 Yog.0 2
15 Ice Carver 1
16 Wyldside 2
17 Gabriel Santiago: Consummate Professional 1
18 Account Siphon 2
19 Easy Mark 3
20 Forged Activation Orders 3
21 Inside Job 3
22 Special Order 3
23 Lemuria Codecracker 2
24 Desperado 1
25 Aurora 2
26 Femme Fatale 2
27 Ninja 2
28 Sneakdoor Beta 2
29 Bank Job 2
30 Crash Space 2
31 Data Dealer 1
32 Decoy 2
33 Kate "Mac" McCaffrey: Digital Tinker 1
34 Diesel 3
35 Modded 2
36 The Maker's Eye 3
37 Tinkering 3
38 Akamatsu Mem Chip 2
39 Rabbit Hole 2
40 The Personal Touch 2
41 The Toolbox 1
42 Battering Ram 2
43 Gordian Blade 3
44 Magnum Opus 2
45 Net Shield 2
46 Pipeline 2
47 Aesop's Pawnshop 1
48 Sacrificial Construct 2
49 Infiltration 3
50 Sure Gamble 3
51 Crypsis 3
52 Access to Globalsec 3
53 Armitage Codebusting 3
54 Haas-Bioroid: Engineering the Future 1
55 Accelerated Beta Test 3
56 Adonis Campaign 3
57 Aggressive Secretary 2
58 Archived Memories 2
59 Biotic Labor 3
60 Shipment from Mirrormorph 2
61 Heimdall 1.0 2
62 Ichi 1.0 3
63 Viktor 1.0 2
64 Rototurret 2
65 Corporate Troubleshooter 1
66 Experiential Data 2
67 Jinteki: Personal Evolution 1
68 Nisei MK II 3
69 Project Junebug 3
70 Snare! 3
71 Zaibatsu Loyalty 1
72 Neural EMP 2
73 Precognition 2
74 Cell Portal 2
75 Chum 2
76 Data Mine 2
77 Neural Katana 3
78 Wall of Thorns 3
79 Akitaro Watanabe 1
80 NBN: Making News 1
81 AstroScript Pilot Program 2
82 Breaking News 2
83 Anonymous Tip 2
84 Closed Accounts 2
85 Psychographics 2
86 SEA Source 2
87 Ghost Branch 3
88 Data Raven 3
89 Matrix Analyzer 3
90 Tollbooth 3
91 Red Herrings 2
92 SanSan City Grid 1
93 Weyland Consortium: Building a Better World 1
94 Hostile Takeover 3
95 Posted Bounty 2
96 Security Subcontract 1
97 Aggressive Negotiation 2
98 Beanstalk Royalties 3
99 Scorched Earth 2
CA Corp Actions 1
CC Corp Clicks 1
RA Runner Actions 1
RC Runner Clicks 1
100 Shipment from Kaguya 2
101 Archer 2
102 Hadrian's Wall 2
103 Ice Wall 3
104 Shadow 3
105 Research Station 2
106 Priority Requisition 3
107 Private Security Force 3
108 Melange Mining Corp 2
109 PAD Campaign 3
110 Hedge Fund 3
111 Enigma 3
112 Hunter 2
113 Wall of Static 3

2012 Android Netrunner What Lies Ahead

RELEASED IN DECEMBER 2012
1 Whizzard: Master Gamer
2 Spinal Modem
3 Imp
4 Morning Star
5 Cortez Chip
6 Peacock
7 ZU.13 Key Master
8 The Helpful AI
9 Plascrete Carapace
10 Haas-Bioroid: Stronger Together
11 Mandatory Upgrades
12 Janus 1.0
13 Ash 2X3ZB9CY
14 Braintrust
15 Snowflake
16 Restructured Datapool
17 TMI
18 Project Atlas
19 Caduceus
20 Draco

2013 Android Netrunner A Study in Static

RELEASED IN MARCH 2013
61 Disrupter
62 Force of Nature
63 Scrubber
64 Doppelganger
65 Crescentus
66 Deus X
67 All-nighter
68 Inside Man
69 Underworld Contact
70 Green Level Clearance
71 Hourglass
72 Dedicated Server
73 Bullfrog
74 Uroboros
75 Net Police
76 Weyland Consortium: Because We Built It
77 Government Contracts
78 Tyrant
79 Oversight AI
80 False Lead

2013 Android Netrunner Creation and Control

RELEASED IN JULY 2013
1 Cerebral Imaging: Infinite Frontiers
2 Custom Biotics: Engineered for Success
3 Next Design: Guarding the Net
4 Director Haas' Pet Project
5 Efficiency Committee
6 Project Wotan
7 Sentinel Defense Program
8 Alix T4LB07
9 Cerebral Overwriter
10 Director Haas
11 Haas Arcology AI
12 Thomas Haas
13 Bioroid Efficiency Research
14 Successful Demonstration
15 Heimdall 2.0
16 Howler
17 Ichi 2.0
18 Minelayer
19 Viktor 2.0
20 Zed 1.0
21 Awakening Center
22 Tyr's Hand
23 Gila Hands Arcology
24 Levy University

25 Server Diagnostics
26 Bastion
27 Datapike
28 Rielle "Kit" Peddler: Transhuman
29 The Professor: Keeper of Knowledge
30 Exile: Streethawk
31 Escher
32 Exploratory Romp
33 Freelance Coding Contract
34 Scavenge
35 Levy AR Lab Access
36 Monolith
37 Feedback Filter
38 Clone Chip
39 Omni-drive
40 Atman
41 Cloak
42 Dagger
43 Chakana
44 Cyber-Cypher
45 Paricia
46 Self-modifying Code
47 Sahasrara
48 Inti
49 Professional Contacts
50 Borrowed Satellite
51 Ice Analyzer
52 Dirty Laundry
53 Daily Casts
54 Same Old Thing
55 The Source

2013 Android Netrunner Cyber Exodus

RELEASED IN FEBRUARY 2013
41 Nerve Agent
42 Joshua B.
43 Emergency Shutdown
44 Muresh Bodysuit
45 Snitch
46 Chaos Theory: Wunderkind
47 Test Run
48 Dinosaurus
49 Personal Workshop
50 Public Sympathy
51 Project Vitruvius
52 Viper
53 Edge of World
54 Sunset
55 Marked Accounts
56 Pop-up Window
57 Woodcutter
58 Commercialization
59 Private Contracts
60 Chimera

2013 Android Netrunner Future Proof

RELEASED IN JUNE 2013
101 Retrieval Run
102 Darwin
103 Data Leak Reversal
104 Faerie
105 Mr. Li
106 Indexing
107 R&D Interface
108 Deep Thought
109 New Angeles City Hall
110 Eli 1.0
111 Ruhr Valley
112 Ronin
113 Midori
114 NBN: The World Is Yours*
115 Project Beale
116 Midseason Replacements
117 Flare
118 Dedicated Response Team
119 Burke Bugs
120 Corporate War

2013 Android Netrunner Humanity's Shadow

RELEASED IN MAY 2013
81 Surge
82 Xanadu
83 Andromeda: Dispossessed Ristie
84 Networking
85 HQ Interface
86 Pheromones
87 Quality Time
88 Replicator
89 Creeper
90 Kraken
91 Kati Jones
92 Eve Campaign
93 Rework
94 Whirlpool
95 Hokusai Grid
96 Data Hound
97 Bernice Mai
98 Salvage
99 Simone Diego
100 Foxfire

2013 Android Netrunner Mala Tempora

RELEASED IN DECEMBER 2013
41 Reina Roja: Freedom Fighter
42 Deep Red
43 Knight
44 Running Interference
45 Expert Schedule Analyzer
46 Grifter
47 Torch
48 Woman in the Red Dress
49 Raymond Flint
50 Isabel McGuire
51 Hudson 1.0
52 Accelerated Diagnostics
53 Unorthodox Predictions
54 Sundew
55 City Surveillance
56 Snoop
57 Ireress
58 Power Shutdown
59 Paper Wall
60 Interns

2013 Android Netrunner Opening Moves

RELEASED IN SEPTEMBER 2013
1 Frame Job
2 Pawn
3 Rook
4 Hostage
5 Gorman Drip v1
6 Lockpick
7 False Echo
8 Motivation
9 John Masanori
10 Project Ares
11 NEXT Bronze
12 Celebrity Gift
13 Himitsu-Bako
14 Character Assassination
15 Jackson Howard
16 Invasion of Privacy
17 Geothermal Fracking
18 Swarm
19 Cyberdex Trial
20 Grim

2013 Android Netrunner Second Thoughts

RELEASED ON NOVEMBER 2013
21 Bishop
22 Scheherazade
23 Hard at Work
24 Recon
25 Copycat
26 Leviathan
27 Eureka!
28 Record Reconstructor
29 Prepaid VoicePAD
30 Wotan
31 Hellion Alpha Test
32 Clone Retirement
33 Swordsman
34 Shipment from SanSan
35 Muckraker
36 The Cleaners
37 Elizabeth Mills
38 Off the Grid
39 Profiteering
40 Restructure

2013 Android Netrunner Trace Amount

RELEASED IN JANUARY 2013
21 Vamp
22 Liberated Account
23 Satellite Uplink
24 E3 Feedback Implants
25 Compromised Employee
26 Notoriety
27 Snowball
28 Dyson Mem Chip
29 Encryption Protocol
30 Sherlock 1.0
31 Jinteki: Replicating Perfection
32 Fetal AI
33 Trick of Light
34 Sensei
35 Big Brother
36 ChiLo City Grid
37 Power Grid Overload
38 Amazon Industrial Zone
39 Executive Retreat
40 Freelancer

2014 Android Netrunner All That Remains

81 Bifrost Array 3
82 Sagittarius 3
83 Hostile Infrastructure 3
84 Gemini 3
85 License Acquisitionr 3
86 Daily Business Show 3
90 Snatch and Grab 3
91 Merlin 3
92 Shell Corporation 3
93 Ekomind 3
94 Cerberus "Cuj.0" H3 3
95 Leela Patel 3
96 Cerberus "Rex" H2 3
97 Zona Sul Shipping 3
98 Cybsoft MacroDrive 3
99 Cerberus "Lady" H1 3
100 Utopia Shard 3

2014 Android Netrunner Double Time

RELEASED IN MARCH 2014
101 Singularity
102 Queen's Gambit
103 Dyson Fractal Generator
104 Silencer
105 Savoir-faire
106 Fall Guy
107 Power Nap
108 Paintbrush
109 Lucky Find
110 Gyri Labyrinth
111 Reclamation Order
112 Broadcast Square
113 Corporate Shuffle
114 Caprice Nisei
115 Shinobi
116 Marker
117 Hive
118 Witness Tampering
119 NAPD Contract
120 Quandary

2014 Android Netrunner Fear and Loathing

RELEASED IN FEBRUARY 2014
81 Quest Completed
82 Hemorrhage
83 Tallie Perrault
84 Executive Wiretaps
85 Blackguard
86 CyberSolutions Mem Chip
87 Alpha
88 Omega
89 Blackmail
90 Blue Level Clearance
91 Strongbox
92 Toshiyuki Sakai
93 Yagura
94 Restoring Face
95 Market Research
96 Wraparound
97 GRNDL: Power Unleashed
98 Vulcan Coverup
99 GRNDL Refinery
100 Subliminal Messaging

2014 Android Netrunner Honor and Profit

1 Harmony Medtech: Biomedical Pioneer
2 Nisei Division: The Next Generation
3 Tennin Institute: The Secrets Within
4 House of Knives
5 Medical Breakthrough
6 Philotic Entanglement
7 The Future Perfect
8 Chairman Hiro
9 Mental Health Clinic
10 Psychic Field
11 Shi.Kyu016b
12 Tenma Line
13 Cerebral Cast
14 Medical Research Fundraiser
15 Mushin No Shin
16 Inazuma
17 Komainu
18 Pup
19 Shiro
20 Susanoo-no-Mikoto
21 NeoTokyo Grid
22 Tori Hanzu014d
23 Plan B
24 Guard
25 Rainbow
26 Diversified Portfolio
27 Fast Track
28 Iain Stirling: Retired Spook
29 Ken "Express" Tenma: Disappeared Clone
30 Silhouette: Stealth Operative
31 Calling in Favors
32 Early Bird
33 Express Delivery
34 Feint
35 Legwork
36 Planned Assault
37 Logos
38 Public Terminal
39 Unregistered S&W '35
40 Window
41 Alias
42 Breach
43 Bug
44 Gingerbread
45 Grappling Hook
46 Passport
47 Push Your Luck
48 Security Testing
49 Theophilius Bagbiter
50 Tri-maf Contact
51 Mass Install
52 Q-Coherence Chip
53 Overmind
54 Oracle May
55 Donut Taganes

2014 Android Netrunner The Source

101 Helium-3 Deposit 3
102 Errand Boy 3
103 IT Department 3
104 Markus 1.0 3
105 Industrial Genomics 3
106 Turtlebacks 3
107 Shoot the Moon 3
108 Troll 3
109 Virgo 3
110 Utopia Fragment 3
111 Excalibur 3
112 Self--destruct 3
113 Incubator 3
114 Ixodidae 3
115 Code Siphon 3
116 Collective Consciousness 3
117 Sage 3
118 Bribery 3
119 Au Revoir 3
120 Earthrise Hotel 3

2014 Android Netrunner True Colors

RELEASED IN JANUARY 2014
61 Keyhole
62 Activist Support
63 Lawyer Up
64 Leverage
65 Garrote
66 LLDS Processor
67 Sharpshooter
68 Capstone
69 Starlight Crusade Funding
70 Rex Campaign
71 Fenris
72 Panic Button
73 Shock!
74 Tsurugi
75 TGTBT
76 Sweeps Week
77 RSVP
78 Curtain Wall
79 Punitive Counterstrike
80 Veterans Program

2014 Android Netrunner Up and Over

61 Architect 3
62 Peak Efficiency 3
63 Labyrinthine Servers 3
64 Ashigaru 3
65 Mamba 3
66 Reversed Accounts 3
67 Universal Connectivity Fee 3
68 Blue Sun: Powering the Future 3
69 Changeling 3
70 Reuse 3
71 Hades Fragment 3
72 Docklands Crackdown 3
73 Inject 3
74 Origami 3
75 Fester 3
76 Autoscripter 3
77 Switchblade 3
78 Trade-In 3
79 Astrolabe 3
80 Angel Arena 3

2014 Android Netrunner Upstalk

1 Domestic Sleepers
2 NEXT Silver
3 Lotus Field
4 Mutate
5 Near-Earth Hub: Broadcast Center
6 Primary Transmission Dish
7 Midway Station Grid
8 The Root
9 Taurus
10 Mother Goddess
11 Galahad
12 Bad Times
13 Cyber Threat
14 Lamprey
15 Paper Tripping
16 Power Tap
17 Nasir Meidan: Cyber Explorer
18 Social Engineering
19 Leprechaun
20 Eden Shard

2014 Android Netrunner The Valley

1 Clot
2 Paige Piper
3 Adjusted Chronotype
4 Spike
5 Enhanced Vision
6 Gene Conditioning Shoppe
7 Synthetic Blood
8 Traffic Jam
9 Symmetrical Visage
10 Brain-Taping Facility
11 NEXT Gold
12 Jinteki Biotech
13 Genetic Resequencing
14 Cortex Lock
15 Valley Grid
16 Bandwidth
17 Predictive Algorithm
18 Capital Investors
19 Negotiator
20 Tech Startup
12A The Brewery
12B The Greenhouse
12C The Tank

2015 Android Netrunner Breaker Bay

21 Hacktivist Meeting 3
22 Off-Campus Apartment 3
23 Career Fair 3
24 Dorm Computer 3
25 Hayley Kaplan 3
26 Game Day 3
27 Comet 3
28 Study Guide 3
29 London Library 3
30 Tyson Observatory 3
31 Beach Party 3
32 Research Grant 3
33 Turing 3
34 Crick 3
35 Recruiting Trip 3
36 Blacklist 3
37 Gutenberg 3
38 Student Loans 3
39 Meru Mati 3
40 Breaker Bay Grid 3

2015 Android Netrunner Chrome City

41 Immolation Script 3
42 Skulljack 3
43 Turntable 3
44 Chrome Parlor 3
45 Titanium Ribs 3
46 Crowbar 3
47 Net-Ready Eyes 3
48 Analog Dreamers 3
49 Brain Cage 3
50 Cybernetics Division 3
51 Self-destruct Chips 3
52 Lab Dog 3
53 Oaktown Grid 3
54 Ryon Knight 3
55 Clairvoyant Monitor 3
56 Lockdown 3
57 Little Engine 3
58 Oaktown Renovation 3
59 Corporate Town 3
60 Quicksand 3

2015 Android Netrunner The Underway

61 Faust 3
62 Street Peddler 3
63 Armand Geist Walker 3
64 Drive By 3
65 Forger 3
66 Shiv 3
67 Gang Sign 3
68 Muertos Gang Member 3
69 Chameleon 3
70 Hyperdriver 3
71 Test Ground 3
72 Defective Brainchips 3
73 Allele Repression 3
74 Marcus Batty 3
75 Expose 3
76 Pachinko 3
77 Underway Renovation 3
78 Contract Killer 3
79 Spiderweb 3
80 Underway Grid 3

2015 Android Netrunner The Valley

1 Clot 3
2 Paige Piper 3
3 Adjusted Chronotype 3
4 Spike 3
5 Enhanced Vision 3
6 Gene Conditioning Shoppe 3
7 Synthetic Blood 3
8 Traffic Jam 3
9 Symmetrical Visage 3
10 Brain-Taping Facility 3
11 NEXT Gold 3
12 Jinteki Biotech 3
13 Genetic Resequencing 3
14 Cortex Lock 3
15 Valley Grid 3
16 Bandwidth 3
17 Predictive Algorithm 3
18 Capital Investors 3
19 Negotiator 3
20 Tech Startup 3
12A The Brewery 3
12B The Greenhouse 3
12C The Tank 3

1997 Babylon 5 Premier Edition

COMPLETE SET (446)	150.00	300.00
BOOSTER BOX (24 PACKS)	50.00	60.00
BOOSTER PACK (8 CARDS)	2.00	3.00
STARTER DECK (60 CARDS)	20.00	30.00
RELEASED IN DECEMBER 1997		
1 A Brighter Future R	1.00	2.50
2 A Good Bluff C	.15	.40
3 A Rising Power C	.15	.40
4 Accident C	.20	.50
5 Adira Tyree	.20	.50
6 Affirm Alliance	.40	1.00
7 Affirmation Of Peace	.25	.60
8 Affirmation Of Power	.25	.60
9 Alliance C	.15	.40
10 Alliance Of Races	.40	1.00
11 Approval Of The Grey	.40	1.00
12 Armed Resistance U	.30	.75
13 Armistice C	.15	.40
14 As It Was Meant To Be R	1.00	2.50
15 Ashan	.25	.60
16 Assault Troops U	.30	.75
17 Assigning Blame	.30	.75
18 Attacking Pawns C	.15	.40
19 Avert Incident C	.15	.40
20 Babylon 5 Unrest R	1.00	2.50
21 Backroom Dealing U	.30	.75
22 Balance	.20	.50
23 Battle Tested U	.30	.75
24 Bester R	3.00	8.00
25 Bio-Weapon Discovery R	1.25	3.00
26 Black Market U	.30	.75
27 Blockade R	.75	2.00
28 Blood Oath U	.30	.75
29 Book Of G'Quan	.40	1.00
30 Border Raid	.40	1.00
31 Campaign For Support C	.15	.40
32 Carn Mollari	.25	.60
33 Carpe Diem R	3.00	8.00
34 Casualty Reports R	1.25	3.00
35 Catherine Sakai U	.30	.75
36 Censure U	.30	.75
37 Centauri Agent	.30	.75
38 Centauri Aide	.20	.50
39 Centauri Captain	.25	.60
40 Centauri Prime	.30	.75
41 Centauri Telepath C	.15	.40
42 Change Of Plans C	.20	.50
43 Changing Opinion C	.15	.40
44 Chaos Reigns C	.15	.40
45 Chrysalis U	.25	.60
46 Colonial Fleet - Centauri	.40	1.00
47 Colonial Fleet - Human	.40	1.00
48 Colonial Fleet - Minbari	.40	1.00
49 Colonial Fleet - Narn	.40	1.00
50 Combat Experience C	.15	.40
51 Commerce Raiding U	.30	.75
52 Commercial Telepaths U	.30	.75
53 Compatible Goals U	.30	.75
54 Competing Interests R	1.25	3.00
55 Complete Support U	.30	.75
56 Concealed Weapon C	.25	.60
57 Concentrated Effort C	.15	.40

Card	Low	High
58 Condemn Deportations C	.15	.40
59 Conflicting Desires R	.75	2.00
60 Conflicting Loyalties R	.75	2.00
61 Confusion In Chaos C	.15	.40
62 Consolidated Position R	.75	2.00
63 Contact With Shadows C	.40	1.00
64 Contact With Vorlons	.40	1.00
65 Coordinated Fire C	.15	.40
66 Counterintelligence R	.75	2.00
67 Court The Rebellious C	.15	.40
68 Covert Allies R	.75	2.00
69 Crisis Of Self U	.30	.75
70 Crusade R	1.00	2.50
71 Crystal Cities	.30	.75
72 Cut Supply Lines C	.25	.60
73 Cynthia Torqueman U	.30	.75
74 Damage Control Team R	1.00	2.50
75 Dan Randall C	.15	.40
76 Decisive Tactics	.25	.60
77 Declaration Of War	.25	.60
78 Deep Space Fleet - Centauri	.30	.75
79 Deep Space Fleet - Human	.40	1.00
80 Deep Space Fleet - Minberi C	.40	1.00
81 Deep Space Fleet - Narn	.40	1.00
82 Defame Ambassador C	.20	.50
83 Defense In Depth U	.40	1.00
84 Delenn	.30	.75
85 Delenn Transformed R	1.25	3.00
86 Demonstrative Victory R	.75	2.00
87 Despair R	.75	2.00
88 Destiny Fulfilled	.30	.75
89 Develop Relationship U	.40	1.00
90 Dhaliri U	.30	.75
91 Diplomatic Advantage R	.75	2.00
92 Diplomatic Blunder C	.15	.40
93 Diplomatic Corps C	.15	.40
94 Diplomatic Immunity C	.15	.40
95 Disaffected Centauri R	1.00	2.50
96 Disaffected Human R	1.00	2.50
97 Disaffected Minbari R	1.00	2.50
98 Disaffected Narn R	1.00	2.50
99 Disenchantment U	.30	.75
100 Disgrace R	1.00	2.50
101 Dishonor	.20	.50
102 Draal	.30	.75
103 Draft U	.40	1.00
104 Drazi Sunhawk C	.20	.50
105 Drigo	.40	1.00
106 Du'Nar U	.50	1.25
107 Du'Rog C	.15	.40
108 Durlan C	.15	.40
109 Early Warning	.40	1.00
110 Earth	.25	.60
111 Elric R	1.25	3.00
112 Emergency Military Aid C	.15	.40
113 Emperor Turhan R	2.00	5.00
114 Energy Mines	.40	1.00
115 Enrage U	.30	.75
116 Establish Base U	.40	1.00
117 Euphrates Treaty	.40	1.00
118 Expeditionary Fleet - Centauri	.40	1.00
119 Expeditionary Fleet - Human	.40	1.00
120 Expeditionary Fleet - Minbari	.40	1.00
121 Expeditionary Fleet - Narn	.40	1.00
122 Exploit Opportunities	.30	.75
123 Exploitation C	.15	.40
124 Exploration C	.60	1.50
125 Extended Contacts C	.15	.40
126 Extreme Sanction U	.30	.75
127 Finish The War	.40	1.00
128 First Battle Fleet - Centauri	.40	1.00
129 First Battle Fleet - Human	.30	.75
130 First Battle Fleet - Minbari	.50	1.25
131 First Battle Fleet - Narn	.40	1.00
132 Fixed In Their Ways U	.40	1.00
133 Fleet Of The Line R	2.00	5.00
134 Fleet Support Base	.30	.75
135 Fleets On The Border C	.20	.50
136 Focus Your Efforts U	.30	.75
137 For My People C	.20	.50
138 For The Common Good C	.30	.75
139 For The Good Of All	.40	1.00
140 Forced Commitment R	.75	2.00
141 Forced Evolution R	1.50	4.00
142 Forced Impairment R	1.50	4.00
143 Forces Collide R	1.25	3.00
144 Frederick Lantz	.40	1.00
145 Free The Souls R	1.00	2.50
146 G'Drog C	.20	.50
147 G'Kar	.15	.40
148 G'Sten R	.40	1.00
149 Garrison Fleet U	.40	1.00
150 General Franklin U	.30	.75
151 General Hague	1.25	3.00
152 Glory R	.75	2.00
153 Government Opposition R	2.00	5.00
154 Grey Council Fleet R	.40	1.00
155 Grievance U	.30	.75
156 Growth In Chaos C	1.25	3.00
157 Guilt U	.30	.75
158 Gunboat Diplomacy	.30	.75
159 Harvest Souls R	.75	2.00
160 Hate Crime U	.30	.75
161 Heavy Fleet R	2.00	5.00
162 Hedronn	.40	1.00
163 Hidden Agent	.25	.60
164 Hidden Knowledge	.40	1.00
165 Higher Calling C	.15	.40
166 Hire Raiders C	.15	.40
167 Homeworld Fleet - Centauri	.40	1.00
168 Homeworld Fleet - Human	.40	1.00
169 Homeworld Fleet - Minbari	.40	1.00
170 Homeworld Fleet - Narn	.40	1.00
171 Hour Of The Wolf U	.40	1.00
172 Human Agent	.30	.75
173 Human Aide	.25	.60
174 Human Captain	.25	.60
175 Humanitarian Aid C	.20	.50
176 Hunted	.40	1.00
177 Hunter, Prey C	.15	.40
178 Immolan V U	.30	.75
179 Immortality Serum R	1.50	4.00
180 Imperial Telepaths R	1.25	3.00
181 Imperialism C	.15	.40
182 In The Line Of Duty U	.20	.50
183 Inevitable Destiny R	1.25	3.00
184 Infiltrate And Exploit U	.30	.75
185 Influential Lords U	.40	1.00
186 Internal Strife C	.15	.40
187 Interstellar Corporation C	.15	.40
188 Intolerable Interference U	.30	.75
189 Intrigues Mature C	.20	.50
190 Ipsha Battleglobe U	.25	.60
191 ISN U	.30	.75
192 Isolated U	.40	1.00
193 Isolationism U	.40	1.00
194 It Will Be His Undoing R	1.25	3.00
195 Ja'Doc	.60	1.50
196 Jason Ironheart R	2.50	6.00
197 Jeffrey Sinclair	.40	1.00
198 Jha'Dur R	2.00	5.00
199 John Sheridan R	3.00	8.00
200 Judgment By Success U	.30	.75
201 Kalain	.20	.50
202 Kha'Mak	.25	.60
203 Kidnapping	.25	.60
204 Knowledge Is Power	.40	1.00
205 Knowledge Of Shadows C	.20	.50
206 Knowledge Of The Soul U	.30	.75
207 Ko'Dath	.25	.60
208 Kosh Naranek R	2.00	5.00
209 Lack Of Subtlety C	.15	.40
210 Lady Ladira U	.30	.75
211 Lady Morella	.25	.60
212 Lamentations	.25	.60
213 Latent Telepath C	.15	.40
214 Leading The Races C	.15	.40
215 Learning Experience C	.15	.40
216 Left Vulnerable R	1.00	2.50
217 Lennier	.40	1.00
218 Level The Playing Field 3+9	.25	.60
219 Limited Strike	.40	1.00
220 Liquidating Assets C	.25	.60
221 Lockdown C	.25	.60
222 Londo Mollari	.25	.60
223 Long Term Investment C	.15	.40
224 Lord Kiro U	.40	1.00
225 Lord Refa U	.30	.75
226 Lord Valo C	.15	.40
227 Loss Of Face C	.15	.40
228 Loss Of Support U	.30	.75
229 Lovell C	.15	.40
230 Luis Santiago R	2.50	6.00
231 Luxuries Of Homeworld U	.40	1.00
232 Lyndisty C	.15	.40
233 Lyta Alexander	.25	.60
234 Maintain The Peace R	1.25	3.00
235 Marcus Cole R	2.50	6.00
236 Markab Fleet R	1.25	3.00
237 Mars Colony	.30	.75
238 Martyr R	1.25	3.00
239 Mary Ann Cramer C	.15	.40
240 Mass Drivers U	.30	.75
241 Meddling With Others U	.30	.75
242 Medical Assistance	.30	.75
243 Meditation C	.25	.60
244 Merchandising B5 C	.15	.40
245 Miagi Hidoshi	.40	1.00
246 Michael Garibaldi	.40	1.00
247 Military Cadre C	.15	.40
248 Military Telepaths U	.30	.75
249 Minbar	.40	1.00
250 Minbari Agent	.25	.60
251 Minbari Aide	.25	.60
252 Minbari Captain	.30	.75
253 Minbari Protectorate U	.50	1.25
254 Minbari Telepath	.25	.60
255 Mines U	.40	1.00
256 Minister Malachi R	2.00	5.00
257 Moral Quandary C	.15	.40
258 Morden R	2.00	5.00
259 Motivated Leaders R	.75	2.00
260 Mr. Adams U	.30	.75
261 Muddy The Waters C	.15	.40
262 N'Grath	.40	1.00
263 Na'Far U	.30	.75
264 Na'Ka'Leen Feeder C	.15	.40
265 Na'Kal	.30	.75
266 Na'Toth	.40	1.00
267 Narn Agent	.40	1.00
268 Narn Aide	.40	1.00
269 Narn Captain	.40	1.00
270 Narn Homeworld	.40	1.00
271 Narn Rabble U	1.00	2.50
272 Negotiated Surrender R	.50	1.25
273 Neroon U	.30	.75
274 Neutrality Treaty C	.15	.40
275 Never Again	.30	.75
276 News Of Defeat U	.30	.75
277 News Of Galactic Import C	.30	.75
278 Nightmares U	.30	.75
279 No Escape R	1.25	3.00
280 Non-Aggression Pact C	.15	.40
281 Non-Aligned Support U	.30	.75
282 Not Meant To Be R	2.50	6.00
283 Observers R	1.00	2.50
284 Older But Wiser C	.15	.40
285 Order Above All R	1.50	4.00
286 Overworked C	.40	1.00
287 Parliament Of Dreams R	.75	2.00
288 Paying For Sins R	.75	2.00
289 Peace In Our Time	.40	1.00
290 Peacekeeping U	.25	.60
291 Personal Enemies U	.25	.60
292 Personal Involvement	.40	1.00
293 Personal Protection U	.30	.75
294 Personal Sacrifice	.40	1.00
295 Picket Fleet - Centauri	.40	1.00
296 Picket Fleet - Human	.40	1.00
297 Picket Fleet - Minbeni	.40	1.00
298 Picket Fleet - Narn	.40	1.00
299 Planetary Defenses C	.15	.40
300 Political Realignment U	.40	1.00
301 Popular Support	.40	1.00
302 Power Politics	.40	1.00
303 Power Posturing R	.75	2.00
304 Precision Strike U	.40	1.00
305 Prolonged Talks R	1.00	2.50
306 Prophecy	.40	1.00
307 Protests R	1.00	2.50
308 Proxima III U	.40	1.00
309 Psi Attack U	.30	.75
310 Psi Bodyguard	.25	.60
311 Psi Corps Intelligence	.40	1.00
312 Psi Interrogation C	.15	.40
313 Public Apology R	.75	2.00
314 Pulling Strings C	.20	.50
315 Purge The Disloyal U	.30	.75
316 Quadrant 14	.30	.75
317 Quadrant 37 U	.30	.75
318 Rabble Rousers U	.30	.75
319 Racial Hatred R	.75	2.00
320 Ragesh III	.40	1.00
321 Raid Shipping U	.30	.75
322 Rally The People R	1.25	3.00
323 Rally To The Cause C	.20	.50
324 Ramming R	1.00	2.50
325 Ranger Strike Team U	.30	.75
326 Rangers Surveillance R	1.25	3.00
327 Rathenn R	2.00	5.00
328 Recalled To Service R	1.00	2.50
329 Refugees	.30	.75
330 Religious Caste U	.40	1.00
331 Renowned Victory	.30	.75
332 Repairing The Past	.30	.75
333 Rescue U	.30	.75
334 Reserve Fleet U	.30	.75
335 Retribution	.30	.75
336 Revenge	.40	1.00
337 Reverse Advances R	1.25	3.00
338 Rise Of The Republic	.40	1.00
339 Rise To Power	.30	.75
340 Rivalry	.30	.75
341 Rogue Soul Hunter R	1.25	3.00
342 Saber Rattling U	.30	.75
343 Sabotage	.25	.60
344 Salvage Yard R	1.25	3.00
345 Sanctions C	.15	.40
346 Sandra Hiroshi C	.15	.40
347 Sarah U	.40	1.00
348 Second Battle Fleet - Centauri	.50	1.25
349 Second Battle Fleet - Human	.50	1.25
350 Second Battle Fleet - Minbari	.50	1.25
351 Second Battle Fleet - Narn	.50	1.25
352 Secondary Control R	.75	2.00
353 Secondary Experience	.25	.60
354 Secret Police U	.25	.60
355 Secret Strike R	1.50	4.00
356 Secret Vorlon Aid C	.20	.50
357 Security Training U	.30	.75
358 Seduction C	.20	.50
359 Seizing Advantage R	1.25	3.00
360 Self Doubt C	.15	.40
361 Senator Voudreau U	.30	.75
362 Servants Of Order	.20	.50
363 Shadow Assault U	.40	1.00
364 Shadow Strike U	.30	.75
365 Shakat R	1.50	4.00
366 Shal Mayan	.25	.60
367 Short Term Goals	.40	1.00
368 Short Term Investment C	.15	.40
369 Shunned U	.30	.75
370 Skeletons In The Closet R	1.25	3.00
371 Sleeper Personality	.40	1.00
372 Sleeping Z'ha'dum R	2.00	5.00
373 Sneak Attack C	.25	.60
374 Sortie C	.15	.40
375 Soul Hunter U	.30	.75
376 Special Ops C	.15	.40
377 Spin Doctors R	.75	2.00
378 Sponsor Rebels U	.40	1.00
379 Stealth Technology R	1.50	4.00
380 Stephen Franklin	.50	1.25
381 Stop Hostilities	.40	1.00
382 Strafing Run C	.15	.40
383 Strategic Reassignment C	.15	.40
384 Strength In Adversity U	.30	.75
385 Strike Fleet U	.60	1.50
386 Subliminal Influence U	.30	.75
387 Successful Manipulation U	.30	.75
388 Supplement Security	.20	.50
389 Support Babylon 5	.50	1.25
390 Support Of The Mighty U	.50	1.25
391 Susan Ivanova	.40	1.00
392 Ta'Lon	.40	1.00
393 Talia Winters	.30	.75
394 Technological Espionage C	.20	.50
395 Telepathic Scan	.25	.60
396 Temptations C	.20	.50
397 Terrorist Bombings U	.30	.75
398 Test Their Mettle	.30	.75
399 The Eye R	3.00	8.00
400 The Great Machine R	2.50	6.00
401 The Hope Of Peace U	.30	.75
402 The Opposition Rises C	.15	.40
403 The Price Of Power	.25	.60
404 Thenta Makur R	2.50	6.00
405 Third Battle Fleet - Centauri R	.75	2.00
406 Third Battle Fleet - Minbari U	2.00	5.00
407 Total War R	1.25	3.00
408 Trade Pact	.25	.60
409 Trade Windfall C	.25	.60
410 Transfer Point To U	.30	.75
411 Triluminary U	.30	.75
412 Tu'Pari R	2.50	6.00
413 Under Pressure U	.40	1.00
414 Underworld Connections	.30	.75
415 United Front	.30	.75
416 Universe Today Feature C	.15	.40
417 Unrecognized Data C	.15	.40
418 Upgraded Defenses	.60	1.50
419 Urza Jaddo	.30	.75
420 Utility Fleet - Centauri C	.40	1.00
421 Utility Fleet - Human C	.40	1.00
422 Utility Fleet - Narn C	.40	1.00
423 Vendetta R	.75	2.00
424 Victory In My Grasp	.30	.75
425 Vir Cotto	.40	1.00
426 Vital Interests R	1.00	2.50
427 Vorlon Enhancement R	2.00	5.00
428 Vorlon Rescue R	.75	2.00
429 Vree Saucers R	1.25	3.00
430 War By Popular Decree C	.15	.40
431 War College C	.15	.40
432 War Hero	.25	.60
433 Warleader Shakiri R	3.00	8.00
434 Warleader's Fleet R	2.00	5.00
435 Warren Keffer C	.15	.40
436 Warrior Caste R	.75	2.00
437 Wear And Tear U	.30	.75
438 What Do You Want? C	.25	.60
439 Who Are You? C	.20	.50
440 Wind Swords U	.40	1.00
441 Witness Protection R	1.25	3.00
442 Working Relationship U	.30	.75
443 Wounded R	1.00	2.50
444 You Are Not Ready	.75	2.00
445 You Know My Reputation	.40	1.00
446 Zack Allen U	.40	1.00

1998 Babylon 5 Deluxe Edition

Card	Low	High
COMPLETE SET (380)	200.00	250.00
BOOSTER BOX (24 PACKS)	30.00	40.00
BOOSTER PACK (8 CARDS)	1.25	2.00
RELEASED ON		
1 A Brighter Future R1	1.25	3.00
2 A Good Bluff C	.15	.40
3 A Rising Power C	.15	.40
4 Accident C	.15	.40
5 Adira Tyree	.25	.60
6 Affirmation Of Power	.25	.60
7 Alliance C	.25	.60
8 Approval Of The Grey	.25	.60
9 Armed Resistance U	.30	.75
10 Armistice C	.15	.40
11 As It Was Meant To Be R	3.00	8.00
12 As It Was Meant To Be - misprint R		
13 Assault Troops U	.30	.75
14 Attacking Pawns C	.15	.40
15 Avert Incident C	.15	.40
16 Babylon 5 Unrest R3	1.00	2.50
17 Backroom Dealing U	.30	.75
18 Balance	.30	.75
19 Battle Tested U	.30	.75
20 Bester R1	3.00	8.00
21 Bio-Weapon Discovery R1	1.25	3.00
22 Black Market U	.50	1.25
23 Blockade R1	1.00	2.50
24 Blood Oath U	.30	.75
25 Border Raid	.30	.75
26 Campaign For Support C	.15	.40
27 Carpe Diem R1	2.50	6.00
28 Casualty Reports R1	.75	2.00
29 Catherine Sakai U	.30	.75
30 Censure U	.40	1.00
31 Centauri Agent	.20	.50
32 Centauri Aide	.20	.50
33 Centauri Captain	.20	.50
34 Centauri Telepath C	.15	.40
35 Change Of Plan C	.15	.40
36 Changing Of Plans C	.15	.40
37 Changing Opinion C	.20	.50
38 Chaos Reigns C	.15	.40
39 Chrysalis U	.25	.60
40 Colonial Fleet - Centauri	.30	.75
41 Colonial Fleet - Human	.30	.75
42 Colonial Fleet - Minbari	.25	.60
43 Colonial Fleet - Narn	.30	.75
44 Combat Experience C	.15	.40
45 Commerce Raiding U	.40	1.00
46 Commerical Telepaths U	.40	1.00
47 Compatible Goals U	.30	.75
48 Competing Interests R1	1.25	3.00
49 Complete Support U	.30	.75
50 Concealed Weapon C	.40	1.00
51 Concentrated Effort C	.30	.75
52 Condemn Deportations C	.30	.75
53 Conflicting Desires R1	.75	2.00
54 Conflicting Loyalties R1	.75	2.00
55 Confusion In Chaos C	.15	.40
56 Consolidated Position R1	.75	2.00
57 Contact With Shadows C	.30	.75
58 Contact With Vorlons C	.30	.75
59 Coordinated Fire C	.20	.50
60 Counterintelligence R1	.75	2.00
61 Court The Rebellious C	.15	.40
62 Covert Allies R1	1.00	2.50
63 Crisis Of Self U	.30	.75
64 Crusade R1	.75	2.00
65 Cut Supply Lines C	.15	.40
66 Cynthia Torqueman U	.50	1.25
67 Damage Control Team R1		
68 Dan Randall C	.15	.40
69 Declaration Of War	.40	1.00
70 Deep Space Fleet - Centauri	.40	1.00
71 Deep Space Fleet - Human	.40	1.00
72 Deep Space Fleet - Minberi C	.25	.60
73 Deep Space Fleet - Narn	.40	1.00
74 Defame Ambassador C	.15	.40
75 Defense In Depth U	.75	2.00
76 Delenn Transformed R1	2.00	5.00
77 Demonstrative Victory R1	.75	2.00
78 Despair R1	.75	2.00
79 Destiny Fulfilled	.20	.50
80 Develop Relationship U	.40	1.00
81 Dhaliri U	.30	.75
82 Diplomatic Advantage R1	.75	2.00
83 Diplomatic Blunder C	.30	.75
84 Diplomatic Corps C	.15	.40
85 Diplomatic Immunity C	.15	.40
86 Disaffected Centauri R3	1.25	3.00
87 Disaffected Human R3	1.25	3.00
88 Disaffected Minbari R3	1.25	3.00
89 Disaffected Narn R3	1.25	3.00
90 Disenchantment U	.40	1.00
91 Disgrace R1	.75	2.00
92 Draft U	.30	.75
93 Drazi Sunhawk C	.20	.50
94 Du'Nar U	.50	1.25
95 Du'Rog C	.20	.50
96 Durlan C	.30	.75
97 Early Warning	.30	.75
98 Elric R1	1.50	4.00
99 Emergency Military Aid C	.15	.40
100 Emperor Turhan R1	2.50	6.00
101 Energy Mines	.30	.75
102 Enrage U	.30	.75
103 Establish Base U	.30	.75
104 Exploit Opportunities	.40	1.00
105 Exploitation C	.15	.40
106 Extended Contacts C	.15	.40
107 Extreme Sanction U	.40	1.00
108 Finish The War	.40	1.00
109 First Battle Fleet - Centauri	.50	1.25
110 First Battle Fleet - Human	.40	1.00
111 First Battle Fleet - Minberi	.40	1.00
112 First Battle Fleet - Narn	.40	1.00
113 Fixed In Their Ways U	.30	.75
114 Fleet Of The Line R1	2.50	6.00
115 Fleet Support Base	.25	.60
116 Fleets On The Border C	.20	.50
117 Focus Your Efforts U	.40	1.00
118 For My People C	.25	.60
119 For The Common Good C	.30	.75
120 For The Good Of All	.30	.75
121 Forced Commitment R1	.75	2.00
122 Forced Evolution R1	1.50	4.00
123 Forced Impairment R3	2.00	5.00
124 Forces Collide R3	1.00	2.50
125 Frederick Lantz	.40	1.00
126 Free The Souls R1	.75	2.00
127 G'Drog C	.20	.50
128 G'Sten R1	1.50	4.00
129 Garrison Fleet U	.30	.75
130 General Franklin U	.30	.75
131 General Hague	.30	.75
132 Glory R1	1.00	2.50
133 Government Opposition R1	1.00	2.50
134 Grey Council Fleet R1	2.50	6.00
135 Grievance U	.40	1.00
136 Growth In Chaos C	.30	.75
137 Guilt U	.40	1.00
138 Gunboat Diplomacy	.30	.75
139 Harvest Souls R1	1.00	2.50
140 Hate Crime U	.30	.75
141 Heavy Fleet R1	2.00	5.00
142 Hidden Agent	.30	.75
143 Hidden Knowledge	.25	.60
144 Higher Calling C	.30	.75
145 Hire Raiders C	.25	.60
146 Hour Of The Wolf U	.30	.75
147 Human Agent	.30	.75
148 Human Aide	.40	1.00
149 Human Captain	.25	.60
150 Humanitarian Aid C	.30	.75
151 Hunted	.30	.75
152 Hunter, Prey C	.15	.40
153 Immolan V U	.30	.75
154 Imperial Telepaths R1	1.25	3.00
155 Imperialism C	.30	.75
156 In The Line Of Duty U	.50	1.25
157 Inevitable Destiny R1	.75	2.00
158 Infiltrate And Exploit U	.40	1.00
159 Influential Lords U	.30	.75
160 Internal Strife C	.20	.50
161 Interstellar Corporation C	.15	.40
162 Intolerable Interference U	.15	.40
163 Intrigues Mature C	.15	.40
164 Ipsha Battleglobe U	.40	1.00
165 ISN U	.30	.75
166 Isolated U	.25	.60
167 Isolationism U	.25	.60
168 It Will Be His Undoing R3	1.00	2.50
169 Ja'Doc	.50	1.25
170 John Sheridan R1	5.00	12.00
171 Judgment By Success U	.30	.75
172 Kha'Mak	.30	.75
173 Knowledge Is Power	.40	1.00
174 Knowledge Of Shadows C	.20	.50
175 Knowledge Of The Soul U	.40	1.00
176 Kosh Naranek R1	3.00	8.00
177 Lack Of Subtlety C	.30	.75
178 Lady Ladira U	.40	1.00
179 Lamentations	.30	.75
180 Latent Telepath C	.15	.40
181 Leading The Races C	.15	.40

182 Learning Experience C .15 .40
183 Left Vulnerable R1 .75 2.00
184 Liquidating Assets C .15 .40
185 Lockdown C .15 .40
186 Long Term Investment C .15 .40
187 Lord Kiro U .30 .75
188 Lord Refa U .40 1.00
189 Lord Valo C .15 .40
190 Loss Of Face C .15 .40
191 Loss Of Support U .40 1.00
192 Lovell C .15 .40
193 Luis Santiago R1 2.50 6.00
194 Luxuries Of Homeworld U .50 1.25
195 Lyndistry C .15 .40
196 Maintain The Peace R1 1.00 2.50
197 Marcus Cole R1 2.00 5.00
198 Markab Fleet R1 1.00 2.50
199 Martyr R1 1.00 2.50
200 Mary Ann Cramer C .15 .40
201 Mass Drivers U .30 .75
202 Meddling With Others U .30 .75
203 Medical Assistance .40 1.00
204 Meditation C .30 .75
205 Merchandising B5 C .25 .60
206 Military Cadre C .30 .75
207 Military Telepaths U .50 1.25
208 Minbari Agent .40 1.00
209 Minbari Aide .30 .75
210 Minbari Captain .30 .75
211 Minbari Protectorate U .30 .75
212 Mines U .30 .75
213 Minister Malachi R1 2.00 5.00
214 Moral Quandary C .15 .40
215 Morden R1 3.00 8.00
216 Motivated Leaders R1 .75 2.00
217 Mr. Adams U .20 .50
218 Muddy The Waters C .15 .40
219 Na'Far U .75 2.00
220 Na'Ka'Leen Feeder C .15 .40
221 Narn Agent .40 1.00
222 Narn Aide .30 .75
223 Narn Captain .40 1.00
224 Narn Rabble U .30 .75
225 Negotiated Surrender R1 .75 2.00
226 Neroon U .30 .75
227 Neutrality Treaty C .15 .40
228 News Of Defeat U .30 .75
229 News Of Galactic Import C .20 .50
230 Nightmares U .30 .75
231 No Escape R1 .75 2.00
232 Non-Aggression Pact C .15 .40
233 Non-Aligned Support U .40 1.00
234 Not Meant To Be R3 2.50 6.00
235 Observers R1 .75 2.00
236 Older But Wiser C .15 .40
237 Order Above All R1 2.50 6.00
238 Overworked C .15 .40
239 Parliament Of Dreams R1 .75 2.00
240 Paying For Sins R1 .75 2.00
241 Peace In Our Time .40 1.00
242 Peacekeeping U .40 1.00
243 Personal Enemies U .50 1.25
244 Personal Involvement .30 .75
245 Personal Protection U .30 .75
246 Personal Sacrifice .30 .75
247 Picket Fleet - Centauri .30 .75
248 Picket Fleet - Human .40 1.00
249 Picket Fleet - Minbari .30 .75
250 Picket Fleet - Narn .30 .75
251 Planetary Defenses C .15 .40
252 Political Realignment U .30 .75
253 Power Posturing R1 .75 2.00
254 Power Posturing - Text From Covert Allies R1
255 Precision Strike U .30 .75
256 Prolonged Talks R1 1.00 2.50
257 Prophecy .30 .75
258 Protests R1 .75 2.00
259 Proxima III U .40 1.00
260 Psi Attack U .40 1.00
261 Psi Bodyguard .30 .75
262 Psi Interrogation C .15 .40
263 Public Apology R1 1.00 2.50
264 Pulling Strings C .15 .40
265 Purge The Disloyal U .30 .75
266 Quadrant 14 .40 1.00
267 Quadrant 37 U .50 1.25
268 Rabble Rousers U .30 .75
269 Racial Hatred R1 .75 2.00
270 Ragesh III .30 .75
271 Raid Shipping U .50 1.25
272 Rally The People R1 1.50 4.00
273 Rally To The Cause C .15 .40
274 Ramming R1 1.25 3.00
275 Ranger Strike Team U .40 1.00
276 Rangers Surveillance R1 1.25 3.00
277 Rathenn R1 1.50 4.00
278 Recalled To Service R1 2.00 5.00
279 Refugees .25 .60
280 Religious Caste U .30 .75
281 Renowned Victory .20 .50
282 Repairing The Past .30 .75
283 Rescue U .40 1.00
284 Reserve Fleet U .40 1.00
285 Retribution .20 .50
286 Reverse Advances R1 1.25 3.00
287 Rise To Power .30 .75
288 Rivalry .25 .60
289 Rogue Soul Hunter R1 1.25 3.00
290 Saber Rattling U .30 .75
291 Sabotage .30 .75
292 Salvage Yard R1 1.25 3.00
293 Sanctions C .15 .40
294 Sandra Hiroshi C .20 .50
295 Sarah U .30 .75
296 Second Battle Fleet - Centauri .40 1.00
297 Second Battle Fleet - Human .40 1.00
298 Second Battle Fleet - Minbari .40 1.00
299 Second Battle Fleet - Narn .40 1.00
300 Secondary Control R1 .75 2.00
301 Secondary Experience .30 .75
302 Secret Police U .50 1.25
303 Secret Strike R1 2.00 5.00
304 Secret Vorlon Aid C .15 .40
305 Security Training U .40 1.00
306 Seduction C .15 .40
307 Seizing Advantage R1 2.00 5.00
308 Self Doubt C .15 .40
309 Senator Voudreau U .25 .60
310 Servants Of Order .30 .75
311 Shadow Assault U .40 1.00
312 Shadow Strike U .40 1.00
313 Shakat R1 1.50 4.00
314 Shal Mayan .25 .60
315 Short Term Goals .40 1.00
316 Short Term Investment C .15 .40
317 Shunned U .30 .75
318 Skeletons In The Closet R1 1.00 2.50
319 Sleeper Personality .30 .75
320 Sleeping Z'Ha'Dum R1 2.00 5.00
321 Sneak Attack C .15 .40
322 Sortie C .30 .75
323 Soul Hunter U .30 .75
324 Special Ops C .15 .40
325 Spin Doctors R1 1.00 2.50
326 Sponsor Rebels U .30 .75
327 Stealth Technology R1 1.50 4.00
328 Stop Hostilities .40 1.00
329 Strafing Run C .15 .40
330 Strategic Reassignment C .15 .40
331 Strength In Adversity U .30 .75
332 Strike Fleet U .30 .75
333 Subliminal Influence U .30 .75
334 Successful Manipulation U .30 .75
335 Support Babylon 5 .20 .50
336 Support Of The Mighty U .40 1.00
337 Technological Espionage C .25 .60
338 Telepathic Scan .40 1.00
339 Temptations C .20 .50
340 Terrorist Bombings U .30 .75
341 Test Their Mettle .25 .60
342 The Hope Of Peace U .30 .75
343 The Opposition Rises C .15 .40
344 The Price Of Power .40 1.00
345 Thenta Makur R1 2.00 5.00
346 Third Battle Fleet - Centauri R1 2.00 5.00
347 Third Battle Fleet - Minbari U .30 .75
348 Total War R1 1.25 3.00
349 Trade Pact .20 .50
350 Trade Windfall C .15 .40
351 Transfer Point To U .30 .75
352 Triluminary U .30 .75
353 Tu'Pari R1 2.50 6.00
354 Under Pressure U .40 1.00
355 United Front .40 1.00
356 Universe Today Feature C .15 .40
357 Unrecognized Data C .20 .50
358 Utility Fleet - Centauri C .40 1.00
359 Utility Fleet - Human C .25 .60
360 Utility Fleet - Narn C .40 1.00
361 Vendetta R1 .75 2.00
362 Victory In My Grasp .25 .60
363 Vital Interests R3 1.00 2.50
364 Vorlon Enhancement R1 2.00 5.00
365 Vorlon Rescue R1 .75 2.00
366 Vree Saucers R1 1.25 3.00
367 War By Popular Decree C .15 .40
368 War College C .25 .60
369 War Hero .30 .75
370 Warleader Shakiri R1 2.50 6.00
371 Warleader's Fleet R1 2.50 6.00
372 Warren Keffer C .15 .40
373 Warrior Caste R1 1.00 2.50
374 Wear And Tear U .40 1.00
375 What Do You Want? C .15 .40
376 Who Are You? C .25 .60
377 Wind Swords U .40 1.00
378 Witness Protection R1 .75 2.00
379 Working Relationship U .30 .75
380 Wounded R1 .75 2.00
381 You Are Not Ready .40 1.00
382 You Know My Reputation .40 1.00
383 Zack Allen U .40 1.00

1998 Babylon 5 The Shadows Expansion

COMPLETE SET (203) 100.00 200.00
BOOSTER BOX (24 PACKS) 40.00 50.00
BOOSTER PACK (8 CARDS) 1.25 2.00
1 A Final Statement R .75 2.00
2 A Moment Of Beauty U .40 1.00
3 Act Of War C .15 .40
4 Additional Force R 1.50 4.00
5 Aiding The Shadows C .15 .40
6 Aiding The Vorlons C .15 .40
7 Ambassador Kosh R 2.50 6.00
8 Ambitious Captain C .15 .40
9 Ancient Rivals U .30 .75
10 Annex Neutral World R 2.00 5.00
11 Assassination Device R 1.00 2.50
12 Associates Revealed U .15 .40
13 At Peak Performance U .40 1.00
14 Atmospheric Fighters C .15 .40
15 Attack Babylon 5 R 3.00
16 Block Progress C .15 .40
17 Bloodied But Unbowed C .15 .40
18 Body Armor U .30 .75
19 Border World U .30 .75
20 Brother Theo C .15 .40
21 Build Infrastructure U .50 1.25
22 Bureaucracy U .30 .75
23 Calenn R 3.00
24 Calling The Shots R 1.00 2.50
25 Casualties C .15 .40
26 Catastrophic Damage U .40 1.00
27 Centauri Beta I R .75 2.00
28 Change Of Direction R 1.50 4.00
29 Commander Ivanova U .75 2.00
30 Conquered Holding U .40 1.00
31 Consumed By Shadows R 1.50 4.00
32 Convincing Words C .15 .40
33 Corrupted Destiny U .30 .75
34 Coup De Grace R 1.50 4.00
35 Covering Weaknesses R 1.50 4.00
36 Damaged From Within R 1.50 4.00
37 Debt Of Gratitude C .15 .40
38 Dedicated Follower R 3.00
39 Delay The War C .15 .40
40 Directing Events C .15 .40
41 Disciple of Light R 3.00
42 Disruption C .15 .40
43 Elder Races Triumph U .40 1.00
44 Eliminate Threats R .75 2.00
45 Emergency Repairs C .15 .40
46 Emperor Cartagia R 2.00 5.00
47 Entil'Zha R 2.50 6.00
48 Extermination U .30 .75
49 Factional Inertia R .75 2.00
50 Fast Learner R 1.50 4.00
51 Followers Of G'Quan R 3.00
52 Force The Issue C .15 .40
53 Forging Alliances R .75 2.00
54 Freedom Of Choice R .75 2.00
55 Gather Rebels R .75 2.00
56 Glitch C .15 .40
57 Government Aid R .75 2.00
58 Government Hostility U .40 1.00
59 Grey Council Servitor U .40 1.00
60 Growing Skepticism R .75 2.00
61 Healing Artifact R 1.00 2.50
62 Heavy Resistance R 1.50 4.00
63 Held Back R 1.00 2.50
64 Heralds Of The Grey R 1.50 4.00
65 Hidden Corruption R .75 2.00
66 Hidden Safehouse C .15 .40
67 High Level Connections U .30 .75
68 Hollow Victory R .75 2.00
69 Impasse C .15 .40
70 In Chaos, Uncertainty R 1.50 4.00
71 In The Spotlight R .75 2.00
72 Information Overload R 1.50 4.00
73 Internal Opposition U .40 1.00
74 Into Their Own U .40 1.00
75 Knowledge, Then Action R .75 2.00
76 Lashing Out R .75 2.00
77 Learn Their Weakness R .75 2.00
78 Leaving The Past U .40 1.00
79 Liberating Resources U .40 1.00
80 Looking Ahead R 1.50 4.00
81 Lord Mollari R 2.00 5.00
82 Lost In Shadows R 1.50 4.00
83 Low Morale U .30 .75
84 Loyal Guardsmen U .40 1.00
85 Managed Growth R 3.00
86 Manifest Destiny R .75 2.00
87 Military Buildup U .40 1.00
88 Minbari Fighting Pike U .40 1.00
89 Mindwipe R 3.00
90 Minister Virini U .75 2.00
91 Misdirected Force U .75 2.00
92 Mobilize Reserves C .15 .40
93 Modern Refit C .15 .40
94 Monks R 3.00
95 Mr. Morden R 3.00 8.00
96 Muster Support U .40 1.00
97 Mysterious Protections R .75 2.00
98 Na'Mel U .40 1.00
99 New Opportunities R 1.00 2.50
100 New Priorities R 3.00
101 Nightwatch Agent C .15 .40
102 Nightwatch Enforcers U .30 .75
103 No Alternatives U .40 1.00
104 Not Alone R 1.50 4.00
105 Not In Vain C .15 .40
106 Observation Post U .75 2.00
107 Obstacles To Victory R 3.00
108 Over The Brink R .75 2.00
109 Peaceful Solutions R .75 2.00
110 Permanent Wound R .75 2.00
111 Personal Insult C .15 .40
112 Political Pull R .75 2.00
113 Portents U .40 1.00
114 PPG Rifle U .40 1.00
115 Preeminence R 2.00 5.00
116 Prejudice Grows U .75 2.00
117 Presidential Coup R 1.50 4.00
118 Prey On The Weak C .15 .40
119 Prove Your Worth R 1.50 4.00
120 Psionic Pacification R .75 2.00
121 Public Outcry C .15 .40
122 Puppeteer R 3.00 8.00
123 Raising The Stakes R .75 2.00
124 Rampage U .40 1.00
125 Ranger Operations R .75 2.00
126 Rapid Recovery C .15 .40
127 Rebuilding Effort C .15 .40
128 Recalled R .75 2.00
129 Recover And Regroup R .75 2.00
130 Reducing Risk U .30 .75
131 Reeling From The Blows U .40 1.00
132 Refusal To Yield R .75 2.00
133 Reluctant Allies R .75 2.00
134 Removed From Power C .15 .40
135 Reverse Engineering U .40 1.00
136 Search For Direction C .15 .40
137 Sebastian R 1.50 4.00
138 Seeds Of Anarchy U .40 1.00
139 Senator Young R 1.50 4.00
140 Shadow Aid U .30 .75
141 Shadow Medallion R 1.50 4.00
142 Shadow Retribution R .75 2.00
143 Shadow Ship U .40 1.00
144 Sigma 957 R .75 2.00
145 Slow Poison U .40 1.00
146 Slow Recovery C .15 .40
147 Sowing Unrest C .15 .40
148 Special Intelligence R 3.00
149 Spread Unrest R .75 2.00
150 Squandered Chances C .15 .40
151 Stagnation R .75 2.00
152 Statement Of Position U .40 1.00
153 Status Quo R 1.50 4.00
154 Stim Addiction R .75 2.00
155 Stolen Spoils R 3.00
156 Stripped Bare R 1.50 4.00
157 Support Fleet - Centauri C .15 .40
158 Support Fleet - Human C .15 .40
159 Support Fleet - Minbari C .15 .40
160 Support Fleet - Narn C .15 .40
161 Survey In Force U .40 1.00
162 Sworn To Shadows R 1.50 4.00
163 Taking Credit R .75 2.00
164 Taralenn II R 3.00
165 Telekinesis R .75 2.00
166 Temporary Aid C .15 .40
167 Test Of Merit U .75 2.00
168 The Long Night C .15 .40
169 The Lure Of Shadow R .75 2.00
170 The Vorlons Respond R .75 2.00
171 The White Star R 1.50 4.00
172 The Young Races Rise R .75 2.00
173 Their Own Destiny C .15 .40
174 Things To Come C .15 .40
175 To Fight Legends U .40 1.00
176 To Stand Alone R 1.50 4.00
177 To The Victor R .75 2.00
178 Tolonius VII U .30 .75
179 Too Predictable U .40 1.00
180 Trivial Gains C .15 .40
181 Troubles Brewing C .15 .40
182 Twisting The Knife U .30 .75
183 Uncertain Followers C .15 .40
184 Uncertain Futures R .75 2.00
185 Underground Resistance C .15 .40
186 Undermine Trust R 1.50 4.00
187 Unheralded Losses R .75 2.00
188 Unsung Hero R 2.00 5.00
189 Va'Kal R .75 2.00
190 Vorlon Cruiser U .40 1.00
191 Vorlon Protection U .40 1.00
192 Vorlon Proxy C .15 .40
193 Vorlon Space R 3.00
194 Vorlons Ascendent C .15 .40
195 Walkabout R .75 2.00
196 We Can't Allow That C .15 .40
197 When Duty Calls R .75 2.00
198 William Morgan Clark R 2.00 5.00
199 Withdrawal C .15 .40
200 Z'Ha'Dum Awakened R 1.50 4.00
201 Za'Thras R .75 2.00
202 Zath'ras C .15 .40
203 Zathras' U .30 .75

1999 Babylon 5 Psi Corps Expansion

COMPLETE SET (196) 80.00 150.00
BOOSTER BOX (24 PACKS) 20.00 30.00
BOOSTER PACK (8 CARDS) 1.00 1.50
1 A Better Place R 1.50 4.00
2 A New Era C .15 .40
3 A Time For Peace U .30 .75
4 Abbut U .30 .75
5 Acclaim C .15 .40
6 Acknowledge Legitimacy U .30 .75
7 Administrator Drake .20 .50
8 Afraid Of The Dark U .30 .75
9 Age Of Exploration C .15 .40
10 Alfred Bester R 4.00 10.00
11 Alisa Beldon C .15 .40
12 Anarchy R 1.50 4.00
13 Anti-Telepath Virus R 2.00 5.00
14 Arms Race C .15 .40
15 At Any Cost U .30 .75
16 Balus R 1.50 4.00
17 Be Seeing You .15 .40
18 Bester .20 .50
19 Bester's Black Omega R 1.50 4.00
20 Black Omega Auxiliary .25 .60
21 Black Omega Fighters .30 .75
22 Black Omega Pilot .30 .75
23 Black Omega Squadron U .30 .75
24 Blackmail .20 .50
25 Block C .15 .40
26 Bloodhound .20 .50
27 Build Bridges C .15 .40
28 Burnt From Both Ends C .15 .40
29 Burnt Out C .15 .40
30 Byron R 2.50 6.00
31 Cease-Fire C .15 .40
32 Centauri Festival U .30 .75
33 Challenge Psi Corps U .30 .75
34 Chen Hikaru .30 .75
35 Come Join Us .15 .40
36 Commerical Telepaths .25 .60
37 Conspiracy C .15 .40
38 Continued Progress U .30 .75
39 Convene The Grey Council R 1.50 4.00
40 Cyborg Reconstruction R 2.00 5.00
41 Cynthia And Rosa U .30 .75
42 Danger Sense .15 .40
43 Dark Talia R 3.00 8.00
44 David C .15 .40
45 Diplomatic Recognition C .15 .40
46 Direct Link C .15 .40
47 Divide And Conquer U .30 .75
48 Don't You Trust Me? C .15 .40
49 Doomed Conspiracy R 2.00 5.00
50 Drop Your Barriers .15 .40
51 Dust C .15 .40
52 Earth .15 .40
53 Ego Boost C .15 .40
54 Elite Black Omega R 1.50 4.00
55 Empathy .20 .50
56 Exercises Of The Mind .15 .40
57 Expanded Network .25 .60
58 Expendable U .30 .75
59 Exposed C .15 .40
60 Forget Something? R 1.50 4.00
61 Front Page Exposure U .30 .75
62 Gestalt R 1.50 4.00
63 Good To Go U .30 .75
64 Gordon .20 .50
65 Greed U .30 .75
66 Guerillas U .30 .75
67 Harriman Gray .40 1.00
68 Hidden Hand C .15 .40
69 Hole In Your Mind U .50 1.25
70 Homeworld Fleet .25 .60
71 Hunting The Blips R 2.00 5.00
72 I'd Die First U .30 .75
73 Informant R 1.50 4.00
74 Insufficient Support C .15 .40
75 Internal Disruptions U .30 .75
76 Irrelevant R 1.50 4.00
77 Is That The Whole Truth? C .15 .40
78 Isdrell R 1.50 4.00
79 Jason' Gift R 1.50 4.00
80 Jecinda U .30 .75
81 Jonathan Harris U .30 .75
82 Juphar Trkider U .30 .75
83 Katz R 2.00 5.00
84 Kelsey .25 .60
85 Korrinine R 1.50 4.00
86 Last Ditch Effort C .15 .40
87 Laurel Takashima R 1.50 4.00
88 Lavindra R 1.50 4.00
89 Level The Playing Field .15 .40
90 Like Unto The Gods U .30 .75
91 Lindstrom C .15 .40
92 Lise Hampton C .15 .40
93 Living Legends U .30 .75
94 Make Them Angry C .20 .50
95 Manipulate The Masters R 2.00 5.00
96 Mass Rioting R 2.00 5.00
97 Master Manipulation U .30 .75
98 Master Of Deception U .40 1.00
99 Master Plan .15 .40
100 Matthew Stoner .20 .50
101 Military Telepaths .15 .40
102 Mind Games .20 .50
103 Minds That Matter C .15 .40
104 Mindwalkers U .30 .75
105 Misdirection R 1.50 4.00
106 Miss Constance C .15 .40
107 Mistaken Identity C .15 .40
108 Mother Ship Alpha R 2.00 5.00
109 Movekk U .30 .75
110 My Hands Are Tied R 1.50 4.00
111 Negotiation Deadline U .30 .75
112 Nejokk C .15 .40
113 Night Of The Long Knives R 2.00 5.00
114 No Surprises C .15 .40
115 Nobody Can Stop Us .30 .75
116 Not Without A Fight U .30 .75
117 Nowhere But Down R 1.50 4.00
118 Obey .15 .40
119 Open Season R 2.00 5.00
120 Oqmrritkz C .15 .40
121 Ostracized U .30 .75
122 Our Last, Best Hope R 1.50 4.00
123 Overwhelming Emotions R 1.50 4.00
124 Pain .15 .40
125 Personal Quest C .15 .40
126 Picket Fleet .25 .60
127 Political Firestorm C .15 .40
128 Proxima III .15 .40
129 Psi Academy C .15 .40
130 Psi Attack .15 .40
131 Psi Bodyguard .15 .40
132 Psi Corps Intelligence .15 .40
133 Psi Suppressors C .15 .40
134 Psionic Sabotage C .15 .40
135 Psychic Blunder C .15 .40
136 Pundits U .30 .75
137 Punitive Sanctions C .15 .40
138 Religious Festival C .15 .40
139 Repairing The Past .20 .50
140 Reparations R 2.50 6.00
141 Reprogrammer U .40 1.00
142 Reprogramming Team U .30 .75
143 Resigned To His Fate U .30 .75
144 Revenge Is Sweet C .15 .40
145 Rogue C .15 .40
146 Saboteurs C .15 .40
147 Sanctity Of The Mind C .15 .40
148 Sara C .15 .40
149 Say What They Want C .15 .40
150 Secret Police .20 .50
151 Sector 90 U .30 .75
152 Seeing Shadows U .30 .75
153 Seeking Knowledge R 1.50 4.00
154 Sh'Sak R 1.25 3.00
155 Star Chamber U .30 .75
156 Steal Skills .30 .75
157 Stealing Secrets R 1.50 4.00
158 Stirring Rebuke U .30 .75
159 Strike Back R 1.50 4.00
160 Syria Planum .20 .50
161 Tactical Error U .30 .75

162 Talia Winters .25 .60
163 Team Player U .30 .75
164 Telepath Colony U .30 .75
165 Telepath For Hire C .15 .40
166 Telepath Hunter U 1.50 4.00
167 Telepath Recruiters R 1.00
168 Telepathic Revenge C .15 .40
169 Telepathic Scan .20 .50
170 That's The Spirit U .30 .75
171 The Badge And The Gloves .40 1.00
172 The Corps Is Mother .40 1.00
173 The Growing Conspiracy U .30 .75
174 The Mind's Eye .15 .40
175 The Spider's Web C .15 .40
176 They Are Not For You R 2.00 5.00
177 They're Just Mundanes R 2.00 5.00
178 Thirteen R 1.25 3.00
179 Thomas U .40 1.00
180 Thought Police R 1.50 4.00
181 Trade Pact .15 .40
182 Tunnel Of Life And Death R 1.50 4.00
183 Unauthorized Scan C .15 .40
184 Underground Leader R 2.00 5.00
185 Underground Railroad U .30 .75
186 Underutilized Resources U .30 .75
187 Universal Enemy R 1.50 4.00
188 Utility Fleet .15 .40
189 Visions In Time R 1.50 4.00
190 Wade R 2.00 5.00
191 War Of Information C .15 .40
192 Wastelands .30 .75
193 We Are Both Damned U .30 .75
194 We Think Alike U .30 .75
195 William Edgars R 1.00 2.50
196 Zathras R 1.50 4.00

1999 Babylon 5 Severed Dreams Expansion

COMPLETE SET (150) 60.00 120.00
BOOSTER BOX (24 PACKS) 120.00 150.00
BOOSTER PACK (8 CARDS) 6.00 8.00
1 50 Credits A Week C .15 .40
2 A Shot In The Dark R 1.25 3.00
3 A World Gone Mad U .30 .75
4 Alexander R 1.25 3.00
5 Alien Scum C .15 .40
6 Alyt U .30 .75
7 Alyt Neroon R 1.50 4.00
8 Anti-Psi Training C .15 .40
9 Assume Authority R 1.00 2.50
10 Attache U .40 1.00
11 Attache Cotto R 1.50 4.00
12 Attack The Underlings C .30 .75
13 Between You And The Abyss R 1.00 2.50
14 Breaching Pod C .15 .40
15 Cannot Run Out Of Time U .30 .75
16 Captain Sheridan - Contingencies R 2.00 5.00
17 Captain Sheridan - Extra Card R 1.50 4.00
18 Captain Sinclair R 1.50 4.00
19 Carve Up The Galaxy U .30 .75
20 Citizen G'Kar R 2.00 5.00
21 Cocksure U .30 .75
22 Compensation U .30 .75
23 Councilor Na'Far R 1.50 4.00
24 Courtly Intrigue C .20 .50
25 Cult Of Personality U .30 .75
26 Deep Agent C .15 .40
27 Deeron C .15 .40
28 Defuse The Situation U .30 .75
29 Delenn - Lennier R 1.50 4.00
30 Delenn - Promote R 1.50 4.00
31 Delenn - Transformer R 1.50 4.00
32 Den'sha R 1.00 2.50
33 Desperate Measures U .30 .75
34 Disinformation U .30 .75
35 Do As You Are Told R 1.00 2.50
36 Dogfight U .40 1.00
37 Domestic Concerns C .15 .40
38 Doomed Expedition U .30 .75
39 Double-Cross C .15 .40
40 Draal The Caretaker R 1.25 3.00
41 Dwindling Resources R 1.25 3.00
42 Efficiency Engineers C .15 .40
43 Entil'zha Delenn R 1.50 4.00
44 Evacuation C .15 .40
45 Executive Aide U .30 .75
46 Eye Of The Storm R 1.00 2.50
47 Facing Oblivion C .15 .40
48 Fifth Column U .30 .75
49 Flashback R 1.00 2.50
50 Foiled Scheme C .15 .40
51 Force Them Back U .30 .75
52 Friendliness And Forgotten C .15 .40
53 G'Kar R .40 1.00
54 G'Kar Foresaken R 2.00 5.00
55 Giant Fusion Bomb U 1.50 4.00
56 Gravity Well C .15 .40
57 Handy Dandy Micro Helper R 1.25 3.00
58 Head On A Pike C .15 .40
59 Hello, Old Friend U .40 1.00
60 Honored Position U .30 .75
61 How Dare You? U .30 .75
62 Incentives C .15 .40
63 Information Control U .30 .75
64 Jane R 1.25 3.00
65 Journalistice Integrity C .15 .40
66 Kha'Ri Citadel R 1.25 3.00
67 Lady Dagger R 1.50 4.00
68 Lady Mariel U .30 .75
69 Lady Timov U .30 .75
70 Lise Hampton Edgars U .30 .75
71 Londo Mollari - Diplomat R 2.00 5.00
72 Londo Mollari - Gambler R 1.50 4.00
73 Londo's Wives U .30 .75
74 Major Krantz C .15 .40
75 Malcontent C .15 .40
76 Man For All Seasons R 1.25 3.00
77 Mass Carnage R 1.25 3.00
78 Mister Allan R 1.50 4.00
79 Mister Welles R 1.00 2.50
80 Mutual Understanding U .30 .75
81 Natural Born Leader C .15 .40
82 Nay-Sayer C .15 .40
83 Nest Of Vipers U .30 .75
84 Nightwatch Collaborators U .30 .75
85 No One Returns U .30 .75
86 Not The One U .30 .75
87 Now He's Ready C .15 .40
88 Nuclear Bluff U .30 .75
89 Number One R 1.25 3.00
90 Offer A Position C .15 .40
91 Our Own People First C .20 .50
92 Oversight Committee U .30 .75
93 Overwhelmed C .15 .40
94 Paparazzi C .15 .40
95 Pariah U .30 .75
96 Partnership For Peace C .15 .40
97 Penultimate Revenge U .30 .75
98 Pestilence, Famine, Death U .30 .75
99 Pierce Macabee U .30 .75
100 Predestination U .30 .75
101 Prime Minister Refa R 1.50 4.00
102 Psi World R 1.50 4.00
103 Psychopath C .15 .40
104 Quartermaster U .15 .40
105 Question Authority C .15 .40
106 Ranger Lennier R 1.50 4.00
107 Rapid Aging U .30 .75
108 Redeemed U .30 .75
109 Resist Control C .15 .40
110 Right Makes Might U .30 .75
111 Rising Star U .30 .75
112 Senator King U .30 .75
113 Shining Beacon In Space R 1.25 3.00
114 Silent Majority U .30 .75
115 Sniper C .15 .40
116 Snoop C .15 .40
117 Steal Babylon 4 C .15 .40
118 Suicide Run C .15 .40
119 Sycophant C .15 .40
120 Tacticians U .30 .75
121 Taking Sides C .15 .40
122 The Conspiracy Deepens C .15 .40
123 The Hive U .30 .75
124 The Messiah Effect R 1.00 2.50
125 The One R 1.25 3.00
126 The Path To Peace C .15 .40
127 They're Killing Us U .30 .75
128 Thug C .15 .40
129 Time Jump R 1.25 3.00
130 Time Stabilizer C .15 .40
131 Toast To Victory C .15 .40
132 Tonia Wallis C .15 .40
133 Trakis R 1.50 4.00
134 Triple-Cross R 1.25 3.00
135 Under Our Protection U .30 .75
136 Unstuck In Time R 1.25 3.00
137 Valen's War R 1.25 3.00
138 VIP Involvement R 1.25 3.00
139 War Crimes Trial R 1.25 3.00
140 Warriors Council C .15 .40
141 Watch Your Back C .15 .40
142 We Die For The One U .30 .75
143 Why Are You Here? R 1.00 2.50
144 Why Are You Hitting Me? C .15 .40
145 With Us Or Against Us C .15 .40
146 Written In The Stars C .15 .40
147 Xenophobia C .15 .40
148 You Have A Destiny U .30 .75
149 You Three Are One R 1.50 4.00
150 Zathras Who Was R 1.25 3.00

2000 Babylon 5 Crusade Expansion

COMPLETE SET (159) 200.00 300.00
BOOSTER BOX (24 PACKS) 200.00 250.00
BOOSTER PACK (9 CARDS) 8.00 10.00
RELEASED IN OCTOBER 2000
1 A Call For Help R 1.25 3.00
2 A Crusade For A Cure C .20 .50
3 A Crusade For A Legacy C .12 .30
4 A Crusade For Knowledge C .20 .50
5 A Crusade For Profit C .12 .30
6 A Dying People C .12 .30
7 A Good Lead C .20 .50
8 A Warning R 1.50 4.00
9 Above It All R 1.50 4.00
10 Accommodations C .15 .40
11 Age Of Conquest R 1.50 4.00
12 Agents Durkani And Lyssa R 2.00 5.00
13 Ain't I A Stinker? UR 5.00 12.00
14 Alien Takeover U .40 1.00
15 All In The Cards R 1.50 4.00
16 Alliance Superfleet R 2.00 5.00
17 Alwyn U .40 1.00
18 Ancient Data Crystal R 1.50 4.00
19 Andre Sabbat U .30 .75
20 Apocalypse Box U .30 .75
21 Apriori Flentak And Nix R 1.50 4.00
22 Archaeologist D. Taylor U .40 1.00
23 Arsenal Of Yesterdays C .20 .50
24 Automated Fleet U .40 1.00
25 Bio-Adaptive Shielding C .20 .50
26 Blaylock R 2.00 5.00
27 Bruder U .60 1.50
28 Captain Daniels U .50 1.25
29 Captain Lochley - Closeup UR 5.00 12.00
30 Captain Lochley - Sitting UR 6.00 15.00
31 Collaboration R 1.50 4.00
32 Collar Gun U .30 .75
33 Corporations Go On U .30 .75
34 Death Incarnate C .12 .30
35 Death Of A Planet R 2.00 5.00
36 Death Of Culture U .50 1.25
37 Detailed Data Analysis C .30 .75
38 Dire Consequences R 2.00 5.00
39 Dr. Sarah Chambers - Brown Smock UR 6.00 15.00
40 Dr. Sarah Chambers - Purple Smock UR 5.00 12.00
41 Duel To The Death C .15 .40
42 Dureena Nafeel - Peering Out Of A Hole UR 5.00 12.00
43 Dureena Nafeel - Standing UR 5.00 12.00
44 Electron Incantation U .30 .75
45 Elizabeth Trent R 2.00 5.00
46 EVA Salvaging U .40 1.00
47 Everything Has A Price R 2.00 5.00
48 Excalibur R 4.00 10.00
49 Exodus R 1.50 4.00
50 Explore Vorlon Space R 1.50 4.00
51 Faces In Stone U .40 1.00
52 Far Reaching Schemes R 1.25 3.00
53 Final Destiny U .30 .75
54 Fireball C .12 .30
55 First Contact Protocols U .30 .75
56 Forced Down R 2.00 5.00
57 Galen - Holding Fire UR 6.00 15.00
58 Galen - With Hood And Staff UR 5.00 12.00
59 Galen's Crystal Ball U .30 .75
60 Galen's Magic Rock R 2.00 5.00
61 Galen's Ship R 2.50 6.00
62 Galen's Staff C .12 .30
63 General Ivanova R 5.00 12.00
64 Genius Loci R 1.50 4.00
65 Ghost Ship C .12 .30
66 Goods And Services C .12 .30
67 High-Tech Weapons C .12 .30
68 Holo-Demons R 1.50 4.00
69 Holo-Dragon R 2.00 5.00
70 Homunculus C .20 .50
71 How To Succeed In Business R 2.00 5.00
72 Hyperspace Getaway C .12 .30
73 Illegal Raid U .30 .75
74 Invisibility U .30 .75
75 IPX Official C .25 .60
76 Isabelle R 1.50 4.00
77 Isabelle's Quest R 2.00 5.00
78 Jacob Redway U .30 .75
79 John Matheson - Blue/Black Uniform UR 6.00 15.00
80 John Matheson - Grey/Red Uniform UR 6.00 15.00
81 Kevin Sprach U .40 1.00
82 Kulan U .50 1.25
83 Lemm Uh'Ekim C .20 .50
84 Leonard Anderson U .30 .75
85 Lieutenant Carr U .30 .75
86 Lieutenant Tewart C .15 .40
87 Lise Hampton Edgars Garibaldi R 2.00 5.00
88 Lorkans C .15 .40
89 M. Garibaldi, CEO R 10.00 25.00
90 Main Gun U .30 .75
91 Marata Fleet C .25 .60
92 Mars Conference UR 5.00 12.00
93 Matthew Gideon - Blue/Black Uniform UR 6.00 15.00
94 Matthew Gideon - Grey/Red Uniform UR 6.00 15.00
95 Max Eilerson - Close Up UR 5.00 12.00
96 Max Eilerson - Sitting On Ledge UR 5.00 12.00
97 Meddling With The Unknown C .20 .50
98 Monopoly U .30 .75
99 Mr. Jones C .15 .40
100 Nantech Plague U .30 .75
101 Natchok Var U .30 .75
102 Navigator Robertson C .20 .50
103 New Team C .15 .40
104 New Uniforms C .20 .50
105 Not Dead Yet R 1.50 4.00
106 Nova Dreadnoughts R 12.00 30.00
107 Nowhere To Hide R 1.50 4.00
108 Null Field C .15 .40
109 Onslaught U .30 .75
110 Opportunity Knocks C .12 .30
111 Organelle Transfer C .12 .30
112 Out Of My Sky C .20 .50
113 Personal Crusade C .12 .30
114 Pieces Of The Puzzle C .12 .30
115 Portrait Of The Past C .12 .30
116 Pro Zeta Corporation U .30 .75
117 Probes C .12 .30
118 Protected C .12 .30
119 Psychic Projection C .12 .30
120 Quarantine U .30 .75
121 Quick To Anger U .30 .75
122 Record Returns U .30 .75
123 Red Tape U .30 .75
124 Refuge C .12 .30
125 Reign Of Terror C .12 .30
126 Relaxation R 1.50 4.00
127 Repeating Lasers U .30 .75
128 Retributive Strike R 2.00 5.00
129 Robert Conner C .30 .75
130 Samuel Drake U .40 1.00
131 Serendipity C .20 .50
132 Shady Dealings C .15 .40
133 Sogayu U .40 1.00
134 Something Always Happens U .30 .75
135 Special Agent Kendarr UR 25.00 60.00
136 Surprising Allies U .30 .75
137 Survivor's Guilt U .40 1.00
138 Tactical Nuke C .12 .30
139 Techno-Virus R 1.50 4.00
140 The Circle Is Joined R 2.50 6.00
141 The Fen C .12 .30
142 The Tech U .40 1.00
143 The Truth Is Out C .12 .30
144 Thieves' Guild U .30 .75
145 Tomorrow's Children R 1.50 4.00
146 Trace Miller U .30 .75
147 Trial By Fire U .30 .75
148 Trulann U .30 .75
149 Ulterior Motives C .25 .60
150 Undercover Investigation C .20 .50
151 Victory R 3.00 8.00
152 Warlock Destroyers U .30 .75
153 We'll Take Over U .40 1.00
154 Well Of Forever U .40 1.00
155 Who's Your Little Pak'ma'ra? UR 6.00 15.00
156 Working Together U .30 .75
157 Yabc Floba R 2.00 5.00
158 Yellow Journalism U .40 1.00
159 You Are Expendable C .12 .30

2000 Babylon 5 Wheel Of Fire Expansion

COMPLETE SET (152) 100.00 200.00
BOOSTER BOX (24 PACKS) 120.00 150.00
BOOSTER PACK (9 CARDS) 5.00 6.00
1 Agitation U .30 .75
2 Airlock Mishap C .20 .50
3 All Alone In The Night C .15 .40
4 Alliance Fleet R 1.50 4.00
5 And So It Begins U .30 .75
6 Attack The Shadows C .15 .40
7 Barren Worlds R 1.50 4.00
8 Black Rose Killer C .15 .40
9 Blow The Jump Gate U .30 .75
10 Blue Narn R 1.50 4.00
11 Brakiri Priest R 1.25 3.00
12 Bread And Circuses U .40 1.00
13 Breaking News C .15 .40
14 But We're Your Allies C .15 .40
15 Captain Ivanova R 1.50 4.00
16 Chief Allan R 2.00 5.00
17 Conquest Fleet U .40 1.00
18 Contest The Presidency C .15 .40
19 Cooperative Measure C .15 .40
20 Coplann U .40 1.00
21 Corporate Connections R 2.00 5.00
22 Cosmopolis U .30 .75
23 Councilor La'Shan U .40 1.00
24 Crawling Chaos C .15 .40
25 Dangerous Game C .15 .40
26 Dark Legacy U .30 .75
27 Declaration Of Principles C .15 .40
28 Destroy Them From Within U .30 .75
29 Disillusioned Garbaldi R 1.50 4.00
30 Doctor Sheridan R 1.25 3.00
31 Drakh Armada R 2.50 6.00
32 Drakh Entire U .30 .75
33 Drakh Mothership U .75 2.00
34 Drakh Raiders C .15 .40
35 Drazi Merchant C .15 .40
36 Drone Fleet R 1.50 4.00
37 Elizabeth Lochley - Cost 10 R 2.00 5.00
38 Elizabeth Lochley - Nightwatch R 2.00 5.00
39 Emperor Mollari II - Old UR 5.00 12.00
40 Emperor Mollari II - Young UR 4.00 10.00
41 Emperor Refa R 1.50 4.00
42 Errand Of Mercy U .40 1.00
43 Espers R 1.50 4.00
44 Expelled C .15 .40
45 Feast Of Lights R 1.50 4.00
46 Flying Fortress U .50 1.25
47 Foment Discord C .15 .40
48 Force Omega U .50 1.25
49 Forell C .15 .40
50 Free Trade C .15 .40
51 G'Obel R .40 1.00
52 General Na'Tok U .30 .75
53 Gerontocracy U 1.50 4.00
54 Guilds U .40 1.00
55 Hindsight R 2.00 5.00
56 Interstellar Alliance C .15 .40
57 ISA President C .15 .40
58 It Stops Here R 1.50 4.00
59 Ivory Towers C .15 .40
60 Kill Them All C .15 .40
61 King Arthur R 1.50 4.00
62 Kirrin U .30 .75
63 Kullenbrak R 1.25 3.00
64 Lady Na'Toth R 1.25 3.00
65 Lazarenn U .40 1.00
66 League Spokesbeing U .40 1.00
67 Legacy Of Power R 1.50 4.00
68 Let The Galaxy Burn C .15 .40
69 Lieutenant Corwin R 1.50 4.00
70 Llort Bodyguard C .15 .40
71 Lyta Released R 2.50 6.00
72 Main Battlefleet R 1.50 4.00
73 Major Lianna Kemmer U .30 .75
74 Manish'tushu U .30 .75
75 Master Of Darkness C .15 .40
76 Media Circus R 1.50 4.00
77 Medical Database C .15 .40
78 Megalopolis U .30 .75
79 Minister Chorlini U .30 .75
80 Miziri Tal R 1.50 4.00
81 Mutual Defense C .15 .40
82 My Good Friend U .40 1.00
83 Napar'ishu C .15 .40
84 Newton's Third Law R 1.50 4.00
85 Nug/Ulg U .40 1.00
86 Open Aggression R 2.00 5.00
87 Opportunism R 1.25 3.00
88 Organic Technology U .40 1.00
89 Outfoxed C .15 .40
90 Pak'ma'ra's Hump C .15 .40
91 Point Of No Return C .15 .40
92 Power Of Darkness C .15 .40
93 Power Supreme U .40 1.00
94 President Sheridan R 2.00 5.00
95 Prohibited Area C .15 .40
96 Proof Of Genocide U .30 .75
97 Psychedelic Program C .15 .40
98 Psychic Trauma C .15 .40
99 Pull From Behind C .15 .40
100 Renegade Telepath U .40 1.00
101 Resist The Vorlons C .15 .40
102 Rimush R 1.50 4.00
103 Roam The Stars U .30 .75
104 Round Table U .30 .75
105 Rule By The Masses U .30 .75
106 Schism R 2.00 5.00
107 Search For A Home U .40 1.00
108 Secret And Arrogant C .15 .40
109 Seeds Of Destruction R 1.50 4.00
110 Shadow Of A Shadow R 1.50 4.00
111 Shai Alyt Neroon R 1.50 4.00
112 Shar'kali U .40 1.00
113 Sharrukin R 2.50 6.00
114 Shine In The Night C .15 .40
115 Shiv'kala R .40 1.00
116 Signs And Portents U 1.50 4.00
117 Soldier Of Darkness R 1.50 4.00
118 Something In The Air C .15 .40
119 Starfire Wheel R 2.00 5.00
120 State Visit U .40 1.00
121 Strange Happenings C .20 .50
122 Subvert The Nexus U .50 1.25
123 Surgeon Of Darkness U .30 .75
124 Surgical Strike R 1.50 4.00
125 Terror Tactics U .30 .75
126 The Chosen Ones U .30 .75
127 The Corps Is Father U .40 1.00
128 The First One C .15 .40
129 The Rangers C .15 .40
130 The Regent R 1.50 4.00
131 The Secret Masters C .15 .40
132 The Trap Is Sprung U .40 1.00
133 There Is Danger, Remember R 1.50 4.00
134 Touched By Vorlons U .30 .75
135 Treachery R 1.50 4.00
136 Tyranny Enthroned R 1.50 4.00
137 United We Stand U .30 .75
138 Unity C .15 .40
139 Universal Policeman C .15 .40
140 Ur'nammu C .15 .40
141 Vorlon UR 15.00 40.00
142 Vorlon Renegade UR 5.00 12.00
143 We Are One C .15 .40
144 We Have Always Been Here U .30 .75
145 We Say It's Over C .15 .40
146 Wheel Of Fire R 1.50 4.00
147 Who Do You Serve? U .30 .75
148 Win-Win Schemes C .15 .40
149 Wisdom Of G'Quan U .30 .75
150 Work Of The Wicked C .15 .40
151 Wushmeshkeshlep Fo U .40 1.00
152 You Have No Power Here R 2.00 5.00

2009 Battle Spirits Call of the Core

COMPLETE SET (149) 30.00 80.00
BOOSTER BOX (32 PACKS) 30.00 60.00
BOOSTER PACK (8 CARDS) 1.25 2.50
RELEASED ON AUGUST 14, 2009
1 Gora C .10 .20
2 Rokceratops C .10 .20
3 Teranosaber C .10 .20
4 The Scout Dragno C .10 .20
5 Eyeburn C .10 .20
6 Meral C .10 .20
7 Hummerdrake C .10 .20
8 Metalburn C .10 .20
9 Volc-Baboon C .10 .20
10 Chakrambat C .10 .20
11 Dragsaurus U .20 .50
12 Tryswordon C .10 .20
13 Taurusknight C .10 .20
14 The Shaman Dragno R .40 1.00
15 Spinoaxe C .10 .20
16 Skelton-Jaw U .20 .50
17 Lanceraptor C .10 .20
18 Lizardman C .10 .20
19 Jurassickle C .10 .20
20 The BladeDragon Steelanodon U .20 .50
21 The FlameDragon Ma-Gwo MR 1.25 3.00
22 The Sickle Fool-Joker R .75 2.00
23 The Fire LithoGraphica Phoenixious MR 1.25 3.00
24 The Dragon Diamat R .75 2.00
25 The DragonicFortress Giga MR 2.00 5.00
26 Foger C .10 .20
27 Will-Orb C .10 .20
28 Skulldevil C .10 .20
29 Rib-Reaper C .10 .20
30 Grip-Hands C .10 .20
31 Death-Haides C .10 .20
32 Gawrm C .10 .20
33 Disaster C .10 .20
34 Bi-Python U .20 .50
35 Bone-Gladiator C .10 .20
36 Sha-Zoo C .10 .20
37 Illusiona C .10 .20
38 Skel-Viper C .10 .20
39 The Mysteryman Dionaeman C .10 .20
40 Darkwitch R .40 1.00
41 Cobraiga C .10 .20
42 Mistweasel C .10 .20
43 Draculious R .40 1.00
44 The PhantomBull Smowg U .20 .50
45 The Ripper Headless C .10 .20
46 The PhantomDragon Sheyron MR 1.25 3.00
47 The Witch Naja R .40 1.00
48 The PrincessVampire Vampiles U .20 .50
49 The Phantom Horseman MR 1.25 3.00
50 Beatbeetle C .10 .20
51 Flyingmirage C .10 .20
52 Pelileaf C .10 .20
53 Leavwolf C .10 .20
54 Shockeater C .10 .20
55 Emeant C .10 .20
56 Matchra C .10 .20
57 Gularva C .10 .20
58 Hercules-Geo C .10 .20
59 Shidafukurou C .10 .20

60 Eagrass C .10 .20
61 Apewhip R .40 1.00
62 Hungrytree R .40 1.00
63 Emeraldscissor C .10 .20
64 Ziga-Wasp C .10 .20
65 Killikabut C .10 .20
66 Stagrove U .20 .50
67 Swallowivy U .20 .50
68 The BlastTiger Tigald U .20 .50
69 The AirMaster Aquilers C .10 .20
70 The MeteoriteArmor Monoqueiroz C .10 .20
71 The Charger Blanboar R .40 1.00
72 Gowsilvia MR 1.25 3.00
73 The GaudyFeather Vulpelture MR 1.25 3.00
74 Warrior-Gun C .10 .20
75 IceDroid C .10 .20
76 Ray-Bullet C .10 .20
77 Baby-Loki C .10 .20
78 The AutoLady Mani C .10 .20
79 Rainbowpapillon C .10 .20
80 Fenrircannon C .10 .20
81 The SilverScale Nithhoggr C .10 .20
82 Ur-Dine C .10 .20
83 Rabicrysta C .10 .20
84 Gatlingstand C .10 .20
85 Elephantite U .20 .50
86 Queen-Valkyrie C .10 .20
87 Metaldy-Bug U .20 .50
88 Towermittcrab C .10 .20
89 Dualcannon-Bell C .10 .20
90 Kell-Blindi U .20 .50
91 The Artifact Laguna U .20 .50
92 The CarrierWhale Mobileflow C .10 .20
93 The ShieldSpirit Dis MR 1.25 3.00
94 Gran-Dolbalkan R .40 1.00
95 The ArmoredBeast Bear-Gelmir MR 1.25 3.00
96 The AutoEmpress Sol R .40 1.00
97 The SteelWyvern R .40 1.00
98 The Burning Battlefield U .20 .50
99 The Canyon Where Sage lives U .20 .50
100 The Ruby Sun C .10 .20
101 The Ancient Dragon Territory C .10 .20
102 The Lost of Old Castle C .10 .20
103 The Swamp of Drain Life U .20 .50
104 The Historic Battlefield of the Cursed R .40 1.00
105 The Shackles of Doom U .20 .50
106 The Hermit Wise Tree R .40 1.00
107 The Fruit of Life U .20 .50
108 The Anthill U .20 .50
109 The Hill of Violent Wind C .10 .20
110 The Timeless Ice Field U .20 .50
111 The Diamond Moon C .10 .20
112 The Castle of Eternal Snow U .20 .50
113 The Invaded Silver Snow C .10 .20
114 Buster Spear R .40 1.00
115 Awaken C .10 .20
116 Offensive Aura C .10 .20
117 Double Draw C .10 .20
118 Call of Lost C .10 .20
119 Burst Fire C .10 .20
120 Buster Phalanx U .20 .50
121 Flame Dance C .10 .20
122 Flame Tempest R .40 1.00
123 Return Draw C .10 .20
124 Cemetery Aura U .20 .50
125 Deadly Balance C .10 .20
126 Shadow Elixir U .20 .50
127 Killer Telescope C .10 .20
128 Chaos Draw R .40 1.00
129 Poison Shoot C .10 .20
130 Changing Cores C .10 .20
131 Dark Coffin C .10 .20
132 Storm Draw C .10 .20
133 Wild Power C .10 .20
134 Binding Thorn C .10 .20
135 Power Aura C .10 .20
136 Gather Forces U .20 .50
137 Relation Soul C .10 .20
138 Hand Reverse U .20 .50
139 Feather Barrier C .10 .20
140 Binding Woods R .40 1.00
141 Invisible Cloak R .40 1.00
142 Pure Elixir C .10 .20
143 Divine Chain R .40 1.00
144 Silent Wall U .20 .50
145 Defensive Aura C .10 .20
146 Dream Ribbon C .10 .20
147 Dream Chest C .10 .20
148 Leak Drive C .10 .20
149 Attack Shift C .10 .20
X1 The DragonEmperor Siegfried XR 6.00 15.00
X2 The SevenShogun Desperado XR 6.00 15.00
X3 The Duke Kingtaurus XR 6.00 15.00
X4 The ImpregnableFortress Odin XR 6.00 15.00

2009 Battle Spirits Rise of the Angels

COMPLETE SET (111) 30.00 60.00
BOOSTER BOX (32 PACKS) 30.00 60.00
BOOSTER PACK (8 CARDS) 1.25 2.50
RELEASED ON NOVEMBER 13, 2009
1 Lizardedge C .10 .20
2 The Acrobat Juggline U .20 .50
3 Dinohound C .10 .20
4 Orcaria C .10 .20
5 The Charger Dragno C .10 .20
6 Pteratomahawk C .10 .20
7 The RiseDragon Balmung C .10 .20
8 Fisdragoon C .10 .20
9 The DragonBuster Archeorni C .10 .20
10 The LavaDragon Plesios R .40 1.00
11 Zwei-Howle C .10 .20
12 The Conqueror Cendragos MR 1.00 2.50
13 Bat-Bat C .10 .20
14 Phantasma C .10 .20
15 Humpdump C .10 .20
16 Slimy C .10 .20
17 Mummella C .10 .20
18 Top Supra C .10 .20
19 Bottom Desuper C .10 .20
20 Lady-Frankelly U .20 .50
21 The SkullKnight Zo-Goin C .10 .20
22 The Marquis Cocytus R .40 1.00
23 The TwinSnake Hydram C .10 .20
24 The General Bloody-Caesar MR 1.00 2.50
25 Sheep man C .10 .20
26 MachG C .10 .20
27 Caprihorn C .10 .20
28 Xscissors C .10 .20
29 Bathopper C .10 .20
30 The Soldier Ant U .20 .50
31 Scorpede C .10 .20
32 Dachono C .10 .20
33 The CavalryBeast Sleiphorse C .10 .20
34 The OldSage Trenton C .10 .20
35 The DarkFeather Yatagross R .40 1.00
36 The Great Kaiseleon MR 1.00 2.50
37 Sphereroid C .10 .20
38 The Buckler Langlies C .10 .20
39 The Sacred Mjolnir C .10 .20
40 Lobsterk C .10 .20
41 Liorider C .10 .20
42 Skuldia C .10 .20
43 Arma-Dillo C .10 .20
44 The CannonArtifact Megarock C .10 .20
45 The ShieldDragon Fevnir MR 1.00 2.50
46 Wingur C .10 .20
47 The AutoPriest Freyr U .20 .50
48 The DragonTank Earthguard R .40 1.00
49 Piyon C .10 .20
50 Koristal C .10 .20
51 Chunpopo C .10 .20
52 Chagamaru U .20 .50
53 The Fairy Tanya C .10 .20
54 Pom C .10 .20
55 Chauw C .10 .20
56 Arcanabeast-Ken C .10 .20
57 The FairyQueen Ti-Tanya U .20 .50
58 Pentan C .10 .20
59 Lom C .10 .20
60 The Clown Clan C .10 .20
61 The Angelia Angu C .10 .20
62 Porkne C .10 .20
63 The HellDog Cerru-Berus R .40 1.00
64 The Melodybird Crewc C .10 .20
65 The BlossomChild Lip R .40 1.00
66 Arcanadoll-Pan C .10 .20
67 The Angelia Virchu MR 1.00 2.50
68 The whiteTiger Huck C .10 .20
69 The BlackTiger Kuron C .10 .20
70 Arcanaprince-Obero U .20 .50
71 The PreciousBeast Carbulc R .40 1.00
72 Trickster MR 1.00 2.50
73 The Kaiser Empereur U .20 .50
74 The BalloonMan Barball C .10 .20
75 The GreatAngelia Principearl MR 1.00 2.50
76 The Ancient Fault C .10 .20
77 The Plateau of Duel U .20 .50
78 The Evil Coffin U .20 .50
79 The Forest of Amethyst C .10 .20
80 The Limestone Cave of Emerald C .10 .20
81 The Budding Plain U .20 .50
82 The Artifact Plant C .10 .20
83 The Corridor of Mirrors U .20 .50
84 The Blessed Sanctuary C .10 .20
85 The Topaz Meteor R .40 1.00
86 The Spiral Tower C .10 .20
87 The Sealed Spellbook R .40 1.00
88 Cross Fire C .10 .20
89 Spirit Link C .10 .20
90 Mind Flare U .20 .50
91 Seventh Crimson R .40 1.00
92 Energy Drain C .10 .20
93 Mind Control R .40 1.00
94 Bloody Rain U .20 .50
95 Sacrifice C .10 .20
96 Divine Wind U .20 .50
97 Nature Forces C .10 .20
98 Cast Off C .10 .20
99 Life Chain R .40 1.00
100 Invincible Shield C .10 .20
101 Reflection Armor C .10 .20
102 White Potion U .20 .50
103 Reload Cores R .40 1.00
104 Additional Color C .10 .20
105 Great Wall C .10 .20
106 Royal Potion C .10 .20
107 Time Reap C .10 .20
108 Magic Book R .40 1.00
109 Angel Voice C .10 .20
110 Heavy Gate C .10 .20
111 Spirit Illusion U .20 .50
X5 The TwinRowdy Diranos XR 6.00 15.00
X6 The SevenShogun Destlord XR 6.00 15.00
X7 The Gigantic Thor XR 6.00 15.00
X8 The ArcAngelia Mikafar XR 6.00 15.00

2009 Battle Spirits Roaring Heaven's Door

COMPLETE SET (21)
RELEASED ON
ONLY RELEASED IN JAPAN
ALSO KNOWN AS SD02
1 The Mysterious Beast Pooxan C .20
2 Misail C .20
3 The Angelia Dunamis C .20
4 The Sacred Beast Haktak U .50
5 The Angelia Cherubim R
6 The Assassin Weaseve C .20
7 The Dog Policeman Bernald C .20
8 The Rhino Mousquetair Grhinos C .20
9 The Beast Commander Kuyultha C .20
10 The Roaring Swordsmaster Lowen MR
11 The Beast Prince Bahamunt U .50
12 The Heaven's Door U .50
13 The Generate Altar C .20
14 The Magic Control Tower U .50
15 Friendly Power C .20
16 Wing Boots R
17 Strong Draw U .50
18 The Brave Colonel Dragron C .20
19 The Dark Knight Schwart C .20
20 The Rainbow Wings Jewelg C .20
21 The Beast Machine Sai-Drill C .20

2010 Battle Spirits Ascension of Dragons

COMPLETE SET (156) 50.00 100.00
BOOSTER BOX (32 PACKS) 30.00 60.00
BOOSTER PACK (8 CARDS) 1.25 2.50
RELEASED ON MAY 5, 2010
1 Kunanomi C .10 .20
2 Chamelewhip C .10 .20
3 DarkGoradon C .10 .20
4 DarkDinohound C .10 .20
5 Chain-Dragon C .10 .20
6 The ZombieDragon Zom-Sauru U .20 .50
7 The Guardsman Dragno U .20 .50
8 The AncientDragon Ba-Gaw MR 1.50 4.00
9 The FlameEmperor Kujaraku C .10 .20
10 The ThunderDragon El-Clair R .40 1.00
11 The Tyrant Fuhjaus MR 1.25 3.00
12 Banshee C .10 .20
13 Skulldemon C .10 .20
14 Shadowjuggler C .10 .20
15 Cyclo-Winder C .10 .20
16 The FallenAngelia Azel U .20 .50
17 Hellwitch C .10 .20
18 The WaterSnake Seaserpenta U .20 .50
19 Headless Carriage C .10 .20
20 The DarkDragon Ops-Curite R .40 1.00
21 The Vampire Dampeel R .40 1.00
22 The KingSnake Quetzalcoatl MR 1.25 3.00
23 Giraffen C .10 .20
24 Duckle C .10 .20
25 Fal-Condor C .10 .20
26 BlackMachG C .10 .20
27 Alligade U .20 .50
28 Sevenspot U .20 .50
29 BlackMonoqueiroz C .10 .20
30 The AppetiteFlower Bug-Lesia C .10 .20
31 The GroundDragon Fon-Daxion R .40 1.00
32 The SpearBeetle Lucanidos R .40 1.00
33 The CrustaceanFighter Longhorn MR 1.25 3.00
34 Vidohunir C .10 .20
35 Berserker-Magnum C .10 .20
36 Oddsay C .10 .20
37 The ArmoredBeast Helth-Rune U .20 .50
38 The Reconnaissance Magni C .10 .20
39 The JewelBug Scaravell U .20 .50
40 The ArmoredBeast Gullin-Bullsty C .10 .20
41 Fenrircannon Mk-II C .10 .20
42 The BeastMaster Dvergr C .10 .20
43 The Valkyrie-Hildr MR 1.25 3.00
44 The SkyDragon Le-Ciel R .40 1.00
45 The IceGoddess Frigg MR 1.25 3.00
46 The Fairy Dorothy C .10 .20
47 Wiseless-Scarecrow U .20 .50
48 DarkPiyon C .10 .20
49 The BlackFairy Ti-Tanya C .10 .20
50 Heartless-Tin U .20 .50
51 Arcanabeast-Hart C .10 .20
52 The Postman Pentan C .10 .20
53 The Angelia Throne R .40 1.00
54 Arcanasoldier-Cinq C .10 .20
55 The LightDragon Lumiere R .40 1.00
56 Braveless-Leo C .10 .20
57 The GreatAngelia Seraphy MR 1.25 3.00
58 The RatMan Zurich C .10 .20
59 The Pharmacist Girmamarl C .10 .20
60 The Soldier Gustav C .10 .20
61 The BattleBeast Jacker C .10 .20
62 The ApeMan Mongoku U .20 .50
63 The Two-Sword Ambrose C .10 .20
64 Ugarurum C .10 .20
65 The Spinner Har?elicite C .10 .20
66 The CatLady Abyssinia C .10 .20
67 Dra-Golem U .20 .50
68 Iron-Golem C .10 .20
69 The Illusionist Mirage C .10 .20
70 The BattleBeast Diatryma C .10 .20
71 Steam-Golem C .10 .20
72 Rabirabi C .10 .20
73 The SeaDragon Courant-Marin R .40 1.00
74 The ChimeraDragon Hydrus R .40 1.00
75 The LegendaryGiant Jude MR 1.25 3.00
76 The BombSoldier Dragno C .10 .20
77 The MysteriousFox Cubic U .20 .50
78 The ScarletDragonRider Rosso R .40 1.00
79 The UnicornDragon Volsung U .20 .50
80 The Dictator Volcanos MR 1.25 3.00
81 Sandman C .10 .20
82 Fallenpaladin C .10 .20
83 The PurpleDragonRider Violet R .40 1.00
84 The EvilAdmiral Negapluto U .20 .50
85 Pineappopotamus C .10 .20
86 The SeaHorse Kelpie C .10 .20
87 The Yojinbo Antman U .20 .50
88 The ViridianDragonRider Grun R .40 1.00
89 Armetcrab C .10 .20
90 Pantomeister C .10 .20
91 The WhiteDragonRider Albus R .40 1.00
92 The EvilDeity Big-Loki U .20 .50
93 The IceWitch Hel MR 1.25 3.00
94 The Angelia Kleio C .10 .20
95 The Princess- Snowwhite U .20 .50
96 Arcanafighter-Quatre C .10 .20
97 The YellowDragonRider Flavum R .40 1.00
98 Dwarf-Seven C .10 .20
99 The BattleBeast Babeaver C .10 .20
100 Bronze-Golem C .10 .20
101 The GiantKnight Aldous MR 1.25 3.00
102 Mithril-Golem C .10 .20
103 The BlueDragonRider Azure R .40 1.00
104 The IronHammer Oswald U .20 .50
105 The Airspace of Pterosaurs C .10 .20
106 The Seven Dragons' Throne C .10 .20
107 The Shadow Street C .10 .20
108 The King Snake Nest C .10 .20
109 The Whirlwind Ravine U .20 .50
110 The Strong-Dominated Earth C .10 .20
111 The Inviolable Sanctuary C .10 .20
112 The Steel Forest U .20 .50
113 The Miraculous Hill C .10 .20
114 The Spring of Full Magical Powers C .10 .20
115 The Ancient Arena U .20 .50
116 The Heart-Buster Huge Slope C .10 .20
117 The Victory Stand of the Glory C .10 .20
118 The Ruby Empty Sky C .10 .20
119 The Amethyst Empty Sky C .10 .20
120 The Emerald Empty Sky C .10 .20
121 The Diamond Empty Sky C .10 .20
122 The Topaz Empty Sky C .10 .20
123 The Sapphire Empty Sky C .10 .20
124 Great Link C .10 .20
125 The Ring of Nibelungen C .10 .20
126 Lightning Ballista R .40 1.00
127 Dragons' Rush C .10 .20
128 Merciful Release C .10 .20
129 Danse Macabre C .10 .20
130 Venom Shot U .20 .50
131 Inferno Eyes R .40 1.00
132 Forest Aura C .10 .20
133 Full Charge C .10 .20
134 Ground Howling R .40 1.00
135 Jungle Law C .10 .20
136 Mist Curtain C .10 .20
137 Dream Hand C .10 .20
138 High Ether C .10 .20
139 Glacial Breath R .40 1.00
140 Trick Prank C .10 .20
141 Gleam Hope C .10 .20
142 Judgment Lights R .40 1.00
143 Straight Flush U .20 .50
144 Switch Hitter C .10 .20
145 Lead Wall U .20 .50
146 Magic Drill C .10 .20
147 Massive Up C .10 .20
148 Nexus Repair C .10 .20
149 Tidal Tide R .40 1.00
150 Warning Attack C .10 .20
151 Absorb Symbol C .10 .20
152 Branch Lock C .10 .20
153 Eternal Shield C .10 .20
154 Chorus Birds C .10 .20
155 Magic Spanner C .10 .20
156 Potential Power U .20 .50
X13 The DarkDragonEmperor Siegfried XR 6.00 15.00
X14 The SevenShogun Pandemium XR 6.00 15.00
X15 The Emperor Kaiseratlas XR 6.00 15.00
X16 The MobileFortress Castle-Golem XR 6.00 15.00
X17 The PhantomLord Rean XR 6.00 15.00
X18 The HugeBeastLord Behedoth XR 6.00 15.00

2010 Battle Spirits Awakening of the Heavens

1 Rainydle C
2 The WingDragman Pteradia C
3 Basilizard C
4 The FuryRockWyvern Dragorock C
5 The HalberdBraver Arc R
6 La-Diablord U
7 The Astrologist Dragron R
8 The BladeDinosaur Bragasaur U
9 The SwordDragonEmperor Ex-Calibus MR
10 Ashtal C
11 Necrow C
12 Plasbat C
13 The FortuneTeller Deasha C
14 The ScytheBraver Zanba R
15 Brionagon U
16 The HellBraver Deathcarabia U
17 The HellBeastMan Zabuligan R
18 The HighPriestess Lilu-Succubus MR
19 Spearmink C
20 Gulyver C
21 The BladeBraver Volza R
22 BlackCaracalossom C
23 Rakudacho C
24 Dyrfangs U
25 The Elder Buchi-Energy U
26 The StingBeast Matsunoarashi R
27 The BlastMarquis Kokatleaf MR
28 The Artifact Velind C
29 Kigna-Swan C
30 The Sacred Laevateinn C
31 The BowBraver Ullr R
32 Hail-Garf C
33 The ChiefLibrarian Saga U
34 Durackdahl U
35 The SteelWingFish Orcanon MR
36 The MachineryMonster Giga-Therium R
37 Hippocampoo C
38 The CherryBlossomFairy Ouka C
39 The Macaroni Pentan C
40 The LilyFairy Yuly C
41 The SwordBraver Ryute R
42 Pao-Peir U
43 The Penpress U
44 The GreatAngelia Tron R
45 The HolyEmperorBeast Sphin-Cross MR
46 The PantherMan Berserkas C
47 The Merman Apkareel C
48 Silver-Golem C
49 Cannon-Golem C
50 Galadolg U
51 The AxeBraver Coyo R
52 The Fencer Falconia U
53 Island-Golem R
54 The PhoenicDeity Phoenix-Golem MR
55 The Meteor Stream Nightsky C
56 The Fall of Meteorite C
57 The Decayed Swamp C
58 The Darkness Church C
59 The Hill of Big Windmill C
60 The Ruins of Strange shaped Rocks C
61 The Gears Plains C
62 The Necklace of Brisingamen C
63 The SecretFlower Garden C
64 The Healing Fountain C
65 The Golem Factory C
66 The Historic Assault Field C
67 Meteor Fall C
68 Felarl Slash U
69 Reborn Flame C
70 Black Ritual C
71 Dirty Fist C
72 Turon Slash U
73 Warlwind C
74 Needle Shot C
75 Fordia Slash U
76 Diamond Strike C
77 Life Saving C
78 Maclarn Slash U
79 Bloom Flute C
80 No Entry C
81 Lunar Slash U
82 Nexus Attack C
83 Wirian Slash U
84 Arms Impact C
x25 The StarEmperorDragon Meteorwurm XR
x26 The BladeKingBeast Byak-Garo XR
x27 The ArcAngelia Isfiel XR
x28 The GiantEmperor Alexander XR

2010 Battle Spirits Dawn of the Ancients

COMPLETE SET (196) 50.00 100.00
BOOSTER BOX (32 PACKS) 30.00 60.00
BOOSTER PACK (8 CARDS) 1.25 2.50
RELEASED ON SEPTEMBER 10, 2010
1 The FanDragon Sordes C .10 .20
2 Dimetrodoron C .10 .20
3 Wyarm C .10 .20
4 The DragonicFortress Megaron C .10 .20
5 Redcap C .10 .20
6 Blindsnake C .10 .20
7 Gastoras U .20 .50
8 The MischievousFairy Imp C .10 .20
9 The QueenVampire Carmilla MR 1.50 4.00
10 Pollu?&Castar C .10 .20
11 Gengoron C .10 .20
12 Mothleaf C .10 .20
13 The GodTree Dionaeus MR 1.25 3.00
14 The SaberTiger Xen-Fu U .20 .50
15 The Artifact Embla C .10 .20
16 The GunKnight Heavybarrel C .10 .20
17 The CoralCrab Siomanekid U .20 .50
18 The GiantMobile Ymir C .10 .20
19 Shesas U .20 .50
20 The MorningFairy Napalco C .10 .20
21 The GreatAngelia Sophia MR 1.50 4.00
22 LittleKnight-Lancelot C .10 .20
23 The ChimeraDinosaur Dinozaur C .10 .20
24 The WolfMan Wolfy C .10 .20
25 MCPanther U .20 .50
26 Erimakilizard C .10 .20
27 Katanakasago C .10 .20
28 Ankillersaurus C .10 .20
29 The Infantry Dragon C .10 .20
30 Tartargar C .10 .20
31 The FireDragon Windrake U .20 .50
32 Styrahorn C .10 .20
33 The ThunderEmperorDragon Siegwurm MR 1.25 3.00
34 Bone-Dog C .10 .20
35 Komoribrella C .10 .20
36 The HellFighter Balam C .10 .20
37 The DoubleHead Snake U .20 .50
38 The HellFencer Berith R .40 1.00
39 Skunks C .10 .20
40 Hacchidori C .10 .20
41 Amenborg C .10 .20
42 The HeavyArmoredBug Caterbarga U .20 .50
43 The Hunter Kingghepardo R .40 1.00
44 Momongul C .10 .20
45 Hitodem C .10 .20
46 The Sacred Gungnir C .10 .20
47 Glasscargot C .10 .20
48 The Artifact Droiden C .10 .20
49 The CentaurusSoldier Atrithr U .20 .50
50 The ArmoredBeast Skoll C .10 .20
51 The IronKnight Yggdrasill MR 1.25 3.00
52 Ovirapt C .10 .20
53 Iguaknife C .10 .20
54 The FierceHeadBeast Horngrizzly C .10 .20
55 The Decurion Dragron C .10 .20
56 The DinosaurPrincess Jura C .10 .20
57 Sabecaulus C .10 .20
58 The ShamshirDinosaur Parasaur U .20 .50
59 The Scabbardfish Espada C .10 .20
60 The CloudBladeDragon Swordlagoon C .10 .20
61 The BattleAxe Apollodinos R .40 1.00
62 The IronScorpionDragon Scord-Goran R .40 1.00
63 The HugeDinosaur Giganoton MR 1.25 3.00
64 Pigeonheadless C .10 .20
65 Smoggoat C .10 .20
66 Straysoul C .10 .20
67 Bronzemaiden C .10 .20
68 The HellAirMan Buney C .10 .20
69 The Werewolf Loup-Gawrou C .10 .20
70 The HellMusician Mur C .10 .20

71 Skullgoyle C .10 .20
72 The SnakeEmpress Medousa U .20 .50
73 The ChopSword Shadowslicer R .40 1.00
74 The DarkBishop Baculus R .40 1.00
75 The HellKnight Andra MR 1.25 3.00
76 Mepon C .10 .20
77 Caracalossom C .10 .20
78 Gazellecaid C .10 .20
79 Gabunohashi C .10 .20
80 Maparrot U .20 .50
81 The Worker Antman C .10 .20
82 Mitsujarashi C .10 .20
83 Woodykong C .10 .20
84 The Baron Jacobino C .10 .20
85 The IronFist Cactusgaroo R .40 1.00
86 Tsukushinmoa R .40 1.00
87 The FangTree Rafflesio MR 1.25 3.00
88 TwinFairies Hugin?Munin C .10 .20
89 Senzangou C .10 .20
90 The FloatingFish Molamola C .10 .20
91 The ChiefMaid Fulla C .10 .20
92 The ArmoredBeast Audhumla C .10 .20
93 The AutoMarine Seerauber U .20 .50
94 The ShieldSoldier Balder C .10 .20
95 Reindeer C .10 .20
96 Tonbeaul C .10 .20
97 The KeyMaul Valgrind R .40 1.00
98 The ShineDragonPalace Breidhablic R .40 1.00
99 The SilverWolfEmperor Gagnrathr MR 1.25 3.00
100 Pyorit C .10 .20
101 The SnowKiddie Yeti C .10 .20
102 Gremly C .10 .20
103 The Chick Pentan C .10 .20
104 The FortuneTeller Pentan C .10 .20
105 Laserpanda C .10 .20
106 Cotton-Candele C .10 .20
107 The CatKnight Cait-Sith R .40 1.00
108 ArcanaKing-Charle MR 1.25 3.00
109 ArcanaKnight-Hex C .10 .20
110 The CleverBeast Iberix U .20 .50
111 The GreatAngelia Fanim MR 1.25 3.00
112 Dolphino C .10 .20
113 The BattlingBeast Zouuchi C .10 .20
114 The GolemCraftEngineer Gatan C .10 .20
115 Mantigore U .20 .50
116 Block-Golem C .10 .20
117 The MuscleBraggart Humphrey C .10 .20
118 The WeaponDealer Goron-Garan C .10 .20
119 The Tactician Shoujouji C .10 .20
120 Tsathoggua C .10 .20
121 The BlastingGiant Douglas MR 1.25 3.00
122 The HeavyJavelin Morgan R .40 1.00
123 The HugeGiant Eurytos MR 1.25 3.00
124 The Great Ancient Dragon's Jaw U .20 .50
125 The Remain of Scaffold U .20 .50
126 The Thorny Colosseum U .20 .50
127 The Eternal Glacier Palace U .20 .50
128 The Empire of Pentan U .20 .50
129 The Sacred Torch scorched the Sky R .40 1.00
130 The Big Lavafalls C .10 .20
131 The Cursed Shrine R .40 1.00
132 The Wriggle Catacomb C .10 .20
133 The Earth of Fertility R .40 1.00
134 The Cape in the Red Sky C .10 .20
135 The Protection of Sacred Artifacts C .10 .20
136 The Burning Canyon C .10 .20
137 The Ruby Volcanic Bombs C .10 .20
138 The Deity in the Sacred Mountains U .20 .50
139 The Digged Tombstone C .10 .20
140 The Depths of the Darkness U .20 .50
141 The Doom Coffin C .10 .20
142 The Forest of the Sacred Conifer C .10 .20
143 The Storm Highland U .20 .50
144 The Fruit of Wise Tree C .10 .20
145 The Infinite Mother Ship U .20 .50
146 The Lighthouse of Hope C .10 .20
147 The Invaded Castle C .10 .20
148 The Chaotic Magic Laboratory C .10 .20
149 The Opened Spellbook C .10 .20
150 The Phantom Paradise U .20 .50
151 The Intentional Scuffle C .10 .20
152 The Battle?ield enclosed by the Chains C .10 .20
153 The Honorable Fight U .20 .50
154 Synchronicity C .10 .20
155 Transmigration R .40 1.00
156 Soul Crash R .40 1.00
157 Reanimate C .10 .20
158 God Speed R .40 1.00
159 Brave Charge C .10 .20
160 Crystal Aura R .40 1.00
161 Icicle Assault C .10 .20
162 Three Cards C .10 .20
163 Nexus Blockade R .40 1.00
164 CircularSaw Arm C .10 .20
165 Victory Fire R .40 1.00
166 Extra Draw U .20 .50
167 Sudden Death Draw C .10 .20
168 Curse Enchant U .20 .50
169 Carry Cores C .10 .20
170 Emerald Boost U .20 .50
171 Blizzard Wall R .40 1.00
172 Armor Purge U .20 .50
173 Buster Javelin C .10 .20
174 Excavation U .20 .50
175 Lightning Aura C .10 .20
176 Trident Flare R .40 1.00
177 Burial Draw C .10 .20
178 Level Drain C .10 .20
179 Bloody Coffin U .20 .50
180 Counter Curse R .40 1.00
181 Savage Power C .10 .20
182 Thorn Prison R .40 1.00
183 Mistral Core C .10 .20
184 Speed Star U .20 .50
185 Chivalry U .20 .50
186 Avalanche Aura C .10 .20
187 Holy Elixir C .10 .20
188 White Hole R .40 1.00
189 Second Sight C .10 .20
190 Discontinue U .20 .50
191 Archaic Smile R .40 1.00
192 Imagine Field C .10 .20
193 Reclamation C .10 .20
194 Muscle Charge C .10 .20
195 Maximum Break U .20 .50
196 Demolish R .40 1.00
X19 The SacredEmperor Siegfrieden XR 6.00 15.00
X20 The GreatArmoredLord Deathtaurus XR 6.00 15.00
X21 The Deity Catastrophedragon XR 6.00 15.00
X22 The SevenShogun Beelzebeat XR 6.00 15.00
X23 The Providence Hououga XR 6.00 15.00
X24 The ArmoredSacred Walhalance XR 6.00 15.00

2010 Battle Spirits Descent of the Astral Dragons Eight

1 Shamcaesar C
2 Bracchio the Longneck Saurian C
3 Shurikeraptor C
4 Eusthedia C
5 Diphorza U
6 Yashium U
7 Duald C
8 Ares Dragoon, Dragonlord of Mars MR
9 Tornadra C
10 Vandalizer the Conqueror Dragon R
11 Onigumon C
12 Anteater C
13 Dragonaga the Magic Swordsnake C
14 Maris the Dark Knight U
15 Logan C
16 Jawscythe U
17 Gaim the Hell Musketer C
18 El Kraken C
19 Kronoboros, Dragonlord of Saturn MR
20 Hydrogen the Water Snake R
21 Mothpede C
22 Musgazemi C
23 Luckiwi C
24 KAMOMÖWE C
25 Herajigusa C
26 Nogan the Veteran U
27 Unpyru the Young Musha U
28 Matangol C
29 Nobunagard Zeusis, dragonlord of Jupiter MR
30 Antman Shogun R
31 Djungaree C
32 Gadphant C
33 Northen Bear'd C
34 Chimaeron the Armored Beast C
35 Eir, Goddess of the Silver Frost U
36 Crystell the Crystal Fish C
37 Emperadol U
38 Bolverg the Black Spear mech MR
39 Bianco Tiga C
40 Hogale, Aircraft Carrier Whale R
41 Tin Soldier C
42 Charadrius C
43 Kikasaal C
44 Pentan Forest Elf C
45 Sabrina the Dark Witch C
46 Princess of Dragon Wizardry MR
47 Rogue the Red-Hooded Fairy U
48 Power the Angel C
49 Fairy Priestess Andromeda MR
50 Nue the Thunder God Beast R
51 Raygallop the Battle Beast C
52 Gobli-Gobli the Lumerjack C
53 Bertram the Guardian Deity C
54 Locomo Golem C
55 Glarkie C
56 Mongokuu the Azure Sage U
57 Dear'd the Stagman C
58 Mercuris Serpent, Dragonlord of Mercury MR
59 Fort Golem U
60 Orion the Jäger Giant R
61 Buster Dragon the Sword-Armored Drake C
62 Phoenix Cannon the Artillery Phoenixdrake R
63 Ballistar the Javelin beast C
64 Gepalberd the Skeletank C
65 Hedgebolg C
66 Pendragon, Exalted Snake King MR
67 Shiba the Karakuri Dog C
68 Beam beetle C
69 Kakurane the Thousand-Blade Bird R
70 Alfothr the Armored horse C
71 Fenrir Cannon Type B C
72 Sabershark R
73 Angeldoll C
74 Kumatta the Mascot U
75 Oniyurin C
76 Bazooka Arms C
77 Gyokuryuun C
78 Ammead the Sacred Armorbeast R
79 The Towering Table Mountains C
80 The Flame Crystal U
81 Canyons of the Blazing Warstar Mars C
82 The Sextant Astronomical Observatory C
83 Ancient Wargrounds of the Shining Devilstar Saturn U
84 Mouth of Truth & Lies C
85 The Floating Rock Mass C
86 Great Fortress of the Giantstar Jupiter C
87 A Breath of Life on the Battlefield U
88 Heavens-Piercing Castle Tower C
89 Frozen Moon Lake U
90 Aerial Coral Reef C
91 The SoapyLakeshore C
92 Flower Gardens of the Glimmering Morningstar Venus C
93 The Ticking Floral Clock U
94 Unfinished Ancient Battleship-Keel C
95 Colosseum of the Swift Wisdomstar Mercury U
96 Flag of the Ultimate Champion C
97 Brave Aura C
98 Revival Draw C
99 Southern Cross Flame R
100 Brave Cementery C
101 Hanged Man R
102 Core Steal C
103 Growing Sword C
104 Triangle Trap R
105 Life Charge C
106 Protection Aura C
107 Silent Lock C
108 Lunatic Seal R
109 Shining Arrow C
110 Knockout C
111 Hand Typhoon R
112 Nexus Extension C
113 Orion Power C
114 Eridanus Flood R
X01 Gaiasura the Phantomstar Dragonlord XR
X02 Piscesgalleon, Twinfish Lord of Pirates ZXR
X03 Cancered the Warlord Crustacean ZXR
X04 Strike-Siegwurm the Moonlight Dragon XR
X05 Venulucider, Fallen Angel Dragonlord XR
X06 Scorspear the Divine Scorpion Knight ZXR

2010 Battle Spirits Fusion Dragon of the Sun

1 Bladra C
2 Stegolas the Swordsaurian C
3 Morgesaurus U
4 Gulnar the Horned Beast C
5 Bighorn C
6 Sieg-Apollodragon the Solarwyrm MR
7 Balgunner the Cannon Dragon C
8 Groungirus the armored Shelldragon R
9 Paradise of Flames C
10 Brave Draw U
11 Sagitta Flame R
12 Elginius the Battle Dragon C
13 Carpenter Chief Mccoy U
14 Sea Serpender the Astral Leviathan U
15 Cerbelord the Fang Emperor U
16 Olympsia Stadium C
17 Blue Splash C

2010 Battle Spirits Scars of Battle

BOOSTER BOX (32 PACKS) 30.00 60.00
BOOSTER PACK (8 CARDS) 1.25 2.50
1 The FireSpirit Salamandert C .10 .20
2 Edgehog C .10 .20
3 The Assassin Dragno C .10 .20
4 Brontrident C .10 .20
5 Enchu C .10 .20
6 Runkaphorhynchus C .10 .20
7 Flame-Elk U .20 .50
8 The BladeDragon Stegorasaurus C .10 .20
9 The FireBlower Melt C .10 .20
10 The BlackDragon Vritra R .40 1.00
11 The DinoCavalry Diridalus MR 1.25 3.00
12 The GrandBishop Levia R .40 1.00
13 Hellscorpio C .10 .20
14 Fish-Skull C .10 .20
15 The EvilGrass Mindragora C .10 .20
16 The InvisibleMan Eclear C .10 .20
17 The GhostCaptain Silvershark C .10 .20
18 Blackwraith C .10 .20
19 The EvilTactician Hellmia U .20 .50
20 Mega-HumDum C .10 .20
21 The Count Wyhl C .10 .20
22 The DarkReefDiva Seiren R .40 1.00
23 The ArtificialCreature No.44 U .20 .50
24 The VampireKnight Nosferat MR 1.50 4.00
25 Stagscissor C .10 .20
26 The WoodenSpirit Dryadena C .10 .20
27 Fullmingo U .20 .50
28 Mogrunner C .10 .20
29 Machfly C .10 .20
30 The Master Rainer Bros. C .10 .20
31 The BlackWind Panther C .10 .20
32 The Spider Arachnet U .20 .50
33 The Beatpriest C .10 .20
34 The FightingBird Bishamon C .10 .20
35 The GoldenFlower Zonne-Bloem R .40 1.00
36 The GodBird Peagod MR 1.25 3.00
37 Ratatoscr C .10 .20
38 Angelafish C .10 .20
39 The Piper Heimdall C .10 .20
40 Ver-Thandia C .10 .20
41 The Artifact Asc C .10 .20
42 The SeaCreature Dugong C .10 .20
43 Holaruri C .10 .20
44 The Metal Surtr R .40 1.00
45 The SilverFox Hati R .40 1.00
46 The Unicorn Einhorn C .10 .20
47 The CrystalGoddess Freyr U .20 .50
48 The ArmoredSnake Mithgarth MR 1.25 3.00
49 Mycanaen C .10 .20
50 Kinokonoko C .10 .20
51 Dongurin C .10 .20
52 Frog Fisher C .10 .20
53 The HundredFaces Flatface U .20 .50
54 Arcanadoll-Tria C .10 .20
55 Gomazarashi C .10 .20
56 Ochogo C .10 .20
57 Jellfy C .10 .20
58 The Fairy Tinguly C .10 .20
59 Arcanabeast-Paira U .20 .50
60 Rumpkin C .10 .20
61 The StrawberryGirl Strawberi C .10 .20
62 Chihuahl C .10 .20
63 Ponysus C .10 .20
64 The RoseLady Barossa R .40 1.00
65 The Angelia Curio R .40 1.00
66 The Angelia Archre MR 1.25 3.00
67 Arcanaprincess-Un U .20 .50
68 Forthros C .10 .20
69 The Rockhopper Pentan U .20 .50
70 The GreatAngelia Exsia MR 1.25 3.00
71 The BattlingBeast Bulltop C .10 .20
72 The Pikeman Jeffrey C .10 .20
73 Stone-Statue C .10 .20
74 The BattlingBeast Doben C .10 .20
75 The DogMan Murdoch C .10 .20
76 The ClawSword Lazarus C .10 .20
77 The AssaultSoldier Norman C .10 .20
78 The Berserk Troll C .10 .20
79 The StaffOfficer Foxin C .10 .20
80 Rock-Golem C .10 .20
81 The GiganticCentaurusSoldier Danston C .10 .20
82 Sharkhammer C .10 .20
83 The BearMan Beard C .10 .20
84 The GiganticCat Blynx U .20 .50
85 Wood-Golem C .10 .20
86 The Repairer Baran-Baran U .20 .50
87 The BattlingBeast Rhino-Ceros C .10 .20
88 The FortressCrasher Dennis C .10 .20
89 Deep-Arnold C .10 .20
90 The DragonSlayBlade Guy U .20 .50
91 The BattlingBeast Bun-Ffalo C .10 .20
92 The GroundSupporter Francis U .20 .50
93 The BuffaloMan Bulltania C .10 .20
94 The Weaponsmith Bagin U .20 .50
95 The Conjurer Oliver R .40 1.00
96 The GiantKing Randolph MR 1.25 3.00
97 The BirdMan R .40 1.00
98 The BattleDragon Wyvern MR 1.25 3.00
99 The IronFist Tiga C .10 .20
100 The WeaponCollector MR 1.25 3.00
101 Volcano-Golem R .40 1.00
102 The Outlaw Wasteland U .20 .50
103 The Middle of Hard Battle C .10 .20
104 The Crossroads of Destiny U .20 .50
105 The Dark Reef Sea Area C .10 .20
106 The Sea of Trees in Dark Green U .20 .50
107 The Endless Horizon C .10 .20
108 The High Sky Covered by Metal U .20 .50
109 The Earth of Aurora C .10 .20
110 The Sacred Place in Falling Stars C .10 .20
111 The Child's Room in Midnight U .20 .50
112 The Kingdom of Cards C .10 .20
113 The Absorption Triumphal Arch R .40 1.00
114 The Rampart of Sapphire U .20 .50
115 The Collapse of Battle Line C .10 .20
116 The Loss of Heroes R .40 1.00
117 The H.Q. filled with Fighting Spirits C .10 .20
118 Fourth Draw R .40 1.00
119 Buster Lance C .10 .20
120 Flame Cyclone C .10 .20
121 Double Hearts R .40 1.00
122 Fall Down C .10 .20
123 Necromancy C .10 .20
124 Poison Mist C .10 .20
125 Weakness U .20 .50
126 Potion Berry U .20 .50
127 Ivy Cage C .10 .20
128 Multiple Cores C .10 .20
129 Flock Recovery C .10 .20
130 Möbius Loop R .40 1.00
131 United Power C .10 .20
132 Perfect Guard C .10 .20
133 High Elixir R .40 1.00
134 Puppet String C .10 .20
135 Escape Route C .10 .20
136 Focus Light C .10 .20
137 Four Cards U .20 .50
138 Teleport Change R .40 1.00
139 Same Tired R .40 1.00
140 Shining Magic U .20 .50
141 Build Up C .10 .20
142 Salvage C .10 .20
143 Blitz C .10 .20
144 Magic Hammer C .10 .20
145 Scramble C .10 .20
146 Nexus Register C .10 .20
147 Golem Craft R .40 1.00
148 Construction U .20 .50
149 Delta Crash U .20 .50
X9 The SavageKnight Hercules XR 6.00 15.00
X10 The IceBeast Mam-Morl XR 6.00 15.00
X11 The ArcAngelia Valiero XR 6.00 15.00
X12 The GiantHero Titus XR 6.00 15.00

2010 Battle Spirits Solar Brave

1 Soulhorse C
2 The Magician Dragonaga U
3 The HellLionKnight Marbalion U
4 The ForestBird Sekkohkiji C
5 Hinawazaru U
6 The BushinBeast Tigerd-Shingen U
7 Igua-Buggy C
8 The CannonBeast Glypdon U
9 The ArtifactDragon Swordrander U
10 Izuna C
11 The ElectricFairy Birit U
12 The ThunderBeast Raijoule U
13 The BlackWingDragon Burn-Crow U
14 The BladeWolf Beo-Wulf U
15 The BeastArmor Megabison U
16 The HeavenHornBeast Bicorn U
17 The Old Devil's Castle C
18 The Immovable Headquarters C
19 The Impregnable Fortress C
20 The Crown of the Starlit Sky C
21 Grim Reaper U
22 Greedy Cores R
23 Grass Trap U
24 Rapid Wind R
25 Magic Boost U
26 Mirage Coat R
27 Elec Trick U
28 Thunder Branch R
29 The SunDragon Sieg-Apollodragon MR
30 The SunDragon Sieg-Apollodragon MR
31 The SunDragon Sieg-Apollodragon MR
32 The SunDragon Sieg-Apollodragon MR

2010 Battle Spirits The Storms of War

1 Dinonychusaw C
2 The CaptureUnit Pteradia C
3 DarkAnkillersaurus C
4 The Dinoman Tyrannoid U
5 The BraveGeneral Catapuldos C
6 The ThunderDragonRider Rayblitz R
7 The PyroclasticDragon Prometeors U
8 The BlackEmperorDragon Darkwurm R
9 The FieldMarshalEmperor Dragron MR
10 Demo-Bone C
11 The HellWolf Armon C
12 The DarkSkulldemon C
13 Andrealphas C
14 The HellGeneral Amaimon C
15 The DarkDragonRider Sabna-Rook U
16 The HellSerpentineMan Botis R
17 The SkeletonSnake Skullpione MR
18 The SupremeDarkKnight Schwart MR
19 Emeantman C
20 Dio-Mantis C
21 BlackAmenborg C
22 Mangoose C
23 The AirCommodore Geran R
24 The GroundDragonRider Vespeniar U
25 The Queen Antreine R
26 The HeavyArmoredBug Goliearth U
27 The ShiningWings Jewelg MR
28 Lampsquid C
29 The Narwhal Monokerock U
30 The Artifact Fjalar C
31 The HellSacred Gungnir C
32 The ResourcefulGeneral Gondlir C
33 The GuardianBeast Snopard U
34 The SkyDragonRider Platinam R
35 The ArtifactBeast Sai-Drigan MR
36 The MachineDeity Inphenit-Wols MR
37 Kikimora C
38 The CatGirl Annie C
39 DarkChunpopo C
40 The Angelia Olifia C
41 The DogGeneral Cu-Sith C
42 The Angelia Salaty U
43 The LightDragonRider Arcanajoker R
44 ArcanaQueen-Pallas U
45 The Braver Phoenixpentan MR
46 The BattleBeast Babyrouza C
47 The PigMan Chohakkai U
48 BlackUgarurum C
49 The BeastPriest Ganes C
50 Bokrugar C
51 The VeteranGeneral Dogu-Golem C
52 The SeaDragonRider Vang-Tholomew U
53 The ReverieBonze Sanzorl R
54 The ChimeraSacredBeast Cthulhum MR
55 The ImperialDragoon's Round Table U
56 The Sunstone Shrine C
57 The Red Sand Glass C
58 The Reverse Pyramid Fields U
59 The Sacred Totem Pole C
60 The Anthill of the Earth U
61 The Resonant Tuning Fork Tower R
62 The Gravity Dimension Engine C
63 The Winner's Green Field C
64 The PhoenixCalibur C
65 The Gogyo Temple C
66 The Ruins of the Seabed R
67 Dragon Scramble C
68 Meteor Storm R
69 Judgment Flare C
70 Turn Inferno C
71 Victim C
72 Mind Break R
73 Lightning Speed C
74 Sniping Blast C
75 Dark Power C
76 Ambush Blocker C
77 Infinity Shield C
78 Destruction Barrier U
79 Cat's Eye C
80 Magic Mirror U
81 Royal Straight Flush U
82 Grow Up C
83 Break Burst C
84 Chimera Assault U
x29 The MasterDragonRider Dark-Crimson XR
x30 The SevenShogun Asmodios XR
x31 The GreatKing Blacktaurus XR
x32 The Wing Deity Grand-Woden XR
x33 The FallenAngelia Mikafar XR
x34 The GodMadeSoldier Orichalcum-Golem XR

2010 Battle Spirits Supernova Supremacy

1 Yoroilizardon C
2 Futabanea C
3 The HornDinoman Drakkhen C
4 The VampireDragon Wybat U
5 The GalaxyDragon Andrometeors U
6 The SnakeDragon King-Gorgo C
7 The WildBeast Cruger C
8 The FlameEmperor Agniffon MR
9 The BlazeEmperor Arc R
10 Kitsunaby C
11 The ShieldKnight Guardner U
12 Bogies U
13 Mimizukurow C
14 The DarkKnight Bors C
15 The JailBeast Gashabers C
16 The DarkKnight Mordred MR
17 The DragonPhoenixDeity Baaral MR
18 The DarknessEmperor Zanba R
19 Ookuchiba C
20 Yamiyanma C

21 The Mononofu Impalar C
22 The Viscount Minoba U
23 The FortressWorm Raliba C
24 The GiantHornCastle Elasmos U
25 The Ninja Sarutobe MR
26 The Captain Dreadnought MR
27 The JungleEmperor Volza R
28 The Artifact Galar C
29 The ArmoredBeast Oozuchi C
30 The Guardian Hlin U
31 The GuardianGiantBeast Galaparzo C
32 The FlyingIronBeast Gale-Fokker C
33 The LanceKnight Gautr U
34 The Valkyrie Gna C
35 The GiantBeastEmperor Smidlord MR
36 The BlizzardEmperor Ullr R
37 Pooka C
38 The LilybellFairy Tinka C
39 Detective Pentan C
40 Iwasaal C
41 Aspidochelun U
42 The FairyKnight Peter U
43 Clockdile C
44 The FairyPrincess Hama-Dryas MR
45 The ShiningEmperor Ryute R
46 The Gatekeeper Alparkar C
47 The SharkMan Sangojaw U
48 The BombBeast Bonnacorn C
49 The FlameLizard Cthugma C
50 The Diva Canary C
51 The DragonArmorGiant Ozias U
52 Forest-Golem C
53 The BlacksmithKing Cyc-Bros MR
54 The StormEmperor Coyo R
55 The Reincarnation Valley C
56 The Star Creation Place C
57 The Shadow Hiding Clock Tower U
58 The Grimoire Bookshelf C
59 The Jade Shrine C
60 The Green Big Tree U
61 The Sanctuary protected by GiantBeast C
62 The Spring of Norn U
63 The Flower Palace C
64 The Flying Ark U
65 The Great Workshop of the Meisters C
66 The Awakening Fortress Castle C
67 Big Bang Energy U
68 Land Mine C
69 Flame Gust R
70 Elimination C
71 Immortal Draw C
72 Shadow Blade R
73 On the Edge C
74 Forest Charge C
75 Wind Shear R
76 Emergency C
77 Iceberg C
78 Healing Circle R
79 Character Lost C
80 Exhaust Nexus C
81 Somersault Turn R
82 Transformation R
83 Blessing Cores C
84 Dragonic Howling U
X35 The SupernovaDragon Siegwurm-Nova XR
X36 The SevenShogun Beldegaulle XR
X37 The DoomKnightLord Ragna-Rock XR
X38 The ImpregnableKnightLord Odin Type-X XR
X39 The MagicalEmpress Ambrocius XR
X40 The HeelGiant Titus-the-Black XR

2011 Battle Spirits Bakuretsu No Hadou

1 Nodeppo C
2 Piledraco C
3 Kamapagos C
4 Ashigaryu C
5 Goemon-Thief-Dragon R
6 Archer-Dragon U
7 Ogre-Dragon C
8 DarkKnight-Dragon MR
9 The ReptileMaster Momochidile U
10 Honejika C
11 Ginroukaku C
12 Kinkokaku C
13 The DarkKnight Florence C
14 Okapien C
15 Kotsugaizi R
16 Boatrictor U
17 Kouenko R
18 Taikotsubo MR
19 Yanadokugar C
20 Zougaomushi C
21 Nouzenserval C
22 Ma-Bachou C
23 Konohazukuro C
24 Barbary-Chouhi R
25 Tarandows C
26 Kumatakanwu U
27 Caucasus-Ryohu-Beetle MR
28 Flow-Zacco C
29 Mibrock-Patrol U
30 Serizawand-Duck C
31 Gilles-de-Rais C
32 La-Hire C
33 Mibrock-the-One MR
34 Brontarl C
35 The FrostedTreeDragon Silver-Rime C
36 The IceSaint Jeanne-da-Arc R
37 Town Musicians of Brepentan C
38 ClubSorcerer-Scarecrow C
39 The Angelia of Grimm Rapunzel C
40 HeartKnight-Tin C
41 The Angelia of Grimm Redhood U
42 The Angelia of Grimm Cinderella R
43 SpadeBeast-Leo C
44 DiamondPrincess-Dorothy MR
45 The GreatAngelia of Olimpics Ophiel MR
46 Sakebibird C
47 The Guardman Pug C
48 Gugalanar C
49 Humbabar C
50 Guymail-Hydra R
51 Shuddomeli C
52 Enkidu-Golem U
53 Illuyankash C
54 The AncientBeastKing Gilgamesh MR
55 Armstronger C
56 Shilgator MR
57 Kotetsu-Tiger R
58 Satellide-Bird R
59 Kaimeiju R
60 Technohyude R
61 The Dark Clowdy Ogre Island C
62 The Grand Sight Gale U
63 The Soul Fishing Place C
64 The Hanged Gogyo Mountain U
65 The Peach Garden of Oath C
66 The Flying Barrier U
67 The Tower of Ice Saint C
68 The Stairway Mountains U
69 The Seven Bridge C
70 The Urtext of Creativity U
71 The Island of Ocean Master C
72 The Kingdom between Two Rivers U
73 Aggressive Rage C
74 Explosion Sword R
75 Scapegoat U
76 Beat Burst C
77 Toughness Recovery C
78 Descent Burst U
79 Moonbow Cloak U
80 Dimension Sword C
81 Magic-of-Oz C
82 Magia Geflüster U
83 Clash-the-Babylon U
84 Exhausted Guard C
X1 The ExplosionHero Lord-Dragon-Bazzel XR
X2 Gyukotsumaou XR
X3 The RetsuHero Seiryubi XR
X4 The CharismaHero Mibrock-Braver XR
X5 Arcanamaster-Oz XR
X6 The MountainsDragon Yamatanohydra XR

2011 Battle Spirits Burst Heroes

1 Ohdoran C
2 Salamantle C
3 One-Kengo C
4 Dos-Monkey C
5 TwinBlade-Dragon U
6 Ikazuchi-Wurm R
7 The HeroDragon Lord-Dragon MR
8 Armaditokage C
9 Kiji-Toria C
10 The SeaDragon Cima-Creek R
11 The HeroEmperor DeitySword C
12 The HeroEmperor DeityShield C
13 Burst Draw C
14 Burst Cross R
15 Burst Flame U
16 Burst Wall U
17 Burst Storm U

2011 Battle Spirits The Golden Earth

1 Touchbet-Monkey C
2 Pygmygator C
3 Firefansaur C
4 Hanzo-Shinobi-Dragon R
5 The HollowBeast Champbongor C
6 Golhorn-Eagle C
7 Zenith-Dragoon R
8 Paladin-Dragon U
9 The HollowDragonEmperor Catastrophedragon MR
10 Gasfrog C
11 Meerbat C
12 Werewolf-Comman C
13 Elefog C
14 The HellHollowBeast Ibos U
15 The VampireLady Ethelfleda U
16 The DarkKnight Gawain R
17 Empress-Youqueen MR
18 The PhantomBeastEmperor Ten-Qoo C
19 Dal-Eagle C
20 Pandal C
21 The HollowSoldier Aoi-Subin C
22 Anagumad-Devil U
23 Takeno-Saigar C
24 Guan-Choun R
25 Kahyoton C
26 The TacticianBird Shokatsuryo R
27 The HollowProvidence Hououga MR
28 Fenneborac C
29 Zugani C
30 The LoveGoddess Lofn U
31 The HollowBeast Glassbear U
32 Snowflaken C
33 Chimera-Debri C
34 Milbrock-Genious MR
35 The WarSacred Mega-Tyr C
36 The HollowMachineEmperor Inphenit-Wols MR
37 Kudagitsunen C
38 Arcanabeast-Jack C
39 The Priest Pentan C
40 Nekomarda C
41 The Angelia Liyulel U
42 The Angelia of Olimpics Aratron C
43 Shogunpentan R
44 The Angelia Sakuel R
45 The HollowBeastEmperor Sphin-Cross MR
46 Rammer-Golem C
47 Punkmouse C
48 The FishermanMaster Zigorou C
49 Tsundog-Golem U
50 Grenade-Golem C
51 The HollowSeaBeast Emehydral U
52 The HeavenMarshall Chohakkai R
53 Kojirond-Golem MR
54 The HollowGolemEmperor Phoenix-Golem MR
55 Matadora C
56 Knight-Anole C
57 Kamen-Fukurou C
58 Double-Camel C
59 Starham C
60 Bandit-Arms C
61 The Cradle of Baby Dragon C
62 The Ganryujima Island U
63 The Hanged Old Castle C
64 The Evil Gate to the Thanatos U
65 The Great River and the Precipice U
66 The Infinite Stairway of the Deserted Temple C
67 The Snow Crystal Tree C
68 The Fortress Metropolis Naumann City R
69 The Lunar Court U
70 The Blowing Lollipop Uplands C
71 The Giant's Stamp Lake C
72 The Whirling Big Channel U
73 Transmigration Flame C
74 Triple Draw U
75 Bloody Rondo C
76 Vampiric Nail R
77 Heat Ride C
78 Burst Stratagem U
79 Provocation U
80 Triple Stab R
81 Royal Bible C
82 Moonlight Punish U
83 Swallow Counter C
84 Burst Fist R
X1 The KatanaHero Musashied-Ashliger XR
X2 The HollowEmperor Netherd-Baaral XR
X3 The BirdWarEmperor Suzacross-Soso XR
X4 The MachineBeastFortress Naumannguard XR
X5 The LightHero LunaArk-Kaguya XR
X6 The IronHero Saigord-Golem XR

2011 Battle Spirits King of the Starlit Sky

1 Hiquick C
2 The ArmoredDinoman Ankylong C
3 Chamaelopus C
4 Phobos-Dragon C
5 The RudeSaurus Dirano-Rex R
6 The Flame Beast Fioryx C
7 The PantherDragon Pandolancer U
8 The DinomanKing Megalo-Saur MR
9 Kemurisu C
10 Skullizard C
11 The Assassin Dragonaga C
12 Jainagant C
13 Skullion U
14 The DarkKnight Agravain C
15 The HellGovernor Hagen R
16 The CurseKing Dragonaga MR
17 Anaguma-Kosuke C
18 Modzu C
19 Corocorn U
20 Bushbabe C
21 Saizorong U
22 Yang-Ogre C
23 Mountain-Seikai R
24 The BushinBeast Deerl-Yukimura MR
25 Ammoknights C
26 Kigna-Swan MK-II C
27 Moonshouuo C
28 The OathGoddess Var U
29 The SwordHorse Granim C
30 Leathalweapondragon R
31 The RainbowDragon Auroria R
32 The LightSpeedKnight Hermod MR
33 Knockmole C
34 Minogamen C
35 The Angelia of Olimpics Och U
36 The StarBird Kuhija U
37 Princepentan C
38 The Witch Tarangda C
39 The SacredBeast Barrong R
40 The VenusDragonDeity Venu-Feather MR
41 Chootah C
42 Night-Gaun C
43 The Birdman Ikarosh C
44 The Minstrel Orphe R
45 The GiantCaptain Iason C
46 Shantarg U
47 The GreatDeepSea Norg-Dens MR
48 The AncientBattleship Argo-Golem MR
49 Irritaban C
50 The ShineDragon Shine-Blazer U
51 Zuganake C
52 Evilglider MR
53 Mokubaoh C
54 Hyo-Katchu R
55 The HeavyArmoredBrave Shield-Dragon Mk-II U
56 Hawk-Breaker MR
57 Poppor C
58 Chihyu R
59 Forbbid-Vulture C
60 Tres-Beluga R
61 The Coronation Volcano C
62 The Shining Galaxy U
63 The Bloody Artifact C
64 The Palace of Snake Believers U
65 The Oclant Small Shrine U
66 The Great Tree of Life C
67 The Light Guiding Tower C
68 The Faraway Satellite Cannon U
69 The Starry Sky Concert Hall C
70 The Constellation Barrier C
71 The Port of Giants C
72 The Unfinished Ancient Battleship:Compass U
73 Burning Sun C
74 Zodiac Conduct R
75 Snake Slave C
76 Assasinate U
77 Breeze Ride C
78 Never Give Up C
79 Vanishing Day U
80 Crescent Howling C
81 Dream Seal U
82 Pegasus Flap C
83 Galaxy Eternal Requiem C
84 Argo Attack U
X1 The ShineCentaurusDeity Sagitto-Apollodragon ZXR
X2 The SnakeMasterDeity Asklepiooze XR
X3 The SephirothicSheepDeity Sephiro-Aries ZXR
X4 The MachineLionDeity Strikewurm-Leo ZXR
X5 The KylinStarBeast Rean XR
X6 The GiantBraver Perseus XR

2011 Battle Spirits Legend of Dragon Heroes

1 Ryzard C
2 Kakyuso C
3 Scartooth C
4 Lesser-Dragsaurus C
5 Hinoshishi U
6 King-Goradon C
7 Kagutsuchidragoon C
8 Pentaceratop C
9 Warrior-Dragon U
10 The FangBeastEmperor Kintarogue-Bear R
11 The FlameDragonDevil Ma-Gwo MR
12 Straw-Puppet C
13 The Rogue Sha-Zoo C
14 Labolas C
15 Todar C
16 Shikitsuru C
17 The SmokeWolf Noroshi C
18 Both-Hands C
19 Shuten-Doga U
20 Nasuno-Archer R
21 The VioletPhoenix Fognix MR
22 The TwinPhantomDragon Sheyron MR
23 Kacchumushi C
24 Tsuchigo C
25 Mushamega C
26 Tamamush C
27 Monshiroran C
28 Ruriruri C
29 Musha-Geo C
30 Grant-Benkei MR
31 Musha-Apewhip R
32 Yatsunokanzo U
33 The GreatTreeGuardian Blanboar R
34 Three-Legger C
35 Raccoonguard C
36 Icemaiden Mk-II C
37 Ezono-Owl C
38 The Shooter Vali C
39 Mibrock-Soldier R
40 The BraveArtifact Ryudroid U
41 Buster-Fenriccannon C
42 The IronArtifact Modi C
43 The MoonLightPrincess Mani MR
44 The GlacialDragon Glaceus R
45 Goristal C
46 Pam C
47 Martiusagi C
48 The SwallowtailFairy Nami C
49 The Butler Pentan C
50 Yaley C
51 Arcanabeastqueen C
52 Tamamonoin R
53 The Angelia of Olimpics Hagith U
54 The GreatAngelia Angu MR
55 Mystic-Himiko MR
56 Chacopecca C
57 Deepfisher C
58 The BattledogBeast Siderope C
59 Repairing-Ceros C
60 Tindalo-Hound C
61 Yagyurd-Jubel R
62 Rock-Golem-Custom C
63 Cuelebrei C
64 Revolutiing-Zeyon R
65 Kurofune-Golem U
66 The FistMaster Tiga MR
67 Lagian C
68 Stolast C
69 Taranty C
70 Diyadokari C
71 Trumpn C
72 Gurangatch C
73 The Red Keyhole-Shaped Tumulus C
74 The Thousand Knowledge Canyon C
75 The Fortified City of Flame Dragon U
76 The Pentagram Castle C
77 The Leaning Tower of Corpse U
78 The Wraith's Ruins C
79 The Green Gojo Bridge C
80 The Ancient Forest C
81 The Stumpcity of God Tree U
82 The Pentagon Stronghold C
83 The Freezing WaterFalls C
84 The Permafrost Capital C
85 The Admiring Pipe Organ C
86 The Destiny Roulette U
87 The Empire of Pentan:the Capital Empereur C
88 The Sapphire Huge Labyrinth U
89 The Exploding Submarine Volcano C
90 The Fearless City on the Ship C
91 Double Blaster C
92 Blaze Slash U
93 Revelation Aura C
94 Critical Burst R
95 Violet Funeral U
96 Curse of Hades R
97 Instantaneous Shoot C
98 Dark Reborn C
99 Arms Shock C
100 Storm Attack R
101 Last Stand C
102 Tornade Burst R
103 Crystallize Illusion U
104 Dream Spiral C
105 Glacial Slash R
106 Recovered Core C
107 Dream Prayer U
108 Magical Light C
109 Altar Mirage C
110 Disaster Wind R
111 Execution Destroy C
112 Sealing Maelstrom C
113 Exclusion Horn U
114 Thunder Burst R
x01 The DragonHero Sieg-Yamato-Fried XR
X02 The CurseHero Chaotic-Seimei XR
x03 The WindHero Dorcus-Ushiwaka XR
x04 The IceHero Mibrock-Baragan XR
X05 The SacredBird An-Zur XR
X06 The MalevolentDeity Nyarla-Trap XR

2011 Battle Spirits Roar of the Moon

1 Veloci-Harpe C
2 Dsungareap C
3 The ArmoredDinoman Gaston C
4 Dragon-Pheasant C
5 The StarHornBeast Unigaunt C
6 The DragonBrawler Ardi-Baron R
7 The FlameDragonDeity Mars-Dragoon MR
8 Grand-Dragcastle U
9 Swordoll C
10 Gagamoth C
11 Mummybird C
12 The ChariotEmperor Dirgan U
13 The DarkKnight Kay C
14 The CorpseKnight Verium C
15 The PlutoDragonDeity Krono-Hades MR
16 The CorpseGiant Gi-Gasha R
17 Kanshakukorogashi C
18 Jakonezu C
19 Kunoichijorou U
20 The Spearhead Siberza U
21 Kojuu-Kamakirou R
22 The SunlightMusha Genji-Bolta C
23 The ShinobiMaster Udou C
24 The EvilJupiterDragon Nobunagard-Sechst MR
25 Zaneegun C
26 Uriborg C
27 The ArtifactGuards Chrysanthe MK-VIII R
28 Sailfish C
29 The IceLady Snotra C
30 The Artifact Forseti U
31 Mechaniffon C
32 The HeavyBootsEmperor Vidar MR
33 Kogumaru C
34 The Astronomer Pentan C
35 The Angelia of Olimpics Phul C
36 The StarDog Pomeran C
37 The Angelia of Olimpics Bethor C
38 The Angelia of Olimpics Phaleg C
39 The ClownPrincess Trickster MR
40 The UranusDragonDeity Slei-Caelus MR
41 Stagger C
42 Hinoki-Golem C
43 The Hunter Condrad C
44 Shumongo C
45 The BlackBeastKing Cepheus U
46 Nata-Golem C
47 The NeptuneDragonDeity Tri-Mercurius MR
48 Captain-Orcard R
49 Amphisbaenar R
50 The ChargingMachineDragon Archaelancer C
51 The Exoskeleton Bone-Loader U
52 Death-Haze C
53 Oodsutsunanafushi C
54 Manekicat MR
55 Gecko-Glider R
56 Jet-Ray U
57 Hydrandea C
58 The DivineBird Thunder-Bird U
59 Shoggoleth C
60 Vulcan-Arms R
61 The Birthplace of the Sword U
62 The Steam-Breathing Mountains C
63 The Brigade's Skyscraper C
64 The House of the Idol U
65 The Wooded Castle Tower U
66 The Gate of the Giant Trees C
67 The Moonlight Gathering Tower U
68 The Light Sacred Sword C
69 The Ruler Mountains C
70 The Heaven's Stairway R
71 The Unfinished Ancient Battleship: Sail U
72 The Pirate King's Treasure Island C
73 Nexus Collapse C
74 Starry Draw U
75 Bootes Call C
76 Brave Break R
77 Insect Aura C
78 Cassiopeia Seal R
79 Absolute Strike C
80 Vacuum Symbol R
81 Melodious Harp C
82 Seventh Heaven R
83 Magic Lamp C
84 Mercury Goblet U
x1 The BullDragonDeity Dragonic-Taurus ZXR
x2 The EvilCapricomusDeity Stein-Bolg ZXR
x3 The MonoeyeBushin Mantics-Masamune XR
x4 The MoonlightDragonDeity Lunatech-Strikewurm XR

x5 The ValkyrieVirgoDeity Vielje ZXR
x6 The PirateKing Leviadan XR

2011 Battle Spirits Scorching Sun

1 Volgames C
2 Cometwyarm C
3 Aquilam C
4 Prominencewyvern U
5 The IronHeadDinoman Pachycephalon C
6 The LeoDragonPrince Leogulus C
7 The ShiningEmperor Heliosdragon MR
8 The BurstDragon Dragonicbeard R
9 Smokeloco C
10 The Dark Knight Gaheris C
11 Flyskull U
12 The HellArmor Zepar C
13 Glasyahound U
14 The RipperPrincess Azalea C
15 The PlutoSacredBeast Inferd-Hades MR
16 The EvilEyeEmperor Zenas MR
17 Mushatsubame C
18 Yakuyanagi C
19 Danderabbit C
20 Onmyoyamasemi C
21 Gokurakucho U
22 Wolvy C
23 Totemowl C
24 The BushinBird Birdy-Kenshin MR
25 Karugamode C
26 Thousandneedle C
27 The SeaCarrier Njord U
28 The ArtifactBird Hresvelgr C
29 Streamotter C
30 Dolphing U
31 The Valkyrie-Mist C
32 The UranusSacredBeast Slei-Uranus MR
33 Nijinoko C
34 The StarHorse Colutte C
35 The HandicraftFairy Lepra C
36 The NetherWitch Helen U
37 Hipogrifee C
38 The HeavenStarHorse Pegaseeda C
39 The Angelia Tiael R
40 The SacredBeast Hikyu MR
41 Clay-Golem C
42 The Pirate Raccorsair C
43 Tower-Golem C
44 Shell-Golem C
45 MC Gingar U
46 The RoaringArm Todon C
47 The NeptuneSacredBeast Tri-Poseidos MR
48 Centaurus-Golem R
49 Jambi-Olepis U
50 The ClawDragon Powered-Tusker C
51 Evil-Fisher C
52 The EvilGun Vesper R
53 Karmula One C
54 The SpearBird Spineed-Hayato R
55 Janome-Shielder C
56 The StarSwordShuttle Polar-Caliber MR
57 Butterhorn C
58 The DivineBowBird Perytorn U
59 Recycle-Arms C
60 The ThunderSacredArtillery Cannon-Arms R
61 The Star Altar U
62 The Oort Dragon's Nest C
63 The Doomsday Drawn Canvas C
64 The Dark Sacred Sword U
65 The Starry Sky Pasture C
66 The Discovered World Tree U
67 The Great Wall of the White Shield R
68 The Pure Milky Way U
69 The Golden Belfry U
70 The Drifting Zero Gravity Island C
71 The PillarRocks' Aquapolis C
72 The Unfinished Ancient Battleship: Stern U
73 Buster Hammer C
74 Solar Breaker R
75 Totentanz C
76 Sharing Pain R
77 Star Cradle R
78 Brave Flash C
79 Reboot Code C
80 Delta Barrier R
81 Lightning Delivery C
82 Wig Bind R
83 Lead Voice U
84 Solid Body C
X01 The SunDragonDeity Rising-Apollodragon XR
X02 The StarSlayerDragon Darkwurm-Nova XR
X03 The StarKnight Hercules? XR
X04 The WaterCarrierDeity Aqua-Elysion ZXR
X05 The MagicalTwinsDeity Geminize ZXR
X06 The BalanceDeity Libra-Golem ZXR

2012 Battle Spirits 20

1 Shichinomus C
2 The FlameShieldGuardian Corona-Dragon R
3 Halberdnix C
4 Sintal-Saur C
5 Quicksand-Dragon C
6 The DemonFlameBladeMaster Schmald C
7 Slave-GaiAsura MR
8 Nebula-Dragon U
9 The DestructionDinosaur Dino-Breaker MR
10 Keylizard C
11 Smogpecker C
12 Bone-Tops C
13 The DarkShieldGuardian Nagan R
14 The HellMonk Fraulow C
15 Knight-Headless C
16 Wybone U
17 The TenSwordsSaint Cobraja MR
18 The WingedSnake Anaconga U
19 Somarin C
20 Kengokiji C
21 Yagoisobana C
22 The WindShieldGuardian Tobimaru R
23 Shinjulius C
24 Byakko-Hayato C
25 The GreenSwordBladeMaster Waonoshin U
26 Shinobi-Chuuhi U
27 Amaranth-Piper MR
28 The ImperialMachine Oath-Me C
29 Saterat C
30 The IceShieldGuardian Ohshin R
31 Missilis C
32 The IceEdgeBladeMaster Brigitt U
33 Nega-Kerberos U
34 Nega-Sabretiger MR
35 Nega-Springer C
36 The HeavyArmoredKnight Gol-Mack MR
37 The Angelia Spiele C
38 Cupid C
39 The LightShieldGuardian Edith R
40 Vanillap C
41 The Angelia Prima U
42 The PrincessAngelia Etoile C
43 The MadBeast Kyuuki C
44 The Swordsman Pentan U
45 The ImaginaryDragonEmperor Gilant MR
46 Doratfish C
47 The OceanShieldGuardian Giles R
48 Tatsuno-Draco C
49 Kamoone U
50 Datas of Trident C
51 The RoughSeaBladeMaster Akashi C
52 The Shaman Sangojaw C
53 The StrangeSeaCreature Shiporeep C
54 The WarGeneral Patroclus MR
55 Turok-Cephale C
56 HotJupiter-Dragon R
57 Snakers C
58 Skullplane U
59 Susukinkei R
60 Karakuribatta C
61 The ImperialMachine Messenger MR
62 Catapuseal C
63 Urvancle C
64 Angelegg U
65 Cyclo-Arms C
66 Konohaganin R
67 The Volcanic Canyon C
68 The Corroding Big Waterfall C
69 The Cumulo-Nimbus Mountain Range C
70 The Mirror Surface World Entrance C
71 The Light Shooting Hill C
72 The Ocean Master's Giant Mouth U
73 Power Boost C
74 Shining Flame C
75 Spiral Vein R
76 Death Accompany C
77 Wind Pressure C
78 Absorb Power U
79 Darkness Aura C
80 Perfect Repair U
81 Steal Heart R
82 Lightning Attack C
83 Call of the Deep U
84 Finishing Blow C
85 The FlashDragonEmperor TheEnd-Dragonis XR
86 The BlackCorpseKing Baldanders XR
87 The BirdBushin Shishigui XR
88 The BlackHeavenFox Nega-Ninetail XR
89 The ArcAngelia Raraphael XR
90 The ShinraNagarjuna Leaf-Shidora XR
91 The OffensiveSkullBlade Executioners XR
92 The LightWingsDivineBlade Angelicfeather XR
93 The ArcAngelia Raraphael XR
94 The BlackCorpseKing Baldanders XR

2012 Battle Spirits Blue Charge

1 The Giant Platoon C
2 The GreatFist Roger C
3 The HeavyJavelinGiant Lance C
4 The BattleMaul Gordon C
5 The TwoHeadedDragonTamer Bernard R
6 The DemonBladeMaster Colvis R
7 Loader-Arms C
8 The Ironwall Giant Fortress U
9 The GiantEmperor Alexander-XIII XR

2012 Battle Spirits Dark Rush

1 Shuraikun C
2 Bobcats C
3 Dark-Caribou C
4 Rhinogold C
5 Dark-Gadphant C
6 Bran-Falcon C
7 Bear-Polar U
8 Wise-Monkey U
9 The HuntingMachineBeast Silver-Jackal U
10 Dark-Uranus MR
11 Jet-Gannet C
12 The Underground Lake of the Ice Sword U
13 The Lost Crystal U
14 Wind Wall U
15 Dream Horizon U
16 Burst Break R
X1 The DarkEmperor Ninetail-Dark XR
X2 The MidnightSunTreasuredSword Midnight-Sun XR

2012 Battle Spirits Great Clash of Heroes

1 Therizino C
2 The GuardianBeast Sisinga C
3 Asassin-Dragon R
4 Basa-Razan C
5 The GuardianBeast Sisingini C
6 Gunner-Dragon MR
7 Yaksamori C
8 Monk-Dragon U
9 The FireBeast Hanu-Marg R
10 Camelot Pawn C
11 Zombie-Snake U
12 The DarkKnight Lamorak R
13 Don-Diegod MR
14 The HellLibrarian Dantalian C
15 Towermingo U
16 The DarkQueen Guinevere C
17 The DarkKnight Perceval C
18 The HellMask Zorro MR
19 Togarinezumin C
20 Bufumot C
21 The SteedGeneral Mugali R
22 The SteedGeneral Chilaun C
23 The SteedGeneral Boorchu C
24 The SteedGeneral Boroqul C
25 The GreaterIncect Riock U
26 The BigChief Jamuqa C
27 The WingBeast Spa-Ruda R
28 Meyeria C
29 Bat-Holliday U
30 Wild-Horn C
31 Geronimond MR
32 Armadidragon C
33 Outlaw-Kid C
34 Sheriff-Eagle R
35 Buffalong-Bill U
36 The HolyGroundGigantBeast Bellroc C
37 Homuncu C
38 The Angelia of Grimm Gretel C
39 The Angelia of Grimm Hansel C
40 The Poet Pentan U
41 Clock-Lycao C
42 The TwinAngelia Melodiel C
43 The Creator Grimm-Wilhelm R
44 The Creator Grimm-Jacob MR
45 Doktor-Faust MR
46 Shaggai-Bug C
47 Otherfellom C
48 The BraveGeneral Leonidas R
49 Gladdy-Squalo C
50 Augusdos U
51 Meteorite-Golem C
52 The LightningGeneral Hanni-Val U
53 Tyrantor-Nero C
54 Dictator-Caesar MR
55 Drake-Baya C
56 The HolySwordDragon Ex-Wyvern C
57 Gearzelle MR
58 Gun-Horse R
59 Zacka-Panzer U
60 Chariot-Arms C
61 The War History Monolith U
62 The Highest Mountain Top C
63 The Spirit Tower in the Sea C
64 The Twilight Camelot U
65 The Great Blue Steppe C
66 The Islands dotting the Emerald Sea C
67 The Great Beast Forest C
68 The O.K. Corral C
69 The Candy Residence U
70 The Walpurgis Night C
71 The Sapphire Highway U
72 The Caldron of Destory and Create C
73 Heroic Entry C
74 Burst Saviour U
75 Mark-of-Zorro R
76 Crystal Crack C
77 Boerte Salkhi U
78 Thunderstorm C
79 Windspout U
80 Kidzuna Blade C
81 Verweile C
82 Panic Voice R
83 Iron Phanlanx C
84 Dictator Legion R
X01 The SuperHero Lord-Dragon-Saviour XR
X02 The KnightsEmperor Avalo-Paladion XR
X03 The BlueSkyHero Kung-Wolf XR
X04 The GlacialHero Lord-Dragon-Glazar XR
X05 The HolyEvilEmperor Mephist-Pheles XR
X06 The ChaosEmperor Otherthoth XR

2012 Battle Spirits Green Rush

1 The SpearSoldier Antman C
2 Takeyanma C
3 Inegobatta C
4 DarkZiga-Wasp C
5 Tarancedar R
6 The TwinBladeInsect Nogogirafa MR
7 The FlyingShelledInsect Nitokugawata C
8 Insects Assemble U
9 The ArmoredWoodGod Herac-Dinus XR

2012 Battle Spirits Ken Mau Sekai

1 Bari-Burn C
2 Fencer Dragon C
3 Arjunas C
4 Ryu-Radha C
5 Drag-Krisnar R
6 Tsukuyomidragoon U
7 Vajranga C
8 The RubyDragon Volgand U
9 Swordmaster-Dragon MR
10 Mudoolo C
11 Camelot Knight C
12 The DarkKnight Aglovale C
13 Smokujira C
14 Chainviper C
15 The DarkKnight Palomides U
16 The DarkKnight Lancelot MR
17 The HellSoarBeast Fur-Fool C
18 The AmethystSnake Zaum U
19 Terimuck C
20 Giraffer C
21 Pixiefalco U
22 Tarzania Great R
23 Junebird C
24 Elestera C
25 Rai-Shuyu MR
26 Jadobaljar R
27 The EmeraldBird Aldeed U
28 Stream-Caribou C
29 Litten-Bikken C
30 Todorl C
31 The FertileGodess Gefion C
32 Viking-Leiv MR
33 Railgunfish U
34 Red-Erik C
35 The DiamondBattleship Drednorg U
36 King-Harald MR
37 Capyppa C
38 Calmion-Cat C
39 Irus-Bird C
40 The Shaman Rio C
41 The Angelia Grayel C
42 Amazonis-Girl U
43 The SacredBeast Seg MR
44 Amazonis-Queen R
45 The TopazQueen Felneit U
46 OryxThievs C
47 The BattleBeast Camerune C
48 The BearMan Ratesied C
49 Roc-Aladdin MR
50 Rhantegoth C
51 The PantherMan Alibaba U
52 The ArabianKnight Sind-Bird R
53 The SapphireHydra Shtrodorm U
54 Majin-Golem C
55 Yasakani-Wing C
56 Aroundizar R
57 Gyokuzeeg MR
58 Osebering C
59 Horus-Jeter U
60 Jinn-Arms U
61 The Divine Flame Takamagahara R
62 The Wandering Sky Temple C
63 The Evil Grail C
64 The Lake of the Dead U
65 The Beast Paradise C
66 The Fruit of Saint Tree C
67 The Freezing Fjord C
68 The Faraway Ground U
69 The Range of Royal Crypts C
70 The Unexplored City in Jungle C
71 The Opened Rock Door C
72 The Lamp of Wish C
73 Ardor Flame C
74 Burst Sword U
75 Strangle Fog R
76 Round Table Knights C
77 Wild Wing C
78 War Cry U
79 Freezing Parry C
80 Kveldúlfr R
81 Nefer Uarbe C
82 Reversible Spark R
83 Abrakadabra C
84 Triangle Ban R
X01 The SwordHero Sieg-Susano-Fried XR
X02 The KnightHero Swordius-Arthur XR
X03 The FangEmperor Byakgalord-Sonken XR
X04 The WolfMachineDeity Ragna-Fenrir XR
X05 The BeautyHero Cleopatras XR
X06 The ArabianKnightEmpress Sahrzad XR

2012 Battle Spirits Purple Rush

1 Amethysbat C
2 Bone-Cat C
3 Bone-Bison C
4 Zombie-Hawk U
5 The CorpseDragonEarl Decoux-Lon MR
6 The DeathBeastOfficial Deathlion R
7 Shadow-Maden C
8 Soul Reap C
9 The WickedDragonKing Cursedragon XR

2012 Battle Spirits Seiken Jidai

1 Doku-Lizard C
2 Mogeira C
3 Sprite-Dragoon C
4 Dimorpho C
5 Cleric-Dragon U
6 Kefaredagger R
7 Staba-Dragon C
8 Death-Mattock C
9 The MeteorBladeMaster Damasques U
10 The NineBladeDragon Spinozanbar MR
11 The HeavenStarDragon Quasar-Dragon MR
12 Tsubasa-Tsupai C
13 DarkDemo-Bone C
14 DarkSwordoll C
15 Mitransnake R
16 Clionet C
17 The Snake Sideron C
18 Victroller C
19 The HellStrikeArm Gushion C
20 The ShadowBladeMaster Blackpard U
21 The VampireMarquis Bezalel MR
22 DarkSkullpione U
23 Grass-Owl C
24 DarkMachG C
25 DarkDio-Mantis C
26 Fosser C
27 Ougononikuwaga U
28 Hagoromochou C
29 Kigashilight C
30 Ougi-Enshou R
31 Tokiiroshidare C
32 The DestructionDragonfly Habilong R
33 The TenSwordsSaint Murasame MR
34 Riverdolphin C
35 Gerenuuk C
36 The ImperialMachine Viking-No.1 U
37 Armor-Fish C
38 The ImperialMachine Curiosity C
39 Pegashione C
40 The TenSwordsSaint Vol-Cougar MR
41 Azara-Burg C
42 The ArmoredFortress Sawback-Turtle U
43 The SilverGoddess Arianrod C
44 The HighSpeedMachineBeast Oseloder R
45 Chocorone C
46 Hakkubishin C
47 The SleepingFlowerFairy Filly C
48 Airavata U
49 The Angelia Miransa C
50 Ray-Fawn C
51 The MadBeast Konton U
52 The Angelia Snipal C
53 The TenSwordsSaint Ruchell MR
54 The Sage Pentan U
55 Pelldea MR
56 The BattleBeast Wao C
57 The Defender of Light Adrian C
58 Kuramen C
59 The Warrior of Light Gaius C
60 Minota-Corse U
61 The Fighter of Light Randall C
62 The Knight of Light Hope U
63 Marble-Golem C
64 The TenSwordsSaint Egbert R
65 The StrangeOceanEmpress Rescura U
66 Maze-Hydra MR
67 Gaimimus C
68 The ElectricArtifactDragon Transfer-Dragon U
69 Hihi-Bone C
70 The ArmoredBattleship Blade-Hind R
71 Bumble C
72 Akkeshigumo R
73 The GunMachine Toradoll R
74 The GunBeast Aquidry C
75 Kongoushouki C
76 Jackkuri C
77 Fuscina-Arms C
78 The SeaCreature Gulon C
79 The Three Star View Towers C
80 The Bisecting Active Volcano C
81 The Crumbling Uroko Mountain C
82 The Bone Forest of Wandering Souls U
83 The Snake's Castle Gate C
84 The Candle Tower of Life C
85 The Pouring Clear Stream C
86 The Shinobi's Hidden Village C
87 The Stronghold of the Demonic Insect U
88 The Beast's Ice Cavern C
89 The Fortress Cube U
90 The Inverse Tower of Frozen Icicle C
91 The Ferris Wheel of Heaven Wings C
92 The Feast of the Pastry Forest C
93 The Nekoron Mountain R
94 The Never Ending Aqueduct R
95 The Lit Three-Pronged Lighthouse C
96 The Sea Monster Infested Ocean C
97 Charge Aura C
98 Red Ray C
99 Flame Field R
100 Dead End Field C
101 Hell's Birthday C
102 Purple Haze R
103 Emerald Field C
104 Turbulence C
105 Binding Ivy U
106 Ice Age Shield R
107 Regain C
108 Recovery Rush C
109 Angelic Pressure C
110 Divine Field R
111 Reversal Point C
112 Ocean Field C
113 Double Biceps C
114 Poseidon Crash R
X01 The TenSwordsSaint Starblade-Dragon XR
X02 The NetherThreeGiants Bergason-Bordeaux XR
X03 The BlackInsectDemonlord Diabolica-Mantis XR
X04 The GoldenKnightLord Fin-Maclan XR
X05 The ArcAngelia Gabrielen XR
X06 The BattleRadiantGod Soldnerg XR
X07 The BlackInsectDemonBlade Usubakagero XR
X08 The BlueWaterGreatSword Maelstrom XR
X09 The BattleRadiantGod Soldnerg XR
X10 The BlackInsectDemonlord Diabolica-Mantis XR

2012 Battle Spirits Shining Charge

1 Light-Bladra C
2 Glory-Guardler C
3 Mirage-Wyvern U
4 The SteamDragon Seasmoker C
5 Bronze-Wurm C
6 Mon-Dosun C
7 The FirewhirlDragon Firestorm U
8 Dragon-Annura C
9 Sunpillar-Dragon U
10 The StormDragon Supercell-Dragoon MR
11 Dustwhirl C
12 The Magma Spouting Star City U
13 The Dragon Shuttle to the Heavens U
14 Twin Flame C
15 Fire Wall U
16 Charge Draw R
X1 The ShineDragon Shining-Dragon XR
X2 The ShiningSacredSword Shining-Sword XR
X3 The ShineDragon Shining-Dragon XR
X4 The ShineDragon Shining-Dragon XR

2012 Battle Spirits Yellow Charge

1 The Angelia Pathiel C
2 The Angelia Machael C
3 The Angelia Archiel C
4 The Angelia Axela R
5 The Angelia Plastiel MR
6 Angeloid C
7 Ascencion Zero C

8 Magical Draw U
9 The BattleAngelia Excel XR

2013 Battle Spirits 21

1 Yamabakka C
2 WolfDragon C
3 Combopelta C
4 Herbig-Wyvern U
5 Blade-Pteras C
6 The LongArmBlade Master Asuquina U
7 The RychlyColoredDragon Peacock-Wyvern MR
8 Garunotaurus C
9 The WarCranDragon Meishunosaurus MR
10 Marshbil C
11 Jangohebi C
12 Bone-Boar U
13 The PhantomThiefBat Bunnygirl C
14 The GrimSnake Boomsnake MR
15 The DeathBladeMaster Durabone U
16 Death-Hydra R
17 The HellPatroller Valfared C
18 The CorpseBeastLord Bone-Cousseraux MR
19 Quick-Mosqui C
20 Harimoguri C
21 The CraneStar Alnair R
22 The WaterBug Gengrass U
23 Mandrahora C
24 Kurotaenhawk C
25 The GreatGrassBird Sotetsunia-Condor MR
26 The CrimsonInsect Benikamikiran C
27 The TenSwordSaint Gohonkaku MR
28 Prod-Falcon C
29 Rishiakirin U
30 The CrimsonGoddess Mach U
31 The Sacred Gaebolg C
32 The HoundMachine Asterio-Venera 9 C
33 The ImperialMachine Geneshield C
34 The ClairvoyantMachineDeity Diareen MR
35 Nega-Kangaroo C
36 The TenSwordSaint Zanba-Kong MR
37 Kamelonpan C
38 Vodyanoi C
39 The Angelia Lissele U
40 Gatobelpas C
41 Adopentan & Charl C
42 The TenSwordsSaint Narashimha MR
43 Darklberix U
44 The MadBeast Toukotsu C
45 The Angelia of Beauty Caphopeia R
46 Yanakurage C
47 The SuperHumanGiant Adolphus C
48 Ryuuguushi C
49 The SeaCarver Napoleo C
50 Gel-Gorth C
51 Dark-Squalo C
52 The TenSwordSaint Burd-Sainos MR
53 The StarEater Yashiganid U
54 The GiantHero Heraclas R
55 Gornic-Eagle C
56 Pterastone U
57 The HellBeastRider Shitori R
58 Gargoylas C
59 Karakuripelican C
60 The InsectivoreGrass Drosella U
61 The SatelliteMachine Pioneer V C
62 The CrossArrowBeast Cross-Bongo C
63 GurumiPanda C
64 BurikiTiger U
65 Dive-Arms C
66 The DeepSeaDragon Lovliss U
67 The Apollonia Cavern Temple C
68 The Dark Coffin Cave C
69 The Big Tree of Ryuketsu U
70 The Fiana Aircraft Carrier City U
71 The Four Cloud Retreat C
72 The Coral Sea of Trees U
73 Burning Force R
74 Volcanic Break C
75 Deadly Hex U
76 Soul Slide C
77 Velotical Wind C
78 Binding Web R
79 Eternal Defense C
80 White Out R
81 Surprise Slap U
82 Life Dream R
83 Sapphire Erode C
84 Raging Sea R
85 The ShiningSunDragonEmperor Shining-Dragon-Ark XR
86 The DoubleHeadedDragonKing Bi-Jaou XR
87 The BlackWoodDeity Kuwaga-Ravna XR
88 The SpearLighMachineDeity Kugel-Horn XR
89 The SpearLighMachineDeity Kugel-Horn XR
90 The LandBeastDeity Behemoth XR
91 The StrangeSeaCreatureGod Dist-Ruction XR
92 The StrangeSeaCreatureGod Dist-Ruction XR
93 The SkyLightSword Crown-Solar XR
94 The AbyssGiantSword Abyss-Apocalypse XR

2013 Battle Spirits 22

1 Pistojasaurus C
2 Alphataceratops C
3 Prophet-Dragon R
4 Khopeshpterus C
5 Photon-Dragon C
6 The BlackSwordDragon Rexbeat-Saura U
7 The ArmoredDragon Edmontsword U
8 Gearattacker-Dragon C
9 The BladeStar Messiah-Dragon MR
10 Bone-Dile C
11 The DarkArtsWarrior Shax C
12 The CorpseDemon Imp U
13 Segurousnake C
14 The Magician Hakuja U
15 Mummy-Phant C
16 The WitchBladeMaster Prisila MR
17 Bone-Bear C
18 The DemonKing Balor R
19 Genin-Suzume C
20 Araigoya C
21 Chuunin-Tsubame C
22 Kabutozemi C
23 Mega-Neura R
24 Jounin-Tonbi U
25 The WindBladeMaster Muramasa MR
26 Ghost-Mantis C
27 The LittleConquerorBird Sonsahawk U
28 Calibera U
29 DarkDober C
30 The TransparentGleamTurtle Matamata C
31 The CrystalDragon Sillimanite R
32 The ImperialMachine Mariner No.2 C
33 Jakou-Cat MR
34 The TacticSacred Conan-Barr R
35 DarkBison C
36 The IceBladeMaster Morrigan U
37 Kamuweasel C
38 Rollmaimai C
39 The MadBeast Toutetsu C
40 The TreasureGuard Zlatorog C
41 Al-Mi'raj C
42 Harpy-Girl MR
43 The HolyAngelia Etoile C
44 The HeavenBladeMaster Kiriel R
45 The SpaceTimeWitch Grandes C
47 Atlach-Nacha C
48 The ZealousGiant Dean C
49 The SeaPrince Eon U
50 The SeaEmperor Ivan MR
51 Pumauros C
52 The OldBladeMaster Tigris R
53 The CalamityGeneral Ngurias C
54 Imperial-Hydra R
55 The StarDragon Stardust-Caliburn R
56 The KillerArmoredDragon Rugops U
57 Skull-Garuda C
58 Saw-Snake C
59 Ootoki Kite C
60 Scissor Catcus U
61 The ImperialMachine Hullnote No. 1 C
62 The BeastBomb Manatee-Marauder MR
63 Pentan Brave C
64 Sweets Fighter C
65 Blue-Arms C
66 Coral-Jaguar U
67 The Sacred Sword of the Mountain Rage C
68 The Mausoleum of Ten Thousand Spirits C
69 The Hidden Village of Light Fang C
70 The Floating Island on the Mercury Sea C
71 The Rose Garden Dyed in Red C
72 The Atraia Sea Empire U
73 Generate Fire C
74 Flame Disaster U
75 Soul Ripper R
76 Triple Deadly C
77 Shining Shadow C
78 Binding Branch C
79 Crystal Field U
80 Phase Change R
81 Dreaming Butterfly U
82 Life Revolution R
83 Abyss Break R
84 Resolution C
85 The PrimitiveKing Gigano-Rex XR
86 The NetherThreeGiants Thunder-Million XR
87 The LightFangPhoenix Rekkumaru XR
88 The DarkKingMachineBeast Darkness-Griffon XR
89 The EvilSacredBeast Chaos-Pegasuros XR
90 The SeaEmperorGiant Durazam XR
91 The HurricaneTwinBlade Kamui-Hayate XR
92 The FantasyHeavenBlade Twilight-Fantasia XR

2013 Battle Spirits 23

1 The FanBladeDragon Dimetron C
2 The DinosaurSwordsSaint Dracorex R
3 Shining-Bladra C
4 Souen-Dragoon C
5 The MeteorSwordsSaint Shootingstar U
6 Guardian-Dragon C
7 Silver-Wurm C
8 The NebulaDragon Andromeda-Dragon MR
9 Kokasutorikera C
10 Wingwinder U
11 Amethysnake C
12 The WolfKnight Loup-Gar C
13 The WhiteSnakeSwordsSaint Albinaga MR
14 Bone-Ceros C
15 The WhiteRiderDragon White-Pendragon C
16 The DeathGodSwordsSaint Darkness-Mare R
17 Shadow-Aldius C
18 The WickedBoneDragonEmperor Bone-Titanoks U
19 The WaterShinobi Gamon C
20 Yoroibatta C
21 Mushatanuki C
22 The FireShinobi Hashibiro MR
23 Grace Caterpiller C
24 The NightButterflySwordsSaint Morphonight R
25 The ShinobiBird Juichi C
26 The SwordsSaintMasterShinobi Jiraiya U
27 The FortressWorm Fort-Caucasus U
28 Anagpanzer C
29 The ImperialMachine Ranger No. 6 C
30 The GunStrikeKnight Maclir C
31 The HeavenSwordsSaint Fisuel MR
32 The BlackGoddess Nemhain C
33 The ArmoredSwordsSaint Minotauros U
34 Nega-Typhon MR
35 Clubman-AT R
36 The GreatImperialMachine ISS C
37 The DancingWitch Maya C
38 The AdventureAngelia Charl R
39 The Adventurer Adopentan C
40 The PuppeteerAngelia Mariel C
41 The Angelia of Light Dariel C
42 Caprinmel C
43 The ShadowMoonSwordsSaint Amalthea MR
44 The IceFireSwordsSaint Sphiel U
45 The WaterDragonDeity Galgios C
46 Atraisoldier C
47 Migo C
48 Falcopanther C
49 The BoarMan Boaboa C
50 The AbyssalSwordsSaint Shubu-Nigura R
51 The Blacksmith Beta C
52 The SwordsSaintGeneral Firanda MR
53 Timbertoll C
54 The OceanEmperorGiantSoldier Atraia-Golem U
55 The SunBlade Cardinal-Sun U
56 The BlazeMoonBlade Scarlet-Moon U
57 Zaguna-Orix C
58 The DemonSword Deathscythe U
59 Hanmyoru C
60 The JadeKodachi Nichirinmaru MR
61 Phantom Jetter C
62 The AuroraBlade Soulbreaker R
63 The HaloBlade Angelhalo R
64 The AnnihilationAngelia Nephilim U
65 The OceanEmperorBlade Triwave R
66 Hydra-Arms C
67 The Eternal Deity Capital C
68 The Underground Empire of Lies C
69 The Bug-Inviting Bewitching Flower Tower U
70 The Rocket City C
71 The St. Mikatar Cathedral C
72 Warning of the Heaven Shrine U
73 Dino Reborn C
74 Sword Raid R
75 Dead Sword C
76 Vanishing Core C
77 Quickly Sword R
78 Grass Bind C
79 Counter Sword C
80 Back Attack U
81 Thunder Wall C
82 Dancing Sword U
83 Spinning Sword U
84 Deep Sea Illusion C
85 The DragonShineDeity Shining-Dragon-Overray XR
86 The WhiteSnakeEmperor Aldius-Viper XR
87 The ButterflyEmpress Grace-Papillon XR
88 The TwinGunMachineDeity Dirum-Dyna XR
89 The ArcAngelia Avrielle XR
90 The AbyssalTwinDragon Hastark XR
91 The True Sword of Judgment Truth-Eden XR
92 The FlashSoulBlade Lightning-Shion XR
93 The DragonShineDeity Shining-Dragon-Overray XR
94 The WhileSnakeEmperor Aldius-Viper XR

2013 Battle Spirits 24

1 Ryuuman-Crow C
2 Vaijiriaxe C
3 The FistBeast Kinguru C
4 Ryuuman-Phoenix R
5 Allocanosaurus C
6 Ryuuman-Vulca C
7 Sleam-Tricera C
8 Eclipse-Dragon U
9 Flame-Gundragna C
10 Ryuuman-Blade MR
11 One-Eyed Demon C
12 GasRabbit C
13 ThirdEyes-Snake C
14 Tsuchigudemon C
15 Batknight MR
16 Kasugacoil C
17 Mezudemon C
18 The HellBeastKIng Othello U
19 The DeadSnakeDragon Kanon R
20 Axemoth C
21 Yoroikarasu C
22 Yoroifukuru C
23 Saberhornet C
24 Swordpuma R
25 Kanabun C
26 Swordcoyote U
27 Knighteagle MR
28 Scorpioknight C
29 The MilleniumBeast Behemoth-Cedar U
30 Automaticgunner C
31 AquaAnemonefish C
32 Cyber-Shepherd C
33 Groshlizard C
34 The 90th Tank Mobile C
35 Garnetdragon MR
36 Burst Turtle C
37 Scrapmammoth C
38 The SkyFortressEmperor King-Fortress R
39 Wyvernberyl C
40 Ottheno C
41 KodaMouse C
42 The Diva Asia MR
43 The Diva Marika U
44 Cocatrice C
45 The Diva Coco C
46 The Knight Pentan C
47 The WingedBeast WingBehemoth R
48 The Diva Mirefa U
49 Drian C
50 Quartz-Golem C
51 The GiantNavigator Dobby C
52 Riot-Golem C
53 Caravel-Golem R
54 The PirateGiant Kidd U
55 Bearcentaurus R
56 Galleon-Golem C
57 The SharkDrake Sharkhydra C
58 Ultimate-Dragsaurus C
59 Ultimate-Pteratomahawk U
60 The UltimateBishop Levia MR
61 Ultimate-Sha-Zoo C
62 Ultimate-Darkwitch C
63 Ultimate Zo-Goin R
64 Ultimate-Quetzalcoatl U
65 Ultimate-Zigawisp C
66 Ultimate-Geo C
67 Ultimate-Trenton R
68 Ultimate-Embla C
69 Ultimate-Fenrir R
70 Ultimate-Freyr U
71 Ultimate-Koristal C
72 Ultimate-Angu C
73 Ultimate-Sophia MR
74 Ultimate-Emperur C
75 Ultimate-Rock-Golem U
76 Ultimate-Mongoku C
77 Ultimate-Iron-Golem C
78 Ultimate-Randolph MR
79 Pterifighter C
80 ArmoredHarley C
81 Kuwagatank C
82 Busterfalcon21 C
83 WingArrow C
84 Robs-Arms C
85 The Prelude to Destruction C
86 The Burnt Out Battlefield C
87 The Hell City Caina R
88 The Battlefield of Thousand Spears C
89 The Twisting Dangaro Mountains R
90 The Fruit of Life Rookery C
91 The Icy Ruins Sky Rio C
92 The Fortress Metropolis of Eternal Snow C
93 The Stage where Angels Descend C
94 The Sealed Witchcraft Library C
95 The Sapphire Sculpture C
96 The Forgotten Triumphal Arch R
97 Brave Destruction C
98 Judgement Call C
99 Flame Breeze U
100 Death Massacre U
101 Soul Burst C
102 Demon's Puppet C
103 Cycle Power C
104 Binding Creeper R
105 Shadow Leaf C
106 Ultimate Wall C
107 Dream Nebula R
108 Suppression U
109 Battle Cancel C
110 Saint Breeze R
111 Ultimate Plasma U
112 Clear Edge C
113 Overdrive C
114 Break Grind C
115 The ConvictionDownfallDragon Judgement-Dragonis XR
116 The NetherThreeGiants Queen-Merduk XR
117 Ultimate-Siegfrieden XR
118 Ultimate-Desperado XR
119 Ultimate-Kaiseratlus XR
120 The UltimateGiant Ultimate-Thor XR
121 Ultimate-Mikafar XR
122 Ultimate-Castle Golem XR

2013 Battle Spirits Darkness Fang

1 Pinacochasaurus C
2 DarkDinonychusaw C
3 The SwordDragon Stegodita U
4 Bronswordsaurus C
5 The FeatherDragon Pedpenner U
6 The ViolentDragon Ranbeos U
7 Pteraslasher C
8 Monoforcesaurus U
9 The PiercingDragon Styragon MR
10 Lancemosaurus C
11 The ArmedMachineDragon Silveed C
12 The Primeval Forest U
13 The Dark Galaxy of Dust C
14 Jurac Flame C
15 Dino Crisis R
16 Rush Draw U
17 The DarkDragon Dark-Tyrannosaura XR
18 The DarknessDemonSword Dark-Blade XR

2013 Battle Spirits Dream Booster

1 Ryuuman-Hammer C
2 Gozdemon C
3 Satoridemon MR
4 HananoMantis C
5 Sawgrizzly MR
6 Heavy-Tankmobile T-75 C
7 Tourmalinedragoon MR
8 NemeaLeon C
9 The Angelia Daruel R
10 Brigatine-Golem C
11 Frigate-Golem R
12 Flame Bust C
13 Death Burst C
14 Resonance Burst C
15 Ryuuman-Godbreaker XR
16 Burst Barrier C
17 The SeaDragon Cima-Creek R
18 Dictator-Caesar MR
19 Doktor-Faust MR
20 The BeautyHero Cleopatras XR
21 Tarzania-Great R
22 The IronHero Saigord-Golem XR
23 The KatanaHero Musashied-Ashliger XR
24 The Angelia of Grim Cinderella XR
25 The IceHero Mibrock-Baragan XR
26 The CurseHero Chaotic-Seimei XR
27 The WindHero Dorcus-Ushiwaka XR
28 The FangBeastEmperor Kintarogue-Bear R

2013 Battle Spirits Eris the Morning Star

1 Haneppo C
2 The Fairy Mona C
3 The Angelia Iver C
4 The Angelia Aester C
5 The Angelia Gourette C
6 The Fairy Actia U
7 The Angelia Lyell U
8 Ultimate-Kleio C
9 Ultimate-Virchu U
10 Ultimate-Exsia MR
11 The Fortress Above the Clouds of Eirein U
12 Yellow Alert C
13 Symphonic Burst R
14 Burst Snap C
15 Angel Strike U
16 Reversal Force U
17 Ultimate-Valiero XR

2013 Battle Spirits SD 19

1 Fizard C
2 Mugendra U
3 Rookie-Ryuuman C
4 Buzz-Ryuuman C
5 Edge-Wolf C
6 Dragoknight C
7 Aizendragon C
8 Ultimate-Goradon U
9 The UltimateSoldier Dragno U
10 Ultimate Ma-Gwo MR
11 The Village of Hunters U
12 The Red Dawn Sky U
13 Neo-Double Draw R
14 Blazing Burst C
15 Flame Spark U
16 Neo-Flame Tempest C
X01 Ultimate-Siegfried XR

2013 Battle Spirits SD 20

1 Missilemobile C
2 Mugendra U
3 Defenzard C
4 Shieldmobile C
5 Troopermobile C
6 Wingsoldier C
7 WhiteJetDragon C
8 UltimateCannon-Bell U
9 Ultimate-Asc U
10 Ultimate-Surtr MR
11 The Rowgard Northern Instructions Bureau U
12 The Falling World U
13 Ultimate Power C
14 Burst Shield U
15 Last Revelion C
16 Blitz Order R
17 Ultimate-Odin XR

2013 Battle Spirits Zero the Hurricane

1 SpiAnt C
2 Ladybird C
3 Claw Fox C
4 NokogiruKuwaga C
5 Vald-Jaeger C
6 Mugendragon U
7 Gradytiger C
8 Ultimate-Tigald U
9 Ultimate-Monoqueiroz U
10 Ultimate-Xen-Fu MR
11 The Clouded Highlands U
12 The Great Tree on Lush Grounds U
13 Triangle Burst R
14 High Stampede C
15 Neo-Hand Reverse C
16 Neo-Binding Thorn U
17 Ultimate-Kingtaurus XR

2014 Battle Spirits 25

1 Debris-Zard C
2 Moonbow-Dragon C
3 The Survivor Neo-Ark C
4 Ryuuman-Tiger C
5 Dark Matter Dragon R
6 Ryuuman-Lightning MR
7 The BurstFireElephant Maximus C
8 The DinosaurAircraftCarrier Apato U
9 The LeonKnight Arocain C
10 Bone-Sabertiger C
11 The Survivor Visargo C
12 Rune Master Naga C
13 The EvilMarquis Focalor U
14 The ChevalLancer Erigale U
15 The EvilBull Morax C
16 Darkwurm-Nova-Remnant R
17 The Hellwitch Aini MR
18 Hakubisword C
19 SaberSeseri C
20 The Survivor Fugue C
21 Rikaospada MR
22 Lucky Cat C
23 Night Ibis R
24 Dandolion U
25 The BladeEmperorInsect Grande-Kuwaga C
26 The Soldier Hrungnir C
27 Tank-Mobil-Hetzer C
28 The Survivor Ur-Defender C
29 Star Drian C
30 Grey Garm C
31 Sunstone-Dragon R
32 Mobile-Golem C
33 The FatePrincessDeity Verthandy MR
34 Hisui-Cannon-Dragon U
35 The Angelia Wizel C
36 Ceryneiar C
37 The Survivor Angelia Mael C
38 The Investigator Asia R
39 Claydon C
40 The Diva Raquel MR

41 The DaughterAngelia Ashael MR
42 The HolyKnight Pentan U
43 Mechanic-Corgi C
44 Gekko-Golem C
45 The ApprenticePirate Terry C
46 The Survivor Buddy C
47 The GinatSwordsman Archbold C
48 The BattleBird Parakeet C
49 The GiantMusketeer Clifford MR
50 Adamant-Golem U
51 The GiantDeity Junius R
52 Ultimate-Siegwurm R
53 Ultimate-Ex-Calibus MR
54 Ultimate-Baculus U
55 Ultimate-Berith U
56 Ultimate-Caracolossom U
57 Ultimate-Amenborg U
58 Ultimate-Monokerock U
59 Ultimate-Yggdrasil R
60 Ultimate-Salaty R
61 Ultimate-Cu-Sith U
62 Ultimate-Galadolg U
63 Ultimate-Lowen U
64 The Planet Celtic Cross C
65 The Dark Capital Antenora C
66 The Fruit of Emerald Agrimony C
67 The Armored City of Shieldonia C
68 The Armored Dragon's Hunting Ground U
69 The Golden Wings of Pipe Organ C
70 The Three Headed Dragon Pirate Flag C
71 The Rare Metal Mine C
72 Neo-Aggressive-Rage C
73 Neo-Call-Of-Lost C
74 Brave Cremation C
75 Neo-Poison Shoot C
76 Wind Circle C
77 Binding Scale R
78 White Crack C
79 Neo-Dream Ribbon R
80 Power Down R
81 Golden Counter C
82 Support Flag C
83 Random Bomb U
84 The ArmoredDragonBattleship Enterprise XR
85 The OceanEmperorGiant Duran-Kidd XR
86 Ultimate-Gai-Asura XR
87 Ultimate-Beelzebeat XR
88 Ultimate-Byak-Garo XR
89 Ultimate-Grand-Woden XR
90 Ultimate-Isfiel XR
91 Ultimate-Orichalcum-Golem XR

2014 Battle Spirits 26

1 Starry-Ryuuman C
2 Drago-Speeder C
3 The Ptera Fighter C
4 Aroblader C
5 Pleiades-Rockdragon C
6 The FlameDragonGeneral Ifrit U
7 Ryuuman-Fantasista R
8 The EmperorDragon Kaiserdragon MR
9 Smogsheep C
10 Hornviper C
11 Jibakku-Armor C
12 Linksmoker C
13 Bone-Ritter C
14 The EvilRitter Kilmedeath U
15 The CorpseDustGeneral Mukuro R
16 Queen-Nightmare MR
17 Tsurugimukade C
18 The ShellWarrior Tendo C
19 Purokiwan U
20 Silva-Yanma C
21 The NorthWindWolf BoreasWolf R
22 The ShellBladeGeneral Legioss MR
23 The HuntingBladeBeast Carla-Hound C
24 Tank-Mobile-Leopard C
25 Amber-Leon C
26 The FlamePrincessDeity Skuld MR
27 The MachineGunDeity HeimCannon C
28 The UnicornMachine Unicorn R
29 The WhiteKnightGeneral Sigdfor U
30 OnyxDragon-Rider C
31 Purimuppo C
32 Radon C
33 The FairyPrincess Perfume MR
34 The Angelia Nursel C
35 The LadyDiva Guriffa-D'Arc U
36 The FairyGeneral Gloria R
37 The MarineBeast Cetus R
38 The TraditionalDiva Marika MR
39 The Helmsman Isaac C
40 The Defender Nupia C
41 The ViceCaptain Chester U
42 The StarOceanPirate Perseus MR
43 The BladeWolf Jigen C
44 The CatManSwashbuckler Birman R
45 The PirateGeneral Edward C
46 The RubyFlameDragon Hinoko U
47 The DevilEmperor David U
48 The EmeraldPhoenix Nix U
49 The ElectricGodEmperor Train U
50 The HolyPegasus Sky U
51 The SapphireBeastEmperor Panzer U
52 The GunAstralArmored Baldo-Lizard C
53 The BirdAstralArmored Shisobird MR
54 The DevilAstralArmored Flybeat C
55 The SnakeAstralArmored Snakers U
56 The EarthAstralArmored Foxstar C
57 The SkyAstralArmored Eaglet MR
58 The SwordAstralArmored Swordfish C
59 The ShieldAstralArmored Shieldtank C
60 The RabbitAstralArmored Rabitta C
61 The VirgoAstralBrave VirgoBrave R
62 The ShipAstralArmored BraveArgo C
63 The ScorpioAstralArmored BraveScorpio R
64 The Gainarock Big Canyon C
65 The Shrine of Supernova U
66 The Tolomaela Streets of Grief C
67 The Alver Prairie C
68 The Spacetime Bonding Point A-01 C
69 The Norandy Absolute Defense Line U
70 The Soluje Hill C
71 The Thunder Seas C
72 Cannonball R
73 Crimson Flare C
74 Core Drain U
75 Forbidden Grave C
76 High Pressure U
77 Ultimate Wind C
78 Ultimate Laser R
79 Anti Brave Barrier C
80 Illusion Mirror R
81 Changeling C
82 Thunder Tactics C
83 Impact Roar C
84 The ShellPriest Shirokabuto XR
85 The PhantomPrincessDeity Echidna XR
86 Ultimate-Siegwurm-Nova XR
87 Ultimate-Ragna-Rock XR
88 The NextGenerationBeastKing Liodras XR
89 The PiscesAstralArmored BravePisces XR
90 The CancerAstralArmored BraveCancer XR
91 The WaterCarrierAstralArmored BraveAquarius XR

2014 Battle Spirits 27

1 Ryuuman-Skysword C
2 Homuraitachi C
3 Ryuuman-Landaxe C
4 The RowdyEmperor Tees-Dragon U
5 The WiseDragon Chiron MR
6 Ryuuman-Raylancer R
7 The LionDeityGeneral Shieldragon C
8 Hyades-Dragon C
9 Thun-Daemon C
10 The FallenKnight Ariel C
11 The FallenKnight Ramiel C
12 The SnakePriests Briesnake C
13 The FallenKnight Arioch U
14 The EvilDeityGeneral Wiene C
15 The FallenKnight Azazel R
16 Death-King-Snake C
17 Mongoose Sword C
18 The Bird of WesterlyWinds Zeefalcon C
19 The GodBird Hansa U
20 The ShellBrawler Muguri C
21 The SextantSword of Ruti-Author R
22 The BlueDeityGeneral Lapis-Jaguar C
23 The FourShellHeaven Aogami C
24 The GoldenShellEmperor Rosenberg MR
25 Beam-Arashi C
26 TankMobil-Sherman C
27 Turquoise-Dragon C
28 TankMobil-M6 C
29 The CarrierEmperor Ridefencer C
30 The SteelDeityGeneral FortElk C
31 The FatePrincessDeity Urd MR
32 TankMobil-Tiger R
33 Shinryuu C
34 Chocodra C
35 The Cape Pentan C
36 Reiki C
37 The SmallSaint Romeda MR
38 The FairyMercenary Drury C
39 The BraveDeityGeneral Ou-Ryute U
40 The DivaEarl Coco R
41 The GiantShip's Doctor Gordon C
42 Anmodora C
43 The AcrobaticsSoldier Fock C
44 The BeastmanKnight Waterbuck C
45 The RubyBeardGiant Barbaros MR
46 The SeaDeityGeneral Elephandar U
47 The WindGeneral Erigyius C
48 The Giant Cepheus C
49 Flame-Cougar U
50 Ultimate-Catastrophedragoon U
51 The DemonPrincess Bizak R
52 Ultimate-Baaral U
53 Shubarian-Husky R
54 Ultimate-Hououga U
55 The BattleMaiden Valkyrie MR
56 Ultimate-Wols U
57 The SuperAngelia Pafuel U
58 Ultimate-Sphin Cross U
59 The BeastGeneral Cheedas R
60 Ultimate-Phoenix-Golem U
61 The BraveAstralArmored Boll-Bear C
62 The GuardianAstralArmored Equu-Leus C
63 The CapricorniusAstralArmored BraveCapricorn MR
64 The WhiteAstralArmored Cygnus-Wing C
65 The AriesAstralArmored BraveAries MR
66 The BraveAstralArmored Leo-Minor C
67 The HeavenAstralArmored Blanc-Pegase C
68 The TwinsAstralArmored BraveGemini R
69 The DogAstralArmored Tossa-Sirius C
70 The Heaven Piercing Ballista C
71 The Ancient Capital Giudecca of Souls C
72 The Forest of Unstoppable Winds C
73 The Finoble Streets of Everlasting Winter C
74 The Star View Observatory C
75 The Military Port City Austere R
76 The Beast Mountain C
77 Bullet Fire R
78 Lightning Poison U
79 Bird Wind R
80 Seventh Force U
81 Dream Bomb R
82 Defense Nebula C
83 Mad Operation U
84 The DarkKnightLord Nemesis XR
85 The GrandAdmiral Claudius XR
86 The HolyDragonEmperor Ultimate-Savior XR
87 The GodWolfTempestar XR
88 Ultimate-Rean XR
89 The SagittariusAstralArmored Brave-Sagittarius XR
90 The LeoAstralArmored LeoBrave XR
91 The LibraAstralArmored BraveLibra XR

2014 Battle Spirits 28

1 Ryuuman-Doshatto C
2 Whitehole-Dragon U
3 Ryuuman-Infinity C
4 Red Fox R
5 Magatsu-Dragoon C
6 Pterawachsen C
7 Cape Rocker C
8 Ryuuman-Oceanrod C
9 General-Dragon MR
10 Living Gargoyle C
11 The HellSorecere Seere C
12 The FallenKnight Tums C
13 Phantom Hound C
14 Bone-Deer C
15 The FallenPrincess Elsha MR
16 Jungle Crow Demon C
17 The FallenKnight Orcus R
18 The BlackCorpseDragon Shadoruga U
19 BladeG R
20 The FourShellSky Kamejuuji C
21 Tanugurin C
22 Knife Cicada C
23 The FourShellSky Hotaruhime C
24 Cancerd-Reverse C
25 The FourShellSky Daikoku U
26 Chiwawanko C
27 Raideen-Wolf MR
28 Mechaoko-Jo C
29 Leading-Orix R
30 Mechatoris C
31 The FateGod Norn C
32 Strikewurm-Leo-Reverse C
33 Noisy Raven C
34 The HeavyCruiserMachine Peacocruiser MR
35 TankMobil-Maus C
36 Tick Tick Rabbit C
37 Tick Tick Raccoon Dog C
38 The Diva Marl U
39 The Trainee Cape Pentan C
40 Princess-Hachikazuki C
41 The SacredBeast Kaichi C
42 The FairyScholar Sakia C
43 The DivaAdmiral Mirefa R
44 The GunAngelia Canon MR
45 The Beast Ocelot C
46 Twin Neck Hydra C
47 The Beast Coyote U
48 The PirateCaptain Edgar C
49 The PirateOfficer Cephas MR
50 The BeastAmur R
51 The GiantSeaCreature Stellard C
52 Crystalhydra C
53 Ultimate-Assassin-Dragon U
54 The BlazeUltimateSky Ryuuman-Burst U
55 The DarkUltimateSky Ibis U
56 Ultimate-Lancelot R
57 Ultimate-Shokatsuryo U
58 The LightningUltimateSky Thunder-Wolf U
59 Ultimate-Geronimond U
60 The SteelUltimateSky Golden-Buffalo U
61 The WaterUltimateSky Princess-Oto U
62 Ultimate-Chocodra MR
63 Ultimate-Elguinius U
64 Ultimate-Caeser MR
65 The BeastUltimateSky Yukihyodor U
66 The Votive Deity Sword C
67 The Lost Paradise C
68 The Dominating Shell Sky Castle C
69 The Jigurazu Steel Grassland C
70 The Far Away Moon World C
71 The Treasures of the Ocean Empire C
72 Ground Break C
73 Ultimate Flame C
74 Burst Venom C
75 Ultimate Deadly U
76 Beetle Storm C
77 Binding Root R
78 Mist World U
79 Shut Out C
80 Bubbly Confuse C
81 Imaginary Gate R
82 Swallow Tail R
83 Gordias Wave C
84 The FirstShellEmperor XR
85 The EvilStarMachineDeity Loki XR
86 Ultimate-Mugendragon XR
87 Ultimate-Arthur XR
88 Ultimate-Seiryubi XR
89 The NextGenerationMachineBeast Blizza-Liger XR
90 Ultimate-Kaguya XR
91 Ultimate-Drian XR
92 The FourShellSky Kamejuuji C
93 The FourShellSky Kamejuuji C
94 The FourShellSky Kamejuuji C
95 The FourShellSky Kamejuuji C
96 The FourShellSky Kamejuuji C

2014 Battle Spirits 29

1 Dragonhead C
2 Ryuuman-Lux C
3 Mononyx U
4 The HotBloodedSwordsSaint Ryuuman-Burncolor MR
5 Beardeagle C
6 Megido-Dragon R
7 The SixGiantEmperor Scarlet-Dragline C
8 Asklesnake C
9 The FallenKnight Mammon C
10 The FallenKnight Sin C
11 The Investigator Fric C
12 The SwordsSaintDevil Gaap MR
13 Gothic-Grave R
14 The SixGiantEmperor Bone-Centaurus C
15 Hosoakuwaga C
16 Nekojaran C
17 Tategamiwolf C
18 The Investigator Laten C
19 The SwordsSaintBeetle Tenagakogane U
20 The GodMonkey Ete MR
21 The SixGiantEmperor Gigas-Antman C
22 Seahorse-Tanker C
23 The Investigator Euro C
24 Foxsaber C
25 The HeroSwordsSaint Sigurd MR
26 Shieldrhinos C
27 Malachite-Dragon U
28 The SixGiantEmperor Diblodocus C
29 Booblack C
30 The MagicTrainee Cape Pentan C
31 The Angelia Miselle C
32 The SwordsSaintmusician Olivier MR
33 The Angelia Marchell C
34 The SixGiantEmperor Ziz C
35 The Beast Skylark C
36 The DragonCraftsman Gaga C
37 The Investigator Nord C
38 The PirateGunner Harvey R
39 The SwordsSaintSeaCreature Swordhydra U
40 The SixGiantEmperor Albion C
41 The DragonSwordsSaint Ryuuman-Masteredge U
42 Ultimate-Dark-Tyrannosaura MR
43 The FallenSwordsSaint Moloch U
44 Ultimate-Bone-Tops U
45 The ShellSwordsSaint Bullmeister U
46 Ultimate-Hashibiro U
47 The SwordsSaintCarrier Frey U
48 Ultimate-Sillimanite R
49 The SwordsSaint Angelia Momoel U
50 Ultimate-Izuna U
51 Ultimate-Behemoth MR
52 The BirdSwordsSaint Peregrine R
53 Ultimate-Imperialhydra U
54 The NextGenerationGiant Brybar U
55 The AstralKnightSpear Gacrux R
56 The PoisonSnakeScythe Alphard C
57 The DragonBow Rastaban U
58 The AttackClaw Adhara C
59 The AstralBeastSpear Sirius R
60 The LionShieldArmor Regulus C
61 The AstralGun Fomalhaut U
62 The AstralSacredStaff Spica U
63 The VenusDeitySword VenusSaber R
64 The TwinBlade Regale-Edge C
65 The MercuryDeitySword Mercury-Blade MR
66 The Ground Drilling Stone Sword C
67 The Skewered Forest C
68 The Jade Old Tree C
69 Deck Mountain C
70 The Rythmic Concert Hall C
71 The Sleeping Sword Emperor's Mausoleum C
72 Flame Saw U
73 Ultimate Resurrection C
74 Sword Breaker C
75 Core Lost R
76 Binding Tree C
77 Ultimate Tornado U
78 Dimension Shield C
79 Dream Blizzard R
80 Absolute Zero R
81 Heaven's Punish C
82 Hammer Impact C
83 Imperial Burst C
84 The ArcAngelia Saint D'Arc XR
85 The GiantSwordSaint Eaglen XR
86 The UltimateShineDeity Ultimate-Overray XR
87 The FallenKnightDeity Saturn XR
88 Ultimate-Mantis XR
89 Ultimate-Griffon XR
90 The MarsDeitySword MarsBringer XR
91 The SnakeEmperorAstralArmored BravePiooze XR

2014 Battle Spirits 30

1 The Survivor Ryuuman-Falco C
2 The Investigator Ozzania C
3 The BladeBristleDragon Yutyrannus C
4 King-Vulture U
5 The DeitySwordDragon Falchion R
6 Ryuuman-Koenig MR
7 Bone-Scout C
8 The Survivor Shieldritter R
9 Bone-Bird U
10 The EvilSpear Shutori C
11 Bone-Griffon C
12 Darkness-Count C
13 The FallenKnight Beliard U
14 Shiramusu C
15 Ubataman C
16 Gomadra MR
17 The SpearUserHornets R
18 The Survivor Kouroko C
19 The DeityCat Shillong C
20 The BeastShellMan Maximus U
21 The Survivor Snowrabi C
22 Bugilance C
23 The ArmoredEvilDragon Fafner C
24 Airraid-Eagle U
25 The ArmoredSwordsman Blizzard C
26 Tank-Mobil KV-2 C
27 The SurvivolAngelia Kurcel U
28 The SingingInvestigator Asia C
29 The MagicSwordsman Cape Pentan C
30 The Angelia Pomoel C
31 The ConductorAngelia Maestel R
32 The CrimsonButterflyWitch Yonaguni C
33 The SeaSacredBeast Leviard C
34 The Survivor Beebird C
35 Atlaia-Hydra R
36 Byakhee C
37 The AbyssalBeast Abyssshark MR
38 The ThunderPirate Kidd U
39 Vulcan-Bison C
40 The InvestigatorTrainee Lolo C
41 The FlameSwordsSaint Ryuuman-Swordwing U
42 Ryuuman-Swordbreaker U
43 The SkeletonSwordsSaint Exoskull MR
44 Blade Panther U
45 The DeityWolf Ben-Gaul MR
46 The ArmoredFortress Taimait U
47 The DawnMachineDeity Dellingr U
48 White Fox MR
49 The SwordDancePriestess Maiel U
50 The GunGreatAngelia Fiel MR
51 Bastet U
52 R'lyeh Golem U
53 The HeavySwordsSaint Moonbear U
54 The UltimateQueen Antarc MR
55 The AstralShieldSword Arcturus C
56 The BigAxe Aldebaran R
57 The SnakeAstralWhip Sabik C
58 The SaturnDeitySword SaturnSlave R
59 The AstralHillHalberd Benetnasch C
60 The AstralBattleStick Algieba C
61 The MoonlightDeitySword WingOfLuna R
62 The HeavenAstralBlade Schedar C
63 The AstralLyreFan Vega C
64 The KeelStick Canopus C
65 The AstralBayonet Antares R
66 The Red Dragon Sword Detector C
67 The TwinSnake Sword Detector C
68 The Crystal Sword Detector C
69 The Heaven Wings Sword Detector C
70 The Giant Ocean Sword Detector C
71 The Reverse Continent C
72 Burning Sword C
73 Flame Meteor C
74 Dark Matter U
75 Necro Blight R
76 Needle Ride U
77 Leaf Bind C
78 Fuge Blast C
79 Dream Glacier R
80 Elemental Burn C
81 Feather Lock C
82 Abyssal Counter R
83 Greed Thunder C
84 The SwordDeityWarrior Ryuuman-Godsword XR
85 The SwordShellEmperor Actaeon XR
86 The MachineWorldSerpentDragon Jörmungandr XR
87 Ryuuman-the-Formula XR
88 Ultimate-Thunder-Million XR
89 Ultimate-Avrielle XR
90 Ultimate-Leaf-Seadra XR
91 The JupiterDeitySword JupiterSaber XR

2014 Battle Spirits Dazzling Ultimate King

1 Ultimate-Bladra C
2 Ultimate-Swordmaster-Dragon R
3 Ultimate-Soulhorse U
4 Ultimate-Don-Diegod R
5 Ultimate-Sekkohkiji U
6 Ultimate-Grant-Benkei R
7 Ultimate-Igua-Buggy U
8 Ultimate-Sunk-Shine R
9 The UltimateMarshal Ultimate-Lay-Saurer MR
10 Ultimate-Hipogrifee U
11 Ultimate-Tamamoin R
12 Ultimate-Sea-Serpendar U
13 Ultimate-Gordias MR
14 Ultimate-Orion R
15 The UltimateExplosion Ultimate-Bazzel XR
16 The CorpseKing Ultimate-Gi-Gasha XR
17 Ultimate-Onikuwaga XR
18 Ultimate-Trickster XR

2014 Battle Spirits Dazzling Ultimate King Promos

19 Ultimate-Lord-Dragon
20 Ultimate-Glazar
21 Ex-One-Kengo
22 Ex-Dos-Monkey
23 Ex-Kiji-Toria

2014 Battle Spirits Diva Booster

1 Ran-Blasear MR
2 The SmileGirl Ran-Blasear C
3 Rabi-Darin C
4 The PrettyGirl Rabi-Darin R
5 Saya-Shine U
6 The PureWhiteVirgo Saya-Shine R
7 Seina-Ryumin C
8 The RetsuQueen Seina-Ryumin U
9 Noah-Felur MR
10 Hilda-Margaret C
11 The PuppetIdol Hilda-Margaret U
12 Delis-Pertio C
13 The IdolSevenShogun Delis-Pertio R
14 Millia-Thunde C
15 The IdolThreeGiants Millia-Thunde R
16 Fongneena U
17 The PassionDancer Fongneena R
18 Leafa-Sears C
19 The ShinraSinger Leafa-Sears U
20 Ortina-Clan U
21 The WhiteWing Ortina-Clan R
22 Ryune-Mato U
23 The PentanLover Raquel C
24 Prim-Angu C
25 The Holiday Asia U
26 The Diva Angu U
27 The Diva Avrielle MR
28 The Diva Catleya R
29 The Diva Vielje R
30 Golden Wing Mic C

31 KigurumiPentan C
32 SoloWing U
33 The Diva's Holiday C
34 The Diva Stage U
35 The Fan's Thanksgiving C
36 Twin Performance C
37 Sweet Heart C
38 Diva Medley R
39 Heartbeat U
40 The SuperStarIdol Noah-Felur XR
41 The Song Princess Priestess Ryune-Mato XR
42 The Diva Trickster XR

2014 Battle Spirits Full Throttle Acceleration

1 The Giant Soldier Mucius C
2 The Dark Warrior Cleitus C
3 The Giant Teacher Aristotle C
4 The Knight General Philotas C
5 The Charger Bucephalas U
6 The Brave General Crateros C
7 Mugendragon-Nova U
8 The Sword General Sution U
9 The Knowledge General Ptolemios MR
10 The Retsu General Antinogus U
11 The Capital of Alexandria C
12 The Gate of Gargando C
13 King's Command R
14 Flood Stream U
15 Muscle Wall C
16 Spark Burst C
17 Ultimate-Alexander XR

2014 Battle Spirits New Sun

1 Thrust-Shepherd C
2 Ryuuman-Charger C
3 Ryuuman-Wisword U
4 Ryuuman-Rebellion C
5 Testarossa-Dragon U
6 Ultimate-Bronze-Wurm C
7 Ryuuman-Skyhigh C
8 Ultimate-Dracorex MR
9 The FireLance Altair C
10 The MarsHatchet Elnath C
11 The Burning Sacred Place of Dragons U
12 The Big Flagship Dragonic C
13 Fatal Draw C
14 Dragonic Wall C
15 Sunbreaker R
16 Ultimate-Ark XR
17 The SunDeitySword Sol-Calibur XR

2014 Battle Spirits SD27

1 Pixilizard C
2 Wyvern-Vera C
3 Eridanus-Dragon C
4 The PirateDeity Piscegalleon XR
5 The CancerBushin Cancerd XR
6 The ScorpioKnight Scor-Spear XR
7 The WaterCarrierDeity Aqua-Elysion XR
8 The MagicalTwinsDeity Geminize XR
9 The BalanceDeity Libra-Golem XR
10 The BullDragonDeity Dragonic-Taurus XR
11 The EvilCapricornusDeity Stein-Bolg XR
12 The ValkyrieVirgoDeity Vielje XR
13 The ShineCentaurusDeity Sagitto-Apollodragon XR
14 The SpehirothicSheepDeity Sephiro-Aries XR
15 The MachineLionDeity Strikewurm-Leo XR
16 The GenesisDragon Bayer MR
17 The GenesisDragon Ptolemy XR
18 The UltimateStar Ultimate-Zodiac XR
19 The GalacticStarBlade Zodiacsword XR
20 The TimeGuardian Horolo-Gium MR

2014 Battle Spirits SD28

1 Gigantea-Kamakiri C
2 Kokuwan C
3 Usubaageha C
4 Akagane U
5 Gorongoro C
6 The LightSwordsSaint Dorsalis U
7 Koganehime C
8 The ToughSwordsSaint Rubeet C
9 The Last Emperor MR
10 The WingedBlade Glide C
11 The AstralBeastSword Procyon C
12 The JadeSword Detector U
13 Counter Bind C
14 Exhaust End C
15 Ultimate Gain R
16 Ultimate-Ushiwaka XR
17 The EarthDeitySword Gianohoko XR

2014 Battle Spirits SD29

1 War Lizard C
2 Mushadaryu C
3 OsodePtera C
4 Jinraidragon C
5 Night Sky Dragon C
6 Shippuudragon C
7 Mushadraco C
8 Murakumodragon U
9 The Rookie Hirinmaru U
10 The WildMusha Ma-Zu MRR
11 The Fierce Dragon Castle C
12 The No.13 East Capital C
13 Flame Sword Strie U
14 Douburyuu Draw U
15 Crimson Flame R
16 Burst Wall U
17 Sengoku-Gurendragon XR
18 The Steel Blade Dragon Calyvorous C
19 Sengoku-Siegfried XR
20 The Deity Catastrophedragon XR
21 The Hollow Dragon Emperor Catastrophedragon MRR
22 The Twin Horn Dragon Doubhorn C
23 Burst Draw C

2014 Battle Spirits Ultimate Full Throttle

1 Rukbart-Dragon C
2 Aschera-Dragon U
3 The StarBowDragon Chaos-Wyvern U
4 Meteordrian U
5 One-Kengo C
6 Kagutsuchidragoon C
7 The FlameDragonDemon Ma-Gwo MR
8 Ultimate-Shurikeraptor U
9 Flame Blast R
10 Energy Burst U
11 The MilkDipperDragon Blazing-Dragon XR
12 Ultimate-Sagitto-Apollodragon XR
13 The DragonHero Sieg-Yamato-Fried XR
14 The TenSwordSaint Starblade-Dragon XR

2015 Battle Spirits 31

1 Mushalizard C
2 Yaibird C
3 Hiendragon C
4 Haganewurm C
5 The DemonMusha Raizan MR
6 Homuracheetah C
7 The Commander Ryuuman U
8 Samurai-Dragon MR
9 Yoroistego C
10 Sengoku-Tiger R
11 The FireGeneralDragon Gouen C
12 The RedBladeDragon The-Heat U
13 Gas Owl C
14 The Shikigami Houriki C
15 The RedOgre Bakuzou C
16 The FallenMusha Bone C
17 The ArmoredWarOgre Rashou MR
18 Headlessritter C
19 The VampireSorceror Hiten R
20 The CorruptPriest Kokugou C
21 Kemurizaru U
22 Violet Smoke Dragon C
23 The Shikigami Zanki C
24 The KingOgre Naraku U
25 The ArmoredMothShinobi Hopper C
26 Uzulucky C
27 The WindDemon Shinobilica C
28 The ArmoredMothShinobi Tokkuriwasp C
29 The WindDemon Ninkouchu R
30 The StrangeFangShinobi Rappanther C
31 The ArmoredMothShinobi Shurikabuto U
32 The ArmoredMothShinobi Kusarikama C
33 The StrangeFangShinobi Kokurou U
34 The StrangeWarriorPriest Zoum MR
35 Eldermoose C
36 The ArmoredMothGreatShinobi Bekkou MR
37 Ashigaru Warrior C
38 Cutter Swallow C
39 The CleverMachineDog Setadog C
40 The CleverMachineMusha Saiun U
41 The GenjiEightKnights HikasuDefender C
42 The Blizzard Gozen C
43 The CleverMachineGeneral Shigure R
44 The GenjiEightKnights UsuganeStriker MR
45 The CleverMachineGeneral Gyouten C
46 Brittlelizard C
47 The GunBeastMachine Liomael C
48 The GiantArmCleverMachineMusha Rakan U
49 One-Eyed Kid C
50 Karakasa Man C
51 Kappappa C
52 Wankoma C
53 The SengokuPrincess Ruri U
54 Zashiki Girl C
55 The SengokuAngelia Mushael C
56 Kashaneko R
57 Nurikabe C
58 The SengokuPrincess Raika C
59 The SengokuPrincess Trickster MR
60 DoroTurbo C
61 The GreenBird Douji C
62 The BuddhaSculptor Pagug C
63 Kanikong C
64 The BlueSeas Douji C
65 The WhiteSky Douji C
66 Yarisquid C
67 The Red Swords WisdomKing R
68 The PurifyingKnowledge WisdomKing C
69 Nautilus Golem C
70 The Blue Seas Wisdom King MR
71 The MasterFencerBeastman Gaou C
72 The Salvation WisdomKing U
73 The DragonArmor Dragmaru C
74 The ArmoredFlyingDragon Oosodelgar R
75 Origamibird C
76 Origamihorse R
77 Hagurama C
78 Karakuriookami U
79 The ArmoredTank Hitterkabuto C
80 The ArmoredWing Fighter C
81 Oborogissha C
82 Oukitsuru C
83 The TwinDragonBoat Hydraship C
84 Jet Karura R
85 The Land of Sharp Valleys C
86 No. 17 Stone River U
87 The Battleground of Thousand Spears U
88 No. 3 Rock Hand C
89 No. 22 Silent Hill C
90 The Blowing Whirlwind C
91 No. 1 North Sea Road C
92 The Castle of Clever Machines R
93 The House of the Lost C
94 No. 38 Love Princess C
95 No. 34 Large Island U
96 The Thousand Space Kannon Temple C
97 Soul Aura C
98 Conflagration Slash R
99 Soul Draw C
100 Shikigami of the Dead C
101 Flux Curse Administratoin C
102 Soul Shoot C
103 Body Flicker Technique R
104 Wind Release Technique C
105 Body Substitution Technique C
106 Time Rewind C
107 Impregnable Wall U
108 Dream Bubble R
109 Yellow Recover U
110 Tousenbo Wall R
111 Fireball Attack C
112 Mantra Draw R
113 Blue Strike Blaze C
114 Hydro Exposure Dragon C
115 The SengokuDragon Souldragon XR
116 The DarkArtsMagician Ogma XR
117 The ArmoredMothHead Kuwagaslayer XR
118 The GreatCleverMachineMusha Kongou XR
119 The SengokuPrincess Nayuta XR
120 The SupremeRealmWisdomKing Nirvana XR
121 The SixAbsoluteDeities Greedy-Death-Gal-Vados XR
122 The SixAbsoluteDeities Impenetrable Chrome-Riservar XR
123 The HeadVassal Akatsukidragon Promo
124 The VassalOgre Shiki Promo
125 The HeadVassal Kimadara Promo
126 The VassalMusha Tokikaze Promo
127 The VassalTengu Coppa Promo
128 The VassalWisdomKing Rudra Promo

2015 Battle Spirits 32

1 Tsunotanu C
2 The WesternMusha Hakurai C
3 Tsunobazuku C
4 The Cub Tiger C
5 The SwordsWarDragon Muramasa-Dragon R
6 Sanzokku-Bear C
7 The MushaDragon Rindou C
8 The FightingWarDragon Chougen U
9 The BlazingBeastGeneral Gurenberos MR
10 Soul Ogre C
11 Onmyou Child U
12 Purple Smoke Boar C
13 The ShikiOgreDeity Shuukai C
14 The Mystic Simon C
15 The ShikiOgreDeity Garan C
16 Purple Smoke Tiger U
17 The Necromancer Yakumo R
18 The ReversePriestess Rinne MR
19 Thornant C
20 The StrangeFangShinobi Momonja C
21 The WindDemon Sasakunai C
22 The WindDemon Greyknight U
23 The StrangeFang Shinobi Jagan U
24 The ArmoredMothShinobi Lunihel R
25 The StrangeFangShinobi Kangaroo C
26 The ArmoredMothShinobu Ooshio C
27 The WindDemonGreatShinobi Tokizane MR
28 The GunSoldier Tanegashima C
29 The CleverMachineDog Kishudog C
30 Ashigaru Spear C
31 The CleverMachineMusha S23 C
32 The GenjiEightKnights TsukikazuLancer C
33 The CleverMachineTactician Shimokaze MR
34 Cuprinckelizard U
35 The GenjiEightKnights HizamaruBuster R
36 The CleverMachineFortress Hakugain U
37 Keukegen C
38 The SengokuPrincess Mizuki C
39 The SengokuPrincess Charl MR
40 Yuki Girl U
41 Kinshachi C
42 The BiwaSwordsman Bokuboku C
43 The SengokuPrincess Kuzunoha U
44 The YoukaiBeast Noue R
45 The SengokuPrincess Kuon MR
46 The YellowSnake Douji C
47 The MasterBlacksmith Kamemitsu C
48 The FiveSacred Douji MR
49 The Sea Dragon WisdomKing C
50 The Bull HermitPriest C
51 Gandala-Hydra C
52 The Purple Lotus WisdomKing U
53 Hoojiro-Tiger R
54 The Iron Fist WisdomKing U
55 The ArmorDragonBlade Gouten U
56 The FlameDragonKatana Onimaru R
57 Origamimonkey C
58 The ArmoredBird Khirenjack R
59 The TortoiseShellBeast Kabutogame C
60 Himeneko MR
61 Gohou-Golem C
62 No. 6 Mountain Shape C
63 No. 32 Island Route R
64 The Purple Smoke Valley C
65 No. 25 Grow Celebration C
66 The Castle Tower Dock C
67 No. 42 Long Cape C
68 The Flowering Yellow Castle Gates C
69 No. 11 Tip Ball U
70 The Lotus Blossom Pagoda R
71 No. 26 Capital Capital C
72 Flame Slash R
73 Blazing Roar C
74 Dark Initiation C
75 Illusion Soul Extraction U
76 Tatami Flip Technique C
77 Spiral Needle U
78 Limited Barrier U
79 Force Cloak R
80 Yourai Spark C
81 Divine Spirit Beam C
82 Kannon Thousand Fists U
83 Crush and Build C
X01 The SengokuHero Gyuumonji XR
X02 The DivineSpiritKing Amehoshi-no-Mikoto XR
X03 The WindDemonHead Shinobiou XR
X04 The CleverMachineCommander Tycoon XR
X05 The YoukaiGeneral Kashaneko-IXA XR
X06 The LotusMonarch Senju XR
XX01 The SixAbsoluteDeities Harvest-Thearth XR
XX02 The SixAbsoluteDeities Affection El-Rafil XR

2015 Battle Spirits BSC 18

1 The OrangeSmile Ran-Blaesar C
2 The GreenBambina Rabi-Darin U
3 The GreyAngel Saya-Shine C
4 Rola-Byaklan U
5 The PurpleTiger Rola-Byaklan MR
6 Pollon-Sagiita U
7 The TrySailor Delis-Pertio C
8 The InnocentWave Millia-Thunde U
9 The SplashDancer Fongneena U
10 Rose-Berry R
11 The IdolQueen Rose-Berry MR
12 Garnet-Ruti C
13 The SummerBreezeDancer Garnet-Ruti R
14 Leona-Rikebloom C
15 The ShyLion Leona-Rikebloom U
16 Wendy Keito C
17 The PowerfulDog Wendy-Keito C
18 Dia-Lune C
19 The LadyCrocodile Dia-Lune C
20 Sephi-Aries C
21 The FluffySheep Sephi-Aries MR
22 Chyu R
23 The CowGirly Chyu U
24 Cassy-Leim C
25 The NorthenQueen Cassy-Leim U
26 Ney-Rantail R
27 The ObsidianMaiden Ney-Rantail MR
28 Diana-Fleur U
29 The ShadyHoliday Seina-Ryumin R
30 The DarkNightBreeze Seina-Ryumin C
31 Mai-Asuka C
32 The PhantomPrincess Mai-Asuka U
33 The Diva Romeda MR
34 The Diva Canon R
35 The UltimateStyle Raquel MR
36 Santa Costume C
37 Golden Wing V R
38 Welcome to Pentanland C
39 The Backstage U
40 The Galaxy Expo C
41 Costume Change C
42 Healing Melody C
43 Mischievous Angel C
44 Cute x Cute U
45 Diva Symphony R
46 The CrimsonShooter Pollon-Sagiita XR
47 The RavenGoddess Diana-Fleur XR
48 The TopIdol Trickster XR
49 The TwinStarDivas Laila Sisters Promo X
50 The WisdomBladeDiva Agrs Promo X

2015 Battle Spirits BSC 19

1 Destoroyah (Juvenile Form) C
2 Destoroyah (Juvenile Form) C
3 Destoroyah (Juvenile Form) C
4 Destoroyah (Juvenile Form) C
5 Destoroyah (Juvenile Form) C
6 Ebirah (2004) R
7 Minilla (2004) C
8 Anguirus (2004) R
9 Little Godzilla C
10 Baragon C
11 Dorat C
12 Rodan (2004) U
13 Monster X U
14 Gigan (2004) U
15 Godzilla Junior C
16 Destoroyah (Aggregate Form) U
17 Fire Rodan R
18 Thousand Year Dragon King Ghidorah R
19 Kaiser-Ghidorah MR
20 Orga MR
21 Fairy Mothra C
22 Kamacuras C
23 Mothra (Larva Form) (1992) C
24 King Caesar (2004) C
25 Megaguirus MR
26 Biollante (Rose Form) R
27 Mothra U
28 Biollante (Final Form) MR
29 Armor Mothra MR
30 Battra (Larva Form) C
31 Battra MR
32 Land Moguera C
33 Star Falcon C
34 Super X3 C
35 MOGUERA U
36 MechaGodzilla (1974) C
37 Jet Jaguar (1973) U
38 New Gotengo R
39 MechaGodzilla (1993) R
40 Modified Gigan (2004) U
41 Type-3 Kiryu MR
42 Mecha-King Ghidorah R
43 Garuda C
44 The Crystal Zone U
45 The Planet Gorath U
46 The Time of Awakening U
47 The Infant Island C
48 The MechaGodzilla Hangar U
49 The G Summit C
50 Gravity Beam U
51 Oxygen Destroyer R
52 Mothra's Emergence R
53 Mothra's Song U
54 Shintoshin Collapse U
55 Type-3 Absolute Zero Cannon R
56 All Arms Attack R
57 King Ghidorah (1991) XR
58 SpaceGodzilla XR
59 Destoroyah (Final Form) XR
60 Mothra (1992) XR
61 Modified Type-3 Kiryu XR
62 Godzilla Promo X
63 Gozilla (2000) Promo X
64 Orga (Phase 1) Promo

2015 Battle Spirits BSC 20

1 The SengokuGoldDragon Ragou XR
2 The BattleArrowDragon Byouha U
3 The FerociousDragonGeneral Hagundragon MR
4 The OgreDeity Basara XR
5 Bone-Weasel C
6 The BlueFlamesWisdomKing Agnius XR
7 The StrangeFangShinobi Tachikazewolf U
8 The FlameSacredBeast Homurawolf MR
9 The SwordArmedGeneral Ash-Lion R
10 The HornetKing Fong-Need XR
11 The ArmoredMothShinobi Tobikage R
12 Verdant Release Technique C
13 The CleverMachineBeast Shoujou C
14 The CleverMachineBeast Yoroiphant U
15 Moon Rabbit U
16 The Cobalt Mitsumataorochi MR
17 The ArmorFalcon Suiran-Hawk MR
18 The SnakeArtsMagician Zuda U
19 The Necromancer Mumei R
20 The WindDemon Amatsuba U
21 The CleverMachineMusha Zantetsu U
22 The CleverMachineMusha Shiranui R
23 Fuurin C
24 Inugami R
25 The BlueSwords WisdomKing U
26 The SengokuPrincess Anko C

2015 Battle Spirits SD 31

1 The ArmoredMothShinobi Nomikage C
2 The ArmoredMothShinobi Namitento C
3 The NinjaMaster Higurashi C
4 The StrangeFangShinobi Katanazelle C
5 Shinobikogane U
6 The ArmoredMothShinobi Girizou C
7 The WindDemon Benimatoi U
8 The ArmoredFangShinobi Sendoukitsune C
9 The WindDemonGreatShinobi U
10 The ShinobiCommander Kurohagane MR
11 The StrangeFangGreatShinobi Hyousouga U
12 Teppounanafushi C
13 Earth Release Technique C
14 Thousand Shuriken U
15 Double Body Swap R
16 The WhirlwindNinja Kirikage XR

2005 Bella Sara Gold Series

1 Bello
2 Birdy
3 Blackie
4 Charlie
5 Dina
6 Dusty
7 Dynamo
8 eagle
9 Filippa
10 Flame
11 Fox
12 Freja
13 Friends
14 Grey
15 Hercules
16 Hunter
17 Jewel
18 Joker
19 Jonathan
20 Karna
21 Leonardo
22 Magic
23 Mandalay
24 Maxi
25 Mermaid
26 Minelle
27 Mystery
28 Nanna
29 Nikita
30 Rain
31 Rose
32 Roxy
33 Shadow
34 Shakira
35 Sham
36 Shaman
37 Shine
38 Skipper
39 Sky
40 Spottie
41 Star
42 Stella
43 Storm
44 Thunder
45 Toffee
46 Treasure
47 Trudy
48 Unicorn

2005 Bella Sara Silver Series

1 Angel
2 Beauty
3 Bella
4 Bliss
5 Butterfly
6 Coco
7 Diamond
8 Dixie
9 Domino
10 Donna
11 Flame

12 Flipper
13 Flower
14 Jewel
15 Jojo
16 Jolly
17 Joy
18 Kiki
19 Lucas
20 Lucky
21 Mandalay
22 Micado
23 Misla
24 Misty
25 Moonlight
26 Niki
27 Pegasus
28 Pink Lady
29 Rain
30 Rainbow
31 Saga
32 Sandy
33 Sarah
34 Scarlett
35 Shaman
36 Silver
37 Speedy
38 Spirit
39 Starlight
40 Sugar
41 Sunny
42 Thunder
43 Twins
44 Walter
45 Yellow

2006 Bella Sara Copper Series

1 Aries C
2 Artemis C
3 Balto C
4 Bellisimo C
5 Bifrost C
6 Colour C
7 Cookie C
8 Daisy C
9 Diablo C
10 Dino C
11 Dodo C
12 Dreamer C
13 Fiona C
14 Friends Forever C
15 Geisha C
16 Ghost C
17 Halloween C
18 Honey C
19 Hummingbird C
20 King C
21 Kini C
22 Kio C
23 Kira C
24 Lotte C
25 Luna C
26 Minty C
27 Montana C
28 Pedro C
29 Ricky C
30 Rocky C
31 Safire C
32 Santos C
33 Silas C
34 Skywalker C
35 Stardust C
36 Starfighter C
37 Starfly C
38 Sunset C
39 Sunshine C
40 Sweety C
41 Tiffi C
42 Tikka C
43 Tokker C
44 Wavebreaker C
45 Wonder C
46 Yin and Yang C
47 Zargo C
48 Zikka C
49 Grooming R
50 Halter R
51 Hoof Care R
52 Jodhpurs R
53 Jumping Saddle R
54 Riding Boots R
55 Riding Hat R
56 Riding Lessons R
57 Rug R
58 Training Saddle R

2007 Bella Sara 1st Series

COMPLETE SET (55)	30.00	50.00
BOOSTER BOX (36)	40.00	80.00
1 Artemis	.40	1.00
2 Beauty	.40	1.00
3 Blackie	.40	1.00
4 Charlie	.40	1.00
5 Dynamo	.25	.60
6 Eagle	.25	.60
7 Flame	.75	2.00
8 Ghost	.50	1.25
9 Grey	.25	.60
10 Halloween	.50	1.25
11 Hercules	.60	1.50
12 Honey	.60	1.50
13 Jojo	.25	.60
14 Jonathan	.15	.40
15 King	.60	1.50
16 Kio	.15	.40
17 Leonardo	.40	1.00
18 Lucas	.25	.60
19 Luna	.60	1.50
20 Moonlight	1.50	4.00
21 Nanna	.40	1.00
22 Nikita	.40	1.00
23 Pedro	.25	.60
24 Rose	2.00	5.00
25 Saga	.40	1.00
26 Santos	.25	.60
27 Sarah	.40	1.00
28 Shadow	.50	1.25
29 Shakira	.15	.40
30 Skipper	.75	2.00
31 Star	.40	1.00
32 Starfighter	.15	.40
33 Sunny	.15	.40
34 Sweety	.50	1.25
35 Walter	.15	.40
36 Yellow	.15	.40
37 Bella	.15	.40
38 Bellisimo	.15	.40
39 Bello	.15	.40
40 Fiona	.15	.40
41 Jewel	3.00	8.00
42 Rain	.15	.40
43 Shaman	.15	.40
44 Thunder	.15	.40
45 Yin and Yang	2.00	5.00
46 Grooming	.15	.40
47 Halter	1.00	2.50
48 Hoof Care	.60	1.50
49 Jodhpurs	2.00	5.00
50 Jumping Saddle	5.00	12.00
51 Riding Boots	2.50	6.00
52 Riding Hat	1.50	4.00
53 Riding Lesson	1.50	4.00
54 Blanket	1.50	4.00
55 Training Saddle	1.50	4.00

2007 Bella Sara 1st Series Foil

F1 Bella	4.00	10.00
F2 Bellisimo	5.00	12.00
F3 Bello	5.00	12.00
F4 Fiona	5.00	12.00
F5 Jewel	4.00	10.00
F6 Rain	8.00	20.00
F7 Shaman	4.00	10.00
F8 Thunder	4.00	10.00
F9 Yin and Yang	4.00	10.00

2007 Bella Sara 2nd Series

BOOSTER BOX (36)	25.00	50.00
1 Alibi	2.00	5.00
2 Artemis	.15	.40
3 Beauty	.40	1.00
4 Blackie	.75	2.00
5 Bosi	.75	2.00
6 Cantaro	.25	.60
7 Cascadeur	1.50	4.00
8 Charlie	.40	1.00
9 Yung	.50	1.25
10 Chung	2.50	6.00
11 Colour	1.25	3.00
12 Dynamo	.15	.40
13 Eagle	.50	1.25
14 Feng	.50	1.25
15 Filippa	.40	1.00
16 Flame	.40	1.00
17 Friends	.75	2.00
18 Grey	.25	.60
19 Halloween	.50	1.25
20 Hercules	.40	1.00
21 Honey	.30	.75
22 Jojo	.15	.40
23 Jonathan	.40	1.00
24 King	.15	.40
25 Kio	.15	.40
26 Konfu	.50	1.25
27 Leonard	.40	1.00
28 Leonardo	.25	.60
29 Lucas	.15	.40
30 Lucky Light	.20	.50
31 Luna	1.50	4.00
32 Macon	1.00	2.50
33 Mandalay	.75	2.00
34 Ming	1.00	2.50
35 Misty	.30	.75
36 Moonlight	.30	.75
37 Mushu	1.50	4.00
38 Nanna	.15	.40
39 Nikita	.50	1.25
40 Ninja	.60	1.50
41 Peace	.15	.40
42 Pedro	.15	.40
43 Pink Lady	.15	.40
44 Rose	1.25	3.00
45 Saga	.30	.75
46 Santos	.25	.60
47 Sarah	.15	.40
48 Sasha	.40	1.00
49 Shakira	.15	.40
50 Sheng	2.00	5.00
51 Skipper	.40	1.00
52 Sokki	1.25	3.00
53 Star	.40	1.00
54 Sung	.15	.40
55 Tai	2.00	5.00
56 Walter	.15	.40
57 Yasmin	1.25	3.00
58 Yellow	.30	.75
59 Angel	.15	.40
60 Balto	.20	.50
61 Bella	.15	.40
62 Bellisimo	.20	.50
63 Bello	2.00	5.00
64 Cajus	1.50	4.00
65 Dino	1.25	3.00
66 Fiona	1.00	2.50
67 Flipper	1.50	4.00
68 Freja	2.00	5.00
69 Hummingbird	1.00	2.50
70 Jewel	.40	1.00
71 Lancelot	2.00	5.00
72 Mermaid	1.25	3.00
73 Misla	2.00	5.00
74 Parlez	2.00	5.00
75 Pegasus	.75	2.00
76 Rain	1.00	2.50
77 Roxy	.75	2.00
78 Shaman	2.50	6.00
79 Spottie	2.50	6.00
80 Tao	1.25	3.00
81 Thunder	.60	1.50
82 Tiffi	1.25	3.00
83 Treasure	1.25	3.00
84 Wavebreaker	4.00	10.00
85 Yin and Yang	1.50	4.00
86 Grooming	2.00	5.00
87 Halter	2.00	5.00
88 Hoof Care	2.00	5.00
89 Jodhpurs	2.50	6.00
90 Jumping Saddle	3.00	8.00
91 Riding Boots	2.00	5.00
92 Riding Hat	1.25	3.00
93 Riding Lesson	1.25	3.00
94 Blanket	2.00	5.00
95 Training Saddle	1.25	3.00
96 Flying Horseshoe	3.00	8.00
97 Treasure Key	3.00	8.00

2007 Bella Sara 2nd Series Foil

F1 Angel		8.00
F2 Balto		8.00
F3 Bella		30.00
F4 Bellisimo		10.00
F5 Bello		10.00
F6 Cajus		12.00
F7 Dino		
F8 Fiona		25.00
F9 Flipper		12.00
F10 Freja		12.00
F11 Hummingbird		10.00
F12 Jewel		20.00
F13 Lancelot		
F14 Mermaid		
F15 Misla		12.00
F16 Parlez		
F17 Pegasus		
F18 Rain		
F19 Roxy		10.00
F20 Shaman		
F21 Spottie		6.00
F22 Tao		
F23 Thunder		
F24 Tiffi		
F25 Treasure		
F26 Wavebreaker		
F27 Yin and Yang		10.00

2007 Bella Sara Ancient Lights

BOOSTER BOX (36)	30.00	60.00
1 Achilles	.15	.40
2 Aphaia	.15	.40
3 Aphrodite	.15	.40
4 Aurora	.15	.40
5 Bukefalos	.15	.40
6 Ceres	.15	.40
7 Clio	.15	.40
8 Cupid	.15	.40
9 Cybele	.15	.40
10 Demeter	.15	.40
11 Diana	.15	.40
12 Echo	.15	.40
13 Eirene	.15	.40
14 Epona	.15	.40
15 Flora	.15	.40
16 Gaia	.15	.40
17 Graia	.15	.40
18 Hera	.15	.40
19 Hestia	.15	.40
20 Juno	.15	.40
21 Jupiter	.15	.40
22 Opis	.15	.40
23 Pandora	.15	.40
24 Persephone	.15	.40
25 Selene	.15	.40
26 Thalia	.15	.40
27 Urania	.15	.40
28 Vesta	.15	.40
29 Amor	5.00	12.00
30 Apollo	2.00	5.00
31 Athena	.15	.40
32 Bella	.15	.40
33 Eurynome	.15	.40
34 Fiona	.15	.40
35 Hecate	.15	.40
36 Iris	.15	.40
37 Janus	1.00	2.50
38 Jewel	.15	.40
39 Naiad	1.00	2.50
40 Neptune	2.50	6.00
41 Nike	.15	.40
42 Thunder	.15	.40
43 Triton	.15	.40
44 Uranus	.15	.40
45 Venus	1.50	4.00
46 Aphrodite's Gown	1.25	3.00
47 Apollo's Lyre	.75	2.00
48 Athena's Chariot	2.00	5.00
49 Mercury's Boots	1.25	3.00
50 Moonlight Tiara	1.25	3.00
51 Olympic Statue	1.50	4.00
52 Poseidon's Trident	1.50	4.00
53 Squirrel Sentinel	1.50	4.00
54 Triton's Horn	1.25	3.00
55 Vulcan's Horseshoes	1.25	3.00

2007 Bella Sara Ancient Lights Shiny

S1 Amor	8.00	20.00
S2 Apollo		
S3 Athena		
S4 Bella		
S5 Eurynome		
S6 Fiona	5.00	12.00
S7 Hecate		
S8 Iris		
S9 Janus		
S10 Jewel	4.00	10.00
S11 Naiad		
S12 Neptune	5.00	12.00
S13 Nike		
S14 Thunder		
S15 Triton	4.00	10.00
S16 Uranus		
S17 Venus	6.00	15.00

2007 Bella Sara Mythology

1 Achilles C
2 Aphaia C
3 Aphrodite C
4 Aurora C
5 Bosi C
6 Brisi C
7 Bukefalos C
8 Ceres C
9 Charlie C
10 Clio C
11 Colour C
12 Cupid C
13 Cybele C
14 Danu C
15 Demeter C
16 Diana C
17 Donn C
18 Echo C
19 Eirene C
20 Embarr C
21 Epona C
22 Firewalker C
23 Flora C
24 Fylgie C
25 Gaia C
26 Graia C
27 Hera C
28 Hestia C
29 Iduna C
30 Juno C
31 Jupiter C
32 Kelpie-Pooka C
33 Mandalay C
34 Mjolnir C
35 Moonlight C
36 Mystery C
37 Opis C
38 Pandora C
39 Persephone C
40 Rauni C
41 Rhiannon C
42 Rimfaxe C
43 Saga C
44 Selene C
45 Skipper C
46 Sleipnir C
47 Sokki C
48 Star C
49 Thalia C
50 Thor C
51 Urania C
52 Urania C
53 Vesta C
54 Viking C
55 Walter C
56 Yasmin C
57 Amor R
58 Apollo R
59 Athena R
60 Balto R
61 Bella R
62 Bella R
63 Bello R
64 Bifrost R
65 Conall R
66 Eurynome R
67 Fiona R
68 Fiona R
69 Froya R
70 Hecate R
71 Iceking R
72 Iris R
73 Janus R
74 Jewel R
75 Jewel R
76 Jonas R
77 Lakehorse R
78 Melusine R
79 Misla R
80 Naiad R
81 Neptune R
82 Nike R
83 Ran R
84 Signy R
85 Skinfaxe R
86 Thunder R
87 Thunder R
88 Triton R
89 Uranus R
90 Venus R
91 Antique Flowerpot R
92 Anvil & Hammer R
93 Aphrodite's Gown R
94 Apollo's Lyre R
95 Athena's Chariot R
96 Horseshoe Water Fountain R
97 Lawn Gnome R
98 Lilac Gazebo R
99 Mercury's Boots R
100 Moonlight Tiara R
101 Olympic Statue R
102 Poseidon's Trident R
103 Primrose Lamppost R
104 Shade Tree R
105 Squirrel Sentinel R
106 Triton's Horn R
107 Vulcon's Horseshoes R
108 Weathervane R
109 Winged Horse Statue R
110 Wishing Well R

2007 Bella Sara Mythology Shiny

S1 Amor
S2 Apollo
S3 Athena
S4 Balto
S5 Bella
S6 Bella
S7 Bello
S8 Bifrost
S9 Conall
S10 Eurynome
S11 Fiona
S12 Fiona
S13 Froya
S14 Hecate
S15 Iceking
S16 Iris
S17 Janus
S18 Jewel
S19 Jewel
S20 Jonas
S21 Lakehorse
S22 Melusine
S23 Misla
S24 Naiad
S25 Neptune
S26 Nike
S27 Ran
S28 Signy
S29 Skinfaxe
S30 Thunder
S31 Thunder
S32 Triton
S33 Uranus
S34 Venus

2007 Bella Sara Northern Lights

BOOSTER BOX (36)	30.00	60.00

1 Bosi
2 Brisi
3 Charlie
4 Colour
5 Danu
6 Donn
7 Embarr
8 Firewalker
9 Fylgie
10 Iduna
11 Kelpie-Pooka
12 Mandalay
13 Mjolnir
14 Moonlight
15 Mystery
16 Rauni
17 Rhiannon
18 Rimfaxe
19 Saga
20 Skipper
21 Sleipnir
22 Sokki
23 Star
24 Thor
25 Urd
26 Viking
27 Walter
28 Yasmin
29 Balto
30 Bella
31 Bello
32 Bifrost
33 Conall
34 Fiona
35 Froya
36 Iceking
37 Jewel
38 Jonas
39 Lakehorse
40 Melusine
41 Misla
42 Ran
43 Signy
44 Skinfaxe
45 Thunder
46 Antique Flowerpot
47 Anvil & Hammer
48 Horseshoe Water Fountain
49 Lawn Gnome
50 Lilac Gazebo
51 Primrose Lamppost
52 Weathervane
53 Shade Tree
54 Winged Horse Statue
55 Wishing Well

2007 Bella Sara Northern Lights Shiny

S1 Balto
S2 Bella
S3 Bello
S4 Bifrost
S5 Conall
S6 Fiona
S7 Froya

S8 Iceking
S9 Jewel
S10 Jonas
S11 Lakehorse
S12 Melusine
S13 Misla
S14 Ran
S15 Signy
S16 Skinfaxe
S17 Thunder

2007 Bella Sara Wise Warriors

1 Alibi C
2 Bandi C
3 Bosi C
4 Calato C
5 Camelot C
6 Cantaro C
7 Cascadeur C
8 Channa C
9 Ching C
10 Chung C
11 Djengis C
12 Fend C
13 Isak C
14 Konfu C
15 Lancelot C
16 Leonard C
17 Louie C
18 Macron C
19 Medusa C
20 Mountain Climber C
21 Ninja C
22 Nuna C
23 Parlez C
24 Pini C
25 Prince C
26 Raimondo C
27 Resident C
28 Rubin C
29 Sheng C
30 Skeleton C
31 Sokki C
32 Sonet C
33 Sorel C
34 Stribes C
35 Sun C
36 Sung C
37 Tai C
38 Tao C
39 Yasmin C
40 Zombie C
41 Flying Horse Show R
42 Grooming R
43 Hoof Care R
44 Jodhpurs R
45 Jumping Saddle R
46 Riding Boots R
47 Riding Lessons R
48 Rug R
49 Training Saddle R
50 Treasure Key R

2007 Bella Sara Wise Warriors Shiny

F1 Cajus
F2 Lucky Light
F3 Ming
F4 Mushu
F5 Peace

2008 Bella Sara Baby Bella

BOOSTER BOX (36) 30.00 60.00
1 Aegis
2 Alexander
3 Amor & Venus
4 Apollo & Athena
5 Arim
6 Asteria
7 Barleycorn
8 Bellerophon
9 Briar
10 Brine
11 Ceranna
12 Charlemagne
13 Charlie & Mandalay
14 Dart
15 Delight
16 Ebenos
17 Emberic
18 Farfalla
19 Harmony
20 Helia
21 Hercules & Hecate
22 Iceking & Nyx
23 Iceprince
24 Khrysor
25 Komenos
26 Larena
27 Leonardo & Sarah
28 Mariannis
29 Mira
30 Mjolnir & Iduna
31 Moonbeam
32 Moonphantom
33 Moonsprite
34 Pirouette
35 Prisma
36 Pythia
37 Reif
38 Royce & Pink Lady
39 Snowflake
40 Sunbeam
41 Tumbleweed
42 Uranus & Anemone
43 Whimsy
44 Addis
45 Balto & Juno
46 Bella
47 Bellisimo
48 Bello & Bella
49 Beran & Rosebriar
50 Bifrost & Colour
51 Bluebell
52 Bukefalos & Mireldis
53 Calyx
54 Celesta
55 Ceratos & Nanna
56 Cherub
57 Chromasia
58 Chryso & Sasha
59 Cirra
60 Embarr & Freja
61 Fiona
62 Flame & Nike
63 Flipper & Ondine
64 Janie
65 Jewel
66 Kora
67 Mistral
68 Murttie
69 Pavonne
70 Pegasus & Roxy
71 Petal
72 Primrose
73 Ruskin
74 Skipper & Flora
75 Starfrost
76 Summit
77 Thunder
78 Toboggan
79 Treasure & Edana
80 Wodan
81 Bella's Bubble Wand
82 Bifrost Skyglider
83 Crystal Fishbowl
84 Dress-Up Doll
85 Jewel's Music Box
86 Lullaby Panda
87 Sound Spinner
88 Sparkle Skywriter
89 Star Top
90 Surprise Box
91 Waterpearl Tadpole
92 Zephyros Kite

2008 Bella Sara Baby Bella Shiny

S1 Addis
S2 Balto & Juno
S3 Bella
S4 Bellisimo
S5 Bello & Bella
S6 Beran & Rosebriar
S7 Bifrost & Colour
S8 Bluebell
S9 Bukefalos & Mireldis
S10 Calyx
S11 Celesta
S12 Ceratos & Nanna
S13 Cherub
S14 Chromasia
S15 Chryso & Sasha
S16 Cirra
S17 Embarr & Freja
S18 Fiona
S19 Flame & Nike
S20 Flipper & Ondine
S21 Janie
S22 Jewel
S23 Kora
S24 Mistral
S25 Murttie
S26 Pavonne
S27 Pegasus & Roxy
S28 Petal
S29 Primrose
S30 Ruskin
S31 Skipper & Flora
S32 Starfrost
S33 Summit
S34 Thunder
S35 Toboggan
S36 Treasure & Edana
S37 Wodan

2008 Bella Sara Magical Friends

BOOSTER BOX (36) 30.00 60.00
1 Anigan
2 Arelus
3 Atalaya
4 Azuro
5 Beau
6 Blossom
7 Bonnie
8 Brumby
9 Connora
10 Donnecha
11 Dreki
12 Dyni
13 Edda
14 Felise
15 Giasa
16 Greenlock
17 Icehorn
18 Kitty
19 Kounari
20 Lukan
21 Madeja
22 Nieva
23 Nori
24 Nuala
25 Pelagos
26 Petri
27 Rosebriar
28 Sabelle
29 Savros
30 Scotty
31 Serilda
32 Socorro
33 Tigrine
34 Tugo
35 Virstan
36 Waterpearl
37 Zephan
38 Anemone
39 Ara
40 Autumn
41 Bathylas
42 Bella
43 Beran
44 Cate
45 Ceratos
46 Cha Ye
47 Chryso
48 Cindra
49 Edana
50 Faith
51 Faxon
52 Fiona
53 Hai Sheng
54 Ivy
55 Jaida
56 Jewel
57 Kallista
58 Kendra
59 Lien
60 Lillova
61 Mellonie
62 Mireldis
63 Morewyn
64 Nerise
65 Nyx
66 Obrylin
67 Ondine
68 Phoenix
69 Quinly
70 Royce
71 Seraphia
72 Sleetmane
73 Thunder
74 Tricksy
75 Angelic Cavy
76 Citrustack
77 Cycargot
78 Finling
79 Flitterwyrm
80 Regal Strider
81 Steampoppo
82 Tomtomme
83 Treblix
84 Tunnel Runner
85 Twig Hare
86 Verdant Liona

2008 Bella Sara Magical Friends Shiny

S1 Anemone
S2 Ara
S3 Autumn
S4 Bathylas
S5 Bella
S6 Beran
S7 Cate
S8 Ceratos
S9 Cha Ye
S10 Chryso
S11 Cindra
S12 Edana
S13 Faith
S14 Faxon
S15 Fiona
S16 Hai Sheng
S17 Ivy
S18 Jaida
S19 Jewel
S20 Kallista
S21 Kendra
S22 Lien
S23 Lillova
S24 Mellonie
S25 Mireldis
S26 Morewyn
S27 Nerise
S28 Nyx
S29 Obrylin
S30 Ondine
S31 Phoenix
S32 Quinly
S33 Royce
S34 Seraphia
S35 Sleetmane
S36 Thunder
S37 Tricksy

2008 Bella Sara Native Lights

BOOSTER BOX (36) 30.00 60.00
1 Abenaki
2 Absaroke
3 Akama
4 Apache
5 Arapaho
6 Chiricahua
7 Cochiti
8 Comanche
9 Hidatsa
10 Huron
11 Inuit
12 Kiowa
13 Lenape
14 Lumbee
15 Menominee
16 Mohawk
17 Paiute
18 Pawnee
19 Pima
20 Ponca
21 Seneca
22 Shawnee
23 Shoshone
24 Tewa
25 Tlingit
26 Wasco
27 Wichita
28 Yakama
29 Anisinabe
30 Bella
31 Blackfeet
32 Cheyenne
33 Chumash
34 Fiona
35 Jewel
36 Laguna
37 Lakota
38 Navajo
39 Nimiipuu
40 Osage
41 Santee
42 Seminole
43 Thunder
44 Tsimshian
45 Zuni
46 Doll
47 Dreamcatcher
48 Drum
49 Headdress
50 Horse Blanket
51 Mandala
52 Moccasins
53 Soapstone Carving
54 Turquoise Necklace
55 Water Jug

2008 Bella Sara Native Lights Shiny

S1 Anisinabe
S2 Bella
S3 Blackfeet
S4 Cheyenne
S5 Chumash
S6 Fiona
S7 Jewel
S8 Laguna
S9 Lakota
S10 Navajo
S11 Nimiipuu
S12 Osage
S13 Santee
S14 Seminole
S15 Thunder
S16 Tsimshian
S17 Zuni

2009 Bella Sara Bella's Ball

BOOSTER BOX (36) 30.00 60.00
1 Aheron
2 Amia
3 Ariadne
4 Bella
5 Bellisimo
6 Bello
7 Bryda
8 Cara
9 Clio
10 Diamond
11 Dowager
12 Empress
13 Epona
14 Fiona
15 Firebright
16 Gracie
17 Halloween
18 Harmony
19 Hellevi
20 Honu
21 Icarus
22 Jewel
23 King
24 Knight
25 Lien
26 Lukan
27 Mahina
28 Memory
29 Merrydancer
30 Mikiko
31 Mireldis
32 Nightingale
33 Nike
34 Ondine
35 Oracle
36 Parlez
37 Pepper
38 Peregrine
39 Rodin
40 Rosamund
41 Rosebriar
42 Sapphirine
43 Socorro
44 Sophie
45 Star
46 Thunder
47 Tramontane
48 Treasure
49 Valkrist
50 Valor
51 Charm Bracelet
52 Fairystone
53 Keepsake Chest
54 Sandhaven
55 Starstone

2009 Bella Sara Bella's Ball Shiny

S1 Aheron
S2 Amia
S3 Ariadne
S4 Bella
S5 Bellisimo
S6 Bello
S7 Bryda
S8 Cara
S9 Clio
S10 Diamond
S11 Dowager
S12 Empress
S13 Epona
S14 Fiona
S15 Firebright
S16 Gracie
S17 Halloween
S18 Harmony
S19 Hellevi
S20 Honu
S21 Icarus
S22 Jewel
S23 King
S24 Knight
S25 Lien
S26 Lukan
S27 Mahina
S28 Memory
S29 Merrydancer
S30 Mikiko
S31 Mireldis
S32 Nightingale
S33 Nike
S34 Ondine
S35 Oracle
S36 Parlez
S37 Pepper
S38 Peregrine
S39 Rodin
S40 Rosamund
S41 Rosebriar
S42 Sapphirine
S43 Socorro
S44 Sophie
S45 Star
S46 Thunder
S47 Tramontane
S48 Treasure
S49 Valkrist
S50 Valor
S51 Charm Bracelet
S52 Fairystone
S53 Keepsake Chest
S54 Sandhaven
S55 Starstone

2009 Bella Sara Royalty

BOOSTER BOX (36) 30.00 60.00
1 Alina
2 Anemone
3 Aviva
4 Bella
5 Brine
6 Brioso
7 Cantaro
8 Cirra
9 Coral
10 Corcel
11 Cosima
12 Dane
13 Donnecha
14 Ebenos
15 Edana
16 Farah
17 Faris
18 Fiona
19 Gracie
20 Haku
21 Hilario
22 Honora
23 Hummingbird
24 Jajali
25 Jewel
26 Kahuna
27 Kitty
28 Kona
29 Kora
30 Magic
31 Mahalo
32 Mahina
33 Nasim
34 Nieva
35 Nike
36 Peka Peka
37 Shamal
38 Shanti
39 Sirocco
40 Sleetmane
41 Snowdreamer
42 Spottie
43 Starunna
44 Thora
45 Thunder
46 Treasure
47 Uranus
48 Valdespar
49 Zephyros
50 Sara
51 Airistos Castle
52 Islandar Castle
53 Rolandsgaard Castle
54 Shahazar Castle
55 Valeryk Castle

2009 Bella Sara Royalty Shiny

S1 Alina
S2 Anemone
S3 Aviva
S4 Bella
S5 Brine
S6 Brioso
S7 Cantaro
S8 Cirra
S9 Coral
S10 Corcel
S11 Cosima
S12 Dane
S13 Donnecha
S14 Ebenos
S15 Edana
S16 Farah
S17 Faris
S18 Fiona
S19 Gracie
S20 Haku
S21 Hilario
S22 Honora
S23 Hummingbird
S24 Jajali
S25 Jewel
S26 Kahuna
S27 Kitty
S28 Kona
S29 Kora
S30 Magic
S31 Mahalo
S32 Mahina
S33 Nasim
S34 Nieva
S35 Nike
S36 Peka Peka
S37 Shamal
S38 Shanti
S39 Sirocco
S40 Sleetmane
S41 Snowdreamer
S42 Spottie
S43 Starunna
S44 Thora
S45 Thunder
S46 Treasure
S47 Uranus
S48 Valdespar
S49 Zephyros
S50 Sara
S51 Airistos Castle
S52 Islandar Castle
S53 Rolandsgaard Castle
S54 Shahazar Castle
S55 Valeryk Castle

2009 Bella Sara Treasures

BOOSTER BOX (36) 30.00 60.00
1 Aheron
2 Amia
3 Ariadne
4 Bella
5 Bellisimo
6 Bello
7 Bryda
8 Cara
9 Clio
10 Diamond
11 Dowager
12 Empress
13 Epona
14 Fiona
15 Firebright
16 Gracie
17 Halloween
18 Harmony
19 Hellevi
20 Honu
21 Icarus
22 Jewel
23 King
24 Knight
25 Lien
26 Lukan
27 Mahina
28 Memory
29 Merrydancer
30 Mikiko
31 Mireldis
32 Nightingale
33 Nike
34 Ondine
35 Oracle
36 Parlez
37 Pepper
38 Peregrine
39 Rodin
40 Rosamund
41 Rosebriar
42 Sapphirine
43 Socorro
44 Sophie
45 Star
46 Thunder
47 Tramontane
48 Treasure
49 Valkrist
50 Valor
51 Charm Bracelet
52 Fairystone
53 Keepsake Chest
54 Sandhaven
55 Starstone

2009 Bella Sara Treasures Shiny

S1 Aheron
S2 Amia
S3 Ariadne
S4 Bella
S5 Bellisimo
S6 Bello
S7 Bryda
S8 Cara
S9 Clio
S10 Diamond
S11 Dowager
S12 Empress
S13 Epona
S14 Fiona
S15 Firebright
S16 Gracie
S17 Halloween
S18 Harmony
S19 Hellevi
S20 Honu
S21 Icarus
S22 Jewel
S23 King
S24 Knight
S25 Lien
S26 Lukan
S27 Mahina
S28 Memory
S29 Merrydancer
S30 Mikiko
S31 Mireldis
S32 Nightingale
S33 Nike
S34 Ondine
S35 Oracle
S36 Parlez
S37 Pepper
S38 Peregrine
S39 Rodin
S40 Rosamund
S41 Rosebriar
S42 Sapphirine
S43 Socorro
S44 Sophie
S45 Star
S46 Thunder
S47 Tramontane
S48 Treasure
S49 Valkrist
S50 Valor
S51 Charm Bracelet
S52 Fairystone
S53 Keepsake Chest
S54 Sandhaven
S55 Starstone

2010 Bella Sara Moonfairies

BOOSTER BOX (24) 30.00 60.00
1 Alamar
2 Albion
3 Ambrosia
4 Anigan
5 Anthea
6 Beetlejape
7 Chortlebones
8 Fiona
9 Flipper
10 Gherkin
11 Janie
12 Jewel
13 Lillova
14 Maypop
15 Merrow
16 Minty
17 Mireldis
18 Moonfairy
19 Moonphantom
20 Moonsprite
21 Mote
22 Murttie
23 Nike
24 Nimblewit
25 Ondine
26 Phoebe
27 Pink Lady
28 Quinly
29 Royce
30 Sirena
31 Sylphie
32 Thunder
33 Tiara
34 Ticklebit
35 Tricksy
36 Trumbeau
37 Twee
38 Twinklehop
39 Willownix
40 Bella & Sara
41 Soot & Colm
42 Twig & Deru
43 Wings & Emma
44 Avalynn
45 Ivenna & Myrfor
46 Fairy Globe
47 Fairy Door
48 Fiary Court
49 Awakening
50 Lovers Reunited
51 Moonstone
52 Riding on Moonbeams
53 Feywynd Castle
54 Moonfairy Found
55 Fairytale Wedding

2010 Bella Sara Moonfairies Shiny

S1 Alamar
S2 Albion
S3 Ambrosia
S4 Anigan
S5 Anthea
S6 Beetlejape
S7 Chortlebones
S8 Fiona
S9 Flipper
S10 Gherkin
S11 Janie
S12 Jewel
S13 Lillova
S14 Maypop
S15 Merrow
S16 Minty
S17 Mireldis
S18 Moonfairy
S19 Moonphantom
S20 Moonsprite
S21 Mote
S22 Murttie
S23 Nike
S24 Nimblewit
S25 Ondine
S26 Phoebe
S27 Pink Lady
S28 Quinly
S29 Royce
S30 Sirena
S31 Sylphie
S32 Thunder
S33 Tiara
S34 Ticklebit
S35 Tricksy
S36 Trumbeau
S37 Twee
S38 Twinklehop
S39 Willownix
S40 Bella & Sara
S41 Soot & Colm
S42 Twig & Deru
S43 Wings & Emma
S44 Avalynn
S45 Ivenna & Myrfor
S46 Fairy Globe
S47 Fairy Door
S48 Fiary Court
S49 Awakening
S50 Lovers Reunited
S51 Moonstone
S52 Riding on Moonbeams
S53 Feywynd Castle
S54 Moonfairy Found
S55 Fairytale Wedding

2010 Bella Sara Sunflowers

BOOSTER BOX (24) 30.00 60.00
1 Autumn
2 Beran
3 Bluebell
4 Bluefiddle
5 Briar
6 Buttercup
7 Calyx
8 Camellia
9 Cattail
10 Cayenna
11 Ceratos
12 Cinnamon
13 Dewsparkle
14 Dowager
15 Fiona
16 Flora
17 Foxglove
18 Foxtail
19 Generosity
20 Hawthorn
21 Jewel
22 Larkspur
23 Lavender
24 Lotus
25 Nike
26 Nutmeg
27 Oracle
28 Petal
29 Reed
30 Rosebriar
31 Saffron
32 Shasta Daisy
33 Snapdragon
34 Sunflower
35 Tarragon
36 Thunder
37 Violet
38 Waterlily
39 Bella & Sara
40 Seraphia & Tyri
41 Soot & Colm
42 Twig & Deru
43 Wings & Emma
44 Ivenna & Myrfor
45 Johan
46 Intruder
47 Emma & Friends
48 Pool of Reflection
49 First Petal
50 Wolf Attack
51 Family Reunion
52 Sunstone
53 Rainbow Path
54 Flower Maze
55 Petalhome

2010 Bella Sara Sunflowers Shiny

S1 Autumn
S2 Beran
S3 Bluebell
S4 Bluefiddle
S5 Briar
S6 Buttercup
S7 Calyx
S8 Camellia
S9 Cattail
S10 Cayenna
S11 Ceratos
S12 Cinnamon
S13 Dewsparkle
S14 Dowager
S15 Fiona
S16 Flora
S17 Foxglove
S18 Foxtail
S19 Generosity
S20 Hawthorn
S21 Jewel
S22 Larkspur
S23 Lavender
S24 Lotus
S25 Nike
S26 Nutmeg
S27 Oracle
S28 Petal
S29 Reed
S30 Rosebriar
S31 Saffron
S32 Shasta Daisy
S33 Snapdragon
S34 Sunflower
S35 Tarragon
S36 Thunder
S37 Violet
S38 Waterlily
S39 Bella & Sara
S40 Seraphia & Tyri
S41 Soot & Colm
S42 Twig & Deru
S43 Wings & Emma
S44 Ivenna & Myrfor
S45 Johan
S46 Intruder
S47 Emma & Friends
S48 Pool of Reflection
S49 First Petal
S50 Wolf Attack
S51 Family Reunion
S52 Sunstone
S53 Rainbow Path
S54 Flower Maze
S55 Petalhome

2010 Bella Sara Sunflowers Motion

L1 Sara & Bella
L2 Foxglove & Foxtail
L3 Flora & Bluebell
L4 Saffron & Lavender
L5 Sunflower & Petelhome
L6 Wings & Emma

2012 Bella Sara Herds from North of North

1 Bella & Sara
2 Penny Inkwell
3 Nike
4 Allegra
5 Cindra
6 Uranus
7 Jewel
8 Chumash
9 Edana
10 Kora
11 Fiona
12 Nasim
13 Shanti
14 Sirocco
15 Thunder
16 Nieva
17 Sleetmane
18 Starunna
19 Sunflower
20 Bluefiddle
21 Foxglove
22 Lavender
23 Moonfairy
24 Ambrosia
25 Mireldis
26 Mote
27 Starlight
28 Andromeda
29 Star
30 Tycho
31 Pantheon
32 Amor
33 Guinevere
34 Saturna
35 Elemyn
36 Colour
37 Jubilee
38 Lien
39 Mustang
40 Lakota
41 Tlingit
42 Zabarius
43 Ivanna & Myrfor
44 Airistos Castle
45 Dawnstar Castle
46 Feywynd Castle
47 Ice Castle
48 Islandar Castle
49 Parthamane Castle
50 Petalhome Castle
51 Rolandsgaard Castle
52 Shahazar Castle
53 Styginmoor Castle
54 Valeryk Castle
55 Wildscape Castle

2001 Buffy the Vampire Slayer Pergamum Prophecy Preview

COMPLETE SET (6)	1.00	2.50
1 Alley C	.10	.25
2 Sunnydale High School Lobby C	.10	.25
3 Breaking the Bones U	.30	.75
4 Principal Snyder U	.30	.75
5 Manacles R	.60	1.50
6 Hide Until It Goes Away R	.60	1.50

2001 Buffy the Vampire Slayer Pergamum Prophecy

COMPLETE SET (200)	80.00	150.00
BOOSTER BOX (36 PACKS)	30.00	60.00
BOOSTER PACK (12 CARDS)	1.50	3.00
1 Feeding Time C	.10	.20
2 From the Ashes of Five Dead C	.10	.20
3 Young Frankenstein C	.10	.20
4 Facing Your Fear C	.10	.20
5 Welcome to the Harvest C	.10	.20
6 Abduction C	.10	.20
7 Body Switch C	.10	.20
8 On Patrol C	.10	.20
9 A Quick Jaunt to the Funeral Home C	.10	.20
10 Cheerleader Tryouts C	.10	.20
11 Oh, May Queen C	.10	.20
12 Mayhem at the Bronze C	.10	.20
13 A Dead Cheerleader Is a Good Cheerleader C	.10	.20
14 You Can Trust the Technopagan C	.10	.20
15 The Bronze C	.10	.20
16 Weatherly Park Bike Trail C	.10	.20
17 Natalie French's Cellar C	.10	.20
18 The Nest C	.10	.20
19 Pool of Blood C	.10	.20
20 Streets of Sunnydale C	.10	.20
21 Mausoleum C	.10	.20
22 Power Station C	.10	.20
23 Public Restroom C	.10	.20
24 Sunnydale School Hallways C	.10	.20
25 Animal Intensity C	.10	.20
26 Varsity Training C	.10	.20
27 Electrical Tunnels Schematic C	.10	.20
28 Empty Puppet Case C	.10	.20
29 Number 1 Alternate C	.10	.20
30 Testosterone C	.10	.20
31 Priority Check C	.10	.20
32 Two Gun Woo C	.10	.20
33 New Kid On The Block C	.10	.20
34 Demon Theory C	.10	.20
35 Feast on Virgins C	.10	.20
36 Overhand Toss C	.10	.20
37 Wooly-Headed Liberal Thinking C	.10	.20
38 My Spider-Sense Is Tingling C	.10	.20
39 Aaack! Spiders! C	.10	.20
40 The CPR Thing C	.10	.20
41 Watch Zebras Mating C	.10	.20
42 Not Prepared for Farrah Hair C	.10	.20
43 Bow Before the Idiot Box C	.10	.20
44 Thrown to the Hyenas C	.10	.20
45 Hit the Streets C	.10	.20
46 The Old Madison Body Switch U	.20	.50
47 Primal Urges U	.20	.50
48 Reviving the Master U	.20	.50
49 Festival of Saint Vigeous U	.20	.50
50 Turn Them On Each Other U	.20	.50
51 Hyenas in the Principal's Office U	.20	.50
52 Never Kill a Boy on the First Date U	.20	.50
53 When Good Mothers Go Bad U	.20	.50
54 Why Yes, I am a Praying Mantis U	.20	.50
55 Parent Teacher Night U	.20	.50
56 Billy Palmer U	.20	.50
57 Cordelia U	.20	.50
58 Jenny Calendar U	.20	.50
59 Owen Thurman U	.20	.50
60 Sid U	.20	.50
61 Xander U	.20	.50
62 Jesse U	.20	.50
63 Andrew Borba U	.20	.50
64 Catherine Madison U	.20	.50
65 Chris Epps U	.20	.50
66 Claw U	.20	.50
67 Fritz U	.20	.50
68 Luke U	.20	.50
69 Moloch, the Corruptor U	.20	.50
70 Natalie French U	.20	.50
71 The Ugly Man U	.20	.50
72 The Pack U	.20	.50
73 The Three U	.20	.50
74 Marc, The Organ Stealer U	.20	.50
75 Absalom U	.20	.50
76 Dr. Gregory U	.20	.50
77 Joyce Summers U	.20	.50
78 Coach Herrold U	.20	.50
79 Mitch U	.20	.50
80 Harmony U	.20	.50
81 Hank Summers U	.20	.50
82 Blayne Mall U	.20	.50
83 Amber Grove U	.20	.50
84 Sunnydale High School Library U	.20	.50
85 1630 Revello Drive (Summer's House) U	.20	.50
86 Tunnels U	.20	.50
87 Madison House U	.20	.50
88 Sunnydale Funeral Home U	.20	.50
89 Cemetary U	.20	.50
90 Hyena Exhibit U	.20	.50
91 Sunnydale High School Computer Lab U	.20	.50
92 CRD U	.20	.50
93 Sunnydale School Lawn U	.20	.50
94 Warehouse U	.20	.50
95 Watcher Training U	.20	.50
96 Off-the-charts Smart U	.20	.50

Card	Low	High
97 Expert on the Weird U	.20	.50
98 Babe-li-tude U	.20	.50
99 Power of the Black Mass U	.20	.50
100 Technopaganism U	.20	.50
101 Scully Me U	.20	.50
102 Demonology 101 U	.20	.50
103 Gone Binary U	.20	.50
104 Morning Person U	.20	.50
105 Pack Rat U	.20	.50
106 Fast Pace U	.20	.50
107 Stake & Crossbow U	.20	.50
108 Lucky 19 Baseball Jersey U	.20	.50
109 May Queen Dress U	.20	.50
110 Tome of Moloch U	.20	.50
111 Fire Axe U	.20	.50
112 Ring of Prophecy U	.20	.50
113 Bat Sonar U	.20	.50
114 Metal Robot Body U	.20	.50
115 Sledgehammer U	.20	.50
116 Sentient Cheerleading Trophy U	.20	.50
117 Giles-mobile U	.20	.50
118 An Innocent Guillotine U	.20	.50
119 Hair Flip U	.20	.50
120 Book Learning U	.20	.50
121 Creep Factor U	.20	.50
122 Vampire Embrace U	.20	.50
123 Cafeteria Soylent Green U	.20	.50
124 Dig Up The Corpses U	.20	.50
125 Stake 'em High U	.20	.50
126 I Quit U	.20	.50
127 Computer Invasion U	.20	.50
128 Clumsy Fingers U	.20	.50
129 Lounging About With Imbeciles U	.20	.50
130 A Friend In Need U	.20	.50
131 Trading Clothing U	.20	.50
132 Talent Show U	.20	.50
133 Oh, the 'Other' Cemetery U	.20	.50
134 Offer of Ugly Death U	.20	.50
135 Shaky on the Dismount U	.20	.50
136 Trans-possession R	1.00	2.50
137 Hot Dog Surprise R	1.00	2.50
138 Cricket Snack R	1.00	2.50
139 A Boy and His Guillotine R	1.00	2.50
140 I Robot, You Jane R	1.00	2.50
141 The Master Returns R	1.00	2.50
142 Pergamum Prophecy R	1.00	2.50
143 The Talent Show Must Go On R	1.00	2.50
144 Nightmares of Mine R	1.00	2.50
145 Demonic Smackdown R	1.00	2.50
146 Angel R	1.00	2.50
147 Angel R	1.00	2.50
148 Buffy Summers R	1.00	2.50
149 Rupert Giles R	1.00	2.50
150 Rupert Giles R	1.00	2.50
151 Willow Rosenberg R	1.00	2.50
152 Willow Rosenberg R	1.00	2.50
153 Collin, the Annointed One R	1.00	2.50
154 Collin, the Annointed One R	1.00	2.50
155 Darla R	1.00	2.50
156 Drusilla R	1.00	2.50
157 Drusilla R	1.00	2.50
158 Spike R	1.00	2.50
159 Spike R	1.00	2.50
160 The Master R	1.00	2.50
161 Sunnydale High School Auditorium R	1.00	2.50
162 Lair of the Master R	1.00	2.50
163 Hospital R	1.00	2.50
164 Football Field R	1.00	2.50
165 Real Literary-like R	1.00	2.50
166 Spellcasting Dolls R	1.00	2.50
167 Pergamum Codex R	1.00	2.50
168 Ashes of Five Dead R	1.00	2.50
169 Supernatural Boost R	1.00	2.50
170 Self-Referential Humor R	1.00	2.50
171 Go Home and Listen to Country Music R	1.00	2.50
172 Circle of Kayless R	1.00	2.50
173 Alone R	1.00	2.50
174 Inside Joke R	1.00	2.50
175 Superior Fighting R	1.00	2.50
176 Master Bones R	1.00	2.50
177 Run, Fast R	1.00	2.50
178 Join the Pep Squad R	1.00	2.50
179 Decisions, Decisions R	1.00	2.50
180 Sunset R	1.00	2.50
181 The Master UR	4.00	10.00
182 Buffy Summers UR	6.00	15.00
183 The Dead Have Risen UR	5.00	12.00
184 Primal Connection UR	6.00	15.00
185 Angel F	1.50	4.00
186 Buffy Summers F	1.50	4.00
187 Rupert Giles F	1.50	4.00
188 Willow Rosenberg F	1.50	4.00
189 Collin, the Annointed One F	1.50	4.00
190 Drusilla F	1.50	4.00
191 Spike F	1.50	4.00
192 The Master F	1.50	4.00
193 Buffy F	1.50	4.00
194 Giles F	1.50	4.00
195 Willow F	1.50	4.00
196 Angel F	1.50	4.00
197 The Master F	1.50	4.00
198 Collin F	1.50	4.00
199 Spike F	1.50	4.00
200 Drusilla F	1.50	4.00

2001 Buffy the Vampire Slayer Pergamum Prophecy First Patrol

Card	Low	High
COMPLETE SET (5)	4.00	10.00
1 Buffy Summers FP R	2.00	5.00
2 Buffy Summers FP F	1.50	4.00
3 Spike FP F	1.25	3.00
4 Buffy FP F	1.50	4.00
5 Spike FP F	1.25	3.00

2002 Buffy the Vampire Slayer Angel's Curse Preview

Card	Low	High
COMPLETE SET (3)	.60	1.25
Pre1 Forceful Persuasion C	.10	.25
Pre2 Home Again U	.30	.75
Pre3 Lily R	.60	1.50

2002 Buffy the Vampire Slayer Angel's Curse

Card	Low	High
COMPLETE SET (125)	50.00	100.00
BOOSTER BOX (36 PACKS)	15.00	30.00
BOOSTER PACK (12 CARDS)	.75	1.50
1 Bad Eggs C	.10	.20
2 Die Young and Stay Pretty C	.10	.20
3 Love Sucks C	.10	.20
4 Death Stalks the Dream C	.10	.20
5 Coach Marin C	.10	.20
6 Dalton C	.10	.20
7 50's Time Capsule C	.10	.20
8 Dragon's Cove Magic Shop C	.10	.20
9 Ethan's Costume Shop C	.10	.20
10 Sunset Club C	.10	.20
11 Body of a Dead Cheerleader C	.10	.20
12 Gypsy Curse C	.10	.20
13 Machiavellian Ingenuity C	.10	.20
14 Ritual of Restoration C	.10	.20
15 Spike's Car C	.10	.20
16 The Look C	.10	.20
17 Tweed Mail C	.10	.20
18 Wisdom C	.10	.20
19 PDA C	.10	.20
20 Something Weird C	.10	.20
21 The Plan C	.10	.20
22 A Lover's Gift C	.10	.20
23 Angry Mob C	.10	.20
24 Anywhere But Here C	.10	.20
25 Confrontation C	.10	.20
26 Cut From the Same Cloth C	.10	.20
27 Going Goth C	.10	.20
28 Hot Sheets C	.10	.20
29 Soda Machine Raid C	.10	.20
30 Total Lecture Overload C	.10	.20
31 Tremors C	.10	.20
32 Unwelcome Surprise C	.10	.20
33 A Soul's Revenge U	.20	.50
34 An American Werewolf in Sunnydale U	.20	.50
35 New Dad in Town U	.20	.50
36 Something Fishy This Way Comes U	.20	.50
37 The Dark Age U	.20	.50
38 Amy Madison U	.20	.50
39 Billy Fordham U	.20	.50
40 Cameron Walker U	.20	.50
41 Der Kindestod U	.20	.50
42 Doug Perren U	.20	.50
43 Ethan Rayne U	.20	.50
44 Gill Monster U	.20	.50
45 Kendra U	.20	.50
46 Oz U	.20	.50
47 Oz U	.20	.50
48 Ted Buchanan U	.20	.50
49 Willy U	.20	.50
50 Xander U	.20	.50
51 Army Base U	.20	.50
52 Sunnydale City Morgue U	.20	.50
53 Willy's Bar U	.20	.50
54 Black Lagoon Aromatherapy U	.20	.50
55 Diana's Touch U	.20	.50
56 Mummy's Seal U	.20	.50
57 Tattoo Remover (Acid) U	.20	.50
58 Video Camera U	.20	.50
59 Wavering Power U	.20	.50
60 Weapon's Expert U	.20	.50
61 A Fervant Wish U	.20	.50
62 Immolation-O-Gram U	.20	.50
63 B.O. U	.20	.50
64 Bad Alcohol U	.20	.50
65 Blind Panic U	.20	.50
66 Box of Goodies U	.20	.50
67 Choke Hold U	.20	.50
68 Competition Appraisal U	.20	.50
69 Desperate Maneuvers U	.20	.50
70 Fatal Recovery U	.20	.50
71 Gathering of Scoobies U	.20	.50
72 Grounded U	.20	.50
73 Henchmen-R-Us U	.20	.50
74 Homeric Insensitivity U	.20	.50
75 Hypnotic Grasp U	.20	.50
76 Master of Ceremonies U	.20	.50
77 No More Soul U	.20	.50
78 Slay Industries U	.20	.50
79 Surprise U	.20	.50
80 Here's How You Eat It U	.20	.50
81 Visions U	.20	.50
82 What Comes Around … U	.20	.50
83 It's The End of the World As We Know It R	1.00	2.50
84 Jigsaw Judge R	1.00	2.50
85 Ritual of Eligor R	1.00	2.50
86 Angel R	1.00	2.50
87 Angelus R	1.00	2.50
88 Angelus R	1.00	2.50
89 Buffy Summers R	1.00	2.50
90 Collin, The Annointed One R	1.00	2.50
91 Cordelia R	1.00	2.50
92 Drusilla R	1.00	2.50
93 Jenny Calendar R	1.00	2.50
94 Kendra R	1.00	2.50
95 Principal Snyder R	1.00	2.50
96 Rupert Giles R	1.00	2.50
97 Spike R	1.00	2.50
98 The Judge R	1.00	2.50
99 The Master R	1.00	2.50
100 Uncle Enyos R	1.00	2.50
101 Willow Rosenberg R	1.00	2.50
102 Natural History Museum R	1.00	2.50
103 Vampire Mansion R	1.00	2.50
104 Claddagh Ring R	1.00	2.50
105 Disembodied Arm R	1.00	2.50
106 Mr. Pointy R	1.00	2.50
107 Orb of Thesulah R	1.00	2.50
108 Rocket Launcher R	1.00	2.50
109 Silver Locket R	1.00	2.50
110 What Doesn't Kill You … R	1.00	2.50
111 Death R	1.00	2.50
112 Slayer's Burden R	1.00	2.50
113 Breaking Free R	1.00	2.50
114 Concealed Weapon R	1.00	2.50
115 Finding Your Destiny R	1.00	2.50
116 Flashy Swordfight R	1.00	2.50
117 Hypnotism R	1.00	2.50
118 Vampiric Expertise R	1.00	2.50
119 Ritual of Acathla R	1.00	2.50
120 St. Du Lac Mausoleum UR	15.00	30.00
121 Wrath of Angelus UR	15.00	30.00
122 Xander F	.75	2.00
123 Kendra F	.75	2.00
124 Cordelia F	.75	2.00
125 Angelus F	.75	2.00

2002 Buffy the Vampire Slayer Class of '99 Preview

Card	Low	High
1 Initiative Commandos C	.10	.25
2 UC Sunnydale Commons C	.10	.25
3 Espresso Pump U	.30	.75
4 Freshman Year U	.30	.75
5 Maggie Walsh R	.60	1.50
6 Riley Finn R	.60	1.50

2002 Buffy the Vampire Slayer Class of '99

Card	Low	High
COMPLETE SET (254)	120.00	250.00
BOOSTER BOX (36 PACKS)	20.00	40.00
BOOSTER PACK (12 CARDS)	1.00	2.00
1 Dead Man's Party C	.10	.20
2 Homecoming C	.10	.20
3 Eliminati Vamps C	.10	.20
4 Hellhound C	.10	.20
5 Percy West C	.10	.20
6 Scott Hope C	.10	.20
7 The Harbingers C	.10	.20
8 April Fools Dress Ship C	.10	.20
9 Boiler Room C	.10	.20
10 Faith's Motel C	.10	.20
11 Garden Shed C	.10	.20
12 Eliminati Swords C	.10	.20
13 Formal Wear C	.10	.20
14 Holy Hand Grenade C	.10	.20
15 Living Flame C	.10	.20
16 Maps and Stuff C	.10	.20
17 Slayer Kryptonite C	.10	.20
18 Witch Pez Dispenser C	.10	.20
19 Cross-Referencing C	.10	.20
20 Demonology, Ph.D C	.10	.20
21 Knife Practice C	.10	.20
22 Necronomenclature C	.10	.20
23 Slayer's Fortitude C	.10	.20
24 Slayer's Training C	.10	.20
25 Spells, Cursies and Whammies C	.10	.20
26 Telekinesis C	.10	.20
27 Telepathic Block C	.10	.20
28 Tutoring C	.10	.20
29 Birthday Tradition C	.10	.20
30 Caught in the Crossfire C	.10	.20
31 Come to the Dark Side C	.10	.20
32 Disciplinary Council C	.10	.20
33 Locker Search C	.10	.20
34 All's Well That Ends Well C	.10	.20
35 Big Bang C	.10	.20
36 Book Cramming C	.10	.20
37 Book Learning C	.10	.20
38 Cluck-Cluck C	.10	.20
39 Creep Factor C	.10	.20
40 Discovery C	.10	.20
41 Don't Get Killed C	.10	.20
42 Dramatic Irony C	.10	.20
43 Drive Like Crazy C	.10	.20
44 Group Support C	.10	.20
45 Hair Flip C	.10	.20
46 If at First You Don't Succeed C	.10	.20
47 Knowledge is Power C	.10	.20
48 Manic-Depressive Chick C	.10	.20
49 Neat Freak C	.10	.20
50 Off My Game C	.10	.20
51 Full-On Monster Fighting C	.10	.20
52 Prom C	.10	.20
53 Testosterone C	.10	.20
54 The Help of the Merry Men C	.10	.20
55 Tranquilized C	.10	.20
56 Untrustworthy C	.10	.20
57 Vampire Embrace C	.10	.20
58 Want, Take, Have C	.10	.20
59 And Hell Follows Him U	.20	.50
60 Fairy Tales are Real U	.20	.50
61 Gingerbread U	.20	.50
62 Hell's Angel U	.20	.50
63 Price of True Evil U	.20	.50
64 Tento di Cruciamentum U	.20	.50
65 Through the Demon Portal U	.20	.50
66 Amy Madison U	.20	.50
67 Angel U	.20	.50
68 Anyanka U	.20	.50
69 Buffy Summers U	.20	.50
70 Faith U	.20	.50
71 Faith U	.20	.50
72 Hansel and Gretal U	.20	.50
73 Jack O'Toole U	.20	.50
74 Pat U	.20	.50
75 Jonathan Levenson U	.20	.50
76 Ken U	.20	.50
77 Lunch Lady U	.20	.50
78 Mr. Trick U	.20	.50
79 Oz U	.20	.50
80 Pete U	.20	.50
81 Rupert Giles U	.20	.50
82 Tucker Wells U	.20	.50
83 Wesley Wyndam-Pryce U	.20	.50
84 Willow Rosenberg U	.20	.50
85 Xander Harris U	.20	.50
86 Hell U	.20	.50
87 Sporting Goods Store U	.20	.50
88 Sunnydale Arms U	.20	.50
89 Balthazar's Amulet U	.20	.50
90 Disturbing Features U	.20	.50
91 Faith's Knife U	.20	.50
92 Haphazard Bomb U	.20	.50
93 Killer of the Dead U	.20	.50
94 Love Tattoo U	.20	.50
95 Tranquilizer Gun U	.20	.50
96 Channeled Aggresion U	.20	.50
97 Charming U	.20	.50
98 Gourmet Cuisine U	.20	.50
99 Homecoming Queen U	.20	.50
100 Invulnerability U	.20	.50
101 Scoring Well U	.20	.50
102 Warding U	.20	.50
103 In the Past U	.20	.50
104 Young at Heart U	.20	.50
105 Bad Girls Part 1 U	.20	.50
106 Band Candy Part 1 U	.20	.50
107 Graduation Day Part 1 U	.20	.50
108 Lover's Walk Part 1 U	.20	.50
109 The Zeppo Part 1 U	.20	.50
110 Donel U	.20	.50
111 I Quit U	.20	.50
112 Lust For Her Death U	.20	.50
113 Modern Day Vampire U	.20	.50
114 Preparing for Ascension U	.20	.50
115 Slayer's Lust U	.20	.50
116 Unknown Outcome U	.20	.50
117 Ascension of Olivikan R	1.00	2.50
118 Commencement Ceremonies R	1.00	2.50
119 Flamma Vitae R	1.00	2.50
120 Angel R	1.00	2.50
121 Angel R	1.00	2.50
122 Anyanka R	1.00	2.50
123 Balthazar R	1.00	2.50
124 Buffy Summers R	1.00	2.50
125 Buffy Summers R	1.00	2.50
126 Cordelia R	1.00	2.50
127 Faith R	1.00	2.50
128 Faith R	1.00	2.50
129 Faith R	1.00	2.50
130 Faith R	1.00	2.50
131 Gwendolyn Post R	1.00	2.50
132 Mayor Richard Wilkins III R	1.00	2.50
133 Mayor Richard Wilkins III R	1.00	2.50
134 Mr. Trick R	1.00	2.50
135 Oz R	1.00	2.50
136 Rupert Giles R	1.00	2.50
137 Spike R	1.00	2.50
138 The First R	1.00	2.50
139 The Master R	1.00	2.50
140 Vamp Willow R	1.00	2.50
141 Willow R	1.00	2.50
142 Xander R	1.00	2.50
143 Band Candy Warehouse R	1.00	2.50
144 Fountain Quad R	1.00	2.50
145 Box of Gavrok R	1.00	2.50
146 Candy Bars R	1.00	2.50
147 Glove of Myhnegon R	1.00	2.50
148 Compound Bow R	1.00	2.50
149 Mask of Ovu Mobani R	1.00	2.50
150 Symbol of Anyanka R	1.00	2.50
151 Tome of Mediocrity R	1.00	2.50
152 Verbal Non-Verbal R	1.00	2.50
153 Eventful Combat R	1.00	2.50
154 Initiation R	1.00	2.50
155 Bad Girls Part 2 R	1.00	2.50
156 Band Candy Part 2 R	1.00	2.50
157 Graduation Day Part 2 R	1.00	2.50
158 Lover's Walk Part 2 R	1.00	2.50
159 The Zeppo Part 2 R	1.00	2.50
160 A Crazy Plan R	1.00	2.50
161 Ambushed R	1.00	2.50
162 Been There, Killed That R	1.00	2.50
163 Bored Now R	1.00	2.50
164 Crushing Blow R	1.00	2.50
165 Demon in Sheep's Clothing R	1.00	2.50
166 Kicking Demon A$$ R	1.00	2.50
167 Make It A Double R	1.00	2.50
168 Raising the Stakes R	1.00	2.50
169 Rivalry R	1.00	2.50
170 Three-some R	1.00	2.50
171 A Thing F	.60	1.50
172 Class Protector F	.60	1.50
173 Demon Hunting F	.60	1.50
174 Morality Lecture F	.60	1.50
175 Slayer's Handiwork F	.60	1.50
176 Mobile Tracking System F	.60	1.50
177 Quality Rage F	.60	1.50
178 Black Hat F	.60	1.50
179 Caught Off Guard F	.60	1.50
180 Hidden Allies F	.60	1.50
181 Lover's Return F	.60	1.50
182 Spring Madness F	.60	1.50
183 The Big Night F	.60	1.50
184 Young, Fast and Hot-Blooded F	.60	1.50
185 Beauty and the Beast F	.60	1.50
186 Bring Me My Amulet F	.60	1.50
187 One Man Army F	.60	1.50
188 Return of The First F	.60	1.50
189 Slayerfest F	.60	1.50
190 Lunch Special F	.60	1.50
191 Doppelgangland F	.60	1.50
192 Power of the Wish F	.60	1.50
193 Start the Juicer F	.60	1.50
194 Wish Granted F	.60	1.50
195 Larry Blaisdell F	.60	1.50
196 Zachary Kralik F	.60	1.50
197 Bizarro Blood Bottling Plant F	.60	1.50
198 Bizarro Bronze F	.60	1.50
199 Bizarro Streets of Sunnydale F	.60	1.50
200 Bizarro Sun Cinema F	.60	1.50
201 Bizarro Sunnydale High School F	.60	1.50
202 Bizarro Sunnydale School Library F	.60	1.50
203 Deserted Cabin F	.60	1.50
204 Eye of Rat F	.60	1.50
205 Hallway Scene-making F	.60	1.50
206 Major Wiggins F	.60	1.50
207 Trade Talks F	.60	1.50
208 Fast Food F	.60	1.50
209 Out of Options F	.60	1.50
210 The Wish Part 1 F	.60	1.50
211 The Wish Part 2 F	.60	1.50
212 Blood and Crumpets F	.60	1.50
213 Broken Wishes F	.60	1.50
214 Clarion Call F	.60	1.50
215 I Love This Part F	.60	1.50
216 I'm A Blood Sucking Fiend F	.60	1.50
217 Oh Fff… F	.60	1.50
218 Oz Watch F	.60	1.50
219 Tiny Victory F	.60	1.50
220 Watching Playtime F	.60	1.50
221 Who Do You Work For F	.60	1.50
222 Wish: The Weirding F	.60	1.50
223 Angel F	.60	1.50
224 Anyanka F	.60	1.50
225 Buffy Summers F	.60	1.50
226 Bizarro Buffy F	.60	1.50
227 Cordelia F	.60	1.50
228 Faith F	.60	1.50
229 Kakistos F	.60	1.50
230 Mayor Richard Wilkins III F	.60	1.50
231 Mr. Trick F	.60	1.50
232 Oz F	.60	1.50
233 Rupert Giles F	.60	1.50
234 The Master F	.60	1.50
235 Vamp Willow F	.60	1.50
236 Vamp Xander F	.60	1.50
237 Willow F	.60	1.50
238 Xander F	.60	1.50
239 Buffy/Riley F	.60	1.50
240 Xander/Anya F	.60	1.50
241 Angel/Spike F	.60	1.50
242 Willow/Tara F	.60	1.50
243 The Mayor/Kathy F	.60	1.50
244 Mr. Trick/Harmony F	.60	1.50
245 Kakistos/Maggie Walsh F	.60	1.50
246 Faith/Adam F	.60	1.50
247 Vamp Willow/Vamp Xander F	.60	1.50
249 The Master/Anyanka F	.60	1.50
251 Oz/Buffy Bizarro Land F	.60	1.50
253 Giles/Cordelia F	.60	1.50
255 City Hall UR	20.00	40.00
256 Books of Ascension UR	20.00	40.00
257 Day of Ascension UR	20.00	40.00
258 Calling in the Heavy Artillery UR	20.00	40.00

2002 Buffy the Vampire Slayer Class of '99 First Patrol

Card	Low	High
COMPLETE (5)		
124 Buffy Summers FP R	2.00	5.00
225 Buffy Summers FP F	1.50	4.00
228 Faith FP F	1.25	3.00
239 Buffy FP F	1.50	4.00
246 Faith FP F	1.25	3.00

2004 Call of Cthulhu Arkham Edition

C3 Blackwood Associate C
C5 Blackwood File Clerk C
C7 Freelance Occultist C
R6 Federal Agent R
R8 G-Men R
R9 Grizzled Vet R
U1 Thomas F. Malone U
U2 Beat Cop U
U4 Blackwood Detective U
C10 Hardboiled Detective C
C11 Hired Muscle C
C15 Mystic Courage C
C17 Police Raid C
C22 Shotgun Blast C
C29 Police Station C
C30 Tommygun C
C34 Etnobiologist C
C37 Laboratory Assistant C
C40 Rare Book Researcher C
C41 Strange Librarian C
C42 Two-fisted Archeologist C
C44 Binding C
C49 Powder of Ibn-Ghazi C
C50 Radical Therapy C
C54 Thaumaturgical Prodigies, Rev. Phillip's Expose C
C57 M.U. Administration Building C
C61 Clover Club Bouncer C
C63 Discreet Physician C
C64 Freelance Reporter C
C69 O'Bannion Enforcer C
C70 O'Bannion Gunsels C
C76 Desperation C
C80 Intimidate C
C81 Persuasive Friends C
C86 Clover Cartage Co. C
C90 Lucky Cigarette Case C
C94 Elder Shoggoth C
C97 Knight of the Void C
F01 The Dreams of Kingsport F
F02 The Horror of the Past F
F03 The Arkham Willows F
F04 The Forgotten Sepulchre F
F05 The Thing at the Gate F
F06 The Secret of the North Woods F
F07 The Innsmouth Threat F
F08 The Terror out of Dunwich F
F09 The Well F
F10 The Crooked Manse F

F11 Investigator Domain 1 F
F12 Investigator Domain 2 F
F13 Investigator Domain 3 F
F14 Mythos Domain 1 F
F15 Mythos Domain 2 F
F16 Mythos Domain 3 F
R12 Special Operative R
R19 Search Warrant R
R20 Shakedown! R
R21 Short Fuse R
R23 Agency Stakeout R
R26 Dockside Speakeasy R
R27 Mayor's Office R
R32 Sir William Brinton R
R35 Expedition Leader R
R38 Mad Genius R
R39 Mysterious Benefactor R
R45 Against the Darkness R
R47 Dangerous Experiment R
R48 Find Gate R
R53 Book of Eibon, Hyperborean Grimoire R
R55 The Necronomicon, The Book of the Mad Arab R
R59 Miskatonic Commons R
R62 Courier R
R65 Hired Mystic R
R71 Syndicate Agent R
R73 Gangster's Moll R
R75 Burning the Midnight Oil R
R79 Forced Foreclosure R
R82 The Rip'Off R
R84 Arkham Docks R
R87 Elder Sign Pendant R
R88 First Bank of Arkham R
R91 Cthulhu, The Great Old One R
R93 Ancient Deep One R
R98 Lurking Star Spawn R
U13 Task Force U
U14 Hair of the Worm U
U16 Playing with Fire U
U18 Preemptive Strike U
U24 Blackwood Office U
U25 Dead Man's Alley U
U28 Patrol Wagon U
U31 Professor Armitage U
U33 Arkham Psychologist U
U36 Field Researcher U
U43 Visiting Professor U
U46 Crafting the Elder Sign U
U51 Unearthing the Ancients U
U52 Undocumented Expedition U
U56 Celaeno Fragments, The Life's Work of Doctor Shrewsbury U
U58 M.U. Science Building U
U60 Miskatonic Library U
U66 Hit Squad U
U67 Investigative Reporter U
U68 Mob Lieutenant U
U72 Syndicate Troubleshooter U
U74 Behind Closed Doors U
U77 Exposed! U
U78 Extortion U
U83 Arkham Advertiser U
U85 Assassination Contract U
U89 Hit List U
U92 Adult Deep One U
U95 Haunter of the Dark U
U96 Keeper of the Golden Path U
U99 Mature Deep One U
C101 Shoggoth Unbound C
C102 Son of the Sleeper C
C103 Young Deep One C
C107 Helpless, Hopeless, and Doomed C
C108 Primal Fear C
C112 Unnatural Stealth C
C118 Silver Twilight Lodge C
C119 The Innsmouth Look C
C122 Academy Patron C
C126 Keeper of the Yellow Sign C
C127 Mad Artist C
C130 Street Scholar C
C131 Thrill Killer C
C137 Committed C
C140 Song of Hastur C
C142 Xanthophobia C
C144 Academy of the Mad C
C146 Pallid Mask C
C154 Disciple of the Gate C
C156 Fire Vampire Swarm C
C159 Nightgaunt Sentry C
C160 Render of Veils C
C163 Shambling Zombie C
C170 Rite of the Broken Stone C
C171 Sacrificial Gate C
C172 Unspeakable Resurrection C
C175 Key of Tawil At-Umr C
C179 Temple of Yog-Sothoth C
C182 Adult Cthonian C
C184 Daugther of the Goat C
C185 Degenerate Ghoul C
C187 Hungry Dark Young C
C191 Mi-Go Worker C
C197 Burrowing Beneath C
C202 Horrid Mutation C
C203 Regeneration C
C206 Rite of Rebirth C
C209 The Witch House C
C212 Inside Information C
C213 Startling Discovery C
C216 Unhealthy Curiosity C
C217 .45 Pistols C
C218 Arkham Asylum C
C227 Independence Square C
C232 Packard C
C233 Shadows Fall C
C234 Shadows Fall Away C
C235 Eldritch Nexus C
R100 Proto-Shoggoth R
R104 Deep One Assault R
R106 Driven by Madness R
R109 Ritual Sacrifice R
R114 Cthaat Aquadingen, Lore of the Sunken Masters R
R115 Marked by the Ancients R
R120 Undersea Treasures R
R121 Hastur, The King in Yellow R
R124 Ghost R
R125 High Priest of Hastur R
R133 Yellow Muse R
R135 Behind the Pallied Mask R
R138 Mass Hysteria R
R141 Unspeakable Revelations R
R143 Carcossa R
R148 The Unnamable House R
R149 Unaussprechliche Kulten, Von Juntz's Dark Masterpieces R
R151 Yog-Sothoth, The Key and the Gate R
R153 Foul Dimensional Shambler R
R157 High Priest of the Key R
R158 Hound of Tindalos R
R164 Burnout R
R166 Dream Messenger R
R168 Mystic Backlash R
R173 Blackmoor Estate R
R178 Temple of Ramasekva R
R180 Warded Flesh R
R181 Shub-Niggurath, The Black Goat of the Woods R
R183 Cyclopean Dhole R
R189 Mi-Go Scientist R
R192 Rampaging Dark Young R
R193 Slavering Gug R
R195 Birthing a Thousand Young R
R200 From Beneath R
R205 Altar of the Blessed R
R208 The Charnel Gate R
R210 Witch-Mark R
R211 Even Death May Die R
R214 The Stars Are Right R
R215 To the Last Breath R
R219 Blasted Heath R
R220 Country Store R
R223 Dimensional Rift R
R230 Nightmare Hours R
R231 North Church R
R239 To See Another Day R
R240 True Magick, Theophilus Wren's Taxonomy R
U105 Dreams of a Sunken City U
U110 The Great Old One Rises! U
U111 Touched by the Sleeper U
U113 Blessing of Cthulhu U
U116 R'lyeh, City of Dreams U
U117 Shadowed Reef U
U123 Byakhee Servant U
U128 Byakhee Raider U
U129 Priestess of the Yellow Sign U
U132 Werewolf U
U134 Agoraphobia U
U136 Byakhee Attack U
U139 Power Drain U
U145 Glasser Art Gallery U
U147 The King in Yellow, The Notorious Play U
U150 Victoria's Loft U
U152 Bloated Star Vampire U
U155 Guardian Elder Thing U
U161 Servant of the Key U
U162 Vampire Stalker U
U165 Dread Curse of Azathoth U
U167 Gathering at the Stones U
U169 Rending the Veil U
U174 Haunted Graveyard U
U176 Pnakotic Manuscripts, Book of Unknown Origin U
U177 Red Gate Mound U
U186 Flying Polyp Scout U
U188 Mi-Go Commander U
U190 Mi-Go Warrior U
U194 Slithering Formless Spawn U
U196 Bound by the Black Mother U
U198 Caught in the Dreamlands U
U199 Fertility Rites U
U201 Horns of the Black Goat U
U204 Trapped in the Labyrinth U
U207 Shadowed Woods U
U221 Crimson Dawn U
U222 Curiosity Shoppe U
U224 Forgotten Temple U
U225 Gentleman's Club U
U226 Ghoul Warrens U
U228 Infested Cemetary U
U229 Miskatonic Antiquities Collection U
U236 Sword of Ramasekva U
U237 Terrors in the Dark U
U238 The Orient Express U

2004 Call of Cthulhu Unspeakable Tales

C4 Off-Duty Patrolman C
C6 Special Operations Team C
C7 Street-Smart Rookie C
R1 Agent Jerry Holland, Undercover Fed R
R3 Back Alley Sawbones R
R8 Backup R
U2 Inspector John Legrasse, Cop in the Know U
U5 Paranormal Specialist U
U9 Calling in the Feds U
C10 Fear of God C
C11 Forced Entry C
C16 Field Office C
C20 Antiquities Consultant C
C22 Cryptozoologist C
C25 Reclusive Researcher C
C26 Arcane Insight C
C29 Purification C
C34 Government Grant C
C37 Bag Man C
C38 Clover Club Torch Singer C
C40 Nosy Columnist C
C46 Like a Moth C
C49 Underworld Contacts C
C50 Alhazrad Lamp C
C57 Guardian Shoggoth C
C59 Master of Silver Twilight C
C61 Ravager from the Deep C
C63 Arise, Children of Dagon! C
C64 Prophecies Revealed C
C72 Thrall of Cthulhu C
C74 Academy Prodigy C
C75 Artist in Residence C
C76 Bound Byakhee C
C80 Embracing the Abyss C
C81 Madness Takes Its Toll C
C89 Sedated C
C92 Arcane Initiate C
C93 Nightgaunt Servant C
C96 Unstoppable Hound C
C98 Calling down the Ancients C
R12 On Ice R
R14 Beneath the Burning Sun R
R15 Blackwood Safehouse R
R19 Steve Clarney, Soldier of Fortune R
R21 Campus Security R
R28 Open Gate R
R30 Research Expedition R
R31 Restless and Wary R
R36 The Light of Reason R
R39 Freelance Photographer R
R42 Sneak Thief R
R44 Double-Cross R
R45 Framed! R
R53 Syndicate Support R
R54 Velma's Restaurant R
R55 Cthulhu, High Priest of R'lyeh R
R56 Dagon, Father of the Deep R
R62 Aquatic Ambush R
R67 Swallowed by the Sea R
R70 Lair of the Deep Ones R
R71 Temple of Dagon R
R73 Hastur, the Unspeakable R
R78 Spawn of Hastur R
R83 On Byakhee Wings R
R85 Unspeakable Oath R
R86 Aldebaran Ascendant R
R88 Private Studio R
R91 Yog-Sothoth, In Whom the Spheres Meet R
R94 Servant from Out of Time R
R99 Opening the Limbo Gate R
U13 Pray for Dawn U
U17 Martial Law U
U18 Shotgun U
U23 Local Historian U
U24 Professor of Metaphysics U
U27 Breakthrough! U
U32 Atwood Science Hall U
U33 Dusty Manuscripts U
U35 Realms Beyond Reason U
U41 O'Bannion Thug U
U43 Syndicate Liaison U
U47 Panic U
U48 Spinning the Story U
U51 O'Bannion Warehouse U
U52 Slander and Libel U
U58 Lord of Y'ha-nthlei U
U60 Star Spawn Priest U
U65 Rite of the Chosen One U
U66 Sacrificial Offerings U
U68 Dreams of the Sleeping Priest U
U69 Forgotten Isle U
U77 Lunatic Shade U
U79 Vessel of Hastur U
U82 Mindblast U
U84 Psychotic Break U
U87 Plague of Madness U
U90 Victoria's Ballroom U
U95 Spell-bound Shoggoth U
U97 Wizard of Yog-Sothoth U
C100 Opening the Third Eye C
C107 Gate Box C
C111 Forest Sister C
C113 The Mother's Messenger C
C115 Wily Goat-spawn C
C116 A Time to Reap C
C120 Curiosity's Price C
C122 Boarding House C
C132 Fighting Blind C
C135 A Higher Purpose C
C138 Blind Spots C
R103 Warping of Time R
R105 Cabala of Saboth, Book of Angels R
R108 The Doors of Time R
R109 Shub-Niggurath, The All-Mother R
R112 Mi-Go Scout R
R117 A Time to Sow R
R118 Alien Excavation R
R125 The Mother's Womb R
R126 Under the Cloak of Darkness R
R127 Dabbler in the Unknown R
R129 Lore Keeper R
R131 Scurrying Rat-Thing R
R133 Prophecies Fulfilled R
R134 Strange Inheritance R
R137 Arkham Library R
R139 Occult Shop R
R145 Train Station R
U101 Peer Into the Future U
U102 Seal of Isis U
U104 Beyond the Gates U
U106 Forbidden Shrine U
U110 Albino Goat-spawn U
U114 Watcher of the Woods U
U119 Bred to Survive U
U121 Shocking Transformation U
U123 Consecrated Lands U
U124 Ghoulish Growth U
U128 Freelance Agent U
U130 Military Advisor U
U136 Arkham Historical Society U
U140 The Darkness Recedes U
U141 Master Plans U
U142 Motorcycle U
U143 Private Charter U
U144 Sniper Rifle U

2004 Call of Cthulhu Yithian Deck

Y1 Pnakotic Elder
Y2 Great Race Scientist
Y3 Yithian Soldier
Y4 Master of Time and Space
Y5 Displaced
Y6 Library at Pnakotus
Y7 Traveller of Aeons

2005 Call of Cthulhu Forbidden Relics

C2 Blackwood Occultist C
C5 Police Detective C
C7 Treasury Agent C
R1 Norman Blackwood, Sr. The Old Man R
R4 Hired Gun R
R9 Cleaning House R
U3 Femme Fatale U
U6 Task Force Captain U
U8 Burning Away the Darkness U
C11 Cover Fire C
C13 Working a Hunch C
C16 Lightning Gun C
C21 Fringe Researcher C
C22 Graduate Assistant C
C25 Back to the Vaults C
C27 Dr. Carson's Treatment C
C33 Glass of Mortlan C
C34 Sarcenic Rituals C
C38 Continental Agent C
C39 Extortionist C
C43 Cut the Power C
C44 Get On Yer Feet! C
C52 Plutonian Drug C
C53 Stuck in the Slammer C
C56 Color from the Stars C
C57 Innsmouth Troublemaker C
C61 Tcho-Tcho Emissary C
C66 Silver Twilight Indoctrination C
C67 The Great Summoning C
C71 Idol from R'lyeh C
C73 Bearer of the Yellow Sign C
C77 Performance Artist C
C81 Infected by Madness C
C84 Wrack C
C86 Chime of Tezchapt C
C88 Life of the Mind C
C92 Humble Supplicant C
C94 Restless Dead C
C95 Servant of Nodens C
C99 Cloak of Tawil At-Umr C
R12 Strike the Shepherd R
R14 Fire of Asshurbanipal R
R17 Neighborhood Gin Joint R
R23 Parapsychologist R
R24 Strange Visitors R
R28 Frenzied Research R
R30 Tapping the Shadow Fund R
R31 Brazier of Nodens R
R35 Secret File R
R37 Etienne-Laurent de Marigny R
R41 Society Page Editor R
R45 Going to Ground R
R48 Worse For The Wear R
R49 Icon of the Nameless Pharaoh R
R54 Syndicate Intelligent Report R
R58 Keeper of the Ancient Ways R
R60 Spawn of Cthulhu R
R62 A Grand Aquatic Destiny R
R63 Calling the Great Priest R
R68 Sacrificial Altar R
R69 Deep One Outpost R
R75 Messenger from Hali R
R76 Mysterious Mentor R
R82 Unsettling Visions R
R83 Voice of Ra R
R85 Bone Pipes of Madness, The True Music of the Spheres R
R90 The Hidden Gallery R
R91 Elder Thing Scientist R
R93 Master of Key R
R98 Chant of Thoth R
U10 Comprehending the Horror U
U15 Crime Lab U
U18 On the Mean Streets U
U19 Professor William Dyer U
U20 Campus Gumshoe U
U26 Cloud Memory U
U29 Mist of Releh U
U32 Academic Conference U
U36 Vaughn's Diary U
U40 Rum Runner U
U42 Triggerman U
U46 Payback U
U47 The Best Bias Money Can Buy U
U50 Breaking and Entering U
U51 Cathouse U
U55 Blasphemous Hybrid U
U59 Priest of Dagon U
U64 Overwhelmed by Nightmares U
U65 Rubbed Out U
U70 Giving Thanks U
U72 Inner Sanctum U
U74 Broken Vessels U
U78 Servant of the Oath U
U79 Dissolve U
U80 Implant Fear U
U87 Condemned Theater U
U89 Still Life Exhibition U
U96 Star Vampire Minion U
U97 Wandering Dimensional Shambler U
C101 Journey to the Other Side C
C107 Glass of Leng C
C113 Star-Summoned Dhole C
C114 The Mother's Hand C
C119 Hands of Colubra C
C120 The Reaping C
C122 Mi-Go Brain Case C
C124 The Mother's Kiss C
C131 Mad Zealot C
C133 Treasure Hunter C
C140 Fetch Stick C
R103 Turning the Silver Key R
R104 Shining Trapezohedron R
R105 Dark Texts R
R109 Alien Researcher R
R112 Spawn from K'n-Yan R
R115 Beneath the Harvest Moon R
R117 From the Womb Reborn R
R121 Everlasting Chalice R
R125 Watkins Family Plot R
R127 Curiousity Collector R
R130 Guru of the Forgotten Way R
R135 Mi-Go Web Armor R
R136 Sword of St. Jerome R
R137 Decrepit Mausoleum R
R138 Draught of Phan R
R141 Incomprehensible Machine R
R144 Time for Discretion R
U100 Dampen Light U
U102 Sanctify the Stone U
U106 Enchanted Cane U
U108 Shadows and Reflections U
U110 Ancient Guardian U
U111 Mrs. Watkin's Boarder U
U116 Deflect Harm U
U118 Gathering Influence U
U123 Poisonous Fog U
U126 Watkins Root Cellar U
U128 Eternal Serpent U
U129 Grim Avenger U
U132 Ravenous Hunting Horror U
U134 Worlds Torn Asunder U
U139 Enchanted Silver Blade U
U142 Private Research Facility U
U143 Tcho-Tcho Talisman U
U145 Zanthu Tablet U

2005 Call of Cthulhu Masks of Nyarlathotep

C2 T-Men C
C3 Brotherhood Street Runner C
C4 Decommissioned Officer C
C9 Adoration of Ma'at C
R1 Captain Isoge Taro, Imperial Japanese Captain R
R8 Unexpected Ally R
U5 Peeler U
U6 Tribal Elder U
U7 Undercover Agent U
C12 Taking No Chances C
C15 Mask of Law C
C20 Natural Philosopher C
C21 American Ambassador C
C22 Brotherhood Researcher C
C27 Adoration of Thoth C
C29 Slumming C
C33 Mask of Wisdom C
C38 Street Preacher C
C39 Brotherhood Interrogator C
C43 Patsy C
C45 Adoration of Maahes C
C46 Cooking the Books C
C51 Mask of Coin C
C56 The Thing in the Fog C
C57 Brotherhood Torturer C
C61 Shoggoth-Twsha C
C63 Adoration of Apep C
C64 Driven to Destruction C
C70 Deathless Mask C
C74 Twin of You C
C76 Brotherhood Visionary C
C77 Court Jester C
C81 Adoration of Yhtill C
C83 Despair C
C88 Flayed Mask C
C92 Fishers from Outside C
C94 Brotherhood Acolyte C
C95 Cannibal Ghast C
C99 Adoration of Upuaut C
R10 Back to Basics R
R11 Scouring the Earth R
R16 Ammo Dump R
R18 The Old Neighborhood R
R19 Mu Hsein, Classical Scholar R
R24 Heterodox Physicist R
R28 Measureless to Man R
R31 Seven Cryptical Books of Hsan, Lost Masterpiece R
R34 Hotel Chelsea R
R35 New Research R
R37 Jack 'Brass' Brady, Steeped in Violence R
R40 Chemist R
R48 Sleight of Hand R
R49 Livre d'Ivon, Eibon in du Nord's Translation R
R52 Calling in Favors R
R53 Unlicensed Garage R
R55 Carl Stanford, Deathless Fanatic R
R58 Cora Infection R
R65 Into the Deep R
R67 Terrible Beauty R
R68 R'lyeh Text * R
R71 Secret Murders R
R73 Hildred Castaigne R
R79 Forgotten Ones R
R84 Mass Hallucination R

R85 That Which is Not R
R86 Revelations of Hali R
R90 Spreading the Disease R
R91 Ho Fong R
R93 Alchemist R
U13 Time Bomb U
U14 Unmasking Cowardice U
U17 Deathtrap U
U23 Classicist U
U25 Itinerant Scholar U
U26 Soothsayer U
U30 Unavoidable Delay U
U32 Unmasking Treachery U
U36 Open for Inspection U
U41 Fixer U
U42 Gang Boss U
U44 Rambling Man U
U47 Eye for an Eye U
U50 Unmasking Shame U
U54 Up for Grabs U
U59 Leech Mother U
U60 Ocean Crawlers U
U62 Skin Weed U
U66 Sea Change U
U69 Unmasking Cruelty U
U72 Sleep of Reason U
U75 Book Publisher U
U78 Demon Lover U
U80 Language Virus U
U82 Ancestral Voices U
U87 Unmasking Idiocy U
U89 Irrational Means U
U96 Insubstantial Insect U
U97 Shantak Mount U
U98 Teller of Tales U
C100 Aklo Sabaoth C
C106 Pharaoic Mask C
C110 Small Ghouls C
C113 Brotherhood Procurer C
C115 Obscene Polyp C
C117 Adoration of Hetheru C
C119 Ever Growing C
C123 Triune Mask C
C134 Serpent from Yoth C
C144 The Unreflecting Mirror C
C145 Yithian Rifle C
R103 The Wave Function R
R104 The Goddess of the Black Fan R
R107 Expectancy R
R109 M'weru R
R114 Interstellar Visitor R
R120 Thanks Be to Shudd-M'ell R
R121 The Mother's Bounty R
R125 Fungal Colony R
R126 Lake of Glaaki R
R127 Jackson Elias R
R130 Nyarlathotep R
R135 Carne Vale R
R138 Strange Aeons R
R140 Gray Dragon Island R
R141 Limehouse Docks R
R142 Massa di Requiem per Shuggay R
R143 The Ju-Ju House R
U101 Haunted Mists U
U102 Stone of the Heart U
U105 Unmasking Hubris U
U108 Unstable Energies U
U111 Black Wind U
U112 Bright Young Thing U
U116 Worms of the Earth U
U118 Cuttings from the Same Branch U
U122 Unmasking Corruption U
U124 Caressed by Y'Golonac U
U128 Shugoron U
U129 The Dweller in Darkness U
U131 Black Wind Zealot U
U132 Independent Operator U
U133 Magus U
U136 Moving the Scenery U
U137 Simple Kindness U
U139 City of the Great Race U

2006 Call of Cthulhu Kingsport Dreams

21 The Terrible Old Man, Ancient Hermit
22 Neil's Curiosity Shop, Collection of Bizarre Antiquities
23 Thomas Olney, Traveler with a Purpose
24 The Hall School, Institution of Higher Learning
25 William Bain, The One
26 The Seventh House on the Left, Avoid at all Costs
27 St. Erasmus' Home for Mariners, Retirement Community or worse?
28 Called to the Sea
29 Charles Dexter Ward, Unfortunate Fool
30 Artists Colony
31 Visitor from the Spheres
32 Dreams in Limbo
33 Basil Elton, Lighthouse Keeper
34 Thunder in the East
35 Mentor to Vaughn, Without Equal
36 Nodens, Potent and Archaic
37 Tulzscha, The Green Flame
38 Granny Orne, Tough Old Bird
39 607 Walter Street, Dockside Property
40 The Rope and Anchor Tavern, Seedy and Rundown

2008 Call of Cthulhu Ancient Horrors

1 Safari Hunter
2 Ammunitions Expert
3 Mr. Ngambe, Urban Investigator
4 Cafeteria Lady
5 Norm Grzbowski, Football Coach
6 Professor Albert Wilmarth, On Sabbatical
7 Richard Finchington III, Exotic Collector
8 Demented Caretaker
9 Island Hermit
10 Bokrug, The Great Water Lizard
11 Ghatanothoa, Lord of the Volcano
12 Aspiring Artist
13 Atlach-Nacha, The Spider God
14 Bringer of Fire
15 Cthuga, Fiery Conflagration
16 Tcho-Tcho Tribe
17 Opener of the Gate
18 Nyogtha, The Sentient Void
19 Ghoulish Worshipper
20 Dark Druid

2008 Call of Cthulhu The Antediluvian Dreams

41 Repo Man
42 Dynamite
43 Howard Ludvinski, Visiting Artist
44 Academic Obfuscation
45 Brazen Hoodlum
46 Blackball Jim, Pool Hustler
47 Vengeful Mob
48 Nocturnal Scavenger
49 Muddy Waters
50 Long-Dead Prince, Ancient Royalty
51 Infernal Obsession
52 The Sleepwalker, Trapped by Nightmare
53 Across Dimensions
54 Gibbering Soul
55 Ghoulish Thrill Seeker
56 Eat the Dead
57 The Cornered Man, andquot;Like an Animalandquot;
58 Secret Stiletto
59 Antediluvian Dreams
60 Ask Questions Later

2008 Call of Cthulhu At the Mountains of Madness

1 Captain George Thorfinnsen, Veteran Whaler
2 The Barque Miskatonic, Sturdy Transport
3 Professor Lake, Obsessed with Footprints
4 Notebook Sketches, Crude but Salient
5 Heavy Furs
6 Specimen Bags
7 Hand Camera
8 Cave Mouth
9 Giant Albino Penguin, Antarctic Monstrosity
10 White Out
11 Polar Mirage
12 Forgotten Shoggoth
13 Reawakened Elder Thing
14 Antarctic Yeti
15 Snow Graves
16 Alaskan Sledge Dog
17 Hypothermia
18 Polar Fog
19 Antarctic Wind
20 Realm of Ice and Death

2008 Call of Cthulhu The Horror Beneath the Surface

21 Marshall Greene, Too Old For This
22 Hand Restraints
23 Hapless Graduate Student
24 Scholarly Plagiarist
25 Chess Prodigy
26 Fugitive Scientist
27 Vengeful Hit
28 Arkham Advertiser Archives
29 Silver Twilight Temptress
30 A Single Path
31 Wandering Inmate
32 Local Brew
33 Unfathomable Elder Thing
34 Book of Eibon, Mind Bending Revelations
35 Mind Eater
36 Under the Porch
37 Tithe Collector
38 Beneath the Surface, Eurekaand#33;
39 With a Fine Toothed Comb
40 The Endless Investigation

2008 Call of Cthulhu In Memory of Day

21 The Captain, Dreamlands Navigator
22 Prize Pistol
23 Daybreak!
24 Obsessive Insomniac
25 Dreamlore Documents
26 Clover Club Regular
27 Forcibly Removed
28 Day of the Deep Ones
29 Curse of Darkness
30 The Seventy Steps, Of Light Slumber
31 The Seven Hundred Steps, Of Deeper Slumber
32 Enraged Gug
33 City of Gugs, Beneath the Earth
34 Ghoul Spawn
35 Back From the Dead
36 Secretive Zoog
37 The Enchanted Wood
38 Kaman-Thah, Priest of the Dreamlands
39 Nasht, Priest of the Dreamlands
40 Slime Mold

2008 Call of Cthulhu In the Dread of Night

41 Nathaniel Elton, Questing for Cathuria
42 Night Raid!
43 Dreamlands Scholar
44 Night Class
45 Petty Thief
46 Ritual Initiation
47 Dreamlands Fanatic
48 Midnight Rendezvous
49 The Cavern of Flame, Gateway to the Dreamlands
50 Dream Parasite
51 Laboring Gug
52 Great Stone Circle
53 Ghoulish Predator
54 Dhole Attack!
55 Ancient Zoog
56 Zoog Burrow
57 The Night, Darkness Incarnate
58 Dream Dagger
59 Blasphemous Dreams
60 Assist Dreamer

2008 Call of Cthulhu Journey to Unknown Kadath

101 Agency Bodyguard
102 The White Ship, Smooth and Silent
103 Twila Katherine Price, Queen of Unknown-Kadath
104 Dreaming of the Past
105 Gregory Gry, Shadow of his Former Self
106 Raking the Pot
107 Mnomquah's Serpent
108 Mnomquah, The Moon God
109 Keeper of Dreams, Mind Breaker
110 Magah Bird
111 Gug Sentinel
112 The Tower of Koth, Passage to the Underworld
113 Dhole Ant-Lion
114 Dark Contagion
115 Stealthy Zoog
116 The Cats of Ulthar
117 Nyarlathotep, The Black Pharaoh
118 The Light Side of the Moon
119 The Dark Side of the Moon
120 Unknown Kadath, Home of the Other Gods

2008 Call of Cthulhu The Path to Y'ha-nthlei

71 Shadow Sorceress
101 Confident Rookie
102 Military Bike
103 Field Researcher
104 Changing the Names
105 Expendable Muscle
106 False Papers
107 Julia Brown, Oddly Amphibious
108 Eye of the Deep
109 Scalethorn Asylum, Amphibious Fort
110 The Thing Behind You, Turn around
111 Brain Transplant
112 Hideous Guardian
113 Idol of the Abomination
114 Binding Worm
115 Unspeakable Transformation
116 Old Sea Dog
117 Conspiracy Theorist
118 Strange Delusions
119 Foiled!
120 The Path to Y'ha-nthlei

2008 Call of Cthulhu Search for the Silver Key

61 John Henry Price, Cold and Paternal
62 Price Manor
63 Randolph Carter, King of Ilek-Vad
64 Arcane Translation
65 King Kuranes, Ruler of Celephais
66 The Back Room
67 Cerenerian Deep One
68 Dark Quagmire
69 Victoria's Protege
70 Devolution
71 Guardian of the Key
72 The Silver Key, Unlocking the way
73 Ghoulish Hag
74 The Vale of Pnath
75 Halflings of D'haz
76 Curious Zoog
77 Cryptic Writings
78 Guardian Pillar
79 The Book of Black Stones
80 Dreamlands Eclipse

2008 Call of Cthulhu Sleep of the Dead

81 Sleep Therapist
82 Behind Bars
83 The Woman of His Dreams
84 Horrid Dreams
85 Clover Club Executive
86 Clover Club Cardroom, Parlor of Higher Stakes
87 Princess Zura, The Flower of the Charnel Garden
88 In an Unmarked Grave
89 Ward Phillips, Obsessed Recluse
90 Dreams Within Dreams
91 Wandering Gug
92 Ascension to Zura
93 Shuggob, Ghoul Sage
94 Mi-Go Dreams
95 Inconspicuous Zoog
96 Basilisk
97 Richard Upton Pickman, Venerable Ghoul
98 Moon-Beast Captain
99 Moon-Beast Galley
100 The Sleep of the Dead

2008 Call of Cthulhu The Spawn of the Sleeper

1 Government Exorcist
2 Interrogation Center
3 Dr. Carson, Fringe Psychologist
4 Rabbit's Foot
5 Sleeping Pills
6 Trent Dixon, Workaholic
7 Underground Asylum
8 Emerging Deep One
9 Called by Azathoth
10 Erich Zann, Strange Virtuoso
11 Spawn of the Sleeper
12 Terrifying Visage
13 Bloodthirsty Zealot
14 Touched with Madness
15 Grim Wraith
16 The Black Goat's Rage
17 Julia Brown, Insomniac
18 Those Without Faces
19 Sleepless Nights
20 The Underwater Conspiracy

2008 Call of Cthulhu The Terror of the Tides

61 Agency Groundskeeper
62 A Call for Help
63 Shortsighted Librarian
64 Pagan Hall, Science Department
65 Arcane Grifter
66 Midnight Alley, No Shelter from the Storm
67 The Terror of the Tides
68 Bite Marks
69 Stealthy Byakhee
70 Coffee House
72 Path of Blood
73 Dimensional Worm
74 Summoning Circle
75 Descendant of Eibon, Master of the Black Arts
76 Clever Zoog
77 Struggling Artist
78 Total Eclipse
79 Stealing the Glory
80 Fountain of Youth

2008 Call of Cthulhu The Thing from the Shore

81 Unorthodox Psychologist
82 Endless Interrogation
83 Literature Professor
84 Summer Classes
85 Friend of the Family
86 Tear Gas
87 The Thing from the Shore
88 Communal Shower
89 Shadow Company, Ghastly Regiment
90 Vaporous Isle
91 Nebulous Ooze
92 Domestic Sacrifice
93 Insect Swarm
94 Open Grave
95 Campaign Chief
96 Samantha Grace, Incompetent Secretary
97 Obsessive Inmate
98 Parallel Universe
99 The Spawn of Madness
100 Unorthodox Tactics

2008 Call of Cthulhu Twilight Horror

1 Night-shift Security
2 Flood Lights
3 Twila Katherine Price, Lost in a Dream
4 Dream Diary
5 Gregory Gry, Muckraker
6 Clover Club Deck
7 Beings of Ib
8 Everlasting Night
9 Sweet Dreams
10 Nightmares!
11 Puj-Dunk, Gug Chieftain
12 Twilight Gate
13 Twilight Cannibal
14 Dhole Tunnel
15 Furtive Zoog
16 Twilight Ritual
17 The Day Dreamer
18 Dreamlands Wanderer
19 The Rays of Dawn, Cleansing Light
20 The Setting Sun, The Light Fails

2009 Call of Cthulhu Core Set

1 Thomas F. Malone, Haunted Police Detective
2 Kirby O'Donnell, Adventurer Abroad
3 Local Sheriff
4 Paul LeMond, Tormented Psychic
5 Professor Hermann Mulder, Bureau Consultant
6 Monster Hunter
7 Undercover Security
8 Hired Muscle
9 Freelance Occultist
10 Blackwood File Clerk
11 Peeler
12 T-Men
13 G-Men
14 Shotgun
15 Patrol Wagon
16 Shotgun Blast
17 Short Fuse
18 Torch the Joint!
19 Small Price to Pay
20 Working a Hunch
21 Professor Albert Wilmarth, Folklore Expert
22 Dr. Ali Kafour, Middle Eastern Scholar
23 Steve Clarney, Soldier of Fortune
24 Professor Nathaniel Peaslee, Scholar of the Arcane
25 Anthropology Advisor
26 Visiting Author
27 Mad Genius
28 Strange Librarian
29 Laboratory Assistant
30 Itinerant Scholar
31 Natural Philosopher
32 Student Archaeologist
33 Celano Fragments, The Life's Work of Dr. Shrewsbury
34 Open for Inspection
35 Atwood Science Hall
36 Binding
37 Feast of Famine
38 Restless and Wary
39 Dr. Carson's Treatment
40 Unearthing the Ancients
41 Cthulhu, The Great Old One
42 Dagon, Father of the Deep
43 Keeper of the Golden Path
44 Guardian Shoggoth
45 Shadow-spawned Hunting Horror
46 Ravager from the Deep
47 Innsmouth Troublemaker
48 Adult Deep One
49 Ocean Crawlers
50 Lord of the Silver Twilight
51 Mature Deep One
52 Young Deep One
53 Sleep of Reason
54 Sword of Y'ha-tallo
55 Shadowed Reef
56 Deep One Assault
57 Pulled Under
58 Get it Off!
59 Sacrificial Offerings
60 Touched by the Sleeper
61 Jack Brass Brady, Steeped in Violence
62 Dr. Marinus Bicknell Willett, Lost but Determined
63 Richard Upton Pickman, Genius Painter
64 Bag Man
65 Clover Club Bouncer
66 Clover Club Torch Singer
67 Triggerman
68 Syndicate Liaison
69 Hard Case
70 Patsy
71 Extortionist
72 Freelance Photographer
73 Dutch Courage
74 Cathouse
75 Alhazred Lamp
76 Like A Moth
77 Panic
78 Get on Yer Feet!
79 Low Blow
80 Legacy of Ramses
81 Hastur, The King in Yellow
82 Victoria Glasser, The Society Hostess
83 Yellow Muse
84 Demon Lover
85 Thing from the Stars
86 Messenger from Beyond
87 Performance Artist
88 Byakhee Servant
89 Predatory Byakhee
90 Bearer of the Yellow Sign
91 Ghost
92 Mad Artist
93 Victoria's Loft
94 Sedated
95 Byakhee Attack
96 Agoraphobia
97 Scotophobia
98 Despair
99 Blind Submission
100 Power Drain
101 Yog-Sothoth, In Whom the Spheres Meet
102 Servant from Out of Time
103 Son of Yeb
104 Living Mummy
105 Fishers from Outside
106 Cannibal Ghast
107 Spell-bound Shoggoth
108 Arcane Initiate
109 Guardian Elder Thing
110 Hound of Tindalos
111 Disciple of the Gate
112 Servant of Nodens
113 Forbidden Shrine
114 Blackmoor Estate
115 Journey to the Other Side
116 Opening the Limbo Gate
117 A Single Glimpse
118 Gathering at the Stones
119 Unspeakable Resurrection
120 Dampen Light
121 Shub-Niggurath, The All Mother
122 Y'Golonac, The Obscenity
123 Priestess of Bubastis
124 Slavering Gug
125 Forest Sister
126 Ancient Guardian
127 Small Ghouls
128 Watcher of the Woods
129 Mi-Go Scout
130 Mi-Go Warrior
131 Hungry Dark Young
132 Degenerate Ghoul
133 Shadowed Woods
134 Ghoul Taint
135 Altar of the Blessed
136 Regeneration
137 Burrowing Beneath
138 Horrid Mutation
139 Bred to Survive
140 Shocking Transformation
141 Mystic Bounty Hunter
142 Freelance Agent
143 .45 Pistols
144 Political Demonstration
145 Overzealous Initiate
146 Arkham Asylum
147 Moving the Scenery
148 Military Advisor
149 Serpent from Yoth
150 Tcho-Tcho Talisman
151 Inside Information
152 Dabbler in the Unknown
153 Gentleman's Club
154 Eldritch Nexus
155 The Bootleg Whiskey Cover-Up
156 Nowhere to Hide
157 The Shadow out of Time
158 Opening Night
159 Ancient Apocrypha

160 The Call of Cthulhu
161 Through the Gates
162 Rotting Away
163 Frozen in Time
164 Dreamwalkers
165 The Other Path

2010 Call of Cthulhu Aspirations of Ascension

61 Special Agent Clarkston, Can't be bought
62 Secret Service Agent
63 G-AAMX, Gypsy Moth
64 Lurking Deep One
65 Devil's Reef, Gate to Hell
66 Y'ha-nthlei Statue
67 Shadow Eater
68 Devoured by Shadow
69 Obscure Linguist
70 Rush Week
71 Ia! Ia! Shudde M'ell
72 Wolf Hunger
73 Master of Blades
74 Reckless Assault
75 Elder Binding
76 Johnny Valone, The Godfather
77 Johnny V's Dame
78 Glaaki, The Inhabitant of the Lake
79 Servants of Glaaki
80 Initiation of Glaaki

2010 Call of Cthulhu The Cacophony

101 Out of the Darkness
102 Bloodbath
103 Springfield M1903
104 Disguised Threat
105 Feeding Frenzy
106 The Cave on the Hill, Local Landmark
107 Lost to the Madness
108 Fledgling Byakhee
109 Stone Calendar
110 Uneasy Translator
111 Harry Houdini, Escape Artist
112 Behind the Door
113 Forgiveness?
114 Shub-Niggurath, Dark Mistress of the Woods
115 Examining the Optic Nerve
116 Safe House
117 Tattooed Thug
118 The View from Within
119 Reckless Elder Thing
120 Bird Demon

2010 Call of Cthulhu The Gleaming Spiral

81 Trial Judge
82 Catastrophic Explosion
83 While He Sleeps
84 Slave to the Undivided Mind
85 Moonbound Byakhee
86 Unhealthy Fixation
87 Scalpel
88 Jamie Winthrop, Whiz Kid
89 Lecturing Historian
90 Full Ride Scholarship
91 Shudde M'ell, The Burrower Beneath
92 Telepathic Chthonian
93 Ground Tremors
94 Meticulous Scribe
95 Unscrupulous Acquisitionist
96 Disturbing Auction
97 Degenerate Gambler
98 Scandal
99 Many-angled Thing
100 Hermetic Text

2010 Call of Cthulhu Initiations of the Favored

41 New Recruit
42 Arrest Warrant
43 Horrific Shoggoth
44 Ghatanotha, Out Of The Aeons
45 Bloated Leng Spider
46 Come With Us
47 Board of Directors
48 Zeiss Model C
49 Trampling Dark Young
50 Slime Covered Dhole
51 Grasping Chthonian
52 Protector of Secrets
53 Wealthy Sponsor
54 Ritual of Power
55 Satchel of the Void
56 Thief for Hire
57 Southside Speakeasy, Hidden Business
58 Expensive Guitar
59 Constricting Elder Thing
60 Evolving Shoggoth

2010 Call of Cthulhu Murmurs of Evil

21 Machete
22 Apprentice Monster Hunter
23 Shrine to Yig, Worship of an Ancient Evil
24 Ravenous Piranhas
25 Feathered Serpent
26 Obsessive Playwright
27 Harbinger of Insanity
28 Erin Moirai, Biology Student
29 Searching the Reserves
30 The Painted Corpse
31 Tattoo Parlor
32 Crowbar
33 Mi-Go Caretaker
34 Specimen Room
35 Mi-Go Brain Cylinder
36 Veronica Frost, Elegant but Deadly
37 Tattoo Artist
38 Trophy Room

2010 Call of Cthulhu The Order of the Silver Twilight

1 Sister Sofia, Nun with a Gun
2 Call for Backup
3 Distraught Shopkeeper
4 An Offer You Can't Refuse
5 Dr. Bartlett, Conspiracy Theorist
6 Pnakotic Manuscripts, Mind Expanding Ideas
7 Faceless Abductor
8 Curse of the Putrid Husk
9 Collector of Sacrifices
10 Come to the Altar
11 Sweet Old Lady
12 Old Man of the Woods
13 Joe Sargent, Rattletrap Bus Driver
14 In the Wake of the Sleeper
15 Neutral Ground
16 Clifton Rosenberg, Mastermind
17 Senator Nathaniel Rhodes, Adept Politician
18 Lord Jeffrey Farrington, Mysterious Benefactor
19 Silver Twilight Enforcer
20 Keeper of the Silver Sphere
21 Young Initiate
22 Arcane Hunter
23 Knight of the Outer Void
24 High Wizard of the Order
25 Lodge Librarian
26 Disgruntled Chef
27 Dedicated Butler
28 Mayor Atkinson, Resourceful Manipulator
29 Devious Architect
30 Lodge Barkeep
31 Failed Initiate
32 The Groundskeeper
33 Silver Twilight Collector
34 Lodge Housekeeper
35 Terrors for the Lodge
36 Silver Twilight Lodge, Nexus of Power
37 Key to the Inner Sanctum
38 Crescent Blade
39 Sigil of the Order
40 The Oubliettes, Secret Chambers
41 Ritual of the Construct, Mystical Summons
42 Ritual of the Lance, Utter Annihilation
43 Crystal of the Elder Things, Radiant Gem
44 Initiation
45 Lodge Meeting
46 Dark Secrets of the Order
47 Secret Handshake
48 You Know Too Much
49 Unbound!
50 Fine Dining
51 Ritual of Summoning, Horrific Methods
52 Steal the Soul
53 Pose Mundane
54 Friendly to the Order
55 Brazier Enchantment

2010 Call of Cthulhu Perilous Trials

21 Educated Officer
22 Cover Up
23 Deep One Stowaway
24 Disguised Serpent Man
25 Sinister Clerk
26 Twisted Choreographer
27 Horrifying Daydreams
28 Medical Student
29 Dean of Admissions
30 Flux Stabilizer
31 Predator of the Night
32 One of the Thousand
33 Rich Widow
34 Master Artificer
35 The Silver Lance, Hallowed Weapon
36 Spirit Dagger
37 Thomas Bannano, andquot;Tommy Bananasandquot;
38 Gang Warfare
39 Stalking Hound
40 A Gate Opens

2010 Call of Cthulhu Screams from Within

81 Border Patrol Guard
82 Police Headquarters
83 Sledgehammer
84 River of Serpents
85 Yig, Father of Serpents
86 Dangerous Inmate
87 Thing from Nightmare
88 Cultist Journal Sketches
89 Professor Smith, Alone With His Secrets
90 M.U. Museum of Natural History
91 Archaeological Dig Site
92 Losing the Trail
93 Riding Shotgun
94 Chupacabra
95 Feeding Time
96 Kidnapping 101
97 A Sight for Sore Eyes
98 Blind Fighting
99 Yog-Sothoth, Lord of Time and Space
100 Spiritual Guidance

2010 Call of Cthulhu Secrets of Arkham

1 Agency Medic
2 Paranormal Specialist
3 Lightning Gun
4 Norman Blackwood, Jr., Scholarly Detective
5 Beneath the Burning Sun
6 Femme Fatale
7 Scientific Text
8 Visiting Professor
9 The Necronomicon, The Book of the Mad Arab
10 Soothsayer
11 Misinformation
12 Professor Armitage, Venerable Librarian
13 Elite Hit Squad
14 Hired Mystic
15 Forced Foreclosure
16 Intimidate
17 Anarchist
18 Fixer
19 Mi-Go Surgeon
20 Mi-Go Commander
21 Rampaging Dark Young
22 Albino Goat-spawn
23 Ageless Mi-Go
24 The Mother's Hand
25 Hydra, Mother of the Deep
26 Lord of Y'ha-nthlei
27 Primal Fear
28 Carl Stanford, Deathless Fanatic
29 Deep One Rising
30 Giving Thanks
31 Things in the Ground
32 Calling Down the Ancients
33 Gatekeeper
34 Hermetic Scholar
35 Chant of Thoth
36 Wizard of Yog-Sothoth
37 Poltergeist
38 Carcosa, Palace of the Tattered King
39 Messenger from Hali
40 Writhing Wall
41 Infected by Madness
42 Implant Fear
43 Feint
44 Diseased Sewer Rats
45 Magnifying Glass
46 Azathoth, The Blind Idiot God
47 Seeker of Mysteries
48 The Greatest Fear
49 Terrors in the Dark
50 Dimensional Rift
51 The Secrets of Arkham
52 They Come at Night
53 Obsessive Research
54 Change of Plans
55 The Terror out of Dunwich
56 The Innsmouth Threat
57 The Thing at the Gate
58 The Secret of the North Woods
59 The Dreams of Kingsport
60 The Well

2010 Call of Cthulhu The Spoken Covenant

41 Museum Security
42 Intervention
43 Priest of Two Faiths
44 Labyrinth of a Dead City
45 Stygian Idol
46 Hastur, Lord of Carcosa
47 The Yellow Sign
48 Swooping Byakhee
49 Broken Glasses
50 Under the Microscope
51 M.U. Chem Lab
52 The Guardian of the Key
53 Drunken Hallucinations
54 Mi-Go Laboratory
55 Mi-Go Guard
57 Bound and Gagged
58 Bootlegging Operation
59 Flying Polyps
60 All are One

2010 Call of Cthulhu That Which Consumes

101 Unlikely Informant
102 Fire Extinguisher
103 Somnambulant Dreamer
104 Misguided Dreams
105 Final Note
106 Painful Reflection
107 Elder Sign Parchment, Scroll of Nodens
108 Forbidden Knowledge
109 Sinkhole!
110 Bast's Hunt
111 The Mage Known as Magnus, Master of the Arcane Arts
112 Crooked Treasurer
113 Ritual of Inferno, Uncontrolled Destruction
114 Rumormill
115 Strung Up!
116 You're Outta Here!
117 Sleepin' wit' da Fishes
118 Flesh Ward
119 A Gift of Knowledge
120 Fist of Yog-Sothoth

2010 Call of Cthulhu The Twilight Beckons

1 Obsessive Detective
2 Holy Rosary
3 Evidence Locker
4 Bloodthirsty Star Spawn
5 Underneath the Surface
6 Gaze of Ghatanothoa
7 Demented Phrenologist
8 Germaphobia
9 Professional Counselor
10 Experiment Subject #613b
11 Harvesting Mi-Go
12 Inter-dimensional Transporter
13 Dr. Baker, Chief of Medicine
14 Zealous Secretary
15 Errand Boy
16 Expulsion from the Order
17 Small Time Magician
18 Clover Club Bootlegger
19 Intruder from Beyond
20 Prism of Many Views, Endless Visions

2010 Call of Cthulhu The Wailer Below

61 Sam Archer, Private Investigator
62 Exploring the Ruins
63 Degenerate Serpent Cultist
64 Cthulhu, Lord of R'lyeh
65 Deep One Scout
66 Renowned Sculptor
67 Wraith
68 Field Research Station
69 Derby Hall, M.U. Dormitory
70 Museum Curator
71 Taming the Storm
72 Getaway Vehicle
73 Feasting Ghouls
74 Optic Warehouse
75 Smugglers
76 Eyes in a Jar
77 Meat Wagon
78 Curse of the Stone
79 Doppelganger
80 Cultist of the Key

2010 Call of Cthulhu Whispers in the Dark

1 James Logan, Ready for Anything
2 Flanking Maneuver
3 Backwater Deep One
4 Brood of Yig
5 Crazed Arsonist
6 Nightstalker
7 The Sirens of Hell
8 Focused Art Student
9 Perpetual Silence
10 The Locked Door
11 The Red-Gloved Man, He Was Never There
12 The Yuggoth Contract, Nefarious Pact
13 Ferocious Dark Young
14 Empty Sockets
15 Tyler Scindere, Bounty Hunter
16 Want Ads
17 The Laundromat, More Than It Seems
18 Hunting Nightgaunt
19 Casting off the Skin
20 Speak to the Dead

2011 Call of Cthulhu The Breathing Jungle

2 Shriven and Resolute
49 The Second Chancers, Doing Bad for Good
50 Eliot Ness' Handcuffs, A New Symbol of Justice
51 Eater from the Depths, It Hungers
52 Monophobia
53 Obsessive Sychphant
54 Pervasive Silence
55 Vaage Randers, Master of Tactics
56 Eryn Cochwyn, Curious and Precocious
57 Disc of Itzamna, Protective Amulet
58 Diligent Study
59 Jaguar Warrior
60 Voice of the Jungle
61 Dirk Sharpe, Acquisitions
62 Erasmus Manor, The Necromancer
63 The Doorway, Extra-dimensional Exit
64 Arcane Tampering
65 Border Runners
67 Reclaimed Servant
68 Lethargic Miasma

2011 Call of Cthulhu Conspiracies of Chaos

41 Mr. Grey, Corrupt Politician
42 The Blackwood Conspiracy
43 Seeker of the Profane
44 A Conspiracy of Scholars
45 Tragic Celebrity
46 The Underground Conspiracy
47 Mutant Spawn, (Soft and Cuddly.)
48 The R'lyeh Conspiracy
49 Shrieking Byakhee
50 The Hidden Conspiracy
51 Blood Magician
52 The Ritual Conspiracy
53 Displaced Cthonian
54 Dreamlands Conspiracy
55 Ol' Lazy Eyes, Inbred but not Inept
56 Crazy Eddie, Don't call him Ed
57 Flare Gun
58 Kitab Al-Azif, The Original Necronomicon
59 Broken Space, Broken Time
60 Beneath the Mire

2011 Call of Cthulhu Curse of the Jade Emperor

29 Inspector Li Flint, With Pride and Care
30 Thorough Search
31 Jade Salesman
32 Ophidian Blight
33 Jiang Shi, The Restless Dead
34 The Guzheng, Item of Ill Fortune
35 Palpable Unhappiness
36 Harlan Earnstone, Historical Theorist
37 Blackmarket Artifact
38 Mi-Go Observer
39 Forms of the Ether
40 Initiate of Huang Hun
41 Hidden Agenda
42 Tzu San Niang, Like A Ghost
43 Mr. David Pan, Red Pole
44 Lady Lu Chu, Death Follows
45 Living Ink, A Questionable Boon
46 Forcing the Truth
47 Key-seeker
48 Hound of Dragons

2011 Call of Cthulhu Dunwich Denizens

61 Canine Guardian
62 Development Camp
63 Professor Rice, Stocky and Iron Grey
64 Professor Morgan, Lean and Youngish
65 Professor Armitage, Old and White-bearded
66 Hack Journalist
67 Ancient Gold
68 Noises in the Hills
69 Devil's Hop Yard, Bleak and Blasted
70 Feathery Watchers
71 Cold Spring Glen, Unsettlingly Desolate
72 The Dunwich Horror, Bigger 'n a barn
73 Wilbur Whateley, Preternaturally Intelligent
74 Sentinel Hill, Where Your Doom Awaits
75 Lavinia Whateley, Somewhat Deformed
76 The Stone on the Peak, That Shocking Altar-Stone
77 Whateley's Diary, Cryptic Text
78 Pocket Telescope
79 The Bootleg Whiskey Cover-Up
80 Negotium Perambulans in Tenebris

2011 Call of Cthulhu Ebla Restored

41 Paid Informant
42 Black Maria
43 Dr. Wentworth Moore, Dark Supplicant
44 Cthaat Aquadingen, Things of the Water
45 The Carpathian, Tomb Raider
46 Alyssa Graham, Speaker to the Dead
47 The Parlor, Where Truths are Revealed
48 Professor of Folklore
49 Dr. Mya Badry, Medical Examiner
50 Karin Marley, Night Witch
51 Corrupted Midwife
52 Book of Iod, Hostiam Sanguinis Virtus
53 Lodge Defenses
54 Pass Grip of a Master
55 Thomas Fleming, Financial Wizard
56 The Penthouse, Fortune's Reward
57 Shoshana Hatch, Warped and Warping
58 The Gate of The Silver Key, Convergence of Space-Time
59 Library of Nalanda, Site of Celestial Learning
60 A Fortunate Accident

2011 Call of Cthulhu Into Tartarus

89 Alexander Pallas, Wrong Place, Right Time
90 Phoebe Kotas, Impertinent and Inquisitive
91 Attack Dogs
92 Timely Intervention
93 The Cult of Bathos, Near Mindless Devotion
94 Scylla's Well, Unfathomable Depths
95 The Spirit of Mania, Breaker of Minds
96 Stygian Eye, It Seduces with Promises of Power
97 Archaeology Interns
98 Mask of Sthenelus, Image of Nobility
99 Child of Argus
100 Mi-Go Skull, Revered Remnant
101 Master of the Myths
102 Vacant Servant
103 The Red Threshold
104 Sons of Hermes
105 Fortifying Ouzo
106 Pawn Broker
107 Breaking the Ward
108 Ritual of Bellephar

2011 Call of Cthulhu Lost Rites

61 Jenica Capra, Police Psychic
62 Daemonolatreia, Witchhunter's Guide
63 Brother James Xavier, The Jesuit
64 Descendent of Yig
65 The Warrens, Despair-ridden Tenement
66 Danni Devine, Mercurial and Mischievous
67 Maureen de Garmeaux, Method Actress
68 The King In Yellow Folio, Cursed Manuscript
69 Watchful Naturalist
70 Combing the Archives
71 Into The Woods
72 Abhorrent Spore
73 Lodge Neophyte
74 O.E.S. Ring
75 Fence
76 Lookout
77 Servant to the Elder Things
78 Feral Elder Thing
79 Library of Ebla, The First Library of Man
80 Professor Zeus, Shrewd Archivist

2011 Call of Cthulhu Never Night

69 Jacques Artois, Surprisingly Insightful
70 Recovered Icebreaker
71 Silent Mover
72 Burden Bearer
73 Temple of R'lyeh, Frozen in Time
74 Horrific Light
75 Deranged Sailor
76 Apeirophobia
77 Expert Cartographer
78 Magnetic Spike
79 The Forgotten Explorer
80 Even Here She Dwells
81 The Three Listeners, Ardent Supporters
82 Eon Chart, Map of the Spheres
83 Ice Shaft
84 James Crusher, Short Fused
85 Premature Detonation
86 Tunnel Lurker
87 Enslaved Yeti
88 Dark Sarcophagus, Holder of Unearthly Remains

2011 Call of Cthulhu Seekers of Knowledge

1 Board of Trustees, Overseeing the Future
2 Whitton Greene, Restricted Collection Bookhunter
3 Richard Pike, Here to Help
4 Roald Ellsworth, Intrepid Explorer
5 Brette Wulffsen, Nothing but Trouble
6 Doctor Bancroft, Military Historian
7 Matthew Alexander, Dark Companion
8 James Cookie Fredericks, Controversial Explorer
9 Lucas Tetlow, Eternal Curator
10 Maurice Diggs, Eldritch Theorist

11 Eschatologist
12 Catacombs Docent
13 Arctic Ethnologist
14 Cub Reporter
15 Alternative Historian
16 Ghost Hunter
17 Overworked Graduate Student
18 Campus Security Guard
19 College Prospect
20 Sports Scholarship
21 Protected by the Elder Sign
22 Station Eismitte, Mid-Ice Polar Station
23 Cylinders of Kadatheron, Knowledge of Ib
24 Mu, The Cradle of Civilization
25 Atlantis, Came to a Catastrophic End
26 Ultima Thule, Beyond the Known World
27 Ipiutak, The Bone City
28 Apocalyptic Visions, Prophecies of the Ancients
29 A Voros Hal'l Jon, Prophecy of the Lost
30 Reading the Star Signs
31 Daring Buju
32 Por V 1:20, and they shall fall to their knees
33 Zero Visibility
34 Protecting the Anirniq
35 Plan B
36 Expert Testimony
37 Fraternal Ties
38 The Claret Knight, Her Sworn Champion
39 Aliki Zoni Uperetria, Resourceful Servant
40 Amaranth, Opener of Ways
41 Er'nrawr, Death and Entropy Manifest
42 Hamu IV 1:13, The heavens speak the Truth
43 The Company, Arm of the Shadow Government
44 Por XV 14:19, drowned upon the altar
45 Cthylla, Secret Spawn of Cthulhu
46 Hamu XX 15:14, The Chimes of Bedlam mark the hour.
47 N'yog-Sothep, The Nameless Mist
48 Hanyalt's 7:13, She will give birth to madness
49 Nug, Blasphemy in the Night Sky
50 Hanyalt's 1:9, The young shall replace the old.
51 Carl Stanford, Sinister, not necessarily Evil
52 Hanyalt's 12:3, The horn blew and the hordes came.
53 Peter Clover, Playing the Odds
54 Lev'l 15:13, The secrets were written in the stars.
55 Umr at-Tawil, Most Ancient

2011 Call of Cthulhu Shadow of the Monolith

109 Dr. Henshaw, Too Close to the Truth
110 Unforeseen Setback
111 Family of Fishers
112 Out of Season Monsoon
113 Painter of Delusion
114 Seeker of the Songlines
115 The Musk Crow's Wind
116 Doctor Marama Riwhi, Warrior of the Mind
117 Deciphered History
118 Kau'uli Warriors
119 Wooden Homunculus
120 Mask of Rakinui, Symbol of Power
121 Taste of Lifeblood
122 Magnus Stiles, Blood Mage
123 Necessary Evil
124 The Sanguine Watcher, He Sees What Is Not There
125 Outback Poacher
126 Naval Tactics
127 The Betrayer, Playing All Sides
128 Song of Charybdis

2011 Call of Cthulhu The Shifting Sands

1 The Opened Door
2 The 9th Plague
3 The Second Dragon
4 Within the Ice
5 Come the Dreamtime
6 Heart of the Labyrinth
7 Congress of the Keys
8 Chaos Unleashed
9 Village of Ash
10 A New Challenge
11 The Heirloom
12 The Seventh Gate
13 John and Jessie Burke, Relentless in Pursuit
14 Federal Vault
15 Aziz Chatuluka, A Danger to all Mankind
16 Khopesh of the Abyss, Manifested Malice
17 Master of Amulets
18 Guardian Beast, Servant of Serapis
19 Professor Sam Campbell, Erudite Archeologist
20 The Cthonian Stone, Stygian Waymark
21 Magarta Kiss, Starry-eyed Lover
22 Desertification
23 Nigel St. James, Lodge Recruiter
24 The Deodand, Cutting Threads
25 Nassor, Alamut Operative
26 Written in Blood, Unbreakable Contract
27 The Large man, Shorn But Patient
28 Canopic Jar, Vessel of Souls

2011 Call of Cthulhu Spawn of Madness

1 Shadow Team
2 Torch the Joint
3 Omega Alumnus
4 Unspeakable Research
5 Danny O'Bannion's Crony
6 Gun Runner's Club
7 Cthuloid Spawn
8 The Sleeper Awakens!
9 Obscene Byakhee
10 Altar of Madness
11 Elder Thing
12 Revelation of the Spheres
13 Dreamlands Messenger
14 Glimpse of the Void
15 Student of the Profane
16 Ghost of Perdition
17 Arkham Inmate
18 Artifact of the Lost Cities
19 Written in the Sky
20 The Greatest Fear

2011 Call of Cthulhu Touched by the Abyss

101 Elena Belskaia, Always Prepared
102 Shadow War
103 The Necronomicon: Simon Translation, Simon Translation
104 Ancient Plans
105 Naaginn
106 The Marked
107 In the Court of the Dragon
108 The Necronomicon: Petrus de Dacia Translation, Petrus de Dacia Translation
110 Faculty Advisor
111 Arthur Todd, Possessed and Typhlotic
112 The Necronomicon: Olaus Wormius Translation, Olaus Wormius Translation
113 Lord of the Woods, Avatar of Shub-Niggurath
114 Adept of the Second Order
115 From the First Degree to the Last
116 Street Tough
117 The Necronomicon: George Hay Translation, George Hay Translation
118 The Night Job
119 The Grand Design
109A Surprising Find
109B Pushed into the Beyond

2011 Call of Cthulhu The Unspeakable Pages

81 St. Amabilis, For the Criminally Insane
82 Dr. Cornelius Rose, Criminal Profiler
83 Padma Amrita, Cold-blooded Charmer
84 Urumi
85 The Necronomicon, Owlswick Translation
86 Kaleidoscope of Calyptra
87 Named by the Unnameable
88 The Great Library of Celaeno, Knowledge from a Distant Star
89 Eryn Cochwyn, Disturbingly Insightful
90 The Necronomicon, Al Azif
91 Ya-te-veo
92 The Three Bells, The Sound of the Dark
93 Ritual of Exclusion
94 Magical Theorist
95 The Necronomicon, John Dee Translation
96 Inside Man
97 On the Run
98 Tindalos Alpha
99 The Necronomicon, Theodorus Philetas Translation
100 Pulled from the Beyond

2011 Call of Cthulhu Words of Power

21 Teodor Corvin, Guardian of the Faith
22 Cover Me!
23 Shadowy Figure
24 Dragged into the Deep
25 Deranged Diva
26 Song of Suffering
27 Research Assistant
28 Infirmary
29 Black Dog
30 Maleficium
31 Sarah Van Shaw, Lodge Warden
32 Knight of the Eclipse
33 Miranda Keeper, Antiquities Trader
34 Sergeant Donnelly, Corrupt Cop
35 O'Bannion's Ledger, Keeping Score
36 George Rogers, Obsessed Devotee
37 Houngan Seydou, Remover of Obstacles
38 Eltdown Shards, Book of Hidden Things
39 Library of Pergamum, Place of Ancient Wisdom
40 Marcus Jamburg, Finder of Lost Things

2011 Call of Cthulhu Written and Bound

1 Customs Agent
2 Flush them Out
3 Uroborus, Fang of Yig
4 Sibilant Cry
5 Elise Warren, Lady in Waiting
6 Whisper in the Wind
7 Sonje Olson, Truth Seeker
8 Dr. Laban Shrewsbury, Extra-dimensional Anthropologist
9 Celaeno Fragments, Book of Books
10 Lucas Corn, Scarecrow of a Man
11 Feed Her Young
12 Chauncey Swann, Eldritch Acquisitionist
13 Nathan Wick, Master of Initiation
14 T'tka Halot, Umbral Codex
15 Jon Pechon, Man with a Plan
16 Go Underground
17 Elder Thing Scavenger
18 Walk the Path
19 Library of Alexandria, Repository of Philosophies
20 Hall of Champions, Honoring Warriors Past and Present

2013 Call of Cthulhu Denizens of the Underworld

1 Naomi O'Bannion, Ruthless Tactician
2 Melisande LeBeau, Playing with Fire
3 O'Bannion's Inner Council, Blood is Thicker
4 Tommy Malloy, The Big Palooka
5 Lena Di Boerio, Occult Consultant
6 Jacob Finnegan, In Over His Head
7 Henry Knoll, A Real Wiseguy
8 Martin Herring, Quick Kip
9 Isaac Miles, Willing to Lend an Ear
10 Clover Club High Roller
11 Clover Club Ringer
12 Clover Club Pit Boss
13 Numbers Runner
14 Fall Guy
15 Marine Salvager
16 Cat Burglar
17 Crooked Attorney
18 Hatchet Man
19 Wheelman
20 The Clover Club, Den of Iniquity
21 Danny O'Bannion's Office, Now Hiring
22 Under Cover of Darkness
23 House Advantage
24 City Map
25 Concrete and Chains
26 Indebted
27 Length of Pipe
28 La Bella Luna, Seedy Restaurant
29 Made Man
30 Immurement
31 On the Lam
32 Reallocate
33 Forced Compliance
34 Pay Tribute
35 Turf War
36 Roll the Dice
37 A Cunning Ruse
38 Wandering Tinker
39 Zstylzhemgni, Matriarch of Swarms
40 Sarnath, Too Proud
41 Outmaneuvered
42 Special Agent Callahan, Always Gets His Man
43 Deep Undercover
44 Robert Friendly, Disgruntled Dockworker
45 Calculated Mutation
46 Jeff Harson, Manic Musician
47 Hali's Directive
48 Elijah Conrad, Distinguished Alumnus
49 Strategic Planning
50 Bill Strauss, Blessed of Shub-Niggurath
51 Ambush
52 Josef Meiger, Metaphysicist
53 Hoarding Knowledge
54 Sebastion Blake, Attuned to the Universe
55 Mind Swap

2013 Call of Cthulhu The Key and the Gate

1 Jeanne D'Ys, The Demoiselle
2 Claude Owen, Trying to Conquer Death
3 Nadine Eskiy, The Namer
4 Nikola Tesla, Man Out of Time
5 Wilbur Whateley, Scion of Yog-Sothoth
6 Professor Nathaniel Peaslee, Alien Intelligence
7 Fthaggua, Regent of the Fire Vampires
8 Yog-Sothoth, All-In-One
9 Lost Oracle
10 Wentshukumishiteu
11 Hungry Star Vampire
12 Quantum Theorist
13 Decrepit Wizard
14 Hand of Aforgomon
15 Yithian Scout
16 Keeper of the Great Library
17 Scholar from Yith
18 Scientist from Yith
19 Displaced
20 One-In-All
21 Elder Chasm, Abyssal Rift
22 Frozen Time
23 Rite of the Silver Key, Ritual of the Profane
24 Ys, Swallowed By The Sea
25 Rite of the Silver Gate, Rending Space-Time
26 De Vermis Mysteriis, Signs of the Black Stars
27 Lost City of Pnakotus, Source of Forgotten Lore
28 Dark Passenger
29 Song of the Spheres
30 Summon Spectral Hunter
31 Temporal Slip
32 Mists of Lethe
33 Calling the Williwaw
34 Vortex of Time
35 Studying the Void
36 Return to Yith
37 Interstellar Migration
38 Prepared Alienist
39 Visions of the Future's Past
40 Will of Azathoth, The Edicts of Madness
41 Eidolon
42 Norman Blackwood, Sr., Crafty Veteran
43 Franklin Automobile
44 Castro, Immensely Aged Mestizo
45 Cyclopean Stone, Horrifying Monolith
46 Sieur Piriou Louis, Hastur's Huntsman
47 The Tattered Cloak, Regalia Dementia
48 Andrew-Chapman, Boon Companion
49 Nepenthe
50 Slenderman, Feaster Upon the Innocent
51 The Festival, Bringer of Strange Joy
52 B. Ramsdale Brown, Well Connected
53 The Black Stone, Leyline Nexus
54 Arsene Renard, Gentleman Thief
55 Burglar Tools

2013 Call of Cthulhu Terror in Venice

1 Abbess Allegria Di Biase, Most Blessed
2 Pious Carabiniere
3 Church Operative
4 San Marco Basilica, The Church of Gold
5 The Iron Cross, Symbol of Authority
6 Hand of Fate
7 Don Lagorio, Secret Servant
8 Poleman
9 San Giorgio in Alga, No Longer Abandoned
10 Flooded Vault
11 Swimming in the Deep
12 Solar Eclipse
13 Doctor Lomboso, Finder of Madness
14 Cunning Mascherаro
15 San Servolo, Refuge from Reality
16 Return to Carcosa
17 At Night they Roam
18 The Unspeakable Oath
19 Bruno Carioli, Hatching a Plan
20 Urban Trailblazer
21 Puzzled Exchange Student
22 Medico Della Peste
23 Desperate Search
24 Mass Hysteria
25 Death Comes for All
26 Purity of Purpose
27 The Guardian
28 Before the Fast
29 Unending Festivities
30 The Mage's Machinations
31 The Supernal Prism, Holy Shard
32 The Plague Stone, Sweet Release
33 Malocchio, An Eye for Death
34 Savio Corvi, Dark Lurker
35 Ghoulish Scavenger
36 Baleful Reveler
37 Dark Rebirth
38 Untimely Burial
39 Elisabetta Magro, High Servant of the Order
40 Guardian of Dawn
41 Zanni
42 Hermetic Seal
43 Volto
44 Look to the Future!
45 Cascio Di Boerio, Don Morto
46 Restless Caporione
47 Carnevale Sentinel
48 Bauta
49 The Gold Pocket Watch, Stealing Time
50 Early Start
51 Tenebrous Nightgaunt
52 Salvatore Neri, Master of Illusion
53 Devious Nightgaunt
54 The Black
55 Fleeting Guise

2015 Call of Cthulhu For the Greater Good

1 Interrogator
2 Supernatural Investigator
3 Overworked Bureaucrat
4 Officer Gibson
5 Relentless Stalker
6 Dr. Christine Marie, Forensic Psychologist
7 Intelligence Agent
8 King John, Overburdened Detective
9 Keen-eyed Detective
10 Warrant Officer
11 Peerless Tracker
12 Grete Wagner, The Purifier
13 Crooked Cop
14 Veteran Monster Hunter
15 Military Attaché
16 Lieutenant Wilson Stewart, Logistical Genius
17 Karl Heinrich, Haunted Commander
18 General Edward Irving
19 Hunters of Ardenne
20 The Foundation, Shield of Humanity
21 Snowmobile
22 By the Book
23 Under Surveillance
24 St. Hubert's Key
25 Armored Car
26 Motor Pool
27 Red Tape
28 Bending the Rules
29 Mano-a-Mano
30 All-Points-Bulletin
31 Raid!
32 The Usual Suspects
33 The Great Work
34 The Anderson Building
35 The Blackwood Initiative
36 Iod, The Hunter of Souls
37 Tommy Gun
38 Ice Storm
39 Caleb Orison
40 Non-Euclidean Geometry
41 Bedlam Boys
42 Under the Yellow Sign
43 Jeremiah Kirby
44 Excavation Site
45 Restless Mi-Go
46 Lit by Death-Fire
47 Sgt. Logan Terry
48 Sir Jon Scott, Noble Philospher
49 August Lindquist, Elegant and Elusive
50 Deciphered Reality
51 Sigil of Doom
52 Escaped Convict
53 On the Take
54 Obsessive Elder Thing
55 Tear in Time

2015 Call of Cthulhu The Thousand Young

1 Handmaid
2 Ambushing Ghoul
3 Restless Dead
4 Jean Deveraeux, Shadow Mage
5 Bayou Shaman
6 Mi-Go Worker
7 Frenzied Ghoul
8 Keelut
9 Baka
10 Baleful Dark Young
11 Elspeth Baudin, Discerning and Discriminating
12 René Bonvillain, Rougarou
13 Rend, Tattered Ghoul
14 Marsh Gug
15 Smoke Serpent
16 Mysterious Philanthropist
17 Lady Esprit, Dangerous Bokor
18 Xlizxcte-Oonth, Lord of the Mi-Go
19 Baron Samedi, Lord of the Cemetery
20 Yeb, Blasphemy in the Night Sky
21 Ancient Chthonian, Father of Worms
22 Dark Sargassum
23 Shub-Niggurath, The Dark Mother
24 Ghoul Tunnels
25 The Black Goat's Milk
26 French Quarter, Vieux Carré
27 Gris-gris
28 The Grim Monolith, Last Landmark
29 Favor of Eshu, Dark Blessing
30 Twisted Consecration
31 Sudden Cyclone
32 Iä! Iä!
33 Birthing a Thousand Young
34 Pervasive Toxemia
35 Ankou, Death's Hand
36 Nyarlathotep, The Crawling Chaos
37 The Archmage's Attaché, Ensorcelled Valise
38 Gregory Lean, Finder of Lost Things
39 Faubourg Marigny, Elysian Fields
40 The Bloody Tongue, The Thing that Howls at the Moon
41 Broadmoor, Out of the Marshes
42 The Thing in the Yellow Mask, The High Priest not to be Named
43 Tremé, Back of Town
44 Harley Warren, Author of Tales of Terror
45 Audubon, University District
46 Lodge Applicant
47 Thule Zealot
48 Walter Fitzpatrick, Sinister Messiah
49 Garden District, Antebellum Wealth
50 Ritual of Expulsion
51 Call the Custodes
52 Phineas Taylor, Carnival Huckster
53 Irish Channel, The River Front
54 Kruschtya Equation, Mathematical Formula of the Gods
55 9th Ward, By the Water

2007 Chaotic Dawn of Perim

COMPLETE SET (232)		
BOOSTER BOX (24 PACKS)	40.00	80.00
BOOSTER PACK (	2.50	5.00
RELEASED ON JUNE 24, 2004		
1 Arias C	.10	.25
2 Attacat U	.20	.50
3 Blazier SR		
4 Blügon R	.30	.75
5 Bodal C	.10	.25
6 Crawsectus SR	5.00	12.00
7 Donmar R	.30	.75
8 Dractyl C	.10	.25
9 Frafdo U	.20	.50
10 Gespedan C	.10	.25
11 Heptadd UR		
12 Intress SR		
13 Laarina U	.20	.50
14 Maglax U	.20	.50
15 Maxxor UR		
16 Najarin R	.30	.75
17 Owis SR		
18 Psimion C	.10	.25
19 Rellim U	.20	.50
20 Slurhk C	.10	.25
21 Staluk R	.30	.75
22 Tangath Toborn SR		
23 Tartarek R	.30	.75
24 Velreth U	.20	.50
25 Vidav C	.10	.25
26 Xaerv U	.20	.50
27 Yokkis SR		
28 Zalic R	.30	.75
29 Barath Beyond SR		
30 Borth-Majar SR		
31 Chaor UR		
32 Dardemus C	.10	.25
33 Drakness SR		
34 Ghuul C	.10	.25
35 Grook U	.20	.50
36 Hail Storm SR		
37 Kerric U	.20	.50
38 Khybon U	.20	.50
39 Klasp R	.30	.75
40 Krekk C	.10	.25
41 Kughar C	.10	.25
42 Lord Van Bloot UR		
43 Magmon R	.30	.75
44 Miklon C	.10	.25
45 Nauthilax U	.20	.50
46 Pyrithion R	.30	.75
47 Rarran U	.20	.50
48 Rothar R	.30	.75
49 Skithia U	.20	.50
50 Skreeth R	.30	.75
51 Solvis R	.30	.75
52 Takinom SR		
53 Toxis U	.20	.50
54 Ulmar SR		
55 Xield SR		
56 Zaur C	.10	.25
57 Ekuud R	.30	.75
58 Formicidor C	.10	.25
59 Galin U	.20	.50
60 Hota U	.20	.50
61 Ibiaan U	.20	.50
62 Junda C	.10	.25
63 Kannen R	.75	2.00
64 Kebna U	.20	.50
65 Lhad C	.10	.25
66 Lore SR	1.50	4.00
67 Mallash R	.30	.75
68 Odu-Bathax R	1.25	3.00
69 Skartalas C	.10	.25
70 Valanii Levaan U	.20	.50
71 Wamma C	.10	.25
72 Ario R	.30	.75

73 Biondu C .10 .25
74 Brathe U .20 .50
75 Malvadine U .20 .50
76 Marquis Darini R .30 .75
77 Prince Mudeenu SR 6.00 15.00
78 Qwun C .10 .25
79 Shimmark U .20 .50
80 Siado C .10 .25
81 Sobtjek U .20 .50
82 Tiaane R 2.50 6.00
83 Ubliqun R .30 .75
84 Uro C .10 .25
85 Vinta U .20 .50
86 Zhade C .10 .25
87 Allmageddon SR
88 Ash Torrent U .20 .50
89 Coil Crush SR 2.00 5.00
90 Degenervate R .30 .75
91 Delerium C .10 .25
92 Ektospasm C .10 .25
93 Ember Swarm U .20 .50
94 Evaporize R .30 .75
95 Fearocity SR 2.00 5.00
96 Flame Orb SR
97 Flash Kick U .20 .50
98 Flash Mend R .30 .75
99 Flashwarp C .10 .25
100 Frost Blight SR 3.00 8.00
101 H'earring U 1.50 4.00
102 Hive Call R .30 .75
103 Incinerase R .30 .75
104 Inferno Gust U .20 .50
105 Iron Balls SR 2.50 6.00
106 Lavalanche SR
107 Lightning Burst U .20 .50
108 Lucky Shot UR 5.00 12.00
109 Megaroar UR 3.00 8.00
110 Mirthquake R .30 .75
111 Paral-Eyes R .30 .75
112 Pebblestorm C .10 .25
113 Power Pulse R .30 .75
114 Quick Exit C .10 .25
115 Rip Tide U .20 .50
116 Rock Wave SR
117 Rustoxic U .20 .50
118 Shadow Strike C .10 .25
119 Shriek Shock C .10 .25
120 Skeletal Strike R .30 .75
121 Sleep Sling R .30 .75
122 Sludge Gush SR 2.50 6.00
123 Spirit Gust C .10 .25
124 Squeeze Play U .20 .50
125 Steam Rage C .10 .25
126 Telekinetic Bolt SR 2.50 6.00
127 Thunder Shout C .10 .25
128 Tornado Tackle R .30 .75
129 Torrent of Flame C .10 .25
130 Toxic Gust SR 3.00 8.00
131 Unsanity U .20 .50
132 Velocitrap C .10 .25
133 Vine Snare U .20 .50
134 Viperlash R .30 .75
135 Windslash U .20 .50
136 Aqua Shield SR
137 Cyclance R .30 .75
138 Diamond of Vlaric R .30 .75
139 Dragon Pulse C .10 .25
140 Elixir Of Tenacity C .10 .25
141 Flux Bauble R .30 .75
142 Gauntlets of Might C .10 .25
143 Liquilizer R 1.25 3.00
144 Mipedian Cactus SR 5.00 12.00
145 Mowercycle C .10 .25
146 Mugician's Lyre C .10 .25
147 Nexus Fuse SR 4.00 10.00
148 Orb of Foresight R .30 .75
149 Phobia Mask U .20 .50
150 Prism of Vacuity U .20 .50
151 Pyroblaster R .30 .75
152 Ring of Na'arin C .10 .25
153 Riverland Star SR 4.00 10.00
154 Skeletal Steed U .20 .50
155 Spectral Viewer R .30 .75
156 Staff of Wisdom C .10 .25
157 Stone Mail UR 10.00 25.00
158 Talisman of the Mandiblor SR 3.00 8.00
159 Torrent Krinth U .20 .50
160 Torwegg U .20 .50
161 Viledriver U .20 .50
162 Vlaric Shard U .20 .50
163 Whepcrack SR
164 Windstrider SR
165 Decrescendo C .10 .25
166 Ember Flourish U .20 .50
167 Fortissimo SR
168 Geo Flourish U .20 .50
169 Interlude of Consequence SR
170 Minor Flourish C .10 .25
171 Song of EmberNova R .30 .75
172 Song of Futuresight C .10 .25
173 Song of GeoNova R .30 .75
174 Song of Truesight C .10 .25
175 Cascade Symphony R .30 .75
176 Hymn of the Elements C .10 .25
177 Mugic Reprise UR 2.50 6.00
178 OverWorld Aria SR
179 Refrain of Denial SR
180 Song of Focus U .20 .50
181 Song of Resurgence U .20 .50
182 Song of Stasis R .30 .75
183 Canon of Casualty U .20 .50
184 Discord of Disarming U .20 .50
185 Melody of Malady SR
186 Refrain of Denial (OverWorld) SR 2.00 5.00
187 Song of Asperity R .30 .75
188 Song of Fury R .30 .75
189 Song of Revival (UnderWorld) UR 8.00 20.00
190 Song of Treachery C .10 .25
191 Chorus of the Hive C .10 .25
192 Refrain of Denial (OverWorld/UnderWorld) U .20 .50
193 Song of Mandiblor SR 2.50 6.00
194 Song of Resistance U .20 .50
195 Song of Surprisal C .10 .25
196 Song of Symmetry R .30 .75
197 Fanfare of the Vanishing R .30 .75
198 Melody of Mirage R .30 .75
199 Notes of Neverwhere C .10 .25
200 Song of Deflection UR 4.00 10.00
201 Song of Recovery U .20 .50
202 Trills of Diminution C .10 .25
203 Castle Bodhran SR
204 Castle Pillar UR 2.50 6.00
205 Cordac Falls C .10 .25
206 Cordac Falls Plungepool C .10 .25
207 Crystal Cave U .20 .50
208 Doors of the Deepmines U .20 .50
209 Dranakis Threshold SR 6.00 15.00
210 Everrain U .20 .50
211 Eye of the Maelstrom U .20 .50
212 Fear Valley U .20 .50
213 Forest of Life C .10 .25
214 Gigantempopolis U .20 .50
215 Glacier Plains SR
216 Gloomuck Swamp C .10 .25
217 Gothos Tower R .30 .75
218 Iron Pillar SR
219 Kiru City R .30 .75
220 Lake Ken-I-Po UR 4.00 10.00
221 Lava Pond R .30 .75
222 Mipedim Oasis R .30 .75
223 Mount Pillar R .30 .75
224 Ravanaugh Ridge C .10 .25
225 Riverlands U .20 .50
226 Runic Grove C .10 .25
227 Stone Pillar SR
228 Storm Tunnel C .10 .25
229 Stronghold Morn SR
230 UnderWorld City SR 10.00 25.00
231 UnderWorld Colosseum R .30 .75
232 Wooden Pillar SR 3.00 8.00

2008 Chaotic Rise of the Oligarch

COMPLETE SET (100) 80.00 150.00
BOOSTER BOX (24 PACKS) 40.00 80.00
BOOSTER PACK 2.50 5.00
RELEASED IN JANUARY 2009
1 Aivenna SR 6.00 15.00
2 Arrthoa R .30 .75
3 Attacat, Tactical Aide C .10 .25
4 Biakan U .20 .50
5 Gimwei R .30 .75
6 Hune Paltanin SR 1.25 3.00
7 Najarin, Fluidmorphers' Foe UR 1.50 4.00
8 Blaaxa SR 1.50 4.00
9 Harmonies of the Wind R .30 .75
10 Khybon, The Renegade U .20 .50
11 Nivenna SR 5.00 12.00
12 Stelgar R 2.00 5.00
13 Takinom, The Shadowknight UR 1.50 4.00
14 Tasqa C .10 .25
15 Agrino Jaldar R .30 .75
16 Aureban SR 1.50 4.00
17 Dhilas U .20 .50
18 Fliandar UR 8.00 20.00
19 Klencka C .10 .25
20 Tarbok C .10 .25
21 Wamma, Hive Ordnance SR 2.00 5.00
22 Appelai U .20 .50
23 Epitrinne SR 1.50 4.00
24 Glost R 1.25 3.00
25 H'earring, Tainted R .30 .75
26 Otinee C .10 .25
27 Rasbma Darini SR 1.00 2.50
28 Taffial R .30 .75
29A Aa'une the Oligarch, Avatar UR 1.50 4.00
29B Aa'une the Oligarch, Projection UR 1.50 4.00
30 Aer'dak R .60 1.50
31 Anger'keem C .10 .25
32 Bahrakatan, The Coralsmith UR 20.00 50.00
33 Dror'niq U .20 .50
34 Fal'makin C .10 .25
35 Fla'gamp SR 2.50 6.00
36 Ikub'ra C .10 .25
37 Jus'hebban C .10 .25
38 Lam'inkal C .10 .25
39 Mik'banin U .20 .50
40 Mock'adyn C .10 .25
41 Nunk'worn SR 5.00 12.00
42 Phelphor, of the Deep U .20 .50
43 Ri'oha R .30 .75
44 Rol'doi C .10 .25
45 Siril'ean's Lair R .30 .75
46 Vitar'zu U .20 .50
47 Aftermath Feint R .30 .75
48 Caustic Cascade U .20 .50
49 Electric Rain SR .75 2.00
50 Fire Stream C .10 .25
51 Fluidmight C .10 .25
52 Force Balls U .20 .50
53 Invader's Tactics R .30 .75
54 Kha'rall Crush C .10 .25
55 Marksman's Preparation U .20 .50
56 Mightswing U .20 .50
57 Petrifying Power C .10 .25
58 Poison Steam C .10 .25
59 Rage of Aa'une R .30 .75
60 Rancorous Projection SR 6.00 15.00
61 Sandstrike U .20 .50
62 Solar Flare R .30 .75
63 Supercooled Rain SR 4.00 10.00
64 Swarming Destruction U .20 .50
65 Tainted Thunderstorm R .30 .75
66 Tidal Surge C .10 .25
67 Baton of Aa'une U .20 .50
68 Dractyl Scales C .10 .25
69 Kha'rall Amber Shard U .20 .50
70 Kha'rall Chime Shard U .20 .50
71 Kha'rall Freshwater Shard R .30 .75
72 Kha'rall Magma Shard R .30 .75
73 Kha'rall Shard of the Tidal Crest UR 8.00 20.00
74 Liquid Thought Evaporator R .30 .75
75 Phobia Plates SR 3.00 8.00
76 Vial of Liquid Thought C .10 .25
77 Sound of Noise SR 1.25 3.00
78 Vexing Waveform R .30 .75
79 Intress' Healing Ballad R .30 .75
80 Kopond's Composition R .30 .75
81 Mindproof March R .30 .75
82 Headmaster Ankhyja UR .75 2.00
83 Calling of Aa'une SR 4.00 10.00
84 Curemorph Chords C .10 .25
85 Decelerating Requiem U .20 .50
86 Denial Refrain of the Deep C .10 .25
87 Mightsingers Requiem U .20 .50
88 Requiem of Fear U .20 .50
89 Requiem of Lost Minds U .20 .50
90 Unheard Melody UR 5.00 12.00
91 Frozen Fire U .20 .50
92 Kiru City Tunnels U .20 .50
93 Psi-fanger's Shelf SR 1.50 4.00
94 Royal Mipedian Academy of Melee Arts R .30 .75
95 Siril'ean, The Songthief UR .75 2.00
96 Skeletal Springs U .20 .50
97 The Coralsmithy R .30 .75
98 The Oligarch's Path C .10 .25
99 The Rao'Pa Sahkk Chimegrid C .10 .25
100 The Training Grounds UR 1.50 4.00

2008 Chaotic Silent Sands

COMPLETE SET (100) 80.00 150.00
BOOSTER BOX (24 PACKS) 40.00 80.00
BOOSTER PACK 2.50 5.00
RELEASED IN JUNE 2008
1 Arbeid U .20 .50
2 Clodor C .10 .25
3 Hifdan U .20 .50
4 Iparu UR 10.00 25.00
5 Kalt C .10 .25
6 Karraba SR 1.50 3.00
7 Kinnianne Ambassador to the Mipedians SR 5.00 12.00
8 Olkiex SR 1.25 3.00
9 Viqtarr R .30 .75
10 Wytod R .30 .75
11 Atrapol C .10 .25
12 Kopond SR 4.00 10.00
13 Phelphor SR 4.00 10.00
14 Vyll U .20 .50
15 Zapetur R .30 .75
16 Hammerdoom Chantcaller Assimilated SR 4.00 10.00
17 Kolmo Assimilated SR 4.00 10.00
18 Lobanne U .20 .50
19 Makrabon C .10 .25
20 Raznus Assimilated R .30 .75
21 Blazvatan UR 1.50 4.00
22 Bylkian R .30 .75
23 Drimesse C .10 .25
24 Enre-Hep UR 10.00 25.00
25 Ere C .10 .25
26 Fivarth SR 3.00 8.00
27 Gnarlus SR 5.00 12.00
28 Lanker U .20 .50
29 Melke C .10 .25
30 Na-inna C .10 .25
31 Ranun U .20 .50
32 Saand U .20 .50
33 Titanix U .20 .50
34 Uboraan R .30 .75
35 Xelfe R .30 .75
36 Apoc-eclipse UR 2.00 5.00
37 Arborsmash C .10 .25
38 Blaze Barrage SR .75 2.00
39 Blind Fury U .20 .50
40 Cyclone Slam SR 1.50 4.00
41 Dexterous Storm C .10 .25
42 Elemental Oxidation SR 2.50 6.00
43 Enlightened Tenacity C .10 .25
44 Fear Fight U .20 .50
45 Force Strike C .10 .25
46 Hampering Winds U .20 .50
47 Harnessed Rage R .30 .75
48 Heptagon Hail UR 10.00 25.00
49 Hurlicane R .30 .75
50 Hydro Balls C .10 .25
51 Liquescent Swirl R .30 .75
52 Matagore U .20 .50
53 Mind Strike C .10 .25
54 Progressive Speed C .10 .25
55 Purifying Mud SR 2.00 5.00
56 Reactive Resolution R .30 .75
57 Reckless Defeat U .20 .50
58 Reckless Reproach R .30 .75
59 Rot Cloud R .30 .75
60 Slashclaw SR 1.50 4.00
61 Stupefying Tide U .20 .50
62 Symmetry Slam R .30 .75
63 Trampling Tackle U .20 .50
64 Twister of Elements SR 2.00 5.00
65 Web Cocoon C .10 .25
66 Challor SR 1.25 3.00
67 The Doomhammer UR 15.00 40.00
68 Entropy Modulator C .10 .25
69 Heptadd's Crown R .30 .75
70 Hunter's Lure U .20 .50
71 Lightning Canister C .10 .25
72 Ravita Flower C .10 .25
73 Reality Field Generator R .30 .75
74 Warbeast Power Leash SR .75 2.00
75 Wind Whip U .20 .50
76 Strain of Clarity U .20 .50
77 Void Dirge C .10 .25
78 Echoes of Empty Hands U .20 .50
79 Rhyme of the Reckless R .30 .75
80 Song of the Dyad C .10 .25
81 Strain of the Tide SR 1.25 3.00
82 Song of Desperation R .30 .75
83 Strain of Ash U .20 .50
84 Melody of Parasitic Mayhem U .20 .50
85 Strain of Infection R .30 .75
86 Armament Adagio C .10 .25
87 Fighters' Fanfare UR 6.00 15.00
88 Hymn of Teleportation SR 1.25 3.00
89 Strain of Expensive Delusions R .30 .75
90 Tune of Xerium U .20 .50
91 Catacombs of the Conjurors R .30 .75
92 Forest of Life During Aichlyys U .20 .50
93 The Hunter's Perimeter U .20 .50
94 Indigo Grove SR 2.00 5.00
95 Iparu Jungle UR 2.50 6.00
96 Mipedian Dew Farm C .10 .25
97 Mipedim Lounge SR 1.50 4.00
98 Mipedim Mirage R .30 .75
99 OverWorld Embassy at Mipedim C .10 .25
100 Rao'Pa Sahkk The Ocean with No Water C .10 .25

2008 Chaotic Zenith of the Hive

COMPLETE SET (100) 80.00 150.00
BOOSTER BOX (24 PACKS) 40.00 80.00
BOOSTER PACK 2.50 5.00
1 Aggroar C .10 .25
2 Garv R .30 .75
3 Hune Marquard U .20 .50
4 Lomma SR 8.00 20.00
5 Raznus Ambassador to the Danians SR 5.00 12.00
6 Geltod C .10 .25
7 Hammerdoom Chantcaller UR 25.00 60.00
8 Illazar SR 4.00 10.00
9 Kamangareth U .20 .50
10 Narfall U .20 .50
11 Ornathor C .10 .25
12 Slufurah R .30 .75
13 Strikto R .30 .75
14 Swassa U .20 .50
15 Ultadur SR 5.00 12.00
16 Balaan C .10 .25
17 Bierk R .30 .75
18 Daj Huun C .10 .25
19 Dasalin U .20 .50
20 Dubin C .10 .25
21 Faash U .20 .50
22 Illexia, The Danian Queen UR 1.50 4.00
23 Jaal U .20 .50
24 Kelvedran C .10 .25
25 Khavakk R .30 .75
26 Khritlaan SR 3.00 8.00
27 Mahrrant SR 1.25 3.00
28 Ramarhvir, the Danian Hivebringer UR 10.00 25.00
29 Tassanil R .30 .75
30 Yondaf R .30 .75
31 Arkanin U .20 .50
32 Dibanni R .30 .75
33 Kolmo SR 6.00 15.00
34 Munnari C .10 .25
35 Ribbian SR .50 1.25
36 Accelerated Unity C .10 .25
37 Acid Wash SR 1.00 2.50
38 Danihilation U .20 .50
39 Dessicate the Land U .20 .50
40 Elementalist's Psy-Blast U .20 .50
41 Freeze Flash C .10 .25
42 Gear Grind R .30 .75
43 Granite Balls R .30 .75
44 Hive-phoon C .10 .25
45 Infight SR 2.00 5.00
46 Malevolent Blast U .20 .50
47 Mandiblor Might SR .50 1.25
48 Muge's Edge R .30 .75
49 Mugician Steal SR 1.50 4.00
50 Pillar Quake R .30 .75
51 Reverberate C .10 .25
52 Scout's Strike C .10 .25
53 Strike of the Meek UR 6.00 15.00
54 Sunder Ground U .20 .50
55 Terraport R .30 .75
56 Danian Carapace SR 1.25 3.00
57 Elementalist Pauldrons R .30 .75
58 Ice Cloak R .30 .75
59 Mandiblor Crown C .10 .25
60 Scout's Monocular C .10 .25
61 Stingblade Prototype SR 4.00 10.00
62 Supercharged Alterant U .20 .50
63 Sword of Khy'at U .20 .50
64 Telebracers SR 2.50 6.00
65 Ur-Shard UR 5.00 12.00
66 Composition of Concentration C .10 .25
67 Defender's Song U 8.00 20.00
68 Momental Virtuosity R .30 .75
69 Prelude of Protection C .10 .25
70 Recurring Rescue SR .50 1.25
71 Cascading Rondo SR .50 1.25
72 Dissonance of Distraction C .10 .25
73 Elemental Denial U .20 .50
74 Hive Destruction U .20 .50
75 Serenade of Subordinance R .30 .75
76 Danian Element Choral R .30 .75
77 Elemental Elegy SR .50 1.25
78 Hive Unsung R .30 .75
79 Infectious Melody U .20 .50
80 Purge Dirge UR 1.50 4.00
81 Song of Encompassing C .10 .25
82 Song of Resilience C .10 .25
83 Gear Glissando C .10 .25
84 Melodic Might SR 8.00 20.00
85 Song of Shelter R .30 .75
86 Switch Riff U .20 .50
87 Casters' Warsong U .20 .50
88 Chorus of Cothica UR 1.50 4.00
89 Forgotten Origins SR .75 2.00
90 Melody of the Meek R .30 .75
91 The Barracks R .30 .75
92 Carnival of Confusion UR 5.00 12.00
93 The Darkened Dunes SR 2.00 5.00
94 Grand Hall of Muge's Summit SR 3.00 8.00
95 Mount Pillar Reservoir C .10 .25
96 Oipont's Lookout R .30 .75
97 OverWorld Embassy at Mount Pillar U .20 .50
98 Queen's Gate C .10 .25
99 Sands of the Unseen U .20 .50
100 Sha-Kree Flats SR 1.50 4.00

2015 Crusaders of Lornia Defenders of the City

ROWPD01 Troublemaker Ricky :G:
ROWPD02 Waitress Nikki :G:
ROWPD03 Gancell, Emor Citizen :G:
ROWPD04 Benthar, Emor City Guard :G:
ROWPD05 Haldur, Emor Officer :G:
ROWPD06 Patron of Emor :G:
ROWPD07 Ventara, Little Café Server :G:
ROWPD08 Gildorien, Knight of Emor :G:
ROWPD09 Tabishian Blade :R:
ROWPD10 Sidearm :R:
ROWPD11 Miscalculated Assault :R:
ROWPD12 Tabishian Spear :R:
ROWPD13 Hero's Aura :R:
ROWPD14 Destined Connection :R:
ROWPD15 Tabishian Greed :R:
ROWPD16 Ricky's Favorite Drink :W:
ROWPD17 Tabishian Exchange :W:
ROWPD18 Basic :W:
ROWPD37 forced eviction :R:
ROWPD38 Nope! :R:
ROWPD39 Chemical X-5 :B:
ROWPD40 Spare Battery :B:
ROWPD41 Hidden Greed :B:

2015 Crusaders of Lornia Remnants of Worlds Past

COMPLETE SET (80) 120.00 250.00
BOOSTER BOX (20 PACKS) 60.00 80.00
BOOSTER PACK (10 CARDS) 2.00 4.00
RELEASED ON NOVEMBER 20, 2015
ROWP001 Destruction of the Masses RR :W: 50.00 100.00
ROWP002 Immortal Hydra LR :G: 6.00 15.00
ROWP003 Ricky Ascended R :G: .40 1.00
ROWP004 Fallen Incarnate LR :G: 6.00 15.00
ROWP005 God Aura LR :R: 15.00 40.00
ROWP006 Emor Power Station XR :B: 4.00 10.00
ROWP007 Changing Sides LR :W: 12.00 30.00
ROWP008 Silent Death R :G: 2.00 5.00
ROWP009 Infeckterz Commander XR :G: 5.00 12.00
ROWP010 EMP XR :R: 2.50 6.00
ROWP011 Infeckterz Apocalypse XR :R: 6.00 15.00
ROWP012 The First Law XR :R: 2.50 6.00
ROWP013 Jeeraudo Paradise LR :B: 5.00 12.00
ROWP014 Remnants of Lornia XR :W: 5.00 12.00
ROWP015 Genji's Hideaway XR :W: 6.00 15.00
ROWP016 Accipitridae XR :W: 6.00 15.00
ROWP017 Basic Fighter R :G: .40 1.00
ROWP018 Gilthorne, Captain of the Emor City Guard C :G: .10 .25
ROWP019 Infeckterz Reservist C :G: .10 .25
ROWP020 Gas Guzzler R :G: .40 1.00
ROWP021 Crydorian Empress R :G: 2.00 5.00
ROWP022 To The Dump! R :R: 1.00 2.50
ROWP023 Big Force Gun R :R: .40 1.00
ROWP024 Take Point R :R: .40 1.00
ROWP025 Ectovolution C :R: .10 .25
ROWP026 Infeckterz Power Cell R :B: 1.50 4.00
ROWP027 BRAINS! R :B: 1.00 2.50
ROWP028 Tactical Asset R :W: .40 1.00
ROWP029 Resource Refinery R :W: 2.00 5.00
ROWP030 Breaking Even R :W: 1.50 4.00
ROWP031 Wandering Black Knight C :G: .10 .25
ROWP032 Dragon of White Flames C :G: .10 .25
ROWP033 Demonic Scavenging Knight R :G: 1.00 2.50
ROWP034 Mini Armorender C :G: .10 .25
ROWP035 Resource Finder C :G: .10 .25
ROWP036 Emor City Private XR :G: 8.00 20.00
ROWP037 Skilled Swordsman C :G: .10 .25
ROWP038 Steel Golem C :G: .10 .25
ROWP039 Stoned Golem C :G: .10 .25
ROWP040 Swift Striker C :G: .10 .25
ROWP041 Unstable Neutralizer C :G: .10 .25
ROWP042 Weapons Supplier C :G: .10 .25
ROWP043 Young Ricky C :G: .10 .25
ROWP044 Infeckterz Soldier C :G: .10 .25
ROWP045 Infeckterz Nurse C :G: .10 .25
ROWP046 Brittle Golem C :G: .10 .25
ROWP047 Archaic Dragon C :G: .10 .25
ROWP048 United Enforcer C :G: .10 .25
ROWP049 Switch-aroo C :G: .10 .25
ROWP050 Shady Miner C :G: .10 .25
ROWP051 Crydor Aristocrat C :G: .10 .25
ROWP052 Viral Infeckterz C :G: .10 .25
ROWP053 Dangeropus C :G: .10 .25
ROWP054 Cuddlefish C :G: .10 .25
ROWP055 Atatar, Rennok Ambassador C :G: .10 .25
ROWP056 Hallox, Ponduran Medic C :G: .10 .25
ROWP057 Infeckterz Abomination C :G: .10 .25
ROWP058 Diana, Jeeraudo Delegate C :G: .10 .25
ROWP059 Dragaby, Emor's Little Dormant Dragon C :G: .10 .25
ROWP060 Mazakala, Tabishian Magistrate C :G: .10 .25
ROWP061 Emirg, Slumlord of Emor C :G: .10 .25
ROWP062 Infeckterz Reliever C :G: .10 .25
ROWP063 Safe From Assault C :R: .10 .25
ROWP064 Xortix Oil Well C :R: .10 .25
ROWP065 Fuel Exchange C :R: .10 .25
ROWP066 Revert C :R: .10 .25
ROWP067 Ricky's Scooter C :R: .10 .25

Card		
ROWP068 Maylik's Ego LR :R:	12.00	30.00
ROWP069 Lifelong Friends C :R:	.10	.25
ROWP070 Lifeforce Syphon C :R:	.10	.25
ROWP071 For the Cause C :R:	.10	.25
ROWP072 Pulled From Action C :R:	.10	.25
ROWP073 Bitten C :R:	.10	.25
ROWP074 Tabishian Force Field C :R:	.10	.25
ROWP075 Cease and Desist C :R:	.10	.25
ROWP076 Emor, La Cité Éternale C :R:	.10	.25
ROWP077 Super Power Boost C :B:	.10	.25
ROWP078 Super Shield Pump C :B:	.10	.25
ROWP079 Hold it! C :B:	.10	.25
ROWP080 Rennok Support Initiative C :B:	.10	.25
ROWPPR1 Guardian of Lornia RR :G: PROMO	25.00	60.00

2015 Crusaders of Lornia Zombie Invasion

ROWPD19 Raught, Infeckterz Juggernaut :G:
ROWPD20 Infeckterz Patient Zero :G:
ROWPD21 Ponduran Solider :G:
ROWPD22 Infeckterz Harvester :G:
ROWPD23 Infeckterz Soul Dragger :G:
ROWPD24 Rising Infeckterz :G:
ROWPD25 Infeckterz Shaman :G:
ROWPD26 Dishonored Infeckterz :G:
ROWPD27 Ponduran Sentry :R:
ROWPD28 Infeckterz plague :R:
ROWPD29 Infeckterz Sacrifice :R:
ROWPD30 Infeckterz Rebirth :R:
ROWPD31 fuel of life :R:
ROWPD32 RISE!!! :R:
ROWPD33 Infeckterz Infusion :R:
ROWPD34 Special Talents :W:
ROWPD35 Corpse Collector :W:
ROWPD36 Basic :W:
ROWPD37 Forced Eviction :R:
ROWPD38 Nope! :R:
ROWPD39 Chemical X-5 :B:
ROWPD40 Spare Battery :B:
ROWPD41 Hidden Greed :B:

1998 Deadlands Doomtown Episodes 1 and 2

1 A Price on His Head R
2 And Stay Down! R
3 Arson C
4 Bad Tequila C
5 Bluff R
6 Brawl C
7 Bucket Brigade C
8 Caught With yer Pants Down R
9 Cave-in R
10 Cheatin' Varmint C
11 Claim Jumper C
12 Clean Up the Town C
13 Crack Shot R
14 Dead Man's Hand R
15 Diversion C
16 Don't Like Yer Looks R
17 Double Dealin' C
18 Drawing a Bead R
19 Dust Devil R
20 Extortion R
21 Fanning the Hammer C
22 Framed R
23 Friends in Low Places C
24 Getting' outta Hand R
25 Giddyup! C
26 Git! R
27 Grave Robbin' R
28 Gremlins R
29 Haunting C
30 Head 'em Off at the Pass C
31 Headsman's Axe R
32 Hell's Fury R
33 Ignore 'im C
34 Just a Graze C
35 Lady Luck R
36 Lynch Mob R
37 Nice Boots, Chief R
38 Out of Ammo R
39 Pannin' for Gold R
40 Quickdraw C
41 Raid C
42 Run Outta Town C
43 Scalpin' R
44 Shortcut R
45 Snake Eyes R
45 Earthquake R
46 Sun in Yer Eyes C
47 Warrant C
48 Yellow Belly R
49 Yer all Chicken! R
50 Abandoned Mine R
51 Blacksmith C
52 Casino Morongo C
53 Claims Office R
54 Colorado Lode R
55 Dispatch Office C
56 Dragon's Nest Strike R
57 Drop in the Ocean Strike C
58 Exchange Office C
59 Foale's Folly C
60 Fu Leng's Laundry & tailoring R
61 Golden Mare Hotel R
62 Graveyard R
63 Henry's Hole C
64 Hideout R
65 Jail R
66 Lad Saloon R
67 Miner's Union House R
68 Nasty Doc's R
69 Old Moon Saloon C
70 Perry's Pawnshop R
71 Pharmacy R
72 Photographer Shop C
73 Pike's Puddle Mine C
74 Pony Express C
75 Rock Ridge Mine R
76 Sam's General Store C
77 San Simeon Mine C
78 Schoolhouse C
79 Scrapyard R
80 Spirit of Kentucky Shaft C
81 St. Martin's Chapel R
82 The 1st Bank of Gomorra R
83 The Alright Corral C
84 The Courthouse R
85 The Desert Rose Lode C
86 The Golden Crack R
87 The Slaughterhouse C
88 The Tree R
89 The Undertaker's C
90 Tombstone Dispatch Branch Office C
91 Town Hall R
92 Wishing Well C
93 Arizona Jane R
94 Benny Hibbs C
95 Black Jack F
96 Bob Bidwell C
97 Cassidy Greene C
98 Charlie Landers C
99 Clell Miller C
100 Cletus Peacock C
101 Cordelia "Corky" Hendricks C
102 Deputy John Templeton R
103 Eddie Bellows R
104 Erik Zarkov R
105 Father Juan Navarro C
106 Fineas von Landingham R
107 Hangin' Judge Gabriel R
108 Hector Casparo C
109 Humphrey Walters R
110 J.P. Coleman F
111 Jessie Freemont C
112 Lilith Vandekamp R
113 Lucky Ted C
114 Marcus Perriwinkle C
115 Meredith Singleton R
116 Mick Caples C
117 Nash Bilton R
118 Nate Hunter R
119 Oswald Hardinger F
120 Prof. Susan Franklin C
121 Rachel Sumner R
122 Robert Holmes C
123 Sandra Harris C
124 Silas Peacock C
125 Spike Dougan R
126 Tao Cheng "T.C." C
127 Vampiric Dance Hall Girl R
128 Victor Navarro C
129 A Coach Comes to Town C
130 Christmas Day R
132 Easter Sunday C
133 Eurika! C
134 Founder's Day R
135 Full Moon R
136 Heavy Rain C
137 The Sabbath R
138 Bullet-Proof Vest C
139 Dynamite Launcher R
140 Gatling Pistol R
141 Kenny C
142 Mechanical Horse C
143 New Hat C
144 Pearl-Handled Revolver C
145 Pinto C
146 Prof. Parnham's Miracle Elixir C
147 Ray Gun R
148 Roan C
149 Rocket Pack R
150 Still R
151 Sweaty Dynamite C
152 Winchester Rifle C
153 Blackjacks F
154 Collegium F
155 Law Dogs F
156 Joker R

1998 Deadlands Doomtown Episode 3

1 A Secret Tunnel C
2 Ace in the Hole R
3 Ambush C
4 Friends in High Places R
5 Get a Rope R
6 Get on Your Feet! C
7 Jail Break R
8 Overtime C
9 Pinned Down C
10 Pistol Whip R
11 Refuse to Fall C
12 Rooftop Sniper C
13 Bob's Fix-it Shop R
14 Equipment Shop R
15 Hell's End Mine R
16 Ignacio's Exotics C
17 One Eyed Ike's Weapons Locker C
18 Orphanage R
19 Red Hill Hotel C
20 Scooter's Lift Winch C
21 Smiley's Shaft C
22 The Docks R
23 The Good Doctor C
24 Top of the World Lode R
25 …And Scooter R
26 Austin Stoker C
27 Big Jake… C
28 Dr. Reginald Branson C
29 Ezzie C
30 Flint Parker R
31 Gerald Klippstein C
32 Gordo Andrade R
33 Gunther Hapworth R
34 Howard Findley F
35 Jim MacNeil C
36 Judge Henry Warwick C
37 Max Baine R
38 Red Crow R
39 Reverend Simon MacPherson R
40 Robert Northrop R
41 Sir Whitmore R
42 The Twitch C
43 Tom O'Reilly C
44 Government Audit C
45 It Was a Mountain Lion R
46 The Fair Comes to Town R
47 The Temperance Army C
48 Bomb R
49 Flamethrower C
50 Gatling Gun R
51 Holy Wheel Gun C
52 Sweetrock F

1998 Deadlands Doomtown Episode 4

1 Deputize C
2 Foreclosure C
3 Forgery C
4 His Back Was to Me C
5 It's Just Coal… C
6 Manitou's Revenge R
7 Nowhere to Run C
8 Sheriff's Watchin' C
9 Smith & Robards Delivery R
10 Stray Lead C
11 The Witching Hour R
12 They Just Pay Better 'N You R
13 Yer Cheatin' Too! R
14 Barkum & Barkum Attorneys C
15 Callahan's Ditch C
16 King Willy's Mother Lode C
17 Lord Grimely's Manor R
18 Pacific Maze Railstation R
19 Sunnyside Hotel R
20 The Clock Tower R
21 Basil Whateley R
22 Billy No-Neck R
23 Bronco Bjork Gutmansen C
24 Buckets Nelson C
25 Byron St. James R
26 Delores Whateley R
27 Eagle Rock C
28 Ezekiel Whateley C
29 Moses Whateley-Braun C
30 Nicodemus Whateley R
31 Pierre Fontaine C
32 Sam Horowitz C
33 Saul Whateley C
34 Sheila Mirabella R
35 Unknown Hooded Figure R
36 Werewolf R
37 Werner Braun R
38 Wilhelmina Whateley F
39 Circus Sideshow C
40 Independence Day R
41 Missing Children R
42 Samhain R
43 Greased Lightning Pill R
44 Shotgun C
45 Blood Curse R
46 Helpin' Hand C
47 Mind Twist R
48 Missed Me! R
49 Shadow Walk C
50 Soul Blast C
51 Texas Twister C
52 Whateley Family Estate F

1998 Deadlands Doomtown Episode 5

1 Bounty Hunter R
2 Double Time C
3 Hat Gun R
4 Hot Lead Flyin' C
5 Human Shield C
6 Reserves R
7 Rumors C
8 Snakebite C
9 Take Ya With Me C
10 Throw Down R
11 War Paint R
12 Deadland R
13 Fish Ridge Mine R
14 Icehouse R
15 Miss Coutreau's C
16 On the Side Strike C
17 Thunder Gulch Strike C
18 Water's Edge Strike C
19 Weaponsmith R
20 Benjamin Nightsinger C
21 Charlie Flatbush C
22 Crazy Quilt R
23 Danny Hamilton R
24 Elizabeth King C
25 Feather-In-His-Hair C
26 Harold Longfellow C
27 Ian Spencer-Whitney R
28 John Bloody Knife R
29 Joseph Eyes-Like-Rain F
30 Lawrence Goodman C
31 Little Running Bear R
32 Singing Feather C
33 The Amazing Xemo C
34 Tioga Joe R
35 Walkin' Dead C
36 Walks-in-Footprints R
37 Whiskey Nick R
38 Wise Cloud C
39 Labor Dispute R
40 New Science Magazine C
41 The 1st Bank is Robbed! R
42 Total Eclipse R
43 Bow and Arrow C
44 Pembroke's Analysis of Hoyle R
45 Corporeal Twist R
46 Shadow Man R
47 Sioux Union F
48 Calming Spirits R
49 Curse C
50 Lightning Strike R
51 Medicine C
52 Strength of the bear C

1998 Deadlands Doomtown Episode 6

1 Bum Rush C
2 Burn 'Em Down C
3 Chinese Day Laborers R
4 Church Raisin' R
5 Crippled C
6 Kidnapping C
7 Luck of the Draw C
8 Night Haunt R
9 No Funny Stuff C
10 Red Spade R
11 Tattoo R
12 The Fear C
13 Green-Eye Saloon C
14 Harlot's Haven Strike C
15 Howlin' Hollow R
16 Ike's Strike C
17 Library R
18 Smiling Lizard Lode R
19 The Lucky Dog Lode C
20 Becky Henrick R
21 Buster Madison C
22 Captain Sim Yut-San F
23 Chin Wei-Lun R
24 Finnegan O'Malley C
25 Gyonshee R
26 Hank Gallagher C
27 Jebediah Whateley R
28 Little Mountain R
29 Marko Muscovich C
30 Maze Dragon R
31 Mitobu C
32 Mortimer Jones C
33 Nelson Roberts R
34 Po Yu R
35 Richard Boothe C
36 Sun Shu-Jen R
37 Wall Crawler C
38 Xiong "Wendy" Cheng C
39 Coleman is Killed! C
40 Election Day R
41 Long Arm of the Law R
42 Stampede R
43 Air Gun R
44 Buffalo Rifle C
45 Maze Runner R
46 Mustang C
47 Sacred Tomahawk R
48 Hunch R
49 Phantom Fingers C
50 The Maze Rats F
51 Rain Dance R
52 Speed of the Wolf C

1998 Deadlands Doomtown Episode 7

1 Derringer C
2 Friendly Game C
3 Hired Guns R
4 Marked Cards R
5 Massacre at High Noon R
6 Mimic C
7 Take Cover R
8 That's Two pair C
9 Yellow Traitor! C
10 Den of Eastern Delights R
11 Flophouse C
12 Lucky Horseshoe Lode R
13 Strike Experiment #1 C
14 Tent City (Chinese Workers) C
15 The Barber's Shop R
16 The Bathhouse C
17 The Mission House R
18 Town Well C
19 Billy Iron Horse R
20 Bobo LeVeux R
21 Cheyenne Bottoms C
22 Envy C
23 Father Juan Nevarro Exp. R
24 Joe Larson C
25 Kansas City Kara C
26 Katie Karl F
27 Little Running Bear Exp. C
28 Los Ojos Del Dios R
29 Nicodemus Whateley Exp. R
30 Rails Richardson R
31 Raymond Armstrong C
32 Reverend Simon MacPherson Exp. R
33 Robert Northrop Exp. R
34 Zeke Beauchamp C
35 Jack Guns Down Spike R
36 Spike Kills Eureka C
37 Chrono Accelerator C
38 Holdout Knife C
39 Hoyle's Book, 1769 Ed. R
40 Nicodemus' Deck R
41 Quick-draw Holster C
42 Stoker's Sabre R
43 Unholy Symbol R
44 Puppet C
45 Sacrifice C
46 Blackjacks R
47 The Texas Rangers F
48 Death's Head Joker R
49 Apache Devil Dancers R
50 Ask the Spirits C
51 Repel Manitou C
52 Spirit Warrior R
53 Summon Spirit R

1998 Deadlands Doomtown Episode 8

1 Bottom Dealin' R
2 Chilling Effect C
3 Degeneration C
4 Drinks On the House R
5 Good Stiff Drink R
6 Home Sweet Home R
7 Lost Faith C
8 Smoke Signals C
9 Swapped Decks R
10 That'll Leave a Scar C
11 Gomorra Gazette C
12 Knot Mine C
13 Machinist's Shop R
14 Raven's Crevasse R
15 Stuffed to the Gills Strike R
16 The Carpenter's Shop C
17 The Dentist's Office C
18 The Guilded Feather R
19 Avarice R
20 Benjamin Dean R
21 Captain Sim Yut-San Exp. R
22 Chester Nero C
23 Cort Williams C
24 Erik Zarkov Exp. R
25 Gus Gallagher C
26 Johnny Quaid R
27 Josef Nicolai Rocescu R
28 Nash Bilton Exp. R
29 Philip Blackmoor C
30 Sister Mary Jebediah C
31 The Ghost F
32 Tombstone Frank C
33 Will O' the Wisp C
34 William Olson C
35 Drought C
36 Magnetic Poles Realign C
37 Major Earthquake R
38 Nate Hunter Is Elected Sherrif R
39 Duplicator R
40 Hardinger's Blueprints R
41 Martyr's Cross R
42 Pair of Six-Shooters C
43 Tin Shield C
44 Calm R
45 Censure R
46 Consecrate Armament C
47 Holy Roller R
48 Lay On Hands R
49 Test Of Faith C
50 The Agency F
51 Call Weather C
52 Turtle's Shell C

1998 Deadlands Doomtown Episode 9

1 Any One of Ya! R
2 Blueprints R
3 Dumb Luck C
4 I Got the Pistols… C
5 Jackelope Stampede C
6 Seductress R
7 Supplies From Back East R
8 Tastes Like Chicken C
9 We've Got Ya Surrounded C
10 Buffalo Chip Saloon C
11 Legal Offices of _____ R
12 Lonesome Willow Strike C
13 Look Homeward Mine R
14 Stagecoach Office R
15 Surveyor's Office C
16 The Gaping Maw Strike C
17 The Intelligence Shop R
18 Barthalomew Prospectus R
19 Black Jack Exp. R
20 Camille Sinclair C
21 Elijah F
22 Flam C
23 Flim C
24 Gluttony R
25 Idleness R
26 J.P. Coleman Exp. R
27 Lechery C
28 Mordecai Whateley R
29 Mr. Slate C
30 Pox Walker C
31 Pride C
32 Skin Shifter C
33 SUZY 309 R
34 Wrath R
35 Dealer's Choice C
36 Eureka! C
37 Los Diablos Stampede R
38 Revival Comes to Town R
39 Bowie Knife C
40 Coleman's Badge R
41 Jack's Right Shooter R
42 Sonic Destabilization Ray C
43 Bolts O' Doom C
44 Babble On C
45 Confession C
46 Exorcism R
47 Inspiration R
48 Sanctify C
49 Smite R
50 Snake Handlin' R
51 The Flock F

1999 Deadlands Doomtown Mouth of Hell

1 ...Today, I Am C
2 A Few Custom Modifications R
3 Aim For the Head C
4 Arcane Protection R
5 Auction C
6 Bad to the Bone C
7 Blaze of Glory R
8 Blue Moon U
9 Caught in the Crossfire C
10 Claws C
11 Devil's Touch C
12 Fall Guy C
13 Ferryman's Fee C
14 Field Test C
15 Fight Like A Man C
16 Hiding in the Bushes C
17 High Noon R
18 Horse Thief C
19 Hostile Takeover C
20 Manitou's Control R
21 Mirror, Mirror R
22 Night Haunt Attack C
23 Nightmare C
24 No End in Sight C
25 Only Winged 'Em C
26 Pickpocket R
27 Red-Handed C
28 Ritual Scars C
29 Sauce for the Gander C
30 Secret Bomb C
31 Secret Identity C
32 Shootin' From the Hip C
33 Stitchin' U
34 Takin' Cover R
35 This Round is on Us C
36 Throw Your Weight Around C
37 Trick Shootin' C
38 Two Hands, Two Guns C
39 Unnatural Selection U
40 You're Not Fast Enough... C
41 You're With Me C
42 1st Baptist Church of Gomorra C
43 2nd Bank of Gomorra U
44 Bat's Breath Mine C
45 Bookstore R
46 Bottleneck Mine C
47 Elysium Fields Mine R
48 Fortune-Teller's Shop R
49 Fountain C
50 Holmes' Workshop R
51 Hunter's Moon Strike C
52 Miss Greene's Room U
53 New Moon Saloon U
54 New Town Hall C
55 Razor-Cliff Mine C
56 Run-Down Lot C
57 Secret Lab R
58 Sweetrock Smoking Lounge R
59 Tack and Harness Shop C
60 The Back Room C
61 The Cooper C
62 The Labyrinth Mine C
63 The Lode R
64 The Side Pocket Billiard Hall C
65 The Steam Tunnel Lode C
66 The T and Q Cattle Ranch C
67 Theatre R
68 Whiskey Nick's Joint C
69 Alfred Barkum, Sr. C
70 Alice Chamberlain C
71 Angus McFadden C
72 Bladed Fist C
73 Bogie Man C
74 Bone Fiend C
75 Brownsville Jack C
76 Clell Miller Exp. R
77 Dark Beast C
78 Darren Titus U
79 Deer Eater R
80 Deputy Dave Montreal U
81 Deputy Milo Powell C
82 Desmond Quentin C
83 Ferret's Eye C
84 Flim Exp. R
85 Freddy Fast Hands U
86 Glom U
87 Howard Findley Exp. F
88 Ironteeth C
89 Jacob the Healer C
90 James Hastings U
91 Jeb Parker C
92 John the Doomsayer U
93 Julius Bailey F
94 Katie Karl Exp. R
95 Lucifer Whateley U
96 Marcus Perriwinkle Exp. U
97 Mary the Wanderer C
98 McCracken Brothers C
99 Melissa Thomas C
100 Montana Holland C
101 Mr. Bones C
102 Mr. Prim C
103 Peevie C
104 Phillip Goodson R
105 Pit Wasp Swarm C
106 Po Yu Exp. R
107 Redbrook C
108 Robert Holmes Exp. R
109 Sally Daniels C
110 Shouting Tom C
111 Singing Feather Exp. R
112 Sister Mary Jebediah Exp. R
113 Skunky Swade C
114 Spike Dougan Exp. R
115 Stone Man C
116 Strikes A Hawk U
117 Tao Cheng ("T.C.") Exp. R
118 Terrormental R
119 Unknown Hooded Figure Exp. R
120 Walter Ponds U
121 Wave Shadow C
122 William Badson R
123 Xiong "Wendy" Cheng Exp. F
124 Austin Saves Father Juan R
125 Coleman Returns C
126 Culling of the Blessed R
127 Ghost Infestation R
128 Ghost Train U
129 Meredith Kills The Hooded Figure R
130 Rachel Murders Warwick R
131 Riot C
132 Sleeping With Shadows U
133 Sumner's Revenge U
134 Tapped Out C
135 The Motherlode Is Found R
136 Undead Miners C
137 Weapons Tax C
138 Acid Gun U
139 Bull Whip C
140 Choking Gas C
141 Double-barreled Shotgun C
142 Dream Catcher R
143 Ectoplasmic Calcifier R
144 Electrostatic Pump Gun U
145 Findley's Quill Pen R
146 Rocket Boots C
147 Sawed-off Shotgun C
148 Slumber Needle C
149 Telescopic Pistol Sight U
150 Time Vision Goggles R
151 Warwick's Gavel R
152 Bash C
153 Dark Protection C
154 Groom C
155 Kentucky Windage C
156 Martyr's Mirror R
157 Pact with Darkness U
158 Sympathy for the Devil R
159 Extra Room C
160 Guard Dog House C
161 Armor Of Righteousness R
162 Battle Hymn C
163 Benediction C
164 Burnt Offerin' C
165 Clear Out! R
166 Cloak R
167 Dervish C
168 Devil's Plaything U
169 Interpret Vision C
170 Water to Wine C
171 Law Dogs- Hunter's Office F
172 Collegium- The New Front F
173 Sweetrock- Western Corporate Office F
174 Back To Nature R
175 Bind Spirit R
176 Clumsiness C
177 False Face C
178 Invisibility R
179 Sticks to Snakes U
180 The Spirits Flee R
181 Vision Quest C

1999 Deadlands Doomtown Pine Box

1 A Secret Tunnel U
2 Ace in the Hole R
3 Ambush U
4 And Stay Down! R
5 Arson C
6 Bad Tequila C
7 Between the Shoulderblades FR
8 Bluff R
9 Bounty Hunter U
10 Brawl C
11 Bucket Brigade C
12 Bum Rush U
13 Burn 'Em Down U
14 Bushwhacked FR
15 Cheatin' Varmint C
16 Claim Jumper U
17 Clean Up the Town C
18 Crack Shot U
19 Dead Man's Hand R
20 Deputize C
21 Derringer C
22 Diversion C
23 Double Dealin' C
24 Drinks On the House R
25 Dust Devil R
26 Fanning the Hammer U
27 Foreclosure U
28 Framed R
29 Friendly Game U
30 Friends in Low Places C
31 Get a Rope U
32 Giddyup! C
33 Git! R
34 Head 'em Off at the Pass C
35 Headsman's Axe R
36 Hell's Commin' With Me FR
37 Hell's Fury R
38 His Back Was to Me C
39 Jackelope Stampede U
40 Just a Graze U
41 Kidnapping U
42 Lady Luck U
43 Manitou's Revenge R
44 Nice Boots, Chief U
45 No Funny Stuff C
46 Out of Ammo U
47 Pistol Whip U
48 Quickdraw U
49 Raid C
50 Red Spade R
51 Refuse to Fall U
52 Reserves U
53 Rumors C
54 Scalpin' R
55 Shortcut U
56 Snake Eyes R
57 Snakebite C
58 Sun in Yer Eyes C
59 Takin' Precautions FR
60 Throw Down U
61 Unlucky Charm FR
62 War Paint R
63 Warrant C
64 Yellow Belly R
65 Abandoned Mine R
66 Barkum & Barkum Attorneys U
67 Bob's Fix-it Shop U
68 Buffalo Chip Saloon C
69 Burial Ground FR
70 California Queen FR
71 Callahan's Ditch C
72 Casino Morongo U
73 Colorado Lode R
74 Deadland R
75 Den of Eastern Delights R
76 Dispatch Office C
77 Dragon's Nest Strike R
78 Drop in the Ocean Strike C
79 Fish Ridge Mine R
80 Foale's Folly C
81 Fu Leng's Laundry & tailoring U
82 Golden Mare Hotel R
83 Graveyard U
84 Green-Eye Saloon C
85 Hell's End Mine U
86 Howlin' Hollow R
87 Jail U
88 King Willy's Mother Lode C
89 Lad Saloon R
90 Legal Offices of _____ R
91 Look Homeward Mine R
92 Lucky Horseshoe Lode U
93 Miss Coutreau's C
94 Old Moon Saloon C
95 On the Side Strike C
96 Orphanage U
97 Pacific Maze Railstation R
98 Pike's Puddle Mine C
99 Pony Express U
100 Red Hill Hotel U
101 Rock Ridge Mine R
102 San Simeon Mine C
103 Schoolhouse U
104 Scooter's Lift Winch U
105 Smiling Lizard Lode R
106 Spirit of Kentucky Shaft C
107 St. Martin's Chapel U
108 Strike Experiment #1 C
109 Stuffed to the Gills Strike R
110 Sunnyside Hotel R
111 Surveyor's Office U
112 The 1st Bank of Gomorra R
113 The Alright Corral U
114 The Barber's Shop U
115 The Clock Tower U
116 The Courthouse U
117 The Dentist's Office U
118 The Docks U
119 The Gaping Maw Strike C
120 The Guilded Feather R
121 The Intelligence Shop R
122 The Mission House U
123 The Slaughterhouse U
124 The Tree U
125 The Undertaker's U
126 Thunder Gulch Strike C
127 Tombstone Dispatch Branch Office U
128 Town Hall R
129 Town Well C
130 Water's Edge Strike C
131 Weaponsmith R
132 ...And Scooter U
133 Arizona Jane U
134 Austin Stoker R
135 Avarice R
136 Barthalomew Prospectus U
137 Basil Whateley R
138 Benjamin Dean U
139 Benny Hibbs C
140 Big Jake... U
141 Billy Iron Horse U
142 Billy No-Neck U
143 Black Jack Exp. R
144 Bob Bidwell C
145 Buckets Nelson Exp. F
146 Buster Madison U
147 Byron St. James R
148 Captain Sim Yut-San Exp. R
149 Cassidy Greene C
150 Charlie Flatbush C
151 Charlie Landers C
152 Chester Nero U
153 Chin Wei-Lun R
154 Clell Miller C
155 Cletus Peacock C
156 Cordelia "Corky" Hendricks U
157 Cort Williams C
158 Danny Hamilton F
159 Deputy John Templeton R
160 Delores Whateley F
161 Eagle Rock C
162 Eddie Bellows R
163 Elijah Exp. F
164 Envy C
165 Erik Zarkov Exp. R
166 Ezekiel Whateley C
167 Ezzie U
168 Father Juan Nevarro Exp. R
169 Fineas von Landingham U
170 Flim U
171 Gerald Klippstein Exp. F
172 Gluttony R
173 Gunther Hapworth U
174 Hector Casparo U
175 Howard Findley R
176 Humphrey Walters R
177 Idleness U
178 J.P. Coleman Exp. R
179 Jebediah Whateley U
180 Jessie Freemont C
181 Jim MacNeil Exp. F
182 Joe Larson C
183 John Bloody Knife R
184 Johnny Quaid R
185 Josef Nicolai Rocescu R
186 Joseph Eyes-Like-Rain R
187 Judge Henry Warwick U
188 Kansas City Kara U
189 Katie Karl R
190 Lawrence Goodman C
191 Lechery C
192 Lilith Vandekamp R
193 Little Running Bear Exp. U
194 Los Ojos Del Dios U
195 Marcus Perriwinkle C
196 Marko Muscovich C
197 Max Baine C
198 Maze Dragon R
199 Meredith Singleton R
200 Mick Caples C
201 Mitobu C
202 Moses Whateley-Braun C
203 Mr. Slate C
204 Nash Bilton Exp. R
205 Nate Hunter Exp. F
206 Nelson Roberts R
207 Nicodemus Whateley Exp. R
208 Oswald Hardinger R
209 Po Yu U
210 Pox Walker U
211 Pride C
212 Prof. Susan Franklin C
213 Rachel Sumner Exp. F
214 Rails Richardson C
215 Raymond Armstrong C
216 Reverend Simon MacPherson Exp. R
217 Richard Boothe C
218 Robert Holmes C
219 Robert Northrop Exp. R
220 Sam Horowitz U
221 Sandra Harris C
222 Saul Whateley U
223 Singing Feather C
224 Sir Whitmore U
225 Sister Mary Jebediah U
226 Sun Shu-Jen R
227 Tao Cheng "T.C." C
228 The Ghost Exp. F
229 The Twitch U
230 Tioga Joe Exp. F
231 Tombstone Frank U
232 Unknown Hooded Figure R
233 Vampiric Dance Hall Girl R
234 Victor Navarro C
235 Walkin' Dead U
236 Walks-in-Footprints R
237 Wall Crawler C
238 Werewolf U
239 Wilhelmina Whateley R
240 Wise Cloud C
241 Wrath R
242 Xiong "Wendy" Cheng C
243 Zeke Beauchamp C
244 A Coach Comes to Town C
245 All Saints Day FR
246 Dealer's Choice C
247 Drought C
248 Easter Sunday C
249 Eurika! U
250 Eureka! U
251 Founder's Day U
252 Full Moon U
253 Government Audit U
254 It Was a Mountain Lion R
255 Labor Dispute U
256 Long Arm of the Law R
257 Los Diablos Stampede R
258 Magnetic Poles Realign C
259 Stampede R
260 The Fair Comes to Town U
261 The Sabbath R
262 Buffalo Rifle U
263 Bullet-Proof Vest C
264 Flamethrower U
265 Gatling Pistol U
266 Ghost Rock Detector FR
267 Holdout Knife C
268 Kenny C
269 Mustang C
270 New Hat C
271 Pair of Six-Shooters U
272 Pearl-Handled Revolver C
273 Pinto C
274 Prof. Parnham's Miracle Elixir C
275 Ray Gun U
276 Roan C
277 Rocket Pack R
278 Shotgun C
279 Sonic Destabilization Ray C
280 Sweaty Dynamite U
281 Tin Shield U
282 Unholy Symbol R
283 Winchester Rifle C
284 Blood Curse R
285 Demon's Eye FR
286 Helpin' Hand C
287 Mind Twist R
288 Phantom Fingers U
289 Puppet C
290 Shadow Walk U
291 Soul Blast C
292 Texas Twister U
293 Babble On C
294 Consecrate Armament C
295 Exorcism R
296 Holy Roller U
297 Inspiration R
298 Lay On Hands U
299 Sacrifice C
300 Smite R
301 Blackjacks F
302 Collegium F
303 Law Dogs F
304 Sioux Union F
305 Sweetrock F
306 The Agency F
307 The Flock F
308 The Maze Rats F
309 The Texas Rangers F
310 Whateley Family Estate F
311 Death's Head Joker R
312 Joker R
313 Apache Devil Dancers R
314 Lightning Strike U
315 Medicine C
316 Speed of the Wolf U
317 Spirit Warrior R
318 Strength of the Bear U
319 Summon Spirit R
320 Turtle's Shell C

1999 Deadlands Doomtown A Reaping of Souls

1 A Legal Deck C
2 A Slight Cough C
3 A Stiff Fine C
4 Ambition U
5 Assault on the Whateleys R
6 Attitude C
7 Bankrupt Morals C
8 Bounty U
9 Bribin' the Town Council R
10 Collegium Sinks the Typhoon R
11 Dominion C
12 Eureka's Rage C
13 Good Kharma C
14 Grace C
15 Hard Labor C
16 I Want A Raise U
17 Insurance Policy C
18 Last Will C
19 Let's Take It Outside C
20 Mines Reopen U
21 Miss Me? R
22 My Fight's With You C
23 Nemesis R
24 Paper Money C
25 Puny Mortals! R
26 Quick Reload C
27 Relic U
28 Renovations C
29 Speaking With the Dead R
30 Teamwork C
31 Tricky Spirits C
32 Vermin Problem C
33 Voice O' the Damned R
34 War of Words C
35 What Have You Done Lately? C
36 What This Town Needs Is... C
37 Wither R
38 Worse'n I Thought R
39 Bakery C
40 Circle K Ranch C
41 Cracked Bone Strike U
42 Dance Hall C
43 Dead Man's Laughter Lode U
44 Gomorra Volunteer Fire Brigade C
45 Gypsy's Tent U
46 Helga's Wafflehaus C
47 Hitched Buggy Strike C
48 Lighthouse C
49 Lord Grimely's Manor Exp. R
50 Lumberyard C
51 Mental Hospital U
52 Muddy Brown Strike C
53 Ninth Circle Mine C
54 No-Tell Hotel R
55 Observatory U
56 Penny Arcade C
57 Polecat Saloon C
58 Reserve Judgement Strike C
59 Rough and Tumble Saloon C
60 Sea of Sorrows Mine C
61 Shark's Grin Lode R
62 Sheriff's Shaft C
63 Shootin' Range C
64 Strike Experiment #2 C
65 Tailor C
66 The Horse Doctor C
67 U.S. Army Enlistment Office R
68 Water Tower R
69 ...And Scooter Exp. U

70 Ainsley Cunningham C
71 Armitage the Damned R
72 Austin Stoker Exp. R
73 Benjamin Dean Exp. R
74 Big Jake… Exp. U
75 Boom-Boom O'Bannon C
76 Cassandra C
77 Chester Nero Exp. U
78 Deputy John Templeton Exp. R
79 Devil Bats C
80 Dexter Simpson C
81 Doctor Duvalier C
82 Elizabeth King Exp. C
83 Elmo Schacci C
84 Ely Parker C
85 Enoch Whateley C
86 Envy Exp. R
87 Ezzie Exp. R
88 Fineas Von Landingham Exp. R
89 Hope In Winter C
90 Jessie Freemont Exp. U
91 John Bloody Knife Exp. R
92 Los Ojos Del Dios Exp. F
93 Lukas Owens C
94 Mae Parker C
95 Malrog Whateley C
96 Max Baine Exp. R
97 Meredith Singleton Exp. U
98 Miss Lily C
99 Poison Woman C
100 Raven Smiles C
101 Sammy Childs C
102 Sandra Harris Exp. R
103 Saul Whateley Exp. R
104 Sin Eater C
105 Squish-Eye Samantha C
106 Sun Shu-Jen Exp. R
107 SUZY 309 Exp. R
108 The Jinx C
109 The Taskmaster U
110 Timmy Derrick C
111 Tzipporah Whateley U
112 Vampiric Dance Hall Girl Exp. R
113 Victor Navarro Exp. R
114 Wilhelmina Whateley Exp. F
115 Windows Derek C
116 Wise Cloud Exp. U
117 Wrath Exp. F
118 A Score is Settled R
119 All Harroweds' Eve C
120 All Souls' Day C
121 Army of Gremlins U
122 Austin Kills John Bloody Knife R
123 Dead Walk the Earth C
124 Harvest Moon C
125 Home is Where Nothin' Happens C
126 Inheritance C
127 Knicknevin R
128 Quarantine C
129 Strangers Among Us C
130 The Gate is Opened R
131 The Madman's Secret R
132 Vampire Ambush C
133 Ammo Belt C
134 Bank Draft C
135 Blue Jeans C
136 Bolt-Action Rifle C
137 Chainsaw C
138 Mystical Bag U
139 Pale Horse R
140 Pocket Watch C
141 Radar R
142 The Ammo-Matic R
143 The Evidence C
144 Tool Belt C
145 Trick Deck C
146 Walkin' Stick C
147 Whateley Family Bible R
148 Zapper U
149 Black Cat C
150 Fleeting Memories R
151 Knicknevin's Deal R
152 Mirror, Mirror U
153 Nightmare Realm C
154 Soul In A Bottle R
155 Suzy Goes Berserk C
156 Balcony C
157 Basement C
158 Bedrock C
159 Bulletproof Glass R
160 Complaint Window R
161 Conveyor Belt C
162 Iron Gate C
163 Long Hallways C
164 Rope Bridge C
165 Runnin' Water C
166 Second Story U
167 Weapons Locker C
168 Confusion R
169 Fire and Brimstone U
170 Light of the Lord C
171 Locust Swarm C
172 Snow In July R
173 Welcome To Hell R
174 The Coalition F
175 The Flock- Children Of Armageddon F
176 The Whateleys- Extended Family F
177 Fool's Joker R
178 Coyote's Laugh R
179 Eagle's Sight C
180 Flash Flood R
181 War Party U

1999 Deadlands Doomtown Revelations

1 Audience C
2 Bloody Face R
3 Born Under a Strange Star C
4 Both Barrels C
5 Con Game Gone Bad C
6 Cover Fire C
7 Double or Nothin' R
8 Dud Round C
9 Embezzlement R
10 Feedin' Time R
11 Flamin' Barrels C
12 Fresh Horses R
13 Funeral Procession R
14 Ham-Handed Play R
15 Here Comes the Cavalry C
16 Hot-loaded Rounds C
17 Intimidation R
18 It's Just You and Me C
19 Lost in the Badlands C
20 Low Profile C
21 Mark of Man C
22 Misdirection C
23 Monopoly R
24 No Mint Juleps Here R
25 Panic Attack C
26 Postal Fine C
27 Rats In Gomorra C
28 Run, You Coward! R
29 Shallow Grave R
30 Shotgun Wedding R
31 Sleep o' the Dead R
32 Stoker versus Knicknevin C
33 Supernatural Smarts C
34 Supernatural Speed C
35 Termite Infestation C
36 Tinker C
37 Together at Last R
38 Trackin' Teeth R
39 Along the Way Strike C
40 Archaeological Dig C
41 Boardinghouse C
42 Boat Yard C
43 Buster's Gambling Hall C
44 Candy Shop C
45 Cobbler Shop C
46 End of Time Lode C
47 Far Away Strike R
48 Foreclosed Folly Strike C
49 Gadget Warehouse R
50 Glassmaker C
51 Grendel's Eye Strike C
52 Horse Racetrack C
53 Investment Broker R
54 Museum R
55 Nick's Never Closes C
56 Papa's Lode Strike R
57 Scared Stiff Saloon R
58 Seventh-Sign Strike R
59 Storage Shed R
60 Tailoring Shop C
61 Trading Post C
62 Western Union Offices R
63 Abel Owens C
64 Alexander Whale R
65 Alfred Barkum, Jr. C
66 Arizona Jane Exp. R
67 Billy No-Neck Exp. R
68 Black Jack Exp.2 F
69 Bobo Leveux Exp. R
70 Buster Madison Exp. R
71 Cain Regen C
72 Chao Li C
73 Charlie Flatbush Exp. R
74 Chinese Ogre C
75 Christopher Hill C
76 Denton Filmore C
77 Dr. Lawrence C
78 Dr. Reginald Branson Exp. R
79 Dread Wolf Pack C
80 Eagle Rock Exp. C
81 Faminite C
82 Father Terrance C
83 Francis Whateley R
84 Gus Gallagher Exp. R
85 Harold Longfellow Exp. F
86 Headless Horseman C
87 Hoodoo C
88 Humphrey Walters Exp. R
89 Idleness Exp. C
90 Jenny Cooper C
91 Joseph Eyes-Like-Rain Exp. F
92 Killer Kerry C
93 Mad Dog Campbell C
94 Mark Preston C
95 Nate Hunter Exp.2 R
96 Nebuchadnezzar C
97 Nelson Roberts Exp. R
98 The Pennsylvania Kid C
99 Pride Exp. R
100 Prof. Susan Franklin Exp. R
101 Reggie Cornell C
102 Richard Boothe Exp. R
103 Sam Horowitz Exp. R
104 Seldon Harrison C
105 Sheila Mirabella Exp. R
106 Shigetoshi Hohiro R
107 Silas Peacock Exp. C
108 Skunky Swade Exp. R
109 Spirit's Eyes C
110 Sun In His Eyes C
111 The Drifter R
112 The Missionary R
113 Thunderbird R
114 Tomb Guardian R
115 Two Birds Chirping R
116 Wendigo Garrison C
117 White Horse C
118 Battle for Lord Grimeley's R
119 Battle Plan C
120 Boxin' Match C
121 Burning of the Whateley Estate R
122 Eye of the Storm F
123 Ghost Rock Fever R
124 Joseph's Return C
125 Purging of the Golden Mare C
126 Saloon's on Fire C
127 Stand Alone, Die Alone R
128 Statute 32 of the Penal Code R
129 Tax Season C
130 Clock Strikes Thirteen R
131 The End is Nigh C
132 The House Always Wins C
133 Wrath O' God R
134 Autogyro R
135 Auto-Incendiary Bullets C
136 Bone-Tipped Bullets C
137 Cold-Iron Bullets C
138 Deer-Stalkin' Hat R
139 Holy Bullets R
140 Infared Spectacles C
141 Lemat Pistol C
142 Magic Bus R
143 Magnum Bullets C
144 Mask C
145 Peace Pipe R
146 Pipe C
147 Psychic Projector R
148 Reckoner's Bullet R
149 Roll of Dimes R
150 Silver Bullets C
151 Spare Chamber R
152 Spurs C
153 Looking Glass C
154 Mark of Death R
155 Mark of Famine C
156 Mark of Pestilence C
157 Mark of War R
158 Stayin' Put C
159 Brewery R
160 Faro Table C
161 Front Porch C
162 Gas Lamp R
163 Homeless Joe R
164 Piano Player C
165 Pump R
166 Sidewalk C
167 Stained-Glass Windows C
168 Fifth Bowl C
169 First Bowl C
170 Fourth Bowl R
171 Guide C
172 Last Rites C
173 Second Bowl C
174 Seventh Bowl R
175 Sixth Bowl R
176 Third Bowl C
177 Maze Rats- Landed Rats F
178 Blackjacks- Stoker's Alliance F
179 Sioux Union- War Party F
180 Blood Oath R
181 Horned Owl's Fury C
182 Nature's Wrath C

1999 Deadlands Doomtown Shootout at High Noon

1 Bad Tequila F BJ/LD
2 Burn 'Em Down F BJ
3 Clean Up the Town F LD
4 Crack Shot F BJ
5 Don't Like Yer Looks F BJ
6 Dust Devil F BJ
7 Friends in High Places F BJ/LD
8 Friends in Low Places F BJ
9 Grave Robbin' F BJ
10 Ignore 'im F BJ
11 It's Just Coal… F BJ/LD
12 Out of Ammo F BJ/LD
13 Pinned Down F LD
14 Pistol Whip F BJ/LD
15 Reserves F BJ/LD
16 Rumors F BJ/LD
17 Seductress F BJ
18 Sun in Yer Eyes F LD
19 Warrant F LD
20 Buffalo Chip Saloon F BJ
21 Callahan's Ditch F BJ
22 Casino Morongo F BJ
23 Fu Leng's Laundry & tailoring F LD
24 Golden Mare Hotel F BJ
25 Gomorra Gazette F LD
26 Harlot's Haven Strike F BJ
27 Henry's Hole F LD
28 Lad Saloon F LD
29 Legal Offices of _____ F BJ
30 Miss Coutreau's F BJ
31 On the Side Strike F BJ
32 Pony Express F LD
33 Spirit of Kentucky Shaft F BJ
34 Sunnyside Hotel F BJ
35 The Barber's Shop F LD
36 The Courthouse F LD
37 The Dentist's Office F LD
38 The Desert Rose Lode F LD
39 The Guilded Feather F LD
40 The Gaping Maw Strike F BJ
41 The Intelligence Shop F BJ
42 The Lucky Dog Lode F LD
43 Top of the World Lode F LD
44 Town Well F BJ
45 Water's Edge Strike F LD
46 Billy No-Neck F BJ
47 Black Jack Exp. F BJ
48 Charlie Flatbush F LD
49 Charlie Landers F BJ
50 Corky Hendricks Exp. F LD
51 Deputy John Templeton F LD
52 Eddie Bellows Exp. F BJ
53 Father Juan Navarro F BJ
54 Flint Parker F BJ
55 Gordo Andrade F BJ
56 Hangin' Judge Gabriel F LD
57 Lilith Vandekamp F BJ
58 Nash Bilton F LD
59 Nate Hunter F LD
60 Rachel Sumner F BJ
61 Tao Cheng "T.C." F LD
62 William Olson F LD
63 Xiong "Wendy" Cheng F LD
64 Bowie Knife F BJ/LD
65 Martyr's Cross F BJ/LD
66 New Hat F BJ/LD
67 Pair of Six-Shooters F BJ/LD
68 Pearl-Handled Revolver F BJ/LD
69 Quick-draw Holster F BJ/LD
70 Shotgun F BJ/LD
71 Winchester Rifle F BJ/LD
72 Blackjacks F BJ
73 Law Dogs F LD

2000 Deadlands Doomtown Ashes to Ashes

1 Close Shave U
2 Confederate Hunter R
3 Defendin' What's Yours R
4 Dehydration R
5 Down The Barrel… R
6 Fireworks Distraction C
7 Fisticuffs C
8 Greasin' Palms R
9 Guilt by Association C
10 Hired Help R
11 I Gotcha Covered C
12 Knicknevin's Legacy R
13 Last Meal C
14 Lazy Sunday C
15 Listen Up! C
16 Lost Horizon C
17 Mesa Checkpoint C
18 Move Along U
19 Oh No, You Don't! U
20 One Good Turn… U
21 Play It Again U
22 Publicity Stunt U
23 Puttin' the Heat On U
24 Red Tape R
25 Spiritual Pawn U
26 The North End C
27 This Don't Involve You C
28 Twist of Fate R
29 Waylaid R
30 Welcome Home U
31 Who Are You, Again? C
32 Yer Not Welcome Here! R
33 Accountant U
34 Art Gallery U
35 Bleeding Vein R
36 Candlestick Maker C
37 Cerulean Cove Mining Operation R
38 Confederate Barracks U
39 Derailed Cafe U
40 Elijah's Parish C
41 Fate's Warning Strike R
42 Fine China Shop C
43 Hundred Yearling Ranch U
44 Hydro-Accelerator C
45 Jeweler C
46 Leaning Rock Strike C
47 Leather and Saddle Shop C
48 Mosley's Maw U
49 New Dunwitch Casino R
50 Nick's And Nack's R
51 Nolan's Smithy C
52 Road House C
53 Rounders Diamond U
54 Spiritual Society Enclave R
55 Tea and Tobacco Shop R
56 The Jaded Jackalope U
57 Toll Bridge U
58 Toy Shop C
59 Union Train Depot R
60 Wyrm Hill R
61 Adrian Townsend U
62 Alastor the Executioner R
63 Army of the Dead C
64 Astoreth Whateley U
65 Barthalomew Prospectus Exp. R
66 Billy Iron Horse Exp. R
67 Brigadier-General Patterson F
68 Chupacabra R
69 Cort Williams Exp. F
70 Cynthia Kingston U
71 Delilah Darby-Scorne C
72 Deputy Dave Montreal Exp. R
73 Dustin Halloway U
74 Enrique Alonso C
75 Erik Zarkov Exp. 2 R
76 Far-Away Fred U
77 Flesh Mob R
78 Freddy Fast-Hands Exp. R
79 Gandy Dancer C
80 Hangin' Judge R
81 Isaiah "Holdout" Curwen U
82 Jacynth Ambrose C
83 Jesse Radcliffe U
84 Jonah Wheeler U
85 Joseph Moon U
86 Juliet "Jewel" Sumner R
87 Lord Ripley Scorne C
88 Lucifer Whateley Exp. R
89 Mad Wolf Striding U
90 Maurice Foster C
91 Max Baine Exp. 2 F
92 Megan Mallory U
93 Melissa Thomas Exp. R
94 Nadia Krasnova C
95 Natalie Sherman U
96 Quon Lin U
97 Reverend C.A. Johnson C
98 Rex Handlen U
99 Rhett Caufield C
100 Santana Tate R
101 Scott Pierce U
102 Sergeant Sean Slade C
103 The Crucible U
104 The Snitch C
105 Thedrick Whateley C
106 Town Drunk C
107 Vance Donovan R
108 Weeping Crow C
109 Wendigo Garrison Exp. R
110 Calm Before the Storm C
111 Gareth Comes To Town R
112 Heat Wave U
113 Military Occupation C
114 New Town, New Rules R
115 Recall Orders R
116 Speakin' With the Dead C
117 Spectral Visitors C
118 Spit And Vinegar R
119 Stumbling Into the Badlands U
120 Unexpected Guest U
121 Anahuac Staff C
122 Blood Money C
123 Formal Duds U
124 Gris-Gris U
125 Hand Cart C
126 Investment Machine C
127 Penny Farthing C
128 Personal Safe U
129 Printing Press R
130 Quickdraw Sling R
131 Spirit Pipe R
132 Steam-Powered Crane R
133 Whiskey Flask U
134 White Shire R
135 Bad Blood R
136 Brimstone C
137 Deal With the Devil U
138 Drawin' A Blank U
139 Corporate Headquarters R
140 Demon's Den C
141 Founder's Memorial U
142 Gatling Emplacement R
143 Harvesting Plots U
144 Indoor Plumbing R
145 Rats In the Walls C
146 Secret Passages C
147 Union Armory U
148 Path of the Righteous R
149 Prophecy U
150 Roll The Dice… C
151 The Lord Provides U
152 Sweetrock- Gomorra Ltd. Rail Line F
153 Texas Rangers- Dixie Rails F
154 The Agency- Union Blue F
155 Astoreth's Rage U
156 Harmony of the Heavens C
157 Higher Learning U
158 Unfinished Business R

2000 Deadlands Doomtown Boot Hill

1 A Legal Deck C
2 A Secret Tunnel U
3 Ace in the Hole R
4 Ambition U
5 Ambush U
6 And Stay Down! R
7 Arcane Protection R
8 Arson C
9 Bad Tequila C
10 Bad to the Bone C
11 Bankrupt Morals C
12 Bounty Hunter U
13 Bucket Brigade C
14 Bum Rush U
15 Burn 'Em Down U
16 Claim Jumper U
17 Claws C
18 Clean Up the Town C
19 Cover Fire C
20 Crack Shot U
21 Deputize C
22 Don't Like Yer Looks R
23 Double Dealin' C
24 Dumb Luck C
25 Dust Devil R2
26 Eureka's Rage C
27 Fanning the Hammer C2
28 Flamin' Barrels C
29 Foreclosure U
30 Friends in Low Places C2
31 Funeral Procession R
32 Giddyup! C2
33 Head 'em Off at the Pass C1
34 Headsman's Axe R
35 Hostile Takeover C
36 Jackelope Stampede U
37 Just a Graze U
38 Kidnapping U
39 Lady Luck U
40 Manitou's Control R

41 Manitou's Revenge R
42 Massacre at High Noon R
43 Mines Reopen U
44 Miss Me? R
45 Nice Boots, Chief U
46 No Funny Stuff C
47 No Mint Juleps Here R
48 Only Winged 'Em C
49 Out of Ammo U
50 Pinned Down C
51 Pistol Whip U
52 Refuse to Fall U
53 Relic U
54 Reserves U
55 Rumors C
56 Shallow Grave R
57 Sheriff's Watchin' C
58 Shortcut U
59 Sleep o' the Dead R
60 Snake Eyes R
61 Snakebite C
62 Stitchin' U
63 Sun in Yer Eyes C
64 Take Ya With Me C
65 Termite Infestation C
66 That'll Leave a Scar C
67 Trackin' Teeth R
68 War Paint R
69 Warrant C
70 Wither R
71 2nd Bank of Gomorra U
72 Abandoned Mine R
73 Barkum & Barkum Attorneys U
74 Bookstore R
75 Callahan's Ditch C
76 Colorado Lode R
77 Dead Man's Laughter Lode U
78 Deadland R
79 Den of Eastern Delights R
80 Dispatch Office C
81 Dragon's Nest Strike R
82 Drop in the Ocean Strike C
83 Elysium Fields Mine R
84 Fish Ridge Mine R
85 Foale's Folly C
86 Fortune-Teller's Shop R
87 Golden Mare Hotel R
88 Graveyard U
89 Green-Eye Saloon C
90 Gypsy's Tent U
91 Hell's End Mine U
92 Howlin' Hollow R
93 Jail U
94 King Willy's Mother Lode C
95 Lad Saloon R
96 Legal Offices of _____ R
97 Mental Hospital U
98 Miss Greene's Room U
99 New Moon Saloon U
100 New Town Hall C
101 Observatory U
102 Pacific Maze Railstation R
103 Pike's Puddle Mine C
104 Red Hill Hotel U
105 Rock Ridge Mine R
106 Run-Down Lot C
107 San Simeon Mine C
108 Shark's Grin Lode R
109 Smiley's Shaft C
110 Smiling Lizard Lode R
111 Spirit of Kentucky Shaft C
112 St. Martin's Chapel U
113 Strike Experiment #1 C
114 Stuffed to the Gills Strike R
115 Surveyor's Office U
116 The 1st Bank of Gomorra R
117 The Alright Corral U
118 The Barber's Shop U
119 The Clock Tower U
120 The Courthouse U
121 The Dentist's Office U
122 The Docks U
123 The Lode R
124 The Mission House U
125 The Slaughterhouse U
126 The Tree U
127 The Undertaker's U
128 Tombstone Dispatch Branch Office U
129 Top of the World Lode R
130 Town Well C
131 Buckets Nelson C
132 ...And Scooter Exp. U
133 Abel Owens C
134 Alice Chamberlain C
135 Arizona Jane Exp. R
136 Barthalomew Prospectus R
137 Benjamin Dean U
138 Big Jake... Exp. U
139 Billy No-Neck Exp. R
140 Black Jack Exp. R
141 Bobo LeVeux R
142 Buster Madison Exp. R
143 Cain Regen C
144 Camille Sinclair C
145 Captain Sim Yut-San Exp. R
146 Cassandra C
147 Chao Li C
148 Charlie Flatbush Exp. R
149 Charlie Landers C
150 Chester Nero Exp. U
151 Clell Miller C2
152 Cort Williams C
153 Darren Titus U
154 Deer Eater R
155 Deputy Dave Montreal U
156 Deputy John Templeton Exp. R
157 Desmond Quentin C
158 Doctor Duvalier C
159 Delores Whateley R
160 Dr. Reginald Branson C
161 Dread Wolf Pack C
162 Eagle Rock Exp. C
163 Erik Zarkov R
164 Ezzie U
165 Faminite C
166 Father Juan Navarro C
167 Father Terrance C
168 Fineas Von Landingham Exp. R
169 Gerald Klippstein C
170 Glom U
171 Gus Gallagher Exp. R
172 J.P. Coleman Exp. R
173 James Hastings U
174 Jebediah Whateley U
175 Jenny Cooper C
176 Jessie Freemont Exp. U
177 Katie Karl F
178 Los Ojos Del Dios R
179 Lucifer Whateley U
180 Marcus Perriwinkle C
181 Max Baine C
182 Meredith Singleton Exp. U
183 Mr. Bones C
184 Nate Hunter Exp.2 R
185 Nebuchadnezzar C
186 Nelson Roberts Exp. R
187 Nicodemus Whateley R
188 Peevie C
189 Po Yu Exp. R
190 Prof. Susan Franklin Exp. R
191 Raven Smiles C
192 Raymond Armstrong C
193 Reggie Cornell C
194 Richard Boothe Exp. R
195 Robert Northrop Exp. R
196 Sam Horowitz Exp. R
197 Saul Whateley Exp. R
198 Shigetoshi Hohiro R
199 Shouting Tom C
200 Silas Peacock Exp. C
201 Singing Feather Exp. R
202 Sister Mary Jebediah Exp. R
203 Skunky Swade C
204 Strikes A Hawk U
205 The Drifter R
206 Thunderbird R
207 Two Birds Chirping R
208 Tzipporah Whateley U
209 Unknown Hooded Figure R
210 Victor Navarro Exp. R
211 Walkin' Dead U
212 Walks-in-Footprints R
213 Wall Crawler C
214 Walter Ponds U
215 Wendigo Garrison C
216 William Olson C
217 Windows Derek C
218 Wise Cloud Exp. U
219 Xiong "Wendy" Cheng C
220 A Coach Comes to Town C
221 Army of Gremlins U
222 Dealer's Choice C
223 Drought C
224 Eureka! U
225 Founder's Day U
226 Full Moon U
227 Ghost Infestation R
228 Ghost Rock Fever R
229 Ghost Train U
230 Government Audit U
231 Harvest Moon C
232 Long Arm of the Law R
233 Riot C
234 Sleeping With Shadows U
235 Stampede R
236 Sumner's Revenge U
237 The Sabbath R
238 Wrath O' God R
239 Frank F
240 Acid Gun U
241 Autogyro R
242 Bowie Knife C
243 Corky's Sidearm F
244 Dragon's Claw F
245 Dream Catcher R
246 Electrostatic Pump Gun U
247 Electrothermic Entropy Projector F
248 Flamethrower U
249 Holy Bullets R
250 Infared Spectacles C
251 Kenny C
252 Magnum Bullets C
253 Mr. Prim's Bust F
254 New Hat C
255 Pair of Six-Shooters U
256 Pearl-Handled Revolver C
257 Pocket Watch C
258 Rachel's Sidearm F
259 Raven's Chop F
260 Ray Gun U
261 Roan C
262 Rocket Pack R
263 Shotgun C
264 Sister Mary's Shotgun F
265 Sweaty Dynamite U
266 The Evidence C
267 The Hooded Figure's Scythe F
268 Tin Shield U
269 Unholy Symbol R
270 Whateley Family Bible R
271 Winchester Rifle C
272 Zapper U
273 Blood Curse R
274 Kentucky Windage C
275 Knicknevin's Deal R
276 Looking Glass C
277 Mirror, Mirror U
278 Nightmare Realm C
279 Pact with Darkness U
280 Puppet C
281 Soul Blast C
282 Sympathy for the Devil R
283 Texas Twister U
284 Bedrock C
285 Brewery R
286 Homeless Joe R
287 Pump R
288 Runnin' Water C
289 Second Story U
290 Stained-Glass Windows C
291 Armor Of Righteousness R
292 Burnt Offerin' C
293 Fire and Brimstone U
294 Inspiration R
295 Lay On Hands U
296 Locust Swarm C
297 Sacrifice C
298 Blackjacks F
299 Collegium- The New Front F
300 Law Dogs- Hunter's Office F
301 Maze Rats- Landed Rats F
302 Sioux Union F
303 Sweetrock- Western Corporate Office F
304 The Agency F
305 The Texas Rangers F
306 The Whateleys- Extended Family F
307 Death's Head Joker R
308 Fool's Joker R
309 Joker R
310 Apache Devil Dancers R
311 Blood Oath R
312 Coyote's Laugh R
313 Medicine C
314 Speed of the Wolf U
315 Spirit Warrior R
316 Sticks to Snakes U
317 Summon Spirit R
318 The Spirits Flee R

2000 Deadlands Doomtown Eye for an Eye

1 Agoraphobia C
2 Between the Cracks C
3 Bring It Down! U
4 Claustrophobia C
5 Clean Getaway U
6 Construction Crew U
7 Desperate Measures U
8 Distracted! R
9 Divided Loyalties U
10 Ethics Aside... R
11 Eyes That Cannot See U
12 Faulty Pipes R
13 First To Fall U
14 Flight Of Angels C
15 Get Off My Land! C
16 Giddyup! C
17 Hiding Out U
18 I Gotta Stake in This! C
19 Inner Strength U
20 Insult to Injury C
21 It's For Her Own Good C
22 Jam! U
23 Just What I Need C
24 Last Request R
25 Life of the Party U
26 Lyin' In Wait R
27 Mercy R
28 Midnight Snack U
29 Nyctophobia C
30 One Eyed Jacks are Wild C
31 Phantoms C
32 Rescue Operation R
33 Run 'Em Down! U
34 Sewing Circle C
35 Shave and a Haircut C
36 This'll Teach You R
37 Trouble There, Buck? R
38 Under The Gun U
39 We've Got Hostages R
40 You're Comin' With Us! R
41 You've Got This Comin'! C
42 Ammunitionist U
43 Blasted Prairie U
44 Bloodsport Arena C
45 Channel Fort R
46 Confessional U
47 Deep in the Earth Shaft C
48 Elephant Hill Mausoleum U
49 Exploratory Trench C
50 Freak Show U
51 New Pony Express Office R
52 O'Reilly's Five & Dime R
53 Power Plant C
54 Prison Factory R
55 Prospectus' Secret Workshop R
56 Registry U
57 Salvage Operation U
58 Strikers' Shaft C
59 The C.S.A. Ourobouros R
60 The Perch C
61 Watering Hole C
62 Abel Owens Exp. R
63 Andrew Garret C
64 Animate Hand F
65 April Segarra U
66 Barney Brash C
67 Bites the Hand C
68 Cain Regen Exp. R
69 Charlie Landers Exp. U
70 Darren Titus Exp. U
71 David Hope R
72 Deputy Tophet C
73 Doctor Duvalier Exp. R
74 Doctor Hardstrom U
75 Eagle Rock Exp. 2 F
76 Elijah Exp. 2 F
77 Evan Childes U
78 Father Terrance Exp. R
79 Ghost of My Father U
80 Gnosis C
81 Guardian Angel C
82 Haborym C
83 Jack Brash C
84 Jack Whateley U
85 Jenny Cooper Exp. R
86 Jolinaxas R
87 Jordan Caldwell U
88 Juliet "Jewel" Sumner Exp. R
89 Lillith U
90 Lt. Colonel Frederick Sykes C
91 Min Su Tao C
92 Moloch C
93 Mr. Applegate, Esq. U
94 Mr. Slate Exp. R
95 Old Scratch U
96 Oswald Hardinger Exp. R
97 Perdition R
98 Rachel Sumner Exp. 2 F
99 Raymond Armstrong Exp. U
100 Requiem C
101 Rooster Beenz C
102 Seeking Fury C
103 Sheriff Syn C
104 Shigetoshi Hohiro Exp. R
105 Simon Lambeth R
106 Sin Je U
107 Sister Mercy Winters U
108 Thunderbird Exp. R
109 Two Birds Chirping Exp. U
110 Tzipporah Whateley Exp. R
111 William Rose C
112 Zeke Hillard C
113 All God's Children R
114 Auxiliumortis U
115 Cadaverus Mobilis U
116 Guy Fawkes Day R
117 Poker Night R
118 Rustlers R
119 Working Out the Details C
120 Chip R
121 Bioengineering R
122 Brimstone Bullets R
123 Clovis The Devilbunny U
124 Eagle Bow R
125 Flashfire Bullets C
126 Hatchet C
127 Lucifer's Cane R
128 Lynchin' Noose U
129 Magic Bus V. 2.0 (Death Bus) C
130 Pandora's Box R
131 Sabtabiel's Remains R
132 Screamers U
133 Soul Blast Cannon U
134 Stallion C
135 The Good Book R
136 Three-Card Monte C
137 Three-Piece Suit U
138 Banish U
139 Faustian Deal R
140 Spirit Walk C
141 Abomination Pit U
142 Interior Decorating C
143 Night Sentry U
144 No Way Out! C
145 Recruiter R
146 Sepulcher R
147 Sewer Tunnels U
148 Spring Cleaning U
149 Well Of Souls R
150 Brush with Death C
151 Draw! U
152 Mysterious Ways R
153 Blackjacks- Rachel's Gang F
154 Lost Angels F
155 Sioux- Spirit Warriors F
156 Breath of the Spirits C
157 The Beast Within R
158 War Cry U

2001 Deadlands Doomtown Do Unto Others

1 ...Or after Three?
2 34 Days Without a Bath
3 A Job Well Done
4 Bait and Switch
5 Blood of Gold
6 Burnin' the Midnight Oil
7 Crossfire
8 Crumbling Dam
9 Cup of Joe
10 Discipline
11 Don't Look
12 Drunken Monkey Technique
13 Eyes in the Back of My Head
14 Faith
15 Fear
16 Flying Claw
17 Gaping Maw
18 Ghost Dance
19 Greed
20 Greener Pastures
21 Honor
22 Is This Your Card?
23 It's That Simple
24 Jade King Stance
25 Leopard and Her Cubs
26 Little Shaky there, Pardner?
27 Lost in the Crowd
28 Manhunt
29 Mantis Pinch
30 Mob Justice
31 Not So Fast!
32 Not Who You Were Expectin'?
33 Now, is That on Three...?
34 Oops...
35 Out of Range
36 Overawe
37 Palm of Prevention
38 Plague of Locusts
39 Quick Getaway
40 Reason
41 Rebel Pride
42 Second Shadow
43 Seizing the Pearl of Death
44 Spirit Bond
45 Step Back to Ward Off Monkey
46 Tai Ch'l Technique
47 The Gauntlet
48 Turnabout's Fair Play
49 Watch the Floor
50 What's that Ticking...?
51 Wing Chun Technique
52 Yankee Pride
53 You Goin' Somewhere?
54 You Lookin' For This?
55 Automaton Factory
56 Bilton Protection Agency
57 Boomtown of Soddum
58 Collegium Airstrip
59 Davidson Consulting
60 Duvalier's Field Office
61 Eye Doctor
62 Fickle Fortune Strike
63 Gulgoleth
64 Gun Shop
65 Iron Dragon Arsenal
66 Lyle's Aquatic Emporium
67 Lyndon Station
68 Pocket Strike
69 Shady Jake's
70 Shouting Tom's Tunnel
71 Smiling Lizard Lode Exp.
72 Strike Experiment #3.1
73 The Master's Dojo
74 The Troupe
75 The Undermaze
76 Victory Springs
77 Vigilance Ranch
78 Water Lou's
79 Andra Miles
80 Animate Hand
81 Ashlar Mayfair
82 Bill Jefferson
83 Bloody Ones
84 Bob Bidwell Exp.
85 Bradley Sloane
86 Brigadier-General Patterson Exp.
87 Capt. Allen Graham
88 Carson Gage
89 Chao Li Exp.
90 Charity
91 Chen Li
92 Chiang Shen
93 Deluge
94 Deputized Civilian
95 Dirt-Faced Figueroa
96 Edward Randolph III
97 Elizabeth Goldstein
98 Ezra Whateley
99 Fallen Minion
100 Fineas Von Landingham Exp. 2
101 Gareth
102 Gordo Andrade Exp.
103 Grady Murdock
104 Harley, Son of David
105 Howard Findley Exp. 2
106 Jason "The Kid" Jung
107 Jebediah Whateley Exp.
108 Judge Fayllen Wells
109 Karl Rundgren
110 Killer Kerry Exp.
111 Kyle Conrad
112 Light Stalker
113 Lt. Colonel Devon Graves
114 Mary the Wanderer Exp.
115 Master Chan
116 Master Sergeant Eric Case
117 Nash Bilton Exp. 2
118 Nicodemus Whateley Exp. 2
119 Oliver Kingsley
120 Peevie Exp.
121 Peter Motambu
122 Po Yu Exp. 2
123 Private Daniel Phelts
124 Prof. Sarah Wings
125 Professor Crowe
126 Rev. Noah Whateley
127 Robert Jones
128 Roughneck Mack
129 Running Moose
130 Ruth Whateley
131 Security Guard
132 Shi Kuan
133 Silver Wolf
134 Sister Leila
135 Solomon

136 Steve Elfinbein
137 Tabitha
138 Teresa Howe
139 The 37th Chamber
140 The Amazing Xemo Exp.
141 The Ancients
142 The Bloodless
143 The Lurking Fear
144 The Swarm
145 Theodore White
146 Timmy Derrick Exp.
147 Tucker Hastings
148 Vampiric Dance Hall Girl
149 Widow Withers
150 William Rose Exp.
151 Windows Derek Exp.
152 Yung Kim
153 Zombie Miners
154 ...Before the Dawn
155 Enter the Dragon
156 It's Always Darkest...
157 Old Friends Come Knockin'
158 Startin' Over
159 The Last Kingdom
160 The Quarantine Ends!
161 The Sky is Falling
162 Union Withdrawal
163 Ascendance
164 Bi-Plane
165 Consecrated Bullets
166 Dim Eyes
167 Ghostrock Cannon
168 Gift of the Thunderbird
169 Hang Glider
170 Kang's Pride
171 Katie Karl's Calibrated Pistols
172 Oswald's New Chair
173 Pepper Box Hold-Out
174 R.H. II
175 Roger and Spencer .44
176 The Claw
177 The Damacles
178 Wild Dingos
179 Cardsharp
180 Imprisonment
181 Jinx
182 Phantasm
183 Silver-Tongued Devil
184 Unearthly Beacon
185 Caroline
186 Chain Gang
187 Disrepair
188 Hardinger-One
189 Previous Tennant
190 Sprinkler System
191 Watering Trough
192 Dust to Dust
193 Collegium- Wasatch Rails
194 Maze Rats- Iron Dragon
195 Whateleys- Black Circle
196 Dream Walk
197 Horse Whispers
198 Sacred Ground
199 Secret Paths

1998-01 Deadlands Doomtown Promos

1 Hit Me
2 No Mas
3 Readin' the Stars
4 Start Again
5 Stop the Presses
6 Big Doc's Casino
7 Bounty Hunter (virtual)
8 Crawford Talmadge
9 Harrowed Kenny
10 Lilith Vanderkamp Exp.
11 Raymond Armstrong
12 Eureka!
13 Eye of the Storm
14 Strange Days
15 Jack's Left Shooter
16 Lucky Rabbit's Foot
17 Blackjacks
18 Collegium
19 Law Dogs- Mob Justice (virtual)
20 Law Dogs
21 Lost Angels - Guardian Angels (virtual)
22 Sioux Union
23 Sweetrock
24 The Agency
25 The Flock
26 The Maze Rats
27 The Texas Rangers
28 Whateley Family Estate
29 Joker

2014 Dice Masters Avengers vs. X-Men

1 Beast, Big Boy Blue S
2 Beast, Genetic Expert S
3 Beast, Mutate #666 S
4 Captain America, American Hero S
5 Captain America, Natural Leader S
6 Captain America, Star-Spangled Avenger S
7 Hulk, Anger Issues S
8 Hulk, Annihilator S
9 Hulk, Jade Giant S
10 Human Torch, Flame On S
11 Human Torch, Matchstick S
12 Human Torch, Playing with Fire S
13 Iron Man, Inventor S
14 Iron Man, Philanthropist S
15 Iron Man, Playboy S
16 Spider-Man, Tiger S
17 Spider-Man, Webhead S
18 Spider-Man, Webslinger S
19 Storm, African Princess S
20 Storm, Goddess of the Plains S
21 Storm, Ro S
22 Thor, Legendary Warrior S
23 Thor, Lord of Asgard S
24 Thor, Odinson S
25 Distraction, Basic Action Card S
26 Focus Power, Basic Action Card S
27 Force Beam, Basic Action Card S
28 Gearing Up, Basic Action Card S
29 Inner Rage, Basic Action Card S
30 Invulnerability, Basic Action Card S
31 Power Bolt, Basic Action Card S
32 Smash!, Basic Action Card S
33 Take Cover, Basic Action Card S
34 Thrown Car, Basic Action Card S
35 Angel, High Ground C
36 Black Widow, Natural C
37 Colossus, Unstoppable C
38 Cyclops, Slim C
39 Deadpool, Assassin C
40 Doctor Doom, Reed Richards' Rival C
41 Doctor Octopus, Megalomaniac C
42 Doctor Strange, Sorcerer Supreme C
43 Gambit, Ace in the Hole C
44 Ghost Rider, Johnny Blaze C
45 Green Goblin, Goblin-Lord C
46 Hawkeye, Longbow C
47 Loki, Trickster C
48 Magneto, Former Comrade C
49 Mr. Fantastic, Brilliant Scientist C
50 Mystique, Unknown C
51 Nick Fury, Mr. Anger C
52 Nightcrawler, Fuzzy Elf C
53 Nova, Quasar C
54 Phoenix, Ms. Psyche C
55 Professor X, Principal C
56 Punisher, McRook C
57 Rogue, Anna Raven C
58 Silver Surfer, Silverado C
59 Thing, Ever-Lovin' Blue-Eyed C
60 Venom, Eddie Brock C
61 War Machine, Combat Comrade C
62 Wolverine, Wildboy C
63 Mjolnir, Fist of the Righteous C
64 Vibranium Shield, One of a Kind C
65 Angel, Avenging Angel U
66 Beast, Kreature U
67 Captain America, Sentinel of Liberty U
68 Colossus, Russian Bear U
69 Cyclops, If Looks Could Kill U
70 Deadpool, Jack U
71 Doctor Doom, Nemesis U
72 Doctor Octopus, Fully Armed U
73 Doctor Strange, Master of the Mystic Arts U
74 Gambit, Le Diable Blanc U
75 Ghost Rider, Spirit of Vengeance U
76 Hawkeye, Br'er Hawkeye U
77 Hulk, Green Goliath U
78 Human Torch, Johnny Storm U
79 Iron Man, Billionaire U
80 Loki, Illusionist U
81 Magneto, Holocaust Survivor U
82 Mystique, Shapeshifter U
83 Nick Fury, WWII Veteran U
84 Nightcrawler, Abandoned U
85 Nova, Buckethead U
86 Phoenix, Redd U
87 Professor X, Powerful Telepath U
88 Punisher, Vigilante U
89 Rogue, Anna Marie U
90 Silver Surfer, Sentinel U
91 Spider-Man, Wall-Crawler U
92 Storm, Wind-Rider U
93 Thing, Grim Ben U
94 Thor, God of Thunder U
95 Venom, Mac Gargan U
96 War Machine, Parnell Jacobs U
97 Mjolnir, Forged by Odin U
98 Vibranium Shield, Irreplaceable U
99 Angel, Soaring R
100 Black Widow, Killer Instinct R
101 Colossus, Piotr Rasputin R
102 Cyclops, Scott Summers R
103 Deadpool, Chiyonosake R
104 Doctor Doom, Victor R
105 Doctor Octopus, Mad Scientist R
106 Doctor Strange, Probably a Charlatan R
107 Gambit, Cardsharp R
108 Ghost Rider, Brimstone Biker R
109 Green Goblin, Norman Osborn R
110 Hawkeye, Robin Hood R
111 Loki, Gem-Keeper R
112 Magneto, Sonderkommando R
113 Mr. Fantastic, The Invincible Man R
114 Mystique, Could Be Anyone R
115 Nick Fury, Patch R
116 Nightcrawler, Circus Freak R
117 Nova, The Human Rocket R
118 Phoenix, Jeannie R
119 Professor X, Charles Francis Xavier R
120 Punisher, Big Nothing R
121 Rogue, Can't Touch This R
122 Silver Surfer, Sky-Rider R
123 Thing, Idol of Millions R
124 Venom, Angelo Fortunado R
125 War Machine, James Rhodes R
126 Wolverine, Formerly Weapon Ten R
127 Mjolnir, Thor's Hammer R
128 Vibranium Shield, Cap's Protection R
129 Black Widow, Tsarina SR
130 Green Goblin, Gobby SR
131 Mr. Fantastic, Elastic SR
132 Wolverine, Canucklehead SR

2014 Dice Masters Marvel Organized Play

1 Teamwork LE
2 Rally! LE
3 Deflection LE
4 Teleport LE
5 Collateral Damage LE
6 Takedown LE
7 Thor, The Might LE
8 Spider-Man, The Amazing LE
9 Wolverine, Walking His Own Path LE
10 Colossus LE
11 Iron Man, Phoenix Buster LE
12 Cyclops, Phoenix Force LE
13 Phoenix Force, Force of Nature LE

2014 Dice Masters Uncanny X-Men

1 Angel, Air Transport S
2 Angel, Inspiring S
3 Angel, Superhero S
4 Cyclops, Optic Blast S
5 Cyclops, Overlook S
6 Cyclops, Superhero S
7 Iceman, Cryokinetic S
8 Iceman, Robert Louis Drake S
9 Iceman, Too Cool for Words S
10 Juggernaut, Cain Marko S
11 Juggernaut, Unstoppable S
12 Juggernaut, Archvillain S
13 Kitty Pryde, Ariel S
14 Kitty Pryde, Sprite S
15 Kitty Pryde, Shadowcat S
16 Magneto, Field Control S
17 Magneto, Will to Live S
18 Magneto, Archvillain S
19 Quicksilver, Pietro Maximoff S
20 Quicksilver, Thanks to Isotope E S
21 Quicksilver, Former Villain S
22 Wolverine, The Best There Is S
23 Wolverine, Not Very Nice S
24 Wolverine, Superhero S
25 Ambush S
26 Enrage S
27 Feedback S
28 Imprisoned S
29 Possession S
30 Reckless Melee S
31 Relentless S
32 Selective Shield S
33 Take That, Villain! S
34 Transfer Power S
35 Ant-Man, Biophysicist C
36 Apocalypse, Awakened C
37 Bishop, Omega Squad C
38 Black Panther, Wakanda Chief C
39 Cable, Man of Action C
40 Captain America, Special Ops C
41 Emma Frost, Archvillain C
42 Falcon, Samuel Wilson C
43 Iron Man, Upright C
44 Magik, Illyana Rasputina C
45 Marvel Girl, Telekinetic C
46 Mister Sinister, Archvillain C
47 Mystique, Ageless C
48 Namor, The Sub-Mariner C
49 Professor X, Recruiting Young Mutants C
50 Psylocke, Betsy Braddock C
51 Pyro, Saint-John Allerdyce C
52 Red Hulk, Thunderbolt Ross C
53 Sabretooth, Something to Prove C
54 Scarlet Witch, Wanda Maximoff C
55 Sentinel, Mutant Hunter C
56 She-Hulk, Jennifer Walters C
57 Spider-Man, Hero for Hire C
58 Storm, Weather Witch C
59 Toad, Tongue Lashing C
60 Vision, Density Control C
61 X-23, Scent of Murder C
62 Cerebro, Cybernetic Intelligence C
63 Angel, Air Transport U
64 Ant-Man, Pym Particles U
65 Apocalypse, Archvillain U
66 Bishop, Branded a Mutant U
67 Black Panther, T'Challa U
68 Cable, Techno-Organic U
69 Captain America, "Follow Me!" U
70 Cyclops, Field Leader U
71 Falcon, Recon U
72 Iceman, Mister Friese U
73 Juggernaut, Kuurth U
74 Kitty Pryde, Just a Phase U
75 Magik, Lightchylde U
76 Magneto, Hellfire Club U
77 Marvel Girl, Superhero U
78 Mister Sinister, Nasty Boy U
79 Mystique, Raven Darkholme U
80 Namor, Atlantean U
81 Professor X, Founder U
82 Psylocke, Ninjutsu U
83 Pyro, Pyrokinetic U
84 Quicksilver, Villainous U
85 Red Hulk, a.k.a. Rulk U
86 Sabretooth, Survivor U
87 Sentinel, Archvillain U
88 She-Hulk, Lady Liberator U
89 Storm, Superhero U
90 Toad, Sniveling Servant U
91 Vision, Android U
92 Wolverine, Antihero U
93 X-23, Assassin U
94 Cerebro, Supercomputer U
95 Ant-Man, The Insect World R
96 Apocalypse, Time of Testing R
97 Bishop, XSE R
98 Black Panther, Diversion R
99 Cable, Time Traveller R
100 Captain America, Superhero R
101 Emma Frost, Graceful R
102 Falcon, Air Strike R
103 Iron Man, Superhero R
104 Magik, Redflag #133 R
105 Marvel Girl, Telepath R
106 Mister Sinister, Nathaniel Essex R
107 Mystique, Alias: You R
108 Namor, Imperius Rex R
109 Professor X, Trainer R
110 Psylocke, Kwannon the Assassin R
111 Pyro, Uncontrolled R
112 Red Hulk, Superhero R
113 Sabretooth, Superpowered R
114 Scarlet Witch, Unity Squad R
115 Sentinel, Robot R
116 She-Hulk, Superhero R
117 Spider-Man, Spider Sense R
118 Storm, Lady Liberator R
119 Toad, Mortimer Toynbee R
120 Vision, Victor Shade R
121 X-23, Killing Machine R
122 Cerebro, Mutant Hunter R
123 Emma Frost, Hellfire Club SR
124 Iron Man, Industrialist SR
125 Scarlet Witch, Controls Probability SR
126 Spider-Man, Superhero SR

2015 Dice Masters Avengers Age of Ultron

1 Black Widow, Natasha S
2 Black Widow, Spy S
3 Black Widow, Cold Warrior S
4 Captain America, Super Soldier S
5 Captain America, The First Avenger S
6 Captain America, Man out of Time S
7 Hawkeye, Formerly Ronin S
8 Hawkeye, Clint S
9 Hawkeye, Trick shot S
10 Hulk, Smash! S
11 Hulk, Bruce Banner S
12 Hulk, Big Green Bruiser S
13 Iron Man, Big Man S
14 Iron Man, Genius S
15 Iron Man, Invincible S
16 Thor, Not Who You Expected? S
17 Thor, Goddess of Thunder S
18 Thor, Worthy S
19 Ultron, Bringing Order S
20 Ultron, Peacekeeper Gone Wrong S
21 Ultron, Creation S
22 Vision, Phasin S
23 Vision, Ultron's Spy S
24 Vision, Negotiator S
25 Assemble S
26 Call them Out! S
27 Coordinated Strike S
28 Enslavement S
29 Hulk Out S
30 Infiltrate S
31 Nasty Plot S
32 Ready to Rocket! S
33 Surprise Attack S
34 The Oppression Begins S
35 Baron Zemo, Helmut J. Zemo C
36 Beast, Dr. Hank McCoy C
37 Black Widow, Oktober C
38 Bucky, James Buchanan Barnes C
39 Captain America, Symbol of Freedom C
40 Captain Marvel, Maj. Carol Danvers C
41 Captain Universe, Tamara Devoux C
42 Daredevil, Matthew Murdock, Attorney-at-Law C
43 Enchantress, Amora C
44 Gamora, Assassin C
45 Giant Man, Dr. Henry Pym C
46 Groot, Reincarnated C
47 Hawkeye, What Kind of Arrow? C
48 Hulk, Gamma Powered C
49 Hyperion, Eternal C
50 Iron Man, Tinhead C
51 Jocasta, Titanium Body C
52 Kang, The Conqueror C
53 Loki, Loki Laufeyson C
54 Loki's Scepter, Magic C
55 Maria Hill, Avengers Liaison C
56 Moondragon, Heather Douglas C
57 Nick Fury, Sgt. Fury C
58 Odin, The All-Father C
59 Pepper Potts, Personal Secretary of Tony Stark C
60 Phil Coulson, Inspirational Leader C
61 Red Skull, Johann Schmidt C
62 Rocket Raccoon, "Blam! Murdered you!" C
63 S.H.I.E.L.D. Agent, Level 6 Access C
64 S.H.I.E.L.D. Helicarrier, Iliad C
65 Spider-Woman, Jessica Drew C
66 Starhawk, Stakar Ogord C
67 Star-Lord, Peter Jason Quill C
68 Thanos, Courting Death C
69 Thor, Thunderer C
70 Ultron, New World Order C
71 Ultron Drone, 01000100 01101001 01100101 C
72 Vision, Punisher C
73 Wasp, The Winsome Wasp C
74 Wonder Man, Simon Williams C
75 Baron Zemo, Master of Evil U
76 Beast, Bouncing Blue Beast U
77 Bucky, Cap's Sidekick U
78 Captain Marvel, Human/Kree Hybrid U
79 Captain Universe, Uni-Power U
80 Daredevil, Man Without Fear U
81 Enchantress, Manipulator U
82 Gamora, Raised by Thanos U
83 Giant Man, Original Avenger U
84 Groot, Protector U
85 Hyperion, Avenger U
86 Jocasta, Wife of Ultron U
87 Kang, Rama-Tut U
88 Loki, Trickster God U
89 Loki's Scepter, Mind Control U
90 Maria Hill, Trained Agent U
91 Moondragon, Dragon of the Moon U
92 Nick Fury, Life Model Decoy U
93 Odin, Gungnir U
94 Pepper Potts, CEO of Stark Industries U
95 Phil Coulson, Man with the Plan U
96 Red Skull, Embodiment of Evil U
97 Rocket Raccoon, Weapons Expert U
98 S.H.I.E.L.D. Agent, You're Not Cleared For That U
99 S.H.I.E.L.D. Helicarrier, Argonaut U
100 Spider-Woman, Playing Both Sides U
101 Starhawk, The One Who Knows U
102 Star-Lord, Reluctant Prince U
103 Thanos, The Mad Titan U
104 Ultron Drone, 1 of a Million U
105 Wasp, Bio-Electric Blasts U
106 Wonder Man, Ionic Energy U
107 Baron Zemo, Thunderbolt R
108 Beast, Not Your Average Pretty Face R
109 Bucky, Soldier R
110 Captain Marvel, Inspiration R
111 Daredevil, Guardian of Hell's Kitchen R
112 Enchantress, Hypnotic R
113 Gamora, Deadliest Woman In The Universe R
114 Giant Man, Pym Particles R
115 Hyperion, Atomic Vision R
116 Kang, Time-Ship R
117 Loki, Agent of Asgard R
118 Loki's Scepter, Piercing R
119 Maria Hill, Director of S.H.I.E.L.D. R
120 Moondragon, Daughter of the Destroyer R
121 Nick Fury, Schemes Upon Schemes R
122 Odin, Asgardian Monarch R
123 Pepper Potts, Stark International R
124 Phil Coulson, Expert Recruiter R
125 Red Skull, "Hail Hydra!" R
126 Rocket Raccoon, Smartest Mammal In The D'ast Galaxy R
127 S.H.I.E.L.D. Agent, Need to Know Basis R
128 S.H.I.E.L.D. Helicarrier, Odyssey R
129 Spider-Woman, Pheromones R
130 Starhawk, Precognitive R
131 Star-Lord, Element Gun R
132 Ultron Drone, Swarm of Destruction R
133 Wasp, Founding Avenger R
134 Wonder Man, Movie Star R
135 Captain Universe, Enigma Force SR
136 Groot, We Are Groot SR
137 Jocasta, Patterned After Janet SR
138 Thanos, Infinite SR
139 Magneto, Magnetic Monster SR
140 Red Skull, Undying Evil SR
141 Gladiator, Intergalactic Terror SR
142 Electro, Cooked Meat SR

2015 Dice Masters Dungeons and Dragons Battle for Faerun

COMPLETE SET W/O S (138) 100.00 200.00
1 Beholder, Minion Aberration S
2 Beholder, Apprentice Aberration S
3 Beholder, Master Aberration S
4 Blue Dragon, Minion Dragon S
5 Blue Dragon, Apprentice Dragon S
6 Blue Dragon, Master Dragon S
7 Gelatinous Cube, Minion Ooze S
8 Gelatinous Cube, Apprentice Ooze S
9 Gelatinous Cube, Master Ooze S
10 Green Dragon, Minion Dragon S
11 Green Dragon, Apprentice Dragon S
12 Green Dragon, Master Dragon S
13 Halfling Thief, Minion Harper S
14 Halfling Thief, Apprentice Emerald Enclave S
15 Halfling Thief, Master Zhentarim S
16 Human Paladin, Minion Order of the Gauntlet S
17 Human Paladin, Apprentice Harper S
18 Human Paladin, Master Lords Apprentice S
19 Troll, Minion Humanoid S
20 Troll, Apprentice Humanoid S
21 Troll, Master Humanoid S
22 Vampire, Minion Undead S
23 Vampire, Apprentice Undead S
24 Vampire, Master Undead S
25 Beholder, Lesser Aberration C 1.50 4.00
26 Blue Dragon, Lesser Dragon C 1.00 2.50
27 Carrion Crawler, Lesser Aberration C .12 .30
28 Copper Dragon, Lesser Dragon C .60 1.50
29 Dracolich, Lesser Undead Dragon C .12 .30
30 Drow Assassin, Lesser Humanoid C .12 .30
31 Dwarf Cleric, Lesser Order of the Gauntlet C .12 .30
32 Elf Wizard, Lesser Harper C .50 1.25
33 Frost Giant, Lesser Elemental C .12 .30
34 Gelatinous Cube, Lesser Ooze C 1.00 2.50
35 Green Dragon, Lesser Dragon C 1.25 3.00
36 Half-Dragon, Lesser Humanoid C .12 .30
37 Half-Orc Fighter, Lesser Emerald Alliance C .60 1.50
38 Halfling Thief, Lesser Lords Alliance C 1.50 4.00
39 Human Paladin, Lesser Emerald Enclave C 1.25 3.00
40 Invisible Stalker, Lesser Elemtal C .12 .30
41 Kobold, Lesser Humanoid C .75 2.00
42 Manticore, Lesser Beast C .50 1.25
43 Mind Flayer, Lesser Humanoid C .40 1.00
44 Minotaur, Lesser Humanoid C .50 1.25
45 Mummy, Lesser Undead C .60 1.50
46 Orc, Lesser Humanoid C .60 1.50
47 Owlbear, Lesser Beast C .12 .30
48 Pit Fiend, Lesser Fiend C .12 .30
49 Purple Worm, Lesser Beast C .12 .30
50 Red Dragon, Lesser Dragon C .60 1.50
51 Skeleton, Lesser Undead C .12 .30
52 Stirge, Lesser Beast C .60 1.50
53 Tarrasque, Lesser Aberration C .75 2.00
54 Treant, Lesser Beast C .12 .30
55 Troll, Lesser Humanoid C 1.50 4.00
56 Umber Hulk, Lesser Beast C 1.00 2.50

57 Unicorn, Lesser Beast C .12 .30
58 Vampire, Lesser Undead C 1.50 4.00
59 Wererat, Lesser Lycanthrope C .12 .30
60 Zombie, Lesser Undead C .12 .30
61 Magic Helmet, Lesser Gear C .12 .30
62 Magic Sword, Lesser Gear C .12 .30
63 Limited Wish, Lesser Spell C .12 .30
64 Prismatic Spray, Lesser Spell C .12 .30
65 Carrion Crawler, Greater Aberration U 1.50 4.00
66 Copper Dragon, Greater Dragon U 1.50 4.00
67 Dracolich, Greater Undead Dragon U 2.00 5.00
68 Drow Assassin, Greater Humanoid U 1.50 4.00
69 Dwarf Cleric, Greater Emerald Enclave U 1.50 4.00
70 Elf Wizard, Greater Order of the Gauntlet U 1.50 4.00
71 Frost Giant, Greater Elemental U .20 .50
72 Half-Dragon, Greater Humanoid U 1.50 4.00
73 Half-Orc Fighter, Greater Lords Alliance U 1.50 4.00
74 Invisible Stalker, Greater Elemental U 1.50 4.00
75 Kobold, Greater Humanoid U 1.25 3.00
76 Manticore, Greater Beast U .20 .50
77 Mind Flayer, Greater Humanoid U .20 .50
78 Minotaur, Greater Humanoid U 2.00 5.00
79 Mummy, Greater Undead U 1.25 3.00
80 Orc, Greater Humanoid U .20 .50
81 Owlbear, Greater Beast U 1.50 4.00
82 Pit Fiend, Greater Fiend U .20 .50
83 Purple Worm, Greater Beast U 1.50 4.00
84 Red Dragon, Greater Dragon U 2.00 5.00
85 Skeleton, Greater Undead U .20 .50
86 Stirge, Greater Beast U 1.50 4.00
87 Tarrasque, Greater Aberration U .20 .50
88 Treant, Greater Beast U 1.25 3.00
89 Umber Hulk, Greater Beast U .20 .50
90 Unicorn, Greater Beast U 1.25 3.00
91 Wererat, Greater Lycanthrope U 2.00 5.00
92 Zombie, Greater Undead U 1.25 3.00
93 Magic Helmet, Greater Gear U 1.50 4.00
94 Magic Sword, Greater Gear U 1.50 4.00
95 Limited Wish, Greater Spell U .75 2.00
96 Prismatic Spray, Greater Spell U 1.50 4.00
97 Carrion Crawler, Paragon Aberration R .75 2.00
98 Copper Dragon, Paragon Dragon R 2.00 5.00
99 Dracolich, Paragon Undead Dragon R 3.00 8.00
100 Drow Assassin, Paragon Humanoid R 2.50 6.00
101 Dwarf Cleric, Paragon Lords Alliance R 3.00 8.00
102 Elf Wizard, Paragon Zhentarim R 2.50 6.00
103 Frost Giant, Paragon Elemental R .75 2.00
104 Half-Dragon, Paragon Humanoid R 2.00 5.00
105 Half-Orc Fighter, Paragon Zhentarim R 2.00 5.00
106 Invisible Stalker, Paragon Elemental R 2.00 5.00
107 Kobold, Paragon Humanoid R 2.00 5.00
108 Manticore, Paragon Beast R .75 2.00
109 Minotaur, Paragon Humanoid R .75 2.00
110 Mummy, Paragon Undead R 2.00 5.00
111 Orc, Paragon Humanoid R 2.00 5.00
112 Owlbear, Paragon Beast R .75 2.00
113 Pit Fiend, Paragon Fiend R 2.00 5.00
114 Purple Worm, Paragon Beast R 2.00 5.00
115 Skeleton, Paragon Undead R 1.50 4.00
116 Treant, Paragon Beast R 2.00 5.00
117 Umber Hulk, Paragon Beast R 2.00 5.00
118 Unicorn, Paragon Beast R 2.00 5.00
119 Wererat, Paragon Lycanthrope R .75 2.00
120 Zombie, Paragon Undead R 1.50 4.00
121 Magic Helmet, Paragon Gear R 3.00 8.00
122 Magic Sword, Paragon Gear R .75 2.00
123 Limited Wish, Paragon Spell R 2.50 6.00
124 Prismatic Spray, Paragon Spell R .75 2.00
125 Mind Flayer, Epic Humanoid SR 12.00 30.00
126 Red Dragon, Epic Dragon SR 10.00 25.00
127 Stirge, Epic Beast SR 10.00 25.00
128 Tarrasque, Epic Aberration SR 8.00 20.00
129 Blessing, Basic Action Card S
130 Charm, Basic Action Card S
131 Cone of Cold, Basic Action Card S
132 Dimension Door, Basic Action Card S
133 Finger of Death, Basic Action Card S
134 Fireball, Basic Action Card S
135 Magic Missile, Basic Action Card S
136 Polymorph, Basic Action Card S
137 Resurrection, Basic Action Card S
138 Stinking Cloud, Basic Action Card S

2015 Dice Masters Justice League

COMPLETE SET W/O S (138) 120.00 250.00
1 Batman, Bruce Wayne S
2 Batman, The Dark Knight S
3 Batman, World's Greatest Detective S
4 Darkseid, God of Apokolips S
5 Darkseid, In Search of Anti-Life S
6 Darkseid, Immortal S
7 Deathstroke, Slade Wilson S
8 Deathstroke, The Terminator S
9 Deathstroke, Villain for Hire S
10 Green Arrow, Oliver Queen S
11 Green Arrow, The Battling Bowman S
12 Green Arrow, The Emerald Archer S
13 Martian Manhunter, J'onn J'onzz S
14 Martian Manhunter, Founding Member S
15 Martian Manhunter, John Jones S
16 Superman, Man of Steel S
17 Superman, Last Son of Krypton S
18 Superman, Kal-El S
19 Wonder Woman, Daughter of Zeus S
20 Wonder Woman, Warrior Princess S
21 Wonder Woman, Champion of Themyscira S 25.00 60.00
22 Zatanna, Zatanna Zatara S
23 Zatanna, Actual Magician S
24 Zatanna, Stage Magician S
25 Anger Issues S
26 Casualties S
27 Fist of Fury S
28 Phantom Zone S
29 Pick Your Battles S
30 Righteous Charge S
31 Save Civilians S
32 Shockwave S
33 Villainous Pact S
34 Vulnerability S
35 Aquaman, Arthur Curry C .12 .30
36 The Atom, Ray Palmer C .12 .30
37 Batarang, Tool of the Bat C .12 .30
38 Batman, The Caped Crusader C .12 .30
39 Black Manta, David C .12 .30
40 Blue Beetle, Jaime Reyes C .12 .30
41 Booster Gold, Michael Jon Carter C .12 .30
42 Brainiac, Terror of Kandor C .12 .30
43 Captain Cold, Leonard Snart C .12 .30
44 Catwoman, Selina Kyle C .12 .30
45 Cheetah, Cursed Archaeologist C .12 .30
46 Constantine, Antihero C .12 .30
47 Cyborg, Vic Stone C .12 .30
48 Darkseid, Omega Beams C .12 .30
49 Deadman, Boston Brand C .12 .30
50 Deathstroke, Weapons Master C 1.50 4.00
51 Firestorm, Jason and Ronnie C .12 .30
52 The Flash, Barry Allen C .12 .30
53 Green Arrow, Former Mayor C .12 .30
54 Green Lantern, Hal Jordan C .12 .30
55 Harley Quinn, Dr. Harleen Quinzel C 15.00 40.00
56 Hawkman, Thanagarian C .12 .30
57 The Joker, Unpredictable C .12 .30
58 Katana, Tatsu Yamashiro C .12 .30
59 Lantern Power Ring, Energy Projection C .12 .30
60 Lex Luthor, Power Suit C .12 .30
61 Martian Manhunter, Green Martian C .12 .30
62 Red Tornado, Rannian C .12 .30
63 Robin, Boy Wonder C .12 .30
64 Shazam!, Billy Batson C .12 .30
65 Sinestro, Instills Fear C .12 .30
66 Solomon Grundy, Born on a Monday C .12 .30
67 Stargirl, Courtney Whitmore C .12 .30
68 Superman, Not a Bird or a Plane C 1.50 4.00
69 Swamp Thing, Dr. Alec Holland C .12 .30
70 Vibe, Francisco Ramon C .12 .30
71 Vixen, Mari McCabe C .12 .30
72 Wonder Woman, Princess Diana C .12 .30
73 Zatanna, Backwards Magic C .12 .30
74 Aquaman, King of Atlantis U 1.50 4.00
75 The Atom, Subatomic Superhero U 1.25 3.00
76 Batarang, Instrument of Distraction U .20 .50
77 Black Canary, Crime-Fighter U 3.00 8.00
78 Black Manta, Deep Sea Deviant U .20 .50
79 Blue Beetle, Magically Infused U .20 .50
80 Booster Gold, Glory-Seeking Showboat U .20 .50
81 Brainiac, Collector of Worlds U .20 .50
82 Captain Cold, Leonard Wynters U .20 .50
83 Cheetah, Powered by Urkartaga U .20 .50
84 Constantine, Con Artist U 4.00 10.00
85 Cyborg, Expectionally Gifted U 1.50 4.00
86 Deadman, Possessive Talents U 1.50 4.00
87 Firestorm, Atom Rearranger U 2.50 6.00
88 The Flash, Speedster U 3.00 8.00
89 Green Lantern, Willpower U 1.50 4.00
90 Harley Quinn, Femme Fatale U 1.50 4.00
91 Hawkman, World's Fiercest Attacker U .20 .50
92 The Joker, Clown Prince of Crime U .20 .50
93 Katana, Outsider U .20 .50
94 Lantern Power Ring, Energy Constructs U .20 .50
95 Lex Luthor, Former President U .20 .50
96 Red Tornado, Lab Creation U 1.25 3.00
97 Robin, Circus Star U 1.25 3.00
98 Shazam!, Wisdom of Solomon U 1.50 4.00
99 Sinestro, Order Through Fear U 1.50 4.00
100 Solomon Grundy, Died on a Saturday U 1.25 3.00
101 Stargirl, Yankee Poodle Fangirl U 1.25 3.00
102 Swamp Thing, Plant Elemental U .20 .50
103 Vibe, Paco U 1.25 3.00
104 Vixen, Healing Factor U .20 .50
105 The Atom, Science Advisor R 2.50 6.00
106 Aquaman, Orin R 2.00 5.00
107 Batarang, From Wayne Enterprises R 2.00 5.00
108 Black Canary, Canary Cry R 3.00 8.00
109 Black Manta, Artificial Gills R 1.50 4.00
110 Blue Beetle, High School Hero R 1.50 4.00
111 Booster Gold, High Publicity Hijinks R .75 2.00
112 Brainiac, Twelfth-Level Intelligence R 2.00 5.00
113 Captain Cold, Master of Absolute Zero R 2.00 5.00
114 Catwoman, Femme Fatale R 2.00 5.00
115 Cheetah, Dr. Barbara Ann Minerva R 2.00 5.00
116 Cyborg, Mentor R 2.00 5.00
117 Deadman, Embracing Life R 1.50 4.00
118 Firestorm, Matter Master R 2.50 6.00
119 Green Lantern, Brightest Day R 3.00 8.00
120 Harley Quinn, Psychopathic Psychiatrist R 4.00 10.00
121 Hawkman, Carter Hall R 2.50 6.00
122 The Joker, Red Hood R 3.00 8.00
123 Katana, Soultaker Sword R 2.50 6.00
124 Lantern Power Ring, Flight R 2.00 5.00
125 Lex Luthor, Billionaire Industrialist R 2.50 6.00
126 Red Tornado, Android R 2.00 5.00
127 Robin, Acrobatic Adolescent R 6.00 15.00
128 Shazam!, Strength of Hercules R 2.00 5.00
129 Sinestro, Sinestro Corps Leader R 2.50 6.00
130 Solomon Grundy, Buried on a Sunday R 2.00 5.00
131 Stargirl, Star-Spangled Kid R 2.00 5.00
132 Swamp Thing, Part of The Green R 3.00 8.00
133 Vibe, Formerly Hardline R 2.50 6.00
134 Vixen, Animal Mimicry R 2.50 6.00
135 Black Canary, Dinah Laurel Lance SR 10.00 25.00
136 Catwoman, Nine Lives SR 12.00 30.00
137 Constantine, Hellblazer SR 20.00 50.00
138 The Flash, Connected to the Speed Force SR 12.00 30.00

2004 Digimon CCG Eternal Courage

DD015 Joe U
DD016 Sora C
DD017 Takato C
DD018 Digimon Emperor U
DD019 T.K. U
DD020 Mimi C
DD021 Tai U
DM067 Betamon C
DM068 Candlemon C
DM069 Aurumon C
DM070 Prariemon C
DM071 Rinkmon C
DM072 Lynxmon C
DM073 Kuwagamon C
DM074 Aquilamon U
DM075 Stingmon U
DM076 ExVeemon HOLO
DM077 Flamedramon HOLO
DM078 Kurisarimon HOLO
DM079 Boarmon C
DM080 Greymon C
DM081 Opossummon U
DM082 Leomon HOLO
DM083 Shakkoumon HOLO
DM084 Silphymon HOLO
DM085 Rapidmon G
DM086 MagnaAngemon U
DM087 Dinobeemon C
DM088 Angewomon HOLO
DM089 Taomon G
DM090 WereGarurumon HOLO
DM091 WarGrowlmon C
DM092 Infermon G
DM093 Paildramon R
DM094 Valkyrimon Super
DM095 MegaGargomon G
DM096 Seraphimon Super
DM097 GranKuwagamon HOLO
DM098 Magnadramon HOLO
DM099 Vikemon HOLO
DM100 Sakuyamon Super
DM101 WarGreymon HOLO
DM102 Diaboromon Super
DM103 Imperialdramon (Fighter Mode) G
DM104 Gallantmon (Crimson Mode) Super
DV005 Grani U
MD017 Digital Bandage C
MD018 Ice Arrow C
MD019 The Aegis C
MD020 Digidote C
MD021 Fire Crystal C
MD022 Digital Gate C
MD023 Excalibur C
MD024 Positron Laser C
MD025 Collapsed Control Spire C
MD026 Giga Claws C
MD027 King Device U
MD028 Rook Device U
MD029 Knight Device U
MD030 Sacred Fruit HOLO

2004 Digimon CCG Hybrid Warriors

COMPLETE SET (60)
BOOSTER BOX ()
BOOSTER PACK ()
RELEASED ON
DD022 Koji R .30 .75
DD023 Rika U .20 .50
DD024 Takuya R .30 .75
DD025 Henry U .20 .50
DD026 Zoe R .30 .75
DD027 J.P. R .30 .75
DD028 Tommy R
DM105 Floramon C .10 .25
DM106 Calumon C .10 .25
DM107 Tentomon C .10 .25
DM108 Palmon C .10 .25
DM109 Otamamon C .10 .25
DM110 Biyomon C .10 .25
DM111 Doggymon C .10 .25
DM112 Veedramon C .10 .25
DM113 Ikkakumon C .10 .25
DM114 Birdramon C .10 .25
DM115 Kabuterimon C .10 .25
DM116 Devimon C .10 .25
DM117 Snimon C .10 .25
DM118 Moosemon C .10 .25
DM119 Nefertimon C .10 .25
DM120 Garudamon C .10 .25
DM121 Zudomon U .20 .50
DM122 MegaKabuterimon U .20 .50
DM123 MegaSeadramon U .20 .50
DM124 Andromon U .20 .50
DM125 WaruMonzaemon U .20 .50
DM126 Lillymon U .20 .50
DM127 Imperialdramon (Paladin Mode) U 2.50 6.00
DM128 Kerpymon U .40 1.00
DM129 MetalSeadramon U .75 2.00
DM130 HerculesKabuterimon U .40 1.00
DM131 Puppetmon U .20 .50
DM132 Rosemon U .20 .50
DM133 Omnimon R 5.00 12.00
DM134 Agunimon G 20.00
DM135 BurningGreymon G
DM136 Lobomon G
DM137 KendoGarurumon G
DM138 Kumamon G
DM139 Korikakumon G 15.00
DM140 Beetlemon G 15.00
DM141 MetalKabuterimon G 10.00
DV006 Spirit R 1.25 3.00
DV007 D-Tector Digivice U .20 .50
MD031 Data Point Charger U .20 .50
MD032 Attack Restriction C .12 .30
MD033 Data Point Charger 2 U .20 .50
MD034 Protective Plug-In C .12 .30
MD035 Data Sucking C .12 .30
MD036 Machine Crush U .20 .50
MD037 Skipping Chip U .20 .50
MD038 Digivolve Duplication C .12 .30
MD039 Trapping Chip C .12 .30
MD040 Resource Control Tower C .12 .30
MD041 Companion Plug-In C .12 .30
MD042 Sacrifice Laser U .20 .50
MD043 Mandatory Shutdown C .12 .30
MD044 Energy Plug-In C .12 .30

2004 Digimon CCG Starter Set 1 Eternal Courage

DD001 Tai U
DD002 Sora R
DD003 Mimi U
DD004 Joe C
DD005 Cody C
DD006 Takato U
DD007 Rika C
DM001 Impmon R
DM002 Labramon U
DM003 Monodramon C
DM004 Renamon C
DM005 Kokuwamon C
DM006 Veemon R
DM007 Patamon U
DM008 ToyAgumon C
DM009 Guilmon C
DM010 Hagurumon C
DM011 Keramon U
DM012 Lopmon C
DM013 Renamon C
DM014 Salamon C
DM015 Kokuwamon C
DM016 Veemon R
DM017 Chuumon C
DM018 Guilmon C
DM019 DemiDevimon U
DM020 Seasarmon U
DM021 Sethmon U
DM022 Turuiemon U
DM023 Gatomon U
DM024 Kyubimon U
DM025 BomberNanimon U
DM026 ExVeemon R
DM027 Growlmon R
DM028 Gargomon R
DM029 Vikaralamon R
DM030 Makuramon R
DM031 Mihiramon R
DM032 Antylamon R
DM033 Gallantmon HOLO
DV001 D-3 Digivice R
DV002 D-Terminal R
MD001 Red Virus Bean U
MD002 Green Virus Bean U
MD003 Yellow Virus Bean U
MD004 Battle Tomahawk R
MD005 Control Spire U
MD006 Evil Chip U
MD007 Aero Wing U
MD008 Miracle Ruby R

2004 Digimon CCG Starter Set 2 Eternal Courage

DD008 Matt U
DD009 Izzy C
DD010 Davis U
DD011 Yolei C
DD012 T.K. C
DD013 Kari R
DD014 Henry U
DM034 Lucemon R
DM035 Agumon C
DM036 Gotsumon C
DM037 Gabumon U
DM038 Gomamon U
DM039 Armadillomon U
DM040 Elecmon U
DM041 Wormmon C
DM042 Terriermon C
DM043 Agumon U
DM044 Goburimon C
DM045 Gizamon C
DM046 Wormmon C
DM047 Hawkmon C
DM048 Kunemon C
DM049 Muchomon C
DM050 Mushroomon C
DM051 Gabumon C
DM052 Terriermon U
DM053 Garurumon U
DM054 Shadramon U
DM055 BlackGargomon U
DM056 BlackGrowlmon U
DM057 Angemon R
DM058 Youkomon U
DM059 Ankylomon R
DM060 Gekomon R
DM061 Greymon R
DM062 MetalGreymon R
DM063 Volcanomon R
DM064 Cerberusmon R
DM065 Karatenmon R
DM066 MetalGarurumon HOLO
DV003 D-Power Digivice R
DV004 D-Terminal R
MD009 Spiritual Crystal U
MD010 Magical Ring U
MD011 Big Bang Hammer R
MD012 Gatling Arm R
MD013 Golden Shield U
MD014 Rapid Arrow U
MD015 Platinum Sword R
MD016 Mysterious Wand U

2005 Digimon CCG Generations

DD029 Izzy C
DD030 Kari U
DD031 Matt U
DM142 Bearmon C
DM143 Penguinmon C
DM144 SnowAgumon C
DM145 Dokunemon C
DM146 Tsukaimon C
DM147 Psychemon C
DM148 Gazimon C
DM149 Sagittarimon C
DM150 Raidramon C
DM151 Gargomon C
DM152 GoldVeedramon C
DM153 Deltamon C
DM154 Bucchiemon C
DM155 Allomon C
DM156 Mothmon C
DM157 Bullmon C
DM158 Flamedramon C
DM159 Honeybeemon C
DM160 Shurimon C
DM161 Myotismon U
DM162 BlackRapidmon U
DM163 MetalTyrannomon U
DM164 Cyberdramon U
DM165 PileVolcanomon U
DM166 AncientGreymon R
DM167 AncientGarurumon R
DM168 Lucemon (Fallen Mode) U
DM169 Panjyamon U
DM170 Kazemon R
DM171 KaiserLeomon R
DM172 Rhihimon R
DM173 MetalKabuterimon R
DM174 Aldamon G
DM175 Beowolfmon G
DM176 RhinoKabuterimon G
DM177 KaiserGreymon G
DM178 MagnaGarurumon G
DM179 Fanglongmon G
DM180 Beelzemon (Bluster Mode) G
DM181 Susanomon G
DM182 Lucemon (Shadowlord Mode) G
DV008 Blade & Cannon U
DV009 Destruction & Regeneration U
DV010 D-Tector Digivice U
DV011 D-3 Digivice R
MD045 Rival Deleter C
MD046 Super Energy Charger U
MD047 Digi-Digit Codes U
MD048 Energy Drink U
MD049 Iron Dagger U
MD050 Attack Blocker C
MD051 Data Absorber U
MD052 Guardian Pyramid C
MD053 Amplifier C
MD054 Android Virus C
MD055 Cure Box C
MD056 Detection Device C
MD057 Bottomless Lake U
MD058 D-Protector C

2005 Digimon CCG Operation X

DM217 Dorumon C
DM218 Lopmon C
DM219 Agumon C
DM220 Ryudamon C
DM221 FanBeemon C
DM222 Hawkmon C
DM223 Strabimon C
DM224 Dorugamon C
DM225 Dexdorugamon C
DM226 Ginryumon C
DM227 Leomon C
DM228 Puteranomon C
DM229 Reptiledramon C
DM230 Waspmon C
DM231 Monochromon C
DM232 Truiemon C
DM233 Brimpmon C
DM234 Tortomon C
DM235 Greymon C
DM236 DoruGreymon U
DM237 DexdoruGreymon U
DM238 CannonBeemon U
DM239 Assaultmon C
DM240 SkullGreymon U
DM241 Grademon U
DM242 MetalTyrannomon U
DM243 WereGarurumon U
DM244 Hisyarumon U
DM245 Dinotigermon R
DM246 Gigaseadramon R
DM247 Megidramon R
DM248 Gaiomon R
DM249 Chaosdramon R
DM250 Dinorexmon R
DM251 Phoenixmon G
DM252 TigerVespamon G
DM253 Dexmon G
DM254 Imperialdramon (Paladin Mode) G
DM255 DexDorgoramon G
DM256 Owryumon G
DM257 Dorugoramon G
DV017 X-Vitamin U
DV018 X-Drink U
DV019 X Antibody U
DV020 X Antibody PF R
MD070 Hacking U
MD071 Dome City C
MD072 Mysterious Land C
MD073 Holy Waterdrop U
MD074 Sky Wing U
MD075 Metal Parts C
MD076 Secret Leaf R
MD077 Magnetic Motor R
MD078 Dark Gate U
MD079 STR-MAX U
MD080 Armor Crusher R
MD081 Digi-Fish C
MD082 Power Hammer U

MD083 Snow Crystal C
MD084 Ancient Digital World U
MD085 Digital World in Danger! C
MD086 Stop the X-Program! C
MD087 Artificial Terminal C
MD088 New Digital World C
MD089 Ancient Garden C

2005 Digimon CCG Starter Set 3 Royal Knights

DM183 Agumon C
DM184 Agumon C
DM185 Gabumon C
DM186 Gabumon C
DM187 Guilmon C
DM188 Guilmon C
DM189 Veemon C
DM190 Veemon C
DM191 Veedramon C
DM192 Veedramon C
DM193 Magnamon G
DM194 Growlmon C
DM195 Growlmon C
DM196 Garurumon C
DM197 Garurumon C
DM198 Greymon C
DM199 Greymon C
DM200 ChaosDramon U
DM201 Garudamon U
DM202 WereGarurumon U
DM203 Knightmon U
DM204 AeroVeedramon U
DM205 WarGrowlmon U
DM206 Silphymon U
DM207 Mistymon U
DM208 Grademon U
DM209 Omnimon G
DM210 Gallantmon G
DM211 UlforceVeedramon G
DM212 LordKnightmon G
DM213 Dunasmon G
DM214 Alphamon G
DM215 WarGreymon R
DM216 MetalGarurumon R
DV012 Digimon Accelerator R
DV013 Digivice 01 R
DV014 D-3 Digivice R
DV015 D-3 Digivice U
DV016 Digi-Egg of Miracle U
MD059 Knight Spear C
MD060 Omni Blade C
MD061 Legend Sword C
MD062 Colosseum U
MD063 Frontier C
MD064 Online Remover U
MD065 Miracle Stone C
MD066 Beast Shield U
MD067 Fairy Sword C
MD068 Burning Wing C
MD069 Digi-Canceler U

2001 Digimon Digi-Battle Series 4

Bo163 Guilmon C
Bo164 Growlmon U
Bo165 WarGrowlmon G
Bo166 Terriermon C
Bo167 Gargomon U
Bo168 Rapidmon G
Bo169 Renamon C
Bo170 Kyubimon U
Bo171 Taomon G
Bo172 Paildramon R
Bo173 Imperialdramon (DM) G
Bo174 Imperialdramon (FM) G
Bo175 Aquilamon C
Bo176 Silphymon U
Bo177 Valkyrimon R
Bo178 Ankylomon U
Bo179 Shakkoumon R
Bo180 Vikemon R
Bo181 Dinobeemon U
Bo182 GranKuwagamon G
Bo183 Mummymon R
Bo184 Arukenimon R
Bo185 Honeybeemon C
Bo186 Depthmon C
Bo187 Gargoylemon C
Bo188 Rinkmon C
Bo189 Harpymon C
Bo190 Flybeemon C
Bo191 Allomon C
Bo192 Pteramon C
Bo193 Boarmon C
Bo194 Baromon R
Bo195 Mantaraymon C
Bo196 Rhinomon R
Bo197 Prairiemon C
Bo198 Stegomon C
Bo199 Tylomon C
Bo200 Lynxmon C
Bo201 Maildramon C
Bo202 Archelomon C
Bo203 Nohemon R
Bo204 Bullmon R
Bo205 Data Duplication C
Bo206 Platinum Sword C
Bo207 Golden Shield C
Bo208 D-Terminal C
Bo209 Sacred Fruit R
Bo210 Control Spire R
Bo211 Spirits of Nature U
Bo212 Guardians of the Wind U
Bo213 Group of the Unknown U
Bo214 Savers of the Deep Blue U
Bo215 Soldiers of Nightmares U
Bo216 Empires of Precious Metals U

2002 Digimon Digi-Battle Series 5

Bo217 Keramon C
Bo218 Impmon C
Bo219 Kurisarimon U
Bo220 Doggymon C
Bo221 Leomon C
Bo222 Infermon R
Bo223 BlackWarGrowlmon R
Bo224 Karatenmon R
Bo225 Mihiramon R
Bo226 Antylamon R
Bo227 Diaboromon G
Bo228 Armageddemon G
Bo229 BlackWarGreymon R
Bo230 Jijimon R
Bo231 MarineAngemon R
Bo232 Omnimon R
Bo233 Imperialdramon (PM) R
Bo234 Ebonwumon G
Bo235 Zhuqiaomon G
Bo236 Azulongmon G
Bo237 Baihumon G
Bo238 Sagittarimon U
Bo239 Kangarumon C
Bo240 Kongoumon C
Bo241 Searchmon C
Bo242 Quetzalmon C
Bo243 Rabbitmon C
Bo244 Swanmon C
Bo245 Kabukimon U
Bo246 Butterflymon C
Bo247 Goatmon C
Bo248 Opossummon U
Bo249 Pipismon U
Bo250 Ponchomon U
Bo251 Mothmon C
Bo252 Manbomon U
Bo253 Tocanmon C
Bo254 Peacockmon C
Bo255 Sepikmon C
Bo256 Elephantmon U
Bo257 Frogmon C
Bo258 Sheepmon C
Bo259 Seahomon U
Bo260 Chameleonmon C
Bo261 Offensive V C
Bo262 Digi-O C
Bo263 Collapsed Control Spire C
Bo264 Power Charger C
Bo265 The Aegis R
Bo266 Miracle Ruby R
Bo267 Digi-Egg Booster A U
Bo268 Digi-Egg Booster B U
Bo269 Reverse U
Bo270 Special Bandage C

2002 Digimon Digi-Battle Series 6

Bo271 Labramon C
Bo272 Monodramon C
Bo273 Lucemon G
Bo274 Seasarmon C
Bo275 Coelamon C
Bo276 Ebidramon C
Bo277 Youkomon C
Bo278 BlackGargomon C
Bo279 GoldVeedramon G
Bo280 Gekomon C
Bo281 Turuiemon C
Bo282 Mephistomon C
Bo283 BlackRapidmon C
Bo284 Cerberusmon C
Bo285 Volcanomon U
Bo286 Vikaralamon U
Bo287 Makuramon U
Bo288 GrapLeomon R
Bo289 Lillymon U
Bo290 Apokarimon (CM) G
Bo291 VenomMyotismon U
Bo292 Gulfmon R
Bo293 Apokarimon U
Bo294 Ophanimon G
Bo295 Megidramon R
Bo296 Goldramon R
Bo297 HiAndromon R
Bo298 BlackMegaGargomon U
Bo299 Pharohmon R
Bo300 Anubismon R
Bo301 Gallantmon (with Grani) G
Bo302 Justimon G
Bo303 Beelzemon U
Bo304 Milleniummon R
Bo305 Change-Up C
Bo306 Digital Gate C
Bo307 Spiritual Crystal C
Bo308 Training Gear C
Bo309 Lightspeed Arrow C
Bo310 Trinity Attack R
Bo311 Digi-Beetle C
Bo312 Spiritual Ring C
Bo313 Spiritual Wand C
Bo314 Rapid Arrow C
Bo315 Fire Crystal C
Bo316 Excalibur C
Bo317 Knight Device R
Bo318 Gatling Arm C
Bo319 Giga Claws U
Bo320 Positron Laser U
Bo321 Rook Device R
Bo322 King Device R
Bo323 Grani U
Bo324 Beelze Motorcycle U

2002 Digimon Digi-Battle Starter Decks

St01 Agumon
St02 Greymon
St03 Biyomon
St04 Birdramon
St05 Gabumon
St06 Garurumon
St07 Tentomon
St08 Kabuterimon
St09 Palmon
St10 Togemon
St11 Gomamon
St12 Ikkakumon
St13 Patamon
St14 Angemon
St15 Nanimon
St16 Unimon
St17 Centarumon
St18 Kunemon
St19 Dokugumon
St20 Musyamon
St21 Kimeramon
St22 Rockmon
St23 Gotsumon
St24 Otamamon
St25 Tortomon
St26 Starmon
St27 Gekomon
St28 MegaKabuterimon
St29 Triceramon
St30 Piximon
St31 Okuwamon
St32 SkullGreymon
St33 HerculesKabuterimon HOLO
St34 SaberLeomon HOLO
St35 Dolphmon
St36 Coelamon
St37 Octomon
St38 Zudomon
St39 MarineDevimon
St40 Pukumon
St41 Candlemon
St42 DemiDevimon
St43 Apemon
St44 Wizardmon
St45 Bakemon
St46 Mammothmon
St47 WereGarurumon
St48 SkullMeramon
St49 Red Offensive
St50 Yellow Offensive
St51 Green Offensive
St52 Blitz
St53 Metal Attack
St54 Counter Attack!
St55 To Champion
St56 Ultra Digivolve HOLO
St57 Downgrade
St58 Digi-Duel
St59 Digivice Red
St60 Digivice Green & Yellow
St61 Digivice Red & Green
St62 Digivice Yellow
St63 Hagurumon
St64 Kokuwamon
St65 SnowAgumon
St66 Goburimon
St67 SnowGoburimon
St68 Muchomon
St69 Tankmon
St70 Deputymon
St71 Mekanorimon
St72 Clockmon
St73 Guardromon
St74 FlareRizamon
St75 Thundermon
St76 Veedramon
St77 Soulmon
St78 Hyogamon
St79 Piddomon
St80 WaruMonzaemon
St81 BigMamemon
St82 Knightmon
St83 Cyberdramon
St84 WarGreymon HOLO
St85 MetalGarurumon HOLO
St86 Red Power Bean
St87 Green Power Bean
St88 Power-Up Floppy Disk
St89 Dark Network
St90 Digidote
St91 Digivice Vaccine
St92 Digivice Data&Virus
St93 Betamon
St94 Dokunemon
St95 Psychemon
St96 Tsukaimon
St97 ModokiBetamon
St98 PlatinumSukamon HOLO
St99 MoriShellmon
St100 Ninjamon
St101 NiseDrimogemon
St102 ShellNumemon
St103 Devidramon
St104 Vegiemon
St105 MudFrigimon
St106 Zassomon
St107 Yanmamon
St108 SandYanmamon
St109 ShogunGekomon
St110 Vermilimon
St111 Vademon
St112 Brachiomon
St113 Gigadramon
St114 Tekkamon
St115 Babamon HOLO
St116 Yellow Power Bean
St117 Terra Firma
St118 Evil Chip
St119 Secret Crush
St120 Resist Downgrade
St121 Digivice Vaccine&Data
St122 Digivice Virus
St123 Guilmon
St124 Terriermon
St125 Lopmon
St126 Agumon
St127 Chuumon
St128 Growlmon
St129 Gargomon
St130 Gatomon
St131 Sethmon
St132 Moosemon
St133 BomberNanimon
St134 WarGrowlmon
St135 Rapidmon
St136 Angewomon
St137 Orochimon
St138 Gallantmon HOLO
St139 MegaGargomon HOLO
St140 Imperialdramon (DM)
St141 Magnadramon
St142 Rosemon
St143 D-Power Digivice Red
St144 D-Power Digivice Green/Yellow
St145 Metal Armor
St146 Shining Digivolution
St147 Deffensive C
St148 Offensive B
St149 Effect P
St150 Aero Wing
St151 Big Bang Hammer
St152 Super Charger
St153 Renamon
St154 Veemon
St155 Gomamon
St156 DemiDevimon
St157 Candlemon
St158 Kyubimon
St159 BlackGrowlmon
St160 Magnamon
St161 Orcamon
St162 Devimon
St163 Seadramon
St164 Taomon
St165 Myotismon
St166 SkullSatamon
St167 LadyDevimon
St168 MarineDevimon
St169 Sakuyamon HOLO
St170 Malomyotismon HOLO
St171 Creepymon
St172 Preciomon
St173 D-Power Digivice Red/Green
St174 D-Power Digivice Yellow
St175 Armor Duplication
St176 Digivolution E
St177 Offensive W
St178 Offensive H
St179 Offensive F
St180 Battle Tomahawk
St181 Grapple Chip
St182 Max Charger

2001-02 Digimon Digi-Battle Bandai Promos

DMEX Gallantmon (CM)
DPC3 Digi-Trinity
DPR1 Impmon
DPX1 Guilmon
DPX2 Renamon
DPX3 Terriermon
DPY1 WarGrowlmon
DPY2 Taomon
DPY3 Rapidmon
DMMG1 Gallantmon
DMMG2 MegaGargomon
DMMG3 Sakuyamon
DPower D-Power

2002 Digimon D-Tector Series 1

DT001 Agumon C
DT002 Gabumon C
DT003 Guilmon C
DT004 Gotsumon C
DT005 Kokuwamon C
DT006 Gizamon C
DT007 Greymon C
DT008 Garurumon C
DT009 Growlmon C
DT010 Shellmon C
DT011 Kuwagamon C
DT012 Deputymon C
DT013 Numemon C
DT014 Thundermon C
DT015 Starmon C
DT016 MetalGreymon C
DT017 WereGarurumon U
DT018 WarGrowlmon U
DT019 Etemon U
DT020 SkullGreymon U
DT021 Orochimon U
DT022 Kimeramon U
DT023 Cyberdramon U
DT024 WarGreymon U
DT025 MetalGarurumon R
DT026 Gallantmon R
DT027 BlackWarGreymon R
DT028 Justimon R
DT029 Phoenixmon R
DT030 Ophanimon R
DT031 Omnimon R
DT032 Gallantmon (Crimson Mode) R
DT065 Agunimon UR
DT066 Lobomon UR
DT067 Kumamon UR
DT068 Beetlemon UR
DT069 Kazemon UR
DT070 BurningGreymon UR
DT071 KendoGarurumon UR
DT072 Korikakumon UR
DT073 MetalKabuterimon UR
DT074 Zephyrmon UR

2002 Digimon D-Tector Series 2

DT033 Veemon C
DT034 Wormmon C
DT035 Terriermon C
DT036 Kunemon C
DT037 Mushroomon C
DT038 Elecmon C
DT039 ExVeemon C
DT040 Stingmon C
DT041 Gargomon C
DT042 Frigimon C
DT043 Ogremon C
DT044 Leomon C
DT045 Gesomon C
DT046 Nanimon C
DT047 Vegiemon C
DT048 Paildramon C
DT049 Dinobeemon U
DT050 Rapidmon U
DT051 MarineDevimon U
DT052 Mummymon U
DT053 Arukenimon U
DT054 Mephistomon U
DT055 Imperialdramon U
DT056 GranKuwagamon U
DT057 MegaGargomon R
DT058 Machinedramon R
DT059 Goldramon R
DT060 MarineAngemon R
DT061 Gulfmon R
DT062 Seraphimon R
DT063 Imperialdramon (Fighter Mode) R
DT064 Beelzemon (Bluster Mode) R
DT075 Agunimon UR
DT076 Lobomon UR
DT077 Kumamon UR
DT078 Beetlemon UR
DT079 Kazemon UR
DT080 BurningGreymon UR
DT081 KendoGarurumon UR
DT082 Korikakumon UR
DT083 MetalKabuterimon UR
DT084 Zephyrmon UR

2002 Digimon D-Tector Series 3

DT085 Agumon C
DT086 Gabumon C
DT087 Guilmon C
DT088 Veemon C
DT089 Wormmon C
DT090 Terriermon C
DT091 Greymon C
DT092 Garurumon C
DT093 Growlmon C
DT094 ExVeemon C
DT095 Stingmon C
DT096 Gargomon C
DT097 Leomon C
DT098 MetalGreymon U
DT099 WereGarurumon U
DT100 WarGrowlmon U
DT101 SkullGreymon U
DT102 Paildramon U
DT103 Dinobeemon U
DT104 Rapidmon U
DT105 WarGreymon U
DT106 MetalGarurumon U
DT107 Gallantmon R
DT108 Justimon R
DT109 Imperialdramon R
DT110 GranKuwagamon R
DT111 MegaGargomon R
DT112 Machinedramon R
DT113 Imperialdramon (Fighter Mode) R
DT114 Beelzemon (Bluster Mode) R
DT115 Omnimon R
DT116 Gallantmon (Crimson Mode) R
DT117 Agunimon UR
DT118 Lobomon UR
DT119 Kumamon UR
DT120 Beetlemon UR
DT121 Kazemon UR
DT122 AncientGreymon UR
DT123 AncientGarurumon UR
DT124 AncientMegatheriummon UR
DT125 AncientBeetlemon UR
DT126 AncientKazemon UR

2003 Digimon D-Tector Series 4

DT127 Monodramon C
DT128 Patamon C
DT129 Keramon C
DT130 ToyAgumon C
DT131 Goburimon C
DT132 Strikedramon C
DT133 Angemon C
DT134 Kurisarimon C
DT135 Rockmon C
DT136 Wizardmon C
DT137 Snimon U
DT138 Tankmon U
DT139 Guardromon U
DT140 MagnaAngemon U

DT141 Infermon U
DT142 Grapleomon U
DT143 Myotismon U
DT144 Cerberusmon U
DT145 Karatenmon U
DT146 Volcanomon U
DT147 SkullScorpiomon U
DT148 Andromon U
DT149 Diaboromon R
DT150 SaberLeomon R
DT151 VenomMyotismon R
DT152 Millenniummon R
DT153 KingEtemon R
DT154 HiAndromon R
DT155 Megidramon R
DT156 Azulongmon R
DT157 Baihumon R
DT158 Ebonwumon R
DT159 Zhuqiaomon R
DT160 Armageddemon R
DT161 ZeedMillenniummon R
DT162 MaloMyotismon R
DT163 Grumblemon UR
DT164 Gigasmon UR
DT165 Arbormon UR
DT166 Petaldramon UR
DT167 Mercurymon UR
DT168 Sephirothmon UR
DT169 Lanamon UR
DT170 Calmaramon UR
DT171 Duskmon UR
DT172 Velgremon UR
DT177 Agunimon UR
DT178 Lobomon UR
DT179 Kumamon UR
DT180 Beetlemon UR
DT181 Kazemon UR
DT182 Loweemon UR
DT183 BurningGreymon UR
DT184 KendoGarurumon UR
DT185 Korikakumon UR
DT186 MetalKabuterimon UR
DT187 Zephyrmon UR
DT188 KaiserLeomon UR
DT189 AncientGreymon UR
DT190 AncientGarurumon UR
DT191 AncientMegatheriummon UR
DT192 AncientBeetmon UR
DT193 AncientIrismon UR
DT194 AncientSphinxmon UR
DT196 Susanoomon UR
DT200 Imperialdramon (Paladin Mode) UR

2002 Digimon D-Tector Promos

BS001 Guilmon HOLO
DV001 Omnimon

2008 Dinosaur King Colossal Team Battle

DKTB001 Relentless Tyrannosaurus SR
DKTB002 Mapusaurus GR
DKTB003 Mad Carcharodontosaurus SR
DKTB004 Prowling Daspletosaurus C
DKTB005 Yangchuanosaurus C
DKTB006 Prowling Acrocanthosaurus C
DKTB007 Alpha Gorgosaurus C
DKTB008 Ampelosaurus GR
DKTB009 Roaring Amargasaurus SR
DKTB010 Cetiosaurus SR
DKTB011 Sunrise Shunosaurus C
DKTB012 Swift Suchomimus C
DKTB013 Wading Nemegtosaurus C
DKTB014 Alpha Irritator C
DKTB015 Pentaceratops GR
DKTB016 Rampaging Anchiceratops SR
DKTB017 Albertaceratops SR
DKTB018 Roaming Arrhinoceratops C
DKTB019 Diceratops C
DKTB020 Water's Edge Eucentrosaurus C
DKTB021 Centrosaurus C
DKTB022 Euoplocephalus GR
DKTB023 Gigantspinosaurus C
DKTB024 Grazing Tarchia SR
DKTB025 Tuojiangosaurus C
DKTB026 Polacanthus C
DKTB027 Pack Protector Dacentrurus SR
DKTB028 Pinacosaurus C
DKTB029 Saurolophus GR
DKTB030 Charonosaurus C
DKTB031 Charging Lambeosaurus SR
DKTB032 Spotted Anatotitan C
DKTB033 Edmontosaurus C
DKTB034 Guardian Fukuisaurus GR
DKTB035 Leaellynasaura Healer C
DKTB036 Megaraptor GR
DKTB037 Majungasaurus C
DKTB038 War Cry Ceratosaurus C
DKTB039 Gallimimus C
DKTB040 Rugops SR
DKTB041 Indosuchus C
DKTB042 Troodon SR
DKTB043 Dino Stomp C
DKTB044 Stalemate Breaker C
DKTB045 Counterattack C
DKTB046 Pet Pounce C
DKTB047 Spying C
DKTB048 Distraction C
DKTB049 Overextended Attack C
DKTB050 Pile On C
DKTB051 Desperate Strike C
DKTB052 Mega Backup C
DKTB053 Meteor Strike SR
DKTB054 Flames of Victory C
DKTB055 Ultimate Firestorm SR
DKTB056 Super Tidal Wave SR
DKTB057 Whirlpool Renewal GR
DKTB058 Stalemate Splash C
DKTB059 Ultimate Torrent SR
DKTB060 Electric Cascade GR
DKTB061 Bolt of Vengeance C
DKTB062 Ultimate Shock Blast SR
DKTB063 Super Earth Barrier SR
DKTB064 Sacrificial Slam GR
DKTB065 Victory Crater C
DKTB066 Ultimate Earthquake SR
DKTB067 Super Nature's Revenge SR
DKTB068 Rejuvenating Light SR
DKTB069 Standoff Swipe C
DKTB070 Ultimate Treetop Toss SR
DKTB071 Super Cyclone SR
DKTB072 Vanquishing Vortex GR
DKTB073 Gust of Vengeance C
DKTB074 Ultimate Wind Scythe SR
DKTB075 Max Taylor SR
DKTB076 Rex Owen SR
DKTB077 Zoe Drake C
DKTB078 Ursula C
DKTB079 Ed C
DKTB080 Zander C
DKTB081 Terry C
DKTB082 Spiny (Battle Mode) GR
DKTB083 Spiny C
DKTB084 Chomp C
DKTB085 Tank (Battle Mode) GR
DKTB086 Tank C
DKTB087 Paris (Battle Mode) GR
DKTB088 Paris C
DKTB089 Ace (Battle Mode) GR
DKTB090 Ace C
DKTB091 Mapusaurus CR
DKTB092 Mad Carcharodontosaurus CR
DKTB093 Ampelosaurus CR
DKTB094 Roaring Amargasaurus CR
DKTB095 Pentaceratops CR
DKTB096 Rampaging Anchiceratops CR
DKTB097 Euoplocephalus CR
DKTB098 Saurolophus CR
DKTB099 Guardian Fukuisaurus CR
DKTB100 Megaraptor CR

2008 Dinosaur King SD

DKSS001 Tyrannosaurus SR
DKSS002 Daspletosaurus C
DKSS003 Abelisaurus C
DKSS004 Abelisaurus C
DKSS005 Acrocanthosaurus C
DKSS006 Siamotyrannus C
DKSS007 Alioramus C
DKSS008 Shunosaurus C
DKSS009 Patagosaurus C
DKSS010 Styracosaurus C
DKSS011 Anchiceratops C
DKSS012 Arrhinoceratops C
DKSS013 Triceratops C
DKSS014 Eucentrosaurus C
DKSS015 Zuniceratops C
DKSS016 Ankylosaurus C
DKSS017 Fukuisaurus C
DKSS018 Ceratosaurus C
DKSS019 Tail Slam C
DKSS020 Attack Boost C
DKSS021 Defense Boost C
DKSS022 Dino Swing C
DKSS023 Fire Power C
DKSS024 Thunder Power C
DKSS025 Surprise Ally C
DKSS026 Surprise Technique C
DKSS027 Absorb Power C
DKSS028 Volcano Burst C
DKSS029 Electric Charge C
DKSS030 Max Taylor OS
DKSS031 Rex Owen OS
DKSS032 Dr. Z OS

2008 Dinosaur King SD 2 Dino Slash

DKS2001 Zuniceratops C
DKS2002 Pouncing Irritator C
DKS2003 Centrosaurus C
DKS2004 Minmi C
DKS2005 Savannah Monoclonius C
DKS2006 Eucentrosaurus C
DKS2007 Achelousaurus C
DKS2008 Swift Udanoceratops C
DKS2009 Mighty Diceratops C
DKS2010 Udanoceratops C
DKS2011 Jungle Saltasaurus C
DKS2012 Alpha Arrhinoceratops C
DKS2013 Arrhinoceratops C
DKS2014 Shantungosaurus C
DKS2015 Anchiceratops C
DKS2016 Prowling Daspletosaurus C
DKS2017 Utahraptor C
DKS2018 Pentaceratops C
DKS2019 Charging Styracosaurus C
DKS2020 Dino Stomp C
DKS2021 Attack Boost C
DKS2022 Defense Boost C
DKS2023 Dino Swing C
DKS2024 Diving Press C
DKS2025 Thunder Power C
DKS2026 Surprise Ally C
DKS2027 Surprise Technique C
DKS2028 Knockout Blast C
DKS2029 Elemental Tag Team C
DKS2030 Static Surge C
DKS2031 Plasma Anchor C
DKS2032 Chomp C
DKS2033 Chomp (Dinotector) SR
DKS2034 Thundering Styracosaurus C
DKS2035 Max Taylor C

2008 Dinosaur King Series 1

DKCG001 Carcharodontosaurus GR
DKCG002 Daspletosaurus C
DKCG003 Torvosaurus C
DKCG004 Abelisaurus SR
DKCG005 Acrocanthosaurus C
DKCG006 Giganotosaurus C
DKCG007 Rajasaurus C
DKCG008 Metriacanthosaurus C
DKCG009 Tarbosaurus SR
DKCG010 Siamotyrannus C
DKCG011 Alioramus C
DKCG012 Albertosaurus C
DKCG013 Gorgosaurus GR
DKCG014 Spinosaurus SR
DKCG015 Titanosaurus C
DKCG016 Amargasaurus GR
DKCG017 Baryonyx SR
DKCG018 Shunosaurus C
DKCG019 Dicraeosaurus SR
DKCG020 Saltasaurus C
DKCG021 Suchomimus C
DKCG022 Camarasaurus SR
DKCG023 Patagosaurus C
DKCG024 Nemegtosaurus C
DKCG025 Opisthocoelicaudia C
DKCG026 Irritator GR
DKCG027 Gondwanatitan C
DKCG028 Pachyrhinosaurus GR
DKCG029 Anchiceratops C
DKCG030 Torosaurus SR
DKCG031 Arrhinoceratops C
DKCG032 Triceratops C
DKCG033 Chasmosaurus SR
DKCG034 Udanoceratops C
DKCG035 Eucentrosaurus C
DKCG036 Monoclonius C
DKCG037 Achelousaurus SR
DKCG038 Zuniceratops C
DKCG039 Brachyceratops C
DKCG040 Einiosaurus GR
DKCG041 Saichania SR
DKCG042 Stegosaurus GR
DKCG043 Tarchia C
DKCG044 Edmontonia C
DKCG045 Gastonia SR
DKCG046 Ankylosaurus C
DKCG047 Nodosaurus C
DKCG048 Kentrosaurus SR
DKCG049 Dacentrurus C
DKCG050 Sauropelta SR
DKCG051 Lexovisaurus C
DKCG052 Wuerhosaurus GR
DKCG053 Talarurus C
DKCG054 Minmi C
DKCG055 Parasaurolophus SR
DKCG056 Lambeosaurus C
DKCG057 Altirhinus GR
DKCG058 Shantungosaurus C
DKCG059 Anatotitan SR
DKCG060 Iguanodon C
DKCG061 Corythosaurus C
DKCG062 Maiasaura SR
DKCG063 Tsintaosaurus SR
DKCG064 Brachylophosaurus C
DKCG065 Fukuisaurus C
DKCG066 Muttaburrasaurus GR
DKCG067 Camptosaurus C
DKCG068 Ouranosaurus C
DKCG069 Carnotaurus SR
DKCG070 Utahraptor GR
DKCG071 Ceratosaurus C
DKCG072 Deltadromeus C
DKCG073 Afrovenator SR
DKCG074 Neovenator C
DKCG075 Allosaurus C
DKCG076 Sinraptor SR
DKCG077 Monolophosaurus C
DKCG078 Szechuanosaurus C
DKCG079 Piatnitzkysaurus SR
DKCG080 Liliensternus C
DKCG081 Dilophosaurus GR
DKCG082 Velociraptor C
DKCG083 Tail Slam C
DKCG084 Attack Boost C
DKCG085 Defense Boost C
DKCG086 Diving Press C
DKCG087 Sand Storm C
DKCG088 Dino Swing C
DKCG089 Stomping Hammer C
DKCG090 Grind Away C
DKCG091 Atomic Bomb C
DKCG092 Fire Power C
DKCG093 Water Power C
DKCG094 Thunder Power C
DKCG095 Earth Power C
DKCG096 Grass Power C
DKCG097 Wind Power C
DKCG098 Venom Fang C
DKCG099 Final Fury C
DKCG100 Kamikaze Tackle C
DKCG101 Surprise Ally C
DKCG102 Surprise Technique C
DKCG103 Absorb Power C
DKCG104 Battle Recharge SR
DKCG105 Pin Down C
DKCG106 Knockout Blast SR
DKCG107 Fire Cannon C
DKCG108 Blazing Spin C
DKCG109 Fire Bomb C
DKCG110 Lava Storm SR
DKCG111 Jaws of Flame GR
DKCG112 Supernova GR
DKCG113 Water Sword C
DKCG114 Aqua Whip C
DKCG115 Tragic Sphere C
DKCG116 Vital Soak SR
DKCG117 Acid Rain GR
DKCG118 Flash Flood GR
DKCG119 Lightning Strike C
DKCG120 Thunder Bazooka C
DKCG121 Lightning Spear C
DKCG122 Energy Spike SR
DKCG123 Voltage Boost GR
DKCG124 Electric Aura GR
DKCG125 Earthquake C
DKCG126 Mole Attack C
DKCG127 Spike Arrows C
DKCG128 Boulder Crush GR
DKCG129 Deep Canyon GR
DKCG130 Survival Instinct SR
DKCG131 Egg Blaster C
DKCG132 Metal Wing C
DKCG133 Big Foot Assault C
DKCG134 Emerald Cure SR
DKCG135 S.O.S. GR
DKCG136 Overgrowth C
DKCG137 Razor Wind C
DKCG138 Ninja Attack C
DKCG139 Tornado Toss C
DKCG140 Hurricane Strike SR
DKCG141 Roaring Tempest GR
DKCG142 Whirlwind GR
DKCG143 Max Taylor SR
DKCG144 Rex Owen SR
DKCG145 Zoe Drake C
DKCG146 Dr. Z SR
DKCG147 Ursula C
DKCG148 Ed C
DKCG149 Terry (Battle Mode) GR
DKCG150 Terry C
DKCG151 Chomp (Battle Mode) GR
DKCG152 Chomp C
DKCG153 Tyrannosaurus CR
DKCG154 Spinosaurus CR
DKCG155 Styracosaurus CR
DKCG156 Saichania CR
DKCG157 Stegosaurus CR
DKCG158 Parasaurolophus CR
DKCG159 Carnotaurus CR
DKCG160 Utahraptor CR

2009 Dinosaur King Alpha Dinosaurs Attack

DKAA001 Alpha Acrocanthosaurus GR
DKAA002 Alpha Rajasaurus C
DKAA003 Fierce Yangchuanosaurus SR
DKAA004 Ferocious Torvosaurus GR
DKAA005 Yangchuanosaurus C
DKAA006 Prowling Acrocanthosaurus C
DKAA007 Alpha Gorgosaurus C
DKAA008 Alpha Amargasaurus GR
DKAA009 Grazing Titanosaurus C
DKAA010 Alpha Suchomimus C
DKAA011 Razor-tooth Baryonyx SR
DKAA012 Jungle Saltasaurus C
DKAA013 Peaceful Patagosaurus SR
DKAA014 Pouncing Irritator C
DKAA015 Alpha Triceratops GR
DKAA016 Alpha Chasmosaurus C
DKAA017 Wandering Torosaurus SR
DKAA018 Mighty Diceratops C
DKAA019 Swift Udanoceratops SR
DKAA020 Savannah Monoclonius C
DKAA021 Alpha Einiosaurus C
DKAA022 Alpha Ankylosaurus GR
DKAA023 Alpha Kentrosaurus C
DKAA024 Plated Edmontonia SR
DKAA025 Roadblock Ankylosaurus C
DKAA026 Startled Nodosaurus SR
DKAA027 Iron Spine Sauropelta C
DKAA028 Alpha Wuerhosaurus C
DKAA029 Alpha Lambeosaurus GR
DKAA030 Excited Altirhinus SR
DKAA031 Alpha Iguanodon C
DKAA032 Nesting Maiasaura SR
DKAA033 Olorotitan C
DKAA034 Starving Brachylophosaurus C
DKAA035 Alpha Ouranosaurus C
DKAA036 Alpha Ceratosaurus GR
DKAA037 Alpha Allosaurus C
DKAA038 Swift Afrovenator C
DKAA039 City Stalker Allosaurus SR
DKAA040 Eustreptospondylus GR
DKAA041 Sprinting Piatnitzkysaurus SR
DKAA042 Alpha Dilophosaurus C
DKAA043 Elemental Tag Team C
DKAA044 Reckless Charge C
DKAA045 D-Team Attack SR
DKAA046 Alpha Gang Attack SR
DKAA047 Alpha Dice SR
DKAA048 Alpha Explosion C
DKAA049 Alpha Droids C
DKAA050 Banana Trap SR
DKAA051 Flame Fang SR
DKAA052 Mega Fireball C
DKAA053 Raging Inferno C
DKAA054 Aquatic Assault SR
DKAA055 Mega Geyser C
DKAA056 Water Spout C
DKAA057 Paralyzing Shock SR
DKAA058 Mega Bolt C
DKAA059 Electric Toss C
DKAA060 Quartz Slam SR
DKAA061 Mega Crush C
DKAA062 Boulder Blast C
DKAA063 Big Backup SR
DKAA064 Mega Healing C
DKAA065 Magical Shot C
DKAA066 Wind Slicer SR
DKAA067 Mega Whirlwind C
DKAA068 Twisting Tornado C
DKAA069 Max Taylor C
DKAA070 Rex Owen C
DKAA071 Zoe Drake C
DKAA072 Dr. Taylor C
DKAA073 The D-Team GR
DKAA074 Dr. Z C
DKAA075 Laura & Rod SR
DKAA076 The Alpha Gang GR
DKAA077 Seth SR
DKAA078 Helga C
DKAA079 Terry C
DKAA080 Terry (Battle Mode) GR
DKAA081 Spiny C
DKAA082 Spiny (Battle Mode) GR
DKAA083 Chomp C
DKAA084 Chomp (Battle Mode) GR
DKAA085 Tank C
DKAA086 Tank (Battle Mode) GR
DKAA087 Paris C
DKAA088 Paris (Battle Mode) GR
DKAA089 Ace C
DKAA090 Ace (Battle Mode) GR
DKAA091 Alpha Acrocanthosaurus CR
DKAA092 Fierce Yangchuanosaurus CR
DKAA093 Grazing Titanosaurus CR
DKAA094 Razor-tooth Baryonyx CR
DKAA095 Alpha Chasmosaurus CR
DKAA096 Wandering Torosaurus CR
DKAA097 Plated Edmontonia CR
DKAA098 Startled Nodosaurus CR
DKAA099 Excited Altirhinus CR
DKAA100 Sprinting Piatnitzkysaurus CR

2009 Dinosaur King Black Dinosaur Rampage

DKBD001 Black Tyrannosaurus GR
DKBD002 SauropHaganax SR
DKBD003 Wild Daspletosaurus C
DKBD004 Forest Camo Abelisaurus C
DKBD005 Alpha Giganotosaurus SR
DKBD006 Roaring Metriacanthosaurus C
DKBD007 Lurking Alioramus C
DKBD008 Black Spinosaurus GR
DKBD009 Seismosaurus C
DKBD010 Futabasaurus C
DKBD011 Placid Cetiosaurus C
DKBD012 Alpha Amargasaurus SR
DKBD013 Majestic Camarasaurus GR
DKBD014 Swamp Opisthocoelicaudia C
DKBD015 Black Pentaceratops GR
DKBD016 Charging Styracosaurus SR
DKBD017 Snow-Peak Pachyrhinosaurus C
DKBD018 Alpha Arrhinoceratops SR
DKBD019 Squall Line Diceratops C
DKBD020 Beachcomber Achelousaurus C
DKBD021 Stormcaller Brachyceratops C
DKBD022 Black Saichania GR
DKBD023 Ruin Guard Stegosaurus C
DKBD024 Alpha Sauropelta SR
DKBD025 Sandstorm Gastonia C
DKBD026 Thirsty Kentrosaurus C
DKBD027 Boulder Bash Lexovisaurus GR
DKBD028 Dune Climber Talarurus C
DKBD029 Black Saurolophus GR
DKBD030 Charging Saurolophus C
DKBD031 Prairie Shantungosaurus C
DKBD032 Oasis Iguanodon C
DKBD033 Alpha Tsintaosaurus SR
DKBD034 Baby Maiasaura GR
DKBD035 Lost Valley Muttaburrasaurus C
DKBD036 Black Megaraptor GR
DKBD037 Lost Megaraptor SR
DKBD038 Leaping Utahraptor C
DKBD039 High Noon Deltadromeus C
DKBD040 Alpha Sinraptor SR
DKBD041 Gale-force Monolophosaurus C
DKBD042 Raging Velociraptor C
DKBD043 Poison Mist C
DKBD044 Surge of Strength C
DKBD045 Elemental Elite C
DKBD046 Elemental Team-Up C
DKBD047 Black Rampage SR
DKBD048 Black Roar C
DKBD049 Fire Scorcher GR
DKBD050 Super Alpha Droids C
DKBD051 Alpha Sonar C
DKBD052 Alpha Blast C
DKBD053 Searing Lava C
DKBD054 Drowning Deluge C
DKBD055 Static Surge C
DKBD056 Rumbling Roll C
DKBD057 Nature's Harmony C
DKBD058 Breakneck Blitz C
DKBD059 Steam Blast SR
DKBD060 Boiling Bite GR
DKBD061 Gushing Geyser SR
DKBD062 Erosion Sword GR
DKBD063 Electric Ivy SR
DKBD064 Spark of Life GR
DKBD065 Crystal Flame SR
DKBD066 Bedrock Blaze GR
DKBD067 Leaf Tornado SR
DKBD068 Spore Storm GR
DKBD069 Lightning Twister SR
DKBD070 Whip Shock GR
DKBD071 Max Taylor C
DKBD072 Rex Owen C
DKBD073 Zoe Drake C
DKBD074 Dr. Owen SR
DKBD075 Dr. Z C
DKBD076 Seth SR
DKBD077 Dr. Taylor C
DKBD078 Helga C
DKBD079 Terry C
DKBD080 Terry (Battle Mode) SR

DKBD081 Spiny C
DKBD082 Spiny (Battle Mode) SR
DKBD083 Chomp C
DKBD084 Chomp (Battle Mode) SR
DKBD085 Tank C
DKBD086 Tank (Battle Mode) SR
DKBD087 Paris C
DKBD088 Paris (Battle Mode) SR
DKBD089 Ace C
DKBD090 Ace (Battle Mode) SR
DKBD091 Black Tyrannosaurus CR
DKBD092 Saurophaganax CR
DKBD093 Futabasaurus CR
DKBD094 Snow-Peak Pachyrhinosaurus CR
DKBD095 Spiny (Battle Mode) CR
DKBD096 Terry (Battle Mode) CR
DKBD097 Tank (Battle Mode) CR
DKBD098 Paris (Battle Mode) CR
DKBD099 Chomp (Battle Mode) CR
DKBD100 Ace (Battle Mode) CR

2009 Dinosaur King Dinotector Showdown

DKDS001 Spectral Armor Mapusaurus GR
DKDS002 Ferocious Mapusaurus SR
DKDS003 Spectral Armor Torvosaurus SR
DKDS004 Roman Torvosaurus C
DKDS005 Wild Giganotosaurus C
DKDS006 Curious Tarbosaurus C
DKDS007 Hunting Gorgosaurus C
DKDS008 Spectral Armor Jobaria GR
DKDS009 Jobaria SR
DKDS010 Spectral Armor Shunosaurus SR
DKDS011 Roman Shunosaurus C
DKDS012 Swamp Dicraeosaurus C
DKDS013 Lake Lurker Patagosaurus C
DKDS014 Rapid Irritator C
DKDS015 Thundering Styracosaurus GR
DKDS016 Brave Pentaceratops SR
DKDS017 Storming Arrhinoceratops C
DKDS018 Spectral Armor Diceratops SR
DKDS019 Enraged Diceratops C
DKDS020 Barking Achelousaurus C
DKDS021 Thundercaller Zuniceratops C
DKDS022 Tunneling Euoplocephalus GR
DKDS023 Mountain Gigantspinosaurus SR
DKDS024 Spectral Armor Edmontonia SR
DKDS025 Caribbean Edmontonia C
DKDS026 Splashing Kentrosaurus C
DKDS027 Crag Climber Dacentrurus C
DKDS028 Resting Wuerhosaurus C
DKDS029 Noble Parasaurolophus GR
DKDS030 Lanzhousaurus SR
DKDS031 Spectral Armor Shantungosaurus SR
DKDS032 Enraged Shantungosaurus C
DKDS033 Brawny Iguanodon C
DKDS034 Friendly Tsintaosaurus C
DKDS035 Wandering Ouranosaurus C
DKDS036 Spectral Armor Megaraptor GR
DKDS037 Surprise Attack Megaraptor SR
DKDS038 Spectral Armor Majungasaurus SR
DKDS039 Roman Majungasaurus C
DKDS040 Screeching Neovenator C
DKDS041 Gladiator Piatnitzkysaurus C
DKDS042 Racing Liliensternus C
DKDS043 Deinonychus GR
DKDS044 Therizinosaurus GR
DKDS045 Knockout Blast C
DKDS046 Final Fury C
DKDS047 Tail Slam C
DKDS048 Broadside Bash SR
DKDS049 Call for Backup SR
DKDS050 Black Howl SR
DKDS051 Alpha Ambush SR
DKDS052 Burning Dash C
DKDS053 Ultimate Fire C
DKDS054 Searing Flames SR
DKDS055 Ocean Panic C
DKDS056 Ultimate Water C
DKDS057 Rising Tide SR
DKDS058 Plasma Anchor C
DKDS059 Ultimate Thunder C
DKDS060 Static Sphere SR
DKDS061 Rock Roller C
DKDS062 Ultimate Earth C
DKDS063 Stone Shield SR
DKDS064 Emerald Garden C
DKDS065 Ultimate Leaf C
DKDS066 Nature Burst SR
DKDS067 Hurricane Beat C
DKDS068 Ultimate Wind C
DKDS069 Turbo Tackle SR
DKDS070 Max Taylor C
DKDS071 Rex Owen GR
DKDS072 Zoe Drake SR
DKDS073 Ursula C
DKDS074 Ed GR
DKDS075 Zander SR
DKDS076 Shear (Sheer) C
DKDS077 Foolscap C
DKDS078 Gabbro (Gavro) C
DKDS079 Terry C
DKDS080 Terry (Dinotector) GR
DKDS081 Spiny C
DKDS082 Spiny (Dinotector) GR
DKDS083 Chomp C
DKDS084 Chomp (Dinotector) GR
DKDS085 Tank C
DKDS086 Tank (Dinotector) GR
DKDS087 Paris C
DKDS088 Paris (Dinotector) GR
DKDS089 Ace C
DKDS090 Ace (Dinotector) GR
DKDS091 Jobaria CR
DKDS092 Mountain Gigantspinosaurus CR
DKDS093 Deinonychus CR
DKDS094 Therizinosaurus CR
DKDS095 Terry (Dinotector) CR
DKDS096 Spiny (Dinotector) CR
DKDS097 Chomp (Dinotector) CR
DKDS098 Tank (Dinotector) CR
DKDS099 Paris (Dinotector) CR
DKDS100 Ace (Dinotector) CR

2010 Dinosaur King Spectral Armor Shock

SAS001 City Stalker Saurophaganax GR
SAS002 Destructive Mapusaurus SR
SAS003 Spectral Armor Yangchuanosaurus SR
SAS004 Fiery Daspletosaurus SR
SAS005 Razor-tooth Abelisaurus C
SAS006 Scary Giganotosaurus C
SAS007 Pack Hunter Albertosaurus C
SAS008 Spectral Armor Titanosaurus colberti (Isisaurus) GR
SAS009 Titanosaurus colberti (Isisaurus) SR
SAS010 Shoreline Titanosaurus SR
SAS011 Swamp Futabasaurus C
SAS012 Hammerer Saltasaurus C
SAS013 Sheltered Camarasaurus C
SAS014 Starving Opisthocoelicaudia C
SAS015 Radiant Pentaceratops GR
SAS016 Spectral Armor Pachyrhinosaurus SR
SAS017 Pachyrhinosaurus C
SAS018 Energetic Torosaurus SR
SAS019 Assertive Chasmosaurus C
SAS020 Playful Udanoceratops C
SAS021 Twilight Centrosaurus C
SAS022 Spectral Armor Euoplocephalus GR
SAS023 Growling Euoplocephalus SR
SAS024 Hidden Gigantspinosaurus C
SAS025 Howling Tarchia C
SAS026 Spectral Armor Lexovisaurus SR
SAS027 Persian Lexovisaurus C
SAS028 Howling Talarurus C
SAS029 Depot Saurolophus GR
SAS030 Grazing Charonosaurus SR
SAS031 Prairie Lambeosaurus C
SAS032 Summit Anatotitan C
SAS033 Searching Maiasaura C
SAS034 Leaping Brachylophosaurus SR
SAS035 Mysterious Leaellynasaura C
SAS036 Prowling Megaraptor GR
SAS037 Spectral Armor Afrovenator SR
SAS038 Tempest Afrovenator SR
SAS039 Shouting Rugops C
SAS040 Wary Allosaurus C
SAS041 Roaming Monolophosaurus C
SAS042 Pouncing Troodon C
SAS043 Cryolophosaurus GR
SAS044 Pawpawsaurus GR
SAS045 Aura Excavator C
SAS046 Confusing Leap C
SAS047 Simulation C
SAS048 Cranial Comet C
SAS049 Shadow Power C
SAS050 Glow of Life C
SAS051 Elemental Bonus C
SAS052 Kamikaze Tackle SR
SAS053 Spying C
SAS054 Tyrannical Charge C
SAS055 Fire Cannon SR
SAS056 Aquatic Harpoon C
SAS057 Tragic Sphere SR
SAS058 Crackling C
SAS059 Thunder Bazooka SR
SAS060 Crystal Shards C
SAS061 Earthquake SR
SAS062 Regenerating Whip C
SAS063 Big Foot Assault SR
SAS064 Rumbling Storm C
SAS065 Ninja Attack SR
SAS066 The D-Team SR
SAS067 The Alpha Gang SR
SAS068 Seth C
SAS069 Spectre GR
SAS070 Gabbro (Gavro) C
SAS071 Foolscap C
SAS072 Shear (Sheer) C
SAS073 Terry C
SAS074 Terry (DinoTector) GR
SAS075 Spiny C
SAS076 Spiny (DinoTector) GR
SAS077 Chomp C
SAS078 Chomp (DinoTector) GR
SAS079 Tank C
SAS080 Tank (DinoTector) GR
SAS081 Paris C
SAS082 Paris (DinoTector) GR
SAS083 Ace C
SAS084 Ace (DinoTector) GR
SAS085 Gigas C
SAS086 Spectral Armor Gigas SR
SAS087 Armatus C
SAS088 Spectral Armor Armatus SR
SAS089 Maximus C
SAS090 Spectral Armor Maximus SR
SAS091 Fiery Daspletosaurus CR
SAS092 Titanosaurus colberti (Isisaurus) CR
SAS093 Howling Tarchia CR
SAS094 Grazing Charonosaurus CR
SAS095 Tempest Afrovenator CR
SAS096 Cryolophosaurus CR
SAS097 Pawpawsaurus CR
SAS098 Spectral Armor Gigas CR
SAS099 Spectral Armor Armatus CR
SAS100 Spectral Armor Maximus CR

2010 Dinosaur King Time Warp Adventures

DKTA001 Terrifying Tyrannosaurus GR
DKTA002 Spectral Armor Carcharodontosaurus SR
DKTA003 Chinese Carcharodontosaurus SR
DKTA004 Fearsome Yangchuanosaurus C
DKTA005 Berserk Acrocanthosaurus C
DKTA006 Wandering Rajasaurus C
DKTA007 Roaring Alioramus C
DKTA008 Hunting Spinosaurus GR
DKTA009 Fearless Ampelosaurus C
DKTA010 Spectral Armor Baryonyx SR
DKTA011 Japanese Baryonyx C
DKTA012 Pouncing Suchomimus SR
DKTA013 Curious Nemegtosaurus C
DKTA014 Oasis Gondwanatitan C
DKTA015 Spectral Armor Pentaceratops GR
DKTA016 Racing Anchiceratops C
DKTA017 Grazing Pachyrhinosaurus C
DKTA018 Serene Triceratops SR
DKTA019 Spectral Armor Achelousaurus SR
DKTA020 Thundering Eucentrosaurus C
DKTA021 Herd Leader Einiosaurus C
DKTA022 Solid Saichania GR
DKTA023 Fierce Stegosaurus C
DKTA024 Spectral Armor Tuojiangosaurus GR
DKTA025 Traveling Tuojiangosaurus SR
DKTA026 Sure-footed Nodosaurus SR
DKTA027 Cliff Lexovisaurus C
DKTA028 Riverbed Pinacosaurus C
DKTA029 Spectral Armor Lanzhousaurus GR
DKTA030 Prosaurolophus SR
DKTA031 Downtown Altirhinus C
DKTA032 Chinese Shantungosaurus SR
DKTA033 Twilight Corythosaurus C
DKTA034 Wary Fukuisaurus C
DKTA035 Forest Camo Camptosaurus C
DKTA036 Mist Hunter Carnotaurus GR
DKTA037 Pouncing Utahraptor SR
DKTA038 Whirling Ceratosaurus C
DKTA039 Cautious Afrovenator C
DKTA040 Spectral Armor Gojirasaurus SR
DKTA041 Gojirasaurus C
DKTA042 Hunting Dilophosaurus(?)* C
DKTA043 Pachycephalosaurus GR
DKTA044 Megalosaurus GR
DKTA045 Gladiator Headbutt C
DKTA046 Tropical Tackle C
DKTA047 Zen Crush C
DKTA048 Samurai Power C
DKTA049 Rippling Roar C
DKTA050 Desperate Dash SR
DKTA051 Team Trample C
DKTA052 Fiery Rage SR
DKTA053 Volcanic Eruption SR
DKTA054 Fire Bomb C
DKTA055 Spectral Shockwave SR
DKTA056 Swirling Vortex SR
DKTA057 Aqua Whip C
DKTA058 Attack Burst SR
DKTA059 Energizing Sparks SR
DKTA060 Lightning Strike C
DKTA061 Quake Saber SR
DKTA062 Quicksand Drain SR
DKTA063 Spike Arrows C
DKTA064 Swinging Smash SR
DKTA065 Green Impulse SR
DKTA066 Metal Wing C
DKTA067 Spectral Hurricane Beat SR
DKTA068 Stealth Slash SR
DKTA069 Razor Wind C
DKTA070 Max Taylor C
DKTA071 Rex Owen C
DKTA072 Zoe Drake C
DKTA073 Ursula C
DKTA074 Ed C
DKTA075 Zander C
DKTA076 Gabbro (Gavro) C
DKTA077 Foolscap C
DKTA078 Shear (Sheer) C
DKTA079 Terry C
DKTA080 Terry (Dinotector) GR
DKTA081 Spiny C
DKTA082 Spiny (Dinotector) GR
DKTA083 Chomp C
DKTA084 Chomp (Dinotector) GR
DKTA085 Tank C
DKTA086 Tank (Dinotector) GR
DKTA087 Paris C
DKTA088 Paris (Dinotector) GR
DKTA089 Ace C
DKTA090 Ace (Dinotector) GR
DKTA091 Terrifying Tyrannosaurus CR
DKTA092 Pouncing Suchomimus CR
DKTA093 Serene Triceratops CR
DKTA094 Traveling Tuojiangosaurus CR
DKTA095 Prosaurolophus CR
DKTA096 Chinese Shantungosaurus CR
DKTA097 Pouncing Utahraptor CR
DKTA098 Gojirasaurus CR
DKTA099 Pachycephalosaurus CR
DKTA100 Megalosaurus CR

2006 Doctor Who Battles in Time Exterminator

RELEASED ON SEPTEMBER 20, 2006
1 The 10th Doctor R
2 The Empty Child C
3 Robot Spider C
4 Coffa C
5 Chained Dalek C
6 The Editor C
7 Gelth Ambassador Blue SR
8 Adam Mitchell C
9 Gwyneth bridging the rift C
10 Slitheen Blon Fel Fotch Pasameer-Day SR
11 Mr Pakoo C
12 Mickey Smith C
13 Anne Droid C
14 Henry Van Statten C
15 Jackie Tyler C
16 Charles Dickens C
17 Hovering Dalek R
18 Auton Bride C
19 Nurse zombie inactive C
20 Harriet Jones C
21 Face of Boe C
22 Scholar C
23 Dr Constantine C
24 Lynda Moss C
25 Oliver Charles C
26 Nancy C
27 Margaret Blaine C
28 Cathica Santini Khadeni C
29 Cassandra's Surgeon 1 C
30 Imperial Dalek Guard 1 SR
31 Child Auton C
32 Pete Tyler C
33 Pig Pilot C
34 Simmons C
35 Mrs Peace Zombie R
36 Platform 1 Staff C
37 Gelth Ambassador Red SR
38 Rose Tyler R
39 Gwyneth (normal) C
40 Jabe R
41 Auton Mickey's Head C
42 Captain Jack R
43 Mutated Dalek R
44 Mr Sneed zombie C
45 General Asquith C
46 Male Programmer C
47 Reaper C
48 Raffalo C
49 Joseph Green C
50 Robot spider group C
51 Controller (under Dalek control) C
52 Damaged Dalek C
53 Jagrafess of the Holy Hadrojassic Maxarodentoe C
54 Cassandra's Surgeon 2 C
55 Suki Macrae Cantrell (Eva Saint Julienne) C
56 Lady Cassandra O'Brien Dot Delta Seventeen R
57 The Steward C
58 Female Programmer C
59 Nestene Consciousness C
60 The Moxx of Balhoon R
61 Nurse Zombie C
62 Controller (free of Dalek control) C
63 Lute C
64 Male Auton C
65 Mrs Pakoo C
66 Chula zombie C
67 Sycorax SR
68 Dalek R
69 Cal 'Sparkplug' MacNannovich C
70 Slitheen Sip Fel Fotch Pasameer-Day SR
71 The Dalek Emperor D full casing SR
72 Antiplastic C
73 Gas Leak R
74 TARDIS UR
75 Code 9 C
76 Forcefield R
77 Security Scan C
78 Sonic Screwdriver R
79 Unlimited Credit C
80 Pickled Eggs SR
81 Regeneration UR
82 Satellite 5 C
83 Platform One C
84 Skinsuit UR
85 Dalek Buster UR
86 Werewolf Power UR
87 Krillitane Evolution UR
88 Milo C
89 Pilot Fish Group C
90 Sarah Jane Smith C
91 Diseased Woman C
92 King Louis XV C
93 Sycorax Warrior C
94 Krillitane 1 R
95 Captain Reynolds C
96 Harriet Jones PM C
97 Werewolf C
98 Hop Pyleen Brother 1 C
99 K-9 attack mode C
100 Father Angelo C
101 Arthur the Horse C
102 Info-Spike Nurse C
103 Frau Clovis C
104 Scholar 2 C
105 Clockwork Woman 1 C
106 Mr Parsons C
107 Sycorax Leader C
108 Warrior Monk C
109 Hop Pyleen Brother 2 C
110 Kenny C
111 Matron Casp R
112 Flora C
113 Pilot Fish 1 C
114 Rodrick C
115 Robot Eye C
116 Lady Isobel MacLeish C
117 Pilot Fish 2 C
118 Indra Ganesh C
119 Imperial Dalek Guard 2 R
120 Novice Hame C
121 Ghosts C
122 Adherents of the Repeated Meme C
123 Jake Simmonds C
124 The Host C
125 Diseased Man SR
126 Jackie Tyler (from a parallel universe) C
127 Reinette C
128 TARDIS Key C
129 Mr Redpath Zombie C
130 Clockwork Man C
131 Scottish Steward C
132 Mr Wagner C
133 President C
134 Alex C
135 Parallel Pete Tyler R
136 Laser Cutter Dalek C
137 Major Blake C
138 Clockwork Woman 2 C
139 Cyber Leader R
140 The Beast C
141 Ambassador 1 C
142 Mrs Moore C
143 The Wire C
144 Broken K-9 C
145 Mr Sneed C
146 Cal's Companion C
147 Headmaster Finch C
148 Danny Llewellyn C
149 Trine-E C
150 Sir Robert MacLeish C
151 Dr Constantine Chula Zombie C
152 Ambassador 2 C
153 Magpie C
154 Krillitane 2 C
155 Eddie Connolly C
156 Cyberman Group R
157 Scooti Manista C
158 Ood Group C
159 Ricky Smith C
160 School Children C
161 Zu-Zana C
162 Cybus Victim C
163 Tommy Connolly C
164 Toby Possessed R
165 Mr Crane C
166 Killer Christmas Tree C
167 Krillitane 3 C
168 Sanctuary Base Six Guard 1 C
169 Cyber Controller SR
170 Possessed Ood 1 C
171 Sister Jatt C
172 Sycorax Group C
173 Crabtree C
174 Zachary Cross Flane C
175 Frozen Suki C
176 Info-spiked Adam C
177 9th Doctor R
178 Graske R
179 Cure all C
180 Victor Kennedy C
181 Cyberman attacking R
182 Diana Goddard C
183 Slitheen Egg C
184 Imperial Dalek Guard Group R
185 Possessed Ood 2 C
186 Yvonne Hartman C
187 Unmasked Clockwork Man C
188 The Hoix C
189 Bridget Sinclair C
190 Nina C
191 Emperor Dalek Mutant C
192 Dinner Lady C
193 Detective Inspector Bishop C
194 Ida Scott C
195 Queen Victoria C
196 Reaper Group C
197 Mr Skinner C
198 Ill Doctor C
199 Fixed K-9 R
200 White Patient C
201 Pilot Fish 3 C
202 Slitheen Group C
203 Mr Skinner Absorbed C
204 Cyberman Electro-Attack R
205 Toby Zed C
206 Scholar 3 C
207 Exterminate C
208 Broken Clock C
209 Dalek Invasion C
210 Musical Weapon C
211 Sycorax Whip C
212 Possessed Drawing C
213 Info-Spiked Cathica C
214 John Lumic C
215 Scholar 4 C
216 Dalek Thay C
217 Slitheen Ship C
218 Koh-I-Noor Diamond C
219 New Earth Hospital C
220 Jack's Ship C
221 Krillitane Oil C
222 Cassandra as a Human C
223 Possessed Ood 3 C
224 Cyberman in pain C
225 Elton Pope C
226 Duke of Manhattan C
227 Dalek Caan C
228 Kel C
229 Slitheen 1 C
230 Torchwood Scientist 1 C
231 Chip C
232 Danny Bartock C
233 Cyberman C
234 Chloe Webber C
235 Ood C
236 Transporter C
237 Dr Rajesh Singh C
238 Abzorbaloff R
239 Cassandra as Chip C
240 Dalek Rabe C
241 Jefferson C
242 Adeola C
243 Slitheen 2 C
244 Faceless Person C
245 Matt C

246 Cyber Controller On The Move C
247 WWII Bomb C
248 Sycorax Ship C
249 Basic: 0 C
250 Torchwood ID C
251 Newsfeed C
252 Trish Webber C
253 Ursula Blake C
254 Sanctuary Base Six Guard 2 C
255 Dalek Sec R
256 Gareth C
257 Torchwood Scientist 2 C
258 The Wire Feeding C
259 Auton Attack C
260 The Beast C
261 SS Madame de Pompadour C
262 Sycorax Sword C
263 Slash Attack C
264 Victor Kennedy's Cane C
265 3D glasses C
266 Body Swap C
267 Clockwork Weapon C
268 Mobile Phone C
269 Nanogenes C
270 Full Moon C
271 Lumic's Airship C
272 Wolf Vision C
273 Sucker Attack C
274 Airships C
275 Genesis Ark C

2007 Doctor Who Battles in Time Annihilator

RELEASED ON FEBRUARY 21, 2007
276 Time Vortex Doctor R
277 Graske Group C
278 Clockwork Woman 3 C
279 Frozen Cyber Army C
280 Cassandra as Rose C
281 Gas Mask C
282 Magna Clamp C
283 Dalek Vision R
284 Dalek Uncovered UR
285 Mark of the Beast C
286 Trapped Slitheen C
287 Forest of Cheem C
288 Cyber Army C
289 Rose Tyler with Fire Extinguisher C
290 Genesis Ark Daleks C
291 Beastly Possession UR
292 Cyber Smasher R
293 Ood Power R
294 Rocket Ship C
295 Bad Wolf SR
296 Yvonne Hartman Cyber Rebel R
297 Diseased Group C
298 Clive Finch C
299 10th Doctor with Sonic Screwdriver R
300 Graske 2 SR
301 Clockwork Teleport SR
302 Prison of the Beast C
303 Cyber Brain C
304 Final Broadcast R
305 Gelth Possession C
306 Legion of the Beast C
307 Jake Simmonds Parallel Soldier C
308 Rita Connolly C
309 Cat Nurse Group C
310 Margaret Blaine Unmasking C
311 Black Hole C
312 Cyber Slicing Machine C
313 Krillitane Chips C
314 Clockwork Injection C
315 Hand Print Activation C
316 Parallel Soldier C
317 Clockwork Robot Group C
318 Rose Tyler Krillitane Oil C
319 The Beast on Fire SR
320 Cult of Skaro R
321 Mistletoe C
322 Cybus Communicator C
323 Disguise R
324 Temporal Rift C
325 Fire Extinguisher C
326 Matron Casp (Infected) C
327 Scholar Group C
328 Donna Noble C
329 Sycorax Army C
330 Bliss C
331 Torchwood R
332 Hologram SR
333 Cave Painting C
334 Danger of Infection C
335 Dalek Shield C
336 Auton Deactivated C
337 Cyber Leader Blast Attack C
338 10th Doctor Ghostbusting C
339 Racnoss Empress Attacking R
340 Rose Tyler Trapped by the Wire C
341 Disease Pod C
342 Cyber Buster UR
343 Ood Possession C
344 Telescope Light Chamber C
345 Self Destruct C
346 Lance Bennett C
347 Jabe Using her Scanner C
348 Pilot Fish Unmasked C
349 Destroyed Dalek C
350 The Doctor Space Explorer C
351 Energy Source C
352 Skasas Paradigm C
353 Beast Hologram SR
354 Sycorax Unmasking UR
355 Double Extermination C
356 Cyberghosts R
357 Pilot Fish Group Unmasked C
358 Cassandra Drying Out C
359 Sycorax Slave C
360 Ursula Blake Absorbed C
361 Slitheen Zapper R
362 Tractor Beam C
363 Huon Particles R
364 Energy Ball C
365 Biodamper C
366 Racnoss Empress C
367 Dalek Underwater Mode C
368 Gelth Zombie Attack C
369 Pilot Fish Under Racnoss Control C
370 Sip Fel Fotch Pasameer-Day Slitheen Unmasking C
371 Sycorax Mask C
372 Bauble Bombs C
373 TARDIS Crash C
374 Cyberman Defeater C
375 Martha Jones R

2007 Doctor Who Battles in Time Daleks vs. Cybermen

RELEASED ON MAY 16, 2007
DVC01 Dalek Mutant C
DVC02 Cyber Controller C
DVC03 Dalek (With Buzz-Saw Weapon) C
DVC04 Cyberman (Electro-Attack) C
DVC05 Damaged Dalek C
DVC06 Cyberman In Pain C
DVC07 Dalek (Exterminator Attack) C
DVC08 Cyberman C
DVC09 Dalek (Sucker Attack) C
DVC10 Cyberman (Demolisher) C
DVC11 Dalek Emperor C
DVC12 Advance Guard C
DVC13 Dalek Sec Hybrid C
DVC14 Cyber Controller (Attacking) C
DVC15 Dalek (Underwater Mode) C
DVC16 Cyberman Group C
DVC17 Dalek Sec R
DVC18 Cyber Leader R

2007 Doctor Who Battles in Time Invader

RELEASED ON SEPTEMBER 5, 2007
0 Dalek Blaster UR
376 Sun-Possessed Doctor R
377 Carrionite 1 C
378 Morgenstern C
379 Pig Laszlo C
380 Professor Lazarus C
381 Plasmavore (Suck Attack) C
382 Dalek Sec Mutant R
383 Face of Boe (Saving New New York) C
384 Mother Doomfinger R
385 New New York Businessman C
386 Son of Mine R
387 Sally Sparrow C
388 Professor Yana C
389 Lilith C
390 Pharmacist 1 C
391 Weeping Angel 1 C
392 Captain Jack C
393 Toclafane C
394 Refugee 1 C
395 Judoon Captain SR
396 Solomon C
397 Mother Bloodtide C
398 Pharmacist 2 C
399 Pig Slave 1 SR
400 Francine Jones C
401 Jeremy Baines C
402 Judoon Trooper 1 C
403 Martha Jones (Mood Patched) C
404 Carrionite 2 C
405 Padra Toc Shafe Cane C
406 Albert Dumfries C
407 Weeping Angel 2 C
408 Face of Boe (dying) C
409 Mother of Mine C
410 Time Lord 1 C
411 Tish Jones C
412 Sally Calypso C
413 Lilith as a Hag C
414 Korwin McDonnell C
415 Joan Redfern C
416 Futurekind Chieftain C
417 Carrionite 3 SR
418 Malcolm Wainwright C
419 William Shakespeare C
420 Macra 1 C
421 Lois C
422 Lazarus Creature C
423 Mr Stoker C
424 Toclafane (Attacking) C
425 Light Storm Tenth Doctor SR
426 Milo C
427 Carrionite Pair R
428 Professor Lazarus Reborn C
429 Kathy Nightingale C
430 Daughter of Mine C
431 SS Pentallian R
432 Traffic Jam C
433 Radiation Blast R
434 Dalek Embryo C
435 Bliss Mood Patch C
436 Fob Watch C
437 Judoon Unmasking UR
438 Macra Grip C
439 Carrionite Puppet C
440 Vortex Manipulator Teleport C
441 Lucy Cartwright C
442 Harry Saxon R
443 Dev Ashton C
444 Tallulah C
445 Judoon Trooper 2 C
446 Dolly Bailey C
447 Pig Slave 2 C
448 Tenth Doctor Frozen C
449 Farmer Clark C
450 Macra 2 C
451 Lady Thaw C
452 Tom Milligan C
453 Sun-Possessed Korwin Mc Donnell SR
454 Pale Woman C
455 Human Dalek 1 C
456 Drained Lady Thaw C
457 Scarecrow 1 C
458 Old Novice Hame C
459 Shakespearean Actor C
460 Judoon (Scanning) C
461 Empire State Building Foreman C
462 Weeping Angel (Feral State) SR
463 Pharmacist 3 C
464 Professor Lazarus Resurrected C
465 Clive Jones C
466 Family of Blood Weapon R
467 Escape Pod R
468 Wallpaper Warning C
469 Laser Screwdriver R
470 Mutant Attack C
471 Judoon Ship C
472 Happy Mood Patch R
473 Valiant R
474 Lazarus Mutation UR
475 Door Hacker C
476 Will Kempe C
477 Macra Group C
478 Age-accelerated Tenth Doctor SR
479 Human Dalek 2 C
480 Lazarus Monster (attacking) R
481 Time Lord Citadel C
482 Archangel Network C
483 Fob Watch Attack C
484 Stasis Chamber C
485 Toclafane Invasion C
486 Judoon Justice C
487 Life Force Drain C
488 New New York Senate C
489 Journal of Impossible Things C
490 Magnetic Overload C
491 Refugee Group C
492 Larry Nightingale C
493 Father of Mine C
494 Lucy Saxon C
495 Slab C
496 Cheen C
497 Richard Burbage C
498 Human Dalek 3 C
499 Julia Swales C
500 Scarecrow Group C
501 Timey-Wimey Detector C
502 GMD C
503 Master Statue C
504 Carrionite Transformation UR
505 New New York Car C
506 Genetic Transfer C
507 Countdown C
508 Vortex Manilpulator C
509 Letter from Kathy Wainwright C
510 Sun Blast UR
511 Wiggins C
512 Brannigan R
513 Disguised Plasmavore C
514 Human Dalek Army C
515 Scarecrow 2 R
516 Erina Lissak C
517 Weeping Angel (Attacking) R
518 Leo Jones C
519 Toclafane (Sphere Open) SR
520 Wiry Woman C
521 Shakespeare (under Carrionite Influence) C
522 Mr Diagoras C
523 Tim Latimer (as a War Veteran) C
524 Sun-Possesed Ashton R
525 Phillips C
526 TARDIS Crew SR
527 Time Lord Novice C
528 Scarecrow 3 C
529 Tanya C
530 Captain Jack (in chains) C
531 Gamma Strike C
532 Lucy Saxon (one year on) C
533 Tenth Doctor (aged 100 years) C
534 Pig Slave 3 C
535 Riley Vashtee C
536 Valerie Brannigan C
537 Queen Elizabeth I C
538 Judoon Trooper 3 C
539 Laszlo C
540 Tim Latimer C
541 Lilith with Puppet C
542 Creet C
543 Billy Shipton (as an old man) C
544 The Master with Laser Screwdriver C
545 John Smith C
546 Blink UR
547 Solar Fuel Ejection C
548 Sleep Patch C
549 Judoon Scanner C
550 Open Fob Watch C
551 Rocket Base C
552 Chipped TARDIS Key C
553 Carrionite Flight C
554 Saxon Campaign C
555 Judoon Fleet C
556 Peter Streete C
557 Kath McDonnell C
558 Dalek Sec Hybrid (Chained) R
559 The Famiy of Blood C
560 Chantho C
561 Time Lord 2 C
562 Cameraman C
563 Vivien Rook C
564 Untempered Schism C
565 Martha Jones (Resistance Fighter) C
566 Carrionite Group C
567 Professor Docherty C
568 Futurekind 1 C
569 Orin Scannell C
570 Bedlam Jailer C
571 Pig Slave Group C
572 Hutchinson C
573 Billy Shipton C
574 Toclafane group C
575 Jenny C
576 Refugee 2 C
577 Captain Jack with Vortex Manipulator R
578 Headmaster Rocastle C
579 Futurekind 2 C
580 Lynley C
581 Judoon Group C
582 Abi Lerner C
583 Dalek Sec Hybrid SR
584 Sinister Woman C
585 Macra 3 C
586 The Master's Regeneration UR
587 Cricket Ball C
588 Laz Labs R
589 Honesty Mood Patch C
590 Compensation Form C
591 Missile C
592 Psychic Connection C
593 Vivien Rook's Message C
594 Crystal Ball C
595 Tooth Identification C
596 President Winters C
597 Time Lord 3 C
598 Ben Wainwright C
599 Martha (in disguise) C
600 The Master R

2008 Doctor Who Battles in Time Devastators

RELEASED ON SEPTEMBER 3, 2008
826 Fifth Doctor (Time Crashed) C
827 Newborn Adipose C
828 High Priestess C
829 General Cobb C
830 Astrid Peth C
831 Natural Ood C
832 Agatha Christie C
833 Matron Cofelia C
834 Major Domo C
835 River Song C
836 Jethro Cane C
837 General Staal (The Undefeated) C
838 Footman C
839 Luke Rattigan C
840 Natural Ood (Caged) C
841 Titanic Steward C
842 Captain Jack (TARDIS Crew) C
843 Proper Dave (Animated Skeleton) R
844 Kess C
845 Jenny C
846 Davenport C
847 Red-Eye Ood 1 C
848 Val Cane C
849 Tenth Doctor (with Luggage) C
850 Pompeii Slaves C
851 Martha Jones (TARDIS Crew) C
852 Atmos Worker 1 C
853 Bannakaffalatta C
854 Penny Carter C
855 Pyrovile C
856 Doctor Ryder C
857 Messaline Soldier 1 C
858 Vespiform C
859 Professor Hobbes C
860 Morvin and Foon C
861 Halo Weapon C
862 Water Pistol C
863 Adipose Pendant C
864 Clone Machine C
865 River Song's Diary C
866 Firestone Necklace C
867 Progenation Machine C
868 Sontaran War Room C
869 Subwave Network C
870 Suit Creature Attack UR
871 Giant Ood Brain C
872 Captain Hardaker C
873 Doctor Martha Jones C
874 Shadow Proclamation C
875 Gable SR
876 Sister Spurrina C
877 Rabid Ood (Attacking) C
878 Biff Cane C
879 Private Ross Jenkins C
880 Carter C
881 Sontaran Squad C
882 Lady Eddison C
883 Tenth Doctor (with Jenny) C
884 General Sanchez C
885 Red-Eye Ood 2 C
886 Anita C
887 Dalek Caan (Scarred by Time War) C
888 Captain Price C
889 Ood Delta 50 (Dying) C
890 Donna Noble (TARDIS Crew) C
891 Sontaran Wrist Device R
892 Marble Circuit (Activated) C
893 Halpen's Communicator C
894 Titanic Teleport Bracelet C
895 Sonic Boom C
896 Pyrovile Attack UR
897 River Song's Squareness Gun C
898 Atmos GPS C
899 The Source SR
900 Magnifying Glass C
901 Astrid Peth (Sacrifice) C
902 Clone R
903 Caecilius C
904 The Hostess C
905 Greeves C
906 Hath Group C
907 Sister Spurrina (with Sacrificial Knife) C
908 Supreme Dalek C
909 Private Harris C
910 Duplicate Doctor (TARDIS Crew) C
911 Adipose Ship C
912 Shore Leave C
913 Sontaran Teleport UR
914 Ood Ball Attack SR
915 River Song's Sonic Screwdriver R
916 Bad Wolf Effect UR
917 Swagger Stick C
918 Psychic Powers C
919 Power Drain C
920 Hath Respirator C
921 Christopher C
922 River Song (with Sonic Screwdriver) C
923 Klineman Halpen C
924 Martha Jones (Sontaran Clone) C
925 Ella McAvoy C
926 Davros (Creator of the Daleks) SR
927 Miss Foster R
928 Red-Eye Ood Group R
929 Rose Tyler (Traveller through the Void) R
930 Messaline Soldier 2 C
931 Albino Servant C
932 Evelina (Entranced) C
933 Sontaran 1 C
934 Dee Dee Blasco C
935 Rabid Ood C
936 Strackman Lux C
937 Crucible Dalek 1 C
938 Fortune Teller C
939 Lady Eddison (in 1886) C
940 Shadow Proclamation Judoon C
941 Ood Sales Rep C
942 River Song (Saved) R
943 Kess (Attacking) C
944 Martha Jones (Being Cloned) C
945 Professor Peach C
946 Sky Silvestry (Possessed) R
947 Stallholder C
948 Enslaved Ood 1 C
949 Donna Noble (Investigator) C
950 Max Capricorn C
951 Mount Vesuvius C
952 Sonic Pen R
953 Luke Smith C
954 Security Camera C
955 Warp Star R
956 Sontaran Ship C
957 Vespiform Transformation UR
958 Dalek Crucible C
959 Tenth Doctor's Hand SR
960 Parthenogenesis Detector C
961 Foon Van Hoff C
962 Solana Mercurio C
963 Joyful Adipose R
964 Rattigan Academy Students C
965 Pyrovile Soldier C
966 Wilfred Mott C
967 Titanic Passenger C
968 Ood Sigma C
969 Miss Chandrakala (in 1886) C
970 Cline C
971 Tenth Doctor (TARDIS Crew) C
972 Sontaran 2 C
973 Charlotte Abigail Lux C
974 Old Woman C
975 K-9 R
976 Electro Blast C
977 Sontaran War Console C
978 Sky Silvestry C
979 Donna Noble (Wrong Turn) C
980 Supreme Dalek (Flanked by Daleks) C
981 Other Dave C
982 Shadow Architect C
983 Sister Thalina C
984 Heavenly Host Army C
985 Private Gray C
986 Enslaved Ood 2 C
987 Penny Carter (Tied Up) C
988 Quintus C
989 Reverend Golightly C
990 Donna McAvoy C
991 Heavenly Host (Flying Attack) C
992 Ood Transformation UR
993 Adipose Industries R
994 Ancient Scroll C
995 Vespiform Vision SR
996 Atmospheric Converter C
997 Ood Hind-Brain C
998 Max Capricorn (Portrait) C
999 Bad Wolf Warning
1000 Davros and Dalek C
1001 Adipose Group C
1002 Donna Noble (Prepared for the Cold) C
1003 Lucius Dextrus C
1004 Suzette C
1005 Rose Tyler (TARDIS Crew) C
1006 Rickston Slade C
1007 Natural Ood (Singing) C
1008 Soothsayer C
1009 Davros (with Dalek Caan) C
1010 Miss Chandrakala C
1011 Time Crash C
1012 SS Titanic R
1013 Adipose Computer SR
1014 Temple of Sibyl C

1015 Adipose Pills C
1016 Detonation Pack C
1017 Electromagnetic Pulse SR
1018 Osterhagen Key R
1019 Sontaran Pod C
1020 Donna Noble (with Time Lord Consciousness) R
1021 Midshipman Alonso Frame C
1022 Matella C
1023 Martha Jones (Project Indigo) R
1024 Escaped Adipose C
1025 Kess (with Whip) C
1026 Mr Copper C
1027 Atmos Worker 2 C
1028 The Two Doctors R
1029 Sibylline Sisterhood C
1030 Sontaran 3 C
1031 Miss Evangelista C
1032 Gwen Cooper C
1033 Enslaved Ood Group C
1034 Roger Curbishley C
1035 Mickey Smith (TARDIS Crew) C
1036 Claude C
1037 Crucible Dalek 2 C
1038 Proper Dave C
1039 Pyrovile 3 C
1040 Heavenly Host (Flying) R
1041 Sylvia Noble C
1042 Tenth Doctor (with Water Pistol) C
1043 Claire C
1044 Commander Skorr (The Bloodbringer) C
1045 Rickston Slade (Survivor) C
1046 Matron Cofelia (with Adipose Computer) C
1047 Doctor Moon C
1048 Colonel Hugh Curbishley C
1049 Jackie Tyler (TARDIS Crew) C
1050 Natural Ood Group C
1051 Project Indigo C
1052 Detonator C
1053 Sontaran Ship (Attack Mode) R
1054 Davros (Raging) C
1055 Adipose Escape C
1056 Vespiform Sting R
1057 Mechanical Claw C
1058 Shrine C
1059 Celery C
1060 Video Message C
1061 Pyrovile Group C
1062 Morvin Van Hoff C
1063 Robina Redmond C
1064 Pyrovile (Breathing Fire) SR
1065 Bartle C
1066 Pack C
1067 General Staal (Full Uniform) R
1068 Evelina C
1069 Heavenly Host (Being Reprogrammed) C
1070 Sarah Jane Smith (TARDIS Crew) C
1071 Duplicate Doctor (with Catalyser) R
1072 Driver Joe C
1073 Colonel Mace C
1074 Harriet Jones (Former Prime Minister) C
1075 Davros (Time War Survivor) SR

2008 Doctor Who Battles in Time Sarah Jane Adventures

SJA00 Introductory card
SJA01 Sarah Jane Smith (and friends)
SJA02 Mrs Wormwood
SJA03 Commander Kaagh
SJA04 The Gorgon
SJA05 The Trickster (with the Graske)
SJA06 Slitheen
SJA07 General Kudlak
SJA08 Odd Bob
SJA09 Mr Smith
SJA10 The Brigadier

2008 Doctor Who Battles in Time Ultimate Monsters

RELEASED ON MARCH 5, 2008
601 Broton C
602 Cyberman (From Our Universe) R
603 God Of Ragnarok C
604 Glass Dalek R
605 Icthar C
606 Alpha Centauri C
607 Ancient Haemovore SR
608 Cyberman (Invading Earth) C
609 Davros C
610 Drathro C
611 Fendahl Core R
612 Black Dalek C
613 Ice Warrior C
614 Exxilon Antibody R
615 Gundan Robot C
616 Autons (Carnival Disguise) C
617 Head Of Stengos C
618 D84 C
619 Aggedor C
620 Draconian C
621 Eldred (Female Form) C
622 Exxilon Group C
623 Axon Man C
624 Guardian Of Uxarieus C
625 Azal C
626 Heavenly Host R
627 Dragon Laser Gun C
628 Bok C
629 Dalek Mutant (Dying) C
630 Bellal C
631 Husk 1 C
632 Draconian Group C
633 Empty Child (Attacking) C
634 Fendahleen C
635 Antiman SR
636 Camouflaged Cyberman C
637 Azaxyr C
638 Cryon R
639 Racnoss Empress (Invading) C
640 Giant Maggot C
641 Gods Of Ragnarok R
642 Auton Scout C
643 Cyberman (Awakening) R
644 Axon Girl C
645 Sisters Of Plenitude C
646 Hand Of Eldrad C
647 Cyber Android C
648 Haemovore 1 C
649 Clockwork Woman (Unmasked) C
650 Foamasi C
651 Cyber Leader (Our Universe) C
652 Cessair Of Diplos C
653 Scarecrow Army C
654 Cheetah Person C
655 Linx C
656 Davros (As Emperor Dalek) SR
657 Kronos C
658 Tetrap C
659 Raston Robot R
660 Axon Eye C
661 Hieronymous C
662 Mags C
663 The Master (Emaciated Form) C
664 Omega (First Appearance) C
665 Sharaz Jek C
666 The Master (Pre-Regeneration) SR
667 Terileptil (Firing) C
668 Drashig C
669 Mutt C
670 Mummy C
671 Sycorax Leader (Swordfighting) C
672 Vervoid (Human Hybrid) C
673 Sea Devil C
674 Izlyr C
675 Eldrad (Attacking) R
676 Special Weapon Dalek R
677 Zygon C
678 Max Capricorn C
679 Nimon C
680 Marcus Scarman (Possessed) C
681 Axon Monster C
682 Linx (Attacking) C
683 Lazarus Creature (Rampaging) C
684 Rutan C
685 Orgon C
686 Mogarian Group R
687 Husk 2 C
688 Sii C
689 Krynoid (Human Hybrid) C
690 Mr Sin C
691 Cult Of Skaro (In New York) C
692 Nemesis Statue R
693 Foamasi Group C
694 Cyberman Guard C
695 Kraals C
696 Axon Family R
697 Mestor C
698 Styre C
699 Doomfinger (Touch Of Death) C
700 Scaroth's Ship C
701 Coronic Acid Attack C
702 Source Manipulator R
703 Sarcophagus C
704 Axonite C
705 Dalek Gas Attack C
706 Vionesium Bombs R
707 Laseron Probe C
708 Yeti Control Sphere R
709 Exxilon City Root R
710 Cyber Leader (Armed) R
711 Silurian C
712 Sutekh SR
713 Jagrafess (Attacking) C
714 Sauvix C
715 Mandrel C
716 Davros (Energy Attack) R
717 Pirate Captain C
718 Krynoid (Attacking House) C
719 Werewolf (Howling) C
720 Vervoid C
721 Morbius C
722 Reptile Areta C
723 Axon Monster Group C
724 War Machine C
725 Weeping Angel Group C
726 Distillation Chamber C
727 Sontaran Unmasking UR
728 Osiran War Missile C
729 Fendahl Skull C
730 Alien Ambassador UR
731 Davros (As The Great Healer) C
732 Scaroth C
733 Sun-Possessed Korwin (Unmasked) R
734 V3 (Attacking) C
735 Vervoid Group C
736 Sensorites C
737 Priest Of Uxarieus C
738 Haemovore 2 C
739 Giant Maggot Group C
740 Mechanoid C
741 Sharaz Jek (Unmasked) C
742 Ogri C
743 Pig Slave (Attacking) C
744 The Destroyer C
745 Haemovore Group C
746 Marshman C
747 Omega (Second Appearance) C
748 Eldrad (Male Form) C
749 Cryon (Attacking) C
750 Zygon Group SR
751 Ood (In Pursuit) C
752 Stike C
753 Magnus Greel C
754 The Malus C
755 Kroll C
756 Sontaran Group C
757 The Lukoser C
758 Mandrel Group C
759 Trin-E & Zu-Zana C
760 Monarch C
761 Bannakaffalatta R
762 Davros And Daleks C
763 Cheetah Group C
764 Terileptil Android C
765 Ogron Group C
766 Omega (Projection) SR
767 Tranquil Repose Daleks C
768 Melkur C
769 Yeti C
770 Zarbi C
771 Unfiltered Sunlight UR
772 Ragnarok Eye SR
773 Giant Brain C
774 Raston Robot Attack C
775 Sonic Booster C
776 Self-Destruct Button C
777 Terileptil Escape Pod C
778 Rouge Cyberman C
779 Carrionite (Escaping) C
780 Sea Devil Group C
781 Xeraphin C
782 Renegade Daleks (Attacking) C
783 Cassandra's Brain C
784 Terileptil Android (Dressed As Death) C
785 Tetraps (Sleeping) C
786 Imperial Dalek (Attacking) C
787 Robot K1 R
788 Wolfweeds C
789 Mother Of Mine (Trapped) C
790 Tractator Group C
791 Dalek Shuttlecraft C
792 Nimon Capsule C
793 Sutekh's Gift Of Death C
794 Sontaran Translator Unit C
795 Cyber Bomb C
796 Nestene Energy Unit C
797 Cyberscope C
798 Scaroth's Time Machine UR
799 Space Freighter C
800 Macra Claws UR
801 The Gravis C
802 Voc Robot Group R
803 Wirrn C
804 Tetrap Group C
805 The Great One C
806 Vorus C
807 Father Of Mine (Trapped) C
808 Marshman Group C
809 Cyberman (From Parallel World) C
810 Terileptil Group C
811 Magnus Greel (Unmasked) C
812 Omega's Creature C
813 Mummy Group C
814 Heavenly Host (Attacking) C
815 Terileptil SR
816 Max Capricorn (With Heavenly Hosts) SR
817 Soliton Gas Machine C
818 SV7 C
819 Primord C
820 Dragon C
821 Bannakaffalatta (Sacrificing Himself) C
822 Mutt Group C
823 Lord Kiv C
824 The Borad C
825 The Master (With Toclafane) R

2004 Duel Masters

1 Chilias, the Oracle R
2 Dia Nork, Moonlight Guardian R
3 Emerald Grass C
4 Frei, Vizier of Air U
5 Gran Gure, Space Guardian VR
6 Holy Awe R
7 Iere, Vizier of Bullets C
8 Iocant, the Oracle U
9 La Ura Giga, Sky Guardian C
10 Lah, Purification Enforcer R
11 Laser Wing R
12 Lok, Vizier of Hunting U
13 Miele, Vizier of Lightning C
14 Moonlight Flash U
15 Rayla, Truth Enforcer VR
16 Reusol, the Oracle C
17 Ruby Grass U
18 Senatine Jade Tree C
19 Solar Ray C
20 Sonic Wing C
21 Szubs Kin, Twilight Guardian R
22 Toel, Vizier of Hope U
23 Aqua Hulcus C
24 Aqua Knight R
25 Aqua Soldier U
26 Aqua Vehicle C
27 Brain Serum U
28 Candy Drop C
29 Crystal Memory R
30 Faerie Child U
31 Hunter Fish C
32 Illusionary Merfolk U
33 King Coral U
34 King Ripped-Hide VR
35 Marine Flower C
36 Phantom Fish C
37 Revolver Fish U
38 Saucer-Head Shark R
39 Seamine VR
40 Spiral Gate C
41 Teleportation R
42 Tropico R
43 Unicorn Fish R
44 Virtual Tripwire C
45 Black Feather, Shadow of Rage C
46 Bloody Squito C
47 Bone Assassin, the Ripper C
48 Bone Spider U
49 Creeping Plague R
50 Dark Clown R
51 Dark Raven, Shadow of Grief U
52 Dark Reversal U
53 Death Smoke C
54 Ghost Touch C
55 Gigaberos R
56 Gigagiele R
57 Gigargon VR
58 Masked Horror, Shadow of Scorn U
59 Night Master, Shadow of Decay R
60 Skeleton Soldier, the Defiled C
61 Stinger Worm U
62 Swamp Worm U
63 Terror Pit R
64 Vampire Silphy VR
65 Wandering Braineater C
66 Writhing Bone Ghoul C
67 Armored Walker Urherion U
68 Artisan Picora C
69 Bolshack Dragon VR
70 Brawler Zyler C
71 Burning Power C
72 Chaos Strike R
73 Crimson Hammer C
74 Deadly Fighter Braid Claw C
75 Draglide R
76 Explosive Fighter Ucarn R
77 Fatal Attacker Horvath C
78 Fire Sweeper Burning Hellion C
79 Gatling Skyterror VR
80 Immortal Baron, Vorg C
81 Magma Gazer R
82 Meteosaur U
83 Nomad Hero Gigio R
84 Onslaughter Triceps U
85 Rothus, the Traveler R
86 Stonesaur U
87 Super Explosive Volcanodon U
88 Tornado Flame U
89 Aura Blast R
90 Bronze-Arm Tribe C
91 Burning Mane C
92 Coiling Vines U
93 Dimension Gate C
94 Dome Shell U
95 Fear Fang C
96 Forest Hornet U
97 Golden Wing Striker C
98 Mighty Shouter C
99 Natural Snare R
S1 Hanusa, Radiance Elemental SR
S2 Urth, Purifying Elemental SR
S3 Aqua Sniper SR
S4 King Depthcon SR
S5 Deathliger, Lion of Chaos SR
S6 Zagaan, Knight of Darkness SR
S7 Astrocomet Dragon SR
S8 Scarlet Skyterror SR
S9 Deathblade Beetle SR
100 Pangaea's Song U
101 Poisonous Dahlia U
102 Poisonous Mushroom U
103 Red-Eye Scorpion R
104 Stampeding Longhorn R
105 Steel Smasher C
106 Storm Shell R
107 Thorny Mandra VR
108 Tower Shell VR
109 Tri-horn Shepherd R
110 Ultimate Force C
S10 Roaring Great-Horn SR

2004 Duel Masters Evo Crushinators of Doom

1 Diamond Cutter U
2 Ethel, Star Sea Elemental VR
3 Fonch, the Oracle C
4 Laguna, Lightning Enforcer R
5 Larba Geer, the Immaculate U
6 Logic Cube C
7 Magris, Vizier of Magnetism C
8 Phal Eega, Dawn Guardian R
9 Reso Pacos, Clear Sky Guardian C
10 Spiral Grass R
11 Wyn, the Oracle U
12 Aqua Bouncer R
13 Aqua Shooter C
14 Corile C
15 Crystal Lancer U
16 Hypersquid Walter R
17 King Nautilus R
18 Plasma Chaser VR
19 Recon Operation C
20 Scissor Eye C
21 Stained Glass U
22 Thought Probe U
23 Amber Piercer R
24 Chaos Worm U
25 Critical Blade C
26 Dark Titan Maginn VR
27 General Dark Fiend R
28 Gigastand C
29 Gray Balloon, Shadow of Greed U
30 Horrid Worm C
31 Lost Soul U
32 Marrow Ooze, the Twister C
33 Poison Worm R
34 Armored Cannon Balbaro U
35 Bolzard Dragon VR
36 Bombersaur R
37 Burst Shot U
38 Cavalry General Curatops U
39 Dogarn, the Marauder R
40 Engineer Kipo C
41 Galsaur C
42 Metalwing Skyterror R
43 Mini Titan Gett C
44 Rumble Gate C
45 Barkwhip, the Smasher U
46 Elf-X R
47 Essence Elf C
48 Fortress Shell R
49 Leaping Tornado Horn C
50 Mana Crisis U
51 Rainbow Stone C
52 Rumbling Terahorn R
53 Silver Axe C
54 Silver Fist U
55 Xeno Mantis VR
S1 Ladia Bale, the Inspirational SR
S2 Crystal Paladin SR
S3 Ultracide Worm SR
S4 Armored Blaster Valdios SR
S5 Fighter Dual Fang SR

2004 Duel Masters Rampage of the Super Warriors

1 Alek, Solidity Enforcer R
2 Aless, the Oracle C
3 Boomerang Comet U
4 Lena, Vizier of Brilliance C
5 Logic Sphere R
6 Ra Vu, Seeker of Lightning U
7 Raza Vega, Thunder Guardian R
8 Sieg Balicula, the Intense VR
9 Sparkle Flower U
10 Sundrop Armor C
11 Ur Pale, Seeker of Sunlight C
12 Angler Cluster C
13 Aqua Deformer R
14 Emeral C
15 Flood Valve U
16 King Neptas R
17 King Ponitas U
18 Legendary Bynor VR
19 Liquid Scope C
20 Psychic Shaper R
21 Shtra C
22 Stinger Ball U
23 Baraga, Blade of Gloom U
24 Bone Piercer C
25 Eldritch Poison U
26 Gamil, Knight of Hatred R
27 Ghastly Drain R
28 Hang Worm, Fetid Larva U
29 Jack Viper, Shadow of Doom VR
30 Mudman C
31 Scratchclaw R
32 Snake Attack C
33 Wailing Shadow Belbetphlo C
34 Armored Warrior Quelos U
35 Baby Zoppe C
36 Blaze Cannon R
37 Boltail Dragon R
38 Explosive Dude Joe C
39 Flametropus R
40 Muramasa, Duke of Blades U
41 Searing Wave U
42 Snip Striker Bullraizer C
43 Uberdragon Jabaha VR
44 Volcanic Arrows C
45 Aurora of Reversal R
46 Dawn Giant R
47 Gigamantis VR
48 Mana Nexus U
49 Masked Pomegranate U
50 Pouch Shell U
51 Psyshroom R
52 Raging Dash-Horn C
53 Roar of the Earth C
54 Sniper Mosquito C
55 Sword Butterfly C
S1 Miar, Comet Elemental SR
S2 Chaos Fish SR
S3 Giriel, Ghastly Warrior SR
S4 Garkago Dragon SR
S5 Earthstomp Giant SR

2004 Duel Masters Shadow Clash of Blinding Night

1 Alcadeias, Lord of Spirits VR
2 Astral Warper VR
3 Trox, General of Destruction VR
4 Dobougyser, Giant Rock Beast VR
5 Supporting Tulip VR
6 Aeris, Flight Elemental R
7 Amber Grass C
8 Fu Reil, Seeker of Storms U
9 Full Defensor R
10 Gulan Rias, Speed Guardian C
11 Kolon, the Oracle C
12 Milieus, the Daystretcher U
13 Mist Rias, Sonic Guardian U
14 Ouks, Vizier of Restoration R
15 Re Bil, Seeker of Archery U
16 Sarius, Vizier of Suppression C
17 Screaming Sunburst U
18 Whisking Whirlwind C
19 Aqua Guard C
20 Aqua Jolter C
21 Clone Factory C
22 Hunter Cluster U
23 Hydro Hurricane R
24 Keeper of the Sunlit Abyss C

25 Marinomancer R
26 Smile Angler R
27 Chains of Sacrifice R
28 Darkpact C
29 Gigabolver U
30 Gregoria, Princess of War R
31 Gregorian Worm C
32 Locomotiver U
33 Mongrel Man U
34 Photocide, Lord of the Wastes R
35 Purple Piercer C
36 Shadow Moon, Cursed Shade C
37 Skeleton Thief, the Revealer C
38 Soul Gulp U
39 Volcano Smog, Deceptive Shade U
40 Blasto, Explosive Soldier C
41 Chaotic Skyterror R
42 Kamikaze, Chainsaw Warrior C
43 Magmarex R
44 Mega Detonator R
45 Missile Boy U
46 Pippie Kuppie C
47 Sword of Malevolent Death U
48 Ancient Giant R
49 Cannon Shell C
50 Dew Mushroom U
51 Exploding Cactus C
52 Mystic Inscription R
53 Sword of Benevolent Life R
54 Three-Eyed Dragonfly U
55 Torcon C
S1 Rimuel, Cloudbreak Elemental SR
S2 King Aquakamui SR
S3 Ballom, Master of Death SR
S4 Galklife Dragon SR
S5 Niofa, Horned Protector SR

2005 Duel Masters Epic Dragons of Hyperchaos

1 Kuukai, Finder of Karma VR
2 Aqua Ranger VR
3 Megaria, Empress of Dread VR
4 Magmadragon Jagalzor VR
5 Kachua, Keeper of the Icegate VR
6 Dracobarrier U
7 Laser Whip U
8 Lunar Charger C
9 Migalo, Vizier of Spycraft C
10 Misha, Channeler of Suns C
11 Nariel, the Oracle R
12 Sasha, Channeler of Suns R
13 Sol Galla, Halo Guardian C
14 Solar Grass U
15 Thrumiss, Zephyr Guardian R
16 Aqua Grappler R
17 Candy Cluster C
18 Eureka Charger C
19 Grape Globbo C
20 Illusion Fish C
21 Lalicious U
22 Marine Scramble R
23 Prowling Elephish U
24 Vikorakys R
25 Wave Lance U
26 Corpse Charger C
27 Cranium Clamp R
28 Dimension Splitter U
29 Gachack, Mechanical Doll U
30 Gigaclaws C
31 Motorcycle Mutant U
32 Necrodragon Galbazeek R
33 Necrodragon Giland C
34 Scream Slicer, Shadow of Fear R
35 Tyrant Worm C
36 Bruiser Dragon U
37 Furious Onslaught R
38 Kyrstron, Lair Delver R
39 Magmadragon Melgars C
40 Missile Soldier Ultimo C
41 Rocketdive Skyterror U
42 Slaphappy Soldier Galback R
43 Torpedo Skyterror C
44 Totto Pipicchi C
45 Volcano Charger U
46 Bakkra Horn, the Silent C
47 Carbonite Scarab R
48 Coliseum Shell U
49 Dracodance Totem U
50 Muscle Charger U
51 Quixotic Hero Swine Snout C
52 Root Charger R
53 Senia, Orchard Avenger C
54 Terradragon Gamiratar R
55 Terradragon Regarion C
S1 Nastasha, Channeler of Suns SR
S2 Emperor Quazla SR
S3 Super Necrodragon Abzo Dolba SR
S4 Überdragon Bajula SR
S5 Super Terradragon Bailas Gale SR
11j Nariel, the Oracle R

2005 Duel Masters Stomp-A-Trons of Invincible Wrath

1 Invincible Aura VR
2 Lu Gila, Silver Rift Guardian VR
3 Aeropica VR
4 Invincible Technology VR
5 Invincible Abyss VR
6 Tank Mutant VR
7 Invincible Cataclysm VR
8 Valiant Warrior Exorious VR
9 Invincible Unity VR
10 Splinterclaw Wasp VR
11 Adomis, the Oracle U
12 Arc Bine, the Astounding R
13 Ballas, Vizier of Electrons C
14 Bonds of Justice R
15 Chekicul, Vizier of Endurance C
16 Chen Treg, Vizier of Blades C
17 Cosmogold, Spectral Knight R
18 Dava Torey, Seeker of Clouds U
19 Forbos, Sanctum Guardian Q R
20 Gariel, Elemental of Sunbeams R
21 Kanesill, the Explorer C
22 Lightning Grass C
23 Moontear, Spectral Knight U
24 Protective Force U
25 Rain of Arrows U
26 Razorpine Tree U
27 Sphere of Wonder C
28 Telitol, the Explorer R
29 Vess, the Oracle C
30 Yuluk, the Oracle C
31 Aqua Rider C
32 Energy Stream C
33 Fort Megacluster R
34 Hazard Crawler U
35 King Triumphant R
36 Kyuroro R
37 Madrillon Fish C
38 Midnight Crawler R
39 Mystic Dreamscape U
40 Neon Cluster U
41 Overload Cluster U
42 Promephius Q C
43 Raptor Fish R
44 Ripple Lotus Q R
45 Shock Hurricane U
46 Sopian C
47 Spiral Gate C
48 Steam Star C
49 Thrash Crawler U
50 Zepimeteus C
51 Bazooka Mutant U
52 Cursed Pincher C
53 Death Smoke C
54 Frost Specter, Shadow of Age R
55 Future Slash U
56 Gigagriff U
57 Gnarvash, Merchant of Blood R
58 Grave Worm Q R
59 Grim Soul, Shadow of Reversal C
60 Grinning Axe, the Monstrosity C
61 Intense Evil R
62 Junkatz, Rabid Doll C
63 Lone Tear, Shadow of Solitude C
64 Lupa, Poison-Tipped Doll U
65 Proclamation of Death U
66 Schuka, Duke of Amnesia R
67 Skullcutter, Swarm Leader U
68 Tentacle Worm C
69 Vile Mulder, Wing of the Void R
70 Zorvaz, the Bonecrusher C
71 Armored Decimator Valkaizer R
72 Armored Scout Gestuchar C
73 Automated Weaponmaster Machai C
74 Badlands Lizard R
75 Bazagazeal Dragon R
76 Choya, the Unheeding C
77 Cocco Lupia U
78 Comet Missile U
79 Crisis Boulder R
80 Cutthroat Skyterror U
81 Legionnaire Lizard C
82 Migasa, Adept of Chaos U
83 Phantom Dragon's Flame C
84 Picora's Wrench C
85 Pyrofighter Magnus C
86 Q-tronic Gargantua R
87 Rikabu's Screwdriver R
88 Rumblesaur Q U
89 Spastic Missile U
90 Torchclencher C
91 Bliss Totem, Avatar of Luck U
92 Cantankerous Giant U
93 Carrier Shell C
94 Charmilia, the Enticer R
95 Clobber Totem R
96 Dimension Gate C
97 Factory Shell Q R
98 Faerie Life C
99 Feather Horn, the Tracker U
S1 Craze Valkyrie, the Drastic SR
S2 Laveil, Seeker of Catastrophe SR
S3 Crystal Jouster SR
S4 Q-tronic Hypermind SR
S5 Daidalos, General of Fury SR
S6 Phantasmal Horror Gigazald SR
S7 Bolmeteus Steel Dragon SR
S8 Lava Walker Executo SR
S9 Cliffcrush Giant SR
100 Forbidding Totem R
101 Garabon, the Glider C
102 Illusory Berry C
103 Innocent Hunter, Blade of All U
104 Living Citadel Vosh R
105 Mighty Bandit, Ace of Thieves C
106 Mystic Treasure Chest R
107 Pangaea's Will U
108 Paradise Horn U
109 Slumber Shell C
110 Trench Scarab C
S10 Ultra Mantis, Scourge of Fate SR

2005 Duel Masters Survivors of the Megapocalypse

1 La Byle, Seeker of the Winds VR
2 King Mazelan VR
3 Sinister General Damudo VR
4 Bladerush Skyterror Q VR
5 Obsidian Scarab VR
6 Ballus, Dogfight Enforcer Q U
7 Calgo, Vizier of Rainclouds C
8 Gallia Zohl, Iron Guardian Q C
9 Glory Snow R
10 Kulus, Soulshine Enforcer C
11 La Guile, Seeker of Skyfire U
12 Le Quist, the Oracle C
13 Snork La, Shrine Guardian R
14 Syforce, Aurora Elemental R
15 Thunder Net U
16 Aqua Surfer U
17 Divine Riptide R
18 Lurking Eel C
19 Miracle Quest U
20 Pokolul R
21 Sea Slug R
22 Solidskin Fish C
23 Spikestrike Ichthys Q C
24 Split-Head Hydroturtle Q U
25 Steel-Turret Cluster C
26 Gigakail U
27 Gigaling Q C
28 Gigazoul C
29 Horned Mutant U
30 Jewel Spider C
31 Scheming Hands U
32 Skullsweeper Q R
33 Slime Veil R
34 Vashuna, Sword Dancer R
35 Wisp Howler, Shadow of Tears C
36 Blazosaur Q C
37 Bolgash Dragon U
38 Bombat, General of Speed U
39 Cannoneer Bargon R
40 Cataclysmic Eruption R
41 Cyclone Panic U
42 Kip Chippotto C
43 Rikabu, the Dismantler C
44 Ruthless Skyterror C
45 Twin-Cannon Skyterror R
46 Ambush Scorpion C
47 Balloonshroom Q U
48 Bloodwing Mantis R
49 Brutal Charge R
50 Crow Winger C
51 Enchanted Soil U
52 Moon Horn U
53 Nocturnal Giant R
54 Scissor Scarab C
55 Smash Horn Q C
9m Glory Snow R
S1 Syrius, Firmament Elemental SR
S2 King Tsunami SR
S3 Death Cruzer, the Annihilator SR
S4 Billion-Degree Dragon SR
S5 Avalanche Giant SR

2005 Duel Masters Thundercharge of Ultra Destruction

1 Gandar, Seeker of Explosions VR
2 King Benthos VR
3 Battleship Mutant VR
4 Armored Transport Galiacruse VR
5 Spinning Totem VR
6 Bex, the Oracle C
7 Geoshine, Spectral Knight U
8 Justice Jamming R
9 Kizar Basiku, the Outrageous R
10 Lightning Charger U
11 Miracle Portal C
12 Pulsar Tree R
13 Rodi Gale, Night Guardian C
14 Rom, Vizier of Tendrils C
15 Rondobil, the Explorer U
16 Aqua Agent C
17 Aqua Fencer R
18 Biancus R
19 Cetibols C
20 Curious Eye U
21 Garatyano C
22 Riptide Charger U
23 Splash Zebrafish U
24 Titanium Cluster C
25 Trenchdive Shark R
26 Dream Pirate, Shadow of Theft C
27 Gezary, Undercover Doll C
28 Gigabuster R
29 Hopeless Vortex R
30 Phantasmal Horror Gigazabal R
31 Propeller Mutant C
32 Scalpel Spider U
33 Three-Faced Ashura Fang U
34 Vacuum Gel C
35 Venom Charger U
36 Apocalypse Vise R
37 Astronaut Skyterror C
38 Cratersaur U
39 Energy Charger U
40 Gazarias Dragon C
41 Kipo's Contraption R
42 Kooc Pollon C
43 Otherworldly Warrior Naglu U
44 Valkrowzer, Ultra Rock Beast R
45 Wild Racer Chief Garan C
46 Brood Shell U
47 Cryptic Totem R
48 Freezing Icehammer C
49 Fruit of Eternity U
50 Launch Locust C
51 Mulch Charger U
52 Popple, Flowerpetal Dancer C
53 Stinger Horn, the Delver C
54 Tangle Fist, the Weaver R
55 World Tree, Root of Life R
S1 Siri, Glory Elemental SR
S2 Cosmic Nebula SR
S3 Crath Lade, Merciless King SR
S4 Sky Crusher, the Agitator SR
S5 Headlong Giant SR

2005 Duel Masters Zakira's Dragon Commander Power-Up Pack

5 Frost Specter, Shadow of Age R
7 Necrodragon Bagrazard R
10 Gigajiras R
11 Scratchclaw R
28 Locomotiver U
29 Necrodragon Zekira U
30 Dimension Splitter U
31 Venom Worm U
32 Lost Soul U
33 Venom Charger U
44 Melnia, the Aqua Shadow U
47 Slash and Burn U
60 Steel-Turret Cluster C
61 Sopian C
62 Angler Cluster C
63 Fist Blader C
65 Reconstruction Man C
66 Cursed Pincher C
67 Trixo, Wicked Doll C
69 Horrid Worm C
71 Grinning Axe, the Monstrosity C
73 Propeller Mutant C
74 Zombie Carnival C
77 Snake Attack C
78 Darkpact C
79 Critical Blade C
83 Quakesaur C
85 Pyrofighter Magnus C
S1 Necrodragon Bazradyuda SR

2006 Duel Masters Arc Seraphim Reverser

2 Soldarios, Holy Emperor VR
11 Laser Wing R
19 Solar Ray C
38 Sandal, Spirit Knight R
39 Assault Champion R
41 Farmahat, Emperor of Spirits U
55 Dandy Eggplant C
66 Ragmal, Spirit Knight U
73 Saiya, Spirit Knight C
74 Rahars, Spirit Knight C

2006 Duel Masters Blastplosion of Gigantic Rage

1 Evil Incarnate VR
2 Heavyweight Dragon VR
3 Diamondia, the Blizzard Rider VR
4 Miraculous Snare VR
5 Miraculous Truce VR
6 Asra, Vizier of Safety C
7 Baraid, the Explorer U
8 Belix, the Explorer R
9 Engbelt, the Spydroid C
10 Lamiel, Destiny Enforcer R
11 Merlee, the Oracle U
12 Nial, Vizier of Dexterity C
13 Solar Trap C
14 Yuliana, Channeler of Suns R
15 Aqua Trickster U
16 Emergency Typhoon C
17 Fantasy Fish R
18 Lucky Ball U
19 Melodic Hunter C
20 Revival Soldier C
21 Squawking Lunatron R
22 Time Scout C
23 Warped Lunatron R
24 Baira, the Hidden Lunatic C
25 Beratcha, the Hidden Glutton C
26 Gazer Eyes, Shadow of Secrets R
27 Hazaria, Duke of Thorns R
28 Jagila, the Hidden Pillager U
29 Morbid Medicine U
30 Roulette of Ruin R
31 Saliva Worm C
32 Spinning Terror, the Wretched C
33 Bonfire Lizard U
34 Brad's Cutter C
35 Eviscerating Warrior Lumez R
36 Gankloak, Rogue Commando C
37 Hysteria Lizard U
38 Jabaha's Automaton R
39 Lockdown Lizard R
40 Sapian Tark, Flame Dervish C
41 Ten-Ton Crunch C
42 Hazard Hopper U
43 Hearty Cap'n Polligon C
44 Macho Melon U
45 Ninja Pumpkin C
46 Quillspike Rumbler C
47 Rainbow Gate C
48 Rollicking Totem R
49 Royal Durian R
50 Skyscraper Shell R
51 Rise and Shine U
52 Live and Breathe U
53 Hide and Seek U
54 Slash and Burn U
55 Reap and Sow U
S1 Warlord Ailzonius SR
S2 Klujadras SR
S3 Miraculous Plague SR
S4 Miraculous Meltdown SR
S5 Miraculous Rebirth SR
52e Live and Breathe U

2006 Duel Masters The Dragonic Nova

1 Spell Del Fin, Light Divine Dragon VR
2 Blue Divine Dragon Spell Grand Blue VR
3 Babelginus, Demonic Dragon VR
4 Super Dragonic Spirit Volgailsak VR
5 Legendary Sante Gat De Paco VR
6 Spirit Rider Muse Rubul R
7 Poppi Luck R
8 Reverse Tone R
9 Blue Divine Dragon Melrosgalb R
10 Time-Space Worker Time Changer R
11 Collapse Wave R
12 Necrodragon Daft Head R
13 Opening of Purgatory R
14 Connected Dragonic Poison R
15 Infinity Dragon R
16 Heat-Fight Brave Maducas R
17 The Universe Gate R
18 Terradragon Geographanis R
19 Pure Grand Swordsman Inos R
20 Blossom Shower R
21 Optic Comet Asteroid Main U
22 Light Divine Dragon Sebuns U
23 Flash Armor U
24 Ice Comet Asteroid Raiser U
25 Sealed Devil Gorgonshack U
26 Dragon Lab U
27 Dark Comet Asteroid Gellum U
28 Sealed Devil Aogrun U
29 Hand of Underworld U
30 Flame Comet Asteroid Gauss SR
31 Dragon's Steward Nyanpatta U
32 Bomber Doll U
33 Ground Comet Asteroid Gaia U
34 Spirit Rider Hamern Dalia U
35 Evolution Egg U
36 Spirit Rider Soul Denan C
37 Spirit Rider Dumar C
38 Revitalize Electric Soldier Energion C
39 Celestrial Arc C
40 Sealed Devil Demigorun C
41 Lip Woppe C
42 Armored Mecha Czarbolt C
43 Future Capsule C
44 Necrodragon Halverd C
45 Sensing Dragoon C
46 Sealed Devil Vines C
47 Serial Dragon Formation C
48 Flaming Jet Dragon C
49 Roppo Roppo C
50 Pop Rubin C
51 Decopin Crash C
52 Terradragon Geobreed C
53 Docganru Pine C
54 Forest Singer Kerodinans C
55 Little Eyes Growth C
S1 Ultimate Galaxy Universe SR
S2 Supernova Petelgius Final Cannon SR
S3 Necrodragon Guljeneraid SR
S4 Supernova Apollonus Dragerion SR
S5 Supernova Uranus Ninetails SR

2006 Duel Masters Fatal Brood of Infinite Ruin

1 Glena Vuele, the Hypnotic VR
2 Marching Motherboard VR
3 Azaghast, Tyrant of Shadows VR
4 Balesk Baj, the Timeburner VR
5 Vreemah, Freaky Mojo Totem VR
6 Betrale, the Explorer U
7 Cosmic Wing C
8 Cyclolink, Spectral Knight C
9 Jil Warka, Time Guardian C
10 Kalute, Vizier of Eternity C
11 Micute, the Oracle R
12 Mihail, Celestial Elemental R
13 Nexus Charger R
14 Tra Rion, Penumbra Guardian U
15 Unified Resistance U
16 Abduction Charger R
17 Emperor Maroll R
18 Hokira U
19 Impossible Tunnel C
20 Kelp Candle C
21 Scout Cluster C
22 Submarine Project U
23 Tekorax U
24 Tentacle Cluster C
25 Zeppelin Crawler R
26 Acid Reflux, the Fleshboiler C
27 Bat Doctor, Shadow of Undeath C
28 Gabzagul, Warlord of Pain R
29 Grinning Hunger U
30 Ice Vapor, Shadow of Anguish R
31 Necrodragon Izorist Vhal U
32 Slash Charger R
33 Trixo, Wicked Doll C
34 Venom Worm U
35 Zombie Carnival C
36 Aerodactyl Kooza C
37 Blizzard of Spears R
38 Fists of Forever U
39 Gigio's Hammer U
40 Quakesaur C
41 Relentless Blitz C
42 Shock Trooper Mykee R
43 Simian Warrior Grash R
44 Snaptongue Lizard U
45 Steam Rumbler Kain C
46 Cavern Raider C
47 Dance of the Sproutlings C
48 Mana Bonanza R
49 Silvermoon Trailblazer U
50 Solid Horn C
51 Storm Wrangler, the Furious R
52 Terradragon Anrist Vhal R
53 Vine Charger U
54 Whip Scorpion C
55 Whispering Totem U
S1 Petrova, Channeler of Suns SR
S2 Aqua Master SR

S3 Stallob, the Lifequasher SR
S4 Magmadragon Ogrist Vhal SR
S5 Stratosphere Giant SR

2006 Duel Masters Grand Devil Finisher

1 Azelzard, Dark Emperor SR
25 Fuuma Garmagias R
53 Death Smoke C
56 Fuuma Raum U
58 Vise Cyclone U
63 Terror Pit R
87 Hekisario Dragoon C
92 Storium, Light Ray Doll C
93 Fuuma Erigoul C

2006 Duel Masters Shockwaves of the Shattered Rainbow

1 Balza, Seeker of Hyperpearls VR
2 Ryudmila, Channeler of Suns VR
3 King Oquanos VR
4 Gajirabute, Vile Centurion VR
5 Kejila, the Hidden Horror VR
6 Gaulezal Dragon VR
7 Carnival Totem VR
8 Tanzanyte, the Awakener VR
9 Bombazar, Dragon of Destiny VR
10 Techno Totem VR
11 Berochika, Channeler of Suns U
12 Bulglut, the Spydroid U
13 Clearlo, Grace Enforcer U
14 Ferrosaturn, Spectral Knight C
15 Flohdani, the Spydroid C
16 Glais Mejicula, the Extreme R
17 Ikaz, the Spydroid R
18 Kaemira, the Oracle C
19 Lemik, Vizier of Thought C
20 Logic Cube C
21 Messa Bahna, Expanse Guardian C
22 Pala Olesis, Morning Guardian R
23 Poltalester, the Spydroid R
24 Rapid Reincarnation R
25 Solar Ray C
26 Static Warp U
27 Tulk, the Oracle C
28 Aqua Strummer C
29 Ardent Lunatron U
30 Battery Cluster C
31 Buoyant Blowfish U
32 Charge Whipper R
33 Crystal Spinslicer R
34 Fluorogill Manta C
35 Milporo C
36 Mystic Magician R
37 Pinpoint Lunatron U
38 Recon Operation C
39 Siren Concerto U
40 Spiral Gate C
41 Tide Patroller C
42 Torpedo Cluster C
43 Transmogrify R
44 Zaltan R
45 Benzo, the Hidden Fury C
46 Death Smoke C
47 Dedreen, the Hidden Corrupter U
48 Gigamente U
49 Gigandura R
50 Hourglass Mutant C
51 Infernal Command C
52 Mikay, Rattling Doll C
53 Mummy Wrap, Shadow of Fatigue C
54 Nightmare Invader C
55 Pierr, Psycho Doll U
56 Spark Chemist, Shadow of Whim R
57 Spinal Parasite U
58 Uliya, the Entrancer R
59 Upheaval R
60 Venom Capsule C
61 Zero Nemesis, Shadow of Panic R
62 Armored Raider Gandaval R
63 Brad, Super Kickin' Dynamo C
64 Burnwisp Lizard R
65 Colossus Boost C
66 Cragsaur C
67 Explosive Trooper Zalmez U
68 Forced Frenzy C
69 Hurlosaur R
70 Mezger, Commando Leader C
71 Minelord Skyterror R
72 Mykee's Pliers C
73 Phantom Dragon's Flame C
74 Siege Roller Bagash C
75 Smash Warrior Stagrandu R
76 Supersonic Jet Pack U
77 Taunting Skyterror U
78 Vorg's Engine U
79 Adventure Boar C
80 Ancient Horn, the Watcher U
81 Bubble Scarab R
82 Earth Ripper, Talon of Rage R
83 Faerie Life C
84 Hustle Berry C
85 Jiggly Totem C
86 Karate Potato U
87 Legacy Shell C
88 Sabermask Scarab C
89 Scowling Tomato C
90 Shaman Broccoli R
91 Soulswap R
92 Sporeblast Erengi U
93 Terradragon Cusdalf R
94 Thirst for the Hunt C
95 Twitch Horn, the Aggressor U
96 Aqua Skydiver R
97 Estol, Vizier of Aqua U
98 Tajimal, Vizier of Aqua U
99 Melnia, the Aqua Shadow U
S1 Elixia, Pureblade Elemental SR
S2 Hawkeye Lunatron SR
S3 Hurricane Crawler SR
S4 Necrodragon Bryzenaga SR
S5 Core-Crash Lizard SR
S6 Ultimate Dragon SR
S7 Bodacious Giant SR
S8 Terradragon Dakma Balgarow SR
S9 Bluum Erkis, Flare Guardian SR
100 Pointa, the Aqua Shadow U
101 Soderlight, the Cold Blade R
102 Dolmarks, the Shadow Warrior R
103 Galek, the Shadow Warrior U
104 Ulex, the Dauntless U
105 Gonta, the Warrior Savage U
106 Tagtapp, the Retaliator R
107 Wind Axe, the Warrior Savage U
108 Lukia Lex, Pinnacle Guardian R
109 Sanfist, the Savage Vizier U
110 Skysword, the Savage Vizier U
S10 Deklowaz, the Terminator SR

2006 Duel Masters Thrash of the Hybrid Megacreatures

1 Kilstine, Nebula Elemental VR
2 Extreme Crawler VR
3 Necrodragon Jagraveen VR
4 Punch Trooper Bronks VR
5 Soul Pheonix, Avatar of Unity VR
6 Ularus, Punishment Elemental R
7 Cosmic Darts R
8 Typhoon Crawler R
9 Meloppe R
10 Gigavrand R
11 Steamroller Mutant R
12 Whirling Warrior Malian R
13 Mechadragon's Breath R
14 Pincer Scarab R
15 Radioactive Horn, the Strange R
16 Agira, the Warlord Crawler R
17 Hydrooze, the Mutant Emperor R
18 Phantomach, the Gigatrooper R
19 Nemonex, Bajula's Robomantis R
20 Comet Eye, The Spectoral Spud R
21 Valkyer, Starstorm Elemental U
22 Cloned Deflector U
23 Cloned Spiral U
24 Enigmatic Cascade U
25 Gigabalza U
26 Cloned Nightmare U
27 Muramasa's Knife U
28 Cloned Blade U
29 Wingeye Moth U
30 Cloned Spike-Horn U
31 Electro Explorer Syrion U
32 Sea Mutant Dormel U
33 Gigappi Ponto U
34 Buzz Betocchi U
35 Spectoral Horn Glitalis U
36 Bigole, the Explorer C
37 Mizoy, the Oracle C
38 Belmol, the Explorer C
39 Pharzi, the Oracle C
40 Tropic Crawler C
41 Funky Wizard C
42 Wily Carpenter C
43 Frantic Chieftain C
44 Necrodragon Zalva C
45 Gigarayze C
46 Windmill Mutant C
47 Gigaslug C
48 Flame Trooper Goliac C
49 Hypersprint Warior Uzesol C
50 Peppi Pepper C
51 Gandaval's Stapler C
52 Copper Locust C
53 Turtle Horn, the Imposing C
54 Fever Nuts C
55 Uncanny Turnip C
S1 Terradragon Arque Delacerna SR
S2 Wise Starnoid, Avatar of Hope SR
S3 Cruel Naga, Avatar of Fate SR
S4 Death Phoenix, Avatar of Doom SR
S5 Aura Pegasus, Avatar of Life SR

2006 Duel Masters Tyranno Drake Crusher

2 Todoroki Riyuu, Fire Bird Dragon VR
17 Roubanrei of Impact R
30 Perionbris Dragoon R
38 Fists of Forever U
44 Rumble Gate C
48 Iron Command Dragoon C
49 Smashblow Dragoon C
60 Igars Dragoon U
62 One-Hit Hero Honoo U
98 Shot Wheel of Meizrazen C
101 Suza of Gale C

2013 Duel Masters 1st Deck Oracle Dash

1 Alternative, Sacred Cavalry C
2 Macuil, Fighter of Truth C
3 Zorro Star, Izanai Tactician C
4 Quilt, Inca of Blending C
5 Cardamom, Loss of Comfort C
6 Tumeric, Floating Apparition C
7 Divine Punishment of Heaven C
8 Saicho, Enlightenment Oracle R
9 Corteo, Spirit Knight R
10 Terror Pit R
11 Inferno Sign R
12 Magris, Vizier of Magnetism C
13 Darkness Southern C
14 Intense Digging Twist C

2013 Duel Masters 1st Deck Outrage Dash

1 Crossfire, Wicked Millionaire R
2 Geega, Thrilling Drill C
3 Roadster, Double Blast C
4 Pulsar, Trans Suction R
5 Zettsu, Bird Cage C
6 Beyond the Beyond C
7 Railgun, Akashic Force C
8 Intense Vacuuming Twist R
9 Dacity Dragoon, Explosive Beast R
10 Aqua Surfer U
11 Lucky Ball U
12 Emergency Typhoon C
13 Spiral Gate C
14 Hot Spring Crimson Meow C

2013 Duel Masters Black Box Pack

1 Trueking Vivaldi VR
2 GENJI Double Cross, Blastdragon VR
3 Codecommand Death Marriage VR
4 Positron Sign R
5 Rapid Reincarnation R
6 Aqua Melge R
7 Infernal Death Sunrise R
8 Geometeus Infinite Dragon R
9 Delacroix, Heroine of Liberation R
10 Goemonkey! Snake-Handed Boss R
11 Manly Pepper R
12 Great Reversal of Reality and Death R
13 Red Scorpion, Electro-mech R
14 Saberfili, the Paladin U
15 Kushinada, Light Weapon U
16 Aqua Jester Loupe U
17 Hogan Blaster U
18 Sandpit Man U
19 Burial Worm, the Burying Insect U
20 Disturbing Chuusa U
21 Mystery Hippo U
22 Ochappi, Pure Hearted Faerie U
23 Super Infernal Gate Smash R
24 Gaga Pikarian C
25 Sol Habaki, Apocalyptic Sage C
26 Tulk, the Oracle C
27 Aqua Advisor C
28 Cebu Aquman Jr. C
29 Filler Robo Concurion C
30 Fuuma Vines C
31 Zabi Claw, Dark Warrior C
32 Change of Mind! Bakel, Cloud Ogre C
33 Self-Destructing Gil Poser C
34 Fighting Musubi C
35 Geo Horn, the Lively C
36 Jasmine, Mist Faerie C
37 Marauder Deis Drive C
38 Yattare Pippi C
S1 Truename Arashi Tiger SR
S2 Truekaiser Max Adrenaline SR
S3 Dolgazer, Veteran of Hard Battle SR
1-b Heaven Eleven 8210 Style, Spirit of Reversal
2-b DASH Leader Greg
3-b Trueshinra Premium Chirico Moon
4-b Parlock -Confront the Conspiracy
5-b Come On Victory
6-b Sigurros
7-b Black Insect Magistrate
8-b Dark Jios, Lord of Dark Dragons
9-b Ultra Man
10-b Duema Ogre! Kikuchi, Assistant Instructor
11-b Game On! Kiriluda Family!
12-b Uberdragon Bajulaterra
13-b Uberdragon Fighbird
14-b Storm Double Cross, Blastdragon
15-b Tatsurion
16-b Bolshack Corodragon
17-b Katsuta Kiriluda, Curry Bread Boy
18-b Shobu Aini
19-b Mr. Matsumoto
20-b Go Duel Brothers
21-b Great Waste
22-b 1st Lt. Pen Pen, Special Forest Commander
23-b Knights of Cobalt, Spirit of Protean
24-b Nero Gryphis, Mystic Light Emperor
25-b Hot Spring Sabaki, Fire Water Sword
26-b Ballcadeia NEX, Lord of Demon Dragons
27-b Ballcadeia NEX, Lord of Demon Dragons
28-b Thunder Moon, the Enlightened SR
29-b Supernova Venus la Saint Mother SR
30-b Gabriella, Holy Princess SR
31-b Alephtina, Spiritual Princess SR
32-b Supernova Betelgeuse Final Cannon SR
33-b King Tsunami SR
34-b Cyber A Irons SR
35-b Aqua Master SR
36-b Ballom Emperor, Lord of Demons SR
37-b Beginning Romanoff, Lord of the Demonic Eye SR
38-b Crath Lade, Merciless King SR
39-b Necrodragon Guljeneraid SR
40-b Zagaan, Knight of Darkness SR
41-b Bolshack Cross NEX SR
42-b Bolmeteus Steel Dragon SR
43-b Supernova Bigbang Anastathis SR
44-b Baban Ban Ban, Earth's Blessing SR
45-b Wise Starnoid, Avatar of Hope SR
46-b Alcadeias, Lord of Spirits VR
47-b Perfect Galaxy, Spirit of Immortality VR
48-b Orochi, of the Hidden Blade VR
49-b Evil Incarnate VR
50-b Jack Viper, Shadow of Doom VR
51-b Dulanzames, Jet-Black War Demon VR
52-b Death Arcadia, Devil Saint VR
53-b Glider Man VR
54-b Bolmeteus Sapphire Dragon VR
55-b GENJI Double Cross, Blastdragon VR
56-b Xenon Da Vinci, Master of Space VR
57-b Diamondia, the Blizzard Rider VR
58-b Shaman Totem VR
59-b Victory Apple VR
60-b Miraculous Snare VR
61-b Ballforce, the Demonic Holy Spirit VR
62-b Bombazar, Dragon of Destiny VR
63-b Corteo, Spirit Knight R
64-b Perfect Madonna, Light Weapon R
65-b Moritz, the Spydroid R
66-b Mestapo, the Patroller R
67-b Slowly Chain R
68-b Cosmic Darts R
69-b Marshall Queen R
70-b Aqua Surfer R
71-b Aqua Surfer R
72-b Aqua Surfer R
73-b Aqua Surfer R
74-b Divine Riptide R
75-b Streaming Shaper R
76-b Death Gate, Gate of Hell R
77-b Terror Pit R
78-b Ghastly Drain R
79-b Raging Dragon Lord R
80-b Curiosity Princess Pudding R
81-b Shaman Broccoli R
82-b Aurora of Reversal R
83-b Brutal Charge R
84-b Codename Ethan R
85-b Last Violence R
86-b Mist Rias, Sonic Guardian R
87-b Iocant, the Oracle R
88-b Cocco Lupia R
89-b Cocco Lupia R
90-b Cocco Lupia R
91-b Cocco Lupia R
92-b Capricorn, Earth's Reflection R
93-b Ancient Horn, the Watcher U
94-b Falconer, Lightfang Ninja C
95-b Aqua Strummer C
96-b Medetine, New Year Electro-knight C
97-b Energy Stream C
98-b Necrodragon Zalva C
99-b Benzo, the Hidden Fury C
100-b Jenny, the Dismantling Puppet C
101-b Jenny, the Dismantling Puppet C
102-b Bind Shadow, Shadow of Bondage C
103-b Nyanjiro, Treasure Cat C
104-b Bronze-Arm Tribe C
105-b Dandy Eggplant C
106-b Raging Bamboo C
107-b Pixie Cocoon C
108-b Faerie Life C
109-b Faerie Life C
110-b Faerie Life C
111-b Faerie Life C

2013 Duel Masters The Book of Oracle

1 Devo, Twin Horse Left God
2 Kraft Werk, Twin Heaven Right God
3 Pearljam, Faerie Left God U
4 Nirvana, Spirit Knight Right God U
5 Izumo U
6 New Wave, End of the Century
7 Truename Academian
8 Truename Rihanna Glory
9 Sun Tzu, Satori's Art of War
10 Ikkyu, Izanai's Sacrificial Mind
11 Triple ZERO, Secret Hell
12 Hagoromo, Izanai's Divine Light
13 Oracle Jewel of Control
14 Chief De Baula, Machine King of Mystic Light R
15 DNA Spark R
16 Death Gate, Gate of Hell R
17 Terror Pit C
18 Prelude of Horror U
19 Ragmal, Spirit Knight U
20 Skysword, the Savage Vizier U
21 Pixie Life C

2013 Duel Masters The Book of Outrage

1 Hurricane, Crossfire
2 Arashi, Crossboy
3 Katsu Tonfa, Secret EX
4 Lobby, Cho Alchemy C
5 Katsudon, Kung Fu Dragon C
6 Volks, Bastard Core
7 Wagen, Master Decoy
8 Ikari, Hustle Commander C
9 Canis, Wonderful One C
10 Dio Jeep, Death Lion
11 Rage Crystal of Injustice
12 Prometheus, Splash Axe
13 Aqua Surfer C
14 Intense Vacuuming Twist C
15 Rothus, the Traveler C
16 Super Flaming Hell's Scrapper C
17 Rumbling Terahorn C
18 Scramble Typhoon C
19 Qurian C
20 Bronze-Arm Tribe C
21 Faerie Life C

2013 Duel Masters Episode 2 Great Miracle

1 Iggy Special, Climax of the End VR
2 Truename Tiger Legend VR
3 Truemechaking Thunderbird Re: VR
4 Royal Straight Flush Kaiser VR
5 Doyagaou VR
6 LOVE x HATE, Secret Cruelty R
7 Tatebue Yahho, Holy Heaven Guardian R
8 Rhapsody, Golden Fighter R
9 Ranchun, Bulk Guardian R
10 Script R
11 Pepper, Golden Fighter R
12 Aqua PTA R
13 Dokurobe, Regiment Guardian R
14 Funk, Golden Fighter R
15 Cut Cake, Evil Guidance of Heaven Descent R
16 Clap, Golden Fighter R
17 Truename Nidogiri Ragon R
18 Big Pan Daddy R
19 Handsome R
1S Maitreya, Canon's Farewell Promo
20 Curry Giant R
21 Pudding, Reversal Princess U
22 Megagyoron, Graveyard Guardian U
23 Fuwatto U
24 Gutche, Mystery Guardian U
25 Heaven's Thunder U
26 King Langley U
27 Summer's Day Spiral C
28 Usuwarai U
29 Honenbe, Skeletal Guardian U
2S Idolmaster Leo Promo
30 Squid, Assassination Guardian U
31 Moel, Love Attack U
32 Missile Burst G U
33 Kabayaki Giant U
34 Silva, Golden Fighter U
35 Pandakko Panda U
36 Noumen C
37 Kyumanomee, Support Guardian C
38 Tattsume, Rednose Guardian C
39 Quick Spark C
3S Katsuta Kiriluda, Curry Bread Boy Promo
40 Aqua Study C
41 Insert Wing, Clothing Interceptor C
42 Cyclone Clear, Clothing Cleaner C
43 Eternal Brain C
44 Scissor Hands, Shadow of Cutting C
45 Ball Man C
46 Doll Finn, Burial Guardian C
47 Nyanko Hand of Hell C
48 Dosukoi C
49 Onidotsuki, Hammer Rascal C
4S Violent Children Promo
50 Ukka Lizard C
51 Dash Repeat C
52 Tatakai no Jingi C
53 Nepenthes Assault C
54 Large Gathering! Acorn Army C
55 Pixie Life C
5S Kubrick, Spiral Accelerator Promo
6S Karre Ganejar, Metal Lamp Djinn Promo
7S Forever Princess, An Eternity to Rule Them Promo
S1 Back to the Ore, Zenith of Ten Tail SR
S2 Trueking Viola Sonata SR
S3 Trueking Wagner SR
S4 Trueking Viva La Revolution SR
S5 Onishura, Golden Twins SR
V1 Shangri-La, Climax of Cruelty VICR
V2 Kiramaru, Great Miracle VICR
11m Pepper, Golden Fighter R
21m Pudding, Reversal Princess U
31m Moel, Love Attack U
34m Silva, Golden Fighter U
37m Kyumanomee, Support Guardian C
46m Doll Finn, Burial Guardian C
49m Onidotsuki, Hammer Rascal C
O1-O2 Ganjin, Messiah's Oracle SCR
O2-O2 Mustang, Royal Destroyer SCR

2013 Duel Masters Episode 3 Dead and Beat

1 Amakusa, Izanai's Spirit VR
2 Testa Rossa, Ji Aggressive VR
3 Yakedo Sasetara VR
4 Majikkuma Taki, Byte Hell VR
5 Stroganoff, Mantra of Flashing Seal VR
6 Jesus Mary Chain, True Flashing Right God R
7 Bloody Valentine, Holy Princess Left God R
8 Steel, Ultra Defense R
9 Perfect Lily, Purity Devotee R
10 Diva Live, Light Weapon Trick R
11 Akaschic, Knowledge Keeper R
12 Lobby Spiral Moonsault R
13 Paranormal, Task Produce R
14 Bhutan Judgment R
15 Dan Crowley, Infinity Shot R
16 Zeroyon, the Chicken Race R
17 Salix, Coleman R
18 Global Navigation R
19 Shining Kinji, Gonbuto Treasure R
20 God Wall, God Trick U
21 Sunsun, Get Treasure R
22 Mangan, Talking Guard U
23 Shizuku, Water Byte U
24 Time Paradox, Blue the Blue U
25 Kooman, Hell Prince U
26 Ginger, True Flash Believer U
27 Falcon Bomber, Rocket Dash U
28 Dodonga Don, Injustice Trick U
29 Kinjiro, Gonbuto Mash U
30 Hepatica, Snow Crusher U
31 Loyalty, Izanai's Light Machine U
32 Garlic, Izanai's Divine Dragon U
33 Assist of Advance and Onslaught U
34 Pamyu Pamyun, Circus Believer C
35 Frill, Mantra of Compassion C
36 Nike Optic C
37 Alice, Code Breaker C
38 Volbick, Mecha Soldier C
39 Niyare Get, Zero Trick C
40 Honetan, Bone Surface Puppet C
41 Inutan, Hound Puppet C
42 Pet Puppet, Puppet Trick C
43 Jigokugulma, Explosive Priest C
44 Pokotusu Kabu, Clap Scrap C
45 Cobra, Snake Man Show C
46 Katsudon ã•ŒI'll do it!ã•? C
47 Oshamambe, Bonbon Believer C
48 Nagare Okami C

49 Nigawarai C
50 Lalala Life, Faerie Trick C
51 Chai and Silk, Familia's Light Machine C
52 Assist of Compassion and Mercy C
53 Assist of Knowledge and Weakness C
54 Assist of Chaos and Fist Attack C
55 Dojiko, Courage Faerie C
6m Jesus Mary Chain, True Flashing Right God R
7m Bloody Valentine, Holy Princess Left God R
9m Perfect Lily, Purity Devotee R
S1 Shoegazer, Bright Deity SR
S2 Alexandrite, Amazing Arrow SR
S3 Gospel, Oracle King SR
S4 Death Shuteron, Hell's Funeral Service SR
S5 Forever Meteor, Matchless Dragonmech SR
V1 Bruce, Dead or Alive VICR
V2 Jackie, Infinity Beat VICR
15m Dan Crowley, Infinity Shot R
20m God Wall, God Trick U
23m Shizuku, Water Byte U
25m Kooman, Hell Prince U
27m Falcon Bomber, Rocket Dash U
37m Alice, Code Breaker C
50m Lalala Life, Faerie Trick C
V1a Bruce, Dead or Alive VICR
V1b Bruce, Dead or Alive VICR
V1c Bruce, Dead or Alive VICR
V2a Jackie, Infinity Beat VICR
V2b Jackie, Infinity Beat VICR
V2c Jackie, Infinity Beat VICR

2013 Duel Masters Episode 3 Rage vs. God

1 Daft Punk, Lord of Demons Right God VR
2 Justice, Lord of Spirits Left God VR
3 Michaelangelo, Cosmo Beauty VR
4 Iron Rose, Full Metal VR
5 Robin Hood, Mutcha Alchemy VR
6 Matrix, Hirame Kick VR
7 Scream, Blood Pit VR
8 Cromwell, Iron Cannon VR
9 Titan Giant VR
10 Misstina, Protection Lotus Faerie VR
11 Strokes, Explosive Right God R
12 Libertines, Fuuma Left God R
13 Silence Topaz R
14 Jetstone, Over Size Dome R
15 Fleece, Satori's Whirlwind R
16 Sufeeko, Spirit Knight R
17 Gods Ceremonial Light R
18 Aqua Spellblue R
19 Ikari, Hustle Commander R
20 Bakubaku Crawler R
21 Ragnarok, the Clock R
22 Quattro Brain R
23 Shadow, Phantom Blood R
24 Phantom, Rose Blossom R
25 Screwmar, Decaying Scar Commander R
26 Undeux Trois, Darkness Princess R
27 Devil Hand R
28 Crunch Shield R
29 Ngoro Ngoro, Blastdragon R
30 Oneezemu, Nobile Brother R
31 Infernal Affair, the Explosive R
32 Testa Rossa, of the Heat R
33 Katsudon Break, Secret Fist R
34 Public Enemy R
35 Deirinojikan R
36 Canis, Wonderful One C
37 Pudding, Domineering Princess R
38 Magnolia, Satori's Fertility U
39 Mystery Cube R
40 Pearljam, Faerie Left God U
41 Massive Attack, Battle Attacking Right God U
42 Square Pusher, Fantasy Left God U
43 Nirvana, Spirit Knight Right God U
44 Izumo U
45 Nichiren, Izanai's Invitation U
46 Nike, Cosmo Cosmos U
47 Pail, Izanai's Spirit Knight U
48 Ika Ikaga, Excess Guardian U
49 Vernelight, Hard Guard U
50 Glorious Tactics U
51 Lobby, Cho Alchemy U
52 Milk, Satori's Salvation U
53 Akadashi, Izanai's Battle Attack U
54 Nebula, Finalist Chain U
55 Duet Spiral R
56 Bhutan, Piggy Blues U
57 Rettoidd, Demonic Dragon U
58 Garam Masala, Izanai's Fuuma U
59 Fuuma Huma U
60 Leatherface, Texas Chainsaw U
61 Katsudon, Kung Fu Dragon U
62 Daidara, Izanai's Explosion U
63 Otokodama, the Explosive U
64 Moped, Positiro Cannon U
65 Dekodekopin U
66 Goromaru, Horn Horn U
67 Erasou, Satori's Resonance U
68 Aurora, Izanai's Invitation U
69 Frog, Jumping Jack U
70 Rokusodonta, Primitive Elephant U
71 Balbora, Spirit Knight C
72 Disukun, the Patroller C
73 Schreiber, Apostle of Strictness C
74 Guard Gainor, Electro Troop C
75 Cotton, Deep Faith C
76 Achorite, Start Dash C
77 Duet Spark C
78 Shockingly Switch-on C
79 Ikasuze Crawler C
80 Sky Force, Blue Divine Dragon C
81 Anchor Captain C
82 Aqua Sharks C
83 Parlock -Final Voyage- C
84 Mypad, Start Dash C
85 Double Reset Punch C
86 Peeping Peeking C
87 Skabox, the Hidden Dissapointment C
88 Fuuma Dekarabia C
89 Hettakuso Sax C
90 Sansho, Satori's Secret Maneuver C
91 Uza Darley, Shadow of Laziness C
92 BloodRayne, Start Dash C
93 Harvest of Bhutan C
94 Like a Rolling Storm C
95 Hot Finger, the Explosive C
96 Onibore, Drilling Brother C
97 Dump Tank, Silent Assassin C
98 Nine, Zero Zero C
99 Oil Bow, Satori's Passion C
S1 Velvet, Flash Priest SR
S2 Impact Rigger, Sky Elemental SR
S3 Cyber W Spiral SR
S4 Marshall Crawler SR
S5 British, Hell Blues SR
S6 Marjoram, Messiah's Revival SR
S7 Diehard Ryusei of Invincibility SR
S8 Schumacher, New World SR
S9 Global, Matterhorn SR
V1 Yomi, Humanity God VICR
V2 Katsuking, Kung Fu Shogun VICR
100 Topgear, Start Dash C
101 Evil Immediate Decapitation, Secret Injustice C
102 Rock'n Roll, Battlefield C
103 Terradragon Garagyagas C
104 Koala Fighter C
105 Uncomprosing Shallot C
106 Rendan, Gentleman Faerie C
107 Konchiwan, Luck-Pusher C
108 Kerasas, Start Dash C
109 Goromaru Communication C
110 Guard Lesson -Beginner- C
15m Fleece, Satori's Whirlwind R
19m Ikari, Hustle Commander R
21m Ragnarok, the Clock R
27m Devil Hand R
37m Pudding, Domineering Princess R
40m Pearljam, Faerie Left God U
41m Massive Attack, Battle Attacking Right God U
44m Izumo U
61m Katsudon, Kung Fu Dragon U
73m Schreiber, Apostle of Strictness C
98m Nine, Zero Zero C
S10 Lupus, Full Armor SR
V1a Yomi, Humanity God VICR
V1b Yomi, Humanity God VICR
V1c Yomi, Humanity God VICR
V2a Katsuking, Kung Fu Shogun VICR
V2b Katsuking, Kung Fu Shogun VICR
V2c Katsuking, Kung Fu Shogun VICR
101m Evil Immediate Decapitation, Secret Injustice C
108m Kerasas, Start Dash C

2013 Duel Masters Episode 3 Ultra Victory Master

1 Detroit Techno, Sacred Demon VR
2 Brahmin, Mantra Pope VR
3 Electraglide, Fallen Left God VR
4 Metamorphose, Demon Right God VR
5 Kaiser Prince, Flame Dragon Prince VR
6 British ROCK, Shentonginus R
7 Lance of Tonginus R
8 Michaela Jenne, Miss Universe R
9 Stonegord, General Guard R
10 Alice, Chaos Witch R
11 Maple Syrup, Izanai's Puppet R
12 Vossradish, Mantra's Admiral R
13 Katsuking GANG, Victorage Caliber R
14 Ultimate Outrage Legend R
15 Dekaburu, Izanai's Bonds R
16 Shantsuai, Inga's Transgression R
17 Crossfire the 2nd, Billionaire R
18 Faerie Shower R
19 Curse of Resurrection and Clash R
20 Bhutan POP, Shenton U
21 Wired, Spirit Knight Right God U
22 Duralumin, Eccentric Wall U
23 Love Parade, Light Weapon Left God U
24 Stephen Jones, Eccentric Wall U
25 Wickerman, Eccentric Wall U
26 Katsudon GO!, Victorage R
27 Bombardier 4000, Eccentric Wall U
28 Trafalgar, Eccentric Wall U
29 Pepper, Oracle Guardian U
30 Conflict of Defense and Slashing U
31 Carol's Flying Live U
32 Terraform. Kenda Magic U
33 Donide Rattera, Matchless Divine Destruction U
34 Pudding, Shining Nyan Nyan C
35 Twill, Inga's Miko U
36 Ultimate Defense Command Code 777 U
37 Patchigi, Mench Gantsuke C
38 Frappuccino, Karma's Freeze C
39 Wakame Zeal, Mystery Monk C
40 Brain Typhoon C
41 Torikabuto, Familia's Disintegration C
42 Kinako, Familia's Defenseless C
43 Pokapoka Hammer C
44 Koenig, Burning Ring C
45 Punska C
46 Flame Suicide Bomb C
47 Eagle, the Chief C
48 Ice, Glacier Faerie C
49 Cobble, Familia's Bonds C
50 Gattsuri Gattsuman C
51 Inuhakka, Inga's Mamorukami C
52 Doination, Explosive Spirit Knight C
53 Testa Rossa, Heartbeat Heat C
54 Erekiter, Biribiri Yard C
55 Allium, Iron Chef C
6m British ROCK, Shentonginus (Mode Change) R
S1 Robin Champ, Orichalcum Wizard SR
S2 Mastermind SR
S3 Global Rise, Show Must Go-on SR
S4 Meteorite Ryusei the Flash SR
S5 Testa Rossa, Last Burning SR
V1 Ultra Knight Punk, Shentury VICR
V2 Katsumaster, Outrage Victory VICR
13m Katsuking GANG, Victorage Caliber (Mode Change) R
18m Faerie Shower (Mode Change) R
20m Bhutan POP, Shenton (Mode Change) U
21m Wired, Spirit Knight Right God (Mode Change) U
23m Love Parade, Light Weapon Left God (Mode Change) U
26m Katsudon GO!, Victorage (Mode Change) R
46m Flame Suicide Bomb (Mode Change) C
51m Inuhakka, Inga's Mamorukami (Mode Change) C
53m Testa Rossa, Heartbeat Heat (Mode Change) C
V1a Ultra Knight Punk, Shentury VICR
V1b Ultra Knight Punk, Shentury VICR
V1c Ultra Knight Punk, Shentury VICR
V2a Katsumaster, Outrage Victory VICR
V2b Katsumaster, Outrage Victory VICR
V2c Katsumaster, Outrage Victory VICR

2013 Duel Masters Katsuking and Treasures of Legend

1 Marduk, Unstoppable
2 Berserk, Sanctuary Guarding
3 Jormungand, Thor Hammer
4 Ultramotion Rage Crystal
5 Katsuking MAX, Outlaw Caliber
6 Don Katsudon, Outlaw
7 Cyber A Irons SR
8 Bolshack Cross NEX SR
9 Eternal Meteor Kaiser SR
10 Bolbalzak Ex SR
11 Insight Indigo Kaiser VR
12 Deepsea Searcher VR
13 Amaterasu, Founder of the Blue Wolves R
14 Intense Vacuuming Twist R
15 Eureka Program R
16 GILL Supergalactic Dragon R
17 Natural Snare R
18 Shrine of Rebirth U
19 Aqua Burster C
20 Jasmine, Mist Faerie C
21 Seventh Tower C
22 Faerie Life C

2013 Duel Masters Strongest Strategy Perfect 12

1 5000GT, Riot
2 Miragino, the Face Up C
3 Tant, Sword Bat C
4 Balzark, Sword Flash Fortress C
5 Intense Vacuuming Twist C
6 Scramble Typhoon C
7 Wily Carpenter C
8 Acid, New Century VICR
9 Truename Shuramaru C
10 Aizen, Canon's Divine Abyss C
11 Rasha, Enlightenment Wandering C
12 Prelude of Horror U
13 Niyare U
14 Bega, Vizier of Shadow C
15 Inga Lupia C
16 Saga, God of Destruction C
17 Earth Eternity Gate C
18 Aku, Ultimate God SR
19 God Saga VR
20 Zen, Transcendent God VR
21 Project God U
22 Chopin, Dragon King C
23 Mendelssohn C
24 Bolmeteus Steel Dragon SR
25 Ogre Kaiser Destruction C
26 Tornado Shiva Double Cross, Blastdragon C
27 Cocco Lupia C
28 Eco Aini C
29 Christopher, Dark Knight C
30 Discovery, Recruiter C
31 Carol, Gokigen Shout C
32 Max, Crimson Blade Lord VR
33 Kodamanma, Gil Gil Puppet C
34 Deadly Fighter Braid Claw C
35 Pipippi, Electro-Riser C
36 Codename Build Leone C
37 Silver Glory, Invincible Fortress C
38 Perfect Madonna, Light Weapon C
39 Heaven's Gate C
40 Lord Reis, Spirit of Wisdom C
41 Murmur, Apostle of the Formation C
42 Webius, the Patroller C
43 Beginning Romanoff, Lord of the Demonic Eye C
44 Varz Romanoff, Dark Lord of Demons C
45 Master Weapon - All Yes C
46 Lost Soul C
47 Primal Scream C
48 Jenny, the Dismantling Puppet C
49 Ghost Touch C
50 Cyber A Irons C
51 Streaming Shooter C
52 Crystal Memory C
53 Eureka Program C
54 Hustle Castle C
55 Aqua Librarian C
56 Energy Stream C
57 Babelginus, Demonic Dragon C
58 Algo Bardiol, Devil Admiral C
59 Super Trash Train, Fuuma Devil C
60 Fuuma Balzoo C
61 Fuuma Gorgonshack C
62 Maxval, Electro-Fuuma C
63 Fuuma Mehlwasp C
64 Amaterasu, Founder of the Blue Wolves C
65 Noble Enforcer C
66 Sanctuary of the Mother C
67 Mystic Treasure Chest C
68 The Grave of Angels and Demons C
69 Mystic Dreamscape C
70 Fortune Slot C
71 Necrodragon Odol Needle C
72 Counterattacking Silent Spark C
73 Death Gate, Gate of Hell C
74 Blazing Tiger, Crimson Lord C
75 Leaf Storm Trap C
76 Super Explosive Duel Fire C
77 Riku, the Oracle C
78 Ochappi, Pure Hearted Faerie C
79 Faerie Gift C
80 Faerie Miracle C
81 Child Festival of Faerie Fire C
82 Faerie Crystal C
83 Faerie Life C
84 Jasmine, Mist Faerie C
01-07 Falconer, Lightfang Ninja C
02-07 Zerokage, Lightfang Lord C
03-07 Baiken, Blue Dragon of the Hidden Blade C
04-07 Orochi, of the Hidden Blade C
05-07 Genius Janit, of the Hidden Blade C
06-07 Hanzou, Menacing Phantom C
07-07 Dark Sanji, Darkfang Ninja C

2013 Duel Masters Virtueless Royal

1 Parlock, Sacred Prayer R
2 Humanity, Nameless God R
3 Pearl, Merimeri Mary R
4 Atlantis, Deepsea Evangelist R
5 Kareiko, Karma's Banned Technique R
6 Valiant, Illusion Infinite R
7 Inka, Karma's Curse Crest R
8 Triple Gentle Volcano, Flaming Jet R
9 Romanoff Guard U
10 Bjork, Satori's Baula U
11 Starback, Karma's Harm U
12 Outrage Egg U
13 Skullrider, Skull Skill U
14 Bhutan Reincarnation U
15 Colnago, Brave Claw U
16 Super Move! Dragon Flame U
17 Pudding Princess, Pandora Celeb U
18 Vermillion Pressure Live U
19 Wendigo Apache, Izanai's Blank C
20 Hopeless Charger U
21 Carina, Izanai's Mantra C
22 Oratulk, Familia's Prophecy C
23 Lady Parlock, Pirate Shaman C
24 Viblo Blade, Hulcus Range C
25 Myoga, Familia's Yamikamu C
26 Soul Address C
27 DeLorean, Flat Lighter C
28 Poppi, Yatarou Soul C
29 Arima and Kicker, Quiche Ban Ban C
30 Hormone, Maxim Bronze C
S1 Rave Diabolos, Holy Damned Festival SR
S2 New Order, Demonic Eye Right God SR
S3 Vitalic, Sword Flash Left God SR
S4 Galaxy, Mister Perfect SR
S5 Terminator, End of the Future SR
S6 Ryusei, Ex Revolver SR
S7 Concorde, Valkyrie Earth SR
S8 Codeless Sorge Thirteen SR
V1 Progre Sapphire, Divine Blue Brightness VICR
V2 Gaial, King of Kaiser VICR

2013 Duel Masters White Zenith Pack

1 Truename Cyber O Holy C
2 Truename Bolmeteus Zero Dragon C
3 Truename Megapounder Mack C
4 Truename Platinum Arm Tribe C
5 Truename Academian C
6 Truename Shuramaru C
7 Truename Rihanna Glory C
8 Lionel Finale, Zenith of Lion VR
9 Codefight Zekia Ex Makina VR
10 Truename Hadesgil Skill VR
11 Maximum the Max, Zenith of Military R
12 Saicho, Satori's Oracle R
13 Nothing Zero, Secret Destruction R
14 Zenith Clutch Destiny R
15 Zero Egg of Zenith R
16 Marching Tristone R
17 Hungry Giant R
18 Prelude of Horror U
19 Psycho Horror, Feeling of Falsehood C
20 Yosakoi, Leader of Spirits U
21 King Acer U
22 Energy Zero U
23 Necrodragon Onbashi Raon U
24 Messa Danjiri Dragon U
25 Zondag Giant U
26 Breaking Right Smith C
27 Notre Dame, Vizier of Illusion Shield C
28 De Baula Charger C
29 Tweet C
30 Eureka Charger C
31 Zero Point Man C
32 Harakkadan, Jetblack Guardian C
33 Onikirimaru C
34 Zero Lupia C
35 Sleeping Fool Tanukichi-san C
36 Faerie Crystal C
S1 Utopia Ever, Zenith of Destruction SR
S2 VAN Beethoven, Zenith of Fighting SR
V1 Kaiser Demon Fang, Zenith of Certain Victory VICR

2014 Duel Masters Battle Passion Dragon

1 Batoraio, Victory Blastdragon
2 GENJI Double Cross, Blastdragon C
3 Uberdragon Sunburst NEX C
4 Batrash Knuckle, Blastdragon
5 Gyanobazuga Dragon
6 Fuji Thunder, Sacred Dragon
7 Hazel Bryne, Explosive Lance
8 Blazing Tiger, Crimson Lord C
9 Smash Warrior Stagrandu C
10 Super Flaming Hell's Scrapper C
11 Game On! Charger C
12 Spear Lupia C
13 Drill Trap C
14 Onikirimaru C
15 Piara Heart C
16 Lyla Litta C

2014 Duel Masters Burning Dragon Sword Gaial

1 Gaial Kaiser
Gaial King Dragon, Raging Dragon Lord C
2 Gaial, Leader Dragon Sword
Gaiban, Furious Leader Dragon
3 Batocross Battle, Passion Dragon
4 Zark Taiser, Passion Admiral
5 Axel Kaiser Thunderclap C
6 Gaimusou, Angry Hero
7 Gaial Zero C
8 Bakuadorgan, Passion Dragon
9 Hyperspatial Shooting Hole C
10 Next Charger
11 Bolshack Dragon, the Temporal Blaze
Bolshack Möbius, Victory Awakened C
12 Truekaiser Max Adrenaline C
13 Ogre Kaiser Destruction C
14 Glenmolt, Dragon Edge C
15 Reckless Cut Scrapper C
16 Take-jin, Dragon King Keep C
17 Boost, Crimson Lord
Gaial King Dragon, Raging Dragon Lord C
18 Dragonic Pippi
Gaial King Dragon, Raging Dragon Lord C
19 Glee Gee Horn, Passion Sword
Little Big Horn, Passion Dragon C
20 Meteor Charger C

2014 Duel Masters Crystal Memory Dragon

1 iQ Cloypaedia, Dragon Symbol
2 Trigram, Zero-order Dragon Formula
3 Vilvisvid, Ultra Flash
4 Assassin Greed, Aqua Agent
5 Aqua Sonicwave
6 Zolul, Aqua Combatant
7 Aqua Surfer R
8 Aqua Evoluter U
9 Aqua Blade, Blue Wolf C
10 Aqua Strummer C
11 Aqua Hulcus C
12 Aqua Vehicle C
13 Aqua, Teacher C
14 Spiral Gate C

2014 Duel Masters Dragon Edge of Destruction Diabolos

1 Diabolos Double Zeta, Temporal Demon Dragon
Devil Diabolos Double Zeta, Ultimate Awakened VICR
2 Diabolos, Prison Dragon Edge
Diajigoku, Demon Dragon of Destruction VICR
3 Ganaldonal, Wrath Demon Dragon
4 Gravemott, Gravestone Demon Dragon
5 Olzekia, Temporal Sword General
Galactica Olzekia, the Decapitator Awakened C
6 Urami Hades, Curse Hero
7 Necrodragon Abayo Shabayo C
8 Zabi Barrel, Western Doll C
9 Hyperspatial Emperor Hole C
10 Punish Charger
11 Bone Dance Charger C
12 Dias Zeta, the Temporal Suppressor
Diabolos Zeta, Annihilation Awakened C
13 Thunder Blade, Wolf Tiger C
14 Dulanzames, Jet-Black War Demon C
15 Black Ganveet, Temporal Soldier
Darkness Ganveet, the Assassin Awakened C
16 Ulvorof, Dragon Edge R
17 Hyperspatial Romanoff Hole C
18 Terror Pit C
19 Death Gate, Gate of Hell C
20 Batou Shoulder, Shadow of Fiction C
21 Jenny, the Suicide Doll C
22 Discald, Misfortune Demon Sickle
Doclald, Misfortune Demon Dragon C

2014 Duel Masters Dragon Solutions Gaiginga

1 Espowaru, Heaven's Dragon Spirit VR
2 Seal Do Leiy, Protection Hero VR
3 Descartes Q, Logic Hero VR
4 Fz Oscilloscope, Dragment Symbol VR
5 Tsumitobatsu, Misfortune Hero VR
6 Superbia, Pride Demon Dragon VR
7 Gaigensui, Striking Hero VR
8 Civil Ward, Passion Dragon VR
9 Tyranno Venom, Chain Ruler VR
10 Otoma=Kutto, Fang Hero VR
11 Shakuseal, Replenish Dragon Elemental R
12 Sullivan, Guidance Dragon Elemental R
13 Everrose, Dragon Edge R
14 Ribulamira, Mirror Wings R
15 Zodiac, Chanting Cathedral R
16 Dragon's Sign R
17 Bs Borapal, Dragment Symbol R
18 Metal Avenger, Dragon Edge R
19 X2 Armor Franz, Dragment Symbol R
20 Dragment Formation R
21 Dragment Answer R
22 Pythagoras, Geometry Squadron R
23 Awaltia, Greed Demon Dragon R
24 Glatoni, Gluttony Demon Dragon R
25 Ulvorof, Dragon Edge R
26 Doterabara, Phantom Mirror R
27 Fusshisshi the Invulnerable R
28 Demon Wolf, Howling Moonlight Castle R

29 Tyrant Dairanto, Passion Dragon R
30 Batornado, Passion Dragon R
31 Glenmolt, Dragon Edge R
32 Hibiki, Explosive Mirror R
33 Miracle Burst Shot R
34 Take-jin, Dragon King Keep R
35 Alakunesaura, Mystery Dieter R
36 Sasoris, Dragon Edge R
37 Miralles, Mirror Style R
38 Jurapi, Chain Asylum R
39 Euru=Nambucca, Antique Dragon Ruins R
40 Get Wild R
41 Fulomairam, Protection Dragon Elemental U
42 Kachaldy, Lightbeam Dragon Elemental U
43 Coccolua, Holy Dragon Wings U
44 Sutantiguna, Electric Power Wings U
45 Urovelia, Divine Dragon Spear
Ultimaria, Divine Dragon Elemental U
46 Justice Plan U
47 JJ Avarspela, Dragment Symbol U
48 Powered Mirror, Aqua Teacher U
49 Rococo, Aqua Birdman U
50 Raija, Aqua Ninja U
51 Multiply, Double Dragon Gun
Nb Leibniz, Dragment Symbol U
52 Energy Formation U
53 Hachinosu Batchikuma U
54 Buttagila, Bone Sever Demon Dragon U
55 Cocco Docco U
56 Pork Beef U
57 Discald, Misfortune Demon Sickle
Doclald, Misfortune Demon Dragon U
58 Deadly Love U
59 Fiddich, Explosive Master U
60 Kulbuzetto, Passion Dragon U
61 Motrack, Explosive Striker U
62 Cocotchi, Quick Explosion U
63 Glee Gee Horn, Passion Sword
Little Big Horn, Passion Dragon U
64 Passionate Training U
65 Pteratox, Large Wing Chain U
66 Eggsaura, Nourishing Egg U
67 Pia, Cocco Style U
68 Hihhi, Decoy Style U
69 Togetops, Tricera Impact
Butssubu Tops, Multilateral Impact U
70 Ancient Trap U
71 Nouvelle Baula, White Wall Dragon Elemental C
72 Akyoora, Crossing Wings C
73 Aries, Dragon Edge C
74 Andorom, Chanting Wings C
75 Vuanie, Guarding Wings C
76 Firumie, Rescuing Wings C
77 Lau, Blue Sky Wings C
78 Justice Curtain C
79 St Flask Beaker, Dragment Symbol C
80 Pu Fibonacci, Dragment Symbol C
81 Gambalander, Dragon Edge C
82 Isorock, Aqua Captain C
83 Newton, Aqua Pilot C
84 Cosmo, Aqua Superman C
85 Spiral Formation C
86 Flashing Hero Rush C
87 Merimeri Chainsaw C
88 Nuigul Gulgul C
89 Ulgilando, Betrayal Demon Dragon C
90 Docloscal, Dragon Edge C
91 Chusha Jusha C
92 Taigamaito, Bomb Devil C
93 Bonbaku Bonbon C
94 Encounter with Old Friends C
95 Jurinarena, Passion Dragon C
96 Kilkeran, Second Class Explosion Soldier C
97 Adobekk, Explosive Flow Boy C
98 Storas Ira, Dragon Edge C
99 Maccaran, Explosive Flame Shooter C
S1 Zeek Cavalie, Dragon King of Spirits SR
S2 Sr Spellcyclica, Dragment Symbol SR
S3 Dead Ryusei, Eternal Demonic Dragon SR
S4 Fulboko Donacle, Ultra Passion SR
S5 Wald Brachio, Absolute World King SR
V1 Perfect, Immortal Lance
Everlast, Destiny King VICR
V2 Evidence, Truth Gun
Q.E.D., Dragon Elemental King VICR
V3 Go To Hell, Annihilator Blade
Deathshiraz, Demonic Corrupt King VICR
V4 Judaina, Jurassic Hammer
Saurpio, Ancient King VICR
100 Dalmoa, Explosive Heat Blade C
101 Meteor Charger C
102 Explosive Swordplay, Sweltering Heat Tricks C
103 Mammothdon, Proboscidean C
104 Bongora, Kraft Style C
105 Bulzasso, Chain Style C
106 Kerosuke, Dragon Edge C
107 Nam=Daeddo, Bronze Style C
108 Irokero, Poison Style C
109 Faerie Life C
110 Berserker Time C
VV1 Gaiheart, Galaxy Sword
Gaiginga, Passionate Star Dragon DV

2014 Duel Masters Dragon Souls Festival

1 Alcadeias D, Lord of Dragon Spirits VR
2 Bell Hell De Linne, Footprint Demon Dragon VR
3 Codename Bazagaze Ragon VR
4 Balga Raizou, the Super-Heavenly Nova VR
5 Joan Mizell, Revolution Spear
D'Arc-en-Ciel, Holy Spear Dragon Elemental
6 Og Amate Radial, Dragment Symbol
7 Toratouluf, Thundering Demon Dragon
8 Redbull Muscle, Uber Passion
9 Quattrodon, Four Fanged
10 Koltiolu, Scale Dragon Elemental R
11 Poppi Lucky R
12 Bg Newton Dedicated Panzer, Dragment Symbol R
13 Veil Babylonia, Blue Divine Dragon R
14 THE FINAL Kaiser R
15 Überdragon Bajula, the 2nd R
16 Kyrstron, Lair Delver R
17 Sanctuary of the Mother R
18 Seventh, Light Divine Dragon U
19 Heaven's Double Tail U
20 Dragon Lab U
21 Dimension Splitter U
22 Dark Lupia C
23 Jajarn Kaiser U
24 Gaial Axel
25 Chopin, Dragon King
26 Ragmatox, Poison Class U
27 Petorozu, Nobility Dragon Elemental C
28 Aries, Dragon Edge C
29 North Grande, Blue Divine Dragon C
30 Lip Woppe C
31 Dragment Slot C
32 Koshigahevu, Sloth Demon Dragon C
33 Lunar Kuroro C
34 Taimando Tsukute, Passion Dragon C
35 Yakou, Nocturnal Demon C
36 Terradragon Geobreed C
37 Hakooshideedi, Hidden Earthkind C
S1 Chirico Cubic, First Model Dragon Emperor SR
S2 Dorballom D, Demon Dragon King SR
S3 Brachio Yaiba, Honorful Oni Blade SR
V1 Lionel, Lion Zenith Dragon VICR
V2 Gaial Mobius, Victory Emperor VICR

2014 Duel Masters Episode 3 Omega Climax

1 Max, Rage Crystal VR
2 Omega, Oracle Jewel VR
3 Shiranai, Mantra's Roaring VR
4 Dionysus, the Earth VR
5 Robby Mikeran Global, Friends Power VR
6 Fashion Monster, Izanai's Artisan R
7 Britney Stasis, Stagnation Believer R
8 Pacific Rim, World Reset R
9 The Stop, Armageddon R
10 Block Party, Wicked Emperor Right God R
11 Bumbershoot, Wicked Queen Left God R
12 Amitabha Hand R
13 Outlander, Ultimate Bancho R
14 Glenmalt, Explosive Swordsman C
15 Third-Eye Giant R
16 Everest, Izanai's Earth R
17 Shackle Erma, Fuuma Saint R
18 Prin, My Graduation R
19 Azami, Heavy Baby R
20 Trance, Sacred Strange U
21 Kigunashion, Pure White Wings U
22 Nagool and Kabool, Double Chance U
23 Olive Oil, Karma's Burial U
24 Robby Robin, Mechanko Friends C
25 Kakky and Kesshy, Double Chance U
26 Bhutan Jackson, Thriller Dance U
27 Tenmenjan, Pinch Hitter Loss U
28 Katsudon DASH, God Eater U
29 Cholochu, Forty Body U
30 Outrage Team Exile U
31 Yukki, Kigurumi Faerie U
32 Makunoka and Nukunoka, Double Chance U
33 Star Pippi U
34 Nike Mikeran, Lovely Friends C
35 Kohaku, Go Straight C
36 Biribiri Twin Thunder C
37 Arujil, Flash Makai C
38 Elysium, Go Straight C
39 Bat Mask, Aqua Warrior C
40 Drop Geega Drill C
41 Vanilla Beans, Fuuma Priest C
42 Elm Street, Go Straight C
43 Chile, Bloody Believer C
44 Bokkan and Dokkun, Double Chance C
45 Big Pulsar, Trade Succession C
46 Choinori, Go Straight C
47 Dondon and Panpan, Double Chance C
48 Goromaru Global, Baribari Friends C
49 Rhino, Go Straight C
50 Pottsun C
51 Ready to Duel C
52 Taki's Majikkuma Show C
53 Cobalt Hulcus, Cyber Savage C
54 Chaser, Dark Taiga C
55 Pulp Fiction, Masuya Moon Knife C
9m The Stop, Armageddon R
S1 Crossover Yomi, New Sacred God SR
S2 Java Jack, Ultra Flash SR
S3 Death Metal Punk, Dance Spear SR
S4 Zorro A Star, Mantra's Prison Break SR
S5 Ryusei, the End of Conclusion SR
V1 God Izumo, Lawless Godkind VICR
V2 Katsumugen, Climax VICR
14m Glenmalt, Explosive Swordsman C
18m Prin, My Graduation R
21m Kigunashion, Pure White Wings U
26m Bhutan Jackson, Thriller Dance U
28m Katsudon DASH, God Eater U
30m Outrage Team Exile U
39m Bat Mask, Aqua Warrior C
48m Goromaru Global, Baribari Friends C
V1a God Izumo, Lawless Godkind VICR
V1b God Izumo, Lawless Godkind VICR
V1c God Izumo, Lawless Godkind VICR
V2a Katsumugen, Climax VICR

2014 Duel Masters Fantasista 12

1 Dorago the Great, Dragon World VICR
2 Jackpot Batoriser C
3 Balga Raiser, the Dragonic Meteor C
4 Cerulean Dagger Dragon C
5 Bolmeteus Steel Dragon C
6 Infinity Dragon C
7 Cheering Pippi C
8 Baradios, Lord of Dragon Spirits C
9 Valhait, Lucky Dragon Elemental C
10 Codeking Number Nine C
11 Truename Baulion C
12 Perfect Galaxy, Spirit of Immortality C
13 True Heaven's C
14 DNA Spark C
15 Destolonely, Dragon King Demon C
16 Futureless, Demonic Dragon of Despair C
17 Vice Kaiser Zeta, the Vengeance C
18 Dark Lucifer, Demonic Eyed Gunman C
19 Olzekia, General of Decapitation C
20 Infernal Death Sunrise C
21 Wicked Soul Reincarnation C
22 Ryusei In The Dark C
23 Codename Dread Blood C
24 Necrodragon Devolution C
25 Bone Dance Charger C
26 Necrodragon Guljeneraid C
27 School Man C
28 BloodRayne, Start Dash C
29 Dragment Sword C
30 Super Spell Great Blue, the Blue Tide C
31 Invincible Technology C
32 Aqua Spellblue C
33 Transmogrify C
34 Hogan Blaster C
35 Brain Storm C
36 Triprex, Growth King C
37 Buon, Saver Style C
38 Kachua, Keeper of the Icegate C
39 Terradragon Mildgarmus C
40 Terradragon Balgazarmas C
41 Terradragon Drapi C
42 Eco Aini C
43 Valkerios G Kaiser C
44 Codename Valkyrie Ragon C
45 Bocco Lupia C
46 Bolshack NEX C
47 Cocco Lupia C
48 Flaming Jet Dragon C
49 Topgear, Start Dash C
50 Bonsowaru, Dragon Elemental Admiral C
51 Sajitorio, Indomitable Wings C
52 Jil Warka, Time Guardian C
53 Ika Ikaga, Excess Guardian C
54 Murmur, Apostle of the Formation C
55 Gunes Valkyrie, Holy Vizier C
56 Acroite, Start Dash C
57 Ekspelion, Dragment Symbol Lp C
58 Retweet, Aqua Warden C
59 Aqua Jester Loupe C
60 Mypad, Start Dash C
61 Aqua Guard C
62 Eureka Charger C
63 Energy Stream C
64 Boaroje, Miracle Style C
65 Nyasu, Courtney Style C
66 Courtney, Summer Breeze Faerie C
67 Super Move! Absolute Despair!! C
68 Kerasas, Start Dash C
69 Jasmine, Mist Faerie C
70 Faerie Miracle C
71 Namename Nameko C
72 Pure White Blueprint C
73 Matsurida Wasshoi C
74 Noumen C
75 Wendigo Apache, Izanai's Blank C
76 Dunas, Spirit Knight C
77 Father Earth C
78 Necrodragon Odol Needle C
79 Heaven's Gate C
80 Ragnarok, the Clock C
81 Death Gate, Gate of Hell C
82 Super Flaming Hell's Scrapper C
83 Natural Snare C
84 Super Explosive Duel Fire C

2014 Duel Masters Heavenly Justice Dragon

1 Vibros Heaven, Lord of Dragon Spirits
2 Valhalla Knight, Domination Dragon Elemental
3 Almil, Rebirth Elemental
4 Baronarde, Glorious Wings
5 Yuppal, Binding Guardian C
6 Valhalla Magic
7 Corteo, Spirit Knight C
8 Mist Rias, Sonic Guardian C
9 Peace Lupia C
10 Parshia, the Explorer C
11 Gaga Pikarian C
12 Notre Dame, Vizier of Illusion Shield C
13 Webius, the Patroller C

2014 Duel Masters Treasures of Pure Wicked God and Izumo's Counterattack

1 Summer Sonic, Light Weapon Left God
2 Lollapalooza, Spirit Knight Left God
3 Oracle Dream Jewel
4 Loud Park, True Flashing Right God
5 Glastonbury, Fuuma Right God
6 Izumo, Super Godkind
7 Big Day Out, Holy Evil Demon
8 Rising Sun, Holy Evil Elemental
9 Spice Queens, Inga's Holy Evil
10 Cyber N World SR
11 Aqua Surfer R
12 Energy Stream C
13 Terror Pit R

2015 Force of Will The Castle of Heaven and the Two Towers

COMPLETE SET (105) 55.00 85.00
BOOSTER BOX (36 PACKS) 120.00 160.00
BOOSTER PACK (10 CARDS) 5.00 8.00
RELEASED ON FEBRUARY 13, 2015
TAT001 Breath of the God C .10 .20
TAT002 Caterina, the Saint of Fantasy U .10 .25
TAT003 Don Quijote, the Wandering Knight R .10 .25
TAT004 Grimm, the Avenger of Fairy Tales SR .30 .50
TAT005 Guardian of Tower C .10 .20
TAT006 Jeanne d'Arc, the Awakening Purity SR .25 .40
TAT007 Jump to the Sky C .10 .20
TAT008 Light of Lumia U .10 .25
TAT009 Longinus, the Holy Lance C .10 .20
TAT010 Lumiel, the Tower of Hope R .10 .25
TAT011 March of Saints C .10 .20
TAT012 Pure Spirit of Fantasy C .10 .20
TAT013 Realm of Pure Spirits U .25 .40
TAT014 Sacred Princess of Guidance R 1.50 2.25
TAT015 Sacred Scepter of Exorcism U .10 .25
TAT016 Seeking Sky Soldier C .10 .20
TAT017 Sleeping Beauty R .10 .25
TAT018 The Queen's Butler C .10 .20
TAT019 Beowulf, the Blazing Wolf C .15 .30
TAT020 Big-Bang Revolution C .10 .20
TAT021 Card Soldier Diamond C .10 .20
TAT022 Card Soldier Heart C .10 .20
TAT023 Dragon King's Flame R .10 .25
TAT024 Duel of Truth C .30 .50
TAT025 Endless War U .10 .25
TAT026 Falltgold, the Dragoon R 3.50 5.00
TAT027 Forced Growth C .10 .20
TAT028 Fthaggua, the Flame Spirit R .10 .25
TAT029 Gliding Dragon Knight C .10 .20
TAT030 Kusanagi Sword C .10 .20
TAT031 Little Dread, the Fake Red Moon SR .75 1.25
TAT032 Rapid Decay U .10 .25
TAT033 Realm of the Dragon King R .10 .25
TAT034 Redbird of Omen U .10 .25
TAT035 Wicked Witch of the West U .10 .25
TAT036 Yamata-no-Orochi, the Eight Disasters SR .60 1.00
TAT037 Alice in Wonderland R 2.25 3.25
TAT038 Alice's World R .10 .25
TAT039 Cheshire Cat, the Grinning Remnant SR 8.00 12.00
TAT040 Crossroad of Worlds U .10 .25
TAT041 Destructive Flow C .10 .20
TAT042 Dreams of Wonderland R .10 .25
TAT043 Humpty Dumpty SR .30 .50
TAT044 Little Mermaid of Tragic Love U .10 .25
TAT045 Mad Hatter U .10 .25
TAT046 Mad Tea-Party U .10 .25
TAT047 March Hare R .10 .25
TAT048 Riina, the Girl with Nothing C .10 .20
TAT049 Seashore Fisherman C .10 .20
TAT050 Shallows Giant Dolphin C .10 .20
TAT051 Sleeping Rat C .10 .20
TAT052 Star Money C .10 .20
TAT053 Whirlpool of Knowledge C .10 .20
TAT054 Witch's Dagger C .10 .20
TAT055 Brainless Scarecrow C .10 .20
TAT056 Cowardly Lion C .10 .20
TAT057 Crimson Girl in the Sky R 5.00 7.00
TAT058 Dorothy, the Lost Girl R .10 .25
TAT059 Dragonslayer C .10 .20
TAT060 Evolution of Limits C .10 .20
TAT061 Gardea, the Guardian Dragon of Heaven SR .10 .25
TAT062 Glinda, the Fairy SR .50 .75
TAT063 Guide of Heaven U .10 .25
TAT064 Heartless Tin Man C .10 .20
TAT065 Oz, the Great Wizard U .10 .25
TAT066 Oz's Magic U .10 .25
TAT067 Portal of Truth C .10 .20
TAT068 Realm of Evolution U .10 .25
TAT069 Refarth, the Castle in Heaven R .40 .75
TAT070 Silver Shoes C .10 .20
TAT071 Wolf in the Sky C .10 .20
TAT072 Xeex the Ancient Magic R 1.25 1.50
TAT073 Al-Haber, the Tower of Despair R .10 .25
TAT074 Card Soldier Club C .10 .20
TAT075 Card Soldier Spade C .10 .20
TAT076 Death Sentence from the Queen C .10 .20
TAT077 Demon's Curse C .10 .20
TAT078 Ebony Devil C .10 .20
TAT079 Ebony Prophet R 1.25 1.75
TAT080 Elder Things U .10 .25
TAT081 Joker's Suit C .10 .20
TAT082 Laplacia, the Demon of Fate SR .10 .25
TAT083 Mephistopheles, the Abyssal Tyrant SR .75 1.15
TAT084 Necronomicon U .10 .25
TAT085 Neithardt, the Demon Knight U .10 .25
TAT086 Queen of Hearts R .10 .25
TAT087 Spire Shadow Drake C .10 .20
TAT088 Stoning to Death R .60 1.00
TAT089 Summoning Art of Alhazred U .10 .25
TAT090 Whisper from the Abyss C .10 .20
TAT091 Almerius, the Levitating Stone SR 3.50 5.00
TAT092 Feethsing, the Holy Wind Stone SR 1.25 1.75
TAT093 Grusbalesta, the Sealing Stone SR 4.00 6.00
TAT094 Magic Stone of Blasting Waves R 2.00 3.00
TAT095 Magic Stone of Dark Depth R 1.75 2.25
TAT096 Magic Stone of Gusting Skies R 2.00 3.50
TAT097 Magic Stone of Light Vapors R 1.00 1.50
TAT098 Magic Stone of Scorched Bales R 2.00 3.00
TAT099 Milest, the Ghostly Flame Stone SR 1.25 2.00
TAT100 Moojdart, the Fantasy Stone SR 1.25 1.75
TAT101 Magic Stone of Light C .10 .20
TAT102 Magic Stone of Flame C .10 .20
TAT103 Magic Stone of Water C .10 .20
TAT104 Magic Stone of Wind C .10 .20
TAT105 Magic Stone of Darkness C .10 .20

2015 Force of Will The Crimson Moon's Fairy Tale

COMPLETE SET (105) 40.00 70.00
BOOSTER BOX (36 PACKS) 80.00 100.00
BOOSTER PACK (10 CARDS) 2.00 3.00
RELEASED ON FEBRUARY 13, 2015
CMF001 Aesop, the Prince's Tutor U .10 .25
CMF002 Blinded Prince C .10 .20
CMF003 Clothes Tailor C .10 .20
CMF004 Dream of Juliet C .40 .75
CMF005 Grimm, the Fairy Tale Prince R .10 .25
CMF006 Holy Grail C .10 .20
CMF007 Jeweled Branch of Horai U .10 .25
CMF008 Juliet, the Hope SR .10 .20
CMF009 King's Servant C .10 .20
CMF010 Knight of Loyalty C .10 .20
CMF011 Light of Hope C .10 .20
CMF012 Light Palace, the King's Castle R .10 .25
CMF013 Pandora, Girl of the Box
Pandora of Light R 1.00 1.50
CMF014 Rapunzel, the Long-Haired Princess SR .10 .25
CMF015 Return to Stories U .10 .25
CMF016 Silver Stake C .10 .20
CMF017 Tell a Fairy Tale R .10 .25
CMF018 The Emperor with New Clothes U .10 .25
CMF019 Tinker Bell, the Spirit R .10 .25
CMF020 Basket of Little Red C .10 .20
CMF021 Bloody Moon R .10 .25
CMF022 Clockwork Apple Bomb C .10 .20
CMF023 Commander of Wolves R .10 .25
CMF024 Gilles de Rais, the Golden Dragon SR .75 1.25
CMF025 Granny by the Fireplace C .10 .20
CMF026 Hunter in Black Forest C .20 .35
CMF027 Little Red Riding Hood R 2.00 3.50
CMF028 Loup-Garou, the New Moon SR .60 1.00
CMF029 Moon Night Pouncer U .10 .25
CMF030 Murderous Snowman C .10 .20
CMF031 Poison Apple C .30 .50
CMF032 Purifying Fire U .30 .50
CMF033 Red Hot Iron Shoes C .10 .20
CMF034 Robe of Fire-Rat U .40 .60
CMF035 Seven Dwarfs C .10 .20
CMF036 Snow White R 2.00 3.50
CMF037 Wolf-Haunted in Black Forest U .10 .25
CMF038 Thunder R 1.50 2.25
CMF039 Archer of the Crescent Moon C .10 .20
CMF040 Charles VII U .10 .25
CMF041 Deep Ones SR .10 .25
CMF042 Five Challenges C .10 .20
CMF043 Hamelin's Pied Piper R .10 .25
CMF044 Heavenly Feathered Robe U .10 .25
CMF045 Inquisition R .10 .25
CMF046 Knight of the New Moon C .10 .20
CMF047 Nameless Girl R 1.25 2.00
CMF048 One-Inch Boy C .10 .20
CMF049 Pale Moon R .10 .25
CMF050 Rabbit Kick U .10 .25
CMF051 Rat Catcher's Pipe C .10 .20
CMF052 Seer of the Blue Moon R 3.00 4.00
CMF053 Servant of Kaguya C .10 .20
CMF054 Squirmer of the Dark C .10 .20
CMF055 Stone Bowl of Buddha U .10 .25
CMF056 Swordsman of the Full Moon SR .75 1.25
CMF057 Voice of the False God C .10 .20
CMF058 Absolute Cake Zone C .40 .60
CMF059 Aramis, the Three Musketeers U .10 .25
CMF060 Athos, the Three Musketeers SR .50 .75
CMF061 Christie, the Wind Tracker R 1.25 2.00
CMF062 Cottage of Cakes R .10 .25
CMF063 Cowrie of Swallows U .10 .25
CMF064 Crucifix C .10 .20
CMF065 Elvish Bowman C .10 .20
CMF066 Elvish Exorcist C .10 .20
CMF067 Elvish Priest C .60 1.00
CMF068 Fina, the Silver Player R .10 .25
CMF069 Gretel U 1.25 1.75
CMF070 Hansel SR .10 .25
CMF071 Law of Silence R .10 .25
CMF072 Musketeer's Bayonet C .10 .20
CMF073 Porthos, the Three Musketeers C .10 .20
CMF074 Puss in Boots R 1.00 1.50
CMF075 Siege Warfare C .10 .20
CMF076 Silver Bullet U .10 .25
CMF077 Alucard, the Dark Noble R 3.00 4.50
CMF078 Alvarez, the Demon Castle R .10 .25
CMF079 Black Coffin of Vampires C .10 .20
CMF080 Bloodsucking Impulse C .10 .20
CMF081 Carmilla, the Queen of Vampires SR 1.50 2.50
CMF082 Cinderella, the Ashen Maiden SR .75 1.25
CMF083 Deadman Prince C .10 .20
CMF084 Jewels on Dragon's Neck U .10 .25
CMF085 Lora, the Blood Speaker U .75 1.25
CMF086 Midnight Bell C .10 .20
CMF087 Pandora, Girl of the Box
Pandora of Dark R 1.00 1.50
CMF088 Pumpkin Witch C .10 .20
CMF089 Resurrection of Vampire U .10 .25
CMF090 Romeo, the Despair U .10 .25
CMF091 Servant of Vampire C .10 .20
CMF092 Slipper of Cinderella C .10 .20
CMF093 Spiral of Despair R .75 1.15
CMF094 Vampire Bat C .10 .20
CMF095 Vampire's Staff R .10 .25
CMF096 Magic Stone of Black Silence R 1.25 2.00
CMF097 Magic Stone of Deep Wood R 1.25 2.00
CMF098 Magic Stone of Hearth's Core R 1.25 2.00
CMF099 Magic Stone of Heat Ray R 1.25 2.00
CMF100 Magic Stone of Heaven's Rift R 1.25 2.00
CMF101 Magic Stone of Darkness C .10 .20
CMF102 Magic Stone of Flame C .10 .20
CMF103 Magic Stone of Light C .10 .20
CMF104 Magic Stone of Water C .10 .20
CMF105 Magic Stone of Wind C .10 .20

2015 Force of Will The Millennia of Ages

COMPLETE SET (50) 8.00 15.00
BOOSTER BOX (36 PACKS) 40.00 50.00
BOOSTER PACK (10 CARDS) 3.00 5.00
RELEASED ON JULY 24, 2015

Card	Low	High
MOA001 Almerius, the Magus of Light R	.10	.25
MOA002 Duet of Light C	.10	.20
MOA003 Grimm, the Heroic King of Aspiration U	.40	.75
MOA004 Kaguya, the Tale of the Bamboo Cutter SR	.10	.25
MOA005 Lumia, the Saint Lady of World Rebirth U	.10	.25
MOA006 Pandora, the Princess of History Chanter U	.10	.25
MOA007 Pandora's Box of Hope C	.10	.20
MOA008 Shining Bamboo C	.10	.20
MOA009 Temporal Spell of Millennia C	.10	.20
MOA010 Zero, the Flashing Mage-Warrior R	.10	.25
MOA011 Ame-no-Habakiri C	.30	.50
MOA012 Blazer, the Awakener R	.10	.25
MOA013 Cthugha, the Living Flame U	1.25	1.75
MOA014 Emissary of Another Dimension U	.10	.25
MOA015 Fetal Movement in Outer World C	.10	.20
MOA016 Ghostflame C	.10	.20
MOA017 Little Red, the Hope of Millennia R	.10	.25
MOA018 Milest, the Invisible Ghostly Flame SR	.10	.25
MOA019 Susanowo, the Ten-Fist Sword U	.60	1.00
MOA020 Wormhole C	.10	.20
MOA021 Alice's Pursuit C	.10	.20
MOA022 Alice's Soldier U	.10	.25
MOA023 Emperor of Millennia U	.10	.25
MOA024 House of the Old Man C	.10	.20
MOA025 Lunya, the Liar Girl R	.10	.25
MOA026 Moojdart, the Queen of Fantasy World SR	.10	.25
MOA027 Moon Incarnation C	.10	.20
MOA028 Oracle of Tsukuyomi U	.10	.25
MOA029 Purplemist, the Fantasy Dragon R	.10	.25
MOA030 Transparent Moon C	.10	.20
MOA031 Bastet, the Elder God U	.10	.25
MOA032 Christie, the Warden of Sanctuary U	.10	.25
MOA033 Fiethsing, the Elvish Oracle R	.10	.25
MOA034 Hansel and Gretel U	.10	.25
MOA035 Leaves of Yggdrasil C	.10	.20
MOA036 Liberate the World C	.10	.20
MOA037 Melfee, the Successor of Sacred Wind R	.10	.25
MOA038 Refarth, the Wind Castle C	.10	.20
MOA039 Scheherazade, the Teller of the Crimson Moon SR	.10	.25
MOA040 Wind of Gods C	.10	.20
MOA041 Aria, the Last Vampire U	.10	.25
MOA042 Book of Elbon C	.10	.20
MOA043 Dark Pulse C	.10	.20
MOA044 Eibon, the Mage R	.10	.25
MOA045 Grusbalesta, the Keeper of Magic Stones SR	.10	.25
MOA046 Hazzard, the Dark Forest Augur U	.10	.25
MOA047 Mephistopheles, the Demon Collaborator U	.10	.25
MOA048 Mount Immortal C	.10	.20
MOA049 Nyarlathotep, the Usurper R	.60	1.00
MOA050 Ritual of Millennia C	.10	.20

2015 Force of Will The Millennia of Ages Foil

Card	Low	High
MOA001 Almerius, the Magus of Light R	.10	.25
MOA002 Duet of Light C	.10	.20
MOA003 Grimm, the Heroic King of Aspiration U	.10	.25
MOA004 Kaguya, the Tale of the Bamboo Cutter SR	.10	.25
MOA005 Lumia, the Saint Lady of World Rebirth U	.40	.60
MOA006 Pandora, the Princess of History Chanter U	.75	1.00
MOA007 Pandora's Box of Hope C	.10	.20
MOA008 Shining Bamboo C	.10	.20
MOA009 Temporal Spell of Millennia C	.10	.20
MOA010 Zero, the Flashing Mage-Warrior R	.10	.25
MOA011 Ame-no-Habakiri C	1.25	1.75
MOA012 Blazer, the Awakener R	.10	.25
MOA013 Cthugha, the Living Flame U	3.00	4.00
MOA014 Emissary of Another Dimension U	.10	.25
MOA015 Fetal Movement in Outer World C	.50	.75
MOA016 Ghostflame C	.10	.20
MOA017 Little Red, the Hope of Millennia R	.10	.25
MOA018 Milest, the Invisible Ghostly Flame SR	.10	.25
MOA019 Susanowo, the Ten-Fist Sword U	1.25	1.75
MOA020 Wormhole C	.10	.20
MOA021 Alice's Pursuit C	.30	.50
MOA022 Alice's Soldier U	.30	.50
MOA023 Emperor of Millennia U	.10	.25
MOA024 House of the Old Man C	.10	.20
MOA025 Lunya, the Liar Girl R	.10	.25
MOA026 Moojdart, the Queen of Fantasy World SR	.10	.25
MOA027 Moon Incarnation C	.10	.20
MOA028 Oracle of Tsukuyomi U	.30	.50
MOA029 Purplemist, the Fantasy Dragon R	.10	.25
MOA030 Transparent Moon C	.10	.20
MOA031 Bastet, the Elder God U	.75	1.25
MOA032 Christie, the Warden of Sanctuary U	.10	.25
MOA033 Fiethsing, the Elvish Oracle R	.10	.25
MOA034 Hansel and Gretel U	.10	.25
MOA035 Leaves of Yggdrasil C	.10	.20
MOA036 Liberate the World C	.10	.20
MOA037 Melfee, the Successor of Sacred Wind R	.10	.25
MOA038 Refarth, the Wind Castle C	.10	.20
MOA039 Scheherazade, the Teller of the Crimson Moon SR	.10	.25
MOA040 Wind of Gods C	.10	.20
MOA041 Aria, the Last Vampire U	.10	.25
MOA042 Book of Elbon C	.75	1.15
MOA043 Dark Pulse C	.15	.30
MOA044 Eibon, the Mage R	.10	.25
MOA045 Grusbalesta, the Keeper of Magic Stones SR	.10	.25
MOA046 Hazzard, the Dark Forest Augur U	.10	.25
MOA047 Mephistopheles, the Demon Collaborator U	.10	.25
MOA048 Mount Immortal C	.10	.20
MOA049 Nyarlathotep, the Usurper R	1.25	1.75
MOA050 Ritual of Millennia C	.10	.20

2015 Force of Will The Moon Priestess Returns

Card	Low	High
COMPLETE SET (105)	35.00	60.00
BOOSTER BOX (36 PACKS)	70.00	90.00
BOOSTER PACK (10 CARDS)	3.00	5.00
RELEASED ON APRIL 24, 2015		
MPR001 I, the Pilot R	.10	.25
MPR002 Abel, the Avenger of Gods SR	.25	.40
MPR003 Accede the Light C	.10	.20
MPR004 Apostle of Paradise C	.10	.20
MPR005 Book of Genesis U	.10	.25
MPR006 Genesis Creation R	.10	.25
MPR007 Holy Warrior of Hope C	.10	.20
MPR008 Jekyll, the Order U	.10	.25
MPR009 Mind Reading Fox U	.10	.25
MPR010 Pandora, the Weaver of Myth R	.60	1.00
MPR011 Ragnarok, the Divine Sword of Savior R	.25	.40
MPR012 Savior of Splendor U	.10	.25
MPR013 Seal of Grimmia C	.10	.20
MPR014 Sign to the Future C	.25	.40
MPR015 Speaker of Creation C	.10	.20
MPR016 Sweet Rose C	.10	.20
MPR017 The Little Prince SR	.40	.60
MPR018 White Spirit C	.10	.20
MPR019 Akashic Records of Eternal Flame R	.10	.25
MPR020 Apostle of Cain C	.10	.20
MPR021 Apostle of Creation R	1.50	2.00
MPR022 Black Goat C	.10	.20
MPR023 Blazer, the Eater of Dimensions SR	1.00	1.50
MPR024 Bullet of Envy C	.10	.20
MPR025 Cain Complex U	.10	.25
MPR026 Crime and Punishment C	.10	.20
MPR027 Eden, the Crimson Garden U	.10	.25
MPR028 Forty Thieves C	.10	.20
MPR029 Glyph of Unkill C	.10	.20
MPR030 Jabal, the Grandsire of Nomads C	.10	.20
MPR031 Jubal, the Grandsire of Musicians U	.10	.25
MPR032 Shubb-Niggurath, the Goddess of Fertility SR	.20	.35
MPR033 Spawn of Blazer C	.10	.20
MPR034 Split Heaven and Earth R	1.25	1.75
MPR035 The First Lie U	.10	.25
MPR036 The Hound of Tindalos R	.10	.25
MPR037 Apollosphere, the Moon Lance R	.10	.25
MPR038 Campanella, the Milky Way Moon SR	.30	.50
MPR039 Dark Shining Swordsman C	.10	.20
MPR040 Elixir of Immortality C	.10	.20
MPR041 Etna, the Snow Queen SR	.50	.80
MPR042 Fallen Comet R	.10	.25
MPR043 Glimpse of Kaguya R	.40	.75
MPR044 Joyful Bird-Catcher C	.10	.20
MPR045 Kai, the Frozen Heart U	.10	.25
MPR046 Moon Princess of Stellar Wars R	.60	1.00
MPR047 Moonglow Bird C	.10	.20
MPR048 Pilot of Universe C	.10	.20
MPR049 Shooting Star U	.10	.25
MPR050 The Milky Way C	.10	.20
MPR051 Total Eclipse C	.10	.20
MPR052 Tsukuyomi, the Moon City U	.10	.25
MPR053 Yang Mage of Decrescent U	.10	.25
MPR054 Yin Mage of Increscent C	.10	.20
MPR055 Aladdin's Lamp R	.10	.25
MPR056 Ali Baba, The Earnest Worker C	.10	.20
MPR057 Art of Sinbad C	.10	.20
MPR058 Barrier Field U	.10	.25
MPR059 Djinn, the Spirit of Lamp R	.10	.25
MPR060 Exceed, the Ancient Magic U	.25	.40
MPR061 Familiar of Holy Wind C	.60	1.00
MPR062 Fiethsing, the Magus of Holy Wind SR	2.00	3.00
MPR063 Flying Carpet C	.10	.20
MPR064 Liberator of Wind R	1.50	2.00
MPR065 Morgiana, the Wise Servant U	.60	1.00
MPR066 Open Sesame C	.10	.20
MPR067 Rukh C	.10	.20
MPR068 Sinbad, the Windrider Merchant SR	.30	.50
MPR069 Stories Told in 1001 Nights R	.10	.25
MPR070 Survivor of Heaven Castle C	.10	.20
MPR071 Wind Dagger C	.10	.20
MPR072 Wiseman of Winds U	.10	.25
MPR073 Acolyte of Darkness C	.10	.20
MPR074 Awakening at the End R	.10	.25
MPR075 Bind of Gravity C	.10	.20
MPR076 Black Miasma C	.10	.20
MPR077 Black Moon U	.10	.25
MPR078 Byakhee, the Winged Lady R	.50	.75
MPR079 Call of Cthulhu C	.10	.20
MPR080 Fiend of Dark Pyre R	1.25	2.00
MPR081 Hyde, the Chaos U	.10	.25
MPR082 King in Yellow C	.20	.35
MPR083 Phantasm of Void C	.10	.20
MPR084 Shantak C	.10	.20
MPR085 Sheharyar, the Distrust King U	.10	.25
MPR086 Shining Trapezohedron R	.10	.25
MPR087 Void Blast U	.10	.25
MPR088 Yellow Sign C	.10	.20
MPR089 Yog-Sothoth, the Dark Myth SR	.60	1.00
MPR090 Zero, the Magus of Null SR	1.50	2.25
MPR091 Alice, the Guardian of Dimensions R	.60	1.00
MPR092 Apollobreak, the Moon Blast R	.10	.25
MPR093 Flame of Outer World R	2.75	3.50
MPR094 Gherta, the Tear of Passion R	.10	.25
MPR095 Giovanni, the Lonely Child R	.10	.25
MPR096 Hastur, the Unspeakable R	1.00	1.50
MPR097 Seth, the Arbiter R	.60	1.00
MPR098 Little Red, the Pure Stone SR	4.00	6.00
MPR099 Magic Stone of Moon Light R	1.50	2.00
MPR100 Magic Stone of Moon Shade R	2.50	3.00
MPR101 Magic Stone of Darkness C	.10	.20
MPR102 Magic Stone of Flame C	.10	.20
MPR103 Magic Stone of Light C	.10	.20
MPR104 Magic Stone of Water C	.10	.20
MPR105 Magic Stone of Wind C	.10	.20

2015 Force of Will The Seven Kings of the Lands

Card	Low	High
COMPLETE SET (105)	50.00	100.00
BOOSTER BOX (36 PACKS)	70.00	90.00
BOOSTER PACK (10 CARDS)	2.00	5.00
UNLISTED C	.12	.30
UNLISTED U	.25	.60
UNLISTED R	.40	1.00
RELEASED ON SEPTEMBER 15, 2015		
SKL001 Arla, the Winged Lord R	.40	1.00
SKL002 Bai Hu, the Sacred Beast R	.40	1.00
SKL003 Bedivere, the Restorer of Souls SR	.75	2.00
SKL004 Blessed Holy Wolf C	.12	.30
SKL005 Celestial Wing Seraph SR	.75	2.00
SKL006 Dignified Seraph U	.25	.60
SKL007 Faria, the Sacred Queen R	.75	2.00
SKL008 Give Wings C	.12	.30
SKL009 Gwiber, the White Dragon U	.25	.60
SKL010 Heavenly Garden of Armalla R	.60	1.50
SKL011 Herald of the Winged Lord C	.12	.30
SKL012 Invigoration of the Winged Lord R	.40	1.00
SKL013 Little Angel of Armalla C	.12	.30
SKL014 Order of Sacred Queen C	.12	.30
SKL015 Protection of the Seraph C	.12	.30
SKL016 Protective Barrier U	.25	.60
SKL017 Wingman of Armalla C	.12	.30
SKL018 Alice's Little Assault Force C	.12	.30
SKL019 Certo, the Blazing Volcano U	.60	1.50
SKL020 Dragoon of Certo C	.12	.30
SKL021 Draig, the Red Dragon U	.25	.60
SKL022 Familiar of Primogenitor C	.12	.30
SKL023 Fear of Battle C	.12	.30
SKL024 Flame Cat C	.12	.30
SKL025 Flame King's Shout C	.12	.30
SKL026 Gareth, the Dauntless Knight U	.25	.60
SKL027 Melgis, the Flame King R	.40	1.00
SKL028 Ouroboros, the Snake of Reincarnation SR	.60	1.50
SKL029 Phantom of Primogenitor R	.40	1.00
SKL030 Shadow Flame C	.12	.30
SKL031 Snow White, the Valkyrie of Passion SR	1.00	3.00
SKL032 War Dance of the Valkyries U	.25	.60
SKL033 Zhu Que, the Sacred Beast R	.40	1.00
SKL034 Alice's Castling C	.20	.50
SKL035 Alice's Little Scout C	.12	.30
SKL036 Charm of the Princess R	.40	1.00
SKL037 Cinderella, the Valkyrie of Glass SR	1.00	3.00
SKL038 Euryale, the Dark Eye of Blindness U	.25	.60
SKL039 Foresee C	.12	.30
SKL040 Heat Gaze C	.12	.30
SKL041 Medusa, the Dead Eye of Petrification SR	.75	2.00
SKL042 Petrifying Gaze U	.25	.60
SKL043 Sailor of Shangri-La C	.12	.30
SKL044 Shangri-La, the Paradise on the Ocean R	.40	1.00
SKL045 Squire of the Ocean Lady C	.12	.30
SKL046 Stheno, the Evil Eye of Temptation U	.25	.60
SKL047 Trader of Shangri-La C	.12	.30
SKL048 Valentina, the Princess of Love R	2.50	10.00
SKL049 Xuan Wu, the Sacred Beast R	.40	1.00
SKL050 Afanc, the Phantom Beast U	.25	.60
SKL051 Alice's Little Guardian C	.12	.30
SKL052 Behemoth, the Earth Eater R	.40	1.00
SKL053 Blessing of Yggdrasil C	.12	.30
SKL054 Branch of Yggdrasil C	.12	.30
SKL055 Elite Commander U	.25	.60
SKL056 Guardian of the Forest C	.12	.30
SKL057 Herald of the Beast Lady C	.12	.30
SKL058 Keen Sense U	.25	.60
SKL059 Pricia, the Beast Lady R	5.00	12.00
SKL060 Qing Long, the Sacred Beast SR	1.25	3.00
SKL061 Rapid Growth C	.12	.30
SKL062 Ratatoskr, the Spirit of Yggdrasil SR	1.50	4.00
SKL063 Sissei, the Ancient Forest R	.40	1.00
SKL064 Sprint of the Beast Lady R	.40	1.00
SKL065 Sprinting Wolf C	.12	.30
SKL066 Arthur, the Dead Lord of Vengeance SR	2.00	5.00
SKL067 Dark Purge C	.12	.30
SKL068 Endless Night U	.25	.60
SKL069 Forbidden Spell of the Undead Lord R	.40	1.00
SKL070 Herald of the Undead Lord C	.12	.30
SKL071 Hunter of Souls C	.12	.30
SKL072 Merlin, the Wizard of Distress R	.40	1.00
SKL073 Necromancy of the Undead Lord C	.12	.30
SKL074 Niflheim, the Realm of the Dead R	.40	1.00
SKL075 Persephone, the Nether Empress SR	.60	1.50
SKL076 Prowler of Niflheim C	.12	.30
SKL077 Rezzard, the Undead Lord R	2.50	6.00
SKL078 Scion of Ancient Lore U	.25	.60
SKL079 Soulhunt C	.12	.30
SKL080 Soulless Soldier C	.12	.30
SKL081 Underground Dragger U	.25	.60
SKL082 Charging Assaulter C	.20	.50
SKL083 Clockwork Scout Plane C	.12	.30
SKL084 Clockwork Soldiers C	.12	.30
SKL085 Imitation Dragon U	.25	.60
SKL086 Leginus, the Mechanical City U	.25	.60
SKL087 Machina, the Machine Lord R	3.00	8.00
SKL088 March of the Machine Lord U	.25	.60
SKL089 Power Supply Team C	.12	.30
SKL090 Special Armor U	.25	.60
SKL091 Winding Mender C	.12	.30
SKL092 Alice, the Girl in the Looking Glass R	.40	1.00
SKL093 Alice, the Girl in the Looking Glass R	.40	1.00
SKL094 Blazer Gill Rabus R	.40	1.00
SKL095 Artemis, the God's Bow R	.40	1.00
SKL096 Deathscythe, the Life Reaper R	.40	1.00
SKL097 Deep Blue, the Phantom Board R	.50	1.25
SKL098 Gleipnir, the Red Binding of Fate R	.40	1.00
SKL099 Horn of Sacred Beasts R	.40	1.00
SKL100 Marybell, the Steel Doll R	.40	1.00
SKL101 Darkness Magic Stone C	.12	.30
SKL102 Fire Magic Stone C	.12	.30
SKL103 Light Magic Stone C	.12	.30
SKL104 Water Magic Stone C	.12	.30
SKL105 Wind Magic Stone C	.12	.30

2015 Force of Will The Twilight Wanderer

Card	Low	High
COMPLETE SET (104)	50.00	100.00
RELEASED ON DECEMBER 11, 2015		
TTW001 Alice, Girl of the Lake/Alice, Fairy Queen R	2.00	5.00
TTW002 Alice's Little Supply Force C	.10	.25
TTW003 Arthur Pendragon, King of the Round Table SR	.75	3.00
TTW004 Elaine, the Fairy U	.20	.50
TTW005 Fairy of the Lake C	.10	.25
TTW006 Galahad, The Son of God	.20	.50
TTW007 Gawain, the Knight of the Sun R	.40	1.00
TTW008 Gloria's Castle Town R	.40	1.00
TTW009 Grand Cross R	.40	1.00
TTW010 Justice of God's Sword C	.10	.25
TTW011 Light Sprite C	.10	.25
TTW012 Nimue, the Fairy U	.20	.50
TTW013 Perceval, the Seeker of Holy Grail R	.75	2.00
TTW014 Pride of Knights C	.10	.25
TTW015 Protection of the Fairies C	.10	.25
TTW016 The Final Word U	.20	.50
TTW017 Viviane, Lady of the Lake SR	1.00	2.50
TTW018 Young Knight of Gloria C	.10	.25
TTW019 Barrier of Flame R	.40	1.00
TTW020 Beat of the Phoenix Wings R	.40	1.00
TTW021 Burn to Cinders C	.10	.25
TTW022 Caldera-Born Dragon U	.20	.50
TTW023 Flame Dragon Commandant U	.20	.50
TTW024 Flame Sprite C	.10	.25
TTW025 Flamewing Wyvern C	.10	.25
TTW026 Flash of Demon Sword C	.10	.25
TTW027 Guinevere, the Jealous Queen R	.75	3.00
TTW028 Hector de Maris, the Acolyte of Mad Demon U	.20	.50
TTW029 Lancelot, the Knight of Mad Demon R	.75	2.00
TTW030 Magic Matchstick C	.10	.25
TTW031 Phoenix, the Flame of the World SR	.75	2.00
TTW032 Sylvia Gill Palarilias Sylvia Gill Palarilias (J) R	3.00	8.00
TTW033 Sylvia's Clanmate C	.10	.25
TTW034 Sylvia's Roar U	.20	.50
TTW035 The Little Match Girl SR	.50	1.25
TTW036 Whelp Drake C	.10	.25
TTW037 Adombrali, the Unfathomable SR	1.50	4.00
TTW038 All Consuming Suspiscion C	.10	.25
TTW039 Hera, Goddess of Jealousy R	.75	2.00
TTW040 Insomniac Dormouse C	.10	.25
TTW041 Invasion Ship, Golden Hind R	.40	1.00
TTW042 Laying the Foundation C	.10	.25
TTW043 Leviathan, the First of the Sea SR	.50	1.25
TTW044 Maritime Lookout C	.10	.25
TTW045 Valentina, Plotting Lord of the Seas / Overlord of the Seven Lands, Valentina R	2.00	5.00
TTW046 Sane Hatter U	.20	.50
TTW047 Send Back C	.10	.25
TTW048 September Hare U	.20	.50
TTW049 Suseri-hime, Goddess of Passion R	.40	1.00
TTW050 The Overlord's Baptism R	.40	1.00
TTW051 The Overlord's Invasion Party U	.20	.50
TTW052 Valentina's Zealot C	.10	.25
TTW053 Wall of Ideas U	.20	.50
TTW054 Water Sprite C	.10	.25
TTW055 Beastly Attack C	.10	.25
TTW056 Drop of Yggdrasil C	.10	.25
TTW057 Familiar of Refrain C	.10	.25
TTW058 Final Forfeit U	.20	.50
TTW059 Fruit of Yggdrasil C	.10	.25
TTW060 Holy Ground of the Four Sacred Beasts R	.40	1.00
TTW061 Hraesvelgr, Drinker of Death R	.40	1.00
TTW062 Pricia, Beast Queen in Hiding SR	.50	1.25
TTW063 Reflect, Child of Potential Refrain, Child of Convergence R	4.00	10.00
TTW064 Rewriting Laws C	.10	.25
TTW065 Servant of Reflect C	.10	.25
TTW066 Spell-Weaver Elf U	.20	.50
TTW067 Spirit of Yggdrasil U	.20	.50
TTW068 The Beast Queen's Counterattack R	.40	1.00
TTW069 The Beast Queen's Guardian U	.20	.50
TTW070 Vedfolnir, Eraser of Wind R	.40	1.00
TTW071 Wind Sprite C	.10	.25
TTW072 Ziz, the Bird that Envelopes the Sky SR	.50	1.25
TTW073 Barrier of Shadows		1.00
TTW074 Black Ribbon	.10	.25
TTW075 Dance of the Shadows U	.20	.50
TTW076 Girl in Twilight Garb R	4.00	10.00
TTW077 Dark Alice's Familiar C	.10	.25
TTW078 Dark Alice's Shadow Warrior C	.10	.25
TTW079 Dark Arla, the Shadow Wing U	.20	.50
TTW080 Dark Faria, Shadow Princess of Ebony SR	1.50	3.00
TTW081 Dark Melgis, the Shadow Flame U	.20	.50
TTW082 Dark Rezzard, the Dying Shadow R	.40	1.00
TTW083 Elisabeth, Shadow Princess of Blood SR	.60	1.50
TTW084 Jeanne d'Arc, Shadow Princess of Purity R	.40	1.00
TTW085 Progenitor Demon C	.10	.25
TTW086 Recollection of Dystopia R	.40	1.00
TTW087 Shadow Assassin C	.10	.25
TTW088 Shadow Doppelganger U	.20	.50
TTW089 The Scorn of Dark Alice	.10	.25
TTW090 Unseen Pressure	.10	.25
TTW091 Dark Machina, Gliding Shadow R	.40	1.00
TTW092 Deployable Defense Device U	.20	.50
TTW093 Mass Produced Giant Land Mine C	.10	.25
TTW094 Mechanical Knight C	.10	.25
TTW095 Mechanical Sprite C	.10	.25
TTW096 Change the World, Orb of Illusion R	1.50	4.00
TTW097 Excalibur, The God's Sword	.40	1.00
TTW098 Excalibur, the Spirit God's Sword R	.40	1.00
TTW099 Laevateinn, the Demon Sword R	.40	1.00
TTW100 Schrödinger, the Fallen Black Cat R		1.00
TTW101 Fairy's Memoria R	1.25	3.00
TTW102 Ruler's Memoria R	5.00	6.00
TTW103 Sacred Beast's Memoria R		1.00
TTW104 Shadow's Memoria R		1.00
TTW105 Unyielding Flame's Memoria R		1.00
TTW106 Darkness Magic Stone NR	.10	.25
TTW107 Fire Magic Stone NR	.10	.25
TTW108 Light Magic Stone NR	.10	.25
TTW109 Water Magic Stone NR	.10	.25
TTW110 Wind Magic Stone NR	.10	.25

2016 Force of Will The Moonlit Savior

Card	Low	High
COMPLETE SET (105)	60.00	120.00
BOOSTER BOX (36 PACKS)	70.00	90.00
BOOSTER PACK (10 CARDS)	2.00	3.00
*FOIL: .75X TO 2X BASIC CARDS		
RELEASED ON MARCH 11, 2016		
TMS001 Angel of Wisdom, Cherudim U	.25	.60
TMS002 Crescent Moon Magician R	.40	1.00
TMS003 Friend from Another World, Kaguya R	2.50	10.00
TMS004 Holy Moon of Pure Nights U	.25	.60
TMS005 Izanagi, Keeper of the Seal SR	.60	1.50
TMS006 Kaguya's Premonition C	.20	.50
TMS007 Knight of the Solstice R	.40	1.00
TMS008 Luminescent Bamboo Bullet R	.40	1.00
TMS009 Lunar Ibis C	.20	.50
TMS010 Moonbreeze Fairy C	.20	.50
TMS011 Pale Savior C	.20	.50
TMS012 Seal of Shining Bamboo C	.20	.50
TMS013 Shining Strike U	.25	.60
TMS014 Temple Monk C	.20	.50
TMS015 Tristan, the Knight of Sorrow C	.20	.50
TMS016 Tsukuyomi Noble SR	1.25	3.00
TMS017 Veteran Master C	.20	.50
TMS018 Athena, Titan of Revenge SR	1.50	4.00
TMS019 Blazing Metropolis, Vell-Savaria U	.25	.60
TMS020 Blessing of Athena C	.20	.50
TMS021 Demonflame U	.25	.60
TMS022 Infernal Spirit of Vell-Savaria C	.20	.50
TMS023 Keeper of the Future, Skuld SR	1.00	2.50
TMS024 Keeper of the Past, Urthr R	.40	1.00
TMS025 Keeper of the Present, Verdandi R	.60	1.50
TMS026 Memory of Disappearance R	.40	1.00
TMS027 Memory of Flame C	.20	.50
TMS028 Mordred, the Traitor U	.25	.60
TMS029 Rukh Egg C	.20	.50
TMS030 Spirit of Certo C	.20	.50
TMS031 The Observer R	2.50	6.00
TMS032 Time Traveling Emissary C	.20	.50
TMS033 Torching the Timeline C	.20	.50
TMS034 Vell-Savarian Dragon U	.25	.60
TMS035 Dance of Inspiration C	.20	.50
TMS036 Drill Sergeant R	.40	1.00
TMS037 Dying Swallow U	.25	.60
TMS038 Flower Kingdom U	.25	.60
TMS039 Magic Conductor's Baton C	.20	.50
TMS040 Muse, Celestial of Music SR	1.00	2.50
TMS041 Musician of Shangri-La C	.20	.50
TMS042 Peasant Revolt C	.30	.75
TMS043 Prison in the Lunar Lake C	.20	.50
TMS044 Puppet Soldier C	.20	.50
TMS045 Shion's Hymn R	.40	1.00
TMS046 Songstress of Shangri-La R	3.00	8.00
TMS047 The Flower Prince U	.25	.60
TMS048 Thumbelina R	.40	1.00
TMS049 Valentina, Puppet Monarch SR	.50	1.25
TMS050 Valentina's Resistance U	.25	.60
TMS051 Wererabbit of the Aqua Moon C	.20	.50
TMS052 Ambush! C	.20	.50
TMS053 Avatar of the Seven Lands, Alice SR	1.25	3.00
TMS054 Child of the Forest C	.20	.50
TMS055 Foment of the World Tree R	.40	1.00
TMS056 Heart Stirring Sage U	.25	.60
TMS057 Huanglong, Leader of the Four Sacred Beasts SR	.60	1.50
TMS058 Kujata, Sacred Ox R	.40	1.00
TMS059 Moonbreeze Elf C	.20	.50
TMS060 Pricia's Call to Action C	.20	.50
TMS061 Rhythm of Life C	.20	.50
TMS062 Servant to the Sacred Moon C	.20	.50
TMS063 Timekeeper Elf U	.25	.60
TMS064 Wall of Wind U	.25	.60
TMS065 Wind-Secluded Refuge U	.25	.60
TMS066 Wolf in the Moonlight C	.20	.50
TMS067 World Tree Protector R	.40	1.00
TMS068 Yggdrasil, the World Tree R	3.00	8.00
TMS069 Auspicious Bird of the Black Moon C	.20	.50
TMS070 Black Moon Fairy C	.20	.50
TMS071 Call of the Primogenitor C	.20	.50
TMS072 Conqueror of the Black Moon, Gill Lapis Uber R	130.00	180.00
TMS072 Conqueror of the Black Moon, Gill Lapis R	4.00	10.00
TMS073 Demon of the Black Moon, Lilith R	.40	1.00
TMS074 Demonic Commander R	.40	1.00
TMS075 Fallen Angelic Destroyer, Lucifer SR	1.50	4.00
TMS076 Fallen Hero U	.25	.60
TMS077 Izanami, the Sealed Terror SR	.60	1.50
TMS078 Izanami's Curse U	.25	.60
TMS079 Knight's Shade C	.20	.50
TMS080 Nighttime Raiders C	.20	.50
TMS081 Pitch Black Moon U	.25	.60
TMS082 Silencing Spell C	.20	.50
TMS083 Space-Time Collapse R	.60	1.50
TMS084 The Executioner C	.20	.50
TMS085 Witch of the Night U	.25	.60
TMS086 Magic Screw C	.20	.50
TMS087 Marybell, Insane Self-Aware Machine R	.40	1.00
TMS088 Pricia, Pursuant of Exploding Flame R	.50	1.25
TMS089 Seal of Wind and Light R	.40	1.00
TMS090 Space-Time Anomaly C	.20	.50
TMS091 Blade of the Seven Lands, Excalibur X R	.60	1.50
TMS092 Heavenly Instrument, Hydromonica R	1.00	2.50
TMS093 Illusory Demonic Globe, The Earth R	.60	1.50
TMS094 Interdimensional Vessel, Apollo R	1.00	2.50
TMS095 Orb of Disaster, Ifrit Glass R	.60	1.50
TMS096 Black Moon's Memoria R	.40	1.00
TMS097 Disaster's Memoria R	1.00	2.50
TMS098 Hymnal's Memoria R	.60	1.50
TMS099 Moonbreeze's Memoria R	.40	1.00
TMS100 Yggdrasil's Memoria R	.40	1.00
TMS101 Darkness Magic Stone NR	.20	.50
TMS102 Fire Magic Stone NR	.20	.50
TMS103 Light Magic Stone NR	.20	.50
TMS104 Water Magic Stone NR	.20	.50
TMS105 Wind Magic Stone NR	.20	.50

2016 Force of Will Battle for Attoractia

Card	Low	High
COMPLETE SET (111 CARDS)	750.00	1200.00
BOOSTER BOX (36 PACKS)	80.00	110.00
BOOSTER PACK (10 CARDS)	2.50	6.00
UNLISTED C	.10	.30
UNLISTED U	.10	.30
UNLISTED R	.20	.60
RELEASED ON JULY 1ST, 2016		
BFA001 Avalon Illusionary Home of Knights U	.10	.30

BFA002 Bors Returned Adventurer R .20 .60
BFA003 Circle of Trust U .10 .30
BFA004 Fairy of Sacred Vision U .10 .30
BFA005 Gathering of Fairies C .10 .25
BFA006 Guardian Angel Raphael R .20 .60
BFA007 Interdimensional Escape R .50 1.25
BFA008 Kaguya Rabbit Princess of the Lunar Halo SR .75 2.00
BFA009 Last People of Gloria C .10 .25
BFA010 Life Profiteering Priest C .10 .25
BFA011 Rabbit of Moonlit Nights U .10 .30
BFA012 Rabbit Trap C .10 .25
BFA013 Reflective Water Shield C .10 .25
BFA014 Sacred Knight of the North C .10 .25
BFA015 Sacred Knight of the South C .10 .25
BFA016 Alisaris Avatar of Destruction SR .25 .75
BFA017 Battle for Attoractia R .20 .60
BFA018 Blood Boil C .10 .25
BFA019 Blood Covered War Axe C .10 .25
BFA020 Bloodfire Dragon U .10 .30
BFA021 Enraged Knight C .10 .25
BFA022 Flame Soldier of Volga C .10 .25
BFA023 Flame Trap C .10 .25
BFA024 Lapis Beast of Flame C .10 .25
BFA025 Napping Lion U .10 .30
BFA026 Ring of Fate U .10 .30
BFA027 Sanguine Arena U .10 .30
BFA028 True Successor of Certo Volga R .20 .60
BFA029 VellSavarian Apparition C .10 .25
BFA030 Ywain Knight of Lions R .20 .60
BFA031 Bulwark Architect C .10 .25
BFA032 CrocoShark U 2.00 5.00
BFA033 CrocoShark Crossing U .10 .30
BFA034 Disassembly Line U .10 .30
BFA035 Down the Drain C .10 .25
BFA036 Engineer of Leginus C .10 .25
BFA037 Fairy Flower Extract C .10 .25
BFA038 Machine Sympathizer R .20 .60
BFA039 Queens Envoy C .10 .25
BFA040 Separation of Body and Soul C .10 .25
BFA041 Set Free R .20 .60
BFA042 Shion Liberator of ShangriLa SR .25 .75
BFA043 Spectating Magician C .10 .25
BFA044 Technician of Leginus U .10 .30
BFA045 Titania Prideful Queen R .20 .60
BFA046 Alices Little Decoy C .10 .25
BFA047 Earthbound Wingman C .10 .25
BFA048 Escort of the Fairy King C .10 .25
BFA049 Hare of Inaba SR .25 .75
BFA050 High Speed Dash R .20 .60
BFA051 Home of the Wingmen U .10 .30
BFA052 Midsummers Night King Oberon R .20 .60
BFA053 Moonbreeze Rabbit U .10 .30
BFA054 Protection of Alice C .10 .25
BFA055 Song of the Fairy King U .10 .30
BFA056 Survivors of Sissei C .10 .25
BFA057 The Last Drop C .10 .25
BFA058 TimeGazer Elf U .10 .30
BFA059 Wing Trap C .10 .25
BFA060 Yggdor Beast of the World R .20 .60
BFA061 Black Moonbeam R .75 2.00
BFA062 Collapsing World U .10 .30
BFA063 Corrosion C .10 .25
BFA064 Covert Operative C .10 .25
BFA065 Death Trap C .10 .25
BFA066 Eyes In The Darkness C .10 .25
BFA067 Fairy Shadow U .10 .30
BFA068 Hades Lord of the Dead SR .25 .75
BFA069 Lapis Dark Beast C .10 .25
BFA070 Lapis Dark Storm C .10 .25
BFA071 Melder Last of the Dead R .20 .60
BFA072 Messenger Familiar C .10 .25
BFA073 Remnants of Niflheim C .10 .25
BFA074 Riza First of the Dead R .20 .60
BFA075 Rotting Black Moon Dragon U .10 .30
BFA076 Alice of Light Alice of Shadow SR .25 .75
BFA077 Lars Inheritor of the Sacred Spirit•Glorian Princess of Water Charlotte SR .25 .75
BFA078 Reflect the Beginning of Time•Refrain the End of Ages SR .50 1.25
BFA079 Slayer of the Overlord Pricia•Possessor Princess of Love Valentina SR 1.50 4.00
BFA079 Slayer of the Overlord Pricia•Possessor Princess of Love Valentina Uber R 150.00 300.00
BFA080 Interdimensional Monarch Gill Lapis•Space Time Pursuer Gill Lapis SR .50 1.25
BFA081 Attoractia Dimension of the Seven Kings Illusory Demonic Globe Attoractia R .20 .60
BFA082 Artificial Moon U .10 .30
BFA083 Dummy Doll U .10 .30
BFA084 Machine Lab of Leginus R .20 .60
BFA085 Mariabellas Work C .10 .25
BFA086 Remote Control Beast C .10 .25
BFA087 Remote Control Golem R .20 .60
BFA088 Small Assistant Mariabella SR .75 2.00
BFA089 The RoBox C .10 .25
BFA090 TickTock Automaton C .10 .25
BFA093 Memoria of the Seven Lands•Machina Clever Researcher Uber R 120.00 180.00
BFA093 Memoria of the Seven Lands•Machina Clever Researcher R 3.00 8.00
BFA094 Memoria of the Seven Lands•Arla Guardian of the Skies R 2.00 5.00
BFA094 Memoria of the Seven Lands•Arla Guardian of the Skies Uber R 120.00 180.00
BFA095 Memoria of the Seven Lands Razzard Dark Necromancer R 2.00 5.00
BFA095 Memoria of the Seven Lands Razzard Dark Necromancer Uber R 120.00 180.00
BFA096 Call to Actions Memoria R .50 1.25
BFA097 Brutal Conquerors Memoria R .50 1.25
BFA098 Aloof Researchers Memoria R .50 1.25
BFA099 First Flights Memoria R .75 2.00
BFA100 Sorrowful Necromancys Memoria R .50 1.25
BFA101 Darkness Magic Stone NR .10 .25
BFA102 Fire Magic Stone NR .10 .25
BFA103 Light Magic Stone NR .10 .25
BFA104 Water Magic Stone NR .10 .25
BFA105 Wind Magic Stone NR .10 .25
BFA091• Memoria of the Seven Lands•Faria Chosen Girl R 3.00 8.00
BFA091• Memoria of the Seven Lands•Faria Chosen Girl Uber R 120.00 180.00
BFA092• Memoria of the Seven Lands•Melgis Conqueror of Flame R 2.50 6.00
BFA092• Memoria of the Seven Lands•Melgis Conqueror of Flame Uber R 120.00 180.00

2016 Force of Will Battle for Attoractia Foil

COMPLETE SET (150 CARDS) 900.00 1650.00
BOOSTER BOX (36 PACKS) 80.00 110.00
BOOSTER PACK (10 CARDS) 2.50 6.00
UNLISTED C .25 .75
UNLISTED U .25 .75
UNLISTED R .40 1.00
RELEASED ON JULY 1ST, 2016
BFA001 Avalon Illusionary Home of Knights U .25 .75
BFA002 Bors Returned Adventurer R .40 1.00
BFA002 Bors Returned Adventurer R Full Art 1.50 4.00
BFA003 Circle of Trust U .25 .75
BFA004 Fairy of Sacred Vision U .25 .75
BFA005 Gathering of Fairies C .25 .75
BFA006 Guardian Angel Raphael R Full Art 3.00 8.00
BFA006 Guardian Angel Raphael R .40 1.00
BFA007 Interdimensional Escape R 1.50 4.00
BFA007 Interdimensional Escape R Full Art 3.00 8.00
BFA008 Kaguya Rabbit Full Art 2.00 5.00
BFA008 Kaguya Rabbit Princess of the Lunar Halo SR .75 2.00
BFA009 Last People of Gloria C .25 .75
BFA010 Life Profiteering Priest C .25 .75
BFA011 Rabbit of Moonlit Nights U .25 .75
BFA012 Rabbit Trap C .25 .75
BFA013 Reflective Water Shield C .25 .75
BFA014 Sacred Knight of the North C .25 .75
BFA015 Sacred Knight of the South C .25 .75
BFA016 Alisaris Avatar of Destruction SR .75 2.00
BFA016 Alisaris Avatar of Destruction SR Full Art 5.00 12.00
BFA017 Battle for Attoractia R .40 1.00
BFA017 Battle for Attoractia R Full Art 1.50 4.00
BFA018 Blood Boil C .25 .75
BFA019 Blood Covered War Axe C .25 .75
BFA020 Bloodfire Dragon U .25 .75
BFA021 Enraged Knight C .25 .75
BFA022 Flame Soldier of Volga C .25 .75
BFA023 Flame Trap C .25 .75
BFA024 Lapis Beast of Flame C .25 .75
BFA025 Napping Lion U .25 .75
BFA026 Ring of Fate U .25 .75
BFA027 Sanguine Arena U .25 .75
BFA028 True Successor of Certo Volga R Full Art 1.50 4.00
BFA028 True Successor of Certo Volga R .40 1.00
BFA029 VellSavarian Apparition C .25 .75
BFA030 Ywain Knight of Lions R Full Art 1.50 4.00
BFA030 Ywain Knight of Lions R .40 1.00
BFA031 Bulwark Architect C .25 .75
BFA032 CrocoShark U 2.50 6.00
BFA033 CrocoShark Crossing U .25 .75
BFA034 Disassembly Line U .25 .75
BFA035 Down the Drain C 1.00 2.50
BFA036 Engineer of Leginus C .25 .75
BFA037 Fairy Flower Extract C .75 2.00
BFA038 Machine Sympathizer R .40 1.00
BFA038 Machine Sympathizer R Full Art 1.50 4.00
BFA039 Queens Envoy C .25 .75
BFA040 Separation of Body and Soul C .25 .75
BFA041 Set Free R Full Art 1.50 4.00
BFA041 Set Free R .40 1.00
BFA042 Shion Liberator of ShangriLa SR .75 2.00
BFA042 Shion Liberator of ShangriLa SR Full Art 2.50 6.00
BFA043 Spectating Magician C .25 .75
BFA044 Technician of Leginus U .25 .75
BFA045 Titania Prideful Queen R 2.00 5.00
BFA045 Titania Prideful Queen R Full Art 5.00 12.00
BFA046 Alices Little Decoy C .25 .75
BFA047 Earthbound Wingman C .25 .75
BFA048 Escort of the Fairy King C .25 .75
BFA049 Hare of Inaba SR Full Art 1.50 4.00
BFA049 Hare of Inaba SR .75 2.00
BFA050 High Speed Dash R Full Art 1.50 4.00
BFA050 High Speed Dash R .40 1.00
BFA051 Home of the Wingmen U .25 .75
BFA052 Midsummers Night King Oberon R Full Art 3.00 8.00
BFA052 Midsummers Night King Oberon R .40 1.00
BFA053 Moonbreeze Rabbit U .25 .75
BFA054 Protection of Alice C .25 .75
BFA055 Song of the Fairy King U .25 .75
BFA056 Survivors of Sissei C .25 .75
BFA057 The Last Drop C .25 .75
BFA058 TimeGazer Elf U .25 .75
BFA059 Wing Trap C .25 .75
BFA060 Yggdor Beast of the World R Full Art 1.50 4.00
BFA060 Yggdor Beast of the World R .40 1.00
BFA061 Black Moonbeam R Full Art 3.00 8.00
BFA061 Black Moonbeam R 1.50 4.00
BFA062 Collapsing World U .25 .75
BFA063 Corrosion C .25 .75
BFA064 Covert Operative C .25 .75
BFA065 Death Trap C .25 .75
BFA066 Eyes In The Darkness C .25 .75
BFA067 Fairy Shadow U .25 .75
BFA068 Hades Lord of the Dead SR Full Art 1.50 4.00
BFA068 Hades Lord of the Dead SR .75 2.00
BFA069 Lapis Dark Beast C .25 .75
BFA070 Lapis Dark Storm C .25 .75
BFA071 Melder Last of the Dead R .40 1.00
BFA071 Melder Last of the Dead R Full Art 2.50 6.00
BFA072 Messenger Familiar C .25 .75
BFA073 Remnants of Niflheim C .25 .75
BFA074 Riza First of the Dead R Full Art 1.50 4.00
BFA074 Riza First of the Dead R .40 1.00
BFA075 Rotting Black Moon Dragon U .25 .75
BFA076 Alice of Light Alice of Shadow SR .75 2.00
BFA076 Alice of Light Alice of Shadow SR Full Art 5.00 12.00
BFA077 Lars Inheritor of the Sacred Spirit•Glorian Princess of Water Charlotte SR Full Art 1.50 4.00
BFA077 Lars Inheritor of the Sacred Spirit•Glorian Princess of Water Charlotte SR .75 2.00
BFA078 Reflect the Beginning of Time•Refrain the End of Ages SR .75 2.00
BFA078 Reflect the Beginning of Time•Refrain the End of Ages SR Full Art 1.50 4.00
BFA079 Slayer of the Overlord Pricia•Possessor Princess of Love Valentina Uber R 150.00 300.00
BFA079 Slayer of the Overlord Pricia•Possessor Princess of Love Valentina SR .75 2.00
BFA079 Slayer of the Overlord Pricia•Possessor Princess of Love Valentina SR Full Art 4.00 10.00
BFA080 Interdimensional Monarch Gill Lapis•Space Time Pursuer Gill Lapis SR .75 2.00
BFA080 Interdimensional Monarch Gill Lapis•Space Time Pursuer Gill Lapis SR Full Art 2.00 5.00
BFA081 Attoractia Dimension of the Seven Kings Illusory Demonic Globe Attoractia R Full Art 1.50 4.00
BFA081 Attoractia Dimension of the Seven Kings Illusory Demonic Globe Attoractia R .40 1.00
BFA082 Artificial Moon U .25 .75
BFA083 Dummy Doll U .25 .75
BFA084 Machine Lab of Leginus R Full Art 1.50 4.00
BFA084 Machine Lab of Leginus R .40 1.00
BFA085 Mariabellas Work C 1.25 3.00
BFA086 Remote Control Beast C 1.50 4.00
BFA087 Remote Control Golem R Full Art 5.00 12.00
BFA087 Remote Control Golem R .50 1.25
BFA088 Small Assistant Mariabella SR Full Art 10.00 25.00
BFA088 Small Assistant Mariabella SR .75 2.00
BFA089 The RoBox C .75 2.00
BFA090 TickTock Automaton C .25 .75
BFA093 Memoria of the Seven Lands•Machina Clever Researcher R Full Art 3.00 8.00
BFA093 Memoria of the Seven Lands•Machina Clever Researcher Uber R 120.00 180.00
BFA093 Memoria of the Seven Lands•Machina Clever Researcher R .40 1.00
BFA094 Memoria of the Seven Lands•Arla Guardian of the Skies Uber R 120.00 180.00
BFA094 Memoria of the Seven Lands•Arla Guardian of the Skies R Full Art 4.00 10.00
BFA094 Memoria of the Seven Lands•Arla Guardian of the Skies R .40 1.00
BFA095 Memoria of the Seven Lands Razzard Dark Necromancer R Full Art 4.00 10.00
BFA095 Memoria of the Seven Lands Razzard Dark Necromancer R .40 1.00
BFA095 Memoria of the Seven Lands Razzard Dark Necromancer Uber R 120.00 180.00
BFA096 Call to Actions Memoria R .75 2.00
BFA096 Call to Actions Memoria R Full Art 3.00 8.00
BFA097 Brutal Conquerors Memoria R .40 1.00
BFA097 Brutal Conquerors Memoria R Full Art 1.50 4.00
BFA098 Aloof Researchers Memoria R 1.50 4.00
BFA098 Aloof Researchers Memoria R Full Art 3.00 8.00
BFA099 First Flights Memoria R .40 1.00
BFA099 First Flights Memoria R Full Art 5.00 12.00
BFA100 Sorrowful Necromancys Memoria R .60 1.50
BFA100 Sorrowful Necromancys Memoria R Full Art 1.50 4.00
BFA101 Darkness Magic Stone NR .25 .75
BFA102 Fire Magic Stone NR .25 .75
BFA103 Light Magic Stone NR .25 .75
BFA104 Water Magic Stone NR .25 .75
BFA105 Wind Magic Stone NR .25 .75
BFA091• Memoria of the Seven Lands•Faria Chosen Girl R .40 1.00
BFA091• Memoria of the Seven Lands•Faria Chosen Girl R Full Art 4.00 10.00
BFA091• Memoria of the Seven Lands•Faria Chosen Girl Uber R 120.00 180.00
BFA092• Memoria of the Seven Lands•Melgis Conqueror of Flame R .40 1.00
BFA092• Memoria of the Seven Lands•Melgis Conqueror of Flame Uber R 120.00 180.00
BFA092• Memoria of the Seven Lands•Melgis Conqueror of Flame R Full Art 3.00 8.00

2016 Force of Will Curse of the Frozen Casket

COMPLETE SET (106 CARDS) 150.00 200.00
BOOSTER BOX (36 PACKS) 80.00 110.00
BOOSTER PACK (10 CARDS) 3.00 5.00
UNLISTED C .15 .25
UNLISTED U .15 .25
UNLISTED R .20 .30
RELEASED ON SEPTEMBER 9TH, 2016
CFC001 Dreaming Girl Wendy R .60 1.00
CFC002 Dreams of Flight C .15 .25
CFC003 Escape from Crisis C .15 .25
CFC004 Eternal Boy Peter Pan SR 1.25 2.00
CFC005 Fairy of Neverland C .15 .25
CFC006 Glorius the Silver Knight SR 4.00 5.00
CFC007 Glorius Summoned Soldier C .15 .25
CFC008 Neverland the Parallel World U .15 .25
CFC009 Pandora the Hope Weaving Queen R .20 .30
CFC010 Pandoras Mark of Hope U .15 .25
CFC011 Pumpkin Carriage U .15 .25
CFC012 Retelling Stories C .15 .25
CFC013 Safeguard of the Light Palace C .15 .25
CFC014 Storytelling Bard C .15 .25
CFC015 Zero Six Sage of Light R 10.00 15.00
CFC015 Zero Master of the Magic Saber R 10.00 15.00
CFC016 Zeros Familiar U .30 .50
CFC017 Zeros Magic Light R 1.00 1.50
CFC018 Ancient Heartfelt Fire U .30 .50
CFC019 Combat Wizard of Altea C .15 .25
CFC020 Demon of the Crest Namblot SR 1.50 2.00
CFC021 Dragon Knight of Altea C .15 .25
CFC022 Fairy Tale Library Alexandria U .15 .25
CFC023 Fiery Chariot Red Boy SR 1.50 2.00
CFC024 Flame Dragon of Altea R .40 .60
CFC025 Introspective Jutsu C .15 .25
CFC026 Invitation of Disaster R .60 1.00
CFC027 Mars Fortuneteller of the Fire Star R 8.00 10.00
CFC027 Mars Dark Commander of Fire R 8.00 10.00
CFC028 Sacred Radiant Soul U .15 .25
CFC029 Spirit of Fire C .15 .25
CFC030 Stalking Tiger in the Woods C .15 .25
CFC031 The Ox King U .15 .25
CFC032 Tiger Charge C .15 .25
CFC033 Tiger Lily Tribal Princess R .30 .50
CFC034 Tiny Reconnaissance Drake C .15 .25
CFC035 Altea Nation of Dark Magics U .15 .25
CFC036 Ancient Automation R .30 .50
CFC037 Captain Hook the Pirate R 1.25 1.75
CFC038 Charlotte The Mage of Sacred Spirit R 10.00 13.00
CFC038 Charlotte Determined Girl R 10.00 13.00
CFC039 Charlottes Protector C .15 .25
CFC040 Charlottes Water Transformation Magic U .15 .25
CFC041 Cheshire Cat Guide to the Mysterious World SR 5.00 6.00
CFC042 Guide to the Ancient Ice Wall C .15 .25
CFC043 Lumia Saint of World Awakening SR 1.50 2.00
CFC043 Lumia Sealed in the Frozen Casket SR 1.50 2.00
CFC044 Melt to Nothing C .15 .25
CFC045 Mermaid of Neverland C .15 .25
CFC046 Rabbit of the Aqua Moon U .30 .50
CFC047 Return to the Moon Wererabbit C .15 .25
CFC048 Rising from the Depths R .60 1.00
CFC049 Shackles of Ice U .15 .25
CFC050 Stargazing Fortune Teller C .15 .25
CFC051 Summon from Memoria C .15 .25
CFC052 Bird of Paradise Dancing in the Sky R .60 1.00
CFC053 Cloning Magic C .15 .25
CFC054 Crea Musician of Wind R .30 .50
CFC055 Elf of the Gusty Hills C .15 .25
CFC056 Favorable Winds C .15 .25
CFC057 Flying Cloud U .15 .25
CFC058 Heavenly Gust R 1.00 1.50
CFC059 Magic Born Vegetation C .15 .25
CFC060 Magic Stone Analysis C .15 .25
CFC061 Protector of the Forest C .15 .25
CFC062 Red Riding Hood SR 4.00 6.00
CFC063 Secluded Elven Village Amonsulle U .25 .40
CFC064 Sha Wujing U .25 .40
CFC065 Sorceress of Heavenly Wind Melfee SR 5.00 7.00
CFC066 Great Sky Sage Sun Wukong R 8.00 10.00
CFC066 The Monkey King Born from Stone R 8.00 10.00
CFC067 Wiseman of Amonsulle C .15 .25
CFC068 Zhu Bajie U .15 .25
CFC069 Alhazreds Zealot C .15 .25
CFC070 An Encounter With Cthulhu C .15 .25
CFC071 Azathoth Hunter of Reality SR .75 1.00
CFC072 Creature from Chaos C .15 .25
CFC073 Eternal Recurrence R .60 1.00
CFC074 Mad Oni C .15 .25
CFC075 Oni Governor U .15 .25
CFC076 Priest of Darkness Abdul Alhazred R .30 .50
CFC077 Princess of the Dragon Palace Otohime R .30 .50
CFC078 Resonance of Madness C .15 .25
CFC079 Rinka Second Daughter of the Mikage SR 3.75 4.15
CFC080 Servant of the Mikage C .15 .25
CFC081 The Black Treasure Box U .25 .40
CFC082 The Gate of the Silver Key U .15 .25
CFC083 The Nameless Mist C .15 .25
CFC084 Umr atTawil Master of 1000 Keys R 8.00 10.00
CFC084 YogSothoth the Chaos of 1000 Doors R 8.00 10.00
CFC085 Urashima Taro U .15 .25
CFC086 Magic Stone of Black Silence R 2.00 3.00
CFC087 Magic Stone of Blasting Waves R 2.00 3.00
CFC088 Magic Stone of Dark Depth R 2.00 3.00
CFC089 Magic Stone of Deep Wood R 2.00 3.00
CFC090 Magic Stone of Gusting Skies R 3.00 4.00
CFC091 Magic Stone of Hearths Core R 2.00 3.00
CFC092 Magic Stone of Heat Ray R 2.00 3.00
CFC093 Magic Stone of Heavens Rift R 1.00 1.50
CFC094 Magic Stone of Light Vapors R 1.50 2.00
CFC095 Magic Stone of Scorched Bales R 2.00 3.00
CFC096 Darkness Magic Stone C 1.00 2.00
CFC097 Fire Magic Stone C 1.00 2.00
CFC098 Light Magic Stone C 1.00 2.00
CFC099 Water Magic Stone C 1.00 2.00
CFC100 Wind Magic Stone C 1.00 2.00

2016 Force of Will Curse of the Frozen Casket Foil

COMPLETE SET (106 CARDS) 160.00 225.00
BOOSTER BOX (36 PACKS) 80.00 110.00
BOOSTER PACK (10 CARDS) 3.00 5.00
UNLISTED C .30 .50
UNLISTED U .40 .75
UNLISTED R .60 1.00
RELEASED ON SEPTEMBER 9TH, 2016
CFC001 Dreaming Girl Wendy R .60 1.00
CFC002 Dreams of Flight C .30 .50
CFC003 Escape from Crisis C .30 .50
CFC004 Eternal Boy Peter Pan SR .60 1.00
CFC005 Fairy of Neverland C .30 .50
CFC006 Glorius the Silver Knight SR .60 1.00
CFC007 Glorius Summoned Soldier C .30 .50
CFC008 Neverland the Parallel World U .40 .75
CFC009 Pandora the Hope Weaving Queen R .60 1.00
CFC010 Pandoras Mark of Hope U .40 .75
CFC011 Pumpkin Carriage U .40 .75
CFC012 Retelling Stories C .30 .50
CFC013 Safeguard of the Light Palace C .30 .50
CFC014 Storytelling Bard C .30 .50
CFC015 Zero Master of the Magic Saber R 15.00 20.00
CFC015 Zero Six Sage of Light R 15.00 20.00
CFC016 Zeros Familiar U 4.50 6.00
CFC017 Zeros Magic Light R 2.00 3.00
CFC018 Ancient Heartfelt Fire U .40 .75
CFC019 Combat Wizard of Altea C .30 .50
CFC020 Demon of the Crest Namblot SR .60 1.00
CFC021 Dragon Knight of Altea C .30 .50
CFC022 Fairy Tale Library Alexandria U .40 .75
CFC023 Fiery Chariot Red Boy SR .60 1.00
CFC024 Flame Dragon of Altea R .60 1.00
CFC025 Introspective Jutsu C .30 .50
CFC026 Invitation of Disaster R .60 1.00
CFC027 Mars Dark Commander of Fire R 8.00 10.00
CFC027 Mars Fortuneteller of the Fire Star R 8.00 10.00
CFC028 Sacred Radiant Soul U .40 .75
CFC029 Spirit of Fire C .30 .50
CFC030 Stalking Tiger in the Woods C .30 .50
CFC031 The Ox King U .40 .75
CFC032 Tiger Charge C .30 .50
CFC033 Tiger Lily Tribal Princess R .60 1.00
CFC034 Tiny Reconnaissance Drake C .30 .50
CFC035 Altea Nation of Dark Magics U .40 .75
CFC036 Ancient Automation R .60 1.00
CFC037 Captain Hook the Pirate R 1.50 2.00
CFC038 Charlotte Determined Girl R 8.00 10.00
CFC038 Charlotte The Mage of Sacred Spirit R 8.00 10.00
CFC039 Charlottes Protector C .30 .50
CFC040 Charlottes Water Transformation Magic U 2.75 3.25
CFC041 Cheshire Cat Guide to the Mysterious World SR .60 1.00
CFC042 Guide to the Ancient Ice Wall C .30 .50
CFC043 Lumia Sealed in the Frozen Casket SR .60 1.00
CFC043 Lumia Saint of World Awakening SR .60 1.00
CFC044 Melt to Nothing C .30 .50
CFC045 Mermaid of Neverland C .30 .50
CFC046 Rabbit of the Aqua Moon U 1.25 2.00
CFC047 Return to the Moon Wererabbit C .30 .50
CFC048 Rising from the Depths R .60 1.00
CFC049 Shackles of Ice U .40 .75
CFC050 Stargazing Fortune Teller C .30 .50
CFC051 Summon from Memoria C .30 .50
CFC052 Bird of Paradise Dancing in the Sky R .60 1.00
CFC053 Cloning Magic C .30 .50
CFC054 Crea Musician of Wind R .60 1.00
CFC055 Elf of the Gusty Hills C .30 .50
CFC056 Favorable Winds C .30 .50
CFC057 Flying Cloud U .40 .75
CFC058 Heavenly Gust R 1.00 1.50
CFC059 Magic Born Vegetation C .30 .50
CFC060 Magic Stone Analysis C .30 .50
CFC061 Protector of the Forest C .30 .50
CFC062 Red Riding Hood SR .60 1.00
CFC063 Secluded Elven Village Amonsulle U .40 .75
CFC064 Sha Wujing U .40 .75
CFC065 Sorceress of Heavenly Wind Melfee SR .60 1.00
CFC066 The Monkey King Born from Stone R 8.00 10.00
CFC066 Great Sky Sage Sun Wukong R 8.00 10.00
CFC067 Wiseman of Amonsulle C .30 .50
CFC068 Zhu Bajie U .40 .75
CFC069 Alhazreds Zealot C .30 .50
CFC070 An Encounter With Cthulhu C .30 .50
CFC071 Azathoth Hunter of Reality SR .60 1.00
CFC072 Creature from Chaos C .30 .50
CFC073 Eternal Recurrence R .60 1.00
CFC074 Mad Oni C .30 .50
CFC075 Oni Governor U .40 .75
CFC076 Priest of Darkness Abdul Alhazred R .60 1.00
CFC077 Princess of the Dragon Palace Otohime R .60 1.00
CFC078 Resonance of Madness C .30 .50
CFC079 Rinka Second Daughter of the Mikage SR .60 1.00
CFC080 Servant of the Mikage C .30 .50
CFC081 The Black Treasure Box U .40 .75
CFC082 The Gate of the Silver Key U .40 .75
CFC083 The Nameless Mist C .30 .50
CFC084 YogSothoth the Chaos of 1000 Doors R 8.00 10.00
CFC084 Umr atTawil Master of 1000 Keys R 8.00 10.00
CFC085 Urashima Taro U .40 .75
CFC086 Magic Stone of Black Silence R 2.00 3.00
CFC087 Magic Stone of Blasting Waves R 2.00 3.00
CFC088 Magic Stone of Dark Depth R 2.00 2.50
CFC089 Magic Stone of Deep Wood R 2.00 3.00
CFC090 Magic Stone of Gusting Skies R 3.50 4.00
CFC091 Magic Stone of Hearths Core R 2.00 3.00
CFC092 Magic Stone of Heat Ray R 2.00 3.00
CFC093 Magic Stone of Heavens Rift R 1.00 2.00
CFC094 Magic Stone of Light Vapors R 2.00 2.50
CFC095 Magic Stone of Scorched Bales R 2.00 3.00
CFC096 Darkness Magic Stone C .30 .50
CFC097 Fire Magic Stone C .30 .50
CFC098 Light Magic Stone C .30 .50
CFC099 Water Magic Stone C .30 .50
CFC100 Wind Magic Stone C .30 .50

2015 Force of Will Vingolf Engage Knights

VIN001001 Abe no Seimei NR
VIN001002 Achilles NR
VIN001003 Breath of the God NR
VIN001004 Duet of Light NR
VIN001005 Emperor Guangwu of Han NR
VIN001006 Hammurabi NR
VIN001007 Hannibal Barca R
VIN001008 Jeanne d'Arc NR
VIN001009 Louis XIV NR
VIN001010 March of Saints NR
VIN001011 Pride of Knights NR
VIN001012 Siegfried NR
VIN001013 Silver Stake NR
VIN001014 Tutankhamun NR
VIN001015 Xuanzang Sanzang NR
VIN001016 Alexander R
VIN001017 Banzai Attack NR
VIN001018 Calamity Jane NR
VIN001019 Crime and Punishment NR
VIN001020 King Ashoka NR
VIN001021 Kleitos NR
VIN001022 Kusanagi Sword NR
VIN001023 Lu Bu NR
VIN001024 Musashi Miyamoto NR
VIN001025 Pachacuti NR
VIN001026 Rapid Decay NR
VIN001027 Saladin NR
VIN001028 Sun Tzu NR
VIN001029 Thunder NR
VIN001030 William Wallace NR

VIN001031 Aqua Magic ~Tempest~ NR
VIN001032 Captain Cook NR
VIN001033 Colombus NR
VIN001034 Hanzo Hattori NR
VIN001035 Julius Caesar R
VIN001036 Marco Polo NR
VIN001037 Napoleon NR
VIN001038 Paracelsus NR
VIN001039 Dreams of Wonderland NR
VIN001040 Glimpse of Kaguya NR
VIN001041 Soji Okita NR
VIN001042 Tai Gong Wang NR
VIN001043 Vainamoinen NR
VIN001044 Whirlpool of Knowledge NR
VIN001045 Witch's Dagger NR
VIN001046 Archimedes NR
VIN001047 Art of Sinbad NR
VIN001048 Attila NR
VIN001049 D'Artagnan NR
VIN001050 Darwin NR
VIN001051 Evolution of Limits NR
VIN001052 Genghis Khan NR
VIN001053 Geronimo NR
VIN001054 Law of Silence NR
VIN001055 Minamoto no Yoshitsune R
VIN001056 Pyotr I NR
VIN001057 Silver Shoes NR
VIN001058 Timur NR
VIN001059 William Tell NR
VIN001060 Wind of Gods NR
VIN001061 Binding Chain NR
VIN001062 Dante NR
VIN001063 Demon's Curse NR
VIN001064 Edward, the Black Prince NR
VIN001065 Faust NR
VIN001066 Michizane Sugawara NR
VIN001067 Mozart NR
VIN001068 Nobunaga Oda NR
VIN001069 Nostradamus NR
VIN001070 Rasputin NR
VIN001071 Ritual of Millennia NR
VIN001072 Solomon NR
VIN001073 Stoning to Death NR
VIN001074 Tunnel Vision NR
VIN001075 Vlad Tepes R
VIN001076 Leonardo da Vinci NR
VIN001077 Ryoma Sakamoto NR
VIN001078 Shakespeare NR
VIN001079 Socrates NR
VIN001080 Magic Stone of Black Silence NR
VIN001081 Magic Stone of Blasting Waves NR
VIN001082 Magic Stone of Dark Depth NR
VIN001083 Magic Stone of Deep Wood NR
VIN001084 Magic Stone of Gusting Skies NR
VIN001085 Magic Stone of Hearth's Core NR
VIN001086 Magic Stone of Heat Ray NR
VIN001087 Magic Stone of Heaven's Rift NR
VIN001088 Magic Stone of Light Vapors NR
VIN001089 Magic Stone of Scorched Bales NR
VIN001090 Darkness Magic Stone NR
VIN001091 Fire Magic Stone NR
VIN001092 Light Magic Stone NR
VIN001093 Water Magic Stone NR
VIN001094 Wind Magic Stone NR
VIN001006SR Hammurabi SR
VIN001001SR Abe no Seimei SR
VIN001002SR Achilles SR
VIN001005SR Emperor Guangwu of Han SR
VIN001008SR Jeanne d'Arc SR
VIN001009SR Louis XIV SR
VIN001012SR Siegfried SR
VIN001014SR Tutankhamun SR
VIN001015SR Xuanzang Sanzang SR
VIN001018SR Calamity Jane SR
VIN001020SR King Ashoka SR
VIN001021SR Kleitos SR
VIN001023SR Lu Bu SR
VIN001024SR Musashi Miyamoto SR
VIN001025SR Pachacuti SR
VIN001027SR Saladin SR
VIN001028SR Sun Tzu SR
VIN001030SR William Wallace SR
VIN001032SR Captain Cook SR
VIN001033SR Colombus SR
VIN001034SR Hanzo Hattori SR
VIN001036SR Marco Polo SR
VIN001037SR Napoleon SR
VIN001038SR Paracelsus SR
VIN001041SR Soji Okita SR
VIN001042SR Tai Gong Wang SR
VIN001043SR Vainamoinen SR
VIN001046SR Archimedes SR
VIN001048SR Attila SR
VIN001049SR D'Artagnan SR
VIN001050SR Darwin SR
VIN001052SR Genghis Khan SR
VIN001053SR Geronimo SR
VIN001056SR Pyotr I SR
VIN001058SR Timur SR
VIN001059SR William Tell SR
VIN001062SR Dante SR
VIN001064SR Edward, the Black Prince SR
VIN001065SR Faust SR
VIN001066SR Michizane Sugawara SR
VIN001067SR Mozart SR
VIN001068SR Nobunaga Oda SR
VIN001069SR Nostradamus SR
VIN001070SR Rasputin SR
VIN001072SR Solomon SR
VIN001076SR Leonardo da Vinci SR
VIN001077SR Ryoma Sakamoto SR
VIN001078SR Shakespeare SR
VIN001079SR Socrates SR

2016 Force of Will Vingolf 2 Valkryia Chronicles

COMPLETE SET (95 CARDS) 40.00 60.00
RELEASED ON JULY 29TH, 2016
VIN002001 Alica Gunther J R 1.25 3.00
VIN002001 Alica Melchiott• R 1.25 3.00
VIN002002 Clementia Forster NR .10 .30
VIN002003 Edy Nelson NR .10 .30
VIN002004 Elshan Flower NR .10 .30
VIN002005 FirstAid NR .10 .30
VIN002006 Flak Jacket NR .10 .30
VIN002007 Homer Peron NR .10 .30
VIN002008 Irene Ellet NR .10 .30
VIN002009 Jann Walker NR .10 .30
VIN002010 Lynn NR .10 .30
VIN002011 Marina Wulfstan NR .10 .30
VIN002012 Martha Lipponen NR .10 .30
VIN002013 Susie Evans NR .10 .30
VIN002014 Symbol of Peace NR .10 .30
VIN002015 Welvar Glenn NR .10 .30
VIN002016 Alfons Avclair NR .10 .30
VIN002017 Amy Apple NR .10 .30
VIN002018 Bombardment NR .10 .30
VIN002019 Carisa Contzen NR .10 .30
VIN002020 Clarissa Callaghan NR .10 .30
VIN002021 Courageous Stand NR .10 .30
VIN002022 Frederica Lipps NR .10 .30
VIN002023 Gusurg NR .10 .30
VIN002024 Imca NR .10 .30
VIN002025 Kurt Irving NR .10 .30
VIN002026 Large Explosion NR .10 .30
VIN002027 Leila Peron NR .10 .30
VIN002028 Margit Ravelli NR .10 .30
VIN002029 Riela Marcellis J R .75 2.00
VIN002029 Riela Marcellis• R .75 2.00
VIN002030 Rielas Lance NR .10 .30
VIN002031 Alicia Melchiott J R 1.25 3.00
VIN002031 Alicia Melchiott• R 1.25 3.00
VIN002032 Alicias Lance NR .10 .30
VIN002033 Brigette Rosie Stark NR .10 .30
VIN002034 Cordelia Gi Randgriz NR .10 .30
VIN002035 Eleanor Varrot NR .10 .30
VIN002036 Faldio Landzaat NR .10 .30
VIN002037 Isara Gunther NR .10 .30
VIN002038 Kreis Czherny NR .10 .30
VIN002039 Largo Potter NR .10 .30
VIN002040 Maurits Con Borg NR .10 .30
VIN002041 Momentary Respite NR .10 .30
VIN002042 Sniping From The Blind Spot NR .10 .30
VIN002043 The Carefree Three NR .10 .30
VIN002044 Welkin Gunther NR .10 .30
VIN002045 Zaka NR .10 .30
VIN002046 Alexis Hilden NR .10 .30
VIN002047 Aliasse J R 1.50 4.00
VIN002047 Aliasse• R 1.50 4.00
VIN002048 Aliasses Lance NR .10 .30
VIN002049 Anisette Nelson NR .10 .30
VIN002050 Avan Hardins NR .10 .30
VIN002051 Cosette Coalhearth NR .10 .30
VIN002052 Bulletproof Barrier NR .10 .30
VIN002053 Destructive Assult NR .10 .30
VIN002054 Juliana Everhart NR .10 .30
VIN002055 Lavinia Lane NR .10 .30
VIN002056 Margari NR .10 .30
VIN002057 Marion Siegbahn NR .10 .30
VIN002058 Power of Unity NR .10 .30
VIN002059 Rene Randall NR .10 .30
VIN002060 Zeri NR .10 .30
VIN002061 Audrey Gassenarl NR .10 .30
VIN002062 Baldren Gassenarl NR .10 .30
VIN002063 Berthold Gregor NR .10 .30
VIN002064 Dahav NR .10 .30
VIN002065 Dirk Gassenarl NR .10 .30
VIN002066 Gilbert Gassenarl NR .10 .30
VIN002067 Hammer of the Valkyrur NR .10 .30
VIN002068 Lydia Agthe NR .10 .30
VIN002069 Maximilian NR .10 .30
VIN002070 Radi Iaeger NR .10 .30
VIN002071 Ragnide Gas NR .10 .30
VIN002072 Schemes of the Empire NR .10 .30
VIN002073 Selvaria Bles• R 1.25 3.00
VIN002073 Selvaria Bles J R 1.25 3.00
VIN002074 Selvarias Lance NR .10 .30
VIN002075 Zig NR .10 .30
VIN002076 Class Gs Tank NR 2.00 5.00
VIN002077 Edelweiss NR 1.50 4.00
VIN002078 Imperial Tank NR 1.25 3.00
VIN002079 Nameless Tank NR 1.50 4.00
VIN002080 Ragnite NR 1.50 4.00
VIN0020xx Magic Stone of Hearths Core NR .75 2.00
VIN0020xx Water Magic Stone NR .10 .30
VIN0020xx Magic Stone of Heavens Rift NR .75 2.00
VIN0020xx Magic Stone of Dark Depth NR .75 2.00
VIN0020xx Darkness Magic Stone NR .10 .30
VIN0020xx Magic Stone of Blasting Waves NR .75 2.00
VIN0020xx Magic Stone of Scorched Bales NR .75 2.00
VIN0020xx Magic Stone of Heat Ray NR .75 2.00
VIN0020xx Wind Magic Stone NR .10 .30
VIN0020xx Magic Stone of Gusting Skies NR 1.25 3.00
VIN0020xx Light Magic Stone NR .10 .30
VIN0020xx Magic Stone of Deep Wood NR .75 2.00
VIN0020xx Fire Magic Stone NR .10 .30
VIN0020xx Magic Stone of Black Silence NR .75 2.00
VIN0020xx Magic Stone of Light Vapors NR .75 2.00

1995 Galactic Empires New Empires

A1 Medical Scanner C
A1 Strategy C
A2 Logic C
A3 Deviant U
A4 Bionic Enhancement C
A4 Assault Rifle U
A4 Artifact - War Medal of Yorl U
A4 Demolition Expertise U
A5 Mind Mold Symbionts R
A5 Battle Suit U
A5 Anarchist R
A6 Promotion R
A6 Mental Anguish R
A6 Double Agent R
A7 Miscreant V
A8 Duo-Brain V
B2 Ancient Ruins C
B3 Heavy Planetary Shield U
B5 Tufor Science Platform U
B5 Penal Colony R
B6 Hospital R
B6 Evil Temple V
B7 Spiritual Temple U
B8 Manufacturing Plant V
B9 Repair Base V
C1 Sysop R
C2 Cyber-Programmer C
C3 Media Personality C
C3 Green Fighter Pilot C
C3 Escaped Prisoner U
C4 Intelligence Officer U
C4 Cyber Mage R
C4 Teamster C
C4 Lieutenant U
C6 Slave Trader V
C6 Cyber Mage V
C6 Prophet R
C6 Bureaucrat U
C6 Tactician R
C6 Ace Fighter Pilot R
C7 Tactical Officer V
C7 Android R
C7 Research Developer V
C8 Spiritual Leader V
D1 Phase Dragoness R
D3 Plasma Dragoness V
D4 Magus Dragoness U
D6 Astral Dragoness V
D6 Vortex Dragoness V
D7 Neutrino Dragoness V
D8 Undead Dragoness V
E1 Explosive Mine C
E3 Radial Dish C
E3 Clydon Energy Armor U
E5 Robotic Crew C
E5 Defense Grid V
E6 Stasis Mine V
E7 Phaser Magnifier Refit V
E7 Cloning Device V
E8 Mechad Network Interface V
E8 Mine Deployment System V
H2 Supersonic Flow C
H3 Magnetic Cloud C
H3 Cyber Disturbance U
H4 Star Quake U
H4 Gravity Pocket U
H6 Alfven Wave R
H6 Cosmic Cyclone V
H7 Distortion Pocket V
L2 Lucky Mine Explosion C
L3 Aurora Effect V
L3 Intoxication U
L4 Parallel Universe C
L6 Artifact - Krebiz Monolith V
L6 Artifact - Dragon Gem of Protection R
L6 Command Disjunction U
L7 Artifact - Star Gate V
L8 Artifact - Galactic Prism V
M2 Skullets U
M2 Rat Infestation C
M2 Vymezies Particle C
M3 Scandig Blob U
M3 Phantom U
M3 Phase Rats C
M4 Vymezies Matter U
M4 The Soulless U
M5 Tectonic Burrower U
M5 Symnergenic Cloud R
M6 Vymezies Blaze R
M6 Void Angel R
M7 Cyber Mites R
M8 Redgelon V
M9 Skull Reaper V
O3 Illness - Aldibrik Ailment (NE) U
O4 Illness - Space Deterioration U
O4 False Distress Call U
O5 Orbital Decay U
O5 Cerebral Void U
O6 Political Clout R
O8 Structural Degeneration V
O8 Tarragym Effect R
O9 Ship Collision R
S1 P.O.T. Armed Launch C
S2 Tufor Escort R
S2 P.O.T. Escort R
S2 Scorpead Frigate U
S2 Nagiridni Pirate Scout U
S2 Clydon Ultra-Light Cruiser U
S2 Scorpead Escort U
S3 Tufor Cutter U
S3 Clydon Light Star Cruiser R
S3 Scorpead Destroyer U
S3 P.O.T. Science Cutter R
S3 P.O.T. Frigate U
S3 Tufor Light Fighter Carrier (NE) R/C
S4 P.O.T. Destroyer U
S4 Scorpead Minesweeper R
S4 Refueler R
S4 Tufor Destroyer R
S4 Scorpead Science Ship U
S4 Tufor Mine Layer R
S4 Clydon Medium Star Cruiser V
S4 Tufor Research Scout R
S4 P.O.T. Minesweeper R
S4 Tufor Light Cruiser R
S5 Scorpead Light Cruiser R
S5 Super Tanker V
S5 P.O.T. Medium Cruiser R
S5 Emergency Rescue Ship R
S5 Clydon War Cruiser - War Cruiser R
S5 P.O.T. Light Cruiser V
S5 Bolaar Heavy Cargo Express V
S5 Clydon Heavy Star Cruiser V
S5 Tufor Heavy Cruiser V
S5 P.O.T. Scout Cruiser R
S5 Nagiridni Pirate Destroyer R/U
S5 P.O.T. Command Cruiser R
S5 P.O.T. Heavy Cruiser V
S5 Scorpead Scout Cruiser R
S6 Clydon Man-o-War - Man-o-war V
S6 Tufor Fighter Carrier V
S6 Scorpead Command Cruiser V
S6 P.O.T. Fighter Carrier V
S6 Tufor Command Launch V
S6 Tufor Mine Cruiser V
S6 Independant Pirate Cruiser U
S6 Nagiridni Pirate Cruiser V
S6 Scorpead Heavy Cruiser V
S7 P.O.T. Battlecruiser V
S7 Vektrean Dreadnought V
S7 Scorpead Battlecruiser V
S7 Tufor War Cruiser V
S8 Scorpead Dreadnought V
S8 Tufor Dreadnought V
S8 P.O.T. Dreadnought V
S9 Tufor Battleship V
S9 P.O.T. Battleship V
S9 Scorpead Battleship V
T1 Energy Moon C
T2 Captured Moon C
T3 Vacation Planet R
T3 Minor Planet - Bosheegh Minor Planet C
T3 Agro Moon C
T3 Blayok Protostar C
T3 Periodic Comet - Rom's Comet C
T4 Obelisk System C
T5 System - Penteir System R
T5 Planet - Zambarez Planet U
T5 Dependency World R
T5 Pirate System R
T6 System - Femerazi System U
T7 Sensor Planet V
T7 Comet - Scorpead Comet of Lore V
T8 Plasmatic Nebula V
T9 Gas Giant - Blookerak Gas Giant V
A10 Techno-Sorcerer S
B10 Tufor Operations Base S
C10 Supreme Leader S
C10 Legendary Pirate Captain S
M10 Zaggoth Mordeth S
M10 Zaggoth Guardian S
O10 Time Portal S
T10 Clydon Super-Massive Planet S
R/A4 Genetic Mutation C
R/A7 Cyborg Death V
R/A9 Accidental Evolution V
R/C2 Science Officer C
R/C6 Administrator U
R/C9 Master Spy V
R/E1 Civilian Transporter C
R/E2 Transport Shuttle C
R/E3 Phaser Fighter U
R/E4 Transporter Mine U
R/E4 Monster Defense System U/R
R/E6 Tactical Fighter V
R/E8 Assault Fighter V
R/E9 Hologram V
R/H7 Interstellar Plasma R
R/L4 Scientifically Enhance Tectonic Plate Structure U
R/M1 Sextaraan Web Crawlers C
R/O5 Warning Buoy R
R/O6 Devolution R
R/S1 Clydon War Craft R
R/S1 Clydon Science Craft R
R/S1 Clydon Mine Craft U
R/S1 Clydon Scout Craft U
R/S2 Clydon Carrier Craft U
R/S2 Clydon Battle Craft V
R/A10 Avatar S
R/C10 Yorl the Forsaken S

1995 Galactic Empires Powers of the Mind

A1 Infestation Inhibitor U
A2 Opposite Extension U
A2 Evolving Terrain V
A2 Filarian Infester U
A2 Cyber Mage Implant R
A3 Techno-Psy U
A3 Star Walker U
A4 Filarian Infester R
A4 Derranged Psy U
A5 Psy Training R
A5 Mental Inspiration U
A5 Filarian Mind Lord R
A6 Filarian Infester R
A7 Filarian Infester V
A7 Arduous Study R
A7 Safe Haven V
A7 Projected Infestation R
A8 Filarian Infester V
B1 Personal Base U
B2 Psy Outpost U
B2 Warehouse V
B3 Psy Training Site R
B4 Psy Pyramid R
B5 Data Bank R
B5 Psycanti Projection Station R
B5 Energy Storage Facility V
B6 Visonic Ruins R
B7 Central Galactic Bank V
B8 Psy Control Base V
B9 Psy Meditation Base V
C3 Psy Healer U
C5 Psyber Mage R
C6 Rogue Couple R
C6 CFO R
C8 CEO V
C8 Psy Marine V
D4 Psy Dragoness U
E4 Psybot U
E6 Psycanti Plane Enhancement V
E7 Technical Display V
E7 Dragon Muzzle R
E7 Dragon Harness R
E8 Psybot V
E8 Psy Relay R
F1 Minor Terrain Field R
F1 Electro-Field U
F2 Lesser Healing Field U
F2 Corporeal Field U
F3 Field of Minor Wilding U
F3 Field of Power U
F4 Psycanti Field U
F4 Visonic Field U
F4 Field of Channeling R
F4 Terrain Field V
F5 Stellar Field V
F6 Field of Matter R
F6 Techno-Field R
F7 Healing Field V
F7 Field of Death V
F8 Temporal Field U
F8 Field of Chaos R
F9 Mind Field V
F9 Interstellar Field V
H1 Divergence of Psy U
H3 Plasma Vortex U
H5 Cosmic String R
H7 Quantum Decay V
H8 Quasi-Particle V
H8 Quark V
L6 Artifact - Scepter of Time V
M1 Psychotic Sludge U
M4 Psychotic Sludge R
M6 Material Evil R
M8 Psy Entrantrix V
M9 Huge Invinco Guardian V
O1 Psy Disease U
O1 Fighter Support U
O2 Comet Control U
O2 Psy Mutation U
O4 Stupefy U
O4 Entertaining Pastime R
O4 Impending Chaos U
O6 Hypnotic Trance V
O6 Desolation U
O8 Visonic Control Bore V
O8 Illness - Psychic Burnout - Psychic Burnout V
O9 Discovery of Discoveries V
O9 Psycanti Conflagration V
P1 Psycanti Muse U
P1 Visonic Pledge U
P1 Visonic Muse U
P1 Psycanti Pledge U
P2 Visonic Apprentice U
P2 Psycanti Apprentice U
P2 Visonic Empath U
P2 Psycanti Empath U
P3 Visonic Kineticist R
P3 Psycanti Practitioner U
P3 Psycanti Occultist R
P4 Visonic Practitioner U
P4 Psycanti Kineticist R
P4 Psycanti Defender V
P4 Visonic Occultist R
P5 Psycanti Apostle R
P5 Visonic Apostle R
P6 Visonic Defender V
P6 Visonic Paladin V
P6 Psycanti Commandant V
P7 Visonic Duelist R
P7 Psycanti Duelist R
P8 Visonic Commandant V
P8 Psycanti Paladin V
P9 Visonic Sub-Master V
P9 Psycanti Sub-Master V
S1 Personal Cruiser U
T2 Psy Moon U
T4 Planet - Visonic Homeworld R
T5 Planet - Psycanti Planetesimal R
T5 Small Planet - Planet Govessera V
T7 Undiscovered System V
T8 Trinary System - Psyvis System V
C10 Chakan: The Forever Man S
L10 Political Intrigue S
P10 Psycanti Master S
P10 Visonic Master S
R/A1 Mind Shield U
R/A4 Scroll Of Viskaras U
R/A4 Mind Guard U
R/A5 Psy Seduction R
R/A6 Psionic Enhancement R
R/B8 Citadel V
R/C1 Informant R
R/E1 Terrain Attack Shuttle U
R/F5 Field of Viscaras R
R/M5 Corporeal Traveler R
R/M9 Corporeal Defender V
R/O1 Atmospheric Evasion U
R/O2 Field Transferal V
R/O2 Visonic Interference U
R/O3 Psycanti Deception U
R/O3 Mind Turning U
R/O5 Exploration Mission V
R/O5 Parasitic Augmentation R

R/05 Psy Responder R
R/05 Mind Turning R
R/06 Psionic Soothing R
R/06 Breached City R
R/06 Parasitic Dispersion R
R/07 Inoperative Gravity R
R/08 Squadron Crash V
R/08 Mind Turning V
R/T2 Asteroid Shield R

1995 Galactic Empires Time Gates

A2 Temporal Shifter U
A3 Mirror Skinned Phaser Eel U
A5 Monster Halt R
A5 Aurora Borealis R
A5 Temporal Comprehension R
B8 Repair Supply Base V
C1 Suark Breed U
C2 Suark Breed U
C3 Cryogenic Convict U
C3 Suark Breed R
C4 Suark Breed R
C4 Cybersist U
C4 Temporal Mechanic V
C4 Invasion Force U
C5 Time Merchant V
C5 Suark Breed R
C6 Suark Breed V
C7 Criminal Judge V
D6 Time Dragoness R
E2 Time Capsule U
E4 Time Capsule R
E6 Time Capsule V
E7 Space-Time Portal R
E7 Temporal Shuttle U
E8 Time Machine V
E8 Starburst Accelerator V
E8 Phaser Distorter V
E8 Time Shield V
E9 Future Ship V
E9 Temporal Fighter U
H5 Space-Time Diversion U
H5 Time Wave U
H6 Temporal Ion Storm R
H7 Time Wave R
H7 Time Tornado R
H8 Anti-Time Mine Field R
H9 Time Wave V
H9 Time Intrusion V
L2 Sequential Continuum U
L5 Temporal Loophole R
L6 Anti-Time Exchange R
L8 Artifact - Timeglass V
L8 Well of Time V
L8 Headquarters Overhaul V
L8 Modified Timeline V
L8 Frayed Time Spindle V
L9 Discard Equivalency V
L9 Timeline Alteration V
M3 Research Mandator U
M4 Cybercyst U
M4 Suark Beast U
M5 Time Fiend R
M6 Time Thief R
M6 Time Guardian R
O2 Early Shipment U
O2 Future Transmission U
O2 Base Relocation U
O3 Accelerated Burn U
O4 Flood C
O5 Time Expansion U
O6 Galacticnet R
O6 Crew Capture R
O6 Accelerated Aging R
O6 Wreckage Survivors R
O7 Quantum Occurrence R
O8 Repeat Fire V
O8 Ante Accelerator V
O9 Catastrophic Repetition V
S1 Time Ship U
S3 Time Ship R
S5 Time Ship V
T2 Time Enclave U
T6 Time Enclave R
T6 Out of Phase World R
B10 Dyson Sphere S
C10 Time Knight S
C10 Father of Time S
L10 Timeline Reversal S
C1/9 Time Knight V
C2/8 Time Knight V
C3/7 Time Knight V
C4/6 Time Knight V
C5/5 Time Knight V
C6/4 Time Knight V
C7/3 Time Knight V
C8/2 Time Knight V
C9/1 Time Knight V
M2/8 Temporal Snake U
M4/6 Temporal Snake R
M6/4 Temporal Snake V
R/A2 Premonition U
R/A8 Time Lore V
R/C1 Janitor R
R/C4 Trophy Hunter U
R/C5 Veterinarian R
R/C6 Time Assault Team R
R/C9 Temporal Engineer V
R/E2 Stasis Canister U
R/E3 Temporal Transporter U
R/E6 Distortion Generator U
R/E7 Temporal Transporter V
R/E7 Time Screen R
R/E7 Time Gap Generator R
R/E8 Base Thrusters R
R/H5 Entity Swap R
R/H5 Time Trap U
R/H7 Time Typhoon V
R/H7 Stellar Gas Cloud R
R/H8 Star Well V
R/L1 Unlucky Crew Action U
R/L3 Time Exchange U
R/L5 Time Evacuation R
R/L7 Temporal Correction R
R/L8 Vacuum Effect V
R/L8 Twist of Fate V
R/L9 Suspended Animation V
R/M4 Time Keeper U
R/O1 Time Skip U
R/O1 Intercept Action U
R/O1 Past Transmission U
R/O1 Time Compression U
R/O2 Shipping Delays (03/10) R
R/O2 Shipping Delays (02/10) R
R/O2 Shipping Delays (10/10) R
R/O2 Shipping Delays (01/10) R
R/O2 Shipping Delays (09/10) R
R/O2 Discard Delay U
R/O2 Shipping Delays (05/10) R
R/O2 Shipping Delays (08/10) R
R/O2 Shipping Delays (07/10) R
R/O2 Dream State U
R/O2 Shipping Delays (06/10) R
R/O2 Shipping Delays (04/10) R
R/O3 Time Switch U
R/O3 Instant Reaction U
R/O3 Crinkled Timeline U
R/O3 Lost In Space U
R/O4 Discard Exchange U
R/O4 Cessation of Events U
R/O6 Time Jump R
R/O6 Resource Theft R
R/O6 Cessation of Engagement U
R/O6 Time Gate U
R/O6 Continuum Disorder R
R/O7 Cessation of Production R
R/O7 Out of Season U
R/O8 Time Discrepancy U
R/O8 Cessation of Fire V
R/O8 Cessation of Time R
R/O8 Reserve Call Up V
R/S1 Ship from the Future U
S2/8 Tranoan Frigate V
S3/7 Tranoan Destroyer V
S4/6 Tranoan Time Ship V
S5/5 Tranoan Time Cruiser V
S6/4 Tranoan Battlecruiser V
S7/3 Tranoan Dreadnought V

1995 Galactic Empires Universe Edition

A1 Lesser Automaton U
A1 Infestation Inhibitor U
A1 Strategy C
A2 Slick Bargainer V
A2 Logic C
A2 Hand Held Weapon U
A3 Landing Officer U
A3 Automaton R
A3 Tri-Millennia Molting R
A4 Hot Nobelium R
A5 Greater Automaton V
A5 Mind Mold Symbionts R
A5 Aurora Borealis R
A5 Anarchist R
A5 Ancient Molting V
A5 Battle Suit U
A5 Mental Inspiration U
A6 Mental Anguish R
A6 Double Agent R
A6 Omniscience V
A7 Miscreant V
A7 Eon Molting V
A7 Safe Haven V
A8 Duo-Brain V
A8 Spiritual Guidance U
A9 Dragon Automaton V
B1 Personal Base U
B1 Military Outpost C
B1 Planetary Shield C
B2 Fighter Garrison U
B2 Ancient Ruins C
B2 Defensive Satellites C
B3 Space Station U
B3 Power Generation Platform R
B3 Heavy Planetary Shield U
B3 Repair Skid U
B3 Tufor Mine Platform C
B4 Spiritual Temple C
B4 Research Base U
B4 Base Station R
B4 Planetary Phaser Base U
B5 Penal Colony R
B5 Administrative Facility R
B5 Data Bank R
B6 Battlestation R
B6 Hospital R
B6 Evil Temple V
B7 Academy V
B7 Central Galactic Bank V
B8 Manufacturing Plant V
B8 Shipyard V
B9 Repair Base V
B9 Starbase V
C1 Boarding Party C
C1 Sysop R
C1 Confidential Coordinating First Chief Executive Deputy Assistant to the..... U
C1 Indirigan Female R
C2 Helmsman C
C2 Ensign U
C2 Engineer U
C2 Ordnance Officer U
C2 Cyber-Programmer C
C2 Mercenary C
C3 Nurse U
C3 Escaped Prisoner U
C3 Boarding Party U
C4 Corrupt Politician U
C4 Teamster C
C4 Navigator R
C4 Lieutenant U
C4 Boarding Party R
C4 Bounty Hunter U
C4 Spiritual Leader R
C4 Cyber Mage R
C4 Temporal Mechanic V
C5 Time Merchant V
C5 Captain U
C5 Suicide Squad R
C5 Weapons Officer R
C5 Quartermaster V
C5 Ambassador V
C6 Clone V
C6 CFO R
C6 Rogue Couple R
C6 Ancient Spacefarer V
C6 Operations Officer - Ops R
C6 Ace Fighter Pilot R
C6 Squadron Commander R
C6 Base Commander V
C6 Mercenary R
C6 Tactician R
C6 Bureaucrat U
C6 Prophet R
C7 Android R
C7 Research Developer V
C7 Tactical Officer V
C7 Criminal Judge V
C7 Boarding Party V
C7 Mystic Wanderer V
C7 Saboteur R
C8 General V
C8 Commodore V
C8 Spiritual Leader V
C8 Assassin V
C8 Rear Admiral V
C8 CEO V
C9 Marauder V
C9 Admiral V
D1 Scintillating Dragoness R
D2 Oort Dragoness V
D3 Quark Dragoness V
D3 Plasma Dragoness V
D4 Radiation Dragoness V
D5 Void Dragoness V
D5 Hydrogen Dragoness V
D6 Neutrino Dragoness V
D6 Astral Dragoness V
D7 Neutron Dragoness V
D8 Undead Dragoness V
D8 Moon Dragoness V
D8 Time Dragoness V
D9 Ether Dragoness V
D9 Nebula Dragon V
E1 Distribution Node R
E1 Probe C
E1 Explosive Mine C
E1 Cargo C
E1 Krebiz Armor R
E1 Shield Refit U
E1 Escape Pod C
E2 Nuclear Mine C
E2 Tram Refit C
E2 Repulsion Beam V
E2 Phaser Refit (UE) C
E3 Heavy Weapon Refit U
E3 Reserve Power R
E3 Heavy Shield Refit R
E3 Krebiz Armor R
E4 Heavy Phaser Refit U
E4 Shuttle Bomb U
E4 Tram Refit U
E4 Survey Shuttle U
E4 Stellar Map V
E5 Defense Grid V
E5 Antimatter Mine V
E5 Planetary Transportation C
E5 Distribution Nodes U
E6 Super Computer R
E6 Stasis Mine V
E6 Heavy Weapon Refit R
E6 Warp Field Destabilization Gun V
E6 Sabot Sequencer V
E7 Mine Rack V
E7 Temporal Shuttle U
E7 Phaser Magnifier Refit V
E7 Argonian Strobe V
E8 Mechad Network Interface V
E8 Energy Flux Mode Enhancement - Argonian Energy Flux Mode Enhancement V
E9 Distribution Nodes V
G1 Time Manipulation C
G2 Survey Mission C
G3 Rescue Attempt C
G4 Solitude C
H1 Divergence of Psy U
H1 Time Warp V
H1 Dust Cloud C
H1 Divergent Anomaly C
H2 Meteor Shower U
H2 Supersonic Flow C
H2 Ion Storm C
H2 Gravity Wave C
H3 Small Mine Field U
H3 Quasar R
H3 Pulsar C
H3 Radioactive Dust Cloud U
H3 Cyber Disturbance U
H4 Cosmic Rays R
H4 Warp Funnel U
H4 Gravity Pocket U
H5 Ion Storm R
H5 EM Burst U
H6 Large Minefield R
H6 Alfven Wave R
H6 Crab Pulsar R
H6 Type II Supernova V
H6 Cosmic Cyclone V
H7 Time Tornado R
H7 Distortion Pocket V
H7 Maelstrom V
H8 Quark V
H8 Gravity Pocket V
H9 Time Intrusion V
H9 Tuforeous Dead Zone V
H9 Dimensional Portal V
H9 Time Wave V
L2 Warp Engine Breech R
L3 Pirate's Cache U
L3 Aurora Effect V
L4 Lucky Shield Repair R
L4 Cursed Alien Artifact U
L4 Navigational Error V
L6 Artifact - Krebiz Monolith V
L7 Alien Artifact R
L7 Expeditious Reserves V
L8 Modified Timeline V
L8 Artifact - Galactic Prism V
L8 Frayed Time Spindle V
L9 Lost Fleet V
L9 Accelerated Timeline V
M1 Small Phaser Eel C
M1 Research Defiler R
M2 Snare Vines C
M2 Planet Gouge C
M3 Alien Parasites U
M3 Shield Fiend C
M3 Phase Rats C
M3 Shadow U
M3 Invinco Guardian C
M3 Scandig Blob U
M4 Space Dragon U
M4 Harvesters V
M4 Vymezies Matter U
M4 Spacetacean R
M5 Zarom R
M5 Tectonic Burrower U
M5 Occumbus R
M5 Astromorph R
M5 Ship Mimic V
M6 Visilikiy's Eye R
M6 Void Angel R
M6 Seductress R
M6 Mind Control Beast V
M6 Time Thief R
M7 Tri-lateral Textangula V
M7 Juggernaut V
M7 Cyber Mites R
M8 Ship Collector V
M8 Redgelon V
M9 Kraken V
M9 Huge Invinco Guardian V
O1 Illness C
O2 Comet Impact R
O2 Serious Hull Breach R
O2 Natural Disaster U
O2 Gold Vein C
O3 Wandering Desire R
O3 Offensive Electronic Warfare C
O3 Illness - Aldibrik Ailment (UE) U
O3 Bureaucracy U
O4 Forced Retreat U
O4 Entertaining Pastime R
O4 False Distress Call U
O4 Information Leak U
O4 Flood C
O5 Political Upheaval V
O5 Insanity (UE) R
O5 Terraforming V
O6 Labor Strikes V
O6 Political Clout R
O6 Broken Supply Lines R
O6 Accelerated Aging R
O7 Interplanetary Conflict V
O7 Surprise Attack V
O7 False Intelligence Report R
O7 Capital Revitalization V
O7 Quantum Occurrence R
O8 Self Destruction V
O8 Structural Degeneration V
O8 Planetary Revolt V
O8 Economic Crises V
O8 Technological Breakthrough V
O8 Plague V
O8 Computer Virus V
O8 Tarragym Effect R
O9 Illness (UE) V
O9 Ship Collision R
O9 Insanity (UE) V
O9 Discovery of Discoveries V
O9 Alliance Treaty V
S1 Fleet Freighter (Left) C
S2 Mechad Escort R
S2 Vektrean Frigate C
S2 Scorpead Escort U
S2 Corporate Frigate U
S2 Fleet Tug R
S2 Clydon Ultra-Light Cruiser U
S2 Independent Freighter U
S2 Argonian Escort - Argonian Warm Front Escort R
S2 Corporate Escort U
S2 P.O.T. Escort R
S2 Space Yacht U
S2 Police Cutter U
S2 Tufor Escort R
S3 Argonian Frigate - Argonian Sunspot Frigate U
S3 Krebiz Escort Ship R
S3 Scorpead Destroyer U
S3 Vektrean Destroyer U
S3 P.O.T. Frigate U
S3 Tufor Light Fighter Carrier (UE) R/C
S3 Independent Tug V
S3 Krebiz Minesweeper R
S3 Tufor Cutter U
S3 Corporate Destroyer U
S3 P.O.T. Science Cutter R
S3 Clydon Light Star Cruiser R
S3 Mechad Destroyer U
S4 Scorpead Minesweeper R
S4 Vektrean Light Cruiser U
S4 Tufor Research Scout R
S4 P.O.T. Minesweeper R
S4 Clydon Medium Star Cruiser V
S4 Corporate Minesweeper R
S4 Refueler R
S4 Argonian Minesweeper - Argonian Sleet Minesweeper V
S4 Mechad Scout Cruiser R
S4 Argonian Scout Cruiser - Argonian Cumulonimbus Scout Cruiser R
S4 Corporate Light Cruiser R
S4 Argonian Destroyer - Argonian Blizzard Destroyer R
S4 Local Police Ship R
S4 P.O.T. Destroyer U
S4 Tufor Light Cruiser R
S4 Independent Pirate Ship R
S4 Tufor Destroyer R
S4 Argonian Assault Carrier - Argonian Galestorm Assault Carrier R
S4 Mechad Medium Cruiser R
S4 Krebiz Light Carrier U
S4 Scorpead Science Ship U
S5 Clydon Heavy Star Cruiser V
S5 Tufor Heavy Cruiser V
S5 P.O.T. Heavy Cruiser V
S5 Scorpead Scout Cruiser R
S5 Emergency Rescue Ship R
S5 Corporate Scout Cruiser R
S5 P.O.T. Light Cruiser V
S5 Argonian Heavy Cruiser - Argonian Typhoon Heavy Cruiser V
S5 Clydon War Cruiser - War Cruiser R
S5 Scorpead Light Cruiser R
S5 Krebiz Scout Ship U
S5 Mechad Heavy Cruiser R
S5 Indirigan Destroyer - Indirigan Nomads Destroyer U
S5 Mechad Minesweeper R
S5 Ore Carrier R
S5 Vektrean Heavy Cruiser U
S5 P.O.T. Scout Cruiser R
S5 Argonian Light Cruiser - Argonian Whirlwind Light Cruiser R
S6 Corporate Heavy Cruiser V
S6 Tufor Command Launch V
S6 Indirigan Light Cruiser R
S6 Mechad Battlecruiser V
S6 Mechad Command Cruiser V
S6 Krebiz Command Ship R
S6 Vektrean Spy Cruiser R
S6 Scorpead Heavy Cruiser V
S6 Scorpead Command Cruiser V
S6 Krebiz Heavy Cruiser V
S6 P.O.T. Fighter Carrier V
S6 Tufor Mine Cruiser V
S6 Vektrean Battlecruiser V
S6 Argonian Command Cruiser - Argonian Tornado Command Cruiser V
S6 Luxury Liner V
S6 Clydon Man-o-War - Man-o-war V
S6 Tufor Fighter Carrier V
S6 Garbage Scow U
S7 Tufor War Cruiser V
S7 Argonian Battlecruiser - Argonian Hurricane Battlecruiser (UE) V
S7 P.O.T. Battlecruiser V
S7 Scorpead Battlecruiser V
S7 Mechad Dreadnought V
S7 Corporate Command Cruiser V
S7 Vektrean Dreadnought V
S7 Argonian Heavy Carrier - Argonian Ionstorm Heavy Carrier V
S7 Krebiz Battlecruiser V
S7 Corporate Battlecruiser V
S8 Krebiz Heavy Carrier V
S8 Corporate Dreadnought V
S8 Scorpead Dreadnought V
S8 Argonian Dreadnought - Argonian Nova Dreadnought V
S8 Tufor Dreadnought V
S8 P.O.T. Dreadnought UE/NE
S8 Mechad Battleship V
S9 Krebiz Battleship V
S9 Argonian Battleship - Argonian Star Cluster Battleship V
S9 Scorpead Battleship V
S9 Corporate Battleship V
S9 Tufor Battleship V
S9 P.O.T. Battleship V
T1 Large Asteroid C
T1 Planetary Storm U
T1 Captured Satellite C
T1 Apollo Body C
T1 Small Moon C
T2 Comet - Biruk's Comet C
T2 Oort Cloud U
T2 Ionized Particle Field C
T2 Moon - Populated Moon C
T2 Artificial Satellite U
T3 Periodic Comet - Rom's Comet C
T3 Dragon Hole U
T3 Vacation Planet R
T3 Armory Moon C

T3 Planet - Crystal Planet C
T3 Moon (UE) C
T3 Ice Moon C
T3 Asteroid Belt - Benakis Asteroid Belt C
T3 Planet - Sigry III U
T3 Dragon Egg C
T3 Repair Moon C
T3 Brown Dwarf U
T3 Protostar C
T4 Planet - Podekkur Prime C
T4 Supernova Remnant U
T4 Gaia Planet R
T4 Small System - Rabuff Locttoor C
T4 Small Moon - Aldibrik Munitions Plant R
T4 Distant Sun C
T4 Forming System C
T4 Small Planet - Bolaar IV U
T5 Nebula - Homecloud Nebula V
T5 Star R
T5 Ring System R
T5 Pirate System R
T5 System - Penteir System R
T5 Dragon Cave R
T5 Small System - The Cramannerak System U
T5 Dependency World R
T5 Small System - Hcsuar-Drahcir System C
T5 Planet - Candor II U
T5 Twin Planets - Verkirsh I & II R
T5 Planet - Zambarez Planet U
T5 Planet - Vektrea Prime R
T6 Comet - Sochess Comet R
T6 System - Gorgochok System V
T6 Black Hole R
T6 Globular Cluster R
T6 Planet - Vorn Ringed Gas Giant V/V/V/R
T6 Asteroid Field R
T7 System - Argo V
T7 Comet - Scorpead Comet of Lore V
T7 Undiscovered System V
T7 Planet - Krebizar V
T7 Sensor Planet V
T7 Quantum Black Hole C
T8 System - Mechad System V
T8 Plasmatic Nebula V
T8 System - The Scandig System V
T8 Dragon Lair V
T9 Planet - Corporate Homeworld V
T9 Gas Giant - Blookerak Gas Giant V
T9 Dragon Lair V
A10 Artificial Landmass S
C10 Legendary Officer S
C10 Spiritual Leader S
E10 Hypercube S
H10 Time Warp S
L10 Galactic Armageddon S
M10 Time Keeper S
O10 Toxic Waste Spill S
S10 Explosive Ore Carrier S
T10 Intergalactic Void S
HQ25 P.O.T. Sector HQ V
HQ25 Corporate Sector HQ V
HQ25 Clydon Sector HQ V
HQ25 Vektrean Sector HQ V
HQ25 Scorpead Sector HQ V
HQ25 Argonian Sector HQ V
HQ25 Tufor Sector HQ V
HQ25 Dragon Sector HQ V
HQ25 Mechad Sector HQ V
HQ25 Krebiz Sector HQ V
R/A4 Mind Guard U
R/A6 Captain's Bluff V
R/A8 Time Lore V
R/B8 Citadel V
R/C1 Crewman C
R/C1 Bar Tender R
R/C1 Informant R
R/C1 Starving Artist V
R/C4 Trophy Hunter U
R/C4 Security Officer U
R/C4 Science Officer C
R/C4 Marine U
R/C5 Mutineer V
R/C6 Science Officer R
R/C6 Planetary Leader R
R/C6 Damage Control Team R
R/C6 Telepath V
R/C6 Administrator U
R/C6 Commando R
R/C6 Spy R
R/C7 Doctor R
R/D6 Solar Dragoness V
R/E1 Terrain Attack Shuttle U
R/E1 False Mine U
R/E2 Transporter C
R/E2 Tractor Beam R
R/E3 Stealth Fighter U
R/E3 Shuttlecraft (Right) C
R/E3 Shuttlecraft (Left) C
R/E3 Emergency Power R
R/E3 Temporal Transporter U
R/E4 Heavy Shuttlecraft U
R/E4 Transporter Mine U
R/E4 Hull Rotation - Argonian Hull Rotation V
R/E5 Fighter R
R/E6 Distortion Generator U
R/E6 Tactical Fighter V
R/E7 Heavy Fighter V
R/E8 Assault Fighter V
R/E9 Hologram V
R/H7 Time Typhoon V
R/H7 Interstellar Plasma R
R/L1 Lucky Crew Action C
R/L2 Phaser Malfunction U
R/L3 Unlucky Targeting R
R/L3 Transporter Malfunction U
R/L3 Repair Malfunction R
R/L4 Miscommunications V
R/L4 Scientifically Enhance Tectonic Plate Structure U
R/L4 Shuttle Malfunction U
R/L4 Monster Overstrike V
R/L4 Unsuccessful Minesweeping U
R/L4 Monster Healing R
R/L5 Heavy Weapons Backfire R
R/L5 Defensive Override R
R/L6 Distress Beacon R
R/L6 Lucky Maneuver V
R/L7 Anomaly Portal V
R/L7 Temporal Correction R
R/L8 Advanced Preparedness V
R/L8 Targeting Error V
R/L8 Demigod Diversion V
R/L8 Twist of Fate V
R/L9 Suspended Animation V
R/M1 Sextaraan Web Crawlers C
R/M3 Space Vertigo C
R/M4 Time Keeper U
R/M9 Luck Demon V
R/O1 Intercept Action U
R/O1 Sun Spot U
R/O2 Shipping Delays (02/10) R
R/O3 Crinkled Timeline U
R/O3 Offensive/Defensive Electronic Warfare U
R/O3 Defensive Electronic Warfare U
R/O3 Instant Reaction U
R/O4 Repair Delivery V
R/O5 Volatile Terrain C
R/O5 Tactical Retreat R
R/O5 Evasive Maneuvers R
R/O6 Breached City R
R/O7 Scientific Breakthrough V
R/O7 Out of Season U
R/O8 Alien Love Interest R
R/O8 Emergency Damage Control V
R/O8 Time Discrepancy U
R/O8 Mind Turning V
R/S1 Clydon Science Craft R
R/S1 Ship from the Future U
R/S1 Clydon Mine Craft U
R/S1 Clydon War Craft R
R/S2 Clydon Carrier Craft U
R/S2 Clydon Battle Craft V
R/T2 Asteroid Shield R
T/B5 Vektrean Asteroid Outpost R
T/B9 Vektrean Asteroid Starbase V
T/H2 Plasma Field C

1996 Galactic Empires Advanced Technology

A3 Drone Clydon U
A4 Executive Position U
A4 Mechanization U
A5 Blood Clydon R
A6 Officer's Saber R
A6 Vektrean Leadership R
A7 Bolaar Negotiator V
A7 Automation V
A7 Imperial Clydon V
A8 Vektrean Loyalty V
B1 Anti-Starcraft R
B2 Freighter Station U
B2 Border Post R
B3 Patrol Ship Support Base U
B4 Border Station V
B4 Espionage Satellite U
B4 Heavy Weapons Platform R
B6 Armory Base V
B8 Power Generation Complex R
C4 Deck Crew R
C5 Alien Technology Expert U
C7 Military Police V
C8 Intergalactic Grave Robbers V
E1 Ship Upgrade U
E1 Armor System Refit U
E1 Patrol Capsule Refit U
E2 Ammo Reserve V
E2 Ship Upgrade R
E2 Heavy Patrol Capsule Refit V
E3 Armor System Refit R
E3 Patrol Scout Refit R
E3 Hyperspace Detonator Refit R
E3 Dragon Saddle R
E3 Clydon Energy Armor U
E4 Battery U
E4 Fusion Mine V
E4 Command & Control Center R
E6 Variable Plasma Refit V
E6 Vektrean Command Override V
E6 Distortion Cannon Refit R
E7 Cloning Device V
E7 Shield Penetration Refit V
E8 Fuser (AT) V
E8 Tractor Beam V
E8 Tufor Mine Accelerator V
E8 EWACS Shuttlecraft V
E9 Time Alteration Device V
E9 Plasma Stream Accelerator V
E9 Unit Overhaul V
F6 Research Field U
H1 Cosmic Cataclysm V
H3 Hyperspace Vortex U
H5 Hyperspace Vortex R
H9 Shield Resonance Wave V
I1 Solitary Station U
I2 Projection Station U/V
I3 Fighter Installation U
L5 Energy Flux V
L9 Demobilization V
M1 Space Remora R
M3 Space Remora R
M5 Space Remora V
O3 Mining Expedition U
O4 Gaseous Degeneration R
O4 Invasion R
O6 Merchant Ship V
O6 Corporate Influence R
P9 Il'ith I'karnas V
S1 Mechad Patrol Scout U
S1 Corporate Patrol Ship R
S1 Tufor Patrol Scout U
S1 Tufor Mine Patrol Ship U
S1 Patrol Ship U
S1 Corporate Patrol Scout U
S1 Bolaar Patrol Ship (AT) U
S1 Tufor Patrol Ship R
S1 Argonian Patrol Ship U
S1 Vektrean Patrol Ship U
S1 Mechad Patrol Ship U
S1 Mechad Patrol Ship Leader R
S1 Scorpead Patrol Ship U
S1 P.O.T. Patrol Launch U
S2 P.O.T. Troop Transport U
S2 Argonian Troop Ship U
S2 Munition Processing Ship U
S2 Corporate Troop Ship U
S2 Krebiz Cargo Capsule U
S2 Tufor Troop Ship U
S2 Repair Tug R
S3 Mechad Infiltration Unit U
S3 P.O.T. Spy Cutter U
S3 Scorpead Spy Ship U
S3 Ship of the Ancients R
S3 P.O.T. Star Frigate - Tequan Star Frigate U
S3 Scorpead Troop Ship R
S3 Patrol Ship Tender U
S3 Corporate Carrier U
S3 Krebiz Dreadnought Carrier V
S4 Bolaar Spy Scout U
S4 P.O.T. Star Destroyer - Tequan Star Destroyer U
S4 Salvage Ship R
S5 Bolaar Boarding Cruiser R
S5 Mechad Patrol Support Ship - Patrol Support Ship R
S5 P.O.T. Light Star Cruiser - Centaurian Light Star Cruiser R
S5 P.O.T. Command Cruiser R
S5 Argonian Spy Ship R
S5 P.O.T. Star Cruiser - Peladine Star Cruiser R
S5 Corporate Spy Ship R
S5 Tufor Spy Ship R
S7 Patrol Ship Courier V
S7 Krebiz King Kraken V
S7 Vacater Heavy Cruiser V
S7 Scorpead Battle Carrier V
S8 Vacater Battle Cruiser V
S9 Vacater Dreadnought V
S9 Mechad Juggernaut V
E10 Targeting Systems S
S10 Argonian Flagship S
S10 Tufor Flagship S
S10 Corporate Flagship S
S10 Indirigan Supercarrier S
S10 P.O.T. Flagship S
B/S2 Light Battle Sled U
B/S4 Battle Sled R
R/A4 Thick Shelled Crab U
R/A7 Improved Automaton R
R/C1 Tour Guide C
R/C1 Landing Signal Officer U
R/E1 Pseudo Capsule U
R/E1 Formation Lights R
R/E4 Monster Defense System U/R
R/E6 Oscillating Transporter R
R/F5 Guardian Field R
R/F7 Protection Field V
R/L7 Transporter Malfunction V
R/L8 Shuttle Malfunction V
R/L9 Murphy's Law V
R/M4 Minor Luck Demon R
R/O3 Fighter Defense System V
R/O6 Strobe Malfunction R
R/O6 Red Tape R
R/O6 Mine Deployment Failure V
R/O6 Mine Defenses V
R/O6 Distortion Cannon Failure R
R/O7 Shield Penetration Failure R
R/O8 Variable Plasma Overload V
R/O9 Equipment Malfunction V
R/S1 Clydon Spy Warcraft U
R/S1 Clydon Troop Warcraft U
R/S1 Base Relocation Tug U
R/S2 Clydon Boarding Warcraft R
T/B6 Vektrean Asteroid Station V

1996 Galactic Empires Allied Forces

B3 Developed Outpost R
B4 Planetary Shield - Ecosphere R
C5 Liege - Noble Liege R
E1 Phaser Overload Device V
E6 Swarm Bolt Accelerator R
E6 Plasmatic Pulse Devise V
H1 Ion Storm - Positron Storm V
H3 Pocket Supernova V
O4 Fleet Disjunction V
O6 Fleet Disjunction -
S1 Paraloid Scout Craft R
S1 Paraloid Munition Craft R
S1 Shon-ti Patrol Ship V
S1 Luxury Gig V
S1 Paraloid Armed Craft R
S2 Tarra'ki Escort R
S2 Paraloid Troop Craft R
S2 Pakta'don Frigate V
S2 Drone Ore Freighter V
S2 Troop Ship V
S2 Trochilidae Escort V
S2 Treglean Attrition Frigate V
S2 Tarra'ki Attrition Frigate V
S2 Paraloid Patrol Cruiser R
S2 Leopan Heavy Patrol Ship V
S2 Pakta'don Escort V
S2 Shon-ti Frigate V
S2 Shon-ti Escort V
S2 Drone Escort V
S2 Erodi Science Craft R
S3 Drone Patrol Support Ship R
S3 Drone War Freighter V
S3 Pakta'don Destroyer V
S3 Paraloid Light Storm Cruiser R
S3 Tarra'ki Attrition Destroyer V
S3 Erodi Scout Destroyer R
S3 Shon-ti Heavy Destroyer V
S3 Tarra'ki Scout V
S3 Tramp Freighter R
S3 Trochilidae Minesweeper V
S3 Treglean Attrition Destroyer V
S3 Tarra'ki Spy Destroyer V
S3 Trochilidae Swift Destroyer V
S3 Treglean Escort V
S3 War Ship V
S4 Drone Converter R
S4 Pakta'don Minesweeper R
S4 Paraloid Medium Star Cruiser R
S4 Shon-ti Defender Cruiser R
S4 Erodi Light War Cruiser V
S4 Treglean Science Vessel V
S4 Corporate Pirate Assault Destroyer V
S4 Trochilidae Light Cruiser V
S4 Tarra'ki War Destroyer V
S4 Shon-ti Attrition Cruiser V
S4 Erodi Light Nova Cruiser V
S4 Treglean War Cruiser R
S4 Erodi Light Cruiser V
S4 Trochilidae Scout Cruiser R
S4 Tarra'ki Light Carrier R
S4 Pakta'don Troop Ship V
S4 Trochilidae Heavy Escort V
S4 Treglean Police Ship V
S5 Leopan Patrol Support Ship V
S5 Trochilidae Medium Cruiser V
S5 Independent Trader V
S5 Treglean Minesweeper R
S5 Trochilidae Command Ship R
S5 Tarra'ki Medium Cruiser V
S5 Tarra'ki Heavy Escort V
S5 Erodi Command Cruiser R
S5 Pakta'don Spy Cruiser R
S5 Independent Pirate Raider V
S5 Drone Deflector Cruiser V
S5 Treglean Police Cruiser V
S5 Drone Heavy Escort V
S5 Erodi Heavy Cruiser V
S5 Paraloid Heavy Storm Cruiser R
S5 Shon-ti Command Cruiser R
S5 Pakta'don Light Cruiser V
S5 Shon-ti Light Cruiser V
S5 Fictitious Ship R
S6 Tarra'ki Command Cruiser R
S6 Treglean Heavy Scout V
S6 Trochilidae Heavy Troop Ship R
S6 Bolaar Command Cruiser V
S6 Treglean Heavy Cruiser V
S6 Trochilidae Heavy Cruiser V
S6 Tarra'ki Heavy War Cruiser V
S6 Shon-ti Heavy Cruiser R
S6 Pakta'don Heavy Cruiser V
S6 Corporate Pirate Stealth Raider V
S6 Pakta'don Command Ship R
S6 Armed Tug R
S6 Erodi Heavy War Cruiser V
S6 Drone Bombardment Cruiser V
S6 Drone Command Ship R
S6 Paraloid Man-at-Arms R
S7 Shon-ti Battlecruiser R
S7 Drone Heavy Deflector V
S7 Drone Heavy Bombardier V
S7 Trade Ship V
S7 Pakta'don Battlecruiser R
S7 Heavy War Cruiser V
S7 Trochilidae Battlecruiser V
S7 Treglean Command Cruiser R
S7 Erodi Battlecruiser V
S8 Bolaar Battleship V
T2 Dust Belt R
T3 Ionized Particle Field R
T4 Planetary Debris R
T5 Event Horizon R
T5 Neutron Star R
T5 Twin Moons R
T6 Star Cluster - Omega Centauri R
T6 Binary Star R
T7 Asteroid - Massive Asteroid R
T7 Planet - Shon-ti Swarm Homeground R
T7 Planet - Trochilidae Homeworld R
T9 Erodi Destabilized Zone R
T9 Nebula - Tarra'ki Homecloud Expanse R
T9 Pakta'don Plasmatic Cloud R
HQ25 Tarra'ki Sector HQ V
HQ25 Treglean Weapon Group Rules V
HQ25 Shon-ti Sector HQ V
HQ25 Pakta'don Pulse Phaser Rules V
HQ25 Paraloid Sector HQ V
HQ25 Drone Special Ship System Rules V
HQ25 Erodi Sector HQ V
HQ25 Trochilidae Sector HQ V
HQ25 Shon-ti Swarm Bolt Rules V
HQ25 Noble Sector HQ - Noble Amassed Fleet V
HQ25 Tarra'ki Aux. Shields & Positron Emitter Rules V
HQ25 Drone Sector HQ V
HQ25 Treglean Sector HQ V
HQ25 Erodi Ion and Nova Cannon Rules V
HQ25 Noble Sector HQ - Noble Reclaimed Space V
HQ25 Paraloid Rules V
HQ25 Pakta'don Sector HQ V
HQ25 Trochilidae Maneuvering Thruster Rules V
R/E3 Shield Synchronizer R
R/E6 Noble Fighter R
R/M2 Ionized Phaser Eel V
R/M6 Ionized Phaser Eel V
R/S1 Emergency Rescue Ship V

1996 Galactic Empires Comedy Club on the Far Side of the Galaxy

A1 Steak Sauce (3/4) U
A1 Steak Sauce (4/4) U
A1 Steak Sauce (1/4) U
A1 Steak Sauce (2/4) U
A1 [Ace of Clubs] U
A1 Ace of Clubs U
A3 Admiral's Rear (4/4) U
A3 Admiral's Rear (3/4) U
A3 Admiral's Rear (2/4) U
A3 Admiral's Rear (1/4) U
A4 Chakan's Hat U
A7 Face Paint U
B1 Eat at Joe's (4/4) U
B1 Eat at Joe's (3/4) U
B1 Eat at Joe's (1/4) U
B1 Eat at Joe's (2/4) U
B2 Donut Shop U
B3 Arduous Study (4/4) U
B3 Arduous Study (1/4) U
B3 Arduous Study (3/4) U
B3 Arduous Study (2/4) U
B4 Home Base U
B5 Cinema U
B6 Defensive Satellites U
C1 Pizza Delivery Alien - P.D.A. (1/4) U
C1 Used Spaceship Dealer - A.K.A. Bob (2/4) U
C1 Used Spaceship Dealer - A.K.A. Bob (1/4) U
C1 Pizza Delivery Alien - P.D.A. (2/4) U
C1 Used Spaceship Dealer - A.K.A. Bob (3/4) U
C1 The Ensign in the Red Shirt U
C1 Pizza Delivery Alien - P.D.A. (3/4) U
C1 Used Spaceship Dealer - A.K.A. Bob (4/4) U
C1 Pizza Delivery Alien - P.D.A. (4/4) U
C2 Mime U
C3 Mime U
C4 Night Club Comedian (3/4) U
C4 Night Club Comedian (2/4) U
C4 Night Club Comedian (1/4) U
C4 Mad Scientist U
C4 Night Club Comedian (4/4) U
C4 The Commodores U
C6 Mime U
C6 Night Club Comedian U
C8 Heckler U
C9 Mime U
D5 Kung Fu Dragon U
H1 The Old Switcheroo U
H7 Either Dragoness U
I1 Road Sign (1/2) U
I1 Coffee House (1/4) U
I1 Sign Post (3/4) U
I1 Coffee House (3/4) U
I1 Road Sign (2/2) U
I1 Sign Post (1/4) U
I1 Coffee House (2/4) U
I1 Sign Post (4/4) U
I1 Coffee House (4/4) U
I1 Sign Post (2/4) U
I2 Kitty Cat Club (3/4) U
I2 Fast Food Franchise (3/4) U
I2 Fast Food Franchise (4/4) U
I2 Kitty Cat Club (1/4) U
I2 Kitty Cat Club (4/4) U
I2 Fast Food Franchise (2/4) U
I2 Fast Food Franchise (1/4) U
I2 Kitty Cat Club (2/4) U
I3 The Club (2/4) U
I3 The Club (3/4) U
I3 The Club (4/4) U
I3 Bouncer Training Facility U
I3 The Club (1/4) U
I4 Gentlealien's Club (2/4) U
I4 Captain's Bluff (2/4) U
I4 Gentlealien's Club (3/4) U
I4 Lobster Market U
I4 Gentlealien's Club (4/4) U
I4 Captain's Bluff (3/4) U
I4 Gentlealien's Club (1/4) U
I4 Captain's Bluff (4/4) U
I4 Captain's Bluff (1/4) U
I4 Lead Balloon Factory U
I5 Comet Control U
I5 Bob's Used Spaceship Lot U
I6 Psychiatric Ward (4/4) U
I6 Psychiatric Ward (1/4) U
I6 Psychiatric Ward (2/4) U
I6 Psychiatric Ward (3/4) U
I7 Clown College (4/4) U
I7 Clown College (1/4) U
I7 Clown College (2/4) U
I7 Clown College (3/4) U
I8 Casino U
I9 Sahnadrei's Weapon Shop U
L3 Twist of Fate II U
L8 Call it Good U
L9 What's This Button For? (1/4) U
L9 What's This Button For? (2/4) U
L9 What's This Button For? (4/4) U
L9 What's This Button For? (3/4) U
M1 Space Penguin U
M2 Space Penguin U
M4 Space Penguin U
M5 Mime Control Beast U
O3 Sabot Tour U
O7 Poker Night U
O7 We Have Special Plans for this Card U
S3 Lobster Boat U
S6 Protest Ship U

T3 Planet - Rubber Ball Planet U
T4 Comet - Out of Control Comet U
T4 Rock Lobster U
T5 Planet - Mime Homeworld U
T5 Planet - Earth U
T6 In Phase World U
T6 Planet - Garbage Planet U
T7 Nebula - Lobster Nebula U
T8 8-Ball U
T8 Planet - Salt Water World U
C10 Night Club Comedian S
I10 The Comedy Club on the Far Side of the Galaxy S
C5/5 Mime Knight U
HQ25 Comedy Club Sector HQ U
O/B1 Kenobi U
R/A1 Mime Pajamas U
R/A2 Speaking Part (4/4) U
R/A2 Speaking Part (1/4) U
R/A2 Speaking Part (2/4) U
R/A2 Speaking Part (3/4) U
R/A4 Holographic Mime U
R/A6 Soft Chewy Center of the Planet U
R/C1 Barmaid (2/4) U
R/C1 Sales Representative U
R/C1 Game Designer - Wanna-be Game Designer U
R/C1 Barmaid (4/4) U
R/C1 Barmaid (3/4) U
R/C1 Super Model U
R/C1 Barmaid (1/4) U
R/C8 Groupie U
R/E1 Shuttlebus U
R/E1 The Club U
R/E2 Clown Car - Clown Car Shuttle (3/4) U
R/E2 Mime Protection Chamber - MP Chamber U
R/E2 Clown Car - Clown Car Shuttle (1/4) U
R/E2 Clown Car - Clown Car Shuttle (4/4) U
R/E2 Clown Car - Clown Car Shuttle (2/4) U
R/E3 Molecular Transporter U
R/E4 Derelict Fighter C
R/E5 Mime Rack U
R/H2 Warp Funnel Cakes U
R/H5 Time Accelerant (1/4) U
R/H5 Time Accelerant (3/4) U
R/H5 Time Accelerant (2/4) U
R/H5 Time Accelerant (4/4) U
R/L2 Time Hiccup U
R/L2 You Missed Me By That Much U
R/L2 Time Gait U
R/L5 Unlucky Mime Explosion (2/4) U
R/L5 Lucky Mime Explosion (2/4) U
R/L5 Unlucky Mime Explosion (3/4) U
R/L5 Unlucky Mime Explosion (4/4) U
R/L5 Lucky Mime Explosion (3/4) U
R/L5 Unlucky Mime Explosion (1/4) U
R/L5 Lucky Mime Explosion (4/4) U
R/L5 Lucky Mime Explosion (1/4) U
R/M3 Money Hungry Weasels U
R/O4 Mime Intrusion (3/4) U
R/O4 Mime Intrusion (4/4) U
R/O4 Mime Intrusion (1/4) U
R/O4 Mime Intrusion (2/4) U
R/S1 Ship From The Present U
T/A1 Shameless Argonian Sunbathing Nude U
R/C10 Master Mime S
R/O10 And Now For Something Completely Different S
36C/C3/6 Buffy the Time Knight Slayer (2/4) U
36C/C3/6 Buffy the Time Knight Slayer (4/4) U
36C/C3/6 Buffy the Time Knight Slayer (3/4) U
36C/C3/6 Buffy the Time Knight Slayer (1/4) U
R/T/B1/9 Vektrean Asteroid Outhouse U

1996 Galactic Empires Galactic Invaders

A3 Eclipse Position V
A3 Primitive Society U
A4 Tranquility U
A4 Officer Training V
A4 Planet Rise U
A4 War Effort U
A4 Hostile Environ Automaton U
A4 Solar Flare U
A5 Solar Corona (2/2) V
A5 Solar Corona (1/2) V
A5 Fire Breathing U
A5 Eclipse Position V
A6 Senior Officer Training V
A7 Solar Disk U
A7 Spiritual Familiar V
B3 Weather Satellite U
B3 Biodome U
B4 Flight School U
B5 Penal Correction Station U
B5 Isolated Base U
B5 J'xar Jump Base - Jx Jump Base U
B6 Castle Rognar V
B6 Mechad Power Base U
B6 Cloning Station U
B7 Krebiz Capsule Base V
B7 Clydon Warcraft Base U
B7 Bolaar Pirate Base V
B7 P.O.T. Centaurian Base V
B7 Corporate Defender Base - Corporate Economic Base V
B7 Zedan Invasion Base U
B7 Defender Base V
B8 Heavy Defender Base - Defender Base V
B8 P.O.T. Tequan Base V
B8 Corporate Economic Base V
C1 Survivalist U
C1 Cadet U
C1 Leopan Raiding Pilot V
C2 Leopan Raiding Pilot V
C3 J'xar Gravitic Engineer V
C4 Secret Service Alien U
C4 Intergalactic Terrorist U
C4 Soldier of Fortune U
C4 Base Engineer U
C5 Mystic V
C6 Zedan Shifter V
C7 Treglean Fleet Coordinator V
C8 Mystic V
C9 Zedan Infiltrator V
D1 Orgon Seed U
D1 Patrol Orgonism R
D2 Orgonism R
D2 Orgon Sprig U
D3 Large Patrol Orgonism U
D3 Orgon Groth R
D3 Orgon Amalgemate U
D4 Orgon Sludge R
D4 Orgon Slath R
D5 Orgon Mire R
D5 Orgon Slag R
D6 Orgon Attacher R
D6 Orgon Engulfer V
D7 Orgon Consumer V
D8 Orgon Straith V
D8 Orgon Slime V
D9 Orgon Blob V
E1 Observation Window U
E1 Personal Fighter U
E2 Satellite D/R System U
E3 Ore Shuttle U
E3 Orbital Mine U
E4 Thermographic Display (1/2) V
E4 Energy Panels U
E4 Target Acquisition Link (2/2) V
E4 Sensor Mine U
E4 Thermographic Display (2/2) V
E4 Transgate Stabilizers V
E4 Mining Drone U
E4 Target Acquisition Link (1/2) V
E5 Technical Readout (2/2) V
E5 Clydon Warcraft Dock U
E5 Technical Readout (1/2) V
E6 Phaser Bolt System V
E8 Transgate Stabilizers V
G3 Prisoners U
G4 Leopan Capture Mission U
H3 Space-Time Rift V
H4 Sublight Debris V
H4 Global Lava U
H4 Space-Time Rift V
H5 Quantum Flare U
H6 Surface Explosions V
H6 Spatial Disjunction U
H6 Surface Vortex U
H6 Star Spindle V
H7 Sublight Debris V
H9 Star Spindle V
I2 Tavern U
I4 Timeless City U
I5 Leisure Station U
L3 Gauntlet of Time - Artifact - Gauntlet of Time V
L9 Parallel Timesight V
M1 Geko Gnats V
M2 Geko Gnats V
M4 Andromeda Beast U
M5 Boarding Beast U
M8 Battalisk V
N3 Traveler U
O3 Tight Maneuver U
O4 Starship Insurance V
O4 Orgonic Frenzy U
O5 Strafing Attack U
O5 Fighter Combat Training U
O6 Starship Insurance V
O6 Demotion U
O7 Vacation U
O8 Space Hallucination - Insanity - Space Hallucination V
O8 Hallucinatory Space - Insanity - Hallucinatory Space V
S1 Zedan Patrol Ship - ZDI Patrol Ship V
S1 Gekonauak Hornet (1/2) V
S1 Gekonauak Hornet (2/2) V
S1 J'xar Armed Jumpship - J'x Guardian Class R
S1 Zedan Patrol Scout - ZDI Patrol Scout U
S2 Gekonauak Stinger U
S2 J'xar Minesweeper Jumpship - J'x Pyre Class U
S2 Zedan Escort - ZDI Escort U
S2 J'xar Troop Ship - J'x Falchion Class U
S2 J'xar Medium Jumpship - J'x Avenger Class R
S2 Zedan Light Scout - ZDI Light Scout U
S3 Freighter - Andromeda Bound Freighter U
S3 J'xar Heavy Jumpship - J'x Protector Class U
S3 Gekonauak Swarmer U
S3 Gekonauak Needle R
S3 J'xar Jump Launcher - J'x Slingshot Class C
S3 Gekonauak Wasp R
S3 Zedan Troop Ship - ZDI Troop Ship U
S3 Zedan Destroyer - ZDI Destroyer U
S4 Gekonauak Apprentice R
S4 J'xar Light Cruiser - J'x Dagger Class C
S4 Heavy Freighter - Andromeda Bound Freighter U
S4 Zedan Light Cruiser - ZDI Dagger Light Cruiser R
S4 Gekonauak Kamikaze U
S4 J'xar Scout - J'x Sentry Class U
S4 Treglean Destroyer U
S4 Converted Freighter - War Ship U
S4 Zedan Minesweeper - ZDI Minesweeper U
S4 Zedan Heavy Destroyer - ZDI Heavy Destroyer R
S4 Gekonauak Trainee R
S5 Gekonauak Subwarrior R
S5 Survey Cruiser - Andromeda Bound Cruiser U
S5 Zedan Patrol Ship Tender - ZDI Patrol Ship Tender R
S5 Gekonauak Worker V
S5 Zedan Carrier - ZDI Carrier U
S5 J'xar Assault Cruiser - J'x Bowman Class R
S5 Zedan War Cruiser - ZDI War Cruiser R
S5 Treglean Light Cruiser U
S5 J'xar Science Cruiser - J'x Allied Class U
S5 Gekonauak Soldier U
S5 Treglean Carrier U
S6 J'xar Command Cruiser - J'x Scepter Class V
S6 Gekonauak Commander V
S6 J'xar Heavy Cruiser - J'x Cavalry Class R
S6 Zedan Command Cruiser - ZDI Command Cruiser V
S6 Zedan Spy Cruiser - ZDI Spy Cruiser V
S6 Gekonauak Warrior V
S6 Command Cruiser - Andromeda Bound Cruiser U
S6 Krebiz Light Defender V
S7 Leopan Troop Ship U
S7 Gekonauak Queen V
S7 Battlecruiser - Andromeda Bound Cruiser U
S7 J'xar Battlecruiser - J'x Lance Class V
S7 Zedan Battlecruiser - ZDI Battlecruiser V
S7 Geko Samurai V
S7 Munitions Cruiser - Andromeda Bound Cruiser U
S7 Argonian Defender - Cold Snap Defender U
S7 Colony Ship V
S7 Krebiz Heavy Defender V
S7 Zedan Survey Cruiser - ZDI Survey Cruiser U
S8 Leopan Dreadnought U
S8 Gekonauak Shogun Warrior V
S8 J'xar Dreadnought - J'x Lance Class V
S8 Treglean Dreadnought V
S8 Zedan Dreadnought - ZDI Dreadnought V
S8 Gekonauak King V
S9 Leopan Battleship U
S9 Zedan Battleship - ZDI Battleship V
S9 Colony Ship V
S9 J'xar Battleship - J'x Halberd Class V
T1 Moon - Tiny Moon V
T1 Lagrange Point V
T2 Dark Mountain V
T2 Barren Moon U
T3 Moon - Dimensional Moon U
T3 Moon - Treglean Moon U
T4 Moon - Gekonauak Moon V
T4 Vacation Planet - Vacation Planet Golf World U
T4 Dark Mountain V
T4 Planet - Conquered Planet V
T5 Planet - ZDI Random Colony V
T5 Globule V
T6 Nebula - Orion Nebula U
T6 Sun - Craft Site V
T6 Planet - Treglean Outpost U
T7 Planet - Gekonauak Outpost V
H10 Extreme Conflict S
S10 Zedan Flagship S
S10 J'xar Flagship - J'x Excaliber Class Flagship S
E8/2 Tranoan Time Bomb V
HQ25 Zedan Sector HQ V
HQ25 Orgon Sector HQ V
HQ25 Gekonauak Sector HQ V
HQ25 J'xar Sector HQ V
HQ25 Aqaaran Sector HQ V
R/A1 Personal Transportation V
R/A3 Sneak Attack V
R/A4 Sneak Attack V
R/A7 Personal Transportation V
R/A8 Orgon Seporation V
R/C5 Rescue Specialist U
R/E2 Base Responder V
R/E5 Krebiz Fighter - Krebiz Krill-F Fighter U
R/E5 Hazard Transceiver U
R/E6 Mechad Virus Fighter U
R/E6 Scorpead Stinger V
R/E9 Mechad Core Fighter V
R/L6 Spontaneous Explosion U
R/O4 Temporary Insanity V
R/O5 Fleet Maneuver U
R/O6 Surprise Maneuver U
R/O6 Temporary Insanity V
R/O6 Crash Maneuver U
T/S2 Vektrean Asteroid Freighter - Vektrean Freighter U
B2/S1 Scout Patrol Craft V
B3/S1 Fighter Base - Aqaaran Fighter Base U
B4/S2 Flight Craft U
B4/S3 Surface Craft V
B5/S3 Submersible V
B6/S2 Outpost Craft V
B6/S3 Holdtast Ship V
B7/S5 Command Post V
B8/S4 Battlepost - Aqaaran Battlepost V
B9/S6 Star Base - Aqaaran Star Base V
R/L10 Emergency Evacuation S
S2/B1 Patrol Craft V
S3/B1 Carrier Craft - Aqaaran Carrier Craft U
S4/B2 Light Craft V
S4/B3 Water Tanker V
S4/B3 Destroyer V
S5/B2 Defender Craft V
S5/B3 Submarine V
S6/B5 Heavy Craft V
S7/B2 Producer V
S7/B5 Command Craft V
S8/B4 Dreadnought Craft - Aqaaran Dreadnought Craft V
S9/B6 Battlecraft - Aqaaran Battlecraft V
B10/S6 Sun Base S
S10/B6 Aqaaran Flagship S

1996 Galactic Empires Persona

A1 Lunar Eclipse U
A2 Advanced Specimen U
A2 Methane Atmosphere U
A2 Ascension U
A3 Terrestrial Overgrowth U
A3 Insurrection U
A3 Alien Love U
A3 Solar Eclipse V
A4 Perfect Specimen V
A5 Resources Management - Personnel Department U
A5 Genetic Variant V
A5 I'm a Persona U
A5 Corporate Gold Card U
A6 Breeder V
A8 Quicksand V
A8 Royal Indirigan Tattoo V
A9 Antimatter Equivalent V
B5 Galactic Credit Bureau V
B5 Floating City U
B6 City of Forever U
C1 Cook U
C1 Jester - Noble Jester U
C1 Speedy Delivery Alien U
C1 Luck Guy U
C1 Visionary U
C2 Bodyguard U
C2 Radioactive Being U
C2 Squire - Noble Squire U
C2 Mad Chemist U
C3 Hydroponic Technician - Gardener U
C3 Indirigan Female V
C3 Corporate Employee U
C3 Scout - Noble Scout U
C3 Negotiator U
C3 Construction Team U
C3 Garbage Man U
C4 Robber Baron - Noble Robber Baron V
C4 Pioneer V
C4 Chef U
C5 Tecnopilot U
C5 Marquis - Noble Marquis V
C5 Renegade Science Officer V
C5 Countess - Noble Countess V
C5 Cybernetic Engineer V
C5 Senior Helmsman V
C6 Explorer V
C6 Earl - Noble Earl V
C6 Indirigan Chieftain - Licifrous V
C6 Viscount - Noble Viscount V
C6 Flight Deck Supervisor V
C7 Warcraft Coordinator V
C7 Indirigan Chieftain - Urvill V
C7 Margrave - Noble Margrave V
C7 Indirigan Chieftain - Lone Wolf V
C7 Electronic Warfare Specialist - EW Specialist V
C7 Thane - Noble Thane V
C7 Indirigan Chieftain - Murinca V
C8 Master Navigator V
C8 Millionaire V
C8 Leopan Technologist V
C8 Laird - Noble Laird V
C8 J'xar High Guard - J'x Yr'llite High Guard V
C8 First Sergeant V
C8 Chief Engineer V
C8 Logistics Officer V
C9 Senior Admiral V
C9 Grand Chieftain - Marchias V
C9 Imperial General - Clydon Imperial General V
C9 Indirigan Chieftain - Noaha V
C9 Zedan Chief Assassin - ZDI Chief Assassin V
C9 Sovereign - Noble Sovereign V
D4 Research Dragoness U
D6 Overwatch Dragon U
E2 Crystalline Detection Matrix U
E3 Boring Probe U
E3 Fluctuating Stasis Mine U
E3 Defensive Aircraft U
E3 Research Probe U
E4 Tranquilizer Mount U
E5 Boomerang Racks U
E5 Surface Probe V
E5 Parasite Torpedoes V
E5 Mainframe System - Desiree' V
E5 Phaser Targeting Refit V
E6 Plasma Phasers U
E6 Assault Tank V
E6 Ancient Control Network U
E9 Adamantine Hull - Sound Construction V
E9 Perpetual Motion Device V
F3 Installation Field U
G4 Espionage V
G6 Ancient Studies U
H3 Nuclear Incident U
H6 Drag Racing U
I4 VGW Hall - Veterans of Galactic Wars Hall U
I6 Teleportation Station U
I6 Ixubermorth Citadel V
I7 Ancient's Library V
I9 Theme Park V
L4 Skeleton Crew U
L5 Weapons Security U
L6 Artifact - Spiritual Symbol U
L6 Reserve Cruiser V
L8 Ancients Portal V
L9 Artifact - Empire Constitution V
M1 Terask U
M1 Party Animals U
M2 Offspring U
M4 Planet Gouge U
M6 Research Mandator V
M7 Mind Thief V
M7 Allizdog U
M9 World Collector V
M9 Prehistoric Space Beast V
O2 Firesuit Malfunction U
O4 Suicide Mission U
O4 Peace Treaty U
O4 Amphibian Desire U
O4 Riot U
O5 Infinite Potential U
O5 Coffee Break U
O7 Intergalactic Transgate V
O7 Reestablish Territory U
O8 Galactic Depression V
P7 Endri K'tal V
P8 Htim' V
P9 Sa'meh E'no V
S3 Galactic Parcel Ship U
S5 Troop Freighter V
S5 Lone Wolf Destroyer U
S6 J'xar Heavy Carrier - J'x Quiver Class V
S6 Lone Wolf Command Cruiser U
S7 Lone Wolf Police Cruiser V
S7 Clydon Flagship V
S8 Lone Wolf Battlecruiser V
S9 Lone Wolf Dreadnought V
T4 Planet - Vektrea Minor U
T5 Asteroid - Repair Asteroid V
T5 Dragon Sun U
T6 Planet - Nagir XII U
T6 Filarian Moon - Infested Moon V
T7 Planet - Zedan Regional Colony V
T7 Planetoid - Argonian Fighter Planetoid V
T7 Moon - Scorpead Dominated Moon V
T7 System - Vektrea System V
T7 System - Clydon System V
T7 Free Trade Zone U
T7 Planet - Krebiz Homeland V
T8 System - Tufor System V
T8 Planet - Leopan Operations Planet V
T8 Refuge - Aqaaran Aquatic Refuge V
T8 Planet - P.O.T. Element Capital V
T8 System - Bolaar Covert System V
T9 Planet - J'xar Transgalactic Gate V
T9 Planet - Mechad Planet - Arretia V
T9 System - Corporate System V
C10 War Prophet S
E10 Dark Circuitry S
G10 Salvage Mission S
A5/5 Time Knight's Scepter V
B/S6 Battlesled V
C6/6 Time Monarch V
R/A1 Perseverance U
R/A3 Indirigan Tattoo V
R/A4 Secret Agent Alien V
R/C1 Street People U
R/C1 Flight Attendant U
R/C1 Cryptologist U
R/C2 Emergency Maintenance Team - Emer. Maintenance Team' U
R/C2 Gorilla Warfare Specialists U
R/C4 Duke - Noble Duke U
R/C5 Knight - Noble Knight V
R/C6 Knight Templar - Noble Knight Templar V
R/C6 Marine - Marine Major V
R/C8 Communication Supervisor V
R/C9 Grand Time Keeper - Sir Thomas Seth V
R/E5 Psycanti Fighter - Psycanti Intellect Fighter U
R/E5 J'xar Fighter - J'xar Jump Fighter U
R/E5 Filarian Fighter - Filarian Needle Fighter U
R/E5 Clydon Fighter U
R/E5 Visonic Fighter - Visonic Probe Fighter U
R/E6 Aqaaran Fighter - Aqaaran Cavalier Fighter U
R/E6 Zedan Fighter U
R/E6 Bolaar Fighter U
R/E6 Tufor Fighter U
R/E6 Vektrean Fighter U
R/E6 Leopan Fighter - Leopan Claw Fighter U
R/E7 Indirigan Fighter - Indirigan Gypsy Fighter U
R/E7 Corporate Fighter U
R/E8 Sound Construction V
R/E9 Argonian Fighter - Argonian Heavy Gail Fighter U
R/M3 Jungle Moths U
R/O1 Aqaaran Holy Day U
R/O2 Jungle Love U
R/O3 Space Sickness - Illness - Space Sickness U
R/O3 Metamorphosis U
R/O3 Instant Reaction U
R/O5 Reserve Lock U
R/O5 Aqaaran Disjunction U
R/O6 Pendulum Effect U
R/O9 Pendulum Defect V
R/S3 Clydon Heavy Warcraft V
R/A10 Rebel Leader S
T/B10 Vektrean Asteroid Flagstar S
R/E6/4 Tranoan Fighter - Tranoan Time Fighter U

1996 Galactic Empires Piracy

A1 Spiritual Ascension U
A3 Covert Operations U
A4 Planescape U
A4 Utopia V
A5 Peace Mission V
A6 Pirate Currency U
A6 Hostile Terrain U
A6 Espionage Training V
A6 Dragon Rider V
A6 Gaia Separation U
A7 Urbanization U
A7 Defended Territory V
A7 Tomb Of The Far Side Pharaoh V
A8 White Nobelium V
A9 Filarian Overlord V
B1 Pirate Outpost U
B3 Electronic Warfare Base U
B3 Forgotten Ruins U
B3 Leopan Stealth Satellite U
B4 Police Headquarters U
C1 Tax Collector U
C2 Pirate Engineer U
C2 Civilian Captain C/U
C3 Orbital Engineer V
C3 Rogue Cop U
C3 Leopan Raiding Party U
C3 Mind Programmer U
C4 Buccaneer V
C4 Pirate Captain R/V
C5 Clan Boss V
C5 Leopan Raiding Captain U
C6 Master Pirate U
C6 Slave Trader V
C6 Mind Programmer V
C7 Leopan Raiding Party V
C8 Not-So-Supreme Leader V
D4 Burrowing Dragoness U
D4 Rogue Dragoness U
D5 Energy Dragoness V
D7 Cyber Dragoness V

D8 Surface Dragoness V
E4 Main Bridge U
E4 Illegal Cargo U
E4 Cargo Hold U
E5 Infiltration Array V
E5 Dual Launch Tubes U
E6 Deflection/Transfer Device (Clydon) V
E6 Degeneration Device V
E6 Shroud Web V
E6 Deflection/Transfer Device (Bolaar/Pir) V
E9 Shroud V
F4 Warp Field U
G2 Celestial Comet U
G5 Archeology V
G5 Pirate Raid U
G5 Raiding Fleet U
H4 Solar Winds U
H4 Sargassos U
H4 Gravity Well U
H4 Temporal Repetition U
H5 System Degeneration V
H5 Power Outage U
H6 Defensive Mine Field V
H8 Toroidal Black Hole V
I2 Projection Station U/V
I4 Minor Religious Installation U
I5 Gunnery Station V
I8 Major Religious Installation V
L5 Ice Age U
L6 Pirate's Cache U
L6 Navigational Error V
M2 Dimensional Dementia U
M5 Pirate Wench V
M6 Pirate's Parrot V
M7 Ghost Fleet V
M7 Space Illness U
M8 Tectonic Marauder V
M8 Creature From The Black Hole V
O2 Travel Agency U
O2 Social Combat U
O4 Raiding Mission U
O4 Wandering Desire U
O5 Planetary Raid V
O5 Pirate Activity U
O6 Blockade V
O6 Technological Breakthrough V
O6 Reinvestment V
O7 Terradeforming V
O9 Gravitational Pull V
S1 Bolaar Patrol Ship (Pir) U
S1 Corporate Pirate Patrol Ship U
S1 Corporate Pirate Patrol Scout U
S1 Leopan Patrol Ship U
S2 Corporate Pirate Tug U
S2 Bolaar Ultra-Light Raider (Pir) U
S2 Leopan Scout Frigate U
S2 Leopan Troop Ship U
S2 Corporate Pirate Raider U
S3 Independent Pirate Ship U
S3 Leopan Minesweeper U
S3 Leopan Destroyer U
S3 Bolaar Medium Raider (Pir) U
S3 Bolaar Light Pirate Raider (Pir) U
S3 Corporate Pirate Stealth Destroyer U
S4 Leopan Light Cruiser U
S4 Corporate Pirate Landing Cruiser U
S4 Corporate Pirate Light Cruiser U
S4 Leopan War Cruiser V
S4 Archeology Ship U
S4 Bolaar Stealth Raider (Pir) U
S4 Corporate Pirate Light Enforcer U
S4 Vicious Six Fleet Survey Cruiser V
S4 Bolaar Cargo Express U/R
S4 Leopan Carrier Cruiser U
S5 Nagiridni Pirate Destroyer R/U
S5 Vicious Six Destroyer (Right) V
S5 Corporate Pirate Spy Ship U
S5 Vicious Six Destroyer (Left) V
S5 Leopan Stealth Raiding Ship V
S5 Corporate Pirate Heavy Cruiser U
S5 Leopan Command Cruiser V
S5 Independent Pirate Ship V
S5 Corporate Pirate Assault Cruiser V
S5 Leopan Heavy Cruiser U
S5 Trade Ship V
S5 Bolaar Heavy Cargo Express V
S6 Bolaar Battlecruiser (Pir) R/V
S6 Corporate Pirate Battlecruiser V
S6 Nagiridni Pirate Cruiser V
S6 Funeral Cruiser V
S6 Leopan Battlecruiser V
S6 Police Cruiser V
S6 Corporate Pirate Enforcer V
S7 Corporate Pirate Stealth Cruiser V
S7 Vicious Six Heavy Cruiser V
S7 Bolaar Dreadnought V
S7 Leopan Heavy War Cruiser V
S7 Vicious Six Command Cruiser V
S8 Vicious Six Dreadnought V
S8 Lost Pirate Ship V
S8 Bolaar Flagship V
S8 Nagiridni Pirate Battlecruiser V
S9 Renegade Ship V
T1 Microscopic Black Hole U
T1 Small Moon - Hidden Moon U
T2 Star U
T2 Planet Of Ill Repute U
T2 Forgotten Planet U
T2 Small Moon - Corporate Moon U
T3 Pirate Nebula U
T4 Planet - Nrutas U
T4 Planet - Muckstra U
T5 Planet - Atoll U
T5 Moon - Storage Moon U
T5 System - Moon System U
T6 Moon - Oversized Moon U
T6 Dragon Eggs - Dragon Eggs In Orbit V
T6 Planet - Virgin Planet V
T6 Planet - Shrouded Planet V
T6 Planet - Bolaar II V
T6 Pirate's Horde V
T6 Nebula - Dragon Nebula V
T6 System - Indirigan Former Homeworld V
T7 Dragon Lair V
T7 Nebula - Leopan Nebula V
T7 Pirate Alcove V
T7 Planet - Water World V
T8 Planet - Massive Ore Planet V
T9 Shinnicera V
C10 Privateer S
L10 Galactic Cataclysm S
O10 General Quarters S
S10 Gohest's Pirate Ship - The Ghost Lord S
HQ25 Leopan Sector HQ V
HQ25 Bolaar Sector HQ V
R/A1 Change Of Identity U
R/A3 Undercover Agent U
R/A4 Pirate's Hook V
R/A4 Walk The Plank V
R/C1 Transporter Chief U
R/C4 Spy U
R/E3 Shroud Web Device U
R/E4 Multi-Purpose Phasers (Indirigan) R/V*
R/E4 Multi-Purpose Phasers (Bolaar) R/V*
R/E5 Pirate Fighter U
R/E7 Holographic Simulator V
R/E8 Phaser Resonator V
R/L2 Armor System Failure V
R/L2 Hasty Retreat U
R/L5 Civil War V
R/M2 Avian Dragon U
R/M8 Time Defiler V
R/M8 Temporal Conscience V
R/O2 Early Warning U
R/O4 Early Warning U
R/O4 Formation Maneuver V
R/O5 Stolen Technology U
R/S3 Gohest's Rescue Launch - The Hazy Ghost U
R/T2 Asteroids U
R/T2 Camouflage World V
T/B3 Vektrean Asteroid Satellite U
T/B6 Vektrean Asteroid Station V
T4/6 Moon - Tranoan Moon U
T7/3 Planet - Tranoan Homeworld V
R/E10 Docking Ring S

2002 Game of Thrones Flight of Dragons

1 Capture U
2 Resilience C
3 Jory Cassel U
4 Maester Luwin R
5 Roose Bolton R
6 Ser Rodrick Cassel U
7 Dreadfort Guard C
8 Flayed Men C
9 Winterfell Cavalry C
10 Winterfell Recruit U
11 The Dreadfort R
12 Northern Borderlands C
13 Winterfell Armory R
14 Complacence C
15 King's Spider R
16 Grand Maester Pycelle U
17 Jalabhar Xho C
18 Ser Balon Swann U
19 Ser Gregor Clegane R
20 Agent of the Lion U
21 Circle of Spies C
22 House Courtesan C
23 Chataya's R
24 Lannisport Treasury C
25 Marbrand Estates R
26 Stokeworth Estates U
27 Blessing of R'hllor C
28 The Onion Knight R
29 Ser Cortnay Penrose U
30 Asshaii Initiate C
31 Field Sergeant C
32 House Florent Rearguard C
33 Lost Captain U
34 Red Sorceress U
35 Shadow Assassin R
36 The Stone Drum R
37 Dragon Battlements C
38 Lookout Tower U
39 Recruiting Tent R
40 Support of Harlaw U
41 Terror of the Seas R
42 Andrik the Unsmiling U
43 Balon Greyjoy R
44 The Reader R
45 House Harlaw Pikeman C
46 Ironmen Raiders U
47 Ship's Bosun C
48 The Dead Walking C
49 Great Wyk R
50 Ten Towers R
51 Ironman's Bay R
52 Longship Raider C
53 Longship Reserves C
54 Tower of Pyke U
55 House Targaryen U
56 Stormborn R
57 Arakh U
58 Blood Steed C
59 Bloodrider U
60 Dragon Fear C
61 Unburnt U
62 Black Hatchling. C
63 Daenerys Targaryen U
64 Drogon R
65 Green Hatchling C
66 Jhogo U
67 Khal Drogo U
68 Rhaegal R
69 Ser Jorah Mormont R
70 Strong Belwas R
71 Viserion R
72 Viserys Targaryen R
73 White Hatchling C
74 Crone of Vaes Dothrak R
75 Dothraki Horselord U
76 Dothraki Skirmisher C
77 Handmaid C
78 Khalasar Horsemen C
79 Maegi R
80 Pentoshi Guildmaster U
81 Qartheen Merchant C
82 The Unsullied U
83 Astapor R
84 Meereen R
85 Qarth R
86 Vaes Dothrak U
87 Daznak's Pit C
88 Great Pyramid C
89 Quartheen Bazaar U
90 Temple of the Graces C
91 Formal Petition R
92 Skulduggery U
93 Anguy The Archer U
94 Beric Dondarrion R
95 Littlefinger U
96 Mord U
97 Syrio Forel R
98 The Mad Huntsman U
99 Tom Sevenstrings U
100 Archmaester R
101 Initiate of the Citadel C
102 Lyseni Assassin R
103 Maester of Oldtown U
104 Mountain Skirmisher C
105 Squire C
106 Lys R
107 Street of Silk R
108 Constant Rebuilding R
109 Countermeasures R
110 Dragon Flight R
111 Endless Bureaucracy U
112 Endless Endurance U
113 Endless Raid U
114 Endless Vigil U
115 Fire and Blood C
116 Harder and Stronger C
117 Hidden Agenda C
118 Immolate C
119 Lethal Counterattack R
120 Open Revolt R
121 Perished in Flame U
122 Price of Failure U
123 Quick as a Snake C
124 Recovery U
125 Retreat U
126 Ritual of R'hllor R
127 Salvage C
128 Secrets of Oldtown R
129 Seen in the Flames C
130 Shifting Plans C
131 Stalwart Defender C
132 Stranglehold R
133 Subterfuge C
134 The Lion's Claws R
135 True Queen's Decree R
136 Waking the Dragon U
137 Whirlwind Assault U
138 Assault on King's Landing U
139 Calm over Westeros R
140 Focused Offense U
141 Oath of Fealty U
142 Old Intrigues R
143 Outmaneuver R
144 Regroup U
145 Treacherous Passage R

2002 Game of Thrones Sea of Storms

1 Bite of the Wolf C
2 Skinchanger R
3 Greatjon Umber R
4 Rickard Karstark U
5 Robb Stark R
6 Septon Chayle C
7 Ser Edmure Tully U
8 Host of Bear Isle C
9 Host of Riverrun C
10 House Manderly Knight U
11 House Mormont Knight C
12 Wolf Pack C
13 Whispering Wood U
14 Winterfell Castle R
15 Winterfell Great Hall U
16 Northland Keep U
17 Winterfell Sept U
18 Blackmail C
19 Powerless C
20 Shame U
21 Widow's Wail R
22 Cersei Lannister U
23 Janos Slynt R
24 Ser Kevan Lannister U
25 Ser Lancel Lannister R
26 Host of Lannisport C
27 House Marbrand Maester R
28 House Westerling Courtier C
29 Queen's Spies U
30 Small Council Retainer C
31 Spider's Whisperer C
32 Lannisport U
33 Lannisport Brothel U
34 Merchant Guildhall R
35 Chosen One U
36 Lightbringer R
37 Shadow's Touch C
38 Edric Storm C
39 Salladhor Saan U
40 Selyse Baratheon C
41 Ser Axel Florent R
42 Shireen Baratheon C
43 Stannis Baratheon R
44 Deckhand C
45 Envoy of Dragonstone C
46 Fleet Captain R
47 Host of Dragonstone C
48 Dragonstone Castle U
49 Dragonstone Port R
50 Fury U
51 King Robert's Hammer U
52 Walls of Westeros R
53 HOUSE GREYJOY U
54 Conquer R
55 Drowned God's Blessing C
56 Aeron Damphair R
57 Asha Greyjoy U
58 Balon Greyjoy U
59 Dagmer Cleftjaw R
60 Euron Crow's Eye R
61 Gorold Goodbrother R
62 Maester Wendamyr C
63 Theon Greyjoy U
64 Victarion Greyjoy U
65 Drowned Men C
66 Host of Ten Towers C
67 House Blacktyde Guardsman R
68 Looters C
69 Oarsman U
70 Priest of the Drowned God C
71 Sea Captain U
72 Septon of Ten Towers C
73 Longship "Black Wind" U
74 Longship "Great Kraken" U
75 Longship "Iron Victory" R
76 Longship "Silence" U
77 The Seastone Chair R
78 Bloody Keep C
79 Gatehouse C
80 Nagga's Ribs C
81 The Iron Mines U
82 The Lonely Lights R
83 The Sea Tower C
84 Bodyguard C
85 Healing Expertise R
86 Knight of Flowers U
87 Ser Jaime Lannister R
88 Ser Barristan Selmy R
89 Ser Boros Blount U
90 Ser Mandon Moore U
91 Ser Meryn Trant U
92 Ser Preston Greenfield R
93 Thoros of Myr R
94 Ulfgor son of Ulf U
95 Vargo Hoat C
96 Bloody Mummers U
97 Burned Men C
98 Headsman C
99 Kingswood Bandit C
100 Stone Crows U
101 Sworn Brother U
102 White Sword Tower R
103 King's Gate R
104 Mountains of the Moon R
105 River Gate R
106 Training Grounds R
107 Balon's Rebellion R
108 Berserker Fury U
109 By Right of Succession C
110 Chaos in Conflict U
111 Crimson and Gold C
112 Guile U
113 Hail of Arrows C
114 Heart of the Stag R
115 House Arrest R
116 Inheritance R
117 Kings in the North U
118 Kingsmoot R
119 Last Defense of the North C
120 Lords of the Narrow Sea R
121 Massacre U
122 Muster U
123 Plunder C
124 Preparing for Winter R
125 Rise of the Kraken U
126 Risen from the Sea C
127 Safeguard R
128 Superior Claim C
129 Superior Politics C
130 Superior Tactics C
131 Swords and Sails U
132 The Lion's Cunning R
133 The Storm God's Wrath R
134 Tithe R
135 We Do Not Sow C
136 Blockade R
137 Building Orders U
138 Here to Serve U
139 Holding the Trident R
140 Longships of the Iron Fleet U
141 Noose and Swordpoint U
142 Political Disaster R
143 Power and Wealth R
144 The Red God's Blessing U
145 Valar Morghulis R

2003 Game of Thrones Ice and Fire

1 The Wolf King R
2 Loyalty C
3 Seal of the Wolf R
4 Ward U
5 Winterfell Watchtower U
6 Arya Stark U
7 Catelyn Stark U
8 Eddard Stark U
9 Jon Snow R
10 Sansa Stark R
11 Septa Mordane U
12 Horsemen of the North C
13 Host of Karhold R
14 House Tully Footsoldier C
15 Lookout C
16 Men of Greywater Watch U
17 Scouting Party C
18 Standard Bearer C
19 The Great Host R
20 Winterfell Reserves R
21 Karhold R
22 Bell Tower C
23 Guard's Hall C
24 Hunter's Gate C
25 Northern Reserves R
26 Sparring Yard U
27 Winterfell Alehouse U
28 Winterfell Heart Tree C
29 The Queen Regent R
30 Alleys and Whispers U
31 Being Watched C
32 Goldsmith C
33 Seal of the Lion R
34 Taken Hostage U
35 Cersei Lannister U
36 Joffrey Baratheon R
37 Ser Jaime Lannister U
38 The Tickler U
39 Tyrion Lannister U
40 Tywin Lannister R
41 Brothel Madam R
42 Castellan of Harrenhal R
43 Courtesan of Highgarden C
44 Host of Golden Tooth Keep C
45 House Marbrand Envoy C
46 Lanniport Moneylender C
47 Red Keep Guard C
48 Ser Stafford's Host U
49 Tax Collector R
50 Turncoat C
51 Casterly Rock U
52 Lord Tywin's Chambers R
53 Dangerous Mines C
54 Golden Gallery C
55 Golden Tooth Keep R
56 Sept of Lannisport U
57 The People's Favorite R
58 Called To Glory U
59 Gargoyle Sentinels U
60 Popularity C
61 Seal of the Stag R
62 Visited by Shadows C
63 Melisandre R
64 Patchface R
65 Renly Baratheon U
66 Robert Baratheon U
67 Ser Davos Seaworth R
68 Stannis Baratheon U
69 Bastard of Robert C
70 Galley Captain R
71 Herald of the Rose C
72 House Celtigar Emissary U
73 House Tactician R
74 Knight Commander C
75 Lord Renly's Host C
76 Maester of Dragonstone C
77 Pirate Crew U
78 Red Zealots C
79 Lord Stannis' Chambers R
80 Storm's End R
81 Dragonstone Courtyard C
82 Sea Dragon Tower C
83 Shipbreaker Bay U
84 Storm's End Battlements U
85 King of the Isles R
86 Salt King C
87 Seal of the Kraken R
88 Ship's Navigator U
89 Under Siege U
90 Aeron Damphair R
91 Asha Greyjoy U
92 Balon Greyjoy U
93 Euron Crow's Eye R
94 Theon Greyjoy U
95 Axemen of Old Wyk C
96 Drumbeater U
97 Harlaw Rebel C
98 Longship Navigator C
99 Maester of Harlaw C
100 Maester of Pyke R
101 Host of the Isles R
102 Oarsman C
103 Sea Raiders C
104 Seasoned Raider U
105 Longship of Pyke U
106 Isle of Pyke R
107 Lord Balon's Chambers R
108 Saltcliffe R
109 Longship Marauder C
110 Sea Bridge C
111 The Iron Mines U
112 The Sea Tower C
113 Mother of Dragons R
114 Annexed U

115 Blood of the Dragon U
116 Queen's Bounty C
117 Seal of the Dragon R
118 Black Hatchling C
119 Daario U
120 Daenerys Targaryen U
121 Drogon R
122 Green Hatchling C
123 Magister Illyrio R
124 Rhaegal R
125 Rhakaro U
126 Ser Barristan Selmy U
127 Viserion R
128 White Hatchling C
129 Dothraki Bowman C
130 Dothraki Chargers C
131 Freed Men U
132 Great Khalassar R
133 Meereenese Pit Fighter C
134 Slave Trader C
135 Illyrio's Estate R
136 Lady Daenerys' Chambers R
137 Daznak's Pit C
138 House of Warlocks C
139 Pentoshi Guildhall U
140 Qartheen Trader's Guild U
141 Hand of the King R
142 Bodyguard C
143 Court Advisor C
144 Court Messenger C
145 Court Soldier C
146 Benjen Stark R
147 Bronn U
148 Conn Son of Corrat U
149 Varys R
150 Ambassador of Red Keep U
151 Camp Follower C
152 King Robert's Hammer U
153 Jousting Knight U
154 King's Fool C
155 Raw Recruit C
156 Rumormonger C
157 Aegon's Hill R
158 The Sharp Point R
159 Harrenhal R
160 The Iron Throne R
161 Gate of Dragons U
162 Gate of the Gods U
163 Iron Gate U
164 King's Hall R
165 Lion Gate U
166 Old Gate U
167 The Roseroad C
168 The Searoad C
169 The Wall R
170 Training Grounds R
171 Arya's Whisper C
172 Concession U
173 Consumed by Flame C
174 Cut Supply Lines U
175 Dance with Dragons R
176 Denounced U
177 Fear Cuts Deeper than Swords C
178 Fleeting Loyalty U
179 Fortify R
180 The Eyrie R
181 Heed the Call! C
182 Humiliation C
183 Immolate C
184 Intimidate U
185 King's Man C
186 Kings of Salt and Rock R
187 Martyrdom R
188 Mummer's Farce C
189 Never Surrender! R
190 No Prisoners R
191 Nothing to Hide U
192 Only Thought Dead U
193 Distraction C
194 Pillage C
195 Put to the Sword C
196 Put to the Torch C
197 Relentless Attack R
198 Risen from the Sea C
199 Ruse R
200 Secrets of the North U
201 Calling the Reserves U
202 Surrender U
203 Tears of Lys C
204 Fire and Blood C
205 The Dragon's Rage R
206 The Horn that Wakes the Sleepers U
207 The Kings of Winter R
208 The Kraken Surfaces! C
209 The Lion Pounces! C
210 The Rains of Castemere R
211 The Spider's Web R
212 The Stag Charges! C
213 The Storm Kings U
214 The Walls Have Ears U
215 The Will of R'hllor U
216 The Wolf Howls! C
217 Treachery C
218 Veins of Gold U
219 Weathering the Storm R
220 Word of R'hllor R
221 Alliance
222 Blaze of Glory R
223 Building Orders U
224 Call to the Throne R
225 Catastrophe R
226 Clash of Kings
227 Dark Forces U
228 Filthy Accusations
229 Fleets of Dragonstone
230 Game of Thrones
231 Herding the Masses R
232 Royal Decree R
233 Longships of the Iron Fleet
234 Mad King's Legacy U
235 Marched to the Wall
236 Mining the Rock U
237 No More Games! R
238 Valar Morghulis R
239 Rank Upon Rank U
240 Reach of the Kraken U
241 Rushed Attack U
242 Secrets and Lies
243 Secure on the Throne R
244 Storm of Swords
245 Summons U
246 The Killing Cold R
247 Threat from the North U
248 Uneasy Peace R
249 Wardens of the North
250 Wildfire Assault U
251 Baratheon/Greyjoy Alliance
252 Lannister/Greyjoy Alliance
253 Lannister/Targaryen Alliance
254 Stark/Baratheon Alliance
255 Stark/Targaryen Alliance
256 House Baratheon
257 House Greyjoy
258 House Lannister
259 House Stark
260 House Targaryen

2003 Game of Thrones Ice and Fire Premium

G1 HOUSE GREYJOY
G2 Building Orders
G3 Here to Serve
G4 Longships of the Iron Fleet
G5 Rushed Attack
G6 The Tide Brings Home the Kraken
G7 Threat from the North
G8 Wildfire Assault
G9 Aeron Damphair
T1 HOUSE TARGARYEN
T2 Assault on King's Landing
T3 Filthy Accusations
T4 Game of Thrones
T5 Mad King's Legacy
T6 Noose and Swordpoint
T7 Outmaneuver
T8 Summons
T9 Black Hatchling
G10 Andrik the Unsmiling
G11 Anguy the Archer
G12 Asha Greyjoy
G13 Axemen of Old Wyk
G14 Balon Greyjoy
G15 Drowned Zealot
G16 Drumbeater
G17 Initiate of the Citadel
G18 Looters
G19 Maester of Harlaw
G20 Master of Oldtown
G21 Maester Wendamyr
G22 Septon of the Isles
G23 Ship's Bosun
G24 The Mad Huntsman
G25 Theon Greyjoy
G26 Victarion Greyjoy
G27 Bloody Keep
G28 Gatehouse
G29 Longship "Black Wind"
G30 Longship "Great Kraken"
G31 Longship "Silence"
G32 Longship Raider
G33 The Sea Tower
G34 The Sea Tower
G35 The Sea Tower
G36 Tower of Pyke
G37 Conquer
G38 Court Messenger
G39 Court Soldier
G40 Drowned God's Blessing
G41 Support of Harlaw
G42 Kiss of the Red God
G43 Massacre
G44 Recovery
G45 Rise of the Kraken
G46 Risen from the Sea
G47 Superior Claim
G48 Superior Tactics
G49 Tithe
G50 We Do Not Sow
T10 Danaerys Targaryen
T11 Dothraki Bowman
T12 Dothraki Horselord
T13 Drogon
T14 Green Hatchling
T15 Handmaid
T16 Khal Drogo
T17 Knight of Flowers
T18 Ser Barristan Selmy
T19 Ser Boros Blount
T20 Ser Mandon Moore
T21 Ser Meryn Trant
T22 Slave Trader
T23 Sworn Brother
T24 The Unsullied
T25 Vargo Hoat
T26 Viserys Targaryen
T27 White Hatchling
T28 Daznak's Pit
T29 Daznak's Pit
T30 Daznak's Pit
T31 Great Pyramid
T32 House of Warlocks
T33 Quartheen Bazaar
T34 Qartheen Trader's Guild
T35 Temple of the Graces
T36 Vaes Dothrak
T37 Arakh
T38 Blood of the Dragon
T39 Bloodrider
T40 Court Advisor
T41 Unburnt
T42 Denounced
T43 Fire from the Skies
T44 Immolate
T45 Muster
T46 Perished in Flame
T47 Price of Failure
T48 Put to the Torch
T49 Superior Politics
T50 Whirlwind Assault

2003 Game of Thrones Throne of Blades

1 Ghost R
2 Grey Wind R
3 Lady U
4 Nymeria U
5 Summer R
6 Mark of the Wolf C
7 Ser Edmure Tully U
8 The Blackfish R
9 Ambassador of the Wolf U
10 House Tully Knight C
11 Kennel Master R
12 Knight of the Red Fork C
13 Septon of Winterfell C
14 Riverrun R
15 The Iron Throne U
16 Woods of the North C
17 Ford on the Trident C
18 Winterfell Kennels U
19 Heavy Taxes R
20 Ridicule C
21 Raff the Sweetling U
22 The Hound R
23 Ambassador of the Lion U
24 Corrupt Councilman C
25 Envoy of Highgarden R
26 Footmen of the Reach C
27 Gossiping Bard R
28 House Herald U
29 Highborn U
30 Lurkers at Harrenhal R
31 Septon of Lannisport C
32 Council Bureaucrat U
33 The Iron Throne U
34 Deep Ore Vein C
35 Secret Passage C
36 Street of Splendor R
37 Ever Vigilant C
38 The Dragon's Mouth U
39 True King C
40 Knight of Flowers R
41 Ambassador of the Stag U
42 Celtigar Bannerman C
43 House Celtigar Retainer R
44 Masked Sorceress U
45 Mistress of Shadows R
46 Red Devotee C
47 Royal Guard U
48 Septon of Dragonstone C
49 Soldier of the Light R
50 Pyre of the False Gods R
51 The Iron Throne U
52 Gates of Storm's End C
53 Estates of Highgarden U
54 Trade Port R
55 Discretion U
56 Heart of Iron C
57 Naval Tactician R
58 Dagmer Cleftjaw R
59 Ambassador of the Kraken U
60 Deep Sea Buccaneers C
61 Drowned Convert U
62 Great Axe Warrior R
63 Grizzled Shiphand C
64 Iron Raiders U
65 Privateer R
66 Saltcliffe Captain C
67 Septon of Pyke C
68 The Iron Throne U
69 Destroyer Fleet R
70 Flagship C
71 Salt Mines R
72 Straits of Blazewater Bay U
73 Blood of my Blood U
74 Khal R
75 Khaleesi's Favor C
76 Grey Worm R
77 Quaithe of the Shadow R
78 Ambassador of the Dragon U
79 Dothraki Screamers C
80 Eastern Mercenary U
81 Pureborn C
82 Qartheen Cutpurse C
83 Servitors of the Thirteen U
84 Thundering Cavalry R
85 Warlock of Qarth R
86 Balerion R
87 The Iron Throne U
88 City of Bones C
89 Graveyard of the Gods C
90 House of the Undying U
91 Lordship C
92 Power Behind the Throne U
93 Scroll and Seal U
94 High Septon R
95 Janos Slynt U
96 Maester Aemon R
97 Yoren R
98 Disgraced Lordling C
99 Lord Tyrion's Host U
100 Mountain Warriors U
101 Petty Noble C
102 Ranging Party C
103 Septon of King's Landing C
104 Great Sept of Baelor R
105 The Red Keep R
106 The Shadow Tower R
107 Jousting Arena U
108 Crushing Victory C
109 Cutting the Braid U
110 Dark Prophecy R
111 Famine R
112 Funeral Pyre C
113 Insult to Injury C
114 Lightning Raid C
115 Maester's Conclave U
116 Oath of the Drowned God R
117 Sorefoot King R
118 Ours is the Old Way U
119 Overwhelming Numbers C
120 Peace Envoys U
121 Prosperity and Plenty C
122 Rally to the Throne R
123 Rampage R
124 Show of Strength R
125 King's Gallows U
126 Starve them Out! C
127 Mining U
128 The Gold Price C
129 The Iron Price U
130 The Seven's Blessing U
131 The Sword in the Darkness U
132 Thrown to the Wolves R
133 Trickery R
134 Turning the Tide U
135 Twisting the Blade R
136 Valiant Protector C
137 Wedding Gift C
138 Against the Common Foe R
139 Forced March R
140 Fortified Position U
141 Plans within Plans U
142 Rule by Decree U
143 Spending the Winter Stores U
144 Stalemate R
145 The Others are Massing R

2003 Game of Thrones Wildling Assault

WA1 Mance Rayder
WA2 Lord of Bones
WA3 Wildling Tent
WA4 Mammoth
WA5 Giant
WA6 Wildling Horde
WA7 Wildling

2004 Game of Thrones Crown of Suns

1 Hunted C
2 Frostbite U
3 Maege Mormont R
4 Robb Stark R
5 Castellan of Winterfell R
6 Direwolf Pup C
7 Dreadfort Turncloaks U
8 Footmen of Bear Island C
9 Host of the Bear R
10 Riverrun Messenger C
11 Wild Hare U
12 Forgotten Path U
13 Littlefinger's Advice C
14 Power of the Message R
15 Myrcella Lannister R
16 Ser Amory Lorch R
17 Ambitious Sellsword U
18 Gregor's Dogs C
19 Impulsive Lordling C
20 Marching Dogs U
21 Mummer Troupe C
22 War Profiteer U
23 Lord Tywin's Hall R
24 Coin Mint U
25 Shadow's Blessing U
26 Edric Storm R
27 Herald of Storm's End C
28 Pirate of the Stormlands U
29 Priestess of the Light C
30 Renly's Reserves R
31 Ser Axell's Guard C
32 Sorceress' Shadow U
33 True Believers R
34 Vanguard of the Rose C
35 The Valyrian R
36 Dragonstone Vault U
37 Bad Seed R
38 Gone Soft U
39 Brigand of Old Wyk U
40 Doomed Longshipman C
41 Euron's Crew C
42 Ward of Pyke U
43 Kingsmoot Candidate U
44 Storm Raiders R
45 Watchers of Ten Towers C
46 Longship "Iron Victory" R
47 Kingsmoot Grounds R
48 Treacherous Shoals C
49 Breaker of Shackles R
50 Under Their Shadow R
51 Aggo U
52 Xaro Xhoan Daxos R
53 Agent in Westeros U
54 Horseback Archers C
55 Lecherous Suitor U
56 Qartheen Fanatic C
57 Shadow Conjurer C
58 Slavemasters U
59 Warriors with Braids Uncut C
60 Young Ko R
61 Attainted C
62 Condemned C
63 Imprisoned C
64 Seal of the Sun R
65 Student of the Viper R
66 War Spear U
67 Areo Hotah R
68 Arianne Martell U
69 Ellaria Sand U
70 Nymeria Sand U
71 Obara Sand U
72 Doran Martell R
73 The Red Viper R
74 Greenblood Trader U
75 Handmaiden of Sunspear C
76 Host of Sunspear R
77 Host of Yronwood C
78 House Dayne Knight C
79 House Messenger C
80 Maester of Sunspear R
81 Nymeria Sand's Entourage C
82 Riders of the Boneway U
83 Spearmaiden U
84 Ghaston Grey U
85 Sunspear U
86 The Old Palace R
87 The Spear Tower R
88 Tower of the Sun R
89 Palace Fountains C
90 Water Gardens C
91 House Martell C
92 Martell/Targaryen Alliance C
93 Martell/Stark Alliance C
94 Bastard C
95 Enforced Loyalty R
96 Alayaya R
97 Ser Arys Oakheart R
98 Emissary of the Red Keep R
99 Errand Boy U
100 Fawning Courtier C
101 Merchant of Whispers U
102 Queen's Assassin C
103 Bandit Lord R
104 Watcher in the Walls C
105 Market Street C
106 Overcrowded Boroughs R
107 Small Council Chamber U
108 Blood for Blood C
109 Bran the Builder's Legacy U
110 By Force of Surprise C
111 Call Their Bluff U
112 Fifty Four Turns R
113 Greater Glory Calls U
114 In Robert's Servitude U
115 Infiltrate U
116 Lord Tywin's Cunning C
117 Make Haste! C
118 Narrow Escape U
119 Naval Superiority R
120 Nightfire R
121 No Good Deed Goes Unpunished R
122 Open Intrigues U
123 Pariah C
124 Ambush from the Plains C
125 Preemptive Vengeance R
126 Promise Me... R
127 Quit their Claim R
128 Ravage U
129 Scorpions in your Bed U
130 Spirited Charge U
131 The Bear and the Maiden Fair R
132 The Viper's Bite C
133 Their Betrayal Runs Deep R
134 Unbowed, Unbent, Unbroken C
135 Vengeance for Elia! R
136 What is Dead Cannot Die C
137 Young Wolf's Justice C
138 Attend the King U
139 Building Contract U
140 Burning Bridges U
141 Nothing Left to Lose R
142 Personal Vendettas R
143 Recruiting Season R
144 To the Spears! R
145 Violent Storms U

2004 Game of Thrones Tourney of Swords

1 Blue Steel Dirk R
2 Chestnut Courser U
3 On Arya's List C
4 Sansa's Favor C
5 Greatjon Umber R
6 Jory Cassel U
7 The Smalljon U
8 Knight of the Blue Fork C
9 Knight of the Green Fork R
10 Master of Shackles C
11 Northern Champion U
12 Trident Defender C
13 Umber Reinforcements R
14 Practice Yard U
15 Winterfell Tourney Grounds R
16 Cersei's Favor C
17 Enthralled C
18 Ill-Tempered Destrier U
19 The Strangler R
20 Ser Meryn Trant U
21 Archery Champion C
22 Court Retainer C

23 Gregor's Retainer R
24 Last-Minute Entrant R
25 Queen's Champion U
26 Tavern Braggart C
27 Vigilant Watchman U
28 Lannisport Tourney Grounds R
29 Perfectly Respectable Inn U
30 Waiting Area R
31 Ancestral Sword R
32 Crowd-Pleaser U
33 Mare In Heat U
34 Margaery's Favor C
35 Offer of Pardon C
36 Servant of R'hllor R
37 Knight of Flowers U
38 Ser Emmon Cuy U
39 Ser Guyard Morrigen R
40 Ser Parmen Crane U
41 Bearer of the Light C
42 Fair-Weather Knight R
43 Tourney Knight C
44 Vanguard Lancer C
45 Storm's End Tourney Grounds R
46 Asha's Contempt C
47 Practiced Disdain U
48 Wild Garron U
49 Torch and Oil R
50 Andrik the Unsmiling U
51 The Knight R
52 Assassin of Pyke C
53 Berserk Axeman C
54 Champion of Pyke U
55 Sneaking Cutthroat R
56 Warrior of the Old Way C
57 Banner Ship C
58 Proving Grounds R
59 Stormy Coastline R
60 Swift Reinforcements U
61 Ancient Arakh R
62 Plains Rider R
63 Black Charger U
64 Daenerys' Favor C
65 Fleeing the Flames C
66 Dothraki Scout U
67 Dragonbone Archer C
68 Hired Guards C
69 Killer of the Wounded R
70 Meereen Champion U
71 Pentoshi Mercenaries C
72 Pike Phalanx U
73 Sworn Defender R
74 Meereen Tourney Grounds R
75 Myrish Villa U
76 Desert Palfrey U
77 Double-Pointed Spear R
78 Ellaria's Favor C
79 Poisoned Javelin U
80 Seduced by Arianne C
81 Darkstar U
82 Doran Martell U
83 Champion of Starfall R
84 Corrupt Disciple C
85 Deadly Lover R
86 Dornish Cavalier C
87 Master of the Spear U
88 Southron Skirmisher C
89 Sunspear Tourney Grounds R
90 The Boneway R
91 Behind the White Shield U
92 Mystery Knight C
93 Silver Link Attained U
94 The Queen's Seal C
95 Beric Dondarrion U
96 Ser Barristan Selmy R
97 Ser Jaime Lannister R
98 Ser Osmund Kettleblack U
99 Ser Preston Greenfield U
100 Thoros of Myr R
101 Newly-Chained Maester C
102 Tourney Equipment Boy C
103 Tourney Magistrate C
104 The Red Keep R
105 Tourney Office U
106 Harrenhal Tourney Grounds R
107 King's Pavilion R
108 Any Knight can Make a Knight R
109 Archery Contest C
110 Claim of the South C
111 Defend the Innocent C
112 Dracarys! U
113 For Casterly Rock! U
114 For Lyanna! U
115 For the Drowned God! U
116 For Winterfell! U
117 Guard the King's Secrets C
118 I Am But a Woman C
119 Jousting Contest C
120 Kill them All C
121 Littlefinger's Meddling R
122 Looking for Rubies U
123 Massed Charge C
124 Melee Contest C
125 Melted Down and Reforged R
126 Obey the King C
127 Queen of Love and Beauty R
128 Resort to Cheating R
129 See who is Stronger R
130 The Dragon Does Not Fear R
131 The Wealth of the Isles R
132 Tourney Season U
133 Trial by Battle U
134 Vengeance! U
135 Wolf King's Charge R
136 You Murdered Her Children R
137 Your Life for His... U
138 All Eyes on the Contest U
139 Blood Will Tell R
140 Grand Melee R
141 The Art of Seduction R
142 Tourney Duel R
143 Your Reputation Precedes You U
144 Knights of the Realm U
145 The Kingsguard U

2005 Game of Thrones Reign of Kings

1 Crown of Winter R
2 Guardians of the North C
3 Sworn Duty U
4 Robb Stark R
5 Child Heir R
6 Crannogmen of the Neck U
7 Feral Direwolf C
8 Greatjon's Cousin U
9 Knight of the Rills U
10 Riverland Horseman C
11 Robb's Cavalry R
12 Stark Councilor U
13 Winterfell Guardsman C
14 Throne of Winterfell R
15 Weirwood Grove C
16 Crown of Seven Kingdoms R
17 Ser Ilyn Payne R
18 A Way with Words C
19 Watched Too Closely U
20 Joffrey Baratheon R
21 Ser Kevan Lannister R
22 Cersei's Pawn C
23 Lannisport Merchant U
24 Lannister Councilor U
25 Master of Whisperers U
26 Red Keep Servant R
27 Scholar of Intrigues C
28 Scholar of Poisons C
29 Andal Monument C
30 Cersei's Bedchamber U
31 Crown of Azor Ahai R
32 Alliance with Highgarden R
33 Born to be King U
34 Burning Heart Tunic C
35 Salladhor Saan U
36 Stannis Baratheon R
37 Baratheon Councilor U
38 House Florent Convert U
39 King's Scribe C
40 Knight of Summer C
41 Shadow Army C
42 Sister of the Flames R
43 Throne of Dragonstone R
44 Blackwater Bay U
45 Boar Hunting Grounds C
46 Crown of Pyke R
47 Sign of the Kraken C
48 Son of the Sea Wind U
49 Balon Greyjoy R
50 Dagmer Cleftjaw U
51 Boarding Party C
52 Balon's Follower U
53 Greyjoy Councilor U
54 Asha Greyjoy C
55 Black Wind's Crew R
56 Thrice-Drowned Veteran C
57 The Seastone Chair R
58 Saltwater Cape R
59 Cliffs of the Sea God U
60 Island Transport C
61 Crown of Meereen R
62 Illyrio's Loyalty R
63 Under the Guild's Sway R
64 Wisdom of the East C
65 Daenerys Targaryen R
66 Astapori Guildmaster U
67 Bejeweled Assassin C
68 Dragon-Worshipper R
69 Drogo's Bloodrider U
70 Naathi Handmaiden C
71 Targaryen Councilor U
72 Targaryen Loyalist C
73 Throne of Meereen R
74 Meereen Audience Chamber C
75 Worm River U
76 Crown of Sunspear R
77 Arianne's Suitor U
78 Arrogance of Dorne C
79 Herald of Sunspear R
80 Tyene Sand U
81 Dornish Princeling U
82 Jealous Paramour C
83 Martell Councilor U
84 Dornish Outcast C
85 Spiteful Bastard C
86 Maiden of Starfall R
87 Throne of Sunspear R
88 Blood Orange Grove C
89 Rhoynar Monument R
90 Scorching Deserts U
91 Hand of the King R
92 Blood Ties U
93 Master of Coin C
94 Protector of the Realm C
95 Littlefinger R
96 Varys R
97 Black Walder U
98 Roslin Frey R
99 Frey Lordling C
100 Ulf Son of Umar C
101 Keeper of the Seven U
102 Tyrion's Bodyguard C
103 Conn Son of Corrat U
104 Flea Bottom R
105 The Iron Throne R
106 House Crypt U
107 Heart Tree Grove U
108 A King's Blood U
109 Burn and Pillage C
110 Tyrion's Cunning U
111 Hidden Poison U
112 Public Execution R
113 The Truth Revealed R
114 Twist of Fate C
115 A Deadly Game U
116 Avenge the Princess C
117 Blood and Glory U
118 Conflicting Orders C
119 Contempt for the Weak U
120 Coronation Ceremony R
121 Enforce the Law C
122 Hidden in the Crypt U
123 Melisandre's Sermon U
124 Glory of R'hllor R
125 Promise the World C
126 Terrorize the Shores U
127 Punish the Guilty C
128 Swing the Sword C
129 Taking Credit C
130 Balon's Edict C
131 Two Steps Ahead U
132 Wrath of the Dragon R
133 Wrath of the Kraken R
134 Wrath of the Lion R
135 Wrath of the Stag R
136 Wrath of the Sun R
137 Wrath of the Wolf R
138 Wardens of the East R
139 Wardens of the North R
140 Wardens of the South R
141 Wardens of the West R
142 The Small Council U
143 The War of Five Kings U
144 Heir to the Iron Throne U

2005 Game of Thrones Song of Twilight

1 Grey Wind R
2 Lady R
3 Nymeria U
4 Summer R
5 Trident Reinforcements C
6 Aemon's Correspondant C
7 Edmure's Van C
8 Grim Defender U
9 Sullen Recruit U
10 Icy Moat U
11 Mole Town Brothel R
12 Reinforced Walls C
13 Gold for Bribes R
14 In Love with Cersei C
15 Podrick Payne R
16 Ser Jacelyn Bywater R
17 Frey Outrider C
18 Cersei's Attendant U
19 Exiled Asshai Courtesan U
20 Kingsroad Merchant Master U
21 Sacrificial Envoy C
22 Slynt's Man C
23 Lannisport Archives U
24 Undefended Port R
25 Devan Seaworth R
26 Edric Storm R
27 The Lord's Assassin C
28 Blackwater Captain U
29 Guardsman of the Arbor C
30 Robert's Squire U
31 Stannis's Cavalry C
32 Stannis's Personal Guard U
33 Caverns of Storm's End R
34 Crackclaw Point Tower R
35 Melisandre's Garden C
36 Salladhor's Merchant Vessel U
37 Gevin Harlaw R
38 Stygg R
39 Sea God's Disciple C
40 Balon's Retainer U
41 Bay of Ice Buccaneers C
42 Cotter Pyke's Men U
43 Euron's Servant U
44 Seagard Looter C
45 Damphair's Chambers C
46 Fjords of Ironman's Bay R
47 Goodbrother Interceptor U
48 Pyke Drydocks R
49 Festering Wound C
50 Horse Whip U
51 Ser Jorah's Storybooks R
52 Brown Ben Plumm R
53 Haggo R
54 Qotho R
55 Blue-Lipped Warlock C
56 Bloodthirsty Khal U
57 Dany's Handmaiden U
58 Minor Khalasar C
59 Narrow Sea Trader C
60 Westerosi Informant U
61 Delicate Stomach C
62 Hooked Spear R
63 Vainglorious U
64 Darkstar R
65 Nymeria Sand R
66 Son of the Red Viper C
67 Doran's Honor Guard C
68 Far-Seeing Scholar U
69 House Dayne Skirmisher C
70 Oberyn's Lover U
71 Prince's Loyalist U
72 Remote Oasis R
73 First Ranger U
74 Longclaw R
75 Lord of Harrenhal U
76 War Band Leader U
77 Black Raven C
78 Court Counsel C
79 War Counsel C
80 Bone Axe R
81 Allyn Crowkiller R
82 Craster U
83 Dalla U
84 Donal Noye R
85 Grenn U
86 Harma Dogshead R
87 Jarmen Buckwell R
88 Maester Aemon U
89 Ryk "Longspear" R
90 Samwell Tarly R
91 Thoren Smallwood R
92 Tormund Giantsbane R
93 Blackmailing Servant C
94 Bringer of Ill Tidings U
95 Harbringer of Woes U
96 Ranger Scout C
97 The Stranger's Septon C
98 Vanguard Herald U
99 Wandering Crow C
100 Wildling Rabble C
101 Young Spearwife C
102 Craster's Keep R
103 Westwatch-by-the-Bridge R
104 Bay of Ice R
105 Camps on the Milkwater U
106 Greywater Swamp C
107 Oxcross U
108 Stronghold on the Wall U
109 The Frozen Shore C
110 My Life for Conquest R
111 My Life for Honor R
112 My Life for Justice R
113 My Life for Love R
114 My Life for the Lord R
115 My Life for Vengeance R
116 As Sunlight Fades C
117 Cracks in the Wall U
118 Crumbled to Dust R
119 Grisly Resurrection U
120 Hope Fades with Twilight R
121 I Am a Bloodthirsty Man U
122 Kill the Crows! C
123 King Balon's Command C
124 King Robert's Command C
125 Last Battle at the Wall R
126 Lord Eddard's Command C
127 Massing at Twilight C
128 Prince Doran's Command C
129 Queen Cersei's Command C
130 Queen Daenerys's Command C
131 Straw Men U
132 Take Off Your Collars! U
133 The Crow is a Tricksy Bird U
134 The Others Take Your Honor! U
135 The Pack Survives U
136 The Watch Has Need! C
137 There Are No Men Like Me U
138 This is the Season! U
139 Twilight Brings Hope R
140 Wraiths in the Midst R
141 Defenders of the Realm R
142 Wildling Assault R
143 The Wildling Horde U
144 Threat from the East U
145 Defenders of the North U

2006 Game of Thrones House of Thorns

1 Chipped Poleaxe C
2 In Eddard's Name U
3 Donella Hornwood R
4 Rickard Karstark U
5 Dreadfort Sentinels C
6 Flayer of Men R
7 Karhold Master at Arms C
8 The Bastard's Recruits U
9 Ramparts of Winterfell R
10 Tywin Lannister R
11 In Robert's Name U
12 Support of the King C
13 Selyse Baratheon U
14 Ser Axell's Man C
15 Sister of Fire R
16 Blockade Runner R
17 Driftwood Cudgel C
18 Hooked Trident R
19 Invoking the Kraken U
20 Maester Wendamyr U
21 Grey Garden Master-at-Arms R
22 House Harlaw Tactician C
23 Ironborn Raiders U
24 Island Defenders R
25 Pirate of Pyke C
26 Saltwater Scholar C
27 Veteran Looters U
28 Shatterstone R
29 Horseback Discipline R
30 Horselord's Bow C
31 In Drogo's Name U
32 Magister Illyrio U
33 Xaro Xoan Daxos R
34 Dothraki Guide U
35 Dothraki Youth C
36 Poison Merchant R
37 Scavenger of the Free Cities C
38 Seeker from the Shadow C
39 Pentoshi Palace U
40 Vaes Tolorro R
41 In Oberyn's Name U
42 Polished Longaxe C
43 Reckless R
44 Quentyn Martell R
45 Tyene Sand U
46 Belated Messenger U
47 Guardian of the Way U
48 House Dayne Courier C
49 Lord Anders' Honor Guard R
50 Maester at Yronwood C
51 Oldtown Apprentice R
52 Vigilant Dornishman C
53 Banner of the Rose C
54 Favorite Among Favorites U
55 Heat Exhaustion C
56 Protection of Highgarden U
57 Rose Perfume C
58 Seduced by the Rose R
59 Sun Stroke R
60 Butterbumps U
61 Knight of Flowers U
62 Mace Tyrell U
63 Margaery Tyrell R
64 The Queen of Thorns R
65 Reek U
66 Roose Bolton U
67 Ser Garlan Tyrell U
68 Steelshanks Walton R
69 The Bastard of Bolton R
70 Willas Tyrell U
71 Summer Sea Brigands R
72 Bringers of Dread C
73 Seeress of Shadows U
74 Highgarden's Finest R
75 House Tyrell Bannermen R
76 House Tyrell Envoy C
77 Knight of the Reach C
78 Men of the Mander C
79 Purposeful Imposters C
80 Roseroad Watchmen C
81 Selfless Scoundrels C
82 Trader on Ironman's Bay R
83 Highgarden R
84 The Dreadfort R
85 The Pleasure Barges U
86 The Weeping Water U
87 Home Ground C
88 Olenna's Study U
89 Rose Garden C
90 Secluded Coast C
91 The Shield Islands R
92 Rusted Sword C
93 Declaration of War U
94 Allegiance U
95 Left R
96 Ramsey's Betrothed R
97 Right R
98 False Septon U
99 Courier Captain R
100 Dreadfort Defender C
101 Garden Caretaker C
102 Keeper of Oaths U
103 Septon of the Shadows C
104 Unorthodox Priest R
105 Wardens of the Reach U
106 Decadent Brothel C
107 Homeland Fiefdom U
108 Mander Ford R
109 A Web of Thorns R
110 Breaking the Siege C
111 Choke R
112 Deception C
113 Dothraki Fury C
114 Edict of the Prince R
115 Endless Ambition R
116 Fleeting Restoration R
117 Hefty Tariff U
118 Hidden Chambers U
119 Holding Tactics R
120 Invocation of Birth C
121 Olenna's Cunning R
122 Opportunistic Thrust U
123 Preemptive Politics C
124 Put to the Question R
125 Resolve of the Kraken C
126 Roles Reversed C
127 Supernatural Supplication C
128 Taxing the Poor R
129 Terminal Schemes C
130 The Rich Get Richer C
131 Trip to the Market R
132 Ulterior Motive U
133 Warden of the South U
134 Shadows and Spiders U
135 Growing Strong U
136 Scouring the Vaults U
137 Winter Storm U
138 Waste Their Time R
139 Roadblock R
140 Final Sacrifice R

2006 Game of Thrones Song of Night

1 High Treason R
2 Many Leeches C
3 Hodor R
4 Osha R
5 Ser Rodrik Cassel U
6 Dreadfort Captain U
7 Greywater Watchmen U
8 Riverriders C
9 Robb's Sworn Swords R
10 Chained Defenders C
11 Followers of the Wolf C
12 The White Knife U
13 Deepwood Motte R
14 Swamps of the Neck U
15 Icefields C
16 A Better Offer R
17 Obsessed with Power C

18 Varys' Advice C
19 Bronn U
20 Grand Maester Pycelle R
21 Ser Adam Marbrand R
22 Bronn's Retainer C
23 Defender of King's Landing R
24 House Brax Footmen U
25 Lion Lord C
26 Master of Spies U
27 Horde of the Halfman C
28 Fair Isle U
29 Shores of the Blackwater R
30 Shores of the Tumblestone U
31 Oathkeeper R
32 Fate Accepted C
33 The Bastard of Nightsong R
34 Ser Axel Florent U
35 Army of Light R
36 Faithless Follower C
37 Ser Garlan's Batallion C
38 Keeper of the Stag C
39 Stannis' Northern Cavalry C
40 Traitorous Lord U
41 Cape Wrath U
42 Mouth of the Blackwater R
43 Command Tent R
44 Fields of Storm's End U
45 Sallador's Escort C
46 Blessed by Iron C
47 Allanys Greyjoy U
48 Captain Bluetooth R
49 Asha's Raiders U
50 Cleftjaw's Pillagers C
51 Damphair's Followers R
52 Drowned Marauder U
53 Euron's Advisor R
54 Goodbrother's Recruit C
55 King Euron's Horde R
56 Kraken Conquerors C
57 Isle of Orkmont U
58 Torrhen's Keep R
59 Blacktyde Longship C
60 The Stony Shore U
61 Courted by Xaro C
62 Aggo R
63 Oznak zo Pahl U
64 The Titan's Bastard R
65 Braavosi Pirates R
66 Gutter Child C
67 Partisan of the Dragon C
68 Grey Worm's Strongest R
69 Illyrio's Guard U
70 Qartheen Tax Collector U
71 The Freed Folk C
72 Fields of Ghiscar R
73 Gates of Meereen U
74 Lyseni Trade Cog C
75 New Ghis U
76 Of Oberyn's Blood R
77 Taste of Blood C
78 Edric Dayne R
79 Harmen Uller U
80 Dornish Confessor C
81 Rider of Starfall U
82 Lord Yronwood's Spears C
83 Prince Doran's Advisor C
84 Champion of the Sun C
85 Standard Bearer of the Viper R
86 Tower Guard R
87 The Dornish Marches R
88 Scars of the Boneway U
89 The Winding Wall C
90 The Triple Gate U
91 Dragonglass Dagger U
92 Savior of Westeros U
93 Coldhands R
94 Cotter Pyke R
95 Denys Mallister R
96 Terrible Crow C
97 Fickle Merchant R
98 Mance's Men C
99 Ravens from the Wall C
100 Force of the Watch R
101 Ranger's Vanguard C
102 Ser Waymar Royce U
103 Small Paul U
104 Mad Doomsayer U
105 Fist of the First Men R
106 Land of Perpetual Winter U
107 Gorge in the Frostfangs U
108 The Haunted Forest C
109 Skirling Pass R
110 Against the Nameless Other U
111 Azor Ahai Reborn C
112 Baratheon at the Wall U
113 Dark Fate U
114 Death from the Mists C
115 Rejected R
116 Hold Out! C
117 Returned from Winter's Claws C
118 Greyjoy at the Wall U
119 He Calls It Thinking C
120 I Vowed It Thrice C
121 I Am You Writ Small C
122 Justice has been Served R
123 Lannister at the Wall U
124 Martell at the Wall U
125 Mother Have Mercy R
126 No One Can Defend the North R
127 Risen from the Cold U
128 Show Trial R
129 Stark at the Wall U
130 Mind this, Nuncle C
131 Targaryen at the Wall U
132 A Feast for Crows R
133 The Last Night is Near R
134 The Long Night Awakens R
135 The Power of Blood R
136 These are my Children C
137 They Cannot Pass C
138 Through the Wall U
139 That's what Kings are For R
140 The Cold Grasp of Death U
141 Feast or Famine R
142 Flee to the Wall U
143 Summon the Realm U
144 Sacrificed to the Others R
145 The First Snow of Winter R

2007 Game of Thrones House of Talons

1 Vale Pact R
2 Wolfswood Ranger C
3 Catelyn Stark U
4 The Blackfish R
5 Alayne Stone U
6 Northern Minstrel R
7 Riverland Mob U
8 The Bastard's Host C
9 Umber Bannerman C
10 Siege Tower R
11 Dreadfort Dungeon U
12 Tyrion's Revenge R
13 Red Hand C
14 Crawn Son of Calor U
15 Gunthor Son of Gurn U
16 Timett Son of Timett R
17 Tyrion Lannister R
18 Tribes of the Vale C
19 The Inn at the Crossroads U
20 Vale Pact R
21 Stannis's Ambition C
22 Ser Robar Royce R
23 Maester Pylos U
24 The Red Queen's Host C
25 Visiting Dignitary U
26 Hallowed Ground U
27 The Rainwood R
28 Vale Pact R
29 Dagmer Cleftjaw R
30 Defiant Sister C
31 Dowered Daughter U
32 Fleet of the Isles C
33 Galley Thralls U
34 Sharp-Eyed Lookout R
35 Student of the Higher Mysteries U
36 Longship "Sea Song" R
37 Crow's Nest C
38 Derelict Hulk U
39 Vale Pact R
40 Under the Dragon's Wing C
41 Viserys's Arrogance U
42 Captain Groleo U
43 Daario Naharis R
44 Braavosi Harbormaster R
45 Dismounted Longbowmen C
46 Jorah's Cohorts C
47 Traveling Jeweler U
48 True Queen's Harbinger U
49 Drogo's Pyre R
50 Dawn U
51 Vale Pact R
52 Doran Martell R
53 Coastal Trader R
54 Displaced Dornishman U
55 Dornish Reserves C
56 Nomadic Harlot U
57 Soldier of Starfall C
58 Wandering Tutor U
59 The Prince's Pass R
60 The Vaith C
61 Conflicted Conscience C
62 Obsidian Dragon U
63 Brothel Guard U
64 Shadow Child C
65 Eyrie Bowman C
66 Guardian of the Motte U
67 Maritime Sneakthief R
68 Nan's Ghost C
69 Salty's Shadow C
70 Sellsword Company R
71 Vale Ward R
72 Wandering Holy Man R
73 The Saltspear U
74 The Stepstones U
75 Woods of the Vale R
76 Behind the Walls U
77 Bowl of Brown U
78 Defender of the Vale C
79 Incognito U
80 Mountain Mule C
81 Sky Cell R
82 Ghost of High Heart R
83 Littlefinger R
84 Lysa Arryn U
85 Maester Colemon U
86 Marillion U
87 Mord U
88 Nestor Royce R
89 Robert Arryn R
90 Rorge R
91 Ser Vardis Egen U
92 Bronze Yohn Royce R
93 Despotic Steward U
94 Granary Overseer C
95 Guardian of the Bloody Gate C
96 High Road Patrol U
97 Knights of the Vale U
98 Lord Jon's Man C
99 Lords' Declarant Bannermen C
100 Septon at the Eyrie C
101 Vale Lordling C
102 The Eyrie R
103 The Moon Door R
104 The Vale of Arryn U
105 Forgotten Dungeon U
106 The Flint Cliffs R
107 The Riverroad R
108 The Sea of Dorne R
109 Vale Granary C
110 Waycastle C
111 Allies of Necessity C
112 Aloof and Apart R
113 Closeted Learning C
114 Contemplated Engagement C
115 Fate and Foresight R
116 Feed It to the Goats U
117 Fled to the Vale C
118 From East and West C
119 Gathering of the Clans R
120 Lion in a Cage U
121 Make Him Fly! C
122 On the Sly U
123 Split Loyalties U
124 Stocking the Summer Seat C
125 Easily Misled C
126 Summer Storm U
127 Tales of Immortality U
128 Temporary Disgrace U
129 That's Worth Another Kiss R
130 The Hard Truth C
131 The Power of Deceit R
132 The Power of Fear R
133 The Power of Honor R
134 The Shield That Guards R
135 As High as Honor U
136 Kings of Mountain and Vale U
137 Our Mountain, Our Goat R
138 Prove One's Worth R
139 Trial by Battle U
140 Wardens of the East R

2008 Game of Thrones Ancient Enemies

21 Ten Towers
22 Areo Hotah
23 Die for Your King!
24 Questioned Claim
25 Fury of the Wolf
26 Fury of the Lion
27 Fury of the Stag
28 Fury of the Kraken
29 Fury of the Dragon
30 Fury of the Sun
31 Bear Island
32 Turncloak Mercenaries
33 Toll Gate
34 King's Champion
35 Drowned Prophet
36 Salt Wife
37 Dragon Thief
38 Dragon Bite
39 Field Spikes
40 Bringers of Law

2008 Game of Thrones Change of Seasons

41 The Long Winter
42 Taxed Dry
43 Burning Sword
44 The Long Summer
45 Demon's Dance
46 Shadow Stalker
47 Wintertime Marauders
48 Theon Greyjoy
49 Maester Aemon
50 Southron Scavengers
51 Walder Frey
52 Secret Hideout
53 The Lion's Law
54 Vigilant Stag
55 Thuggish Tactics
56 Dragon Attack
57 A Game of Cyvasse
58 Den of the Wolf
59 A Time for Ravens
60 Unconventional Warfare

2008 Game of Thrones Clash of Arms Promos

19 Qualthe of the Shadows
20 Maester Caelotte
22 Permutation of Power
26 Marked for Ransom

2008 Game of Thrones Song of Summer

1 Kings of Summer
2 Black Raven
3 Summer Tax
4 Fishing Net
5 Dragon Sight
6 Jeyne Westerling
7 Priestess of the Pyre
8 Selyse Baratheon
9 Summer's Champion
10 Scavengers of the Sea
11 Fairweather Followers
12 Red Warlock
13 Starfall Bannerman
14 Maester of the Sun
15 Knights of the Sun
16 Carrion Bird
17 Lion's Gate
18 Summer Port
19 Open Market
20 A Song of Summer

2009 Game of Thrones Scattered Armies

101 Desperate Looters
102 Depleted Host
103 Northern Cavalry Flank
104 Northern Infantry
105 Weary Swordsmen
106 Tommen Baratheon
107 Exhausted Horsemen
108 Stormland Scavengers
109 Weathered Crew
110 Pirates of Orkmont
111 Destitute Horde
112 Desert Exiles
113 Men With No King
114 Retreat and Regroup
115 Missing Recruit
116 Spy in Their Midst
117 Beguiled Bodyguard
118 Winter Reserves
119 Summer Reserves
120 Summer Encampment

2009 Game of Thrones Secrets and Spies

81 Jeyne Poole
82 Cannot be Bribed, Cannot be Bought
83 Qyburn
84 Littlefinger
85 Death by Payne
86 Knight of Flowers
87 Small Council Chamber
88 Ancient Mariner
89 Shore Leave
90 King's Landing Assassin
91 Shadow Prophet
92 Visenya's Hill
93 Aegon's Legacy
94 Dornish Diplomat
95 The Broken Spear
96 Backroom Bribery
97 Varys
98 Ser Osmund Kettleblack
99 King's Landing
100 City of Spies

2009 Game of Thrones Time of Trials

21 Catelyn Stark
22 Septa Mordane
23 Storm Dancer
24 Cersei Lannister
25 Gold Cloaks
26 A Fistful of Coppers
27 Sweet Cersei
28 Moon Boy
29 Abandoned Forge
30 Balon Greyjoy
31 Balon's Rebellion
32 Street Waif
33 Tears of Lys
34 The Shadow of the East
35 Flea Bottom Scavenger
36 Lost Oasis
37 The Hound
38 Condemned by the Council
39 Twilight Market
40 City of Sin

2010 Game of Thrones King in the North

41 Reek
42 Imposter!
43 Timett Son of Timett
44 The Burned Men
45 Tyrion's Enforcers
46 Vale Scavenger
47 Hidden Vale Pass
48 Rise of the Mountain Clans
49 Ser Eldon Estermont
50 Black Amethysts
51 Island Smuggler
52 Driftwood Crown
53 Blood-Crazed Screamer
54 Wedding Feast
55 Lost Spearman
56 Patience
57 Lem Lemoncloak
58 Lady Stoneheart
59 Knights of the Hollow Hill
60 Stoic Resolve

2010 Game of Thrones Of Snakes and Sand

81 Steelshanks Walton
82 The Weeping Water
83 Tribeless Vagabond
84 Tyrion's Thug
85 Shadow Enchantress
86 King Robert's Debt
87 Bloodthirsty Crew
88 Refurbished Hulk
89 Jhogo
90 Jhogo's Whip
91 Tyene Sand
92 Nymeria Sand
93 Bastard Daughter
94 Blood of the Viper
95 Alchemist's Shop
96 His Viper Eyes
97 Jack-be-Lucky
98 Orphaned Recruit
99 Gossip and Lies
100 Bungled Orders

2010 Game of Thrones Song of Silence

61 Steelshanks' Reserves
62 In Ramsay's Name
63 Son of the Mist
64 Ill-Begotten Spoils
65 Stormlands Smuggler
66 Massey's Hook
67 Euron Crow's Eye
68 Cragorn
69 Euron's Mongrel
70 Horn of Dragons
71 Longship Silence
72 River Raid
73 Horseback Hunters
74 The Womb of the World
75 Silent Assassin
76 Poisoned Knife
77 The Mad Huntsman
78 Hollow Hill
79 Whispers from the Hill
80 Retaliation!

2010 Game of Thrones Sword in the Darkness

41 Jon Snow
42 Feigned Retreat
43 Greedy Councilor
44 Favors from on High
45 Salladhor's Crew
46 The Iron Throne
47 Margaery Tyrell
48 Naval Escort
49 Stalwart Shield
50 The Hatchlings' Feast
51 House Dayne Squire
52 Starfall
53 Builder of the Watch
54 A Sword in the Darkness
55 Longclaw
56 Orell the Eagle
57 Crow Killers
58 Over the Wall
59 The Builders
60 At The Wall

2011 Game of Thrones Mask of the Archmaester

80 Dragonstone Watchtower
81 Lonely Hills
83 House Payne Enforcer
84 Restrict and Restrain
85 Ser Jon Fossoway
86 Starfall Cavalry
87 Iron Fleet Raiders
88 Iron Lore
89 Bloodrider
90 House of Shadow
91 We Light the Way
92 Oberyn's Guile
93 The Mad Mouse
94 Archmaester Marwyn
95 Citadel Law
96 Iron Link
97 The Archmaester's Wrath
98 Rickon Stark
99 Black Iron Link
100 War of Attrition

2012 Game of Thrones Harsh Mistress

61 Maege Mormont
62 Hall of Dragons
63 Volantis Inn
64 Pentoshi Manor
65 Watcher of the Nightfire
66 The Nightfort
67 Ghost of Winterfell
68 Longship Red Jester
69 Captured Cog
70 Maester Myles
71 Rhoynar Emissary
72 The Windblown
73 The Golden Company
74 Dragon Egg
75 Great Pyramid of Meereen
76 Myr
77 Tyrosh
78 Much and More
79 Men of Honor
80 Men of Duty

2012 Game of Thrones House of Black and White

81 Arya Stark
82 The House of Black and White
83 Poisoned Coin
84 I Am No One
85 Dockside Brothel
86 Dragonbone Dagger
87 Enslaved
88 Northern Encampment
89 Banner Bearer
90 Freed Galley
91 Cowed
92 Noyne
93 Qhoyne
94 Lhorulu
95 Company of the Cat
96 Long Lances
97 Greyscale
98 Execution
99 Men of Pride
100 The Pale Mare

2012 Game of Thrones Poisoned Spear

101 Ser Kyle Condon
102 Northern Courser
103 House Clegane Outlaw
104 Andal Charger
105 Dragonstone Convert
106 Highgarden Destrier
107 The Sparr
108 Drowned Crewman

109 Isle Garron
110 Sorrowful Man
111 True Queen's Loyalist
112 Dothraki Stallion
113 The Red Viper
114 Rhoynish Steed
115 Poisoned Spear
116 Heavy Taxes
117 Seal of the Crown
118 Isle of Faces
119 Twist of Fate
120 Across the Summer Sea

2012 Game of Thrones Roll of the Dice

101 The Bastard's Boys
102 Ramsay's Hunting Dogs
103 Rhymes with Meek
104 Walk of Shame
105 The Second Sons
106 Snowed In
107 Glamor of Fire
108 Outfitted for War
109 Sacrificed to Two Gods
110 Flood Waters
111 Old Bill Bone
112 Greenblood Merchant
113 Outthought
114 Deceit
115 The Brazen Beasts
116 Meereenese Fighting Pit
117 Dragonbone Bow
118 Little and Less
119 House of Dreams
120 Lead by Example

2013 Game of Thrones Fire and Ice

21 Ser Imry Florent
22 Ser Garlan Tyrell
23 The Kingsroad
24 Balon Greyjoy
25 Longship Great Kraken
26 Damphair's Drowned
27 King's Landing Guard
28 Tommen Baratheon
29 The Kingsroad
30 Ellaria Sand
31 Oberyn's Shield Bearer
32 The Long Plan
33 Bran Stark
34 Winterfell
35 Green Dream
36 Khal Drogo
37 Slaver's Bay
38 Dothraki Vanguard
39 A Song of Fire
40 A Song of Ice

2013 Game of Thrones Journey's End

101 King's Landing Dromon
102 Qarl the Maid
103 Ten Towers Longship
104 Longship Nightflyer
105 Arms of the Kraken
106 Shores of the Mander
107 Huntress
108 Fury
109 House Manderly Escort
110 Trident Guard
111 Call of the Three-Eyed Crow
112 Starfall Skirmisher
113 Choosing the Spear
114 Venomous Manticore
115 Randyll Tarly
116 Cape Wrath
117 The Tattered Prince
118 Blessed by the Maiden
119 Supported by the Smith
120 Favored by the Warrior

2013 Game of Thrones Turn of the Tide

61 House Clegane Brigands
62 Sitting the Iron Throne
63 Raiders of Orkmont
64 Deepwood Motte
65 Seized
66 Blackcrown Knights
67 Dale Seaworth
68 Shores of the Blackwater
69 Riders of Karhold
70 Passing the Wall
71 Host of the Boneway
72 Greenblood Vessel
73 Shores of the Summer Sea
74 Dothraki Outrider
75 Braided Screamers
76 Port at Slaver's Bay
77 Margaery Tyrell
78 Blazewater Bay
79 Blackwater Rush
80 King's Landing Coup

2014 Game of Thrones Ancestral Home

61 Renly Baratheon
62 Lyseni Captain
63 Warden of the South
64 Great Wyk
65 King of the Isles
66 Set Sail
67 Tyrion Lannister
68 The Westerlands
69 Warden of the West
70 Dorne Loyalist
71 Prince of Dorne
72 Hoster Tully
73 The Blackfish
74 Warden of the North
75 Horselord
76 Daenerys Targaryen

77 Khal
78 Harrenhal
79 The Brave Companions
80 Dark Wings, Dark Words

2014 Game of Thrones Hidden Agenda

101 Maester Cressen
102 Mace Tyrell
103 Riches of the Reach
104 Gran Goodbrother
105 Longship Maiden's Bane
106 Euron's Favor
107 Grand Maester Pycelle
108 Tywin's Favor
109 Lashing Out
110 Southron Heiress
111 Secret Schemes
112 Littlefinger
113 Alleras
114 Sansa Stark
115 Robb's Favor
116 Viserion
117 Drogon
118 Rhaegal
119 Bloodthirst
120 Summoned by the Conclave

2014 Game of Thrones Spoils of War

1 Conquest
2 Defiance
3 Seasoned Smuggler
4 Bitterbridge
5 Right of Conquest
6 Enraged Crewman
7 The Reaver's Song
8 Frey Armsmen
9 Traitor
10 Doran Martell
11 Spy from Starfall
12 You Murdered Her Children
13 Catelyn Stark
14 Show of Force
15 Aegon Targaryen
16 Lysono Maar
17 Theon Greyjoy
18 Tycho Nestoris
19 Seizing the Prize
20 Crossing the Mummer's Ford

2015 Game of Thrones Deadly Game

21 Brienne of Tarth
22 Offer of a Peach
23 Warrior of Note
24 Thunderer
25 8 Command the Winds
26 Ulf Son of Umar
27 Moon Brother Harriers
28 Vale Encampment
29 Tyene Sand
30 The Red Mountains
31 A Secret Mission
32 Tytos Blackwood
33 Raventree Elite
34 Seagard
35 Khal Drogo
36 Irri
37 Mya Stone
38 The Eyrie
39 Taken Captive
40 Fallen from Favor

2015 Game of Thrones Time for Wolves

61 Ser Emmon Cuy
62 Camp Follower
63 Renly's Pavilion
64 Iron Fleet Pillager
65 Salt and Iron
66 The Mountain Clan Horde
67 Clan Scout
68 Obella Sand
69 Doran's Solar
70 A Hidden Game
71 Alayne Stone
72 Volley of Arrows
73 Aggo
74 Lesser Ko
75 Horse Gate
76 Lysa Arryn
77 Petyr Baelish
78 Lyn Corbray
79 Knights Declarant
80 A Time for Wolves

2004 InuYasha Tetsusaiga

COMPLETE SET (266) 120.00 200.00
BOOSTER BOX (12 PACKS) 7.50 15.00
BOOSTER PACK (10 CARDS) 1.00 2.00
RELEASED ON OCTOBER 20, 2004
1 Warriors C .10 .25
2 Archers C .10 .25
3 Ms. Ikeda C .10 .25
4 Mayu Ikeda C .10 .25
5 Teacher C .10 .25
6 Wolves C .10 .25
7 Crows C .10 .25
8 Child Villager C .10 .25
9 Mistress Centipede C .10 .25
10 Bone Vulture C .10 .25
11 Troubled Villager C .10 .25
12 Manten's Girls C .10 .25
13 Militia C .10 .25
14 Kagome's Mom C .10 .25
15 Clay Warriors C .10 .25
16 Souls C .10 .25
17 Builders C .10 .25
18 Samurai C .10 .25
19 Village Matron C .10 .25
20 Old Villager C .10 .25
21 High Priest C .10 .25
22 Spider Head C .10 .25
23 Imps C .10 .25
24 Hurt Bandit C .10 .25
25 Demons C .10 .25
26 Little Vixen C .10 .25
27 Bandits C .10 .25
28 Village Mother C .10 .25
29 Princess Tsuyu's Lord C .10 .25
30 Hiyoshimaru, Nobunaga's Monkey C .10 .25
31 Inuyasha, the Young Hanyou C .10 .25
32 Kagome's Grandfather C .10 .25
33 Scared Bandit C .10 .25
34 Righteous Anger C .10 .25
35 Protected, Yet Never Known To It's Protector C .10 .25
36 Deadly Claws C .10 .25
37 Evil Ritual C .10 .25
38 Tag Team C .10 .25
39 Enchanted Sleep C .10 .25
40 Speed Demon C .10 .25
41 Pulling the Strings C .10 .25
42 You've Been a Naughty, Naughty Girl C .10 .25
43 At What Cost C .10 .25
44 Try Something New C .10 .25
45 She Hit It! C .10 .25
46 Die Stinking Toad! C .10 .25
47 Forget Ye Differences C .10 .25
48 Full Moon C .10 .25
49 Priorities C .10 .25
50 Look, I Got One! C .10 .25
51 I'm Not Impressed C .10 .25
52 Ambush C .10 .25
53 Inuyasha's Destructive Path C .10 .25
54 Call of the Wild C .10 .25
55 Stampede C .10 .25
56 Rioting in the Streets C .10 .25
57 Vile Intent C .10 .25
58 Running Engagement C .10 .25
59 Going to the Other Side C .10 .25
60 All You Need is the Ground C .10 .25
61 Things to Come C .10 .25
62 Mob Mentality C .10 .25
63 Torches C .10 .25
64 Sword C .10 .25
65 The First Shard C .10 .25
66 Spear C .10 .25
67 School Girl Outfit C .10 .25
68 Bow C .10 .25
69 Pieces of the Puzzle C .10 .25
70 Yura's Hair C .10 .25
71 Black Pearl C .10 .25
72 Hiten's Lightning Pike C .10 .25
73 Yura's Sword C .10 .25
74 Gamajiro's Shard C .10 .25
75 Shampoo C .10 .25
76 Manten's Shards C .10 .25
77 Kikyo's Ashes C .10 .25
78 Spirit Wards C .10 .25
79 Flashlight C .10 .25
80 Fireworks C .10 .25
81 The Last Hut on the Left C .10 .25
82 A Bloody Nest C .10 .25
83 Sacred Tree C .10 .25
84 Bone Eater's Well C .10 .25
85 Lord Toad's Castle C .10 .25
86 Officer U .20 .50
87 Commanders U .20 .50
88 Samurai Lord U .20 .50
89 Inuyasha, Human U .20 .50
90 Samurai, Loyal Yojimbo U .20 .50
91 Gamajiro U .20 .50
92 Sleeping Guard U .20 .50
93 Beta Wolf U .20 .50
94 Princess Tsuyu U .20 .50
95 Sota U .20 .50
96 Carrion Crow U .20 .50
97 Puppet Villagers U .20 .50
98 Steel Wasps U .20 .50
99 Veteran Samurai U .20 .50
100 Veteran Soldier U .20 .50
101 Hiten, Enraged Demon U .20 .50
102 Jaken, Sesshomaru's Pawn U .20 .50
103 Manten, Bald Demon U .20 .50
104 Yuka, Kagome's friend U .20 .50
105 Kikyo U .20 .50
106 Satoru Ikeda U .20 .50
107 Kaede, Village Priestess U .20 .50
108 Ayumi, Kagome's Friend U .20 .50
109 Inuyasha's Mother U .20 .50
110 Eri, Kagome's Friend U .20 .50
111 Nazuna U .20 .50
112 Kaede, the Young Brat U .20 .50
113 Demon Carrion Crow U .20 .50
114 Big Villager U .20 .50
115 Buyo U .20 .50
116 Sesshomaru's Demon U .20 .50
117 Militia Commander U .20 .50
118 Shippo, the Shapeshifter U .20 .50
119 General U .20 .50
120 Cursed Noh Mask U .20 .50
121 Nobunaga U .20 .50
122 Kagome Higurashi U .20 .50
123 Great Wolf, the Alpha Male U .20 .50
124 Boot to the Head U .20 .50
125 Falling U .20 .50
126 Final Strike U .20 .50
127 Energy Whip U .20 .50
128 Give Me My Clothes! U .20 .50
129 Father's Legacy U .20 .50
130 Look What I Found U .20 .50
131 Looting U .20 .50
132 Always Gotta Be the Nice Guy U .20 .50
133 Preparation U .20 .50
134 Fox Fire U .20 .50
135 A Brother's Wrath U .20 .50
136 The Power of Humans U .20 .50
137 Battle Cry U .20 .50
138 Sit!!!! U .20 .50
139 Take That! U .20 .50
140 Sesshomaru's Poisoned Claw U .20 .50
141 You Stinking Toad! U .20 .50
142 Strength By Numbers U .20 .50
143 Poison U .20 .50
144 Blades of Blood U .20 .50
145 Monkey on Your Back U .20 .50
146 See You in Hell U .20 .50
147 Caught in a Web U .20 .50
148 Destruction U .20 .50
149 Manten's Cleaver U .20 .50
150 Manten's Fox Pelt U .20 .50
151 Jewel Keychain U .20 .50
152 Sesshomaru's Robe U .20 .50
153 Shard of the Cursed Noh Mask U .20 .50
154 Kaede's Bow U .20 .50
155 Priest Garb U .20 .50
156 Hiten's Armor U .20 .50
157 Giant Cleaver U .20 .50
158 Inuyasha's Necklace U .20 .50
159 Imprisoning Chains U .20 .50
160 Sesshomaru's Armor U .20 .50
161 Hiten's Shards U .20 .50
162 Hiten's Fire Wheel Shoes U .20 .50
163 Inuyasha's Father's Tomb U .20 .50
164 Gateway to Hell U .20 .50
165 Kaede's Village U .20 .50
166 Higurashi Storage Room U .20 .50
167 Outlaw's Lair U .20 .50
168 War Camp U .20 .50
169 Wild Dog Shrine U .20 .50
170 Border of the Spirit World U .20 .50
171 Un-Mother R .75 2.00
172 Myoga R .75 2.00
173 Soul Piper, Eyes Open R .75 2.00
174 Villagers R .75 2.00
175 Kikyo, Guardian of the Jewel R .75 2.00
176 Inuyasha, Demonic Half Breed R .75 2.00
177 Kagome Outlaw Boss R .75 2.00
178 Kagome, Kikyo Reincarnated R .75 2.00
179 The Hella Nasty Crow R .75 2.00
180 Manten, Loyal Brother R .75 2.00
181 Kagome, the Archer R .75 2.00
182 Sesshomaru, Aristocratic Assassin R .75 2.00
183 Jaken R .75 2.00
184 Hiten, Demon Warrior R .75 2.00
185 Shippo, Master of Fox Fire R .75 2.00
186 Hojo R .75 2.00
187 Yura of the Demon Hair R .75 2.00
188 Kagome, the Student R .75 2.00
189 Urasue R .75 2.00
190 Head Spider Head R .75 2.00
191 Possessed Bandit Leader R .75 2.00
192 Soul Piper, Eyes Closed R .75 2.00
193 Inuyasha, Kagome's Protector R .75 2.00
194 This Human is Going to Kick Your â•¦ R .75 2.00
195 Okay Boss R .75 2.00
196 Survival of the Fittest R .75 2.00
197 Get Undressed R .75 2.00
198 I Think I Want To Touch Them R .75 2.00
199 I'll Never Let You Go R .75 2.00
200 Charge R .75 2.00
201 Blessing R .75 2.00
202 What? Broken? R .75 2.00
203 Bath Time R .75 2.00
204 Shard Shower R .75 2.00
205 Hairspray Flamethrower R .75 2.00
206 You Think He Likes You? R .75 2.00
207 Hiten's Destructive Ways R .75 2.00
208 You Tried To Kill Me! R .75 2.00
209 Defeated R .75 2.00
210 Yura's Flawless Snatch R .75 2.00
211 The Thunder Brother's Anger R .75 2.00
212 Thank You For Showing Me Mercy R .75 2.00
213 New Age Technology R .75 2.00
214 I Leave Them to You R .75 2.00
215 Kikyo's Legacy R .75 2.00
216 Where am I? R .75 2.00
217 My Power Is What it is R .75 2.00
218 Evil Things are Amidst R .75 2.00
219 Caretakers of the Shrine R .75 2.00
220 Sit! Sit! Sit! Sit! R .75 2.00
221 Caught Red Handed R .75 2.00
222 Let Go of Me R .75 2.00
223 I didn't Say Get Naked! R .75 2.00
224 Get Off Ye Duff R .75 2.00
225 Halt! R .75 2.00
226 Be as One R .75 2.00
227 Oh-Me-Oh-My! R .75 2.00
228 Yura's Comb R .75 2.00
229 Tetsusaiga R .75 2.00
230 The Cursed Noh Mask R .75 2.00
231 Staff of Two Heads R .75 2.00
232 Inuyasha's Ball R .75 2.00
233 Kagome's Backpack R .75 2.00
234 Hiten's & Manten's Thunder Cloud R .75 2.00
235 Kagome's Bow R .75 2.00
236 Shippo's Top R .75 2.00
237 Tetsusaiga's Sheath R .75 2.00
238 Medic Kit R .75 2.00
239 Kagome's Bicycle R .75 2.00
240 Robe of the Fire Rat R .75 2.00
241 Yura's Skull R .75 2.00
242 Sacred Arrow R .75 2.00
243 Urasue's Scythe R .75 2.00
244 Kagome's Birthday present R .75 2.00
245 Kikyo's Bow R .75 2.00
246 Spirit Sutra R .75 2.00
247 Resting Place R .75 2.00
248 Kagome's Junior High R .75 2.00
249 Samurai War Camp R .75 2.00
250 Hospital R .75 2.00
251 Tokyo R .75 2.00
252 Yura's Lair R .75 2.00
253 Higurashi Shrine R .75 2.00
254 Thunder Brother's Battle Ground R .75 2.00
255 Blast Land R .75 2.00
256 Inuyasha, the Feudal Warrior UR 3.00 8.00
257 Kikyo, Reborn UR 4.00 10.00
258 Sesshomaru, Transformed UR 4.00 10.00
259 Enraged UR 3.00 8.00
260 Burst of Power UR 3.00 8.00
261 Here He Comes to Save the Day! UR 3.00 8.00
262 Returning Home UR 3.00 8.00
263 Tetsusaiga, Transformed UR 3.00 8.00
264 Inuyasha, Sota's Hero PROMO 1.00 2.50
265 Iron Reaver Soul Stealer PROMO 1.00 2.50
266 Shard From the Jewel of Four Souls PROMO 1.00 2.50
HO Miroku HR 10.00 20.00

2005 InuYasha Jaki

COMPLETE SET (119) 30.00 80.00
BOOSTER BOX (12 PACKS) 5.00 12.00
BOOSTER PACK (10 CARDS) .60 1.50
RELEASED IN MAY 2005
1 Flesh Eating Demon, Baby C .10 .25
2 Birds of Paradise C .10 .25
3 Naraku's Poison Insects, 2 C .10 .25
4 Flesh Eating Demon, Adult C .10 .25
5 Head of the Birds of Paradise C .10 .25
6 Inuyasha, Night of the New Moon C .10 .25
7 Jinenji's Mom C .10 .25
8 Kaijinbo, Evil Sword Smith C .10 .25
9 Koharu, Miroku's Admirer C .10 .25
10 Ginta, Member of the Wolf Demon Tribe C .10 .25
11 A-Un, Sesshomaru's Two-Headed Dragon C .10 .25
12 Totosai, Tetsusaiga's Creator C .10 .25
13 Totosai's Flying Three-Eyed Cow C .10 .25
14 Hakkaku, Member of the Wolf Demon Tribe C .10 .25
15 Bruised, Bloody and Broken C .10 .25
16 Evil Doings C .10 .25
17 Power Exit C .10 .25
18 Looking Out for You C .10 .25
19 Naraku's Cage C .10 .25
20 Taking Aim C .10 .25
21 Whatcha Getting So Angry for? C .10 .25
22 Hammer of the Armory C .10 .25
23 Koga's Jewel Shards C .10 .25
24 Mark of Onigumo C .10 .25
25 Nest of Eggs C .10 .25
26 Goshinki, Sword Breaker C .10 .25
27 Hojo, the Perfect Guy C .10 .25
28 Jinenji, the Gentle Giant C .10 .25
29 Judgmental Villagers C .10 .25
30 Kikyo's Soul Stealers C .10 .25
31 Sango, the Relentless C .10 .25
32 Samurai of Fortune C .10 .25
33 Massacre C .10 .25
34 Cat and Dog C .10 .25
35 Demonic Anger C .10 .25
36 Dragon Eyes C .10 .25
37 Holy Power C .10 .25
38 Soul Discharge C .10 .25
39 Take a Look in the Mirror C .10 .25
40 They Still Desire Her Life C .10 .25
41 Transformation C .10 .25
42 Vanquished C .10 .25
43 The Little People! C .10 .25
44 The Soul Moves On C .10 .25
45 Slayer's Heart C .10 .25
46 Koga, Speed Demon U .20 .50
47 Shippo, Master Artist U .20 .50
48 Kageromaru, Spawn of Naraku U .20 .50
49 Jaken, Evil's Comedian U .20 .50
50 How Did This Happen? U .20 .50
51 Wrath of Koga U .20 .50
52 Kagome, Innocent Warrior U .20 .50
53 Kagome, the Incarnate U .20 .50
54 They Were Dead!? U .20 .50
55 Kirara, Scared Helper U .20 .50
56 Was I Dreaming? U .20 .50
57 Miroku, Perverted Monk U .20 .50
58 Sango, Female Warrior U .20 .50
59 Evil Lurks U .20 .50
60 Sesshomaru, Wanderer U .20 .50
61 Kaede, the Counselor U .20 .50
62 Inuyasha, Master of the Wind Scar U .20 .50
63 AAAHHHH! GET IT AWAY! U .20 .50
64 Kagura, Wind Mistress U .20 .50
65 Kanna, Soul Stealer U .20 .50
66 Kanna, Spawn of Naraku U .20 .50
67 Kikyo, Wandering Soul U .20 .50
68 Kikyo, Free to Hate U .20 .50
69 Sesshomaru, Weilder of Tokijin U .20 .50
70 Naraku, Mastermind U .20 .50
71 Shippo, the Dreamer U .20 .50
72 Pull Yourself Together! U .20 .50
73 Juromaru, Spawn of Naraku U .20 .50
74 Naraku's Evil U .20 .50
75 No Rest for the Wicked U .20 .50
76 Some Things Never Change U .20 .50
77 The Birds U .20 .50
78 Things Don't Look Good for Our Hero U .20 .50
79 Den of Wolves U .20 .50
80 Kagura, Spawn of Naraku U .20 .50
81 Staff of Two Heads, Jaken's Power U .20 .50
82 Kagura's Fan U .20 .50
83 Tenseiga, the Sword of Life U .20 .50
84 Camp Site U .20 .50
85 Jenenji's Farm U .20 .50
86 Rin, Obedient Child R .75 2.00
87 He Sounds Like a Real Psycho R .75 2.00
88 Incoming! R .75 2.00
89 Nosey Little Thing R .75 2.00
90 What the Five Fingers Say R .75 2.00
91 The Wind Scar R .75 2.00
92 Koga's Rage R .75 2.00
93 I Grow Tired of These Deceptions R .75 2.00

94 Workin' the Looks R .75 2.00
95 Is That All You Got? R .75 2.00
96 To Battle! R .75 2.00
97 Our Little Secret R .75 2.00
98 Surprise R .75 2.00
99 Legendary Archers R .75 2.00
100 Where's the Party? R .75 2.00
101 That's Random R .75 2.00
102 Three's Company R .75 2.00
103 Shippo's Shroom R .75 2.00
104 Whirlwind Slice R .75 2.00
105 Moment of Compassion R .75 2.00
106 Terrorize R .75 2.00
107 What's Going On? R .75 2.00
108 Wolves Mate for Life R .75 2.00
109 It's a Lot Heavier... R .75 2.00
110 Wait... R .75 2.00
111 Totosai's Weapon Smithy R .75 2.00
112 The Miasma R .75 2.00
113 Naraku's New Castle R .75 2.00
114 Kanna's Mirror R .75 2.00
115 Bow and Arrow R .75 2.00
116 Inuyasha, the Demon Within UR 4.00 10.00
117 Naraku, Deceptive Demon UR 4.00 10.00
118 Koga, the Furious UR 4.00 10.00
119 Tokijin, the Evil Sword UR 4.00 10.00
199 I'll Never Let You Go PROMO 1.00 2.50
260 Burst of Power PROMO 1.00 2.50
H1 Muso HR .75 2.00
H2 Tsubaki HR .75 2.00

2005 InuYasha Jaki Shippo's Slideshow

COMPLETE SET (10) 6.00 15.00
SS1 There Once Was a Dog... 1.25 3.00
SS2 The Dog Was Protective of the Cat... 1.25 3.00
SS3 The Wolf 1.25 3.00
SS4 The Birds Hurt the Wolf... 1.25 3.00
SS5 The Dog 1.25 3.00
SS6 The Dog Wanted to Kill the Wolf... 1.25 3.00
SS7 But the Cat Protected the Wolf... 1.25 3.00
SS8 The Dog Was a REAL Jerk... 1.25 3.00
SS9 The Cat 1.25 3.00
SS10 So the Cat Ran Down a Well... 1.25 3.00

2005 InuYasha Kassen

COMPLETE SET (119) 30.00 80.00
BOOSTER BOX (12 PACKS) 5.00 12.00
BOOSTER PACK (10 CARDS) .60 1.50
RELEASED ON NOVEMBER 8, 2005
1 Cat of the Panther Tribe, 1 C .10 .25
2 Cat of the Panther Tribe, 2 C .10 .25
3 Cat of the Panther Tribe, 3 C .10 .25
4 Bat Demon Tribe Member, 1 C .10 .25
5 Bat Demon Tribe Member, 2 C .10 .25
6 Bat Demon tribe member, 3 C .10 .25
7 Wolf, Koga's Companion C .10 .25
8 Torako C .10 .25
9 Kagome, Happy to be Home C .10 .25
10 Shiori's Mom C .10 .25
11 Naraku's Poison Insects, 3 C .10 .25
12 Inuyashaâ„¢, the Little Half-Demon C .10 .25
13 Soul Collectors C .10 .25
14 Master Muso C .10 .25
15 Little Monk, Muso's Companion C .10 .25
16 Bandit General C .10 .25
17 Myoga, Enraged Flea C .10 .25
18 Kuranosuke C .10 .25
19 Enraged Villager C .10 .25
20 Royakan, Willing Helper C .10 .25
21 Bandits, Villain Soldiers C .10 .25
22 Buyo, Playful Kitty C .10 .25
23 Hachi, Raccoon Demon C .10 .25
24 Eri, Caring Friend C .10 .25
25 Yuka, Caring Friend C .10 .25
26 Bunza, Senior Apprentice C .10 .25
27 Kirara, Peaceful Companion C .10 .25
28 Totosai, Old Fool C .10 .25
29 Kaede, Village Protector C .10 .25
30 Nanafushi C .10 .25
31 Quick Slash C .10 .25
32 In Command C .10 .25
33 Prisoners of War C .10 .25
34 She is the One C .10 .25
35 What are You Thinking? C .10 .25
36 Quick Strikes C .10 .25
37 Koga's Fury C .10 .25
38 Attack of the Bat Demons of Doom C .10 .25
39 Dumbfounded C .10 .25
40 Engaged in Battle C .10 .25
41 Playing Cards C .10 .25
42 Shippo's Crayons C .10 .25
43 Stolen Shards C .10 .25
44 Smoke Bomb C .10 .25
45 Steak C .10 .25
46 Sesshomaru, Son of the Dog Leader U .20 .50
47 Inuyasha, Son of the Dog Leader U .20 .50
48 Muso, Faceless Demon U .20 .50
49 Ginta, Fierce Wolf Demon U .20 .50
50 Jaken, Imp Commander U .20 .50
51 Rin, Child Follower U .20 .50
52 No-Man U .20 .50
53 Kohaku, Slave of Naraku U .20 .50
54 Kagome, Gossiping School Girl U .20 .50
55 Miroku, the Modern Gentleman U .20 .50
56 Tsukuyomaru, Father of the Bat Demons U .20 .50
57 Miroku, Flirtatious Wandering Monk U .20 .50
58 Koga, New Leader of the Wolf Demon Tribe U .20 .50
59 Sango, Passionate Demon Slayer U .20 .50
60 Soten, Little Thunder Sister U .20 .50
61 Karan, Deva of the Panther Tribe U .20 .50
62 Shuuran, Deva of the Panther Tribe U .20 .50
63 Toran, Deva of the Panther Tribe U .20 .50
64 Kagura, Mistress of Betrayal U .20 .50
65 Naraku's Demons U .20 .50
66 Shippo, Brave Warrior U .20 .50
67 Kikyo, Forgotten Soul U .20 .50
68 Koga, Guy of Your Dreams U .20 .50
69 Koryu, Lightning Cloud Dragon U .20 .50
70 Naraku, Man of Many Demons U .20 .50
71 Wind Scar, Inuyashaâ„¢'s Weapon U .20 .50
72 Naraku's Power U .20 .50
73 Playful Siblings U .20 .50
74 Blown Away U .20 .50
75 Wake Up U .20 .50
76 Laughing Acorns U .20 .50
77 The Bat Demons are Coming! U .20 .50
78 Walking Home U .20 .50
79 Shuffling Cards U .20 .50
80 Sudden Strike U .20 .50
81 Panther Demon Tribe's Castle U .20 .50
82 Royakan's Cave U .20 .50
83 Kagome's Bedroom U .20 .50
84 Kagome's Living Room U .20 .50
85 Well Placed Trap U .20 .50
86 Ocean U .20 .50
87 Beach Front U .20 .50
88 Country Road U .20 .50
89 Cave of the Bat Demon Tribe U .20 .50
90 Jaken, Master Thief R .75 2.00
91 Shippo, Master Duelist R .75 2.00
92 Naraku, Master of Demons R .75 2.00
93 Kikyo, Fading Soul R .75 2.00
94 Taigokumaru, Grandfather of the Bat Demons R .75 2.00
95 Shiori, Princess of the Bat Demons R .75 2.00
96 Shunran, Member of the Panther Tribe R .75 2.00
97 Power Over the Elements R .75 2.00
98 Gone Fishing R .75 2.00
99 Enter the Panther R .75 2.00
100 I'm a Genius R .75 2.00
101 Watching from Afar R .75 2.00
102 Overjoyed R .75 2.00
103 The Long Walk Home R .75 2.00
104 Loyal Followers R .75 2.00
105 True Power R .75 2.00
106 Preparing for Battle R .75 2.00
107 FINISH HIM! R .75 2.00
108 He Has Ears R .75 2.00
109 Consumed Souls R .75 2.00
110 The Heart of Onigumo R .75 2.00
111 Shikon Jewel Nearly Completed R .75 2.00
112 Blood Coral Crystal R .75 2.00
113 Tetsusaiga, Red R .75 2.00
114 City Street R .75 2.00
115 Village R .75 2.00
116 King of the Panther Tribe UR 4.00 10.00
117 Muso, Heart of Onigumo UR 4.00 10.00
118 Ready for War UR 3.00 8.00
119 Just Ask for Help UR 3.00 8.00
H1 Inuyasha HR 10.00 20.00
H2 Kagome HR 7.50 15.00

2005 InuYasha Kassen Legendary Foes

COMPLETE SET (10) 6.00 15.00
LF1 Yura, LF 1.25 3.00
LF2 Kotatsu, LF 1.25 3.00
LF3 Hiten, LF 1.25 3.00
LF4 Manten, LF 1.25 3.00
LF5 Sesshomaru, LF 1.25 3.00
LF6 Naraku, LF 1.25 3.00
LF7 Juromaru, LF 1.25 3.00
LF8 Kageromaru, LF 1.25 3.00
LF9 Ryukotsusei, LF 1.25 3.00
LF10 Demon Carrion Crow, LF 1.25 3.00

2005 InuYasha Kassen Promos

COMPLETE SET (9) 5.00 12.00
KP1 Ayame, Koga's Fiancee 1.00 2.50
KP2 Kagome, Protector of the Shikon Jewel 1.00 2.50
KP3 Rin, Follower of Sesshomaru 1.00 2.50
KP4 Kikyo, Master Archer 1.00 2.50
KP5 Inuyasha, Battle Ready 1.00 2.50
KP6 Rampage of Destruction 1.00 2.50
KP7 One on One 1.00 2.50
KP8 Karan, Soldier of the Panther Tribe 1.00 2.50
KP9 Determined 1.00 2.50

2005 InuYasha Kijin

COMPLETE SET (140) 40.00 80.00
BOOSTER BOX (12 PACKS) 15.00 30.00
BOOSTER PACK (10 CARDS) 1.50 3.00
RELEASED ON FEBRUARY 2, 2005
1 Hachi, Miroku's Friend C .10 .25
2 Taromaru C .10 .25
3 Ink Demon, 1 C .10 .25
4 Ink Demon, 2 C .10 .25
5 Jaken, Little Bundle of Evil C .10 .25
6 Kikyo, the Tragic Soul C .10 .25
7 Kohaku, the Young Demon Slayer C .10 .25
8 Miroku's Grandfather C .10 .25
9 Myoga, the Loyal Friend C .10 .25
10 Onigumo, the Helpless Foe C .10 .25
11 Villain Soldier C .10 .25
12 Oppressed Villager C .10 .25
13 Slayer, Mace and Trident C .10 .25
14 Three Eyed Wolf, Aggressive C .10 .25
15 Three Eyed Wolf, Enraged C .10 .25
16 Water God, the Evil Water Spirit C .10 .25
17 Sayo, Young Village Girl C .10 .25
18 A Girl and Her Cat C .10 .25
19 A Girl and Her Dog C .10 .25
20 Buried Alive C .10 .25
21 Defensive Stance C .10 .25
22 Hold On C .10 .25
23 I'll Be Taking That... C .10 .25
24 I'll Find Him Yet C .10 .25
25 Look What We Found! C .10 .25
26 The Group's All Here C .10 .25
27 Miroku's Wind Tunnel C .10 .25
28 On Guard C .10 .25
29 Overpowered C .10 .25
30 Quick Hands C .10 .25
31 She Hit it Again! C .10 .25
32 Shippos Everywhere C .10 .25
33 Trapped in a Shack C .10 .25
34 Tricked C .10 .25
35 What? He Stopped It? C .10 .25
36 Miroku's Staff C .10 .25
37 Monk's Ball of Dragon C .10 .25
38 Newspaper C .10 .25
39 Painting C .10 .25
40 Prayer Beads C .10 .25
41 Stolen Souls C .10 .25
42 Sutra Beads C .10 .25
43 Valuables C .10 .25
44 Shrine of the Water God C .10 .25
45 Slayers' Battleground C .10 .25
46 Ayumi, Kagome's Friend Until the End U .20 .50
47 Demon Worm Charmer U .20 .50
48 Yuka, Kagome's Friend Until the End U .20 .50
49 Kotatsu U .20 .50
50 Kaede, the Village Protector U .20 .50
51 Kagome's Grandfather, Her Personal Secretary U .20 .50
52 Kagome, Priestess in Training U .20 .50
53 Kagome, Sickly Beauty U .20 .50
54 Kirara, Sango's Companion U .20 .50
55 Kirara, Transformed U .20 .50
56 Miroku, the Cursed Monk U .20 .50
57 Mushin, the Old Drunk U .20 .50
58 Naraku's Poison Insects U .20 .50
59 Naraku, Nemesis U .20 .50
60 Villager, Battle Ready U .20 .50
61 Royakan, Protector of the Forest U .20 .50
62 Shippo, the Demon Child U .20 .50
63 Sango's Father, Demon Slayer U .20 .50
64 Axe Wielder, Slayer U .20 .50
65 Sota, Fighting Game Fanboy U .20 .50
66 The Water Goddess U .20 .50
67 Village Head Master U .20 .50
68 Weasel Demon U .20 .50
69 Eri, Kagome's Friend Until the End U .20 .50
70 Big Sit U .20 .50
71 Do You Want Him to Look? U .20 .50
72 Face-off U .20 .50
73 Kikyo's Kiss U .20 .50
74 Thinking of You U .20 .50
75 On the Run U .20 .50
76 Shippo's Item Technique U .20 .50
77 Will You Have My Children? U .20 .50
78 Hiraikotsu U .20 .50
79 Hive of Poison Insects U .20 .50
80 Miroku's Jewel Shard U .20 .50
81 Naraku's Baboon Mask U .20 .50
82 Sesshomaru's Arm U .20 .50
83 Text Books U .20 .50
84 The Mask of a Slayer U .20 .50
85 The Trident of the Water Goddess U .20 .50
86 Massacred Village U .20 .50
87 Naraku's Castle U .20 .50
88 Resting House U .20 .50
89 Rice Fields U .20 .50
90 Village by the Mountain U .20 .50
91 Inuyasha, Master of the Tetsusaiga R .75 2.00
92 Kohaku, Servant of Naraku R .75 2.00
93 Miroku, the Lady Killer R .75 2.00
94 Naraku, the Spirit of Onigumo R .75 2.00
95 Sango, the Demon Slayer R .75 2.00
96 Sesshomaru, the Evil Brother R .75 2.00
97 The Reflecting Shower R .75 2.00
98 Blush R .75 2.00
99 Brighter Days R .75 2.00
100 Child Sacrifice R .75 2.00
101 Deep Thought R .75 2.00
102 Destructive Force R .75 2.00
103 Game Over R .75 2.00
104 How Can We Thank You? R .75 2.00
105 Kikyo's Embrace R .75 2.00
106 Massive Destruction R .75 2.00
107 My Intentions Were Honorable R .75 2.00
108 Overwhelmed R .75 2.00
109 Overwhelming Odds R .75 2.00
110 She's Creeping Me Out R .75 2.00
111 Stuffed R .75 2.00
112 The Best Healing Herb R .75 2.00
113 The Most Powerful Human of Her Time R .75 2.00
114 What a Dale! R .75 2.00
115 What are You Doing? R .75 2.00
116 What Strange People R .75 2.00
117 What's That Look For? R .75 2.00
118 Wolf in Your Mouth R .75 2.00
119 Barrier R .75 2.00
120 Blessed Idol R .75 2.00
121 Shikon Jewel - Half Completed R .75 2.00
122 A Field of Flowers R .75 2.00
123 Armory of the Slayers R .75 2.00
124 Cave of the Shikon Jewel R .75 2.00
125 Crater R .75 2.00
126 Field of Dead Bodies R .75 2.00
127 Hot Springs R .75 2.00
128 Lake of the Water God R .75 2.00
129 Onigumo's Cave R .75 2.00
130 Village in the Valley R .75 2.00
131 Inuyasha, Enraged Demon UR 4.00 10.00
132 A Tragic Death UR 4.00 10.00
133 Burned UR 3.00 8.00
134 On the Move UR 4.00 10.00
135 Midoriko, Creator of the Shikon Jewel PROMO 1.00 2.50
136 Sango, the Scarred Warrior PROMO 1.00 2.50
137 The Eye of Naraku PROMO 1.00 2.50
138 Downtown Tokyo PROMO 1.00 2.50
182 Sesshomaru, Aristocratic Assassin PROMO 1.00 2.50
263 Tetsusaiga, Transformed PROMO 1.00 2.50
H1 Koga HR 10.00 20.00
H2 Kagura HR 10.00 20.00

2005 InuYasha Kijin Legends

COMPLETE SET (11) 6.00 15.00
LS1 Inuyasha LEG 1.25 3.00
LS2 Jaken LEG 1.25 3.00
LS3 Kikyo LEG 1.25 3.00
LS4 Kagome LEG 1.25 3.00
LS5 Kirara LEG 1.25 3.00
LS6 Kohaku LEG 1.25 3.00
LS7 Miroku LEG 1.25 3.00
LS8 Naraku LEG 1.25 3.00
LS9 Sango LEG 1.25 3.00
LS10 Sesshomaru LEG 1.25 3.00
LS11 Yura LEG 1.25 3.00

2005 InuYasha Yokai

COMPLETE SET (123) 30.00 60.00
BOOSTER BOX (12 PACKS) 5.00 12.00
BOOSTER PACK (10 CARDS) .60 1.50
1 Inuyasha, Human at Heart C .10 .25
2 Scared Village Woman C .10 .25
3 Bandit Soldier C .10 .25
4 Village Grandpa C .10 .25
5 Serina, Young Ninja C .10 .25
6 Shippo, Shape Changing Fox C .10 .25
7 Bandit Wench C .10 .25
8 School Teacher C .10 .25
9 Kirara, House Cat C .10 .25
10 Smiling Bandit C .10 .25
11 Gatenmaru, Human C .10 .25
12 Young Village Bully C .10 .25
13 Village Wealthy Man C .10 .25
14 Lizard Demon C .10 .25
15 Demon Horde C .10 .25
16 Kikyo, the Lost Soul C .10 .25
17 Kagome's Mom, Loving Mother C .10 .25
18 Jaken, Loyal Servant C .10 .25
19 Shikigami C .10 .25
20 Shikigami Inuyasha C .10 .25
21 Shikigami Kagome C .10 .25
22 Totosai, Sword Maker C .10 .25
23 Rin, Young Follower C .10 .25
24 Demon Eye C .10 .25
25 Tsubaki's Demon C .10 .25
26 Buyo, the Fat Cat C .10 .25
27 Ninja, 1 C .10 .25
28 Ninja, 2 C .10 .25
29 Suzuna, Young Ninja Girl C .10 .25
30 Struggle C .10 .25
31 Bloody Rage C .10 .25
32 Injured During Battle C .10 .25
33 Stop Fighting C .10 .25
34 Torn Apart C .10 .25
35 Angered Beyond Belief C .10 .25
36 You'll Be Sorry C .10 .25
37 AHHHHH C .10 .25
38 Take That You Demon! C .10 .25
39 Glaring Evil C .10 .25
40 He Can't Be Dead! C .10 .25
41 Big Rolling Rock C .10 .25
42 Candle C .10 .25
43 Enchanted Bracelet C .10 .25
44 Demon Tree Fruit C .10 .25
45 Soda C .10 .25
46 Ryukotsusei, Father's Old Enemy U .20 .50
47 Tokajin, Transformed U .20 .50
48 Tokajin, Human U .20 .50
49 Kagome, #1 Student U .20 .50
50 Shippo, the Playful Fox U .20 .50
51 Kirara, Enraged Protector U .20 .50
52 Myoga, Little Bloodsucker U .20 .50
53 Satsuki, Shippo's First Love U .20 .50
54 Sango, Slayer of Demons U .20 .50
55 Hojo, a Fool in Love U .20 .50
56 Momiji, Little Priestess Girl U .20 .50
57 Miroku, Quick-Handed Monk U .20 .50
58 Kanna, Follower of Naraku U .20 .50
59 Sesshomaru, Lord of Demons U .20 .50
60 Tsubaki, Young Priestess U .20 .50
61 Botan, the Little Priestess U .20 .50
62 Koga, Wolf Leader U .20 .50
63 Miroku, Single U .20 .50
64 Kagome, Innocent U .20 .50
65 Sango, the Skilled Warrior U .20 .50
66 Coyote Demon U .20 .50
67 Kagome, Bathing Beauty U .20 .50
68 Bandit Brutality U .20 .50
69 Where are You? U .20 .50
70 Trouble Sleeping U .20 .50
71 Retreat! U .20 .50
72 Vanity U .20 .50
73 Matters of the Heart U .20 .50
74 Getting Along? U .20 .50
75 Crushed U .20 .50
76 Sake U .20 .50
77 Bath Towel U .20 .50
78 Food U .20 .50
79 Shippo's Sucker U .20 .50
80 Dried Potatoes U .20 .50
81 Tokajin's Trap U .20 .50
82 Valley Settlement U .20 .50
83 Forest Path U .20 .50
84 Woodland Valley U .20 .50
85 Cliff Side U .20 .50
86 Ryukotsusei, Demon Awakened R .75 2.00
87 Gatenmaru, Transformed R .75 2.00
88 Naraku, Master of Deception R .75 2.00
89 Kagura, Follower of Naraku R .75 2.00
90 Tsubaki, Old Priestess R .75 2.00
91 Inuyasha, Bodyguard R .75 2.00
92 The Demon Tree R .75 2.00
93 Raging Into Battle R .75 2.00
94 Slay Rin R .75 2.00
95 Exhausted R .75 2.00
96 Sucking Your Life Away R .75 2.00
97 Unspoken Feelings R .75 2.00
98 Mind Your Own Business R .75 2.00
99 Ninja Vanish R .75 2.00
100 The Aftermath of a Legendary Battle R .75 2.00
101 Awkward Moments R .75 2.00
102 Discussing Other People's Lives R .75 2.00
103 You're Alive R .75 2.00
104 My Hero R .75 2.00
105 Tetsusaiga's Sheath, Inuyasha's Protector R .75 2.00
106 Hojo's Gift R .75 2.00
107 Bedroom R .75 2.00
108 Riverside R .75 2.00
109 The Bandit's Hideout R .75 2.00
110 Wacdnald R .75 2.00
111 Gravesite of the Slayers R .75 2.00
112 Busted R .75 2.00
113 Making Plans R .75 2.00
114 Let Me Go Home R .75 2.00
115 Evil's Awakening R .75 2.00
116 Epic Battle UR 4.00 10.00
117 Inuyasha, Demon with a Heart UR 4.00 10.00
118 Peaceful Times UR 4.00 10.00
119 Out of Control UR 3.00 8.00
183 Jaken PROMO 1.00 2.50
187 Yura, of the Demon Hair PROMO 1.00 2.50
193 Inuyasha, Kagome's Protector PROMO 1.00 2.50
261 Here He Comes to Save the Day! PROMO 1.00 2.50
H1 Karan HR .75 2.00
H2 Inuyasha's Father HR .75 2.00

2005 InuYasha Yokai Chibi

COMPLETE SET (10) 6.00 15.00
CB1 Kagome, Chibi 1.25 3.00
CB2 Shippo, Chibi 1.25 3.00
CB3 Kikyo, Chibi 1.25 3.00
CB4 Miroku, Chibi 1.25 3.00
CB5 Sesshomaru, Chibi 1.25 3.00
CB6 Inuyasha, Chibi 1.25 3.00
CB7 Inuyasha, Human Chibi 1.25 3.00
CB8 Sango, Chibi 1.25 3.00
CB9 Sango, Slayer Chibi 1.25 3.00
CB10 Koga, Wolf Chibi 1.25 3.00

2006 InuYasha Saisei

COMPLETE SET (158) 40.00 80.00
BOOSTER BOX (12) 5.00 12.00
BOOSTER PACK (10) .60 1.50
1 Naraku's Poison Insects, 4 C .10 .25
2 Kirara, Protector of Sango C .10 .25
3 Nazuna, Little Demon Hunter C .10 .25
4 Royakan, Wolf Demon C .10 .25
5 Kikyo, Forgotten Hero C .10 .25
6 Kaede, Old Warrior C .10 .25
7 Sage, Tokajin's Mentor C .10 .25
8 Muso, Ravager of Villages C .10 .25
9 Bat Demon Tribe Member, 4 C .10 .25
10 Kaede, Master Archer C .10 .25
11 Soul Piper C .10 .25
12 Mistress Centipede, Evil Demon C .10 .25
13 Cursed Noh Mask, Evil Demon C .10 .25
14 A-Un, Follower of Sesshomaru C .10 .25
15 Crows, 2 C .10 .25
16 Gamajiro, Evil Toad Demon C .10 .25
17 Sesshomaru's Demon, Follower of Sesshomaru C .10 .25
18 Torako, Bunza's Friend C .10 .25
19 Mayu Ikeda, Mischievous Soul C .10 .25
20 Shikigami, 2 C .10 .25
21 Hakkaku. Warrior of the Wolf Demon Tribe C .10 .25
22 School Teacher, Kagome's Nightmare C .10 .25
23 Ink Demon, 3 C .10 .25
24 White Wolf C .10 .25
25 Ayame, Koga's Bride to Be C .10 .25
26 Imps, 1 C .10 .25
27 Imps, 2 C .10 .25
28 Imps, 3 C .10 .25
29 Kaijimbo, Forger of Tokijin C .10 .25
30 Giant Soul Collector C .10 .25
31 Shikigami, Demon Serpent C .10 .25
32 Bunza's Father C .10 .25
33 Northern Tribe Wolf Leader C .10 .25
34 Birds of Paradise, 2 C .10 .25
35 Inuyasha, Injured C .10 .25
36 Kagome, Tender Soul C .10 .25
37 Tsubaki's Demon, Deadly Predator C .10 .25
38 Kikyo, Patient Soul C .10 .25
39 Miroku, the Thoughtful C .10 .25
40 Shippo, Little Demon Fox C .10 .25
41 Naraku, Master of Evil C .10 .25
42 Hachi, Friend of Miroku C .10 .25
43 Hair Demon C .10 .25
44 Cat of the Panther Tribe, 4 C .10 .25
45 Samurai Warrior C .10 .25
46 Inuyasha's Destructive Path C .10 .25
47 Attack of the Spirit Puppets C .10 .25
48 Don't Tell Me C .10 .25
49 Goosebumps C .10 .25
50 Family Curse C .10 .25
51 Awake C .10 .25
52 Wink C .10 .25
53 Lecher C .10 .25
54 Tender Moments C .10 .25
55 I'm Not Crying C .10 .25
56 Cursed Shikon Jewel C .10 .25
57 Slayer Weapons C .10 .25
58 Fake Jewel Shard C .10 .25
59 Alarm Clock C .10 .25
60 Stew C .10 .25
61 Inuyasha's Mother, Loving Soul U .20 .50
62 Jaken, Follower of Sesshomaru U .20 .50
63 Kohaku, Sango's Little Brother U .20 .50
64 Tokajin, Evil Mage U .20 .50
65 Muso, Soul of Onigumo U .20 .50
66 Urasue, Evil Witch U .20 .50
67 Onigumo, Future Villain U .20 .50
68 Totosai's Flying Three-Eyed Cow U .20 .50
69 Taigokumaru, Leader of the Bat Demons U .20 .50
70 Kagome, Koga's Love Interest U .20 .50
71 Koga, Protector of Kagome U .20 .50
72 Naraku's Puppet U .20 .50
73 Sesshomaru, Full Blooded Demon U .20 .50
74 Shippo, Battle Ready U .20 .50
75 Hojo, Kagome's Friend U .20 .50
76 Myoga, Terrified Flea U .20 .50
77 Koga, Hero of the Wolf Demon Tribe U .20 .50

78 Sota, Helpful Brother U .20 .50
79 Shunran, Deva of the Panther Tribe U .20 .50
80 Demon U .20 .50
81 Yura, Master of Puppets U .20 .50
82 Hachi, Shape Changing Raccoon U .20 .50
83 Totosai, Old Sword Maker U .20 .50
84 Ryukotsusei, Deadly Demon U .20 .50
85 Jaken, Critical Thinker U .20 .50
86 Tsubaki, Old Witch U .20 .50
87 Myoga, Old Friend U .20 .50
88 Policeman U .20 .50
89 Toran, Warrior of the Panther Tribe U .20 .50
90 Shuuran, Warrior of the Panther Tribe U .20 .50
91 Archery Training U .20 .50
92 Fighting Over a Girl U .20 .50
93 Goofing Around U .20 .50
94 Righteous Strike U .20 .50
95 Weakling U .20 .50
96 Coward U .20 .50
97 Deflection U .20 .50
98 We Will Protect You U .20 .50
99 Eavesdropping U .20 .50
100 Nightmares About Homework U .20 .50
101 Pinned U .20 .50
102 Famished U .20 .50
103 What Do Women Really Like??? U .20 .50
104 I Will Cause Your Demise U .20 .50
105 Generations U .20 .50
106 Priestess Traps U .20 .50
107 Sacred Saki and Charms U .20 .50
108 Iron Work Hammer U .20 .50
109 Naraku's Lair U .20 .50
110 Subway U .20 .50
111 Sango, Peaceful Traveler R .75 2.00
112 Kikyo, Supernatural Beauty R .75 2.00
113 Goshinki, Spawn of Naraku R .75 2.00
114 Inuyasha, Protector of Kagome R .75 2.00
115 Sango, Worried Sister R .75 2.00
116 Inuyasha, Sota's Hero R .75 2.00
117 Kanna, Naraku's Servant R .75 2.00
118 Naraku, the Mastermind R .75 2.00
119 Goodies R .75 2.00
120 Scissors R .75 2.00
121 Rock R .75 2.00
122 Paper R .75 2.00
123 Sucking Up R .75 2.00
124 Menacing Evil R .75 2.00
125 Learning New Techniques R .75 2.00
126 Sigh R .75 2.00
127 Enraged R .75 2.00
128 Strong Punch R .75 2.00
129 Followers R .75 2.00
130 Play Time R .75 2.00
131 Remembering Her R .75 2.00
132 I'm Honored R .75 2.00
133 The Dead Walk R .75 2.00
134 Girl Talk R .75 2.00
135 You Look Like Her R .75 2.00
136 A Deal With a Bat R .75 2.00
137 Halt! R .75 2.00
138 Scared of Not Talking R .75 2.00
139 They're so Cute R .75 2.00
140 Treasures R .75 2.00
141 Baggage R .75 2.00
142 School Hallway R .75 2.00
143 Kagome's Junior High R .75 2.00
144 Kagome's Refrigerator R .75 2.00
145 Classroom R .75 2.00
146 Graveyard R .75 2.00
147 Jealous R .75 2.00
148 Cover Up R .75 2.00
149 Down the Well R .75 2.00
150 Clash of Power R .75 2.00
151 Kagome, Traveler Through Time UR 4.00 10.00
152 Sesshomaru, Intimidating Adversary UR 4.00 10.00
153 Shunran, Panther Tribe Deva UR 4.00 10.00
154 Kagura, Temptress of Evil UR 5.00 12.00
155 Thank You Great Lord UR 3.00 8.00
156 You Were Worried UR 3.00 8.00
157 Tetsusaiga, Transformed UR 4.00 10.00
158 Things Never Change UR 3.00 8.00
H1 The Three Sprites of the Monkey God HR 10.00 20.00
H2 Kawaramaru HR 10.00 20.00

2006 InuYasha Saisei Timeless Champions

COMPLETE SET (10) 6.00 15.00
TC1 Inuyasha, TC 1.25 3.00
TC2 Kagome, TC 1.25 3.00
TC3 Miroku, TC 1.25 3.00
TC4 Sango, TC 1.25 3.00
TC5 Shippo, TC 1.25 3.00
TC6 Kirara, TC 1.25 3.00
TC7 Koga, TC 1.25 3.00
TC8 Kikyo, TC 1.25 3.00
TC9 Inuyasha, Human TC 1.25 3.00
TC10 Kohaku, TC 1.25 3.00

2006 InuYasha Saisei Promos

COMPLETE SET (9) 5.00 12.00
P1 Inuyasha, Skilled Warrior PROMO 1.00 2.50
P2 Naraku, Puppet Master PROMO 1.00 2.50
P3 Sesshomaru, Diabolical Brother PROMO 1.00 2.50
P4 Relaxing PROMO 1.00 2.50
P5 Forward Charge PROMO 1.00 2.50
P6 Kikyo, Sacred Jewel Protector PROMO 1.00 2.50
P7 Meditation PROMO 1.00 2.50
P8 Kagome, Guardian of the Shikon Jewel PROMO1.00 2.50
P9 What Test? PROMO 1.00 2.50

2006 InuYasha Shimei

COMPLETE SET (119) 25.00 50.00
BOOSTER BOX (12 PACKS) 5.00 12.00
BOOSTER PACK (10 CARDS) .60 1.50
RELEASED ON JUNE 14, 2006
1 Rats C .10 .25
2 Tesso C .10 .25
3 Kuroro C .10 .25
4 Two-Tailed Kittens C .10 .25
5 Wolves, 2 C .10 .25
6 Clay Warriors, 2 C .10 .25
7 Gamajiro, Evil Demon C .10 .25
8 Madam Exorcist C .10 .25
9 Demon Head C .10 .25
10 Hitomi C .10 .25
11 Turtle Demon C .10 .25
12 Buyo, Happy Kitty C .10 .25
13 Mushin, the Old Monk C .10 .25
14 Angry Villagers C .10 .25
15 Hachi, as Miroku C .10 .25
16 Soldier C .10 .25
17 Surprised Outlaws C .10 .25
18 Kansuke, Mad Killer C .10 .25
19 Village Women C .10 .25
20 Myoga, Faithful Friend C .10 .25
21 Ginta, Follower of Koga C .10 .25
22 Sota, Boy in Love C .10 .25
23 Koume C .10 .25
24 Hakkaku, Follower of Koga C .10 .25
25 Kirara, Sango's Pet C .10 .25
26 Orochimaru, Evil Demon C .10 .25
27 Gyuoh, Evil Demon C .10 .25
28 Kawaramaru, Leader of the Clay Warriors C .10 .25
29 Summoned Clay Warrior C .10 .25
30 Rin, Friend of Jaken C .10 .25
31 A Friendly Conversation C .10 .25
32 Hard Strike C .10 .25
33 Tight Grip C .10 .25
34 Sneaking a Peek C .10 .25
35 Quick Reflexes C .10 .25
36 Don't Catch a Cold C .10 .25
37 Taken by Force C .10 .25
38 Stuck to a Stone C .10 .25
39 Forceful Strike C .10 .25
40 Watching Over Her C .10 .25
41 Fish C .10 .25
42 Soccer Ball C .10 .25
43 Mermaid Scale C .10 .25
44 Chips C .10 .25
45 Water Bottle C .10 .25
46 Enju, Urasue's Child U .20 .50
47 Jaken, Friend of Rin U .20 .50
48 Koga, Leader of the Wolf Demon Tribe U .20 .50
49 Onigumo, Villain U .20 .50
50 Kansuke, Aging Outlaw U .20 .50
51 The Three Sprites of the
Monkey God, Playful Kids U .20 .50
52 Monkey God U .20 .50
53 Kagura, Evil Demon U .20 .50
54 Kagome, Showing the Roast U .20 .50
55 Sango, Friend of Kirara U .20 .50
56 Sango, Demon Hunter U .20 .50
57 Hachi, Friendly Raccoon U .20 .50
58 Shippo, Master Gamer U .20 .50
59 Miroku, Ready for Battle U .20 .50
60 Kagome, Master Archer U .20 .50
61 Sesshomaru, Menacing Demon U .20 .50
62 Kaede, Village Leader U .20 .50
63 Moth Demon U .20 .50
64 Naraku, Evil Demon U .20 .50
65 Inuyasha, Wearing a Hat U .20 .50
66 Inuyasha, Aggravated U .20 .50
67 Kanna, Evil Demon U .20 .50
68 Kikyo, Wandering Priestess U .20 .50
69 Fake Shikon Jewel U .20 .50
70 The Monkey God's Stone U .20 .50
71 Dagger U .20 .50
72 Beautiful Valley U .20 .50
73 Bandit Camp U .20 .50
74 Stream U .20 .50
75 Trail Into Village U .20 .50
76 Abandoned Shrine U .20 .50
77 Grassy Trail U .20 .50
78 Cliff U .20 .50
79 Cave of the Priestess U .20 .50
80 A Place to Sleep U .20 .50
81 The Night Sky U .20 .50
82 Come On U .20 .50
83 A Helping Hand U .20 .50
84 Family Dinner U .20 .50
85 All Tied Up U .20 .50
86 Promise Under the Rainbow U .20 .50
87 Relieved U .20 .50
88 Don't Be Fooled U .20 .50
89 I Was So Worried About You U .20 .50
90 Shopping U .20 .50
91 Naraku, Menacing Demon R .75 2.00
92 Sesshomaru, Silent Warrior R .75 2.00
93 Jaken, Serving Lord Sesshomaru R .75 2.00
94 Miroku, Flattering Monk R .75 2.00
95 Koga, Inuyasha's Rival R .75 2.00
96 Kawaramaru, Ruthless Leader R .75 2.00
97 Inuyasha, Master Hunter R .75 2.00
98 Following the Scent R .75 2.00
99 Overwhelmed With Happiness R .75 2.00
100 Waiting R .75 2.00
101 The Power of Prayer R .75 2.00
102 Lord Sesshomaru R .75 2.00
103 Playing With Toys R .75 2.00
104 Which One is Which? R .75 2.00
105 Keeping Warm R .75 2.00
106 Deal With It R .75 2.00
107 Determined Slayer R .75 2.00
108 I Need Help R .75 2.00
109 Deadly Poison R .75 2.00
110 Jeweled Souls R .75 2.00
111 I'm Late! R .75 2.00
112 Be Quiet R .75 2.00
113 Fake Shikon Jewel Club R .75 2.00
114 Bomb R .75 2.00
115 Swarm R .75 2.00
116 Inuyasha, Quick to Attack UR 5.00 12.00
117 Explosion UR 3.00 8.00
118 She's Just Saying That UR 3.00 8.00
119 Brute Force UR 4.00 10.00
H1 Jakotsu HR 10.00 20.00
H2 Bankotsu HR 10.00 20.00

2006 InuYasha Shimei Memories

COMPLETE SET (10) 6.00 15.00
M1 Approaching the Well 1.25 3.00
M2 He Was Here? 1.25 3.00
M3 Reunited 1.25 3.00
M4 A Reflection of One's Self 1.25 3.00
M5 Shot in the Heart 1.25 3.00
M6 Remembering the Fallen 1.25 3.00
M7 Being Bashful 1.25 3.00
M8 A Moment of Peace 1.25 3.00
M9 Happy Birthday 1.25 3.00
M10 A Special Occasion 1.25 3.00

2006 InuYasha Tousou

COMPLETE SET (119) 25.00 50.00
BOOSTER BOX (12) 5.00 12.00
BOOSTER PACK (10) .60 1.50
RELEASED IN OCTOBER 2006
1 Inuyasha, Feudal Hero C .10 .25
2 Miroku, Feudal Hero C .10 .25
3 Kagome, Feudal Hero C .10 .25
4 Sango, Feudal Hero C .10 .25
5 Shippo, Feudal Hero C .10 .25
6 Kirara, Feudal Hero C .10 .25
7 Naraku, Powerful Foe C .10 .25
8 Sesshomaru, Powerful Foe C .10 .25
9 Jaken, Sesshomaru's Loyal Companion C .10 .25
10 Kikyo, Feudal Hero C .10 .25
11 Village Man C .10 .25
12 Kohaku, Naraku's Pawn C .10 .25
13 Koga, Warrior of the Wolf Demon Tribe C .10 .25
14 Kagura, Naraku's Pawn C .10 .25
15 Northern Wolf Tribe Warriors C .10 .25
16 Ayame, Princess of the Northern Wolf Tribe C .10 .25
17 Naraku's Poison Insects, 5 C .10 .25
18 Gun Battalion C .10 .25
19 Province Lord C .10 .25
20 Myoga, Traveling Flea C .10 .25
21 Koyuki, Snow Maiden C .10 .25
22 Shintaro's Sister C .10 .25
23 Cavalryman C .10 .25
24 Rin, Little Girl C .10 .25
25 Jinenji, Half Demon C .10 .25
26 Village Boy C .10 .25
27 Naraku's Poison Insects, 6 C .10 .25
28 Kanna, Naraku's Pawn C .10 .25
29 Kyokotsu, Member of the Band of Seven C .10 .25
30 Mukotsu, Member of the Band of Seven C .10 .25
31 Stay Back C .10 .25
32 Breaking the Barrier C .10 .25
33 How Dare You? C .10 .25
34 I Want Them C .10 .25
35 Off to War C .10 .25
36 Laughing Mushrooms C .10 .25
37 Keep Your Hands Off My Wolves! C .10 .25
38 Surprise Attack C .10 .25
39 Daydreaming C .10 .25
40 Wire Trap C .10 .25
41 Matchlock Rifle C .10 .25
42 Sleeping Potion C .10 .25
43 Myoga's Special Potion C .10 .25
44 Shintaro's Staff C .10 .25
45 Ointment C .10 .25
46 Wolf, 3 U .20 .50
47 Wolf Tribe Elder U .20 .50
48 Ginkotsu, Member of the Band of Seven U .20 .50
49 Kyokotsu, Warrior of the Band of Seven U .20 .50
50 Kikyo, Supernatural Priestess U .20 .50
51 Suikotsu, Good Doctor U .20 .50
52 Inuyasha, the Victor U .20 .50
53 Suikotsu, Member of the Band of Seven U .20 .50
54 Renkotsu, Member of the Band of Seven U .20 .50
55 Warlord General U .20 .50
56 Renkotsu, Member of the Band of Seven U .20 .50
57 Elder of the Northern Wolf Tribe U .20 .50
58 Battalion Leader U .20 .50
59 Kohaku, Follower of Naraku U .20 .50
60 Suikotsu, Warrior of the Band of Seven U .20 .50
61 Inuyasha, Kagome's Hero U .20 .50
62 Mukotsu, Poison Master of the Band of Seven U .20 .50
63 Guard U .20 .50
64 Sango, Last Living Slayer U .20 .50
65 Miroku, Carefree Monk U .20 .50
66 Shintaro U .20 .50
67 Kagome, Reincarnated Priestess U .20 .50
68 Ginkotsu, Warrior of the Band of Seven U .20 .50
69 Shippo, Helpful Friend U .20 .50
70 Jakotsu, Member of the Band of Seven U .20 .50
71 You're So Adorable U .20 .50
72 Die! U .20 .50
73 Surrounded U .20 .50
74 Tormented U .20 .50
75 Paralysis U .20 .50
76 I Made it Worse! U .20 .50
77 Executed U .20 .50
78 Are You Okay? U .20 .50
79 It's Not Fair U .20 .50
80 Burying the Dead U .20 .50
81 Ginkotsu's Jewel Shard U .20 .50
82 Special Restorative U .20 .50
83 Tainted Jewel Shard U .20 .50
84 Suikotsu's Claws U .20 .50
85 Mukotsu's Poison U .20 .50
86 Hijiri Island U .20 .50
87 Bamboo Forest U .20 .50
88 Tomb of the Band of Seven U .20 .50
89 Renkotsu's Workshop U .20 .50
90 Mount Hakurei U .20 .50
91 Warlord General, Military Mastermind R .75 2.00
92 Renkotsu, Tactician of the Band of Seven R .75 2.00
93 Jakotsu, Warrior of the Band of Seven R .75 2.00
94 Suikotsu, Mercenary of the Band of Seven R .75 2.00
95 Sesshomaru, Skilled Warrior R .75 2.00
96 Inuyasha, Wielder of Tetsusaiga R .75 2.00
97 Koga, Fierce Wolf Demon R .75 2.00
98 He Smelled of Corpses and Graveyard Soil R .75 2.00
99 Clash of Swords R .75 2.00
100 Sucking Out the Poison R .75 2.00
101 He Will Die... He Won't Die... R .75 2.00
102 Fun at the Hot Springs R .75 2.00
103 It's Just One Promise R .75 2.00
104 Approaching Danger R .75 2.00
105 Looking for Koga R .75 2.00
106 Abducted R .75 2.00
107 Strong Slash R .75 2.00
108 You and I Share Similar Fates R .75 2.00
109 Ginkotsu Self Destructs R .75 2.00
110 Koga's Determination R .75 2.00
111 That's Enough R .75 2.00
112 Jumping Out of the Way R .75 2.00
113 Banryu R .75 2.00
114 Jakotsuto R .75 2.00
115 Saint Hakushin's Amulet R .75 2.00
116 Bankotsu, Leader of the Band of Seven UR 4.00 10.00
117 Miroku, Warrior Monk UR 4.00 10.00
118 Saving an Old Love UR 5.00 12.00
119 Breakthrough UR 3.00 8.00
H1 Saint Hakushin HR 10.00 20.00
H2 Naraku, Reborn HR 10.00 20.00

2006 InuYasha Tousou Weapons

COMPLETE SET (10) 6.00 15.00
W1 Tetsusaiga 1.25 3.00
W2 Tenseiga 1.25 3.00
W3 Tokijin 1.25 3.00
W4 Hiraikotsu 1.25 3.00
W5 Miroku's Staff 1.25 3.00
W6 Kagome's Bicycle 1.25 3.00
W7 Kagome's Backpack 1.25 3.00
W8 Jewel of Four Souls 1.25 3.00
W9 Banryu 1.25 3.00
W10 Jakotsuto 1.25 3.00

2006 InuYasha Tousou Promos

COMPLETE SET (7) 3.00 8.00
P1 Bankotsu, Warrior of the Band of Seven P 1.00 2.50
P2 Kohaku, Tragic Soul P 1.00 2.50
P3 Koga, Wolf Commander P 1.00 2.50
P4 Bankotsu's Lightning Attack P 1.00 2.50
P5 Sango, Fearless Warrior P 1.00 2.50
P6 Clash P 1.00 2.50
P7 Inuyasha, Rushing into Battle P 1.00 2.50

2007 InuYasha Keshin

COMPLETE SET (119) 25.00 50.00
BOOSTER BOX (12 PACKS) 15.00 30.00
BOOSTER PACK (10 CARDS) 1.50 3.00
RELEASED ON FEBRUARY 28, 2007
1 Naraku's Demons, 2 C .10 .25
2 The Little Fox Demons C .10 .25
3 Naraku's Demons, 3 C .10 .25
4 Kohaku, Controlled by Naraku C .10 .25
5 Chokyukai's Brides C .10 .25
6 Yuka, Kagome's Classmate C .10 .25
7 Kagome's Mom, Caring Mother C .10 .25
8 Renkotsu, Warrior of the Band of Seven C .10 .25
9 Jakotsu, Soldier of the Band of Seven C .10 .25
10 Suikotsu, Maniac of the Band of Seven C .10 .25
11 Bankotsu, Strongest of the Band of Seven C .10 .25
12 Mimisenri C .10 .25
13 Kagome, Willing Helper C .10 .25
14 Sango, Feudal Warrior C .10 .25
15 Shippo, Quick Little Fox Demon C .10 .25
16 Chokyukai, Direct Descendant of Chohakkai C .10 .25
17 Sagojo, Descendant of Sagojo C .10 .25
18 Goku, Descendant of Songoku C .10 .25
19 Koga, Kagome's Protector C .10 .25
20 Kagura, Naraku's Incarnation C .10 .25
21 Kanna, Naraku's Incarnation C .10 .25
22 Kirara, Cat Demon of Two Tails C .10 .25
23 Kikyo, Powerful Priestess C .10 .25
24 Eri, Stern Director C .10 .25
25 Ayumi, Music Conductor C .10 .25
26 Sesshomaru, Inuyasha's Older Brother C .10 .25
27 Miroku, Feudal Traveler C .10 .25
28 Mizuki C .10 .25
29 Kaede, Elder Priestess C .10 .25
30 Kagome's Grandfather, Old Priest C .10 .25
31 Sins of the Past C .10 .25
32 Good Friends C .10 .25
33 May You Rest in Peace C .10 .25
34 Giving in to Temptation C .10 .25
35 Farewell Old Friend C .10 .25
36 The First Meeting C .10 .25
37 A Big Disappointment C .10 .25
38 Incinerated by the Fire Cannon C .10 .25
39 Drying Off C .10 .25
40 I Refuse to Die C .10 .25
41 Renkotsu's Blast Cannon C .10 .25
42 Robe of the Fire Rat, Inuyasha's Armor C .10 .25
43 Fire Bomb C .10 .25
44 Kanna's Mirror, Her Weapon C .10 .25
45 Groceries C .10 .25
46 Inuyasha, Kikyo's Past Love U .20 .50
47 Sango, Feudal Traveler U .20 .50
48 Naraku, Revealed U .20 .50
49 Rin, Child in Wonder U .20 .50
50 Inuyasha, Looking Sad U .20 .50
51 Shippo, the Transformer U .20 .50
52 Kagome, in a Play U .20 .50
53 Hojo, in a Play U .20 .50
54 Inuyasha, Modern U .20 .50
55 Naraku's Demons, 4 U .20 .50
56 Inuyasha, Purified U .20 .50
57 Infant, Spawn of Naraku U .20 .50
58 Miroku, Roaming Monk U .20 .50
59 Jakotsu, Band of Seven Warrior U .20 .50
60 Renkotsu, Deceptive Member of the Band of Seven U .20
.50
61 Bankotsu, Band of Seven Warrior U .20 .50
62 Yuka, the Cook U .20 .50
63 Ayumi, Strict Leader U .20 .50
64 Eri, Determined U .20 .50
65 Ginta, Koga's Companion U .20 .50
66 Hakkaku, Koga's Companion U .20 .50
67 Kagome's Grandfather, Demon Fighter U .20 .50
68 Sota, the Soul Stealer U .20 .50
69 Koga, Demon Wolf Tribe Warrior U .20 .50
70 Clumps of Flesh U .20 .50
71 Knockout Strike U .20 .50
72 New Found Power U .20 .50
73 Born Again U .20 .50
74 Holding on Tight U .20 .50
75 Cooking Class U .20 .50
76 Chokyukai's Abducted Brides U .20 .50
77 Silence U .20 .50
78 I'll Defend You U .20 .50
79 They are Both Stupid U .20 .50
80 There is Still Hope for This Child U .20 .50
81 Chinese Sutra U .20 .50
82 Necklace of Flowers U .20 .50
83 Staff U .20 .50
84 Scalpel U .20 .50
85 Naraku's Tainted Shard U .20 .50
86 Banryu, Demon Powered U .20 .50
87 Cultural Festival U .20 .50
88 Convenience Store U .20 .50
89 Chokyukai's Lair U .20 .50
90 All Knowing U .20 .50
91 Kikyo, Elegant Priestess R .75 2.00
92 Naraku, Transformed R .75 2.00
93 Chokyukai, Stealer of Women R .75 2.00
94 Infant, Controller of Hearts R .75 2.00
95 Inuyasha, the Proud R .75 2.00
96 Kagome, Feudal Traveler R .75 2.00
97 Bankotsu, Last of the Band of Seven R .75 2.00
98 Sesshomaru, Roaming Demon R .75 2.00
99 Saint Hakushin, Living Buddha R .75 2.00
100 Support from the Family R .75 2.00
101 My Lost Love R .75 2.00
102 Save Him Inuyasha! R .75 2.00
103 Thinking R .75 2.00
104 Deadly Hit R .75 2.00
105 Running Into the Windscar R .75 2.00
106 Uppercut R .75 2.00
107 Shut Your Trap! R .75 2.00
108 It's No Ones Fault But Your Own R .75 2.00
109 The Heart Scar R .75 2.00
110 I Hate You! R .75 2.00
111 At a Loss R .75 2.00
112 It's Cold R .75 2.00
113 When Will They Be Back? R .75 2.00
114 Kagome's House R .75 2.00
115 Chokyukai's Tiara R .75 2.00
116 Naraku, Master of Manipulation UR 4.00 10.00
117 Shippo, Master Fox Demon UR 4.00 10.00
118 Damn You! UR 5.00 12.00
119 An Unimaginable Loss UR 3.00 8.00
H1 Sesshomaru HR 10.00 20.00
H2 Sango HR 10.00 20.00

2007 InuYasha Keshin Feudal Voices Autographs

STATED PRINT RUN 170 SER. #'d SETS
FV1 Inuyasha, Feudal Hero 30.00 60.00
FV2 Sango, the Demon Slayer 12.00 25.00
FV3 Sesshomaru, Wanderer 12.00 25.00
FV4 Shippo, the Shapeshifter 12.00 25.00
FV5 Miroku, Warrior Monk 12.00 25.00
FV6 Koga, Protector of Kagome 12.00 25.00

2007 InuYasha Keshin Feudal Warriors

COMPLETE SET (10) 6.00 15.00
FW1 Inuyasha 1.25 3.00
FW2 Sesshomaru 1.25 3.00
FW3 Naraku 1.25 3.00
FW4 Kagome 1.25 3.00
FW5 Miroku 1.25 3.00
FW6 Sango 1.25 3.00
FW7 Kikyo 1.25 3.00
FW8 Muso 1.25 3.00
FW9 Kagura 1.25 3.00
FW10 Koga 1.25 3.00

2007 InuYasha Keshin Players Choice Autographs

UNPRICED DUE TO SCARCITY
PC1 Inuyasha/20
PC2 Koga/20
PC3 Halt!/10

2007 InuYasha Keshin Promos

COMPLETE SET (7) 4.00 10.00
P1 Infant, the Heart of Naraku P 1.00 2.50
P2 Naraku, Master of Deception P 1.00 2.50
P3 Saint Hakushin, Manipulated by Naraku P 1.00 2.50
P4 Naraku, Vile Demon P 1.00 2.50
P5 Shippo, in Love P 1.00 2.50
P6 Miroku's Curse P 1.00 2.50
P7 Sit Inuyasha! P 1.00 2.50

2007 InuYasha Tensei

COMPLETE SET (80) 30.00 60.00
BOOSTER BOX (12 PACKS) 15.00 30.00
BOOSTER PACK (10 CARDS) 1.50 3.00
RELEASED ON JUNE 6, 2007
1 Sara, Young Princess C .10 .25
2 Genbu, Ninja of the Darkness C .10 .25
3 Byakko, Ninja of the Snow C .10 .25
4 Seiryu, Ninja of the Moon C .10 .25
5 Suzaku, Ninja of the Flower C .10 .25
6 Chief Slayer C .10 .25
7 Hoshiyomi, Demon Ninja C .10 .25
8 Bird Demons, 1 C .10 .25
9 Bird Demons, 2 C .10 .25
10 Bird Demons, 3 C .10 .25
11 Hakudoshi, the Horrible C .10 .25
12 Akitoki Hojo, Hojo's Ancestor C .10 .25

13 Mezu, the Stone Gate Keeper C .10 .25
14 Gozu, the Stone Gate Keeper C .10 .25
15 Paper Thin Demon C .10 .25
16 Rengokuki, Entei's First Master C .10 .25
17 Kwannon, Salamander Demon C .10 .25
18 Entei, the Untamed C .10 .25
19 Demon Ninja Shadow Hold C .10 .25
20 The Band of Seven C .10 .25
21 Ninja Kite C .10 .25
22 Priestess Amulet C .10 .25
23 Ken Blade C .10 .25
24 Kon Blade C .10 .25
25 Byakko, Transformed U .20 .50
26 Suzaku, Flamboyant Ninja U .20 .50
27 Seiryu, Transformed U .20 .50
28 Genbu, Transformed U .20 .50
29 Saint Hijiri the Holy One U .20 .50
30 Tsubaki, Cursed Priestess U .20 .50
31 Tsukiyomi, Samurai Priestess U .20 .50
32 Shippo, Kagome's Protector U .20 .50
33 Bird Demons, 4 U .20 .50
34 Inuyasha, Protector of Kagome's Heart U .20 .50
35 Princess Abi, Princess of the Bird Demons U .20 .50
36 Kirara, Companion of Sango U .20 .50
37 Kagome, Mushin's Maid U .20 .50
38 Sango, Miroku's Love Interest U .20 .50
39 Miroku, Sentimental Monk U .20 .50
40 Sesshomaru, Master of Tenseiga U .20 .50
41 Sara, the Woman Who Loved Sesshomaru U .20 .50
42 Intoxicated U .20 .50
43 Akitoki Hojo, Protector of Kagome U .20 .50
44 Demon Ninja Doppleganger Techinque U .20 .50
45 Attack of the Bird Demons of Doom U .20 .50
46 Wounded U .20 .50
47 How Long Do You Intend to Hide? U .20 .50
48 Sack! U .20 .50
49 Shippo, the Master Fox Demon U .20 .50
50 Tomb of Inuyasha's Father U .20 .50
51 Possessed Shrine U .20 .50
52 Princess Abi, Bird Master R .75 2.00
53 Inuyasha, Heroic Champion R .75 2.00
54 Hoshiyomi, Leader of the Demon Ninja R .75 2.00
55 Entei, Raging Demon Horse R .75 2.00
56 Sesshomaru, Silent Demon R .75 2.00
57 Naraku, Wicked Demon R .75 2.00
58 Hakudoshi, Entei's Rider R .75 2.00
59 Demon Ninja Shadow Incarnation R .75 2.00
60 Preparing the Ceremony R .75 2.00
61 Naraku's Grip R .75 2.00
62 Regenerating R .75 2.00
63 He Proposed R .75 2.00
64 What Do You Want to Give Me? R .75 2.00
65 Hakudoshi R .75 2.00
66 Kikyo R .75 2.00
67 Sesshomaru, Warrior of the Feudal Era P 1.00 2.50
68 Miroku, Sango's Protector P 1.00 2.50
69 Koga, Protector of Kagome's Heart P 1.00 2.50
70 Naraku's Mark R .75 2.00
71 Could She Be? R .75 2.00
72 The Naginata of Kenkon R .75 2.00
73 Trident of Naraku's Bones R .75 2.00
74 River Bank R .75 2.00
75 Believe Us! UR 3.00 8.00
76 Princess Abi, Bird Demon Princess UR 5.00 12.00
77 Hakudoshi, Naraku's Incarnation UR 4.00 10.00
78 Kanna UR 4.00 10.00
79 The Cost of War UR 4.00 10.00
80 Tekkei UR 4.00 10.00

2007 InuYasha Tensei Classics

COMPLETE SET (10) 6.00 15.00
C1 Miroku, Lecherous Monk (Saisei #IYP4) 1.25 3.00
C2 Inuyasha, Helpful Friend (Saisei #0P3) 1.25 3.00
C3 Kagome (Kassen #H2) 1.25 3.00
C4 Sesshomaru, Rival Brother (Saisei #IYP3) 1.25 3.00
C5 Rin, Follower of Sesshomaru (Kassen #KP3) 1.25 3.00
C6 Yura, Master of Puppets (Saisei #81) 1.25 3.00
C7 Halt! (Saisei #137) 1.25 3.00
C8 Waking Up (Saisei #0p1) 1.25 3.00
C9 Watching Each Others Back (Saisei #PR4) 1.25 3.00
C10 Naraku's Evil Influence (Saisei #0P2) 1.25 3.00

2007 InuYasha Tensei Feudal Voices Autographs

STATED PRINT RUN 170 SER. #'d SETS
FV1 Bankotsu, Band of Seven 10.00 20.00
FV2 Kagura 10.00 20.00
FV3 Jaken, Friend of Rin 10.00 20.00
FV4 Kikyo, Legends 12.00 25.00
FV5 Hakudoshi, Spawn of Naraku 10.00 20.00
FV6 Naraku, Deceptive Demon 20.00 40.00

2007 InuYasha Tensei Players Choice Autographs

UNPRICED DUE TO SCARCITY
PC1 Just Ask For Help/20
PC2 Naraku, Reborn/20
PC3 Kikyo, Fading Soul/20
PC4 A Tragic Death (Kijin #104) /20
PC5 Yura, Master of Puppets (Saisei #81) /20
PC6 Kikyo/20
PC7 You Were Worried (Saisei #156) /10
PC8 Koga, the Furious (Jaki #118) /10
PC9 Sesshomaru, Rival Brother (Saisei #IYP3) /10
PC10 Miroku, Lecherous Monk (Saisei #IYP4) /10
PC11 Inuyasha, Helpful Friend (Saisei #0P3) /10
PC12 Naraku's Evil Influence (Saisei #0P2) /10
PC13 Hakudoshi (Keshin #10) /10
PC14 Kanna/10

2012 Kaijudo Evo Fury

COMPLETE SET (61) 20.00 50.00
BOOSTER BOX (24 PACKS) 30.00 40.00
BOOSTER PACK (9 CARDS) 1.00 2.00
RELEASED ON NOVEMBER 3, 2012
1 Chasm Entangler C .30 .75
2 Cloudwalker Drone C .10 .25
3 Cobalt, the Storm Knight VR .40 1.00
4 Halon, Paragon of Light U .20 .50
5 Helios Rings C .10 .25
6 Photon Squad C .10 .25
7 Prism-Blade Enforcer U .30 .75
8 Recharge R .30 .75
9 Shock Sentinel R .30 .75
10 Starwing U .20 .50
11 Twilight Commander R .30 .75
12 Aquatic Expulsion R .30 .75
13 Cyber Sprite C .30 .75
14 Cyber Trader C .10 .25
15 Emperor Axon U .20 .50
16 Forklift Tank Glu-urrgle VR .40 1.00
17 King Neptas R .75 2.00
18 Neuron's Oracle R .30 .75
19 Rapids Lurker Wwhhshrll C .10 .25
20 Reef Gladiator U .60 1.50
21 Search the Depths C .10 .25
22 Sopan, Cyber Renegade U .20 .50
23 Chimera Tyrant R .30 .75
24 Gigabolver C .10 .25
25 Gigazanda C .10 .25
26 Hydra Medusa U .75 2.00
27 Locomotivator U .20 .50
28 Olgate, Knight of Shadow R .30 .75
29 Return from Beyond R .30 .75
30 Scavenging Chimera U .40 1.00
31 Screeching Scaradorable VR 3.00 8.00
32 Slyth C .10 .25
33 Swampstench Worm C .10 .25
34 Big Hissy VR .40 1.00
35 Blastforge Captain R .30 .75
36 Cliffcutter C .10 .25
37 Drakon Warchief U .20 .50
38 Gunwing Dragon U .20 .50
39 Heat Seekers C .10 .25
40 Jet-Thrust Darter C .60 1.50
41 Jetflame Bodyguard C .30 .75
42 Laser-Arm Drakon U .20 .50
43 Lava Leaper R .30 .75
44 Twin-Cannon Maelstrom R .30 .75
45 Bronze-Arm Sabertooth U .30 .75
46 Forsett, Heroic Shaman R .30 .75
47 Granite Avenger R .30 .75
48 Illusory Berry C .10 .25
49 Lepidos the Ancient VR .40 1.00
50 Moonhowler Tribe C .10 .25
51 Prickleback C .40 1.00
52 Reap and Sow C .30 .75
53 Silver Fist U .20 .50
54 Snapclaw U .20 .50
55 Tendril Grasp R .40 1.00
D1 Ra-Vu the Stormbringer SR 1.00 2.50
S1 Orion, Radiant Fury SR 3.00 8.00
S2 Emperor Neuron SR 8.00 20.00
S3 Tekamora the Wretched SR .75 2.00
S4 Evo Fury Tatsurion SR 1.25 3.00
S5 Flamespike Tatsurion SR 1.50 4.00

2012 Kaijudo Rise of the Duel Masters

COMPLETE SET (182) 30.00 80.00
BOOSTER BOX (24 PACKS)
BOOSTER PACK (9 CARDS)
RELEASED ON SEPTEMBER 7, 2012
1 Argus, Vigilant Seer C .10 .25
2 Astinos, the Cloud Knight R .30 .75
3 Blinder Beetle C .30 .75
4 Covering Fire C .40 1.00
5 Current Charger R .30 .75
6 Grand Gure, Tower Keeper VR .40 1.00
7 Halon U .20 .50
8 Jade Monitor C .10 .25
9 Keeper of Clouds U .20 .50
10 Keeper of Dawn R .30 .75
11 Keeper of Twilight R .30 .75
12 Logic Cube U .40 1.00
13 Luminar C .10 .25
14 Magris the Magnetizer C .40 1.00
15 Nimbus Scout C .10 .25
16 Orbital Observer U .20 .50
17 Paladio, Patrol Leader U .20 .50
18 Perimeter Drone U .20 .50
19 Portal Tech R .30 .75
20 Rally the Reserves U .30 .75
21 Razorpine Tree R .30 .75
22 Regroup U .20 .50
23 Seer Serpent VR .40 1.00
24 Shaw K'Naw R .30 .75
25 Spyweb Scurrier U .20 .50
26 Stalker Sphere C .10 .25
27 Starlight Strategist R .30 .75
28 Stormspark Blast R 2.50 6.00
29 Strobe Flash C .10 .25
30 Sun-Stalk Seed C .10 .25
31 Sunshock C .10 .25
32 Thunder Cruiser C .30 .75
33 Urth, the Overlord VR .40 1.00
34 Aqua Commando U .20 .50
35 Aqua Knight R .30 .75
36 Aqua Seneschal C .10 .25
37 Aqua Soldier C .10 .25
38 Buoyant Blowfish C .10 .25
39 Crystal Memory R .75 2.00
40 Finbarr, Council of Logos U .20 .50
41 Fluorogill Manta C .10 .25
42 Frogzooka U .20 .50
43 Hokira, Council of Logos R .30 .75
44 Hydro Spy U .20 .50
45 Hydrobot Crab U .20 .50
46 Ice Blade C .10 .25
47 Ice Launcher C .10 .25
48 King Bullfang R .30 .75
49 King Coral R .75 2.00
50 King Nautilus VR .40 1.00
51 King Pontias U .20 .50
52 Knowledge Warden C .10 .25
53 Logos Scan C .10 .25
54 Memory Swarm C .10 .25
55 Midnight Crawler VR .40 1.00
56 Milporo, Council of Logos R .30 .75
57 Predict C .10 .25
58 Queen Orion VR .40 1.00
59 Reef Prince Glu-urrgle R .30 .75
60 Reef-Eye C .10 .25
61 Rusalka, Aqua Chaser U .60 1.50
62 Spy Mission U .20 .50
63 Steam Star Grapplog C .10 .25
64 Teleport U .20 .50
65 Thought Probe R .30 .75
66 Veil Vortex R .30 .75
67 Acid-Tongue Chimera U .20 .50
68 Black Feather of Shadow Abyss R .30 .75
69 Bone Blades C .10 .25
70 Brain Squirmer C .10 .25
71 Dark Return U .20 .50
72 Death Smoke U .60 1.50
73 Draxar, the Soul Crusher C .10 .25
74 Dream Pirate U .20 .50
75 Fumes C .10 .25
76 Gigargon R .30 .75
77 Gigastand U .50 1.25
78 Gorgeon, Shadow of Gluttony U .20 .50
79 Grave Scrounger C .10 .25
80 Grave Worm Hatchling C .10 .25
81 Horrid Stinger U .20 .50
82 Kronkos, General of Fear R .30 .75
83 Marrow Ooze C .30 .75
84 Quakes the Unclean C .10 .25
85 Razorkinder Puppet VR .40 1.00
86 Roton the Destroyer R .30 .75
87 Rupture Spider U .20 .50
88 Scaradorable of Gloom Hollow R 8.00 20.00
89 Scaradorable the Hunter VR .40 1.00
90 Skeeter Swarmer C .30 .75
91 Skull Cutter C .40 1.00
92 Skull Shatter R .30 .75
93 Specter Claw C .40 1.00
94 Terror Pit R 2.00 5.00
95 Trox, General of Destruction VR .40 1.00
96 Venom Worm C .10 .25
97 Voidwing R .30 .75
98 Writhing Bone Ghoul U .20 .50
99 Zagaan, the Bone Knight R .30 .75
100 Badlands Lizard U .20 .50
101 Barrage U .30 .75
102 Blastforge Slaver U .20 .50
103 Blaze Belcher C .50 1.25
104 Bolgash Dragon VR .40 1.00
105 Bolshack Dragon R .30 .75
106 Bolt-Tail Dragon R .30 .75
107 Comet Missile C .10 .25
108 Draglide the Swiftest C .10 .25
109 Drakon Weaponsmith C .10 .25
110 Flame Aura C .10 .25
111 Flametropus R .30 .75
112 Gatling Skyterror C .10 .25
113 Gilaflame the Assaulter VR 1.25 3.00
114 Hyperspeed Dragon R .40 1.00
115 Kenina the Igniter C .10 .25
116 Legionnaire Lizard R .30 .75
117 Little Hissy U .20 .50
118 Magma Madness R .30 .75
119 Meteosaur U .20 .50
120 Moorna, Gatling Dragon VR .40 1.00
121 Om Nom Nom U .20 .50
122 Overcharge U .20 .50
123 Pyro Trooper C .10 .25
124 Rock Bite C .10 .25
125 Simian Trooper Grash C .10 .25
126 Skycrusher's Elite R .30 .75
127 Snaptongue Lizard U .20 .50
128 Stonesaur C .10 .25
129 Super Bazooka Volcanodon U .20 .50
130 Tornado Flame R .30 .75
131 Tracer Rounds R .30 .75
132 Vorg C .10 .25
133 Ambush Scorpion C .10 .25
134 Brave Giant U .20 .50
135 Breach the Veil U .20 .50
136 Bronze-Arm Tribe C .10 .25
137 Carnivorous Dahlia U .20 .50
138 Deathblade Beetle VR .40 1.00
139 Drifting Toadstool U .20 .50
140 Essence Elf C .10 .25
141 Fear Fang C .10 .25
142 Forest Hornet C .10 .25
143 Gasbag C .10 .25
144 Gigahorn Charger R .30 .75
145 Karate Carrot U .20 .50
146 Launcher Locust R .30 .75
147 Mana Storm R 2.00 5.00
148 Manabind U .20 .50
149 Mighty Shouter VR .40 1.00
150 Power Surge U .20 .50
151 Raging Goliant U .30 .75
152 Razorhide C .10 .25
153 Red-Eye Scorpion R .30 .75
154 Return to the Soil C .10 .25
155 Roaming Bloodmane VR .40 1.00
156 Root Trap R 1.00 2.50
157 Rumbling Terrasaur C .10 .25
158 Shell Dome R .30 .75
159 Sniper Mosquito C .10 .25
160 Splinterclaw Wasp R .30 .75
161 Sprout C .40 1.00
162 Stampeding Longhorn R .30 .75
163 The Great Arena R .50 1.25
164 Thorny Creeper C .10 .25
165 Three-Eyed Dragonfly C .10 .25
D1 Dark Scaradorable SR 1.00 2.50
D2 Wrist-Rockets Tatsurion SR .40 1.00
S1 Ra-Vu, Seeker of Lightning SR 2.50 6.00
S2 Radiant, the Lawbringer SR .40 1.00
S3 Sasha, Channeler of Light SR .40 1.00
S4 Hovercraft Glu-urrgle SR 3.00 8.00
S5 King Tsunami SR .40 1.00
S6 Waterspout Gargoyle SR 1.25 3.00
S7 Death Liger, Lion of Chaos SR .40 1.00
S8 Diabrost, Shadow Marshal SR .40 1.00
S9 Megaria, the Collector SR .40 1.00
S10 Crimson Wyvern SR 1.50 4.00
S11 Meteor Dragon SR .40 1.00
S12 Tatsurion the Unchained SR 2.50 6.00
S13 Bestial Rage Tatsurion SR .75 2.00
S14 Earthstomp Giant SR .40 1.00
S15 Xeno Mantis SR .75 2.00

2012 Kaijudo Tatsurion vs. Razorkinder Battle Deck

COMPLETE SET (45) 8.00 20.00
RELEASED ON JUNE 27, 2012
1 Aqua Seneschal C .10 .25
2 Frogzooka U .20 .50
3 Hydro Spy U .20 .50
4 Hydrobot Crab U .20 .50
5 Ice Blade C .10 .25
6 King Nautilus VR .40 1.00
7 King Pontias U .20 .50
8 Reef-Eye C .10 .25
9 Spy Mission U .20 .50
10 Teleport U .20 .50
11 Bone Blades C .10 .25
12 Brain Squirmer C .10 .25
13 Death Smoke U .30 .75
14 Dream Pirate U .20 .50
15 Fumes C .10 .25
16 Gigargon R .30 .75
17 Grave Worm Hatchling C .10 .25
18 Horrid Stinger U .20 .50
19 Skeeter Swarmer C .10 .25
20 Skull Cutter C .10 .25
21 Terror Pit R 2.00 5.00
22 Zagaan, the Bone Knight R .30 .75
23 Blaze Belcher C .10 .25
24 Comet Missile C .50 1.25
25 Draglide the Swiftest C .10 .25
26 Flametropus R .30 .75
27 Gatling Skyterror C .10 .25
28 Little Hissy U .20 .50
29 Overcharge U .20 .50
30 Pyro Trooper C .10 .25
31 Rock Bite C .10 .25
32 Simian Trooper Grash C .10 .25
33 Tornado Flame R .30 .75
34 Ambush Scorpion C .10 .25
35 Brave Giant U .20 .50
36 Bronze-Arm Tribe C .40 1.00
37 Essence Elf C .10 .25
38 Raging Goliant U .20 .50
39 Return to the Soil C .10 .25
40 Roaming Bloodmane VR .40 1.00
41 Root Trap R 1.25 3.00
42 Rumbling Terrasaur C .10 .25
43 Sprout C .50 1.25
S1 Razorkinder SR .40 1.00
S2 Tatsurion SR .40 1.00

2012 Kaijudo The Dojo Edition

COMPLETE SET (61) 12.00 30.00
BOOSTER BOX (24 PACKS) 30.00 40.00
BOOSTER PACK (9 PACKS) 1.00 2.00
RELEASED ON JULY 24, 2012
1 Blinder Beetle C .10 .25
2 Grand Gure, Tower Keeper VR .30 .75
3 Keeper of Clouds C .10 .25
4 Keeper of Dawn R .25 .60
5 Keeper of Twilight R .25 .60
6 Luminar C .10 .25
7 Regroup U .20 .50
8 Shaw K'Naw R .40 1.00
9 Star Lantern U .20 .50
10 Sun-Stalk Seed C .10 .25
11 Sunshock C .10 .25
12 Aqua Commando U .20 .50
13 Aqua Soldier C .10 .25
14 Fluorogill Manta C .10 .25
15 Hydro Spy U .20 .50
16 Ice Blade C .10 .25
17 King Bullfang R .25 .60
18 Logos Scan C .10 .25
19 Potato Gun Glu-urrgle VR .30 .75
20 Reef Prince Glu-urrgle R .25 .60
21 Veil Vortex R .25 .60
22 Vikorakus U .20 .50
23 Acid-Tongue Chimera U .20 .50
24 Black Feather of Shadow Abyss R .25 .60
25 Brain Squirmer C .10 .25
26 Ghost Spy U .20 .50
27 Gigargon R .25 .60
28 Skeeter Swarmer C .10 .25
29 Skull Cutter C .10 .25
30 Specter Claw C .10 .25
31 Terror Pit R 1.25 3.00
32 Trox, General of Destruction VR .30 .75
33 Writhing Bone Ghoul U .20 .50
34 Bolt-Tail Dragon R .25 .60
35 Chain-Lash Tatsurion R .40 1.00
36 Comet Missile C .30 .75
37 Draglide the Swiftest C .10 .25
38 Drakon Weaponsmith C .10 .25
39 Gatling Skyterror C .10 .25
40 Gilaflame the Assaulter VR 1.25 3.00
41 Little Hissy U .20 .50
42 Om Nom Nom U .20 .50
43 Super Bazooka Volcanodon U .20 .50
44 Tornado Flame R .25 .60
45 Brave Giant U .20 .50
46 Chief Many-Tribes U .20 .50
47 Deathblade Beetle VR .30 .75
48 Forest Hornet C .10 .25
49 Karate Carrot U .20 .50
50 Razorhide C .40 1.00
51 Root Trap R .75 2.00
52 Rumbling Terrasaur C .10 .25
53 Splinterclaw Wasp R .25 .60
54 Sprout C .30 .75
55 Stampeding Longhorn R .25 .60
D1 Quillspike Tatsurion SR .40 1.00
S1 Alcadeus, Winged Justice SR .40 1.00
S2 King Tsunami SR .40 1.00
S3 Bat-Breath Scaradorable SR 4.00 10.00
S4 Lord Skycrusher SR 2.50 6.00
S5 Terradragon Regarion Doom SR 4.00 10.00

2013 Kaijudo Clash of the Duel Masters

COMPLETE SET (122) 40.00 100.00
BOOSTER BOX (24 PACKS) 30.00 40.00
BOOSTER PACK (9 CARDS) 1.00 2.00
RELEASED ON MAY 24, 2013
1 Azuri, the Dawnbreaker VR .40 1.00
2 Beliqua the Ascender C .10 .25
3 Citadel Magistrate R .30 .75
4 Citadel Steward U .20 .50
5 Containment Field C .10 .25
6 Halo Hawk C .10 .25
7 Keeper of Laws R 6.00 15.00
8 Lars, Virtuous Imager U .20 .50
9 Rain-Cloud Kraken C .10 .25
10 Rodi Gale, Night Guardian U .20 .50
11 Shimmerwing C .10 .25
12 Spire Zealot U .20 .50
13 Thunder Reaper C .10 .25
14 Zone Defense R .30 .75
15 Aeropica C .10 .25
16 Aqua Rider C .10 .25
17 Aqua-Ranger Commander U .20 .50
18 Cyber Cyclones U .20 .50
19 Cyber Lord Corile U .20 .50
20 Cybergrid Bandit C .10 .25
21 Glu-urrgle 2.0 R .30 .75
22 Hazard Crawler R .40 1.00
23 King Poseidon VR .40 1.00
24 Mark of Tritonus R .30 .75
25 Queen Sargasso C .10 .25
26 Reef Scout C .10 .25
27 Tenuous Trove C .10 .25
28 Time Rime U .20 .50
29 Arachnoir of Cobweb Cavern C .10 .25
30 Cave Gulper C .10 .25
31 Dreadhusk C .10 .25
32 Fanged Horror C .10 .25
33 Gregoria the Malevolent R .30 .75
34 Gregoria's Fortress R .30 .75
35 Mesmerize U .20 .50
36 Shapeshifter Scaradorable VR 1.00 2.50
37 Skeleton Soldier C .10 .25
38 Soul Schism U .20 .50
39 Spectral Mummy U .20 .50
40 Suffocate R .30 .75
41 Thunder Grub U .20 .50
42 Toxic Fog C .10 .25
43 Assault Dragon R .30 .75
44 Blade-Rush Wyvern C .10 .25
45 Blastforge Bruiser C .10 .25
46 Chaotic Skyterror C .10 .25
47 Drill Storm U .20 .50
48 Ember-Eye U .20 .50
49 Flame Spinner U .20 .50
50 Jump Jets C .10 .25
51 Kaboom! R .30 .75
52 Magma Dragon Melgars VR .40 1.00
53 Mark of Infernus R .30 .75
54 Redscale Drakon C .10 .25
55 Scaled Impaler U .20 .50
56 Toolbot C .10 .25
57 Chief Thorn-Bringer R .40 1.00
58 Deepwood Druid C .10 .25
59 Ironvine Dragon VR .40 1.00
60 Jackalax C .10 .25
61 Lumbering Elderwood U .20 .50
62 Mana Tick U .20 .50
63 Noble Rumbling Terrasaur R .30 .75
64 Reinforce C .10 .25
65 Saber Mantis C .10 .25
66 Shaman Broccoli C .10 .25
67 Shardhide Tusker C .10 .25
68 Silver Axe U .20 .50
69 Slumbering Titan R .30 .75
70 Spore Siren U .20 .50
71 Aqua Strider C .30 .75
72 Crusader Engine R .30 .75
73 Elevan the Seeker R .30 .75
74 Memory Keeper C .10 .25
75 Panopter VR .40 1.00
76 Piercing Judgment R .75 2.00
77 Sunspout Quartz U .20 .50
78 Wave Lancer U .20 .50
79 Blade Seer U .20 .50
80 Dawnflower Quartz U .20 .50
81 Fullmetal Lemon C .40 1.00
82 Humonculon the Blaster R 1.50 4.00
83 Oathsworn Call R .40 1.00
84 Starseed Squadron VR .40 1.00
85 Suncloak Protector R .30 .75
86 Sword Horned C .10 .25
87 Cryptic Worm C .10 .25
88 Featherfin Stalker R .40 1.00
89 Freakish Test Subject U .20 .50
90 Grip of Despair R .30 .75
91 Ramis the Cloaked C .10 .25
92 Seacurse Quartz U .20 .50
93 Skarvos the Assassin R .30 .75

94 Spelljacker VR .40 1.00
95 Baron Burnfingers R .30 .75
96 Chasmblaze Quartz U .20 .50
97 Galzak of Shadow Pass VR .40 1.00
98 Haunted Mech C .10 .25
99 Kronax the Brutal R .30 .75
100 Lizard-Skin Puppet U .20 .50
101 Oozing Lavasaur C .10 .25
102 Soul Vortex R .30 .75
103 Cindermoss Quartz U .20 .50
104 Fight R .30 .75
105 Gorim the Striker R .30 .75
106 Lotus Warrior U .20 .50
107 Smolderhorn C .10 .25
108 Steamtank Kryon VR .60 1.50
109 Tatsurion the Champion R .30 .75
110 Weaponized Razorcat C .10 .25
D1 General Finbarr SR 3.00 8.00
D2 General Skycrusher SR 1.50 4.00
S1 Sasha the Observer SR .75 2.00
S2 King Tritonus SR 8.00 20.00
S3 Death Liger, Apex Predator SR .75 2.00
S4 Infernus the Immolator SR 6.00 15.00
S5 The Hive Queen SR 8.00 20.00
S6 Truthseeker Forion SR .40 1.00
S7 Guardian Akhal-Teek SR 2.00 5.00
S8 Squillace Scourge SR 8.00 20.00
S9 Shadeblaze the Corruptor SR 4.00 10.00
S10 Tatsurion the Relentless SR 2.50 6.00

2013 Kaijudo Dragon Master Collection Kit

2-CARD SET ISSUED W/DRAGON MASTER KIT
RELEASED ON FEBRUARY 19, 2013
1 Necrodragon of Vile Ichor SR .40 1.00
2 Hammer Dragon Foulbyrn SR .40 1.00

2013 Kaijudo DragonStrike Infernus

COMPLETE SET (60) 30.00 80.00
BOOSTER BOX (24 PACKS) 30.00 40.00
BOOSTER PACK (9 CARDS) 1.00 2.00
RELEASED ON MARCH 15, 2013
1 Arachnopod R .25 .60
2 Aurora Valkyrie U .20 .50
3 Canyon Skimmer C .10 .25
4 Defense Mode C .10 .25
5 Gemini Dragon R .40 1.00
6 Lux U .60 1.50
7 Lyra, the Blazing Sun VR 5.00 12.00
8 Reflector Cannon R .25 .60
9 Spark Cage U .20 .50
10 Storm Seeker C .10 .25
11 Vectro Scout C .10 .25
12 Bottle of Wishes R .25 .60
13 Coral-Claw C .10 .25
14 Dragon of Reflections R .30 .75
15 Emperor Dendrite U .20 .50
16 Eye of the Tides C .10 .25
17 Kindrix the Psionic VR .30 .75
18 Logos Lookout C .10 .25
19 Man o' Warden U .20 .50
20 Nix U .30 .75
21 Queen Taniwha R .25 .60
22 Trial and Error C .10 .25
23 Ancient Grave Worm U .20 .50
24 Boneraffle Dragon R .40 1.00
25 Devouring Smog U .20 .50
26 Dreadclaw, Dark Herald VR .30 .75
27 Drooling Worm C .10 .25
28 Gloom Tomb C .20 .50
29 Grudge Weaver U .30 .75
30 Patchwork Surgeon R .25 .60
31 Ripper Reaper R 1.00 2.50
32 Toothed Grubling C .10 .25
33 Umbra U .40 1.00
34 Bagash U .20 .50
35 Blastforge Dragon C .10 .25
36 Branca the Treacherous C .20 .50
37 Burnclaw the Relentless U .30 .75
38 Dragon's Breath R .25 .60
39 Explosive Infantry C .20 .50
40 Hammer Fist C .10 .25
41 Herald of Infernus R 2.50 6.00
42 Kenina U .40 1.00
43 Ragefire Tatsurion VR .30 .75
44 Spellbane Dragon R .30 .75
45 Belua U .20 .50
46 Copper Locust C .10 .25
47 Dauntless Tusker R .30 .75
48 Energize C .20 .50
49 Ensnare R .25 .60
50 Hornblade Dragon R .25 .60
51 Manapod Beetle C .20 .50
52 Sok'ran the Untamed VR .30 .75
53 Steel Hammer C .10 .25
54 The Swarmleader U .20 .50
55 Treetop Dragon U .20 .50
S1 Andromeda of the Citadel SR 15.00 40.00
S2 Issyl of the Frozen Wastes SR 1.00 2.50
S3 Dracothane of the Abyss SR 6.00 15.00
S4 Infernus the Awakened SR 8.00 20.00
S5 Kurragar of the Hordes SR 6.00 15.00

2013 Kaijudo Invasion Earth

COMPLETE SET (91) 50.00 120.00
BOOSTER BOX (24 PACKS) 20.00 30.00
BOOSTER PACK (9 CARDS) .75 1.25
RELEASED ON NOVEMBER 8, 2013
1 Arc Ward U .20 .50
2 Detain C .10 .25
3 Graviton Generator U .20 .50
4 Haven's Elite VR 1.00 2.50
5 Ion Cruiser C .10 .25
6 Sunmote Field R .30 .75
7 Sunwhip Sentry R .30 .75
8 Aqua Trickster C .10 .25
9 Engulf C .10 .25
10 Guardian Rusalka U .20 .50
11 King Barnacle R .30 .75
12 Morphing Pod R .30 .75
13 Seneschal, Choten's Lieutenant VR .40 1.00
14 Veil Slip U .20 .50
15 Chimera Predator C .10 .25
16 Ravenous Web-Leg R .30 .75
17 Sickly Larva U .20 .50
18 Snake Trap C .10 .25
19 Spinning Terror R .40 1.00
20 Vile Malvictus VR .60 1.50
21 Wandering Brain-Eater U .20 .50
22 Aerial Bombardment R .30 .75
23 Blastforge Marauder R .30 .75
24 Drakon Upstart C .10 .25
25 Flame Fangs U .20 .50
26 Galsaur VR .60 1.50
27 Manic Mechanic U .20 .50
28 Ricochet Shot C .10 .25
29 Broadsword Butterfly C .10 .25
30 Cultivate C .10 .25
31 Defiant Shaman U .20 .50
32 Mark of Almighty Colossus R .30 .75
33 Nurturing Hive U .20 .50
34 Tricky Turnip VR 3.00 8.00
35 Tusked Shouter R .30 .75
36 Choten's Stalker Sphere C .10 .25
37 Fallen Keeper U .20 .50
38 Luminar Unleashed VR .40 1.00
39 Reverberate R 1.00 2.50
40 Skyvolt Mech C .10 .25
41 Corvus Dragon R .30 .75
42 Lamp-Lighter C .10 .25
43 Mad Watcher C .10 .25
44 Panic and Disorder U .20 .50
45 Bodyguard Vorg C .10 .25
46 Crash and Burn U .20 .50
47 Dawnblaze Patrol C .10 .25
48 Volcano Dervish R .30 .75
49 Beam Bloom U .20 .50
50 Chief Toko R .30 .75
51 Hunter Sphere C .10 .25
52 Stratus Beetle C .10 .25
53 Emergency Protocol R .30 .75
54 Essence Shade C .10 .25
55 Fate's Hand U .20 .50
56 Sabotage Worm C .10 .25
57 The Reviled VR .60 1.50
58 Ballistic Skyterror C .10 .25
59 Blitz Commando R .30 .75
60 Cyber Trooper C .10 .25
61 Frantic Blast U .20 .50
62 Bad Apple VR 2.50 6.00
63 Bronze-Arm Renegade C .10 .25
64 Crystal Pulse U .20 .50
65 Tainted Quartz C .10 .25
66 Telanar, the Stormer R .30 .75
67 Boom Skull C .10 .25
68 Flamespine Ravager VR .60 1.50
69 Infernal Taskmaster R .30 .75
70 Lava-Tube Crawler C .10 .25
71 XT-4 Brutefist U .20 .50
72 Cackling Fiend C .10 .25
73 Fearfeather the Scavenger VR .40 1.00
74 Looming Devourer R .30 .75
75 Shadow Strike U .20 .50
76 Skulking Cypress C .10 .25
77 Armored Sentinel U .20 .50
78 Corporal Pepper C .10 .25
79 Emblazoned Giant C .10 .25
80 Victory Gunner R .60 1.50
D1 Vicious Squillace Scourge SR 2.00 5.00
S1 Cassiopeia Starborn SR 15.00 40.00
S2 Warbringer Poseidon SR 6.00 15.00
S3 Megaria, the Deceiver SR 8.00 20.00
S4 Napalmeon the Conquering SR 5.00 12.00
S5 Almighty Colossus SR 10.00 25.00
S6 Dark-Seer Jurlon SR 10.00 25.00
S7 Major Ao SR 8.00 20.00
S8 Elder Titan Auralia SR 2.00 5.00
S9 General Charzon SR 3.00 8.00
S10 Tatsurion the Brawler SR 1.50 4.00

2013 Kaijudo Shattered Alliances

Complete Set (91) 40.00 100.00
BOOSTER BOX (24 PACKS) 20.00 30.00
BOOSTER PACK (9 CARDS) .75 1.25
RELEASED ON SEPTEMBER 13, 2013
1 Blade Barrier C .10 .25
2 Blinder Beetle Prime R 1.25 3.00
3 Heliosphere C .10 .25
4 Mark of Eternal Haven R .30 .75
5 Ra-Vu the Indomitable VR .40 1.00
6 Replicator Patrol C .10 .25
7 Repulse U .20 .50
8 Sentrus U .20 .50
9 Angler Cluster C .10 .25
10 Aqua-Reflector Nomulos R .30 .75
11 Bladefish C .10 .25
12 Cyber Scamp R 1.50 4.00
13 Deep Mind Probe C .10 .25
14 Finbarr's Dreadnought VR .40 1.00
15 Phase Scout U .20 .50
16 Recon Mission U .20 .50
17 Curse-Eye Black Feather R .30 .75
18 Dagger Doll C .10 .25
19 Doomblast Scaradorable VR .40 1.00
20 Gaunt Boneweaver U .20 .50
21 Ghost Bite C .10 .25
22 Maddening Whispers VR .40 1.00
23 Mark of Kalima R .30 .75
24 Tygrif C .10 .25
25 Blastforge Scrapper C .10 .25
26 Blazetrail Gilaflame R .30 .75
27 Cinder Fist C .10 .25
28 Magma Ram U .20 .50
29 Onslaught Trooper R .30 .75
30 Skycrusher's Volcano-Ship VR .40 1.00
31 Skytalon Harrier U .20 .50
32 Sledgehammer Slammer C .10 .25
33 Dawn Giant VR .40 1.00
34 Headstrong Wanderer C .10 .25
35 Jarbala Keeper C .10 .25
36 Monstrify C .10 .25
37 Ninja Pumpkin R .30 .75
38 Striding Hearthwood R .30 .75
39 Transforming Totem U .20 .50
40 Wild Growth U .20 .50
41 Calamity Bell R .30 .75
42 Glimmergloom Quartz U .20 .50
43 Lost Patrol C .10 .25
44 Serpens, the Spirit Shifter VR .60 1.50
45 Spire Puppet C .10 .25
46 Slingwing C .10 .25
47 Tar Gusher U .20 .50
48 Zoltara the Mercenary R .30 .75
49 Axos the Avenger R .30 .75
50 Blitzer-Mech Falkora VR .60 1.50
51 Flamewing Phoenix U .20 .50
52 Metal Max C .10 .25
53 Plasma Pincer C .10 .25
54 Prototype Gunship C .10 .25
55 Starforge Quartz U .20 .50
56 Sunstrike R .30 .75
57 Aqua Trooper XJ-3 C .10 .25
58 Flamespitter U .20 .50
59 Flame-Vent Diver C .10 .25
60 Frostburn Quartz U .20 .50
61 Krazzix the Volatile VR .40 1.00
62 Mar-Blurpa the Weaponsmith R .30 .75
63 Scalding Surge R .30 .75
64 Unstable Rockhound C .10 .25
65 Bloomwarden C .10 .25
66 Crystalize R .30 .75
67 Kivu, Ingenious Shaman VR 1.25 3.00
68 Lore-Strider U .20 .50
69 Mistvine Quartz U .20 .50
70 Oktuska the Infused R .30 .75
71 Squall Darter C .10 .25
72 Wavebreaker Tribe C .10 .25
73 Cavernmold Quartz U .20 .50
74 Foul Mana R .30 .75
75 Goop Striker C .10 .25
76 Haunted Harvest C .10 .25
77 Masked Gravewing U .20 .50
78 Obsidian Death VR .40 1.00
79 Skaak the Stinger R .30 .75
80 Terror Hound C .10 .25
D1 Death Liger the Justicar SR 1.25 3.00
S1 Eternal Haven SR 15.00 40.00
S2 King Alboran SR 1.00 2.50
S3 Queen Kalima SR 10.00 25.00
S4 Forgelord Vesuvius SR .60 1.50
S5 Wildstrider Ramnoth SR 5.00 12.00
S6 Twilight Archon SR 6.00 15.00
S7 Dragon Knight Volaron SR 4.00 10.00
S8 Heretic Prince Var-rakka SR 4.00 10.00
S9 Borran, the Reality Shaper SR 2.00 5.00
S10 Khordia, the Soul Tyrant SR 4.00 10.00

2013 Kaijudo Triple Strike

Complete Set (25) 5.00 12.00
RELEASED ON JULY 12, 2013
1 Aqua Seneschal C .10 .25
2 Bottle of Wishes R .30 .75
3 Crystal Memory R 1.25 3.00
4 Fluorogill Manta C .10 .25
5 Logos Scan C .10 .25
6 Reef-Eye C .10 .25
7 Black Feather of Shadow Abyss R .30 .75
8 Bone Blades C .10 .25
9 Dream Pirate U .20 .50
10 Razorkinder SR .40 1.00
11 Skull Shatter R .30 .75
12 Terror Pit R 1.50 4.00
13 Bolshack Dragon R .30 .75
14 Comet Missile C .30 .75
15 Dragon's Breath R .30 .75
16 Hyperspeed Dragon R .30 .75
17 Meteosaur U .20 .50
18 Moorna, Gatling Dragon VR .40 1.00
19 Rock Bite C .10 .25
20 Tornado Flame R .75 2.00
21 Grip of Despair R .30 .75
22 Soul Vortex R .30 .75
D1 Magnet Mech Glu-urrgle SR .40 1.00
D2 Feral Scaradorable SR .40 1.00
D3 Rampaging Tatsurion SR .40 1.00

2014 Kaijudo The 5 Mystics

COMPLETE SET (60)
BOOSTER BOX (36 PACKS)
BOOSTER PACK (14 CARDS)
RELEASED ON MARCH 14, 2014
1 Arcane Warden U .20 .50
2 Beacon Drone C .10 .25
3 Caelum Skysworn R .75 2.00
4 Cerulean Core C .10 .25
5 Haven's Command U .20 .50
6 Lightning Sniper C .10 .25
7 Luminous Shieldwing R .40 1.00
8 Radiant Purification VR 2.00 5.00
9 Restrain C .10 .25
10 Solar Helix U .20 .50
11 Captain Orwellia C .10 .25
12 Captive Squill C .10 .25
13 Hypergrid Hacker U .20 .50
14 Liquid Compulsion VR 1.50 4.00
15 Neural Helix U .20 .50
16 Octobot Infiltrator U .20 .50
17 Queen Riptide R .60 1.50
18 Saucer-Head Shark U .20 .50
19 Sawtooth Cyclone C .10 .25
20 The Mystic of Water R .50 1.25
21 Absolute Darkness VR 2.00 5.00
22 Eager Cleaver C .10 .25
23 Harbringer of the Void R .60 1.50
24 Night Haunt U .20 .50
25 Nightmare Helix U .20 .50
26 Rib Collector C .10 .25
27 Scourge Lord U .20 .50
28 Terrorfang Clinger C .10 .25
29 The Mystic of Darkness R 1.00 2.50
30 Vengeful Blast C .10 .25
31 Absolute Incineration VR 3.00 8.00
32 Blaze Helix U .20 .50
33 Bluescale Drakon C .10 .25
34 Doomcannon Mech U .20 .50
35 Lavanator 3000 C .10 .25
36 Morkaz the Defiant R 1.25 3.00
37 Sparkspine Lizard U .20 .50
38 The Disassembler C .10 .25
39 The Mystic of Fire R 2.00 5.00
40 Waylay C .10 .25
41 Blademane C .10 .25
42 Broodmother R .60 1.50
43 Jarbala Swordbreaker C .10 .25
44 Rampage C .10 .25
45 Seedpod Puffer C .10 .25
46 Sledgefoot U .20 .50
47 Swift Regeneration VR 2.00 5.00
48 Taunting Totem U .20 .50
49 The Mystic of Nature R 2.50 6.00
50 Verdant Helix U .10 .25
51 Twilight Worm R 1.00 2.50
52 Fornax, the Juggernaut R .60 1.50
53 Deathtongue Leech R 1.50 4.00
54 Vectron Crawler R 1.50 4.00
55 Magmaclysm Rex R 2.00 5.00
S1 The Mystic of Light SR 6.00 15.00
S2 Psychic Predator Rusalka SR 15.00 40.00
S3 Soul-Devourer Black Feather SR 6.00 15.00
S4 Humonguru SR 8.00 20.00
S5 Overlord Sargon SR 6.00 15.00

2014 Kaijudo Booster Brawl

COMPLETE SET (3) 8.00 20.00
RELEASED ON FEBRUARY 21, 2014
1 Kolani, Dragon Oracle 3.00 8.00
2 Spire Widow 4.00 10.00
3 Krakatoa the Shattered 3.00 8.00

2014 Kaijudo Quest for the Gauntlet

COMPLETE SET (171)
BOOSTER BOX (36 PACKS)
BOOSTER PACK (14 CARDS)
RELEASED ON MAY 30, 2014
1 Battlesworn Seer U
2 Blinder Beetle C
3 Citadel Knight U
4 Cloudweave R
5 Commissar Soris U
6 Eternity Pulse R
7 Eye Spy C
8 Flux Drone U
9 Garrison Duty C
10 General Dorzim VR
11 Glare of Sanction U
12 Harmony Wing U
13 Hover-Talon C
14 Ironwill Tree R
15 Laser Drone C
16 Magistrate Jazuri R
17 Magris the Magnetizer U
18 Nova Cruiser C
19 Penlarc C
20 Photon Weaver C
21 Reactor Sphere C
22 Safe Passage C
23 Sentinel Orb C
24 Sky-Ring Captain C
25 Skybound Keeper C
26 Spire Keeper C
27 Stratus Dart C
28 Strobe Flash C
29 Sunstorm Dreadnought U
30 The Arbiter VR
31 Aqua Initiate C
32 Aqua Inquisitor U
33 Aqua Scout C
34 Citizen Tokori U
35 Cryo-Nucleus U
36 Cyber Lord Wakiki R
37 Ethereal Agent VR
38 Gobblemaw U
39 Hydro Spy C
40 Hydrobot Nautilus C
41 Icebelly Blowfish C
42 Kalorth, Lord of Tides VR
43 Mind Core U
44 Ocean Ravager R
45 Outpost Sentry U
46 Pincer-Fin C
47 Reef Kraken C
48 Scavenging Cenophor R
49 Scrutinize C
50 Shore Chomper U
51 Snapping Eel C
52 Steadfast Vorwhal C
53 Stockade Virus C
54 Temporal Tinkering C
55 Thought Collective U
56 Tide Angler C
57 Tide Seer C
58 Veil Bubble C
59 Wave Spears R
60 Whirlpool Warden C
61 Attic Reaper C
62 Baleful Drummer R
63 Cavern Snapper C
64 Creeping Heap C
65 Cursed Phantom C
66 Den Gorger U
67 Dream Pirate C
68 Eldritch Lightning C
69 Forsaken Puppet U
70 Fumes C
71 Gloom-Hollow Taskmaster U
72 Gloomlurker Drask C•
73 Gorgalisk C
74 Grave Call C
75 Grievous Strike U
76 Horrific Tick C
77 Horror Box R
78 Lurking Skull Cutter C
79 Mindwrack Moth U
80 Mr. Smiles C
81 Oblivion Knight R
82 Ravenous Whiptongue U
83 Shadowblade Conqueror U
84 Shanok, the Soul Harvester VR
85 Skrap Skull C
86 Snakebite C
87 Terror Pit R
88 Underworld Stalker VR
89 Venomancer C
90 Vile Reanimator C
91 Blastforge Sweeper C
92 Bloodbound Dragon U
93 Convoy Runner C
94 Drakon Mercenary C
95 Dropship Commando U
96 Ember Adept C
97 Firemane Dragon R
98 Flame Auger U
99 Kenina the Igniter C
D1 Beastlord Rulchor SR
S1 Caius of Cloud Legion SR
S2 Regent Sasha SR
S3 Change-o-bot Glu-urrgle SR
S4 Exalarc, Grand Metachron SR
S5 Grand Manipulator Agaryx SR
S6 Trox the Merciless SR
S7 Supreme Dragon Bolshack SR
S8 Warmaster Tatsurion SR
S9 Boulderfist the Pulverizer SR
100 Krakus the Dominator R
101 Laserize C
102 Megacannon Renegade C
103 Railgun Raptor C
104 Rally Bot C
105 Relentless Vanguard C
106 Restless Conflagration VR
107 Rocket Hawk C
108 Scrapheap Hunter U
109 Searing Spears U
110 Sergeant Maddox U
111 Shock Trooper C
112 Siege Dragon C
113 Slagcannon Grunt U
114 Technoraptor C
115 Thundering Clap C
116 Torhelm, Stomper Elite R
117 Tornado Flame R
118 Volcano Trooper U
119 Warchief Kyo VR
120 Wreck Mech C
121 Allure U
122 Amberhorn C
123 Anjak, the All-Kin VR
124 Ardu Ranger C
125 Ardu Totem C
126 Barbed Crusher C
127 Bronze-Arm Gladiator U
128 Bronze-Arm Tribe C
129 Charging Greatclaw R
130 Colonel Corn C
131 Cumulofungus U
132 Grasslands Goliath U
133 Hunter Blossom C
134 Huntmaster Taegrin U
135 Instill Might C
136 Mesa Behemoth R
137 Moss Giant C
138 Pouncing Crickant C
139 Predatory Snapdragon U
140 Rapscallion C
141 Root Trap R
142 Shouter, Paragon of Nature VR
143 Sigil of Primacy U
144 Snarling Craghorn C
145 Sprout C
146 Sumo Artichoke R
147 Sun-Clan Tortoise U
148 Vine Bind C
149 Violet Puffer C
150 Woolly Tusker C
151 Sky Shark R
152 Eye of Inquisition R
153 Solstar Commander R
154 Battlebred Defender R
155 Mind Censor R
156 Flame Serpent R
157 Hydrobot Scarab R
158 Zombie Backhoe R
159 Johnny Darkseed R
160 Thunderaxe Shaman R
S10 Voksa, Herd Matriarch SR

2014 Kaijudo Vortex

COMPLETE SET (171)
BOOSTER BOX (36 PACKS)
BOOSTER PACK (14 CARDS)
RELEASED ON AUGUST 29, 2014
1 Aerial Arcavore C
2 Ancient Keeper C

3 Ardent Observer C
4 Aurora Scout C
5 Bewildering Blast U
6 Bolt-Hawk U
7 Citadel Judge R
8 Cloud Grappler C
9 Empyrean Overseer U
10 Galvanize U
11 Hydrus the Oathbound VR
12 Intrepid Invader C
13 Justice Archon C
14 Karstara the Warder R
15 Overshields R
16 Perseus Dragon R
17 Phase Generator C
18 Prelaie of Wind C
19 Radion Sphere C
20 Regent's Attendant C
21 Salvation Reckoner R
22 Scroll Orb C
23 Skyforce Adjutant U
24 Spark Drone C
25 Stormstrike Enforcer C
26 Sunshock C
27 Superia-Citadel Militia C
28 Temple Lantern U
29 Virtuous Alcadeus VR
30 Zephyr Keeper U
31 Aeronaut Glu-urrgle VR
32 Aqua Infiltrator U
33 Aqua Swordsman C
34 Cloaked Saboteur C
35 Cranky Leviathan U
36 Cyber Savant C
37 Deep-Currents Drifter U
38 Dreamfish C
39 Emperor Palata U
40 Garglevision C
41 Hydrobot Elite C
42 Hypnobot C
43 Master Trader Cephelia R
44 Metroplex Operative U
45 Metroplex Scout C
46 Optic Cell C
47 Rip Swirl C
48 Runemaster Zyr VR
49 Spy Mission C
50 Spy Tide C
51 Tarvox the Voracious R
52 Teleportation Equation U
53 Tide Gulper C
54 Time Tethers C
55 Tusked Nautiloid R
56 Veil Vortex R
57 Void Seer C
58 Wave Skimmer C
59 Wavecrest Crawler U
60 Waveforce Seer R
61 Agent of Lies C
62 Batter-Axe C
63 Bloated Gatekeeper U
64 Chasm Gigabolver C
65 Darkbolt C
66 Decay C
67 Deteriorate C
68 Foul Cave Worm C
69 Gloom Wraith C
70 Gregoria's Guile U
71 Grim Specter C
72 Gullet Ghost C
73 Hollow Worm R
74 Ichor Spider C
75 Joko, Lunatic Chimp VR
76 Legionnaire Corpse C
77 Lethal Lockbox U
78 Malphalgus the Tormenter R
79 Megaria's Trapheap C
80 Nether Tactician R
81 Prowling Chimera C
82 Rite of Revival U
83 Shredmane R
84 Sinister Scheme U
85 Slithering Phantasm U
86 Soul Reflection R
87 Timelost Phantom VR
88 Vicious Coffer C
89 Vile Piercer U
90 Wraith Hound C
91 Ammo Train U
92 Artillery Dragon C
93 Ashen Tribute C
94 Battering Monolith C
95 Blade-Rush Wyvern C
96 Blaze Darter C
97 Cannonade Dragon R
98 Flaming Arrow Volley U
99 Furywing Trooper U
D1 Dragon Engine Glu-urrgle SR
S1 Toronok the Voidshaper SR
S2 The Chronarch SR
S3 Baelgor, Accursed Dragon SR
S4 Krogon, Blazing Devastation SR
S5 Eternal Gaia Dragon SR
S6 Ulphonas, Fendish Overlord SR
S7 Drakomech Commander SR
S8 Krotork, the Mirror SR
S9 Worldwaker Omgoth SR
100 Hydragon C
101 Igniss U
102 Jack, the Hammer C
103 Jetpack Thug C
104 Kuth the Dervish R
105 Lava Burst C
106 Lava Racer U
107 Meteor Rider U
108 Mighty Stomp U
109 Mischievous Fire-Chick C
110 Quetaro the Gladiator R
111 Raging Firebrand C
112 Raptor-Ace Valko C
113 Rothos the Destroyer R
114 Runes of Fortune R
115 Rygar the Tank VR
116 Sandstorm Prowler C
117 Sledge Bot C
118 Smoldering Brute C
119 Stormdiver C
120 Wildfire Valkyrie R
121 Ancestor Bear U
122 Ardu Cloudstrider C
123 Bronze-Arm Fanatic U
124 Colossal Avenger C
125 Creeper Snare C
126 Daunting Presence U
127 Duke Durian C
128 Earthbond Giant R
129 Embolden U
130 Field Marshal Cornucopia VR
131 Granite Titan C
132 Grove Protector U
133 Horned Chameleon C
134 Jarbala Hatchery R
135 Leafwing Totem C
136 Lumbering Coliseum C
137 Lunar Boar U
138 Lurking Orchid U
139 Moonhowler Hunter R
140 Muk'tak, Lifespark Guide VR
141 Pesky Pineapple C
142 Ringleader Radish C
143 Ritual of Challenge R
144 Ragonite the Obliterator R
145 Runestone Goliath C
146 Savage Spawn C
147 Solstice Chanter C
148 Sprite's Gift C
149 Trapdoor Tunneler C
150 Warren Shaman C
151 Cetus the Augur R
152 Wave Keeper U
153 Brave Shalloteer U
154 Radiant Blinderhorn R
155 Abyssal Scavenger U
156 Magglekax R
157 Bile Raptor U
158 Taksha, Scourge Gunner VR
159 Arachnomech R
160 Riot Sprite U
S10 Scaradorable the Behemoth SR

2012-13 Kaijudo Promos

P1Y1 Draglide the Swiftest
(issued in Bull Rush deck at WPN stores)
P2Y1 Aqua Seneschal
(issued in Wal-Mart Rise of the Duel Masters packs)
P3Y1 Blinder Beetle
(issued in Wal-Mart Rise of the Duel Masters packs)
P4Y1 Blaze Belcher
(issued in Wal-Mart Rise of the Duel Masters packs)
P5Y1 Fumes
(issued in Wal-Mart Rise of the Duel Masters packs)
P6Y1 Razorhide
(issued in Wal-Mart Rise of the Duel Masters packs)
P7Y1 Mighty Shouter, the Shaman
(issued at Kaijudo League 2012, 9/12-10/12)
P8Y1 Flare Inhibitor
(issued at Kaijudo League 2012, 9/12-10/12)
P9Y1 Moorna the Vengeful
(issued at Kaijudo League 2012, 9/12-10/12)
P10Y1 Mother Virus
(issued at Kaijudo League 2012, 11/12-12/12)
P11Y1 Impalicus
(issued at Kaijudo League 2012, 11/12-12/12)
P12Y1 Sparkblade Protector
(issued at Kaijudo League 2012, 11/12-12/12)
P13Y1 Bronze-Arm Sabertooth
(issued at Summer 2013 Kaijudo Championship)
P14Y1 Kenina the Igniter
(issued in Creatures Unleashed DVD)
P15Y1 Old Man Winter
(2012 Holiday)
P16Y1 Thorn Dragon
(issued at DragonStrike Infernus premiere)
P17Y1 Cybersphere Dragon
(issued at DragonStrike Infernus premiere)
P18Y1 Dorado, Golden Dragon
(issued at Kaijudo Duel Day, 4/13)
P19Y1 Billion-Degree Dragon
(issued at Kaijudo Duel Day, 4/13)
P20Y1 Herald of Infernus
(issued in DragonStrike DVD)

2013-14 Kaijudo Promos

P1Y2 Memory Swarm
(issued in Darkness of Heart DVD)
P2Y2 Wild Sky Sword
(issued at Clash of the Duel Masters premiere)
P3Y2 Fault-Line Dragon
(issued at Clash of the Duel Masters premiere)
P4Y2 Grybolos the Gatherer
(issued at May 2013 Kaijudo Duel Day)
P5Y2 Saracon, Storm Dynamo
(issued at May 2013 Kaijudo Duel Day)
P6Y2 Sprout
(issued at June 2013 Kaijudo Duel Day)
P7Y2 Magris the Magnetizer
(issued at August 2013 Kaijudo Duel Day)
P8Y2 Veil Stalker
(issued at Shattered Alliances premiere)
P9Y2 Ba'kaar Frostwing
(issued at Shattered Alliances premiere)
P10Y2 Necrose, Nightmare Bloom
(issued at September 2013 Kaijudo Duel Day)
P11Y2 Cyber Walker Kaylee
(issued at October 2013 Kaijudo Duel Day)
P12Y2 Forgotten Chief
(issued at Invasion Earth premiere)
P13Y2 Skraven, Draconic Reaper
(issued at Invasion Earth premiere)
P14Y2 Enslaved Flametropus
(issued at November 2013 Kaijudo Duel Day)
P15Y2 Shaman of the Vigil
(issued at December 2013 Kaijudo Duel Day)
P16Y2 Ember Titan
(issued at January 2014 Kaijudo Duel Day)
P17Y2 Gilded Archon
(issued at February 2014 Kaijudo Duel Day)
P18Y2 Snow Fort
(2013 Holiday)
P19Y2 Fullmetal Lemon
(issued at Kaijudo Master Challenge 2014)
P20Y2 Reckoning
(issued at The 5 Mystics premiere)
P21Y2 Wavebreaker Shaman
(issued at The 5 Mystics premiere)
P22Y2 Cyber Seer
(issued at March 2014 Kaijudo Duel Day)

2007 Kingdom Hearts

COMPLETE SET (91)
1 SORA - Level 1 U
2 SORA - Level 2 U
3 SORA - Level 3 U
4 DONALD DUCK - Level 1 C
5 DONALD DUCK - Level 2 C
6 DONALD DUCK - Level 3 U
7 GOOFY - Level 1 C
8 GOOFY - Level 2 C
9 GOOFY - Level 3 U
10 ALADDIN - Level 1 C
11 ALADDIN - Level 2 U
12 ALADDIN - Level 3 R
13 ARIEL - Level 1 R
14 ARIEL - Level 2 R
15 ARIEL - Level 3 R
16 SIMBA - Level 2 R
17 SIMBA - Level 3 R
18 SIMBA - Level 4 R
19 GENIE - Level 2 U
20 GENIE - Level 3 U
21 GENIE - Level 4 R
22 BAMBI - Level 2 U
23 BAMBI - Level 3 U
24 BAMBI - Level 4 R
25 DUMBO - Level 2 U
26 DUMBO - Level 3 U
27 TINKER BELL - Level 2 R
28 FIRE - Level 2 C
29 FIRA - Level 3 U
30 FIRAGA - Level 4 R
31 BLIZZARD - Level 2 C
32 BLIZZARA - Level 3 U
33 BLIZZAGA - Level 4 R
34 THUNDER - Level 2 C
35 THUNDARA - Level 3 U
36 THUNDAGA - Level 4 R
37 CURE - Level 1 C
38 PUMPKINHEAD C
39 LIONHEART U
40 LADY LUCK U
41 DIVINE ROSE C
42 OATHKEEPER R
43 SHADOW - Level 1 C
44 BOUNCYWILD - Level 1 C
45 SOLDIER - Level 1 C
46 RED NOCTURNE - Level 2 U
47 BLUE RHAPSODY - Level 2 U
48 YELLOW OPERA - Level 2 U
49 GREEN REQUIEM - Level 2 U
50 BARREL SPIDER - Level 3 C
51 LARGE BODY - Level 3 C
52 SEA NEON - Level 4 C
53 WIGHT KNIGHT - Level 5 R
54 GARGOYLE - Level 6 C
55 PIRATE - Level 6 C
56 WIZARD - Level 7 R
57 WYVERN - Level 8 R
58 TRAVERSE TOWN - Level 3 C
59 TRAVERSE TOWN - Level 1 C
60 TRAVERSE TOWN - Level 2 C
61 WONDER LAND - Level 2 R
62 DEEP JUNGLE - Level 2 R
63 AGRABAH - Level 2 R
64 HALLOWEEN TOWN - Level 1 R
65 SORA - Level 1 SR
66 SORA - Level 2 SR
67 SORA - Level 3 SR
68 DONALD DUCK - Level 1 SR
69 DONALD DUCK - Level 2 SR
70 DONALD DUCK - Level 3 SR
71 GOOFY - Level 1 SR
72 GOOFY - Level 2 SR
73 GOOFY - Level 3 SR
74 ALADDIN - Level 1 SR
75 ALADDIN - Level 2 SR
76 ALADDIN - Level 3 SR
77 ARIEL - Level 1 SR
78 ARIEL - Level 2 SR
79 ARIEL - Level 3 SR
80 SIMBA - Level 2 SR
81 SIMBA - Level 3 SR
82 SIMBA - Level 4 SR
83 GENIE - Level 2 SR
84 GENIE - Level 3 SR
85 GENIE - Level 4 SR
86 BAMBI - Level 2 SR
87 BAMBI - Level 3 SR
88 BAMBI - Level 4 SR
89 DUMBO - Level 2 SR
90 DUMBO - Level 3 SR
91 TINKER BELL - Level 2 SR

2007 Kingdom Hearts A Darkness Awakened

COMPLETE SET (128)
1 Riku - Level 3 R
2 Donald Duck - Level 4 SR
3 Goofy - Level 4 SR
4 Jack Skellington - Level 1 C
5 Jack Skellington - Level 2 U
6 Jack Skellington - Level 3 R
7 Sally - Level 0 R
8 The Mayor - Level 0 C
9 Zero - Level 0 U
10 Beast - Level 1 C
11 Beast - Level 2 U
12 Beast - Level 3 R
13 Hercules - Level 1 C
14 Hercules - Level 2 U
15 Hercules - Level 3 R
16 Peter Pan - Level 1 C
17 Peter Pan - Level 2 U
18 Peter Pan - Level 3 R
19 Pluto - Level 0 C
20 Chip & Dale - Level 0 SR
21 Broom - Level 0 U
22 Huey - Level 0 C
23 Dewy - Level 0 C
24 Louie - Level 0 C
25 Jiminy Cricket - Level 0 C
26 King Triton - Level 2 SR
27 Winnie the Pooh - Level 0 R
28 Tidus - Level 0 U
29 Selphie - Level 0 U
30 Wakka - Level 0 U
31 Yuffie - Level 2 R
32 Leon - Level 4 R
33 Moogle - Level 1 R
34 Mushu - Level 2 C
35 Mushu - Level 3 U
36 Mushu - Level 4 R
37 Dumbo - Level 4 C
38 Tinker Bell - Level 3 R
39 Tinker Bell - Level 4 R
40 Cura - Level 2 U
41 Curaga - Level 4 R
42 Gravity - Level 2 C
43 Gravira - Level 3 U
44 Graviga - Level 4 R
45 Stop - Level 4 C
46 Stopra - Level 5 U
47 Stopga - Level 6 R
48 Aero - Level 2 C
49 Fairy Harp - U
50 Olympia - U
51 Metal Chocobo - U
52 Oblivion - U
53 Soul Eater - R
54 Power Wild - Level 2 C
55 White Mushroom - Level 2 C
56 Air Soldier - Level 2 C
57 Pot Spider - Level 3 R
58 Bandit - Level 3 C
59 Screwdiver - Level 4 C
60 Fat Bandit - Level 4 U
61 Angel Star - Level 4 C
62 Stealth Sneak - Level 4 R
63 Aquatank - Level 5 R
64 Air Pirate - Level 5 C
65 Pot Centipede - Level 5 U
66 Search Ghost - Level 5 U
67 Behemoth - Level 5 R
68 Invisible - Level 5 U
69 Darkball - Level 6 C
70 Guard Armor (Arm) - Level 5 C
71 Guard Armor (Leg) - Level 6 C
72 Guard Armor (Body) - Level 7 U
73 Defender - Level 7 C
74 Parasite Cage - Level 7 R
75 Darkside - Level 8 U
76 Queen of Hearts - Level 8 U
77 Hades - Level 8 U
78 Clayton - Level 8 U
79 Jafar - Level 8 U
80 Ursula - Level 8 R
81 Oogie Boogie - Level 8 R
82 Captain Hook - Level 8 R
83 Maleficent - Level 8 R
84 Destiny Islands - Level 1 R
85 Disney Castle - Level 1 R
86 Wonderland - Level 1 C
87 Wonderland - Level 3 U
88 Olympus Coliseum - Level 2 R
89 Olympus Coliseum - Level 3 U
90 Atlantica - Level 2 U
91 Halloween Town - Level 2 R
92 Halloween Town - Level 3 C
93 Neverland - Level 1 C
94 Hundred Acre Wood - Level 0 SR
95 Hollow Bastion - Level 3 C
96 End of the World - Level 3 SR
97 Riku - Level 3 SR
98 Jack Skellington - Level 3 SR
99 Sally - Level 0 SR
100 Beast - Level 1 SR
101 Beast - Level 2 SR
102 Beast - Level 3 SR
103 Hercules - Level 1 SR
104 Hercules - Level 2 SR
105 Hercules - Level 3 SR
106 Peter Pan - Level 1 SR
107 Peter Pan - Level 2 SR
108 Peter Pan - Level 3 SR
109 Winnie the Pooh - Level 0 SR
110 Yuffie - Level 2 SR
111 Leon - Level 4 SR
112 Moogle - Level 1 SR
113 Dumbo - Level 4 SR
114 Tinker Bell - Level 3 SR
115 Tinker Bell - Level 4 SR
116 Soul Eater - SR
117 Behemoth - Level 5 SR
118 Parasite Cage - Level 7 SR
119 Queen of Hearts - Level 8 SR
120 Hades - Level 8 SR
121 Clayton - Level 8 SR
122 Jafar - Level 8 SR
123 Ursula - Level 8 SR
124 Oogie Boogie - Level 8 SR
125 Captain Hook - Level 8 SR
126 Maleficent - Level 8 SR
127 Destiny Islands - Level 1 SR
128 Disney Castle - Level 1 SR

2008 Kingdom Hearts Light and Darkness

COMPLETE SET (92)
2 Riku - Level 2 U
3 Dark Riku - Level 3 R
4 Ansem - Level 10 SR
5 Kairi - Level 0 R
6 Donald Duck - Level 3 U
7 Goofy - Level 3 U
8 Hercules - Level 3 U
9 Aladdin - Level 4 R
10 Ariel - Level 4 C
11 Peter Pan - Level 3 U
12 Beast - Level 3 U
13 Merlin - Level 3 U
14 Fairy Godmother - Level 2 SR
15 Alice - Level 0 R
16 The Cheshire Cat - Level 2 R
17 The White Rabbit - Level 0 U
18 Phil - Level 1 U
19 Jasmine - Level 0 R
1R Riku - Level 3 R
1U Sora - Level 2 U
20 Abu - Level 0 C
21 Pinocchio - Level 1 R
22 Geppetto - Level 0 U
23 Sebastian - Level 0 U
24 Flounder - Level 0 U
25 Wendy - Level 0 R
26 Winnie the Pooh - Level 1 R
27 Piglet - Level 0 U
28 Owl - Level 0 R
29 Roo - Level 0 C
30 Aerith - Level 2 SR
31 Cloud - Level 4 SR
32 Sephiroth - Level 4 SR
33 Simba - Level 1 U
34 Genie - Level 1 SR
35 Bambi - Level 1 U
36 Dumbo - Level 1 U
37 Tinker Bell - Level 0 R
38 Aerora - Level 4 C
39 Aeroga - Level 5 R
40 Magic Lamp - C
41 Magic Carpet - C
42 Smasher - C
43 Save the King - U
44 Warhammer - C
45 Herc?s Shield - C
46 Morning Star - C
47 Lord Fortune - R
48 Ultima Weapon - SR
49 Soldier - Level 1 C
50 Gigant Shadow - Level 1 C
51 Black Fungus - Level 1 U
52 Tornado Step - Level 1 U
53 Creeper Plant - Level 2 C
54 Bit Sniper - Level 4 C
55 Rare Truffle - Level 4 C
56 Crescendo - Level 5 R
57 Sheltering Zone - Level 6 C
58 Trickmaster - Level 7 R
59 Battleship - Level 8 C
60 Jafar-Genie - Level 8 SR
61 Dragon Maleficent - Level 9 SR
62 Olympus Coliseum - Level 1 C
63 Deep Jungle - Level 3 C
64 Agrabah - Level 1 R
65 Agrabah - Level 3 R
66 Monstro - Level 1 U
67 Monstro - Level 2 R
68 Atlantica - Level 1 C
69 Atlantica - Level 3 C
70 Never Land - Level 2 R
71 Fairy Godmother - Level 2 R
72 Dark Riku - Level 3 SR
73 Crescendo - Level 5 SR
74 Trickmaster - Level 7 SR
75 Kairi - Level 0 SR
76 Aladdin - Level 4 SR
77 Alice - Level 0 SR
78 The Cheshire Cat - Level 2 SR
79 Jasmine - Level 0 SR
80 Pinocchio - Level 1 SR
81 Wendy - Level 0 SR
82 Winnie the Pooh - Level 1 SR
83 Owl - Level 0 SR
84 Tinker Bell - Level 0 SR
85 Aeroga - Level 5 SR
86 Lord Fortune - SR
87 Agrabah - Level 1 SR
88 Agrabah - Level 3 SR
89 Monstro - Level 2 SR
90 Never Land - Level 2 SR
91 The King - Level 0 SR

2009 Kingdom Hearts Break of Dawn

COMPLETE SET (162)
1 Sora - Level 1 U
2 Sora - Level 2 R
3 Sora - Level 3 SR
4 Sora (Valor Form) - Level 3 SR
5 Sora (Wisdom Form) - Level 3 SR
6 Ansem - Level 10 SR
7 Axel - Level 2 U
8 Xaldin - Level 2 U
9 Roxas - Level 1 SR
10 Kairi - Level 2 U
11 Mickey Mouse - Level 1 SR
12 Minnie Mouse - Level 1 SR
13 DiZ - Level 1 SR
14 Captain Pete - Level 0 SR
15 Donald Duck - Level 1 C
16 Donald Duck - Level 3 U
17 Donald Duck - Level 4 R
18 Goofy - Level 1 C
19 Goofy - Level 3 U
20 Goofy - Level 4 R
21 Merlin - Level 3 U
22 Hayner - Level 1 U
23 Olette - Level 1 C
24 Pence - Level 1 U
25 Alice - Level 0 SR
26 Hercules - Level 1 C
27 Hercules - Level 2 U
28 Hercules - Level 3 R
29 Megara - Level 0 C
30 Phil - Level 1 U
31 Pegasus - Level 2 C
32 Aladdin - Level 1 C
33 Aladdin - Level 2 U
34 Aladdin - Level 3 R
35 Jasmine - Level 1 SR
36 Abu - Level 1 C
37 Iago - Level 0 C
38 Pinocchio - Level 1 R
39 Ariel - Level 1 C
40 King Triton - Level 2 U
41 Jack Skellington - Level 1 C
42 Jack Skellington - Level 2 U
43 Jack Skellington - Level 4 SR
44 Sally - Level 1 U
45 Zero - Level 1 C
46 Dr. Finkelstein - Level 2 R
47 The Mayor - Level 0 C
48 Peter Pan - Level 1 C
49 Beast - Level 3 R
50 Will Turner - Level 2 U
51 Elizabeth Swann - Level 1 U
52 Jack Sparrow - Level 3 R
53 Ping - Level 1 C
54 Mulan - Level 2 U
55 Mushu - Level 2 C
56 Simba - Level 3 R
57 Selphie - Level 1 U
58 Yuffie - Level 2 SR
59 Leon - Level 4 SR
60 Fuu - Level 1 C
61 Rai - Level 1 U
62 Vivi - Level 1 C
63 Seifer - Level 2 U
64 Auron - Level 4 SR
65 Genie - Level 4 R
66 Bambi - Level 3 U
67 Tinker Bell - Level 2 C
68 Fire - Level 2 C
69 Fira - Level 3 U
70 Firaga - Level 4 R
71 Blizzard - Level 2 C
72 Blizzard - Level 3 U
73 Blizzaga - Level 4 R
74 Thunder - Level 2 C
75 Thundara - Level 3 U
76 Thundaga - Level 4 R
77 Aero - Level 2 C
78 Gravity - Level 2 C
79 Cure - Level 1 C
80 Stop - Level 3 C
81 Kingdom Key - R
82 Olympia - U
83 Wishing Lamp - U
84 Decisive Pumpkin - U
85 Lamp - C
86 Rings - U
87 Spear - C
88 Whirli-Goof - C
89 Comet - C
90 Bushido - U
91 Shooting Star - U
92 Red Rocket - U
93 Shadow - Level 1 C
94 Oathkeeper - C
95 Bouncywild - Level 1 C
96 Soldier - Level 1 C
97 Oblivion - C
98 Shock - Level 1 C
99 Barrel - Level 1 C
100 Dusk - Level 1 C
101 Samurai - Level 1 C
102 Creeper Plant - Level 2 C
103 Powerwild - Level 2 C
104 Pot Spider - Level 2 R
105 Pete - Level 2 SR
106 Mr. Smee - Level 2 U
107 Undead Pirate - Level 2 C
108 Assassin - Level 2 C
109 Barrel Spider - Level 3 C
110 Bandit - Level 3 C
111 Large Body - Level 3 C
112 Pain - Level 3 U
113 Panic - Level 3 U
114 Dragoon - Level 3 U
115 Angel Star - Level 4 C
116 Search Ghost - Level 4 R
117 Sea Neon - Level 4 C
118 Stealth Sneak - Level 4 U
119 Bit Sniper - Level 4 C
120 Fat Bandit - Level 4 C
121 Lock - Level 4 C
122 Aqualank - Level 5 U
123 Invisible - Level 5 U
124 Air Pirate - Level 5 C
125 Pot Centipede - Level 5 R
126 Phantom - Level 5 SR
127 Barbossa - Level 5 U
128 Gargoyle - Level 6 C
129 Pirate - Level 6 C
130 Behemoth - Level 6 SR
131 Crescendo - Level 6 R
132 Cerberus - Level 6 SR
133 Cave of Wonders Guardian - Level 6 U
134 Wizard - Level 7 R
135 Defender - Level 7 C
136 Parasite Cage - Level 7 SR
137 Hydra - Level 7 C
138 Queen of Hearts - Level 7 U
139 Darkside - Level 8 U
140 Wyvern - Level 8 R
141 Jafar-Genie - Level 8 SR
142 Hades - Level 8 SR
143 Destiny Islands - Level 2 SR
144 Twilight Town - Level 2 C
145 Twilight Town - Level 3 R
146 Olympus Coliseum - Level 1 C
147 Olympus Coliseum - Level 2 C
148 Olympus Coliseum - Level 3 U
149 Agrabah - Level 1 C
150 Agrabah - Level 2 U
151 Agrabah - Level 3 C
152 Monstro - Level 1 U
153 Halloween Town - Level 1 U
154 Halloween Town - Level 2 C
155 Halloween Town - Level 3 C
156 Neverland - Level 1 C
157 Hundred Acre Wood - Level 1 R
158 Hollow Bastion - Level 2 C
159 End of the World - Level 2 SR
160 Port Royal - Level 1 U
161 Port Royal - Level 2 C
162 Timeless River - Level 1 C

2003 Knights of the Zodiac A New Era of Heroic Legends

F011 The 5 Ancient Peaks in the Rozan Mountains U
F012 Graveyard of the Cloth U
F013 Mediterranean Islands U
F014 Aries Palace U
F015 Taurus Palace U
F016 Gemini Palace U
F017 Cancer Palace U
F018 Leo Palace U
K037 Seiya in Sagittarius Cloth G
K038 Chamaleon June C
K039 Ophiuchus Shina R
K040 Centaurus Babel C
K041 Perseus Argol C
K042 Crow Jamian C
K043 Auriga Capella C
K044 Cerberus Dante C
K045 Canis Major Sirius C
K046 Musca Dios C
K047 Hercules Argethi C
K048 Sagitta Tremy C
K049 Kiki R
K050 Aries Mu R
K051 Taurus Aldebaran G
K052 Secret Gemini Knights G
K053 Cancer Mephisto H
K054 Libra Dohko R
K055 Leo Aioria U
K056 Leo Aioria H
K057 Virgo Shaka S
K058 Scorpio Miro S
K059 Sagittarius Aioros H
K060 Ohko C
K061 Master of Sanctuary, Ares H
P011 Truth of Athena C
P012 Kidnap the Princess U
P013 The Shield of Medusa C
P014 Steel Knights C
P015 Dangerous Crisis C
P016 A Thousand Days War C
P017 Golden Arrow U
T035 Pegasus Rolling Crush U
T036 Dragon's Roar U
T037 Aurora Thunder Attack R
T038 Rolling Defense U
T039 Flying Phoenix H
T040 Babel's Flame C
T041 Flying Saucer C
T042 Black Wing C
T043 Ball and Chain C
T044 Gorgon's Kick C
T045 Dead End Fly C
T046 Korne Horse C
T047 Phantom Arrow C
T048 Great Horn R
T049 Another Dimension R
T050 Underworld Portal Confinement R
T051 Lightning Bolt R
T052 Tenbuhoring R
T053 Rikudorinne U
T054 Great Tiger Whirlwind C

2003 Knights of the Zodiac Perilous Conquest

F006 Lord Nobu's Mansion U
F007 Jamir U
F008 Grande Foundation U
F009 The Island of Spirits U
F010 The Princess' Hideaway U
K019 Pegasus Seiya H
K020 Dragon Shiryu U
K021 Swan Hyoga R
K022 Andromeda Shun H
K023 Phoenix Ikki U
K024 Bear Geki C
K025 Hydra Ichi C
K026 Wolf Nachi C
K027 Docrates C
K028 Crystal Knight U
K029 Lacerta Misty U
K030 Hound Asterion U
K031 Black Swan C
K032 Black Phoenix C
K033 Gyste C
K034 Jellyfish C
K035 Tatsumi C
K036 Gigas C
P006 Tournament Breaks Out! U
P007 Sunrei C
P008 Cloth Repair U
P009 Revival Phoenix U
P010 Handsome Silver Knight U
T018 Pegasus Meteor Punch R
T019 Rozan's Rising Dragon Blow R
T020 Ring of Ice C
T021 Thunder Wave U
T022 Phantom Demon U
T023 Crushing Bear C
T024 Fang of Poison C
T025 Hercules Fist Attack C
T026 Marble Tripper U
T027 Million Ghost Attack C
T028 Diamond Dust C
T029 Black Blizzard C
T030 Black Phantom Demon C
T031 Punch C
T032 Punch C
T033 Kick C
T034 Kick C

2003 Knights of the Zodiac Power of the Constellation

F001 Sanctuary U
F002 Hoshinoko School U
F003 Grande Arena U
F004 Mayhem Valley U
F005 Sunken Ship U
K001 Pegasus Seiya R
K002 Dragon Shiryu H
K003 Swan Hyoga U
K004 Andromeda Shun U
K005 Phoenix Ikki H
K006 Unicorn Jab C
K007 Lionet Ban C
K008 Eagle Marin U
K009 Ophiuchus Shina U
K010 Blaze Knight C
K011 Cetus Morris U
K012 Tarantula Arakune C
K013 Black Pegasus C
K014 Black Dragon C
K015 Black Andromeda C
K016 Sea Serpent C
K017 Dolphin C
K018 Cassios C
P001 Truth of Shina C
P002 Pegasus vs Dragon U
P003 Stolen Gold Cloth U
P004 Fears of Black Meteor U
P005 Miho U
T001 Pegasus Meteor Punch U
T002 The Shield of Dragon C
T003 Diamond Dust R
T004 Nebula Chain R
T005 Unicorn Gallop C
T006 Thunder Cobra U
T007 Fire Screw C
T008 Air Fist C
T009 Cetus Spouting Bomber U
T010 Tarantula Net C
T011 Black Meteor Punch C
T012 Fist of Black Dragon C
T013 Black Nebula Chain C
T014 Punch C
T015 Punch C
T016 Kick C
T017 Kick C

2004 Knights of the Zodiac Mythological Forces

F019 Starting Point to Greece C
F020 Master of Sanctuary's Room U
F021 Virgo Palace U
F022 Libra Palace U
F023 Scorpio Palace U
F024 Sagittarius Palace U
F025 Capricorn Palace U
F026 Aquarius Palace U
F027 Pisces Palace U
K062 Pegasus Seiya C
K063 Dragon Shiryu C
K064 Swan Hyoga C
K065 Andromeda Shun C
K066 Phoenix Ikki C
K067 Eagle Marin R
K068 Sky Cloth Sho U
K069 Marine Cloth Ushio U
K070 Land Cloth Daichi U
K071 Lotus Agora C
K072 Pavo Shiba C
K073 Cepheus Arbiore C
K074 Leda C
K075 Spica C
K076 Aries Mu G
K077 Cancer Mephisto R
K078 Leo Aioria H
K079 Libra Dohko H
K080 Scorpio Miro R
K081 Sagittarius Aioros S
K082 Capricorn Shura H
K083 Aquarius Camus H
K084 Pisces Aphrodite G
K085 Spartan C
K086 Ophiuchus Shin's Men C
P018 Seika's Memory C
P019 Seventh Sense C
P020 Entrustment C
P021 Rose Corridor C
P022 The Shield of Athena H
P023 Athena S
T055 Pegasus Meteor Punch U
T056 Rozan Dragon Ultimate Attack H
T057 Aurora Raid R
T058 Nebula Stream R
T059 Nebula Storm C
T060 Double Nebula Chain U
T061 Nen Riky C
T062 Lightning Plasma C
T063 Tenma Kofuku U
T064 Kaan U
T065 Libra's Weapon C
T066 Scarlet Needle R
T067 Atomic Thunder Bolt R
T068 Excalibur C
T069 Aurora Raid U
T070 Freezing Coffin C
T071 Scarlet Rose C
T072 Pirhana Rose U
T073 Royal Demon Rose U
T074 Rush C

1995 Legend of the Five Rings Imperial

COMPLETE SET (309)	120.00	250.00
RELEASED IN OCTOBER 1995		
1 Agasha Tamori C	.10	.20
2 Air Dragon R	.75	2.00
3 Akodo Kage U	.20	.50
4 Akodo Toturi R	3.00	8.00
5 Alhundro Cornejo U	.20	.50
6 Alliance U	.20	.50
7 Ambush R	2.50	6.00
8 Ancestral Sword of the Crab F	1.50	4.00
9 Ancestral Sword of the Crane F	2.50	6.00
10 Ancestral Sword of the Dragon F	3.00	8.00
11 Ancestral Sword of the Lion F	2.50	6.00
12 Ancestral Sword of the Phoenix F	2.50	6.00
13 Ancestral Sword of the Unicorn F	2.50	6.00
14 Animate the Dead U	.20	.50
15 Apprentice R	.60	1.50
16 Archers C	.10	.20
17 Armor of Sun-Tao U	.20	.50
18 Armor of the Golden Samurai U	.20	.50
19 Asahina Tamako U	.20	.50
20 Asahina Tomo C	.10	.20
21 Asako Yasu R	.40	1.00
22 Avoid Fate R	2.00	5.00
23 Barbican U	.20	.50
24 Battering Ram Crew U	.20	.50
25 Bayushi Kachiko R	10.00	20.00
26 Bayushi Togai R	.40	1.00
27 Be Prepared to Dig Two Graves R	1.25	3.00
28 Biting Steel C	.10	.20
29 Blackmail R	5.00	10.00
30 Blacksmith C	.10	.20
31 Blazing Arrows U	.20	.50
32 Block Supply Lines C	.10	.20
33 Bloodsword C	.10	.20
34 Bloom of the White Orchid R	1.25	3.00
35 Bon Festival U	.20	.50
36 Bountiful Harvest R3	.75	2.00
37 Breach of Etiquette U	.20	.50
38 Break Morale C	.10	.20
39 Brilliant Victory C	.10	.20
40 Call Upon The Wind C	.10	.20
41 Careful Planning C	.10	.20
42 Castle of Water C	.10	.20
43 Celestial Alignment R	.40	1.00
44 Charge C	.10	.20
45 Chrysanthemum Festival R	1.50	4.00
46 Climbing Gear U	.20	.50
47 Cloak of Night R	.75	2.00
48 Contentious Terrain C	.10	.20
49 Copper Mine C	.10	.20
50 Counterattack U	.20	.50
51 Counterspell U	.20	.50
52 Crystal Katana C	.10	.20
53 Daidoji Uji C	.10	.20
54 Dance Troupe U	.20	.50
55 Dead Walk The Earth R	.60	1.50
56 Deadly Ground C	.10	.20
57 Debt of Honor R	.40	1.00
58 Demon-Bride of Fu Leng R	3.00	8.00
59 Diamond Mine U	.20	.50
60 Dispersive Terrain C	.10	.20
61 Doji Hoturi R	2.00	5.00
62 Doji Yosai C	.10	.20
63 Dragon Helm U	.20	.50
64 Dragon of Fire R	1.25	3.00
65 Earth Dragon R	.75	2.00
66 Earthquake U	.20	.50
67 Elemental Ward U	.20	.50
68 Emergence of the Tortoise R	.40	1.00
69 Emperor's Peace U	.20	.50
70 Encircled Terrain C	.10	.20
71 Energy Transference C	.10	.20
72 Entrapping Terrain C	.10	.20
73 Evil Feeds Upon Itself U	.20	.50
74 Evil Portents R3	5.00	10.00
75 Explosives U	.20	.50
76 Famous Poet C	.10	.20
77 Fan of Command R	.40	1.00
78 Fantastic Gardens U	.20	.50
79 Feign Death R	2.50	6.00
80 Feint R	.75	2.00
81 Fire Breather R	.40	1.00
82 Fires of Purity U	.20	.50
83 Fist of Osano-Wo R	.75	2.00
84 Flight of Dragons U	.20	.50
85 Focus R	2.50	6.00
86 Forest C	.10	.20
87 Forgotten Tomb R	.40	1.00
88 Fort On A Hill R	.75	2.00
89 Foxwife R	1.25	3.00
90 Frenzy U	.20	.50
91 Fury of Osano-Wo C	.10	.20
92 Gaijin Mercenaries R	.40	1.00
93 Geisha Assassin R3	2.50	6.00
94 Ginawa C	.10	.20
95 Glimpse of the Unicorn U	.20	.50
96 Go Master C	.10	.20
97 Goblin Chuckers C	.10	.20
98 Goblin Mob C	.10	.20
99 Goblin Warmonger C	.10	.20
100 Gold Mine C	.10	.20
101 Greater Mujina U	.20	.50
102 Hawk Riders R	.40	1.00
103 Hawks and Falcons C	.10	.20
104 Heart of the Inferno R	2.50	6.00
105 Heavy Cavalry U	.20	.50
106 Heavy Infantry U	.20	.50
107 Heichi Chokei C	.10	.20
108 Hida Amoro U	.20	.50
109 Hida Kisada R	3.00	8.00
110 Hida Sukune C	.10	.20
111 Hida Tampako C	.10	.20
112 Hida Tsuru U	.20	.50
113 Hida Yakamo (Crab Clan Oni) R	3.00	8.00
114 Hida Yakamo R	2.50	6.00
115 Hisa C	.10	.20
116 Honorable Seppuku C	.10	.20
117 Horiuchi Shoan C	.10	.20
118 Hurricane U	.20	.50
119 Iaijitsu Challenge C	.10	.20
120 Iaijitsu Duel C	.10	.20
121 Ide Tadaji R	.40	1.00
122 Ikoma Ujiaki R	.75	2.00
123 Immortal Steel R	.75	2.00
124 Imperial Acrobats R	.75	2.00
125 Imperial Gift R	3.00	8.00
126 Imperial Quest R	.75	2.00
127 Inheritance R1	5.00	10.00
128 Intersecting Highways C	.10	.20
129 Investigation R	.75	2.00
130 Iris Festival R	2.50	6.00
131 Iron Mine C	.10	.20
132 Isawa Kaede U	.20	.50
133 Isawa Tadaka U	.20	.50
134 Isawa Tomo U	.20	.50
135 Isawa Tsuke R	2.50	6.00
136 Isawa Uona C	.10	.20
137 Iuchi Daiyu U	.20	.50
138 Iuchi Karasu U	.20	.50
139 Iuchi Takaai R	.40	1.00
140 Jade Bow C	.10	.20
141 Jade Works C	.10	.20
142 Kakita Toshimoko R	3.00	8.00
143 Kakita Yinobu U	.20	.50
144 Kakita Yoshi R	1.25	3.00
145 Kakita Yuri U	.20	.50
146 Kharmic Strike U	.20	.50
147 Ki-Rin R	1.50	4.00
148 Kitsu Toju C	.10	.20
149 Kitsuki Yasu R	1.50	4.00
150 Kolat Assassin U	.20	.50
151 Kolat Infiltrator U	.20	.50
152 Kolat Master R	2.50	6.00
153 Kolat Servant U	.20	.50
154 Kuni Yori U	.20	.50
155 Kyoso no Oni U	.20	.50
156 Legendary Victory U	.20	.50
157 Lesser Mujina C	.10	.20
158 Light Cavalry C	.10	.20
159 Light Infantry C	.10	.20
160 Look into the Void C	.10	.20
161 Market Place C	.10	.20
162 Marries a Barbarian U	.20	.50
163 Marsh Troll U	.20	.50
164 Martyr U	.20	.50
165 Mask of the Oni U	.20	.50
166 Master of the Tea Ceremony R	.40	1.00
167 Master Smith U	.20	.50
168 Matsu Agetoki U	.20	.50
169 Matsu Gohei C	.10	.20
170 Matsu Hiroru U	.20	.50
171 Matsu Imura U	.20	.50
172 Matsu Tsuko R	5.00	10.00
173 Matsu Yojo C	.10	.20
174 Meditation C	.10	.20
175 Medium Cavalry C	.10	.20
176 Medium Infantry C	.10	.20
177 Mercy R	.40	1.00
178 Mirumoto Daini C	.10	.20
179 Mirumoto Hitomi C	.10	.20
180 Mirumoto Sukune U	.20	.50
181 Mists of Illusion U	.20	.50
182 Miya Yoto U	.20	.50
183 Moat C	.10	.20
184 Morito C	.10	.20

185 Morito Tokei C .10 .20
186 Moshi Wakiza C .10 .20
187 Moto Tsume U .20 .50
188 Naga Bowmen U .20 .50
189 Naga Bushi C .10 .20
190 Naga Shugenja C .10 .20
191 Naga Spearmen U .20 .50
192 Naga Warlord C .10 .20
193 Naginata C .10 .20
194 Naka Kuro R 2.00 5.00
195 Necromancer U .20 .50
196 Night Medallion R .40 1.00
197 Ninja Genin U .20 .50
198 Ninja Shapeshifter U .20 .50
199 Ninja Spy C .10 .20
200 Ninja Stronghold R 5.00 10.00
201 Ninja Thief U .20 .50
202 Oath of Fealty C .10 .20
203 Occult Murders U .20 .50
204 Occupied Terrain C .10 .20
205 Ogre Bushi U .20 .50
206 Oni no Akuma R 2.00 5.00
207 Oni no Shikibu U .20 .50
208 Oni no Tsuburu U .20 .50
209 Oracle of Earth R .40 1.00
210 Oracle of Fire R1 1.25 3.00
211 Oracle of Water R1 .60 1.50
212 Oracle of Wind R1 .40 1.00
213 Otaku Kamoko C .10 .20
214 Outflank C .10 .20
215 Pearl Divers C .10 .20
216 Peasant Revolt U .20 .50
217 Personal Champion R .40 1.00
218 Plague U .20 .50
219 Poisoned Weapon R 2.00 5.00
220 Port C .10 .20
221 Proposal of Peace R .60 1.50
222 Rally Troops C .10 .20
223 Rallying Cry C .10 .20
224 Ratling Bushi U .20 .50
225 Ratling Pack C .10 .20
226 Reflective Pool R .75 2.00
227 Refuse Advantage R .75 2.00
228 Remorseful Seppuku C .10 .20
229 Resist Magic R .75 2.00
230 Retired General C .10 .20
231 Retreat U .20 .50
232 Ring of Air U .20 .50
233 Ring of Earth U .20 .50
234 Ring of Fire U .20 .50
235 Ring of the Void U .20 .50
236 Ring of Water U .20 .50
237 Rise of the Phoenix R .75 2.00
238 Sacrificial Altar U .20 .50
239 Sake Works U .20 .50
240 Samurai Cavalry R .40 1.00
241 Samurai Warriors R .40 1.00
242 Sanctified Temple C .10 .20
243 Sanzo C .10 .20
244 School of Wizardry R1 3.00 8.00
245 Scout C .10 .20
246 Scribe R .40 1.00
247 Secrets on the Wind U .20 .50
248 Shadow Samurai R .40 1.00
249 Shady Dealings U .20 .50
250 Shame U .20 .50
251 Shiba Katsuda C .10 .20
252 Shiba Tsukune C .10 .20
253 Shiba Ujimitsu R 1.50 4.00
254 Shinjo Hanari U .20 .50
255 Shinjo Yasamura C .10 .20
256 Shinjo Yokatsu R 2.00 5.00
257 Shuriken of Serpents C .10 .20
258 Shuten Doji U .20 .50
259 Silver Mine C .10 .20
260 Skeletal Troops C .10 .20
261 Small Farm C .10 .20
262 Sneak Attack R3 6.00 12.00
263 Solar Eclipse R .40 1.00
264 Spearmen C .10 .20
265 Spirit Guide R 1.25 3.00
266 Stables C .10 .20
267 Star of Laramun U .20 .50
268 Strength of Purity U .20 .50
269 Summon Faeries C .10 .20
270 Summon Swamp Spirits U .20 .50
271 Summon Undead Champion R .40 1.00
272 Superior Tactics C .10 .20
273 Temple of the Ancestors U .20 .50
274 Terrible Standard of Fu Leng R .40 1.00
275 Test of Honor R 5.00 10.00
276 Test of Stone U .20 .50
277 Test of the Emerald Champion R .40 1.00
278 The Ancestral Home of the Lion .60 1.50
279 The Deafening War Drums of Fu Leng R .40 1.00
280 The Egg of P'an Ku R 5.00 10.00
281 The Esteemed House of the Crane .60 1.50
282 The Jade Hand R .60 1.50
283 The Mountain Keep of the Dragon .60 1.50
284 The Provincial Estate of the Unicorn .60 1.50
285 The Sacred Temple of the Phoenix .60 1.50
286 The War Fortress of the Crab .60 1.50
287 Togashi Hoshi R 1.50 4.00
288 Togashi Mitsu U .20 .50
289 Togashi Yokuni R 5.00 10.00
290 Togashi Yoshi U .20 .50
291 Toku C .10 .20
292 Torrential Rain R 2.50 6.00
293 Touch of Death R 1.50 4.00
294 Trade Route U .20 .50
295 Traversable Terrain C .10 .20
296 Unexpected Allies U .20 .50
297 Unscalable Walls C .10 .20
298 Void Dragon R 3.00 8.00
299 Walking the Way U .20 .50
300 Water Dragon R 1.50 4.00
301 Way of Deception U .20 .50
302 Wind Born Speed C .10 .20
303 Winds of Change U .20 .50
304 Wings of Fire C .10 .20
305 Wyrm Riders U .20 .50
306 Yasuki Taka C .10 .20
307 Yogo Junzo R 2.00 5.00
308 Yotsu Seiki C .10 .20
309 Zombie Troops U .20 .50

1996 Legend of the Five Rings Anvil of Despair

COMPLETE SET (152)
RELEASED IN DECEMBER 1996
1 A Hidden Fortress U .20 .50
2 A Moment of Truth R .40 1.00
3 A Prophecy Fulfilled R .40 1.00
4 A Thunder's Sacrifice R .40 1.00
5 Agasha Koishi C .10 .20
6 Akodo Kage (Experienced) R .75 2.00
7 Ancestral Shrines of Otosan Uchi C .10 .20
8 Arrival of the Emerald Champion R 1.25 3.00
9 As the Shadow Falls U .20 .50
10 At the Last Moment C .10 .20
11 Basecamp C .10 .20
12 Battlefield of Shallow Graves C .10 .20
13 Bayushi Kachiko (Experienced) R 2.50 6.00
14 Bayushi Tangen C .10 .20
15 Benevolent Protection of Shinsei C .10 .20
16 Blood Oath C .10 .20
17 Bo Stick C .10 .20
18 Candle of the Void U .20 .50
19 Cornered C .10 .20
20 Corrupted Energies U .20 .50
21 Corrupted Silver Mine C .10 .20
22 Corruption of the Harmonies U .20 .50
23 Cremation U .20 .50
24 Daidoji Sembi C .10 .20
25 Daidoji Uji (Experienced) R .40 1.00
26 Daisho Technique C .10 .20
27 Defender From Beyond C .10 .20
28 Disarmament C .10 .20
29 Disfavored R .40 1.00
30 Disrupted Resources R .40 1.00
31 Doom of Fu Leng R 1.50 4.00
32 Drum of Water U .20 .50
33 Duty to the Clan U .20 .50
34 Duty to the Empire R .40 1.00
35 Elemental Vortex U .20 .50
36 Emperor's Protection U .20 .50
37 Essence of Fire C .10 .20
38 Essence of the Void C .10 .20
39 Essence of Water C .10 .20
40 Fields of Asahina Temple C .10 .20
41 Fight to the Setting Sun C .10 .20
42 Forests of Shinomen C .10 .20
43 Fortified Coast U .20 .50
44 Fu Leng's Horde R .40 1.00
45 Garden of Purification C .10 .20
46 Golden Obi of the Sun Goddess R .75 2.00
47 Hammer of Earth U .20 .50
48 Hida Unari C .10 .20
49 Hida Yakamo (Experienced Crab Clan Oni) R 1.50 4.00
50 Hiraiko U .20 .50
51 Hoseki C .10 .20
52 Hotogitsu U .20 .50
53 Ichiin C .10 .20
54 Ikoma Kimura C .10 .20
55 Imperial Honor Guard U .20 .50
56 Imperial Taxation U .20 .50
57 Inaccessible Region U .20 .50
58 Isawa Osugi U .20 .50
59 Isawa Tsuke (Experienced) R .60 1.50
60 Kaiu Pass U .20 .50
61 Kaiu Utsu U .20 .50
62 Kakita Shijin U .20 .50
63 Kamoto R .60 1.50
64 Kasuga Kyogi U .20 .50
65 Kisada's Blockade R .40 1.00
66 Kolat Instigator R 1.50 4.00
67 Kolat Interference U .20 .50
68 Kusatte Iru R .40 1.00
69 Kyojin U .20 .50
70 Lies, Lies, Lies... U .20 .50
71 Mantle of Fire U .20 .50
72 Matsu Seijuro U .20 .50
73 Mikaru C .10 .20
74 Mikio U .20 .50
75 Minor Shugenja C .10 .20
76 Monsoon U .20 .50
77 Mountain of the Seven Thunders R .60 1.50
78 Naga Guard C .10 .20
79 Night Battle C .10 .20
80 Oni no Tadaka C .10 .20
81 Otaku Baiken C .10 .20
82 Peasant Defense C .10 .20
83 Pitch and Fire C .10 .20
84 Plague Infested Region U .20 .50
85 Plague Skulls R .75 2.00
86 Political Dissent R .40 1.00
87 Possession R .40 1.00
88 Prophecy of the Hero R .40 1.00
89 Qakar U .20 .50
90 Radakast C .10 .20
91 Ratling Conjurer C .10 .20
92 Refugees C .10 .20
93 Retirement U .20 .50
94 Return of Fu Leng R 2.00 5.00
95 Rise, Brother U .20 .50
96 River Region C .10 .20
97 Scorched Earth C .10 .20
98 Shallow Victory R .40 1.00
99 Shashakar (Experienced Naga Shugenja) R .75 2.00
100 Shinjo Morito (Experienced Morito) R .60 1.50
101 Shinjo Yasoma U .20 .50
102 Shiryo no Akodo R .40 1.00
103 Shiryo no Bayushi R .40 1.00
104 Shiryo no Hiruma R .40 1.00
105 Shiryo no Isawa R .40 1.00
106 Shiryo no Kakita R .40 1.00
107 Shiryo no Shinjo R 1.25 3.00
108 Shiryo no Togashi R .40 1.00
109 Slander U .20 .50
110 Spiritual Presence C .10 .20
111 Stall Until Sunrise C .10 .20
112 Stealing the Soul U .20 .50
113 Stifling Wind C .10 .20
114 Strategic Victory U .20 .50
115 Summon Nightstalker U .20 .50
116 Suzume Mukashino C .10 .20
117 Takuan R .40 1.00
118 Tapestry of Air U .20 .50
119 Tessen C .10 .20
120 The Blood Feud R .40 1.00
121 The Bronze Gong of the Hantei R .40 1.00
122 The Celestial Pattern U .20 .50
123 The Darkest Day U .20 .50
124 The Face of Fear C .10 .20
125 The Perfect Gift R .40 1.00
126 The Tao of the Naga R .40 1.00
127 The Way of Air U .20 .50
128 The Way of Earth U .20 .50
129 The Way of Fire U .20 .50
130 The Way of Water U .20 .50
131 There is No Hope R .60 1.50
132 To Avenge Our Ancestors R .40 1.00
133 To Do What We Must U .20 .50
134 To the Last Man R 1.25 3.00
135 Togashi Kokujin R 1.25 3.00
136 Togashi Yama U .20 .50
137 Togashi Yokuni (Experienced) R 1.50 4.00
138 Tomb of Iuchiban R .40 1.00
139 Torturous Terrain C .10 .20
140 Toturi (Experienced) R 1.25 3.00
141 Toturi's Army Box .60 1.50
142 Trading Grounds C .10 .20
143 Training Grounds C .10 .20
144 Travelling Poet C .10 .20
145 Treacherous Terrain C .10 .20
146 Tsukuro R .75 2.00
147 Valley of the Shadow R .40 1.00
148 Watchtower C .10 .20
149 Wetlands C .10 .20
150 Yodin R .40 1.00
151 Yogo Ichiba U .20 .50
152 Yogo Junzo's Army Box 1.25 3.00

1996 Legend of the Five Rings Battle of Beiden Pass

1 The War Fortress of the Crab
2 The Mountain Keep of the Dragon
3 Hida Amoro
4 Hida Kisada (Unique)
5 Hida Sukune
6 Hida Tampako
7 Hida Tsuru
8 Hida Yakamo (Unique)
9 Hida Yakamo
10 Kuni Yori
11 Yasuki Nokatsu
12 Doji Kuwanan
13 Agasha Tamori
14 Mirumoto Hitomi
15 Mirumoto Sukune
16 Mirumoto Taki
17 Togashi Rinjin
18 Togashi Yoshi
19 Mirumoto Daini
20 Matsu Chokoku
21 Isha
22 Shiba Katsuda
23 Shosuro Taberu
24 Dairya (Unique)
25 Ginawa
26 Morito Tokei
27 Toku
28 Toturi (Unique)
29 Otaku Kamoko
30 Shinjo Hanari
31 Shinjo Tsuburo
32 Dragon of Fire (Unique)
33 Goblin Warmonger
34 Heichi Chokei
35 Kumo
36 Kyoso no Oni
37 Moshi Wakiza
38 Moto Tsume
39 Ninja Spy
40 Ogre Bushi
41 Sanzo
42 The Monstrous War Machine of Fu Leng (Unique)
43 Yotsu Seiki
44 Archers
45 Goblin Chuckers
46 Goblin Mob
47 Heavy Infantry
48 Lesser Oni
49 Light Infantry
50 Medium Cavalry
51 Medium Infantry
52 Scout
53 Shield Wall
54 Spearmen
55 Skeletal Troops
56 Zombie Troops
57 Blacksmiths
58 Bushi Dojo
59 Diamond Mine
60 Famous Poet
61 Gambling House
62 Gold Mine
63 Go Master
64 Hawks and Falcons
65 Iron Mine
66 Jade Works
67 Merchant Caravan
68 Retired General
69 Sanctified Temple
70 Small Farm
71 Alliance
72 Emperor's Peace
73 Glimpse of the Unicorn
74 Solar Eclipse
75 The Rising Sun
76 The Unexpected Allies (Experienced)
77 Ancestral Armor of the Dragon
78 Ancestral Sword of the Crab
79 Crystal Arrow
80 Crystal Katana
81 Naginata
82 No-Dachi
83 Biting Steel
84 Blood of Midnight
85 Earthquake
86 Summon Undead Champion
87 The Fire From Within
88 Tomb of Jade
89 Torrential Rain
90 Another Time
91 Block Supply Lines
92 Careful Planning
93 Charge
94 Contentious Terrain
95 Corrupted Ground
96 Deadly Ground
97 Diversionary Tactics
98 Encircled Terrain
99 Entrapping Terrain
100 Explosives (Experienced)
101 Frenzy
102 He's Mine!
103 Iaijutsu Challenge
104 Iaijutsu Duel
105 Kolat Assassin
106 Oath of Fealty
107 Outflank
108 Rallying Cry
109 Ring of Air
110 Ring of Earth
111 Ring of Fire
112 Ring of the Void
113 Ring of Water
114 Strength of Purity
115 Superior Tactics
116 Test of Might
117 The Turtle's Shell
118 Wounded in Battle

1996 Legend of the Five Rings Emerald Edition

1 The Ancestral Home of the Lion F
2 The Esteemed House of the Crane F
3 The Mountain Keep of the Dragon F
4 The Provincial Estate of the Unicorn F
5 The Sacred Temple of the Phoenix F
6 The War Fortress of the Crab F
7 Hida Amoro U
8 Hida Kisada (Unique) R
9 Hida Sukune C
10 Hida Tampako C
11 Hida Tsuru U
12 Hida Yakamo (Unique) R
13 Hida Yakamo R
14 Kuni Yori U
15 Yasuki Taka C
16 Asahina Tamako U
17 Asahina Tomo C
18 Daidoji Uji C
19 Doji Hoturi (Unique) R
20 Doji Yosai C
21 Kakita Toshimoko (Unique) R
22 Kakita Yinobu U
23 Kakita Yoshi R
24 Kakita Yuri U
25 Agasha Tamori C
26 Kitsuki Yasu R
27 Mirumoto Daini C
28 Mirumoto Hitomi C
29 Mirumoto Sukune U
30 Togashi Hoshi (Unique) R
31 Togashi Mitsu U
32 Togashi Yokuni (Unique) R
33 Togashi Yoshi U
34 Akodo Kage U
35 Ikoma Ujiaki R
36 Kitsu Motso (Unique) R
37 Kitsu Toju C
38 Matsu Agetoki U
39 Matsu Gohei C
40 Matsu Imura U
41 Matsu Tsuko (Unique) R
42 Matsu Yojo C
43 Moshi Wakiza C
44 Naga Abomination (Unique) R
45 Naga Shugenja C
46 Naga Warlord C
47 Asako Yasu R
48 Isawa Kaede U
49 Isawa Tadaka U
50 Isawa Tomo U
51 Isawa Tsuke R
52 Isawa Uona C
53 Shiba Katsuda C
54 Shiba Tsukune C
55 Shiba Ujimitsu (Unique) R
56 Bayushi Hisa C
57 Bayushi Kachiko (Unique) R
58 Bayushi Togai R
59 Shosuro Hametsu R
60 Ginawa C
61 Morito Tokei C
62 Naka Kuro (Unique) R
63 Toku C
64 Toturi (Unique) R
65 Horiuchi Shoan C
66 Ide Tadaji (Unique) R
67 Iuchi Daiyu U
68 Iuchi Karasu U
69 Iuchi Takaai R
70 Otaku Kamoko C
71 Shinjo Hanari U
72 Shinjo Yasamura C
73 Shinjo Yokatsu (Unique) R
74 Air Dragon (Unique) R
75 Alhundro Cornejo U
76 Dragon of Fire (Unique) R
77 Earth Dragon (Unique) R
78 Goblin Warmonger C
79 Heichi Chokei C
80 Ki-Rin (Unique) R
81 Kolat Servant U
82 Kyoso no Oni U
83 Matsu Hiroru U
84 Miya Yoto U
85 Morito C
86 Moto Tsume U
87 Necromancer U
88 Ninja Shapeshifter U
89 Ninja Spy C
90 Ogre Bushi U
91 Oni no Akuma R
92 Oni no Shikibu U
93 Oni no Tsuburu U
94 Sanzo C
95 Shuten Doji U
96 The Demon Bride of Fu Leng R
97 Void Dragon (Unique) R
98 Water Dragon (Unique) R
99 Yogo Junzo (Unique) R
100 Yotsu Seiki C
101 Barbican U
102 Blacksmiths C
103 Copper Mine C
104 Dance Troupe U
105 Diamond Mine U
106 Famous Poet C
107 Fantastic Gardens U
108 Forest C
109 Forgotten Tomb R
110 Fort on a Hill R
111 Gold Mine C
112 Go Master C
113 Hawks and Falcons C
114 Imperial Acrobats R
115 Iron Mine C
116 Jade Works C
117 Marketplace C
118 Master of the Tea Ceremony R
119 Master Smith U
120 Moat C
121 Ninja Stronghold R
122 Oracle of Earth R
123 Oracle of Fire R
124 Oracle of Water R
125 Oracle of Wind R
126 Pearl Divers U
127 Port C
128 Retired General U
129 Sacrificial Altar U
130 Sake Works C
131 Sanctified Temple C
132 School of Wizardry R
133 Silver Mine C
134 Small Farm C
135 Stables C
136 Temple of the Ancestors U
137 Trade Route U
138 Unscalable Walls C
139 Alliance U
140 Bloom of the White Orchid R
141 Bon Festival U
142 Celestial Alignment R
143 Chrysanthemum Festival R
144 Dead Walk the Earth R
145 Emergence of the Tortoise R
146 Emperor's Peace U
147 Evil Feeds Upon Itself U
148 Glimpse of the Unicorn U
149 Hurricane U
150 Imperial Gift R
151 Imperial Quest R
152 Inheritance R
153 Iris Festival R
154 Occult Murders U
155 Peasant Revolt U
156 Plague U
157 Proposal of Peace R
158 Rise of the Phoenix R
159 Solar Eclipse R
160 Test of Stone U
161 Test of the Emerald Champion R
162 Unexpected Allies U
163 Ancestral Armor of Crab Clan FE
164 Ancestral Armor of Crane Clan FE
165 Ancestral Armor of Dragon Clan FE
166 Ancestral Armor of Lion Clan FE
167 Ancestral Armor of Phoenix Clan FE
168 Ancestral Armor of Unicorn Clan FE
169 Ancestral Standard of the Crab FO
170 Ancestral Standard of the Crane FO
171 Ancestral Standard of the Dragon FO
172 Ancestral Standard of the Lion FO

173 Ancestral Standard of the Phoenix FO
174 Ancestral Standard of the Unicorn FO
175 Bloodsword C
176 Climbing Gear U
177 Crystal Katana C
178 Dragon Helm U
179 Fan of Command R
180 Jade Bow C
181 Mask of the Oni U
182 Naginata C
183 Night Medallion R
184 Shuriken of Serpents U
185 Terrible Standard of Fu Leng R
186 The Armor of Sun Tao U
187 The Armor of the Golden Samurai U
188 The Deafening War Drums of Fu Leng R
189 The Jade Hand R
190 The Star of Laramun R
191 Apprentice R
192 Archers C
193 Battering Ram Crew U
194 Fire Breather R
195 Foxwife R
196 Gaijin Mercenaries R
197 Goblin Chuckers C
198 Goblin Mob C
199 Greater Mujina U
200 Hawk Riders R
201 Heavy Cavalry U
202 Heavy Infantry U
203 Lesser Mujina C
204 Light Cavalry C
205 Light Infantry C
206 Marsh Troll U
207 Medium Cavalry C
208 Medium Infantry C
209 Naga Bowmen U
210 Naga Bushi C
211 Naga Spearmen U
212 Ninja Genin U
213 Personal Champion R
214 Ratling Bushi U
215 Ratling Pack C
216 Samurai Cavalry R
217 Samurai Warriors R
218 Scout C
219 Scribe R
220 Shadow Samurai R
221 Skeletal Troops C
222 Spearmen C
223 Spirit Guide R
224 Wyrm Riders U
225 Zombie Troops U
226 Animate the Dead U
227 Biting Steel C
228 Call Upon the Wind C
229 Castle of Water C
230 Cloak of Night R
231 Counterspell U
232 Earthquake U
233 Elemental Ward U
234 Energy Transference C
235 Fires of Purity U
236 Heart of the Inferno R
237 Immortal Steel R
238 Look Into the Void C
239 Mists of Illusion U
240 Reflective Pool R
241 Secrets on the Wind U
242 Summon Faeries C
243 Summon Swamp Spirits U
244 Summon Undead Champion R
245 The Fist of Osano Wo R
246 The Fury of Osano-Wo C
247 Torrential Rain R
248 Touch of Death R
249 Walking the Way R
250 Wind Born Speed C
251 Winds of Change U
252 Wings of Fire C
253 Ambush R
254 Avoid Fate R
255 Be Prepared to Dig Two Graves R
256 Blackmail R
257 Blazing Arrows U
258 Block Supply Lines C
259 Bountiful Harvest R
260 Breach of Etiquette U
261 Break Morale C
262 Brilliant Victory C
263 Careful Planning C
264 Charge C
265 Contentious Terrain C
266 Counterattack U
267 Deadly Ground C
268 Debt of Honor R
269 Dispersive Terrain C
270 Encircled Terrain C
271 Entrapping Terrain C
272 Evil Portents R
273 Explosives U
274 Feign Death R
275 Feint R
276 Flight of Dragons U
277 Focus R
278 Frenzy U
279 Geisha Assassin R
280 Honorable Seppuku C
281 Iaijutsu Challenge C
282 Iaijutsu Duel C
283 Intersecting Highways C
284 Investigation R
285 Kharmic Strike U
286 Kolat Assassin U
287 Kolat Infiltrator U
288 Kolat Master R
289 Legendary Victory U
290 Marries A Barbarian U
291 Martyr U
292 Meditation C
293 Mercy R
294 Ninja Thief U
295 Oath of Fealty C
296 Occupied Terrain C
297 Outflank C
298 Poisoned Weapon R
299 Rallying Cry C
300 Rally Troops C
301 Refuse Advantage R
302 Remorseful Seppuku C
303 Resist Magic R
304 Retreat U
305 Ring of Air U
306 Ring of Earth U
307 Ring of Fire U
308 Ring of the Void U
309 Ring of Water U
310 Shady Dealings U
311 Shame U
312 Sneak Attack R
313 Strength of Purity U
314 Superior Tactics C
315 Test of Honor R
316 The Egg of P'an Ku R
317 Traversable Terrain C
318 Way of Deception U

1996 Legend of the Five Rings Forbidden Knowledge

COMPLETE SET (150) 30.00 80.00
BOOSTER BOX (46 PACKS) 75.00 150.00
BOOSTER PACK (11 CARDS) 2.00 4.00
RELEASED IN AUGUST 1996
1 A Black Scroll is Opened U .20 .50
2 A Terrible Oath R 1.50 4.00
3 Akiyoshi C .10 .20
4 Akodo Godaigo R .60 1.50
5 An Untold Cost R .60 1.50
6 Ancestral Sword of Hantei R 2.00 5.00
7 Armor of Earth R 1.00 2.50
8 Artificer C .10 .20
9 Asako Oyo U .20 .50
10 Bandit Hideout C .10 .20
11 Battlements of Matsu Castle R .60 1.50
12 Bayushi Baku U .20 .50
13 Bayushi Shoju R 2.00 5.00
14 Beiden Pass U .20 .50
15 Black Market C .10 .20
16 Black Wind From The Soul R 1.50 4.00
17 Bog Hag C .10 .20
18 Brash Hero C .10 .20
19 Bribery U .20 .50
20 Bushi Dojo C .10 .20
21 Calling the Elements C .10 .20
22 Chasing the Wind R .40 1.00
23 Courage of the Seven Thunders U .20 .50
24 Crossroads C .10 .20
25 Crushing Attack U .20 .50
26 Dairya (Experienced) R .75 2.00
27 Dark Daughter of Fu Leng R .40 1.00
28 Dealing With Shadows U .20 .50
29 Delicate Calculations C .10 .20
30 Disharmony C .10 .20
31 Diversionary Tactics C .10 .20
32 Doji Kuwannan C .10 .20
33 Dragon Sword is Broken U .20 .50
34 Dripping Poison U .20 .50
35 Enlightenment C .10 .20
36 Family Loyalty R .40 1.00
37 Farmlands C .10 .20
38 Fearful Populace U .20 .50
39 Flatlands C .10 .20
40 Fu Leng's Steeds U .20 .50
41 Fusaki C .10 .20
42 Garotte U .20 .50
43 Goblin Berserkers C .10 .20
44 Gunsen of Water R .60 1.50
45 Hazardous Ground C .10 .20
46 Higher Ground C .10 .20
47 Ide Daikoku R .40 1.00
48 Ikoma Tsanuri U .20 .50
49 Ikoma Ujiaki (Experienced) R .40 1.00
50 Imperial Funeral U .20 .50
51 Isawa Natsune C .10 .20
52 Isawa Uona (Experienced) R .40 1.00
53 Jade Strike C .10 .20
54 Kaiu Kenru C .10 .20
55 Kaiu Suman U .20 .50
56 Kakita Foruku U .20 .50
57 Kakita Toshimoko (Experienced) R 1.50 4.00
58 Katana of Fire R .40 1.00
59 Kemmei C .10 .20
60 Kolat Saboteur R .40 1.00
61 Kolat Whisperer R .60 1.50
62 Kotaro R .40 1.00
63 Kuni Wastelands R 1.50 4.00
64 Kuni Yori (Experienced) R .40 1.00
65 Lesser Oni C .10 .20
66 Mantis Budoka U .20 .50
67 Mantis Samurai U .20 .50
68 Matsu Toshiro C .10 .20
69 Mempo of the Void R .75 2.00
70 Merchant Caravan C .10 .20
71 Mirumoto Daini (Experienced) R 1.25 3.00
72 Mountain Pass C .10 .20
73 Moving the Shadow C .10 .20
74 Nemesis U .20 .50
75 Ningyo C .10 .20
76 Ninja Kidnapper U .20 .50
77 No-Dachi C .10 .20
78 Not this Day! U .20 .50
79 Ogre Warriors R .40 1.00
80 Oni no Akeru U .20 .50
81 Oni no Jimen U .20 .50
82 Oni no Kaze U .20 .50
83 Oni no Mizu U .20 .50
84 Oni no Seiryoku U .20 .50
85 Oni no Taki-Bi U .20 .50
86 Passing on the Soul U .20 .50
87 Pearl of Wisdom R .40 1.00
88 Personal Standard C .10 .20
89 Pikemen C .10 .20
90 Plains of Otosan Uchi R 1.25 3.00
91 Purity of the Seven Thunders R .75 2.00
92 Qarash U .20 .50
93 Ramash C .10 .20
94 Reserve Movement U .20 .50
95 Return of the Fallen Lord R .75 2.00
96 Reversal of Fortunes U .20 .50
97 Ride Until Dawn R .40 1.00
98 Scorn C .10 .20
99 Seikua C .10 .20
100 Seize the Day R .40 1.00
101 Shahadet (Experienced Naga Warlord) R .60 1.50
102 Sharing the Strength of Many C .10 .20
103 Shield Wall U .20 .50
104 Shinjo Mosaku U .20 .50
105 Shinjo Sadato C .10 .20
106 Spoils of War R .40 1.00
107 Strength of the Earth U .20 .50
108 Strike at the Roots C .10 .20
109 Strike with No-Thought U .20 .50
110 Swamplands C .10 .20
111 The Arrow Knows the Way R 2.50 6.00
112 The Coward's Way U .20 .50
113 The Doji Plains U .20 .50
114 The Elements' Fury U .20 .50
115 The Emerald Armor R .75 2.00
116 The Eye of Shorihotsu U .20 .50
117 The Final Breath C .10 .20
118 The Fires That Cleanse U .20 .50
119 The First Shout C .10 .20
120 The Gates of Hida Castle R 1.25 3.00
121 The Imperial Standard R 1.50 4.00
122 The Iron Citadel R 1.50 4.00
123 The Isawa Woodlands U .20 .50
124 The Kaiu Walls U .20 .50
125 The Kakita Palisades R .40 1.00
126 The Path to Inner Peace C .10 .20
127 The People's Expense C .10 .20
128 The Price of War U .20 .50
129 The Ruined Keep of Fu Leng R .60 1.50
130 The Second Shout C .10 .20
131 The Shinjo Parade Grounds R .40 1.00
132 The Third Shout U .20 .50
133 The Togashi Bastion R .40 1.00
134 The Towers of Isawa Castle R .40 1.00
135 The Wasting Disease R 2.00 5.00
136 Those Who Stand Alone C .10 .20
137 Tides of Battle R .40 1.00
138 Togashi Mikoto C .10 .20
139 Togashi Rinjin U .20 .50
140 Tsuruchi C .10 .20
141 Unfettered Attack U .20 .50
142 Virtues of Command U .20 .50
143 Walking Horror of Fu Leng R 1.00 2.50
144 Wheel of Fate U .20 .50
145 Whispering Winds C .10 .20
146 Wind-Borne Slumbers U .20 .50
147 Yari of Air R .40 1.00
148 Yogo Asami C .10 .20
149 Yogo Junzo (Experienced) R 1.50 4.00
150 Your Life Is Mine R .75 2.00

1996 Legend of the Five Rings Shadowlands

COMPLETE SET (155) 30.00 80.00
RELEASED IN MAY 1996
1 A Gift of Honor R .60 1.50
2 A Stout Heart U2 .20 .50
3 Accessible Terrain C .10 .20
4 Ancient Spear of the Naga F 2.00 5.00
5 Another Time C .10 .20
6 Arrows from the Woods C .10 .20
7 Ashigaru C .10 .20
8 Ashlim U2 .20 .50
9 Balash C .10 .20
10 Bayushi Aramoro U2 .20 .50
11 Bayushi Goshiu U2 .20 .50
12 Bayushi Hisa C .10 .20
13 Bayushi Kyoto R .60 1.50
14 Bayushi Supai R .40 1.00
15 Bayushi Tomaru C/F .10 .20
16 Blood of Midnight C .10 .20
17 Call to Arms U2 .20 .50
18 Change of Loyalty R .40 1.00
19 Confusion at Court C .10 .20
20 Contemplate the Void C .10 .20
21 Corrupted Ground C .10 .20
22 Corrupted Iron Mine C .10 .20
23 Court Jester U2 .20 .50
24 Crystal Arrow C .10 .20
25 Dark Divination R 2.00 5.00
26 Dark Oracle of Air R .60 1.50
27 Dark Oracle of Earth R .60 1.50
28 Dark Oracle of Fire R .60 1.50
29 Dark Oracle of Water R 2.00 5.00
30 Darkness Feeds... R .60 1.50
31 Dashmar R .60 1.50
32 Defend Your Honor C/U1 .40 1.00
33 Desperate Measures R 2.50 6.00
34 Doji Hoturi (Experienced) R 1.50 4.00
35 Doji House Guard U2 .20 .50
36 Doom of the Crab U2 .20 .50
37 Doom of the Crane U2 .20 .50
38 Doom of the Dragon U2 .20 .50
39 Doom of the Lion U2 .20 .50
40 Doom of the Naga U2 .20 .50
41 Doom of the Phoenix U2 .20 .50
42 Doom of the Scorpion U2 .20 .50
43 Doom of the Unicorn U2 .20 .50
44 Earthworks C .10 .20
45 Enough Talk! U2 .20 .50
46 Evil Ward U2 .20 .50
47 False Alliance R .60 1.50
48 Final Charge R .40 1.00
49 Force of Will C .10 .20
50 Forced March U2 .20 .50
51 Gambling House C .10 .20
52 Garegoso no Bakemono R .60 1.50
53 Geisha House C .10 .20
54 Goblin Shaman C .10 .20
55 Gust of Wind U2 .20 .50
56 Han-Kyu U2 .20 .50
57 He's Mine! C .10 .20
58 Hida House Guard U2 .20 .50
59 Hida O-Ushi R .75 2.00
60 Himura Kage U2 .20 .50
61 His Most Favored R 2.00 5.00
62 Ikiryo C .10 .20
63 Ikoma Kaoku U2 .20 .50
64 Impassable Terrain C .10 .20
65 Imperial Levying R .75 2.00
66 Isawa Tadaka (Experienced) R .40 1.00
67 Isha C .10 .20
68 Jade Arrow U2 .20 .50
69 Jade Goblet U2 .20 .50
70 Kakita Torikago C .10 .20
71 Kakita Yogoso U2 .20 .50
72 Kitsu Motso R 1.00 2.50
73 Kolat Oyabun U2 .20 .50
74 Kumo C .10 .20
75 Levy Troops U1 .60 1.50
76 Mamoru U2 .20 .50
77 Mantis Bushi R .60 1.50
78 Mara U2 .20 .50
79 Matsu Chokoku C .10 .20
80 Matsu House Guard U2 .20 .50
81 Minor Oni Servant R .75 2.00
82 Mirumoto Hitomi (Experienced) U2 .20 .50
83 Mirumoto House Guard U2 .20 .50
84 Mirumoto Taki C .10 .20
85 Mountain Goblin C .10 .20
86 Nageteppo U2 .20 .50
87 New Year's Celebrations R .40 1.00
88 Obsidian Mirror R .60 1.50
89 Oni no Ogon R 1.00 2.50
90 Oni no Ogon U2 .20 .50
91 Oni no Sanru U2 .20 .50
92 Otaku Kamoko (Experienced) U2 .20 .50
93 Otaku Kojiro R .75 2.00
94 Pearl Bed C .10 .20
95 Pennaggolan C .10 .20
96 Plague Zombies C .10 .20
97 Plea of the Peasants U2 .20 .50
98 Porcelain Mask of Fu Leng R .60 1.50
99 Qamar R .60 1.50
100 Rampant Plague R .60 1.50
101 Ratling Conscripts C .10 .20
102 Ratling Scavenger C .10 .20
103 Ratling Thief U2 .20 .50
104 Setsuban Festival R .60 1.50
105 Shabura U2 .20 .50
106 Shadowlands Madmen R .40 1.00
107 Shadowlands Sickness U2 .20 .50
108 Shadowmadness U2 .20 .50
109 Shagara C .10 .20
110 Shapeshifting R 1.00 2.50
111 Shiba House Guard U2 .20 .50
112 Shiba Tetsu C .10 .20
113 Shinjo House Guard U2 .20 .50
114 Shinjo Tsuburo C .10 .20
115 Shosuro Hametsu F .60 1.50
116 Shosuro Taberu U/F .40 1.00
117 Shosuro Tage R .75 2.00
118 Skeletal Archers C .10 .20
119 Soshi Bantaro C/F .10 .20
120 Stale Wind U2 .20 .50
121 Strike at the Tail R .60 1.50
122 Suspended Terrain C .10 .20
123 Sympathetic Energies C .10 .20
124 Temple of Bishamon C .10 .20
125 Terrible Standard of Fu Leng R .40 1.00
126 Test of Might C .10 .20
127 Tetsubo C .10 .20
128 The Broken Sword of the Scorpion F 1.50 4.00
129 The Code of Bushido U2 .20 .50
130 The Falling Darkness R .40 1.00
131 The Festering Pit of Fu Leng R 1.50 4.00
132 The Fire From Within U2 .20 .50
133 The Hidden Temples of the Naga 1.00 2.50
134 The Hooded Ronin R .60 1.50
135 The Laughing Monk C .10 .20
136 The Nameless One U2 .20 .50
137 The Obsidian Hand R 1.50 4.00
138 The Rising Sun R .40 1.00
139 The Ruined Fortress of the Scorpion .20 .50
140 The Turtle's Shell U2 .20 .50
141 Threat of War R .40 1.00
142 Thunder Dragon R 1.00 2.50
143 Togashi Gaijutsu R .75 2.00
144 Tomb of Jade C .10 .20
145 Touch of Despair R .75 2.00
146 Touch of Fu Leng R .75 2.00
147 Twist of Fate R .40 1.00
148 Utter Defeat R 3.00 8.00
149 Wakizashi C .10 .20
150 Warhorses C .10 .20
151 When Darkness Draws Near R .40 1.00
152 Winning Kachiko's Favor R .75 2.00
153 Wounded in Battle C .10 .20
154 Yasuki Nokatsu C .10 .20
155 Yuki no Onna C/F .10 .20

1997 Legend of the Five Rings Crimson and Jade

1 A Glimpse of the Soul's Shadow C .10 .20
2 A Samurai's Fury R 2.00 5.00
3 A Spirit of Water C .10 .20
4 Agasha Heizo C .10 .20
5 Along the Coast at Midnight R .40 1.00
6 An Oni's Fury U .20 .50
7 Ancestral Guidance R .40 1.00
8 Ancestral Weapons of the Mantis F 1.00 2.50
9 Antidote U .20 .50
10 Architects of the Wall R .50 1.25
11 Are You With Me? U .20 .50
12 Armor of the Shadow Warrior R .60 1.50
13 Armory C1 .10 .20
14 Asahina Tomo (Experienced) R .60 1.50
15 Ashamana C .10 .20
16 Bad Kharma R .60 1.50
17 Bandit Gang C .10 .20
18 Barbarian Horde R .75 2.00
19 Bayushi Tasu U .20 .50
20 Borderland U .20 .50
21 Breaking Blow U .20 .50
22 Bridged Pass C1 .10 .20
23 Brotherhood of Shinsei .40 1.00
24 Brothers of Thunder U .20 .50
25 Carrier Pigeon C .10 .20
26 Catching the Wind's Favor C .10 .20
27 Chime of Harmony C .10 .20
28 Chinoko U .20 .50
29 Clan Banner R .60 1.50
30 Clan Heartland R 1.25 3.00
31 Corrupted Copper Mine C .10 .20
32 Counterfeit U .20 .50
33 Courier C .10 .20
34 Cowardice U .20 .50
35 Dance of the Elements U .20 .50
36 Deploy Reserves U .20 .50
37 Disrupt the Aura C .10 .20
38 Divine the Future U .20 .50
39 Doji Reju C .10 .20
40 Double Chi C .10 .20
41 Dragon's Teeth C .10 .20
42 Engineering Crew C1 .10 .20
43 Extortion R 2.00 5.00
44 Fiery Wrath R .50 1.25
45 Fight for My Favor U .20 .50
46 Fist of the Earth C .10 .20
47 Forced Alliance R .50 1.25
48 Forest of Thorns U .20 .50
49 Fresh Horse U .20 .50
50 Genzo R .60 1.50
51 Gift of the Wind C .10 .20
52 Ginawa (Experienced) R 1.25 3.00
53 Hida Yakamo (Experienced) R 1.25 3.00
54 Hiruma Yoshi C .10 .20
55 Historian C1 .10 .20
56 Hitoshi C1 .10 .20
57 Hyobe U .20 .50
58 Ikoma Ryozo U .20 .50
59 Incense of Concentration U .20 .50
60 Inner Fire U .20 .50
61 Isawa Norikazu R .60 1.50
62 Isawa Tomo (Experienced) U .20 .50
63 Island Wharf C .10 .20
64 Iuchi Daiyu (Experienced) R .60 1.50
65 Kado C .10 .20
66 Kakita Ichiro U .20 .50
67 Kanbe C1 .10 .20
68 Kenku Teacher C .10 .20
69 Kenku U .20 .50
70 Kenshin's Helm U .20 .50
71 Kitsu Motso (Experienced) R .60 1.50
72 Know Your Enemy R .50 1.25
73 Koichi C .10 .20
74 Kolat Bodyguard U .20 .50
75 Kolat's Favor U .20 .50
76 Light of the Sun Goddess U .20 .50
77 Lost Valley C1 .10 .20
78 Mantis Clan Shugenja U .20 .50
79 Masasue C .10 .20
80 Master of the Rolling River U .20 .50
81 Matsu Goemon C .10 .20
82 Mine Riots U .20 .50
83 Moto Sada C1 .10 .20
84 Moto Tsume (Experienced) R 2.00 5.00
85 Mounts C .10 .20
86 Mukami C .10 .20
87 Naming the True Evil R .60 1.50
88 Narrow Ground C .10 .20
89 New Taxes U .20 .50
90 Night of a Thousand Fires U .20 .50
91 Nobuo U .20 .50
92 Norio C .10 .20
93 Ogre Outlaw U .20 .50
94 One Koku C .10 .20
95 Oni no Chi U .20 .50
96 Oni no Genso C1 .10 .20
97 Oni Warding R .50 1.25
98 Orochi R .75 2.00
99 Osano-Wo's Breath U .20 .50
100 Pearl-Encrusted Staff R .60 1.50
101 Peasant Levies C .10 .20
102 Prayer Shrines C .10 .20
103 Robes of Shinsei U .20 .50
104 Ryosei C .10 .20
105 Secluded Ravine C1 .10 .20
106 Severed from the Emperor R 1.00 2.50
107 Shabura (Experienced) R .60 1.50
108 Shadow of the Dark God U .20 .50
109 Shalasha U .20 .50
110 Shiba Shingo C .10 .20

111 Shinjo Rojin C .10 .20
112 Shinjo Tashima U .20 .50
113 Shinsei's Shrine R .60 1.50
114 Shiryo no Agasha R .40 1.00
115 Shiryo no Doji R .60 1.50
116 Shiryo no Hida R .60 1.50
117 Shiryo no Matsu R .60 1.50
118 Shiryo no Otaku R .60 1.50
119 Shiryo no Shiba R .60 1.50
120 Shiryo no Shosuro R .60 1.50
121 Shosuro Sadato C .10 .20
122 Soshi Bantaro (Experienced) R .75 2.00
123 Stand Against the Waves C .10 .20
124 Stand Firm C .10 .20
125 Strength of My Ancestors C .10 .20
126 Strike of Flowing Water C .10 .20
127 Suana U .20 .50
128 Summons from Beyond U .20 .50
129 Sunken City R .40 1.00
130 Superior Strategist R 1.50 4.00
131 Takao U .20 .50
132 Takuni C1 .10 .20
133 Taro C .10 .20
134 Temple of Osano-Wo F .60 1.50
135 Tetsuya R .75 2.00
136 The Battle at Isawa Palace U .20 .50
137 The Death of Tsuko R .50 1.25
138 The Fault is Mine C .10 .20
139 The Great Bear R .60 1.50
140 The Hooded Ronin (Experienced) R .75 2.00
141 The Purity of Shinsei R .40 1.00
142 The Touch of Shinsei R .60 1.50
143 The Wrath of Osano-Wo C .10 .20
144 The Yasuki Estates C1 .10 .20
145 Togashi Jodome U .20 .50
146 Togashi Mitsu (Experienced) R .60 1.50
147 Tokiuji C .10 .20
148 Toturi's Fan R .75 2.00
149 Tradeposts of the Mantis C1 .10 .20
150 Tsunami U .20 .50
151 Tsuo C .10 .20
152 Tunnel System C1 .10 .20
153 Visage of the Void U .20 .50
154 Void Strike U .20 .50
155 Winter Warfare R 1.50 4.00
156 Wisdom the Wind Brings U .20 .50
157 Yasuki Kojiro U .20 .50
158 Yoritomo R 1.25 3.00
159 Yoritomo's Alliance .60 1.50
160 You Walk With Evil R 1.50 4.00
161 Yugoro R .75 2.00

1997 Legend of the Five Rings Obsidian Edition

1 The Ancestral Home of the Lion F
2 The Esteemed House of the Crane F
3 The Mountain Keep of the Dragon F
4 The Provincial Estate of the Unicorn F
5 The Sacred Temple of the Phoenix F
6 The War Fortress of the Crab F
7 Hida Amoro U
8 Hida Kisada (Unique) R
9 Hida Sukune C
10 Hida Tampako C
11 Hida Tsuru U
12 Hida Yakamo (Unique) R
13 Hida Yakamo R
14 Kuni Yori U
15 Yasuki Taka C
16 Asahina Tamako U
17 Asahina Tomo C
18 Daidoji Uji C
19 Doji Hoturi (Unique) R
20 Doji Yosai C
21 Kakita Toshimoko (Unique) R
22 Kakita Yinobu U
23 Kakita Yoshi R
24 Kakita Yuri U
25 Agasha Tamori C
26 Kitsuki Yasu R
27 Mirumoto Daini C
28 Mirumoto Hitomi C
29 Mirumoto Sukune U
30 Togashi Hoshi (Unique) R
31 Togashi Mitsu U
32 Togashi Yokuni (Unique) R
33 Togashi Yoshi U
34 Akodo Kage U
35 Ikoma Ujiaki R
36 Kitsu Motso (Unique) R
37 Kitsu Toju C
38 Matsu Agetoki U
39 Matsu Gohei C
40 Matsu Imura U
41 Matsu Tsuko (Unique) R
42 Matsu Yojo C
43 Moshi Wakiza C
44 Naga Abomination (Unique) R
45 Naga Shugenja C
46 Naga Warlord C
47 Asako Yasu R
48 Isawa Kaede U
49 Isawa Tadaka U
50 Isawa Tomo U
51 Isawa Tsuke R
52 Isawa Uona C
53 Shiba Katsuda C
54 Shiba Tsukune C
55 Shiba Ujimitsu (Unique) R
56 Bayushi Hisa C
57 Bayushi Kachiko (Unique) R
58 Bayushi Togai R
59 Shosuro Hametsu R
60 Ginawa C
61 Morito Tokei C
62 Naka Kuro (Unique) R
63 Toku C
64 Toturi (Unique) R
65 Horiuchi Shoan C
66 Ide Tadaji (Unique) R
67 Iuchi Daiyu C
68 Iuchi Karasu U
69 Iuchi Takaai R
70 Otaku Kamoko C
71 Shinjo Hanari U
72 Shinjo Yasamura C
73 Shinjo Yokatsu (Unique) R
74 Air Dragon (Unique) R
75 Alhundro Cornejo U
76 Dragon of Fire (Unique) R
77 Earth Dragon (Unique) R
78 Goblin Warmonger C
79 Heichi Chokei C
80 Ki-Rin (Unique) R
81 Kolat Servant U
82 Kyoso no Oni U
83 Matsu Hiroru U
84 Miya Yoto U
85 Morito C
86 Moto Tsume U
87 Necromancer U
88 Ninja Shapeshifter U
89 Ninja Spy C
90 Ogre Bushi U
91 Oni no Akuma R
92 Oni no Shikibu U
93 Oni no Tsuburu U
94 Sanzo C
95 Shuten Doji U
96 The Demon Bride of Fu Leng R
97 Void Dragon (Unique) R
98 Water Dragon (Unique) R
99 Yogo Junzo (Unique) R
100 Yotsu Seiki C
101 Barbican U
102 Blacksmiths C
103 Copper Mine C
104 Dance Troupe U
105 Diamond Mine U
106 Famous Poet C
107 Fantastic Gardens U
108 Forest C
109 Forgotten Tomb R
110 Fort on a Hill R
111 Gold Mine C
112 Go Master C
113 Hawks and Falcons C
114 Imperial Acrobats R
115 Iron Mine C
116 Jade Works C
117 Marketplace C
118 Master of the Tea Ceremony R
119 Master Smith U
120 Moat C
121 Ninja Stronghold R
122 Oracle of Earth R
123 Oracle of Fire R
124 Oracle of Water R
125 Oracle of Wind R
126 Pearl Divers U
127 Port C
128 Retired General U
129 Sacrificial Altar U
130 Sake Works C
131 Sanctified Temple C
132 School of Wizardry R
133 Silver Mine C
134 Small Farm C
135 Stables C
136 Temple of the Ancestors U
137 Trade Route U
138 Unscalable Walls C
139 Alliance U
140 Bloom of the White Orchid R
141 Bon Festival U
142 Celestial Alignment R
143 Chrysanthemum Festival R
144 Dead Walk the Earth R
145 Emergence of the Tortoise R
146 Emperor's Peace U
147 Evil Feeds Upon Itself U
148 Glimpse of the Unicorn U
149 Hurricane U
150 Imperial Gift R
151 Imperial Quest R
152 Inheritance R
153 Iris Festival R
154 Occult Murders U
155 Peasant Revolt U
156 Plague U
157 Proposal of Peace R
158 Rise of the Phoenix R
159 Solar Eclipse R
160 Test of Stone U
161 Test of the Emerald Champion R
162 Unexpected Allies U
163 Ancestral Armor of the Crab Clan FE
164 Ancestral Armor of the Crane Clan FE
165 Ancestral Armor of the Dragon Clan FE
166 Ancestral Armor of the Lion Clan FE
167 Ancestral Armor of the Phoenix Clan FE
168 Ancestral Armor of the Unicorn Clan FE
169 Ancestral Standard of the Crab FO
170 Ancestral Standard of the Crane FO
171 Ancestral Standard of the Dragon FO
172 Ancestral Standard of the Lion FO
173 Ancestral Standard of the Phoenix FO
174 Ancestral Standard of the Unicorn FO
175 Bloodsword C
176 Climbing Gear U
177 Crystal Katana C
178 Dragon Helm U
179 Fan of Command R
180 Jade Bow C
181 Mask of the Oni U
182 Naginata C
183 Night Medallion R
184 Shuriken of Serpents U
185 Terrible Standard of Fu Leng R
186 The Armor of Sun Tao U
187 The Armor of the Golden Samurai U
188 The Deafening War Drums of Fu Leng R
189 The Jade Hand R
190 The Star of Laramun R
191 Apprentice R
192 Archers C
193 Battering Ram Crew U
194 Fire Breather R
195 Foxwife R
196 Gaijin Mercenaries R
197 Goblin Chuckers C
198 Goblin Mob C
199 Greater Mujina U
200 Hawk Riders R
201 Heavy Cavalry U
202 Heavy Infantry U
203 Lesser Mujina C
204 Light Cavalry C
205 Light Infantry C
206 Marsh Troll U
207 Medium Cavalry C
208 Medium Infantry C
209 Naga Bowmen U
210 Naga Bushi C
211 Naga Spearmen U
212 Ninja Genin U
213 Personal Champion R
214 Ratling Bushi U
215 Ratling Pack C
216 Samurai Cavalry R
217 Samurai Warriors R
218 Scout C
219 Scribe R
220 Shadow Samurai R
221 Skeletal Troops C
222 Spearmen C
223 Spirit Guide R
224 Wyrm Riders U
225 Zombie Troops U
226 Animate the Dead U
227 Biting Steel C
228 Call Upon the Wind C
229 Castle of Water C
230 Cloak of Night R
231 Counterspell U
232 Earthquake U
233 Elemental Ward U
234 Energy Transference C
235 Fires of Purity U
236 Heart of the Inferno R
237 Immortal Steel R
238 Look Into the Void C
239 Mists of Illusion U
240 Reflective Pool R
241 Secrets on the Wind U
242 Summon Faeries C
243 Summon Swamp Spirits U
244 Summon Undead Champion R
245 The Fist of Osano Wo R
246 The Fury of Osano-Wo C
247 Torrential Rain R
248 Touch of Death R
249 Walking the Way R
250 Wind Born Speed C
251 Winds of Change U
252 Wings of Fire C
253 Ambush R
254 Avoid Fate R
255 Be Prepared to Dig Two Graves R
256 Blackmail R
257 Blazing Arrows U
258 Block Supply Lines C
259 Bountiful Harvest R
260 Breach of Etiquette U
261 Break Morale C
262 Brilliant Victory C
263 Careful Planning C
264 Charge C
265 Contentious Terrain C
266 Counterattack U
267 Deadly Ground C
268 Debt of Honor R
269 Dispersive Terrain C
270 Encircled Terrain C
271 Entrapping Terrain C
272 Evil Portents R
273 Explosives U
274 Feign Death R
275 Feint R
276 Flight of Dragons U
277 Focus R
278 Frenzy U
279 Geisha Assassin R
280 Honorable Seppuku C
281 Iaijutsu Challenge C
282 Iaijutsu Duel C
283 Intersecting Highways C
284 Investigation R
285 Kharmic Strike U
286 Kolat Assassin U
287 Kolat Infiltrator U
288 Kolat Master R
289 Legendary Victory U
290 Marries A Barbarian U
291 Martyr U
292 Meditation C
293 Mercy R
294 Ninja Thief U
295 Oath of Fealty C
296 Occupied Terrain C
297 Outflank C
298 Poisoned Weapon R
299 Rallying Cry C
300 Rally Troops C
301 Refuse Advantage R
302 Remorseful Seppuku C
303 Resist Magic R
304 Retreat U
305 Ring of Air U
306 Ring of Earth U
307 Ring of Fire U
308 Ring of the Void U
309 Ring of Water U
310 Shady Dealings U
311 Shame U
312 Sneak Attack R
313 Strength of Purity U
314 Superior Tactics C
315 Test of Honor R
316 The Egg of P'an Ku R
317 Traversable Terrain C
318 Way of Deception U

1997 Legend of the Five Rings Scorpion Clan Coup Scroll 1

COMPLETE SET (53) 10.00 15.00
BOOSTER BOX (46 PACKS)
BOOSTER PACK (11 CARDS)
RELEASED IN DECEMBER 1997
1 A Samurai Never Stands Alone C .10 .20
2 Agasha's Illusion U .20 .50
3 Ancestral Sword of the Scorpion U .20 .50
4 Armor of Osano-Wo C .10 .20
5 Arrival of the Unicorns C .10 .20
6 Bayushi Dozan C .10 .20
7 Bayushi Kachiko (Inexperienced) U .20 .50
8 Bayushi Shoju (Inexperienced) F 2.00 5.00
9 Bayushi Yokuan U .20 .50
10 Behind Night's Shadow U .20 .50
11 Cavalry Raiders C .10 .20
12 Daikua C .10 .20
13 Divinitory Pool C .10 .20
14 East Wall of Otosan Uchi U .20 .50
15 Flood C .10 .20
16 Freezing the Lifeblood C .10 .20
17 Garrison C .10 .20
18 Hantei the 38th U .20 .50
19 Hatsuko C .10 .20
20 Hiruma's Last Breath U .20 .50
21 Imperial Palace Guard U .20 .50
22 Isawa Tomo's Portal U .20 .50
23 Ishikawa U .20 .50
24 Iuchi Katta C .10 .20
25 Jurojin's Touch C .10 .20
26 Lieutenant Morito U .20 .50
27 Lions Attack the Crane U .20 .50
28 Musubi U .20 .50
29 Plains Above Evil C .10 .20
30 Political Distraction C .10 .20
31 Political Mistake U .20 .50
32 Robbing the Dead C .10 .20
33 Sanado U .20 .50
34 Shinjo Yokatsu U .20 .50
35 Shioda C .10 .20
36 Shosuro Ikawa C .10 .20
37 Soshi Taoshi U .20 .50
38 Soshi Ujemi U .20 .50
39 South Wall of Otosan Uchi U .20 .50
40 Storehouses C .10 .20
41 Streets of Otosan Uchi F .60 1.50
42 The 38th Hantei Falls U .20 .50
43 The Endless Well U .20 .50
44 The Exalted Ugu C .10 .20
45 The First Scroll is Opened U .20 .50
46 The Secret Entrance C .10 .20
47 The Shadow Stronghold of the Bayushi F .50 1.25
48 The Soul Goes Forth C .10 .20
49 The Unclean Cut C .10 .20
50 Through the Waterways U .20 .50
51 Toturi is Drugged U .20 .50
52 War Wagon C .10 .20
53 Yogo Shidachi C .10 .20

1997 Legend of the Five Rings Time of the Void

COMPLETE SET (229) 80.00 150.00
BOOSTER BOX (46 PACKS) 150.00 250.00
BOOSTER PACK (11 CARDS) 3.50 7.00
RELEASED IN SEPTEMBER 1997
1 A Good Day To Die U1 .20 .50
2 A Moment of Clarity U1 .20 .50
3 A Moment of Truth R .60 1.50
4 A Soul of Thunder U .20 .50
5 A Test of Courage C1 .10 .20
6 Agasha Gennai C .10 .20
7 Agasha Tunnels C1 .10 .20
8 Akiyoshi (Experienced) U1 .20 .50
9 Akodo Tactical School R1 .75 2.00
10 al-Hazaad U1 .20 .50
11 al-Rashid C1 .10 .20
12 An Exhibition C1 .10 .20
13 Ancestral Standard of the Scorpion R1 .75 2.00
14 Ancient Armor of the Qamar R1 .75 2.00
15 As Far as the Eye Can See R1 .60 1.50
16 Asako Ishio U .20 .50
17 Asako Togama C1 .10 .20
18 Ashan C1 .10 .20
19 Augury R1 1.50 4.00
20 Battle Standard of Shinsei R1 .60 1.50
21 Battle Standard of the Mantis R1 .60 1.50
22 Battle Standard of the Naga R1 .60 1.50
23 Bayushi Goshiu (Experienced) R 1.50 4.00
24 Bayushi Hisa (Experienced) U .20 .50
25 Bayushi Kachiko (Experienced 2) R1 5.00 10.00
26 Bayushi Marumo C .10 .20
27 Bend Like A Reed C1 .10 .20
28 Berserkers C1 .10 .20
29 Bonds of Darkness R1 .50 1.25
30 Burning Your Essence R1 1.25 3.00
31 Chi Strike R .50 1.25
32 Concealed Weapon R1 .60 1.50
33 Contested Ground C1 .10 .20
34 Coordinated Fire C1 .10 .20
35 Corrupt Geisha House C .10 .20
36 Corrupt Gold Mines C .10 .20
37 Corrupt Stables C .10 .20
38 Corrupted Region C1 .10 .20
39 Counting the Lost U1 .20 .50
40 Crystal Gate C .10 .20
41 Curse of the Jackal C .10 .20
42 Dark Lord's Favor C1 .10 .20
43 Dashmar (Experienced) U1 .20 .50
44 Depth of the Void U1 .20 .50
45 Destiny Has No Secrets C1 .10 .20
46 Disenlightenment R .40 1.00
47 Distractions of the Flesh C1 .10 .20
48 Doji Chomei C .10 .20
49 Doji Hoturi (Experienced 2) R1 6.00 12.00
50 Doji Kuwanan (Experienced) U .20 .50
51 Doji Shizue C1 .10 .20
52 Doji Yosai (Experienced) R .40 1.00
53 Elite Heavy Infantry U .20 .50
54 Elite Light Infantry C1 .10 .20
55 Elite Medium Infantry C1 .10 .20
56 Enlightened Ruler R1 .60 1.50
57 Enlistment U1 .20 .50
58 Eshru C .10 .20
59 Essence of Air U1 .20 .50
60 Essence of Earth U1 .20 .50
61 Factionism R1 .60 1.50
62 Familiar Surroundings C1 .10 .20
63 Fatal Mistake R1 .60 1.50
64 Festival of Long Sticks R1 .40 1.00
65 Final Stand R .40 1.00
66 Flight of Doves U1 .20 .50
67 Flying Carpet R1 .60 1.50
68 Fog C1 .10 .20
69 For the Empire U1 .20 .50
70 Forgiveness C .10 .20
71 Gaijin Merchant U .20 .50
72 Gekkai U1 .20 .50
73 Goblin Madcaps C1 .10 .20
74 Goblin Sneaks C1 .10 .20
75 Goblin War Standard C .10 .20
76 Goblin Wizard C1 .10 .20
77 Harima U1 .20 .50
78 Heavy Mounted Infantry U .20 .50
79 Hida Amoro (Experienced) U1 .20 .50
80 Hida O-Ushi (Experienced) R 1.25 3.00
81 Hida Tadashiro C .10 .20
82 Hida War College R1 .60 1.50
83 Hida Yakamo (Experienced 2) F .60 1.50
84 Hizuka C .10 .20
85 Horde of Fu Leng C1 .10 .20
86 Horsebowmen C1 .10 .20
87 I Believed in You... C1 .10 .20
88 Ikoma Tsanuri (Experienced) R1 .50 1.25
89 In Time of War U .20 .50
90 Isawa Suma C .10 .20
91 Isawa Tadaka (Experienced 2) F 1.00 2.50
92 Isawa Uona (Experienced 2) U1 .20 .50
93 Isha (Experienced) R .40 1.00
94 Iuchi Karasu (Experienced) U .20 .50
95 Izaku Library C .10 .20
96 Jade Dragon R 1.25 3.00
97 Jiujitsu Duel U1 .20 .50
98 Junzo's Battle Standard R1 .60 1.50
99 Kage (Experienced 2 Akodo Kage) R1 .60 1.50
100 Kakita Kenjutsu School R1 .75 2.00
101 Kakita Yoshi (Experienced) U1 .20 .50
102 Kappuksu (Experienced Goblin Warmonger) U .20 .50
103 Kaze-Do C .10 .20
104 Kitsu Okura C1 .10 .20
105 Kitsu Toju (Experienced) U1 .20 .50
106 Know the School C1 .10 .20
107 Kolat Spy C1 .10 .20
108 Komaro C1 .10 .20
109 Kuni Sensin C1 .10 .20
110 Kyujutsu C1 .10 .20
111 Lady Kitsune C1 .10 .20
112 Legions of Fu Leng C .10 .20
113 Lessons from the Past C1 .10 .20
114 Light Mounted Infantry C1 .10 .20
115 Matsu Agetoki (Experienced) R .40 1.00
116 Matsu Gohei (Experienced) U .20 .50
117 Matsu Hiroru (Experienced) R1 .75 2.00
118 Matsu Turi C .10 .20
119 Mighty Protection R1 .75 2.00
120 Mikio (Experienced) U1 .20 .50
121 Mirumoto Hitomi (Experienced 2) R1 1.00 2.50
122 Mirumoto Yukihira U .20 .50
123 Moshi Wakiza (Experienced) U1 .20 .50
124 Mounted Spearmen C1 .10 .20
125 Mujina Chieftain C1 .10 .20
126 Mujina Miners U1 .20 .50
127 Mystical Terrain C .10 .20
128 Necromancer (Experienced) R 1.00 2.50
129 Ninja Stalkers U .20 .50
130 Nogoten's Bow U .20 .50
131 Obsidian Blade C .10 .20
132 Offer of Fealty C1 .10 .20
133 One With the Elements C1 .10 .20
134 Oni no Ianwa R1 .60 1.50
135 Oni no Pekkle C1 .10 .20
136 Oni no Ugulu C1 .10 .20
137 Oracle of the Void R1 .60 1.50
138 Otaku Kamoko (Experienced 2) R1 1.50 4.00

139 Plans Within Plans U1 .20 .50
140 Qamar (Experienced) R1 .40 1.00
141 Radakast (Experienced) U .20 .50
142 Rebuilding the Kaiu Walls U .20 .50
143 Regions of Rokugan U1 .20 .50
144 Rest, My Brother U .20 .50
145 River Delta U1 .20 .50
146 Ruins of the Isawa Library R1 .60 1.50
147 Ryokan's Sword C .10 .20
148 Sailors C1 .10 .20
149 Salute of the Samurai R1 .60 1.50
150 Sanctified Ground C1 .10 .20
151 Seikua (Experienced) R .40 1.00
152 Shahadet's Legion R .75 2.00
153 Shiba Tsukune (Experienced) R1 .60 1.50
154 Shinjo Hanari (Experienced) R .60 1.50
155 Shinjo Riding Stables R1 1.50 4.00
156 Shinjo Sanetama C .10 .20
157 Shinjo Shirasu C1 .10 .20
158 Shinjo Yasamura (Experienced) U1 .20 .50
159 Shinobi U1 .20 .50
160 Shiryo no Asahina R 1.00 2.50
161 Shiryo no Asako R .40 1.00
162 Shiryo no Ide R .40 1.00
163 Shiryo no Ikoma R .75 2.00
164 Shiryo no Kaiu R .60 1.50
165 Shiryo no Mirumoto R .60 1.50
166 Shiryo no Yogo R .75 2.00
167 Shiryo no Yoritomo R .40 1.00
168 Shosuro Hametsu (Experienced) U1 .20 .50
169 Stance of the Mountain C1 .10 .20
170 Strength of Osano-Wo C .10 .20
171 Strength of the Dark One U1 .20 .50
172 Strike Without Striking U1 .20 .50
173 Surrender U1 .20 .50
174 Swamp Goblins C1 .10 .20
175 Sysh C1 .10 .20
176 Taquar C1 .10 .20
177 Teeth of the Serpent U .20 .50
178 The 12th Black Scroll R1 5.00 10.00
179 The Ancestral Home of the Lion U1 .20 .50
180 The Brotherhood of Shinsei U1 .20 .50
181 The Darkest Magics R1 .75 2.00
182 The Esteemed House of the Crane U1 .20 .50
183 The Great Walls of Kaiu Box 1.50 4.00
184 The Heavy Shadow of Fear U1 .20 .50
185 The Hero's Triumph U .20 .50
186 The Hidden Heart of Iuchiban R1 1.50 4.00
187 The Hidden Temples of the Naga U1 .20 .50
188 The Light of Amaterasu C .10 .20
189 The Longest Night R1 1.25 3.00
190 The Mountain Keep of the Dragon U1 .40 1.00
191 The Path of Wisdom R 2.50 6.00
192 The Phoenix is Reborn U1 .20 .50
193 The Plains of Amaterasu U1 .20 .50
194 The Provincial Estate of the Unicorn U1 .20 .50
195 The Ruined Fortress of the Scorpion U1 .20 .50
196 The Ruins of Isawa Castle Box .60 1.50
197 The Sacred Temples of the Phoenix U1 .20 .50
198 The Scorpion's Sting R1 .75 2.00
199 The Sight of Death U .20 .50
200 The Time is Now U1 .20 .50
201 The Touch of Amaterasu U .20 .50
202 The Twelve Ronin R .75 2.00
203 The War Fortress of the Crab U1 .20 .50
204 The Yoritomo Alliance U1 .20 .50
205 To Save an Empire R1 .60 1.50
206 Today We Die R1 1.25 3.00
207 Togashi Kama C1 .10 .20
208 Togashi Testing Grounds R1 .40 1.00
209 Togashi Yokuni (Experienced 2) R 1.50 4.00
210 Togashi Yoshi (Experienced) U1 .20 .50
211 Toku (Experienced) U .20 .50
212 Toturi (Experienced 2) R1 2.00 5.00
213 Toturi's Army U1 .20 .50
214 Toturi's Battle Standard R1 .60 1.50
215 Toturi's Last Stand R1 .50 1.25
216 Toturi's Tactics R1 3.00 8.00
217 Troops from the Woods C1 .10 .20
218 Tsuyu C .10 .20
219 Unattuned U .20 .50
220 Untrustworthy U1 .20 .50
221 Warrior Monks U .20 .50
222 Wedge R1 2.50 6.00
223 Yasuki Taka (Experienced) U .20 .50
224 Yodin (Experienced) R1 .50 1.25
225 Yogo Junzo's Army U1 .20 .50
226 Yogo Oshio C1 .10 .20
227 Yoritomo (Experienced) R1 1.00 2.50
228 Yoritomo's Armor R1 .75 2.00
229 Your Last Mistake U1 .20 .50

1998 Legend of the Five Rings The Hidden Emperor Episode 1

COMPLETE SET (53) 8.00 20.00
RELEASED IN JUNE 1998
1 A Time for Mortal Men C .10 .20
2 Aiki Tactics R2 .50 1.25
3 Blackened Sky U4 .20 .50
4 Broken Guard R2 .40 1.00
5 Chasing Osano-Wo C .10 .20
6 Concealed Archers C .10 .20
7 Cricket C .10 .20
8 Daidoji Rekai C .10 .20
9 Dai-kyu of Anekkusai U4 .20 .50
10 Damesh C .10 .20
11 Day and Night R3 .40 1.00
12 Elite Spearmen C .10 .20
13 Flanking Maneuver C .10 .20
14 Flee the Darkness U4 .20 .50
15 Fu Leng's Skull R 1.25 3.00
16 Grove of the Five Masters U5 .20 .50
17 Hasame C .10 .20
18 Haunted Lands C .10 .20
19 Heart of the Shinomen Forest F .40 1.00
20 Heart of the Shinomen Forest R .40 1.00
21 Hiruma Castle U5 .20 .50
22 Ikudaiu C .10 .20
23 Imperial Legion U4 .20 .50
24 Journey to the Burning Sands U4 .20 .50
25 Kakita Yoshi (Experienced 2) R3 .50 1.25
26 Kyoso no Oni (Experienced) R2 .50 1.25
27 Master's Tactics R3 .40 1.00
28 Mizu-Do C .10 .20
29 Mukami (Experienced) U5 .20 .50
30 Naga Apprentice U4 .20 .50
31 Naga Storm Mirumoto Mountain U4 .20 .50
32 Naka Kuro (Experienced) R2 .40 1.00
33 Open Fields C .10 .20
34 Otaku Tetsuko C .10 .20
35 Otomu Banu U5 .20 .50
36 Political Marriage U4 .20 .50
37 Ralish C .10 .20
38 Rebuilding the Empire U4 .20 .50
39 Scouting Team C .10 .20
40 Selection of the Chancellor U5 .20 .50
41 Shahadet (Experienced 2 Naga Warlord) F .50 1.25
42 Shinjo Yokatsu (Experienced) R2 .50 1.25
43 Shiryo no Hoturi R2 1.25 3.00
44 Shiryo no Tsuko R2 .75 2.00
45 Show Me Your Stance U5 .20 .50
46 Takuan (Experienced) R2 .75 2.00
47 The Hidden Emperor R2 .60 1.50
48 The Hiruma Dojo C .10 .20
49 The Jade Throne R .60 1.50
50 The Mountains Below Kyuden Hitomi C .10 .20
51 The People's Hero C .10 .20
52 The Scorpion Children C .10 .20
53 Tidal Land Bridge R2 1.25 3.00

1998 Legend of the Five Rings The Hidden Emperor Episode 2

COMPLETE SET (53) 8.00 20.00
RELEASED IN JULY 1998
1 Ancestral Duty R2 .40 1.00
2 Betrayal U5 .20 .50
3 Chitatchikkan U4 .20 .50
4 Daidoji Tsumerai C .10 .20
5 Deadly Message U4 .20 .50
6 Double Agent R3 .40 1.00
7 Doubt R2 .40 1.00
8 Drawing Fire C .10 .20
9 Flooded Pass C .10 .20
10 Ginawa (Experienced 2) R3 1.00 2.50
11 Hitomi (Experienced 3 Mirumoto Hitomi) F 1.25 3.00
12 Hitomi Akuai C .10 .20
13 Hitomi Tashima (Experienced Shinjo Tashima) U5 .20 .50
14 Hitsu-do C .10 .20
15 Imperial Ambassadorship R2 .50 1.25
16 Iuchi Shahai C .10 .20
17 Kirazo C .10 .20
18 Ki-Rin's Shrine R2 .50 1.25
19 Kisada's Funeral U5 .20 .50
20 Kitsune Diro C .10 .20
21 Kyuden Hitomi F .50 1.25
22 Kyuden Hitomi R1 .50 1.25
23 Meishodo Amulet C .10 .20
24 Mystic Ground C .10 .20
25 Ninja Mystic (Experienced Hoseki) R2 .40 1.00
26 Norikazu's Ravings U5 .20 .50
27 Palisades C .10 .20
28 Purging the House R2 .40 1.00
29 Rise Again! U4 .20 .50
30 Root the Mountain C .10 .20
31 Ryoko Owari R2 .60 1.50
32 Shinjo's Breath U4 .20 .50
33 Shinsei's Fan C .10 .20
34 Shireikan U4 .20 .50
35 Shiryo no Tadaka R2 .75 2.00
36 Shosuro Nishiko U5 .20 .50
37 Slap the Wave R2 .50 1.25
38 Sting of the Wasp C .10 .20
39 Suspicions U4 .20 .50
40 Tattered Ear Tribe C .10 .20
41 Tattooed Men R2 .60 1.50
42 Tattooing Chamber R2 .60 1.50
43 Tchickchuk C .10 .20
44 The Bayushi Provinces C .10 .20
45 The Daini (Experienced 2 Mirumoto Daini) R2 1.25 3.00
46 The Dragon's Heart R3 .50 1.25
47 The Search Begins U5 .20 .50
48 The Shinjo Stockades C .10 .20
49 The Song of Blood C .10 .20
50 Token of Jade C .10 .20
51 Veil of Shadows U4 .20 .50
52 Writ of the Magistrate U4 .20 .50
53 Yoritomo Hogosha U4 .20 .50

1998 Legend of the Five Rings The Hidden Emperor Episode 3

COMPLETE SET (55) 12.00 30.00
RELEASED IN AUGUST 1998
1 Abandoning the Fortunes U5 .20 .50
2 Aramoro (Experienced Bayushi Aramoro) U4 .20 .50
3 Ascension of the Mantis R1 .60 1.50
4 Banish All Shadows R3 2.50 6.00
5 Empty Words U4 .20 .50
6 Enlightened Tutor U5 .20 .50
7 Face of Ninube C .10 .20
8 Fields of the Morning Sun C .10 .20
9 Finding the Balance R2 .40 1.00
10 Fortified Infantry C .10 .20
11 Ginawa (Experienced) R1 1.25 3.00
12 Grasp the Earth Dragon R2 .60 1.50
13 Hitomi Kazaq C .10 .20
14 Hitomi Kokujin (Experienced) R2 2.50 6.00
15 Hold This Ground C .10 .20
16 Hoshi Eisai C .10 .20
17 Hoshi Maseru C .10 .20
18 Ikoma Ryozo (Experienced) R3 .40 1.00
19 Kamoko's Charge U4 .20 .50
20 Kobune Crew U4 .20 .50
21 Kuni Utagu C .10 .20
22 Kuni Yori (Experienced 2) R2 .50 1.25
23 Let Your Spirit Guide You R3 2.00 5.00
24 Mercy Shrouds the Earth C .10 .20
25 Monastery R2 .50 1.25
26 Moto Soro U4 .20 .50
27 Move to the Bushes R2 .40 1.00
28 Mushin C .10 .20
29 Not While I Breathe U4 .20 .50
30 Otaku Meadows C .10 .20
31 Restoring the Doji Treasury U4 .20 .50
32 Retired Wasp General C .10 .20
33 River Bridge of Kaiu C .10 .20
34 Ryoku U4 .20 .50
35 Sacrifices For Our Future U5 .20 .50
36 Seppun Kossori C .10 .20
37 Shiryo no Kisada R2 .50 1.25
38 Stand or Run U4 .20 .50
39 Suzume Yugoki U5 .20 .50
40 Takao's Jingasa C .10 .20
41 The Dark Sanctuary R2 .60 1.50
42 The Efforts of the Clan R2 .40 1.00
43 The Grey Crane (Experienced 2 Kakita Toshimoko) R2 2.00 5.00
44 The Hiruma Dojo R1 .40 1.00
45 The House of Tao F .75 2.00
46 The House of Tao R1 .75 2.00
47 The New Way C .10 .20
48 The Touch of the Lands C .10 .20
49 Togashi Hoshi (Experienced) F 1.25 3.00
50 Torii Shrine U5 .20 .50
51 Trusted Counsel U4 .20 .50
52 Tsuchi-Do C .10 .20
53 Tsuruchi's Arrow R2 .50 1.25
54 Umi Amaterasu C .10 .20
55 Where Shinsei Stood C .10 .20

1998 Legend of the Five Rings The Hidden Emperor Episode 4

COMPLETE SET (52) 8.00 20.00
RELEASED IN SEPTEMBER 1998
1 A Dark Foretelling R .40 1.00
2 Akodo Hall of Ancestors R .40 1.00
3 Arrow from the Ranks C .10 .20
4 Asako Hosigeru C .10 .20
5 Bayushi Technique U .20 .50
6 Desperate Wager R 1.50 4.00
7 Die Tsuchi C .10 .20
8 Doji Shizue (Experienced) R 1.25 3.00
9 Doom of the Brotherhood U .20 .50
10 Festival of the River of Stars R .40 1.00
11 Flattery C .10 .20
12 Funeral Pyre C .10 .20
13 Goblin War Truck U .20 .50
14 Goldsmith C .10 .20
15 Hida Yasamura (Experienced 2 Shinjo Yasamura) R 1.25 3.00
16 Hitomi Technique U .20 .50
17 Ide Ashijun C .10 .20
18 Itako U .20 .50
19 Kitsuki Evidence C .10 .20
20 Kitsuki Kaagi U .20 .50
21 Kitsuki Kaagi's Journal U .20 .50
22 Kolat Geisha C .10 .20
23 Lay of the Land R .40 1.00
24 Lessons from Kuro R .50 1.25
25 Malekish C .10 .20
26 Matsu Ketsui R .40 1.00
27 Mujina Tricks C .10 .20
28 Ninja Saboteur R .50 1.25
29 Noble Sacrifice R .50 1.25
30 Oni no Gekido U .20 .50
31 Otaku Kamoko (Experienced 3) F 2.50 6.00
32 Otaku Xieng Chi U .20 .50
33 Philosopher C .10 .20
34 Plains of Foul Tears C .10 .20
35 Refuge of the Three Sisters U .20 .50
36 Ronin Dojo C .10 .20
37 Ryosei (Experienced) U .20 .50
38 Shinjo Groomsman R .60 1.50
39 Shinjo Technique U .20 .50
40 Shinjo Tsuburo (Experienced) R .40 1.00
41 Shiryo no Moto R .40 1.00
42 Takuan Technique U .20 .50
43 The Boundless Depths of Water U .20 .50
44 The Great Feast U .20 .50
45 The Iuchi Plains C .10 .20
46 The Kami Watch Over Me U .20 .50
47 The Naga Akasha R .40 1.00
48 The Utaku Palaces F .75 2.00
49 The Power of Incompleteness C .10 .20
50 The Price of Failure C .10 .20
51 Walk Through the Mountains C .10 .20
52 War Dogs R .50 1.25

1998 Legend of the Five Rings The Hidden Emperor Episode 5

COMPLETE SET (52) 8.00 20.00
RELEASED IN OCTOBER 1998
1 A Stone Circle C6 .10 .20
2 Akodo Dagger R2 .50 1.25
3 Basher's Club U4 .20 .50
4 Battle Hardened R2 .40 1.00
5 Bayushi Aramasu U4 .20 .50
6 Bayushi Yojiro (Experienced) U5 .20 .50
7 Blade of Secrets R3 .50 1.25
8 Corrupted Jade Sliver U4 .20 .50
9 Doom of Toturi C1 .10 .20
10 Drawing Out the Darkness U4 .20 .50
11 Facing Your Devils C5 .10 .20
12 Flaming Ground U4 .20 .50
13 Hida Technique U5 .20 .50
14 Hitomi Kobai R2 .75 2.00
15 Holy Home Village C6 .10 .20
16 Imperial Edicts C5 .10 .20
17 Island Barricades U5 .20 .50
18 Island of Silk R2 .40 1.00
19 Iuchi Karasu (Experienced 2) U4 .20 .50
20 Jama Suru C6 .10 .20
21 Kouta C9 .10 .20
22 Kuni Mokuna's Guide R2 .50 1.25
23 Kyuden Yoritomo F .75 2.00
24 Large Farm C5 .10 .20
25 March of the Alliance R2 .50 1.25
26 Matsu Hiroru (Experienced 2) R2 1.25 3.00
27 Matsu Turi (Experienced) U4 .20 .50
28 Naga Pearl Guardian C6 .10 .20
29 One Life, One Destiny R2 .60 1.50
30 Out of the Shadows C6 .10 .20
31 Ratling Hordes C6 .10 .20
32 Ratling Villages C6 .10 .20
33 Salt the Earth C6 .10 .20
34 Sanzo (Experienced) R1 .40 1.00
35 Shiba Technique U4 .20 .50
36 Shiryo no Nodotai R2 .50 1.25
37 Shiryo no Osano-Wo R2 .40 1.00
38 Shrine of Osano-Wo R2 .50 1.25
39 Silk Works C5 .10 .20
40 Takao (Experienced) U4 .20 .50
41 Take the Initiative C5 .10 .20
42 The Great Silence U4 .20 .50
43 The Otaku Stables Burn R2 .50 1.25
44 The Way of Death U4 .20 .50
45 Unrequited Love C6 .10 .20
46 Wasp Archers R2 .60 1.50
47 When Dark Winds Howl U4 .20 .50
48 Yoritomo (Experienced 2) F 1.50 4.00
49 Yoritomo Nodoteki C6 .10 .20
50 Yoritomo Technique U4 .20 .50
51 Yoritomo Yukue R3 .75 2.00
52 Zokujin C5 .10 .20

1998 Legend of the Five Rings The Hidden Emperor Episode 6

COMPLETE SET (52) 8.00 20.00
RELEASED IN NOVEMBER 1998
1 700 Soldier Plain U5 .20 .50
2 A Pure Stroke R2 .40 1.00
3 Battle Maidens C5 .10 .20
4 Big Stink U4 .20 .50
5 Blackened Claws C6 .10 .20
6 Chi Protection C6 .10 .20
7 Cleansing Bell C6 .10 .20
8 Coordinated Strike R2 .60 1.50
9 Cultists C5 .10 .20
10 Daidoji Karasu R2 .50 1.25
11 Daisoji Osen C6 .10 .20
12 Death of the Ki-Rin R2 2.00 5.00
13 Dharma Technique U4 .20 .50
14 Doji Kuwannon (Experienced 2) F 1.50 4.00
15 Doom of the Alliance U4 .20 .50
16 Eshru (Experienced) R2 1.25 3.00
17 Haunted U4 .20 .50
18 Hida O-Ushi (Experienced 2) R2 .60 1.50
19 Hitomi Reju (Experienced Doji Reju) U4 .20 .50
20 Hoshi Wayan C6 .10 .20
21 Ikoma Technique U4 .20 .50
22 Isawa Norikazu (Experienced) R2 .50 1.25
23 Kachiko's Fan U5 .20 .50
24 Kakita Ariteko C5 .10 .20
25 Kakita Technique U4 .20 .50
26 Kansen U4 .20 .50
27 Legacy of the Dark One U4 .20 .50
28 Makashi U4 .20 .50
29 Makoto R2 .50 1.25
30 Oni no Akuma (Experienced) U4 .20 .50
31 Otaku Steed C6 .10 .20
32 Prophet's Tower U4 .20 .50
33 Ratling Nest C5 .10 .20
34 Ratling Spy C6 .10 .20
35 Shiryo no Tetsuya R2 .40 1.00
36 Shosuro Chian C6 .10 .20
37 Silk Farm C5 .10 .20
38 Speak with the Voices of the Dead R2 .40 1.00
39 Storms of War C5 .10 .20
40 Teach the Mountain R3 .40 1.00
41 The Iron Cranes C5 .10 .20
42 The Iron Fortress of the Daidoji F .75 2.00
43 The Silk Road C6 .10 .20
44 Togashi's Daisho R2 .40 1.00
45 Tohaku C5 .10 .20
46 Trapping Tactics C6 .10 .20
47 Tutor R2 .40 1.00
48 Unrelenting Terror R2 .75 2.00
49 Valley of the Two Generals R3 .50 1.25
50 War in the Shadowlands R2 .50 1.25
51 Way of Shadow U4 .20 .50
52 Wisdom Gained U4 .20 .50

1998 Legend of the Five Rings Jade Edition

1 The Ancient Halls of the Lion
2 The Brotherhood of Shinsei
3 The Esteemed House of the Crane
4 The Great Walls of Kaiu
5 The Hidden Temples of the Naga
6 The Mountain Keep of the Dragon
7 The Provincial Estate of the Unicorn
8 The Ruins of Isawa Castle
9 The Shadowlands Horde
10 The Shadow Stronghold of the Bayushi
11 The Yoritomo Alliance
12 Toturi's Army
13 Hida O-Ushi (Experienced) R
14 Hida Tadashiro C
15 Hida Unari U
16 Hida Yakamo (Experienced 2) R
17 Hiruma Yoshi C
18 Kaiu Suman U
19 Yasuki Nokatsu C
20 Yasuki Taka (Experienced) U
21 Asahina Tamako U
22 Daidoji Sembi C
23 Daidoji Uji (Experienced) R
24 Doji Chomei U
25 Doji Kuwanan (Experienced) R
26 Doji Reju C
27 Doji Shizue C
28 Kakita Yoshi R
29 Agasha Gennai C
30 Agasha Tamori C
31 Hitomi (Experienced 2) R
32 Hitomi Kokujin (Unique) R
33 Kitsuki Yasu R
34 Mirumoto Daini (Experienced) R
35 Mirumoto Sukune U
36 Mirumoto Taki C
37 Togashi Mitsu
38 Ikoma Kaoku U
39 Ikoma Ryozo U
40 Ikoma Tsanuri (Experienced) R
41 Kitsu Motso R
42 Kitsu Okura C
43 Matsu Agetoki (Experienced) R
44 Matsu Goemon C
45 Matsu Seijuro U
46 Moshi Wakiza (Experienced) R
47 Mukami C
48 Ryosei C
49 Tsuruchi U
50 Yoritomo (Experienced) R
51 Yoritomo Kamoto R
52 Yoritomo Kanbe U
53 Yoritomo Masasue U
54 Yoritomo Takuni C
55 Yoritomo Tsuyu U
56 Heichi Chokei C
57 Hizuka C
58 Komaro C
59 Suana U
60 Yodin (Experienced) R
61 Yoshi (Experienced) U
62 Ashamana C
63 Balash C
64 Isha (Experienced) U
65 Qamar (Experienced) R
66 Radakast (Experienced) U
67 Shahadet (Experienced) R
68 Shalasha C
69 Shashakar (Experienced) R
70 Isawa Norikazu (Unique) R
71 Isawa Osugi (Unique) U
72 Shiba Tsukune (Experienced) R
73 Bayushi Aramoro U
74 Bayushi Yokuan R
75 Ginawa (Experienced) R
76 Matsu Hiroru (Experienced) R
77 Mitsu (Experienced) R
78 Naka Kuro (Unique) R
79 Takuan R
80 Toku (Experienced) U
81 Iuchi Karasu (Experienced) U
82 Iuchi Katta U
83 Otaku Baiken C
84 Otaku Kamoko (Experienced 2) R
85 Shinjo Morito (Experienced) R
86 Shinjo Sanetama C
87 Shinjo Shirasu C
88 Shinjo Yokatsu (Unique) R
89 Hoseki U
90 Kage (Experienced 2) R
91 Kappuksu U
92 Kuni Yori R
93 Kyoso no Oni U
94 Ninja Shapeshifter U
95 Ninja Spy C
96 Ogre Bushi U
97 Oni no Akuma (Unique) R
98 Sanzo C
99 Togashi Hoshi (Unique) R
100 Clan Heartland R
101 Crossroads C
102 Farmlands C
103 Flatlands C
104 Fortified Coast U
105 Inaccessible Region U
106 Mountain Pass C
107 Plains Above Evil U
108 River Delta U
109 Swamplands C
110 Barbican U
111 Basecamp C
112 Black Market
113 Blacksmiths C
114 Bridged Pass U
115 Bushi Dojo U
116 Charter of the Crab Clan
117 Charter of the Crane Clan
118 Charter of the Dragon Clan
119 Charter of the Lion Clan
120 Charter of the Mantis Clan
121 Charter of the Phoenix Clan
122 Charter of the Scorpion Clan
123 Charter of Toturi's Army
124 Charter of the Unicorn Clan
125 Copper Mine C
126 Corrupt Geisha House
127 Corrupted Iron Mine
128 Corrupted Silver Mine
129 Diamond Mine U
130 Fantastic Gardens U
131 Forest C
132 Gambling House U
133 Garrison U
134 Geisha House C
135 Gold Mine C
136 Go Master C
137 Hawks and Falcons C
138 Iron Mine C
139 Island Wharf C

140 Jade Works C
141 Marketplace C
142 Master Smith U
143 Oracle of Earth R
144 Oracle of Fire R
145 Oracle of the Void R
146 Oracle of Water R
147 Oracle of Wind R
148 Pearl Bed C
149 Pearl Divers U
150 Pitch and Fire C
151 Port C
152 Prayer Shrines C
153 Retired General U
154 Sanctified Temple C
155 School of Wizardry R
156 Silver Mine
157 Small Farm C
158 Stables C
159 Treaty with the Naga
160 Unscalable Walls C
161 Vows of the Brotherhood
162 Writings of Kuni Yori
163 Alliance U
164 Architects of the Wall R
165 Chrysanthemum Festival R
166 Corruption of the Harmonies U
167 Emperor's Peace U
168 Evil Feeds Upon Itself U
169 Glimpse of the Unicorn U
170 Hurricane U
171 Imperial Gift R
172 Inheritance R
173 Iris Festival R
174 Occult Murders U
175 Peasant Revolt U
176 Proposal of Peace R
177 Rise of the Phoenix R
178 Test of the Emerald Champion R
179 The Tao of the Naga R
180 Unexpected Allies U
181 Armor of Osano-Wo R
182 Bloodsword U
183 Climbing Gear U
184 Fan of Command R
185 Jade Bow C
186 Naginata C
187 Night Medallion R
188 No-Dachi C
189 Shuriken of Serpents U
190 Tetsubo C
191 The Armor of Sun Tao U
192 The Armor of the Golden Samurai R
193 The Star of Laramun R
194 Wakizashi C
195 A Glimpse of the Soul's Shadow U
196 Ancestral Guidance R
197 Catching the Wind's Favor C
198 Double Chi C
199 Fist of the Earth C
200 Freezing the Lifeblood U
201 Fury of the Earth C
202 Gift of the Wind C
203 Kaze-do C
204 Led From the True Path R
205 Master of the Rolling River U
206 One with the Elements U
207 Piercing the Soul U
208 Strength of My Ancestors C
209 The Purity of Shinsei R
210 The Sight of Death U
211 The Soul Goes Forth U
212 The Touch of Amaterasu R
213 The Wrath of Osano-Wo C
214 Touching the Soul U
215 Unattuned R
216 Void Strike U
217 Archers C
218 Ashigaru C
219 Battering Ram Crew R
220 Elite Heavy Infantry R
221 Elite Light Infantry U
222 Elite Medium Infantry U
223 Heavy Cavalry U
224 Heavy Infantry U
225 Imperial Honor Guard R
226 Imperial Palace Guard R
227 Kenku Teacher U
228 Light Cavalry C
229 Light Infantry C
230 Mantis Budoka R
231 Mantis Bushi R
232 Medium Cavalry C
233 Medium Infantry C
234 Mounts U
235 Naga Bowmen U
236 Naga Bushi C
237 Naga Guard C
238 Naga Spearmen U
239 Ninja Genin R
240 Ogre Warriors R
241 Ratling Bushi U
242 Ratling Conscripts C
243 Ratling Pack C
244 Samurai Cavalry R
245 Samurai Warriors R
246 Scout C
247 Shield Wall U
248 Skeletal Troops C
249 Spearmen C
250 Spirit Guide R
251 Swamp Spirits C
252 Zombie Troops U
253 A Moment of Truth R
254 Accessible Terrain C
255 Along the Coast at Midnight R
256 Ambush R
257 Arrows from the Woods C
258 Avoid Fate R
259 Block Supply Lines C
260 Bountiful Harvest R
261 Breach of Etiquette U
262 Brilliant Victory C
263 Careful Planning C
264 Charge C
265 Confusion at Court C
266 Contentious Terrain C
267 Counterattack U
268 Crushing Attack R
269 Daisho Technique U
270 Deadly Ground C
271 Defenders of the Realm U
272 Defend Your Honor U
273 Dispersive Terrain C
274 Diversionary Tactics C
275 Enlightenment U
276 Enough Talk! R
277 Entrapping Terrain C
278 Explosives R
279 Focus R
280 Frenzy U
281 Geisha Assassin R
282 He's Mine! C
283 Higher Ground U
284 Iaijutsu Challenge C
285 Iaijutsu Duel C
286 Investigation R
287 Kharmic Strike U
288 Kolat Assassin U
289 Kolat Interference R
290 Kolat Master R
291 Lies, Lies, Lies... R
292 Marries A Barbarian U
293 Narrow Ground C
294 Ninja Kidnapper R
295 Ninja Thief U
296 Oath of Fealty C
297 Outflank C
298 Poisoned Weapon R
299 Rallying Cry U
300 Refugees C
301 Remorseful Seppuku U
302 Resist Magic R
303 Retreat R
304 Ring of Air U
305 Ring of Earth U
306 Ring of Fire U
307 Ring of the Void U
308 Ring of Water U
309 Rise, Brother R
310 Shame U
311 Sneak Attack R
312 Street to Street U
313 Strength of Purity U
314 Strike With No-Thought R
315 Superior Tactics C
316 Test of Honor R
317 Test of Might C
318 The Code of Bushido R
319 The Final Breath U
320 The Turtle's Shell R
321 Traversable Terrain C
322 Treacherous Terrain C
323 Way of Deception R
324 Wounded in Battle U
325 Biting Steel U
326 Secrets on the Wind R
327 Stifling Wind U
328 The Fires That Cleanse R
329 Touch of Death R
330 Walking the Way R

1998 Legend of the Five Rings Scorpion Clan Coup Scroll 2

COMPLETE SET (50) 6.00 12.00
RELEASED IN JANUARY 1998
1 A Vision of Truth U .20 .50
2 Agasha Nabe C .10 .20
3 Arrival of the Unicorns C .10 .20
4 Ashina Uojin C .10 .20
5 Bayushi Dairu U .20 .50
6 Bayushi House Guard U .20 .50
7 Bayushi Kyono C .10 .20
8 Bayushi Yojiro C .10 .20
9 Defenders of the Realm C .10 .20
10 Disloyalty C .10 .20
11 Doji Satsume U .20 .50
12 Fury of the Earth C .10 .20
13 Gift of Fealty U .20 .50
14 Hasagawa C .10 .20
15 Hida Matyu C .10 .20
16 Hojatsu's Blade C .10 .20
17 Iaijutsu Art C .10 .20
18 Isawa Sze U .20 .50
19 Kappa C .10 .20
20 Kuroshin's Prayer U .20 .50
21 Led from the True Path U .20 .50
22 Lieutenant Daini U .20 .50
23 Lieutenant Uji U .20 .50
24 Matsu Hokitare C .10 .20
25 Matsu Tsuko (Inexperienced) U .20 .50
26 Monk Advisors C .10 .20
27 My Enemy's Weakness U .20 .50
28 Ninja Shapeshifter (Inexperienced) U .20 .50
29 North Wall of Otosan Uchi U .20 .50
30 One Man's Honor U .20 .50
31 Piercing the Soul C .10 .20
32 Plain of Fast Troubles C .10 .20
33 Ranbe U .20 .50
34 Rear Guard C .10 .20
35 Shazaar C .10 .20
36 Shinjo Goshi C .10 .20
37 Shoju's Armor U .20 .50
38 Soshi's Curse C .10 .20
39 The Dragon Pearl U .20 .50
40 The Face of My Enemy U .20 .50
41 The Fair Voice of Lies U .20 .50
42 The Kharmic Wheel Spins U .20 .50
43 The Moment Before the Strike C .10 .20
44 The Purity of Kitsu U .20 .50
45 The Ruby of Iuchiban U .20 .50
46 The True Lands U .20 .50
47 Touching the Soul C .10 .20
48 Trading Port C .10 .20
49 West Wall of Otosan Uchi U .20 .50
50 When Men Stand Divided C .10 .20

1998 Legend of the Five Rings Scorpion Clan Coup Scroll 3

COMPLETE SET (52) 6.00 12.00
RELEASED IN FEBRUARY 1998
1 A Final Duel U .20 .50
2 A Greater Destiny U .20 .50
3 Acolyte Kaede U .20 .50
4 Agasha Mumoko C .10 .20
5 Agasha's Mirror C .10 .20
6 Akodo Hari C .10 .20
7 Akodo Ikawa C .10 .20
8 Akodo Matoko U .20 .50
9 Akodo Toturi (Inexperienced) F .60 1.50
10 All Distances Are One C .10 .20
11 Asahina's Breath U .20 .50
12 Bayushi's Labyrinth U .20 .50
13 Fires of Retribution C .10 .20
14 Give Me Your Hand U .20 .50
15 Heartbeat Drummers C .10 .20
16 Hida Kisada (Inexperienced) U .20 .50
17 Hiruma Osuno C .10 .20
18 Isawa Ujina U .20 .50
19 Isawa's Helm U .20 .50
20 Jitte C .10 .20
21 Kaiu Castle U .20 .50
22 Kyudo C .10 .20
23 Lieutenant Sukune U .20 .50
24 Lieutenant Tsanuri U .20 .50
25 Mirror Image C .10 .20
26 Mirumoto Satsu U .20 .50
27 Obi of Protection U .20 .50
28 Plains of the Emerald Champion C .10 .20
29 Quarry C .10 .20
30 Shiba Kyo C .10 .20
31 Street to Street C .10 .20
32 Streets of Otosan Uchi C .10 .20
33 Subversion U .20 .50
34 Sunabe C .10 .20
35 Suru's Mempo U .20 .50
36 Swamp Spirits C .10 .20
37 Tell the Tale C .10 .20
38 The Ancient Halls of the Lion F .40 1.00
39 The Courage of Osano-Wo U .20 .50
40 The Crab Arrive C .10 .20
41 The Fog of War C .10 .20
42 The Fortune's Wisdom C .10 .20
43 The Hub Villages C .10 .20
44 The Master Painter U .20 .50
45 The People's Champion U .20 .50
46 The Shiba Fortification U .20 .50
47 The Soul of Akodo U .20 .50
48 The Soul of Shiba U .20 .50
49 The Temples of Shinsei U .20 .50
50 The World Stood Still U .20 .50
51 Whispers of the Land C .10 .20
52 Yazaki C .10 .20

1999 Legend of the Five Rings Ambition's Debt

COMPLETE SET (213) 50.00 100.00
RELEASED IN NOVEMBER 1999
1 A Chance Meeting U .20 .50
2 Akodo Fields U .20 .50
3 Armorer C .10 .20
4 As the Shadow Falls Foil .20 .50
5 Asahina Dorai (Experienced) R .50 1.25
6 Asahina Tsukiyoka C .10 .20
7 Ashigaru Levies C .10 .20
8 Ashlim Foil .20 .50
9 Ashlim (Experienced) R .50 1.25
10 Assault on Otosan Uchi U .20 .50
11 At'tok'tuk Sensei R 1.50 4.00
12 Baby Ki-Rin R .50 1.25
13 Bakeneko C .10 .20
14 Barracks C .10 .20
15 Bayushi Aramasu (Experienced) R .50 1.25
16 Bayushi Urei C .10 .20
17 Be the Mountain C .10 .20
18 Beiden Pass Foil .20 .50
19 Bitter Destiny R .50 1.25
20 Bloodspeaker's Deal U .20 .50
21 Bokken C .10 .20
22 Botsumoku C .10 .20
23 Bridged Pass Foil .10 .20
24 Calm Winds U .20 .50
25 Carpenter Pass U .20 .50
26 Celestial Gift U .20 .50
27 Chi Strike Foil .40 1.00
28 Concede Defeat C .10 .20
29 Corrupt Gold Mines Foil .60 1.50
30 Costly Alliance C .10 .20
31 Critical Duel C .10 .20
32 Dangerous Terrain C .10 .20
33 Dark Energy R .50 1.25
34 Darkness Within C .10 .20
35 Dead Eyes U .20 .50
36 Death of Onnotangu R .60 1.50
37 Declaration of War U .20 .50
38 Defensible Position C .10 .20
39 Den of Spies U .20 .50
40 Denying the Emperor R .50 1.25
41 Dirty Politics R 1.50 4.00
42 Disfavored Foil .40 1.00
43 Disharmony Foil .10 .20
44 Dragon Sword is Broken Foil .20 .50
45 Dragon's Strength R .40 1.00
46 Dying Effort R .50 1.25
47 Entrench U .20 .50
48 Exile's Road R .50 1.25
49 Family Shrine C .10 .20
50 Fatal Mistake Foil .50 1.25
51 Finding the Harmony U .20 .50
52 Footsteps of Madness R .50 1.25
53 Forethought R .50 1.25
54 Forgotten Lands R .60 1.50
55 Fortune's Turn C .10 .20
56 Forward, March! C .10 .20
57 Goblin Berserkers Foil .10 .20
58 Goblin Wizard Foil .10 .20
59 Goju Utsuei C .10 .20
60 Greensnake C .10 .20
61 Guardian of the Rift R .40 1.00
62 Gyosho U .20 .50
63 Hale's Heart R .50 1.25
64 Hida Amoro (Experienced 2) R .75 2.00
65 Hida Sukune Foil .10 .20
66 Hida Yakamo (Experienced 3) F .60 1.50
67 Hirariko (Experienced) R .50 1.25
68 Hiruma Sensei R .40 1.00
69 Honor, Bah! R .40 1.00
70 Honor's Cost U .20 .50
71 Hoshi Kumonosu U .20 .50
72 Ichiro Kihongo U .20 .50
73 Ikoma Ryozo (Experienced 2) F .50 1.25
74 Ikoma Sensei U .20 .50
75 Ikoma Tsanuri (Experienced 2) R 1.50 4.00
76 Ikoma Yosei U .20 .50
77 Ikudaiu (Experienced) R 1.25 3.00
78 Imperial Highway C .10 .20
79 Imperial Summons C .10 .20
80 In Search of the Future C .10 .20
81 Infantry Square C .10 .20
82 Inner Fire Foil .20 .50
83 Isawa Kaede (Experienced 2) R 1.25 3.00
84 Isawa Mitori U .20 .50
85 Issut C .10 .20
86 Judgement of Toshiken U .20 .50
87 Kage (Experienced 4 Akodo Kage) R .60 1.50
88 Kage Sensei U .20 .50
89 Kakita Aihara U .20 .50
90 Kakita Ichiro (Experienced) Foil 1.25 3.00
91 Kakita Teacher U .20 .50
92 Kitsune Diro (Experienced) R 1.25 3.00
93 Kolat Bookkeeping U .20 .50
94 Kukanchi C .10 .20
95 Kuro Sensei R .75 2.00
96 Kuro's Fire R 3.00 8.00
97 Large Shrine C .10 .20
98 Last Stand Plain C .10 .20
99 Lessons from the Past Foil .10 .20
100 Lookout Mountain C .10 .20
101 Mantis Marine Troops R .75 2.00
102 Matsu Daoquan C .10 .20
103 Matsu Mori C .10 .20
104 Moetechi C .10 .20
105 Morikage R .50 1.25
106 Moto Soro (Experienced) R .50 1.25
107 Naga Spies U .20 .50
108 Night of Three Stars C .10 .20
109 Ningyo Foil .20 .50
110 Nio Sensei R 1.25 3.00
111 Norikazu Sensei R .50 1.25
112 Nue C .10 .20
113 Oath of Courage U .20 .50
114 Obake U .20 .50
115 Olyah U .20 .50
116 Ono U .20 .50
117 Orschat C .10 .20
118 Otomo Shishi C .10 .20
119 Overconfidence C .10 .20
120 Oyuchi U .20 .50
121 Parade Ground Practice C .10 .20
122 Pikemen Foil .10 .20
123 Plague of Locusts U .20 .50
124 Plague Zombies Foil .10 .20
125 Plains of the Emerald Champion Foil .10 .20
126 Poisoned C .10 .20
127 Poisoned Honor C .10 .20
128 Political Distraction Foil .10 .20
129 Poor Health U .20 .50
130 Ratling Archers U .20 .50
131 Ravine C .10 .20
132 Recovering the True Tao U .20 .50
133 River Around the Hill C .10 .20
134 Roshungi U .20 .50
135 Ruantek C .10 .20
136 Sake Works Foil .20 .50
137 Savaged Fields U .20 .50
138 Scorpion Courtiers R .50 1.25
139 Seppun Mashita C .10 .20
140 Shadow Beast C .10 .20
141 Shakoki Dogu R .60 1.50
142 Shiba Kyukyo C .10 .20
143 Shiba Odoshi U .20 .50
144 Shinjo Shono C .10 .20
145 Shipyard C .10 .20
146 Shiryo no Kaze R .40 1.00
147 Shiryo no Takuan R .75 2.00
148 Shiryo no Yasuki R .40 1.00
149 Shiyokai U .20 .50
150 Shooting Star Strike U .20 .50
151 Shosuro Dojo R .50 1.25
152 Shosuro Yodoka U .20 .50
153 Shugenja Students U .20 .50
154 Sorrow's Path C .10 .20
155 Soshi Taoshi Foil .20 .50
156 Stand Firm Foil .10 .20
157 Storm of Arrows C .10 .20
158 Strong Words U .20 .50
159 Suana (Experienced) R .40 1.00
160 Summoning the Moon R .50 1.25
161 Suspended Terrain Foil .10 .20
162 Swifter Arrow U .20 .50
163 Sympathetic Energies Foil .20 .50
164 Tactical Maneuvers U .20 .50
165 Tangen's Lies R 1.00 2.50
166 Temple Guard U .20 .50
167 The Arrow Knows the Way Foil 2.00 5.00
168 The Damned C .10 .20
169 The Fallen Lion Fortress R .50 1.25
170 The Festering Pit of Fu Leng Foil 1.50 4.00
171 The Fire from Within Foil .40 1.00
172 The Gates to Jigoku R .50 1.25
173 The Ikoma Histories U .20 .50
174 The Kitsu Tombs F 1.00 2.50
175 The Legion of Two Thousand R 1.50 4.00
176 The New Akasha F .75 2.00
177 The Path of Akodo U .20 .50
178 The Prophecies R .50 1.25
179 The Spawning Ground F .60 1.50
180 The Sun in Shadow U .20 .50
181 To Avenge Our Ancestors Foil .40 1.00
182 Togashi Hoshi (Experienced 2) R 1.00 2.50
183 Togashi Jodome Foil .20 .50
184 Togashi Shinseken U .20 .50
185 Tohaku (Experienced) R 1.25 3.00
186 Toichi U .20 .50
187 Tonbo Toryu C .10 .20
188 Toturi's Treatise U .20 .50
189 Touching the Void U .20 .50
190 Trading Grounds Foil .20 .50
191 Troll Raiders U .20 .50
192 Troops from the Woods Foil .10 .20
193 Tsuruchi's Legion R 1.25 3.00
194 Twenty-Seven Days of Darkness U .20 .50
195 Uncertainty C .10 .20
196 Undead Cavalry C .10 .20
197 Unmaker's Shadow R .40 1.00
198 Void's Path R .50 1.25
199 War Weary U .20 .50
200 Way of the Zukojin C .10 .20
201 Woodland Reserves C .10 .20
202 Yabanjin Horsemen C .10 .20
203 Yasuki Nokatsu (Experienced) R/F .40 1.00
204 Yasuki Taka (Experienced 2) R .60 1.50
205 Yokai no Junzo F .50 1.25
206 Yokatsu (Experienced 2 Yokatsu) R .75 2.00
207 Yori Sensei R .40 1.00
208 Yoritomo Chujitsu U .20 .50
209 Yoritomo Furikae C .10 .20
210 Yoritomo Sensei U .20 .50
211 Yoshi (Experienced 2 Togashi Yoshi) R 1.25 3.00
212 Yoshi Sensei U .20 .50
213 Yosuchi C .10 .20

1999 Legend of the Five Rings Honor Bound

COMPLETE SET (206) 50.00 100.00
BOOSTER BOX (48 PACKS) 100.00 200.00
BOOSTER PACK (11 CARDS) 2.50 5.00
RELEASED IN JUNE 1999
1 A New Teacher R .40 1.00
2 A Stout Heart Foil .20 .50
3 Abresax R .75 2.00
4 Akodo's Leadership R .75 2.00
5 Amnesia U .20 .50
6 An Empty Victory R .40 1.00
7 Ancient Sage C .10 .20
8 Another Time Foil .20 .50
9 Asahina Tomo Foil .10 .20
10 Asako Provinces C .10 .20
11 Awakening Shakoki Dogu C .10 .20
12 Bad Kharma Foil .50 1.25
13 Bandit Attack C .10 .20
14 Bandit Raids U .20 .50
15 Barricades C .10 .20
16 Bayushi Dozan Foil .10 .20
17 Bayushi Eiyo C .10 .20
18 Bayushi Goshiu (Experienced 2) R .75 2.00
19 Bayushi Hisa (Experienced 2) R .50 1.25
20 Bayushi Kachiko (Experienced 3) F 2.50 6.00
21 Benefices of the Emperor R .75 2.00
22 Black Pearl R .75 2.00
23 Bleeding the Elements U .20 .50
24 Blessing Upon the Lands C .10 .20
25 Bloodstrike R 2.00 5.00
26 Builders C .10 .20
27 Burn It Down C .10 .20
28 Command Staff U .20 .50
29 Court Jester Foil .20 .50
30 Curse of the Rot Within C .10 .20
31 Daidoji Kedamono C .10 .20
32 Dairya (Experienced 2) R .60 1.50
33 Dark Bargains U .20 .50
34 Darkness Beyond Darkness U .20 .50
35 Dashmar (Experienced 2) R .50 1.25
36 Deep Forest U .20 .50
37 Doji Adoka C .10 .20
38 Dragon's Claw Katana U .20 .50
39 Dragon's Teeth Foil .10 .20
40 Elite Pikemen C .10 .20
41 Energy Terrain C .10 .20
42 Extortion Foil 2.00 5.00
43 Face of the Nameless R 2.00 5.00
44 False Alliance Foil .40 1.00
45 Familiar Surroundings Foil .10 .20
46 Famine U .20 .50
47 Fear's Bane C .10 .20
48 Feydn Rafiq C .10 .20
49 Firestorm Legion R .50 1.25
50 Flameseeker C .10 .20

Card	Low	High
51 Flashing Blades U	.20	.50
52 Force of Honor C	.10	.20
53 Force of Will Foil	.20	.50
54 Forest Fire C	.10	.20
55 Forgotten Lesson R	.40	1.00
56 Fortress of the Dragonfly C	.10	.20
57 Ghedai C	.10	.20
58 Gift of the Maker U	.20	.50
59 Gohei's Daisho R	.60	1.50
60 Goju Stalkers U	.20	.50
61 Hasame (Experienced) R	.50	1.25
62 Hassuk's Golden Bow C	.10	.20
63 Hida O-Ushi (Experienced 3) F	.75	2.00
64 Hida Tsuru Foil	.20	.50
65 High Morale C	.10	.20
66 Hiruma Yugure C	.10	.20
67 Hiruma Zunguri C	.10	.20
68 Hitomi Kagetora U	.20	.50
69 Hitomi's Defeat U	.20	.50
70 Hizuka (Experienced) R	.50	1.25
71 Hojyn U	.20	.50
72 Horsebowmen Foil	.10	.20
73 Hoshi Wayan (Experienced) R	.50	1.25
74 Hoshi's Challenge U	.20	.50
75 Ikoma Ken'o U	.20	.50
76 Isawa Norikazu (Experienced 2) R	.75	2.00
77 Isawa Tanayama (Experienced Necromancer) R	.50	1.25
78 Iuchi Shahai (Experienced) R	1.25	3.00
79 Kabuki Theater Troupe U	.20	.50
80 Kaede Sensei R	3.00	8.00
81 Kaimetsu-Uo's Ono C	.10	.20
82 Kakita Kaiten U	.20	.50
83 Kakita's The Sword R	3.00	8.00
84 Kenshinzen R	1.25	4.00
85 Kisada Sensei U	.20	.50
86 Kitsu Osen (Experienced Daidoji Osen) R	.50	1.25
87 Kolat Apprentice R	.50	1.25
88 Kolat Duplicate R	1.25	3.00
89 Kuni Yasashii C	.10	.20
90 Kuni Yori (Experienced 3) F	.75	2.00
91 Lord Moon's Bones R	2.00	5.00
92 Lord Moon's Smile R	1.00	2.50
93 Low Morale C	.10	.20
94 Mantis Fleet C	.10	.20
95 Master of Bushido U	.20	.50
96 Master Painter Foil	.20	.50
97 Matsu Morishigi C	.10	.20
98 Matsu Toshiro Foil	.40	1.00
99 Mercenaries C	.10	.20
100 Mirumoto Uso C	.10	.20
101 Mirumoto's Niten U	.20	.50
102 Moment of Brilliance U	.20	.50
103 Monopoly U	.20	.50
104 Monsoon Season U	.20	.50
105 Moto Tsume (Experienced 2) R	.75	2.00
106 Moto Yesugai U	.20	.50
107 Mountains of the Phoenix C	.10	.20
108 Ninja Mimic U	.20	.50
109 Ninja Mystic (Experienced 2 Hoseki) R	.50	1.25
110 Nishiko (Experienced Shosuro Nishiko) R	.60	1.50
111 Nunchaku U	.20	.50
112 Oh-chi'chek C	.10	.20
113 Okura is Released U	.20	.50
114 One Life, One Action C	.10	.20
115 Oni no Okura U	.20	.50
116 Oseuth U	.20	.50
117 Otomo Yayu C	.10	.20
118 Palace of the Emerald Champion R	.50	1.25
119 Pincer Attack C	.10	.20
120 Plans Within Plans Foil	1.25	3.00
121 Porthungluin U	.20	.50
122 Pressure C	.10	.20
123 Return of the Kami R	.40	1.00
124 Rik'tik'tichek U	.20	.50
125 Rodrigo C	.10	.20
126 Rugged Ground C	.10	.20
127 Sabotage U	.20	.50
128 Saigorei U	.20	.50
129 Sanctified Ground Foil	.10	.20
130 Seppun Nakao U	.20	.50
131 Sepulcher of Bone F	.60	1.50
132 Setsuban Festival Foil	.40	1.00
133 Shadowlands Sickness Foil	.20	.50
134 Shiba Kyo Foil	.10	.20
135 Shiba Ningen U	.20	.50
136 Shiba Raigen C	.10	.20
137 Shiba Shingo Foil	.20	.50
138 Shinjo's Judgement R	.50	1.25
139 Shoju Sensei R	1.50	4.00
140 Shosuro Taberu (Experienced) R	.75	2.00
141 Shosuro Taushui C	.10	.20
142 Shurin Storms R	.60	1.50
143 Silence U	.20	.50
144 Silent War U	.20	.50
145 Skeletal Archers Foil	.20	.50
146 Slaughter of the Imperial Court R	.40	1.00
147 Soshi Jomyako C	.10	.20
148 Soshi Jujun C	.10	.20
149 Souls of the Betrayed R	.50	1.25
150 Stain Upon the Soul U	.20	.50
151 Stance of the Mountain Foil	.10	.20
152 Stars Scatter U	.20	.50
153 Stress U	.20	.50
154 Sword of the Emerald Champion R	.60	1.50
155 Swordmaster C	.10	.20
156 Temple of Blood C	.10	.20
157 Temple to Shinsei U	.20	.50
158 The Citadel of the Hiruma F	.40	1.00
159 The Emperor's Lands U	.20	.50
160 The Emperor's Left Hand U	.20	.50
161 The Emperor's Right Hand U	.20	.50
162 The Empty Pyre U	.20	.50
163 The Enemy of My Enemy U	.20	.50
164 The Fair Voice of Lies Foil	.20	.50
165 The False Tao R	.40	1.00
166 The Final Breath Foil	.10	.20
167 The First Scroll is Opened Foil	.20	.50
168 The Head of My Enemy R	.40	1.00
169 The Kaiu Forge U	.20	.50
170 The Kaiu Walls Foil	.20	.50
171 The Master of Five R	.60	1.50
172 The Tower of the Yogo F	.60	1.50
173 The Unquiet Grave of Hida Amoro C	.10	.20
174 The Wind's Truth C	.10	.20
175 Thy Master's Will R	.40	1.00
176 Tiger's Teeth U	.20	.50
177 Tomb of Iuchiban Foil	.40	1.00
178 Tomb of Jade Foil	.20	.50
179 Torn From the Past U	.20	.50
180 Toshimoko Sensei R	1.50	4.00
181 Toturi is Drugged Foil	1.50	4.00
182 Toturi Sensei R	.60	1.50
183 Treachery and Deceit R	.75	2.00
184 Trenches C	.10	.20
185 Tribute to Your House R	.75	2.00
186 Tunnel System Foil	.20	.50
187 Uji Sensei U	.20	.50
188 Uragirimono C	.10	.20
189 Victory at Hiruma Castle R	.40	1.00
190 Volcano R	.50	1.25
191 Volturnum R	.50	1.25
192 Way of the Void R	.60	1.50
193 Wetlands Foil	.10	.20
194 Whispers of Twilight C	.10	.20
195 Whistling Arrows U	.20	.50
196 Wide Terrain U	.20	.50
197 Will of the Emperor C	.10	.20
198 Within Your Soul C	.10	.20
199 Yakamo's Funeral R	.60	1.50
200 Yogo Shidachi Foil	.60	1.50
201 Yokatsu Sensei R	.40	1.00
202 Yokuni Sensei U	.20	.50
203 Yoritomo Denkyu C	.10	.20
204 Yoritomo Komori U	.20	.50
205 Yoritomo Masasue (Experienced) R	.50	1.25
206 Yoshun C	.10	.20

1999 Legend of the Five Rings The Hidden Emperor: The Dark Journey Home

Card	Low	High
COMPLETE SET (154)	30.00	80.00
BOOSTER BOX (48 PACKS)	100.00	200.00
BOOSTER PACK (11 CARDS)	2.50	5.00
RELEASED IN FEBRUARY 1999		
1 A Dark Moment C	.10	.20
2 A Glimpse Beyond R	.40	1.00
3 A Kolat Revealed U	.20	.50
4 Agasha Gennai (Experienced) R	.50	1.25
5 Agasha Kusabi U	.20	.50
6 Aka Mizu-umi U	.20	.50
7 Ambition R	2.00	5.00
8 Arrow of the Four Winds R	.40	1.00
9 Arrowroot Tattoo U	.20	.50
10 Asahina Dorai C	.10	.20
11 Ashigaru Archers C	.10	.20
12 Ashigaru Spearman C	.10	.20
13 Assassins C	.10	.20
14 Balash (Experienced) U	.20	.50
15 Battlements C	.10	.20
16 Bayushi Areru C	.10	.20
17 Bells of the Dead C	.10	.20
18 Black Finger River C	.10	.20
19 Blessings of Isawa U	.20	.50
20 Blood Arrows of Yajinden C	.10	.20
21 Bonsai Garden C	.10	.20
22 Centipede Tattoo U	.20	.50
23 Chochu U	.20	.50
24 Clay Horse C	.10	.20
25 Contemplation C	.10	.20
26 Contested Holding R	1.25	3.00
27 Crane Tattoo U	.20	.50
28 Creating the Monkey Clan U	.20	.50
29 Crystal Nagamaki U	.20	.50
30 Daidoji Rekai (Experienced) R	.50	1.25
31 Dangai C	.10	.20
32 Deeds, Not Words U	.20	.50
33 Disgraced U	.20	.50
34 Disobedience R	.40	1.00
35 Dragon Tattoo U	.20	.50
36 Dragonfly Tattoo U	.20	.50
37 Dragon's Tail Star U	.20	.50
38 Emergence of the Masters C	.10	.20
39 Eternal Halls of the Shiba F	.40	1.00
40 Falling Star Strike C	.10	.20
41 Final Haiku R	.50	1.25
42 Firebird Falls R	.50	1.25
43 Full Moon Tattoo U	.20	.50
44 Glimpse of Kage U	.20	.50
45 Goju Adorai F	1.25	3.00
46 Golden Sun Plain R	2.00	5.00
47 Heavy Ground C	.10	.20
48 Held Terrain R	.50	1.25
49 Heroic Opportunities R	.50	1.25
50 Hida Rohiteki C	.10	.20
51 Hidden Blade R	.60	1.50
52 Hiruma Osuno (Experienced) R	1.50	4.00
53 Hitomi Dajan C	.10	.20
54 Hitomi Iyojin U	.20	.50
55 Hitomi Juppun U	.20	.50
56 Hitomi Nakuso U	.20	.50
57 Hoshi Maseru (Experienced) U	.20	.50
58 Hunted U	.20	.50
59 Ikoma Gunjin U	.20	.50
60 Isawa Hochiu U	.20	.50
61 Isawa Kaede (Experienced) R	1.50	4.00
62 Isawa Taeruko C	.10	.20
63 Kage (Experienced 3 Akodo Kage) R	.50	1.25
64 Kharma U	.20	.50
65 Kitsu Sanako U	.20	.50
66 Kitsuki Iyekao C	.10	.20
67 Kitsuki's Coin R	.40	1.00
68 Kolat Agent C	.10	.20
69 Kolat Recruiter R	1.50	4.00
70 Let Him Escape R	.60	1.50
71 Lion Tattoo U	.20	.50
72 Lion's Pride R	1.25	3.00
73 Lord Moon's Blood R	.75	2.00
74 Loss of Face C	.10	.20
75 Magic Mud U	.20	.50
76 Maho-Tsukai R	.50	1.25
77 Mamoru U	.20	.50
78 Mantis House Guard U	.20	.50
79 Mantle of the Jade Champion R	.50	1.25
80 Master of Destiny R	.50	1.25
81 Matsu Toki U	.20	.50
82 Moshi Hito C	.10	.20
83 Moto Amadare C	.10	.20
84 Moto Fanatics U	.20	.50
85 Mountain Tattoo U	.20	.50
86 Nightmares of Iuchiban R	.50	1.25
87 Ninja Infiltrator (Experienced Sanado) R	.60	1.50
88 Ninja Questioner U	.20	.50
89 Ninja Shadow-Walker C	.10	.20
90 Ninja Tricks U	.20	.50
91 Ninube Ogoku C	.10	.20
92 Osari Plains C	.10	.20
93 Phoenix Tattoo U	.20	.50
94 Pillaging C	.10	.20
95 Plain of Desperate Evil U	.20	.50
96 Poison Dartgun C	.10	.20
97 Pride C	.10	.20
98 Proud Words C	.10	.20
99 Purity of Spirit C	.10	.20
100 Ratling Scout C2	.10	.20
101 Rebuilding the Temples R	.40	1.00
102 Retired Advisor R	.50	1.25
103 Rise from the Ashes U	.20	.50
104 River of the Dark Moon R	.40	1.00
105 River of the Last Stand R	.40	1.00
106 Ropp'tch'tch R	.50	1.25
107 Seppun Toshiken R	.50	1.25
108 Shadow Brand C	.10	.20
109 Shadowlands Contagion R	1.25	3.00
110 Shadowlands Marsh U	.20	.50
111 Shiba Gensui C	.10	.20
112 Shiba Tetsu (Experienced) U	.20	.50
113 Shiba Tsukune (Experienced 2) F	.50	1.25
114 Shinko Kamiko (Experienced Pennagolan) R	.50	1.25
115 Shiryo no Goju R	.40	1.00
116 Shiryo no Kuni R	.40	1.00
117 Shiryo no Yurei R	.50	1.25
118 Shosuro (Experienced Ninja Shapeshifter) R	1.25	3.00
119 Shotai R	.60	1.50
120 Siege C	.10	.20
121 Slidge C	.10	.20
122 Smoke and Mirrors U	.20	.50
123 Stagnation C	.10	.20
124 Stand Together R	.50	1.25
125 Steep Terrain C	.10	.20
126 Strike of Silent Waters U	.20	.50
127 Tattooed U	.20	.50
128 Tausha C	.10	.20
129 Test of the Jade Champion R	.40	1.00
130 The Agasha Join the Phoenix R	.50	1.25
131 The Agasha Libraries C	.10	.20
132 The Age of Man U	.20	.50
133 The Daimyo's Command R	.40	1.00
134 The Dark Path of Shadow F	1.25	3.00
135 The Edge of the Shinomen Forest C	.10	.20
136 The Palace of Otosan-Uchi F	1.25	3.00
137 The Path Not Taken R	1.50	4.00
138 The Wave Men R	.50	1.25
139 Threat C	.10	.20
140 Tiger Tattoo U	.20	.50
141 Toku (Experienced 2) R2	.75	2.00
142 Toritaka Genzo (Experienced Genzo) R	.40	1.00
143 Toturi the First (Experienced 3) F	1.50	4.00
144 Toturi's Return U	.20	.50
145 Touch the Lands C	.10	.20
146 Treacherous Pass C	.10	.20
147 Tsuruchi (Experienced) R	.50	1.25
148 Twilight Mountains R	.60	1.50
149 Twisting Ravine C	.10	.20
150 Tzurui U	.20	.50
151 Virtuous Heart C	.10	.20
152 Warstained Fields C	.10	.20
153 Winds and Fortunes U	.20	.50
154 Yotsu Seou C	.10	.20

1999 Legend of the Five Rings Pearl Edition

Card
1 A Glimpse of the Soul's Shadow U
2 A Moment of Truth R
3 Accessible Terrain C
4 Agasha Gennai C
5 Agasha Tamori C
6 Alliance U
7 Along the Coast at Midnight R
8 Ambush R
9 Ancestral Guidance R
10 Archers C
11 Architects of the Wall R
12 Armor of Osano-Wo R
13 Arrows from the Woods C
14 Asahina Tamako U
15 Ashamana C
16 Ashigaru C
17 Avoid Fate R
18 Balash C
19 Barbican U
20 Basecamp C
21 Battering Ram Crew R
22 Bayushi Aramoro U
23 Bayushi Yokuan R
24 Biting Steel U
25 Black Market
26 Blacksmiths U
27 Block Supply Lines C
28 Bloodsword U
29 Bo Stick
30 Bountiful Harvest R
31 Breach of Etiquette U
32 Bridged Pass U
33 Brilliant Victory C
34 Bushi Dojo U
35 Careful Planning C
36 Catching the Wind's Favor C
37 Charge! C
38 Chrysanthemum Festival R
39 Clan Heartland R
40 Climbing Gear U
41 Confusion at Court C
42 Contentious Terrain C
43 Coordinated Fire
44 Copper Mine C
45 Cornered
46 Corrupt Geisha House
47 Corrupted Iron Mine
48 Corrupted Silver Mine
49 Corruption of the Harmonies U
50 Counterattack U
51 Crossroads C
52 Crushing Attack R
53 Daidoji Sembi C
54 Daidoji Uji
55 Daidoji Uji (Experienced) R
56 Daisho Technique U
57 Deadly Ground C
58 Defend Your Honor U
59 Defenders of the Realm U
60 Diamond Mine U
61 Dispersive Terrain C
62 Diversionary Tactics C
63 Doji Chomei U
64 Doji Kuwanan
65 Doji Kuwanan (Experienced) R
66 Doji Reju C
67 Doji Shizue C
68 Double Chi C
69 Earthquake
70 Elite Heavy Infantry R
71 Elite Light Infantry U
72 Elite Medium Infantry U
73 Emperor's Peace U
74 Encircled Terrain
75 Enlightenment U
76 "Enough Talk!" R
77 Entrapping Terrain C
78 Evil Feeds Upon Itself U
79 Explosives (Experienced) R
80 Fan of Command R
81 Fantastic Gardens U
82 Farmlands C
83 Fist of the Earth C
84 Flatlands C
85 Focus R
86 Forest C
87 Fortified Coast U
88 Freezing the Lifeblood U
89 Frenzy U
90 Fury of the Earth C
91 Gambling House U
92 Garrison U
93 Geisha Assassin R
94 Geisha House C
95 Gift of the Wind C
96 Ginawa
97 Ginawa (Experienced) R
98 Glimpse of the Unicorn U
99 Go Master C
100 Goblin Sneaks
101 Goblin Wizard
102 Gold Mine C
103 Hawks and Falcons C
104 He's Mine! C
105 Heavy Cavalry U
106 Heavy Infantry U
107 Heichi Chokei C
108 Hida O-Ushi R
109 Hida Tadashiro C
110 Hida Unari U
111 Hida Yakamo (Experienced 2) R
112 Higher Ground U
113 Hiruma Yoshi C
114 Hitomi (Experienced 2) R
115 Hitomi Kokujin (Unique) R
116 Hizuka C
117 Hoseki U
118 Hurricane U
119 Iaijutsu Challenge C
120 Iaijutsu Duel C
121 Ikoma Kaoku U
122 Ikoma Ryozo U
123 Ikoma Tsanuri (Experienced) R
124 Imperial Gift R
125 Imperial Honor Guard R
126 Imperial Palace Guard R
127 Inaccessible Region U
128 Inheritance R
129 Inner Fire
130 Investigation R
131 Iris Festival R
132 Iron Mine C
133 Isawa Norikazu (Unique) R
134 Isawa Osugi (Unique) U
135 Isha C
136 Isha (Experienced) U
137 Island Wharf C
138 Iuchi Karasu
139 Iuchi Karasu (Experienced) U
140 Iuchi Katta U
141 Jade Bow C
142 Jade Works C
143 Kage (Experienced 2) R
144 Kaiu Suman U
145 Kakita Yoshi R
146 Kappuksu U
147 Kaze-do C
148 Kenku Teacher U
149 Kharmic Strike U
150 Kitsu Motso R
151 Kitsu Okura C
152 Kitsuki Yasu R
153 Kolat Assassin U
154 Kolat Interference R
155 Kolat Master R
156 Komaro C
157 Kuni Yori
158 Kuni Yori (Experienced) R
159 Kyoso no Oni U
160 Led From the True Path R
161 Lies, Lies, Lies R
162 Light Cavalry C
163 Light Infantry C
164 Mantis Budoka R
165 Mantis Bushi R
166 Marketplace C
167 Marries A Barbarian U
168 Master of the Rolling River U
169 Master Smith U
170 Matsu Agetoki
171 Matsu Agetoki (Experienced) R
172 Matsu Goemon C
173 Matsu Hiroru (Experienced) R
174 Matsu Seijuro U
175 Matsu Turi
176 Medium Cavalry C
177 Medium Infantry C
178 Mirumoto Daini
179 Mirumoto Daini (Experienced) R
180 Mirumoto Sukune U
181 Mirumoto Taki C
182 Mitsu (Experienced) R
183 Morito
184 Moshi Wakiza
185 Moshi Wakiza (Experienced) R
186 Mountain Pass C
187 Mounts U
188 Mukami C
189 Naga Bowmen U
190 Naga Bushi C
191 Naga Guard C
192 Naga Shugenja
193 Naga Spearmen U
194 Naga Warlord
195 Naginata C
196 Naka Kuro (Unique) R
197 Narrow Ground C
198 Nemesis
199 Night Battle
200 Night Medallion R
201 Ninja Genin R
202 Ninja Kidnapper R
203 Ninja Shapeshifter U
204 Ninja Spy C
205 Ninja Thief U
206 No-Dachi C
207 Oath of Fealty C
208 Occult Murders U
209 Ogre Bushi U
210 Ogre Warriors R
211 One with the Elements U
212 Oni no Akuma (Unique) R
213 Oracle of Earth R
214 Oracle of Fire R
215 Oracle of the Void R
216 Oracle of Water R
217 Oracle of Wind R
218 Otaku Baiken C
219 Otaku Kamoko
220 Otaku Kamoko (Experienced 2) R
221 Outflank C
222 Pearl Bed C
223 Pearl Divers U
224 Peasant Levies
225 Peasant Revolt U
226 Piercing the Soul U
227 Pitch and Fire C
228 Plains Above Evil U
229 Poisoned Weapon R
230 Port C
231 Prayer Shrines C
232 Proposal of Peace R
233 Qamar (Experienced) R
234 Radakast (Experienced) U
235 Rallying Cry U
236 Ratling Bushi U
237 Ratling Conscripts C
238 Ratling Pack C
239 Refugees C
240 Remorseful Seppuku U
241 Resist Magic R
242 Retired General U
243 Retreat R
244 Ring of Air U
245 Ring of Earth U
246 Ring of Fire U
247 Ring of the Void U
248 Ring of Water U
249 Rise of the Phoenix R
250 Rise, Brother R
251 River Delta U
252 Ryokan's Sword
253 Ryosei C
254 Samurai Cavalry R
255 Samurai Warriors R
256 Sanctified Temple C

257 Sanzo C
258 School of Wizardry R
259 Scout C
260 Secrets on the Wind R
261 Shahadet (Experienced) R
262 Shalasha U
263 Shame U
264 Shashakar (Experienced) R
265 Shiba Tsukune C
266 Shiba Tsukune (Experienced) R
267 Shield Wall U
268 Shinjo Morito (Experienced) R
269 Shinjo Sanetama C
270 Shinjo Shirasu C
271 Shinjo Yokatsu (Unique) R
272 Shuriken of Serpents U
273 Silver Mine
274 Skeletal Troops C
275 Small Farm C
276 Sneak Attack R
277 Spearmen C
278 Spirit Guide R
279 Stables C
280 Stand Against the Waves
281 Stand Firm
282 Stifling Wind U
283 Street to Street U
284 Strength of My Ancestors C
285 Strength of Purity U
286 Strike With No-Thought R
287 Suana U
288 Superior Tactics C
289 Swamp Spirits C
290 Swamplands C
291 Takuan R
292 Test of Honor R
293 Test of Might C
294 Test of the Emerald Champion R
295 Tetsubo C
296 Tetsuya's Bo
297 The Ancient Halls of the Lion
298 The Armor of Sun Tao U
299 The Armor of the Golden Samurai U
300 The Brotherhood of Shinsei
301 The Code of Bushido R
302 The Daidoji Yari
303 The Esteemed House of the Crane
304 The Final Breath U
305 The Fires That Cleanse R
306 The Great Walls of Kaiu
307 The Hidden Temples of the Naga
308 The Hiruma Tetsubo
309 The Ikoma Tessen
310 The Isawa Naginata
311 The Isha's Yumi
312 The Kitsune Nagamaki
313 The Lost Ono of Osano-Wo
314 The Mirumoto Wakizashi
315 The Mountain Keep of the Dragon
316 The Otaku Nageyari
317 The Provincial Estate of the Unicorn
318 The Purity of Shinsei R
319 The Ruins of Isawa Castle
320 The Shadow Stronghold of the Bayushi
321 The Shadowlands Horde
322 The Sight of Death U
323 The Soul Goes Forth U
324 The Star of Laramun R
325 The Tao of the Naga R
326 The Touch of Amaterasu R
327 The Turtle's Shell R
328 The Wrath of Osano-Wo C
329 The Yogo Jitte
330 The Yoritomo Alliance
331 There is No Hope
332 Togashi Hoshi (Unique) R
333 Togashi Mitsu
334 Toku
335 Toku (Experienced) U
336 Toturi's Army
337 Toturi's Daisho
338 Touch of Death R
339 Touching the Soul U
340 Traversable Terrain C
341 Treacherous Terrain C
342 Tsuruchi U
343 Oni no Ugulu
344 Unattuned R
345 Unexpected Allies U
346 Unscalable Walls C
347 Void Strike U
348 Wakizashi C
349 Walking the Way R
350 Way of Deception R
351 Wounded in Battle U
352 Yasuki Nokatsu C
353 Yasuki Taka (Experienced) U
354 Yodin (Experienced) R
355 Yoritomo (Experienced) R
356 Yoritomo Kamoto R
357 Yoritomo Kanbe U
358 Yoritomo Masasue U
359 Yoritomo Takuni C
360 Yoritomo Tsuyu U
361 Yoshi (Experienced) U
362 Zombie Troops U

1999 Legend of the Five Rings Siege of Sleeping Mountain

14 Another Time C
DragonD02 Hitomi (Experienced 3)
DragonD04 Gold Mine
DragonD06 Mirumoto Taki
DragonD07 Mirumoto Bujun
DragonD09 Hitomi Akuai
DragonF00 The Mountain Keep of the Dragon
DragonF06 Kolat Assassin
DragonF07 Iaijutsu Duel
DragonF08 No-Dachi
DragonF09 Ninja Thief
DragonF11 Bountiful Harvest
DragonF15 Iaijutsu Challenge
DragonF21 Outflank
NagaD09D1 Damesh
old14 Takao
old19 Qamar (Unique)
old26 Hoshi (Unique)
old54 Charge!
old55 Explosives (Experienced)
ToturiD01 Ginawa
ToturiD03 Toku
ToturiD04 Takuan
ToturiD05 Hasame
ToturiD13 Seppun Hotaitaka
ToturiF00 The Palace of Otosan Uchi
ToturiF04 Heavy Infantry
ToturiF08 The Turtle's Shell
BhoodD3 Jade Works
BhoodF2 Careful Planning
NagaD02 Naga Warlord
NagaD04 Forest
NagaD05 Shagara
NagaD06 Pearl Bed
NagaD08 Balash
NagaD10 Naga Shugenja
NagaF00 The Naga Stronghold
NagaF03 Spearmen
NagaF06 Naga Bowmen
NagaF07 Arrows from the Woods
NagaF18 Naga Spearmen
BhoodD00 The House of Tao
BhoodD02 Shioda
BhoodD04 Prayer Shrines
BhoodD05 Small Farm
BhoodD06 Ikudaiu
BhoodD07 Hawks and Falcons
BhoodD08 Large Farm
BhoodD09 Kirazo
BhoodD12 Hoshi Eisai
BhoodD14 Sanctified Temple
BhoodF00 Ring of the Void
BhoodF01 Falling Star Strike
BhoodF03 Light Infantry
BhoodF04 Strength of My Ancestors
BhoodF05 Mushin
BhoodF06 Naga Bushi
BhoodF09 Ryoku
BhoodF10 Medium Infantry
BhoodF11 Naginata
BhoodF12 Sneak Attack
BhoodF19 Block Supply Lines
DragonD3 Hitomi Kobai
ToturiD2 Basecamp

2000 Legend of the Five Rings Fire and Shadow

COMPLETE SET (220)	40.00	80.00
BOOSTER BOX (48 PACKS)	40.00	80.00
BOOSTER PACK (11 CARDS)	1.25	2.50
RELEASED IN MARCH 2000		
1 Agasha Fujita U	.15	.40
2 Akui Cliffs C	.10	.20
3 Ambush Strategist C	.10	.20
4 Ancestors Possess the Living R	.30	.75
5 Asako Kaushen U	.15	.40
6 Asako Sagoten C	.10	.20
7 Ascendence R	.75	2.00
8 Ashalan Sandsmith C	.10	.20
9 Assuming the Championship R	.30	.75
10 Bayushi Aramasu (Experienced 2) R	.30	.75
11 Bayushi Aramoro (Experienced 2) R	.40	1.00
12 Bayushi Muraisan C	.10	.20
13 Belyezn Rafiq U	.15	.40
14 Bend Like A Reed Foil	.40	1.00
15 Blade of Kaiu U	.15	.40
16 Blood and Darkness R	.30	.75
17 Blood of Midnight Foil	.60	1.50
18 Bloodstained Rage C	.10	.20
19 Bonds of Darkness Foil	.60	1.50
20 Bridge to Jigoku R	.30	.75
21 Brothers of Thunder Foil	.60	1.50
22 Burden of the Word R	.30	.75
23 Burning Your Essence Foil	2.00	5.00
24 Campsite U	.15	.40
25 Capturing the Soul R	1.25	3.00
26 Chasing the Shadow R	.40	1.00
27 Come One At A Time C	.10	.20
28 Command of the Kami U	.15	.40
29 Corrupted Dojo C	.10	.20
30 Corrupted Ground Foil	.60	1.50
31 Crab Cavalry R	.30	.75
32 Crisis in Command C	.10	.20
33 Cross-Clan Wedding R	.30	.75
34 Crow Tattoo U	.15	.40
35 Dakosho C	.10	.20
36 Dangerous Choices R	.30	.75
37 Dark Energies Run Red U	.15	.40
38 Decoy R	.30	.75
39 Defeat the Reserves C	.10	.20
40 Den of Mujina U	.15	.40
41 Disenlightenment Foil	.75	2.00
42 Divided Loyalties R	.30	.75
43 Djahab U	.15	.40
44 Doji Chomei (Experienced) R	.30	.75
45 Doji Jiro C	.10	.20
46 Elemental Attunement R	.30	.75
47 Emerald Magistrates R	.30	.75
48 Emmissary of the Ivory Kingdoms U	.15	.40
49 Eternal Darkness U	.15	.40
50 Far From the Empire R	.30	.75
51 Fate's Merciful Hand U	.15	.40
52 Fearful Presence U	.15	.40
53 Fearsome Strength U	.15	.40
54 Feeding on Flesh R	.30	.75
55 Fields of the Dead C	.10	.20
56 Final Words R	.30	.75
57 Fu Leng's Steeds Foil	.75	2.00
58 Gift of the Emperor R	.40	1.00
59 Goblin War Standard Foil	.60	1.50
60 Grandfather's Jaw C	.10	.20
61 Hanoshi C	.10	.20
62 Hantei Sensei U	.15	.40
63 Harsh Lessons C	.10	.20
64 Heart of the Damned C	.10	.20
65 Heimin Village U	.15	.40
66 Hida Nezu U	.15	.40
67 Hida Rohiteki (Experienced) R	.30	.75
68 Hidden From the Empire C	.10	.20
69 His Tsu C	.10	.20
70 Hitomi Bujun (Experienced Mirumoto Bujun) R	.30	.75
71 Honorable Sacrifice U	.15	.40
72 House of Contracts C	.10	.20
73 Hummingbird Tattoo U	.15	.40
74 Hurricane Initiates C	.10	.20
75 Ide Buodin C	.10	.20
76 Ikoma Gunjin (Experienced) R	.30	.75
77 Imperial Surveyor C	.10	.20
78 Iron Mountain F	.30	.75
79 Isawa Toiko C	.10	.20
80 Jian U	.15	.40
81 Journey to Otosan Uchi C	.10	.20
82 Kachiko Calls to Thunder U	.15	.40
83 Kachiko's Promises R	.30	.75
84 Kaiu Endo C	.10	.20
85 Kaiu Seige Engine C	.10	.20
86 Kakita Ichiro (Experienced) R	.30	.75
87 Kemmei Foil	.60	1.50
88 Kitsu Gongsun U	.15	.40
89 Kitsu Huiyuan R	.30	.75
90 Kitsu R	.30	.75
91 Kitsu Sensei R	.30	.75
92 Kitsuki Mizuochi U	.15	.40
93 Kitsune Shudo C	.10	.20
94 Kitsune Tsuke C	.10	.20
95 Know the Evil U	.15	.40
96 Koichi Foil	.75	2.00
97 Kolat Assistance R	.30	.75
98 Kumo (Experienced) R	.30	.75
99 Kyuden Kitsune F	.30	.75
100 Last Refuge U	.15	.40
101 Last Words C	.10	.20
102 Mack'uk C	.10	.20
103 Maintain Balance C	.10	.20
104 Mantis Isles U	.15	.40
105 Mara (Experienced) R	.40	1.00
106 Masamune Katana C	.10	.20
107 Master of the Tea Ceremony Foil	.60	1.50
108 Matsu Suhada C	.10	.20
109 Mine Cave-in U	.15	.40
110 Mirumoto Songui C	.10	.20
111 Mirumoto Sukune (Experienced) F	.30	.75
112 Mirumoto Watanubo U	.15	.40
113 Mirumoto Yuyake C	.10	.20
114 Mismanaged Troops U	.15	.40
115 Miya Yuritogen U	.15	.40
116 Miya's Sasumata R	.30	.75
117 Mohai U	.15	.40
118 Moto Notu R	.50	1.25
119 Moto Ride to the Shadowlands R	.30	.75
120 Moto Toyotomi U	.15	.40
121 Mountain of the Seven Thunders Foil	1.00	2.50
122 My Life For Yours U	.15	.40
123 Never Yield U	.15	.40
124 New Beginnings U	.15	.40
125 Night Battle Foil	.75	2.00
126 Ninja Shadow-Walker (Experienced) R	.30	.75
127 Ninja-to R	.60	1.50
128 Of One Mind U	.15	.40
129 One Last Battle R	.30	.75
130 Oni no Kamu Foil	2.00	5.00
131 Oni no Megada C	.10	.20
132 Oni no Okura (Experienced) R	.30	.75
133 Oracle of Thunder R	.30	.75
134 Oskuda U	.15	.40
135 Otaku Xieng Chi (Experienced) R	.30	.75
136 Owned U	.15	.40
137 Pearl Magic C	.10	.20
138 Peasant Levies Foil	.60	1.50
139 Pestilance C	.10	.20
140 Pitfall C	.10	.20
141 Primal Rage U	.15	.40
142 Proud Heritage C	.10	.20
143 Provision Storehouse C	.10	.20
144 Purusha C	.10	.20
145 Ranbe Foil	1.50	4.00
146 Ratling Youth U	.15	.40
147 Relief C	.10	.20
148 Remember What You Have Seen C	.10	.20
149 Remember Your Oath R	.30	.75
150 Return of Myth U	.15	.40
151 Return of the True Champion U	.15	.40
152 Rights of the Challenged C	.10	.20
153 Road of Dust U	.15	.40
154 Robes of Shinsei Foil	.75	2.00
155 Run For Your Life C	.10	.20
156 Ryosei (Experienced 2) F	.30	.75
157 Ryoshun's First Gift C	.10	.20
158 Sanctified Blade C	.10	.20
159 Sanjuro C	.10	.20
160 Satsume Sensei U	.15	.40
161 Scrolls of Norikazu R	.40	1.00
162 Secluded Ravine Foil	1.50	4.00
163 Seppun Sensei U	.15	.40
164 Seppun Toshiken (Experienced) R	.40	1.00
165 Shabura Foil	.60	1.50
166 Shadowlands Madmen Foil	1.50	4.00
167 Shagara Foil	1.50	4.00
168 Shahadet's Legion Foil	1.50	4.00
169 Sharpest Blade R	.30	.75
170 Shasyahkar R	.30	.75
171 Shiba Gensui (Experienced) R	.75	2.00
172 Shiba Katsuda Foil	1.50	4.00
173 Shifting Ground U	.15	.40
174 Shi-Khan Wastes U	.15	.40
175 Shinjo Sadato Foil	2.00	5.00
176 Shinobi Corruption U	.15	.40
177 Shioda Foil	.60	1.50
178 Shipping Lanes C	.10	.20
179 Shokansuru U	.15	.40
180 Shosuro Technique R	.30	.75
181 Shrine of the Dragon Champion C	.10	.20
182 Single Combat C	.10	.20
183 Skeletal Elite R	.40	1.00
184 Skirmisher's Pike C	.10	.20
185 Slaughter of the Land U	.15	.40
186 Sleeping Lake R	.30	.75
187 Soul's Sacrifice U	.15	.40
188 Spectral Guide U	.15	.40
189 Spirit of the Bright Eye U	.15	.40
190 Spreading the Shadow U	.15	.40
191 Stepping Between the Cracks R	.40	1.00
192 Stifling Wind Foil	1.50	4.00
193 Sunken City Foil	1.50	4.00
194 Sword of the Sun R	.75	2.00
195 Taka Sensei R	.30	.75
196 Takao (Experienced 2) F	.30	.75
197 Tattoo of the Night Sky U	.15	.40
198 Tax Collector C	.10	.20
199 Temple of Divine Influence R	.40	1.00
200 Temples of the Crow F	.30	.75
201 The Celestial Pattern Foil	1.50	4.00
202 The Dark Moto Sensei R	.40	1.00
203 The Face of Fear Foil	1.50	4.00
204 The Price of War Foil	1.50	4.00
205 The Twelve Ronin Foil	1.50	4.00
206 Third Mask of Iuchiban R	.30	.75
207 Togashi Jodome (Experienced) R	.40	1.00
208 Toritaka Kitao C	.10	.20
209 Trade Route Foil	.75	2.00
210 Tricked C	.10	.20
211 Triumphant Victory R	.30	.75
212 Tsuruchi (Experienced 2) R	.40	1.00
213 Ujina Tomo C	.10	.20
214 Venerable Stature C	.10	.20
215 Warrior Monks Foil	1.50	4.00
216 White Shore Plain U	.15	.40
217 Yabanjin Sorceror C	.10	.20
218 Yoritomo Okan U	.15	.40
219 Yoritomo Refuses the Throne U	.15	.40
220 Yotsu Sabieru U	.15	.40

2000 Legend of the Five Rings Heroes of Rokugan

COMPLETE SET (27)	25.00	60.00
RELEASED IN MAY 2000		
1 Anvil of Despair F	2.00	5.00
2 Atarasi's Armor F	3.00	8.00
3 Celestial Dragon F	4.00	10.00
4 Cherry Blossom Festival F	1.25	3.00
5 Goju Yume F	1.50	4.00
6 Gusai F	1.50	4.00
7 Hida Osano-Wo F	6.00	15.00
8 Isawa Ijime F	1.25	3.00
9 Judgement F	4.00	10.00
10 Kakita Rensei F	4.00	10.00
11 Land of the Dead F	.75	2.00
12 Matsu Hitomi F	1.50	4.00
13 Mirumoto Tokeru F	4.00	10.00
14 Miya Mashigai F	.75	2.00
15 One Virtue and Seventy Faults F	.60	1.50
16 Otaku Shiko F	2.00	5.00
17 Qatol F	3.00	8.00
18 Revealing the Ancient Wisdom F	.75	2.00
19 Rezan F	.75	2.00
20 Seppun Murayasu F	.75	2.00
21 Shinsei's Riddle F	.75	2.00
22 Shosuro Furuyari F	2.50	6.00
23 Someisa F	.75	2.00
24 Spirit Legion F	.60	1.50
25 The First Oni F	4.00	10.00
26 Warrens of the Nezumi F	1.25	3.00
27 Yasuki Kaneko F	3.00	8.00

2000 Legend of the Five Rings Soul of the Empire

COMPLETE SET (205)	80.00	150.00
BOOSTER BOX (48 PACKS)	50.00	100.00
BOOSTER PACK (11 CARDS)	1.50	3.00
RELEASED IN JUNE 2000		
1 Air Dragon (Experienced) R1	2.00	5.00
2 Amoro's Honor U2	.25	.60
3 Armor of the Ebony Samurai U2	.40	1.00
4 Armor of the Monkey Clan U1	.25	.60
5 Armor of the Twilight Mountains C1	.10	.20
6 Armored Steeds C1	.10	.20
7 Ashina Archers R2	.60	1.50
8 Ashida C1	.10	.20
9 Ashigaru C1	.40	1.00
10 Bayushi Aramoro (Experienced 3) R2	1.50	4.00
11 Bayushi Goshiu (Experienced 3) R2	2.00	5.00
12 Bayushi Hisa (Experienced 3) U1	1.25	3.00
13 Bayushi Ikita C2	.10	.20
14 Bayushi Meharu C1	.10	.20
15 Bhakarash C1	.10	.20
16 Bide Your Time C2	.10	.20
17 Blessing of the Celestial Heavens C2	.10	.20
18 Blood Rite R2	1.25	3.00
19 Bloodstained Forest U1	.25	.60
20 Bokatu C1	.10	.20
21 Brothers in Blood R2	1.25	3.00
22 Burning the Ashes C1	1.00	2.50
23 Cavalry C2	.40	1.00
24 Cavalry Screen C2	.10	.20
25 Chains of Jigoku U1	1.25	3.00
26 City of Empty Dreams C2	.10	.20
27 City of Living Flames C2	.10	.20
28 City of Loyalty C2	.10	.20
29 City of Tears C2	.10	.20
30 City of White Clouds C2	.10	.20
31 Cornering Maneuver C2	.10	.20
32 Daidoji Rekai (Experienced 2) R2	1.25	3.00
33 Daidoji Technique U2	.40	1.00
34 Dairya (Experienced 3) R1	1.00	2.50
35 Dark Plains U2	.25	.60
36 Deadly Fright C2	.10	.20
37 Death-Seeker Technique U2	.20	.50
38 Defenders of the Wall R2	.60	1.50
39 Devastation C2	.10	.20
40 Doji Benku C1	.10	.20
41 Doji Kuwannon (Experienced 2) F	1.00	2.50
42 Draft Notice C1	.10	.20
43 Dragon of Fire (Experienced) R1	1.25	3.00
44 Dragon's Tooth R2	.60	1.50
45 Earth Dragon (Experienced) R1	1.00	2.50
46 Elder Goju C1	.10	.20
47 Empty Crevasse C1	.10	.20
48 Eternal Halls of the Shiba U1	1.25	3.00
49 Eyes Shall Not See C1	.10	.20
50 Farmer C2	.40	1.00
51 Fearful Soul C2	.10	.20
52 Fields of Courage U2	.25	.60
53 Fields of the Moon U2	.25	.60
54 Firefly Tattoo U2	.40	1.00
55 For My Clan U2	.25	.60
56 Fortified Ground U2	.25	.60
57 From Broken Ground C2	.10	.20
58 Fulfilling My Duty C2	.10	.20
59 Fully Armed C2	.10	.20
60 Ginawa (Experienced 3) R2	.60	1.50
61 Glory Grounds C1	1.00	2.50
62 Goju Adorai (Experienced) R2	1.00	2.50
63 Half-Beat Strike R2	1.00	2.50
64 Heavy Barde R2	.60	1.50
65 Hida Tsuru (Experienced) R2	1.00	2.50
66 Hiruma Abun C1	.10	.20
67 Hitomi Iyojin (Experienced) R2	.60	1.50
68 Hoshi Eisai (Experienced) U1	.60	1.50
69 Hoshi Eisai (Experienced) U1	.60	1.50
70 Hoshi Sensei R1	.60	1.50
71 Hoshi Wayan (Experienced 2) R2	.60	1.50
72 Hoturi Sensei R2	.60	1.50
73 Hurlspit Goblins U2	.25	.60
74 Ide Tadaji (Experienced) U1	.25	.60
75 Imperial Wedding U2	.25	.60
76 Increased Production C2	.10	.20
77 Into the Heavens U1	.25	.60
78 Iron Mountain U1	1.00	2.50
79 Isawa Tomo (Experienced 2) U1	1.00	2.50
80 Jal-Pur Raiders U1	.25	.60
81 Jama Suru (Experienced) U1	1.00	2.50
82 Kaede's Tears R2	.60	1.50
83 Kage (Experienced 5 Akodo Kage) R1	1.00	2.50
84 Kakita Kryuko C2	.10	.20
85 Kakita Yoshi (Experienced 3) U1	1.00	2.50
86 Karmic Link U2	.25	.60
87 Katana of the Twilight Mountains C1	.10	.20
88 Keda C2	.10	.20
89 Kingdom of Ghosts C2	.10	.20
90 Kitsu Motso (Experienced 2) R2	1.00	2.50
91 Kolat Chambers U2	.25	.60
92 Kolat Courtiers U1	.20	.50
93 Kosaten Shiro F	1.25	3.00
94 Kosaten Shiro U1	1.25	3.00
95 Kyoso No Oni (Experienced 2) R2	1.25	3.00
96 Kyuden Kitsune U1	1.25	3.00
97 Lessons of Honor U2	.20	.50
98 Lost Souls R1	1.25	3.00
99 Magistrate's Blade U2	.25	.60
100 Master Courtier U2	1.25	3.00
101 Matsu Agetoki (Experienced 2) R2	1.00	2.50
102 Matsu Domotai C2	.10	.20
103 Mat'tck C1	.10	.20
104 Mirumoto Taki (Experienced) U1	1.00	2.50
105 Moon and Sun U1	.40	1.00
106 Moto Chargers C1	.10	.20
107 Moto Gaheris F	1.00	2.50
108 Moto Tsugi C2	.10	.20
109 Mujina C1	.40	1.00
110 Mukami (Experienced 2) R2	.60	1.50
111 Naga C2	.40	1.00
112 Naga Vipers U1	.40	1.00
113 Naka Kuro (Experienced 2) R2	1.25	3.00
114 Nature Provides C1	.10	.20
115 Ninja Mystic (Experienced 3 Hoseki) R2	.60	1.50
116 Ninja Shadow-Walker (Experienced 2) U1	1.25	3.00
117 Nori Farm C1	.10	.20
118 Norikesh C2	.10	.20
119 Northern Provinces of the Moto F	1.25	3.00
120 Northern Provinces of the Moto U1	1.25	3.00
121 Oni no Byoki U1	.40	1.00
122 Oni no Gorusei C2	.10	.20
123 Oni no Okura (Experienced 2) U2	1.00	2.50
124 Oni Podling R2	.60	1.50
125 Orochi Tattoo U2	.40	1.00
126 Otaku Kamoko (Experienced 4) R1	2.50	6.00
127 Otaku Sahijir C1	.10	.20
128 Otomo Sensei R2	.60	1.50
129 Otomo Towers U1	.25	.60
130 O-Ushi Sensei R1	1.00	2.50
131 O-Ushi's Hammer R1	1.00	2.50
132 Overwhelm C2	.10	.20
133 Passage of Time U2	.40	1.00
134 Past Glories U1	.25	.60
135 Political Favors C1	.10	.20
136 Public Ridicule U1	.25	.60
137 Question Without an Answer R2	.60	1.50
138 Rank Hath Privilege R2	1.00	2.50
139 Ratling Pack C1	.40	1.00

140 Rebirth of the Dark Daughter U2 .25 .60
141 Regional Travel Papers C1 .10 .20
142 Restoring the Age of Myth U1 .25 .60
143 Return of Thunder U2 .25 .60
144 Riding Yari U1 .20 .50
145 Ruined Earth R1 1.00 2.50
146 Ryoshun's Last Words C2 .10 .20
147 Seppun Toshiken (Experienced 2) R2 .60 1.50
148 Shadow Assassins C1 .10 .20
149 Shadowed Wastes U2 .25 .60
150 Shiba Kiku C2 .10 .20
151 Shiba Tsukune (Experienced 3) R2 .60 1.50
152 Shinjo Hanari (Experienced 2) R2 1.00 2.50
153 Shirasu Sensei R1 6.00 15.00
154 Shiryo no Chiroku R1 1.00 2.50
155 Shiryo no Gohei R1 1.00 2.50
156 Shiryo no Hantei R1 1.00 2.50
157 Shiryo no Kunliu R1 1.00 2.50
158 Shrine of the Dead C1 .10 .20
159 Shrines of the Emperor U1 .25 .60
160 Sniping U2 .40 1.00
161 Something Worth Dying For U2 .25 .60
162 Son of the Clan C2 .10 .20
163 Soul of the Empire U2 .25 .60
164 Spy Network C1 .10 .20
165 Steel and Iron R2 .60 1.50
166 Strike from Behind R2 .60 1.50
167 Suana (Experienced 2) R2 1.00 2.50
168 Swamp Marsh U2 .20 .50
169 Temples of the Crow U1 1.25 3.00
170 Temples of the New Tao C1 .10 .20
171 Tetsuya Sensei R2 .60 1.50
172 The Citadel of the Hiruma U1 2.00 5.00
173 The Dark Path of Shadow U1 1.25 3.00
174 The Emperor Returns U2 .40 1.00
175 The Grey Crane 2.50 6.00
(Experienced 3 Kakita Toshimoko) R1
176 The Kitsu Tombs U1 1.25 3.00
177 The New Akasha U1 1.25 3.00
178 The Spawning Ground U1 1.25 3.00
179 The Sun Returns R2 1.50 4.00
180 The Towers of the Yogo U1 1.50 4.00
181 Thunder Dragon (Experienced) R1 1.25 3.00
182 Time of Destiny U2 .25 .60
183 Togashi Mitsu (Experienced 2) R1 1.00 2.50
184 Togashi Mitsu F .40 1.00
185 Togashi Senai C2 .10 .20
186 Toku (Experienced 3) U1 1.00 2.50
187 Toritaka Mariko C2 .10 .20
188 Toturi the First (Experienced 4 Toturi) F .40 1.00
189 Travelling Caravan C1 .10 .20
190 Tsunami Legion R2 .60 1.50
191 Undead C1 .40 1.00
192 Vigilant Keep of the Monkey F 1.00 2.50
193 Vigilant Keep of the Monkey U1 1.00 2.50
194 Void Dragon (Experienced) R1 1.25 3.00
195 Void Guard U1 .25 .60
196 Water Dragon (Experienced) R1 1.00 2.50
197 When Spirits Walked U1 .25 .60
198 Where the Sun Walked R2 .60 1.50
199 Yaro C1 .10 .20
200 Yasuki Nokatsu (Experienced 2) U1 .25 .60
201 Yodin Sensei R2 .60 1.50
202 Yoritomo (Experienced 3) R2 1.00 2.50
203 Yoritomo Furukae (Experienced) U1 .25 .60
204 Yotsu Shoku C1 .10 .20
205 Z'orr'tek C1 .10 .20

2000 Legend of the Five Rings The Spirit Wars

COMPLETE SET (202) 80.00 150.00
BOOSTER BOX (36) 150.00 250.00
BOOSTER PACK (15) 5.00 10.00
RELEASED IN NOVEMBER 2000
1 Akodo Ginawa (Experienced 4 Ginawa) R1 2.50 6.00
2 Akodo Ijiasu U2 .30 .75
3 Akodo Quehao R2 1.25 3.00
4 Akodo Sensei U1 .30 .75
5 Amaterasu's Furnace U2 .20 .50
6 Ancestral Dictate U2 .20 .50
7 Ancestral Protection R2 .60 1.50
8 Ancient Knowledge U1 .30 .75
9 Arriving at the Imperial Gates U2 .20 .50
10 Asako Misao U2 .20 .50
11 Asako Riders R2 .60 1.50
12 Back Banner C1 .10 .20
13 Battle at White Shore Plain C2 .20 .50
14 Battle of Drowned Honor C2 .10 .20
15 Battle of Quiet Winds C2 .10 .20
16 Battle of Shallow Waters C2 .10 .20
17 Bayushi Baku (Experienced) R2 .60 1.50
18 Bayushi Paneki C2 .10 .20
19 Bayushi Yojiro (Experienced 2) R1 1.50 4.00
20 Beginning and End R2 .60 1.50
21 Birth of the Anvil R1 1.25 3.00
22 Birth of the Sword R1 1.25 3.00
23 Birth of the Wolf R1 1.00 2.50
24 Bitter R2 2.00 5.00
25 Bronze Lantern R2 .60 1.50
26 Call the Spirit R2 .60 1.50
27 Chou-Sin C2 .10 .20
28 Clay Soldiers C2 .10 .20
29 Cliff of Golden Tears U2 .20 .50
30 Crab Tattoo R2 .60 1.50
31 Cursed Ground U1 .60 1.50
32 Daidoji Hachi C1 .10 .20
33 Dark Secrets C2 .10 .20
34 Devastation of Beiden Pass C/R .20 .50
35 Doji Kurohito U2 .20 .50
36 Doji Meihu U2 .20 .50
37 Doji Reju (Experienced 2) R1 4.00 10.00
38 Doji Reju (Experienced 2) R1 3.00 8.00
39 Dragon Dancers C1 .10 .20
40 Earthquake at Otosan Uchi R1 .60 1.50
41 East Wall of Otosan Uchi (Experienced) R1 .60 1.50
42 Elite Light Infantry F .10 .20
43 Elite Medium Infantry F .10 .20
44 Emperor's Under-Hand R1 4.00 10.00
45 Emperor's Favor R1 .60 1.50
46 Empress's Guard R2 1.25 3.00
47 Evil Feeds Upon Itself F .10 .20
48 Fall of the Alliance R1 .60 1.50
49 Fall on Your Knees R2 1.50 4.00
50 Fallen Ground C2 .20 .50
51 Fallen Legion U2 .20 .50
52 Fields of Darkness C1 .10 .20
53 Fields of the Sun R1 1.25 3.00
54 Giuniko C1 .60 1.50
55 Great Crater R1 .60 1.50
56 Guard the House C2 .10 .20
57 Hantei XVI F .30 .75
58 Hesitation U2 .20 .50
59 Hida Hio C2 .10 .20
60 Hida Kuon C2 .10 .20
61 Hida Kuroda C2 .10 .20
62 Hida Sukune (Experienced 2) R1 3.00 8.00
63 Hida Tsuneo R1 2.50 6.00
64 Hitomi's Glare R2 .60 1.50
65 Honorable R2 2.50 6.00
66 Ide Gokun U2 .20 .50
67 Ikoma Tsai C2 .10 .20
68 Imperial Census R1 2.50 6.00
69 Infantry Charge C2 .10 .20
70 Inkyo C1 .10 .20
71 Intelligence Agent U2 .30 .75
72 Interruption U2 .30 .75
73 Iron Mempo C1 .10 .20
74 Isawa Metigaru C1 .10 .20
75 Isawa Nakamuro C1 .10 .20
76 Kaiu Sensei R2 .60 1.50
77 Kakita Kaiten (Experienced) R2 .60 1.50
78 Kamoko's Constellation R1 1.25 3.00
79 Kitsu Deijiko C2 .10 .20
80 Kitsune C1 .10 .20
81 Knowing Lands and Giving Trees U1 .30 .75
82 Kohuri C2 .10 .20
83 Kuni Utagu (Experienced) R1 2.50 6.00
84 Lady of the Forest Sensei U1 .30 .75
85 Lalesha C1 .10 .20
86 Last Gift C2 .10 .20
87 Lay the Blame C2 .10 .20
88 Let the Spirit Move You C1 .10 .20
89 Lsinyuan C1 .10 .20
90 Luring Tactics U2 .30 .75
91 Mara's Farewell C2 .10 .20
92 Master Smith Ascends C1 .10 .20
93 Matsu Goemon F .10 .20
94 Mirumoto Ukira C2 .10 .20
95 Mirumoto Uso (Experienced) R2 .60 1.50
96 Miya Dosonu U2 .30 .75
97 Miya Sensei R2 .60 1.50
98 Miya Yemi U2 2.50 6.00
99 Mizuichi C2 .10 .20
100 Mokoto U2 .20 .50
101 Morito (Experienced 2 Morito) R1 1.25 3.00
102 Mortal Flesh U1 .20 .50
103 Moshi Shanegon U2 .30 .75
104 Moto Hideyo C1 .10 .20
105 Moto Technique R2 .60 1.50
106 Moto Vordu C2 .10 .20
107 Moving the Wind U1 .30 .75
108 Nage-yari C1 .10 .20
109 New Kimono C1 .10 .20
110 Nightmare C2 .20 .50
111 Noble Halls of the Akodo F .30 .75
112 Noekam U2 .20 .50
113 North Wall of Otosan Uchi (Experienced) R1 .60 1.50
114 Obsidian Statues R1 .60 1.50
115 Old Debts C2 .10 .20
116 Oni no Fushiki C1 .60 1.50
117 Oni no Yamaso C1 .10 .20
118 Oni Spawn C2 .10 .20
119 Otomo Dsichi R1 1.25 3.00
120 Otomo Hoketuhime C1 .10 .20
121 Personal Sacrifice C2 .10 .20
122 Poorly Placed Garden C1 1.00 2.50
123 Quiet Tombs C1 .10 .20
124 Ratling Scroungers R2 .60 1.50
125 Return for Training U2 1.25 3.00
126 Revealing the Bastard R1 .60 1.50
127 Revering the Past R1 1.25 3.00
128 Right to Rule R1 1.25 3.00
129 Roshungi (Experienced) R2 .60 1.50
130 Ruin and Devastation U1 .20 .50
131 Saigorei (Experienced) R2 .60 1.50
132 Scaring the Masses U2 .30 .75
133 Scholarship C2 .10 .20
134 Shasyahkar (Experienced) R2 .60 1.50
135 Shaunasea U2 .20 .50
136 Shiba Aikune C2 .10 .20
137 Shiba Ningen (Experienced) R1 1.25 3.00
138 Shinjo Shono (Experienced) R2 .60 1.50
139 Shiryo no Ch'i R1 1.00 2.50
140 Shiryo no Hotei R2 .60 1.50
141 Shiryo no Nyoko R1 1.25 3.00
142 Shiryo no Rohata R1 1.25 3.00
143 Shiryo no Shoju R1 2.50 6.00
144 Shiryo no Taisa R1 1.25 3.00
145 Shiryo no Ujik-hai R1 1.25 3.00
146 Shosuro Chian (Experienced) R1 2.50 6.00
147 Shrine of the Evening Star R1 .10 .20
148 Shrine of the Spirits F .30 .75
149 Shuriken C1 .30 .75
150 Sign of Weakness U2 .30 .75
151 Signal Corps U2 .20 .50
152 Simple Huts C1 .30 .75
153 Snow Crane Tattoo R2 1.25 3.00
154 Sodegarami C1 .10 .20
155 Soshi Angai U2 .20 .50
156 Soul Sword C1 .10 .20
157 South Wall of Otosan Uchi (Experienced) R1 1.25 3.00
158 Spirit Bells U2 .20 .50
159 Spirit Hounds C2 .10 .20
160 Star-Filled Steel U2 .20 .50
161 Sumai Match R1 1.50 4.00
162 Suzume Roshi C1 .10 .20
163 Suzume Sensei U1 .40 1.00
164 Taikon U2 .20 .50
165 Tamori Chosai C1 .10 .20
166 Tamori Shaitung U2 .20 .50
167 Te'tik'kir C1 .10 .20
168 Temptation C2 .10 .20
169 Three-Stone River U2 .30 .75
170 Through the Flames C2 .10 .20
171 Togashi Mio C1 .10 .20
172 Torii Arch C1 .10 .20
173 Torii Tattoo C2 .10 .20
174 Towers of the Asako F .30 .75
175 Treaty U1 .30 .75
176 Tsi Yoji U2 .20 .50
177 Tsuko Sensei F .30 .75
178 Tsuko's Heart U2 .20 .50
179 Tsuruchi Okame C1 .20 .50
180 Turn of Fate U2 .20 .50
181 Uidori U2 .20 .50
182 Undead Legion U2 .20 .50
183 Uona Sensei F .30 .75
184 Usagi Gohei U2 .20 .50
185 Utaku Yu-Pan U2 .20 .50
186 Wall of Bones C1 .10 .20
187 War Paints R2 .60 1.50
188 Warriors of the Great Climb U2 .20 .50
189 Wasp Sensei U1 .40 1.00
190 Weapons Cache C2 .10 .20
191 West Wall of Otosan Uchi (Experienced) R1 .60 1.50
192 Where Tsanuri Fell R2 .40 1.00
193 Witch Hunt U2 .30 .75
194 Witch Hunter's Accusation U2 .30 .75
195 Wutho U2 .60 1.50
196 Yakamo's Smile R2 .60 1.50
197 Yeiseo C1 .10 .20
198 Yoee'trr U2 .60 1.50
199 Yokai no Mizushai R2 .60 1.50
200 Yoritomo Aramasu R1 4.00 10.00
201 Yoritomo Kitao C2 .10 .20
202 Yoritomo Yukue R1 1.25 3.00

2000 Legend of the Five Rings Storms Over Matsu Palace

old2 The Provincial State of the Unicorn
old5 Ikoma Tsunari
LionD08D1 Kitsu Okura
old13 Otaku Xieng Chi
old16 Shinjo Yasamura
old29 Unexpected Allies (Experienced)
UnicornD01 Silk Works
UnicornD04 Stables
UnicornD06 Otaku Kamoko
UnicornD08 Shinjo Hanari
UnicornD09 Glimpse of the Unicorn
UnicornD11 Kabuki Theater Troupe
UnicornD14 Moto Yesugai
UnicornD15 Retired General
UnicornD16 Shinjo Sadato
UnicornD18 New Year's Celebration
UnicornD23 Iuchi Daiyu
UnicornF01 Heavy Cavalry
UnicornF02 Medium Cavalry
UnicornF05 Horsebowmen
UnicornF06 Mounted Spearmen
UnicornF08 Higher Ground
UnicornF09 Careful Planning
UnicornF12 Block Supply Lines
UnicornF13 Another Time
UnicornF15 Heart of the Inferno
UnicornF17 Stifling Wind
UnicornF18 Strike at the Tail
UnicornF24 Deadly Ground
LionD01 Copper Mine
LionD02 Jade Works
LionD03 Small Farm
LionD04 Large Farm
LionD05 Matsu Morishigi
LionD06 Matsu Suhada
LionD13 Akodo Matoko
LionD14 Matsu Ketsui
LionD18 Hurricane
LionD19 Hawks and Falcons
LionD23 Ikoma Gunjin
LionF00 The Ancestral Home of the Lion
LionF01 Heavy Infantry
LionF03 Medium Infantry
LionF05 Spearmen
LionF06 Light Infantry
LionF07 Bloodstained Forest
LionF08 Charge
LionF09 Fog
LionF10 Iaijutsu Duel
LionF11 Focus
LionF14 Entrapping Terrain
LionF16 Ikoma Technique
LionF19 The Fires That Cleanse
LionF20 Strength of Purity
LionF21 Diversionary Tactics

2000 Legend of the Five Rings Top Deck Booster Pack

1b Arrows from the Woods
2b Careful Planning
3b Charge
4b Contentious Terrain
5b Deadly Ground
6b Diversionary Tactics
7b Doji Kuwanan
8b Fist of the Earth
9b Hida Tampako
10b Hitomi Dajan
11b Iaijutsu Duel
12b Isawa Sze
13b Matsu Ketsui
14b Otaku Kamoko
15b Outflank
16b Shosuro Yudoka
17b Strength of My Ancestors
18b Strength of Purity
19b The Wrath of Osano-Wo
20b Wounded in Battle

2001 Legend of the Five Rings A Perfect Cut

COMPLETE SET (156) 30.00 80.00
BOOSTER BOX (48 PACKS) 20.00 40.00
BOOSTER PACK (11 CARDS) 1.00 2.00
RELEASED IN SEPTEMBER 2001
1 A Desperate Act C2 .10 .20
2 A Matter of Pride U .20 .50
3 A Plague Spreads U .20 .50
4 Acquiring Favor U .60 1.50
5 Advance Scout U .20 .50
6 Akodo Setai C2 .10 .20
7 Anekkusai's Feathers C2 .10 .20
8 Asahina Handen U .20 .50
9 Banner Guard C2 .10 .20
10 Bayushi Tai U .20 .50
11 Bayushi Tasagore F .75 2.00
12 Blazing Sun U .20 .50
13 Blood Madness R 1.00 2.50
14 Breaking Concentration R 1.00 2.50
15 By Will of the Wind R 1.00 2.50
16 Cast Down the Meek C2 .10 .20
17 Command Group C4 .10 .20
18 Connecting Walls C2 .10 .20
19 Contemplation of Osano-Wo R 1.00 2.50
20 Contingency Planning R 1.00 2.50
21 Crab Recruiter R .60 1.50
22 Crane Tradesman R .60 1.50
23 Daidoji Megumi C2 .10 .20
24 Dairu no Shiryo R .60 1.50
25 Dairya's Cackling Skull R .60 1.50
26 Defensive Duty C2 .10 .20
27 Diplomatic Apprentice C2 .10 .20
28 Doji Kurohito (Experienced) F .60 1.50
29 Elemental Shock U .20 .50
30 Endless Deluge R .60 1.50
31 Family Tactics C2 .10 .20
32 Fire and Air C2 .10 .20
33 Fortify U .20 .50
34 Fukurokujin Seido U .20 .50
35 Furious Strike R .60 1.50
36 Guard House C2 .10 .20
37 Hida Kagore U .20 .50
38 Hida Kuon (Experienced) F .40 1.00
39 Hida Reiha C2 .10 .20
40 Hiruma Todori C2 .10 .20
41 Hunter C2 .10 .20
42 Hyakute no Oni U .20 .50
43 Iaijutsu Lesson C2 .10 .20
44 Ide Michisuna R .60 1.50
45 In Light of Darkness U .20 .50
46 Inside Agent U .20 .50
47 Interesting Sticks U .25 .60
48 Isawa Hochiu (Experienced) R .60 1.50
49 Isawa Nakamuro (Experienced) R .60 1.50
50 Isawa Nodotai U .25 .60
51 Kaeru Kenko U .20 .50
52 Kaiu Hosaru U .20 .50
53 Kakita Duelling Academy F .60 1.50
54 Kakita Gosha U .20 .50
55 Kayobun U .20 .50
56 Kitsune Taro C2 .10 .20
57 Kokoro C2 .10 .20
58 Kukan-do U .20 .50
59 Kyuden Hida F .40 1.00
60 Lion Scout R .60 1.50
61 Mapped Region C2 .10 .20
62 Matsu Domotai (Experienced) R .60 1.50
63 Matsu Hyun C2 .10 .20
64 Matsu Kenji R .60 1.50
65 Matsu Kenseiko U .20 .50
66 Memorial C2 .10 .20
67 Mining Foreman C2 .10 .20
68 Minor Illusions R 1.00 2.50
69 Mirumoto Junnosuke U .20 .50
70 Mirumoto Taiu C2 .10 .20
71 Miya Heikichi R .60 1.50
72 Moto Chen R 1.00 2.50
73 Moto Reijiro U .20 .50
74 Mujina Gang C2 .10 .20
75 Nagamaki C2 .10 .20
76 Needed at the Wall U .20 .50
77 No One Wins U .20 .50
78 Omoni C2 .10 .20
79 Open Arms C2 .10 .20
80 Osoreru no Oni C2 .10 .20
81 Outmaneuvered by Force U .25 .60
82 Outmaneuvered in Court U .25 .60
83 Persuasion R .60 1.50
84 Phoenix Library R .60 1.50
85 Plum Tree Training Ground U .20 .50
86 Political Warfare U .20 .50
87 Prepared for the Enemy C2 .10 .20
88 Preparing the Edge U .20 .50
89 Rain of Emeralds U .20 .50
90 Reassert One's Mettle C2 .10 .20
91 Retired Sohei C2 .10 .20
92 Returned to the Pit R .60 1.50
93 Ronin at the Wall C2 .10 .20
94 Scorpion Distractor R .60 1.50
95 Seppun Isei U .20 .50
96 Shadowlands Bastion R .60 1.50
97 Shallow Graves C2 .10 .20
98 Shiba Mirabu R .60 1.50
99 Shiba Unasagi C2 .10 .20
100 Shinjo Sanraku C2 .10 .20
101 Shinsei's Smile R .60 1.50
102 Shosuro Gardens F .40 1.00
103 Shosuro Higatsuku U .25 .60
104 Shosuro Yasuko C2 .10 .20
105 Show of Strength R .60 1.50
106 Snowy Fields C2 .10 .20
107 Sohei R .60 1.50
108 Soshi Tishi C2 .10 .20
109 Speed of the Waterfall U .20 .50
110 Spyglass U .20 .50
111 Stand as Stone U .20 .50
112 Stand Your Ground C2 .10 .20
113 Standing Tall C2 .10 .20
114 Strong Guard U .20 .50
115 Summoning the Gale C2 .10 .20
116 Tachi U .20 .50
117 Taijikku U .20 .50
118 Taiko no Shiryo R .60 1.50
119 Tainted Bushi U .20 .50
120 Tamori Chieko C2 .10 .20
121 Tampako no Shiryo R .60 1.50
122 Tea House C2 .10 .20
123 Temple of the Dragon R .60 1.50
124 The Enemy You Deserve R .60 1.50
125 The Great Climb C2 .10 .20
126 The Greatest Cost U .25 .60
127 The Hand of Thunder R .60 1.50
128 The Power of Nothing R .60 1.50
129 The Wolf Speaks R .60 1.50
130 Thuk-Kigi's War Machine R .60 1.50
131 Thunder Calls to Fortune R .60 1.50
132 Togashi Iroshi U .20 .50
133 Togashi Satsu R .60 1.50
134 Too Much Too Soon U .20 .50
135 Training Dojo U .20 .50
136 Training Exercises C2 .10 .20
137 Traitor's Grove R .60 1.50
138 Tsudao's Challenge U .20 .50
139 Tsuno Kurushimi U .25 .60
140 Tsuno Ravagers R .60 1.50
141 Tsuno Squad U .20 .50
142 Twenty Goblin Winter R .60 1.50
143 Unavoidable Destiny R .60 1.50
144 Unexpected Assault R .60 1.50
145 Unexpected Confrontation R .60 1.50
146 Unicorn Marketeer R .60 1.50
147 Unspeakable Preparations U .20 .50
148 Usagi Kashira C2 .10 .20
149 Utaku Mu Dan C2 .10 .20
150 While the Empire Watches U .20 .50
151 Yasuki Heikichi C2 .10 .20
152 Yasuki Palaces R 4.00 10.00
153 Yasuki Palaces R 2.50 6.00
154 Yogoso no Shiryo R .60 1.50
155 Yoritomo Kitao (Experienced) R .60 1.50
156 Yoshi's Fan R .60 1.50

2001 Legend of the Five Rings An Oni's Fury

COMPLETE SET (156) 30.00 60.00
BOOSTER BOX (48 PACKS) 25.00 50.00
BOOSTER PACK (11 CARDS) 1.00 2.00
RELEASED IN DECEMBER 2001
1 A New Legacy R .60 1.50
2 Aikune's Wrath R 1.00 2.50
3 Akodo Koun U .20 .50
4 Akodo Senke C .10 .20
5 An Error in Orders R .60 1.50
6 Ancestral Shrine C .10 .20
7 Armor of Shadows .60 1.50
(Experienced Armor of the Shadow Warrior) R
8 Asako Itaru U .20 .50
9 Asako Shuntaro C .10 .20
10 Ashigaru Barracks U .20 .50
11 Ashigaru Hordes C .10 .20
12 Bayushi Ambushers U .20 .50
13 Bayushi Paneki (Experienced) R 1.25 3.00
14 Bayushi Shixiang C .10 .20
15 Benefactor C .10 .20
16 Blacksteel Blade C .10 .20
17 Blue Skies C .10 .20
18 Brightest Winter U .20 .50
19 Burning the Tombs R 1.00 2.50
20 Carpenter Wall Falls U .20 .50
21 Cascading Fire C .10 .20
22 Celestial Vision U .20 .50
23 Child of the Last Wish U .20 .50
24 Citadel of Daigotsu F 1.25 3.00
25 City of Night R 1.00 2.50
26 Cleared Grounds U .20 .50
27 Coastal Region U .20 .50
28 Complications R 1.00 2.50
29 Consecrate the Land C .10 .20
30 Daidoji Enai C .10 .20
31 Daidoji Gudeta U .20 .50
32 Daikyu U .20 .50
33 Darkest Winter U .20 .50
34 Dirty Scum! R .60 1.50
35 Doji Yasuyo (Experienced) R .60 1.50
36 Elegant Kimono U .20 .50
37 Engage the Enemy R .60 1.50
38 Everpresent Fear U .20 .50
39 Follow the Path U .20 .50
40 Fox Nagamaki U .20 .50
41 Friendly Traveler Village C .10 .20
42 Frontal Assault C .10 .20
43 Gaijutsu no Shiryo R .60 1.50
44 Harvest Time U .20 .50
45 Hasty Exploitation C .10 .20
46 Hida Sakamoto R .60 1.50
47 Hida Sunao U .20 .50
48 Hiruma Archers U .20 .50
49 Hiruma Nichi C .10 .20
50 Hitomi Akuai (Experienced) R .60 1.50
51 Hitomi Kagetora (Experienced) F 1.00 2.50
52 Hoshi's Claw U .20 .50

53 Hoturi's Blade U .20 .50
54 House of the Red Lotus C .10 .20
55 Ikoma Fudai U .20 .50
56 Imperial Scrutiny U .20 .50
57 Inner Wall C .10 .20
58 Isawa Ihara R .60 1.50
59 Iuchi Lixue R .60 1.50
60 Kaiu Ryojiro C .10 .20
61 Kaneka's Advance C .10 .20
62 Kharmic Unison C .10 .20
63 Ki-Rin's Shrine (Experienced) R .60 1.50
64 Kitsu Dejiko (Experienced) R 1.00 2.50
65 Kitsuki Remata U .20 .50
66 Kitsune Gohei R .60 1.50
67 Kiyomi U .20 .50
68 Know the Enemy R .60 1.50
69 Know the Truth R .60 1.50
70 Kuni Kiyoshi U .20 .50
71 Lion Warcats U .30 .75
72 Lobbyist C .10 .20
73 Logistics Problem U .20 .50
74 Lost Glories U .20 .50
75 Mantis Raiders R .60 1.50
76 Masume Wakizashi C .10 .20
77 Matsu Shinya C .10 .20
78 Mirumoto Tsuge C .10 .20
79 Miya Hatori R .60 1.50
80 Moment in the Sun R .60 1.50
81 Moshi Kalani U .20 .50
82 Moto Chagatai (Experienced) F .60 1.50
83 Moto Vordu (Experienced) R .60 1.50
84 Moto Wardogs U .20 .50
85 Moto Zhijuan U .20 .50
86 Naga Tattoo U .20 .50
87 Naka Tokei (Experienced Morito Tokei) R .60 1.50
88 Natsune no Shiryo R .60 1.50
89 New Emerald Champion R .60 1.50
90 Nezumi Technique C .10 .20
91 Osoreru no Oni (Experienced) R 1.25 3.00
92 Otomo Motoshi C .10 .20
93 Poetry Contest R .60 1.50
94 Por'ee-rep C .10 .20
95 Power C .10 .20
96 Quench the Ashes R .60 1.50
97 Remember the Mountain C .10 .20
98 Rewards of Rank C .10 .20
99 Ruins of the Kappa R .60 1.50
100 Rumors U .20 .50
101 Sacred Tunnels U .20 .50
102 Sanshu Denki U .20 .50
103 Seeking the Master R .60 1.50
104 Seeping Darkness U .20 .50
105 Shatter the Elements U .20 .50
106 Shiba Aikune (Experienced) R .60 1.50
107 Shiba Arai C .10 .20
108 Shinjo Huang C .10 .20
109 Shinmaki Monastery C .10 .20
110 Shintao Library C .10 .20
111 Shiro Ide F 1.00 2.50
112 Shiro Mirumoto F .60 1.50
113 Show No Fear C .10 .20
114 Slaughter the Scout C .10 .20
115 Sleepless Nights C .10 .20
116 Soshi Eiji U .20 .50
117 Spider Tattoo U .20 .50
118 Stolen Records C .10 .20
119 Sun Kiles U .20 .50
120 Sun Tao's Tessen R .60 1.50
121 Taking the Wall U .20 .50
122 Tamori Hiroko C .10 .20
123 Tetsuko no Shiryo R .60 1.50
124 The Calm of Shinsei U .20 .50
125 The Company You Keep C .10 .20
126 The First Legion R .60 1.50
127 The Jaws of Defeat C .10 .20
128 The Jaws of Victory C .10 .20
129 The Masters Imprisoned R .60 1.50
130 The Oracle Awakens R .60 1.50
131 The Price of Innocence C .10 .20
132 The Thunder's Clap U .20 .50
133 Thunder of the Earth C .10 .20
134 Toturi Miyako C .10 .20
135 Tsukune Ascends R .60 1.50
136 Tsukune's Choice U .20 .50
137 Tsuno Attack U .20 .50
138 Tsuno Scouts U .20 .50
139 Tsuno Takuma C .10 .20
140 Usagi Ozaki R .60 1.50
141 Using the Land C .10 .20
142 Vengeance U .20 .50
143 Vordu's Discovery C .10 .20
144 Word of the Anvil R .60 1.50
145 Word of the Bastard R .60 1.50
146 Word of the Sword R .60 1.50
147 Word of the Wolf R .60 1.50
148 Written in Blood R .60 1.50
149 Yakamo's Armor R .60 1.50
150 Yasuki Hachi (Experienced) R .60 1.50
151 Yasuki Nishi U .20 .50
152 Yogo Koji C .10 .20
153 Yogo Tjeki R .60 1.50
154 Yokubo F 1.25 3.00
155 Yoritomo Katoa C .10 .20
156 Yoshimitsu no Yokai R .60 1.50

2001 Legend of the Five Rings Gold Edition

1 A Glimpse of the Soul's Shadow U
2 A Samurai Never Stands Alone U
3 A Samurai's Fury R
4 A Stout Heart U
5 Accessible Terrain C
6 Akodo Ginawa (Experienced 4) R
7 Akodo Ijiasu U
8 Akui Cliffs U
9 Alliance U
10 Ambush R
11 Ambush Strategist U
12 An Empty Victory R
13 Ancestral Shrines of Otosan Uchi U
14 Another Time C
15 Archers C
16 Armored Steeds U
17 Armory U
18 Arrowroot Tattoo U
19 Arrows from the Woods C
20 Asahina Archers R
23 Asahina's Breath R
25 Ashigaru Archers C
26 Ashigaru Spearmen C
27 Avoid Fate U
28 Bandit Hideout U
29 Barbican U
30 Barricades U
31 Yamaso no Oni C
32 Battering Ram Crew U
33 Battle Maidens U
38 Bayushi Paneki C
41 Bayushi Yojiro (Experienced 2) R
43 Be Prepared to Dig Two Graves R
44 Bend Like a Reed C
45 Big Stink R
46 Biting Steel C
47 Black Finger River U
48 Blackened Claws U
49 Blackened Sky U
50 Blacksmiths U
51 Blade of Kaiu U
52 Block Supply Lines C
53 Blood of Midnight U
54 Blood Rite R
55 Bloodstained Forest U
56 Wakizashi C
57 Borderland U
58 Brash Hero C
59 Bridged Pass C
60 Burning Your Essence R
61 Bushi Dojo C
62 Call to Arms U
63 Campsite U
64 Candle of the Void U
65 Careful Planning C
66 Celestial Alignment R
67 Charge C
68 Chasing Osano-Wo C
69 Chime of Harmony C
70 Chrysanthemum Festival R
71 Cleansing Bell C
72 Come One at a Time C
73 Confusion at Court C
74 Contentious Terrain C
75 Copper Mine
76 Corrupted Iron Mine C
77 Corrupted Silver Mine C
78 Corrupted Ground C
79 Corruption of the Harmonies U
80 Costly Alliance U
81 Counterattack U
84 Crane Tattoo U
85 Crossroads C
86 Crystal Katana C
87 Yasuki Hachi C
89 Daidoji Rekai (Experienced 2) R
91 Deadly Ground C
92 Dealing With Shadows U
93 Deathseeker Technique
94 Diamond Mine U
95 Dai Tsuchi U
96 Dispersive Terrain C
97 Diversionary Tactics C
100 Doji Kurohito R
102 Double Chi U
104 Dragon Tattoo U
105 Dragon's Claw Katana U
106 Dragon's Teeth C
107 Drum of Water U
108 Duty to the Clan U
109 Earthquake U
110 Earthworks C
111 Elite Pikemen C
112 Elite Spearmen C
113 Encircled Terrain C
114 Energy Transference C
115 Enough Talk! U
116 Entrapping Terrain C
118 The Arrow Knows the Way R
119 Eyes Shall Not See U
120 Facing Your Devils C
121 False Alliance U
122 Familiar Surroundings C
123 Famine U
124 Famous Poet U
125 Fan of Command R
126 Fantastic Gardens U
127 Farmlands C
130 Fields of the Morning Sun U
131 Fight to the Setting Sun C
132 Finding the Harmony U
133 Fires of Purity U
134 Fires of Retribution C
135 Firestorm Legion R
136 Fist of the Earth C
137 Flatlands C
138 Flattery U
139 Focus R
140 For the Empire U
141 Forest C
142 Forests of Shinomen C
143 Forgotten Tomb U
144 Fortress of the Dragonfly C
145 Frenzy U
147 Gambling House U
148 Garrison U
149 Geisha Assassin R
150 Geisha House
151 Gift of the Wind C
152 Glimpse of the Unicorn U
153 Go Master C
154 Goblin Madcaps C
155 Goblin Mob C
156 Goblin Sneaks C
157 Goblin Warmonger C
158 Goblin Wizard C
159 Gold Mine
161 Goldsmith U
162 Hammer of Earth U
163 Hawks and Falcons C
164 He's Mine! C
165 Heartbeat Drummers C
166 Heavy Cavalry U
167 Heavy Infantry U
169 Hida Hio C
171 Hida Kuon U
172 Hida Kuroda U
178 High Morale C
179 Higher Ground U
180 Hiruma's Last Breath R
181 Historian U
185 Hitomi Technique
186 Hitsu-do C
187 Honorable Seppuku C
188 Horsebowmen C
189 Hoshi Wayan (Experienced 2) R
190 Hummingbird Tattoo U
191 Hurricane U
192 I Believed in You U
193 Iaijutsu Challenge C
194 Iaijutsu Duel C
195 Ikiryo C
198 Ikoma Tsai U
199 Imperial Funeral R
200 Imperial Gift R
201 Imperial Honor Guard R
202 Inaccessible Region U
203 Inner Fire U
204 Investigation R
205 Iron Mine
206 Iron Mountain
207 Isawa Nakamuro C
209 Isawa Taeruko C
212 Izaku Library U
213 Jade Bow C
214 Jade Works C
215 Judgment of Toshiken U
216 Kabuki Theater Troupe U
217 Kaede's Tears R
221 Kakita Kyruko C
222 Kakita Technique
224 Kamoko's Constellation R
225 Thuk-Kigi (Experienced) R
226 Kaze-do C
227 Kharmic Strike U
229 Kitsu Dejiko C
231 Kolat Assassin U
232 Kolat Master R
233 Kosaten Shiro
234 Kumo C
235 Kuni Utagu (Experienced) R
236 Kuni Utagu C
237 Kyoso no Oni (Experienced) R
238 Kyoso no Oni U
239 Kyuden Hitomi
240 Lady Kitsune C
241 Large Farm C
242 Last Stand Plain U
243 Lesser Mujina C
244 Lesser Oni C
245 Let Your Spirit Guide You R
246 Lies, Lies, Lies... U
247 Light Cavalry C
248 Light Infantry C
249 Light Mounted Infantry C
251 Lion's Pride R
252 Look into the Void C
253 Lookout Mountain C
254 Low Morale C
256 Magic Mud U
257 Mantis Bushi R
258 Mantle of Fire U
259 Mantle of the Jade Champion R
261 Marries A Barbarian U
262 Master of the Rolling River U
263 Master of the Tea Ceremony U
264 Matsu Domotai C
270 Matsu Hataki C
271 Meditation C
272 Medium Cavalry C
273 Medium Infantry C
277 Mirumoto Ukira C
280 Mizu-do C
281 Moat C
282 Moto Fanatics U
283 Moto Hideyo C
286 Moto Vordu C
287 Mountain Pass C
288 Mountain Tattoo U
289 Mushin C
290 Ghedai C
291 Naginata C
292 Narrow Ground C
293 Nemesis U
294 New Year's Celebration R
295 Night Battle C
296 Ninja Spy C
297 Ninja Thief U
298 No-Dachi C
299 Noekam U
300 Northern Provinces of the Moto
301 Oath of Fealty C
302 Occult Murders U
303 Ogre Bushi U
304 Ogre Warriors R
305 One Life, One Action C
306 Tsuburu no Oni U
307 Ono C
314 Outflank C
315 Dragon Dancers U
316 Pearl Divers U
317 Peasant Revolt U
318 Personal Champion R
319 Personal Standard C
321 Towers of the Asako
322 Pitch and Fire C
323 Plain of Fast Troubles C
324 Plains Above Evil U
325 Plains of Otosan Uchi R
326 Poison Dartgun U
327 Poisoned C
328 Poisoned Weapon R
329 Political Dissent U
330 Poorly Placed Garden U
331 Porcelain Mask of Fu Leng R
332 Port U
333 Proposal of Peace R
334 Provision Storehouse C
335 Rallying Cry C
336 Ratling Bushi U
338 Ratling Pack C
339 Ratling Scout C
340 Te'tik'kir C
341 Refugees C
342 Remorseful Seppuku C
343 Resist Magic R
344 Retired General C
345 Retired Wasp General U
346 Retirement R
347 Riding Yari U
348 Ring of Air U
349 Ring of Earth U
350 Ring of Fire U
351 Ring of the Void U
352 Ring of Water U
353 Rise of the Phoenix R
354 River Region U
355 Road of Dust U
357 Ruantek C
358 Ryoshun's Last Words U
359 Sacrificial Altar U
360 Salt the Earth U
361 Samurai Warriors R
362 Sanctified Temple C
364 Scout C
365 Secluded Ravine C
366 Secrets on the Wind U
368 Setsuban Festival R
370 The Shadowlands Horde
371 Shadowlands Marsh U
372 Shame U
373 Shiba Aikune C
377 Asako Misao U
379 Shiba Technique
380 Shiba Tsukune C
381 Shiba Tsukune (Experienced 3) R
382 Shield Wall U
385 Shinjo Shono (Experienced) R
386 Shinjo Shono C
388 Shinjo Technique
390 Shosuro Yudoka U
391 Shrine of the Dragon Champion U
392 Silk Farm C
393 Silk Works C
394 Silver Mine
395 Skeletal Troops C
396 Slander U
397 Sludge C
398 Small Farm C
399 Sneak Attack R
400 Solar Eclipse R
401 Sorrow's Path C
402 Soshi Angai U
403 Soshi's Curse U
404 Spearmen C
405 Spirit Guide R
406 Stables
407 Stand Against the Waves C
408 Stand Firm C
409 Stifling Wind U
410 Storehouses U
411 Street to Street C
412 Streets of Otosan Uchi R
413 Strength of My Ancestors C
414 Strength of Purity U
415 Strength of the Earth U
416 Strike at the Tail R
417 Strike of Flowing Water C
418 Superior Strategist R
419 Superior Tactics C
420 Surrender U
421 Suspended Terrain C
422 Suspicions U
423 Swamp Marsh U
424 Swamplands C
425 Take the Initiative C
426 Tamori Chosai C
427 Tamori Shaitung U
428 Tapestry of Air U
430 Temple of Bishamon U
431 Temples of the New Tao U
432 Tessen U
433 Test of Might C
434 Test of Stone U
435 Test of the Emerald Champion R
436 Test of the Jade Champion R
437 The Ancient Halls of the Lion
438 The Celestial Pattern R
439 The Citadel of the Hiruma
440 The Code of Bushido R
441 The Damned U
442 The Edge of Shinomen Forest C
443 The Endless Well R
444 The Face of Fear U
445 The Fire from Within U
446 The Fires That Cleanse R
447 The Fury of Osano-Wo C
448 Great Crater R
449 The Great Walls of Kaiu
450 The Hiruma Dojo C
451 The Imperial Standard R
452 The Iron Fortress of the Daidoji
453 The Iuchi Plains C
454 The Kaiu Forge U
456 The Price of War U
457 Regions of Rokugan U
458 The Rising Sun R
459 The Ruined Keep of Fu Leng R
460 The Shadow Stronghold of the Bayushi
461 The Soul of Shiba R
462 The Spawning Ground
463 The Towers of the Yogo
464 The Turtle's Shell R
465 The Utaku Palaces
466 The Wind's Truth C
467 The Wrath of Osano-Wo C
468 Those Who Stand Alone U
469 To Do What We Must U
470 To the Last Man R
471 Togashi Hoshi (Experienced 2) R
472 Tomb of Jade C
473 Torrential Rain R
474 Touch of Death R
475 Touching the Soul U
476 Trade Route U
477 Trading Grounds C
478 Training Grounds C
479 Traveling Caravan C
480 Treacherous Terrain C
481 Trenches C
482 Tunnel System U
483 Umi Amaterasu C
486 Unscalable Walls C
487 Untrustworthy U
488 Utaku Xieng Chi U
489 Utaku Xieng Chi (Experienced) R
490 Utaku Yu-Pan U
491 Walking the Way U
492 Wall of Bones U
493 Warhorses C
494 War-Stained Fields C
495 Watchtower C
496 Way of Deception U
497 Wetlands C
498 When Darkness Draws Near U
499 White Shore Plain U
500 Winds of Change U
503 Yuki no Onna C
504 Zokujin U
505 Zombie Troops U
506 A Test of Courage C
507 The Armor of Sun Tao U
509 Dead Eyes
510 Deeds, Not Words U
511 Defend Your Honor U
512 Delicate Calculations U
513 Fist of Osano-Wo R
514 Flee the Darkness U
515 Iaijutsu Art C
516 Imperial Ambassadorship R
517 Imperial Edicts C
518 In Search of the Future C
519 In Time of War U
520 Overconfidence C
521 Purity of Spirit C
522 Purity of the Seven Thunders R
523 Ryokan's Sword C
524 Shadowlands Sickness U
525 Shokansuru U
526 Shosuro Technique
527 Single Combat U
528 The Emperor's Left Hand U
529 The Emperor's Right Hand U
530 The Noble Halls of the Akodo
531 Tides of Battle U
532 Uncertainty C
534 Way of Death
535 Mountain of the Seven Thunders R
536 Akodo Kaneka
537 Toturi Tsudao
538 Hantei Naseru
539 Toturi Sezaru
old21 Asahina Sekawa (Soul Asahina Tamako) U
old22 Asahina Kimita (Soul Asahina Tomo) U
old24 Asako Ryoma (Soul Asako Yasu) U
old34 Bayushi Churai (Soul Bayushi Dozan) C
old35 Bayushi Kaukatsu (Soul B.Goshiu) R
old36 Bayushi House Guard (Unique) R
old37 Bayushi Sunetra (Soul Bayushi Mamuro) C
old39 Bayushi Kamnan (Soul B.Tomaru) U
old40 Bayushi Norachai (Soul B.Yojiro) C
old42 Shosuro Aroru (Soul Bayushi Yokuan) U
old82 Celestial Sword of the Crab (Unique)
old83 Celestial Sword of the Crane (Unique)
old88 Doji Yasuyo (Soul Doji Kuwanan) C
old90 Shahai (Unique) R
old98 Doji House Guard (Unique) R
old99 Kakita Noritoshi (Soul Doji Jiro) C
old101 Doji Nagori (Soul Doji Shizue) C

old103 Celestial Sword of the Dragon (Unique)
old117 Eternal Halls of Shiba
old128 Festering Pit of Fu Leng (Unique) R
old129 Fields of the Dead U
old146 Satoshi (Soul Fusaki) C
old160 Golden Obi of the Sun Goddess (Unique) R
old168 Hida Tenshu (Soul Hida Amoro) U
old170 Hida House Guard (Unique) R
old173 Hiruma Tatsuya (Soul Hida Nezu) U
old174 Hida Rohiteki R
old175 Hiruma Masagaro (Soul Hiruma Kage) C
old176 Toritaka Tatsune (Soul Hida Tadashiro) C
old177 Hida Yasuhiro (Soul Hida Unari) C
old182 Togashi Nyima (Soul Hitomi Iyojin) C
old183 Togashi Genshuo (Soul Hitomi Juppun) U
old184 Hitomi Vedau (Soul Hitomi Kagetora) U
old196 Akodo Tadenori (Soul Ikoma Gunjin) U
old197 Ikoma Sume (Soul Ikoma Kaoku) U
old208 Agasha Hamanari (Soul I.Norikazu)(U.) R
old210 Isawa Riake (Soul Isawa Tomo) U
old211 Horiuchi Shem-Zhe (Soul Iuchi Takaai) U
old218 Kaiu Umasu (Soul Kaiu Utsu) U
old219 Kakita Kaiten R
old220 Kakita Atoshi (Soul Kakita Torikago) U
old223 Kakita Nanami (Soul Kakita Yuri) U
old228 Ki-Rin (Unique) R
old230 Kitsune Ryukan (Soul Kitsune Shudo) C
old250 Celestial Sword of the Lion (Unique)
old255 Nir'um'tuk (Soul Mack'uk) C
old260 Market Place
old265 Matsu House Guard (Unique) R
old266 Matsu Ketsui (Unique) R
old267 Ikoma Otemi (Soul Matsu Mori) C
old268 Matsu Nimuro (Soul Matsu Tsuko) (Uni) R
old270 Matsu Hataki (Soul Matsu Turi) C
old274 Mirumoto Temoru (Soul M. Hitomi) C
old275 Mirumoto House Guard (Unique) R
old276 Mirumoto Daisuke (Soul M. Sukune) U
old278 Mirumoto Rosanjin (Soul M. Taki) C
old279 Mirumoto Uso R
old284 Moto Chagatai (Soul Moto Soro) C
old285 Moto Kadu-kai (Soul Moto Toyotami) U
old308 Oracle of Earth (Unique) U
old309 Oracle of Fire (Unique) U
old310 Oracle of the Void (Unique) U
old311 Oracle of Water (Unique) U
old312 Oracle of Wind (Unique) U
old313 Gakochun (Soul Orschat) C
old320 Celestial Sword of the Phoenix (Unique)
old337 Rattling Conjurer C
old356 Zin'tch (Soul Ropp'tch'tch) (Unique) R
old363 Celestial Sword of the Scorpion (Unique)
old367 Ukuro (Soul of Seikua) C
old369 Yakamo's Claw (Unique)
old374 Shiba House Guard (Unique) R
old375 Shiba Kai (Soul Shiba Katsuda) C
old376 Shiba Yoma (Soul Shiba Kyukyo) U
old378 Shiba Ningen R
old383 Shinjo Maku (Soul Shinjo Hanari) U
old384 Shinjo House Guard (Unique) R
old387 Shinjo Osema (Soul Shinjo Tashima) C
old389 Shosuro Turaki (Soul Shosuro Taushui) C
old429 Kan'ok'tichek (Soul of Tchickchuk) C
old455 Isawa Sayuri (Soul Nameless One) (Uni) R
old484 Unexpected Allies (Experienced) U
old485 Celestial Sword of the Unicorn (Unique)
old501 Hida Wukau (Soul Yasuki Nokatsu) C
old502 Yoee'tr U
old508 Bayushi Kwanchai (Soul B.Tangen) C
old533 Voitagi (Soul Uragirimono) C
old540 Doji Tanitsu (Soul Kakita Yoshi) U
old541 Hoshi Eisai R

2002 Legend of the Five Rings 1,000 Years of Darkness

COMPLETE SET (94) 100.00 200.00
RELEASED IN SEPTEMBER 2002
1 A Fallen Friend .40 1.00
2 A Wish Granted 1.25 3.00
3 Another Hero Falls 1.50 4.00
4 Aramoro's Promise 3.00 8.00
5 Asako Kinyue 1.25 3.00
6 Ashalan Blade 1.25 3.00
7 Ashura 2.00 5.00
8 Bayushi Aramoro (Experienced KYD) 3.00 8.00
9 Birth of the New Hantei 1.00 2.50
10 Bloodspeaker's Altar 1.25 3.00
11 Burial Mound .60 1.50
12 Candas 1.25 3.00
13 Chamber of the Dark Council 1.00 2.50
14 Child of Fu Leng 1.25 3.00
15 Chithith 2.00 5.00
16 Chuda Retainer 1.25 3.00
17 Daidoji Uji (Experienced 2) 3.00 8.00
18 Dark Emperor's Blessing 1.00 2.50
19 Dark Ring of Air 1.00 2.50
20 Dark Ring of Earth 1.00 2.50
21 Dark Ring of Fire 3.00 8.00
22 Dark Ring of the Void 1.00 2.50
23 Dark Ring of Water 1.25 3.00
24 Dim Mak .40 1.00
25 Everyone Dies .40 1.00
26 False Scroll .60 1.50
27 Gifts and Favors 1.00 2.50
28 Goju Hitomi (Experienced 3 Mirumoto Hitomi) 2.00 5.00
29 Hakumei 1.00 2.50
30 Hantei Kachiko (Experienced 3 Bayushi Kachiko) 10.00 25.00
31 Hantei the 39th 4.00 10.00
32 Hellbeast 1.00 2.50
33 Heroic Sacrifice 1.50 4.00
34 Hida Yakamo (Experienced 3 KYD) 8.00 20.00
35 Hitomi's Choice 1.00 2.50
36 Honzo .40 1.00
37 Horiochi Shoan (Experienced) 1.25 3.00
38 Hoturi the Heartless (Experienced 3 Doji Hoturi) 8.00 20.00
39 I Give You My Name 1.25 3.00
40 Ikoma Ujiaki (Experienced 2 KYD) 1.00 2.50
41 Importune Kami 3.00 8.00
42 Isawa Tsuke (Experienced 2) 2.50 6.00
43 Ishada 1.25 3.00
44 Island Sanctuary .40 1.00
45 Kage (Experienced 3 KYD Akodo Kage) 1.00 2.50
46 Kuni Osaku 1.00 2.50
47 Kuni Yori (Experienced 2 KYD) 1.25 3.00
48 Kuruma Date 1.00 2.50
49 Kuruma Seiro 1.00 2.50
50 Lesser of Two Evils 1.00 2.50
51 Matsu Masutaro 2.00 5.00
52 Moto Kumari .40 1.00
53 Mountain of Shadows 1.00 2.50
54 Musha 1.25 3.00
55 Obsidian and Jade .40 1.00
56 Obsidian Magistrate 1.25 3.00
57 Obsidian Mine .40 1.00
58 Oracle of Thunder (Experienced) 1.25 3.00
59 Otaku Kamoko (Experienced 3 KYD) 3.00 8.00
60 Parasitic Oni .40 1.00
61 Pick Your Battles 2.00 5.00
62 Pointless Sacrifice 1.00 2.50
63 Radakast (Experienced 2) 1.00 2.50
64 Ray of Hope .40 1.00
65 Ruins of Otosan Uchi 1.25 3.00
66 Seppun Matsuo 1.50 4.00
67 Shahai no Yokai 1.00 2.50
68 Sharp-Sharp Stick 1.00 2.50
69 Shashakar (Experienced 2) 1.25 3.00
70 Shiba Tsukune (Experienced 2 KYD) 1.25 3.00
71 Shosuro Nabukazo 1.00 2.50
72 Snak .40 1.00
73 Soul of the Grand Master .40 1.00
74 Swallowed by the Sea 1.00 2.50
75 Tadaka's Last Wish 1.00 2.50
76 Tadaka's Sacrifice 1.00 2.50
77 The Darkest Shadow 1.00 2.50
78 The Imperial Palace of Fu Leng 8.00 20.00
79 The Jade Hand (Experienced) 2.00 5.00
80 The Maw 1.25 3.00
81 The Thunders Fall 1.25 3.00
82 Togashi Mitsu (Experienced 2 KYD) 2.00 5.00
83 Togashi Sunshen 1.00 2.50
84 Togashi's Prison 1.00 2.50
85 Toku (Experienced 2 KYD) 1.00 2.50
86 Tosekiki 1.00 2.50
87 Toturi (Experienced 3 KYD) 12.00 30.00
88 Toturi's Defeat .40 1.00
89 Toturi's Grave 1.25 3.00
90 Usagi Masashi .40 1.00
91 Vengeful Kami .40 1.00
92 Yogo Junzo (Experienced 2) 3.00 8.00
93 Yoritomo (Experienced 2 KYD) 12.00 30.00
94 Zanshar .40 1.00

2002 Legend of the Five Rings Broken Blades

COMPLETE SET (156) 25.00 60.00
BOOSTER BOX (48 PACKS) 20.00 40.00
BOOSTER PACK (11 CARDS) 1.00 2.00
RELEASED IN AUGUST 2002
1 A Time for Action U .20 .50
2 Agasha Chieh C .10 .20
3 Akodo Fumio C .10 .20
4 Akodo Hakuseki U .20 .50
5 Akodo Yobi U .40 1.00
6 Ancient Promise U .20 .50
7 Armor of the Mountain U .20 .50
8 Asahina Sekawa (Experienced) R 1.25 3.00
9 Asako Bairei R 1.00 2.50
10 At Your Command C .10 .20
11 Badge of Purity C .10 .20
12 Banzai Charge C .10 .20
13 Bayushi Katai C .10 .20
14 Bayushi Yaro C .10 .20
15 Berserker Rage R 1.25 3.00
16 Blessed Dojo C .10 .20
17 Blessed Ward C .10 .20
18 Blood in the Shinomen U .20 .50
19 Boundless Sight R 1.25 3.00
20 Brilliant Armor C .10 .20
21 Burning Blade C .10 .20
22 Choke the Soul R 1.00 2.50
23 Chukandomo R 1.25 3.00
24 City of Gold U .20 .50
25 Conscription R 1.00 2.50
26 Consumption C .10 .20
27 Corruption's Price C .10 .20
28 Cut Them Off U .25 .60
29 Daidoji Heizo C .10 .20
30 Daidoji Merchants U .40 1.00
31 Dangerous Extremes R .60 1.50
32 Dark Oracle of Air R .60 1.50
33 Deep in Meditation R .60 1.50
34 Devout Acolyte C .10 .20
35 Dirty Fighting C .10 .20
36 Doji Akiko R .60 1.50
37 Doji Jotaro C .10 .20
38 Draw Them Out C .10 .20
39 Embargo U .20 .50
40 Entrenchment U .20 .50
41 Falcon Messengers C .10 .20
42 Field of Amaterasu C .10 .20
43 Gaheris No Shiryo R .60 1.50
44 Garen U .20 .50
45 Gunso C .10 .20
46 Harsh Winter R .60 1.50
47 Hida Advisor U .20 .50
48 Hida Kuon (Experienced 2) F .40 1.00
49 Hida Reiha (Experienced) R .60 1.50
50 Hida Tokichiro C .10 .20
51 Hiruma Ryuichi C .10 .20
52 Hitomi Eichiko U .20 .50
53 Hitomi Hogai U .40 1.00
54 Honor Is My Blade U .20 .50
55 Hound of the Lost U .20 .50
56 I Give You My Sword U .20 .50
57 Iaijutsu Technique R .60 1.50
58 Ide Sadanobu C .10 .20
59 Ikoma Otemi (Experienced) R 1.00 2.50
60 Iron Defenders U .10 .20
61 Isawa Izumi C .10 .20
62 Isawa Yoriko U .20 .50
63 Iuchi Hari U .20 .50
64 Jade Vein C .10 .20
65 Jotei R 1.25 3.00
66 Kaelung R .60 1.50
67 Katsu C .10 .20
68 Kisada's Fist R .60 1.50
69 Kisada's Shrine R .60 1.50
70 Kozue U .25 .60
71 Lady Moon's Curse C .10 .20
72 Lesser Shrine C .10 .20
73 Lobbyists U .20 .50
74 Loyal Yojimbo C .10 .20
75 Maho Bujin U .20 .50
76 Make Your Choice C .10 .20
77 Matsu Makiko C .10 .20
78 Mirumoto Shokan C .10 .20
79 Moshi Jukio R .60 1.50
80 Moth Tattoo U .20 .50
81 Moto Kubulai F 1.25 3.00
82 Muchitsujo R 1.25 3.00
83 My Father's Weapon C .10 .20
84 Mystic Dojo C .10 .20
85 No More Games, Yasuki U .20 .50
86 Ogre Hag R .60 1.50
87 Open the Waves C .10 .20
88 Open Warfare U .40 1.00
89 Overwhelmed R .60 1.50
90 Paddock U .20 .50
91 Palm Strike R .60 1.50
92 Path of the Dragon Star U .20 .50
93 Perfect Silence R .60 1.50
94 Petition Forgiveness U .20 .50
95 Pirate Wharf U .20 .50
96 Plumb the Darkness U .20 .50
97 Port Town C .10 .20
98 Private Augury U .20 .50
99 Quest for Guidance R .60 1.50
100 Ravenous Podlings R .60 1.50
101 Razor's Edge Dojo F .40 1.00
102 Relentless Assault U .20 .50
103 Rice Paddy U .20 .50
104 Righteous Protection R .60 1.50
105 Rising Sun Tattoo U .25 .60
106 Run Him Down U .25 .60
107 Sacred Gong C .10 .20
108 Sailors for Hire C .10 .20
109 Sampan C .10 .20
110 Scroll Cache R 1.25 3.00
111 Seas of Shadow R .60 1.50
112 Seductive Kansen R .60 1.50
113 Seiko No Shiryo R .60 1.50
114 Shadow Dragon U .25 .60
115 Shiba Hayoto U .20 .50
116 Shinjo Inoue C .10 .20
117 Shinjo Noriyori U .20 .50
118 Shiro Shinjo F .40 1.00
119 Shosuro Yudoka (Experienced) F .40 1.00
120 Shrine of Stone R .60 1.50
121 Slaying Fields C .10 .20
122 Solitary Engagement U .20 .50
123 Stand Aside U .20 .50
124 Tamori Shiatung (Experienced) R .60 1.50
125 Tamori Shukuen C .10 .20
126 Ten Thousand As One U .20 .50
127 The Dark Daughter's Caress R .60 1.50
128 The Importunate Vu C .10 .20
129 The Shadowed Tower of the Shosuro F .40 1.00
130 The Shogun's Fealty U .25 .60
131 The Steel Throne R .60 1.50
132 The Wolf's Proposal U .20 .50
133 Three-Pronged Assault C .10 .20
134 Time of Loyalty R .60 1.50
135 Tonfa C .10 .20
136 Toturi's Shrine R .60 1.50
137 Trade Hub C .10 .20
138 Traveling Merchants U .20 .50
139 Tsuruchi Heishiro C .10 .20
140 Tsuruchi Yutaka C .10 .20
141 Twisted Forest C .10 .20
142 Uona No Shiryo R .60 1.50
143 Veteran Bushi U .20 .50
144 We Will Have Revenge R 1.00 2.50
145 White Stag Burns R .60 1.50
146 Will of Air R .60 1.50
147 Will of Earth R .60 1.50
148 Will of Fire R .60 1.50
149 Will of Water R .60 1.50
150 Yasuki Jinn-Kuen U .20 .50
151 Yasuki Palaces R 1.25 3.00
152 Yogo Hatsumi U .20 .50
153 Yogo Tjeki (Experienced) R 1.00 2.50
154 Yoritomo Kumiko R 1.25 3.00
155 Yoritomo Soetsuko U .25 .60
156 Yoshi No Shiryo R .60 1.50

2002 Legend of the Five Rings Dark Allies

COMPLETE SET (161) 30.00 80.00
BOOSTER BOX (48 PACKS) 20.00 40.00
BOOSTER PACK (11 CARDS) 1.00 2.00
RELEASED IN APRIL 2002
1 Agetoki no Shiryo R 1.00 2.50
2 Aid of the Grand Master U .40 1.00
3 Akodo Jusho U .20 .50
4 Akodo Map R .60 1.50
5 Akodo Ninsei U .20 .50
6 Asahina Keitaro U .20 .50
7 Asahina's Blessing R 1.00 2.50
8 Asako Hirariko (Experienced 2 Hirariko) F 1.25 3.00
9 Asako Misao (Experienced) R 1.00 2.50
10 Asako Yuya U .20 .50
11 Auspicious House R .60 1.50
12 Baku no Oni C .10 .20
13 Bayushi Hirono C .10 .20
14 Bayushi Norachai (Experienced) R 1.00 2.50
15 Bayushi Ogura C .10 .20
16 Bayushi Toru U 1.00 2.50
17 Be the Breeze C .10 .20
18 Bitter Vengeance R .60 1.50
19 Blackened Honor U .20 .50
20 Blade of Truths R 1.25 3.00
21 Boastful Proclamation U .20 .50
22 Break the Wave C .10 .20
23 Celestial Sword of the Mantis R 2.00 5.00
24 City of Lightning F 1.00 2.50
25 City of the Lost C .10 .20
26 Clear Water Village C .10 .20
27 Construction Crew R 1.00 2.50
28 Court Intrigue R .60 1.50
29 Cowardly Conscripts U .20 .50
30 Curse of Weakness U .20 .50
31 Deep Earth Sanctum R .60 1.50
32 Defend Yourself! U .20 .50
33 Doji Kazo R 1.00 2.50
34 Doji Midoru C .10 .20
35 Doji Okakura C .10 .20
36 Doji Seishiro U .25 .60
37 Doomsayers U .20 .50
38 Drain the Soul U .20 .50
39 Draw From Within R 1.00 2.50
40 Ebbing Strength R .60 1.50
41 Face Me! U .25 .60
42 Faith In My Clan R 1.25 3.00
43 Gale Force Winds R .60 1.50
44 Gift of the Water Dragon C .10 .20
45 Goblin Slingers C .10 .20
46 Goju Kyoden U .20 .50
47 Grim Mempo C .10 .20
48 Heavy Armor C .10 .20
49 Hida Hitoshi C .10 .20
50 Hida Kosho U .40 1.00
51 Hida Shara C .10 .20
52 Hiruma Slayers U .25 .60
53 Hitomi Maya U .20 .50
54 Honor's Lesson Dojo R .60 1.50
55 Hoshi Tadao U .20 .50
56 Hoshi Takeji C .10 .20
57 House of Fates R .60 1.50
58 Ik'krt U .25 .60
59 Ikoma Fujimaro F .25 .60
60 Ikoma Goro C .10 .20
61 Inspiration C .10 .20
62 Isawa Maasaki C .10 .20
63 It's a Trap! U .20 .50
64 Ivory Isles Mercenaries C .10 .20
65 Jagged Earth C .10 .20
66 Junnosuke (Experienced Mirumoto Junnosuke) R .60 1.50
67 Kabuki Mask R .60 1.50
68 Kaiu Namboku R .60 1.50
69 Kanbe no Shiryo R .60 1.50
70 Kaneka's Blockade R .60 1.50
71 Kaneka's Strength U .20 .50
72 Kawaru Coins R .60 1.50
73 Ki-Rin's Blessing U .20 .50
74 Kitsu Hisashi C .10 .20
75 Koan C .10 .20
76 Kobune Port C .10 .20
77 Kyojin's Blade U .20 .50
78 Kyuden Agasha F .40 1.00
79 Lies C .10 .20
80 Light a Candle C .10 .20
81 Light of the Kami C .10 .20
82 Living Death R .60 1.50
83 Lost Souls R .60 1.50
84 Make Them Pay R 1.25 3.00
85 Massive Power R .60 1.50
86 Mirumoto Zenko C .10 .20
87 Miya Gensaiken (Experienced Oni no Pekkle) R1.00 2.50
88 Moshi Junichi F .25 .60
89 Moshi Mogai F .40 1.00
90 Moto Chaozhu R .60 1.50
91 Moto Feng U .20 .50
92 Moto Quing C .10 .20
93 Moto Steed C .10 .20
94 Naishi R 1.00 2.50
95 Naseru's Strength U .20 .50
96 New Formation U .20 .50
97 Nikushimi R 1.00 2.50
98 No Failure R .60 1.50
99 No Hiding Place C .10 .20
100 Omen U .20 .50
101 One Sword C .10 .20
102 Oni Horde U .20 .50
103 Patience U .20 .50
104 Personal Sohei R .60 1.50
105 Pillaged R .60 1.50
106 Raise the Dead R .60 1.50
107 Restless Zokujin C .10 .20
108 Roaming Caravan U .20 .50
109 Ronin Village R 1.00 2.50
110 Rubble of Beiden Pass U .20 .50
111 Selecting the Chancellor U .20 .50
112 Sezaru's Mask R .60 1.50
113 Sezaru's Strength U .20 .50
114 Shackled Oni C .10 .20
115 Shiba Ilami C .10 .20
116 Shiba's Shrine R .60 1.50
117 Shinjo Xushen U .20 .50
118 Shinsei's Staff C .10 .20
119 Shiro Matsu F 1.00 2.50
120 Short Season R .60 1.50
121 Shosuro Koneko U .20 .50
122 Shrieking Mujina C .10 .20
123 Shrine of Reverse Fortunes R .60 1.50
124 Soshi Kiyo U .20 .50
125 Strength in Unity C .10 .20
126 Taken Unawares C .10 .20
127 Tamori Yamabushi C .10 .20
128 Teeth of Osano-Wo R 1.25 3.00
129 Te'tik'kir (Experienced) R .60 1.50
130 The Future Laid Bare U .20 .50
131 The Wandering Monk C .10 .20
132 Thunder's Kiss C .10 .20
133 T'k C .10 .20
134 Togashi Matsuo R .60 1.50
135 Toturi Koshei U .20 .50
136 Trusted Advisor U .20 .50
137 Tsudao's Strength U .20 .50
138 Tsuno Nintai C .10 .20
139 Tsuruchi Hiro F .25 .60
140 Tsuruchi Nobumoto F .40 1.00
141 Uji no Shiryo R .60 1.50
142 Unprepared R 1.25 3.00
143 Unlested Troops U .20 .50
144 Utaku Keyo C .10 .20
145 Vengeful Ronin U .20 .50
146 Veteran Samurai R 1.25 3.00
147 Violence Behind Courtliness City C .10 .20
148 Voice of the Shiryo U .20 .50
149 Wall of Steel U .20 .50
150 Wasp Tattoo U .20 .50
151 Wave Tattoo U .20 .50
152 Whistling Bulb Arrow C .10 .20
153 Wikki'thich-hie A'tck R .60 1.50
154 Yoritomo Gombei U .20 .50
155 Yoritomo Heishiro C .10 .20
156 Yoritomo Ikemoto U .20 .50
157 Yoritomo Naizen F .40 1.00
158 Yoritomo Sen F .25 .60
159 Yoritomo Sumio C .10 .20
160 Yoritomo's Kama R .60 1.50
161 You Are Weak C .10 .20

2002 Legend of the Five Rings The Fall of Otosan Uchi

1 A Champion's Strike R 1.25 3.00
2 A New Path U .20 .50
3 Agasha Oshu C .10 .20
4 Agasha Yubisaki U .20 .50
5 Aid of the Fortunes U .20 .50
6 Akodo Tsuri U .20 .50
7 Ambush Pits C .10 .20
8 Armed and Ready C .10 .20
9 Arrow of Purity C .10 .20
10 Balance in Nothingness U .40 1.00
11 Bayushi Kaukatsu (Experienced) R 1.25 3.00
12 Bayushi Seiryo C .10 .20
13 Bayushi Sharaku U .20 .50
14 Beachhead U .20 .50
15 Blood Money U .20 .50
16 Bonds of Fate C .10 .20
17 Broken Words U .20 .50
18 Carrion's Breath C .10 .20
19 Chaldera R 1.00 2.50
20 Ch'tppu'kich R .60 1.50
21 Consuming Darkness R 1.00 2.50
22 Daidoji Ekiken C .10 .20
23 Dark Eyes on the Wall R .60 1.50
24 Denkyu no Shiryo R .60 1.50
25 Dojo Raiden R .60 1.50
26 Dotanuki C .10 .20
27 Earthly Yearnings U .20 .50
28 Eye of the Needle C .10 .20
29 Far and Wide U .20 .50
30 Favor for a Favor R .60 1.50
31 Fields of Grain U .20 .50
32 Fires of the Phoenix R .60 1.50
33 Footman's Yari C .10 .20
34 Forgery R .60 1.50
35 Forward Guard C .10 .20
36 Fury of the Damned U .20 .50
37 Glick C .10 .20
38 Hand of the Shogun R .60 1.50
39 Hida Ishi U .20 .50
40 Hida Yagimaki C .10 .20
41 Hideo Spawn U .25 .60
42 Hiruma Tatsuzo R 1.00 2.50
43 Hitaka U .20 .50
44 Hoshi Chuichi F (Dragon) 1.25 3.00
45 H-Tach'ch U .20 .50
46 Hungry Ghost U .20 .50
47 Hunting Cabin R .60 1.50
48 Hurricane Tattoo U .20 .50
49 Ikoma Kyuso U .20 .50
50 Imperial Messenger U .20 .50
51 Imperial Proclamation C .10 .20
52 Inferno R .60 1.50
53 Informant R .60 1.50
54 Isawa Nodotai (Experienced) R .60 1.50
55 Iuchi Huasha U .20 .50
56 Jester R .60 1.50
57 Kaeru Contracter C .10 .20
58 Kaiu Tasuku C .10 .20
59 Kakita Instructor R .60 1.50
60 Kakita Munemori U .20 .50
61 Kakita Nakazo F (Crane) 1.00 2.50
62 Kakita Yariga C .10 .20
63 Kansen Haunting U .20 .50
64 Keen Eye U .25 .60
65 Kirei C .10 .20
66 Kiseru C .10 .20
67 Kitsu Juri R .60 1.50
68 Kjgkt R .60 1.50
69 Konetsu R 1.25 3.00
70 Kukojin (Experienced 2 Hitomi Kukojin) R .60 1.50
71 Kyofu (Experienced Hida Kuroda) R 1.25 3.00
72 Kyuden Doji F (Crane) .60 1.50
73 Kyuden Gotei F (Mantis) .60 1.50
74 Led Into Darkness C .10 .20

75 Legendary Strength C .10 .20
76 Let Courage Guide Me U .20 .50
77 Lost Ashigaru C .10 .20
78 Master Sculptor C .10 .20
79 Mastu Reishiko C .10 .20
80 Matsu Masakado C .10 .20
81 Menhari-gata R 1.00 2.50
82 Mirumoto Tachiyama U .20 .50
83 Mirumoto's Haori U .20 .50
84 Moneylender R 1.00 2.50
85 Monkey Magistrates U .20 .50
86 Moshi Hinome C .10 .20
87 Moto Sanpao C .10 .20
88 Moto Tsusung U .20 .50
89 Mystic R .60 1.50
90 Now Face Me U .20 .50
91 Ogre Hordes C .10 .20
92 Omoidasu C .10 .20
93 One Will Fall U .20 .50
94 Perfect Attunement R .60 1.50
95 Pile of Stones C .10 .20
96 Playing With Madness C .10 .20
97 Precise Orders R .60 1.50
98 Private Dojo U .25 .60
99 Pulse of the Black River U .20 .50
100 Purity C .10 .20
101 Recruiting Drive C .10 .20
102 Run For Your Lives! U .20 .50
103 Scouting Maneuvers U .20 .50
104 Shahai's Fan U .20 .50
105 Shiba Takeishi C .10 .20
106 Shiba Yoma (Experienced) R .60 1.50
107 Shinjo Horsebow C .10 .20
108 Shinjo Rao C .10 .20
109 Shinjo Shono (Experienced 2) R .60 1.50
110 Shiro Tamori F (Dragon) .60 1.50
111 Shosuro Miyo C .10 .20
112 Show of Good Faith R 1.25 3.00
113 Shrine of the Moon U .20 .50
114 Shrine of the Sun U .40 1.00
115 Snake Tattoo U .20 .50
116 Song of Corruption R .60 1.50
117 Soshi Kiyo (Experienced) R .60 1.50
118 Storm Legion R .60 1.50
119 Strike at the Soul U .20 .50
120 Summon the Dead R .60 1.50
121 Superior Swordplay C .10 .20
122 Tamori Tsukiro C .10 .20
123 Tempting Kansen U .20 .50
124 Terror U .20 .50
125 The Anvil's Blessing R .60 1.50
126 The Deathless U .20 .50
127 The Seppun Temples R .60 1.50
128 The Shadow's Claw R 2.00 5.00
129 The Time Is Not Right U .20 .50
130 Third Whisker Warren C .10 .20
131 Togashi Kansuke C .10 .20
132 Togashi's Shrine R .60 1.50
133 Traveling Ronin R 1.25 3.00
134 Trickster Spirits C .10 .20
135 Tsuno Blade U .20 .50
136 Tsuno House Guard R .60 1.50
137 Tsuno Sochi C .10 .20
138 Tsuruchi Hunters C .25 .60
139 Tsuruchi Technique C .10 .20
140 Tsuruchi Terao C .10 .20
141 Tsutomo no Shiryo R .10 .20
142 Unicorn Striders C .60 1.50
143 Unquiet Spirits R .10 .20
144 Unraveling C .60 1.50
145 Using the Wish R .10 .20
146 Vengeful Dead U .60 1.50
147 Watanabe Builders C .20 .50
148 Wazinu no Yokai R .10 .20
149 Wear Him Down U .60 1.50
150 Whispers R .20 .50
151 Words Cut Like Steel R .60 1.50
152 Yasuki Yukinga U .60 1.50
153 Yokutsu no Shiryo R .20 .50
154 Yoritomo Kililae U .60 1.50
155 Yoritomo Komori (Experienced) F (Mantis) .20 .50
156 Yoritomo Yoyonagi R .60 1.50

2002 Legend of the Five Rings L5R Experience

1 Glimpse of the Unicorn
2 Jade Works
9 Asahina Kimita
14 Yasuki Hachi
16 Contentious Terrain
17 Diversionary Tactics
18 Duty to the Clan
19 Entrapping Terrain
1b Archers
20 High Morale
21 Iaijutsu Challenge
22 Iaijutsu Duel
24 Elite Spearmen
25 Light Infantry
26 Medium Infantry
28 Naginata
29 Wakizashi
2b Armory
30 Hitsu-Do
31 Purity of Spirit
32 Strength of My Ancestors
3b Asahina Handen
42 Small Farm
43 Bayushi Churai
48 Soshi Angai
50 Charge
53 Kolat Assassin
54 Rallying Cry
57 Ashigaru Archers
58 Heavy Infantry
61 Spearmen
62 Dai Tsuchi
63 Jade Bow
64 Kaze-do
65 Remember the Mountain
7b Bayushi Kwanchai
8b Bayushi Paneki
9b Bayushi Shixiang
10b Bayushi Tai
11b Block Supply Lines
15b Daidoji Enai
16b Daidoji Gudeta
18b Doji Nagori
19b Doji Yasuyo
20b Dragon's Claw Katana
23b Encircled Terrain
25b Geisha House
32b In Time of War
35b Kabuki Theater Troupe
38b Kosaten Shiro
40b Marketplace
43b Port
44b Provision Storehouse
48b Sanctified Temple
49b Silk Works
50b Slander
55b Test of Might
56b The Hiruma Dojo
57b The Towers of the Yogo
58b Toturi Sezaru
61b You are the Crane Clan...
62b You are the Scorpion Clan...

2003 Legend of the Five Rings Diamond Edition

1 Are You With Me? U
2 Birth of the Anvil R
3 Birth of the Sword R
4 Boastful Proclamation
5 Boundless Sight R
6 Celestial Alignment R
7 Chrysanthemum Festival R
8 Doom of the Dark Lord R
9 Far From the Empire R
10 The Heavy Shadow of Fear U
11 Imperial Ambassadorship
12 Imperial Quest U
13 In Time of War U
14 Kachiko's Promises R
15 The Shogun's Fealty
16 Moon and Sun U
17 My Enemy's Weakness R
18 Naga Storm Mirumoto Mountain U
19 New Emerald Champion R
20 Norikazu's Ravings U
21 Poetry Contest
22 Proposal of Peace
23 Regions of Rokugan
24 Restoring the Doji Treasury U
25 Shadow of the Dark God U
26 Wisdom Gained U
27 Blacksmiths C
28 Copper Mine
29 Daidoji Merchants U
30 Devout Acolyte C
31 Dragon Dancers
32 Fantastic Gardens U
33 Geisha House
34 Gifts and Favors
35 Gold Mine
36 Grove of the Five Masters U
37 Honor's Lesson Dojo R
38 House of the Red Lotus C
39 Iron Mine
40 Ki-Rin's Shrine U
41 Ki-Rin's Shrine (Experienced) U
42 Kisada's Shrine R
43 Kobune Port
44 Lion Scout R
45 Marketplace
46 Master of Bushido C
47 Master Painter U
48 Oracle of the Void U
49 Phoenix Library R
50 Treasure Hoard
51 Rice Paddy C
52 Sanctified Temple
53 Scorpion Distracter R
54 Shackled Oni C
55 Shadowlands Bastion R
56 Shinmaki Monastery C
57 Shokansuru
58 Shrine Of Stone U
59 Silk Works C
60 Silver Mine
61 Simple Huts C
62 Stables
63 Tangen's Lies U
64 Trading Grounds
65 Unicorn Marketeer R
66 Hida Hitoshi C
67 Hida Kosho U
68 Hida Kuon (Experienced 3)
69 Hida Reiha (Experienced) R
70 Hida Shara C
71 Hida Sunao C
72 Hida Tenshu C
73 Hida Isamu R
74 Hida Utaemon U
75 Hiruma Todori C
76 Kuni Tansho U
77 Kaiu Hisayuki C
78 Hiruma Ashihei C
79 Daidoji Gudeta U
80 Daidoji Akagi U
81 Doji Gombei C
82 Doji Jotaro C
83 Doji Kurohito (Experienced 2)
84 Doji Nagori C
85 Doji Domotai C
86 Doji Tanitsu (Experienced 2) R
87 Kakita Gosha C
88 Kakita Mai C
89 Kakita Mai (Experienced) R
90 Kakita Masazumi C
91 Kakita Korihime (Experienced) R
92 Hitomi Daisetsu C
93 Hoshi Wayan (Experienced 2) R
94 Kitsuki Iweko U
95 Togashi Teijo C
96 Mirumoto Gonkuro C
97 Mirumoto Tsuge C
98 Hitomi Mae C
99 Tamori Chieko C
100 Tamori Hiroko C
101 Tamori Shaitung C
102 Tamori Shaitung (Experienced) R
103 Togashi Jusai U
104 Togashi Satsu (Experienced)
105 Akodo Tadenori C
106 Akodo Yobi U
107 Ikoma Sume C
108 Matsu Ikari C
109 Akodo Kurako U
110 Akodo Mino (Experienced) R
111 Matsu Aoiko C
112 Matsu Mabuchi C
113 Matsu Kenji R
114 Matsu Nimuro (Experienced)
115 Matsu Michiho C
116 Matsu Atasuke C
117 Akodo Shigetoshi U
118 Yoritomo Chimori C
119 Yoritomo Hiroya C
120 Moshi Kalani C
121 Moshi Amika C
122 Tsuruchi Hiro C
123 Tsuruchi Hiro (Experienced) R
124 Tsuruchi Nobumoto C
125 Tsuruchi Isunori C
126 Yoritomo Ukyo U
127 Yoritomo Kumiko (Experienced)
128 Yoritomo Masasue (Experienced) R
129 Yoritomo Sen C
130 Yoritomo Kajiko U
131 Agasha Chieh C
132 Asako Naokazu C
133 Isawa Ihara U
134 Isawa Toshiji C
135 Isawa Moriko U
136 Isawa Yoriko U
137 Isawa Washichi (Experienced 2) R
138 Shiba Bunjaku C
139 Shiba Mirabu (Experienced 2)
140 Agasha Seruma C
141 Shiba Danjuro C
142 Shiba Tsukimi C
143 Ik'krt C
144 Kan'ok'ticheck (Experienced)
145 Pep'trchek C
146 Nir'um'tuk C
147 Ratling Conjuror C
148 Ratling Scavenger C
149 Ashi U
150 Ruantek C
151 T'k C
152 Te'tik'kir (Experienced) R
153 Yoee'trr C
154 Ep'kee U
155 Zin'tch R
156 Bayushi Tsimaru (Experienced) R
157 Shosuro Toson (Experienced) U
158 Shosuro Toson C
159 Bayushi Churai C
160 Bayushi Kaukatsu R
161 Bayushi Sunetra (Experienced)
162 Bayushi Tai C
163 Shosuro Higatsuku C
164 Bayushi Shunko C
165 Soshi Angai C
166 Shosuro Maru C
167 Yogo Soto C
168 Yogo Tjeki R
169 Fushiki no Oni C
170 Gekido no Oni C
171 Goblin Wizard C
172 Iuchiban
173 Jama Suru (Experienced) R
174 Chuda Masaru C
175 Kukanchi C
176 Seppun Jin (Experienced 3) R
177 Kyoso no Oni U
178 Mohai U
179 Ogre Bushi U
180 Voitagi C
181 Yosuchi C
182 Air Dragon R
183 Chiang-Tsu R
184 Earth Dragon R
185 Fire Dragon R
186 Utagawa C
187 Ki-Rin R
188 The Mad Ronin R
189 Thunder Dragon R
190 Koto C
191 Void Dragon R
192 Water Dragon R
193 Iuchi Najato C
194 Moto Chagatai C
195 Moto Chagatai (Experienced 2)
196 Moto Kadu-kai U
197 Moto Reijiro C
198 Moto Zhijuan C
199 Shinjo Noriyori U
200 Shinjo Reizo C
201 Shinjo Yushiro C
202 Shinjo Xushen C
203 Shinjo Nakaga (Experienced) R
204 Utaku Etsumi (Experienced) R
205 Utaku Tama C
206 700 Soldier Plain C
207 City Of Gold C
208 Farmlands C
209 Fields of the Moon U
210 Fields of the Sun U
211 Mapped Region C
212 Mystic Ground C
213 Plains Above Evil C
214 Plains of Otosan Uchi R
215 Ratling Village C
216 Refuge of the Three Sisters C
217 Road of Dust C
218 Ryoko Owari R
219 Secluded Ravine C
220 Shadowlands Marsh U
221 Shinsei's Shrine U
222 Sorrow's Path C
223 Temples of the New Tao C
224 Tidal Land Bridge U
225 Utaku Meadows C
226 Valley of the Two Generals U
227 Violence Behind Courtliness City C
228 Along the Coast at Midnight U
229 Ambush R
230 Ashigaru Levies C
231 Assuming the Championship R
232 Avoid Fate U
233 Battlefield of Shallow Graves C
234 Be Prepared to Dig Two Graves R
235 Call to Arms C
236 Carrier Pigeon C
237 Come One at a Time C
238 Concede Defeat C
239 Confusion at Court C
240 Contested Holding R
241 Corrupted Ground
242 Retribution C
243 Rhetoric C
244 The Daimyo's Command R
245 Desperate Wager R
246 Destiny has No Secrets C
247 Dirty Politics U
248 Diversionary Tactics C
249 Dying Effort U
250 The Egg of P'an Ku R
251 The Emperor Returns U
252 Encircled Terrain C
253 Enough Talk! C
254 Explosives U
255 The Face of Fear C
256 Face of Ninube C
257 Faith in my Clan R
258 Fall on Your Knees U
259 Feign Death R
260 Focus R
261 For the Empire C
262 Geisha Assassin R
263 Honor's Cost C
264 I Believed in You U
265 Iaijutsu Challenge C
266 Iaijutsu Lesson
267 Imperial Edicts C
268 In Search of the Future C
269 Kamoko's Charge C
270 Kharmic Strike U
271 Kolat Assassin U
272 Kolat Recruiter R
273 Let Your Spirit Guide You R
274 Loyal Yojimbo C
275 Luring Tactics U
276 Moment of Brilliance C
277 Narrow Ground C
278 Nezumi Technique
279 Ninja Kidnapper R
280 Ninja Thief C
281 No Hiding Place C
282 Open Warfare U
283 Outmaneuvered by Force C
284 Outmaneuvered in Court C
286 Overwhelmed U
287 The Path of Wisdom R
288 Plans Within Plans R
289 Political Distraction C
290 The Price of Innocence C
291 Primal Rage U
292 Spearhead C
293 Refugees C
294 Relentless Assault U
295 Remorseful Seppuku C
296 Return for Training C
297 Scroll Cache R
298 Shame U
299 Shosuro Technique
300 Show Me Your Stance C
301 Smoke and Mirrors U
302 Sneak Attack R
303 Soul's Sacrifice C
304 Stand or Run C
305 Peasant Vengeance C
306 Strength of Purity C
307 Strike at the Tail
308 Superior Strategist R
309 Suspended Terrain C
310 A Test of Courage C
311 Test of Might C
312 Three-Stone River C
313 Time of Destiny U
314 Today We Die R
315 Touching the Void C
316 Treachery and Deceit U
317 Tribute to Your House R
318 Tsuruchi Technique
319 Twisted Forest C
320 Uncertainty C
321 Unrequited Love C
322 Wedge R
323 White Shore Plain
324 White Stag Burns U
325 Wounded in Battle C
326 Akodo House Guard
327 Ashigaru Archers C
328 Ashigaru Hordes C
329 Ashigaru Spearmen C
330 Chitatchikkan C
331 Command Staff U
332 Courier C
333 Decoy R
334 Diplomatic Apprentice C
335 Elite Spearmen C
336 Empress's Guard R
337 Firestorm Legion U
338 Fortified Infantry C
339 Goblin Slingers C
340 Gunso C
341 Heavy Cavalry C
342 Heavy Infantry C
343 Heavy Mounted Infantry C
344 Hiruma Archers C
345 Hiruma House Guard
346 Hoshi House Guard
347 Imperial Honor Guard U
348 Isawa House Guard
349 Kakita House Guard
350 Kenshinzen R
351 Kobune Crew U
352 The Legion of Two Thousand R
353 Light Mounted Infantry C
354 Mantis Bushi U
355 Mantis Raiders C
356 Minor Shugenja C
357 Moto Steed C
358 Clay Horse C
359 Ogre Elite
360 Ogre Warriors U
361 Oni Horde U
362 Byoki no Oni C
363 Ratling Archers C
364 Ratling Bushi C
365 Ratling Scroungers U
366 Shireikan C
367 Shosuro House Guard
368 Skeletal Troops C
369 Spearmen C
370 Spirit Guide R
371 Tattered Ear Watcher
372 Tsuruchi's Legion U
373 Untested Troops C
374 Utaku House Guard
375 Veteran Bushi U
376 Veteran Samurai U
377 War Dogs U
378 Warrior Monks C
379 Yoritomo House Guard
380 Armor of Earth R
381 Blackened Claws U
382 Blade of Secrets R
383 Blade of Truths R
384 Bone of the Tattered Ear Tribe
385 Bronze Lantern U
386 Celestial Sword of the Crab
387 Celestial Sword of the Crane
388 Celestial Sword of the Dragon
389 Celestial Sword of the Lion
390 Celestial Sword of the Mantis
391 Celestial Sword of the Phoenix
392 Celestial Sword of the Scorpion
393 Celestial Sword of the Unicorn
394 Chukandomo R
395 Corrupted Jade Sliver C
396 Dai Tsuchi C
397 Daikyu U
398 Dragon Pearl R
399 The Emerald Armor R
400 Fan of Command U
401 Gunsen of Water R
402 The Imperial Standard R
403 Lessons from Kuro U
404 Mempo of the Void R
405 My Father's Weapon C
406 Obsidian Mirror U
407 Ruby of Iuchiban R
408 Takao's Jingasa C
409 Thuk-Kigi's War Machine R
410 Yakamo's Claw
411 Yoritomo's Kama R
412 Yoshi's Fan R
413 Aid of the Grand Master C
414 Bloodstrike R
415 Chasing Osano-Wo C
416 Dharma Technique U
417 Double Chi C
418 Feeding on Flesh U
419 Fist of the Earth C
420 Flee the Darkness C
421 Freezing the Lifeblood C
422 Mercy Shrouds the Earth C
423 Palm Strike R
424 Purity of Spirit C
425 Ryoshun's Last Words U
426 Touching the Soul U
427 Written in Blood R

428 Ring of Air U
429 Ring of Earth U
430 Ring of Fire U
431 Ring of the Void U
432 Ring of Water U
433 Amnesia U
434 Cloak of Night R
435 Contemplate the Void C
436 Doom of Fu Leng R
437 Earthquake C
438 Emergence of the Masters C
439 Fear's Bane C
440 Fire and Air
441 The Fire from Within C
442 The Fires That Cleanse R
443 Fist of Osano-Wo R
444 Force of Will C
445 The Kami Watch Over Me U
446 Kuro's Fire R
447 Look into the Void C
448 Purity of the Seven Thunders R
449 Ryoshun's First Gift C
450 Sympathetic Energies C
451 Tomb of Jade C
452 Walking the Way U
453 Kyuden Hida
454 Razor's Edge Dojo
455 Kakita Dueling Academy
456 Kyuden Doji
457 House of Tao
458 Shiro Mirumoto
459 Kyuden Ikoma
460 Kenson Gakka
461 Kyuden Gotei
462 Castle of the Wasp
463 Morning Glory Castle
464 Kyuden Agasha
465 Tch'tch Warrens
466 Warrens of the Nezumi
467 The Shadowed Tower Of The Shosuro
468 The Towers of the Yogo
469 The Spawning Ground
470 Temple of the Ninth Kami
471 Northern Provinces of the Moto
472 Shiro Shinjo
473 Court Intrigue
474 Berserker Rage R
475 Dragon's Strength U
476 Left Hand of the Emperor
477 Right Hand of the Emperor
478 Underhand of the Emperor
479 Voice of the Emperor
480 Black Heart of the Empire
481 Occult Murders
482 New Year's Celebration
483 Obsidian Mine
484 Block Supply Lines C
485 The Hiruma Dojo C
486 Shiba Ningen (Experienced) R
487 To Do What We Must C
488 Slaughter the Scout C
old398 The Dragon Pearl R
old2590 Doji Masazumi C
old2591 Kakita Rei (Experienced) R
old489a Utz! C
old490a Overconfidence
oldDE01 A New Wall Promo

2003 Legend of the Five Rings Heaven and Earth

COMPLETE SET (157) 30.00 80.00
BOOSTER BOX (48 PACKS) 30.00 60.00
BOOSTER PACK (11 CARDS) 1.00 2.00
RELEASED IN APRIL 2003
1 A Game of Go U .20 .50
2 A New Guardian U .20 .50
3 Accept With Honor C .10 .20
4 Akodo Rokuro C .10 .20
5 Akodo Tekkan R 1.25 3.00
6 Akodo's No-Dachi R .60 1.50
7 Ancestral Reverence R .60 1.50
8 Aramasu's Ashes R 1.25 3.00
9 Arms Merchant C .10 .20
10 Asahina Itoeko C .10 .20
11 Asako Toshi F (Phoenix) .60 1.50
12 Ashigaru Fishermen C .10 .20
13 Avalanche Tattoo U .20 .50
14 Bane of the Anvil U .20 .50
15 Bane of the Bastard U .25 .60
16 Bane of the Sword U .20 .50
17 Bane of the Wolf U .20 .50
18 Bar the Gates U .20 .50
19 Bayushi Eitarou U .20 .50
20 Bayushi Tai (Experienced) R .60 1.50
21 Blade of Slaughter U .20 .50
22 Blessed Sword C .10 .20
23 Burning Smoke C .10 .20
24 By Steel Redeemed U .20 .50
25 Celestial Imbalance U .20 .50
26 Channeling Void U .20 .50
27 Chuk'tek U .20 .50
28 Chunigo U .20 .50
29 Cove of Cursed Blades R .60 1.50
30 Crab Builders R .60 1.50
31 Critical Moment U .20 .50
32 Crude Blade C .10 .20
33 Daigotsu F (Lion, Phoenix, Shadowlands) .25 .60
34 Dark Covenant R .60 1.50
35 Dark Oracle of the Void R .60 1.50
36 Darkness Rising R .60 1.50
37 Delicate Negotiation C .10 .20
38 Deploy Scouts C .10 .20
39 Desertion U .20 .50
40 Doji Jurian U .20 .50
41 Doji Okakura (Experienced) R .60 1.50
42 Embrace the Elements R .60 1.50
43 Escape from Shadow R 1.00 2.50
44 For the Clan R .60 1.50
45 Garden of Serenity U .20 .50
46 Gargelara C .10 .20
47 Goshiu no Shiryo R .60 1.50
48 Heart of Rokugan C .10 .20
49 Hida Benjiro C .10 .20
50 Hida Hitoshi (Experienced) R .60 1.50
51 Hida War Banner C .10 .20
52 Hiruma Tsukiko C .10 .20
53 Honor's Ground C .10 .20
54 Hoshi Yoson C .10 .20
55 House of the First Stone C .10 .20
56 Ide Tang U .20 .50
57 Ikoma Fudai (Experienced) F .60 1.50
58 Ikoma Tomaru R .60 1.50
59 Introspection R 2.50 6.00
60 Isawa Junichiro C .10 .20
61 Iuchi Yue R .60 1.50
62 Jade Katana C .10 .20
63 Jade Pikemen U .20 .50
64 Jade Yari U .20 .50
65 Kaiu Waotaka U .20 .50
66 Kakita Chiyeko C .10 .20
67 Kakita Dojo U .25 .60
68 Kakita Soichi R .60 1.50
69 Kanashimi F 1.00 2.50
70 Kanji of Power U .20 .50
71 Katana of the Moon R .60 1.50
72 Kaze-no-kami's Blessing C .10 .20
73 Kikage Zumi Initiates C .20 .60
74 Kitsuki Tadashi C .10 .20
75 Kokujin's Daisho R .60 1.50
76 Kuni Rihito U .20 .50
77 Kyuden Ikoma F (Lion) .60 1.50
78 Lessons From Earth R 1.00 2.50
79 Loyalty Renewed R .60 1.50
80 Mask of the Maw (Experienced Mask of the Oni) R 1.25 3.00
81 Master of the Bells C .10 .20
82 Matsu Watako U .20 .50
83 Military Advisor C .10 .20
84 Mirumoto Kyuzo R .60 1.50
85 Morning Glory Castle F (Phoenix) .60 1.50
86 Moto Chaozhu (Experienced) R .60 1.50
87 Nairu no Oni C .10 .20
88 Noh Theater Troupe U .20 .50
89 Observe the Enemy U .20 .50
90 Obsidian Mempo of Fu Leng R .60 1.50
91 Once and Again R .60 1.50
92 Oracle of Blood U .20 .50
93 Otomo Ambassador C .10 .20
94 Outrider R .60 1.50
95 Poison Marsh U .20 .50
96 Puppet Theater Troupe U .20 .50
97 Purification R .60 1.50
98 Ransom Hostage C .10 .20
99 Rebuilt Temple U .20 .50
100 Rekai's Harriers C .10 .20
101 Rend the Soul R 2.00 5.00
102 Righteous Conviction U .20 .50
103 Sand Garden C .10 .20
104 Shamate Pass R .60 1.50
105 Shiba Gyukudo U .20 .50
106 Shiba Mirabu (Experienced) R .60 1.50
107 Shiba Yobei C .10 .20
108 Shifting Earth C .10 .20
109 Shinjo Guan C .10 .20
110 Shinjo Slings R .60 1.50
111 Shosuro Kamatari C .10 .20
112 Shrine to Benten R 1.25 3.00
113 Shrine to Bishamon R 1.00 2.50
114 Shrine to Daikoku R 1.25 3.00
115 Shrine to Ebisu R .60 1.50
116 Shrine to Fukurokujin R 1.25 3.00
117 Shrine to Hotei R .60 1.50
118 Shrine to Jurojin U .20 .50
119 Siege Towers U .20 .50
120 Sinister Transformation C .10 .20
121 Soshi Aki R .60 1.50
122 Soshi Natsuo C .10 .20
123 Steel Fan C .10 .20
124 Stolen Relics U .20 .50
125 Stone Hand Adepts C .10 .20
126 Strange Travelers R .60 1.50
127 Subterfuge C .10 .20
128 Sunda Mizu Dojo C .10 .20
129 Superior Stance R .60 1.50
130 Sycophant C .10 .20
131 Tattoo of the Void U .20 .50
132 Tax Collection R .60 1.50
133 Tear Away the Darkness U .20 .50
134 Temple of the Ninth Kami F (Shadowlands) .60 1.50
135 Tengoku's Gates C .10 .20
136 The Demon Skull U .20 .50
137 The Mountain Does Not Move C .10 .20
138 The Topaz Armor C .10 .20
139 The White Guard U .20 .50
140 Tireless Assault C .10 .20
141 Togashi Kinuko U .20 .50
142 Togashi Tashishai U .20 .50
143 Toshimoko no Shiryo R .60 1.50
144 Tsudao's Tanto R .60 1.50
145 Tsuno Kira U .20 .50
146 Tsurayuki U .20 .50
147 Tsuruchi Ichiro R .60 1.50
148 Tsuruchi Kaii U .20 .50
149 Tsuruchi Sho C .10 .20
150 Unexpected Strike R .60 1.50
151 Unspoken Threats U .20 .50
152 Utaku Yisheng C .10 .20
153 Volcanic Fields C .10 .20
154 Wholeness of Self U .20 .50
155 Wikki'thich-hie G'ni'ch R .60 1.50
156 Yoritomo Toyozo C .10 .20
157 Zashiki Warashi U .20 .50

2003 Legend of the Five Rings Reign of Blood

COMPLETE SET (157)
BOOSTER BOX (48 PACKS) 30.00 60.00
BOOSTER PACK (11 CARDS) 1.00 2.00
RELEASED IN DECEMBER 2003
1 Acolytes of Air C .10 .20
2 Agasha Chieh (Experienced) F (Phoenix) 1.25 3.00
3 Akodo Ieshigi U .20 .50
4 Akodo Maiko C .10 .20
5 Asahina Nahomi C .10 .20
6 Asahina Nizomi C .10 .20
7 Asako Genjo U .20 .50
8 Asako Katsuhito C .10 .20
9 Barley Farm C .10 .20
10 Battle-Hardened C .10 .20
11 Bayushi Atsuki (Experienced Shosuro Furuyari) R 1.25 3.00
12 Bayushi Shintaro U .20 .50
13 Birth and Death R .60 1.50
14 Blade of Penance R 1.25 3.00
15 Bleak Portents R 1.25 3.00
16 Blessing of the Dragon C .10 .20
17 Blood and Chaos R .60 1.50
18 Blood Armor C .10 .20
19 Blood Command R .60 1.50
20 Blood Pact C .10 .20
21 Blood-Soaked Ground R 1.00 2.50
22 Bloodspeaker Sanctum U .20 .50
23 Bloodspeaker Students C .10 .20
24 Bloodspeaker's Tools R .60 1.50
25 Bloodstained Peasants C .10 .20
26 Bones of the Fallen C .10 .20
27 Break the Line C .10 .20
28 Burning Blood C .10 .20
29 Calculate Strength U .20 .50
30 Chuda Agent C .10 .20
31 Ciphered Scroll R .60 1.50
32 City of Remembrance F (Phoenix) 1.00 2.50
33 Cloud the Soul C .10 .20
34 Corrupt Officials U .20 .50
35 Crystal Mine C .10 .20
36 Curse R .60 1.50
37 Daidoji Sabaru U .30 .75
38 Death's Caress C .10 .20
39 Ebb and Flow R .60 1.50
40 Essence of Gaki-do R .60 1.50
41 Eye of Iuchiban R .60 1.50
42 Fan of the Grand Master U .20 .50
43 Fires of Dishonor U .20 .50
44 From Every Side C .10 .20
45 Hakai R 1.25 3.00
46 Harsh Crossing R .60 1.50
47 Harvest of Death R .60 1.50
48 Heaven's Wrath U .20 .50
49 Hero's Grave U .20 .50
50 Hida Katai C .10 .20
51 Hida Soh U .20 .50
52 Hidden Retreat C .10 .20
53 Hiruma Rikiya C .10 .20
54 Hitomi Dojo U .20 .50
55 Honor and Glory U .20 .50
56 Honor's Gift C .10 .20
57 Hope in Shadows R .60 1.50
58 Horsemaster R .60 1.50
59 Hoshi Oki C .10 .20
60 Ide Haichang C .10 .20
61 Inazuma Blade R .60 1.50
62 Inexorable March U .20 .50
63 Inkyo Teacher U .20 .50
64 Inkyo's Jingasa U .20 .50
65 Isawa Jun C .10 .20
66 Isawa Ochiai R .60 1.50
67 Iuchi Katsumi C .10 .20
68 Iuchi Tudev U .20 .50
69 Jade Shortage R .60 1.50
70 Jigoku's Rage R 1.25 3.00
71 Kakita Matabei R 1.25 3.00
72 Kakita Nichira U .20 .50
73 Kitsu Tomoe U .20 .50
74 Kouken Blade U .20 .50
75 Kuni Jiyuna U .20 .50
76 Kuroiban Advisor U .20 .50
77 Mark of the Ninth Kami R .60 1.50
78 Matsu Takenao C .10 .20
79 Matsu Taniko R .60 1.50
80 Migawari C .10 .20
81 Mirumoto Kenzo U .20 .50
82 Mirumoto Mareshi F (Dragon) 1.50 4.00
83 Moshi Kekiesu U .20 .50
84 Moto Najmudin F (Unicorn) 1.00 2.50
85 Move the Earth U .20 .50
86 Nemuranai Arms C .10 .20
87 Omen (Experienced) R .60 1.50
88 Our Darkest Hour R .60 1.50
89 Pit of Blood R .60 1.50
90 Poison the Land C .10 .20
91 Poisoned Kiss U .20 .50
92 Political Interference R 1.00 2.50
93 Purification R .60 1.50
94 Purity of the Heavens U .20 .50
95 Quarantined R .60 1.50
96 Rain of Blood R .60 1.50
97 Reflect the Spirit R .60 1.50
98 Reichin's Helm U .20 .50
99 Reinforced Cavalry U .20 .50
100 Reinforced Infantry U .20 .50
101 Reinforcements R 1.25 3.00
102 Renewed Energy U .20 .50
103 Ride the Way C .10 .20
104 Rising Shadows C .10 .20
105 Rising Terror U .20 .50
106 Search For Advantage U .20 .50
107 Sezaru's Gift R .60 1.50
108 Shadowed Terrain R .60 1.50
109 Shield of Blood R .60 1.50
110 Shinden Horiuchi F (Unicorn) .60 1.50
111 Shirasu no Shiryo F (Unicorn) .60 1.50
112 Shosuro Haru C .10 .20
113 Shrine of Fu Leng R .60 1.50
114 Shrine of Humility R .60 1.50
115 Shrine of the Eternal U .20 .50
116 Shukumei U .20 .50
117 Silence the Future R .60 1.50
118 Skub C .10 .20
119 Smite the Blood U .20 .50
120 Soshi Uidori U .20 .50
121 Speed of the Plains U .20 .50
122 Spirit Drums R .60 1.50
123 Steel on Steel C .60 1.50
124 Strange Alliance C .10 .20
125 Strategic Crossroad C .10 .20
126 Strength in Numbers U .20 .50
127 Stymied R .60 1.50
128 Suchiro no Oni C .10 .20
129 Suitengu's Uncertainty U .20 .50
130 Swift as the Wind U .20 .50
131 Taint the Land R .60 1.50
132 Talented Apprentice C .10 .20
133 Tamori Nobuyoki C .10 .20
134 Tamori's Furnace R .60 1.50
135 Tch'rikch C .10 .20
136 Temples of the Snake R .60 1.50
137 Test of Magic R .60 1.50
138 The Death of Tadaji U .20 .50
139 The Temple of Hoshi F (Dragon) 1.00 2.50
140 The Voice's Command R .60 1.50
141 Togashi Shozo U .20 .50
142 Tsuruchi Amane C .10 .20
143 Tsuruchi Fusako U .20 .50
144 Tsuruchi's Flame U .20 .50
145 Two Souls, One Destiny C .10 .20
146 Utaku Xiulian U .20 .50
147 Vigilant Witch Hunter U .20 .50
148 Way of the Willow C .10 .20
149 Where the Kami Walk U .20 .50
150 Witch Hunter's Amulet C .10 .20
151 Woodlands U .20 .50
152 Worthy Gift R .60 1.50
153 Yajinden R 2.50 6.00
154 Yasuki Trader C .10 .20
155 Yogo Hiroji C .10 .20
156 Yoritomo Kitao (Experienced 2) R 1.00 2.50
157 Yoritomo Utemaro C .10 .20

2003 Legend of the Five Rings Training Grounds

LionD6D14 Matsu Mabuchi
ShadowD01 Obsidian Mine
ShadowD04 Seppun Jin (Experienced 3)
ShadowD07 Voitagi (Experienced)
ShadowD11 Bawaru no Oni
ShadowD13 Run For Your Lives!
ShadowD15 Plains of Otosan Uchi
ShadowD16 Ogre Bushi
ShadowD18 Proposal of Peace
ShadowD22 Voitagi
ShadowD23 Oblivion's Gate
ShadowD24 Fushiki no Oni
ShadowD26 Shadowlands Bastion
ShadowD27 Gekido no Oni
ShadowD30 Akodo's Grave
ShadowD31 Nairu no Oni
ShadowD35 Kyoso no Oni
ShadowD37 Ashura
ShadowD39 Shackled Oni
ShadowD41 Farmlands
ShadowD42 Shadowlands Marsh
ShadowD43 Far From the Empire
ShadowD44 Chuda Masaru
ShadowD47 Kukanchi
ShadowD48 Yosuchi
ShadowF00 The Spawning Ground
ShadowF01 Parasitic Oni
ShadowF03 The Face of Fear
ShadowF06 Corrupted Jade Sliver
ShadowF07 Test of Might
ShadowF08 Along the Coast at Midnight
ShadowF09 Primal Rage
ShadowF15 Retribution
ShadowF19 Kirei
ShadowF23 Armor of Earth
ShadowF30 Blackened Claws
ShadowF31 For the Empire
ShadowF33 Tsuno Blade
ShadowF34 Sneak Attack
ShadowF36 Wanton Destruction
ShadowF40 Hideo Spawn
ShadowF41 Blade of Secrets
ShadowF42 Goblin Slingers
ShadowF44 Oni Horde
ShadowF46 Diversionary Tactics
ShadowF49 Feign Death
ShadowF00b Black Heart of the Empire
LionD00 Right Hand of the Emperor
LionD01 Temples of the New Tao
LionD02 Shrine to Fukurokujin
LionD08 Birth of the Sword
LionD09 Shrine to Daikoku
LionD10 Ashigaru Fort
LionD12 Matsu Aoiko
LionD15 Matsu Kenji
LionD16 Matsu Hyun (Experienced)
LionD18 Akodo Shigetoshi
LionD24 Matsu Reishiko
LionD28 Matsu Ferishi
LionD30 Akodo Tadenori
LionD33 Rice Paddy
LionD34 Dragon Dancers
LionD37 Copper Mine
LionD38 Violence Behind Courtliness City
LionD40 Gifts and Favors
LionD41 700 Soldier Plain C
LionD42 Boastful Proclamation
LionD43 Doom of the Dark Lord
LionD45 Sanctified Temple
LionD46 Akodo Yobi
LionD49 Akodo Kurako
LionF00 Kenson Gakka
LionF01 Strength of Purity
LionF02 Omoidasu
LionF05 White Shore Plain
LionF08 Ring of Water
LionF10 Volcanic Fields
LionF14 Luring Tactics
LionF19 Steadfast Bushi
LionF21 Spearmen
LionF23 Ring of Earth
LionF26 Gunsen of Water
LionF27 Deathseeker's Glory
LionF29 Gunso
LionF30 Officers' Council
LionF32 Tireless Assault
LionF33 Peasant Vengeance
LionF35 Spearhead
LionF37 Veteran Bushi
LionF41 Lessons from Kuro
LionF43 Elite Spearmen
LionF45 Shireikan
LionF47 Superior Strategist
LionF48 Battlefield of Shallow Graves
Shadow17 Corrupted Dojo

2003 Legend of the Five Rings Winds of Change

COMPLETE SET (155)
BOOSTER BOX (48 PACKS) 50.00 100.00
BOOSTER PACK (11 CARDS) 1.50 3.00
RELEASED IN AUGUST 2003
1 A Champion's Heart U .20 .50
2 Akodo Sarasa U .20 .50
3 Akodo Tadenori (Experienced) R 1.00 2.50
4 Akodo's Grave C .10 .20
5 Asahina Barako U .20 .50
6 Asako Shiwasu C .10 .20
7 Ashigaru Fort C .10 .20
8 Banner of Heroes R .60 1.50
9 Barren Fields C .25 .60
10 Bawaru no Oni C .10 .20
11 Bayushi Aotora U .20 .50
12 Bayushi Kwanchi (Experienced) R 1.25 3.00
13 Bayushi Rei C .10 .20
14 Bloodied Ground R .60 1.50
15 Castle of the Wasp F (Mantis) .60 1.50
16 Chu-rochu C .10 .20
17 Clarity of Purpose C .10 .20
18 Commanding Favor R 1.25 3.00
19 Contingency Plans U .20 .50
20 Control the Field C .60 1.50
21 Corrupted Dojo U .10 .20
22 Court Chambers R .20 .50
23 Daidoji Akimasa C .60 1.50
24 Damning Evidence R .20 .50
25 Dark Soul Mask R .60 1.50
26 Dark Wings C .60 1.50
27 Defend Your Master U .10 .20
28 Dismissed U .20 .50
29 Doji Tanitsu (Experienced) R .10 .20
30 Domotai's Sacrifice R .60 1.50
31 Edict of Glory U .60 1.50
32 Edict of Judgement U .20 .50
33 Eloquence R .20 .50
34 Field of Glorious Slaughter C .10 .20
35 Fine Steed U .10 .20
36 Fruitless Combat C .20 .50
37 Gaki C .10 .20
38 Gempukku C .10 .20
39 Ghul Lord U .10 .20
40 Hachi's Legion U .20 .50
41 Hands of the Tides U .20 .50
42 Heimin Laborers U .10 .20
43 Hida Hoitsu C .20 .50
44 Hida Sozen C .10 .20
45 Hida Wukau (Experienced) F (Crab) .30 .75
46 Hiruma Tracker C .10 .20
47 Hitomi Kichi U .10 .20
48 Honored Sensei U .20 .50
49 Hospitality R .20 .50
50 Ichido no Shiryo R2 .60 1.50
51 Ik'krt (Experienced) F (Ratling) .60 1.50
52 Ikoma Korin C 1.00 2.50
53 Inspired Troops C .20 .50
54 Invasion U .10 .20
55 Isawa Fosuta R .10 .20
56 Isawa Wazuka U .60 1.50
57 Judgment of the Kami U .10 .20
58 Kaede's Fan R .10 .20
59 Kaiu Village R .60 1.50
60 Kakita Hirotada U .60 1.50
61 Kakita Rekkusu C .20 .50
62 Karo U .25 .60
63 Kharmic Vengeance R .25 .60
64 Kitsu Tanoyame U .60 1.50
65 Kitsuki Kiyushichi R .20 .50
66 Kitsuki Mizuochi R .60 1.50
67 Kitsune House Guard R .60 1.50
68 Korjagun U .10 .20
69 Koten F (Crab) .20 .50
70 Kyuden Tonbo R .20 .50
71 Mastermind U .10 .20
72 Mat'chek U .20 .50
73 Matsu Ferishi C .20 .50
74 Meditation Chamber C .10 .20
75 Mirumoto Ryosaki C .10 .20

76 Mirumoto Takeo C	.10	.20
77 Miya Shoin R	.10	.20
78 Monkey House Guard R	.60	1.50
79 Moshi Eihime U	.60	1.50
80 Moshi Yoshinaka F (Mantis)	.20	.50
81 Moto Genki C	1.00	2.50
82 Moto Latomu U	.10	.20
83 No Mercy R	.25	.60
84 Oblivion's Gate R	.20	.50
85 Officers' Council U	.60	1.50
86 Official Papers U	.20	.50
87 Omoni (Experienced) R	.20	.50
88 Otomo Taneji C	.20	.50
89 Ox House Guard R	.10	.20
90 Peasant Vengeance C	.60	1.50
91 Personal Librarian C	.20	.50
92 Petty Insults U	.10	.20
93 Poisoned Thread C	.20	.50
94 Political Entanglements R	.10	.20
95 Promotion to the Court R	1.25	3.00
96 Prophets C	.60	1.50
97 Provincial Governor U	.10	.20
98 Radiant Staff R	.20	.50
99 Rage C	.60	1.50
100 Reserve Commander C	.20	.50
101 Retribution C	.10	.20
102 Rhetoric C	.10	.20
103 Ruins of Yotsu Dojo U	.10	.20
104 Running Engagement C	.20	.50
105 Ryouko U	.10	.20
106 Sacred Grove R	.40	1.00
107 Sashimono C	.60	1.50
108 Seek the Path C	.10	.20
109 Settozai R	.10	.20
110 Sharing Strength C	1.25	3.00
111 Shiba Emiri C	.10	.20
112 Shinjo Haruko U	.10	.20
113 Shinjo Xushen (Experienced) R	.20	.50
114 Soshi Seika U	.10	.20
115 Soshi Tabito C	.20	.50
116 Sound Strategy R	.10	.20
117 Spearhead C	1.00	2.50
118 Stable Master U	.10	.20
119 Stay Your Blade C	.20	.50
120 Steadfast Bushi C	.10	.20
121 Stern Reprimand U	.10	.20
122 Storm Heart R	.20	.50
123 Strange Politics U	2.50	6.00
124 Strike Like the Wind U	.20	.50
125 Suzume House Guard R	.10	.20
126 Tadaka's Children U	.60	1.50
127 Tainted Dreams C	.20	.50
128 Taut Bowstrings U	.10	.20
129 Tch'tch Warrens F (Ratling)	.20	.50
130 The Four Winds March R	.60	1.50
131 The Future is Unwritten U	1.25	3.00
132 The New Order R	.20	.50
133 The Outer Darkness R	.60	1.50
134 The Shogun's Barracks R	.60	1.50
135 The World is Empty U	.60	1.50
136 Time to Pay the Price R	.20	.50
137 Traitor's Reward U	.20	.50
138 Treachery R	.20	.50
139 Tsudao's Chambers R	.60	1.50
140 Tsuruchi Tasaku C	.30	.75
141 Twist the World U	.10	.20
142 Untouched Temple U	.20	.50
143 Utaku Qsi-Tsing C	.20	.50
144 Utz! C	.10	.20
145 Wait and See R	.10	.20
146 Weight of the Heavens R	.60	1.50
147 Well Prepared C	.60	1.50
148 Wretches U	.10	.20
149 Writ of Conscription U	.20	.50
150 Writ of Justice R	.20	.50
151 Writ of Peace U	.60	1.50
152 Yasu no Shiryo R	.20	.50
153 Yasuki Namika R	.60	1.50
154 Yoritomo Manobu R	.30	.75
155 Yoritomo Yorikane C	.30	.75

2004 Legend of the Five Rings Dawn of the Empire

COMPLETE SET (108)	40.00	80.00
1 Akodo F	2.00	5.00
2 Akodo Mirotai F	.40	1.00
3 Amaterasu's Blessing F	.40	1.00
4 Ancient Armor F	.40	1.00
5 Ancient Battlefield F	1.00	2.50
6 Ancient Sword F	.40	1.00
7 Asako Moharu F	.40	1.00
8 Asako Yogo F	1.00	2.50
9 A'tck F	1.25	3.00
10 Batlul F	1.00	2.50
11 Bayushi F	2.00	5.00
12 Bayushi Nissho F	.40	1.00
13 Bayushi's Mask F	1.00	2.50
14 Blood Calls to Blood F	.40	1.00
15 Broken Sword of the Lion F	1.00	2.50
16 Call of Thunder F	1.25	3.00
17 Chamber of the Damned F	.40	1.00
18 Deeds of My Ancestors F	.40	1.00
19 Depths of Jigoku F	.40	1.00
20 D'nir'ch F	.40	1.00
21 Doji F	2.00	5.00
22 Doji Hayaku F	.40	1.00
23 Doji Konishiko (Experienced 7) F	2.00	5.00
24 Eclipse F	.40	1.00
25 Enmity F	.40	1.00
26 Extermination F	.40	1.00
27 Eye of the Emperor F	.40	1.00
28 Fall from the Heavens F	.40	1.00
29 Fallen Thunder F	.40	1.00
30 Family Library F	1.00	2.50
31 Fu Leng F	2.00	5.00
32 Fu Leng's Sword F	2.50	6.00
33 Golden Mirror F	1.00	2.50
34 Hantei F	2.50	6.00
35 Hantei Genji F	1.25	3.00
36 Hida Atarasi (Experienced 7) F	3.00	8.00
37 Hida F	1.00	2.50
38 Hiruma F	1.25	3.00
39 Hole in the Sky F	.40	1.00
40 I Can Swim F	.40	1.00
41 Ide F	1.00	2.50
42 Ikoma F	1.25	3.00
43 Into the Darkness F	2.00	5.00
44 Isawa (Experienced 7) F	1.25	3.00
45 Isawa Ariminhime F	.40	1.00
46 Isawa's Last Wish (Inexperienced) F	.40	1.00
47 Isawa's Scrolls F	.40	1.00
48 Kaimetsu-Uo F	1.00	2.50
49 Kaiu Fortress F	.40	1.00
50 Kaiu Norio F	.40	1.00
51 Kakita F	5.00	12.00
52 Kanashimi Toshi F	1.25	3.00
53 Kan'chek F	.40	1.00
54 Kindari F	.40	1.00
55 Ki-Rin's Exodus F	.40	1.00
56 Legion of the Kami F	.40	1.00
57 Lesson of Thunder F	.40	1.00
58 Matsu (Experienced 7) F	2.00	5.00
59 Men of Cunning F	.40	1.00
60 Mirumoto (Experienced 7) F	3.00	8.00
61 Mirumoto Hojatsu F	1.00	2.50
62 Mountains of Exile F	.40	1.00
63 Muhomono F	.40	1.00
64 Mutsuhito F	1.25	3.00
65 One Thousand Years of Peace F	.40	1.00
66 Oni no Hatsu Suru F	.40	1.00
67 Onnotangu's Hand (Inexperienced Obsidian Hand) F	.40	1.00
68 Otaku (Experienced 7) F	1.50	4.00
69 P'an Ku F	5.00	12.00
70 Rebirth of the Dark Kami F	.40	1.00
71 Sacred Arena F	.40	1.00
72 Scribing the Tao F	.40	1.00
73 Sculpting Flesh F	.40	1.00
74 Seppun Hill F	.60	1.50
75 Shiba F	4.00	10.00
76 Shinjo Bairezu F	4.00	10.00
77 Shinjo F	.40	1.00
78 Shinjo's Courage F	.40	1.00
79 Shinsei F	1.00	2.50
80 Shinsei's Legion F	1.00	2.50
81 Shosuro (Experienced 7) F	4.00	10.00
82 Shrine of Discussion F	.40	1.00
83 Souls of the Fallen F	.40	1.00
84 Spirit Made Flesh F	.40	1.00
85 Standing Stones F	.40	1.00
86 Student of the Tao F	.40	1.00
87 Tashrak F	1.00	2.50
88 Temples of Gisei Toshi F	1.50	4.00
89 Test of the Kami F	1.00	2.50
90 The Death of Ryoshun F	4.00	10.00
91 The Emperor's Blessing F	.40	1.00
92 The First Dojo F	.40	1.00
93 The First Oni (Inexperienced) F	1.25	3.00
94 The First Wedding F	2.00	5.00
95 The Lying Darkness F	.40	1.00
96 The Tao F	.40	1.00
97 Togashi F	2.00	5.00
98 Togashi Kaiteru F	.40	1.00
99 Tora F	.40	1.00
100 Troll War Band F	.40	1.00
101 Unmei F	.40	1.00
102 Until I Understand F	.40	1.00
103 Wako F	.40	1.00
104 War Chariot F	.40	1.00
105 Way of the Horse and Bow F	.40	1.00
106 Where Gods Have Fallen F	.40	1.00
107 Yobanjin Fortress F	.40	1.00
108 Yogo (Experienced Asako Yogo) F	2.00	5.00

2004 Legend of the Five Rings The Hidden City

COMPLETE SET (156)	30.00	80.00
BOOSTER BOX (48 PACKS)	20.00	40.00
BOOSTER PACK (11 CARDS)	1.00	2.00
RELEASED IN APRIL 2004		
1 A Favor Returned C	.10	.20
2 A Samurai's Anger C	.10	.20
3 Akodo Dagurasu R	.60	1.50
4 Akodo Dojo U	.20	.50
5 Akodo Minako U	.20	.50
6 Akodo Tadenori (Experienced) F (Lion)	2.00	5.00
7 Anvil of Earth R	.60	1.50
8 Archer Squad U	.20	.50
9 Armed Brigade U	.20	.50
10 Asako Soun C	.10	.20
11 Battlefield Messenger C	.10	.20
12 Bayushi Adachi U	.20	.50
13 Bayushi Kamnan (Experienced) R	1.25	3.00
14 Bayushi Motomu U	.20	.50
15 Blade of Fury C	.10	.20
16 Bleeding Grounds U	.20	.50
17 Blessings of Steel R	1.00	2.50
18 Blind Honor R	1.00	2.50
19 Blocked Ground C	.10	.20
20 Brilliant Soul U	.20	.50
21 Brothers in Arms U	.20	.50
22 Brutal Confrontation R	1.25	3.00
23 Cautious Advance R	.60	1.50
24 Chee'trr C	.10	.20
25 Chizuko U	.20	.50
26 Ch'krit C	.10	.20
27 Daidoji Kikaze R	1.00	2.50
28 Daidoji Tani C	.10	.20
29 Daigotsu Dojo U	.20	.50
30 Daigotsu Meguro C	.20	.50
31 Daigotsu Toru U	.20	.50
32 Daisho of Water R	1.50	4.00
33 Deathseeker's Oath U	.20	.50
34 Delayed March C	.10	.20
35 Demanding Gunso U	.20	.50
36 Deranged Mujina U	.20	.50
37 Desperate Conscripts C	.10	.20
38 Direct Assault R	1.00	2.50
39 Disciplined Infantry C	.10	.20
40 Doji Asano C	.10	.20
41 Doji Yasuyo (Experienced 2) R	.60	1.50
42 Drunken Mantis U	.20	.50
43 Endless Horde U	.20	.50
44 Er'chi-check U	.20	.50
45 Essence of Yomi C	.10	.20
46 Exhaustion R	.60	1.50
47 Expert Archers C	.10	.20
48 Explored Territory C	.10	.20
49 Failure of Duty R	1.00	2.50
50 Family Token C	.10	.20
51 Family War Banner R	.60	1.50
52 Fire and Water C	.10	.20
53 Fire in the Hidden City C	.10	.20
54 Fortress of Thunder R	.60	1.50
55 Fortune's Gift R	.60	1.50
56 From Nowhere R	.60	1.50
57 Fudoshi C	.10	.20
58 Fushin R	.60	1.50
59 Geisha Network U	2.50	6.00
60 Glassblower R	.60	1.50
61 Gleaming Wakizashi R	.60	1.50
62 Go In Disgrace U	.20	.50
63 Goju Arai C	.10	.20
64 Gold Buys Security R	.60	1.50
65 Hada Daizu C	.60	1.50
66 Hardy Infantry R	.10	.20
67 Hasty Barricades C	.20	.50
68 Heart of a Hero U	.10	.20
69 Heart of Bushido C	.60	1.50
70 Hero's Banner R	.10	.20
71 Hida Enko R	.60	1.50
72 Hida Sosuke C	.10	.20
73 Hiruma Todori (Experienced) F (Crab)	.60	1.50
74 Ichiro's Yumi C	.10	.20
75 Ignominious End U	.20	.50
76 Ikm'atch-tek R	.60	1.50
77 Iron Pillar C	.10	.20
78 Ith-ik C	.10	.20
79 Iuchi Katamari U	.20	.50
80 Kaiu Kamura U	.20	.50
81 Kakita Kaneo U	.20	.50
82 Kaneka R	.60	1.50
83 Kareido no Oni U	.20	.50
84 Killing Fields C	.10	.20
85 Kiss of the Scorpion R	.60	1.50
86 Knife in the Dark C	.10	.20
87 Legacy of My Ancestors R	.60	1.50
88 Lotus at Dusk R	.60	1.50
89 Marching Column C	.10	.20
90 Matsu Fujiwe C	.10	.20
91 Matsu Ryoichi C	.10	.20
92 Mirumoto Arai U	.20	.50
93 Mirumoto Daisho C	.10	.20
94 Mirumoto Kei U	.20	.50
95 Mirumoto Satoe C	.10	.20
96 Moto Gurban C	.10	.20
97 Moto Taidjut C	.10	.20
98 Naka Tokei (Experienced 2) R	.60	1.50
99 Outer Walls C	.10	.20
100 Peasant Laborers R	.60	1.50
101 Pillar of Flesh R	1.00	2.50
102 Piolitical Adjunct U	.20	.50
103 Purloined Letters U	.20	.50
104 Quartermaster C	.10	.20
105 Ratling Raider R	.60	1.50
106 Retired Master U	.20	.50
107 Scrutiny's Sweet Sting R	.60	1.50
108 Seasoned Cavalry U	.30	.75
109 Secluded Outpost R	6.00	15.00
110 Seeds of the Void R	.60	1.50
111 Senpent Scimitar C	.10	.20
112 Set'tchr'too U	.20	.50
113 Shakuhachi of Air R	.60	1.50
114 Shameless Slander U	.20	.50
115 Shiba Aikune (Experienced 2) R	.60	1.50
116 Shiba Koseki C	.10	.20
117 Shiba Marihito U	.20	.50
118 Shiba Toshiki U	.20	.50
119 Shining Example U	.20	.50
120 Shinjo Jinturi R	.60	1.50
121 Shiranai Toshi F (Lion)	1.25	3.00
122 Shosuro Mikado C	.10	.20
123 Shosuro Osamito C	.10	.20
124 Shrine of Compassion R	.60	1.50
125 Shrine of Courage R	1.25	3.00
126 Shrine of Duty R	.60	1.50
127 S'ktcha F (Ratling)	1.25	3.00
128 Strategic Assassin C	.10	.20
129 Summon Air Kami U	.20	.50
130 Summon Earth Kami U	.20	.50
131 Summon Fire Kami U	.20	.50
132 Summon Water Kami U	.20	.50
133 Tamori Minoru C	.10	.20
134 Tani Hitokage F (Crab)	1.25	3.00
135 Tek'teki-tek U	.20	.50
136 Ten Thousand Swords C	.20	.50
137 The Iron Legion R	.60	1.50
138 The Legions Charge U	.30	.75
139 The Meeting Place F (Ratling)	1.25	3.00
140 The Pull of Destiny U	.20	.50
141 The Shogun's Armory R	.60	1.50
142 Third Whisker Mine U	.20	.50
143 Togashi Tsuri R	.60	1.50
144 Trade District R	.60	1.50
145 Tsuruchi Arishia C	.10	.20
146 Tsuruchi Mochisa U	.20	.50
147 Tsuruchi Nobumoto (Experienced) R	.60	1.50
148 Turn of Fortune R	.60	1.50
149 Usagi Rangers C	.10	.20
150 Utaku Jamaira U	.30	.75
151 War Council U	.20	.50
152 We Know U	.20	.50
153 Well-Tended Farm U	1.25	3.00
154 Yobanjin Wyrm R	.60	1.50
155 Yoritomo Mie C	.10	.20
156 Yumi of Fire R	.60	1.50

2004 Legend of the Five Rings Web of Lies

COMPLETE SET (156)	30.00	80.00
BOOSTER BOX (48 PACKS)	40.00	80.00
BOOSTER PACK (11 CARDS)	1.25	2.50
RELEASED IN DECEMBER 2004		
1 Agasha Miyoshi C	.10	.20
2 Akodo Kitaka C	.10	.20
3 Akodo Kuemon C	.10	.20
4 Akodo Rokku U	.20	.50
5 Anchor the Line U	.20	.50
6 Aramasu's Pride F (Mantis)	.60	1.50
7 Asahina Sekawa (Experienced 2) R	.60	1.50
8 Asako Hirotsugu C	.10	.20
9 Asako Kinuye (Experienced) F (Phoenix)	.60	1.50
10 Baraunghar Amulet U	.20	.50
11 Bayushi Paneki (Experienced 2) R	1.25	3.00
12 Bayushi Shusui C	.10	.20
13 Bishamon's Fury U	.20	.50
14 Blade of the Master R	.60	1.50
15 Blood Pearl U	.20	.50
16 Brand of Fire and Thunder C	.10	.20
17 Cavalry Reserves U	.20	.50
18 Chirtk R	.60	1.50
19 Circle of Steel C	.10	.20
20 City of Blood F (Phoenix)	.60	1.50
21 Cunning of Daidoji C	.10	.20
22 Daidoji Setsuko U	.20	.50
23 Daidoji Takihiro C	.10	.20
24 Daigotsu R	1.25	3.00
25 Defining the Essence C	.10	.20
26 Distant Keep U	.20	.50
27 Doji Saori C	.10	.20
28 Doji Takeji C	.10	.20
29 False Trail R	1.25	3.00
30 Few Against Many R	2.50	6.00
31 Fields of Pyrrhic Victory R	1.50	4.00
32 Forward Sentries C	.10	.20
33 Fury of Hida C	.10	.20
34 Fury of Steel R	.60	1.50
35 Glory of Mirumoto C	.10	.20
36 Glory of the Shogun R	.60	1.50
37 Gong of the Righteous Emperor U	.20	.50
38 Gozoku Influence C	.10	.20
39 Gozoku Pawn R	1.25	3.00
40 Gunsen-gata U	.20	.50
41 Henshin's Amulet U	.20	.50
42 Hida Atsumori U	.20	.50
43 Hida Rikyu C	.10	.20
44 Hida Shara (Experienced) R	.60	1.50
45 Hiruma Oda U	.20	.50
46 Hordes of the Nezumi C	.10	.20
47 Hoshi Masote U	.20	.50
48 House of the Spring Chrysanthemum U	.20	.50
49 I Am Ready R	.60	1.50
50 Ik'krt (Experienced 2) R	.60	1.50
51 Ikoma Korin (Experienced) R	.60	1.50
52 Invincible Legions R	1.00	2.50
53 Isawa Sachi U	.20	.50
54 Isawa Sezaru R	.60	1.50
55 Jade Stores U	.20	.50
56 J'uma Jirushi R	.60	1.50
57 Kaeru Fields R	.60	1.50
58 Kaiu Kazu C	.10	.20
59 Kakita Benkei R	.60	1.50
60 Kanjiro U	.20	.50
61 Kinuye's Garden U	.20	.50
62 Kitsuku Yojimbo U	.20	.50
63 Kiyune's Blood U	.20	.50
64 Kobune Scout C	.10	.20
65 Kuni Kiyoshi (Experienced) R	.60	1.50
66 Legendary Confrontation R	2.50	6.00
67 Lessons of Pain C	.10	.20
68 Living Blade Dojo R	.60	1.50
69 Make Your Stand C	.10	.20
70 Mak'irtch C	.10	.20
71 Matsu Mieko C	.10	.20
72 Mirumoto Gukochi C	.10	.20
73 Mirumoto Kenzo (Experienced) R	.60	1.50
74 Mirumoto Takige C	.10	.20
75 Misdirection R	1.50	4.00
76 Morisue U	.20	.50
77 Moshi Hinome (Experienced) R	.60	1.50
78 Moto Latomu (Experienced) F (Unicorn)	1.25	3.00
79 Moto Ogedei R	.60	1.50
80 Muketsu C	.10	.20
81 Mura Sabishii Toshi U	.25	.60
82 Natsumono U	.20	.50
83 No Victory U	.25	.60
84 Ogre Mage C	.10	.20
85 Oni Lair U	.60	1.50
86 Passion R	.60	1.50
87 Peasant Defenders R	.60	1.50
88 Poetry U	.20	.50
89 Political Outcast R	.60	1.50
90 Rage of Matsu C	.10	.20
91 Rain of Death C	.10	.20
92 Remember's Stick U	.20	.50
93 Roadside Shrine U	.20	.50
94 Ronin Swordsman R	.60	1.50
95 Sapphire Strike R	1.00	2.50
96 Savagery of Moto C	.10	.20
97 Secured Ground R	.60	1.50
98 Seige Engine U	.60	1.50
99 Shadow Harrier R	.10	.20
100 Shadow of Shosuro C	.60	1.50
101 Shahai (Experienced) R	.60	1.50
102 Shattered Focus R	.10	.20
103 Shinjo Loruko C	.20	.50
104 Shinjo Suboto U	.10	.20
105 Shinjo Turong C	.20	.50
106 Shiny Treasure U	.20	.50
107 Shore Commander U	.20	.50
108 Shosuro Infiltrator U	.20	.50
109 Shosuro Saemon U	.20	.50
110 Shosuro Taki U	.10	.20
111 Shosuro Tsuyoshi C	.20	.50
112 Silent Warriors U	.20	.50
113 Soul of the Clan R	.60	1.50
114 Storm of Isawa C	.10	.20
115 Stranglehold U	.20	.50
116 Suitengu's Surge C	.10	.20
117 Sword of Gales C	.10	.20
118 Swordmaster Dojo U	.20	.50
119 Swordmaster's Wakizashi U	.20	.50
120 Tamori Watoshu U	.20	.50
121 Tangen Sensei R	.60	1.50
122 Tch'wik U	.20	.50
123 Tears of Blood R	.60	1.50
124 Tejina's Blessings U	.20	.50
125 Tengoku Acolyte U	.20	.50
126 The Fortunes Smile R	3.00	8.00
127 The Khol Wall F (Unicorn)	.60	1.50
128 The Last Prophecy R	.60	1.50
129 The Tribeless U	.20	.50
130 Tik'tek C	.10	.20
131 Togashi Matsuo (Experienced) R	.60	1.50
132 Toturi Kurako (Experienced Akodo Kurako) R	.60	1.50
133 Tsuma Dojo R	.60	1.50
134 Tsuruchi Armband U	.20	.50
135 Tsuruchi Etsui C	.10	.20
136 Tsuruchi Iyaken C	.10	.20
137 Tsuruchi Shiroko F (Mantis)	.60	1.50
138 Tsuruchi's Retreat U	.20	.50
139 Umasu Sensei R	.60	1.50
140 Uso Sensei R	.60	1.50
141 Utaku Tarako C	.10	.20
142 Victory or Death R	1.25	3.00
143 Wardens C	.10	.20
144 Warrior Pilgrim U	.20	.50
145 Way of Sincerity U	.20	.50
146 Weapon Rack C	.10	.20
147 Weigh the Cost C	.10	.20
148 Well-Laid Plains (sic) R	.60	1.50
149 Wrath of the Storm C	.10	.20
150 Writ of Commendation C	.10	.20
151 Writ of Obligation C	.10	.20
152 Writ of Requisition R	.60	1.50
153 Yogo Rieko R	.60	1.50
154 Yoritomo Matsoru U	.20	.50
155 Yoritomo Tokaro C	.10	.20
156 Z'chkir C	.10	.20

2004 Legend of the Five Rings Wrath of the Emperor

COMPLETE SET (156)	50.00	100.00
BOOSTER BOX (48 PACKS)	20.00	40.00
BOOSTER PACK (11 CARDS)	1.00	2.00
RELEASED IN AUGUST 2004		
1 Agasha Tomioko C	.10	.20
2 Akodo Sanuro C	.10	.20
3 Akodo Tsuyumi U	.20	.50
4 Ambush at Sea C	.10	.20
5 Ambush Duel U	.20	.50
6 Archer Towers C	.10	.20
7 Archer's Row U	.30	.75
8 Armor of Sacrifice R	.60	1.50
9 Army of Jigoku U	.20	.50
10 Asako Bairei R	.60	1.50
11 Asako Tsukuro U	.30	.75
12 Ashigaru Armor C	.10	.20
13 Bamboo Forest R	.60	1.50
14 Bayushi Baku (Experienced 2) F (Scorpion)	.60	1.50
15 Bayushi Muhito C	.10	.20
16 Bayushi Toho U	.20	.50
17 Bayushi's Knives U	.20	.50
18 Beiden Shadows U	.20	.50
19 Binding Kharma R	1.25	3.00
20 Blade of the Meek U	.30	.75
21 Blood Frenzy U	.20	.50
22 Bloodspeaker Ambush U	.20	.50
23 Brother of Lightning C	.10	.20
24 Chinamire no Oni U	.20	.50
25 Chuda Mishime C	.10	.20
26 Companion Spirit R	2.00	5.00
27 Contagion U	.20	.50
28 Courtly Sabotage R	1.00	2.50
29 Crippled Bone Runner C	.10	.20
30 Crush the Unworthy C	.10	.20
31 Curse of Blood R	1.00	2.50
32 Daidoji Kumi C	.10	.20
33 Daidoji Ryunosuke U	.20	.50
34 D'gr'n-ki C	.10	.20
35 Divide and Conquer U	.20	.50
36 Do Not Delay the Inevitable C	.10	.20
37 Exquisite Armor C	.10	.20
38 Fall Before the Master U	.20	.50
39 Fierce Bushi C	.10	.20
40 For the Lady C	.10	.20
41 Fury of the Dark Lord R	2.00	5.00
42 Fury of the Wolf C	.10	.20
43 Goemon's Ascension R	.60	1.50
44 Gozoku Sensei U	.30	.75
45 Hand of Vengeance U	.20	.50
46 Hida Horii U	.20	.50
47 Hida Sobu U	.20	.50
48 Hida Tonoji U	.20	.50
49 Hida's Formation U	.20	.50
50 Hiruma Tokito C	.10	.20
51 Hitomi Suguhara C	.10	.20

Card	Low	High
52 Horiuchi Nobane C	.10	.20
53 Hoshi Akiyama R	1.50	4.00
54 Hoshi Ishida U	.30	.75
55 House of the Jade Princess U	.20	.50
56 Ide Tang (Experienced) R	.60	1.50
57 Ikoma Hasaku C	.10	.20
58 Ikoma Masote U	.20	.50
59 Ikoma Tsai (Experienced) R	1.00	2.50
60 Isawa Sueno U	.20	.50
61 Iuchi Ryoi U	.20	.50
62 Iuchiban Sensei U	.20	.50
63 Iuchiban's Citadel F (Shadowlands)	.60	1.50
64 Jak-ir't U	.20	.50
65 Jigoku Sensei R	.60	1.50
66 Kaimetsu-uo's Blade C	.10	.20
67 Kakita Noritoshi (Experienced) F (Crane)	2.50	6.00
68 Kakita Tamura U	.30	.75
69 Kakita Totani C	.10	.20
70 Katsu F (Shadowlands)	1.25	3.00
71 Knife in the Darkness U	.30	.75
72 Kuni Tansho (Experienced) R	1.25	3.00
73 Kuni Yae C	.10	.20
74 Kyuden Bayushi F (Scorpion)	1.00	2.50
75 Layered Armor C	.10	.20
76 Many-Temple Master U	.20	.50
77 Marital Instruction R	1.25	3.00
78 Megumi (Experienced Daidoji Megumi) R	.60	1.50
79 Mercy in Battle C	.10	.20
80 Mihoko Sensei R	.60	1.50
81 Mirumoto Kaiji U	.20	.50
82 Mirumoto Narumi C	.10	.20
83 Mirumoto Rosanjin (Experienced) R	1.25	3.00
84 Moshi Mogai (Experienced) R	1.00	2.50
85 Motivation R	1.25	3.00
86 Moto Chen (Experienced) R	.60	1.50
87 Murder in the Streets C	.10	.20
88 Musaboru no Oni C	.10	.20
89 Musume Mura U	1.00	2.50
90 Ninja Mentor U	.30	.75
91 One Tribe U	.20	.50
92 Otomo Spokesman U	.20	.50
93 Patronage C	.10	.20
94 Peasant Weapons U	.20	.50
95 Purge the Weak C	.10	.20
96 Ratling Guide C	.10	.20
97 Ratling Nameseeker C	.10	.20
98 Rich Coffers C	.10	.20
99 Sai no Oni R	.60	1.50
100 Scroll Satchel C	.10	.20
101 Setai Sensei R	.60	1.50
102 Sezaru's Punishment C	.10	.20
103 Shiba Hayama C	.10	.20
104 Shiba Tsukimi (Experienced) R	1.00	2.50
105 Shifting Fortunes R	1.25	3.00
106 Shinjo Isuto U	.20	.50
107 Shinjo Riders C	.10	.20
108 Shiro Giri F (Crane)	1.00	2.50
109 Shi-Tien Yen-Wang Temple C	.10	.20
110 Shosoku Sensei R	.60	1.50
111 Shosuro Hokii U	.20	.50
112 Shosuro Naname C	.10	.20
113 Siege-Breakers C	.10	.20
114 Sla'Yerr U	.20	.50
115 Snow-Covered Pass C	.10	.20
116 Someisa Sensei R	.60	1.50
117 Souls in Harmony U	.20	.50
118 Spirits and Steel U	.20	.50
119 Strength From Weakness U	.20	.50
120 Strike and Move U	.20	.50
121 Strike With No Shadow R	2.00	5.00
122 Supply Lines U	.20	.50
123 Suru's Mempo (Experienced) R	1.00	2.50
124 Swamp Harriers C	.10	.20
125 Tadaji Sensei R	1.00	2.50
126 Tamago R	1.25	3.00
127 Temple of Initiation R	.60	1.50
128 Tenshu Sensei R	1.00	2.50
129 Te'tik'kir (Experienced 2) R	1.00	2.50
130 The Barbarian Wall R	1.00	2.50
131 The Iron Citadel (Experienced) R	.60	1.50
132 The Same Old Tricks C	.10	.20
133 The Tribes Gather C	.10	.20
134 Tishi Sensei R	1.00	2.50
135 To the Forests U	.20	.50
136 Tomorrow Sensei R	1.00	2.50
137 Touching the Elements C	.10	.20
138 Tower of the Ningyo R	1.00	2.50
139 Trading House C	.10	.20
140 Troublesome Bureaucrat R	1.25	3.00
141 Tsuruchi Okame (Experienced) R	1.00	2.50
142 Tsuruchi Renshi C	.10	.20
143 Unleash the Demons R	.60	1.50
144 Utaku Rishimaru C	.10	.20
145 Veteran Spearman R	.60	1.50
146 Victory of the Wolf U	.20	.50
147 War on the Plains R	.60	1.50
148 Wikki'thich-hie Z-ee R	1.25	3.00
149 Wrath of the Bloodspeaker R	.60	1.50
150 Wrath of the Emperor R	.60	1.50
151 Yasuki Hachi (Experienced 2) R	1.50	4.00
152 Yogo Baisetsu U	.40	1.00
153 Yoma Sensei R	.60	1.50
154 Yoritomo Egumi C	.10	.20
155 Yoritomo Hotako U	.20	.50
156 Yoritomo Katoa (Experienced) R	1.00	2.50

2005 Legend of the Five Rings Code of Bushido

Card	Low	High
COMPLETE SET (156)	30.00	80.00
BOOSTER BOX (48 PACKS)	40.00	80.00
BOOSTER PACK (11 CARDS)	1.25	2.50
RELEASED IN AUGUST 2005		
1 Agasha Fumihiro R	1.00	2.50
2 Akatch C	.10	.20
3 Akodo Bakin R	1.00	2.50
4 Akodo Chikatusa U	.20	.50
5 Akodo Mokichi C	.10	.20
6 Akodo Moromao R	1.00	2.50
7 Baraunghar Tactics R	.60	1.50
8 Bayushi Bokatsu R	1.25	3.00
9 Bayushi Fujio C	.10	.20
10 Bayushi Hikaru U	.20	.50
11 Bayushi Kan U	.20	.50
12 Bayushi Shun R	1.25	3.00
13 Bayushi's Feint U	.20	.50
14 Border Skirmish U	.20	.50
15 Cast Out U	.20	.50
16 Chikka-tek U	.20	.50
17 Chuda Isoruko C	.10	.20
18 Chuda Kyuwa R	1.00	2.50
19 Chuda Ruri C	.10	.20
20 Compassion R	.60	1.50
21 Countermove R	1.25	3.00
22 Courage R	2.00	5.00
23 Courtesy R	.60	1.50
24 Crippled Bone Blade C	.10	.20
25 Czinn'tch R	1.00	2.50
26 Daidoji Nichiren U	.20	.50
27 Daidoji Tae U	.20	.50
28 Daidoji Teika R	.60	1.50
29 Daidoji Uji (Experienced 3) R	.60	1.50
30 Daigotsu Soetsu U	.20	.50
31 Daigotsu Yajinden (Experienced Yajinden) R	1.00	2.50
32 Dark Fate R	1.00	2.50
33 Devoured By the Sea U	.20	.50
34 Disavowed U	.20	.50
35 Doji Koin U	.20	.50
36 Doji Midoru F (Crane)	.20	.50
37 Doji Nio C	.10	.20
38 Doji Ranmaru C	.10	.20
39 Doji Soh C	.10	.20
40 Duty R	1.50	4.00
41 Emikek U	.20	.50
42 Expanding Territory U	.20	.50
43 Extended Maneuvers C	.10	.20
44 Goblin Swarm U	.20	.50
45 Governor's Quarters R	.60	1.50
46 Guilt By Association C	.10	.20
47 Hida Kosedo C	.10	.20
48 Hida Renga U	.20	.50
49 Hida Takuji R	1.25	3.00
50 Hida Yachi C	.10	.20
51 Hiruma Hiroji U	.20	.50
52 Hiruma Takaaki U	.20	.50
53 Hiruma Tama C	.10	.20
54 Hitomi Kobai (Experienced) R	.60	1.50
55 Hitomi Morimasa R	.60	1.50
56 Honesty R	.60	1.50
57 Honor R	.60	1.50
58 Hoshi Kaelung (Experienced Kaelung) R	.60	1.50
59 Hyotaru U	.20	.50
60 Ichiro Yojimbo C	.10	.20
61 Ikoma Chikao F (Lion)	.60	1.50
62 Ikoma Itagi U	.20	.50
63 Iron Hand Strike C	.10	.20
64 Isawa Eitoku U	.20	.50
65 Isawa Kimi C	.10	.20
66 Isawa Suzuko C	.10	.20
67 Isawa Tsune C	.10	.20
68 Iuchi Lixue (Experienced) R	.60	1.50
69 Iuchi Umeka C	.10	.20
70 Kagami no Oni C	.10	.20
71 Kaimetsu-uo's Formation C	.10	.20
72 Kaiu Haku R	.60	1.50
73 Kaiu Sugimoto (Experienced Keeper of Earth) R	.60	1.50
74 Kakita Kiyonobu R	.60	1.50
75 Keep the Peace U	.20	.50
76 Kensaku C	.10	.20
77 Kiii C	.10	.20
78 Kitsuki Hakihime C	.10	.20
79 Kitsuki Nagiken R	.60	1.50
80 Kitsuki Raichi C	.10	.20
81 K'mee U	.20	.50
82 Kobushi U	.20	.50
83 Kyuden Otomo F (Crane)	.60	1.50
84 Manithith R	.60	1.50
85 Masahigi's Blade R	.60	1.50
86 Matsu Arinori C	.10	.20
87 Matsu Eishi U	.20	.50
88 Matsu Okyoito C	.10	.20
89 Matsu Sanraku R	.60	1.50
90 Midnight Blades C	.10	.20
91 Minikui no Oni R	.60	1.50
92 Mirumoto Bokkai U	.20	.50
93 Mirumoto Etsuya U	.20	.50
94 Mirumoto Kiyohira U	.20	.50
95 Moshi Hitaka R	.60	1.50
96 Moto Hideyo (Experienced) R	.60	1.50
97 Moto Ichezo U	.20	.50
98 Moto Jippensha C	.10	.20
99 Moto Kinnojo R	.60	1.50
100 Moto Rumiko U	.20	.50
101 Nem'tek R	.60	1.50
102 Nezumi Migration U	.20	.50
103 Nimm'k U	.20	.50
104 Nomi U	.20	.50
105 O'chin C	.10	.20
106 Passage Between Worlds C	.10	.20
107 Peasant Uprising C	.10	.20
108 Righteous Fury C	.10	.20
109 Rise of the Shogun R	.60	1.50
110 Ryoken R	1.50	4.00
111 Scouring the Shadows C	.10	.20
112 Seal the Way R	.60	1.50
113 Shiba Denbe C	.10	.20
114 Shiba Ningen (Experienced 2) R	.60	1.50
115 Shiba Shinsaku U	.20	.50
116 Shiba Yoshimi U	.20	.50
117 Shinjo Irosuko C	.10	.20
118 Shinjo Natsume U	.20	.50
119 Shinjo Shria C	.10	.20
120 Shiro no Soshi F (Scorpion)	1.25	3.00
121 Shiro no Yojin F (Lion)	1.25	3.00
122 Shorihotsu's Blessing C	.10	.20
123 Shosuro Hisashi C	.10	.20
124 Shosuro Kinji C	.10	.20
125 Shosuro Madoka R	.60	1.50
126 Shosuro Nakaga (Experienced Shinjo Nakaga) F (Scorpion)	.60	1.50
127 Shosuro Oniji U	.20	.50
128 Sincerity R	.60	1.50
129 Skirt the Edge U	.20	.50
130 Strike at the Head R	.60	1.50
131 Sucking Mire U	.20	.50
132 Sunder the Darkness R	.60	1.50
133 Tactics of the Bear R	.60	1.50
134 Tamafune C	.10	.20
135 Tamori Konoyoe C	.10	.20
136 Tasu no Oni U	.20	.50
137 Tempest Island Initiate C	.10	.20
138 The Emperor's Defense C	.10	.20
139 The Emperor's Justice U	.20	.50
140 The Lion's Roar C	.10	.20
141 The Master Redeemed R	1.00	2.50
142 The Obsidian Halls of the Lost U	.30	.75
143 The Wolf's Mercy U	.20	.50
144 Threads of Fate C	.10	.20
145 Tsuruchi Masanori C	.10	.20
146 Usagi Retainer C	.10	.20
147 Wayward Attack U	.20	.50
148 We Stand Ready U	.20	.50
149 Will of the Elements U	.20	.50
150 Writ of the Anvil R	.60	1.50
151 Yasuki Miliko U	.20	.50
152 Yoritomo Buntaro R	.60	1.50
153 Yoritomo Kaigen R	.60	1.50
154 Yoritomo Kiroto U	.20	.50
155 Yoritomo Kumita C	.10	.20
156 Yoritomo Okitsugu U	.20	.50

2005 Legend of the Five Rings Enemy of my Enemy

Card	Low	High
COMPLETE SET (156)	30.00	80.00
BOOSTER BOX (48 PACKS	40.00	80.00
BOOSTER PACK (11 CARDS)	1.25	2.50
RELEASED IN APRIL 2005		
1 Advance Forces U	.20	.50
2 Agasha Kushojin C	.10	.20
3 Akodo Sadahige C	.10	.20
4 Ancestral Standard of the Lion Clan (Experienced) R	.60	1.50
5 Armor of Tengoku C	.10	.20
6 Ashigaru Conscripts C	.10	.20
7 Awaken the Eighth R	1.25	3.00
8 Bayushi Kaibara U	.20	.50
9 Bayushi Saya C	.10	.20
10 Bayushi Shinzo U	.20	.50
11 Bayushi Sunetra (Experienced 2) R	1.00	2.50
12 Bayushi Tsimaru (Experienced) R	.60	1.50
13 Blazing Arrow C	.10	.20
14 Blight of War C	.10	.20
15 Celestial Road R	.60	1.50
16 Charge of the First Legion U	.20	.50
17 Chi'kel U	.20	.50
18 Clash of Steel R	1.00	2.50
19 Cleansing Spirit U	.20	.50
20 Clumsy Ambush C	.10	.20
21 Complex Maneuvers R	1.25	3.00
22 Contest of Iaijutsu C	.10	.20
23 Contest of Power C	.10	.20
24 Contest of Testimony C	.10	.20
25 Contest of Wealth C	.10	.20
26 Control the Roads U	.20	.50
27 Crown of the Amethyst Champion U	.20	.50
28 Curio Shop C	.10	.20
29 Daidoji Armor C	.10	.20
30 Daidoji Gunso C	.10	.20
31 Daidoji Shihei C	.10	.20
32 Darkwater Bay U	.20	.50
33 Diplomatic Retreat C	.10	.20
34 Doji Akiko (Experienced) R	.60	1.50
35 Doji Choshi U	.20	.50
36 Doji Maseru (Experienced) R	.60	1.50
37 Doji Ran U	.20	.50
38 Doji Reju (Experienced 3) R	.60	1.50
39 Embrace the Stone U	.20	.50
40 Emma-O's Amulet R	.60	1.50
41 Equal Match R	.60	1.50
42 Excellence R	.60	1.50
43 Fire on the Sea R	.60	1.50
44 Fires of Battle U	.20	.50
45 Flag Messengers C	.10	.20
46 Foolish Words R	.60	1.50
47 Fortified Camp C	.10	.20
48 Fu Leng's Tomb (Experienced Forgotten Tomb) R	.60	1.50
49 Gohei Sensei R	.60	1.50
50 Harmony in Chaos C	.10	.20
51 Hasaiki no Oni C	.10	.20
52 Hida Kisada (Experienced) R	.60	1.50
53 Hida Nari U	.20	.50
54 Hida Sadaharu (Experienced) F (Crab)	1.00	2.50
55 Hiruma Tokimune C	.10	.20
56 Hohiro U	.20	.50
57 Ide Bantu U	.20	.50
58 Ikm'atch-tek (Experienced) R	.60	1.50
59 Ikoma Yasuko (Experienced Shosuro Yasuko) R	.60	1.50
60 Imbue Chi C	.10	.20
61 Imperial Artificer C	.10	.20
62 Iron Warriors R	.60	1.50
63 Isawa Jumon U	.20	.50
64 Isawa Kazushi C	.10	.20
65 Jade Tetsubo C	.10	.20
66 Kaiu Natsukiwa C	.10	.20
67 Kakita Osei C	.10	.20
68 Kedamono Sensei R	.60	1.50
69 Kharmic Confrontation R	1.00	2.50
70 Kitsuki Otojiro C	.10	.20
71 Kr'chan C	.10	.20
72 Ku'chek C	.10	.20
73 Kuni Nakanu's Journals U	.20	.50
74 Kuni Okichi U	.20	.50
75 Legacy of Dragons U	.20	.50
76 Matsu Aoiko (Experienced) R	.60	1.50
77 Matsu Nanako C	.10	.20
78 Matsu Robun U	.25	.60
79 Matsu Takuya U	.20	.50
80 Meeting the Keepers R	2.50	6.00
81 Midnight Raid U	.20	.50
82 Mirumoto Hakahime C	.10	.20
83 Mirumoto Hirohisa U	.20	.50
84 Mirumoto Yuichi U	.20	.50
85 Morale Officer C	.10	.20
86 Moto Akikazu U	.20	.50
87 Moto Gonnohyoe R	.60	1.50
88 Moto Hanzhi (Experienced) R	.60	1.50
89 Munemitsu no Oni R	.60	1.50
90 Ninja Sabotage U	.20	.50
91 O'kichit F (Ratling)	.60	1.50
92 Oni-Daikyu R	1.50	4.00
93 Opportunists C	.10	.20
94 Osaju's Lifeblood U	.20	.50
95 Outmaneuvered by Tactics U	.25	.60
96 Personal Assassin U	.20	.50
97 Plague of Insects U	.20	.50
98 Rama Singh U	.25	.60
99 Ratling Trackers C	.10	.20
100 Rezan (Experienced) R	.60	1.50
101 Rite of Travel R	.60	1.50
102 Rosoku R	.60	1.50
103 Sacrifice of Pawns R	1.25	3.00
104 Sadance Contest C	.10	.20
105 Sap the Spirit U	.20	.50
106 Scour the Earth C	.10	.20
107 Seikitsu Mountains U	.20	.50
108 Sentei no Oni R	2.00	5.00
109 Seppun Toshiaki U	.25	.60
110 Sezaru Returns U	.20	.50
111 Shadow of Amaterasu U	.20	.50
112 Shiba Naoya U	.20	.50
113 Shiba Yoma (Experienced 2) R	.60	1.50
114 Shining Son R	.60	1.50
115 Shinjo Fuyuko C	.10	.20
116 Shinjo Tsuyoshi C	.10	.20
117 Shiro Kitsuki F (Dragon)	1.00	2.50
118 Shosuro Adeiko C	.10	.20
119 Shrine of Thwarted Destiny C	.10	.20
120 Sinister Rebirth R	.60	1.50
121 Soften the Resistance C	.10	.20
122 Sohei Guardian C	.10	.20
123 Stagnant Ground R	.60	1.50
124 Stinging Insects R	.60	1.50
125 Strange Magics R	.60	1.50
126 Suiteiru no Oni (Experienced) R	.60	1.50
127 Tamori Shiki (Experienced) F (Dragon)	.60	1.50
128 Temple of Persistence F (Crab)	1.00	2.50
129 The Bear Returns R	1.25	3.00
130 The Better Gift U	.20	.50
131 The Hidden Heart of Iuchiban (Experienced) R	.60	1.50
132 The Shogun's Command R	.60	1.50
133 The Snake Speaks U	.20	.50
134 The Steel Throne (Experienced) U	.20	.50
135 Three Storms U	.20	.50
136 Tighten Patrol U	.20	.50
137 To Seek the Truth U	.20	.50
138 Togashi Ieshigi (Experienced Akodo Ieshigi) R	.60	1.50
139 Tortoise Ambassador R	.60	1.50
140 Tsuruchi Risako R	.60	1.50
141 Tsuruchi Shunso C	.10	.20
142 Tsusung Sensei R	.60	1.50
143 Unfamiliar Ground C	.10	.20
144 Untested Scouts C	.10	.20
145 Wandering Budoka R	6.00	15.00
146 Warrens of the One Tribe F (Ratling)	1.00	2.50
147 Writ of Command U	.20	.50
148 Writ of Restriction U	.20	.50
149 Yobanjin Alliance U	.25	.60
150 Yojireru no Oni C	.10	.20
151 Yoriki C	.10	.20
152 Yoritomo Bokkai U	.20	.50
153 Yoritomo Naizen (Experienced) R	.60	1.50
154 Yoritomo Shumei C	.10	.20
155 Yoritomo Suketsune U	.20	.50
156 Zamalash U	.20	.50

2005 Legend of the Five Rings Lotus Edition

RELEASED IN OCTOBER 2005

1 28
2 145
3 144
4 46
5 60
6 114
7 82
8 26
9 81
10 142
11 121
12 2
13 3
14 155
15 10
16 49
17 51
18 52
19 141
20 48
21 120
22 121
23 126
24
25 12
26 25
27 Kobune Port
28 Kyuden Tonbo R
29 Large Farm C
30 Lesser Shrine U
31 Marketplace
32 143
33 56
34 88
35 105
36 110
37 111
38 126
39 104
40 144
41 79
42 21
43 22
44 23
45 24
46 25
47 26
48 29
49 30
50 39
51 50
52 96
53 101
54 103
55 57
56 42
57 105
58 97
59 28
60 82
61 23
62 107
63 117
64 119
65 135
66 106
67 4
68 78
69 34
70 95
71 4
72 134
73 137
74 139
75 140
76 141
77 142
78 27
79 136
80 146
81 143
82 148
83 138
84 147
85 57
86 60
87 29
88 76
89 30
90 87
91 86
92
93 77
94
95 Doji Seo C
96 59
97 31
98 89
99 151
100 150
101 64
102 87
103 66
104 149
105 65
106
107 52
108 88
109 51
110 91
111 151
112 154
113 153
114 4
115 58
116 60
117 61
118 62
119 150
120 57
121 59
122 5
123 152
124 71
125 72
126 109
127 12
128 105
129 106
130 110
131 111
132 X5
133 X7
134 11
135 14

136 13
137 18
138 20
139 1
140 16
141 19
142 17
143 3
144 2
145 14
146 149
147 X2
148 X3
149 15
150 56
151 94
152 2
153 3
154 147
155 80
156 127
157 104
158 5
159 115
160 109
161 116
162 8
163 18
164 13
165 12
166 14
167 16
168 13
169 19
170 20
171 15
172 16
173 18
174 17
175 10
176 8
177 41
178 124
179 6
180 75
181 70
182 19
183 32
184 63
185 12
186 27
187 32
188 29
189 149
190 89
191 108
192 96
193 146
194 84
195 11
196 18
197 21
198 22
199 1
200 76
201 6
202 23
203 2
205 9
206
207 3
208 75
209 7
210 156
211 157
212 118
213
214 11
215 22
216 35
217
218 33
219 34
220 44
221 58
222 45
223 48
224 35
225 Kiss of the Scorpion R
226 54
227 65
228 66
229 68
230 69
231 71
232 72
233 98
234 91
235 92
236 55
237 99
238 100
239 101
240 65
241 113
242 116
243 117
244 118
245 119
246 129
247 103
248 7
249 8
250 122
251 13
252 Knife in the Darkness U
253 74
254 Low Morale C
255 84
256 77
257 11
258 1
259 148
260 128
261 75
262 102
263 130
264 40
265 123
266 111
267 92
268 90
269 144
270 14
271 85
272 Kolat Insurgent C
273 148
274 9
275 40
276 2
277 98
278 83
279 107
280 97
281 64
282 100
283 76
284 103
285 113
286 120
287 124
288 125
289 143
290 140
291 141
292 142
293 19
294 20
295 99
296 10
297 33
298 36
299 37
300 41
301
302 43
303 147
304 46
305 47
306 59
307 83
308 73
309 86
310 94
311 100
312 X6
313 1
314 146
315 15
316 21
317
318
319 6
320 17
321 6
322 7
323 21
324 27
325 31
326 74
327 90
328 53
329 123
330 131
331 70
332 Kuruma Dale R
333 73
334 54
335 Lion's Pride U
336 X8
337 50
338 49
339 19
340 139
341 136
342 55
343 42
344 38
345 26
346 20
347 11
348 91
349 93
350 108
351 114
352 7
353 31
354 38
355 99
356 30
357 67
358 104
359 110
360 122
361 132
362 133
363 63
364 39
365 102
366 97
367 81
368 86
369 68
370 102
371 89
372 134
373 5
374
375 18
376 9
377 25
378 88
379 106
380 152
381 5
382 115
383 67
384 X4
385 101
386 109
387
388 5
389 7
390 129
391 130
392 131
393 132
394 133
395 1
396 47
397 95
398 96
399 127
400 66
401 Kuro's Fire R
402 43
403 79
404 44
405 112
406 45
407 13
408 Masagaro Sensei
409 Kedamono Sensei
410 67
411 125
412 95
413 Kanjiro Sensei
414 93
415 54
416 94
417
418 Kyuden Toketsu
419 17
420 Kyuden Otomo
421 80
422 69
423 8
424 36
425 10
426 159
427 37
428 69
429 56
430 70
431 16
433 9
434 87
435 71
436 72
437 77
438 24
439 Left Hand of the Emperor
440 128
441
442 10
443 145
444 Kettei
445 145
446 92
447 64
448 112
449 12
450 55
451 9
452 53
453 4
454
455
456 85
457 24
458 Kyoryoku
459 135
460 Doji Kurohito (Experienced 3)
461 90
462 6
463 15
464 X1
465 Kan'ok'ticheck (Experienced 2)
466 14
467 62
468 74
469 8
470 Doji Saori
471 Kakita Osei
472 107
473 16
474 108
475 17
476 A Champion's Heart
477 4
478 158
479 61
480 62
481 93
482
483
484 98
485
486 15
704 3
F02 58
F03 61
F04 73
F05 Doji Koin
F06 Doji Nio
F07 Doji Ran
F08 Doji Ranmaru
F09 Doji Takeji
F10 137
F11 138
F12 28
F13 63
F14 78
431b 68

2005 Legend of the Five Rings Lotus Edition Promos

1 A Favor Returned
2 A Hero's Courage
3 A Hero's Name
4 A Hero's Tale
5 Arrival of the Phoenix
6 Ayamari
7 Battle at the Tomb
8 Bayushi Paneki (Experienced 3)
9 Brilliant Artisan
10 Call of Destiny
11 City Guard
12 Clan Standard
13 Daigotsu (Experienced)
14 Danjuro's Legion
15 Dark Divination (Experienced)
16 Desperate Defense
17 Diamond
18 District Governor
19 Doji Domotai (Experienced 2)
20 Emerald
21 Emerald Competitor
22 Favor of the Emerald Champion
23 Favor of the Jade Champion
24 Fighting in the Streets
25 Fireworks
26 Gift of the Shogun
27 Gifts and Favors
28 Gold
29 Hida Kuon (Experienced 4)
30 House of the Blue Tanuki
31 Imperial
32 Jade
33 Kadano's Map
34 Kan'ok'ticheck (Experienced 2)
35 Kaneka's Reserves
36 Kitsuki Scrutiny
37 Kitsune Den
38 Legion of the Sapphire Chrysanthemum
39 Lion Rout the Unicorn
40 Lotus
41 Lotus Blade
42 Luxurious Silk
43 Mantle of the Jade Champion (Experienced)
44 Matsu Yoshino (Experienced)
45 Moto Chagatai (Experienced 4)
46 Nanashi Mura
48 Oath to the Empire
49 Obsidian
50 Ordered Retreat
51 Osami
52 Pearl
53 Private Trader
54 Purifying Rite
56 Ruthless Advance
57 Satoru
58 Sezaru's Choice
59 Shiba Mirabu (Experienced 3)
60 Shiga
61 Shourido
62 Soul of Bushido
63 Spearhead
64 Standard Bearers
65 Strength of Darkness
76 Strict Training
77 Sushi Stand
78 The Emerald Armor (Experienced)
80 The Race Begins
82 The Unclean
84 Togashi Satsu (Experienced 3)
85 Tomb of the Seven Thunders
86 Trail of Deception
87 Trials of Jade
88 Tsi Zutaka
89 Tsukotu
90 Ujina Kadano
91 Unexpected Resistance
92 Writ of the Herald
93 Yoritomo Kumiko (Experienced 2)
13-Jan Strength of the Crab
13-Feb Strength of the Crane
13-Mar Strength of the Dragon
13-Apr Strength of the Lion
13-May Strength of the Mantis
13-Jun Strength of the Nezumi
13-Jul Strength of the Phoenix
13-Aug Strength of the Scorpion
13-Sep Strength of the Shadowlands
13-Oct Strength of the Unicorn
13-Nov The Wanderer (Experienced)
13-Dec The Ronin (Experienced)
13-13 The Mystic (Experienced)
Proxy-F47 Ninja Token
Proxy-F55 Ratling Token

2006 Legend of the Five Rings Drums of War

COMPLETE SET (156)	40.00	100.00
BOOSTER BOX (48 PACKS)	50.00	100.00
BOOSTER PACK (11 CARDS)	1.50	3.00
RELEASED IN MAY 2006		
1 Agasha Chisuzu U	.20	.50
2 All Things Have A Price U	.20	.50
3 Arms Smugglers U	.50	1.25
4 Asahina Hira	1.00	2.50
(Experienced Keeper of the Void) R		
5 Asahina Sekawa (Experienced 3) R	.60	1.50
6 Asako Meisuru C	.10	.20
7 Awaken the Sins U	.20	.50
8 Back to Back U	.20	.50
9 Bayushi Lineage U	.20	.50
10 Bayushi Muhito R	1.00	2.50
11 Blade of Hubris R	2.50	6.00
12 Blessed Yumi C	.10	.20
13 Border Conflict U	.20	.50
14 Broad Front R	4.00	10.00
15 Broken Shinbone Warren C	.10	.20
16 Buying Time U	.20	.50
17 City of the Rich Frog R	1.25	3.00
18 Corrupt Jade Vein U	.20	.50
19 Crane Detachment C	.10	.20
20 Crippling Cut U	.40	1.00
21 Crossroads of Destiny C	.10	.20
22 Daigotsu Kaikou U	.30	.75
23 Daigotsu Masami C	.10	.20
24 Daigotsu Rekai	1.25	3.00
(Experienced 3 Daidoji Rekai) R		
25 Dark Moto Steed U	.20	.50
26 Deadly Melee R	1.25	3.00
27 Doji Chieri C	.10	.20
28 Doji Lineage U	.20	.50
29 Dragon's Heart Dojo F (Dragon)	1.00	2.50
30 Eager to Fight R	2.00	5.00
31 Embrace the Darkness C	.10	.20
32 Exchange Destiny C	.10	.20
33 Face to Face C	.10	.20
34 Fields of Mercy R	1.00	2.50
35 Flying Leap C	.10	.20
36 Forest Thickets C	.10	.20
37 Gates of Jigoku U	.20	.50
38 Goblin Healer C	.10	.20
39 Goblin Sapper U	.30	.75
40 Gosoku Strategies U	.60	1.50
41 Gozoku Distraction R	.20	.50
42 Gozoku Meddling U	.20	.50
43 Grasp Destiny C	.10	.20
44 Guarded by Chi R	.60	1.50
45 Heigai	1.25	3.00
(Experienced 5 Akodo Ginawa) F (Lion)		
46 Heroic Feat C	.10	.20
47 Hida Daizu (Experienced) R	.60	1.50
48 Hida Harou U	.20	.50
49 Hida Kaihei U	.20	.50
50 Hida Kengo C	.10	.20
51 Hida Nichie C	.10	.20
52 Hida Students R	.60	1.50
53 Hitomi Mineyo C	.20	.50
54 Hitomi Sugahara	1.00	2.50
(Experienced) F (Dragon)		
55 Hitomi Tatsumi U	.20	.50
56 Hitomi Tsubo C	.10	.20
57 Horiuchi Wakiza C	.10	.20
58 Ichiro Kihongo (Experienced) U	.20	.50
59 Ikoma Fujimaro (Experienced) R	.60	1.50
60 Ikuei U	.25	.60
61 Immobile Stance R	1.25	3.00
62 Isawa Aiya R	.60	1.50
63 Joy of Plunder U	.20	.50
64 Junghar Encampment F (Unicorn)	1.00	2.50
65 Kakita Daiki C	.10	.20
66 Kakita Korihime (Experienced) U	.20	.50
67 Kaneka's Conflict C	.10	.20
68 Kitsu Fukashi U	.20	.50
69 Kitsu Katsuko U	.20	.50
70 Kitsu Lineage U	.20	.50
71 Kituski Orika C	.10	.20
72 Kokujin's Daisho (Experienced) R	.60	1.50
73 Kyofu (Experienced 2 Hida Kuroda) R	1.25	3.00
74 Lasy Moon's Prophecy U	.20	.50
75 Lateral Maneuver U	.20	.50
76 Legion of the Sapphire Shrysanthemum R	.60	1.50
77 Lion Detachment C	.10	.20
78 Mantis Detachment U	.20	.50
79 Mark of the Taine C	.10	.20
80 Matsu Benika C	.10	.20
81 Matsu Lineage C	.10	.20
82 Matsu Yokuya C	.10	.20
83 Memories of the Lost U	.20	.50
84 Mockery R	2.00	5.00
85 Moto Wasaka U	.20	.50
86 Municipal Roads C	.10	.20
87 Naseru's Conflict C	.10	.20
88 Nintai (Experienced Tsuno Nintai) R	.60	1.50
89 Omoni (Experienced 2) R	.60	1.50
90 Path of Jigoku U	.20	.50
91 Phoenix Detachment U	.20	.50
92 Porcelain Mask of Fu Leng	.60	1.50
(Experienced 2) R		
93 Precise Strike C	.10	.20
94 Reckless Pursuit C	.10	.20
95 Reinforcements Arrive R	2.00	5.00
96 Relief Troops C	.10	.20
97 Re-outfitting C	.10	.20
98 Run or Die C	.10	.20
99 Second Doom of the Lion R	.60	1.50
100 Second Doom of the Phoenix R	.60	1.50
101 Serene Patrol C	.10	.20
102 Set'tch'chet U	.25	.60
103 Sezaru's Burden R	.60	1.50
104 Sezaru's Conflict U	.20	.50

105 Shadow on the Court U	.20	.50
106 Shadowed Path to Victory U	.20	.50
107 Shamed by Valor R	1.25	3.00
108 Shattered Defenses C	.10	.20
109 Shiba Arihiro U	.20	.50
110 Shiba Danjuro (Experienced) R	.60	1.50
111 Shiba Gyousei C	.10	.20
112 Shiba's Promise R	.60	1.50
113 Shinbone Pack U	.25	.60
114 Shinbone Warrior C	.10	.20
115 Shinjo Dun C	.10	.20
116 Shinjo Shono (Experienced 3) F (Unicorn)	1.25	3.00
117 Shinsei's Crow R	.60	1.50
118 Shosuro Maru (Experienced) R	.60	1.50
119 Shosuro Nakako C	.10	.20
120 Shosuro Rishou U	.20	.50
121 Shosuro Yudoka (Experienced 2) U	.20	.50
122 Shoulder to Shoulder C	.10	.20
123 Silent Kill U	.20	.50
124 Smuggler Agent R	.60	1.50
125 Song of Steel C	.10	.20
126 Soshi Shuuko C	.10	.20
127 Spiked Tetsubo C	.10	.20
128 Supply Smugglers C	.10	.20
129 Tanuki Spirit U	.20	.50
130 Tawagoto (Experienced) R	.60	1.50
131 Tch'tek C	.10	.20
132 The Hall of Ancestors F (Lion)	1.25	3.00
133 The Shogun's Guard R	.60	1.50
134 Togashi Mitsu (Experienced 3) R	.60	1.50
135 Toturi Miyako (Experienced) R	.60	1.50
136 Toturi's Battle Standard (Experienced) R	.60	1.50
137 Tsukuri R	6.00	15.00
138 Tsuruchi Chikuma U	.25	.60
139 Tsuruchi Jougo C	.10	.20
140 Turn the Tide R	1.25	3.00
141 Unexpected Resources R	.60	1.50
142 Unstoppable Force R	.60	1.50
143 Utaku Uzuki R	.60	1.50
144 Utaku Yasuha U	.20	.50
145 Vengeance Cannot Wait R	.60	1.50
146 Visions of Doom U	.20	.50
147 Void Dragon (Experienced 2) R	.60	1.50
148 Water Is My Steed R	.60	1.50
149 Weighted Yari C	.10	.20
150 Yasuki Gakuto U	.20	.50
151 Yoee'tr (Experienced) R	.60	1.50
152 Yoritomo Bunmei C	.10	.20
153 Yoritomo Hanayo U	.25	.60
154 Yoritomo Kitao (Experienced 3) R	.60	1.50
155 Yoritomo Yashinko R	2.50	6.00
156 Yotsu Dojo C	.10	.20

2006 Legend of the Five Rings Path of Hope

COMPLETE SET (156)	40.00	100.00
BOOSTER BOX (48 PACKS)	50.00	100.00
BOOSTER PACK (11 CARDS)	1.50	3.00
RELEASED IN JANUARY 2006		
1 A Hero's Gift U	.20	.50
2 A Life for a Life R	.60	1.50
3 Abandoned C	.10	.20
4 Accusation U	.60	1.50
5 Agasha Shaku R	.60	1.50
6 Air Dragon (Experienced 2) R	1.00	2.50
7 Akodo Michio C	.10	.20
8 Akodo Nariaki U	.20	.50
9 Akodo Terumoto R	1.25	3.00
10 Akutenshi's Tribute C	.10	.20
11 Allegiance to the Emperor C	.10	.20
12 Allegiance to the Shogun C	.10	.20
13 Always Ready U	.20	.50
14 Arrival of the Obsidian Champion R	1.25	3.00
15 Arrogance R	1.50	4.00
16 Baraunghar Technique C	.10	.20
17 Bayushi Kageki (Experienced Mad Ronin) R	1.00	2.50
18 Bayushi Kaneo C	.10	.20
19 Bayushi Moyotoshi U	.20	.50
20 Bayushi Shumpei U	.20	.50
21 Blood and Steel U	.20	.50
22 Blossoming Conflict R	.60	1.50
23 Castle Gate R	1.25	3.00
24 Castle Towers C	.10	.20
25 Castle Walls C	.10	.20
26 Chitik R	1.50	4.00
27 Chuda Hankyu R	2.00	5.00
28 Conscriptors R	1.00	2.50
29 Conserve Your Strength C	.10	.20
30 Counsel of the Keepers U	.20	.50
31 Courtly Scholars U	.20	.50
32 Credit Where Due C	.10	.20
33 Daidoji Naito C	.10	.20
34 Daigotsu Fumiaki U	.10	.20
35 Daigotsu Ogiwara U	.20	.50
36 Dark Feeding C	.20	.50
37 Doji Fujie U	.10	.20
38 Doji Jun'ai (Experienced Keeper of Water) R	.20	.50
39 Doji Kazo (Experienced) U	.60	1.50
40 Doji Munabu C	.20	.50
41 Draw Your Blade R	8.00	20.00
42 Eyes of the Serpent C	.10	.20
43 Favor to the Dragon U	.20	.50
44 Favor to the Horde U	.20	.50
45 Favor to the Scorpion U	.20	.50
46 Favorable Terrain C	.10	.20
47 Fields of Foolish Pride R	1.25	3.00
48 Flee from Tomorrow R	.60	1.50
49 Forest Cleansing R	1.50	4.00
50 Forest Killer Cavern C	.10	.20
51 Fortress of the Bear F (Crab)	1.25	3.00
52 Fuhao's Shadow U	.20	.50
53 Golden Obi of the Sun Goddess (Experienced) R	.60	1.50
54 Gr'tik-er C	.10	.20
55 Heart of the Mountain U	.20	.50
56 Hida Hiyao C	.10	.20
57 Hida Iseki F (Crab)	.40	1.00
58 Hida Takuma U	.20	.50
59 Hida Uneki U	.20	.50
60 Hida War Cry R	.60	1.50
61 Hiruma Hino C	.10	.20
62 Hiruma Hitaken R	.60	1.50
63 Hisaki R	.60	1.50
64 Homecoming C	.10	.20
65 Honor Guard C	.10	.20
66 Hoshi Masujiro U	.30	.75
67 House of the White Jade Fan U	.20	.50
68 Howl of the Wolf U	.20	.50
69 I Know That Trick R	4.00	10.00
70 Ide Jiao U	.20	.50
71 Isawa Sata U	.20	.50
72 Isawa Tanaka U	.20	.50
73 Isawa Tomita C	.10	.20
74 Iwase C	.10	.20
75 Jade Petal Tea U	.20	.50
76 Kakita Tsuken (Experienced Keeper of Fire) F (Crane)	.60	1.50
77 Kharmic Struggle R	.60	1.50
78 Kitsuki Ryushi R	.60	1.50
79 Kitsuki Seiji C	.10	.20
80 Kukojin (Experienced 3) R	.60	1.50
81 Kukojin's Temptation R	1.25	3.00
82 Kuni's Eye U	.20	.50
83 Kyoso's Hunters U	.20	.50
84 Letter of Confession C	.10	.20
85 Lone Magistrate U	.20	.50
86 Matsu Hirake U	.20	.50
87 Matsu Shimei C	.10	.20
88 Matsu Yoshino R	1.00	2.50
89 Mirumoto Chojiro C	.10	.20
90 Mirumoto Masae (Experienced Keeper of Air) R	.60	1.50
91 Mishakene C	.10	.20
92 Mitsu's Return R	.60	1.50
93 Moshi Sayako U	.20	.50
94 Moto Kang U	.20	.50
95 Moto Tsume (Experienced 3) F (Shadowlands)	2.00	5.00
96 N'ck C	.10	.20
97 Night Crystal Scepter C	.10	.20
98 Obsidian Riders R	.60	1.50
99 P-o'tch U	.20	.50
100 Preparation C	.10	.20
101 Proof of Dishonor U	.20	.50
102 Prosperous Plains City F (Crane)	1.00	2.50
103 Rapid Deployment C	.10	.20
104 Repair Crew U	.20	.50
105 Righteous Doshin C	.10	.20
106 Sachi's Defiance C	.10	.20
107 Scrutiny of the Wasp U	.20	.50
108 Second Doom of the Crab R	.60	1.50
109 Second Doom of the Crane R	.60	1.50
110 Secret from the Mantis U	.20	.50
111 Secrets from the Ratling U	.20	.50
112 Seeking Within C	.10	.20
113 Selfless Courage R	.60	1.50
114 Shiba Fugimori R	.60	1.50
115 Shiba Riza C	.10	.20
116 Shinjo Senhao R	.60	1.50
117 Shinjo Wei R	.60	1.50
118 Shinjo Xie C	.10	.20
119 Shinjo's Arrow R	.60	1.50
120 Shosuro Mikado (Experienced) R	.60	1.50
121 Shosuro Toma C	.10	.20
122 Shuten Doji's Fury R	2.00	5.00
123 Storm Rider Explorer R	1.25	3.00
124 Tainted Whispers C	.10	.20
125 Tawagoto C	.10	.20
126 Tchree U	.20	.50
127 Temple of the General U	.20	.50
128 Temple of the Lotus U	.20	.50
129 Ten Thousand Temples U	.20	.50
130 Test His Mettle C	.10	.20
131 Test of Loyalty C	.10	.20
132 The Bitter Shadow of Shame R	2.00	5.00
133 The Death of Akiko R	.60	1.50
134 The Halls of the Damned F (Shadowlands)	1.25	3.00
135 The Kami's Blessing U	.20	.50
136 The Tail Strikes U	.20	.50
137 The War of Fire and Thunder R	.60	1.50
138 Thunder and Steel U	.20	.50
139 Togashi Razan U	.20	.50
140 Tsuken's Blade C	.10	.20
141 Tsuruchi Chae R	.60	1.50
142 Tsuruchi Dokuo C	.10	.20
143 Tsuruchi Kaya C	.10	.20
144 Unexpected Testimony R	.60	1.50
145 Unity of Purpose U	.20	.50
146 Utaku Mihua C	.10	.20
147 Valiant Stand U	.20	.50
148 Wareta no Oni R	.60	1.50
149 Water Dragon (Experienced 2) R	.60	1.50
150 Weakened Defenses C	.10	.20
151 Wisdom and Courage U	.20	.50
152 Wrath of the Keepers R	.60	1.50
153 Wretched Mercenary C	.10	.20
154 Yoritomo Ietsuna U	.20	.50
155 You Are Too Late R	.60	1.50
156 Y'tchee R	.60	1.50

2006 Legend of the Five Rings Rise of the Shogun

COMPLETE SET (155)	40.00	100.00
BOOSTER BOX (48 PACKS)	40.00	80.00
BOOSTER PACK (11 CARDS)	1.25	2.50
RELEASED IN SEPTEMBER 2006		
1 A Dragon's Caress R	.60	1.50
2 Advance with Glory C	.10	.20
3 Akodo Meyo C	.10	.20
4 Akodo Osamu R	2.00	5.00
5 Allegiance to the Dark Lord C	.30	.75
6 Ancestral Ground C	.10	.20
7 Asahina Aoshi R	.60	1.50
8 Asahina Beniha U	.40	1.00
9 Asako Bairei (Experienced 2) R	1.25	3.00
10 Asako Makito U	.20	.50
11 Assembly Grounds C	.10	.20
12 Bamboo Thickets U	.20	.50
13 Battle Maiden Troop R	1.50	4.00
14 Bayushi Iyona C	.10	.20
15 Bayushi Kwanchi (Experienced 2) F (Scorpion)	1.50	4.00
16 Bayushi Shaiga C	.10	.20
17 Bayushi Takaharu U	.20	.50
18 Blackmailed Bride R	2.50	6.00
19 Bounty of the Clan U	.20	.50
20 Bow Your Head! C	.10	.20
21 Breeding Season U	.20	.50
22 Broken Wave City F (Mantis)	1.00	2.50
23 Call Upon the Dead C	.10	.20
24 Calling the East Wind R	1.25	3.00
25 Castle Barracks C	.10	.20
26 Chuda Ikumi C	.10	.20
27 Consumed by Five Fires C	.10	.20
28 Control R	2.00	5.00
29 Crab Detachment C	.10	.20
30 Daigotsu Eiya U	1.25	3.00
31 Daigotsu Makishi C	.10	.20
32 Daigotsu's Discipline U	.20	.50
33 Dark Harmony U	.20	.50
34 Deathseeker Troop C	.10	.20
35 Deeds of Honor C	.10	.20
36 Delaying Column C	.10	.20
37 Determination R	2.50	6.00
38 Doji Domotai (Experienced 2) R	1.25	3.00
39 Doji Ichita C	.10	.20
40 Doji Otoya C	.10	.20
41 Dragon Detachment U	.20	.50
42 Earth Becomes Sky U	.30	.75
43 East Hub Village R	1.25	3.00
44 Fan and Sword U	.20	.50
45 Fields of Honor C	.10	.20
46 Fire Maple Mempo U	.20	.50
47 Glorious Mission C	.10	.20
48 Golden Oriole Wakizashi U	.20	.50
49 Hachiwari R	.20	.50
50 Hida Benjiro (Experienced) R	.60	1.50
51 Hida Wakou U	.40	1.00
52 Hida War Drums R	.60	1.50
53 Hiruma Sakimi C	.10	.20
54 Hitomi Chishou C	.10	.20
55 Honored Hostage U	.30	.75
56 Horiushi Nobane R	1.00	2.50
57 Hunted Down C	.10	.20
58 Ik'chda C	.10	.20
59 Infamous Deeds C	.10	.20
60 Insight R	1.50	4.00
61 Inspired Strategy U	1.00	2.50
62 Isawa Angai (Experienced Soshi Angai) F (Phoenix)	2.00	5.00
63 Isawa Emori C	.10	.20
64 Isawa Seiga C	.10	.20
65 Itch'choo C	.10	.20
66 Iuchi Bitomu C	.10	.20
67 Jade Figurine C	.10	.20
68 Kaimetsu-Ou's Lineage U	.20	.50
69 Kaiu Sadao C	.10	.20
70 Kakita Kaisei U	.20	.50
71 K'chee R	.60	1.50
72 Kisada's Banishment U	.30	.75
73 Knowledge R	3.00	8.00
74 Kokujin Akae U	.20	.50
75 Kokujin Konetsu R	.60	1.50
76 Kuni Daigo R	1.00	2.50
77 Kuni Fumitake U	.20	.50
78 Kuroiban Compound U	.20	.50
79 Kyoden's Technique C	.10	.20
80 Legion of Pain R	1.50	4.00
81 Lightning Strike R	.60	1.50
82 Matsu Bunka U	.20	.50
83 Matsu Gakuya C	.10	.20
84 Matsu Yoshino (Experienced) R	.60	1.50
85 Matsu Yufu U	.20	.50
86 Merchant's Wagon U	.60	1.50
87 Mirumoto Taishuu C	.10	.20
88 Moshi Sakae U	.20	.50
89 Ninube Chisai U	.20	.50
90 North Hub Village R	1.50	4.00
91 Obsidian Dragon R	1.25	3.00
92 Obsidian Figurine C	.10	.20
93 Oh-krch U	.20	.50
94 One-Sided Melee U	.20	.50
95 Oni no Akuma (Experienced 2) R	1.25	3.00
96 Pale Oak Castle F (Phoenix)	.60	1.50
97 Paper Lantern Festival C	.10	.20
98 Passing the Mssage U	.30	.75
99 Path of Pain C	.10	.20
100 Perfection R	1.25	3.00
101 Rally the Ranks C	.10	.20
102 Rampage R	1.25	3.00
103 Ratling Truthseeker U	.20	.50
104 Rising Tensions U	.20	.50
105 River Crossing C	.10	.20
106 Rosoku's Urn R	.60	1.50
107 Rout C	.10	.20
108 Scorpion Detachment U	.20	.50
109 Second Doom of the Dragon R	.60	1.50
110 Second Doom of the Scorpion R	.60	1.50
111 Shadowlands Ambassador U	.20	.50
112 Shiba Jouta U	.20	.50
113 Shogun's Advisors R	2.50	6.00
114 Shosuro Atesharu U	.30	.75
115 Slayer's Vial C	.10	.20
116 Soshi Tabito (Experienced) R	.60	1.50
117 South Hub Village R	.60	1.50
118 Steep Slopes C	.10	.20
119 Strength of the Forge R	1.50	4.00
120 Strength R	.60	1.50
121 Strike of the Dragon U	.30	.75
122 Stronger than Steel R	.60	1.50
123 Tamori Emina R	1.00	2.50
124 Tamori Futaba U	.30	.75
125 Tchik R	.60	1.50
126 The City of Lies F (Scorpion)	.60	1.50
127 The End is Near R	.60	1.50
128 The Hammer of Kaiu C	.10	.20
129 The Price of Loyalty R	2.00	5.00
130 The Rolling Tides U	.20	.50
131 The Shogun's Left Hand R	.60	1.50
132 The Shogun's Peace U	.20	.50
133 The Shogun's Right Hand R	.60	1.50
134 Tiger's Mouth C	.10	.20
135 Togashi Kadoma U	.30	.75
136 Togashi Satsu (Experienced 3) R	2.00	5.00
137 Tok-ik U	.20	.50
138 Toku Butaku C	.10	.20
139 Torii no Orochi U	.20	.50
140 Tortoise Shell Armor R	.60	1.50
141 Treacherous Plains R	.60	1.50
142 Treacherous Sands U	.60	1.50
143 Tsuruchi Chion C	.10	.20
144 Tsuruchi Futoshi U	.20	.50
145 Usagi Genchi C	.10	.20
146 Utaku Gyonwan U	.20	.50
147 Utaku Lineage U	.20	.50
148 Utaku Tayoi C	.10	.20
149 Utaku Wakiken U	.20	.50
150 Utaku Yu-Pan (Experienced) R	.60	1.50
151 West Hub Village R	1.00	2.50
152 Will R	2.50	6.00
153 Yoritomo Ryouta C	.10	.20
154 Yoritomo Singh (Experienced Rama Singh) F (Mantis)	.60	1.50
155 Yoritomo Tadame R	1.25	3.00

2006 Legend of the Five Rings Test of Enlightenment

COMPLETE SET (124)	120.00	200.00
RELEASED IN JULY 2006		
1 A Clan Divided F	.75	2.00
2 A Clan United F	.75	2.00
3 A Long Journey F	.40	1.00
4 A Quest Abandoned F	.40	1.00
5 A Sage's Counsel F	.40	1.00
6 A Scorpion's Wisdom F	.40	1.00
7 Achirin (Experienced) F	1.25	3.00
8 Agasha Miyoshi (Experienced) F	1.25	3.00
9 Aikido Demonstration F	.75	2.00
10 Akifumi F	.75	2.00
11 Akodo Anshiro (Experienced) F	1.25	3.00
12 Akodo Bakin (Experienced) F	1.25	3.00
13 Akodo Kuemon (Experienced) F	1.50	4.00
14 Akodo Natsu (Experienced) F	1.25	3.00
15 Akodo Rokuro (Experienced) F	1.50	4.00
16 Asahina Yoshino (Experienced) F	1.25	3.00
17 Asako Takakazu (Experienced) F	1.25	3.00
18 Banzai Cry F	1.25	3.00
19 Bay of Green Coral F	1.25	3.00
20 Bayushi Adachi (Experienced) F	3.00	8.00
21 Bayushi Bokatsu (Experienced) F	1.50	4.00
22 Bayushi Kan (Experienced) F	3.00	8.00
23 Bayushi Saya (Experienced) F	1.50	4.00
24 Bayushi Shinzo (Experienced) F	2.50	6.00
25 Boisterous Soldiers F	1.25	3.00
26 Brothers in Arm F	3.00	8.00
27 Cautious Escort F	.75	2.00
28 Chikka-tek (Experienced) F	1.25	3.00
29 Chuda Ruri (Experienced) F	3.00	8.00
30 Curfew Declared F	.75	2.00
31 Daidoji Akagi (Experienced) F	1.25	3.00
32 Daidoji Setsuko (Experienced) F	1.25	3.00
33 Daigotsu Fumiaki (Experienced) F	3.00	8.00
34 Daigotsu Soetsu (Experienced) F	3.00	8.00
35 Destined Enemies F	.75	2.00
36 Diving Pool F	.40	1.00
37 Doji Saori (Experienced) F	3.00	8.00
38 Doji Seo (Experienced) F	4.00	10.00
39 Eager Students F	.75	2.00
40 Elemental Arrow F	1.25	3.00
41 Ep'kee (Experienced) F	.40	1.00
42 Festival of Inari F	.40	1.00
43 Fragrant Waters F	.75	2.00
44 Gaijin Writings F	.75	2.00
45 Gift of Rice F	.75	2.00
46 Gran-otik (Experienced) F	.75	2.00
47 Hard Pressed F	.75	2.00
48 Hida Nari (Experienced) F	1.25	3.00
49 Hida Sosuke (Experienced) F	2.00	5.00
50 Hida Sozen (Experienced) F	3.00	8.00
51 Hiruma Oda (Experienced) F	4.00	10.00
52 Hitomi Kazu (Experienced) F	1.25	3.00
53 Hoshi Masote (Experienced) F	2.00	5.00
54 Ikoma Kosaku (Experienced) F	1.25	3.00
55 Inspiring Leadership F	.40	1.00
56 Isawa Kimi (Experienced) F	1.25	3.00
57 Isawa Sawao (Experienced) F	1.25	3.00
58 Itsume F	.40	1.00
59 Iuchi Umeka (Experienced) F	1.25	3.00
60 Journey's Beginning F	.40	1.00
61 Journey's End F	.40	1.00
62 Kaiu Haku (Experienced) F	1.25	3.00
63 Kakita Funaki (Experienced) F	4.00	10.00
64 K'mee (Experienced) F	.75	2.00
65 Komori Junsaku F	.40	1.00
66 Kuni Okichi (Experienced) F	2.00	5.00
67 Kyoso no Oni (Experienced 3) F	1.50	4.00
68 Mantle of Flame F	.75	2.00
69 Mirumoto Bokkai (Experienced) F	1.25	3.00
70 Mirumoto Gonkuro (Experienced) F	3.00	8.00
71 Mirumoto Hakahime (Experienced) F	1.25	3.00
72 Monastary Classroom F	.40	1.00
73 Moshangoru (Experienced) F	.75	2.00
74 Moshi Amika (Experienced) F	2.00	5.00
75 Moshi Kekiesu (Experienced) F	2.00	5.00
76 Moto Akikazu (Experienced) F	1.25	3.00
77 Moto Rumiko (Experienced) F	2.00	5.00
78 Muketsu (Experienced) F	2.50	6.00
79 Mystic Waterfall F	1.25	3.00
80 Nagisa F	.40	1.00
81 Partake of the Fire F	1.25	3.00
82 Qolsa F	.40	1.00
83 Reckless Charge F	.40	1.00
84 Rosoku Sensei F	6.00	15.00
85 Sacred Hillside F	.40	1.00
86 Seeking Enlightenment F	.75	2.00
87 Shiba Denbe (Experienced) F	.75	2.00
88 Shiba Yoshimi (Experienced) F	.75	2.00
89 Shinjo Wei (Experienced) F	1.50	4.00
90 Shosuro Dazai (Experienced) F	3.00	8.00
91 Sisters of the Elements F	.75	2.00
92 Snow-Blocked Pass F	.75	2.00
93 Strength of the Crab F	.40	1.00
94 Strength of the Crane F	.40	1.00
95 Strength of the Dragon F	.40	1.00
96 Strength of the Lion F	.40	1.00
97 Strength of the Mantis F	.40	1.00
98 Strength of the Nezumi F	.40	1.00
99 Strength of the Phoenix F	.40	1.00
100 Strength of the Scorpion F	.40	1.00
101 Strength of the Shadowlands F	.40	1.00
102 Strength of the Unicorn F	.40	1.00
103 Sumotori Arena F	.40	1.00
104 Teaching Stick F	.40	1.00
105 Test of Enlightenment F	.40	1.00
106 The Darkened Path F	.40	1.00
107 The Dragon's Talons F	.40	1.00
108 The Mystic (Experienced Isawa Sezaru) F	1.50	4.00
109 The Ronin (Experienced Kaneka) F	2.00	5.00
110 The Wanderer (Experienced Emperor Toturi III) F	.75	2.00
111 The Way of Will F	.40	1.00
112 Togashi Nyima (Experienced) F	.75	2.00
113 Tsuruchi Arishia (Experienced) F	1.50	4.00
114 Tsuruchi Terao (Experienced) F	2.00	5.00
115 Tuftuf Sake House F	1.50	4.00
116 Unexpected Find F	1.25	3.00
117 Utaku Keyo (Experienced) F	1.50	4.00
118 Utaku Tarako (Experienced) F	2.00	5.00
119 Wanderers Revealed F	1.25	3.00
120 Wandering Pilgrim F	.75	2.00
121 Writ of the Elements F	.40	1.00
122 Yoritomo Chimori (Experienced) F	.75	2.00
123 Yoritomo Iongi (Experienced) F	.75	2.00
124 Z'chkir (Experienced) F	.75	2.00

2006 Legend of the Five Rings Training Grounds 2

RELEASED IN JULY 2006
542 Hoshi Kaelung
543 Hoshi Masujiro
594 Togashi Ieshige
2DDD Hitomi Sugihara
CraneF14F Obi of Silence
DragonD00 Voice of the Emperor
DragonD03 Mirumoto Mareshi (Experienced)
DragonD04 A New Wall
DragonD13 Temple to Shinsei
DragonD14 Togashi Kazuki
DragonD15 Puppet Theater Troupe
DragonD17 Wisdom Gained
DragonD18 Kitsuki Hakihime
DragonD19 Tamori Aoki
DragonD22 City Of Gold
DragonD24 Secluded Village
DragonD26 Togashi Satsu (Experienced 2)
DragonD27 Swordmaster Dojo
DragonD29 Secluded Waystation
DragonD31 Second Doom of the Crane
DragonD32 Temples of the New Tao C
DragonD33 Togashi Masujiro
DragonD35 Gold Mine
DragonD36 Tamori Konoye
DragonD37 Tower of the Ningyo
DragonD38 War of Silk and Steel
DragonD39 Tsuma Dojo
DragonD40 Mirumoto Gonkuro
DragonD41 Togashi Razan
DragonD44 A Favor Returned C
DragonF00 Dragon's Heart Dojo
DragonF04 Abandoned
DragonF05 Yogen
DragonF06 Tattooed Acolytes
DragonF08 Ring of Earth
DragonF10 The People's Champion
DragonF11 Sneak Attack
DragonF12 Spearmen
DragonF15 Palm Strike
DragonF16 Hoshi House Guard
DragonF17 Charge of the Baraunghar
DragonF19 Threads of Fate
DragonF20 The Kami's Blessing
DragonF24 Meeting the Keepers
DragonF25 Ring of Air
DragonF28 Explored Territory
DragonF32 Companion Spirit
DragonF33 Stay Your Blade
DragonF34 Refugees
DragonF35 Duty
DragonF36 Will of the Elements
DragonF37 Be Prepared to Dig Two Graves
DragonF39 Brutal Confrontation
DragonF41 The Future is Unwritten
DragonF42 Tsuruchi Technique

DragonF43 Mark of Oblivion
CraneD00 Left Hand of the Emperor
CraneD01 Daidoji Shihei
CraneD02 Ten Thousand Temples
CraneD09 Kabuki Theater Troupe
CraneD12 Asahina Yoshino
CraneD14 A Soul of Thunder
CraneD15 Quartermaster
CraneD16 Doji Domotai
CraneD17 Doji Midoru (Experienced)
CraneD18 Asahina Kasai
CraneD19 Venerable Master
CraneD22 Living Blade Dojo
CraneD23 Wisdom of the Keepers
CraneD24 Doji Domotai (Experienced)
CraneD25 Daidoji Uji (Experienced 3)
CraneD29 Shrine to Hotei
CraneD30 Regions of Rokugan
CraneD32 House of the Fallen Blossom
CraneD33 Doji Seo
CraneD34 Tsuno Swamps
CraneD35 Boastful Proclamation
CraneD36 Diplomatic Retreat
CraneD38 Mura Sabishii Toshi
CraneD39 Daidoji Takihiro
CraneD40 Daidoji Nichiren
CraneD41 Marketplace
CraneD42 Daidoji Akagi
CraneD43 Doji Nio
CraneD44 Gifts and Favors
CraneF00 Prosperous Plains City
CraneF02 Well-Laid Plans
CraneF03 Rosoku's Staff
CraneF04 Ring of Fire
CraneF07 Doji House Guard
CraneF12 Ring of the Void
CraneF17 Weigh the Cost
CraneF19 Silent Warriors
CraneF22 Cunning of Daidoji
CraneF24 Disavowed
CraneF26 Ring of Water
CraneF27 First and Final Strike
CraneF28 Battlefield of Shallow Graves
CraneF29 Daidoji Gunso
CraneF30 Explosives
CraneF31 Tomodachi
CraneF32 No Victory
CraneF33 Impromptu Duel
CraneF34 Ambush
CraneF35 To Do What We Must
CraneF36 Heavily Engaged
CraneF37 Saboteur
CraneF38 Honor's Cost C
CraneF39 Mountains of the Phoenix
CraneF40 Return for Training
CraneF41 Conserve Your Strength
CraneF42 Overwhelmed

2007 Legend of the Five Rings Khan's Defiance

COMPLETE SET (156) 80.00 150.00
BOOSTER BOX (48 PACKS)
BOOSTER PACK (11 CARDS)
RELEASED IN JANUARY 2007
1 A Noble End U .20 .50
2 A Soldier's Fate R 1.25 3.00
3 A Soldier's Spirit U .20 .50
4 Advance Position C .10 .20
5 Aka-Name C .10 .20
6 Akodo Hachigoro U .40 1.00
7 Akodo Shigetoshi R .50 1.25
8 Allies Become Enemies C .10 .20
9 Asahina Hideki C .10 .20
10 Asako Juro C .10 .20
11 Asako Keiki U .20 .50
12 Badge of Authority C .10 .20
13 Bayushi Hisako C .10 .20
14 Bayushi Kaukatsu (Experienced 2) R .50 1.25
15 Bayushi Maemi U .20 .50
16 Bayushi Yumita U .20 .50
17 Birth of the Blood Heir U .20 .50
18 Blade of Guile R 1.25 3.00
19 Blanketed Forest R 1.50 4.00
20 Broken Lines U .20 .50
21 Churoburo U .20 .50
22 Cool Heads Prevail U .25 .60
23 Coward! R 3.00 8.00
24 Crippled Bone Berserker U .20 .50
25 Crushing Blow U .20 .50
26 Daidoji Kikaze R .50 1.25
27 Daidoji Yaichiro U .20 .50
28 Daigotsu Rekai 1.50 4.00
(Experienced 4 Daidoji Rekai) R
29 Dishonored Vassal U .20 .50
30 Dissent C .10 .20
31 Doji Doukohito C .10 .20
32 Doji Nagori (Experienced) F (Crane) 1.50 4.00
33 Doomed Intentions R 8.00 20.00
34 Fire Dragon (Experienced 2) R 1.25 3.00
35 Fist and Blade C .10 .20
36 Flanking Action R 4.00 10.00
37 Flanking Assault C .10 .20
38 Flash of Steel R 6.00 15.00
39 Frenzied Charge R 2.00 5.00
40 Gathering Darkness U .20 .50
41 Governor's Court R 8.00 20.00
42 Gutobo C .10 .20
43 Harmonious Temple U .20 .50
44 Hch-tik U .20 .50
45 Hida Dayu C .10 .20
46 Hida Ikkaku U .20 .50
47 Hida Rikyu (Experienced) F (Crab) 2.00 5.00
48 Hida Yaheiko U .40 1.00
49 Hidden Warrens C .10 .20
50 High Courts C .10 .20
51 Hitomi Shiori U .20 .50
52 Hitsu Taeruko U .20 .50
53 Hoshi Noritada C .10 .20
54 Houhou U .20 .50
55 Hunting the Prophet U .20 .50
56 Ideal Conditions C .10 .20
57 Ikoma Hanshiro C .10 .20
58 Imperial Magistrates C .10 .20
59 Impressive Resiliance R 1.25 3.00
60 Insolence Punished R 5.00 12.00
61 Iuchi Eiji U .20 .50
62 Jikagun C .10 .20
63 Kaiu Shiro F (Crab) .40 1.00
64 Kakita Noriko U .20 .50
65 Kitsu Ineko U .20 .50
66 Kitsune Tsutaro U .20 .50
67 Kumade C .10 .20
68 Lacquered Armor U .25 .60
69 Matsu Benika (Experienced) R .75 2.00
70 Matsu Yoshike C .10 .20
71 Mirumoto Rosanjin (Experienced 2) F .50 1.25
72 Mirumoto Taikishi C .10 .20
73 Moto Chagatai (Experienced 4) R 1.25 3.00
74 Moto Chen (Experienced 2) R .50 1.25
75 Mytchokan C .10 .20
76 Nairu no Oni (Experienced) R .50 1.25
77 Nezumi Vengeance U .20 .50
78 Ok'kantich C .10 .20
79 Old Alliances C .10 .20
80 One Final March C .10 .20
81 One More Sacrifice U .20 .50
82 Ordered Retreat C .75 2.00
83 Overflowing Fields R .75 2.00
84 Ox Sentry C .10 .20
85 Peaceful Discourse R 1.25 3.00
86 Pep'trchek (Experienced) F (Ratling) 1.50 4.00
87 Pincers and Tail C .10 .20
88 Purge the Unclean C .10 .20
89 Recruiting Allies R 1.25 3.00
90 Restoring Order C .10 .20
91 Reverence for Chikushudo R 2.00 5.00
92 Revolutionaries U .20 .50
93 Ruthless Advance U 1.50 4.00
94 Sachika C .30 .75
95 Sasada C .10 .20
96 Scouring the Village C .10 .20
97 Seasoned Deckhand U .30 .75
98 Second Doom of the Unicorn R .30 .75
99 Seeking the Way R 2.00 5.00
100 Seiden Sanzo R 2.50 6.00
101 Shiba Aikune (Experienced 3) R .50 1.25
102 Shiba Daizan C .10 .20
103 Shinbone Warpack R .50 1.25
104 Shinjo Isuke U .20 .50
105 Shinjo Saihan C .10 .20
106 Shizuka Toshi F (Crane) .60 1.50
107 Shosuro Aroru R .50 1.25
108 Silent Solace U .20 .50
109 Snowy Overlook C .10 .20
110 Soshi Idaurin C .10 .20
111 Soul of Battle U .20 .50
112 Soul of the Winds U .25 .60
113 Standing Fast R 1.25 3.00
114 Strength in Certainty R 2.50 6.00
115 Strike the Base R 1.25 3.00
116 Strike the Center U .40 1.00
117 Strike the Summit C .10 .20
118 Surprise Attack C .10 .20
119 Take the Charge R 1.50 4.00
120 Tamori Nakamuro .50 1.25
(Experienced 2 Isawa Nakamuro) R
121 Tamori Wotan U .20 .50
122 Temple Acolytes C .10 .20
123 Temple of Unity R 1.25 3.00
124 The Brotherhood's Influence R .50 1.25
125 The Elements' Path C .10 .20
126 The Empress' Address R 1.25 3.00
127 The General Falls U .20 .50
128 The Kami's Embrace U .20 .50
129 The Khan's Gambit U .20 .50
130 The Lesser Evil C .10 .20
131 The Portals Open U .20 .50
132 The Winter Warren F (Ratling) .25 .60
133 Togashi Tsuri (Experienced) R .75 2.00
134 Touch of Ice C .10 .20
135 Tsuruchi Ayame U .20 .50
136 Tsuruchi Etsui (Experienced) R .75 2.00
137 Tsuruchi Gidayu C .10 .20
138 Two-Front War R .50 1.25
139 Umi-Bozu U .20 .50
140 Unexpected Betrayal R 4.00 10.00
141 Unexpected News R .50 1.25
142 Unshakable R 3.00 8.00
143 Unstoppable Power U .20 .50
144 Utaku Nayan C .10 .20
145 Valley of Heroes R .50 1.25
146 Veteran Warrior C .10 .20
147 Vik-sch'tok U .20 .50
148 Watch Commander R .75 2.00
149 Wave Man U .25 .60
150 Wrath of the People R .50 1.25
151 Yasuki Jinn-Kuen (Experienced) R .50 1.25
152 Yoritomo Isoshi U .20 .50
153 Yoritomo Utemaro R .50 1.25
154 You Die With Me! C .10 .20
155 Yukari no Onna C .10 .20
156 Yuki no Onna's Wrath U .20 .50

2007 Legend of the Five Rings Samurai

1 A New Wall R 2.00 5.00
2 A Terrible Oath R .50 1.25
3 A Test of Courage C .10 .20
4 Akodo Seiichi U .25 .60
5 Akodo Shunori C .10 .20
6 Akodo Terumoto R 1.25 3.00
7 Akodo's Grave C .10 .20
8 Akuma no Oni (Experienced 2) R .50 1.25
9 Ambush R 1.00 2.50
10 Ancestral Ground F .10 .20
11 Arrival of the Emerald Champion R 1.50 4.00
12 Arrival of the Obsidian Champion R 1.25 3.00
13 Arrow of Purity C .10 .20
14 Arrows from the Woods C .10 .20
15 Asahina Beniha U .60 1.50
16 Asako Meisuru C .10 .20
17 Asako Takakazu (Experienced) R .30 .75
18 Ashigaru Conscripts C .10 .20
19 Ashigaru Spearmen C .10 .20
20 Banish All Shadows R 3.00 8.00
21 Battlefield of Shallow Graves C .10 .20
22 Bayushi Eisaku C .10 .20
23 Bayushi Hisato C .10 .20
24 Bayushi Hisoka R 1.00 2.50
25 Bayushi Iyona F .25 .60
26 Bayushi Kurumi C .10 .20
27 Bayushi Muhito U .20 .50
28 Bayushi Nomen U .20 .50
29 Bayushi Paneki (Experienced 4) F 3.00 8.00
30 Bayushi Saya C .10 .20
31 Bayushi Tsimaru (Experienced) R 1.00 2.50
32 Beiden Pass U .20 .50
33 Berserkers U .20 .50
34 Blade of Hubris R 3.00 8.00
35 Block Supply Lines C .10 .20
36 Border Skirmish U .25 .60
37 Boshanai U .25 .60
38 Brand of Fire and Thunder C .10 .20
39 Brash Hero C .10 .20
40 Brilliant Victory C .10 .20
41 Brothers in Arms (Experienced) R .20 .50
42 Brothers in Arms C 1.00 2.50
43 Burn it Down U .30 .75
44 Call of Thunder R .50 1.25
45 Castle Barracks C .10 .20
46 Castle Gate R 1.00 2.50
47 Castle of Water C .10 .20
48 Castle Walls C .10 .20
49 Ceremonial Armor U .25 .60
50 Chuda Hankyu R 1.00 2.50
51 Chuda Hiroe C .10 .20
52 Chuda Ikumi C .10 .20
53 Chuda Kyuwa R 1.50 4.00
54 Chuda Rintaro U .20 .50
55 Circle of Steel F .25 .60
56 City of the Rich Frog R 1.00 2.50
57 Cleansing Spirit U .25 .60
58 Combined Efforts F .10 .20
59 Commanding Favor R .50 1.25
60 Companion Spirit U .20 .50
61 Compassion U .20 .50
62 Concealed Archers U .25 .60
63 Consumed by Five Fires C .10 .20
64 Contested Ground C .10 .20
65 Control R 2.00 5.00
66 Control the Field C .10 .20
67 Copper Mine F .25 .60
68 Cornering Maneuver U .25 .60
69 Corrupt Adjunct U .20 .50
70 Corrupt Officials U .20 .50
71 Countermove R 1.25 3.00
72 Courage U 1.00 2.50
73 Courtesy U .30 .75
74 Crippling Cut U .25 .60
75 Crossroads Fortress F .50 1.25
76 Cut Them Off U .25 .60
77 Daidoji Akagi C .10 .20
78 Daidoji Eitoku C .10 .20
79 Daidoji Gunso F .10 .20
80 Daidoji Nagiko R .50 1.25
81 Daigotsu (Experienced 2) F 3.00 8.00
82 Daigotsu Gyoken C .10 .20
83 Daigotsu Kaikou U .40 1.00
84 Daigotsu Masami F .25 .60
85 Daigotsu Meguro C .10 .20
86 Daruma C .10 .20
87 Deception's Veil Dojo F 1.00 2.50
88 Defining the Essence C .10 .20
89 Desperate Wager R .50 1.25
90 Determination R 6.00 15.00
91 Diplomatic Apprentice F .25 .60
92 Dirty Politics R .50 1.25
93 Doji Ayano U .25 .60
94 Doji Domotai (Experienced 3) F 2.50 6.00
95 Doji Hakuseki C .10 .20
96 Doji Jotaro C .10 .20
97 Doji Jun'ai R .50 1.25
98 Doji Koin U .20 .50
99 Doji Seo F .10 .20
100 Doji Sesshu R 1.00 2.50
101 Draw Your Blade R 6.00 15.00
102 Duty U .50 1.25
103 Eager to Fight R 1.25 3.00
104 Earth Becomes Sky U .20 .50
105 Eastern Hub Port F .60 1.50
106 Encircled Terrain C .10 .20
107 Enlistment U .20 .50
108 Essence of Gaki-do R .50 1.25
109 Essence of Water F .10 .20
110 Explored Territory C .10 .20
111 Extended Maneuvers C .10 .20
112 Failure of Duty R .50 1.25
113 False Alliance R .30 .75
114 False Trail R .50 1.25
115 Family Library U .60 1.50
116 Fan of Command U .25 .60
117 Farmlands C .10 .20
118 Few Against Many R 3.00 8.00
119 First and Final Strike C .10 .20
120 Flight of Doves U .25 .60
121 Focus R .50 1.25
122 Forest Cleansing R 1.25 3.00
123 Forest Killer Cavern C .10 .20
124 Forewarning U .50 1.25
125 Fortified Camp C .10 .20
126 Frenzy F .10 .20
127 Fury of the Dark Lord R 1.00 2.50
128 Geisha House F .25 .60
129 Glory of the Shogun R .50 1.25
130 Goblin Chuckers U .20 .50
131 Gold Mine F .25 .60
132 Greater Sacrifice U .25 .60
133 Hachiwari U .25 .60
134 Heavy Infantry C .10 .20
135 Hida Daizu (Experienced) R .10 .20
136 Hida Daizu C .50 1.25
137 Hida Genichi C .10 .20
138 Hida Hiyao U .20 .50
139 Hida Kaoru C .10 .20
140 Hida Kuon (Experienced 5) F 2.50 6.00
141 Hida Sozen (Experienced) R .50 1.25
142 Hida Takuji R 1.25 3.00
143 Hired Killer U 2.50 6.00
144 Hiruma Aki U .20 .50
145 Hiruma Tama C .10 .20
146 Hitsu-do U .25 .60
147 Honesty U .25 .60
148 Honor U .25 .60
149 House of the Fallen Blossom R 1.00 2.50
150 Hunger of the Earth C .10 .20
151 I Am Ready R .50 1.25
152 Ikoma Akiyama C .10 .20
153 Ikoma Yasuko 1.00 2.50
(Experienced Shosuro Yasuko) R
154 Imbue Chi C .10 .20
155 Immobile Stance R 1.00 2.50
156 Imperial Summons C .10 .20
157 Impromptu Duel C .10 .20
158 In Time of War U .20 .50
159 Inner Fire U .25 .60
160 Insight R 2.00 5.00
161 Iron Mine F .10 .20
162 Isawa Eitoku U .20 .50
163 Isawa Kyoko C .20 .50
164 Isawa Ochiai (Experienced) F .50 1.25
165 Isawa Oharu C .10 .20
166 Isawa Takesi U .25 .60
167 Isawa Umeko F .25 .60
168 Iuchi Umeka C .10 .20
169 Kabuki Theater Troupe U .20 .50
170 Kaiu Hisayuki U .20 .50
171 Kaiu Jurobei C .10 .20
172 Kaiu Sadao F .25 .60
173 Kakita Hideo C .10 .20
174 Katsu (Experienced) R 1.00 2.50
175 Kitsu Katsuko U .20 .50
176 Kitsuki Ryushi R 1.00 2.50
177 Kitsuki Taiko U .20 .50
178 Kitsune Den R 1.00 2.50
179 Kiyomi U .25 .60
180 Knife in the Darkness U .25 .60
181 Knowledge R 5.00 12.00
182 Kobune Port F .10 .20
183 Kobune Scout C .10 .20
184 Kobushi U .25 .60
185 Kodomo U .20 .50
186 Koutetsu Chikara F .50 1.25
187 Koutetsu Iyoku F .50 1.25
188 Koutetsu Kabe F .50 1.25
189 Koutetsu Kyuui F .50 1.25
190 Koutetsu Meiyo F 2.50 6.00
191 Koutetsu Mukei F 2.00 5.00
192 Koutetsu Sessou F .50 1.25
193 Koutetsu Shinri F 1.25 3.00
194 Koutetsu Unabara F .50 1.25
195 Kyoso no Oni (Experienced 3) R .20 .50
196 Kyoso no Oni U 1.50 4.00
197 Kyuden Asako F .50 1.25
198 Kyuden Ashinagabachi F 1.00 2.50
199 Kyuden Wasuremono F .40 1.00
200 Lesser Shrine U .20 .50
201 Lies, Lies, Lies... U .25 .60
202 Light Infantry C .10 .20
203 Lion's Pride U .20 .50
204 Mantis Detachment U .20 .50
205 Marketplace F .10 .20
206 Master of the Rolling River U .25 .60
207 Matsu Aoiko (Experienced) R .50 1.25
208 Matsu Benika C .10 .20
209 Matsu Bunka F .25 .60
210 Matsu Robun C .10 .20
211 Matsu Takeko C .10 .20
212 Matsu Yoshino (Experienced 2) F 2.50 6.00
213 Matsu Yulu U .20 .50
214 Menhari-gata R .75 2.00
215 Michio C .10 .20
216 Mirumoto Chojiro C .10 .20
217 Mirumoto Ichizo C .10 .20
218 Mirumoto Mareshi (Experienced) R .50 1.25
219 Mirumoto Taishuu C .25 .60
220 Misdirection R 1.00 2.50
221 Morale Officer C .10 .20
222 Moshi Amika C .10 .20
223 Moshi Euiko C .10 .20
224 Moto Akikazu C .10 .20
225 Moto Chagatai (Experienced 5) F .50 1.25
226 Moto Suren U .20 .50
227 Moto Taban U .20 .50
228 Mountain Summit Temple F .50 1.25
229 Mountains of the Phoenix C .10 .20
230 Mountain's Shadow Dojo F 1.00 2.50
231 Muketsu (Experienced) R 1.25 3.00
232 Never Stand Alone U .25 .60
233 No Hiding Place C .10 .20
234 Obsidian Dragon R 1.25 3.00
235 Ogre Warriors U .20 .50
236 Omoni (Experienced 2) R .50 1.25
237 Oni-Daikyu R .75 2.00
238 Outer Walls C .10 .20
239 Palm Strike R .50 1.25
240 Peasant Vengeance C .10 .20
241 Pekkle no Oni U .10 .20
242 Perfect Attunement R .50 1.25
243 Perfection R 1.25 3.00
244 Pokku U .25 .60
245 Political Interference R .50 1.25
246 Private Trader F .50 1.25
247 Proposal of Peace R .30 .75
248 Purge the Weak C .10 .20
249 Rapid Deployment C .10 .20
250 Raze to the Ground U .50 1.25
251 Razor of the Dawn Castle F 1.00 2.50
252 Refugees C .10 .20
253 Reinforce the Gates U .25 .60
254 Resumed Hostilities C .10 .20
255 Retribution U .25 .60
256 Rich Coffers U .25 .60
257 Righteous Doshin C .10 .20
258 Righteous Fury C .10 .20
259 Ring of Air U .25 .60
260 Ring of Earth U .25 .60
261 Ring of Fire U .25 .60
262 Ring of the Void U .25 .60
263 Ring of Water U .25 .60
264 Roshungi U .20 .50
265 Rosoku's Staff R .50 1.25
266 Rout C .10 .20
267 Ruins of Otosan Uchi R .50 1.25
268 Salute of the Samurai U .20 .50
269 Sap the Spirit U .25 .60
270 Seat of Power F .25 .60
271 Secluded Village C .10 .20
272 Secluded Waystation C .25 .60
273 Seikitsu Mountains U .20 .50
274 Severed From the Emperor R 1.25 3.00
275 Shiba Arihiro U .20 .50
276 Shiba Fugimori R 1.00 2.50
277 Shiba Ikku C .10 .20
278 Shiba Miiko C .10 .20
279 Shiba Ningen (Experienced 2) R 1.00 2.50
280 Shinjo Horsebow C .10 .20
281 Shinjo Kadonomaro U .60 1.50
282 Shinjo Meikoku C .10 .20
283 Shinjo Xushen (Experienced) R .50 1.25
284 Shinjo's Courage R 1.50 4.00
285 Shinomen Marsh F .25 .60
286 Shinsei's Last Hope U .20 .50
287 Shizuka Toshi F .60 1.50
288 Shosuro Adeiko U .25 .60
289 Shosuro Uyeda C .10 .20
290 Shout of Challenge C .10 .20
291 Shout of Defiance C .10 .20
292 Shout of Victory U .60 1.50
293 Shrine of the Sun U .25 .60
294 Shrine to Bishamon R .75 2.00
295 Shrine to Fukurokujin R 2.50 6.00
296 Shrine to Osano-Wo R 1.25 3.00
297 Shuten Doji's Fury R 1.50 4.00
298 Silence the Future R .50 1.25
299 Silver Mine F .25 .60
300 Sincerity U .25 .60
301 Skub U .25 .60
302 Sneak Attack R 2.50 6.00
303 Sorrows Path U .20 .50
304 Spearhead U .10 .20
305 Stables F .25 .60
306 Stay Your Blade C .10 .20
307 Stone Breaker R .50 1.25
308 Strength of the Forge R 3.00 8.00
309 Strength R 1.00 2.50
310 Strike of the Dragon U .25 .60
311 Superior Strategist R 2.00 5.00
312 Supply Outpost U .25 .60
313 Supply Smugglers F .25 .60
314 Sword of Victory C .10 .20
315 Tactical Advisors C .10 .20
316 Tactical Maneuvers R 1.50 4.00
317 Tamori Konoye F .10 .20
318 Temple of the Seekers F .25 .60
319 Temple to Shinsei F .25 .60
320 Temples of Gisei Toshi R 3.00 8.00
321 Test of the Emerald Champion U .20 .50
322 Test of the Jade Champion U .20 .50
323 Tetsu Kama Mura F .50 1.25
324 The Agasha Foundries F .50 1.25
325 The Arrow Knows the Way R 1.25 3.00
326 The Bitter Shadow of Shame R 2.50 6.00
327 The Crab's Strength F .30 .75
328 The Crane's Strength F .30 .75
329 The Dragon's Strength F .30 .75
330 The End is Near R .30 .75
331 The Fires that Cleanse U .25 .60
332 The Fortunes Smile R 5.00 12.00
333 The Hall of Ancestors F 1.00 2.50
334 The Kami's Blessing U .25 .60
335 The Lion's Strength F .30 .75
336 The Mantis's Strength F .30 .75
337 The Maw's Grave R 1.50 4.00
338 The Path Not Taken R .75 2.00
339 The Phoenix's Strength F .30 .75
340 The Ruined City F .60 1.50
341 The Scorpion's Strength F .60 1.50
342 The Seventh Tower F .60 1.50
343 The Shogun's Peace U .20 .50
344 The Spider's Lair F .30 .75
345 The Spider's Strength F .30 .75
346 The Temple of Death F .60 1.50
347 The Unicorn's Strength F .30 .75
348 The Utaku Plains F .60 1.50
349 Three Man Alliance Plain C .10 .20
350 Three-Stone River F .30 .75
351 Tides of Battle F .25 .60

352 Togashi Ieshige (Experienced Akodo Ieshige) R .50 1.25
353 Togashi Jomei C .10 .20
354 Togashi Kazuki U .20 .50
355 Togashi Masujiro U .20 .50
356 Togashi Miyoko C .10 .20
357 Togashi Satsu (Experienced 4) F 2.50 6.00
358 Togashi's Shrine R .50 1.25
359 Touch of Death R 2.00 5.00
360 Traveling Ronin R .50 1.25
361 Tsi Blade C .10 .20
362 Tsuburu no Oni U .20 .50
363 Tsuruchi Kansuke C .10 .20
364 Tsuruchi Kaya U .20 .50
365 Tsuruchi Mitsuzuka C .10 .20
366 Tsuruchi Mochisa F .25 .60
367 Tsuruchi Nobumoto (Experienced) R .50 1.25
368 Tsuruchi Okame (Experienced) R .50 1.25
369 Turn of Fortune R 1.50 4.00
370 Turn the Tide R .75 2.00
371 Unfamiliar Ground F .25 .60
372 Unfortunate Incident C .10 .20
373 Unrequited Love F .25 .60
374 Unspoken Threats U .25 .60
375 Untested Scouts C .10 .20
376 Unwavering Assault C .10 .20
377 Utaku Genshi R 2.50 6.00
378 Utaku Kohana C .10 .20
379 Utaku Meadows C .10 .20
380 Utaku Tama F .25 .60
381 Utaku Tayoi C .10 .20
382 Utaku Yu-Pan (Experienced) R 1.00 2.50
383 Utter Defeat R 1.50 4.00
384 Venerable Master R 1.25 3.00
385 Wako C .10 .20
386 Walking the Way U .60 1.50
387 Wandering Budoka R 6.00 15.00
388 Wandering Scout U .20 .50
389 Wardens C .10 .20
390 Wareta no Oni R .50 1.25
391 Warrior Challenge C .10 .20
392 We Stand Ready U .20 .50
393 Wedge R 1.25 3.00
394 Weigh the Cost C .10 .20
395 Well Prepared F .10 .20
396 Will R 2.50 6.00
397 Winter Storm R 1.00 2.50
398 Winter Warfare R 1.00 2.50
399 Wisdom Gained U .20 .50
400 Wisdom of the Keepers U .20 .50
401 Wounded in Battle F .10 .20
402 Wrath of Osano-Wo C .10 .20
403 Wretched Mercenary F .10 .20
404 Writ of Restriction U .25 .60
405 Yobanjin Alliance U .20 .50
406 Yobanjin Fortress R 1.00 2.50
407 Yogo Rieko R .50 1.25
408 Yoritomo Eriko U .20 .50
409 Yoritomo Naizen (Experienced 2) F 1.25 3.00
410 Yoritomo Okitsugu U .20 .50
411 Yoritomo Saburo C .10 .20
412 Yoritomo Tadame R 1.25 3.00

2007 Legend of the Five Rings Stronger Than Steel

COMPLETE SET (156) 40.00 100.00
BOOSTER BOX (48 PACKS) 50.00 100.00
BOOSTER PACK (11 CARDS) 1.50 3.00
RELEASED IN OCTOBER 2007
1 A Gruesome Display U .20 .50
2 A Lion's Roar U .20 .50
3 A Matter of Honor R .75 2.00
4 Agasha Tamaki C .10 .20
5 Akodo Hiroyuki F 2.00 5.00
6 Akodo Katsumoto R .75 2.00
7 Asahina Ekei R 1.25 3.00
8 Asako Bairei (Experienced 3) R 1.25 3.00
9 Asako Eichiro C .10 .20
10 Bairei's Vigil R .50 1.25
11 Bayushi Arunsa U .20 .50
12 Bayushi Ryuzaburo R .50 1.25
13 Bayushi Shinobu C .10 .20
14 Blade of the Kansen U .20 .50
15 Brilliant Rebirth Temple F .75 2.00
16 Budoka's Tonfa C .10 .20
17 Calling in Favors U .20 .50
18 Choose Your Ground C .10 .20
19 Chuda Genkei C .10 .20
20 Chutaro C .10 .20
21 City Gate C .10 .20
22 Clan Estate U .30 .75
23 Crosswinds Cut Style R .75 2.00
24 Daidoji Kojima U .20 .50
25 Daidoji Naoshige C .10 .20
26 Daigotsu Junichi U .20 .50
27 Daigotsu Susumu R .60 1.50
28 Dastardly Tactics C .10 .20
29 Datsue-ba U .20 .50
30 Death of Virtue Style R .75 2.00
31 Devious Explorer C .10 .20
32 Disgraced Ronin C .10 .20
33 Doji Armor R .75 2.00
34 Doji Masako R .50 1.25
35 Doji Nobuhide R .75 2.00
36 Drawing in the Strike C .10 .20
37 Establishing a Foothold U .20 .50
38 Evenly Matched C .10 .20
39 Failure to Your Daimyo U .20 .50
40 Falling Leaf Strike C .10 .20
41 Fight As One C .10 .20
42 Furious Assault C .10 .20
43 Gagoze no Oni C .10 .20
44 Gaijin Utensil C .10 .20
45 Goju Ryuu R 1.50 4.00
46 Gujo Odori C .10 .20
47 Gunso Atshushi R .75 2.00
48 Gunso Chitose R 2.50 6.00
49 Gunso Hirobumi R .75 2.00
50 Haiku School C .10 .20
51 Heart of the Katana Style R .50 1.25
52 Heated Discussion U .20 .50
53 Hida Fumetsu R .50 1.25
54 Hida Itsuma C .10 .20
55 Hida Kashin R 1.25 3.00
56 Hiromasa R .60 1.50
57 Hiruma Aya R .50 1.25
58 Hisao U .20 .50
59 Hojatsu's Legacy Style R .75 2.00
60 Honor is Power U .20 .50
61 Horiuchi Yoko C .10 .20
62 Houritsu Mura F .75 2.00
63 Ide Eien U .20 .50
64 Ikoma Tatsunori R .50 1.25
65 Isawa Emori F 1.25 3.00
66 Isawa Kajibara U .20 .50
67 Isawa's Air U .20 .50
68 Isawa's Blood U .20 .50
69 Isawa's Earth U .20 .50
70 Isawa's Fire U .20 .50
71 Isawa's Void U .20 .50
72 Isawa's Water U .20 .50
73 Justly Earned Victory R 4.00 10.00
74 Kafu C .10 .20
75 Kakita Amakuni C .10 .20
76 Kakita Kensho-in U .20 .50
77 Katashi C .10 .20
78 Kitsu Tenshin U .20 .50
79 Kitsune Aiko C .10 .20
80 Kolat Forgery U .20 .50
81 Kuni Takaniro U .20 .50
82 Kuni Umibe U .20 .50
83 Kusari-Gama U .30 .75
84 Longshoremen U .20 .50
85 Matsu Kameko C .10 .20
86 Matsu Sakaki U .20 .50
87 Mirumoto Ryosaki (Experienced) R .50 1.25
88 Mirumoto Yozo C .30 .75
89 Moshi Taya U .20 .50
90 Moto Chai R .75 2.00
91 Mysterious Deaths R 1.25 3.00
92 Noburo C .10 .20
93 O-shiken C .10 .20
94 Overwhelming Speed U .20 .50
95 Paper to Steel C .20 .50
96 Paragon of Honor C .10 .20
97 Parley C .10 .20
98 Power of Innocence R .75 2.00
99 Power of the Masters U .20 .50
100 Powerful Accusation C .10 .20
101 Private Whispers R .60 1.50
102 Red Leaf Cut U .40 1.00
103 Respected Mentor C .10 .20
104 Ruthless Bandits U .20 .50
105 Sentei no Oni U .20 .50
106 Seppun Detachment R .75 2.00
107 Shiba Fusaburu U .20 .50
108 Shiba Rae R 1.25 3.00
109 Shinjo Kurimoko C .10 .20
110 Shinjo Turong (Experienced) R .75 2.00
111 Shosuro Kyuichi R 2.00 5.00
112 Shosuro Takuro C .10 .20
113 Silent Movements U .20 .50
114 Single Strike Style R 1.25 3.00
115 Soshi Ukon U .20 .50
116 Soul Strike C .10 .20
117 Splendid Phoenix Style R .75 2.00
118 Storm's Eye Style R .75 2.00
119 Strength in Shadow Style R .75 2.00
120 Strength of Paragons C .10 .20
121 Superior Positioning R .60 1.50
122 Surveying the Land C .10 .20
123 Tamori Sugi U .20 .50
124 Temple of the Righteous Emperor C .10 .20
125 The Heavens Are Watching U .20 .50
126 The Hundred-Hand Strike R 3.00 8.00
127 The Rashana R 1.25 3.00
128 The Throne Stands Empty U .20 .50
129 Tight Quarters C .10 .20
130 Togashi Kanaye R 1.25 3.00
131 Togashi Remi C .10 .20
132 Togashi Shichi U .20 .50
133 Toritaka Kaiketsu C .10 .20
134 Toshi Ranbo R .50 1.25
135 True Strength R .75 2.00
136 Tsuruchi Amaya R .60 1.50
137 Tsuruchi Fuyu U .20 .50
138 Tsuruchi Masako R .50 1.25
139 Unbroken Blade Style R .75 2.00
140 Unexpected Intimidation R 1.50 4.00
141 Unexpected Reinforcements C .10 .20
142 Unproven Guardian C .10 .20
143 Unseen Assailant U .20 .50
144 Unseen Valor U .20 .50
145 Use the Wind C .10 .20
146 Utaku Etsuko R .50 1.25
147 Utaku Saber R 1.25 3.00
148 Utaku Takai U .10 .20
149 Vigilance Keep F .75 2.00
150 Vision of P'an Ku U .20 .50
151 Wasp Bow U .30 .75
152 Watching the Battle C .10 .20
153 Yajuu no Oni U .20 .50
154 Yogo Honami R .50 1.25
155 Yoritomo Daishiro F 2.00 5.00
156 Yoritomo Kane C .10 .20

2007 Legend of the Five Rings The Emerald and Jade Champions

COMPLETE SET (52) 80.00 150.00
RELEASED IN DECEMBER 2007
1 Akasha (Experienced 2) F 3.00 8.00
2 Bayushi Arashii F .60 1.50
3 Bayushi Norachai (Experienced 2) F 2.50 6.00
4 Brisk Economy F .60 1.50
5 Caught in the Act F 2.50 6.00
6 Daigotsu Eiya (Experienced) F 2.50 6.00
7 Daigotsu Kanpeki F 2.50 6.00
8 Daigotsu Sachio F 1.00 .25
9 Death at the Mikado F 1.25 3.00
10 Doji Toyoaki F .60 1.50
11 Doji Yasuyo (Experienced 3) F 6.00 15.00
12 Emerald Champion's Mempo F 4.00 10.00
13 Hida Haruko F 2.00 5.00
14 Hida Sozen (Experienced 2) F 8.00 20.00
15 Hida Yagimaki (Experienced) F 1.00 2.50
16 Hiruma Todori (Experienced 2) F 2.50 6.00
17 Ikoma Otemi (Experienced 3) F 2.50 6.00
18 Isawa Kokuten F 1.25 3.00
19 Kabuki Show F 1.25 3.00
20 Kakita Noritoshi (Experienced 2) F 4.00 10.00
21 Kitsuki Iweko (Experienced) F 2.00 5.00
22 Magistrate Station F 1.50 4.00
23 Matsu Robun (Experienced) F 2.50 6.00
24 Matsu Yoshifumi F 1.50 4.00
25 Meanwhile… F .60 1.50
26 Mikado Invitation F 1.25 3.00
27 Mirumoto Agito F .60 1.50
28 Mirumoto Narumi (Experienced) F 2.50 6.00
29 Miya's Mercy F .60 1.50
30 Moto Hotei F .60 1.50
31 Night Silk Poison F 2.00 5.00
32 Ribbon of Success F .60 1.50
33 Shiba Danjuro (Experienced 2) F 3.00 8.00
34 Shiba Yoma (Experienced 3) F 2.50 6.00
35 Shosuro Jimen (Experienced) F 3.00 8.00
36 Test of Etiquette F .60 1.50
37 Test of Investigation F .60 1.50
38 Test of Law F .60 1.50
39 Test of Leadership F .60 1.50
40 Test of Martial Ability F .60 1.50
41 Test of Ressources F .60 1.50
42 The Kami's Justice F 1.25 3.00
43 The Khan F 10.00 25.00
44 The Mikado F 1.25 3.00
45 The Saga of Taki F 1.25 3.00
46 Tsuruchi Etsui (Experienced 2) F 1.50 4.00
47 Tsuruchi Kaya (Experienced) F 1.50 4.00
48 Tsuruchi Ki (Experienced) F 1.25 3.00
49 Unauthorized Duel F 2.50 6.00
50 Utagawa (Experienced) F 3.00 8.00
51 Wheels within Wheels F 1.25 3.00
52 Yoritomo Kazuma F 1.25 3.00

2007 Legend of the Five Rings The Truest Test

COMPLETE SET (156) 40.00 100.00
BOOSTER BOX (48 PACKS) 50.00 100.00
BOOSTER PACK (11 CARDS) 1.50 3.00
RELEASED IN MAY 2007
1 A Legion of One C .10 .20
2 Akegarasu U .10 .20
3 Akodo Shinichi U .40 1.00
4 Allegations U .20 .50
5 Anvil of Despair (Experienced) R .50 1.25
6 Asako Masamichi C .10 .20
7 Assigning Blame R 5.00 12.00
8 Astonishing Resiliance R 2.00 5.00
9 Bakemono Warpack C .10 .20
10 Bayushi Kosaku C .10 .20
11 Bayushi Tomo C .10 .20
12 Beginning Arbitrations C .10 .20
13 Berserker's Charge U .20 .50
14 Blunting the Charge C .10 .20
15 Brand of Cowardice C .10 .20
16 Castle Moat U .20 .50
17 Ceremony of Planting U .10 .20
18 Chuda Chiaki U .30 .75
19 Chuda Eiichi U .20 .50
20 Clan Heirloom C .10 .20
21 Courage in Death R 2.50 6.00
22 Cowardly Rabble C .10 .20
23 Cursed Gift U .20 .50
24 Daidoji Gempachi R 1.25 3.00
25 Daidoji Murasaki C .10 .20
26 Daigotsu Hidetsugu U .20 .50
27 Daigotsu Iemitsu C .10 .20
28 Daigotsu Yajinden (Experienced 2) F .75 2.00
29 Da'na'tch U .20 .50
30 Dark Inheritance U .20 .50
31 Dawn of the Spider U .10 .20
32 Death After Life R 1.50 4.00
33 Death Poem C .10 .20
34 Denounced on Stage U 2.00 5.00
35 Desperate Gambit U .20 .50
36 Devoted Yojimbo U .20 .50
37 Doji Hitomaro C .10 .20
38 Double Bind C .10 .20
39 Earthen Guardians U .20 .50
40 Echoes of Disgrace R 2.50 6.00
41 Etsushi R 1.25 3.00
42 Failure of Courage C .10 .20
43 Fight Another Day R .75 2.00
44 Find a Way Through It C .10 .20
45 For the Fallen R 1.25 3.00
46 Forgotten Battleground C .10 .20
47 Funeral Rites C .10 .20
48 Fusami R .60 1.50
49 Gate Guardsman U .20 .50
50 Gift of the Lady C .10 .20
51 Glory in Death R 1.25 3.00
52 Goju Zeshin U .20 .50
53 Gumbai-Uchiwa C .10 .20
54 Hashi no Oni R .50 1.25
55 Hida Kozen U .20 .50
56 Hida Masatari U .20 .50
57 Hida Otoya R 1.25 3.00
58 Hida Tsuburu C .10 .20
59 Hiruma Shotoku C .10 .20
60 Honor in Death R 1.50 4.00
61 Honorable Rebirth R 1.25 3.00
62 Hope from Death R .75 2.00
63 Horiuchi Rikako R 1.25 3.00
64 Ikoma Noda C .10 .20
65 Ikoma Uchito R .75 2.00
66 I-m'jek C .10 .20
67 Inferno's Tooth C .10 .20
68 Inspire Courage C .10 .20
69 Inspire Excellence R 1.25 3.00
70 Inspire Fear C .10 .20
71 Inspire Obediance U .20 .50
72 Inspire Reverence U .20 .50
73 Iron Tetsubo C .20 .50
74 Isawa Chinatsu C .10 .20
75 Isawa Sawao (Experienced 2) R 1.25 3.00
76 Isawa Tokiko U .20 .50
77 Kakita Komachi U .10 .20
78 Kan'ok'tichek (Experienced 3) R .50 1.25
79 Kanshi U .20 .50
80 Kazumasa R .50 1.25
81 Kharma in Death R .75 2.00
82 Kitsuki Berii C .10 .20
83 K'mee (Experienced 2) R 1.25 3.00
84 K'mee's Jingasa U .20 .50
85 Kokujin Buncho C .10 .20
86 Krn'n C .10 .20
87 Kuni Ochiyo R 1.25 3.00
88 Let Them Fight Their Dead R 1.25 3.00
89 Lion Advisor R .50 1.25
90 Lion Mempo R .50 1.25
91 Loyalty, Unto Death R 1.50 4.00
92 Masakazu R .75 2.00
93 Master Saleh C .10 .20
94 Matsu Fumiyo R 1.50 4.00
95 Matsu Ouka C .10 .20
96 Matsu Shoken U .10 .20
97 Merciless Death R 1.50 4.00
98 Mirumoto Jaizuru U .20 .50
99 Mirumoto Kei (Experienced) F 2.00 5.00
100 Moshi Kiyomori U .10 .20
101 Moshi Minami U .20 .50
102 Moto Jin-sahn F 2.50 6.00
103 Moto Yong-tai U .10 .20
104 Naoharu R .75 2.00
105 Naseru's Funeral R .60 1.50
106 Picker of Bones C .10 .20
107 Prepared Defense U .20 .50
108 Preparing Stockpiles C .10 .20
109 Profit from Death R .50 1.25
110 Purity in Death R .75 2.00
111 Reclamation U .20 .50
112 Redeployment U .20 .50
113 Requisitioned Troops C .10 .20
114 Ronin Scout U .20 .50
115 Sake House Brawl C .10 .20
116 Samarhad (Experienced) U .20 .50
117 Second Doom of the Dark Lord R .50 1.25
118 Shameful Tactics U .20 .50
119 Share the Blame C .10 .20
120 Shiba Sotatsu U .10 .20
121 Shiro Usagi R .50 1.25
122 Shosuro Jimen R .75 2.00
123 Shosuro Maru (Experienced 2) R .60 1.50
124 Shosuro Masanori U .20 .50
125 Soshi Korenaga U .20 .50
126 Soul Jar R 2.50 6.00
127 Spider Heavy Regulars C .10 .20
128 Summon Maseru no Oni R 2.50 6.00
129 Summoned to Justice U .75 2.00
130 Tadaka no Oni
(Experienced Oni no Tadaka) R .50 1.25
131 Tales of Battle R 1.25 3.00
132 Tempered Resurrection U .20 .50
133 Tetsu Kama Mura F 1.25 3.00
134 The Dessicated C .10 .20
135 The Khan's Shining Horde F .75 2.00
136 The Price of Weakness U .20 .50
137 The Quelsaurth R .75 2.00
138 The Spider's Lair F .75 2.00
139 Togashi Kisu C .10 .20
140 Togashi Wirro U .10 .20
141 Traveling Magistrate U .20 .50
142 Triumph of Courage C .10 .20
143 True Artistry U .20 .50
144 Tsukai-sagasu R 1.25 3.00
145 Tsuruchi Ki C .10 .20
146 Ujina Saionji C .10 .20
147 Unicorn Wardogs U .10 .20
148 Usagi Heiji C .10 .20
149 Utaku Fujiko C .10 .20
150 Utaku Remi C .10 .20
151 Vengeful Shadows U .20 .50
152 Wandering Sohei U .20 .50
153 We Join the Ancestors R 1.25 3.00
154 Yoritomo Harada C .10 .20
155 Yoritomo Kurei R 1.25 3.00
156 Yoritomo Sachina R .75 2.00

2007 Legend of the Five Rings Tomorrow

RELEASED IN MARCH 2007
1 Barracks of the Damned
2 Tao of Fu Leng
3 Kakita's Edge
4 Kakita's First Blade
5 Togashi's Devoted
6 Jade Mirror
7 Shiryo no Matsu (Experienced)
8 Ancestral Urn
9 Naseru's Last Words
10 Candle of Shadows
11 Ring of the Phoenix
12 Egg of the Void
13 Tomorrow
14 Tomorrow's Hourglass
15 The Blasted Lands
16 Essence of Jigoku
18 The Scarab Case
19 Kamoko's Avatar
20 Heavenly Kobune of Suitengu
21 Shinsei's Tomb
22 A New Wall R
23 All Things Have A Price
24 Arms Smugglers
25 Black Heart of the Empire
26 Dark Lord's Favor
27 Emma-O's Amulet
28 Encircled Terrain
29 Explosives
30 Fields of Foolish Pride
31 Forest Killer Cavern
32 Gifts and Favors
33 Golden Obi of the Sun Goddess (Experienced)
34 Hired Killer
35 Kanashimi Toshi
36 Mak'irtch
37 Mark of Oblivion
38 Outer Walls
39 Refugees
40 Reinforce the Gates
41 Rich Coffers
42 Shinbone Pack
43 Shinbone Warrior
44 Test of Honor
45 The First Wedding
46 The Last Prophecy
47 The Price of Power
48 Three-Stone River
49 Timely Arrival
50 Tomorrow Sensei
51 Ku'chek
52 Warrens of the One Tribe
53 Whispered Rumors
54 Yotsu Dojo
55 Zamalash
517 Monkey Man

2008 Legend of the Five Rings Honor's Veil

COMPLETE SET (156) 40.00 100.00
BOOSTER BOX (48) 50.00 100.00
BOOSTER PACK (11) 1.50 3.00
RELEASED IN FEBRUARY 2008
1 A Common Goal U .20 .50
2 A Generous Offer R 1.25 3.00
3 A Lord's Compassion C .10 .20
4 A Priest's Courtesy U .20 .50
5 A Prophet Revealed U .10 .20
6 A Warrior's Courtesy U .20 .50
7 Advantageous Climate C .10 .20
8 Akodo Bakin (Experienced 2) R .30 .75
9 Akodo Nakama R 1.00 2.50
10 Ancestral Sword of the Ki-Rin R .30 .75
11 Arranged Marriage C .10 .20
12 Asako Nagami U .10 .20
13 Asp Warriors U .10 .20
14 Bayushi Eisaku (Experienced) F .50 1.25
15 Bayushi Kosugi U .10 .20
16 Bayushi Nomen (Experienced) R 1.00 2.50
17 Binding Contract U .10 .20
18 Blessings of the Death Lords U .10 .20
19 Borrowed Advisors C .10 .20
20 Brute Force R 4.00 10.00
21 Clear Signals U .20 .50
22 Consecrating the Temple R .30 .75
23 Cornered Market U .20 .50
24 Court Invitation C .10 .20
25 Daidoji Takihiro (Experienced) F .50 1.25
26 Daidoji Zoushi C .10 .20
27 Daigotsu Hirata R 1.25 3.00
28 Daigotsu Masahiko C .10 .20
29 Daigotsu Ryudo C .10 .20
30 Daigotsu Sahara R 1.25 3.00
31 Daigotsu Takayasu C .10 .20
32 Daigotsu Usharo C .10 .20
33 Daimyo's Blade R .60 1.50
34 Darling of the Season U .10 .20
35 Desolate Plains U .10 .20
36 Doji Jorihime U .10 .20
37 Doji Tsubakita C .10 .20
38 Duel to the Death R 1.50 4.00
39 Elaborate Preparations U .20 .50
40 Essence of Jade Dragon C .10 .20
41 Exchange of Hostages R .50 1.25
42 Exchanging Civilities C .10 .20
43 Famous Bazaar R 8.00 20.00
44 Gaining Momentum C .10 .20
45 Gaki of Desire C .10 .20
46 Gempukku Blade C .10 .20
47 Gempukku Ceremony C .10 .20
48 Gift Armor R 1.00 2.50
49 Gunso Kinta R 1.00 2.50
50 Gunso Shiraki R 1.00 2.50
51 Gunso Tabarou R 1.00 2.50
52 Hazardous Ford R .50 1.25
53 Hida Lineage U .20 .50
54 Hidden Dragon Temple R .50 1.25
55 Hidden Scandal C .10 .20
56 Hidden Sword Ronin U .20 .50
57 Hidekazu C .10 .20
58 High Temple of Toshi Ranbo C .10 .20
59 Hiruma Aki (Experienced) R 1.50 4.00
60 Hiruma Ikage C .10 .20
61 Horiuchi Meimei C .10 .20
62 Hummingbird Wings R 2.00 5.00
63 Ide Towako U .10 .20
64 Ide Yusuke U .10 .20
65 Ikoma Hodota U .10 .20
66 Impeccable Nobility C .10 .20
67 Inspecting the Charts C .10 .20
68 Inspiring Speech R .50 1.25
69 Isawa Mizuhiko U 1.00 2.50

70 Isawa Shokuta C .10 .20
71 Kaiu Genji U .10 .20
72 Kaiu Taru R 3.00 8.00
73 Kakita Senko U .10 .20
74 Kakita Tsukao R 1.25 3.00
75 Kata Training Grounds U .10 .20
76 Kayomasa R 1.25 3.00
77 Kishida U .10 .20
78 Kitsu Nariyumi C .10 .20
79 Kitsuki Kouri U .10 .20
80 Kitsuki Taiko (Experienced) F 1.25 3.00
81 Kitsune Mizuru C .10 .20
82 Kitsune Ryukan (Experienced) R .30 .75
83 Kuni Bachida C .10 .20
84 Kyuden Kyotei F 1.25 3.00
85 Kyuden Miya R .30 .75
86 Luxurious Gift U .10 .20
87 Manipulation U .20 .50
88 Martyr and Pawn U .20 .50
89 Matsu Fukiki U .10 .20
90 Matsu Nao C .10 .20
91 Mirumoto Katsutoshi U .10 .20
92 Mirumoto Satobe R 1.25 3.00
93 Mirumoto Toraizo C .10 .20
94 Miya Anzai C .10 .20
95 Morning Frost Castle F 1.25 3.00
96 Moto Choon-yei R .30 .75
97 Moto Masakage C .10 .20
98 Muddy Sandals U .30 .75
99 My Ancestors' Strength R .50 1.25
100 Northern Hub Village Shipwrights U .10 .20
101 Odori Dance U .20 .50
102 Oni Mura U .10 .20
103 Otomo Lineage U .20 .50
104 Passing Judgement U .20 .50
105 Perilous Ground C .10 .20
106 Poisoned Gift U .10 .20
107 Pokku's Raiders C .10 .20
108 Polite Discussion C .10 .20
109 Puppet Master R 2.00 5.00
110 Resilient Naginata U .10 .20
111 Respect Among Warriors C .10 .20
112 Return to the Heavens R .30 .75
113 Shattered Peaks C .10 .20
114 Shiba Maroyo C .10 .20
115 Shiba Sakishi R .60 1.50
116 Shiba Tsukimi (Experienced 2) R .50 1.25
117 Shikage no Oni R .30 .75
118 Shosuro Chihiro C .10 .20
119 Shosuro Lineage U .20 .50
120 Shosuro Masato C .10 .20
121 Shosuro Mizuno U .10 .20
122 Skilled Quartermaster R 1.25 3.00
123 Snow Riders R 2.50 6.00
124 Solid Defense R 1.50 4.00
125 Solving the Riddle U .20 .50
126 Sparrow Clan Aide C .10 .20
127 Sun Doru R .30 .75
128 Swift Counterattack R 2.50 6.00
129 Swift Punishment R .50 1.25
130 Teardrop Island R .60 1.50
131 Tempest of Osano-Wo U .10 .20
132 The Balance Shifts U .10 .20
133 The Champion's Guidance R .30 .75
134 The House of False Hope F 1.00 2.50
135 The Spider's Shadow R .30 .75
136 The Strength of Allies C .10 .20
137 To Serve Justice C .10 .20
138 To the Last Breath C .10 .20
139 Togashi Keitori C .10 .20
140 Tonfajutsu C .10 .20
141 Torch's Flame Flickers C .10 .20
142 Tsuruchi Takeba U .10 .20
143 Unbiased Advice U .20 .50
144 Under Suspicion C .10 .20
145 Ungrateful Host R .50 1.25
146 Utaku Keiko R 2.00 5.00
147 Versatile Army R 3.00 8.00
148 Winter Ravager C .10 .20
149 Wolf Legion U .10 .20
150 Wolf's Little Lesson U .20 .50
151 Yarijutsu R 4.00 10.00
152 Yasuki Tenzo U .10 .20
153 Yoritomo Hotako (Experienced) R 1.25 3.00
154 Yoritomo Jera U .10 .20
155 Yoritomo Yagami C .10 .20
156 Yoritomo Yoyonagi (Experienced) R .30 .75

2008 Legend of the Five Rings The Heaven's Will

COMPLETE SET (166) 80.00 150.00
BOOSTER BOX (48 PACKS) 50.00 100.00
BOOSTER PACK (11 CARDS) 1.50 3.00
RELEASED IN OCTOBER 2008
1 Adepts of Mighty Pokku C .10 .20
2 Agasha Iwarou U .10 .20
3 Aggressive Landing C .10 .20
4 Akodo Hijikata R .60 1.50
5 Akodo Shinichi (Experienced) F 1.25 3.00
6 Akodo Tadatoshi U .10 .20
7 Armor of Light R1 1.50 4.00
8 Asako Juro (Experienced) R .50 1.25
9 Assassin's Strike C .10 .20
10 Bayushi Gaho C .10 .20
11 Bayushi Irishi U .10 .20
12 Bayushi Kasata C .10 .20
13 Bayushi Kurumi (Experienced) R 2.50 6.00
14 Beloved of the Clan R 3.00 8.00
15 Blessed Tessen C .10 .20
16 Blighted Region R .50 1.25
17 Broken Reef Keep F 1.25 3.00
18 Bronze Memorial R .75 2.00
19 Chagatai's Legion R .50 1.25
20 Chuda Mishime (Experienced) R1 3.00 8.00
21 Chuda Shikyo U .10 .20
22 Claiming the Throne U .10 .20
23 Consecration R .60 1.50
24 Daidoji Awao U .10 .20
25 Daidoji Barashi R 1.50 4.00
26 Daigotsu Kurai C .10 .20
27 Daigotsu Meguro (Experienced) R .50 1.25
28 Daigotsu Sendo R 1.25 3.00
29 Daigotsu Shiraki U .10 .20
30 Dance of the Kami U .10 .20
31 Decisive Strike U .10 .20
32 Decree of Peace U3 .10 .20
33 Defensive Tactics U .20 .50
34 Deftly Wielded U3 .20 .50
35 Desperate Plea R1 1.50 4.00
36 Discretionary Valor U .20 .50
37 Doji Hiromi U3 .10 .20
38 Dojo Applicants R .75 2.00
39 Eku C .10 .20
40 Entangling Terrain C .10 .20
41 Estate Halls U .10 .20
42 Fall of Greatness R .50 1.25
43 Flame of Truth C3 .10 .20
44 Flanked by Nightmares R 4.00 10.00
45 Footman's Pike R .50 1.25
46 Fortified Fields C3 .10 .20
47 Fortune's Favor U .10 .20
48 Fubiri no Oni U .10 .20
49 Gentle Blade of Winter U .20 .50
50 Glukku C .10 .20
51 Great Falls Castle F 1.25 3.00
52 Hand of Osano-Wo R 1.50 4.00
53 Hateful Curse R .50 1.25
54 Hida Kaoru (Experienced) R .60 1.50
55 Hida Ubogin R 1.25 3.00
56 Hiruma Moshiro C .10 .20
57 Hiruma Tabarou U .10 .20
58 Hold! R .75 2.00
59 Holy Site R1 .50 1.25
60 Ideal Grounds U .20 .50
61 Ikoma Okita C .10 .20
62 Imperial City Guards C3 .10 .20
63 Isawa Chishaki R .60 1.50
64 Isawa Naki C3 .10 .20
65 Isawa Ochiai (Experienced 2) R1 .50 1.25
66 Isawa Uhiko U3 .10 .20
67 Iuchi Konyo U .10 .20
68 Kaiu Seison R .50 1.25
69 Kakita Hideo (Experienced) R .60 1.50
70 Kakita Hideshi C .10 .20
71 Kakita Idzuki R 2.50 6.00
72 Kakita Toma C .10 .20
73 Katana of Twilight R1 5.00 12.00
74 Keen Blade U3 .10 .20
75 Keeping Enemies Close U .20 .50
76 Kimogen U .10 .20
77 Kitsu Yutaro U .10 .20
78 Kitsuki Rai F 2.00 5.00
79 Kitsuki Taji C .10 .20
80 Kitsune Hisano R 1.25 3.00
81 Kuni Tanin C3 .10 .20
82 Kuri C3 .10 .20
83 Kuronada U .40 1.00
84 Laborious Effort U3 .20 .50
85 Let Them Run C .10 .20
86 Masu C .10 .20
87 Matsu Hatsuyo R 1.25 3.00
88 Matsu Mikura C .10 .20
89 Might of Paragons R 1.25 3.00
90 Mirumoto Akio R 3.00 8.00
91 Moshi Amarante U .10 .20
92 Moshi Mareo C .10 .20
93 Moto Soonshin R .75 2.00
94 Musha Shugyo R1 2.00 5.00
95 My Ally's Strength C .10 .20
96 My Enemy's Mercy R 2.00 5.00
97 No Escape U .20 .50
98 Offered Gift R .50 1.25
99 Old Rivalries R1 4.00 10.00
100 Only the Well-Trained Listen R 4.00 10.00
101 Ornate Armor C3 .10 .20
102 Pack Tactics C .10 .20
103 Peaceful Interlude C3 .10 .20
104 Political Influence R 1.50 4.00
105 Powerful Blow R 4.00 10.00
106 Ramifications U .20 .50
107 Regroup and Redeploy C .10 .20
108 Reprimand C .10 .20
109 Resurgence R 1.50 4.00
110 Roaring to Shake Heaven C .10 .20
111 Sacrificial Lands U .20 .50
112 Seeking the Path R 1.50 4.00
113 Seiko C3 .10 .20
114 Seppun Miharu R .60 1.50
115 Shelter for Refugees U .20 .50
116 Shiba Morihiko C .10 .20
117 Shikibu no Oni 1.50 4.00
(Experienced Oni no Shikibu) R1
118 Shinjo Aniji C .10 .20
119 Shinjo Joyung R .75 2.00
120 Shinjo Kirita U .10 .20
121 Shosuro Hihiko R 4.00 10.00
122 Shosuro Kiemon U3 .10 .20
123 Silent Rot R 2.50 6.00
124 Skin of the Naga R .50 1.25
125 Small Estate C .10 .20
126 Stalemate R .75 2.00
127 Stolen Blade U3 .20 .50
128 Strength in Simplicity C .10 .20
129 Strength of my Father C3 .10 .20
130 Sublime Peacock Stance C .10 .20
131 Subtle Reminder U .20 .50
132 Swift Darkness U .20 .50
133 Sword Saint Shrine C .10 .20
134 Tamori Akeno U .10 .20
135 The Earth's Wrath U .10 .20
136 The Slow Death R 4.00 10.00
137 Threat of Execution U .20 .50
138 Tiger Climbing Mountain C .10 .20
139 Togashi Chiko U .10 .20
140 Togashi Dai C .10 .20
141 Togashi Miyoko (Experienced) R .50 1.25
142 Transcendence of Flesh R 1.50 4.00
143 Traveling Smugglers C .10 .20
144 Tsuruchi Shisuken C .10 .20
145 Underhanded Attack U .20 .50
146 Undermining Command U .20 .50
147 Undignified Death R 4.00 10.00
148 Unpleasant Discovery U3 .20 .50
149 Utaku Jisoo C .10 .20
150 Utaku Kohana (Experienced) R .60 1.50
151 Venerable Plains of the Ikoma F 1.50 4.00
152 Veteran Advisor R 1.50 4.00
153 Victory March C .20 .50
154 Viper Tattoo U .20 .50
155 Wakened Dead U .10 .20
156 Wandering Ronin R .75 2.00
157 Ward of the Kami C .10 .20
158 Wary Peace C .10 .20
159 Wrack the Soul C .10 .20
160 Yakamo's End U .20 .50
161 Yasuki Takai U3 .10 .20
162 Yogo Koji (Experienced) R1 2.00 5.00
163 Yoritomo Joben U .10 .20
164 Yoritomo Saburo (Experienced) R .60 1.50
165 Yoritomo Tadame (Experienced) F 1.25 3.00
166 Yoshe C .10 .20

2008 Legend of the Five Rings The Imperial Gift Part 1

RELEASED IN JANUARY 2009
1 As the Breakers F
2 Call Forth the Dead F
3 Consecration of Steel F
4 Daigotsu Bundoru F
5 Daku no Oni F
6 Dance of the Winds F
7 Discovering Lost Lore F
8 Drinking One's Life F
9 Facilitation F
10 Fubatsu Blade F
11 Game of Sincerity F
12 Hida Manoru F
13 Hitofu F
14 Imperial Couriers F
15 Intercession F
16 Isawa Itsuoko F
17 Kakita Taminoko F
18 Matsu Notsuo F
19 Military Assessment F
20 One Thousand Years of Darkness F
21 Osano-Wo's Rebuke F
22 Race for the Throne F
23 Regional Treasurer F
24 Sacred Valley F
25 Saga of the Clan War F
26 Saga of the Four Winds F
27 Scholarly Attendant F
28 Scorpion Clan Coup F
29 Shosuro Miyoto F
30 Togashi Cunoken F
31 Tsuruchi Saya F
32 Utaku Kioko F
33 War Against the Darkness F
34 War of Spirits F
35 War-Torn Plains F
36 What Is Yet to Come F

2008 Legend of the Five Rings Ultimate Clan Pack: Crab

1 Crab Master F3
2 Enraged Assault F1
3 Front Gate F1
4 Heroic Defiance F3
5 Hida Fujiki F1
6 Kaiu Kirino F1
7 Kuni Josuke F3
8 Masakari F3
9 Men at Arms F4
10 Rampart Sentries F3
11 Siege Engine F1

2008 Legend of the Five Rings Ultimate Clan Pack: Crane

1 A Surprising Tale F Crane
2 Artisan Academy F1
3 Crane Levies F4
4 Crane Master F3
5 Daidoji Arrows F3
6 Daidoji Jitawa F1
7 Doji Noburo F3
8 Kakita Katsuro F1
9 Shielding the Command Group F1
10 Signal Fan F3
11 Writ of Protection F1

2008 Legend of the Five Rings Ultimate Clan Pack: Dragon

1 Brothers of Jade F3
2 Contemplation of Destiny F1
3 Dragon Master F3
4 Gong of the High House F1
5 Militia Recruit F4
6 Mirumoto Yoma-shi F1
7 Mountain's Heart Blade F1
8 Temple Sentries F3
9 Togashi Chikato F3
10 Togashi Ikumu F1

2008 Legend of the Five Rings Ultimate Clan Pack: Lion

1 Akodo Tomio F1
2 College of War F1
3 Hidden Reserves F3
4 Ikoma Bugoro F3
5 Ikoma Reinforcements F4
6 Impenetrable Front F3
7 Lion Master F3
8 Matsu Takehiko F1
9 My Gradfather's Blade F1
10 Otemi's Technique F1
11 O-Yoroi F3

2008 Legend of the Five Rings Ultimate Clan Pack: Mantis

1 Archers Unleashed F3
2 Conscript Sailors F1
3 Courageous Yoriki F3
4 Dissension F1
5 Equipment Storage F1
6 Kitsune Tsuke F3
7 Mantis Master F3
8 New Recruit F4
9 Tsuruchi Kimita F1
10 Tsuruchi Longbow F3
11 Yoritomo Omura F1

2008 Legend of the Five Rings Ultimate Clan Pack: Phoenix

1 Agasha Orito F3
2 Blessed Library F1
3 Elemental Mastery F1
4 Isawa Idomu F1
5 Legion of Flame Armor F3
6 Phoenix Master F3
7 Ritual Standard F1
8 Shiba Ryugo F1
9 Shielded by Fire F3
10 Summon the Council F3
11 Young Defender F4

2008 Legend of the Five Rings Ultimate Clan Pack: Scorpion

1 House of the Rising Sun F1
2 Onnotangu's Memory F1
3 Phial of Poison F3
4 Poison Sake F3
5 Scorpion Master F3
6 Shadow Games F3
7 Shosuro Nikai F1
8 Shosuro Seibei F1
9 Soshi Iaike F3
10 The Wind Whispers F1
11 Toshi Ranbo Guard F4

2008 Legend of the Five Rings Ultimate Clan Pack: Spider

1 Ashigaru Defender F4
2 Chuda Naotake F1
3 Daigotsu Keigo F3
4 Dawn of the Dead F1
5 Fuyuzare F1
6 House of the Dead F1
7 Obsidian Armor F3
8 Shattered Morale F3
9 Spider Master F3
10 The Kansen's Shadow F1
11 Venomous Steel F3

2008 Legend of the Five Rings Ultimate Clan Pack: Unicorn

1 Baraunghar Scouts F3
2 Custom Barding F1
3 Ide Shinji F3
4 Kurimoko's Recruits F4
5 Moto Horsebow F3
6 Moto Kunio F1
7 The Moto Feint F1
8 Trident Formation F3
9 Unicorn Master F3
10 Utaku Arisa F1
11 Western Outpost F1

2008 Legend of the Five Rings Words and Deeds

COMPLETE SET (166) 80.00 150.00
BOOSTER BOX (48 PACKS) 50.00 100.00
BOOSTER PACK (11 CARDS) 1.50 3.00
RELEASED IN MAY 2008
1 A Warrior's Patience R 1.50 4.00
2 Agasha Sanami C .10 .20
3 Akodo Itoku R 4.00 10.00
4 Akodo Sadahige (Experienced) R .50 1.25
5 An Act of Disdain R 1.00 2.50
6 Armor of Command C .10 .20
7 Armor of Toshigoku U .20 .50
8 Arrogant Dismissal C .10 .20
9 Asahina Keitaro (Experienced) R .50 1.25
10 Asahina Naoki R 2.50 6.00
11 Asakao Bushiken C .10 .20
12 Bayushi Chikayo C .10 .20
13 Bayushi Ikkou C .10 .20
14 Bayushi Ryouya R 1.50 4.00
15 Bayushi Tenbin R 2.00 5.00
16 Bayushi Yusui U .20 .50
17 Behind Enemy Lines C .10 .20
18 Besieged R 1.50 4.00
19 Black and White U .20 .50
20 Black Silk Castle F .50 1.25
21 Blade of Awe R 1.25 3.00
22 Blade of Spirit R 1.00 2.50
23 Brink of Exhaustion R 1.25 3.00
24 Celestial Unrest U .10 .20
25 Chuda Jinsei U .20 .50
26 Contested Ownership C .10 .20
27 Coordinated Movement R 1.00 2.50
28 Coronation of Jade R .50 1.25
29 Crude Trap R 5.00 12.00
30 Customized Armor R 1.00 2.50
31 Daidoji Teruo C .10 .20
32 Daigotsu Gyoken (Experienced) R 2.00 5.00
33 Daigotsu Harushi C .10 .20
34 Daigotsu Masisha U .20 .50
35 Daimyo's Vassals R .50 1.25
36 Darkness Unleashed U .20 .50
37 Death Trance R 1.00 2.50
38 Demented Craftsmen U .10 .20
39 Devastating Blow R .50 1.25
40 Differences Between Us U .20 .50
41 Dissolution U .20 .50
42 Diverting the Reserves U .20 .50
43 Doji Ayano (Experienced) R .50 1.25
44 Doji Chitose U .10 .20
45 Doji Sakurako U .10 .20
46 Duel of Champions R 1.25 3.00
47 Failure of Diplomacy U .20 .50
48 Fatina R 1.50 4.00
49 Final Sacrifice U .20 .50
50 Follow the Flame C .10 .20
51 Fortified Cavalry U .20 .50
52 Glorious Path to Victory C .10 .20
53 Gunso Hiroshi R 1.25 3.00
54 Gunso Kisho R 1.25 3.00
55 Gunso Raiden R .60 1.50
56 Hamstrung R 4.00 10.00
57 Heaven's Fire U .20 .50
58 Hida Bachiatari C .20 .50
59 Hida Fubatsu U .10 .20
60 Hida Manabu C .10 .20
61 Hida Nichie (Experienced) R .50 1.25
62 Hiruma Kaikawa C .10 .20
63 Hub of Commerce C .10 .20
64 Hurried Gempukku U .20 .50
65 I Will Not Die Alone! U .20 .50
66 Ikoma Asa U .30 .75
67 Inspirational Address C .10 .20
68 Insurmountable Obstacle U .30 .75
69 Inu C .10 .20
70 Isawa Kyoko (Experienced) R .60 1.50
71 Isawa Miniko U .10 .20
72 Isawa Wakasa R 1.00 2.50
73 Iuchi Ietsuna U .20 .50
74 Jinako U .20 .50
75 Kaiu Shoichi R 1.00 2.50
76 Kakita Michihiro C .10 .20
77 Kata of the North Wind R 1.00 2.50
78 Keeping the Peace C .10 .20
79 Kensai's Blade C .10 .20
80 Kitsuki Mayako U .10 .20
81 Kitsuki Nagiken (Experienced) R .60 1.50
82 Kitsune Engo C .10 .20
83 Kote U .10 .20
84 Kuni Daigo (Experienced) F 1.25 3.00
85 Lightening the Load U .20 .50
86 Maga-yari C .20 .50
87 Masterpiece U .20 .50
88 Masters of Steel R 1.25 3.00
89 Matsu Daichi C .10 .20
90 Matsu Takeko (Experienced) R .50 1.25
91 Matsu Ushio U .10 .20
92 Matsu Yosa C .10 .20
93 Michio (Experienced) F 2.00 5.00
94 Militia Training Ground R 1.25 3.00
95 Mirumoto Atsushi U .10 .20
96 Mirumoto Otohiko R .60 1.50
97 Mirumoto Toshiyuki C .10 .20
98 Moshi Chuuya U .10 .20
99 Moto Yong-tai (Experienced) R .50 1.25
100 Muduro no Oni U .20 .50
101 Mukku C .10 .20
102 Naseru's Private Journal R .50 1.25
103 One After Another R .60 1.50
104 Otomo Ouga C .20 .50
105 Patron of the Arts C .10 .20
106 Pokku (Experienced) R 1.25 3.00
107 Prized Farmlands C .10 .20
108 Questionable Patron C .10 .20
109 Reckless Abandon U .20 .50
110 Reihado Shinsei R .60 1.50
111 Rejoining the Fight U .20 .50
112 Remote Farms C 1.00 2.50
113 Removing the Advantage U .20 .50
114 Rewards of Experience R 1.50 4.00
115 Rising Lava Strike U .20 .50
116 Secret Passages C .10 .20
117 Seized Assets C .10 .20
118 Selfless Politics U .20 .50
119 Shameful Injury C .10 .20
120 Shiba Erena R 2.00 5.00
121 Shiba Ritsuo U .20 .50
122 Shinjo Genya C .10 .20
123 Shinjo Naota C .10 .20
124 Shinjo Shono (Experienced 4) F 1.00 2.50
125 Shinjo T'sao U .20 .50
126 Shiotome U .20 .50
127 Shosuro Hirubumi C .10 .20
128 Skilled Defense C .10 .20
129 Song of the World R 1.25 3.00
130 Soshi Tishi (Experienced) R .50 1.25
131 Sowing Suspicion C .10 .20
132 Speed of the Sea C .10 .20
133 Spider Abbot R .60 1.50
134 Strength of Arms C .10 .20
135 Swift Sword Cut U .20 .50
136 Tadaka's Mirror C .10 .20
137 Tale of Tsukuro R 10.00 25.00
138 Taoist Archer R .10 .20
139 Tengoku's Justice C .30 .75
140 Tetsuo C 1.50 4.00
141 The Emperor's Road R .10 .20
142 The Fall of Shiro Moto U .10 .20
143 The Final Wave C 1.00 2.50
144 The Great Carpenter Wall F 1.50 4.00
145 The Jackal's Kiss R 1.25 3.00
146 The Last One R .20 .50
147 The Mountain's Feet U 5.00 12.00
148 The Third Yasuki War R .60 1.50
149 The Western Steppes F 1.00 2.50
150 Togashi Binya C .10 .20

151 Togashi Hogai (Experienced Hitomi Hogai) R 1.50 4.00
152 Touch of the Infinite R .50 1.25
153 Tsuruchi Akinobu C .10 .20
154 Tsuruchi Taiga U .10 .20
155 Ujina Ukita C .10 .20
156 Unwanted Mediation C .10 .20
157 Usurpation R 3.00 8.00
158 Utaku Fusae R .60 1.50
159 Web of Pain C .10 .20
160 Wrist Lock U .60 1.50
161 Ying and Yang C .10 .20
162 Yobanjin Mercenaries C .10 .20
163 Yoritomo Eriko (Experienced) R .50 1.25
164 Yoritomo Fushu R .60 1.50
165 Yoritomo Han-ku R .50 1.25
166 Zanaru C .10 .20

2009 Legend of the Five Rings Celestial Edition

RELEASED IN JUNE 2009
1 A Legion of One F
2 A New Year R
3 A Time for Action R
4 A Walking Death R
5 A Warrior's Patience R
6 Acrobat Troupe R
7 Advance Position C
8 Agasha Ueda C
9 Aggressive Landing C
10 Akodo Sadahige (Exp) R
11 Akodo Sagashite C
12 Akodo Seiichi U
13 Akodo Shigetoshi (Exp) F
14 Akodo Shinichi (Exp) R
15 Akodo Shunori C
16 Akodo's Grave C
17 Akuma no Oni (Exp) R
18 Allegations U
19 Ambush R
20 Armor of Command C
21 Arrival of the Emerald Champion R
22 Arrival of the Obsidian Champion R
23 Asako Katashi U
24 Bamboo Harvesters F
25 Barley Farm U
26 Battle Maiden Troop U
27 Battle of Drowned Honor C
28 Bayushi Arashii F
29 Bayushi Eisaku C
30 Bayushi Eisaku (Exp) R
31 Bayushi Jutsushi U
32 Bayushi Kurumi C
33 Bayushi Kurumi (Exp) R
34 Bayushi Maemi U
35 Bayushi Paneki (Exp) F
36 Bayushi Sakai C
37 Beloved of the Clan R
38 Berserkers U
39 Black Hearts, Red Blades C
40 Blade of Guile R
41 Blanketed Forest R
42 Blessed Tessen C
43 Blowdarts C
44 Border Keep F
45 Border Village C
46 Boshanai U
47 Castle of Water C
48 Celestial Alignment R
49 Celestial Vision U
50 Central Castle F
51 Ceremonial Armor U
52 Charge C
53 Chasing Osano-Wo U
54 Chuda Hiroe C
55 Chuda Shuzo U
56 City of Tears F
57 Claiming the Throne U
58 Clan Estate U
59 Consumed by Five Fires C
60 Control R
61 Convenient Disaster U
62 Copper Mine F
63 Corrupt Officials U
64 Countermove R
65 Counting House C
66 Courage U
67 Courtesy U
68 Daidoji Kimpira F
69 Daidoji Sakihiko C
70 Daidoji Yaichiro U
71 Daidoji Zoushi C
72 Daigotsu (Exp) F
73 Daigotsu Gyoken U
74 Daigotsu Gyoken (Exp) R
75 Daigotsu Hirata R
76 Daigotsu Setsuko C
77 Daigotsu Taizo F
78 Dance of the Kami U
79 Darkness Unleashed U
80 Datsue-ba U
81 Decree of Peace U
82 Deeds and Words R
83 Defensive Screen R
84 Desolate Plains U
85 Diamond Mine U
86 Discretionary Valor U
87 Disfavored R
88 Dissolution U
89 Doji Armor R
90 Doji Ayano U
91 Doji Ayano (Exp) R
92 Doji Domotai (Exp) F
93 Doji Hatashi C
94 Doji Senta C
95 Dragon's Guard City F
96 Dramatic Assassination U
97 Drawing in the Strike C
98 Duty U
99 Echoes of Disgrace R
100 Elaborate Preparations U
101 Encircled Terrain C
102 Enough Talk! C
103 Essence of Gaki-do R
104 Extended Maneuvers C
105 Failure of Courage C
106 Falling Leaf Strike U
107 Family Keep C
108 Famous Bazaar R
109 Farmlands U
110 Favor to the Horde U
111 Festival of Cherry Blossoms U
112 Fields of the Dead F
113 Fight As One F
114 Final Sacrifice U
115 Flanked by Nightmares R
116 Flight of Doves U
117 Follow the Flame C
118 Forests of Shinomen U
119 Forewarning U
120 From Every Side C
121 Fueling the Flames U
122 Fury of the Dark Lord R
123 Geisha House F
124 Gift Armor R
125 Goblin Chuckers U
126 Gold Mine F
127 Greater Sacrifice C
128 Gumbai-Uchiwa C
129 Gunso C
130 Gutobo C
131 Hamstrung R
132 Hand of Osano-Wo R
133 Heavenly Blade of the Crane F
134 Heavenly Daisho of the Dragon F
135 Heavenly Jumonji-yari of the Lion F
136 Heavenly Kama of the Mantis F
137 Heavenly Lance of the Unicorn F
138 Heavenly Ninja-to of the Scorpion F
139 Heavenly Tetsubo of the Crab F
140 Heavenly Yari of the Phoenix F
141 Heavy Infantry U
142 Heroic Feat C
143 Hida Bachiatari U
144 Hida Eijiko U
145 Hida Kaoru C
146 Hida Kuon (Exp) F
147 Hida Masatari C
148 Hida Ogano C
149 Hida War Drums R
150 Hidden Moon Dojo F
151 Hidden Scandal C
152 Hiruma Aki U
153 Hiruma Aki (Exp) R
154 Hiruma Gohachiro C
155 Hiruma Masato F
156 Hiruma Seiko C
157 Hisao U
158 Hitsu-do C
159 Hold! R
160 Holy Site R
161 Houhou U
162 Hurlspit Goblins U
163 I Am Ready R
164 I Will Not Die Alone! U
165 Ikoma Toraji C
166 Impeccable Nobility U
167 Imperial Ambassadorship R
168 Imperial Artificer C
169 Imperial Census R
170 Imperial City Guards C
171 Imperial Decree F
172 Impressive Resilience R
173 Impromptu Duel F
174 Inferno R
175 Inheriting an Heirloom U
176 Insight R
177 Inspire Fear F
178 Insurmountable Obstacle U
179 Iron Mine F
180 Isawa Akihiro C
181 Isawa Emori (Exp) R
182 Isawa Kyoko C
183 Isawa Kyoko (Exp) R
184 Isawa Mizuhiko C
185 Isawa Nakajima C
186 Iuchi Xiong C
187 Jinako U
188 Justly Earned Victory R
189 Kaiu Taru R
190 Kakita Hideo U
191 Kakita Hideo (Exp) R
192 Kakita Idzuki R
193 Kakita Okirou U
194 Kata of the North Wind R
195 Kayomasa R
196 Keen Blade U
197 Kitsuki Berii C
198 Kitsuki Taiko U
199 Kitsuki Taiko (Exp) R
200 Kitsune Den R
201 Kitsune Mizuru C
202 Knife in the Darkness U
203 Know Your Center C
204 Kobune Port F
205 Kobushi U
206 Kuni Daigo (Exp) R
207 Kuronada U
208 Kyuden Hida F
209 Large Farm U
210 Last Gift C
211 Light Infantry C
212 Manipulation U
213 Marketplace F
214 Master Saleh C
215 Matsu Fumiyo R
216 Matsu Mari U
217 Matsu Mikura F
218 Matsu Satsune C
219 Matsu Ushio U
220 Matsu Yosa C
221 Michio (Exp) R
222 Mirumoto Ichizo C
223 Mirumoto Ino C
224 Mirumoto Kei (Exp) F
225 Mirumoto Minawa U
226 Mirumoto Satobe R
227 Monkey Magistrates U
228 Moshi Kamiya U
229 Moto Chen (Exp) F
230 Moto Choon-yei R
231 Moto Qu Yuan C
232 Moto Taban U
233 Mountains of the Phoenix C
234 Mujina Gang C
235 Nagataka C
236 Never Stand Alone U
237 Offered Gift R
238 Omoni (Exp) R
239 One After Another R
240 Oni-Daikyu R
241 Outer Walls C
242 Palm Strike R
243 Peaceful Discourse R
244 Peasant Vengeance F
245 Permanent Encampment U
246 Pillars of Virtue F
247 Pokku U
248 Pokku (Exp) R
249 Pokku's Raiders C
250 Power of Innocence R
251 Precise Strike F
252 Private Shrine U
253 Private Whispers R
254 Ramifications U
255 Reinforce the Gates U
256 Relief C
257 Resilient Naginata U
258 Restoring Order C
259 Retribution U
260 Return to the Heavens R
261 Rich Coffers U
262 Ride Through the Night U
263 Ring of Air U
264 Ring of Earth U
265 Ring of Fire U
266 Ring of the Void U
267 Ring of Water U
268 Rise, Brother U
269 Rout C
270 Ruthless Advance U
271 Secluded Outpost R
272 Seeking the Path R
273 Seiden Sanzo R
274 Selfless Politics U
275 Settling the Homeless C
276 Seven Fold Palace F
277 Seven Seas Port F
278 Seven Stings Keep F
279 Shame Never Dies U
280 Shameful Injury C
281 Shameful Tactics U
282 Shattered Peaks Castle F
283 Shiba Fusaburu U
284 Shiba Morihiko F
285 Shiba Rae R
286 Shiba Tsukimi (Exp) F
287 Shikage no Oni R
288 Shikibu no Oni R
289 Shinjo Hwarang C
290 Shinjo Naota C
291 Shinomen Marsh F
292 Shio no Oni U
293 Shiro Daidoji F
294 Shosuro Mizuno U
295 Shosuro Tomoko U
296 Shrine of Champions F
297 Shrine to Hotei R
298 Silent Rot R
299 Silver Mine F
300 Sinister Bisento of the Spider F
301 Sneak Attack R
302 Snow Riders R
303 Song of the World R
304 Soshi Ganrou C
305 Souls of Virtue U
306 Spearhead U
307 Spearmen C
308 Stables F
309 Steadfast Bushi U
310 Steel on Steel C
311 Strength of the Bamboo U
312 Summon Maseru no Oni R
313 Swift Counterattack R
314 Swift Sword Cut U
315 Tactical Advisors C
316 Tamori Wotan F
317 Taoist Archer R
318 Temple to Shinsei U
319 Tetsu Kama Mura F
320 Tetsuo C
321 The Field of the Winds F
322 The Height of Courage C
323 The Hundred-Hand Strike R
324 The Last One R
325 The New Order U
326 The Shadowed Dojo F
327 The Slow Death R
328 The Utaku Plains F
329 The Wrath of Osano-Wo C
330 Those Who Stand Alone C
331 Threat of Execution U
332 Tiger Climbing Mountain C
333 Togashi Gato C
334 Togashi Miyoko (Exp) R
335 Togashi Shiori U
336 Togashi Taro U
337 Toku's Grave R
338 Tonfajutsu F
339 Toshi Ranbo R
340 Toturi's Tactics R
341 Touch of Death R
342 Touch of Ice C
343 Touch of the Infinite R
344 Tower of the Ningyo R
345 Trade District R
346 Traitor's Grove U
347 Traveling Ronin R
348 Tsuruchi Omori C
349 Tsuruchi Sanjo C
350 Turn The Tide R
351 Twice-Cutting Spirit C
352 Umi-Bozu U
353 Unexpected Intimidation R
354 Unfamiliar Ground U
355 Unfortunate Incident F
356 Unicorn War Dogs U
357 Unproven Guardian C
358 Unstoppable Force R
359 Unstoppable Power U
360 Untested Scouts C
361 Unwavering Assault C
362 Utaku Anhui U
363 Utaku Keiko R
364 Utaku Kohana C
365 Utaku Kohana (Exp) R
366 Utaku Meadows C
367 Utaku Tayoi F
368 Venerable Plains of the Ikoma F
369 Vengeance Cannot Wait R
370 Versatile Army R
371 Veteran Advisor R
372 Viper Tattoo U
373 Walking the Way U
374 Wandering Scout U
375 War Dogs U
376 We Stand Ready F
377 Wedge R
378 Weigh the Cost C
379 Will R
380 Wisdom Gained U
381 Wisdom of the Keepers U
382 Writ of Restriction U
383 Wyrm Riders C
384 Yarijutsu R
385 Yogo Rieko R
386 Yoritomo Eriko U
387 Yoritomo Han-ku R
388 Yoritomo Joben F
389 Yoritomo Kurei R
390 Yoritomo Naizen (Exp) F
391 Yoritomo Okitsugu U
392 Yoritomo Saburo C
393 Yoritomo Saburo (Exp) R
394 Yoritomo Suwa C
395 Yukari no Onna U
396 Zanaru C
397 Celestial Mempo of the Crab Clan F
398 Celestial Mempo of the Crane Clan F
399 Celestial Mempo of the Dragon Clan F
400 Celestial Mempo of the Lion Clan F
401 Celestial Mempo of the Mantis Clan F
402 Celestial Mempo of the Phoenix Clan F
403 Celestial Mempo of the Scorpion Clan F
404 Celestial Mempo of the Unicorn Clan F

2009 Legend of the Five Rings Death at Koten

1 A False Accusation F3 1.00 2.50
2 A Magistrate's Blade F3 1.00 2.50
3 Akodo Tsudoken F1 1.25 3.00
4 Asako Fosu F1 1.50 4.00
5 Blind Rage F3 1.00 2.50
6 Cavalry Tactics F3 1.25 3.00
7 Censure of Thunder F3 .75 2.00
8 Chuda Seiki F1 2.50 6.00
9 Chugo Seido F3 2.00 5.00
10 Civil Discussion F3 .60 1.50
11 Conspiracy F1 .40 1.00
12 Court Attendants F3 .75 2.00
13 Crippling Strike F3 .60 1.50
14 Daidoji Inada F3 .40 1.00
15 Daigotsu Rasetu F3 .75 2.00
16 Dance of Flames F3 .60 1.50
17 Defensive Nature F3 1.25 3.00
18 Demonic Possession F3 .40 1.00
19 Desperate Battle F3 1.00 2.50
20 Doji Kishio F3 .40 1.00
21 Doomed Undertaking F3 .40 1.00
22 Dragon Attendants F3 .40 1.00
23 Essence of Destruction F1 1.50 4.00
24 Essence of Evil F3 .40 1.00
25 Expected Arrival F3 .60 1.50
26 Exposing Secrets F3 .60 1.50
27 Fatal Error F3 .60 1.50
28 Final Duty F3 8.00 20.00
29 Forward Camp F3 .40 1.00
30 Friendly Traveler Sake F3 .75 2.00
31 Hanayashiki F3 .40 1.00
32 Hida Hachimoto F1 1.25 3.00
33 Hida Kagura F3 .40 1.00
34 Hiruma Akio F3 .40 1.00
35 I Do Not Die So Easily! F3 .60 1.50
36 Ikoma Ryudo F3 .75 2.00
37 Imperial Adjudication F3 3.00 8.00
38 Imperial Arrival F1 .40 1.00
39 Isawa Kumai F3 .40 1.00
40 Isawa Mariko F3 .75 2.00
41 Kakita Aichiko F1 1.00 2.50
42 Kakita Tasaka F3 .40 1.00
43 Kitsuki Umibe F3 .40 1.00
44 Matsu Shunran F3 1.25 3.00
45 Matsu Youko F3 .75 2.00
46 Mirumoto Eikaru F3 .40 1.00
47 Momiji F3 .75 2.00
48 Moshi Enju F3 .75 2.00
49 Moto Rena F1 1.00 2.50
50 Moto Sihung F3 .40 1.00
51 Mutual Hatred F3 .75 2.00
52 Nosioc no Oni F3 .75 2.00
53 Order of Venom F3 .40 1.00
54 Presenting Papers F3 .40 1.00
55 Preserving Honor F3 .75 2.00
56 Ritual of Binding F3 .75 2.00
57 Ritual of Summoning F3 1.50 4.00
58 Scouting Ahead F3 1.00 2.50
59 Searching the Libraries F3 .75 2.00
60 Seppun Blade F3 6.00 15.00
61 Seppun Tashime F3 1.25 3.00
62 Shadowed Steel F1 .40 1.00
63 Shiba Kosoku F3 .60 1.50
64 Shinjo Ji-tae F3 .40 1.00
65 Shinjo Kai Ki F3 .40 1.00
66 Shosuro Takuma F3 .40 1.00
67 Suikotsu F3 1.25 3.00
68 Tamori Shaiko F1 2.00 5.00
69 The Loss of the Soul F1 1.25 3.00
70 The Second Death of Kisasda F1 .40 1.00
71 The Sensei F3 .40 1.00
72 The Student F3 .40 1.00
73 The Water Dragon's Favor F3 .40 1.00
74 Togashi Sho F3 1.00 2.50
75 Training Maneuvers F3 .75 2.00
76 Tsudo no Oni F3 1.25 3.00
77 Tsuruchi Suzuki F3 .75 2.00
78 United F3 .75 2.00
79 Unleashed Fury F3 .40 1.00
80 Veiled Menace F3 .75 2.00
81 Yasuki Tijaki F3 .40 1.00
82 Yogo Kazunori F1 5.00 12.00
83 Yoritomo Iwata (Experienced) F1 .40 1.00
84 Yoritomo Iwata F3 1.50 4.00

2009 Legend of the Five Rings Glory of the Empire

COMPLETE SET (166) 120.00 250.00
BOOSTER BOX (48 PACKS) 50.00 100.00
BOOSTER PACK (11 CARDS) 1.50 3.00
RELEASED IN JANUARY 2009
1 A Game of Sadane U2 .30 .75
2 A Rival Eliminated C2 .10 .20
3 Akaru no Oni C2 .10 .20
4 Akodo Hiroshi U2 .20 .50
5 Akodo Yanagi C2 .10 .20
6 An Imperial Marriage U2 .20 .50
7 Armor of the Heavens R2 4.00 10.00
8 Armor of the Ryu R1 10.00 25.00
9 Asako Kanta U2 .20 .50
10 Asako Serizawa R2 1.25 3.00
11 Asako Suda R2 1.25 3.00
12 Balanced Yari C3 .10 .20
13 Bayushi Hirose R2 5.00 12.00
14 Bayushi Ishikura R2 .75 2.00
15 Bayushi Shigeru R2 2.50 6.00
16 Buoyed by the Kami U2 .20 .50
17 Burned Village C2 .10 .20
18 Cavalry Officer C2 .10 .20
19 Certain Death C2 .10 .20
20 Changing Paths R2 2.50 6.00
21 Chrysanthemum Blossom C2 .10 .20
22 City of Tears F (Phoenix) 2.50 6.00
23 Clan Rivalries C3 .10 .20
24 Daidoji Murata U2 .20 .50
25 Daidoji Reita R2 1.50 4.00
26 Daigotsu Buroki R2 2.50 6.00
27 Daigotsu Churo C2 .10 .20
28 Daigotsu Minoko U2 .20 .50
29 Daigotsu Yuhmi R2 1.25 3.00
30 Daigotsu Zenshi R2 2.50 6.00
31 Dangerous Reconnaissance R2 2.00 5.00
32 Deadly Orders C2 .10 .20
33 Death Ravagers U3 .20 .50
34 Desperation Strikes U3 .20 .50
35 Discrete Retreat R2 3.00 8.00
36 Doji Hariya R2 2.50 6.00
37 Doji Numata C2 .10 .20
38 Doji Odaka F (Crane) 4.00 10.00
39 Endless Road C2 .10 .20
40 Eradicate All Doubt U2 .20 .50
41 First-Hand Account C2 .10 .20
42 Five Harmonies Blend U2 .20 .50
43 Fluid Formation U2 .20 .50
44 Fubatsu No-Dachi R2 .75 2.00
45 Furu no Oni R2 1.25 3.00
46 Games of Court R1 1.25 3.00
47 Goju Asagi C2 .10 .20
48 Half-Breath Strike R2 2.00 5.00
49 Hasty Exit R2 1.50 4.00
50 Hida Hikita R2 2.50 6.00
51 Hida Tatsuma R2 2.50 6.00
52 Hida Togeriso U2 .20 .50
53 Hida Yumiya U2 .20 .50
54 Hiruma Rohitsu C3 .10 .20
55 Hongo U2 .20 .50
56 Honor & Steel U2 .20 .50
57 Honor the Ancestors U3 .20 .50
58 House of Exotic Goods C2 .10 .20
59 I Carry Two Blades! C3 .10 .20

60 Ikoma Hagio R2 1.50 4.00
61 Ikoma Tomoi R2 1.25 3.00
62 Imperial Decree C2 .10 .20
63 Imperial Elite Guard C2 .10 .20
64 Imperial Intercession C2 .10 .20
65 Incredible Resilience R1 3.00 8.00
66 Inexplicable Challenge R2 5.00 12.00
67 Isawa Yutako C2 .10 .20
68 Iuchi Hotaru R2 1.50 4.00
69 Kaiu Kyoka F (Crab) 1.50 4.00
70 Kakita Omori C2 .10 .20
71 Kakita Takashima U3 .20 .50
72 Kami Unleashed R2 8.00 20.00
73 Kincho the Sixth C2 .10 .20
74 Kitsuki Kenichi C2 .10 .20
75 Kitsuki Tsuboko R2 2.00 5.00
76 Kitsune Ando U3 .20 .50
77 Kuni Sagara C2 .10 .20
78 Layered Plates R2 2.50 6.00
79 Legion of Death R2 1.25 3.00
80 Low Stance R2 10.00 25.00
81 Magistrate's Accusation U2 .20 .50
82 Malevolent Kappa C3 .10 .20
83 Matsu Ishigaki C2 .10 .20
84 Matsu Misato R2 2.50 6.00
85 Matsu Naomasa U2 .20 .50
86 Might of the Shadowlands U2 .20 .50
87 Mirumoto Ishino R2 3.00 8.00
88 Mirumoto Kuroki C3 .10 .20
89 Mirumoto Takehiro U2 .20 .50
90 Mokku C2 .20 .50
91 Moonless Riders R1 1.50 4.00
92 Moshi Awako R2 2.00 5.00
93 Moshi Nakata R2 1.25 3.00
94 Moto Juncheng C2 .10 .20
95 Moto Xiao R1 2.00 5.00
96 Mounting a Defense R2 2.00 5.00
97 Night of the Blood Moon U2 .20 .50
98 Ogre Savagery C2 .10 .20
99 Oishi R1 4.00 10.00
100 Open Shore Market C2 .10 .20
101 Oyumi R2 2.50 6.00
102 Paths of Honor & Glory R2 2.50 6.00
103 Phantom Blade Kata R2 1.50 4.00
104 Piercing the Heavens U2 .20 .50
105 Power Corrupting R2 2.50 6.00
106 Pragmatism R2 1.25 3.00
107 Public Garden R2 1.25 3.00
108 Raising Heaven's Banner C2 .10 .20
109 Reinforced Border U2 .20 .50
110 Revered Sensei U2 .20 .50
111 Riding the Clouds C3 .10 .20
112 Ronin Brotherhood R2 8.00 20.00
113 Sakarah C2 .10 .20
114 Scouring Flood C2 .10 .20
115 Seeking the Ancestors U3 .20 .50
116 Selfless Devotion C2 .10 .20
117 Servitors of Stone U2 .20 .50
118 Setting Sun Strike R2 2.00 5.00
119 Seven Fold Palace F (Crane) 2.50 6.00
120 Shattered Peaks Castle F (Crab) 2.50 6.00
121 Shiba Ikokawa F (Phoenix) 2.50 6.00
122 Shiba Raiden U2 .20 .50
123 Shiba Shigenobu C2 .10 .20
124 Shinjo Ki-Chang R2 2.50 6.00
125 Shinjo Ming-Ii U2 .20 .50
126 Shinjo Shinlao C3 .10 .20
127 Shisa Infestation R1 2.50 6.00
128 Shosuro Nitsu C2 .10 .20
129 Shosuro Takagi U2 .20 .50
130 Shukku U2 .20 .50
131 Siege Tactics C2 .10 .20
132 Soshi Mayumi C3 .10 .20
133 Spin the Karmic Wheel C2 .10 .20
134 Split the Reed U2 .20 .50
135 Strength of the Dead C2 .10 .20
136 Student of Ninjutsu C2 .10 .20
137 Subtle Corruption U2 .20 .50
138 Temple of Tsukune U2 .40 1.00
139 Terasaka U2 .20 .50
140 The Call of Battle C3 .10 .20
141 The Kharmic Cycle U2 .20 .50
142 The Sea's Lightning U3 .20 .50
143 The Winds' Favor R2 2.00 5.00
144 Thunder's Favor U2 .20 .50
145 Togashi Nakahara R1 1.50 4.00
146 Togashi Osawa U2 .20 .50
147 Traditions of Steel U2 .20 .50
148 Traveling Peddler R2 12.00 30.00
149 Tsuruchi Onaka C2 .10 .20
150 Undone by Truth R2 6.00 15.00
151 Unexpected Arrival R2 8.00 20.00
152 Unexplained Illness U2 .20 .50
153 Unpredictable Strategy R2 8.00 20.00
154 Unsavory Practices U2 .20 .50
155 Unworthy Rivals U2 .20 .50
156 Utaku Elite Guard U2 .20 .50
157 Utaku Yumiko U3 .20 .50
158 War Encampment C2 .10 .20
159 Winter Solstice R1 1.50 4.00
160 Winter's Embrace R1 1.50 4.00
161 Word of Fire R2 2.50 6.00
162 Word of Heaven U3 .20 .50
163 Wrath of the Elements C2 .10 .20
164 Yogo Fujitani U3 .20 .50
165 Yoritomo Kisho U2 .20 .50
166 Yoritomo Sunagawa R2 1.50 4.00

2009 Legend of the Five Rings Path of the Destroyer

COMPLETE SET (166) 40.00 80.00
BOOSTER BOX (48 PACKS 50.00 100.00
BOOSTER PACK (11 CARDS) 1.50 3.00
RELEASED IN AUGUST 2009
1 Agasha Asai U .15 .40
2 Akodo Dosei C .10 .25
3 Akodo Masao C .10 .25
4 Akodo Nagataka U .15 .40
5 Akodo Shunori R .30 .75
6 Akodo's Guidance C .10 .25
7 Apprentice Shinobi U .15 .40
8 Armor of Legacy R .30 .75
9 Asako Hoshimi C .10 .25
10 Asako Misako C .10 .25
11 Assault Riders C .10 .25
12 Bare Ground C .10 .25
13 Bayushi Hisoka 6.00 15.00
(Experienced) F (Scorpion)
14 Bayushi Komiya R .30 .75
15 Bayushi Minoru C .10 .25
16 Bayushi Saka U .15 .40
17 Bayushi's Guidance U .15 .40
18 Besieged Borderland C .10 .25
19 Border Ambush C .10 .25
20 Breath of the Heavens U .15 .40
21 Brothers in Harmony C .10 .25
22 Burn the Towers C .10 .25
23 Calm Before Death U .15 .40
24 Chagatai's Armor R .30 .75
25 Channeling Jigoku's Essence R .30 .75
26 Chikara (Experienced) R .30 .75
27 Cleansing the Path U .15 .40
28 Consuming the Flesh U .15 .40
29 Crushing Strength C .10 .25
30 Daidoji Kirimi C .10 .25
31 Daidoji Yorio U .15 .40
32 Daigotsu Gahseng R .30 .75
33 Daigotsu Isoroku U .15 .40
34 Daigotsu Susumu 1.00 2.50
(Experienced) F (Spider)
35 Deflection R .40 1.00
36 Deployed Reinforcements U .15 .40
37 Desporate Rush R 4.00 10.00
38 Desperate Throw C .10 .25
39 Disarm U .15 .40
40 Doji Bukita R .30 .75
41 Doji Shikana C .10 .25
42 Doji Tsubota R .30 .75
43 Doji's Guidance C .10 .25
44 Dutiful Apprentice R .30 .75
45 Earth's Embrace U .15 .40
46 Eternal Armor U .15 .40
47 Expendable Resources R .30 .75
48 First to Fall C .10 .25
49 Force of Law R .30 .75
50 Forging the Gift U .15 .40
51 Fu Leng's Guidance C .10 .25
52 Gakku C .10 .25
53 Greater Good C .10 .25
54 Hand of the Jade Dragon R .30 .75
55 Hand of the Obsidian Dragon R .50 1.25
56 Hida Fosuko U .15 .40
57 Hida Ikarukani R .50 1.25
58 Hida Kitamura C .10 .25
59 Hida Suteru R .30 .75
60 Hida Tobashi R .30 .75
61 Hida's Guidance U .15 .40
62 Hidden Route R .30 .75
63 Hiruma Hidora U .15 .40
64 Ikoma Tobikuma R .30 .75
65 Impossible Force R .30 .75
66 Inspirational Victory U .15 .40
67 Isawa Fosuta (Experienced) R .30 .75
68 Isawa Mizuhiko (Experienced) R .30 .75
69 Kaiu Smithy U .15 .40
70 Kakita Kensho-in (Experienced) R .30 .75
71 Kakita Sadaka U .15 .40
72 Kata of the Concealed Blade U .15 .40
73 Kitsuki Yodo R .30 .75
74 Kitsune Iwarou U .15 .40
75 Last Stand U .15 .40
76 Laughter of the Flames C .10 .25
77 Laying in Wait R .30 .75
78 Lead By Example R .50 1.25
79 Legion of Toshigoku R .50 1.25
80 March Beyond Hope C .10 .25
81 Masserah C .10 .25
82 Master the Body R .50 1.25
83 Matsu Benika (Experienced 2) R .30 .75
84 Matsu Kasei U .15 .40
85 Might of the Kami R .30 .75
86 Mirumoto Kondo U .15 .40
87 Mirumoto Washizuka U .15 .40
88 Misleading Wasteland C .10 .25
89 Monstrous Might C .10 .25
90 Moshi Chuuna U .15 .40
91 Moto Chiang (Experienced) R .30 .75
92 Moto Jin-sahn (Experienced) F (Unicorn) 3.00 8.00
93 Moto Kang's Sword R .30 .75
94 Moto Paisei C .10 .25
95 Mountain Watch Keep F (Unicorn) 1.50 4.00
96 Nerve Strike U .15 .40
97 Nightshade Touch U .15 .40
98 One Soul's Strength U .15 .40
99 Overwhelming Pressure U .15 .40
100 Palace of Crimson Shadows F (Scorpion) 1.50 4.00
101 Pull the String R 6.00 15.00
102 Seeking the Guilty C .10 .25
103 Selfless Defense C .10 .25
104 Seven Waves Mercenaries R .30 .75
105 Sharpened Naginata C .10 .25
106 Shiba Ningen (Experienced 3) R .30 .75
107 Shiba Sakaki U .15 .40
108 Shiba Yukihito R .40 1.00
109 Shiba's Guidance C .10 .25
110 Shielded by Tempest U .15 .40
111 Shinjo Hansu R .30 .75
112 Shinjo Rina U .15 .40
113 Shinjo Scouts U .15 .40
114 Shinjo Tae-hyun C .10 .25
115 Shinjo's Guidance U .15 .40
116 Shosuro Ohba U .15 .40
117 Shosuro Sogetsu C .10 .25
118 Soshi Yoshihara R .60 1.50
119 Speed of the Blade R .30 .75
120 Spiteful Obstruction C .10 .25
121 Storm-filled Sails C .10 .25
122 Strategic Strike R 6.00 15.00
123 Strength in Honor U .15 .40
124 Strength in Terror U .15 .40
125 Suitengu's Gateway R .30 .75
126 Sympathy for the Assaulted U .15 .40
127 Synchronized Attack C .10 .25
128 Talisman of Chikushudo R .30 .75
129 Talisman of Gaki-do R .30 .75
130 Talisman of Meido R .30 .75
131 Talisman of Tengoku R .30 .75
132 Tempered No-Dachi U .15 .40
133 Test of Sincerity U .15 .40
134 The Direct Approach C .10 .25
135 The Earth Answers C .10 .25
136 The Fingers of Bone F (Spider) .75 2.00
137 The Fire Answers U .15 .40
138 The Lost Path R .40 1.00
139 Thorough Preparations C .10 .25
140 Togashi Akagi C .10 .25
141 Togashi Kazuki (Experienced) R .30 .75
142 Togashi Satsu (Experienced 5) R .30 .75
143 Togashi Shintaro C .10 .25
144 Togashi's Guidance U .15 .40
145 Torao C .10 .25
146 Tsuruchi Mochisa (Experienced) R .30 .75
147 Tsuruchi Nabeta C .10 .25
148 Udo U .15 .40
149 Unclean Sacrifice R .30 .75
150 Unshakable Resolve C .10 .25
151 Untaken C .10 .25
152 Untrained Scouts C .10 .25
153 Useful Connections R .30 .75
154 Utaku Hana U .15 .40
155 Uzaki no Oni R .40 1.00
156 Walk in Shadows R .40 1.00
157 Wall of Honor R 6.00 15.00
158 Wandering Caravan C .10 .25
159 Whispers of the Dying Moon R .30 .75
160 Whispers of the Dying Sun R .60 1.50
161 Wrath of the Thunder C .10 .25
162 Yasuki Otsuka U .15 .40
163 Yoritomo Eihiko C .10 .25
164 Yoritomo Souhiko R .30 .75
165 Yoritomo Utemaro (Experienced 2) R .30 .75
166 Yoritomo's Guidance U .15 .40

2009 Legend of the Five Rings The Imperial Gift 2

COMPLETE SET (82) 15.00 30.00
RELEASED IN AUGUST 2009
1 A Samurai's Soul F .40 1.00
2 Akodo Kurogane F .50 1.25
3 Arugai no Oni F 1.00 2.50
4 Back to the Front F .20 .50
5 Bayushi Kayama F .20 .50
6 Bayushi Shihaken F .20 .50
7 Bayushi Tsubaki F .20 .50
8 Breath of the Dragon F .40 1.00
9 Chuda Fukuzo F .20 .50
10 Collapsing Bridge F .20 .50
11 Daidoji Harada F .20 .50
12 Daigotsu Oki F 1.00 2.50
13 Daigotsu Shinjitsu F .50 1.25
14 Delayed Arrival F .20 .50
15 Do Not Turn Your Back! F .20 .50
16 Doji Kato F .75 2.00
17 Dutiful Yojimbo F .20 .50
18 Earthen Blade F .40 1.00
19 Elite Archers F .20 .50
20 Espionage F .20 .50
21 Fall Back! F .20 .50
22 Family Histories F .20 .50
23 Fields of Battle F .20 .50
24 For My Brothers! F .20 .50
25 Forward Reconnaissance F .50 1.25
26 Frontline Encampment F .20 .50
27 Heavy Regulars F .20 .50
28 Hida Rokurota F .30 .75
29 Hida Shinko F .30 .75
30 Hiruma Etsuro F .30 .75
31 Ikoma Igawa F .40 1.00
32 Incapacitated F .20 .50
33 Infamous Blade F .20 .50
34 Iron Fan F .20 .50
35 Isawa Reido F .20 .50
36 Isawa Tanaka F .50 1.25
37 Iuchi Kota F .40 1.00
38 Kakita Toshiro F .20 .50
39 Kitsuki Hanbei F .75 2.00
40 Kyogen F .20 .50
41 Lost Traveler Castle F .60 1.50
42 Mastery of the Blade F .20 .50
43 Midnight Assault F .20 .50
44 Military Alliance F .40 1.00
45 Mirumoto Ayabe F .20 .50
46 Moshi Takako F .50 1.25
47 My Father's Shrine F .30 .75
48 Natsu Mansaiko F .20 .50
49 Obfuscation F .40 1.00
50 Outmatched F .40 1.00
51 Pokupo F .50 1.25
52 Prayer for Guidance F .20 .50
53 Prepared for Death F .20 .50
54 Rejuvenating Vapors F .30 .75
55 Ruthless Determination F .30 .75
56 Seppun Heavy Infantry F .30 .75
57 Shiba Nobuyuki F .20 .50
58 Shinjo Kodama F .30 .75
59 Simple Merchants F .75 2.00
60 Suitengu's Embrace F .20 .50
61 Smuggler's Port F .20 .50
62 Spearmen Legion F .20 .50
63 Straw Horse F .20 .50
64 Sunrise Keep F .10 2.50
65 Tamori Masako F .20 .50
66 The Cresting Wave F .20 .50
67 The Stone Discovered F .20 .50
68 Throwing Knives F .40 1.00
69 Thunderous Report F .40 1.00
70 Timely Assisance F .20 .50
71 Token of Destiny F .30 .75
72 Traveling Wardens F 1.00 2.50
73 Tsuruchi Oguri F .60 1.50
74 Undefended Border F .20 .50
75 Under Cover of Night F .20 .50
76 Under Seige F .20 .50
77 Utaku Yanai F .40 1.00
78 Village Guardian F .50 1.25
79 Well-Defender Border F .20 .50
80 Wrathful Defense F .20 .50
81 Yari F .20 .50
82 Yoritomo Sasake F .20 .50

2010 Legend of the Five Rings Empire at War

COMPLETE SET (166) 50.00 100.00
BOOSTER BOX (48 PACKS) 50.00 100.00
BOOSTER PACK (11 CARDS) 1.50 3.00
RELEASED IN SEPTEMBER 2010
1 A Stain Cleansed R 2.50 6.00
2 Akodo Areru C .10 .25
3 Akodo Kusamoto R .50 1.25
4 Alter History R 1.50 4.00
5 Ancient Tome U .15 .40
6 Asako Ayako U .15 .40
7 Attuned to the Elements U .15 .40
8 Bakunai U .15 .40
9 Battle Fatigue R .30 .75
10 Bayushi Darisu U .15 .40
11 Bayushi Himaru C .10 .25
12 Bayushi Jutsushi (Experienced) R .30 .75
13 Bayushi Kahoku R 1.25 3.00
14 Bayushi Miyako 1.25 3.00
(Experienced 2 Toturi Miyako) Fixed
15 Bayushi Shigehiro C .10 .25
16 Bishamon's Guidance R 1.50 4.00
17 Bitter Lies Student U .15 .40
18 Blade of Perfection C .10 .25
19 Bridging the Gap C .10 .25
20 Clan Conflict C .10 .25
21 Conscript Troops C .10 .25
22 Crossing the Forbidden Sea U .15 .40
23 Daidoji Arima C .10 .25
24 Daidoji Yaichiro (Experienced) R .30 .75
25 Daigotsu Akihime U .15 .40
26 Daigotsu Hotako .40 1.00
(Experienced 2 Yoritomo Hotako) R
27 Daigotsu Shaiko .30 .75
(Experienced Tamori Shaiko) R
28 Dangerous Indulgence R .30 .75
29 Death is Not the End U .15 .40
30 Distractions in Court R 2.50 6.00
31 Dockside Market C .10 .25
32 Doji Kusari R .30 .75
33 Doji Shikishi R .75 2.00
34 Doji Tajihi U .15 .40
35 Doji Umakai C .10 .25
36 Dove Tattoo U .15 .40
37 Downhill Assault U .15 .40
38 Earthen Fist C .10 .25
39 Ekichu no Oni R 3.00 8.00
40 Elemental Disciple C .10 .25
41 Endless Rain U .15 .40
42 Essence of Death C .10 .25
43 Farthest Fortress Fixed .75 2.00
44 Fearless Defense R .75 2.00
45 Feign Weakness C .10 .25
46 Fertile Plains U .15 .40
47 Final Confrontation U .15 .40
48 Fire on My Command R .40 1.00
49 Fires of the Heart U .15 .40
50 Flood the Earth U .15 .40
51 Flow of the Water C .10 .25
52 Force of Spirit R 1.00 2.50
53 Fortified Docks C .10 .25
54 Fortress of Blackened Sight Fixed 1.50 4.00
55 Fortune Favors the Bold U .15 .40
56 Fury of Suitengu U .15 .40
57 Goju Katsume C .10 .25
58 Hands of Stone U .15 .40
59 Hida Benjiro (Experienced 2) R .40 1.00
60 Hida Maruken U .15 .40
61 Hida Shikoujin R 1.00 2.50
62 Hidden Entrance U .15 .40
63 Hidden Valley U .15 .40
64 Hired Thugs C .10 .25
65 Hiroshi's Legion R .50 1.25
66 Hiruma House Guard (Experienced) R .30 .75
67 Hiruma Ikuya U .15 .40
68 Hiruma Todori (Experienced 3) R .30 .75
69 Honorable Death U .15 .40
70 Hozumi R .40 1.00
71 Ichiro Kaagi C .10 .25
72 Ikoma Hagio (Experienced) R .30 .75
73 Ikoma Toruken R .30 .75
74 Immovable Object R .30 .75
75 Imperial Orders U .15 .40
76 In the Heart of Battle C .10 .25
77 Invincible Determination U .15 .40
78 Isawa Kimi (Experienced 2) R .30 .75
79 Isawa Shioki R .30 .75
80 Isawa Takahiro U .15 .40
81 Isawa Toshio C .10 .25
82 Iuchi Jadaran C .10 .25
83 Kaiu Futaro C .10 .25
84 Kakita Mimaro U .15 .40
85 Kitsuki Nakai C .10 .25
86 Knowledge of the Land U .15 .40
87 Koji C .10 .25
88 Kuni Shikehime C .10 .25
89 Matsu Kinihara U .15 .40
90 Matsu Misuka C .10 .25
91 Matsu Otsuko U .15 .40
92 Merciless Tactics C .10 .25
93 Mirumoto Asakazu R .30 .75
94 Mirumoto Kalen U .15 .40
95 Mirumoto Kenzo (Experienced 2) Fixed 1.25 3.00
96 Mirumoto Tobushi C .10 .25
97 Moshi Yuriko U .15 .40
98 Moto Hunters R 4.00 10.00
99 Moto Munoru C .10 .25
100 Moto Shanyu U .15 .40
101 Mountainous Region C .10 .25
102 Mysterious Ailment U .15 .40
103 Night Watchers U .15 .40
104 One with the World U .15 .40
105 Osano-Wo's Guidance R .40 1.00
106 Otomo Seimi R .75 2.00
107 Outsider Keep Fixed 1.00 2.50
108 Paid Off C .10 .25
109 Perfect Aim R .40 1.00
110 Preparing the Bodies C .10 .25
111 Protect the Caravan C .10 .25
112 Rekai's Yumi R .50 1.25
113 Rus'tik'tik C .10 .25
114 Savagery C .10 .25
115 Secured Borders C .10 .25
116 Shameful and Cowardly R 8.00 20.00
117 Shatter the Line C .10 .25
118 Shiba Goto C .10 .25
119 Shiba Morihiko (Experienced) R .40 1.00
120 Shinjo Dun (Experienced) Fixed .30 .75
121 Shinjo Jalair R .30 .75
122 Shinjo's Children C .10 .25
123 Shinran C .10 .25
124 Shosuro Ritsuko U .15 .40
125 Smoke Cover R .40 1.00
126 Sought for Justice R .60 1.50
127 Stable Ground C .10 .25
128 Startling Attack R .30 .75
129 Stay Put C .10 .25
130 Stripped Armor C .10 .25
131 Sudden Rebuke U .15 .40
132 Sudden Strike R .30 .75
133 Sullied Gift C .10 .25
134 Superior Mobility R 8.00 20.00
135 Takaikabe Mura U .15 .40
136 Talisman of Jigoku R .30 .75
137 Tamori Kuroko U .15 .40
138 The Art of Ninjutsu U .15 .40
139 The Law's Strength U .15 .40
140 The Unmaking R 1.00 2.50
141 Timely Save R .30 .75
142 Togashi Furai R .40 1.00
143 Travel Light C .10 .25
144 Tsuruchi Chiko U .15 .40
145 Tsuruchi Nobumoto (Experienced 2) R .30 .75
146 Tsuruchi Shisuken (Experienced) R .40 1.00
147 Tsuruchi's Legacy R .40 1.00
148 Ugaro R .30 .75
149 Ultimate Sacrifice R 6.00 15.00
150 Under Arrest U .15 .40
151 Undying Warriors U .15 .40
152 Unmoving as the Mountain C .10 .25
153 Unnatural Flood R .30 .75
154 Unstoppable Cut R .60 1.50
155 Untouchable Escort U .15 .40
156 Utaku Fujiko (Experienced) R .50 1.25
157 Utaku Jin-lao U .15 .40
158 Waylay the Messenger Gong Studios .30 .75
159 Weight of Numbers R .30 .75
160 Whirlwind U .15 .40
161 Wooden Barricade C .10 .25
162 Wrath R .40 1.00
163 Yagimaki's Fist R 4.00 10.00
164 Yoritomo Kaemon C .10 .25
165 Yoritomo Manzo R .50 1.25
166 Yoritomo Rai C .10 .25

2010 Legend of the Five Rings The Harbinger

COMPLETE SET (176) 30.00 60.00
BOOSTER BOX (48 PACKS) 50.00 100.00
BOOSTER PACK (11 CARDS) 1.50 3.00
RELEASED IN JANUARY 2010
1 A Cleansing Death U .15 .40
2 A Paragon's Strength R .75 2.00
3 Advanced Spellcraft U .15 .40
4 Agasha Kusadao C .10 .25
5 Akodo Kin C .10 .25
6 Akodo Ryozo R .30 .75
7 Akodo Senichi R .30 .75
8 Akodo Senzo U2 .15 .40
9 Akodo Shigo R .30 .75
10 Alert the Guard U2 .15 .40
11 Allure of Jigoku U .15 .40
12 Apprehending the Villain C .10 .25
13 Arjuna Singh U2 .15 .40
14 Arranged Guilt R .30 .75
15 Arrows Do Not Falter U .15 .40
16 Asahina Ekei (Experienced) R .30 .75
17 Asako Mokichi U .15 .40
18 Assaults Without Finesse U .15 .40
19 Aura of Malice C .10 .25
20 Bakemono Pups C .10 .25
21 Banish All Doubt R .30 .75
22 Bayushi Hikoko U .15 .40
23 Bayushi Kindebu C .10 .25
24 Bayushi Mago U .15 .40
25 Bayushi Momochi C .10 .25
26 Bayushi Suboru R .30 .75
27 Blades of the Fallen Phoenix U .15 .40

28 Border Pass C .10 .25
29 Br'nn C .10 .25
30 Burn the Village R .30 .75
31 Chain and Sword R .30 .75
32 Chikara C .10 .25
33 Chuda Atsuro U2 .15 .40
34 Civility R .40 1.00
35 Cowed by Wisdom U .15 .40
36 Daidoji Bolan C .10 .25
37 Daidoji Yuki R .30 .75
38 Daigotsu Azuma U .15 .40
39 Daigotsu Koneru C .10 .25
40 Daigotsu Yuhmi (Experienced) R .30 .75
41 Dance of Blades R .30 .75
42 Deceit and Subterfuge U .15 .40
43 Determined Force R .75 2.00
44 Doji Kazuo C .10 .25
45 Doji Nenkai R .30 .75
46 Dutiful Cavalry C .10 .25
47 Elite Guard C .10 .25
48 Emma-O's Guidance R .30 .75
49 Enticement R .30 .75
50 Extensive Training R .30 .75
51 Farmlands Conscripts C .10 .25
52 Flash of Bright Wings C .10 .25
53 Flashy Technique C .10 .25
54 Flawless Assassin U .15 .40
55 Fortitude U .15 .40
56 Fudo C .10 .25
57 Furumaro R .50 1.25
58 Generosity R .30 .75
59 Groves of Stone C .10 .25
60 Heaven's Tears R .30 .75
61 Heavy Elite R .50 1.25
62 Hida Harou R .30 .75
63 Hida Hebi U .15 .40
64 Hida Kosho (Experienced) R .30 .75
65 Hiruma Gondo C .10 .25
66 Hiruma Shigeo U .15 .40
67 Hiruma Toshio R .30 .75
68 Hold Them Off R .30 .75
69 Hope Against Hope U .15 .40
70 Imperial Outpost U .15 .40
71 In Aikune's Name R .30 .75
72 Intimidating Stance U2 .15 .40
73 Isawa Mitsuko R .30 .75
74 Isawa Takashi R .30 .75
75 Isawa Takino U .15 .40
76 Junghar Legion C .10 .25
77 Kakita Kado U .15 .40
78 Kakita Reisei U2 .15 .40
79 Ki-Rin Tattoo U .15 .40
80 Kitsuki Suiha U .15 .40
81 Knowledge from Within R 1.25 3.00
82 Last Line of Defense U .15 .40
83 Last Step Castle F (Dragon) .40 1.00
84 Learn by Doing U .15 .40
85 Let None Draw Near C .10 .25
86 Masakazu (Experienced) F (Phoenix) 1.25 3.00
87 Maseru no Oni C .10 .25
88 Matsu Akuto C .10 .25
89 Matsu Kita U .15 .40
90 Maws of Stone C .10 .25
91 Mirumoto Bokusui C .10 .25
92 Mirumoto Dakotsu U2 .15 .40
93 Mirumoto Ichizo (Experienced) R .30 .75
94 Mirumoto Meisetsu C .10 .25
95 Mirumoto Shiki F (Dragon) .40 1.00
96 Morru C .10 .25
97 Moshi Kazue C .10 .25
98 Moshi Sayoko (Experienced) F (Mantis) 1.25 3.00
99 Moto Chuluun C .10 .25
100 Moto Kang (Experienced) R .30 .75
101 Moto Kushi C .10 .25
102 Naggru C .10 .25
103 Negotiations at Court C .10 .25
104 Newly-Discovered Mine U .15 .40
105 No Hope C .10 .25
106 Offices of the Emerald Magistrates C .10 .25
107 One with the Flame R .30 .75
108 Oyo Seido C .10 .25
109 Pacify C .10 .25
110 Pawn of Corruption C .10 .25
111 Peasant Armor C .10 .25
112 Phantom Blade C .10 .25
113 Pinned Down U2 .15 .40
114 Poorly Chosen Allies C .10 .25
115 Prayer to Hotei U .15 .40
116 Prepare for the Worst R .30 .75
117 Preserving What Was Lost C .10 .25
118 Reinforce the Line U .15 .40
119 Riding in Harmony C .10 .25
120 Roaring Sky U2 .15 .40
121 Sadamune Blade U .15 .40
122 Saving Kazumasa C .10 .25
123 Scout Armor C .10 .25
124 Search for Survivors R .30 .75
125 Senseki Province C .10 .25
126 Seppun Tashime (Experienced) R .30 .75
127 Shadow Plays U2 .15 .40
128 Shiba Allies C .10 .25
129 Shiba Ikuko C .10 .25
130 Shinjo Emiko U .15 .40
131 Shinjo Yamauchi R .30 .75
132 Shosuro Akemi R .30 .75
133 Sister of the Sun R .30 .75
134 Snow-Swept Summit C .10 .25
135 Soshi Miroki R .30 .75
136 Spider Cultist U .15 .40
137 Spinning Heel Kick C .10 .25
138 Spirit of Maigo no Musha C .10 .25
139 Stand Down! R .30 .75
140 Stolen Property C2 .10 .25
141 Storm-Forged Blade C .10 .25
142 Strengthening Protection U .15 .40
143 Strike from the Shadows R 2.50 6.00
144 Subtle Sting R .30 .75
145 Talisman of Maigo no Musha R .30 .75
146 Talisman of Toshigoku R .30 .75
147 Tamago (Experienced 2 Matsu Nimuro) R 2.00 5.00
148 Temporary Truce R .30 .75
149 The Badgers Live U .15 .40
150 The Dead Do Not Rest U .15 .40
151 The Dread Kar R .30 .75
152 The Eighth Legion R .30 .75
153 The Light of Justice U .15 .40
154 The Thriving Light R 1.50 4.00
155 The Walking Dead C .10 .25
156 The Wrath of Kali-Ma R .30 .75
157 Thunder Dragon Bay F (Mantis) .40 1.00
158 Togashi Kyoshi R .30 .75
159 Toritaka Okabe C .10 .25
160 Travel Swiftly R .30 .75
161 Tsuruchi Gosho U .15 .40
162 Twin Soul Temple F (Phoenix) 1.50 4.00
163 Utaku Gunso U .15 .40
164 Utaku Tairu R .30 .75
165 Utaku Toshie U .15 .40
166 Utogu no Oni C .10 .25
167 Vigilant Eyes C .10 .25
168 Wander Among the Stars R .30 .75
169 Wanyudo R .30 .75
170 Wartime Allies U .15 .40
171 Wind-Borne Aid C .10 .25
172 Yojimbo's Glory U .15 .40
173 Yoritomo Eita C .10 .25
174 Yoritomo Takara R .30 .75
175 Yoritomo Tatsuhiko R .30 .75
176 Yuhmi no Oni R .30 .75

2010 Legend of the Five Rings The Plague War

COMPLETE SET (176) 40.00 80.00
BOOSTER BOX (48 PACKS) 50.00 100.00
BOOSTER PACK (11 CARDS) 1.50 3.00
RELEASED IN MAY 2010
1 A Pure Heart C2 .10 .25
2 A Tranquil Mind U2 .15 .40
3 Agasha Gifu U2 .15 .40
4 Agasha Kitsuki's Ashes R2 .50 1.25
5 Air Dragon's Guidance R2 .40 1.00
6 Akodo Kuma C2 .10 .25
7 Ao-bozu R2 .40 1.00
8 Ao-bozu's Blade C1 .10 .25
9 Asako Bairei (Experienced 4) R2 .30 .75
10 Asijin's Legacy C2 .10 .25
11 Bayushi Eiyu U4 .15 .40
12 Bayushi Keirei R2 2.50 6.00
13 Bayushi Shigeo U2 .15 .40
14 Bayushi Sorii C2 .10 .25
15 Blessings of Sky C2 .10 .25
16 Caught Unawares R2 .50 1.25
17 Choose Your Fight C2 .10 .25
18 Chuda Kanashi U2 .15 .40
19 Chuda Mishime (Experienced 2) R2 .30 .75
20 Chuda Otsu C2 .10 .25
21 Claw and Shell R2 6.00 15.00
22 Claws of the Wolf C2 .10 .25
23 Cold Hands, Stone Heart U2 .15 .40
24 Concealed Scroll R2 .40 1.00
25 Cricket Tattoo U2 .15 .40
26 Daidoji Akagi (Experienced 2) R2 .30 .75
27 Daidoji Gisei U2 .15 .40
28 Daidoji Kyorai U2 .15 .40
29 Daigotsu Arima C2 .10 .25
30 Daigotsu Setsuko (Experienced) R2 .30 .75
31 Daigotsu Shimekiri U2 .15 .40
32 Dance of the Void U2 .15 .40
33 Deathly Aura R2 2.00 5.00
34 Deception Revealed U2 .15 .40
35 Defenders of Nanashi C2 .10 .25
36 Doji Gotobo C2 .10 .25
37 Doji Hakuseki (Experienced) F (Crane) .50 1.25
38 Doji Tadanori C2 .10 .25
39 Dutiful Cavalry C1 .10 .25
40 Earth Dragon's Guidance R2 .30 .75
41 Earthen Tetsubo C1 .10 .25
42 East Wind Riders C2 .10 .25
43 Excellent Armor U4 .15 .40
44 Farmland Conscripts C1 .10 .25
45 Feinting Position U2 .15 .40
46 Fire Blossom U4 .15 .40
47 Fire Dragon's Guidance R2 .30 .75
48 Flow of the Elements C2 .10 .25
49 Foolish Pride U4 .15 .40
50 Fortress of the Forgotten F (Crab) .50 1.25
51 Great Hall of Records F (Lion) 1.00 2.50
52 Gutobo (Experienced) R2 .30 .75
53 Hariya's Blade C1 .10 .25
54 Hasty Evaluation C2 .10 .25
55 Heedless Assault R2 .30 .75
56 Hida Demopen R2 .30 .75
57 Hida Kichiro U2 .15 .40
58 Hida Satoshi C2 .10 .25
59 Hida Shimonai U4 .15 .40
60 Hida Tenshi C2 .10 .25
61 Hida Yaheiko (Experienced) F (Crab) 1.25 3.00
62 Hiruma Sniper U2 .15 .40
63 Honor & Strength U2 .15 .40
64 Honor's Hope C2 .10 .25
65 Hundred-Fold Cut U4 .15 .40
66 Ide Kin C2 .10 .25
67 Ikoma Satoru R2 .40 1.00
68 Imaishi R2 .30 .75
69 Impetuous Challenge C2 .10 .25
70 Inexorable Defeat U2 .15 .40
71 Infantry Follower C1 .10 .25
72 Innuendo C2 .10 .25
73 Inugami U2 .15 .40
74 Iron Gauntlet Brothers R2 .30 .75
75 Isawa Hachiko C2 .10 .25
76 Isawa Ochiai (Experienced 3) R2 .40 1.00
77 Isawa Shun U2 .15 .40
78 Iweko's Journals R2 .40 1.00
79 Karatsu C2 .10 .25
80 Kitsu Iwao U2 .15 .40
81 Kitsuki Yukari U2 .15 .40
82 Masked in Shadows R2 .30 .75
83 Matsu Haruya C2 .10 .25
84 Matsu Kenji (Experienced) R2 .30 .75
85 Matsu Mikura (Experienced) F (Lion) .30 .75
86 Matsu Nishijo U4 .15 .40
87 Mirumoto Haru C2 .10 .25
88 Mirumoto Mori R2 1.25 3.00
89 Mountain Herd C2 .10 .25
90 Mountain Storehouse U2 .15 .40
91 Mouth of the Plague C2 .10 .25
92 Murerous Intent C2 .10 .25
93 My Life Is Yours R2 1.50 4.00
94 Narrow Cliffs C2 .10 .25
95 Nature's Embrace C2 .10 .25
96 Nitoru C2 .10 .25
97 On All Sides U4 .15 .40
98 Only Actions Speak R2 6.00 15.00
99 Oppression C2 .10 .25
100 Order of the Wooden Blade R2 .40 1.00
101 Overpower Assault R2 2.00 5.00
102 Part the Waves C2 .10 .25
103 Patrolling the Roads U2 .15 .40
104 Plagued Terrain U2 .15 .40
105 Precious Burden C2 .10 .25
106 Proper Deference R2 .40 1.00
107 Province Assaulted U4 .15 .40
108 Questionable Charity C2 .10 .25
109 Radiant Steel U2 .15 .40
110 Reckless Confrontation U2 .15 .40
111 Relentless Conviction R2 1.00 2.50
112 Remember Their Valor C2 .10 .25
113 Rise Corrupted U2 .15 .40
114 Rising Sun Blade R2 3.00 8.00
115 Sarassa U2 .15 .40
116 Scouting Far Afield R2 1.50 4.00
117 Seawatch Castle F (Crane) 1.25 3.00
118 Selfless Yojimbo C1 .10 .25
119 Shadow's Talon R2 .75 2.00
120 Shiba Kotaro C2 .10 .25
121 Shinjo Dong-Min C2 .10 .25
122 Shinjo Hee-Young R2 .30 .75
123 Shinjo Ki-Chang (Experienced) R2 .30 .75
124 Shosuro Orikasa R2 .30 .75
125 Shosuro Rokujo C2 .10 .25
126 Shune R2 .30 .75
127 Silent Struggle U2 .15 .40
128 Simple Men C2 .10 .25
129 Spirit of Gaki-do C1 .10 .25
130 Stand as One R2 .30 .75
131 Stare Into the Void R2 .30 .75
132 Strength of Will R2 .40 1.00
133 Successful Bounty U2 .15 .40
134 Talisman of Sakkaku R2 .30 .75
135 Talisman of Yomi R2 .30 .75
136 Talisman of Yume-do R2 .30 .75
137 Tamori Shimura R2 .30 .75
138 Tennyo R2 .30 .75
139 Tetsu Kama Mine U2 .15 .40
140 Tetsubo of Earth U2 .15 .40
141 The Blessed Herd U2 .15 .40
142 The Cost of Pride R2 6.00 15.00
143 The Cursed Dead C2 .10 .25
144 The Master's Guard U2 .15 .40
145 The Oni's Footsteps C2 .10 .25
146 The Quiet Death C2 .10 .25
147 The Serpent's Deception U2 .15 .40
148 The Silent Blade U2 .15 .40
149 The Trap is Sprung! R2 .30 .75
150 The Walking Dead C1 .10 .25
151 The Wind Never Stops R2 1.00 2.50
152 Thoughtful Present C2 .10 .25
153 Thunder's Blessing C2 .10 .25
154 Togashi Kanmu U2 .15 .40
155 Togashi Konishi R2 .30 .75
156 Toshi Ranbo Guard C1 .10 .25
157 Touch of the Flames R2 .30 .75
158 Triumph Before Battle U2 .15 .40
159 Trust the Void R2 .30 .75
160 Tsai-tsu C2 .10 .25
161 Tsuruchi Gidayu (Experienced) R2 .30 .75
162 Tsuruchi Kuze C2 .10 .25
163 Tsuruchi Ogata R2 .30 .75
164 Tsuruchi Ohashi R2 .30 .75
165 Two Men At A River C2 .10 .25
166 Unexpected Sympathy C2 .10 .25
167 Unimpeachable Name U2 .15 .40
168 Unwavering Commitment U2 .15 .40
169 Utaku Kana U4 .15 .40
170 Utaku Yu-Pan (Experienced 2) R2 .30 .75
171 Void Dragon's Guidance R2 .75 2.00
172 Water Dragon's Guidance R2 .30 .75
173 Whispers of the Forgotten R2 .50 1.25
174 Yogo Rieko (Experienced) R2 .50 1.25
175 Yoritomo Chiako C2 .10 .25
176 Yoritomo Tahei U2 .15 .40

2010 Legend of the Five Rings Battle of Kyuden Tonbo

RELEASED IN SEPTEMBER 2010
1 Akodo's Guidance
2 Togashi's Guidance
3 I Am Ready
4 Triumph Before Battle
5 Wisdom Gained
6 Akodo's Grave
7 Bamboo Harvesters
8 Barley Farm
9 Border Keep
10 Border Village
11 Chugo Seido
12 Copper Mine
13 Counting House
14 Diamond Mine
15 Expendable Resources
16 Famous Bazaar
17 Frontline Encampment
18 Gold Mine
19 Kaiu Smithy
20 Permanent Encampment
21 Rich Coffers
22 Temple to Shinsei
23 Tetsu Kama Mine
24 Traveling Peddler
25 Togashi Akagi
26 Togashi Kanmu
27 Togashi Konishi
28 Togashi Kyoshi
29 Togashi Osawa
30 Togashi Satsu (Experienced 5)
31 Togashi Shintaro
32 Togashi Shiori
33 Togashi Taro
34 Akodo Kuma
35 Akodo Masao
36 Akodo Ryozo
37 Akodo Sadahige (Experienced)
38 Akodo Senzo
39 Matsu Benika (Experienced 2)
40 Matsu Haruya
41 Matsu Mari
42 Matsu Mikura
43 Matsu Ushio
44 Farmlands
45 Mountain Storehouse
46 Berserkers
47 Elite Guard
48 Order of the Wooden Blade
49 Spearmen
50 War Dogs
51 Fubatsu No-Dachi
52 Gumbai-Uchiwa
53 Scout Armor
54 Seppun Blade
55 Tempered No-Dachi
56 Ring of Air
57 Ring of Earth
58 Ring of the Void
59 Ring of Water
60 A Cleansing Death
61 A Legion of One
62 Burn the Village
63 Caught Unawares
64 Chasing Osano-Wo
65 Cold Hands, Stone Heart
66 Crushing Strength
67 Deployed Reinforcements
68 Final Duty
69 Fire Blossom
70 First to Fall
71 Greater Sacrifice
72 Hitsu-Do
73 Honor's Hope
74 Justly Earned Victory
75 Kami Unleashed
76 Laughter of the Flames
77 Laying in Wait
78 Low Stance
79 Maws of Stone
80 Palm Strike
81 Scouting Far Afield
82 Sneak Attack
83 Spinning Heel Kick
84 Strength of the Bamboo
85 Swift Counterattack
86 Unpredictable Strategy
87 Will
88 Pillars of Virtue
89 Great Hall of Records
90 Inspire Fear
248 Inspire Fear
TIF1 The Imperial Favor

2010 Legend of the Five Rings Celestial Edition 15th Anniversary

1 Doom of the Dark Lord Promo
2 Emperor's Peace Promo
3 Evil Feeds Upon Itself Promo
4 Imperial Gift Promo
5 Inheritance Promo
6 Iris Festival Promo
7 Black Market Promo
8 Infernal Mempo of the Spider Clan
9 Sanctified Temple Promo
11 Hida Yakamo (Hero) Promo
12 Hida Yakamo (Oni) Promo
13 Kuni Yori (Experienced) Promo
14 Daidoji Uji Promo
15 Doji Hoturi (Experienced) Promo
16 Doji Reju Promo
17 Wisdom Gained U
18 Wisdom of the Keepers U
19 Togashi Mitsu Promo
20 Togashi Satsu (Experienced) Promo
21 Togashi Yokuni (Experienced) Promo
22 Akodo Kage (Experienced) Promo
23 Matsu Agetoki Promo
24 Matsu Gohei Promo
25 Tamago Promo
26 Tsuruchi Promo
27 Tsuruchi Etsui (Experienced) Promo
28 Yoritomo (Experienced 2) Promo
29 Yoritomo Utemaro Promo
30 Naga Abomination Promo
31 Ninja Shapeshifter Promo
32 Ninja Spy Promo
33 Isawa Sezaru Promo
34 Isawa Tadaka Promo
35 Isawa Tsuke Promo
36 Kaneka Promo
37 Kan'ok'ticheck (Experienced) Promo
38 Bayushi Aramoro Promo
39b Bayushi Kachiko Promo
40 Bayushi Kaukatsu Promo
41 Bayushi Saya Promo
42 Daigotsu Promo
43 Moto Tsume Promo
45 Yogo Junzo Promo
47 Ginawa Promo
48 Toku Promo
49 Void Dragon Promo
50 Moto Akikazu Promo
50b Fields of the Dead (CE)
51 Moto Chagatai (Experienced 4) Promo
52 Moto Gaheris (Experienced) Promo
53 Otaku Kamoko Promo
54 Musume Mura Promo
55 Shinsei's Shrine Promo
55b Hida Kuon (Experienced 6)
56 Hida Masatari C
56b Brothers in Arms Promo
57 Shinsei's Crow Promo
57b Hida Kisada (Imperial) Promo
58 The Twelve Ronin Promo
59 Wandering Budoka Promo
59b Hiruma Aki (Experienced) R
60 Bloodsword Promo
61 The Egg of P'an Ku Promo
62 The Jade Hand Promo
63 Night Medallion Promo
63b Kaiu Taru R
64 Tao of Fu Leng Promo
65 I Give You My Name Promo
66 Secrets on the Wind Promo
67 Another Time Promo
68 Avoid Fate Promo
68b Iaijutsu Duel Promo
68c Gakku C
69 Bountiful Harvest Promo
70 Breach of Etiquette Promo
71 Brutal Confrontation Promo
72 Come One at a Time Promo
73 Confusion at Court Promo
74 Counterattack Promo
75 Crushing Attack Promo
76 Dark Lord's Favor Promo
77 Deadly Ground Promo
78 Deeds, Not Words Promo
79 Doomed Intentions Promo
79b Kitsuki Taiko (Experienced) R
80 Entrapping Terrain Promo
81 Evil Portents Promo
82 Fall on Your Knees Promo
82b Besieged Borderland C
83 Focus Promo
84 For the Empire Promo
85 Geisha Assassin Promo
86b Hired Killer Promo
87 His Most Favored Promo
88 Iaijutsu Challenge Promo
8b Merchant Caravan Promo
90 Into the Darkness Promo
91 Kharmic Strike Promo
92 Kolat Assassin Promo
93 Kolat Master Promo
93b Akodo Seiichi U
94 Marries a Barbarian Promo
95 Ninja Kidnapper Promo
96 Ordered Retreat Promo
97 Overwhelmed Promo
98 Poisoned Weapon Promo
99 Rallying Cry Promo
100 Scroll Cache Promo
102 Show of Good Faith Promo
103 Stand Against the Waves Promo
104 Stay Your Blade Promo
105 Storm Heart Promo
105b Oni no Akuma Promo
107 Tell the Tale Promo
108 The People's Champion Promo
109 To Do What We Must Promo
110 Wedge Promo
114 Yoritomo Saburo C
117 Agasha Ueda C
125 Superior Tactics Promo
127 Shiba Morihiko
132 Bayushi Eisaku (Experienced) R
140 Toturi Promo
143 Chuda Hiroe C
178 Shikibu no Oni (Experienced) R
17b Kakita Toshimoko (Experienced) Promo
18b Mirumoto Hitomi Promo
205 Black Hearts, Red Blades C
232 Flanked by Nightmares R
251 Kata of the North Wind R
252 Knife in the Darkness U
25b Clan Estate U
278 Shameful Tactics U
300 Unexpected Intimidation R
303 Unstoppable Force R
342 Doji Armor R
353 Hida War Drums R
354 Keen Blade U
378 Kyuden Hida
380 Seven Fold Palace
381 Shiro Daidoji
384 Central Castle
385 Venerable Plains of the Ikoma
386 Dragon's Guard City
394 The Field of the Winds
395 The Utaku Plains
1 of 9 Celestial Mempo of the Crab Clan
2 of 9 Celestial Mempo of the Crane Clan

3 of 9 Celestial Mempo of the Dragon Clan
5 of 9 Celestial Mempo of the Lion Clan
6 of 9 Celestial Mempo of the Mantis Clan
7 of 9 Celestial Mempo of the Phoenix Clan
8 of 9 Celestial Mempo of the Scorpion Clan
9 of 9 Celestial Mempo of the Unicorn Clan

2010 Legend of the Five Rings The Imperial Gift 3

RELEASED IN AUGUST 2010
1 A Life for a Soul
2 Celestial Distavor
3 Exotic Goods
4 Strategic Keep
5 Hida Mochitoko
6 Kuni Iyedo
7 Asahina Okimoto
8 Kakita Furegami
9 Mirumoto Miyami
10 Tamori Ochimo
11 Akodo Tetsuru
12 Kitsu Marimi
13 Yoritomo Gazuke
14 Yoritomo Kakeko
15 Agasha Yuhiko
16 Shiba Kyushi
17 Bayushi Orijitte
18 Shosuro Nishu
19 Fettered Minion
20 Kazuwaru
21 Iuchi Quan
22 Shinjo Liu Ying
23 Seasoned Ronin
24 Tarui
25 Coordinated Assault
26 Demand Obedience
27 Deny the Darkness
28 Deny the Horde
29 Faint Praise
30 Howls of the Dead
31 Ominous Battlefield
32 Opportunistic Advance
33 Planned Adversity
34 Shadowed Words
35 Shattered Stone Kata
36 Sohei's Duty
37 Subversive Whispers
38 Succumb to Vice
39 Ambitious Merchant
40 Aspiring Ronin
41 Awakened Blade
42 Fearsome Mempo
43 Shelter of the Earth
44 Steed of the Ebbing Tides

2011 Legend of the Five Rings Before the Dawn

COMPLETE SET (163) 50.00 100.00
BOOSTER BOX (48 PACKS) 60.00 120.00
BOOSTER PACK (11 CARDS) 2.50 4.00
RELEASED IN MAY 2011
1 A Champion in Court C .10 .25
2 A Dragon's Favor U .20 .50
3 A Gentle Word U .20 .50
4 A Simple Yari C .10 .25
5 Advanced Warning C .10 .25
6 Akodo Ashiko U .20 .50
7 Akodo Kobi (Exp) F .75 2.00
8 Akodo Tezuka C .10 .25
9 Amazing Feat R .30 .75
10 Anger Management R .30 .75
11 Asahina Nanae C .10 .25
12 Asako Heiwa U .20 .50
13 Asako Izuna C .10 .25
14 Ascending the Ranks U .20 .50
15 Ashigaru Elite R .30 .75
16 Ashigaru Recruits C .10 .25
17 Bayushi Ebara U .20 .50
18 Bayushi Shibata C .10 .25
19 Bayushi Suwabe U .20 .50
20 Beautiful Host U .20 .50
21 Beyond the Line C .10 .25
22 Bird of Prey C .10 .25
23 Brothers in Battle U .20 .50
24 Brothers of Goemon U .20 .50
25 Chuda Kiuchi U .20 .50
26 Consuming Weakness C .10 .25
27 Control the Board U .20 .50
28 Crimson Shadow Armor C .10 .25
29 Daidoji Masafuni U .20 .50
30 Daigotsu Bukaro U .20 .50
31 Daigotsu Miki C .10 .25
32 Daigotsu Yajinden (Exp) R .30 .75
33 Death, Defeated U .20 .50
34 Defending Their Home C .10 .25
35 Destructive Priorities R 3.00 8.00
36 Detained R 1.50 4.00
37 Disgraceful Conduct R 1.00 2.50
38 Dismissing the Cur R 3.00 8.00
39 Disrupting Communication C .10 .25
40 Doji Shigeyuki U .20 .50
41 Drawing on the Mountain U .20 .50
42 Ebisu's Honesty R .75 2.00
43 Ember's Final Fire U .20 .50
44 En'you C .10 .25
45 Erosion R .75 2.00
46 Favors R 6.00 15.00
47 Fear Me! R 4.00 10.00
48 Firm Censure C .10 .25
49 Fledgling Ashigaru C .10 .25
50 Forging Destiny U .20 .50
51 Fury of a Mob R 2.50 6.00
52 Genji's Students U .20 .50
53 Goju Genin C .10 .25
54 Goju Sawaki U .20 .50
55 Headbutt U .20 .50
56 Hida Defenders U .20 .50
57 Hida Fujita R .60 1.50
58 Hida Yamadera U .20 .50
59 Hiruma Akio (Exp) F .60 1.50
60 Horse Archers R 1.50 4.00
61 Hunger R .30 .75
62 Ikoma Ayumu R 1.00 2.50
63 Ikoma Shinohara U .20 .50
64 Indomitable Home C .10 .25
65 Iron Will R 6.00 15.00
66 Isawa Kaname R 1.50 4.00
67 Isawa Sakonoko F .40 1.00
68 Iuchi Kota (Exp) R .30 .75
69 Iuchi Yupadi U .20 .50
70 Kaiu Iemasa R .30 .75
71 Kaiu Nakano U .20 .50
72 Kakita Munemori (Exp) R .30 .75
73 Kakita Nara R .60 1.50
74 Kakita Yasunori U .20 .50
75 Kitsuki Fujimura U .20 .50
76 Komori Taruko C .10 .25
77 Kunji C .10 .25
78 Kyuden Hida (Exp) F .30 .75
79 Kyuden Hida Survivor C .10 .25
80 Matsu Kaido R .40 1.00
81 Measure of Devotion U .20 .50
82 Mirumoto Houken C .10 .25
83 Mirumoto Inokuchi U .20 .50
84 Mirumoto Yozo (Exp) R .30 .75
85 Moshi Umiko U .20 .50
86 Moto Hailung C .10 .25
87 Necessary Evil R 1.50 4.00
88 Never Enough Soldiers R .30 .75
89 Nijugun C .10 .25
90 No Time for Games C .10 .25
91 Oathsworn Deathseeker C .10 .25
92 Of One Instant C .10 .25
93 Omigawa C .10 .25
94 One Action, Two Strikes R 1.25 3.00
95 placeholder C .10 .25
96 Pride of the Hand C .10 .25
97 Raido no Oni C .10 .25
98 Readied Steel R 2.50 6.00
99 Reckless Rush C .10 .25
100 Record of Failure R .60 1.50
101 Revenge U .20 .50
102 Rocky Terrain C .10 .25
103 Rumormonger U .20 .50
104 Saibankan's Justice R 1.50 4.00
105 Scars of War U .20 .50
106 Seaside Bazaar R 6.00 15.00
107 Seek the Stain C .10 .25
108 Shadow Tactics C .10 .25
109 Shamate Keep F .30 .75
110 Shiba Jouta (Exp) R .30 .75
111 Shiba Ryuba U .20 .50
112 Shinjo Byung C .10 .25
113 Shinjo Dak-ho U .20 .50
114 Shosuro Toson (Exp) R .30 .75
115 Shosuro Tsuji C .10 .25
116 Show of Restraint U .20 .50
117 Sly Deciever U .20 .50
118 Soshi Komiko R 2.50 6.00
119 Spirit of the Blade C .10 .25
120 Spirit of the Shadows C .10 .25
121 Spirit of the Truth C .10 .25
122 Spirit of the Warrior C .10 .25
123 Stockpiled Resources U .20 .50
124 Stolen Merchandise R 3.00 8.00
125 Stone-Hewed Shrine U .20 .50
126 Strength of the Mountain R .30 .75
127 String of Victories U .20 .50
128 Taishuu R .30 .75
129 Takayuki C .10 .25
130 Tamori Shosei U .20 .50
131 Temple of Purity F .30 .75
132 The Agony of her Gaze R .30 .75
133 The Crimson Mark R .75 2.00
134 The Great Death R 1.00 2.50
135 The Killing Grounds C .10 .25
136 The Price of Honor R .40 1.00
137 The Red Hunger C .10 .25
138 The Second Feint R .75 2.00
139 The Sound of Thunder U .20 .50
140 The Spirit of Knowledge C .10 .25
141 The Tapestry Perceived U .20 .50
142 The World Disappears R .75 2.00
143 Thoughts of Wind C .10 .25
144 Togashi Sakata R 1.25 3.00
145 Too Close to Home U .20 .50
146 Tsi Weapon C .10 .25
147 Tsubute C .10 .25
148 Tsunami Tattoo U .20 .50
149 Tsuruchi Yashiro C .10 .25
150 Unorthodox Attack R 6.00 15.00
151 Utaku Eun-ju C .10 .25
152 Utaku Tairu (Exp) R .30 .75
153 Vigilant Riders U .20 .50
154 Visage of the Orochi C .10 .25
155 Words of Consecration R 1.50 4.00
156 Wrathful Dead C .10 .25
157 Xijkt C .10 .25
158 Yasuki Dokansuto C .10 .25
159 Yoritomo Sachina (Exp) R .40 1.00
160 Yoritomo Singh (Exp) R .30 .75
161 Yoritomo Tarao U .20 .50
162 Yoritomo Zinan U .20 .50
163 Temple of the Seven Fortunes C .10 .25

2011 Legend of the Five Rings The Dead of Winter

COMPLETE SET (165) 40.00 80.00
BOOSTER BOX (48 PACKS) 30.00 60.00
BOOSTER PACK (11 CARDS) 1.00 2.00
RELEASED IN JANUARY 2011
1 1,000 Cuts Technique R 2.00 5.00
2 Agasha Kamarou C .10 .25
3 Agasha Kokiden U .20 .50
4 Akodo Ebiro U .20 .50
5 Akodo Raemon R .50 1.25
6 Akodo Seiichi (Exp) R .30 .75
7 All Water Flows C .10 .25
8 Ancestral Temple R .40 1.00
9 Aramasu's Vigilance F .40 1.00
10 Archery Unit C .10 .25
11 Armor of the Loyal Son R .40 1.00
12 Asahina Beniha (Exp) F 1.00 2.50
13 Asako Hitsuko R .75 2.00
14 Atone Through Life U .20 .50
15 Awed Witness R 2.00 5.00
16 Balance in Water U .20 .50
17 Bayushi Azumamoru U .20 .50
18 Bayushi Jou U .20 .50
19 Bayushi Muhito (Exp) R .30 .75
20 Bayushi Saito C .10 .25
21 Bestial Rage U .20 .50
22 Calculated Offensive C .10 .25
23 Castle of Earth C .10 .25
24 Cavalry for Hire R .30 .75
25 Chuda Inisi R .30 .75
26 Compromised U .20 .50
27 Concentrated Fire R .30 .75
28 Consumption by Fire R 1.00 2.50
29 Controlling the Seas U .20 .50
30 Corrupt Governor U .20 .50
31 Crippling Weather C .10 .25
32 Croplands C .10 .25
33 Daidoji Kagami C .10 .25
34 Daidoji Sadayori R .30 .75
35 Daigotsu Gahseng (Exp) R .30 .75
36 Daigotsu Sahara (Exp) F .30 .75
37 Daisho C .10 .25
38 Dark Oracle of Fire (Exp) R 3.00 8.00
39 Dependable Gear C .10 .25
40 Doji Nukada C .10 .25
41 Doji Shikatsu U .20 .50
42 Draw Attention U .20 .50
43 Drawing the Void C .10 .25
44 Ekibyogami's Spite R .40 1.00
45 Embassy of the Crane F 1.00 2.50
46 Endless Stamina C .10 .25
47 Favor of Artisans C .10 .25
48 Fifth Wind Cavalry R .50 1.25
49 Fosuta no Oni C .10 .25
50 Guardian of Earth U .20 .50
51 Guided by Honor U .20 .50
52 Hachigoro U .20 .50
53 Heroic Inspiration R .75 2.00
54 Hida Akeno C .10 .25
55 Hida Desora C .10 .25
56 Hida Eijiko (Exp) R .30 .75
57 Hida Tokido U .20 .50
58 Hida Yiu U .20 .50
59 Hidden in the Shadows C .10 .25
60 Hunting the Daughter R 1.50 4.00
61 Iainuki C .10 .25
62 Ieyoshi C .10 .25
63 Ignoble Demise Event U .20 .50
64 Impromptu Weapon U .20 .50
65 Inari's Blessing R .30 .75
66 Infamous Strike R 1.25 3.00
67 Inspired Devotion U .20 .50
68 Isawa Furiko R .75 2.00
69 Isawa Kumai (Exp) R .30 .75
70 Isawa Kuniki U .20 .50
71 Iuchi Katamari (Exp) R .30 .75
72 Jimen's Decree Event R .30 .75
73 Kakita Noritoshi (Exp) R .40 1.00
74 Kakita Yosuga U .20 .50
75 Karyuudo C .10 .25
76 Katahide C .10 .25
77 Khol Regulars U .20 .50
78 Kitsuki Bokuko U .20 .50
79 Know the Terrain R .30 .75
80 Kuni Kiyoshi (Exp) R .30 .75
81 Kyuden Suzume F .30 .75
82 Lack of Vigilance Event U .20 .50
83 Leaked Information U .20 .50
84 Legendary Feud R 1.00 2.50
85 Matsu Amuro U .20 .50
86 Matsu Ato C .10 .25
87 Matsu Fumiyo (Exp) R 1.00 2.50
88 Matsu Sako C .10 .25
89 Midnight Shadows C .10 .25
90 Mirumoto Hojatsu (TDoW) R .60 1.50
91 Mirumoto Kijima C .10 .25
92 Mirumoto Tsubasa U .20 .50
93 Moshi Kalani (Exp) R .50 1.25
94 Moshi Kinyo C .10 .25
95 Moto Jeng-Yun R .60 1.50
96 Muscle and Steel R 1.25 3.00
97 No Pure Breaths R .50 1.25
98 Open Emotion R .40 1.00
99 Out of Nowhere R 1.00 2.50
100 Panther Tattoo R .30 .75
101 Preparedness R 2.00 5.00
102 Preserve Your Forces C .10 .25
103 Private Farm C .10 .25
104 Public Records C .10 .25
105 Pure Breath R .30 .75
106 Rain of Justice R 2.50 6.00
107 Rally Through Sacrifice U .20 .50
108 Reach Across the World C .10 .25
109 Reckless Assault C .10 .25
110 Retired Magistrates U .20 .50
111 Second-Hand Goods R .30 .75
112 Seppun Ujifusa C .10 .25
113 Serene Brother U .20 .50
114 Shatter the Wave U .20 .50
115 Shiba Gohiko C .10 .25
116 Shinjo Chu-Yeung U .20 .50
117 Shinjo Hwarang (Exp) R .30 .75
118 Shinjo Meng-Do C .10 .25
119 Shinjo Tobasa C .10 .25
120 Shosuro Jimen (Exp) R .75 2.00
121 Shosuro Shigemasa R .60 1.50
122 Shuriken and Smoke R 1.50 4.00
123 Snow-Covered Plain C .10 .25
124 Snowy Plains C .10 .25
125 Soshi Hirotsugu C .10 .25
126 Southern Blockade R .40 1.00
127 Stand Alone Event U .20 .50
128 Stealing the Essence U .20 .50
129 Stone Guardian U .20 .50
130 Strike Quickly C .10 .25
131 Subversive Influence R .40 1.00
132 Takaharu U .20 .50
133 Tamori Wotan (Exp) R .40 1.00
134 Taxing the Scum U .20 .50
135 Temple of Redemption U .20 .50
136 Temporizing Ground C .10 .25
137 The Fires of War R 1.50 4.00
138 The Kami's Whisper R .40 1.00
139 The Shadow Court U .20 .50
140 The Testament of Fire U .20 .50
141 Togashi Okamoto C .10 .25
142 Togashi Shiori (Exp) R .40 1.00
143 Toritaka Horoiso R .50 1.25
144 Touch of Thunder R .40 1.00
145 Treacherous Defile C .10 .25
146 Tsangusuri C .10 .25
147 Tsume Spearmen C .10 .25
148 Tsuruchi Daikyu U .20 .50
149 Tsuruchi Seisha U .20 .50
150 Tsuruchi Toboro R .30 .75
151 Ujisato R .50 1.25
152 Unnatural Hunger R 1.00 2.50
153 Utaku Liu-Xeung U .20 .50
154 Vigorous Sparring U .20 .50
155 Waves Rush to the Shore U .20 .50
156 Well Scouted Target U .20 .50
157 Winter Pilgrimage C .10 .25
158 Winter Siege R .40 1.00
159 With My Last Breath C .10 .25
160 Words Have Strength U .20 .50
161 Yoritomo Ai C .10 .25
162 Yoritomo Aranai (Mantis) U .20 .50
163 Yoritomo Aranai (Spider) U .20 .50
164 Yoritomo Elhiko (Exp) F .30 .75
165 Yukataka no Onna U .20 .50

2011 Legend of the Five Rings Forgotten Legacy

RELEASED IN JULY 2011
1 Ryoshun's Guidance
2 Assault in the Jungle
3 Burning Dreams
4 Willing Spirits
5 Ageless Shrine
6 Bamboo Harvesters (Experienced)
7 Border Keep (Experienced)
8 Colonial Harbor
9 Hida Fubatsu (Experienced)
10 Hiruma Nikaru
11 Toritaka Chokichi
12 Yasuki Daiki
13 Asahina Shigemitsu
14 Daidoji Takichi
15 Doji Hakuseki (Experienced 2)
16 Doji Rengetsu
17 Kitsuki Nubane
18 Mirumoto Kojinrue
19 Tamori Kazushige
20 Togashi Osawa (Experienced)
21 Akodo Tsudoken (Experienced)
22 Ikoma Tsukasa
23 Kitsu Kagako
24 Matsu Koyama
25 Kitsune Hisano (Experienced)
26 Moshi Sasako
27 Tsuruchi Nobukatsu
28 Yoritomo Haruhiko
29 Asako Chukage
30 Asako Kaitoko
31 Asako Karachu
32 Shiba Sawaken
33 Bayushi Higaonna
34 Bayushi Toshimo
35 Shosuro Aroru (Experienced 2)
36 Shosuro Makiko
37 Daigotsu Gyoken (Experienced 2)
38 Daigotsu Murota
39 Ninube Shiho
40 Yamazaki
41 Iuchi Abodan
42 Moto Xiao (Experienced)
43 Shinjo Junpei
44 Utaku Ji-Yun
45 The Dark Naga
46 The Shakash
47 The Sleepless One
48 The Second City
49 Hunter of Harmony
50 Scourge of the Sea
51 The Vengeful
52 Black Pearl (Experienced)
53 Cursed Relic
54 Pearl of Embers
55 Pearl of Rage
56 The Mountain's Power
57 Thunder's Wrath
58 Wind of the Moon
59 A Game of Dice
60 A Yojimbo's Duty
61 Accidental Confession
62 Asset Denial
63 Broken Alliance
64 Cast Aside the Weak
65 Consideration
66 Creating Order
67 Duel of Haiku
68 Economic Repercussions
69 Entrenched Position
70 Feint & Strike
71 Fruitless Search
72 Grateful Reward
73 Gripped by Terror
74 Heart of Darkness
75 Honor Never Falls
76 Intimidation
77 Never Beyond My Reach
78 Oblivious
79 Pearls & Spirits
80 Petty Squabbles
81 Returning Home
82 Rise of the Dark Naga
83 Seeking the Truth
84 Siege Volley
85 Steadfast Defense
86 Sundering Strike
87 Sword for Hire
88 The Perfect Moment
89 Wanted for Questioning
90 The Forgotten Temple
ProxyF1 Hisano's Guide

2011 Legend of the Five Rings Second City

Kyuden Kitsune Stronghold
RELEASED IN SEPTEMBER 2011
1 Blessings of the Shi-Tien Yen-Wang R
2 Jurojin's Blessing R
3 Formal Apology U
4 Harsh Choices R
5 Rebuilding Kyuden Hida U
6 Times of Strife U
7 War Weariness U
8 Archery Range C
9 Red Crane Dojo U
10 Remote Village C
11 Slanderer R
12 Temple of Hotei C
13 Tranquil Garden U
14 Hida Mimori C
15 Hida Mochitoko R
16 Hiruma Tensin U
17 Kaiu Watsuki C
18 Yasuki Jinn-Kuen R
19 Yasuki Tsujiken U
20 Asahina Munefusa C
21 Daidoji Ebizo U
22 Daidoji Yuki R
23 Doji Dainagon C
24 Doji Yoshitada R
25 Kakita Maratai U
26 Kitsuki Horume R
27 Mirumoto Ezuno C
28 Mirumoto Yumaru R
29 Tamori Ruya
30 Tamori Yayu U
31 Togashi Hizumi U
32 Togashi Meiyu C
33 Akodo Kakihara C
34 Akodo Kamina U
35 Ikoma Sugo C
36 Kitsu Akai R
37 Kitsu Fukui U
38 Matsu Kasei R
39 Kitsune Ohsuki
40 Kitsune Tokoru C
41 Moshi Tomeno C
42 Tsuruchi Yakusho U
43 Yoritomo Emoto R
44 Yoritomo Minori U
45 Yoritomo Sakuma R
46 Agasha Kodo U
47 Asako Moeru C
48 Asako Rikate R
49 Isawa Kojiro C
50 Isawa Mitsuko R
51 Shiba Kudome U
52 Bayushi Kahoku
53 Bayushi Nori U
54 Shosuro Hawado U
55 Shosuro Rin R
56 Shosuro Ritoru C
57 Soshi Neiru C
58 Yogo Adi R
59 Daigotsu Bolana U
60 Daigotsu Hotako R
61 Daigotsu Shikenuro C
62 Fukuzo R
63 Goju Yurishi U
64 Sutigu C
65 Moto Jun-Ni R
66 Moto Ming-Gwok C
67 Shinjo Kinto U
68 Shinjo Sanenari C
69 Utaku Liu-Xeung R
70 Utaku Mai U
71 Keppo C
72 Kuronada R
73 Sea Troll Predator C
74 Shikaro C
75 Takasho R
76 Overgrown Grove C
77 Quagmire U
78 Shinden Shorai R
79 Champion of Thunder R
80 Elite Sentry R
81 Fading Shadows C
82 Legion of the Bat U
83 Moto Gunso C

84 Singh Remnants U
85 Blade of Champions R
86 Flesh Cutter Arrows C
87 Fubatsu Plate C
88 Nightingale Blade R
89 Satoshi's Dual Warfans U
90 Bo of Water C
91 Control Your Destiny U
92 Essence of Undeath C
93 Intervening Spirit U
94 Katana of Fire R
95 Mastering the Elements R
96 Rage of the Spirits C
97 Stormless Fury U
98 Strength of the Tsunami R
99 Taming the Beast C
100 The Earth Flows C
101 Winds of Dismissal R
102 A Fugitive Apprehended U
103 A Quiet Transaction U
104 Again! U
105 Ancient Feud C
106 Barred Passage U
107 Basic Lesson C
108 Bonds of Coin U
109 Bow Before My Will U
110 Brawl R
111 Costly Opportunity C
112 Discovering a Conspiracy R
113 Dislodge the Foe R
114 Dispensing Justice R
115 Disreputable Deal R
116 Effortless Counterattack R
117 Engulfing Flames U
118 Goju Plot U
119 Great Sacrifice R
120 Hasty Fortifications C
121 Hibernation U
122 Improved Defenses U
123 Insulting Gesture R
124 Interference C
125 Know No Fear U
126 Know Their Minds R
127 Nakanu Technique C
128 Never Safe U
129 On the Hunt R
130 Redoubled Attack C
131 Scandalous Rumors U
132 Scavenging Party U
133 Shiotome Plains C
134 Silent Terror U
135 Skipping the Puddle R
136 Spirit of the Berserker C
137 Spirit of the Duelist C
138 Spirit of the Monk C
139 Spirit of the Paragon C
140 Spirit of the Scout C
141 Spirit of the Yojimbo C
142 Strategic Sacrifice U
143 Superior Reach R
144 Surety of Purpose R
145 Tales of Dishonor R
146 The Weakness of Man R
147 Tireless Efforts C
148 To First Blood C
149 Unexpected Support U
150 Visitation U
151 Volcano Tattoo U
152 Wrathful Ancestor R
153 Your Clan Needs You! R
154 Dragon's Breath Castle
156 Law of Darkness Dojo
Proxy1 Questionable Resources C
Proxy2 Lion Ancestor C
Proxy3 Ohsuki's Sparrow C
Proxy4 Tokoru's Bear C
Proxy5 Flame Katana C
Proxy6 Water Bo C

2011 Legend of the Five Rings War of Honor

RELEASED IN JUNE 2011
1 Birth of the Sword
2 Emissary of the Ivory Kingdoms
3 Enlistment
4 Imperial Ambassadorship
5 Military Alliance
6 Welcome Home
7 Wisdom Gained
8 Acrobat Troupe
9 Temple to the Ancestors
10 Bamboo Harvesters
11 Border Keep
12 Border Village
13 Copper Mine
14 Diamond Mine
15 Disreputable House
16 Expendable Resources
17 Family Library
18 Geisha House
19 Gold Mine
20 Large Farm
21 Permanent Encampment
22 Rich Coffers
23 Shinsei's Tomb
24 Shrine to Fukurokujin
25 Silver Mine
26 Simple Men
27 Small Farm
28 Temple of Harmony
29 Temple to Shinsei
30 The Seekers' Temple
31 Traveling Peddler
32 War Encampment
33 Togashi Akagi
34 Togashi Chiko
36 Togashi Kanmu
37 Togashi Nakahara
38 Togashi Oki
39 Togashi Shiori
40 Togashi Taro
41 Akodo Dosei
42 Ikoma Toraji
43 Matsu Fumiyo
44 Matsu Mansaiko
45 Matsu Miyahara
46 Matsu Nishijo
47 Matsu Sakaki
48 Matsu Yosa
49 Agasha Asai
50 Agasha Gifu
51 Asako Hoshimi
52 Asako Meisuru
53 Isawa Akihiro
54 Isawa Kyoko
55 Isawa Kyoko (Experienced)
56 Isawa Naki
57 Bayushi Hikoko
58 Bayushi Hirose
59 Bayushi Jutsushi
60 Bayushi Maemi
61 Bayushi Saka
62 Bayushi Shigeo
63 Bayushi Sorii
65 Soshi Tabito (Experienced)
66 Akodo Regulars
67 Ashigaru Conscripts
68 Deathseeker Troop
69 Hired Legion
70 Ronin Brotherhood
71 A Samurai's Soul
72 Blades of the Fallen Phoenix
73 Ring of Air
74 Ring of Earth
75 Ring of Flame
77 Ring of Water
78 Consumed by Five Fires
79 Fury of the Sea
80 Groves of Stone
81 Heaven's Tears
82 Shielded by Tempest
83 Tempest of Flame
84 The Storm Within
85 A Warrior's Wisdom
86 Allegations
87 Begone, Fool!
88 Black and White
89 Block Supply Lines
90 Changing Paths
91 Charge
92 Chasing Osano-Wo
93 Chokehold
94 Cold Hands, Stone Heart
95 Courtesy
96 Dance of the Void
97 Desperate Mediation
98 Embracing Virtue
99 Fist and Blade
100 Fortuitous Alliance
101 From Every Side
102 Game of Sincerity
104 Magistrate's Accusation
105 My Enemy's Mercy
106 Paths of Honor & Glory
107 Prideful Allies
108 Ramifications
109 Relentless Conviction
110 Restoring Order
111 Seeking the Guilty
112 Settling the Homeless
113 Shameful Death
114 Shameful Rebuke
115 Spinning Heel Kick
116 Stagnation
117 Striking Through the Void
118 The Lion's Charge
119 The Wrath of Osano-Wo
120 Unpredictable Strategy
121 Unstoppable Power
122 Viper Tattoo
123 Wall of Honor
124 Tetsu Kama Mura
125 Venerable Plains of the Ikoma
126 City of Tears (GotE)
127 Seven Stings Keep
52b Glorious Path to Victory
83b Ring of the Void
97b Soshi Idaurin
113b Togashi Gato

2012 Legend of the Five Rings Embers of War

RELEASED IN MAY 2012
1 Hotei's Contentment R
2 Lady Matsu's Rage R
3 Gaining Advantage R
4 Growing Hostility U
5 In Search of Guidance U
6 The Scorpion Wall is Finished U
7 Shrine to Nimuro U
8 Staging Grounds C
9 Surveillance Outpost C
10 Temple Fortress C
11 Temple to the Elements C
12 Terraced Farm C
13 Hida Bakishi C
14 Hida Osote U
15 Hiruma Moritoki C
16 Kaiu Onizuka R
17 Kaiu Tojikana U
18 Yasuki Makoto R
19 Asahina Konomi C
20 Daidoji Akeha R
21 Daidoji Narizane U
22 Kakita Gonji U
23 Kakita Kae R
24 Kakita Kenta C
25 Kitsuki Daisuke (Experienced) R
26 Kitsuki Jakuei U
27 Mirumoto Hikaro U
28 Mirumoto Kouzei C
29 Tamori Seiken C
30 Togashi Rikyou R
31 Akodo Tamisu U
32 Akodo Uehara C
33 Ikoma Hakige R
34 Ikoma Shika (Experienced)
35 Ikoma Sido C
36 Ikoma Yamahatsu U
37 Kitsu Miro R
38 Kitsune Haruki U
39 Moshi Tomiko C
40 Tsuruchi Shichiro U
41 Tsuruchi Shigekazu C
42 Tsuruchi Tomaru (Experienced) R
43 Yoritomo Kanaye R
44 Asako Kikugoro U
45 Asako Megu R
46 Isawa Koiso R
47 Isawa Mina C
48 Isawa Sanetomo U
49 Shiba Toshisugo C
50 Bayushi Kazutoshi (Experienced) U
51 Bayushi Nomen (Experienced 2) C
52 Bayushi Tenzan U
53 Shosuro Ryoichi C
54 Shosuro Ietsuno R
55 Soshi Yoshihara (Experienced) R
56 Daigotsu Kazuko U
57 Daigotsu Susaiken U
58 Daigotsu Takayasu (Experienced)
59 Daigotsu Tenbatsu C
60 Goju Gochiso C
61 Shadow Dragon (Experienced 2) R
62 Sugihara R
63 Gozaru no Oni U
64 Itoku (Experienced) R
65 Makito (Experienced) R
66 Rata C
67 Rokku (Experienced) R
68 Sakti C
69 Tokiko (Experienced) R
70 Iuchi Yuri C
71 Moto Isul C
72 Moto Rani (Experienced) R
73 Shinjo Hayan U
74 Shinjo Junpei (Experienced)
75 Shinjo Sarang U
76 Utaku Lishan R
77 Low Market U
78 The Distant Reaches U
79 Ashigaru Guards C
80 Field Messenger C
81 Flanking Unit R
82 Hiromi's Vassals R
83 Home Guard C
84 Murderous Thieves C
85 Ninja Guards U
86 Village Raiders U
87 Armor of the Uruwashii U
88 Celestial Sword of the Lion (Experienced)
89 Celestial Sword of the Unicorn (Experienced)
90 Dazzling Attire C
91 Pillowbook U
92 Sankaku-Yari C
93 Shamsir C
94 Splintered Weapon U
95 The Ancestral Sword of Hantei (Experienced)
96 Centering the Soul U
97 Damning Ceremony U
98 Delving into History R
99 Extending Influence U
100 Illusory Defense R
101 Incite the Phantoms C
102 Inescapable Snare C
103 Mara's Touch C
104 Ochiai's Bravery R
105 Sudden Guardian U
106 The Menacing Sky R
107 The Swell of Strength C
108 A Weak Poison C
109 Astonishing Accusation R
110 Broken Cipher C
111 Deadly Discipline U
112 Deep Snows C
113 Exploited Advantage U
114 Games of Will C
115 Greasing the Wheels C
116 Help from the Shadows U
117 Honest Assessment U
118 Inciting Mistrust R
119 Indecision U
120 Inexorable R
121 Killing Intent C
122 Moving and Unmoving R
123 Perfect Sacrifice R
124 Perplexing Guests U
125 Phantom Visage R
126 Pillar Tattoo U
127 Power of Strength R
128 Preceding Reputation C
129 Precision R
130 Preserving Forces C
131 Pronouncement of Guilt R
132 Reckless Duel R
133 Request Authorization R
134 Riddle of Rebirth R
135 Ride the Breeze R
136 Scouting the Pass R
137 Searching for Answers R
138 Secret Reserve C
139 Seeking the Question U
140 Sheathing the Sword C
141 Stand as the Mountain U
142 Stuck in Rokugan C
143 Surrounded! U
144 Tactical Trap U
145 The Bite of Winter C
146 The Cycle of Vengeance C
147 The Heir's Wrath R
148 The Host's Advantage U
149 The Snow Has Teeth C
150 Thick Marsh R
151 Too Much for Mortals U
152 Two Fronts U
153 Unsafe Passage U
154 Unstoppable Strike R
155 Yojimbo Assemble R
156 You Are Unworthy U
157 The Marshalling Fields
158 The Plain of Glass
159 The Ki-Rin's Path
ProxyF1 Lion Ancestor C
ProxyF2 Haruki's Deer C
ProxyF3 Assassin C
ProxyF4 Emerald Magistrate C
ProxyF5 Fresh Recruit C
ProxyF6 Guest C

2012 Legend of the Five Rings Emperor Edition

RELEASED IN FEBRUARY 2012
1 Akodo's Guidance
2 Bayushi's Guidance
3 Daigotsu's Guidance
4 Doji's Guidance
5 Hida's Guidance
6 Shiba's Guidance
7 Shinjo's Guidance
8 Togashi's Guidance
9 Yoritomo's Guidance
10 Abandoning the Fortunes R
11 Alter History R
12 Benefices of the Emperor R
13 Boastful Proclamation U
14 Cherry Blossom Festival R
15 Cross-Clan Wedding R
16 Delayed Arrival C
17 Disgrace R
18 Glory of the Shogun R
19 Imperial Gift R
20 Moon and Sun R
21 Naoharu's Gift R
22 Rebuilding the Empire R
23 Successful Bounty U
24 Suspicions R
25 Wisdom Gained U
26 Akodo's Grave C
27 Bamboo Harvesters
28 Border Keep
29 Chugo Seido R
30 Copper Mine
31 Deeds and Words R
32 Falling Rain Dojo U
33 Family Library U
34 Fortifications C
35 Geisha House
36 Gold Mine
37 Governor's Court R
38 Iron Mine
39 Kobune Port
40 Large Farm U
41 Luxurious Silk R
42 Marketplace
43 Moneylender R
44 Prosperous Village C
45 Public Records C
46 Rugashi Bazaar U
47 Shinomen Marsh
48 Shrine to Hachiman R
49 Silk Works C
50 Silver Mine
51 Small Farm C
52 Stables
53 Temples of Gisei Toshi R
54 Traveling Peddler R
55 Venerable Master R
56 Well-Tended Farm U
57 Hida Bushotsu C
58 Hida Horu
59 Hida Kisada
60 Hida Komatsu R
61 Hida Takeuchi C
62 Hida Watari R
63 Hiruma Nitani U
64 Kaiu Esumi U
65 Kaiu Hideaki R
66 Kaiu Kawachi U
67 Kuni Shinoda C
68 Toritaka Shishido C
69 Yasuki Jekku U
70 Yasuki Tanimura U
71 Yasuki Tono C
72 Asahina Keigo U
73 Asahina Kitiaru R
74 Asahina Michiru U
75 Asahina Yasutora C
76 Daidoji Kenshi C
77 Daidoji Tametaka C
78 Doji Atsumichi U
79 Doji Genshin C
80 Doji Makoto
81 Doji Shunya U
82 Doji Tatsuki
83 Kakita Genshi U
84 Kakita Kazan R
85 Kakita Seishi C
86 Kakita Tadanobu R
87 Kitsuki Daisuke U
88 Kitsuki Kinaro C
89 Kitsuki Yataku R
90 Mirumoto Gobashi C
91 Mirumoto Ichizo R
92 Mirumoto Katagi R
93 Mirumoto Reiyu U
94 Mirumoto Shikei
95 Tamori Kusugi U
96 Tamori Muzu U
97 Tamori Tomaru C
98 Togashi Korimi U
99 Togashi Torazu
100 Togashi Tsukagi C
101 Tsai-tsu C
102 Akodo Dairuko
103 Akodo Kano R
104 Akodo Kisho
105 Akodo Makotai R
106 Akodo Suoh C
107 Ikoma Natsu U
108 Ikoma Shika C
109 Ikoma Shinju U
110 Kitsu Sorano C
111 Kitsu Suki C
112 Kitsu Tamasine U
113 Matsu Arata U
114 Matsu Hachiro C
115 Matsu Hana R
116 Matsu Yuuto U
117 Kitsune Denhei U
118 Kitsune Gina U
119 Kitsune Kohaki C
120 Moshi Madoka C
121 Moshi Yokohime U
122 Tsuruchi Isas C
123 Tsuruchi Kosoko C
124 Tsuruchi Samuru R
125 Tsuruchi Tomaru U
126 Unmei R
127 Yoritomo Doho C
128 Yoritomo Hama R
129 Yoritomo Hiromi
130 Yoritomo Nakoshi
131 Yoritomo Naoto U
132 Agasha Ryo C
133 Asako Niou C
134 Asako Nobunori U
135 Asako Rinshi C
136 Asako Tsunefusa U
137 Asako Ume R
138 Asako Yorisada U
139 Isawa Kimi R
140 Isawa Norimichi R
141 Isawa Shunsuko C
142 Isawa Tamaki
143 Isawa Tomohiro U
144 Shiba Katakén C
145 Shiba Sansesuke U
146 Shiba Tsukimi
147 Bayushi Hurunayi C
148 Bayushi Irezu U
149 Bayushi Kahoku R
150 Bayushi Manami C
151 Bayushi Mitsuo
152 Bayushi Nitoshi
153 Bayushi Rentatsu R
154 Bayushi Waru U
155 Bayushi Yasashiku C
156 Shosuro Kameyoi U
157 Shosuro Konishi C
158 Shosuro Koshiba C
159 Shosuro Rokuta U
160 Shosuro Tanzaki U
161 Soshi Yorimi R
162 Daigotsu Aya R
163 Daigotsu Gyoken
164 Daigotsu Ishibashi U
165 Daigotsu Kanpeki
166 Daigotsu Kendo C
167 Daigotsu Matsuda C
168 Daigotsu Misaki U
169 Daigotsu Negishi C
170 Goju Kobashi U
171 Goju Oyoto C
172 Ninube Onchi U
173 Nishimura R
174 Ohaba U
175 Sandayu C
176 Tetsuo R
177 Chuda Niiro C
178 Ekichu no Oni R
179 Genmyo C
180 Nosloc no Oni R
181 Otomo Demiyah U
182 Qalyar C
183 Seppun Washi C
184 Suiteiru no Oni R*
185 Ugulu no Oni R
186 Yung R
187 Iuchi Shunshi R
188 Moto Naleesh
189 Moto Rani C
190 Moto Shigeru U
191 Moto Shunsuke U
192 Moto Taha C
193 Moto Tetsuo U
194 Shinjo Baeshuko C
195 Shinjo Eun-Sahng U
196 Shinjo Horibe

197 Shinjo Itao C
198 Shinjo Ki-Chang R
199 Shinjo Taeken C
200 Utaku Ryoko U
201 Utaku Tsukiko R
202 Blighted Region R
203 Kaiu Village R
204 Plains of Otosan Uchi R
205 Refuge of the Three Sisters U
206 Ten Thousand Temples U
207 Apprentice Shinobi U
208 Asahina House Guard
209 Asako House Guard
210 Bandit Gang C
211 Goju House Guard
212 Hiruma Sniper U
213 Ikiryo C
214 Ikoma House Guard
215 Kaiu House Guard
216 Khol Regulars U
217 Legion of Pain R
218 Moto House Guard
219 Outriders C
220 Shinjo's Children C
221 Soshi House Guard
222 Stalking Tiger R
223 Tamori House Guard
224 Tsuruchi House Guard
225 Utaku Elite Guard U
226 Veteran Advisor R
227 Veteran Skirmishers C
228 Village Guardian C
229 Armor of the Heavens R
230 Blade of Perfection C
231 Chrysanthemum Blossom C
232 Clan Standard R
233 Gift Armor R
234 Kensai's Blade C
235 Maga-yari C
236 Modifications R
237 Reserve Weapon U
238 Sasumata R
239 Spiked Tetsubo C
240 Tsuruchi Daikyu U
241 Ring of Air U
242 Ring of Earth U
243 Ring of Fire U
244 Ring of the Void U
245 Ring of Water U
246 Capturing the Soul R
247 Chikushudo's Trickery R
248 Cleansing the Path U
249 Conflagration U
250 Consecration R
251 Contemplate the Void C
252 Hanabi R
253 I Give You My Name R
254 Obscured Pathways U
255 Scouring Flood C
256 Seeking the Way R
257 Summon Swamp Spirits U
258 The Kami's Blessing U
259 Thunder's Favor U
260 Unnatural Flood R
261 Walking the Way U
262 Warded Paths U
263 A Forefather's Vengeance U
264 A Paragon's Strength R
265 A Pure Stroke C
266 A Stain Cleansed R
267 A Time for Mortal Men C
268 Ambush R
269 Ancestral Protection R
270 Aramoro's Promise U
271 At Any Cost R
272 Awed Witness R
273 Back to the Front C
274 Bad Kharma R
275 Banish All Doubt R
276 Bend like a Reed C
277 Besieged R
278 Blind Rage U
279 Block Supply Lines C
280 Breath of the Heavens U
281 Burn the Towers C
282 Caught In The Act R
283 Caught Unawares R
284 Confusion at Court C
285 Control the Field C
286 Dangerous Indulgence R
287 Deadly Orders C
288 Deception Revealed U
289 Duel of Serpents U
290 Encircled Terrain C
291 Extended Maneuvers C
292 Face of Ninube C
293 Fall Back! C
294 Falling Leaf Strike C
295 Feign Death R
296 Fields of Mercy R
297 Final Confrontation U
298 Flooded Pass C
299 Focus R
300 Footsteps of Madness R
301 Fortitude U
302 Gold and Steel U
303 Guided by Honor U
304 Hard Pressed U
305 He's Mine! C
306 Heart of Rokugan C
307 Heavily Engaged C
308 Hidden Defenses C
309 Hundred-Fold Cut U
310 Immovable Object R
311 In the Heart of Battle C
312 Incapacitated C
313 Inexplicable Challenge R
314 Inspired Devotion U
315 Introspection R
316 Knife in the Darkness U
317 Martial Instruction R
318 Meeting the Keepers R
319 Murderous Intent C
320 My Enemy's Mercy R
321 Mysterious Deaths R
322 Nerve Strike U
323 Ninja Tricks U
324 No Hiding Place C
325 Ogre Savagery C
326 One Koku C
327 Opportunistic Advance U
328 Oyo's Second Lesson U
329 Paid Off C
330 Plans Within Plans R
331 Prepared for Death C
332 Preserving Honor R
333 Relentless Conviction R
334 Remember Your Ancestors C
335 Rend the Soul R
336 Retribution U
337 Rhetoric C
338 Rumors Travel R
339 Sacrifice of Pawns R
340 Sanctioned Duel R
341 Selfless Defense C
342 Shadows Walk U
343 Shameful Injury C
344 Snake Tattoo U
345 Sneak Attack R
346 Sniping U
347 Solid Defense R
348 Soul's Sacrifice C
349 Spinning Heel Kick C
350 Stay Put C
351 Steel on Steel C
352 Strategic Strike R
353 Strength in Terror U
354 Strength of Purity C
355 Summoned to Justice U
356 Superior Opponent C
357 Surprise Attack C
358 Tell the Tale C
359 The Compassion of the Unicorn
360 The Courage of the Mantis
361 The Courtesy of the Crane
362 The Duty of the Crab
363 The Empress' Address R
364 The Fires of War R
365 The Height of Courage C
366 The Honesty of the Phoenix
367 The Honor of the Lion
368 The Law's Strength U
369 The Light of Justice U
370 The Loyalty of the Scorpion
371 The Power of a Word U
372 The Power of One U
373 The Serpent's Deception U
374 The Shadow Court U
375 The Sincerity of the Dragon
376 The Slow Death R
377 The Strength of the Spider
378 The Trap is Sprung! R
379 Torch's Flame Flickers C
380 Treachery and Deceit U
381 Twist of Fate R
382 Undetectable Enemy U
383 Unimpeachable Name U
384 Unseen Assailant U
385 Useful Connections R
386 Veiled Menace U
387 Vigilant Eyes C
388 Wall of Honor R
389 Well Prepared C
390 White Shore Plain U
391 Words Have Strength U
392 Carpenter Castle
393 Halls of the Forgotten
394 Kyuden Hida
395 Yasuki Palaces
396 Hidden Falls Dojo
397 Kyuden Otomo
398 Shinden Asahina
399 The Aerie
400 Dragon's Breath Castle
401 Foothills Keep
402 Pillars of Virtue
403 Watchful Eye Dojo
404 Eternal Victory Dojo
405 Halls of Memory
406 Shamate Keep
407 The Golden Plains
408 Kalani's Landing
409 Koshin Keep
410 Kyuden Kitsune
411 Suitengu's Torch
412 Library of Rebirth
413 Shiro Shiba
414 Temple of Purity
415 Waystation of the Path
416 Law of Darkness Dojo
417 Midday Shadow Court
418 Shiro Chugo
419 The Otoro Estate
420 Keep of the Dead
421 Steel Soul Dojo
422 The Shadow's Lair
423 The Spider's Web
424 Palace of the Breaking Dawn R
425 Journey's End Keep
426 Plains of the Maiden
427 The Khan's Estate
428 The Temple of Death
Draft1 The Governor's Estate PR
Proxy1 Lion Ancestor PR
Proxy2 Denhei's Snake PR
Proxy3 Gina's Fox PR
Proxy4 Rokuta's Apprentice PR
Proxy5 The Walking Dead PR
Proxy6 Venerated Sensei PR
Proxy7 Witness PR
Proxy8 Dak-ho's Men PR
Proxy9 Dutiful Cavalry PR
Proxy10 Farmlands Conscripts PR
Proxy11 Infantry Follower PR
Proxy12 Kobashi's Spawn PR
Proxy13 Kyuden Hida Scout PR
Proxy14 Mounted Ashigaru PR
Proxy15 Nakanu's Creations PR
Proxy16 Suiteieru's Podling PR
Proxy17 Swamp Spirit PR
Proxy18 Kaiu Armor PR
Proxy19 Tsi Weapon PR
Proxy20 Yasunori's Gift PR
Proxy21 Plain of Gold PR

2012 Legend of the Five Rings Emperor Edition Promos

1 Akodo Dairuko
2 Akodo Kakihara
3 Akodo Kamina
4 Ambush
5 Ancient Armor of the Qamar (Experienced)
6 Asahina House Guard
7 Asahina Michiru
8 Asako Heiwa
9 Asako House Guard
10 Asako Moeru
11 Bar Fight
12 Battle Standard of the Naga (Experienced)
13 Bayushi Nitoshi
14 Bayushi Tenzan
15 Bayushi Waru
16 Bokken of the Ruby Champion
17 Border Market
18 Brothers in Battle
19 Charter of the Legion of Two Thousand
20 Chikara (Experienced 2)
21 Closing the Gap
22 Daidoji Ebizo
23 Daigotsu Bukaro
24 Daigotsu Kanpeki (Experienced)
25 Daigotsu Tenbatsu
26 Dark Naga Scouts
27 Den of Iniquity
28 Doji Dainagon
29 Doji Genshin
30 Doji Makoto
31 Encircled Terrain
32 Ever-Winter Copse
33 Expansion
34 Exquisite Blade
35 Forgotten Outpost
36 Fudo (Experienced)
37 Gakku (Experienced)
38 Goju House Guard
39 Goju Yurishi
40 Govern the Land
41 Gozu
42 Gozu's Guide
43 Heart of Fudo (Experienced)
44 Hida Kisada (Emperor)
45 Hida Mimori
46 Hiruma Nitani
47 Hofukushu's Vengeance
48 Ikoma House Guard
49 Ikoma Shinju
50 Imperial Charter
51 Interesting Plains
52 Isawa Kojiro
53 Iuchi Yupadi
54 Jade Embrace
55 Jungle Stockade
56 Kaiu Esumi
57 Kaiu House Guard
58 Ki no Oni
59 Kimono of the Turquoise Champion
60 Kitsu Akai
61 Kitsuki Daisuke
62 Kitsune Tokoru
63 Know No Fear
64 Legendary Rivalry
65 Mahatsu
66 Mantle of the Jade Champion (Experienced 2)
67 Mantle of the Onyx Champion
68 Mempo of the Amethyst Champion
69 Might of the Sun
70 Mirumoto Kouzei
71 Mirumoto Shikei
72 Moshi Tomiko
73 Moto House Guard
74 Moto Isul
75 Moto Naleesh
76 No Hiding Place
77 Omigawa
78 Patchwork Armor
79 Peace
80 Plantation
81 Profits
82 Public Room
83 Quicksand
84 Re-fortification
85 Renewal
86 Resurrection
87 Retired Sensei
88 Revenge
89 Ritual Dagger
90 Ritual of Sacrifice
91 Sea & Sky
92 Second City Dojo
93 Seppun Ichigo
94 Seppun Ritsharu
95 Shiba Toshisugo
96 Shiba Tsukimi (Experienced 4)
97 Shinjo Horibe
98 Shosuro Kameyoi
99 Shosuro Konishi
100 Sinkhole
101 Six-Ring Sword
102 Small Farm
103 Soshi House Guard
104 Steel on Steel
105 Suitengu's Blessing
106 Tales of Valor
107 Tamori House Guard
108 Tamori Potion
109 Tamori Tomaru
110 Tess'kss
111 The Amethyst Championship
112 The Arcane Cloak of the Chameleons
113 The Blade of the Balash
114 The Blessed Mantle of the Greensnakes
115 The Deciding Moment
116 The Emerald Armor (Experienced 2)
117 The Emerald Championship
118 The Height of Courage
119 The Isha's Yumi (Experienced)
120 The Ivory Sword
121 The Jade Championship
122 The Obsidian Armor
123 The Obsidian Championship
124 The Onyx Championship
125 The Pearl-Encrusted Staff of the Cobras (Experienced)
126 The Ruby Championship
127 The Sacred Rosary of the Constrictors
128 The Topaz Armor (Experienced)
129 The Topaz Championship
130 The Turquoise Championship
131 The Wall is Breached
132 The Yari of the Shabura
133 Through the Breach
134 Togashi Torazu
135 Treasure Hunter
136 Tsuruchi House Guard
137 Tsuruchi Tomaru
138 Uta
139 Utaku Mai
140 Verdant Jungle
141 Village Guardian
142 Well Protected
143 Wildfire
144 Winter Sled
145 Yasuki Tsujiken
146 Yoritomo Hiromi
147 Yoritomo Tarao

2012 Legend of the Five Rings Seeds of Decay

RELEASED IN OCTOBER 2012
1 Akuma's Power U
2 Megumi's Guidance R
3 Dark Experiments U
4 Incredible Tragedy U
5 Offering Reverence U
6 Starting on the Path R
7 Farmer's Market C
8 Hachi's Revenge R
9 Incense Mill C
10 Overlooked Palace U
11 Second City Port U
12 Small Library C
13 Temple to Fudo C
14 Hida Kaiji U
15 Hiruma Nitani (Experienced) R
16 Hiruma Sawai C
17 Kaiu Okaru C
18 Yasuki Baiko U
19 Yasuki Tsujiken (Experienced) R
20 Asahina Akikusa R
21 Asahina Tsugio C
22 Daidoji Kitahime R
23 Doji Mitsuru U
24 Doji Yuka U
25 Kakita Yusugi C
26 Kitsuki Minori C
27 Mirumoto Houken (Experienced) R
28 Mirumoto Michi U
29 Tamori Takeshi U
30 Tamori Tamoko R
31 Togashi Hiroto C
32 Togashi Noboru
33 Akodo Hotaka R
34 Akodo Michitsu U
35 Ikoma Aimi U
36 Ikoma Masumi C
37 Kitsu Kouki C
38 Matsu Koyama (Experienced) R
39 Kitsune Merihiko R
40 Moshi Ino U
41 Thunder Dragon (Experienced 2) R
42 Tsuruchi Kohrogi C
43 Tsuruchi Nobukatsu (Experienced)
44 Yoritomo Akukiho U
45 Yoritomo Iwashi C
46 Asako Chukage (Experienced) R
47 Asako Jukko C
48 Asako Kijo C
49 Asako Rikate (Experienced) R
50 Isawa Momoko U
51 Shiba Iaimiko U
52 Bayushi Makubesu C
53 Bayushi Mugoshi U
54 Bayushi Shibata (Experienced) R
55 Shosuro Hawado (Experienced)
56 Soshi Kodanshi C
57 Yogo Heijin R
58 Yogo Ugimori U
59 Daigotsu Yamato C
60 Daigotsu Yutaka U
61 Goju Asuka U
62 Goju Yurishi (Experienced) R
63 Masayoshi C
64 Ninube Hajime R
65 Chuda Seki C
66 Mukudori R
67 Naka Mahatsu (Experienced) R
68 Otomo Suikihime R
69 Seppun Nagi R
70 Tanemono C
71 Zansho C
72 Moto Aoi U
73 Moto Miyu C
74 Moto Taigo R
75 Shinjo Katsuo C
76 Utaku Chikako R
77 Utaku Hironori U
78 Tested Land U
79 Cavalry Detachment U
80 Horseback Warriors R
81 O-Yoroi Troops U
82 Ronin Ambushers C
83 Water Spider Adept C
84 Aka-beko C
85 Blades of the Black Dragon R
86 Celestial Sword of the Dragon (Experienced)
87 Celestial Sword of the Mantis (Experienced)
88 Celestial Sword of the Scorpion (Experienced)
89 Hato-gurama U
90 Kama C
91 Ki-Uso U
92 Light Armor C
93 The Deciding Moment R
94 Mining Apparatus R
95 Moksha Patam U
96 Okesa-goma C
97 Sandalwood Incense C
98 Unparalleled Sword C
99 Deafening Thunder U
100 Extend the Soul's Boundaries R
101 Immolation C
102 Master of Beasts U
103 Nature's Wrath U
104 Peace of the Kami U
105 Scent of Dishonor R
106 Step Through the Void U
107 Suitengu's Path C
108 The Earth's Strength R
109 Advanced Intelligence R
110 An Insult Answered U
111 Black Marketeering R
112 Brotherhood Schism U
113 Ceaseless Vigil U
114 Courting Trouble C
115 Debt to the Kaiu C
116 Defensive Blockade C
117 Determined Challenge R
118 Dragon Tattoo (Experienced) C
119 Dubious Resources C
120 Embracing Battle U
121 Exchange of Letters U
122 Exquisite Gifts C
123 Fair Warning U
124 Grappling the Snake R
125 Harsh Taskmaster R
126 Imperial Protection U
127 Incriminating Testimony C
128 Ingenuity R
129 Learning R
130 Manipulate Energies U
131 Martial Manipulation R
132 Metsubushi R
133 Military Promotion C
134 My Lord's Favor U
135 Only a Shadow U
136 Out of My Sight! C
137 Requesting Reinforcements R
138 Ruthless Onslaught U
139 Sentinel Spirit R
140 Sharing Gossip U
141 Shield Formation C
142 Shifting Terrain U
143 Sound the Retreat R
144 Sticks and Stones C
145 Testimony U
146 The Arrow's Eye C
147 Turning Away U
148 Turning the Story C
149 Two Hands R
150 Two Slings R
151 Unexpected Obstacle C
152 Unsettling Doubts R
153 Urgency R
154 Vengeful Dismissal C
155 Virtuous Charity R
156 Wide Valley R
157 Monastery of New Thought
158 Aramasu's Legacy
159 The Castle of Order
ProxyF1 Merihiko's Swarm C
ProxyF2 Ninja C
ProxyF3 Detached Personality C
ProxyF4 Your Name is Mine C
ProxyF5 Ronin Follower C
ProxyF6 Masayoshi's Blade C

2012 Legend of the Five Rings The Shadow's Embrace

RELEASED IN JULY 2012
1 The Moon's Imperative
2 The Sun's Aspiration
3 Discovering the Temple
4 Distant Expansion
5 On
7 Wartime Preparations
8 Fortress of Lidless Eyes
9 Humble Farm
10 Platinum Mine
11 Sheltered Port
12 Small-Time Bully
13 Versatile Farm
14 Whispering Archive
15 Chiisai
16 Hida Bakari
17 Hiruma Hikazu
18 Hiruma Nikaru (Experienced)
19 Kaiu Fumiko
20 Kuni Renyu
21 Yasuki Ikke
22 Asahina Keigo (Experienced)
23 Daidoji Sosuke
24 Daidoji Tsunehiko
25 Kakita Ichigiku
26 Kakita Saki
27 Kakita Tadanobu (Experienced)
28 Kazehime
29 Kitsuki Yoyugi
30 Mirumoto Mitoshi
31 Mirumoto Rokai
32 Shugorei
33 Togashi Kasuru
34 Togashi Korimi (Experienced)
35 Akodo Furu
36 Ikoma Shuji
37 Kitsu Kanae
38 Kitsu Sorano (Experienced)
39 Matsu Rika
40 Zlkyt
41 Kitsune Kichi
42 Moshi Rukia
43 Tsuruchi Kosoko (Experienced)
44 Yoritomo Ebumi
45 Yoritomo Kanahashi
46 Yoritomo Tsang
47 Agasha Kurou
48 Asako Hayate
49 Asako Jirou
50 Isawa Hinata
51 Natsumi
52 Shiba Kudome (Experienced)
53 Shiba Shirou
54 Bayushi Misaki
55 Bayushi Tarou
56 Bayushi Waru (Experienced)
57 Shosuro Keirei (Experienced)
58 Shosuro Nobu
59 Shosuro Ryoken
60 Daigotsu Arakan
61 Daigotsu Rafu
62 Goju Bunoro
63 Kenta
64 M'rika
65 Yamazaki (Experienced)
66 Atosa
67 Chuda Hitaka (Experienced)
68 Niiro no Oni
69 Quelsa
70 Sanzoko
71 Iuchi Haruma
72 Longtooth (Experienced)
73 Moto Morio
74 Shinjo Jong-Ho
75 Shinjo Min-Hee
76 Utaku Sung-Ki
77 Fallow Lands
78 Natural Aviary
79 Clearing Crew
80 Elephant Caravan
81 Heavy Chargers
82 Lookout
83 Native Guide
84 Nikutai
85 Shieldman
86 Wasteland Scout
87 Blood of the Preserver
88 Celestial Sword of the Crab (Experienced)
89 Celestial Sword of the Crane (Experienced)
90 Celestial Sword of the Phoenix (Experienced)
91 Pure Strike Blade
92 The String of the Colonies
93 The Victor
94 Vanquisher's Armor
95 Vanquisher's Blades
96 Beseech Sakkaku
97 Channel the Moon
98 Our Ancestor's Call
99 Purify the Soul
100 Set the Fields Aflame
101 The Earth's Hunger
102 The Wave Persists
103 Thunder's Stamina
104 Touch the Emptiness
105 Ward of Air
106 Yari of Air (Experienced)
107 Your Heart's Enemy
108 Burning Fury
109 Captured Convict
110 Cowed and Defeated
111 Crippled Sensei
112 Crowded Streets
113 Deep Roots
114 Defensive Grill
115 Direct the Path
116 Duel to First Blood
117 Easy Persuasion
118 Fields of Victory
119 Forge Your Soul
120 Forged Documents
121 Forthrightness
122 Grief
123 I Cast Two Shadows
124 Kitsuki Methods
125 Kuon's Legacy
126 Lessons Never Forgotten
127 Methodical Questioning
128 Never Afraid
129 One Shout
130 Overcome Adversity
131 Paralyzing Touch
132 Power of the Night
133 Preserving Beauty
134 Pure Intent
135 Regret
136 Running Battle
137 Scorn the Weak
138 Serenity in Air
139 Shinobi Assault
140 Social Grace
141 Spiritual Manipulation
142 Steady Resolve
143 Strong Defenses
144 Subtle Games
145 Sudden Movement
146 Tactical Assault
147 The Game Has Changed
148 The Lesson of Earth
149 Theological Indecision
150 Thuggish Techniques
151 Two-Fold Virtue
152 Unexpected
153 Unfortunate Hesitation
154 Unstable Ground
155 Void Tattoo
156 Watchers in the Dark
157 Bishamon's Tower
158 Twin Forks City
159 The New Foundries

2013 Legend of the Five Rings Aftermath

RELEASED IN DECEMBER 2013
1 Chagatai's Wrath U
2 The Inevitable Grasp of Conquest U
3 The Ways of Sensei Wu U
4 Changing the Game R
5 Into the Wastes R
6 Marriage of the Emerald Champion U
7 Purge of Fudoism U
8 The Asahina's Shame C
9 Exotic Market C
10 House of Prophecy R
11 Jade Pearl Inn R
12 Nexus of Lies C
13 Suana Dojo R
14 Well-Defended Farm C
15 Yukihime's Hot Springs C
16 Hida Kaiji (Experienced) R
17 Hida Kurabi R
18 Hiruma Koru C
19 Kaiu Esumi (Experienced) U
20 Kaiu Gorobei C
21 Yasuki Jiro U
22 Asahina Umehiko U
23 Daidoji Gensai R
24 Daidoji Tametaka (Experienced 2) R
25 Doji Kurohime C
26 Doji Tatsuki (Experienced) U
27 Kakita Ujirou C
28 Kitsuki Miroken C
29 Mirumoto Hatsuto C
30 Mirumoto Kalen (Experienced) R
31 Tamori Shinji R
32 Togashi Noboru (Experienced 2) U
33 Togashi Obote U
34 Akodo Kano (Experienced) U
35 Akodo Uehara (Experienced) R
36 Ikoma Takakura C
37 Kitsu Tamao U
38 Matsu Miura R
39 Matsu Ryohei C
40 Kitsune Merihiko (Experienced) R
41 Kitsune Yamazaru U
42 Moshi Ikako C
43 Tsuruchi Shusaku C
44 Yoritomo Toganin R
45 Yoritomo Yashinko (Experienced) U
46 Asako Misora C
47 Isawa Ikariya R
48 Isawa Tsumaro R
49 Natsumi (Experienced) U
50 Shiba Heirai C
51 The Broken Man U
52 Bayushi Dijuro U
53 Bayushi Jin-e R
54 Bayushi Mifuyu C
55 Bayushi Wateru U
56 Shosuro Chizuru C
57 Shosuro Takazaki R
58 The Sorrow (Experienced) U
59 Daigotsu Chiboshi U
60 Daigotsu Endo R
61 Daigotsu Kanpeki (Experienced 2) R
62 Goju Obayashi C
63 Nonaka C
64 Susumu Takada U
65 Isidoros C
66 Iweko Seiken R
67 Iweko Shibatsu R
68 Kitsune Kichi (Experienced) U
69 Usui C
70 Ide Mutsuken U
71 Iuchi Wattu R
72 Moto Paikao U
73 Shinjo Kinto (Experienced 2) R
74 Shinjo Sujikaro C
75 Utaku Sakiko C
76 Band of Brothers R
77 Black Riders R
78 Commander's Steed C
79 Court Scribe R
80 Disciples of Ganesh U
81 Floating Reserve C
82 Front Rank Troops U
83 Legion of the Fallen U
84 Legulus's Legion R
85 Long-Range Scouts U
86 Seasoned Ashigaru C
87 Senior Infantry Legion C
88 Dagger of Crystal Wind R
89 Fortune's Charm U
90 Khalimpeh-jiak R
91 Ningen's 'Treatise on the Nezumi' U
92 Ominous Armor C
93 Stonemason's Hammer C
94 Tankoji C
95 Tiger Claw R
96 Tsujiken's Coin U
97 Versatile Blade R
98 Banished from the Realm U
99 Blistering Rain R
100 Chikushudo's Infusion U
101 Drawing on All Things U
102 Hitomi's Devotion R
103 Mystical Augmentation C
104 Reverse Fate U
105 Sailor's Warning R
106 Searing Siege R
107 The Earth's Armor U
108 The Wind's Champion C
109 Yojimbo of Earth R
110 A Moving Battle R
111 A Small Favor C
112 A Warrior's Brutality C
113 Absolution U
114 Banzai! C
115 Benediction C
116 Breaking the Rhythm C
117 Concealed Reserves R
118 Demonstrating Technique R
119 Desire U
120 Directing the Battle R
121 Dying Remonstration U
122 Expanding the Gardens R
123 Expensive Achievement C
124 Find Your Center U
125 Grasp the Swords U
126 Hold the Walls C
127 Knowledge and Power U
128 Lonely Battlefield C
129 Lost Equipment C
130 Lost in Transit C
131 Marshal Your Strength C
132 Mercantile Conflict R
133 Move the Troops R
134 Never Without a Weapon C
135 Planted Evidence R
136 Provoked Violence U
137 Respect U
138 Return to Action U
139 Sleight of Hand R
140 Steal an Advantage U
141 Strategic Withdrawal C
142 Suffer the Consequences C
143 The Legion's Might R
144 The Way of the World U
145 Thoughtless Sacrifice R
146 Two Steady Breaths U
147 Unchecked Fury R
148 Unholy Strike C
149 Unpleasant Truths U
150 Unseemly Alliance C

2013 Legend of the Five Rings Coils of Madness

RELEASED IN MAY 2013
1 Fudo's Assurances
2 Hantei's Guidance
3 P'an Ku's Madness
4 An Empire of Madness
5 An End to Hostilities
6 Dark Audience
7 Rampant Paranoia
8 Riot in the Second City
9 The Second Battle of Beiden Pass
10 The Empire's Foe Exposed
11 The Madness Spreads
12 Bamboo Harvesters (Experienced 2)
13 Border Keep (Experienced 2)
14 Colonial Dojo
15 Colonial Temple
16 Fudoist Advisor
17 Questionable Merchant
18 Recruitment Station
19 Suikihime's Chambers
20 Temple of Madness
21 Temple of Tengen
22 Hida O-Ushi
23 Hiruma Nikaru, the Flesh Eater (Experienced 2)
24 Kasuga Aizawa, the Razor's Edge
25 Kuni Renyu (Experienced 2)
26 Nishoji, the Steel-Eyed
27 Yasuki Tono (Experienced)
28 Asukai, the Tireless
29 Doji Hakuseki (Experienced 3)
30 Doji Hoturi
31 Kakita Hideo, the Fallen Keeper (Experienced 2)
32 Kakita Ichigiku (Experienced)
33 Suzume Shindo, the Final Blade
34 Kimura, Forgiver of Sins
35 Kitsuki Daisuke (Experienced 2)
36 Kitsuki Kinaro (Experienced)
37 Togashi Mitsu
38 Togashi Noboru, the Shattered Star (Experienced)
39 Usagi Seki, the Untouchable
40 Akodo Tsudoken (Experienced 2)
41 Ikoma Aimi (Experienced)
42 Ikoma Natsu (Experienced)
43 Jikoji, Fist of Stone
44 Matsu Nimuro (Experienced 2)
45 Morito Inoue, Scourge of the Plains
46 Moshi Tomiko (Experienced)
47 Okazaki, Breaker of Wills
48 Tochiko, the Jagged Tusk of Death
49 Tsuruchi
50 Yoritomo Kanaye (Experienced)
51 Yoritomo Minori (Experienced)
52 Asako Chukage (Experienced 2)
53 Asako Kaitoko (Experienced)
54 Hamuro, the Wise
55 Isawa Tsuke (Experienced)
56 Shiba Iaimiko (Experienced)
57 Tonbo Inuyama, the Eye of Tomorrow
58 Bayushi Kachiko (Experienced)
59 Bayushi Kahoku (Experienced 2)
60 Bayushi Nitoshi (Experienced)
61 Rokkaku, Master of Scrolls
62 Shosuro Kameyoi (Experienced)
63 Daigotsu Arakan (Experienced)
64 Daigotsu Gyoken (Experienced 3)
65 Susumu Kuroko
66 Toku Saiga, the Metal Storm
67 Yunmen, the Whisper
68 Akumasa
69 Asako Usohara
70 Asp Skirmisher
71 Hantei XVI
72 Ichiro Otani, the Stone Breaker
73 Iuchi Takaki
74 Kokujin
75 Otomo Suikihime, Queen of Fools (Experienced)
76 P'an Ku (Experienced)
77 Sengmai, the Unbreakable
78 Takujin
79 The Dark Naga (Experienced)
80 The Shakash (Experienced)
81 Tsi Hayamizu, the Hand of Steel
82 Zansho (Experienced)
83 Iuchi Karasu
84 Komori Miyano, the Shadow Wing
85 Moto Ming-Gwok (Experienced)
86 Moto Taigo, the Skull Taker (Experienced)
87 Shinjo Tselu (Experienced)
88 Tsiang, the Benevolent
89 Aberrations
90 Fudo's Fiends
91 Lone Sentry
92 Maddened Horde
93 Naga Remnants
94 Reconnaissance Scouts
95 Shinobi Vassal
96 Thunderous Legion
97 Armor of the Mad
98 Blood of the Preserver (Experienced)
99 Heart of Fudo (Experienced 2)
100 Justice of the Crane
101 Koan's Jingasa
102 Koan's Robes
103 Koan's Scroll Satchel
104 Koan's Staff
105 Parangu
106 The Egg of P'an Ku (Experienced)
107 False Ring of Air
108 False Ring of Earth
109 False Ring of Fire
110 False Ring of the Void
111 False Ring of Water
112 Among the Clouds
113 Blade of Storms
114 Flame Lash
115 Hidden Power
116 Koan's Whisper
117 Soul of Earth
118 Tempest of Air
119 Typhoon Surge
120 A Magistrate Falls
121 Death of the Winds
122 Deliberations
123 Delicate Gamble
124 Fires of Turmoil
125 Invocation
126 Looming Danger
127 Moments of Destiny
128 No Way Out
129 Overwhelming Chaos
130 Strength in the Earth
131 Strength of the Divine
132 Suikihime's Sanction
133 Temple Grounds
134 The Heavens' Blessing
135 The Tale of the Disgraced
136 Unbearable Weight
137 Foothold of the Mad
138 The False Path
139 Hiruma Ogata PR
140 Daidoji Adachi PR
141 Mirumoto Kazuya PR
142 Ikoma Ayumi PR
143 Yoritomo Tonogi PR
144 Isawa Ryuzo PR
145 Yogo Katsuta PR
146 Nishiguchi PR
147 Moto Xin PR

2013 Legend of the Five Rings Emperor Edition Gempukku

1 Buried Treasures
2 Purveyor of Questionable Goods
3 Tattoos & Trinkets
4 The Daidoji Marketplace
5 The Ide Caravan
6 The Merchant's District
7 The Mystical Merchant
8 The Quartermaster's Depot
9 The Yasuki Peddler
10 Hida Yamadera (Experienced)
11 Doji Dainagon (Experienced)
12 Togashi Korimi (Experienced 2)
13 Jade's Roar (Experienced)
14 Moshi Madoka (Experienced)
15 Kunji (Experienced)
16 Shosuro Hawado (Experienced 2)
17 Daigotsu Negishi (Experienced)
18 Shinjo Byung (Experienced)

2013 Legend of the Five Rings Gates of Chaos

RELEASED IN SEPTEMBER 2013
1 Blood of Shahai U
2 A Fever in the Blood C
3 Journey's End Siege R
4 Riding to the Rescue U
5 Abundant Farmlands C
6 Coastal Pearl Bed C
7 Exquisite Silk Works R
8 Fudoist Temple C
9 Glassworks U
10 Imperial Explorer's Dojo R
11 Jade Mine R
12 Productive Mine R
13 Slave Pits R
14 The Breeding Ground C
15 The Tower of Vigilance U
16 Hida Gojiro U
17 Hida Tadama U
18 Kaiu Sokakaze C
19 Toritaka Chokichi (Experienced) R
20 Toritaka Iabuchi R
21 Yasuki Daisuki C
22 Asahina Kitiaru (Experienced) R
23 Asahina Shigemitsu (Experienced) U
24 Daidoji Soken C
25 Daidoji Tametaka (Experienced) U
26 Daidoji Tobei R
27 Doji Razan U
28 Kitsuki Nakai (Experienced) U
29 Mirumoto Bojan C
30 Mirumoto Katagi (Experienced) R
31 Mirumoto Omero C
32 Tamori Jinai R
33 Togashi Noritada U
34 Akodo Dairuko (Experienced) R
35 Akodo Kamina (Experienced) U
36 Akodo Nojima C
37 Ikoma Ayumu (Experienced) U
38 Ikoma Jeiku C
39 Kitsu Ririko R
40 Kitsune Yuko C
41 Moshi Rukia (Experienced) U
42 Moshi Sasako (Experienced) U
43 Tsuruchi Gombei C
44 Yoritomo Hiromi (Experienced) R
45 Yoritomo Mikaru R
46 Asako Itukube R
47 Asako Karachu (Experienced) R
48 Isawa Hajime C
49 Isawa Koizumi C
50 Isawa Norimichi (Experienced) U
51 Shiba Tsurao U
52 Bayushi Amorie C
53 Bayushi Manami (Experienced) U
54 Shosuro Nigawa U
55 Soshi Kodanshi (Experienced) R
56 Yogo Nobukai C
57 Yogo Takashi R
58 Daigotsu Kikumura C
59 Daigotsu Ryuko R
60 Lao-she C
61 M'rika (Experienced) U
62 Ninube Onchi (Experienced) R
63 Susumu Haikaro U
64 Abdollah U
65 Boyoh Mercenary C
66 Chuda Hikano U
67 Hoshoku-sha C
68 Legulus R
69 The Lost Colossus C
70 Ide Hinobu C
71 Moto Daiken C
72 Shinjo Kinto (Experienced) U
73 Shinjo Tselu (Experienced 2) R
74 Shinjo Yoshie R
75 Utaku Sayaka U
76 Aulus U
77 Camel Mounts R
78 Clay Kshatriya R
79 Elephant Cavalry R
80 Enslaved Djinn R
81 Frontier Farmer C
82 Kamalakar's Harem U
83 Scholarly Hermit C
84 Spawn of Vritra U
85 Spitting Llama U
86 The Bestial Ones C
87 Yodotai Legionnaire C
88 Divination Bowl U

89 Kshatriya Artifacts U
90 Lantern Oil C
91 Lost Blade of the Maharaja R
92 Map of the Northern Colonies C
93 Red Hunger's Fang R
94 Seppun's Blessed Blade C
95 Shard of the Great Death's Bones U
96 Translated Story of Shaharazad C
97 Watersteel Sword U
98 Befriend the Tides R
99 Cast Aside Appearances R
100 Constructing the Self R
101 Focus on the Flame R
102 Gates of Chikushudo U
103 Kiyoshi's Wrath R
104 My Ancestor's Steed U
105 Poison the Cup U
106 Steal the Candle's Flame C
107 Study the Wheel C
108 The Tao of Fudo R
109 The Thunder Resounds U
110 A Doomseeker's Tomb U
111 A New Perspective U
112 A Welcome Reprieve U
113 Allied Efforts C
114 Ashalan Ambush U
115 Boiling Point U
116 Chaos of Battle C
117 Claiming the Ruins R
118 Defensive Formation C
119 Exotic Farmlands U
120 Friends in the Jungle U
121 Hidden Storehouse of House Rafiq R
122 Holding Cells U
123 Honor Replaces Rage C
124 Iaijutsu Dojo U
125 Ivinda Village R
126 Ivory Magistrate Outpost U
127 Lakeside Retreat C
128 Lessons from the Heralds R
129 Looting the Ruins C
130 Lost Caravan U
131 Merchant Patronage C
132 Mukudori's Wisdom C
133 New Cavalry Tactics R
134 Nubane's Defense U
135 Outnumbered C
136 Practicing Kata C
137 Recovering What Was Lost R
138 Ritual Preparation C
139 Sorrowful Prayer R
140 Strength of the Bear R
141 Tactical Setback C
142 The Crystal Tears R
143 The Eternal Rainbows C
144 The False Route R
145 The Final Lesson R
146 The Tomb of Sun Tao U
147 Trade Embargo R
148 Uncovering Treasures C
149 Unexpected Discovery C
150 Unsettling Gathering R

2013 Legend of the Five Rings Torn Asunder

RELEASED IN FEBRUARY 2013
1 Hachiman's Prowess R
2 Kurohito's Perfection R
3 A Dangerous Game U
4 Harbingers of War R
5 Rejected Mediation U
6 Revelations R
7 Unseasonable Weather U
8 Damaged Port C
9 Green Lake Dojo U
10 Hero's Memorial U
11 Merchant Outpost C
12 Miryoku no Shima R
13 The Forgotten Bay Dojo C
14 The Tachikaze C
15 Vast Paddy Fields C
16 Hida Chiyurei C
17 Hiruma Ikeuchi U
18 Kaiu Nagai C
19 Kuni Renyu (Experienced) R
20 Kuni Shinoda (Experienced) R
21 Yasuki Daito U
22 Asahina Akahiko C
23 Asahina Nanae (Experienced) R
24 Daidoji Ibara C
25 Doji Iza U
26 Doji Kazuo (Experienced) R
27 Doji Tatsuzo U
28 Mirumoto Kojinrue (Experienced) R
29 Mirumoto Kyoshiro U
30 Mirumoto Yonekura C
31 Mirumoto Yozo (Experienced 2) R
32 Tamori Tsuchiya U
33 Togashi Mihato C
34 Akodo Chiyo R
35 Ikoma Satoru (Experienced) R
36 Ikoma Shizuka U
37 Kitsu Miwa U
38 Matsu Sango C
39 Matsu Yoshito C
40 Kitsune Yuribara U
41 Moshi Ira U
42 Yoritomo Harumi R
43 Yoritomo Hofu C
44 Yoritomo Naoto (Experienced) R
45 Yoritomo Tansen C
46 Asako Izuna (Experienced) R
47 Asako Kyuudo C
48 Asako Suzukaze U
49 Isawa Hibana R
50 Isawa Mizuhama C
51 Shiba Tetsaka U
52 Bayushi Hamada U
53 Bayushi Kazutoshi (Experienced 2) R
54 Bayushi Wakui U
55 Shosuro Makiko (Experienced) R
56 Shosuro Tanihara C
57 Soshi Shinoko C
58 Daigotsu Arare C
59 Daigotsu Botana (Experienced) R
60 Daigotsu Hashibei U
61 Daigotsu Shiraume C
62 Fubuko U
63 Ninube Tsukau R
64 Chuda Kaito C
65 Chun C
66 Mumoku no Oni U
67 Riku R
68 Seppun Ryota U
69 Iuchi Shaocheng C
70 Moto Ogaru C
71 Shinjo Sihung U
72 Shinjo Tselu R
73 Utaku Ji-Yun (Experienced) R
74 Utaku Suying U
75 Kokure's Lands R
76 Brothers of the Great Lake U
77 Cavalry Flankers C
78 Destrier C
79 Disciples of Master Coin R
80 Goju Kaxt U
81 Oriole Imperial Vanguard R
82 Sycophants R
83 Uji's Saboteurs U
84 Chiyurei's Axe C
85 Kage's Teachings R
86 Paneki's Mask R
87 Renyu's Wrath R
88 Sturdy Armor C
89 Thunder Bow U
90 Anchored in Earth U
91 Blood of Isawa's Tribe R
92 Blood Wave R
93 Earth's Protection C
94 Opening the Veil U
95 Path to Inner Peace C
96 Read the Essence U
97 Scorching Lash C
98 The Sky's Barrier R
99 The Thunderer's Protection U
100 Unbound Essence R
101 Witness the Untold U
102 A Cleansing Breath C
103 A Close Call C
104 A Threat Enacted R
105 Ambush Tactics C
106 Avenging the Fallen U
107 Bamboo Tattoo U
108 Bonds of Hospitality R
109 Calling the Darkness C
110 Charge Into Danger U
111 Courteous Gift C
112 Defensive Stance C
113 Drain of Effort U
114 Duty Over All Things U
115 Eye of the Sword R
116 Forest Cover R
117 Forgotten Teachings C
118 Frozen in Place C
119 Generational Gap C
120 Harbor-of-Kalani's Landing R
121 Harmony U
122 Imperial Deployment U
123 Improper Papers R
124 Imprudent Misstep U
125 In the Right R
126 Kitsuki Judgment R
127 Martyr's Call U
128 Mutual Support C
129 Nocturnal Attack R
130 Now We Are Enemies C
131 Overpower C
132 Pierce the Tapestery U
134 Recruitment Effort C
135 Scandalous Gossip U
136 Shifting Waves U
137 Spiritual Coalescence U
138 Spoils of Exploration R
139 Suck the Marrow U
140 Sudden Blockade C
141 Tactical Sacrifice R
142 The Last Move R
143 The Passing of Tradition U
144 Touch of the Night U
145 Truce C
146 Trusting Instinct C
147 Vital Pathways R
148 Warded Premises C
149 Without Mercy R
150 Journey's End Keep (Experienced) R
101b Ready the Defenses C

2014 Legend of the Five Rings Ivory Edition

RELEASED ON MARCH 24, 2014
1 A Time for Action R
2 Alliance U
3 Glimpse of the Unicorn U
4 Military Alliance (Unique) U
5 Political Standoff R
6 Severed from the Emperor R
7 Wisdom Gained (Unique) U
8 Akodo Dojo C
9 Ashigaru Fort C
10 Brilliant Cascade Inn R
11 Carrion's Breath C
12 Clear Water Village U
13 Collapsing Bridge C
14 Copper Mine
15 Counting House U
16 Deeds and Words R
17 Deep Harbor C
18 Family Library U
19 Famous Bazaar R
20 Farmer's Market U
21 Frontline Encampment C
22 Geisha House
23 Gold Mine
24 Haiku School U
25 Heavy Infantry Dojo R
26 Hida Advisor U
27 House of Exotic Goods U
28 House of the Red Lotus C
29 Humble House R
30 Imperial Dojo R
31 Iron Mine
32 Jade Works C
33 Jiramu's Court R
34 Kabuki Theater Troupe C
35 Kaeru Contractor U
36 Kobune Port
37 Marketplace
38 Merchant Atoll R
39 Poorly Placed Garden U
40 Rice Paddy C
41 Roaming Caravan C
42 School of Wizardry R
43 Secluded Outpost R
44 Secluded Shrine U
45 Shinomen Marsh
46 Shrine to Hachiman R
47 Silver Mine
48 Slanderer R
49 Small-Time Bully R
50 Stables
51 Tea House U
52 Temple of Harmony U
53 Temple to the Elements C
54 Vast Paddy Fields U
55 Vengeful Populace R
56 Wandering Caravan C
57 Yasuki Trader C
58 Hida Ayahi R
59 Hida Kisada, the Little Bear (Experienced)
60 Hida Reigoro U
61 Hida Saiyuki U
62 Hida Toranosuke R
63 Hiruma Fujito C
64 Hiruma Itta U
65 Hiruma Moritoki C
66 Hiruma Tsurao C
67 Kaiu Nakagawa R
68 Kuni Tomokazu C
69 Yasuki Makoto R
70 Yasuki Tono U
71 Asahina Umeko C
72 Daidoji Kinta U
73 Daidoji Tametaka U
74 Daidoji Tanshi U
75 Daidoji Ujirou R
76 Doji Dainagon C
77 Doji Etsuki U
78 Doji Katata R
79 Doji Makoto, the Smiling Blade (Experienced)
80 Doji Shirarou R
81 Doji Soeka R
82 Kakita Amiki C
83 Kakita Ibara C
84 Mirumoto Higaru U
85 Mirumoto Hikuryo R
86 Mirumoto Niwa C
87 Mirumoto Nokkai C
88 Mirumoto Shikei, the Laughing Dragon (Experienced)
89 Mirumoto Tsukazu C
90 Mirumoto Yasushi R
91 Tamori Katsumi U
92 Tamori Seiken C
93 Tamori Shaisen U
94 Togashi Ango R
95 Togashi Korimi U
96 Togashi Ogure R
97 Akodo Dairuko, the Steel Lion (Experienced 2)
98 Akodo Kenaro U
99 Ikoma Ichimoko C
100 Ikoma Shika C
101 Ikoma Yoshimoko R
102 Kitsu Miro R
103 Kitsu Suki U
104 Matsu Agai C
105 Matsu Choiko U
106 Matsu Misato R
107 Matsu Morito R
108 Matsu Rutaro U
109 Matsu Tayuko C
110 Kitsune Kohaki C
111 Kitsune Parumba U
112 Moshi Madohime C
113 Sasada C
114 Tsuruchi Gosho U
115 Tsuruchi Kaito R
116 Tsuruchi Natsuki R
117 Tsuruchi Rin C
118 Yoritomo Hiromi, the Growing Storm (Experienced 2)
119 Yoritomo Ichido R
120 Yoritomo Matsuo R
121 Yoritomo Takuya U
122 Yoritomo Teihiko U
123 Agasha Kyokuta C
124 Asako Sadaki R
125 Isawa Amihiko R
126 Isawa Hibana R
127 Isawa Kamiko U
128 Isawa Kosea C
129 Isawa Kouka U
130 Isawa Shunryu, the Infinite Eye (Unique)
131 Isawa Uzuyumi U
132 Shiba Eraki C
133 Shiba Michiki C
134 Shiba Myoushi U
135 Shiba Tsukimi, the Blind Phoenix (Experienced 5) R
136 Bayushi Akane U
137 Bayushi Dakatsu C
138 Bayushi Masashi C
139 Bayushi Meiko C
140 Bayushi Nitoshi, the Poison Mask (Experienced 2)
141 Bayushi Shizuka U
142 Bayushi Toshimo R
143 Shosuro Hotaka R
144 Shosuro Keiichi U
145 Shosuro Rokujo C
146 Shosuro Tagiso R
147 Shosuro Tosaku U
148 Yogo Honami R
149 Daigotsu Geiko R
150 Daigotsu Kanpeki, the Shadow Emperor (Experienced 3)
151 Daigotsu Konishi U
152 Daigotsu Meguro C
153 Daigotsu Onosaka C
154 Daigotsu Roburo U
155 Hiyamako C
156 Ninube Shiho R
157 Sandayu C
158 Suikotsu R
159 Susumu Neya U
160 Susumu Yanada R
161 Tairao U
162 Dainiko R
163 Gekido no Oni U
164 Hatsu Suru no Oni R
165 Horobei C
166 Karyuudo C
167 Komori Taruko C
168 Minikui no Oni R
169 Myuken C
170 Noekam U
171 Ogre Bushi C
172 Otomo Demiyah U
173 Yotsu Shinzai C
174 Ide Kotono U
175 Ide Okinomi U
176 Iuchi Chiwa U
177 Iuchi Honma C
178 Moto Alagh R
179 Moto Chinua U
180 Moto Naleesh, the Living Goddess (Experienced)
181 Moto Okano C
182 Moto Ulagan R
183 Shinjo Okiau C
184 Shinjo Tobita C
185 Utaku Hyo-Yeon R
186 Utaku Izimi R
187 Ashigaru Spearmen C
188 Baraunghar Scouts R
189 Bounty Hunter U
190 Brothers of Jade U
191 Chagatai's Legion R
192 Court Attendants R
193 Expert Archers C
194 Firestorm Legion U
195 Heavy Cavalry U
196 Heavy Infantry C
197 Incendiary Archers R
198 Iweko Honor Guard R
199 Kikage Zumi Initiates C
200 Legion of Toshigoku R
201 Light Cavalry C
202 Light Infantry C
203 Medium Cavalry U
204 Medium Infantry C
205 Oriole Imperial Vanguard R
206 Plague Zombies U
207 Shield Wall U
208 Skeletal Troops C
209 Souls of the Fallen R
210 Sparrow Clan Aide U
211 Spearmen C
212 Spearmen Cavalry R
213 The Desiccated U
214 The White Guard C
215 Tsukai-sagasu R
216 Watch Commander R
217 Wyrm Riders U
218 Akodo Kaiken C
219 Ancestral Armor of the Crab Clan (Experienced)
220 Ancestral Armor of the Crane Clan (Experienced)
221 Ancestral Armor of the Dragon Clan (Experienced)
222 Ancestral Armor of the Lion Clan (Experienced)
223 Ancestral Armor of the Mantis Clan (Experienced)
224 Ancestral Armor of the Phoenix Clan (Experienced)
225 Ancestral Armor of the Scorpion Clan (Experienced)
226 Ancestral Armor of the Spider Clan (Unique)
227 Ancestral Armor of the Unicorn Clan (Experienced)
228 Ashalan Blade R
229 Blessed Sword C
230 Do-Maru U
231 Dotanuki C
232 Exquisite Nagamaki of the Fox Clan U
233 Gumbai-Uchiwa C
234 Haramaki-do R
235 Heavy Yari U
236 Hellbeast R
237 Light Yari C
238 Naginata C
239 Oriole Katana C
240 Record of Failure R
241 Regal Furisode R
242 Reinforced Parangu C
243 Sadamune Blade U
244 Spiked Tetsubo C
245 Storm-Forged Blade C
246 Tsuruchi Longbow R
247 Utaku's Destiny R
248 Ring of Air (Unique) U
249 Ring of Earth (Unique) U
250 Ring of Fire (Unique) U
251 Ring of the Void (Unique) U
252 Ring of Water (Unique) U
253 Akagi Sensei U
254 Akikazu Sensei U
255 Gidayu Sensei U
256 Hojatsu Sensei U
257 Jutsushi Sensei U
258 Mahatsu Sensei U
259 Rae Sensei U
260 Satoru Sensei U
261 Tetsuo Sensei U
262 Todori Sensei U
263 Ancestral Aid C
264 Deafening Thunder C
265 Fire and Air C
266 Fueling the Flames U
267 In Awe of the Earth C
268 Overwhelming Power C
269 Secrets on the Wind U
270 Seeking the Way R
271 Servitors of Stone C
272 Shielded by Tempest U
273 Suitengu's Embrace U
274 Summon Undead Champion R
275 Touch of Death R
276 Touch the Emptiness R
277 Walking the Way U
278 Ward of Air R
279 Words of Consecration R
280 A Champion's Strike R
281 A Champion's Tactics C
282 A Ready Soul U
283 A Stout Heart C
284 Advance Warning C
285 Aligned with the Elements R
286 Ambush R
287 Ambush Pits U
288 Army Like a Tide C
289 Ascendance R
290 Back to the Front C
291 Banish All Shadows R
292 Blanketed Forest R
293 Blind Honor R
294 Block Supply Lines C
295 Come One at a Time U
296 Confusion at Court C
297 Contentious Terrain C
298 Coward! R
299 Defensive Grill R
300 Destiny Has No Secrets C
301 Determined Challenge R
302 Discretionary Valor C
303 Disrupting the Rhythm C
304 Do Not Delay! C
305 Encircled Terrain C
306 Everpresent Fear U
307 Faint Praise C
308 Fall Back! C
309 Favors R
310 Feared Duelist R
311 Fearful Volley U
312 Final Sacrifice C
313 Flashy Technique C
314 Focus R
315 For the Fallen R
316 Higher Ground C
317 Imperial Summons U
318 In Stillness, Forge the Soul C
319 Incapacitated C
320 Inexplicable Challenge R
321 Insight R
322 Inspired Devotion U
323 Investigation R
324 Journey's End R
325 Kharmic Strike U
326 Men of Cunning R
327 Mist U
328 My Lord's Favor C
329 Oath of Fealty U
330 Okura Is Released U
331 Open Emotion R
332 Oppression U
333 Pack Tactics U
334 Palm Strike R
335 Ramifications U
336 Reprisal C
337 Resist Magic R
338 Ruthless Determination C
339 Sanctioned Duel R
340 Sneak Attack R
341 Soul's Sacrifice U
342 Stand Or Run C
343 Strength of my Father C
344 Sudden Movement R
345 Swift Sword Cut U
346 The Company You Keep U
347 The Greater Threat C
348 The Sun Returns R
349 The Turtle's Shell R
350 The Wrath of Osano-Wo C
351 Today We Die R
352 Tonfajutsu U
353 Treachery and Deceit U
354 Unassailable Defense U
355 Uncertainty C
356 Uncovering the Culprit R
357 Unwelcome Supervision R

358 Versatile Army R
359 Vigilant Eyes C
360 Wary Peace C
361 Weakness Exposed U
362 Wheels within Wheels R
363 Wounded in Battle U
364 The Impregnable Fortress of the Crab
365 The Exquisite Palace of the Crane
366 The Remote Monastery of the Dragon
367 The Honorable Garrison of the Lion
368 The Fruitful Port of the Mantis
369 The Eternal Temple of the Phoenix
370 The Shadowed Estate of the Scorpion
371 The Sinister Citadel of the Spider
372 The Golden Plains of the Unicorn
2727 Gates of the Second City PR

2014 Legend of the Five Rings Siege Heart of Darkness

RELEASED IN SEPTEMBER 2014
1 Hour of the Boar
2 Hour of the Dog
3 Hour of the Dragon
4 Hour of the Goat
5 Hour of the Hare
6 Hour of the Horse
7 Hour of the Monkey
8 Hour of the Ox
9 Hour of the Rat
10 Hour of the Rooster
11 Hour of the Serpent
12 Hour of the Tiger
13 Breeding Grounds
14 Clutch of Eggs
15 Pearl Cache
16 Treacherous Growth
17 Askett
18 The Dark Naga, the Heart of Darkness (Experienced 2)
19 The Niskara
20 The Qeltash
21 The Quelsa, the Forbidden Jakla (Experienced)
22 The Riddiqesh
23 The Shakash, the Will of the Knot (Experienced 2)
24 The Sleepless One, Keeper of the Pearl (Experienced)
25 The Teskath
26 Corrupted Wildlife
27 Asp Spear
28 The Akasha (Unique)
29 Baseless Rage
30 Brutal Strike
31 Cursed Resolve
32 Gathering
33 Inevitability
34 Malevolence
35 Serpent Tunnels
36 Warlord's Command
37 Knot of Serpents
38 Asp Warrior
T1 Peasant District
T2 Artisan District
T3 Merchant District
T4 Temple District
T5 Military District
T6 Imperial District

2014 Legend of the Five Rings The Coming Storm

RELEASED ON JUNE 9, 2014
1 Auspicious Arrival R
2 Denial U
3 The Blessing R
4 Alchemy Lab C
5 Bookkeeper U
6 Bountiful Fields C
7 Carpenter Shrine U
8 Cloth Market C
9 Defensive Memorial C
10 Expansive Range C
11 Hotei's Smile C
12 House of Disgrace R
13 Kaiu Engineers C
14 Shigekawa's Court U
15 Summer Court U
16 Temple of Serenity U
17 Temple of the Heavenly Crab R
18 Tunnel Network R
19 Voice of Experience C
20 Hida Zaiberu C
21 Hiruma Maiko C
22 Kuni Shinoda, Advisor to the Jade Champion (Experienced 2) R
23 Toritaka Isai U
24 Yasuki Aitoko U
25 Yasuki Shairei R
26 Daidoji Ryushi U
27 Daidoji Sutebo R
28 Doji Natsuyo C
29 Kakita Burei C
30 Kakita Jikeru R
31 Kakita Mitohime U
32 Kitsuki Kira R
33 Gates of the Second City PR
34 Mirumoto Takanori U
35 Tamori Junya U
36 Tamori Touya C
37 Togashi Yayoi R
38 Akodo Iketsu R
39 Ikoma Keisuke C
40 Ikoma Shungo U
41 Kitsu Asato U
42 Kitsu Leiko R
43 Matsu Marii C
44 Kitsune Beiko U
45 Moshi Raiko C
46 Tsuruchi Hikari C
47 Tsuruchi Yashiro, Defender of the Obsidian Blades (Experienced) R
48 Yoritomo Shotsuo U
49 Yoritomo Yusuke R
50 Isawa Genma R
51 Isawa Kaname, Advisor to the Ruby Champion (Experienced) R
52 Isawa Kido C
53 Isawa Muira U
54 Shiba Kakei C
55 Shiba Yuuchi U
56 Bayushi Akagi R
57 Bayushi Fuyuko U
58 Bayushi Jinn-Ja R
59 Bayushi Kotomuri C
60 Shosuro Kayo U
61 Shosuro Sadao C
62 Daigotsu Atsushi C
63 Daigotsu Teruo R
64 Nao C
65 Sora U
66 Susumu Mizuki U
67 Susumu Takuan R
68 Aikiren U
69 Oneiyara C
70 Pataraku no Oni R
71 Seppun Teshan C
72 Zenathaar R
73 Ide Aragaki U
74 Ide Kosaka R
75 Moto Erdene U
76 Moto Qorin C
77 Shinjo Ajasu, Topaz Champion C
78 Utaku Saiken R
79 Assault Unit R
80 Battle Attendants C
81 Cavalry Escort C
82 Defensive Miko C
83 Mobile Troops U
84 Personal Guard U
85 Profiteer U
86 Samurai Lancers C
87 Traveling Ronin (Experienced) R
88 Yomanri Archers C
89 Zikyt's Family C
90 Aramasu's Mask R
91 Awakened Naginata U
92 Bishamon's Bow U
93 Bo of Ritual Blessings R
94 Jiramu's Wakizashi C
95 Kaiu Axe C
96 Kikko U
97 Osano-wo's Bow C
98 Singing Blade U
99 Sohei's Ono R
100 Tested Blade C
101 Untested Blade C
102 Aranai Sensei U
103 Suikihime Sensei U
104 Fear the Thunder C
105 Interrupt the Void's Flow R
106 Legacy of Tadaka C
107 Look Into the Soul U
108 Sinful Dreams R
109 The Dragon's Breath U
110 The Dragon's Talon R
111 The Swell of the Storm C
112 Visions of Darkness U
113 A Growing Rift R
114 Arrival of the Ivory Champion R
115 Bitter Lies Technique U
116 Bleak Lands C
117 Bonds of Service C
118 Contained at Court U
119 Death from Above C
120 Defending the City C
121 Deny the False Form C
122 Discovering the Anvil of Earth R
123 Discovering the Daisho of Water U
124 Discovering the Seeds of the Void R
125 Discovering the Shakuhachi of Air U
126 Inspired Leadership R
127 Iron and Stone U
128 Kharmic Threat U
129 Losing Favor C
130 Merciless Assault C
131 Open Roads U
132 Persuasive Tactics C
133 Proper Equipment C
134 Punishing Blow R
135 Relentless U
136 Relocating the Court R
137 Scout Training C
138 Signal the Scouts U
139 Strength in Subtlety R
140 Strike as the Earth C
141 Strike as the Wind C
142 Sudden Storm U
143 Swan Technique U
144 Taken Hostage C
145 The Eternal Chase C
146 Thousand Year Rivalry U
147 Unsanctioned Strike U
148 Way of the Crab R
149 Way of the Crane R
150 Way of the Dragon R
151 Way of the Lion R
152 Way of the Mantis R
153 Way of the Phoenix R
154 Way of the Scorpion R
155 Way of the Spider R
156 Way of the Unicorn R
33b Mirumoto Reiji C
ProxyF1 Small Holding PR
ProxyF4 Beiko's Bear PR
ProxyF5 Parumba's Boar PR
ProxyF6 Yamazaru's Monkey PR
ProxyF7 Ashalan PR
ProxyF8 Baraunghar Scout PR
ProxyF10 Champion PR
ProxyF12 Ivory Champion PR
ProxyF13 Kichi's Shadow Badger PR
ProxyF14 Major Illusion PR
ProxyF15 Minor Illusion PR
ProxyF16 Oni Hatchling PR
ProxyF17 Onyx Oni PR
ProxyF18 Tower Guard PR
ProxyF19 Tsumaro's Illusion PR
ProxyF20 Undead Champion PR
ProxyF21 Zombie PR
ProxyF22 Clay Yojimbo PR
ProxyF23 Goblin Follower PR
ProxyF24 Kiba PR
ProxyF25 Light Follower PR
ProxyF26 Lion Follower PR
ProxyF27 Little Elephant PR
ProxyF28 Medium Cavalry Follower PR
ProxyF29 Medium Follower PR
ProxyF30 Peasant PR
ProxyF31 Armor PR
ProxyF32 Unexpected Weapon PR

2015 Legend of the Five Rings The Currency of War

RELEASED ON JANUARY 5, 2015
1 Contested Market
2 Counting House
3 Family Library
4 Farmer's Market
5 Fortified Docks
6 Frontline Encampment
7 House of Exotic Goods
8 Kabuki Theater Troupe
9 Kobune Port
10 Marketplace
11 Second City Harbor
12 Small Library
13 Temple Fortress
14 Daidoji Kinta
15 Daidoji Taenaru
16 Daidoji Tametaka
17 Daidoji Tanshi
18 Doji Shimada
19 Kakita Ibara
20 Kakita Izumiko
21 Kakita Mitohime
22 Tsuruchi Jinrai
23 Tsuruchi Satou
24 Tsuruchi Taito
25 Yoritomo Raiden
26 Yoritomo Teihiko
27 Yoritomo Yakuwa
28 Tarui
29 Ashigaru Archers
30 Medium Infantry
31 Sons of Gusai
32 Sparrow Clan Aide
33 A Samurai's Soul
34 Akodo Kaiken
35 Reinforced Parangu
36 Singing Blade
37 A Warrior's Brutality
38 Advance Warning
39 Allied Efforts
40 Another Time
41 Back to the Front
42 Block Supply Lines
43 Breaking the Rhythm
44 Destiny Has No Secrets
45 Discretionary Valor
46 Drawing First Blood
47 Fall Back!
48 Incapacitated
49 Planned Departure
51 Ruthless Determination
52 Startling Lessons
53 Steal an Advantage
54 Strength of my Father
55 The Eternal Chase
56 The Esteemed Palace of the Crane
58 The Fruitful Port of the Mantis
37b Ritual Preparation

2014 Legend of the Five Rings A Line in the Sand

RELEASED ON SEPTEMBER 28, 2014
1 Abdication R
2 The Samurai Caste Divides R
3 The Serpent War R
4 Coastal Lane R
5 Colonial Market C
6 Contested Market C
7 Hanamachi C
8 House of Floating Petals R
9 House of Loose Silk C
10 House of the Floating Lotus C
11 Kumite Grounds U
12 Lonely Dojo U
13 Momiji's Chambers U
14 Musha-Gaeshi C
15 Second City Harbor C
16 Second City Market U
17 The Inner Ring C
18 The Ivory Courtroom U
19 Hida Kozan, Voice of the Empress (Unique) R
20 Hida Kurima C
21 Hiruma Daizen U
22 Kuni Araizen C
23 Yasuki Hora R
24 Yasuki Nakura U
25 Daidoji Hirota C
26 Daidoji Natsuki R
27 Daidoji Takeda U
28 Kakita Ariyoshi R
29 Kakita Mariko U
30 Kakita Shinichi C
31 Mirumoto Futoro C
32 Mirumoto Jaikei C
33 Mirumoto Saiko U
34 Tamori Ginrao U
35 Tamori Wataru R
36 Togashi Shao R
37 Akodo Niito R
38 Ikoma Akinari U
39 Ikoma Genichi C
40 Kitsu Junsuke R
41 Kitsu Watanabe U
42 Matsu Rishou C
43 Kitsune Nakumi U
44 Kitsune Satoko R
45 Tsuruchi Kaitaru C
46 Tsuruchi Taito U
47 Yoritomo Dairu C
48 Yoritomo Haruna R
49 Agasha Beiru C
50 Isawa Kaisei R
51 Isawa Orinoko R
52 Isawa Waiko U
53 Shiba Tuoko U
54 Shiba Yinfuo C
55 Bayushi Atsuto U
56 Bayushi Yasunari C
57 Shosuro Kiyofumi C
58 Shosuro Yasumasa U
59 Soshi Kitaiko R
60 Yogo Gingo R
61 Daigotsu Jemaru C
62 Goju Saido R
63 Marimako C
64 Susumu Jaru R
65 Susumu Tanjin U
66 Yasi U
67 Akenohoshi, the Dancer C
68 Harukaze, the Confidant R
69 Momiji, the Madam U
70 Natsumi, the Socialite U
71 Oboro, the Liar R
72 Suzune, the Coy C
73 Ide Ryou R
74 Iuchi Kalsang C
75 Moto Alani R
76 Moto Kyouaku-Inu U
77 Shinjo Shimikoto C
78 Utaku Kimiono U
79 Colonial Conscripts U
80 Dark Naga Ambusher C
81 Dragon Elite Inkyo R
82 Front Line Fodder C
83 Ichigo's Guard C
84 Legion of the Khan R
85 Mercenary Guard U
86 Mounted Skirmishers C
87 Pursuit Riders U
88 Sons of Gusai C
89 Spider Elite Sohei R
90 Talented Maiko U
91 Aranai's Armor U
92 Aranai's Kama C
93 Crude Dai-kyu U
94 Ensorcelled Longsword R
95 Heirloom Tanto C
96 Hidden Dagger U
97 Official Sanction U
98 Opportune Weapon C
99 Shikomizue C
100 Shinai U
101 Staff of the Raja's Court R
102 Stockpiled Weapon C
103 Toshigoku's Blade R
104 Kobi Sensei U
105 Sachina Sensei U
106 Tanizaki Sensei U
107 Yung Sensei U
108 Burning Spirit U
109 Guidance in War R
110 Impassable Waters U
111 Light of the Morning Sun R
112 Past and Future U
113 See the Soul's Past R
114 Stones of Purity C
115 Suspending Wind R
116 Thundering Waves C
117 A Kensai's Art C
118 A Kensai's Victory R
119 A Kensai's Will U
120 Banishing Breath C
121 Benefits of Honor R
122 Beset from All Sides R
123 Calculated Risk R
124 Casting Aside Honor R
125 Combat at Court C
126 Diplomacy Breaks Down R
127 Disappearing World Style U
128 Familiar Terrain C
129 Fearless Devotion C
130 Flight of No Mind C
131 Hidden Machinations U
132 Ideological Differences C
133 Long Term Fruition R
134 Not Yet Finished U
135 Ornery U
136 Planned Departure C
137 Press the Advantage U
138 Progressive R
139 Redirecting Rage R
140 Sanctioned Declaration C
141 Show No Mercy R
142 Show of Power C
143 Spirited Dispute R
144 Startling Lessons C
145 Step Into the Fray C
146 Streets of the Second City C
147 Strength Remains R
148 Strike First C
149 Strike to Both Sides C
150 Traditionalist R
151 Uncovered Plans R
152 Untouched Lands C
153 Unwavering Resolve U
154 Victory Through Deference R
155 Your Past U
156 Your True Nature U
157 Kagako Sensei P
158 Koiso Sensei P
159 Kuroko Sensei P
160 Ohsuki Sensei P
161 Shibata Sensei P
162 Tadanobu Sensei P
163 Takeru Sensei P
164 Tamoko Sensei P
165 Tsujiken Sensei P
Proxy-F14 Nakumi's Fox P
Proxy-F17 Asako Ontaiko P
Proxy-F25 Kikuchiyo P
Proxy-F45 Wataru's Potion P

2014 Legend of the Five Rings The New Order

RELEASED ON DECEMBER 1, 2014
1 Devastating Betrayal R
2 Seclusion U
3 Contemplative Shrine C
4 Delicate Forge R
5 Developed Quarry C
6 Earthborn Temple C
7 House of No Tomorrow U
8 Jade Bazaar U
9 Lane of Immorality R
10 Missing Caravan U
11 Otomo Bureaucrat C
12 Plain Library C
13 Protected Temple C
14 Remote Temple R
15 Rich Vein U
16 Shrine of the Colonies U
17 The Toil of Zokujin C
18 Weapon Artist C
19 Hida Ayameko C
20 Hida Kenjiro U
21 Hida O-Win R
22 Hiruma Toshi C
23 Kaiu Akemi, the Diplomat U
24 Yasuki Makoto, Imperial Advisor (Experienced) R
25 Daidoji Nozomi R
26 Daidoji Tomomi U
27 Daidoji Yurei R
28 Doji Shimada C
29 Doji Takato, the Manipulator C
30 Kakita Daitsu U
31 Mirumoto Touya R
32 Mirumoto Tsukino C
33 Mirumoto Yoritama U
34 Tamori Chikyu U
35 Tamori Daishu C
36 Togashi Gozato, the Wise Monk R
37 Akodo Raikitsu R
38 Akodo Yuyama C
39 Ikoma Ayumi (Experienced) U
40 Kitsu Suzaki R
41 Matsu Hachiro (Experienced) U
42 Matsu Misato, the Hatamoto C
43 Kitsune Gorikki U
44 Kitsune Yoshioka R
45 Tsuruchi Satou U
46 Yoritomo Nishigori R
47 Yoritomo Raiden C
48 Yoritomo Yakuwa C
49 Isawa Fujigawa U
50 Isawa Nomura R
51 Isawa Tenkawa, the Scholar R
52 Kyuji C
53 Shiba Kintaro, the Remembered C
54 Shiba Koshiba U
55 Bayushi Aggushi & Bayushi Janqu R
56 Bayushi Irezu (Experienced) C
57 Bayushi Iyashi, Lady Sorrow U
58 Shosuro Yamazaki, the Master Courtier U
59 Yogo Chijin R
60 Yogo Gorobei C
61 Daigotsu Takahide R
62 Gyushi Kageto C
63 Kokujin Dairu, Student of the Dark Lotus U
64 Kokujin Kuchika, Blood of the Dark Lotus C
65 Susumu Issei R
66 Susumu Kengo U
67 Banished C
68 Br'nn (Experienced) C
69 Iweko Miaka, the Princess (Unique) R
70 Keppo (Experienced) R
71 Masajiro U
72 The Abbot (Experienced 3) R
73 Ide Hideshi, Topaz Champion R
74 Ide Igo U
75 Moto Chizura C
76 Moto Nergui R
77 Moto Tadasu U
78 Shinjo Saeki C
79 Anonymous Monk R
80 Bound Spirit U
81 Boyoh Spearmen C
82 Gifted Officer C
83 Hachiro's Legion C
84 Jovial Ronin C
85 Nezumi Remnants C
86 Shinjo Archers U
87 Trained Horsemen R
88 Trained Swordsmen R

89 Unliving Legion R
90 Victorious Wave Men U
91 Akumato U
92 Demolisher R
93 Forge Hammer U
94 Iron Armor U
95 Raiden O-Tsuchi R
96 Saikatsu C
97 Takatsume U
98 Taketori C
99 Tessen of the Tsunami Legion R
100 Token of Affection U
101 Tsuruchi Hankyu C
102 Uguisu C
103 Unfinished Blade C
104 Bushido's Scourge C
105 Fearsome Visage of the Earth C
106 Fierce Blood of the Earth R
107 Final Ruin R
108 Fire Kami's Greed U
109 Grasp the Mind R
110 Purification of the Heart U
111 Strength of the Fifth Ring R
112 Touch of Lightning U
113 A Desperate Struggle C
114 A Good Death U
115 A New Alliance R
116 Battle of Wits U
117 Besieged Fortifications U
118 Brazen Disregard R
119 Bring them Forward C
120 Cautious Contemplation R
121 Courage Beyond Question C
122 Dirty Tricks U
123 Drawing First Blood U
124 Emerald Ascension R
125 Escalating Violence C
126 Honed to a Razor's Edge U
127 In Defense C
128 Jade Ascension R
129 New Factors C
130 No One of Consequence C
131 Obsidian Ascension R
132 Ongoing Division C
133 Open Ground C
134 Overwhelming Offense R
135 Priestly Feud R
136 Return to Your Feet U
137 Scouting Amid the Snow U
138 Self and No Self R
139 Serenity R
140 Sinister Deception C
141 Springing the Ambush C
142 Stay Behind Me U
143 Sulphurous Swamps U
144 The Soul of Man R
145 The Thrill of Daring U
146 Two Swords, One Cut C
147 Undermining the Otomo R
148 Undone by the Enlightened R
149 Unexpected Attack C
150 Unforeseen Cost R
151 Valiant Defense C
152 We Are Not Yet Beaten C
153 Zazen Meditation C
154 Brotherhood Sensei U
155 Seppun Tasuke U
156 Shika Sensei U
Proxy-F34 Zombie Follower P
Proxy-F8 Yoshioka's Elephant P

2015 Legend of the Five Rings Thunderous Acclaim

RELEASED ON JULY 21, 2015
1 A Vision Imparted R
2 Coronation Festival R
3 Exodus of the Spider U
4 Architect C
5 Ashigaru Farmland R
6 Bamboo Irrigation U
7 Borderless Fields C
8 Combat Drill Field U
9 Daikura U
10 Garrison Hub C
11 Hasty Defenses U
12 Heisha C
13 Isolated Farmlands C
14 Mess Hall C
15 Officer's Lodge R
16 Padis Dojo R
17 Peaceful Retreat U
18 Rhetorician C
19 Veteran's Farmland C
20 Hida Toranosuke (Experienced) R
21 Kaiu Gizen U
22 Kaiu Otogou R
23 Kuni Igarasu C
24 Kuni Soseki U
25 Toritaka Suppon C
26 Daidoji Kuraou C
27 Doji Buredo C
28 Doji Hoshihana U
29 Doji Moro U
30 Kakita Iwari R
31 Kakita Shinichi (Experienced) R
32 Kitsuki Akito C
33 Kitsuki Mizukabe U
34 Mirumoto Higaru (Experienced) R
35 Tamori Hirakura R
36 Tamori Mabasu U
37 Togashi Tameko C
38 Akodo Kano, Master Tactician (Experienced 2) R
39 Akodo Naotaka U
40 Akodo Toshigure C
41 Ikoma Kiyomako C
42 Matsu Hideyuki U
43 Matsu Kaori R
44 Kitsune Narako U
45 Moshi Kyan C
46 Tsuruchi Akira R
47 Yoritomo Kinshikirai C
48 Yoritomo Kyunan U
49 Yoritomo Minoko R
50 Asako Kazuki R
51 Asako Nashimoto U
52 Isawa Fujisawa U
53 Isawa Hibana (Experienced) R
54 Isawa Nobuo C
55 Shiba Hano C
56 Bayushi Chizuken C
57 Bayushi Fuyuko (Experienced) R
58 Bayushi Tenburo R
59 Shosuro Kanako C
60 Shosuro Wayari U
61 Soshi Mumoshi U
62 Chuda Teraiko C
63 Daigotsu Kanpeki, Unleashed (Experienced 4) R
64 Daigotsu Onita U
65 Daigotsu Tomiyama C
66 Goju Kenteiru U
67 Ninube Aitso R
68 Ashigaru Gunso C
69 Banished (Experienced) R
70 Kenturo U
71 Seppun Omihiru C
72 Venerable Spirit R
73 Moto Baatar C
74 Shinjo Chairei C
75 Shinjo Tsung-min R
76 Utaku Masako U
77 Utaku Sakiko (Experienced) R
78 Utaku Zo Sia U
79 Caravan Guards C
80 Conscription Officer R
81 Fresh Recruits C
82 Hirakura's Attendant C
83 Junghar Regulars R
84 Legion of the Ninth Kami R
85 Razorfang R
86 Shiotome Patrol C
87 The Thundering Death C
88 Village Defenders U
89 Box of Secrets R
90 Fang of Vengeance C
91 Flawless Naginata U
92 Inevitable Victory R
93 Kano's Tessen U
94 Master Bowman's Yumi U
95 Matched Daisho C
96 Poisoned Shuriken U
97 Reinforced Yari U
98 Shield of the Honored Soul U
99 Swordcatcher R
100 Fangs of the Heavens C
101 Nourished by Fallen Leaves U
102 Numinous Mantra U
103 On Storm-Borne Wings U
104 Seeking Answers R
105 Stepping Behind The Tapestry R
106 Terrible Revelations R
107 The Spaces In-Between U
108 Tracing with the Mountain's Finger C
109 Trick of Moon's Light U
110 Veil of Water C
111 Warning Flame C
112 A Breed Apart C
113 Accepting the Choice R
114 Amethyst Adjunct R
115 An Honored Guest C
116 Battlefield Challenge R
117 Be Silent! C
118 Caught Among Thieves U
119 Confounding Departure C
120 Darkness Inside R
121 Dense Jungle C
122 Dissension in Command C
123 Distracting Paranoia U
124 Immaterial Weapons C
125 Inexorable Advance U
126 Intimidation Tactic R
127 Ivory Ascendance R
128 Kharma's First Form U
129 Leave It Abandoned U
130 Narrow Passage C
131 Not the End C
132 Ominous Rumors R
133 Onyx Ascendance R
134 Ruby Ascendance U
135 Secret Alliances R
136 Strength of the Torrent R
137 Strike of the Obsidian Blade C
138 Sundered Blade U
139 Swifter than Sight R
140 Terrorizing Ambush C
141 The Dark Sword's Lunacy U
142 The Indignity of Arrest C
143 The Looming Darkness R
144 The Price of Shame C
145 Turquoise Adjunct R
146 Unexpected Valor C
147 Unforgivable U
148 Unseemly Brawl C
149 Unwanted Tutelage C
150 Virtuous Victory C
151 Walking with the Water R
152 Walls of Death R
153 Hikahime Sensei U
154 Hira Sensei U
155 Ichigo Sensei U
156 Yajinden Sensei U

2015 Legend of the Five Rings Twenty Festivals

1 A New Year R
2 Enlistment (Unique) U
3 Into the Wastes R
4 Return of Myth U
5 Short Season R
6 The Heavens Are Watching U
7 The New Order (Unique) U
8 Beautiful Host U
9 Blessed Dojo U
10 Blessed Herbalist C
11 Coastal Pearl Bed C
12 Colonial Temple C
13 Distracted Sentries C
14 Elemental Library C
15 Forgotten Legacy U
16 Fortified Docks U
17 Forward Encampment C
18 Fudoist Temple U
19 Honored Sensei C
20 Jade Mine R
21 Kaiu-Built Defenses R
22 Labor Crew C
23 Miryoku no Shima R
24 Mystic Dojo U
25 Nexus of Lies C
26 Personal Dojo R
27 Platinum Mine U
28 Puppet Theater Troupe U
29 Questionable Market C
30 Reserve Commander C
31 Secret Dojo C
32 Slave Pits R
33 Small Library C
34 Suana Dojo R
35 Temple Fortress U
36 Temple of Destiny R
37 The Blessed Herd C
38 The Obsidian Dojo C
39 Throes of Madness R
40 Trading Grounds U
41 Traveling Market U
42 Yukihime's Hot Springs U
43 Hida Iguchi C
44 Hida Kurabi R
45 Hida Taisho C
46 Hida Zaiburo U
47 Hiruma Raikohime R
48 Kaiu Burei U
49 Kaiu Daikohime R
50 Kaiu Gorobei U
51 Kaiu Watsuki (Experienced) F
52 Kuni Chutsu C
53 Kuni Harakibi U
54 Kuni Renyu (Experienced 3) F
55 Kuni Yairao C
56 Toritaka Iabuchi R
57 Asahina Hirakane R
58 Daidoji Hiroteru R
59 Daidoji Taenaru C
60 Doji Masachika C
61 Doji Norime U
62 Doji Senkiku C
63 Doji Tashihime U
64 Kakita Akitomo R
65 Kakita Hikai U
66 Kakita Ikura (Unique) F
67 Kakita Izumiko U
68 Kakita Mitsumichi C
69 Kakita Ujirou (Experienced) F
70 Shune R
71 Kitsuki Einosuke C
72 Kitsuki Goichi U
73 Kitsuki Masamitsu C
74 Mirumoto Akifumi R
75 Mirumoto Eisuke C
76 Mirumoto Rikiya C
77 Mirumoto Tsuda, Emerald Champion (Experienced) F
78 Tamori Jinai R
79 Tamori Seiken (Experienced) F
80 Tamori Shoko U
81 Tamori Tsunemi U
82 Togashi Kasuru R
83 Togashi Taiki R
84 Togashi Tsukagi U
85 Akodo Eirasu U
86 Akodo Hio U
87 Akodo Kenaro (Experienced) F
88 Akodo Naikiru R
89 Akodo Shaido C
90 Akodo Taiketsu U
91 Ikoma Noritsu R
92 Ikoma Sairei C
93 Matsu Ataruko R
94 Matsu Chizuki (Unique) F
95 Matsu Iairimi C
96 Matsu Karoko R
97 Matsu Kelasu U
98 Matsu Seijuko C
99 Moshi Ikako (Experienced) F
100 Moshi Karuiko C
101 Moshi Yokohime U
102 Sarassa C
103 Tsuruchi Arayo R
104 Tsuruchi Jinrai C
105 Yoritomo Juriken U
106 Yoritomo Kuniken U
107 Yoritomo Matsuo (Experienced) F
108 Yoritomo Minoro R
109 Yoritomo Nintai R
110 Yoritomo Saitsuko U
111 Yoritomo Tsuhime C
112 Yoritomo Waito R
113 Agasha Shikeno C
114 Agasha Tameko U
115 Asako Hiribe R
116 Asako Misora U
117 Asako Tsunetsusa (Experienced) F
118 Isawa Akime R
119 Isawa Haruge C
120 Isawa Ikariya R
121 Isawa Kageharu C
122 Isawa Mochiko U
123 Isawa Nairuko U
124 Isawa Uzuyumi (Experienced) F
125 Shiba Danjiro C
126 Shiba Kiyomichi R
127 Bayushi Aibako C
128 Bayushi Junko U
129 Bayushi Katsue R
130 Bayushi Manora U
131 Bayushi Mifuyu C
132 Bayushi Saikaku R
133 Bayushi Sunetsu U
134 Bayushi Toshimo (Experienced) F
135 Shosuro Longji U
136 Shosuro Orikasa R
137 Shosuro Saigyo C
138 Shosuro Sakura (Unique) F
139 Soshi Kodanshi C
140 Soshi Rei R
141 Daigotsu Atsushi (Experienced) F
142 Daigotsu Hachiko C
143 Daigotsu Hayigi R
144 Daigotsu Kendo C
145 Daigotsu Ryuko R
146 Daigotsu Shaoru U
147 Daigotsu Zenshi R
148 Goju Kumoru R
149 Goju Mitsuru U
150 Goju Yurishi (Experienced 2) F
151 Kokujin Gunjao C
152 Lao-shc C
153 Naibu U
154 The Twisted One U
155 Air Dragon (Experienced 3) R
156 Chaldera R
157 Earth Dragon (Experienced 2) R
158 Enomoto C
159 Fire Dragon (Experienced 3) R
160 Fushiki no Oni U
161 Haikitsu U
162 Kung-an U
163 Moto Daigoro R
164 Ninja Shapeshifter U
165 Otomo Terumoto C
166 Ratling Raider R
167 Seasoned Ronin C
168 Tarui C
169 Tonbo Jairyu R
170 Void Dragon (Experienced 3) R
171 Voltagi C
172 Water Dragon (Experienced 3) R
173 Iuchi Daitoru C
174 Moto Aikenro R
175 Moto Paikao U
176 Moto Taigo, Shogun (Experienced 2) F
177 Moto Yao-tsu U
178 Moto Zaitsuta U
179 Shinjo Hamura U
180 Shinjo Jalendu R
181 Shinjo Jao-shen C
182 Shinjo Nobunaga C
183 Shinjo Tae-hyun (Experienced) F
184 Shinjo Zhi-tae R
185 Utaku Kazue R
186 Utaku Sakiko C
187 Amoral Wave Men R
188 Ashigaru Archers C
189 Band of Brothers R
190 Camel Mounts R
191 Diplomatic Apprentice C
192 Elite Spearmen C
193 Enslaved Djinn R
194 Fearless Heavy Cavalry U
195 Fearless Heavy Infantry U
196 Fearless Light Cavalry C
197 Fearless Light Infantry C
198 Fearless Medium Cavalry C
199 Fearless Medium Infantry C
200 Front Rank Troops U
201 Fudoshi U
202 Goblin Chuckers U
203 Gunso C
204 Hidden Reserves R
205 Iron Defenders C
206 Karo C
207 Lookout R
208 Mounted Support R
209 Ninja Guards U
210 Personal Instructor R
211 Ratling Archers C
212 Shugenja Aide R
213 The Unquiet Moto R
214 Young Battlecat C
215 Zaiko U
216 A Samurai's Soul C
217 Bisento R
218 Eternal Armor U
219 Farmer's Kama U
220 Fubatsu Blade U
221 Ichiro's Yumi U
222 Lacquered Armor U
223 Lost Blade of the Maharaja R
224 Ominous Armor U
225 Ouma-Jinushi U
226 Polvora Cache R
227 Red Hunger's Fang R
228 Seppun's Blessed Blade C
229 Tachi U
230 Throwing Knives C
231 Tiger Claw R
232 Versatile Blade R
233 Wooden Nunchaku C
234 Ring of Air (Unique) U
235 Ring of Earth (Unique) U
236 Ring of Fire (Unique) U
237 Ring of the Void (Unique) U
238 Ring of Water (Unique) U
239 Armor of the Emperor C
240 Conflagration C
241 Divide Into Ash U
242 Earth's Embrace C
243 Favor of the Air Spirits U
244 Frozen Tomb U
245 Heart Thunder C
246 Hitomi's Devotion R
247 Kiyoshi's Wrath R
248 Mark of Heaven's Favor R
249 Pull of the Tides C
250 Reach Across the World U
251 Sailor's Warning R
252 See The Many Faces R
253 Steal the Candle's Flame C
254 Summon Water Kami U
255 The Mountain's Feet U
256 The Thunder Resounds U
257 Thunder Dragon's Child U
258 Thunderer's Embrace C
259 Typhoon Surge U
260 A Lion's Roar U
261 A Test of Courage C
262 A Warrior's Brutality C
263 Absolution U
264 Accessible Terrain C
265 Alliance Threatened U
266 An Act of Disdain R
267 Art of the Iai R
268 Assassin's Strike U
269 Awed Witness R
270 Balance in Nothingness U
271 Banzai! C
272 Brazen Challenge C
273 Breaking the Rhythm C
274 Bridging the Gap C
275 Brush The Arrow Aside R
276 Building Contract R
277 Civil Discussion R
278 Clash of Blades R
279 Concealed Archers C
280 Conservation C
281 Control R
282 Death of the Winds R
283 Defend Your Honor U
284 Defensive Technique R
285 Desperate Sacrifice R
286 Diligent Care U
287 Directing the Battle R
288 Explored Territory C
289 False Trail R
290 Feign Death R
291 Feinting Maneuver R
292 Fist of the Earth C
293 Gaining an Edge U
294 Gempukku U
295 Grasp the Swords U
296 Hidden Storehouse of House Rafiq R
297 Hidden Strength U
298 Hold the Walls C
299 Holding Cells C
300 Interference C
301 Ivory Magistrate Outpost C
302 Knife in the Darkness U
303 Lakeside Retreat C
304 Legendary Victory U
305 Lookout Post R
306 Lost in Transit C
307 Mastery of Chikujo U
308 Mercantile Conflict R
309 Mutual Support C
310 Needed at the Wall U
311 Outmaneuvered by Force C
312 Pacify C
313 Poison Sake R
314 Powerful Motivation R
315 Preserving Forces C
316 Public Arrest U
317 Pure Intent C
318 Purity of Spirit C
319 Rank Hath Privilege R
320 Rewards of Experience R
321 Sake House Brawl C
322 Scour the Unworthy C
323 Selfless Politics C
324 Show Me Your Stance C
325 Smoke and Mirrors U
326 Spinning the Web R
327 Standing Fast R
328 Startling Kiai C
329 Steal an Advantage U
330 Strategic Withdrawal C
331 Superior Defense R
332 Superior Tactics U
333 Test of Character R
334 Test of Sincerity U
335 The Call of Battle C
336 The Code of Bushido R
337 The Emperor's Road R
338 The Eternal Rainbows C
339 The Path of Wisdom R
340 Unexpected Testimony R
341 Unexplained Illness U
342 Unholy Strike C
343 Unrequited Love U

344 Unsafe Passage U
345 Usurpation R
346 Walking with the Earth R
347 Walking with the Fire R
348 Warranted Search C
349 Wedge R
350 You Walk with Evil R
351 Aroru Sensei P
352 Chukage Sensei P
353 Chuuna Sensei P
354 Daigo Sensei P
355 Dijuro Sensei U
356 Hakuseki Sensei P
357 Kiyoteru Sensei U
358 Mahatsu Sensei U
359 Sahara Sensei P
360 Seijuro Sensei P
361 Taitaken Sensei U
362 Tselu Sensei P
363 Yodo Sensei P
364 The Unassailable Fortress of the Crab F
365 The Esteemed Palace of the Crane F
366 The Fortified Monastery of the Dragon F
367 The Grand Halls of the Lion F
368 The Fruitful Port of the Mantis F
369 The Majestic Temple of the Phoenix F
370 The Shadowed Estate of the Scorpion F
371 The Hidden Bastion of the Spider F
372 The Endless Plains of the Unicorn F
391 Gates of the Second City P

2001 Lord of the Rings The Fellowship of the Ring

COMPLETE SET (365) 50.00 100.00
BOOSTER BOX (36 PACKS) 25.00 50.00
BOOSTER PACK (11 CARDS) 1.00 2.00
RELEASED ON NOVEMBER 6, 2001
1C2 The One Ring, The Ruling Ring .12 .30
1C3 Axe Strike .12 .30
1C4 Battle Fury .12 .30
1C5 Cleaving Blow .12 .30
1C6 Delving .12 .30
1C7 Dwarf Guard .12 .30
1C8 Dwarven Armor .12 .30
1C9 Dwarven Axe .12 .30
1R1a The One Ring, Isildur's Bane 1.25 3.00
1R1b The One Ring, Isildur's Bane
TENGWAR
1C10 Dwarven Heart .12 .30
1C11 Farin, Dwarven Emissary .12 .30
1C18 Halls of My Home .12 .30
1C19 Here Lies Balin, Son of Fundin .12 .30
1C20 Let Them Come! .12 .30
1C21 Lord of Moria .12 .30
1C24 Stairs of Khazad-dum .12 .30
1C25 Still Draws Breath .12 .30
1C26 Their Halls of Stone .12 .30
1C32 Border Defenses .12 .30
1C37 Defiance .12 .30
1C39 Elf-song .12 .30
1C41 Elven Bow .12 .30
1C42 Elven Cloak .12 .30
1C43 Far-seeing Eyes .12 .30
1C52 Lightfootedness .12 .30
1C53 Lorien Elf .12 .30
1C58 The Seen and the Unseen .12 .30
1C59 Shoulder to Shoulder .12 .30
1C61 Songs of the Blessed Realm .12 .30
1C67 Uruviel, Maid of Lorien .12 .30
1C68 The White Arrows of Lorien .12 .30
1C76 Intimidate .12 .30
1C78 Mysterious Wizard .12 .30
1C82 Risk a Little Light .12 .30
1C84 Sleep, Caradhras .12 .30
1C85 Strength of Spirit .12 .30
1C86 Treachery Deeper Than You Know .12 .30
1C92 Armor .12 .30
1R13a Gimli, Son of Gloin .60 1.50
1R13b Gimli, Son of Gloin TENGWAR
1R15 Gimli's Helm 1.00 2.50
1R16 Greatest Kingdom of My People .60 1.50
1R22 Mithril Shaft .60 1.50
1R23 Nobody Tosses a Dwarf .75 2.00
1R28 Wealth of Moria .60 1.50
1R30a Arwen, Daughter of Elrond 1.50 4.00
1R30b Arwen, Daughter of Elrond
TENGWAR
1R33 Bow of the Galadhrim 1.50 4.00
1R34 Celeborn, Lord of Lorien .60 1.50
1R35 The Council of Elrond .60 1.50
1R36 Curse Their Foul Feet! .60 1.50
1R38 Double Shot 6.00 12.00
1R40 Elrond, Lord of Rivendell 1.00 2.50
1R45 Galadriel, Lady of Light .60 1.50
1R47 Gwemegil 1.00 2.50
1R49 The Last Alliance of Elves and Men 1.00 2.50
1R50a Legolas, Greenleaf 1.50 4.00
1R50b Legolas, Greenleaf TENGWAR
1R55 The Mirror of Galadriel .60 1.50
1R62 The Splendor of Their Banners .60 1.50
1R66 The Tale of Gil-galad 1.00 2.50
1R69 Albert Dreary, Entertainer From Bree .60 1.50
1R71 Durin's Secret .60 1.50
1R72a Gandalf, Friend of the Shirefolk 1.25 3.00
1R72b Gandalf, Friend of the Shirefolk
TENGWAR
1R75 Glamdring .60 1.50
1R79 The Nine Walkers .60 1.50
1R80 Ottar, Man of Laketown .60 1.50
1R81 Questions That Need Answering .60 1.50
1R83a Servant of the Secret Fire 1.25 3.00
1R83b Servant of the Secret Fire TENGWAR
1R87 A Wizard Is Never Late 1.50 4.00
1R88 An Able Guide .60 1.50
1R89a Aragorn, Ranger of the North 1.25 3.00
1R89b Aragorn, Ranger of the North
TENGWAR
1R90 Aragorn's Bow 1.50 4.00
1R93 Arwen's Fate .60 1.50
1R95 Blade of Gondor 1.00 2.50
1R96a Boromir, Lord of Gondor 1.25 3.00
1R96b Boromir, Lord of Gondor TENGWAR
1R99 Change of Plans .60 1.50
1U12 Gimli, Dwarf of Erebor .30 .75
1U17 Grimir, Dwarven Elder .30 .75
1U27 Thrarin, Dwarven Smith .30 .75
1U29 Ancient Enmity .30 .75
1U31 Asfaloth .30 .75
1U44 Foul Creation .30 .75
1U46 Gift of Boats .30 .75
1U48 Haldir, Elf of the Golden Wood .30 .75
1U51 Legolas, Prince of Mirkwood .30 .75
1U54 Mallorn-trees .30 .75
1U56 Orophin, Lorien Bowman .30 .75
1U57 Rumil, Elven Protector .30 .75
1U60 Silinde, Elf of Mirkwood .30 .75
1U63 Stand Against Darkness .30 .75
1U64 Support of the Last Homely House .30 .75
1U65 Swan-ship of the Galadhrim .30 .75
1U70 Barliman Butterbur .30 .75
Prancing Pony Proprietor
1U73 Gandalf's Cart .30 .75
1U74 Gandalf's Pipe .30 .75
1U77 Let Folly Be Our Cloak .30 .75
1U91 Aragorn's Pipe .30 .75
1U94 Athelas .30 .75
1U97 Boromir, Son of Denethor .30 .75
1U98 Boromir's Cloak .30 .75
1C101 Coat of Mail .12 .30
1C102 Dagger Strike .12 .30
1C103 Elendil's Valor .12 .30
1C104 Eregion's Trails .12 .30
1C106 Gondor's Vengeance .12 .30
1C107 Great Shield .12 .30
1C110 Pathfinder .12 .30
1C116 Swordarm of the White Tower .12 .30
1C117 Swordsman of the Northern Kingdom .12 .30
1C119 What Are They? .12 .30
1C121 Bred for Battle .12 .30
1C122 Breeding Pit .12 .30
1C133 Saruman's Ambition .12 .30
1C134 Saruman's Chill .12 .30
1C138 Saruman's Snows .12 .30
1C141 Their Arrows Enrage .12 .30
1C144 Uruk Bloodlust .12 .30
1C145 Uruk Brood .12 .30
1C146 Uruk Fighter .12 .30
1C149 Uruk Messenger .12 .30
1C150 Uruk Rager .12 .30
1C151 Uruk Savage .12 .30
1C152 Uruk Shaman .12 .30
1C154 Uruk Soldier .12 .30
1C156 Uruk Warrior .12 .30
1C157 Uruk-hai Armory .12 .30
1C158 Uruk-hai Raiding Party .12 .30
1C160 Uruk-hai Sword .12 .30
1C168 Drums in the Deep .12 .30
1C171 Frenzy .12 .30
1C174 Goblin Backstabber .12 .30
1C176 Goblin Marksman .12 .30
1C177 Goblin Patrol Troop .12 .30
1C179 Goblin Scavengers .12 .30
1C180 Goblin Scimitar .12 .30
1C182 Goblin Spear .12 .30
1C184 Goblin Wallcrawler .12 .30
1C185 Goblin Warrior .12 .30
1C187 Host of Thousands .12 .30
1C191 Moria Scout .12 .30
1C192 Pinned Down .12 .30
1C193 Plundered Armories .12 .30
1C196 They Are Coming .12 .30
1C197 Threat of the Unknown .12 .30
1C201 Unfamiliar Territory .12 .30
1C248 Forces of Mordor .12 .30
1C255 Mordor's Strength .12 .30
1C261 Orc Ambusher .12 .30
1C266 Orc Chieftain .12 .30
1C268 Orc Inquisitor .12 .30
1C269 Orc Scimitar .12 .30
1C271 Orc Soldier .12 .30
1C273 The Ring's Oppression .12 .30
1C277 Shadow's Reach .12 .30
1C278 Strength Born of Fear .12 .30
1C281 Under the Watching Eye .12 .30
1C283 You Bring Great Evil .12 .30
1C286 Bounder .12 .30
1C287 Extraordinary Resilience .12 .30
1C290 Frodo, Son of Drogo .12 .30
1C294 Hobbit Appetite .12 .30
1C295 Hobbit Farmer .12 .30
1C296 Hobbit Intuition .12 .30
1C297 Hobbit Party Guest .12 .30
1C298 Hobbit Stealth .12 .30
1C299 Hobbit Sword .12 .30
1C300 Longbottom Leaf .12 .30
1C303 Merry, From O'er the Brandywine .12 .30
1C304 Noble Intentions .12 .30
1C305 Old Toby .12 .30
1C306 Pippin, Friend to Frodo .12 .30
1C311 Sam, Son of Hamfast .12 .30
1C312 Sorry About Everything .12 .30
1C315 Stout and Sturdy .12 .30
1C317 There and Back Again .12 .30
1C326 Westfarthing .12 .30
1C331 Ettenmoors .12 .30
1C337 Council Courtyard .12 .30
1C346 Moria Lake .12 .30
1C349 The Bridge of Khazad-dum .12 .30
1C351 Galadriel's Glade .12 .30
1C354 Anduin Wilderland .12 .30
1C356 Anduin Banks .12 .30
1C362 Summit of Amon Hen .12 .30
1P364 Gandalf, The Grey Wizard .40 1.00
1P365 Aragorn, King in Exile .40 1.00
1R100 The Choice of Luthien .60 1.50
1R111 Pursuit Just Behind .60 1.50
1R114a The Saga of Elendil 1.00 2.50
1R114b The Saga of Elendil TENGWAR
1R115 Strength of Kings .60 1.50
1R118 Valiant Man of the West .60 1.50
1R120 Alive and Unspoiled .60 1.50
1R123 Caradhras Has Not Forgiven Us .60 1.50
1R124 Cruel Caradhras .60 1.50
1R125 Greed .60 1.50
1R127a Lurtz, Servant of Isengard .75 2.00
1R127b Lurtz, Servant of Isengard TENGWAR
1R128 Lurtz's Battle Cry
1R129 The Misadventure of Mr. Underhill .60 1.50
1R131 Orthanc Assassin .60 1.50
1R132 Parry .60 1.50
1R137 Saruman's Reach .60 1.50
1R139 Savagery to Match Their Numbers 1.25 3.00
1R140 Spies of Saruman .60 1.50
1R143 Troop of Uruk-hai .75 2.00
1R147 Uruk Guard .60 1.50
1R148 Uruk Lieutenant 1.25 3.00
1R14a Gimli's Battle Axe .60 1.50
1R14b Gimli's Battle Axe TENGWAR
1R155 Uruk Spy .60 1.50
1R163 Ancient Chieftain .60 1.50
1R165a Cave Troll of Moria 1.50 4.00
Scourge of the Black Pit
1R165b Cave Troll of Moria
Scourge of the Black Pit TENGWAR
1R166 Cave Troll's Hammer .60 1.50
1R167 Denizens Enraged .60 1.50
1R169 The End Comes .60 1.50
1R170 Fool of a Took! .60 1.50
1R172 Goblin Archer .75 2.00
1R173 Goblin Armory 5.00 10.00
1R175 Goblin Domain .60 1.50
1R183 Goblin Swarms 1.50 4.00
1R186 Guard Commander .60 1.50
1R189 Lost to the Goblins .60 1.50
1R190 Moria Axe .75 2.00
1R195 Relics of Moria .60 1.50
1R199 Troll's Keyward .75 2.00
1R200 The Underdeeps of Moria .60 1.50
1R204 All Veils Removed .60 1.50
1R205 Beauty Is Fading .60 1.50
1R206 Bent on Discovery .60 1.50
1R208 Black Steed .60 1.50
1R210 Dark Whispers .60 1.50
1R212 Fear .60 1.50
1R214 In the Ringwraith's Wake .60 1.50
1R216 Morgul Blade .60 1.50
1R217 Morgul Gates 2.50 6.00
1R221 The Pale Blade .60 1.50
1R224 Return to Its Master .75 2.00
1R228 The Twilight World .60 1.50
1R229 Ulaire Attea, Keeper of Dol Guldur 1.25 3.00
1R230 Ulaire Cantea 1.50 4.00
Lieutenant of Dol Guldur
1R236 Ulaire Toldea, Messenger of Morgul 1.25 3.00
1R237a The Witch-king, Lord of Angmar .75 2.00
1R237b The Witch-king,
Lord of Angmar TENGWAR
1R240 Band of the Eye .60 1.50
1R243 Despair .60 1.50
1R244 Desperate Defense of the Ring 1.25 3.00
1R245 Desperate Measures .60 1.50
1R246 Enduring Evil .75 2.00
1R247 Enheartened Foe .60 1.50
1R250 Hate 1.50 4.00
1R252 The Irresistible Shadow .60 1.50
1R253 Journey Into Danger .60 1.50
1R254 Mordor Enraged .60 1.50
1R256a Morgul Hunter .60 1.50
1R256b Morgul Hunter TENGWAR
1R259 Morgul Warden .60 1.50
1R263 Orc Banner .60 1.50
1R264 Orc Bowmen 2.50 6.00
1R265 Orc Butchery .60 1.50
1R272 Orc War Band .60 1.50
1R276 Seeking Its Master .60 1.50
1R279 Thin and Stretched .60 1.50
1R282 The Weight of a Legacy .60 1.50
1R284 Bilbo, Retired Adventurer .60 1.50
1R288 Farmer Maggot, Chaser of Rascals .60 1.50
1R289 Frodo, Old Bilbo's Heir .75 2.00
1R291 The Gaffer, Sam's Father .60 1.50
1R302 Merry, Friend to Sam .60 1.50
1R307 Pippin, Hobbit of Some Intelligence .60 1.50
1R308 Power According to His Stature 2.50 6.00
1R310 Sam, Faithful Companion .60 1.50
1R313 Sting 1.25 3.00
1R314 Stone Trolls .60 1.50
1R318 Thror's Map .60 1.50
1U105 Foes of Mordor .30 .75
1U108 No Stranger to the Shadows .30 .75
1U109 One Whom Men Would Follow .30 .75
1U112 Ranger's Sword .30 .75
1U113 A Ranger's Versatility .30 .75
1U126 Hunt Them Down! .30 .75
1U130 No Ordinary Storm .30 .75
1U135 Saruman's Frost .30 .75
1U136 Saruman's Power .30 .75
1U142 Traitor's Voice .30 .75
1U153 Uruk Slayer .30 .75
1U159 Uruk-hai Rampage .30 .75
1U161 Wariness .30 .75
1U162 Worry .30 .75
1U164 Bitter Hatred .30 .75
1U178 Goblin Runner .30 .75
1U181 Goblin Sneak .30 .75
1U188 The Long Dark .30 .75
1U194 Relentless .30 .75
1U198 Through the Misty Mountains .30 .75
1U202 What Is This New Devilry? .30 .75
1U203 All Blades Perish .30 .75
1U207 Black Breath .30 .75
1U209 Blade Tip .30 .75
1U211 Drawn to Its Power .30 .75
1U213 Frozen by Fear .30 .75
1U215 The Master's Will .30 .75
1U218 Nazgul Sword .30 .75
1U219 The Nine Servants of Sauron .30 .75
1U220 Not Easily Destroyed .30 .75
1U222 Paths Seldom Trodden .30 .75
1U223 Relentless Charge .30 .75
1U225 Sword of Minas Morgul .30 .75
1U226 Their Power Is in Terror .30 .75
1U227 Threshold of Shadow .30 .75
1U231a Ulaire Enquea, Lieutenant of Morgul .30 .75
1U231b Ulaire Enquea
Lieutenant of Morgul TENGWAR
1U232 Ulaire Lemenya, Lieutenant of Morgul .30 .75
1U233 Ulaire Nelya, Lieutenant of Morgul .30 .75
1U234 Ulaire Nertea, Messenger of Dol Guldur .30 .75
1U235 Ulaire Otsea, Lieutenant of Morgul .30 .75
1U238 Wreathed in Shadow .30 .75
1U239 All Thought Bent on It .30 .75
1U241 Curse From Mordor .30 .75
1U242 The Dark Lord's Summons .30 .75
1U249 Gleaming Spires Will Crumble .30 .75
1U251 A Host Avails Little .30 .75
1U257 Morgul Skirmisher .30 .75
1U258 Morgul Skulker .30 .75
1U260 The Number Must Be Few .30 .75
1U262 Orc Assassin .30 .75
1U267 Orc Hunters .30 .75
1U270 Orc Scouting Band .30 .75
1U274 Sauron's Defenses .30 .75
1U275 Seeking It Always .30 .75
1U280 Tower Lieutenant .30 .75
1U285 Bilbo's Pipe .30 .75
1U292 The Gaffer's Pipe .30 .75
1U293 Halfling Deftness .30 .75
1U301 Master Proudfoot, Distant Relative of Bilbo .30 .75
1U309 Rosie Cotton, Hobbiton Lass .30 .75
1U316 A Talent for Not Being Seen .30 .75
1U319 Bag End .30 .75
1U320 East Road .30 .75
1U321 Farmer Maggot's Fields .30 .75
1U322 Green Dragon Inn .30 .75
1U323 Green Hill Country .30 .75
1U324 The Prancing Pony .30 .75
1U325 Shire Lookout Point .30 .75
1U327 Bree Gate .30 .75
1U328 Bree Streets .30 .75
1U329 Breeland Forest .30 .75
1U330 Buckleberry Ferry .30 .75
1U332 Midgewater Marshes .30 .75
1U333 Midgewater Moors .30 .75
1U334 Trollshaw Forest .30 .75
1U335 Weatherhills .30 .75
1U336 Weathertop .30 .75
1U338 Ford of Bruinen .30 .75
1U339 Frodo's Bedroom .30 .75
1U340 Rivendell Terrace .30 .75
1U341 Rivendell Valley .30 .75
1U342 Rivendell Waterfall .30 .75
1U343 Balin's Tomb .30 .75
1U344 Dwarrowdelf Chamber .30 .75
1U345 Mithril Mine .30 .75
1U347 Moria Stairway .30 .75
1U348 Pass of Caradhras .30 .75
1U350 Dimrill Dale .30 .75
1U352 Lothlorien Woods .30 .75
1U353 Anduin Confluence .30 .75
1U355 Silverlode Banks .30 .75
1U357 Brown Lands .30 .75
1U358 Pillars of the Kings .30 .75
1U359 Shores of Nen Hithoel .30 .75
1U360 Emyn Muil .30 .75
1U361 Slopes of Amon Hen .30 .75
1U363 Tol Brandir .30 .75

2002 Lord of the Rings Mines of Moria

COMPLETE SET (122) 15.00 30.00
BOOSTER BOX (36 PACKS) 20.00 40.00
BOOSTER PACK (11 CARDS) 1.00 2.00
RELEASED ON MARCH 6, 2002
2C2 Disquiet of Our People .12 .30
2C5 Flurry of Blows .12 .30
2C6 Fror, Gimli's Kinsman .12 .30
2C9 Great Works Begun There .12 .30
2R1 Beneath the Mountains .60 1.50
2R7 Gloin, Friend to Thorin .60 1.50
2U3 Dwarven Bracers .30 .75
2U4 Endurance of Dwarves .30 .75
2U8 Golden Light on the Land .30 .75
2C10 Hand Axe .12 .30
2C14 Till Durin Wakes Again .12 .30
2C21 Erland, Advisor to Brand .12 .30
2C23 Gandalf's Wisdom .12 .30
2C24 Hugin, Emissary from Laketown .12 .30
2C26 Speak Friend and Enter .12 .30
2C29 Wizard Staff .12 .30
2C35 Natural Cover .12 .30
2C37 Sentinels of Numenor .12 .30
2C40 Demands of the Sackville-Bagginses .12 .30
2C42 Goblin Man .12 .30
2C44 No Business of Ours .12 .30
2C47 Uruk Scout .12 .30
2C51 The Balrog, Durin's Bane .12 .30
2C55 Dark Places .12 .30
2C58 Foul Tentacle .12 .30
2C60 Goblin Bowman .12 .30
2C61 Goblin Flankers .12 .30
2C62 Goblin Pursuer .12 .30
2C63 Goblin Reinforcements .12 .30
2C64 Goblin Scrabbler .12 .30
2C65 Goblin Spearman .12 .30
2C69 Old Differences .12 .30
2C88 Memory of Many Things .12 .30
2C89 Orc Scout .12 .30
2C90 Orc Taskmaster .12 .30
2C91 Southern Spies .12 .30
2C95 Vile Blade .12 .30
2C99 Deft in Their Movements .12 .30
2R11 Make Light of Burdens .60 1.50
2R12 Realm of Dwarrowdelf .60 1.50
2R15 What Are We Waiting For? .60 1.50
2R19 Release the Angry Flood .60 1.50
2R20 Secret Sentinels .60 1.50
2R22 Gandalf's Staff .60 1.50
2R25 Jarnsmid, Merchant from Dale .60 1.50
2R27 Staff Asunder .60 1.50
2R32 Flaming Brand 1.25 3.00
2R36 No Mere Ranger .60 1.50
2R38 Shield of Boromir .60 1.50
2R39 Beyond the Height of Men .60 1.50
2R43 Lurtz's Sword .60 1.50
2R45 Too Much Attention .60 1.50
2R46 Uruk Captain .60 1.50
2R49 Archer Commander .75 2.00
2R50 The Balrog's Sword .60 1.50
2R52a The Balrog, Flame of Udun .60 1.50
2R52b The Balrog, Flame of Udun
TENGWAR
2R53 Cave Troll's Chain .60 1.50
2R57 Final Cry .60 1.50
2R66 Huge Tentacle .60 1.50
2R73 Watcher in the Water .75 2.00
Keeper of Westgate
2R74 Whip of Many Thongs .60 1.50
2R75 Bill Ferny, Swarthy Sneering Fellow 1.00 2.50
2R77 His Terrible Servants .60 1.50
2R80 Stricken Dumb .60 1.50
2R84 Ulaire Nelya, Ringwraith in Twilight .60 1.50
2R85 The Witch-king, Lord of the Nazgul 1.50 4.00
2R86 Wraith-world .60 1.50
2R93 Tower Assassin .60 1.50
2R94 Verily I Come .60 1.50
2R97 Consorting With Wizards .60 1.50
2U13 Tidings of Erebor .30 .75
2U16 A Blended Race .30 .75
2U17 Dismay Our Enemies .30 .75
2U18 Hosts of the Last Alliance .30 .75
2U28 Wielder of the Flame .30 .75
2U30 You Cannot Pass! .30 .75
2U31 Blood of Numenor .30 .75
2U33 Flee in Terror .30 .75
2U34 Gondor Will See It Done .30 .75
2U41 Evil Afoot .30 .75
2U48 Wizard Storm .30 .75
2U54 Dark Fire .30 .75
2U56 Fill With Fear .30 .75
2U59 Foul Things .30 .75
2U67 Moria Archer Troop .30 .75
2U68 Must Do Without Hope .30 .75
2U70 Power and Terror .30 .75
2U71 Throw Yourself in Next Time .30 .75
2U72 Troubled Mountains .30 .75
2U76 Helpless .30 .75
2U78 It Wants to be Found .30 .75
2U79 Resistance Becomes Unbearable .30 .75
2U81 They Will Find the Ring .30 .75
2U82 Ulaire Attea, The Easterling .30 .75
2U83 Ulaire Enquea, Ringwraith in Twilight .30 .75
2U87 The Eye of Sauron .30 .75
2U92 Spies of Mordor .30 .75
2U96 Bilbo, Well-spoken Gentlehobbit .30 .75
2U98 Dear Friends .30 .75
2C101 Filibert Bolger, Wily Rascal .12 .30
2C102a Frodo, Reluctant Adventurer .12 .30
2C102b Frodo, Reluctant Adventurer
TENGWAR
2C104 Merry, Horticulturalist .12 .30
2C110 Pippin, Mr. Took .12 .30
2C114 Sam, Proper Poet .12 .30
2C117 Town Center .12 .30
2C119 Hollin .12 .30
2P121 Gimli, Dwarf of the Mountain-race .40 1.00
2P122 Gandalf, The Grey Pilgrim .40 1.00
2R100 Fearing the Worst .60 1.50
2R105a Mithril-coat .75 2.00
2R105b Mithril-coat TENGWAR
2R108 O Elbereth! Gilthoniel! .75 2.00
2R109 Orc-bane .60 1.50
2R112 A Promise 2.50 6.00
2R113 Red Book of Westmarch .60 1.50
2U103 Hobbit Sword-play .30 .75
2U106 Nice Imitation .30 .75
2U107 Not Feared in Sunlight .30 .75
2U111 Practically Everyone Was Invited .30 .75
2U115 Hobbiton Party Field .30 .75
2U116 Hobbiton Woods .30 .75
2U118 Great Chasm .30 .75
2U120 Valley of the Silverlode .30 .75

2002 Lord of the Rings Realms of the Elf-Lords

COMPLETE SET (122) 20.00 40.00
BOOSTER BOX (36 PACKS) 20.00 40.00
BOOSTER PACK (11 CARDS) 1.00 2.00
RELEASED ON JUNE 19, 2002
3C6 Storm of Argument .12 .30
3R1 Book of Mazarbul .60 1.50
3R3 Mines of Khazad-Dum .60 1.50
3R8 Arwen, Lady Undomiel .60 1.50
3U2 Gimli's Pipe .30 .75
3U4 A Royal Welcome .30 .75
3U5 Song of Durin .30 .75
3U7 Arwen, Elven Rider .30 .75
3U9 Beren and Luthien .30 .75
3C11 Cast It Into the Fire! .12 .30

Card	Low	High
3C14 Erestor, Chief Advisor to Elrond	.12	.30
3C16 Friends of Old	.12	.30
3C22 Master of Healing	.12	.30
3C28 Voice of Nimrodel	.12	.30
3C30 Deep in Thought	.12	.30
3C31 Depart Silently	.12	.30
3C32 Fireworks	.12	.30
3C33 His First Serious Check	.12	.30
3C36 Unknown Perils	.12	.30
3C37 Answering the Cries	.12	.30
3C43 Might of Numenor	.12	.30
3C48 We Must Go Warily	.12	.30
3C49 Abandoning Reason for Madness	.12	.30
3C51 Coming for the Ring	.12	.30
3C55 Isengard Axe	.12	.30
3C56 Isengard Forger	.12	.30
3C59 Isengard Shaman	.12	.30
3C62 Isengard Worker	.12	.30
3C63 One of You Must Do This	.12	.30
3C69 Saruman, Servant of the Eye	.12	.30
3C70 Servants to Saruman	.12	.30
3C74 Uruk Raider	.12	.30
3C76 Dangerous Gamble	.12	.30
3C78 Hide and Seek	.12	.30
3C84 They Will Never Stop Hunting You	.12	.30
3C87 The Dark Lord Advances	.12	.30
3C90 Hand of Sauron	.12	.30
3C94 Orc Butcher	.12	.30
3C95 Orc Guard	.12	.30
3C98 Orc Swordsman	.12	.30
3R13 Elrond, Herald to Gil-galad	1.25	3.00
3R15 Forests of Lothlorien	.60	1.50
3R17 Galadriel, Lady of the Golden Wood	.60	1.50
3R19 Gift of the Evenstar	.60	1.50
3R21 Long-knives of Legolas	2.00	5.00
3R23 Nenya	.60	1.50
3R27 Vilya	.60	1.50
3R29 Betrayal of Isengard	.60	1.50
3R34 Narya	1.00	2.50
3R38 Aragorn, Heir to the White City	.60	1.50
3R39 Banner of the White Tree	.75	2.00
3R40 Citadel of Minas Tirith	.75	2.00
3R41 Gondor Bowmen	2.00	5.00
3R42 Horn of Boromir	.60	1.50
3R44 The Shards of Narsil	.75	2.00
3R50 Can You Protect Me From Yourself?	.60	1.50
3R52 A Fell Voice on the Air	.60	1.50
3R54 Hollowing of Isengard	.60	1.50
3R64 Orc Commander	.60	1.50
3R65 Orc Overseer	.60	1.50
3R66 Orthanc Berserker	.60	1.50
3R67 The Palantir of Orthanc	.60	1.50
3R68 Saruman, Keeper of Isengard	.60	1.50
3R71 Tower of Orthanc	.60	1.50
3R77 Depths of Moria	.60	1.50
3R80 Such a Little Thing	.60	1.50
3R81 Gates of the Dead City	.60	1.50
3R85 Too Great and Terrible	.60	1.50
3R91 His Cruelty and Malice	.60	1.50
3R93 Morgul Slayer	.60	1.50
3R99 Orc Trooper	.60	1.50
3U10 Calaglin, Elf of Lorien	.30	.75
3U12 Dinendal, Silent Scout	.30	.75
3U18 Galdor, Councilor From the West	.30	.75
3U20 Golradir, Councilor of Imladris	.30	.75
3U24 Phial of Galadriel	.30	.75
3U25 Saelbeth, Elven Councilor	.30	.75
3U26 Something Draws Near	.30	.75
3U35 Trust Me as You Once Did	.30	.75
3U45 Some Who Resisted	.30	.75
3U46 Still Sharp	.30	.75
3U47 Voice of Rauros	.30	.75
3U53 Hate and Anger	.30	.75
3U57 Isengard Retainer	.30	.75
3U58 Isengard Servant	.30	.75
3U60 Isengard Smith	.30	.75
3U61 Isengard Warrior	.30	.75
3U72 Trapped and Alone	.30	.75
3U73 The Trees Are Strong	.30	.75
3U75 Uruk Ravager	.30	.75
3U79 Malice	.30	.75
3U82 News of Mordor	.30	.75
3U83 The Ring Draws Them	.30	.75
3U86 Ulaire Otsea, Ringwraith in Twilight	.30	.75
3U88 Get Off the Road!	.30	.75
3U89 Gleaming in the Snow	.30	.75
3U92 Massing in the East	.30	.75
3U96 Orc Pillager	.30	.75
3U97 Orc Slayer	.30	.75
3C101 Orc Warrior	.12	.30
3C108 Frying Pan	.12	.30
3C109 Meant to Be Alone	.12	.30
3C111 Old Noakes, Purveyor of Wisdoms	.12	.30
3C112 Seek and Hide	.12	.30
3C114 Three Monstrous Trolls	.12	.30
3C117 Gates of Argonath	.12	.30
3C118 The Great River	.12	.30
3P121 Legolas, Son of Thranduil	.40	1.00
3P122 Boromir, Defender of Minas Tirith	.40	1.00
3R102 Our List of Allies Grows Thin	.60	1.50
3R103 Terrible as the Dawn	.60	1.50
3R104 Tower of Barad-dur	.75	2.00
3R105 Why Shouldn't I Keep It?	.60	1.50
3R110 Melilot Brandybuck, Merry Dancer	.60	1.50
3R113 The Shire Countryside	1.00	2.50
3U100 Orc Veteran	.30	.75
3U106 Bill the Pony	.30	.75
3U107 Frodo's Pipe	.30	.75
3U115 Caras Galadhon	.30	.75
3U116 Eregion Hills	.30	.75
3U119 House of Elrond	.30	.75
3U120 Wastes of Emyn Muil	.30	.75

2002 Lord of the Rings The Two Towers

Card	Low	High
COMPLETE SET (365)	50.00	100.00
BOOSTER BOX (36 PACKS)	25.00	50.00
BOOSTER PACK (11 CARDS)	1.00	2.00
RELEASED ON NOVEMBER 6, 2002		
4C2 The One Ring, The Ruling Ring	.12	.30
4C3 Anger	.12	.30
4C4 Band of Wild Men	.12	.30
4C5 Burn Every Village	.12	.30
4C7 Dark Fury	.12	.30
4R1A The One Ring, Answer To All Riddles	7.50	15.00
4R1B The One Ring Answer To All Riddles TENGWAR		
4R6 Constantly Threatening	.60	1.50
4U8 Death to the Strawheads	.30	.75
4U9 Dunlending Arsonist	.30	.75
4C10 Dunlending Brigand	.12	.30
4C12 Dunlending Madman	.12	.30
4C14 Dunlending Ransacker	.12	.30
4C15 Dunlending Ravager	.12	.30
4C16 Dunlending Robber	.12	.30
4C17 Dunlending Savage	.12	.30
4C18 Dunlending Warrior	.12	.30
4C21 Hillman Band	.12	.30
4C25 Hillman Tribe	.12	.30
4C26 Iron Axe	.12	.30
4C37 War Cry of Dunland	.12	.30
4C42 Best Company	.12	.30
4C44 Courtesy of My Hall	.12	.30
4C49 Gimli, Unbidden Guest	.12	.30
4C50 Here Is Good Rock	.12	.30
4C51 Khazad Ai-menu	.12	.30
4C56 Search Far and Wide	.12	.30
4C64 Elven Sword	.12	.30
4C67 Fereveldir, Son of Thandronen	.12	.30
4C68 Ferevellon, Son of Thandronen	.12	.30
4C70 Flashing Steel	.12	.30
4C71 Haldir, Emissary of the Galadhrim	.12	.30
4C74 Legolas, Elven Comrade	.12	.30
4C76 Lorien Guardian	.12	.30
4C78 Lorien Swordsman	.12	.30
4C83 Supporting Fire	.12	.30
4C85 Thandronen, Veteran Protector	.12	.30
4C87 Valor	.12	.30
4C90a Gandalf, The White Wizard	.12	.30
4C90b Gandalf, The White Wizard TENGWAR		
4C93 Have Patience	.12	.30
4C97 Long I Fell	.12	.30
4C98 Mithrandir, Mithrandir!	.12	.30
4R19A Hides	3.00	8.00
4R19B Hides TENGWAR		
4R20 Hill Chief	.60	1.50
4R22 Hillman Horde	.60	1.50
4R23 Hillman Mob	.60	1.50
4R29 No Refuge	.60	1.50
4R30 No Retreat	.60	1.50
4R32 Ravage the Defeated	.60	1.50
4R33 Saruman, Rabble-rouser	1.50	4.00
4R35 Wake of Destruction	.60	1.50
4R39 Wild Man Raid	.60	1.50
4R40 Wulf, Dunlending Chieftain	.60	1.50
4R41 Axe of Erebor	.75	2.00
4R45 Dwarven Foresight	.60	1.50
4R46 Ever My Heart Rises	.60	1.50
4R48 Gimli, Lockbearer	.60	1.50
4R52 My Axe Is Notched	.60	1.50
4R54 Rest by Blind Night	.60	1.50
4R55 Restless Axe	.60	1.50
4R58 Alliance Reforged	.60	1.50
4R61 Company of Archers	1.25	3.00
4R65 Erethon, Naith Lieutenant	.60	1.50
4R69 Final Count	.60	1.50
4R72 Killing Field	.60	1.50
4R73A Legolas, Dauntless Hunter	.60	1.50
4R73B Legolas, Dauntless Hunter TENGWAR		
4R75 Lembas	1.00	2.50
4R79 Night Without End	.60	1.50
4R84 Sword-wall	.60	1.50
4R89 Gandalf, Greyhame	.75	2.00
4R91 Gandalf's Staff, Walking Stick	.60	1.50
4R92 Grown Suddenly Tall	.60	1.50
4R94 Hearken to Me	1.00	2.50
4R95 Into Dark Tunnels	.60	1.50
4U11 Dunlending Looter	.30	.75
4U13 Dunlending Pillager	.30	.75
4U24 Hillman Rabble	.30	.75
4U27 Living Off Rock	.30	.75
4U28 No Defense	.30	.75
4U31 Over the Isen	.30	.75
4U34 Secret Folk	.30	.75
4U36 War Club	.30	.75
4U38 Wild Man of Dunland	.30	.75
4U43 Come Here Lad	.30	.75
4U47 From the Armory	.30	.75
4U53 Quick As May Be	.30	.75
4U57 Stout and Strong	.30	.75
4U59 Arrow and Blade	.30	.75
4U60 Blades Drawn	.30	.75
4U62 Elven Bow	.30	.75
4U63 Elven Brooch	.30	.75
4U66 Feathered	.30	.75
4U77 Lorien Is Most Welcome	.30	.75
4U80 Ordulus, Young Warrior	.30	.75
4U81 Pengedhel, Naith Warrior	.30	.75
4U82 Strength of Arms	.30	.75
4U86 Thonnas, Naith Captain	.30	.75
4U88 Behold the White Rider	.30	.75
4U96 Keep Your Forked Tongue	.30	.75
4U99 Roll of Thunder	.30	.75
4C102 Task Was Not Done	.12	.30
4C104 Treebeard, Oldest Living Thing	.12	.30
4C105 Under the Living Earth	.12	.30
4C109 Aragorn, Heir of Elendil	.12	.30
4C112 Boromir's Gauntlets	.12	.30
4C113 Curse Them	.12	.30
4C115 Defend It and Hope	.12	.30
4C117 Faramir, Son of Denethor	.12	.30
4C122 Gondorian Ranger	.12	.30
4C128 New Errand	.12	.30
4C129 Pathfinder	.12	.30
4C130 Ranger of Ithilien	.12	.30
4C131 Ranger's Bow	.12	.30
4C134 Sword of Gondor	.12	.30
4C135 War and Valor	.12	.30
4C137 Attack on Helm's Deep	.12	.30
4C141 Beyond Dark Mountains	.12	.30
4C142 Broad-bladed Sword	.12	.30
4C145 Cloud of Arrows	.12	.30
4C151 Ferocity	.12	.30
4C153 Grima, Son of Galmod	.12	.30
4C156 Kill Them Now	.12	.30
4C165 Orthanc Warrior	.12	.30
4C175 Still They Came	.12	.30
4C178 Unferth, Grima's Bodyguard	.12	.30
4C180 Uruk Besieger	.12	.30
4C181 Uruk Chaser	.12	.30
4C183 Uruk Crossbowman	.12	.30
4C184 Uruk Defender	.12	.30
4C185 Uruk Fanatic	.12	.30
4C187 Uruk Foot Soldier	.12	.30
4C189 Uruk Plains Runner	.12	.30
4C190 Uruk Pursuer	.12	.30
4C191 Uruk Rear Guard	.12	.30
4C192 Uruk Regular	.12	.30
4C193 Uruk Runner	.12	.30
4C195 Uruk Seeker	.12	.30
4C196 Uruk Spear	.12	.30
4C197 Uruk Stalker	.12	.30
4C198 Uruk Stormer	.12	.30
4C204 Uruk-hai Marauder	.12	.30
4C206 Uruk-hai Patrol	.12	.30
4C207 Uruk-hai Raiding Party	.12	.30
4C210 We Are the Fighting Uruk-hai	.12	.30
4C212 Weary	.12	.30
4C221 Desert Spearman	.12	.30
4C222 Desert Warrior	.12	.30
4C224 Easterling Axeman	.12	.30
4C226 Easterling Guard	.12	.30
4C227 Easterling Infantry	.12	.30
4C228 Easterling Lieutenant	.12	.30
4C235 Gathering to the Summons	.12	.30
4C239 Men of Rhun	.12	.30
4C241 On the March	.12	.30
4C248 Southron Bowman	.12	.30
4C252 Southron Scout	.12	.30
4C254 Southron Soldier	.12	.30
4C255 Southron Spear	.12	.30
4C258 Southron Wanderer	.12	.30
4C260 Whirling Strike	.12	.30
4C265 Elite Rider	.12	.30
4C266 Eomer, Sister-son of Theoden	.12	.30
4C270 Eowyn, Lady of Rohan	.12	.30
4C273 Fight for the Villagers	.12	.30
4C277 Guma, Plains Farmer	.12	.30
4C278 Heavy Chain	.12	.30
4C281 Hlafwine, Village Farmhand	.12	.30
4C283 Horse of Rohan	.12	.30
4C286 Rider of Rohan	.12	.30
4C287 Rider's Mount	.12	.30
4C288 Rider's Spear	.12	.30
4C291 Sword of Rohan	.12	.30
4C292 Theoden, Son of Thengel	.12	.30
4C297 Work for the Sword	.12	.30
4C298 Brace of Coneys	.12	.30
4C302 Frodo, Tired Traveller	.12	.30
4C306 Hobbit Sword	.12	.30
4C308 Knocked on the Head	.12	.30
4C310 Merry, Learned Guide	.12	.30
4C314 Pippin, Woolly-footed Rascal	.12	.30
4C316 Sam, Samwise the Brave	.12	.30
4C319 Severed His Bonds	.12	.30
4C321 Swiftly and Softly	.12	.30
4C322 Warmed Up a Bit	.12	.30
4P364A Aragorn, Wingfoot	.40	1.00
4P364B Aragorn, Wingfoot TENGWAR		
4P365 Theoden, Lord of the Mark	.40	1.00
4R100A Shadowfax	.60	1.50
4R100B Shadowfax TENGWAR		
4R103A Treebeard, Earthborn	.60	1.50
4R103B Treebeard, Earthborn TENGWAR		
4R106 Well Met Indeed	.60	1.50
4R107 Windows in a Stone Wall	.60	1.50
4R111 Boromir, My Brother	.60	1.50
4R116 Faramir, Captain of Gondor	.60	1.50
4R118 Faramir's Bow	2.00	5.00
4R119 Faramir's Cloak	.60	1.50
4R120 Forbidden Pool	.60	1.50
4R121 Forests of Ithilien	.60	1.50
4R124 Help in Doubt and Need	.60	1.50
4R125 Henneth Annun	.60	1.50
4R133 Ruins of Osgiliath	.60	1.50
4R139 Banished	.60	1.50
4R140 Beyond All Hope	.60	1.50
4R144 Burning of Westfold	.60	1.50
4R146 Come Down	.60	1.50
4R149 Driven Back	.60	1.50
4R150 Elite Crossbowmen	.75	2.00
4R154A Grima, Wormtongue	1.25	3.00
4R154B Grima, Wormtongue TENGWAR		
4R157 Leechcraft	.60	1.50
4R158 Lieutenant of Orthanc	.60	1.50
4R160 Mauhur, Patrol Leader	.60	1.50
4R162 New Power Rising	.60	1.50
4R163 No Dawn for Men	.60	1.50
4R164 Orthanc Champion	.75	2.00
4R166 The Palantir of Orthanc Seventh Seeing-stone	.60	1.50
4R167 Pillage of Rohan	.60	1.50
4R168 Race Across the Mark	.60	1.50
4R169 Ranged Commander	.60	1.50
4R171 Rest While You Can	.60	1.50
4R172 Rohan Is Mine	.60	1.50
4R173A Saruman, Black Traitor	1.00	2.50
4R173B Saruman, Black Traitor TENGWAR		
4R174 Saruman's Staff, Wizard's Device	.75	2.00
4R176A Ugluk, Servant of Saruman	.75	2.00
4R176B Ugluk, Servant of Saruman TENGWAR		
4R177 Ugluk's Sword	.60	1.50
4R179 Uruk Assault Band	.60	1.50
4R186 Uruk Follower	.60	1.50
4R199 Uruk Trooper	.60	1.50
4R200 Uruk Vanguard	.75	2.00
4R203 Uruk-hai Horde	.60	1.50
4R209 Volley Fire	.60	1.50
4R211 Weapons of Isengard	1.50	4.00
4R213 What Did You Discover?	.60	1.50
4R214 Where Has Grima Stowed It?	.60	1.50
4R215 Wounded	.60	1.50
4R218 Desert Legion	.75	2.00
4R219A Desert Lord	2.50	6.00
4R219B Desert Lord TENGWAR		
4R223 Discovered	.60	1.50
4R225A Easterling Captain	.75	2.00
4R225B Easterling Captain TENGWAR		
4R229 Easterling Skirmisher	.60	1.50
4R231 Eastern Emyn Muil	.60	1.50
4R237 Ithilien Wilderness	.60	1.50
4R238 Men of Harad	.60	1.50
4R240 New Fear	1.00	2.50
4R243 Rapid Fire	.75	2.00
4R244 Regiment of Haradrim	.60	1.50
4R245 Southron Archer	.75	2.00
4R246 Southron Assassin	.60	1.50
4R247 Southron Bow	.75	2.00
4R251 Southron Fighter	.60	1.50
4R256 Southron Troop	.60	1.50
4R257 Southron Veterans	.60	1.50
4R259 Vision From Afar	2.00	5.00
4R261 Wrath of Harad	.60	1.50
4R262 Aldor, Soldier of Edoras	.60	1.50
4R267 Eomer, Third Marshal of Riddermark	1.50	4.00
4R269 Eothain, Scout of the Mark	.60	1.50
4R271 Eowyn, Sister-daughter of Theoden	.60	1.50
4R272 Eowyn's Sword	.75	2.00
4R274 Firefoot	1.00	2.50
4R279 Helm! Helm!	.60	1.50
4R284 King's Mail	.60	1.50
4R289A Simbelmyne	1.50	4.00
4R289B Simbelmyne TENGWAR		
4R290 Supplies of the Mark	.60	1.50
4R293 Valleys of the Mark	.60	1.50
4R294 Weapon Store	.75	2.00
4R299 Cliffs of Emyn Muil	.75	2.00
4R300 Escape	1.00	2.50
4R301A Frodo, Courteous Halfling	.60	1.50
4R301B Frodo, Courteous Halfling TENGWAR		
4R303 Frodo's Cloak	.60	1.50
4R304 Get On and Get Away	.60	1.50
4R307 Impatient and Angry	.60	1.50
4R311 Merry, Unquenchable Hobbit	.60	1.50
4R313 Pippin, Just a Nuisance	.60	1.50
4R315 Sam, Frodo's Gardener	.60	1.50
4R317 Sam's Pack	.60	1.50
4U101 Stump and Bramble	.30	.75
4U108 Wizardry Indeed	.30	.75
4U110 Arrows Thick in the Air	.30	.75
4U114 Damrod, Ranger of Ithilien	.30	.75
4U123 Hard Choice	.30	.75
4U126 Ithilien Trap	.30	.75
4U127 Mablung, Soldier of Gondor	.30	.75
4U132 Ranger's Sword, Blade of Aragorn	.30	.75
4U136 Advance Uruk Patrol	.30	.75
4U138 Band of Uruk Bowmen	.30	.75
4U143 Brought Back Alive	.30	.75
4U147 Covering Fire	.30	.75
4U148 Down to the Last Child	.30	.75
4U152 Get Back	.30	.75
4U155 Haunting Her Steps	.30	.75
4U159 Many Riddles	.30	.75
4U161 Men Will Fall	.30	.75
4U170 Ranks Without Number	.30	.75
4U182 Uruk Crossbow Troop	.30	.75
4U188 Uruk Hunter	.30	.75
4U194 Uruk Searcher	.30	.75
4U201 Uruk Veteran	.30	.75
4U202 Uruk-hai Band	.30	.75
4U205 Uruk-hai Mob	.30	.75
4U208 Vengeance	.30	.75
4U216 Arrow From the South	.30	.75
4U217 Desert Lancers	.30	.75
4U220 Desert Soldier	.30	.75
4U230 Easterling Trooper	.30	.75
4U232 Elite Archer	.30	.75
4U233 Fearless	.30	.75
4U234 Flanking Attack	.30	.75
4U236 Howl of Harad	.30	.75
4U242 Raiders From the East	.30	.75
4U249 Southron Commander	.30	.75
4U250 Southron Explorer	.30	.75
4U253 Southron Sentry	.30	.75
4U263 Brego	.30	.75
4U264 Ceorl, Weary Horseman	.30	.75
4U268 Eomer's Spear	.30	.75
4U275 Forth Eorlingas!	.30	.75
4U276 Fortress Never Fallen	.30	.75
4U280 Herugrim	.30	.75
4U282 An Honorable Charge	.30	.75
4U285 Leod, Westfold Herdsman	.30	.75
4U295 Weland, Smith of the Riddermark	.30	.75
4U296 Well Stored	.30	.75
4U305 Good Work	.30	.75
4U309 Light Shining Faintly	.30	.75
4U312 Mind Your Own Affairs	.30	.75
4U318 Seven We Had	.30	.75
4U320 Store-room	.30	.75
4U323 East Wall of Rohan	.30	.75
4U324 Eastemnet Downs	.30	.75
4U325 Eastemnet Gullies	.30	.75
4U326 Horse-country	.30	.75
4U327 Plains of Rohan	.30	.75
4U328 The Riddermark	.30	.75
4U329 Western Emyn Muil	.30	.75
4U330 Derndingle	.30	.75
4U331 Eastfold	.30	.75
4U332 Fangorn Forest	.30	.75
4U333 Plains of Rohan Camp	.30	.75
4U334 Rohirrim Village	.30	.75
4U335 Uruk Camp	.30	.75
4U336 Wold of Rohan	.30	.75
4U337 Barrows of Edoras	.30	.75
4U338 Golden Hall	.30	.75
4U339 Stables	.30	.75
4U340 Streets of Edoras	.30	.75
4U341 Throne Room	.30	.75
4U342 Westemnet Plains	.30	.75
4U343 Ered Nimrais	.30	.75
4U344 Westemnet Hills	.30	.75
4U345 White Mountains	.30	.75
4U346 White Rocks	.30	.75
4U347 Deep of Helm	.30	.75
4U348 Deeping Wall	.30	.75
4U349 Helm's Gate	.30	.75
4U350 Hornburg Courtyard	.30	.75
4U351 Hornburg Parapet	.30	.75
4U352 Caves of Aglarond	.30	.75
4U353 Great Hall	.30	.75
4U354 Hornburg Armory	.30	.75
4U355 Cavern Entrance	.30	.75
4U356 Hornburg Causeway	.30	.75
4U357 King's Room	.30	.75
4U358 Ring of Isengard	.30	.75
4U359 Wizard's Vale	.30	.75
4U360 Fortress of Orthanc	.30	.75
4U361 Orthanc Balcony	.30	.75
4U362 Orthanc Library	.30	.75
4U363 Palantir Chamber	.30	.75

2003 Lord of the Rings Battle of Helm's Deep

Card	Low	High
COMPLETE SET (128)	25.00	50.00
BOOSTER BOX (36 PACKS)	25.00	50.00
BOOSTER PACK (11 CARDS)	1.00	2.00
RELEASED MARCH 12, 2003		
5C6 Defending the Keep	.12	.30
5R3 Leaping Blaze	.60	1.50
5R4 Wild Men of the Hills	.60	1.50
5R5 Baruk Khazad	.60	1.50
5R7 Gimli, Skilled Defender	.60	1.50
5U1 Dunlending Rampager	.30	.75
5U2 Dunlending Renegade	.30	.75
5U8 Horn of Helm	.30	.75
5U9 More to My Liking	.30	.75
5C14 That Is No Orc Horn	.12	.30
5C17 Forest Guardian	.12	.30
5C24 Gollum, Nasty Treacherous Creature	.12	.30
5C27 Poor Wretch	.12	.30
5C28 Smeagol, Old Noser	.12	.30
5C30 We Must Have It	.12	.30
5C32 Citadel of the Stars	.12	.30
5C33 City Wall	.12	.30
5C35 Gondorian Knight	.12	.30
5C36 Knight of Gondor	.12	.30
5C37 Men of Numenor	.12	.30
5C40 Take Cover	.12	.30
5C43 War Must Be	.12	.30
5C52 Isengard Flanker	.12	.30
5C53 Isengard Rider	.12	.30
5C61 Uruk Engineer	.12	.30
5C62 Uruk Sapper	.12	.30
5C65 Warg	.12	.30
5C66 Warg-master	.12	.30
5C67 Warg-rider	.12	.30
5C68 Wolf-voices	.12	.30
5C73 Mumak	.12	.30
5C74 Southron Marcher	.12	.30
5C75 Southron Runner	.12	.30
5C76 Southron Traveler	.12	.30
5C81 Ecglaf, Courageous Farmer	.12	.30
5C83 Household Guard	.12	.30
5C85 Let Us Be Swift	.12	.30
5C88 Rohirrim Bow	.12	.30
5C90 Rohirrim Scout	.12	.30
5C91 Rohirrim Shield	.12	.30
5C93 Theoden, King of the Golden Hall	.12	.30
5C97 Gate Soldier	.12	.30
5C98 Gate Trooper	.12	.30
5C99 Gate Veteran	.12	.30
5R11 Break the Charge	.60	1.50
5R16 Down From the Hills	.60	1.50
5R18 Fury of the White Rider	.60	1.50
5R19 Lindenroot, Elder Shepherd	.60	1.50
5R21 Be Back Soon	.60	1.50
5R25A Gollum, Stinker	2.00	5.00
5R25B Gollum, Stinker TENGWAR		
5R29A Smeagol, Slinker	.60	1.50
5R29B Smeagol, Slinker TENGWAR		
5R31 Alcarin, Warrior of Lamedon	.60	1.50
5R39 Stone Tower	.60	1.50
5R41 These Are My People	.60	1.50
5R46 Berserk Savage	.60	1.50
5R47 Berserk Slayer	.60	1.50
5R49 Devilry of Orthanc	.60	1.50
5R50 Foul Horde	.60	1.50
5R51 Grima, Chief Counselor	.60	1.50
5R56 Saruman, Master of Foul Folk	.60	1.50
5R58 Sharku, Warg-captain	.60	1.50

5R59 Sharku's Warg .75 2.00
5R69 Wolves of Isengard .60 1.50
5R70 Army of Haradrim .60 1.50
5R71 Company of Haradrim .60 1.50
5R72 Desert Stalker .60 1.50
5R78 War Mumak 1.25 3.00
5R82 Gamling, Warrior of Rohan .60 1.50
5R84 I Am Here .60 1.50
5R86 No Rest for the Weary .60 1.50
5R89 Rohirrim Helm .60 1.50
5R94 Thundering Host .60 1.50
5R95 Dead Marshes .60 1.50
5R96 Eye of Barad-Dur .60 1.50
5U10 Balglin, Elven Warrior .30 .75
5U12 Legolas' Sword .30 .75
5U13 Taurnil, Sharp-eyed Bowman .30 .75
5U15 Birchseed, Tall Statesman .30 .75
5U20 Turn of the Tide .30 .75
5U22 Evil-smelling Fens .30 .75
5U23 Follow Smeagol .30 .75
5U26 Look at Him .30 .75
5U34 Fall Back .30 .75
5U38 Rally Point .30 .75
5U42 Turgon, Man of Belfalas .30 .75
5U44 Battering Ram .30 .75
5U45 Berserk Rager .30 .75
5U48 Black Shapes Crawling .30 .75
5U54 Isengard Scimitar .30 .75
5U55 Isengard Scout Troop .30 .75
5U57 Scaling Ladder .30 .75
5U60 Siege Engine .30 .75
5U63 Uruk-hai Berserker .30 .75
5U64 War-warg .30 .75
5U77 Strength in Numbers .30 .75
5U79 Armory .30 .75
5U80 Arrow-slits .30 .75
5U87 Parapet .30 .75
5U92 Sigewulf, Brave Volunteer .30 .75
5C106 Orc Infantry .12 .30
5C108 Orc Pursuer .12 .30
5C109 Orc Runner .12 .30
5C117 You Must Help Us .12 .30
5P121 Legolas, Archer of Mirkwood .40 1.00
5P122 Eowyn, Daughter of Eomund .40 1.00
5R100A Grishnakh, Orc Captain 2.00 5.00
5R100B Grishnakh, Orc Captain TENGWAR
5R102 Morannon .60 1.50
5R103 Orc Captain .60 1.50
5R112 No Help for It .60 1.50
5R113 No Use That Way .60 1.50
5R116A Sting, Baggins Heirloom 1.50 4.00
5R116B Sting, Baggins Heirloom TENGWAR
5R123 Baruk Khazad .40 1.00
5R124 Break the Charge .40 1.00
5R125 Foul Horde .40 1.00
5R126 Army of Haradrim .40 1.00
5R127 Rohirrim Helm .40 1.00
5R128 Thundering Host .40 1.00
5U101 I'd Make You Squeak .30 .75
5U104 Orc Cutthroat .30 .75
5U105 Orc Fighter .30 .75
5U107 Orc Patrol .30 .75
5U110 Teeth of Mordor .30 .75
5U111 Frodo, Master of the Precious .30 .75
5U114 Rare Good Ballast .30 .75
5U115 Sam, Nice Sensible Hobbit .30 .75
5U118 Hornburg Wall .30 .75
5U119 Nan Curunir .30 .75
5U120 Caverns of Isengard .30 .75

2003 Lord of the Rings Ents of Fagorn

COMPLETE SET (128) 15.00 30.00
BOOSTER BOX (36 PACKS) 20.00 40.00
BOOSTER PACK (11 CARDS) 1.00 2.00
RELEASED ON JULY 2, 2003
6C1 Bound By Rage .12 .30
6C2 Dunlending Elder .12 .30
6C3 Dunlending Footmen .12 .30
6C4 Dunlending Headman .12 .30
6C5 Dunlending Reserve .12 .30
6R6 Hill Clan .60 1.50
6R7 Ready to Fall .75 2.00
6U8 Too Long Have These Peasants Stood .30 .75
6U9 Lend Us Your Aid .30 .75
6C10 Suspended Palaces .12 .30
6C12 Agility .12 .30
6C17 Forewarned .12 .30
6C21 Naith Longbow .12 .30
6C27 Ent Avenger .12 .30
6C29 Ent Moot .12 .30
6C33 Quickbeam, Bregalad .12 .30
6C34 Roused .12 .30
6C37 Treebeard, Guardian of the Forest .12 .30
6C38 Don't Follow the Lights .12 .30
6C40 Gollum, Old Villain .12 .30
6C42 Nasty, Foul Hobbitses .12 .30
6C43 Not Listening .12 .30
6C45 Smeagol, Poor Creature .12 .30
6C47 You're a Liar and a Thief .12 .30
6C48 Anborn, Skilled Huntsman .12 .30
6C52 Garrison of Osgiliath .12 .30
6C53 Mortal Men .12 .30
6C56 Trust .12 .30
6C59 Banner of Isengard .12 .30
6C65 Isengard Artisan .12 .30
6C67 Isengard Journeyman .12 .30
6C69 Isengard Plodder .12 .30
6C71 Isengard Tinker .12 .30
6C72 Rohirrim Traitor .12 .30
6C81 Southron Invaders .12 .30
6C95 Hrethel, Rider of Rohan .12 .30
6C97 We Left None Alive .12 .30
6C98 Banner of the Eye .12 .30
6C99 Corpse Lights .12 .30
6R11 Toss Me .60 1.50
6R15 Elrond, Keeper of Vilya .60 1.50
6R18 Galadriel, Keeper of Nenya .60 1.50
6R23 Naith Warband .60 1.50
6R26 Enraged .75 2.00
6R28 Ent Horde .60 1.50
6R30 Gandalf, Mithrandir .60 1.50
6R31 Glamdring, Lightning Brand .60 1.50
6R35 Skinbark, Fladrif .60 1.50
6R39 Don't Look at Them .75 2.00
6R41 Master Broke His Promise .60 1.50
6R44 Safe Paths .60 1.50
6R46 They Stole It .75 2.00
6R49 Ancient Roads .60 1.50
6R50 Aragorn, Defender of Free Peoples .75 2.00
6R55 Ring of Barahir .60 1.50
6R57 Agents of Orthanc .60 1.50
6R60 Berserk Butcher .60 1.50
6R62 Fires and Foul Fumes .60 1.50
6R68 Isengard Mechanics .60 1.50
6R74 Sharku, Vile Marauder .60 1.50
6R76 The Balrog, Terror of Flame and Shadow 1.25 3.00
6R77 Durin's Tower .60 1.50
6R78 Easterling Army 1.00 2.50
6R80 Southron Archer Legion .60 1.50
6R82 Trample .60 1.50
6R85 Sword of Dol Guldur .60 1.50
6R88A Ulaire Toldea, Winged Sentry 1.00 2.50
6R88B Ulaire Toldea, Winged Sentry TENGWAR
6R89 Winged and Ominous .60 1.50
6R92 Eomer, Rohirrim Captain .60 1.50
6R94 Hama, Doorward of Theoden .60 1.50
6R96 News From the Mark .60 1.50
6U13 Arwen, Evenstar of Her People .30 .75
6U14 Banner of Elbereth .30 .75
6U16 Forearmed .30 .75
6U19 Gift of Foresight .30 .75
6U20 Must Be a Dream .30 .75
6U22 Naith Troop .30 .75
6U24 Boomed and Trumpeted .30 .75
6U25 Crack Into Rubble .30 .75
6U32 Host of Fangorn .30 .75
6U36 Threw Down My Enemy .30 .75
6U51 Banner of Westernesse .30 .75
6U54 Perilous Ventures .30 .75
6U58 Assault Ladder .30 .75
6U61 Desertion .30 .75
6U63 Gnawing, Biting, Hacking, Burning .30 .75
6U64 Iron Fist of the Orc .30 .75
6U66 Isengard Builder .30 .75
6U70 Isengard Tender .30 .75
6U73 Scaffolding .30 .75
6U75 Twisted Tales .30 .75
6U79 Easterling Polearm .30 .75
6U83 Fell Beast .30 .75
6U84 Spied From Above .30 .75
6U86 Ulaire Lemenya, Winged Hunter .30 .75
6U87 Ulaire Nertea, Winged Hunter .30 .75
6U90 Banner of the Mark .30 .75
6U91 Blood Has Been Spilled .30 .75
6U93 Ever the Hope of Men .30 .75
6C100 Dead Ones .12 .30
6C102 Gate Sentry .12 .30
6C108 Wisp of Pale Sheen .12 .30
6C111 Kept Safe .12 .30
6C112 Long Slow Wrath .12 .30
6P121 Faramir, Ithilien Ranger .60 1.50
6P122 The Witch-king, Deathless Lord .60 1.50
6R101 Gate Picket .60 1.50
6R103 Gate Troll .60 1.50
6R106 Troll of Udun .60 1.50
6R109 Held .60 1.50
6R113 Merry, Impatient Hobbit .60 1.50
6R114 Pippin, Hastiest of All .60 1.50
6R123 Enraged 1.00 2.50
6R124 Skinbark, Fladrif .60 1.50
6R125 Don't Look at Them 1.50 4.00
6R126 Ancient Roads .75 2.00
6R127 Isengard Mechanics .60 1.50
6R128 Gate Troll .60 1.50
6U104 Orc Insurgent .30 .75
6U105 Peril .30 .75
6U107 Troll's Chain .30 .75
6U110 It Burns Us .30 .75
6U115 Rocks of Emyn Muil .30 .75
6U116 Westfold .30 .75
6U117 Meduseld .30 .75
6U118 Hornburg Hall .30 .75
6U119 Valley of Saruman .30 .75
6U120 Saruman's Laboratory .30 .75

2003 Lord of the Rings The Return of the King

COMPLETE SET (367) 75.00 150.00
BOOSTER BOX (36 PACKS) 25.00 50.00
BOOSTER PACK (11 CARDS) 1.00 2.00
RELEASED ON NOVEMBER 5, 2003
7C1 The One Ring, The Ruling Ring .12 .30
7C4 Calculated Risk .12 .30
7C6 Gimli, Faithful Companion .12 .30
7R5 Dark Ways .75 2.00
7R7 Gimli, Feared Axeman .60 1.50
7R9 Gimli's Battle Axe, Trusted Weapon 1.00 2.50
7U3 Battle Tested .30 .75
7U8 Gimli's Armor .30 .75
7C11 Out of Darkness .12 .30
7C20 Defiance .12 .30
7C23 Into the West .12 .30
7C26 Legolas, Nimble Warrior .12 .30
7C29 Still Needed .12 .30
7C30 Uncertain Paths .12 .30
7C31 All Save One .12 .30
7C34 Echoes of Valinor .12 .30
7C36 Gandalf, Defender of the West .12 .30
7C40 Have Patience .12 .30
7C41 Intimidate .12 .30
7C46 Peace of Mind .12 .30
7C51 Undaunted .12 .30
7C52 Wizard Staff .12 .30
7C53 Captured by the Ring .12 .30
7C59 Gollum, Vile Creature .12 .30
7C62 It's Mine .12 .30
7C65 Never .12 .30
7C72 Smeagol, Hurried Guide .12 .30
7C75 Sweeter Meats .12 .30
7C76 Very Nice Friends .12 .30
7C81 Aragorn, Captain of Gondor .12 .30
7C82 Cirion .12 .30
7C83 City of Men .12 .30
7C84 Dagger Strike .12 .30
7C86 Denethor, Wizened Steward .12 .30
7C89 Duty of Two .12 .30
7C90 Faramir, Stout Captain .12 .30
7C92 First Level .12 .30
7C96 Gondorian Captain .12 .30
7C99 Great Gate .12 .30
7R10 Loyalty Unshaken 1.00 2.50
7R12 Preparations 1.00 2.50
7R16 Arwen, Fair Elf Maiden .60 1.50
7R17 Asfaloth, Elven Steed 1.00 2.50
7R18 Bow of the Galadhrim, Gift of Galadriel .60 1.50
7R21 Elrond, Elven Lord .75 2.00
7R22 Hope Comes .60 1.50
7R24 Leaving Forever .60 1.50
7R25 Legolas, Fearless Marksman .60 1.50
7R27 Mirkwood Bowman .60 1.50
7R28 Shadow Between 1.25 3.00
7R2a The One Ring, Such a Weight to Carry 3.00 8.00
7R2b The One Ring, Such A Weight To Carry TENGWAR
7R32 The Board Is Set .60 1.50
7R33 Citadel to Gate .60 1.50
7R37 Gandalf, Manager of Wizards 1.50 4.00
7R38 Gandalf's Staff, Focus of Power 1.25 3.00
7R39 Glamdring, Elven Blade 1.25 3.00
7R43 Light the Beacons .60 1.50
7R44 Moment of Respite 1.25 3.00
7R48 Stay This Madness .60 1.50
7R50 Terrible and Evil 1.50 4.00
7R56 The Dead City .60 1.50
7R57 Fat One Wants It .60 1.50
7R58 Gollum, Plotting Deceiver .60 1.50
7R61 Hobbitses Are Dead 1.25 3.00
7R63 Let Her Deal With Them 1.25 3.00
7R66 No Safe Places .60 1.50
7R67 Plotting 1.25 3.00
7R68 Scouting .60 1.50
7R69 Secret Paths .60 1.50
7R70 Serving the Precious .60 1.50
7R71 Smeagol, Always Helps 1.25 3.00
7R73 Sneaking! 1.25 3.00
7R74 So Polite .60 1.50
7R80 Anduril, King's Blade 1.00 2.50
7R85 Denethor, Steward of the City .60 1.50
7R87 Derufin .60 1.50
7R91 Faramir, Wizard's Pupil .60 1.50
7R95 Gondor Still Stands .60 1.50
7R97 Gondorian Merchant .60 1.50
7U13 Reckless Pride .30 .75
7U14 Slaked Thirsts .30 .75
7U15 Ancient Blade .30 .75
7U19 Careful Study .30 .75
7U35 Fool's Hope .30 .75
7U42 King's Advisor .30 .75
7U45 Numenor's Pride .30 .75
7U47 Sharpen Your Swords .30 .75
7U49 Steadfast Champion .30 .75
7U54 Clever Hobbits .30 .75
7U55 Days Growing Dark .30 .75
7U60 Heavy Burden .30 .75
7U64 Nasty .30 .75
7U77 We Hates Them .30 .75
7U78 Where Shall We Go .30 .75
7U88 Dervorin .30 .75
7U93 Footman's Armor .30 .75
7U94 Gondor Bow .30 .75
7U98 Gondorian Sword .30 .75
7C105 I Will Go .12 .30
7C106 Ingold .12 .30
7C108 Knight's Spear .12 .30
7C111 Man the Walls .12 .30
7C115 Ranger of Minas Tirith .12 .30
7C116 Ranger of Osgiliath .12 .30
7C117 Reckless Counter .12 .30
7C118 Second Level .12 .30
7C121 Stout Resistance .12 .30
7C124 Targon .12 .30
7C130 Dark Tidings .12 .30
7C131 Desert Fighter .12 .30
7C132 Desert Nomad .12 .30
7C133 Desert Runner .12 .30
7C135 Desert Sneak .12 .30
7C137 Desert Spearman .12 .30
7C139 Easterling Aggressor .12 .30
7C140 Easterling Assailant .12 .30
7C141 Easterling Attacker .12 .30
7C142 Easterling Blademaster .12 .30
7C144 Easterling Ransacker .12 .30
7C149 Great Beasts .12 .30
7C150 Harsh Tongues .12 .30
7C153 Mumakil of the Harad .12 .30
7C154 New Strength Came Now .12 .30
7C155 Raider Bow .12 .30
7C156 Raider Halberd .12 .30
7C161 Southron Brigand .12 .30
7C172 Troop of Haradrim .12 .30
7C173 War Towers .12 .30
7C184 More Unbearable .12 .30
7C186 Morgul Axe .12 .30
7C189 Morgul Cur .12 .30
7C192 Morgul Hound .12 .30
7C193 Morgul Lackey .12 .30
7C194 Morgul Mongrel .12 .30
7C196 Morgul Predator .12 .30
7C198 Morgul Ruffian .12 .30
7C199 Morgul Soldier .12 .30
7C200 Morgul Spawn .12 .30
7C201 Morgul Spearman .12 .30
7C208 There Came a Cry .12 .30
7C209 Too Late .12 .30
7C220 War Long Planned .12 .30
7C222 Deor .12 .30
7C225 Elite Rider .12 .30
7C226 Enraged Horseman .12 .30
7C229 Eowyn, Restless Maiden .12 .30
7C235 Guthlaf, Herald .12 .30
7C237 His Golden Shield .12 .30
7C240 Long Spear .12 .30
7C243 Morning Came .12 .30
7C246 Rohirrim Guard .12 .30
7C247 Rohirrim Herdsman .12 .30
7C248 Rohirrim Javelin .12 .30
7C253 Swift Steed .12 .30
7C256 They Sang as They Slew .12 .30
7C257 Veteran Horseman .12 .30
7C259 Wind in His Face .12 .30
7C262 Above the Battlement .12 .30
7C263 Anguish .12 .30
7C265 Besieging Pike .12 .30
7C273 Gorgoroth Garrison .12 .30
7C275 Gorgoroth Pillager .12 .30
7C276 Gorgoroth Ransacker .12 .30
7C277 Gorgoroth Sapper .12 .30
7C285 Mordor Defender .12 .30
7C287 Mordor Guard .12 .30
7C288 Mordor Regular .12 .30
7C290 Mordor Soldier .12 .30
7C291 Mordor Trooper .12 .30
7C296 Orc Brood .12 .30
7C297 Orc Butcher .12 .30
7C298 Orc Chaser .12 .30
7C299 Orc Destroyer .12 .30
7C300 Orc Fanatic .12 .30
7C303 Orc Pursuer .12 .30
7C304 Orc Rager .12 .30
7C312 Siegecraft .12 .30
7C313 Some Secret Art of Flame .12 .30
7C315 Tower Walkway .12 .30
7C317 Frodo, Hope of Free Peoples .12 .30
7C319 Hobbit Sword .12 .30
7C320 Merry, Rohirrim Squire .12 .30
7C322 Noble Intentions .12 .30
7C323 Pippin, Sworn to Service .12 .30
7C326 Sam, Needer of Vittles .12 .30
7P364 Aragorn, Driven by Need 1.00 2.50
7P365 Eomer, Valiant Warchief .40 1.00
7R100 Greatest Stronghold .60 1.50
7R101 Guarded .60 1.50
7R103 Hearts Raised .75 2.00
7R104 Hidden Knowledge .60 1.50
7R112 Noble Leaders 3.00 8.00
7R113 Pippin's Armor .60 1.50
7R114 Pippin's Sword .60 1.50
7R119 Seventh Level .60 1.50
7R122 Strong and Old .60 1.50
7R127 Vorondil .60 1.50
7R129 Bold Men and Grim 1.00 2.50
7R143 Easterling Footman .60 1.50
7R145 Easterling Regiment .60 1.50
7R148 Fierce in Despair 1.00 2.50
7R152 Mumak Commander .60 1.50
7R158 Rout .60 1.50
7R159 Small Hope 2.00 5.00
7R163 Southron Chieftain .60 1.50
7R164 Southron Conqueror .60 1.50
7R165 Southron Intruder .60 1.50
7R166 Southron Leader .60 1.50
7R167 Southron Marksmen .75 2.00
7R169 Surging Up .60 1.50
7R170 Suzerain of Harad .60 1.50
7R177 Feel His Blade .60 1.50
7R179 Ghastly Host .60 1.50
7R180 Gorbag, Lieutenant of Cirith Ungol 1.00 2.50
7R181 Held Ground .60 1.50
7R182 Loathsome .60 1.50
7R183 Mind and Body .75 2.00
7R188 Morgul Brute 5.00 10.00
7R191 Morgul Detachment .75 2.00
7R197 Morgul Regiment .60 1.50
7R204 Out of Sight and Shot 1.25 3.00
7R205 Put Forth His Strength .60 1.50
7R206 Stronghold of Minas Morgul .75 2.00
7R210 Ulaire Attea, Wraith on Wings 1.25 3.00
7R211a Ulaire Cantea, Faster Than Winds .75 2.00
7R211b Ulaire Cantea, Faster Than Winds
TENGWAR
7R213 Ulaire Lemenya, Assailing Minion .60 1.50
7R215 Ulaire Nelya, Assailing Minion .60 1.50
7R219 Ulaire Toldea, Wraith on Wings 1.00 2.50
7R221a The Witch-king, Morgul King .75 2.00
7R221b The Witch-king, Morgul King
TENGWAR
7R223 Death They Cried .60 1.50
7R227a Eomer, Skilled Tactician .75 2.00
7R227b Eomer, Skilled Tactician
TENGWAR
7R228 Eowyn, Dernhelm .60 1.50
7R230 Eowyn's Sword, Dernhelm's Blade 1.25 3.00
7R232 Firefoot, Eomer's Steed .60 1.50
7R233 Grimbold, Marshal of Rohan 1.00 2.50
7R236 Herugrim, Sword of the Mark .60 1.50
7R239 Leowyn .60 1.50
7R241 Merry's Armor .75 2.00
7R242 Merry's Sword .75 2.00
7R249 Seeking New Foes .60 1.50
7R250 Snowmane .60 1.50
7R251 Stern People .60 1.50
7R255 Theoden, Rekindled King .60 1.50
7R260 Windfola .60 1.50
7R261 With Strength to Fight 1.00 2.50
7R266 Breached .60 1.50
7R267 Din of Arms 1.00 2.50
7R268 Encirclement .60 1.50
7R269 Fires Raged Unchecked .60 1.50
7R274 Gorgoroth Officer .60 1.50
7R279 Gorgoroth Troop 1.25 3.00
7R283 Legions of Morgul .60 1.50
7R284 Mordor Assassin .60 1.50
7R286 Mordor Fighter .60 1.50
7R306 Orc Seeker .60 1.50
7R308 Rally the Host .60 1.50
7R311 Siege Commander .60 1.50
7R314 Stronghold of Cirith Ungol .60 1.50
7R316 Troop Tower 2.00 5.00
7R318 Frodo, Wicked Masster! .60 1.50
7R321a Merry, Swordthain .75 2.00
7R321b Merry, Swordthain TENGWAR
7R324a Pippin, Wearer of Black and Silver 1.00 2.50
7R324b Pippin, Wearer of Black and Silver
TENGWAR
7R325 Pressing On .60 1.50
7R327 Sam, Resolute Halfling .60 1.50
7R79a Anduril, Flame of the West 5.00 10.00
7R79b Anduril, Flame of the West TENGWAR
7U102 Hasty Repairs .30 .75
7U107 Iorlas .30 .75
7U109 Long Prepared .30 .75
7U110 Madril, Faramir's Aide .30 .75
7U120 Stand to Arms .30 .75
7U123 Support of the City .30 .75
7U125 Third Level .30 .75
7U126 Unexpected Visitor .30 .75
7U128 While We Yet Live .30 .75
7U134 Desert Scout .30 .75
7U136 Desert Soldier .30 .75
7U138 Desert Villain .30 .75
7U146 Easterling Sergeant .30 .75
7U147 Easterling Veteran .30 .75
7U151 Hosts Still Unfought .30 .75
7U157 Red Wrath .30 .75
7U160 Southron Bandit .30 .75
7U162 Southron Captain .30 .75
7U168 Southron Thief .30 .75
7U171 Thrice Outnumbered .30 .75
7U174 Called .30 .75
7U175 Corrupt .30 .75
7U176 Disposable Servants .30 .75
7U178 Foul Clutches .30 .75
7U185 Morgul Answers .30 .75
7U187 Morgul Brawler .30 .75
7U190 Morgul Destroyer .30 .75
7U195 Morgul on the March .30 .75
7U202 Morgul Whelp .30 .75
7U203 Nazgul Scimitar .30 .75
7U207 Their Power Is in Terror .30 .75
7U212 Ulaire Enquea, Faster Than Winds .30 .75
7U214 Ulaire Lemenya, Wraith on Wings .30 .75
7U216 Ulaire Nelya, Black-Mantled Wraith .30 .75
7U217 Ulaire Nertea, Black-Mantled Wraith .30 .75
7U218 Ulaire Otsea, Black-Mantled Wraith .30 .75
7U224 Elfhelm, Marshal of Rohan .30 .75
7U231 Fey He Seemed .30 .75
7U234 Guarded Fastness .30 .75
7U238 Knights of His House .30 .75
7U244 Mustering for Battle .30 .75
7U245 Riding Armor .30 .75
7U252 Strong Arms .30 .75
7U254 Theoden, Leader of Spears .30 .75
7U258 White Hot Fury .30 .75
7U264 Army of Udun .30 .75
7U270 Gorgoroth Attacker .30 .75
7U271 Gorgoroth Axeman .30 .75
7U272 Gorgoroth Engineer .30 .75
7U278 Gorgoroth Soldier .30 .75
7U280 Great Peril of Fire .30 .75
7U281 Great Siege-towers .30 .75
7U282 Host of Udun .30 .75
7U289 Mordor Savage .30 .75
7U292 Mordor Veteran .30 .75
7U293 Mordor Warrior .30 .75
7U294 Orc Archer Troop .30 .75
7U295 Orc Assault Band .30 .75
7U301 Orc Marauder .30 .75
7U302 Orc Officer .30 .75
7U305 Orc Savage .30 .75
7U307 Orc Stalker .30 .75
7U309 Rope and Winch .30 .75
7U310 Sauron's Hatred .30 .75
7U328 Slow-kindled Courage .30 .75
7U329 Dunharrow Plateau .30 .75
7U330 Edoras Hall .30 .75
7U331 Isengard Ruined .30 .75
7U332 Rohirrim Road .30 .75
7U333 Sleeping Quarters .30 .75
7U334 Steps of Edoras .30 .75
7U335 King's Tent .30 .75
7U336 Rohirrim Camp .30 .75
7U337 West Road .30 .75
7U338 Beacon of Minas Tirith .30 .75
7U339 Hall of the Kings .30 .75
7U340 Tower of Ecthelion .30 .75
7U341 Anduin Banks .30 .75
7U342 Osgiliath Fallen .30 .75
7U343 Pelennor Plain .30 .75
7U344 City Gates .30 .75
7U345 Pelennor Flat .30 .75
7U346 Minas Tirith Fifth Circle .30 .75
7U347 Minas Tirith First Circle .30 .75
7U348 Minas Tirith Fourth Circle .30 .75
7U349 Minas Tirith Second Circle .30 .75
7U350 Minas Tirith Seventh Circle .30 .75
7U351 Minas Tirith Sixth Circle .30 .75
7U352 Minas Tirith Third Circle .30 .75
7U353 Osgiliath Crossing .30 .75

7U354 Pelennor Grassland .30 .75
7U355 Ruined Capitol .30 .75
7U356 Cross Roads .30 .75
7U357 Morgul Vale .30 .75
7U358 Morgulduin .30 .75
7U359 Northern Ithilien .30 .75
7U360 Dagorlad .30 .75
7U361 Haunted Pass .30 .75
7U362 Narchost .30 .75
7U363 Slag Mounds .30 .75

2004 Lord of the Rings Mount Doom

COMPLETE SET (124) 20.00 40.00
BOOSTER BOX (36 PACKS) 25.00 50.00
BOOSTER PACK (11 CARDS) 1.00 2.00
RELEASED ON JULY 14, 2004
10R1 Great Day, Great Hour .60 1.50
10R3 More Yet to Come .60 1.50
10R7 Celeborn, Lord of the Galadhrim .60 1.50
10R8 Cirdan, The Shipwright 2.00 5.00
10U2 Memories of Darkness .30 .75
10U4 Aegnor, Elven Escort .30 .75
10U5 Arwen, Echo of Luthien .30 .75
10C10 Fleet-footed .12 .30
10C16 Gathering Wind .12 .30
10C24 Unabated in Malice .12 .30
10C27 Dead Man of Dunharrow .12 .30
10C30 End of the Game .12 .30
10C31 Every Little is a Gain .12 .30
10C34 Last Throw .12 .30
10C36 Cast Unto the Winds .12 .30
10C37 Corsair Boatswain .12 .30
10C41 Easterling Pillager .12 .30
10C42 Far Harad Mercenaries .12 .30
10C49 Southron Fanatic .12 .30
10C50 Southron Savage .12 .30
10C52 Under Foot .12 .30
10C55 Cirith Ungol Soldier .12 .30
10C56 Cirith Ungol Warrior .12 .30
10C61 Houses of Lamentation .12 .30
10C62 Morgul Banner-bearer .12 .30
10C64 Stooping to the Kill .12 .30
10C65 Swarming Like Beetles .12 .30
10C66 Ten Times Outnumbered .12 .30
10C76 Advance Marauder .12 .30
10C77 Advance Regular .12 .30
10C79 Barren Land .12 .30
10C80 Beaten Back .12 .30
10C81 Cirith Ungol Guard .12 .30
10C84 Cirith Ungol Sentry .12 .30
10C85 Flames Within .12 .30
10C86 Gorgoroth Keeper .12 .30
10C87 Gorgoroth Swarm .12 .30
10C90 Mordor Brute .12 .30
10C91 Mordor Fiend .12 .30
10R11 Galadriel, Lady Redeemed .60 1.50
10R13 Phial of Galadriel, Star-glass .60 1.50
10R14 Borne Far Away .60 1.50
10R17 Out of the High Airs 1.25 3.00
10R18 Treebeard, Keeper of the Watchwood .60 1.50
10R19 A Dark Shape Sprang .60 1.50
10R21 Gollum, Mad Thing .60 1.50
10R23 Shelob, Her Ladyship 2.50 6.00
10R25a Aragorn, Elessar Telcontar .75 2.00
10R25b Aragorn, Elessar Telcontar TENGWAR
10R28 Denethor, Lord of Minas Tirith .60 1.50
10R29 Drawing His Eye .60 1.50
10R38 Corsair Brute .60 1.50
10R40 Easterling Berserker .60 1.50
10R45 Mumak Chieftain 1.25 3.00
10R46 Quelled .60 1.50
10R48 Seasoned Leader 1.25 3.00
10R51 Stampeded .60 1.50
10R58 Dark Swooping Shadows .60 1.50
10R59 Gorbag, Covetous Captain .60 1.50
10R60 Gorbag's Sword .60 1.50
10R63 Morgul Vanguard .60 1.50
10R67 Ulaire Cantea, Thrall of the One .60 1.50
10R68 Ulaire Enquea, Thrall of the One 5.00 10.00
10R6a Arwen, Queen of Elves and Men .75 2.00
10R6b Arwen, Queen of Elves and Men TENGWAR
10R71 Ulaire Toldea, Thrall of the One .60 1.50
10R72 Eowyn, Lady of Ithilien .60 1.50
10R75 Advance Captain .75 2.00
10R88a Gothmog, Lieutenant of Morgul 1.25 3.00
10R88b Gothmog, Lieutenant of Morgul TENGWAR
10R89 Gothmog's Warg .60 1.50
10R94 Orc Ravager .60 1.50
10R95 Orc Slaughterer .60 1.50
10R99 Shagrat, Captain of Cirith Ungol .60 1.50
10R9a Elrond, Venerable Lord .60 1.50
10R9b Elrond, Venerable Lord TENGWAR
10U12 Glimpse of Fate .30 .75
10U15 Brooding on Tomorrow .30 .75
10U20 Final Strike .30 .75
10U22 Reclaim the Precious .30 .75
10U26 Cursed of Erech .30 .75
10U32 Fifth Level .30 .75
10U33 Hardy Garrison .30 .75
10U35 Suffered Much Loss .30 .75
10U39 Corsair Ruffian .30 .75
10U43 Field of the Fallen .30 .75
10U44 High Vantage .30 .75
10U47 Rallying Call .30 .75
10U53 Black Marshal .30 .75
10U54 Cirith Ungol Scavenger .30 .75
10U57 Cirith Ungol Watchman .30 .75
10U69 Ulaire Lemenya, Thrall of the One .30 .75
10U70 Ulaire Nelya, Thrall of the One .30 .75
10U73 Fell Deeds Awake .30 .75
10U74 Unyielding .30 .75
10U78 Advance Scout .30 .75
10U82 Cirith Ungol Patroller .30 .75
10U83 Cirith Ungol Sentinel .30 .75
10U92 Mordor Pillager .30 .75
10U93 Mordor Wretch .30 .75
10U96 Rank and File .30 .75
10U97 The Ring is Mine! .30 .75
10U98 Ruinous Hail .30 .75
10C102 Uruk Axe .12 .30
10C103 Window of the Eye .12 .30
10C106 Chance Observation .12 .30
10C107 Great Heart .12 .30
10C109 Make Haste .12 .30
10C110 A Marvel .12 .30
10C112 Nine-fingered Frodo and the Ring of Doom .12 .30
10C113 Orc Armor .12 .30
10P121 Frodo, Resolute Hobbit 2.00 5.00
10P122a Sam, Great Elf Warrior .75 2.00
10P122b Sam, Great Elf Warrior TENGWAR
10R100 Speak No More to Me .60 1.50
10R101 Troll of Cirith Gorgor 2.00 5.00
10R104 Birthday Present .75 2.00
10U105 Brave and Loyal .30 .75
10U108 A Light in His Mind .30 .75
10U111 Narrow Escape .30 .75
10U114 Shadowplay .30 .75
10U115 Slunk Out of Sight .30 .75
10U116 The Tale of the Great Ring .30 .75
10U117 Base of Mindolluin .30 .75
10U118 Pelennor Prairie .30 .75
10U119 Steward's Tomb .30 .75
10U120 Watchers of Cirith Ungol .30 .75

2004 Lord of the Rings Reflections

COMPLETE SET (52) 40.00 80.00
BOOSTER BOX (24 PACKS) 50.00 100.00
BOOSTER PACK (11 CARDS) 2.50 5.00
RELEASED ON MAY 12, 2004
9R1 The One Ring, The Binding Ring 1.25 3.00
9R2 Freca, Hungry Savage 2.00 5.00
9R3 Durin III, Dwarven Lord 5.00 10.00
9R4 Gimli, Bearer of Grudges 1.50 4.00
9R5 Linnar, Dwarven Lord .40 1.00
9R6 Ring of Accretion .40 1.00
9R7 Ring of Fury 3.00 8.00
9R8 Ring of Guile .40 1.00
9R9 Ring of Retribution .40 1.00
9R10 Sindri, Dwarven Lord .40 1.00
9R11 Uri, Dwarven Lord .40 1.00
9R12 Aiglos 2.50 6.00
9R13 Elven Rope .40 1.00
9R14 Galadriel, Bearer of Wisdom 1.50 4.00
9R15 Gil-galad, Elven High King 5.00 10.00
9R16 Glorfindel, Revealed in Wrath 1.25 3.00
9R17 Knife of the Galadhrim 1.25 3.00
9R18 Merry's Dagger .40 1.00
9R19 Narya, Ring of Fire .40 1.00
9R20 Nenya, Ring of Adamant .40 1.00
9R21 Pippin's Dagger .40 1.00
9R22 Strands of Elven Hair .40 1.00
9R23 Vilya, Ring of Air .40 1.00
9R24 Ent Draught .40 1.00
9R25 Huorn .40 1.00
9R26 Radagast, The Brown 5.00 10.00
9R27 Sent Back .40 1.00
9R28 Gollum, Dark as Darkness 1.25 3.00
9R29 Slippery as Fishes 2.00 5.00
9R30 Smeagol, Bearer of Great Secrets 1.25 3.00
9R31 Boromir, Bearer of Council 2.00 5.00
9R32 Elendil, The Tall 1.00 2.50
9R33 Isildur, Bearer of Heirlooms 1.50 4.00
9R34 Narsil, Blade of the Faithful 2.00 5.00
9R35 Sapling of the White Tree .40 1.00
9R36 Scroll of Isildur .40 1.00
9R37 Seeing Stone of Minas Anor .40 1.00
9R38 Seeing Stone of Orthanc .40 1.00
9R39 Library of Orthanc .40 1.00
9R40 Sack of the Shire .40 1.00
9R41 Host of Moria, Legion of the Underdeeps 2.50 6.00
9R42 Ring of Asperity .40 1.00
9R43 Ring of Ire .75 2.00
9R44 Ring of Rancor .40 1.00
9R45 Horn of the Mark .40 1.00
9R46 The Red Arrow .40 1.00
9R47 Ithil Stone 2.50 6.00
9R48 Sauron, The Lord of the Rings 5.00 10.00
9R49 Bilbo, Bearer of Things Burgled .75 2.00
9R50 Everyone Knows .40 1.00
9R51 Goldberry, River-daughter .40 1.00
9R52 Tom Bombadil, The Master .75 2.00

2004 Lord of the Rings Seige of Gondor

COMPLETE SET (122) 20.00 40.00
BOOSTER BOX (36 PACKS) 25.00 50.00
BOOSTER PACK (11 CARDS) 1.00 2.00
RELEASED ON MARCH 10, 2004
8C1 Aggression .12 .30
8C5 Gimli, Counter of Foes .12 .30
8C6 Honed .12 .30
8R2 Battle in Earnest .60 1.50
8R3 Blood Runs Chill 2.50 6.00
8R7 Unheard of .60 1.50
8U4 Counts But One .30 .75
8U8 Wish For Our Kinfolk .30 .75
8U9 A Grey Ship .30 .75
8C10 Legolas, Elven Stalwart .12 .30
8C14 A Fool .12 .30
8C22 Hidden Even From Her .12 .30
8C26 Shelob, Last Child of Ungoliant .12 .30
8C28 Spider Poison .12 .30
8C30 Web .12 .30
8C31 At His Command .12 .30
8C34 Faramir, Defender of Osgiliath .12 .30
8C35 Fourth Level .12 .30
8C39 Knight of Dol Amroth .12 .30
8C40 Knight's Mount .12 .30
8C41 Oathbreaker .12 .30
8C47 Stronger and More Terrible .12 .30
8C48 Swept Away .12 .30
8C50 Black Sails of Umbar .12 .30
8C52 Corsair Ballista .12 .30
8C53 Corsair Buccaneer .12 .30
8C54 Corsair Freebooter .12 .30
8C55 Corsair Gunners .12 .30
8C58 Corsair Plunderer .12 .30
8C61 Haradwaith .12 .30
8C63 Line of Defense .12 .30
8C66 Wind That Sped Ships .12 .30
8C74 Morgul Ambusher .12 .30
8C75 Morgul Creeper .12 .30
8C76 Morgul Lurker .12 .30
8C87 Eomer, Keeper of Oaths .12 .30
8C89 Fury of the Northmen .12 .30
8C90 No Living Man .12 .30
8R11 Life of the Eldar .60 1.50
8R12 Reckless We Rode .60 1.50
8R15a Gandalf, Leader of Men 1.25 3.00
8R15b Gandalf, Leader of Men TENGWAR
8R20 Saved From the Fire 5.00 10.00
8R21 Shadowfax, Greatheart .60 1.50
8R24 Promise Keeping 1.25 3.00
8R25a Shelob, Eater of Light 1.25 3.00
8R25b Shelob, Eater of Light TENGWAR
8R27 Smeagol, Slippery Sneak .60 1.50
8R32 Catapult .60 1.50
8R33 Elessar's Edict .60 1.50
8R36 Garrison of Gondor 1.50 4.00
8R37 Imrahil, Prince of Dol Amroth .60 1.50
8R38a King of the Dead, Oathbreaker 1.25 3.00
8R38b King of the Dead, Oathbreaker TENGWAR
8R43 Shadow Host .75 2.00
8R49 Black Numenorean 1.50 4.00
8R51a Castamir of Umbar 1.50 4.00
8R51b Castamir of Umbar TENGWAR
8R57a Corsair Marauder 3.00 8.00
8R57b Corsair Marauder TENGWAR
8R62 Heavy Axeman .60 1.50
8R65 Ships of Great Draught 3.00 8.00
8R67 Between Nazgul and Prey 2.00 5.00
8R68 Beyond All Darkness .75 2.00
8R70 Black Flail .75 2.00
8R72 Gothmog, Morgul Commander 1.00 2.50
8R77 Morgul Squealer .75 2.00
8R81 Ulaire Otsea, Thrall of the One .60 1.50
8R84 The Witch-king, Black Captain 1.00 2.50
8R88 Eowyn's Shield .60 1.50
8R91 Rohirrim Army .75 2.00
8R92 Theoden, Tall and Proud 1.00 2.50
8R93 Called Away .60 1.50
8R95 Gorgoroth Assassin 1.00 2.50
8R96 Gorgoroth Berserker .60 1.50
8U100 Gorgoroth Servitor .30 .75
8U107 Their Marching Companies .30 .75
8U110 Morgai Foothills .30 .75
8U112 Song of the Shire .30 .75
8U117 The Dimholt .30 .75
8U118 City of the Dead .30 .75
8U119 Crashed Gate .30 .75
8U120 Osgiliath Channel .30 .75
8U13 Shake Off the Shadow .30 .75
8U16 Let Us Not Tarry .30 .75
8U17 Mighty Steed .30 .75
8U18 Not the First Halfling .30 .75
8U19 On Your Doorstep .30 .75
8U23 Larder .30 .75
8U29 Still Far Ahead .30 .75
8U42 A Path Appointed .30 .75
8U44 Sixth Level .30 .75
8U45 Sleepless Dead .30 .75
8U46 Spectral Sword .30 .75
8U56 Corsair Lookout .30 .75
8U59 Corsair War Galley .30 .75
8U60 Haradrim Marksman .30 .75
8U64 Mumakil .30 .75
8U69 Black Dart .30 .75
8U71 Flung Into the Fray .30 .75
8U73 Mastered By Madness .30 .75
8U78 Streaming to the Field .30 .75
8U79 Ulaire Attea, Thrall of the One .30 .75
8U80 Ulaire Nertea, Thrall of the One .30 .75
8U82 Unhindered .30 .75
8U83 Winged Mount .30 .75
8U85 Charged Headlong .30 .75
8U86 Doom Drove Them .30 .75
8U94 Gorgoroth Agitator .30 .75
8U97 Gorgoroth Breaker .30 .75
8U98 Gorgoroth Looter .30 .75
8U99 Gorgoroth Patrol .30 .75
8C101 Gorgoroth Stormer .12 .30
8C102 Great Hill Troll .12 .30
8C104 Morgai .12 .30
8C106 Siege Troop .12 .30
8C109 Closer and Closer He Bent .12 .30
8C111 So Fair, So Desperate .12 .30
8C114 Straining Towards Us .12 .30
8C116 We Shall Meet Again Soon .12 .30
8P121 Merry, Noble Warrior .40 1.00
8P122 Pippin, Guard of Minas Tirith .40 1.00
8R103a Grond, Hammer of the Underworld 1.00 2.50
8R103b Grond, Hammer of the Underworld TENGWAR
8R105 Olog-hai of Mordor .75 2.00
8R108 Troll of Gorgoroth, Abomination of Sauron .75 2.00
8R113 Sting, Bane of the Eight Legs 1.25 3.00
8R115 Unheeded .75 2.00

2004 Lord of the Rings Shadows

COMPLETE SET (266) 20.00 40.00
BOOSTER BOX (36 PACKS) 20.00 40.00
BOOSTER PACK (11 CARDS) 1.00 2.00
RELEASED ON NOVEMBER 3, 2004
11C4 Battle to the Last .12 .30
11C5 Dwarven Embassy .12 .30
11C7 Farin, Emissary of Erebor .12 .30
11R1a The One Ring, The Ring of Rings 2.50 6.00
11R1b The One Ring, The Ring of Rings TENGWAR
11R9 Gimli's Battle Axe, Vicious Weapon .60 1.50
11S2 The One Ring, The Ruling Ring .40 1.00
11U3 Axe of Khazad-dum .30 .75
11U6 Fallen Lord .30 .75
11U8 Gimli, Lively Combatant .30 .75
11C13 On Guard .12 .30
11C19 Farewell to Lorien .12 .30
11C27 Woodland Sentinel .12 .30
11C31 Final Account .12 .30
11C36 Inspiration .12 .30
11C39 Prolonged Struggle .12 .30
11C46 Master Commands It .12 .30
11C62 Madril, Ranger of Ithilien .12 .30
11C63 Much-needed Rest .12 .30
11C71 Bold and Cunning .12 .30
11C72 Column of Easterlings .12 .30
11C73 Corps of Harad .12 .30
11C76 Easterling Shield Wall .12 .30
11C79 Fearsome Dunlending .12 .30
11C83 Force of Harad .12 .30
11C85 Horde of Harad .12 .30
11C86 Invading Haradrim .12 .30
11C88 Legion of Harad .12 .30
11C89 Long Battle Bow .12 .30
11C93 Patroller of Haradrim .12 .30
11C94 Pavise .12 .30
11C98 Rampaging Easterling .12 .30
11R10 Grimir, Dwarven Emissary .60 1.50
11R11 Hall of Our Fathers .60 1.50
11R14 Well-equipped .60 1.50
11R17 Elven Marksmanship .60 1.50
11R22 Legolas, Woodland Emissary .60 1.50
11R23 Legolas' Bow .60 1.50
11R24 Might of the Elf-lords .60 1.50
11R30 Erland, Dale Counselor .75 2.00
11R34 Gandalf's Staff, Ash-Staff .60 1.50
11R35 Glamdring, Foe-hammer 1.25 3.00
11R42 Gollum, Skulker .60 1.50
11R43 Horribly Strong .75 2.00
11R44 Incited .60 1.50
11R48 Not Yet Vanquished .60 1.50
11R50 Safe Passage .60 1.50
11R51 Smeagol, Scout and Guide .60 1.50
11R54a Aragorn, Strider 2.50 6.00
11R54b Aragorn, Strider TENGWAR
11R57a Boromir, Hero of Osgiliath 1.25 3.00
11R57b Boromir, Hero of Osgiliath TENGWAR
11R60 The Highest Quality .60 1.50
11R66 Well-traveled 1.00 2.50
11R68 Armored Easterling .60 1.50
11R70 Bloodthirsty .60 1.50
11R75 Easterling Host .60 1.50
11R78 Elevated Fire 1.50 4.00
11R81 Fletcher of Harad .60 1.50
11R91 Oath Sworn .60 1.50
11R96 Precision Targeting .75 2.00
11S18 Elven Scout .40 1.00
11S20 The Lady's Blessing .40 1.00
11S21 Legolas, Companion of the Ring .40 1.00
11S32 G for Grand .40 1.00
11S33a Gandalf, Leader of the Company .75 2.00
11S33b Gandalf, Leader of the Company TENGWAR
11S53 Aragorn, Guide and Protector .40 1.00
11S56 Battle Cry .40 1.00
11S64 Pledge of Loyalty .60 1.50
11S65 Ranger of Westernesse .40 1.00
11S77 Elder of Dunland .40 1.00
11S82 Footman of Dunland .40 1.00
11S84 Harad Standard-bearer .40 1.00
11S90 Man of Bree .40 1.00
11S92 Overrun .40 1.00
11S95 Poleaxe .40 1.00
11S97 Raging Dunlending .40 1.00
11U12 Mountain Homestead .30 .75
11U15 Arwen, Staunch Defender .30 .75
11U16 Blade of Lindon .30 .75
11U25 Nocked .30 .75
11U26 Uncertain Future .30 .75
11U28 The Art of Gandalf .30 .75
11U29 Ease the Burden .30 .75
11U37 New Authority .30 .75
11U38 New-awakened .30 .75
11U40 Shadowfax, Unequaled Steed .30 .75
11U41 Frenzied Attack .30 .75
11U45 Led Astray .30 .75
11U47 No End of Wickedness .30 .75
11U49 One Good Turn Deserves Another .30 .75
11U52 Strange and Terrible .30 .75
11U55 Armor of the Citadel .30 .75
11U58 Bow of Minas Tirith .30 .75
11U59 Gondorian Blade .30 .75
11U61 Houses of Healing .30 .75
11U67 Archer of Harad .30 .75
11U69 Axeman of Harad .30 .75
11U74 Detachment of Haradrim .30 .75
11U80 Ferocious Haradrim .30 .75
11U87 Lathspell .30 .75
11U99 Squad of Haradrim .30 .75
11C101 Swarthy Bree-lander .12 .30
11C102 Throng of Harad .12 .30
11C103 Warrior of Dunland .12 .30
11C107 Barbarous Orc .12 .30
11C111 Champion Orc .12 .30
11C113 Cutthroat Orc .12 .30
11C120 Entrapping Orc .12 .30
11C121 Foraging Orc .12 .30
11C122 Frenzied Orc .12 .30
11C125 Isengard Underling .12 .30
11C127 Mocking Goblin .12 .30
11C128 Mordor Scimitar .12 .30
11C129 Mountain Orc .12 .30
11C131 Orc Miscreant .12 .30
11C132 Orkish Smith .12 .30
11C136 Prowling Orc .12 .30
11C140 Strength in Shadows .12 .30
11C148 Hrothlac, Man of Rohan .12 .30
11C155 Riding Like the Wind .12 .30
11C157 Rush of Steeds .12 .30
11C162 Crouched Down .12 .30
11C167 Incognito .12 .30
11C168 Merry, Loyal Companion .12 .30
11C169 The More, The Merrier .12 .30
11C192 Isengard Sword .12 .30
11C195 Murderous Uruk .12 .30
11C196 Our Foes Are Weak .12 .30
11C198 Patrol of Uruk-hai .12 .30
11C199 Relentless Uruk .12 .30
11C200 Ruthless Uruk .12 .30
11C201 Sentinel Uruk .12 .30
11C202 Squad of Uruk-hai .12 .30
11C203 Swarming Uruk .12 .30
11C204 Tyrannical Uruk .12 .30
11C206 Watchman Uruk .12 .30
11R100 Strange-looking Men .60 1.50
11R108 Beastly Olog-hai 1.25 3.00
11R119 Emboldened Orc 1.00 2.50
11R123a Goblin Hordes 6.00 12.00
11R123b Goblin Hordes TENGWAR
11R133 Orkish Worker .60 1.50
11R134 Persistent Orc .60 1.50
11R135 Porter Troll 1.00 2.50
11R141 Undisciplined .60 1.50
11R143 Watchful Orc .75 2.00
11R147 Gamling, Defender of the Hornburg .60 1.50
11R154 Riders of the Mark .60 1.50
11R158 Sword Rack .60 1.50
11R165 Habits of Home .60 1.50
11R170 Pippin, Brave Decoy .60 1.50
11R171 Salt from the Shire .60 1.50
11R173 Sting, Weapon of Heritage .75 2.00
11R177 Army of Uruk-hai .60 1.50
11R179 Brawling Uruk .60 1.50
11R181 Determined Uruk .60 1.50
11R184 Force of Uruk-hai .60 1.50
11R186 Furious Uruk .60 1.50
11R194 Lurtz, Minion of the White Wizard .75 2.00
11R205 Vigilant Uruk .60 1.50
11R207 Dark Powers Strengthen .60 1.50
11R211 Keening Wail 1.25 3.00
11R214 The Pale Blade, Sword of Flame .60 1.50
11R216 A Shadow Rises .60 1.50
11R217 Shapes Slowly Advancing .75 2.00
11R219 Ulaire Attea, Second of the Nine Riders .60 1.50
11R224 Ulaire Otsea, Seventh of the Nine Riders .75 2.00
11R226a The Witch-king, Captain of the Nine Riders 3.00 8.00
11R226b The Witch-king, Captain of the Nine Riders TENGWAR
11S112 Conquered Halls .40 1.00
11S115 Denizen of Khazad-dum .40 1.00
11S116 Denizen of Moria .40 1.00
11S117 Denizen of the Black Pit .40 1.00
11S126 Marauding Orcs .40 1.00
11S130 Orc Hammer .40 1.00
11S138 Skulking Goblin .40 1.00
11S142 Unyielding Goblin .40 1.00
11S146 Eowyn, Shieldmaiden of Rohan .40 1.00
11S150 Rally Cry .40 1.00
11S152 Riddermark Soldier .40 1.00
11S153 Rider's Spear .40 1.00
11S160 War Now Calls Us .40 1.00
11S161 Concerning Hobbits .40 1.00
11S164 Frodo, Protected by Many .40 1.00
11S166 Hobbit Sword .40 1.00
11S174 Sworn Companion .40 1.00
11S176 Unharmed .40 1.00
11S178 Bloodthirsty Uruk .40 1.00
11S180 Brutality .40 1.00
11S183 Feral Uruk .40 1.00
11S187 Furor .40 1.00
11S188 Hounding Uruk .40 1.00
11S190 Invincible Uruk .40 1.00
11S193 Lookout Uruk .40 1.00
11S209 Drawn to its Power .40 1.00
11S213 Moving This Way .40 1.00
11S215 Riders in Black .40 1.00
11S220 Ulaire Cantea, Fourth of the Nine Riders .40 1.00
11S221 Ulaire Lemenya, Fifth of the Nine Riders .40 1.00
11S222 Ulaire Nelya, Third of the Nine Riders .60 1.50
11S223 Ulaire Nertea, Ninth of the Nine Riders .40 1.00
11S225 Ulaire Toldea, Eighth of the Nine Riders .40 1.00
11S228 Anduin Confluence .60 1.50
11S229 Barazinbar .40 1.00
11S230 Buckland Homestead .40 1.00
11S231 Caras Galadhon .40 1.00
11S232 Cavern Entrance .40 1.00
11S233 Chamber of Mazarbul .40 1.00
11S234 Crags of Emyn Muil .40 1.00
11S236 East Road .40 1.00
11S237 Ettenmoors .40 1.00
11S238 Expanding Marshland .40 1.00
11S239 Fangorn Glade .40 1.00
11S240 Flats of Rohan .40 1.00
11S241 Fortress of Orthanc .40 1.00
11S242 Green Dragon Inn .40 1.00
11S243 Harrowdale .40 1.00
11S245 Helm's Gate .40 1.00
11S247 Moria Guardroom .40 1.00
11S248 Moria Stairway .40 1.00
11S249 Neekerbreekers' Bog .75 2.00
11S250 North Undeep .40 1.00
11S251 Old Forest Road .40 1.00
11S252 Osgiliath Reclaimed .40 1.00
11S253 Pelennor Fields .40 1.00
11S254 Pelennor Flat .40 1.00
11S255 Pinnacle of Zirakzigil .40 1.00
11S256 The Prancing Pony .40 1.00
11S257 Rohan Uplands .40 1.00
11S258 Slag Mounds .40 1.00
11S259 Stables .40 1.00
11S260 Trollshaw Forest .40 1.00
11S261 Valley of the Silverlode .40 1.00
11S262 Watch-tower of Cirith Ungol .40 1.00

11S263 West Gate of Moria .40 1.00
11S264 Westemnet Village .40 1.00
11S265 Window on the West .40 1.00
11S266 Woody-End .60 1.50
11U104 Whistling Death .30 .75
11U105 Wielding the Ring .30 .75
11U106 Armed for Battle .30 .75
11U109 Bladed Gauntlets .30 .75
11U110 Bound to its Fate .30 .75
11U114 Demoralized .30 .75
11U118 Dread and Despair .30 .75
11U124 Hill Orc .30 .75
11U137 Scurrying Goblin .30 .75
11U139 Spurred to Battle .30 .75
11U144 Border Patrol .30 .75
11U145 Eomer, Guardian of the Eastmark .30 .75
11U149 Protecting the Hall .30 .75
11U151 Riddermark Javelin .30 .75
11U156 Rohirrim Mount .30 .75
11U159 Theoden, King of the Eorlingas .30 .75
11U163 Farmer Maggot, Hobbit of the Marish .30 .75
11U172 Sam, Steadfast Friend .30 .75
11U175 A Task Now to Be Done .30 .75
11U182 Devastation .30 .75
11U185 Fortitude .30 .75
11U189 Intimidating Uruk .30 .75
11U191 Isengard Siege Bow .30 .75
11U197 Overpowering Uruk .30 .75
11U208 Dark Wings .30 .75
11U210 Hatred Stirred .30 .75
11U212 Lost in the Woods .30 .75
11U218 Surrounded by Wraiths .30 .75
11U227 Anduin Banks .30 .75
11U235 Dammed Gate-stream .30 .75
11U244 Heights of Isengard .30 .75
11U246 Mere of Dead Faces .30 .75

2004 Lord of the Rings Shadows Foil

COMPLETE SET (18) 15.00 30.00
RELEASED ON NOVEMBER 3, 2004
11RF1 The One Ring, The Ring of Rings F 2.00 5.00
11RF2 Elven Marksmanship F 1.25 3.00
11RF3 Legolas, Woodland Emissary F .60 1.50
11RF4 Glamdring, Foe-hammer F 1.50 4.00
11RF5 Gollum, Skulker F .60 1.50
11RF6 Smeagol, Scout and Guide F .75 2.00
11RF7 Aragorn, Strider F 2.00 5.00
11RF8 Bloodthirsty F .60 1.50
11RF9 Fletcher of Harad F .75 2.00
11RF10 Porter Troll F 1.00 2.50
11RF11 Undisciplined F .60 1.50
11RF12 Gamling, Defender of the Hornburg F .60 1.50
11RF13 Sword Rack F .60 1.50
11RF14 Salt from the Shire F .75 2.00
11RF15 Brawling Uruk F .60 1.50
11RF16 Lurtz, Minion of the White Wizard F .75 2.00
11RF17 The Pale Blade, Sword of Flame F .75 2.00
11RF18 The Witch-king, Captain of the Nine Riders F3.00 8.00

2005 Lord of the Rings Black Rider

COMPLETE SET (194) 20.00 40.00
BOOSTER BOX (36 PACKS) 20.00 40.00
BOOSTER PACK (11 CARDS) 1.00 2.00
RELEASED ON MARCH 18, 2005
12C4 Durability .12 .30
12C6 Dwarven Skill .12 .30
12C7 Dwarven Warrior .12 .30
12C8 His Father's Charge .12 .30
12R9 Loud and Strong .60 1.50
12U1 Argument Ready to Hand .30 .75
12U2 Belt of Erebor .30 .75
12U3 A Clamour of Many Voices .30 .75
12U5 Dwarven Bracers .30 .75
12C16 Attunement .12 .30
12C20 Orophin, Brother of Haldir .12 .30
12C22 Rumil, Brother of Haldir .12 .30
12C31 Mysterious Wizard .12 .30
12C32 Salve .12 .30
12C33 The Terror of His Coming .12 .30
12C34 Traveled Leader .12 .30
12C40 There's Another Way .12 .30
12C44 Concealment .12 .30
12C45 Confronting the Eye .12 .30
12C46 Elendil's Valor .12 .30
12C52 Tireless .12 .30
12C53 Valorous Leader .12 .30
12C59 Covetous Easterling .12 .30
12C60 Crazed Hillman .12 .30
12C61 Crooked Townsman .12 .30
12C64 Enraged Southron .12 .30
12C67 Goaded to War .12 .30
12C70 Hemmed In .12 .30
12C77 War Trident .12 .30
12C78 Wrathful Hillman .12 .30
12C84 Bloodstained Field .12 .30
12C87 Goblin Aggressor .12 .30
12C88 Great Cost .12 .30
12C92 Orc Dreg .12 .30
12C93 Orc Footman .12 .30
12C95 Orc Skulker .12 .30
12C96 Orc Spear .12 .30
12C98 Orc Tormentor .12 .30
12R10 No Pauses, No Spills 5.00 10.00
12R17a Elrond, Witness to History 1.25 3.00
12R17b Elrond, Witness to History TENGWAR
12R18 Hadafang 1.25 3.00
12R19 Long-knives of Legolas .60 1.50
12R26 Discoveries .60 1.50
12R27 Gandalf, The White Rider .60 1.50
12R28 Gandalf's Hat .60 1.50
12R30 Jarnsmid, Barding Emissary .60 1.50
12R35a Watch and Wait 1.50 4.00
12R35b Watch and Wait TENGWAR
12R37 Come Away .60 1.50
12R38 From Deep in Shadow .60 1.50
12R42 Blade of Gondor, Sword of Boromir .75 2.00
12R47 Faramir, Dunadan of Gondor .60 1.50
12R48 Faramir's Sword .75 2.00
12R54a Saruman, of Many Colours .75 2.00
12R54b Saruman, of Many Colours TENGWAR
12R56 Castamir of Umbar, Corsair Vandal .75 2.00
12R57 Corrupted Spy .60 1.50
12R68 Grima, Betrayer of Rohan .60 1.50
12R69 Harrying Hillman .60 1.50
12R72 Messenger's Mount .60 1.50
12R74 Mumak Rider 2.00 5.00
12R75 Poisonous Words .60 1.50
12R79 The Balrog, The Terror of Khazad-dum 1.00 2.50
12R80 Whip of Many Thongs, Weapon of Flame and Shadow 1.25 3.00
12R81 Abiding Evil .75 2.00
12R82 Barrage .75 2.00
12R83 The Beckoning Shadow .60 1.50
12R85 Cave Troll of Moria, Savage Menace 1.25 3.00
12R86 Cave Troll's Hammer, Unwieldy Cudgel .60 1.50
12R91 Orc Artisan .60 1.50
12S55 Brutal Easterling .40 1.00
12S65 Frenzied Dunlending .40 1.00
12S73a The Mouth of Sauron, Messenger of Mordor.40 1.00
12S73b The Mouth of Sauron, Messenger of Mordor TENGWAR
12U11 Nobody Tosses a Dwarf .30 .75
12U12 Proud and Able .30 .75
12U13 Sharp Defense .30 .75
12U14 Stalwart Support .30 .75
12U15 Thrarin, Smith of Erebor .30 .75
12U21 Refuge .30 .75
12U23 Seclusion .30 .75
12U24 Taking the High Ground .30 .75
12U25 Betrayal of Isengard .30 .75
12U29 Introspection .30 .75
12U36 With Doom We Come .30 .75
12U39 Not Alone .30 .75
12U41 Treacherous Little Toad .30 .75
12U43 Boromir, Defender of Minas Tirith .30 .75
12U49 Gondorian Steed .30 .75
12U50 Guardian .30 .75
12U51 Invigorated .30 .75
12U58 Countless Companies .30 .75
12U62 Dunlending Zealot .30 .75
12U63 Easterling Banner-bearer .30 .75
12U66 Gathering Strength .30 .75
12U71 Last Days .30 .75
12U76 Trail of Terror .30 .75
12U79 The Balrog, The Terror of Khazad-dum TENGWAR
12U89 Mordor Aggressor .30 .75
12U90 Morgul Tormentor .30 .75
12U94 Orc Sapper .30 .75
12U97 Orc Strategist .30 .75
12U99 Pitiless Orc .30 .75
12C102 Scavenging Goblins .12 .30
12C106 Vile Goblin .12 .30
12C107 Aldred, Eored Soldier .12 .30
12C109 Challenging the Orc-host .12 .30
12C110 Cleaving a Path .12 .30
12C114 For the Mark .12 .30
12C115 Golden Glimmer .12 .30
12C121 Flotsam and Jetsam .12 .30
12C122 Home and Hearth .12 .30
12C123 Hope is Kindled .12 .30
12C134 Advancing Uruk .12 .30
12C137 Breeding Pit Conscript .12 .30
12C142 Merciless Uruk .12 .30
12C143 Quelling Force .12 .30
12C145 Shingle in a Storm .12 .30
12C146 Strange Device .12 .30
12C149 Uruk Common .12 .30
12C153 Uruk Pikeman .12 .30
12C159 Weapon of Opportunity .12 .30
12C160 Worthy of Mordor .12 .30
12C164 Echo of Hooves .12 .30
12C168 Nazgul Blade .12 .30
12C172 Steed of Mordor .12 .30
12C177 Ulaire Nelya, Black Hunter .12 .30
12C178 Ulaire Nertea, Black Horseman .12 .30
12C181 Unending Life .12 .30
12C182 Unimpeded .12 .30
12R100 Rallying Orc 3.00 8.00
12R101 Retribution 2.00 5.00
12R105 Troll's Keyward, Keeper of the Beast 1.00 2.50
12R108 Cast Out .60 1.50
12R111 Coif .75 2.00
12R116 Haethen, Veteran Fighter .75 2.00
12R118 The Mouth of Sauron, Lieutenant of Barad-dur 1.25 3.00
12R119 Bilbo, Melancholy Hobbit .60 1.50
12R120 Diversion .60 1.50
12R124 Long Live the Halflings .60 1.50
12R127 Pippin, Hobbit of Some Intelligence .60 1.50
12R128 A Promise 1.00 2.50
12R129 Rosie Cotton, Barmaid .75 2.00
12R139 Broken in Defeat .60 1.50
12R141 Dark Alliance .60 1.50
12R150 Uruk Decimator .60 1.50
12R154 Uruk Slaughterer .60 1.50
12R155 Uruk Zealot .60 1.50
12R156 Uruk-hai Guard .60 1.50
12R157 Uruk-hai Troop .60 1.50
12R162 Dark Approach 7.50 15.00
12R163 Dark Temptation 1.00 2.50
12R169 Sauron's Gaze .60 1.50
12R171 Shadowy Mount 1.25 3.00
12R173 Ulaire Attea, Black Predator .60 1.50
12R174a Ulaire Cantea, Black Assassin 1.50 4.00
12R174b Ulaire Cantea, Black Assassin TENGWAR
12R175 Ulaire Enquea, Black Threat .75 2.00
12R179 Ulaire Otsea, Black Specter .60 1.50
12R183 The Witch-king, Black Lord 1.25 3.00
12S113 Eored Warrior .40 1.00
12S125 Measure of Comfort .40 1.00
12S126 No Worse for Wear .40 1.00
12S133 Tolman Cotton, Farmer of Bywater .40 1.00
12S144 Saruman, Agent of the Dark Lord .40 1.00
12S151 Uruk Desecrator .40 1.00
12S152 Uruk Dominator .40 1.00
12S187 Emyn Muil .40 1.00
12S188 Hill of Sight .40 1.00
12S189 Hobbiton Market .40 1.00
12S190 Northern Pelennor .40 1.00
12U103 Storming the Ramparts .30 .75
12U104 Taunt .30 .75
12U112 Eomer, Eored Leader .30 .75
12U117 Leofric, Defender of the Mark .30 .75
12U130 Simple Living .30 .75
12U131 Stand Together .30 .75
12U132 Sudden Fury .30 .75
12U135 Barbaric Uruk .30 .75
12U136 Berserker Torch .30 .75
12U138 Broken Heirloom .30 .75
12U140 Crushing Uruk .30 .75
12U147 Suppressing Uruk .30 .75
12U148 Tempest of War .30 .75
12U158 Vicious Uruk .30 .75
12U161 Black Rider .30 .75
12U165 In the Ringwraith's Wake .30 .75
12U166 Lingering Shadow .30 .75
12U167 Minas Morgul Answers .30 .75
12U170 Sense of Obligation .30 .75
12U176 Ulaire Lemenya, Black Enemy .30 .75
12U180 Ulaire Toldea, Black Shadow .30 .75
12U184 The Witch-king's Beast, Fell Creature .30 .75
12U185 The Angle .30 .75
12U186 The Bridge of Khazad-dum .30 .75
12U191 Shores of Nen Hithoel .30 .75
12U192 Slopes of Orodruin .30 .75
12U193 Starkhorn .30 .75
12U194 Wold Battlefield .30 .75

2005 Lord of the Rings Black Rider Legends Foil

COMPLETE SET (18) 20.00 40.00
RELEASED ON MARCH 18, 2005
12RF1 Elrond, Witness to History F 1.50 4.00
12RF2 Hadafang F 2.50 6.00
12RF3 Gandalf, The White Rider F .75 2.00
12RF4 Faramir, Dunadan of Gondor F 1.00 2.50
12RF5 Faramir's Sword F 1.25 3.00
12RF6 Castamir of Umbar, Corsair Vandal F 2.00 5.00
12RF7 Grima, Betrayer of Rohan F .60 1.50
12RF8 The Balrog, The Terror of Khazad-dum F 1.50 4.00
12RF9 Cave Troll of Moria, Savage Menace F 5.00 10.00
12RF10 Orc Artisan F 1.25 3.00
12RF11 The Mouth of Sauron, Lieutenant of Barad-dur F 1.25 3.00
12RF12 Bilbo, Melancholy Hobbit F .60 1.50
12RF13 Uruk Zealot F .60 1.50
12RF14 Dark Approach F 7.50 15.00
12RF15 Ulaire Attea, Black Predator F .60 1.50
12RF16 Ulaire Cantea, Black Assassin F 3.00 8.00
12RF17 Ulaire Enquea, Black Threat F 1.00 2.50
12RF18 The Witch-king, Black Lord F 2.50 6.00

2005 Lord of the Rings Black Rider Legends Masterworks Foil

COMPLETE SET (9) 25.00 50.00
RELEASED ON MARCH 18, 2005
12O1 Gandalf, The White Rider O 5.00 10.00
12O2 Faramir, Dunadan of Gondor O 5.00 10.00
12O3 Faramir's Sword O 3.00 8.00
12O4 The Balrog, The Terror of Khazad-dum O 5.00 10.00
12O5 Dark Approach O 7.50 15.00
12O6 Ulaire Attea, Black Predator O 3.00 8.00
12O7 Ulaire Cantea, Black Assassin O 6.00 12.00
12O8 Ulaire Enquea, Black Threat O 3.00 8.00
12O9 The Witch-king, Black Lord O 7.50 15.00

2005 Lord of the Rings Bloodlines

COMPLETE SET (194) 100.00 200.00
BOOSTER BOX (36 PACKS) 30.00 60.00
BOOSTER PACK (11 CARDS) 1.25 2.50
RELEASED ON AUGUST 12, 2005
13C2 Awkward Moment .12 .30
13C6 Honoring His Kinfolk .12 .30
13C7 Sorrow Shared .12 .30
13R1 Arod, Rohirrim Steed 1.50 4.00
13R5a Gimli, Lord of the Glittering Caves 2.00 5.00
13R5b Gimli, Lord of the Glittering Caves TENGWAR
13R8 Subterranean Homestead .60 1.50
13S9 Arwen, Reflection of Luthien .40 1.00
13U3 Deep Hatred .30 .75
13U4 Dwarf-lords .30 .75
13C12 City of the Trees .12 .30
13C13 Crashing Cavalry .12 .30
13C14 Final Shot .12 .30
13C16 Inside a Song .12 .30
13C21 Many Miles .12 .30
13C23 Shrouded Elf .12 .30
13C24 Sprang Forth Nimbly .12 .30
13C25 Standing Tall .12 .30
13C29 Dasron, Merchant from Dorwinion .12 .30
13C30 Fear and Great Wonder .12 .30
13C32 For a While Less Dark .12 .30
13C35 No Colour Now .12 .30
13C39 Return to Us .12 .30
13C41 Strange Meeting .12 .30
13C47 Duality .12 .30
13C51 It's My Birthday .12 .30
13C54 Out of All Knowledge .12 .30
13C66 Faramir, Prince of Ithilien .12 .30
13C68 Guarded City .12 .30
13C69 Heirs of Gondor .12 .30
13C73 Kingsfoil .12 .30
13C77 Tradesman From Lebennin .12 .30
13C82 Bring Down the Wall .12 .30
13C83 Caravan From the South .12 .30
13C87 Driven From the Plains .12 .30
13C90 Easterling Runner .12 .30
13C96 Merciless Dunlending .12 .30
13C97 Pirate Cutthroat .12 .30
13R10 Asfaloth, Swift Blossom .60 1.50
13R11 Celeborn, The Wise 1.00 2.50
13R15 Galadriel, Sorceress of the Hidden Land .75 2.00
13R18 Legolas, of the Grey Company 1.25 3.00
13R22 Secluded Homestead .75 2.00
13R26 Take Up the Bow 1.00 2.50
13R33 Gandalf, Bearer of Obligation 2.00 5.00
13R36 The Palantir of Orthanc, Recovered Seeing Stone 1.25 3.00
13R37 Pallando, Far-travelling One 5.00 10.00
13R38 Radagast, Tender of Beasts 2.00 5.00
13R40 Shadowfax, Roaring Wind .60 1.50
13R42 Traveler's Homestead .75 2.00
13R44 Chasm's Edge 1.25 3.00
13R46a Deagol, Fateful Finder .75 2.00
13R46b Deagol, Fateful Finder TENGWAR
13R48 Fishing Boat .75 2.00
13R49 Gladden Homestead 1.25 3.00
13R57 Trap Is Sprung .75 2.00
13R58 Wild Light of Madness 1.25 3.00
13R59 Aragorn, Isildur's Heir 1.00 2.50
13R63 Brego, Loyal Steed 1.25 3.00
13R64 Denethor, Last Ruling Steward 1.00 2.50
13R65 Elendil, High-King of Gondor 6.00 12.00
13R76 Storied Homestead 1.00 2.50
13R78 Alatar Deceived .75 2.00
13R80 Radagast Deceived .60 1.50
13R81 Staff of Saruman, Fallen Istar's Stave 1.25 3.00
13R84 Corsair Champion .75 2.00
13R86 Desert Wind 1.00 2.50
13R93 Harmless 1.25 3.00
13S20 Lorien Protector .40 1.00
13S62 Boromir, Doomed Heir .40 1.00
13S74 Rally the Company .40 1.00
13S85 Cruel Dunlending .40 1.00
13S99 Stragglers .40 1.00
13U17 Kindreds Estranged .30 .75
13U19 Let Fly .30 .75
13U27 Wells of Deep Memory .30 .75
13U28 Alatar, Final Envoy .30 .75
13U31 The Flame of Anor .30 .75
13U34 Look to My Coming .30 .75
13U43 Vapour and Steam .30 .75
13U45 Cunningly Hidden .30 .75
13U50 Gollum, Her Sneak .30 .75
13U52 Little Snuffler .30 .75
13U53 Naked Waste .30 .75
13U55 Smeagol, Simple Stoor .30 .75
13U56 Softly Up Behind .30 .75
13U60 Away on the Wind .30 .75
13U61 Banners Blowing .30 .75
13U67 Guard of the White Tree .30 .75
13U70 Hope Renewed .30 .75
13U71 Isildur, Heir of Elendil .30 .75
13U72 Kings' Legacy .30 .75
13U75 Stewards' Legacy .30 .75
13U79 Pallando Deceived .30 .75
13U88 Dunlending Patriarch .30 .75
13U89 Dunlending Trapper .30 .75
13U91 Fires Brightly Burning .30 .75
13U92 Grima, Footman of Saruman .30 .75
13U94 Howdah .30 .75
13U95 Lying in Wait .30 .75
13U98 Southron Murderer .30 .75
13C102 Worn Battleaxe .12 .30
13C107 Expendable Servants .12 .30
13C111 Massing Strength .12 .30
13C113 Orc Line-breaker .12 .30
13C116 Orc Reaper .12 .30
13C119 Underdeeps Denizen .12 .30
13C120 Unforgiving Depths .12 .30
13C121 Whatever Means .12 .30
13C125 Ferthu Theoden Hal .12 .30
13C127 Freely Across Our Land .12 .30
13C129 Hamstrung .12 .30
13C132 Merchant of Westfold .12 .30
13C133 Riddermark Tactician .12 .30
13C134 Ride With Me .12 .30
13C145 Don't Let Go .12 .30
13C147 Faith in Friendship .12 .30
13C157 Westfarthing Businessman .12 .30
13C159 Assault Denizen .12 .30
13C160 Cavern Denizen .12 .30
13C161 Endless Assault .12 .30
13C162 Enemy Without Number .12 .30
13C163 Entranced Uruk .12 .30
13C164 Fearless Approach .12 .30
13C168 Uruk Aggressor .12 .30
13C172 Uruk Outrider .12 .30
13C173 Uruk Reserve .12 .30
13C175 Uruk Tactician .12 .30
13C176 War Machine .12 .30
13C184 Ulaire Nertea, Servant of the Shadow .12 .30
13R101 Voice of the Desert, Southron Troop 2.00 5.00
13R104 Chamber Patrol 1.00 2.50
13R108 Forced March .75 2.00
13R112a Orc Crusher 1.50 4.00
13R112b Orc Crusher TENGWAR
13R115 Orc Raid Commander .75 2.00
13R117 Ordnance Grunt 3.00 8.00
13R123 Eomer, Heir to Meduseld 1.00 2.50
13R126 Firefoot, Mearas of the Mark 7.50 15.00
13R136 Snowmane, Noble Mearas 1.00 2.50
13R137a Theoden, The Renowned 3.00 8.00
13R137b Theoden, The Renowned TENGWAR
13R138 Theodred, Second Marshal of the Mark 2.00 5.00
13R139 Wind-swept Homestead .60 1.50
13R140 Sauron, Dark Lord of Mordor 3.00 8.00
13R141 Sceptre of the Dark Lord 1.50 4.00
13R142 Bilbo, Aged Ring-bearer 2.00 5.00
13R143 Bill the Pony, Dearly-loved 1.00 2.50
13R149 Frodo, Frenzied Fighter 3.00 8.00
13R152 Humble Homestead 1.00 2.50
13R153 Mithril-coat, Dwarf-mail 1.00 2.50
13R155 Phial of Galadriel, The Light of Earendil 1.00 2.50
13R156a Sam, Bearer of Great Need .75 2.00
13R156b Sam, Bearer of Great Need TENGWAR
13R158 Assault Commander .75 2.00
13R169 Uruk Blitz 1.25 3.00
13R171 Uruk Invader .60 1.50
13R174a Uruk Rogue 1.00 2.50
13R174b Uruk Rogue TENGWAR
13R178 Dark Fell About Him .75 2.00
13R180 Shadow in the East .60 1.50
13R182 Ulaire Enquea, Sixth of the Nine Riders 2.00 5.00
13S100 Vicious Dunlending .40 1.00
13S109 Howling Orc .40 1.00
13S114 Orc Plains Runner .40 1.00
13S118 Picket Denizen .40 1.00
13S186 Caves of Aglarond .75 2.00
13S189 Crossroads of the Fallen Kings .75 2.00
13S191 Fords of Isen .40 1.00
13S192 The Great Gates .40 1.00
13U103 Always Threatening .30 .75
13U105 Defiled .30 .75
13U106 Enemy Upon Enemy .30 .75
13U110 Isengard Informant .30 .75
13U122 Bitter Tidings .30 .75
13U124 Eowyn, Restless Warrior .30 .75
13U128 Hama, Captain of the King's Guard .30 .75
13U130 Hurried Barrows .30 .75
13U131 King's Board .30 .75
13U135 Rider's Bow .30 .75
13U144 Daddy Twofoot, Next-door Neighbor .30 .75
13U146 Everything but My Bones .30 .75
13U148 Fates Entwined .30 .75
13U150 Frodo Gamgee, Son of Samwise .30 .75
13U151 The Gaffer, Master Gardener .30 .75
13U154 New Chapter .30 .75
13U165 Isengard Infiltrator .30 .75
13U166 New Enemy .30 .75
13U167 Signs of War .30 .75
13U170 Uruk Distractor .30 .75
13U177 Weapons of Control .30 .75
13U179 From Hideous Eyrie .30 .75
13U181 They Came From Mordor .30 .75
13U183 Ulaire Lemenya, Servant of the Shadow .30 .75
13U185 Abandoned Mine Shaft .30 .75
13U187 City of Kings .30 .75
13U188 Courtyard Parapet .30 .75
13U190 Doors of Durin .30 .75
13U193 Isenwash .30 .75
13U194 Redhorn Pass .30 .75

2005 Lord of the Rings Bloodlines Legends Foil

COMPLETE SET (18) 30.00 60.00
RELEASED ON AUGUST 12, 2005
13RF1 Celeborn, The Wise F 2.00 5.00
13RF2 Galadriel, Sorceress of the Hidden Land F .75 2.00
13RF3 Legolas, of the Grey Company F 3.00 8.00
13RF4 Gandalf, Bearer of Obligation F 2.50 6.00
13RF5 Pallando, Far-travelling One F 3.00 8.00
13RF6 Deagol, Fateful Finder F 1.25 3.00
13RF7 Aragorn, Isildur's Heir F .75 2.00
13RF8 Denethor, Last Ruling Steward F 1.50 4.00
13RF9 Voice of the Desert, Southron Troop F 1.50 4.00
13RF10 Chamber Patrol F 1.00 2.50
13RF11 Orc Crusher F 1.50 4.00
13RF12 Eomer, Heir to Meduseld F .75 2.00
13RF13 Theoden, The Renowned F 1.25 3.00
13RF14 Sauron, Dark Lord of Mordor F 6.00 12.00
13RF15 Frodo, Frenzied Fighter F 3.00 8.00
13RF16 Sam, Bearer of Great Need F 2.50 6.00
13RF17 Uruk Blitz F .75 2.00
13RF18 Uruk Rogue F 1.50 4.00

2005 Lord of the Rings Bloodlines Legends Masterworks Foil

COMPLETE SET (9) 50.00 100.00
RELEASED ON AUGUST 12, 2005
13O1 Celeborn, The Wise O 7.50 15.00
13O2 Galadriel, Sorceress of the Hidden Land O10.00 20.00
13O3 Legolas, of the Grey Company O 15.00 30.00
13O4 Gandalf, Bearer of Obligation O 10.00 20.00
13O5 Pallando, Far-traveling One O 12.00 25.00
13O6 Aragorn, Isildur's Heir O 10.00 20.00
13O7 Denethor, Last Ruling Steward O 7.50 15.00
13O8 Eomer, Heir to Meduseld O 7.50 15.00
13O9 Theoden, The Renowned O 10.00 20.00

2006 Lord of the Rings Expanded Middle-Earth

COMPLETE SET (15) 20.00 40.00
14R1 Dain Ironfoot, King Under the Mountain 2.00 5.00
14R2 Elladan, Son of Elrond 5.00 10.00
14R3 Elrohir, Son of Elrond 6.00 12.00
14R4 Gildor Inglorion, of the House of Finrod 1.25 3.00
14R5 Brand, King of Dale 2.00 5.00
14R6 Grimbeorn, Beorning Chieftain 5.00 10.00
14R7 Duilin, Ranger from Blackroot Vale 1.25 3.00
14R8 Duinhir, Tall Man of Blackroot Vale 1.25 3.00
14R9 Halbarad, Ranger of the North 2.50 6.00
14R10 Furious Hillman 1.25 3.00
14R11 Swarming Hillman 1.25 3.00
14R12 Half-troll of Far Harad 1.50 4.00
14R13 Horror of Harad 1.25 3.00
14R14 Uruk-hai Healer 1.25 3.00
14R15 Uruk-hai Scout 1.25 3.00

2006 Lord of the Rings The Hunters

COMPLETE SET (194) 200.00 300.00
BOOSTER BOX (36 PACKS) 50.00 100.00
BOOSTER PACK (11 CARDS) 2.00 4.00
RELEASED ON JUNE 9, 2006
15C5 Gimli, Eager Hunter .12 .30
15C8 Sturdy Stock .12 .30
15R1 The One Ring, The Ring of Doom 12.00 25.00
15R6 Gloin, Son of Groin 3.00 8.00
15R9 Well-crafted Armor 1.25 3.00
15S2 The One Ring, The Ruling Ring .40 1.00
15U3 Chamber of Records .30 .75
15U4 The Fortunes of Balin's Folk .30 .75

15U7 Heavy Axe	.30	.75
15C10 Whatever End	.12	.30
15C13 Elven Bow	.12	.30
15C14 Elven Warrior	.12	.30
15C15 Focus	.12	.30
15C23 Point Blank Range	.12	.30
15C25 Sword of the Fallen	.12	.30
15C28 Ent Avenger	.12	.30
15C45 Hurry Hobbitses	.12	.30
15C46 Nice Fish	.12	.30
15C48 Release Them	.12	.30
15C59 Dunedain of the South	.12	.30
15C60a Forth the Three Hunters! DWARVEN	.12	.30
15C60b Forth the Three Hunters! ELVEN	.12	.30
15C60c Forth the Three Hunters! GONDOR	.12	.30
15C62 Ithilien Blade	.12	.30
15C65 No Quicker Path	.12	.30
15C68 Ranger's Cloak	.12	.30
15C69 Silent Traveler	.12	.30
15C71 Unyielding Ranger	.12	.30
15C73 Bold Easterling	.12	.30
15C75 Courageous Easterling	.12	.30
15C77 Easterling Scout	.12	.30
15C80 Great Axe	.12	.30
15C82 Grousing Hillman	.12	.30
15C83 Hunting Herdsman	.12	.30
15C91 Ravaging Wild Man	.12	.30
15C93 Swarthy Hillman	.12	.30
15C97 Beasts of Burden	.12	.30
15R11 Arwen, She-Elf	5.00	10.00
15R12 Dinendal, Mirkwood Archer	5.00	10.00
15R19 Legolas, of the Woodland Realm	6.00	12.00
15R22 The Mirror of Galadriel, Dangerous Guide	2.00	5.00
15R24 Spied From Afar	1.25	3.00
15R29 Gandalf, Powerful Guide	7.50	15.00
15R29P Gandalf, Powerful Guide PROMO	5.00	10.00
15R30 Leaflock, Finglas	6.00	12.00
15R33 One Last Surprise	1.50	4.00
15R34 Quickbeam, Hastiest of All Ents	2.50	6.00
15R36 Shepherd of the Trees	5.00	10.00
15R38 Treebeard, Enraged Shepherd	6.00	12.00
15R40 Connected by Fate	.75	2.00
15R42 Desperate Move	1.50	4.00
15R43 Gollum, Hopeless	2.50	6.00
15R47 Not This Time!	5.00	10.00
15R49 Smeagol, Wretched and Hungry	1.25	3.00
15R53 Unseen Foe	3.00	8.00
15R55 Aragorn, Thorongil	6.00	12.00
15R56 Aragorn's Bow, Ranger's Longbow	12.00	25.00
15R58 Decorated Barricade	2.00	5.00
15R64 Madril, Defender of Osgiliath	1.50	4.00
15R70 Tremendous Wall	1.00	2.50
15R72 Bill Ferny, Agent of Saruman	6.00	12.00
15R74 Chieftain of Dunland	2.00	5.00
15R76 Destroyed Homestead	1.00	2.50
15R84 Last Gasp	1.50	4.00
15R86 Mumak Commander, Giant Among the Swertings	6.00	12.00
15R87 Primitive Savage	1.50	4.00
15R99 Black Land Chieftain	1.50	4.00
15S18 Legolas, Fleet-footed Hunter	.40	1.00
15S54 Aragorn, Swift Hunter	.40	1.00
15S95 Battlefield Recruit	.40	1.00
15S96 Battlefield Veteran	.40	1.00
15U16 Gift of the Evenstar, Blessed Light	.30	.75
15U17 Haldir, Sentry of the Golden Wood	.30	.75
15U20 Lorien's Blessing	.30	.75
15U21 Mighty Shot	.30	.75
15U26 Uruviel, Woodland Maid	.30	.75
15U27 Be Gone!	.30	.75
15U31 Mellon!	.30	.75
15U32 Momentous Gathering	.30	.75
15U35 Shadow of the Wood	.30	.75
15U37 Skinbark, Elder Ent	.30	.75
15U39 Called to Mordor	.30	.75
15U41 Controlled by the Ring	.30	.75
15U44 Herbs and Stewed Rabbit	.30	.75
15U50 Something Slimy	.30	.75
15U51 Sudden Strike	.30	.75
15U52 Swear By the Precious	.30	.75
15U57 Damrod, Dunadan of Gondor	.30	.75
15U61 Gondorian Prowler	.30	.75
15U63 Mablung, Ranger of Ithilien	.30	.75
15U66 No Travellers In This Land	.30	.75
15U69 Portico	.30	.75
15U78 Engrossed Hillman	.30	.75
15U79 Enraged Herdsman	.30	.75
15U81 Grieving the Fallen	.30	.75
15U85 Lying Counsel	.30	.75
15U88 Pursuing Horde	.30	.75
15U89 Rapid Reload	.30	.75
15U90 Rapt Hillman	.30	.75
15U92 Savage Southron	.30	.75
15U94 Wandering Hillman	.30	.75
15U98 Black Gate Sentry	.30	.75
15C100 Black Land Commander	.12	.30
15C101 Black Land Observer	.12	.30
15C103 Black Land Runner	.12	.30
15C105 Black Land Spy	.12	.30
15C107 Desolation Orc	.12	.30
15C108 Destructive Orc	.12	.30
15C110 Isengard Marauder	.12	.30
15C116 Scouting Orc	.12	.30
15C120 Veteran War Chief	.12	.30
15C121 Brilliant Light	.12	.30
15C125 Eowyn, Willing Fighter	.12	.30
15C127 Grim Trophy	.12	.30
15C130 Horseman of the North	.12	.30
15C131 Our Inspiration	.12	.30
15C133 Rider's Mount	.12	.30
15C136 Rohirrim Axe	.12	.30
15C143 Community Living	.12	.30
15C144 Frodo, Weary From the Journey	.12	.30
15C145 Hobbit Sword	.12	.30
15C147 Hobbiton Farmer, Lover of Pipeweed	.12	.30
15C149 Merry, The Tall One	.12	.30
15C150 No Visitors	.12	.30
15C151 Pippin, The Short One	.12	.30
15C156 Charging Uruk	.12	.30
15C157 Chasing Uruk	.12	.30
15C158 Covetous Uruk	.12	.30
15C161 Hunting Uruk	.12	.30
15C167 Pursuing Uruk	.12	.30
15C169 Seeking Uruk	.12	.30
15C176 Uruk Village Assassin	.12	.30
15C178 Uruk Village Stormer	.12	.30
15C179 Violent Hurl	.12	.30
15R104 Black Land Shrieker	2.50	6.00
15R109 Gorbag, Filthy Rebel	2.50	6.00
15R112 Mountain-troll	7.50	15.00
15R117 Tower Troll	3.00	8.00
15R119 Unreasonable Choice	1.25	3.00
15R122 Burial Mounds	1.25	3.00
15R123 Eomer, Horsemaster	3.00	8.00
15R124 Eomer's Spear, Trusty Weapon	3.00	8.00
15R135 Rohan Worker	1.00	2.50
15R141 Sturdy Shield	1.25	3.00
15R146 Hobbiton Brewer, Maker of Fine Ales	5.00	10.00
15R148 Little Golden Flower	2.00	5.00
15R152 Relaxation	2.00	5.00
15R154 Second Breakfast	1.25	3.00
15R155 Advancing Horde	2.00	5.00
15R162 Lurtz, Now Perfected	2.00	5.00
15R163 Lurtz's Sword, Mighty Longsword	1.00	2.50
15R165 Merciless Berserker	1.25	3.00
15R170 Sentry Uruk	1.50	4.00
15R172 Ugluk, Ugly Fellow	7.50	15.00
15R173 Ugluk's Sword, Weapon of Command	1.50	4.00
15R174 Uruk Cavern Striker	.75	2.00
15R180 With All Possible Speed	1.50	4.00
15R182 A Shadow Fell Over Them	1.50	4.00
15R184 Ulaire Attea, Desirous of Power	1.25	3.00
15R185 Ulaire Lemenya, Eternally Threatening	5.00	10.00
15R186 Ulaire Nelya, Fell Rider	.75	2.00
15R193 Mount Doom	3.00	8.00
15S126 Gamling, The Old	.40	1.00
15S138 Rohirrim Soldier	.40	1.00
15S164 Mauhur, Relentless Hunter	.40	1.00
15S171 Tracking Uruk	.40	1.00
15U102 Black Land Overlord	.30	.75
15U106 Coordinated Effort	.30	.75
15U111 Moria Menace	.30	.75
15U113 Orkish Camp	.30	.75
15U114 Orkish Hunting Spear	.30	.75
15U115 Pummeling Blow	.30	.75
15U118 Unmistakable Omen	.30	.75
15U128 Haleth, Son of Hama	.30	.75
15U129 Horse of Great Stature	.30	.75
15U132 Last Days of My House	.30	.75
15U134 Rohan Stable Master	.30	.75
15U137 Rohirrim Doorwarden	.30	.75
15U139 Rohirrim Warrior	.30	.75
15U140 Spear of the Mark	.30	.75
15U142 Swift Stroke	.30	.75
15U153 Sam, Innocent Traveler	.30	.75
15U159 Defensive Rush	.30	.75
15U160 Following Uruk	.30	.75
15U166 Poised for Assault	.30	.75
15U168 Searching Uruk	.30	.75
15U175 Uruk Infantry	.30	.75
15U177 Uruk Village Rager	.30	.75
15U181 Later Than You Think	.30	.75
15U183 They Feel the Precious	.30	.75
15U187 Anduin River	.30	.75
15U188 Breeding Pit of Isengard	.30	.75
15U189 City Gates	.30	.75
15U190 East Wall of Rohan	.30	.75
15U191 Gate of Mordor	.30	.75
15U192 Isengard Ruined	.30	.75
15U194 Westfold Village	.30	.75

2006 Lord of the Rings The Hunters Legends Foil

COMPLETE SET (18)	50.00	100.00
RELEASED ON JUNE 9, 2006		
15RF1 The One Ring, The Ring of Doom F	30.00	60.00
15RF2 Well-crafted Armor F	2.00	5.00
15RF3 Legolas, of the Woodland Realm F	3.00	8.00
15RF4 The Mirror of Galadriel, Dangerous Guide F	1.25	3.00
15RF5 Gandalf, Powerful Guide F	7.50	15.00
15RF6 One Last Surprise F	.75	2.00
15RF7 Quickbeam, Hastiest of All Ents F	5.00	10.00
15RF8 Smeagol, Wretched and Hungry F	2.50	6.00
15RF9 Aragorn, Thorongil F	10.00	20.00
15RF10 Madril, Defender of Osgiliath F	2.00	5.00
15RF11 Black Land Chieftain F	1.25	3.00
15RF12 Gorbag, Filthy Rebel F	2.00	5.00
15RF13 Eomer, Horsemaster F	3.00	8.00
15RF14 Sentry Uruk F	1.00	2.50
15RF15 Ulaire Attea, Desirous of Power F	2.50	6.00
15RF16 Ulaire Lemenya, Eternally Threatening F	5.00	10.00
15RF17 Ulaire Nelya, Fell Rider F	1.00	2.50
15RF18 Mount Doom F	7.50	15.00

2006 Lord of the Rings The Hunters Legends Masterworks Foil

COMPLETE SET (9)		
RELEASED ON JUNE 9, 2006		
15O1 Legolas, of the Woodland Realm O	25.00	50.00
15O2 Gandalf, Powerful Guide O	15.00	30.00
15O3 Quickbeam, Hastiest of All Ents O	12.00	25.00
15O4 Aragorn, Thorongil O	30.00	60.00
15O5 Madril, Defender of Osgiliath O	15.00	30.00
15O6 Eomer, Horsemaster O	10.00	20.00
15O7 Ulaire Attea, Desirous of Power O	12.00	25.00
15O8 Ulaire Lemenya, Eternally Threatening O	10.00	20.00
15O9 Ulaire Nelya, Fell Rider O	10.00	20.00

2006 Lord of the Rings The Wraith Collection

COMPLETE SET (6)	7.50	15.00
16R1 Barrow-wight Stalker	1.50	4.00
16R2 Candle Corpses	1.50	4.00
16R3 Covetous Wisp	1.50	4.00
16R4 Dead Faces	1.50	4.00
16R5 Spirit of Dread	1.50	4.00
16R6 Undead of Angmar	1.50	4.00

2007 Lord of the Rings Ages End

COMPLETE SET (40)	20.00	40.00
RELEASED IN JUNE 2007		
19P1 The One Ring, The Great Ring		
19P2 Gimli, Opinionated Guide		
19P3 Still Twitching		
19P4 That's Two!		
19P5 Army Long Trained		
19P6 Arwen, Royal Maiden		
19P7 Legolas, Skeptical Guide		
19P8 Gandalf, Wise Guide		
19P9 Stern Words		
19P10 Gollum, Threatening Guide		
19P11 Smeagol, Pitiable Guide		
19P12 Aragorn, Well-traveled Guide		
19P13 Boromir, Destined Guide		
19P14 Not Bound To His Fate		
19P15 Strength In My Blood		
19P16 Grima, Servant of Another Master		
19P17 Urgency		
19P18 The Balrog, Demon of Might		
19P19 Reaching Tentacle		
19P20 Strong Tentacle		
19P21 Watcher in the Water, Many-Tentacled Creature		
19P22 Pit Troll		
19P23 Troll of the Deep, Cave Troll		
19P24 Brought Down From Inside		
19P25 Eomer, Eored Captain		
19P26 Eowyn, Lady of the Mark		
19P27 Sauron's Might		
19P28 Frodo, Little Master		
19P29 Merry, Resolute Friend		
19P30 Pippin, Steadfast Friend		
19P31 Rabbit Stew		
19P32 Sam, Loyal Friend		
19P33 Lurtz, Resilient Captain		
19P34 In Twilight		
19P35 Ulaire Attea, Dark Predator		
19P36 Ulaire Enquea, Dark Threat		
19P37 Ulaire Lemenya, Dark Enemy		
19P38 Ulaire Nertea, Dark Horseman		
19P39 Ulaire Toldea, Dark Shadow		
19P40 The Witch-king, Dark Lord		

2007 Lord of the Rings Rise of Saruman

COMPLETE SET (148)	200.00	300.00
BOOSTER BOX (36 PACKS)		
BOOSTER BOX (11 CARDS)		
RELEASED ON MARCH 1, 2007		
17R2 Balin Avenged	1.50	4.00
17R4 Ring of Artifice	6.00	12.00
17R6 Thorin III, Stonehelm	6.00	12.00
17S7 Elven Guardian	.60	1.50
17U1 Armor of Khazad	.40	1.00
17U3 Dwarven Stratagem	.40	1.00
17U5 Axe- Work	.40	1.00
17U8 Hearth and Hall	.40	1.00
17U9 Lothlorien Guides	.40	1.00
17C46 Pandemonium	.12	.30
17C51 Stampeding Madman	.12	.30
17C53 Stampeding Savage	.12	.30
17C54 Stampeding Shepherd	.12	.30
17C55 Sunland Guard	.12	.30
17C57 Sunland Skirmisher	.12	.30
17C59 Sunland Trooper	.12	.30
17C60 Sunland Warrior	.12	.30
17C62 Vengeful Savage	.12	.30
17C63 Vengeful Wild Man	.12	.30
17C64 Vengeful Pillager	.12	.30
17C66 Wildman's Oath	.12	.30
17C68 Chaotic Clash	.12	.30
17C69 Cry and Panic	.12	.30
17C70 Feral Ride	.12	.30
17C72 Orkish Assassin	.12	.30
17C75 Orkish Dreg	.12	.30
17C78 Orkish Footman	.12	.30
17C80 Orkish Lackey	.12	.30
17C81 Orkish Maurader	.12	.30
17C83 Orkish Runner	.12	.30
17C85 Orkish Traveler	.12	.30
17C92 Vicious Warg	.12	.30
17R13 The World Ahead	5.00	10.00
17R17 Gandalf, Returned	12.00	25.00
17R18 Glamdring, Orc Beater	2.00	5.00
17R20 Gwaihir, The Windlord	6.00	12.00
17R23 Scintillating Bird	.75	2.00
17R24 Shadowfax, Greatest of the Mearas	6.00	12.00
17R27 Anduril, Sword That Was Broken	6.00	12.00
17R28 Faramir, Bearer of Quality	7.50	15.00
17R29 Faramir's Bow, Ithilien Longbow	3.00	8.00
17R31 Narsil, Forged by Telchar	5.00	10.00
17R36 Throne of Minas Tirith	5.00	10.00
17R37 Saruman, Instigator of Insurrection	5.00	10.00
17R38 Saruman, Servant of Sauron	6.00	12.00
17R39 Throne of Isengard	1.25	3.00
17R41 Ceremonial Armor	2.50	6.00
17R43 Easterling Sneak	1.50	4.00
17R44 Grima's Dagger	1.25	3.00
17R45 In the Wild Men's Wake	2.50	6.00
17R49 Stampeding Chief	3.00	8.00
17R52 Stampeding Ransacker	2.00	5.00
17R56 Sunland Scout	1.50	4.00
17R58 Sunland Sneak	2.00	5.00
17R61 Sunland Weaponmaster	5.00	10.00
17R65 Vengeful Primitive	.75	2.00
17R67 A Defiled Charge	3.00	8.00
17R71 Grishnakh, Treacherous Captain	6.00	12.00
17R73 Orkish Berserker	1.25	3.00
17R74 Orkish Cavalry	2.50	6.00
17R76 Orkish Fiend	2.00	5.00
17R79 Orkish Invader	2.50	6.00
17R82 Orkish Rider	2.00	5.00
17R84 Orkish Scout	2.50	6.00
17R86 Orkish Veteran	3.00	8.00
17R87 Orkish Warg-master	2.50	6.00
17R89 Relentless Warg	6.00	12.00
17R93 Aragorn, Defender of Rohan	6.00	12.00
17R95 Eomer, Northman	6.00	12.00
17R96 Eowyn, Northwoman	6.00	12.00
17R98 Throne of the Golden Hall	3.00	8.00
17R99 Hama, Northman	1.50	4.00
17S11 Orophin, Silvan Elf	.60	1.50
17S12 Rumil, Silvan Elf	.60	1.50
17S30 Madril, Loyal Lieutenant	.60	1.50
17S33 Ranger of the White Tree	.60	1.50
17S35 Soldier's Cache	.60	1.50
17S48 Saruman, Coldly Still	.60	1.50
17U10 Namarie	.40	1.00
17U14 Weapons of Lothlorien	.40	1.00
17U15 A New Light	.40	1.00
17U16 Barliman Butterbur, Red-Faced Landlord	.40	1.00
17U19 Guidance of the Istari	.40	1.00
17U21 Long-stemmed Pipe	.40	1.00
17U22 Meneldor, Misty Mountain Eagle	.40	1.00
17U25 The Sap is in the Bough	.40	1.00
17U26 Woodland Onod	.40	1.00
17U32 Nimble Attack	.40	1.00
17U34 Spirit of the White Tree	.40	1.00
17U40 Beast of War	.40	1.00
17U42 Easterling Dispatcher	.40	1.00
17U47 Primitive Brand	.40	1.00
17U50 Stampeding Hillsman	.40	1.00
17U77 Orkish Flanker	.40	1.00
17U88 Orkish Warrior	.40	1.00
17U90 Rider's Gear	.40	1.00
17U91 Threatening Warg	.40	1.00
17U94 Dispatched with Haste	.40	1.00
17U97 For Death and Glory	.40	1.00
17C113 Deathly Roar	.12	.30
17C118 Vile Pit	.12	.30
17C119 White Hand Aggressor	.12	.30
17C120 White Hand Attacker	.12	.30
17C122 White Hand Butcher	.12	.30
17C125 White Hand Enforcer	.12	.30
17C126 White Hand Guard	.12	.30
17C127 White Hand Intruder	.12	.30
17C128 White Hand Invader	.12	.30
17C130 White Hand Scout	.12	.30
17C131 White Hand Slayer	.12	.30
17C133 White Hand Trooper	.12	.30
17C134 White Hand Vanquisher	.12	.30
17C136 White Hand Warrior	.12	.30
17R102 Theoden, Northman, King of Rohan	1.50	4.00
17R105 Throne of the Dark Lord	3.00	8.00
17R114 Land Had Changed	2.00	5.00
17R116 Saruman, Master of the White Hand	3.00	8.00
17R121 White Hand Berserker	2.00	5.00
17R123 White Hand Captain	1.50	4.00
17R124 White Hand Destroyer	2.50	6.00
17R129 White Hand Legion	1.50	4.00
17R132 White Hand Taskmaster	2.00	5.00
17R135 White Hand Veteran	2.50	6.00
17R137 You Do Not Know Fear	5.00	10.00
17R139 Ulaire Cantea, Duplicitous Assassin	6.00	12.00
17R140 Ulaire Enquea, Duplicitous Lieutenant	3.00	8.00
17R141 Ulaire Otsea, Duplicitous Specter	5.00	10.00
17R142 Ring of Savagery	2.50	6.00
17R143 Ring of Terror	6.00	12.00
17R144 The Witch-king, Conqueror of Arthedain	3.00	8.00
17S115 Saruman, Curunir	.60	1.50
17U100 Into the Caves	.40	1.00
17U101 Soldier of Rohan	.40	1.00
17U103 Where Now the Horse	.40	1.00
17U104 Warrior of Rohan	.40	1.00
17U106 Halfling Leaf	.40	1.00
17U107 Merry, In the Bloom of Health	.40	1.00
17U108 Hornblower Leaf	.40	1.00
17U109 Pippin, In the Bloom of Health	.40	1.00
17U110 Southfarthing Leaf	.40	1.00
17U111 Southlinch Leaf	.40	1.00
17U112 Blade of the White Hand	.40	1.00
17U117 Spear of the White Hand	.40	1.00
17U138 You Do Not Know Pain	.40	1.00
17U145 Dol Guldur	.40	1.00
17U146 Falls of Rauros	.40	1.00
17U147 Imladris	.40	1.00
17U148 Nurn	.40	1.00

2007 Lord of the Rings Rise of Saruman Legends Foil

COMPLETE SET (18)	120.00	250.00
RELEASED ON MARCH 1, 2007		
17RF1 Ring of Artifice F	7.50	15.00
17RF2 Glamdring, Orc Beater F	7.50	15.00
17RF3 Shadowfax, Greatest of the Mearas F	20.00	40.00
17RF4 Gwaihir, The Windlord F	10.00	20.00
17RF5 Anduril, Sword That Was Broken F	12.00	25.00
17RF6 Faramir, Bearer of Quality F	30.00	60.00
17RF7 Narsil, Forged by Telchar F	12.00	25.00
17RF8 Throne of Minas Tirith F	7.50	15.00
17RF9 Throne of Isengard F	15.00	30.00
17RF10 Stampeding Chief F	10.00	20.00
17RF11 Orkish Invader F	12.00	25.00
17RF12 Aragorn, Defender of Rohan F	10.00	20.00
17RF13 Throne of the Golden Hall F	12.00	25.00
17RF14 Theoden, Northman, King of Rohan F	15.00	30.00
17RF15 Throne of the Dark Lord F	15.00	30.00
17RF16 Ulaire Otsea, Duplicitous Specter F	15.00	30.00
17RF17 Ring of Savagery F	15.00	30.00
17RF18 Ring of Terror F	7.50	15.00

2007 Lord of the Rings Rise of Saruman Legends Masterworks Foil

UNPRICED DUE TO SCARCITY		
17O1 Shadowfax, Greatest of the Mearas O		
17O2 Gwaihir, The Windlord O		
17O3 Throne of Minas Tirith O		
17O4 Aragorn, Defender of Rohan O		
17O5 Throne of the Golden Hall O		
17O6 Theoden, Northman, King of Rohan O		
17O7 Ulaire Otsea, Duplicitous Specter O		
17O8 Ring of Savagery O		
17O9 Ring of Terror O		

2007 Lord of the Rings Treachery and Deceit

COMPLETE SET (140)	200.00	350.00
BOOSTER BOX (36 PACKS)		
BOOSTER PACK (11 CARDS)		
RELEASED IN MAY 2007		
18C3 Thorin's Harp	.25	.60
18C9 Elven Defender	.25	.60
18R1 Gimli, Sprinter	3.00	8.00
18R4 Arwen's Bow	3.00	8.00
18R5 Arwen's Dagger	3.00	8.00
18R6 Back to the Light	5.00	10.00
18R7 Celebring, Elven-smith	2.50	6.00
18U2 Run Until Found	.40	1.00
18U8 Elven Armaments	.40	1.00
18C16 Miruvore	.25	.60
18C17 Woodhall Elf, Exile	.25	.60
18C19 Drawn to Full Height	.25	.60
18C20 Ents Marching	.25	.60
18C22 Librarian, Keeper of Ancient Texts	.25	.60
18C36 Time for Food	.25	.60
18C39 Armor of the White City	.25	.60
18C44 Defenses Long Held	.25	.60
18C49 Faramir's Company	.25	.60
18C51 For Gondor!	.25	.60
18C56 Ranger of the South	.25	.60
18C57 Shield of the White Tree	.25	.60
18C65 Declined Business	.25	.60
18C68 Harry Goatleaf	.25	.60
18C70 Ill News Is An Ill Guest	.25	.60
18C72 Ruffian	.25	.60
18C73 Rough Man of the South	.25	.60
18C74 Squint-eyed Southerner	.25	.60
18C77 Whisper in the Dark	.25	.60
18C84 Orkish Ax	.25	.60
18C85 Orkish Aggressor	.25	.60
18C87 Orkish Breeder	.25	.60
18C88 Orkish Defender	.25	.60
18C89 Orkish Headsman	.25	.60
18C90 Orkish Skirmisher	.25	.60
18C91 Orkish Sneak	.25	.60
18C94 Cast From the Hall	.25	.60
18R11 Galadriel's Silver Ewer	7.50	15.00
18R12 Gil-galad, High King of the Noldor	15.00	30.00
18R13 Glorfindel, Eldarin Lord	6.00	12.00
18R14 Haldir, Warrior Messenger	2.50	6.00
18R15 Lembas Bread	3.00	8.00
18R18 Beorning Axe	6.00	12.00
18R24 Our Time	3.00	8.00
18R26 Radagast's Herb Bag	6.00	12.00
18R28 Countless Cords	2.50	6.00
18R29 Deceit	3.00	8.00
18R31 It Draws Him	2.50	6.00
18R32 Not Easily Avoided	5.00	10.00
18R34 Shelob, Menace	6.00	12.00
18R35 Sting of Shelob	3.00	8.00
18R38 Aragorn, Heir to the Throne of Gondor	7.50	15.00
18R40 Boromir, Proud and Noble Man	6.00	12.00
18R41 Crown of Gondor	3.00	8.00
18R42 Denethor, On the Edge of Madness	2.00	5.00
18R43 Denethor's Sword	2.00	5.00
18R47 Elendil's Army	3.00	8.00
18R48 Faramir, Captain of Ithilien	6.00	12.00
18R50 The Faithful Stone	5.00	10.00
18R52 Gondorian Servant, Denethor's Handman	2.50	6.00
18R53 Horn of Boromir, The Great Horn	5.00	10.00
18R54 Isildur, Sword-Bearer	6.00	12.00
18R55 Ranger of the North	2.00	5.00
18R59 Watcher at Sarn Ford, Ranger of the North	3.00	8.00
18R66 Fleet of Corsair Ships	2.50	6.00
18R67 Grima, Witless Worm	6.00	12.00
18R69 Henchman's Dagger	2.00	5.00
18R71 Mumakil Commander, Bold and Grim	2.50	6.00
18R76 Treachery	2.50	6.00
18R80 Gothmog, Morgul Leader	7.50	15.00
18R81 Gothmog's Warg, Leader's Mount	3.00	8.00
18R82 Grond, Forged With Black Steel	5.00	10.00
18R83 Gruesome Meal	3.00	8.00
18R95 Eomer's Bow	2.50	6.00
18R96 Erkenbrand's Horn	3.00	8.00
18R97 Erkenbrand's Shield	6.00	12.00
18R98 Fall back to Helm's Deep	3.00	8.00
18R99 Gamling, Dutiful Marshal	2.50	6.00
18U10 Elven Supplies	.40	1.00
18U21 Last Stand	.40	1.00
18U23 One-Upsmanship	.40	1.00
18U25 Perspective	.40	1.00
18U27 Ship of Smoke	.40	1.00
18U30 Enemy in Your Midst	.40	1.00
18U33 Set Up	.40	1.00
18U37 Trusted Promise	.40	1.00
18U45 Dunadan's Bow	.40	1.00
18U46 Disarmed	.40	1.00
18U58 Soldier's Cache	.40	1.00
18U60 Corsair Boarding Axe	.40	1.00
18U61 Corsair Bow	.40	1.00
18U62 Corsair Grappling Hook	.40	1.00
18U63 Corsair Halberd	.40	1.00
18U64 Corsair Scimitar	.40	1.00
18U75 Ted Sandyman, Chief's Men's Ally	.40	1.00
18U78 Destroyers and Usurpers	.40	1.00
18U79 Frenzy of Arrows	.40	1.00
18U86 Orkish Archer Troop	.40	1.00
18U92 War Preparations	.40	1.00
18U93 Wary Orc	.40	1.00
18C101 Precise Attack	.25	.60
18C103 Rohirrim Recruit	.25	.60
18C106 A Dragon's Tale	.25	.60

18C109 Make a Run For It .25 .60
18C116 Fury of the Evil Army .25 .60
18C117 Ghastly Wound .25 .60
18C124 White Hand Attacker .25 .60
18C125 White Hand Exorciser .25 .60
18C128 White Hand Mystic .25 .60
18C129 White Hand Sieger .25 .60
18C131 White Hand Uruk .25 .60
18R100 Gamling's Horn 3.00 8.00
18R102 Rohirrim Diadem 2.50 6.00
18R105 Theoden, Ednew 3.00 8.00
18R107 Fredegar Bolger, Fatty 5.00 10.00
18R112 Scouring of the Shire 7.50 15.00
18R113 Sting, Elven Long Knife 5.00 10.00
18R114 Cleaved 3.00 8.00
18R115 Final Triumph 3.00 8.00
18R118 Lurtz, Halfling Hunter 5.00 10.00
18R119 Lurtz's Bow, Black-Fletch Bow 5.00 10.00
18R122 Shagrat, Tower Captain 5.00 10.00
18R126 White Hand Marchers 2.00 5.00
18R127 White Hand Marshal 6.00 12.00
18R133 Pull of the Ring 2.50 6.00
18U104 Surrendered Weapons .40 1.00
18U108 Golden Perch Ale .40 1.00
18U110 Prized Lagan .40 1.00
18U111 Robin Smallburrow, Shirriff Cock-Robin .40 1.00
18U120 New Forges Built .40 1.00
18U121 Pikes Upon Pikes .40 1.00
18U123 Tracking the Prize .40 1.00
18U130 White Hand Traveler .40 1.00
18U132 All Life Flees .40 1.00
18U134 Doorway to Doom .40 1.00
18U135 Foot of Mount Doom .40 1.00
18U136 Mithlond .40 1.00
18U137 Morannon Plains .40 1.00
18U138 Sirannon Ruins .40 1.00
18U139 Steward's Tomb .40 1.00
18U140 Streets of Bree .40 1.00

2007 Lord of the Rings Treachery and Deceit Legends Foil

COMPLETE SET (18) 120.00 200.00
RELEASED IN MAY 2007
18RF1 Arwen's Bow F 10.00 20.00
18RF2 Arwen's Dagger F 7.50 15.00
18RF3 Galadriel's Silver Ewer F 10.00 20.00
18RF4 Beorning Axe F 15.00 30.00
18RF5 Radagast's Herb Bag F 10.00 20.00
18RF6 Shelob, Menace F 7.50 15.00
18RF7 Crown of Gondor F 7.50 15.00
18RF8 Denethor's Sword F 7.50 15.00
18RF9 Watcher at Sarn Ford, Ranger of the North F7.50 15.00
18RF10 Gothmog, Morgul Leader F 10.00 20.00
18RF11 Erkenbrand's Horn F 10.00 20.00
18RF12 Erkenbrand's Shield F 7.50 15.00
18RF13 Rohirrim Diadem F 7.50 15.00
18RF14 Theoden, Ednew F 7.50 15.00
18RF15 Fredegar Bolger, Fatty F 7.50 15.00
18RF16 Sting, Elven Long Knife F 10.00 20.00
18RF17 Shagrat, Tower Captain F 7.50 15.00
18RF18 Pull of the Ring F 10.00 20.00

2007 Lord of the Rings Treachery and Deceit Legends Masterworks Foil

COMPLETE SET (9) 150.00 300.00
RELEASED IN MAY 2007
1801 Beorning Axe O 25.00 50.00
1802 Radagast's Herb Bag O 25.00 50.00
1803 Crown of Gondor O 25.00 50.00
1804 Denethor's Sword O 25.00 50.00
1805 Watcher at Sarn Ford, Ranger of the North O20.00 40.00
1806 Erkenbrand's Horn O 20.00 40.00
1807 Erkenbrand's Shield O 25.00 50.00
1808 Rohirrim Diadem O 20.00 40.00
1809 Pull of the Ring O 20.00 40.00

2014 Lord of the Rings The Antlered Crown

137 Erkenbrand
138 Warden of Helm's Deep
139 The Day's Rising
140 Captain of Gondor
141 Booming Ent
142 Ride Them Down
143 Shadows Give Way
144 Don't Be Hasty!
145 Waters of Nimrodel
146 Treebeard
147 Battle for Dunland
148 The Raven Clan
149 The Last Stage
150 Chief Turch
151 Raven Chief
152 Raven Chief's Camp
153 Raven Warrior
154 Raven Skirmisher
155 Raven War-camp
156 Raven Village
157 Dunland Battlefield
158 Raven Country
159 Raising the Cry
160 Fierce Folk
161 Driven Back

2014 Lord of the Rings Celebrimbor's Secret

112 Galadriel
113 Heir of Mardil
114 Orophin
115 Henneth Annûn Guard
116 Charge of the Rohirrim
117 Galadriel's Handmaiden
118 Mirror of Galadriel
119 Wandering Ent
120 Cloak of Lórien
121 Nenya
122 The Ruins of Ost-in-Edhil
123 The Enemy's Servant
124 Bellach
125 The Orcs' Search
126 The Secret Chamber
127 Celebrimbor's Mould
128 Bellach's Scout
129 Prowling Orc
130 Ruined Plaza
131 Collapsed Tower
132 Ancient Foundation
133 City Remains
134 Discovered!
135 Desecrated Ruins
136 Spies from Mordor

2015 Lord of the Rings The Lost Realm

1 Aragorn
2 Halbarad
3 Weather Hills Watchman
4 Dunedain Hunter
5 Sarn Ford Sentry
6 Warden of Annuminas
7 Ranger Summons
8 Tireless Hunters
9 Expert Trackers
10 Heir of Valandil
11 Athelas
12 Secret Vigil
13 Star Brooch
14 Gather Information
15 Ranger of the North
16 Iârion
17 Orc War Party
18 Chetwood Forest
19 Borders of Bree-land
20 Outlying Homestead
21 Sudden Assault
22 Surprising Speed
23 Orc Rearguard
24 Rescue Iârion
25 Cornered Orc
26 Amon Forn
27 Weathered Hilltop
28 Exposed Ridge
29 Sheltered Valley
30 Concealed Orc-camp
31 Ice Storm
32 Find Shelter
33 Thaurdir
34 Thaurdir's Damned
35 Baleful Shade
36 Broken Battlements
37 Norbury Tombs
38 Fornost Square
39 Haunted Keep
40 Deadmen's Gate
41 Unnatural Fog
42 The Shadow World
43 Angmar Orc
44 Angmar Marauder
45 Angmar Captain
46 Orc Ambush
47 Rugged Country
48 Shrouded Hills
49 Pressing Needs
50 Weight of Responsibility
51 Lost in the Wilderness
52 Biting Wind
53 Freezing Blast
54 Cold from Angmar
55 Make Camp
56 Ruins of Arnor
57 Ancient Causeway
58 Tragic Discovery
59 Search the Ruins
60 Dead Lord
61 Cursed Dead
62 Restless Evil
63 Seal the Tomb
64 Terror of the North
65 Dark Sorcery
66 Heavy Curse
67 The Power of Angmar
68 Stop the War Party
69 Scattered Among the Hills
70 Cornered Animals
71 Hunting the Orcs
73 The Shades of Angmar
74 A Fell Wraith

2016 Luck and Logic Growth and Genesis

COMPLETE SET (137 CARDS) 200.00 400.00
BOOSTER BOX (20 PACKS) 55.00 85.00
BOOSTER PACK (7 CARDS) 2.00 5.00
UNLISTED C .10 .30
UNLISTED U .20 .75
RELEASED ON JUNE 24TH, 2016
BT01001EN Power of Bonds Tamaki SP 80.00 120.00
BT01001EN Power of Bonds Tamaki SR 20.00 40.00
BT01001EN Power of Bonds Tamaki RR 10.00 25.00
BT01002EN Six Fists Sena RR 1.50 4.00
BT01002EN Six Fists Sena SR 3.00 8.00
BT01003EN Yellow Dragon of Rage Tamaki RR 5.00 12.00
BT01003EN Yellow Dragon of Rage Tamaki SR 8.00 20.00
BT01004EN Full Force Strike Sena R .75 2.00
BT01005EN Carange Leg, Sena R 1.25 3.00
BT01006EN Achieving Her Goal Sena R .75 2.00
BT01007EN In a Rush Tamaki R 1.50 4.00
BT01008EN Girl that Likes Sweets Xiaolin R 2.50 6.00
BT01009EN Smile of Satisfaction, Tamaki U .20 .75
BT01010EN Beyond the Battle Sena U .20 .75
BT01011EN Summoned by the Ocean Tamaki U .60 1.25
BT01012EN Counter Current Shock Tamaki U .60 1.50
BT01013EN Permeating Willpower Sena U .20 .75
BT01014EN Skilled Writing Tamaki U .40 1.00
BT01015EN Personification of Battle Asura U .20 .75
BT01016EN Incomplete Talent Xiaolin U .50 1.25
BT01017EN Repelling Dragon Scale Tamaki C .10 .30
BT01018EN Musical Performance Training Tamaki C.10 .30
BT01019EN Establishing the Target Tamaki C .10 .30
BT01020EN Monitoring Tamaki C .10 .30
BT01021EN The Decision to Protect Sena C .10 .30
BT01022EN In a Hurry Sena C .10 .30
BT01023EN A Little Relaxation Tamaki C .10 .30
BT01024EN Working Hard Asura C .10 .30
BT01025EN Successor Divine Music Otohime C .10 .30
BT01026EN Speak with My Fists U .50 1.25
BT01027EN Defense Tactics Lecture C .10 .30
BT01028EN Dragon Cradle PxR 2.50 6.00
BT01029EN Blood Bath Coliseum PxC .10 .30
BT01030EN Artistic Aquarium PxC .10 .30
BT01031EN Forbidden Overtrance Yoshichika RR2.00 5.00
BT01031EN Forbidden Overtrance Yoshichika SR3.00 8.00
BT01032EN Crushing Evil, Yoshichika SR 3.00 8.00
BT01032EN Crushing Evil, Yoshichika RR 2.00 5.00
BT01032EN Crushing Evil, Yoshichika SP 8.00 20.00
BT01033EN Going to Hades Mejiko SR 5.00 12.00
BT01033EN Going to Hades Mejiko RR 4.00 10.00
BT01034EN Full of Conviction Yoshichika R .75 2.00
BT01035EN Leaving Behind Her Grudge Mejiko R .75 2.00
BT01036EN Belief in the Occult Mejiko R 1.25 3.00
BT01037EN Ready to Go Yoshichika R .75 2.00
BT01038EN Fierce God Rasetsu R .75 2.00
BT01039EN Rapid Fall Mejiko U .20 .75
BT01040EN Brief Victory Yoshichika U .20 .75
BT01041EN Flash of Demon Yoshichika U .20 .75
BT01042EN One Sided Trance Mejiko U .20 .75
BT01043EN First Trance Yoshichika U .20 .75
BT01044EN Errands in the Early Afternoon Yoshichika U .40 1.00
BT01045EN Genius Monk of Great Envy Huang Huang U .20 .75
BT01046EN Fondly Remembering Rasetsu U .20 .75
BT01047EN Dispelling Secret Technique Yoshichika C .10 .30
BT01048EN Invisible Sword Stroke Yoshichika C .10 .30
BT01049EN Rosary of Sorrow Mejiko C .10 .30
BT01050EN Swordswoman Yoshichika C .10 .30
BT01051EN Twin Fine Blades Yoshichika C .10 .30
BT01052EN Girl that Senses the Supernatuarl Mejiko C .10 .30
BT01053EN Intracerebral Simulation Yoshichika C.10 .30
BT01054EN Enjoying Life Huang Huang C .10 .30
BT01055EN Beautiful Master Fencer Hibana C .10 .30
BT01056EN Unforeseen Summoning U .20 .30
BT01057EN Fighting Trance C .10 .30
BT01058EN Age of Civil Wars PxR 1.25 3.00
BT01059EN Mega Heavy Hard Luck PxC .10 .30
BT01060EN Sword to Sword PxC .10 .30
BT01061EN Super Tiger Claw Chloe SR 8.00 20.00
BT01061EN Super Tiger Claw Chloe RR 8.00 20.00
BT01061EN Super Tiger Claw Chloe SP 25.00 50.00
BT01062EN Reserved Fighting Ashley RR 1.00 2.50
BT01062EN Reserved Fighting Ashley SR 2.00 5.00
BT01063EN White Tiger Fist Chloe SR 5.00 12.00
BT01063EN White Tiger Fist Chloe RR 3.00 8.00
BT01064EN Stirring Up Trouble Chloe R .75 2.00
BT01065EN Driving Them Away Ashley R .75 2.00
BT01066EN Indulging in Reading Ashley R .75 2.00
BT01067EN Counterattack Commence Chloe R 1.50 4.00
BT01068EN Free Spirited Daiga R 1.50 4.00
BT01069EN Complete Devotion Ashley U .20 .75
BT01070EN Solid Armor Ashley U .20 .75
BT01071EN Concentration of Mind Chloe U .20 .75
BT01072EN Attack from the Trees Chloe U .60 1.50
BT01073EN Differing Ideals Ashley U .20 .75
BT01074EN Full Speed Patrol Chloe U .50 1.25
BT01075EN Strength to Smash Boulders Daiga U .20 .75
BT01076EN Jade of the Cliffs U .20 .75
BT01077EN Meal Before Battle Chloe C .10 .30
BT01078EN Trident Wielder Chloe C .10 .30
BT01079EN Cautious and Careful Ashley C .10 .30
BT01080EN Seaside Guard Chloe C .10 .30
BT01081EN Sprinting Chloe C .10 .30
BT01082EN Daydreaming Maiden Ashley C .10 .30
BT01083EN Returning to Supreme Bliss Chloe C .10 .30
BT01084EN Midday Drink Jade C .10 .30
BT01085EN Calm Time Fyrill C .10 .30
BT01086EN Barrier of Shadows U .20 .30
BT01087EN Goddess of the Waterfront C .10 .30
BT01088EN Golden Exercise PxR 1.50 4.00
BT01089EN Last Survivor PxC .10 .30
BT01090EN Slow Wave PxC .10 .30
BT01091EN Longbow in the Moonlight Aoi SR 20.00 40.00
BT01091EN Longbow in the Moonlight Aoi RR 10.00 25.00
BT01092EN Going at Dusk Sieghard RR 1.25 3.00
BT01092EN Going at Dusk Sieghard SR 2.00 5.00
BT01093EN Extreme Destruction of Boxes Aoi RR2.50 6.00
BT01093EN Extreme Destruction of Boxes Aoi SR3.00 8.00
BT01094EN Mastery of the Air Leap Aoi R .75 2.00
BT01095EN Soaring in Blue Skies Sieghard R .75 2.00
BT01096EN Youth of Sincerity Sieghard R .75 2.00
BT01097EN Full Bodied Sweets Aoi R 1.25 3.00
BT01098EN Lotta of the Sativa R 1.00 2.50
BT01099EN Breakthrough at the Speed of Sound Sieghard U .20 .75
BT01100EN Continuation of Combat Aoi U .20 .75
BT01101EN Eyes of the Skies Sieghard U .20 .75
BT01102EN Wings to the Future Sieghard U .20 .75
BT01103EN Taut Bow Aoi U .20 .75
BT01104EN Busy Morning Aoi U .50 1.25
BT01105EN Lucia of the Swallowblacks U .20 .75
BT01106EN Body Guard Lotta U .75 2.00
BT01107EN Three Steps Ahead Aoi C .10 .30
BT01108EN Tempest of Destruction Aoi C .10 .30
BT01109EN First Flight Sieghard C .10 .30
BT01110EN Buffalo Form Aoi C .10 .30
BT01111EN Bunny Style Aoi C .10 .30
BT01112EN Dress Up Doll Sieghard C .10 .30
BT01113EN Archery Uniform Aoi C .10 .30
BT01114EN Smiling in the Spirit World Lucia C .10 .30
BT01115EN Melchi of Spring Anticipation C .10 .30
BT01116EN Non Standard U .20 .30
BT01117EN Vow to Pass Over Dimensions C .10 .30
BT01118EN Lunatic Burst PxR 3.00 8.00
BT01119EN Tornado Disco PxC .10 .30
BT01120EN Milky Paradise PxC .10 .30
BT01G001EN Chloe Maxwell SCR 30.00 60.00
BT01G002EN Tamaki Yurine SCR 80.00 120.00

2016 Luck and Logic Growth and Genesis Foil

BT01009EN Smile of Satisfaction, Tamaki U .75 2.00
BT01010EN Beyond the Battle Sena U .75 2.00
BT01011EN Summoned by the Ocean Tamaki U 1.00 2.50
BT01012EN Counter Current Shock Tamaki U 1.00 2.50
BT01013EN Permeating Willpower Sena U .75 2.00
BT01014EN Skilled Writing Tamaki U .75 2.00
BT01015EN Personification of Battle Asura U .75 2.00
BT01016EN Incomplete Talent Xiaolin U .75 2.00
BT01017EN Repelling Dragon Scale Tamaki C .40 1.00
BT01018EN Musical Performance Training Tamaki C.40 1.00
BT01019EN Establishing the Target Tamaki C .40 1.00
BT01020EN Monitoring Tamaki C .40 1.00
BT01021EN The Decision to Protect Sena C .40 1.00
BT01022EN In a Hurry Sena C .40 1.00
BT01023EN A Little Relaxation Tamaki C .40 1.00
BT01024EN Working Hard Asura C .40 1.00
BT01025EN Successor Divine Music Otohime C .40 1.00
BT01026EN Speak with My Fists U .75 2.00
BT01027EN Defense Tactics Lecture C .75 2.00
BT01028EN Dragon Cradle PxR 4.00 10.00
BT01029EN Blood Bath Coliseum PxC .40 1.00
BT01030EN Artistic Aquarium PxC .40 1.00
BT01039EN Rapid Fall Mejiko U .75 2.00
BT01040EN Brief Victory Yoshichika U .75 2.00
BT01041EN Flash of Demon Yoshichika U .75 2.00
BT01042EN One Sided Trance Mejiko U .75 2.00
BT01043EN First Trance Yoshichika U .75 2.00
BT01044EN Errands in the Early Afternoon Yoshichika U .75 2.00
BT01045EN Genius Monk of Great Envy Huang Huang U .75 2.00
BT01046EN Fondly Remembering Rasetsu U .75 2.00
BT01047EN Dispelling Secret Technique Yoshichika C .40 1.00
BT01048EN Invisible Sword Stroke Yoshichika C .40 1.00
BT01049EN Rosary of Sorrow Mejiko C .40 1.00
BT01050EN Swordswoman Yoshichika C .40 1.00
BT01051EN Twin Fine Blades Yoshichika C .40 1.00
BT01052EN Girl that Senses the Supernatuarl Mejiko C .40 1.00
BT01053EN Intracerebral Simulation Yoshichika C.40 1.00
BT01054EN Enjoying Life Huang Huang C .40 1.00
BT01055EN Beautiful Master Fencer Hibana C .40 1.00
BT01056EN Unforeseen Summoning U .75 2.00
BT01057EN Fighting Trance C .40 1.00
BT01058EN Age of Civil Wars PxR 2.00 5.00
BT01059EN Mega Heavy Hard Luck PxC .40 1.00
BT01060EN Sword to Sword PxC .40 1.00
BT01069EN Complete Devotion Ashley U .75 2.00
BT01070EN Solid Armor Ashley U .75 2.00
BT01071EN Concentration of Mind Chloe U .75 2.00
BT01072EN Attack from the Trees Chloe U 1.50 4.00
BT01073EN Differing Ideals Ashley U .75 2.00
BT01074EN Full Speed Patrol Chloe U .75 2.00
BT01075EN Strength to Smash Boulders Daiga U .75 2.00
BT01076EN Jade of the Cliffs U .75 2.00
BT01077EN Meal Before Battle Chloe C .40 1.00
BT01078EN Trident Wielder Chloe C .40 1.00
BT01079EN Cautious and Careful Ashley C .40 1.00
BT01080EN Seaside Guard Chloe C .40 1.00
BT01081EN Sprinting Chloe C .40 1.00
BT01082EN Daydreaming Maiden Ashley C .40 1.00
BT01083EN Returning to Supreme Bliss Chloe C .40 1.00
BT01084EN Midday Drink Jade C .40 1.00
BT01085EN Calm Time Fyrill C .75 2.00
BT01086EN Barrier of Shadows U .75 2.00
BT01087EN Goddess of the Waterfront C .40 1.00
BT01088EN Golden Exercise PxR 2.00 5.00
BT01089EN Last Survivor PxC .40 1.00
BT01090EN Slow Wave PxC .40 1.00
BT01099EN Breakthrough at the Speed of Sound Sieghard U .75 2.00
BT01100EN Continuation of Combat Aoi U .75 2.00
BT01101EN Eyes of the Skies Sieghard U .75 2.00
BT01102EN Wings to the Future Sieghard U .75 2.00
BT01103EN Taut Bow Aoi U .75 2.00
BT01104EN Busy Morning Aoi U .75 2.00
BT01105EN Lucia of the Swallowblacks U .75 2.00
BT01106EN Body Guard Lotta U 2.00 5.00
BT01107EN Three Steps Ahead Aoi C .40 1.00
BT01108EN Tempest of Destruction Aoi C .40 1.00
BT01109EN First Flight Sieghard C .40 1.00
BT01110EN Buffalo Form Aoi C .40 1.00
BT01111EN Bunny Style Aoi C .40 1.00
BT01112EN Dress Up Doll Sieghard C .40 1.00
BT01113EN Archery Uniform Aoi C .40 1.00
BT01114EN Smiling in the Spirit World Lucia C .40 1.00
BT01115EN Melchi of Spring Anticipation C .40 1.00
BT01116EN Non Standard U .75 2.00
BT01117EN Vow to Pass Over Dimensions C .40 1.00
BT01118EN Lunatic Burst PxR 4.00 10.00
BT01119EN Tornado Disco PxC .40 1.00
BT01120EN Milky Paradise PxC .40 1.00
BT01G001EN Chloe Maxwell SCR 30.00 60.00
BT01G002EN Tamaki Yurine SCR 80.00 120.00

2000 Mitos y Leyendas El Reto

1 Odin R
2 Espada Real SF
3 Argonautas V
4 Rey Mono V
5 Grootslang R
6 Gorgonas V
7 Guerrero Jaguar C
8 Lámpara Mágica SF
9 Pegaso C
10 Grifo V
11 Ser Abominable R
12 Búfalo Blanco C
13 Tesoro del Rey SF
14 Trauko R
15 Seth V
16 Ogro V
17 Vampiro C
18 Demonio R
19 Centauro V
20 gnomos Burlones C
21 Fruto Sagrado SF
23 Escudo Real SF
24 Ek Chuah V
25 Prometeo V
26 Talos V
27 Mara V
28 Caleuche C
29 Tagaro y Suque V
2b Oráculo de Delfos O
30 Los Titanes V
31 Hutzilopochtli C
32 Gárgola V
33 Joyas de la Corona SF
34 Unicornio C
35 Pájaro de Trueno V
36 Perseo C
37 Sirenas C
38 Sátiro V
39 Final del Arcoiris SF
40 Hefesto C
41 Sko Yo V
42 Lothar C
43 Atlas V
44 Khnum V
45 Armadura Dorada SF
46 Cancerbero C
47 Thor V
48 Manuk V
49 Kornos C
50 Rosa de los Vientos SF
51 Sisiutil V
52 Hombre de Piedra V
53 Baal V
54 Busyip C
55 Dragón Medieval R
56 Gilgamesh V
57 Gigante Andino V
58 Ninfas C
59 Ave Fénix V
60 Cáliz Sagrado SF
61 Oannes V
62 Tentenvilu-Coicoivilu V
63 Amazonas R
64 Hadas V
65 Cíclope C
67 Anubis V
68 Hombre Lobo V
69 Fenrir C
6b Monedas de Oro SF
70 Kali V
71 Marduk C
72 Lilith V
73 Diamante Turquesa SF
74 Viracocha C
75 Osiris V
76 Medusa R
77 Nibelungos V
78 Anchimallen C
79 Estatua de Oro SF
80 Ymir V
81 Hadas Guerreras V
82 Loki V
83 Icaro V
84 Duende V
85 Xolotl C
86 Bárbaro V
87 Vishnu V
88 Isis V
89 La Quimera V
90 gnomo V
91 Pan-Gu V
92 Beowulf V
93 Portal Celestial SF
94 Aquiles V
95 El Basajaun C
96 Caballero Blanco V
97 Invunche C
98 Vikingo V
99 Serpiente Emplumada C
100 Esfinge V
101 Jinas C
102 Kordrag R
103 Arpía C
104 Hydra V
105 Kel-Essuf V
106 Hércules C
107 Caballero Negro R
108 Chon-chon C
109 Vampiro Oriental V
110 Pincoya C
111 Minas del Rey Salomón SF
112 Bruja Carabusse C
113 Haiwatha V
114 Zeus R
115 Poseidón V
116 Minotauro V
117 Cizin R
118 Merlin R
119 Melusina V
120 Berserker V
121 Hades C
122 Cuerno de la Abundancia SF
123 Brujo Chilote V
124 Zusano V
125 Eshu V

126 El Alicanto V
127 Mirhra C
128 Shiva V
129 Maui V
130 Hermes C
131 Indra V
132 Isthar C
133 Izanamie Izanagi V
134 Apolo C
135 Tlaloc V
136 Kirshna C
137 Odiseo R
138 Kasewats V
139 Sir Galahad V
140 Caballo de Troya C
141 Sigurd R
142 Rey Midas C
143 Orejona C
144 Mimi V
145 Yggdrasil C
146 Quetzalcoatl V
147 Dragón Oriental R
148 Humbaba C
149 Kelpie V
150 Hait V
151 Kraker V
152 Matador de Dragón C
153 Hombre Pájaro V
154 Rey Arturo R
155 Hubahpu y Xbalanque V
156 Guillermo Tell V
157 Balder V
158 Sir Gawain V
159 Hada Viviana V
160 Sedna V
161 Caja de Pandora R
162 Walkirias R
163 Afrodita V
164 Fu Hi V
165 Milloalobo V
166 Nugua V
167 Cernunno V
168 Horus V
169 Dragón C
170 Conejo Escriba V
171 Goblins V
172 Wondjinas V
173 Pixies V
174 Narciso V

2000 Mitos y Leyendas Mundo Gotico

1 Pozo del Juramento R
2 Hombre de Poca Fe R
3 Dominacion R
4 Cremacion C
5 Vigilia de Armas C
6 Prueba de Fuego C
7 Marcas de guerra V
8 Lucha de Golems R
9 Licantropia R
10 Ofuscacion V
11 Arlequin C
12 Oraculo Zingaro C
13 Mordida V
14 Luna Llena R
15 Custodio V
16 Estigma R
17 Stribog C
18 Daimon V
19 Macara de jade R
20 Mascara de Oro R
21 Eclipse de Dragon R
22 Dama de Hierro V
23 Justos por Pecadores R
24 Incubo V
25 Amanecer C
26 Presencia Maligna R
27 Tragedia V
28 Tumba del Caballero C
29 Rappagan-Mekabx R
30 Juego eterno V
31 Yelmo R
32 Escudo Hiperboreo R
33 Guadaña V
34 Hacha de enoch V
35 Guantelete R
36 Ballesta V
37 Espada Envenenada V
38 Anima Negra V
39 Dagas Krish V
40 Martillo y estacas V
41 Totem de la Fecundidad R
42 Totem del Vacio R
43 Totem de sangre V
44 Totem de la iluminacion V
45 Totem del genesis V
46 Totem del Olvido C
47 Totem de la Desesperanza R
48 Totem ultimo V
49 Totem de fuego V
50 Totem de vitalidad V
51 Knochen C
52 Dragon de Sombra V
53 Magnus V
54 Lupo V
55 Licantropo V
56 Jauria R
57 Guevadan R
58 Golem SF
59 Golem sombrio V
60 Espectro V
61 Zombies V
62 Hechicera V
63 Campesina V
64 Pastor V
65 Draco V
66 Salamandra V
67 Triton V
68 Bestia V
69 Abominacion V
70 Igor V
71 Kain C
72 Kasim R
73 Conde Shatten R
74 Ekimmu V
75 Strix V
76 Hiedra Espino R
77 Ryurik C
78 Falsa Cautiva V
79 Fetiche C
80 Khan C
81 Lesther V
82 Rasputin R
83 Nosferatu V
84 Moiras V
85 Issler V
86 Xamedhi V
87 Natasha V
88 Enjambre V
89 Mesalina V
90 Lucy V
91 Monje de Dri-Ling R
92 Casandra V
93 Roy R
94 Silver R
95 Krana R
96 Corazon de Leon R
97 Tribunal V
98 Scarlet V
99 Puritano R
100 Selena R
101 Armstrong V
102 Niamh V
103 Daphne y Gregor V
104 Exorcista V
105 Zara V
106 Zara V
107 Kemsa V
108 Karl V
109 Linna V
110 Emboscada V
111 Bafometh SF
112 Codice SF
113 Sortija SF
114 Rosal Silvestre SF
115 Castillo Sombrio SF
116 Cripta SF
117 Agua Sagrada SF
118 Raza Nocturna SF
119 Corona Imperial SF
120 Baculo SF
121 Dragon de Rubi SF
122 Catedral SF
123 Candelabro SF
124 Escudo de Cazador SF
125 Escudo de Vampiro SF
126 Campanas del Alba SF

2001 Mitos y Leyendas La Ira del Nahual

1 Anchancho C
2 Yanomami C
3 Auca C
4 Toki C
5 Flechero C
6 Ira del Nahual R
7 Ix Chebel Yax C
8 Pachamama R
9 Ix Tabai V
10 Sacrificio Humano R
11 K ak Na R
12 Machitun R
13 Sotz Na R
14 IX Chel V
15 Xochi Vaoyotl R
16 Ch Ayin Na C
17 Cataratas del Iguazú R
18 Revolución de los Objetos R
19 Rito del Dorado R
20 Reducción de Cabeza V
21 Mascara del Sol C
22 Sacrificio Gladiatorio C
23 Iniciación Guerrera C
24 Camaxtle V
25 Tonatiuh R
26 Cacería del Peyolt C
27 Huascar y Atahualpa R
28 Macuñ V
29 Ah Puch C
30 Xochiquetzal V
31 Tótem de Perro C
32 Tótem del Cóndor R
33 Tótem de Conejo V
34 Tótem del Aguila R
35 Tótem de Guanaco C
36 Tótem de Cocodrilo C
37 Tótem del Mono R
38 Tótem de Jaguar C
39 Tótem del Puma R
40 Tótem de Serpiente C
41 Insignia de Toqui V
42 Atlatl V
43 Tepoztopilli V
44 Boleadoras V
45 Cerbatana C
46 Honda V
47 Macahuitl V
48 Maza V
49 Arco y Flechas C
50 Tecpatl C
51 Cueva de quicavi V
52 Huitzil C
53 Machi C
54 Inca Yupanqui R
55 Tacan V
56 Pahuahtun C
57 Itzam Na C
58 Nanahuatzin R
59 Kenos V
60 Cin Teotl V
61 Wiraqocha C
62 Huehue Teotl C
63 Kalku R
64 Runa Urutruagu R
65 Apuilla C
66 Kukulcan V
67 Inti R
68 Tezcaltlipoca C
69 Joon V
70 Cipatqivil y Oxmoco R
71 Cunas V
72 Tlaloques R
73 Galvarino C
74 Cangrejos C
75 Tzitzimime C
76 Huracán R
77 Rumiñahui V
78 Caupolicán C
79 Chaco R
80 Guajiro V
81 Cabracán R
82 Guerrero Aguila V
83 Lautaro C
84 Etsa V
85 Karib V
86 Cihuate Teotl R
87 Ñamandu V
88 Peri Pillan C
89 Umoara R
90 Aclhuatl R
91 Tlacatecolotl R
92 Centzon Totochtin V
93 Ahu Kin R
94 Quetzalcoatl Retorna V
95 Chasqui R
96 Tlazolteotl R
97 Tsachila V
98 Killa V
99 Shuar V
100 Moctezuma V
101 Basilisco V
102 Camahueto V
103 Cuchivilu R
104 Cuero C
105 Caballo Marino V
106 Amaru V
107 Chinivilu V
108 Cuauhteomoc C
109 Puchao R
110 Tesoro de Guayacán R
111 Trapelacucha SF
112 Collar de Mani SF
113 Naricuera SF
114 Señor de Sipan SF
115 Uxmal SF
116 Machu Pichu SF
117 Zampoña SF
118 Tzolkin SF
119 Cráneo de Cristal SF
120 Trutruca SF
121 Puerta del sol Tahuanacu SF
122 Nazca SF
123 Columnas de Thulan SF
124 Tenochtitlan SF
125 El Dorado SF
126 Ciudad de los Cesares SF

2001 Mitos y Leyendas Ragnarok

1 Los Eddas R
2 Matador de gigantes R
3 Galdar R
4 Juramento de los Heroes R
5 Naglfar R
6 Espina Somnoliente R
7 Nidavellir R
8 Lanza de Odin R
9 Martillo de Thor R
10 Guantes de Hierro R
11 Hodur R
12 Hermod R
13 Nanna R
14 Nyord R
15 Maghi R
16 Hel R
17 Gigantes de Fuego R
18 Brokk R
19 Gigantes de Hielo R
20 Nidhogg R
21 Draugar R
22 Ejercito Enano R
23 Garm R
24 Geri y Freki R
25 Hymir R
26 Ratatosk R
27 Gandalf R
28 Dawn R
29 Vola R
30 Ragnar Lodbrog R
31 Einheryar R
32 Egil Skalla Grimsson R
33 Nott R
34 Mani R
35 Sol R
36 Dagur R
37 Elfos Arqueros C
38 Hyrronkkin C
39 Waldganger C
40 Esposas de los Furibundos C
41 Nidos de Pesadilla C
42 Herfyoturr C
43 Amuleto de Thor C
44 Forja de Enanos C
45 Astucia de Loki C
46 Metamorfosis de Loki C
47 Mirada Berserker C
48 Sacrificio de Odin C
49 Amor de Valkyria C
50 Espiritus de la Niebla C
51 Fimbultyr C
52 Draupnir C
53 Alfheim C
54 Vanaheim C
55 Asgard C
56 Niflheim C
57 Helheim C
58 Yotunheim C
59 Zapatos de Hierro C
60 Gambantein C
61 Arco de Ullr C
62 Espada de Frey C
63 Frigg C
64 Modi C
65 Baldur C
66 Hugin y Munin C
67 Yormungand C
68 Aegir C
69 Vavtrudnir C
70 Byleist C
71 Sleipnir C
72 Rugnir C
73 Surt V
74 Trivaldi V
75 Cuernos de Adumla V
76 Runas V
77 Fuente de Mimir V
78 Suplicio de Loki V
79 Hidromiel V
80 Holmgang V
81 Fuente de Urd V
82 Cadena Gleipnir V
83 Fuente de Hvergelmir V
84 Funeral Vikingo V
85 Midgard V
86 Muspellsheimm V
87 Cinturon de Thor V
88 Hacha Danesa V
89 Yelmo Escandinavo V
90 Niorun V
91 Eir V
92 Sif V
93 Heimdal V
94 Freya V
95 Idunn V
96 Bragi V
97 Nerthus V
98 Frey V
99 Ullr V
100 Yord V
101 Snotra V
102 Tyr C
103 Forseti V
104 Kvasir V
105 Vidar V
106 Skadi V
107 Tyra V
108 Fenoeiself V
109 Hraesvelg V
110 Mimir V
111 Gyallarhorn SF
112 Halatafl SF
113 Drakkar SF
114 Ataud de Marfil SF
115 Arqueta de Oro SF
116 Collar Brising SF
117 Martillo Amuleto SF
118 Calendario Runico SF
119 Rimkalk SF
120 Armadura de Valkyria SF
121 Escudo SF
122 Codex Runicus SF
123 Puente Bifrost SF
124 Piedras Runicas SF
125 Carro de Oseberg SF
126 Trono de Odin SF

2002 Mitos y Leyendas Espiritu de Dragon

1 Hotei R
2 Hoori R
3 Sarutahiko R
4 Iha Naga R
5 Hachiman R
6 Jurojin R
7 Kojin R
8 Fukurukujo R
9 Okuni Nushi R
10 Oho Yama R
11 Ninigi no Mikoto R
12 Amatsu Mara C
13 Sengen C
14 Inari C
15 Susano Wa C
16 Ryujin C
17 Izanami C
18 Kagutsuchi C
19 Bishamon C
20 Benten C
21 Raiden C
22 Amateratsu R
23 Daikoku V
24 Hoderi V
25 Momotaro V
26 Fujin V
27 Uzume V
28 Suku Na Biko V
29 Da Yu V
30 Izanagi V
31 Raiko V
32 Tsuki Yumi V
33 Ebisu V
34 San Xing V
35 Huang Fei Hu V
36 Huang Di V
37 Li Tien V
38 Yu Ren V
39 Lan Cai He V
40 Lao Tse V
41 Yuan Shueh V
42 Niu Wa V
43 Cai Shen V
44 Fu Xi C
45 Sha Heshang C
46 Guan Ti C
47 Heng-O C
48 Wang Mu Niang Niang C
49 He Xian Gu C
50 Fan Kui C
51 Lei Kung C
52 Shen Yi C
53 Sun Wu Kung C
54 Lu Dong Pin C
55 Panku R
56 Men Shen R
57 Kuei Xing R
58 Zhang Guo Lao R
59 Han Xiang Zi R
60 Zhong Kui R
61 Tsao Guojiu R
62 Han Zhongli R
63 Tien Mu R
64 Yu Huang R
65 Li Tie Guai R
66 Baije V
67 Mono de Hierro R
68 Yama Bushi R
69 Nemuri Kyoshiro R
70 Huang Zhong R
71 Zato Ichi R
72 Lin Kuei R
73 Geisha R
74 Ma Chao R
75 Shiro Amakusa R
76 Cao Cao R
77 Kunoichi R
78 Guan Yu C
79 Liu Bei C
80 Yagyu Jubei C
81 Hattori Hanzo C
82 Zhang Fei C
83 Tammo C
84 Miyamoto Musashi C
85 Hua Mu Lan C
86 Tomoe Gozen C
87 Sasaki Kojiro C
88 13 Heroes R
89 Benkei V
90 Zhao Yun V
91 Jimmu Tenno V
92 Pa Yu Feng V
93 47 Ronin V
94 Nomi No Sukune V
95 Shue Yuen V
96 Li Sou V
97 Bai Yu Feng V
98 Shinobi V
99 Wong Fei Hung V
100 Gallo Celestial R
101 Oni R
102 Geon Si R
103 Cienpies R
104 Bruja de la Montana R
105 Xing Tien R
106 Ninyo R
107 Konaki Jiji R
108 Gui R
109 Kappa R
110 Lung C
111 Gui Xian C
112 Fu C
113 Baku C
114 Feng-Huang C
115 Tchi Yeu C
116 Kitsune C
117 Yosei C
118 Tanuki C
119 Chiang Shih C
120 Serpiente Blanca V
121 Kilin V
122 Yurei V
123 Kong Kong V
124 Nurikabe V
125 Tengu V
126 Grulla V
127 Isun Boshi V
128 Rukuru Kubi V
129 Shachihoko V
130 Jujitsu R
131 Bushido R
132 Kayakujutsu R
133 Feng Shui R
134 Dokuenjutsu R
135 Kawarimi R
136 Chi Kung R
137 Pak Hok Cha R
138 Marca del Tigre R
139 Sepukku R
140 Kyudo R
141 Asesino del Emperador R
142 Pao Chuan Fa R

143 Kage Aruki Jutsu R
144 Saimin no Jutsu R
145 Kibidango R
146 Iaido R
147 Okinawa Te R
148 Kendo R
149 Saku Arai R
150 Niten Ichi Ryu C
151 Acupuntura C
152 Descubrir al zorro C
153 I Ching C
154 Tche Ma Tien C
155 Kage Bun Shin No Jutsu C
156 Lung Chuan-Fa C
157 tecnica de un dedo C
158 Yabusame C
159 Kitsune-Tsuki C
160 Ken Nage C
161 Fu Chuan-Fa C
162 Yingzhao Chuan-Fa C
163 Tradicion Viva C
164 Banquete Japones C
165 Viaje al Oeste C
166 Tang Lang Chuan-fa C
167 Ge Xiang Weng C
168 Palma de Hierro C
169 Kage Gakure Jutsu C
170 Banquete Chino V
171 Cha No Yu V
172 Kyusho V
173 Sake V
174 Nukewaza V
175 Marca de Dragon V
176 Zui Chuan Fa V
177 Dispositivo Espinoso V
178 Vencer sin Luchar V
179 tecnica de la Media luna V
180 Hombres de Madera V
181 She Chuan Fa V
182 Entrenamiento en Pilares V
183 Duelo de Espadas V
184 Kamasama No Jutsu V
185 Entrenar Multitudes V
186 Makimono V
187 Cometa V
188 Hou Chuan Fa V
189 Yuki Onna V
190 Perla de Dragon V
191 Chien V
192 Kun V
193 Monte Kun Lun V
194 Pa Kua Tai Chi C
195 Kan C
196 Sun C
197 Li C
198 Ken R
199 Tui R
200 Chen R
201 Pala de Monje R
202 Kabuto R
203 Yoroi R
204 Sai R
205 Bo R
206 Fu Tao R
207 Espada Celestial C
208 Kusari Gama C
209 Shuriken C
210 Escudo y Espada C
211 Katana C
212 Guan Dao C
213 Tetsu-Bishi C
214 Coraza China R
215 Gao Jie Bien V
216 Martillo Shaolin V
217 Nanigata V
218 Kunai V
219 Shuko V
220 Nunchaku V
221 Gran Muralla SF
222 Monedas Imperiales SF
223 Abaco SF
224 Templo de la Armonia SF
225 Calabaza del Inmortal SF
226 Origami SF
227 Teatro nov no SF
228 Bonsai SF
229 Kiku SF
230 Sakura SF
231 Ching His SF
232 Templo Shaolin SF
233 Yasakani SF
234 Teatro Kabuki SF
235 Sello Imperial de Jade SF
236 Go SF

2002 Mitos y Leyendas La Cofradia

1 Arpia C
2 Ah Puch C
3 Cancerbero C
4 Bufalo Blanco C
5 Berserker C
6 Aquiles C
7 Apolo C
8 Anchimallen C
9 Conde Shatten C
10 Guevadan C
11 Guantelete C
12 Grifo C
13 Fenrir C
14 Estigma C
15 Eclipse de Dragon C
16 Corazon de Leon C
17 Dominacion C
18 Hadas C
19 Hait C
20 Hades C
21 Licantropia C
22 Kasim C
23 Justos por Pecadores C
24 Invunche C
25 Escudo Hiperboreo C
26 Lucha de Golems C
27 Luna Llena C
28 Prueba de Fuego C
29 Pozo del Juramento C
30 Hombre de Poca Fe C
31 Pegaso C
32 Ogro C
33 Ninfas C
34 Minotauro C
35 Mascara de Oro C
36 Puritano C
37 Yelmo C
38 Xolotl C
39 Viracocha C
40 Vigilia de Armas C
41 Unicornio C
42 Totem de la Fecundidad C
43 Totem de Cocodrilo C
44 Totem del Olvido C
45 Shuar C
46 Serpiente Emplumada C
47 Sacrificio Gladiatorio C
48 Rasputin C
49 Diamante Turquesa SF
50 Baculo SF
51 Trutruca SF
52 Tenochtitlan SF
53 Sortija SF
54 Portal Celestial SF
55 Nariguera SF
56 Monedas de Oro SF
57 Lampara Magica SF
58 Escudo de Vampiro SF
59 Cripta SF
60 Collar de Mani SF
61 Caliz Sagrado SF
62 Catedral SF
63 Uxmal SF
64 Abominacion R
65 Enjambre R
66 Duende R
67 Cremacion R
68 Cuchivilu R
69 Brujo Chilote R
70 Arlequin R
71 Anubis R
72 Espada Real R
73 Hombre Lobo R
74 Golem Sombrio R
75 Hechicera R
76 Kemsa R
77 Kak Na R
78 Kain R
79 Inti R
80 Igor R
81 Killa R
82 Knochen R
83 Triton R
84 Trauko R
85 Totem del Mono R
86 Thor R
87 Stribog R
88 Sotz Na R
89 Salamandra R
90 Sacrificio Humano R
91 Ryurik R
92 Pastor R
93 Oraculo R
94 Odin R
95 Natasha R
96 Mesalina R
97 Merlin R
98 Melusina R
99 Medusa R
100 Maui R
101 Magnus R
102 Zusano R
103 Zara R
104 Amaru V
105 Basilisco V
106 Caballo Marino V
107 Chinivilu V
108 Centauro V
109 Cachorro V
110 Ballesta V
111 Baal V
112 Anima Negra V
113 Daphne y Gregor V
114 Dragon de Sombra V
115 Guerrero Aguila V
116 Gorgonas V
117 Gnomos Burlones V
118 Exorcista V
119 Espectro V
120 Espada Envenenada V
121 Esfinge V
122 Emboscada V
123 Hadas Guerreras V
124 Haiwatha V
125 Osiris V
126 Nosferatu V
127 Niamh V
128 Moiras V
129 Martillo y Estacas V
130 Mara V
131 Manuk V
132 Loki V
133 Linna V
134 Lilith V
135 Lesther V
136 Khnum V
137 Karl V
138 Karib V
139 Hefesto V
140 Honda V
141 Incubo V
142 Icaro V
143 Pan-Gu V
144 Perseo V
145 Tsachila V
146 Tragedia V
147 Totem de Conejo V
148 Strix V
149 Sisiutil V
150 La Quimera V
151 Sirenas V
152 Wondjinas V
153 Xamedhi V
154 Ymir V
155 Zombies V
156 Caceria del Peyotl C
157 Chon-chon C
158 Huehueteotl C
159 Kel-Essuf C
160 Totem del Guanaco C
161 Totem de Perro C
162 Tezcatlipoca C
163 El Alicanto R
164 Fetiche R
165 Vikingo R
166 Revolucion de los Objetos R
167 Oraculo Zingaro R
168 Monje de Kri-Ling R
169 Walkirias R
170 Rugdraige V

2003 Mitos y Leyendas Cruzadas

237 Ricardo Corazón de León R
238 Federico Barbarroja R
239 Felipe II R
240 Claymore R
241 Torre de Campaña R
242 Saladino R
243 Arca de la Alianza R
244 Jerusalén R
245 Mezquita de Damasco R
246 Siroco R
247 Fantasmas del Desierto R
248 Pedro el Ermitaño R
249 Gitanos R
250 La Llama Fría R
251 Ma arrat An-Numan R
252 Bernardo de Clairvaux R
253 Sir Robin De Locksley R
254 Jaques de Molay R
255 Mercaderes R
256 Cruz Templaria R
257 Simón de Montfort C
258 Ivanhoe C
259 Caballero Hospitalario C
260 Caballero Teuton C
261 Caballero Templario C
262 Duque Enrico Dandolo C
263 Basilio II Bulgaroktonos C
264 Sir Beufort C
265 Sir Vergenio C
266 Hermano Lazarus C
267 Capitán Imperial C
268 Maza de Guerra C
269 Escudo Templario C
270 Lanza de Justa C
271 Espada Templaria C
272 Ballesta Franca C
273 San Juan de Acre C
274 Bizancio C
275 Templo del Desierto C
276 Traficante de Esclavos C
277 Cruzada de los Niños C
278 Joyero C
279 Falso Tesoro C
280 Edessa C
281 Balduino V
282 Conrado III V
283 Duque Godofredo V
284 Luis IX El Santo V
285 Leonor de Aquitania V
286 Caballería Pesada V
287 Infante V
288 Cimitarra Dorada SF
289 Tancredo V
290 Alejo V
291 Curandera V
292 Mina de Diamantes SF
293 Cimitarra V
294 Aceite Hirviendo V
295 Antioquia V
296 Gente Escorpión V
297 Espejismo V
298 Grito de Guerra V
299 Ataque a Traición V
300 Cruzada de los Pobres V

2003 Mitos y Leyendas Espada Sagrada

1 Rey Arturo Pendragón R
2 Reina Guinivere R
3 Sir Lancelot R
4 Sir Gawein R
5 Sir Pérsival R
6 Sir Tristán R
7 Sir Galahad R
8 Príncipe Valiant R
9 Lady Dawn R
10 El Obispo de Londinium R
11 Sir Boores R
12 Cornelius de York R
13 Josofones R
14 Sir Bedivere R
15 El gran Wyrm R
16 Dragón de Magma R
17 Dragón de Eter R
18 Dragón Demonio R
19 Dragón de Luz R
20 Dragón de Aire R
21 Dragón del Agua R
22 Dragón de Plata R
23 Dragón Cobrizo R
24 Dragón de Bronce R
25 Kernuac El Cazador R
26 Dragón Nube R
27 Basoon R
28 Oberon R
29 Titania R
30 Mago Merlín R
31 Mordred R
32 Morgana R
33 Belial el Bestial R
34 La Dama del Lago R
35 Alto Druida R
36 Las Tres Hermanas R
37 El Poeta R
38 Puck R
39 Each Usige R
40 Ellyllon R
41 Plaga R
42 La Traición de Lancelot R
43 ¡Desleal! R
44 Bola de Fuego R
45 Transmutación R
46 Fe sin Limite R
47 Dragón Dorado R
48 Cuna de Dragones R
49 La Mirada de Mordred R
50 Santo Grial R
51 Una R
52 Capa de Invisibilidad R
53 Ataque Sorpresa R
54 Aulladores Blancos R
55 Ataque de Aliento R
56 La espada en la Piedra R
57 Atraer la Tormenta R
58 Barco R
59 Caballo Lunar R
60 Stonehage R
61 Tótem Maldito R
62 Tótem de Fe R
63 Tótem de Runas Elficas R
64 Tótem de la Ultima Canción R
65 Woodhage R
66 El Circulo Eterno R
67 Excalibur R
68 Espada de Cristal R
69 Escudo Sidhe R
70 Malla de Mitril R
71 La Lanza de los Dioses R
72 Armadura del Sol R
73 Espada Dragón R
74 Llewelyn, Voz de Plata C
75 Sir Owen C
76 Lady Rachel C
77 Sir Gabriel C
78 Isolda C
79 Lord Fergus Macloud C
80 Sir Wesley C
81 Sir Badallor C
82 Loth C
83 Sir Baldwin C
84 Sir Lionel C
85 Sir Héctor C
86 Sir Sagregor C
87 Dragón Montaña C
88 Tortuga Dragón C
89 Dragón Espía C
90 Darg, el Semi Dragón C
91 Org, el Hechicero C
92 Dragón Negro C
93 Dragón Nival C
94 Dragón de Mercurio C
95 Monta Dragones C
96 Wyvern C
97 Draco Esmeralda C
98 Draco Conjurador C
99 Serpentino C
100 Mulvan, el Dragón C
101 Lord Elfo C
102 Lady Shee Dia C
103 Greenknight C
104 Bruja Anis C
105 Banshee C
106 Pooka C
107 Elfo Oscuro C
108 Nixx C
109 Lobos de Avalon C
110 Pixie C
111 Kelpie C
112 Bane C
113 Ettin C
114 San Jorge y el Dragón C
115 Cuatro Fuertes Vientos C
116 Misil Mágico C
117 Flecha Ácida C
118 Congelar C
119 Nombrado Caballero C
120 Estampida C
121 Cuna de Gusanos C
122 Pergamino Mágico C
123 La Piedra de los Sueños C
124 Justa C
125 El Juicio de Dios C
126 Incinerar C
127 Favor de la Corte C
128 Knockers C
129 Brownie C
130 Urisk C
131 Legado del Bosque C
132 Producir Terremoto C
133 Tótem del Errante C
134 Tótem Goblin C
135 Tótem de Cristal C
136 Tótem Alquímico C
137 Oldhage C
138 Tótem de Nwyre C
139 Tótem del Conjurador C
140 Armadura Completa C
141 Hacha de Batalla C
142 Botas Elficas C
143 Espada Dentada C
144 Mandoble C
145 Scotish C
146 Morning Star C
147 Kay V
148 Halconero Real V
149 piqueros V
150 Caballería Ligera V
151 Comisario V
152 Guardián Real V
153 Campesino V
154 Sir Gareth V
155 Sir Thomas V
156 Sir Ducan V
157 Sir Mador del Portal V
158 Sir Gaerin, El Blanco V
159 Sir Jason de la Sangre V
160 Duque Thurk Bloodline V
161 Aghast, el Dragón V
162 Draco Sangre V
163 Atha-Uk V
164 Guerreros del Dragón V
165 Bárbaros Enfurecidos V
166 Dragón Nodriza V
167 Dragonel V
168 Bandidos Pictos V
169 Draco Águila V
170 Cultistas del Dragón V
171 Caballeros Pictos V
172 Dregon V
173 Rávido V
174 Goblin V
175 Hobglobin V
176 Arquero Elfo V
177 Ciervo Sagrado V
178 Duendes V
179 Goblin Conjurador V
180 Armada Elfica V
181 Talsoi V
182 Hijas del Caldero V
183 Galeb Duhr V
184 Otyugh V
185 Boggart V
186 Brag V
187 Asesinos en la corte V
188 Camino a Ávalon V
189 Cantrip V
190 Nombrado Escudero V
191 Grig V
192 Talismán Celta V
193 Juglares V
194 Hechizo de niebla V
195 Yermo V
196 Funeral para un Amigo V
197 Dioses en la Sombra V
198 El Juez V
199 Ataque Dragón V
200 Relatos en la Mesa Redonda V
201 Leprechaun V
202 Bugbear V
203 Ser Incorpóreo V
204 Gwyllion V
205 Vegetación Animada V
206 Alquimista V
207 Tótem Celta V
208 Tótem de Bossus V
209 Tótem de Hobgoblin V
210 Tótem de las Alas Eternas V
211 Tótem del Draco V
212 Argusthat V
213 Tótem del Alba V
214 Espada Larga V
215 Caballo de Batalla V
216 Caballo Ligero V
217 Dardos Envenenados V
218 Catapulta V
219 Espada Corta V
220 Alabarda V
221 Codex Arturicus SF
222 Azor SF
223 Pergamino de Bardo SF
224 Tierras Cultivadas SF
225 Herrero SF
226 Carruaje de Plata SF
227 Escudo de Familia SF
228 Tesoro Celta SF
229 Votos Sagrados SF
230 Árbol de los Viejos Dioses SF
231 Anillo Faerie SF
232 Joyería Picta SF
233 Collar de Dragón SF
234 Flota Mercante SF
235 Mesa Redonda SF
236 El Mercado de Camelot SF

2003 Mitos y Leyendas Helenica

1 Gaia R
2 Helios R
3 Eolo R
4 El Gran Zeus R
5 Hera R
6 Poseidon R

7 El Oscuro Hades R
8 Apolo R
9 Dionisio R
10 Thanatos R
11 Atenea R
12 Ares R
13 Eros R
14 Heracles R
15 Ulises R
16 Teseo R
17 Aristoteles R
18 Jason R
19 Dafne R
20 Orfeo R
21 Paris R
22 Alejandro Magno R
23 Penelope R
24 Castor R
25 Polux R
26 Edipo R
27 Aquiles R
28 Tifon R
29 Los Titanes R
30 Rea R
31 Atlas R
32 Cronos R
33 Oceano R
34 Kampe R
35 Selene R
36 Hiparion R
37 Prometeo R
38 Nocturnbros R
39 Eos R
40 Tea R
41 Expulsion de Titanes R
42 Maldicion de Hera R
43 Rayos R
44 Teleute R
45 Arde Troya R
46 Caballo de Troya R
47 Ira Ignea R
48 Invocar Luz R
49 Almas de Estigia R
50 Olimpiadas R
51 La Ira de Tifon R
52 Vellocino de Oro R
53 Urano R
54 Alas de Icaro R
55 Termofilas R
56 Hogar de Demonios R
57 Doce Pruebas R
58 Nacimiento de Pegaso R
59 Misterio de la Esfinge R
60 Tridente de los Mares R
61 Xiphos R
62 Hoz de Cronos R
63 Escudo de Atenea R
64 Casco de Hades R
65 Jabalina R
66 Martillo de Hefestos R
67 Monte Olimpo R
68 Tartaro R
69 Campos Elisios R
70 Atenas R
71 Esparta R
72 Arcadia R
73 Atlantida R
74 Hermes C
75 Artemisa C
76 Afrodita C
77 Hestia C
78 HECATAE C
79 Demetrios C
80 Fenix C
81 Europa C
82 Nemesis C
83 Hefestos C
84 Piton C
85 Demeter C
86 Caronte C
87 Temistocles C
88 Pericles C
89 Yolao C
90 Platon C
91 Sisifo el Hechicero C
92 Idmon el Adivino C
93 Calais y Cetes C
94 Amazonas Guerreras C
95 Hector C
96 Socrates C
97 Epicureo, el Sabio C
98 Belerofonte C
99 Ptolomeo C
100 Homero C
101 Ciclopes C
102 Mnemoisine C
103 Asteria C
104 Las Musas C
105 Titan C
106 Quimera C
107 Ladon C
108 Nessos C
109 Hecatoncheires C
110 Ketos C
111 Equidna C
112 Hidra de Lernea C
113 Dragon Custodio C
114 Furias C
115 Pasion de Zeus C
116 Raza de Pigmeos C
117 Antropolagos C
118 Isla de las Sirenas C
119 Iris C
120 Caliope C
121 Refugiados C
122 Medicina de Hipocrates C
123 Veneno Sagrado C
124 Entrenamiento Espartano C
125 Red de Aracne C
126 Templo de Medusa C
127 Fuego Griego C
128 Proteus C
129 Tormenta de Fuego C
130 Forja de Hefestos C
131 Locura de Heracles C
132 Cadenas de Andromeda C
133 Llamar al Fuego C
134 Espada de Infanteria C
135 Espada Macedonia C
136 Espada Noble C
137 Escudo Ateniense C
138 Espada de Caballeria C
139 Tormento C
140 Totem de Fenix C
141 Templo de Apolo C
142 Casa de Hestia C
143 Partenon C
144 Alejandria C
145 Templo de la Cazadora C
146 Templo de la gran Hera C
147 Meleagro V
148 Pandora V
149 Falange V
150 Mercenario Hoplita V
151 Ajax V
152 Medea V
153 Helena V
154 Sacerdotisa V
155 Maestro de Armas V
156 Felipo V
157 Atalanta V
158 Hilas V
159 Agammenon V
160 Anceo V
161 Lycaon V
162 Persefone V
163 Nereidas V
164 Triton V
165 Cibeles V
166 Alastor V
167 Boreas V
168 Lyssa V
169 Sileno V
170 Pan V
171 Psyche V
172 Nike V
173 Morfeo V
174 Cerbero V
175 Palias V
176 Talos V
177 Phorkys V
178 Telchines V
179 Cecrope V
180 Basilisco Griego V
181 Ixxion V
182 Epimeteo V
183 Pholo V
184 Coloso V
185 Minotauro de Creta V
186 Las Grayas V
187 Lamia V
188 Flota Helenica V
189 Nyx V
190 Homunculus V
191 Hipocampo V
192 Hipalectrycon V
193 Los Gorilai V
194 Casta de Gigantes V
195 Perros Tindalos V
196 Aspidoquelon V
197 Anakelades V
198 Alkyon V
199 Mercaderes Fenicios V
200 Estirge V
201 Serpiente de Bronce V
202 Bestia del Caos V
203 Cantobele V
204 Gente Insecto V
205 Caballo de Pesadilla V
206 Satiros Libres V
207 Lanza Espartana V
208 Yelmo Arcadio V
209 Daga Griega V
210 Brazaletes V
211 Sandalias de Hermes V
212 Pertiga V
213 Arco y Flechas Dorios V
214 Totem de Equidna V
215 Templo de Gaia V
216 Altar de Cronos V
217 Altar de Ares V
218 Templo Perdido V
219 Santuario de Poseidon V
220 Santuario Familiar V
221 Ofrenda a los Dioses R
222 Anfiteatro SF
223 Comedia SF
224 La Iliada R
225 La Odisea SF
226 Escultores SF
227 Galeras SF
228 Jardin de las Hesperides SF
229 Antorcha Olimpica R
230 Aves Exoticas SF
231 Corona de Laureles SF
232 El Agora SF
233 Dones de Hades SF
234 Viñas SF
235 Frontera Oriental SF
236 Lira SF

2003 Mitos y Leyendas Imperio

237 Julio Cesar R
238 Espartaco R
239 Cesar Augusto R
240 Júpiter R
241 Jano R
242 Neptuno R
243 Leucrota R
244 Dragón Ceniza R
245 Constantino C
246 Calígula C
247 Nerón C
248 Marte C
249 Las Erinias C
250 Venus C
251 Mercurio C
252 Dragón Oscuro C
253 Gigante de la Niebla C
254 Manticora C
255 Deva V
256 Legionario V
257 Pretoriano V
258 Gladiador V
259 Minerva V
260 Ondinas V
261 Vulcano V
262 Criaturas del Caos V
263 Atlante V
264 Hipogrifo V
265 Pantera de Niebla V
266 Gladius R
267 Maquinaria de Guerra R
268 Yelmo de Legionario V
269 Escudo Romano C
270 Armadura Legionaria C
271 Ariete C
272 Pilum C
273 Daga Envenenada V
274 Red de Gladiador V
275 Coliseo R
276 Templo de Júpiter R
277 Tótem Etrusco C
278 Catacumbas V
279 Panteón C
280 Termas V
281 Murallas de Adriano V
282 Rómulo y Remo R
283 Ambrosía R
284 Ataque de Aníbal R
285 El Vesubio R
286 Formación de Tortuga R
287 Los Caminos de Roma V
288 Conspiradores C
289 Nombrado Emperador C
290 Ataque Fulminante C
291 Animales del Circo C
292 Tribus Germanas V
293 Hunos V
294 Celtas del Oeste V
295 Carrera de Carros V
296 ¡Rebelión! V
297 Aceite de Oliva SF
298 Arcas del Imperio SF
299 Águila Imperial SF
300 Festín SF

2004 Mitos y Leyendas Dominios de Ra

1 Colosos Hititas Promo
1 Amon R
2 Relampago Arcano Promo
2 Ptah R
3 Osiris R
3 Dendera Promo
4 Horus R
4 Seshat Promo
5 Apophis R
6 Seth R
7 Ra R
8 Anubis R
9 Bastet R
10 Isis R
11 Geb R
12 Nut R
13 Shu R
14 Am-Heh R
15 Akenathon R
16 Tutmosis III R
17 Ramses II R
18 Nefertiti R
19 Amenofis II R
20 Seti R
21 Tutankamon R
22 Snofru R
23 Kefren R
24 Keops R
25 Micerinos R
26 Djoser R
27 Narmer R
28 Imoteph R
29 Bahiti R
30 Meskhenet R
31 Asheru R
32 Osorkhon el Grande R
33 Werin el Poseido R
34 Takelot R
35 Qer-Her R
36 Tuthu R
37 Kiya R
38 Yunet R
39 Kawit R
40 Suma R
41 Aton R
42 Alas de Horus R
43 Momificacion R
44 Arenas en Fuego R
45 La Letania de Ra R
46 Juicio a los Muertos R
47 Osiris ha Muerto R
48 Venganza R
49 Qadesh R
50 Lamento de Isis R
51 Gran Guardian R
52 Flechas de Lava R
53 Jinetes de Fuego R
54 Denwen R
55 Barca Dorada R
56 Ojos de Serpiente R
57 Purificar Escencias R
58 Aliento de Anubis R
59 Demonio de Piedra R
60 Hacha Sagrada R
61 Mandoble de Seth R
62 Sakraham R
63 Lanza de Osiris R
64 Carro Real R
65 Espada Diamante R
66 Garras de Bronce R
67 Guiza R
68 Abu Simbel R
69 Amarna R
70 Akeru R
71 Nubia R
72 Karnak R
73 Luxor R
74 Sobek C
75 Neftis C
76 Montu C
77 Maat C
78 Kepreth C
79 Hathor C
80 Knum C
81 Toth C
82 Neith C
83 Nejbet C
84 Sacmis C
85 Uadyet C
86 Tueris C
88 Nefertari C
89 Sesotris C
90 Sesotris III C
91 Hateshesput C
92 Mentuhopet C
93 Horemheb C
94 Escorpion C
95 Ahmosis el de fuego C
96 Virrey Setau C
97 Marenptah C
98 Smedes C
99 Shosheng C
100 Shebaka C
101 Dagi C
102 Gua C
103 Umm C
104 Zaliki C
105 Anpu C
106 Ramla C
107 Acero C
108 Penumbra C
109 Pili C
110 Panya C
111 Qaa C
112 Uni C
113 Yii C
114 Cárcel para el mal C
115 Sokar-Wesir C
116 Can Seth C
117 La Vision C
118 Hijos de Anubis C
119 Hititas C
120 Sombras Areneras C
121 Moldear la Realidad C
122 Misil de Montu C
123 Cobras de Luz C
124 Ser de Arena C
125 Gnam-Gnam C
126 Rechazar la Sombra C
127 Duelo de Dezzi Ah C
128 Barro Sanador C
129 Controlar el Mercado C
130 Destruir Mercado C
131 Mineros del Lapislazuli C
132 Producir Caos C
133 Guardian de Apophis C
134 Daga de Bastet C
135 Espada Miliciana C
136 Escudo Miliciano C
137 Dezzi Ah C
138 Vengativa C
139 Espada Nubia C
140 Tebas C
141 Beni Hassam C
142 Valle de los Reyes C
143 Deir El-Bahari C
144 Valle de las Reinas C
145 Colosos de Memnon C
146 Lago de la Vida C
147 Wepwawet V
148 Tefnut V
149 Selkis V
150 Satis V
151 Aken V
152 Khonsu V
153 Hike V
154 Kek y Kauket V
155 Hapi V
156 Renenutet V
157 Heqet V
158 Mahu V
159 Aman V
160 Pepi I V
161 Montuhopet II V
162 Sehetepibre V
163 Salitis el Usurpador V
164 Kamose V
165 Medjay V
166 Guerreros Egipcios V
167 Visir V
168 Radjedef V
169 Sinuhe el Viajero V
170 Yey V
171 Kah el Protector V
172 Surero V
173 Astronomo V
174 Dogir V
175 Femi V
176 Nathifa V
177 Ipy V
178 Hechicero Errante V
179 Traductor de Palacio V
180 Escribano V
181 Ipi-Ha-Ishutet V
182 Jarha V
183 Iuput V
184 Bennu V
185 Asceta del Nilo V
186 Monje de Aton V
187 Vastago de Anubis V
188 El perdon de Ra V
189 Dardos de Montu V
190 Abrir la Boca V
191 Trueno de Seth V
192 Nieblas de Anubis V
193 Duelo en el Desierto V
194 Caceria de Hipopotamo V
195 Badu-Badu V
196 Sacerdotiza Corrupta V
197 Hambre de Apophis V
198 Momia Andante V
199 Dioses del Arbol V
200 Sept V
201 Subach V
202 Tou tou V
203 Bas-Pef V
204 Halcon Sagrado V
205 Hatmeyth V
206 No mas Juegos V
207 Arco de Satis V
208 Daga de Seth V
209 Honda Milisiana V
210 Hacha de Trabajo V
211 Espada de Guardian V
212 Jabalina Milesiana V
213 Baston de Hequet V
214 Debod V
215 Dones del Nilo V
216 Templo Sombrio V
217 Esfinge de Guiza V
218 Templo de Isis V
219 Mastabas V
220 Saqqara V
221 Poema a Nefertari SF
222 Escarabeo SF
223 Corona Faraonica SF
224 Diadema SF
225 Libro de los Muertos SF
226 Libro de las Cavernas SF
227 Senet SF
228 Sarcofago Sagrado SF
229 Amkh SF
230 Latigo y Baston SF
231 Libro de la Tierra SF
232 Juguetes Infantiles SF
233 Fieras Domesticas SF
234 Hipopotamo Sagrado SF
235 Poetas de la Corte V
236 Piedra Roseta SF

2004 Mitos y Leyendas Encrucijada

237 Cleopatra VII R
238 Ptolomeo II R
239 Cleomenes de Naukratis R
240 Marco Antonio R
241 Alejandro II R
242 Neferite I R
243 Dario el Grande R
244 Haquika R
245 Oseye R
246 Bengay R
247 Demoledor de Amon R
248 Iuwlot R
249 Nuh R
250 Zazamoukh R
251 Aker R
252 Ament R
253 Oraculo de Botu R
254 Baal-zaphon R
255 Mafedet R
256 Reshep R
257 Shay R
258 Cadena Espiritual R
259 Festin Impio R
260 Aullido de Furia R
261 Invocar Chacales R
262 Vuelta a lo Primordial R
263 Jugar con las llamas R
264 Cobra de Cripta R
265 Adios belleza R
266 Hienas Asesinas R
267 Destrozar la Mente R
268 Islas filas R
269 Kabasha R
270 Dakka R
271 Wadi-el Sabua R
272 Kom Ombo R
273 Mandoble de Horus R
274 Sedienta R

275 Yelmo Alejandrino R
276 Hacha Guardiana R
277 Escudo de la Tormenta R
278 Ojo Udyat R
279 Biblioteca eterna R
280 Tocador R
281 Amyrteos C
282 Guerrero Etiope C
283 Capitan de Guardia C
284 Hijo de Amon C
285 Cambyses C
286 Euergeter I C
287 Philometor C
288 Airlea C
289 Aldara C
290 Absalon C
291 Chanoch C
292 Ayu C
293 Ksathra C
294 Adolfo C
295 Qetesh C
296 Min C
297 Nefertum C
298 Serapis C
299 Aesma Daeva C
300 Asto Vidatu C
301 Rashnu C
302 Anillo de Rashnu C
303 Usar el viento Este C
304 Muerte Roja C
305 Usar la Vision C
306 Levantar las Aguas C
307 Muro de Espinas C
308 Limpiar Conjuro C
309 Langostas C
310 Furia Irracional C
311 Arrancar el Alma C
312 Corromper Campeon C
313 Templo de Amon C
314 Totem del Sudan C
315 Santuario de Hapi C
316 Piramide Curvada C
317 Jardin Sagrado C
318 Lanza del Caos C
319 Daga de Bote C
320 Arco Persa C
321 Espada Colosal C
322 Corcel Egipcio C
323 Taharga V
324 Kush V
325 Teo V
326 Pedubaste I V
327 Lathyros V
328 Cleopatra Berenis V
329 Neos Dionisios V
330 Olabisi V
331 Oad V
332 Las Zesiro V
333 Urbi V
334 Tirano de las Arenas V
335 Neema V
336 Chike de la Sombra V
337 As el Halcon V
338 Patise y Pihor V
339 Heret-Kau V
340 Ihy V
341 Mehen V
342 Ta-Bitjet V
343 Weneg alma de Ra V
344 Llamar Avispas V
345 Aves de la Noche V
346 Amor o Traicion V
347 Guia Espiritual V
348 Llamar al gran Canibal V
349 Migraciones Beduinas V
350 Pastores del Nilo V
351 Gatos Sagrados V
352 Los Ojos de la Muerte V
353 Caricia Inmortal V
354 Expulsar Sacerdotes V
355 Necropolis Popular V
356 Templo a Ptolomeo V
357 Osar Ibrim V
358 Meidum V
359 Esna V
360 Baston de Aker V
361 Mandoble de Tifon V
362 Lagrima V
364 Cimitarra Persa V

2004 Mitos y Leyendas Hijos de Daana

1 Daana R
2 El Dagda Mor R
3 Midyir R
4 Ogma R
5 Ethain R
6 Angus Og R
7 Lugh R
8 Nuada Brazo de Plata R
9 Brigit R
10 Diancecht R
11 Epona R
12 Tutatis R
13 Belenos R
14 Mananaun R
15 Balor R
16 Devorador de Almas R
17 Wyrm Ahismal R
18 Demonio de Tara R
19 Laegerie R
20 Filborgs R
21 Duergar R
22 Abbey Lubber R
23 Bean Sidhe R
24 Slaugh R
25 Tethra R
26 General Corb R
27 Cethilion R
28 Cuchulain R
29 Vincegeratorix R
30 Bodicea R
31 Conn R
32 Fergus R
33 Finn Mac Cool R
34 Bolgos R
35 Taliesin R
36 Mathgen el Mago R
37 Figol el Druida R
38 Dianan y Bechulle R
39 Amergin el Druida R
40 Averix el Sabio R
41 Ojo Asesino R
42 Cambiar de Forma R
43 Hijos de Lir R
44 Raudo Surcador Marino R
45 Maldicion Danaan R
46 Fuego Magico R
47 Despertar Oscuro R
48 Caldero de la Abundancia R
49 Piedra del Destino R
50 Caceria Salvaje R
51 Corte Seelie R
52 Corte Unseelie R
53 Voz de la Tierra R
54 Derribar Montañas R
55 Levantar a los Muertos R
56 Bola de Energia R
58 Manzanas de la Vida R
59 Llama Marina R
60 Espada de la Luz R
61 Lanza de la Victoria R
62 Espada del Abismo R
63 Carro Celta R
64 Escudo Batersse R
65 Gae Bolga R
66 Lanza de Fuego R
67 Tier-Na-Oge R
68 Tier-Na-Moe R
69 Moy-Mell R
70 Tier-Fo-Tonn R
71 Pais sin Luz R
72 Ty Newydd R
73 Avalon R
74 Morrigan C
75 Gobniu C
76 Niña de la Suerte C
77 Cian C
78 Unicornio Sidhe C
79 Arawn C
80 Sidhe Guerrero C
81 Zorro de Fuego C
82 Dylan C
83 Lir C
84 Dama Blanca C
85 Gente Roble C
86 Cernunnos C
87 Cangrejo Oscuro C
88 Guerrero Fomor C
89 Mastin Oscuro C
90 Capas Rojas C
91 Druida Oscuro C
92 Orcos C
93 Kurick, el Picto C
94 Merodeador C
95 Tumulario C
96 Demonio del Viento C
97 Willowrong, el Dragon C
98 Gibberling C
99 Gusano de Hielo C
100 Unicornio Oscuro C
101 Myrdrin C
102 Druida de Man C
103 Brennos C
104 Guerrero Celtibero C
105 Guerrero Fianna C
106 Galatas C
107 Cristasiros C
108 Conary Mor C
109 Mac Cecht C
110 Lomma el Tonto C
111 Eochy C
112 Aibric C
113 Amada de los Bosques C
114 Golpear la Raiz C
115 Cuna de Hadas C
116 Nombrado Campeon C
117 Discipulos C
118 Piedra de Maldicion C
119 Exilio C
120 Abrir Portal C
121 Eclipse Siniestro C
122 ¿Se Cae el Cielo? C
123 Destino de Campeon C
124 Sajones C
125 Semhain C
126 Cazador Oscuro C
127 Carreras de Carman C
128 Paz Entre Hermanos C
129 Escudo y Refugio C
130 Bendecir las Armas C
131 Anillo de Fe C
132 Cuervos de Batalla C
133 Crear Talisman C
134 Espada Gala C
135 Espada Britanica C
136 Lanza Celta C
137 Escudo Solar C
138 Cota de Mayas C
139 Falcata C
140 Doncellas Alegres C
141 Men-An-Tol C
142 Piedras Azules C
143 Roble Sagrado C
144 Totem Sidhe C
145 Totem Fomor C
146 Hogar de Paz C
147 Dainone Sidhe V
148 Driadas V
149 Firdarring V
150 Benefactora V
151 Gregosh V
152 Cluricaun V
153 Leanan Sidhe V
154 Gnomo Irlandes V
155 Blodeuwedd V
156 Gwynn V
157 Hada Subterranea V
158 Neit V
159 Merrows V
160 Demoledor Fomoriano V
161 Ogro Guerrero V
162 Señor Oscuro V
163 Ainseil V
164 Bodach V
165 Bruja Gris V
166 Baba Yaga V
167 Kobold V
168 Perro Fomor V
169 Lagarto Oropel V
170 Draco Obsidiana V
171 Ingcel Solo un Ojo V
172 Gusano de Limerick V
173 Gobhaun Saor V
174 Cathbadh el Druida V
175 Connal Cernach V
176 Cu Roi, el Mago V
177 Maeb V
178 Fedelma V
179 Maeldum V
180 Skatcha V
181 Oisin V
182 Ambiorix V
183 Ovate V
184 Bardo V
185 Guerreras Britanicas V
186 Coperos V
187 Scots V
188 Canto Nocturno V
189 Duelo de Poetas V
190 Fuegos Fatuos V
191 Raza Oculta V
192 Huevo del Engaño V
193 Guardian Incesante V
194 Resplandecer V
195 Ira de los Elementos V
196 Fantasmas Aulladores V
197 Luz Esmeralda V
198 Broche de la Invisibilidad V
199 Armadura de Espiritus V
200 Lanza de Relampago V
201 Capa de Curacion V
202 Avenida de los Muertos V
203 El Gran Vuelo V
204 Reconocer el Honor V
205 Reunión de Druidas V
206 Serpientes Negras V
207 Rodela V
208 Hacha Ligera V
209 Escudo Largo V
210 Yelmo de Batalla SF
211 Espada Lusitana V
212 Arco Sidhe V
213 Honda y Misil C
214 Menhir V
215 Hogar de Gnomos V
216 Torre de Cristal V
217 Penhros-Feilw V
218 Totem de Balor V
219 Alesia V
220 Santuario Fianna V
221 Arpa Sagrada SF
222 Torc SF
223 Leche de Unicornio SF
224 Estatua Sagrada SF
225 Cerveza Negra SF
226 Whisky SF
227 Bouzouki Irlandes SF
228 Tierras Altas SF
229 Pendientes SF
230 Comerciante Galo SF
231 Jardines de Tier-Na-Moe SF
232 Marmita Druida SF
233 Hoz de Oro SF
234 Medallon SF
235 Corona de Campeon SF
236 Tejedora SF

2004 Mitos y Leyendas Tierras Altas

237 Macha R
238 Arianrhod R
239 Dewi R
240 Mogons R
241 Cerridwen R
242 Math R
243 Macda Tho R
244 Oengus R
245 Gronw Pebyr R
246 Gruagash R
247 Sonriente R
248 La Serpiente Negra R
249 La Serpiente Roja R
250 Bridei R
251 Fergus Mor Maceric R
252 Aedan Mac Gabrain R
253 Aed R
254 Brian O Grady R
255 Pwyll R
256 Pryderi R
257 Kenneth I R
258 Ejercito de la Noche R
259 Hijos de Plata R
260 Despertar R
261 Sacrificio R
262 La Traición de Mac Alpin R
263 Envenenar la Tierra R
264 Cuatro Aceros R
265 Animar los Elementos R
266 León Blanco R
267 La Cabeza del Mal R
268 Dalriada R
269 Ulster R
270 Tótem del León R
271 Caledonia R
272 Orkney R
273 Espada Lunar R
274 Arabar R
275 Eclipse R
276 Espada Necrofagia R
277 Yelmo Carnivoro R
278 Ogham C
279 Gaitas SF
280 Carmix SF
281 Finvarra C
282 Cliodna C
283 Creide C
284 Ratis C
285 Donn C
286 Nechtan C
287 Nemhain C
288 Dando C
289 Gusano de Lambton C
290 Bocan C
291 Talurc C
292 Hombre Vacío C
293 Necrófagos C
294 Carroñeros C
295 Aed Finn C
296 Ruthven C
297 Ogilvie C
298 Aethelfrid C
299 Niall C
300 Myghin C
301 Lilias C
302 Robar la Memoria C
303 Alma Animal C
304 Crear Necrófagos C
305 Las Tres Olas C
306 Tatuaje C
307 Forja Siniestra C
308 La Caída C
309 Levantar Castillo C
310 Las Tres Plagas C
311 Ácido de Gusano C
312 Red de Plata C
313 Fuente del Saber C
314 Tótem Salvaje C
315 Santuario de Math C
316 Santuario del Norte C
317 Templo de Gruagash C
318 Sigian Dubh C
319 Dirk C
320 Targe C
321 Gran Espada C
322 Caballo de Arrastre C
323 Roane V
324 Ghillie Dhu V
325 Spunky V
326 Ashrays V
327 Facham V
328 Boobrie V
329 Fenodoree V
330 Ly Erg V
331 Cailleac V
332 Hombre Azul V
333 Cultista Picto V
334 Fanático Picto V
335 Hechiceros del Caos V
336 Tropa Esqueleto V
337 Domhnall V
338 Duque Owen V
339 Montañes V
340 Sanador V
341 Guerrero Scot V
342 macCallum V
343 MacInnes V
344 Sidhes del Bosque V
346 Temor V
347 Behir V
348 Fantasmas Dorados V
349 Cazador Invisible V
350 Tácticas de Guerra V
351 Cadenas Eternas V
352 Colmillos de Plata V
353 Ejército del Sur V
354 Aguilas Azules V
355 Tótem de la Serpiente V
356 Campo de Juego V
357 Tótem de Macha V
358 Gwann V
359 Totem de Dewi V
360 Espada Picta V
361 Martillo Pesado V
362 Hacha Doble V
363 Sigian Dei V
364 Yelmo Scot V

2005 Mitos y Leyendas Barbarie

1 Aldaric R
2 Teodoric I R
3 Odoacro R
4 Widukind R
5 Clodoveo R
6 Carlomagno R
7 Carlos Martel R
8 Atila R
9 Genseric R
10 Justiniano I R
11 Belisario R
12 Aetius R
13 Teodosio I, El Grande R
14 Recaredo R
15 Darmer R
16 Wotán R
17 Seaxneat R
18 Frigue R
19 Svarog R
20 Tiw R
21 Sif R
22 Fanfir R
23 Drachenstein R
24 El Knucker R
25 Haat R
26 Darak de la Sombra R
27 Amatista R
28 Chmarnik R
29 Erix el Bretón R
30 Hada Melusina R
31 Sigfried R
32 Glaistig R
33 Gurlukh R
34 Havfrue y Havmand R
35 Beowulf R
36 Grendel R
37 Crom Gruach R
38 Tarasca R
39 Dominador R
40 Bisclavret R
41 Dhampir R
42 Focalor R
43 Furfur R
44 Chalons R
45 Derrocar R
46 Emergen las Sombras R
47 Licantropía R
48 Alianza R
49 Saqueo R
50 Descargar Magia R
51 Sacrificio a Wotán R
52 Ordalía R
53 Morbo Gótico R
54 Primera Sangre R
55 Ejército de Almas R
56 Relámpagos R
57 Los Cuervos de Wotán R
58 Cacería de Demonios R
59 Humillación R
60 Inmunidad al Aliento R
61 Poitiers R
62 Tótem de Darmer R
63 Altar de Wotán R
64 Tótem Báltico R
65 Nido de Plaga R
66 Las Manos de Wotán R
67 Los Ojos de Perkuna R
68 Sagrado Valhalla R
69 Ciudad Sagrada R
70 Godesberg R
71 Templo de Uppsala R
72 Aquitania R
73 Armas Alanas R
74 Espada Visigoda R
75 Yelmo Godo R
76 Escudo Godo R
77 Balmung R
78 Espada Anglosajona R
79 Martillo de Darmer R
80 Arco Huno R
81 Spatha R
82 Espada Franca R
83 Alboin C
84 Khagan C
85 Arquero Alano C
86 Gundobad C
87 Roderic C
88 Rosamund C
89 Gepidae C
90 Grodlon C
91 Comandante Bizantino C
92 Magnus Maximus C
93 Anthemius C
94 Cazador de Demonios C
95 Caza Recompensas C
96 Valens C
97 Brunilda C
98 Vali C
99 Nerthus C
100 Tuisto C
101 Hellia C
102 Freyr C
103 Aegir C
104 Drac C
105 Kovo El Destructor C
106 Dragón Subterráneo C
107 Celeste C
108 Anfibisena C
109 Stihi C
110 Graully C
111 Huldra C
112 Brechta C
113 Cwn Annwn C
114 Rusalje C
115 Gob Rey de Gnomos C
116 Ku Rey de Enanos C
117 Basadone C
118 Mustélido Gigante C
119 Kludde C
120 Gunawulf C
121 Sicario del Pozo C

122 Varcolac C
123 Krvopijak C
124 Eurynomos C
125 Ataque Draugar C
126 Pesca Fantástica C
127 La Canción de Rolando C
128 Mal Acero C
129 Sin Sobrevivientes C
130 Cambiantes C
131 Esferas de Fuego C
132 Misil Helado C
133 Conjuro de Hambre C
134 Fundir Tesoro C
135 Piratería C
136 Muro de Flechas C
137 Gorgades C
138 Los Dones de Annwn C
139 Cazar Habergeis C
140 Llamar al Halstraub C
141 Crear Rebis C
142 Cuerpo de Cometa C
143 Vuelo Siniestro C
144 Templo del Dragón C
145 Irminsul C
146 Tótem Subterráneo C
147 Tótem de la Madre C
148 Tuonela C
149 Horgr C
150 Kalevala C
151 Los Muros de Justiniano C
152 Los Huesos del Behemot C
153 Midgard C
154 Río de Lava C
155 Armadura Goda C
156 Escudo Sajón C
157 Yelmo Nórdico C
158 Jannadiche C
159 Espada Bizantina C
160 Hacha Goda C
161 Espada Capadocia C
162 Siete Demonios C
163 Baakhandor C
164 Trebuchet C
165 Kniva V
166 Invasor Juto V
167 Horsa el Sajón V
168 Pelayo de Asturias V
169 Athal el Noble V
170 Leovigildo V
171 Requila V
172 Romulus Augustus V
173 Respendial V
174 Magistrado V
175 Fuerzas de Choque V
176 Vengador V
177 Arsenio V
178 Zeno V
179 Ukko V
180 Tuoni V
181 Perkele V
182 Idun V
183 Marzanna V
184 Chernobog V
185 Kupala V
186 Dracónico Bestial V
187 Herren Sugue V
188 Balaur V
189 Chalkydri V
190 Azhi Dahaka V
191 Nimbu V
192 Dragón Carroñero V
193 Elfos del Norte V
194 Ellefolk V
195 Gegetones V
196 Elemental del Hielo V
197 Elemental del Fuego V
198 Elemental del Bosque V
199 Arlik V
200 Becut V
201 Ankout V
202 Serafín Corrupto V
203 Grilo Salvaje V
204 Ayperos V
205 Kuzlak V
206 Larvae V
207 Ataque Jettins V
208 Canción de Lorelei V
209 Salamandra V
210 Hombre Jabalí V
211 Borrones Blancos V
212 Mirada de Dragón V
213 Contaminar las Aguas V
214 Comercio Clandestino V
215 Herida Superficial V
216 Bufón Espía V
217 Asesino Oculto V
218 Lemures V
219 Tecnología Inútil V
220 Miedo a la Sombra V
221 Tropas Congeladas V
222 Matrimonio Arreglado V
223 El Beso de Letzel V
224 Tierra de Luderec V
225 Pacto de Sangre V
226 Totem Eslavo V
227 Tótem de la Fuerza V
228 Árbol de Sangre V
229 Campamento V
230 Pequeño Feudo V
231 Morkies V
232 Salón de Espejos V
233 Fogata de Poetas V
234 Fortaleza Arrasada V
235 Hogar Ellefolk V
236 Tótem Caníbal V
237 Mazo Ligero V
238 Espada Germánica V
239 Espada Vándala V
240 Mazo Calavera V
241 Espada de Bretaña V
242 Botas Francas V
243 Bombardas Dragonas V
244 Espada Burgundia V
245 Hacha de Enano V
246 Espada de Alboin V
247 Piel de Oso SF
248 Aguila Real V
249 Botín Huno SF
250 Códex Germánico SF
251 Liber Iudicorum SF
252 Daga Dorada SF
253 Corona de Plata SF
254 Perro Alano SF
255 Obras Clásicas SF
256 Lex Sálica SF
257 Copa Calavera SF
258 Arte Religioso SF
259 Anillo Papal SF
260 Carta a la Amada SF

2005 Mitos y Leyendas Vendaval

1 Atahualpa R
2 Huascar R
3 Manco Capac R
4 Sinchi Roca R
5 Sapa Inca R
6 Caupolican R
7 Cazador Yanomami R
8 Lautaro R
9 Guarani R
10 Tume Arandu R
11 Viracocha R
12 Mama Quilla R
13 Mama Cocha R
14 Inti R
15 Siete Monstruos R
16 Caicai Vilu R
17 Cherruve R
18 Meuler R
19 Basilisco Chilote R
20 Pillan R
21 Ngechen R
22 Jurupari R
23 Kren R
24 Shompalahue R
25 Cherufes R
26 Wekufes R
27 Huecuvo R
28 Escuchar el Bosque R
29 Guillatun R
30 Puma Rampante R
31 Tomar Pucara R
32 Forma de Jaguar R
33 Nombrar Magistrado R
34 Caleuche R
35 Caballo de Agua R
36 Tierra de Diablos R
37 Trempulcahue R
38 Vencer Veneno R
39 Malas Astucias R
40 Cuzco R
41 Machu Pichu R
42 Nazca R
43 Chungara R
44 Rehue R
45 Cueva de Salamanca R
46 Budi R
47 Signo Toqui R
48 Maza De Estrella R
49 Hacha Inca R
50 Boleadora R
51 Chueca R
52 Lanza de Inti R
53 Baculo Marino R
55 Capitan Inca C
56 Guerrero de Elite C
57 Guardia del Emperador C
58 Embarcacion R
59 Cazador Yagan C
60 Kaweshkar C
61 Karana C
62 Pacha Mama C
63 Yastay C
64 Mama Oclla C
65 Urcuguary C
66 Apo C
67 Anaconda Tej C
68 Cuchivilu C
69 Chinifilu C
70 Oriflama C
71 Huentreyao C
72 Nguenco C
73 Shenu C
74 Carcancho C
75 Llorona C
76 La Fiura C
77 La Calchona C
78 Flechero C
79 Umoara C
80 Hashbi C
81 Kawtcho C
82 Flor de Hielo C
83 Incendiar el Pasado C
84 Frutos Magicos C
85 Invasion al Altiplano C
86 Alma de Condor C
87 Quicavi C
88 Aconcagua C
89 Tierra Celeste C
90 Tumba Volcanica C
91 Pozos de Luna C
92 Muelle de Muertos C
93 Hacha Cortante C
94 Arco Amazonico C
95 Honda C
96 Armadura Inca C
97 Yelmo Inca C
98 Baston de Viajero C
99 Flechas Magicas C
100 Virgen del Templo V
101 Ayar Anca V
102 Ayar Cachi V
103 Ayar Ushu V
104 Mama Cura V
105 Aoinkenk V
106 kolla V
107 Hombre Tiwanaku V
108 Curandera Quichua V
109 Abaanqui V
110 Pombero V
111 Apu Illapu V
112 Mama Huaco V
113 Chasca Coyllur V
114 Constrictor Gigante V
115 Piuchen V
116 Dragon Austral V
117 Antu Fuche V
118 Antu Kuche V
119 Camahueto V
120 Yoalox V
121 Millalobo V
122 Invunche V
123 El Coo V
124 Ruende V
125 La Voladora V
126 Tau V
127 Unu Pashukuti V
128 Domo y Lituche V
129 Canoeros V
130 Ritos de Iniciacion V
131 Cruzar el Fuego V
132 Viaje Astral V
133 Duelo de Brujos V
134 Anchimalen V
135 Demonios Olvidados V
136 Invocar Bestia Negra V
137 Alhue V
138 Pucara V
139 Santuario Amazonico V
140 Tiwanaku V
141 Totem Mapuche V
142 Santuario Inca V
143 Cueva de Fantasmas V
144 Tierra del Fuego V
145 Maza Circular V
146 Escudo Inca V
147 Lanza de Vigilante V
148 Poncho V
149 Cerbatana y Dardo V
150 Baculo Imperial V
151 Armas de Brujo V
152 Las Armas del Creador V
153 Tesoro de los Cesares SF
154 Cadena Infernal SF
155 Minas Imperiales SF
156 Dones de Tau SF
157 Plumas Nobles SF
158 Tenten Vilu R
159 Trauko R
160 Colo-colo R
161 La luz De Inti R
162 Soldados Cañari C
163 La Añañuca C
164 Selk nam C
165 Pihuychen C
166 Hueñauca C
167 La Brujería C
168 Manta-Manta C
169 Saire, Agua y Lluvia C
170 Caminos del Inca C
171 Macuñ C
172 Seres de La mañana C
173 Ciudad Cesares C
174 Lanza Cañari C
175 Poràsÿ V
176 Vilpoñi V
177 Hombres Serpientes V
178 Ad-Mapu V
179 Cazar Ñandu V
180 Comercio Inca SF
58b Magnate Inca C

2006 Mitos y Leyendas Bestiario

1 Chukack SP R
2 Orias SP R
4 Nemain SP R
5 Simargl SP R
6 Espectro de Dragon SP R
7 Arlequin SP R
8 Dominacion SP R
9 Luna Llena SP R
10 Minas de Gruash SP R
11 Parkhusa SP R
12 Hanan'el SP R
13 Makara SP R
14 Dentalion SP R
15 Hombre Pantera SP R
16 Flechero SP R
17 Cienpies SP R
18 Atraer la Tormenta SP R
19 Tótem Goblin SP R
20 Demonio SP R
21 Nosferatu SP R
22 Cultista Picto SP R
23 Demonio de Tara SP R
24 Draco Fulgor SP R
25 La Llama Fria SP R
26 Cocratea R
27 Barack R
28 Chukack R
29 Okenuth R
30 Dragón Canibal R
31 Gran Tiamath R
32 Dragón del Foso R
33 Draconico Dorado R
34 Escupe Brazas R
35 Uthuthu R
36 Ik-al-marin R
37 Malafar R
38 Baalzebu R
39 Malphas R
40 Malthus R
41 Mammon R
42 Marax R
43 Marbas R
44 Marchosias R
45 Nakkin R
46 Zagan R
47 Mephistopheles R
48 Orias R
49 Taranis R
50 Nemain R
51 Maahes R
52 Mania R
53 Mantus R
54 Amatsu Mikaboshi R
55 Mara el Mentiroso R
56 Cariocecus R
57 Ereshkigal R
58 Vlad Tepes R
59 Kingu R
60 Mummu R
61 Pikullos R
62 Gran Bestuk R
63 Marowit R
64 Simargl R
65 Julana R
66 Los Mokoi R
67 Yama R
68 Chon - Chon R
69 Hombre de Poca Fe R
70 Prueba de Fuego R
71 Gorgonas R
72 Kel-Essuf R
73 Espectro de Dragon R
74 Medusa R
75 Dearg Diulai R
76 Arlequin R
77 Kain R
78 Knochen R
79 Rappagan-Mekkak R
80 Ryurik R
81 Conde Shatten R
82 Dominacion R
83 Eclipse de Dragon R
84 Estigma R
85 Justos por Pecadores R
86 Luna Llena R
87 Arbol de la Justicia R
88 Blaghu R
89 Totem del vacio R
90 Totem de la Desesperanza R
91 Totem Lunar R
92 Minas de Gruash R
93 Moy-Mell R
94 Hellfire R
95 Goetia R
96 Laguna de los muertos R
97 Tótem de la Sangre R
98 Fetiche R
99 Escudo Hiperboreo R
100 Anima Negra R
101 Dama de Hierro R
102 Guadaña R
103 Marcas de Guerra R
104 Akhadia R
105 Parkhusa R
106 La Última Garra R
107 Gashilion R
108 Zirnitra C
109 Abuhuza C
110 Draco Acerino C
111 Taranto C
112 Dragón Golem C
113 Draconico Viajero C
114 Dragón Niebla C
115 Wyrm Colosal C
116 Wyrm Celeste C
117 Guinon C
118 Gomory C
119 Fata siniestra C
120 Gremlins C
121 Hanan'el C
122 Grigori C
123 Incubo de pozo C
124 Sucubo del pozo C
125 Salmac C
126 Samael C
127 Tonga Hiti C
128 Makara C
129 Mahisha C
130 Yama Uba C
131 Yeti C
132 Dentalion C
133 Danyul C
134 Decarabia C
135 Jack O'Lattern C
136 Drudes C
137 Uttuku C
138 Vapula C
139 Lilitu C
140 Vampiro del Desierto C
141 Guifred Estruch C
142 Conde Strucc C
143 Erzsébet Báthory C
144 Gilles de Rais C
145 Licantropo de Plata C
146 Hombre Pantera C
147 Lix Tetrax C
148 Guraldon C
149 Cocoraceo C
150 Esposas de los Furibundos C
151 Sacrificio de Odin C
152 Sacrificio Humano C
153 Reduccion de Cabeza C
154 Flechero C
155 Ix Tabai C
156 Chiang Shi C
157 Cienpies (Invocar Bestia Negra) C
158 Lung C
159 Serpiente Blanca C
160 Yurei C
161 Dragon de Eter C
162 Belial el Bestial C
163 Puck C
164 Plaga C
165 Atraer la Tormenta C
166 Se cae el Cielo C
167 Bane C
168 Ataque de Dragón C
169 Tótem de Magma C
170 Castillo Sombrio C
171 Cueva de Quicavi C
172 Tótem Maldito C
173 Tótem Goblin C
174 Tótem Hobgoblin C
175 Totem Fomor C
176 Tótem Salvaje C
177 Cadenas Eternas C
178 Tótem de la Serpiente C
179 Tótem de Balor C
180 Espada del Abismo C
181 Golem C
182 Ayajak C
183 Armadura Vampiro C
184 Escudo de las Nieves C
185 Espada del Cuervo C
186 La Armadura del Oso C
187 Escudo Vampiro C
188 Armadura Viva C
189 Catapulta Infernal C
190 Demonio V
191 Gargola V
192 Nosferatu V
193 Falsa Cautiva V
194 Alimaña V
195 Hechicera V
196 Issler V
197 Salome V
198 Cultista Picto V
199 Hechiceros del Caos V
200 Ly Erg V
201 Carroñeros V
202 Gusano de Lambton V
203 Necrofagos V
204 Oengus V
205 Bean Sidhe V
206 Bruja Gris V
207 Demoledor Fomoriano V
208 Demonio de Tara V
209 Fantasmas Aulladores V
210 Fedelma V
211 General Corb V
212 Laegerie V
213 Morrigan V
214 Orcos V
215 Org, el Hechicero V
216 Slaugh V
217 Unicornio Oscuro V
218 Noctumbros V
219 Quimera V
220 Triton V
221 Mortus V
222 Draco Fulgor V
223 Xuan V
224 Draco Imperial V
225 Draco Cristal V
226 Ilina Inferna V
227 Ilina Sanguinea V
228 Ilinia Ignea V
229 Yatu V
230 Gawigawen V
231 La Llama Fria V
232 Marrat an Numan V
233 El Oscuro Hades V
234 Thanatos V
235 Aquiles V
236 Almas de Estigia V
237 Nemesis V
238 Antropofagos V
239 Alastor V
240 Perros Tindalos V
241 Avenida de los muertos V
242 Caldero de la Abundancia V
243 Corte Unseelie V
244 Despertar Oscuro V
245 Devorador de Almas V
247 Levantar a los Muertos V
248 Merodeador V
249 Bridei V
250 Hombre Vacio V
251 Robar la memoria V
252 Tartaro V
253 Tótem de Medusa V
254 Totem de Hierro V
255 Quien lo ve todo V
256 Árbol del Caos V

257 Dolmen del Sacrificio V
258 Puerta del hades V
259 Sanf V
260 Tótem Hiperboreo V
261 Santuario Vampírico V
262 Yelmo Carnivoro V
263 Forja Siniestra V
264 Daga Bebedora V
265 Yelmo del Caos V
266 Armadura Amatista V
267 Puas Retractiles V
268 Masa de Ogro V
269 Canilleras Doradas V
270 Arco del Hades V
271 Estaca V
272 Bafometh O
273 Codice O
274 Hacha Danesa O
275 Dones de Hades O
276 Candelabro O
277 Collar de Dragon O
278 Mascara de Oro O
279 Yelmo O
280 Fragua O
281 Pacto O
282 Tatuaje Lupino O
283 Ojo de cristal O
284 Codex Licantropo O
285 Bezoar O
2SP Malafar SP R
45b Nakkin R
177b Cadenas Eternas C
216b Tethra V
276b Candelabro O
278b Máscara de Oro O

2006 Mitos y Leyendas Heroes

1 Nintu SP R
2 Duberdicus SP R
3 Dziewanna SP R
4 Cormac mac Airt SP R
5 Skalla-Grimm SP R
6 Gisli el Bandido SP R
7 Cassivellaunus SP R
8 Taira no Kiyomori SP R
9 Teletransportación Limitada SP R
10 Invasión de Almas SP R
11 Exorcismo Avanzado SP R
12 Humm SP R
13 Unicornio Montura SP R
14 Grifo Montura SP R
15 Hierodule SP R
16 Troll de Skaga SP R
17 Metatron SP R
18 Vespasiano SP R
19 Alto Rey SP R
20 Espíritus del Agua SP R
21 Achianabul SP R
22 Sandbag SP R
23 Warcrie SP R
24 Babieca SP R
25 Pendiente Pirata SP R
26 Gilgamesh R
27 Llew R
28 Arduinna R
29 Bodb Dearg R
30 Glanis el Inmortal R
31 Aplu R
32 Aeon R
33 Sucellus R
34 Nintu R
35 Duberdicus R
36 Badhbh Catha R
37 Alaunos el Magno R
38 Padre Lobo R
39 Shamash R
40 Maia R
41 Dziewanna R
42 Camulus R
43 Cormac mac Airt R
44 Skalla-Grimm R
45 Eirikr Hákonarson R
46 Gisli el Bandido R
47 Cassivellaunus R
48 Taira no Kiyomori R
49 Akechi Mitsuhidec R
50 Uther Pendragón R
51 Sir Breunor le Noir R
52 Sir Constantine R
53 Sir Griflet R
54 Encarcelar el Mal R
55 Teletransportación Limitada R
56 Invocar Anfibios R
57 Cortar la Sombra R
58 Invasión de Almas R
59 War Spasm R
60 Camino a la Noche R
61 Sumisión R
62 Forjar Katana R
63 Exorcismo Avanzado R
64 Caminar por la Telaraña R
65 Duelo Celestial R
66 Barrera Esmeralda R
67 Tótem de la Gloria Eterna R
68 Tótem de la Flama R
69 Boconnath R
70 Humm R
71 Henge Eterno R
72 Espada Deva R
73 Unicornio Montura R
74 Grifo Montura R
75 Lanza del Bufalo R
76 Sir Olivier C
77 Otton C
78 Guy de Bourgogne C
79 Guillaume de Palerme C
80 Haokah C
81 Sin C
82 Kan Loan C
83 Rongo C
84 Akitha C
85 Hierodule C
86 Gothi C
87 Sacerdote del Troll C
88 Troll de Skaga C
89 Sidhe Aventurero C
90 Sidhe Rojo C
91 Uriel C
92 Metatron C
93 Orestes C
94 Vespasiano C
95 Tiberio C
96 Electra C
97 Oniwabanshu C
98 Fujibayashi Sabuji C
99 Offa C
100 Sláine C
101 Sir Aglovale C
102 Sir Pelleas C
103 Sir Palamades el Sarraceno C
104 Sir Gingalian el Desconocido C
105 Bombardear Abadía C
106 Fuego negro C
107 Invocar la gran Cacería C
108 Alto Rey C
109 Llamada de los Fianna C
110 Bendecir las Armas C
111 Romper Amuleto C
112 Domar Bestias C
113 Consejo de la Triple Diosa C
114 Espíritus del Agua C
115 Achianabul C
116 Burlar las trampas C
117 Sandbag C
118 Ataque Arboreo C
119 Llamas de Sargón C
120 Anima Lumina R
121 Larimia C
122 Trollkyrka R
123 Arena de Gladiadores C
124 Hacha de los Bosques C
125 Yelmo de Bisonte C
126 Cruzado Bizantino V
127 Paladín de Bruenas V
128 Akilhar V
129 Paladín Leal V
130 Deva León V
131 Na Tuk Kong V
132 Zalmoxis de Dacia V
133 Menrva la Etrusca V
134 Hija de Plata V
135 Lara V
136 Rasiel V
137 Casiel V
138 Caminante Azul V
140 Benwulf V
141 Kunoichi V
142 McBeth V
143 Portador del Martillo V
144 Elfo Plateado V
145 Lingura V
146 Domina Dragones V
147 Sir Jonas V
148 Sir Cador V
149 Hoel V
150 Daniel von Blumenthal V
151 La hoguera V
152 Lágrimas Vitales V
153 Vitalia V
154 Bebida Fomor V
155 Flecha Danaan V
156 Recibir laureles V
157 Duelo Invernal V
159 Banquete de Dragón V
160 Saquear al Caido V
161 Tres Lunas V
162 Salón del Jazmín V
163 Jardín Imperial V
164 Templo Deva V
165 Babieca V
166 Pistola de Rueda V
167 Lengua Plata O
168 Perla Negra O
169 Jaula dorada O
170 Collar de Huesos O
171 Esfera de Cristal O
172 Brazalete Germano O
173 Pintura Sagrada O
174 Calaca de invocación O
175 Pendiente Pirata O

2006 Mitos y Leyendas Hordas

1 Kublai Khan R
2 Genghis Khan R
3 Marco Polo R
4 Tengri R
5 Soldado Mameluko R
6 Jalair R
7 Hoelum R
8 Borte R
9 Whang Khan R
10 Gu R
11 Kalgama R
12 Las Kikimoras R
13 Los Kormos R
14 Losum R
15 Manzachiri R
16 Mecin R
17 Jamuka R
18 Togrul R
19 Subutai R
20 Noyons R
21 Shah Ala ad-Din Muhammad R
22 Msislav el Valeroso R
23 Halych R
24 Li-Dewang R
25 Emperador Bing R
26 La Furia de Khan R
27 Veneno Tartaro R
28 Asalto al Muro R
29 Enfrentar a los Cruzados R
2b Genghis Khan R
30 Dominio del Sol R
31 Tigres de Guerra R
32 Lobos del Volga R
33 Magos de la Corte R
34 Ataque a Cipango R
35 Muerte a la Serpiente R
36 La caída de Persia R
37 Sombras de la Tierra R
38 Ujan-buthan-ke R
39 Samarcanda R
40 Ciudad Nómade R
41 Templo Budista R
42 Moscú R
43 Santuario de Tendri R
44 Espada de Temujin Khan R
45 Escudo de Temujin Khan R
46 Montura dorada R
47 Caballo Mongol R
48 Ivailio C
49 Alexander Nevski C
50 Mikhail Yaroslavich C
51 Uzbeg Khan C
52 Batu Khan C
53 Akhmat Khan C
54 Andrés II de Hungría C
55 Erlik el Eclipse C
56 Solovei C
57 Sug ási C
58 Tien-Kou C
59 Ilja Muromec C
60 Campeón Celestial C
61 Kirm C
62 Surãle C
63 O Ogusa C
64 Tepegöz C
65 Uker C
66 Chaka C
67 Nogai Khan C
68 Jochi C
69 Chagatai Khan C
70 Caballero Germano C
71 Öljeitü C
72 Ivan II Ivanovich C
73 Padre de Demonios C
74 Negulathos C
75 Soborno C
76 Llamar Fantasmas C
77 Hunubornos C
78 Sikhonn C
79 Batalla de Legnica C
80 Seguir la Corriente C
81 Entrada al Templo C
82 Juh C
83 Curación con barro C
84 Emboscar al traidor C
85 Suelo Canibal C
86 Tierra bestias C
87 Hogar en la Tormenta C
88 Templo Nestoriano C
89 Tangut C
90 Jorezm C
91 Elefante de Guerra C
92 Espada de Jinete C
93 Armadura Mongol C
94 Arco Mongol C
95 Jinete Tártaro V
96 Cruzado Georgiano V
97 Loto V
98 Vurus-Vut V
99 Bodisatva V
100 Herbalista V
101 Emisario de Wudang V
102 Misionero Nestoriano V
103 Misionero Franciscano V
104 Xingitan V
105 Xia V
106 Xu V
107 Xianglu V
108 Turán V
109 Uzut V
110 Xiwagmu V
111 Jabe V
112 Mongka Khan V
113 Sorghaghtani Bek V
114 Guerrero Manchur V
115 Libertador Ming V
116 Soldados del Viet V
117 Tropas de Samarcanda V
118 Tribus del Desierto V
119 Caballero de la Gran Casa V
120 Sacrificios por el Khan V
121 Caravanas Comerciales V
122 Competencia de caballos V
123 Carga de Elefantes V
124 El favor de los Xhindi V
125 Huanihuai V
126 Llamar a los Gophet V
127 La horda Azul V
128 La horda Dorada V
129 La horda Blanca V
130 Linh V
131 Aliento de Ma V
132 Hijo de las Tormentas V
133 Altar Estepario SF
134 Yurt V
135 Reinos Kerait V
136 Merv V
137 La Gran Bilar V
138 Rinoceronte de Guerra V
139 Armadura Persa V
140 Daga Mongol V
141 Red de Cazador V
142 Yak SF
143 Trono de Kublai SF
144 Habitación Dorada SF
145 Dadivas SF
146 Aguila Sagrada O
147 Rutas Comerciales O
148 Buda Dorado O
149 Cultivo de Arroz O
150 Estatuilla de Jade O

2006 Mitos y Leyendas Reino de Acero

1 Mio Cid Campeador R
2 Joan D'Arc R
3 Robert De Bruce R
4 Tarik R
5 Henry V R
6 Otto I El Grande R
7 Luis el Piadoso R
8 Yngvi R
9 Tharapita R
10 Perún R
11 Bealdor R
12 Eostre R
13 Alvis el Enano R
14 Sciapodi R
15 Duhons R
16 Gigante Agripiano R
17 Stribog IV R
18 Bestla R
19 Smok Wawelski R
20 Chair Salée R
21 Al R
22 Cocadrille R
23 Loki R
24 Kraken C
25 Goin R
26 Dommon R
27 Garm R
28 Veles R
29 Nidhogg R
30 Hagen de Borguen R
31 Andras R
32 Infantes de Carrión R
33 Shax R
34 Dinabuc R
35 William Wallace R
36 Björn Ironside R
37 Alfonso X R
38 Fernando el Magno R
39 Conan de Bretaña R
40 Harold Godwinson R
41 Lothair R
42 William el Conquistador R
43 Nombrarse Emperador R
44 Guerra de Cien Años R
45 Reconquista R
46 Cruzada Oscura R
47 Asalto R
48 Pestilencia R
49 Emboscada de Artilleros R
50 Agonía R
51 Carnaval R
52 Honoris Salve R
53 Ataque Vikingo R
54 ¡Infieles! R
55 Pacto Impío R
56 Impuestos R
57 Agravio R
58 Rebelión en el Feudo R
59 Nacimiento en el Mal R
60 Licantropos Orientales R
61 Travesía Imposible R
62 Alfein R
63 Yggdrasil R
64 Praga R
65 Île de la Cité R
66 Ducado de Luxemburgo R
67 Toledo R
68 Valencia la Mayor R
69 Edimburgo R
70 Castillo de Dublin R
71 Westminster R
72 Skåneland R
73 Colada R
74 Tizona R
75 Mangonel R
76 Balista R
77 Bombarda R
78 Guantes de Thor R
79 Cinturón de Thor R
80 Ribaud R
81 Veuglaire R
82 Escudo de Borgoña R
83 Alfonso VI de Castilla C
84 Carlos V de Francia C
85 Widewut C
86 Egill Skallagrímsson C
87 Caballero de Santiago C
88 Dievas C
89 Ilmarinen C
90 Moderdekai Alas de Acero C
91 Oiger el Danés C
92 Bruteno C
93 Obispo Marino C
94 Pikne C
95 Na Amhuisgean C
96 Sherkano C
97 Orchera C
98 Blanar C
99 Alp C
100 Vanatuhi C
101 Loviatar C
102 Xanochoy C
103 Sarkany C
104 Fannakendlor C
105 Otso C
106 Marool C
107 Adremelech C
108 Príncipe Negro C
109 Juan I Tzimisces C
110 Isaac II Angelus C
111 Leonardo C
112 Muló C
113 Liuvgat C
114 Los Koerakoonlased C
115 Angantyr C
116 Leif Eriksson C
117 Brian Boru C
118 Urraca de Castilla C
119 Irene de Atenas C
120 Auseklis C
121 Las Mathe C
122 Tirante El Blanco C
123 Caballeros de Calatrava C
124 Caballeros de Dobrin C
125 Fiesta de Klabers C
126 Nube de muerte C
127 Peste Negra C
128 Hechiceras del Norte C
129 Aquelarre C
130 Travesuras C
131 Domar Hipogrifo C
132 Doncella del Camino C
133 Duelo de Guerra C
134 Traductor C
135 Cae Constantinopla C
136 Negocios con Herishef C
137 La promesa de Tirante C
138 Hechizar al Fuath C
139 Familiares C
140 Buguel Noz C
141 Odisea por los Mares C
142 Bigorne C
143 Asesinato en la Corte C
144 Alcázar de Segovia C
145 Castillo de Tarascón C
146 Cahir Castle C
147 Alhambra C
148 Castelo Guimaraéz C
149 Abadía de Cluny C
150 Jumieges C
151 Monte Athos C
152 Monte San Miguel C
153 Santa Caterina C
154 Tótem de Svetovid C
155 Espadón Morges C
156 Bastarda Normanda C
157 Alabarda Burgundia C
158 Proto Fusil C
159 Escudo Imperial C
160 Ballesta Francesa C
161 Partisana C
162 Armadura Pesada C
163 Guanteletes C
164 Arco Inglés C
165 Digenis Acritas V
166 Bertrand du Guesclin V
167 Orvar-Odd V
168 Hermanos de la Espada V
169 Radagast V
170 Dazbog V
171 Saxo Gramaticus V
172 Honnid V
173 Astolfo V
174 Blemmyes V
175 Guerrero Feerico V
176 Leshy V
177 Diale V
178 Bergfolk V
179 Lange Wapper V
180 Hors V
181 Jarilo V
182 Lado y Lada V
183 Antolpphs V
184 Grand'Goule V
185 Bis V
186 Mahwot V
187 Salumargo V
188 Agares V
189 Flauros V
190 Navi V
191 Carabuncle V
192 Albinach V
193 Carlos de Navarra, el Mal V
194 Aliana V
195 Yanidor V
196 Amli V
197 Callicantzaroi V
198 Dachanavar V
199 Erdmannchen V
200 Arngrim V
201 Hjalmar V
202 Simeon I V
203 Yekuno Amlak V
204 Osman I C
205 Mokosh V
206 Golliardo V
207 Quema Textos V
208 Ataque del Bosque V
209 Pájaros de Hielo V
210 Vuelo Sobrenatural V
211 Compañía de Teatro V
212 Ataques Mongoles V
213 Envenenar la Hoja V

214 Traficante de Tesoros V
215 Refugiados Bizantinos V
216 Hechiceras Jannish V
217 Gente Abeja V
218 Polkran V
219 Tumbas de Portunes V
220 Prepolnica V
221 Matines cazadores V
222 Caballo Alado V
223 Toro de Agua V
224 Tentaculos de Fuego V
225 Invisibilidad Chirriante V
226 Torre de Londres V
227 Califato de Cordoba V
228 Chateau de Vincennes V
229 Katzenelnbogen V
230 Castillo de Limerick V
231 Dolbadarn V
232 Ewloe V
233 Donan V
234 Warwick V
235 Fuerte Medieval V
236 Muelle Drakkar C
237 Escudo de la Orden V
238 Caballo Armado V
239 Hacha Eslava V
240 Francisca V
241 Espada Normanda V
242 Mandoble Franco V
243 Escudo Castellano V
244 Escudo de León V
245 Yelmo de Arquero V
246 Armadura Ligera. V
247 Corona Imperial SF
248 Corona Otomana SF
249 Rescate Monetario SF
250 Monedas Imperiales SF
251 Parche de Irene SF
252 Tierras Domadas SF
253 Liber Monstruorum SF
254 Siete Partidas SF
255 Obra del Amadis SF
256 Textos Goticos SF
257 Arte Bizantino SF
258 Estela Báltica SF
259 Penacho SF
260 Estandarte SF
192b Albinach V

2007 Mitos y Leyendas Codigo Samurai

1 Ryujin UR
2 Minamoto no Yoritomo UR
3 Seiwa Genji UR
4 Nihon koryu jūjutsu UR
5 Amatseratsu SP R
6 Izanagi e Izanami SP R
7 Sennin SP R
8 Dogen Kissen SP R
9 Kitsune SP R
10 Kirin SP R
11 Bakemono SP R
12 Shimma Kunoichi SP R
13 Bojutsu SP R
14 Espíritus Negros SP R
15 Haiku SP R
16 Kusanagi SP R
17 Agua SP R
18 Tanuki SP R
19 Takeda Shingen SP R
20 Mon Moshi SP R
21 Ashikaga Takauji R
22 Yoshimitsu R
23 Hattori Hanzō R
24 Amatseratsu R
25 Suzanoo R
26 Izanagi e Izanami R
27 Ookuninushi R
28 Sennin R
29 Dogen Kissen R
30 Basho R
31 Akusen R
32 Kitsune R
33 Rai Ju R
34 Kagu-tsuchi R
35 Raiden R
36 Baku R
37 Tengu R
38 Nue R
39 Kirin R
40 Tatsu R
41 Shokuin R
42 Hai Ryu R
43 Yasha R
44 Kiyohime R
45 Futen R
46 Yaamma Ten R
47 Nuke Kubi R
48 Bakemono R
49 Yurei R
50 Tsuchigumo R
51 Oda Nobunaga R
52 Aka Oni R
53 Ao Oni R
54 Ōnamuji R
55 Princesa Yakami R
56 Jubei R
57 Masamune R
58 Haohmaru Musashi R
59 Shoki R
60 Shimma Kunoichi R
61 Karima Kunoichi R
62 Tokugawa Leyasu R
63 Hōjō Tokimasa R
64 Miyamoto Musashi R
65 Kushinada R
66 Seppuku R
67 Dominar los Vientos R
68 Nacimiento del Dragón R
69 Espíritus Shugenjas R
70 Sazen R
71 Manipular Ki R
72 Dominar al Dragón R
73 Cambiaformas Salvajes R
74 Tsunami R
75 Bojutsu R
76 Juegos de la Corte R
77 Duelo de Kenjutsu R
78 La Fuerza del Agua R
79 Empujar el Viento R
80 Deshonor R
81 Espíritus Negros R
82 Ceremonía del Té R
83 Iado R
84 Sombras Ninja R
85 Canción Geisha R
86 Haiku R
87 Teatro Kabuki R
88 Edo R
89 Nagoya R
90 Onomichi R
91 Yamotsu R
92 Monte Fuji R
93 Kinkakuji R
94 Katsura R
95 Palacio de Kioto R
96 Daibutsu de Kamakura R
97 Kusanagi R
98 Katana Amatseratsu R
99 Daisho Tokugawa R
100 Kinton R
101 Tokugawa Yoshimune C
102 Yamamoto Tsunetomo C
103 Teruhime C
104 Kaguya Hime C
105 Tennin C
106 Shukongoshin C
107 Ama no Uzume C
108 Ikkaku Sennin C
109 Ikkyu Sojun C
110 Koun Ejo C
111 Morihei Ueshiba C
112 Momotaro C
113 Katuri Umin C
114 Chodorio C
115 Kintaro C
116 Mitsume Kozo C
117 Kappa C
118 Tenaga C
119 Howo C
120 Kai Sai C
121 Ka Ryu C
122 Ri Ryu C
123 Ichimoku C
124 Yuki Onna C
125 Hitoban C
126 Ubume C
127 Neko Mata C
128 Hyttoko C
129 Gaki Botoke C
130 Rokudaijin C
131 Genjuro Makoto C
132 Oni Canibal C
133 Hari Onaga C
134 Issun Boshi C
135 Kato Kiyomasa C
136 Kusunoki Masashige C
137 Onna gugeisha C
138 Tomoe Gozen C
139 Taira C
140 Takeda Shingen C
141 Cuarenta y Siete Ronin C
142 Aochi Shigetsuna C
143 Uesugi Kenshin C
144 Hosokawa Garasha C
145 Dama de Rojo C
146 Teatro Bunraku C
147 Teatro Noh C
148 Venganza Geisha C
149 Oku no Hosomichi C
150 Kyudo C
151 Técnica de Doble Espada C
152 Asesinato a Traición C
153 Caligrafía C
154 Sumai C
155 Kashima no Tachi C
156 Montura Ryu me C
157 Emboscada en el Templo C
158 Técnica del Remo C
159 Tierra C
160 Aire C
161 Fuego C
162 Agua C
163 Sueño del Vacio C
164 Azuchi C
165 Bitshu C
166 Castillo Hachigata C
167 Castillo Hachioji C
168 Palacio Katsura C
169 Ginkakuji C
170 Pagoda Yasaka C
171 Yari C
172 Sais C
173 Naginata C
174 Toyotomi Hideyoshi V
175 Jaraiya V
176 Tsuname V
177 Konohana V
178 Ohoyamatsumi V
179 Tanuki V
180 Fujin V
181 Hachiman V
182 Keisan Yokin V
183 Senkio V
184 Seiobo V
185 Hibagon V
186 Shōjō V
187 Shiyoku V
188 Shinriku V
189 Kinchizo V
190 Jiuri V
191 Takujiu V
192 Teirei V
193 Basan V
194 Tatsumaki V
195 Shozan no Shin V
196 Ryuja Sama V
197 Shosuda no baba V
198 Shugenju Oni V
199 Orochimaru V
200 Otoroshi V
201 Shiga V
202 Jikininki V
203 Sazae Oni V
204 Demonio Ninja V
205 Oni Bushi V
206 Kawata el Ronin V
207 Shokuza no Baba V
208 Okiku V
209 Tokugawa Hidetada V
210 Go-Yozei V
211 Konoe V
212 Daimyo Lujurioso V
213 Yasuke V
214 Yagyū Munenori V
215 Yojimbo V
216 Arcabucero Imperial V
217 Marinero Yoritomo V
218 Shinsengumi V
219 Magia de Cristal V
220 Técnica de Shuriken V
221 Waka Sensei V
222 Forja de Kokitsune Maru V
223 Triunfo del Escorpión V
224 La Nave Negra V
225 Escupir Fuego V
226 Herida Viciosa V
227 Beso Venenoso V
228 Fantasmas Hambrientos V
229 Encender Katana V
230 Tatuaje Sagrado V
231 Proyección de Sombras V
232 Recolectores de Perlas V
233 Kamikaze V
234 Kendo V
235 Drenar a distancia V
236 Sekei Tei V
237 Santuario Shinto V
238 Santuario Toshogu V
239 Daibutsu de Nara V
240 Asakusa Kannon V
241 Nijo V
242 Horyuji V
243 Sanjusangendo V
244 Shuriken V
245 Kyu V
246 Tanto V
247 Máscara de Jade O
248 Mon Oda O
249 Mon Moshi O
250 Mon Tokugawa O
251 Crisantemo Imperial O
252 Bonzai O
253 Campana Zen O
254 Pez Koi O
255 Shamisen O
256 Kimono O
257 Ikebana O
258 Nikko-Bori O
259 Origami O
260 Yatay O

2007 Mitos y Leyendas Corsarios

1 Sir Francis Drake UR
2 Jugando con el Diablo UR
3 Merrow-SP R
4 Cetus-SP R
5 Sida al Hurra-SP R
6 La Garse-SP R
7 Tragado por el mar-SP R
8 Mar sin Piratas-SP R
9 Ruinas de la Atlántida-SP R
10 Parche Pirata-SP R
11 Rusla de Noruega R
12 Sida al Hurra R
13 Ravenau de Lusan R
14 Oshun R
15 Reverendo Padre Labat R
16 Aycayía R
17 Oya R
18 Bakunawa R
19 Rahab R
20 Forneus R
21 Cecaelia R
22 Merrow R
23 Capitán Devil R
24 Hendrick Brouwer R
25 Lady Mary Killigrew R
26 Cornelius Essex R
27 Henry Every R
28 Jane de Belleville R
29 María Pita R
30 Antonia María de Soto R
31 Bruno Mauricio Zabala R
32 Almirante Howards R
33 Ann Mills R
34 Thomas Cavendish R
35 Jaula de Almas R
36 Locura Oceánica R
37 Tragado por el Mar R
38 Tráfico de Esclavos R
39 Repartir Ganancias R
40 Mar sin Piratas R
41 Apuesta R
42 Lluvia de Estrellas R
43 Navío condenado R
44 Nombrado Gobernador R
45 Libertaria R
46 Ruinas de la Atlántida R
47 Gully R
48 Swivelgun R
49 La Garse R
50 Satisfaction R
51 Parche Pirata R
52 Carta Marina R
53 Bernard Claesen Speirdyke C
54 Guillermo de Orange C
55 Reina de Anjouan C
56 Atargatis C
57 Thomas Gage C
58 Rusalki C
59 Sedna C
60 Tannin C
61 Yofune-Nushi C
62 Aughisky C
63 Hombre azul de Minch C
64 Cetus C
65 Phineas Bunce C
66 Edward Collier C
67 Captain Yeats C
68 Miguel Henríquez C
69 John Morris C
70 Elizabeth Shirland C
71 Duque de Alba C
72 Diego Grillo "El Mulato" C
73 Andrés del Pos C
74 Sir Francis Verney C
75 Christopher Winter C
76 Deborah Sampson C
77 Sin Viento C
78 Desposar Princesa C
79 Entierro en el Mar C
80 Golem de coral C
81 Invocar tormentas C
82 Astillero C
83 Mercado de Esclavos C
84 Forado C
85 Limpiando las Aguas C
86 Despilfarro C
87 Estrecho de Magallanes C
88 Mar de Sargazos C
89 Granada C
90 Mortero Naval C
91 Flying Dragon C
92 Fancy C
93 Arcón C
94 Grog C
95 Pata de Palo C
96 Etienne Moreau V
97 Ranavalona Manjaka I V
98 Capitán Desmarris V
99 O-Wata-Tsu-Mi V
100 Fray Juan de Barrenechea V
101 Asrai V
102 Tien Hou V
103 Damballah V
104 Oshunmare V
105 Bunyip V
106 Shellycoat V
107 Spriggans V
108 Edward Low V
109 Joseph Bradley V
110 Dixey Bull V
111 Thomas Cocklyn V
112 Israel Hands V
113 David Herriot V
114 Manuel Rivero Pardal V
115 Marqués de Castelfuerte V
116 José Fernando de Abascal V
117 John Taylor V
118 Edward Vernon V
119 Lawrence Washington V
120 Oficio Divino V
121 Reparaciones V
122 Naturalista V
123 Pierna por Oro V
124 Escorbuto V
125 Reclutar Tripulación V
126 Sin Timón V
127 Crónica V
128 Colonizar V
129 Pasado pirata V
130 Ensenada de Ocrakoud V
131 Sallee V
132 Broadsword V
133 Carronada V
134 Lanfranco V
135 Revenge V
136 Aquamarina V
137 Carta en la botella V
138 Barril de Provisiones V
139 Munición V
140 Mascota V
142 Oliver la Bouche R
143 Alexander Sellkirk C

2007 Mitos y Leyendas Dominvs

518II Go Promo
CR10140SP Parche Pirata-SP R
CR19140II Rahab R
CR20140II Forneus R
CR42140II Lluvia de Estrellas R
CR52140II Carta Marina R
CR54140II Guillermo de Orange C
CR58140II Rusalki C
CR62140II Aughisky C
CR74140II Sir Francis Verney C
CR77140II Sin Viento C
CR80140II Golem de coral C
CR95140II Pata de Palo C
CR98140II Capitán Desmarris V
CS10260SP Kirin SP R
CS13260SP Bojutsu SP R
CS17260SP Agua SP R
CS20260SP Mon Moshi SP R
CS22260II Yoshimitsu R
CS40260II Tatsu R
CS41260II Shokuin R
CS44260II Kiyohime R
CS45260II Futen R
CS51260II Oda Nobunaga R
CS52260II Aka Oni R
CS56260II Jubei R
CS62260II Tokugawa Leyasu R
CS74260II Tsunami R
CS84260II Sombras Ninja R
CS99260II Daisho Tokugawa R
HC20160II Diego Portales R
HC38160II Cruzar la Cordillera R
HC63160II Hilarión Daza C
HC67160II Mariano Osorio C
HE25175SP Pendiente Pirata SP O
HE85175II Hierodule C
KA19140II Mujina R
KA20140II Emma R
KA21140II Ningyo R
KA25140II Tenjō-Name R
KA46140II Corcel Espectral R
KA62140II Shachi Hoko C
KA65140II Goryō C
KA74140II Amakuni C
KA93140II Yamato Takeru V
PI10240SP Rehén-SP R
PI62240II Motín R
PI75240II Fondo de Mar R
PI79240II Golden Hind R
PI88240II Corte de Nereidas C
PI89240II Ondinas C
VE41180SP Trempulcahue SP R.
BE160285II Yurei C
BE202285II Gusano de Lambton V
BE213285II Morrigan V
BE2285SPII Malafar SP R
CR102140II Tien Hou V
CR104140II Oshunmare V
CR106140II Shellycoat V
CR124140II Escorbuto V
CR131140II Sallee V
CR137140II Carta en la botella V
CR139140II Munición V
CS121260II Ka Ryu C
CS1260URII Ryujin UR
CS142260II Aochi Shigetsuna C
CS149260II Oku no Hosomichi C
CS153260II Caligrafía C
CS165260II Bitshu C
CS169260II Ginkakuji C
CS189260II Kinchizo V
CS196260II Ryuja Sama V
CS198260II Shugenju Oni V
CS199260II Orochimaru V
CS200260II Otoroshi V
CS219260II Magia de Cristal V
CS222260II Forja de Kokitsune Maru V
CS228260II Fantasmas Hambrientos V
CS241260II Nijo V
CS247260II Máscara de Jade O
CS249260II Mon Moshi O
CS255260II Shamisen O
CS258260II Nikko-Bori O
CS266260II Ken Nage Promo
CS3260URII Seiwa Genji UR
CS4260URII Nihon koryu jūjutsu UR
CS9260SPII Kitsune SP R
EC0151SPII Gaita SP R
EC050150SP Armadillo SP R
HC112160II Orosimbo Barboza V
HC128160II Pacificación de la Araucania V
HC155160II Salitre O
HC158160II Aurora de Chile O
HC159160II Primer Escudo O
HC162160II Goleta Ancud Promo
HC164160II Abordaje SP Promo
HC167160II Principe De Los Caminos Promo
HE106175II Fuego Negro C
HE120175II Anima Lumina C
HE128175II Akilhar V
HE161175II Tres Lunas V
HE167175II Lengua Plata O
KA110140II Minamoto no Hiromasa V
KA1140URII Tsukuyomi UR
KA128140II Kusarigamajutsu V
KA129140II Tenjosan V
KA134140II Ukiyo-e O
KA135140II Amenonuhoko O
KA140140II Taiko O
KA8140SPII Mujina SP R
PI130240II Encuentro con tritones C
PI163240II Iris V
PI169240II El Hombre Marin V
PI198240II Bloque de Hielo V
PI229240II Mascarón de Proa O
PI245240II Samuel Axe Promo
PI246240II John Walden Promo
PI3240SPII Anne Dieu-Le-Veut-SP R
PI6240SPII Anne Bonny-SP R
PI9240SPII Trípoli-SP R
TR1936 Caligrafía - SP R

CS205260 Oni Bushi V
IM240238 Guillaume de Favy Promo
IM241238 Travesía Imposible Promo
TR1136Il Oda Nobunaga - SP R
TR1336Il Tsunami - SP R
TR1736Il Shamisen - SP R
TR1836Il Tenjo Name - SP R
TR2136Il Gran Kraken - SP R
TR2236Il Barbarroja - SP R
TR2336Il Samuel Bellamy - SP R
TR2436Il Lemanja - SP R
TR2736Il ¡Sin Dios ni Ley! R
TR2936Il Golden Hind - SP R
TR3636Il Triada R

2007 Mitos y Leyendas Heroes la Gloria Tiene su Pricio

1 Bernardo OHiggins UR
2 Manuel Rodríguez UR
3 Balmaceda SP R
4 Arturo Prat SP R
5 Diego Portales SP R
6 Luis Carrera SP R
7 Duelo a Siete Pasos SP R
8 Plaza de Armas SP R
9 Sable de Caballería SP R
10 Escudo Nacional SP R
11 Balmaceda R
12 Arturo Prat R
13 José Miguel Carrera R
14 San Martín R
15 Ignacio Carrera Pinto R
16 Ramón Freire R
17 Isabel Riquelme R
18 Manuel Blanco Encalada R
19 Manuel Baquedano R
20 Diego Portales R
21 Luis Carrera R
22 Juan José Carrera R
23 Juan MacKenna R
24 Ambrosio OHiggins R
25 Paula Jaraquemada R
26 Javiera Carrera R
27 Lord Cochrane R
28 Mateo de Toro y Zambrano R
29 Desastre de Rancagua R
30 Abrazo de Maipú R
31 Abordaje R
32 Escape R
33 Cancha Rayada R
34 Camuflaje R
35 Duelo a siete pasos R
36 Francotirador R
37 Embestida R
38 Cruzar la Cordillera R
39 Sable de Caballería R
40 Corvo R
41 Balloneta larga R
42 Huáscar R
43 Esmeralda R
44 El Blanco R
45 Cañón de Largo Alcance R
46 Cañón Naval R
47 Casa Colorada R
48 Plaza de Armas R
49 Virreinato R
50 Morro de Arica R
51 Carlos Condell C
52 Aníbal Pinto C
53 Benjamín Vicuña Mackenna C
54 José Joaquín Prieto C
55 Camilo Henríquez C
56 Los Pincheira C
57 Manuel Bulnes C
58 Manuel Montt C
59 Antonio Varas C
60 Domingo Santa María C
61 Vicente Benavides C
62 Grau C
63 Hilarión Daza C
64 Fernando VII C
65 Gabino Gaínza C
66 Francisco de la Lastra C
67 Mariano Osorio C
68 Anselmo de la Cruz C
69 Francisco Antonio Pinto C
70 Andrés de Santa Cruz C
71 Juramento Lautarino C
72 Asilo C
73 Fusilamiento C
74 Saltar del Caballo C
75 Montoneros C
76 Mala Pólvora C
77 Toma del Morro C
78 Extracción del Salitre C
79 Declaración de Independencia C
80 Junta de Gobierno C
81 Emboscada C
82 Chupilca del Diablo C
83 Fusil Grass Cheatelleray C
84 Remington Rolling Block C
85 Yatagan C
86 Smith & Wesson C
87 Cobadonga C
88 La Independencia C
89 Bergantín Aguila C
90 Bergantín Pueyrredón C
91 Faenadora Ballenera C
92 Metralla Naval C
93 Cañón de Corto Alcance C
94 Telégrafo C
95 Mineral de Chañarcillo C
96 Fundición de Guayacán C
97 Pisagua C
98 Nieblas C
99 Humberstone C
100 Santa Laura C
101 Francisco Bilbao V
102 Simón Bolívar V
103 Juan Martínez de Rozas V
104 Manuel de Salas V
105 Andrés Bello V
106 Miguel Zañartu V
107 José Ignacio Zenteno V
108 Mariano Egaña V
109 Juan Gregorio de las Heras V
110 Hipolito Villegas V
111 Jorge Montt V
112 Orosimbo Barboza V
113 Ramón Barros Luco V
114 Pedro Montt V
115 Francisco de Miranda V
116 Rafael Maroto V
117 Rodriguez Aldea V
118 Pérez-Cotapo V
119 Gandarillas V
120 Bernardo de Monteagudo V
121 Zapadores V
122 Batallón Chacabuco V
123 Carga V
124 Pirquineros V
125 Extracción de Carbón V
126 Toma de Valdivia V
127 Revuelta Indígena V
128 Pacificación de la Araucania V
129 Quemar la ciudad V
130 Duelo de Navajas V
131 Esconder a los Patriotas V
132 Escuadra Independentista V
133 Kropatscheck V
134 Carabina Evans V
135 Fusil Grass Styer V
136 Pistola de Chispa V
137 Fragata Lautaro V
138 Fragata Warren V
139 Bergatín Potrillo V
140 Fragata Perla V
141 Caldera Naval V
142 El Marte V
143 El relámpago V
144 El furioso V
145 Fundición de Huanchaca V
146 Iglesia de San Francisco V
147 Cabildo Abierto V
148 Cerro Huelén V
149 Encayadero Chilote V
150 Hacienda Riquelme V
151 Escudo Nacional O
152 Bandera Patria Vieja O
153 Estrella Solitaria O
154 Bandera Transición O
155 Salitre O
156 Carbón Piedra O
157 Escarapela Nacional O
158 Aurora de Chile O
159 Primer Escudo O
160 Monitor Araucano O

2007 Mitos y Leyendas Katana

1 Tsukuyomi UR
2 Ryugu-jo UR
3 Vara de Trueno SP R
4 Flujo de Fuego SP R
5 Minamoto no Yoshitomo SP R
6 Itsumaden SP R
7 Ebisu SP R
8 Mujina SP R
9 Jimmu SP R
10 Regalia Imperial SP R
11 Ninigi-no-Mikoto R
12 Amitabha R
13 Abe no Seimei R
14 Hidari Jingoro R
15 Tamamo-no-Mae R
16 Zashiki-warashi R
17 Ami-Kiri R
18 Karakasa-obake R
19 Mujina R
20 Emma R
21 Ningyo R
22 Ushi Oni R
23 Negoro-no-ushi-oni R
24 Noppera-bō R
25 Tenjō-name R
26 Soga no Umako R
27 Príncipe Shōtoku R
28 Himiko R
29 Gemmei R
30 Jimmu R
31 Ono no Imoko R
32 Emperatriz Suiko R
33 Fujiwara no Fuhito R
34 Kōshō R
35 Lobo de Tinieblas R
36 Espíritu Ainu R
37 Magia de Sangre R
38 Kashoga R
39 Kodo R
40 Bendición de La Pureza R
41 Barrera Elemental R
42 Levantar a los Espíritus R
43 Máscara de Muerte R
44 Vara de Trueno R
45 Rechazo Mágico R
46 Corcel Espectral R
47 Kofukuji R
48 La Corte del Norte R
49 La Corte del Sur R
50 Daitō de Nara R
51 Shōtō Sagrado R
52 Príncipe Ōjin C
53 Regente Jingū C
54 Bishamon-ten C
55 Sōjōbō C
56 Miko C
57 Sōgen-bi C
58 Azuki-arai C
59 Sune-kosuri C
60 Urashima Tarō C
61 Sarutahiko Ohkami C
62 Shachi Hoko C
63 Toyotama-hime C
64 Sugawara no Michizane C
65 Goryō C
66 Onryō C
67 Kogon C
68 Kōmyō C
69 Minamoto no Yoshitomo C
70 Hoori C
71 Minamoto no Tametomo C
72 Fujiwara no Nobuyori C
73 Emperador Takakura C
74 Amakuni C
75 Taira no Shigehira C
76 Flujo de Fuego C
77 Tormenta Ácida C
78 Anillo de Manos C
79 Coro Ultraterreno C
80 Ventana Astral C
81 Armonía Defensiva C
82 Orbe Abrazante C
83 Invocar Centinela C
84 Red Mental C
85 Túnica de curación C
86 Flecha Precisa C
87 Garza de la Incertidumbre C
88 Isla de Shikoku C
89 Santuarios de Ise C
90 Camino de Nakasendo C
91 Kogarasu Maru C
92 Ken C
93 Yamato Takeru V
94 Ebisu V
95 Benzaiten V
96 Kukai V
97 Bodhisena V
98 Kameosa V
99 Kashambo V
100 Tsukumo-gami V
101 Hito-dama V
102 Wani-Gushi V
103 Gusano Cienpies V
104 Suppon-no-yūrei V
105 Umi-bōzu V
106 Itsumaden V
107 Ninja Matsudaira V
108 Masako Naishinnō V
109 Chūai V
110 Minamoto no Hiromasa V
111 Hozoin Kakuzenbo V
112 Tatsumi Sankyo V
113 Yamauchi Kazutoyo V
114 Minamoto no Yoshitsune V
115 Araki Mataemon V
116 Minamoto no Noriyori V
117 Higo Ko-ryu V
118 Hontai Yoshin-ryu V
119 Isshin-ryū V
120 Kito-ryu V
121 Ono-ha Itto-ryu V
122 Tatsumi-ryu V
123 Battōjutsu V
124 Tessenjutsu V
125 Feroz Constrictor V
126 Adivinación V
127 Ira Bakemono V
128 Kusarigamajutsu V
129 Tenjosan V
130 Fuentes Termales V
131 Rashomon V
132 Tessen V
133 Kusarigama V
134 Ukiyo-e O
135 Amenonuhoko O
136 Regalia Imperial O
137 Gohei O
138 Shisa O
139 O-fuda O
140 Taiko O

2007 Mitos y Leyendas Piratas

1 Henry Morgan UR
2 El Holandés Errante UR
3 Anne Dieu-Le-Veut-SP R
4 Davy Jones-SP R
5 Sirena-SP R
6 Anne Bonny-SP R
7 Bloque de Hielo- SP R
8 Ataque Submarino-SP R
9 Tripoli-SP R
10 Rehén-SP R
11 Anne Dieu-Le-Veut R
12 Maurycy Beniowski R
13 Samuel Bellamy R
14 Lemanja R
15 Eustace el Monje R
16 Ictiocentauro R
17 Sirena R
18 Eolos R
19 Manannan R
20 Hydra R
21 Leviatán R
22 Montura de Vahana R
23 Arpía R
24 Gran Kraken R
25 Davy Jones R
26 Bernard Fokke R
27 Pirata sin Cabeza R
28 Barbossa R
29 John Hawkins R
30 Piet Hein R
31 Benito Soto Aboal R
32 Bartolomeo "el Portugués" R
33 Roche Brasiliano R
34 Jean-David Nau el Olonés R
35 James Plantain R
36 Bartholomew Roberts R
37 Edward Teach "Barbanegra" R
38 Grace O'Malley R
39 Anne Bonny R
40 John Rackham R
41 Edward England R
42 Mary Read R
43 Capitán Misson R
44 Álvaro de Bazán R
45 Juan Martínez de Recalde R
46 Blas de Lezo R
47 Robert Maynard R
48 Sir Hyde Parker R
49 Robert Blake R
50 John Byron R
51 Cantó de las Sirenas R
52 Blasfemia R
53 Alma por Viento R
54 Caminar por la Tabla R
55 Desterrado al Olvido R
56 Condenado a la Horca R
57 Naufragio R
58 Enterrar Tesoro R
59 Lucha de Cañones R
60 Fin del Mundo R
61 Asalto a puerto R
62 Motín R
63 Aparición R
64 Rendición R
65 Duelo R
66 Espolonear R
67 Tormenta R
68 Ataque Submarino R
69 Desembarco R
70 Isla Tortuga R
71 Cabo Buena Esperanza R
72 Archipiélago Juan Fernández R
73 Port Royal R
74 Trípoli R
75 Fondo de Mar R
76 Hacha de Abordaje R
77 Alfanje R
78 Artillería R
79 Golden Hind R
80 Barco de Oseberg R
81 Santísima Trinidad R
82 Queen Anne's Revenge R
83 Jean Ango C
84 Pierre Le Moyne DIberville C
85 James Cook C
86 Kabeiro C
87 Obispo de Plasencia C
88 Corte de Nereidas C
89 Ondinas C
90 Ogeno C
91 Nereo C
92 Dragón de Ares C
93 Caribdis C
94 Naga C
95 Afang C
96 Escila C
97 Dem Bones C
98 Capitán Sandovate C
99 Ocean-Born Mary C
100 Stede Bonnet "El Bufón" C
102 Dirk Chivers C
103 Christopher Condent C
104 William Kidd C
105 Olivier Levasseur C
106 Lancelot Blackburne C
107 Pierre Le Grand C
108 Capitán Bournano C
109 Charlotte de Berry C
110 Howell Davies C
111 Alexander Exquemelin C
112 Jean Florin C
114 Jean Lafitte C
116 Pedro Menéndez de Avilés C
117 Capitán Juan Fandiño C
118 Juan Francisco de la Bodega y Quadra C
119 Nathaniel Butler C
120 Wimund C
121 Tobias Bridge C
122 Sussex Camock C
123 Patente de Corso C
124 Navío a la Vista C
125 Músicos a Bordo C
126 Captura de barco C
127 Tripulación fantasma C
128 Código de Conducta C
129 Pleamar C
130 Encuentro con tritones C
131 Defensa del fuerte C
132 Victoria C
133 Elevar Anclas C
134 A la deriva C
135 Elección de Capitán C
136 Ejecución C
137 Maldición C
138 Vuelta al Mundo C
139 Indulto Real C
140 Tierra a la vista C
141 Hombre al Agua C
142 Isla Sulú C
144 Madagascar C
145 Mazalquivir C
146 Costa Malabar C
147 Isla de Pascua C
148 Lanza de Abordaje C
149 Arcabuz C
150 Falconete C
151 Galeón C
152 Drakkar C
153 Fragata C
154 Clipper Inglés C
155 Hubert de Brienne V
156 François Joseph Paul V
157 Jean-François de La Pérouse V
158 Losna V
159 Santero V
160 Espumero V
161 Delfín V
162 Eurybia V
163 Iris V
164 Morgawr V
165 Kun V
166 Ekhidna V
167 Alom-begwi-no-sis - V
168 Selkie V
169 El Hombre Marin V
170 Old Stormalong V
171 Rannamaari V
172 Queen Mary's sisters C
173 Klein Henszlein V
174 Jan de Bouff V
176 Hendrick Jacobszoon Lucifer V
177 Jacques de Sores V
178 John Ward V
179 Thomas Anstis V
180 Klaus Störtebeker V
181 Awilda V
182 Cord Widderich V
183 Olivier van Noort V
185 Laurens de Graff V
187 Fanny Campbell V
188 Francisco de Camargo V
189 Luis de Córdova y Córdova V
190 Ching Shih V
191 James Lancaster V
192 Woodes Roger V
193 William Goodson V
194 Arthur Herbert V
195 Comida Rancia V
196 Castigo Ejemplar V
197 Cruz del Sur V
198 Bloque de Hielo V
200 Ballena a Estribor V
201 Trueque V
202 Fondeo V
203 Disfraz V
204 Prisionero V
205 Noche sin Luna V
206 Perdidos V
207 Enjuiciamiento V
208 Polizonte V
209 Bloqueo de Puerto V
210 Herida de Guerra V
211 Condecoración V
212 Despliegue de velas V
213 Bote Salvavidas V
214 Nueva Orleans V
215 Surat V
216 China meridional V
217 Argel V
218 Panamá V
219 Coquimbo V
220 Rapier V
221 Mosquete V
222 Cañón Tigre V
223 Goleta V
224 Carabela V
225 Ballenero V
226 Bergantín V
227 Mapa del Tesoro O
228 Garfio O
229 Mascarón de Proa O
230 Jelly Roger O
231 Pólvora O
232 Botella de Ron O
233 Bitácora O
234 Brújula O
235 Catalejo O
236 Doblón O
237 Oro Azteca O
238 Joyas de la Corona O
239 Boston Newsletter O
240 Rehén O
242 William R
247 Hallazgo C

2008 Mitos y Leyendas Duna

1 Simbad UR
2 Sherezade UR
3 Ahura Mazda - SP R
4 Arenero - SP R
5 Battuta - SP R
6 Abrete Sésamo - SP R
7 Despertar al genio - SP R
8 Bagdad - SP R
9 Shamsir - SP R
10 Lampara maravillosa - SP R
11 Ali Babá R
12 Aladino R
13 Ahura Mazda R
14 Angra Mainyu R
15 Schariar R
16 Efreeti R
17 El Genio de la Lámpara R
18 Kujata R
19 Zarik R
20 Bahamut R
21 Azhi Dahaka R
22 Aesma Daeva R

23 Azhakul Amo del Fuego R
24 Roc R
25 Zahak R
26 Kod-Hassam R
27 Cassim R
28 Thraetaona R
29 Baltuta R
30 Kamaralzaman R
31 Badroulbadour R
32 Morgiana R
33 Amr ibn al-Aas R
34 Shajar al-Durr R
35 Abrete Sésamo R
36 Fuego Celestial R
37 Mil Historias R
38 Cuarenta ladrones R
39 Vuelo en alfombra R
40 Despertar al genio R
41 Viaje en Sueños R
42 Enviar a otra dimension R
43 Magia maghrebín R
44 Cimitarra en polvo R
45 Bagdad R
46 Harem R
47 Teber R
48 Kaskara R
49 Takouba R
50 Shamsir R
51 Alfombra mágica de Tangu R
52 Lampara maravillosa R
53 An-Nasir C
54 Al-Mustarshid C
55 Anahita C
56 Allatum C
57 Schazaman C
58 Marrashi C
59 Glypt C
60 Datin C
61 Zurbon C
62 Arenero C
63 Azi Sruvara C
64 Zovvutos C
65 Homa C
66 Djinn Oscuro C
67 Araña hechicera C
68 Hashshashin C
69 Komesh C
70 Marzabán C
71 Reina Dihja C
72 Campeón Sassanida C
73 Gazaleh C
74 Jann C
75 Al-Kamil C
76 Qalawun C
77 Cegar al monstruo C
78 Venganza Bezarra C
79 Presa del Araf C
80 Metamorfosis magica C
81 Golems de cadenas C
82 A merced de los monos C
83 Ataque ghul C
84 Danza del Sable C
85 Mefites de Fuego C
86 Mefites de Agua C
87 Magreb C
88 Damasco C
89 Kilic C
90 Talwar C
91 Allanje noble C
92 Pértiga Mameluca C
93 Fuego Sagrado C
94 Piedra Safiro C
95 Ojo de Rubí C
96 Jafar al-Barmaki V
97 Uthman V
98 Dena V
99 Atur V
100 Abu Nuwas V
101 Loxo V
102 Karkadann V
103 Genio del Anillo V
104 Verethraga V
105 Dragón de Lava V
106 Azi Visapa V
107 Grell V
108 Julijuimus V
109 Gambol V
110 Daojinn V
111 Los Yazata V
112 Profeta Oscuro V
113 Beréberes V
114 Arquero Turco V
115 Gushtasp V
116 Budur V
117 Celma V
118 Orhan I V
119 Princesa Aixa V
120 Hechizo del Caos V
121 Comerciantes Orientales V
122 Sacrificios para All-Uza V
123 Vuelo en roc V
124 Invocacion equivocada V
125 Geomancia V
126 Busqueda de la lampara V
127 Guardia de eunucos V
128 Mefites de Arena V
129 Mefites de barro V
130 Templo Sufi V
131 Oasis V
132 Yelmo Otomano V
133 Mallas Turcas V
134 Tombak V
135 Porta Llamas V
136 Huevo de Roc V
137 Narguile V
138 Anfora de Aceites V
139 Halcón Laggar V
140 Camello V
141 Duna Promo
142 A Promo
143 Carlos Martel Promo
144 Ataque Vikingo Promo
145 Adios Belleza Promo

2008 Mitos y Leyendas Inmortales

1 Cronos UR
2 Dragón Dorado UR
3 Leshy-SP R
4 Dragón Nival-SP R
5 Huracan-SP R
6 Guinevere-SP R
7 Los Cuervos de Wotán-SP R
8 Alas de Horus-SP R
9 Tierra Celeste-SP R
10 Biblioteca Eterna-SP R
11 Jacques de Molay R
12 Joan D Arc R
13 Sigfried R
14 Atenea R
15 Helios R
16 Zeus R
17 Inti R
18 Ra R
19 Haquika R
20 Figol El Druida R
21 Curandera R
22 Mago Merlín R
23 Leshy R
24 Donn R
25 Oberon R
26 Armada Élfica R
27 MacDaTho R
20 Daana R
29 Gran Cabrakán R
30 Dragón de Magma R
31 Balaur R
32 Chair Salee R
33 Grendel R
34 Cherufe R
35 Gruagash R
36 Manzachiri R
37 Loki R
38 Balor R
39 Thanatos R
40 Apophis R
41 Morgana R
42 Mordred R
43 Atila R
44 Espartaco R
45 Marco Antonio R
46 Julio César R
47 Fergus R
48 Cuchulainn R
49 Carlos Martel R
50 Conan de Bretaña R
51 Guinevere R
52 Rey Arturo Pendragón R
53 Moctezuma R
54 Saladino R
55 ¡Desleal! R
56 Fe sin Límite R
57 Caleuche R
58 Cacería de Demonios R
59 Relámpagos R
60 Capa de Invisibilidad R
61 Licántropos Orientales R
62 Rómulo y Remo R
63 Ataque Vikingo R
64 Adios Belleza R
65 Invocar Chacales R
66 Nombrarse Emperador R
67 Caballo Lunar R
68 La Traición de MacAlpin R
69 Alas de Horus R
70 Juicio de Dios R
71 Relámpago Arcano R
72 Ataque a Cipango R
73 Furia de Cabrakán R
74 Monte Olimpo R
75 Tlillán-Tlapallán R
76 Tótem de Nwyre R
77 Guiza R
78 Machu Pichu R
79 Avalon R
80 Excalibur R
81 Balmung R
82 Derribador Olmeca R
83 Maquinaria de Guerra R
84 Mercaderes R
85 Letanía R
86 Jeroglífico Maya R
87 Mío Cid Campeador C
88 Marco Polo C
89 Federico Barbarroja C
90 Ares C
91 Tengri C
92 Ptah C
93 Anubis C
94 Pacha Mama C
95 Bahiti C
96 Mama Ocla C
97 Demoledor de Amón C
98 Arquero Elfo C
99 Las Kikimoras C
100 Gente Roble C
101 Mathgen El Mago C
102 Ettin C
103 Atlas C
104 Eirix El Bretón C
105 Balam Quitze C
106 Oriflama C
107 Dragón Demonio C
108 Fanfir C
109 La Brujería C
110 Kobold C
111 Noctumbros C
112 Leucrota C
113 Hades C
114 Xolotl C
115 Tifón C
116 Huracán C
117 Darío El Grande C
118 Genghis Khan C
119 Nerón C
120 Pridery C
121 Cakixia C
122 Heracles C
123 Aed Finn C
124 Alejandro Magno C
125 Uni C
126 Alejo C
127 Ulises C
128 Sir Gabriel C
129 Duque Godofredo C
130 Sir Galahad C
131 Vuelta a lo Primordial C
132 Mal Acero C
133 Mineros de Lápislazuli C
134 Sajones C
135 Joyero C
136 Urisk C
137 Arde Troya C
138 Sacrificio a Wotán C
139 Trempulcahue C
140 Levantar Castillo C
141 Buitres de Cizin C
142 Ataque Fulminante C
143 Tentáculos del Abismo C
144 Abrir la Tierra C
145 Trampa de Enredaderas C
146 Letanía de Ra C
147 Las Fauces C
148 Maldición Tolteca C
149 Tótem de León C
150 Chichen Itzá C
151 Tenochtitlán C
152 Tierra Celeste C
153 Atlántida C
154 Tártaro C
155 Hacha de Batalla C
156 Morning Star C
157 Red de Gladiador C
158 Coloso Hitita C
159 Códex Arturicus C
160 Ofrenda a los Dioses C
161 Antorcha Olímpica C
162 Biblioteca Eterna C
163 Luis el Piadoso V
164 Otton El Grande V
165 Caballero Templario V
166 Ogma V
167 Tutatis V
168 Tonantzin V
169 Horus V
170 Neptuno V
171 Bruja de la Selva V
172 Nuh V
173 Takelot V
174 Ilmarinen V
175 Unicornio Sidhe V
176 Venus V
177 Imoteph V
178 Atlante V
179 Beowulf V
180 Brigit V
181 Macha V
182 Los Chaobs V
183 Celeste V
184 Dragón Nival V
185 Orcos V
186 Tropa Esqueleto V
187 Hueñauca V
188 Haat V
189 Focalor V
190 Darak de la Sombra V
191 Vanatuhi V
192 Fannakeldorn V
193 Dhampir V
194 Bisclavret V
195 Aldara V
196 Ajax V
197 Teseo V
198 William Wallace V
199 Olger el Danés V
200 Conn V
201 Gladiador V
202 Oseye V
203 Akenathon V
204 Itzanma V
205 Henry V V
206 Sir Persival V
207 Producir Caos V
208 Atón V
209 La Cruzada de los Pobres V
210 Cantrip V
211 Grito de Guerra V
212 Impuestos V
213 Escuchar el Bosque V
214 Frutos Mágicos V
215 Raza de Pigmeos V
216 Red de Aracné V
217 Inmunidad al Aliento V
218 Los Cuervos de Wotán V
219 Poitiers V
220 Ordalía V
221 Morbo Gótico V
222 Arenas en Fuego V
223 Levantar a los Muertos V
224 Nazca V
225 Tótem Mapuche V
226 Casa de Hestia V
227 Círculo Eterno V
228 Esparta V
229 Gladius V
230 Escudo Celestial V
231 Armadura de Águila V
232 Cráneo de Cristal V
233 Estatuilla de Jade V
234 Festín V
235 Dádivas V
236 Aceite de Oliva O
237 Mesa Redonda V
238 Cruz Templaria V

2008 Mitos y Leyendas Insurgentes

1 Emiliano Zapata UR
2 Porfirio Díaz UR
3 Doroteo Arango - SP R
4 Álvaro Obregón - SP R
5 Emilio P. Campa - SP R
6 Adelita - SP R
7 Constitución de 1917 - SP R
8 Decena Trágica - SP R
9 Ciudad de México - SP R
10 Tequila - SP R
11 Francisco Villa R
12 Francisco I. Madero R
13 Genovevo de la O R
14 Venustiano Carranza R
15 Pablo González R
16 Pascual Orozco R
17 Hermanos Magón R
18 Salvador Escalante R
19 Carmen Serdán R
20 Adelita R
21 Ambrosio Figueroa R
22 Benjamín Hill R
23 Álvaro Obregón R
24 Victoriano Huerta R
25 Félix Díaz R
26 Manuel González Cosío R
27 Manuel M. Diéguez R
28 Henry Lane Wilson R
29 Benjamín Argumedo R
30 John Joseph Pershing R
31 Emilio P. Campa R
32 Bernardo Reyes R
33 Cándido Aguilar R
34 José Inés Salazar R
35 Convención Nacional Revolucionaria R
36 Huelga de Cananea R
37 Partido Liberal R
38 Decena Trágica R
39 Asesinato de Zapata R
40 Soldaderas R
41 Los Rurales R
42 Ferrocarril Central Mexicano R
43 Plan de San Luis R
44 Constitución de 1917 R
45 Ciudad de México R
46 Monumento a Villa R
47 Madsen R
48 Lewis R
49 Colt R
50 Dinamita R
51 Bandera de México R
52 Tequila R
53 Gustavo A. Madero C
54 Aquiles Serdán C
55 Toribio Ortega C
56 Manuel Palafox C
57 Rómulo Figueroa C
58 Juan M. Banderas C
59 Dolores Jiménez y Muro C
60 Juana Belén Gutiérrez de Mendoza C
61 Luis Moya C
62 Juan Medina C
63 Felipe Ángeles C
64 Plutarco Elías Calle C
65 Manuel Mondragón C
66 Los Intelectuales C
67 Rodolfo Herreros C
68 Ramón Corral C
69 Toribio Esquivel Obregón C
70 Francisco León de la Barra C
71 Pedro Lascuráin C
72 Francisco Vásquez Gómez C
73 Juan Andreu Almazán C
74 Higinio Aguilar C
75 Aureliano Blanquet C
76 John Lind C
77 Invasión a Veracruz C
78 Plan de Ayala C
79 Plan de Chihuahua C
80 Plan de Agua Prieta C
81 Plan de Guadalupe C
82 Corrido de la Revolución C
83 Batalla de Celaya C
84 Combate Aeronaval de Topolobampo C
85 Rebelión de Acayucán C
86 Persecución Clerical C
87 Zacatecas C
88 Petrolera Faja de Oro C
89 Vicker C
90 Mondragón M1908 C
91 St. Chamond-Mondragón C
92 Anillo Pastoral C
93 Busto de Bonaparte C
94 Prensa Revolucionaria C
95 Peso C
96 Serapio Rendón V
97 Belisario Domínguez V
98 José Garibaldi V
99 Adolfo Gurrión V
100 Antonio Soto y Gama V
101 Praxedis Guerrero V
102 José Vasconcelos V
103 Herminia Galindo V
104 María Arias Bernal V
105 Librado Rivera V
106 Los Yaquis V
107 Roque González V
108 Francisco Carvajal V
109 Los Científicos V
110 Juan N. Méndez V
111 La Aristocracia V
112 Adolfo de la Huerta V
113 Enrique Gorostieta y Velarde V
114 Ignacio Luis Vallarta V
115 Pelagio de Labastida V
116 Manuel Romero Rubio V
117 Francisco Cárdenas V
118 Felipe Neri Jiménez V
119 Manuel María de Zamacona V
120 Presidencia Interina V
121 Intervención Estadounidense V
122 Ejecución Masiva V
123 Incidente de Tampico V
124 Batalla de El Ébano V
125 Ley Agrícola V
126 Levantamiento Campesino V
127 Abandono de Torreón V
128 Reclutamiento V
129 Exilio V
130 Palacio Bellas Artes V
131 Presa de Necaxa V
132 Schneider-Canet V
133 Carabina 30-30 V
134 Algodón V
135 Telégrafo V
136 Guitarra V
137 Sombrero V
138 Pulque V
139 Maíz V
140 Canana V

2008 Mitos y Leyendas Invasion

1 Leónidas UR
2 Oráculo de Delfos UR
3 Aquiles - SP R
4 Niké - SP R
5 Medusa - SP R
6 Lluvia de Flechas - SP R
7 Dios de la Guerra - SP R
8 Sarisa - SP R
9 Gran Camino Real - SP R
10 Manzana de la Discordia - SP R
11 Ares Miaiphonos R
12 Eris R
13 Niké R
14 Spenta Mainyu R
15 Mithra R
16 Medea R
17 Tiresias R
18 Pitia del Oráculo R
19 Zaratustra R
20 Magi R
21 Ismenios R
22 Ladon R
23 Python R
24 Abathur R
25 Azi Raooita R
26 Ekhidna R
27 Circe R
28 Medusa R
29 Simurgh R
30 Asto Vidatu R
31 Gaumata R
32 Amestris R
33 Aquemenes R
34 Los Inmortales R
35 Hidarnes R
36 Artabano R
37 Temístocles R
38 Euribíades R
39 Dienekes R
40 Aquiles R
41 Héctor de Troya R
42 Perseo R
43 Menelao R
44 Leda R
45 Cástor y Polux R
46 Helena de Esparta R
47 Agamenón R
48 Heródoto R
49 Jerjes I R
50 Artemisia de Halicarnaso R
51 Darío I R
52 Megabizo II R
53 Kaveh R
54 Rustam R
55 Batalla de las Termópilas R
56 Phálanx R
57 La agogé R
58 Batalla Naval de Salamina R
59 Invocar a los Espartoi R
60 Caída de Babilonia R
61 Lluvia de Flechas R
62 Favor de Atenea R
63 Travesía de Argonautas R
64 Los Treinta Tiranos R
65 Ocupación de Atenas R
66 Tierra y Agua R
67 Invocar a Amesha Spentas R
68 Dios de la Guerra R
69 Invocar a los Daevas R
70 Canto de Karshipta R
71 Adam Kasia R

72 Embajadores al Foso R
73 Dinastía Aqueménida R
74 Paso de las Termópilas R
75 Templo de Apolo R
76 Persépolis R
77 Santuario de Artemisa R
78 Peloponeso R
79 Templo de Rustam R
80 Helepolis R
81 Fuego Griego R
82 Trirreme R
83 Galera de Guerra R
84 Cofre de Python R
85 Ares Espartano R
86 Shahnameh R
87 Enio C
88 Hypnos C
89 Themis C
90 Vala C
91 Izha C
92 Moiras C
93 Io C
94 Ferdowsi C
95 Éforo Espartano C
96 Briseida C
97 Kholkikos C
98 Sybaris C
99 Aithiopios C
b2 Fuego Sagrado Promo
b3 Xoon uan té Promo
b4 El Genio de la Lámpara Promo
100 Asdeev C
101 Ganj * C
102 Dev C
103 Aracne C
104 Cidoimos C
105 Agas C
106 Aka Manah C
107 Artajerjes I C
108 Gergis C
109 Jeh C
110 Aspamistres C
111 Pantea C
112 Súbditos Fenicios C
114 Kriatos C
115 Atenades de Traquia C
116 Hipólita C
117 Pausanias C
118 Paris de Troya C
119 Príamo C
120 Hoplitas C
121 Espartoi C
122 Tíndaro C
123 Cadmo C
124 Andrómeda C
125 Artabazo C
126 Mardonio C
127 Arash C
128 Ciro II el Grande C
129 Vanant C
130 Geus-Urvan C
131 Batalla de Maratón C
132 Grito de Alala C
133 Furia de los Macas C
134 Gran Retra C
135 Regresar como Héroe C
136 Ataque Nocturno C
137 Inspirado por Musas C
138 Apóthetas C
139 Imperio Corrupto C
140 Ofrenda a Apolo C
141 Rapto de Europa C
142 Compra de Mujeres C
143 Furia de Titanes C
144 Dominio de Drug C
145 Frashegird C
146 Surcando el Vouruskasha C
147 Guía mi Alma C
148 Guardián Fravashis C
149 Tumba de Ciro C
150 Acrópolis C
151 Cerámico C
152 Puerta de las Naciones C
153 Colonia Griega en Oriente C
154 La Apadana C
155 Sarisa C
156 Manus Ferrea C
157 Pentecotera C
158 Tessarakonteres C
159 Piedras Abraxas C
160 Tablillas de la Fortaleza C
161 Manzana de la Discordia C
162 Rhyton de Oro C
163 Ahurani V
164 Pasifae (griega) V
165 Burijas V
166 Nairyosangha V
167 Hebe V
168 Ancianos de Lesjé V
169 Plutarco V
170 Arda Viraf V
171 Yima V
172 Adarbad Mahraspandan V
173 Nemeios V
174 Dragones de Medea V
175 Ezhdeha V
176 Draco Thespiakos V
177 Ketos Troias V
178 Campe V
179 Fobos & Deimos V
180 Argos V
181 Demrusch V
182 Gandarewa V
183 Tritantacmes V
184 Domador Diwe V
185 Datis V
186 Mercenarios Egipcios V
187 Cambises II V
188 Efialtes de Tesalia V
189 Trasíbulo V
190 Cleómenes III V
191 Creso V
192 Esquilo V
193 Alejandro y Antigono de Esparta V
194 Gorgo V
195 Pirrón V
196 Guerreros Tebanos V
197 Alejandro I Filoheleno V
198 Cinisca V
199 Licurgo V
200 Ilotas V
201 Ariabigne V
202 Manuchihr V
203 Harmamitras y Titeo V
204 Abrocomes V
205 Artaintes V
206 Masistes V
207 Conquista de Babilonia V
208 Guerra del Peloponeso V
209 Misterios Eleusinos V
210 Fiestas Carneas V
211 Huir de Atenas V
212 Comercio Mediterráneo V
213 Huida Deshonrosa V
214 Remeros V
215 Imperdonable Cobardía V
216 Vigías Hippeis V
217 Cripteia V
218 Fracaso Naval Persa V
219 Puente de Barcas V
220 Levantamiento Jonio V
221 Cantando el Peán V
222 Hipomancia V
223 Influjo Bushyasta V
224 Monte Taigeto V
225 Gran Camino Real V
226 Inscripción Mortuoria V
227 Oráculo de Dodona V
228 Leuce V
229 Arqueros y Carros Persas V
230 Galera Egipcia V
231 Birremes V
232 Semillas Gao-kerena V
233 Dárico V
234 Inscripción del Harén V
235 Brazalete Aqueménida V
236 Prótomes de Artemisa V
237 Herramientas Quirúrgicas V
238 Arte Persa V
239 Papiro Mágico Griego V
240 Espejo Oscuro V
241 Invasión Promo
242 Venganza Persa Promo
243 Astval-Ereta Promo
244 Milcíades Promo
245 Sacrificio Espartano Promo
246 Troya Promo
247 Demoledor de Jerjes I Promo
248 Máscara de Agamenón Promo

2008 Mitos y Leyendas Origenes

1 La Tirana UR
2 Onkolxón UR
3 Quitralpique R
4 Okori R
5 Kalku R
6 Canto Chamánico R
7 Absorber Konkaspi R
8 Pukará de Quitor R
9 Lanza de Soortes R
10 Keen Yenkán R
11 Hotu Matua R
12 Quitralpique R
13 Calchaquí R
14 Umoara R
15 Kwonnyip R
16 Yonolpe R
17 Elal R
18 Kamshout R
19 Yatiri R
20 Yekamush R
21 Xoon Waiuwin R
22 Ivi Atua R
23 Amaru R
24 Alicanto R
25 Ballena de la Luz R
26 Xóchem R
27 Kuanip R
28 Kenos R
29 Kré y Kréen R
30 Make Make R
31 Wekufe R
32 Jalpén R
33 Ayayema R
34 Xaxax R
35 Creación de Temaukel R
36 Hain R
37 Xoon uan té R
38 Xoon Unitern R
39 Tapatí R
40 Nguillatún R
41 Canto Chamánico R
42 Caos del Viento R
43 Absorber Konkaspi R
44 Protección de Yastay R
45 Tierra del fuego R
46 Hiva R
47 Lanza de Soortes R
48 Flechas Xoon R
49 Clava R
50 Maza de metal R
51 Keen Yenkán R
52 Kava Kava R
53 Purén C
54 Matatoa C
55 Weichafe C
56 Táiyin C
57 Okori C
58 Los Chinchorro C
59 Wari Katuri C
60 Klöketen C
61 Xoon del Kréen C
62 Laika C
63 Maori Rongo Rongo C
64 Kalku C
65 Wangulén C
66 Jurasi C
67 Mwono C
68 Huayrapuca C
69 Tangata Manu C
70 Llacolén C
71 Licarayén C
72 Soortes C
73 Kaskoyuk C
74 Uoke el Devastador C
75 Pihuychen C
76 Peripillán C
77 Eclipse Lunar C
78 Competencias Chamánicas C
79 Sacrificio de Calafate C
80 Ira de Mamacocha C
81 Ceremonia del Hombre Pájaro C
82 Yincihaua C
83 Siete Exploradores C
84 Concentrar Mana C
85 Wilancha C
86 Mamiña C
87 Ngill Chenmaywe C
88 Volcán Licancabur C
89 La Chume C
90 Pinkullo C
91 Kóchil C
92 Maza Mapuche C
93 Cacho de Camahueto C
94 Tableta de Rapé C
95 Llancas C
96 Lican-Antay V
97 Tangata Honui V
98 Ariacca V
99 Héroé Kolla V
100 Talimeoat y Kaichin V
101 Millantú V
102 Santagua V
103 Léjes V
104 Owurkan V
105 Cutica V
106 Machi Ermitaña V
107 Tonko V
108 Cheter V
109 Mailkus V
110 Alhue V
111 Alaraco V
112 Los Payachatas V
113 Mata-Ko-Iro V
114 Ava Rei Púa V
115 Yacurmana V
116 Cuero V
117 Chon Chon V
118 Umpillay V
119 Aku Aku V
120 Nómades V
121 Aringa Ora V
122 Ana O Keke V
123 Sueño Premonitorio V
124 Pachallampe V
126 Ceremonia de los Aros V
127 Carrera del Chasqui V
128 Cueva del Inca V
129 Entierros V
130 Pukará de Quitor V
131 Tulor V
132 Puntas de Jabalinas V
133 Cuerdas de Sargazo V
134 Cuchillo de Ballena V
135 Arpón V
136 Polvo Rojo V
137 Geoglifos V
138 Momia Chinchorro C
139 Jarro Pato V
140 Cebil V
141 Origenes Promo
142 Haru y Sasan Promo
27b Espíritu Kotaix R

2013 My Little Pony Premiere

COMPLETE SET (211) 250.00 400.00
BOOSTER BOX (36 PACKS) 60.00 90.00
BOOSTER PACK (12 CARDS) 2.50 3.50
1 Rainbow Dash Flier Extraordinaire :B: F 6.00 15.00
2 Applejack Steadfast Farmpony :O: F 5.00 12.00
3 Pinkie Pie Party Animal :K: F 4.00 10.00
4 Twilight Sparkle Faithful Student :P: F 3.00 8.00
5 Rarity Dazzling Fashionista :W: F 4.00 10.00
6 Fluttershy Beastmaster :Y: F 3.00 8.00
7 Jetstream All Heart :B: C .10 .25
8 Cerulean Skies Skyward Soarer :B: C .10 .25
9 Finish Line Jammer :B: U .20 .50
10 Wild Fire Speed Racer :B: R 1.50 4.00
11 Cloudchaser Flexible Flier :B: R 4.00 10.00
12 Emerald Green Cider Aficionado :B: C .10 .25
13 Holly Dash Flighty Filly :B: F 3.00 8.00
14 Pegasus Royal Guard Elite Sentry :B: C .10 .25
15 Rainbow Dash Weather Leader :B: U .20 .50
16 Rainbowshine Cloud Wrangler :B: C .10 .25
17 Scootaloo Creature Catcher :B: R 1.00 2.50
18 Spike Baby Dragon :B: R 1.00 2.50
19 Solar Wind Enterprising Astronomer :B: R 1.00 2.50
20 Sweetie Sunrise Early Riser :B: C .10 .25
21 Gala Appleby Refined Farmer :O: R 1.00 2.50
22 Apple Cobbler Headstrong :O: C .10 .25
23 Applejack Plant Leader :O: C .10 .25
24 Applejack Barn Raiser :O: R 1.25 3.00
25 Auntie Applesauce Gum Flapper :O: U .20 .50
26 Cherry Jubilee Queen of the Hill :O: F 3.00 8.00
27 Coco Crusoe Thick Skinned :O: R 1.00 2.50
28 Granny Smith Apple Elder :O: C .10 .25
29 Igneous Rock Pebble Pusher :O: C .10 .25
30 Drill Bit Destruction Worker :O: C .10 .25
31 Full Steam Smoke Stacked :O: R 1.25 3.00
32 Silver Spanner Nuts for Bolts :O: R 1.00 2.50
33 Red Gala Favorite Cousin :O: C .10 .25
34 Sunny Smiles Iconic Friend :O: R 1.00 2.50
35 Night Watch Vigilant Patrol :O: R 1.00 2.50
36 Apple Brown Betty Pastry Chef :K: C .10 .25
37 Berry Dreams Pom-Pom Pony :K: C .10 .25
38 Big Top Silly Pony :K: F 4.00 10.00
39 Charged Up Energizer Pony :K: R .75 2.00
40 Dance Fever Disco King :K: C .10 .25
41 Lucky Streak One in a Million :K: R 1.25 3.00
42 Flitter Ribbion Wielder :K: C .10 .25
43 Goldengrape Popular Punster :K: R 1.25 3.00
44 High Spirits Life Enthusiast :K: C .10 .25
45 Pinkie Pie Pinkie Responsibility Pie :K: R 1.25 3.00
46 Pinkie Pie Ice Cutter :K: C .10 .25
47 Pinprick Pop Star :K: R .60 1.50
48 Ol' Salt Salt Blocked :K: U .20 .50
49 Snips and Snails Dynamic Duo :K: R .60 1.50
50 Surprise Party Pegasus :K: R .60 1.50
51 Apple Stars Fruit Prodigy :P: R .50 1.25
52 Professor Neigh Algebraic! :P: C .10 .25
53 Bright Bulb Seasoned Strategist :P: R 2.50 6.00
54 Comet Tail Hale Bopper :P: C .10 .25
55 Mint Jewelup a Cut Above :P: C .10 .25
56 Gyro Poindexter :P: R 1.25 3.00
57 Lemony Gem Sour Grapes :P: R 1.00 2.50
58 Mayor Mare Elected Official :P: C .10 .25
59 Rare Find A Real Gem :P: R .75 2.00
60 Blue Moon Ol' Blue Eyes :P: C .10 .25
61 Spring Forward Companionable Filly :P: R 2.50 6.00
62 Sunny Rays One Bright Mare :P: R 1.25 3.00
63 Lady Justice Judge and Jury :P: F 2.50 6.00
64 Twilight Sparkle All-Team Organizer :P: C .10 .25
65 Action Shot Shutterbug :W: R 1.25 3.00
66 Big Shot Wildlife Photographer :W: R .60 1.50
67 Featherweight Editor-in-Chief :W: R .50 1.25
68 Fiddly Faddle Country Twang :W: R .40 1.00
69 Eff Stop Muckraker :W: R 1.00 2.50
70 Vidala Swoon Mane Manager :W: F 2.50 6.00
71 Hoity Toity Vogue Authority :W: C .10 .25
72 Savoir Fare Snooty Server :W: R .75 2.00
73 Pearly Stitch Crotchety Crocheter :W: C .10 .25
74 Lotus Blossom Sauna Expert :W: R 1.25 3.00
75 Rising Star In the Spotlight :W: C .10 .25
76 Noteworthy Humdinger :W: C .10 .25
77 Rarity Nest Weaver :W: U .20 .50
78 Royal Riff Songster :W: C .10 .25
79 Sugar Twist Twister Sister :W: C .10 .25
80 Amethyst Star Animal Leader :Y: C .10 .25
81 Blue Jay Warbler :Y: C .10 .25
82 Falcon Fast and Furious :Y: R 2.50 6.00
83 Fluttershy Guidance Counselor :Y: R 1.00 2.50
84 Fluttershy Animal Team :Y: U .20 .50
85 Forest Owl Novice Assistant :Y: C .10 .25
86 House Mouse Little Pipsqueak :Y: C .10 .25
87 Hummingway Fine Feathered Friend :Y: F 2.50 6.00
88 Lilac Links Superstitious :Y: R 1.25 3.00
89 Mane Cureall Veteran Vet :Y: R .75 2.00
90 Mr. Beaverton Beaverteeth Dam Builder :Y: R .40 1.00
91 Mr. Breezy Fan Fan :Y: R .75 2.00
92 Opalescence Curtain Shredder :Y: C .10 .25
93 Sea Swirl Porpoiseful :Y: R 2.50 6.00
94 Winona On the Scent :Y: C .10 .25
95 Spread Your Wings C .10 .25
96 Getting Hooves Dirty F 2.50 6.00
97 Dig Deep F 1.50 4.00
98 Apples and Oranges F 2.50 6.00
99 Royal Guidance C .10 .25
100 Sweet and Kind F 2.50 6.00
101 Good Hustle R .50 1.25
102 A Bully and a Beast :O: U .20 .50
103 A Touch of Refinement :W: U .20 .50
104 A Vision of the Future :K: R .40 1.00
105 Assertiveness Training R .50 1.25
106 Back Where you Began :P: R 1.50 4.00
107 Creme de la Creme :W: U .20 .50
108 Critter Cavalry :Y: U .20 .50
109 Double-check the Checklist :P: U .20 .50
110 Downright Dangerous :K: U .20 .50
111 Duck and Cover :O: U .20 .50
112 Eeyup :O: R .75 2.00
113 Here's Your Invitation! :K: U .20 .50
114 Let's Get This Party Started :K: U .20 .50
115 Fears Must be Faced :B: U .20 .50
116 Nurture With Knowledge :Y: U .20 .50
117 Gotta Go Fast :B: R .75 2.00
118 Stand Still! :W: R 1.00 2.50
119 Straighten Up and Fly Right R .60 1.50
120 Swing Into Action :B: U .20 .50
121 Team Effort R .60 1.50
122 The Big Guns R .60 1.50
123 The Horror! The Horror! :Y: U .20 .50
124 Spike, Take a Letter :P: U .20 .50
125 Undercover Adventure R .60 1.50
126 Watch in Awe :P: U .20 .50
127 What Went Wrong :B: U .20 .50
128 Whoa There Nelly! :O: R .50 1.25
129 Working Together R .50 1.25
130 Yay! :Y: U .20 .50
131 Assault Cake :K: R .75 2.00
132 Carousel Boutique :W: R .75 2.00
133 Tangled Coiffure :W: R .40 1.00
134 Critter Cuisine :Y: U .20 .50
135 Fighting for Friendship :P: C .10 .25
136 Foal Free Press :B: C .10 .25
137 Focused Study :P: U .20 .50
138 Golden Oak Library :P: R .60 1.50
139 Hard Hat :O: U .20 .50
140 Lead Pony Badge :B: U .20 .50
141 Marvelous Chapeau :W: U .20 .50
142 Outshine Them All :P: U .20 .50
143 Ridiculous Outfit :K: U .20 .50
144 Rubber Chicken :K: C .10 .25
145 Sweet Apple Acres :O: R .75 2.00
146 Picnic Lunch :Y: R .75 2.00
147 The Ponyville Express :W: U .20 .50
148 Too Many Bandages :Y: U .20 .50
149 Too Much Pie :O: U .20 .50
150 Tricksy Hat :P: U .20 .50
151 Two Bits :B: R 2.00 5.00
152 Ahuizotl R 1.25 3.00
153 Brown Parasprite C .10 .25
154 Flam U .20 .50
155 Flim U .20 .50
156 Parasprite Swarm R 1.25 3.00
157 Purple Parasprite C .10 .25
158 Timberwolf U .20 .50
159 Wild Manticore U .20 .50
160 Yellow Parasprite C .10 .25
161 A Thorn in His Paw :Y: C .10 .25
162 Avalanche! :O: C .10 .25
163 Kitchen au Flambe :W: C .10 .25
164 Bunny Breakout :Y: U .20 .50
165 Bunny Stampede :Y: C .10 .25
166 The Problem with Parasprites :B: C .10 .25
167 Clearing Gloomy Skies :B: U .20 .50
168 Cloudbursting :B: U .20 .50
169 Adventures in Foalsitting :K: C .10 .25
170 Emergency Dress Order :W: U .20 .50
171 795 Wing Power :B: U .20 .50
172 Mean Meanie Pants :K: C .10 .25
173 Hungry Hungry Caterpillars :O: C .10 .25
174 I Can Fix It! :W: C .10 .25
175 I Need Answers :P: U .20 .50
176 It's a Twister! :B: U .20 .50
177 It's Alive! :P: U .20 .50
178 Looking for Trouble :B: C .10 .25
179 May the Best Pet Win :Y: U .20 .50
180 Who is Gabby Gums :W: C .10 .25
181 Not Enough Pinkie Pies :K: C .10 .25
182 Monitor EVERYTHING! :P: C .10 .25
183 Monster of a Minotaur :Y: C .10 .25
184 My Pinkie Sense is Tingling :K: U .20 .50
185 Maybes are for Babies :K: U .20 .50
186 Fashion Feast :W: U .20 .50
187 Parasprite Pandemic :P: C .10 .25
188 Ponyville in a Bottle :P: C .10 .25
189 Raze This Barn :O: U .20 .50
190 Runaway Cart :O: U .20 .50
191 Save Sweet Apple Acres :O: U .20 .50
192 Special Delivery! :K: U .20 .50
193 Ponynapped! :W: U .20 .50
194 This Way, Little Ones :Y: U .20 .50
195 Want It, Need It! :O: U .20 .50
196 Wrapping up Winter :P: U .20 .50
197 Dr. Hooves Unblinking :B: UR 10.00 25.00
198 Rainbow Dash Winged Wonder :B: UR 25.00 50.00
199 Big Mac Immense Apple :O: UR 10.00 25.00
200 Ship Shape Heavy Lifter :O: UR 4.00 10.00
201 Lyra Heartstrings Bonafide :K: UR 10.00 25.00
202 Screwy Barking Mad :K: UR 8.00 20.00
203 Twilight Sparkle Ursa Vanquisher :P: UR 15.00 40.00
204 Zecora Everfree Guru :P: UR 10.00 25.00
205 Octavia Virtuoso :W: UR 10.00 25.00
206 Rarity Truly Outrageous :W: UR 25.00 50.00
207 Philomena Bird of a Feather :Y: UR 6.00 15.00
208 Princess Celestia Ray of Sunshine :Y: UR 12.00 30.00
209 Heart's Desire UR 15.00 40.00
210 Nightmare Moon UR 25.00 50.00
211 Fluttershy Monster Tamer :Y: UR 8.00 20.00

2013 My Little Pony Premiere Foil

F1 Rainbow Dash Flier Extradinaire :B: F 6.00 15.00
F2 Applejack Steadfast Farmpony :O: F 2.50 6.00
F3 Pinkie Pie Party Animal :K: F 2.00 5.00
F4 Twilight Sparkle Faithful Student :P: F 2.00 5.00
F5 Rarity Dazzling Fashionista :W: F 2.00 5.00
F6 Fluttershy Beastmaster :Y: F 2.00 5.00
F7 Finish Line Jammer :B: U 1.25 3.00
F8 Wild Fire Speed Racer :B: R 2.50 6.00
F9 Rainbow Dash Weather Leader :B: U 1.50 4.00
F10 Rainbowshine Cloud Wrangler :B: C 1.25 3.00
F11 Spike Baby Dragon :B: R 1.50 4.00
F12 Applejack Plant Leader :O: C 1.25 3.00
F13 Applejack Barn Raiser :O: R 1.50 4.00
F14 Auntie Applesauce Gum Flapper :O: U 1.25 3.00
F15 Granny Smith Apple Elder :O: C 1.25 3.00
F16 Drill Bit Destruction Worker :O: C 1.25 3.00
F17 Berry Dreams Pom-Pom Pony :K: C 1.25 3.00
F18 Pinkie Pie Pinkie Responsibility Pie :K: R 3.00 8.00
F19 Pinkie Pie Ice Cutter :K: C 1.25 3.00
F20 Pinprick Pop Star :K: R 1.50 4.00
F21 Professor Neigh Algebraic! :P: C 1.25 3.00
F22 Gyro Poindexter :P: R 2.00 5.00
F23 Rare Find a Real Gem :P: R 1.50 4.00
F24 Twilight Sparkle All-Team Organizer :P: C 1.25 3.00
F25 Featherweight Editor-in-Chief :W: R 1.50 4.00
F26 Rarity Nest Weaver :W: U 1.25 3.00
F27 Fluttershy Guidance Counselor :Y: R 2.00 5.00
F28 Fluttershy Animal Team :Y: U 1.25 3.00
F29 Lilac Links Superstitious :Y: R 1.50 4.00
F30 Winona on the Scent :Y: C 1.25 3.00
F31 Assertiveness Training R 1.25 3.00
F32 Let's Get This Party Started :K: U 1.25 3.00
F33 Straighten Up and Fly Right R 1.50 4.00
F34 Undercover Adventure R 1.50 4.00
F35 Working Together R 1.25 3.00
F36 Carousel Boutique :W: R 1.50 4.00
F37 Golden Oak Library :P: R 1.50 4.00

- F38 Sweet Apple Acres :O: R 1.50 4.00
- F39 Picnic Lunch :Y: R 1.25 3.00
- F40 Ahuizotl R 2.00 5.00
- F41 Parasprite Swarm R 2.00 5.00

2013 My Little Pony Premiere Promos

- PF1 Rainbow Dash to the Rescue 15.00 40.00
- PF4 Twilight Sparkle Research Student 4.00 10.00
- PF8 Eeyup 3.00 8.00
- PF12 Assault Cake 6.00 15.00

2009 Naruto Emerging Alliance

- COMPLETE SET (145) 50.00 100.00
- BOOSTER BOX (24 PACKS) 50.00 100.00
- BOOSTER PACK (10 CARDS) 2.00 5.00
- RELEASED IN OCTOBER 2009
- J496 Art of Ink Mist U .20 .50
- J497 Ninja Art: Super Beast Scroll R .75 2.00
- J498 Fire Style: Phoenix Flower Jutsu R .75 2.00
- J499 Self-Destruct Doppelganger R .75 2.00
- J500 Water Style: Water Shark Bomb Jutsu SR 10.00 25.00
- J501 Detonating Kunai C .10 .25
- J502 Sealing Jutsu: Breaking the Lions Roar SR 3.00 8.00
- J503 Flamethrower U .20 .50
- J504 Secret White Move: Chikamatsu?s Ten Puppets R .75 2.00
- J505 Partial Expansion Jutsu U .20 .50
- J506 Ninja Art: Shadow Stitching SR 3.00 8.00
- J507 Reanimation Ninjutsu U .20 .50
- J508 Secret Red Move: Performance of a Hundred Puppets R .75 2.00
- J509 Critical Wound C .10 .25
- J510 Getting Ready U .20 .50
- J511 Sense of Fear SR 4.00 10.00
- J512 Assimilation C .10 .25
- J513 Tricky Move C .10 .25
- J514 Ninja Art: Super Beast Scroll Rat U .20 .50
- J515 Wood Style Transformation C .10 .25
- J516 Striking Multi Shadow Snakes Jutsu U .20 .50
- J517 Formation! R .75 2.00
- J518 Revealing the True Face C .10 .25
- J519 Earth Style: Rending Piercing Fang SR 3.00 8.00
- J520 Ultimate Art U .20 .50
- J521 Ten Thousand Snakes Wave U .20 .50
- J522 Wood Style Jutsu: Wooden Lock Wall C .10 .25
- J523 Wood Clone Jutsu C .10 .25
- J524 Summoning Jutsu: Triple Rashomon R .75 2.00
- J525 Chakra Cannon U .20 .50
- J526 Thunder Funeral: Feast of Lightning U .20 .50
- J527 Unique Skill U .20 .50
- J528 Razor Chain C .10 .25
- J529 Sonic Attack C .10 .25
- J530 Super Sonic Slicing Wave C .10 .25
- J531 Stealing Chakra R .75 2.00
- J532 Twining Limbs C .10 .25
- J533 Bone Transformation C .10 .25
- J534 Bone Guard C .10 .25
- J535 Supplement of Energy U .20 .50
- J536 Wood Style Jutsu: Four Pillars Prison Jutsu U.20 .50
- J537 Visual Jutsu R .75 2.00
- J538 Giant Rasengan R .75 2.00
- J539 Crow Clone Jutsu R .75 2.00
- J540 Long Sword Shark Skin U .20 .50
- M455 Rules for Medical Ninjas R .75 2.00
- M456 Search Party C .10 .25
- M457 Piggyback C .10 .25
- M458 Filling Up the Open Spot R .75 2.00
- M459 100 Hot-Blooded C .10 .25
- M460 Fellowship C .10 .25
- M461 Tears for a Friend C .10 .25
- M462 Constricting Bind U .20 .50
- M463 Bad Dream R .75 2.00
- M464 Control by Fear C .10 .25
- M465 Transmitter U .20 .50
- M466 Lunchbox U .20 .50
- M467 Shake Hands U .20 .50
- M468 Meaning of Comrade C .10 .25
- M469 Tenchi Bridge C .10 .25
- M470 Releasing the Sealed Power U .20 .50
- M471 Compressed Chakra C .10 .25
- M472 A Sign of Revival U .20 .50
- M473 The best pair C .10 .25
- M474 Hiding U .20 .50
- M475 Check U .20 .50
- M476 Fateful Encounter C .10 .25
- M477 Super Bushy-Brow C .10 .25
- M478 Ninja Info Card R .75 2.00
- M479 Pressure R .75 2.00
- M480 Captivity R .75 2.00
- M481 Precious Student C .10 .25
- M482 The Ones Who Have the Same Eyes U .20 .50
- M483 Meaning of Life C .10 .25
- M484 Impersonation U .20 .50
- M485 Medical Ninja U .20 .50
- M486 Sealing Barrier R .75 2.00
- M487 A New Squad R .75 2.00
- M488 Surprise Training C .10 .25
- M489 Invitation to the Darkness U .20 .50
- M490 Picture Book C .10 .25
- M491 Discord C .10 .25
- M492 Secret Meeting C .10 .25
- M493 Commemorative Photo U .20 .50
- M494 Pledge under a Starry Sky C .10 .25
- M495 Respective Dreams C .10 .25
- M496 Underground Organization U .20 .50
- M497 Advisors U .20 .50
- M498 Prelude to an End U .20 .50
- M499 Intellectual Strategy R .75 2.00
- N590 Kakashi Hatake & Might Guy U .20 .50
- N591 Naruto Uzumaki (Tailed Beast Mode) SR 10.00 25.00
- N592 Naruto Uzumaki C .10 .25
- N593 Sakura Haruno C .10 .25
- N594 Sai R 1.00 2.50
- N595 Ino Yamanaka C .10 .25
- N596 Shikamaru Nara C .10 .25
- N597 Choji Akimichi C .10 .25
- N598 Yamato R .75 2.00
- N599 Shizune C .10 .25
- N600 Danzo R .75 2.00
- N601 Chiyo U .20 .50
- N602 Matsuri C .10 .25
- N603 Mikoshi C .10 .25
- N604 Tobi R 1.50 4.00
- N605 Sasori (Possesion Mode) R .75 2.00
- N606 Kabuto Yakushi SR 5.00 12.00
- N607 Orochimaru SR 5.00 12.00
- N608 Naruto Uzumaki & Sai R .75 2.00
- N609 Anbu (The Foundation) R .75 2.00
- N610 Homura Mitomon U .20 .50
- N611 Koharu Utatane U .20 .50
- N612 The First Hokage SR 5.00 12.00
- N613 The Second Hokage SR 5.00 12.00
- N614 Haku (Childhood) C .10 .25
- N615 Kabuto Yakushi R .75 2.00
- N616 Naruto Uzumaki & Yamato SR 4.00 10.00
- N617 Dosu Kinuta C .10 .25
- N618 Zaku Abumi C .10 .25
- N619 Kin Tsuchi C .10 .25
- N620 Kimimaro (Childhood) U .20 .50
- N621 Dosu Kinuta, Zaku Abumi & Kin Tsuchi U .20 .50
- N622 Anko Mitarashi C .10 .25
- N623 Ranmaru C .10 .25
- N624 Manda R .75 2.00
- N625 Raiga Kurosuki R .75 2.00
- N626 The Demon Brothers Gouzu C .10 .25
- N627 The Demon Brothers Meizu C .10 .25
- N628 Shimon Hijiri U .20 .50
- N629 Misumi Tsurugi C .10 .25
- N630 Yoroi Akado C .10 .25
- N631 Ino Yamanaka C .10 .25
- N632 Naruto Uzumaki R .75 2.00
- N633 Rock Lee & Tortoise Ninja U .20 .50
- N634 Shikamaru Nara SR 10.00 25.00
- N635 Choji Akimichi C .10 .25
- N636 Shizune & Tonton U .20 .50
- N637 Sasuke Uchiha C .10 .25
- N638 Gaara of the Desert (Possessed Mode) SR 4.00 10.00
- N639 Sakura Haruno & Sai R .75 2.00
- N640 Might Guy SR 3.00 8.00
- N641 Kankuro & Black Ant U .20 .50
- N642 Temari R .75 2.00
- N643 Itachi Uchiha R 1.50 4.00
- N644 Kisame Hoshigaki R .75 2.00

2009 Naruto Fateful Reunion

- COMPLETE SET (156) 60.00 120.00
- BOOSTER BOX (24 PACKS) 60.00 120.00
- BOOSTER PACK (10 CARDS) 3.00 6.00
- RELEASED IN MAY 2009
- C047 Teuchi C .10 .25
- C048 Takamaru C .10 .25
- J450 Radio C .10 .25
- J451 A Thousand Years of Death R .75 2.00
- J452 Snatching the Weapon C .10 .25
- J453 Giant Shuriken U .20 .50
- J454 Multi Shadow Clone Taijutsu U .20 .50
- J455 Copy Ninjutsu C .10 .25
- J456 Mirror Reflection Jutsu R .75 2.00
- J457 Button Hook Entry C .10 .25
- J458 Detonating Clay Centipede C .10 .25
- J459 Mangekyo Sharingan SR 3.00 8.00
- J460 Water Style: Five Hungry Sharks SR 3.00 8.00
- J461 Five-Seal Barrier U .20 .50
- J462 Sealing Jutsu: Nine Phantom Dragons C .10 .25
- J463 Simultaneous Attacks U .20 .50
- J464 Assault Blade R .75 2.00
- J465 Medical Ninjutsu U .20 .50
- J466 Iron Sand: Scattered Showers C .10 .25
- J467 Iron Sand: Unleash C .10 .25
- J468 Body Manipulation C .10 .25
- J469 Concealed Weapon C .10 .25
- J470 Chakra Shield C .10 .25
- J471 Poison Smoke U .20 .50
- J472 Power of the Cursed Blood C .10 .25
- J473 8 Trigrams Palms Rotation C .10 .25
- J474 Scope C .10 .25
- J475 Fire Style: Fire Ball Jutsu U .20 .50
- J476 Illusion by Genjutsu U .20 .50
- J477 A Treasure Puppet U .20 .50
- J478 Continuous Firing of Poison Needles R .75 2.00
- J479 Hallucination by Genjutsu R .75 2.00
- J480 Perfect Defense R .75 2.00
- J481 Continuous Shuriken Attacks C .10 .25
- J482 Water Style: Exploding Water Shock Wave R .75 2.00
- J483 Clean Hit R .75 2.00
- J484 Clay Clone C .10 .25
- J485 Shadow Clone Jutsu U .20 .50
- J486 Genjutsu: Sylvan Fetters R .75 2.00
- J487 Crescent Moon Dance C .10 .25
- J488 Human Boulder C .10 .25
- J489 Genjutsu Negation U .20 .50
- J490 Ino-Shika-Cho Formation R .75 2.00
- J491 Trap C .10 .25
- J492 Spinning Kick C .10 .25
- J493 Demon Illusion: Death Mirage Jutsu R .75 2.00
- J494 Detonating Clay Signature Technique R .75 2.00
- J495 Rasengan SR 3.00 8.00
- M412 Mission of Capturing the Missing Pet Tora R.75 2.00
- M413 Lottery C .10 .25
- M414 Fulfilling the Quota C .10 .25
- M415 Buying Time R .75 2.00
- M416 Cruel Irony C .10 .25
- M417 Eliminating the Alliance U .20 .50
- M418 Weak Remembrance C .10 .25
- M419 Uncovered Trick C .10 .25
- M420 Control of the Nine-Tailed C .10 .25
- M421 Ubiquitous U .20 .50
- M422 Evil Spirit U .20 .50
- M423 Whim U .20 .50
- M424 Puppet Show R .75 2.00
- M425 Quota U .20 .50
- M426 The Ones Wriggling in the Dark C .10 .25
- M427 Messenger C .10 .25
- M428 Eight Ninja Dogs R .75 2.00
- M429 Sealing the Tailed Beast U .20 .50
- M430 Threat of the Tailed Beasts C .10 .25
- M431 Successive Kazekage U .20 .50
- M432 Detecting the Enemy C .10 .25
- M433 Unhealed Wound R .75 2.00
- M434 Bad Omen U .20 .50
- M435 Kazekage in Custody C .10 .25
- M436 Hidden Village of the Wind R .75 2.00
- M437 Long Awaited Reunion C .10 .25
- M438 Overflowing Fighting Spirits C .10 .25
- M439 New Hokage Rock C .10 .25
- M440 Misunderstanding U .20 .50
- M441 Dark Ritual U .20 .50
- M442 Reinforcement from Sand C .10 .25
- M443 Substitute R 3.00 8.00
- M444 Tactic against Genjutsu C .10 .25
- M445 Unstable Ground R .75 2.00
- M446 Report C .10 .25
- M447 4 Times Faster U .20 .50
- M448 Fellow and Loneliness SR 3.00 8.00
- M449 Losing Control of Chakra C .10 .25
- M450 Eternal Rivalry R .75 2.00
- M451 Beginning of the New Chronicle R .75 2.00
- M452 Corps in Black U .20 .50
- M453 Successive Hokage U .20 .50
- M454 Sleeping in the Open U .20 .50
- N522 Naruto Uzumaki (Tailed Beast Mode) SR 8.00 20.00
- N523 Sakura Haruno R .75 2.00
- N527 Kakashi Hatake R .75 2.00
- N528 Kiba Inuzuka R .75 2.00
- N529 Shino Aburame R .75 2.00
- N530 Hinata Hyuga U .20 .50
- N531 Ino Yamanaka U .20 .50
- N532 Choji Akimichi U .20 .50
- N533 Kotetsu Hagane U .20 .50
- N534 Izumo Kamizuki U .20 .50
- N535 Kidomaru C .10 .25
- N536 Jirobo C .10 .25
- N537 Sakon C .10 .25
- N538 Tayuya C .10 .25
- N539 Chiyo SR 5.00 12.00
- N540 Father and Mother U .20 .50
- N541 Deidara U .20 .50
- N542 Sasori SR 8.00 20.00
- N543 The 3rd Kazekage SR 6.00 15.00
- N544 Sasori (Puppet Mode) SR 3.00 8.00
- N545 Hanabi Hyuga C .10 .25
- N546 Neji Hyuga U .20 .50
- N547 Sasuke Uchiha N-548 .10 .25
- N548 Sasuke Uchiha SR 10.00 25.00
- N549 Neji Hyuga & Hinata Hyuga R .75 2.00
- N550 Sasuke Uchiha & Orochimaru SR 10.00 25.00
- N551 Shino Aburame & Kiba Inuzuka R 2.50 6.00
- N552 Sasori & Deidara R .75 2.00
- N553 Ino Yamanaka U .20 .50
- N554 Anko Mitarashi R .75 2.00
- N555 Jiraiya C .10 .25
- N556 Shizune R .75 2.00
- N557 Rock Lee N-558 .20 .50
- N558 Orochimaru U .20 .50
- N559 Naruto Uzumaki U .20 .50
- N560 Neji Hyuga SR 10.00 25.00
- N561 Hinata Hyuga U .20 .50
- N562 Tenten R .75 2.00
- N563 Naruto Uzumaki U .20 .50
- N564 Sasuke Uchiha U .20 .50
- N565 Rock Lee R .75 2.00
- N566 Naruto Uzumaki U .20 .50
- N567 Kakashi Hatake (Anbu Days) U .20 .50
- N568 Neji Hyuga U .20 .50
- N569 Temari R .75 2.00
- N570 Tsunade U .20 .50
- N571 Rock Lee U .20 .50
- N572 Kakashi Hatake & Might Guy R .75 2.00
- N573 Kakashi Hatake & Pakkun R .75 2.00
- N574 Kiba Inuzuka & Akamaru R 1.50 4.00
- N575 Naruto Uzumaki C .10 .25
- N576 Neji Hyuga R .75 2.00
- N577 Tenten U .20 .50
- N578 Shikamaru Nara SR 5.00 12.00
- N579 Sakura Haruno ST .40 1.00
- N580 Kakashi Hatake ST .40 1.00
- N581 Itachi Uchiha ST .40 1.00
- N582 Rock Lee ST .40 1.00
- N583 Ninja Dog Squad (All Gathered) ST .40 1.00
- N584 The 5th Kazekage ST .40 1.00
- N585 Jiraiya ST .40 1.00
- N586 The 5th Hokage ST .40 1.00
- N587 Orochimaru ST .40 1.00
- N588 Naruto Uzumaki STSR 2.00 5.00
- N589 Sasuke Uchiha STSR 2.00 5.00

2009 Naruto Foretold Prophecy

- COMPLETE SET (177) 60.00 120.00
- BOOSTER BOX (24 PACKS) 40.00 80.00
- BOOSTER PACK (10 CARDS) 2.00 4.00
- RELEASED IN DECEMBER 2009
- C049 Taruho U .20 .50
- C050 Susuki U .20 .50
- C051 Miroku R 1.25 3.00
- J541 Tongfa C .10 .25
- J542 Dynamic Action U .20 .50
- J543 Storm by Rasengan ST .40 1.00
- J544 Destructive Swing C .10 .25
- J545 Fast Capture R 1.00 2.50
- J546 Power of Sharingan U .20 .50
- J547 Fire Style: Fire Ball Jutsu C .10 .25
- J548 Burst of Lightning Blade U .20 .50
- J549 Assault of Snakes C .10 .25
- J550 Ecdysis C .10 .25
- J551 Sand Arm R 1.00 2.50
- J552 Giant Sand Shield C .10 .25
- J553 Heaven Kick of Pain U .20 .50
- J554 Chakra Thread C .10 .25
- J555 Leaf Hurricane R 1.25 3.00
- J556 Priestess's Bell C .10 .25
- J557 Chocolate Bomb!! U .20 .50
- J558 Hidden Lotus U .20 .50
- J559 Super Chakra Rasengan R 1.25 3.00
- J560 Shadow Mirror Body Transfer Art U .20 .50
- J561 Monstrous Warriors U .20 .50
- J562 Water Style: Surface Slicer U .20 .50
- J563 Combination Ninjutsu C .10 .25
- J564 Chakra Infusion R 1.00 2.50
- J565 Wind Style: Divine Down-Current C .10 .25
- J566 Earth Style: Petrifying Jutsu U .20 .50
- J567 Youth at Full Power! C .10 .25
- J569 Great Leaf Flash U .20 .50
- J570 Radiant Energy C .10 .25
- J571 Ninja Art: Super Beast Scroll Falcon C .10 .25
- J572 Ninja Art: Super Beast Scroll Snake U .20 .50
- J573 Snake Sword ST .40 1.00
- J574 Mulitple Striking Shadow Snake R 1.50 4.00
- J575 Chidori Stream SR 5.00 12.00
- J576 Sickle Chain C .10 .25
- J577 Weapon Control! Tensasai U .20 .50
- J578 Antidote C .10 .25
- J579 8 Trigrams Hazan Strike C .10 .25
- J580 Fist of Anger C .10 .25
- J581 Cherry Blossom Impact SR 5.00 12.00
- J582 Detonating Clay C .10 .25
- J583 Gentle Fist U .20 .50
- J584 Emergency Meeting U .20 .50
- J585 Giving Ones Best C .10 .25
- J586 Thousand Arms Manipulation U .20 .50
- J587 Wood Style: Four Pillars House Jutsu C .10 .25
- J588 Massive Iron Sand Attack U .20 .50
- J589 Kamui SR 5.00 12.00
- J590 8 Trigrams Air Palm C .10 .25
- J591 Glare of Snake U .20 .50
- J592 Power of the Evil C .10 .25
- J593 Special Power C .10 .25
- J594 Sealing the Evil U .20 .50
- J595 Ink Clone Jutsu C .10 .25
- J596 Running on the Water U .20 .50
- J597 Stock C .10 .25
- J598 Chakra Knife U .20 .50
- J599 Wood Style: Domed Wall C .10 .25
- J600 Revival of the Dead R 1.00 2.50
- J601 Interrogation C .10 .25
- M500 Leaf Academy U .20 .50
- M501 Reunion of Destiny C .10 .25
- M502 Betrayal R 1.25 3.00
- M503 Sacrifice C .10 .25
- M504 Target of the Vengeance C .10 .25
- M505 Lack of Sensitivity R 1.25 3.00
- M506 Luxurious Meal C .10 .25
- M507 Temporary Squad C .10 .25
- M508 The Priestess Who Seals the Evil ST .40 1.00
- M509 Beyond the Time C .10 .25
- M510 Changed Prophecy C .10 .25
- M511 Competition R 1.00 2.50
- M512 Retiring Character R 1.00 2.50
- M513 Surprise Attack from a Mysterious Enemy R1.00 2.50
- M514 Powerless C .10 .25
- M515 Punishment U .20 .50
- M516 Not Again U .20 .50
- M517 Cold Eyes U .20 .50
- M518 Heart-to-Heart Communication C .10 .25
- M519 Weird Picture Book U .20 .50
- M520 Fake Smile R 1.00 2.50
- M521 Internal Trouble U .20 .50
- M522 Secret Mission U .20 .50
- M523 Buddy System R 1.00 2.50
- M524 Search for a Member U .20 .50
- M525 A Tail C .10 .25
- M526 Necklace of the First Hokage U .20 .50
- M527 Master of the Weapons R 1.00 2.50
- M528 Inherited Kekkei Genkai C .10 .25
- M529 Dummy U .20 .50
- M530 Member List R 1.00 2.50
- M531 Impatient Feeling U .20 .50
- M532 Earth Style: Hidden Mole Jutsu C .10 .25
- M533 Jealousy C .10 .25
- M534 Bashfulness SR 6.00 15.00
- M535 Deep-Rooted Organization R 1.00 2.50
- M536 Deeply Cut Wound U .20 .50
- M537 Approaching Shadow of a Snake R 1.00 2.50
- M538 Crying in Vain R 1.00 2.50
- M539 The Power to Seal the Disaster U .20 .50
- M540 Not Another Step! R 1.00 2.50
- M541 Firm Union U .20 .50
- M542 Will of the Third Hokage C .10 .25
- M543 Sharpening the Blade C .10 .25
- M544 Big Help C .10 .25
- M545 Leaf Hospital SR 5.00 12.00
- M546 Destiny of the Clan U .20 .50
- M547 Approaching Showdown SR 5.00 12.00
- M548 Threat of the State 2 R 1.00 2.50
- M549 Leaf Police Force ST .40 1.00
- N645 Shion (Awakened) ST .40 1.00
- N646 Kusuna R 1.50 4.00
- N647 Shizuku U .20 .50
- N648 Setsuna U .20 .50
- N649 Gitai C .10 .25
- N650 The Nine-Tailed Fox Spirit R 1.25 3.00
- N651 Naruto Uzumaki C .10 .25
- N652 Sakura Haruno U .20 .50
- N653 Sasuke Uchiha R 5.00 12.00
- N654 Sai R 1.25 3.00
- N655 Yamato SR 10.00 25.00
- N656 Kiba Inuzuka U .20 .50
- N657 Shino Aburame C .10 .25
- N658 Hinata Hyuga U .20 .50
- N659 Hiashi Hyuga U .20 .50
- N660 Akamaru U .20 .50
- N661 The 5th Kazekage R 1.00 2.50
- N662 Kankuro R 1.00 2.50
- N663 Ebizo U .20 .50
- N664 Sasori (Childhood) U .20 .50
- N665 Deidara U .20 .50
- N666 Orochimaru SR 6.00 15.00
- N667 Kabuto Yakushi R 1.25 3.00
- N668 Sasuke Uchiha SR 10.00 25.00
- N669 Naruto Uzumaki STSR 2.00 5.00
- N670 Sasuke Uchiha STSR 2.00 5.00
- N671 Sai ST .40 1.00
- N672 Sakura Haruno C .10 .25
- N673 Sasori & The 3rd Kazekage R 1.25 3.00
- N674 Shikamaru Nara U .20 .50
- N675 Kakashi Hatake R 1.00 2.50
- N676 Itachi Uchiha ST .40 1.00
- N677 Yamato R 1.25 3.00
- N678 Baki R 3.00 8.00
- N679 Temari C .10 .25
- N680 Jiraiya ST .40 1.00
- N681 Tsunade C .10 .25
- N682 Orochimaru U .20 .50
- N683 Konohamaru ST .40 1.00
- N684 Naruto Uzumaki & Jiraiya R 2.00 5.00
- N685 Sakura Haruno & Tsunade SR 6.00 15.00
- N686 Naruto Uzumaki & Yamato C .10 .25
- N687 Naruto Uzumaki & Sai ST .40 1.00
- N688 Naruto Uzumaki & Shion R 1.25 3.00
- N689 Shion ST .40 1.00
- N690 Yomi ST .40 1.00
- N691 The Fourth Kazekage SR 6.00 15.00
- N692 Giant Ninja Toad ST .40 1.00
- N693 Giant Snake U .20 .50
- N694 Tonton C .10 .25
- N695 Tortoise Ninja C .10 .25
- N696 Giant Tiger C .10 .25
- N697 Kakashi Hatake (Childhood) C .10 .25
- N698 The Third Hokage (Childhood) U .20 .50
- N699 Koharu Utatane (Childhood) C .10 .25
- N700 Homura Mitomon (Childhood) C .10 .25
- N701 The Fourth Hokage (Childhood) C .10 .25
- N702 The Fourth Hokage (Younger Days) SR 10.00 25.00
- N703 Neji Hyuga (Childhood) C .10 .25
- N704 Tekka Uchiha ST .40 1.00
- N705 Inabi Uchiha ST .40 1.00
- N706 Yashiro Uchiha ST .40 1.00
- N707 Elder of Hyuga Clan U .20 .50
- N708 Iruka Umino (Childhood) C .10 .25

2009 Naruto A New Chronicle

- COMPLETE SET (172) 75.00 150.00
- BOOSTER BOX (24 PACKS) 50.00 100.00
- BOOSTER PACK (10 CARDS) 2.50 5.00
- RELEASED IN FEBRUARY 2009
- J387 Sexy Jutsu R .75 2.00
- J388 New Pervy Ninjutsu R .75 2.00
- J389 Revealing the Ending C .10 .25
- J390 Make-Out Tactics C .10 .25
- J391 Brainwash Jutsu U .20 .50
- J392 Forbidden Word C .10 .25
- J393 Iron-Armed U .20 .50
- J394 Wind Scythe Jutsu R .75 2.00
- J395 Sand Shield C .10 .25
- J396 Leaf Rising Wind U .20 .50
- J397 Nunchaku C .10 .25
- J398 Opening the Eight Inner Gates R .75 2.00
- J399 Asakujaku SR 10.00 25.00
- J400 Giant Rasengan SR 6.00 15.00
- J401 Genjutsu C .10 .25
- J402 Mission File C .10 .25
- J403 Detonating Clay Eagle U .20 .50
- J404 Detonating Clay Bird U .20 .50
- J405 Detonating Clay Spider U .20 .50
- J406 Detonating Clay Signature Technique R 1.50 4.00
- J407 Cleanup U .20 .50
- J408 Water Style: Exploding Water Shock Wave U .20 .50
- J409 Water Prison Jutsu R .75 2.00
- J410 Shark Skin R .75 2.00
- J411 Impersonation Jutsu U .20 .50
- J412 Explosive Blade C .10 .25
- J413 Puppet Master Jutsu U .20 .50
- J414 Absolute Defense U .20 .50
- J415 Sand Prison U .20 .50
- J416 Sand Coffin SR 5.00 12.00
- J417 Detoxification C .10 .25
- J418 Deadly Poison R 1.50 4.00
- J419 Emission of Chakra R .75 2.00
- J420 Compound Jutsu C .10 .25
- J421 8 Trigrams Air Palm R 2.50 6.00
- J422 Arhat Fist R .75 2.00
- J423 Spider Bow: Fierce Rip R .75 2.00
- J424 Deadly Combination Attack R .75 2.00
- J425 Demon Flute: Chains of Fantasia U .20 .50
- J426 Threat of the Puppets C .10 .25
- J427 Substitution by Insects C .10 .25
- J428 Concealed Weapon U .20 .50
- J429 Gentle Fist Style: 8 Trigrams 64 Palms R .75 2.00
- J430 Shadow Strangle Jutsu U .20 .50
- J431 Poison Needles U .20 .50
- J432 Dispatch of Anbu U .20 .50
- J433 Angry Fist U .20 .50
- J434 Striking Shadow Snake U .20 .50
- J435 Reaper Death Seal R .75 2.00
- J436 Shadow Clone Jutsu R .75 2.00
- J437 Summoning Jutsu C .10 .25
- J438 Playing Possum Jutsu C .10 .25
- J439 Liquid Bullets R .75 2.00
- J440 Air Bullets R .75 2.00
- J441 Sealing Jutsu: Fire Seal C .10 .25
- J442 Anbu Mask U .20 .50
- J443 Knockout Blow U .20 .50
- J444 Opening the Byakugan C .10 .25
- J445 Wolf Fang Over Fang C .10 .25
- J446 Larch Dance U .20 .50
- J447 Substitution by Puppet R .75 2.00
- J448 Capture C .10 .25
- J449 Fire Style: Fire Ball Jutsu C .10 .25
- M364 Dangerous Intruder U .20 .50

M365 New leader of the Village U	.20	.50
M366 Round-Table Conference C	.10	.25
M367 Sending Off C	.10	.25
M368 Growth of the Two R	.60	1.50
M369 Existence of Tailed Beast U	.20	.50
M370 Powerful Help C	.10	.25
M371 Art is an explosion! R	.60	1.50
M372 Akatsuki Gathered C	.10	.25
M373 The ones who interrupt C	.10	.25
M374 Revenge for My Son C	.10	.25
M375 Sasori of the Red Sand R	3.00	8.00
M376 Playing Dead U	.20	.50
M377 Heroic Whirl Wind R	.60	1.50
M378 Tyrannical Storm R	.60	1.50
M379 West Gate, North Gate C	.10	.25
M380 South Gate, East Gate C	.10	.25
M381 The one who lives within SR	6.00	15.00
M382 Raid By Anbu U	.20	.50
M383 Teacher and pupils C	.10	.25
M384 Great Memory C	.10	.25
M385 A Mark U	.20	.50
M386 Arbitration R	.60	1.50
M387 Oath of Vengeance U	.20	.50
M388 Welling Up Red Chakra C	.10	.25
M389 Secret of Uchiha Clan U	.20	.50
M390 On the Stump C	.10	.25
M391 Debt R	1.25	3.00
M392 A Preach C	.10	.25
M393 Found You! C	.10	.25
M394 Wonderful Days U	.20	.50
M395 Wager C	.10	.25
M396 A Gift U	.20	.50
M397 BBQ R	3.00	8.00
M398 Preparation C	.10	.25
M399 Ino-Shika-Cho Trio U	.20	.50
M400 Inuzuka Clan U	.20	.50
M401 Ichiraku Noodle Shop R	.60	1.50
M402 Chase U	.20	.50
M403 Creeping Up Dark Clouds U	.20	.50
M404 Agony of the Strong C	.10	.25
M405 Numbness U	.20	.50
M406 Archrival U	.20	.50
M407 Ultimate Two-Step Program C	.10	.25
M408 Invitation to the Evil U	.20	.50
M409 Escape C	.10	.25
M410 Apology C	.10	.25
M411 Long Awaited Reinforcements R	1.50	4.00
N461 Kankuro SR	12.00	30.00
N462 Temari R	.50	1.25
N463 Yura C	.10	.25
N464 Baki U	.20	.50
N465 The Fifth Kazekage SR	8.00	20.00
N466 Naruto Uzumaki U	.20	.50
N467 Sakura Haruno R	1.25	3.00
N468 Iruka Umino U	.20	.50
N469 Konohamaru C	.10	.25
N470 Moegi C	.10	.25
N471 Udon C	.10	.25
N472 Ebisu C	.10	.25
N473 Kakashi Hatake SR	8.00	20.00
N474 Might Guy R	1.25	3.00
N475 Rock Lee R	1.25	3.00
N476 Neji Hyuga U	.20	.50
N477 Tenten U	.20	.50
N478 Itachi Uchiha SR	8.00	20.00
N479 Kisame Hoshigaki R	1.25	3.00
N480 Deidara SR	12.00	30.00
N481 Sasori SR	12.00	30.00
N482 Zetsu SR	6.00	15.00
N483 Gaara of the Desert U	.20	.50
N484 Crow U	.20	.50
N485 Black Ant U	.20	.50
N486 Salamander U	.20	.50
N487 Ebizo U	.20	.50
N488 Chiyo R	1.50	4.00
N489 Cipher Corps U	.20	.50
N490 Naruto Uzumaki C	.10	.25
N491 Sakura Haruno C	.10	.25
N492 Rock Lee U	.20	.50
N493 Hinata Hyuga C	.10	.25
N494 Naruto Uzumaki & Gaara of the Desert SR	8.00	20.00
N495 Temari & Kankuro SR	10.00	25.00
N496 Sasuke Uchiha U	.20	.50
N497 Naruto Uzumaki U	.20	.50
N498 Kiba Inuzuka C	.10	.25
N499 Ninja Dog Squad C	.10	.25
N500 Hinata Hyuga & Hiashi Hyuga U	.20	.50
N501 Sasori & Kisame Hoshigaki SR	8.00	20.00
N502 Itachi Uchiha & Deidara SR	6.00	15.00
N503 Double Headed Wolf R	1.25	3.00
N504 Kiba Inuzuka & Akamaru R	1.25	3.00
N505 Kotetsu Hagane C	.10	.25
N506 Kurenai Yuhi U	.20	.50
N507 Genma Shiranui C	.10	.25
N508 Hayate Gekko U	.20	.50
N509 Hanabi Hyuga C	.10	.25
N510 Kankuro U	.20	.50
N511 Shino Aburame R	4.00	10.00
N512 Ninja Dog Squad (All Gathered) C	.10	.25
N513 Neji Hyuga C	.10	.25
N514 Inoichi Yamanaka R	1.25	3.00
N515 Shikaku Nara R	2.50	6.00
N516 Choza Akimichi R	1.25	3.00
N517 Gen Aburame R	1.25	3.00
N518 Hiashi Hyuga R	1.25	3.00
N519 Choji Akimichi C	.10	.25
N520 Deidara U	.20	.50
N521 Sasori U	.20	.50

2010 Naruto Broken Promise

COMPLETE SET (157)	50.00	100.00
BOOSTER BOX (24 PACKS)	50.00	100.00
BOOSTER PACK (10 CARDS)	2.50	5.00
RELEASED IN MARCH 2010		
C052 Lady Haruna R	.40	1.00
C053 Momiji R	.40	1.00
C054 Chikara U	.20	.50
C055 Uroko U	.20	.50
J602 Summoning Jutsu: Ninja Dogs C	.10	.25
J603 Special Kunai C	.10	.25
J604 Chidori SR FOIL	8.00	20.00
J605 White Fang's Blade C	.10	.25
J606 Sharingan Kunai R	1.00	2.50
J607 Detonating Clay: Mysterious Bird C	.10	.25
J608 Tsukuyomi U	.20	.50
J609 Chakra Slice U	.20	.50
J610 Mental Fatigue R	.40	1.00
J611 Water Style: Water Dragon Jutsu R	1.00	2.50
J612 Striking Shadow Snake R	.40	1.00
J613 Counter R	1.00	2.50
J614 Infuriation R	.40	1.00
J615 Wood Style: Tree Bind Eternal Burial U	.20	.50
J616 Sharpness of the Weapon U	.20	.50
J617 Intrustion C	.10	.25
J618 Sharingan of Tears C	.10	.25
J619 Change in Chakra Form C	.10	.25
J620 Change in Chakra Nature R	.40	1.00
J621 Power of the Clones C	.10	.25
J622 Power of the Meteorite U	.20	.50
J623 Summoning Jutsu: Air Fish C	.10	.25
J624 Magnetic Power C	.10	.25
J625 Rasengan R	.40	1.00
J626 Genjutsu U	.20	.50
J627 Space Created by Genjutsu R	.40	1.00
J628 Canceling Tone C	.10	.25
J629 Dragon Eyes: Fang Release: Dark Sword U	.20	.50
J630 Wind Slicer C	.10	.25
J631 Wind Scythe Jutsu U	.20	.50
J632 Soaring Shot Sword C	.10	.25
J633 Wood Style: Great Forest Jutsu SR	3.00	8.00
J634 Inflow of Chakra U	.20	.50
J635 Chidori Stream R	1.25	3.00
J636 Water Style: Bubbling Water C	.10	.25
J637 Flower Shuriken: Burning Petals and Fallen Leaves C	.10	.25
J638 Exposing the Hideout R	.40	1.00
J639 High Speed Hand Signs C	.10	.25
J640 Fear by Genjutsu SR	12.00	30.00
J641 Release of Fury SR FOIL	2.50	6.00
J642 Trump card R	.40	1.00
J643 Beast Transformation C	.10	.25
J644 Beast Mimicry Ninja Art: Man Beast Clone C	.10	.25
M585 Succeeded Will of Fire R	.40	1.00
M586 Beauty and Intelligence R	.40	1.00
M587 Chakra Paper C	.10	.25
M588 Earth Style: Rampart of Flowing Soil C	.10	.25
M589 BBQ House "Barbe-Q" C	.10	.25
M590 Recollection C	.10	.25
M591 Restricted Jutsu U	.20	.50
M592 Tears of Determination R	.40	1.00
M593 Shogi Match SR	5.00	12.00
M594 A Snake Hiding in the Dark R	.40	1.00
M595 Infiltration C	.10	.25
M596 Reconfirmation of the Mission R	.40	1.00
M597 Skeleton Key U	.20	.50
M598 Smile of the Two C	.10	.25
M599 Retreat C	.10	.25
M600 Fire Temple C	.10	.25
M601 Group Lesson R	.75	2.00
M602 Messenger Ninjas C	.10	.25
M603 Lullaby U	.20	.50
M604 Showy Entrance U	.20	.50
M605 Tracking Mission C	.10	.25
M606 Clear Tone Carries in the Sunset C	.10	.25
M607 Picture of Their Dreams C	.10	.25
M608 My First Fellow C	.10	.25
M609 Favor to Ask U	.20	.50
M610 Visiting Kakashi in the Hospital U	.20	.50
M611 Narrow Escape R	.40	1.00
M612 Seeing Through Distance U	.20	.50
M613 A Gift from a Friend U	.20	.50
M614 Pressing R	.40	1.00
M615 Imaginary Monster C	.10	.25
M616 Last Message U	.20	.50
M617 Efficient Training SR FOIL	5.00	12.00
M618 Determination of Men SR	3.00	8.00
M619 Water Style: Waterfall Basin Jutsu C	.10	.25
M620 Reconnoitering Party C	.10	.25
N709 Kakashi Hatake (Boyhood) SR FOIL	10.00	25.00
N710 Rin U	.20	.50
N711 Obito Uchiha SR FOIL	12.00	30.00
N712 The Fourth Hokage SR	10.00	25.00
N713 Kakkou U	.20	.50
N714 Taiseki C	.10	.25
N715 Mahiru C	.10	.25
N716 Zetsu U	.20	.50
N717 Tobi U	.20	.50
N718 Orochimaru (Childhood) R	1.50	4.00
N719 Jiraiya (Childhood) R	1.25	3.00
N720 Tsunade (Childhood) R	1.50	4.00
N721 Chiriku C	.10	.25
N722 Hana Inuzuka U	.20	.50
N723 Haimaru Brothers C	.10	.25
N724 Yoshino Nara R	1.25	3.00
N725 Shin C	.10	.25
N726 Naruto Uzumaki (Student) U	.20	.50
N727 Sasuke Uchiha (Student) U	.20	.50
N728 Sakura Haruno (Student) U	.20	.50
N729 Sakura Haruno & Hinata Hyuga R	.40	1.00
N730 Shikamaru Nara & Kakashi Hatake SR	5.00	12.00
N731 Kakashi Hatake (Teacher) U	.20	.50
N732 Asuma Sarutobi C	.10	.25
N733 Yugito Ni'i R	.40	1.00
N734 Two Tails SR	5.00	12.00
N735 Sasori & Zetsu U	.20	.50
N736 Deidara & Tobi U	.20	.50
N737 Itachi Uchiha SR FOIL	4.00	10.00
N738 Kankuro R	.75	2.00
N739 Temari R	.40	1.00
N740 Yugao Uzuki U	.20	.50
N741 Kakashi Hatake C	.10	.25
N742 Kakashi Hatake & Pakkun C	.10	.25
N743 Kiba Inuzuka C	.10	.25
N744 Kiba Inuzuka & Akamaru C	.10	.25
N745 The First Hokage & Yamato R	.40	1.00
N746 Naruto Uzumaki U	.20	.50
N747 Naruto Uzumaki (Tailed Beast Form) SR FOIL	4.00	10.00
N748 Sasuke Uchiha U	.20	.50
N749 The Third Hokage C	.10	.25
N750 Advisor of the Sand C	.10	.25
N751 Rock Lee & Neji Hyuga U	.20	.50
N752 Ino Yamanaka C	.10	.25
N753 Ziga C	.10	.25
N754 Ruiga U	.20	.50
N755 Renga R	.40	1.00
N756 Mizuki (Transformed) C	.10	.25
N757 Raiga Kurosuki U	.20	.50
N758 Ranmaru C	.10	.25
N759 Lord Sagi C	.10	.25
N760 Chishima C	.10	.25
N761 Amachi (Sea Monster) U	.20	.50
N762 Anko Mitarashi & Orochimaru U	.20	.50
N763 Isaribi (Sea Monster) U	.20	.50
N764 Rampageous Pig C	.10	.25
N765 Hotarubi C	.10	.25
N767 Natsuhi U	.20	.50
N768 The 3rd Hoshikage U	.20	.50
N769 Shiso C	.10	.25
N770 Yotaka C	.10	.25
N771 Naruto Uzumaki C	.10	.25
N772 Hinata Hyuga C	.10	.25
N773 Choji Akimichi C	.10	.25
N774 Ino Yamanaka U	.20	.50
N775 Might Guy (Afro) R	.40	1.00
N776 Anbu U	.20	.50
N777 Yakumo Kurama U	.20	.50
N778 Gantetsu C	.10	.25
N779 Menma C	.10	.25
N780 Hoki U	.20	.50
N781 Kujaku C	.10	.25
N782 Ryugan C	.10	.25
N783 Suiko C	.10	.25

2010 Naruto Fangs of the Snake

COMPLETE SET (132)	50.00	100.00
BOOSTER BOX (24 PACKS)	50.00	100.00
BOOSTER PACK (10 CARDS)	2.50	5.00
RELEASED IN AUGUST 2010		
J706 Hokage Style: Elder Jutsu R	.40	1.00
J707 Explosive Kunai U	.20	.50
J708 Summoning Jutsu: Projectile Weapons U	.20	.50
J709 Wood Style: Tree Bind Eternal Burial SR	5.00	12.00
J710 Shikamaru's Judgement U	.20	.50
J711 Flying Swallow C	.10	.25
J712 Awakening the Byakugan U	.20	.50
J713 Genjutsu of Pain! R	.40	1.00
J714 Following the Trail C	.10	.25
J715 Veterinary Meds U	.20	.50
J716 Take Down U	.20	.50
J717 Backed into a Corner R	.40	1.00
J718 Quick Reflex U	.20	.50
J719 Revenge C	.10	.25
J720 Reading Movement U	.20	.50
J721 Expert Kunai C	.10	.25
J722 Wind Style: Toad Water Pistol U	.20	.50
J723 Collaboration Ninjutsu! Wind Style: Toad Flame Bombs! R	.40	1.00
J724 Multi Shadow Clone Jutsu U	.20	.50
J725 Summoning Jutsu SR	5.00	12.00
J726 Collateral Damage U	.20	.50
J727 Clone Tactics U	.20	.50
J728 Snake Transformation Jutsu C	.10	.25
J729 Transference Ritual U	.20	.50
J730 Curse Mark Activation U	.20	.50
J731 Sword Charge C	.10	.25
J732 Chidori Lance U	.20	.50
J733 Multi Striking Shadow Snake R	.40	1.00
J734 Chidori Sword U	.20	.50
J735 Snake Bind U	.20	.50
J736 Elemental Defense R	.40	1.00
J737 Sand Cocoon U	.20	.50
J738 Puppet Master Jutsu U	.20	.50
J739 Iron-Armed Punch C	.10	.25
J740 Iron Sand: Unleash! R	.40	1.00
J741 Wind Style: Rasen Shuriken U	.20	.50
J742 Flamethrower U	.20	.50
M670 Team Asuma C	.10	.25
M671 Master of Weapons U	.20	.50
M672 Comparative Strengths C	.10	.25
M673 Student and Sensei R	.40	1.00
M674 Kakuzu's Abilities R	.40	1.00
M675 Shelter from the Shifting Sands R	.40	1.00
M676 Surprise Help R	.40	1.00
M677 Rapid Communication U	.20	.50
M678 Scouting Party R	.40	1.00
M679 Master of Genjutsu U	.20	.50
M680 Hidden Leaf Veterinary Hospital U	.20	.50
M681 Sync Dance U	.20	.50
M682 Desperate Training U	.20	.50
M683 Relaxation U	.20	.50
M684 Silent Prayer R	.40	1.00
M685 Well Fed U	.20	.50
M686 Enveloping Chakra U	.20	.50
M687 Animal Contract U	.20	.50
M688 Chakra Molding U	.20	.50
M689 Spread Talons U	.20	.50
M690 Friendship from Sorrow U	.20	.50
M691 Formation of Hebi R	.40	1.00
M692 Controlling the Curse U	.20	.50
M693 Sasori's Feelings U	.20	.50
M694 Puppet Fight: 10 VS 100! R	.40	1.00
M695 Kankuro's Puppet Show R	.40	1.00
M696 Shinobi of the Sand U	.20	.50
M697 Sakura's Desire R	.40	1.00
M698 Battle over the Barrier R	.40	1.00
N883 Neji Hyuga C	.10	.25
N884 Hanabi Hyuga C	.10	.25
N885 Choji Akimichi C	.10	.25
N886 Shikamaru Nara C	.10	.25
N887 Hinata Hyuga C	.10	.25
N888 Ino Yamanaka C	.10	.25
N889 Neji Hyuga R	.40	1.00
N890 Zetsu C	.10	.25
N891 Asuma Sarutobi SR	6.00	15.00
N892 Yamato R	.40	1.00
N893 Deidara R	.40	1.00
N894 The First Hokage SR	6.00	15.00
N895 Neji Hyuga & Hinata Hyuga R	.40	1.00
N896 Urushi C	.10	.25
N897 Guruko C	.10	.25
N898 Kiba Inuzuka C	.10	.25
N899 Sasuke Uchiha C	.10	.25
N900 Big Bark Bull C	.10	.25
N901 Obito Uchiha C	.10	.25
N902 Biscuit C	.10	.25
N903 Kotetsu Hagane C	.10	.25
N904 Hayate Gekko C	.10	.25
N905 Tobi C	.10	.25
N906 Kakashi Hatake (Anbu Days) SR	10.00	25.00
N907 Itachi Uchiha SR	8.00	20.00
N908 Gamakichi C	.10	.25
N909 Gamatatsu C	.10	.25
N910 Gamariki C	.10	.25
N911 Naruto Uzumaki C	.10	.25
N912 Gama C	.10	.25
N913 Rock Lee C	.10	.25
N914 The Fourth Hokage R	.40	1.00
N915 Might Guy U	.20	.50
N916 Sai R	.40	1.00
N917 Konohamaru Ninja Squad C	.10	.25
N918 Anko Mitarashi C	.10	.25
N919 Naruto Uzumaki SR	6.00	15.00
N920 Kidomaru C	.10	.25
N921 Jirobo C	.10	.25
N922 Tayuya C	.10	.25
N923 Kabuto Yakushi SR	6.00	15.00
N924 Suigetsu Hozuki R	1.50	4.00
N925 Karin C	.10	.25
N926 Jugo C	.10	.25
N927 Kimimaro C	.10	.25
N928 Kimimaro (Childhood) C	.10	.25
N929 Sakon C	.10	.25
N930 Anko Mitarashi (Childhood) C	.10	.25
N931 Sasuke Uchiha R	.40	1.00
N932 Orochimaru (Snake Form) SR	6.00	15.00
N933 Kimimaro & Jugo R	.40	1.00
N934 Sasuke Uchiha (State 2) SR	12.00	30.00
N935 Gaara of the Desert C	.10	.25
N936 Kankuro C	.10	.25
N937 Matsuri (Childhood) C	.10	.25
N938 Temari C	.10	.25
N939 Advisor of the Sand C	.10	.25
N940 Sakura Haruno C	.10	.25
N941 Black Ant, Crow, & Salamander R	.40	1.00
N942 Chiyo R	.40	1.00
N943 Kurenai Yuhi R	.40	1.00
N944 Unkai Kurama U	.20	.50
N945 Hiruko SR	6.00	15.00
N946 Katsuyu SR	6.00	15.00
N947 Sasori (Puppet Mode) R	.40	1.00
N948 Gaara of the Desert & Temari R	.40	1.00

2010 Naruto Fierce Ambitions Tin

N145 Gaara of the Desert	.30	.75
N370 The Third Hokage	.30	.75
N372 The Fifth Hokage	.30	.75
N453 Itachi Uchiha	.50	1.25
N461 Kankuro	.50	1.25
N473 Kakashi Hatake	.30	.75
N480 Deidara	.30	.75
N495 Temari & Kankuro	.30	.75
NUS020 Rock Lee	.50	1.25
NUS040 Shikamaru Nara & Asuma Sarutobi	.30	.75

2010 Naruto Path of Pain

COMPLETE SET (112)	50.00	100.00
BOOSTER BOX	50.00	100.00
BOOSTER PACK	2.50	5.00
J743 Detonating Clay: C2 Dragon U	.20	.50
J744 Detonating Clay: Snake C	.10	.25
J745 Detonating Clay: Mines U	.20	.50
J746 Detonating Clay: C3 Ohako U	.20	.50
J747 Detonating Clay: C4 Karura SR	5.00	12.00
J748 Clay Clone Jutsu U	.20	.50
J749 Lightning Blade F	2.00	5.00
J750 Mangekyou Sharingan SR	6.00	15.00
J751 Anticipation U	.20	.50
J752 Fatigue C	.10	.25
J753 Tracking Orders U	.20	.50
J754 Animal Transformation U	.20	.50
J755 Leaf Hurricane U	.20	.50
J756 Eight Inner Gates R	.40	1.00
J757 Primary Lotus SR	6.00	15.00
J758 Severe Leaf Hurricane C	.10	.25
J759 Toad Mouth Trap U	.20	.50
J760 Piggyback R	.40	1.00
J761 Fire Style: Searing Migraine U	.20	.50
J762 Striking Shadow Snake U	.20	.50
J763 Striking Multi Shadow Snakes Jutsu R	.40	1.00
J764 Chidori C	.10	.25
J765 Chakra Punch C	.10	.25
J766 Righteous Anger U	.20	.50
J767 Kick of Anger! U	.20	.50
J768 Palm Healing R	.40	1.00
J769 Coordination R	.40	1.00
J770 The Fangs of Pain U	.20	.50
J771 The Wings of Pain R	.40	1.00
J772 Rinnegan SR	5.00	12.00
M699 Intellectual Strategy U	.20	.50
M700 Sharpened Skills R	.40	1.00
M701 Strategy Scroll U	.20	.50
M702 Rooftop Standoff U	.20	.50
M703 Past Lessons C	.10	.25
M704 Reaper Death Seal R	.40	1.00
M705 Sacrifice U	.20	.50
M706 Supervised Training U	.20	.50
M707 Denka & Hina U	.20	.50
M708 Burst of Power R	.40	1.00
M709 Tailed Beast Unleashed U	.20	.50
M710 Surprise Ability C	.10	.25
M711 Promise to Return U	.20	.50
M712 Kakashi's Test U	.20	.50
M713 The Great Naruto Bridge R	.40	1.00
M714 Suigetsu's Joy R	.40	1.00
M715 Power of State 2 U	.20	.50
M716 Pledge under a Setting Sun F	2.00	5.00
M717 Barrier Preparation R	.40	1.00
M718 Perfect Chakra Control C	.10	.25
M719 Delicate Operation U	.20	.50
M720 Reflection R	.40	1.00
M721 The Time of Pain R	.40	1.00
M722 The City of Pain R	.40	1.00
N949 Detonating Clay Minion C	.10	.25
N950 Ino Yamanaka C	.10	.25
N951 Kikunojou C	.10	.25
N952 Yurinojou C	.10	.25
N953 Shikamaru Nara C	.10	.25
N954 Tenten U	.20	.50
N955 Chiriku U	.20	.50
N956 Yamato U	.20	.50
N957 Deidara SR•	6.00	15.00
N958 Deidara & Tobi R	.40	1.00
N959 Pakkun U	.20	.50
N960 Uhei C	.10	.25
N961 Shiba C	.10	.25
N962 Akino C	.10	.25
N963 Sasuke Uchiha C	.10	.25
N964 Kotetsu Hagane C	.10	.25
N965 Monkey King Enma R	.40	1.00
N966 Kakashi Hatake F	2.00	5.00
N967 Itachi Uchiha C	.10	.25
N968 The Third Hokage SR	5.00	12.00
N969 Might Guy R	.40	1.00
N970 Rock Lee & Might Guy R	.40	1.00
N971 Naruto Uzumaki (Taijutsu) C	.10	.25
N972 Izumo Kamizuki C	.10	.25
N973 Iruka Umino C	.10	.25
N974 Ninja Tortoise U	.20	.50
N975 Naruto Uzumaki C	.10	.25
N976 Naruto Uzumaki (Nine-Tail's Cloak) R	.40	1.00
N977 Jiraiya U	.20	.50
N978 The Fourth Hokage R	.40	1.00
N979 Doki C	.10	.25
N980 Karin C	.10	.25
N981 Tayuya (State 1) C	.10	.25
N982 Suigetsu Hozuki C	.10	.25
N983 Jugo (State 1) C	.10	.25
N984 Anko Mitarashi F	2.00	5.00
N985 Orochimaru R•	.40	1.00
N986 Sasuke Uchiha U	.20	.50
N987 Kabuto Yakushi (Possessed Mode) R	.40	1.00
N988 Tayuya (State 2) U	.20	.50
N989 Kakuzu (Soul Form) SR	6.00	15.00
N990 Kamatari C	.10	.25
N991 Sakura Haruno C	.10	.25
N992 Rin C	.10	.25
N993 Temari C•	.10	.25
N994 Chiyo U	.20	.50
N995 Shizune U	.20	.50
N996 Kurenai Yuhi R	.40	1.00
N997 Tsunade U	.20	.50
N998 Shukaku SR	6.00	15.00
N999 Konan C	.10	.25
N1000 Pain (Deva Path) SR	12.00	25.00
N1001 Giant Chameleon C	.10	.25
N1002 Giant Chimera C	.10	.25
N1003 Pain (Animal Path) C	.10	.25
N1004 Pain (Petra Path) U	.20	.50
N1005 Sasuke Uchiha STSR		
N1006 Naruto Uzumaki STSR		

2010 Naruto Tournament Pack 1

COMPLETE SET (60)	40.00	80.00
BOOSTER BOX (24)	60.00	120.00
BOOSTER PACK	3.00	6.00
RELEASED IN AUGUST 2010		
J697 Expansion Jutsu: Super Slap!	.20	.50
J698 Fire Style: Fireball Jutsu	.50	1.25
J699 Lightning Blade Single Slash	.75	2.00
J700 Ninja Art: Super Beast Scroll Lion	.40	1.00
J701 Severe Leaf Hurricane	.20	.50
J702 Water Clone Jutsu	.20	.50
J703 Water Prison Jutsu	.40	1.00
J704 Medical Jutsu: Reanimation	.20	.50
J705 Wind Nature: Chakra Blades	.40	1.00
M665 Shogi Lesson	.20	.50
M666 Make-Out Tactics	.50	1.25
M667 Fierce Rivals	2.50	6.00
M668 Dehydration	.50	1.25
M669 Bonds of Friendship	1.00	2.50
N019 Naruto Uzumaki	.50	1.25
N024 Zabuza Momochi	.50	1.25
N114 Temari	.10	.25
N122 Hayate Gekko	.10	.25
N202 Kisame Hoshigaki	.20	.50
N209 Nawaki	.20	.50
N333 Kakashi Hatake	.10	.25
N336 Tsubaki	.20	.50
N371 The Fourth Hokage	.10	.25
N382 Toki	.75	2.00
N384 Isaribi	.20	.50
N451 Shizune	.10	.25
N511 Shino Aburame	.40	1.00
N547 Sasuke Uchiha	.50	1.25
N571 Rock Lee	.10	.25
N595 Ino Yamanaka	.10	.25
N600 Danzo	.10	.25

N622 Anko Mitarashi .10 .25
N631 Ino Yamanaka .10 .25
N640 Might Guy .10 .25
N864 Choji Akimichi (Childhood) 2.50 6.00
N865 Hinata Hyuga (Childhood) .10 .25
N866 Shikamaru Nara (Childhood) .10 .25
N867 Anbu (Captain) .10 .25
N868 Itachi Uchiha (Anbu Days) .20 .50
N869 Kiba Inuzuka (Childhood) 8.00 20.00
N870 Gamabunta .10 .25
N871 Konohamaru Ninja Squad 8.00 20.00
N872 Rock Lee (Childhood) .10 .25
N873 Giant Spider .10 .25
N874 Rashomon .10 .25
N875 Zabuza Momochi (Younger Days) .40 1.00
N876 Ebisu 6.00 15.00
N877 Gaara of the Desert (Childhood) .10 .25
N878 Sasori .10 .25
N879 Hinata Hyuga 25.00 50.00
N880 Yamato .10 .25
N881 Iruka Umino 8.00 20.00
N882 Konohamaru .10 .25
J696B Byakugan .10 .25
NUS006 Sakura Haruno .20 .50
NUS015 Shikamaru Nara 4.00 10.00
NUS027 Jiraiya .20 .50
NUS035 Haku .10 .25
NUS072 Gamakichi .20 .50
NUS106 Kurenai Yuhi .20 .50

2010 Naruto Tournament Pack 2

COMPLETE SET (64) 20.00 40.00
BOOSTER BOX (24 PACKS) 25.00 50.00
BOOSTER PACK (10 CARDS) 2.00 3.00
RELEASED IN FEBRUARY 2011
J696 Byakugan U .20 .50
J697 Expansion Jutsu: Super Slap! R .40 1.00
J698 Fire Style: Fireball Jutsu R .40 1.00
J699 Lightning Blade Single Slash R .40 1.00
J700 Ninja Art: Super Beast Scroll Lion U .20 .50
J701 Severe Leaf Hurricane U .20 .50
J702 Water Clone Jutsu R .40 1.00
J703 Water Prison Jutsu U .20 .50
J704 Reanimation Ninjutsu R .40 1.00
J705 Chakra Blades U .20 .50
M665 Shogi Lesson R .40 1.00
M666 Make-Out Tactics R .40 1.00
M667 Fierce Rivals R .40 1.00
M668 Dehydration R .40
M669 Bonds of Friendship R .40 1.00
N864 Choji Akimichi (Childhood) C .10 .25
N865 Hinata Hyuga (Childhood) C .10 .25
N866 Shikamaru Nara (Childhood) C .10 .25
N867 Anbu (Captain) R .40 1.00
N868 Itachi Uchiha (Anbu Days) SR 6.00 15.00
N869 Kiba Inuzuka (Childhood) C .10 .25
N870 Gamabunta SR 5.00 12.00
N871 Konohamaru Ninja Squad U .20 .50
N872 Rock Lee (Childhood) C .10 .25
N873 Giant Spider C .10 .25
N874 Rashomon R .40 1.00
N875 Zabuza Momochi (Younger Days) SR 5.00 12.00
N876 Ebisu U .20 .50
N877 Gaara of the Desert (Childhood) C .10 .25
N878 Sasori SR 5.00 12.00
N879 Hinata Hyuga U .20 .50
N880 Yamato SR 6.00 15.00
N881 Iruka Umino C .10 .25
N882 Konohamaru C .10 .25
N1007 Neji Hyuga C .10 .25
N1008 Shikamaru Nara U .20 .50
N1009 Zetsu C .10 .25
N1010 Deidara U .20 .50
N1011 Ibiki Morino U .20 .50
N1012 Shikaku Nara R .40 1.00
N1013 Hidan SR 6.00 15.00
N1014 Tobi C .10 .25
N1015 Itachi Uchiha R .40 1.00
N1016 Kiba Inuzuka U .20 .50
N1017 Sasuke Uchiha C .10 .25
N1018 Raido Namiashi C .10 .25
N1019 Naruto Uzumaki C .10 .25
N1020 Iruka Umino C .10 .25
N1021 Naruto Uzumaki C .10 .25
N1022 Sai R .40 1.00
N1023 Ink Summon U .20 .50
N1024 Jiraiya U .20 .50
N1025 Kisame Hoshigaki SR 5.00 12.00
N1026 Kakuzu SR 5.00 12.00
N1027 Karin U .20 .50
N1028 Haku C .10 .25
N1029 Kimimaro R .40 1.00
N1030 Sasuke Uchiha R .40 1.00
N1031 Mizuki U .20 .50
N1032 Shizune C .10 .25
N1033 Rin C .10 .25
N1034 Gaara of the Desert C .10 .25
N1035 Konan R .40 1.00
N1036 The Fifth Hokage R .40 1.00

2010 Naruto Untouchables Tin

N086 Sasuke Uchiha .40 1.00
N146 Temari .75 2.00
N168 The Second Hokage 1.00 2.50
N224 Naruto Uzumaki .30 .75
N311 Tenten .30 .75
N324 Kisame Hoshigaki .50 1.25
N531 Ino Yamanaka .75 2.00
N567 Kakashi Hatake (Anbu Days) 1.25 3.00
PR063 Kakashi Hatake & Itachi Uchiha 1.25 3.00
PR064 Naruto Uzumaki & Sasuke Uchiha 1.00 2.50
PR065 The Fourth Hokage & Jiraiya 1.50 4.00
NUS005 Sakura Haruno 1.00 2.50

2010 Naruto Will of Fire

COMPLETE SET (177) 60.00 120.00
BOOSTER BOX (24 PACKS) 40.00 80.00
BOOSTER PACK (10 CARDS) 2.50 5.00
RELEASED IN JUNE 2010
C056 Princess Koto U .20 .50
C057 Lord Owashi U .20 .50
C058 Murakumo R .40 1.00
C059 Giant Eagle R .40 1.00
J645 Wind Style: Rasen Shuriken SR 4.00 10.00
J646 Raigo! Thousand Hand Strike! U .20 .50
J647 Burning Ash U .20 .50
J648 Anger of the Tailed Beast U .20 .50
J649 Water Style: Syrup Trap C .10 .25
J650 Earth Style: Earth Pike R .40 1.00
J651 Three-Bladed Scythe C .10 .25
J652 Black Strings U .20 .50
J653 Ritual Circle U .20 .50
J654 High Speed Thinking U .20 .50
J655 Shadow Possession Jutsu U .20 .50
J656 Water Clone Jutsu U .20 .50
J657 Howl U .20 .50
J658 Scattered Thousand Birds Jutsu U .20 .50
J659 Black Sword C .10 .25
J660 Sharing the Pain U .20 .50
J661 Shadow Stitching Jutsu U .20 .50
J662 Attacking on Both Sides C .10 .25
J663 Change in Chakra Nature: Rasengan U .20 .50
J664 Kiss of Death U .20 .50
J665 Combination Jutsu C .10 .25
J666 Super Strength U .20 .50
J667 Transporting the Bodies U .20 .50
J668 Beast Wave: Palm Hurricane U .20 .50
J669 Giant Spider U .20 .50
J670 Labyrinth R .40 1.00
J671 Sharingan Activated R .40 1.00
J672 Illusion caused by the Poisonous Moths R .40 1.00
J673 Super Expansion Jutsu U .20 .50
J674 Fatal Blow U .20 .50
J675 Five Pronged Seal Release C .10 .25
J676 Power of the Red Chakra R .40 1.00
J677 War Cry U .20 .50
J678 Giant Club C .10 .25
J679 Chakra Blade C .10 .25
J680 Shuriken C .10 .25
J681 Art of the Raging Lion's Mane U .20 .50
J682 Concentration U .20 .50
J683 Booby-Trap R .40 1.00
J684 Kunai C .10 .25
J685 Piercing Chidori SR 6.00 15.00
J686 Water Style: Water Shark Bomb Jutsu U .20 .50
J687 Attack from Behind U .20 .50
J688 Hellfire U .20 .50
J689 Exposing the Real Face U .20 .50
J690 Killer Shot U .20 .50
J691 Burst of Shots U .20 .50
J692 Sharp Shooting U .20 .50
J693 Earth Style: Stone Plate Coffin U .20 .50
J694 Earth Style Revival Jutsu: Soil Bodies R .40 1.00
J695 Lightning Style: Earth Slide R .40 1.00
J696 Rasengan R .40 1.00
M624 Bounty C .10 .25
M625 Invasion of the Akatsuki R 1.25 3.00
M626 Ritual R .40 1.00
M627 Scream U .20 .50
M628 Just Like That Hero SR 3.00 8.00
M629 Tragic Destiny SR 4.00 10.00
M630 The Last Moment R .40 1.00
M631 The Top Priority U .20 .50
M632 In the Rain C .10 .25
M633 Loss R .40 1.00
M634 Distraction R .40 1.00
M635 Entrustment U .20 .50
M636 Emergency Call-Up U .20 .50
M637 Reading U .20 .50
M638 The Next Target U .20 .50
M639 Argument U .20 .50
M640 Capture U .20 .50
M641 Strong Bond C .10 .25
M642 Approaching Shadow of Death R .40 1.00
M643 Sudden Entry R .40 1.00
M644 Strategy Meeting R .40 1.00
M645 Stolen Bodies U .20 .50
M646 Fierce Clash U .20 .50
M647 Interruption U .20 .50
M648 Present for the Promotion R .40 1.00
M649 Mid-Night Shogi Match R .40 1.00
M650 Under the Drifting Clouds U .20 .50
M651 Farewell C .10 .25
M652 Taking Over the World R .40 1.00
M653 Violent Emotion U .20 .50
M654 Clue U .20 .50
M655 Scary Story U .20 .50
M656 Rebellion U .20 .50
M657 Shout of Victory U .20 .50
M658 Backup C .10 .25
M659 Hate U .20 .50
M660 Flash Back U .20 .50
M661 Hard Ones to Deal With R .40 1.00
M662 Additional Team Member R .40 1.00
M663 Shock R .40 1.00
M664 Eight Gate Lock Up U .20 .50
N784 Hidan (Cursed Mode) R .40 1.00
N785 Hidan SR 10.00 25.00
N786 Kakuzu SR 8.00 20.00
N787 Kotetsu Hagane C .10 .25
N788 Izumo Kamizuki C .10 .25
N789 Sai C .10 .25
N790 Kurenai Yuhi C .10 .25
N791 Shikamaru Nara SR 6.00 15.00
N792 Ino Yamanaka C .10 .25
N793 Choji Akimichi C .10 .25
N794 Naruto Uzumaki (Childhood) C .10 .25
N795 Sasuke Uchiha (Childhood) C .10 .25
N796 Sakura Haruno (Childhood) C .10 .25
N797 Hinata Hyuga (Student) C .10 .25
N798 Sora C .10 .25
N799 Gozu C .10 .25
N800 Guren R .40 1.00
N801 Kigiri C .10 .25
N802 Kihou C .10 .25
N803 Nurari C .10 .25
N804 Rinji C .10 .25
N805 Yukimaru C .10 .25
N806 Seimei R .40 1.00
N807 Fudo C .10 .25
N808 Fuen C .10 .25
N809 Furido R .40 1.00
N810 Fouka C .10 .25
N811 Kazuma C .10 .25
N812 Tatsuji C .10 .25
N813 Roshi SR 6.00 15.00
N814 Three Tails SR 5.00 12.00
N815 Naruto Uzumaki C .10 .25
N816 Naruto Uzumaki & Jiraiya SR 5.00 12.00
N817 Rock Lee C .10 .25
N818 Gaara of the Desert C .10 .25
N819 Shikamaru Nara & Choji Akmichi R .40 1.00
N820 Hinata Hyuga C .10 .25
N821 Kisame Hoshigaki R .40 1.00
N822 The Second Hokage SR 5.00 12.00
N823 Asuma Sarutobi C .10 .25
N824 Shino Aburame C .10 .25
N825 The First Hokage SR 8.00 20.00
N826 Might Guy C .10 .25
N827 Jiraiya U .20 .50
N828 Kabuto Yakushi R .40 1.00
N829 Sasuke Uchiha C .10 .25
N830 Kakashi Hatake R .40 1.00
N831 Tenten C .10 .25
N832 Kiba Inuzuka C .10 .25
N833 Temari C .10 .25
N834 Tracking Ninja C .10 .25
N835 Ino Yamanaka C .10 .25
N836 Anko Mitrashi C .10 .25
N837 The Fifth Kazekage R .40 1.00
N838 The Third Hokage R .40 1.00
N839 Rock Lee C .10 .25
N840 Sakura Haruno SR 4.00 10.00
N841 Four Souls of Kakuzu R .40 1.00
N842 Tenzo C .10 .25
N843 Tsunade SR 3.00 8.00
N844 Yugito Ni'i R .40 1.00
N845 Fujin C .10 .25
N846 Raijin C .10 .25
N847 Mizuki (Childhood) C .10 .25
N848 Queen Bee C .10 .25
N849 Cursed Warrior C .10 .25
N850 Sea Monster C .10 .25
N851 Shiin C .10 .25
N852 Agira R .40 1.00
N853 Gensho R .40 1.00
N854 Rokkaku C .10 .25
N855 Yagura C .10 .25
N856 Jako C .10 .25
N857 Monju C .10 .25
N858 Shura C .10 .25
N859 Todoroki C .10 .25
N860 Shikamaru Nara & Asuma Sarutobi R .40 1.00
N861 Naruto Uzumaki SR 2.00 5.00
N862 Sakura Haruno C .10 .25
N863 Kakashi Hatake SR 1.50 4.00

2011 Naruto Invasion

COMPLETE SET (120) 40.00 80.00
BOOSTER BOX (24 PACKS) 40.00 80.00
BOOSTER PACK (10 CARDS) 2.50 4.00
J865 Hands Boulder U .20 .50
J866 Earth Style, Mud Wall C .10 .25
J867 Partial Expansion Jutsu U .20 .50
J868 Smoke Pellet Kunai C .10 .25
J869 Shadow Stitching R .40 1.00
J870 Lightning Blade SR 2.00 5.00
J871 Kamui SR 2.50 6.00
J872 Fire Style, Biscuit Firing Jutsu C .10 .25
J873 Fang over Fang R .40 1.00
J874 Lightning Beast Running Jutsu U .20 .50
J875 Sage Art, Amphibian Jutsu U .20 .50
J876 Iron Chain C .10 .25
J877 Lightning Style Shadow Clone R .40 1.00
J878 Lightning Style, Four-Pillar Trap U .20 .50
J879 Rasengan SR 10.00 25.00
J880 Chakra Liquid U .20 .50
J881 Water Whip ST .20 .50
J882 Sticky Webbing C .10 .25
J883 Ninja Art, Grudge Rain R .40 1.00
J884 Wind Blade C .10 .25
J885 Mind Scan C .10 .25
J886 Healing Chakra Transmission R .40 1.00
J887 Finishing Blow U .20 .50
J888 Almighty Push SR 6.00 15.00
J889 Absorption Barrier U .20 .50
M817 Cornered U .20 .50
M818 Information Extraction U .20 .50
M819 Brooding Mood U .20 .50
M820 Betrayal R .40 1.00
M821 Decoding the Message R .40 1.00
M822 Defensive Posture C .10 .25
M823 The Man Who Died Twice U .20 .50
M824 Patriarch R .40 1.00
M825 Lifeflash U .20 .50
M826 Final Moments U .20 .50
M827 The Warhawk R .40 1.00
M828 Heated Argument C .10 .25
M829 Motionless R .40 1.00
M830 The Sage Returns R .40 1.00
M831 Ichiraku Ramen U .20 .50
M832 Hero's Welcome U .20 .50
M833 Feudal Lord's Treasure ST .20 .50
M834 Wager U .20 .50
M835 Struggle U .20 .50
M836 Suspicious Characters R .40 1.00
M837 Hiding C .10 .25
M838 Contemplation ST .10 .25
M839 Outlaws Converge U .20 .50
M840 Revenge R .40 1.00
M841 Floating U .20 .50
M842 Regret R .40 1.00
M843 A Master's Death R .40 1.00
M844 Autopsy Report C .10 .25
M845 The Six Paths U .20 .50
M846 Invasion R .40 1.00
N1270 Shikamaru Nara C .10 .25
N1271 Choji Akimichi C .10 .25
N1272 Shiho C .10 .25
N1273 Hinata Hyuga C .10 .25
N1274 Ino Yamanaka C .10 .25
N1275 Neji Hyuga C .10 .25
N1276 Ibiki Morino U .20 .50
N1277 Tenten SR 2.00 5.00
N1278 Shikamaru Nara R .40 1.00
N1279 Inoichi Yamanaka R .40 1.00
N1280 Choza Akimichi U .20 .50
N1281 Deidara SR 3.00 8.00
N1282 Asuma Sarutobi R .40 1.00
N1283 Kisuke Maboroshi C .10 .25
N1284 Sasuke Uchiha (Childhood) C .10 .25
N1285 Tsukado C .10 .25
N1286 Genma Shiranui C .10 .25
N1287 Monkey King Enma C .10 .25
N1288 Tobi U .20 .50
N1289 Hidan U .20 .50
N1290 Anbu Elite R .40 1.00
N1291 Kakashi Hatake (Boyhood) R .40 1.00
N1292 Sakumo Hatake SR 2.50 6.00
N1293 Kakashi Hatake R .40 1.00
N1294 Ink Leech C .10 .25
N1295 Akaboshi C .10 .25
N1296 Rock Lee C .10 .25
N1297 Ink Snake C .10 .25
N1298 Naruto Uzumaki STSR .75 2.00
N1299 Rock Lee C .10 .25
N1300 Sai U .20 .50
N1301 Shima U .20 .50
N1302 Fukasaku R .40 1.00
N1303 Killer Bee SR 2.50 6.00
N1304 Might Guy ST .10 .25
N1305 Jiraiya SR 3.00 8.00
N1306 Samidare C .10 .25
N1307 Jako C .10 .25
N1308 Karin C .10 .25
N1309 Jugo C .10 .25
N1310 Suigetsu Hozuki C .10 .25
N1311 Haku C .10 .25
N1312 Tayuya C .10 .25
N1313 Sasuke Uchiha STSR .75 2.00
N1314 Jirobo (State 2) R .40 1.00
N1315 Kisame Hoshigaki R .40 1.00
N1316 Kabuto Yakushi R .40 1.00
N1317 Kakuzu R .40 1.00
N1318 Orochimaru R .40 1.00
N1319 Yaoki C .10 .25
N1320 Sakura Haruno (Childhood) C .10 .25
N1321 Crow C .10 .25
N1322 Black Ant C .10 .25
N1323 Shino Aburame SR 3.00 8.00
N1324 Temari C .10 .25
N1325 Salamander U .20 .50
N1326 Sakura Haruno C .10 .25
N1327 Gaara of the Desert R .40 1.00
N1328 Kankuro U .20 .50
N1329 Konan U .20 .50
N1330 Sasori (Puppet Mode) SR 4.00 10.00
N1331 Giant Centipede C .10 .25
N1332 Pain (Animal Path) C .10 .25
N1333 Heretical Icon R .40 1.00
N1334 Pain (Asura Path) R .40 1.00

2011 Naruto Shattered Truth

COMPLETE SET (120) 50.00 100.00
BOOSTER BOX (24 PACKS) 50.00 100.00
BOOSTER PACK (10 CARDS) 2.50 5.00
RELEASED IN APRIL 2011
J802 Ninja Art: Tile Shuriken C .10 .25
J803 Earth Style: Earth Dragon Bomb R .40 1.00
J804 Flying Swallow U .20 .50
J805 Self-Destructing Clay Clone R .40 1.00
J806 Headhunter Jutsu U .20 .50
J807 Fire Style: Fireball Jutsu R .40 1.00
J808 Dispatch of Anbu U .20 .50
J809 Madara's Eye U .20 .50
J810 Fire Style: Great Dragon Flame Jutsu U .20 .50
J811 Overwhelming Power U .20 .50
J812 Feral Rage R .40 1.00
J813 Wire Trap C .10 .25
J814 Kirin SR 6.00 15.00
J815 Chidori R .40 1.00
J816 Snake Sword U .20 .50
J817 Water Style: Raging Waves C .10 .25
J818 Tsuchigumo Style: Forbidden Jutsu Release - Big Bang U .20 .50
J819 Chameleon Jutsu C .10 .25
J820 Infinite Embrace R .40 1.00
J821 Bubble Barrier Jutsu R .40 1.00
J822 Poison Senbon Stream U .20 .50
J823 Amaterasu C .10 .25
J824 Tsukuyomi R .40 1.00
J825 Hologram C .10 .25
J826 Sealing Jutsu: Nine Phantom Dragons R .40 1.00
M749 Raigo's Blessing U .20 .50
M750 Clear Sky R .40 1.00
M751 Team Guy U .20 .50
M752 Senju vs. Uchiha SR 6.00 15.00
M753 World of Earth R .40 1.00
M754 Anbu Assault U .20 .50
M755 World of Fire R .40 1.00
M756 Make-Out Paradise R .40 1.00
M757 Throne of the Uchiha U .20 .50
M758 Last Words U .20 .50
M759 World of Lightning R .40 1.00
M760 Baneful Gaze SR 5.00 12.00
M761 Passing Fates C .10 .25
M762 Cursed Existence R .40 1.00
M763 New Members U .20 .50
M764 Rashomon's Defense U .20 .50
M765 Sasuke's Curse C .10 .25
M766 Eight-Headed Serpent Jutsu U .20 .50
M767 Orochimaru's Goal U .20 .50
M768 World of Water R .40 1.00
M769 World of Wind R .40 1.00
M770 Slug Infestation! U .20 .50
M771 Daydreaming C .10 .25
M772 Dreams of the Past C .10 .25
M773 Void World R .40 1.00
M774 Symbol of the Rogue Ninja R .40 1.00
M775 Chakra Seal U .20 .50
N1102 Choji Akimichi C .10 .25
N1103 Deidara (Younger Days) U .20 .50
N1104 Tenzo (Anbu Days) U .20 .50
N1105 Deidara (C0 Form) R .40 1.00
N1106 Denka C .10 .25
N1107 Hina C .10 .25
N1108 Anbu C .10 .25
N1109 The Thrid Hokage (Younger Days) R .40 1.00
N1110 Anbu U .20 .50
N1111 Madara Uchiha SR 5.00 12.00
N1112 Kakashi Hatake (Anbu Days) U .20 .50
N1113 Itachi Uchiha R .40 1.00
N1114 Susano'o SR 5.00 12.00
N1115 Sai SR 6.00 15.00
N1116 Kushina Uzumaki C .10 .25
N1117 Rock Lee C .10 .25
N1118 Naruto Uzumaki U .20 .50
N1119 Jiraiya U .20 .50
N1120 Anko Mitarashi C .10 .25
N1121 Konohamaru Ninja Corp. C .10 .25
N1122 Minato Namikaze SR 5.00 12.00
N1123 Ninja Art: Tile Shuriken C .40 1.00
N1124 Karin C .10 .25
N1125 Suigetsu C .10 .25
N1126 Jugo C .10 .25
N1127 Sakon (State 1) U .20 .50
N1128 Ukon (State 1) R .40 1.00
N1129 Sasuke Uchiha SR 5.00 12.00
N1130 Rashomon U .20 .50
N1131 Sakon & Ukon (State 2) R .40 1.00
N1132 Harusame C .10 .25
N1133 Utakata R .40 1.00
N1134 Hotaru Katsuragi C .10 .25
N1135 Sakura Haruno C .10 .25
N1136 Konan (Childhood) C .10 .25
N1137 Salamander C .10 .25
N1138 Temari U .20 .50
N1139 Hiruko R .40 1.00
N1140 Sasori U .20 .50
N1141 The 3rd Kazekage R .40 1.00
N1142 Sasori & Hiruko R .40 1.00
N1143 Six Tails SR 6.00 15.00
N1144 Giant Panda C .10 .25
N1145 Zetsu F 2.00 5.00
N1146 Tobi F 2.00 5.00
N1147 Konan F 2.00 5.00
N1148 Sasori F 2.00 5.00
N1149 Deidara F 2.00 5.00
N1150 Kisame Hoshigaki F 2.00 5.00
N1151 Itachi Uchiha STSR .40 1.00
N1152 Pain (Deva Path) STSR .40 1.00
N1153 Kakuzu F 2.00 5.00
N1154 Hidan F 2.00 5.00
N1155 Neji Hyuga C .10 .25
N1156 Hinata Hyuga C .10 .25
N1157 Ino Yamanaka C .10 .25
N1158 Tenten C .10 .25
N1159 Shikamaru Nara U .20 .50
N1160 Yamato C .10 .25
N1161 Asuma Sarutobi C .10 .25
N1162 The 1st Hokage U .20 .50
N1163 Tsume Inuzuka C .10 .25
N1164 Kuromaru C .10 .25
N1165 Kiba Inuzuka C .10 .25
N1166 Akamaru C .10 .25
N1167 Rock Lee C .10 .25
N1168 Naruto Uzumaki C .10 .25
N1169 Might Guy U .20 .50

2011 Naruto Tales of the Gallant Sage

COMPLETE SET (140) 50.00 100.00
BOOSTER BOX (24 PACKS) 50.00 100.00
BOOSTER PACK (10 CARDS) 2.50 5.00
RELEASED IN FEBRUARY 2011
J773 Protective 8 Trigrams 64 Palms U .20 .50
J774 8 Trigrams Palms Rotation C .10 .25
J775 Gentle Fist Style: 8 Trigrams 64 R .40 1.00
J776 8 Trigrams Air Palm U .20 .50
J777 Detonating Kunai C .10 .25
J778 Fire Style: Dragon Flame Jutsu C .10 .25
J779 Eyes of the Betrayer U .20 .50
J780 Echoes of Pain U .20 .50
J781 Sage Art: Bath of Boiling Oil R .40 1.00
J782 Shield Block C .10 .25
J783 Toad Subjugation: Art of the Manipulated Shadow U .20 .50
J784 Sage Art: Kebari Senbon R .40 1.00
J785 Demonic Illusion: Toad Confrontation Singing SR 4.00 10.00
J786 Snake Sword R .40 1.00
J787 Summoning Jutsu: Reanimation SR 6.00 15.00
J788 Digital Phalanx Shrapnel U .20 .50
J789 Spider Bow: Fierce Rip U .20 .50
J790 Spider Armor C .10 .25
J791 Crystal Style: Burst Crystal Dragon C .10 .25

Card	Low	High
J792 Acid Shot C	.10	.25
J793 First-Aid C	.10	.25
J794 Ferocious Punch! U	.20	.50
J795 Puppet Shield U	.20	.50
J796 Puppet Summoning R	.40	1.00
J797 Hydro-pump SR	4.00	10.00
J798 Summoning Jutsu: Pain R	.40	1.00
J799 The Eyes of Pain C	.10	.25
J800 The Hand of Pain R	.40	1.00
J801 The Soul of Pain U	.20	.50
M723 Training in the Moonlight R	.40	1.00
M724 Gentle Fist Style: Eight Trigrams U	.20	.50
M725 End of the Immortal R	.40	1.00
M726 Mover's Jacket C	.10	.25
M727 Follower of Jashin C	.10	.25
M728 Past and Future R	.40	1.00
M729 Scornful Eyes U	.20	.50
M730 Gathering Intel U	.20	.50
M731 Another Mask… U	.20	.50
M732 Doppelganger U	.20	.50
M733 Mount Myoboku R	.40	1.00
M734 Jiraiya's Hermit Dance R	.40	1.00
M735 Tale of the Gallent Jiraya C	.10	.25
M736 Vessel for Dreams R	.40	1.00
M737 Orochimaru's Forbidden Jutsu U	.20	.50
M738 Anko's Memory C	.10	.25
M739 Karin's Anger U	.20	.50
M740 Monster Research R	.40	1.00
M741 Katsuyu's Division R	.40	1.00
M742 Ino's Tears R	.40	1.00
M743 Puppet Master in Training R	.40	1.00
M744 Kankuro's Tenacity U	.20	.50
M745 Rash Decision U	.20	.50
M746 The Ame Orphans R	.40	1.00
M747 A Gift of Pain U	.20	.50
M748 Chakra Paper C	.10	.25
N1037 Neji Hyuga R	.40	1.00
N1037 Neji Hyuga P		
N1038 Hinata Hyuga U	.20	.50
N1039 Ino Yamanaka C	.10	.25
N1039 Ino Yamanaka P		
N1040 Choji Akimichi C	.10	.25
N1041 The First Hokage R	.40	1.00
N1041 The First Hokage P		
N1042 Asuma Sarutobi SR	6.00	15.00
N1042 Asuma Sarutobi P		
N1043 Shikamaru Nara (Suit) C	.10	.25
N1044 Tenten C	.10	.25
N1044 Tenten P		
N1045 Hanabi Hyuga C	.10	.25
N1046 Choji Akimichi & Shikamaru Nara R	.40	1.00
N1047 Hinata Hyuga (Awakened) P		
N1047 Hinata Hyuga (Awakened) C	.10	.25
N1048 Hiashi Hyuga R	.40	1.00
N1049 Protective 8 Trigrams 64 Palms U	.10	.25
N1050 Sasuke Uchiha C	.10	.25
N1051 Hidan P		
N1051 Hidan U	.20	.50
N1052 Akamaru C	.10	.25
N1053 Kakashi Hatake & Yamato P		
N1053 Kakashi Hatake & Yamato R	.40	1.00
N1054 The Third Hokage P		
N1054 The Third Hokage U	.20	.50
N1055 Itachi Uchiha & Sasuke Uchiha R	.40	1.00
N1056 Sasuke Uchiha (Suit) C	.10	.25
N1057 Kakashi Hatake P		
N1057 Kakashi Hatake R	.40	1.00
N1058 Itachi Uchiha U	.20	.50
N1059 Kiba Inuzuka & Akamaru R	.40	1.00
N1060 Kakashi Hatake & The 4th Hokage P		
N1060 Kakashi Hatake & The 4th Hokage SR	5.00	12.00
N1061 Naruto Uzumaki (Tailed Beast Form) R	.40	1.00
N1062 Naruto Uzumaki (Four Tails) P		
N1062 Naruto Uzumaki (Four Tails) R	.40	1.00
N1063 Fukasaku U	.20	.50
N1064 Shima C	.10	.25
N1065 Gamaken C	.10	.25
N1066 Great Toad Sage C	.10	.25
N1067 Jiraiya (Sage Mode) P		
N1067 Jiraiya (Sage Mode) SR	5.00	12.00
N1068 Jiraiya P		
N1068 Jiraiya U	.20	.50
N1069 Rock Lee C	.10	.25
N1070 Killer Bee C	.10	.25
N1071 Naruto Uzumaki (Suit) C	.10	.25
N1072 Sai (Suit) C	.10	.25
N1073 Yahiko (Childhood) C	.10	.25
N1074 Giant Spider C	.10	.25
N1075 Kidomaru (State 1) P		
N1075 Kidomaru (State 1) U	.20	.50
N1076 Karin C	.10	.25
N1077 Suigetsu Hozuki C	.10	.25
N1078 Jugo C	.10	.25
N1079 Kimimaro (State 1) U	.20	.50
N1080 Sasuke Uchiha P		
N1080 Sasuke Uchiha U	.20	.50
N1081 Orochimaru SR	6.00	15.00
N1082 Hanzo the Salamander R	.40	1.00
N1083 Manda U	.20	.50
N1083 Manda P		
N1084 Kidomaru (State 2) R	.40	1.00
N1085 Mini Katsuyu C	.10	.25
N1086 Crow C	.10	.25
N1087 Black Ant C	.10	.25
N1088 Gaara of the Desert (Suit) C	.10	.25
N1089 Father and Mother C	.10	.25
N1090 Chiyo U	.20	.50
N1090 Chiyo P		
N1091 Ebizo C	.10	.25
N1092 Kankuro C	.10	.25
N1093 Monzaemon Chikamatsu SR	5.00	12.00
N1094 Sakura Haruno R	.40	1.00
N1094 Sakura Haruno P		
N1095 Ino Yamanaka C	.10	.25
N1096 Pain & Itachi Uchiha SR	5.00	12.00
N1096 Pain & Itachi Uchiha P		
N1097 Giant Rhino C	.10	.25
N1098 Nagato (Childhood) C	.10	.25
N1099 Pain (Human Path) U	.20	.50
N1100 Pain (Naraka Path) C	.10	.25
N1101 Pain (Asura Path) R	.40	1.00

2011 Naruto Tournament Pack 3

Card	Low	High
COMPLETE SET (60)	20.00	40.00
BOOSTER BOX (24 PACKS)	50.00	100.00
BOOSTER PACK (10 CARDS)	2.50	5.00
RELEASED IN JULY 2011		
J827 Tree Climbing Training U	.20	.50
J828 Standing Alone U	.20	.50
J829 Fire Style: Fireball Jutsu R	4.00	1.00
J830 Chidori SR	5.00	12.00
J831 Wind Style: Rasen Shuriken SR	4.00	10.00
J832 Barrier Battle Arts R	.40	1.00
J833 Deformable Body U•	.20	.50
J834 Blade of the Thunder God R	.40	1.00
J835 Stunning Strike U	.20	.50
J836 Fear of Blood R	.40	1.00
J837 Chakra Manipulation Training U	.20	.50
J838 Money Style: Shadow Clone Jutsu R	.40	1.00
M776 Summoning Weapons R	.40	1.00
M777 After the Battle R	.40	1.00
M778 Old Faces, New Problems R	.40	1.00
M779 Demon's Eyes R	.40	1.00
M780 Clone Training U	.20	.50
M781 Awkward Thinking SR	6.00	15.00
M782 Low Stamina R	.40	1.00
M783 Observer U	.20	.50
M784 Under the Rising Moon U	.20	.50
M785 Fond Memories R	.40	1.00
M786 The Fool & The Elite R	.40	1.00
M787 Money Style: Help Me Jutsu R	.40	1.00
N1170 Hinata Hyuga C	.10	.25
N1171 Shikamaru Nara C	.10	.25
N1172 Neji Hyuga C	.10	.25
N1173 Asuma Sarutobi C	.10	.25
N1174 The 1st Hokage U	.20	.50
N1175 Sasuke Uchiha C	.10	.25
N1176 Kakashi Hatake C	.10	.25
N1177 Itachi Uchiha U	.20	.50
N1178 The 3rd Hokage R	.40	1.00
N1179 Naruto Uzumaki C	.10	.25
N1180 Rock Lee C	.10	.25
N1181 Kushina Uzumaki C	.10	.25
N1182 Killer Bee C	.10	.25
N1183 Sai C	.10	.25
N1184 Naruto Uzumaki (Tailed Beast Form) SR	6.00	15.00
N1185 A R	.40	1.00
N1186 Eight Tails U	.20	.50
N1187 Suigetsu Hozuki C	.10	.25
N1188 Jugo C	.10	.25
N1189 Karin C	.10	.25
N1190 Suigetsu Hozuki C	.10	.25
N1191 Jugo C	.10	.25
N1192 Sasuke Uchiha C	.10	.25
N1193 Orochimaru U	.20	.50
N1194 Sasuke Uchiha (State 2) R	.40	1.00
N1195 Sakura Haruno C	.10	.25
N1196 Gaara of the Desert C	.10	.25
N1197 Kurenai Yuhi C	.10	.25
N1198 Konan U	.20	.50
N1199 Pain (Animal Path) C	.10	.25
N1200 Pain (Preta Path) C	.10	.25
N1201 Pain (Naraka Path) C	.10	.25
N1202 Pain (Human Path) U	.20	.50
N1203 Pain (Asura Path) U	.20	.50
N1204 Pain (Deva Path) U	.20	.50
N1205 Nagato SR	5.00	12.00

2011 Naruto Ultimate Battle Tin

Card	Low	High
PR069 Sasori	.30	.75
PR070 Deidara	.30	.75
PR071 Kakashi Hatake	.30	.75
PR072 Naruto Uzumaki	.30	.75
PR073 Itachi Uchiha	.30	.75
PR074 Sasuke Uchiha	.30	.75

2011 Naruto Weapons of War

Card	Low	High
COMPLETE SET (119)	50.00	100.00
BOOSTER BOX (24 PACKS)	50.00	100.00
BOOSTER PACK (10 CARDS)	2.50	5.00
RELEASED IN OCTOBER 2011		
J839 Byakugan R•	.40	1.00
J840 Deflection C•	.10	.25
J841 Mind Transfer Jutsu U•	.20	.50
J842 Partial Expansion Jutsu R•	.40	1.00
J843 Shadow Possession Jutsu C•	.10	.25
J844 Shuriken C•	.10	.25
J845 Smash C•	.10	.25
J846 Sharingan Eye C•	.10	.25
J847 Mangekyo Sharingan R•	.40	1.00
J848 Fire Style: Dragon Flame Jutsu R•	.40	1.00
J849 Needle Jizo C•	.10	.25
J850 Double Impact U•	.20	.50
J851 Seven Swords Dance R•	.40	1.00
J852 Lariat SR•	6.00	15.00
J853 Chakra Cannon U•	.20	.50
J854 Severe Leaf Hurricane U•	.20	.50
J855 Water Style: Demon Wave R•	.40	1.00
J856 Walking on Water C•	.10	.25
J857 Chidori Lance R•	.40	1.00
J858 Snake Sword SR•	8.00	20.00
J859 Earth Style Barrier: Earth Dome Prison U•	.20	.50
J860 Parasitic Insect Jutsu R•	.40	1.00
J861 Mind Scour C•	.10	.25
J862 Finger Flick R•	.40	1.00
J863 Puppet Master Jutsu C•	.10	.25
J864 Flamethrower U•	.20	.50
M788 Wrath of the Two Tails U•	.20	.50
M789 Leaf Squad Organized! R•	.40	1.00
M790 Sweet Treat U•	.20	.50
M791 Weapons of War R•	.40	1.00
M792 12 Shinobi Guardians R•	.40	1.00
M793 Quicksand C•	.10	.25
M794 Pad C•	.10	.25
M795 Guidance U•	.20	.50
M796 Naruto vs. Sasuke SR•	4.00	10.00
M797 Hokage Rocks U•	.20	.50
M798 Fading Touch R•	.40	1.00
M799 Brotherhood R•	.40	1.00
M800 Sage Training R•	.40	1.00
M801 A Good Book U•	.20	.50
M802 Mad Skillz R•	.40	1.00
M803 Ditched C•	.10	.25
M804 Disaster of the Nine-Tailed Fox Spirit R•	.40	1.00
M805 Just Like That Hero R•	.40	1.00
M806 Fierce Clash U•	.20	.50
M807 Flashback U•	.20	.50
M808 Ambush C•	.10	.25
M809 Right of Succession SR•	4.00	10.00
M810 Teacher and Pupil R•	.40	1.00
M811 Research U•	.20	.50
M812 The Blank Page C•	.10	.25
M813 Sealing Barrier R•	.40	1.00
M814 Ignorance U•	.20	.50
M815 A Gift R•	.40	1.00
M816 Kage of the Leaf U•	.20	.50
N1206 Choji Akimichi C•	.10	.25
N1207 Hinata Hyuga (Kimono) C•	.10	.25
N1208 Tenten (Kimono) C•	.10	.25
N1209 Ino Yamanaka (Kimono) U•	.20	.50
N1210 Neji Hyuga C•	.10	.25
N1211 Shikamaru Nara C•	.10	.25
N1212 Chiriku R•	.40	1.00
N1213 Hinata Hyuga C•	.10	.25
N1214 Deidara R•	.40	1.00
N1215 Yamato R•	.40	1.00
N1216 The 1st Hokage SR•	6.00	15.00
N1217 Akamaru C•	.10	.25
N1218 Kiba Inuzuka C•	.10	.25
N1219 Sasuke Uchiha C•	.10	.25
N1220 Pakkun C•	.10	.25
N1221 Yugao Uzuki U•	.20	.50
N1222 Sasuke Uchiha C•	.10	.25
N1223 Obito Uchiha R•	.40	1.00
N1224 Tobi C•	.10	.25
N1225 Danzo R•	.40	1.00
N1226 Hidan R•	.40	1.00
N1227 Kakashi Hatake U•	.20	.50
N1228 Itachi Uchiha U•	.20	.50
N1229 The 3rd Hokage SR•	4.00	10.00
N1230 Konohamaru C•	.10	.25
N1231 Naruto Uzumaki C•	.10	.25
N1232 Ink Lion C•	.10	.25
N1233 Rock Lee C•	.10	.25
N1234 Naruto Uzumaki (Clone) C•	.10	.25
N1235 Iruka Umino C•	.10	.25
N1236 Sai R•	.40	1.00
N1237 Killer Bee U•	.20	.50
N1238 Anko Mitarashi (Kimono) U•	.20	.50
N1239 Might Guy R•	.40	1.00
N1240 Jiraiya R•	.40	1.00
N1241 The 4th Hokage SR•	10.00	25.00
N1242 Eight Tails R•	.40	1.00
N1243 Orochimaru C•	.10	.25
N1244 Sakon C•	.10	.25
N1245 Karin C•	.10	.25
N1246 Anko Mitarashi R•	.40	1.00
N1247 Suigetsu Hozuki U•	.20	.50
N1248 Jugo (State 1) U•	.20	.50
N1249 Zabuza Momochi SR•	5.00	12.00
N1250 Sasuke Uchiha SR•	15.00	30.00
N1251 The 2nd Hokage SR•	4.00	10.00
N1252 Sakura Haruno (Kimono) C•	.10	.25
N1253 Kankuro C•	.10	.25
N1254 Tonton C•	.10	.25
N1255 Shino Aburame C•	.10	.25
N1256 Sakura Haruno R•	.40	1.00
N1257 Shizune (Kimono) U•	.20	.50
N1258 Kurenai Yuhi R•	.40	1.00
N1259 The 5th Hokage SR•	4.00	10.00
N1260 Kurenai Yuhi (Kimono) R•	.40	1.00
N1261 Tsunade (Kimono) R•	.40	1.00
N1262 Jirobo (State 1) C•	.10	.25
N1263 Kabuto Yakushi C•	.10	.25
N1264 Tayuya C•	.10	.25
N1265 Haku U•	.20	.50
N1266 Temari C•	.10	.25
N1267 Gaara of the Desert C•	.10	.25
N1268 Chiyo U•	.20	.50
N1269 Baki U•	.20	.50

2012 Naruto Avenger's Wrath

Card	Low	High
COMPLETE SET (120)	75.00	150.00
BOOSTER BOX (24 PACKS)	40.00	80.00
BOOSTER PACK (10 CARDS)	2.50	4.00
RELEASED ON SEPTEMBER 7, 2012		
J946 Earth Style: Hidden in Stones U	.20	.50
J947 Earth Style: Mud Wave R	.40	1.00
J948 Paper Bomb C	.10	.25
J949 Spontaneous Tree Summoning SR	12.00	30.00
J950 Narrow Dodge C	.10	.25
J951 Summoning Jutsu U	.20	.50
J952 Simulstrike R	.40	1.00
J953 Izanagi SR	8.00	20.00
J954 Taking a Hostage U	.20	.50
J955 Panic Attack C	.10	.25
J956 Art of the Raging Lion's Mane R	.40	1.00
J957 Shadow Clone Jutsu U	.20	.50
J958 Naruto Uzumaki Barrage U	.20	.50
J959 Chidori Sword R	.40	1.00
J960 Sacrifice U	.20	.50
J961 Chakra Transference C	.10	.25
J962 Mystic Fog Prison C	.10	.25
J963 Savior R	.40	1.00
J964 Wind Style: Vacuum Blade U	.20	.50
J965 Wind Style: Vacuum Bullets R	.40	1.00
J966 Enhanced Shuriken C	.10	.25
J967 Paralyzing Seal C	.10	.25
J968 Wind Style: Vacuum Blast U	.20	.50
J969 Reverse Tetragram Sealing Jutsu SR	10.00	25.00
J970 Chakra Stream U	.20	.50
J971 Unorthodox Weaponry R	.40	1.00
M914 A Quiet Day C	.10	.25
M915 Konoha's Strongest Genin SR	3.00	8.00
M916 Intriguing Story R	.40	1.00
M917 The Ultimate Weapon U	.20	.50
M918 Self Conversation U	.20	.50
M919 Desperate Power R	.40	1.00
M920 Pocket Dimension R	.40	1.00
M921 Face-off U	.20	.50
M922 The Fire Lord C	.10	.25
M923 A Rival's Challenge SR	3.00	8.00
M924 Differing Emotions C	.10	.25
M925 An Old Friend R	.40	1.00
M926 Medicinal Pills C	.10	.25
M927 Stuffed U	.20	.50
M928 Inari's Decision R	.40	1.00
M929 Moment of Weakness U	.20	.50
M930 Turn of Phrase SR	3.00	8.00
M931 Seasick U	.20	.50
M932 Skeleton Panic R	.40	1.00
M933 A Fisherman's Quarry C	.10	.25
M934 The Rogue Jinchuriki C	.10	.25
M935 Sakura's Confession SR	6.00	15.00
M936 Shameful Actions R	.40	1.00
M937 Present from Students C	.10	.25
M938 Kakashi Hatake's Date U	.20	.50
M939 Jotuku Flower R	.40	1.00
M940 Ex-Samurai R	.40	1.00
M941 Strength in Numbers U	.20	.50
M942 The Mediator R	.40	1.00
N1488 Choji Akimichi C	.10	.25
N1489 Hinata Hyuga (Childhood) C	.10	.25
N1490 Neji Hyuga C	.10	.25
N1491 Ino Yamanaka (Childhood) C	.10	.25
N1492 Chushin C	.10	.25
N1493 Tenten C	.10	.25
N1494 Shikamaru Nara U	.20	.50
N1495 Tonbei U	.20	.50
N1496 Ko Hyuga U	.20	.50
N1497 Neji Hyuga U	.20	.50
N1498 Asuma Sarutobi R	.40	1.00
N1499 Yamato R	.40	1.00
N1500 The 1st Hokage SR	8.00	20.00
N1501 Hibachi C	.10	.25
N1502 Akane C	.10	.25
N1503 Tamaki (Childhood) C	.10	.25
N1504 Kiba Inuzuka C	.10	.25
N1505 Nango C	.10	.25
N1506 Sasuke Uchiha U	.20	.50
N1507 Tobi C	.10	.25
N1508 Sasuke Uchiha R	.40	1.00
N1509 Hidan U	.20	.50
N1510 Kakashi Hatake U	.20	.50
N1511 Itachi Uchiha R	.40	1.00
N1512 Madara Uchiha SR	8.00	2.00
N1513 The 6th Hokage SR	12.00	30.00
N1514 The Sage U	.20	.50
N1515 Gameru C	.10	.25
N1516 Kusune C	.10	.25
N1517 Naruto Uzumaki C	.10	.25
N1518 Izumo Kamizuki C	.10	.25
N1519 Rock Lee U	.20	.50
N1520 Naruto Uzumaki U	.20	.50
N1521 Anko Mitarashi U	.20	.50
N1522 Sai U	.20	.50
N1523 Jiraiya R	.40	1.00
N1524 Might Guy R	.40	1.00
N1525 Might Guy and Kakashi Hatake SR	3.00	8.00
N1526 Kanabun C	.10	.25
N1527 Tanishi C	.10	.25
N1528 Karin C	.10	.25
N1529 Haku C	.10	.25
N1530 Suigetsu Hozuki U	.20	.50
N1531 Jugo U	.20	.50
N1532 Kabuto Yakushi U	.20	.50
N1533 Zabuza Momochi R	.40	1.00
N1534 Kisame Hoshigaki R	.40	1.00
N1535 Jugo (State 2) R	.40	1.00
N1536 Orochimaru R	.40	1.00
N1537 Susano'o (Sasuke) SR	25.00	50.00
N1538 Shino Aburame (Childhood) C	.10	.25
N1539 Sakura Haruno U	.20	.50
N1540 Hotaru Katsuragi C	.10	.25
N1541 Temari C	.10	.25
N1542 Gaara of the Desert C	.10	.25
N1543 Inner Sakura R	.40	1.00
N1544 Father and Mother U	.20	.50
N1545 Hiruko U	.20	.50
N1546 Kurenai Yuhi U	.20	.50
N1547 Sasori R	.40	1.00
N1548 Kurenai Yuhi and Asuma Sarutobi R	.40	1.00
N1549 Sakura Haruno and Chiyo R	.40	1.00
N1550 En no Gyoja R	.40	1.00
N1551 Samurai Warrior C	.10	.25
N1552 Mifune R	.40	1.00

2012 Naruto Hero's Ascension

Card	Low	High
COMPLETE SET (132)	80.00	150.00
BOOSTER BOX (24 PACKS)	50.00	80.00
BOOSTER PACK (10 CARDS)	2.50	4.00
RELEASED ON DECEMBER 17, 2012		
C060 Madara Uchiha ST	2.50	6.00
J1000 Wind Style: Rasen Shuriken ST	.40	1.00
J1001 The Mind of Pain ST	.20	.50
J972 Mind Transfer, Puppet Curse Jutsu SR	1.25	3.00
J973 Barrier Ninjutsu U	.20	.50
J974 Interrogation R	.50	1.25
J975 Overwhelming Hunger C	.10	.25
J976 Chidori R	.40	1.00
J977 Threaten C	.10	.25
J978 Body Flicker U	.20	.50
J979 Reaper Death Seal SR	2.00	5.00
J980 Backstab U	.30	.75
J981 Role Reversal R	.40	1.00
J982 Pencil Toss U	.20	.50
(Mull to Four Exclusive Preview)		
J983 Double Lariat SR	2.50	6.00
J984 Unlocking the Seal C	.10	.25
J985 Special Kunai U	.20	.50
J986 Rasengan R	1.50	4.00
J987 Water Prison Shark Dance Jutsu SR	1.25	3.00
J988 Skeletal Control U	.20	.50
J989 Summoning Jutsu: Reanimation SR	4.00	10.00
J990 Water Prison Jutsu C	.10	.25
J991 Voracious Appetite C	.10	.25
J992 Simple Disguise C	.10	.25
J993 Gigantic Fan C	.10	.25
J994 Palm Healing R	.40	1.00
J995 Fungal Power U	.20	.50
J996 Shark Skin C	.10	.25
(Pojo Exclusive Preview)		
J997 The Passion of Youth C	.10	.25
(Pojo Exclusive Preview)		
J998 Almighty Push ST	.50	1.25
J999 Eyes of the Sage ST	.20	.50
M943 Rebuilding the Village U	.20	.50
M944 Great Praise C	.10	.25
M945 The Power of the Trio R	.40	1.00
M946 A Hard Bargain R	.40	1.00
M947 The Future Hokage? U	.20	.50
M948 Out of Control Curse Mark C	.10	.25
M949 Path of the Avenger R	.40	1.00
M950 Shadow of the Leaf U	.30	.75
M951 Jonin's Intervention R	1.50	4.00
M952 Exhaustion U	.20	.50
M953 A Master's Treat U	.20	.50
M954 Disaster of the Nine-Tailed Fox Spirit R	.40	1.00
M955 A Parent's Love R	.40	1.00
M956 Unlocking the Power C	.10	.25
(Mull to Four Exclusive Preview)		
M957 The Evil Within U	.20	.50
M958 The Tailless Beast R	.40	1.00
M959 A New Master U	.20	.50
M960 Dark Aspirations R	.40	1.00
M961 Alliance of Evil U	.20	.50
M962 A Show of Power U	.20	.50
M963 Forceful Persuasion R	.40	1.00
M964 Sakura's Tears R	.40	1.00
M965 Idle Comrades U	.20	.50
M966 What Could Have Been U	.20	.50
M967 Tinker R	.40	1.00
M968 Gathering Herbs R	.40	1.00
M969 Outcast R	.40	1.00
(Pojo Exclusive Preview)		
M970 The Lord's Convene C	.10	.25
(Pojo Exclusive Preview)		
M971 Sparring U	.20	.50
(Pojo Exclusive Preview)		
M972 The Spiral of Pain ST	.40	1.00
M973 Sage's Training Ground ST	.20	.50
M974 Exhaustive Battle ST	.20	.50
M975 The Herald of Pain ST	.20	.50
N1553 Choji Akimichi C	.10	.25
N1554 Ino Yamanaka C	.10	.25
N1555 Tenten C	.10	.25
N1556 Tofu C	.10	.25
N1557 Mikage C	.10	.25
N1558 Shikamaru Nara U	.20	.50
N1559 Hinata Hyuga C	.10	.25
N1560 Zetsu U	.20	.50
N1561 Asuma Sarutobi U	.20	.50
N1562 Neji Hyuga U	.20	.50
N1563 Deidara R	.40	1.00
N1564 The 3rd Tsuchikage SR	1.50	4.00
N1565 Hanabi Hyuga C	.10	.25
N1566 Gentleman Cat C	.10	.25
N1567 Suguro C	.10	.25
N1568 Mr. Ostrich C	.10	.25
N1569 Kiba Inuzuka C	.10	.25
N1570 Sasuke Uchiha C	.10	.25
N1571 Obito Uchiha U	.20	.50
N1572 Tobi C	.10	.25
N1573 Hidan U	.20	.50
N1574 Sasuke Uchiha R	.75	2.00
N1575 Kakashi Hatake (Boyhood) U	.20	.50
N1576 Kakashi Hatake R	1.25	3.00
N1577 Itachi Uchiha R	.40	1.00
N1578 Masked Man SR	8.00	20.00
N1579 Konohamaru C	.10	.25
N1580 Naruto Uzumaki C	.10	.25
N1581 Pakkun C	.10	.25
N1582 Rock Lee U	.20	.50
(Mull to Four Exclusive Preview)		
N1583 Kushina Uzumaki R	.40	1.00
N1584 Izumo Kamizuki U	.20	.50
N1585 Sora R	.40	1.00
N1586 Naruto Uzumaki U	.20	.50
N1587 Sai U	.20	.50
N1588 Killer Bee R	.40	1.00
N1589 Killer Bee (Version 2) SR	10.00	25.00
N1590 The 4th Hokage SR	12.00	30.00
N1591 Gamabunta R	.50	1.25
N1592 Jirobo C	.10	.25
N1593 Karin C	.10	.25
N1594 Suigetsu C	.10	.25
N1595 Jugo U	.20	.50
N1596 Haku R	.40	1.00
N1597 Utakata U	.20	.50
N1598 Kabuto Yakushi U	.20	.50
N1599 Zabuza Momochi R	.40	1.00
N1600 Kisame Hoshigaki C	.10	.25
N1601 Kimimaro R	.40	1.00
N1602 Kabuto Yakushi SR	10.00	25.00
N1603 Kisame Hoshigaki SR	12.00	30.00
N1604 Gaara of the Desert C	.10	.25

Card	Low	High
N1605 Sakura Haruno C	.10	.25
N1606 Kankuro C	.10	.25
N1607 Temari C	.10	.25
N1608 Rin C	.10	.25
N1609 Shino Aburame U	.20	.50
N1610 Temari U	.20	.50
N1611 Sakura Haruno U	.20	.50
N1612 Hiruko R	.40	1.00
N1613 Chiyo U	.20	.50
N1614 Shizune R	.40	1.00
N1615 Kurenai Yuhi R	.40	1.00
N1616 Tsunade SR	3.00	8.00
N1617 Kakuzu R	.40	1.00
(Pojo Exclusive Preview)		
N1618 Naruto Uzumaki (Sage Mode) STSR	4.00	10.00
N1619 Pain (Deva Path) STSR	4.00	10.00
N1620 Jiraiya ST	.20	.50

2012 Naruto Kage Summit

Card	Low	High
COMPLETE SET (120)	150.00	250.00
BOOSTER BOX (24 PACKS)	40.00	80.00
BOOSTER PACK (10 CARDS)	2.50	4.00
RELEASED ON JUNE 22, 2012		
J921 Sporulation Jutsu U	.20	.50
J922 Wood Style: Four Pillar Prison R	.40	1.00
J923 Lava Style: Lava Monster R	.40	1.00
J924 Golem Technique R	.40	1.00
J925 Earth Style: Weighted Boulder C	.10	.25
J926 Particle Style: Atomic Dismantling SR	6.00	15.00
J927 Danzo's Seal C	.10	.25
J928 Lightning Blade U	.20	.50
J929 Genjutsu SR	8.00	20.00
J930 Amaterasu Shield U	.20	.50
J931 Inferno Style: Flame Control R	.40	1.00
J932 Gale Style: Laser Circus R	.40	1.00
J933 Lightning Illusion: Flash Pillar C	.10	.25
J934 Liger Bomb SR	4.00	10.00
J935 Lightning Style Armor R	.40	1.00
J936 Lightning Style: Emotion Wave R	.40	1.00
J937 Water Style: Water Wall C	.10	.25
J938 Cursed Seal Chakra Blast U	.20	.50
J939 Hiramekarei Unleash: Hammer R	.40	1.00
J940 Vapor Style: Solid Fog SR	2.50	6.00
J941 Sand Shield C	.10	.25
J942 Wind Scythe Jutsu R	.40	1.00
J943 Secret Red Technique: Puppet Triad SR	6.00	15.00
J944 Sand Shower Barrage R	.40	1.00
J945 Sand Wall U	.20	.50
M884 Messengers U	.20	.50
M885 The Stone Council SR	6.00	15.00
M886 Five Kage Summit R	.40	1.00
M887 Spoils of War C	.10	.25
M888 Exhaustion R	.40	1.00
M889 Untold Destruction R	.40	1.00
M890 Battle of Attrition R	.40	1.00
M891 New Orders U	.20	.50
M892 The Leaf Council SR	6.00	15.00
M893 Tense Negotiations U	.20	.50
M894 An Honest Discussion C	.10	.25
M895 Power of Suggestion C	.10	.25
M896 Bodyguard's Protection C	.10	.25
M897 Exaggeration R	.40	1.00
M898 For Vengeance U	.20	.50
M899 The Cloud Council SR	6.00	15.00
M900 A Unique Exit U	.20	.50
M901 A Plea U	.20	.50
M902 A Dark Message C	.10	.25
M903 The Mist Council SR	3.00	8.00
M904 Massacre U	.20	.50
M905 The Kage Assassins U	.20	.50
M906 Arrogance R	.40	1.00
M907 Leader of the Bloody Mist U	.20	.50
M908 Grossed Out U	.20	.50
M909 Personal Guard R	.40	1.00
M910 The Sand Council SR	6.00	15.00
M911 Pure of Heart R	.40	1.00
M912 Sneak Attack U	.20	.50
M913 Village Heroes C	.10	.25
N1423 Neji Hyuga C	.10	.25
N1424 Ino Yamanaka C	.10	.25
N1425 Shikamaru Nara C	.10	.25
N1426 Tenten C	.10	.25
N1427 Choji Akimichi ST	.10	.25
N1428 Shikamaru Nara ST	.40	1.00
N1429 Hinata Hyuga ST	.75	2.00
N1430 Zetsu U	.20	.50
N1431 Deidara U	.20	.50
N1432 Akatsuchi R	.40	1.00
N1433 Yamato R	.40	1.00
N1434 Kurotsuchi R	.40	1.00
N1435 The 3rd Tsuchikage SR	8.00	20.00
N1436 Bartender Cat C	.10	.25
N1437 Chainya C	.10	.25
N1438 Sabiru R	.40	1.00
N1439 Sasuke Uchiha C	.10	.25
N1440 Kiba Inuzuka C	.10	.25
N1441 Tobi C	.10	.25
N1442 Hidan U	.20	.50
N1443 Sasuke Uchiha U	.20	.50
N1444 Kakashi Hatake R	.40	1.00
N1445 Itachi Uchiha R	.40	1.00
N1446 The 3rd Hokage SR	12.00	30.00
N1447 Four Tails R	.40	1.00
N1448 Io C	.10	.25
N1449 Shoseki C	.10	.25
N1450 Rock Lee C	.10	.25
N1451 Mabui U	.20	.50
N1452 Ink Mouse U	.20	.50
N1453 Naruto Uzumaki ST	.10	.25
N1454 Sai U	.20	.50
N1455 Cee U	.20	.50
N1456 Might Guy U	.20	.50
N1457 Darui R	.40	1.00
N1458 Ink Bat R	.40	1.00
N1459 The 4th Raikage SR	10.00	25.00
N1460 The Nine-Tailed Fox Spirit R	.40	1.00
N1461 Mist Anbu C	.10	.25
N1462 Suiu C	.10	.25
N1463 Jirobo C	.10	.25
N1464 Tayuya C	.10	.25
N1465 Kidomaru C	.10	.25
N1466 Sakon C	.10	.25
N1467 Jugo (State 1) C	.10	.25
N1468 Suigetsu Hozuki U	.20	.50
N1469 Chojuro U	.20	.50
N1470 Ao R	.40	1.00
N1471 The 5th Mizukage SR	15.00	40.00
N1472 Orochimaru R	.40	1.00
N1473 Zhandou C	.10	.25
N1474 Epidemic Prevention Officer C	.10	.25
N1475 Tonton C	.10	.25
N1476 Shino Aburame C	.10	.25
N1477 Sakura Haruno C	.10	.25
N1478 Temari C	.10	.25
N1479 Sand Anbu U	.20	.50
N1480 Shizune U	.20	.50
N1481 Kankuro ST	.20	.50
N1482 Scorpion R	.40	1.00
N1483 Seven Tails R	.40	1.00
N1484 Temari ST	.40	1.00
N1485 The 5th Kazekage SR	12.00	30.00
N1486 Ino Yamanaka, Shikamaru Nara, and Choji Akimichi STSR	2.00	5.00
N1487 Kankuro, Temari, and Gaara of the Desert STSR	1.50	4.00

2012 Naruto Sage's Legacy

Card	Low	High
COMPLETE SET (120)	100.00	150.00
BOOSTER BOX (24 PACKS)	30.00	50.00
BOOSTER PACK (10 CARDS)	1.00	2.00
RELEASED ON FEBRUARY 10, 2012		
J895 Tailed Beast Sealing R	.40	1.00
J896 Gentle Fist U	.20	.50
J097 Dravery C	.10	.25
J898 Gentle Step: Twin Lion Fists SR	.40	1.00
J899 Mangekyo Sharingan R	.40	1.00
J900 Shadow Windmill C	.10	.25
J901 Crow Clone U	.20	.50
J902 Amaterasu SR	4.00	10.00
J903 Sage Art: Frog Call C	.10	.25
J904 Sage Jutsu: Rasengan Barrage R	.75	2.00
J905 Frog Kumite U	.20	.50
J906 Sage Art: Giant Rasengan R	1.00	2.50
J907 Wind Style: Rasen-Shuriken SR	4.00	10.00
J908 Chidori Lance U	.20	.50
J909 Striking Shadow Snake C	.10	.25
J910 Water Style: Exploding Water Shockwave C	.10	.25
J911 Chakra Stealing C	.10	.25
J912 Bug Shield U	.20	.50
J913 Chakra Scalpel C	.10	.25
J914 Wind Style: Pressure Damage R	.40	1.00
J915 Palm Healing U	.20	.50
J916 Pinned Down U	.20	.50
J917 Chakra Disturbance U	.20	.50
J918 Chakra Drain C	.10	.25
J919 Catastrophic Planetary Devastation SR	5.00	12.00
J920 Demonic Dragon R	.40	1.00
M855 The Hyuga Clan R	1.00	2.50
M856 Determination to Protect U	.20	.50
M857 A Matter of Love R	.40	1.00
M858 Troubling Sign U	.20	.50
M859 The Nara Clan R	.75	2.00
M860 Hyuga Training C	.10	.25
M861 The Inuzuka Clan R	.40	1.00
M862 Leader of the Cats U	.20	.50
M863 The Uchiha Clan R	.40	1.00
M864 Insanity R	.40	1.00
M865 The Strongest One R	.40	1.00
M866 Guardians of the Village R	.40	1.00
M867 Musings of a Hermit U	.20	.50
M868 Nice Guy Pose U	.20	.50
M869 Burden of Hatred C	.10	.25
M870 A Father In Dark Times U	.20	.50
M871 Shadows of the Past SR	3.00	8.00
M872 Angering the Beast R	1.00	2.50
M873 Organization of Peace R	.40	1.00
M874 An Impossible Situation R	.40	1.00
M875 Final Goodbye U	.20	.50
M876 Training in the Rain U	.20	.50
M877 Reminisce R	.75	2.00
M878 The Aburame Clan R	.40	1.00
M879 Chakra Transmission U	.20	.50
M880 Secret Book U	.20	.50
M881 Gedo: Art of Rinne Rebirth SR	3.00	8.00
M882 The True Pain U	.20	.50
M883 Awakening U	.20	.50
N1358 Choji Akimichi C	.10	.25
N1359 Shikamaru Nara C	.10	.25
N1360 Hinata Hyuga C	.10	.25
N1361 Ino Yamanaka C	.10	.25
N1362 TenTen C	.10	.25
N1363 Shikamaru Nara R	.75	2.00
N1364 Zetsu C	.10	.25
N1365 Two Tails U	.20	.50
N1366 Foo U	.20	.50
N1367 Hinata Hyuga SR	10.00	25.00
N1368 Yamato R	1.00	2.50
N1369 Deidara R	.75	2.00
N1370 The First Hokage R	.40	1.00
N1371 Cat Guard C	.10	.25
N1372 Katazu C	.10	.25
N1373 Sasuke Uchiha C	.10	.25
N1374 Kiba Inuzuka C	.10	.25
N1375 Akamaru C	.10	.25
N1376 Pakkun R	.40	1.00
N1377 Tobi C	.10	.25
N1378 Sasuke Uchiha U	.20	.50
N1379 Double Headed Wolf R	.40	1.00
N1380 Kakashi Hatake U	.20	.50
N1381 Itachi Uchiha R	.75	2.00
N1382 Hidan R	.40	1.00
N1383 The 6th Hokage SR	.40	1.00
N1384 Naruto Uzumaki C	.10	.25
N1385 Sekiei C	.10	.25
N1386 Ink Fish C	.10	.25
N1387 Konohamaru C	.10	.25
N1388 Naruto Uzumaki C	.10	.25
N1389 Karui C	.10	.25
N1390 Omoi U	.20	.50
N1391 Ink Eagle U	.20	.50
N1392 Samui R	2.00	5.00
N1393 Gamahiro R	.40	1.00
N1394 Naruto Uzumaki and Jiraiya R	1.50	4.00
N1395 Naruto Uzumaki SR	35.00	70.00
N1396 Naruto Uzumaki R	3.00	8.00
N1397 Unagi C	.10	.25
N1398 Kandachi C	.10	.25
N1399 Karin C	.10	.25
N1400 Jirobo C	.10	.25
N1401 Jugo C	.10	.25
N1402 Suigetsu C	.10	.25
N1403 Haku U	.20	.50
N1404 Five-Tails R	2.50	6.00
N1405 Kimimaro SR	4.00	10.00
N1406 Kisame Hoshigaki U	.20	.50
N1407 Zabuza Momochi U	.20	.50
N1408 Kisame Hoshigaki and Zetsu R	1.50	4.00
N1409 The Second Hokage R	.40	1.00
N1410 Hanare C	.10	.25
N1411 Furufuki C	.10	.25
N1412 Shino Aburame C	.10	.25
N1413 Sakura Haruno C	.10	.25
N1414 Temari C	.10	.25
N1415 Father and Mother C	.10	.25
N1416 Shizune C	.10	.25
N1417 Torune U	.20	.50
N1418 Chiyo R	.75	2.00
N1419 Kurenai Yuhi R	.40	1.00
N1420 Sasori R	.75	2.00
N1421 Tsunade SR	6.00	15.00
N1422 Pain SR	3.00	8.00

2012 Naruto Tournament Pack 4

Card	Low	High
COMPLETE SET (60)	20.00	40.00
BOOSTER BOX (24 PACKS)	40.00	80.00
BOOSTER PACK (10 CARDS)	3.00	5.00
RELEASED IN DECEMBER 2011		
C019 Futaba C	.10	.25
C032 Teyaki Uchiha U	.20	.50
C048 Takamaru C	.10	.25
C059 Giant Eagle R	.40	1.00
J021 Earth Style: Headhunter Jutsu C	.10	.25
J214 Application of the First Stage U	.20	.50
J268 Sand Tsunami R	.40	1.00
J462 Sealing Jutsu: Nine Phantom Dragons C	.10	.25
J890 Formidable Team U	.20	.50
J891 Subdue C	.10	.25
J892 Taijutsu Suit U	.20	.50
J893 Chakra Eater Sword U	.20	.50
J894 Healing U	.20	.50
M080 Sakura's Decision R	.60	1.50
M092 Tide of the Deadly Combat R	.40	1.00
M847 Generations U	.20	.50
M848 Shikamaru's Decision R	5.00	12.00
M849 Eyes of the Betrayer U	.20	.50
M850 Race! C	.10	.25
M851 Dango U	1.50	4.00
M852 Mysterious Warrior SR	2.50	6.00
M853 Twining Limbs C	.10	.25
M854 Genjutsu Adept U	.20	.50
N320 Orochimaru R	.40	1.00
N365 Itachi Uchiha R	.40	1.00
N424 Konohamaru C	.10	.25
N454 Kisame Hoshigaki R	.40	1.00
N488 Chiyo R	.40	1.00
N560 Neji Hyuga R	.40	1.00
N595 Ino Yamanaka C	.10	.25
N635 Choji Akimichi C	.10	.25
N657 Shino Aburame C	.10	.25
N658 Hinata Hyuga C	.10	.25
N675 Kakashi Hatake R	.40	1.00
N711 Obito Uchiha SR	5.00	12.00
N1335 Tenten C	.10	.25
N1336 Neji Hyuga C	.10	.25
N1337 Deidara SR	1.25	3.00
N1338 Sasuke Uchiha C	.10	.25
N1339 Tobi U	.20	.50
N1340 Naruto Uzumaki SR	2.50	6.00
N1341 Rock Lee U	.20	.50
N1342 Iruka Umino C	.10	.25
N1343 Sai U	.20	.50
N1344 Jiraiya R	.40	1.00
N1345 The 4th Hokage R	.40	1.00
N1346 Yukimaru C	.10	.25
N1347 Kabuto Yakushi U	.30	.75
N1348 Gozu C	.10	.25
N1349 Rinji C	.10	.25
N1350 Guren SR	3.00	8.00
N1351 Sasuke Uchiha C	.10	.25
N1352 Rin C	.10	.25
N1353 Utakata C	.10	.25
N1354 Ebisu C	.10	.25
N1355 Sakura Haruno SR	12.00	30.00
N1356 Shizune U	.20	.50
N1357 Gaara of the Desert R	.40	1.00
JUS065 Chidori R	.40	1.00
PRUS010 Sakura Haruno U	.20	.50

2013 Naruto Ultimate Ninja Storm 3

Card	Low	High
COMPLETE SET (120)	120.00	200.00
BOOSTER BOX (24 PACKS)	60.00	90.00
BOOSTER PACK (10 CARDS)	3.50	4.50
RELEASED ON MARCH 9, 2013		
J1002 Golem Technique C	.10	.25
J1003 Lava Style: Quicklime Congealing Jutsu C	.10	.25
J1004 Particle Style: Atomic Dismantling C	.10	.25
J1005 8 Trigrams 64 Palms C	.10	.25
J1006 Cat Fire Bowl R	1.00	2.50
J1007 Shattered Heaven SR	3.00	8.00
J1008 Great Blazing Eruption R	1.00	2.50
J1009 Flame Control Sword R	1.00	2.50
J1010 Yasaka Magatama C	.10	.25
J1011 Summoning: Gedo Statue R	.40	1.00
J1012 Hirudora C	.10	.25
J1013 Hell Stab: One-Finger Spear Hand U	.20	.50
J1014 Tailed Beast Bomb SR	25.00	50.00
J1015 Gale Style: Black Hunting C	.10	.25
J1016 Bashosen's Power C	.10	.25
J1017 Benihisago's Power C	.10	.25
J1018 Five-Mountain Jump U	.20	.50
J1019 Rough Sea Spume U	.20	.50
J1020 Ninja Art: Sickle Fog Jutsu C	.10	.25
J1021 Summoning: Reanimation SR	4.00	10.00
J1022 Freight Bubbles U	.20	.50
J1023 Phosphorus Blast U	.20	.50
J1024 Sand Tsunami C	.10	.25
J1025 Hidden Jutsu: Insect Bog C	.10	.25
J1026 Cherry Blossom Clash R	.60	1.50
J1027 Spirit of the Samurai U	.20	.50
J1028 Helmetsplitter's Rush C	.10	.25
J1029 Fang's Rush C	.10	.25
J1030 Sewing Needle's Rush U	.20	.50
J1031 Master of the 7 Swords R	.75	2.00
J1032 Needle Senbon C	.10	.25
J1033 Spatter's Rush C	.10	.25
M976 Zetsu Army C	.20	.50
M977 Super Sized C	.10	.25
M978 Bloodline Selection U	.20	.50
M979 Masterful User R	.40	1.00
M980 Digging One's Grave C	.10	.25
M981 Strength of Conviction U	.20	.50
M982 Destructive Duo R	.60	1.50
M983 Vengeful Spirit C	.10	.25
M984 Heroic Spirit C	.10	.25
M985 Eight Inner Gates R	.60	1.50
M986 Clash of Ideals SR	5.00	12.00
M987 Lightning Speed U	.20	.50
M988 Axis of Evil U	.20	.50
M989 Bloodline Limit C	.10	.25
M990 Hiding in the Mist U	.20	.50
M991 Indomitable Strength C	.20	.50
M992 Empassioned Speech R	.40	1.00
M993 4 Man Squad C	.10	.25
M994 Furious Tempest R	1.00	2.50
M995 Tailed Beast Transformation R	.75	2.00
M996 Gathering the Beasts U	.40	1.00
M997 Mist's Greatest Swordsmen C	.20	.50
M998 Ninja Alliance SR	3.00	8.00
N1621 Choji Akimichi C	.20	.50
N1622 Ino Yamanaka C	.10	.25
N1623 Tenten C	.10	.25
N1624 Hinata Hyuga C	.10	.25
N1625 Shikamaru Nara C	.10	.25
N1626 Two Tails C	.10	.25
N1627 Neji Hyuga C	.10	.25
N1628 Akatsuchi C	.10	.25
N1629 Kurotsuchi U	.20	.50
N1630 The 3rd Tsuchikage R	.50	1.25
N1631 Kakashi Hatake (Boyhood) C	.20	.50
N1632 Kiba Inuzuka C	.10	.25
N1633 Obito Uchiha C	.10	.25
N1634 Four Tails U	.20	.50
N1635 Kakashi Hatake R	.50	1.25
N1636 Sasuke Uchiha R	2.00	5.00
N1637 Danzo U	.20	.50
N1638 Tobi SR	10.00	25.00
N1639 Rock Lee C	.10	.25
N1640 Cee C	.10	.25
N1641 Naruto Uzumaki C	.10	.25
N1642 Sai C	.10	.25
N1643 Killer Bee R	.50	1.25
N1644 Darui U	.20	.50
N1645 The 4th Raikage R	.60	1.50
N1646 Naruto (9 Tails Cloak) SR	25.00	50.00
N1647 Kabuto Yakushi R	2.00	5.00
N1648 Three Tails U	.40	1.00
N1649 Chojuro U	.20	.50
N1650 Kisame Hoshigaki U	.20	.50
N1651 Ao C	.10	.25
N1652 Five Tails U	.20	.50
N1653 The 5th Mizukage R	1.00	2.50
N1654 Shino Aburame C	.10	.25
N1655 Sakura Haruno SR	6.00	15.00
N1656 Kankuro C	.10	.25
N1657 Six Tails R	1.00	2.50
N1658 Seven Tails R	1.25	3.00
N1659 Temari U	.20	.50
N1660 The 5th Kazekage R	.75	2.00
N1661 Haku C	.10	.25
N1662 Utakata C	.10	.25
N1663 Fuu C	1.00	2.50
N1664 Jinin Akebino C	.20	.50
N1665 Jinpachi Munashi C	.20	.50
N1666 Ameyuri Ringo C	.20	.50
N1667 Kushimaru Kuriarare U	.20	.50
N1668 Mangetsu Hozuki SR	8.00	20.00
N1669 Zabuza Momochi U	.20	.50
N1670 Fuguki Suikazan R	.40	1.00
N1671 Kinkaku C	.10	.25
N1672 Ginkaku C	.10	.25
N1673 Asuma Sarutobi C	.10	.25
N1674 Yugito Ni'i C	.10	.25
N1675 Han C	.20	.50
N1676 Roshi C	.10	.25
N1677 Itachi Uchiha U	.20	.50
N1678 Mifune SR	12.00	30.00
N1679 The 2nd Tsuchikage U	.40	1.00
N1680 The 3rd Raikage R	.75	2.00
N1681 The 4th Kazekage U	.20	.50
N1682 Yagura C	.20	.50
N1683 Nagato SR	12.00	30.00
N1684 Hanzo The Salamander U	.20	.50
N1685 Madara Uchiha SR	10.00	25.00

2005 Neopets Curse of the Maraqua

Card	Low	High
COMPLETE SET (120)	30.00	80.00
RELEASED ON MARCH 15, 2005		
1 The Black Pawkeet HOLO	2.00	5.00
2 Caylis HOLO	2.00	5.00
3 Chasm Beast HOLO	2.00	5.00
4 The Drenched HOLO	2.00	5.00
5 Faerie Circle HOLO	2.00	5.00
6 Garins Redemption HOLO	2.00	5.00
7 Ghost Yurble HOLO	2.00	5.00
8 Goregas HOLO	2.00	5.00
9 Isca HOLO	2.00	5.00
10 Maraquan Chomby HOLO	2.00	5.00
11 Maraquan Krawk HOLO	2.00	5.00
12 Maraquan Paint Brush HOLO	2.00	5.00
13 Maraquan Scorchio HOLO	2.00	5.00
14 Meepit HOLO	2.00	5.00
15 Nereid the Water Faerie HOLO	2.00	5.00
16 One Dubloon Coin HOLO	2.00	5.00
17 Rainbow Pearl HOLO	2.00	5.00
18 Starry Tuskaninny HOLO	2.00	5.00
19 Tears of Caylis HOLO	2.00	5.00
20 Walk the Plank HOLO	2.00	5.00
21 Brown Scorchio R	.30	.75
22 Green Flotsam R	.30	.75
23 Red Krawk R	.30	.75
24 Against the Odds R	.30	.75
25 Angry Giants R	.30	.75
26 Black Pearl R	.30	.75
27 Captain Scarblade R	.30	.75
28 Confusion R	.30	.75
29 Garin the Foolish R	.30	.75
30 Gathow R	.30	.75
31 Island Hasee R	.30	.75
32 Island Negg R	.30	.75
33 King Kelpbeard R	.30	.75
34 Krawk Braggart R	.30	.75
35 Lenny Sorcerer R	.30	.75
36 Lightning Conductor R	.30	.75
37 Maraquan Harp R	.30	.75
38 New Maraqua R	.30	.75
39 Old Maraqua R	.30	.75
40 Petpetpet Swarm R	.30	.75
41 Pollution R	.30	.75
42 Regulation Crossbow R	.30	.75
43 Scorchio Avenger R	.30	.75
44 Screal R	.30	.75
45 Tournament Arena R	.30	.75
46 Trunkard R	.30	.75
47 Whirlpool R	.30	.75
48 White Pearl R	.30	.75
49 Yurble Raider R	.30	.75
50 Zombie Flotsam R	.30	.75
51 Green Scorchio U	.15	.40
52 Yellow Krawk U	.15	.40
53 Yellow Lenny U	.15	.40
54 Apprentice Wand U	.15	.40
55 Benny the Blade U	.15	.40
56 Chomby Genie U	.15	.40
57 Brightvale Castle U	.15	.40
58 Chomby Plushie U	.15	.40
59 Defender of Ador U	.15	.40
60 Florg U	.15	.40
61 Flotsam Hunter U	.15	.40
62 Fyoras Palace Guards U	.15	.40
63 Glowing Babaa U	.15	.40
64 Gnarlas U	.15	.40
65 Gypsys Curse U	.15	.40
66 Jacques the Swift U	.15	.40
67 Jhudoras Bodyguards U	.15	.40
68 Lenny Librarian U	.15	.40
69 Maractite Trident U	.15	.40
70 Mutant Peo U	.15	.40
71 Petrification U	.15	.40
72 Rotten Negg U	.15	.40
73 Scurvy Island U	.15	.40
74 Smite U	.15	.40
75 Smugglers Cove U	.15	.40
76 Swordmaster Talek U	.15	.40
77 Tors Gamble U	.15	.40
78 Tuskaninny Sailor U	.15	.40
79 Underwater Discovery U	.15	.40
80 White Primella U	.15	.40
81 Blue Chomby C	.10	.25
82 Blue Lenny C	.10	.25
83 Blue Yurble C	.10	.25
84 Green Tuskaninny C	.10	.25
85 Green Yurble C	.10	.25
86 Red Flotsam C	.10	.25
87 Red Tuskaninny C	.10	.25
88 Yellow Chomby C	.10	.25
89 Alchemy C	.10	.25
90 Battle of Wits C	.10	.25
91 Blue Cocofizz C	.10	.25
92 Cabbage C	.10	.25
93 Catch! C	.10	.25
94 Chocolate Cybunnies C	.10	.25
95 Coral Bracelet C	.10	.25
96 Coral Fruit C	.10	.25
97 Corrode C	.10	.25
98 Everlasting Porridge C	.10	.25
99 Faerie Tales C	.10	.25
100 Ghoti C	.10	.25
101 Gooseberries C	.10	.25
102 Illusens Faerie Globe C	.10	.25
103 Illusens Potion Book C	.10	.25
104 Iscas Necklace C	.10	.25
105 Juppie Juice C	.10	.25
106 Maractite Armour C	.10	.25
107 Maractite Axe C	.10	.25
108 Maractite Shield C	.10	.25
109 Maractite Sword C	.10	.25

110 Maraquan Jellypops C .10 .25
111 Mazzew C .10 .25
112 Peo C .10 .25
113 Pirate Cutlass C .10 .25
114 Ring of the Deep C .10 .25
115 Sea Anemones C .10 .25
116 Seaweed Omelette C .10 .25
117 Something Will Happen C .10 .25
118 Tribal Headdress C .10 .25
119 Ummagine C .10 .25
120 Water Mote C .10 .25

2005 Neopets Lost Desert

COMPLETE SET (100) 25.00 60.00
BOOSTER BOX ()
BOOSTER PACK ()
RELEASED ON JUNE 10, 2005
1 Baby Jetsam HOLO 2.00 5.00
2 Desert Ruins HOLO 2.00 5.00
3 Faellie HOLO 2.00 5.00
4 Faerie Slorg HOLO 2.00 5.00
5 Fyora Faerie Doll HOLO 2.00 5.00
6 JubJub Performer HOLO 2.00 5.00
7 Lost Desert Paint Brush HOLO 2.00 5.00
8 Moehog Pickpocket HOLO 2.00 5.00
9 Nightsteed HOLO 2.00 5.00
10 Nuria HOLO 2.00 5.00
11 Princess Amira HOLO 2.00 5.00
12 Rainbow Sticky Hand HOLO 2.00 5.00
13 Ruki Patrol HOLO 2.00 5.00
14 Sakhmet City HOLO 2.00 5.00
15 Scamander HOLO 2.00 5.00
16 The Snowager HOLO 2.00 5.00
17 Sophie the Swamp Witch HOLO 2.00 5.00
18 Spotted Kau HOLO 2.00 5.00
19 Tomos HOLO 2.00 5.00
20 Vile Stench of Zal-Bora R .30 .75
21 Yellow Ruki R .30 .75
22 Book of Scarabs R .30 .75
23 Bow of Searing Dawn R .30 .75
24 Everlasting Hiccups R .30 .75
25 Flooding Chamber R .30 .75
26 Forgotten Promise R .30 .75
27 Gebmids R .30 .75
28 Gracklebug R .30 .75
29 Hot Feet R .30 .75
30 JubJub Morphing Potion R .30 .75
31 Nabile R .30 .75
32 Prince Jazan R .30 .75
33 Royal Wedding Ring R .30 .75
34 Ruki Mummy R .30 .75
35 Sakhmet Oasis R .30 .75
36 Sandstorm R .30 .75
37 Scordrax the Furious R .30 .75
38 Swarm of Scamanders R .30 .75
39 Tonu Desert Strider R .30 .75
40 Vanishing City U .15 .40
41 Blue JubJub U .15 .40
42 Blue Tonu U .15 .40
43 Green Jetsam U .15 .40
44 Green Tonu U .15 .40
45 Red Kau U .15 .40
46 Red Moehog U .15 .40
47 Yellow Jetsam U .15 .40
48 Anubis Plushie U .15 .40
49 Bazaar of Wonders U .15 .40
50 Blue Warf U .15 .40
51 Cobrall Dagger U .15 .40
52 Crest of Sakhmet U .15 .40
53 Curse of the Mootix U .15 .40
54 Horace the Poor U .15 .40
55 Jetsam Shark U .15 .40
56 JubJub Bandit U .15 .40
57 Kau Fortune Teller U .15 .40
58 Laziness U .15 .40
59 Megan U .15 .40
60 Moehog Explorer U .15 .40
61 Mummified Negg U .15 .40
62 Plains of Despair U .15 .40
63 Raining Kadoaties U .15 .40
64 Sceptre of Qasala U .15 .40
65 Spirit of the Ruins U .15 .40
66 Stop, Thief! U .15 .40
67 Swarm of Undead U .15 .40
68 Tonu Palace Guard U .15 .40
69 Unsolvable Riddle U .15 .40
70 Wadjet C .10 .25
71 Blue Kau C .10 .25
72 Green Ruki C .10 .25
73 Red JubJub C .10 .25
74 Yellow Moehog C .10 .25
75 Anubis C .10 .25
76 Apis C .10 .25
77 Bagguss C .10 .25
78 Cheery Tomatoes C .10 .25
79 Cursed Strawberries C .10 .25
80 Dead of Night C .10 .25
81 Desert Scimitar C .10 .25
82 Fire Mote C .10 .25
83 Geb C .10 .25
84 Golden Scorchstone C .10 .25
85 Grappling Hook C .10 .25
86 Khonsu C .10 .25
87 Mark of the Scarab C .10 .25
88 Mirage C .10 .25
89 Mutant Bearog C .10 .25
90 Potion of Invisibility C .10 .25
91 Pyramibread C .10 .25
92 Qasalan Tablets C .10 .25
93 Ring of the Lost C .10 .25
94 Ruki Plushie C .10 .25
95 Scorched Negg C .10 .25
96 Spike Trap C .10 .25
97 Tchea Fruit C .10 .25
98 Wheel of Excitement C .10 .25
99 Wheel of Knowledge C .10 .25
100 Yellow Mazzew C .10 .25

2006 Neopets The Haunted Woods

COMPLETE SET (100) 25.00 60.00
RELEASED ON JUNE 18, 2006
1 Aisha Morphing Potion HOLO 2.00 5.00
2 Alien Aisha HOLO 2.00 5.00
3 Archos HOLO 2.00 5.00
4 Baby Cybunny HOLO 2.00 5.00
5 Bruno HOLO 2.00 5.00
6 The Founder HOLO 2.00 5.00
7 Fruity Star Juice HOLO 2.00 5.00
8 Ghost Meepit HOLO 2.00 5.00
9 Ghost Spyder HOLO 2.00 5.00
10 Golden Scratching Post HOLO 2.00 5.00
11 Halloween HOLO 2.00 5.00
12 Ilere of the Woods HOLO 2.00 5.00
13 Illusens Quest HOLO 2.00 5.00
14 Pocket Lab Ray HOLO 2.00 5.00
15 Royal Tonu HOLO 2.00 5.00
16 Sasha the Dancer HOLO 2.00 5.00
17 Sentient Stones HOLO 2.00 5.00
18 Sophie HOLO 2.00 5.00
19 The Taint HOLO 2.00 5.00
20 The Wand of Wishing HOLO 2.00 5.00
21 Anubits R .30 .75
22 Attack Broom R .30 .75
23 Boo! R .30 .75
24 Curing the Plague R .30 .75
25 Dance of the Meepits R .30 .75
26 Evil Trees R .30 .75
27 Lenny Curator R .30 .75
28 Mr. Krawley R .30 .75
29 Rolling Pin R .30 .75
30 Rusty Sloth Clone #11 R .30 .75
31 Shadow Korbat R .30 .75
32 Spotted Tonu R .30 .75
33 Squeezy Spyder R .30 .75
34 Touch of Von Roo R .30 .75
35 Transformation R .30 .75
36 Trick or Treat R .30 .75
37 Werhond R .30 .75
38 Xantan R .30 .75
39 Zombie Acara R .30 .75
40 Zomutt R .30 .75
41 Brown Aisha U .15 .40
42 Pink Cybunny U .15 .40
43 A Tale of Woe U .15 .40
44 Acara Hiker U .15 .40
45 Acara Nurse U .15 .40
46 Air Mote U .15 .40
47 Baby Korbat U .15 .40
48 Bony Grasp U .15 .40
49 Coconut Shy U .15 .40
50 Creeping Shadows U .15 .40
51 Followers of Meow U .15 .40
52 Ghost Lenny U .15 .40
53 Green Warf U .15 .40
54 Grilled Ummagine U .15 .40
55 Gypsy Camp U .15 .40
56 Hall of Heros U .15 .40
57 The Haunted Woods U .15 .40
58 Island Cybunny U .15 .40
59 Krawk Island U .15 .40
60 Mashed Eye Potato U .15 .40
61 Mound of Grulb U .15 .40
62 Mutant Flowper U .15 .40
63 Mutant Hasee U .15 .40
64 Neovia U .15 .40
65 Nova Fruit U .15 .40
66 Reginald U .15 .40
67 Sanity Check U .15 .40
68 Spooky Doughnut U .15 .40
69 Spotted Slorg U .15 .40
70 Ugly Bruno U .15 .40
71 Blue Korbat C .10 .25
72 Brown Cybunny C .10 .25
73 Green Lenny C .10 .25
74 Orange Acara C .10 .25
75 Orange Korbat C .10 .25
76 Red Lenny C .10 .25
77 Red Tonu C .10 .25
78 White Acara C .10 .25
79 White Aisha C .10 .25
80 Yellow Tonu C .10 .25
81 Attack of the Slorgs C .10 .25
82 Blue Babaa C .10 .25
83 Broken Crackers C .10 .25
84 Cybunny Plushie C .10 .25
85 Failed Experiment C .10 .25
86 Familiar C .10 .25
87 Green Meowclops C .10 .25
88 Hide-and-Seek C .10 .25
89 Hissi Oil C .10 .25
90 It Came From Kreludor C .10 .25
91 Light Faerie Doll C .10 .25
92 Noil Gem C .10 .25
93 Pant Devil Sandwich C .10 .25
94 Scary Abandoned Plushie C .10 .25
95 Slymook C .10 .25
96 Test Your Strength C .10 .25
97 Tooth of Goregas C .10 .25
98 Water Faerie Doll C .10 .25
99 Witch's Hat C .10 .25
100 Yellow Snorkle C .10 .25

2006 Neopets Travels in Neopia

COMPLETE SET (200) 60.00 120.00
RELEASED ON MARCH 1, 2006
1 Bag of Neopoints HOLO 1.50 4.00
2 Caylis HOLO 1.50 4.00
3 Cloud Shoyru HOLO 1.50 4.00
4 Darigan Paint Brush HOLO 1.50 4.00
5 Dr. Sloth HOLO 1.50 4.00
6 Eithne HOLO 1.50 4.00
7 Faerie Poogle HOLO 1.50 4.00
8 Faerie Slorg HOLO 1.50 4.00
9 Faerieland HOLO 1.50 4.00
10 Fyora's Wand HOLO 1.50 4.00
11 Hannah the Cursed HOLO 1.50 4.00
12 Hubrid Nox HOLO 1.50 4.00
13 Illusen's Staff HOLO 1.50 4.00
14 Island Angelpuss HOLO 1.50 4.00
15 Island Paint Brush HOLO 1.50 4.00
16 Jhudora HOLO 1.50 4.00
17 Lost Desert Paint Brush HOLO 1.50 4.00
18 Malevolent Sentient Poogle Plushie HOLO 1.50 4.00
19 Maraquan Paint Brush HOLO 1.50 4.00
20 Maraquan Scorchio HOLO 1.50 4.00
21 Meepit HOLO 1.50 4.00
22 Nereid the Water Faerie HOLO 1.50 4.00
23 Nuria HOLO 1.50 4.00
24 Ona HOLO 1.50 4.00
25 Princess Amira HOLO 1.50 4.00
26 Rainbow Paint Brush HOLO 1.50 4.00
27 Sakhmet City HOLO 1.50 4.00
28 Snow Bruce HOLO 1.50 4.00
29 Snow Paint Brush HOLO 1.50 4.00
30 Snowickle HOLO 1.50 4.00
31 Sophie the Swamp Witch HOLO 1.50 4.00
32 Space Faerie HOLO 1.50 4.00
33 Starry Cybunny HOLO 1.50 4.00
34 Starry Paint Brush HOLO 1.50 4.00
35 Taelia the Snow Faerie HOLO 1.50 4.00
36 Tura-Kepek HOLO 1.50 4.00
37 White HOLOasee HOLO 1.50 4.00
38 Ylana Skyfire HOLO 1.50 4.00
39 Zafara Princess HOLO 1.50 4.00
40 Zed Codestone HOLO 1.50 4.00
41 Galactic Green Grundo R .30 .75
42 Green Draik R .30 .75
43 Green Kacheek R .30 .75
44 Red Bori R .30 .75
45 Red Krawk R .30 .75
46 Red Lupe R .30 .75
47 Yellow Kyrii R .30 .75
48 Yellow Meerca R .30 .75
49 Yellow Ruki R .30 .75
50 Acara Treasure Seeker R .30 .75
51 Aisha Shopkeeper R .30 .75
52 Banishment R .30 .75
53 Battle JubJub R .30 .75
54 Blue Sticky Hand R .30 .75
55 Dark Faerie Sisters R .30 .75
56 Eliv Thade R .30 .75
57 Faerie Dust R .30 .75
58 Ghost Korbat R .30 .75
59 Ghost Snowbunny R .30 .75
60 Illusen's Ring R .30 .75
61 Invisible Doglefox R .30 .75
62 Invisible Mynci R .30 .75
63 Ixi Courtier R .30 .75
64 Jeran Plushie R .30 .75
65 Jerdana R .30 .75
66 Jerdana's Orb R .30 .75
67 Jhudora's Storm R .30 .75
68 Kacheek Thief R .30 .75
69 Kreludor R .30 .75
70 Lucky Coin R .30 .75
71 Magic Lottery Ticket R .30 .75
72 Masila R .30 .75
73 New Maraqua R .30 .75
74 Noil R .30 .75
75 Sloth's Master Plan R .30 .75
76 Soup Faerie R .30 .75
77 Space Faerie Circlet R .30 .75
78 Tiki Bomb R .30 .75
79 Vanishing City R .30 .75
80 Xarthab R .30 .75
81 Blue Cybunny U .15 .40
82 Blue Nimmo U .15 .40
83 Blue Skeith U .15 .40
84 Blue Tonu U .15 .40
85 Brown Eyrie U .15 .40
86 Brown Grarrl U .15 .40
87 Green Gelert U .15 .40
88 Green Poogle U .15 .40
89 Green Scorchio U .15 .40
90 Orange Mynci U .15 .40
91 Purple Shoyru U .15 .40
92 Red Kau U .15 .40
93 Red Koi U .15 .40
94 Red Uni U .15 .40
95 Yellow Bruce U .15 .40
96 Yellow Lenny U .15 .40
97 Yellow Pteri U .15 .40
98 Alpine Challenger U .15 .40
99 Apprentice Wand U .15 .40
100 Avalanche U .15 .40
101 Benny the Blade U .15 .40
102 Blue Paint Brush U .15 .40
103 Blumaroo Squire U .15 .40
104 Chomby Plushie U .15 .40
105 Darigan Unii U .15 .40
106 Earth Faerie Leaves U .15 .40
107 Everlasting Apple U .15 .40
108 Faerie Pancakes U .15 .40
109 Gelert Beast Hunter U .15 .40
110 Glowing Babaa U .15 .40
111 Green Paint Brush U .15 .40
112 Grey Faerie U .15 .40
113 Hannah the Usul U .15 .40
114 Illusen's Glade U .15 .40
115 Island Flotsam U .15 .40
116 Kacheek Plushie U .15 .40
117 Kougra Scientist U .15 .40
118 Lower Ice Caves U .15 .40
119 Lupe Defender U .15 .40
120 Lutari Builder U .15 .40
121 Meerca Catapult U .15 .40
122 Moehog Chef U .15 .40
123 Mootix U .15 .40
124 Niptor U .15 .40
125 Pawkeet U .15 .40
126 Quiggle Scout U .15 .40
127 Red Paint Brush U .15 .40
128 Scurvy Island U .15 .40
129 Shadow Hissi U .15 .40
130 Shoyru Plushie U .15 .40
131 Slorg U .15 .40
132 Snowball Cannon U .15 .40
133 Snowball Flurry U .15 .40
134 Starry Negg U .15 .40
135 Trading Post U .15 .40
136 Turmac U .15 .40
137 Warf Rescue Team U .15 .40
138 White Primella U .15 .40
139 Wishing Well U .15 .40
140 Yellow Paint Brush U .15 .40
141 Blue Aisha C .10 .25
142 Blue Blumaroo C .10 .25
143 Blue Kougra C .10 .25
144 Blue Moehog C .10 .25
145 Blue Peophin C .10 .25
146 Blue Wocky C .10 .25
147 Blue Yurble C .10 .25
148 Green Kiko C .10 .25
149 Green Lutari C .10 .25
150 Green Quiggle C .10 .25
151 Green Usul C .10 .25
152 Red Elephante C .10 .25
153 Red Flotsam C .10 .25
154 Red Ixi C .10 .25
155 Red Jetsam C .10 .25
156 Red Tuskaninny C .10 .25
157 Red Zafara C .10 .25
158 Yellow Acara C .10 .25
159 Yellow Buzz C .10 .25
160 Yellow Chomby C .10 .25
161 Yellow Hissi C .10 .25
162 Yellow JubJub C .10 .25
163 Yellow Korbat C .10 .25
164 Yellow Techo C .10 .25
165 Abominable Snowball C .10 .25
166 Anubis C .10 .25
167 Asparagus C .10 .25
168 Babaa C .10 .25
169 Baby Blu C .10 .25
170 Battle Stations C .10 .25
171 Bubble Gun C .10 .25
172 Capture the Snowbunnies C .10 .25
173 Cheesy Pineapple Sticks C .10 .25
174 Coral Bracelet C .10 .25
175 Desert Scimitar C .10 .25
176 Fyora's Blessing C .10 .25
177 Gadgadsbogen C .10 .25
178 Geb C .10 .25
179 Happy Negg C .10 .25
180 Harris C .10 .25
181 Illusen's Charm C .10 .25
182 Island Lei C .10 .25
183 Lab Ray C .10 .25
184 Maractite Shield C .10 .25
185 Mazzew C .10 .25
186 Money Tree Ghosts C .10 .25
187 Pant Devil Attacks C .10 .25
188 Petpetnip C .10 .25
189 Planet Pops C .10 .25
190 Polarchuck C .10 .25
191 Rocket Boots C .10 .25
192 Sceptre of Banishing C .10 .25
193 Something Will Happen C .10 .25
194 Spike Trap C .10 .25
195 Spotted Meowclops C .10 .25
196 Starberry C .10 .25
197 Strawberry Brucicle C .10 .25
198 Tribal Blowgun C .10 .25
199 Wand of Ice C .10 .25
200 Warf Rescue Team C .10 .25

1995 Shadowfist Limited

1 Buro Assassin, Covert Operator C
2 DNA Mage, Occult Scientist C
3 Midnight Whisperer, Abomination C
4 PubOrd Sniper, Cop C
5 Desdemona Deathangel, Abomination R
6 Dr. April Mucosa, Mad Scientist R
7 Homo Omega, Buro Cyborg R
8 Johann Bonengel, BuroPresident R
9 Nirmal Yadav, Supersoldier R
10 Prototype X, Abomination R
11 Tactical Team, Buro Cops R
12 Arcanotechnician, Buro Scientist U
13 Arcanowave Researcher, Scientist U
14 Brain Eater, Abomination U
15 Buro Official, Vile Bureaucrat U
16 Monster Hunter, Timewalker U
17 Mutoid, Abomination U
18 Reconstructed, The, Abomination U
19 Super Soldier, Fanatic Cop U
20 Vivisector, Abomination Scientist U
21 Alpha Beast, Abomination VC
22 PubOrd Officer, Security Cop VC
23 PubOrd Squad, Buro Cops VC
24 Test Subjects, Abominations VC
25 Probability Manipulator R
26 Arcanowave Reinforcer U
27 Reinvigoration Process U
28 Seed of the New Flesh U
29 Abominable Wave C
30 Code Red C
31 Expendable Unit C
32 Imprisoned C
33 Nerve Gas C
34 PubOrd Raid C
35 Superior Technology C
36 Dangerous Experiment R
37 Arcanowave Pulse U
38 Cellular Reinvigoration U
39 Neutron Bomb U
40 Police State U
41 State of Emergency U
42 Abominable Lab C
43 Helix Chewer C
44 Helix Rethread C
45 Brain Bug EQ3200 R
46 Cabinet Minister, Pledged Politician C
47 Gruff Lieutenant, Pledged Cop C
48 Swiss Banker, Pledged Financier C
49 Adrienne Hart, Pledged Martial Artist R
50 Draco, Lodge Enforcer R
51 Mr. X, Lodge Mastermind R
52 Phillipe Benoit, Pledged Assassin R
53 Shell of the Tortoise, Lodge Mastermind R
54 Strike Force, Commandos R
55 Tatsuya Yanai, Lodge Mastermind R
56 Unspoken Name, The, Lodge Chairperson R
57 Vladimir Kovalov, Lodge Mastermind R
58 Web of the Spider, Lodge Mastermind R
59 Church Official, Pledged Operative U
60 Fist of the Bear, Lodge Enforcer U
61 Might of the Elephant, Lodge Enforcer U
62 Military Commandant, Pledged Mastermind U
63 Muckraking Journalist, Pledged Operative U
64 Soul of the Shark, Lodge Mastermind U
65 Sting of the Scorpion, Lodge Assassin U
66 Tooth of the Snake, Lodge Assassin U
67 Undercover Cop, Pledged Operatives U
68 Liquidators, Pledged Enforcers VC
69 Pledged, The, Loyal Initiates VC
70 Student of the Bear, Pledged Martial Artist VC
71 Swat Team, Cop Pawns VC
72 Monkey King U
73 Paper Trail U
74 Political Lock U
75 Tomb of the Beast U
76 Covert Operation C
77 Faked Death C
78 Mole Network C
79 Operation Killdeer C
80 Realpolitik C
81 Bull Market R
82 Roar of the Beast R
83 Suicide Mission R
84 Bite of the Jellyfish U
85 Cry of the Forgotten Ancestor U
86 Hostile Takeover U
87 Subterfuge U
88 Family Estate C
89 Marked for Death C
90 Security C
91 Shadowy Mentor C
92 Seal of the Wheel R
93 Dawn of the Righteous C
94 Healing Earth C
95 Blade Palm U
96 Return to the Center U
97 Alchemist's Lair C
98 Ancient Grove C
99 Armored in Life C
100 Hands Without Shadow C
101 Whirlwind Strike C
102 Death Touch R
103 Shadowfist R
104 Ultimate Mastery R
105 Claw of the Tiger U
106 Contract of the Fox U
107 Dim Mak U
108 Fortune of the Turtle U
109 Chinese Doctor, Wise Physician C
110 Dragon Fighter, Streetfighter C
111 Gadgeteer, Resourceful Techie C
112 Righteous One, Loyal Defender C
113 Capoeira Master, Martial Artist R
114 Iala Mané, Martial Artist R
115 Jack Donovan, Maverick Cop R
116 Johnny Tso, Heroic Gunman R
117 Kar Fai, Kung Fu Master R
118 Mad Dog McCroun, Big Bruiser R
119 Oscar Balbuena, Karate Cop R
120 Redeemed Assassin, Heroic Killer R
121 Shamanistic Lieutenant, Magic Cop R
122 Silver Fist, Cosmopolitan Hero R
123 Zheng Yi Quan, Kung Fu Master R
124 Big Bruiser, Kicker of Butts U
125 Dragon Adept, Versatile Combatant U
126 Masked Avenger, Vigilante Hero U
127 Maverick Cop, Gun-Toting Hero U
128 Old Hermit, Wily Sorcerer U
129 Silver Band, Legion of Supporters U
130 Average Joe, Blue-Collar Hero VC
131 Everyday Hero, Brave Scrapper VC
132 Friends of the Dragon, Dragon Supporters VC
133 Ring Fighter, Martial Artist VC
134 Wind Across Heaven U
135 Back for Seconds C
136 Booby Trap C
137 Final Brawl C
138 Golden Comeback C
139 Last Outpost C
140 Victory for the Underdog C
141 Assassins in Love R
142 Crucible, The R
143 Last Stand R
144 Now You've Made Us Mad U
145 Array of Stunts U
146 Thunder on Thunder U
147 House on the Hill C
148 Training Sequence C
149 Baptism of Fire R
150 Fists of Legend R

151 Bag Full of Guns U
152 Charmed Life U
153 Heroic Conversion U
154 Undercover U
155 Abysmal Horror, Demon C
156 Hopping Vampire, Ancient Monsters C
157 Shadow Creeper, Eunuch Assassin C
158 Walking Corpses, Undead Servitors C
159 White Disciple, Eunuch Sorcerer C
160 Abysmal Daughter, Vampiric Demon R
161 Big Brother Tsien, Demon Hood R
162 Evil Twin, Sinister Sibling R
163 Gao Zhang, Center of the Lotus R
164 Ghostly Seducer, Demon Sorceress R
165 Jueding Shelun, Eunuch Sorcerer R
166 Kan Li, Martial Artist R
167 Mother of Corruption, Demon Queen R
168 Snake Man, Demon R
169 Thing with a 1000 Tongues, Disgusting Demon R
170 Tomb Spirit, Creature R
171 Abysmal Spirit, Ghost Assassin U
172 Gnarled Horror, Demon U
173 Gnarled Marauder, Demon U
174 Imperial Guard, Ancient Cop U
175 Kun Kan, Earth Demon U
176 Walker of the Purple Twilight, Eunuch Sorcerer U
177 Eunuch Underling, Sorcerous Bureaucrat VC
178 Shadowy Horror, Demon VC
179 Sinister Priest, Macabre Sorcerer VC
180 Thorns of the Lotus, Fanatical Archers VC
181 Vassals of the Lotus, Ancient Hoods VC
182 Feast of Souls R
183 Imperial Boon R
184 Chains of Bone U
185 Flood on the Mountain U
186 Dance of the Centipede C
187 Inauspicious Reburial C
188 Tortured Memories C
189 Banish R
190 Shifting Loyalties R
191 Infernal Plague U
192 Infernal Temple C
193 Deathtrap C
194 Demon Within, The C
195 Inexorable Corruption C
196 Sword of Biting C
197 Flying Guillotine R
198 Theft of Fortune R
199 Poison Needles U
200 Sphere of Defilement U
201 Vampiric Touch U
202 Veiling of the Light U
203 City Square, Feng Shui Site R
204 Dragon Mountain, Feng Shui Site R
205 Fox Pass, Feng Shui Site R
206 Hanging Coffins, Feng Shui Site R
207 Kinoshita House, Feng Shui Site R
208 Mourning Tree, Feng Shui Site R
209 Red Lantern Tavern, The, Feng Shui Site R
210 Sacred Heart Hospital, Feng Shui Site R
211 Turtle Beach, Feng Shui Site R
212 Proving Ground, Feng Shui Site U
213 Ancestral Tomb, Feng Shui Site VC
214 Ancient Temple, Feng Shui Site VC
215 Auspicious Termites, Feng Shui Site VC
216 Blessed Orchard, Feng Shui Site VC
217 Cave Network, Feng Shui Site VC
218 Family Home, Feng Shui Site VC
219 Family Restaurant, Feng Shui Site VC
220 Grove of Willows, Feng Shui Site VC
221 Hallowed Earth, Feng Shui Site VC
222 Inner Sanctum, Feng Shui Site VC
223 Jagged Cliffs, Feng Shui Site VC
224 Lily Pond, Feng Shui Site VC
225 Marsh, Feng Shui Site VC
226 Mountain Retreat, Feng Shui Site VC
227 Sacred Ground, Feng Shui Site VC
228 Stone Garden, Feng Shui Site VC
229 Ice Warriors, Netherworld Soldier C
230 Thunder Knights, Netherworld Soldier C
231 King of the Thunder Pagoda, Warlord R
232 Queen of the Ice Pagoda, Mastermind R
233 Gardener, Devoted Follower C
234 Shaolin Warrior, Martial Artist C
235 Chin Ken, Kung Fu Master R
236 Elderly Monk, Sage R
237 Fong Sai Yuk, Martial Artist R
238 Old Master, Kung Fu Master R
239 Quai Li, Spy R
240 Quan Lo, The Perfect Master R
241 Shih Ho Kuai, Martial Arts Master R
242 Sun Chen, Legendary Archer R
243 Tranquil Persuader, Mastermind R
244 Wong Fei Hong, Kung Fu Master R
245 Confucian Sage, Font of Wisdom U
246 General, The, Military Mastermind U
247 Green Monk, Martial Artist U
248 One Hundred Names, Legion of Followers U
249 Orange Monk, Martial Artist U
250 Shaolin Master, Martial Arts Master U
251 Golden Candle Society, Secret Society VC
252 Instrument of the Hand, Martial Artist VC
253 Shaolin Monk, Martial Artist VC
254 Swordsman, Foot Soldier VC
255 Fire in the Lake U
256 Hill of the Turtle U
257 Shifting Tao U
258 Beneficial Realignment C
259 Confucian Stability C
260 Iron and Silk C
261 Mysterious Return C
262 Natural Order C
263 Rigorous Discipline C
264 Difficulty at the Beginning U
265 Into the Light U
266 Onslaught of the Turtle U
267 Positive Chi U
268 Progress of the Mouse U
269 Robust Feng Shui U
270 Shattering Jade U
271 Wind on the Mountain U
272 Shaolin Sanctuary C
273 Power of the Great R
274 Thunder on the Mountain U
275 Orbital Laser Strike C
276 Salvage U
277 Satellite Surveillance U
278 Secret Laboratory C
279 Havoc Suit C
280 Floating Fortress R
281 Combat Aircar U
282 Disintegrator Ray U
283 Fusion Rifle U
284 Fusion Tank U
285 Robot Arm U
286 Dump Warrior, Scavenger / Scrapper C
287 Edge Warrior, Subversive Op C
288 Battlechimp Potemkin, Subversive Leader R
289 $10,000 Man, Jury-Rigged Cyborg U
290 Chromosome Screamer, Escaped Abomination U
291 I Ching R
292 Soul Maze R
293 Spirit Frenzy R
294 Hungry, The U
295 Killing Rain C
296 Shattering Fire C
297 Curtain of Fullness U
298 Larcenous Mist U
299 Scroll of Incantation U
300 Illusory Bridge C
301 Alabaster Javelin U
302 Amulet of the Turtle U
303 Luis Camacho, Vengeful Hood R
304 Nine Cuts, Mercenary Assassin R
305 White Ninja, Assassin R
306 Mysterious Stranger, Netherworld Outcast U
307 Mooks, Mercenary Hoods VC
308 Safehouse R
309 Rackets, The, Hood Edge U
310 Trade Center C
311 Drug Lab, Hood Site R
312 Police Station R
313 Secret Headquarters R
314 Motorcycle C
315 Netherworld Passageway C
316 Really Big Gun C
317 Speed Boat C
318 Sports Car C
319 Water Sword R
320 Attack Helicopter U
321 Explosives U
322 Grenade Launcher U
323 Throwing Star U

1995 Shadowfist Standard

1 Buro Assassin, Covert Operator C
2 DNA Mage, Occult Scientist C
3 Midnight Whisperer, Abomination C
4 PubOrd Sniper, Cop C
5 Desdemona Deathangel, Abomination R
6 Dr. April Mucosa, Mad Scientist R
7 Homo Omega, Buro Cyborg R
8 Johann Bonengel, BuroPresident R
9 Nirmal Yadav, Supersoldier R
10 Prototype X, Abomination R
11 Tactical Team, Buro Cops R
12 Arcanotechnician, Buro Scientist U
13 Arcanowave Researcher, Scientist U
14 Brain Eater, Abomination U
15 Buro Official, Vile Bureaucrat U
16 Monster Hunter, Timewalker U
17 Mutoid, Abomination U
18 Reconstructed, The, Abomination U
19 Super Soldier, Fanatic Cop U
20 Vivisector, Abomination Scientist U
21 Alpha Beast, Abomination VC
22 PubOrd Officer, Security Cop VC
23 PubOrd Squad, Buro Cops VC
24 Test Subjects, Abominations VC
25 Probability Manipulator R
26 Arcanowave Reinforcer U
27 Reinvigoration Process U
28 Seed of the New Flesh U
29 Abominable Wave C
30 Code Red C
31 Expendable Unit C
32 Imprisoned C
33 Nerve Gas C
34 PubOrd Raid C
35 Superior Technology C
36 Dangerous Experiment R
37 Arcanowave Pulse U
38 Cellular Reinvigoration U
39 Neutron Bomb U
40 Police State U
41 State of Emergency U
42 Abominable Lab C
43 Helix Chewer C
44 Helix Rethread C
45 Brain Bug EQ3200 R
46 Cabinet Minister, Pledged Politician C
47 Gruff Lieutenant, Pledged Cop C
48 Swiss Banker, Pledged Financier C
49 Adrienne Hart, Pledged Martial Artist R
50 Draco, Lodge Enforcer R
51 Mr. X, Lodge Mastermind R
52 Phillipe Benoit, Pledged Assassin R
53 Shell of the Tortoise, Lodge Mastermind R
54 Strike Force, Commandos R
55 Tatsuya Yanai, Lodge Mastermind R
56 Unspoken Name, The, Lodge Chairperson R
57 Vladimir Kovalov, Lodge Mastermind R
58 Web of the Spider, Lodge Mastermind R
59 Church Official, Pledged Operative U
60 Fist of the Bear, Lodge Enforcer U
61 Might of the Elephant, Lodge Enforcer U
62 Military Commandant, Pledged Mastermind U
63 Muckraking Journalist, Pledged Operative U
64 Soul of the Shark, Lodge Mastermind U
65 Sting of the Scorpion, Lodge Assassin U
66 Tooth of the Snake, Lodge Assassin U
67 Undercover Cop, Pledged Operatives U
68 Liquidators, Pledged Enforcers VC
69 Pledged, The, Loyal Initiates VC
70 Student of the Bear, Pledged Martial Artist VC
71 Swat Team, Cop Pawns VC
72 Monkey King U
73 Paper Trail U
74 Political Lock U
75 Tomb of the Beast U
76 Covert Operation C
77 Faked Death C
78 Mole Network C
79 Operation Killdeer C
80 Realpolitik C
81 Bull Market R
82 Roar of the Beast R
83 Suicide Mission R
84 Bite of the Jellyfish U
85 Cry of the Forgotten Ancestor U
86 Hostile Takeover U
87 Subterfuge U
88 Family Estate C
89 Marked for Death C
90 Security C
91 Shadowy Mentor C
92 Seal of the Wheel R
93 Dawn of the Righteous C
94 Healing Earth C
95 Blade Palm U
96 Return to the Center U
97 Alchemist's Lair C
98 Ancient Grove C
99 Armored in Life C
100 Hands Without Shadow C
101 Whirlwind Strike C
102 Death Touch R
103 Shadowfist R
104 Ultimate Mastery R
105 Claw of the Tiger U
106 Contract of the Fox U
107 Dim Mak U
108 Fortune of the Turtle U
109 Chinese Doctor, Wise Physician C
110 Dragon Fighter, Streetfighter C
111 Gadgeteer, Resourceful Techie C
112 Righteous One, Loyal Defender C
113 Capoeira Master, Martial Artist R
114 Iala Mané, Martial Artist R
115 Jack Donovan, Maverick Cop R
116 Johnny Tso, Heroic Gunman R
117 Kar Fai, Kung Fu Master R
118 Mad Dog McCroun, Big Bruiser R
119 Oscar Balbuena, Karate Cop R
120 Redeemed Assassin, Heroic Killer R
121 Shamanistic Lieutenant, Magic Cop R
122 Silver Fist, Cosmopolitan Hero R
123 Zheng Yi Quan, Kung Fu Master R
124 Big Bruiser, Kicker of Butts U
125 Dragon Adept, Versatile Combatant U
126 Masked Avenger, Vigilante Hero U
127 Maverick Cop, Gun-Toting Hero U
128 Old Hermit, Wily Sorcerer U
129 Silver Band, Legion of Supporters U
130 Average Joe, Blue-Collar Hero VC
131 Everyday Hero, Brave Scrapper VC
132 Friends of the Dragon, Dragon Supporters VC
133 Ring Fighter, Martial Artist VC
134 Wind Across Heaven U
135 Back for Seconds C
136 Booby Trap C
137 Final Brawl C
138 Golden Comeback C
139 Last Outpost C
140 Victory for the Underdog C
141 Assassins in Love R
142 Crucible, The R
143 Last Stand R
144 Now You've Made Us Mad U
145 Array of Stunts U
146 Thunder on Thunder U
147 House on the Hill C
148 Training Sequence C
149 Baptism of Fire R
150 Fists of Legend R
151 Bag Full of Guns U
152 Charmed Life U
153 Heroic Conversion U
154 Undercover U
155 Abysmal Horror, Demon C
156 Hopping Vampire, Ancient Monsters C
157 Shadow Creeper, Eunuch Assassin C
158 Walking Corpses, Undead Servitors C
159 White Disciple, Eunuch Sorcerer C
160 Abysmal Daughter, Vampiric Demon R
161 Big Brother Tsien, Demon Hood R
162 Evil Twin, Sinister Sibling R
163 Gao Zhang, Center of the Lotus R
164 Ghostly Seducer, Demon Sorceress R
165 Jueding Shelun, Eunuch Sorcerer R
166 Kan Li, Martial Artist R
167 Mother of Corruption, Demon Queen R
168 Snake Man, Demon R
169 Thing with a 1000 Tongues, Disgusting Demon R
170 Tomb Spirit, Creature R
171 Abysmal Spirit, Ghost Assassin U
172 Gnarled Horror, Demon U
173 Gnarled Marauder, Demon U
174 Imperial Guard, Ancient Cop U
175 Kun Kan, Earth Demon U
176 Walker of the Purple Twilight, Eunuch Sorcerer U
177 Eunuch Underling, Sorcerous Bureaucrat VC
178 Shadowy Horror, Demon VC
179 Sinister Priest, Macabre Sorcerer VC
180 Thorns of the Lotus, Fanatical Archers VC
181 Vassals of the Lotus, Ancient Hoods VC
182 Feast of Souls R
183 Imperial Boon R
184 Chains of Bone U
185 Flood on the Mountain U
186 Dance of the Centipede C
187 Inauspicious Reburial C
188 Tortured Memories C
189 Banish R
190 Shifting Loyalties R
191 Infernal Plague U
192 Infernal Temple C
193 Deathtrap C
194 Demon Within, The C
195 Inexorable Corruption C
196 Sword of Biting C
197 Flying Guillotine R
198 Theft of Fortune R
199 Poison Needles U
200 Sphere of Defilement U
201 Vampiric Touch U
202 Veiling of the Light U
203 City Square, Feng Shui Site R
204 Dragon Mountain, Feng Shui Site R
205 Fox Pass, Feng Shui Site R
206 Hanging Coffins, Feng Shui Site R
207 Kinoshita House, Feng Shui Site R
208 Mourning Tree, Feng Shui Site R
209 Red Lantern Tavern, The, Feng Shui Site R
210 Sacred Heart Hospital, Feng Shui Site R
211 Turtle Beach, Feng Shui Site R
212 Proving Ground, Feng Shui Site U
213 Ancestral Tomb, Feng Shui Site VC
214 Ancient Temple, Feng Shui Site VC
215 Auspicious Termites, Feng Shui Site VC
216 Blessed Orchard, Feng Shui Site VC
217 Cave Network, Feng Shui Site VC
218 Family Home, Feng Shui Site VC
219 Family Restaurant, Feng Shui Site VC
220 Grove of Willows, Feng Shui Site VC
221 Hallowed Earth, Feng Shui Site VC
222 Inner Sanctum, Feng Shui Site VC
223 Jagged Cliffs, Feng Shui Site VC
224 Lily Pond, Feng Shui Site VC
225 Marsh, Feng Shui Site VC
226 Mountain Retreat, Feng Shui Site VC
227 Sacred Ground, Feng Shui Site VC
228 Stone Garden, Feng Shui Site VC
229 Ice Warriors, Netherworld Soldier C
230 Thunder Knights, Netherworld Soldier C
231 King of the Thunder Pagoda, Warlord R
232 Queen of the Ice Pagoda, Mastermind R
233 Gardener, Devoted Follower C
234 Shaolin Warrior, Martial Artist C
235 Chin Ken, Kung Fu Master R
236 Elderly Monk, Sage R
237 Fong Sai Yuk, Martial Artist R
238 Old Master, Kung Fu Master R
239 Quai Li, Spy R
240 Quan Lo, The Perfect Master R
241 Shih Ho Kuai, Martial Arts Master R
242 Sun Chen, Legendary Archer R
243 Tranquil Persuader, Mastermind R
244 Wong Fei Hong, Kung Fu Master R
245 Confucian Sage, Font of Wisdom U
246 General, The, Military Mastermind U
247 Green Monk, Martial Artist U
248 One Hundred Names, Legion of Followers U
249 Orange Monk, Martial Artist U
250 Shaolin Master, Martial Arts Master U
251 Golden Candle Society, Secret Society VC
252 Instrument of the Hand, Martial Artist VC
253 Shaolin Monk, Martial Artist VC
254 Swordsman, Foot Soldier VC
255 Fire in the Lake U
256 Hill of the Turtle U
257 Shifting Tao U
258 Beneficial Realignment C
259 Confucian Stability C
260 Iron and Silk C
261 Mysterious Return C
262 Natural Order C
263 Rigorous Discipline C
264 Difficulty at the Beginning U
265 Into the Light U
266 Onslaught of the Turtle U
267 Positive Chi U
268 Progress of the Mouse U
269 Robust Feng Shui U
270 Shattering Jade U
271 Wind on the Mountain U
272 Shaolin Sanctuary C
273 Power of the Great R
274 Thunder on the Mountain U
275 Orbital Laser Strike C
276 Salvage U
277 Satellite Surveillance U
278 Secret Laboratory C
279 Havoc Suit C
280 Floating Fortress R
281 Combat Aircar U
282 Disintegrator Ray U
283 Fusion Rifle U
284 Fusion Tank U
285 Robot Arm U
286 Dump Warrior, Scavenger / Scrapper C
287 Edge Warrior, Subversive Op C
288 Battlechimp Potemkin, Subversive Leader R
289 $10,000 Man, Jury-Rigged Cyborg U
290 Chromosome Screamer, Escaped Abomination U
291 I Ching R
292 Soul Maze R
293 Spirit Frenzy R
294 Hungry, The U
295 Killing Rain C
296 Shattering Fire C
297 Curtain of Fullness U
298 Larcenous Mist U
299 Scroll of Incantation U
300 Illusory Bridge C
301 Alabaster Javelin U
302 Amulet of the Turtle U
303 Luis Camacho, Vengeful Hood R
304 Nine Cuts, Mercenary Assassin R
305 White Ninja, Assassin R
306 Mysterious Stranger, Netherworld Outcast U
307 Mooks, Mercenary Hoods VC
308 Safehouse R
309 Rackets, The, Hood Edge U
310 Trade Center C
311 Drug Lab, Hood Site R
312 Police Station R
313 Secret Headquarters R
314 Motorcycle C
315 Netherworld Passageway C
316 Really Big Gun C
317 Speed Boat C
318 Sports Car C
319 Water Sword R
320 Attack Helicopter U
321 Explosives U
322 Grenade Launcher U
323 Throwing Star U

1996 Shadowfist Flashpoint

1 BuroMil Elite, Perfect Soldiers C
2 BuroMil Grunt, Brutal Soldier C
3 BuroMil Ninja, Shadowy Assassin C
4 Encephalon Screamer, Abomination C
5 Plasma Trooper, BuroMil Cyborg C
6 Pod Trooper, Abomination in a Can C
7 Colonel Griffith, BuroMil Mastermind R
8 Dunwa Saleem, Lodge Traitor R
9 Genghis X, BuroMil Supersoldier R
10 Rhys Engel, Purist Mastermind R
11 Drop Troopers, BuroMil Cyborgs U
12 Purist, Buro Sorcerer U
13 Spawn of the New Flesh, Unstable Abomination U
14 Paradox Cube U
15 Scorched Earth U
16 Napalm Sunrise C
17 Bzzzzt! U
18 Disinformation Packet U
19 Total War U
20 Creche of the New Flesh, Feng Shui Site C
21 Arcanotower 2056 R
22 Arcanotower Now R
23 Arcanoseed, Battleground Site U
24 Buro Godhammer C
25 Arcanostriker U
26 Arcanotank U
27 Arcanoworms U
28 Resistance is Futile! U
29 Mountain Warrior, Pledged Survivor C
30 Student of the Shark, Pledged Hood C
31 Mr. Big, Hood Mastermind R
32 Sam Mallory, Lodge Killer R
33 Bad Colonel, Pledged Hood Warlord U
34 Just a Rat, Lodge Survivor U
35 Leatherback, Lodge Survivor U
36 Open Season U
37 Lodge Politics C
38 We Know Where You Live U
39 Dark's Soft Whisper U
40 Invincible Chi U
41 Wing of the Crane U
42 Drunken Stance C
43 Flying Windmill Kick C
44 Fortuitous Chi C
45 Rain of Fury U
46 Ex-Commando, Dangerous Vet C
47 Gonzo Journalist, Crazed Reporter C
48 Hacker, Gun-Totin' Techie C
49 Jane Q. Public, Girl Next Door C
50 Redeemed Gunman, Reforming Hood C
51 Stunt Man, Gutsy Hombre C
52 Joey Paz, Escrima Master R
53 Johnny Badhair, Wild Man R
54 Little Jim, Rebel Abomination R
55 Melissa Aguelera, Commando Vet R
56 Silver Jet, Secret Warrior R
57 Coffee-Stained Cop, Wily Veteran U
58 Grease Monkey, Gutsy Mechanic U
59 Scrappy Kid, Martial Arts Prodigy U
60 Carnival of Carnage C
61 Dirk Wisely's Gambit C
62 Fighting Spirit C
63 Old Hermit's Gambit C
64 Slo Mo Vengeance C
65 Ting Ting's Gambit C
66 Who's the Big Man Now?! C
67 Let's Book! U
68 Kar Fai's Crib R
69 Both Guns Blazing C
70 Claw of the Dragon C
71 Comrades in Arms C
72 Stolen Police Car C
73 Bloody Horde, Demon Trouble C
74 Claw of Fury, Shadowy Assassin C
75 Vile Prodigy, Infant Demon C
76 Destroyer, Demon Martial Artist U
77 Gibbering Horror, Disgusting Demon U

78 Purist Sorcerer, Buro Infiltrator U
79 Underworld Presence U
80 Cyclone of Knives U
81 Glimpse of the Abyss U
82 Registry of the Damned U
83 Birdhouse Cafe, Feng Shui Site C
84 City Park, Feng Shui Site C
85 Curio Shop, Feng Shui Site C
86 Heart of the Rainforest, Feng Shui Site C
87 Hidden Sanctuary, Feng Shui Site C
88 Night Market, Feng Shui Site C
89 Peacock Summit, Feng Shui Site C
90 Rainforest Grove, Feng Shui Site C
91 Rainforest Temple, Feng Shui Site C
92 Sampan Village, Feng Shui Site C
93 Turtle Island, Feng Shui Site C
94 Rainforest River, Feng Shui Site U
95 Thunder Champion, Netherworld Commandant U
96 Spirit Pole U
97 Fire Sled, Netherworld State C
98 Kung Fu Student, Fledgling Shaolin C
99 Righteous Fist, Martial Artist C
100 Shan Tsu, Shaolin Master R
101 Xiaoyang Yun, Spy Mastermind R
102 Cop on Vacation, Martial Artist U
103 Red Monk, Martial Artist U
104 Virtuous Hood, Martial Artist U
105 Wandering Monk, Martial Artist U
106 Blood of the Valiant C
107 Orange Meditation C
108 Shaolin Surprise C
109 Laughter of the Wind U
110 Smart Missile C
111 CAT Tactics U
112 Doomsday Device U
113 Supercomputer U
114 Tank Warfare U
115 Satellite Intelligence U
116 Hover Tank C
117 MegaTank U
118 Chimpanzer, Cyborg Monkey Tank C
119 Dallas Rocket, Fanatic Guerilla C
120 Just Another Consumer, Scrappy Rebel C
121 Portal Jockey, Redeemed Timewalker C
122 Rocket Scientist, Techie Guerrilla C
123 Gorilla Fighter, Flying Monkey U
124 Trust Me, I've Got a Plan C
125 In Your Face Again C
126 Monkeywrenching C
127 Nuked C
128 Too Much Monkey Business C
129 Hosed U
130 Underground, The U
131 Homemade Tank U
132 Anomaly Spirit, Sorcerous Construct U
133 Mirror Dancer, Netherworld Spirit U
134 Memory Reprocessing U
135 Year of the Rat U
136 Alchemist's Lair C
137 Cheap Punks, Mercenary Hoods C
138 Yakuza Enforcer, Killer Hood C
139 White Ninja, Assassin R
140 Art of War U
141 Killing Ground, Battleground Site C
142 Sniper Nest, Battleground Site C
143 Forty-Story Inferno, Battleground Site U
144 Home Front, The, Battleground Site U
145 Portal in Tower Square, Battleground Site U
146 Pump-Action Shotgun C

1996 Shadowfist Netherworld

1 Capture Squad, Monster Hunters C
2 CHAR, BuroMil Cyborg C
3 Flying Bladder, Netherworld Abomination C
4 Gnarled Attuner, Abomination R
5 Sergeant Blightman, Mutating Soldier R
6 Brain Sucker, Abomination VC
7 Chi Sucker, Netherworld Abomination VC
8 Foul Hatchling, Abomination VC
9 Undercover Agent, Buro Operative VC
10 Biomass Reprocessing Center, Netherworld Site C
11 Agony Grenade C
12 Sucker Rounds C
13 Blade Freak, Mercenary C
14 Triumvirate Dealmaker, Pledged Mastermind C
15 Death Shadow, Mercenary R
16 Reverend RedGlare, Mercenary R
17 Shinobu Yashida, Pledged Master R
18 Soul of the Dragon, Triumvirate Edge C
19 Operation Green Strike C
20 Violet Meditation VC
21 Fox Outfoxed, The U
22 Bao Chou, Avenging Ghost R
23 Golden Gunman, The, Magic Hero R
24 Jason X, Supersoldier R
25 Marisol, Netherworld Mercenary R
26 Prof, The, Mastermind R
27 Serena Ku, Vengeful Hero R
28 Ting Ting, Martial Artist R
29 Bronze Sentinel, Automation VC
30 Netherworld Vet, Portal Crawler VC
31 Flying Kick VC
32 Kiii-YAAAH! VC
33 Surprise, Surprise VC
34 Repulsor Beams C
35 Abysmal Absorber, Netherworld Demon C
36 Abysmal Deceiver, Infiltrator C
37 Abysmal Prince, Demon Bureaucrat Mastermind C
38 Ghost Assassin, Deadly Spirit C
39 Jueding Bao-Fude, Eunuch Sorcerer R
40 Sung Hi, Demon Buro Infiltrator R
41 Tanbi Guiawu, Giant Demon R
42 Wu Ta-Hsi, Eunuch Pledged Infiltrator R
43 Xiu Xie Jiang, Triumvirate Infiltrator R
44 Doomed Lackey, Eunuch Pawn VC
45 Necromantic Conspiracy C
46 Guiyu Zui, Netherworld Demon Site R
47 Locksley Station, Netherworld Feng Shui Site R
48 Ancestral Sanctuary, Netherworld Feng Shui Site U
49 Monkey House, Netherworld Feng Shui Site U
50 Festival Circle, Feng Shui Site VC
51 Field of Tentacles, Netherworld Feng Shui Site VC
52 Fortress of Shadow, Feng Shui Site VC
53 Garden of Bronze, Netherworld Feng Shui Site VC
54 House of Mirrors, Netherworld Feng Shui Site VC
55 Perpetual Motion Machine, Netherworld Feng Shui Site VC
56 Pinball Hall, Netherworld Feng Shui Site VC
57 Ring of Gates, Netherworld Feng Shui Site VC
58 Rust Garden, Netherworld Feng Shui Site VC
59 Wall of a Thousand Eyes, Netherworld Feng Shui Site VC
60 Whirlpool of Blood, Netherworld Feng Shui Site VC
61 Fire Assassin, Netherworld Killer C
62 Fire Martyr, Assassin C
63 Ice Courtier, Sorceress C
64 Ice Shards, Elite Bodyguards R
65 King of the Fire Pagoda, Mastermind R
66 Lord Shi, Netherworld Warrior R
67 Queen of the Darkness Pagoda, Netherworld Mastermind R
68 Butterfly Knight, Thunder Warrior VC
69 Darkness Priestess, Sorceress VC
70 Fire Warriors, Soldiers VC
71 Ice Falcons, Netherworld Spirits VC
72 Ice Healer, Sorceress VC
73 Ice Tiger, Netherworld Spirits VC
74 Soul Diver, Ice Shaman VC
75 Thunder Squire, Netherworld Warrior VC
76 Blanket of Darkness, Netherworld Edge R
77 Counterfeit Heart, Triumvirate Edge R
78 Molten Heart, Triumvirate Edge R
79 Avenging Thunder C
80 Netherworld Return U
81 Sibling Rivalry U
82 Brain Fire VC
83 Mark of Fire VC
84 Darkness Pagoda, Netherworld Site R
85 Fire and Darkness Pavilion, Triumvirate Site R
86 Fire Pagoda R
87 Ice Pagoda, Netherworld Site R
88 Thunder Pagoda, Netherworld Site R
89 Claws of Darkness, Triumvirate State C
90 Enchanted Sword C
91 Flying Crescent C
92 Ice Diadem C
93 Shields of Darkness, Triumvirate State C
94 Thunder Sword R
95 Violet Monk, Martial Artist C
96 Yellow Monk, Martial Artist C
97 Shield of Pure Soul C
98 Heat of Battle VC
99 Storm of the Just VC
100 Green Senshi Chamber, Netherworld Site R
101 Orange Senshi Chamber, Netherworld Site R
102 White Senshi Chamber, Netherworld Site R
103 Yellow Senshi Chamber, Netherworld Site R
104 RedGlare Chapel, Netherworld Site R
105 Desire Manipulator C
106 IKTV Rebroadcast Link, Netherworld State C
107 Gunrunner, Netherworld Hood C
108 Furious George, Flying Monkey R
109 Jamal Hopkins, Mastermind R
110 Orango Tank, Ground-Assault Monkey R
111 Rah Rah Rasputine, Netherworld Cyborg R
112 Gearhead, Saboteur U
113 Demolitions Expert, Rebel Supporter VC
114 Grenade Posse, Netherworld Punks VC
115 Mad Bomber, Netherworld Nutcase VC
116 Resistance Squad, Techie Guerrillas VC
117 Tunnel Ganger, Netherworld Hood VC
118 Burn, Baby, Burn! C
119 Entropy Is Your Friend C
120 Gorilla Warfare, Triumvirate Edge R
121 Death-O-Rama VC
122 New Manifesto VC
123 Chimp Shack VC
124 Tick... Tick... Tick... C
125 Eugene Fo, Sorcerous Hood R
126 Discerning Fire VC
127 Pocket Demon VC
128 Jimmy Wai, Mastermind R
129 Ze Botelho, Lodge Outcast R
130 Dark Traveler, Netherworld Hero VC
131 Displaced, The, Netherworld Rabble VC
132 Faceless, The, Netherworld Rabble VC
133 Losers, The, Netherworld Rabble VC
134 Elevator to the Netherworld R

2000 Shadowfist Throne War

1 Andrea Van de Graaf, Purist Sorceress R
2 Dr. Celeste Carter, Purist Assassin R
3 Oliver Chen, Pledged Saboteur R
4 The Blue Cardinal's Guards, Mercenary Timewalkers U
5 Time Bandits, Netherworld Mercenary Hoods U
6 Competitive Intelligence C
7 Ulterior Motives C
8 Violet Meditation v2 C
9 Flying Sword Stance C
10 Twin Thunder Kick U
11 Dr. John Haynes, Full-Contact Historian R
12 Kar Fai, Kung Fu Master R
13 Final Sacrifice C
14 Open a Can of Whupass Promo
15 Who Wants Some? U
16 Earth Poisoner, Eunuch Geomancer C
17 Elite Guards, Competent Pawns C
18 Palace Guards, Hopeless Pawns C
19 Demon Emperor, Wicked Impersonator R
20 Gao Zhang vPAP, Eunuch Mastermind R
21 Mad Monk, Shaolin Traitor R
22 Seven Evils, Demon Lord R
23 Shi Zi Hu, Eunuch General R
24 The Emperor, Imperial Pawn R
25 Xin Kai Sheng, Sorcerer Emperor Mastermind R
26 Eater of Fortune, Hungry Demon U
27 Evil Twin v2, Sinister Sibling U
28 Two Hundred Knives of Pain, Dangerous Demon U
29 Underworld Tracker, Demon Cop U
30 Flying Sleeves C
31 Inauspicious Return C
32 Die!!! U
33 Infernal Pact U
34 Hall of Brilliance, Feng Shui Site R
35 Imperial Palace R
36 The Dragon Throne U
37 Sinister Accusations U
38 Eagle Mountain, Feng Shui Site C
39 Grizzly Pass, Feng Shui Site C
40 Möbius Gardens, Feng Shui Site C
41 Petroglyphs, Feng Shui Site C
42 Puzzle Garden, Feng Shui Site C
43 Smiling Heaven Lake, Feng Shui Site C
44 Whirlpool of Blood, Netherworld Feng Shui Site C
45 Desolate Ridge, Feng Shui Site U
46 Temple of the Angry Spirits, Feng Shui Site U
47 Darkness Priestess v2, Netherworld Sorceress C
48 Once and Future Champion, Netherworld Hero Promo
49 Blade of Darkness, Netherworld Killer U
50 Darkness Adept, Vicious Sorceress U
51 Obsidian Eye U
52 Black Flag Rebels, Grim Supporters C
53 Righteous Protector, Heroic Monk C
54 Leung Mui, The Black Flag R
55 True Son of Heaven, Shaolin Emperor R
56 Blue Monk, Kung Fu Infiltrator U
57 Wandering Teacher, Shaolin Agent U
58 For China! U
59 Festival of Giants C
60 Peasant Uprising C
61 Cave of a Thousand Banners, Feng Shui Site U
62 Just Another Consumer, Scrappy Rebel C
63 Resistance Squad, Techie Guerrillas C
64 Ba-BOOM!, Unstable Monkey R
65 The Monkey Who Would Be King, Guerrilla Emperor R
66 Titanium Johnson, Cyborg Bruiser R
67 Apes of Wrath, Ornery Monkeys U
68 Napalm Addict, Pyromaniac Anarchist U
69 Payback Time U
70 Scrounging C
71 Weird Science U
72 Who's the Monkey Now? U
73 Discerning Fire C
74 Farseeing Rice Grains C
75 Pocket Demon v2 C
76 Shattering Fire C
77 Sword of the Dragon King U
78 Hsiung-nu Mercenaries, Hired Killers C
79 White Ninja vPAP, Assassin Promo
80 Jui Szu, Outmaneuvered Empress R
81 Bandit Chief, Hood Scum U
82 Bandit Hideout, Battleground Site U
83 Rebel Camp U

2000 Shadowfist Year of the Dragon

1 CDCA Scientist, Overzealous Researcher
2 CHAR, BuroMil Cyborg
3 Homo Omega vPAP, Buro Cyborg
4 Plasma Trooper, BuroMil Cyborg
5 Prototype X, Abomination
6 PubOrd Officer, Security Cop
7 Test Subjects, Abominations
8 Vivisector v2, Abomination Scientist
9 Arcanowave Reinforcer
10 Dangerous Experiment v2
11 Nerve Gas
12 Neutron Bomb
13 Abominable Lab
14 Buro Godhammer
15 Helix Chewer
16 Helix Rethread
17 Draco vPAP, Lodge Enforcer
18 Rat Fink, Lodge Infiltrator
19 Sam Mallory, Lodge Killer
20 Sting of the Scorpion vPAP, Lodge Assassin
21 Student of the Bear, Pledged Martial Artist
22 Student of the Shark, Pledged Hood
23 The Pledged, Loyal Initiates
24 Paper Trail
25 Bull Market
26 Covert Operation v2
27 Mole Network v2
28 Operation Killdeer
29 Suicide Mission
30 Family Estate
31 Shadowy Mentor
32 Blade Palm
33 Violet Meditation v2
34 Hands Without Shadow v2
35 Shadowfist
36 Bronze Sentinel, Righteous Automaton
37 Friends of the Dragon v2, Student Supporters
38 Hacker, Gun-Totin' Techie
39 Jane Q. Public, Girl Next Door
40 Little Jim, Rebel Abomination
41 Maverick Cop, Gun-Toting Hero
42 Netherworld Vet, Portal Crawler
43 Redeemed Gunman, Reforming Hood
44 Ting Ting, Martial Artist
45 Tricia Kwok, Undercover Cop
46 Dirk Wisely's Gambit
47 Final Brawl
48 Golden Comeback
49 Surprise, Surprise
50 House on the Hill
51 Claw of the Dragon
52 Abysmal Absorber, Netherworld Demon
53 Eunuch Underling v2, Sorcerer Bureaucrat
54 Evil Twin v2, Sinister Sibling
55 Four Burning Fists, Demon Martial Artist
56 Kun Kan, Earth Demon
57 Sinister Priest, Macabre Sorcerer
58 Thing with a 1000 Tongues, Disgusting Demon
59 Vassals of the Lotus, Ancient Hoods
60 Walking Corpses, Undead Servitors
61 White Disciple, Eunuch Sorcerer
62 Glimpse of the Abyss
63 Tortured Memories
64 Internal Temple v2
65 Inexorable Corruption
66 Birdhouse Cafe, Feng Shui Site
67 Blessed Orchard, Feng Shui Site
68 Cave Network, Feng Shui Site
69 City Park, Feng Shui Site
70 City Square, Feng Shui Site
71 Curio Shop, Feng Shui Site
72 Festival Circle, Feng Shui Site
73 Field of Tentacles, Netherworld Feng Shui Site
74 Floating Restaurant, Feng Shui Site
75 Fox Pass v2, Feng Shui Site
76 Gambling House, Feng Shui Site
77 Inner Sanctum, Feng Shui Site
78 Jade Valley, Feng Shui Site
79 Jagged Cliffs, Feng Shui Site
80 Kinoshita House v2, Feng Shui Site
81 Nine Dragon Temple, Feng Shui Site
82 Perpetual Motion Machine, Netherworld Feng Shui Site
83 Sacred Heart Hospital, Feng Shui Site
84 Stone Garden, Feng Shui Site
85 Turtle Beach, Feng Shui Site
86 Blue Monk, Kung Fu Infiltrator
87 Gardener, Devoted Follower
88 Golden Candle Society, Secret Society
89 Kung Fu Student, Fledgling Shaolin
90 Red Monk v2, Martial Artist
91 Righteous Fist, Martial Artist
92 Shan Tsu, Shaolin Master
93 The Iron Monkey, Masked Hero
94 Wong Fei Hong vPAP, Kung Fu Master
95 Shield of Pure Soul
96 Blood of the Valiant
97 Confucian Stability
98 Iron and Silk
99 Rigorous Discipline v2
100 Shaolin Sanctuary
101 Satellite Intelligence
102 Robot Arm
103 The Hungry v2
104 Discerning Fire
105 Pocket Demon v2
106 Shattering Fire
107 Amulet of the Turtle v2
108 Secret Headquarters
109 Explosives v2
110 Pump-Action Shotgun v2

2001 Shadowfist Netherworld II Back Through the Portals

1 Arcanorat, Hideous Monster C
2 DNA Mage, Occult Scientist C
3 Midnight Whisperer, Abomination C
4 Colonel Griffith, BuroMil Mastermind R
5 Colonel Richtmeyer, BuroMil Intelligence Officer R
6 Dr. Ally Matthews, Brilliant Scientist R
7 Dr. Curtis Boatman, CDCA Scientist Mastermind R
8 Jeroen Becker, Purist Mastermind R
9 Paradox Beast, Purist Prototype Construct R
10 Simon Draskovic, Cyborg Monster Hunter R
11 Arcanotechnician, Buro Scientist U
12 Conversion Drone, Arcanowave Robot U
13 Swarm of Teeth, Abomination Horde U
14 Expendable Unit C
15 Imprisoned C
16 Biomass Reprocessing Center, Netherworld Site R
17 Helix Scrambler C
18 Ninja Interior Decorators, Hood Geomancers C
19 Swiss Banker, Pledged Financier C
20 The Eastern King, Lodge Mastermind Promo
21 Mr. Red, Backstabbing Bastard R
22 Raven Li, Lodge Troubleshooter R
23 Military Commandant, Pledged Mastermind U
24 Bounty, Killer Edge U
25 Playing Both Ends C
26 Bite of the Jellyfish U
27 Cutting Loose Ends U
28 Pulling Strings U
29 The Hub, Netherworld Site R
30 Hiro Asataka, Ninja Hacker R
31 Suong Xa, Netherworld Hero R
32 The Golden Gunman, Magic Hero R
33 The Prof, Netherworld Mastermind R
34 Wu Ming Yi, Repentant Demon R
35 The New Heroes U
36 Back for Seconds C
37 Going Out in Style U
38 That Which Does Not Kill Me... U
39 The Prof's Gambit U
40 Thunder on Thunder U
41 Ravenous Devourer, Hungry Demon C
42 Je Pai, Seductive Ghost Sorceress R
43 The Bound, Netherworld Horror R
44 The Burning King, Demon Lord R
45 The Strangled Scream, Netherworld Horror R
46 Purist Sorcerer, Buro Infiltrator U
47 Inauspicious Reburial C
48 The Twisted Gardens, Netherworld Demon Site U
49 Hall of Portals, Netherworld Feng Shui Site C
50 Maze of Stairs, Netherworld Feng Shui Site C
51 Obsidian Mountain, Feng Shui Site C
52 Ominous Swamp, Netherworld Feng Shui Site C
53 Ring of Gates, Netherworld Feng Shui Site C
54 Waterfall Sanctuary, Feng Shui Site C
55 Monkey House, Netherworld Feng Shui Site U
56 Phlogiston Mine, Netherworld Feng Shui Site U
57 Proving Ground, Feng Shui Site U
58 Sunless Sea Ruins, Netherworld Feng Shui Site U
59 Tangram Alley, Netherworld Feng Shui Site U
60 Butterfly Knight, Thunder Warrior C
61 Darkness Warriors, Netherworld Soldiers C
62 Fire Acolytes, Netherworld Disciples C
63 Fire Warriors, Netherworld Soldiers C
64 Ice Commandos, Elite Strike Force C
65 Ice Healer, Netherworld Sorceress C
66 Ice Warriors, Netherworld Soldiers C
67 Palm of Darkness, Netherworld Ninja C
68 Skin and Darkness Ravagers, Netherworld Horrors C
69 Thunder Initiate, Netherworld Sorcerer C
70 Thunder Knights, Netherworld Soldiers C
71 Thunder Squire, Netherworld Warrior C
72 Atourina Baktiari, Fire Mastermind R
73 Chiu Fa, Fire Sorcerer R
74 General Fung, Darkness Warrior R
75 King of the Fire Pagoda, Netherworld Mastermind R
76 King of the Thunder Pagoda, Netherworld Warlord R
77 Lucius Centares, Thunder Champion R
78 Once and Future Champion, Netherworld Hero R
79 Queen of the Darkness Pagoda, Netherworld Mastermind R
80 Queen of the Ice Pagoda, Netherworld Mastermind R
81 The Baron, Masked Avenger R
82 Fire Constructs, Netherworld Automatons U
83 Storm Riders, Thunder Warriors U
84 Thunder Champion, Netherworld Commandant U
85 Thunder Valkyries, Warrior Maidens U
86 Fanaticism U
87 Feeding the Fires U
88 Spirit Pole U
89 Blood and Thunder C
90 Brain Fire C
91 Mark of Fire C
92 Netherworld Return C
93 Avenging Thunder U
94 Darkness Falls U
95 Darkness Pagoda, Netherworld Site R
96 Fire Pagoda, Netherworld Site R
97 Ice Pagoda, Netherworld Site R
98 Thunder Pagoda, Netherworld Site R
99 Claws of Darkness, Triumvirate State C
100 Fire Sled, Netherworld State C
101 Ice Shield C
102 Prisoner of the Monarchs C
103 Thunder Lance C
104 Avenging Fire U
105 Fist of Shadow, Netherworld Monk C
106 Hung Hei Kwon, Legendary Martial Artist R
107 Lui Man Wai, Master of the Chambers R
108 Wind on the Mountain U
109 Temple of Boundless Meditation, Netherworld Feng Shui Site R
110 Blue Senshi Chamber, Netherworld Site U
111 Green Senshi Chamber, Netherworld Site U
112 Orange Senshi Chamber, Netherworld Site U
113 Red Senshi Chamber, Netherworld Site U
114 Violet Senshi Chamber, Netherworld Site U
115 White Senshi Chamber, Netherworld Site U
116 Yellow Senshi Chamber, Netherworld Site U
117 Supercomputer U
118 Big Red Button U
119 Smart Gun C
120 Fusion Rifle U
121 Dallas Rocket, Fanatic Guerilla C
122 Junkyard Crawler, Netherworld Scavenger C
123 Low-Rent Cyborg, Self-Made Man C
124 Portal Jockey, Redeemed Timewalker C
125 Furious George, Flying Monkey R
126 Red Don, Techie Mastermind R
127 Adrenaline Junkie, Crazy Bastard U
128 Gorilla Fighter, Flying Monkey U
129 Monkey Boy, Flying Chimp U
130 Entropy is Your Friend U
131 In Your Face Again C
132 Gorilla Encampment C
133 Genocide Lounge, Netherworld Site R
134 Molotov Cocktail Party U
135 Duodenum of Yang Luo, Demon Entrails R
136 Lusignan the Fool, Mysterious Jester R
137 Lusignan's Automaton, Sorcerous Jester R
138 Cloud Walking C
139 Scroll of Incantation U
140 The Dis-Timed, Netherworld Rabble C
141 The Displaced, Netherworld Rabble C
142 Nine Cuts, Shadowy Assassin Promo
143 Man With No Name, Mysterious Stranger R
144 Art of War U
145 The Junkyard, Netherworld Site Promo
146 Lusignan's Tower, Netherworld Site R
147 Blood Fields, Netherworld Battleground Site U
148 Netherworld Portal, Battleground Site U

2001 Shadowfist Shaolin Showdown

1 Commander Corliss, TacOps Officer R
2 Hermes, Purist Agent R
3 TacOps Troopers, BuroMil Elite U
4 Reinvigoration Process v2 U
5 Geoscan Report C
6 Coil of the Snake, Lodge Assassin C
7 Jade Wheel Society, Secret Society C
8 Manchu Officer, Military Commandant C
9 Manchu Soldiers, Imperial Pawns C
10 Order of the Wheel, Secret Society C
11 Monkey Chang, Transformed Martial Artist R
12 General Senggelinqin, Manchu Military Mastermind R
13 Juan "El Tigre" Velasquez, Lodge Killer R
14 Kinoshita, Lodge Chairperson R
15 Mr. X, Lodge Mastermind R
16 Natraj Thalnasser, Lodge Warlord R
17 Rachel McShane, Lodge Enforcer R
18 Senor Ocho, Lodge Assassin R
19 Shinobu Yashida, Pledged Master R
20 The Eastern King v2, Lodge Mastermind R
21 The Unspoken Name, Lodge Chairperson R
22 Yen Song, Shaolin Traitor R
23 Charge of the Rhino, Lodge Enforcer U
24 Fist of the Bear vPAP, Lodge Enforcer U

25 Manchu Bureaucrat, Corrupt Official U
26 Might of the Elephant, Lodge Enforcer U
27 Web of the Spider vPAP, Lodge Mastermind U
28 Faked Death C
29 Realpolitik C
30 Contingency Plans U
31 Lodge Politics U
32 Spider vs. Mantis U
33 Tiger vs. Crane U
34 Year of the Snake U
35 Manchu Garrison C
36 Opium Den, Hood Site U
37 Dark's Soft Whisper C
38 Healing Earth C
39 Shaking the Mountain C
40 Invincible Chi U
41 Ancient Grove C
42 Butterfly Swords C
43 King on the Water C
44 Path of the Praying Mantis C
45 Path of the Storm Turtle C
46 Fortune of the Turtle U
47 Legacy of the Master U
48 Path of the Clever Fox U
49 Path of the Healthy Tiger U
50 Path of the Lurking Rat U
51 Path of the Raging Bear U
52 Point Blockage U
53 The Fox Outfoxed U
54 Walk of a Thousand Steps U
55 Chinese Doctor, Wise Physician C
56 Old Uncle, Martial Artist C
57 Sifu, Martial Arts Teacher C
58 Student of the Dragon, Martial Artist C
59 Big Mack, Bar-Room Brawler R
60 Doctor Shen, Martial Artist R
61 Iala Mane, Blind Master R
62 Katie Kincaid, Gunfighter R
63 Six Bottles Hwang, Drunken Master R
64 Zheng Yi Quan vPAP, Kung Fu Master R
65 Jenny Zheng, Promising Student U
66 Novice Students, Fledgling Martial Artists U
67 Peking Opera Troupe, Kung Fu Acrobats U
68 I Will Avenge You! C
69 Carnival of Carnage C
70 Flying Kick C
71 Kiii-YAAAH! C
72 Time to Kick Ass! Promo
73 Dragon Dojo C
74 Charmed Life U
75 Lai Kuang, Eunuch Sorcerer R
76 Malachi, Purist Agent R
77 Poison Clan Killers, Mercenary Assassins R
78 Feng Kan, Wind Demon U
79 Li Yu, Fire Demon U
80 Shui Yu, Water Demon U
81 Ti Kan, Metal Demon U
82 Underworld Contract U
83 Infernal Plot U
84 Rend Chi U
85 Larcenous Fog C
86 Ancient Monument, Feng Shui Site C
87 Forgotten Shrine, Feng Shui Site C
88 Market Square, Feng Shui Site C
89 Dragon Mountain, Feng Shui Site R
90 Four Sorrows Island, Feng Shui Site R
91 Hartwell Iron Works, Feng Shui Site R
92 Heaven's Peak, Feng Shui Site R
93 Plains of Ash, Feng Shui Site R
94 Primeval Forest, Feng Shui Site U
95 Temple of the Monkey King, Feng Shui Site U
96 Fire Infiltrator, Netherworld Subversive C
97 Jiang Xushen, Fire Infiltrator R
98 Mouth of the Fire Righteous, Netherworld Master R
99 The Inner Fire U
100 Path of the Fire Righteous, Netherworld State C
101 Impoverished Monk, Dedicated Martial Artist C
102 Instrument of the Hand, Martial Artist C
103 Master Swordsman, Righteous Warrior C
104 Peasant Agitator, Disgruntled Commoner C
105 Peasant Leader, Disgruntled Commoner C
106 Peasant Mob, Angry Rabble C
107 Shaolin Student, Fledgling Monk C
108 Swordsman, Foot Soldier C
109 Chen Sho Kung, Master Swordsman R
110 Fong Sai Yuk vPAP, Martial Artist R
111 Gong Wei, Reformed Bandit R
112 Li Sen-Hao, Master of the Mantis Style R
113 Miu Tsui Fa, Butt-Kicking Mom R
114 Old Man Wu, Master of the Monkey Style R
115 Quan Lo, The Perfect Master R
116 Tong Su Yin, Master of the Snake Style R
117 Tsung Jin, Master of the Crane Style R
118 Wei Fong-Yi, Master of the Fox Style R
119 Yen Fan, Pledged Traitor R
120 Master Blacksmith, Industrious Peasant U
121 Dragon Boat Festival Promo
122 Try My Kung Fu! C
123 Into the Light C
124 Shaolin Surprise v2 C
125 Superior Kung Fu C
126 The Dragon Unyielding R
127 Bear vs. Fox U
128 Eagle vs. Snake U
129 Order Out of Chaos U
130 Positive Chi v2 U
131 Robust Feng Shui U
132 Sword Dance U
133 Temple of the Shaolin Dragon, Feng Shui Site R
134 18 Bronze Men U
135 Master Killer U
136 Flying Monkey Squad, Guerrilla Gorillas C
137 Koko Chanel, Master of Monkey Style R
138 Portal Rat, Netherworld Saboteur U
139 Mo' Monkeys, Mo' Problems U
140 Homemade Grenade C
141 Sabotage C
142 Larcenous Mist v2 C
143 Primus, Master of Paradox Promo
144 Two Dragons Inn R
145 Sliding Paper Walls, Battleground Site U
146 Tiger Hook Swords C
147 Elephant Gun Promo
148 Sword of the Master Promo
149 Three Sectional Staff U

2002 Shadowfist 10,000 Bullets

1 Assault Squad, BuroMil Soldiers
2 Blood Reaver, Killer Abomination
3 CDCA Scientist, Overzealous Researcher
4 CHAR, BuroMil Cyborg
5 Genghis X, BuroMil Supersoldier
6 Magog, Unstoppable Abomination
7 Test Subjects, Abominations
8 The Reconstructed, Standard Abominations
9 Vivisector, Abomination Scientist
10 Dangerous Experiment
11 Nerve Gas
12 Neutron Bomb
13 Abominable Lab
14 Arcanotank
15 Buro Godhammer
16 Helix Rethread
17 Bleys Fontaine, Lodge Enforcer
18 Captain Liu, Pledged Cop Mastermind
19 Gruff Lieutenant, Pledged Cop
20 Jaded Cop, Corrupt Pawn
21 Liquidators, Pledged Enforcers
22 Phillippe Benoit, Pledged Assassin
23 Rachel McShane, Lodge Enforcer
24 Student of the Bear, Pledged Martial Artist
25 SWAT Team, Cop Pawns
26 Bull Market
27 Faked Death
28 Mole Network
29 Operation Killdeer
30 Realpolitik
31 Suicide Mission
32 Family Estate
33 Security
34 Shadowy Mentor
35 Blade Palm
36 Healing Earth
37 Flying Sword Stance
38 Hands Without Shadow
39 Everyday Hero, Brave Scrapper
40 Ex-Commando, Dangerous Vet
41 Hacker, Gun-Totin' Techie
42 Johnny Tso, Heroic Gunman
43 Karate Cop, Martial Artist
44 Redeemed Gunman, Reforming Hood
45 Steven Wu, Zen Gunman
46 Ting Ting, Martial Artist
47 Tricia Kwok, Undercover Cop
48 Now You've Made Us Mad
49 Dirk Wisely's Gambit
50 Final Brawl
51 Golden Comeback
52 Kar Fai's Crib
53 Bag Full of Guns
54 Both Guns Blazing
55 Big Brother Tsien, Demon Hood
56 Claw of Fury, Shadowy Assassin
57 Four Burning Fists, Demon Martial Artist
58 Kan Li, Martial Artist
59 Poison Thorns, Dangerous Hoods
60 Sinister Priest, Macabre Sorcerer
61 Tommy Hsu, Hood Sorcerer
62 Vassals of the Lotus, Ancient Hoods
63 Walking Corpses, Undead Servitors
64 White Disciple, Eunuch Sorcerer
65 Die!!!
66 Flying Sleeves
67 Glimpse of the Abyss
68 Tortured Memories
69 Bird Sanctuary, Feng Shui Site
70 Birdhouse Cafe, Feng Shui Site
71 Cave Network, Feng Shui Site
72 City Hospital, Feng Shui Site
73 City Park, Feng Shui Site
74 City Square, Feng Shui Site
75 Curio Shop, Feng Shui Site
76 Family Home, Feng Shui Site
77 Festival Circle, Feng Shui Site
78 Field of Tentacles, Netherworld Feng Shui Site
79 Fireworks Factory, Feng Shui Site
80 Floating Restaurant, Feng Shui Site
81 Fox Pass, Feng Shui Site
82 Gambling House, Feng Shui Site
83 Garden of Bronze, Netherworld Feng Shui Site
84 Golden Mile, Feng Shui Site
85 Hidden Sanctuary, Feng Shui Site
86 Inner Sanctum, Feng Shui Site
87 Jade Valley, Feng Shui Site
88 Kinoshita House, Feng Shui Site
89 Night Market, Feng Shui Site
90 Nightclub, Feng Shui Site
91 Nine Dragon Temple, Feng Shui Site
92 Rust Garden, Netherworld Feng Shui Site
93 Stone Garden, Feng Shui Site
94 Temple of Celestial Mercy, Feng Shui Site
95 Turtle Beach, Feng Shui Site
96 Turtle Island, Feng Shui Site
97 Blade of Darkness, Netherworld Killer
98 Butterfly Knight, Thunder Warrior
99 Darkness Warriors, Netherworld Soldiers
100 Fire Acolytes, Netherworld Disciples
101 Fire Mystic, Netherworld Sorcerer
102 Ice Healer, Netherworld Sorceress
103 Lord Hawksmoor, Thunder Champion
104 Lord Shi, Netherworld Warrior
105 Thunder Bishop, Netherworld Sorcerer
106 The Legacy
107 Avenging Thunder
108 Brain Fire
109 Mark of Fire
110 Claws of Darkness, Triumvirate State
111 Ice Diadem
112 Thunder Sword
113 Blue Monk, Kung Fu Infiltrator
114 Bulletproof Monk, Martial Artist
115 Derek Han, Martial Artist
116 Golden Candle Society, Secret Society
117 Instrument of the Hand, Martial Artist
118 Kung Fu Student, Fledgling Shaolin
119 Shih Ho Kuai, Martial Arts Master
120 The Iron Monkey, Masked Hero
121 Virtuous Hood, Martial Artist
122 Yellow Geomancer, Crafty Monk
123 Shield of Pure Soul
124 Confucian Stability
125 Heat of Battle
126 Iron and Silk
127 Shaolin Sanctuary
128 Tank Warfare
129 Dallas Rocket, Fanatic Guerrilla
130 Edge Warrior, Subversive Op
131 Furious George, Flying Monkey
132 Gorilla Fighter, Flying Monkey
133 Just Another Consumer, Scrappy Rebel
134 Napalm Addict, Pyromaniac Anarchist
135 Professional Killer, Mercenary Hood
136 Resistance Squad, Techie Guerrillas
137 Payback Time
138 Close Call
139 Death-O-Rama
140 Scrounging
141 Street Riot
142 Who's the Monkey Now?
143 Bomb Factory
144 Homemade Tank
145 Discerning Fire
146 Pocket Demon
147 Alabaster Javelin
148 Amulet of the Turtle
149 Arcane Scientist, Initiate of Paradox
150 Cognitive Spirit, Self-Aware Construct
151 Father of Chaos, Spirit of Destruction
152 Inoue Oram, Sorcerer Mastermind
153 Isomorphic Spirit, Paradox Construct
154 Kallisti, Daughter of Entropy
155 Mathemagician, Arcane Student
156 Purist Aspirant, Expendable Lackey
157 Void Sorcerer, Mysterious Geomancer
158 Quantum Sorcery
159 Entropy Sphere
160 Entropy Tap
161 Paradox Garden
162 Pain Feedback
163 Drug Lab, Hood Site
164 Explosives
165 Pump-Action Shotgun, Gun State
166 Sports Car
167 Sub-Machine Gun

2002 Shadowfist Boom Chaka Laka

1 Rocket Man, Cyborg C
2 Superfreak, Abomination R
3 We Have the Technology U
4 Fire in the Sky C
5 Napalm Sunrise C
6 The Suits, Pledged Agents C
7 Max Brunner, Pledged Cop R
8 Serena Chase, Transformed Stone Fox R
9 The Man, Lodge Chairperson R
10 Night Moves U
11 Political Corruption U
12 Dirty Tricks U
13 Fox On the Run U
14 Nuclear Power Plant U
15 Walk on the Wild Side C
16 Nunchuks C
17 Good Ol' Boys, Righteous Rednecks C
18 Maverick Trucker, Blue-Collar Hero C
19 Rookies, Idealistic Cops C
20 Isis Fox, Soul Sister R
21 Jack Hades, Motorcycle Daredevil R
22 John Tower, One Bad Mother R
23 Spencer's Beauties, Foxy Heroines R
24 Taggert, Streetwise Cop R
25 Street Fighter, Martial Artist U
26 We Got the Funk, Superfly Edge U
27 Fast as Lightning C
28 Fists of Fury U
29 Life in the Fast Lane U
30 Big Ass Car, Gas-Guzzling State C
31 Brick House C
32 CB Radio U
33 Real Bad Cat, State of Mind U
34 Vassals of Chin, Hood Martial Artists C
35 The Mantis, Martial Artist Assassin R
36 The Netarious Master Chin, Hood Mastermind R
37 Snake Fighter, Hood Martial Artist U
38 Spies Everywhere U
39 Chin's Criminal Network, Hood Event U
40 Throwdown in Chinatown U
41 Death Ring, Underground Hood Site R
42 The White Leopard Club, Tacky Hood Site R
43 Five Fingers of Death C
44 Evil Master U
45 Disco, Feng Shui Site C
46 Pinball Arcade, Feng Shui Site C
47 Roller Rink, Feng Shui Site C
48 Ice Shaman, Netherworld Sorcerer C
49 Soul Doctor, Ice Priest C
50 Silver Jet, Secret Warrior Promo
51 Ice Vixen, Stone Cold Fox U
52 Ice Totem U
53 Earth, Wind, and Fire U
54 Righteous Bro, Shaolin Brother C
55 Billy Chow, Undercover Shaolin R
56 Fatty Cho, Chubby Cop R
57 Chinese Connection U
58 Everybody Was Kung Fu Fighting U
59 You Have Offended Shaolin! C
60 Smoke on the Water C
61 Swinging With the Hand C
62 Kung Fu Prodigy C
63 Mad Monkey Kung Fu C
64 Outlaw Bikers, Easy Riders C
65 Punks, Anarchist Rebels C
66 Simian Liberation Army, Anarchist Apes C
67 Street Gang, Young Hoods C
68 Che Gorilla, Rebel Mastermind Promo
69 Curtis Graham, Urban Revolutionary R
70 Doctor Zaius, Weird Monkey Scientist R
71 Funky Monkey, Chimp Pimp R
72 Buffalo Soldier, Rasta Rebel U
73 Burn, Baby, Burn! U
74 Do You Feel Lucky, Punk? U
75 Disco Inferno U
76 Stick it to The Man! U
77 The Discombobulator, Weird Science State R
78 Big Daddy Voodoo, Hood Sorcerer R
79 Binary Spirit, Duality Construct C
80 Rama Singh, Freaky Sorcerer R
81 Strange Magic U
82 Time Keeps On Slipping U
83 Da Boys, Hood Enforcers C
84 Claws, Unkillable Hood Bruiser R
85 Mr. Simms, Hood Lieutenant R
86 The Big Boss, Hood Mastermind R
87 Magnum Justice, Cop Edge U
88 Zodiac Lounge, Hood Site R
89 Car Wash U
90 Chop Shop, Hood Site U
91 Big Rig, Truck State C
92 Partners, Cop State C
93 Heavy Machine Gun U

2002 Shadowfist Dark Future

1 Beta Beast, Early Model Abomination C
2 BuroMil Grunt, Brutal Soldier C
3 Raptor Squad, Blood-Thirsty Abominations C
4 The Dogs of War, Veteran Soldiers C
5 Desdemona Deathangel, Abomination R
6 General Olivet, BuroMil Military Mastermind R
7 Jason X, Brainwashed Supersoldier R
8 Johann Bonengel, BuroPresident R
9 Sergeant Blightman, Mutating Soldier R
10 Thing with a 1000 Tongues, Abhorrent Abomination R
11 Assault Drone, Arcanowave Robot U
12 Destroyer Drone, Arcanowave Robot U
13 Spawn of the New Flesh, Unstable Abomination U
14 Tank Commander, BuroMil Officer U
15 Tunneler Drone, Arcanowave Robot U
16 Cellular Reinvigoration C
17 Vivisection Agenda U
18 Fortress Omega R
19 BK97 Attack Chopper C
20 Buro Blue Spear, Gun State C
21 Spirit Shield Generator C
22 BuroMil "Savage", Tank State U
23 Combat Veteran U
24 Just a Rat, Lodge Survivor C
25 Arachnae, Reascended Spider R
26 Dunwa Saleem, Prophet of the Reascension R
27 Louie the Roach, Lodge Survivor R
28 Serket, Reascended Scorpion R
29 Ursus, Reascended Bear R
30 Consumer on the Brink, Disgruntled Everyman C
31 Concourse Godard, Renegade Supersoldier R
32 Dirk Wisely, Man of Action R
33 Johnny Badhair, Wild Man R
34 Master Mechanic, Renegade Techie U
35 Got My Mojo Working C
36 Fake Out U
37 Fallen Heroes U
38 Kar Fai's Last Stand U
39 Kar Fai's Legacy U
40 Borrowed Nuke R
41 Mobile HQ R
42 Legion of the Damned, Undead Soldiers C
43 Destroyer, Demon Martial Artist R
44 Fo Shen, Eunuch Pawn R
45 Corruption U
46 Demon Tank U
47 Fearsome Foe U
48 Gloating Laughter U
49 Hell Charger, Demon State U
50 Coral Reef, Feng Shui Site C
51 Hot Springs, Feng Shui Site C
52 Cataract Gorge, Feng Shui Site R
53 Mount Makarakomburu, Feng Shui Site R
54 The Pinnacles, Feng Shui Site R
55 Identity Chop Shop, Feng Shui Site U
56 Ice Sorceress, Geomancer Mastermind U
57 Thunder Swordsman, Netherworld Knight U
58 Battle Cry C
59 Dark Sacrifice C
60 Snowblind C
61 Blue Mandarin, Deceptive Bureaucrat C
62 Fist of Freedom, Rebel Martial Artist C
63 Rebel Consumer, Freedom Fighter C
64 Shaolin Agent, Undercover Monk C
65 Yung Chang, Master of the Gardeners Promo
66 Master Hao, Superior Martial Artist R
67 Master Gardener, Elderly Geomancer U
68 Defiant Bloom U
69 Superior Mastery U
70 Marauder Gang, Renegade Cyborgs C
71 Marauder Lord, Ruthless Cyborg U
72 Smart Missile U
73 IFF Missiles C
74 Orbital Laser Strike C
75 Spit and Baling Wire C
76 Secret Laboratory C
77 Jet Pack C
78 Newest Model C
79 Replacement Parts C
80 Mark IV Fusion Rifle U
81 MegaTank U
82 Big Macaque Attack, Monkey Horde C
83 Dump Scrounger, Netherworld Scavenger C
84 Jack of All Trades, Resourceful Techie C
85 Simian Sneaker, Primate Saboteur C
86 Funky Monkey, Chimp Pimp Promo
87 Battlechimp Potemkin, Subversive Chimp Mastermind R
88 King Kung, Cyborg Gorilla R
89 Major Hottie, Ex-Buro Operative R
90 FAE Schwartz, Incendiary Fanatic U
91 SAM Simian, Destructive Primate U
92 Close Call C
93 Nuked C
94 Parting Gift C
95 Free Fire Zone, Battleground Site U
96 Homemade Tank C
97 Jury-Rigged Dynamo C
98 Battle-Matic U
99 Chaos Spirit, Volatile Construct C
100 Spirit Guardian U
101 Memory Reprocessing U
102 Alchemist's Lair C
103 Energy Flail U
104 Arcane Scientist, Initiate of Paradox C
105 Memory Spirit, Psychic Construct C
106 Purist Aspirant, Expendable Lackey C
107 Purist Initiate, Student Sorcerer C
108 Void Sorcerer, Mysterious Geomancer C
109 Zen Logician, Esoteric Numerologist C
110 Esteban Vicente, Geomancer Mastermind R
111 Misery Totelben, Insane Musician R
112 Primus, Master of Paradox R
113 Rhys Engel, Purist Mastermind R
114 Hexagram Spirit, Sorcerous Construct U
115 Inoue Oram, Sorcerer Mastermind U
116 Mutator, Probability Spirit U
117 Quantum Sorcery U
118 Entropy Sphere C
119 Entropy Tap C
120 Memory Palace R
121 Temporal Realignment R
122 Chi Reconfiguration U
123 Deja Vu U
124 Paradox Divination U
125 Nexus Tower R
126 Portal Nexus U
127 Killing Ground, Battleground Site C
128 No Man's Land, Battleground Site C
129 Motor Pool U
130 Training Camp, Battleground Site U

2003 Shadowfist Red Wedding

1 Bouncing Benji, Mass-Produced Abomination C
2 BuroMil Scout, Recon Soldier C
3 Loyalty Officer, Buro Soldier C
4 Dr. Jean-Marc Ngubane, Buro Scientist Double Agent R
5 Assassin Bug, Killer Abomination U
6 Black Ops Team, Buro Assassins U
7 Napalm Belcher, Netherworld Abomination U
8 Bio-Salvage U
9 Artillery Strike C
10 War of Attrition U
11 Helix Mine C
12 Tracer Implant, Arcanowave State C
13 Broken Wheel Brigade, Netherworld Soldiers C
14 Jan Zvireci, Pledged Lackey R
15 Jormungandr, Reascended Snake R
16 Kauhuhu, Reascended Shark R
17 Rebecca Dupress, Pledged Mastermind R
18 Reverend RedGlare, Netherworld Mercenary R
19 Corrupt Bookie, Pledged Hood Gambler U
20 Spin Doctoring U
21 The Enemy of my Enemy U
22 Lodge Machinations R
23 Shell Game U
24 Official Harassment C
25 Robbing the Kong R
26 Reluctant Hero, Netherworld Outcast C
27 Scrappy Kid, Martial Arts Prodigy C
28 Bei Tairong, Lodge Traitor R
29 Gus Andropolous, IKTV Reporter R
30 Big Bruiser vPAP, Kicker of Butts U
31 Wandering Hero, Netherworld Ally U
32 Is that all you got? C
33 Ashes of the Fallen C
34 Mano a Mano U
35 Never Surrender U
36 Slo Mo Vengeance U
37 Bring It R
38 Ring of Silver R
39 Ogre, Ancient Monster C
40 Red Dragon Troupe, Sinister Acrobats C
41 Shamanistic Punk, Hood Sorcerer C
42 Jueding Shelun vPAP, Ghost Sorcerer R
43 Ten Thousand Agonies, Demon Lord R
44 Throne of Skulls R
45 Wasting Curse U
46 Bribery C
47 Demonic Plague C
48 Evil Whispers C
49 Verminous Rain C
50 Diamond Beach, Netherworld Feng Shui Site C
51 Dragon Graveyard, Netherworld Feng Shui Site C
52 Stone Dolmens, Feng Shui Site C
53 Stone Spirals, Netherworld Feng Shui Site C
54 Escher Hotel, Netherworld Feng Shui Site R
55 Peacock Summit, Feng Shui Site U
56 Ice Tigers, Netherworld Spirits C

57 Skin and Darkness Zealots, Netherworld Horrors C
58 Thunder Apprentice, Fledgling Sorcerer C
59 Thunder Gladiator, Netherworld Warrior C
60 Akani Hideo, Ice Steward R
61 Bonebreaker Jun, Thunder Dome Champion R
62 Chamberlain, Skin and Darkness Zealot R
63 Fakhir-al-Din, Fire Warlord R
64 Silver Jet vPAP, Secret Warrior R
65 Arena Warrior, Thunder Knight U
66 Armies of the Monarchs U
67 Blood Lust C
68 Transmogrification C
69 Wrath of the Monarchs C
70 Wedding Gifts Promo
71 Contest of Arms U
72 Snowfall U
73 Ice Pavilion, Netherworld Feng Shui Site R
74 The Thunder Dome, Netherworld Site R
75 Ring of Ice R
76 Butterfly Armor, Thunder State U
77 Fire Sword U
78 Buddhist Monk, Martial Artist C
79 Little Grasshopper, Energetic Kid C
80 Xiaoyang Yun, Spy Mastermind R
81 Green Sage, Tough Old Monk U
82 Leaping Tiger Troupe, Shaolin Acrobats U
83 Orange Sage, Wise Monk U
84 Secrets of Shaolin C
85 The Orange Principle C
86 Ornamental Garden U
87 IKTV Special Report C
88 Wave Disruptor C
89 Information Warfare U
90 RedGlare Chapel, Netherworld Site R
91 Mad Scientist, Unorthodox Techie C
92 Two-Face, Punk Anarchists R
93 Brass Monkey, Simian Automaton U
94 Violence Junkies, Crazy Rabble U
95 Black Market Connections R
96 Friends in Low Places R
97 Frag the G! U
98 There's Always One More... C
99 Blow Things Up! C
100 Monkey vs. Robot U
101 Bomb Factory C
102 BoBo Splitter C
103 Chizu U
104 Sonic Reducer U
105 Chi Detachment C
106 Aether Spirit, Invisible Construct C
107 Morphic Spirit, Sorcerous Construct C
108 Paradox, Void Entity R
109 Dr. Timbul Damiri, Fugue Sorcerer U
110 Void, Entropy Spirit U
111 Echo Cancellation U
112 Paradox Garden C
113 Paradigm Recoding U
114 Ho Chen, Master of the Flawless Strike Promo
115 Dark Traveler, Netherworld Hero C
116 The Ickies, Netherworld Rabble C
117 Yakuza Enforcer, Killer Hood C
118 Ninja Six, Enigmatic Agent R
119 Zino the Greek, Netherworld Information Broker R
120 Cassandra, Netherworld Seer U
121 Reverend Zebediah Paine, Demon Hunter U
122 Stand Together U
123 Secret Pact U
124 Uprising U
125 Trade Center C
126 The Bazaar, Netherworld Battleground Site Promo
127 The Forest of Fallen Banners, Netherworld Site R
128 Battle Arena, Battleground Site U
129 Exile Village, Battleground Site U
130 Police Station v2 U

2004 Shadowfist 7 Masters vs. The Underworld

1 Arcanogardener, CDCA Scientist C
2 Buro Scientist, Loyal Researcher U
3 Penal Soldiers, BuroMil Conscripts U
4 Rapid Response Team, PubOrd Cops U
5 Aerial Bombardment C
6 Uncontrolled Mutation C
7 Brain Tap Rifle C
8 Neural Stimulator, Arcanowave State C
9 Arcanoleech U
10 Cobra Clan Stalkers, Transformed Animals C
11 Peacock Clan Warriors, Transformed Animals C
12 Rat Clan Spies, Transformed Animals C
13 Wolf Clan Hunters, Transformed Animals C
14 Grey Mountain, Transformed Elephant Chieftain R
15 Leopard Clan Warriors, Transformed Animals U
16 200 Guys With Hatchets and Ladders U
17 Cry of the Forgotten Ancestor U
18 The Lady or the Tiger? U
19 Shung Dai, Guardian Monk R
20 Wing of the Crane C
21 Buddha's Palm U
22 Celestial Stance R
23 Invincible Earth Sword R
24 Invincible Stance R
25 No Shadow Kick R
26 Phoenix Stance R
27 Master Bowman, Heroic Archer C
28 Ting Ting's Bandits, Righteous Hoods C
29 Tom Donovan, Hard-Boiled Detective Promo
30 Li Mao vPAP, Accidental Hero R
31 Lin, Moon Sorceress R
32 Wu Bin of Turtle Island, Wandering Sorcerer R
33 Wandering Swordsman, Heroic Warrior U
34 Fighting Spirit C
35 Out For Blood C
36 Storming the Gates of Hell U
37 Baptism of Fire U
38 Four Mountains Fist U
39 Ready For Action U
40 Bloody Horde, Demon Trouble C
41 Hopping Vampire, Ancient Monster C
42 Poison Clan Warriors, Hood Martial Artists C
43 Ang Dao the Corrupt, Demon Warrior Promo
44 Cenotaph, Undead Assassin R
45 Desolation, Underworld Demon King R
46 Jiang Fei, Seductive Ghost R
47 Kong Jun She, Master of the Forbidden Stance R
48 Long Axe and Short Axe, Martial Artist Assassins R
49 Miasma, Stealer of Souls R
50 Xiang Kai, Poison Clan Chieftain R
51 Shu Kan, Tree Demon U
52 Feast of Souls R
53 Evil Chanting C
54 Shrieking Witch Heads C
55 Haunted Forest U
56 Terracotta Warriors, Ghost State C
57 Soul Theft U
58 Underworld Gateway U
59 Wall of a Thousand Eyes, Netherworld Feng Shui Site C
60 Jade Palace of the Dragon King, Feng Shui Site R
61 Mountain Fortress, Feng Shui Site U
62 Thousand Sword Mountain, Feng Shui Site U
63 Thunder Captain, Netherworld Knight C
64 Thunder Inquisitor, Netherworld Sorcerer C
65 Sir Gawain, Timewalker Knight R
66 Jaguar Warriors, Elite Darkness Soldiers U
67 Blanket of Darkness, Netherworld Edge R
68 The Book of Wrath, Thunder Edge U
69 The Queen's Wrath, Darkness Event C
70 Combat Courtship U
71 Ice Sword C
72 Shaolin Defender, Guardian Monk C
73 Shaolin Swordsman, Martial Artist C
74 Lui Yu Min, Shaolin Master R
75 Orange Master, Martial Artist U
76 Red Master, Martial Artist U
77 Sword Saint, Spiritual Warrior U
78 Tranquil Persuader, Mastermind U
79 Wandering Monk, Martial Artist U
80 Eight Pillars of Heaven Array U
81 Shaolin vs. Wudang U
82 Know Your Enemy, Kung Fu State C
83 Righteous Heaven Stance C
84 Essence-Absorbing Stance, Kung Fu State U
85 Ape Nuts, Crazy Cyborg Monkeys C
86 Shaolin Monkey, Simian Martial Artist C
87 401k Squad, Mutated Soldiers U
88 Deep-Cover Rebels, Subversive Operatives U
89 Rogue Scientist, CDCA Defector U
90 Hordes of Saboteurs U
91 Kick 'em When They're Down C
92 Monkeywrenching C
93 We Need Bigger Guns! C
94 Netherflitter, Weird Science State C
95 Curtain of Fullness C
96 Killing Rain C
97 Solar Sword C
98 Boundless Heaven Sword R
99 The Celestial Eye R
100 Lunar Sword U
101 Ordinal Spirit, Mathematical Construct C
102 Shadow Legion, Elite Ex-Buro Soldiers C
103 Jenaya Ou, Vengeful Sorcerer R
104 Shards of Warped Reflection, Fractured Construct R
105 Geomantic Spirit, Sorcerous Construct U
106 The Shattered Mirror C
107 Glimpse of Brief Eternity U
108 Material Transcendence C
109 Incarnate Abstraction R
110 Chi Syphon U
111 Wah-Shan Clan Warriors, Martial Arts Students C
112 Wudang Monk, Martial Artist C
113 Li Mao vPAP, Young Master Promo
114 Ghost Wind, Master of the Liquid Sword R
115 Gold Lion, Master of the Wah-Shan Clan R
116 Ho Chen, Master of the Flawless Strike R
117 Red Bat, Master of the Kunlun Clan R
118 Sky Dragon, Master of the Invulnerable Stance R
119 Wu Man Kai, Master of Wudang Mountain R
120 Monsoon, Flying Swordsman U
121 Balanced Harmonies U
122 Beneficent Tao C
123 Kunlun Clan Assault C
124 Monkey Fools the Tiger C
125 Pao Yeh Pao Lo Mi C
126 Unexpected Rescue C
127 Wondrous Illusion U
128 Wudang Mountain, Feng Shui Site U
129 One Thousand Swords C
130 Occult Kung Fu U
131 The Swords Unite U

2004 Shadowfist Two-Fisted Tales of the Secret War

1 Stormtroopers, Brutal Soldiers C
2 Colonel Wilhelm Reiger, Buro Agent R
3 Dr. Klaus Herrbruck, CDCA Scientist R
4 Elsa Winterhagen, Supersoldier R
5 Rocket Team, Heavily-Armed Soldiers U
6 Ubermensch, Superior Soldier U
7 Probability Manipulator R
8 Repression U
9 Sinister Research Promo
10 Blitzkrieg U
11 State of Emergency U
12 Guard Tower, Battleground Site C
13 Rabenfels Castle, Feng Shui Site R
14 Eisenriese C
15 Supersoldier Serum C
16 Zeppelin C
17 G-Man, Pledged Agent C
18 Gangsters, Hood Muscle C
19 Gun Moll, Dishy Hood C
20 Athena, Reascended Owl Mastermind R
21 John Fenris, the Iron Man, Reascended Wolf Hero R
22 Vincent "The Jackal" Benilli, Lodge Hood Mastermind R
23 Hammer Harrison, Hood Bruiser U
24 Bad Colonel, Pledged Hood Warlord U
25 Femme Fatale, Sinister Seductress U
26 Murder By Night C
27 Throw Me the Idol... U
28 Hired Killer C
29 Master of Disguise U
30 Tools Of The Trade U
31 Secret Wisdom of the Ancients U
32 Fortuitous Chi U
33 Captain Jake Molloy, Daredevil Pilot R
34 Dr. Amanda Snow, Treasure Hunter R
35 The Nemesis, Masked Avenger R
36 Tom Donovan, Hard-Boiled Detective R
37 David Maxwell, Man About Town U
38 Heroic Agents, Legion of Supporters U
39 Booby Trap C
40 The Golden Gunman's Gambit C
41 Tough as Nails C
42 Cliffhanger U
43 Damsel in Distress U
44 Lair of the Nemesis, Secret Feng Shui Site R
45 Bullwhip C
46 Running Out of Time C
47 Mask of The Nemesis, Secret Identity State U
48 Hired Bodyguard, Cheap Hood Muscle C
49 Thugs, Hoods C
50 Tong Hatchetman, Red Scorpion Hood C
51 Chang, Red Scorpion Hood Martial Artist R
52 Madame Yen, The Dragon Lady R
53 Yuen Sheng, Red Scorpion Mastermind R
54 Red Scorpion Killers, Hood Martial Artists U
55 Insidious Plan U
56 You Fell Into My Trap! C
57 Hypnotized! C
58 Poisoned! C
59 Necromantic Conspiracy U
60 Deathtrap C
61 Drugged! C
62 Booby-Trapped Tomb, Feng Shui Site C
63 Hidden Tomb, Feng Shui Site C
64 Aztec Pyramid, Feng Shui Site U
65 The Blue Moon Club, Feng Shui Site U
66 Priestess of Itzcoliuhqui, Darkness Sorceress C
67 Teutonic Knights, Thunder Secret Society C
68 Itzcoliuhqui, Undead King R
69 Khalid Al-Haddad, Fire Assassin R
70 Lord Wolfgang Thaler, Thunder Champion R
71 Xitlali, Darkness High Priestess R
72 Aztec Mummy, Undead Guardian U
73 Fire Martyr, Netherworld Assassin U
74 Plots and Intrigues C
75 Ritual of Death, Darkness Event C
76 Tomb of Itzcoliuhqui, Ancient Feng Shui Site U
77 Curse of Itzcoliuhqui, Darkness State C
78 Obsidian Dagger, Darkness State C
79 Rope Bridge, Trap State C
80 The Crystal Skull, Darkness State R
81 Jade Dragon Monk, Mysterious Martial Artist C
82 Swords of Heaven, Secret Society C
83 Kwan Lung-Wei, Jade Dragon Master R
84 Carmen Zhou, Leader of the Swords of Heaven U
85 Charge of the Righteous U
86 Breath of the Dragon C
87 Difficulty at the Beginning U
88 The Red Harvest U
89 Temple of the Jade Dragon, Feng Shui Site R
90 Deadly Hands, Kung Fu State C
91 Scales of the Dragon C
92 The Jade Dragon R
93 Electro-Gauntlet C
94 Tesla Lightning Blaster, Gun State C
95 Invisi-Ray R
96 Disguise Kit U
97 Disintegrator Ray U
98 Tesla Lightning Cannon U
99 Marmojet, Flying Monkey C
100 Resistance Fighters, Partisan Rebels C
101 Wild Gorillas, Primitive Monkeys C
102 Dr. Ivan Vasilovich, Mad Scientist R
103 K'tongo, The White Ape R
104 Rampage! U
105 Torch the Place! C
106 Far Too Much Dynamite C
107 The Ape is Loose! C
108 Year of the Monkey R
109 Stolen Plans U
110 The Underground U
111 Ape City, Jungle Site R
112 X-Ray Specs, Weird Science State U
113 The Ruby Eye U
114 The Ivory Goddess R
115 Faceless Minions, Cultist Swarm C
116 Priest of the Unnameable, Cult Leader C
117 The Unnameable, Spirit of Madness R
118 Sir Arthur Broome, Eccentric Patron U
119 Twisted Horror, Madness Spirit U
120 Voice of the Unnameable, Maniacal Mastermind U
121 They Came Out of Nowhere! C
122 Tortured by Madness! C
123 Ritual of the Unnameable U
124 Mount Erebus, Feng Shui Site R
125 Spirit of the Gun R
126 Lateral Reincarnation Promo
127 Casbah U
128 Seedy Dive, Hood Site U
129 Tommy Gun C
130 Public Enemy No. 1 Promo
131 Spear of Destiny U

2006 Shadowfist Shurikens and Six-Guns

1 Agathon's Deputies, Demon Cops C
2 Agent Tanaka, CDCA Ninja R
3 Anastasia, Orphan Ice Ward R
4 Arcanovirus U
5 Avenging Darkness, Vengeance Spirit U
6 Bait and Switch C
7 Big Red Barn C
8 Black Ophir, Gorilla Bartender R
9 Blasting Crew, Railroad Workers C
10 Blood Eagles, Abomination Scouts C
11 Bloody Herd, Vampire Cattle U
12 Boiler Room, Mad Science Site U
13 BoneChill, Reprogrammed Pawn U
14 Boot Hill U
15 Bountiful Fields U
16 Bridge of Birds U
17 Cavalry Regiment, Horseback Heroes C
18 Celestials, Chinatown Secret Society C
19 Chain Lightning, Thunder Event U
20 Children of the Sharp Knives, Self-Destructive Cultists C
21 Corporate Hacker, Sleep-Deprived Operator C
22 Corrupt Land Agent, Pledged Flim-Flam Man C
23 Covert Operation Promo
24 Coyote Clan Scavengers, Transformed Animals C
25 Crazed Preacher, Dangerous Zealot C
26 Curse of Discord C
27 Dan Dammer, Jammer Slammer, Fanatic Cop Promo
28 Data Theft U
29 Daughter of Flame, Fire Assassin U
30 Demon Whiskey, Rotgut Horde C
31 Detonating Corpses C
32 Devil's Mountain R
33 Devil's Rope Promo
34 Dog Soldiers, Thunder Braves C
35 Donner Lake R
36 Dr. Curtis Boatman, Corporate Scientist Mastermind R
37 Dr. Quentin Higginsbottham, Weirder Scientist R
38 Dust Storm C
39 Echo and Silence, Twin Assassins R
40 Elephant Gun Promo
41 Evacuation: 2066 U
42 Exiled Monk, Shaolin Outcast C
43 Fastest Gun in the West U
44 Fermat's Last Stand U
45 Fermat's Soldiers, Secret Shock Troops U
46 Fire Ants, Deadly Insects C
47 Fire Woman, Crazed Pyromaniac C
48 Fistful of Dollars U
49 Flesh Eater, Bloodthirsty Demon C
50 Frenzy of the Shark, Lodge Killer U
51 Gambler, Lucky Bastard C
52 Gamma Beast, Third-Generation Abomination C
53 The Golden Spike, Railroad Event R
54 Gunboat Diplomacy U
55 Gunslinger, Pledged Assassin C
56 Hideout U
57 High Noon U
58 The Honorable Earl Mason, Hangin' Judge R
59 Hoosegow Jackson, Desperate Outlaw R
60 Horse Thief, Lodge Operator U
61 Huichen Kan, Dust Demon U
62 Hydrophobia C
63 Hyper Alloy Blade C
64 Inconvenient Debt U
65 The Insidious Dr. Fermat, Mad Mathemagician Mastermind R
66 Involuntary Embalming U
67 Isothermal Zodiac, Weird Science Event C
68 The Jackson Gang, Heroic Outlaws U
69 Jessica Ng, Corporate Mastermind R
70 Jessica Ng, CDCA Scientist Promo
71 Jia Baoyu, Lovelorn Shaolin Agent U
72 Johann Bonengel, NeoBuroPresident R
73 Joshua Norton, Emperor of the USA R
74 Just a Scratch C
75 Kunlun Clan Assault Promo
76 Lateral Reincarnation U
77 Liquored Up C
78 Living Legend Promo
79 Mah-Jongg Parlor U
80 Mars Colonist, Expendable Student Promo
81 Math Bomb U
82 Midnight, Demon Horse R
83 Military Commandant, Pledged Mastermind Promo
84 Monkey Pirates, Simian Scalawags U
85 Moonlight Raid C
86 Morse Code Poet, Magical Telegraph Operator C
87 Naikute, Tribal Chief R
88 Netherflitter, Weird Science State U
89 Night Horror, Rogue Abomination C
90 Nihilist, Cybernetic Ninja U
91 Nitro Jack, Unsavory Demolitions Expert R
92 Nothing Happens U
93 One-Eye Chan, Chinatown Elder R
94 Open a Can of Whupass Promo
95 Personality Shard C
96 Pony Express U
97 Potlatch R
98 Prudence Nightingale, Sinister Schoolmarm R
99 Queen of the Ice Pagoda, Netherworld Mastermind Promo
100 Railroad Workers, Steel-Driving Rabble C
101 Rainmaker Floyd, Wandering Con Man R
102 Ranchers, Cowboy Heroes C
103 Redeemed Pirate, Shaolin Sailor U
104 Reinvigoration Seed C
105 Revenge on the Patent Office!, Weird Science Event C
106 Reverend Adam Wither, Evil Preacher R
107 Rise of the NeoBuro U
108 Sacred Wigwam, Thunder Site C
109 Salaryman, Corporate Killer C
110 Scrounging Promo
111 Senoritas, Three Sisters U
112 The Seven, Roving Heroes R
113 Shao the Killer, Master of Dim Mak R
114 Shaolin Hoedown U
115 Sheriff Agathon, Demon Boss R
116 Shurikens C
117 The Silent Cowboy, Six-Gun Shaolin R
118 Simple Paper Fan C
119 Single-Action Devolver, Weird Gun State U
120 Six-Gun C
121 Skin and Darkness Bats, Netherworld Horrors C
122 Song, The Little Dragon, Heir Apparant R
123 The Steam Laundry Company R
124 Steam-Powered Tricycle, Weird Science State C
125 Strange Ore U
126 Street Sweepers, Enhanced Martial Artists C
127 Swift Eagle, Brave Warrior R
128 Texas Jack Cody, Lodge Ranger R
129 Thunder Bird, Mighty Spirit R
130 Thunder in the West U
131 Thunder Stick, Gun State C
132 Triad Punks, Wired Hoods C
133 Two-Headed Horror, Demon State U
134 University Library C
135 Wall Running U
136 Whispers in the Dark C
137 Wild Spirits, Free-Range Constructs C
138 The Willow Bends... C
139 Yippee-Yi-Yo Kiii-YAAAH! U
140 Yosef Halevi, Kabalist Sorcerer R

2007 Shadowfist Critical Shift

1 Acupressure Master, Martial Artist U
2 Anubis, Reascended Jackal R
3 Ape Shall Kill Ape U
4 Arcanomoth, Metamorphic Abomination C
5 Arctic Fortress U
6 Black Belt Rebels, Fanatic Nationalists C
7 Black Helicopter Squad, Pledged Agents C
8 The Blind, Sorcerer Assassin R
9 Botzilla, Behemoth Mechanical Lizard R
10 Bouncing the Rubble U
11 Box of Bones U
12 Bull Market U
13 Burning Man, Fire Secret Agent U
14 Bush Pilot, Rugged Hero C
15 Buzzsaw Arm, Brutal Weapon State U
16 Cannibal Army, Albino Horde C
17 Cannibal's Banquet C
18 Catching Bullets C
19 Cheng Hu Bai, Red Master R
20 Christine Winter, Fractured Sorcerer Prodigy U
21 Cloaca, Demon King of the Hong Kong Sewers R
22 Corporate Warfare U
23 Crane Stance C
24 Cybermod Parlor C
25 Cyborg Mermaid, Aquatic Saboteur U
26 Delay the Inevitable C
27 Demonic Alliance Promo
28 Devendra Chalal, The Burning Hand R
29 Dimitri Lyapunov, Cybernetics Mastermind R
30 Echo Distortion C
31 Elephant Style C
32 Everything Falls Apart U
33 Feral Regression U
34 Flambards, Fire Secret Society C
35 Floating Teeth, Darkness Horrors C
36 Forgotten Temple U
37 Freelance Platoon, Abandoned Pledged Agents C
38 Frenzy Engine, Arcanowave State U
39 Gathering the Fire C
40 General Gog, Abomination Mastermind R
41 Geoffrey Smythe, Cultist Traitor R
42 The Gimp, Nanotech Mutant Promo
43 The Gray, Spirit of Absence R
44 Habbakuk, Floating Feng Shui Site R
45 The Hand of the Underworld, Killer Demon U
46 Harbinger, Secret Herald of the Fire King R
47 Haunted, Ghost State C
48 The Hegemeister, Tank State R
49 Hirake Kazuko, Corporate Mastermind R
50 Hit Squad, Violent Gangsters C
51 Homicide Detective, Jaded Cop U
52 Hot Zone, Wasteland Site U
53 Howling for Blood C
54 Hydroponic Garden, Martian Feng Shui Site C
55 Ice Blessing C
56 Ice Carvers, Netherworld Mystics C
57 Impossible Men, Self-Made Paradoxes U
58 Improvised Weapons C
59 The Inner Garden U
60 Inside Man, Connected Hood U
61 Iron Hands Ma, Rebel Martial Artist U
62 The Iron Palace, Secret Feng Shui Site R
63 Jigsaw Beast, Modular Abomination U
64 Julienne Wong, Political Mastermind R
65 Junior Executive, Corporate Agent C
66 Kamikaze Cosmonauts, Outer-Space Saboteurs C
67 Keeper of Echoes, Recursive Spirit R
68 LaGrange Four, Orbital Feng Shui Site R
69 Lenny Wu, Martial Artist Cop U
70 Li Han, Kung Fu Prodigy R
71 The Library of Souls R
72 Lightning Strike, Thunder Event U
73 malloc(), Resurrected Hacker R
74 The Mark of Evil Promo
75 Mars Colonist, Expendable Student C
76 Master Yuen, Teacher of the Red Principle R
77 Melting Flesh Squad, Unruly Abominations U
78 Ming I's Chosen, Darkness State U
79 Mistress of Blotted Moonlight, Darkness Spirit R
80 Moon Base C
81 Muscle Car, Homemade Tank State U
82 Mystical Cosine U
83 Nanovirus C
84 New Recruits, Netherworld Soldiers C
85 Noriko Watson, Razor Girl Promo
86 Northern Long Fist U
87 Orange Divination U
88 Palace of Virtual Light R
89 Panzer X, Tank State U
90 Petal's Attendant, Eunuch Sorcerer Assassin C
91 Probability Soldiers, Agents of the Uncertainty Principle C
92 Project Apocalypse, Doomsday Site R

93 Rainforest Ruins U
94 Reascension Agenda Promo
95 Reascension Spy, Undercover Salaryman U
96 Rebel Without a Cause, Disaffected Saboteur C
97 Reentry Squad, Space Monkeys U
98 Rei Okamoto, Hacker Mastermind U
99 Reprogramming C
100 Rogue Shaper, Netherworld Mercenary U
101 Sacred Heart Hospital Promo
102 Safety Third! C
103 Scramble Suit, State of the Art Tech U
104 Secret Plans for World Domination U
105 Security Officers, Corporate Cops C
106 Sewer Demon, Noxious Monster U
107 Shadowy Mentor C
108 Shaolin Saboteur, Agent of the Blue Principle C
109 Shard of the Molten Heart, Triumvirate Relic Edge Promo
110 Sidekick, Scrappy Teenager C
111 Silverback, Revolutionary Monkey Leader R
112 Smugglers, Black-Market Operators C
113 Solar Flare C
114 Soul of the Wolf C
115 Squadron-Leader Holz, Retired Soldier R
116 Street Sensei, Hood Martial Artist C
117 Stunt Driving, Death-Defying Event C
118 Summer Fire Palace, Netherworld Site R
119 Symphonic Disciples, Insane Orchestra C
120 Taiko Drummer, Martial Arts Student C
121 Temporal Anomaly U
122 Three Days to Retirement, Cop State U
123 Triumphant Heroes C
124 True Believer, Indoctrinated Pawn C
125 Turbo Boost C
126 Turing Machine, Chi-Hating Silicon C
127 Twelve Thousand Skulls U
128 The Unspoken Name, Pledged Renegade R
129 Wailing Apparition, Vengeful Ghost C
130 Willow Step U
131 Xin Ji Yang, Evil Princess R
132 Xu Mei, The Dragon, Cybernetic Martial Arts Master R
133 Zero-G Sumo, Enhanced Colonist U
134 Zheng Yi Quan, Master of the World R
135 Zhu Maichen, Martial Arts Mastermind R

2009 Shadowfist Empire of Evil

1 36-Legged Horror, Spirit of Persistence U
2 Abomination Serum U
3 Abysmal Behemoth, Demon Steed State U
4 Akamatsu Mitsusuke, Corporate Samurai R
5 Alexandre Chen, Redeemed Monster Hunter R
6 Alpine Squad, Elite Soldiers U
7 Ancient Stone Arch C
8 Andi Di, Rabble Rouser U
9 Arcanowave Feedback C
10 Auspicious Thermite U
11 Awesome Presence U
12 Back in Black C
13 Bamboo Forest C
14 Bandolier of Throwing Knives C
15 Baron Volund, Thunder General R
16 Bending Chi C
17 Blue Master, Martial Artist U
18 Blue Meditation C
19 Bonebow Army, Mercenary Demon Archers U
20 Brave Villagers, Peasant Archers C
21 CDCA Spies, Arcanowave Sorcerers C
22 Cocktail Waiters, Pyromaniac Rabble C
23 Combat Engineer, Military Scientist C
24 Commandant Barkhorn, Rugged Soldier R
25 Compromised Security C
26 Consuming Darkness C
27 Damon Winter, Keeper of Secrets R
28 Dao Biotech Headquarters, Corporate Site R
29 Darkness Golem, Netherworld Nightmare R
30 Data Mining C
31 Delaying Tactics U
32 Desperate Measures C
33 Difficulty at the End of Things C
34 Dr. Hans Wulfjaeger, Disturbing Scientist U
35 Drowning in Blood U
36 Echo Spirit, Reverberating Construct C
37 Embrace of the Snake U
38 Endless Corridor, Netherworld Feng Shui Site U
39 Equal Opportunity Butt-Kicking C
40 Escalation C
41 Evil Brain in a Jar Promo
42 Explosive Motorcycle U
43 Fingertip Razors C
44 Fire Engineers, Netherworld Scholars C
45 Fire Falx, Two-Handed Sword State U
46 Gnarled Annihilator, Killer Abomination R
47 Hanging Gardens R
48 Hell Hound, Servant of Evil U
49 Heroic Converts, Martial Artists U
50 Hiroshi Kata, Wired Martial Artist R
51 Horus, Reascended Falcon R
52 Hunger of the Jackal, Lodge Hood U
53 Imperial Sycophants, Eunuch Toadies C
54 Infernal Army, Immense Demon Horde R
55 Iron Jim Colson, One-Man Gang R
56 Jade Willow, Master of Unyielding Dragon Kung Fu R
57 Jayne Insane, Pyromaniac Cyborg R
58 Johnny Amok, Suicidal Netherworld Mercenary R
59 KFC Promo
60 Kisa Serkov, Doomsday Prophet R
61 Liu Jian Lang, Honorable Eunuch R
62 Machine Warrior, Junk-Eating Cyborg Promo
63 Mars Program Executive, Corporate Scientist U
64 Martyr's Tomb U
65 Meditative Flight, Shaolin State U
66 Mirrored Lake C
67 Mountain Hermit, Taoist Sorcerer U
68 Mountain Monastery, Sanctuary Site C
69 Mountain Sanctuary U
70 NeoBuro Field Medic, Military Doctor C
71 Netherworld Librarian, Ice Scholar C
72 Nomad Army, Bandit Warriors C
73 Origami Handguns, Gun State C
74 Out of the Barrel C
75 Overzealous Assasins U
76 Paradox Archives U
77 Platinum Upgrade, Cybernetic State R
78 Potemkin's Brigade, Loyal Saboteurs U
79 Prefect's Guard, Imperial Cops C
80 Preserving Chi U
81 Probability Shift U
82 Red Tape Assault C
83 Resistance in Numbers U
84 Secret Warrior Training Base, Battleground Site U
85 Shadow Seductress, Darkness Assassin U
86 Shang Bojing, Rebel Leader Promo
87 Shihong, Ghost Martial Artist R
88 Skin and Darkness Hunter, Relentless Horror U
89 Smoke and Mirrors U
90 Spartan Warriors, Netherworld Mercenaries C
91 Spy Network U
92 Stoic Wanderer, Orange Monk C
93 Stolen Thunder C
94 Street Doc, Cybernetics Patch Man C
95 Street Racers, High-Speed Hoods C
96 Strength of the Land U
97 Suicide Squad, Rebel Infiltrators C
98 Superior Tactics, Military Edge U
99 Swordbreaker Rao, Rebel Gladiator Promo
100 Synchronic Beam Emitter, Cybernetic State U
101 Tattooed Man, Mysterious Martial Artist U
102 Tentacles of the Squid, Lodge Enforcers U
103 The Alabaster King, Demon Lord R
104 The Alabaster Palace, Underworld Feng Shui Site R
105 The Becoming R
106 The Blood of Heroes U
107 The Great Wall C
108 The Keeper of Hearts, High Darkness Priestess R
109 The Petrified Man, Netherworld Mercenary R
110 The Price of Progress C
111 The Shangshu Mansion R
112 The She-Wolf, Transformed Animal Warlord R
113 The Spirit of Kongxiangshi, Guardian Ghost R
114 The Stasis Engine, Spirit of Inertia Promo
115 The Wireless, Nightclub Site R
116 The Withering of Souls C
117 The Wrath of Kong, Big Angry Monkey R
118 Thingshot U
119 Tunnel King, Rebel Techie C
120 Uncertainty Spirit, Enigmatic Construct U
121 Under the Knife C
122 Underworld Contacts C
123 Underworld Coronation R
124 Unholy Legionnaires, Undead Soldiers C
125 Vitality Shunt C
126 Weeping Willows U
127 Whelps, Young Transformed Wolves C
128 Willow Warriors, Army of the Treetops C
129 Wisdom of the Owl, Lodge Archivist C
130 Withering Touch C
131 Wriggling Skin Suit, Darkness Event U
132 Xin Ji Yang vPAP, Underworld Queen R
133 Xin Ji Yang vPAP, Center of the Lotus Promo
134 Yuan Chonguan, Mastermind of War R
135 Zen Ritualist, Abstract Geomancer C

1994 Spellfire Master the Magic 0th Edition

1 Waterdeep
2 Menzoberranzan
3 Zhentil Keep R
4 Shadowdale
5 Cormyr
6 Sembia
7 Moonshae Isles
8 Thay
9 Calimshan
10 Pirate Isles
11 Ravens Bluff
12 Great Rift, The
13 Myth Drannor U
14 Vaasa
15 Jungles of Chult
16 High Forest, The
17 Sword Coast
18 Anauroch
19 Impiltur
20 Icewind Dale
21 High Moor, The
22 Rashemen
23 Damara
24 Narfell
25 Dragonspear Castle
26 Daggerdale
27 Darkhold
28 Haunted Hall of Eveningstar R
29 Evermeet
30 Trollmoors, The
31 Berdusk U
32 Tantras U
33 Mulmaster U
34 Hillsfar U
35 Suzail U
36 Arabel U
37 Fortifications U
38 Fortifications U
39 Selune U
40 Peasant Militia U
41 Alias the Sell-Sword U
42 King Azoun IV R
43 Maligor the Red R
44 Elminster the Mage U
45 Drizzt Do'Urden C
46 Midnight, Goddess of Magic R
47 Torg Mac Cei, the Ironlord U
48 Pereghost, The R
49 Bruenor Battlehammer R
50 Marco Volo U
51 Harpers, The C
52 Gnomes of Samek U
53 Adventurers! C
54 War Party C
55 Crime Lord U
56 Adventurers C
57 Jotunslayers, The C
58 Armies of Bloodstone U
59 Iron Legion, The C
60 Tergoz Tenhammer C
61 Myrmidons R
62 Magister, The R
63 Karlott the Shaman U
64 King Halvor II U
65 Pteranadon C
66 Gorgosaurus R
67 Greater Feyr R
68 Cleric of Gond R
69 Cleric of Torm R
70 Cleric of Mask R
71 Drow Matron U
72 Dracolich R
73 Vasos Flameslayer R
74 Allisa of the Mists C
75 Grypht the Saurial U
76 Worden Ironfist R
77 Amarill U
78 Joliet the Rash C
79 Dwarf of Earthfast C
80 Black Courser R
81 Hornhead Saurial C
82 Dagrande U
83 Mind Flayer R
84 Noble Djinni R
85 Hubadai R
86 Intellect Devourer U
87 Shandrill C
88 Triceratops R
89 Cleric of Malar C
90 Airship U
91 Bad Omens C
92 Fortunate Omens C
93 Rod of Shapechange U
94 Dwarven Hammer R
95 Staff of Striking R
96 Horrors of the Abyss U
97 Flameblade R
98 Figurine of Wonderous Power C
99 Cataclysm! U
100 Good Fortune U
101 Surprise Raid C
102 Banner of 1-eyed God C
103 Viperhand U
104 Orb of Doom C
105 Staff of Conjuring C
106 Spell of Formless Horror U
107 Safe Harbor R
108 Labor of Legend C
109 Wand of Light U
110 Elf Galleon R
111 Free City of Greyhawk R
112 Lands of Iuz, The U
113 Pomarj, The
114 Hold of the Sea Princes
115 Yeomanry
116 Blackmoor U
117 Horned Society, The
118 Wolf Nomads, The
119 Sterich
120 Nyrond
121 Veluna
122 Furyondy
123 Great Kingdom R
124 Temple of Elemental Evil U
125 Greyhawk Ruins U
126 Perrenland
127 Keoland
128 Celene
129 Bright Desert, The
130 Theocracy of the Pale
131 Bone March
132 Duchy of Urnst, The
133 Sea Barons, The
134 Bissel C
135 Scarlet Brotherhood, The U
136 Irongate
137 Principality of Ulek C
138 County of Sunndi C
139 Duchy of Tenh C
140 Burneal Forest C
141 Castle Hart C
142 Arms of Horned Society R
143 Arms of Iuz R
144 Arms of Greyhawk R
145 Arms of Great Kingdom R
146 Arms of Furyondy C
147 Arms of Nyrond C
148 Skull Keep C
149 Fortification C
150 Siege! U
151 War Banner C
152 Codex of the Infinite Planes C
153 Crystal of the Ebon Flame U
154 Hordes of Castle Greyhawk R
155 Skeletal Horde C
156 Eye & Hand of Vecna U
157 Orb of Dragonkind U
158 Baba Yaga's Hut U
159 Chariot of Lynx R
160 Cup of Al-Akbar U
161 Rary the Traitor C
162 Mordenkainen R
163 Tysiln San U
164 Otto R
165 Mika the Wolf Nomad R
166 Lolth, the Spider Queen R
167 Iuz the Evil U
168 Mutiny! R
169 Swordwraith R
170 Sysania U
171 Kiara U
172 Hettman Tsurin R
173 Griffon R
174 Sea Zombie R
175 Mist Wolf R
176 Tyrinon U
177 Quagmiela the Dragon U
178 Seragrimm the Just R
179 Skulk R
180 Berserk Fury! R
181 Wolf Nomads C
182 Zadoc R
183 Miles U
184 Trystan C
185 Thorvid R
186 Fairy Madness R
187 Nenioc U
188 Young Gold Dragon C
189 Arch-Druid R
190 Hell Hound U
191 Griffon R
192 Giant Skeleton R
193 Skeleton C
194 Winged Horror U
195 Treants of Grandwood U
196 Rangers of Hornwood C
197 Magical Barding R
198 Border Forts C
199 Ren's Crystal Ball C
200 Falcon Figurine U
201 Transformation C
202 Enslaved! U
203 Siege C
204 Bribery! R
205 Charge! U
206 Magic Sword C
207 Enlarge R
208 Ring of Shooting Stars R
209 Arms of Veluna C
210 Fast Talking! U
211 Flight C
212 Shapechange R
213 Barbarian Raiders R
214 Treasure Fleet R
215 Potion of Fire Breathing R
216 Arms of Shield Lands C
217 Net of Entrapment U
218 Johydee's Mask R
219 Helm of Teleportation R
220 Rod of Dispel Magic U
221 Draj
222 Raam
223 Urik
224 Tyr
225 Gulg U
226 Nibenay U
227 Balic
228 Mud Palace, The U
229 North Ledopolus U
230 South Ledopolus U
231 Altaruk C
232 Salt View C
233 Ogo U
234 Makla U
235 Kalidnay C
236 Arkhold C
237 Salt View C
238 Waverly R
239 Bodach R
240 Giustenal U
241 Yaramuke C
242 Lost Oasis C
243 Grak's Pool C
244 Silver Spring C
245 Bitter Well C
246 Black Waters C
247 Fort Melidor C
248 Dungeon of Gulg C
249 Ziggurat U
250 Temple C
251 Mogadisho's Horde C
252 Assassins U
253 Halfling Mercenaries C
254 War Band C
255 Kank Lancers U
256 Nomad Mercenaries C
257 Gladiators U
258 Rikus U
259 Neeva R
260 Sadira C
261 Agis U
262 Anavias R
263 Vaerhirmana R
264 Herminard C
265 T'kkyl C
266 Azhul the Hasty U
267 Chividal R
268 Bagual C
269 Rowan U
270 Shayira C
271 Ashathra C
272 Stug C
273 Ka'Cha U
274 Galek C
275 Wind Dancers U
276 Water Hunters C
277 Silver Hands U
278 Sky Singers C
279 Silt Stalkers C
280 Night Runners U
281 So-ut R
282 Cistern Fiend C
283 Sloth C
284 Mul Savage R
285 Inhuman U
286 Pyreen R
287 Cha'thrang U
288 Spirit of the Land R
289 Thri-kreen R
290 Wijon C
291 Mikor U
292 Salicia R
293 Zurn U
294 Powell C
295 Baber R
296 Wachter C
297 Foucault U
298 Stef'fa Naf'ski R
299 Captain Kazhal R
300 Dlasva U
301 Tithian R
302 Verrasi U
303 Defiler C
304 Dragon King R
305 Borys R
306 Preserver C
307 Punisher C
308 Gith U
309 Tiger C
310 Orb of Power C
311 Rings of All Seeing U
312 Treasure C
313 Shield of Destruction C
314 Shield of Annihilation U
315 Shield of Devastation C
316 Shield of Wickedness C
317 Shield of Gore U
318 Heartwood Spear, The C
319 Caravan, The C
320 Necklace, The U
321 Elemental Cleric C
322 Elven Archer R
323 Outcast, The R
324 Thugs U
325 Desert Warrior R
326 Desert Warrior R
327 Desert Warrior R
328 Marauder C
329 Shaqat Beetles C
330 Tembo U
331 Fireball C
332 Lightning Bolt C
333 Paralyze C
334 Magic Missile C
335 Wall of Fire C
336 Wall of Iron C
337 Wall of Stone C
338 Wall of Force C
339 Invisibility R
340 Cone of Cold C
341 Sleep C
342 Shield C
343 Fly C
344 Crushing Fist R
345 Anti-Magic Shell R
346 Dispel Magic C
347 Improved Phantasmal Force C
348 Fear R
349 Cure Light Wounds C
350 Cure Serious Wounds C
351 Sticks to Snakes C
352 Blade Barrier R
353 Bless C
354 Sanctuary R
355 Wind Walk R
356 Bark Skin C
357 Charm C
358 Dispel Magic C
359 Darkness C
360 Protection C
361 Chariot of Sustarre C
362 Sunray R
363 Wall of Thorns C
364 Wall of Fire U
365 Holy Word C
366 Raise Dead R
367 Flame Strike U
368 Protection from Lightning C
369 Silence U
370 Invisibility to Undead C
371 Wall of Fog C
372 Forget C
373 Web C
374 Blink C
375 Hold Undead C
376 Charm Monster C
377 Wind of Disenchantment R
378 Black Tentacles U
379 Fire Shield U
380 Ice Storm C
381 Phantasmal Killer R
382 Solid Fog C
383 Animate Dead C
384 Cloudkill C
385 Feebleminded C
386 Magic Jar C
387 Faithful Hound C
388 Passwall C
389 Rock to Mud C
390 Chain Lightning C
391 Death Fog C
392 Death Spell C
393 Disintegrate R
394 Geas C

395 Banishment C
396 Control Undead C
397 Finger of Death C
398 Spell Turning C
399 Ancient Curse R
400 Calm C

1994 Spellfire Master the Magic 1st Edition

125 Sakornia VR
225 Edomira, Red Dragon VR
325 Gloriana VR
425 Gib Ekim VR
525 Neirgral, Green Dragon VR
625 Dagaronzie, Green Dragon VR
725 Feyelsae VR
825 Dragon Rage VR
925 Shalbaal, Red Dragon VR
1025 Delsenora VR
1125 Gib Evets VR
1225 Dori the Barbarian VR
1325 Gib Htimsen VR
1400 Waterdeep
1425 Darbee VR
1525 Aurum, Gold Dragon VR
1625 Halcyon VR
1725 Stryck VR
1825 Alicia VR
1925 Red Zeb VR
2025 Avatar, The VR
2125 Smolder, Red Dragon VR
2225 Lovely Colleen VR
2325 Ember, Red Dragon VR
2400 Menzoberranzan
2425 Andra the Wise VR
2525 Karm, Black Dragon VR
3400 Zhentil Keep R
4400 Shadowdale
5400 Cormyr
6400 Sembia
7400 Moonshae Isles
8400 Thay
9400 Calimshan
10400 Pirate Isles
11400 Ravens Bluff
12400 Great Rift, The
13400 Myth Drannor U
14400 Vaasa
15400 Jungles of Chult
16400 High Forest, The
17400 Sword Coast
18400 Anauroch
19400 Impiltur
20400 Icewind Dale
21400 High Moor, The
22400 Rashemen
23400 Damara
24400 Narfell
25400 Dragonspear Castle
26400 Daggerdale
27400 Darkhold
28400 Haunted Hall of Eveningstar R
29400 Evermeet
30400 Trollmoors, The
31400 Berdusk U
32400 Tantras U
33400 Mulmaster U
34400 Hillsfar U
35400 Suzail U
36400 Arabel U
37400 Fortifications U
38400 Fortifications U
39400 Selune U
40400 Peasant Militia U
41400 Alias the Sell-Sword U
42400 King Azoun IV R
43400 Maligor the Red R
44400 Elminster the Mage U
45400 Drizzt Do'Urden C
46400 Midnight, Goddess of Magic R
47400 Torg Mac Cei, the Ironlord U
48400 Pereghost, The R
49400 Bruenor Battlehammer R
50400 Marco Volo U
51400 Harpers, The C
52400 Gnomes of Samek U
53400 Adventurers! C
54400 War Party C
55400 Crime Lord U
56400 Adventurers C
57400 Jotunslayers, The C
58400 Armies of Bloodstone U
59400 Iron Legion, The C
60400 Tergoz Tenhammer C
61400 Myrmidons R
62400 Magister, The R
63400 Karlott the Shaman U
64400 King Halvor II U
65400 Pteranadon C
66400 Gorgosaurus R
67400 Greater Feyr R
68400 Cleric of Gond R
69400 Cleric of Torm R
70400 Cleric of Mask R
71400 Drow Matron U
72400 Dracolich R
73400 Vasos Flameslayer R
74400 Allisa of the Mists C
75400 Grypht the Saurial U
76400 Worden Ironfist R
77400 Amarill U
78400 Joliet the Rash C
79400 Dwarf of Earthfast C
80400 Black Courser R
81400 Hornhead Saurial C
82400 Dagrande U
83400 Mind Flayer R
84400 Noble Djinni R
85400 Hubadai R
86400 Intellect Devourer U
87400 Shandrill C
88400 Triceratops R
89400 Cleric of Malar C
90400 Airship U
91400 Bad Omens C
92400 Fortunate Omens C
93400 Rod of Shapechange U
94400 Dwarven Hammer R
95400 Staff of Striking R
96400 Horrors of the Abyss U
97400 Flameblade R
98400 Figurine of Wonderous Power C
99400 Cataclysm! U
100400 Good Fortune U
101400 Surprise Raid C
102400 Banner of 1-eyed God C
103400 Viperhand U
104400 Orb of Doom C
105400 Staff of Conjuring C
106400 Spell of Formless Horror U
107400 Safe Harbor R
108400 Labor of Legend C
109400 Wand of Light U
110400 Elf Galleon R
111400 Free City of Greyhawk R
112400 Lands of Iuz, The U
113400 Pomarj, The
114400 Hold of the Sea Princes
115400 Yeomanry
116400 Blackmoor U
117400 Horned Society, The
118400 Wolf Nomads, The
119400 Sterich
120400 Nyrond
121400 Veluna
122400 Furyondy
123400 Great Kingdom R
124400 Temple of Elemental Evil U
125400 Greyhawk Ruins U
126400 Perrenland
127400 Keoland
128400 Celene
129400 Bright Desert, The
130400 Theocracy of the Pale
131400 Bone March
132400 Duchy of Urnst, The
133400 Sea Barons, The
134400 Bissel C
135400 Scarlet Brotherhood, The U
136400 Irongate
137400 Principality of Ulek C
138400 County of Sunndi C
139400 Duchy of Tenh C
140400 Burneal Forest C
141400 Castle Hart C
142400 Arms of Horned Society R
143400 Arms of Iuz R
144400 Arms of Greyhawk R
145400 Arms of Great Kingdom R
146400 Arms of Furyondy C
147400 Arms of Nyrond C
148400 Skull Keep C
149400 Fortification C
150400 Siege! U
151400 War Banner C
152400 Codex of the Infinite Planes C
153400 Crystal of the Ebon Flame U
154400 Hordes of Castle Greyhawk R
155400 Skeletal Horde C
156400 Eye & Hand of Vecna U
157400 Orb of Dragonkind U
158400 Baba Yaga's Hut U
159400 Chariot of Lyrx R
160400 Cup of Al-Akbar U
161400 Rary the Traitor C
162400 Mordenkainen R
163400 Tysiln San U
164400 Otto R
165400 Mika the Wolf Nomad R
166400 Lolth, the Spider Queen R
167400 Iuz the Evil U
168400 Mutiny! R
169400 Swordwraith R
170400 Sysania U
171400 Kiara U
172400 Hettman Tsurin R
173400 Griffon R
174400 Sea Zombie R
175400 Mist Wolf R
176400 Tyrinon U
177400 Quagmiela the Dragon U
178400 Seragrimm the Just R
179400 Skulk R
180400 Berserk Fury! R
181400 Wolf Nomads C
182400 Zadoc R
183400 Miles U
184400 Trystan C
185400 Thorvid R
186400 Fairy Madness R
187400 Nenioc U
188400 Young Gold Dragon C
189400 Arch-Druid R
190400 Hell Hound U
191400 Griffon R
192400 Giant Skeleton R
193400 Skeleton C
194400 Winged Horror U
195400 Treants of Grandwood U
196400 Rangers of Hornwood C
197400 Magical Barding R
198400 Border Forts C
199400 Ren's Crystal Ball C
200400 Falcon Figurine U
201400 Transformation C
202400 Enslaved! U
203400 Siege C
204400 Bribery! R
205400 Charge! U
206400 Magic Sword C
207400 Enlarge R
208400 Ring of Shooting Stars R
209400 Arms of Veluna C
210400 Fast Talking! U
211400 Flight C
212400 Shapechange R
213400 Barbarian Raiders R
214400 Treasure Fleet R
215400 Potion of Fire Breathing R
216400 Arms of Shield Lands C
217400 Net of Entrapment U
218400 Johydee's Mask R
219400 Helm of Teleportation R
220400 Rod of Dispel Magic U
221400 Draj
222400 Raam
223400 Urik
224400 Tyr
225400 Gulg U
226400 Nibenay U
227400 Balic
228400 Mud Palace, The U
229400 North Ledopolus U
230400 South Ledopolus U
231400 Altaruk C
232400 Salt View C
233400 Ogo U
234400 Makla U
235400 Kalidnay C
236400 Arkhold C
237400 Salt View C
238400 Waverly R
239400 Bodach R
240400 Giustenal U
241400 Yaramuke C
242400 Lost Oasis C
243400 Grak's Pool C
244400 Silver Spring C
245400 Bitter Well C
246400 Black Waters C
247400 Fort Melidor C
248400 Dungeon of Gulg C
249400 Ziggurat U
250400 Temple C
251400 Mogadisho's Horde C
252400 Assassins U
253400 Halfling Mercenaries C
254400 War Band C
255400 Kank Lancers U
256400 Nomad Mercenaries C
257400 Gladiators U
258400 Rikus U
259400 Neeva R
260400 Sadira C
261400 Agis U
262400 Anavias R
263400 Vaerhirmana R
264400 Herminard C
265400 T'kkyl C
266400 Azhul the Hasty U
267400 Chividal R
268400 Bagual C
269400 Rowan U
270400 Shayira C
271400 Ashathra C
272400 Stug C
273400 Ka'Cha U
274400 Galek C
275400 Wind Dancers U
276400 Water Hunters C
277400 Silver Hands U
278400 Sky Singers C
279400 Silt Stalkers C
280400 Night Runners U
281400 So-ut R
282400 Cistern Fiend C
283400 Sloth C
284400 Mul Savage R
285400 Inhuman U
286400 Pyreen R
287400 Cha'thrang U
288400 Spirit of the Land R
289400 Thri-kreen R
290400 Wijon C
291400 Mikor U
292400 Salicia R
293400 Zurn U
294400 Powell C
295400 Baber R
296400 Wachter C
297400 Foucault U
298400 Stef'fa Naf'ski R
299400 Captain Kazhal R
300400 Dlasva U
301400 Tithian R
302400 Verrasi U
303400 Defiler C
304400 Dragon King R
305400 Borys R
306400 Preserver C
307400 Punisher C
308400 Gith U
309400 Tiger C
310400 Orb of Power C
311400 Rings of All Seeing U
312400 Treasure C
313400 Shield of Destruction C
314400 Shield of Annihilation U
315400 Shield of Devastation C
316400 Shield of Wickedness C
317400 Shield of Gore U
318400 Heartwood Spear, The C
319400 Caravan, The C
320400 Necklace, The U
321400 Elemental Cleric C
322400 Elven Archer R
323400 Outcast, The R
324400 Thugs U
325400 Desert Warrior R
326400 Desert Warrior R
327400 Desert Warrior R
328400 Marauder C
329400 Shaqat Beetles C
330400 Tembo U
331400 Fireball C
332400 Lightning Bolt C
333400 Paralyze C
334400 Magic Missile C
335400 Wall of Fire C
336400 Wall of Iron C
337400 Wall of Stone C
338400 Wall of Force C
339400 Invisibility R
340400 Cone of Cold C
341400 Sleep C
342400 Shield C
343400 Fly C
344400 Crushing Fist R
345400 Anti-Magic Shell R
346400 Dispel Magic C
347400 Improved Phantasmal Force C
348400 Fear R
349400 Cure Light Wounds C
350400 Cure Serious Wounds C
351400 Sticks to Snakes C
352400 Blade Barrier R
353400 Bless C
354400 Sanctuary R
355400 Wind Walk R
356400 Bark Skin C
357400 Charm C
358400 Dispel Magic C
359400 Darkness C
360400 Protection C
361400 Chariot of Sustarre C
362400 Sunray R
363400 Wall of Thorns C
364400 Wall of Fire U
365400 Holy Word C
366400 Raise Dead R
367400 Flame Strike U
368400 Protection from Lightning C
369400 Silence U
370400 Invisibility to Undead C
371400 Wall of Fog C
372400 Forget C
373400 Web C
374400 Blink C
375400 Hold Undead C
376400 Charm Monster C
377400 Wind of Disenchantment R
378400 Black Tentacles U
379400 Fire Shield U
380400 Ice Storm C
381400 Phantasmal Killer R
382400 Solid Fog C
383400 Animate Dead C
384400 Cloudkill C
385400 Feebleminded C
386400 Magic Jar C
387400 Faithful Hound C
388400 Passwall C
389400 Rock to Mud C
390400 Chain Lightning C
391400 Death Fog C
392400 Death Spell C
393400 Disintegrate R
394400 Geas C
395400 Banishment C
396400 Control Undead C
397400 Finger of Death C
398400 Spell Turning C
399400 Ancient Curse R
400400 Calm C
401420 Discovery of Spellfire R
402420 Magical Champion R
403420 Traitor R
404420 Chaos Shield R
405420 Slave of Tunek R
406420 Phorbes's Scrolls R
407420 Mercenary Gold R
408420 Living Scroll R
409420 Ren's Bell of Death R
410420 Labyrinth Map of Shucc, The R
411420 Annulus R
412420 Scroll of 7 Leagues R
413420 Map of Life R
414420 Supernatural Chill R
415420 Map to a Mercenary Army R
416420 Pit Trap! R
417420 Mind Flayer Lord R
418420 Aurak Draconian Lord R
419420 Ego Coin R
420420 Chest of Many Things R
421440 Gelatinous Cube R
422440 Gatekeeper R
423440 Age of Entropy R
424440 Orb of Green Dragonkind R
425440 Undead Htimsen, The R
426440 Tapestry of the Stag R
427440 Dori the Barbarian's Cape R
428440 Weasel Attack! R
429440 Barbarian's Decree, The R
430440 Abyssal Vortex, The R
431440 Prismal the Outrageous R
432440 Malatra, the Living Jungle R
433440 Mayor Charles Oliver O'Kane R
434440 Bengoukee the Witch Doctor R
435440 Big Chief Bagoomba R
436440 Genie Bottle, The R
437440 Estate Transference R
438440 Starshine R
439440 Starving Artist, The R
440440 King of the Elves, The R

1994 Spellfire Master the Magic 2nd Edition

1400 Waterdeep
2400 Menzoberranzan
3400 Zhentil Keep R
4400 Shadowdale
5400 Cormyr
6400 Sembia
7400 Moonshae Isles
8400 Thay
9400 Calimshan
10400 Pirate Isles
11400 Ravens Bluff
12400 Great Rift, The
13400 Myth Drannor U
14400 Vaasa
15400 Jungles of Chult
16400 High Forest, The
17400 Sword Coast
18400 Anauroch
19400 Impiltur
20400 Icewind Dale
21400 High Moor, The
22400 Rashemen
23400 Damara
24400 Narfell
25400 Dragonspear Castle
26400 Daggerdale
27400 Darkhold
28400 Haunted Hall of Eveningstar R
29400 Evermeet
30400 Trollmoors, The
31400 Berdusk U
32400 Tantras U
33400 Mulmaster U
34400 Hillsfar U
35400 Suzail U
36400 Arabel U
37400 Fortifications U
38400 Fortifications U
39400 Selune U
40400 Peasant Militia U
41400 Alias the Sell-Sword U
42400 King Azoun IV R
43400 Maligor the Red R
44400 Elminster the Mage U
45400 Drizzt Do'Urden C
46400 Midnight, Goddess of Magic R
47400 Torg Mac Cei, the Ironlord U
48400 Pereghost, The R
49400 Bruenor Battlehammer R
50400 Marco Volo U
51400 Harpers, The C
52400 Gnomes of Samek U
53400 Adventurers! C
54400 War Party C
55400 Crime Lord U
56400 Adventurers C
57400 Jotunslayers, The C
58400 Armies of Bloodstone U
59400 Iron Legion, The C
60400 Tergoz Tenhammer C
61400 Myrmidons R
62400 Magister, The R
63400 Karlott the Shaman U
64400 King Halvor II U
65400 Pteranadon C
66400 Gorgosaurus R
67400 Greater Feyr R
69400 Cleric of Torm R
70400 Cleric of Mask R
71400 Drow Matron U
72400 Dracolich R
73400 Vasos Flameslayer R
74400 Allisa of the Mists C
75400 Grypht the Saurial U
76400 Worden Ironfist R
77400 Amarill U
78400 Joliet the Rash C
79400 Dwarf of Earthfast C
80400 Black Courser R
81400 Hornhead Saurial C
82400 Dagrande U
83400 Mind Flayer R
84400 Noble Djinni R
86400 Intellect Devourer U
87400 Shandrill C
88400 Triceratops R
89400 Cleric of Malar C
90400 Airship U
91400 Bad Omens C
92400 Fortunate Omens C
93400 Rod of Shapechange U
94400 Dwarven Hammer R
95400 Staff of Striking R
96400 Horrors of the Abyss U
98400 Figurine of Wonderous Power C
99400 Cataclysm! U
100400 Good Fortune U
101400 Surprise Raid C
102400 Banner of 1-eyed God C
103400 Viperhand U

104400 Orb of Doom C
105400 Staff of Conjuring C
106400 Spell of Formless Horror U
107400 Safe Harbor R
108400 Labor of Legend C
109400 Wand of Light U
110400 Elf Galleon R
111400 Free City of Greyhawk R
112400 Lands of Iuz, The U
113400 Pomarj, The
114400 Hold of the Sea Princes
115400 Yeomanry
116400 Blackmoor U
117400 Horned Society, The
118400 Wolf Nomads, The
119400 Sterich
120400 Nyrond
121400 Veluna
122400 Furyondy
123400 Great Kingdom R
124400 Temple of Elemental Evil U
125400 Greyhawk Ruins U
126400 Perrenland
127400 Keoland
128400 Celene
129400 Bright Desert, The
130400 Theocracy of the Pale
131400 Bone March
132400 Duchy of Urnst, The
133400 Sea Barons, The
134400 Bissel C
135400 Scarlet Brotherhood, The U
136400 Irongate
137400 Principality of Ulek C
138400 County of Sunndi C
139400 Duchy of Tenh C
140400 Burneal Forest C
141400 Castle Hart C
142400 Arms of Horned Society R
144400 Arms of Greyhawk R
145400 Arms of Great Kingdom R
146400 Arms of Furyondy C
147400 Arms of Nyrond C
148400 Skull Keep C
149400 Fortification C
150400 Siege! U
151400 War Banner C
152400 Codex of the Infinite Planes C
153400 Crystal of the Ebon Flame U
154400 Hordes of Castle Greyhawk R
155400 Skeletal Horde C
156400 Eye & Hand of Vecna U
157400 Orb of Dragonkind U
158400 Baba Yaga's Hut U
159400 Chariot of Lyrx R
160400 Cup of Al-Akbar U
161400 Rary the Traitor C
162400 Mordenkainen R
163400 Tysiln San U
164400 Otto R
165400 Mika the Wolf Nomad R
166400 Lolth, the Spider Queen R
167400 Iuz the Evil U
169400 Swordwraith R
170400 Sysania U
171400 Kiara U
172400 Hettman Tsurin R
173400 Griffon R
174400 Sea Zombie R
175400 Mist Wolf R
176400 Tyrinon U
177400 Quagmiela the Dragon U
180400 Berserk Fury! R
181400 Wolf Nomads C
183400 Miles U
184400 Trystan C
185400 Thorvid R
186400 Fairy Madness R
187400 Nenioc U
188400 Young Gold Dragon C
189400 Arch-Druid R
190400 Hell Hound U
192400 Giant Skeleton R
193400 Skeleton C
194400 Winged Horror U
195400 Treants of Grandwood U
196400 Rangers of Hornwood C
198400 Border Forts C
199400 Ren's Crystal Ball C
200400 Falcon Figurine U
201400 Transformation C
202400 Enslaved! U
203400 Siege C
204400 Bribery! R
205400 Charge! U
206400 Magic Sword C
207400 Enlarge R
208400 Ring of Shooting Stars R
209400 Arms of Veluna C
210400 Fast Talking! U
211400 Flight C
212400 Shapechange R
213400 Barbarian Raiders R
214400 Treasure Fleet R
215400 Potion of Fire Breathing R
216400 Arms of Shield Lands C
217400 Net of Entrapment U
220400 Rod of Dispel Magic U
221400 Draj
222400 Raam
223400 Urik
224400 Tyr
225400 Gulg U
226400 Nibenay U
227400 Balic
228400 Mud Palace, The U
229400 North Ledopolus U
230400 South Ledopolus U
231400 Altaruk C
232400 Salt View C
233400 Ogo U
234400 Makla U
235400 Kalidnay C
236400 Arkhold C
237400 Salt View C
240400 Giustenal U
241400 Yaramuke C
242400 Lost Oasis C
243400 Grak's Pool C
244400 Silver Spring C
245400 Bitter Well C
246400 Black Waters C
247400 Fort Melidor C
248400 Dungeon of Gulg C
249400 Ziggurat U
250400 Temple C
251400 Mogadisho's Horde C
252400 Assassins U
253400 Halfling Mercenaries C
254400 War Band C
255400 Kank Lancers U
256400 Nomad Mercenaries C
257400 Gladiators U
258400 Rikus U
259400 Neeva R
260400 Sadira C
261400 Agis U
262400 Anavias R
263400 Vaerhirmana R
264400 Herminard C
265400 T'kkyl C
266400 Azhul the Hasty U
268400 Bagual C
269400 Rowan U
270400 Shayira C
271400 Ashathra C
272400 Stug C
273400 Ka'Cha U
274400 Galek C
275400 Wind Dancers U
276400 Water Hunters C
277400 Silver Hands U
278400 Sky Singers C
279400 Silt Stalkers C
280400 Night Runners U
281400 So-ut R
282400 Cistern Fiend C
283400 Sloth C
284400 Mul Savage R
285400 Inhuman U
286400 Pyreen R
287400 Cha'thrang U
288400 Spirit of the Land R
289400 Thri-kreen R
290400 Wijon C
291400 Mikor U
292400 Salicia R
293400 Zurn U
294400 Powell C
295400 Baber R
296400 Wachter C
297400 Foucault U
298400 Stef'fa Naf'ski R
299400 Captain Kazhal R
300400 Dlasva U
301400 Tithian R
302400 Verrasi U
303400 Defiler C
304400 Dragon King R
305400 Borys R
306400 Preserver C
307400 Punisher C
308400 Gith U
309400 Tiger C
310400 Orb of Power C
311400 Rings of All Seeing U
312400 Treasure C
313400 Shield of Destruction C
314400 Shield of Annihilation U
315400 Shield of Devastation C
316400 Shield of Wickedness C
317400 Shield of Gore U
318400 Heartwood Spear, The C
319400 Caravan, The C
320400 Necklace, The U
321400 Elemental Cleric C
322400 Elven Archer R
323400 Outcast, The R
324400 Thugs U
325400 Desert Warrior R
327400 Desert Warrior R
328400 Marauder C
329400 Shaqat Beetles C
330400 Tembo U
331400 Fireball C
332400 Lightning Bolt C
333400 Paralyze C
334400 Magic Missile C
335400 Wall of Fire C
336400 Wall of Iron C
337400 Wall of Stone C
338400 Wall of Force C
340400 Cone of Cold C
341400 Sleep C
342400 Shield C
343400 Fly C
344400 Crushing Fist R
346400 Dispel Magic C
347400 Improved Phantasmal Force C
348400 Fear R
349400 Cure Light Wounds C
350400 Cure Serious Wounds C
351400 Sticks to Snakes C
352400 Blade Barrier R
353400 Bless C
354400 Sanctuary R
355400 Wind Walk R
356400 Bark Skin C
357400 Charm C
358400 Dispel Magic C
359400 Darkness C
360400 Protection C
361400 Chariot of Sustarre C
362400 Sunray R
363400 Wall of Thorns C
364400 Wall of Fire U
365400 Holy Word C
366400 Raise Dead R
367400 Flame Strike U
368400 Protection from Lightning C
369400 Silence U
370400 Invisibility to Undead C
371400 Wall of Fog C
372400 Forget C
373400 Web C
374400 Blink C
375400 Hold Undead C
376400 Charm Monster C
377400 Wind of Disenchantment R
378400 Black Tentacles U
379400 Fire Shield U
380400 Ice Storm C
382400 Solid Fog C
383400 Animate Dead C
384400 Cloudkill C
385400 Feebleminded C
386400 Magic Jar C
387400 Faithful Hound C
388400 Passwall C
389400 Rock to Mud C
390400 Chain Lightning C
391400 Death Fog C
392400 Death Spell C
393400 Disintegrate R
394400 Geas C
395400 Banishment C
396400 Control Undead C
397400 Finger of Death C
398400 Spell Turning C
400400 Calm C
402420 Magical Champion R
404420 Chaos Shield R
405420 Slave of Tunek R
406420 Phorbes's Scrolls R
407420 Mercenary Gold R
408420 Living Scroll R
409420 Ren's Bell of Death R
410420 Labyrinth Map of Shucc, The R
411420 Annulus R
412420 Scroll of 7 Leagues R
413420 Map of Life R
415420 Map to a Mercenary Army R
416420 Pit Trap! R
417420 Mind Flayer Lord R
418420 Aurak Draconian Lord R
419420 Ego Coin R
420420 Chest of Many Things R

1994 Spellfire Master the Magic Dragonlance

125 Call to Arms! VR
225 Axe of Brotherhood VR
325 Sword of Friendship VR
425 Knights of the Crown VR
525 Knights of the Sword VR
625 Knights of the Rose VR
725 Shield of Huma VR
825 Crossed Blades VR
925 Spirit of the Que-Shu VR
1025 Skull of Fistandantilus VR
1100 Mithas R
1125 Takhisis's Mirror and Staff VR
1225 Takhisis's Mirror and Sword VR
1325 Takhisis's Abyssal Gateway VR
1425 Takhisis's Mirror of Life Trapping VR
1525 Takhisis's Mirror of Underworld Minions VR
1625 Takhisis's Mirror of Revenge VR
1725 Takhisis's Mirror of the Abyssal Warlord VR
1825 Takhisis's Helmet Power VR
1925 Tower of High Sorcery VR
2025 Blessing of the Gods VR
2100 Nordmaar C
2125 Age of Dreams VR
2225 Golden Age, The VR
2325 Haste Spell VR
2425 Flute of Wind Dancing VR
2525 Medallion of Faith VR
3100 Silvanesti C
4100 Goodland U
5100 Khur C
6100 Solamnia R
7100 Sancrist C
8100 Cristyne C
9100 Northern Ergoth C
10100 Southern Ergoth U
11100 Plains of Dust U
12100 Spine of Taladas U
13100 Isle of Selasia U
14100 Thorin C
15100 Reorxcrown Mountains R
16100 Tower of Wayreth R
17100 Lost Citadel, The R
18100 Shoikan Grove C
19100 Inn of the Last Home C
20100 Altar of Mishakal U
21100 Skie, Blue Dragon C
22100 Governor Erann Flowston C
23100 Tika Waylan Majere C
24100 Lord Gunthar, Solamnic Knight U
25100 Kaz the Minotaur C
26100 Crysania C
27100 Maquesta Kar-Thon R
28100 Ladonna, Wizard of the Black Robes U
29100 Justarian, Wizard of the Red Robes U
30100 Dargent, Silver Dragon R
31100 Raistlin Majere, Wizard of the Black Robes R
32100 Fizban the Fabulous R
33100 Takhisis, Queen of Darkness R
34100 Par-Salian, Wizard of the White Robes U
35100 Pyrite, the Ancient Gold Dragon U
36100 Tanis Half-Elven C
37100 Flint Fireforge C
38100 Caramon Majere R
39100 Tasslehoff Burrfoot C
40100 Phudge, the Great Highblup C
41100 Gully Dwarves C
42100 Night of the Eye R
43100 Krynn Minotaurs U
44100 Solamnic Knights C
45100 Brine Dragon R
46100 Kagonesti Elves C
47100 Dimernesti Elves C
48100 Sivak Draconians C
49100 Kapak Draconians U
50100 Aurak Draconians U
51100 Dragonlance U
52100 Staff of Magius U
53100 Shield of Huma C
54100 Nightjewel, The C
55100 Hammer of Kharas C
56100 Blamblower C
57100 Irongnome U
58100 Bupu's Emerald C
59100 Inflatable Flotilla C
60100 Brooch of Imog U
61100 Solamnic Armor R
62100 Dlamar's Ring of Healing R
63100 Wand of Telekinesis R
64100 Flute of Wind Dancing U
65100 Dagger of Night R
66100 Time Shift: Night into Day R
67100 Time Shift: Day into Night R
68100 Antimagic Barrier U
69100 Unnerving Aura C
70100 Strength C
71100 Steel C
72100 Moonlight Madness C
73100 Switch C
74100 Recall U
75100 Tenser's Transformation U
76100 Charm Monster C
77100 Fire Rain C
78100 Stone Water C
79100 Protection from Draconians C
80100 Mishakal's Insistence R
81100 Divine Intervention R
82100 Summon Griffon C
83100 Reflection U
84100 Earth-Walking C
85100 Borrow C
86100 Despair C
87100 Return C
88100 Hazy Image C
89100 Peace C
90100 Double Trouble C
91100 Mishakal Intervenes C
92100 Habbakuk Interferes U
93100 Kiri-Jolith Arrives U
94100 Reorx, the Forge, Walks the Land C
95100 Morgion, God of Disease, Strikes C
96100 Zeboim, the Sea Queen, is Enraged C
97100 Bronze Dragons R
98100 Moon Solinari Waxes R
99100 Moon Lunitari Waxes R
100100 Moon Nuitarti Waxes R

1994 Spellfire Master the Magic Forgotten Realms

125 Thrice Hearty Cup of Balder the Red VR
225 Cold Cup of Calamity VR
325 Vessel of Vaporous Stones VR
425 Mug of the Earthbound VR
525 Hawksflight Grail VR
625 Vessel of Misty Passage VR
725 Teapot of the Golden Tempest VR
825 Ebony Cup of Fate VR
925 Hero's Chalice VR
1025 Day That Will Live in Infamy VR
1100 Tarrasque U
1125 Unusually Good Fortune VR
1225 Apple of His Eye VR
1325 Golden Touch VR
1425 Feather Flight VR
1525 Golden Barter VR
1625 Dagger of Deception VR
1725 Wyrm of Earthwalking VR
1825 Bell of Might VR
1925 Muragh Brilstagg VR
2025 Phase Door VR
2100 Black Bess R
2125 Wine of Eternity VR
2225 Spellblades VR
2325 Netheril VR
2425 Lure of Undermountain VR
2525 Zhentarim Intrigue VR
3100 Caer Allison R
4100 Curse of the Azure Bonds R
5100 Cyrinishad R
6100 Darkwalker War U
7100 Dead Magic Zone U
8100 Horde C
9100 Lady Luck R
10100 Wild Magic Surge R
11100 Coral Kingdom, The C
12100 Halruaa C
13100 Kozakura C
14100 Luiren C
15100 Maztica C
16100 Mulhorand C
17100 Raurin C
18100 Shou Lung C
19100 Blackstaff Tower U
20100 Candlekeep U
21100 High Horn U
22100 Mithril Hall U
23100 Moonwell U
24100 Pook's Palace U
25100 Yulash U
26100 Tower of Ashaba U
27100 Aerial Servant C
28100 Creeping Doom U
29100 Earthquake C
30100 Illusory Fortification C
31100 Quest C
32100 Succor U
33100 Reincarnate R
34100 Ressurection R
35100 Shadow Engines C
36100 Symbol of Hopelessness U
37100 Word of Recall C
38100 Zone of Truth C
39100 Death Link C
40100 Find Familiar C
41100 Great Shout C
42100 Hallucinatory Terrain C
43100 Limited Wish U
44100 Time Stop U
45100 Water Breathing C
46100 Wish R
47100 Deck of Many Things R
48100 Dragonslayer R
49100 Flametongue R
50100 Frostbrand R
51100 Gauntlets of Swimming C
52100 Helm of Water Breathing C
53100 Horn of Blasting U
54100 Ring of Jumping C
55100 Slippers of Spider Climbing C
56100 Vorpal Blade R
57100 Wand of Wonder R
58100 Dragon Throne R
59100 Guenhwyvar R
60100 Hammer of Tyr R
61100 Ring of Winter R
62100 Sword of Cymrych Hugh R
63100 Bloodriders C
64100 Dragonclaw R
65100 Flaming Fist U
66100 Halfling, Inc. U
67100 Kuo Toa C
68100 Locathah C
69100 Mad Monkey R
70100 Ninjas U
71100 Olive Ruskettle U
72100 Orcs of Dragonspear C
73100 Orcs of the Savage Frontier C
74100 Pseudodragon C
75100 Red Wizards C
76100 Sahuagin C
77100 Samurai C
78100 Darkenbeast C
79100 Firbolg C
80100 Iron Golem C
81100 Storm Giant C
82100 Stone Giant C
83100 Werewolf U
84100 Adon C
85100 Erixitl C
86100 Fzoul Chembryl C
87100 Young Robyn C
88100 Ambassador Carrague U
89100 Helm U
90100 Simbul of Aglarond R
91100 Vangerdahast C
92100 Cyric R
93100 Dragonbait C
94100 Khelben "Blackstaff" Arunsun C
95100 Ochimo C
96100 Prince Tristan C
97100 Princess Alusair C
98100 Randal Morn C
99100 Time of Troubles U
100100 Tablets of Fate R

1994 Spellfire Master the Magic Ravenloft

1100 Barovia U
2100 Darkon R
3100 Lamordia C
4100 Mordent C
5100 Kartakass C
6100 Keening U
7100 Tepest C
8100 Verbrek C
9100 Invidia R
10100 Nova Vaasa C
11100 Dementlieu U
12100 Valachan C
13100 Har'Akir C
14100 Souragne C
15100 Sri Raji U
16100 Castle Ravenloft R
17100 Azalin's Graveyard R
18100 Kargat Mausoleum C
19100 Paridon U
20100 Pharaoh's Rest C
21100 Mists C
22100 Dark Powers U

23100 Grand Conjunction C
24100 Harvest Moon R
25100 All Hallow's Eve C
26100 Quirk of Fate R
27100 Disrupted Magic C
28100 Power of the Land U
29100 Spell Book of Drawmij R
30100 City States R
31100 Islands of Terror R
32100 Eyes of the Undead C
33100 Living Ward U
34100 Binding Curse C
35100 Conjure Grave Elemental R
36100 Animate Rock U
37100 Word of Recall C
38100 Glyph of Warding C
39100 Call Lightning C
40100 Prayer C
41100 Turn Undead U
42100 Imbue with Spell Ability C
43100 Insect Plague C
44100 Plane Shift R
45100 Heal R
46100 Shadow Magic C
47100 Shades C
48100 Vampiric Touch C
49100 Hold Person R
50100 Detect Magic U
51100 Augment Undead C
52100 Strahd's Malefic Meld U
53100 Misty Summons R
54100 Neverending Nightmare C
55100 Chill Touch C
56100 Tarokka Deck U
57100 Timepiece of Klorr R
58100 Ring of Regeneration U
59100 Sun Sword C
60100 Blood Coin C
61100 Staff of Mimicry U
62100 Soul Searcher Medal C
63100 Ring of Reversion U
64100 Amulet of the Beast C
65100 Cat of Felkovic C
66100 Apparatus R
67100 Crown of Souls R
68100 Holy Symbol of Ravenkind U
69100 Tapestry of Dark Souls U
70100 Fang of the Nosferatu R
71100 Kargat Vampire C
72100 Wolf Pack C
73100 Flesh Golem U
74100 Ghost Ship R
75100 Strahd Zombies C
76100 Fiend R
77100 Spectre U
78100 Vistani C
79100 Loup-garou U
80100 Werebat C
81100 Mysterious Stranger C
82100 Azalin R
83100 Adam R
84100 Ankhtepot U
85100 Ireena Kolyana C
86100 Dr. Rudolph Van Richten C
87100 Harkon Lukas U
88100 Headless Horseman R
89100 Arijani U
90100 Wilfred Godefroy C
91100 Tiyet C
92100 Sir Hiregaard C
93100 Gabrielle Aderre C
94100 Hags of Tepest C
95100 Sir Edmund Bloodsworth C
96100 High Master Illithid U
97100 Dr. Mordenheim C
98100 Sergei Von Zarovich C
99100 Lord Soth R
100100 Strahd Von Zarovich R

1995 Spellfire Master the Magic 3rd Edition

1400 Waterdeep
2400 Menzoberranzan
3400 Ruins of Zhentil Keep R
4400 Shadowdale
5400 Cormyr
6400 Sembia
7400 Moonshae Isles
8400 Thay
9400 Calimshan
10400 Pirate Isles
11400 Ravens Bluff
12400 The Great Rift
13400 Myth Drannor U
14400 Vaasa
15400 Jungles of Chult
16400 High Forest, The
17400 Sword Coast
18400 Anauroch
19400 Impiltur
20400 Icewind Dale
21400 High Moor, The
22400 Rashemen
23400 Damara
24400 Narfell
25400 Dragonspear Castle
26400 Daggerdale
27400 Darkhold
29400 Evermeet
30400 Trollmoors, The
31400 Berdusk U
32400 Tantras U
33400 Mulmaster U
34400 Hillsfar U
35400 Suzail U
36400 Arabel U
37400 Castle Draw U
38400 Fortifications U
39400 Selune U
40400 Peasant Militia U
41400 Alias the Sell-Sword U
42400 King Azoun IV R
43400 Maligor the Red R
44400 Elminster the Mage U
45400 Drizzt Do'Urden C
46400 Midnight, Goddess of Magic R
47400 Torg Mac Cei, the Ironlord U
48400 Pereghost, The R
50400 Marco Volo U
51400 Harpers, The C
52400 Gnomes of Samek U
53400 Adventurers! C
54400 War Party C
55400 Crime Lord U
56400 Adventurers C
57400 Jotunslayers, The C
58400 Armies of Bloodstone U
59400 Iron Legion, The C
60400 Tergoz Tenhammer C
61400 Myrmidons R
62400 Magister, The R
63400 Karlott the Shaman U
64400 King Halvor II U
65400 Pteranadon C
66400 Gorgosaurus R
67400 Greater Feyr R
69400 Cleric of Torm R
70400 Cleric of Mask R
71400 Drow Matron U
72400 Dracolich R
73400 Vasos Flameslayer R
74400 Allisa of the Mists C
75400 Grypht the Saurial U
76400 Worden Ironfist R
77400 Amarill U
78400 Joliet the Rash C
79400 Dwarf of Earthfast C
80400 Black Courser R
81400 Hornhead Saurial C
82400 Dagrande U
83400 Mind Flayer R
84400 Noble Djinni R
86400 Intellect Devourer U
87400 Shandrill C
89400 Cleric of Malar C
90400 Airship U
91400 Bad Omens C
92400 Fortunate Omens C
93400 Rod of Shapechange U
94400 Dwarven Hammer R
95400 Staff of Striking R
96400 Horrors of the Abyss U
98400 Figurine of Wonderous Power C
99400 Cataclysm! U
100400 Good Fortune U
101400 Surprise Raid C
102400 Banner of 1-eyed God C
103400 Viperhand U
104400 Orb of Doom C
105400 Staff of Conjuring C
106400 Spell of Formless Horror U
107400 Safe Harbor R
108400 Labor of Legend C
109400 Wand of Light U
110400 Elf Galleon R
111400 Free City of Greyhawk R
112400 Lands of Iuz, The U
113400 Pomarj, The
114400 Hold of the Sea Princes
115400 Yeomanry
116400 Blackmoor U
117400 Horned Society, The
118400 Wolf Nomads, The
119400 Sterich
120400 Nyrond
121400 Veluna
122400 Furyondy
123400 Great Kingdom R
124400 Temple of Elemental Evil U
125400 Greyhawk Ruins U
126400 Perrenland
127400 Keoland
128400 Celene
129400 Bright Desert, The
130400 Theocracy of the Pale
131400 Bone March
132400 Duchy of Urnst, The
133400 Sea Barons, The
134400 Hookhill C
135400 Scarlet Brotherhood, The U
136400 Iron Hills
137400 Principality of Ulek C
138400 County of Sunndi C
139400 Duchy of Tenh C
140400 Burneal Forest C
141400 Castle Hart C
142400 Ancient Arms of Horned Society R
144400 Ancient Arms of Greyhawk R
145400 Ancient Arms of Great Kingdom R
146400 Ancient Arms of Furyondy C
147400 Ancient Arms of Nyrond C
148400 Skull Keep C
149400 Fortification C
150400 Siege! U
151400 War Banner C
152400 Codex of the Infinite Planes C
153400 Crystal of the Ebon Flame U
154400 Hordes of Castle Greyhawk R
155400 Lich Conclave C
156400 Eye & Hand of Vecna U
157400 Orb of Dragonkind U
158400 Baba Yaga's Hut U
159400 Chariot of Lyrx R
160400 Cup of Al-Akbar U
161400 Rary the Traitor C
162400 Mordenkainen R
163400 Tysiln San U
164400 Otto R
165400 Mika the Wolf Nomad R
166400 Lolth, the Spider Queen R
167400 Iuz the Evil U
169400 Avatar's Bane R
170400 Sysania U
171400 Kiara U
172400 Hettman Tsurin R
175400 Mist Wolf R
176400 Tyrinon U
177400 Quagmiela the Dragon U
180400 Berserker Wrath R
181400 Wolf Nomads C
183400 Miles U
184400 Trystan C
185400 Thorvid R
187400 Nenioc U
188400 Young Gold Dragon C
189400 Arch-Druid R
190400 Hell Hound U
192400 Skeleton Commander R
193400 Skeleton C
194400 Winged Horror U
195400 Treants of Grandwood U
196400 Rangers of Hornwood C
198400 Border Forts C
199400 Ren's Crystal Ball C
200400 Falcon Figurine U
201400 Transformation C
202400 Slave Revolt U
203400 Bruce's Revenge C
204400 Bribery! R
205400 Charge! U
206400 Kevin's Blade of Doom C
209400 Ancient Arms of Veluna C
210400 Fast Talking! U
211400 Flight C
212400 Shapechange R
213400 Barbarian's Revenge!, The R
214400 Storm at Sea R
216400 Ancient Arms of Shield Lands C
217400 Net of Entrapment U
220400 Rod of Dispel Magic U
221400 Draj
222400 Raam
223400 Urik
224400 Tyr
225400 Gulg U
226400 Nibenay U
227400 Balic
228400 Mud Palace, The U
229400 North Ledopolus U
230400 South Ledopolus U
231400 Altaruk C
232400 Mekillot Mountains C
233400 Ogo U
234400 Makla U
235400 Kalidnay C
236400 Arkhold C
237400 Salt View C
240400 Giustenal U
241400 Yaramuke C
242400 Lost Oasis C
243400 Grak's Pool C
244400 Silver Spring C
245400 Bitter Well C
246400 Black Waters C
247400 Fort Melidor C
248400 Dungeon of Gulg C
249400 Ziggurat U
250400 Temple C
251400 Mogadisho's Horde C
252400 Assassins U
253400 Halfling Mercenaries C
254400 War Band C
255400 Kank Lancers U
256400 Nomad Mercenaries C
257400 Gladiators U
258400 Rikus U
259400 Neeva R
260400 Sadira C
261400 Agis U
262400 Erellika R
263400 Vaerhirmana R
264400 Herminard C
265400 T'kkyl C
266400 Azhul the Hasty U
268400 Bagual C
269400 Rowan U
270400 Shayira C
271400 Ashathra C
272400 Stug C
273400 Ka'Cha U
274400 Galek C
275400 Wind Dancers U
276400 Water Hunters C
277400 Silver Hands Revenge U
278400 Sky Singers C
279400 Silt Stalkers C
280400 Night Runners U
282400 Cistern Fiend C
283400 Sloth C
284400 Mul Savage R
285400 Inhuman U
287400 Cha'thrang U
288400 Spirit of the Land R
289400 Thri-kreen R
290400 Wijon C
291400 Mikor U
293400 Zurn U
294400 Powell C
296400 Wachter C
297400 Foucault U
298400 Stef'fa Naf'ski R
299400 Captain Kazhal R
300400 Dlasva U
301400 Tithian R
302400 Verrasi U
303400 Rogue Defiler of Tyr C
304400 Lion of Urik, The R
305400 Borys the Dragon R
306400 Preserver C
307400 Punisher C
308400 Gith U
309400 Tiger C
310400 Orb of Power C
311400 Rings of All Seeing U
312400 Treasure C
313400 Shield of Destruction C
314400 Shield of Annihilation U
315400 Shield of Devastation C
316400 Shield of Wickedness C
317400 Shield of Gore U
318400 Heartwood Spear, The C
319400 Caravan, The C
320400 Necklace, The U
321400 Elemental Cleric C
322400 Elven Archer R
323400 Outcast, The R
324400 Thugs U
328400 Marauder C
329400 Shaqat Beetles C
330400 Tembo U
331400 Fireball C
332400 Lightning Bolt C
333400 Paralyze C
334400 Magic Missile C
335400 Wall of Fire C
336400 Wall of Iron C
337400 Wall of Stone C
338400 Wall of Force C
340400 Cone of Cold C
341400 Sleep C
342400 Shield C
343400 Fly C
344400 Crushing Fist R
346400 Dispel Magic C
347400 Improved Phantasmal Force C
348400 Fear R
349400 Cure Light Wounds C
350400 Cure Serious Wounds C
351400 Sticks to Snakes C
352400 Blade Barrier R
353400 Bless C
354400 Sanctuary R
355400 Wind Walk R
356400 Bark Skin C
357400 Charm C
358400 Dispel Magic C
359400 Darkness C
360400 Protection C
361400 Chariot of Sustarre C
363400 Wall of Thorns C
364400 Wall of Fire U
365400 Holy Word C
366400 Raise Dead R
367400 Flame Strike U
368400 Protection from Lightning C
369400 Silence U
370400 Improved Invisibility to Undead C
371400 Wall of Fog C
372400 Forget C
373400 Web C
374400 Blink C
375400 Hold Undead C
376400 Charm Monster C
377400 Wind of Disenchantment R
378400 Black Tentacles U
379400 Fire Shield U
380400 Ice Storm C
382400 Solid Fog C
383400 Animate Dead C
384400 Cloudkill C
385400 Feebleminded C
386400 Magic Jar C
387400 Mordenkainen's Faithful Hound C
388400 Passwall C
389400 Rock to Mud C
390400 Chain Lightning C
391400 Death Fog C
392400 Death Spell C
394400 Geas C
395400 Banishment C
396400 Control Undead C
397400 Finger of Death C
398400 Spell Turning C
400400 Calm C

1995 Spellfire Master the Magic Artifacts

120 Mace of Cuthbert VR
220 Death Rock VR
320 Psychometron Nerad VR
420 Silencer of Bodach VR
520 Barab's Goblet Disolusion VR
620 Onad the Weasel VR
720 Lord Blacktree VR
820 Young Strahd VR
920 Killian VR
1020 Ghostly Piper VR
1100 Wand of Orcus R
1120 Forbiddance VR
1220 Bigby's Clenched Fist VR
1320 Fire Charm VR
1420 Thunder Staff VR
1520 Spectral Hand VR
1620 Ariel's Feather Charm VR
1720 Amulet of Spell Protection VR
1820 Amelior's Restraint VR
1920 Smoke Powder Pistol VR
2020 Dragon Font VR
2100 Axe of the Dwarvish Lords C
3100 Iron Flask Tuerny Merciless U
4100 Jacinth of Inestimable Beauty U
5100 Machine of Lum the Mad R
6100 Queen Ehlissa's Marvelous Nightingale C
7100 Sword of Kas U
8100 Talisman of Al'Akbar C
9100 Teeth of Dalhvar-Nar U
10100 All-Knowing Eye Yasmin Sira R
11100 Coin of Jisan the Bountiful C
12100 Seal of Lost Arak R
13100 Crystal of the Ebon Flame C
14100 Obsidian Man of Urik R
15100 Rod of Teeth U
16100 Midnight's Mask of Disguise C
17100 Girdle of Storm Giant Strength C
18100 Hammer of Thunderbolts R
19100 Gauntlets Ogre Power R
20100 Winged Boots C
21100 Rod of 7 Parts, #1 U
22100 Rod of 7 Parts, #2 R
23100 Rod of 7 Parts, #3 U
24100 Rod of 7 Parts, #4 R
25100 Rod of 7 Parts, #5 U
26100 Rod of 7 Parts, #6 R
27100 Rod of 7 Parts, #7 U
28100 Bag of Holding C
29100 Daern's Instant Fortress R
30100 Spellbook R
31100 Plentiful Psionics R
32100 Sorcerer-Kings C
33100 Dark Lords C
34100 Walking Dead, The U
35100 Artifact Vault R
36100 Artifact Champions U
37100 Isolated Worlds C
38100 No Funny Business R
39100 Forbidden Lore C
40100 Cosmic Justice R
41100 Roc C
42100 Kinsle the Druid C
43100 Dragonbane C
44100 Ship of the Sky, The R
45100 Pegasus C
46100 Windrider C
47100 Erica of the Dark Watch C
48100 Dimock the Sprite C
49100 Flying Carpet C
50100 Ariel Anjelique C
51100 Dragon Slayer U
52100 Marilith, Tanar'ri C
53100 Temporal Stasis U
54100 Deflection R
55100 Help! R
56100 Reverse Gravity U
57100 Shift Earth C
58100 Mirror Image U
59100 Ethereality C
60100 Prismatic Spray C
61100 Treasure Vault R
62100 Tupillil C
63100 Kestrel's Keep U
64100 Keep of the Dead C
65100 Spellfire Citadel U
66100 Fire Glyph R
67100 Weakness Glyph U
68100 Lightning Glyph R
69100 Curse Glyph U
70100 Death Glyph C
71100 Dragon Turtle C
72100 Deathstream, Black Dragon C
73100 Zielesch, Ancient Green Dragon U
74100 Dregoth, Undead Dragon-King R
75100 Korgunard the Avangion C
76100 Drawmij U
77100 Klik-Ka'cha C
78100 Mykell, Amythest Great Wyrm C
79100 Hornung the Anarch C
80100 Invisible Stalker U
81100 Erital Kaan-Ipzirel C
82100 Yagno Petrovna C
83100 Goldmoon C
84100 Princess Amber R
85100 Darsson Spellmaker C
86100 Council Aerie U
87100 Shining Lands C
88100 Bluet Spur U
89100 Hell Furnaces C
90100 Euripis C
91100 New Giustenal C
92100 Ancient Kalidnay C
93100 Ur Draxa C
94100 Shault C
95100 Forest Ridge C
96100 Celik R
97100 Lake Island C
98100 Year of Plenty C
99100 Thought Eater C
100100 Deja Vu U

1995 Spellfire Master the Magic Powers

120 Crystal Sphere VR
220 Rock of Bral VR
320 Unipsi VR
420 Inverter, The VR
520 Royal Conscription/Tax Levy VR
620 Fate's Promise VR
720 Bando's Whitestone VR
820 Quill Pen of the Planes VR

920 Tantelear, The VR
1020 Borah's Ring VR
1100 Adjatha, the Spell Drinker U
1120 Shawl of Mordenheim VR
1220 Sirrion's Brooch VR
1320 Psionicist Bracelet VR
1420 Psionicist Anklet VR
1520 Psionatrix VR
1620 Antimagic Cloud VR
1720 Poisoned Water VR
1820 Ultimate Rule Card, The VR
1920 Cosmic Intervention VR
2020 Avatar's Edict VR
2100 Abhorrence of Shapechangers R
3100 Sword of the Avoreen R
4100 Sword of Blackflame U
5100 Sword of the High King R
6100 Dragonsbane U
7100 Post-Hypnotic Suggestion C
8100 Sword of the Black Rose R
9100 Davron Parscall U
10100 Yorgia Sandow C
11100 Roghal Baen U
12100 Kelsur Brighteye C
13100 Rand the Bowyer U
14100 Seveia Shadowmaster C
15100 Rafe Racker U
16100 Jacenelle Traen C
17100 Bilago Lumen U
18100 Dawn d'Ereath C
19100 Phridge C
20100 Seluna Darkenstar U
21100 Kerm of Tyr C
22100 Havrum Riddle U
23100 Lyr of the Mists C
24100 Colum Calder U
25100 Kelaser Redbelt U
26100 Breshkil Logon C
27100 Masara d'Will C
28100 Rayden Valers U
29100 Psychic Storm C
30100 Sandstorm C
31100 Necromantic Wave C
32100 Night of the Blue Moon R
33100 Zepherwind R
34100 Avangion's Protection C
35100 Nullification C
36100 Tuigan Invasion R
37100 Dark Negation R
38100 Caravan Raiders C
39100 Icedawn, Avatar of Auril R
40100 Nightsinger, Avatar of Shar R
41100 Bonemaster, Avatar of Nerull R
42100 Lady of Fate, Avatar of Istus R
43100 Misfortune, Avatar of Ralishaz R
44100 Tempest, Avatar of Zeboim R
45100 Sirrion, Avatar R
46100 Mirror, Mirror C
47100 Rope Trick C
48100 Stasis C
49100 Giant Space Hamster U
50100 Polymorph Other C
51100 Phase Out C
52100 Gith U
53100 Crabman U
54100 Aquatic Elf U
55100 Ixitxachitl U
56100 Kirre U
57100 Locathah Champion U
58100 Living Wall R
59100 Tako U
60100 Earth Elemental U
61100 Skriaxit, Composit Elemental R
62100 Mountain Giant U
63100 Grippli U
64100 Chameleon Power C
65100 Brandobaris's Inversion R
66100 Energy Containment C
67100 Complete Healing C
68100 Wheel of Fate R
69100 Teleport Trigger C
70100 Molecular Rearrangement C
71100 Telekinesis C
72100 Mind Shield C
73100 Molecular Agitation C
74100 Control Wind C
75100 Cause Decay C
76100 Repugnance C
77100 Mind Thrust C
78100 Sea Queen, Avatar of Zeboim R
79100 Kiri, Avatar of Kiri-Jolith R
80100 Shadair Mesker U
81100 Mental Barrier C
82100 Tower of Iron Will C
83100 Intellect Fortress C
84100 Control Flames C
85100 Psychic Storm R
86100 Nullify Magic R
87100 Mind of the Avatar R
88100 Gift of the Avatar R
89100 Intensify C
90100 Summon Planar Creature C
91100 Graft Weapon C
92100 Melt Stone C
93100 Psionic Blast C
94100 Magnify C
95100 Probability Travel C
96100 Banishment C
97100 Create Object C
98100 Psychic Lock C
99100 Life Draining C
100100 Dimentional Door C

1995 Spellfire Master the Magic The Underdark

125 Lazarus, the Drow VR
225 Inflict Pain VR
325 Hoof of Auroch, The VR
425 Ring of Gaxx, The VR
525 Deep, The VR
625 Ultimate Triumvirate, The VR
725 Dispossessed, The VR
825 Cavernous Hall, The VR
925 Underground River VR
1025 Way Out, The VR
1100 UnderAthas C
1125 Triumphant Barbarian, The VR
1225 Minotaur Attacks!, The VR
1325 Cave-in! VR
1425 Mandate of Dori the Barbarian, The VR
1525 Demi-Lich Zyenj, The VR
1625 Minotaur, The VR
1725 Piercer VR
1825 Lurker in the Deep VR
1925 Oogly the Half-Orc VR
2025 Marble Orb, The VR
2100 Unipolar Triumvirate, The C
2125 Sword and Helm of Garion, The VR
2225 Scourge of Mika VR
2325 Drow Assassin VR
2425 Broken Arrow VR
2525 Mindshatter VR
3100 UnderKrynn C
4100 Bipolar Triumvirate, The U
5100 Underdark, The R
6100 Tripolar Triumvirate, The R
7100 UnderToril C
8100 UnderOerth C
9100 UnderDread C
10100 Burning Cavern, The U
11100 Unipolar Cavern, The C
12100 Subterranean Seas U
13100 Bipolar Cavern, The U
14100 North Wind, The C
15100 Tripolar Cavern, The U
16100 Echoes from the Deep R
17100 Cavern of the Gods U
18100 Dread Chamber, The U
19100 God's Plague R
20100 When God's Walk R
21100 Drow Justice R
22100 Memory Moss R
23100 East Wind, The C
24100 Forest Oracle, The U
25100 Mika's Magic Ban U
26100 Mika's Dragon Charm C
27100 Mika's Undead Ward C
28100 Amulet of Protection from Artifacts R
29100 Armor of Dispel Magic C
30100 Cloak of the Gargoyle C
31100 Dori's Obsidian Steed of Wondrous Power U
32100 Goibhniu's Warhammer R
33100 Helmet of Selnor R
34100 Necklass of Protection R
35100 Black Snail of Shnai U
36100 Shovel of Gravedigging C
37100 Hornung's Guess U
38100 Hornung's Baneful Deflector C
39100 Maximillian's Earthen Grasp C
40100 Shattered Glass R
41100 Lorloveim's Creeping Shadow C
42100 Locate Creature U
43100 Summon Lycanthrope C
44100 Mind Fog U
45100 Bloodstone's Spectral Steed C
46100 Summon Undead U
47100 Warband Quest C
48100 Wolf Spirits U
49100 Stalker R
50100 South Wind, The C
51100 Animal Horde R
52100 Elemental Swarm U
53100 Preservation C
54100 Ward Matrix C
55100 Age Dragon R
56100 Mindkiller R
57100 Spacewarp R
58100 Spirit of Power C
59100 West Wind, The C
60100 Tentacle Walls C
61100 Timelessness U
62100 Hovering Road C
63100 Breath of Death C
64100 Unnamed, Avatar of Gruumsh, The R
65100 Faceless One, Avatar of Jubilex, The U
66100 Moradin's Avatar C
67100 Invasion of the Undead U
68100 Red Death, The R
69100 Things That Go Bump In The Night U
70100 Sargonnas C
71100 Uncaring, Avatar of Boccob, The R
72100 Avatar Shar, The U
73100 Baelnorn C
74100 Chitine C
75100 Crypt Servant C
76100 Foulwing C
77100 Gnasher R
78100 Magebane R
79100 Sword Slug C
80100 Skum R
81100 Fey Dwarf C
82100 Corpse Dragon U
83100 Earth Weird C
84100 Gorynych R
85100 Noran C
86100 Gibbering Mouther C
87100 Umber Hulk C
88100 Mind Flayer C
89100 Myconid C
90100 Monster of the Lake R
91100 Belwar Dissengulp C
92100 Jarlaxle C
93100 Ellorelloran C
94100 Zaknafein the Weapons Master C
95100 Baldar Dwellardon C
96100 Fowron, the Giant C
97100 Chantal the Banshee C
98100 Aquilla U
99100 Iseult U
100100 Xontra C

1996 Spellfire Master the Magic 4th Edition

1500 Menzoberranzan U
2500 Ruins of Zentil Keep R
3500 Sembia U
4500 Myth Drannor U
5500 Icewind Dale U
6500 Damara U
7500 Daggerdale U
8500 Evermeet U
9500 Trollmoors, The U
10500 Coral Kingdom, The R
11500 Raurin U
12500 Vilhon Reach, The U
13500 Giant's Run Mountains R
14500 Sterich U
15500 Nyrond U
16500 Furyondy R
17500 Temple of Elemental Evil U
18500 Greyhawk Ruins U
19500 Perrenland U
20500 Duchy of Tenh R
21500 Hell Furnaces U
22500 Free and Independent City of Dyvers U
23500 Spindrift Islands U
24500 Stonefist Hold U
25500 Ull U
26500 Valley of the Mage R
27500 Urik U
28500 Tyr U
29500 Gulg U
30500 Euripis U
31500 New Guistenal R
32500 Ur Draxa U
33500 Shault U
34500 Forest Ridge, The R
35500 Celik U
36500 Lake Island U
37500 Jagged Cliffs, The U
38500 Last Sea, The U
39500 Dragon's Crown Mountains R
40500 Realm of the While Witch U
41500 Battle-Fens, The R
42500 Giantdowns, The U
43500 Sphinx, The U
44500 Mistmoor, The U
45500 Tarvan Waste U
46500 Black Spear Tribes R
47500 Thurazor U
48500 Sielwode, The U
49500 Five Peaks, The U
50500 Cariele U
51500 Boeruine U
52500 Rhuobhe R
53500 Reorxcrown Mountains U
54500 Shining Lands R
55500 Delving, The R
56500 Estwilde U
57500 Blood Sea of Istar U
58500 Enstar R
59500 Bluet Spur R
60500 Arak U
61500 Borca R
62500 Gundarak U
63500 Sithicus U
64500 Nightmare Lands R
65500 Council Aerie U
66500 Milborne R
67500 Isle of Beacon Point, The U
68500 Lair of the Eye Tyrant R
69500 Dancing Hut of Baba Yaga U
70500 Anytown, Anywhere R
71500 Haven of the Undead U
72500 Monastery of Perdien the Damned R
73500 Mulmaster U
74500 Blackstaff Tower U
75500 Candlekeep U
76500 Mithral Hall U
77500 Moonwell U
78500 Nagawater U
79500 Tilverton U
80500 Lhespenbog U
81500 Adderswamp U
82500 Fortification: Rampart U
83500 Fortification: Bastion U
84500 Fortification: Parapet U
85500 Fortification: Bailey U
86500 Fortification: Curtain Wall U
87500 Fortification: Inner Wall U
88500 Fortification: Bulwark U
89500 Fortification: Barricade U
90500 Fortification: Breastwork U
91500 Mud Palace, The U
92500 South Ledopolus U
93500 Ogo U
94500 Arkhold U
95500 Lost Oasis U
96500 Grak's Pool U
97500 Silver Spring U
98500 Black Waters U
99500 Dungeon of Gulg U
100500 Celestial Jewel of Sarimie, The U
101500 Points East Trading Company U
102500 Thorn Throne, The U
103500 Peaceful Seas of Nesirie U
104500 Sarimie's Temple of Fortune U
105500 Boeruine Trading Guild U
106500 Taeghan Outfitters U
107500 Straits of Aerele Shipping U
108500 Grovnekvic Forest U
109500 Madding Springs U
110500 Shark Reef U
111500 Barter U
112500 Dance of the Red Death U
113500 Red Jack U
114500 Red Tide U
115500 Treasure Vault U
116500 Kestrel's Keep U
117500 Keep of the Dead U
118500 Airship U
119500 Cataclysm! U
120500 Good Fortune U
121500 Surprise Raid U
122500 Labor of Legend U
123500 Siege! U
124500 Mutiny! U
125500 Transformation! U
126500 Slave Revolt! U
127500 Bruce's Revenge U
128500 Fast Talking! U
129500 Barbarian's Revenge!, The U
130500 Treasure U
131500 Caravan, The U
132500 Ice Storm U
133500 Solid Fog U
134500 Tarrasque U
135500 Black Bess U
136500 Dead Magic Zone U
137500 Deflection U
138500 Temporal Stasis U
139500 Dragons Rebellious U
140500 Hurricane! U
141500 Call to Arms U
142500 Phantasmal Wolf U
143500 Land Ho! U
144500 Provocation U
145500 Balance of Power U
146500 Assault of Magic U
147500 Psionic Contrition U
148500 Monstrous Intervention U
149500 Land Rebels, The U
150500 Elven Rebirth U
151500 Death of a Hero, The U
152500 Ambush U
153500 Brave Heart U
154500 Torments of Sisyphus, The U
155500 Secret War U
156500 Covert Aid U
157500 Wrath of the Immortals U
158500 Titans Walk the Earth U
159500 Bess's Revenge U
160500 Foreign Wars U
161500 Gales at Sea U
162500 Escape from the Abyss U
163500 Banner of the Two-Eyed God C
164500 Staff of Striking C
165500 Staff of Conjuring C
166500 War Banner C
167500 Falcon Figurine C
168500 Ghost Crystal C
169500 Net of Entrapment C
170500 Orb of Power C
171500 Rings of All Seeing C
172500 Shield of Destruction C
173500 Shield of Annihilation C
174500 Shield of Devastation C
175500 Shield of Wickedness C
176500 Necklace, The C
177500 Dragonslayer C
178500 Gauntlets of Swimming C
179500 Horn of Blasting C
180500 Wand of Wonder C
181500 Drow Slippers C
182500 Midnight's Mask of Disguise C
183500 Girdle of Storm Giant Strength C
184500 Hammer of the Gods C
185500 Gauntles of Golem Strength C
186500 Winged Boots C
187500 Badge of the Wolf Nomads C
188500 Dark Haven C
189500 Spellbook C
190500 Pan's Pipes C
191500 Bagpipes of Drawmij, The C
192500 Ailarond Horn C
193500 Lyre of Arvanaith C
194500 Harp of Kings, The C
195500 Leviathan Horn, The C
196500 Chimes of Chelerie C
197500 Xeno-Xylophone C
198500 Dragon Drums C
199500 Scarab of Protection C
200500 Arrow of Slaying C
201500 Crossbow of Accuracy C
202500 Dagger of Venom C
203500 Javelin of Lightning C
204500 Mace of Disruption C
205500 Scimitar of Speed C
206500 Trident of Fish Command C
207500 Holy Avenger C
208500 Armies of Bloodstone C
209500 Iron Legion, The C
210500 Myrmidons C
211500 Hornhead Saurial C
212500 Mind Flayer C
213500 Intellect Devourer C
214500 Elf Galleon C
215500 Tyrol C
216500 Hell Hound C
217500 Skeletal Lord C
218500 Skeletal Minion C
219500 Treants of the Grandwood C
220500 Mogadisho's Horde Marches On C
221500 Assassins C
222500 Halfling Mercenaries C
223500 Gladiators C
224500 Rowan C
225500 Ashathra C
226500 Slug C
227500 Galek C
228500 Silt Stalkers C
229500 Night Runners C
230500 Athasian Sloth C
231500 Wijon C
232500 Elven Archer C
233500 Marauder C
234500 Shagat Beetles C
235500 Flesh Golem C
236500 Loup-Garou C
237500 Brine Dragon C
238500 Flaming Fist C
239500 Ninjas C
240500 Psuedodragon C
241500 Roc C
242500 Marilith Tanar'ri C
243500 Thought Eater C
244500 Ogre Mage C
245500 Mermaid C
246500 Dreaded Ghost, The C
247500 Clay Golem C
248500 Ki-Rin C
249500 Troll C
250500 Selkie C
251500 Rust Monster C
252500 Displacer Beast C
253500 Drizzt Do'Urden C
254500 Harpers, The C
255500 Helm R
256500 Thorvid C
257500 Hettman Tsurin C
258500 Tyrinon C
259500 Rikus C
260500 Captain Kazhal C
261500 Neeva C
262500 Pereghost, The C
263500 Dracolich C
264500 Stone Giant C
265500 Lich Conclave C
266500 Winged Horror C
267500 Mature Gold Dragon C
268500 Borys the Dragon C
269500 Athasian Cistern Fiend C
270500 Korgunard the Avangion C
271500 Elminster the Mage C
272500 Vangerdahast C
273500 Ambassador Carrague C
274500 Mike the Wolf Nomad C
275500 Mordenkainen C
276500 Drawmij C
277500 Sadira C
278500 Rogue Defiler of Tyr C
279500 Kalid-na R
280500 Amaril C
281500 Clerics of Malar C
282500 Adon C
283500 Sysania C
284500 Nenioc C
285500 Arch-Druid R
286500 Shayira C
287500 Elemental Cleric C
288500 Klik-Ka'Cha C
289500 Photed C
290500 Sharla C
291500 Migrane C
292500 Vitralis C
293500 Larn C
294500 Livekor C
295500 Shayla C
296500 Ssilcroth C
297500 Rumples C
298500 Diamond C
299500 Emerald C
300500 Topaz C
301500 Ruby C
302500 Jacinth C
303500 Amethyst C
304500 Pearl C
305500 Amber C
306500 Aquamarina C
307500 Cyclops C
308500 Ettin R
309500 Formorian Giant C
310500 Fire Giant C
311500 Yumac the Cold R
312500 Pellgrade the Inexorable C
313500 Nemal C
314500 Gloaranor C
315500 Moralin C
316500 Borin Moradinson C
317500 Mallin Dimmerswill C
318500 Arden Glimrock C
319500 Drider C
320500 Eye Tyrant C
321500 Roper C
322500 Malleyahl C
323500 Malaruat C
324500 Maleficent C
325500 Isika C
326500 Merika C
327500 Funerea C
328500 Salurana C
329500 Jella C
330500 Myalasia C
331500 Kit'Kit'Kin C

332500 Beala C
333500 Minerva C
334500 Iserik C
335500 Merik C
336500 Pyre C
337500 Ansalong C
338500 Jarek Halvs C
339500 Moraster C
340500 Kal'Rik'Tik C
341500 Talcon R
342500 Minervan C
343500 Apocalypse C
344500 Harpy, The C
345500 Magian, The R
346500 Serpent C
347500 Chernevik C
348500 Cidre Bint Corina C
349500 Adan El-Mesir C
350500 Rahil the Falcon C
351500 Arlando El-Adaba C
352500 Ancient Dead, The C
353500 Madman Enraged C
354500 Ting Ling C
355500 Death Ship, The C
356500 Lesser Mummy, The C
357500 Bride of Malice C
358500 Vulture of the Core, The C
359500 Fleeing Adventurers C
360500 Bog Monster, The C
361500 Flight C
362500 Shapechange U
363500 Fireball C
364500 Lightning Bolt C
365500 Magic Missle C
366500 Wall of Fire C
367500 Wall of Force C
368500 Cone of Cold C
369500 Crushing Fist C
370500 Dispel Magic C
371500 Wall of Fog C
372500 Fear C
373500 Blink C
374500 Charm Monster C
375500 Black Tentacles C
376500 Death Fog C
377500 Death Spell U
378500 Power Word, Stun C
379500 Spell Turning C
380500 Power Word, Silence C
381500 Death Link U
382500 Limited Wish U
383500 Time Stop U
384500 Wish U
385500 Reverse Gravity C
386500 Mirror Image C
387500 Elminster's Evasion C
388500 Prismatic Sphere C
389500 Re-target C
390500 ESP C
391500 Leomund's Trap C
392500 Misdirection C
393500 Ray of Enfeeblement C
394500 Stinking Cloud C
395500 Sepia Snake Sigil C
396500 Armor C
397500 Sticks to Snakes C
398500 Sanctuary C
399500 Wind Walk C
400500 Dispel C
401500 Raise Dead C
402500 Creeping Doom U
403500 Earthquake U
404500 Shadow Engines C
405500 Faith-Magic Zone C
406500 Ward of Sleep C
407500 Ward of Peace C
408500 Ward of Erebus C
409500 Ward of Lancoon C
410500 Ward of Laius C
411500 Ward of Freedom C
412500 Ward of Ironguarding C
413500 Ward of Ruin C
414500 Ward of the Erinyes C
415500 Animal Friendship C
416500 Command C
417500 Shillelagh C
418500 Aid C
419500 Enthrall C
420500 Fire Trap C
421500 Heat Metal C
422500 Locate Object C
423500 Negative Plane Protection C
424500 Switch Personality C
425500 Superior Invisibility C
426500 Mindlink C
427500 Precognition C
428500 Phobia Amplification C
429500 Body Weaponry C
430500 Lend Health C
431500 Metamorphosis U
432500 Mindwipe C
433500 Jab C
434500 Boot to the Head C
435500 Reversal C
436500 Choke Hold C
437500 Counter C
438500 Rake! C
439500 Tail Slap U
440500 Blind Side! C
441500 Heroic Effort C
442500 Elemental Control C
443500 Fear C
444500 Healing C
445500 Resistance C
446500 Bloodform C
447500 Charm Aura C
448500 Major Resistance C
449500 Wither Touch C
450500 Persuasion C
451500 Ren's Crystal Ball C
452500 Codex of the Infinite Planes C
453500 Eye and Hand of Vecna C
454500 Cup of Al-Akbar C
455500 Ring of Winter, The C
456500 Wand of Orcus C
457500 Axe of Dwarvish Lords C
458500 Guenhwyvar C
459500 Obsidian Man of Urik C
460500 Throne of the Gods, The C
461500 Nature's Throne C
462500 Throne of Bone C
463500 Medusa Throne, The C
464500 Throne of Ice C
465500 Throne of the Seas C
466500 Throne of the Pharaohs C
467500 Emerald Throne, The C
468500 Throne of the Drow C
469500 Elemental Avatar of Earth R
470500 Elemental Avatar of Air R
471500 Elemental Avatar of Water R
472500 Elemental Avatar of Fire R
473500 Garl Glittergold R
474500 Urdlen R
475500 Yondalla the Provider R
476500 Brandobaris R
477500 Corellon Larethian R
478500 Bahgtru R
479500 Great Mother R
480500 Annam R
481500 Remnis R
482500 Cegilune R
483500 Kanchelsis R
484500 Ferrix R
485500 Titania R
486500 Verenestra R
487500 Midnight, Goddess of Magic R
488500 Iuz, Avatar of Evil R
489500 Lolth, the Spider Avatar R
490500 Nobody Wins! C
491500 Rule Lawyer's Delight C
492500 Time of Troubles C
493500 Power of Faith, The C
494500 Forbidden Knowledge C
495500 Circle of Life C
496500 Fair Fight! C
497500 Event Wheel, The C
498500 Backwaters, The C
499500 Master the Magic C
500500 Master Strategist, The C
501520 Flash Flood VR
502520 Netherese Symbol of Power VR
503520 Rengarth Oracle VR
504520 Sea of Dust VR
505520 Caves of Mystery VR
506520 Living Earth, The VR
507520 Painted Hills, The VR
508520 Ethereal Champion VR
509520 Agis's Cairn VR
510520 Throne of the Mountain God VR
511520 Between a Rock and a Hard Place VR
512520 Barbaric Allies VR
513520 Sylvan Pool, The VR
514520 Poor Man's Fort VR
515520 Crystal Dome, The VR
516520 Towers of Menzoberranzan VR
517520 Mystic Passage VR
518520 Blingdenstone Symbol of Power VR
519520 Dragon's Eye Symbol of Power VR
520520 Winner's Cape, The VR

1996 Spellfire Master the Magic Birthright

125 It's Good to be the King VR
225 Shadow World, The VR
325 Forced Conscription VR
425 Sphere of Annihilation VR
525 Vacuous Grimoire VR
625 Manual of Puissant Skill at Arms VR
725 Book of Infinite Spells VR
825 Libram of Ineffable Damnation VR
925 Count of Muden, The VR
1025 Wizardess Carrie, The VR
1100 Roesone C
1125 Pontifex of the Southern Coast, The VR
1225 Olaf the Sly VR
1325 Targoth the Unclean VR
1425 Rhuobhe Manslayer VR
1525 Kaerizen Whiteheart VR
1625 Adara Addlepate VR
1725 Blood of Azrai, The VR
1825 Taxation VR
1925 Diplomacy VR
2025 Blood Challenge! VR
2100 Ilien C
2125 Festival VR
2225 Child's Play VR
2325 Fates, The VR
2425 War Declared! VR
2525 Mebhaigl Surge VR
3100 Spiderfell, The U
4100 Gorgon's Crown, The R
5100 Avanil U
6100 Ghoere R
7100 Tuarhievel C
8100 Mur-Kilad C
9100 Baruk-Azhik R
10100 Impregnable Heart of Haelyn, The C
11100 Tower of the Sword Mage C
12100 Imperial City of Anuire U
13100 Heartland Outfitters, The C
14100 Proudglaive U
15100 Kal-Saitharak R
16100 Magical Source C
17100 Maze of Maalvar the Minotaur, The C
18100 Espionage! C
19100 Chaos! R
20100 Investiture Ceremony C
21100 Forge Ley Line R
22100 Biding Your Time U
23100 In Search of Adventure U
24100 Revolution! C
25100 Kraken Attacks!, The R
26100 Crown of Regency C
27100 Armor of the High King C
28100 Dragon's Teeth C
29100 Bracers of Brachiation C
30100 Ring of Human Influence U
31100 Ring of Spell Storing R
32100 Rod of Lordly Might C
33100 Amulet of Plane Walking C
34100 Cloak of Displacement U
35100 Alertness U
36100 Animal Affinity C
37100 Battlewise R
38100 Courage C
39100 Divine Wrath C
40100 Regeneration U
41100 Touch of Decay U
42100 Unreadable Thoughts C
43100 Death Touch R
44100 Detect Life C
45100 Invulnerability U
46100 Tighmaevril Sword R
47100 Wintering R
48100 Emperor's Crown of Anuire R
49100 Kingstopper R
50100 Bless Land U
51100 Blight C
52100 Investiture C
53100 Control Weather U
54100 Transmute Metal to Wood C
55100 Part Water C
56100 Speak with Monsters C
57100 Summon Insects C
58100 Legion of Dead U
59100 Raze R
60100 Blood Drain C
61100 Otto's Irresistible Dance C
62100 Clone R
63100 Drawmij's Instant Summons U
64100 Gorgon, The R
65100 Spider, The U
66100 Banshegh R
67100 Lamia, The R
68100 Siren, The R
69100 White Witch, The C
70100 Hag, The U
71100 Cerilian Dragon U
72100 Shadow World, The C
73100 Divine Right C
74100 Orogs C
75100 Green Slime R
76100 Nightmare C
77100 Unicorn C
78100 Wraith U
79100 Stirge Swarm R
80100 Ankheg C
81100 Wood Nymph C
82100 Giant Squid U
83100 Lord Cronal C
84100 Grimm Graybeard C
85100 Teodor Profiev C
86100 Darien Avan R
87100 Caliedhe Dosiere C
88100 Tomkin Dross C
89100 Elf Prince Fhileraene, The R
90100 Tie'skar Graecher, the Goblin King C
91100 Noble Outlaw, The R
92100 High Mage Aelies U
93100 Sword Mage, The C
94100 Wizard, The U
95100 Nadia Vasily C
96100 Moergan C
97100 Barak the Dark C
98100 Jana Orel U
99100 Flower of Roesone, The C
100100 Gwenyth the Bard U

1996 Spellfire Master the Magic Draconomicon

125 T'char, Dragon of Flame VR
225 Lair Raid! VR
325 Boreas VR
425 Morcanth Dragontamer VR
525 Cron the Black VR
625 Draconic Allies VR
725 Lernaean Hydra VR
825 Dragon Hatchling VR
925 Dragon Cultist VR
1025 Playing to Lose VR
1100 Rauglothgor's Lair C
1125 Wyvern VR
1225 Charm, the Crystal Dragon VR
1325 Chimera VR
1425 Red Dragon Figurine VR
1525 Saphire the Blue Dragon VR
1625 Glimmer the Brass Dragon VR
1725 Treasure Hoard VR
1825 Dragon's Bones VR
1925 Dragon Skirmish VR
2025 Wyrmblight VR
2100 Dragon Mountain C
2125 Wyrms' Conclave VR
2225 Dragon's Breath VR
2325 Ancient Dragon Magic VR
2425 Underground Lair VR
2525 Dragon's Scale VR
3100 Lair of the Shadowdrake R
4100 Dragonspine Mountains R
5100 Griff Mountains C
6100 Vesve Forest C
7100 Mount Nevermind U
8100 Palanthas C
9100 Mount Deismaar R
10100 Dragon's Hoard R
11100 Dark Depths U
12100 Powers of the Land C
13100 Mistmarsh, The C
14100 Mist Caves, The C
15100 Dragon's Crown C
16100 Council of Wyrms C
17100 Dragon Magic R
18100 Dragon's Graveyard U
19100 Wyrm's Decree C
20100 Dragon Raid! R
21100 Dragon Fear U
22100 Trapped! C
23100 Forced Revolt C
24100 Favorable Winds R
25100 Blessing of Zorquan C
26100 Infyrana the Dragon U
27100 Flame C
28100 Pelath the Bronze Dragon C
29100 Maldraedior, Great Blue Wyrm U
30100 Tamarand, Great Gold Wyrm C
31100 Lareth, King of Justice R
32100 Flashburn C
33100 Fi Lendicol C
34100 Rauglothgor C
35100 Sparkle, Crystal Dragon U
36100 Shadow Dragon R
37100 Greyhawk Dragon U
38100 Flare C
39100 Sleet C
40100 Khisanth U
41100 Cyan Bloodbane U
42100 Verminaard the Dragonmaster R
43100 Celestial Emperor, The R
44100 Tiamat, God of Evil Dragons U
45100 Bahamut, God of Good Dragons U
46100 Astral Spell R
47100 Dragon's Calm U
48100 Humanoid Familiar C
49100 Venomdust C
50100 Firetrail C
51100 Dragon's Death Door C
52100 Cold Curtain C
53100 Summon Dragon C
54100 Dragon Mark U
55100 Meteor Swarm U
56100 Enchanted Flight R
57100 Blessing of Tiamat C
58100 Blessing of Bahamut C
59100 Symbol of Pain C
60100 Symbol of Persuasion C
61100 Symbol of Death R
62100 Confusion C
63100 Find the Path C
64100 True Seeing C
65100 Plague R
66100 Inertial Barrier C
67100 Combat Mind U
68100 Phase C
69100 Death Field C
70100 Ultrablast R
71100 Synaptic Static C
72100 Daydream R
73100 Psychic Blade C
74100 Gauntlets of Combat C
75100 Talisman of the Beast R
76100 Wand of Magic Detection C
77100 Well of Many Worlds U
78100 Wand of Negation R
79100 Maul of the Titans U
80100 Cult of the Dragon R
81100 Undead Dragonrider U
82100 Dragonne C
83100 Faerie Dragon C
84100 Firedrake C
85100 Drake C
86100 Amulet of the Wyrm U
87100 Fang of the Dragon U
88100 Orb of the Eternal Dragon R
89100 Mighty Servant of Leuk-o U
90100 Swoop R
91100 Claw C
92100 Tail Sweep C
93100 Bite R
94100 Breath Weapon I C
95100 Breath Weapon II U
96100 Breath Weapon III R
97100 Swallow Whole U
98100 Evade C
99100 Age of the Dragon R
100100 Battle Must Go On!, The U

1996 Spellfire Master the Magic Nightstalkers

125 Good Triumphs in the End VR
225 Crime Does Not Pay VR
325 Busted! VR
425 Confused Hunchback VR
525 Dark Prophesy VR
625 Dark Dreams VR
725 Celestial Lights VR
825 Mirror of Corruption VR
925 Amulet of Undead Aura VR
1025 Arcane Formula for a Lich VR
1100 Vast Swamp, The R
1125 Bag of Beans VR
1225 Shadowcloak VR
1325 Pavlov's Bell VR
1425 Ring of Lycanthropy VR
1525 Zombie VR
1625 Varney the Vampire VR
1725 Moonbeast VR
1825 Gib Lhadsemlo VR
1925 Gib Hcivonad VR
2025 Gib Reltub VR
2100 Bandit Kingdom, The U
2125 Gib Irod VR
2225 Gib Drawsemaj VR
2325 Gib Aklem VR
2425 Den of Thieves VR
2525 Mad Scientist's Laboratory VR
3100 Mintarn C
4100 Nelanther C
5100 Falkovnia R
6100 Richemulot U
7100 Cromlin U
8100 UnderCerilia C
9100 Vampire's, The U
10100 Thieve's Guild U
11100 Haunted Graveyard R
12100 Guild Shop C
13100 Forgotten Crypt C
14100 Assassin's Guild C
15100 Pristine Tower, The U
16100 Giustenal Ruins R
17100 Hellgate Keep U
18100 Cavern of Ancient Knowledge R
19100 Paying Your Dues C
20100 Moonlight Madness C
21100 Boss Wants a Cut, The U
22100 Dawn of the Dead C
23100 Long Arm of the Law, The R
24100 Wail of the Banshee U
25100 Complete Surprise R
26100 Black Death, The C
27100 Three Card Monte R
28100 Guildmaster, The R
29100 Artemis Entreri U
30100 Daryth of Calimshan C
31100 Storm Silverhand U
32100 Jacqueline Renier C
33100 Ratik Ubel C
34100 Julio, Master Thief of Haslic C
35100 Turin Deathstalker R
36100 Simpkin The Weasel" Furzear U
37100 Phostrek C
38100 Jamlin U
39100 Donval C
40100 El-Hadid U
41100 Kelda Auslawsen C
42100 Moriad C
43100 Uldo Dracobane R
44100 Orcus R
45100 Mask R
46100 Dancing Sword C
47100 Rod of Zombie Mastery C
48100 Whip of Disarming U
49100 Gauntlets of Dexterity U
50100 Wand of Bone R
51100 Book of the Dead R
52100 Heart of Darkness C
53100 Trumpet of Doom R
54100 Herald of Mei Lung C
55100 Back Stab C
56100 Pick Pockets C
57100 Move Silently C
58100 Set Traps C
59100 Hide in Shadows U
60100 Climb Walls C
61100 Detect Noise C
62100 Read Languages C
63100 Use Poison U
64100 Concealed Weapon U
65100 Werebear R
66100 Crawling Claws C
67100 Nemon Hotep C
68100 Shera the Wise C
69100 Winslow the Lich U
70100 Caller in Darkness U
71100 Vampire, The R
72100 Wereshark C
73100 Negative Planar Energy R
74100 Sure Thing, A R
75100 Kaisharga C
76100 Guild Master C
77100 Raaig C
78100 Cat Burglar C
79100 Zombie Horde U
80100 Beggar R
81100 Ancient Dracolich R
82100 Loric the Fence U
83100 Bigby's Dexterous Digits C
84100 Guardian Mist C
85100 Alarm C
86100 Corruption of the Flesh U
87100 Power of Faith R
88100 Find Traps C
89100 Blessed Abundance C
90100 Monster Mount C
91100 Aging C
92100 Cause Despair C
93100 Cause Fear C
94100 Cause Paralysis C
95100 Constitution Drain C
96100 Strength Drain C
97100 Level Drain R
98100 Magic Resistance U
99100 Rapid Regeneration C
100100 Cause Disease R

1996 Spellfire Master the Magic Runes and Ruins

125 Dream Team, The VR
225 Brain Drain VR
325 Toad, The VR

425 Lost Treasure VR
525 Holy Sword Chrysomer VR
625 Manshoon of the Zhentarim VR
725 Undead Regeneration VR
825 Dark Lens, The VR
925 Book of the Damned VR
1025 Horn of Change VR
1100 Isle of the Ape R
1125 Kuroth's Quill VR
1225 Dodge VR
1325 Runes of the Future VR
1425 Cursed Idol VR
1525 Tower of Spirits VR
1625 Gib Kcir VR
1725 Dispel Psionics VR
1825 Psionic Reflection VR
1925 Icon of Magic VR
2025 Nectar of the Gods VR
2100 Forbidden City, The C
2125 Boots of Pharlanghn VR
2225 Crystal Cave, The VR
2325 Fair Princess, The VR
2425 Phylactery, The VR
2525 Portal to Limbo VR
3100 Lost Caverns of Tsojcanth, The C
4100 White Plume Mountain U
5100 Doc's Island C
6100 City of Phlan, The R
7100 Barrier Peaks, The C
8100 Tomb of Horrors C
9100 Demonweb Pits C
10100 Hidden Shrine of Tamoachan, The U
11100 Depths of the Earth, The C
12100 Isle of Dread C
13100 Desert of Desolation R
14100 Glacial Rift, The C
15100 Lendore Isles, The C
16100 Lost City, The U
17100 Village of Orlane U
18100 Sunderhan, Isle of the Slave Lords R
19100 Keep on the Borderlands R
20100 Palace of the Silver Princess C
21100 Labyrinth of Madness C
22100 Village of Hommlet U
23100 Oasis of the White Palm C
24100 Ghost Tower of Inverness C
25100 Vault of the Drow C
26100 Tenser's Castle U
27100 Temple of Death, The C
28100 Bigby the Great R
29100 Tenser the Arch Mage U
30100 Oonga the Ape R
31100 Falx the Silver Dragon C
32100 Lord Robilar C
33100 Phoebus the Lizard Man C
34100 Vecna the Arch Lich R
35100 Kas the Terrible U
36100 Grimslade the Gray C
37100 Ren o' the Blade R
38100 Acerack the Eternal R
39100 Wulfgar C
40100 Jarl the Frost Giant C
41100 King Snurre the Fire Giant C
42100 Queen Frumpy the Fire Giant C
43100 Keeper, The U
44100 Nosnra the Hill Giant C
45100 Ombi the Renegade Dwarf C
46100 Mordenkainen's Disjunction R
47100 Slay Living C
48100 Intercession U
49100 Conjure Earth Elemental U
50100 Conjure Fire Elemental C
51100 Conjure Air Elemental U
52100 Conjure Water Elemental C
53100 Crystalbrittle C
54100 Energy Drain U
55100 Tyranthraxus, The Possessing Spirit R
56100 Coming of the Phoenix C
57100 Forgotten King, The R
58100 Elixir of Life C
59100 Giant Raid! U
60100 Vampire Attacks, The U
61100 Undead Guardian R
62100 Barbarian Charge! C
63100 Psionic Shield U
64100 Volcanic Eruption U
65100 Midas Orb, The C
66100 Invulnerable Coat of Arnd U
67100 Ipsissimo's Black Goose C
68100 Tenser's Crystal Ball C
69100 Albruin C
70100 Blackrazor R
71100 Wave U
72100 Whelm R
73100 Girdle of Dwarvenkind R
74100 Star Gem of Martek: Opal C
75100 Star Gem of Martek: Sapphire U
76100 Star Gem of Martek: Ruby C
77100 Star Gem of Martek: Clear Crystal R
78100 Star Gem of Martek: Amethyst U
79100 Big Giant's Rock C
80100 Huge Giant's Rock C
81100 Enormous Giant's Rock R
82100 Hypnosnake C
83100 Rahaisa, The R
84100 Remorhaz U
85100 Incantrix, The R
86100 Winter Wolf Pack C
87100 Hydra C
88100 Red Dragon U
89100 Rampaging Oni C
90100 Live Ones, The R
91100 Flying Kick C
92100 Haymaker R
93100 Uppercut U
94100 Disarm C
95100 Kidney Punch R
96100 Bear Hug C
97100 Knockdown C
98100 Headlock U
99100 Block C
100100 Monty Haul Campaign, The R

1997 Spellfire Master the Magic Dungeons

125 Winner's Trophy VR
225 Pretty Magical Ring VR
325 Fighting Dirty! VR
425 Dissolution VR
525 Black Hand Thieves' Guild VR
625 Elminster's Intuition VR
725 Fool's Paradise VR
825 Aliki VR
925 Lilac Hesabon VR
1025 Enter Darkness Together VR
1100 Mausoleum of the Zombie Master C
1125 Recorder of Ye Cind VR
1225 Telarie Willowind VR
1325 Llama King, The VR
1425 Necba the Wrathmaker VR
1525 Shan, Karate Master VR
1625 Handmine VR
1725 Builder, The VR
1825 Slorath's Gloves VR
1925 Rary's Apprentice VR
2025 Poor Oriental Lord VR
2100 Dungeon of the King C
2125 Highmaster Illithios VR
2225 Chaos Lord VR
2325 Giant Troll VR
2425 Elyk the Bard VR
2525 Dor Amberglow VR
3100 Lair of Dregoth, the Undead Dragon-King U
4100 Domain of Takhisis, Queen of Darkness C
5100 Undermountain C
6100 Labyrinth of Castle Greyhawk R
7100 Under Castle Strahd C
8100 Palace of the Celestial Light C
9100 Field of the Battle Lord R
10100 Belly of the Beast, The C
11100 Pit of the Mind Lord C
12100 Torture Room, The C
13100 Maze of the Guild C
14100 Carrock of High Magicks R
15100 Enchanted Land, The C
16100 Purveyor of Events U
17100 Spells of the Archmage C
18100 Spells of the Friar C
19100 Spells from the Grave R
20100 Powers from the Savage Land C
21100 Might of the Blood Right C
22100 Song of the Dragonlance R
23100 Bats in the Belfry R
24100 Azure Tower of Onad the Fallen, The R
25100 Beneath Castle Drawmij U
26100 Return of the Dwarven King C
27100 Guildhall, The C
28100 Dragon's Refuge, The U
29100 Cities of the Sun C
30100 Border Post U
31100 Border Garrison R
32100 Ruins of Lololia, The R
33100 Tower by the Sea C
34100 Forgotten Ruins, The C
35100 Hidden Village, The C
36100 Bitter Knoll C
37100 Ogre, The U
38100 Fire Dragon R
39100 Zaranda Star C
40100 Skulker R
41100 Jasper U
42100 Hapless Halfling, The C
43100 Feral Halfling U
44100 Dearlyn Ambersong C
45100 Tyvorg the Frost Giant C
46100 Troglodyte C
47100 Hook Horror C
48100 Lurker in the Earth U
49100 Skull Tumor R
50100 Hero Slayer C
51100 While Weird, The R
52100 Psion Sucker C
53100 Master Illithid U
54100 Bottomless Horror U
55100 Boiling Oil R
56100 Siege Ladder U
57100 Net of Ensnaring R
58100 Battering Ram U
59100 Ballista R
60100 Cannon Ball R
61100 Borer R
62100 Catapult C
63100 Siege Machine C
64100 Sword of Sharpness C
65100 Triton Throne, The C
66100 Flask of Curses C
67100 Crystal Dragon Figurine U
68100 Amulet of the Dragon King U
69100 Breath Charm C
70100 Pearl Pegasus R
71100 Clockwork Ogre U
72100 Amulet of Spell Turning R
73100 Psionic Disintegration R
74100 Magic Draining Field C
75100 Drain Will U
76100 Eat Dirt! C
77100 Vital Blow U
78100 Supernatural Strength C
79100 Create Minion C
80100 Melt Bone U
81100 Death Field U
82100 Con Game R
83100 Legal Loophole C
84100 Tumble Out of Danger U
85100 Broad Jump R
86100 Hijacking R
87100 Fortune Telling C
88100 Gather Information C
89100 Intimidation U
90100 Trailing C
91100 Extension I C
92100 City Shield U
93100 Spectral Dragon C
94100 Ball Lightning U
95100 Drawmij's Beneficent Polymorph U
96100 Animate Gargoyle R
97100 Minions of Darkness C
98100 Conjure Greater Fire Elemental C
99100 Divine Assistance C
100100 What Comes Around Goes Around C

2010 The Spoils Seed II Gloamspike's Revenge

COMPLETE SET (110)	120.00	180.00
BOOSTER BOX (12 PACKS)	60.00	80.00
BOOSTER PACK (13 CARDS)	5.00	7.00
1 Desolate R	6.00	15.00
2 Foment C	.10	.25
3 Hextilda, the Exiled Crone R	.60	1.50
4 Hideous Hexapede of Horror R	.75	2.00
5 Imperial Thaumaturge C	.10	.25
6 Inadequate Wand C	.20	.50
7 Manifest R	4.00	10.00
8 Meat of the Mountain R	.40	1.00
9 Minion of Thabbash C	.10	.25
10 Muddle R	2.00	5.00
11 Nattering Stoopswaggler C	.20	.50
12 Obscene Astrologer C	.40	1.00
13 Otter Floss C	.20	.50
14 Perturb C	.10	.25
15 Redonkulous C	.75	2.00
16 Ritual of the Double Monkey C	.30	.75
17 Titillated Mooncalf C	.10	.25
18 Tumescent Guilt Bladder R	1.25	3.00
19 Verrucose Brains R	.40	1.00
20 Witty Worm C	.10	.25
21 Woadenworm Gloamspike, Thabbashite Prince R	1.00	2.50
22 Alluring Quicksand C	.10	.25
23 Ceremonious Groomer C	.20	.50
24 Clam Hash C	.10	.25
25 Delectable Boon R	2.00	5.00
26 Derelict Seafarer R	1.50	4.00
27 Dowsing Cleric C	.10	.25
28 Dwarvish Grimalkin C	.60	1.50
29 Emissary of Loot C	.10	.25
30 Framptle Tromwibbler, Lord of Bling R	2.00	5.00
31 Gilded Yurt C	1.25	3.00
32 Grandiose Resurrector R	2.00	5.00
33 Gus VanBaymaven R	2.00	5.00
34 Hidden Ruins R	2.00	5.00
35 Lodge Dock Florist R	.75	2.00
36 Melty Cheese C	.10	.25
37 Miraculous Regeneration C	.10	.25
38 Overzealous Excavation R	.75	2.00
39 Prophetic Assistant C	.10	.25
40 Swinish Elder C	.10	.25
41 The Poshernacle R	2.50	6.00
42 Tiny Shiny C	.10	.25
43 313371 C	.10	.25
44 3cc3n7r1c 73chn1c14n C	.10	.25
45 3p1c D00dm4k3r C	.10	.25
46 4rm0r3d 31f C	.40	1.00
47 Accidental Invention R	3.00	8.00
48 Braggadocian Aide C	.10	.25
49 Cantankerous Claywork R	2.50	6.00
50 Clay Node R	2.00	5.00
51 Cock Block R	2.00	5.00
52 Contrabulous Fabtraption R	2.00	5.00
53 Enormous and Uncooperative Golem C	.10	.25
54 G14n7 5p0rk D3f3n53 C	.10	.25
55 Gewgawed Gimcrack R	1.00	2.50
56 Golemizer C	.25	.60
57 Goloam R	.75	2.00
58 Lab of Luxury R	1.25	3.00
59 Recyclable Golem C	.25	.60
60 Research Intern C	.10	.25
61 Rewarding Salvage C	.10	.25
62 Thorough Sanitization C	.10	.25
63 Time Traveler Tourist Trap R	1.25	3.00
64 Ass R	3.00	8.00
65 Burly Assailment R	3.00	8.00
66 Delusive Strumpet C		.50
67 Drygulch C	.40	1.00
68 Epicureous Mammajamma C	.10	.25
69 Fired Hand C	.20	.50
70 I Drink Your Milkshake! R	3.00	8.00
71 Lucky Bastard C	.10	.25
72 Mistaken Identity R	2.50	6.00
73 Muscle Tribe of Danger and Excellence C	.10	.25
74 Mustache Aficionado R	1.25	3.00
75 Party Clowns R	10.00	25.00
76 Peculate R	3.00	8.00
77 Resistance Fighter C	.10	.25
78 Rosy Palmer, and Her Five Friends R	2.50	6.00
79 Roundalicious Breasticles C	.40	1.00
80 Rusty Pickaxe C	.10	.25
81 Smothering Corpulence C	.10	.25
82 Sprint C	.10	.25
83 Uncontrollable Jalopy C	.10	.25
84 Vast Mastabatorium R	1.25	3.00
85 Crest of Deception R	6.00	15.00
86 Crest of Elitism R	6.00	15.00
87 Crest of Greed R	5.00	12.00
88 Crest of Obsession R	6.00	15.00
89 Crest of Rage R	8.00	20.00
90 A Blazing Zero R	5.00	12.00
91 Acidic Phlegm C	.10	.25
92 Aroused Stiffbone C	.40	1.00
93 Ascendant Madcap C	.10	.25
94 Athalamund Mangod, The Iron Fist R	4.00	10.00
95 Barrier of Benevolence C	.10	.25
96 Conscientious Objector R	2.50	6.00
97 Dark Awakening R	8.00	20.00
98 Dying Hero R	2.50	6.00
99 Embittered Cadet C	.10	.25
100 Epic Smackdown R	2.50	6.00
101 Implosive Explosion C	.10	.25
102 Midget Mine C	.10	.25
103 Necromantic Healer C	.20	.50
104 Padamose, Emperor of Marduun R	2.00	5.00
105 Plunging Shriever C	.25	.60
106 Spiky Pumpkin R	1.25	3.00
107 Spry Archer C	.10	.25
108 Surplus Soldier C	.10	.25
109 The Emperor Barduse R	2.00	5.00
110 Vorpal Sword C	.10	.25

2012 The Spoils Seed III Fall of Marmothoa

1 Cowslaw
2 Devilfang Thunderhoof
3 Geiseric, the Souleater
4 God's Autograph
5 Pony Slaystation
6 Spatchcocking
7 The Stone of Shame
8 Anatidaephobia
9 Fecal Urgency
10 Intriguing Mezzanine
11 Port Manteau
12 Prestige Inversion
13 Vilghame Manewaft
14 Ensmallment Ray
15 94r913 My 908570pp3r5
16 Hilarious Refrigerator Alarm
17 Merbegon, the Insatiable Taxidermist
18 Notion Sickness
19 Axeclaw Grandchest
20 Community Chest
21 Delicious Strawberry Flavored Death
22 Fornicaves
23 Iohane, the Convex
24 Ipsighast, the Lustful
25 Unscrupuls of Victory
26 Giada, the Elegant
27 Octo-Ba-Ba, the Devourer
28 Shieldmane Grandchest
29 The Great Wall of Keeping Stuff Out
30 The Stone of Triumph

2013 The Spoils Shade of the Devoured Emperor

COMPLETE SET (130)	150.00	200.00
BOOSTER BOX (12 PACKS)	30.00	50.00
BOOSTER PACK (13 CARDS)	2.00	4.00
1 Anxious Imp C	.10	.25
2 Concentriculation C	.10	.25
3 Contiguous Defalcating Machine R	.40	1.00
4 Elementary Elemental C	.10	.25
5 Expedition Endeavour R	1.25	3.00
6 Forgotten Tentacle U	.25	.60
7 Gloamspike-Gosche Bridge R	1.50	4.00
8 Lugubrian Poacher C	.10	.25
9 Man Shark R	1.50	4.00
10 Mittens of Muffled Thought C	.10	.25
11 Monstrous Lassitude U	.25	.60
12 Neuralyzer Agent C	.10	.25
13 Officially Offensive Overseer U	.25	.60
14 Ping Konk U	.25	.60
15 Quotidian Concealer C	.10	.25
16 Quotidian Transposition C	.10	.25
17 Study Disturbance R	1.50	4.00
18 Tedious TriAdic Truculence R	1.25	3.00
19 Thabbashite Chemist U	.25	.60
20 The Lugubrian Council of Quotidian Affairs R	.75	2.00
21 This, That, and the Other Thing U	.25	.60
22 Underwhelming Performance C	.10	.25
23 Undevoted Gargantuan R	1.25	3.00
24 Violating Ritual U	.25	.60
25 Voidal Trinket U	.25	.60
26 Ancient and Disreputable Law Office R	2.00	5.00
27 Arcane Escrow U	.25	.60
28 Audacious Appraisal U	.60	1.50
29 Auspicious Arrival R	1.50	4.00
30 Contractual Execution C	.10	.25
31 Enlightened Mau U	.25	.60
32 Eustace Padamose-Gristwalter R	2.50	6.00
33 Fallen Quarter-Finalist C	.10	.25
34 Golden Charm R	2.50	6.00
35 Goldmau Sacks Representative U	.25	.60
36 Hassan-i of Thabbash R	6.00	15.00
37 Homewrecker U	.75	2.00
38 Impressionistic Furball C	.10	.25
39 Mau Strategist C	.10	.25
40 Mr. Fetch R	.40	1.00
41 Mushroom Merchant C	.10	.25
42 Negotiation Ceremonies C	.10	.25
43 Pinguid Bodyguard U	.25	.60
44 Purloinering Pirate U	.25	.60
45 Recycling Scheme Facility U	.25	.60
46 Siluriformes Flaxenscale R	5.00	12.00
47 Swindle C	.10	.25
48 Thabbashite Financier C	.10	.25
49 Timid Mau C	.10	.25
50 Underhanded Hang-Out C	.10	.25
51 Unexpected Codicil R	1.50	4.00
52 5n4p C	.10	.25
53 Abandoned Testing Complex U	.25	.60
54 Accumulation Majig C	.10	.25
55 Clockman Junk Picker U	.40	1.00
56 Draconic Luteoderm Suit R	4.00	10.00
57 Elitistmajig C	.10	.25
58 EPM (Extra Powerful Magnetic) Pulse R	2.50	6.00
59 Frickin' Sweet Pogo-Bunny U	.25	.60
60 Gigantitect's Giant Giant R	6.00	15.00
61 Industrious Usage C	.10	.25
62 It's a Trap! U	.25	.60
63 Jo Ciendeilio, M07h3r 0f 1337 R	3.00	8.00
64 M3CHm4n1c 31f C	.10	.25
65 Micromajig Recycling Station C	.10	.25
66 Micromajigmakermachinemajig C	.10	.25
67 Pwny Bomb C	.10	.25
68 R3p347 0ff3nd3r U	.25	.60
69 Reluctant Reconciliation C	.10	.25
70 Rocket Lawnchair R	2.00	5.00
71 Runic Junker R	3.00	8.00
72 Runic Map U	.25	.60
73 Sockem Bot U	.25	.60
74 Stuttershy U	.25	.60
75 Testudine Autoframe R	3.00	8.00
76 Thabbashite Armorer C	.10	.25
77 Backdoor Brigand U	.25	.60
78 Banana Peel C	.10	.25
79 Bottlebeard Brandyshanks R	1.00	2.50
80 Bug Bite C	.10	.25
81 Carnival Ringmaster U	.25	.60
82 Cicibeo the Swift R	4.00	10.00
83 Clockman City Shuffle U	.25	.60
84 Drive By Boobing C	.10	.25
85 Elusive Wolf C	.10	.25
86 Gang Weapon Dealer R	3.00	8.00
87 Gassy Gastornis C	.10	.25
88 Guileful Astucion C	.10	.25
89 Martial Arts Wannabe U	.25	.60
90 Murderous Kleptomaniac R	.40	1.00
91 Numba 1 Stunna! C	.10	.25
92 Opportunistic Pirate U	.25	.60
93 Parkour Hoodlum R	1.50	4.00
94 Sharpey Pointy Lethal Army Tool R	2.00	5.00
95 Sickened Sarcophyle C	.10	.25
96 Sneaker Attack! U	.25	.60
97 Sticky Stealy Hand U	.25	.60
98 Surreptitious Larceny R	1.50	4.00
99 Thabbashite Assailant C	.10	.25
100 Torchlight District R	2.00	5.00
101 Totally Random Kid C	.10	.25
102 Clockman Skydocks R	2.50	6.00
103 Remains of Foreman Pete, the Clock Man U	.25	.60
104 Time to Retire C	.10	.25
105 6r4wny 60dy9u4rd5 U	.25	.60
106 B.A.S.E. Jump U	.25	.60
107 Barracks of Precipitancy R	2.00	5.00
108 Battle-Ready Back-Breaker C	.10	.25
109 Bloating Bask C	.10	.25
110 Bloody Fisted Fanatic C	.10	.25
111 Confrontational Conflagration C	.10	.25
112 Discordant Cadencer C	.10	.25
113 Drill Instructor U	.25	.60
114 Duelist of Surfeit C	.10	.25
115 Fanatical Shriever U	.25	.60
116 Fistfight C	.10	.25
117 Flaming Cube R	2.00	5.00
118 Juice Closet C	.10	.25
119 Juice Sale! C	.10	.25
120 Marauding Madster R	2.50	6.00
121 Rudo Mangod, Dragonweight Champion R	2.50	6.00
122 Rushing Crushing Blockhead U	.25	.60
123 Shade of the Devoured Emperor R	4.00	10.00
124 Shriever Breeding Program R	2.50	6.00
125 Skullcrush Steamroller U	.25	.60
126 Super Shiny Caltrops of DOOM! U	.25	.60
127 Thabbashite Warmonger U	.25	.60
128 Ursine Assassin R	1.50	4.00
129 Warbeast of Thabbash C	.10	.25
130 Words of Glory R	3.00	8.00

2006-13 The Spoils Promos

1 Arrogance
2 ASS Season 1 - Degenerate Molestation
3 ASS Season 1 - Martial Artist
4 ASS Season 1 - Senior Research Assistant
5 ASS Season 1 - Strength In Numbers
6 ASS Season 1 - The Ministry of Other Smaller Ministries

1994 Star Trek Premiere Black Border

COMPLETE SET (363)	120.00	200.00
BOOSTER BOX (36 PACKS)	50.00	100.00
BOOSTER PACK (15 CARDS)	2.00	4.00
UNLISTED C	.10	.25
UNLISTED U	.20	.50
UNLISTED R	.40	1.00
RELEASED ON NOVEMBER 10, 1994		
1 Albert Einstein R	1.25	3.00
14 Anti-Time Anomaly R	.75	2.00
27 B'Etor R	.60	1.50
28 Beverly Crusher R	.60	1.50
33 Borg Ship R	1.50	4.00
34 Bynars Weapon Enhancement R	.60	1.50
43 Crosis R	1.25	3.00
48 Data R	2.00	5.00
50 Deanna Troi R	2.00	5.00
52 Devoras R	.75	2.00
60 Dr. Leah Brahms R	.60	1.50
99 Geordi LaForge R	3.00	8.00
106 Haakona R	.60	1.50
111 Horga'hn R	.75	2.00
138 Investigate Rogue Comet R	.60	1.50
140 Investigate Time Continuum R	.60	1.50
145 Jean-Luc Picard R	5.00	10.00
175 Kurak R	.60	1.50
176 Kurlan Naiskos R	.60	1.50
188 Lwaxanna Troi R	.75	2.00
205 Morgan Bateson R	.60	1.50
237 Q R	1.50	4.00
253 Roga Danar R	2.00	5.00
259 Sarek R	.75	2.00
260 Sarjenka R	.75	2.00
274 Sir Isaac Newton R	1.25	3.00
290 Supernova R	.75	2.00

297 Tam Elbrun R 1.25 3.00
300 Tasha Yar R 2.00 5.00
313 Thomas Riker R 1.50 4.00
325 Tox Uthat R .60 1.50
336 U.S.S. Enterprise R 4.00 10.00
355 Wesley Crusher R 1.25 3.00
357 William T. Riker R 3.00 8.00
359 Worf R 2.00 5.00
361 Wormhole Negotiations R .60 1.50

1994 Star Trek Premiere White Border

COMPLETE SET (363) 60.00 120.00
BOOSTER BOX (36 PACKS)
BOOSTER PACK (15 CARDS)
UNLISTED C
UNLISTED U
UNLISTED R
RELEASED ON DECEMBER 12, 1994
ALSO KNOWN AS ALPHA VERSION
1 Albert Einstein R .75 2.00
14 Anti-Time Anomaly R .50 1.25
27 B'Etor R .40 1.00
28 Beverly Crusher R .40 1.00
33 Borg Ship R 1.00 2.50
34 Bynars Weapon Enhancement R .40 1.00
43 Crosis R .75 2.00
48 Data R 1.25 3.00
50 Deanna Troi R 1.25 3.00
52 Devoras R .50 1.25
60 Dr. Leah Brahms R .40 1.00
99 Geordi LaForge R 2.00 5.00
106 Haakona R .40 1.00
111 Horga'hn R .50 1.25
138 Investigate Rogue Comet R .40 1.00
140 Investigate Time Continuum R .40 1.00
145 Jean-Luc Picard R 2.50 6.00
175 Kurak R .40 1.00
176 Kurlan Naiskos R .40 1.00
188 Lwaxanna Troi R .50 1.25
205 Morgan Bateson R .40 1.00
237 Q R 1.00 2.50
253 Roga Danar R 1.25 3.00
259 Sarek R .50 1.25
260 Sarjenka R .50 1.25
274 Sir Isaac Newton R .75 2.00
290 Supernova R .50 1.25
297 Tam Elbrun R .75 2.00
300 Tasha Yar R 1.25 3.00
313 Thomas Riker R 1.00 2.50
325 Tox Uthat R .40 1.00
336 U.S.S. Enterprise R 2.50 6.00
355 Wesley Crusher R .75 2.00
357 William T. Riker R 2.00 5.00
359 Worf R 1.25 3.00
361 Wormhole Negotiations R .40 1.00

1995 Star Trek Alternate Universe

COMPLETE SET (122) 50.00 100.00
BOOSTER BOX (36 PACKS) 15.00 30.00
BOOSTER PACK (15 CARDS) 1.00 1.50
UNLISTED C .10 .25
UNLISTED U .20 .50
UNLISTED R .75 2.00
RELEASED ON DECEMBER 8, 1995
7 Berlingoff Rasmussen R 1.25 3.00
8 Beverly Picard R 2.00 5.00
15 Commander Tomalak R 2.00 5.00
16 Compromised Mission R 1.50 4.00
19 Cryosatellite R 1.25 3.00
20 Data's Head R 1.50 4.00
25 Devidian Door R 1.50 4.00
29 Echo Papa 607 Killer Drone R 1.50 4.00
40 Future Enterprise UR 30.00 60.00
42 Governor Worf R 1.25 3.00
51 Ian Andrew Troi R 1.25 3.00
58 Jack Crusher R 1.25 3.00
68 Major Rakal R 1.25 3.00
86 Rachel Garrett R 1.50 4.00
98 Samuel Clemens' Pocketwatch R 1.25 3.00
105 Tasha Yar - Alternate R 1.50 4.00
114 U.S.S. Enterprise-C R 1.50 4.00
117 Warped Space R 1.25 3.00

1995 Star Trek Premiere White Border

COMPLETE SET (363) 80.00 150.00
UNLISTED C .10 .25
UNLISTED U .20 .50
UNLISTED R .40 1.00
RELEASED IN JUNE 1995
ALSO KNOWN AS BETA VERSION
1 Albert Einstein R 1.25 3.00
14 Anti-Time Anomaly R .75 2.00
27 B'Etor R .60 1.50
28 Beverly Crusher R .60 1.50
33 Borg Ship R 1.50 4.00
34 Bynars Weapon Enhancement R .60 1.50
43 Crosis R 1.25 3.00
48 Data R 2.00 5.00
50 Deanna Troi R 2.00 5.00
52 Devoras R .75 2.00
60 Dr. Leah Brahms R .60 1.50
99 Geordi LaForge R 3.00 8.00
106 Haakona R .60 1.50
111 Horga'hn R .75 2.00
138 Investigate Rogue Comet R .60 1.50
140 Investigate Time Continuum R .60 1.50
145 Jean-Luc Picard R 5.00 10.00
175 Kurak R .60 1.50
176 Kurlan Naiskos R .60 1.50
188 Lwaxanna Troi R .75 2.00
205 Morgan Bateson R .60 1.50
237 Q R 1.50 4.00
253 Roga Danar R 2.00 5.00
259 Sarek R .75 2.00
260 Sarjenka R .75 2.00
274 Sir Isaac Newton R 1.25 3.00
290 Supernova R .75 2.00

297 Tam Elbrun R 1.25 3.00
300 Tasha Yar R 2.00 5.00
313 Thomas Riker R 1.50 4.00
325 Tox Uthat R .60 1.50
336 U.S.S. Enterprise R 4.00 10.00
355 Wesley Crusher R 1.25 3.00
357 William T. Riker R 3.00 8.00
359 Worf R 2.00 5.00
361 Wormhole Negotiations R .60 1.50

1996 Star Trek Introductory Two-Player Game

1 A Good Place to Die C
2 Admiral McCoy P
3 Admiral Picard P
4 Avert Danger C
5 Cargo Rendezvous C
6 Commander Data P
7 Commander Troi P
8 Data Laughing P
9 Distress Mission C
10 Gault C
11 Gi'ral P
12 Gravesworld C
13 Homeward C
14 Hostage Situation C
15 Ja'rod P
16 Mogh P
17 Reopen Dig C
18 Reported Activity C
19 Sensitive Search C
20 Spock P
21 Survey Instability C

1996 Star Trek Q Continuum

COMPLETE SET (121) 25.00 60.00
BOOSTER BOX (36) 20.00 40.00
BOOSTER PACK (18) 1.00 2.00
UNLISTED C .10 .25
UNLISTED U .20 .50
UNLISTED R .75 2.00
RELEASED IN OCTOBER 1996
15 Data's Body R 1.25 3.00
19 Doppelganger R 1.25 3.00
25 Galen R 1.25 3.00
43 Juliana Tainer R 1.25 3.00
46 Katherine Pulaski R 1.25 3.00
48 Keiko O'Brien R 1.25 3.00
54 Lal R 1.25 3.00
56 Madam Guinan R 1.25 3.00
65 Mortal Q R 1.50 4.00
112 U.S.S. Stargazer R 1.50 4.00
118 Yuta R 1.25 3.00

1997 Star Trek The Fajo Collection

COMPLETE SET (18) 30.00 60.00
COMMON CARD 2.00 5.00
RELEASED ON DECEMBER 31, 1997

1997 Star Trek First Anthology

COMPLETE SET (6) 8.00 20.00
COMMON CARD 2.00 5.00
RELEASED IN JUNE 1997

1997 Star Trek First Contact

COMPLETE SET (130) 40.00 80.00
BOOSTER BOX (30 PACKS) 30.00 60.00
BOOSTER PACK (9 CARDS)) 2.00 3.00
UNLISTED C .10 .25
UNLISTED U .20 .50
UNLISTED R .60 1.50
RELEASED ON DECEMBER 17, 1997
6 Admiral Hayes R .75 2.00
8 Alyssa Ogawa R .75 2.00
13 Assimilate Homeworld R 1.00 2.50
21 Beverly Crusher R 1.50 4.00
27 Borg Queen R .75 2.00
32 Data R 2.00 5.00
35 Deanna Troi R 1.25 3.00
44 Espionage Mission R .75 2.00
50 Geordi LaForge R 1.50 4.00
56 Jean-Luc Picard R 2.00 5.00
62 Lily Sloane R .75 2.00
79 Phoenix R .75 2.00
82 Primitive Culture R 1.00 2.50
83 Queen's Borg Cube R 1.50 4.00
84 Queen's Borg Sphere R .75 2.00
86 Regenerate R 2.00 5.00
87 Reginald Barclay R .75 2.00
89 Retask R 1.00 2.50
93 Scout Encounter R 1.00 2.50
96 Shipwreck R .75 2.00
103 Stop First Contact R .75 2.00
104 Strict Dress Code R .75 2.00
109 Theta-Radiation Poisoning R .75 2.00
121 U.S.S. Enterprise-E R 3.00 8.00
122 Undetected Beam-In R .75 2.00
123 Visit Cochrane Memorial R .75 2.00
125 Wall of Ships R 1.00 2.50
127 William T. Riker R 1.50 4.00
128 Worf R 1.50 4.00
129 Zefram Cochrane R 1.00 2.50

1998 Star Trek Deep Space Nine

COMPLETE SET (277) 80.00 150.00
BOOSTER BOX (30 PACKS)
BOOSTER PACK (9 CARDS)
UNLISTED C
UNLISTED U
UNLISTED R
RELEASED ON JULY 23, 1998
1 Aamin Marritza R .60 1.50
6 Airlock R .60 1.50
7 Aldara R .60 1.50
11 Altovar R .60 1.50
20 Automated Security System R .75 2.00
21 Bajoran Civil War R 1.00 2.50
30 Bareil Antos R .75 2.00
31 Baseball R .75 2.00
32 Benjamin Sisko R 2.00 5.00
34 Boheeka R .60 1.50
35 Borad R .60 1.50
36 Bo'Rak R .60 1.50
38 Camping Trip R .60 1.50
44 Central Command R .75 2.00
45 Cha'Joh R 1.00 2.50
46 Chamber of Ministers R .60 1.50
47 Changeling Research R .60 1.50
50 Colonel Day R .60 1.50
56 Cure Blight R .60 1.50
59 Danar R .75 2.00
60 Deep Space Nine / Terok Nor R 6.00 15.00
61 Defiant Dedication Plaque R 1.25 3.00
64 D'Ghor R .60 1.50
65 DNA Clues R .60 1.50
72 Dukat R 2.00 5.00
74 Duranja R .60 1.50
75 Elim Garak R 2.00 5.00
77 Enabran Tain R 1.00 2.50
79 Entek R .60 1.50
88 Establish Tractor Lock R .60 1.50
99 Garak Has Some Issues R 1.00 2.50
100 Garak's Tailor Shop R .60 1.50
102 General Krim R .60 1.50
104 Gilora Rejal R .60 1.50
105 Going to the Top R 2.00 5.00
107 Grilka R 1.00 2.50
108 Groumall R .75 2.00
110 Harvester Virus R .75 2.00
115 HQ: Return Orb to Bajor R 1.00 2.50
120 I.K.C. Toh'Kaht R 1.00 2.50
126 Investigate Rumors R .60 1.50
130 Jadzia Dax R 2.00 5.00
132 Jake and Nog R 1.50 4.00
133 Jaro Essa R .60 1.50
135 Julian Bashir R 2.00 5.00
137 Kai Opaka R .60 1.50
141 Karina R .75 2.00
143 Kira Nerys R 1.50 4.00
145 Korinas R .75 2.00
147 Kovat R .75 2.00
149 Lenaris Holem R .60 1.50
151 Li Nalas R .60 1.50
155 Makbar R 1.00 2.50
156 Martus Mazur R .60 1.50
162 Mora Pol R .60 1.50
163 Morka R .60 1.50
164 Mysterious Orb R .75 2.00
166 Natima Lang R .75 2.00
168 Neela R .75 2.00
169 No Loose Ends R .60 1.50
172 Odo R 2.00 5.00
177 Orb Fragment R .60 1.50
181 Pallra R .60 1.50
185 Plain, Simple Garak R 1.00 2.50
186 Plans of the Obsidian Order R .75 2.00
187 Plans of the Tal Shiar R .75 2.00
188 Prakesh R .60 1.50
192 Protouniverse R .60 1.50
195 Pup R .60 1.50
199 Razka Karn R .60 1.50
202 Recruit Mercenaries R .60 1.50
208 Rescue Personnel R .60 1.50
210 Retaya R .60 1.50
216 Ruwon R .60 1.50
217 Sakonna R .60 1.50
218 Saltah'na Clock R .60 1.50
224 Secret Compartment R .60 1.50
226 Seismic Quake R .60 1.50
227 Selveth R .60 1.50
228 Shakaar Edon R .60 1.50
232 Sorus R .60 1.50
236 Surmak Ren R .75 2.00
238 Symbiont Diagnosis R .60 1.50
239 System 5 Disruptors R .60 1.50
240 Tahna Los R .60 1.50
242 Tekeny Ghemor R .75 2.00
243 The Three Vipers R .60 1.50
244 The Walls Have Ears R 1.00 2.50
248 Tora Ziyal R .60 1.50
249 Toran R .60 1.50
250 Trauma R .60 1.50
256 Turrel R .60 1.50
259 U.S.S. Yangtzee Kiang R .60 1.50
263 Vakis R .75 2.00
267 Vedek Winn R .60 1.50
275 Yeto R .60 1.50
276 Zef'No R .60 1.50
277 U.S.S. Defiant PREVIEW 6.00 15.00

1998 Star Trek Official Tournament Sealed Deck

COMPLETE SET (20) 10.00 20.00
COMMON CARD .75 2.00
RELEASED ON MAY 14, 1998

1998 Star Trek Starter Deck II

COMPLETE SET (8) 4.00 8.00
COMMON CARD .75 2.00
RELEASED ON DECEMBER 16, 1998

1999 Star Trek Blaze of Glory

COMPLETE SET (130) 30.00 60.00
BOOSTER BOX (30 PACKS) 100.00 150.00
BOOSTER PACK (9 CARDS) 4.00 6.00
UNLISTED C .10 .25
UNLISTED U .20 .50
UNLISTED R .60 1.50
RELEASED ON AUGUST 10, 1990
3 Admiral Ross R .75 2.00
11 Blood Oath R .75 2.00
16 Chief O'Brien R 1.25 3.00
31 E-Band Emissions R .75 2.00
32 Elim R 1.00 2.50
48 I.K.C. Koraga R 1.00 2.50
49 I.K.C. Lukara R 1.00 2.50
50 I.K.C. Negh'Var R 1.00 2.50
52 Impersonate Captive R .75 2.00
56 Jadzia Dax R 1.50 4.00
62 Koloth R .75 2.00
63 Kor R .75 2.00
68 Locutus' Borg Cube R 1.25 3.00
69 Long Live the Queen R .75 2.00
71 Maximum Firepower R 1.50 4.00
73 Miles O'Brien R 1.50 4.00
78 Odo Founder R .75 2.00
86 Picard Maneuver R .75 2.00
95 Quark Son of Keldar R .75 2.00
96 Riker Wil R .75 2.00
98 Ro Laren R .75 2.00
110 Sword of Kahless R .75 2.00
114 Target These Coordinates R 1.25 3.00
121 Torture R .75 2.00
122 U.S.S. Thunderchild R 1.25 3.00
129 Worf Son of Mogh R 1.25 3.00

1999 Star Trek Blaze of Glory Foil

COMPLETE SET (18) 40.00 80.00
COMMON CARD 1.50 4.00
RELEASED ON AUGUST 18, 1998
2 Elim URF 6.00 15.00
7 Jadzia Dax URF 6.00 15.00
10 Kor SRF 3.00 8.00
12 La Forge Impersonator SRF 3.00 8.00
13 Locutus' Borg Cube URF 6.00 15.00
14 Maximum Firepower SRF 3.00 8.00
15 Odo Founder SRF 3.00 8.00
16 Riker Wil URF 6.00 15.00
17 Sword of Kahless SRF 3.00 8.00
18 U.S.S. Thunderchild SRF 3.00 8.00

1999 Star Trek The Dominion

COMPLETE SET (130) 50.00 100.00
BOOSTER BOX (30 PACKS) 50.00 100.00
BOOSTER PACK (9 CARDS) 2.50 5.00
UNLISTED C .10 .25
UNLISTED U .20 .50
UNLISTED R .60 1.50
RELEASED ON JANUARY 20, 1999
1 10 and 01 R .75 2.00
24 D'deridex Advanced R 1.50 4.00
27 Empok Nor R .75 2.00
36 Founder Leader R .75 2.00
42 Goran'Agar R .75 2.00
44 I.K.C. Rotarran R .75 2.00
61 Keldon Advanced R 1.25 3.00
65 Kira Founder R .75 2.00
73 Martok Founder R .75 2.00
74 Martok R 1.50 4.00
76 Michael Eddington R .75 2.00
80 O'Brien Founder R .75 2.00
81 Office of the President R .75 2.00
82 Office of the Proconsul R .75 2.00
111 The Great Hall R .75 2.00
112 The Great Link R .75 2.00
119 U.S.S. Defiant R 3.00 8.00
124 Weyoun R 1.25 3.00

1999 Star Trek Enhanced First Contact

COMPLETE SET (16) 30.00 60.00
COMMON CARD 2.00 5.00
RELEASED ON JANUARY 13, 1999

1999 Star Trek Rules of Acquisition

COMPLETE SET (130) 20.00 40.00
BOOSTER BOX (30 PACKS) 15.00 30.00
BOOSTER PACK (9 CARDS) 1.00 1.50
UNLISTED C .10 .25
UNLISTED U .20 .50
UNLISTED R .60 1.50
RELEASED ON DECEMBER 1, 1999
9 Alaura R 1.25 3.00
11 Apnex R 1.25 3.00
12 Arandis R 1.25 3.00
21 Brunt R 1.25 3.00
26 Chula: The Door R .75 2.00
28 Continuing Committee R .75 2.00
32 Deyos R .75 2.00
37 Elizabeth Lense R 1.00 2.50
50 Gaila R 1.00 2.50
51 George Primmin R 1.00 2.50
54 Gral R .75 2.00
55 Grand Nagus Gint R 1.25 3.00
56 Grand Nagus Zek R 1.25 3.00
58 Hagath R 1.00 2.50
61 Ikat'ika R .75 2.00
65 Ishka R .75 2.00
69 Kasidy Yates R .75 2.00
71 Krajensky Founder R .75 2.00
77 Kukalaka R .75 2.00
79 Leeta R 1.25 3.00
83 Malhar'du R 1.00 2.50
85 Margh R 1.00 2.50
87 Morn R .75 2.00
89 Naprem R 1.00 2.50
93 Nog R 1.25 3.00
96 Orion Syndicate Bomb R .75 2.00
107 Quark R 2.50 6.00
108 Quark's Bar R 1.25 3.00
110 Quark's Treasure R .75 2.00
112 Rom R 1.25 3.00
116 Senator Cretak R 1.25 3.00
128 U.S.S. Sao Paulo R 1.25 3.00
130 Writ of Accountability R .75 2.00

2000 Star Trek Enhanced Premiere

COMPLETE SET (21) 20.00 40.00
COMMON CARD 2.00 5.00
RELEASED IN NOVEMBER 2000

2000 Star Trek Mirror Mirror

COMPLETE SET (131) 30.00 60.00
BOOSTER BOX (30 PACKS) 20.00 40.00
BOOSTER PACK (11 CARDS) 1.00 2.00
UNLISTED C .10 .25
UNLISTED U .20 .50
UNLISTED R .60 1.50
RELEASED ON DECEMBER 6, 2000
2 A Fast Ship Would be Nice R .75 2.00
10 Kelvan Show of Force R .75 2.00
14 The Guardian of Forever R .75 2.00
27 Mirror Terok Nor (Front) | (Reverse) R+ 2.00 5.00
29 Terran Rebellion HQ R .75 2.00
46 Construct Starship R .75 2.00
49 Bareil R+ 1.25 3.00
53 Overseer Odo R+ 1.50 4.00
56 The Intendant R+ 1.25 3.00
57 Weyoun of Borg R+ 1.50 4.00
61 Security Chief Garak R+ 1.50 4.00
64 Captain Bashir R+ 1.25 3.00
65 Captain Dax R+ 1.25 3.00
66 Chief Engineer Scott R+ 1.25 3.00
67 Chief Navigator Chekov R+ 1.25 3.00
68 Chief Surgeon McCoy R+ 1.25 3.00
69 Comm Officer Uhura R+ 1.25 3.00
74 First Officer Spock UR 20.00 40.00
75 Jake Sisko R+ 1.25 3.00
76 James Tiberius Kirk R+ 2.00 5.00
80 Marlena Moreau R+ 1.25 3.00
82 Mr. Tuvok R 1.00 2.50
83 Nurse Chapel R+ 1.25 3.00
85 Security Chief Sulu R+ 1.25 3.00
86 Smiley R+ 1.25 3.00
88 Mr. Brunt R+ 1.25 3.00
89 Mr. Nog R+ 1.25 3.00
90 Mr. Quark R+ 1.25 3.00
91 Mr. Rom R+ 1.25 3.00
94 Regent Worf R+ 1.25 3.00
102 Ezri R+ 1.25 3.00
103 Fontaine R+ 1.25 3.00
104 Mr. Sisko R+ 1.50 4.00
105 Professor Sisko R+ 1.25 3.00
107 Thomas Paris R .75 2.00
109 Commander Charvanek R+ 1.25 3.00
115 Bajoran Warship R .75 2.00
118 Defiant R+ 2.00 5.00
120 I.S.S. Enterprise R+ 1.50 4.00
127 Regency 1 R .75 2.00

2000 Star Trek Reflections

COMPLETE SET (105)
COMMON CARD .40 1.00
BOOSTER BOX (36) 40.00 80.00
BOOSTER PACK (18) 2.00 4.00
1 Borg Queen URF 25.00 50.00
2 D'deridex Advanced SRF 2.00 5.00
3 Keldon Advanced SRF 2.00 5.00
4 10 and 01 SRF 1.25 3.00
5 100,000 Tribbles (Clone) BTF 3.00 8.00
6 Admiral Riker BTF 6.00 15.00
10 Barclay's Protomorphosis Disease SRF 1.00 2.50
12 Benjamin Sisko SRF 3.00 8.00
14 B'Etor SRF 1.25 3.00
15 Beverly Crusher SRF 2.00 5.00
16 Beverly Picard SRF 1.50 4.00
17 Borg Ship SRF 2.50 6.00
18 Bynars Weapon Enhancement SRF 1.50 4.00
19 Central Command SRF 1.00 2.50
21 Chamber of Ministers SRF 1.25 3.00
24 Cytherians SRF 1.00 2.50
26 Data SRF 2.50 6.00
27 Data's Head SRF 1.00 2.50
28 Dathon SRF 1.00 2.50
29 Deanna Troi SRF 2.50 6.00
31 Devidian Door SRF 2.00 5.00
33 Dr. Telek R'Mor BTF 2.50 6.00
34 Dukat SRF 2.00 5.00
35 Elim Garak SRF 1.00 2.50
36 Espionage Mission SRF 1.00 2.50
37 Founder Leader SRF 1.00 2.50
38 Future Enterprise URF 50.00 100.00
39 Galen SRF 1.25 3.00
41 Geordi La Forge SRF 1.50 4.00
43 Governor Worf SRF 1.00 2.50
44 Gowron SRF 1.00 2.50
45 Gowron of Borg BTF 2.50 6.00
46 Horga'hn SRF 1.00 2.50
54 Jadzia Dax SRF 2.00 5.00
55 Jean-Luc Picard URF 30.00 60.00
56 Julian Bashir SRF 2.00 5.00
60 Kira Nerys SRF 2.50 6.00
62 Kurlan Naiskos SRF 1.00 2.50
64 Lursa SRF 1.00 2.50
65 Madam Guinan SRF 1.00 2.50
67 Major Rakal SRF 1.00 2.50
68 Martok SRF 1.50 4.00
72 Odo SRF 1.50 4.00
73 Office of the President SRF 1.00 2.50
74 Office of the Proconsul SRF 1.00 2.50
78 Q SRF 1.00 2.50
79 Queen's Borg Cube SRF 1.25 3.00
80 Regenerate SRF 1.25 3.00
84 Roga Danar SRF 1.00 2.50
86 Sela SRF 1.00 2.50
87 Seven of Nine CTF 4.00 10.00
92 Tasha Yar-Alternate SRF 1.25 3.00
93 The Great Hall SRF 1.00 2.50
94 The Great Link SRF 1.00 2.50
97 U.S.S Defiant URF 20.00 40.00
98 U.S.S. Enterprise SRF 1.25 3.00
101 Weyoun SRF 1.50 4.00
102 William T. Riker SRF 1.50 4.00
103 Worf SRF 1.00 2.50

2000 Star Trek Second Anthology

COMPLETE SET (6) 2.50 6.00
COMMMON CARD .75 2.00
RELEASED ON MARCH 15, 2000

2000 Star Trek The Trouble with Tribbles

COMPLETE SET (141) 30.00 60.00
BOOSTER BOX (30 PACKS) 20.00 40.00
BOOSTER PACK (11 CARDS) 1.00 2.00
UNLISTED C .10 .25
UNLISTED U .20 .50
UNLISTED R .60 1.50
RELEASED ON AUGUST 9, 2000
4 Executive Authorization R .75 2.00
22 Deep Space Station K-7 R .75 2.00
40 Council of Warriors R .75 2.00
43 First Minister Shakaar R+ 1.25 3.00
46 Third of Five R+ 1.25 3.00
48 Kira R+ 1.50 4.00
51 Thot Gor R+ 1.25 3.00
55 Captain Kirk R+ 2.00 5.00
56 Dr. McCoy UR 2.50 6.00
57 Dulmer R+ 1.25 3.00
58 Ensign Checkov R+ 1.50 4.00
59 Ensign O'Brien R+ 1.25 3.00
60 Lt. Bailey R+ 1.25 3.00
61 Lt. Bashir R+ 1.50 4.00
63 Lt. Dax R+ 1.50 4.00
67 Lt. Sulu R+ 1.50 4.00
68 Lt. Uhura R+ 1.50 4.00
70 Lucsly R+ 1.25 3.00
71 Mr. Scott R+ 1.50 4.00
72 Mr. Spock R+ 2.00 5.00
75 Lumba R+ 1.25 3.00
77 Arne Darvin R+ 1.25 3.00
85 Barry Waddle R+ 1.25 3.00
88 Grebnedlog R+ 1.25 3.00
90 Odo R+ 1.25 3.00
92 Worf R+ 1.25 3.00
96 Keras R+ 1.25 3.00
97 The Centurion R+ 1.25 3.00
98 Velal R+ 1.25 3.00
102 Stolen Attack Ship R 1.00 2.50
103 Breen Warship R 1.00 2.50
104 Dominion Battleship R 1.00 2.50
105 Weyoun's Warship R 1.00 2.50
108 Starship Enterprise R+ 2.00 5.00
110 I.K.C. Gr'oth R+ 1.25 3.00
111 I.K.C. Ning'tao R .75 2.00
117 Breen Energy-Dampening Weapon R 1.00 2.50
132 10,000 Tribbles (Go) R+ .75 2.00
133 10,000 Tribbles (Poison) R+ .75 2.00
134 10,000 Tribbles (Rescue) R+ .75 2.00
135 100,000 Tribbles (Clone) R+ .75 2.00
136 100,000 Tribbles (Discard) R+ .75 2.00
137 100,000 Tribbles (Rescue) R+ .75 2.00

2000 Star Trek The Trouble with Tribbles Federation Starter Deck

COMPLETE SET (13) 1.50 4.00
RELEASED ON AUGUST 9, 2000
1 Alyssa Ogawa (FC) R .75 2.00
2 Archer (Prem) C .10 .25
3 Chula: The Abyss (BoG) R .60 1.50
4 Chula: The Lights (BoG) C .10 .25
5 Fleet Admiral Shanthi (Prem) U .20 .50
6 Hazardous Duty (BoG) C .10 .25
7 Male's Love Interest (Prem) C .10 .25
8 Medical Kit (Prem) C .10 .25
9 Montgomery Scott (AU) C .10 .25
10 Plasmadyne Relay (QC) C .10 .25
11 Security Precautions (QC) C .10 .25
12 Starfleet Type I Phaser (BoG) C .10 .25
13 Thomas McClure (FC) U .20 .50

2000 Star Trek The Trouble with Tribbles Klingon Starter Deck

COMPLETE SET (14) 1.50 4.00
UNLISTED C .10 .25
UNLISTED U .20 .50
UNLISTED R 1.00 2.50
RELEASED ON AUGUST 9, 2000

2000 Star Trek Voyager

COMPLETE SET (201) 125.00 175.00
BOOSTER BOX (30 PACKS) 25.00 50.00
BOOSTER PACK (11 CARDS) 1.25 2.50
UNLISTED C .10 .25
UNLISTED U .20 .50
UNLISTED R .60 1.50
RELEASED ON MAY 23, 2001
13 Hull Breach R .75 2.00
30 Barzan Wormhole R 1.25 3.00
59 Caretaker's Array R .75 2.00
66 Vidiian Boarding Claw R .75 2.00
67 War Council R .75 2.00
74 Quinn R 1.25 3.00
112a Tabor BLUE R 1.25 3.00
112b Tabor PLUM R 1.25 3.00
113a Seska DK RED R 1.25 3.00
113b Seska PURPLE R 1.25 3.00
115a B'Elanna Torres BLUE R 3.00 8.00
115b B'Elanna Torres GOLD R 3.00 8.00
117a Chakotay BLUE R 3.00 8.00
117b Chakotay GOLD R 3.00 8.00
120 Harry Kim R 1.50 4.00
122 Kathryn Janeway R 2.50 6.00
123a Lon Suder BLUE R 2.00 5.00
123b Lon Suder GOLD R 2.00 5.00
126a Maxwell Burke BLUE R 2.00 5.00
126b Maxwell Burke GOLD R 2.00 5.00
131a Rudolph Ransom BLUE R 2.00 5.00
131b Rudolph Ransom GOLD R 2.00 5.00
132 Samantha Wildman R .75 2.00
134 The Doctor R 1.50 4.00
136 Tom Paris R 1.50 4.00
137 Tuvok R 1.50 4.00
138 Vorik R .75 2.00
143 Culluh R .75 2.00
148 Karden R 1.25 3.00
164a Kes BLUE R 1.50 4.00
164b Kes GOLD R 1.50 4.00
167a Neelix BLUE R 1.50 4.00
167b Neelix GOLD R 1.50 4.00
170 Penk R 1.25 3.00
171a Seven of Nine BLUE R 6.00 15.00
171b Seven of Nine GOLD R 25.00 50.00
173 The Pendari Champion UR 15.00 30.00
174 Dr. Telek R'Mor R .75 2.00
192a U.S.S. Equinox BLUE R 1.25 3.00
192b U.S.S. Equinox GOLD R 1.25 3.00
194 U.S.S. Voyager R 2.50 6.00
197 Kazon Warship R 1.25 3.00
199 Vidiian Cruiser R 1.25 3.00

2001 Star Trek The Borg

COMPLETE SET (131) 80.00 150.00
BOOSTER BOX (30 PACKS) 15.00 30.00
BOOSTER PACK (11 CARDS 1.00 1.50
UNLISTED C .10 .25
UNLISTED U .20 .50
UNLISTED R .65 1.50
RELEASED ON SEPTEMBER 19, 2001
9 The Weak Will Perish R .75 2.00
24 Unicomplex R+ .75 2.00
50 Borg Queen R+ 3.00 8.00
55 Fifth R+ .75 2.00
56 First R+ .75 2.00
57 Four of Nine R+ .75 2.00
60 Second R+ .75 2.00
61 Seven of Nine R+ 1.50 4.00
64 Third and Fourth R+ .75 2.00
65 Three of Nine R+ .75 2.00
66 Two of Nine R+ .75 2.00
69 Deanna Troi R+ 1.25 3.00
70a Equinox Doctor BLUE R+ 3.00 8.00
70b Equinox Doctor GOLD R+ 3.00 8.00
72 Reginald Barclay UR 10.00 20.00
78 Donik R+ .75 2.00
80a Hajur DK BLUE R+ 3.00 8.00
80b Hajur GOLD R+ 3.00 8.00
86 Karr R+ .75 2.00
88 Notok R+ 1.00 2.50
101 B'Elanna R+ 1.25 3.00
102 Captain Chakotay R+ 1.25 3.00
104a Icheb BLUE R+ 2.00 5.00
104b Icheb GOLD R+ 2.00 5.00
105 Kes R+ .75 2.00
108a Marika BLUE R+ 1.50 4.00
108b Marika GOLD R+ 1.50 4.00
109a Mezoti BLUE R+ 1.50 4.00
109b Mezoti GOLD R+ 1.50 4.00
110 One R+ 1.00 2.50
111a Orum GOLD R+ 2.00 5.00
111b Orum GREEN R+ 2.00 5.00
113a Rebi and Azan BLUE R+ 1.50 4.00
113b Rebi and Azan GOLD R+ 1.50 4.00
114a Riley Frasier BLUE R+ 1.50 4.00
114b Riley Frasier GOLD R+ 1.50 4.00
122 Borg Queen's Ship R .75 2.00
123 Borg Tactical Cube R .75 2.00
124a U.S.S. Prometheus BLUE R+ 10.00 20.00
124b U.S.S. Prometheus GREEN R+ 10.00 20.00
128 I.K.C. Voq'leng R+ .75 2.00
129 Liberty R+ .75 2.00
131a U.S.S. Dauntless BLUE R+ 6.00 15.00
131b U.S.S. Dauntless GOLD R+ 6.00 15.00

2001 Star Trek Holodeck Adventures

COMPLETE SET (131) 60.00 125.00
BOOSTER BOX (30) 25.00 50.00
BOOSTER PACK (11) 1.25 2.50
UNLISTED C .10 .25
UNLISTED U .20 .50
UNLISTED R .60 1.50
RELEASED ON DECEMBER 21, 2001
12 Your Galaxy is Impure R .75 2.00
51a Iden DK BLUE R+ 2.50 6.00
51b Iden PLUM R+ 2.50 6.00
53 Crell Moset R+ .75 2.00
57a Kejal DK BLUE R+ 2.50 6.00
57b Kejal PURPLE R+ 2.50 6.00
64 Admiral J.P. Hanson R+ .75 2.00
65 Boothby R+ 1.25 3.00
67 Edward Jellico R+ .75 2.00
68 Ezri Dax R+ 2.00 5.00
69 Lewis Zimmerman R+ .75 2.00
73 The E.C.H. R+ .75 2.00
74a Weiss BLUE R+ 2.50 6.00
74b Weiss DK BLUE R+ 2.50 6.00
76 B'Elanna Daughter of Miral R+ 1.25 3.00
77 Chancellor Gowron R+ .75 2.00
81 Anastasia Komananov R+ 1.25 3.00
82 Arachnia R+ 1.25 3.00
84 Buster Kincaid R .75 2.00
85 Captain Proton R+ 1.25 3.00
87 Chaotica R .75 2.00
91 Dixon Hill UR 25.00 50.00
92 Dr. Noah R+ 1.25 3.00
93 Duchamps R+ 1.25 3.00
94 Durango R+ .75 2.00
96 Falcon R+ 1.25 3.00
98 Frank Hollander R+ .75 2.00
99 John Watson R+ 1.25 3.00
100 Leonardo da Vinci R .75 2.00
106 Mr. Garak R+ .75 2.00
110 Professor Honey Bare R+ 1.50 4.00
111 Professor Moriarty R+ .75 2.00
113 Secret Agent Julian Bashir R+ 1.25 3.00
114 Sheriff Worf R+ 1.25 3.00
115 Sherlock Holmes R+ 1.25 3.00
119 Vic Fontaine R+ .75 2.00
121 Praetor Neral R+ .75 2.00
129a Olarra DK BLUE R+ 6.00 15.00
129b Olarra GOLD R+ 6.00 15.00

2002 Star Trek The Motion Pictures

COMPLETE SET (131) 100.00 200.00
BOOSTER BOX (30 PACKS) 100.00 200.00
BOOSTER PACK (11 CARDS) 4.00 8.00
UNLISTED C .10 .25
UNLISTED U .20 .50
UNLISTED R .60 1.50
RELEASED ON APRIL 17, 2002
27 What Does God Need With A StarshipR .75 2.00
35 Admiral Kirk R+ 3.00 8.00
36 Amanda Grayson R+ .75 2.00
37 Ambassador Sarek R+ .75 2.00
38 Captain Spock R+ 1.50 4.00
40 Captain Sulu R+ 1.25 3.00
41 Carol Marcus R .75 2.00
43 Commander Chekov R+ 1.25 3.00
45 Commander Uhura R+ 1.25 3.00
46 David Marcus R .75 2.00
49 Dr. Chapel R+ 1.25 3.00
50 Dr. McCoy R+ 1.25 3.00
51 Ensign Tuvok R .75 2.00
56 James T. Kirk UR 30.00 60.00
57 John Harriman R+ .75 2.00
61 Mr. Scott R+ 1.25 3.00
62 Saavik R+ 1.25 3.00
68 Willard Decker R+ .75 2.00
71 Captain Kang R+ 1.25 3.00
73 Chancellor Gorkon R+ .75 2.00
74 Colonel Worf R+ 1.25 3.00
75 General Chang R+ 1.50 4.00
83 Krase R+ .75 2.00
84 Kruge R+ .75 2.00
92a Dr. Gillian Taylor BLUE R+ 10.00 20.00
92b Dr. Gillian Taylor GOLD R+ 10.00 20.00
93 Dr. Tolian Soran R+ 1.25 3.00
97 Khan R+ 1.50 4.00
102 Ru'afo R+ 1.25 3.00
110a H.M.S. Bounty BLUE R+ 15.00 30.00
110b H.M.S. Bounty RED R+ 15.00 30.00
112 Starship Enterprise R+ 1.50 4.00
113 Starship Excelsior R+ 1.25 3.00
114 U.S.S. Enterprise-A R+ 1.50 4.00
120 I.K.C. Kla'Diyus R+ 1.25 3.00
121 Kronos One R+ 1.25 3.00
126a U.S.S. Reliant BLUE R+ 20.00 40.00
126b U.S.S. Reliant GOLD R+ 20.00 40.00

2002 Star Trek Premiere

COMPLETE SET (415) 200.00 500.00
BOOSTER BOX (30 PACKS) 40.00 80.00
BOOSTER PACK (11 CARDS) 2.00 4.00
RELEASED ON DECEMBER 8, 2002
ALSO KNOWN AS SECOND EDITION
1C2 Aggressive Behavior .10 .30
1C3 Alien Abduction .10 .30
1C5 Armus Roulette .10 .30
1C7 Assassination Attempt (1E) .10 .30
1C8 Authenticate Artifacts (1E) .10 .30
1R1 A Living Death 1.50 4.00
1R4 Antedean Assassins (1E) 1.50 4.00
1R6 Assassin's Blade 1.50 4.00
1R9 Automated Weapons (1E) 1.50 4.00
1C11 Blended .10 .30
1C12 Bynars' Password .10 .30
1C13 Captain's Holiday (1E) .10 .30
1C14 Center of Attention .10 .30
1C15 Chula: Echoes .10 .30
1C17 Command Decisions (1E) .10 .30
1C18 Console Overload .10 .30
1C20 Damaged Reputation (1E) .10 .30
1C21 Dangerous Liaisons .10 .30
1C28 Graviton Ellipse (1E) .10 .30
1C30 Impressive Trophies .10 .30
1C35 Maglock .10 .30
1C36 Magnetic Field Disruptions (1E) .10 .30
1C37 Microbrain (1E) .10 .30
1C39 Nanite Attack (1E) .10 .30
1C40 None Shall Pass .10 .30
1C43 Pinned Down (1E) .10 .30
1C47 Quarren Labor Shortage .10 .30
1C49 Skullduggery .10 .30
1C51 Sympathetic Magic (1E) .10 .30
1C53 Temptation (1E) .10 .30
1C55 The Moon's a Window to Heaven .10 .30
1C56 Trabe Grenade .10 .30
1C59 Vastly Outnumbered (1E) .10 .30
1C63 Cardassian Phaser Pistol .10 .30
1C64 Engineering Kit .10 .30
1C66 Klingon Disruptor Pistol .10 .30
1C67 Medical Kit .10 .30
1C69 Romulan Disruptor Pistol .10 .30
1C71 Starfleet Type-2 Phaser .10 .30
1C74 A Treasure Beyond Comparison .10 .30
1C78 BaH! (1E) .10 .30
1C80 Battle Drills (1E) .10 .30
1C85 Days of Atonement .10 .30
1C87 Engage Cloak .10 .30
1C94 Let Honor Guide You (1E) .10 .30
1R22 Debris Field 1.50 4.00
1R23 Drumhead 1.50 4.00
1R25 Equipment Malfunction 1.50 4.00
1R26 Explosive Decompression (1E) 1.50 4.00
1R27 Gravimetric Distortion 1.50 4.00
1R29 Hunter Gangs 1.50 4.00
1R31 Invidium Leak (1E) 1.50 4.00
1R34 Limited Welcome 1.50 4.00
1R38 Misguided Activist 1.50 4.00
1R41 Ornaran Threat (1E) 1.50 4.00
1R45 Primitive Culture 1.50 4.00
1R50 Stellar Core Fragment (1E) 1.50 4.00
1R54 Tense Negotiations (1E) 1.50 4.00
1R57 Triage (1E) 1.50 4.00
1R60 Wavefront (1E) 1.50 4.00
1R72 Tricorder 1.50 4.00
1R73 A Chance for Glory (1E) 1.50 4.00
1R75 Astrometrics Lab (1E) 1.50 4.00
1R79 Bajoran Gratitude Festival 1.50 4.00
1R86 Diplomatic Overture (1E) 1.50 4.00
1R88 Feast on the Dying 1.50 4.00
1R89 For All Our Sons 1.50 4.00
1R90 How Would You Like a Trip to Romulus? 1.50 4.00
1R95 Line of Defense (1E) 1.50 4.00
1R97 No Love for the Spoon Heads 1.50 4.00
1S16 Chula: Pick One to Save Two .10 .30
1S24 Enemy Boarding Party .10 .30
1S32 Kelvan Show of Force .10 .30
1S33 Kolaran Raiders (1E) .10 .30
1S42 Personal Duty (1E) .10 .30
1S82 Brutal Struggle (1E) .10 .30
1S83 Cry "Havoc!" (1E) .10 .30
1U10 Berserk Changeling .10 .30
1U19 Contamination .10 .30
1U44 Planetary Survey (1E) .10 .30
1U46 Pursuit Just Behind (1E) .10 .30
1U48 Recurring Injury (1E) .10 .30
1U52 Systems Diagnostic (1E) .10 .30
1U58 Unscientific Method .10 .30
1U61 Alien Gambling Device .10 .30
1U62 Bajoran Phaser Pistol .10 .30
1U65 Engineering PADD .10 .30
1U68 Medical Tricorder .10 .30
1U70 Science PADD .10 .30
1U76 Awaiting Trial (1E) .10 .30
1U77 Back-flush Bussard Collectors .10 .30
1U81 Blind Spot (1E) .10 .30
1U84 D'Arsay Archive .10 .30
1U91 Inspiring Leader .10 .30
1U92 Just Like Old Times (1E) .10 .30
1U93 Labor Camp (1E) .10 .30
1U96 Nelvana Trap (1E) .10 .30
1U98 No Peace in Our Time (1E) .10 .30
1U99 Nothing That Happens is Truly Random .10 .30
1C101 Order of the Bat'leth .10 .30
1C118 To Boldly Go .10 .30
1C129 Kevin Uxbridge .10 .30
1C134 Pursuit Course .10 .30
1C140 Shady Resources .10 .30
1C206 Wormhole Negotiations .10 .30
1C209 Benjamin Sisko, .10 .30
The Emissary of the Prophets (1E)
1C210 Brilgar (1E) .10 .30
1C213 Hazar .10 .30
1C214 Jabara (1E) .10 .30
1C224 Shakaar Edon, Resistance Leader (1E) .10 .30
1C226 Trazko, Hired Muscle (1E) .10 .30
1C233 Darhe'el, The Butcher of Gallitep (1E) .10 .30
1C236 Elim Garak, Agent of the Obsidian Order (1E) .10 .30
1C240 Gilora Rejal, Subspace Researcher (1E) .10 .30
1C246 Makbar, Chief Archon (1E) .10 .30
1C248 Ocett, Dogged Rival (1E) .10 .30
1C249 Parn (1E) .10 .30
1C250 Rogesh (1E) .10 .30
1C253 Andrea Brand, Academy Superintendent (1E) .10 .30
1C254 Bandee (1E) .10 .30
1C257 Beverly Crusher, Chief Medical Officer (1E) .10 .30
1C259 Data, Aspirer (1E) .10 .30
1C264 Gideon Seyetik, Great Terraformer (1E) .10 .30
1C272 Leyton, Chief of Starfleet Operations .10 .30
1C273 Lian T'su (1E) .10 .30
1C275 Luther Sloan, Man of Secrets .10 .30
1C277 Miles O'Brien, Chief of Operations .10 .30
1C279 Nog, Eager Cadet .10 .30
1C280 Paulson (1E) .10 .30
1C282 Robin Lefler, Mission Specialist .10 .30
1C283 Seth Mendoza (1E) .10 .30
1C284 T'Lara (1E) .10 .30
1C286 Tasha Yar, Chief of Security (1E) .10 .30
1C291 Worf, Strategic Operations Officer .10 .30
1C294 Bo'rak, Klingon Intelligence Agent .10 .30
1C297 Gowron, Leader of the High Council .10 .30
1C300 Kahlest, GhojmoH of Worf (1E) .10 .30
1C306 Koroth, High Cleric of Boreth (1E) .10 .30
1C311 Martok, Soldier of the Empire .10 .30
1C314 Nu'Daq, Tenacious Rival (1E) .10 .30
1C315 T'vis (1E) .10 .30
1C316 Vorax (1E) .10 .30
1C318 Altovar, Vindictive Criminal (1E) .10 .30
1C319 Berild (1E) .10 .30
1C322 Chorgan, Leader of the Gatherers (1E) .10 .30
1C324 Dathon, Speaker of Tama (1E) .10 .30
1C326 Etana Jol, Ktarian Operative (1E) .10 .30
1C328 Grathon Tolar, Hologram Forger (1E) .10 .30
1C329 Grenis (1E) .10 .30
1C332 Kamala, The Perfect Mate (1E) .10 .30
1C333 Kolos (1E) .10 .30
1C335 Marouk, Sovereign of Acamar (1E) .10 .30
1C338 Nel Apgar, Temperamental Researcher (1E) .10 .30
1C339 Pran Tainer, Atrean Seismologist (1E) .10 .30
1C340 Rabal (1E) .10 .30
1C344 Serova, Warp Field Theorist (1E) .10 .30
1C345 Soto .10 .30
1C346 Sunad (1E) .10 .30
1C348 The Albino, Killer of Children (1E) .10 .30
1C352 Vash, Treasure Hunter (1E) .10 .30
1C354 Alidar Jarok, Conscientious Admiral (1E) .10 .30
1C357 Donatra, Compassionate Patriot (1E) .10 .30
1C359 Hiren, Romulan Praetor (1E) .10 .30
1C361 Lovok, Tal Shiar Colonel .10 .30
1C364 N'Vek, Soldier of the Underground .10 .30
1C365 Noram (1E) .10 .30
1C372 Tal'Aura, Impatient Senator (1E) .10 .30
1C380 Assault Vessel .10 .30
1C381 Bajoran Interceptor .10 .30
1C383 Bralek (1E) .10 .30
1C384 Galor .10 .30
1C392 U.S.S. Enterprise-E, Federation Envoy (1E) .10 .30
1C393 U.S.S. Excelsior .10 .30
1C397 I.K.S. Hegh'ta .10 .30
1C403 I.K.S. Vor'cha .10 .30
1C404 Flaxian Scout Vessel .10 .30
1C405 Miradorn Raider .10 .30
1C406 T'Lani Munitions Ship .10 .30
1C411 Haakona (1E) .10 .30
1R108 Rescue Captives 1.50 4.00
1R113 Taken Prisoner (1E) 1.50 4.00
1R114 Tapestry (1E) 1.50 4.00
1R119 Warrior's Birthright (1E) 1.50 4.00
1R120 Alternate Identity 1.50 4.00
1R121 Amanda Rogers 1.50 4.00
1R123 Comfort Women 1.50 4.00
1R124 Condition Captive 1.50 4.00
1R125 Dimensional Shifting (1E) 1.50 4.00
1R126 Empathic Touch (1E) 1.50 4.00
1R128 Evasive Maneuvers 1.50 4.00
1R133 Protection of the Tal Shiar 1.50 4.00
1R136 Render Assistance 1.50 4.00
1R138 Sensor Sweep 1.50 4.00
1R146 Torture 1.50 4.00
1R207 Anara 1.50 4.00
1R208 Bareil Antos, Esteemed Vedek (1E) 1.50 4.00
1R215 Keeve Falor 1.50 4.00
1R219 Mora Pol, Pioneering Scientist (1E) 1.50 4.00
1R220 Odo, Constable (1E) 1.50 4.00
1R222 Ranjen Koral, Student of B'hala (1E) 1.50 4.00
1R223 Rom, Diagnostic and Repair Technician (1E) 1.50 4.00
1R225 Shandor (1E) 1.50 4.00
1R229 Ari 1.50 4.00
1R234 Daro 1.50 4.00
1R235 Dukat, Military Advisor 1.50 4.00
1R237 Emok (1E) 1.50 4.00
1R238 Enabran Tain, Head of the Obsidian Order 1.50 4.00
1R241 Jerax (1E) 1.50 4.00
1R244 Lemec, Posturing Negotiator (1E) 1.50 4.00
1R245 Madred, Calculating Captor (1E) 1.50 4.00
1R247 Megar (1E) 1.50 4.00
1R251 Altman (1E) 1.50 4.00
1R256 Benjamin Sisko, Defiant Captain 1.50 4.00
1R258 Daniel Kwan (1E) 1.50 4.00
1R260 Davies (1E) 1.50 4.00
1R262 Elizabeth Shelby, Formidable Presence 1.50 4.00
1R265 Hoya (1E) 1.50 4.00
1R266 Jadzia Dax, Science Officer (1E) 1.50 4.00
1R268 Jean-Luc Picard, Explorer 1.50 4.00
1R270 Kalandra, Battlefield Surgeon (1E) 1.50 4.00
1R271 Kathryn Janeway, Wry Admiral 1.50 4.00
1R274 Lopez (1E) 1.50 4.00
1R276 Martin (1E) 1.50 4.00
1R278 Mills (1E) 1.50 4.00
1R285 T'Lor 1.50 4.00
1R287 Van Orton (1E) 1.50 4.00
1R292 B'amara (1E) 1.50 4.00
1R293 B'Etor, Sister of Duras 1.50 4.00
1R295 Dokar (1E) 1.50 4.00
1R301 Kahmis (1E) 1.50 4.00
1R303 Kitrik, "The Tyrant Molor" (1E) 1.50 4.00
1R304 Koloth, D'akturak (1E) 1.50 4.00
1R307 Kroval (1E) 1.50 4.00
1R308 Kurak, Warp Field Specialist 1.50 4.00
1R309 Kurn, Squadron Commander 1.50 4.00
1R310 Lursa, Sister of Duras 1.50 4.00
1R312 Merakt (1E) 1.50 4.00
1R313 Morka, Klingon Intelligence Agent 1.50 4.00
1R317 Acost Jared (1E) 1.50 4.00
1R323 Dallan (1E) 1.50 4.00
1R330 Inad (1E) 1.50 4.00
1R331 Jo'Bril, Patient Schemer (1E) 1.50 4.00
1R336 Marshor 1.50 4.00
1R341 Regana Tosh (1E) 1.50 4.00
1R343 Riva, Respected Mediator (1E) 1.50 4.00
1R347 Temarek (1E) 1.50 4.00
1R349 Togaran (1E) 1.50 4.00
1R351 Ty Kajada, Relentless Investigator 1.50 4.00
1R356 Cretak, Supporter of the Alliance 1.50 4.00
1R360 Jorvas (1E) 1.50 4.00
1R363 Movar, Political General 1.50 4.00
1R366 Sabrun (1E) 1.50 4.00
1R368 Selveth, Tal Shiar Pilot (1E) 1.50 4.00
1R370 Shinzon, Romulan Praetor (1E) 1.50 4.00
1R371 Suran, Ambitious Commander (1E) 1.50 4.00
1R374 Taris, Deceitful Subcommander 1.50 4.00
1R375 Telek R'Mor, Astrophysical Researcher 1.50 4.00
1R377 Thexor (1E) 1.50 4.00
1R378 Tomalak, Beguiling Adversary (1E) 1.50 4.00
1R382 Bajoran Scout Vessel 1.50 4.00
1R387 Prakesh (1E) 1.50 4.00
1R388 Reklar (1E) 1.50 4.00
1R390 U.S.S. Akira 1.50 4.00
1R391 U.S.S. Defiant, Prototype Warship (1E) 1.50 4.00
1R396 U.S.S. Sovereign (1E) 1.50 4.00
1R400 I.K.S. Lukara (1E) 1.50 4.00
1R401 I.K.S. Maht-H'a (1E) 1.50 4.00
1R410 Deranas (1E) 1.50 4.00
1R412 Romulan Scout Vessel 1.50 4.00
1R413 Scimitar, Predator (1E) 1.50 4.00
1R414 Serrola (1E) 1.50 4.00
1R415 Valdore (1E) 1.50 4.00
1S130 Lasting Peace (1E) .10 .30
1S135 Quantum Slipstream Drive .10 .30
1S139 Sermon .10 .30
1S142 Symbol of Devotion .10 .30
1S144 The Tides of Fortune .10 .30
1S147 Twist of Fate (1E) .10 .30
1S160 Deliver Supplies .10 .30
1S166 Excavation .10 .30
1S169 Feldomite Rush .10 .30
1S170 Fissure Research .10 .30
1S171 Geological Survey .10 .30
1S175 Intercept Maquis .10 .30
1S177 Investigate Alien Probe .10 .30
1S179 Investigate Massacre .10 .30
1S182 Investigate Sighting .10 .30
1S186 Military Exercises .10 .30
1S187 Mining Survey .10 .30
1S190 Plague Planet .10 .30
1S194 Rescue Prisoners .10 .30
1S197 Search and Rescue .10 .30

Card	Low	High
1S198 Search for Survivors	.10	.30
1S199 Security Briefing	.10	.30
1S200 Sensitive Search	.10	.30
1S201 Study Cometary Cloud	.10	.30
1S202 Supervise Dilithium Mine (1E)	.10	.30
1S216 Kira Nerys, Colonel Kira (1E)	.10	.30
1S255 Barron (1E)	.10	.30
1S261 Deanna Troi, Guide and Conscience	.10	.30
1S267 Jean-Luc Picard, Argo Pilot	.10	.30
1S288 Wesley Crusher, Prodigy (1E)	.10	.30
1S289 William T. Riker, Number One (1E)	.10	.30
1S290 Worf, Security Detail Leader	.10	.30
1S296 Duras, Son of a Traitor (1E)	.10	.30
1S298 J'Dan	.10	.30
1S299 K'nera, Klingon Defense Force Commander (1E)	.10	.30
1S302 Kang, Honored Warrior	.10	.30
1S350 Tosk, The Hunted (1E)	.10	.30
1S355 Chagrith (1E)	.10	.30
1S362 Mopak	.10	.30
1S369 Shinzon, Capable Commander	.10	.30
1S376 The Viceroy, Shinzon's Protector (1E)	.10	.30
1S389 Vetar (1E)	.10	.30
1S394 U.S.S. Galaxy	.10	.30
1S402 I.K.S. Rotarran, Ship of Tears	.10	.30
1S407 Tamarian Vessel	.10	.30
1U100 Observer from the Obsidian Order	.10	.30
1U102 Peacemaker or Predator? (1E)	.10	.30
1U103 Pierce Their Defenses	.10	.30
1U104 Point Blank Strike	.10	.30
1U105 Precise Attack	.10	.30
1U106 Prejudice and Politics (1E)	.10	.30
1U107 Process Identification (1E)	.10	.30
1U109 Resistance Tactics (1E)	.10	.30
1U110 Romulan Intelligence Network (1E)	.10	.30
1U111 Standard Cardassian Procedure (1E)	.10	.30
1U112 Tactical Planning	.10	.30
1U115 The Orion Underworld (1E)	.10	.30
1U116 The Pillage of Bajor (1E)	.10	.30
1U117 The Reman Mines (1E)	.10	.30
1U122 Arrest Order	.10	.30
1U127 Escape	.10	.30
1U131 Mission Briefing	.10	.30
1U132 Power to the Shields (1E)	.10	.30
1U137 Secret Conspiracy	.10	.30
1U141 Souls of the Dead (1E)	.10	.30
1U143 The Promise	.10	.30
1U145 Ties of Blood and Water	.10	.30
1U148 Abduction Plot (1E)	.10	.30
1U149 Access Relay Station	.10	.30
1U150 Acquire Illicit Explosives	.10	.30
1U151 Amnesty Talks (1E)	.10	.30
1U152 Bajor, Gift of the Prophets	.10	.30
1U153 Cardassia Prime, Hardscrabble World	.10	.30
1U154 Cargo Rendezvous	.10	.30
1U155 Changeling Research	.10	.30
1U156 Chart Stellar Cluster	.10	.30
1U157 Collect Sample	.10	.30
1U158 Colony Preparations	.10	.30
1U159 Cure Blight	.10	.30
1U161 Earth, Cradle of the Federation	.10	.30
1U162 Earth, Home of Starfleet Command	.10	.30
1U163 Eliminate Harvesters	.10	.30
1U164 Encounter at Farpoint (1E)	.10	.30
1U165 Evacuate Colony	.10	.30
1U167 Explore Black Cluster	.10	.30
1U168 Extraction	.10	.30
1U172 Host Metaphasic Shielding Test (1E)	.10	.30
1U173 Hunt for DNA Program	.10	.30
1U174 Iconia Investigation	.10	.30
1U176 Intercept Renegade	.10	.30
1U178 Investigate Coup	.10	.30
1U180 Investigate Rogue Comet	.10	.30
1U181 Investigate Rumors	.10	.30
1U183 Khitomer Investigation	.10	.30
1U184 Kressari Rendezvous	.10	.30
1U185 Medical Relief	.10	.30
1U188 Mouth of the Wormhole, Deep Space 9	.10	.30
1U189 Pegasus Search	.10	.30
1U191 Qo'noS, Heart of the Empire	.10	.30
1U192 Qualor II Rendezvous	.10	.30
1U193 Quest for the Sword of Kahless	.10	.30
1U195 Romulus, Seat of Power	.10	.30
1U196 Runabout Search	.10	.30
1U203 Surgery Under Fire (1E)	.10	.30
1U204 Uncover DNA Clues	.10	.30
1U205 Verify Evidence	.10	.30
1U211 Dohlem (1E)	.10	.30
1U212 Furel, Resistance Fighter (1E)	.10	.30
1U217 Li Nalas, Legend of Bajor (1E)	.10	.30
1U218 Lupaza, Resistance Fighter (1E)	.10	.30
1U221 Opaka, Kai of Bajor	.10	.30
1U227 Weld Ram	.10	.30
1U228 Winn Adami, Kai of Bajor (1E)	.10	.30
1U230 Corbin Entek, Undercover Operations Supervisor	.10	.30
1U231 Damar, Loyal Glinn (1E)	.10	.30
1U232 Danar, Irascible Gul (1E)	.10	.30
1U239 Evek, Attaché to the Demilitarized Zone (1E)	.10	.30
1U242 Joret Dal, Patriotic Visionary	.10	.30
1U243 Kovat, Public Conservator	.10	.30
1U252 Alyssa Ogawa, Enterprise Medical Assistant (1E)	.10	.30
1U263 Geordi La Forge, Chief Engineer	.10	.30
1U269 Julian Bashir, "Frontier" Physician	.10	.30
1U281 Rixx (1E)	.10	.30
1U305 Kor, Dahar Master	.10	.30
1U320 Bhavani (1E)	.10	.30
1U321 Brull, Encampment Leader (1E)	.10	.30
1U325 Durg (1E)	.10	.30
1U327 Galnar (1E)	.10	.30
1U334 Leyor (1E)	.10	.30
1U337 Morn, Barfly	.10	.30
1U342 Retaya, Urbane Poisoner	.10	.30
1U353 Volnoth (1E)	.10	.30
1U358 Dralvak (1E)	.10	.30
1U367 Sela, Mysterious Operative	.10	.30
1U373 Talvin (1E)	.10	.30
1U379 Vreenak, Tal Shiar Chairman	.10	.30
1U385 Keldon	.10	.30
1U386 Keldon Advanced	.10	.30
1U395 U.S.S. Nebula	.10	.30
1U398 I.K.S. K't'inga	.10	.30
1U399 I.K.S. K'Vort	.10	.30
1U408 D'deridex	.10	.30
1U409 D'deridex Advanced	.10	.30

2002 Star Trek Premiere Foil

1R220 Odo, Constable (1E)
1R236 Elim Garak, Agent of the Obsidian Order (1E)
1R267 Jean-Luc Picard, Argo Pilot
1R311 Martok, Soldier of the Empire
1R369 Shinzon, Capable Commander
1R391 U.S.S. Defiant, Prototype Warship (1E)
1R392 U.S.S. Enterprise-E, Federation Envoy (1E)
1R402 I.K.S. Rotarran, Ship of Tears
1R413 Scimitar, Predator (1E)

2003 Star Trek All Good Things

Card	Low	High
COMPLETE SET (40)	600.00	1200.00
RELEASED ON JULY 16, 2003		
1 Environmental Suit P	10.00	25.00
2 Espionage: Bajoran on Dominion P	10.00	25.00
3 Shape-Shift Inhibitor P	10.00	25.00
4 Timepod Ring P	10.00	25.00
5 Treacherous Advice P	10.00	25.00
6 Bluegill Infestation P	10.00	25.00
7 Kobayashi Maru Scenario P	25.00	40.00
8 Strategema P	25.00	40.00
9 Changeling Sweep P	20.00	35.00
10 Dimensional Shifting P	10.00	25.00
11 Empathic Touch P	10.00	25.00
12 Aid Clone Colony P	10.00	25.00
13 In For A Trim P	10.00	25.00
14 Colonel Kira P	50.00	80.00
15 Shandor P	20.00	25.00
16 Admiral Janeway P	10.00	25.00
17 Admiral Riker P	10.00	25.00
18 Christopher Pike P	60.00	100.00
19 Gideon Seyetik P	10.00	25.00
20 Lt. Palmer P	10.00	25.00
21a Miral Paris BLUE P	10.00	25.00
21b Miral Paris RED P	10.00	25.00
22 Raymond Boone P	10.00	25.00
23 Robert DeSoto P	10.00	25.00
24 Yeoman Rand P	30.00	50.00
25 Uri'lash P	30.00	50.00
26 K'Temoc P	10.00	25.00
27 Anij P	10.00	25.00
28 Artim P	10.00	25.00
29 Raimus P	10.00	25.00
30 Sojef P	10.00	25.00
31 Sunad P	10.00	25.00
32 Tournel P	10.00	25.00
33 Weyoun 6 P	10.00	25.00
34 Reklar P	10.00	25.00
35 U.S.S. Drake P	10.00	25.00
36 U.S.S. Grissom P	30.00	50.00
37 U.S.S. Pegasus P	10.00	25.00
38 Calondon P	10.00	25.00
39 Lokirrim Vessel P	10.00	25.00
40 Tsunkatse Ship P	10.00	25.00

2003 Star Trek Call to Arms

Card	Low	High
COMPLETE SET (208)	30.00	80.00
BOOSTER BOX (30 PACKS)	25.00	50.00
BOOSTER PACK (11 CARDS)	1.25	2.50
COMMON CARD	.08	.20
RELEASED ON SEPTEMBER 10, 2003		
3R5 Dangerous Climb (1E)	.40	1.00
3S2 An Old Debt	.20	.50
3S7 DNA Analysis (1E)	.20	.50
3U9 Dressing Down	.20	.50
3R11 Forsaken (1E)	.75	2.00
3R12 Gomtuu Shock Wave (1E)	1.25	3.00
3R19 Overwhelmed	.75	2.00
3R22 Quantum Filament (1E)	.40	1.00
3R31 The Demands of Duty (1E)	.40	1.00
3R34 Abduction	.40	1.00
3R37 Bred For Battle (1E)	.40	1.00
3R38 Building a Bridge (1E)	.40	1.00
3R39 Cavalry Raid	1.00	2.50
3R44 I Don't Like to Lose	.40	1.00
3R46 Jem'Hadar Birthing Chamber	.40	1.00
3R49 Psychological Pressure (1E)	1.25	3.00
3R54 Set Up (1E)	.75	2.00
3R56 Sluggo	.40	1.00
3R57 Steeled By Loss	.40	1.00
3R59 The Blight	.40	1.00
3R60 The Crystalline Entity	.40	1.00
3R61 The Enterprise Incident	.40	1.00
3R62 The Manheim Effect	.40	1.00
3R72 Founder Trap	.60	1.50
3R74 Our Death is Glory To the Founders	1.50	4.00
3R75 Parting Shot	.40	1.00
3R76 Pseudopod	1.50	4.00
3S10 Failure To Communicate (1E)	.20	.50
3S15 Inside Collaborators (1E)	.20	.50
3S16 Justice or Vengeance (1E)	.20	.50
3S21 Psycho-Kinetic Attack (1E)	.20	.50
3S30 Sokath, His Eyes Uncovered	.20	.50
3S36 Borg Cutting Beam	.20	.50
3S70 Analyze	.20	.50
3S82 Assault On Species 8472	.20	.50
3S83 Battle Reconnaissance (1E)	.20	.50
3S86 Destroy Iconian Gateway (1E)	.20	.50
3S92 Founders' Homeworld, Home of the Great Link	.20	.50
3S94 Hunt Alien	.20	.50
3U20 Psychic Receptacle (1E)	.20	.50
3U23 Restricted Area (1E)	.20	.50
3U25 Rogue Borg Ambush	.20	.50
3U26 Secret Identity (1E)	.20	.50
3U28 Skeleton Crew (1E)	.20	.50
3U32 Jem'Hadar Disruptor Pistol	.20	.50
3U35 Adding to Our Perfection	.20	.50
3U40 Changeling Sabotage	.20	.50
3U42 Dissolving the Senate	.20	.50
3U47 Jem'Hadar Strike Force (1E)	.20	.50
3U48 One With the Borg	.20	.50
3U52 Sabotage Program	.20	.50
3U53 Sensing a Trap	.20	.50
3U63 The Trial Never Ended	.20	.50
3U64 The Will of the Collective	.20	.50
3U65 Trial of Faith (1E)	.20	.50
3U66 Under Suspicion	.20	.50
3U68 We're Mutants	.20	.50
3U69 Adapt	.20	.50
3U73 Insult	.20	.50
3U77 Security Sweep (1E)	.20	.50
3U80 You Could Be Invaluable (1E)	.20	.50
3U81 Archanis Dispute	.20	.50
3U84 Camping Trip	.20	.50
3U85 Clash at Chin'toka (1E)	.20	.50
3U87 Destroy Transwarp Hub	.20	.50
3U88 Evade Borg Vessel	.20	.50
3U89 Evade Dominion Squadron (1E)	.20	.50
3U90 Expose Changeling Influence	.20	.50
3U91 Extract Defector	.20	.50
3U93 Harness Omega Particle	.20	.50
3U95 Instruct Advanced Drone	.20	.50
3U96 Mouth of the Wormhole, Terok Nor	.20	.50
3U97 Pacify Warring Factions	.20	.50
3U98 Peaceful Contact	.20	.50
3U99 Plot Invasion	.20	.50
3R112 Kira Nerys, Reformed Collaborator (1E)	.75	2.00
3R113 Odo, Wayward Link (1E)	.60	1.50
3R114 Porta, Advisor to the Emissary	.40	1.00
3R116 Yassim, Zealous Protester	.40	1.00
3R123 Borg Queen, Guardian of the Hive	1.50	4.00
3R132 Locutus, Voice of the Borg	1.50	4.00
3R138 Seven of Nine, Part of the Greater Whole	1.50	4.00
3R141 Damar, Useful Adjutant	.40	1.00
3R143 Dukat, Liberator and Protector (1E)	.60	1.50
3R149 Tora Ziyal, Beloved Daughter (1E)	1.25	3.00
3R150 Bashir Founder, Nefarious Saboteur	.40	1.00
3R151 Borath, Psychological Researcher	.40	1.00
3R155 Ikat'ika, Honorable Warrior (1E)	1.25	3.00
3R159 Kira Founder, Examiner	1.00	2.50
3R166 Remata'Klan, Unit Leader (1E)	.60	1.50
3R171 Weyoun, Loyal Subject of the Dominion (1E)	.75	2.00
3R173 Yelgrun, Blunt Negotiator	.40	1.00
3R174 B'Elanna Torres, Creative Engineer (1E)	.75	2.00
3R175 Jack, Maladjusted Misfit (1E)	.60	1.50
3R176 Lauren, Seductress	.40	1.00
3R177 Michael Eddington, Traitor to Starfleet (1E)	1.25	3.00
3R180 Reginald Barclay, Reclusive Engineer	.60	1.50
3R182 Quark, Resistance Informant (1E)	.75	2.00
3R183 Rom, Undercover Spy (1E)	.60	1.50
3R184 Alexander Rozhenko, Good Luck Charm (1E)	.40	1.00
3R185 Darok, Martok's Aide	.40	1.00
3R186 Kor, Noble Warrior to the End	.40	1.00
3R191 Kasidy Yates, Maquis Smuggler	.40	1.00
3R196 Pardek, Betrayer (1E)	.40	1.00
3R197 Ruwon, Intelligence Analyst (1E)	.40	1.00
3R200 Locutus' Borg Cube	1.25	3.00
3R204 Tenak'talar, Weyoun's Warship (1E)	1.50	4.00
3R205 U.S.S. Defiant, Stolen Warship	2.00	5.00
3R206 I.K.S. Pagh (1E)	.40	1.00
3R207 Xhosa	.40	1.00
3R208 Soterus (1E)	.60	1.50
3S101 Rescue Prisoners of War	.20	.50
3S103 Salvage Borg Ship (1E)	.20	.50
3S104 Salvage Dominion Ship	.20	.50
3S108 Survey Star System	.20	.50
3S110 Unicomplex, Root of the Hive Mind	.20	.50
3S122 Borg Queen, Bringer of Order	.40	1.00
3S124 Calibration Drone (1E)	.40	1.00
3S139 Seven of Nine, Representative of the Hive (1E)	.40	1.00
3S154 Founder Leader, Forbidding Judge	.20	.50
3S158 Kilana, Dissembling Envoy (1E)	.20	.50
3S162 Martok Founder, Poison of the Empire	.20	.50
3S163 Noret'ikar (1E)	.20	.50
3S199 Borg Sphere	.40	1.00
3S202 Jem'Hadar Attack Ship	.20	.50
3U100 Political Intrigue	.20	.50
3U102 Restock Ketracel-White	.20	.50
3U105 Signal for Rescue (1E)	.20	.50
3U106 Stage Bombardment	.20	.50
3U107 Study Rare Phenomenon (1E)	.20	.50
3U109 The Siege of AR-558 (1E)	.20	.50
3U115 Tahna Los, Voice of the Kohn-ma (1E)	.20	.50
3U136 Reclamation Drone (1E)	.20	.50
3U144 Elim Garak, Plain, Simple Taylor (1E)	.20	.50
3U146 Mavek, Science Officer (1E)	.20	.50
3U153 Founder Leader, Beguiling Teacher (1E)	.20	.50
3U157 Keevan, Conniving Liar (1E)	.20	.50
3U160 Limara'Son, Fierce Soldier	.20	.50
3U161 Lovok Founder, Puppet Master	.20	.50
3U170 Weyoun, Instrument of the Founders	.20	.50
3U172 Yak'Talon, Deadly Patroller	.20	.50
3U178 Norah Satie, Starfleet Investigator	.20	.50
3U179 Patrick, Idiot Savant (1E)	.20	.50
3U181 Sarina Douglas, Cataleptic Conundrum (1E)	.20	.50
3U187 Larg, Piece of Baktag (1E)	.20	.50
3U188 Martok, Leader of Destiny (1E)	.20	.50
3U194 Karina, Intelligence Analyst (1E)	.20	.50

2003 Star Trek Energize

Card	Low	High
COMPLETE SET (180)	30.00	80.00
BOOSTER BOX (30 PACKS)	100.00	200.00
BOOSTER PACK (11 CARDS)	4.00	8.00
COMMON CARD	.10	.20
RELEASED ON MAY 21, 2003		
2R2 Casualties of War	.50	1.25
2R9 Face to Face (1E)	.75	2.00
2U1 A Klingon Matter	.20	.50
2U3 Crippling Attack (1E)	.20	.50
2U8 Exposed Power Relay (1E)	.20	.50
2R11 Head to Head (1E)	.50	1.25
2R26 Training Accident	.50	1.25
2R30 Ak'voh	.50	1.25
2R31 Assassination Plot (1E)	1.25	3.00
2R35 Common Ground	.50	1.25
2R36 Complications	.50	1.25
2R37 Confessions in the Pale Moonlight	.50	1.25
2R38 Conscription	.50	1.25
2R40 Deep Roots	.50	1.25
2R41 Disable Sensors (1E)	1.00	2.50
2R49 Machinations	.50	1.25
2R59 Retaliation	.50	1.25
2R61 Shadow Operation	.50	1.25
2R65 Straying from the Path (1E)	.50	1.25
2R67 The Text of the Kosst Amojan	.50	1.25
2R68 Under Scrutiny (1E)	.50	1.25
2R72 Visionary (1E)	.50	1.25
2R81 If Wishes Were Horses	.50	1.25
2R82 Ja'chuq	1.25	3.00
2R83 Powerful Example	.50	1.25
2R85 Relentless	.75	2.00
2R91 Vile Deception	.50	1.25
2U10 Flim-Flam Artist (1E)	.20	.50
2U12 Hired Muscle (1E)	.20	.50
2U17 Picking Up the Pieces (1E)	.20	.50
2U18 Plasma Shock (1E)	.20	.50
2U19 Quaint Technology (1E)	.20	.50
2U22 Stolen Computer Core	.20	.50
2U32 Born for Conquest (1E)	.20	.50
2U33 Brief Reunion	.20	.50
2U42 Ferocity (1E)	.20	.50
2U44 For the Sisko (1E)	.20	.50
2U46 Kotra (1E)	.20	.50
2U50 Mental Discipline (1E)	.20	.50
2U51 Peldor Jol	.20	.50
2U53 Picking Up the Basics	.20	.50
2U55 Political Leverage (1E)	.20	.50
2U62 Sickbay (1E)	.20	.50
2U63 Smuggling Run	.20	.50
2U64 Staunch Determination	.20	.50
2U66 Temba, His Arms Wide	.20	.50
2U70 Unseen Manipulations	.20	.50
2U71 Vast Resources	.20	.50
2U73 We Will Not Surrender (1E)	.20	.50
2U74 Bank Heist	.20	.50
2U76 Diplomatic Masquerade	.20	.50
2U77 Discreet Inquiry	.20	.50
2U80 Honorable Death	.20	.50
2U84 Precautionary Measures (1E)	.20	.50
2U86 Shared Delicacy (1E)	.20	.50
2U87 Stricken Dumb	.20	.50
2U93 We Are Klingon	.20	.50
2U94 Well-Crafted Lure	.20	.50
2U95 Aid Clone Colony	.20	.50
2U96 Athos IV, Maquis Base	.20	.50
2U97 Avert Danger	.20	.50
2U98 Brute Force	.20	.50
2U99 Cargo Haul	.20	.50
2R104 Borum, Selfless Hero (1E)	.50	1.25
2R105 Jaro Essa, Leader of the Circle	.50	1.25
2R106 Kira Nerys, Impassioned Major (1E)	1.25	3.00
2R107 Kurn, Bajoran Security Officer (1E)	.50	1.25
2R108 Leeta, Dabo Girl (1E)	1.25	3.00
2R112 Winn Adami, Devious Manipulator	.50	1.25
2R114 Enabran Tain, Retired Mastermind (1E)	.50	1.25
2R115 Evek, Harsh Interrogator (1E)	.50	1.25
2R120 Chakotay, Freedom Fighter	1.25	3.00
2R121 Ezri Dax, Station Counselor	.75	2.00
2R122 Jake Sisko, Temporal Anchor	.50	1.25
2R125 Keiko O'Brien, School Teacher	.50	1.25
2R127 Michael Eddington, Noble Hero (1E)	.75	2.00
2R128 Miles O'Brien, Transporter Chief	.75	2.00
2R130 Rebecca Sullivan, Resistance Fighter (1E)	1.50	4.00
2R131 Thomas Riker, Defiant Leader (1E)	1.00	2.50
2R135 Drex, Arrogant Warrior	.50	1.25
2R136 K'mpec, Klingon Supreme Commander	.50	1.25
2R138 Kahless, The Unforgettable	.50	1.25
2R139 Kargan, Rash Captain (1E)	.50	1.25
2R142 Konmel, Renegade Warrior	.50	1.25
2R144 Korris, Renegade Captain (1E)	.50	1.25
2R157 Roga Danar, Decorated Subhadar	.75	2.00
2R158 Sakonna, Gunrunner (1E)	.50	1.25
2R161 Galathon, Steadfast Rival	.75	2.00
2R163 Neral, Senate Proconsul	.50	1.25
2R165 Sirol, Diplomatic Adversary (1E)	.50	1.25
2R168 Toreth, Cautious Commander (1E)	.50	1.25
2R169 Kitara (1E)	1.00	2.50
2R170 Aldara (1E)	.75	2.00
2R173 Valjean	.60	1.50
2R174 I.K.S. Qam-Chee (1E)	.75	2.00
2R175 Fortune	.50	1.25
2R178 Khazara (1E)	.75	2.00
2R179 Terix (1E)	.75	2.00
2R180 Trolarak (1E)	.75	2.00
2U100 Investigate Maquis Activity (1E)	.20	.50
2U101 Mine Nebula	.20	.50
2U102 Treat Plague Ship (1E)	.20	.50
2U103 Akorem Laan, Revered Poet (1E)	.20	.50
2U110 The Sirah, The Storyteller	.20	.50
2U111 Varis Sul, Tetrarch of the Paqu (1E)	.20	.50
2U113 Boheeka, Clandestine Connection	.20	.50
2U117 Natima Lang, Professor of Political Ethics (1E)	.20	.50
2U118 Benjamin Sisko, Man of Resolve (1E)	.20	.50
2U119 Cal Hudson, Attache to the Demilitarized Zone	.20	.50
2U123 Joseph Sisko, Creole Chef (1E)	.20	.50
2U124 Julian Bashir, Unnatural Freak	.20	.50
2U132 William Patrick Samuels, Maquis Saboteur (1E)	.20	.50
2U137 Kahless, The Greatest Warrior of Them All (1E)	.20	.50
2U146 M'vil	.20	.50
2U147 Amaros, Earnest Vanguard	.20	.50
2U156 Raimus, Criminal Master	.20	.50
2U162 Mirok, Interphase Researcher (1E)	.20	.50
2U166 T'Rul, Curt Subcommander (1E)	.20	.50
2U171 Guingouin (1E)	.20	.50
2U177 Tama (1E)	.20	.50

2004 Star Trek Fractured Time

Card	Low	High
COMPLETE SET (40)	30.00	80.00
COMMON CARD	.75	2.00
RELEASED ON OCTOBER 13, 2004		
5P2 The Clown: Bitter Medicine (1E)	1.50	4.00
5P3 Tragic Turn	5.00	10.00
5P4 Cardassian Protectorate	1.25	3.00
5R5 Expand the Collective	1.25	3.00
5P10 Quantum Incursions (1E)	1.25	3.00
5P12 Security Drills (1E)	1.50	4.00
5P18 Unyielding	2.00	5.00
5P19 Explicit Orders (1E)	1.50	4.00
5P20 Fitting In (1E)	2.00	5.00
5P22 Kira Nerys, The Intendant	1.25	3.00
5P24 Dukat, Prefect of Bajor	1.25	3.00
5P25 Elim Garak, First Officer of Terok Nor	1.25	3.00
5P28 James T. Kirk, Living Legend	2.00	5.00
5P29 Tasha Yar, Tactical Officer	1.50	4.00
5P30 Worf, First Officer	1.50	4.00
5P31 Korath, Duplicitous Tinkerer	1.25	3.00
5P32 Worf, Regent of the Alliance	1.50	4.00
5P33 Benjamin Sisko, Outlaw (1E)	1.50	4.00
5P34 Daniels, Temporal Enforcers	1.25	3.00
5P35 Miles O'Brien, Smiley	2.50	6.00
5P39 Sphere 634	2.00	5.00
5P40 U.S.S. Enterprise-D, Personal Flagship	3.00	8.00

2004 Star Trek Necessary Evil

Card	Low	High
COMPLETE SET (180)	120.00	200.00
BOOSTER BOX (30 PACKS)	200.00	300.00
BOOSTER PACK (11 CARDS)	6.00	12.00
COMMON CARD	.10	.20
RELEASED ON MARCH 17, 2004		
4R7 Biochemical Hyperacceleration	1.50	4.00
4R9 Broken Captive (1E)	1.25	3.00
4U8 Bleeding to Death (1E)	.20	.50
4R11 Counterinsurgency Program	1.25	3.00
4R18 In Training	1.25	3.00
4R25 Talosian Trial	1.25	3.00
4R27 The Dreamer and the Dream	1.50	4.00
4R28 Tsiolkovsky Infection	2.00	5.00
4R30 Whisper in the Dark	1.25	3.00
4R34 The Sword of Kahless	1.25	3.00
4R35 Accepting the Past	1.50	4.00
4R36 All-Out War	3.00	8.00
4R37 Anything or Anyone	3.00	8.00
4R40 At What Cost?	6.00	12.00
4R44 Caught in the Act	2.00	5.00
4R49 Endangered	3.00	8.00
4R51 Far-Seeing Eyes	2.50	6.00
4R52 Field Studies	1.25	3.00
4R59 Militia Patrol (1E)	1.25	3.00
4R65 Organized Terrorist Activities	7.50	15.00
4R68 Prison Compound (1E)	2.50	6.00
4R70 Ressikan Flute	2.50	6.00
4R71 Running a Tight Ship	1.25	3.00
4R74 Storage Compartment	2.00	5.00
4R78 The Perfect Tool	1.25	3.00
4R79 Thought Maker	2.50	6.00
4R83 You've Always Been My Favorite	5.00	10.00
4R85 Allies on the Inside	2.50	6.00
4R86 Brainwashing	1.25	3.00
4R89 Knowledge and Experience	1.25	3.00
4R94 Outlining the Stakes	1.25	3.00
4R98 The Rite of Emergence	1.25	3.00
4U10 Cave-In	.20	.50
4U12 Dealing With Pressure	.20	.50
4U14 Formal Hearing	.20	.50
4U16 Harsh Conditions	.20	.50
4U22 Renegade Ambush	.20	.50
4U23 Short Circuit (1E)	.20	.50
4U24 Side by Side (1E)	.20	.50
4U29 Ungracious Hosts (1E)	.20	.50
4U33 The Stone of Gol	.20	.50
4U38 Apprehended	.20	.50
4U39 At An Impasse	.20	.50
4U41 Battle Lust	.20	.50
4U42 Biological Distinctiveness	.20	.50
4U47 Deploy the Fleet	.20	.50
4U48 Desperate Sacrifice	.20	.50
4U50 Escaping Detection	.20	.50
4U53 Forcing Their Hand (1E)	.20	.50
4U54 Forever Linked (1E)	.20	.50
4U55 Getting Under Your Skin (1E)	.20	.50
4U60 Misdirection (1E)	.20	.50
4U61 Mission Accomplished (1E)	.20	.50
4U62 More Than Meets the Eye	.20	.50
4U67 Power Shift	.20	.50
4U75 Targeted for Assimilation	.20	.50
4U76 Tempted By Flesh	.20	.50
4U80 Undercover Resource	.20	.50
4U84 Your Fear Will Destroy You	.20	.50
4U88 Indomitable	.20	.50
4U90 Lying in Wait	.20	.50
4U91 Natural Instincts	.20	.50
4U92 One-Upmanship	.20	.50
4U93 Operational Necessity	.20	.50
4U95 Reborn	.20	.50
4R100 Bareil Antos, Opaka's Protector	1.25	3.00
4R102 Dukat, Anjohl Tennan	1.50	4.00
4R103 Kira Meru, Comfort Woman (1E)	1.50	4.00
4R104 Krim, Thoughtful Tactician	1.25	3.00
4R106 Leeta, Rebel Supporter (1E)	2.00	5.00
4R108 Solbor, Faithful Attendant (1E)	2.00	5.00
4R119 Kira Nerys, Iliana Ghemor	2.00	5.00
4R121 Odo, Impartial Investigator	2.00	5.00
4R124 Toran, Ambitious Brute (1E)	1.25	3.00
4R126 Founder Architect (1E)	1.50	4.00
4R130 Odo Founder, Adept Imposter	1.50	4.00
4R131 Rodak'koden (1E)	1.25	3.00
4R133 Beverly Crusher, Chief Physician (1E)	2.50	6.00

4R134 Data, Pinocchio (1E) 2.50 6.00
4R138 Guinan, Listener 1.50 4.00
4R139 Jadzia Dax, Problem Solver (1E) 3.00 8.00
4R140 Jake Sisko, Reporter Behind the Lines 3.00 8.00
4R149 William T. Riker, First Officer (1E) 2.50 6.00
4R150 Worf, Conn Officer 2.50 6.00
4R151 B'Etor, Ambitious Renegade 1.25 3.00
4R152 Jadzia Dax, Sworn Ally (1E) 2.50 6.00
4R154 Lursa, Ambitious Renegade 1.25 3.00
4R155 William T. Riker, Exchange Officer 2.00 5.00
4R157 Crosis, Fanatical Lieutenant 1.25 3.00
4R158 Data, Loyal Brother (1E) 1.25 3.00
4R161 Lore, The One 2.50 6.00
4R165 B'Etor, Romulan Conspirator 1.25 3.00
4R168 Koval, Chairman of the Tal Shiar 1.25 3.00
4R169 Lursa, Romulan Conspirator 1.25 3.00
4R173 Sela, Devious Schemer (1E) 1.25 3.00
4R180 I.K.S. Ning'tao 2.50 6.00
4U101 Day Kannu .20 .50
4U109 Surmak Ren, Medical Administrator .20 .50
4U113 Facilitation Drone .20 .50
4U114 Five of Twelve, Secondary Adjunct of Trimatrix 942 .20 .50
4U115 Reconnaissance Drone (1E) .20 .50
4U116 Aamin Marritza, Honorable Patriot (1E) .20 .50
4U117 Broca, Groveling Lackey .20 .50
4U120 Mila, Trusted Confidante .20 .50
4U122 Rusot, Proud Nationalist (1E) .20 .50
4U123 Seskal, Comrade in Arms .20 .50
4U128 Luaran, Cautious Inspector .20 .50
4U129 O'Brien Founder, Agent Provocateur .20 .50
4U132 Weyoun, Warship Commander .20 .50
4U135 Deanna Troi, Ship's Counselor (1E) .20 .50
4U137 Geordi La Forge, Conn Officer (1E) .20 .50
4U141 Kalita, Maquis Pilot .20 .50
4U143 Lenara Kahn, Wormhole Theorist (1E) .20 .50
4U144 Miles O'Brien, Repair Chief .20 .50
4U148 Tim Watters, Valiant Captain (1E) .20 .50
4U159 Koval, Follower of the One .20 .50
4U166 Bochra, Loyal Centurion .20 .50
4U171 Parem, Special Security (1E) .20 .50
4U176 Tamarith, Reformist (1E) .20 .50
4U178 Talnot .20 .50
4U179 U.S.S. Valiant, Red Squad Training Ship (1E) .20 .50

2004 Star Trek Necessary Evil Foil

COMPLETE SET (18) 150.00 250.00
COMMON CARD 10.00 25.00
RELEASED ON MARCH 17, 2004

2004 Star Trek Reflections 2.0

COMPLETE SET (61) 40.00 80.00
COMMON CARD .10 .30
BOOSTER BOX (24) 30.00 60.00
BOOSTER PACK (18) 1.50 3.00
6P2 Dignitaries and Witnesses (1E) .60 1.50
6P3 Eye to Eye (1E) .60 1.50
6P6 Hard Time (1E) .60 1.50
6P7 Helpless (1E) .60 1.50
6P8 Mr. Tricorder (1E) .60 1.50
6P9 Shipboard Fire (1E) .60 1.50
6P11 Unknown Microorganism (1E) .60 1.50
6P17 Changed History (1E) .60 1.50
6P20 Friction (1E) .60 1.50
6P26 Maquis Raid 1.50 4.00
6P29 Stalling for Time (1E) .60 1.50
6P33 Change of Heart (1E) .60 1.50
6P40 Odo, Curzon Odo (1E) .60 1.50
6P43 Requisitions Drone (1E) .60 1.50
6P46 Gelnon, Aloof Tactician 1.50 4.00
6P47 Ixtana'Rax, Honored Elder (1E) .60 1.50
6P50 Kira Nerys, Starfleet Emissary (1E) .60 1.50
6P51 Santos, Squad Leader .75 2.00
6P53 William T. Riker, Wistful Admiral 3.00 8.00
6P55 Worf, Son of Mogh (1E) 1.50 4.00
6P56 Jean-Luc Picard, Galen (1E) 15.00 30.00
6P57 Vina, Orion Slave Girl (1E) .60 1.50
6P59 Mendak, Duplicitous Admiral 1.50 4.00
6P60 Dominion Battleship (1E) .60 1.50

2004 Star Trek Tenth Anniversary Collection

COMPLETE SET (18) 45.00 100.00
RELEASED ON MAY 3, 2004
0P6 Benjamin Sisko, Shipwright (1E) 2.50 6.00
0P7 Borg Queen, Perfectionist 2.50 6.00
0P8 Dukat, True Cardassian 2.50 6.00
0P9 Kudak'Etan, Arrogant First (1E) 2.50 6.00
0P10 Data, Commanding Officer 2.50 6.00
0P11 Jean-Luc Picard, Starship Captain (1E) 2.50 6.00
0P12 Gowron, Sole Leader of the Empire (1E) 2.50 6.00
0P13 Arctus Baran, Treasure Seeker 2.50 6.00
0P14 Velal, Reluctant Aggressor 2.50 6.00
0P15 Baraka (1E) 2.50 6.00
0P16 Queen's Borg Cube 2.50 6.00
0P17 Naprem 2.50 6.00
0P18 U.S.S. Defiant, Commandeered Warship 2.50 6.00
0P19 U.S.S. Enterprise-D, Explorer 2.50 6.00
0P20 U.S.S. Sutherland 2.50 6.00
0P21 I.K.S. Bortas 2.50 6.00
0P22 Fortune, Raider for Hire (1E) 2.50 6.00
0P23 Rovaran (1E) 2.50 6.00

2005 Star Trek Adversaries Anthology

1R7 Assassination Attempt (1E)
0P16 Queen's Borg Cube
1R39 Nanite Attack (1E)
1R90 How Would You Like a Trip to Romulus?
1R121 Amanda Rogers
1R129 Kevin Uxbridge
1R248 Ocett, Dogged Rival (1E)
1R275 Luther Sloan, Man of Secrets
1R314 Nu'Daq, Tenacious Rival (1E)
1R348 The Albino, Killer of Children (1E)
1R376 The Viceroy, Shinzon's Protector (1E)
1R383 Bralek (1E)
1R401 I.K.S. Maht-H'a (1E)
1R413 Scimitar, Predator (1E, Al)
1U228 Winn Adami, Kai of Bajor (1E)
2R131 Thomas Riker, Defiant Leader (1E)
3R151 Borath, Psychological Researcher
3R205 U.S.S. Defiant, Stolen Warship

2005 Star Trek Strange New Worlds

COMPLETE SET (120) 40.00 100.00
BOOSTER BOX (30 PACKS) 25.00 50.00
BOOSTER PACK (11 CARDS) 1.00 2.00
COMMON CARD .12 .30
RELEASED ON MAY 13, 2005
7R2 Code of Honor .75 2.00
7R4 Entanglement .75 2.00
7R8 Molecular Reversion Field (1E) .75 2.00
7R10 Proximity-Actuated Field .75 2.00
7R15 Where No One Has Gone Before .75 2.00
7R18 Brinkmanship .75 2.00
7R20 Exceed Engine Output .75 2.00
7R23 Provoked Attack .75 2.00
7R25 Rule of Acquisition #6 .75 2.00
7R26 Rule of Acquisition #22 .75 2.00
7R28 Rule of Acquisition #141 .75 2.00
7R29 Rule of Acquisition #144 .75 2.00
7R32 Temporal Incursion .75 2.00
7R36 Ascertain .75 2.00
7R40 Delegated Assignment .75 2.00
7R59 Tekeny Ghemor, Prominent Official .75 2.00
7R61 Goran'Agar, Trusted Commander .75 2.00
7R62 Omet'iklan, Steely Disciplinarian .75 2.00
7R67 Leonard H. McCoy, Remarkable Man .75 2.00
7R69 Montgomery Scott, Relic .75 2.00
7R70 Arridor, Great Sage .75 2.00
7R74 Brunt, FCA Liquidator .75 2.00
7R77 Ishka, Moogie .75 2.00
7R78 Kazago, First Officer .75 2.00
7R81 Leck, Eliminator .75 2.00
7R83 Lurin, Renegade DaiMon .75 2.00
7R89 Quark, True Ferengi .75 2.00
7R92 Sovak, Treasure Hunter .75 2.00
7R93 Taar, Bristling DaiMon .75 2.00
7R94 Zek, The Grand Nagus .75 2.00
7R95 Jean-Luc Picard, Worf's cha'Dich .75 2.00
7R98 B-4, Dangerous Simpleton (1E) .75 2.00
7R101 Ira Graves, Noted Molecular Cyberneticist .75 2.00
7R102 Kivas Fajo, Collector .75 2.00
7R104 Noonien Soong, Often-Wrong .75 2.00
7R109 Tolian Soran, Renegade Scientist .75 2.00
7R111 Vic Fontaine, Vegas Crooner .75 2.00
7R113 Spock, Celebrated Ambassador .75 2.00
7R116 Aurulent .75 2.00
7R118 Kurdon .75 2.00
7R120 Devoras .75 2.00

2006 Star Trek Captain's Log

COMPLETE SET (120) 100.00 200.00
BOOSTER BOX (30 PACKS) 30.00 60.00
BOOSTER PACK (11 CARDS) 1.25 2.50
RELEASED ON OCTOBER 27, 2006
10R2 An Issue of Trust 2.50 6.00
10R3 Armed Search Party (1E) 2.50 6.00
10R6 Contaminating a Culture (1E) 2.50 6.00
10R14 Psionic Attack (1E) 2.50 6.00
10R19 Thermokinetic Explosion 2.50 6.00
10R23 A Sight for Sore Eyes (1E) 2.50 6.00
10R25 Dark Pursuit 2.50 6.00
10R31 Parallel Course 2.50 6.00
10R32 Political Putsch 2.50 6.00
10R33 Rule of Acquisition #16 2.50 6.00
10R35 The Dominion Will Prevail 2.50 6.00
10R36 The Long Journey Home 2.50 6.00
10R37 The Spirit of Kahless 2.50 6.00
10R42 Surprise Snag 2.50 6.00
10R45 Warp Speed Transfer (1E) 2.50 6.00
10R53 Basso Tromac, Smug Subordinate 2.50 6.00
10R56 Second, Neonatal Drone (1E) 2.50 6.00
10R58 Macet, Skeptical Commander (1E) 2.50 6.00
10R66 Harry Kim, Eager to Please (1E) 2.50 6.00
10R70 Kathryn Janeway, Forceful Captain 2.50 6.00
10R75 Matthew Dougherty, Misguided Admiral 2.50 6.00
10R83 The Doctor, Emergency Medical Hologram 2.50 6.00
10R84 Tom Paris, Best Pilot You Could Have 2.50 6.00
10R85 Tuvok, Chief of Security (1E) 2.50 6.00
10R86 Quark, Little Green Man (1E) 2.50 6.00
10R94 Lal, Beloved (1E) 2.50 6.00
10R96 Neelix, Morale Officer (1E) 2.50 6.00
10R98 Tam Elbrun, Prodigal Telepath 2.50 6.00
10R99 Thon 2.50 6.00

2006 Star Trek Captain's Log Foil

COMPLETE SET (18) 50.00 100.00
COMMON CARD 2.50 6.00
RELEASED ON OCTOBER 27, 2006

2006 Star Trek Dangerous Missions

COMPLETE SET (19) 20.00 40.00
COMMON CARD (9R1-9R19) .75 2.00
RELEASED ON SEPTEMBER 1, 2006

2006 Star Trek The Enterprise Collection

COMPLETE SET (18) 20.00 40.00
COMMON CARD .75 2.00
RELEASED ON AUGUST 26, 2006

2006 Star Trek Genesis

COMPLETE SET (27) 20.00 40.00
COMMON CARD .75 2.00
RELEASED ON NOVEMBER 13, 2006

2006 Star Trek To Boldly Go

COMPLETE SET (120) 100.00 250.00
BOOSTER BOX (30 PACKS) 40.00 80.00
BOOSTER PACK (11 CARDS) 1.50 3.00
COMMON CARD .10 .30
RELEASED ON AUGUST 18, 2006
8R1 Agonizing Encounter 2.50 6.00
8R4 Bre'Nan Ritual 2.50 6.00
8R5 Cardassian Processing (1E) 2.50 6.00
8R11 Molecular Mishap 2.50 6.00
8R13 Outclassed 2.50 6.00
8R14 Parallels (1E) 2.50 6.00
8R16 Tactical Disadvantage (1E) 2.50 6.00
8R18 Up The Ante 2.50 6.00
8R20 Zero Hour 2.50 6.00
8R21 Data's Emotion Chip 2.50 6.00
8R28 Dabo! 2.50 6.00
8R32 Distracting Exhibition 2.50 6.00
8R33 Escape Pod 2.50 6.00
8R35 Latinum Storage 2.50 6.00
8R38 Reman Subterfuge 2.50 6.00
8R39 Remarkable Regeneration 2.50 6.00
8R43 Strafing Fire 2.50 6.00
8R46 The Muse 2.50 6.00
8R49 Disinterested Visitant 2.50 6.00
8R51 Temporal Delineation 2.50 6.00
8R65 First, Unstable 2.50 6.00
8R67 Third, Neonatal Drone 2.50 6.00
8R68 Thrax, Chief of Security 2.50 6.00
8R76 Wesley Crusher, Nova Squadron Pilot (1E) 2.50 6.00
8R83 Kieran MacDuff, Executive Officer 2.50 6.00
8R86 Raakin, Dominant Augment 2.50 6.00
8R87 Shran, In Archer's Debt 2.50 6.00
8R88 Silik, Chameleon 2.50 6.00
8R90 Zefram Cochrane, Ready to Make History 2.50 6.00
8R91 Jean-Luc Picard, Bearer of Ill Tidings 2.50 6.00
8R106 Jonathan Archer, Headstrong Captain (1E) 2.50 6.00
8R108 Malcolm Reed, Weapon Expert (1E) 2.50 6.00
8R109 Maxwell Forrest, Starfleet Executive (1E) 2.50 6.00
8R111 Phlox, Alien Physiologist (1E) 2.50 6.00
8R113 Travis Mayweather, Space Boomer (1E) 2.50 6.00
8R115 U.S.S. Ganges, One of the First 2.50 6.00
8R116 U.S.S. Rio Grande, Built to Last 2.50 6.00
8R117 Enterprise, Finally Ready to Swim 2.50 6.00
8R119 Shuttlepod One, Reliable Transport 2.50 6.00

2006 Star Trek To Boldly Go Foil

COMPLETE SET (18) 75.00 180.00
COMMON CARD 4.00 10.00
RELEASED ON AUGUST 18, 2006

2007 Star Trek In a Mirror Darkly

COMPLETE SET (122) 100.00 250.00
BOOSTER BOX (30 PACKS) 200.00 300.00
BOOSTER PACK (11 CARDS) 1.50 3.00
COMMON CARD .12 .30
RELEASED ON JUNE 15, 2007
13R14 Paradan Replicant 3.00 8.00
13R15 Paranoid Escape (1E) 3.00 8.00
13R20 The Dal'Rok 3.00 8.00
13R23 Bigger Tattoo 3.00 8.00
13R26 Captain's Log 3.00 8.00
13R28 Guardians Advice 3.00 8.00
13R29 Necessary Evil (1E) 3.00 8.00
13R32 Sabotaged Transporter 3.00 8.00
13R34 Strange New Worlds (1E) 3.00 8.00
13R35 Temporal Flux Energy Ribbon 3.00 8.00
13R36 The Inner Light (1E) 3.00 8.00
13R39 Unimatrix Zero 3.00 8.00
13R42 Brutal Experiments 3.00 8.00
13R47 Bareil Antos, Petty Thief 3.00 8.00
13R48 Kira Nerys, Resourceful Prisoner (1E) 3.00 8.00
13R50 Odo, Efficient Overseer 3.00 8.00
13R53 Elim Garak, Crafty Underling 3.00 8.00
13R56 Gor, Thot 3.00 8.00
13R58 Pran, Thot 3.00 8.00
13R61 Erika Benteen, Leyton's Adjunct 3.00 8.00
13R65 James T. Kirk, Brutal Barbarian 3.00 8.00
13R67 Leonard H. McCoy, Fiendish Physician 3.00 8.00
13R80 Spock, Man of Integrity 3.00 8.00
13R84 Worf, Defiant Commander 3.00 8.00
13R88 Quark, Simple Barkeep 3.00 8.00
13R90 Grilka, Glorious Lady 3.00 8.00
13R95 Laas, One of the 100 3.00 8.00
13R96 Slar, Gorn Slave Master (1E) 3.00 8.00
13R97 Tuvok, Coldly Logocal Soldier (1E) 3.00 8.00
13R99 Data, From the City of Rateg (1E) 3.00 8.00

2007 Star Trek In a Mirror Darkly Foil

COMPLETE SET (18) 80.00 140.00
RELEASED ON JUNE 15, 2007
13A1 Chula: The Dice 3.00 8.00
13A2 Paranoid Escape (1E) 3.00 8.00
13A3 The Dal'Rok 3.00 8.00
13A4 Temporal Flux Energy Ribbon 3.00 8.00
13A5 Elim Garak, Crafty Underling 3.00 8.00
13A6 Gor, Thot 3.00 8.00
13A7 Pran, Thot 3.00 8.00
13A8 James T. Kirk, Brutal Barbarian 3.00 8.00
13A9 Spock, Man of Integrity 3.00 8.00
0AP11 Stripped Down 3.00 8.00
0AP12 Neras, Slave Girl 3.00 8.00
13A10 Worf, Defiant Commander 3.00 8.00
13A11 Slar, Gorn Slave Master (1E) 3.00 8.00
13A12 Jonathan Archer, Covetous Commander (1E) 3.00 8.00
13A13 T'Pol, Not a Slave 3.00 8.00
13A14 Tykk 3.00 8.00
13A15 U.S.S. Lakota, Modified Starship 3.00 8.00
13A16 Defiant, Mirror Warship 3.00 8.00
13A17 Phoenix, Risen From the Ashes 3.00 8.00
13A18 I.S.S. Enterprise, Terran Flagship (1E) 3.00 8.00

2007 Star Trek These Are the Voyages

COMPLETE SET (122) 150.00 350.00
BOOSTER BOX (30 PACKS) 40.00 80.00
BOOSTER PACK (11 CARDS 1.50 3.00
COMMON CARD .15 .40
RELEASED ON MARCH 6, 2007
12R13 Neural Parasites 4.00 10.00
12R14 No Kill I 4.00 10.00
12R15 Psychokinetic Control (1E) 4.00 10.00
12R17 Swashbuckler at Heart (1E) 4.00 10.00
12R20 Vian Test 4.00 10.00
12R21 Tox Uthat 4.00 10.00
12R31 The Circle 4.00 10.00
12R33 Cascade Virus 4.00 10.00
12R37 Grav-Plating Trap 4.00 10.00
12R45 Four of Nine, Heuristics Drone 4.00 10.00
12R47 Three of Nine, Tactician Drone (1E) 4.00 10.00
12R48 Two of Nine, Translator Drone 4.00 10.00
12R50 Parek, Privileged Legate (1E) 4.00 10.00
12R51 Bashir Founder, Imperturbable Infiltrator 4.00 10.00
12R52 Krajensky Founder, Adversary 4.00 10.00
12R56 B'Elanna Torres, Chief Engineer 4.00 10.00
12R58 Benjamin Sisko, Command Staffer 4.00 10.00
12R60 Chakotay, First Officer 4.00 10.00
12R66 Jadzia Dax, Communications Staffer (1E) 4.00 10.00
12R67 James T. Kirk, Highly-Decorated Captain 4.00 10.00
12R71 Julian Bashir, Medical Staffer (1E) 4.00 10.00
12R72 Leonard H. McCoy, Chief Medical Officer 4.00 10.00
12R78 Montgomery Scott, Chief Engineer 4.00 10.00
12R84 Seven of Nine, Efficient Analyst 4.00 10.00
12R85 Spock, Science Officer 4.00 10.00
12R89 Kang, Vigilant Commander 4.00 10.00
12R91 Koloth, Ingratiating Captain 4.00 10.00
12R92 Kor, Courageous Governor 4.00 10.00
12R98 Dukat, Pah-Wraith Puppet (1E) 4.00 10.00

2007 Star Trek These Are the Voyages Foil

COMPLETE SET (18) 50.00 100.00
COMMON CARD 2.50 6.00
RELEASED ON MARCH 6, 2007

2007 Star Trek What You Leave Behind

COMPLETE SET (122) 75.00 200.00
BOOSTER BOX (30 PACKS) 40.00 80.00
BOOSTER PACK (11 CARDS) 1.50 3.00
COMMON CARD .10 .30
RELEASED ON DECEMBER 20, 2007
14R1 Back to Basics (1E) 2.50 6.00
14R12 Prisoner of the Exile 2.50 6.00
14R14 Spatial Distortions 2.50 6.00
14R15 Stripped Down 2.50 6.00
14R16 Sylvia 2.50 6.00
14R17 The Clown: Guillotine 2.50 6.00
14R18 The Phage 2.50 6.00
14R24 Clarity 2.50 6.00
14R26 Distant Control (1E) 2.50 6.00
14R30 Ghost Stories 2.50 6.00
14R34 In a Mirror, Darkly 2.50 6.00
14R35 Military Assault Command Operations (1E) 2.50 6.00
14R43 U.S.S. Enterprise-J (1E) 2.50 6.00
14R47 Covenant (1E) 2.50 6.00
14R64 Leeta, Union Member 2.50 6.00
14R66 Borg Queen, Obsessed 2.50 6.00
14R67 Data, Tempted by Flesh (1E) 2.50 6.00
14R68 Crell Moset, Notorious Exobiologist 2.50 6.00
14R71 Founder Leader, Single Minded (1E) 2.50 6.00
14R72 Odo, The Great Link's Saviour (1E) 2.50 6.00
14R78 Data, Lucasian Chair 2.50 6.00
14R79 Ezri Dax, Resourceful Counselor 2.50 6.00
14R83 Sarek, Logical Being 2.50 6.00
14R86 The Doctor, Emergency Command Hologram (1E) 2.50 6.00
14R91 Gorkon, Visionary Chancellor 2.50 6.00
14R92 Gowron, Celebrated Leader 2.50 6.00
14R97 Kasidy Yates, Conflicted Captain (1E) 2.50 6.00

2007 Star Trek What You Leave Behind Foil

COMPLETE SET (18) 50.00 100.00
COMMON CARD 2.50 6.00
RELEASED ON DECEMBER 20, 2007

1995 Star Wars Premiere

COMPLETE SET (324) 75.00 150.00
BOOSTER BOX (36 PACKS) 75.00 150.00
BOOSTER PACK (15 CARDS) 3.00 6.00
RELEASED IN DECEMBER 1995
1 5D6-RA-7 (Fivedesix) R1 1.25 3.00
2 Admiral Motti R2 .75 2.00
3 Chief Bast U1 .30 .75
4 Colonel Wulff Yularen U1 .30 .75
5 Commander Praji U2 .30 .75
6 DS-61-2 U1 .30 .75
7 DS-61-3 R1 3.00 8.00
8 Darth Vader R1 10.00 25.00
9 Dathcha U1 .30 .75
10 Death Star Trooper C2 .12 .30
11 Djas Puhr R2 .75 2.00
12 Dr. Evazan R2 .75 2.00
13 EG-6 (Eegee-Six) U2 .30 .75
14 Feltipern Trevagg U1 .30 .75
15 Garindan R2 .75 2.00
16 General Tagge R2 .75 2.00
17 Grand Moff Tarkin R1 3.00 8.00
18 Imperial Pilot C2 .12 .30
19 Imperial Trooper Guard C2 .12 .30
20 Jawa LIGHT C2 .12 .30
21 Kitik Keed'kak R1 1.25 3.00
22 LIN-V8M (Elleyein-Veeateemm) C1 .12 .30
23 Labria R2 .75 2.00
24 Lieutenant Tanbris U2 .30 .75
25 M'iiyoom Onith U2 .30 .75
26 MSE-6 'Mouse' Droid U1 .30 .75
27 Myo R2 .75 2.00
28 Ponda Baba U1 .30 .75
29 Prophetess U1 .30 .75
30 R1-G4 (Arone-Geefour) C2 .12 .30
31 R4-M9 (Arfour-Emmnine) C2 .12 .30
32 Stormtrooper C3 .12 .30
33 Tonnika Sisters R1 1.25 3.00
34 Tusken Raider C2 .12 .30
35 WED-9-M1 'Bantha' Droid R2 .75 2.00
36 Wuher U2 .30 .75
37 Blaster Scope U1 .30 .75
38 Caller LIGHT U2 .30 .75
39 Comlink C1 .12 .30
40 Droid Detector C2 .12 .30
41 Fusion Generator Supply Tanks LIGHT C2 .12 .30
42 Observation Holocam U2 .30 .75
43 Restraining Bolt LIGHT C2 .12 .30
44 Stormtrooper Backpack C2 .12 .30
45 Stormtrooper Utility Belt C2 .12 .30
46 A Disturbance In The Force U1 .30 .75
47 Baniss Keeg C2 .12 .30
48 Blast Door Controls U2 .30 .75
49 Blaster Rack U1 .30 .75
50 Dark Hours U2 .30 .75
51 Death Star Sentry U1 .30 .75
52 Disarmed LIGHT R1 1.25 3.00
53 Expand The Empire R1 1.25 3.00
54 Fear Will Keep Them In Line R2 .75 2.00
55 I Find Your Lack Of Faith Disturbing R1 1.25 3.00
56 I've Lost Artoo! U1 .30 .75
57 Jawa Pack U1 .30 .75
58 Juri Juice R2 .75 2.00
59 Ket Maliss C2 .12 .30
60 Lateral Damage R2 .75 2.00
61 Luke's X-34 Landspeeder U1 .30 .75
62 Macroscan C2 .12 .30
63 Molator R1 1.25 3.00
64 Organa's Ceremonial Necklace R1 1.25 3.00
65 Presence Of The Force R1 1.25 3.00
66 Reactor Terminal U2 .30 .75
67 Send A Detachment Down R1 1.25 3.00
68 Sundown U1 .30 .75
69 Tactical Re-Call R2 .75 2.00
70 Wrong Turn U1 .30 .75
71 Your Powers Are Weak, Old Man R1 1.25 3.00
72 Alter LIGHT U1 .30 .75
73 Boring Conversation Anyway R1 1.25 3.00
74 Charming To The Last R2 .75 2.00
75 Collateral Damage C2 .12 .30
76 Counter Assault C1 .12 .30
77 Dark Collaboration R1 1.25 3.00
78 Dark Jedi Presence R1 4.00 10.00
79 Dark Maneuvers C2 .12 .30
80 Dead Jawa C2 .12 .30
81 Elis Helrot U2 .30 .75
82 Emergency Deployment U1 .30 .75
83 Evacuate? U2 .30 .75
84 Full Scale Alert U2 .30 .75
85 Gravel Storm U2 .30 .75
86 I Have You Now R2 .75 2.00
87 I've Got A Problem Here C2 .12 .30
88 Imperial Barrier DARK C2 .12 .30
89 Imperial Code Cylinder C2 .12 .30
90 Imperial Reinforcements C1 .12 .30
91 It's Worse C2 .12 .30
92 Kintan Strider C1 .12 .30
93 Limited Resources U2 .30 .75
94 Local Trouble R1 1.25 3.00
95 Lone Pilot R2 .75 2.00
96 Lone Warrior R2 .75 2.00
97 Look Sir, Droids R1 1.25 3.00
98 Moment Of Triumph R2 .75 2.00
99 Nevar Yalnal R2 .75 2.00
100 Ommni Box C2 .12 .30
101 Overload C2 .12 .30
102 Physical Choke R1 1.25 3.00
103 Precise Attack C2 .12 .30
104 Scanning Crew C2 .12 .30
105 Sense DARK U1 .30 .75
106 Set For Stun C2 .12 .30
107 Takeel C2 .12 .30
108 Tallon Roll C2 .12 .30
109 The Circle Is Now Complete R1 1.25 3.00
110 The Empire's Back U1 .30 .75
111 Trinto Duaba U1 .30 .75
112 Trooper Charge U2 .30 .75
113 Tusken Scavengers C2 .12 .30
114 Utinni! DARK R1 1.25 3.00
115 Vader's Eye R1 1.25 3.00
116 We're All Gonna Be A Lot Thinner! R1 1.25 3.00
117 Your Eyes Can Deceive You U1 .30 .75
118 Y-wing C2 .12 .30
119 Alderaan DARK R1 1.25 3.00
120 Dantooine DARK U1 .30 .75
121 Death Star: Central Core U2 .30 .75
122 Death Star: Detention Block Corridor C1 .12 .30
123 Death Star: Docking Bay 327 DARK C2 .12 .30
124 Death Star: Level 4 Military Corridor U1 .30 .75
125 Death Star: War Room U2 .30 .75
126 Kessel Run R2 .75 2.00
127 Tatooine DARK C2 .12 .30
128 Tatooine: Cantina DARK R2 .75 2.00
129 Tatooine: Docking Bay 94 DARK C2 .12 .30
130 Tatooine: Jawa Camp DARK C1 .12 .30
131 Tatooine: Jundland Wastes C1 .12 .30
132 Tatooine: Lars' Moisture Farm LIGHT C1 .12 .30
133 Tatooine: Mos Eisley DARK C1 .12 .30
134 Yavin 4 LIGHT C2 .12 .30
135 Yavin 4: Docking Bay LIGHT C2 .12 .30
136 Yavin 4: Jungle DARK U2 .30 .75
137 Black 2 R1 2.50 6.00
138 Black 3 U1 .30 .75
139 Devastator R1 2.50 6.00
140 Imperial-Class Star Destroyer U1 .75 2.00
141 TIE Advanced x1 U2 .30 .75
142 TIE Fighter C2 .12 .30
143 TIE Scout C2 .12 .30
144 Vader's Custom TIE R1 4.00 10.00
145 Bantha U2 .30 .75
146 Lift Tube DARK C2 .12 .30
147 Sandcrawler DARK R2 .75 2.00
148 Ubrikkian 9000 Z001 C2 .12 .30
149 Assault Rifle R2 .75 2.00
150 Blaster Rifle LIGHT C1 .12 .30
151 Boosted TIE Cannon U1 .30 .75
152 Dark Jedi Lightsaber U1 .40 1.00
153 Gaderffii Stick C2 .12 .30
154 Han Seeker R2 .75 2.00
155 Imperial Blaster LIGHT C2 .12 .30
156 Ion Cannon U1 .30 .75
157 Laser Projector U2 .30 .75
158 Light Repeating Blaster Rifle R1 1.25 3.00
159 Luke Seeker R2 .75 2.00
160 Timer Mine DARK C2 .12 .30
161 Turbolaser Battery R2 .75 2.00
162 Vader's Lightsaber R1 3.00 8.00
163 2X-3KPR (Tooex) U1 .30 .75

164 Beru Lars U2 .30 .75
165 Biggs Darklighter R2 .75 2.00
166 BoShek U1 .30 .75
167 C-3PO (See-Threepio) R1 3.00 8.00
168 CZ-3 (Seezee-Three) C1 .12 .30
169 Dice Ibegon R2 .75 2.00
170 Dutch R1 2.50 6.00
171 Figrin D'an U2 .30 .75
172 General Dodonna U1 .30 .75
173 Han Solo R1 5.00 12.00
174 Jawa DARK C2 .12 .30
175 Jek Porkins U1 .30 .75
176 Kabe U1 .30 .75
177 Kal'Falnl C'ndros R1 1.25 3.00
178 LIN-V8K (Elleyein-Veeatekay) C1 .12 .30
179 Leesub Sirln R2 .75 2.00
180 Leia Organa R1 4.00 10.00
181 Luke Skywalker R1 6.00 15.00
182 Momaw Nadon U2 .30 .75
183 Obi-Wan Kenobi R1 4.00 10.00
184 Owen Lars U1 .30 .75
185 Pops U1 .30 .75
186 R2-X2 (Artoo-Extoo) C2 .12 .30
187 R4-E1 (Arfour-Eeone) C2 .12 .30
188 Rebel Guard C2 .12 .30
189 Rebel Pilot C2 .12 .30
190 Rebel Trooper C3 .12 .30
191 Red Leader R1 2.50 6.00
192 Shistavanen Wolfman C2 .12 .30
193 Talz C2 .12 .30
194 WED15-1662 'Treadwell' Droid R2 .75 2.00
195 Wioslea U1 .30 .75
196 Caller DARK U2 .30 .75
197 Electrobinoculars C2 .12 .30
198 Fusion Generator Supply Tanks DARK C2 .12 .30
199 Hydroponics Station U2 .30 .75
200 Restraining Bolt DARK C2 .12 .30
201 Targeting Computer U1 .30 .75
202 Tatooine Utility Belt C2 .12 .30
203 Vaporator C2 .12 .30
204 A Tremor In The Force U1 .30 .75
205 Affect Mind R1 1.25 3.00
206 Beggar R1 1.25 3.00
207 Crash Site Memorial U1 .30 .75
208 Death Star Plans R1 1.25 3.00
209 Demotion R2 .75 2.00
210 Disarmed DARK R1 1.25 3.00
211 Ellorrs Madak C2 .12 .30
212 Eyes In The Dark U1 .30 .75
213 Jawa Siesta U1 .30 .75
214 K'lor'slug R1 1.25 3.00
215 Kessel LIGHT U2 .30 .75
216 Lightsaber Proficiency R1 1.25 3.00
217 Mantellian Savrip R2 .75 2.00
218 Nightfall U1 .30 .75
219 Obi-Wan's Cape R1 1.25 3.00
220 Our Most Desperate Hour R1 1.25 3.00
221 Plastoid Armor U2 .30 .75
222 Rebel Planners R2 .75 2.00
223 Restricted Deployment U1 .30 .75
224 Revolution R1 1.25 3.00
225 Rycar Ryjerd U1 .30 .75
226 Sai'torr Kal Fas C2 .12 .30
227 Special Modifications U1 .30 .75
228 Traffic Control U2 .30 .75
229 Tusken Breath Mask U1 .30 .75
230 Yerka Mig U1 .30 .75
231 You Overestimate Their Chances C1 .12 .30
232 A Few Maneuvers C2 .12 .30
233 Alter DARK U1 .30 .75
234 Beru Stew U2 .30 .75
235 Cantina Brawl R1 1.25 3.00
236 Collision! C2 .12 .30
237 Combined Attack C2 .12 .30
238 Don't Get Cocky R1 1.25 3.00
239 Don't Underestimate Our Chances C1 .12 .30
240 Droid Shutdown C2 .12 .30
241 Escape Pod U2 .30 .75
242 Friendly Fire C2 .12 .30
243 Full Throttle R2 .75 2.00
244 Gift Of The Mentor R1 1.25 3.00
245 Han's Back U2 .30 .75
246 Han's Dice C2 .12 .30
247 Hear Me Baby, Hold Together C2 .12 .30
248 Help Me Obi-Wan Kenobi R1 1.25 3.00
249 How Did We Get Into This Mess? U2 .30 .75
250 Hyper Escape C2 .12 .30
251 I've Got A Bad Feeling About This C2 .12 .30
252 Into The Garbage Chute, Flyboy R2 .75 2.00
253 It Could Be Worse C2 .12 .30
254 Jedi Presence R1 1.25 3.00
255 Krayt Dragon Howl R1 1.25 3.00
256 Leia's Back U2 .30 .75
257 Luke? Luuuuke! U1 .30 .75
258 Move Along... R1 1.25 3.00
259 Nabrun Leids U2 .30 .75
260 Narrow Escape C2 .12 .30
261 Noble Sacrifice R2 .75 2.00
262 Old Ben C2 .12 .30
263 On The Edge R2 .75 2.00
264 Out Of Nowhere U2 .30 .75
265 Panic U1 .30 .75
266 Radar Scanner C2 .12 .30
267 Rebel Barrier C2 .12 .30
268 Rebel Reinforcements C1 .12 .30
269 Return Of A Jedi U2 .30 .75
270 Scomp Link Access C2 .12 .30
271 Sense LIGHT U1 .30 .75
272 Skywalkers R1 1.25 3.00
273 Solo Han R2 .75 2.00
274 Spaceport Speeders U2 .30 .75
275 Surprise Assault C1 .12 .30
276 Thank The Maker R2 .75 2.00
277 The Bith Shuffle C2 .12 .30
278 The Force Is Strong With This One R2 .75 2.00
279 This Is All Your Fault U1 .30 .75
280 Utinni! LIGHT R1 1.25 3.00
281 Warrior's Courage R2 .75 2.00
282 We're Doomed C2 .12 .30
283 Alderaan LIGHT U2 .75 2.00
284 Dantooine LIGHT U1 .30 .75
285 Death Star: Detention Block Control Room U2 .30 .75
286 Death Star: Docking Bay 327 LIGHT C2 .12 .30
287 Death Star: Trash Compactor U1 .30 .75
288 Kessel DARK U2 .30 .75
289 Tatooine LIGHT C2 .12 .30
290 Tatooine: Cantina LIGHT R2 .75 2.00
291 Tatooine: Docking Bay 94 LIGHT C2 .12 .30
292 Tatooine: Dune Sea C1 .12 .30
293 Tatooine: Jawa Camp LIGHTC1 .12 .30
294 Tatooine: Lars' Moisture Farm DARK U2 .30 .75
295 Tatooine: Mos Eisley LIGHT U2 .30 .75
296 Tatooine: Obi-Wan's Hut R1 1.25 3.00
297 Yavin 4: Docking Bay DARK C2 .12 .30
298 Yavin 4: Jungle LIGHT C1 .12 .30
299 Yavin 4: Massassi Throne Room R1 1.25 3.00
300 Yavin 4: Massassi War Room U2 .30 .75
301 Yavin Sentry U2 .30 .75
302 Corellian Corvette U2 .40 1.00
303 Gold 1 R2 .75 2.00
304 Gold 5 R2 .75 2.00
305 Millenium Falcon R1 3.00 8.00
306 Red 1 U1 .30 .75
307 Red 3 R2 .75 2.00
308 X-wing C2 .12 .30
309 Yavin 4 DARK C2 .12 .30
310 Lift Tube LIGHT C2 .12 .30
311 Luke's Back U2 .30 .75
312 Sandcrawler LIGHT R2 .75 2.00
313 SoroSuub V-35 Landspeeder C2 .12 .30
314 Blaster C2 .12 .30
315 Blaster Rifle DARK C2 .12 .30
316 Han's Heavy Blaster Pistol R2 .75 2.00
317 Jedi Lightsaber U1 .30 .75
318 Leia's Sporting Blaster U1 .30 .75
319 Obi-Wan's Lightsaber R1 2.50 6.00
320 Proton Torpedoes C2 .12 .30
321 Quad Laser Cannon U1 .30 .75
322 Tagge Seeker R2 .75 2.00
323 Tarkin Seeker R2 .75 2.00
324 Timer Mine LIGHT C2 .12 .30

1996 Star Wars Hoth

COMPLETE SET (163) 50.00 100.00
BOOSTER BOX (36 PACKS) 50.00 100.00
BOOSTER PACK (15 CARDS) 2.00 4.00
RELEASED IN NOVEMBER 1996
1 AT-AT Driver C2 .12 .30
2 Admiral Ozzel R1 1.25 3.00
3 Captain Lennox U1 .40 1.00
4 Captain Piett R2 1.25 3.00
5 FX-10 (Effex-ten) C2 .12 .30
6 General Veers R1 3.00 8.00
7 Imperial Gunner C2 .12 .30
8 Lieutenant Cabbel U2 .40 1.00
9 Probe Droid C2 .12 .30
10 Snowtrooper C3 .12 .30
11 Snowtrooper Officer C1 .12 .30
12 Wampa R2 1.25 3.00
13 Deflector Shield Generators U2 .40 1.00
14 Evacuation Control U1 .40 1.00
15 Portable Fusion Generator C2 .12 .30
16 Probe Antennae U2 .40 1.00
17 Breached Defenses U2 .40 1.00
18 Death Mark R1 1.25 3.00
19 Death Squadron U1 .40 1.00
20 Frostbite LIGHT C2 .12 .30
21 Frozen Dinner R1 1.25 3.00
22 High Anxiety R1 1.25 3.00
23 Ice Storm LIGHT U1 .40 1.00
24 Image Of The Dark Lord R2 1.25 3.00
25 Imperial Domination U1 .40 1.00
26 Meteor Impact? R1 1.25 3.00
27 Mournful Roar R1 1.25 3.00
28 Responsibility Of Command R1 1.25 3.00
29 Silence Is Golden U2 .40 1.00
30 The Shield Doors Must Be Closed U1 .40 1.00
31 This Is Just Wrong R1 1.25 3.00
32 Too Cold For Speeders U1 .40 1.00
33 Weapon Malfunction R1 1.25 3.00
34 Target The Main Generator R2 1.25 3.00
35 A Dark Time For The Rebellion C1 .12 .30
36 Cold Feet C2 .12 .30
37 Collapsing Corridor R2 1.25 3.00
38 ComScan Detection C2 .12 .30
39 Crash Landing U1 .40 1.00
40 Debris Zone R2 1.25 3.00
41 Direct Hit U1 .40 1.00
42 Exhaustion U2 .40 1.00
43 Exposure U1 .40 1.00
44 Furry Fury R2 1.25 3.00
45 He Hasn't Come Back Yet C2 .12 .30
46 I'd Just As Soon Kiss A Wookiee C2 .12 .30
47 Imperial Supply C1 .12 .30
48 Lightsaber Deficiency U1 .40 1.00
49 Oh, Switch Off C2 .12 .30
50 Our First Catch Of The Day C2 .12 .30
51 Probe Telemetry C2 .12 .30
52 Scruffy-Looking Nerf Herder R2 1.25 3.00
53 Self-Destruct Mechanism U1 .40 1.00
54 Stop Motion C2 .12 .30
55 Tactical Support R2 1.25 3.00
56 That's It, The Rebels Are There! U2 .40 1.00
57 Trample R1 1.25 3.00
58 Turn It Off! Turn It Off! C1 .12 .30
59 Walker Barrage U1 .40 1.00
60 Wall Of Fire U1 .40 1.00
61 Yaggle Gakkle R2 1.25 3.00
62 Hoth DARK U2 .40 1.00
63 Hoth: Defensive Perimeter LIGHT C2 .12 .30
64 Hoth: Echo Command Center (War Room) LIGHT U2 .40 1.00
65 Hoth: Echo Corridor DARK U2 .40 1.00
66 Hoth: Echo Docking Bay LIGHT C2 .12 .30
67 Hoth: Ice Plains C2 .12 .30
68 Hoth: North Ridge LIGHT C2 .12 .30
69 Hoth: Wampa Cave R2 1.25 3.00
70 Ord Mantell LIGHT U2 .40 1.00
71 Stalker R1 4.00 10.00
72 Tyrant R1 3.00 8.00
73 Blizzard 1 R1 2.50 6.00
74 Blizzard 2 R2 1.25 3.00
75 Blizzard Scout 1 R1 2.50 6.00
76 Blizzard Walker U2 .40 1.00
77 AT-AT Cannon U1 .40 1.00
78 Echo Base Operations R2 1.25 3.00
79 Infantry Mine LIGHT C2 .12 .30
80 Probe Droid Laser U2 .40 1.00
81 Vehicle Mine LIGHT C2 .12 .30
82 2-1B (Too-Onebee) R1 1.25 3.00
83 Cal Alder U2 .40 1.00
84 Commander Luke Skywalker R1 6.00 15.00
85 Dack Ralter R2 1.25 3.00
86 Derek 'Hobbie' Klivian U1 .40 1.00
87 Electro-Rangefinder U1 .40 1.00
88 Echo Base Trooper Officer C1 .12 .30
89 Echo Trooper Backpack C2 .12 .30
90 FX-7 (Effex-Seven) C2 .12 .30
91 General Carlist Rieekan R2 1.25 3.00
92 Jeroen Webb U1 .40 1.00
93 K-3PO (Kay-Threepio) R1 1.25 3.00
94 Major Bren Derlin R2 1.25 3.00
95 R2 Sensor Array C2 .12 .30
96 R5-M2 (Arfive-Emmtoo) C2 .12 .30
97 Rebel Scout C1 .12 .30
98 Rogue Gunner C2 .12 .30
99 Romas Lock Navander U2 .40 1.00
100 Shawn Valdez U1 .40 1.00
101 Tamizander Rey U2 .40 1.00
102 Tauntaun Handler C2 .12 .30
103 Tigran Jamiro U1 .40 1.00
104 Toryn Farr U1 .40 1.00
105 WED-1016 'Techie' Droid C1 .12 .30
106 Wes Janson R2 1.25 3.00
107 Wyron Serper U2 .40 1.00
108 Zev Senesca R2 1.25 3.00
109 Artillery Remote R2 1.25 3.00
110 EG-4 (Eegee-Four) C1 .12 .30
111 Hoth LIGHT U2 .40 1.00
112 R-3PO (Ar-Threepio) LIGHT R2 1.25 3.00
112 R-3PO (Ar-Threepio) DARK R2 1.25 3.00
113 Bacta Tank R2 2.00 5.00
114 Disarming Creature R1 1.25 3.00
115 Echo Base Trooper C3 .12 .30
116 E-web Blaster C1 .12 .30
117 Frostbite DARK C2 .12 .30
118 Ice Storm DARK U1 .40 1.00
119 Tauntaun Bones U1 .40 1.00
120 The First Transport Is Away! R1 1.25 3.00
121 Attack Pattern Delta U1 .40 1.00
122 Dark Dissension R1 1.25 3.00
123 Fall Back! C2 .12 .30
124 I Thought They Smelled Bad On The Outside R1 1.25 3.00
125 It Can Wait C2 .12 .30
126 Lucky Shot U1 .40 1.00
127 Nice Of You Guys To Drop By C2 .12 .30
128 One More Pass U1 .40 1.00
129 Perimeter Scan C2 .12 .30
130 Rug Hug R1 1.25 3.00
131 Under Attack U1 .40 1.00
132 Walker Sighting U2 .40 1.00
133 Who's Scruffy-Looking? R1 1.25 3.00
134 You Have Failed Me For The Last Time R1 1.25 3.00
135 You Will Go To The Dagobah System R1 1.25 3.00
136 Hoth Survival Gear C2 .12 .30
137 Hoth: Defensive Perimeter DARK C2 .12 .30
138 Hoth: Echo Command Center (War Room) DARK U2 .40 1.00
139 Hoth: Echo Corridor LIGHT C2 .12 .30
140 Hoth: Echo Docking Bay DARK C2 .12 .30
141 Hoth: Echo Med Lab C2 .12 .30
142 Hoth: Main Power Generators U2 .40 1.00
143 Hoth: North Ridge DARK C2 .12 .30
144 Hoth: Snow Trench C2 .12 .30
145 Ord Mantell DARK C2 .12 .30
146 Medium Transport U2 .40 1.00
147 Rogue 1 R1 2.50 6.00
148 Rogue 2 R2 1.25 3.00
149 Rogue 3 R1 2.50 6.00
150 Snowspeeder U2 .40 1.00
151 Tauntaun C2 .12 .30
152 Anakin's Lightsaber R1 6.00 15.00
153 Atgar Laser Cannon U2 .40 1.00
154 Concussion Grenade R1 1.25 3.00
155 Dual Laser Cannon U1 .40 1.00
156 Golan Laser Battery U1 .40 1.00
157 Infantry Mine DARK C2 .12 .30
158 Medium Repeating Blaster Cannon C1 .12 .30
159 Planet Defender Ion Cannon R2 1.25 3.00
160 Power Harpoon U1 .40 1.00
161 Surface Defense Cannon R2 1.25 3.00
162 Vehicle Mine DARK C2 .12 .30

1996 Star Wars Jedi Pack

COMPLETE SET (11) 3.00 8.00
1 Hyperoute Navigation Chart PM .40 1.00
2 Dark Forces PM .40 1.00
3 Eriadu PM .40 1.00
4 For Luck PM .40 1.00
5 Gravity Shadow PM .40 1.00
6 Han PM .40 1.00
7 Leia PM .40 1.00
8 Luke's T-16 Skyhopper PM .40 1.00
9 Motti PM .40 1.00
10 Tarkin PM .40 1.00
11 Tedn Dahai PM .40 1.00

1996 Star Wars A New Hope

COMPLETE SET (162) 50.00 100.00
BOOSTER BOX (36 PACKS) 50.00 100.00
BOOSTER PACK (15 CARDS) 2.00 4.00
RELEASED IN JULY 1996
1 Advosze C2 .12 .30
2 Captain Khurgee U1 .40 1.00
3 DS-61-4 R2 1.25 3.00
4 Dannik Jerriko R1 1.25 3.00
5 Danz Borin U2 .40 1.00
6 Death Star R2 4.00 10.00
7 Defel C2 .12 .30
8 Greedo R1 3.00 8.00
9 Hem Dazon R1 1.25 3.00
10 IT-O (Eyetee-Oh) R1 1.25 3.00
11 Imperial Commander C2 .12 .30
12 Imperial Squad Leader C3 .12 .30
13 Lirin Car'n U2 .40 1.00
14 Lt. Pol Treidum C1 .12 .30
15 Lt. Shann Childsen U1 .40 1.00
16 Mosep U2 .40 1.00
17 Officer Evax C1 .12 .30
18 R2-Q2 (Artoo-Kyootoo) C2 .12 .30
19 R3-T6 (Arthree-Teesix) R1 1.25 3.00
20 R5-A2 (Arfive-Aytoo) C2 .12 .30
21 Reegesk U2 .40 1.00
22 Reserve Pilot U1 .40 1.00
23 Rodian C2 .12 .30
24 Tech Mo'r U2 .40 1.00
25 Trooper Davin Felth R2 1.25 3.00
26 U-3PO (Yoo-Threepio) R1 1.25 3.00
27 URoRRuR'R'R U2 .40 1.00
28 WED15-I7 'Septoid' Droid U2 .40 1.00
29 Dianoga R2 1.25 3.00
30 Death Star Tractor Beam R2 1.25 3.00
31 Hypo R1 1.25 3.00
32 Laser Gate U2 .40 1.00
33 Maneuver Check R2 1.25 3.00
34 Tractor Beam U1 .40 1.00
35 Astromech Shortage U2 .40 1.00
36 Besieged R2 1.25 3.00
37 Come With Me C2 .12 .30
38 Dark Waters R2 1.25 3.00
39 Hyperwave Scan U1 .40 1.00
40 Imperial Justice C2 .12 .30
41 Krayt Dragon Bones U1 .40 1.00
42 Merc Sunlet C2 .12 .30
43 Program Trap U1 .40 1.00
44 Spice Mines Of Kessel R1 1.25 3.00
45 Swilla Corey C2 .12 .30
46 Tentacle C2 .12 .30
47 There'll Be Hell To Pay U2 .40 1.00
48 Undercover LIGHT U2 .40 1.00
49 Commence Primary Ignition R2 1.25 3.00
50 Evader U1 .40 1.00
51 Ghhhk C2 .12 .30
52 I'm On The Leader R1 1.25 3.00
53 Informant U1 .40 1.00
54 Monnok C2 .12 .30
55 Ng'ok C2 .12 .30
56 Oo-ta Goo-ta, Solo? C2 .12 .30
57 Retract the Bridge R1 1.25 3.00
58 Sniper U1 .40 1.00
59 Stunning Leader C2 .12 .30
60 This Is Some Rescue! U1 .40 1.00
61 We Have A Prisoner C2 .12 .30
62 Death Star Gunner C1 .12 .30
63 Death Star: Conference Room U1 .40 1.00
64 Imperial Holotable R1 1.25 3.00
65 Kashyyyk LIGHTC1 .12 .30
66 Kiffex R1 1.25 3.00
67 Ralltiir LIGHT C1 .12 .30
68 Sandcrawler: Droid Junkheap R1 1.25 3.00
69 Tatooine: Bluffs R1 1.25 3.00
70 Black 4 U2 .40 1.00
71 Conquest R1 4.00 10.00
72 TIE Assault Squadron U1 .40 1.00
73 TIE Vanguard C2 .12 .30
74 Victory-Class Star Destroyer U1 .40 1.00
75 Bespin Motors Void Spider THX 1138 C2 .12 .30
76 Mobquet A-1 Deluxe Floater C2 .12 .30
77 Enhanced TIE Laser Cannon C2 .12 .30
78 Jawa Blaster C2 .12 .30
79 Leia Seeker R2 1.25 3.00
80 Superlaser R2 2.00 5.00
81 URoRRuR'R'R's Hunting Rifle U1 .40 1.00
82 Arcona C2 .12 .30
83 Brainiac R1 2.50 6.00
84 Chewbacca R2 6.00 15.00
85 Commander Evram Lajaie C1 .12 .30
86 Commander Vanden Willard U2 .40 1.00
87 Corellian C2 .12 .30
88 Doikk Na'ts U2 .40 1.00
89 Garouf Lafoe U2 .40 1.00
90 Het Nkik U2 .40 1.00
91 Hunchback R1 1.25 3.00
92 Ickabel G'ont U2 .40 1.00
93 Magnetic Suction Tube DARK R2 1.25 3.00
94 Nalan Cheel U2 .40 1.00
95 R2-D2 (Artoo-Detoo) R2 6.00 15.00
96 R5-D4 (Arfive-Defour) C2 .12 .30
97 RA-7 (Aray-Seven) C2 .12 .30
98 Rebel Commander C2 .12 .30
99 Rebel Squad Leader C3 .12 .30
100 Rebel Tech C1 .12 .30
101 Saurin C2 .12 .30
102 Tiree U2 .40 1.00
103 Tzizvvt R2 1.25 3.00
104 Wedge Antilles R1 6.00 15.00
105 Zutton C1 .12 .30
106 Fire Extinguisher U2 .40 1.00
107 Magnetic Suction Tube LIGHT R2 1.25 3.00
108 Rectenna C2 .12 .30
109 Remote C2 .12 .30
110 Sensor Panel U1 .40 1.00
111 Cell 2187 R1 1.25 3.00
112 Commence Recharging R2 1.25 3.00
113 Eject! Eject! C2 .12 .30
114 Grappling Hook C2 .12 .30
115 Logistical Delay U2 .40 1.00
116 Luke's Cape R1 1.25 3.00
117 M-HYD 'Binary' Droid U1 .40 1.00
118 Scanner Techs U1 .40 1.00
119 Solomahal C2 .12 .30
120 They're On Dantooine R1 1.25 3.00
121 Undercover DARK U2 .40 1.00
122 What're You Tryin' To Push On Us? U2 .40 1.00
123 Attack Run R2 1.25 3.00
124 Advance Preparation U1 .40 1.00
125 Alternatives To Fighting U1 .40 1.00
126 Blast The Door, Kid! C2 .12 .30
127 Blue Milk C2 .12 .30
128 Corellian Slip C2 .12 .30
129 Double Agent R2 1.25 3.00
130 Grimtaash C2 .12 .30
131 Houjix C2 .12 .30
132 I Have A Very Bad Feeling About This C2 .12 .30
133 I'm Here To Rescue You U1 .40 1.00
134 Let The Wookiee Win R1 5.00 12.00
135 Out Of Commission U2 .40 1.00
136 Quite A Mercenary C2 .12 .30
137 Sabotage U1 .40 1.00
138 Sorry About The Mess U1 .40 1.00
139 Wookiee Roar R1 1.25 3.00
140 Y-wing Assault Squadron U1 .40 1.00
141 Clak'dor VII R2 1.25 3.00
142 Corellia R1 1.25 3.00
143 Death Star: Trench R2 1.25 3.00
144 Dejarik Hologameboard R1 1.25 3.00
145 Kashyyyk DARK C1 .12 .30
146 Ralltiir DARK C1 .12 .30
147 Sandcrawler: Loading Bay R1 1.25 3.00
148 Yavin 4: Massassi Ruins U1 .40 1.00
149 You're All Clear Kid! R1 1.25 3.00
150 Gold 2 U1 .40 1.00
151 Red 2 R1 1.25 3.00
152 Red 5 R1 3.00 8.00
153 Red 6 U1 .40 1.00
154 Tantive IV R1 4.00 10.00
155 Yavin 4: Briefing Room U1 .40 1.00
156 Incom T-16 Skyhopper C2 .12 .30
157 Rogue Bantha U1 .40 1.00
158 Bowcaster R2 1.25 3.00
159 Jawa Ion Gun C2 .12 .30
160 Luke's Hunting Rifle U1 .40 1.00
161 Motti Seeker R2 1.25 3.00
162 SW-4 Ion Cannon R2 1.25 3.00

1997 Star Wars Cloud City

COMPLETE SET (180) 50.00 100.00
BOOSTER BOX (60 PACKS) 50.00 100.00
BOOSTER PACK (9 CARDS) 2.00 4.00
RELEASED IN NOVEMBER 1997
1 Ability, Ability, Ability C .12 .30
2 Abyss U .40 1.00
3 Access Denied C .12 .30
4 Advantage R 1.25 3.00
5 Aiiii! Aaa! Agggggggggg! R 1.25 3.00
6 All My Urchins R 1.25 3.00
7 All Too Easy R 1.25 3.00
8 Ambush R 1.25 3.00
9 Armed And Dangerous U .40 1.00
10 Artoo, Come Back At Once! R 1.25 3.00
11 As Good As Gone C .12 .30
12 Atmospheric Assault R 1.25 3.00
13 Beldon's Eye R 1.25 3.00
14 Bespin DARK U .40 1.00
15 Bespin LIGHT U .40 1.00
16 Bespin: Cloud City DARK U .40 1.00
17 Bespin: Cloud City LIGHT U .40 1.00
18 Binders C .12 .30
19 Bionic Hand R 1.25 3.00
20 Blasted Droid C .12 .30
21 Blaster Proficiency C .12 .30
22 Boba Fett R 8.00 20.00
23 Boba Fett's Blaster Rifle R 3.00 8.00
24 Bounty C .12 .30
25 Brief Loss Of Control R 1.25 3.00
26 Bright Hope R 1.25 3.00
27 Captain Bewil R 1.25 3.00
28 Captain Han Solo R 8.00 20.00
29 Captive Fury U .40 1.00
30 Captive Pursuit C .12 .30
31 Carbon-Freezing U .40 1.00
32 Carbonite Chamber Console U .40 1.00
33 Chasm U .40 1.00
34 Chief Retwin R 1.25 3.00
35 Civil Disorder C .12 .30
36 Clash Of Sabers U .40 1.00
37 Cloud Car DARK C .12 .30
38 Cloud Car LIGHT C .12 .30
39 Cloud City Blaster DARK C .12 .30
40 Cloud City Blaster LIGHT C .12 .30
41 Cloud City Engineer C .12 .30
42 Cloud City Sabacc DARK U .40 1.00
43 Cloud City Sabacc LIGHT U .40 1.00
44 Cloud City Technician C .12 .30
45 Cloud City Trooper DARK C .12 .30
46 Cloud City Trooper LIGHT C .12 .30
47 Cloud City: Carbonite Chamber DARK U .40 1.00
48 Cloud City: Carbonite Chamber LIGHT U .40 1.00
49 Cloud City: Chasm Walkway DARK C .12 .30
50 Cloud City: Chasm Walkway LIGHT C .12 .30
51 Cloud City: Dining Room R 1.25 3.00
52 Cloud City: East Platform (Docking Bay) C .12 .30
53 Cloud City: Guest Quarters R 1.25 3.00
54 Cloud City: Incinerator DARK C .12 .30
55 Cloud City: Incinerator LIGHT C .12 .30

- 56 Cloud City: Lower Corridor DARK U .40 1.00
- 57 Cloud City: Lower Corridor LIGHT U .40 1.00
- 58 Cloud City: Platform 327 (Docking Bay) C .12 .30
- 59 Cloud City: Security Tower C .12 .30
- 60 Cloud City: Upper Plaza Corridor DARK C .12 .30
- 61 Cloud City: Upper Plaza Corridor LIGHT U .40 1.00
- 62 Clouds DARK C .12 .30
- 63 Clouds LIGHT C .12 .30
- 64 Commander Desanne U .40 1.00
- 65 Computer Interface C .12 .30
- 66 Courage Of A Skywalker R 1.25 3.00
- 67 Crack Shot U .40 1.00
- 68 Cyborg Construct U .40 1.00
- 69 Dark Approach R 1.25 3.00
- 70 Dark Deal R 1.25 3.00
- 71 Dark Strike C .12 .30
- 72 Dash C .12 .30
- 73 Despair R 1.25 3.00
- 74 Desperate Reach U .40 1.00
- 75 Dismantle On Sight R 1.25 3.00
- 76 Dodge C .12 .30
- 77 Double Back U .40 1.00
- 78 Double-Crossing, No-Good Swindler C .12 .30
- 79 E Chu Ta C .12 .30
- 80 E-3PO R 1.25 3.00
- 81 End This Destructive Conflict R 1.25 3.00
- 82 Epic Duel R 2.00 5.00
- 83 Fall Of The Empire U .40 1.00
- 84 Fall Of The Legend U .40 1.00
- 85 Flight Escort R 1.25 3.00
- 86 Focused Attack R 1.25 3.00
- 87 Force Field R 1.25 3.00
- 88 Forced Landing R 1.25 3.00
- 89 Frozen Assets R 1.25 3.00
- 90 Gambler's Luck R 1.25 3.00
- 91 Glancing Blow R 1.25 3.00
- 92 Haven R 1.25 3.00
- 93 He's All Yours, Bounty Hunter R 1.25 3.00
- 94 Heart Of The Chasm U .40 1.00
- 95 Hero Of A Thousand Devices U .40 1.00
- 96 Higher Ground R 1.25 3.00
- 97 Hindsight R 1.25 3.00
- 98 Hopping Mad R 1.25 3.00
- 99 Human Shield C .12 .30
- 100 I Am Your Father R 1.25 3.00
- 101 I Don't Need Their Scum, Either R 1.25 3.00
- 102 I Had No Choice R 1.25 3.00
- 103 Imperial Decree U .40 1.00
- 104 Imperial Trooper Guard Dainsom U .40 1.00
- 105 Impressive, Most Impressive R 1.25 3.00
- 106 Innocent Scoundrel U .40 1.00
- 107 Interrogation Array R 1.25 3.00
- 108 Into The Ventilation Shaft, Lefty R 1.25 3.00
- 109 It's A Trap! U .40 1.00
- 110 Kebyc U .40 1.00
- 111 Keep Your Eyes Open C .12 .30
- 112 Lando Calrissian DARK R 5.00 12.00
- 113 Lando Calrissian LIGHT R 5.00 12.00
- 114 Lando's Wrist Comlink U .40 1.00
- 115 Leia Of Alderaan R 2.00 5.00
- 116 Levitation Attack U .40 1.00
- 117 Lieutenant Cecius U .40 1.00
- 118 Lieutenant Sheckil R 1.25 3.00
- 119 Lift Tube Escape C .12 .30
- 120 Lobot R 2.50 6.00
- 121 Luke's Blaster Pistol R 1.25 3.00
- 122 Mandalorian Armor R 2.00 5.00
- 123 Mostly Armless R 1.25 3.00
- 124 NOOOOOOOOOOOO! R 1.25 3.00
- 125 Obsidian 7 R 2.00 5.00
- 126 Obsidian 8 R 2.00 5.00
- 127 Off The Edge R 1.25 3.00
- 128 Old Pirates R 1.25 3.00
- 129 Out Of Somewhere U .40 1.00
- 130 Path Of Least Resistance C .12 .30
- 131 Point Man R 1.25 3.00
- 132 Prepare The Chamber U .40 1.00
- 133 Princess Leia R 4.00 10.00
- 134 Projective Telepathy U .40 1.00
- 135 Protector R 1.25 3.00
- 136 Punch It! R 1.25 3.00
- 137 Put That Down C .12 .30
- 138 Redemption R 2.50 6.00
- 139 Release Your Anger R 1.25 3.00
- 140 Rendezvous Point On Tatooine R 1.25 3.00
- 141 Rescue In The Clouds C .12 .30
- 142 Restricted Access C .12 .30
- 143 Rite Of Passage C .12 .30
- 144 Shattered Hope U .40 1.00
- 145 Shocking Information C .12 .30
- 146 Shocking Revelation C .12 .30
- 147 Slave I R 4.00 10.00
- 148 Slip Sliding Away R 1.25 3.00
- 149 Smoke Screen R 1.25 3.00
- 150 Somersault C .12 .30
- 151 Sonic Bombardment U .40 1.00
- 152 Special Delivery C .12 .30
- 153 Surprise R 1.25 3.00
- 154 Surreptitious Glance R 1.25 3.00
- 155 Swing-And-A-Miss U .40 1.00
- 156 The Emperor's Prize R 1.25 3.00
- 157 This Is Even Better R 1.25 3.00
- 158 This Is Still Wrong R 1.25 3.00
- 159 Tibanna Gas Miner DARK C .12 .30
- 160 Tibanna Gas Miner LIGHT C .12 .30
- 161 TIE Sentry Ships C .12 .30
- 162 Treva Horme U .40 1.00
- 163 Trooper Assault C .12 .30
- 164 Trooper Jerrol Blendin U .40 1.00
- 165 Trooper Utris M'toc U .40 1.00
- 166 Ugloste R 1.25 3.00
- 167 Ugnaught C .12 .30
- 168 Uncontrollable Fury R 1.25 3.00
- 169 Vader's Bounty R 1.25 3.00
- 170 Vader's Cape R 1.25 3.00
- 171 We'll Find Han R 1.25 3.00
- 172 We're The Bait R 1.25 3.00
- 173 Weapon Levitation U .40 1.00
- 174 Weapon Of An Ungrateful Son U .40 1.00
- 175 Weather Vane DARK U .40 1.00
- 176 Weather Vane LIGHT U .40 1.00
- 177 Why Didn't You Tell Me? R 1.25 3.00
- 178 Wiorkettle U .40 1.00
- 179 Wookiee Strangle R 1.25 3.00
- 180 You Are Beaten U .40 1.00

1997 Star Wars Dagobah

- COMPLETE SET (181) 50.00 100.00
- BOOSTER BOX (60 PACKS) 50.00 100.00
- BOOSTER PACK (9 CARDS) 1.50 3.00
- RELEASED ON APRIL 23, 1997
- 1 3,720 To 1 C .12 .30
- 2 4-LOM R 2.50 6.00
- 3 4-LOM's Concussion Rifle R 2.00 5.00
- 4 A Dangerous Time C .12 .30
- 5 A Jedi's Strength U .40 1.00
- 6 Anger, Fear, Aggression C .12 .30
- 7 Anoat DARK U .40 1.00
- 8 Anoat LIGHT U .40 1.00
- 9 Apology Accepted C .12 .30
- 10 Asteroid Field DARK C .12 .30
- 11 Asteroid Field LIGHT C .12 .30
- 12 Asteroid Sanctuary C .12 .30
- 13 Asteroids Do Not Concern Me R 1.25 3.00
- 14 Astroid Sanctuary C .12 .30
- 15 Astromech Translator C .12 .30
- 16 At Peace R 1.25 3.00
- 17 Avenger R 4.00 10.00
- 18 Away Put Your Weapon U .40 1.00
- 19 Awwww, Cannot Get Your Ship Out C .12 .30
- 20 Bad Feeling Have I R 1.25 3.00
- 21 Big One DARK U .40 1.00
- 22 Big One LIGHT U .40 1.00
- 23 Big One: Asteroid Cave or Space Slug Belly DARK U .40 1.00
- 24 Big One: Asteroid Cave or Space Slug Belly LIGHT U .40 1.00
- 25 Blasted Varmints C .12 .30
- 26 Bog-wing DARK C .12 .30
- 27 Bog-wing LIGHT C .12 .30
- 28 Bombing Run R 1.25 3.00
- 29 Bossk R 3.00 8.00
- 30 Bossk's Mortar Gun R 2.00 5.00
- 31 Broken Concentration R 1.25 3.00
- 32 Captain Needa R 2.00 5.00
- 33 Close Call C .12 .30
- 34 Closer?! U .40 1.00
- 35 Comm Chief C .12 .30
- 36 Commander Brandei U .40 1.00
- 37 Commander Gherant U .40 1.00
- 38 Commander Nemet U .40 1.00
- 39 Control DARK U .40 1.00
- 40 Control LIGHT U .40 1.00
- 41 Corporal Derdram U .40 1.00
- 42 Corporal Vandolay U .40 1.00
- 43 Corrosive Damage R 1.25 3.00
- 44 Dagobah U .40 1.00
- 45 Dagobah: Bog Clearing R 1.25 3.00
- 46 Dagobah: Cave R 1.25 3.00
- 47 Dagobah: Jungle U .40 1.00
- 48 Dagobah: Swamp U .40 1.00
- 49 Dagobah: Training Area C .12 .30
- 50 Dagobah: Yoda's Hut R 2.00 5.00
- 51 Defensive Fire C .12 .30
- 52 Dengar R 1.25 3.00
- 53 Dengar's Blaster Carbine R 1.25 3.00
- 54 Descent Into The Dark R 1.25 3.00
- 55 Do, Or Do Not C .12 .30
- 56 Domain Of Evil U .40 1.00
- 57 Dragonsnake R 1.25 3.00
- 58 Droid Sensorscope C .12 .30
- 59 Effective Repairs R 1.25 3.00
- 60 Egregious Pilot Error R 1.25 3.00
- 61 Encampment C .12 .30
- 62 Executor R 8.00 20.00
- 63 Executor: Comm Station U .40 1.00
- 64 Executor: Control Station U .40 1.00
- 65 Executor: Holotheatre R 1.25 3.00
- 66 Executor: Main Corridor C .12 .30
- 67 Executor: Meditation Chamber R 1.25 3.00
- 68 Failure At The Cave R 1.25 3.00
- 69 Fear C .12 .30
- 70 Field Promotion R 1.25 3.00
- 71 Flagship R 1.25 3.00
- 72 Flash Of Insight U .40 1.00
- 73 Found Someone You Have U .40 1.00
- 74 Frustration R 1.25 3.00
- 75 Great Warrior C .12 .30
- 76 Grounded Starfighter U .40 1.00
- 77 Han's Toolkit R 1.25 3.00
- 78 He Is Not Ready C .12 .30
- 79 Hiding In The Garbage R 1.25 3.00
- 80 HoloNet Transmission U .40 1.00
- 81 Hound's Tooth R 2.50 6.00
- 82 I Have A Bad Feeling About This R 1.25 3.00
- 83 I Want That Ship R 1.25 3.00
- 84 IG-2000 R 2.00 5.00
- 85 IG-88 R 4.00 10.00
- 86 IG-88's Neural Inhibitor R 2.00 5.00
- 87 IG-88's Pulse Cannon R 2.00 5.00
- 88 Imbalance U .40 1.00
- 89 Imperial Helmsman C .12 .30
- 90 Ineffective Maneuver U .40 1.00
- 91 It Is The Future You See R 1.25 3.00
- 92 Jedi Levitation R 1.25 3.00
- 93 Knowledge And Defense C .12 .30
- 94 Landing Claw R 1.25 3.00
- 95 Lando System? R 1.25 3.00
- 96 Levitation U .40 1.00
- 97 Lieutenant Commander Ardan U .40 1.00
- 98 Lieutenant Suba R 1.25 3.00
- 99 Lieutenant Venka U .40 1.00
- 100 Light Maneuvers R 1.25 3.00
- 101 Location, Location, Location R 1.25 3.00
- 102 Lost In Space R 1.25 3.00
- 103 Lost Relay C .12 .30
- 104 Luke's Backpack R 1.25 3.00
- 105 Mist Hunter R 2.00 5.00
- 106 Moving To Attack Position C .12 .30
- 107 Much Anger In Him R 1.25 3.00
- 108 Mynock DARK C .12 .30
- 109 Mynock LIGHT C .12 .30
- 110 Never Tell Me The Odds C .12 .30
- 111 No Disintegrations! R 1.25 3.00
- 112 Nudj C .12 .30
- 113 Obi-Wan's Apparition R 1.25 3.00
- 114 Order To Engage R 1.25 3.00
- 115 Polarized Negative Power Coupling R 1.25 3.00
- 116 Portable Fusion Generator C .12 .30
- 117 Precision Targeting U .40 1.00
- 118 Proton Bombs U .40 1.00
- 119 Punishing One R 2.00 5.00
- 120 Quick Draw C .12 .30
- 121 Raithal DARK R 1.25 3.00
- 122 Raithal LIGHT U .40 1.00
- 123 Rebel Flight Suit C .12 .30
- 124 Recoil In Fear C .12 .30
- 125 Reflection R 1.25 3.00
- 126 Report To Lord Vader R 1.25 3.00
- 127 Res Luk Ra'auf R 1.25 3.00
- 128 Retractable Arm C .12 .30
- 129 Rogue Asteroid DARK C .12 .30
- 130 Rogue Asteroid LIGHT C .12 .30
- 131 Rycar's Run R 1.25 3.00
- 132 Scramble U .40 1.00
- 133 Shoo! Shoo! U .40 1.00
- 134 Shot In The Dark U .40 1.00
- 135 Shut Him Up Or Shut Him Down U .40 1.00
- 136 Size Matters Not R 1.25 3.00
- 137 Sleen C .12 .30
- 138 Smuggler's Blues R 1.25 3.00
- 139 Something Hit Us! U .40 1.00
- 140 Son of Skywalker R 8.00 20.00
- 141 Space Slug DARK R 1.25 3.00
- 142 Space Slug LIGHT U .40 1.00
- 143 Star Destroyer: Launch Bay C .12 .30
- 144 Starship Levitation U .40 1.00
- 145 Stone Pile R 1.25 3.00
- 146 Sudden Impact U .40 1.00
- 147 Take Evasive Action C .12 .30
- 148 The Dark Path R 1.25 3.00
- 149 The Professor R 1.25 3.00
- 150 There Is No Try C .12 .30
- 151 They'd Be Crazy To Follow Us C .12 .30
- 152 This Is More Like It R 1.25 3.00
- 153 This Is No Cave R 1.25 3.00
- 154 Those Rebels Won't Escape Us C .12 .30
- 155 Through The Force Things You Will See R 1.25 3.00
- 156 TIE Avenger C .12 .30
- 157 TIE Bomber U .40 1.00
- 158 Tight Squeeze R 1.25 3.00
- 159 Transmission Terminated U .40 1.00
- 160 Tunnel Vision U .40 1.00
- 161 Uncertain Is The Future C .12 .30
- 162 Unexpected Interruption R 1.25 3.00
- 163 Vine Snake DARK C .12 .30
- 164 Vine Snake LIGHT C .12 .30
- 165 Visage Of The Emperor R 1.25 3.00
- 166 Visored Vision C .12 .30
- 167 Voyeur C .12 .30
- 168 Warrant Officer M'Kae U .40 1.00
- 169 Wars Not Make One Great U .40 1.00
- 170 We Can Still Outmaneuver Them R 1.25 3.00
- 171 We Don't Need Their Scum R 1.25 3.00
- 172 WHAAAAAAAAAOOOW! R 1.25 3.00
- 173 What Is Thy Bidding, My Master? R 1.25 3.00
- 174 Yoda R 8.00 20.00
- 175 Yoda Stew U .40 1.00
- 176 Yoda, You Seek Yoda R 1.25 3.00
- 177 Yoda's Gimer Stick R 1.25 3.00
- 178 Yoda's Hope U .40 1.00
- 179 You Do Have Your Moments U .40 1.00
- 180 Zuckuss R 2.00 5.00
- 181 Zuckuss' Snare Rifle R 1.25 3.00

1997 Star Wars First Anthology

- COMPLETE SET (6) 3.00 8.00
- 1 Boba Fett PV .75 2.00
- 2 Commander Wedge Antilles PV .75 2.00
- 3 Death Star Assault Squadron PV .75 2.00
- 4 Hit And Run PV .75 2.00
- 5 Jabba's Influence PV .75 2.00
- 6 X-wing Assault Squadron PV .75 2.00

1997 Star Wars Rebel Leaders

- COMPLETE SET (2) 1.25 3.00
- 1 Gold Leader In Gold 1 PM 1.00 2.50
- 2 Red Leader In Red 1 PM 1.00 2.50

1998 Star Wars Enhanced Premiere

- COMPLETE SET (6) 3.00 8.00
- 1 Boba Fett With Blaster Rifle PM .75 2.00
- 2 Darth Vader With Lightsaber PM .75 2.00
- 3 Han With Heavy Blaster Pistol PM .75 2.00
- 4 Leia With Blaster Rifle PM .75 2.00
- 5 Luke With Lightsaber PM .75 2.00
- 6 Obi-Wan With Lightsaber PM .75 2.00

1998 Star Wars Jabba's Palace

- COMPLETE SET (180) 40.00 80.00
- BOOSTER BOX (60 PACKS) 40.00 80.00
- BOOSTER PACK (9 CARDS) 1.00 2.00
- RELEASED IN MAY 1998
- 1 8D8 R 1.25 3.00
- 2 A Gift U .40 1.00
- 3 Abyssin C .12 .30
- 4 Abyssin Ornament U .40 1.00
- 5 All Wrapped Up U .40 1.00
- 6 Amanaman R 1.25 3.00
- 7 Amanin C .12 .30
- 8 Antipersonnel Laser Cannon U .40 1.00
- 9 Aqualish C .12 .30
- 10 Arc Welder U .40 1.00
- 11 Ardon Vapor Crell R 1.25 3.00
- 12 Artoo R 3.00 8.00
- 13 Artoo, I Have A Bad Feeling About This U .40 1.00
- 14 Attark R 1.25 3.00
- 15 Aved Luun R 1.25 3.00
- 16 B'omarr Monk C .12 .30
- 17 Bane Malar R 1.25 3.00
- 18 Bantha Fodder C .12 .30
- 19 Barada R 1.25 3.00
- 20 Baragwin C .12 .30
- 21 Bargaining Table U .40 1.00
- 22 Beedo R 1.25 3.00
- 23 BG-J38 R 1.25 3.00
- 24 Bib Fortuna R 1.25 3.00
- 25 Blaster Deflection R 1.25 3.00
- 26 Bo Shuda U .40 1.00
- 27 Bubo U .40 1.00
- 28 Cane Adiss U .40 1.00
- 29 Chadra-Fan C .12 .30
- 30 Chevin C .12 .30
- 31 Choke C .12 .30
- 32 Corellian Retort U .40 1.00
- 33 CZ-4 C .12 .30
- 34 Den Of Thieves U .40 1.00
- 35 Dengar's Modified Riot Gun R 1.25 3.00
- 36 Devaronian C .12 .30
- 37 Don't Forget The Droids C .12 .30
- 38 Double Laser Cannon R 1.25 3.00
- 39 Droopy McCool R 1.25 3.00
- 40 Dune Sea Sabacc DARK U .40 1.00
- 41 Dune Sea Sabacc LIGHT U .40 1.00
- 42 Elom C .12 .30
- 43 Ephant Mon R 1.25 3.00
- 44 EV-9D9 R 1.25 3.00
- 45 Fallen Portal U .40 1.00
- 46 Florn Lamproid C .12 .30
- 47 Fozec R 1.25 3.00
- 48 Gailid R 1.25 3.00
- 49 Gamorrean Ax C .12 .30
- 50 Gamorrean Guard C .12 .30
- 51 Garon Nas Tal R 1.25 3.00
- 52 Geezum R 1.25 3.00
- 53 Ghoel R 1.25 3.00
- 54 Giran R 1.25 3.00
- 55 Gran C .12 .30
- 56 H'nemthe C .12 .30
- 57 Herat R 1.25 3.00
- 58 Hermi Odle R 1.25 3.00
- 59 Hidden Compartment U .40 1.00
- 60 Hidden Weapons U .40 1.00
- 61 Holoprojector U .40 1.00
- 62 Hutt Bounty R 1.25 3.00
- 63 Hutt Smooch U .40 1.00
- 64 I Must Be Allowed To Speak R 1.25 3.00
- 65 Information Exchange U .40 1.00
- 66 Ishi Tib C .12 .30
- 67 Ithorian C .12 .30
- 68 J'Quille R 1.25 3.00
- 69 Jabba the Hutt R 4.00 10.00
- 70 Jabba's Palace Sabacc DARK U .40 1.00
- 71 Jabba's Palace Sabacc LIGHT U .40 1.00
- 72 Jabba's Palace: Audience Chamber DARK U .40 1.00
- 73 Jabba's Palace: Audience Chamber LIGHT U .40 1.00
- 74 Jabba's Palace: Droid Workshop U .40 1.00
- 75 Jabba's Palace: Dungeon U .40 1.00
- 76 Jabba's Palace: Entrance Cavern DARK U .40 1.00
- 77 Jabba's Palace: Entrance Cavern LIGHT U .40 1.00
- 78 Jabba's Palace: Rancor Pit U .40 1.00
- 79 Jabba's Sail Barge R 2.50 6.00
- 80 Jabba's Sail Barge: Passenger Deck R 1.25 3.00
- 81 Jedi Mind Trick R 1.25 3.00
- 82 Jess R 1.25 3.00
- 83 Jet Pack U .40 1.00
- 84 Kalit R 1.25 3.00
- 85 Ke Chu Ke Kakuta? C .12 .30
- 86 Kiffex R 1.25 3.00
- 87 Kirdo III R 1.25 3.00
- 88 Kithaba R 1.25 3.00
- 89 Kitonak C .12 .30
- 90 Klaatu R 1.25 3.00
- 91 Klatooinian Revolutionary C .12 .30
- 92 Laudica R 1.25 3.00
- 93 Leslomy Tacema R 1.25 3.00
- 94 Life Debt R 1.25 3.00
- 95 Loje Nella R 1.25 3.00
- 96 Malakili R 1.25 3.00
- 97 Mandalorian Mishap U .40 1.00
- 98 Max Rebo R 1.25 3.00
- 99 Mos Eisley Blaster DARK C .12 .30
- 100 Mos Eisley Blaster LIGHT C .12 .30
- 101 Murttoc Yine R 1.25 3.00
- 102 Nal Hutta R 1.25 3.00
- 103 Nar Shaddaa Wind Chimes U .40 1.00
- 104 Nikto C .12 .30
- 105 Nizuc Bek R 1.25 3.00
- 106 None Shall Pass C .12 .30
- 107 Nysad R 1.25 3.00
- 108 Oola R 1.25 3.00
- 109 Ortolan C .12 .30
- 110 Ortugg R 1.25 3.00
- 111 Palejo Reshad R 1.25 3.00
- 112 Pote Snitkin R 1.25 3.00
- 113 Princess Leia Organa R 3.00 8.00
- 114 Projection Of A Skywalker U .40 1.00
- 115 Pucumir Thryss R 1.25 3.00
- 116 Quarren C .12 .30
- 117 Quick Reflexes C .12 .30
- 118 R'kik D'nec, Hero Of The Dune Sea R 1.25 3.00
- 119 Rancor R 2.50 6.00
- 120 Rayc Ryjerd R 1.25 3.00
- 121 Ree-Yees R 1.25 3.00
- 122 Rennek R 1.25 3.00
- 123 Resistance U .40 1.00
- 124 Revealed U .40 1.00
- 125 Saelt-Marae R 1.25 3.00
- 126 Salacious Crumb R 1.25 3.00
- 127 Sandwhirl DARK U .40 1.00
- 128 Sandwhirl LIGHT U .40 1.00
- 129 Scum And Villainy R 1.25 3.00
- 130 Sergeant Doallyn R 1.25 3.00
- 131 Shasa Tiel R 1.25 3.00
- 132 Sic-Six C .12 .30
- 133 Skiff DARK C .12 .30
- 134 Skiff LIGHT C .12 .30
- 135 Skrilling C .12 .30
- 136 Skull U .40 1.00
- 137 Snivvian C .12 .30
- 138 Someone Who Loves You U .40 1.00
- 139 Strangle R 1.25 3.00
- 140 Tamtel Skreej R 2.50 6.00
- 141 Tanus Spijek R 1.25 3.00
- 142 Tatooine: Desert DARK C .12 .30
- 143 Tatooine: Desert LIGHT C .12 .30
- 144 Tatooine: Great Pit Of Carkoon U .40 1.00
- 145 Tatooine: Hutt Canyon U .40 1.00
- 146 Tatooine: Jabba's Palace U .40 1.00
- 147 Taym Dren-garen R 1.25 3.00
- 148 Tessek R 1.25 3.00
- 149 The Signal C .12 .30
- 150 Thermal Detonator R 2.00 5.00
- 151 Thul Fain R 1.25 3.00
- 152 Tibrin R 1.25 3.00
- 153 Torture C .12 .30
- 154 Trandoshan C .12 .30
- 155 Trap Door U .40 1.00
- 156 Twi'lek Advisor C .12 .30
- 157 Ultimatum U .40 1.00
- 158 Unfriendly Fire R 1.25 3.00
- 159 Vedain R 1.25 3.00
- 160 Velken Tezeri R 1.25 3.00
- 161 Vibro-Ax DARK C .12 .30
- 162 Vibro-Ax LIGHT C .12 .30
- 163 Vizam R 1.25 3.00
- 164 Vul Tazaene R 1.25 3.00
- 165 Weapon Levitation U .40 1.00
- 166 Weequay Guard C .12 .30
- 167 Weequay Hunter C .12 .30
- 168 Weequay Marksman U .40 1.00
- 169 Weequay Skiff Master C .12 .30
- 170 Well Guarded U .40 1.00
- 171 Whiphid C .12 .30
- 172 Wittin R 1.25 3.00
- 173 Woolf R 1.25 3.00
- 174 Wortt U .40 1.00
- 175 Wounded Wookiee U .40 1.00
- 176 Yarkora C .12 .30
- 177 Yarna d'al' Gargan U .40 1.00
- 178 You Will Take Me To Jabba Now C .12 .30
- 179 Yoxgit R 1.25 3.00
- 180 Yuzzum C .12 .30

1998 Star Wars Official Tournament Sealed Deck

- COMPLETE SET (18) 4.00 10.00
- 1 Arleil Schous PM .40 1.00
- 2 Black Squadron TIE PM .40 1.00
- 3 Chall Bekan PM .40 1.00
- 4 Corulag DARK PM .40 1.00
- 5 Corulag LIGHT PM .40 1.00
- 6 Dreadnaught-Class Heavy Cruiser PM .40 1.00
- 7 Faithful Service PM .40 1.00
- 8 Forced Servitude PM .40 1.00
- 9 Gold Squadron Y-wing PM .40 1.00
- 10 It's a Hit! PM .40 1.00
- 11 Obsidian Squadron TIE PM .40 1.00
- 12 Rebel Trooper Recruit PM .40 1.00
- 13 Red Squadron X-wing PM .40 1.00
- 14 Stormtrooper Cadet PM .40 1.00
- 15 Tarkin's Orders PM .40 1.00
- 16 Tatooine: Jundland Wastes PM .40 1.00
- 17 Tatooine: Tusken Canyon PM .40 1.00
- 18 Z-95 Headhunter PM .40 1.00

1998 Star Wars Second Anthology

- COMPLETE SET (6) 4.00 10.00
- 1 Flagship Operations PV 1.00 2.50
- 2 Mon Calamari Star Cruiser PV 1.00 2.50
- 3 Mon Mothma PV 1.00 2.50
- 4 Rapid Deployment PV 1.00 2.50
- 5 Sarlacc PV 1.00 2.50
- 6 Thunderflare PV 1.00 2.50

1998 Star Wars Special Edition

- COMPLETE SET (324) 75.00 150.00
- BOOSTER BOX (30 PACKS) 60.00 120.00
- BOOSTER PACK (9 CARDS) 3.00 6.00
- RELEASED IN NOVEMBER 1998
- 1 ISB Operations / Empire's Sinister Agents R 1.00 2.50
- 2 2X-7KPR (Tooex) C .12 .30
- 3 A Bright Center To The Universe U .40 1.00
- 4 A Day Long Remembered U .40 1.00
- 5 A Real Hero R 1.00 2.50
- 6 Air-2 Racing Swoop C .12 .30
- 7 Ak-rev U .40 1.00
- 8 Alderaan Operative C .12 .30
- 9 Alert My Star Destroyer! C .12 .30
- 10 All Power To Weapons C .12 .30
- 11 All Wings Report In R 1.00 2.50
- 12 Anoat Operative DARK C .12 .30

13 Anoat Operative LIGHT C .12 .30
14 Antilles Maneuver C .12 .30
15 ASP-707 (Ayesspee) F .60 1.50
16 Balanced Attack U .40 1.00
17 Bantha Herd R .75 2.00
18 Barquin D'an U .40 1.00
19 Ben Kenobi R 2.00 5.00
20 Blast Points C .12 .30
21 Blown Clear U .40 1.00
22 Boba Fett R 1.50 4.00
23 Boelo R 1.00 2.50
24 Bossk In Hound's Tooth R 1.00 2.50
25 Bothan Spy C .12 .30
26 Bothawui F .60 1.50
27 Bothawui Operative C .12 .30
28 Brangus Glee R .75 2.00
29 Bren Quersey U .40 1.00
30 Bron Burs R .75 2.00
31 B-wing Attack Fighter F .60 1.50
32 Camie R 1.00 2.50
33 Carbon Chamber Testing 1.00 2.50
My Favorite Decoration R
34 Chyler U .40 1.00
35 Clak'dor VII Operative U .40 1.00
36 Cloud City Celebration R 1.00 2.50
37 Cloud City Occupation R 1.25 3.00
38 Cloud City: Casino DARK U .40 1.00
39 Cloud City: Casino LIGHT U .40 1.00
40 Cloud City: Core Tunnel U .40 1.00
41 Cloud City: Downtown Plaza DARK R 1.00 2.50
42 Cloud City: Downtown Plaza LIGHT R 1.00 2.50
43 Cloud City: Interrogation Room C .12 .30
44 Cloud City: North Corridor C .12 .30
45 Cloud City: Port Town District U .40 1.00
46 Cloud City: Upper Walkway C .12 .30
47 Cloud City: West Gallery DARK C .12 .30
48 Cloud City: West Gallery LIGHT C .12 .30
49 Colonel Feyn Gospic R 1.00 2.50
50 Combat Cloud Car F .60 1.50
51 Come Here You Big Coward! C .12 .30
52 Commander Wedge Antilles R 1.00 2.50
53 Coordinated Attack C .12 .30
54 Corellia Operative U .40 1.00
55 Corellian Engineering Corporation R 1.00 2.50
56 Corporal Grenwick R .75 2.00
57 Corporal Prescott U .40 1.00
58 Corulag Operative C .12 .30
59 Coruscant Celebration R .75 2.00
60 Coruscant DARK R 2.50 6.00
61 Coruscant LIGHT R 1.00 2.50
62 Coruscant: Docking Bay C .12 .30
63 Coruscant: Imperial City U .40 1.00
64 Coruscant: Imperial Square R 1.25 3.00
65 Counter Surprise Assault R 1.00 2.50
66 Dagobah U .40 1.00
67 Dantooine Base Operations .75 2.00
More Dangerous Than You Realize R
68 Dantooine Operative C .12 .30
69 Darklighter Spin C .12 .30
70 Darth Vader, Dark Lord Of The Sith R 6.00 15.00
71 Death Squadron Star Destroyer R 1.00 2.50
72 Death Star Assault Squadron R 1.00 2.50
73 Death Star R 1.25 3.00
74 Death Star: Detention Block Control Room C .12 .30
75 Death Star: Detention Block Corridor C .12 .30
76 Debnoli R 1.00 2.50
77 Desert DARK F .60 1.50
78 Desert LIGHT F .60 1.50
79 Desilijic Tattoo U .40 1.00
80 Desperate Tactics C .12 .30
81 Destroyed Homestead R 1.00 2.50
82 Dewback C .12 .30
83 Direct Assault C .12 .30
84 Disruptor Pistol DARK F .60 1.50
85 Disruptor Pistol LIGHT F .60 1.50
86 Docking And Repair Facilities R 1.00 2.50
87 Dodo Bodonawieedo U .40 1.00
88 Don't Tread On Me R 1.00 2.50
89 Down With The Emperor! U .40 1.00
90 Dr. Evazan's Sawed-off Blaster U .40 1.00
91 Draw Their Fire U .40 1.00
92 Dreaded Imperial Starfleet R 1.25 3.00
93 Droid Merchant C .12 .30
94 Dune Walker R 1.25 3.00
95 Echo Base Trooper Rifle C .12 .30
96 Elyhek Rue U .40 1.00
97 Entrenchment R .75 2.00
98 Eriadu Operative C .12 .30
99 Executor: Docking Bay U .40 1.00
100 Farm F .60 1.50
101 Feltipern Trevagg's Stun Rifle U .40 1.00
102 Firepower C .12 .30
103 Firin Morett U .40 1.00
104 First Aid F .60 1.50
105 First Strike U .40 1.00
106 Flare-S Racing Swoop C .12 .30
107 Flawless Marksmanship C .12 .30
108 Floating Refinery C .12 .30
109 Fondor U .40 1.00
110 Forest DARK F .60 1.50
111 Forest LIGHT F .60 1.50
112 Gela Yeens U .40 1.00
113 General McQuarrie R .75 2.00
114 Gold 3 U .40 1.00
115 Gold 4 U .40 1.00
116 Gold 6 U .40 1.00
117 Goo Nee Tay R 1.00 2.50
118 Greeata U .40 1.00
119 Grondorn Muse R .75 2.00
120 Harc Seff U .40 1.00
121 Harvest R 1.25 3.00
122 Heavy Fire Zone C .12 .30
123 Heroes Of Yavin R .75 2.00
124 Heroic Sacrifice U .40 1.00
125 Hidden Base 1.50 4.00
Systems Will Slip Through Your Fingers R
126 Hit And Run R .75 2.00
127 Hol Okand U .40 1.00
128 Homing Beacon R 1.00 2.50
129 Hoth Sentry U .40 1.00
130 Hunt Down And Destroy The Jedi 1.50 4.00
Their Fire Has Gone Out Of The Universe R
131 Hunting Party R 1.00 2.50
132 I Can't Shake Him! C .12 .30
133 Iasa, The Traitor Of Jawa Canyon R .75 2.00
134 IM4-099 F .60 1.50
135 Imperial Atrocity R 3.00 8.00
136 Imperial Occupation / Imperial Control R 1.00 2.50
137 Imperial Propaganda R 3.00 8.00
138 In Range C .12 .30
139 Incom Corporation R .75 2.00
140 InCom Engineer C .12 .30
141 Intruder Missile DARK F .60 1.50
142 Intruder Missile LIGHT F .60 1.50
143 It's Not My Fault! F .60 1.50
144 Jabba R 1.00 2.50
145 Jabba's Influence R .75 2.00
146 Jabba's Space Cruiser R 1.25 3.00
147 Jabba's Through With You U .40 1.00
148 Jabba's Twerps U .40 1.00
149 Joh Yowza R .75 2.00
150 Jungle DARK F .60 1.50
151 Jungle LIGHT F .60 1.50
152 Kalit's Sandcrawler R 1.00 2.50
153 Kashyyyk Operative DARK U .40 1.00
154 Kashyyyk Operative LIGHT U .40 1.00
155 Kessel Operative U .40 1.00
156 Ketwol R .75 2.00
157 Kiffex Operative DARK U .40 1.00
158 Kiffex Operative LIGHT U .40 1.00
159 Kirdo III Operative C .12 .30
160 Koensayr Manufacturing R 1.00 2.50
161 Krayt Dragon R 1.00 2.50
162 Kuat Drive Yards R 1.25 3.00
163 Kuat U .40 1.00
164 Lando's Blaster Rifle R 1.00 2.50
165 Legendary Starfighter C .12 .30
166 Leia's Blaster Rifle R 1.00 2.50
167 Lieutenant Lepira U .40 1.00
168 Lieutenant Naytaan U .40 1.00
169 Lieutenant Tarn Mison R 1.00 2.50
170 Lobel C .12 .30
171 Lobot R 1.00 2.50
172 Local Defense U .40 1.00
173 Local Uprising / Liberation R 1.00 2.50
174 Lyn Me U .40 1.00
175 Major Palo Torshan R 1.00 2.50
176 Makurth F .60 1.50
177 Maneuvering Flaps C .12 .30
178 Masterful Move C .12 .30
179 Mechanical Failure R .75 2.00
180 Meditation R 1.25 3.00
181 Medium Bulk Freighter U .40 1.00
182 Melas R 1.00 2.50
183 Mind What You Have Learned 1.25 3.00
Save You It Can R
184 Moisture Farmer C .12 .30
185 Nal Hutta Operative C .12 .30
186 Neb Dulo U .40 1.00
187 Nebit R 1.00 2.50
188 Niado Duegad U .40 1.00
189 Nick Of Time U .40 1.00
190 No Bargain U .40 1.00
191 Old Times R .75 2.00
192 On Target C .12 .30
193 One-Arm R 1.00 2.50
194 Oppressive Enforcement U .40 1.00
195 Ord Mantell Operative C .12 .30
196 Organized Attack C .12 .30
197 OS-72-1 In Obsidian 1 R 1.00 2.50
198 OS-72-10 R 1.00 2.50
199 OS-72-2 In Obsidian 2 R 1.00 2.50
200 Outer Rim Scout R 1.50 4.00
201 Overwhelmed C .12 .30
202 Patrol Craft DARK C .12 .30
203 Patrol Craft LIGHT C .12 .30
204 Planetary Subjugation U .40 1.00
205 Ponda Baba's Hold-out Blaster U .40 1.00
206 Portable Scanner C .12 .30
207 Power Pivot C .12 .30
208 Precise Hit C .12 .30
209 Pride Of The Empire C .12 .30
210 Princess Organa R 1.25 3.00
211 Put All Sections On Alert C .12 .30
212 R2-A5 (Artoo-Ayfive) U .40 1.00
213 R3-A2 (Arthree-Aytoo) U .40 1.00
214 R3-T2 (Arthree-Teetoo) R 1.00 2.50
215 Raithal Operative C .12 .30
216 Ralltiir Freighter Captain F .60 1.50
217 Ralltiir Operations 1.50 4.00
In The Hands Of The Empire R
218 Ralltiir Operative C .12 .30
219 Rapid Fire C .12 .30
220 Rappertunie U .40 1.00
221 Rebel Ambush C .12 .30
222 Rebel Base Occupation R .75 2.00
223 Rebel Fleet R 1.00 2.50
224 Red 10 U .40 1.00
225 Red 7 U .40 1.00
226 Red 8 U .40 1.00
227 Red 9 U .40 1.00
228 Relentless Pursuit C .12 .30
229 Rendezvous Point R 1.00 2.50
230 Rendili F .60 1.50
231 Rendili StarDrive R 1.00 2.50
232 Rescue The Princess 1.00 2.50
Sometimes I Amaze Even Myself R
233 Return To Base R 1.00 2.50
234 Roche U .40 1.00
235 Rock Wart F .60 1.50
236 Rogue 4 R 1.50 4.00
237 Ronto DARK C .12 .30
238 Ronto LIGHT C .12 .30
239 RR'uruurrr R 1.00 2.50
240 Ryle Torsyn U .40 1.00
241 Rystall R 1.50 4.00
242 Sacrifice F .60 1.50
243 Sandspeeder F .60 1.50
244 Sandtrooper F .60 1.50
245 Sarlacc R 1.00 2.50
246 Scrambled Transmission U .40 1.00
247 Scurrier F .60 1.50
248 Secret Plans U .40 1.00
249 Sentinel-Class Landing Craft F .60 1.50
250 Sergeant Edian U .40 1.00
251 Sergeant Hollis R 1.00 2.50
252 Sergeant Major Bursk U .40 1.00
253 Sergeant Major Enfield R .75 2.00
254 Sergeant Merril U .40 1.00
255 Sergeant Narthax R 1.00 2.50
256 Sergeant Torent R 1.00 2.50
257 S-Foils C .12 .30
258 SFS L-s9.3 Laser Cannons C .12 .30
259 Short-Range Fighters R 1.00 2.50
260 Sienar Fleet Systems R 1.00 2.50
261 Slayn and Korpil Facilities R .75 2.00
262 Slight Weapons Malfunction C .12 .30
263 Soth Petikkin R .75 2.00
264 Spaceport City DARK F .60 1.50
265 Spaceport City LIGHT F .60 1.50
266 Spaceport Docking Bay DARK F .60 1.50
267 Spaceport Docking Bay LIGHT F .60 1.50
268 Spaceport Prefect's Office F .60 1.50
269 Spaceport Street DARK F .60 1.50
270 Spaceport Street LIGHT F .60 1.50
271 Spiral R 1.25 3.00
272 Star Destroyer! R 1.00 2.50
273 Stay Sharp! U .40 1.00
274 Steady Aim C .12 .30
275 Strategic Reserves R 1.00 2.50
276 Suppressive Fire C .12 .30
277 Surface Defense R 1.00 2.50
278 Swamp DARK F .60 1.50
279 Swamp LIGHT F .60 1.50
280 Swoop Mercenary F .60 1.50
281 Sy Snootles R 1.00 2.50
282 T-47 Battle Formation R 1.00 2.50
283 Tarkin's Bounty U .40 1.00
284 Tatooine Celebration R 1.25 3.00
285 Tatooine Occupation R 1.50 4.00
286 Tatooine: Anchorhead F .60 1.50
287 Tatooine: Beggar's Canyon R .75 2.00
288 Tatooine: Jabba's Palace C .12 .30
289 Tatooine: Jawa Canyon DARK U .40 1.00
290 Tatooine: Jawa Canyon LIGHT U .40 1.00
291 Tatooine: Krayt Dragon Pass F .60 1.50
292 Tatooine: Tosche Station C .12 .30
293 Tauntaun Skull C .12 .30
294 Tawss Khaa R .75 2.00
295 The Planet That It's Farthest From U .40 1.00
296 Thedit R 1.00 2.50
297 Theron Nett U .40 1.00
298 They're Coming In Too Fast! C .12 .30
299 They're Tracking Us C .12 .30
300 They've Shut Down The Main Reactor C .12 .30
301 Tibrin Operative C .12 .30
302 TIE Defender Mark I F .60 1.50
303 TK-422 R 1.00 2.50
304 Trooper Sabacc DARK F .60 1.50
305 Trooper Sabacc LIGHT F .60 1.50
306 Uh-oh! U .40 1.00
307 Umpass-stay R .75 2.00
308 Ur'Ru'r R 1.00 2.50
309 URoRRuR'R'R's Bantha R 1.00 2.50
310 Uutkik R 1.00 2.50
311 Vader's Personal Shuttle R 1.00 2.50
312 Vengeance R 1.00 2.50
313 Wakeelmui U .40 1.00
314 Watch Your Back! C .12 .30
315 Weapons Display C .12 .30
316 Wise Advice U .40 1.00
317 Wittin's Sandcrawler R 1.00 2.50
318 Womp Rat C .12 .30
319 Wookiee F .60 1.50
320 Wrist Comlink C .12 .30
321 X-wing Assault Squadron R 1.00 2.50
322 X-wing Laser Cannon C .12 .30
323 Yavin 4 Trooper F .60 1.50
324 Yavin 4: Massassi Headquarters R 1.00 2.50

1999 Star Wars Endor

COMPLETE SET (180) 75.00 150.00
BOOSTER BOX (30 PACKS) 75.00 150.00
BOOSTER PACK (9 CARDS) 3.50 7.00
RELEASED IN JUNE 1999
1 AT-ST Pilot C .12 .30
2 Biker Scout Trooper C .12 .30
3 Colonel Dyer R 1.25 3.00
4 Commander Igar R 1.25 3.00
5 Corporal Avarik U .40 1.00
6 Corporal Drazin U .40 1.00
7 Corporal Drelosyn R 1.25 3.00
8 Corporal Misik R 1.00 2.50
9 Corporal Oberk R 1.25 3.00
10 Elite Squadron Stormtrooper C .12 .30
11 Lieutenant Arnet U .40 1.00
12 Lieutenant Grond U .40 1.00
13 Lieutenant Renz R .75 2.00
14 Lieutenant Watts R 1.25 3.00
15 Major Hewex R .75 2.00
16 Major Marquand R 1.50 4.00
17 Navy Trooper C .12 .30
18 Navy Trooper Fenson R 1.00 2.50
19 Navy Trooper Shield Technician C .12 .30
20 Navy Trooper Vesden U .40 1.00
21 Sergeant Barich R 2.00 5.00
22 Sergeant Elsek U .40 1.00
23 Sergeant Irol R 1.50 4.00
24 Sergeant Tarl U .40 1.00
25 Sergeant Wallen R 1.50 4.00
26 An Entire Legion Of My Best Troops U .40 1.00
27 Aratech Corporation R 1.00 2.50
28 Battle Order U .40 1.00
29 Biker Scout Gear U .40 1.00
30 Closed Door R .75 2.00
31 Crossfire R 3.00 8.00
32 Early Warning Network R .75 2.00
33 Empire's New Order R .75 2.00
34 Establish Secret Base R 1.50 4.00
35 Imperial Academy Training C .12 .30
36 Imperial Arrest Order U .40 1.00
37 Ominous Rumors R .75 2.00
38 Perimeter Patrol R 1.00 2.50
39 Pinned Down U .40 1.00
40 Relentless Tracking R .75 2.00
41 Search And Destroy U .40 1.00
42 Security Precautions R 2.50 6.00
43 Well-earned Command R .75 2.00
44 Accelerate C .12 .30
45 Always Thinking With Your Stomach R 2.50 6.00
46 Combat Readiness C .12 .30
47 Compact Firepower C .12 .30
48 Counterattack R .75 2.00
49 Dead Ewok C .12 .30
50 Don't Move! C .12 .30
51 Eee Chu Wawa! C .12 .30
52 Endor Scout Trooper C .12 .30
53 Freeze! U .40 1.00
54 Go For Help! C .12 .30
55 High-speed Tactics U .40 1.00
56 Hot Pursuit C .12 .30
57 Imperial Tyranny C .12 .30
58 It's An Older Code R .75 2.00
59 Main Course U .40 1.00
60 Outflank C .12 .30
61 Pitiful Little Band C .12 .30
62 Scout Recon C .12 .30
63 Sneak Attack C .12 .30
64 Wounded Warrior R 1.50 4.00
65 You Rebel Scum R 1.00 2.50
66 Carida U .40 1.00
67 Endor Occupation R .75 2.00
68 Endor: Ancient Forest U .40 1.00
69 Endor: Back Door LIGHT U .40 1.00
70 Endor: Bunker LIGHT U .40 1.00
71 Endor: Dark Forest R 2.50 6.00
72 Endor: Dense Forest LIGHT C .12 .30
73 Endor: Ewok Village LIGHT U .40 1.00
74 Endor: Forest Clearing U .40 1.00
75 Endor: Great Forest LIGHT C .12 .30
76 Endor: Landing Platform .12 .30
(Docking Bay) LIGHT C
77 Endor DARK U .40 1.00
78 Lambda-class Shuttle C .12 .30
79 Speeder Bike LIGHT C .12 .30
80 Tempest 1 R .75 2.00
81 Tempest Scout 1 R 1.00 2.50
82 Tempest Scout 2 R 2.00 5.00
83 Tempest Scout 3 R .75 2.00
84 Tempest Scout 4 R 2.50 6.00
85 Tempest Scout 5 R 2.00 5.00
86 Tempest Scout 6 R 2.50 6.00
87 Tempest Scout U .40 1.00
88 AT-ST Dual Cannon R 6.00 15.00
89 Scout Blaster C .12 .30
90 Speeder Bike Cannon U .40 1.00
91 Captain Yutani U .40 1.00
92 Chewbacca of Kashyyyk R .75 2.00
93 Chief Chirpa R 1.00 2.50
94 Corporal Beezer U .40 1.00
95 Corporal Delevar U .40 1.00
96 Corporal Janse U .40 1.00
97 Corporal Kensaric R 1.25 3.00
98 Daughter of Skywalker R 10.00 20.00
99 Dresselian Commando C .12 .30
100 Endor LIGHT U .40 1.00
101 Ewok Sentry C .12 .30
102 Ewok Spearman C .12 .30
103 Ewok Tribesman C .12 .30
104 General Crix Madine R 1.00 2.50
105 General Solo R .75 2.00
106 Graak R .75 2.00
107 Kazak R 1.00 2.50
108 Lieutenant Greeve R .75 2.00
109 Lieutenant Page R 1.50 4.00
110 Logray R .75 2.00
111 Lumat U .40 1.00
112 Mon Mothma R 1.25 3.00
113 Orrimaarko R .75 2.00
114 Paploo U .40 1.00
115 Rabin U .40 1.00
116 Romba R .75 2.00
117 Sergeant Brooks Carlson R .75 2.00
118 Sergeant Bruckman R .75 2.00
119 Sergeant Junkin U .40 1.00
120 Teebo R .75 2.00
121 Threepio R 1.25 3.00
122 Wicket R .75 2.00
123 Wuta U .40 1.00
124 Aim High R 1.00 2.50
125 Battle Plan U .40 1.00
126 Commando Training C .12 .30
127 Count Me In R .75 2.00
128 I Hope She's All Right U .40 1.00
129 I Wonder Who They Found U .40 1.00
130 Insurrection U .40 1.00
131 That's One R .75 2.00
132 Wokling R 6.00 15.00
133 Deactivate The Shield Generator R 1.25 3.00
134 Careful Planning C .12 .30
135 Covert Landing U .40 1.00
136 Endor Operations / Imperial Outpost R 2.50 6.00
137 Ewok And Roll C .12 .30
138 Ewok Log Jam C .12 .30
139 Ewok Rescue C .12 .30
140 Firefight C .12 .30
141 Fly Casual R .75 2.00
142 Free Ride U .40 1.00
143 Get Alongside That One U .40 1.00
144 Here We Go Again R .75 2.00
145 I Have A Really Bad .12 .30
Feeling About This C
146 I Know R 1.25 3.00
147 Lost In The Wilderness R .75 2.00
148 Rapid Deployment R .75 2.00
149 Sound The Attack C .12 .30
150 Surprise Counter Assault R .75 2.00
151 Take The Initiative C .12 .30
152 This Is Absolutely Right R .75 2.00
153 Throw Me Another Charge U .40 1.00
154 Were You Looking For Me? R 4.00 10.00
155 Wookiee Guide C .12 .30
156 Yub Yub! C .12 .30
157 Chandrila U .40 1.00
158 Endor Celebration R .75 2.00
159 Endor: Back Door DARK U .40 1.00
160 Endor: Bunker DARK U .40 1.00
161 Endor: Chief Chirpa's Hut R 3.00 8.00
162 Endor: Dense Forest DARK C .12 .30
163 Endor: Ewok Village DARK U .40 1.00
164 Endor: Great Forest DARK C .12 .30
165 Endor: Hidden Forest Trail U .40 1.00
166 Endor: Landing Platform .12 .30
(Docking Bay) DARK C
167 Endor: Rebel Landing Site (Forest) R 2.50 6.00
168 Rebel Strike Team 1.25 3.00
Garrison Destroyed R
169 Tydirium R 1.25 3.00
170 YT-1300 Transport C .12 .30
171 Chewie's AT-ST R 3.00 8.00
172 Ewok Glider C .12 .30
173 Speeder Bike DARK C .12 .30
174 A280 Sharpshooter Rifle R 2.50 6.00
175 BlasTech E-11B Blaster Rifle C .12 .30
176 Chewbacca's Bowcaster R 2.50 6.00
177 Ewok Bow C .12 .30
178 Ewok Catapult U .40 1.00
179 Ewok Spear C .12 .30
180 Explosive Charge U .40 1.00

1999 Star Wars Enhanced Cloud City

1 4-LOM With Concussion Rifle PM 1.50 4.00
2 Any Methods Necessary PM 2.00 5.00
3 Boba Fett in Slave I PM 1.00 2.50
4 Chewie With Blaster Rifle PM 1.00 2.50
5 Crush The Rebellion PM 1.25 3.00
6 Dengar In Punishing One PM 1.00 2.50
7 IG-88 With Riot Gun PM 3.00 8.00
8 Lando In Millennium Falcon PM 1.00 2.50
9 Lando With Blaster Pistol PM 1.00 2.50
10 Quiet Mining Colony 1.00 2.50
Independent Operation PM
11 This Deal Is Getting Worse All The Time 1.00 2.50
Pray I Don't Alter It Any Further
12 Z-95 Bespin Defense Fighter PM 1.00 2.50

1999 Star Wars Enhanced Jabba's Palace

1 Bossk With Mortar Gun PM 1.00 2.50
2 Boushh PM 1.25 3.00
3 Court Of The Vile Gangster 1.00 2.50
I Shall Enjoy Watching You Die PM
4 Dengar With Blaster Carbine PM 1.00 2.50
5 IG-88 In IG-2000 PM 1.00 2.50
6 Jodo Kast PM 1.50 4.00
7 Mara Jade, The Emperor's Hand PM 10.00 20.00
8 Mara Jade's Lightsaber PM 1.50 4.00
9 Master Luke PM 2.50 6.00
10 See-Threepio PM 1.00 2.50
11 You Can Either Profit By This... 1.00 2.50
Or Be Destroyed PM
12 Zuckuss In Mist Hunter PM 1.25 3.00

2000 Star Wars Death Star II

COMPLETE SET (182) 200.00 300.00
BOOSTER BOX (30 PACKS) 150.00 250.00
BOOSTER PACK (11 CARDS) 5.00 9.00
RELEASED IN JULY 2000
1 Accuser R 1.25 3.00
2 Admiral Ackbar XR 1.25 3.00
3 Admiral Chiraneau R 1.50 4.00
4 Admiral Piett XR 1.00 2.50
5 Anakin Skywalker R 1.00 2.50
6 Aquaris C .12 .30
7 A-wing C .12 .30
8 A-wing Cannon C .12 .30
9 Baron Soontir Fel R 1.50 4.00
10 Battle Deployment R 1.25 3.00
11 Black 11 R 1.00 2.50
12 Blue Squadron 5 U .40 1.00
13 Blue Squadron B-wing R 1.50 4.00
14 Bring Him Before Me 1.00 2.50
Take Your Father's Place R
15 B-wing Attack Squadron R 1.00 2.50
16 B-wing Bomber C .12 .30
17 Capital Support R 1.00 2.50
18 Captain Godherdt U .40 1.00
19 Captain Jonus U .40 1.00
20 Captain Sarkli R 1.00 2.50
21 Captain Verrack U .40 1.00
22 Captain Yorr U .40 1.00
23 Chimaera R 2.50 6.00
24 Close Air Support C .12 .30
25 Colonel Cracken R 1.00 2.50
26 Colonel Davod Jon U .40 1.00
27 Colonel Jendon R 1.00 2.50
28 Colonel Salm U .40 1.00
29 Combat Response C .12 .30

Card	Low	High
30 Combined Fleet Action R	1.00	2.50
31 Commander Merrejk R	1.25	3.00
32 Concentrate All Fire R	1.00	2.50
33 Concussion Missiles DARK C	.12	.30
34 Concussion Missiles LIGHT C	.12	.30
35 Corporal Marmor U	.40	1.00
36 Corporal Midge U	.40	1.00
37 Critical Error Revealed C	.12	.30
38 Darth Vader's Lightsaber R	1.00	2.50
39 Death Star II R	1.25	3.00
40 Death Star II: Capacitors C	.12	.30
41 Death Star II: Coolant Shaft C	.12	.30
42 Death Star II: Docking Bay C	.12	.30
43 Death Star II: Reactor Core C	.12	.30
44 Death Star II: Throne Room R	1.00	2.50
45 Defiance R	1.25	3.00
46 Desperate Counter C	.12	.30
47 Dominator R	1.00	2.50
48 DS-181-3 U	.40	1.00
49 DS-181-4 U	.40	1.00
50 Emperor Palpatine UR	30.00	60.00
51 Emperor's Personal Shuttle R	1.00	2.50
52 Emperor's Power U	.40	1.00
53 Endor Shield U	.40	1.00
54 Enhanced Proton Torpedoes C	.12	.30
55 Fighter Cover R	2.00	5.00
56 Fighters Coming In R	1.00	2.50
57 First Officer Thaneespi R	1.00	2.50
58 Flagship Executor R	1.25	3.00
59 Flagship Operations R	1.00	2.50
60 Force Lightning R	2.00	5.00
61 Force Pike C	.12	.30
62 Gall C	.12	.30
63 General Calrissian R	1.00	2.50
64 General Walex Blissex U	.40	1.00
65 Gold Squadron 1 R	1.00	2.50
66 Gray Squadron 1 U	.40	1.00
67 Gray Squadron 2 U	.40	1.00
68 Gray Squadron Y-wing Pilot C	.12	.30
69 Green Leader R	1.00	2.50
70 Green Squadron 1 R	1.00	2.50
71 Green Squadron 3 R	1.00	2.50
72 Green Squadron A-wing R	1.25	3.00
73 Green Squadron Pilot C	.12	.30
74 Head Back To The Surface C	.12	.30
75 Heading For The Medical Frigate C	.12	.30
76 Heavy Turbolaser Battery DARK C	.12	.30
77 Heavy Turbolaser Battery LIGHT C	.12	.30
78 Home One R	4.00	10.00
79 Home One: Docking Bay C	.12	.30
80 Home One: War Room R	1.25	3.00
81 Honor Of The Jedi U	.40	1.00
82 I Feel The Conflict U	.40	1.00
83 I'll Take The Leader R	2.50	6.00
84 I'm With You Too R	1.50	4.00
85 Imperial Command R	4.00	10.00
86 Inconsequential Losses C	.12	.30
87 Independence R	1.25	3.00
88 Insertion Planning C	.12	.30
89 Insignificant Rebellion U	.40	1.00
90 Intensify The Forward Batteries R	1.00	2.50
91 Janus Greejatus R	1.00	2.50
92 Judicator R	1.50	4.00
93 Karie Neth U	.40	1.00
94 Keir Santage U	.40	1.00
95 Kin Kian U	.40	1.00
96 Launching The Assault R	1.00	2.50
97 Leave Them To Me C	.12	.30
98 Let's Keep A Little Optimism Here C	.12	.30
99 Liberty R	1.25	3.00
100 Lieutenant Blount R	1.00	2.50
101 Lieutenant Endicott U	.40	1.00
102 Lieutenant Hebsly U	.40	1.00
103 Lieutenant s'Too Vees U	.40	1.00
104 Lieutenant Telsij U	.40	1.00
105 Lord Vader R	10.00	20.00
106 Luke Skywalker, Jedi Knight UR	30.00	60.00
107 Luke's Lightsaber R	1.50	4.00
108 Luminous U	.40	1.00
109 Major Haash'n U	.40	1.00
110 Major Mianda U	.40	1.00
111 Major Olander Brit U	.40	1.00
112 Major Panno U	.40	1.00
113 Major Rhymer U	.40	1.00
114 Major Turr Phennir U	.40	1.00
115 Masanya R	1.50	4.00
116 Menace Fades C	.12	.30
117 Mobilization Points C	.12	.30
118 Moff Jerjerrod R	1.00	2.50
119 Mon Calamari DARK C	.12	.30
120 Mon Calamari LIGHT C	.12	.30
121 Mon Calamari Star Cruiser R	1.25	3.00
122 Myn Kyneugh R	1.00	2.50
123 Nebulon-B Frigate U	.40	1.00
124 Nien Nunb R	1.25	3.00
125 Obsidian 10 U	.40	1.00
126 Onyx 1 R	1.25	3.00
127 Onyx 2 U	.40	1.00
128 Operational As Planned C	.12	.30
129 Orbital Mine C	.12	.30
130 Our Only Hope U	.40	1.00
131 Overseeing It Personally R	1.00	2.50
132 Prepared Defenses C	.12	.30
133 Rebel Leadership R	3.00	8.00
134 Red Squadron 1 R	1.00	2.50
135 Red Squadron 4 U	.40	1.00
136 Red Squadron 7 U	.40	1.00
137 Rise, My Friend R	1.00	2.50
138 Royal Escort C	.12	.30
139 Royal Guard C	.12	.30
140 Saber 1 R	6.00	15.00
141 Saber 2 U	.40	1.00
142 Saber 3 U	.40	1.00
143 Saber 4 U	.40	1.00
144 Scimitar 1 U	.40	1.00
145 Scimitar 2 U	.40	1.00
146 Scimitar Squadron TIE C	.12	.30
147 Scythe 1 U	.40	1.00
148 Scythe 3 U	.40	1.00
149 Scythe Squadron TIE C	.12	.30
150 SFS L-s7.2 TIE Cannon C	.12	.30
151 Sim Aloo R	1.00	2.50
152 Something Special Planned For Them C	.12	.30
153 Squadron Assignments C	.12	.30
154 Staging Areas C	.12	.30
155 Strike Planning R	1.00	2.50
156 Strikeforce C	.12	.30
157 Sullust DARK C	.12	.30
158 Sullust LIGHT C	.12	.30
159 Superficial Damage C	.12	.30
160 Superlaser Mark II U	.40	1.00
161 Taking Them With Us R	1.25	3.00
162 Tala 1 R	1.00	2.50
163 Tala 2 R	1.00	2.50
164 Ten Numb R	1.00	2.50
165 That Thing's Operational R	1.00	2.50
166 The Emperor's Shield R	1.00	2.50
167 The Emperor's Sword R	1.00	2.50
168 The Time For Our Attack Has Come C	.12	.30
169 The Way Of Things U	.40	1.00
170 There Is Good In Him I Can Save Him R	1.00	2.50
171 Thunderflare R	1.00	2.50
172 TIE Interceptor C	.12	.30
173 Twilight Is Upon Me R	1.00	2.50
174 Tycho Celchu R	1.25	3.00
175 Visage R	1.00	2.50
176 We're In Attack Position Now R	2.50	6.00
177 Wedge Antilles, Red Squadron Leader R	1.50	4.00
178 You Cannot Hide Forever U	.40	1.00
179 You Must Confront Vader R	1.50	4.00
180 Young Fool R	1.00	2.50
181 Your Destiny C	.12	.30
182 Your Insight Serves You Well U	.40	1.00

2000 Star Wars Jabba's Palace Sealed Deck

Card	Low	High
1 Agents In The Court No Love For The Empire PM	.40	1.00
2 Hutt Influence PM	.40	1.00
3 Jabba's Palace: Antechamber PM	.40	1.00
4 Jabba's Palace: Lower Passages PM	.40	1.00
5 Lando With Vibro-Ax PM	.40	1.00
6 Let Them Make The First Move / My Kind Of Scum Fearless And Inventive PM	.40	1.00
7 Mercenary Pilot PM	.40	1.00
8 Mighty Jabba PM	.40	1.00
9 No Escape PM	.40	1.00
10 Ounee Ta PM	.40	1.00
11 Palace Raider PM	.40	1.00
12 Power Of The Hutt PM	.40	1.00
13 Racing Skiff DARK PM	.40	1.00
14 Racing Skiff LIGHT PM	.40	1.00
15 Seeking An Audience PM	.40	1.00
16 Stun Blaster DARK PM	.40	1.00
17 Stun Blaster LIGHT PM	.40	1.00
18 Tatooine: Desert Heart PM	.40	1.00
19 Tatooine: Hutt Trade Route (Desert) PM	.40	1.00
20 Underworld Contacts PM	.40	1.00

2000 Star Wars Reflections II

Card	Low	High
COMPLETE SET (54)	20.00	50.00
BOOSTER BOX (30 PACKS)	150.00	250.00
BOOSTER PACK (11 CARDS)	5.00	10.00
RELEASED IN DECEMBER 2000		
1 There Is No Try and Oppressive Enforcement PM	.60	1.50
2 Abyssin Ornament and Wounded Wookiee PM	.40	1.00
3 Agents Of Black Sun Vengence Of The Dark Prince PM	.40	1.00
4 Alter and Collateral Damage PM	.60	1.50
5 Alter and Friendly Fire PM	.60	1.50
6 Arica PM	2.00	5.00
7 Artoo and Threepio PM	.60	1.50
8 Black Sun Fleet PM	.40	1.00
9 Captain Gilad Pellaeon PM	.60	1.50
10 Chewbacca, Protector PM	.60	1.50
11 Control and Set For Stun PM	.60	1.50
12 Control and Tunnel Vision PM	1.00	2.50
13 Corran Horn PM	1.50	4.00
14 Dark Maneuvers and Tallon Roll PM	1.00	2.50
15 Dash Rendar PM	1.25	3.00
16 Defensive Fire and Hutt Smooch PM	.40	1.00
17 Do, Or Do Not and Wise Advice PM	.40	1.00
18 Dr Evazan and Ponda Baba PM	.40	1.00
19 Evader and Monnok PM	.60	1.50
20 Ghhhk and Those Rebels Won't Escape Us PM	.40	1.00
21 Grand Admiral Thrawn PM	2.50	6.00
22 Guri PM	1.25	3.00
23 Houjix and Out Of Nowhere PM	.60	1.50
24 Jabba's Prize PM	.40	1.00
25 Kir Kanos PM	.40	1.00
26 LE-BO2D9 [Leebo] PM	.40	1.00
27 Luke Skywalker, Rebel Scout PM	1.00	2.50
28 Mercenary Armor PM	.40	1.00
29 Mirax Terrik PM	.60	1.50
30 Nar Shaddaa Wind Chimes and Out Of Somewhere PM	.40	1.00
31 No Questions Asked PM	.40	1.00
32 Obi-Wan's Journal PM	.40	1.00
33 Ommni Box and It's Worse PM	.40	1.00
34 Out of Commission and Transmission Terminated PM	1.00	2.50
35 Outrider PM	.60	1.50
36 Owen Lars and Beru Lars PM	.40	1.00
37 Path Of Least Resistance and Revealed PM	.40	1.00
38 Prince Xizor PM	1.50	4.00
39 Pulsar Skate PM	.40	1.00
40 Sense and Recoil In Fear PM	.60	1.50
41 Sense and Uncertain Is The Future PM	.60	1.50
42 Shocking Information and Grimtaash PM	.40	1.00
43 Sniper and Dark Strike PM	.40	1.00
44 Snoova PM	1.00	2.50
45 Sorry About The Mess and Blaster Proficiency PM	.60	1.50
46 Stinger PM	.40	1.00
47 Sunsdown and Too Cold For Speeders PM	.40	1.00
48 Talon Karrde PM	.60	1.50
49 The Bith Shuffle and Desperate Reach PM	.40	1.00
50 The Emperor PM	1.50	4.00
51 Vigo PM	1.50	4.00
52 Virago PM	.40	1.00
53 Watch Your Step This Place Can Be A Little Rough PM	.40	1.00
54 Yoda Stew and You Do Have Your Moments PM	.40	1.00

2000 Star Wars Third Anthology

Card	Low	High
COMPLETE SET (6)	4.00	10.00
1 A New Secret Base PM	1.00	2.50
2 Artoo-Detoo In Red 5 PM	1.00	2.50
3 Echo Base Garrison PM	1.00	2.50
4 Massassi Base Operations One In A Million PM	1.00	2.50
5 Prisoner 2187 PM	1.00	2.50
6 Set Your Course For Alderaan The Ultimate Power In The Universe PM	1.00	2.50

2001 Star Wars Coruscant

Card	Low	High
COMPLETE SET (188)	120.00	250.00
BOOSTER BOX (30 PACKS)	300.00	400.00
BOOSTER PACK (11 CARDS)	12.00	15.00
RELEASED IN AUGUST 2001		
1 A Tragedy Has Occurred U	.40	1.00
2 A Vergence In The Force U	.40	1.00
3 Accepting Trade Federation Control U	.40	1.00
4 Aks Moe R	1.25	3.00
5 All Wings Report In and Darklighter Spin R	6.00	15.00
6 Allegations Of Corruption U / Alter DARK U	.40	1.00
7 Alter DARK U	.40	1.00
8 Alter LIGHT U	.40	1.00
9 Another Pathetic Lifeform U	.40	1.00
10 Are You Brain Dead?! R	1.50	4.00
11 Ascertaining The Truth U	.40	1.00
12 Baseless Accusations C	.12	.30
13 Baskol Yeesrim U	.40	1.00
14 Battle Droid Blaster Rifle C	.12	.30
15 Battle Order and First Strike R	1.00	2.50
16 Battle Plan and Draw Their Fire R	1.50	4.00
17 Begin Landing Your Troops U	.40	1.00
18 Blockade Flagship: Bridge R	3.00	8.00
19 Captain Madakor R	1.00	2.50
20 Captain Panaka R	1.00	2.50
21 Chokk U	.40	1.00
22 Control DARK U	.40	1.00
23 Control LIGHT U	.40	1.00
24 Coruscant DARK C	.12	.30
25 Coruscant LIGHT C	.12	.30
26 Coruscant Guard DARK C	.12	.30
27 Coruscant Guard LIGHT C	.12	.30
28 Coruscant: Docking Bay DARK C	.12	.30
29 Coruscant: Docking Bay LIGHT C	.12	.30
30 Coruscant: Galactic Senate DARK C	.12	.30
31 Coruscant: Galactic Senate LIGHT C	.12	.30
32 Coruscant: Jedi Council Chamber R	3.00	8.00
33 Credits Will Do Fine C	.12	.30
34 Darth Maul, Young Apprentice R	15.00	30.00
35 Daultay Dofine R	1.25	3.00
36 Depa Billaba R	1.25	3.00
37 Destroyer Droid R	12.00	25.00
38 Dioxis R	1.00	2.50
39 Do They Have A Code Clearance? R	1.00	2.50
40 Droid Starfighter C	.12	.30
41 Drop! U	.40	1.00
42 Edcel Bar Gane C	.12	.30
43 Enter The Bureaucrat U	.40	1.00
44 Establish Control U	.40	1.00
45 Free Ride and Endor Celebration R	1.50	4.00
46 Freon Drevan U	.40	1.00
47 Gardulla The Hutt U	.40	1.00
48 Graxol Kelvyyn U	.40	1.00
49 Grotto Werribee R	1.25	3.00
50 Gungan Warrior C	.12	.30
51 Horox Ryyder C	.12	.30
52 I Will Not Defer U	.40	1.00
53 I've Decided To Go Back C	.12	.30
54 Imperial Arrest Order and Secret Plans R	3.00	8.00
55 Imperial Artillery R	3.00	8.00
56 Inconsequential Barriers C	.12	.30
57 Insurrection and Aim High R	2.50	6.00
58 Jawa DARK C	.12	.30
59 Jawa LIGHT C	.12	.30
60 Keder The Black R	1.00	2.50
61 Ki-Adi-Mundi U	.40	1.00
62 Kill Them Immediately C	.12	.30
63 Lana Dobreed U	.40	1.00
64 Laser Cannon Battery U	.40	1.00
65 Liana Merian U	.40	1.00
66 Lieutenant Williams U	.40	1.00
67 Little Real Power C	.12	.30
68 Lott Dod R	1.25	3.00
69 Mace Windu R	10.00	20.00
70 Malastare DARK U	.40	1.00
71 Malastare LIGHT U	.40	1.00
72 Mas Amedda U	.40	1.00
73 Master Qui-Gon R	3.00	8.00
74 Masterful Move and Endor Occupation R	2.00	5.00
75 Maul Strikes R	2.00	5.00
76 Maul's Sith Infiltrator R	3.00	8.00
77 Might Of The Republic R	2.50	6.00
78 Mind Tricks Don't Work On Me U	.40	1.00
79 Mindful Of The Future C	.12	.30
80 Motion Supported U	.40	1.00
81 Murr Danod R	1.00	2.50
82 My Lord, Is That Legal? I Will Make It Legal U	.40	1.00
83 My Loyal Bodyguard U	.40	1.00
84 Naboo Blaster C	.12	.30
85 Naboo Blaster Rifle DARK C	.12	.30
86 Naboo Blaster Rifle LIGHT C	.12	.30
87 Naboo Defense Fighter C	.12	.30
88 Naboo Fighter Pilot C	.12	.30
89 Naboo Security Officer Blaster C	.12	.30
90 Naboo DARK U	.40	1.00
91 Naboo LIGHT U	.40	1.00
92 Naboo: Battle Plains DARK C	.12	.30
93 Naboo: Battle Plains LIGHT C	.12	.30
94 Naboo: Swamp DARK C	.12	.30
95 Naboo: Swamp LIGHT C	.12	.30
96 Naboo: Theed Palace Courtyard DARK C	.12	.30
97 Naboo: Theed Palace Courtyard LIGHT C	.12	.30
98 Naboo: Theed Palace Docking Bay DARK C	.12	.30
99 Naboo: Theed Palace Docking Bay LIGHT C	.12	.30
100 Naboo: Theed Palace Throne Room DARK C	.12	.30
101 Naboo: Theed Palace Throne Room LIGHT C	.12	.30
102 Neimoidian Advisor U	.40	1.00
103 Neimoidian Pilot C	.12	.30
104 New Leadership Is Needed C	.12	.30
105 No Civility, Only Politics C	.12	.30
106 No Money, No Parts, No Deal! You're A Slave? U	.40	1.00
107 Nute Gunray R	1.00	2.50
108 Odin Nesloor U	.40	1.00
109 On The Payroll Of The Trade Federation C	.12	.30
110 Orn Free Taa C	.12	.30
111 Our Blockade Is Perfectly Legal U	.40	1.00
112 P-59 R	3.00	8.00
113 P-60 R	1.50	4.00
114 Panaka's Blaster R	1.25	3.00
115 Passel Argente C	.12	.30
116 Phylo Gandish R	1.50	4.00
117 Plea To The Court U	.40	1.00
118 Plead My Case To The Senate Sanity And Compassion U	.40	1.00
119 Plo Koon R	3.00	8.00
120 Queen Amidala, Ruler Of Naboo R	5.00	10.00
121 Queen's Royal Starship R	1.25	3.00
122 Radiant VII R	1.50	4.00
123 Rebel Artillery R	3.00	8.00
124 Republic Cruiser C	.12	.30
125 Reveal Ourselves To The Jedi C	.12	.30
126 Ric Olie R	1.00	2.50
127 Rune Haako R	1.00	2.50
128 Sabe R	1.25	3.00
129 Sache U	.40	1.00
130 Secure Route U	.40	1.00
131 Security Battle Droid C	.12	.30
132 Security Control U	.40	1.00
133 Sei Taria U	.40	1.00
134 Senator Palpatine (head and shoulders) R	3.00	8.00
135 Senator Palpatine (head shot) R	15.00	30.00
136 Sense DARK U	.40	1.00
137 Sense LIGHT U	.40	1.00
138 Short Range Fighters and Watch Your Back! R	2.50	6.00
139 Speak With The Jedi Council R	3.00	8.00
140 Squabbling Delegates R	1.25	3.00
141 Stay Here, Where It's Safe C	.12	.30
142 Supreme Chancellor Valorum R	1.00	2.50
143 Tatooine DARK U	.40	1.00
144 Tatooine LIGHT U	.40	1.00
145 Tatooine: Marketplace DARK C	.12	.30
146 Tatooine: Marketplace LIGHT C	.12	.30
147 Tatooine: Mos Espa Docking Bay DARK C	.12	.30
148 Tatooine: Mos Espa Docking Bay LIGHT C	.12	.30
149 Tatooine: Watto's Junkyard DARK C	.12	.30
150 Tatooine: Watto's Junkyard LIGHT C	.12	.30
151 TC-14 R	1.00	2.50
152 Televan Koreyy R	1.00	2.50
153 Tendau Bendon U	.40	1.00
154 Tey How U	.40	1.00
155 The Gravest Of Circumstances U	.40	1.00
156 The Hyperdrive Generator's Gone We'll Need A New One U	.40	1.00
157 The Phantom Menace R	5.00	10.00
158 The Point Is Conceded C	.12	.30
159 They Will Be No Match For You R	1.00	2.50
160 They're Still Coming Through! U	.40	1.00
161 This Is Outrageous! U	.40	1.00
162 Thrown Back C	.12	.30
163 Tikkes C	.12	.30
164 Toonbuck Toora U	.40	1.00
165 Trade Federation Battleship U	.40	1.00
166 Trade Federation Droid Control Ship R	1.25	3.00
167 Tusken Raider C	.12	.30
168 Vote Now! DARK R	1.00	2.50
169 Vote Now! LIGHT R	1.25	3.00
170 We Must Accelerate Our Plans R	10.00	20.00
171 We Wish To Board At Once R	2.00	5.00
172 We're Leaving C	.12	.30
173 Wipe Them Out, All Of Them U	.40	1.00
174 Yade M'rak U	.40	1.00
175 Yané U	.40	1.00
176 Yarua U	.40	1.00
177 Yeb Yeb Adem'thorn C	.12	.30
178 Yoda, Senior Council Member R	2.50	6.00
179 You Cannot Hide Forever and Mobilization Points R	2.50	6.00
180 You've Got A Lot Of Guts Coming Here R	1.25	3.00
181 Your Insight Serves You Well and Staging Areas R	1.00	2.50
182 Coruscant Dark Side List 1	.12	.30
183 Coruscant Dark Side List 2	.12	.30
184 Coruscant Light Side List 1	.12	.30
185 Coruscant Light Side List 2	.12	.30
186 Coruscant Rule Card 1	.12	.30
187 Coruscant Rule Card 2	.12	.30
188 Coruscant Rule Card 3	.12	.30

2001 Star Wars Reflections III

Card	Low	High
COMPLETE SET (96)	80.00	150.00
BOOSTER BOX (30 PACKS)	250.00	350.00
BOOSTER PACK (11 CARDS)	7.50	15.00
RELEASED IN		
1 A Close Race PM	1.00	2.50
2 A Remote Planet PM	1.00	2.50
3 A Tragedy Has Occured PM	1.25	3.00
4 A Useless Gesture PM	1.00	2.50
5 Aim High PM	1.25	3.00
6 Allegations of Coruption PM	1.00	2.50
7 An Unusual Amount Of Fear PM	1.00	2.50
8 Another Pathetic Lifeform PM	1.00	2.50
9 Armament Dismantled PM	1.00	2.50
10 Battle Order PM	1.00	2.50
11 Battle Plan PM	1.25	3.00
12 Bib Fortuna PM	1.00	2.50
13 Blizzard 4 PM	2.00	5.00
14 Blockade Flagship: Hallway PM	1.00	2.50
15 Blow Parried PM	1.00	2.50
16 Boba Fett, Bounty Hunter PM	6.00	12.00
17 Chewie, Enraged PM	1.50	4.00
18 Clinging To The Edge PM	1.00	2.50
19 Colo Claw Fish DARK PM	1.00	2.50
20 Colo Claw Fish LIGHT PM	1.00	2.50
21 Come Here You Big Coward PM	1.25	3.00
22 Conduct Your Search PM	1.25	3.00
23 Crossfire PM	1.00	2.50
24 Dark Rage PM	1.00	2.50
25 Darth Maul's Demise PM	1.00	2.50
26 Deep Hatred PM	1.00	2.50
27 Desperate Times PM	1.00	2.50
28 Diversionary Tactics PM	1.00	2.50
29 Do They Have A Code Clearance? PM	1.25	3.00
30 Do, Or Do Not PM	1.00	2.50
31 Don't Do That Again PM	1.00	2.50
32 Echo Base Sensors PM	1.25	3.00
33 Energy Walls DARK PM	1.00	2.50
34 Energy Walls LIGHT PM	1.00	2.50
35 Ewok Celebration PM	1.00	2.50
36 Fall Of A Jedi PM	1.00	2.50
37 Fanfare PM	1.00	2.50
38 Fear Is My Ally PM	1.00	2.50
39 Force Push PM	1.25	3.00
40 Han, Chewie, and The Falcon PM	6.00	12.00
41 He Can Go About His Business PM	1.00	2.50
42 Horace Vancil PM	1.00	2.50
43 Inner Strength PM	1.00	2.50
44 Jabba Desilijic Tiure PM	1.00	2.50
45 Jar Jar's Electropole PM	1.00	2.50
46 Jedi Leap PM	1.00	2.50
47 Lando Calrissian, Scoundrel PM	2.00	5.00
48 Lando's Not A System, He's A Man PM	1.00	2.50
49 Leave them to Me PM	1.00	2.50
50 Leia, Rebel Princess PM	2.50	6.00
51 Let's Keep A Little Optimism Here PM	1.00	2.50
52 Lord Maul PM	7.50	15.00
53 Maul's Double-Bladed Lightsaber PM	2.00	5.00
54 Naboo: Theed Palace Generator Core DARK PM	1.00	2.50
55 Naboo: Theed Palace Generator Core LIGHT PM	1.00	2.50
56 Naboo: Theed Palace Generator DARK PM	1.00	2.50
57 Naboo: Theed Palace Generator LIGHT PM	1.00	2.50
58 No Escape PM	1.00	2.50
59 No Match For A Sith PM	1.00	2.50
60 Obi-Wan Kenobi, Jedi Knight PM	1.50	4.00
61 Obi-Wan's Lightsaber PM	1.00	2.50
62 Only Jedi Carry That Weapon PM	1.00	2.50
63 Opee Sea Killer DARK PM	1.00	2.50
64 Opee Sea Killer LIGHT PM	1.00	2.50
65 Oppressive Enforcement PM	1.00	2.50
66 Ounee Ta PM	1.00	2.50
67 Planetary Defenses PM	1.00	2.50
68 Prepare For A Surface Attack PM	1.00	2.50
69 Qui-Gon Jinn, Jedi Master PM	2.50	6.00
70 Qui-Gon's End PM	1.25	3.00
71 Resistance PM	1.00	2.50
72 Sando Aqua Monster DARK PM	1.00	2.50
73 Sando Aqua Monster LIGHT PM	1.00	2.50
74 Secret Plans PM	1.00	2.50
75 Sio Bibble PM	1.00	2.50
76 Stormtrooper Garrison PM	5.00	10.00
77 Strike Blockaded PM	1.00	2.50
78 The Ebb Of Battle PM	1.00	2.50
79 The Hutts Are Gangsters PM	1.00	2.50
80 There Is No Try PM	1.25	3.00
81 They Must Never Again Leave This City PM	1.00	2.50
82 Thok and Thug PM	1.00	2.50
83 Through The Corridor PM	1.00	2.50
84 Ultimatum PM	1.00	2.50
85 Unsalvageable PM	1.00	2.50
86 We'll Let Fate-a Decide, Huh? PM	1.00	2.50
87 Weapon Of A Fallen Mentor PM	1.00	2.50
88 Weapon Of A Sith PM	1.00	2.50
89 Where Are Those Droidekas?! PM	1.00	2.50
90 Wipe Them Out, All Of Them PM	1.00	2.50
91 Wise Advice PM	1.00	2.50
92 Yoda, Master Of The Force PM	5.00	10.00
93 You Cannot Hide Forever PM	1.00	2.50
94 You've Never Won A Race? PM	1.00	2.50
95 Your Insight Serves You Well PM	1.00	2.50
96 Your Ship? PM	1.25	3.00

2001 Star Wars Tatooine

COMPLETE SET (95) 25.00 60.00
BOOSTER BOX (30 PACKS) 50.00 100.00
BOOSTER PACK (11 CARDS) 2.50 5.00
RELEASED IN MAY 2001
1 A Jedi's Concentration C .12 .30
2 A Jedi's Focus C .12 .30
3 A Jedi's Patience C .12 .30
4 A Jedi's Resilience U .40 1.00
5 A Million Voices Crying Out R .75 2.00
6 A Step Backward U .40 1.00
7 Anakin's Podracer R .75 2.00
8 Aurra Sing R 1.50 4.00
9 Ben Quadinaros' Podracer C .12 .30
10 Boonta Eve Podrace DARK R .75 2.50
11 Boonta Eve Podrace LIGHT R .75 2.00
12 Brisky Morning Munchen R .75 2.00
13 Caldera Righim C .12 .30
14 Changing The Odds C .12 .30
15 Daroe R .75 2.00
16 Darth Maul R 1.50 4.00
17 Deneb Both U .40 1.00
18 Don't Do That Again C .12 .30
19 Dud Bolt's Podracer C .12 .30
20 Either Way, You Win U .40 1.00
21 End Of A Reign R .75 2.00
22 Entering The Arena U .40 1.00
23 Eopie C .12 .30
24 Eventually You'll Lose U .40 1.00
25 Fanfare C .12 .30
26 Gamall Wironicc U .40 1.00
27 Ghana Gleemort U .40 1.00
28 Gragra U .40 1.00
29 Great Shot, Kid! R .75 2.00
30 Grugnak U .40 1.00
31 His Name Is Anakin C .12 .30
32 Hit Racer U .40 1.00
33 I Can't Believe He's Gone C .12 .30
34 I Did It! R .75 2.00
35 I Will Find Them Quickly, Master R .75 2.00
36 I'm Sorry R .75 2.00
37 If The Trace Was Correct U .40 1.00
38 Jar Jar Binks R .75 2.00
39 Jedi Escape C .12 .30
40 Join Me! U .40 1.00
41 Keeping The Empire Out Forever R .75 2.00
42 Lathe U .40 1.00
43 Lightsaber Parry C .12 .30
44 Loci Rosen U .40 1.00
45 Losing Track C .12 .30
46 Maul's Electrobinoculars C .12 .30
47 Maul's Lightsaber R .75 2.00
48 Neck And Neck U .40 1.00
49 Ni Chuba Na?? C .12 .30
50 Obi-wan Kenobi, Padawan Learner R 1.00 2.50
51 Padme Naberrie R 2.00 5.00
52 Pit Crews U .40 1.00
53 Pit Droid C .12 .30
54 Podrace Prep U .40 1.00
55 Podracer Collision U .40 1.00
56 Quietly Observing U .40 1.00
57 Qui-Gon Jinn R 1.50 4.00
58 Qui-Gon Jinn's Lightsaber R 1.00 2.50
59 Rachalt Hyst U .40 1.00
60 Sebulba R .75 2.00
61 Sebulba's Podracer R .75 2.00
62 Shmi Skywalker R .75 2.00
63 Sith Fury C .12 .30
64 Sith Probe Droid R 1.00 2.50
65 Start Your Engines! U .40 1.00
66 Tatooine: City Outskirts U .40 1.00
67 Tatooine: Desert Landing Site R .75 2.00
68 Tatooine: Mos Espa DARK C .12 .30
69 Tatooine: Mos Espa LIGHT C .12 .30
70 Tatooine: Podrace Arena DARK C .12 .30
71 Tatooine: Podrace Arena LIGHT C .12 .30
72 Tatooine: Podracer Bay C .12 .30
73 Tatooine: Slave Quarters U .40 1.00
74 Teemto Pagalies' Podracer C .12 .30
75 The Camp C .12 .30
76 The Shield Is Down! R .75 2.00
77 There Is No Conflict C .12 .30
78 Threepio With His Parts Showing R 1.25 3.00
79 Too Close For Comfort U .40 1.00
80 Vader's Anger C .12 .30
81 Watto R 1.25 3.00
82 Watto's Box C .12 .30
83 Watto's Chance Cube U .40 1.00
84 We Shall Double Our Efforts! R .75 2.00
85 What Was It U .40 1.00
86 Yotts Orren U .40 1.00
87 You May Start Your Landing R .75 2.00
88 You Swindled Me! U .40 1.00
89 You Want This, Don't You? C .12 .30
90 You'll Find I'm Full Of Surprises U .40 1.00
91 Tatooine Dark Side List .12 .30
92 Tatooine Light Side List .12 .30
93 Tatooine Rule Card 1 .12 .30
94 Tatooine Rule Card 2 .12 .30
95 Tatooine Rule Card 3 .12 .30

2001 Star Wars Theed Palace

COMPLETE SET (121) 80.00 150.00
BOOSTER BOX (30 PACKS) 400.00 500.00
BOOSTER PACK (11 CARDS) 15.00 20.00
RELEASED IN DECEMBER 2001
FINAL EXPANSION PRODUCT BY DECIPHER
1 3B3-10 U .30 .75
2 3B3-1204 U .30 .75
3 3B3-21 U .30 .75
4 3B3-888 U .30 .75
5 AAT Assault Leader R 1.00 2.50
6 AAT Laser Cannon U .30 .75
7 Activate The Droids C .12 .30
8 After Her! R .75 2.00
9 Amidala's Blaster R .75 2.00
10 Armored Attack Tank U .30 .75
11 Artoo, Brave Little Droid R 1.50 4.00
12 Ascension Guns U .30 .75
13 At Last We Are Getting Results C .12 .30
14 Battle Droid Officer C .12 .30
15 Battle Droid Pilot C .12 .30
16 Big Boomers! C .12 .30
17 Blockade Flaghip R 1.50 4.00
18 Blockade Flagship: .30 .75
Docking Bay DARK U
19 Blockade Flagship: .30 .75
Docking Bay LIGHT U
20 Bok Askol U .30 .75
21 Booma C .12 .30
22 Boss Nass R 1.25 3.00
23 Bravo 1 R .75 2.00
24 Bravo 2 U .30 .75
25 Bravo 3 U .30 .75
26 Bravo 4 U .30 .75
27 Bravo 5 U .30 .75
28 Bravo Fighter R .75 2.00
29 Captain Tarpals R .75 2.00
30 Captain Tarpals' Electropole C .12 .30
31 Captian Daultay Dofine R .75 2.00
32 Cease Fire! C .12 .30
33 Corporal Rushing U .30 .75
34 Dams Denna U .30 .75
35 Darth Maul With Lightsaber R 12.00 25.00
36 Darth Sidious R 25.00 50.00
37 DFS Squadron Starfighter C .12 .30
38 DFS-1015 U .30 .75
39 DFS-1308 R .75 2.00
40 DFS-327 C .12 .30
41 Droid Racks R 1.25 3.00
42 Droid Starfighter Laser Cannons C .12 .30
43 Drop Your Weapons C .12 .30
44 Electropole C .12 .30
45 Energy Shell Launchers C .12 .30
46 Fambaa C .12 .30
47 Fighters Straight Ahead U .30 .75
48 General Jar Jar R 1.25 3.00
49 Get To Your Ships! C .12 .30
50 Gian Speeder C .12 .30
51 Gimme A Lift! R .75 2.00
52 Gungan Energy Shield C .12 .30
53 Gungan General C .12 .30
54 Gungan Guard C .12 .30
55 Halt! C .12 .30
56 I'll Try Spinning R .75 2.00
57 Infantry Battle Droid C .12 .30
58 Invasion / In Complete Control U .30 .75
59 It's On Automatic Pilot C .12 .30
60 Jerus Jannick U .30 .75
61 Kaadu C .12 .30
62 Let's Go Left R .75 2.00
63 Lieutenant Arven Wendik U .30 .75
64 Lieutenant Chamberlyn U .30 .75
65 Lieutenant Rya Kirsch U .30 .75
66 Mace Windu, Jedi Master R 7.50 15.00
67 Master, Destroyers! R 1.00 2.50
68 Multi Troop Transport U .30 .75
69 Naboo Celebration R .75 2.00
70 Naboo Occupation R 1.00 2.50
71 Naboo: Boss Nass's Chambers U .30 .75
72 Naboo: Otoh Gunga Entrance U .30 .75
73 Naboo: Theed Palace Hall U .30 .75
74 Naboo: Theed Palace Hallway U .30 .75
75 No Giben Up, General Jar Jar! R .75 2.00
76 Nothing Can Get Through Are Shield R 1.00 2.50
77 Nute Gunray, Neimoidian Viceroy R 2.00 5.00
78 Officer Dolphe U .30 .75
79 Officer Ellberger U .30 .75
80 Officer Perosei U .30 .75
81 OOM-9 U .30 .75
82 Open Fire! C .12 .30
83 OWO-1 With Backup R 1.25 3.00
84 Panaka, Protector Of The Queen R 2.50 6.00
85 Proton Torpedoes C .12 .30
86 Queen Amidala R 10.00 20.00
87 Qui-Gon Jinn With Lightsaber R 7.50 15.00
88 Rayno Vaca U .30 .75
89 Rep Been U .30 .75
90 Ric Olie, Bravo Leader R .75 2.00
91 Rolling, Rolling, Rolling R 1.00 2.50
92 Royal Naboo Security Officer C .12 .30
93 Rune Haako, Legal Counsel R 1.25 3.00
94 Senate Hovercam DARK R 1.00 2.50
95 Senate Hovercam LIGHT R 1.00 2.50
96 Sil Unch U .30 .75
97 Single Trooper Aerial Platform C .12 .30
98 SSA-1015 U .30 .75
99 SSA-306 U .30 .75
100 SSA-719 R 1.25 3.00
101 STAP Blaster Cannons C .12 .30
102 Steady, Steady C .12 .30
103 Take Them Away C .12 .30
104 Take This! C .12 .30
105 Tank Commander C .12 .30
106 The Deflector Shield Is Too Strong R .75 2.00
107 There They Are! U .30 .75
108 They Win This Round R .75 2.00
109 This Is Not Good C .12 .30
110 Trade Federation Landing Craft C .12 .30
111 TT-6 R 1.00 2.50
112 TT-9 R .75 2.00
113 We Didn't Hit It C .12 .30
114 We Don't Have Time For This R 1.00 2.50
115 We Have A Plan .12 .30
They Will Be Lost And Confused C
116 We're Hit Artoo C .12 .30
117 Wesa Gotta Grand Army C .12 .30
118 Wesa Ready To Do Our-sa Part C .12 .30
119 Whoooo! C .12 .30
120 Theed Palace Dark Side List .12 .30
121 Theed Palace Light Side List .12 .30

2002 Star Wars Attack of the Clones

COMPLETE SET (180) 30.00 80.00
BOOSTER BOX (36 PACKS) 20.00 40.00
BOOSTER PACK (11 CARDS) 1.00 1.50
*FOIL: .75X TO 2X BASIC CARDS
RELEASED IN APRIL 2002
1 Anakin Skywalker (A) R .60 1.50
2 Anakin Skywalker (B) R .60 1.50
3 Assassin Droid ASN-121 (A) R .60 1.50
4 Bail Organa (A) R .60 1.50
5 Battle Fatigue R .60 1.50
6 Boba Fett (A) R .60 1.50
7 Captain Typho (A) R .60 1.50
8 Clear the Skies R .60 1.50
9 Clone Officer R .60 1.50
10 Dark Rendezvous R .60 1.50
11 Dark Side's Command R .60 1.50
12 Dark Side's Compulsion R .60 1.50
13 Darth Sidious (A) R .60 1.50
14 Darth Tyranus (A) R .60 1.50
15 Destruction of Hope R .60 1.50
16 Dexter Jettster (A) R .60 1.50
17 Geonosian Sentry R .60 1.50
18 Hero's Duty R .60 1.50
19 Hero's Flaw R .60 1.50
20 Interference in the Senate R .60 1.50
21 Jango Fett (A) R .60 1.50
22 Jango Fett (B) R .60 1.50
23 Jar Jar Binks (A) R .60 1.50
24 Jedi Call for Help R .60 1.50
25 Jedi Council Summons R .60 1.50
26 Jedi Knight's Deflection R .60 1.50
27 Lama Su (A) R .60 1.50
28 Luxury Airspeeder U .20 .50
29 A Moment's Rest R .60 1.50
30 Naboo Defense Station R .60 1.50
31 Obi-Wan Kenobi (A) R .60 1.50
32 Obi-Wan's Starfighter (A) R .60 1.50
33 Order Here R .60 1.50
34 Padmé Amidala (A) R .60 1.50
35 Padmé Amidala (B) R .60 1.50
36 Padmé's Yacht (A) R .60 1.50
37 Plo Koon (A) R .60 1.50
38 Plot the Secession R .60 1.50
39 Power Dive R .60 1.50
40 Queen Jamillia (A) R .60 1.50
41 R2-D2 (A) R .60 1.50
42 San Hill (A) U .20 .50
43 Second Effort R .60 1.50
44 Seek the Council's Wisdom R .60 1.50
45 Shu Mai (A) U .20 .50
46 Slave I (A) R .60 1.50
47 Spirit of the Fallen R .60 1.50
48 Target the Senator R .60 1.50
49 Taun We (A) R .60 1.50
50 Trade Federation Battleship Core R .60 1.50
51 Tyranus's Edict R .60 1.50
52 Tyranus's Geonosian Speeder (A) R .60 1.50
53 Tyranus's Solar Sailer (A) R .60 1.50
54 Tyranus's Wrath R .60 1.50
55 War Will Follow R .60 1.50
56 Ward of the Jedi R .60 1.50
57 Windu's Solution R .60 1.50
58 Yoda (A) R .60 1.50
59 Yoda's Intervention R .60 1.50
60 Zam Wesell (A) R .60 1.50
61 Acklay U .20 .50
62 Anakin Skywalker (C) U .20 .50
63 Anakin's Inspiration U .20 .50
64 AT-TE Walker 23X U .20 .50
65 AT-TE Walker 71E R .60 1.50
66 Attract Enemy Fire U .20 .50
67 C-3PO (A) U .20 .50
68 Capture Obi-Wan U .20 .50
69 Chancellor Palpatine (A) R .60 1.50
70 Chase the Villain U .20 .50
71 Cheat the Game U .20 .50
72 Cliegg Lars (A) U .20 .50
73 Clone Warrior 4/163 U .20 .50
74 Clone Warrior 5/373 U .20 .50
75 Commerce Guild Droid Platoon U .20 .50
76 Cordé (A) U .20 .50
77 Coruscant Freighter AA-9 (A) U .20 .50
78 Dark Speed U .20 .50
79 Darth Tyranus (B) U .20 .50
80 Departure Time U .20 .50
81 Destroyer Droid, P Series U .20 .50
82 Down in Flames U .20 .50
83 Droid Control Ship U .20 .50
84 Elan Sleazebaggano (A) R .60 1.50
85 Geonosian Guard U .20 .50
86 Geonosian Warrior U .20 .50
87 Go to the Temple U .20 .50
88 Infantry Battle Droid, B1 Series U .20 .50
89 Jango Fett (C) U .20 .50
90 Jawa Sandcrawler U .20 .50
91 Jedi Patrol U .20 .50
92 Kaminoan Guard U .20 .50
93 Kit Fisto (A) U .20 .50
94 Master and Apprentice U .20 .50
95 Naboo Security Guard U .20 .50
96 Naboo Spaceport U .20 .50
97 Nexu U .20 .50
98 Nute Gunray (A) U .20 .50
99 Obi-Wan Kenobi (B) U .20 .50
100 Padmé Amidala (C) U .20 .50
101 Poggle the Lesser (A) U .20 .50
102 Reek U .20 .50
103 Republic Assault Ship U .20 .50
104 Republic Cruiser C .10 .25
105 Shaak Ti (A) U .20 .50
106 Ship Arrival U .20 .50
107 Splinter the Republic U .20 .50
108 Strength of Hate U .20 .50
109 Subtle Assassination U .20 .50
110 Super Battle Droid 8EX U .20 .50
111 Trade Federation Battleship U .20 .50
112 Trade Federation C-9979 U .20 .50
113 Tyranus's Gift U .20 .50
114 Underworld Connections U .20 .50
115 Wat Tambor (A) U .20 .50
116 Watto (A) U .20 .50
117 Weapon Response U .20 .50
118 Wedding of Destiny U .20 .50
119 Yoda (B) U .20 .50
120 Zam's Airspeeder (A) U .20 .50
121 Anakin Skywalker (D) C .10 .25
122 Battle Droid Squad C .10 .25
123 Bravo N-1 Starfighter C .10 .25
124 Chancellor's Guard Squad C .10 .25
125 Clone Platoon C .10 .25
126 Clone Squad C .10 .25
127 Commerce Guild Droid 81 C .10 .25
128 Commerce Guild Starship C .10 .25
129 Corellian Star Shuttle C .10 .25
130 Darth Tyranus (C) C .10 .25
131 Destroyer Droid Squad C .10 .25
132 Droid Starfighter DFS-4CT C .10 .25
133 Droid Starfighter Squadron C .10 .25
134 Droid Starfighter Wing C .10 .25
135 Elite Jedi Squad C .10 .25
136 Flying Geonosian Squad C .10 .25
137 Geonosian Defense Platform C .10 .25
138 Geonosian Fighter C .10 .25
139 Geonosian Squad C .10 .25
140 Gozanti Cruiser C .10 .25
141 Hatch a Clone C .10 .25
142 Hero's Dodge C .10 .25
143 High-Force Dodge C .10 .25
144 Hyperdrive Ring C .10 .25
145 InterGalactic Banking Clan Starship C .10 .25
146 Jango Fett (D) C .10 .25
147 Jedi Starfighter 3R3 C .10 .25
148 Knockdown C .10 .25
149 Lost in the Asteroids C .10 .25
150 Lull in the Fighting C .10 .25
151 Mending C .10 .25
152 N-1 Starfighter C .10 .25
153 Naboo Cruiser C .10 .25
154 Naboo Royal Starship C .10 .25
155 Naboo Senatorial Escort C .10 .25
156 Naboo Starfighter Squadron C .10 .25
157 Obi-Wan Kenobi (C) C .10 .25
158 Padawan's Deflection C .10 .25
159 Padmé Amidala (D) C .10 .25
160 Patrol Speeder C .10 .25
161 Peace on Naboo C .10 .25
162 Pilot's Dodge C .10 .25
163 Recon Speeder U .10 .25
164 Republic Attack Gunship UH-478 C .10 .25
165 Repulsorlift Malfunction C .10 .25
166 Return to Spaceport C .10 .25
167 Rickshaw C .10 .25
168 Slumming on Coruscant C .10 .25
169 Sonic Shockwave C .10 .25
170 Speeder Bike Squadron C .10 .25
171 Starship Refit C .10 .25
172 Surge of Power C .10 .25
173 Swoop Bike C .10 .25
174 Take the Initiative C .10 .25
175 Target Locked C .10 .25
176 Taylander Shuttle C .10 .25
177 Techno Union Starship C .10 .25
178 Trade Federation War Freighter C .10 .25
179 Walking Droid Fighter C .10 .25
180 Zam Wesell (B) C .10 .25

2002 Star Wars A New Hope

COMPLETE SET (180) 30.00 80.00
BOOSTER BOX (36 PACKS) 25.00 50.00
BOOSTER PACK (11 CARDS) 1.50 3.00
*FOIL: .8X TO 2X BASIC CARDS
RELEASED IN OCTOBER 2002
1 Admiral Motti (A) R .60 1.50
2 Beru Lars (A) R .60 1.50
3 Blaster Barrage R .60 1.50
4 Capture the Falcon R .60 1.50
5 Contingency Plan R .60 1.50
6 Dannik Jerriko (A) R .60 1.50
7 Darth Vader (A) R 1.25 3.00
8 Desperate Confrontation R .75 2.00
9 Destroy Alderaan R .60 1.50
10 Dianoga (A) R .60 1.50
11 Disturbance in the Force R .60 1.50
12 It's Not Over Yet R .60 1.50
13 EG-6 Power Droid R .60 1.50
14 Elite Stormtrooper Squad R .60 1.50
15 Figrin D'an (A) R .75 2.00
16 Greedo (A) R .60 1.50
17 Hold 'Em Off R .60 1.50
18 Imperial Blockade R .60 1.50
19 Imperial Navy Helmsman R .60 1.50
20 Imperial Sentry Droid R .60 1.50
21 IT-0 Interrogator Droid R .75 2.00
22 Jawa Leader R .60 1.50
23 Krayt Dragon R .60 1.50
24 Leia's Kiss R .60 1.50
25 Luke Skywalker (B) R .60 1.50
26 Luke Skywalker (A) R .60 1.50
27 Luke's Speeder (A) R .60 1.50
28 Luke's X-Wing (A) R .60 1.50
29 Momaw Nadon (A) R 1.00 2.50
30 Most Desperate Hour R .60 1.50
31 No Escape R .60 1.50
32 Obi-Wan Kenobi (E) R .60 1.50
33 Obi-Wan's Prowess R .60 1.50
34 Obi-Wan's Task R .60 1.50
35 Our Only Hope R .60 1.50
36 Owen Lars (A) R .60 1.50
37 Plan of Attack R .60 1.50
38 Princess Leia (A) R .60 1.50
39 Protection of the Master R .60 1.50
40 R5-D4 (A) R .60 1.50
41 Rebel Crew Chief R .60 1.50
42 Rebel Lieutenant R .60 1.50
43 Regroup on Yavin R .60 1.50
44 Sandtrooper R .60 1.50
45 Starfighter's End R .60 1.50
46 Stormtrooper TK-421 R .60 1.50
47 Strategy Session R .60 1.50
48 Strike Me Down R .60 1.50
49 Surprise Attack R .60 1.50
50 Tantive IV (A) R .60 1.50
51 Tarkin's Stench R .60 1.50
52 TIE Fighter Elite Pilot U .20 .50
53 Tiree (A) R .60 1.50
54 Tractor Beam R .60 1.50
55 URoRRuR'R'R (A) R .60 1.50
56 Imperial Manipulation R .60 1.50
57 Vader's Leadership R .60 1.50
58 Vader's TIE Fighter (A) R .60 1.50
59 Wedge Antilles (A) R .60 1.50
60 Yavin 4 Hangar Base R .60 1.50
61 Astromech Assistance U .20 .50
62 Benefits of Training U .20 .50
63 Biggs Darklighter (A) U .20 .50
64 C-3PO (C) U .20 .50
65 Commander Praji (A) U .20 .50
66 Tatooine Sandcrawler U .20 .50
67 Darth Vader (B) U .20 .50
68 Death Star Hangar Bay U .20 .50
69 Death Star Plans U .20 .50
70 Death Star Scanning Technician U .20 .50
71 Death Star Superlaser Gunner U .20 .50
72 Death Star Turbolaser Gunner U .20 .50
73 Demonstration of Power U .20 .50
74 Devastator (A) U .20 .50
75 Dissolve the Senate U .20 .50
76 Error in Judgment U .20 .50
77 Fate of the Dragon U .20 .50
78 General Dodonna (A) U .20 .50
79 General Tagge (A) U .20 .50
80 Han's Courage U .20 .50
81 Imperial Control Station U .20 .50
82 Imperial Navy Lieutenant U .20 .50
83 Insignificant Power U .20 .50
84 Into the Garbage Chute C .10 .25
85 Jawa U .20 .50
86 Jawa Collection Team U .20 .50
87 Jedi Extinction U .20 .50
88 Jon Dutch Vander (A) U .20 .50
89 Learning the Force U .20 .50
90 Lieutenant Tanbris (A) U .20 .50
91 LIN Demolitionmech U .20 .50
92 Luke Skywalker (C) U .20 .50
93 Luke's Warning U .20 .50
94 Mounted Stormtrooper U .20 .50
95 Mouse Droid U .20 .50
96 Obi-Wan Kenobi (F) U .20 .50
97 Oil Bath U .20 .50
98 Princess Leia (B) U .20 .50
99 R2-D2 (C) U .20 .50
100 Rebel Blockade Runner U .20 .50
101 Rebel Control Officer U .20 .50
102 Rebel Control Post U .20 .50
103 Rebel Marine U .20 .50
104 Rebel Surrender U .20 .50
105 Rebel Trooper U .20 .50
106 Remote Seeker Droid U .20 .50
107 Press the Advantage U .20 .50
108 Stabilize Deflectors U .20 .50
109 Star Destroyer Commander U .20 .50
110 Stormtrooper Charge U .20 .50
111 Stormtrooper DV-692 U .20 .50
112 Stormtrooper Squad Leader U .20 .50
113 Stormtrooper TK-119 U .20 .50
114 Support in the Senate U .20 .50
115 Disrupt the Power System U .20 .50
116 Tatooine Speeder U .20 .50
117 Tusken Sharpshooter U .20 .50
118 Vader's Interference U .20 .50
119 Vader's TIE Fighter (B) U .60 1.50
120 Wuher (A) U .20 .50
121 Air Cover C .10 .25
122 Precise Blast C .10 .25
123 Stay Sharp C .10 .25
124 Carrack Cruiser C .10 .25
125 Darth Vader (C) C .10 .25
126 Death Star Cannon Tower C .10 .25
127 Death Star Guard Squad C .10 .25
128 Domesticated Bantha C .10 .25
129 Flare-S Swoop C .10 .25
130 Ground Support C .10 .25
131 Imperial Detention Block C .10 .25
132 Imperial Star Destroyer C .10 .25
133 Incom T-16 Skyhopper C .10 .25
134 Into Hiding C .10 .25
135 Jawa Squad C .10 .25
136 Jawa Supply Trip C .10 .25
137 Jump to Lightspeed C .10 .25
138 Luke Skywalker (D) C .10 .25
139 Luke's Repairs C .10 .25
140 Moisture Farm C .10 .25
141 Planetary Defense Turret C .10 .25
142 Nowhere to Run C .10 .25
143 Obi-Wan Kenobi (G) C .10 .25
144 Jedi Intervention C .10 .25
145 Obi-Wan's Plan C .10 .25
146 Penetrate the Shields C .10 .25
147 Preemptive Shot C .10 .25
148 Princess Leia (C) C .10 .25
149 Rebel Fighter Wing C .10 .25
150 Rebel Honor Company C .10 .25
151 Rebel Marine Squad C .10 .25
152 Rebel Pilot C .10 .25
153 Rebel Squad C .10 .25

154 Rescue C .10 .25
155 Slipping Through C .10 .25
156 SoroSuub V-35 Courier C .10 .25
157 Synchronized Assault C .10 .25
158 Stormtrooper Assault Team C .10 .25
159 Stormtrooper DV-523 C .10 .25
160 Stormtrooper Patrol C .10 .25
161 Stormtrooper Squad C .10 .25
162 TIE Fighter DS-3-12 C .10 .25
163 TIE Fighter DS-73-3 C .10 .25
164 TIE Fighter DS-55-6 C .10 .25
165 TIE Fighter DS-61-9 C .10 .25
166 TIE Fighter Pilot C .10 .25
167 TIE Fighter Squad C .10 .25
168 Tusken Squad C .10 .25
169 Vader's Grip U .10 .25
170 Victory-Class Star Destroyer C .10 .25
171 Well-Aimed Shot C .10 .25
172 X-wing Red One C .10 .25
173 X-wing Red Three C .10 .25
174 X-wing Red Two C .10 .25
175 X-wing Attack Formation C .10 .25
176 Y-wing Gold One C .10 .25
177 Y-wing Gold Squadron C .10 .25
178 YT-1300 Transport C .10 .25
179 YV-664 Light Freighter C .10 .25
180 Z-95 Headhunter C .10 .25

2002 Star Wars Sith Rising

COMPLETE SET (90) 15.00 40.00
BOOSTER BOX (36 PACKS) 25.00 50.00
BOOSTER PACK (11 CARDS) 1.00 2.00
*FOIL: .75X TO 2X BASIC CARDS
RELEASED IN JULY 2002
1 Aayla Secura (A) R .60 1.50
2 Anakin Skywalker (E) R .60 1.50
3 Aurra Sing (A) R .60 1.50
4 Chancellor Palpatine (B) R .60 1.50
5 Clone Captain R .60 1.50
6 Clone Facility R .60 1.50
7 Darth Maul (A) R .60 1.50
8 Darth Maul (C) R .60 1.50
9 Darth Sidious (B) R .60 1.50
10 Darth Tyranus (D) R .60 1.50
11 Geonosian Picadors R .60 1.50
12 Impossible Victory R .60 1.50
13 Jango Fett (E) R .60 1.50
14 Jedi Bravery R .60 1.50
15 Jedi Starfighter Wing R .60 1.50
16 Jocasta Nu (A) R .60 1.50
17 Mace Windu (A) R .60 1.50
18 Mace Windu (C) R .60 1.50
19 Massiff R .60 1.50
20 Nute Gunray (B) R .60 1.50
21 Republic Drop Ship R .60 1.50
22 Sio Bibble (A) R .60 1.50
23 Sith Infiltrator (A) R .60 1.50
24 Slave I (B) R .60 1.50
25 Super Battle Droid 5TE R .60 1.50
26 Trade Federation Control Core R .60 1.50
27 Tusken Camp R .60 1.50
28 Twilight of the Republic R .60 1.50
29 Unfriendly Fire R .60 1.50
30 Yoda (C) R .60 1.50
31 Aiwha Rider U .20 .50
32 C-3PO (B) U .20 .50
33 Careful Targeting U .20 .50
34 Clever Escape U .20 .50
35 Clone Trooper 6/298 U .20 .50
36 Darth Maul (B) U .20 .50
37 Darth Tyranus (E) U .20 .50
38 Destroyer Droid, W Series U .20 .50
39 Female Tusken Raider U .20 .50
40 Fog of War U .20 .50
41 Geonosian Scout U .20 .50
42 Hailfire Droid U .20 .50
43 Homing Spider Droid U .20 .50
44 Infantry Battle Droid U .20 .50
45 Jedi Heroes U .20 .50
46 Jedi Starfighter Scout U .20 .50
47 Mace Windu (B) U .20 .50
48 Moment of Truth U .20 .50
49 Obi_Wan Kenobi (D) U .20 .50
50 Out of His Misery U .20 .50
51 Padmé Amidala (E) U .20 .50
52 Passel Argente (A) U .20 .50
53 Price of Failure U .20 .50
54 R2-D2 (B) U .20 .50
55 Recognition of Valor U .20 .50
56 Sun Fac (A) U .20 .50
57 Techno Union Warship U .20 .50
58 Trade Federation Offensive U .20 .50
59 Tusken Raider U .20 .50
60 Visit the Lake Retreat U .20 .50
61 Acclamator-Class Assault Ship C .10 .25
62 Aggressive Negotiations C .10 .25
63 Anakin Skywalker (F) C .10 .25
64 AT-TE Troop Transport C .10 .25
65 Battle Droid Assault Squad C .10 .25
66 Brutal Assault C .10 .25
67 Clone Trooper Legion C .10 .25
68 Commerce Guild Cruiser C .10 .25
69 Commerce Guild Spider Droid C .10 .25
70 Concentrated Fire C .10 .25
71 Corsucant Speeder C .10 .25
72 Darth Maul (D) C .10 .25
73 Diplomatic Cruiser C .10 .25
74 Droid Starfighter DFS-1VR C .10 .25
75 Geonosian Artillery Battery C .10 .25
76 Geonosian Defense Fighter C .10 .25
77 Maul's Strategy C .10 .25
78 Mobile Assault Cannon C .10 .25
79 Naboo Starfighter Wing C .10 .25
80 Nubian Yacht C .10 .25
81 Padawan and Senator C .10 .25
82 Reassemble C-3PO C .10 .25
83 Republic LAAT/i Gunship C .10 .25
84 Retreat Underground R .10 .25
85 Run the Gauntlet C .10 .25
86 Senatorial Cruiser C .10 .25
87 Shoot Her or Something C .10 .25
88 Super Battle Droid Squad C .10 .25
89 Suppressing Fire C .10 .25
90 Trade Federation Warship C .10 .25

2003 Star Wars Battle of Yavin

COMPLETE SET (105) 60.00 120.00
BOOSTER BOX (36 PACKS) 30.00 50.00
BOOSTER PACK (11 CARDS) 2.50 5.00
*FOIL: .75X TO 2X BASIC CARDS
RELEASED IN MARCH 2003
1 Artoo's Repairs R 2.00 5.00
2 Blow This Thing R 1.50 4.00
3 Celebrate the Victory R .75 2.00
4 Chariot Light Assault Vehicle R .75 2.00
5 Chewbacca (B) R 4.00 10.00
6 Chewbacca (A) R 4.00 10.00
7 Chief Bast (A) R 2.00 5.00
8 Colonel Wullf Yularen (A) R 2.00 5.00
9 Darth Vader (D) R 4.00 10.00
10 Death Star (A) R 3.00 8.00
11 Death Star (C) R 3.00 8.00
12 Garven Dreis (A) R 1.25 3.00
13 Grand Moff Tarkin (A) R 3.00 8.00
14 Han Solo (B) R 5.00 12.00
15 Han Solo (A) R 4.00 10.00
16 Hero's Potential R .20 .50
17 Jek Porkins (A) R .60 1.50
18 Lieutenant Shann Childsen (A) R 1.25 3.00
19 Luke Skywalker (E) R 4.00 10.00
20 Luke's Skyhopper (A) R .20 .50
21 Luke's X-wing (B) R 2.00 5.00
22 Millennium Falcon (A) R 2.00 5.00
23 Millennium Falcon (B) R 2.00 5.00
24 Millennium Falcon (C) R 2.00 5.00
25 Obi-Wan Kenobi (H) R 4.00 10.00
26 Obi-Wan's Guidance R .75 2.00
27 Princess Leia (D) R 1.25 3.00
28 R2-X2 (A) R 1.25 3.00
29 R2-Q5 (A) R 1.25 3.00
30 Rebel Ground Crew Chief R .75 2.00
31 Second Wave R 1.25 3.00
32 Stormtrooper Commander R 4.00 10.00
33 Vader's Fury R 2.00 5.00
34 X-wing Squadron R 2.00 5.00
35 Your Powers Are Weak R 1.25 3.00
36 Alien Rage U .40 1.00
37 C-3PO (D) U .40 1.00
38 Chewbacca (C) U .40 1.00
39 Commander Willard (A) U .40 1.00
40 Countermeasures U .40 1.00
41 Darth Vader (E) U .40 1.00
42 Death Star (B) U .40 1.00
43 Death Star Trooper U .40 1.00
44 Deflectors Activated U .40 1.00
45 Grand Moff Tarkin (B) U .40 1.00
46 Grand Moff Tarkin (C) U .40 1.00
47 Han Solo (C) U .40 1.00
48 Heavy Fire Zone U .40 1.00
49 Imperial Dewback U .40 1.00
50 Interrogation Droid U .40 1.00
51 Jawa Crawler U .40 1.00
52 Jawa Scavenger U .40 1.00
53 Labria (A) U .40 1.00
54 Let the Wookiee Win U .40 1.00
55 Luke Skywalker (F) U .40 1.00
56 Luke's Speeder (B) U .40 1.00
57 Mobile Command Base U .40 1.00
58 Obi-Wan's Handiwork U .40 1.00
59 Princess Leia (E) U .40 1.00
60 R2-D2 (D) U .40 1.00
61 Rebel Armored Freerunner U .40 1.00
62 Refit on Yavin U .40 1.00
63 Sabers Locked U .40 1.00
64 Stormtrooper KE-829 U .40 1.00
65 Tatooine Hangar U .40 1.00
66 Tusken Raider Squad U .40 1.00
67 Tusken War Party U .40 1.00
68 Untamed Ronto U .40 1.00
69 WED Treadwell U .40 1.00
70 Womp Rat U .40 1.00
71 Accelerate C .20 .50
72 Blast It! C .20 .50
73 Chewbacca (D) C .20 .50
74 Corellian Corvette C .20 .50
75 Creature Attack C .20 .50
76 Luke Skywalker (G) C .20 .50
77 Darth Vader (F) C .20 .50
78 Death Star Turbolaser Tower C .20 .50
79 Dewback Patrol C .20 .50
80 Escape Pod C .20 .50
81 Greedo's Marksmanship C .20 .50
82 Han Solo (D) C .20 .50
83 Han's Evasion C .20 .50
84 Imperial Landing Craft C .20 .50
85 Jawa Salvage Team C .20 .50
86 Juggernaut U .20 .50
87 Star Destroyer C .20 .50
88 Malfunction C .20 .50
89 Outrun C .20 .50
90 Pilot's Speed C .20 .50
91 Rebel Defense Team C .20 .50
92 Sandtrooper Squad C .20 .50
93 Stormtrooper Assault C .20 .50
94 Stormtrooper TK-875 C .20 .50
95 Stormtrooper Platoon C .20 .50
96 Stormtrooper Regiment C .20 .50
97 TIE Defense Squadron C .20 .50
98 TIE Fighter DS-73-5 C .20 .50
99 TIE Fighter DS-29-4 C .20 .50
100 TIE Fighter DS-55-2 C .20 .50
101 Trust Your Feelings C .20 .50
102 Visit to Mos Eisley C .20 .50
103 X-wing Red Squadron C .20 .50
104 X-wing Red Ten C .20 .50
105 Y-wing Gold Two C .20 .50

2003 Star Wars The Empire Strikes Back

COMPLETE SET (210) 100.00 200.00
BOOSTER BOX (36 PACKS) 400.00 550.00
BOOSTER PACK (11 CARDS) 1.25 2.50
*FOIL: .75X TO 2X BASIC CARDS
RELEASED IN NOVEMBER 2003
1 2-1B Medical Droid (A) R 1.25 3.00
2 Admiral Firmus Piett (B) R 1.25 3.00
3 AT-AT Assault Group R 1.25 3.00
4 Avenger (A) R 4.00 10.00
5 Blizzard Force Snowtrooper R 1.25 3.00
6 Blizzard One (A) R 1.25 3.00
7 C-3PO (E) R 1.25 3.00
8 Captain Lorth Needa (A) R 1.25 3.00
9 Carbon Freezing Chamber R 5.00 12.00
10 Chewbacca (E) U 1.25 3.00
11 Chewbacca (G) R 1.25 3.00
12 Dack Ralter (A) R 1.25 3.00
13 Dangerous Gamble R 1.25 3.00
14 Dark Cave R 1.25 3.00
15 Darth Vader (H) R 2.00 5.00
16 Darth Vader (I) R 3.00 8.00
17 Decoy Tactics R 1.25 3.00
18 Desperate Times R 1.25 3.00
19 Echo Base R 3.00 8.00
20 Emperor's Bidding R 1.25 3.00
21 Emperor's Prize R 1.25 3.00
22 Executor (A) R 1.25 3.00
23 Failed for the Last Time R 1.25 3.00
24 Future Sight R 1.25 3.00
25 FX-7 Medical Droid (A) R 1.25 3.00
26 General Carlist Rieekan (A) R 1.25 3.00
27 General Maximilian Veers (B) R 1.25 3.00
28 Go for the Legs R 1.25 3.00
29 Han Solo (G) R 2.00 5.00
30 Jedi Test R 1.25 3.00
31 Jedi's Failure R 1.25 3.00
32 K-3PO (A) R 1.25 3.00
33 Kiss From Your Sister R 1.25 3.00
34 Lando Calrissian (A) R 2.50 6.00
35 Lando Calrissian (D) R 2.50 6.00
36 Lieutenant Wes Janson (A) R 2.00 5.00
37 Lobot (A) R 2.00 5.00
38 Luke Skywalker (J) R 6.00 15.00
39 Luke Skywalker (K) R 5.00 12.00
40 Luke's Snowspeeder (A) R 4.00 10.00
41 Luke's Wrath R 1.25 3.00
42 Luke's X-wing (c) R 2.00 5.00
43 Major Bren Derlin (A) R 1.25 3.00
44 Mara Jade (A) R 1.25 3.00
45 Millennium Falcon (E) R 2.00 5.00
46 Millennium Falcon (F) R 2.00 5.00
47 Millennium Falcon (G) R 2.00 5.00
48 Obi-Wan's Spirit (A) R 1.25 3.00
49 Occupation R 1.25 3.00
50 Parting of Heroes R 1.25 3.00
51 Planetary Ion Cannon R 1.25 3.00
52 Princess Leia (G) R 2.00 5.00
53 Quest for Truth R 1.25 3.00
54 R2-D2 (G) R 1.25 3.00
55 R2-D2's Heroism R 1.25 3.00
56 Rally the Defenders R 1.25 3.00
57 Sacrifice R 1.25 3.00
58 Search for the Rebels R 1.25 3.00
59 Stormtrooper Swarm R 1.25 3.00
60 Streets of Cloud City R 1.25 3.00
61 Toryn Farr (A) R 1.25 3.00
62 Vader's Imperial Shuttle (A) R 2.00 5.00
63 Wampa Cave R 1.25 3.00
64 Wedge Antilles (B) R 4.00 10.00
65 Wedge's Snowspeeder (A) R 4.00 10.00
66 Yoda (F) R 1.25 3.00
67 Yoda (G) R 1.25 3.00
68 Yoda (H) R 1.25 3.00
69 Yoda's Training R 1.25 3.00
70 Zev Senesca (A) R 1.25 3.00
71 3,720 to 1 U .40 1.00
72 Admiral Firmus Piett (A) U .40 1.00
73 Admiral Kendal Ozzel (A) U .40 1.00
74 Outmaneuver Them U .40 1.00
75 All Terrain Troop Transport U .40 1.00
76 Anti-Infantry Laser Battery U .40 1.00
77 Asteroid Field U .40 1.00
78 AT-AT Driver U .40 1.00
79 Blizzard Force AT-ST U .40 1.00
80 Battle the Wampa U .40 1.00
81 Cloud City Penthouse U .40 1.00
82 Cloud City Prison U .40 1.00
83 Bespin Twin-Pod Cloud Car U .40 1.00
84 Blockade U .40 1.00
85 Bright Hope (A) U .40 1.00
86 C-3PO (F) U .40 1.00
87 Change in Destiny U .40 1.00
88 Chewbacca (F) R .40 1.00
89 Darth Vader (G) R .40 1.00
90 Darth Vader (K) U .40 1.00
91 Death Mark U .40 1.00
92 Derek Hobbie Klivian (A) U .40 1.00
93 Don't Get All Mushy U .40 1.00
94 Dragonsnake U .40 1.00
95 Emergency Repairs U .40 1.00
96 Carbon Freeze U .40 1.00
97 Executor Bridge U .40 1.00
98 Executor Hangar U .40 1.00
99 Quicker Easier More Seductive U .40 1.00
100 General Maximilian Veers (A) U .40 1.00
101 Han Enchained U .40 1.00
102 Han Solo (F) U .40 1.00
103 Hoth Icefields U .40 1.00
104 Imperial Fleet U .40 1.00
105 Imperial Misdirection U .40 1.00
106 Jungles of Dagobah U .40 1.00
107 Lambda-Class Shuttle U .40 1.00
108 Lando Calrissian (C) U .40 1.00
109 Leia's Warning U .40 1.00
110 Luke Skywalker (I) U .40 1.00
111 Medical Center U .40 1.00
112 Millennium Falcon (D) U .40 1.00
113 Mynock U .40 1.00
114 Painful Reckoning U .40 1.00
115 Princess Leia (H) U .40 1.00
116 Probe Droid U .40 1.00
117 Probot U .40 1.00
118 R2-D2 (F) U .40 1.00
119 Rebel Fleet U .40 1.00
120 Rebel Hoth Army U .40 1.00
121 Rebel Trenches U .40 1.00
122 Rebel Troop Cart U .40 1.00
123 Redemption (A) U .40 1.00
124 See You In Hell U .40 1.00
125 Self Destruct U .40 1.00
126 Shield Generator U .40 1.00
127 Snowspeeder Rogue Ten U .40 1.00
128 Snowspeeder Squad U .40 1.00
129 Snowtrooper Elite Squad U .40 1.00
130 Stormtrooper Sentry U .40 1.00
131 Surprise Reinforcements U .40 1.00
132 TIE Bomber Pilot U .40 1.00
133 TIE Bomber Squad U .40 1.00
134 TIE Pursuit Pilot U .40 1.00
135 Torture Room U .40 1.00
136 Vader's Call U .40 1.00
137 Vicious Attack U .40 1.00
138 Wampa U .40 1.00
139 Yoda's Hut U .40 1.00
140 725 to 1 C .20 .50
141 All Terrain Armored Transport C .20 .50
142 All Terrain Scout Transport C .20 .50
143 Alter the Deal C .20 .50
144 Antivehicle Laser Cannon C .20 .50
145 Armor Plating C .20 .50
146 Space Slug C .20 .50
147 Blizzard Force AT-AT C .20 .50
148 Precise Attack C .20 .50
149 Belly of the Beast C .20 .50
150 Cloud City Battleground C .20 .50
151 Cloud City Dining Hall C .20 .50
152 Cloud City Landing Platform C .20 .50
153 Bespin System C .20 .50
154 Blizzard C .20 .50
155 Bogwing C .20 .50
156 Close the Shield Doors C .20 .50
157 Darth Vader (J) C .20 .50
158 Vader's Vengeance C .20 .50
159 Dagobah System C .20 .50
160 Explore the Swamps C .20 .50
161 Float Away C .20 .50
162 Force Throw C .20 .50
163 Gallofree Medium Transport C .20 .50
164 Ground Assault C .20 .50
165 Han Solo (E) C .20 .50
166 Han's Attack U .20 .50
167 Han's Promise C .20 .50
168 Hanging Around C .20 .50
169 Hope of Another C .20 .50
170 Hoth Battle Plains C .20 .50
171 Hoth System C .20 .50
172 Imperial II-Class Star Destroyer C .20 .50
173 Jedi Master's Meditation C .20 .50
174 Jedi Trap C .20 .50
175 Kuat Lancer-Class Frigate C .20 .50
176 Kuat Nebulon-B Frigate C .20 .50
177 Lando Calrissian (B) C .20 .50
178 Lando's Repairs C .20 .50
179 Leap into the Chasm C .20 .50
180 Luke Skywalker (H) C .20 .50
181 Meditation Chamber C .20 .50
182 Navy Trooper C .20 .50
183 Princess Leia (F) C .20 .50
184 Probe the Galaxy C .20 .50
185 Rebel Command Center C .20 .50
186 Rebel Escape Squad C .20 .50
187 Rebel Hangar C .20 .50
188 Rebel Trench Defenders C .20 .50
189 Rebel Assault Frigate C .20 .50
190 Dreadnaught Heavy Cruiser C .20 .50
191 Snowspeeder Rogue Two C .20 .50
192 Snowstorm C .20 .50
193 Snowtrooper Heavy Weapons Team C .20 .50
194 Snowtrooper Squad C .20 .50
195 Snowtrooper Guard C .20 .50
196 Imperial II Star Destroyer C .20 .50
197 Strange Lodgings C .20 .50
198 Swamps of Dagobah C .20 .50
199 Tauntaun C .20 .50
200 Tauntaun Mount C .20 .50
201 TIE Bomber EX-1-2 C .20 .50
202 TIE Bomber EX-1-8 C .20 .50
203 TIE Fighter EX-4-9 C .20 .50
204 TIE Fighter OS-72-8 C .20 .50
205 TIE Pursuit Squad C .20 .50
206 Trust Her Instincts C .20 .50
207 Visions of the Future C .20 .50
208 Well-Earned Meal C .20 .50
209 X-wing Rogue Seven C .20 .50
210 Y-wing Gold Six C .20 .50

2003 Star Wars Jedi Guardians

COMPLETE SET (105) 60.00 120.00
BOOSTER BOX (36 PACKS) 120.00 250.00
BOOSTER PACK (11 CARDS) 5.00 7.00
*FOIL: .75X TO 2X BASIC CARDS
RELEASED IN JULY 2003
1 Adi Gallia (A) R 1.25 3.00
2 Anakin Skywalker (H) R 1.25 3.00
3 Aurra Sing (B) R 1.25 3.00
4 Boba Fett (B) R 1.25 3.00
5 Coup de Grace U 1.25 3.00
6 Dark Dreams R 1.25 3.00
7 Darth Maul (E) R 3.00 8.00
8 Darth Sidious (C) R 1.25 3.00
9 Darth Tyranus (F) R 2.00 5.00
10 Eeth Koth (A) R 1.25 3.00
11 Even Piell (A) R 1.25 3.00
12 Furious Charge C 1.25 3.00
13 Gather the Council R 1.25 3.00
14 Guidance of the Chancellor C 1.25 3.00
15 Homing Missile R 1.25 3.00
16 Jango Fett (G) R 1.25 3.00
17 Jedi Council Quorum R 1.25 3.00
18 Jedi Youngling R 1.25 3.00
19 Ki-Adi-Mundi (A) R 1.25 3.00
20 Kouhun R 1.25 3.00
21 Mace Windu (D) R 2.50 6.00
22 Trade Federation Battle Freighter C 1.25 3.00
23 Obi-Wan Kenobi (I) R 1.25 3.00
24 Obi-Wan's Starfighter (B) R 2.00 5.00
25 Oppo Rancisis (A) R 1.25 3.00
26 Padme Amidala (F) R 2.00 5.00
27 Plo Koon (B) R 1.25 3.00
28 R2-D2 (E) R 1.25 3.00
29 Remember the Prophecy R 1.25 3.00
30 Saesee Tiin (A) R 2.00 5.00
31 Senator Tikkes (A) R 1.25 3.00
32 Shaak Ti (B) R 2.00 5.00
33 Shmi Skywalker (A) R 2.00 5.00
34 Slave I (C) R 1.25 3.00
35 Trade Federation Blockade Ship C 1.25 3.00
36 Rapid Recovery R 1.25 3.00
37 Tipoca Training Ground R 1.25 3.00
38 Trade Federation Core Ship C 1.25 3.00
39 Tyranus's Geonosis Speeder (B) C 1.25 3.00
40 Unified Attack U 1.25 3.00
41 Yoda (D) R 5.00 12.00
42 Zam Wesell (D) R 1.25 3.00
43 Zam's Airspeeder (R) R 1.25 3.00
44 Battle Droid Division U .40 1.00
45 Battle Protocol Droid (A) U .40 1.00
46 Call for Reinforcements U .40 1.00
47 Tyranus's Power C .40 1.00
48 Clone Cadet U .40 1.00
49 Coleman Trebor (A) U .40 1.00
50 Corporate Alliance Tank Droid U .40 1.00
51 Coruscant Air Bus U .40 1.00
52 Depa Billaba (A) U .40 1.00
53 Executioner Cart U .40 1.00
54 FA-4 (A) U .40 1.00
55 Jango Fett (F) U .40 1.00
56 Jedi Arrogance U .40 1.00
57 Jedi Training Exercise U .40 1.00
58 Jedi Knight's Survival U .40 1.00
59 Jedi Superiority U .40 1.00
60 Lightsaber Gift U .40 1.00
61 Lightsaber Loss U .40 1.00
62 Neimoidian Shuttle (A) U .40 1.00
63 Obi-Wan Kenobi (J) U .40 1.00
64 Orray U .40 1.00
65 Padme's Yacht (B) U .40 1.00
66 Underworld Investigations C .40 1.00
67 Protocol Battle Droid (A) U .40 1.00
68 Qui-Gon Jinn (B) U .40 1.00
69 Republic Communications Tower U .40 1.00
70 RIC-920 U .40 1.00
71 Sun-Fac (B) U .40 1.00
72 Tactical leadership U .40 1.00
73 Tame the Beast U .40 1.00
74 Train For War U .40 1.00
75 Tyranus's Return U .40 1.00
76 Tyranus's Solar Sailer (B) U .40 1.00
77 Yoda (E) U .40 1.00
78 Zam Wesell (C) U .40 1.00
79 Anakin Skywalker (I) C .20 .50
80 Mobile Artillery Division C .20 .50
81 Captured Reek C .20 .50
82 Clone Fire Team C .20 .50
83 Close Pursuit C .20 .50
84 Darth Tyranus (G) C .20 .50
85 Destroyer Droid Team U .20 .50
86 Diplomatic Barge C .20 .50
87 Droid Deactivation C .20 .50
88 Droid Starfighter Assault Wing C .20 .50
89 Trade Federation Droid Bomber C .20 .50
90 Forward Command Center C .20 .50
91 Geonosian Fighter Escort C .20 .50
92 Gondola Speeder C .20 .50
93 Gunship Offensive C .20 .50
94 Jedi Starfighter Squadron C .20 .50
95 Obi-Wan's Maneuver C .20 .50
96 Plan for the Future C .20 .50
97 Republic Assault Transport C .20 .50
98 Republic Attack Gunship C .20 .50
99 Republic Light Assault Cruiser C .20 .50
100 Republic Hyperdrive Ring C .20 .50
101 Sabaoth Starfighter C .20 .50
102 Scurrier C .20 .50
103 Separatist Battle Droid C .20 .50
104 Shaak C .20 .50
105 Synchronized Systems C .20 .50

2004 Star Wars The Phantom Menace

COMPLETE SET (90) 50.00 100.00
BOOSTER BOX (36 PACKS) 200.00 250.00
BOOSTER PACK (11 CARDS) 1.50 3.00
*FOIL: .75X TO 2X BASIC CARDS
RELEASED IN JULY 2004
1 Ann and Tann Gella (A) R 2.00 5.00
2 Aurra Sing (C) R 1.25 3.00
3 Bongo Sub R 1.25 3.00
4 Boss Nass (A) R 1.25 3.00
5 C-9979 R 1.25 3.00
6 Corridors of Power R 1.25 3.00
7 Dark Woman (A) R 2.00 5.00

8 Darth Maul (F) R	2.00	5.00
9 Duel of the Fates R	1.25	3.00
10 Fambaa Shield Beast R	1.25	3.00
11 Fight on All Fronts R	1.25	3.00
12 Gardulla the Hutt (A) R	1.25	3.00
13 Gas Attack R	1.25	3.00
14 Gungan Grand Army R	1.50	4.00
15 Guardian Mantis (A) R	1.25	3.00
16 In Disguise R	1.25	3.00
17 Jar Jar Binks (B) R	1.25	3.00
18 Jedi Temple R	1.25	3.00
19 Ki-Adi-Mundi (B) R	2.00	5.00
20 Marauder-Class Corvette R	1.25	3.00
21 Negotiate the Peace R	1.25	3.00
22 Nute Gunray (C) R	1.25	3.00
23 Orn Free Taa (A) R	1.25	3.00
24 Otoh Gunga R	1.25	3.00
25 Podracing Course R	1.25	3.00
26 Quinlan Vos (A) R	1.25	3.00
27 Sando Aqua Monster R	1.25	3.00
28 Sith Infiltrator (B) R	1.25	3.00
29 Walking Droid Starfighter R	1.25	3.00
30 Watto's Shop R	1.25	3.00
31 A'Sharad Hett (A) U	1.25	3.00
32 Anakin Skywalker (J) U	3.00	8.00
33 Anakin's Podracer (A) U	2.00	5.00
34 Bravo Starfighter U	.40	1.00
35 Captain Panaka (A) U	.40	1.00
36 Captain Tarpals (A) U	.40	1.00
37 Citadel Cruiser U	.40	1.00
38 Colo Claw Fish U	.40	1.00
39 Discuss It in Committee U	.40	1.00
40 Durge (A) U	.40	1.00
41 Falumpaset U	.40	1.00
42 Gungan Battle Wagon U	.40	1.00
43 Gungan Catapult U	.40	1.00
44 Inferno (A) U	.40	1.00
45 Kaadu Scout U	.40	1.00
46 Let the Cube Decide U	.40	1.00
47 Modified YV-330 (A) U	.40	1.00
48 Naboo System U	.40	1.00
49 Qui-Gon Jinn (D) U	.40	1.00
50 Ric Olié (A) U	.40	1.00
51 Royal Cruiser U	.40	1.00
52 Rune Haako (A) U	.40	1.00
53 Sebulba (A) U	.40	1.00
54 Sebulba's Podracer (A) U	.40	1.00
55 Streets of Theed U	.40	1.00
56 Trade Federation Hangar U	.40	1.00
57 Trade Federation MTT U	.40	1.00
58 Vilmarh Grahrk (A) U	.40	1.00
59 Watto (B) U	.40	1.00
60 Yaddle (A) U	.40	1.00
61 A Bigger Fish C	.20	.50
62 Aayla Secura (B) C	.20	.50
63 Blockade (TPM) C	.20	.50
64 Blockade Battleship C	.20	.50
65 CloakShape Fighter C	.20	.50
66 Darth Sidious (D) C	.20	.50
67 Delta Six Jedi Starfighter C	.20	.50
68 Eopie C	.20	.50
69 Finis Valorum (B) C	.20	.50
70 Flash Speeder C	.20	.50
71 Gian Speeder C	.20	.50
72 Gungan Kaadu Squad C	.20	.50
73 Jedi Transport C	.20	.50
74 Melt Your Way In C	.20	.50
75 Mos Espa C	.20	.50
76 Naboo Pilot C	.20	.50
77 Obi-Wan Kenobi (K) C	.20	.50
78 Opee Sea Killer C	.20	.50
79 Podrace C	.20	.50
80 Qui-Gon Jinn (C) C	.20	.50
81 Sith Probe Droid C	.20	.50
82 Sneak Attack C	.20	.50
83 Swamps of Naboo C	.20	.50
84 TC-14 (A) C	.20	.50
85 Theed Power Generator C	.20	.50
86 Theed Royal Palace C	.20	.50
87 Trade Federation AAT C	.20	.50
88 Trade Federation STAP C	.20	.50
89 Unconventional Maneuvers C	.20	.50
90 Yinchorri Fighter C	.20	.50

2004 Star Wars Return of the Jedi

COMPLETE SET (109)	50.00	100.00
BOOSTER BOX (36 PACKS)	100.00	200.00
BOOSTER PACK (11 CARDS)	3.00	5.00
*FOIL: .75X TO 2X BASIC CARDS		
RELEASED IN OCTOBER 2004		
1 Admiral Ackbar (A) R	1.25	3.00
2 Anakin Skywalker (K) R	1.25	3.00
3 Anakin's Spirit (A) R	1.25	3.00
4 Bargain with Jabba R	1.25	3.00
5 Bib Fortuna (A) R	1.25	3.00
6 Chewbacca (J) R	1.25	3.00
7 Darth Vader (P) R	1.25	3.00
8 Death Star II (B) R	1.25	3.00
9 Emperor Palpatine (E) R	1.25	3.00
10 Endor Imperial Fleet R	1.25	3.00
11 Endor Rebel Fleet R	1.25	3.00
12 Endor Shield Generator R	1.25	3.00
13 Ephant Mon (A) R	1.25	3.00
14 Endor Regiment R	1.25	3.00
15 Free Tatooine R	1.25	3.00
16 Han Solo (K) R	1.25	3.00
17 Home One (A) R	1.25	3.00
18 Honor the Fallen R	1.25	3.00
19 Jabba the Hutt (A) R	1.25	3.00
20 Jabba's Dancers R	1.25	3.00
21 Jabba's Palace R	1.25	3.00
22 Jabba's Spies R	1.25	3.00
23 Lando Calrissian (H) R	1.25	3.00
24 Luke Skywalker (N) R	1.25	3.00
25 Malakili (A) R	1.25	3.00
26 Max Rebo Band (A) R	1.25	3.00
27 Mixed Battlegroup R	1.25	3.00
28 Mon Mothma (A) R	1.25	3.00
29 Nien Nunb (A) R	1.25	3.00
30 Occupied Tatooine R	1.25	3.00
31 Progress Report R	1.25	3.00
32 Rancor R	1.25	3.00
33 Reactor Core R	1.25	3.00
34 Salacious B. Crumb (A) R	1.25	3.00
35 Sarlacc (A) R	1.25	3.00
36 Scythe Squadron (A) R	1.25	3.00
37 Throne Room R	1.25	3.00
38 Trap Door! R	1.25	3.00
39 Vader's Guile R	1.25	3.00
40 Yoda's Spirit (A) R	1.25	3.00
41 Baited Trap U	.40	1.00
42 Boba Fett (H) U	.40	1.00
43 C-3PO (H) U	.40	1.00
44 Captain Lennox (A) U	.40	1.00
45 Chief Chirpa (A) U	.40	1.00
46 Darth Vader (N) U	.40	1.00
47 Desperate Bluff U	.40	1.00
48 Emperor Palpatine (D) U	.40	1.00
49 Ewok Village U	.40	1.00
50 Free Bespin U	.40	1.00
51 Free Endor U	.40	1.00
52 Han Solo (J) U	.40	1.00
53 Ionization Weapons U	.40	1.00
55 Jabba the Hutt (C) U	.40	1.00
56 Jabba's Sail Barge (A) U	.40	1.00
57 Lando Calrissian (I) U	.40	1.00
58 Luke Skywalker (O) U	.40	1.00
59 Millennium Falcon (J) U	.40	1.00
60 Occupied Bespin U	.40	1.00
61 Occupied Endor U	.40	1.00
62 Princess Leia (J) U	.40	1.00
63 R2-D2 (I) U	.40	1.00
64 Rancor Pit U	.40	1.00
65 Red Squadron X-wing U	.40	1.00
66 Skiff U	.40	1.00
67 Vader's Summons U	.40	1.00
68 Wicket W. Warrick (A) U	.40	1.00
69 Wookiee Hug U	.40	1.00
70 Worrt U	.40	1.00
71 A-wing C	.20	.50
72 B-wing C	.20	.50
73 Cantina Bar Mob C	.20	.50
74 Chewbacca (K) C	.20	.50
75 Close Quarters C	.20	.50
76 Elite Royal Guard C	.20	.50
77 Darth Vader (O) C	.20	.50
78 Death Star Battalion C	.20	.50
79 Death Star II (A) C	.20	.50
80 Decoy C	.20	.50
81 Dune Sea C	.20	.50
82 Elite Squad C	.20	.50
83 Emperor Palpatine (C) C	.20	.50
84 Ewok Artillery C	.20	.50
85 Ewok Glider C	.20	.50
86 Fly Casual C	.20	.50
87 Force Lightning C	.20	.50
88 Forest AT-AT C	.20	.50
89 Forest AT-ST C	.20	.50
90 Endor Attack Squad C	.20	.50
91 Forests of Endor C	.20	.50
92 Free Coruscant C	.20	.50
93 Gray Squadron Y-wing C	.20	.50
94 High-Speed Dodge C	.20	.50
95 Imperial Speeder Bike C	.20	.50
96 Imperial-Class Star Destroyer C	.20	.50
97 Jabba's Guards C	.20	.50
98 Lightsaber Throw C	.20	.50
99 Log Trap C	.20	.50
100 Luke Skywalker (M) C	.20	.50
101 Mon Calamari Cruiser C	.20	.50
102 Occupied Coruscant C	.20	.50
103 Oola (A) C	.20	.50
104 Princess Leia (K) C	.20	.50
105 Rebel Scouts C	.20	.50
106 Royal Guards C	.20	.50
107 Scout Trooper C	.20	.50
108 Surprising Strength C	.20	.50
109 TIE Interceptor C	.20	.50
110 Savage Attack C	.20	.50

2004 Star Wars Rogues and Scoundrels

COMPLETE SET (105)	50.00	100.00
BOOSTER BOX (36 PACKS)	40.00	80.00
BOOSTER PACK (11 CARDS)	1.50	3.00
*FOIL: .75X TO 2X BASIC CARDS		
RELEASED IN APRIL 2004		
1 Admiral Firmus Piett (C) R	1.25	3.00
2 Boba Fett (G) R	1.25	3.00
3 Bossk (A) R	1.25	3.00
4 Call For Hunters R	1.25	3.00
5 Chewbacca (I) R	1.25	3.00
6 Commander Nemet (A) R	1.25	3.00
7 Dantooine System R	1.25	3.00
8 Dark Sacrifice R	1.25	3.00
9 Dengar (A) R	1.25	3.00
10 Doctor Evazan (A) R	1.25	3.00
11 Guri (A) R	1.25	3.00
12 Han Solo (I) R	1.25	3.00
13 Het Nkik (A) R	1.25	3.00
14 Hounds Tooth (A) R	1.25	3.00
15 IG-2000 (A) R	1.25	3.00
16 IG-88 (A) R	1.25	3.00
17 Dune Sea Krayt Dragon R	1.25	3.00
18 Lando Calrissian (F) R	1.25	3.00
19 Lando Calrissian (G) R	1.25	3.00
20 Lando's Influence R	1.25	3.00
21 Lobot (B) R	1.25	3.00
22 Mara Jade (B) R	1.25	3.00
23 Millennium Falcon (I) R	1.25	3.00
24 Mist Hunter (A) R	1.25	3.00
25 Modal Nodes (A) R	1.25	3.00
26 Prince Xizor (A) R	1.25	3.00
27 Princess Leia (I) R	1.25	3.00
28 Slave 1 (F) R	1.25	3.00
29 Stinger (A) R	1.25	3.00
30 Take A Prisoner R	1.25	3.00
31 Trash Compactor R	1.25	3.00
32 Virago (A) R	1.25	3.00
33 Yoda (I) R	1.25	3.00
34 Yoda's Lesson R	1.25	3.00
35 Zuckuss (A) R	1.25	3.00
36 4 Lom (A) U	.40	1.00
37 AT-AT U	.40	1.00
38 Bespin Cloud Car Squad U	.40	1.00
39 Big Asteroid U	.40	1.00
40 Boba Fett (F) U	.40	1.00
41 C 3PO (G) U	.40	1.00
42 Chewbacca (H) U	.40	1.00
43 Cloud City Wing Guard U	.40	1.00
44 Darth Vader (M) U	.40	1.00
45 Death Star Control Room U	.40	1.00
46 Garindan (A) U	.40	1.00
47 Greedo (B) U	.40	1.00
48 Han Solo (H) U	.40	1.00
49 Han's Sacrifice U	.40	1.00
50 Holoprojection Chamber U	.40	1.00
51 Human Shield U	.40	1.00
52 Kessel System U	.40	1.00
53 Lando Calrissian (E) U	.40	1.00
54 Lando's Trickery U	.40	1.00
55 Luke Skywalker (L) U	.40	1.00
56 Luke's X-wing (D) U	.40	1.00
57 Millennium Falcon (H) U	.40	1.00
58 Ponda Baba (A) U	.40	1.00
59 Punishing One (A) U	.40	1.00
60 R2-D2 (H) U	.40	1.00
61 Redoubled Effort U	.40	1.00
62 E-3PO (A) U	.40	1.00
63 Slave 1 (E) U	.40	1.00
64 Slave 1 (D) U	.40	1.00
65 Space Slug (RaS) U	.40	1.00
66 Outrider (A) U	.40	1.00
67 Ugnaught U	.40	1.00
68 Vendetta U	.40	1.00
69 Enraged Wampa U	.40	1.00
70 Lars Homestead U	.40	1.00
71 2-1B's Touch C	.20	.50
72 Bantha Herd C	.20	.50
73 Base Guards C	.20	.50
74 Bespin Patrol Cloud Car C	.20	.50
75 Boba Fett (C) C	.20	.50
76 Boba Fett (D) C	.20	.50
77 Boba Fett (E) C	.20	.50
78 Darth Vader (L) C	.20	.50
79 Dash Rendar (A) C	.20	.50
80 Disrupting Strike C	.20	.50
81 Falcon's Needs C	.20	.50
82 Jabba's Death Mark C	.20	.50
83 Kabe (A) C	.20	.50
84 Kyle Katarn (A) C	.20	.50
85 Lando System? C	.20	.50
86 Leebo (A) C	.20	.50
87 Luke's Garage C	.20	.50
88 Luke's Vow C	.20	.50
89 Medium Asteroid C	.20	.50
90 Mos Eisley C	.20	.50
91 Mos Eisley Cantina C	.20	.50
92 Muftak C	.20	.50
93 No Good To Me Dead C	.20	.50
94 Ord Mantell System C	.20	.50
95 Sleen C	.20	.50
96 Small Asteroid C	.20	.50
97 Zutton (A) C	.20	.50
98 Star Destroyer (RaS) C	.20	.50
99 Stormtrooper Detachment C	.20	.50
100 Streets Of Tatooine C	.20	.50
101 Tatooine Desert C	.20	.50
102 Tie Fighter C	.20	.50
103 Tusken Warrior C	.20	.50
104 Unmodified Snowspeeder C	.20	.50
105 X Wing Escort C	.20	.50

2005 Star Wars Revenge of the Sith

COMPLETE SET (110)	50.00	100.00
BOOSTER BOX (36 PACKS)	30.00	60.00
BOOSTER PACK (11 CARDS)	1.25	2.50
*FOIL: .75X TO 2X BASIC CARDS		
RELEASED IN MAY 2005		
1 Anakin Skywalker (M) R	1.25	3.00
2 Bail Organa (B) R	1.25	3.00
3 Chewbacca (M) R	1.25	3.00
4 Commerce Guild Droid 81-X R	1.25	3.00
5 Commerce Guild Starship (ROTS) R	1.25	3.00
6 Coruscant Shuttle R	1.25	3.00
7 Darth Sidious (G) R	1.25	3.00
8 Darth Tyranus (I) R	1.25	3.00
9 Darth Vader (R) R	1.25	3.00
10 Darth Vader (S) R	1.25	3.00
11 Dismiss R	1.25	3.00
12 Droid Security Escort R	1.25	3.00
13 Engine Upgrade R	1.25	3.00
14 Foil R	1.25	3.00
15 Palpatine's Sanctum R	1.25	3.00
16 Grand Moff Tarkin (D) R	1.25	3.00
17 It Just Might Work R	1.25	3.00
18 Jar Jar Binks (C) R	1.25	3.00
19 Lightsaber Quick Draw R	1.25	3.00
20 Mace Windu (F) R	1.25	3.00
21 Mas Amedda (A) R	1.25	3.00
22 Mustafar Battle Grounds R	1.25	3.00
23 Mustafar System R	1.25	3.00
24 Nos Monster R	1.25	3.00
25 Obi-Wan Kenobi (N) R	1.25	3.00
26 Padmé Amidala (G) R	1.25	3.00
27 R4-P17 (A) R	1.25	3.00
28 Rage of Victory R	1.25	3.00
29 Recusant-Class Light Destroyer R	1.25	3.00
30 Republic Fighter Wing R	1.25	3.00
31 Sacrifice the Expendable R	1.25	3.00
32 Separatist Fleet R	1.25	3.00
33 Spinning Slash R	1.25	3.00
34 Strike with Impunity R	1.25	3.00
35 Stubborn Personality R	1.25	3.00
36 Super Battle Droid 7EX R	1.25	3.00
37 Theta-Class Shuttle R	1.25	3.00
38 Unexpected Attack R	1.25	3.00
39 Venator-Class Destroyer R	1.25	3.00
40 Yoda (K) R	1.25	3.00
41 Acclamator II-Class Assault Ship U	.40	1.00
42 AT-AP U	.40	1.00
43 C-3PO (I) U	.40	1.00
44 Chancellor's Office U	.40	1.00
45 Combined Squadron Tactics U	.40	1.00
46 Confusion U	.40	1.00
47 Darth Sidious (F) U	.40	1.00
48 Darth Vader (Q) U	.40	1.00
49 Destroyer Droid, Q Series U	.40	1.00
50 Droid Missiles U	.40	1.00
51 Elite Guardian U	.40	1.00
52 Hardcell-Class Transport U	.40	1.00
53 Jedi Concentration U	.40	1.00
54 Jedi Master's Deflection U	.40	1.00
55 Kashyyyk System U	.40	1.00
56 Naboo Star Skiff U	.40	1.00
57 Nute Gunray (D) U	.40	1.00
58 Obi-Wan Kenobi (L) U	.40	1.00
59 Padmé Amidala (H) U	.40	1.00
60 Patrol Mode Vulture Droid U	.40	1.00
61 GH-7 Medical Droid U	.40	1.00
62 R2-D2 (J) U	.40	1.00
63 Thread The Needle U	.40	1.00
64 Thwart U	.40	1.00
65 Treachery U	.40	1.00
66 Techno Union Interceptor U	.40	1.00
67 Utapau System U	.40	1.00
68 Vehicle Shields Package U	.40	1.00
69 Vehicle Weapons Package U	.40	1.00
70 Yoda (J) U	.40	1.00
71 Anakin Skywalker (L) C	.20	.50
72 Anakin's Starfighter (A) C	.20	.50
73 ARC-170 Starfighter C	.20	.50
74 AT-RT C	.20	.50
75 BARC Speeder C	.20	.50
76 Blaster Pistol C	.20	.50
77 Blaster Rifle C	.20	.50
78 Buzz Droid C	.20	.50
79 Chewbacca (L) C	.20	.50
80 Coruscant Emergency Ship C	.20	.50
81 Darth Sidious (E) C	.20	.50
82 Darth Tyranus (H) C	.20	.50
83 DC0052 Intergalactic Airspeeder C	.20	.50
84 Diving Attack C	.20	.50
85 Droid Battlestaff C	.20	.50
86 Droid Tri-Fighter C	.20	.50
87 Force Dodge C	.20	.50
88 HAVw A6 Juggernaut C	.20	.50
89 Homing Missiles Salvo C	.20	.50
90 IBC Hailfire Droid C	.20	.50
91 Instill Doubt C	.20	.50
92 InterGalactic Banking Clan Cruiser C	.20	.50
93 Jedi Lightsaber C	.20	.50
94 Jedi Piloting C	.20	.50
95 Meditate C	.20	.50
96 Obi-Wan Kenobi (M) C	.20	.50
97 Plo Koon's Starfighter (A) C	.20	.50
98 Power Attack C	.20	.50
99 Republic Assault Gunboat C	.20	.50
100 Security Droid C	.20	.50
101 Sith Lightsaber C	.20	.50
102 STAP Squad C	.20	.50
103 Surge of Strength C	.20	.50
104 Tank Droid C	.20	.50
105 TF Battle Droid Army C	.20	.50
106 Trade Federation Cruiser C	.20	.50
107 Unity of the Jedi C	.20	.50
108 Utapau Sinkhole C	.20	.50
109 Vulture Droid Starfighter C	.20	.50
110 V-wing Clone Starfighter C	.20	.50

2006 Universal Fighting System Soulcalibur III

COMPLETE SET (143)	25.00	60.00
BOOSTER BOX (24 PACKS)	25.00	50.00
BOOSTER PACK (10 CARDS)	1.50	3.00
RELEASED IN APRIL 2006		
1 *Astaroth* StR	.20	.50
2 **Astaroth** SuR	.75	2.00
3 Size Matters R	.20	.50
4 Kulutues SuR	.40	1.00
5 Annihilation U	.20	.50
6 Ax Grave C	.20	.50
7 Demented Moon StR	.20	.50
8 Destruction U	.20	.50
9 Hades Break C	.20	.50
10 Maelstrom Divide U	.20	.50
11 Minotaur Crush C	.20	.50
12 Poseidon Tide Rush R	.20	.50
13 Poseidon Crest R	.20	.50
14 Reverse Spiral R	.20	.50
15 Tornado Shot C	.20	.50
16 Gyulkus StR	.75	2.00
17 Made Not Born U	.20	.50
18 Single Minded C	.20	.50
19 *Cassandra* SuR	.40	1.00
20 **Cassandra** R	.20	.50
21 Angel Step R	.20	.50
22 Digamma Sword & Nemea Shield SuR	.20	.50
23 Angel Press C	.20	.50
24 Dancing Shield U	.20	.50
25 Destined Greatness C	.20	.50
26 Guardian's Judgement R	.20	.50
27 Heaven's Guardian R	.20	.50
28 Holy Purification C	.20	.50
29 Luminance Fall U	.20	.50
30 Seraphim Hammer R	.20	.50
31 Seraphim Heel C	.20	.50
32 Shield Nova U	.20	.50
33 Shooting Star U	.20	.50
34 Angel Twirl R	.20	.50
35 Angelic Protection U	.20	.50
36 Assured Retribution C	.20	.50
37 *Mitsurugi* SuR	.20	.50
38 **Mitsurugi** R	.75	2.00
39 A Perfect Cut R	.20	.50
40 Shishi-Oh SuR	.20	.50
41 Autumn Requiem U	.20	.50
42 Bullet Cutter U	.20	.50
43 Disembowel C	.20	.50
44 Heavenly Prayer R	.20	.50
45 Hem Stitch C	.20	.50
46 Splitting Gold U	.20	.50
47 Stone Wall Thrust R	.20	.50
48 Swift Edge C	.20	.50
49 Twin Splitters C	.20	.50
50 Wheel Kick U	.20	.50
51 Wind Hole Vortex R	.20	.50
52 Masterful Duelist C	.20	.50
53 Tenpu-Kosai-Ryu Kai U	.20	.50
54 Veteran Of 1000 Battles R	.20	.50
55 *Nightmare* SuR	.20	.50
56 **Nightmare** StR	.75	2.00
57 Power Of The Edge R	1.00	2.50
58 Soul Edge SuR	1.25	3.00
59 Dark High Kick U	.20	.50
60 Drop Kick U	.20	.50
61 Earth Divide R	.40	1.00
62 Evil Eye C	.20	.50
63 Gauntlet Bust U	.20	.50
64 Helm Divider C	.20	.50
65 Right Slasher C	.20	.50
66 Shoulder Rush R	1.25	3.00
67 Spin Kick Slash Cross StR	.20	.50
68 Sword Buster C	.20	.50
69 Thrust Throw R	.20	.50
70 Cross Style Mastery U	.20	.50
71 Lost Memories C	.40	1.00
72 Relic's Thrall StR	.75	2.00
73 *Taki* SuR	.40	1.00
74 **Taki** StR	.20	.50
75 Shadow Healing StR	.20	.50
76 Rekki-Maru & Mekki-Maru SuR	1.25	3.00
77 Bamboo Cutter C	.20	.50
78 Blood Scroll R	.20	.50
79 Dark Destroyer U	.20	.50
80 Demon Fangs U	.20	.50
81 Earth Scroll C	.20	.50
82 Heavy Shadow R	.20	.50
83 Lightning Strike U	.20	.50
84 Shadow Banishment R	1.25	3.00
85 Shadow Ripper C	.20	.50
86 Shadow Rush U	.20	.50
87 Shadow Split C	.20	.50
88 Fu-Ma Training StR	.40	1.00
89 Persistence C	.20	.50
90 The Power Of The Gale U	.20	.50
91 *Voldo* SuR	.40	1.00
92 **Voldo** StR	.20	.50
93 Sonic Perception R	.20	.50
94 Manas & Ayas SuR	.75	2.00
95 Asylum Dance R	.20	.50
96 Blade Nail C	.20	.50
97 Blind Dive R	.20	.50
98 Blind Drop C	.20	.50
99 Bloody Drill U	.20	.50
100 Dark Shredder U	.20	.50
101 Demon Elbow U	.20	.50
102 Despair C	.20	.50
103 Running With Scissors StR	.20	.50
104 Scissor Claw C	.20	.50
105 Scorpion Tail U	.20	.50
106 Devotion C	.20	.50
107 Ridiculously Flexible StR	.20	.50
108 Unorthodox Style U	.75	2.00
109 Back Flip R	.20	.50
110 Critical Timing SuR	.60	1.50
111 Replenishment R	.20	.50
112 Sidestep R	.20	.50
113 Soul Reprisal R	.20	.50
114 Start Over SuR	4.00	10.00
115 Viscious Assault U	.20	.50
116 We'll Do It My Way U	.20	.50
117 You Will Not Escape C	.20	.50
118 Close To The Edge SuR	2.00	5.00
119 Enigmatic Maneuvers R	.20	.50
120 Enlightenment SuR	.20	.50
121 Inhuman Fortitude R	.20	.50
122 Guarded Stance R	.20	.50
123 Earth Shatter U	.20	.50
124 Feint C	.20	.50
125 Great Cleave U	.20	.50
126 High Slash C	.20	.50
127 High Thrust U	.20	.50
128 Low Slash U	.20	.50
129 Low Thrust C	.20	.50
130 Rising Ripper U	.20	.50
131 Slash C	.20	.50
132 Spinning Cross Slash R	.20	.50
133 Thrust U	.20	.50
134 Belligerent Aggression C	.20	.50
135 Circle Of Steel C	.20	.50
136 Shake It Off C	.20	.50
137 Focus The Soul U	.20	.50
138 Footwork U	.20	.50
139 Knows No Fear C	.20	.50
140 Material Advantage U	.40	1.00
141 Sublime Contemplation C	.20	.50
142 The Soul Still Burns R	.20	.50
143 Weapon Training U	.20	.50

2006 Universal Fighting System Soulcaliber III A Tale of Swords and Souls

COMPLETE SET (126)		
BOOSTER BOX (24 PACKS)	25.00	50.00
BOOSTER PACK (10 CARDS)	1.50	3.00

RELEASED IN JULY 2006
1 *Ivy* SuR
2 **Ivy** R
3 Kiss From Your Valentine U
4 Valentine SuR
5 Ancient Wheel U
6 Calamity Symphony R
7 Diving Raven U
8 Embrace of Lust R
9 Ivy Sweep C
10 Menace C
11 Poison Ivy C
12 Raven Catcher C
13 Shameless C
14 Spiral Dominance R
15 Spiral Punishment U
16 Troubled Orphan C
17 Unrelated Link U
18 You're Not My Father U
19 *Kilik* SuR
20 **Kilik** R
21 Punishing Defense R
22 Kali-Yuga SuR
23 Bo Rush C
24 Bo Smack Down R
25 Festival of the Damned R
26 Ling Su Upper C
27 Phoenix Flare R
28 Phoenix Roar R
29 Phoenix Tail C
30 Raging Phoenix Soul U
31 Reverse Sheng Su Low Kick U
32 Reverse Waterfall C
33 Sunrise Kick R
34 Atoning For Ancient Sins U
35 Secret Art of Ling-Sheng Su Style C
36 Strength Of Purpose U
37 *Raphael* SuR
38 **Raphael** R
39 Penetrating Lunge R
40 Flambert SuR
41 Assalto Montante R
42 Assalto Montante Cresendo SuR
43 Attack Au Fer C
44 Fendante C
45 Lunging Press U
46 Moulinet C
47 Pirouette Sweep C
48 Stocatta Rampage Crescendo U
49 Sweep Kick C
50 Tondo Reversi U
51 Violent Blood U
52 Cold Blooded Demeanor U
53 Les Rapier Des Sorel U
54 New Found Purpose C
55 *Setsuka* SuR
56 **Setsuka** R
57 Payback U
58 Ugestu Kageuchi SuR
59 Blossom Slicer C
60 Crimson Death U
61 Oiran Rising Heel C
62 Sakura Air Combo R
63 Sakura Twister U
64 Shade Dancer C
65 Shade Roundhouse R
66 Shade Thrust U
67 Shadow Hunter R
68 Winter Funeral C
69 Deceptive Maneuvering C
70 Lightning Reflexes U
71 Shinden Tsushima-ryu Battoujutsu U
72 Underhanded C
73 *Tira* SuR
74 **Tira** R
75 Ring Barrage R
76 Aisel Nedrossel SuR
77 Agrement Double Claw U
78 Beak Break Toss C
79 Blazing Cadenza R
80 Bloody Tale R
81 Cadense Side Kick U
82 Chattering Mandible U
83 Diving Wing Flap C
84 Glass Slippers R
85 Swing Kick U
86 Undertone Rectrix C
87 Warbling Pinion C
88 Constant Motion C
89 Dance of Death U
90 Trickster C
91 *Zasalamel* SuR
92 **Zasalamel** R
93 Diminishing Returns R
94 Hibernation R
95 Mobius Strip R
96 Katziel SuR
97 Adoration of Gilgamesh C
98 Belitsheri's Spear U
99 Enlil's Punishment R
100 Marduk's Thunder U
101 Namtar's Claw R
102 Nergal's Poison Sting C
103 Offering to Kishar C
104 Shamesh The Just C
105 Tiamat's Rampage R
106 Ancient Insight C
107 Original Style U
108 Unknown Force U
109 Dominance SuR
110 Second Wind U
111 Steel's Bane U
112 Turn Loss To Gain U
113 Legendary Blade R
114 Murderous Intent C
115 Temperance R
116 Touch of the Edge C
117 Bell Ringer U
118 High Kick C
119 Straight Throw C
120 Burning Soul U
121 Controlled Rage U
122 Glimpse of Fate C
123 Preparation U
124 Reckless U
125 The Legend Will Never Die U
126 Victorious C

2006 Universal Fighting System Street Fighter

BOOSTER BOX (24 PACKS)	25.00	50.00
BOOSTER PACK (10 CARDS)	1.50	3.00

1 *Chun-Li* SuR
2 **Chun-Li** StR
3 Sankaku Tobi C
4 Yatta! R
5 Backflip Kick U
6 Heel Stomp U
7 Hyakuretsu Kyaku R
8 Kakushu Raku Kyaku U
9 Knee Flip Kick U
10 Koshu To R
11 Senjou Shuu C
12 Senretsukyaku SuR
13 Souren Shou C
14 Spinning Bird Kick StR
15 Tenshin Shuu Kyaku C
16 Determined Pursuit U
17 Interpol Training R
18 Worlds Strongest Woman StR
19 *Dhalsim* SuR
20 **Dhalsim** StR
21 Yoga Teleport R
22 Skull Necklace StR
23 Drill Headthrust R
24 Drill Kick R
25 Yoga Blast StR
26 Yoga Fierce Punch C
27 Yoga Fire U
28 Yoga Flame R
29 Yoga Inferno SuR
30 Yoga Jab U
31 Yoga Roundhouse Kick C
32 Yoga Short Kick C
33 Yoga Strong Punch C
34 Calm Mind C
35 Mystic C
36 Yoga Mastery U
37 *Ken* SuR
38 **Ken** StR
39 Fierce Determination C
40 Ready For You R
41 Flaming Shoryuken StR
42 Fumikomi Mae Geri U
43 Hiza Geri U
44 Hold For A Second Overhead Kick C
45 Inazuma Kakato Wari C
46 Jigoku Guruma U
47 Ken's Hadoken R
48 Ken's Seoi Nage U
49 Ken's Tatsumaki R
50 Shinden Kakato Otoshi U
51 Shoryureppa SuR
52 Charisma C
53 Shotokan Master StR
54 Shotokan Training C
55 *Ryu* SuR
56 **Ryu** StR
57 Finesse StR
58 You Must Defeat Shen Long... R
59 ...To Stand A Chance C
60 Foot Sweep C
61 Jodan Sokuto Geri R
62 Kyuubi Kudaki C
63 Ryu's Hadoken R
64 Ryu's Seoi Nage U
65 Ryu's Shoryuken R
66 Ryu's Tatsumaki R
67 Sakotsu Wari U
68 Shakonetsu Hadoken StR
69 Shinku Hadoken SuR
70 Tomoe Nage U
71 Apt Pupil C
72 Skilled Fighter C
73 **Sagat** R
74 *Sagat* SuR
75 Muay Thai Defence C
76 You Aren't A Warrior... R
77 ...You Are A Beginner U
78 Eye Patch R
79 Ground Tiger Shot R
80 Jumping Knee Kick C
81 Muay Thai Punch C
82 Overhanded Throw U
83 Tiger Genocide SuR
84 Tiger Knee R
85 Tiger Shot R
86 Tiger Uppercut R
87 Champion U
88 Hardened Veteran C
89 Muay Thai Discipline U
90 Size And Speed U
91 **Zangief** R
92 *Zangief* SuR
93 My Strength Is Much Greater Than Yours U
94 Overwhelming Strength R
95 Abdominal Claw U
96 Air Throw U
97 Banishing Punch R
98 Body Press U
99 Double German Suplex R
100 Face Claw U
101 Final Atomic Buster SuR
102 Pile Driver U
103 Russian Double Knee Press U
104 Spinning Lariat R
105 Spinning Pile Driver R
106 Grappler C
107 National Hero R
108 Ring Veteran C
109 Block C
110 Crouch U
111 Dodge C
112 Fighting Spirit C
113 Jump C
114 Power Up SuR
115 Revenge R
116 Reversal SuR
117 Smack Talk R
118 Taunt U
119 Balanced Stance C
120 Crouching Stance U
121 Defensive Stance U
122 Offensive Stance U
123 Close Throw U
124 Fierce Punch U
125 Forward Kick U
126 Quick Elbow C
127 Roundhouse Kick U
128 Short Kick C
129 Strong Punch C
130 Super Kick R
131 Super Punch R
132 Aerial Combatant C
133 Beefy C
134 Experienced U
135 Fools No Pain StR
136 Beginner's Luck C
137 Ground Fighter C
138 Physically Fit U
139 Quick C
140 Scrapper R
141 Signature Style SuR
142 Too Fast To See U
143 Tricky C

2006 Universal Fighting System Street Fighter The Next Level

BOOSTER BOX (24 PACKS)	25.00	50.00
BOOSTER PACK (10 CARDS)	1.50	3.00

RELEASED IN DECEMBER 2006
1 *Akuma* SuR
2 **Akuma** R
3 Ashura Senku R
4 Hyakki Shu U
5 Only the Strong Survive R
6 Goken's Beads SuR
7 Akuma's Close Jab C
8 Akuma's Close Strong Punch C
9 Akuma's Tomoe Nage U
10 Gohadoken SuR
11 Messatsu-Gohado SuR
12 Tatsumaki Zanku kyaku U
13 Tenma Kujin Kyaku C
14 Zugai Hasatsu U
15 Dark Hado U
16 Power and Skill C
17 Unbridled Rage U
18 Unparalleled Skill C
19 *Cammy* SuR
20 **Cammy** R
21 Demolition U
22 Forward Spin Flip C
23 Muscle Memory U
24 Combat Gauntlets SuR
25 Cammy's Forward Kick C
26 Cammy's Jab C
27 Cammy's Jumping Forward Kick C
28 Cannon Drill C
29 Cannon Spike C
30 Hooligan Throw U
31 Spin Drive Smasher SuR
32 Spin Knuckle C
33 Brainwashed R
34 One Track Mind U
35 Perfect Posture C
36 Retribution C
37 *Dudley* SuR
38 **Dudley** R
39 Spun Around R
40 Internal Bleeding SuR
41 Pugilisitic Punishment C
42 Boxing Gloves R
43 Dart Shot C
44 Dudley's Low Fierce Punch R
45 Jet Upper U
46 Liver Blow U
47 Machine Gun Blow U
48 Rocket Uppercut U
49 Slipping Jab C
50 Stomach Blow U
51 Exhaust the Opposition C
52 Honor and Glory C
53 Punching Machine C
54 Years of Tradition C
55 *Fei Long* SuR
56 **Fei Long** R
57 Brooding Dragon U
58 Press Your Advantage U
59 Waterfall's Momentum C
60 Nunchaku U
61 Dragon Arc Kick SuR
62 Fei Long's Close Strong Punch R
63 Fei Long's Jab C
64 Fei Long's Short Kick C
65 Fei Long's Strong Punch U
66 Rekka Ken SuR
67 Rising Dragon Kick U
68 Roundhouse Hop U
69 Business Associate C
70 Kung Fu Stance U
71 Silent Movement R
72 Take You All On C
73 Knocked Out SuR
74 Someone Has Your Back R
75 Sound Advice U
76 Symbol of Authority R
77 Big Punch R
78 Binding Attack SuR
79 Improvised Weapon Attack U
80 Shard Attack SuR
81 Shotokan Fireball U
82 Solid Punch C
83 Barbaric C
84 Do-Gooder C
85 Elementalist U
86 Envy U
87 Friends and Rivals U
88 Grief C
89 Lover U
90 Televised Coverage U

2006 Universal Fighting System Street Fighter World Warriors

BOOSTER BOX (24 PACKS)	25.00	50.00
BOOSTER PACK (10 CARDS)	1.50	3.00

RELEASED IN JULY 2006
1 *Balrog* SuR
2 **Balrog** R
3 Below The Belt C
4 Bob and Weave U
5 Combination of Blows C
6 Buffalo Headbutt C
7 Crazy Buffalo SuR
8 Dash Uppercut R
9 Haymaker R
10 Kidney Blow C
11 Low Dash U
12 Multiple Headbutts R
13 Straight Dash C
14 Turn Punch C
15 Uppercut C
16 Fists of Iron C
17 Float Like A Butterfly C
18 Prize Fighter U
19 *Blanka* SuR
20 **Blanka** R
21 Hop C
22 Seeing You In Action Is A Joke U
23 Slide U
24 Backflip Roundhouse C
25 Backstep Rolling Attack R
26 Electric Thunder R
27 Ground Shave Rolling SuR
28 Headbutt C
29 Overhand Claw C
30 Rake C
31 Rolling Attack R
32 Vertical Rolling Attack R
33 Bestial Fury C
34 Dirty Fighter C
35 Man Beast U
36 Unorthodox Fighting Style U
37 *E.Honda* SuR
38 **E.Honda** R
39 Can't You Do Better Than That C
40 Grounded Stance R
41 Sumo Stance U
42 Bear Hug U
43 Double Sumo Headbutt R
44 Hundred Hand Slap SuR
45 Ohicho Throw R
46 Over the Shoulder Throw U
47 Sumo Headbutt R
48 Sumo Knee To Face U
49 Sumo Smash U
50 Sumo Splash U
51 Sweep U
52 All Muscle C
53 Low Centre Of Gravity C
54 Yokozuna U
55 *Guile* SuR
56 **Guile** R
57 Calculated Strike Of Fury C
58 Man On A Mission R
59 Dog Tags SuR
60 Commando Forward Kick C
61 Double Somersault Kick R
62 Extended Roundhouse Sweep U
63 German Suplex U
64 Knee Bazooka R
65 Laeping Commando Kick C
66 Mid Air German Suplex U
67 Reverse Spin Kick C
68 Somersault Kick R
69 Sonic Boom R
70 Disciplined C
71 Methodical C
72 Army Training U
73 *M.Bison* SuR
74 **M.Bison** R
75 Get Lost... C
76 Psycho Focus SuR
77 ... You Can't Compare C
78 Devil Reverse R
79 Head Press U
80 Head Press Somersault Skull Diver R
81 Jumping Strong Punch C
82 Knee Press Nightmare SuR
83 Psycho Crusher R
84 Psycho Double Knee Press R
85 Psycho Power Punch C
86 Slide Tackle C
87 Spinning Throw U
88 Demon Eyes C
89 Megalomania U
90 Psycho Power U
91 *Vega* SuR
92 **Vega** R
93 Vega's Backflip U
94 Handsome Fighters Never Lose C
95 Not The Face C
96 Vega's Claw R
97 Vega's Mask SuR
98 Pit Arena U
99 Airborne Izuna Drop U
100 Flip Kick C
101 Flying Barcelona Attack R
102 Izuna Drop U
103 Rolling Crystal Flash R
104 Rolling Izuna Drop R
105 Sky High Claw R
106 For The Ladies C
107 Pit Fighter C
108 Viscious U
109 Exertion U
110 Knock Down, Drag Out... C
111 Methodical Fighter SuR
112 To The Bone C
113 Boxing Ring U
114 City Square R
115 Sports Car U
116 Reverse Heel Kick U
117 Stunning Blow C
118 Chicanery U
119 Expanded Options C
120 Loving Devotion C
121 Lower Body Strength C
122 Seeking Answers U
123 Street Brawling U
124 Someone In Your Corner U
125 Unstoppable U
126 Wandering Master U

2007 Universal Fighting System Darkstalkers

BOOSTER BOX (24 PACKS)	40.00	80.00
BOOSTER PACK (10 CARDS)	2.50	5.00

RELEASED IN NOVEMBER 2007
1 *B.B. Hood* R
2 Dark Heart R
3 Basket of Tricks R
4 Cheer and Fire SuR
5 Cool Hunting SuR
6 Tricky Basket C
7 Born to Hunt U
8 Cute and Innocent U
9 Mercenary C
10 *Bishamon* R
11 Roppodo U
12 Hannya and Kien SuR
13 Gedan Kassobaki C
14 Hane Ha C
15 Kirisute Gomen U
16 A Moment Too Late C
17 Contemplation C
18 Countless Days of Killing U
19 *Demitri* R
20 Midnight Bliss SuR
21 Zeltzereich Castle SuR
22 Bat Spin U
23 Chaos Fire C
24 Demon Blast SuR
25 Blood of the Innocent C
26 No Weakness U
27 Power Hungry U
28 Donovan R
29 Into the Iron Maiden U
30 Dhylec SuR
31 Ifreet Sword U
32 Katana O Rakurai U
33 Press of Death U
34 Buddhist Devotion C
35 Containing the Power U
36 Cursed Blood C
37 *Felicia* R
38 Please Help Me R
39 Ball of Yarn SuR
40 Hellcat R
41 Rolling Buckler R
42 Sand Splash C
43 A Singing and Dancing Musical Sister U
44 Purity U
45 Star Power C
46 *J. Talbain* R
47 Full Moon U
48 Phases of the Moon SuR
49 Chijo Beast Rush C
50 Dragon Cannon SuR
51 Moment Slice U
52 Loner C
53 Nobility and Pride U
54 The Beast Within U
55 *Lilith* R
56 Lure the Enemy U
57 Primitive Instinct U
58 Luminous Illusion C
59 Mystic Arrow C
60 Shining Blade SuR
61 Cheerful C
62 Free Will C
63 Self Aware C
64 *Lord Raptor* R

65 Final Performance SuR
66 A Chapter of Tolgaido U
67 Death Phrase U
68 Evil Scream C
69 Ultimate Undead SuR
70 God of Metal C
71 Instant Success C
72 Oral Dead C
73 *Morrigan* R
74 Look into Dreams SuR
75 Seductive Beauty R
76 Cryptic Needle U
77 Valkyrie Turn U
78 Vector Drain U
79 Powers Torn U
80 S Class Noble C
81 Successor to the Throne C
82 *Pyron* R
83 Lying in Wait U
84 Army of Huitzil R
85 Kuchu Soul Smasher C
86 Orbital Blaze SuR
87 Zodiac Fire C
88 Consumer of Planets C
89 Cosmic Being U
90 Pillar of Flame C
91 *Q-Bee* R
92 Deadly Swarm SuR
93 Soul Hive SuR
94 B+R
95 C R C
96 Delta A U
97 Predator's Instincts U
98 Queen of the Hive C
99 Sustained by Souls C
100 *Rikuo* R
101 Pull of the Tides C
102 Egg Clutch R
103 Killer Vortex C
104 Sea Rage SuR
105 Sonic Wave U
106 Bounty of the Sea U
107 Empire's Ruin C
108 King of the Sea C
109 Sasquatch R
110 Jumping In R
111 Stone Mail C
112 Big Cyclone U
113 Big Gulp U
114 ES Super Whirlwind Kick SuR
115 Bigfoot Tribe U
116 Bunches of Bananas U
117 Signs of Friendship U
118 *Victor* R
119 Dense Mass SuR
120 Gerdenheim's Research Notes R
121 Gravitation Knuckle C
122 Gyro Crush C
123 Thunder Break SuR
124 Mockery of Life U
125 Search for Acceptance C
126 Stitched Together U

2007 Universal Fighting System SNK

BOOSTER BOX (24 PACKS)	30.00	60.00
BOOSTER PACK (10 CARDS)	2.00	4.00

RELEASED IN DECEMBER 2006
1 *Alba* R
2 Photographic Memory R
3 Captive Serpent Jab R
4 Luminescent Lash U
5 Seizing the Dragon C
6 Surreptitious Punch of the Thundergod SuR
7 Winds of Pain U
8 Self Made Man C
9 The Devil of Daybreak U
10 *Athena* R
11 Psychic Teleport U
12 Phoenix Arrow U
13 Psycho Ball Attack C
14 Psycho Reflector U
15 Psycho Sword U
16 Shining Crystal Bit SuR
17 E.S.P. C
18 The Eternal Psychic Idol C
19 *Charlotte* R
20 La Roche SuR
21 Crystal Rose R
22 Lance de Lion C
23 Splash Fount R
24 Tri-Slash C
25 Violette Lunge U
26 Master Fencer U
27 Wander Lust C
28 *Galford* R
29 Justice Blade SuR
30 Double Megastrike Heads R
31 Plasma Blade C
32 Replica Attack U
33 Rush Dog R
34 Strike Heads U
35 Mission of Peace C
36 Ninja of Justice C
37 *Gaira* R
38 Namu Abi Dabi SuR
39 Ceiling Slam Grabber R
40 Earthquake Assault C
41 Exploding Euthanasia R
42 Hard Head Grabber U
43 Shout! R
44 Lacks Virtue U
45 Wandering Monk U
46 *Hanzo* R
47 Unnamed Ninja Sword SuR
48 Flying Cicada Dance R
49 Ninja Exploding Dragon Blast R
50 Ninja Shrike Dash U
51 Ninja Windsplitter U
52 True Shrike Dash U
53 Duty Calls U
54 Iga Master U
55 *Haohmaru* StR
56 Fugudoku SuR
57 Crescent Moon Slash U
58 Cyclone Slash C
59 Earthquake Slice StR
60 Judgement Blast Slash R
61 Sake Slash R
62 Fierce Competitor StR
63 Strive for Excellence U
64 *Iori* R
65 Mow The Men Down U
66 Crescent Moon Crunch C
67 Exorcism R
68 Iori's Fire Ball U
69 Rage of the 8 Maidens SuR
70 Winds of Waste R
71 Ancient Arts of Yagami C
72 The Flame of Finality C
73 *Kyo* R
74 Beautiful Purple Flame R
75 427 Torment Trigger R
76 Kyo's Fire Ball C
77 Poison Bite 105 R
78 Serpent Wave SuR
79 Yano Sabi C
80 Ancient Arts of Kusanagi C
81 The Purifying Flame C
82 *Lien* R
83 Lovely Reaper C
84 Assault Type Beta: Al Tarf R
85 Assault Type Epsilon: Atropos C
86 Assault Type Epsilon: Psdterior U
87 Assault Type Lambda: Shaula U
88 Assault Type Iota: Syrma C
89 Homicidal Karate C
90 The Sexy Avenger of the Shadows U
91 *Mai* StR
92 Ninja Arts U
93 Deadly Ninja Bees StR
94 Dragons Flame Romp U
95 Folding Fan Fandango C
96 Nocturnal Plover U
97 Super Deadly Ninja Bees SuR
98 Shiranui Ninja Arts C
99 The Enchanting Ninja Maiden StR
100 *Nagase* R
101 Nagase's Blog U
102 Nagase Spiral R
103 Nagase's Shooting Star U
104 Punishment Mode TYPE: Maximum Spiral C
105 Punishment Mode TYPE: Mega Slash SuR
106 Unrelenting Fire R
107 Battle Disc System U
108 The Ninja Computer Geek U
109 *Nakoruru* R
110 Chichiushi SuR
111 Ambe Yataro R
112 Etelyu Kamui Risse R
113 Kamui Mutsube C
114 Kamui Risse C
115 Lela Mutsube U
116 Idyllic Kamui Kotan U
117 Nature's Defender C
118 *Terry* StR
119 Martial Arts U
120 Burning Knuckle R
121 Buster Wolf StR
122 Power Charge U
123 Power Dunk C
124 Power Wave C
125 Deadly Rage StR
126 The Hero of Southtown C
127 *Ukyo* StR
128 Ukyo's Sword of No Name SuR
129 6 Swallow Flash R
130 Concealed Sabre Snowfall Slash C
131 Concealed Sabre Swallow Swipe StR
132 Ghostly Dashing Slice C
133 Strong Slash Attack C
134 Deathly Ill StR
135 Iaido Sword Style C
136 *Yoshitora* R
137 Nadeshiko SuR
138 Camellias R
139 Hollyhocks C
140 Morning Glories C
141 Pink Blossoms C
142 White Lilies U
143 Carouser C
144 Impetuous U

2007 Universal Fighting System SNK Fortune and Glory

BOOSTER BOX (24 PACKS)	40.00	80.00
BOOSTER PACK (10 CARDS)	2.50	5.00

RELEASED IN AUGUST 2007
1 **Billy** R
2 Come to the Aid R
3 Billy's Staff SuR
4 Club Cruncher C
5 Mighty Whirlwind R
6 Soaring Crackdown Cane U
7 Challenged C
8 Rebellion C
9 The Don's Right Hand Man C
10 **Genjuro** R
11 Uncontrollable Rage U
12 Baio-doku SuR
13 Five Flash Rip C
14 Slash of a Hundred Demons U
15 Triple Death Hack C
16 A Skill for Killing People C
17 Nice Guys Finish Last U
18 The Sword Arts of the Ancient Shadow C
19 **Jubei** R
20 Perfect Form R
21 Steel Tiger and Sukenhiro SuR
22 Geyser Thrust U
23 Moonbeam Slicer SuR
24 Tsunami Sabre C
25 Meaning in Mastery C
26 Modified Shadow Style of Yagyu U
27 Rough and Tumble C
28 **K'** R
29 The Better K' SuR
30 Power Stabilization Glove SuR
31 Crimson Starload R
32 K's Knee Strike U
33 The Trigger U
34 Cold and Haughty C
35 Mysterious Past C
36 Pure Violence U
37 **Luise** R
38 Appreciate the Finer Things in Life U
39 Antique Music Box SuR
40 Quartet of Oblivion U
41 Requiem for a Moth SuR
42 Treacherous Ballade U
43 Linguistics C
44 Schmettering Fighting Performance Arts. C
45 The Dancing Butterfly in a Starry Sky C
46 ***Mai*** R
47 Shiranui Flames U
48 Combat Fan SuR
49 Blossom Storm C
50 Phoenix Dance SuR
51 Rising Dragon Flamefest U
52 Japan's Best! C
53 Unrequited Love U
54 Won't Settle for Second Best C
55 *Nightmare Geese* R
56 Resolution Through Force SuR
57 Eminence SuR
58 Deadly Rave R
59 Homicidal Slam U
60 Shrieking Lightning Shockwave R
61 Ancient Arts of Combat U
62 Ruler of Southtown U
63 The Recurring Nightmare C
64 *Sankuro* R
65 Absurd Strength C
66 The Unbeatable SuR
67 Goshichi C
68 Ippachi U
69 My Tanegashima SuR
70 Overconfident C
71 The Way of the Mightiest C
72 Vanity U
73 *Seth* R
74 Growing Up in the Ghetto R
75 Profitable Opportunity U
76 Cascading Moon U
77 Drifting Moon R
78 Two-Fisted Rising Sun U
79 Rigourous Training U
80 The Art of Self-Defense C
81 The Proud Agent C
82 *Tam Tam* R
83 Rage Gauge SuR
84 Henge Hange Zange SuR
85 Ahaooh Gaboora U
86 Pagona Dios SuR
87 Paguna Paguna U
88 Feral Fury U
89 The Sword That Protects C
90 The Way of the Maya U
91 ***Ukyo*** R
92 Control the Flow SuR
93 Ukyo's Apple SuR
94 Concealed Shallow Swipe U
95 Swordless Sabre Snowfall Slash C
96 Ukyo's Short Slash Attack R
97 Misdirection C
98 Romantic Yearnings U
99 The Sword is One Scary Beast C

2007 Universal Fighting System Soul Calibur III Battle Pack

1 *Siegfried* R
2 **Siegfried** R
3 Chief Hold R
4 Shoulder Charge C
5 Side Hold R
6 Requiem R
7 Armor Breaker U
8 Backspin Slash C
9 Blaze Storm U
10 Maelstrom C
11 Nightmare Killer R
12 Slash Impact C
13 Spinning Phantom Combo R
14 Witch Hunt R
15 Armored Defense U
16 Controlled Rage R
17 Focus the Soul R
18 Heavy Metal U
19 Memory Regained C
20 Two-Handed Style C
21 Victorious R
22 Weapon Training R
23 *Sophitia* R
24 **Sophitia** R
25 Angelic Grace C
26 Divine Champion U
27 Shield Bash U
28 Omega Sword and Elk Shield R
29 Angel Punisher U
30 Angel's Flow C
31 Ascend Splash U
32 Iron Butterfly U
33 Nasty Impale U
34 Sophitia's Guardian's Judgement R
35 Spinning Hilt C
36 Widow Maker R
37 Angelic Protection R
38 Athenian Style C
39 Baker's Daughter U
40 Close Fighter R
41 Inspired U
42 Persistence C
43 Troubled Orphan R
44 You're Not My Father R

2007 Universal Fighting System Soulcalibur III Blades of Fury

BOOSTER BOX (24 PACKS)	30.00	60.00
BOOSTER PACK (10 CARDS)	2.00	3.50

RELEASED IN MAY 2007
1 *Maxi* SuR
2 **Maxi** R
3 Flashy Display U
4 Maxi's Taunt C
5 Pure Soul Loop C
6 Soryuju SuR
7 Dragon Destroyer R
8 Fury SuR
9 Illusion Kick C
10 Lunging Snake C
11 Mark of the Beast U
12 Mark of the Dragon R
13 Snake's Tale C
14 Steel Dragon R
15 Amnesia U
16 Nothing to Lose C
17 Pirate from Ryukyu C
18 Shissen Karihadi U
19 ****Nightmare**** R
20 Soul Wave SuR
21 The Ancient SuR
22 Double Snap Kick C
23 Grim Roundhouse C
24 Hell Slayer U
25 Jade Crusher SuR
26 Grim Stride U
27 Night Side Stance C
28 ****Tira**** R
29 Vimana SuR
30 Canary Waltz C Minor SuR
31 Con Il Legno U
32 Fleeting Scratcher C
33 Groove Disc C
34 Harmonic Wing R
35 Ibis Minuet C
36 Rumbling Robin U
37 *Yun-Seong* R
38 **Yun-Seong** SuR
39 Crane Swoop C
40 Land Walk U
41 White Storm SuR
42 Avenging Claws U
43 Bird of Prey SuR
44 Branding Blade U
45 Burning Sky U
46 Circling Wing U
47 Heaven's Path C
48 Meteor Throw U
49 Ragged Fangs C
50 Twisting Coils C
51 Natural Footwork U
52 Purity of Innocence C
53 Seong Style Longsword U
54 Whereabouts Unknown C
55 *Xianghua* SuR
56 **Xianghua** R
57 Chinese Sword Style C
58 Pure of Heart C
59 Dodge Step U
60 Xianghua's Sword of No Name SuR
61 Beautiful Rhythm U
62 Chicken Kick C
63 Circle Breaker Feint Divide SuR
64 Crescent Flow C
65 Pointing Thrust U
66 Quake Step C
67 Rhythm Break U
68 Yng Dyi Yann U
69 Child Prodigy C
70 Circuitous Prancing U
71 Defender of the Empire U
72 Flashy Blade Work C
73 Hypnotic Misdirection U
74 Masterful Form C
75 Heisheng Jian SuR
76 Claymore R
77 Descending Slash R
78 Foot Spear C
79 Run Through R
80 Sweeping Slash R
81 Upper Slash U
82 Winding Blow U
83 Beautiful Friendship C
84 Gather the Soul U
85 Inner Demons C
86 Regal Bearing U
87 Reminiscent U
88 The Best Defense… R
89 The Curse Broken U
90 Unpredictable R

2007 Universal Fighting System Soulcalibur III Higher Calibur

BOOSTER BOX (24 PACKS)	40.00	80.00
BOOSTER PACK (10 CARDS)	2.50	5.00

RELEASED IN AUGUST 2007
1 ****Astaroth**** R
2 *****Astaroth***** SuR
3 Irresistible Force R
4 Terror Moon SuR
5 Ares Spiral Rage U
6 Ax Volcano C
7 Bear Tamer U
8 Bludgeoning Crush U
9 Bull Low Kick C
10 Canyon Creation SuR
11 Discus Breaker U
12 Hades Cannon R
13 Scourge of Zeus SuR
14 Disciple of War R
15 Glory of Ares C
16 Inhuman Strength C
17 Leverage C
18 Long Reach U
19 ****Cassandra**** SuR
20 *****Cassandra***** R
21 Temporal Ascension R
22 Dark Blade SuR
23 Angel Side Kick U
24 Artemis Dart SuR
25 Cutlass Serendipity C
26 Heaven Lift R
27 Holy Sweeper C
28 Meteor Shower C
29 Tornado Feint U
30 Undertow SuR
31 Zephyros Wheel R
32 Family Values C
33 Intuition U
34 Positional Exploitation U
35 Steel Cage C
36 Tradition of Battle U
37 ****Cervantes**** R
38 *****Cervantes***** SuR
39 Kiss the Gunner's Daughter C
40 Styx SuR
41 The Adrian R
42 Figurehead Break U
43 Genocidal Culverin C
44 Gibbering Torpedo U
45 Iceberg Circular R
46 Killer X R
47 Pirate's Cross U
48 Pirate's Tactics SuR
49 Pressure Astern C
50 Soul Swing SuR
51 Avarice U
52 Bretheren of the Coast C
53 Dead Men Tell No Tales U
54 Pieces of Eight C
55 Cagemaster C
56 False Pretenses C
57 ****Ivy**** R
58 *****Ivy***** SuR
59 Whipcracker R
60 Viper Edge SuR
61 Cursed Mark R
62 Drowning Madness C
63 God Whisper C
64 Lost Pledge C
65 Metal Dancer U
66 Pride U
67 Raven's Egg SuR
68 Stinging Souls U
69 Asylum U
70 Driven Madness U
71 Serpent's Embrace U
72 Soul of Ivy C
73 **Seong Mi-na** R
74 Run Away U
75 Scarlet Thunder SuR
76 Heavy Willow Divide C
77 Mi-na Frankensteiner R
78 Twin Fang Thrust U
79 Eavesdropping U
80 Ling Sheng Su Style Rod C
81 Quick to Anger C
82 ****Voldo**** R
83 *****Voldo***** SuR
84 Super Freak Lunge C
85 Guillotine SuR
86 Blind Slap Spin U
87 Demon Pheromone R
88 Ecstasy C
89 Freak Roll C
90 Gate Prier U
91 Guillotine Scissors U
92 Insanity Trap R
93 Jolly Ripper C
94 Life Sucker SuR
95 Blind Stance C
96 Caliostro Rush U
97 Mantis Crawl U
98 Rat Chaser C
99 Sealed Away U

2007 Universal Fighting System Soulcalibur III Soul Arena

BOOSTER BOX (24 PACKS)	40.00	80.00
BOOSTER PACK (10 CARDS)	2.50	5.00

RELEASED IN FEBRUARY 2007
1 *Abyss* R
2 **Abyss** StR
3 Echoing Roar U
4 Twisting Hearts of Men C
5 Irkalla SuR
6 Abyss's Nergal's Poison Sting C
7 Apsu's Fury C
8 Cosmic Embryo U
9 Enkidu's Grief C
10 Fatal Gravity StR
11 Lilitu's Needle C

12 Lunatic Sin R
13 Nova's Combo U
14 Void Nova C
15 Achieving Your Goals U
16 Eternity of Lifetimes C
17 Inhuman Power StR
18 True Death U
19 *Cervantes* R
20 **Cervantes** StR
21 Immortality U
22 Pirate Raid C
23 Soul Edge & Nirvana SuR
24 Dread Slash StR
25 Eternal Curse U
26 Flying Dutchman C
27 Galleon Sinker U
28 Jolly Roger Hoist C
29 Night Raid C
30 Phantasm Fleet C
31 Suprise Wave U
32 Tornado Swell U
33 Dread Charge C
34 No Quarter StR
35 Soul of Cervantes C
36 The Merchant's Message C
37 *Lizardman* SuR
38 **Lizardman** StR
39 Experiments U
40 Punishing Onslaught C
41 Grudge Ax & Aya Shield SuR
42 Killing Bite U
43 Mezentius Desert Threat StR
44 Mezentius Head Butt C
45 Mezentius Sand Revenger R
46 Mezentius Shield Cannon U
47 Mezentius Style Reptile Rumble C
48 Sandland Predator C
49 Turnus Dune Comet C
50 Turnus Nether Blast StR
51 Awakening U
52 Forsaken U
53 Raise the Shield C
54 Soldier of Sparta C
55 ****Mitsurugi**** SuR
56 *****Mitsurugi***** R
57 Quest to Defeat the Rifle R
58 Shogyusha R
59 Damascus Sword SuR
60 8th Bill of Punishment U
61 Cannon Divide R
62 Double Reaver R
63 Hell Flash R
64 Lantern Divide R
65 Mitsurugi's Phoenix Tail R
66 Rising Knee R
67 Star Fall Eve R
68 Upper Arch R
69 Calm but Deadly R
70 Mist U
71 Silent Step R
72 Son of a Farmer R
73 *Rock* SuR
74 **Rock** R
75 Hesitation C
76 Remember the Past U
77 Onslaught SuR
78 Atomic Drop Maximum R
79 Avalanche Press U
80 Crack Divider C
81 Earth Lifter C
82 Hyper Dynamite Slam C
83 Jumping Tomahawk C
84 Rock Knuckle U
85 Rock Stomp Kick C
86 Ultimate Volcano R
87 Father Figure C
88 Immense Strength U
89 Proven Manhood U
90 Taking the Bait U
91 ****Taki**** SuR
92 *****Taki***** R
93 Melding U
94 Wind Roll R
95 Fuma Kugi SuR
96 Dragon Wheel R
97 Executioner's Curse R
98 Jute Burial R
99 Ninja Cannon U
100 Seal of the Fire Dragon R
101 Shadow Cannon R
102 Stalker Drop R
103 Weaving Blades R
104 Windfall R
105 Demon Hunting R
106 Intuitive Observation R
107 Leave at Dawn U
108 Skilled Ninja R
109 *Talim* SuR
110 **Talim** R
111 Unparalleled Potential U
112 Virtue of the Small U
113 Syi Salika & Loka Luha SuR
114 Blue Sky U
115 Flowing Gale Hook U
116 Icewind Combo C
117 Monsoon Season C
118 Parabolic Sipa R
119 Piggyback Tulison C
120 Rolling Storm U
121 Turning Kali Strikes C
122 Witik Stomp C
123 Deceptive Look U
124 Not the Strongest C
125 Searching for Fragments U
126 Shaman Training U
127 *Yoshimitsu* R
128 **Yoshimitsu** StR
129 Infiltrating SuR
130 Manji Ninjitsu StR
131 Yoshimitsu SuR
132 Firmiana Solor Kick C
133 Jaw Smash U
134 Moon Sault Slayer C
135 Rainbow Drop C
136 Soul Harvest R
137 Spinning Fall Pogo U
138 Spinning Sword C
139 Steel Wind C
140 Turning Suicide StR
141 Chivalrous Thievery C
142 Hidden Base U
143 Dragonfly U
144 Sole Survivor U

2007 Universal Fighting System Street Fighter Extreme Rivals

BOOSTER BOX (24 PACKS) 40.00 80.00
BOOSTER PACK (10 CARDS) 2.50 5.00
RELEASED IN MAY 2007
1 *Cody* SuR
2 **Cody** R
3 I'll Take You On U
4 So Much Work Ahead of Me U
5 Manacles SuR
6 Bad Spray R
7 Bad Stone U
8 Chain Throw U
9 Cody's Stomach Blow C
10 Crack Kick C
11 Criminal Uppercut R
12 Final Destruction SuR
13 Knife Throw C
14 Ruffian Kick U
15 Don't Let Me Down U
16 Heart of Gold C
17 Fighting Frenzy C
18 Short Fuse U
19 *Dee Jay* SuR
20 **Dee Jay** R
21 Close Quarters U
22 Flying Feet C
23 MAXIMUM Wear SuR
24 Dee Jay's Crouching Roundhouse U
25 Dee Jay's Fierce Punch C
26 Dee Jay's Jab C
27 Double Dread Kick U
28 Dread Carnival SuR
29 Hyper Fist R
30 Knee Shot C
31 Max Out U
32 Maximum Jacknife C
33 Familiar Moves C
34 Kickboxing Discipline U
35 Move to the Rhythm C
36 Practice Makes Perfect U
37 *Ibuki* SuR
38 **Ibuki** R
39 Kasumi Gaki R
40 Tsuji Goe U
41 Ibuki's Kunai SuR
42 Bonso Geri C
43 Hien U
44 Kasumi-Suzaku SuR
45 Kazekiri U
46 Kubi Ori C
47 Kunai C
48 Maki Geri U
49 Raida R
50 Tsumuji U
51 Ninjitsu C
52 Shadow Art R
53 Shinobi Tradition C
54 Waste Not U
55 ****Ken**** SuR
56 *****Ken***** R
57 I Wish You Good Luck R
58 Shotokan Knowledge U
59 Red Gi R
60 Ken's Close Fierce Punch C
61 Ken's Close Strong Punch C
62 Ken's Hadoken EXTRA SuR
63 Ken's Jab C
64 Ken's Low Roundhouse C
65 Ken's Shoryuken R
66 Ken's Tatsumaki Senpu Kyaku EXTRA U
67 Ken's Shiden Kakato Otoshi C
68 Shinryuken U
69 Art of Shotokan U
70 Martial Arts Champion C
71 Show-Off C
72 Vast Resources U
73 *R. Mika* SuR
74 **R. Mika** R
75 Evasion Technique R
76 Piling It On SuR
77 Squared Circle SuR
78 Body Splash C
79 Brain Buster C
80 Daydream Headlock C
81 Flying Peach C
82 Heavenly Dynamite SuR
83 Neck Breaker U
84 Paradise Hold U
85 Rainbow Hip Rush U
86 Shooting Peach U
87 Intestinal Fortitude U
88 Roll With the Fall C
89 Star of the Ring U
90 Tendon Strength C

2007 Universal Fighting System Street Fighter Fight for the Future

BOOSTER BOX (24 PACKS) 40.00 80.00
BOOSTER PACK (10 CARDS) 2.50 5.00
RELEASED IN NOVEMBER 2007
1 *Alex* R
2 **Alex** SuR
3 Deadly Grapple U
4 You Can't Escape C
5 Grappling Gloves U
6 N.Y. Subway Station R
7 Flash Chop R
8 Flying Cross Chop C
9 Hyper Bomb SuR
10 Power Bomb SuR
11 Slash Elbow U
12 Spiral D.D.T. U
13 Come into Your Own U
14 Headstrong C
15 Impressive Physique C
16 Physical Fighter C
17 Stay Down U
18 Undefeated C
19 *****Cammy***** R
20 ******Cammy****** SuR
21 Break Free SuR
22 Scarred SuR
23 Combat Boots R
24 Delta Red Insignia SuR
25 Cammy's Low Punch C
26 Cammy's Roundhouse SuR
27 Cannonball Jump U
28 Hooligan Combo U
29 **Spin Drive Smasher** R
30 Thrust Kick U
31 Assassin C
32 Confrontation U
33 Forgotten Memories U
34 Killer Bee C
35 Realizations C
36 Undercover C
37 *******Chun-Li******* R
38 ********Chun-Li******** SuR
39 Aerial Assault R
40 Amazing Acrobatics SuR
41 Interpol Badge SuR
42 Light-footed Stance R
43 Kakashi Ken C
44 Koho Kaiten Kyaku U
45 **Ryusei Raku** U
46 Spinning Bird Kick EXTRA R
47 Tensei-Ranka SuR
48 Yoso Kyaku C
49 Ancestor's Strength U
50 Death from Above C
51 Harness Your Chi U
52 Peace and Harmony U
53 Strike to Maim C
54 Traditional Style C
55 *****Dhalsim***** R
56 Lead a Simple Life R
57 Dhalsim's Turban U
58 Yoga Catch C
59 Yoga Drill Kick U
60 Yoga Legend SuR
61 Journey to Enlightenment U
62 Roam the World C
63 Spiritual Center C
64 **Gen** R
65 Tiger Style U
66 Genhanten SuR
67 Gekiro U
68 Hyakurenko C
69 Shitenshu R
70 A Worthy Death C
71 Failing Health U
72 Kung Fu Master C
73 **Gill** R
74 Resurrection SuR
75 The Illuminati C
76 Cryokenesis C
77 Impact Claw C
78 Seraphic Wing R
79 Illuminati Messiah U
80 Overwhelming Power U
81 Prophesied Leader U
82 *****Guile***** R
83 ******Guile****** SuR
84 Brilliant Escape R
85 Setting Explosives SuR
86 Fatigues R
87 Safu R
88 Flash Kick U
89 Guile's Backfist C
90 **Reverse Spin Kick** C
91 **Somersault Kick** U
92 Sonic Boom Typhoon SuR
93 Standing Roundhouse SuR
94 Daily Routine U
95 Family Ties C
96 Friendship C
97 Man Enough U
98 Military Rank C
99 Patriot U

2007 Universal Fighting System Street Fighter Ryu vs. Akuma Battle Pack

COMPLETE SET (44)
RELEASED IN JULY 2007
1 ****Akuma**** R
2 *****Akuma***** R
3 Instant Hell Murder C
4 Unleashed Demons U
5 Onigami Isle R
6 Akuma's Low Forward Kick U
7 Forward Kick U
8 Go Shoryuken U
9 Hyakki Go Sen R
10 Hyakki Go Tsui U
11 Kongoko-Kuretsuzan R
12 Messatsu-Gorasen U
13 Tenma Go Zanku U
14 Constant Training C
15 Demon Eyes U
16 Done no Wrong U
17 Float like a Butterfly… U
18 Full Power U
19 Live for the Fight C
20 Megalomania U
21 The Raging Demon U
22 Twisted Moral Code U
23 ******Ryu****** R
24 *******Ryu******* R
25 Block C
26 Rejecting the Demons U
27 Shotokan Style C
28 Furinkazan R
29 Kuchu Tatsumaki Senpukyaku EXTRA R
30 Hatobi Kudaki U
31 Ryu's Hadoken EXTRA R
32 Ryu's Shoryuken EXTRA R
33 Ryu's Low Roundhouse U
34 Shinku Tatsumaki Senpukyaku U
35 Tatsumaki Senpukyaku R
36 Beefy C
37 Tricky C
38 Evil Shunned C
39 Grieving for the Master C
40 Inner Mastery U
41 Mortal Strike C
42 Proven U
43 Shotokan Training C
44 The Strongest Fighter C

2007 Universal Fighting System Street Fighter The Dark Path

BOOSTER BOX (24 PACKS) 40.00 80.00
BOOSTER PACK (10 CARDS) 2.50 5.00
RELEASED IN FEBRUARY 2007
1 *Adon* SuR
2 **Adon** R
3 Challenge the Master R
4 Seeking Out C
5 Jackknife Kick R
6 Jaguar Assault SuR
7 Jaguar Kick C
8 Jaguar Revolver U
9 Jaguar Tooth R
10 Kickboxer Fury U
11 Knee Toss C
12 Ultimate U
13 Rising Jaguar U
14 Slice and Dice C
15 Acrobatic Techniques U
16 Cocky C
17 God of Muay Thai U
18 Wai Khru C
19 *Charlie* SuR
20 **Charlie** R
21 One-Armed Manuevers R
22 Reversal Kata U
23 Air Backbreaker U
24 Charlie's Knee Bazooka R
25 Charlie's Somersault Shell R
26 Charlie's Sonic Boom R
27 Crossfire Barrage R
28 Overhead Hop Kick C
29 Sonic Blade SuR
30 Sonic Blitz R
31 Sonic Break R
32 Spinning Back Knuckle SuR
33 Investigations R
34 M.I.A. R
35 Martial Arts Champ C
36 Special Forces Training U
37 ****Chun-Li**** SuR
38 *****Chun-Li***** StR
39 The Fight is Never Over R
40 You've Wasted Enough of My Time StR
41 Spiked Bracelets StR
42 Chun-Li's Forward Kick R
43 Chun-Li's Roundhouse Kick U
44 Double Palm Strike U
45 Hazan Shu C
46 Kaku Kyaku Raku C
47 Kiko-Sho C
48 Kikoken C
49 Ryusei Raku C
50 Sen'en Shu U
51 Legendary Legs U
52 Out for Revenge C
53 Serious Fighter U
54 Strength and Beauty C
55 ****Ryu**** SuR
56 *****Ryu***** StR
57 Ryu's Ashura Senku SuR
58 Consumed StR
59 Denjin Hadoken U
60 Dive Kick C
61 Hado no Kamae C
62 Kuchu Seoi Nage C
63 Messatsu Go Shoryu U
64 Satsui no Hado C
65 Seichu Nidan Tsuki U
66 Senpu Kyaku C
67 Shin Shoryuken StR
68 Shun Goku Satsu U
69 Merciless C
70 Dark Hado (SF04) C
71 Unbound Rage U
72 Untapped Potential U
73 *Rose* SuR
74 **Rose** R
75 Reading the Cards R
76 Crystal Ball SuR
77 Aura Soul Spark R
78 Mega Soul Spark R
79 Mind Blast R
80 Soul Catch R
81 Soul Illusion C
82 Soul Images U
83 Soul Reflect R
84 Soul Slide R
85 Soul Spark U
86 Super Soul Catch R
87 Control the Present R
88 Fortune Teller R
89 Soul Power R
90 Terrible Discovery R
91 *Sakura* SuR
92 **Sakura** R
93 Justice Always Prevails U
94 That Was Cool, Do it Again! SuR
95 Agohani Geri U
96 Batobi Punch C
97 Furiko Upper U
98 Genkotsu Stamp C
99 Jumping Shotei C
100 Midare Zakura U
101 Sakura's Hadoken R
102 Shagami Jab U
103 Sho-Oh-Ken C
104 Shunpu Kyaku R
105 Shotokan C
106 Getting an Education C
107 Repeat Techniques C
108 Well-Traveled R
109 *T. Hawk* SuR
110 **T. Hawk** StR
111 Condor Spirit U
112 Reclaim the Land R
113 Native Heritage U
114 Condor Splash U
115 Double Typhoon R
116 Elbow Smasher U
117 Heavy Body Press R
118 Neck Choke C
119 Overhead Throw C
120 Storm Hammer U
121 The Hawk U
122 Thunderstrike StR
123 Condor Power C
124 Reversal Totem C
125 Son of Arroyo StR
126 Thunderfoot C
127 *Twelve* SuR
128 **Twelve** StR
129 Kabe Haritsuki U
130 Kokku C
131 Let's Go C
132 Perfect U
133 X.C.O.P.Y. StR
134 A.X.E. R
135 B.M.K. U
136 D.R.A. C
137 N.D.L. U
138 X.F.L.A.T. R
139 X.N.D.L. StR
140 00101.01101.00001.01111 U
141 1011.01111C
142 Clones C
143 Doppelgang U
144 Impervious U

2008 Universal Fighting System Darkstalkers Realm of Midnight

BOOSTER BOX (24 PACKS)
BOOSTER PACK (10 CARDS)
RELEASED IN JUNE 2008
1 **Anakaris** R
2 The Price of Foolishness R
3 The Nine Commandments SuR
4 Cobra Blow U
5 Mirror Drop C
6 Pharaoh Split U
7 Eternal Rule C
8 The King of the Golden Kingdom C
9 Ultimate and Immortal U
10 ***Bishamon*** R
11 Preventing the Curse R
12 Accursed Power SuR
13 Jodan Iaigiri U
14 Tsuji Hayate C
15 Tsurane Kiri SuR
16 Lesser of Many Evils C
17 Miserable Existance U
18 Trapped in a Nightmare C
19 ***Demitri*** R
20 Hypnotic Gaze U
21 Vampiric Aura SuR
22 Demon Cradle R
23 Midnight Pleasure SuR
24 Negative Strain U
25 100 Years of Humiliation C
26 Prince of Darkeness U
27 The Thirst Always Wins C
28 **Donovan** R
29 Dark Awakening U
30 Supernatural Heritage SuR
31 Change Immortal SuR
32 Katana O Modosu C
33 Lightning Sword U
34 Fight Fire with Fire C
35 Looking for Peace C
36 The Struggle Within U
37 ****Felicia**** R
38 Feline Ferocity U
39 A Cat's Reflexes SuR

40 Feline Spike SuR
41 Flashing Buckler C
42 Rolling Buckler Uppercut U
43 Feline Grace C
44 Inhuman Senses U
45 Nine Lives C
46 **Hsien-Ko** R
47 Igyo Tenshin no Jutsu R
48 Mei-Lin's Ward SuR
49 Ankipo C
50 Henkoyuki C
51 Tenraiha U
52 Dark Dreams U
53 Darkhunter of the Night C
54 Senjutsu C
55 **Huitzil** R
56 Genocide R
57 Combat Programming SuR
58 Circuit Scrapper R
59 High Plasma Beam U
60 Might Launcher C
61 Dormant for Millions of Years C
62 Program Malfunction U
63 Tool of Destruction U
64 **Jedah** R
65 Soul Absorption R
66 Liquid Form SuR
67 Dio-Cega C
68 Ira-Spinta R
69 Prova-Dei-Cervo U
70 Dark Messiah C
71 Grand Vision U
72 Makai High Noble U
73 ***J. Talbain*** R
74 Feral Cunning U
75 Hidden Beastly Powers SuR
76 Climb Razor C
77 Dark Force: Mirage Body SuR
78 Million Flicker C
79 Antisocial U
80 Fight or Flight U
81 Lone Wolf C
82 ***Morrigan*** R
83 Caught Up in the Moment R
84 Looks That Kill SuR
85 Darkness Blade SuR
86 Shadow Blade C
87 Soul Fist C
88 Alluring Beauty C
89 Irresistable U
90 Without a Care U
91 ***Victor*** R
92 Searching for a Place in the World U
93 Reanimated SuR
94 Great Gerdenheim SuR
95 Mega Spike R
96 Mega Stake C
97 Confused and Lonely U
98 Outsider U
99 Self Sacrifice C

2008 Universal Fighting System SNK Cutting Edge

BOOSTER BOX (24 PACKS)	20.00	40.00
BOOSTER PACK (10 CARDS)	1.25	2.50

RELEASED IN FEBRUARY 2008
1 B. Jenet** R
2 Treasure Hunt R
3 Pirate Ship U
4 Crazy Ivan SuR
5 Harrier Bee C
6 Spiraling Neck Lock C
7 Lillien Knights C
8 LK Arts U
9 The Corsair Under the Skull and Crossbones U
10 Galford*** R
11 One-sided Crush U
12 Ayame's Scarf SuR
13 Machine Gun Dog SuR
14 Overhead Crash U
15 Stardust Drop C
16 Koga Ninja Arts U
17 Seeking a Challenge C
18 Upholding Justice U
19 Haohmaru*** R
20 Offer a Duel R
21 The Blowfish Blade SuR
22 Hiogi C
23 Tenha Fujin Zan U
24 Zankosen C
25 A Samurai's Life C
26 Building a Country C
27 Personal Style R
28 Iori*** R
29 Ostracized SuR
30 Yasakani no Magatama SuR
31 Cleansing Nirvana U
32 Gaishiki Lunar Rebellion C
33 Reverse Flayer R
34 Maniac C
35 Strenuous Training C
36 The Street Life C
37 Kula** R
38 Purpose U
39 Lollipop SuR
40 Critical Cold U
41 Freezing Execution R
42 Ice Coffin R
43 Feelings of Friendship U
44 The Anti K' U
45 The Icicle Doll C
46 Kyo**** R
47 Instinctual Rivalry R
48 Leather Jacket SuR
49 125 Rapids of Rage R
50 Steel Slammer C
51 Wicked Chew R
52 Kenpo U
53 Pyrokinetics U
54 The Red Lotus of the Sun U
55 Kyoshiro** R
56 Graceful Kabuki U
57 Kyoshiro's Naginata SuR
58 Chikemuri Kuruwa SuR
59 Gama Jigoku U
60 Kaen Kyokubu U
61 A Mysterious Figther U
62 Dancing Battle Kabuki U
63 Kabuki Artist C
64 Mai***** R
65 Rejection R
66 Fan Blade SuR
67 Dream Blossoms R
68 Solar Flash Dance SuR
69 Windmill Waster U
70 Ninja Skills C
71 Shiranui-Ryu Ninjutsu U
72 The Gorgeous Team R
73 Nagase*** R
74 Collecting Data R
75 Assassination Arts SuR
76 Nagase Stomp C
77 Nagase's Unrelenting Fire R
78 Punishment Mode-Type: Energy Vacuum SuR
79 Arrogant and Insolent U
80 More Machine than Woman U
81 N-type Human C
82 Ninon* R
83 Puppetry U
84 Doll from Grandma SuR
85 Glory of Sephiroth C
86 Hammer of Demiurges U
87 Melancholic Mercurius C
88 Black Magic C
89 Superior Witch U
90 The Girl Dancing with the Devil U
91 Rera** R
92 Fight to Protect U
93 Dark Chichiushi SuR
94 Imeru Shikite R
95 Okami Ni Noru R
96 Rera Kishima Tek R
97 Exist Within U
98 Polar Opposite U
99 The Darker Side C
100 Rock Howard* R
101 Disdain R
102 Good Looks SuR
103 Demonic Drubbing U
104 Fatal Disruptor U
105 Neo Deadly Rave R
106 Never Give Up U
107 New Information R
108 The Noble Scion of an Odious Bloodline C
109 Yoshitora*** R
110 Bringing the Master to His Knees R
111 Yoshitora's Girlfriends SuR
112 Ichi no Tachi C
113 Yuchoka R
114 Yugao U
115 Once a Student, Now a Soldier U
116 Refusal of Power C
117 Superiority R
118 Yumeji*** R
119 Penance R
120 Yumeji's Sword of No Name SuR
121 Bayonette Lunge C
122 Chobi Jishi U
123 Ninpo Mozu Otoshi U
124 Adopted C
125 Daughter of a Sensei C
126 Soichi Jinmu C
127 About Face SuR
128 Divination U
129 Engineered C
130 Nefarious Deeds C
131 Revitalize SuR
132 Taking Them Down a Level SuR
133 Turnabout SuR
134 Ulterior Motives SuR
135 Addes Syndicate SuR
136 Secret Project R
137 Cool-Headed C
138 Detached C
139 Holding Ground C
140 Light on One's Feet C
141 Low to the Ground C
142 Rookie's Fortune C
143 Take to the Air C
144 Unconventional Martial Arts C

2008 Universal Fighting System SNK Flames of Fame

BOOSTER BOX (24 PACKS)	20.00	40.00
BOOSTER PACK (10 CARDS)	1.25	2.50

RELEASED IN DECEMBER 2008
1 Basara.. R
2 Demon's Scourge U
3 The Evil-Doer Destroyer R
4 Soul of the Beast C
5 Shadow Exit U
6 Friendly Rip SuR
7 Instinctive Sword Swinging C
8 Living Shadow U
9 A Beautiful Nightmare C
10 Billy:. R
11 At a Distance SuR
12 Kid Sister SuR
13 Flaming Mid-Section Club Cruncher C
14 Homing Water Dragon Cane C
15 Super Fire Wheel U
16 Clean Freak R
17 British Subject C
18 Born on Christmas Day C
19 Gaira:. R
20 Amazing Tolerance C
21 Namu Abi Dabi.. SuR
22 Heart Slicer C
23 Butt Slam U
24 Centennipierce Slam R
25 Distractible U
26 Weapons are Unnecessary C
27 Will for the Fight U
28 Kazuki:. R
29 Kazuki's Pyrotechnics U
30 Sujaku SuR
31 Soul Burner U
32 Exploding Death SuR
33 Annihilating Flames C
34 Always Done First R
35 Flames of Disaster U
36 Kazama Ninja Arts C
37 Kim* R
38 Swift Justice C
39 Kim's Dojang SuR
40 Kim's Neck Crunch Drop U
41 Heavenly Phoenix Dancing Stomp R
42 Swooper Kick C
43 The National Tae Kwon Do Treasure U
44 Superlative Gymnast U
45 Karaoke Idol C
46 Nakoruru:. R
47 Nature's Force U
48 Father Bull R
49 Rera Kishi Matek C
50 Annu Mutsube SuR
51 Apenhuchi Kamui Risse C
52 A Means of Self Defense U
53 Dancing Sword Arts C
54 Voice of the Land U
55 Nightmare Geese:. R
56 Forceful Resolution R
57 Self Confidence SuR
58 Double Gale Fist U
59 Evil Illusion Slam C
60 Raising Storm SuR
61 Billiard Player U
62 Meat Eater U
63 Multi-Hobbyist C
64 Ralf* R
65 Homerun! R
66 Decorated for Service R
67 Galactica Phantom SuR
68 Northern Lights Bomb C
69 Vulcan Punch C
70 Connoisseur of Blades U
71 Ikari Warrior C
72 The One May Army U
73 Rock Howard:. R
74 Traveling Man R
75 Gift from a Friend SuR
76 Crack Counter -> Vaulting U
77 Double Cyclone Punch C
78 Neo Raging Storm SuR
79 Culinary Artist U
80 Motorcyclist C
81 Street Baller U
82 Sogetsu.. R
83 High Tide SuR
84 The Blue Dragon SuR
85 Lunar Slash R
86 Moon Glow C
87 Weak Slash C
88 An Efficient Method to Slay People U
89 Aquakinesis U
90 Familial Loyalty C
91 Terry:. R
92 Trolling SuR
93 Jeff's Gloves R
94 Fire Kick U
95 Power Drive C
96 Rising Tackle U
97 Baller U
98 Fast Food Lover U
99 American Made C

2008 Universal Fighting System SNK King of Fighters

COMPLETE SET (99)

BOOSTER BOX (24 PACKS)	20.00	40.00
BOOSTER PACK (10 CARDS)	1.25	2.50

RELEASED IN SEPTEMBER 2008
1 ***Alba*** R
2 God Hand SuR
3 Arrogance SuR
4 Hallowed Slug of the Heavenly Conqueror R
5 Molten Steel U
6 Omnidirectional Cluster Bomb C
7 Chinese Boxing C
8 Keep Your Cool U
9 Natural Leader C
10 *Chae* R
11 Tae Kwon Do Strike R
12 Treasured Gift SuR
13 Furious Feet of the Phoenix U
14 Neck Crunch Drop U
15 Single Wing Slam C
16 Honor Your Dojo C
17 Speak the Truth C
18 The Tae Kwon Do Zephyr U
19 *Fio* R
20 Special Ops SuR
21 Family Tradition SuR
22 K.A.M.I.K.A.Z.E U
23 SPECIAL MISSION: Swing Tomahawk R
24 Terrestrial Heavy Machine Gun C
25 La Superba C
26 Military Combat Arts U
27 The Bespectacled Master Sergeant C
28 ***Hanzo*** R
29 Shadow Strike SuR
30 Preparedness R
31 Demonic Self-Sacrifice Strategem U
32 Enveloping Exorcism U
33 **True Shrike Dash** SuR
34 Fade into Darkness C
35 Iga Legacy C
36 The Ruler of the Shadows U
37 *Jivatma* R
38 Punish the Weak R
39 The Stars Aligned SuR
40 Dark Rending U
41 Divine Folly C
42 Flames of Fate C
43 Approaching Physical Perfection U
44 The Glare from the Abyss C
45 The Ways of Punishment U
46 **Leona** R
47 Military Discipline SuR
48 Explosive Earings SuR
49 Gravity Storm C
50 Moon Slasher U
51 Order Backslash U
52 Heidern's Assassination Arts C
53 Origins Unknown U
54 The Silent Soldier C
55 *Maxima* R
56 Self-diagnosis Program SuR
57 The Maxima Reactor SuR
58 Dynamite Drop R
59 Mongolian – Trample U
60 MX-11 Final Cannon C
61 Altered Mind and Body C
62 M-Style Combat Arts U
63 The Human Weapon of Steel C
64 *Mignon* R
65 Better Under Pressure U
66 Family Heirloom SuR
67 Pony Throw U
68 Thunderbolt C
69 Wind Storm SuR
70 Descended from a Long Line of Witches C
71 The Wielder of Miraculously Mystic Powers U
72 White Magic C
73 *Soiree* R
74 Reckless and Implusive SuR
75 Such a Popular Person SuR
76 Double Mittwoch R
77 Welle Leiten U
78 Zart Zap C
79 Excitable C
80 Shooting Capoera U
81 The Angel of Evening U
82 ***Terry*** R
83 Mark of the Wolf R
84 Ookie SuR
85 Grasping Upper U
86 Power Stream C
87 Power-Charged Elbow U
88 Powerful Style C
89 Return to Southtown U
90 The Legendary Wolf C
91 *Yuri* R
92 Intuitive Innovation U
93 Inner Circle SuR
94 Rising Conquering Crunch C
95 Swallow Slam R
96 Yuri's Super Upper SuR
97 Battle Prowess C
98 Kyokugen Karate U
99 The Kyokugen Karate Innovator U

2008 Universal Fighting System Soulcalibur III Flash of the Blades

COMPLETE SET (99)

BOOSTER BOX (24 PACKS)	20.00	40.00
BOOSTER PACK (10 CARDS)	1.25	2.50

RELEASED IN SEPTEMBER 2008
1 Kilik**** R
2 Lever Bar R
3 Jingu Staff SuR
4 Escaping Bo C
5 Mountain Sweep U
6 Summer Gale SuR
7 Repentance C
8 Soul of Ling-Sheng Su C
9 Stained Honor U
10 Lizardman**** R
11 Feral Shield Rush R
12 Tabarzin SuR
13 Lizard Stamp Kick C
14 Lumber Axe U
15 Mezentius Style Sand Bomb SuR
16 Abomination C
17 Irrevocably Changed C
18 Rapid Ares Style U
19 Mitsurugi******* R
20 Blink of an Eye U
21 Masamune SuR
22 Gates of Hell SuR
23 Prime Moon Shadow C
24 Snap Kick U
25 Bereaved C
26 Commitment to Excellence C
27 Seen it All U
28 Raphael**** R
29 Flurry of Thrusts R
30 Queen's Guard SuR
31 Death Puppet SuR
32 Scarlet Roar U
33 Squalambrato Concierto U
34 Infected C
35 Questionable Motives U
36 Quick and Decisive C
37 Seong Mi-Na*** R
38 Arm's Length R
39 Defender SuR
40 Check Mate U
41 Circular Heaven Slash U
42 Dropping Embrace SuR
43 Hybrid Style U
44 Tenacious C
45 The Bigger They Are... C
46 Setsuka**** R
47 Strike from the Draw U
48 Ridicule SuR
49 Knee Seduction C
50 Vermilion Moon R
51 Willow Splitter U
52 Burning Hatred C
53 Drifter U
54 Quest for Vengeance C
55 Siegfried**** R
56 Armored Charge U
57 Glam SuR
58 Double Grounder U
59 Flying Edge C
60 Unholy Terror SuR
61 Blood Stained Fate C
62 Inner Turmoil C
63 Will of Iron U
64 Sophitia**** R
65 Hard to Catch U
66 Orichalcum SuR
67 Broken Promise SuR
68 Cutlass Europa R
69 Stepping Low Kick C
70 Forethought U
71 Maternal Instincts C
72 Spirit of Athens C
73 Taki******* R
74 Shadow Acrobatics U
75 Kagekiri SuR
76 Hurricane Punishment C
77 Reaping Hook C
78 Strangulation Blade R
79 Ninja Training U
80 Power of the Shadows U
81 Rootless C
82 Talim**** R
83 Powers of the Wind U
84 Side Harpe SuR
85 Diving Wind Kick Throw SuR
86 Mirror Fan Strikes R
87 Shearing Blades U
88 Healer U
89 The Harder They Fall C
90 Wind Dance C
91 Zasalamel R
92 Reincarnation Magic U
93 Ankou SuR
94 Ereshkigal the Ruthless U
95 Sickle of Sin R
96 Tiamat's Frenzy C
97 End it All U
98 Inhuman Perception C
99 The Curse of Immortality C

2008 Universal Fighting System Street Fighter Deadly Ground

COMPLETE SET (99)

BOOSTER BOX (24 PACKS)	25.00	50.00
BOOSTER PACK (10 CARDS)	1.50	3.00

RELEASED IN JUNE 2008
1 ****Adon**** R
2 Enough Trash Talk U
3 Sacred Temple R
4 Adon's Roundhouse U
5 Jaguar Carry C
6 Jaguar Thousand SuR
7 Brash Confidence C
8 Impulsive C
9 Speed and Strength U
10 ********Cammy******** R
11 Deceptive Acrobatics U
12 Cathedral Overlook SuR
13 Cammy's Flying Frankensteiner SuR
14 Killer Bee Assault C
15 Spinning Back Fist R
16 Conditioned Reflexes U
17 Independent Operative C
18 Professional Soldier C
19 ****Charlie**** R
20 Crippling Strike SuR
21 US Air Base SuR
22 Charlie's Fierce Punch C
23 Crossfire Blitz U
24 Knee Gatling C
25 Mentor and a Friend U
26 Undercover Agent U
27 US Intelligence Training C
28 ****E. Honda**** R
29 Purification U
30 Bath House SuR
31 Oni Muso SuR
32 Orochi Crush C
33 Saba Ori C
34 Celebrity U
35 Explosive Power C
36 Voracious Appetite U
37 ****Fei Long**** R
38 Fist of Rage SuR
39 Ancient Battle Ground R
40 Fei Long's Forward Kick C
41 Fei Long's Roundhouse SuR
42 Rekka Shin Ken U
43 Action Hero C
44 Feet of Fury C
45 Make a Difference U
46 ****Ibuki**** R

47 Blinding Speed R
48 Forest Clearing U
49 Sazan U
50 Ura Maki Geri U
51 Yoroi-Doshi SuR
52 Duty to the Clan C
53 Immature U
54 Slim and Athletic C
55 **Juli** R
56 Death Cross Dancing R
57 Twilight Field C
58 Juli's Spin Drive Smasher U
59 Reverse Drive Shaft Break U
60 Sniping Arrow SuR
61 Completely Dominated C
62 Enslaved C
63 Reprogrammed U
64 **Juni** R
65 Psycho Rolling SuR
66 Field of Storms R
67 Juni's Cannon Drill C
68 Juni's Cannon Spike C
69 Juni's Spiral Arrow SuR
70 Abducted C
71 Blind Loyalty U
72 Psycho Style U
73 *Makato* R
74 Rush Down SuR
75 Ancient Training Ground R
76 Hayate C
77 Naruto U
78 Seichusen-Godanzuki SuR
79 Financial Distress C
80 Responsibility U
81 Rindokan C
82 ****Rose**** R
83 Light as a Feather SuR
84 Magic Shop R
85 Aura Soul Throw U
86 Soul Spiral SuR
87 Soul-Piette U
88 Destiny C
89 Motivated U
90 Web of Fate C
91 *****Vega***** R
92 Backslash SuR
93 Cage Arena R
94 Red Impact C
95 Rolling Barcelona Attack U
96 Scarlet Terror R
97 Mentally Unstable U
98 Narcissistic C
99 Sadistic Glee U

2008 Universal Fighting System Street Fighter Domination

COMPLETE SET (144)
BOOSTER BOX (24 PACKS) 40.00 80.00
BOOSTER PACK (10 CARDS) 2.50 5.00
RELEASED IN 2008
1 Akuma****** R
2 Seclusion SuR
3 Kiga Cave U
4 Akuma's Hadoken R
5 Akuma's Shoryureppa R
6 Hurricane Kick U
7 Challenges Only R
8 Sensing Weakness C
9 Tensho Kaireki Jin U
10 Blanka***** R
11 Rock Crush U
12 Anklets SuR
13 Amazon River Run SuR
14 Beast Hurricane R
15 Wild Fang SuR
16 Reunited C
17 Savage Fighter C
18 Separated U
19 Dan** R
20 Dan's Taunt R
21 Championship Belt U
22 Dan's Dragon Punch SuR
23 Dan's Fireball U
24 Still Dragon C
25 Saikyo-ryu C
26 Unorthodox Training U
27 Valuable Experience C
28 Guy* R
29 39th Bushin Master C
30 Orange Gi SuR
31 Hozanto SuR
32 Kagesukui C
33 Kubikari C
34 An Old Friend U
35 Bushinryu Ninpo C
36 The End Justifies the Means C
37 Karin* R
38 Be the Best at Everything U
39 Queen of Victory R
40 Arakuma Inashi C
41 Gurenken U
42 Mujin Kyaku SuR
43 Bitter Rivals C
44 Kanzukiryu Kakutojutsu U
45 Silver Spoon C
46 Ken******* R
47 Taking in Students SuR
48 Sparring Gloves SuR
49 Kama Harai Keri SuR
50 Kuzuryu Reppa R
51 Tsukami Nage U
52 Ken's Shotokan C
53 Prankster R
54 Son of a Tycoon C
55 M. Bison ***** R
56 Expelled Humanity U
57 Psycho Drive SuR
58 Psycho Break Smasher R
59 Psycho Cannon SuR
60 Somersault Skull Diver R
61 Evil Plans U
62 Psychotic Power U
63 Transference U
64 Ryu********* R
65 Escape the Island U
66 White Gi SuR
67 Ryu's Denjin Hadoken C
68 Ryu's Roundhouse U
69 Ryu's Shin Shoryuken R
70 Internal Struggles U
71 Pursued by Many C
72 Quick Study C
73 Sagat**** R
74 Clean Rematch SuR
75 Battle Scarred Chest SuR
76 Super Tiger Ki C
77 Tiger Fury R
78 Tiger Wave R
79 A Powerful Offer U
80 Blinding Rage R
81 Teenage Champion U
82 Sakura**** R
83 Tag Along C
84 School Uniform R
85 Sakura's Shinku Hadoken R
86 Sakura's Shoryuken R
87 Sakura's Tatsumakisenpukyaku U
88 Fighting for Information U
89 Schoolgirl Innocence C
90 Without a Trainer R
91 Sean* R
92 Ken's Training SuR
93 Yellow Gi SuR
94 Dragon Smash C
95 Ryubi Kyaku C
96 Shoryu Cannon SuR
97 A Year's Difference R
98 Black Belt U
99 Brazilian Heritage C
100 Yang** R
101 Work in the Restaurant U
102 Yang's Sneakers SuR
103 Byakko Soshoda U
104 Senkyutai R
105 Toro Zan C
106 Adoration C
107 Bounce Back C
108 Superior Balance U
109 Yun** R
110 Kung-Fu Training C
111 Yun's Cap SuR
112 Nisho Kyaku C
113 Tetsu Zanko C
114 Zessho Hoho U
115 Admiration U
116 Exceptional Poise C
117 Get Up and Go C
118 Zangief***** R
119 Siberian Training C
120 Government Sponsership SuR
121 Air Pile Driver C
122 Flying Power Bomb U
123 Screw Pile Driver SuR
124 Grappling for Glory R
125 In Service to Country U
126 Red Cyclone of Mother Russia U
127 Begin Anew SuR
128 Through the Defenses SuR
129 Turn It On U
130 Yoga Adept R
131 Mysterious Stance SuR
132 Ready for Anything U
133 Ring of Fame R
134 Superhuman Strength R
135 Wisdom from a Confidant U
136 A New Low U
137 Experienced Combatant U
138 Manifest Destiny C
139 No Memories C
140 Popularity C
141 Sting Like a Bee C
142 Tough Outer Shell U
143 Visions of Destiny U
144 Whirlwind C

2008 Universal Fighting System Street Fighter Warriors Dream

COMPLETE SET (99)
BOOSTER BOX (24 PACKS) 25.00 50.00
BOOSTER PACK (10 CARDS) 1.50 3.00
RELEASED IN DECEMBER 2008
1 Alex:: R
2 Fully Recovered U
3 Times Square SuR
4 Air Stampede C
5 Chop U
6 Boomerang Raid R
7 A Clouded Mind C
8 Raw Talent C
9 Dedication U
10 Balrog::: R
11 Stubborn Buffalo C
12 Punching Bag R
13 Face Smasher C
14 Dash Low U
15 Crazy Buffalo** SuR
16 Former Champion C
17 Illegal Maneuvers U
18 Thug U
19 Chun-Li:::: R
20 Calm and Centered U
21 Sworn Vengeance R
22 Hakkei C
23 Yoko Sen Kyaku U
24 Hoyoku-Sen SuR
25 Heart of a Fighter C
26 Keen Insight C
27 Marksman U
28 Dhalsim::: C
29 Your Mind is Known to Me SuR
30 Impossible Contortion R
31 Dhalsim's Crouching Roundhouse C
32 Yoga Headlock U
33 Yoga Flame** SuR
34 Mind Over Matter C
35 Selfless Giving C
36 Look Inward U
37 Elena.. R
38 Flashy Leg Work R
39 A Tradition of Fighting SuR
40 Hand Stand Kick C
41 Lynx Tail U
42 Spinning Beat SuR
43 Light Hearted C
44 Moving On U
45 Warrior Princess U
46 Guile:::. R
47 Just Retribution U
48 Guile's Comb R
49 Guile's Spinning Backfist C
50 Sonic Boom EXTRA SuR
51 Double Somersault Kick** SuR
52 Aim High C
53 Chain of Command U
54 Know Wrong From Right U
55 Hugo* R
56 Perfect Grapple U
57 A Giant of a Man SuR
58 Monster Lariat C
59 Hugo's Body Press R
60 Gigas Breaker SuR
61 Huge Wrestling Army C
62 Hulking Brute C
63 Criminal Past U
64 M. Bison::: R
65 Malevolent Genius U
66 Shadaloo Crime Syndicate SuR
67 M. Bison's Fierce Punch C
68 M. Bison's Jumping Roundhouse C
69 Psycho Crusher EXTRA SuR
70 Past Shrouded in Mystery U
71 Total Global Domination U
72 Charismatic R
73 R. Mika:: R
74 Top Turnbuckle SuR
75 Huge Appetite SuR
76 Hip Buster C
77 Wingless Aeroplane C
78 Sardine's Beach Special R
79 Travel Abroad C
80 Big Dreams U
81 Come Through in the Clinch U
82 Remy* R
83 Power of the Light C
84 Omega Jacket SuR
85 Light of Virtue C
86 Rising Rage Flash U
87 Supreme Rising Rage Flash R
88 Bitter Grudge U
89 Lost a Sister U
90 Vanished Father U
91 T. Hawk:: R
92 Thunder Clap U
93 Ancestor Spirits SuR
94 T. Hawk's Crouching Roundhouse C
95 T. Hawk's Strong Punch C
96 Double Typhoon** R
97 Deceptive Quickness C
98 Take Responsibility C
99 Reclamation U

2009 Universal Fighting System ShadoWar

COMPLETE SET (144)
BOOSTER BOX (24 PACKS) 40.00 80.00
BOOSTER PACK (10 CARDS) 2.50 5.00
RELEASED IN APRIL 2009
1 Zhao Daiyu** R
2 Invoking the Ancients C
3 Unnatural Grace SuR
4 Ritual Magic U
5 Scoll of the Abyss SuR
6 Zhao Daiyu's Poison Touch C
7 Two Deadly Rings Technique SuR
8 Lao Xie's Grinning Death U
9 Twilight Embrace SuR
10 Ancient Ensnaring Sleeve Technique U
11 The Shadow Rises C
12 Respected and Feared C
13 Forbidden Lore U
14 Treacherous Offspring C
15 Her Own Agenda C
16 Intolerant of Failure R
17 The Twilight Witch U
18 Covenant Elder R
19 Ragnar** StR
20 Berserker Rage StR
21 Ymirfang R
22 Stormhammer SuR
23 Shield Breaker C
24 Hammer Uppercut R
25 Cleave C
26 Backhanded Axe Slash C
27 Body Slam U
28 Mighty Knee Strike SuR
29 Crushing Embrace of the Jotun U
30 Jotun's Fury SuR
31 Brooding U
32 Fury of the North C
33 Lives for Battle U
34 Might Makes Right StR
35 In Search of Plunder U
36 Unstoppable Warrior R
37 Astrid StR
38 Warrior's Path C
39 Valkynsverd SuR
40 Reaver's Axe StR
41 Valkyrja's Shield R
42 Odin's Wrath SuR
43 Fierce Twin Slash R
44 Tyr's Warding Smash C
45 Astrid's Wolf Strike U
46 Raven's Claw C
47 Pommel Smash U
48 Bloodied but Unbowed R
49 Resourceful U
50 Queen's Champion C
51 Paying Respect to Your Ancestors SuR
52 Determined U
53 Envoy of the Queen C
54 Relentless StR
55 Zi Mei** StR
56 Willful C
57 Ascending Zephyr R
58 Claws of Chian Tang SuR
59 Autumn's Kiss StR
60 Flying Side Kick C
61 Zi Mei's Wheel Kick U
62 Execution Technique First Rite C
63 Execution Technique Second Rite U
64 Execution Technique Third Rite R
65 Fury of the Ancients SuR
66 Determined to be the Best R
67 Communing with the Ancients U
68 Ruthless C
69 Driven by Fear SuR
70 Always in Motion U
71 Solitary Assassin C
72 Long-Standing Rivalry StR
73 Yi Shan** StR
74 Tien Lei, Iron Thunder StR
75 The Dragon of Mt. Lao R
76 Pendant of the Western Paradise U
77 Monastery of Mt. Lao SuR
78 Dragon Punch StR
79 Yi Shan's Tiger Claw U
80 Yi Shan's Spinning Backfist U
81 Yi Shan's Dragon Tail Leg Sweep C
82 Striking Thunder SuR
83 Rage of the Dragon SuR
84 Dark Past C
85 Repentant Hero C
86 Striving for Perfection C
87 Iron Body Technique U
88 Atoning for the Past R
89 Zhao Family Discipline U
90 Calming the Mind R
91 Lu Chen** R
92 Flowing Strikes R
93 Master's Challenge C
94 Robes of the Grandmaster U
95 Scroll of the Celestial Dawn SuR
96 Chi Disruptor C
97 Crane Strike SuR
98 Lu Chen's Palm Strike U
99 Peaceful Path Hold R
100 Leaping Snap Kick U
101 Wrath of Heaven SuR
102 The Pillar of Heaven U
103 Know When to Talk... U
104 ...and When to Fight C
105 Warrior Poet C
106 Great Teacher C
107 Endless Years of Practice R
108 Venerable U
109 Temujin** R
110 Pillage R
111 Crown of the Forgotten Secret U
112 Wandering Dragon Staff SuR
113 Armor of the Forsaken One R
114 Swooping Hawk Lunge C
115 Grappling Knee Strike U
116 Dragon Lifter R
117 Dragon's Flame SuR
118 Sweeping Tail Strike U
119 Descending Dragon Spear SuR
120 Loves to Talk C
121 Nursing a Grudge U
122 From the Horse, Endurance C
123 Trained Far and Wide U
124 From the Hawk, Alterness C
125 From the Mouse, Humility C
126 The Forgotten Technique U
127 Rashotep** R
128 KNEEL BEFORE ME! SuR
129 Sa, Symbol of Protection C
130 The Double Crown of Egypt SuR
131 Bracers of Horus and Set U
132 The Pharaoh's Crown Strike C
133 Relentless Assault of Set U
134 Flooded-Nile Throw C
135 One-Handed Crocodile Grasp R
136 Sandstorm Throw U
137 Command the Sandstorm SuR
138 Undisputed Ruler U
139 Master of Magic C
140 Dead for One Thousand Years R
141 Jealously-Guarded Secret C
142 Valued but Not Trusted SuR
143 Strength of Ages C
144 Ka Technique U

2009 Universal Fighting System Soulcalibur IV Quest of Souls

COMPLETE SET (99)
BOOSTER BOX (24 PACKS) 30.00 60.00
BOOSTER PACK (10 CARDS) 1.50 3.00
RELEASED IN NOVEMBER 2009
1 Mitsurugi* R
2 Mist Stance U
3 Quick Strike R
4 Shish-Oh * SuR
5 Jyurakudai R
6 Fire Brand SuR
7 Forced Prayer Divide U
8 Full Moon Disembowel SuR
9 Shin Slicer Feint C
10 Steel Slicer R
11 Step Stone Divide U
12 Unrefined C
13 Seeking Perfection R
14 Battle Tested U
15 Needs a Challenge C
16 Deafeated the Rifle C
17 Looking for a Thrill U
18 The Strength Within C
19 Taki* R
20 Possession Stance U
21 Ninja Tactics SuR
22 Rekki-Maru & Mekki-Maru * SuR
23 Tower of Rememberance - Ancient Gate R
24 Assassin's Secret U
25 Assassin's Strike R
26 Crossing the Cliff U
27 Dream Scroll C
28 Ninja Cannon: Fury SuR
29 Seal C
30 Evil Destroyer R
31 No Chance U
32 Musoh-Battoh-Ryu C
33 Assassin's Technique C
34 Quick Exit SuR
35 Loves her Blade U
36 Knows her Objective R
37 Xianghua* R
38 Silent Xia Sheng Stance U
39 Acrobatic SuR
40 Sword of No Name SuR
41 Hall of the Warrior God R
42 Playful Slice SuR
43 Pointing Thrust U
44 Rhythm Hall R
45 Tiao Wu Kick C
46 Twisting Lotus Flow SuR
47 Waterfall R
48 Finding Happiness U
49 Carefree C
50 Lost Partner R
51 Playful U
52 Deceptively Quick C
53 Just Kidding C
54 Pure Hearted U
55 Amy* R
56 Amaryllis Spin U
57 Amy's Sidestep C
58 Albion SuR
59 Ostreinsburg Castle Throne Room SuR
60 Bloody Funeral SuR
61 Flash Needle R
62 Frigid Moon U
63 Hilt Strike U
64 Soaring Dance C
65 Triple Botta in Tempo R
66 Inhuman Speed C
67 Strange Fashion R
68 Loyal at all Costs U
69 To the Ends of the Earth C
70 Cute Prankster C
71 Not Human U
72 Together Again R
73 Yoshimitsu* R
74 Unorthodox Movements SuR
75 Flea U
76 Yoshimitsu * SuR
77 Pavilion R
78 Bad Stomach C
79 Deathcopter Attack SuR
80 Golden Shrine C
81 Mt. Devil Divider SuR
82 Nimbus U
83 Spiral Blade R
84 Leader of the Manjitou U
85 Excellent Thief U
86 Meditating in Battle C
87 Sacrifices for the Cause R
88 Master of Ninjitsu C
89 Risky Fighting Style U
90 Contemplating C
91 Crawling Stance R
92 Bone Crusher C
93 Lower Celtis R
94 Mezentius Style Santana Storm C
95 Rolling Revenge SuR
96 Scale Ram C
97 Ravenous Fighting Style C
98 Sisters of Battle U
99 For Justice U

2009 Universal Fighting System Soulcalibur IV Tower of Souls

COMPLETE SET (144)
BOOSTER BOX (24 PACKS) 30.00 60.00
BOOSTER PACK (10 CARDS) 1.50 3.00
RELEASED IN APRIL 2009
1 Nightmare* StR
2 Soul Wave* StR
3 Hunger for Souls SuR
4 Soul Edge* SuR

5 Tower of Rememberance - Encounter SuR
6 Soul Smasher U
7 Knight Breaker SuR
8 Midnight Launcher R
9 Upper Claw C
10 Dark Bite U
11 Leg Slash C
12 The Azure Knight StR
13 Intimidating Presence C
14 All Life is Prey C
15 Beacon of Evil U
16 Memories that Stain its Armor R
17 Corrupting Force U
18 The Master of Ostrheinsburg U
19 Siegried* StR
20 No Forgiveness! R
21 Base Hold StR
22 Soul Calibur* SuR
23 Tower of Rememberance - Spiral of Time R
24 Double Grounder Beta SuR
25 Reborn Slasher U
26 Reborn Basher StR
27 Rising Hilt U
28 Hilt Impact C
29 Siegfried's Earth Divide SuR
30 Memories of a Nightmare U
31 Chosen by Soul Calibur C
32 Atoning for Wicked Deeds R
33 Needs No Ally C
34 Regretful Existence U
35 Journey of Repentance C
36 Torn Hero U
37 Astaroth* R
38 Stone Skin C
39 Immovable Object R
40 Kulutues* SuR
41 Kunpaetku Shrine - Dream Remnants R
42 Hades Ax U
43 Titan Ax U
44 Hades SuR
45 Bear Fang C
46 Hades Destroyer SuR
47 Astaroth's Body Splash C
48 Black Giant C
49 Enraged Golem U
50 Hungry for Battle U
51 No Longer Controllable U
52 Body Transformed C
53 Anger Towards a God R
54 Laughable C
55 Algol* R
56 Hoping for a Challenge C
57 Pseudo-Soul Calibur R
58 Pseudo-Soul Edge SuR
59 Tower of Rememberance - Degredation R
60 Alaraph Achernar U
61 Alphard Maliki U
62 Alshain Najm SuR
63 Eltanin Nath C
64 Thalthah Qarn C
65 Theemin Menkar U
66 The Hero King U
67 Body of Souls C
68 Father's Tragedy U
69 Temporary Being R
70 Controller of Souls SuR
71 Ancient Fighting Style C
72 Fatherly Love C
73 Cervantes. StR
74 Corrupting Evil SuR
75 Soul Stealing U
76 Acheron & Nirvana SuR
77 Sailor's Rest SuR
78 Wild Storm C
79 High Tide Anchoring U
80 Curse of the Ancient Mariner R
81 Sail Nautilus C
82 Shadow Flare StR
83 Dark Geo Da Ray SuR
84 Feast of Souls C
85 Beyond Humanity U
86 Dread Pirate U
87 Chasing After the Power StR
88 No Mercy R
89 Seeking Treasure C
90 Driven by Ambition C
91 Ivy* StR
92 Frantic Search U
93 Switching Weapon Styles StR
94 Valentine* SuR
95 Ice Coffin of the Sleeping Ancient SuR
96 Raging Gnome SuR
97 Venom Lash U
98 Howling Spirits R
99 Cross Madness StR
100 Evil Sparrow C
101 Razor's Bite C
102 Genius Alchemist C
103 Researching the Past U
104 Soul that Protects U
105 Artificial Soul R
106 Purified Body C
107 Researching Anywhere R
108 Prominent Noblewoman C
109 Tira* R
110 Gloomy Side U
111 Jolly Side U
112 Eiserne Drossel R
113 Ostrheinsburg Castle - Twilight R
114 Menuett Dance SuR
115 Oratorio Halcyon U
116 Shredding Vibrato SuR
117 Swing Kick* C
118 Lowdown Neb U
119 Piercing Talon Strike C
120 Personality Split C
121 Distracting Taunt U
122 Mesmerizing Dance R
123 Keeper of the Watchers C
124 Shattered Persona C
125 Flexible Body SuR
126 Perfect Sense of Balance U
127 Hilde* R
128 Dual-Wielding U
129 Aura of Strength R
130 Glanzende Nova and Frischer Himmel R
131 Wolfkrone Monument SuR
132 Lightning Horn SuR
133 Eagle Talon U
134 Siren's Call R
135 Iron Tower U
136 Dragon Breath U
137 Fire Shadow C
138 Ready for the Battle U
139 Unstoppable Conviction C
140 Hope for One's People C
141 Challenge to Battle SuR
142 Persevering Despite Rejection C
143 Strength of Training C
144 Nobility of the Wolf U

2009 Universal Fighting System Tekken 6

COMPLETE SET (99)		
BOOSTER BOX (24 PACKS)	30.00	60.00
BOOSTER PACK (10 CARDS)	1.50	3.00

RELEASED IN AUGUST 2009
1 Christie Montiero* R
2 Graceful Style C
3 You Have no Rhythm! U
4 Designer Clothes SuR
5 Samba R
6 Slippery Kick C
7 Side Flop U
8 Lunging Brush Fire U
9 Fruit Picker SuR
10 Asfixiante U
11 Knee Thruster R
12 Hoping for the Best C
13 Searching for Family R
14 Brazilian Beauty U
15 Capoeira Style C
16 Relaxing Model C
17 Close Friends C
18 One with the Rhythm R
19 Kazuya Mishima* R
20 Evil Intentions R
21 Destruction in his Wake SuR
22 Kazuya's Gloves SuR
23 Devil Gene SuR
24 Lightning Uppercut SuR
25 Spinning Demon U
26 Double Face Kick R
27 Hell Lancer U
28 Lion Slayer C
29 Demon Slayer U
30 Vengeance C
31 G-Corp Leader U
32 Merciless Fighter C
33 Need to Destroy R
34 Mishima Family Bloodline U
35 Maniacal Laughter C
36 The Hunt is On C
37 King* R
38 Test of Strength SuR
39 Ready to Launch R
40 Jaguar Mask SuR
41 Rolling Sobat R
42 Konvict Kick C
43 Jaguar Straight U
44 Cobra Clutch C
45 Cobra Twist U
46 King's Reverse DDT SuR
47 Flinging Half Nelson R
48 The People's Hero U
49 The Man behind the Mask C
50 King of the Ring U
51 Mexican Sensation` U
52 Enemies now Friends C
53 The Entertainer R
54 Learned from the Best C
55 Nina Williams* R
56 Cold and Indifferent R
57 Proficient Sniper SuR
58 Lethal Fighting Style R
59 Purple Army Suit SuR
60 Head Ringer C
61 Shockwave Palm SuR
62 Sadistic Cupid C
63 Wipe the Floor U
64 Ice Pick SuR
65 Evil Mist U
66 Stoic Assassin U
67 Sworn to Protect C
68 War between Sisters U
69 Sharing a Moment U
70 Unknown Son C
71 Professional Bodyguard C
72 Keep them Down R
73 Paul Phoenix* R
74 Overconfidence R
75 Toughest in the Universe SuR
76 Paul's Gi SuR
77 Hammer of the Gods R
78 The Boot C
79 Phoenix Smasher SuR
80 Turn Thruster R
81 Over the Shoulder C
82 Neutron Bomb U
83 Tandoya U
84 It's Got to be the Hair C
85 Rivalry with a Bear U
86 The Ultimate Team U
87 Financial Troubles C
88 For the Money U
89 Open Road C
90 Best Friends U
91 Mishima Zaibatsu Leader U
92 Tekken Forces SuR
93 Hunt for Jin U
94 Boxing is Life R
95 Recon C
96 Killer Android R
97 Blazing Fist SuR
98 Law's Somersault Kick SuR
99 Gut Drill R

2005 Vampire TES Kindred Most Wanted

1 Allonzo Montoya U
2 Lorrie Dunsirn U
3 Pariah U
4 Amaravati U
5 Basir U
6 Janni U
7 Joe "Boot" Hill U
8 Michael diCarlo U/PG
9 Tariq, The Silent U
10 Vardar Vardarian U
11 Azaneal U/PB
12 Cybele U/PB
13 Elihu U
14 Maureen, Dark Priestess PB
15 Petaniqua U/PB
16 Count Germaine PA
17 Jayne Jonestown PA
18 Ankh-sen-Sutekh U
19 Black Lotus U
20 Cagliostro, The Grand Copht U
21 Kemintiri U
22 Neferu U
23 Reverend Djoser Jones U
24 Sahira Siraj PB
25 Denette Stensen PG
26 Doyle Fincher U
27 Enkidu, The Noah U/PG
28 Janey Pickman U
29 Jeffrey Mullins PG
30 Mitru the Hunter U/PG
31 Phillipe Rigaud U/PG
32 Almodo Giovanni U
33 Ambrogino Giovanni U
34 Benedict Giovanni, Agent PA
35 Carmine Giovanni U
36 Cristobal Ghiberti U
37 Don Michael Antonio Giovanni U
38 Raphaela Giovanni U
39 Black Wallace U
40 Petaniqua U/PB
41 Louhi U
42 Echo PAI
43 Rabbat, The Sewer Goddess PA
44 Black Annis U
45 Alexis Sorokin U/PA
46 Callirus U
47 Devyn U
48 Marion French U
49 Mata Hari U/PA
50 Paul Forrest, False Prophet U
51 Tatiana Stepanova, Alastor U
52 Ransam, The Old Man U
53 L'Epuisette U
54 Valerius Maior, Hell's Fool U/PB
55 Valerius Maior, Hell's Fool U/PB
56 Jane Sims U
57 Sonja Blue U
58 Dylan U
59 Anarch Secession R
60 Anima Gathering C
61 Baal's Bloody Talons R
62 Backflip C
63 Backstep C
64 Bay and Howl R/PG
65 Beretta 9mm C
66 Big Game C/PA
67 Black Sunrise C
68 Bloodstone C
69 Bloodstorm of Chorazin C/PB
70 The Book of Going Forth by Night PB
71 Breath of Thanatos C
72 Bujo R
73 Condemnation: Mute R
74 Confusion of the Eye C/PG
75 The Crocodile Temple R
76 Dead Hand C
77 Deviki Prasanta R
78 Dis Pater R
79 Disengage C
80 Distant Friend R
81 Dr. Marisa Fletcher, CDC R
82 Dual Form R
83 Earthshock C
84 Edged Illusion C
85 Esteem C
86 Fatuus Mastery C
87 FBI Special Affairs Division R
88 Ferraille R
89 Follow the Alpha R
90 Forced March C/PA
91 From a Sinking Ship R
92 Glass Walker Pact R
93 Grasp of the Python C
94 Groundfighting C
95 Haqim's Law: Judgment R
96 Harzomatuili R
97 Haymaker C
98 Heart of the City R
99 Hierophant C
100 Ignore the Searing Flames C/PB
101 Immense Size R
102 Inquisition PG
103 Khabar: Glory C
104 Kingston Penitentiary, Ontario R
105 Learjet C
106 Leathery Hide C/PG
107 Lifeless Tongues R
108 Mercy for Seth C
109 Mind of a Killer R
110 The Name Forgotten R
111 Nightshades C
112 Not to Be R
113 NSA Trio R
114 Ossian R
115 Pack Alpha C
116 Permanency C
117 Phased Motion Detector C
118 Powder of Rigidity PA
119 Priority Shift R
120 Procurer C
121 Projectile C
122 Proxy Kissed C
123 Purification R
124 Rebirth R/PA
125 Red List C/PA
126 Revelation of Despair C
127 Revelation of Wrath R
128 Ruins of Charizel R/PB
129 Samuel Haight R
130 Scalpel Tongue C
131 Selective Silence C
132 Shared Nightmare R
133 Shared Strength R
134 Shilmulo Tarot R
135 Sonar C/PG
136 Soul Decoration C
137 Sudario Refraction R
138 Suppressing Fire C
139 Svadharma C
140 The Textbook Damnation R
141 Threestar Cab Company PA
142 Tranquility R
143 Trophy: Clan Respect R
144 Trophy: Diablerie R
145 Trophy: Discipline R
146 Trophy: Domain R
147 Trophy: Hunting Ground R
148 Trophy: Progeny R
149 Trophy: Retainers R
150 Trophy: Safe Passage R
151 Trophy: Wealth R
152 True Love's Face C
153 Trumped-Up Charges C/PA
154 Truth of a Thousand Lies C
155 Tumnimos C
156 Undue Influence C
157 Undying Thirst R
158 Victim of Habit R
159 Warning Sirens C
160 Waters of Duat C
161 Web of Knives Recruit C
162 Weigh the Heart C
163 Acrobatics PAI2/PG3
164 Aire of Elation PAn2
165 Alastor PAI
166 Ambush PG3
167 Anarch Revolt PAn
168 Anastasz di Zagreb PAI
169 Anathema PAI2
170 Antara PAn
171 Apportation PB
172 Approximation of Loyalty PAn2
173 Archon PAI3
174 Archon Investigation PG
175 Ardan Lane PB
176 Bang Nakh -- Tiger's Claws PAI5
177 Banishment PAn2
178 Behind You! PG2
179 Black Spiral Buddy PG
180 Blood Doll PB3/PG3/PAn2
181 Blood Fury PB3
182 Blur PAI5
183 Bribes PAn3/PAI
184 Bum's Rush PG4/PAI3
185 Burst of Sunlight PB3
186 Call the Great Beast PB
187 Campground Hunting Ground PG
188 Celerity PAI
189 City Gangrel Connections PG
190 Claws of the Dead PG5
191 Closed Session PAI
192 Cohn Rose PB
193 Concealed Weapon PAI3
194 Concordance PB2
195 Conflagration PB3
196 Consignment to Duat PB2
197 Count Germaine U/PAn
198 Depravity PAI
199 D'habi Revenant PB
200 Disarm PAI
201 Diversity PAn2
202 Dreams of the Sphinx PG/PAn
203 Dummy Corporation PB2
205 Ecstasy PB2
206 Elder Impersonation PB2
207 Enchant Kindred PAn3
208 Enhanced Senses PAI3
209 Enticement PB
210 Entrenching PAn
211 Faceless Night PB3
212 Fame PAI
213 Fear of the Void Below PB
214 The Final Nights PAn
215 Finding the Path PB2
216 Flesh of Marble PG3
217 Flurry of Action PG2
218 Force of Will PG
219 Forgotten Labyrinth PAn/PG2
220 Form of Corruption PB
221 Form of Mist PG2
222 Free States Rant PAn3
223 Games of Instinct PG2
224 Gengis PAI
225 Gleam of Red Eyes PG2
226 Govern the Unaligned PAI3
227 Graverobbing PAI
228 Harry Reese PG
229 Hartmut Stover PG
230 Haven Uncovered PAn3
231 Heart of Darkness PB2
232 Heidelberg Castle, Germany PAI
233 Hidden Lurker PAn4
234 Honor the Elders PAn2
235 Iron Glare PAn
236 Jaroslav Pascek PAI
237 Jesús Alcalá PG
238 Juggler PAI
239 Legal Manipulations PB5
240 Life in the City PAn
241 Lost in Crowds PG2
242 Lucas Halton PAI
243 Lucinde, Alastor PAI
244 Madame Guil PAI
245 Major Boon PG
246 Marcus Vitel PAn
247 Marcus Vitel PAn
248 Maria Stone PAn
249 Mask of a Thousand Faces PB2
250 Meat Hook PAI2
251 Media Influence PAn
252 Menele PAI
253 Mighty Grapple PAI
254 Minion Tap PAI3
255 Mob Rule PAn3
256 Muhsin Samir PAI
257 Mylan Horseed (Goblin) PB
258 Nimble Feet PG4
259 Obfuscate PB
260 Owl Companion PG
261 The Path of the Feral Heart PG
262 Potence PAn
263 Praxis Seizure: Barcelona PAI
264 Praxis Seizure: Rome PAI
265 Precognition PAI3
266 Protean PG
267 Psyche! PAI2
268 Psychomachia PB3
269 Pursuit PAn4
270 Pushing the Limit PAI2
271 Quick Meld PG
272 Raven Spy PG
273 Reins of Power PAn
274 Restoration PAn2
275 Restricted Vitae PAn
276 Rutor's Hand PB3
277 Sabbat Threat PAI
278 Scarlet Carson O'Toole PG
279 Second Tradition: Domain PAI3
280 Sense the Sin PB3
281 Seren Sukardi PB
282 Serpentis PB2
283 Shadow Feint PG2
284 Shadow of the Beast PG
285 Sideslip PAI3
286 Skidmark PAn
287 Skin of Steel PAn
288 Skin of the Adder PB
289 Skryta Zyleta PG
290 Slave Auction PAI
291 Sleep Unseen PAn
292 Slum Hunting Ground PAn
293 Soak PAn2/PG2
294 Society of Leopold PAn
295 Spying Mission PB2
296 Steve Booth PAI
297 Stunt Cycle PAn3
298 Stutter-Step PG4
299 Sudden Reversal PAI
300 Superior Mettle PG3
301 Swallowed by the Night PAn3
302 Talons of the Dead PG
303 Taste of Vitae PAn2
304 Temptation PB
305 Theft of Vitae PB6
306 Thrown Gate PAn4
307 Torn Signpost PAI2
308 Undead Strength PAI4
309 Voter Captivation PAn3
310 Vox Senis PAI
311 Wake with Evening's Freshness PAn3/PB5/PG2
312 Warzone Hunting Ground PAn
313 Wolf Companion PG
314 Wolfgang PAn
315 Rötschreck PB

2005 Vampire TES Legacies of Blood

1 .44 Magnum PO3
2 Abebe U
3 Abombwe C
4 Absorb the Mind C
5 Adhiambo U
6 Agru Kabera U
7 Ahrimane Protectorate C
8 Aimee Laroux U
9 Aiyana, The Wolfcatcher U
10 Akunanse Kholo PA2
11 Al-Muntaquim, The Avenger U
12 Alacrity PI3
13 Amavi PA2

14 Ananasi Vampirephile R
15 Ancestor Spirit R
16 Ancestor's Insight C/PO4
17 Ancient Influence PG
18 Ancilla Empowerment PG2
19 Anesthetic Touch C
20 Antoinette Dubois U
21 Aredhel U
22 Aren, Priest of Eshu PG2
23 Armor of Caine's Fury C
24 Armor of Terra R
25 Army of Rats PA2
26 Art's Traumatic Essence R
27 Asanbonsam Ghoul R
28 Ashes to Ashes R
29 Aura Absorption C
30 Aversion C
31 Awe PG
32 Aye C
33 Ayo Igoli U
34 Babalawo Alafin U
35 Banishment PG
36 The Barrens PA/PI
37 Base Hunting Ground PO2
38 Basilisk's Touch R
39 Bastille Opera House R
40 Batsheva PG2
41 Battle Frenzy C
42 Belonging Grants Protection C
43 Bewitching Oration PG4
44 Bima U
45 Bind the Night-Walker R
46 Blessed Audience R
47 Blessing of the Name R
48 Blissful Agony R
49 Blood Doll PA3/PI2/PO2
50 Blood Tears of Kephran PG2
51 Blooding by the Code C
52 Brass Knuckles PG
53 Brick Laying PO2
54 Brother in Arms C
55 Brother's Blood C
56 Bum's Rush PA4
57 Bupe Kuila U
58 Burning Touch C
59 Burning Wrath PG2
60 Canine Horde PA
61 Carrion Crows PA2
62 Catatonic Fear PI2
63 Cats' Guidance PG3
64 Cedric U
65 Celerity PI/PO
66 Cesewayo PO2
67 Chameleon's Colors C
68 Change of Target PG2/PI2
69 Chanjelin Ward R
70 Charming Lobby PG
71 Choir C
72 Circle C
73 Claiming the Body C
74 Cleansing Ritual R
75 Clio's Kiss R
76 Clotho's Gift C
77 Coagulated Entity R
78 Collapse the Arches C
79 Compress C
80 Computer Hacking PA3
81 Concert Tour R
82 Conductor R
83 Consanguineous Boon PG2
84 Conscripted Statue R
85 Conservative Agitation PG5
86 Consume the Dead R
87 Coordinate Attacks C
88 Coroner's Contact R
89 Covincraft C
90 Crawling Chamber C
91 Create Gargoyle R
92 Creeping Infection C
93 Crocodile's Tongue PO3
94 Dame Hollerton U
95 Daring the Dawn PI
96 Darkling Trickery R
97 Dawn Operation PA2
98 The Death of My Conscience PG
99 Death of the Drum C
100 Defender of the Haven R
101 Dela Eden U
102 Demdemeh U
103 Devil-Channel: Back C
104 Devil-Channel: Hands C/PA4
105 Devil-Channel: Throat C/PA4
106 Dirty Contract C
107 Disguised Weapon PO
108 Disputed Territory PG
109 Dolie PA2
110 Domain Challenge PG2
111 Domain of Evernight C
112 Duma Rafiki C
113 Dummy Corporation PG
114 Dust to Dust R
115 Eagle's Sight PO2
116 Earth-Feeder R
117 Earth Swords C
118 Echo of Harmonies R
119 Effective Management PA
120 Effie Lowery U
121 Elder Library PG
122 The Eldest Are Kholo R
123 The Eldest Command Undeath R
124 Elephant Guardian C/PG2
125 Emergency Rations R
126 Enchant Kindred PI5
127 Enforcer C/PO3
128 Engling Fury R
129 Entrancement PI
130 Erebus Mask R
131 Eurayle Gelasia Mylonas U
132 Excellent Thirst R
133 Eye of Unforgiving Heaven U
134 Eze, The Demon Prince U
135 Fae Contortion C
136 Falcon's Eye C
137 Falhu Shibaba U
138 Fast Reaction PO
139 Feral Spirit C
140 Fire on the Mountain R
141 Fish U
142 Flak Jacket PG
143 Flow Within the Mountain R
144 Folderol C
145 Forced Awakening PO4
146 Forced March PI4
147 Fortitude PI
148 Founders of the Ebony Kingdom C
149 Fractured Armament PG
150 Freak Drive PA2
151 Free Fight R
152 Frenzy PO
153 Frozen Object R
154 Ganhuru PI2
155 Gentha Shale U
156 Gestalt R
157 Ghost-Eater R
158 Ghoul Messenger R
159 Giant's Blood PG
160 Gift of Bellona R
161 Glare of Lies C
162 Glutton R
163 Goblinism R
164 The Grandest Trick R
165 Gregory Winter PA
166 Gualtiero Ghiberti U
167 Guardian Angel PO2
168 The Guruhi Are the Land C/PG4
169 Guruhi Kholo PG2
170 Hag's Wrinkles R
171 Hall of Hades' Court R
172 Hanging Fermata C
173 Harass PA3
174 Hasani U
175 Hatchling R
176 Healing Touch C
177 Heaven's Gate C
178 Heidelberg Castle, Germany PI
179 Hermana Hambrienta Mayor C
180 Hermana Hambrienta Menor C
181 Hidden Strength PI4
182 High Aye C
183 High Orun C
184 High Top R
185 Homa U
186 Honorine Ateba PI2
187 Houngan C
188 Hourglass of the Mind R
189 IR Goggles PO
190 Ibn Khaldun, Scholar U
191 Idrissa U
192 Igoli's Loyalty C
193 Improvised Flamethrower PO2
194 Increased Strength PO2
195 Infection R
196 Infernal Pursuit PO
197 Informant R
198 Information Highway PI
199 Iniko, The Black Lion U
200 Inspire Greatness C
201 Instinctive Reaction PA3
202 Internal Recursion R
203 Invoking the Beast C/PA4
204 Iron Glare PG4
205 Ishtarri Kholo PI2
206 Ismitta PO2
207 Jack Dawson U
208 Jibade el-Bahrawi PI2
209 Jubal U
210 Jungle Hunting Ground PA2
211 KRCG News Radio PA
212 Kamaria U
213 Kamau Jafari U
214 Kamiri wa Itherero PA2
215 Kduva's Mask R
216 Kenyatta PI2
217 Kerrie C/PI2
218 Khalu PO2
219 The Kikiyaon U
220 Kine Resources Contested PG3
221 King's Favor PG2
222 Kiss of Lachesis C
223 The Kiss of Ra PI
224 Langa U
225 Lapse C
226 Laptop Computer PA
227 Lazarene Inquisitor R
228 Leapfrog C
229 Legal Manipulations PI3
230 Legendary Vampire PG
231 Legend of the Leopard C
232 Life in the City PA2/PI2
233 Little Mountain Cemetery C
234 Lumumba PG2
235 Maabara R
236 Macoute U
237 Madrigal C
238 Majesty PI2
239 Major Boon PA
240 Manstopper Rounds PO
241 Maria Stone U
242 Marijava Ghoul PI
243 Masai Blood Milk R
244 Maskini U
245 Massassi U
246 Massassi's Honor C
247 Matata U
248 Mbare Market, Harare R
249 Meno Ngari PA2
250 Mina Grotius U
251 Minion Tap PG3
252 Misdirection PI
253 Misrak PO2
254 The Missing Voice C
255 Mob Connections PO
256 Mozambique Allure C
257 Mr. Noir U
258 Muricia U
259 Muricia's Call R
260 My Enemy's Enemy PO2
261 Nangila Were PG2
262 Nehemiah U
263 Neutral Guard R
264 New in Town PO2
265 Nimble Feet PO3
266 Nkechi U
267 Nkule Galadima U
268 No Secrets From the Magaji C
269 Nose of the Hound C
270 Octopod C
271 Ohoyo Hopoksia (Bastet) R
272 Olugbenga U
273 Omme Enberbenight U
274 Onaedo U
275 Orun C
276 Osebo Kholo PO2
277 Otieno U
278 Overseer C/PG
279 Owl Companion PA2
280 Palace Hunting Ground PG2
281 Panacea R
282 Pandora's Whisper C
283 Panya, The Wicked U
284 Paris Opera House R
285 The Parthenon PA
286 The Path of Retribution R
287 The Path of Tears R
288 The Path of the Scorched Heart R
289 Patrol C
290 Peace Treaty PG
291 Peacemaker C
292 Persistent Echo R
293 Phagian U
294 Phantom Speaker C
295 Pherydima U
296 Poker PI2
297 Political Flux PG
298 Political Stranglehold PG
299 Port Hunting Ground PI2
300 Potence PG
301 Pounce C
302 Powerbase: Cape Verde R
303 Powerbase: Tshwane R
304 Predator's Communion C
305 Predator's Mastery C/PA4
306 Predator's Transformation C
307 Prejudice U
308 Procurer PI2
309 Projectile PO3
310 Propaganda PI2
311 Psychic Projection PO
312 Pulse of the Canaille PO
313 Pursuit PO4
314 Pushing the Limit PG2
315 Putrescent Servitude R
316 Quicken Sight PO4
317 Quicksilver Contemplation C
318 Quincy, The Trapper U
319 Raking Talons C
320 Rapid Healing PA
321 Rashiel U
322 Rat's Warning PA2
323 Rayzeel's Song C
324 Razor Bat C
325 Reanimated Corpse C
326 Recurring Contemplation C
327 Redcap Wilder R
328 Redistribution C
329 Regenerative Blood R
330 Reindoctrination C
331 Reliquary: Akunanse Remains PA2
332 Reliquary: Biague PI2
333 Renewed Vigor C
334 Repulsion C
335 Resurrection R
336 Rewind Time R
337 Riddle Phantastique R
338 Rigor Mortis C
339 Riposte PO
340 Rocia U
341 Rock Cat R
342 Rockheart C
343 Roderick Phillips March U
344 Roll C
345 Rolling with the Punches PA3
346 Rosemarie U
347 Rötschreck PA
348 Rowan Ring PI
349 The Rumor Mill, Tabloid Newspaper PG
350 Rumors of Gehenna PA
351 Sanguine Instruction C
352 Sanjo PA2
353 Saulot, The Wanderer U
354 Sayshila U
355 Scalpel Tongue PI3
356 Scry the Hearthstone C
357 Secret Horde PA
358 The Secret Must Be Kept R
359 Secret Passage PI2
360 Sennadurek U
361 Sense Death C
362 Sense Vitality C
363 Shadow of Taint R
364 Shaman R
365 Shasa Abu Badr PI
366 Shell Game C
367 Side Strike PI4
368 Sideslip PI2
369 Sight Beyond Sight R
370 Siren's Lure R
371 Sires Command, Childer Inherit C
372 Skin of Steel PA2
373 Skin of the Chameleon C
374 The Slaughterhouse C
375 Sniper Rifle PO
376 Soar C
377 Sobayifa PG2
378 Social Charm PI5
379 Solomon Batanea U
380 Song of Pan C
381 Song of Serenity PA2
382 Soul of the Earth R
383 Speak with Spirits C
384 Spike-Thrower C
385 Spirit Marionette C
386 Squirrel Balance C
387 Staredown PG3
388 Static Virtue R
389 Steal the Mind R
390 Stone Dog R
391 Stone Quills C
392 Stone Travel C
393 Stonestrength C
394 Storage Annex PG
395 Strange Day R
396 Strength of the Bear C
397 Sudden Reversal PA/PG/PI
398 Summon Spirit Beast R
399 Swarm C
400 Swiftness of the Stag C
401 Swoop R
402 Sword of the Righteous C
403 Tabriz Assembly R
404 Tanginé U
405 Tangle Atropos' Hand R
406 Taste of Vitae PO2
407 Tatu Sawosa PO2
408 Telepathic Tracking PO2
409 Tension in the Ranks PO
410 Terra Incognita C
411 Terror Frenzy PG
412 Thomasso Ghiberti U
413 Those Who Endure Judge C
414 Thrown Gate PO4
415 Thrown Sewer Lid PO5
416 Tier of Souls PA
417 Toreador's Bane R
418 Tourette's Voice C
419 Tracker's Mark C
420 Transfusion C
421 Trap PO
422 Travelers Obey the Tenets R
423 Troglodytia U
424 Truth of Blood C
425 Tsunda U
426 Tupdog C
427 Ubende PI2
428 Uchenna PA2
429 Ugadja PG2
430 Unburdening the Bestial Soul R
431 Uncontrolled Impulse C/PI5
432 Unflinching Persistence PA2
433 Unseen Hibernation C/PA
434 Unwholesome Bond C
435 Urenna Bunu U
436 Uzoma U/PO2
437 Vampiric Speed PI
438 Vengeance of Samiel C
439 Vitae Block R
440 Voter Captivation PG3
441 Vox Domini PA
442 Vulnerability PA
443 Vulture's Buffet R
444 Wake with Evening's Freshness PG2/PI3
445 Walk of Caine C
446 Wamukota U
447 Wanderer's Counsel C
448 Whistling Up the Beast R
449 The Wildebeest R
450 Winged Second R
451 Wise Spider R
452 Withering C
453 Yavu Malebo U
454 Year of Fortune PA
455 Yoruba Shrine R
456 Yseult U
457 Zaire River Ferry R
458 Zhara U
459 Zhenga U
460 Zillah's Valley PG2
461 Zygodat U

2006 Vampire TES Nights of Reckoning

1 Abjure R
2 Angel of Berlin C
3 Anna "Dictatrix11" Suljic U
4 Antithesis C
5 Augur C
6 Béatrice "Oracle171" Tremblay U
7 Blood Cult Awareness Network R
8 Bond C
9 Break the Code R
10 Champion R
11 The Church of Vindicated Faith R
12 Cleave C
13 The Crusader Sword R
14 Determine C
15 Discern C
16 Donate C
17 Earl "Shaka74" Deams U
18 Edge Explosion R
19 Erick "Shophet125" Franco U
20 Expiate R
21 Foresee R
22 François "Warden" Loehr U
23 Hide R
24 Illuminate C
25 Imprison R
26 Inez "Nurse216" Villagrande U
27 Inflict C
28 Inspire R
29 Jack "Hannibal137" Harmon U
30 Jennie "Cassie247" Orne U
31 Jennifer "Flame61" Vidisania U
32 John "Cop90" O'Malley U
33 Leaf "Potter116" Pankowski U
34 Living Wood Staff R
35 Liz "Ticket312" Thornton U
36 Lock C
37 Lupe "Cabbie22" Droin U
38 Maman Boumba U
39 Marion "Teacher193" Perks U
40 Moise Kasavubu R
41 Muse of Flame C
42 Paul "Sixofswords29" Moreton U
43 Pedro Cortez U
44 Peter "Outback295" Rophail U
45 Project R
46 Punish C
47 React with Conviction C
48 Rejuvenate C
49 Respire C
50 The Rose Foundation R
51 Second Sight C
52 Shame C
53 Smite R
54 Strike with Conviction C
55 Surge R
56 Travis "Traveler72" Miller U
57 Unity R
58 Vigil: The Thin Line R
59 Vigilance C
60 Xian "DziDzat155" Quan U

2006 Vampire TES Third Edition

1 Aaron Bathurst V
2 Aksinya Daclau V
3 Alejandro Aguirre PTr
4 Alessandro Garcia PB
5 Andrew Emory V
6 Antón de Concepción V
7 Antonio d'Erlette V
8 Apache Jones PM2
9 Armin Brenner PB2
10 Axel Von Anders V
11 Beauregard Krueller PM2
12 Bela Kardoza V
13 Bill Butler V
14 Blister V
15 Bloodfeud PM
16 Caroline Bishops V
17 Charlie Tyne V
18 Conrad Adoula V
19 Count Vladimir Rustovitch PTz
20 Darvag, The Butcher of Rus V
21 DeSalle V
22 Dominique Santo Paulo V
23 Dr. Julius Sutphen V
24 Droescher One-Eye V
25 Brusilla Euphemia V
26 Duality PTz
27 Elizabeth Westcott PTz
28 Eric Kressida V
29 Ermenegildo, The Rake V
30 Esoara PTr2
31 Fabrizia Contreraz V
32 Father Juan Carlos PB2
33 Frank Litzpar V
34 Frère Marc V
35 Frondator PTr
36 Gabriel de Cambrai V
37 General Perfidio Dios PM
38 Gravitnir V
39 Greensleeves V
40 Guedado V
41 Harold Zettler, Pentex Director PM
42 Hektor PB2
43 Hukros V
44 Humo V
45 Icarus, The Manchurian V
46 Ilias cel Frumos V
47 Isouda de Blaise V
48 Jackie V
49 Jacques Molay V
50 Jaggedy Andy V
51 Jane Sims PTz
52 Janine PTr
53 Jefferson Foster V
54 Jephta Hester V
55 Jonathan Gursel V
56 Joseph Cambridge V
57 Justine Chen, Innocent V
58 Kai Simmons V
59 Keith Moody V
60 Klaus Konrecht V
61 Konrad Fleischer V
62 Ladislas Toth, The Torch PTr
63 Lady Zara Slatikov PTz2
64 Laika PTz2

65 Laszlo Mirac V
66 Lectora V
67 Leila Monroe V
68 Leo Washington V
69 Lernean V
70 Little Willie V
71 Loonar V
72 Lord Aaron Wesley Wilkshire V
73 Lord Vauxhall V
74 Louis de Maisonneuve V
75 Luc V
76 Luca Italicus V
77 Lucubratio PTr2
78 Lucy Markowitz V
79 Lukas V
80 Luke Fellows V
81 Lula Burch V
82 Malabranca V
83 Malgorzała V
84 Marcel de Breau PB
85 Margarite V
86 Mariel St. John V
87 Marta V
88 Mary Johnson V
89 Melinda Galbraith V
90 Melinda Galbraith V
91 Monique Kim V
92 Morrow the Sage V
93 Mostair V
94 Mowgli V
95 Mugur Sabau V
96 Neighbor John V
97 Nickolai, The Survivor V
98 Nostoket V
99 Old Neddacka V
100 Orlando Oriundus V
101 Patrick V
102 Paul Cordwood PTr2
103 Paulo de Castille V
104 Persephone Tar-Anis PM2
105 Polly Kay Fisher V
106 Radu Bistri PTz2
107 Rain V
108 Randel, The Coward V
109 Raphael Catarari V
110 Redbone McCray V
111 Rico Loco V
112 Rodolfo PM
113 Rodrigo V
114 Ryszard V
115 Schuyler V
116 Servius Marius Pustula V
117 Sha-Ennu V
118 Shawnda Dorrit PB
119 Smash PB
120 Stavros V
121 Stick V
122 Tears, The Dark Pierrot V
123 Terrifisto V
124 Titus Camille V
125 Ulrike Rothbart V
126 Uncle George PM
127 Urraca PB2
128 Uta Kovacs PTr2
129 Virginie, Prodigy V
130 White Lily PM
131 Xendil Charmer V
132 Ysador the Foul V
133 Yuri Kerezenski PTz2
134 Abandoning the Flesh R
135 Abbot U
136 Ablative Skin R
137 Acrobatics C/PB3
138 Aid from Bats C
139 Alacrity PB2
140 Amaranth PTz
141 Amusement Park Hunting Ground PB
142 Anarch Revolt U
143 Anarchist Uprising C
144 Apportation C/PTr5
145 Aranthebes, The Immortal PB
146 Archon Investigation U
147 Art Scam R
148 Assault Rifle U
149 Aura of Invincibility PB
150 Aura Reading PTz
151 Auspex PTz
152 Auto-da-fé U
153 Awe R
154 Backstab U
155 Bang Nakh -- Tiger's Claws C
156 Banshee Ironwail R
157 Bauble R
158 Behind You! PM
159 Bewitching Oration PB5
160 Black Forest Base R
161 Black Gloves R
162 Black Metamorphosis R
163 Black Spiral Buddy U
164 Blade of Enoch R
165 Blessing of Chaos PM
166 Blood Doll P2
167 Blood Feast PTz
168 Blood of the Sabbat R
169 Blood Rage PTr3
170 Bloodbath R
171 Blow Torch C
172 Blur C
173 Body Arsenal PTz4
174 Body Flare R
175 Bomb U
176 Bonding PTr4
177 Bonecraft PTz3
178 Boxed In C
179 Brass Knuckles C
180 Breath of the Dragon PTz
181 Bribes PB3
182 Burning Wrath U/PB
183 Burst of Sunlight U
184 Canine Horde PTz
185 Cardinal Benediction U
186 Cardinal Sin: Insubordination U
187 Carrion Crows C
188 Catacombs PM
189 Catatonic Fear U
190 Celerity PB
191 Changeling C/PTz3
192 Cheval de Bataille U
193 Chiropteran Marauder C
194 Claws of the Dead C
195 Cloak the Gathering PM6
196 Club Zombie PTz
197 Codex of the Damned R
198 Coma U
199 Combat Shotgun C
200 Command U
201 Command of the Beast U
202 Communal Haven: Cathedral U
203 Concoction of Vitality PTr
204 Confusion C/PM4
205 Consanguineous Boon C/PB
206 Conservative Agitation C
207 Corrupt Construction C
208 Courier U
209 Cracking the Wall R2
210 Creation Rites U
211 Creepshow Casino PB
212 Crusade: Detroit PB
213 Crusade: New York PM
214 Crusade: Philadelphia PTr
215 Crusade: Pittsburgh PTz
216 Crusade: Rome PB
217 Crusade: Toronto PM
218 Cryptic Rider U
219 Cull the Herd R
220 Danse Macabre C
221 Daring the Dawn R
222 Darkness Within U
223 Darksight C
224 Dauntain Black Magician (Changeling) R
225 Decapitate U
226 Deer Rifle PM
227 Delaying Tactics U
228 Dementation PM
229 Demonstration U
230 Deny PM
231 Deploy the Hand C
232 Depravity U
233 Derange R
234 Direct Intervention U
235 Disarm R
236 Disengage PM2
237 Disputed Territory PB
238 Dissolution U
239 Dodge C
240 Dogs of War U/PB
241 Dominate PTr
242 Dominate Kine PTr
243 Dragon's Breath Rounds U
244 Drain Essence PTr
245 Drawing Out the Beast PTz3
246 Dreams of the Sphinx R2
247 Drum of Xipe Totec R
248 Dummy Corporation PB
249 Eagle's Sight PTz2
250 Effective Management PM
251 Elder Impersonation C/PM2
252 Elysian Fields U
253 Enchant Kindred C
254 Enchanted Marionette PM
255 Enhanced Senses C/PTr3/PTz5
256 Esbat C
257 Escaped Mental Patient U/PM
258 Eternal Vigilance U/PTr
259 Excommunication PTr
260 Eyes of Chaos PM5
261 Faceless Night C
262 Fame PTz
263 Far Mastery R2
264 Fast Hands PB
265 Festivo dello Estinto PTz
266 Fiendish Tongue C
267 Finding the Path PTz
268 Flamethrower U
269 Flash PB5
270 Flurry of Action C
271 Force of Will C
272 Forced Awakening PTz3
273 Foreshadowing Destruction C
274 Forger's Hammer U
275 Forgery C/PTz2
276 Forgotten Labyrinth U
277 Form of Mist C
278 Freak Drive U
279 Frenzy C
280 Frontal Assault U
281 Gang Tactics R
282 Gang Territory R
283 Gangrel Conspiracy R
284 Garrote C
285 Giant's Blood R
286 Glancing Blow C/PM3
287 Golconda: Inner Peace PTr
288 Govern the Unaligned PTr5
289 Graverobbing PTr
290 Grooming the Protégé C
291 Guard Dogs C/PTz3
292 Guardian Angel C
293 Gurchon Hall R2
294 Hand Intervention PTr
295 Harass C/PTr4
296 Harvest Rites U
297 Haven Affinity R
298 Heart of Nizchetus R
299 Helicopter U/PTr
300 Hexaped U
301 Hidden Pathways R
302 High Ground C
303 Honor the Elders C
304 Horrid Form U/PTz2
305 Immortal Grapple U
306 Improvised Flamethrower U
307 Inconnu Tutelage R
308 Increased Strength PB2
309 Infernal Familiar R
310 Infernal Pact R/PTr
311 Information Highway U
312 Information Network R
313 Inner Essence PTz2
314 Instability U
315 Instinctive Reaction C
316 Institution Hunting Ground PM
317 Intimidation R
318 IR Goggles U
319 Iron Glare PB3
320 Ivory Bow R
321 J. S. Simmons, Esq. R
322 Jack of Both Sides PTz
323 Keep It Simple C
324 Kindred Manipulation R
325 Kindred Segregation U
326 Kindred Spirits C/PM5
327 Kine Resources Contested PB6
328 King's Rising C
329 Kraken's Kiss C
330 Leather Jacket C/PB2/PM2
331 Left for Dead R
332 Legacy of Caine R
333 Legwork C
334 Library Hunting Ground PTz
335 Living Manse R
336 Lobotomy R
337 Local 1111 PTz
338 London Evening Star, Tabloid Newspaper PB
339 Lost in Crowds C/PM4
340 Lunatic Eruption R
341 Lupine Assault R
342 Magic of the Smith R
343 Major Boon U
344 Malkavian Game PM
345 Marijava Ghoul U
346 Marked Path R
347 Martial Ritus C
348 Martinelli's Ring R
349 Media Influence C
350 Melange PM
351 Meld with the Land C
352 Mighty Grapple PB
353 Mind Tricks PM2
354 Minor Irritation C
355 Mirror Walk C
356 Mob Connections U
357 Monomancy PTz
358 My Enemy's Enemy U
359 Mylan Horseed (Goblin) R
360 Neighborhood Watch Commander (Hunter) PTz
361 Nephandus (Mage) R
362 New Management R2
363 Nimble Feet PB3
364 Nosferatu Kingdom R
365 NRA PAC R
366 Obedience U
367 Obfuscate PM
368 On the Qui Vive C/PB2/PM2/PTr2
369 Oubliette U
370 Owl Companion PTz
371 Palatial Estate PM
372 Palla Grande R
373 Patronage U
374 Patterns in the Chaos R
375 Peace Treaty C
376 Pentex(TM) Loves You! U
377 Pentex(TM) Subversion U
378 Perfect Clarity R2
379 Perpetual Care C
380 Pier 13, Port of Baltimore U
381 Plasmic Form PTz2
382 Political Antagonist R
383 Political Stranglehold U
384 Political Struggle R
385 Potence PB
386 Power Structure R
387 Powerbase: Barranquilla PTz
388 Powerbase: Mexico City U
389 Powerbase: Montreal R
390 Precognition C/PM3
391 Private Audience C
392 Propaganda U
393 Protected Resources R
394 Psyche! U
395 Pulse of the Canaille U
396 Purchase Pact PTz
397 Purity of the Beast PTr
398 Pursuit C
399 Pushing the Limit C
400 Quick Meld C
401 Quickness R
402 Rabble Razing C
403 Rafastio Ghoul C
404 Rapid Change C
405 Raptor U
406 Rave C
407 Raven Spy PTz3
408 Read Intentions PM3
409 Read the Winds U
410 Reality Mirror R
411 Recruiting Party R
412 Recruitment PTr
413 Recure of the Homeland U/PTr
414 Redirection C/PTr4
415 Regent R
416 Reinforcements PB
417 Reins of Power PTr
418 Resilience U
419 Restoration C
420 Restructure R
421 Revelations U
422 Revenant U/PTz
423 Robert Carter PTr
424 Rolling with the Punches C
425 Rooftop Shadow C
426 Root of Vitality PTz
427 Rumble C/PTz3
428 Rutor's Hand PTr
429 Rötschreck PTz
430 Sabbat Inquisitor U
431 Sabbat Priest C/PB
432 Sacrament of Carnage C
433 San Nicolás de los Servitas R
434 Saturday-Night Special C
435 Sawed-Off Shotgun PM2
436 Scalpel Tongue PB2
437 Scorpion Sting C/PTz2
438 Scouting Mission C
439 Scrounging U
440 Secret Horde PB
441 Secure Haven PM
442 Sengir Dagger PB
443 Sermon of Caine C
444 Shadow Court Satyr (Changeling) R
445 Shadow of the Beast U
446 Shadow Play C
447 Shadow Step R
448 Shadow Strike C
449 Shattered Mirror U
450 Shroud of Night C
451 Sibyl's Tongue R2
452 Sire's Index Finger R
453 Skin Trap U
454 Slaughtering the Herd U
455 Slave Auction R
456 Smiling Jack, The Anarch PTz
457 Song of Serenity C
458 Soul Burn C
459 Soul Gem of Etrius R
460 Special Report C
461 Spirit Summoning Chamber U
462 Spirit's Touch PTr5/PTz2
463 Sport Bike U
464 Spying Mission U
465 Staredown C
466 Starshell Grenade Launcher PB
467 Starvation of Marena PTz4
468 Stealth Ritus C
469 Strained Vitae Supply PTr
470 Stunt Cycle C/PB3
471 Succubus R
472 Sunrise Service R
473 Superior Mettle C
474 Survivalist U
475 Swallowed by the Night C/PM4
476 Sword of Judgment R
477 Talaq, The Immortal PTr
478 Talons of the Dead R
479 Taste of Vitae PB2
480 Telepathic Counter PM4
481 Telepathic Misdirection C/PM2
482 Telepathic Tracking U
483 Telepathic Vote Counting R2
484 Templar C
485 Tension in the Ranks R2
486 Thaumaturgy PTr
487 The Admonitions U
488 The Art of Love U
489 The Art of Pain R
490 The Call PM
491 The Damned U
492 The Hungry Coyote R
493 The Parthenon U
494 The Path of Metamorphosis U
495 The Path of Night U
496 The Path of the Feral Heart U
497 The Rack U
498 The Rumor Mill, Tabloid Newspaper U
499 The Sleeping Mind PTr
500 Theft of Vitae C/PTr6
501 Thoughts Betrayed C
502 Threats PTr4
503 Tier of Souls R
504 Tithings R
505 Torn Signpost PB2
506 Total Insanity C
507 Toy Chest Test PB
508 Transfer of Power R
509 Trap C
510 Tribute to the Master C
511 Uncontrollable Rage U
512 Undead Strength C/PB5
513 University Hunting Ground PTr
514 Using the Advantage R
515 Vagabond Mystic U
516 Vast Wealth U
517 Vendetta R2/PB1
518 Ventrue Investment U
519 Vial of Garou Blood C
520 Vicissitude PTz
521 Visit from the Capuchin R
522 Voice of Madness PM
523 Voter Captivation U/PB2
524 Vox Senis PM
525 Walk of Flame C/PTr4
526 War Ghoul R/PTz
527 War Party U
528 Wash U
529 Waste Management Operation U
530 Weather Control PTr3
531 Weighted Walking Stick U
532 White Phosphorus Grenade U
533 Wolf Companion PTz2
534 Wooden Stake U
535 Yawp Court R
536 Young Bloods R
537 Zillah's Tears C

2007 Vampire TES Lords of the Night

1 Abdelsobek U
2 Accorri Giovanni U
3 Ahmose Chambers U
4 Alu U
5 Anjalika Underwood U
6 Arnulf Jormungandrsson U
7 Bakr U
8 Belle Equitone PS2
9 Bertrand d'Anjou PA2
10 Brian Thompson PR2
11 Chavi Oraczko U
12 Clea Auguste d'Holford U
13 Diego Giovanni U
14 Djuhah, The Bronze Bow U
15 Dmitri Borodin PA2
16 Durga Syn PR2
17 Eric Milliner U
18 Evan Rogers PA2
19 Francis Milliner PG2
20 Ganesh U
21 Gianmaria Giovanni U
22 Giovanni del Georgio U
23 Guillaume Giovanni PG2
24 Gwen Brand U
25 Hafsa, The Watcher U
26 Halim Bey PS2
27 Izhim abd Azrael U
28 Jamal U
29 Jayakumar U
30 Johann Matheson U
31 Kabede Maru U
32 Kashan PA2
33 Kay Polerno U
34 Kiradin PR2
35 Lady Constancia PG2
36 Layla bint-Nadr PA2
37 Lizette PR2
38 Lorenzo Detuono U
39 Luna Giovanni U
40 Marcia Felicia Licinia U
41 Margaret Milliner PG2
42 Maria Kenyon PS2
43 Monty Coven U
44 Nakhthorheb PS2
45 Neel Ramanathan PR2
46 Nunzio Giovanni PG2
47 Ogwon U
48 Paolo Sardenzo U
49 Papa Legba U
50 Pentweret U
51 Phaedyme U
52 Porphyrion U
53 Primo Giovanni PG2
54 Renenet PS2
55 Sajid al Misbah U
56 Seterpenre U
57 Shemti U
58 Sisocharis U
59 Stephen Milliner U
60 Sukainah U
61 Sundervere, The Devil Brahmin PS2
62 Thucimia PA2
63 Vasiliy Vasilevich U
64 Vassily Taltos PR2
65 Agent of Power C
66 AK-47 R
67 Ambulance R
68 Amria PR2
69 Apparition PR4
70 Approximation of Loyalty PS3
71 Armor of Vitality C/PR2
72 Army of Apparitions C/PR
73 Autonomic Mastery U
74 Baal's Bloody Talons PA
75 Bang Nakh -- Tiger's Claws PG3
76 Bestow Vigor R
77 Black Sunrise PA3
78 Blithe Acceptance C/PS2
79 Blood Awakening C/PA3
80 Bloodlust R
81 Brute Force C/PG3
82 Bundi C/PG3
83 Burden the Mind C
84 Call of the Hungry Dead PG3
85 Camera Phone C/PG2
86 Can't Take it with You C
87 Carrion Crows PR3
88 Cave of Apples R
89 Chair of Hades R
90 Charigger, The Axe R
91 Chill of Oblivion PG
92 Chimerstry PR2
93 Clandestine Contract PA4
94 Cloak the Gathering PS2
95 Cobra Fangs R
96 Cold Aura C
97 Command the Legion R
98 Community Justice R
99 Compel the Spirit PG
100 Conceal R
101 Concealed Weapon PG2

102 Condemn the Sins of the Father R
103 Conditioning PG3
104 Confusion of the Eye PS3
105 Deed the Heart's Desire PA2
106 Divine Image U
107 Divine Sign PG2
108 Dominate Kine PG2
109 Dragonbound PA
110 Dream World C/PS4
111 Dummy Corporation PS
112 Ecstasy PS3
113 Edged Illusion PR2
114 Eluding the Arms of Morpheus C/PG2/PS2
115 Enticement PS2
116 Ex Nihilo PG
117 Eyes of Blades R
118 False Resonance C
119 Fantasy World R
120 Fata Amria PR
121 Fata Morgana PR4
122 Fatuus Mastery PR2
123 Fillip C/PR2
124 Flesh Bond C
125 Flurry of Action PA2
126 Forced March PR
127 Forced Vigilance PR2
128 Forearm Block C
129 Forger's Hammer PG
130 Form of Corruption PS
131 Fortune Teller Shop PR
132 Foul Blood PA2
133 Freak Drive PR
134 Free States Rant PA
135 Frontal Assault PA
136 Garrote PA2
137 Gemini's Mirror PA3
138 Giant's Blood PG
139 Gramle C
140 Graverobbing PG
141 Haqim's Law: Judgment PA
142 Haqim's Law: Leadership C/PA
143 Harass PG4
144 Hard Case R
145 Heart's Desire C/PR
146 Hide the Mind R
147 Hierophant PS
148 Ignis Fatuus PR4
149 Immortal Grapple PG2
150 Indomitability PR4
151 Inspire Greatness PG
152 Instinctive Reaction PR3
153 Into Thin Air C/PS2
154 Jack of Both Sides PG2
155 Jericho Founding C
156 Karavalanisha Vrana R
157 Khabar: Glory PA
158 Khazar's Diary (Endless Night) C
159 Khobar Towers, Al-Khubar PS
160 Kpist m/45 U
161 KRCG News Radio PG
162 Kumpania R
163 Lesser Boon R
164 Leverage C/PR2
165 Loss C/PA3
166 Lost in Translation C/PA
167 Majesty PS4
168 Malajit Chandramouli R
169 Mantle of the Moon U
170 Market Square PA
171 Mask of a Thousand Faces PA
172 Mayaparisatya PR2
173 Mental Maze C/PS2
174 Mercury's Arrow C
175 Mesu Bedshet C/PS
176 Mirror Image PR2
177 Mirror's Visage R
178 Mokolé Blood R
179 Monster R
180 Morgue Hunting Ground PG
181 Murmur of the False Will C/PG4
182 Narrow Minds R
183 Necromancy PG
184 Nephren-Ka R
185 Nest of Eagles C/PA2
186 Nightmare Curse PR
187 Nightstick U
188 Occlusion PR4
189 Omael Kuman R
190 Open Dossier C
191 Opium Den PS
192 Owl Companion PR
193 Park Hunting Ground PR
194 Permanent Vacation R
195 Poison the Well of Life R
196 Possession PG
197 Powerbase: Savannah R
198 Powerbase: Zürich R
199 Precision R
200 Preternatural Strength R
201 Promise of 1528 U
202 Provision of the Silsila PA
203 Proxy Kissed PG2
204 Pseudo-Blindness PR2
205 Public Trust C/PS2
206 Pursuit PA4
207 Quick Jab C
208 Quietus PA
209 Raven Spy PR3
210 Ravnos Carnival PR
211 Reckless Agitation C/PG3
212 Resist Earth's Grasp C/PA2
213 Resume the Coil R
214 Retain the Quick Blood R
215 Revelation of Desire PS4
216 Revelation of Despair PS2
217 Revelation of Ecstasy C/PS4
218 Revelation of Wrath PS
219 Rooftop Shadow PA3
220 Scorpion's Touch PA4
221 Secure Haven PS
222 Selective Silence PA4
223 Sense the Savage Way C
224 Serpentis PS
225 Set's Curse R
226 Shadow Feint PA
227 Shambling Hordes PG4
228 Sheepdog R
229 Shell Break C
230 Shroudsight C
231 Siphon PG
232 Skin of Night PR2
233 Slam C/PG2
234 Soak PR3
235 Songs of the Distant Vitae PA
236 Soul Feasting R
237 Spectral Divination PG4
238 Spell of Life C
239 Spying Mission PS2
240 Street Cred C
241 Strike at the True Flesh C
242 Sudario Refraction PG
243 Svadharma PR2
244 Swallowed by the Night PA3
245 Swiss Cut R
246 Sympathetic Agony R
247 Tajdid PA
248 Talith U/PR
249 Target Hand R
250 Target Head R
251 Target Leg R
252 Target Vitals U
253 Taste of Death PA3
254 Taste of Vitae PG2
255 Temple Hunting Ground PS
256 Temptation PS3
257 The Black Throne R
258 The Crocodile Temple PS
259 The Eternal Mask C
260 The Eternals of Sirius U
261 The Jones PS3
262 The Khabar: Honor PA2
263 The Path of Blood PA2
264 The Path of Bone PG2
265 The Path of Paradox PR2
266 The Sargon Fragment PG
267 The Summoning PS
268 Therbold Realty R
269 Torn Signpost PG2
270 Treasured Samadji PR
271 Trochomancy C
272 Trophy: Library R
273 Trophy: No Questions R
274 Trophy: Revered R
275 True Love's Face PS4
276 Truth of a Thousand Lies PS2
277 Truth of Blood PA
278 Tutu the Doubly Evil One (Bane Mummy) PS
279 Tye Cooper R
280 Underbridge Stray U
281 Underworld Hunting Ground PA
282 Undying Tenacity C
283 Unholy Penance C/PS3
284 Urban Jungle R
285 Veil the Legions PS2
286 Vessel PA2/PG2/PR2/PS2
287 Warrant C/PG
288 Wash PS
289 Web of Knives Recruit PA2
290 Week of Nightmares PR
291 Weighted Walking Stick PA3
292 Whispers from the Dead PG2
293 Will-o'-the-Wisp R
294 WMRH Talk Radio PS
295 Zapaderin C/PR2

2007 Vampire TES Sword of Caine

1 Appius Claudius Corvus V
2 Arianne, The Conqueror V
3 Ash Harrison V
4 Carmen V
5 Dr. Morrow, The Skindoctor V
6 Elimelech the Twice-Damned V
7 Fairuza V
8 Gatjil Munyarryun V
9 Hagar Stone V
10 Kestrelle Hayes V
11 Lubomira Hradok V
12 Marge Khan V
13 Nails V
14 Nizzam al-Latif V
15 Ondine "Boudicca" Sinclair V
16 Rashid Stockton V
17 Saul Meira V
18 Shaggydog V
19 Stephen Bateson V
20 Zubeida V
21 Biothaumaturgic Experiment C
22 Black Hand Emissary R
23 Blind Spot C
24 Cadet C
25 Census Taker R
26 Cloak of Blood R
27 Drink the Blood of Ahriman R
28 Drop Point Network R
29 Eccentric Billionaire C
30 Empowering the Puppet King C
31 Enrage C
32 Epiphany R
33 Follow the Blood R
34 Forced Vigilance C
35 Framing an Ancient Grudge R
36 Guarded Rubrics R
37 Hand Contract C
38 Joseph Pander R
39 Liquefy the Mortal Coil R
40 Mantle of the Bestial Majesty R
41 Mustajib C
42 Nocturn C
43 Notorious Brutality C
44 Praetorian Backer R
45 Prison of the Mind R
46 Psychic Assault C
47 Ruins of Ceoris R
48 Sanguinary Wind C
49 Seraph's Second R
50 Tattoo Signal C
51 Taunt the Caged Beast C
52 The Uncoiling R
53 Touch of Pain C
54 Tribunal Judgment R
55 Trophy: Chosen R
56 Truth in Ink C
57 Unexpected Coalition C
58 Veil the Legions C
59 Vermin Channel C
60 Watchtower: The Wolves Feed R

2008 Vampire TES Keepers of Tradition

1 Adana de Sforza PB2
2 Aidan Lyle V
3 Aleister Crowley PM2
4 Alex Wilkins V
5 Allanyan Serata V
6 Alonso Petrodon V
7 Andre LeRoux V
8 Andrew Stuart V
9 Ariadne V
10 Arthur Denholm V
11 Baron Dieudonne V
12 Beetleman V
13 Bela V
14 Benjamin Rose V
15 Bernard, the Scourgo V
16 Beth Malcolm V
17 Bethany Ray V
18 Bloody Mary V
19 Bulscu V
20 Carlak V
21 Cassandra Langely, The Waif PM2
22 César Holfield V
23 Claus Wegener V
24 Count Zaroff V
25 Dmitra Ilyanova V
26 Don Caravelli V
27 Don Cerro V
28 Donald Cargill V
29 Dr. John Dee V
30 Dr. Solomon Grey V
31 Emily Carson V
32 Epikasta Rigatos PT2
33 Eugene PT2
34 Ezra Hawthorne V
35 Fakir al Sidi V
36 Federico di Padua V
37 Fergus Alexander V
38 Florentina Lengauer PM2
39 Foureyes V
40 Frank Weisshadel V
41 Freddy Gage V
42 Gabrielle di Righetti V
43 Garret PB2
44 Gem Ghastly V
45 Gerald Windham V
46 Gotsdam, The Tired Warrior PV2
47 Gracetius V
48 Graham Gottesman V
49 Gunnar V
50 Gustaphe Brunnelle V
51 Gustav Breidenstein PV2
52 Gwendolyn Fleming V
53 Gwyedd V
54 Hardestadt PV2
55 Harold Tanner V
56 Herbert Westin PB2
57 Hiram "Hide" DeVries V
58 Honest Abe V
59 Iris Bennett V
60 Jack Tredegar V
61 Jackson Asher PV2
62 Jann Berger PB2
63 Jeremy "Wix" Wyzchovsky V
64 João Bilé PV2
65 Johan Wrede V
66 Johannes Castelein PV2
67 Josef von Bauren V
68 Joseph DiGiaccomo V
69 Kalila V
70 Karen Suadela V
71 Kateline Nadasdy PT2
72 Keller Thiel V
73 Lillian V
74 Lindsay Yates V
75 Lisé V
76 Lodin (Olaf Holte) V
77 Lord Ephraim Wainwright V
78 Lord Fianna V
79 Lutz von Hohenzollern PM2
80 Lynn Thompson V
81 MacAlister Marshall V
82 Mary Anne Blaire V
83 Masdela V
84 Mictlantecuhtli V
85 Miguel Cordovera V
86 Mistress Fanchon V
87 Montecalme V
88 Morel PM2
89 Nichodemus V
90 Osric Vladislav V
91 Paul Calderone V
92 Pedrag Hasek V
93 Philippe de Marseilles V
94 Portia V
95 Rafael de Corazon PT2
96 Randall V
97 Rathmere V
98 Reginald Moore PB2
99 Reiner Stoschka V
100 Robert Price V
101 Rutor V
102 Ruxandra V
103 Santaleous V
104 Sean Andrews PT2
105 Sergei Voshkov, The Eye V
106 Sheva Carr V
107 Shiloh Marie, Vengeance V
108 Slag V
109 Talbot V
110 Tara V
111 Tarrence Moore V
112 The Ankou V
113 Themistocles V
114 Thomas De Lutrius PT2
115 Tomaine PB2
116 Troius V
117 Tryphosa PM2
118 Tyler McGill V
119 Unmada V
120 Vasily V
121 Victor Donaldson V
122 Vidal Jarbeaux V
123 Viktor, The Night General V
124 Walker Grimes V
125 William Thorbecke V
126 Zane V
127 Zelios V
128 Aaron's Feeding Razor R
129 Abomination R
130 Academic Hunting Ground U
131 Aching Beauty U
132 Agate Talisman C
133 Aid from Bats C
134 Al's Army Apparatus R
135 Alastor R
136 Amaranth U
137 Anarch Troublemaker R
138 Anima Gathering C
139 Approximation of Loyalty C/PT4
140 Arcane Appraiser R
141 Arcane Library R
142 Archon Investigation U
143 Armor of Vitality C/PV4
144 Arms Dealer U
145 Art Museum R
146 Ashur Tablets C
147 Assault Rifle U
148 Asylum Hunting Ground U
149 Aura of Invincibility C/PV3
150 Aura Reading U
151 Auspex PM/PT
152 Backstep C
153 Backways U
154 Bang Nakh -- Tiger's Claws C/PB4
155 Behind You! U
156 Beretta 9mm C/PT5
157 Blade of Enoch R
158 Bleeding the Vine PM
159 Blood Hunt U
160 Blood of Sandman U
161 Blood Weakens R
162 Bomb U
163 Bounty U
164 Bowl of Convergence R/PT
165 Brick Laying C
166 Brujah Justicar R
167 Brute Force C/PB6
168 Bundi C/PB2
169 Burst of Sunlight U
170 Camera Phone C
171 Can't Take it with You C/PV3
172 Carrion Crows C
173 Caseless Rounds U
174 Celerity PB/PT
175 Chain of Command C
176 Change of Target U/PM3
177 Charisma R
178 Charismatic Aura C
179 Charming Lobby U
180 Charnas the Imp R
181 Childling Muse U
182 Claws of the Dead C
183 Cloak the Gathering C
184 Concealed Weapon C/PT2
185 Conditioning C/PV5
186 Contingency Planning PT2
187 Cooler C/PM3
188 Coterie Tactics U
189 Crocodile's Tongue C/PT4
190 Dark Influences U
191 Dark Mirror of the Mind U
192 Dawn Operation U
193 Day Operation R
194 Deep Song C
195 Delaying Tactics U
196 Delivery Truck R
197 Dementation PM
198 Deny PM2
199 Desert Eagle C/PT3
200 Dive into Madness C
201 Diversity C
202 Dominate PV
203 Dominate Kine PV
204 Dragon's Breath Rounds U
205 Drum of Xipe Totec PB
206 Eagle's Sight U/PT3
207 Earthshock C
208 Ecoterrorists R
209 Effective Management U/PM2
210 Elder Kindred Network U
211 Eluding the Arms of Morpheus C
212 Elysium: Storzesco Castle R
213 Elysium: The Arboretum U/PM
214 Elysium: The Palace of Versailles U
215 Empowering the Puppet King C
216 Enkil Cog R
217 Enrage C/PB4
218 Entrancement PT
219 Entrenching PB2
220 Ephor R
221 Esgrima PV2
222 Eyes of Argus C
223 Eyes of Chaos C/PM6
224 Eyes of the Beast C
225 Fame U/PT2
226 Fast Hands U
227 Fifth Tradition: Hospitality U
228 Finding the Path C/PB2
229 First Tradition: The Masquerade R
230 Fleetness C
231 Flesh of Marble U
232 Flurry of Action C
233 Force of Personality C
234 Forced Vigilance C
235 Forgery C/PM5
236 Form of Mist C
237 Fortitude PV
238 Fourth Tradition: The Accounting U/PV3
239 Fragment of the Book of Nod R
240 Freak Drive PV3
241 From a Sinking Ship R
242 Frontal Assault U
243 Gambit Accepted R
244 Gather R
245 Ghoul Retainer U/R
246 Giant's Blood R/PM
247 Glancing Blow C/PM4
248 Golconda: Inner Peace R/PV
249 Graverobbing U
250 Gregory Winter R
251 Harass C/PB5
252 Haymaker PV2
253 Heart of Nizchetus R
254 Heart of the City R
255 Helicopter U
256 Heroic Might U
257 High Ground C
258 High Museum of Art, Atlanta PM
259 Honor the Elders C/PV5
260 Horseshoes C
261 Hostile Takeover R
262 Immortal Grapple U/PB3
263 Improvised Flamethrower U
264 Indomitability C
265 Instability U/PV2
266 Instinctive Reaction C
267 Into Thin Air C/PM6
268 IR Goggles U/PT2
269 Ivory Bow R/PT
270 Jackie Therman R
271 Jake Washington (Hunter) R
272 Justicar Retribution U
273 Keep it Simple C
274 Kevlar Vest U
275 Kindred Intelligence U
276 Kindred Spirits C/PM6
277 Kine Resources Contested C/PT4/PV6
278 King's Rising C
279 KRCG News Radio U/PB
280 Leadership Vacuum R
281 Learjet PM2
282 Leech U
283 Leverage C
284 Liberty Club Intrigue R
285 Life in the City C/PM4
286 Light Intensifying Goggles U
287 Lightning Reflexes R
288 Loki's Gift C
289 Loyal Street Gang U
290 Madness Network R
291 Magazine R
292 Magic of the Smith R
293 Majesty C/PV4
294 Major Boon U/PB2
295 Malkavian Justicar R
296 Malkavian Prank R
297 Mark V PT
298 Martinelli's Ring PV
299 Mask of a Thousand Faces U
300 Meat Hook C
301 Metro Underground U
302 Millicent Smith, Puritan Vampire Hunter R
303 Mind Rape R
304 Minor Boon U
305 Minor Irritation C/PT4
306 Mirror Walk C
307 Momentum's Edge R
308 Monastery of Shadows R
309 Monocle of Clarity R
310 Mouthpiece C
311 Movement of the Slow Body U
312 Muddled Vampire Hunter U
313 Murmur of the False Will C/PV5
314 National Guard Support PV2
315 Neonate Breach C
316 New Carthage R
317 New Management R
318 No Trace C

319 Nocturn Theater R
320 Nod PB
321 Nosferatu Bestial R
322 Nosferatu Justicar R
323 NRA PAC R
324 Obfuscate PM2
325 Old Friends C
326 On the Qui Vive C/PB3/PM3/PT2
327 Ossian R
328 Owl Companion U
329 Papillon U
330 Perfect Paragon U
331 Perfectionist C
332 Persona Non Grata U
333 Petra Resonance R
334 Phased Motion Detector PB
335 Pier 13, Port of Baltimore U
336 Poison Pill PM2
337 Political Ally R
338 Ponticulus R
339 Potence PB
340 Powerbase: Chicago U
341 Powerbase: Montreal R/PV
342 Praxis Seizure: Atlanta PV
343 Praxis Seizure: Chicago PM
344 Praxis Seizure: Houston PT
345 Praxis Seizure: Miami PV
346 Praxis Seizure: Washington, D.C. PT
347 Presence PB/PT/PV
348 Protected Resources R
349 Psyche! U/PB3/PT3
350 Psychic Veil R
351 Public Trust C/PB3/PT6
352 Pursuit C/PT6
353 Quick Meld C
354 Raven Spy U
355 Read Intentions C
356 Rego Motus C
357 Reins of Power C/PV
358 Relentless Pursuit PB3
359 Renegade Garou R
360 Repair the Undead Flesh U
361 Resist Earth's Grasp C/PB5
362 Rowan Ring R
363 Rumors of Gehenna U
364 Scattershot C
365 Scorn of Adonis U
366 Scourge U
367 Scourge of the Enochians R
368 Scrounging U
369 Seal of Veddartha R
370 Second Tradition: Domain U/PV3
371 Seduction C/PV4
372 Sengir Dagger R/PB
373 Sense the Savage Way C
374 Serenading the Kami C
375 Shape Mastery R
376 Shattered Mirror U/PM2
377 Sixth Tradition: Destruction R
378 Slam C/PB4
379 Sleep of Reason C/PM2
380 Sleep Unseen C
381 Slum Hunting Ground U
382 Smiling Jack, The Anarch R
383 Sniper Rifle U/PT3
384 Soak C/PV4
385 Social Ladder R/PV
386 Society of Leopold U/R
387 Sonar C
388 Soul Gem of Etrius R
389 Soul Scan R
390 Special Report C/PV2
391 Specialization R
392 Spirit's Touch C/PM3
393 Spying Mission U/PM4
394 Steadfastness C
395 Still the Mortal Flesh U
396 Storm Sewers R
397 Stunt Cycle C
398 Stutter-Step C/PB4
399 Suppressing Fire PT3
400 Sword of Nuln R
401 Sword of Troile R
402 Tainted Spring R
403 Talbot's Chainsaw R
404 Tapestry of Blood R
405 Target Retainer R
406 Taste of Vitae U/PB3/PT3
407 Taunt the Caged Beast C
408 Telepathic Misdirection C/PT4
409 Temptation of Greater Power R
410 Tension in the Ranks R/PB
411 The Ankara Citadel, Turkey U
412 The Becoming U
413 The Coven PM
414 The Embrace R
415 The Haunting C
416 The Labyrinth U
417 The Oath C
418 The Rack U/PT
419 The Summoning C
420 The Unmasking R
421 Theft of Vitae C
422 Third Tradition: Progeny U
423 Toreador Grand Ball U
424 Toreador Justicar R
425 Torn Signpost U/PB3
426 Torpid Blood R
427 Torrent C
428 Touch of Clarity R
429 Tremere Justicar R
430 Undying Tenacity C
431 Uptown Hunting Ground U
432 Vast Wealth U
433 Veil the Legions C/PM4
434 Veles' Hunt R
435 Veneficorum Artum Sanguis R
436 Ventrue Headquarters U
437 Ventrue Justicar R
438 Vessel PB2/PM2/PT2/PV2
439 Victim of Habit R
440 Villein U
441 Voice of Madness U/PM2
442 Vulnerability U
443 Waiting Game R
444 Walk of Flame C
445 Warsaw Station R
446 Warzone Hunting Ground U
447 Wash U
448 Weather Control U
449 Weighted Walking Stick U/PB3
450 Wendell Delburton (Hunter) R
451 White Nights Massacre R
452 Will of the Council U
453 Winchester Mansion R
454 Wooden Stake U
455 Wrong and Crosswise C
456 XTC-Laced Blood R
457 Year of Fortune C/PB2
458 Zillah's Valley C
459 Zoning Board R
460 Zoo Hunting Ground U

2008 Vampire TES Twilight Rebellion

1 Anarch Convert U
2 Andy U
3 Antoine, The Lost U
4 Calvin Cleaver U
5 Clifton Derrik U
6 Dirk U
7 Jack Drake U
8 Jacob Fermor U
9 Juniper U
10 Laecanus U
11 Lin Jun U
12 Louis Fortier U
13 Marguerite Foccart U
14 Preston Varrick U
15 Reverend Adams U
16 Sean Rycek U
17 T.J. U
18 Tarautas U
19 Toby U
20 Topaz U
21 An Anarch Manifesto C
22 Anonymous Freight C
23 Baseball Bat C
24 Blade Clot R
25 Blood Turnip R
26 Chameleon R
27 Club Illusion R
28 Constant Revolution R
29 CrimethInc. C
30 Crypt's Sons R
31 Detect Authority C
32 Elixir of Distillation C
33 Exclusion Principle C
34 Failsafe R
35 Final Loosening R
36 Garibaldi-Meucci Museum R
37 Grey Thorne R
38 Haven Hunting C
39 Hell-for-Leather C
40 Keystone Kine C
41 Lam Into C
42 Libertas C
43 Monkey Wrench C
44 No Confidence C
45 Open War R
46 Patsy R
47 Piper R
48 Poacher's Hunting Ground R
49 Power of All C
50 Power of One C
51 Revolutionary Council C
52 Shattering R
53 Shoulder Drop C
54 Smear Campaign R
55 Stealing Years R
56 Steely Tenacity C
57 The Framing R
58 The World's a Canvas R
59 Twilight Camp R
60 Zip Line C

2009 Vampire TES Ebony Kingdom

1 Abiku U
2 Abu Nuwasi U
3 Aisata Swanou U
4 Arriette Sylla U
5 Batsheva U
6 Cesewayo U
7 Elizabeth Conde U
8 Fode Kourouma U
9 Jibade el-Bahrawi U
10 Kamiri wa Itherero U
11 Luanda Magere U
12 Lucian, the Perfect U
13 Mamadou Keita U
14 Nana Buruku U
15 Nestor Kaba U
16 Ngozi Ekwensu U
17 Socrate Cidibe U
18 Titi Camara U
19 Umdava U
20 Undele U
21 419 Operation C
22 Aye C
23 Bamba C
24 Bestial Vengeance R
25 Blood Shield R
26 Brutal Influence C
27 Despiral C
28 Devil-Channel: Feet C
29 Dusk Work C
30 Edge of the World R
31 Exile C
32 Familial Bond C
33 Guinea-Bissau Carnival R
34 Hiding in the Open R
35 Ilomba R
36 Impundulu R
37 Invoke Poison Glands C
38 Ishtarri Warlord R
39 Jua Vema C
40 Kufa C
41 Make an Example R
42 Mapatano Utando R
43 Mundane C
44 My Kin Against the World C
45 Neebi C
46 Nkishi R
47 Orun C
48 Pallid C
49 Powerbase: Luanda R
50 Reliquary: Trinket C
51 Remnant of the Endless Storm R
52 Savannah Runner R
53 Sense Vibrations R
54 Supernatural Resistance C
55 Taking the Skin: Minion R
56 Taking the Skin: Vulture R
57 Taming the Beast C
58 The Bitter and Sweet Story R
59 Transcendent Laibon R
60 Tunnel Runner C
61 Unholy Radiance C
62 Well-Marked R

2010 Vampire TES Heirs to the Blood

1 Abebe PSam
2 Al-Muntathir, God's Witness U
3 Alcoan U
4 Andrew Emory PKia
5 Angel Chavarria U
6 Annazir U
7 Anu Diptinatpa U
8 Aredhel PSal
9 Ariel U
10 Arishat U
11 Asguresh U
12 Azrael U
13 Baroque U/PSam2
14 Black Wallace PKia
15 Brigitte Mandisa U
16 Byzar U
17 Cedric PGar2
18 Chaundice U
19 Claus Wegener PGar
20 Dame Hollerton PKia
21 Danylo U
22 Darlene Killian U
23 Dovey Ebfwe U
24 Ermenegildo, The Rake PKia
25 Evil Jensen U
26 Federico di Padua PSam
27 Frank Weisshadel PGar
28 Fustuk U
29 Gavrylo U
30 Greer Worder U
31 Grotesque U2
32 Harlan Graves U
33 Harold Tanner PSam
34 Hector Trelane PGar
35 Helen Fairchild U
36 Hillanvale U
37 Isanwayen U/PKia2
38 Janet Langer U
39 Jefferson Foster PSal
40 Jephta Hester PSal
41 Josette U
42 Jozz U
43 Kyrylo U
44 La Viuda Blanca U
45 Langa PSal
46 Lord Ephraim Wainwright PGar
47 Lord Vauxhall PKia
48 Luca Italicus PKia
49 Lydia, Grand Praetor U
50 Macoute PSam
51 Malachai U
52 Mariel St. John PSal
53 Matthew U
54 Mikael Birkholm U
55 Mordechai Ben-Nun U
56 Morlock U
57 Muhsin Samir PGar
58 Myrna Goldman U
59 Nahum Enosh U
60 Neighbor John PSal
61 Nicomedes U
62 Nitidas U
63 Nkechi PSal
64 Obaluaye U
65 Omme Enberbenight PKia
66 Pavlo U
67 Petra PSam
68 Pherydima PKia
69 Polly Kay Fisher PSal
70 Qawiyya el-Ghaduba U
71 Rashiel PSal
72 Rocia PGar2
73 Roderick Phillips March PKia
74 Rusticus U/PGar2
75 Sahana U
76 Scout Youngwood U
77 Serenna the White U
78 Shahid PSam
79 Shalmath U
80 Silas U
81 Slag PSam
82 Sylvie Helgon U
83 Tanginé P
84 Tanginé P
85 Tarrence Moore PGar
86 The Arcadian U
87 The Horde U2
88 The unnamed U
89 Titus Camille PSal
90 Topaz PSam
91 Toy U
92 Troglodytia PSam
93 Uriel U/PSal2
94 Veejay Vinod U
95 Virginie, Prodigy PKia
96 Volo U
97 Xeper, Sultan of Lepers U
98 Abbot PSal3
99 Absorb the Mind PKia3
100 Agent of Power PSam4
101 Amulet of Temporal Perception R
102 Antediluvian Awakening PGar
103 As the Crow C
104 Aura Absorption PKia4
105 Auspex PSal
106 Autonomic Mastery PKia
107 Barrenness R
108 Baseball Bat PSal5
109 Benefit Performance C
110 Blanket of Night PKia
111 Blessed Resilience R
112 Blessing of the Beast R2
113 Blessing of the Name PSal
114 Blind Spot PKia2
115 Bliss R
116 Blissful Agony PSal
117 Blood Tempering R2
118 Blooding by the Code PSal2
119 Bonding PKia6
120 Brick by Brick C
121 Brother in Arms PSal2
122 Bum's Rush PGar3
123 Camera Phone PSam3
124 Capitalist PKia2
125 Cavalier R
126 Channel 10 PKia
127 Chantry PGar
128 Charge of the Buffalo R
129 Cheat the Fates R
130 Cloak the Gathering PSam4
131 Clockwerx R
132 Code of Samiel R
133 Cold Aura PSam2
134 Command Performance R
135 Compress PSam2
136 Computer Hacking PSam4
137 Conditioning PGar4
138 Coroner's Contact PSam2
139 Corporate Hunting Ground PSal
140 Covincraft PKia2
141 Create Gargoyle PGar
142 Dabbler R
143 Dagger C
144 Darkness Within PKia2
145 Dawn Operation PSal2
146 Death Seeker C/PSal2
147 Decompose R
148 Deep Song PSam2
149 Defender of the Haven PGar
150 Deflection PGar4
151 Depravity PGar
152 Development C
153 Diabolic Lure C
154 Din of the Damned C
155 Dive Bomb C
156 Divine Sign PSam
157 Dominate PKia
158 Draeven Softfoot (Changeling) R
159 Dragonbound PSal
160 Dreams of the Sphinx PSam
161 Dummy Corporation PSam
162 Ears of the Hare C
163 Effective Management PGar2
164 Elder Intervention PSam2
165 Enhanced Senses PSal3
166 Ensconced R
167 Eternal Vigilance PKia
168 Evil Eye C
169 Eye of Unforgiving Heaven PSal
170 Eyes of Argus PSal3
171 Fae Contortion PKia3
172 Faerie Wards C
173 Fame PGar/PSal
174 Fanfare for Elysium R2
175 Flames of the Netherworld C
176 Foldable Machine Gun C
177 Folderol PKia2
178 Fortitude PSal
179 Fractura R
180 Freak Drive PSam2
181 Gift of Sleep C
182 Goblinism PKia
183 Govern the Unaligned PKia6/PSal4
184 Graverobbing P
185 Great Symposium R
186 Greater Curse C
187 Gremlins C
188 Groaning Corpse C
189 Guardian Angel PGar
190 Hag's Wrinkles PSam
191 Harmony R
192 Hatch the Viper R
193 Hatchling PGar
194 Hay Ride R
195 Hexe C
196 Hide the Heart C/PSal2
197 Hive Mind C
198 Horseshoes PSam2
199 Houngan PSam
200 Hunger Moon R
201 I am Legion R
202 Immortal Grapple PGar3
203 Indomitability PSal5
204 Infernal Servitor R2
205 Information Highway PSal
206 J. S. Simmons, Esq. PGar
207 Jar of Skin Eaters C
208 Joumlon's Axe R
209 Journal of Hrorsh R
210 Knotted Cord R
211 Lead Fist C/PGar2
212 Lily Prelude C
213 Little Mountain Cemetery PSam2
214 Lord of Serenity C
215 Lost in Crowds PSam4
216 Loving Agony C
217 Maleficia C
218 Marked Path PSam
219 Masca C
220 Mask of a Thousand Faces PSam2
221 Melange PSal
222 Member of the Entourage R2
223 Mind of the Wilds C
224 Minor Curse R
225 Mole's Tunneling C
226 Momentary Delay C
227 Morphean Blow C
228 Mr. Winthrop PKia
229 Murmur of the False Will PKia4
230 New Moon Sigil R
231 Night Moves PSam3
232 Nocturn PKia2
233 Obedience PKia3
234 Obtenebration PKia
235 Off Kilter C/PSam2
236 Olid Loa R
237 On the Qui Vive PKia3/PSam4
238 Oppugnant Night C
239 Oubliette PKia3
240 Outside the Hourglass C
241 Patagia: Flaps Allowing Limited Flight PSam
242 Patrol PGar4
243 Penitent Resilience C
244 Pocket Out of Time C
245 Political Hunting Ground PKia
246 Potio Martyrium R
247 Pounce PGar2
248 Precognition PSal3
249 Pressing Flesh R
250 Psalm of the Damned C
251 Raking Talons PGar3
252 Rampage PSam
253 Ravager C
254 Raw Recruit R
255 Razor Bat PGar3
256 Reanimated Corpse PSam3
257 Research R
258 Ritual Scalpel R
259 Rock Cat PGar
260 Rockheart PGar4
261 Rumble PSal2
262 Safe Passage C
263 Scarlet Lore R
264 Scobax C
265 Scourge of Alecto C
266 Scry the Hearthstone PGar4
267 Sense Death PSal2
268 Shaal Fragment R
269 Shadow Play PKia4
270 Shadowed Eyes R
271 Shatter the Gate C
272 Shattering Crescendo C
273 Shroud of Absence PKia
274 Slake the Thirst C
275 Slam PGar4
276 Soak PGar4/PSam2
277 Song of Pan PKia
278 Soul of the Earth PGar
279 Spirit Claws R
280 Sport Bike PSam3
281 Steadfastness PSam3
282 Stiff Contempt C
283 Stone Travel PKia6
284 Stonestrength PGar4
285 Striga C
286 Strix R
287 Sudden Reversal PKia
288 Summon History R
289 Sword of the Righteous PSal3
290 Target Vitals PSal3
291 Telepathic Counter PSal2
292 Tend the Flock C
293 Thaumaturgy PGar
294 The Ailing Spirit R
295 The Barrens PGar
296 The Black Beast R
297 The Path of Harmony R
298 The Path of Retribution PSal
299 The Path of Service R
300 The Rising R
301 Thicker than Blood R2
302 Threading the Path of Orpheus R
303 Three's a Crowd C
304 Tinglestripe C/PKia2
305 Torn Signpost PGar3
306 Treat the Sick Mind R
307 Under My Skin C/PSam2
308 Underbridge Stray PSam

Card	Low	High
309 Unflinching Persistence PSal5		
310 Unleash Hell's Fury R		
311 Vaticination C		
312 Veil the Legions PSam4		
313 Veneficti (Mage) R		
314 Vengeance of Samiel PSal3		
315 Vessel PKi/PSI2/PSa2		
316 Villein P2		
317 Virtuosa C		
318 Visionquest C		
319 Voices of the Castle C/PGar2		
320 Wake with Evening's Freshness PGar6/PSal5		
321 Warding the Beast R		
322 Warsaw Station PSam		
323 Wasserschloss Anif, Austria PGar		
324 Wider View C/PKia2		
325 Zaire River Ferry Pkia		

2004 Vs System DC Origins

Card	Low	High
COMPLETE SET (165)	30.00	60.00
BOOSTER BOX (24 CARDS)	15.00	30.00
BOOSTER PACK (14 CARDS)	.75	1.25
*FOIL: .8X TO 2X BASIC CARDS		
RELEASED IN JULY 2004		
1 Alfred Pennyworth, Faithful Friend R	2.00	5.00
2 Azrael, Jean Paul Valley C	.10	.25
3 Barbara Gordon Oracle, Information Network R	1.25	3.00
4 Batman, Caped Crusader C	.10	.25
5 Batman, The Dark Knight R	2.00	5.00
6 Batman, World's Greatest Detective U	.20	.50
7 Cassandra Cain Batgirl, Martial Artist C	.10	.25
8 Catwoman, Selina Kyle C	.10	.25
9 Commissioner Gordon, James Gordon U	.20	.50
10 Dick Grayson Nightwing, High-Flying Acrobat R	2.00	4.00
11 Dick Grayson Nightwing, Defender of Bludhaven C	.10	.25
12 Dick Grayson Robin, Sidekick R	1.25	3.00
13 Dinah Laurel Lance Black Canary, Canary Cry C	.10	.25
14 GCPD Officer, Army C	.10	.25
15 Harvey Bullock, GCPD Detective U	.20	.50
16 Huntress, Helena Rosa Bertinelli C	.10	.25
17 Lady Shiva, Sandra Woosan C	.10	.25
18 Lucius Fox, Wayne Enterprises Executive R	.40	1.00
19 Spoiler, Stephanie Brown U	.20	.50
20 Superman, Big Blue Boy Scout R	2.50	6.00
21 Tim Drake Robin, Young Detective C	.10	.25
22 Batarang U	.20	.50
23 Batcave R	.75	2.00
24 Batmobile R	1.25	3.00
25 Batplane U	.20	.50
26 Bat-Signal U	.20	.50
27 Clocktower C	.10	.25
28 Dynamic Duo U	.20	.50
29 Fizzle R	2.00	5.00
30 GCPD Headquarters U	.20	.50
31 Utility Belt U	.20	.50
32 Wayne Enterprises R	.40	1.00
33 Wayne Manor U	.20	.50
34 Bart Allen Kid Flash, Speedster C	.10	.25
35 Beast Boy, Garfield Logan R	.40	1.00
36 Cassie Sandsmark Wonder Girl, Zeus's Chosen C	.10	.25
37 Connor Kent Superboy, Tactile Telekinetic C	.10	.25
38 Dick Grayson Nightwing, Titan Leader C	.10	.25
39 Donna Troy Wonder Girl, Amazon Warrior R	1.50	4.00
40 Dawn Granger Dove, Agent of Order C	.10	.25
41 Garth Tempest, Atlantean Sorcerer R	2.00	5.00
42 Hank Hall Hawk, Agent of Chaos C	.10	.25
43 Kole, Kole Weathers U	.20	.50
44 Koriand'r Starfire, Alien Princess C	.10	.25
45 Mirage, Miriam Delgado U	.20	.50
46 Omen, Lilith Clay R	.40	1.00
47 Pantha, Subject X-24 C	.10	.25
48 Phantasm, Danny Chase R	.75	2.00
49 Raven, Daughter of Trigon R	1.25	3.00
50 Red Star, Leonid Kovar U	.20	.50
51 Roy Harper Arsenal, Sharpshooter C	.10	.25
52 Terra, Tara Markov R	1.00	2.50
53 Tim Drake Robin, The Boy Wonder C	.10	.25
54 Vic Stone Cyborg, Human Machine C	.10	.25
55 Circle Defense U	.20	.50
56 Heroic Sacrifice R	.75	2.00
57 Liberty Island Base U	.20	.50
58 Optitron R	.75	2.00
59 Tamaran U	.20	.50
60 Teen Titans Go! C	.10	.25
61 Titans Tower U	.20	.50
62 T-Jet U	.20	.50
63 USS Argus R	.40	1.00
64 Bane, The Man Who Broke the Bat C	.10	.25
65 Charaxes, Drury Walker C	.10	.25
66 Firefly, Garfield Lynns R	.60	1.50
67 Harley Quinn, Dr. Harleen Quinzel C	.10	.25
68 Killer Croc, Waylon Jones C	.10	.25
69 Mad Hatter, Jervis Tetch R	.60	1.50
70 Man-Bat, Dr. Robert Langstrom C	.10	.25
71 Matt Hagen Clayface, Man of Clay C	.10	.25
72 Mr. Freeze, Dr. Victor Fries C	.10	.25
73 Mr. Zsasz, Victor Zsasz R	.60	1.50
74 Poison Ivy, Pamela Isley R	.75	2.00
75 Professor Hugo Strange, Psycho-Analyst C	.10	.25
76 Query and Echo, Double Trouble U	.20	.50
77 Ratcatcher, Otis Flannegan U	.20	.50
78 Scarecrow, Professor Jonathan Crane R	1.00	2.50
79 The Joker, Joker's Wild R	1.50	4.00
80 The Joker, Laughing Lunatic C	.10	.25
81 The Joker, The Clown Prince of Crime R	1.25	3.00
82 The Penguin, Oswald Chesterfield Cobblepot C	.10	.25
83 The Riddler, Edward Nygma U	.20	.50
84 Two-Face, Harvey Dent U	.20	.50
85 Ventriloquist Scarface, Arnold Wesker R	.60	1.50
86 Arkham Asylum U	.20	.50
87 Blackgate Prison R	.60	1.50
88 Cracking the Vault R	.40	1.00
89 Fear and Confusion C	.10	.25
90 Kidnapping U	.20	.50
91 No Man's Land U	.20	.50
92 Paralyzing Kiss U	.20	.50
93 Prison Break U	.20	.50
94 Riddle Me This U	.20	.50
95 Rigged Elections R	.60	1.50
96 Assassin Initiate, Army C	.10	.25
97 Bane, Ubu C	.10	.25
98 Dr. Tzin-Tzin, Master of Hypnosis C	.10	.25
99 Hassim, Loyal Retainer U	.20	.50
100 Josef Witschi, Talia's Assistant U	.20	.50
101 Kyle Abbot, Wolf in Man's Clothing C	.10	.25
102 Lady Shiva, Master Assassin R	.60	1.50
103 Malaq, Money Man U	.20	.50
104 Ra's al Ghul, Immortal Villain C	.10	.25
105 Ra's al Ghul, Master Swordsman C	.10	.25
106 Ra's al Ghul, The Demon's Head R	.60	1.50
107 Talia, Daughter of the Demon's Head R	.60	1.50
108 Thuggee, Army C	.10	.25
109 Ubu, Ra's al Ghul's Bodyguard C	.10	.25
110 Whisper A'Daire, Cold-Blooded Manipulator C	.10	.25
111 Clench Virus U	.20	.50
112 Dual Nature R	.40	1.00
113 Flying Fortress U	.20	.50
114 Lazarus Pit C	.10	.25
115 Mountain Stronghold U	.20	.50
116 Remake the World R	.40	1.00
117 The Shrike R	.40	1.00
118 Tower of Babel R	.60	1.50
119 Wheel of Plagues R	.40	1.00
120 Dr. Light, Arthur Light U	.20	.50
121 Gizmo, Mikron O'Jeneus U	.20	.50
122 Jinx, Elemental Sorceress U	.20	.50
123 Mammoth, Baran Flinders R	.40	1.00
124 Neutron, Nat Tryon R	.40	1.00
125 Psimon, Dr. Simon Jones R	.40	1.00
126 Shimmer, Selinda Flinders U	.20	.50
127 The Underworld Star U	.20	.50
128 Deathstroke the Terminator, Slade Wilson R	.75	2.00
129 Black Mask, Roman Sionis U	.20	.50
130 Blackfire, Komand'r R	.40	1.00
131 Brother Blood, Leader of the Church of Blood C	.10	.25
132 Ferak, Army C	.10	.25
133 King Snake, Sir Edmund Dorrance U	.20	.50
134 Lady Vic, Lady Elaine Marsh-Morton U	.20	.50
135 Lightning, Travis Williams U	.20	.50
136 Lockup, Lyle Bolton U	.20	.50
137 The Demon, Jason Blood R	.60	1.50
138 The Demon, Etrigan R	.60	1.50
139 Thunder, Gan Williams U	.20	.50
140 Trigon, The Terrible R	.40	1.00
141 Wildebeest, Army C	.10	.25
142 A Death in the Family R	.40	1.00
143 Airborne Assault U	.20	.50
144 Break You C	.10	.25
145 Combat Reflexes C	.10	.25
146 Concrete Jungle R	.40	1.00
147 Crossbow C	.10	.25
148 Escrima Sticks U	.20	.50
149 Fast Getaway C	.10	.25
150 From the Shadows C	.10	.25
151 Gone But Not Forgotten U	.20	.50
152 GothCorp R	.40	1.00
153 Have a Blast! R	1.25	3.00
154 Hidden Surveillance R	.40	1.00
155 Home Surgery U	.20	.50
156 Last Laugh U	.20	.50
157 Mega-Blast C	.10	.25
158 Museum Heist R	.40	1.00
159 My Beloved U	.20	.50
160 Shape Change U	.20	.50
161 Tag Team C	.10	.25
162 The Brave and the Bold U	.20	.50
163 Total Anarchy R	.40	1.00
164 Twin Firearms U	.20	.50
165 World's Finest C	.10	.25

2004 Vs System Marvel Origins

Card	Low	High
COMPLETE SET (220)	40.00	80.00
BOOSTER BOX (24 PACKS)	20.00	40.00
BOOSTER PACK (14 CARDS)	1.00	2.00
*FOIL: .8X TO 2X BASIC CARDS		
RELEASED IN APRIL 2004		
1 Archangel, Warren Worthington III C	.10	.25
2 Banshee, Sean Cassidy C	.10	.25
3 Beast, Dr. Henry McCoy U	.20	.50
4 Bishop, Lucas Bishop C	.10	.25
5 Colossus, Peter Rasputin C	.10	.25
6 Cyclops, Scott Summers C	.10	.25
7 Cyclops, Slim C	.10	.25
8 Dazzler, Alison Blaire C	.10	.25
9 Forge, Cheyenne Mystic R	.40	1.00
10 Gambit, Remy LeBeau U	.20	.50
11 Havok, Alex Summers R	.40	1.00
12 Iceman, Bobby Drake U	.20	.50
13 Jean Grey, Marvel Girl C	.10	.25
14 Jean Grey, Phoenix Force R	1.00	2.50
15 Longshot, Rebel Freedom Fighter R	.75	2.00
16 Moira MacTaggert, World-Renowned Geneticist R	.40	1.00
17 Nightcrawler, Fuzzy Elf R	1.00	2.50
18 Nightcrawler, Kurt Wagner U	.20	.50
19 Professor X, Charles Xavier C	.10	.25
20 Professor X, World's Most Powerful Telepath R	.50	1.25
21 Psylocke, Betsy Braddock C	.10	.25
22 Rogue, Power Absorption R	.75	2.00
23 Rogue, Powerhouse U	.20	.50
24 Shadowcat, Kitty Pryde C	.10	.25
25 Storm, Ororo Munroe C	.10	.25
26 Storm, Weather Witch R	1.25	3.00
27 Wolverine, Berserker Rage R	1.00	2.50
28 Wolverine, James Howlett U	.20	.50
29 Wolverine, Logan C	.10	.25
30 Cerebro R	1.00	2.50
31 Children of the Atom R	.75	2.00
32 Danger Room U	.20	.50
33 Fastball Special U	.20	.50
34 Muir Island U	.20	.50
35 Professor Xavier's Mansion R	.50	1.25
36 The Blackbird R	.40	1.00
37 X-Corporation U	.20	.50
38 Xavier's Dream R	.50	1.25
39 Xavier's School for Gifted Youngsters U	.20	.50
40 Alicia Masters, Blind Sculptress R	.40	1.00
41 Ant Man, Scott Lang C	.10	.25
42 Crystal, Inhuman C	.10	.25
43 Frankie Raye, Herald of Galactus U	.20	.50
44 Franklin Richards, Child Prodigy R	.50	1.25
45 Ghost Rider, New Fantastic Four R	1.00	2.50
46 Hulk, New Fantastic Four R	1.00	2.50
47 Human Torch, Johnny Storm C	.10	.25
48 Human Torch, Hotshot R	.60	1.50
49 Human Torch, Super Nova U	.20	.50
50 Invisible Woman, The Invisible Girl U	.20	.50
51 Invisible Woman, Sue Storm C	.10	.25
52 Invisible Woman, Sue Richards R	.40	1.00
53 Luke Cage, Hero for Hire U	.20	.50
54 Medusa, Inhuman C	.10	.25
55 Mr. Fantastic, Reed Richards C	.10	.25
56 Mr. Fantastic, Stretch U	.20	.50
57 Mr. Fantastic, Scientific Genius R	.75	2.00
58 She-Hulk, Jennifer Walters U	.20	.50
59 She-Hulk, Green Jeans C	.10	.25
60 She-Thing, Sharon Ventura C	.10	.25
61 Spider-Man, New Fantastic Four R	1.00	2.50
62 Thing, Ben Grimm C	.10	.25
63 Thing, Heavy Hitter R	1.00	2.50
64 Thing, The Ever-Lovin' Blue-Eyed Thing U	.20	.50
65 Wolverine, New Fantastic Four R	1.25	3.00
66 A Child Named Valeria R	.40	1.00
67 Antarctic Research Base R	.40	1.00
68 Baxter Building U	.20	.50
69 Cosmic Radiation R	.50	1.25
70 Fantasticar R	.50	1.25
71 Four Freedoms Plaza R	.40	1.00
72 It's Clobberin' Time! R	1.50	4.00
73 Signal Flare R	.40	1.00
74 The Pogo Plane R	.40	1.00
75 Yancy Street U	.20	.50
76 Avalanche, Dominic Petros U	.20	.50
77 Blob, Fred Dukes C	.10	.25
78 Destiny, Irene Adler C	.10	.25
79 Lorelei, Savage Land Mutate C	.10	.25
80 Magneto, Eric Lehnsherr U	.20	.50
81 Magneto, Master of Magnetism R	1.00	2.50
82 Magneto, Lord Magnus R	1.00	2.50
83 Mastermind, Jason Wyngarde U	.20	.50
84 Mystique, Raven Darkholme U	.20	.50
85 Mystique, Shape-Changing Assassin C	.10	.25
86 Phantazia, Eileen Harsaw C	.10	.25
87 Pyro, St. John Allerdyce C	.10	.25
88 Quicksilver, Pietro Maximoff C	.10	.25
89 Quicksilver, Speed Demon R	.75	2.00
90 Rogue, Anna Raven C	.10	.25
91 Sabretooth, Feral Rage R	.50	1.25
92 Sabretooth, Victor Creed C	.10	.25
93 Sauron, Dr. Karl Lykos C	.10	.25
94 Scarlet Witch, Wanda Maximoff C	.10	.25
95 Toad, Mortimer Toynbee C	.10	.25
96 Unus, Angelo Unuscione U	.20	.50
97 Asteroid M U	.20	.50
98 Avalon Space Station U	.20	.50
99 Genosha R	1.00	2.50
100 Global Domination R	.40	1.00
101 Lost City U	.20	.50
102 Mutant Supremacy R	.50	1.25
103 Savage Land U	.20	.50
104 The Mutant Menace U	.20	.50
105 The New Brotherhood U	.20	.50
106 War On Humanity U	.20	.50
107 Boris, Personal Servant of Dr. Doom R	1.50	4.00
108 Darkoth, Major Desmund Pitt U	.20	.50
109 Doom Guards, Army C	.10	.25
110 Doom-Bot, Army U	.40	1.00
111 Dr. Doom, Diabolic Genius U	.20	.50
112 Dr. Doom, Victor Von Doom C	.10	.25
113 Dr. Doom, Lord of Latveria R	1.25	3.00
114 Dragon Man, Experimental Monster C	.10	.25
115 Kristoff Von Doom, The Boy Who Would Be Doom U	.20	.50
116 Rama-Tut, Pharaoh from the 30th Century R	.40	1.00
117 Robot Destroyer, Army R	.40	1.00
118 Robot Enforcer, Army C	.10	.25
119 Robot Seeker, Army C	.10	.25
120 Robot Sentry, Army C	.10	.25
121 Sub-Mariner, Ally of Doom R	.75	2.00
122 Tibetan Monks, Army C	.10	.25
123 Titania, Mary MacPherran C	.10	.25
124 Victor Von Doom II, Son of Doom U	.20	.50
125 Volcana, Marsha Rosenberg U	.20	.50
126 Bitter Rivals U	.20	.50
127 Doom Triumphant R	.50	1.25
128 Doom's Throne Room R	.20	.50
129 Doomstadt C	.10	.25
130 Faces of Doom U	.20	.50
131 Latveria R	.40	1.00
132 Micro-Size C	.10	.25
133 Mystical Paralysis U	.20	.50
134 Power Compressor R	.40	1.00
135 Reign of Terror R	.50	1.25
136 The Power Cosmic R	.50	1.25
137 Bastion, Leader of Operation: Zero Tolerance R	.75	2.00
138 Boliver Trask, Creator of the Sentinel Program R	.75	2.00
139 Master Mold, Sentinel Supreme R	.75	2.00
140 Nimrod, Mutant Hunter U	.20	.50
141 Senator Kelly, Anti-Mutant Advocate U	.20	.50
142 Sentinel Mark I, Army C	.10	.25
143 Sentinel Mark II, Army C	.10	.25
144 Sentinel Mark IV, Army U	.20	.50
145 Wild Sentinel, Army C	.10	.25
146 Combat Protocols U	.20	.50
147 Micro-Sentinels R	.50	1.25
148 Orbital Sentinel Base U	.20	.50
149 Primary Directive R	.40	1.00
150 Prime Sentinels U	.20	.50
151 Project: Wide Awake U	.20	.50
152 Reconstruction Program C	.10	.25
153 Search and Destroy U	.20	.50
154 South American Sentinel Base U	.20	.50
155 Underground Sentinel Base R	.50	1.25
156 Annihilus, Destroyer of Life R	.40	1.00
157 Blastaar, King of Baluur R	.50	1.25
158 Negative Zone U	.20	.50
159 Skrull Soldier, Army C	.10	.25
160 Super Skrull, Engineered Super-Soldier R	.75	2.00
161 Apocalypse, En Sabah Nur R	1.00	2.50
162 Arcade, Master of Murderworld U	.20	.50
163 Black Tom, Thomas Cassidy C	.10	.25
164 Dark Phoenix, Cosmic Entity R	2.00	5.00
165 Juggernaut, Cain Marko R	1.25	3.00
166 Lady Deathstrike, Yuriko Oyama R	.50	1.25
167 Mojo, Ruler of Mojoworld U	.20	.50
168 Mr. Sinister, Dr. Nathaniel Essex R	.75	2.00
169 Onslaught, Psionic Spawn of Xavier and Magneto R	1.25	3.00
170 Puppet Master, Philip Masters C	.10	.25
171 Random Punks, Army C	.10	.25
172 Spiral, Ricochet Rita C	.10	.25
173 Acrobatic Dodge C	.10	.25
174 Advanced Hardware C	.10	.25
175 Backfire C	.10	.25
176 Base of Operations C	.10	.25
177 Betrayal R	.50	1.25
178 Blind Sided R	.40	1.00
179 Borrowed Blade C	.10	.25
180 Burn Rubber C	.10	.25
181 Charge! U	.20	.50
182 Common Enemy U	.20	.50
183 Cover Fire C	.10	.25
184 Dual Sidearms C	.10	.25
185 Entangle U	.20	.50
186 Fall Back! U	.20	.50
187 Finishing Move C	.10	.25
188 Flame Trap R	.60	1.50
189 Flying Kick C	.10	.25
190 Focused Blast U	.20	.50
191 Foiled R	.75	2.00
192 Friendly Fire U	.20	.50
193 Gamma Bomb R	1.00	2.50
194 Greater of Two Evils R	.50	1.25
195 Heroes United U	.20	.50
196 Ka-Boom! R	1.25	3.00
197 Kevlar Body Armor U	.20	.50
198 Last Stand C	.10	.25
199 Marvel Team-Up U	.20	.50
200 Medical Attention C	.10	.25
201 Mutant Nation U	.20	.50
202 Nasty Surprise C	.10	.25
203 Night Vision U	.20	.50
204 Not So Fast U	.20	.50
205 One-Two Punch C	.10	.25
206 Overload U	.20	.50
207 Overpowered U	.20	.50
208 Personal Force Field U	.20	.50
209 Political Pressure R	.50	1.25
210 Press the Attack U	.20	.50
211 Reconnaissance U	.20	.50
212 Relocation R	.50	1.25
213 Salvage R	.60	1.50
214 Savage Beatdown R	4.00	10.00
215 Surprise Attack C	.10	.25
216 Swift Escape U	.20	.50
217 Team Tactics C	.10	.25
218 Tech Upgrade C	.10	.25
219 Unlikely Allies U	.20	.50
220 Unstable Molecules C	.10	.25

2004 Vs System Superman Man of Steel

Card	Low	High
COMPLETE SET (165)	20.00	40.00
BOOSTER BOX (24 PACKS)	15.00	30.00
BOOSTER PACK (14 CARDS)	.75	1.25
*FOIL: .8X TO 2X BASIC CARDS		
RELEASED IN NOVEMBER 2004		
1 Alpha Centurion, Marcus Aelius C	.10	.25
2 Cir-El Supergirl, Daughter of Tomorrow C	.10	.25
3 Connor Kent Superboy, Kon-El U	.20	.50
4 Dubbilex, DNAlien U	.20	.50
5 Eradicator, Soul of Krypton C	.10	.25
6 Gangbuster, Jose Delgado C	.10	.25
7 Girl 13, Traci Thirteen U	.20	.50
8 Jimmy Olsen, Superman's Pal U	.20	.50
9 John Henry Irons Steel, Peerless Engineer C	.10	.25
10 Kara Zor-El Supergirl, Last Daughter of Krypton C	.10	.25
11 Krypto, Superdog R	.40	1.00
12 Lana Lang, Smallville Sweetheart U	.20	.50
13 Linda Danvers Supergirl, Matrix R	.75	2.00
14 Lois Lane, Star Reporter U	.20	.50
15 Perry White, Chief R	.60	1.50
16 Professor Emil Hamilton, Garrulous Genius C	.10	.25
17 Rose Thorn, Rose Forrest U	.20	.50
18 Scorn, Ceritak C	.10	.25
19 Strange Visitor, Sharon Vance R	.40	1.00
20 Superman, Blue R	.10	.25
21 Superman, Clark Kent C	.40	1.00
22 Superman, Kal-El U	1.50	4.00
23 Superman, Man of Steel R	.10	.25
24 Superman, Red C	.10	.25
25 Superman, Robots Army C	1.25	3.00
26 Cadmus Labs U	.20	.50
27 Daily Planet R	.60	1.50
28 Entropy Aegis Armor R	.40	1.00
29 Fortress of Solitude U	.20	.50
30 Kandor R	.40	1.00
31 Last Son of Krypton R	.60	1.50
32 Man of Tomorrow U	.20	.50
33 Super Speed U	.20	.50
34 X-Ray Vision R	.60	1.50
35 Beautiful Dreamer, Forever People U	.20	.50
36 Big Barda, Barda Free C	.10	.25
37 Big Bear, Forever People C	.10	.25
38 Fastbak, Sky Scorcher C	.10	.25
39 Forager, Bug Warrior C	.10	.25
40 Himon, Enigmatic Researcher U	.20	.50
41 Infinity Man, Drax R	.40	1.00
42 Izaya Highfather, The Inheritor C	.10	.25
43 Lightray, Solis C	.10	.25
44 Lonar, Explorer U	.20	.50
45 Mark Moonrider, Forever People C	.10	.25
46 Metron, Time Traveler C	.10	.25
47 Orion, Dog of War R	.40	1.00
48 Orion, True Son of Darkseid C	.10	.25
49 Scott Free Mister Miracle, Escape Artist R	.60	1.50
50 Serifan, Forever People C	.10	.25
51 Takion Hightfather, Josh Saunders R	.40	1.00
52 Vykin, Forever People U	.20	.50
53 Astro Force R	.75	2.00
54 Dog of War U	.20	.50
55 Escape Artist U	.20	.50
56 Forever People R	.75	2.00
57 New Genesis R	.75	2.00
58 Supercycle U	.20	.50
59 The Prophecy Fulfilled R	.60	1.50
60 The Source R	2.00	5.00
61 Atomic Skull, Joe Martin U	.20	.50
62 Bizarro, Imperfect Duplicate R	1.00	2.50
63 Brainiac 2.5, Vril Dox C	.10	.25
64 Dominus, Tuoni R	.60	1.50
65 Doomsday, Armageddon Creature R	.40	1.00
66 Encantadora, Lourdes Lucero C	.10	.25
67 Eradicator, Doctor David Connor C	.10	.25
68 General Zod, Ruler of Pokolistan R	.40	1.00
69 Gog, Nemesis C	.10	.25
70 Hank Henshaw Cyborg, Evil Imposter R	.60	1.50
71 Hope, Amazon Bodyguard U	.20	.50
72 Intergang, Army U	.20	.50
73 Lex Luthor, Power Armor C	.10	.25
74 Lex Luthor, President Luthor R	1.00	2.50
75 Massacre, Alien Bounty Hunter U	.20	.50
76 Mercy, Amazon Bodyguard C	.10	.25
77 Metallo, John Corben C	.10	.25
78 Mongal, Ruler of Almerac C	.10	.25
79 Mongul, Tyrant of Warworld C	.10	.25
80 Mr. Mxyzptlk, Fifth Dimension Imp U	.20	.50
81 Parasite, Rudy Jones C	.10	.25
82 Prankster, Oswald Loomis U	.20	.50
83 Satanus, Evil Incarnate R	.40	1.00
84 Silver Banshee, Siobhan McDougal C	.10	.25
85 Talia, LexCorp CEO U	.20	.50
86 Winslow Schott Toyman, Crooked Craftsman U	.20	.50
87 Bizarro World R	.40	1.00
88 Brainiac's Ship R	.60	1.50
89 Feeding Time! U	.20	.50
90 Kryptonite R	.60	1.50
91 LexCorp U	.20	.50
92 Revenge Pact R	.60	1.50
93 State of the Union R	.40	1.00
94 Suicide Slums U	.20	.50
95 Toy Soldiers U	.20	.50
96 Warworld R	.40	1.00
97 Amazing Grace, Manipulator R	.40	1.00
98 Bernadeth, Leader of Female Furies C	.10	.25
99 Brimstone, Engine of Destruction R	.40	1.00
100 Darkseid, Lord of Apokolips R	1.00	2.50
101 Darkseid, Uxas U	.20	.50
102 Desaad, Royal Torturer C	.10	.25
103 Devilance, The Pursuer C	.10	.25
104 Glorious Godfrey, Persuader U	.20	.50
105 Gole, Deep Six U	.20	.50
106 Granny Goodness, Everyone's Favorite Granny C	.10	.25
107 Hunger Dogs, Army U	.20	.50
108 Jaffar, Deep Six U	.20	.50
109 Kalibak, Unworthy Son C	.10	.25
110 Kanto, Darkseid's Assassin C	.10	.25
111 Kurin, Deep Six U	.20	.50
112 Shaligo, Deep Six C	.10	.25
113 Slig, Deep Six C	.10	.25
114 Steppenwolf, Darkseid's General C	.10	.25
115 Superman, False Son R	.20	.50
116 Topkick, Parademon Drill Instructor U	.20	.50
117 Trok, Deep Six C	.10	.25
118 Anti-Life Equation R	.40	1.00
119 Apokolips R	.40	1.00
120 Armagetto U	.20	.50
121 Beta Club U	.20	.50
122 Firepits of Apokolips U	.20	.50
123 Granny Loves You U	.20	.50
124 Happiness Home R	.40	1.00
125 Hordes of Apokolips U	.20	.50
126 Omega Beams R	.40	1.00
127 Ride of the Black Racer R	.40	1.00

128 Blood Feud U .20 .50
129 Phantom Zone U .20 .50
130 The Exchange R .40 1.00
131 Barbara Gordon Batgirl, Guardian of Gotham R .75 2.00
132 Jason Todd Robin, Crime Fighter R .75 2.00
133 Spoiler Robin, The Girl Wonder U .20 .50
134 Detective Work R 1.00 2.50
135 Donna Troy Troia, Child of Myth R .75 2.00
136 Roy Harper Speedy, Mercurial Marksman R .40 1.00
137 Wally West Kid Flash, Fastest Teen Alive R .40 1.00
138 New Teen Titans R 1.00 2.50
139 Blockbuster, Roland Desmond U .20 .50
140 Maxie Zeus, God Complex U .20 .50
141 The Joker, Emperor Joker R .75 2.00
142 Smiles, Everyone! R .40 1.00
143 Bronze Tiger, Benjamin Turner U .20 .50
144 Merlyn, Deadly Archer U .20 .50
145 Pit of Madness R .40 1.00
146 The Demon's Head R .40 1.00
147 Charger, Power Conduit U .20 .50
148 Deuce, Miss Perception U .20 .50
149 Imperiex, The Beginning and The End R .40 1.00
150 Back to Back C .10 .25
151 Boom Tube C .10 .25
152 Female Furies C .10 .25
153 Heat Vision C .10 .25
154 I Hate Magic! C .10 .25
155 Men of Steel C .10 .25
156 Metropolis C .10 .25
157 Mother Box U .20 .50
158 Narrow Escape C .10 .25
159 Path of Destruction C .10 .25
160 Phantom Zone Projector U .20 .50
161 Play Time C .10 .25
162 Royal Decree U .20 .50
163 Stopped Cold C .10 .25
164 Super Strength C .10 .25
165 Up, Up, and Away C .10 .25

2004 Vs System Web of Spider-Man

COMPLETE SET (165) 25.00 50.00
BOOSTER BOX (24 PACKS) 20.00 40.00
BOOSTER PACK (14 CARDS) .75 1.50
*FOIL: .8X TO 2X BASIC CARDS
RELEASED IN SEPTEMBER 2004
1 Black Cat, Felicia Hardy C .10 .25
2 Daredevil, The Man Without Fear C .10 .25
3 Madame Web, Cassandra Webb C .10 .25
4 Prowler, Hobie Brown C .10 .25
5 Punisher, Vigilante U .20 .50
6 Solo, James Bourne C .10 .25
7 Spider-Man, Friendly Neighborhood Spider-Man C .10 .25
8 Spider-Man, The Amazing Spider-Man R 1.25 3.00
9 Nova, Richard Rider U .20 .50
10 Daily Bugle U .20 .50
11 ESU Science Lab U .20 .50
12 Spider Senses U .20 .50
13 Twist of Fate U .20 .50
14 Dr. Octopus, Doc Ock R 1.25 3.00
15 Dr. Octopus, Otto Octavius C .10 .25
16 Electro, Maxwell Dillon U .20 .50
17 Green Goblin, Norman Osborn C .10 .25
18 Kraven the Hunter, Sergei Kravinoff C .10 .25
19 Lizard, Dr. Curtis Connors C .10 .25
20 Rhino, Alex O'Hirn C .10 .25
21 Venom, Eddie Brock U .20 .50
22 Vulture, Adrian Toomes C .10 .25
23 Doc Ock's Lab U .20 .50
24 Osborn Industries U .20 .50
25 Sadistic Choice U .20 .50
26 Sinister Salvo U .20 .50
27 Alley-Oop! C .10 .25
28 Crushing Blow C .10 .25
29 Jetpack C .10 .25
30 No Fear C .10 .25
31 Smoke Screen C .10 .25
32 Aunt May, May Parker U .20 .50
33 Black Cat, Master Thief U .20 .50
34 Cardiac, Elias Wirtham U .20 .50
35 Cloak, Tyrone Johnson C .10 .25
36 Dagger, Tandy Bowen U .20 .50
37 Dusk, Cassie St. Commons C .10 .25
38 Ezekiel, Spirit of the Spider C .10 .25
39 Firestar, Hot Stuff R .50 1.25
40 Hornet, Eddie McDonough C .10 .25
41 Human Torch, Friendly Rival C .10 .25
42 Iceman, Cool Customer C .10 .25
43 Jessica Drew Spider-Woman, Venom Blast U .20 .50
44 Julia Carpenter Spider-Woman, Web Weaver R .75 2.00
45 Mary Jane Watson, MJ R 1.25 3.00
46 Mattie Franklin Spider-Woman, Gift of Power U .20 .50
47 Prodigy, Richie Gilmore C .10 .25
48 Puma, Thomas Fireheart C .10 .25
49 Ricochet, Johnny Gallo C .10 .25
50 Rocket Racer, Robert Farrell C .10 .25
51 Scarlet Spider, Ben Reilly C .10 .25
52 Silver Sable, Silver Sablinova C .10 .25
53 Spider-Man, Alien Symbiote C .10 .25
54 Spider-Man, Cosmic Spider-Man R 2.50 6.00
55 Wild Pack, Army C .10 .25
56 Will O' The Wisp, Jackson Arvad R .50 1.25
57 Ace Reporter R .50 1.25
58 Armored Spider Suit U .20 .50
59 Costume Change U .20 .50
60 Fun and Games R .50 1.25
61 Going My Way? U .20 .50
62 Midtown High School C .10 .25
63 My Hero U .20 .50
64 Nice Try! R .50 1.25
65 Spider-Tracer R .50 1.25
66 Sticky Situation U .20 .50
67 Tragic Loss U .20 .50
68 Unexpected Mutation U .20 .50
69 Alistair Smythe, Ultimate Spider Slayer R .50 1.25
70 Beetle, Abner Jenkins C .10 .25
71 Boomerang, Fred Myers C .10 .25
72 Carnage, Cletus Kasady R 1.00 2.50
73 Chameleon, Dmitri Smerdyakov C .10 .25
74 Green Goblin, Altered Ego C .10 .25
75 Hammerhead, Gangster C .10 .25
76 Hobgoblin, Roderick Kingsley C .10 .25
77 Hydro-Man, Morris Bench C .10 .25
78 Jackal, Dr. Miles Warren C .10 .25
79 Kaine, Imperfect Clone C .10 .25
80 Kingpin, Crime Boss R 1.00 2.50
81 Man-Wolf, John Jameson C .10 .25
82 Morbius, Dr. Michael Morbius R 1.00 2.50
83 Mysterio, Quentin Beck R .50 1.25
84 Sandman, William Baker R 1.00 2.50
85 Scorpion, MacDonald Gargan C .10 .25
86 Shocker, Herman Schultz C .10 .25
87 Shriek, Frances Barrison U .20 .50
88 Silvermane, Silvio Manfredi C .10 .25
89 Speed Demon, James Sanders C .10 .25
90 The Rose, Richard Fisk R .50 1.25
91 Tinkerer, Phineas Mason R .50 1.25
92 Tombstone, Lonnie Lincoln R .75 2.00
93 Venom, Alien Symbiote R 2.00 5.00
94 Dangerous Experiment R .75 2.00
95 Fisk Towers R .50 1.25
96 Get Him My Petsss R .50 1.25
97 Goblin Glider U .20 .50
98 Hired Goons C .10 .25
99 Lion's Den C .10 .25
100 Oscorp Board Room U .20 .50
101 Rejuvenation U .20 .50
102 Spider Slayers U .20 .50
103 Archangel, Angel of Death U .20 .50
104 Emma Frost, Headmistress of Xavier's Academy R 1.50 4.00
105 John Proudstar Thunderbird, Apache Warrior U .20 .50
106 Shadowcat, Pride of the X-Men U .20 .50
107 Sunfire, Shiro Yoshida R .50 1.25
108 Aerial Supremacy U .20 .50
109 Bamf! R 1.25 3.00
110 Madripoor U .20 .50
111 Power Nexus R .75 2.00
112 Siege Perilous R .50 1.25
113 Ultimate Sacrifice R 1.25 3.00
114 Silver Surfer, Norrin Radd R 2.50 6.00
115 Wyatt Wingfoot, Keewazi Adventurer U .20 .50
116 Marvel's First Family R .75 2.00
117 Pier 4 R .50 1.25
118 Supernova U .20 .50
119 Mimic, Calvin Rankin R 1.00 2.50
120 Post, Kevin Tremain R .50 1.25
121 Thornn, Feral Hunter U .20 .50
122 Insignificant Threat R .50 1.25
123 Misappropriation U .20 .50
124 Rise to Power R .75 2.00
125 Volcanic Base R .50 1.25
126 Dr. Hauptmann, Diabolic Inventor U .20 .50
127 Purple Man, Zebediah Killgrave U .20 .50
128 Terrax, Tyros R .50 1.25
129 Decoy Program R .50 1.25
130 Devil's Due R .75 2.00
131 Latverian Embassy R .50 1.25
132 Mark II, Number II, Leader Unit R 1.00 2.50
133 Sentinel Mark V, Army C .10 .25
134 Sentinel Mark III, Army C .10 .25
135 Tri-Sentinel, Super Sentinel R .50 1.25
136 Next Generation Technology R .75 2.00
137 Termination Sequence R .75 2.00
138 Wave of Sentinels R .50 1.25
139 Lyja, The Lazerfist U .20 .50
140 Deathlok, Luther Manning R 1.00 2.50
141 J. Jonah Jameson, Sensationalist R .75 2.00
142 Mole Man, Leader of the Moloids U .20 .50
143 Bad Press R .50 1.25
144 Big Bully C .10 .25
145 Breaking Story U .20 .50
146 Clone Saga U .20 .50
147 Com Link U .20 .50
148 Crowd Control C .10 .25
149 Fight to the Finish U .20 .50
150 Flamethrower R .50 1.25
151 Forced Allegiance U .20 .50
152 Grounded C .10 .25
153 Mojoverse C .10 .25
154 Murderworld R 1.00 2.50
155 Pinned U .20 .50
156 Pleasant Distraction U .20 .50
157 Rapier U .20 .50
158 Rise from the Grave R .50 1.25
159 Sinister Six U .20 .50
160 Sonic Gun U .20 .50
161 Sucker Punch U .20 .50
162 Surrounded C .10 .25
163 Thinking Outside the Box R .50 1.25
164 Time Platform R .50 1.25
165 Unmasked U .20 .50

2005 Vs System The Avengers

COMPLETE SET (220) 25.00 50.00
BOOSTER BOX (24 PACKS) 20.00 40.00
BOOSTER PACK (14 CARDS) 1.00 2.00
*FOIL: .8X TO 2X BASIC CARDS
RELEASED IN AUGUST 2005
1 Beast, Furry Blue Scientist C .10 .25
2 Black Panther, T'challa U .20 .50
3 Captain America, Steve Rogers C .10 .25
4 Captain America, Super Soldier R 1.00 2.50
5 Carol Danvers Warbird, Galactic Adventurer C .10 .25
6 Dane Whitman Black Knight, Heroic Paladin C .10 .25
7 Falcon, Sam Wilson C .10 .25
8 Hank Pym Ant Man, Diminutive Hero C .10 .25
9 Hank Pym Giant Man, Towering Titan U .20 .50
10 Hank Pym Goliath, Giant Genius C .10 .25
11 Hank Pym Yellowjacket, Pym Particle Creator C .10 .25
12 Hawkeye, Clinton Barton C .10 .25
13 Hercules, Son of Zeus U .20 .50
14 Hulk, Gamma Rage R .50 1.25
15 Iron Man, Invincible C .10 .25
16 Iron Man, Tony Stark C .10 .25
17 Jarvis, Honorary Avenger R 1.00 2.50
18 Monica Rambeau Captain Marvel, Lady of Light R1.00 2.50
19 Natasha Romanoff Black Widow, Super Spy U .20 .50
20 Quicksilver, Mutant Avenger C .10 .25
21 Rick Jones, A Hero's Best Friend U .20 .50
22 Scarlet Witch, Mistress of Chaos Magic C .10 .25
23 She-Hulk, Gamma Bombshell C .10 .25
24 Thor, God of Thunder R 1.50 4.00
25 Thor, Odinson R 1.50 4.00
26 Vision, Synthetic Humanoid C .10 .25
27 Wasp, Janet Van Dyne-Pym C .10 .25
28 Wonder Man, Simon Williams U .20 .50
29 Avengers Assemble! R 2.00 5.00
30 Avengers Mansion R 1.00 2.50
31 Call Down the Lightning C .10 .25
32 Chaos Magic R .40 1.00
33 Earth's Mightiest Heroes R 1.25 3.00
34 Legendary Battles C .10 .25
35 Mjolnir R .50 1.25
36 Playroom C .10 .25
37 Pym Laboratories U .20 .50
38 Quinjet C .10 .25
39 Repel Attack C .10 .25
40 Repulsor Ray C .10 .25
41 Two Worlds, Team-Up C .10 .25
42 Walk Through Walls R .40 1.00
43 Albert Gaines Nuke, Atomic Powerhouse C .10 .25
44 Amphibian, Kingsley Rice R .40 1.00
45 Ape X, Xina C .10 .25
46 Arcanna, Arcanna Jones C .10 .25
47 Blue Eagle, James Dore Jr. C .10 .25
48 Doctor Decibel, Anton Decibel C .10 .25
49 Doctor Spectrum, Joe Ledger R .50 1.25
50 Foxfire, Olivia Underwood U .20 .50
51 Golden Archer, Wyatt McDonald C .10 .25
52 Haywire, Harold Danforth C .10 .25
53 Hyperion, Mark Milton C .10 .25
54 Hyperion, Sun God R .40 1.00
55 Inertia, Edith Freiberg C .10 .25
56 Lady Lark, Linda Lewis U .20 .50
57 Lamprey, Donald McQuiggan C .10 .25
58 Moonglow, Melissa Hanover C .10 .25
59 Nighthawk, Kyle Richmond C .10 .25
60 Power Princess, The Last Utopian R .40 1.00
61 Power Princess, Zarda C .10 .25
62 Quagmire, Jerome Meyers U .20 .50
63 Redstone, Michael Redstone U .20 .50
64 Shape, Malleable Mutant U .20 .50
65 Skymax, Skrullian Skymaster C .10 .25
66 Thermite, Sam Yurimoto C .10 .25
67 Tom Thumb, Thomas Thompson C .10 .25
68 Whizzer, Stanley Stewart U .20 .50
69 AIDA R .40 1.00
70 Airskimmer C .10 .25
71 Answer the Call C .10 .25
72 Behavior Modification Device, Team-Up C .10 .25
73 Eldritch Power C .10 .25
74 Hibernaculum C .10 .25
75 Other-Earth R .50 1.25
76 Panacea Potion U .20 .50
77 Peace in Our Time U .20 .50
78 Project Utopia R .40 1.00
79 Rocket Central R .40 1.00
80 Squadron City R .40 1.00
81 Supply Line U .20 .50
82 Utopia Isle U .20 .50
83 Beetle Mach 1, Reluctant Hero C .10 .25
84 Beetle Mach 2, Matthew Davis C .10 .25
85 Beetle Mach 3, Repentant Villain U .20 .50
86 Beetle Mach 4, New Team Leader C .10 .25
87 Blizzard, Donny Gill C .10 .25
88 Charcoal, Charles Burlingame C .10 .25
89 Dallas Riordan, Mayoral Aide C .10 .25
90 Dallas Riordan Vantage, Ionic Inheritor C .10 .25
91 Erik Josten Atlas, Ionic Powerhouse R .40 1.00
92 Erik Josten Atlas, Kosmos Convict U .20 .50
93 Genis-Vell Captain Marvel, Son of Mar-Vell R .50 1.25
94 Hawkeye, Leader by Example R .60 1.50
95 Helmut Zemo Citizen V, Tactician C .10 .25
96 Helmut Zemo Citizen V, Warmonger C .10 .25
97 Iron Man Cobalt Man, Avenger in Disguise C .10 .25
98 Jolt, Helen Takahama C .10 .25
99 Joystick, Janice Yanizesh U .20 .50
100 Karla Sofen Meteorite, Celestial Power R .40 1.00
101 Karla Sofen Meteorite, Twin Moonstones R .40 1.00
102 Melissa Gold Songbird, Heroine Unbound C .10 .25
103 Melissa Gold Songbird, Sonic Carapace U .20 .50
104 Ogre, Weaponsmith U .20 .50
105 Paul Ebersol Techno, Gadgeteer C .10 .25
106 Paul Ebersol Techno, Man of Metal C .10 .25
107 Plant Man Blackheath, Samuel Smithers C .10 .25
108 Radioactive Man, Reformed Renegade U .20 .50
109 Speed Demon, Second Chance Speedster U .20 .50
110 A Second Chance U .20 .50
111 Biomodem Satellite U .20 .50
112 Combat Maneuvers C .10 .25
113 Deadly Conspiracy C .10 .25
114 Justice, Like Lightning C .10 .25
115 Marvel's Most Wanted R .40 1.00
116 Mt. Charteris R .40 1.00
117 New Identity R 1.25 3.00
118 Project Liberator R .40 1.00
119 Stormfront-1, Team-Up C .10 .25
120 Thunder Jet C .10 .25
121 Thunderbolts Plaza R .40 1.00
122 V-Wing U .20 .50
123 Win-Lose Deal U .20 .50
124 Beetle, Armorsmith C .10 .25
125 Bulldozer, Wrecking Crew C .10 .25
126 Egghead, Elihas Starr C .10 .25
127 Enchantress, Amora C .10 .25
128 Erik Josten Goliath, Growing Menace C .10 .25
129 Executioner, Scourge of Jotunheim R .40 1.00
130 Grey Gargoyle, Paul Pierre Duval U .20 .50
131 Heinrich Zemo Baron Zemo, Baron of Zeulniz C .10 .25
132 Helmut Zemo Baron Zemo, Uber Enemy U .20 .50
133 Karla Sofen Moonstone, Master Manipulator U .20 .50
134 Klaw, Ulysses Klaw R .50 1.25
135 Marcus Daniels Blackout, Darkbringer C .10 .25
136 Melissa Gold Screaming Mimi, Mimi Schwartz C .10 .25
137 Melter, Bruno Horgan C .10 .25
138 Mr. Hyde, Engine of Destruction C .10 .25
139 Nathan Garrett Black Knight, Corrupt Crusader C .10 .25
140 Paul Ebersol Fixer, Problem Solver R .40 1.00
141 Piledriver, Wrecking Crew C .10 .25
142 Radioactive Man, Chen Lu C .10 .25
143 Scorpion, Fatal Sting U .20 .50
144 Shocker, Vibro-Shock Villain R .40 1.00
145 The Wrecker, Wrecking Crew C .10 .25
146 Thunderball, Wrecking Crew C .10 .25
147 Tiger Shark, Todd Arliss C .10 .25
148 Titania, Vengeful Vixen C .10 .25
149 Ultron Crimson Cowl, Dark Disguise U .20 .50
150 Ultron Ultron 5, Ultimate Evil R .40 1.00
151 Whirlwind, David Cannon U .20 .50
152 Yellowjacket, Rita DeMara C .10 .25
153 Adhesive X U .20 .50
154 Crime Spree C .10 .25
155 Evil Reborn C .10 .25
156 Hard Sound Construct, Construct R .50 1.25
157 Hero's Demise R .50 1.25
158 Mystic Summons C .10 .25
159 Sonic Disruption C .10 .25
160 Stolen Power C .10 .25
161 The Wrecking Crew C .10 .25
162 Under Siege R .40 1.00
163 Unfair Advantage C .10 .25
164 Amenhotep, Dark Pharaoh U .20 .50
165 Baltag, Hand of the Conqueror C .10 .25
166 Growing Man, Kinetic Stimuloid U .20 .50
167 Kang Kross-roads U .20 .50
168 Kang, Earth Mesozoic-24 U .20 .50
169 Kang, Immortus R .40 1.00
170 Kang, Kang Cobra C .10 .25
171 Kang, Kang Kong R .40 1.00
172 Kang, Kang Ransom R .50 1.25
173 Kang, Lord Kang R .40 1.00
174 Kang, Lord of Limbo C .10 .25
175 Kang, Master of Time C .10 .25
176 Kang, Rama Tut U .20 .50
177 Kang, The Conqueror R .40 1.00
178 Kang's Guards, Army U .20 .50
179 Macrobots, Army C .10 .25
180 Tempus, Menace out of Time C .10 .25
181 Game of the Galaxy R .40 1.00
182 Kang, Ultimate Kang C .10 .25
183 Null Time Zone R 1.00 2.50
184 Psyche-Globe U .20 .50
185 Spheres of Solitude U .20 .50
186 The Time Keepers C .10 .25
187 Faces of Evil, Team-Up C .10 .25
188 Justice for All, Team-Up C .10 .25
189 Supreme Sanction, Team-Up C .10 .25
190 A Day Unlike Any Other, Team-Up C .10 .25
191 Avengers Disassembled R .40 1.00
192 Call to Arms C .10 .25
193 Force Field Belt C .10 .25
194 Heroes in Reserve C .10 .25
195 Insect Swarm C .10 .25
196 Might Makes Right C .10 .25
197 Prismatic Shield, Construct C .10 .25
198 Seek Cover C .10 .25
199 Shrink U .20 .50
200 System Failure R .75 2.00
201 United We Stand C .10 .25
202 War of Attrition R .40 1.00
203 Windstorm C .10 .25
204 Polaris, Lorna Dane U .20 .50
205 Framistat U .20 .50
206 Mammomax, Elephant Boy U .20 .50
207 Zorba, Deposed Leader of Latveria R .40 1.00
208 Ahab, Houndkeeper U .20 .50
209 Spider-Man, Peter Parker R 1.25 3.00
210 White Tiger, Hector Ayala U .20 .50
211 Basilisk, Basil Elks U .20 .50
212 Vermin, Sewer Rat U .20 .50
213 Lady Punisher, Lynn Michaels U .20 .50
214 Bring Down the House R .40 1.00
215 Phat, Liv'n Large U .20 .50
216 Mutant of the Year R .50 1.25
217 Hitman, Burt Kenyon U .20 .50
218 Hired Hit R .50 1.25
219 Mortician, Toussaint Morrow U .20 .50
220 Spirits of Vengeance R .40 1.00

2005 Vs System Green Lantern Corps

COMPLETE SET (220) 30.00 60.00
BOOSTER BOX (24 PACKS) 30.00 60.00
BOOSTER PACK (14 CARDS) 1.50 2.50
*FOIL: .8X TO 2X BASIC CARDS
RELEASED IN MAY 2005
1 Abin Sur, Green Lantern of Ungara U .20 .50
2 Alan Scott, Keeper of the Starheart C .10 .25
3 Anti-Green Lantern, Army C .20 .50
4 Anti-Matter Cannon R .10 .25
5 Anti-Matter Universe R .20 .50
6 Anti-Monitor, Architect of Destruction R .10 .25
7 Apokoliptian Hospitality U .10 .25
8 Appa Ali Apsa, Mad God R .10 .25
9 Arisia, Green Lantern of Graxos IV U .10 .25
10 Armies of Qward R 1.50 4.00
11 Azrael Batman, Knightfall U 1.00 2.50
12 Banished to the Anti-Matter Universe U .20 .50
13 Bart Allen Impulse, Hyper-Accelerated U .10 .25
14 Bat's Belfry R .10 .25
15 Battered and Broken U .10 .25
16 Battle of Wills C .10 .25
17 Birthing Chamber U .10 .25
18 Black Hand, Dark-Hearted Villain C .10 .25
19 Blood in the Dark U 1.00 2.50
20 Boodikka, Green Lantern of Bellatrix C .20 .50
21 Book of Oa C .10 .25
22 Breaking Ground, Construct R .10 .25
23 Brik, Green Lantern of Dryad U .20 .50
24 Carol Ferris Star Sapphire, Beloved Enemy C 2.00 5.00
25 Catcher's Mitt, Construct C .20 .50
26 Central Power Battery C .10 .25
27 Ch'p, Green Lantern of H'lven C .10 .25
28 Children of Forever R .10 .25
29 Chopping Block, Construct C .10 .25
30 Coast City C .20 .50
31 Commander, Military Leader of New Genesis R .20 .50
32 Cosmic Conflict C .10 .25
33 Council of Power R .20 .50
34 Damsel in Distress, Construct C .50 1.25
35 Darkseid Undenied R 1.25 3.00
36 Dead-Eye, Qwardian Conglomerate U .20 .50
37 Death of Superman R .30 .75
38 Dimming of the Starheart C .10 .25
39 Dr. Bedlam, Psionic Being R .10 .25
40 Dr. Ebenezer Darrk, Original Leader of the League U .20 .50
41 Dr. Light, Master of Holograms U .10 .25
42 Dr. Polaris, Dr. Neal Emerson C .10 .25
43 Dr. Ub'X, Galactic Conqueror C .75 2.00
44 Elasti-Man, Qwardian Conglomerate C .30 .75
45 Element Man, Qwardian Conglomerate C .10 .25
46 Emerald City, Construct R .10 .25
47 Emerald Dawn U 1.50 4.00
48 Emerald Twilight U .10 .25
49 Empire of Tears U .10 .25
50 Evil Star, Servant of the Star-Band R .10 .25
51 Fatality, Yrra Cynril R .10 .25
52 Femme Fatality U .10 .25
53 Fiero, Qwardian Conglomerate C .20 .50
54 Fifth Dimension R .10 .25
55 Fire Support C .10 .25
56 Fists of the Guardians, Oan Enforcers U .10 .25
57 Force Sphere, Construct C .10 .25
58 From Qward With Hate R 1.25 3.00
59 Frostbite, Qwardian Conglomerate C .10 .25
60 G'Nort, Green Lantern of G'Newt C .20 .50
61 Ganthet, Last Guardian C .20 .50
62 Garth Aqualad, Atlantean Ambassador U .10 .25
63 Gnaxos, Arena Robot C .20 .50
64 Golden Death C .10 .25
65 Goldface, Keith Kenyon C .20 .50
66 Governor Tozad, Planetary Commander U .20 .50
67 Grandmaster, Manhunter Leader R .20 .50
68 Grayven, Son of Darkseid C .10 .25
69 Green Lantern Ring U .20 .50
70 Guardians Reborn U .30 .75
71 Guy Gardner, Strong Arm of the Corps C .30 .75
72 Guy Gardner, Warrior C .30 .75
73 Hal Jordan, Green Lantern of Earth C .10 .25
74 Hal Jordan, Green Lantern of Sector 2814 R .10 .25
75 Hal Jordan, Reborn R .75 2.00
76 Hal Jordan, Parallax R .20 .50
77 Hal Jordan Spectre, Mortal Avatar R .10 .25
78 Hard-Traveling Heroes C .10 .25
79 Harlequin, Molly Mayne-Scott C .10 .25
80 Hector Hammond, Super-Futuristic Mind C .10 .25
81 Helping Hand, Construct C .10 .25
82 Henry King Jr. Brainwave, Psionic Manipulator U1.00 2.50
83 Highmaster, Supreme Leader C .20 .50
84 Hostage Situation R .75 2.00
85 House of El U .10 .25
86 Hush, Mystery Man R .10 .25
87 In Darkest Night U .20 .50
88 In Evil Star's Evil Clutches C .10 .25
89 In Remembrance C .20 .50
90 In the Hands of Qward R .20 .50
91 Invisible Destroyer, Subconscious Entity C .10 .25
92 Jack T. Chance, Green Lantern of Garnet U .10 .25
93 Jackhammer, Construct C .10 .25
94 Jade, Jennifer-Lynn Hayden C .10 .25
95 Jailbird, Construct R .10 .25
96 Jericho, Joseph Wilson R .10 .25
97 John Stewart, Green Lantern of Earth C .10 .25
98 Johnny Quick, Crime Syndicate R .20 .50
99 Katma Tui, Green Lantern of Korugar C 1.00 2.50
100 Kilowog, Green Lantern of Bolovax Vik C .50 1.25
101 Kiman, Chief Weaponer U .10 .25
102 Korugar R .30 .75
103 Kreon, Green Lantern of Tebis C .30 .75
104 Krona, Creator of the Anti-Matter Universe C .10 .25
105 Kyle Rayner, Green Lantern of the Universe C .20 .50

106 Kyle Rayner, Ion R .10 .25
107 Kyle Rayner, Last Green Lantern U .30 .75
108 Lana Lang, Manhunter Sleeper U .30 .75
109 Lantern's Light C .10 .25
110 Lanterns in Love, Construct C .20 .50
111 Legion, He Who Is Many C .20 .50
112 Light Armor, Construct C .30 .75
113 Light Brigade, Construct C .10 .25
114 Living Ink, Construct C .10 .25
115 Locked in Combat C .20 .50
116 Major Disaster, Paul Booker U .10 .25
117 Major Force, Clifford Zmeck C .10 .25
118 Malvolio, Lord of the Green Flame C .10 .25
119 Manhunter Engineer, Army C .10 .25
120 Manhunter Excavator, Army C .10 .25
121 Manhunter Giant, Army C .10 .25
122 Manhunter Guardsman, Army C .10 .25
123 Manhunter Infiltrator, Army C .10 .25
124 Manhunter Lantern, Power Ring Thief C .10 .25
125 Manhunter Protector, Army C .10 .25
126 Manhunter Science C .30 .75
127 Manhunter Sniper, Army C .10 .25
128 Manhunter Soldier, Army C .10 .25
129 Manhunter Spacecraft R .10 .25
130 Manhunter Transphere C .30 .75
131 Mark Shaw, Manhunter C .10 .25
132 Mean Green Machine, Construct U .10 .25
133 Millennium C .50 1.25
134 Mogo R .10 .25
135 Mosaic World C .10 .25
136 Mouse Trap, Construct U .50 1.25
137 Myrwhydden, Mightiest of Mages C .10 .25
138 Nero, Qwardian Puppet R .75 2.00
139 Nero Unleashed C .75 2.00
140 No Evil Shall Escape Our Sight, Construct C .50 1.25
141 No Man Escapes the Manhunters C .20 .50
142 Oa R .20 .50
143 Olapet, Green Lantern of Southern Goldstar C .20 .50
144 Ole!, Construct C .50 1.25
145 Only a Friend Can Betray You C .75 2.00
146 Orinda R .50 1.25
147 Owlman, Crime Syndicate C .20 .50
148 Pan, Manhunter Duplicate R .30 .75
149 Parademons, Army U .30 .75
150 Pest Control, Construct C .20 .50
151 Plans Within Plans C 1.25 3.00
152 Power Armor Elite, Army U .50 1.25
153 Power Ring, Crime Syndicate C .30 .75
154 Power Surge U .30 .75
155 Prison Planet R .20 .50
156 Prisoner of a Mad God R .20 .50
157 Q Energy U .20 .50
158 Q Field C .50 1.25
159 Qward R .20 .50
160 Qwardian Council Hall R .50 1.25
161 Qwardian Pincer C .20 .50
162 Qwardian Watchdog, Gatekeeper U .20 .50
163 Qwardians, Army C .20 .50
164 Ragman, Rory Regan R .30 .75
165 Rain of Acorns, Construct U .30 .75
166 Rebellion on Oa R .50 1.25
167 Recharging the Ring C .50 1.25
168 Reciting the Oath U .20 .50
169 Reign of Terra R .20 .50
170 Remoni-Notra Star Sapphire, Obsessed Warrior Princess C .30 .75
171 Rocket Red, Manhunter Sleeper C .50 1.25
172 Rot Lop Fan, F-Sharp Bell of the Obsidian Deeps C .20 .50
173 S.T.A.R. Labs R .10 .25
174 Salakk, Green Lantern of Slyggia U .10 .25
175 Scarab, Qwardian Conglomerate U 1.25 3.00
176 Sector 2814 U .10 .25
177 Sensei, Martial Arts Master U .20 .50
178 Shadow Creatures, Army U .20 .50
179 Shadows of the Past R .10 .25
180 Shock Troops C .30 .75
181 Sinestro, Lantern in Exile C .10 .25
182 Sinestro, Green Lantern of Korugar R .20 .50
183 Sinestro, Enemy of the Corps R .10 .25
184 Sinestro Defiant C .30 .75
185 Sleeper Agent, Manhunter Sleeper C .10 .25
186 Slipstream, Qwardian Conglomerate C .10 .25
187 Soldiers of New Genesis, Army U .10 .25
188 Solomon Grundy, Born on a Monday C .10 .25
189 Sonar, Dastardly Discord C .10 .25
190 Space Bears, Construct C .20 .50
191 Sl'nlli, Super-Qwardian C .10 .25
192 Starlings, Army U .10 .25
193 Stealing the Light C .10 .25
194 Sturmer, War Dog R .10 .25
195 Superman, Returned U .30 .75
196 Supermanhunter, Kryptonite Armor C .10 .25
197 Superwoman, Crime Syndicate C .10 .25
198 Sweeping Up, Construct C .10 .25
199 Tattooed Man, Abel Tarrant U .10 .25
200 The Fall of Oa R .10 .25
201 The Kent Farm R .10 .25
202 The Manhunters are a Myth R .10 .25
203 The Ring Has Chosen U .10 .25
204 The Shark, T.S. Smith C .10 .25
205 Thunderous Onslaught C .10 .25
206 Tomar Re, Green Lantern of Xudar U .10 .25
207 Tomar Tu, Green Lantern of Xudar C .20 .50
208 Trapped in the Sciencells U .10 .25
209 Two-Face, Split Personality R .20 .50
210 Ultraman, Crime Syndicate C .10 .25
211 Underground Complex U .20 .50
212 Uppercut, Construct C .10 .25
213 Virman Vundabar, Military Leader of Apokolips U .10 .25
214 Weaponers of Qward, Army C .10 .25
215 Willworld R .20 .50
216 Xallarap, Anti-Green Lantern Corps C .20 .50
217 Yellow Impurity C .10 .25
218 Yellow Power Ring U .30 .75
219 Yokal, The Atrocious U .10 .25
220 Zero Hour R 1.00 2.50

2005 Vs System Justice League of America

COMPLETE SET (220) 25.00 50.00
BOOSTER BOX (24 PACKS) 25.00 50.00
BOOSTER PACK (14 CARDS) 1.00 2.00
*FOIL: .8X TO 2X BASIC CARDS
RELEASED IN NOVEMBER 2005
1 Aquaman, Arthur Curry C .10 .25
2 Aquaman, King of the Seven Seas U .20 .50
3 Barry Allen The Flash, Scarlet Speedster R .30 .75
4 Batman, Avatar of Justice C .10 .25
5 Connor Hawke Green Arrow, Son of the Archer U .20 .50
6 Dinah Laurel Lance Black Canary, Blonde Bombshell C .10 .25
7 Elongated Man, Ralph Dibny C .10 .25
8 Faith, The Fat Lady U .20 .50
9 Firestorm, The Nuclear Man U .20 .50
10 Gypsy, Cynthia Reynolds C .10 .25
11 Hal Jordan, Hard-Traveling Hero C .10 .25
12 John Henry Irons Steel, Steel-Drivin' Man C .10 .25
13 John Stewart, Emerald Architect C .10 .25
14 Katar Hol Hawkman, Thanagarian Enforcer C .10 .25
15 Martian Manhunter, Manhunter from Mars R .30 .75
16 Oliver Queen Green Arrow, Hard-Traveling Hero C .10 .25
17 Plastic Man, Eel O'Brian R .30 .75
18 Ray Palmer The Atom, World's Smallest Hero R .30 .75
19 Red Tornado, John Smith C .10 .25
20 Shayera Thal Hawkwoman, Thanagarian Enforcer C .10 .25
21 Snapper Carr, Cool Daddy-O U .20 .50
22 Superman, Avatar of Peace R 1.25 3.00
23 Wonder Woman, Princess Diana C .10 .25
24 Wonder Woman, Avatar of Truth R .40 1.00
25 Zatanna, Zatanna Zatara R .40 1.00
26 Zauriel, Guardian Angel C .10 .25
27 Disband the League U .20 .50
28 Field of Honor U .20 .50
29 Hero's Welcome R .40 1.00
30 Monitor Womb Station R .30 .75
31 New Era R .30 .75
32 Reform the League C .10 .25
33 Roll Call! C .10 .25
34 Satellite HQ C .10 .25
35 Secret Sanctuary U .20 .50
36 Teleport Tube R .30 .75
37 Wall of Will, Construct C .10 .25
38 The Watchtower R .40 1.00
39 Batman, Hidden Crusader C .10 .25
40 Bluejay, Jay Abrams C .10 .25
41 Booster Gold, Michael Jon Carter C .10 .25
42 Captain Atom, Nathaniel Adam C .10 .25
43 Captain Marvel, Billy Batson R .30 .75
44 Catherine Cobert, Embassy Chief U .20 .50
45 Crimson Fox, Vivian and Constance D'Aramis U .20 .50
46 Dinah Laurel Lance Black Canary, Pretty Bird C .10 .25
47 Dr. Fate, Kent Nelson R .30 .75
48 Fire, Beatriz DaCosta C .10 .25
49 Guy Gardner, Egomaniac C .10 .25
50 Ice, Tora Olafsdotter C .10 .25
51 Joseph Jones General Glory, Lady Liberty's Champion C .10 .25
52 Kimiyo Hoshi Dr. Light, Starlight Sentinel C .10 .25
53 L-Ron, Robot Companion U .20 .50
54 Martian Manhunter, J'onn J'onzz U .20 .50
55 Maxwell Lord, Financier C .10 .25
56 Metamorpho, Rex Mason C .10 .25
57 Oberon, Micro Manager U .20 .50
58 Power Girl, Karen Starr R .30 .75
59 Rocket Red #4, Dmitri Pushkin C .10 .25
60 Scott Free Mister Miracle, Man of a Thousand Escapes U .20 .50
61 Silver Sorceress, Laura Cynthia Neilsen C .10 .25
62 Sue Dibny, Charismatic Coordinator C .10 .25
63 Tasmanian Devil, Hugh Dawkins C .10 .25
64 Ted Kord Blue Beetle, Heir of the Scarab C .10 .25
65 BWA HA HA HA HA! R 1.00 2.50
66 The Castle U .20 .50
67 JLI Embassy C .10 .25
68 Justice League Task Force, Team-Up C .10 .25
69 Kooey Kooey Kooey R 1.00 2.50
70 Plasma Blast C .10 .25
71 Running Interference U .20 .50
72 Safety in Numbers U .20 .50
73 Staged Attack C .10 .25
74 UN General Assembly R .40 1.00
75 UN Recognition C .10 .25
76 Abra Kadabra, Citizen Abra U .20 .50
77 Captain Boomerang, George Harkness C .10 .25
78 Circe, Immortal Sorceress C .10 .25
79 Creeping Doom, Army C .10 .25
80 David Clinton Chronos, The Time Thief C .10 .25
81 Dr. Light, Light Shaper R .30 .75
82 Evan McCulloch Mirror Master, Smoke and Mirrors C .10 .25
83 Floronic Man, Alien Hybrid U .20 .50
84 The General, Wade Eiling R .30 .75
85 Illusionary Warriors, Army C .10 .25
86 Infernal Minions, Army C .10 .25
87 Insectoid Troopers, Army C .10 .25
88 IQ, Ira Quimby C .10 .25
89 The Joker, Headline Stealer C .10 .25
90 Lex Luthor, Nefarious Philanthropist U .20 .50
91 Lex Luthor, Evil Incorporated C .10 .25
92 Libra, Alien Conqueror R .30 .75
93 Ocean Master, Son of Atlan C .10 .25
94 Poison Ivy, Deadly Rose R 1.25 3.00
95 Prometheus, Darker Knight C .10 .25
96 Sam Scudder Mirror Master, Reflective Rogue U .20 .50
97 Scarecrow, Psycho Psychologist C .10 .25
98 Shadow-Thief, Carl Sands C .10 .25
99 The Shark, Karshon C .10 .25
100 Tattooed Man, Living Ink C .10 .25
101 Zazzala Queen Bee, Royal Genetrix C .10 .25
102 All Too Easy C .10 .25
103 Criminal Mastermind C .10 .25
104 Gang-Up, Team-Up C .10 .25
105 Hard-Light Storage Tank R .50 1.25
106 Infestation U .20 .50
107 Injustice Gang Satellite R .30 .75
108 Philosopher's Stone R .30 .75
109 Power Siphon R .75 2.00
110 Royal Egg-Matrix U .20 .50
111 Secret Files C .10 .25
112 World War III R .30 .75
113 Captain Boomerang, Digger U .20 .50
114 Captain Cold, Leonard Snart U .20 .50
115 Charaxes, Killer Moth C .10 .25
116 Copperhead, Slithering Assassin C .10 .25
117 Crystal Frost Killer Frost, Cold-Hearted Killer U .20 .50
118 Darkseid, Heart of Darkness C .10 .25
119 Deadshot, Floyd Lawton R .30 .75
120 Dr. Sivana, Thaddeus Bodog Sivana C .10 .25
121 Floronic Man, Jason Woodrue C .10 .25
122 Funky Flashman, Salesman Supreme U .20 .50
123 Gorilla Grodd, Simian Mastermind C .10 .25
124 Hector Hammond, Mind Over Matter C .10 .25
125 Henry King Brainwave, Sinister Psionic C .10 .25
126 James Jesse Trickster, Giovanni Giuseppe C .10 .25
127 Lex Luthor, Criminal Genius R .30 .75
128 Manhunter Clone, Clone of Paul Kirk C .10 .25
129 Mark Desmond Blockbuster, Mindless Brute U .20 .50
130 The Mist, Jonathan Smythe C .10 .25
131 Poison Ivy, Kiss of Death C .10 .25
132 Psycho-Pirate, Roger Hayden R .30 .75
133 Quakemaster, Robert Coleman U .20 .50
134 Remoni-Notra Star Sapphire, Zamoran Champion U .20 .50
135 Scarecrow, Fearmonger C .10 .25
136 Sinestro, Corrupted by the Ring R .30 .75
137 Solomon Grundy, Buried on Sunday R .30 .75
138 Ultra-Humanite, Evolutionary Antecedent C .10 .25
139 The Wizard, William Zard C .10 .25
140 Attend or Die! R .30 .75
141 Divided We Fall R .30 .75
142 Funky's Big Rat Code, Team-Up C .10 .25
143 Gorilla City C .10 .25
144 Mysterious Benefactor U .20 .50
145 The Plunder Plan C .10 .25
146 Quadromobile U .20 .50
147 Sinister Citadel U .20 .50
148 Slaughter Swamp C .10 .25
149 Sorcerer's Treasure R .30 .75
150 Straight to the Grave R 2.50 6.00
151 With Prejudice C .10 .25
152 Justice League Signal Device C .10 .25
153 Magnificent Seven C .10 .25
154 World's Greatest Heroes, Team-Up C .10 .25
155 Amazo, Ivo's Android R .30 .75
156 Despero, Master of the Third Eye C .10 .25
157 Dr. Destiny, John Dee C .10 .25
158 Felix Faust, Infernal Dealmaker U .20 .50
159 Kanjar Ro, Kylaq Defense Minister C .10 .25
160 Mageddon, Weapon of Universal Destruction R .30 .75
161 Neron, Soul Collector R .30 .75
162 Professor Ivo, Anthony Ivo C .10 .25
163 Queen of Fables, Wickedest Witch C .10 .25
164 Rama Khan, Elemental Magician C .10 .25
165 Starro the Conqueror, Intergalactic Starfish R .30 .75
166 T. O. Morrow, Thomas Oscar Morrow U .20 .50
167 Tomorrow Woman, Trojan Telepath R .30 .75
168 Air Strike C .10 .25
169 Atlantean Trident U .20 .50
170 Balance of Power C .10 .25
171 Bulletproof C .10 .25
172 Counterstrike C .10 .25
173 Counterterrorism U .20 .50
174 Crisis on Infinite Earths, Team-Up R 1.50 4.00
175 Death Times Five C .10 .25
176 Death Trap C .10 .25
177 Funeral For a Friend U .20 .50
178 Glass Jaw C .10 .25
179 High-Tech Flare Gun U .20 .50
180 H'ronmeer's Curse R .30 .75
181 Identity Crisis R .30 .75
182 Lair of the Mastermind C .10 .25
183 Lead by Example C .10 .25
184 Membership Drive C .10 .25
185 Midnight Cravings C .10 .25
186 Not on My Watch U .20 .50
187 Nth Metal C .10 .25
188 Rallying Cry! C .10 .25
189 Resistance is Useless C .10 .25
190 Secret Origins R .75 2.00
191 Shake It Off C .10 .25
192 S.T.A.R. Labs Orbital Platform C .10 .25
193 Token Resistance C .10 .25
194 Trial by Fire C .10 .25
195 UN Building, Team-Up C .10 .25
196 Vicarious Living U .20 .50
197 Wheel of Misfortune U .20 .50
198 Mogo, The Living Planet R .30 .75
199 Oliver Queen Green Arrow, Emerald Archer U .20 .50
200 Recharge the Sun R .30 .75
201 Controller Sanction U .20 .50
202 Fatality, Emerald Assassin R .30 .75
203 Chomin, Qwardian Spy U .20 .50
204 General Fabrikant, Qwardian General U .20 .50
205 Matter Convergence R .30 .75
206 Conscription R .30 .75
207 Manhunter Conqueror, Grandmaster U .20 .50
208 War Without End R .30 .75
209 Kelex, Faithful Servant U .20 .50
210 Look-Alike Squad R 1.00 2.50
211 Bizarro Ray U .20 .50
212 Maxima, Empress of Almerac R .30 .75
213 Mobius Chair U .20 .50
214 Valkyra, Valkyrie of New Genesis U .20 .50
215 Die for Darkseid! U .20 .50
216 Mantis, Power Parasite R .30 .75
217 Justice League of Arkham, Team-Up U .20 .50
218 The Creeper, Jack Ryder R .75 2.00
219 Poisoned! U .20 .50
220 Bumblebee, Karen Beecher-Duncan U .20 .50

2005 Vs System Marvel Knights

COMPLETE SET (220) 25.00 50.00
BOOSTER BOX (24 PACKS) 15.00 30.00
BOOSTER PACK (14 CARDS) .75 1.25
*FOIL: .8X TO 2X BASIC CARDS
RELEASED IN FEBRUARY 2005
1 Blade, Eric Brooks R .50 1.25
2 Brother Voodoo, Jericho Drumm C .10 .25
3 Caretaker, Nomadic Mentor C .10 .25
4 Cloak, Child of Darkness C .10 .25
5 Dagger, Child of Light U .20 .50
6 Daredevil, Guardian Devil C .10 .25
7 Daredevil, Matt Murdock R 1.00 2.50
8 Daredevil, Protector of Hell's Kitchen C .10 .25
9 Dr. Strange, Stephen Strange R .40 1.00
10 Elektra, Assassin U .20 .50
11 Elektra, Elektra Natchios C .10 .25
12 Ghost Rider, Danny Ketch R .60 1.50
13 Ghost Rider, Johnny Blaze C .10 .25
14 Hannibal King, Occult Investigator C .10 .25
15 Iron Fist, Danny Rand C .10 .25
16 Iron Fist, Living Weapon C .10 .25
17 Luke Cage, Power Man R .40 1.00
18 Luke Cage, Street Enforcer C .10 .25
19 Micro-Chip, Linus Lieberman C .10 .25
20 Mikado and Mosha, Angels of Destruction C .10 .25
21 Moon Knight, Marc Spector C .10 .25
22 Natasha Romanoff Black Widow, KGB Killer U .20 .50
23 Punisher, Executioner C .10 .25
24 Punisher, Judge R .40 1.00
25 Punisher, Jury U .20 .50
26 Shang Chi, Master of Kung Fu U .20 .50
27 Spider-Man, The Spectacular Spider-Man C .10 .25
28 Stick, Leader of the Chaste U .20 .50
29 Yelena Belova Black Widow, Enemy Agent R .40 1.00
30 Blind Justice R .40 1.00
31 Bring the Pain C .10 .25
32 Crime and Punishment C .10 .25
33 Deposed C .10 .25
34 Head Shot C .10 .25
35 Hell's Kitchen U .20 .50
36 Judge, Jury, and Executioner C .10 .25
37 Midnight Sons C .10 .25
38 Penance Stare U .20 .50
39 Punisher's Armory U .20 .50
40 Quentin Carnival U .20 .50
41 Quick Kill C .10 .25
42 Swan Dive U .20 .50
43 Titanium Sword U .20 .50
44 War Wagon C .10 .25
45 Wild Ride R 2.50 6.00
46 Anarchist, Man of the People R .40 1.00
47 Anarchist, Tike Alicar U .20 .50
48 Battering Ram, Short-Lived Strongman C .10 .25
49 Bloke, Mickey Tork U .20 .50
50 Coach, Manipulative Mentor C .10 .25
51 Corkscrew, Twisted Trainee C .10 .25
52 Dead Girl, Crafty Cadaver C .10 .25
53 Doop, Forward Observer C .10 .25
54 Doop, Ultimate Weapon R .40 1.00
55 El Guapo, Robbie Rodriguez U .20 .50
56 Gin Genie, Beckah Parker C .10 .25
57 La Nuit, Pierre Truffaut C .10 .25
58 Mysterious Fan Boy, Arthur Lundberg C .10 .25
59 Orphan, Good Guy C .10 .25
60 Orphan, Guy Smith C .10 .25
61 Orphan, Mr. Sensitive R .40 1.00
62 Phat, William Reilly R .40 1.00
63 Plazm, Protoplasmic Protagonist C .10 .25
64 Saint Anna, Sympathetic Healer C .10 .25
65 Sluk, Byron Spencer C .10 .25
66 The Spike, Angry Young Mutant C .10 .25
67 U-Go-Girl, Eddie Sawyer U .20 .50
68 U-Go-Girl, Tragic Teleporter U .20 .50
69 Venus Dee Milo, Dee Milo R .40 1.00
70 Venus Dee Milo, Telegenic Teleporter U .20 .50
71 Vivisector, Lunatic Lycanthrope C .10 .25
72 Vivisector, Myles Alfred C .10 .25
73 Zeitgeist, Axel Cluney C .10 .25
74 Dead Weight U .20 .50
75 Doop Cam C .10 .25
76 Falling Stars C .10 .25
77 Glory Hound C .10 .25
78 Go in Swinging U .20 .50
79 Grandstanding U .20 .50
80 Mind Over Matter U .20 .50
81 Missed Drop C .10 .25
82 Nerve Strike C .10 .25
83 Never Give Up! U .20 .50
84 Overexposed C .10 .25
85 Spin Doctoring R .75 2.00
86 Star of the Show R .60 1.50
87 Supporting Role C .10 .25
88 Training Theatre U .20 .50
89 X-Statix Cafe C .10 .25
90 X-Statix HQ R .40 1.00
91 Bullseye, Deadly Marksman R .50 1.25
92 Bullseye, Master of Murder C .10 .25
93 Carbone's Assassins, Army C .10 .25
94 Cobra, Klaus Vorhees C .10 .25
95 Deadpool, Wade Wilson R .50 1.25
96 Death-Stalker, Phillip Sterling C .10 .25
97 Echo, Maya Lopez C .10 .25
98 Jaime Ortiz Damage, Cybernetic Enforcer C .10 .25
99 Jester, Jonathan Powers U .20 .50
100 Jigsaw, Billy Russo U .20 .50
101 Kingpin, The Kingpin of Crime R .40 1.00
102 Kingpin, Wilson Fisk C .10 .25
103 Kirigi, Master Assassin U .20 .50
104 Masked Marauder, Frank Farnum C .10 .25
105 Mr. Code, Masked Malcontent U .20 .50
106 Mr. Fear, Zoltan Drago C .10 .25
107 Mr. Hyde, Calvin Zabo C .10 .25
108 Nuke, Renegade Super Soldier C .10 .25
109 Owl, Leland Owlsley R .50 1.25
110 Roscoe Sweeny, Fixer U .20 .50
111 Saracen, Muzzafar Lambert C .10 .25
112 Sniper, Rich van Burian C .10 .25
113 Stilt-Man, Wilbur Day R .40 1.00
114 The Hand, Army C .10 .25
115 The Rose, Shadowy Lieutenant U .20 .50
116 The Russian, Contract Killer C .10 .25
117 Typhoid Mary, Mary Walker R .40 1.00
118 Vanessa Fisk, Mob Matron C .10 .25
119 Armed Escort C .10 .25
120 Boss of Bosses U .20 .50
121 Drive-by Shooting C .10 .25
122 Face the Master U .20 .50
123 Geraci Family Estate U .20 .50
124 Good Night, Sweet Prince C .10 .25
125 Hand Dojo U .20 .50
126 King Takes Knight R .40 1.00
127 Made Men C .10 .25
128 Marked for Death U .20 .50
129 No Rest for the Wicked C .10 .25
130 Rough House C .10 .25
131 Shakedown C .10 .25
132 Sold Out R .40 1.00
133 The Family C .10 .25
134 Untouchable R .40 1.00
135 Uprising U .20 .50
136 Anton Hellgate, Thanatologist C .10 .25
137 Asmodeus, Duke of Hell U .20 .50
138 Blackheart, Son of Mephisto C .10 .25
139 Blackout, Master of Darkness U .20 .50
140 Centurious, The Soulless Man C .10 .25
141 Deacon Frost, Vampire Master R .50 1.25
142 Dracula, Lord of the Damned C .10 .25
143 Dracula, Vlad Dracula R .50 1.25
144 Lilith, Daughter of Dracula R .40 1.00
145 Marie Laveau, Voodoo Priestess U .20 .50
146 Mephisto, Father of Lies R .40 1.00
147 Mephisto, Soulstealer U .20 .50
148 Morbius, The Living Vampire C .10 .25
149 Nekra, Nekra Sinclair U .20 .50
150 New Blood, Army C .10 .25
151 Nightmare, Dark Lord of Dreams C .10 .25
152 Orb, Drake Shannon R .60 1.50
153 Reaper, Vampire Armageddon C .10 .25
154 Shelob, Queen of Spiders U .20 .50
155 Skinner, Psychotic Shredder C .10 .25
156 Steel Wind, Cyborg Cyclist C .10 .25
157 Suicide, Chris Daniels C .10 .25
158 Tryks, Army C .10 .25
159 Varnae, First Vampire R .40 1.00
160 Vengeance, Michael Badilino C .10 .25
161 Werewolf by Night, Jack Russell C .10 .25
162 Zarathos, Spirit of Vengeance C .10 .25
163 Zodiak, Norman Harrison C .10 .25
164 Black Magic C .10 .25
165 Blood Hunt R .40 1.00
166 Children of the Night C .10 .25
167 Dark Embrace R .40 1.00
168 Dracula's Castle U .20 .50
169 Evil Awakens U .20 .50
170 Gravesite U .20 .50
171 Hypnotic Charms C .10 .25
172 Infernal Gateway U .20 .50
173 Mist Form U .20 .50
174 Shadow Step C .10 .25
175 Strength of the Grave C .10 .25
176 The Darkhold C .10 .25
177 Club Dead C .10 .25
178 Wake the Dead U .20 .50
179 Witching Hour R .40 1.00
180 Blade, The Daywalker C .10 .25
181 Professor X, Mutant Mentor R .50 1.25
182 Elektra, Agent of the Hand C .10 .25
183 Deathwatch, Unrepentant Killer C .10 .25
184 Moving Target C .10 .25
185 Hell's Fury C .10 .25
186 Day of the Dead C .10 .25
187 Blown to Pieces C .10 .25
188 Team X-change R .40 1.00
189 Coalition of Heroes R .40 1.00
190 Honor Among Thieves R .40 1.00
191 Professor X, Mental Master R .50 1.25
192 Outback Stronghold R .40 1.00
193 Valeria, Daughter of Doom R .40 1.00
194 Lockjaw, Inhuman U .20 .50
195 Scarlet Witch, Eldritch Enchantress R .40 1.00
196 Monument to a Madman R .40 1.00
197 Diplomatic Immunity R .40 1.00
198 Hounds of Ahab, Army U .20 .50
199 Mekanix R .40 1.00
200 Frog Man, Eugene Patilio U .20 .50
201 Scarlet Spider Spider-Man, Successor R .50 1.25

202 Swing into Action R .40 1.00
203 The Slingers R .40 1.00
204 Web Shooters R .40 1.00
205 Carrion, Cadaverous Clone U .20 .50
206 Mendel Stromm, Robot Master R .40 1.00
207 Scorpia, Elaine Colls U .20 .50
208 Inside Job R .40 1.00
209 Lacuna, Media Darling C .10 .25
210 Sharon Ginsberg, Corrupt Counsel C .10 .25
211 Advance Recon C .10 .25
212 Marvel Team-Up C .10 .25
213 Medallion of Power R .40 1.00
214 Meltdown C .10 .25
215 Mystic Chain R .50 1.25
216 Mystical Sigil U .20 .50
217 Out of the Darkness C .10 .25
218 Psychoville C .10 .25
219 Team Spirit U .20 .50
220 Weapon of Choice R .50 1.25

2006 Vs System Heralds of Galactus

COMPLETE SET (220) 35.00 75.00
BOOSTER BOX (24 PACKS) 25.00 50.00
BOOSTER PACK (14 CARDS) 1.00 2.00
*FOIL: .8X TO 2X BASIC CARDS
RELEASED IN SEPTEMBER 2006
1 Air-Walker, Gabriel Lan R 2.50 6.00
2 Air-Walker, Harbinger of Despair U .20 .50
3 Destroyer, Soulless Juggernaut C .10 .25
4 Destroyer, Harbinger of Devastation C .10 .25
5 Firelord, Pyreus Kril C .10 .25
6 Firelord, Harbinger of Havoc C .10 .25
7 Frankie Raye Nova, Optimistic Youth C .10 .25
8 Frankie Raye Nova, Soul Searcher C .10 .25
9 Frankie Raye Nova, Harbinger of Death C .10 .25
10 Galactus, The Maker U .20 .50
11 Galactus, Devourer of Worlds R 3.00 8.00
12 Galan, Famished C .10 .25
13 Human Torch, The Invisible Man C .10 .25
14 Morg, Slayer C .10 .25
15 Morg, Corrupt Destroyer C .10 .25
16 Morg, Harbinger of Extinction C .10 .25
17 Plasma, Replacement Herald C .10 .25
18 Red Shift, Rift Walker R 2.00 5.00
19 Silver Surfer, Skyrider of the Spaceways U .75 2.00
20 Silver Surfer, Righteous Protector C .10 .25
21 Silver Surfer, Harbinger of Oblivion R 1.50 4.00
22 Stardust, Merciless Warrior C .10 .25
23 Terrax, The Tamer R .60 1.50
24 Terrax, Harbinger of Ruin R .50 1.25
25 The Fallen One, The Forgotten C .10 .25
26 The Punishers, Army C .10 .25
27 Tyrant, The Original Herald U .20 .50
28 Absorba Shield R .75 2.00
29 Cosmic Necessity U .20 .50
30 Creation of a Herald R 3.00 8.00
31 Elemental Battle C .10 .25
32 Elemental Converters U .20 .50
33 I Hunger R .60 1.50
34 I Must Obey R .40 1.00
35 Inspiring Demise R 1.50 4.00
36 Kindred Spirits U .20 .50
37 Pacification U .20 .50
38 Relentless Onslaught C .10 .25
39 Taa II R .40 1.00
40 The Herald Ordeal, Team-Up C .10 .25
41 The Power Cosmic Unleashed C .10 .25
42 Ultimate Nullifier R .50 1.25
43 Worldeater Apparatus U .20 .50
44 Worldship U .20 .50
45 Admiral Galen Kor, Lunatic Legion C .10 .25
46 Bron Char, Lunatic Legion R .50 1.25
47 Captain Att-Lass, Starforce C .10 .25
48 Clumsy Foulup, Puppet Dictator C .10 .25
49 Colonel Yon-Rogg, Commander of the Helion R .60 1.50
50 Commander Dylon Cir, Lunatic Legion C .10 .25
51 Dr. Minerva, Starforce C .10 .25
52 Korath the Pursuer, Starforce C .10 .25
53 Kree Commandos, Army U .20 .50
54 Kree Public Accusers, Army U .20 .50
55 Kree Soldiers, Army U .20 .50
56 Lieutenant Kona Lor, Lunatic Legion C .10 .25
57 Lunatic Legionnaires, Army U .20 .50
58 Mar-Vell Captain Marvel, Soldier of the Empire C .10 .25
59 Mar-Vell Captain Marvel, Enemy of the Empire C .10 .25
60 Nenora, Skrull Usurper C .10 .25
61 Ronan the Accuser, Starforce C .10 .25
62 Ronan the Accuser, Supreme Public Accuser R .40 1.00
63 Ruul Warrior, Army C .10 .25
64 Sentry #459, Advance Guard C .10 .25
65 Shatterax, Starforce C .10 .25
66 Sintariis, High Kronamaster R .40 1.00
67 Supreme Intelligence, Kree Collective R .40 1.00
68 Supremor, Starforce C .10 .25
69 Talla Ron, Lunatic Legion C .10 .25
70 Ultimus, Starforce C .10 .25
71 Conquered Planet C .10 .25
72 Enemy of the Empire U .20 .50
73 Genetic Destiny U .20 .50
74 Hala C .10 .25
75 Improper Burial U .20 .50
76 Live Kree . . . or Die! U .20 .50
77 Nega-Bands U .20 .50
78 Nega-Bomb R .40 1.00
79 Penal Colony C .10 .25
80 Planet Weapon R .60 1.50
81 Pressed into Service, Team-Up C .10 .25
82 Remnant Fleet C .10 .25
83 Starforce Strike C .10 .25
84 Stargate R 2.50 6.00
85 Strategic Retreat R .40 1.00
86 The Infamous Seven U .20 .50
87 The Lunatic Legion U .20 .50
88 Universal Weapon C .10 .25
89 Ahura, Heir to Attilan C .10 .25
90 Alaris, The Outgoing One C .10 .25
91 Alpha Primitives, Army C .10 .25
92 Black Bolt, Illuminati C .10 .25
93 Black Bolt, King of the Inhumans C .10 .25
94 Black Bolt, Devastating Decree R .50 1.25
95 Crystal, Elementelle C .10 .25
96 Dewoz, Dark Reflection C .10 .25
97 Dinu, Face of Terror C .10 .25
98 Franklin Richards, Creator of Counter-Earth C .10 .25
99 Gorgon, Thundering Hooves R .40 1.00
100 Human Torch, Sparky C .10 .25
101 Invisible Woman, Flame On! C .10 .25
102 Jolen, The Treacherous One U .20 .50
103 Karnak, The Shatterer R .75 2.00
104 Lockjaw, Inhuman's Best Friend U .75 2.00
105 Luna Maximoff, Only Human C .10 .25
106 Maximus the Mad, Mental Manipulator C .10 .25
107 Medusa, Queen of the Inhumans U .20 .50
108 Mr. Fantastic, Illuminati U .20 .50
109 Nahrees, The Negative One C .10 .25
110 Quicksilver, Inhuman by Marriage C .10 .25
111 San, The Alienated One C .10 .25
112 Thing, Rockhead C .10 .25
113 Tonaja, The Responsible One C .10 .25
114 Triton, Aquatic Ambassador R .40 1.00
115 Attilan R .75 2.00
116 Blue Area of the Moon C .10 .25
117 Exploiting the Flaw R .50 1.25
118 Extended Family, Team-Up C .10 .25
119 Final Decree R .40 1.00
120 Himalayan Enclave C .10 .25
121 It's Slobberin' Time! C .10 .25
122 Power Struggle U .20 .50
123 Terragenesis U .20 .50
124 The Great Refuge R 3.00 8.00
125 The Outside World C .10 .25
126 The Royal Guard R 1.50 4.00
127 The Substructure C .10 .25
128 Waking the Ancestors C .10 .25
129 Divinity, Vampiric General U .20 .50
130 Doom-Bot Dr. Doom, Cosmic Thief C .10 .25
131 Doom-Bot Corps, Army C .10 .25
132 Dorma, Atlantean General C .10 .25
133 Dr. Doom, Richards's Rival C .10 .25
134 Dr. Doom, Sorcerous Savant C .10 .25
135 Dr. Doom, Latverian Monarch R .60 1.50
136 Elite Doom Guards, Army C .10 .25
137 Invisible Woman, Baroness Von Doom C .10 .25
138 Iron Man, Illuminati C .10 .25
139 Kang, One of Many U .20 .50
140 Kang, Destiny Warrior R .75 2.00
141 Klaw, Sonic Construct R .40 1.00
142 Lancer, Samantha Dunbar C .10 .25
143 Magneto, Acts of Vengeance C .10 .25
144 Mole Man, Moloid Master U .20 .50
145 Molecule Man, Owen Reece R .40 1.00
146 Moloids, Army C .10 .25
147 Mr. Fantastic, Doom's Adversary U .20 .50
148 Purple Man, Subtle Manipulator U .20 .50
149 Shakti, Mage General C .10 .25
150 Sub-Mariner, Illuminati C .10 .25
151 Technarx, Cyborg General C .10 .25
152 Titania, Temper Tantrum C .10 .25
153 Ultron Ultron 11, Army C .10 .25
154 Valeria Von Doom, Heir to Latveria C .10 .25
155 Armies of Doom U .20 .50
156 Arsenal of Doom C .10 .25
157 Astral Suppression U .20 .50
158 Doom Needs Only Doom C .10 .25
159 Doomed Earth R 1.50 4.00
160 Doomstadt, Castle Doom R 1.25 3.00
161 Expendable Ally R 1.25 3.00
162 For the Glory of Doom!, Team-Up C .10 .25
163 Lust for Power R .40 1.00
164 Mask of Doom U .20 .50
165 Master of Puppets U .20 .50
166 Super Genius C .10 .25
167 The Devil We Know C .10 .25
168 The Enemy Within R .40 1.00
169 Time Thief R 3.00 8.00
170 Unthinkable R .40 1.00
171 Adam Warlock, Protector of the Soul Gem U .20 .50
172 Drax the Destroyer, Protector of the Power Gem R .40 1.00
173 Gamora, Protector of the Time Gem U .20 .50
174 Moondragon, Protector of the Mind Gem C .10 .25
175 Pip the Troll, Protector of the Space Gem U .20 .50
176 Thanos, Protector of the Reality Gem R .40 1.00
177 Gathering the Watch U .20 .50
178 Mind Gem, Infinity Gem C .10 .25
179 Power Gem, Infinity Gem C .10 .25
180 Reality Gem, Infinity Gem R 1.50 4.00
181 Soul Gem, Infinity Gem U .20 .50
182 Soul World U .20 .50
183 Space Gem, Infinity Gem U .20 .50
184 The Infinity Gauntlet R .50 1.25
185 Time Gem, Infinity Gem R .50 1.25
186 Captain America, Skrull Impostor U .20 .50
187 Ethan Edwards, Visitor from Another World C .10 .25
188 Paibok, The Power Skrull C .10 .25
189 Rogue, Total Transformation R .50 1.25
190 Titannus, Alien Conqueror C .10 .25
191 Warskrull, Skrull Infiltrator U .20 .50
192 Wolverine, Skrunucklehead C .10 .25
193 Act of Defiance, Team-Up C .10 .25
194 Alien Insurrection C .10 .25
195 Interstellar Offensive C .10 .25
196 Armageddon R .75 2.00
197 Assault and Battery U .20 .50
198 Barbaric Brawl C .10 .25
199 Battleworld C .10 .25
200 Cannibal Tech C .10 .25
201 Cosmic Order C .10 .25
202 Ego the Living Planet R .40 1.00
203 Intergalactic Summit C .10 .25
204 Sworn Enemies C .10 .25
205 The Kyln C .10 .25
206 The Rapture U .20 .50
207 The Uni-Power C .10 .25
208 Thanos, Alpha and Omega R .40 1.00
209 Barnacle, Acolyte U .20 .50
210 Negative Zone, Shadow Dimension U .20 .50
211 Syphonn, Energy Leech R .50 1.25
212 Carnage, Symbiote Surfer R .60 1.50
213 Dr. Strange, Illuminati U .20 .50
214 Mephisto, Lord of Hell U .20 .50
215 Taskmaster, Mnemonic Assassin U .20 .50
216 O-Force R .40 1.00
217 Katrina Luisa Van Horne Amazon, Unrepentant Hero U .20 .50
218 Haywire, Suicidal Lover R .60 1.50
219 Litterbug, Killer Cockroach U .20 .50
220 Mr. Sinister, Supreme Geneticist U .20 .50

2006 Vs System Infinite Crisis

COMPLETE SET (220) 25.00 50.00
BOOSTER BOX (24 PACKS) 20.00 40.00
BOOSTER PACK (14 CARDS) 1.00 2.00
*FOIL: .8X TO 2X BASIC CARDS
RELEASED IN APRIL 2006
1 Alan Scott Sentinel, Golden Age Guardian R .40 1.00
2 Atom Smasher, Al Rothstein U .20 .50
3 Batman, Earth 2 C .10 .25
4 Black Adam, Ruthless Hero C .10 .25
5 Captain Marvel, Earth's Mightiest Mortal R .40 1.00
6 Carter Hall Hawkman, Eternal Champion C .10 .25
7 Charles McNider Dr. Mid-Nite, Golden Age Academic U .20 .50
8 Chay-Ara Hawkgirl, Eternal Companion C .10 .25
9 Dr. Fate, Lord of Order R .40 1.00
10 Hourman III Hourman, Time Machine U .20 .50
11 Huntress, Earth 2 C .10 .25
12 Jakeem Williams, JJ Thunder U .20 .50
13 Jay Garrick The Flash, Golden Age Speedster R .40 1.00
14 Katar Hol Hawkman, Eternal Hero C .10 .25
15 Kate Spencer Manhunter, Fearless Renegade U .20 .50
16 Kendra Saunders Hawkgirl, Eternal Heroine C .10 .25
17 Michael Holt Mr. Terrific, Renaissance Man C .10 .25
18 Power Girl, Earth 2 C .10 .25
19 Prince Khufu Hawkman, Eternal Warrior C .10 .25
20 Rex Tyler Hourman, Inventor of Miraclo R .40 1.00
21 Richard Tyler Hourman, Man of the Hour U .20 .50
22 Sand, Sanderson Hawkins C .10 .25
23 Stargirl, Courtney Whitmore C .10 .25
24 Superman, Earth 2 C .10 .25
25 Ted Grant Wildcat, Golden Age Pugilist C .10 .25
26 Terry Sloane Mr. Terrific, Golden Age Gold Medalist C .10 .25
27 The Phantom Stranger, Wandering Hero U .20 .50
28 Thunderbolt, Yz R .40 1.00
29 Wesley Dodds The Sandman, Golden Age Gunman U .20 .50
30 Wonder Woman, Earth 2 C .10 .25
31 A Moment of Crisis C .10 .25
32 Advance Warning R .40 1.00
33 Allied Against the Dark C .10 .25
34 Brothers in Arms U .20 .50
35 Double Play U .20 .50
36 Heroic Rescue C .10 .25
37 JSA Headquarters R .40 1.00
38 Justice United, Team-Up C .10 .25
39 Living Legacy U .20 .50
40 Taking Up the Mantle C .10 .25
41 The Rock of Eternity R .75 2.00
42 T-Spheres C .10 .25
43 Black Alice, Lori Zechlin U .20 .50
44 Blackbriar Thorn, Druid of Cymru U .20 .50
45 Blue Devil, Dan Cassidy C .10 .25
46 Blue Devil, Big Blue C .10 .25
47 Captain Marvel, Champion of Magic R .40 1.00
48 Detective Chimp, Bobo T. Chimpanzee C .10 .25
49 Detective Chimp, Shoeless Gumshoe R .40 1.00
50 Dr. Fate, Hector Hall C .10 .25
51 Dr. Occult, Richard Occult C .10 .25
52 Ibis, Prince Amentep C .10 .25
53 June Moon Enchantress, Good Witch R .40 1.00
54 June Moon Enchantress, Bad Witch R .40 1.00
55 Madame Xanadu, Cartomancer U .20 .50
56 Manitou Dawn, Spirit Shaman C .10 .25
57 Nightmaster, Jim Rook C .10 .25
58 Nightmaster, Demon Slayer R .40 1.00
59 Nightshade, Eve Eden C .10 .25
60 Nightshade, Shadow Siren C .10 .25
61 Ragman, Patchmonger U .20 .50
62 Ragman, Redeemer of Souls C .10 .25
63 Rose Psychic, Ghost Detective C .10 .25
64 Shazam, The Sorcerer R .40 1.00
65 The Phantom Stranger, Fallen Angel C .10 .25
66 Witchfire, Rebecca Carstairs C .10 .25
67 Zatanna, Magical Manipulator C .10 .25
68 Zatanna, Showstopper C .10 .25
69 Abjuration, Magic U .20 .50
70 Chimp Detective Agency R .40 1.00
71 Collecting Souls, Magic C .10 .25
72 Conjuration, Magic R .40 1.00
73 Divination, Magic C .10 .25
74 Magical Conduit, Magic U .20 .50
75 Mystical Binding, Magic C .10 .25
76 Spectral Slaughter, Magic R .40 1.00
77 Stepping Between Worlds, Magic C .10 .25
78 The Conclave, Magic R 1.25 3.00
79 The Oblivion Bar U .20 .50
80 True Name, Magic C .10 .25
81 Adrian Chase Vigilante, Street Justice R .40 1.00
82 Ahmed Samsarra, White King U .20 .50
83 Amanda Waller, Queen C .10 .25
84 Annihilation Protocol OMAC Robot, Army C .10 .25
85 Arthur Kendrick, Knight C .10 .25
86 Aspiring Pawn, Army C .10 .25
87 Black Thorn, Elizabeth Thorne U .20 .50
88 Christopher Smith Peacemaker, Obsessed Outlaw U .20 .50
89 Connie Webb, Knight U .20 .50
90 Elimination Protocol OMAC Robot, Army C .10 .25
91 Graziella Reza, Knight C .10 .25
92 Harry Stein, King in Check U .20 .50
93 Huntress, Reluctant Queen C .10 .25
94 Jacob Lee, Knight U .20 .50
95 Maxwell Lord, Black King R .40 1.00
96 Neutralization Protocol OMAC Robot, Army C .10 .25
97 Retrieval Protocol OMAC Robot, Army C .10 .25
98 Roy Harper Arsenal, Knight C .10 .25
99 Sarge Steel, Knight U .20 .50
100 Sasha Bordeaux, Knight C .10 .25
101 Sasha Bordeaux, Autonomous Prototype C .10 .25
102 Surveillance Pawn, Army C .10 .25
103 Valentina Vostok, Negative Woman, Bishop C .10 .25
104 Brother Eye U .20 .50
105 Brother I Satellite U .20 .50
106 Check and Mate! R .40 1.00
107 Checkmate Armory C .10 .25
108 Checkmate Safe House, Team-Up C .10 .25
109 Knight Armor U .20 .50
110 Knightmare Scenario U .20 .50
111 Knights' Gambit R .40 1.00
112 Laser Watch C .10 .25
113 Pawn of the Black King R .40 1.00
114 Rook Control U .20 .50
115 Secret Checkmate HQ C .10 .25
116 Target Acquired C .10 .25
117 Threat Neutralized U .20 .50
118 Traitor to the Cause C .10 .25
119 Alexander Luthor, Duplicitous Doppelganger U .20 .50
120 Alexander Luthor, Insidious Impostor R .40 1.00
121 Alexander Luthor, Diabolical Double C .10 .25
122 Bizarro, ME AM BIZARRO #1 C .10 .25
123 Black Adam, Teth-Adam C .10 .25
124 Black Adam, Lord of Kahndaq R .40 1.00
125 Cheetah, Feral Feline C .10 .25
126 Count Vertigo, Werner Vertigo C .10 .25
127 Deathstroke the Terminator, Lethal Weapon C .10 .25
128 Deathstroke the Terminator, Ultimate Assassin R .40 1.00
129 Dr. Polaris, Force of Nature C .10 .25
130 Dr. Light, Furious Flashpoint U .20 .50
131 Dr. Psycho, Mental Giant C .10 .25
132 Dr. Psycho, Twisted Telepath C .10 .25
133 Fatality, Flawless Victory R .40 1.00
134 Hunter Zolomon Professor Zoom, Sinister Speedster R .40 1.00
135 Ishmael Gregor Sabbac, Malevolent Marvel C .10 .25
136 Mr. Freeze, Brutal Blizzard C .10 .25
137 Sinestro, Villain Reborn C .10 .25
138 Talia, Beloved Betrayer U .20 .50
139 Talia, Daughter of Madness R .40 1.00
140 The Calculator, Noah Kuttler C .10 .25
141 The Calculator, Evil Oracle C .10 .25
142 The Calculator, Crime Broker C .10 .25
143 Weather Wizard, Mark Mardon C .10 .25
144 Zazzala Queen Bee, Mistress of the Hive C .10 .25
145 3 . . . 2 . . . 1 . . . R .40 1.00
146 Arms Deal R .40 1.00
147 Baddest of the Bad U .20 .50
148 Coercion, Team-Up C .10 .25
149 Grand Gesture C .10 .25
150 Join Us or Die U .20 .50
151 No Hope R .40 1.00
152 No Mercy C .10 .25
153 Return Fire! C .10 .25
154 Systematic Torture C .10 .25
155 The Science Spire R .75 2.00
156 Catman, Thomas Blake C .10 .25
157 Cheshire, Jade C .10 .25
158 Deadshot, Dead Aim C .10 .25
159 Fiddler, Isaac Bowin C .10 .25
160 Lex Luthor Mockingbird, Evil Exile U .20 .50
161 Parademon, Apokoliptian Ally C .10 .25
162 Ragdoll, Resilient Rogue C .10 .25
163 Scandal, Savage Spawn C .10 .25
164 Dodge the Bullet R .40 1.00
165 Help Wanted, Team-Up U .20 .50
166 House of Secrets U .20 .50
167 It's Not Over Yet U .20 .50
168 Secret Six Victorious R .40 1.00
169 Harbinger, Multiverse Messenger R .40 1.00
170 Pariah, Herald of Doom R .40 1.00
171 Superboy, Earth Prime R .40 1.00
172 The Monitor, Guardian of the Multiverse R .40 1.00
173 Bart Allen The Flash, Impulsive Speedster R .40 1.00
174 Amulet of Nabu, Fate Artifact C .10 .25
175 Cloak of Nabu, Fate Artifact C .10 .25
176 Helm of Nabu, Fate Artifact C .10 .25
177 Dr. Fate's Tower U .20 .50
178 Fate Has Spoken, Magic R .40 1.00
179 Eclipso, Jean Loring R .40 1.00
180 Jaime Reyes Blue Beetle, High-Tech Hero U .20 .50
181 Mordru, Dark Lord C .10 .25
182 The Spectre, Soulless R .40 1.00
183 Absolute Dominance R .40 1.00
184 Blinding Rage R 1.00 2.50
185 Burning Gaze C .10 .25
186 Death from Above C .10 .25
187 Defend Yourself! C .10 .25
188 Deflection C .10 .25
189 End of All That Is R .40 1.00
190 Epic Battle C .10 .25
191 Forbidden Loyalties, Team-Up C .10 .25
192 I Still Hate Magic! C .10 .25
193 Magical Lobotomy, Magic U .20 .50
194 Multiverse Power Battery U .20 .50
195 Rann C .10 .25
196 Relentless Pursuit C .10 .25
197 Removed from Continuity R .40 1.00
198 Revitalize C .10 .25
199 Thanagar C .10 .25
200 Thanagarian Invasion C .10 .25
201 Transmutation, Magic R .40 1.00
202 Tricked-Out Sports Car C .10 .25
203 Watch the Birdie! C .10 .25
204 Barbara Gordon Oracle, Data Broker R .40 1.00
205 Leslie Thompkins's Clinic U .20 .50
206 Mourn for the Lost U .20 .50
207 Return of Donna Troy U .20 .50
208 Amadeus Arkham, Architect of Insanity U .20 .50
209 The Joker, Permanent Vacation R .60 1.50
210 The Penguin, Arms Merchant U .20 .50
211 Seiobo's Garden R .40 1.00
212 Lois Lane, Earth 2 U .20 .50
213 Lex Luthor, Champion of the Common Man U .20 .50
214 Kilowog, Drill Sergeant U .20 .50
215 Brainiac, Earth 2 U .20 .50
216 Obsidian, Todd James Rice U .20 .50
217 Adam Strange, Champion of Rann R .40 1.00
218 Animal Man, Buddy Baker U .20 .50
219 Mr. Mxyzptlk, Troublesome Trickster R .40 1.00
220 Ultra-Humanite, Metahuman Manipulator R .40 1.00

2006 Vs System Legion of Super-Heroes

COMPLETE SET (220) 30.00 60.00
BOOSTER BOX (24 PACKS) 25.00 50.00
BOOSTER PACK (14 CARDS) 1.00 2.00
*FOIL: .8X TO 2X BASIC CARDS
RELEASED IN DECEMBER 2006
1 Andromeda, Laurel Gand C .10 .25
2 Apparition, Tinya Wazzo C .10 .25
3 Bouncing Boy, Chuck Taine C .10 .25
4 Brainiac 5.1, Querl Dox R .75 2.00
5 Chameleon, Reep Daggle U .20 .50
6 Colossal Boy Leviathan, Gim Allon C .10 .25
7 Cosmic Boy, Rokk Krinn R .75 2.00
8 Dream Girl, Nura Nal R 1.00 2.50
9 Element Lad, Jan Arrah C .10 .25
10 Ferro Lad, Andrew Nolan C .10 .25
11 Jazmin Cullen Kid Quantum, Hero of Xanthu C .10 .25
12 Kara Zor-El Supergirl, Lost in Time U .20 .50
13 Karate Kid, Val Armorr C .10 .25
14 Kinetix, Zoe Saugin C .10 .25
15 Live Wire, Garth Ranzz C .10 .25
16 Mon-el Valor, Lar Gand R .40 1.00
17 R.J. Brande, Philanthropist U .20 .50
18 Saturn Girl, Imra Ardeen R .60 1.50
19 Sensor, Jeka Wynzorr U .20 .50
20 Shrinking Violet Leviathan, Salu Digby U .20 .50
21 Spark, Ayla Ranzz C .10 .25
22 Star Boy, Thom Kallor C .10 .25
23 Sun Boy, Dirk Morgna C .10 .25
24 Timber Wolf, Brin Londo C .10 .25
25 Triad, Luornu Durgo U .20 .50
26 Ultra Boy, Jo Nah U .20 .50
27 Umbra, Tasmia Mallor C .10 .25
28 Wildfire, Drake Burroughs C .10 .25
29 XS, Jenni Ognats C .10 .25
30 Celebrity Status R .60 1.50
31 Flight Ring C .10 .25
32 Foiled Assassination U .20 .50
33 Legion Headquarters C .10 .25
34 Legion of Super-Pets C .10 .25
35 Legion World C .10 .25
36 Let's Go, Legionnaires! C .10 .25
37 Long Live the Legion U .20 .50
38 Many Worlds C .10 .25
39 New Recruits R .75 2.00
40 Past, Present, and Future, Team-Up C .10 .25
41 Science Police Central R .60 1.50
42 Terror Incognita R .75 2.00
43 We Are Legion U .20 .50
44 Youth of Tomorrow, Team-Up C .10 .25
45 Atrophos, Chief Blight Scientist U .20 .50
46 Brainiac 4, Dark Circle Leader C .10 .25
47 Composite Man, Living Weapon R .40 1.00
48 Computo, Rogue Program C .10 .25
49 Computo Mr. Venge, Hidden File C .10 .25
50 Cosmic King, Legion of Super Villains C .10 .25
51 Daxamites, Army C .10 .25
52 Dominators, Alien Invaders C .10 .25
53 Emerald Empress, Fatal Five U .20 .50
54 Emerald Eye, Sentient Artifact C .10 .25
55 Glorith, Seductive Sorceress C .10 .25
56 Lightning Lord, Legion of Super Villains C .10 .25
57 Mano, Fatal Five C .10 .25
58 Mordru, The Merciless C .10 .25
59 Ol-Vir, Legion of Super Villains C .10 .25
60 Ra's al Ghul, Engine of Change C .10 .25
61 Ra's al Ghul Leland McCauley, U.P. President C .10 .25
62 Saturn Queen, Legion of Super Villains C .10 .25
63 Shrinking Violet Emerald Empress, Emerald Vi C .10 .25
64 Starfinger, Char Burrane R .75 2.00
65 Tarik the Mute, Legion of Super Villains C .10 .25
66 Tharok, Fatal Five C .10 .25
67 The Blight, Army U .20 .50
68 The Persuader, Fatal Five R 1.00 2.50
69 Time Trapper, Temporal Manipulator R 1.25 3.00
70 Universo, Vidar R .75 2.00

71 Validus, Fatal Five C .10 .25
72 Altered History C .10 .25
73 Asteroid JS-1967 U .20 .50
74 Chain Lightning C .10 .25
75 Dark Circle Rising U .20 .50
76 Dominated R .40 1.00
77 Earth Enslaved U .20 .50
78 Fatal Five Hundred C .10 .25
79 Five Against One C .10 .25
80 For Khundia! C .10 .25
81 Khundian Warship U .20 .50
82 Legion of the Damned C .10 .25
83 Mutual Enemies U .20 .50
84 Return of the Demon's Head R 1.25 3.00
85 Sorcerous Suppression C .10 .25
86 Tempus Fugit U .20 .50
87 The Sun-Eater R .60 1.50
88 Apokoliptian Zealots, Army C .10 .25
89 Bernadeth, Female Fury U .20 .50
90 Dark Champion, Mockery C .10 .25
91 Dark Firestorm, Mockery C .10 .25
92 Dark Kryptonian Dark Superboy, Mockery R .75 2.00
93 Dark Lantern, Mockery C .10 .25
94 Dark Martian, Mockery C .10 .25
95 Dark Superboy, Mockery R .75 2.00
96 Dark Thanagarian, Mockery C .10 .25
97 Dark Warrior, Mockery C .10 .25
98 Darkseid, 8th Century C .10 .25
99 Darkseid, Apokolips Now R .75 2.00
100 Darkseid, Apokoliptian Oppressor C .10 .25
101 Darkseid, Evil Reborn C .10 .25
102 Darkseid, Nemesis R .75 2.00
103 Gillotina, Female Fury C .10 .25
104 Kara Zor-El Supergirl, Female Fury C .10 .25
105 Knockout, Female Fury C .10 .25
106 Lashina, Female Fury C .10 .25
107 Mad Harriet, Female Fury C .10 .25
108 Malice Vundabar, Female Fury C .10 .25
109 Parademon Elite, Army C .10 .25
110 Speed Queen, Female Fury C .10 .25
111 Stompa, Female Fury R .60 1.50
112 31st Century Apokolips R .50 1.25
113 All Hail Darkseid! U .20 .50
114 Ancient Evils, Team-Up C .10 .25
115 Ancient Throne U .20 .50
116 Created from Hate R 2.50 6.00
117 Curse of Darkness R .40 1.00
118 Dark Fury C .10 .25
119 Dark Matter Drain R .40 1.00
120 Joining the Darkseid, Team-Up C .10 .25
121 No Match for Darkseid R .75 2.00
122 Omega Effect C .10 .25
123 Price of Treason C .10 .25
124 Prophetic Battle C .10 .25
125 Servants of Darkness C .10 .25
126 Shock and Awe U .20 .50
127 Unravel Reality U .20 .50
128 Bart Allen Kid Flash, Heir to the Mantle U .20 .50
129 Bart Allen The Flash, Titans Tomorrow West U .20 .50
130 Beast Boy, Party Animal C .10 .25
131 Beast Boy Animal Man, Titans Tomorrow West C .10 .25
132 Bette Kane Batwoman, Titans Tomorrow East U .20 .50
133 Bumblebee, Titans Tomorrow East C .10 .25
134 Cassie Sandsmark Wonder Girl, Ares's Chosen C .10 .25
135 Cassie Sandsmark Wonder Woman, Titans Tomorrow West C .10 .25
136 Connor Kent Superboy, Inspiration to the Legion C .10 .25
137 Connor Kent Superman, Titans Tomorrow West R .40 1.00
138 Dawn Granger Dove, Avatar of Order C .10 .25
139 Duela Dent Harlequin, The Joker's Daughter C .10 .25
140 Freddy Freeman Captain Marvel, Titans Tomorrow East C .10 .25
141 Holly Granger Hawk, Avatar of Chaos C .10 .25
142 Kid Devil, Eddie Bloomberg C .10 .25
143 Koriand'r Starfire, Tamaranian Princess C .10 .25
144 Lorena Marquez Aquawoman, Titans Tomorrow West R .50 1.25
145 Mia Dearden Speedy, Deadly Aim C .10 .25
146 Raven, Rachel Roth R .50 1.25
147 Raven Dark Raven, Titans Tomorrow West R .75 2.00
148 Rose Wilson The Ravager, Daughter of Deathstroke R .40 1.00
149 Rose Wilson The Ravager, Titans Tomorrow East U .20 .50
150 Terra, Titans Tomorrow East U .20 .50
151 The Herald, Malcolm Duncan C .10 .25
152 Tim Drake Batman, Titans Tomorrow West U .20 .50
153 Tim Drake Robin, Sidekick No More C .10 .25
154 Vic Stone Cyborg, Titans Veteran C .10 .25
155 Vic Stone Cyborg 2.0, Titans Tomorrow East U .20 .50
156 Born of Blood U .20 .50
157 Clash of the Titans C .10 .25
158 First Date C .10 .25
159 Generation Next, Team-Up C .10 .25
160 Hall of Mentors U .20 .50
161 Now You See Me R .40 1.00
162 Order and Chaos U .20 .50
163 Pour It On R 1.00 2.50
164 Tamaranian Garden R .40 1.00
165 Titans Communicator C .10 .25
166 Titans Memorial U .20 .50
167 Titans, Together! R .50 1.25
168 T-Jet, Tamaranian Fighter U .20 .50
169 Donna Troy, Born Again C .10 .25
170 Superboy, Yellow Sun Armor U .20 .50
171 Jason Todd Red Hood, Revived R .40 1.00
172 31st Century Metropolis, Team-Up C .10 .25
173 Awestruck C .10 .25
174 Blinding Light C .10 .25
175 Busted Knee C .10 .25
176 Contact! U .20 .50
177 Cosmic Tuning Fork R 1.50 4.00
178 Death of a Legionnaire C .10 .25
179 Earth 2 U .20 .50
180 Forged in Crisis U .20 .50
181 Furious Assault C .10 .25
182 Furnace of Apokolips C .10 .25
183 Girls' Night Out C .10 .25
184 Legion Lost C .10 .25
185 Level 12 Intelligence R 1.25 3.00
186 Lost in Translation U .20 .50
187 Mobilize R 12.00 30.00
188 Need for Speed R 1.00 2.50
189 Ravaged! U .20 .50
190 Steely Resolve R .40 1.00
191 Substitute Heroes C .10 .25
192 The Future Is Changing C .10 .25
193 Titans of Tomorrow U .20 .50
194 United Planets HQ, Team-Up C .10 .25
195 Crimson Avenger, Jill Carlyle U .20 .50
196 Jack Knight Starman, Knight Past U .20 .50
197 Power Girl, Child of Crisis R 1.25 3.00
198 S.T.R.I.P.E., Pat Dugan U .20 .50
199 Alan Scott, White King U .20 .50
200 Director Bones, D.E.O. U .20 .50
201 Fire, Knight U .20 .50
202 Girl 13 Traci Thirteen, Hex and the City R .40 1.00
203 Mary Marvel, World's Mightiest Girl U .20 .50
204 Otherworldly Battle, Magic R .40 1.00
205 Blüdhaven Destroyed R .40 1.00
206 Chemo, Chemical Golem U .20 .50
207 High Society C .10 .25
208 Harvey Bullock, Bishop R .75 2.00
209 The Riddler, Brain Teaser R .40 1.00
210 Nyssa Raatko, Daughter of the Demon R .60 1.50
211 Solar Powered R 1.00 2.50
212 Brainiac 2.5, Future Intelligence R .60 1.50
213 Shiloh Norman Mister Miracle, Soldier of Victory R .50 1.25
214 Kyle Rayner Ion, Torch Bearer R 1.50 4.00
215 Mongul, Intergalactic Menace R .40 1.00
216 Alexander Luthor, Earth 3 U .20 .50
217 Kate Spencer Manhunter, Vigilante Justice U .20 .50
218 Wally West The Flash, The Fastest Man Alive R .60 1.50
219 Peter Merkel Ragdoll, Malleable Miscreant U .20 .50
220 Owen Mercer Captain Boomerang, Digger's Son U .20 .50

2006 Vs System X-Men

COMPLETE SET (220) 30.00 60.00
BOOSTER BOX (24 PACKS) 30.00 60.00
BOOSTER PACK (14 CARDS) 1.50 2.50
*FOIL: .8X TO 2X BASIC CARDS
RELEASED IN FEBRUARY 2006
1 Archangel, Angel C .10 .25
2 Beast, Feline Geneticist U .20 .50
3 Bishop, XSE Commando C .10 .25
4 Cannonball, Blast Field C .10 .25
5 Changeling, Kevin Sidney R .40 1.00
6 Colossus, Organic Steel U .20 .50
7 Cyclops, Blue Leader C .10 .25
8 Dazzler, Rock Star C .10 .25
9 Emma Frost, Friend or Foe R 1.00 2.50
10 Gambit, Ragin' Cajun U .20 .50
11 Havok, Critical Mass C .10 .25
12 Iceman, Deep Freeze C .10 .25
13 Jean Grey, Red R .40 1.00
14 Jubilee, Jubilation Lee U .20 .50
15 Juggernaut, The Unstoppable U .75 2.00
16 Lockheed, Saurian Sidekick C .10 .25
17 Longshot, Hero of Mojoworld U .20 .50
18 Nightcrawler, Swashbuckler C .10 .25
19 Professor X, Headmaster R 1.50 4.00
20 Psylocke, Armored Empath C .10 .25
21 Rachel Summers Phoenix, Phoenix of the Future R .40 1.00
22 Rogue, Anna Marie C .10 .25
23 Sage, Xavier's Secret Weapon C .10 .25
24 Shadowcat, Kitya C .10 .25
25 Storm, Gold Leader C .10 .25
26 Wolverine, The Best at What He Does C .10 .25
27 Xorn, Shen Xorn C .10 .25
28 Angel of Mercy U .20 .50
29 Blackbird Blue U .20 .50
30 Harry's Hideaway U .20 .50
31 Phoenix Rising R .40 1.00
32 Rebirth C .10 .25
33 SNIKT! R .60 1.50
34 Time Breach R .40 1.00
35 Turnabout C .10 .25
36 Worthington Industries, X-Corp R 1.25 3.00
37 X-Corp: Amsterdam, X-Corp C .10 .25
38 X-Corp: Hong Kong, X-Corp C .10 .25
39 X-Corp: Paris, X-Corp C .10 .25
40 X-Men United, Team-Up C .10 .25
41 X-Treme Maneuver U .20 .50
42 Angel Dust, Adrenaline Junkie U .20 .50
43 Annalee, Mother Hen C .10 .25
44 Ape, Metamorph R .40 1.00
45 Artie, Arthur Maddicks C .10 .25
46 Blow Hard, Windbag U .20 .50
47 Caliban, Mutant Bloodhound C .10 .25
48 Callisto, Morlock Queen C .10 .25
49 Cybelle, Meltdown R .40 1.00
50 Electric Eve, Live Wire C .10 .25
51 Erg, Electric Eye C .10 .25
52 Feral, Maria Callasantos C .10 .25
53 Healer, Life Giver C .10 .25
54 Hemingway, Gene Nation C .10 .25
55 Hump, Servant of Masque U .20 .50
56 Leech, Inhibitor U .20 .50
57 Marrow, Gene Nation C .10 .25
58 Masque, Flesh Shaper U .20 .50
59 Mikhail Rasputin, Morlock Messiah R .40 1.00
60 Piper, Rat Charmer C .10 .25
61 Plague, Deathwalker C .10 .25
62 Postman, Memory Thief U .20 .50
63 Scaleface, Dragon Lady C .10 .25
64 Storm, Leader of the Morlocks C .10 .25
65 Sunder, Callisto's Enforcer C .10 .25
66 Tar Baby, Adhesive Ally C .10 .25
67 The Beautiful Dreamer, Dreamweaver C .10 .25
68 Thornn, Lucia Callasantos R .40 1.00
69 Tommy, Runaway C .10 .25
70 Backs Against the Wall R .40 1.00
71 Bloodhound U .20 .50
72 Bum's Rush C .10 .25
73 Good Samaritan R .40 1.00
74 Morlock Justice U .20 .50
75 Neutralized C .10 .25
76 Retribution C .10 .25
77 Sewer System U .20 .50
78 Shrapnel Blast U .20 .50
79 Subterranean Sanctuary R .40 1.00
80 The Alley U .20 .50
81 The Forsaken, Team-Up C .10 .25
82 The Hill C .10 .25
83 Amelia Voght, Acolyte R .75 2.00
84 Anne-Marie Cortez, Acolyte C .10 .25
85 Avalanche, Freedom Force R .40 1.00
86 Blob, Freedom Force C .10 .25
87 Chrome, Acolyte C .10 .25
88 Colossus, Acolyte U .20 .50
89 Crimson Commando, Freedom Force C .10 .25
90 Destiny, Freedom Force C .10 .25
91 Exodus, Acolyte C .10 .25
92 Fabian Cortez, Acolyte U .20 .50
93 Harry Delgado, Acolyte C .10 .25
94 Joanna Cargill, Acolyte C .10 .25
95 Julia Carpenter, Freedom Force C .10 .25
96 Kleinstock Brothers, Acolyte U .20 .50
97 Magneto, Ruler of Avalon R .50 1.25
98 Mystique, Freedom Force U .20 .50
99 Polaris, Acolyte C .10 .25
100 Pyro, Freedom Force C .10 .25
101 Rem-Ram, Acolyte C .10 .25
102 Sabretooth, Savage Killer R .50 1.25
103 Scanner, Acolyte C .10 .25
104 Senyaka, Acolyte C .10 .25
105 Silver Sabre, Freedom Force C .10 .25
106 Spiral, Freedom Force R .40 1.00
107 Spoor, Acolyte C .10 .25
108 Stonewall, Freedom Force U .20 .50
109 Toad, Hopalong C .10 .25
110 Unuscione, Acolyte U .20 .50
111 Acolyte Body Armor U .20 .50
112 Boot to the Head R .50 1.25
113 Freedom Force C .10 .25
114 Go Down Fighting C .10 .25
115 Hellhound U .20 .50
116 Kill the Flatscans U .20 .50
117 Lying in Wait C .10 .25
118 Planet X, Team-Up C .10 .25
119 Ruins of Avalon R .40 1.00
120 Shake, Rattle, and Roll R .40 1.00
121 Sovereign Superior U .20 .50
122 The Acolytes R .40 1.00
123 Wundagore Citadel C .10 .25
124 Beef, Hellion C .10 .25
125 Bevatron, Hellion C .10 .25
126 Catseye, Hellion U .20 .50
127 Courtney Ross, Once and Future Queen U .20 .50
128 Dark Phoenix, Alien Life Force R .50 1.25
129 Donald Pierce, White Bishop C .10 .25
130 Emma Frost, White Queen C .10 .25
131 Empath, Hellion C .10 .25
132 Firestar, Hellion C .10 .25
133 Friedrich Von Roehm, Black Rook C .10 .25
134 Harry Leland, Black Bishop R .40 1.00
135 Hellfire Club Initiate, Army C .10 .25
136 Hellfire Club Mercenary, Army C .10 .25
137 James Proudstar Thunderbird, Hellion R .40 1.00
138 Jetstream, Hellion C .10 .25
139 Madelyne Pryor, Black Rook C .10 .25
140 Magneto, Black Lord R .40 1.00
141 Mastermind, Dark Dreamer C .10 .25
142 Roberto Da Costa, Heir to the Throne C .10 .25
143 Roulette, Hellion R .40 1.00
144 Sage, Tessa C .10 .25
145 Sebastian Shaw, Black King R .40 1.00
146 Selene, Black Queen C .10 .25
147 Shinobi Shaw, White King C .10 .25
148 Tarot, Hellion C .10 .25
149 Trevor Fitzroy, White Rook R .40 1.00
150 Viper, White Warrior Princess C .10 .25
151 Absolute Power U .20 .50
152 Army of One C .10 .25
153 Cardinal Law C .10 .25
154 Deadly Game R .40 1.00
155 Eminent Domain R .40 1.00
156 Evil Alliance, Team-Up C .10 .25
157 Inner Circle R .40 1.00
158 Join the Club! U .20 .50
159 Massachusetts Academy U .20 .50
160 Power and Wealth R .75 2.00
161 Power Play R .40 1.00
162 Raising Hell C .10 .25
163 Shaw Industries U .20 .50
164 The Hellfire Club C .10 .25
165 Above and Below, Team-Up U .20 .50
166 Blow the Man Down R .50 1.25
167 Chill Out! R .40 1.00
168 Drain Essence C .10 .25
169 Feel the Burn C .10 .25
170 Magnetic Force U .20 .50
171 The Evil Eye C .10 .25
172 Phase Shift C .10 .25
173 Memory Probe C .10 .25
174 Mental Domination U .20 .50
175 Mind Control C .10 .25
176 Psi-Link R .40 1.00
177 Psionic Storm C .10 .25
178 Psychic Armor C .10 .25
179 Psychic Struggle R .40 1.00
180 Immovable C .10 .25
181 Kidney Punch C .10 .25
182 Kill or be Killed C .10 .25
183 Mob Mentality R .40 1.00
184 Momentary Distraction R .40 1.00
185 Pack Tactics C .10 .25
186 Special Delivery U .20 .50
187 Krakoa, Island Monster C .10 .25
188 Multiple Man Jamie Madrox, Army U 1.50 4.00
189 Wolverine, Patch R .40 1.00
190 X-23, Laura Kinney R .50 1.25
191 Alter Density C .10 .25
192 Brave New World, Team-Up C .10 .25
193 District X U .20 .50
194 Enemy of My Enemy R 10.00 25.00
195 Homo Superior C .10 .25
196 Image Inducer C .10 .25
197 Leadership Challenge C .10 .25
198 Mindtap Mechanism U .20 .50
199 Mutant Massacre U .20 .50
200 Mutopia, Team-Up C .10 .25
201 Super Hero Showdown C .10 .25
202 Teamwork U .20 .50
203 Franklin Richards, Trapped in Time R .40 1.00
204 Kristoff Von Doom, Pretender to the Throne R .40 1.00
205 Sentinel Mark VI, Army U .20 .50
206 Toxin, Patrick Mulligan U .20 .50
207 Man-Bull, William Taurens R .40 1.00
208 Black Panther, King of Wakanda U .20 .50
209 Henrietta Hunter, X-Celebrity U .20 .50
210 Doctor Sun, Creator of Project: Mind R .40 1.00
211 Witch Woman, Linda Littletrees U .20 .50
212 Doctor Druid, Anthony Druid U .20 .50
213 Sub-Mariner, Namor U .20 .50
214 Lady Lark, Skylark R .40 1.00
215 Mysterium, Joseph Lightner R .40 1.00
216 Genis-Vell Photon, Transformed U .20 .50
217 Mech Bay R .40 1.00
218 Absorbing Man, Carl Creel R .40 1.00
219 Gargantua, Edward Cobert R .40 1.00
220 Kang, Scarlet Centurion U .20 .50

2007 Vs System DC Legends

COMPLETE SET (273) 50.00 100.00
BOOSTER BOX (24 PACKS) 50.00 100.00
BOOSTER PACK (14 CARDS) 3.00 4.00
*FOIL: .8X TO 2X BASIC CARDS
RELEASED IN DECEMBER 2007
1 Aquaman, Founding Member C .10 .25
2 Aquaman, Lord of Atlantis U .20 .50
3 Aztek, Champion of Quetzalcoatl C .10 .25
4 Barry Allen The Flash, Crimson Tornado R 3.00 8.00
5 Barry Allen The Flash, Founding Member R 1.25 3.00
6 Batman, Founding Member R 5.00 12.00
7 Batman, Justice's Shadow C .10 .25
8 Big Barda, Furious Fatale C .10 .25
9 Black Lightning, Energetic Hero U .20 .50
10 Dinah Laurel Lance Black Canary, New Wings C .10 .25
11 Elongated Man, Stretchable Sleuth U .20 .50
12 Firehawk, Flaming Justice C .10 .25
13 Firestorm, Ronnie Raymond U .20 .50
14 Hal Jordan, Founding Member R 3.00 8.00
15 Hal Jordan, Fearless R 2.50 6.00
16 John Henry Irons Steel, Working Man C .10 .25
17 John Stewart, The Master Builder C .10 .25
18 Katar Hol Hawkman, Death from Above C .10 .25
19 Kendra Saunders Hawkgirl, Thanagarian Heroine C .10 .25
20 Kyle Rayner, Guardian of the Universe U .20 .50
21 Martian Manhunter, Founding Member C .10 .25
22 Martian Manhunter, The Last Martian R 1.25 3.00
23 Oliver Queen Green Arrow, Bullseye C .10 .25
24 Plastic Man, Plastic Fantastic U .20 .50
25 Ray Palmer The Atom, World's Smallest Hero R .40 1.00
26 Red Tornado, Elemental Android C .10 .25
27 Roy Harper Red Arrow, Coming of Age R .75 2.00
28 Superman, Metropolis Marvel R 2.00 5.00
29 Superman, Founding Member R 1.50 4.00
30 Vixen, Tantu Totem C .10 .25
31 Wally West The Flash, Keystone Cop C .10 .25
32 Wonder Woman, Ambassador of Peace R 2.00 5.00
33 Wonder Woman, Founding Member C .10 .25
34 Zatanna, Sucoh Sucop! C .10 .25
35 Sea Creatures, Army R 1.50 4.00
36 Lasso of Truth R .50 1.25
37 Batcomputer, Criminal Database U .20 .50
38 Cadmus Labs U .20 .50
39 Hall of Justice U .20 .50
40 Keystone City U .20 .50
41 Poseidonis R .75 2.00
42 The Watchtower R .40 1.00
43 Atomize R .75 2.00
44 Battle Training C .10 .25
45 Crisis Averted C .10 .25
46 Emerald Rebirth U .20 .50
47 Fearless R .60 1.50
48 From the Darkness R 3.00 8.00
49 Full Throttle R 1.25 3.00
50 Fury of the Amazons R 1.25 3.00
51 Indestructible R 4.00 10.00
52 Intangible R .40 1.00
53 Magnificent Seven C .10 .25
54 Mightiest Heroes R 4.00 10.00
55 New Era R .40 1.00
56 Recharge! R 1.25 3.00
57 Reform the League C .10 .25
58 Stalwart Defense U .20 .50
59 Telepathic Link R .40 1.00
60 Terminal Velocity R 1.00 2.50
61 Truth, Justice, and Peace R .75 2.00
62 Argent, Toni Monetti C .10 .25
63 Bart Allen Kid Flash, Generation Fourth U .20 .50
64 Beast Boy, Garfield Logan R .75 2.00
65 Beast Boy, Freak of Nature C .10 .25
66 Bette Kane Flamebird, Reflex Action C .10 .25
67 Bumblebee, Sonic Sting U .20 .50
68 Cassie Sandsmark Wonder Girl, Might of Atlas C .10 .25
69 Dawn Granger Dove, Teralaya's Chosen C .10 .25
70 Dick Grayson Nightwing, Going it Alone C .10 .25
71 Donna Troy Wonder Girl, Amazon Warrior R .40 1.00
72 Freddy Freeman Captain Marvel Jr., Third in Line C .10 .25
73 Holly Granger Hawk, T'Charr's Chosen U .20 .50
74 Hot Spot, Isaiah Crockett C .10 .25
75 Jericho, Contact! R .40 1.00
76 Kid Devil, Teen Hellion C .10 .25
77 Koriand'r Starfire, Fiery Temper U .20 .50
78 Koriand'r Starfire, X'Hal's Fury R 4.00 10.00
79 Mia Dearden Speedy, Archer's Apprentice C .10 .25
80 Miss Martian, M'gann M'orzz R 1.25 3.00
81 Pantha, Subject X-24 C .10 .25
82 Raven, Demon Spawn C .10 .25
83 Ray Palmer The Atom, Tiny Titan C .10 .25
84 Red Star, Russian Roulette C .10 .25
85 Rose Wilson The Ravager, Redemption Earned U .20 .50
86 Roy Harper Speedy, Mercurial Marksman R .40 1.00
87 Roy Harper Arsenal, Additional Firepower R 1.25 3.00
88 Tim Drake Robin, Titan in Command U .20 .50
89 Tim Drake Robin, Leader of the Pack R .75 2.00
90 Vic Stone Cyborg, Mechanized Mentor C .10 .25
91 Vic Stone Cyborg, Titans Warhorse U .20 .50
92 Zatara, Teen Magician U .20 .50
93 Cybernetic Laser U .20 .50
94 T-Jet, Unique * Titans Transport R .40 1.00
95 Weapon Upgrade R .40 1.00
96 Optitron R .40 1.00
97 Solar Tower C .10 .25
98 Titans Tower U .20 .50
99 Best Friends Forever R .40 1.00
100 Call of the Wild U .20 .50
101 Cunning Strategy R .60 1.50
102 Follow the Leader U .20 .50
103 Graduation Day U .20 .50
104 Headstrong Charge R .40 1.00
105 More Than Just Sidekicks C .10 .25
106 Prodigies U .20 .50
107 Starbolts R .50 1.25
108 Teen Titans Go! C .10 .25
109 Abra Kadabra, Magical Rogue C .10 .25
110 Agamemno, Interplanetary Conqueror R .40 1.00
111 Barracuda, Earth 3 C .10 .25
112 Black Manta, Deepwater Denizen C .10 .25
113 Captain Boomerang, George Harkness C .10 .25
114 Catwoman, Cat o' Nine Tails C .10 .25
115 Circe, Evil Enchantress C .10 .25
116 David Clinton Chronos, Timetwister R .40 1.00
117 Dr. Light, Blinding Flash R .40 1.00
118 Felix Faust, Soulless Mystic C .10 .25
119 Jemm, Son of Saturn U .20 .50
120 Johnny Quick, Earth 3 C .10 .25
121 The Joker, Headline Stealer C .10 .25
122 The Joker, Killer Smile R .75 2.00
123 Lex Luthor, Megalomaniac R 1.50 4.00
124 Lex Luthor, Metropolis Mogul C .10 .25
125 Lex Luthor, The Everyman R .40 1.00
126 Ocean Master, Son of Atlan C .10 .25
127 Owlman, Earth 3 C .10 .25
128 The Penguin, Gentleman of Crime C .10 .25
129 Power Ring, Earth 3 C .10 .25
130 Prometheus, New Year's Evil U .20 .50
131 Scarecrow, Chiroptophobic R .75 2.00
132 The Shade, Ageless Enigma U .20 .50
133 Sinestro, Korugaran Despot C .10 .25
134 Superwoman, Earth 3 C .10 .25
135 Tattooed Man, Art Imitates Life R .40 1.00
136 Ultraman, Earth 3 C .10 .25
137 Vandal Savage, Cro-Magnon Man R .40 1.00
138 White Martian, Earth 3 C .10 .25
139 Zazzala Queen Bee, H.I.V.E. Monarch R .60 1.50
140 Laughing Gas U .20 .50
141 Earth 3 U .20 .50
142 Injustice Gang Satellite R .40 1.00
143 All Too Easy C .10 .25
144 Crime Syndicate of Amerika R 1.50 4.00
145 Criminal Mastermind C .10 .25
146 Evil Genius U .20 .50
147 Gang-Up, Team-Up C .10 .25
148 Injustice for All R .40 1.00
149 The Joke's on You! R .50 1.25
150 Power Siphon R .40 1.00
151 Research and Development R .40 1.00
152 Secret Files C .10 .25
153 Sunburst R .50 1.25
154 Amazo, Power Duplication C .10 .25
155 Basil Karlo Clayface, Slimy Shapeshifter U .20 .50
156 Bizarro, Dark Mirror U .20 .50
157 Black Manta, Underwater Marauder R 1.25 3.00
158 The Calculator, Q.E.D. C .10 .25
159 Charaxes, Moth Monster R 2.00 5.00
160 Cheetah, Barbara Minerva U .20 .50
161 Chemo, Toxic Waste R 2.50 6.00
162 Darkseid, Destroyer of Life C .10 .25
163 Darkseid, Dark God R 1.50 4.00
164 Deadshot, Floyd Lawton R .40 1.00
165 Deathstroke the Terminator, Killing Machine C .10 .25
166 Desaad, Dark Side Therapy R .50 1.25
167 Doomsday, Engine of Destruction R .50 1.25
168 Dr. Polaris, Polar Opposite C .10 .25
169 Dr. Psycho, Demented Dwarf C .10 .25
170 Dr. Sivana, Mad Scientist C .10 .25
171 Fatality, Okaaran Warrior R 1.00 2.50
172 Felix Faust, Dark Bargain U .20 .50

173 Floronic Man, Jason Woodrue C .10 .25
174 Giganta, Rampaging U .20 .50
175 Gorilla Grodd, Grodd Awful C .10 .25
176 Gorilla Grodd, Psionic Simian C .10 .25
177 Ishmael Gregor Sabbac, Deadly Sin R .40 1.00
178 King Shark, Jaws of Death R 1.00 2.50
179 Mark Desmond Blockbuster, Mindless Brute U .20 .50
180 Mr. Freeze, Cold Blooded R .75 2.00
181 Poison Ivy, Intoxicating U .20 .50
182 Psycho-Pirate, Medusa Mask C .10 .25
183 The Riddler, Riddle Me This R 1.25 3.00
184 Shadow-Thief, Umbral Burglar C .10 .25
185 Sinestro, Yellow Lantern R 1.25 3.00
186 Solomon Grundy, Died on a Saturday R .60 1.50
187 Gorilla City C .10 .25
188 Hidden HQ R 1.00 2.50
189 Remote Facility, Non-Unique C .10 .25
190 Acceptable Loss C .10 .25
191 Anger and Hate R .75 2.00
192 Anti-Life R .60 1.50
193 Coup d'Etat R .40 1.00
194 Endgame R .50 1.25
195 Forced Conscription C .10 .25
196 Going Ape U .20 .50
197 Lord of Apokolips U .20 .50
198 Maleficent Meeting C .10 .25
199 Master Plan U .20 .50
200 Monkey See, Monkey Do R .75 2.00
201 Shadow Strike C .10 .25
202 Straight to the Grave R 1.00 2.50
203 Unnatural Selection U .20 .50
204 Cassandra Cain, Daughter of Shiva U .20 .50
205 David Cain, World Class Assassin R .40 1.00
206 Hassim, Loyal Retainer U .20 .50
207 Lady Shiva, Master Assassin R .40 1.00
208 The Mad Dog, Rabid Killer C .10 .25
209 Merlyn, Direct Hit Man R 1.00 2.50
210 Novice Assassin, Army C .10 .25
211 Nyssa Raatko, Maiden of Death C .10 .25
212 Ra's al Ghul, Demon's Head Rising C .10 .25
213 Ra's al Ghul, The Demon's Head R 1.25 3.00
214 Shadow Assassin, Army C .10 .25
215 Shrike, Boone C .10 .25
216 Talia, Heir Apparent C .10 .25
217 Ubu, Ra's al Ghul's Bodyguard C .10 .25
218 The Demon's Quarters R .40 1.00
219 Flying Fortress U .20 .50
220 Lazarus Pit, Non-Unique * Death's Door R .60 1.50
221 Mountain Stronghold, Non-Unique U .20 .50
222 Plague Zone, Non-Unique U .20 .50
223 The Demon's Head R .40 1.00
224 Demonfang C .10 .25
225 Divide and Conquer R .50 1.25
226 Harsh Judgment R .40 1.00
227 Tower of Babel R .40 1.00
228 The Chief, Niles Caulder U .20 .50
229 Elasti-Girl, Rita Farr R .60 1.50
230 Mento, Steve Dayton U .20 .50
231 Negative Man, Larry Trainor U .20 .50
232 Robotman, Cliff Steele C .10 .25
233 Dayton Manor R 1.00 2.50
234 Freak Out R .60 1.50
235 Misfits R .50 1.25
236 Strange Days R .40 1.00
237 Captain Atom, Quantum Energy R .40 1.00
238 The Demon, Etrigan R .50 1.25
239 Imperiex, The Beginning and The End R .40 1.00
240 Lobo, The Main Man R 1.50 4.00
241 Supernova, Daniel Carter R 1.00 2.50
242 Terra, Earth Mover R .50 1.25
243 Twin Firearms U .20 .50
244 Nth Metal C .10 .25
245 Birthing Chamber U .20 .50
246 Coast City C .10 .25
247 Metropolis Reborn, Non-Unique * Team-Up C .10 .25
248 A Better World, Team-Up C .10 .25
249 Blind Sided R 1.25 3.00
250 Blinding Rage R 1.00 2.50
251 Break You C .10 .25
252 Changing Minds, Team-Up C .10 .25
253 Chaos and Villainy, Team-Up C .10 .25
254 Combat Reflexes C .10 .25
255 Death Trap C .10 .25
256 Dirty Tricks R .40 1.00
257 Duty Calls C .10 .25
258 From the Shadows C .10 .25
259 Have a Blast! R 1.00 2.50
260 Hero's Best Friend C .10 .25
261 Heroes of Two Worlds R 2.50 6.00
262 Heroic Effort C .10 .25
263 Home Surgery C .10 .25
264 Judgment Day R .40 1.00
265 Mirror Image R .50 1.25
266 The Multiverse, Team-Up C .10 .25
267 Nasty Surprise C .10 .25
268 Overwhelming Odds C .10 .25
269 Path of Destruction C .10 .25
270 Shape Change U .20 .50
271 Tag Team C .10 .25
272 Total Anarchy R .40 1.00
273 Total Recall, Team-Up U .20 .50

2007 Vs System Marvel Legends

COMPLETE SET (273) 50.00 100.00
BOOSTER BOX (24 PACKS) 30.00 60.00
BOOSTER PACK (14 CARDS) 1.50 2.50
*FOIL: .8X TO 2X BASIC CARDS
RELEASED IN AUGUST 2007
1 Archangel, Aerobalistic C .10 .25
2 Beast, Bookworm R .75 2.00
3 Bishop, Time Cop C .10 .25
4 Blink, Exile C .10 .25
5 Cable, Nathan Summers C .10 .25
6 Cable, Askani'Son U .20 .50
7 Colossus, Tin Man C .10 .25
8 Cyclops, Fearless Leader C .10 .25
9 Domino, Neena Thurman R 1.50 4.00
10 Emma Frost, Ice Queen R 2.50 6.00
11 Forge, Inventor Extraordinaire U .20 .50
12 Gambit, Swamp Rat U .20 .50
13 Havok, Unstable Son C .10 .25
14 Iceman, Frosty C .10 .25
15 Jean Grey, Teen Telepath C .10 .25
16 Jean Grey, Phoenix Rising C .10 .25
17 Jean Grey, Phoenix Force R .60 1.50
18 Jubilee, Mallrat C .10 .25
19 Mimic, Exile R 1.00 2.50
20 Morph, Exile U .20 .50
21 Multiple Man, Army MadroX C .10 .25
22 Nightcrawler, Man of the Cloth C .10 .25
23 Professor X, Idealistic Dreamer C .10 .25
24 Professor X, World's Most Powerful Telepath R .60 1.50
25 Psylocke, Second Skin C .10 .25
26 Rogue, Power Absorption R 1.00 2.50
27 Shadowcat, Phase Shifter R 1.25 3.00
28 Storm, Elemental Goddess C .10 .25
29 Sunfire, Rising Sun C .10 .25
30 Wolverine, Logan C .10 .25
31 Wolverine, Bub R 2.00 5.00
32 Wolverine, Bloodlust U .20 .50
33 X-Man, Nate Grey C .10 .25
34 Cerebro R .40 1.00
35 Muir Island U .20 .50
36 Xavier's Institute of Higher Learning R 4.00 10.00
37 Adamantium Claws R 3.00 8.00
38 Battle Tactics C .10 .25
39 Berserker Rage R 4.00 10.00
40 Bodyslide R 3.00 8.00
41 Children of the Atom R .75 2.00
42 Cleansing Flame R .75 2.00
43 Commanding Nature C .10 .25
44 Fastball Special U .20 .50
45 Healing Factor U .20 .50
46 Sneak Attack R 1.25 3.00
47 Splintering Consciousness U .20 .50
48 Telepathic Suppression R .75 2.00
49 To Me, My X-Men! R 1.25 3.00
50 Turnabout C .10 .25
51 Avalanche, Earthmover R .60 1.50
52 Black Tom, Callous Opportunist C .10 .25
53 Blob, Fred Dukes C .10 .25
54 Blob, Immovable Object U .20 .50
55 Dark Beast, Sinister Reflection R .75 2.00
56 Destiny, Doomsday Diarist U .20 .50
57 Exodus, Bennet du Paris C .10 .25
58 Juggernaut, Champion of Cyttorak C .10 .25
59 Juggernaut, Walking Disaster U .20 .50
60 Juggernaut, Weapon of Mass Destruction R .75 2.00
61 Magneto, Mutant Terrorist C .10 .25
62 Magneto, Mutant Supreme R 1.25 3.00
63 Magneto, Master of Magnetism R .50 1.25
64 Mammomax, Maximus Jensen C .10 .25
65 Mystique, Shapely Shifter U .20 .50
66 Mystique, Shape-Changing Assassin C .10 .25
67 Nocturne, Talia Wagner R 1.00 2.50
68 Phantazia, Eileen Harsaw C .10 .25
69 Post, Harbinger of Onslaught C .10 .25
70 Pyro, St. John Allerdyce C .10 .25
71 Quicksilver, Mercurial Speedster C .10 .25
72 Quicksilver, Speed Demon R .75 2.00
73 Random, Marshall Evan Stone III R 1.00 2.50
74 Rogue, Southern Belle C .10 .25
75 Sabretooth, Genocidal Savage C .10 .25
76 Sabretooth, Feral Rage R .75 2.00
77 Sauron, Mutant Vampire R .75 2.00
78 Scarlet Witch, Mistress of Magic C .10 .25
79 Scarlet Witch, Brotherhood Sister C .10 .25
80 Sentinel Mark VII, Repurposed R 1.25 3.00
81 Toad, Court Jester C .10 .25
82 Unus, Angelo Unuscione U .20 .50
83 Xorn, Champion of Mutantkind R .75 2.00
84 Juggernaut's Helmet U .20 .50
85 Asteroid M U .20 .50
86 Genosha R 1.00 2.50
87 Underground Resistance R 2.50 6.00
88 A Human Juggernaut R .60 1.50
89 Avalanched! C .10 .25
90 Betrayal Most Foul R .50 1.25
91 Eviscerate C .10 .25
92 Immovable Object C .10 .25
93 Insignificant Threat R .60 1.50
94 Iron Extraction R 1.25 3.00
95 Metallic Assault R .60 1.50
96 Pecking Order U .20 .50
97 Sibling Support C .10 .25
98 The Next Brotherhood R 2.50 6.00
99 Unstoppable R 1.50 4.00
100 Xorn's Takeover R .40 1.00
101 Black Cat, Thrillseeker C .10 .25
102 Black Panther, Silent Stalker C .10 .25
103 Black Widow, Femme Fatale R 1.25 3.00
104 Blade, Vampire Slayer R 1.25 3.00
105 Captain America, Loyal Patriot R 2.00 5.00
106 Cloak, Shadowmaster R .50 1.25
107 Dagger, Lightbringer C .10 .25
108 Daredevil, Fearless Survivor C .10 .25
109 Daredevil, Hornhead C .10 .25
110 Deadgirl, Dead Again? U .20 .50
111 Dr. Strange, Master of the Mystic Arts C .10 .25
112 Echo, Masterless Samurai R 1.00 2.50
113 Elektra, Masterless Assassin R 2.50 6.00
114 Ghost Rider, The Devil's Rider C .10 .25
115 Ghost Rider, Spirit of Vengeance U .20 .50
116 Ghost Rider, Danny Ketch R .75 2.00
117 Hulk, Savage Hulk R 1.50 4.00
118 Iron Fist, Hired Hero C .10 .25
119 Luke Cage, Hired Hero C .10 .25
120 Marvel Boy, Noh-Varr U .20 .50
121 Moon Knight, Knight of Khonshu C .10 .25
122 Morbius, Biochemical Bloodsucker U .20 .50
123 Nick Fury, Col. Nicholas Fury R 1.00 2.50
124 Punisher, Suicide Run C .10 .25
125 Punisher, Guns Blazing U .20 .50
126 Punisher, Angel of Death R 2.00 5.00
127 Shang Chi, Martial Master R .50 1.25
128 Spider-Man, Webhead C .10 .25
129 Spider-Man, Outlaw C .10 .25
130 The Sentry, Forgotten Hero U .20 .50
131 Vengeance, Spirit of Vengeance C .10 .25
132 White Tiger, Angela Del Toro C .10 .25
133 Wolverine, Covert Predator C .10 .25
134 Brass Grill C .10 .25
135 Desert Eagle C .10 .25
136 M60s U .20 .50
137 Scattergun R .75 2.00
138 Wheels of Vengeance R .75 2.00
139 Dark Alley C .10 .25
140 Anguish of the Innocent R .60 1.50
141 Bring the Pain C .10 .25
142 Chain of Vengeance U .20 .50
143 Defensive Formation R 1.00 2.50
144 Encircle R .75 2.00
145 Neighborhood Watch, Team-Up C .10 .25
146 Penance Stare U .20 .50
147 Quick Kill C .10 .25
148 Reload R .75 2.00
149 Sniper Shot R 1.25 3.00
150 Wild Ride R 2.00 5.00
151 Ant-Man, King of the Hill C .10 .25
152 Crystal, Inhuman Elemental C .10 .25
153 Dr. Strange, Ally of The Four R 1.25 3.00
154 Frankie Raye, Johnny's Flame C .10 .25
155 Franklin Richards, Child of the Cosmos C .10 .25
156 Ghost Rider, Rider on the Storm C .10 .25
157 H.E.R.B.I.E., Robot Nanny R .75 2.00
158 Hulk, The Fantastic Hulk C .10 .25
159 Human Torch, Matchstick U .20 .50
160 Human Torch, Nova Blast C .10 .25
161 Human Torch, Flame On! R .75 2.00
162 Invisible Woman, Walking on Air C .10 .25
163 Invisible Woman, First Lady of the Fantastic Four C .10 .25
164 Invisible Woman, Sight Unseen U .20 .50
165 Invisible Woman, Shield of The Four R .75 2.00
166 Luke Cage, Steel-Hard Skin R 1.25 3.00
167 Luke Cage, Paid in Full C .10 .25
168 Lyja, Mrs. Johnny Storm R .60 1.50
169 Medusa, Red R .75 2.00
170 Mr. Fantastic, Stringbean C .10 .25
171 Mr. Fantastic, Critical Thinker U .20 .50
172 Mr. Fantastic, Dimensional Explorer C .10 .25
173 Namorita, Atlantean Warrior Princess R .75 2.00
174 Nathaniel Richards, Temporal Traveler R .75 2.00
175 She-Hulk, Single Green Lawyer C .10 .25
176 Silver Surfer, Norrin Radd R .75 2.00
177 Spider-Man, Power and Responsibility U .20 .50
178 Sub-Mariner, Uncertain Ally U .20 .50
179 Thing, Idol O'Millions C .10 .25
180 Thing, Heavy Hitter R .50 1.25
181 Thing, The Ever-Lovin' Blue-Eyed Thing U .20 .50
182 Uatu the Watcher , He Who Watches U .20 .50
183 Valeria Richards, Child of Light and Darkness U .20 .50
184 Fantasticar 2.0 R .60 1.50
185 Future Technology R .60 1.50
186 Unstable Molecular Suit C .10 .25
187 Four Freedoms Plaza R .75 2.00
188 Pier 4 R .50 1.25
189 Clobberin' Pine! R .75 2.00
190 Eureka! R .60 1.50
191 Family of Four R 1.25 3.00
192 Firewall U .20 .50
193 Force Field Projection R 1.50 4.00
194 Heat Wave R .75 2.00
195 Invisibility U .20 .50
196 It's Clobberin' Time! R .75 2.00
197 Reed and Sue C .10 .25
198 Signal Flare R .75 2.00
199 Stretch Out U .20 .50
200 Torch and Thing C .10 .25
201 Boris, Personal Servant of Dr. Doom R 1.00 2.50
202 Doom-Bot, Army U .20 .50
203 Doom-Bot II, Army C .10 .25
204 Dr. Doom, Diabolic Genius U .20 .50
205 Dr. Doom, Gypsy King C .10 .25
206 Dr. Doom, Fearsome Monarch U .20 .50
207 Dr. Doom, Lord of Latveria R .50 1.25
208 Dragon Man, Experimental Monster C .10 .25
209 Dreadnought Tank, Arsenal of Doom R .75 2.00
210 Pacifier Robot, Army C .10 .25
211 Puppet Master, Overprotective Father R .75 2.00
212 Swarm Bots, Army C .10 .25
213 Ultron, Army C .10 .25
214 Armor of Doom R .75 2.00
215 Faces of Doom U .20 .50
216 Fervent Research R 1.25 3.00
217 Mystical Paralysis U .20 .50
218 Robotic Offensive U .20 .50
219 Sacrificial Pawn C .10 .25
220 Supersize C .10 .25
221 The Power Cosmic R .40 1.00
222 Gladiator, Praetor of the Imperial Guard R .50 1.25
223 Lilandra, Majestrix of the Shi'ar R .75 2.00
224 Shi'ar Soldier, Army C .10 .25
225 Apocalypse, The Fittest R .75 2.00
226 Bullseye, #1 with a Bullet U .20 .50
227 Deadpool, Interminable Terminator U .20 .50
228 Holocaust, Nemesis R .75 2.00
229 Mr. Sinister, Visionary Geneticist U .20 .50
230 Omega Red, Cold War Commando R .75 2.00
231 Onslaught, Psionic Spawn of Xavier and Magneto R .75 2.00
232 Random Punks, Army C .10 .25
233 Stryfe, X-Cutioner C .10 .25
234 Frag Grenade C .10 .25
235 Katana C .10 .25
236 Mandroid Prototype R .50 1.25
237 Med Kit U .20 .50
238 Steel Girder R .75 2.00
239 Three-Ton Boulder R .40 1.00
240 Construction Site C .10 .25
241 Evil Lair U .20 .50
242 Research Facility C .10 .25
243 Unstable Ground R .50 1.25
244 Assorted Aliases R 1.25 3.00
245 Burn Rubber C .10 .25
246 Combat Veteran U .20 .50
247 Crushing Blow C .10 .25
248 Dealing with the Devil, Team-Up U .20 .50
249 Devastating Blow C .10 .25
250 Finishing Move C .10 .25
251 For Great Justice! C .10 .25
252 Fortify C .10 .25
253 Forward Assault C .10 .25
254 Gamma Bomb R .40 1.00
255 Heroes of the City, Team-Up C .10 .25
256 Marvel Crossover, Team-Up C .10 .25
257 Mental Blast C .10 .25
258 Mobilize R 6.00 15.00
259 Monkey Business R 1.25 3.00
260 New and Improved R 2.00 5.00
261 New Mutations U .75 2.00
262 Only Human R 2.50 6.00
263 Overwhelming Force U .75 2.00
264 RAT-TAT-TAT R .50 1.25
265 Reset R 1.50 4.00
266 Rigged Explosives R 1.25 3.00
267 Savage Beatdown R 5.00 12.00
268 Secret Identity R 1.00 2.50
269 Shrink U .20 .50
270 Strange Bedfellows, Team-Up U .20 .50
271 Swift Escape U .20 .50
272 The 198, Team-Up C .10 .25
273 The Greater Threat, Team-Up C .10 .25

2007 Vs System Marvel Team-Up

COMPLETE SET (220) 30.00 60.00
BOOSTER BOX (24 PACKS) 20.00 40.00
BOOSTER PACK (14 CARDS) 1.00 2.00
*FOIL: .8X TO 2X BASIC CARDS
RELEASED IN FEBRUARY 2007
1 Aunt May, Golden Oldie U .20 .50
2 Black Cat, Nine Lives C .10 .25
3 Blade, Nightstalker U .20 .50
4 Captain America, Heroic Paragon C .10 .25
5 Daredevil, New Kingpin C .10 .25
6 Darkhawk, Chris Powell C .10 .25
7 Elektra, Leader of the Hand C .10 .25
8 Frank Drake, Nightstalker C .10 .25
9 Ka-Zar, Lord Kevin Plunder C .10 .25
10 Luke Cage, Neighborhood Watch C .10 .25
11 Man-Thing, Theodore Sallis U .20 .50
12 Mattie Franklin, Reserve Webhead C .10 .25
13 Michael Collins Deathlok, Schizophrenic Cyborg C .10 .25
14 Night Thrasher, Dwayne Michael Taylor C .10 .25
15 Phil Urich Green Goblin, Lunatic Laugh U .20 .50
16 Punisher, Frank Castle U .20 .50
17 The Sentry, Golden Guardian of Good R .40 1.00
18 Shanna the She-Devil, Shanna O'Hara Plunder C .10 .25
19 Sleepwalker, Rick Sheridan R .40 1.00
20 Speedball, Robert Baldwin C .10 .25
21 Spider-Man, Stark's Protege R 1.25 3.00
22 Spider-Man, The Sensational Spider-Man R .75 2.00
23 Spider-Man, Parasitic Host C .10 .25
24 Spider-Man, Spider-Hulk C .10 .25
25 Spider-Man, The Amazing Bag-Man C .10 .25
26 Venom, Lethal Protector C .10 .25
27 Wolverine, Canucklehead C .10 .25
28 Zabu, Constant Companion C .10 .25
29 Catch You Later! U .20 .50
30 Down, but Not Out U .20 .50
31 Drink This! R .40 1.00
32 Empire State University R 1.25 3.00
33 Feminine Wiles U .20 .50
34 Gift Wrapped R 1.50 4.00
35 Indebted R 1.50 4.00
36 Need a Lift? U .20 .50
37 Ring of Fire U .20 .50
38 Spider-Sense Tingling! C .10 .25
39 Spider-Signal U .20 .50
40 Spider-Mobile, Unique C .10 .25
41 Stark Tower, Team-Up C .10 .25
42 Target Practice C .10 .25
43 Trial by Jury R .50 1.25
44 Archangel, New Defender C .10 .25
45 Beast, New Defender U .20 .50
46 Brunnhilde Valkyrie, Barbara Norriss C .10 .25
47 Devil-Slayer, Eric Simon Payne R .40 1.00
48 Dr. Strange, Founding Father R .75 2.00
49 Dr. Strange, Sorcerer Supreme R .60 1.50
50 Gargoyle, Isaac Christians C .10 .25
51 Hawkeye, Loud Mouth R .60 1.50
52 Hellcat, Patsy Walker C .10 .25
53 Howard the Duck, Master of Quack-Fu C .10 .25
54 Hulk, Grumpy Green Goliath C .10 .25
55 Hulk, Strongest One There Is R .50 1.25
56 Iceman, New Defender U .20 .50
57 Jack of Hearts, Jack Hart C .10 .25
58 John Walker U.S. Agent, Loose Cannon C .10 .25
59 Johnny Blaze Ghost Rider, Damned C .10 .25
60 Kyle Richmond Nighthawk, Heart of the Team C .10 .25
61 Professor X, Illuminati C .10 .25
62 Richard Rider Nova, Xandarian Nova Corps C .10 .25
63 Samantha Parrington Valkyrie, Chooser of the Slain R 1.50 4.00
64 Silver Surfer, Prodigal Herald U .20 .50
65 Silver Surfer, Earthbound C .10 .25
66 Sub-Mariner, Neptune's Fist C .10 .25
67 Sub-Mariner, King of Atlantis C .10 .25
68 Tania Belinskya Red Guardian, Cold Warrior C .10 .25
69 Wendell Vaughn Quasar, Protector of the Universe C .10 .25
70 Wong, Mystical Manservant R 1.50 4.00
71 Astral Projection U .20 .50
72 Banished to the Abyss U .20 .50
73 The Arrival R 2.00 5.00
74 The Book of the Vishanti U .20 .50
75 Consulting the Orb U .20 .50
76 Crimson Bands of Cyttorak R .50 1.25
77 Defenders Defend! U .20 .50
78 Eye of Agamotto, Unique R .40 1.00
79 Imperius Rex! C .10 .25
80 One-Man Rampage R .50 1.25
81 The Order R .75 2.00
82 Sanctum Sanctorum U .20 .50
83 Secret Defenders, Team-Up C .10 .25
84 Soul Survival U .20 .50
85 Star-Crossed C .10 .25
86 Teleportation Ring, Unique C .10 .25
87 Zzzax Attax! C .10 .25
88 Albert Malik Red Skull, Axis of Evil C .10 .25
89 Answer, Aaron Nicholson R .75 2.00
90 Black Tarantula, Carlos LaMuerto U .20 .50
91 Bullseye, Assassin for Hire C .10 .25
92 Carnage, Psychopath R .75 2.00
93 Chameleon, Man of Many Faces C .10 .25
94 Dr. Octopus, Master of Evil R .60 1.50
95 Electro, Shock Jock U .20 .50
96 Francis Klum Mysterio, Mutant Magician C .10 .25
97 Fusion, Markley C .10 .25
98 Gog, Alien Menace R .40 1.00
99 Harry Osborn Green Goblin, Unfortunate Son C .10 .25
100 Jason Macendale Hobgoblin, Possessed Lunatic C .10 .25
101 Lizard, Voracious Predator R .60 1.50
102 Maguire Beck Mad Jack, Jack o' Lantern C .10 .25
103 Nitro, Robert Hunter R .40 1.00
104 Razorfist, Sociopathic Mercenary C .10 .25
105 Rhino, Unstoppable Force C .10 .25
106 Slyde, Jalome Beacher C .10 .25
107 Spider-Man Robot, Timespinner C .10 .25
108 Spider-Slayer V.X., Arachnid Hunter C .10 .25
109 Spot, Dr. Jonathan Ohnn C .10 .25
110 Swarm, Fritz von Meyer U .20 .50
111 Trapster, Peter Petruski C .10 .25
112 Venom, Mac Gargan C .10 .25
113 Venom, The Hunger C .10 .25
114 Vulture, Aerial Stalker C .10 .25
115 Alien Symbiote, Unique C .10 .25
116 Breakout U .20 .50
117 The Contract, Team-Up C .10 .25
118 Demonic Association U .20 .50
119 The Enforcers R .40 1.00
120 Gotcha! C .10 .25
121 The Great Game U .20 .50
122 Hidden Cache R .40 1.00
123 Legacy of Evil U .20 .50
124 Legion of Losers C .10 .25
125 Planet of the Symbiotes U .20 .50
126 Ravencroft Institute R .40 1.00
127 Sand Trap U .20 .50
128 Spider Hunt R .60 1.50
129 Suffocation C .10 .25
130 The Vault U .20 .50
131 Baron Mordo, Karl Amadeus Mordo C .10 .25
132 Black Rose, Roxanne Simpson U .20 .50
133 Blackheart, Black King R .60 1.50
134 Chthon, Demon of the Darkhold U .20 .50
135 Doppelganger, Killer Clone C .10 .25
136 Dormammu, Dread Dormammu C .10 .25
137 The Dwarf, Soul Broker U .20 .50
138 Dweller-in-Darkness, Fear Lord C .10 .25
139 Ebenezer Laughton Scarecrow, Undead Lunatic C .10 .25
140 Illyana Rasputin Magik, Queen of Limbo C .10 .25
141 Madelyne Pryor, Goblyn Queen U .20 .50
142 Meatmarket, Lilin C .10 .25
143 Mephisto, pheles C .10 .25
144 The Mindless Ones, Army C .10 .25
145 Modred the Mystic, Servant of Chthon C .10 .25
146 Morlun, Totem Hunter C .10 .25
147 N'astirh, Liege of Limbo C .10 .25
148 The N'Garai, Army C .10 .25
149 Noble Kale, Lord of Hell R .40 1.00
150 Pilgrim, Lilin C .10 .25
151 Queen Lilith, Den Mother C .10 .25
152 Satana, Hellstrom C .10 .25
153 Shathra, Sharon Keller C .10 .25
154 Shuma-Gorath, He Who Sleeps but Shall Awake R .40 1.00
155 Thanos, Courting Death R .40 1.00
156 Umar, Sorceress Sublime R .40 1.00
157 Zarathos, Demon of Fire C .10 .25
158 Book of Cagliostro U .20 .50
159 Dark Bargain R .40 1.00
160 Dark Designs C .10 .25
161 The Dark Dimension, Non-Unique C .10 .25
162 Death's Embrace R 1.50 4.00
163 Demonic Embryo C .10 .25
164 Dimensional Rift R .60 1.50
165 In Limbo U .20 .50

166 Mausoleum, Non-Unique C .10 .25
167 Midnight Massacre R .50 1.25
168 Netherworld Gift U .20 .50
169 Ritual Sacrifice, Team-Up C .10 .25
170 Siege of Darkness C .10 .25
171 Strange Love U .20 .50
172 Surtur's Anvil U .20 .50
173 Transformation C .10 .25
174 Undead Legions R .50 1.25
175 Battlestar, Lemar Hoskins R .40 1.00
176 Chen, Amy Chen C .10 .25
177 Crippler, Carl Striklan C .10 .25
178 Dominic Fortune, Soldier of Fortune U .20 .50
179 Fin, Intruders C .10 .25
180 Man-Eater, Intruders C .10 .25
181 Paladin, Intruders R .40 1.00
182 Powell, Southern Charm U .20 .50
183 Quentino, Raul Quentino U .20 .50
184 Sandman, Intruders U .20 .50
185 Silver Sable, World's Deadliest Mercenary R .40 1.00
186 Wild Pack Recruit, Army U .20 .50
187 Bounty Hunt U .20 .50
188 Capture Net U .20 .50
189 Stealthcraft, Team-Up C .10 .25
190 Alyosha Kravinoff, Son of Kraven C .10 .25
191 Deadpool, Merc With a Mouth R .60 1.50
192 Demogoblin, Disembodied Demon C .10 .25
193 Dr. Doom, Just Reward R .40 1.00
194 Hellstorm, Son of Satan C .10 .25
195 Moon Knight, Fist of Khonshu C .10 .25
196 Morbius, Shadow of the Vampire R .40 1.00
197 Against All Odds R .75 2.00
198 Big Leagues R 4.00 10.00
199 Burns at the Touch C .10 .25
200 He Who Watches U .20 .50
201 The Illuminati C .10 .25
202 Justice Is Served! C .10 .25
203 Marvel Crossover, Team-Up C .10 .25
204 Poker Night C .10 .25
205 Rabbit Fire C .10 .25
206 We Had a Team-Up, Team-Up C .10 .25
207 What Are Friends For? C .10 .25
208 Cassandra Nova, Genocidal Tendencies U .20 .50
209 Damocles Base R 1.00 2.50
210 Dark Beast, McCoy U .20 .50
211 Ego Gem, Unique ? Infinity Gem U .20 .50
212 Hulk, Joe Fixit U .20 .50
213 Monster Island R .40 1.00
214 New Baxter Building U .20 .50
215 Quicksilver, Terrigenesis Rebirth U .20 .50
216 Ronan the Accuser, Exiled U .20 .50
217 Super Skrull, Kl'rt R .40 1.00
218 The B Team R .40 1.00
219 The Annihilation Wave R .40 1.00
220 The Void, Robert Reynolds R .40 1.00

2007 Vs System World's Finest

COMPLETE SET (220) 30.00 60.00
BOOSTER BOX (24 PACKS) 40.00 80.00
BOOSTER PACK (14 CARDS) 2.00 3.00
*FOIL: .8X TO 2X BASIC CARDS
RELEASED IN JULY 2007
1 Bibbo Bibbowski, Barroom Brawler U .20 .50
2 Brahma, Supermen of America C .10 .25
3 The Guardian, Jim Harper U .20 .50
4 Hiro Okamura Toyman, Whiz-Kid C .10 .25
5 John Henry Irons Steel, Armor Aura C .10 .25
6 John Henry Irons Steel, Steel Works U .20 .50
7 Kara Zor-El Flamebird Kandorian Vigilante C .10 .25
8 Kara Zor-El Supergirl, Claire Connors R 1.00 2.50
9 Kelex, Caretaker of the Fortress C .10 .25
10 Krypto, Guard Dog of El C .10 .25
11 Lois Lane, Reporter Extraordinaire U .20 .50
12 Loser, Supermen of America C .10 .25
13 Maximum, Supermen of America C .10 .25
14 Natasha Irons Steel, Unlikely Alloy C .10 .25
15 The Newsboy Legion, Army C .10 .25
16 Outburst, Supermen of America C .10 .25
17 Power Girl Nightwing, Kandorian Vigilante C .10 .25
18 Pyrogen, Supermen of America R .75 2.00
19 Superman, Man of Tomorrow C .10 .25
20 Superman, Deterrent Force R 2.00 5.00
21 Superman, Last Son of Krypton R 2.00 5.00
22 Superman, Bulletproof R 1.25 3.00
23 Vartox, Hero of Tynola U .20 .50
24 White Lotus, Supermen of America C .10 .25
25 Wonder Woman, Deflection Diva R .75 2.00
26 City of Tomorrow, Team-Up C .10 .25
27 Kandor, City in a Bottle U .20 .50
28 Smallville U .20 .50
29 Desperate Sacrifice U .20 .50
30 Double Team C .10 .25
31 Early Edition R .60 1.50
32 For the Man Who Has Everything R .60 1.50
33 Future Friends C .10 .25
34 Good Boy! C .10 .25
35 Home Sweet Home U .20 .50
36 Impervious U .20 .50
37 Iron Will C .10 .25
38 Soaring to New Heights C .10 .25
39 Alfred Pennyworth, Faithful Friend R .60 1.50
40 Batman, Problem Solver U .20 .50
41 Batman, Twilight Vigilante C .10 .25
42 Bat-Mite, #1 Fan R .75 2.00
43 Batmobile, Burn Rubber U .20 .50
44 Commissioner Gordon, Gotham Central U .20 .50
45 Crispus Allen, Gotham Central C .10 .25
46 Gotham Central S.W.A.T., Army C .10 .25
47 Harvey Bullock, Gotham Central C .10 .25
48 Kate Kane Batwoman, Katherine the Younger R 1.00 2.50
49 Maggie Sawyer, Gotham Central C .10 .25
50 The Question, Victor Sage U .20 .50
51 Renee Montoya, Gotham Central U .20 .50
52 Tim Drake Robin, Flying Solo C .10 .25
53 Two-Face, Jekyll and Hyde C .10 .25
54 Batman and the Outsiders R 1.25 3.00
55 Bat-Signal U .20 .50
56 Batman, Cape and Cowl R .75 2.00
57 Gotham Central U .20 .50
58 Bat Got Your Tongue? R .60 1.50
59 Batcave, Crime-Fighting Lab U .20 .50
60 Good Cop, Good Cop C .10 .25
61 The Hook-Up, Team-Up C .10 .25
62 Interrogate R .60 1.50
63 Nine Lives U .20 .50
64 Taking Aim R .60 1.50
65 Barbara Gordon Oracle, Hacker Elite C .10 .25
66 Barbara Gordon Oracle, Inside Information U .20 .50
67 Cassandra Cain, Death's Daughter C .10 .25
68 Catwoman, Feline Fatale C .10 .25
69 Dinah Laurel Lance Black Canary, Cry in the Dark C .10 .25
70 Gypsy, Illusionary Operative U .20 .50
71 Huntress, Vicious Vigilante C .10 .25
72 Lady Blackhawk, Zinda Blake R .60 1.50
73 Lady Shiva, Jade Canary C .10 .25
74 Savant, Brian Durlin C .10 .25
75 Ted Grant Wildcat, Nine Lives C .10 .25
76 Vixen, Mari Jiwe McCabe C .10 .25
77 Aerie One U .20 .50
78 Birds of a Feather C .10 .25
79 Cry for Blood C .10 .25
80 Black Lightning, Jefferson Pierce C .10 .25
81 Dick Grayson Nightwing, Renegade C .10 .25
82 Dick Grayson Nightwing, Rough Justice U .20 .50
83 Faust, Sebastian Faust U .20 .50
84 Freddy Freeman Captain Marvel Jr. , CM3 C .10 .25
85 Geo-Force, Brion Markov C .10 .25
86 Grace, Grace Choi C .10 .25
87 Grace, The Bouncer U .20 .50
88 Halo, Gabrielle Doe C .10 .25
89 Huntress, Harsh Mistress C .10 .25
90 Indigo, Paranoid Android C .10 .25
91 Jade, Emerald Beacon C .10 .25
92 Katana, Tatsu Yamashiro U .20 .50
93 Katana, Soultaker R .60 1.50
94 Kimiyo Hoshi Dr. Light, Sunburst R .75 2.00
95 Koriand'r Starfire, Royal Temper C .10 .25
96 Looker, Emily Briggs C .10 .25
97 Metamorpho, The Element Man C .10 .25
98 Owen Mercer Captain Boomerang Jr., Prodigal Son C .10 .25
99 Roy Harper Arsenal, Ladies' Man C .10 .25
100 Shift, Knockoff R .60 1.50
101 Technocrat, Geoffrey Barron C .10 .25
102 Terra, Little Sis R 1.00 2.50
103 Thunder, Anissa Pierce C .10 .25
104 Thunder, Heavy Duty C .10 .25
105 Wylde, Charlie Wylde C .10 .25
106 Pequod, Unique U .20 .50
107 Brooklyn HQ R .60 1.50
108 Markovia U .20 .50
109 Optitron Corporation U .20 .50
110 Batman, Dark Knight Returned U .20 .50
111 Betrayal of Trust U .20 .50
112 Booze Elementals C .10 .25
113 Fighting the Liar C .10 .25
114 Get It Done U .20 .50
115 Hell Breaks Loose C .10 .25
116 Incognito C .10 .25
117 The Insiders, Team-Up C .10 .25
118 Recruiting Drive R .75 2.00
119 Scorched Earth C .10 .25
120 Soul Slicer U .20 .50
121 Taking Out the Trash U .20 .50
122 Anarky, Lonnie Machin U .20 .50
123 Basil Karlo Ultimate Clayface, Mud Pack R .60 1.50
124 Batarang, Cutting Edge R 1.00 2.50
125 Batzarro, World's Worst Detective U .20 .50
126 Calendar Man, Julian Gregory Day U .20 .50
127 Catwoman, Jewel Thief C .10 .25
128 Charaxes, Drury Walker C .10 .25
129 Crime Doctor, Bradford Thorne C .10 .25
130 Firefly, Burning Desire C .10 .25
131 Great White, Warren White C .10 .25
132 Harley Quinn, Mr. J's Girl C .10 .25
133 The Joker, Crazy for You R .75 2.00
134 The Joker, Out of His Mind R 1.25 3.00
135 The Joker Red Hood, The Man Who Laughs U .20 .50
136 KGBeast, Anatoli Knyazev C .10 .25
137 Killer Croc, Cannibal C .10 .25
138 Mad Hatter, Mad as a Hatter U .20 .50
139 Matt Hagen Clayface, Mud Pack C .10 .25
140 Mr. Freeze, Cold Shoulder C .10 .25
141 Mr. Zsasz, Scar Tissue C .10 .25
142 The Penguin, Crime's Early Bird C .10 .25
143 Poison Ivy, Venomous Vixen C .10 .25
144 The Riddler, Multiple Choice U .20 .50
145 Scarecrow, Fear and Loathing R .60 1.50
146 Sondra Fuller Clayface, Mud Pack C .10 .25
147 Tally Man, Tax Time R .60 1.50
148 Two-Face, Heads or Tails C .10 .25
149 Arkham Asylum, Team-Up R .60 1.50
150 Blackgate Prison, Maximum Security U .20 .50
151 All Locked Up C .10 .25
152 Beside Myself R .60 1.50
153 Burn Baby Burn C .10 .25
154 Hush Baby C .10 .25
155 It's a Hard Life R .60 1.50
156 Money Talks R .60 1.50
157 Pick a Card R .75 2.00
158 Usual Suspects U .20 .50
159 Alexandra Allston Parasite, Power Drain C .10 .25
160 Atomic Skull, Cursed R .60 1.50
161 Bizarro, Bizarro World's Finest R .75 2.00
162 Brainiac 12, Upgrade Complete C .10 .25
163 Brainiac 13, B-13 C .10 .25
164 Darkseid, The Omega U .20 .50
165 Doomsday, Evolution Advanced C .10 .25
166 Hank Henshaw Cyborg, Manhunter Grandmaster U .20 .50
167 Indigo, Brainiac 8 R .75 2.00
168 Kryptonite Man, K. Russell Abernathy C .10 .25
169 Lex Luthor, Master Manipulator R 1.25 3.00
170 Lex Luthor, Sinister Scientist C .10 .25
171 Livewire, Leslie Willis C .10 .25
172 Manchester Black, Union Jack C .10 .25
173 Maxima, Warrior Queen C .10 .25
174 Metallo, Kryptonite Heart C .10 .25
175 Mongul, Son of the Tyrant C .10 .25
176 Mr. Mxyzptlk, Felonious Fiend R .60 1.50
177 Natasha Irons Starlight, Everyman Project U .20 .50
178 Preus, Citizen's Patrol C .10 .25
179 Professor Emil Hamilton Ruin, Power Suit R .60 1.50
180 Satanus, Colin Thornton U .20 .50
181 Solaris, Tyrant Sun R 1.00 2.50
182 Terra-Man, Toby Manning C .10 .25
183 Ultraman, Despot of Kandor C .10 .25
184 Winslow Schott Toyman, Child's Play C .10 .25
185 Graveyard of Solitude U .20 .50
186 Battle for Metropolis U .20 .50
187 Bizarro Brawl R .60 1.50
188 Dimensional Deal, Team-Up C .10 .25
189 Executive Privilege R .75 2.00
190 Fatal Weakness R 1.00 2.50
191 Future Shock C .10 .25
192 Hidden Agenda R .60 1.50
193 Hostile Takeover C .10 .25
194 Imprisoned in the Source R .60 1.50
195 Knowledge Is Power U .20 .50
196 Never-Ending Battle C .10 .25
197 Obey or Die! R .75 2.00
198 World's Worstest, Team-Up C .10 .25
199 At Their Finest R .60 1.50
200 Best of the Best R 1.25 3.00
201 Brains and Brawn R 1.00 2.50
202 Phantom Zone U .20 .50
203 Power Armor C .10 .25
204 Stryker's Island R .60 1.50
205 Batter Up! C .10 .25
206 Batzarro Beatdown R .60 1.50
207 Certifiable R .60 1.50
208 Chilly Reception R .60 1.50
209 Crackshot C .10 .25
210 Engine of Change U .20 .50
211 Gorilla Warfare C .10 .25
212 Jack-in-the-Box R .75 2.00
213 SKREEEEEEE! C .10 .25
214 Spirit of Nabu, Magic U .20 .50
215 Standoff U .20 .50
216 Tied Down C .10 .25
217 Training Day, Team-Up C .10 .25
218 Truth and Justice, Team-Up C .10 .25
219 Matter-Eater Lad, Tenzil Kem U .20 .50
220 Deathstroke the Terminator, Wolf in Bat's Clothing U .20 .50

2008 Vs System Marvel Universe

COMPLETE SET (330) 50.00 100.00
BOOSTER BOX (24 PACKS) 30.00 60.00
BOOSTER PACK (14 CARDS) 2.00 3.00
*FOIL: .8X TO 2X BASIC CARDS
RELEASED IN JUNE 2008
1 Bill Foster Goliath, Secret Avenger R .75 2.00
2 Black Panther, Secret Avenger C .10 .25
3 Cable, Secret Avenger R .75 2.00
4 Captain America, The Patriot Secret Avenger C .10 .25
5 Captain America, Champion License R 2.00 5.00
6 Captain America, Living Legend R 1.50 4.00
7 Captain America, Sentinel of Liberty R 1.50 4.00
8 Cloak, Secret Avenger U .20 .50
9 Dagger, Secret Avenger C .10 .25
10 Dr. Strange, Secret Avenger R 1.50 4.00
11 Echo Ronin, Secret Avenger C .10 .25
12 Falcon, Secret Avenger C .10 .25
13 Hawkeye Ronin, Secret Avenger U .20 .50
14 Hercules, Secret Avenger C .10 .25
15 Hulkling, Teddy Altman Young Avenger C .10 .25
16 Human Torch, Secret Avenger C .10 .25
17 Invisible Woman, Secret Avenger C .10 .25
18 Iron Fist Daredevil, Imposter Secret Avenger U .20 .50
19 Iron Fist, Secret Avenger C .10 .25
20 Jessica Drew Spider-Woman Secret Avenger U .20 .50
21 Kate Bishop Hawkeye, Young Avenger R .75 2.00
22 Luke Cage, Secret Avenger U .20 .50
23 Patriot, Elijah Bradley - Young Avenger C .10 .25
24 Punisher, Secret Avenger R 1.00 2.50
25 Speed, Thomas Shepard Young Avenger U .20 .50
26 Spider-Man, Secret Avenger R 1.50 4.00
27 Stature, Cassandra Lang Young Avenger U .20 .50
28 Storm, Secret Avenger C .10 .25
29 Vision, Young Avenger R .75 2.00
30 Wiccan, William Kaplan Young Avenger U .20 .50
31 Wolverine, Secret Avenger R 1.50 4.00
32 Captain America's Shield, Null R 1.50 4.00
33 Electron Scrambler, Null R .75 2.00
34 Safe House No. 23, Team-Up U .20 .50
35 Above the Law, Null U .20 .50
36 Atlantis, Null R .75 2.00
37 Avengers Forever, Null U .20 .50
38 Avengers Reassembled, Null R 2.00 5.00
39 The Big Three, Null C .10 .25
40 Charging Star, Null R 1.50 4.00
41 Final Justice, Null U .20 .50
42 Hard to Kill, Null C .10 .25
43 Liberating Number 42, Null C .10 .25
44 Reckless Youth, Null R .75 2.00
45 Secret Avengers, Team-Up C .10 .25
46 Shield Slash, Null C .10 .25
47 Stars and Stripes, Null U .20 .50
48 Switching Sides, Null U .20 .50
49 Thou Art No Thor!, Null R .75 2.00
50 Young Avengers, Null C .10 .25
51 Beetle Mach, Discharged C .10 .25
52 Blizzard, Frosty Friend U .20 .50
53 Bullseye, Lester R 1.25 3.00
54 Bullseye, Closer to God R 1.25 3.00
55 Genis-Vell Photon, Cosmic Threat C .10 .25
56 Green Goblin, Insanity Unleashed C .10 .25
57 Green Goblin, Director of the Thunderbolts C .10 .25
58 Helmut Zemo Baron Zemo Master of the Moonstones R .75 2.00
59 Joystick, Fun and Games U .20 .50
60 Karla Sofen Moonstone Uncertain Loyalty C .10 .25
61 Karla Sofen Moonstone Field Commander U .20 .50
62 Lady Deathstrike, Opportunistic Killer C .10 .25
63 Melissa Gold Songbird, Caged Angel C .10 .25
64 Radioactive Man, Containment Suit R 1.00 2.50
65 Radioactive Man Sheep in Wolf's Clothing U .20 .50
66 Speed Demon, Whizzer U .20 .50
67 Speedball Penance, Pain Monger C .10 .25
68 Speedball Penance Repentant Masochist R .75 2.00
69 Swordsman, Andreas Von Strucker C .10 .25
70 Taskmaster, Super Hero Trainer C .10 .25
71 Venom, Faithless Monster U .20 .50
72 Venom, Blood-Eater C .10 .25
73 The T-Wagon, Null U .20 .50
74 The Zeus, Unique R .75 2.00
75 Thunderbolts Mountain, Null R .75 2.00
76 Collect Them All!, Null R 1.00 2.50
77 Dangerous Liason, Null R .75 2.00
78 Faith In Monsters, Null U .20 .50
79 Ruthless Agression, Null C .10 .25
80 Sanctioned Killers, Team-Up C .10 .25
81 Speedball Is Dead, Null U .20 .50
82 Unregistered Combatants, Null R .75 2.00
83 The Wrong Stuff, Team-Up C .10 .25
84 Ares, Mighty Avenger R 1.00 2.50
85 Bishop, Agent of S.H.I.E.L.D. U .20 .50
86 Blade, Independant Contractor U .20 .50
87 Cape-Killers Unit, Army Agent of S.H.I.E.L.D. U .20 .50
88 Carol Danvers Ms. Marvel, Mighty Avenger C .10 .25
89 Daisy Johnson, Agent of S.H.I.E.L.D. C .10 .25
90 Deadpool, Independant Contractor C .10 .25
91 Doc Samson, Agent of S.H.I.E.L.D. C .10 .25
92 Dum-Dum Dugan, Howling Commando C .10 .25
93 Eric O'Grady Ant Man, Fugitive at Large C .10 .25
94 Hank Pym Yellowjacket, Initiative Instructor U .20 .50
95 Iron Man, Mighty Avenger R 2.00 5.00
96 Iron Man, Director of S.H.I.E.L.D. U .20 .50
97 Jessica Drew Spider-Woman, Agent of S.H.I.E.L.D. - HYDRA C .10 .25
98 Justice, Vance Astrovik C .10 .25
99 Life Model Decoy, More Human Than Human R 1.00 2.50
100 Maria Hill, Deputy Commander of S.H.I.E.L.D. C .10 .25
101 Mar-Vell Captain Marvel, Warden of Prison Alpha C .10 .25
102 Mr. Fantastic, Haunted Genius C .10 .25
103 Natasha Romanoff Black Widow, Mighty Avenger U .20 .50
104 Nick Fury, Director of S.H.I.E.L.D. R 1.00 2.50
105 S.H.I.E.L.D. Agents, Army Agent of S.H.I.E.L.D. C .10 .25
106 Sentinel Squad O*N*E*, Army U .20 .50
107 The Sentry, Mighty Avenger R .75 2.00
108 Sharon Carter, Agent 13 Agent of S.H.I.E.L.D. C .10 .25
109 She-Hulk, Agent of S.H.I.E.L.D. C .10 .25
110 Spider-Man, Unmasked R 1.00 2.50
111 Squirrel Girl, Doreen Green U .20 .50
112 Thing, Conscientious Objector R .75 2.00
113 Thor, Cyborg Clone R .75 2.00
114 Tigra, Greer Grant Nelson C .10 .25
115 War Machine Director of the Initiative C .10 .25
116 Wasp, Mighty Avenger U .20 .50
117 Wolverine, Agent of S.H.I.E.L.D. HYDRA U .20 .50
118 Wonder Man, Mighty Avenger R .75 2.00
119 Yelena Belova Black Widow, Agent of S.H.I.E.L.D. - HYDRA R .75 2.00
120 Extremis Upgrade, Null U .20 .50
121 Hulkbuster Armor, Null R 1.00 2.50
122 Power Dampeners, Null U .20 .50
123 S.H.I.E.L.D. Flying Car, Null U .20 .50
124 Godseye Satellite, Null U .20 .50
125 Negative Zone, Non-Unique Prison Alpha R .75 2.00
126 S.H.I.E.L.D. Helicarrier, Null R 1.00 2.50
127 Stark Armory, Null R .75 2.00
128 Company of Heroes, Null U .20 .50
129 I'm a Futurist, Null R .75 2.00
130 The Initiative, Team-Up C .10 .25
131 License to Kill, Null R .75 2.00
132 Out for Justice, Null C .10 .25
133 S.T.A.R. Squad, Null U .20 .50
134 Scarlet Spiders, Null U .20 .50
135 Secret War, Team-Up C .10 .25
136 Security Clearance, Null R .75 2.00
137 You're Under Arrest!, Null R .75 2.00
138 A.I.M. Agents, Army - A.I.M. C .10 .25
139 Arnim Zola, The Bio-Fanatic Raid U .20 .50
140 Baron Strucker, Baron Wolfgang Von Strucker - HYDRA C .10 .25
141 Crossbones, Brock Rumlow - Raid C .10 .25
142 Doctor Faustus, Johann Fennhoff - Raid U .20 .50
143 Elektra, Pawn of the Gorgon - HYDRA U .20 .50
144 The Gorgon, Tomi Shishido - HYDRA R .75 2.00
145 The Hand, Army - HYDRA U .20 .50
146 Head Case, Sean Madigan - A.I.M. R .75 2.00
147 The Hood, Prince of Pistols C .10 .25
148 HYDRA Recruit, Army - HYDRA C .10 .25
149 James Barnes Winter Soldier, Communist Puppet - Raid R 1.00 2.50
150 Kingpin, War Profiteer - HYDRA U .20 .50
151 M.O.D.O.K., Mobile Organism Designed Only for Killing - A.I.M. C .10 .25
152 Mandarin, Tem Borjigan R .75 2.00
153 Master Man, Max Lohmer - Raid U .20 .50
154 MODOC Squad, Army - A.I.M. C .10 .25
155 Red Skull, Aleksander Lukin - Raid C .10 .25
156 Red Skull, Johann Shmidt - HYDRA C .10 .25
157 Red Skull, Master of Creation C .10 .25
158 Scientist Supreme, Monica Rappaccini - A.I.M. U .20 .50
159 Silver Samurai, Kenuichio Harada - HYDRA R .75 2.00
160 Sin, Synthia Schmidt - Raid C .10 .25
161 The Sleeper, Doomsday Device - Raid R .75 2.00
162 Viper, Madame Hydra - HYDRA U .20 .50
163 Cosmic Cube, Null R .75 2.00
164 Death Warrant, Null R 1.00 2.50
165 Satan Claw, Null U .20 .50
166 Fortress Yashida, Null U .20 .50
167 HYDRA Armageddon Carrier, Null R .75 2.00
168 Underground Laboratory, Null R .75 2.00
169 Acts of Vengeance, Null U .20 .50
170 Assault on Hellicarrier 13, Null U .20 .50
171 Cold Storage, Null R .75 2.00
172 Cut Off One Head..., Null R .75 2.00
173 Double Agent!, Team-Up C .10 .25
174 Enemies of the State, Null C .10 .25
175 Hail Hydra!, Team-Up C .10 .25
176 New King in Town, Null U .20 .50
177 Ninjas! Ninjas! Ninjas!, Null R .75 2.00
178 Radically Advanced, Null U .20 .50
179 Archangel, Champion U .20 .50
180 Brood, Brood Creature 2 of 6 C .10 .25
181 Caiera, The Oldstrong U .20 .50
182 Elloe Kaifi, Slave of the Empire U .20 .50
183 Hiroim, The Shamed C .10 .25
184 Hulk, Exile C .10 .25
185 Hulk, Green Scar R 1.50 4.00
186 Hulk, Gladiator C .10 .25
187 Hulk, The Green King C .10 .25
188 Hulk, Sakaar'Son C .10 .25
189 Hulk, Worldbreaker R 1.00 2.50
190 Korg, Kronan Warrior U .20 .50
191 Mastermind Excello, Amadeus Cho R 1.00 2.50
192 Miek, The Unhived C .10 .25
193 Rick Jones, Monster's Best Friend C .10 .25
194 The Great Arena, Null R .75 2.00
195 Imperial Dreadnaught, Null C .10 .25
196 Sakaar, Null R .75 2.00
197 Bloodsport, Null U .20 .50
198 The End of the World, Null R .75 2.00
199 Fight or Die!, Null U .20 .50
200 Hulk Red, Null U .20 .50
201 Hulk Smash, Null R 5.00 12.00
202 Righteous Anger, Null R .75 2.00
203 The Strongest One There Is, Null U .20 .50
204 Warbound to the End, Null R 1.00 2.50
205 World War Hulk, Team-Up .20 .50
206 Annihilus, Anti-Matter Master C .10 .25
207 Annihilus, The Living Death That Walks R .75 2.00
208 Blastaar, The Living Bomb Burst R .75 2.00
209 The Centurians, Army C .10 .25
210 Currs, Army U .20 .50
211 Ravenous, Steward of Annihilus U .20 .50
212 Seekers, Army C .10 .25
213 Skreet, Chaos Mite C .10 .25
214 Thanos, The Mad Titan R 1.00 2.50
215 Cosmic Control Rod, Unique U .20 .50
216 Negative Zone, Non-Unique - Gateway R .75 2.00
217 Negative Zone, Non-Unique - Harvester of Sorrows C .10 .25
218 Negative Zone, Non-Unique - Seat of Annihilation C .10 .25
219 Gift for Death, Null R .75 2.00
220 Swarm of Annihilus, Null R .75 2.00
221 Wave of Destruction, Null R .75 2.00
222 Beta Ray Bill, Simon Walters - Omega Flight R 1.50 4.00
223 John Walker U.S. Agent, Omega Flight R .75 2.00
224 Julia Carpenter Arachne, Omega Flight C .10 .25
225 Sasquatch, Walter Langrowski - Omega Flight C .10 .25
226 Talisman, Elizabeth Twoyoungmen - Omega Flight C .10 .25
227 Weapon Omega, Michael Pointer - Omega Flight R .75 2.00
228 Alpha Flight: Reborn, Null R 1.25 3.00
229 Omega Flight, Team-Up C .10 .25
230 Black Bolt, Protector of the Space Gem U .20 .50
231 Dr. Strange, Protector of the Soul Gem U .20 .50
232 Iron Man, Protector of the Reality Gem U .20 .50
233 Mr. Fantastic, .10 .25

Protector of the Power Gem C
234 Professor X, .20 .50
Protector of the Mind Gem U
235 Sub-Mariner, .20 .50
Protector of the Time Gem U
236 Atlantis Attacks!, Null C .10 .25
237 Undisclosed Location, Non-Unique U .20 .50
238 The 100 Ideas, Null U .20 .50
239 Clandestine Operations, Null R 1.50 4.00
240 The Elektra Situation, Null R 1.00 2.50
241 Essence of Zom, Null R .75 2.00
242 The Infinity Gauntlet, Null R 1.00 2.50
243 Realm of the Mind, Null U .20 .50
244 Secret Government, Null U .20 .50
245 Silent War, Null R .75 2.00
246 Loki, Loki Laufeyson R .75 2.00
247 Thor, Donald Blake R .75 2.00
248 The Reckoning, Null U .20 .50
249 Sub-Mariner, The Avenging Son U .20 .50
250 Atlantean Warriors, Army U .20 .50
251 Magneto, House of M C .10 .25
252 Quicksilver, House of M R 1.00 2.50
253 Scarlet Witch, House of M R .75 2.00
254 Dr. Doom, Future Perfect U .20 .50
255 Tortune Chamber, Null U .20 .50
256 I Am Doom, Null C .10 .25
257 Silver Surfer, The Silver Savage U .20 .50
258 Black Bolt, Enemy Within C .10 .25
259 James Barnes Bucky, Kid Commando R 1.00 2.50
260 Kang, Non-Unique - .20 .50
Time Warrior U
261 Kang Iron Lad, Non-Unique - .75 2.00
Young Avenger R
262 Punisher, Captain America R 1.00 2.50
263 Aaron Stack, Hater of Fleshy Ones U .20 .50
264 The Captain, .20 .50
Can't Remember His Real Name U
265 Elsa Bloodstone, Foulmouthed Bombshell U .20 .50
266 Monica Rambeau, I Was An Avenger U .20 .50
267 Tabitha Smith, Zomg! U .20 .50
268 Ultron, Ultron Prime R .75 2.00
269 Spider-Girl, Daughter of Spider-Man U .20 .50
270 Cammi, Annoying Sidekick U .20 .50
271 Drax the Destroyer, Titan Slayer U .20 .50
272 Phyla-Vell Quasar, .10 .25
Protector of the Universe C
273 Richard Rider Nova Centurion, .20 .50
Keeper of the Worldmind U
274 Ronan the Accuser, Kree Emporer U .20 .50
275 Star-Lord, Peter Quill R .75 2.00
276 Super Skrull, Noble Sacrifice U .20 .50
277 Maverick, Christoph Nord R .75 2.00
278 Sabretooth, Government Assassin U .20 .50
279 Wolverine, Weapon 10 U .20 .50
280 Professor X, Mutant Benefactor U .20 .50
281 Abomination, Emil Blonsky U .20 .50
282 Adam Warlock, Savior of the Universe R .75 2.00
283 Aegis, Lady of All Sorrows R .75 2.00
284 The Beyonder, Inhuman R .75 2.00
285 Death, The Second Force .75 2.00
of the Universe R
286 Fin Fang Foom, .75 2.00
He Whose Limbs Shatter Mountains R
287 James Barnes Captain America, .20 .50
Legacy Reborn U
288 James Barnes Winter Soldier, 1.00 2.50
Out in the Cold R
289 Layla Miller, She Knows Stuff U .20 .50
290 Nick Fury, Off the Grid U .20 .50
291 Skaar, Son of Hulk U .20 .50
292 Tenebrous, Of the Darkness R .75 2.00
293 Quantum Bands, Unique C .10 .25
294 Alias Investigations, Null U .20 .50
295 Asgard, Null C .10 .25
296 The Raft, Null U .20 .50
297 Agents of H.A.T.E., Null C .10 .25
298 Annihilating Conquest, Null U .20 .50
299 Carrying the Torch, Null R 2.00 5.00
300 Casualty of War, Null C .10 .25
301 Code White, Null U .20 .50
302 Collateral Damage, Null C .10 .25
303 Death of the Dream, Null U .20 .50
304 Empire's End, Null U .20 .50
305 Flattened, Null C .10 .25
306 Frog of Thunder, Null R .75 2.00
307 Grudge Match, Null C .10 .25
308 Heroes for Hire, Team-Up C .10 .25
309 House of M, Null C .10 .25
310 Hunt for Nitro, Null C .10 .25
311 I Got 'Em All, Null R .75 2.00
312 Invasion Plans, Null C .10 .25
313 Lay Down With Dogs, Null U .20 .50
314 Losing the Argument, Null C .10 .25
315 Messiah Complex, Null C .10 .25
316 My Name is Peter Parker..., Null R 1.50 4.00
317 No Retreat, No Surrender, Null C .10 .25
318 Now I'm Fighting Dirty, Null C .10 .25
319 Outmatched, Null C .10 .25
320 Public Outcry, Null C .10 .25
321 Rogue Squadron, Null U .20 .50
322 She-Hulk Smash!, Null U .20 .50
323 Sleeper Cells, Null R .75 2.00
324 Slobberknocker, Null C .10 .25
325 The Stamford Incident, Null U .20 .50
326 Superhuman Registration Act, Team-Up R 2.00 5.00
327 Trouble With Dinosaurs, Null R 1.00 2.50
328 Uncertain Legacy, Null R 1.00 2.50
329 Underground Movement, Team-Up R .75 2.00
330 What If?, Team-Up C .10 .25

2004 WarCry Chivalry and Deceit Bretonia vs. Skaven

1 Clanrats of the Warlord Clans C
2 Clawspeck's Night Runners C
3 Grey Seer Thanquol and Boneripper U
4 Queekpest's Stenchmonks C
5 Stikstik Bloodbone U
6 Stikstik's Giant Rats C
7 Stikstik's Throat Rippers C
8 Warlock Skriskrivet U
9 Sacred Standard of the Horned Rat U
10 Battle Plan C
11 Battlefield Orders U
12 Blessings of the Lady C
13 Boundless Faith U
14 Critical Strike U
15 Cunning Raid C
16 Empower Weapon U
17 Faithful Devotion C
18 Fireball C
19 Full Charge C
20 Furious Charge R
21 Grim Resolution U
22 Hold Your Ground! U
23 Immortal Charge C
24 Iron Fist U
25 Life is Cheap U
26 Look Out, Sir! U
27 One for One C
28 One Last Charge C
29 Overwhelming Numbers C
30 Sacrificial Unit U
31 Stare Into the Face of Death C
32 Strength of Honor U
33 Sweeping Flank Maneuver U
34 When They Least Expect It U
35 Banner of Terror U
36 Enchanted Armor U
37 Lance of Piercing U
38 Sword of Striking C
39 Adaltrud's Scrappers C
40 Angelburg's Volunteers C
41 King Louen Leoncouer U
42 Knights of the Lady's Banner C
43 Knights of Winged Valor U
44 Leoncouer's Defenders of the Realm U
45 Leoncouer's Lancers C
46 The Battle Pilgrims C
47 The White Mistress U
48 The Grail Shield U

2004 WarCry Legions of Chaos

1 Archaon's Blood Horde U
2 Archaon's Vanguard C
3 Bilith's Madmen C
4 Crom's Chosen U
5 D'aggorn's Chosen U
6 Grunt Trollskinner R
7 Rack of the Damned C
8 Styrkaar of the Sortsvinaer R
9 Swords of Chaos C
10 The Brides of Styrkaar U
11 Zoekarl, Bringer of Darkness (foil)
12 Archers of Nightbreeze R
13 Beastlord Rakarth of Karrond Kar (foil)
14 Rikhaine's Black Maidens C
15 Rikhaine's Dark Sisters C
16 Rikhaine's Foot C
17 Rikhaine's Vengeance R
18 Rikhaine's Wrath R
19 Saerith, Bride of Haasek U
20 Da Pump Pump Truck R
21 Facebeater's Big Stick Smashaz U
22 Gobbo Elfchasers C
23 Grimgor's Spikey Boyz R
24 Ozol's Netterboyz U
25 Ozol's Snotling Swarm U
26 Ozol's Squig Chasers C
27 Zahubu, Exalted of Gork (foil)
28 Throt the Unclean (foil)
29 Summon Daemon R
30 And Then Comes Darkness U
31 Armed and Dangerous C
32 As Heroes Kill, Flags Fall U
33 Attack the Scouts U
34 Battlefield Veteran U
35 Blessing R
36 Breaking Their Spirit U
37 Bretonnian Resolve U
38 Call in the Reserves U
39 Channel Your Power C
40 Charge of the Knights Panther U
41 Clean Up the Dead R
42 Coordinated Battle Plans C
43 Cunning Battle Plans U
44 Cutting Through the Reserves R
45 Defense of the Empire C
46 Epic Duel R
47 Escape Through the Sewers C
48 Fight Until Dawn R
49 Fire on them Both U
50 Follow My Lead R
51 Franz's Charge C
52 Franz's Regroup C
53 Glorious Melee R
54 Hordes of the North U
55 Huss' Arrival R
56 Inner Strength R
57 Into the Fray U
58 It's not the Blade, but the Soldier C
59 Jasenland's Rolling Charge C
60 Keep them Pinned C
61 Magic Currents U
62 March of the Damned C
63 Overtake Them! U
64 Own the Battlefield C
65 Rain Hell Upon Them! U
66 Re-equip R
67 Relentless March R
68 Remember Your Training! U
69 Scouting Skirmish R
70 Siphoned Power C
71 Strike When They are Weak C
72 Take Up the Charge C
73 Taunting Tactics C
74 The Bretonnian Fields of Battle U
75 The Faithful Fear Not U
76 The Fight Belongs to the Soldier C
77 The Hand of Chaos R
78 The Judgment of Sigmar U
79 The Triumph of Huss R
80 To Our Last Man R
81 Unexpected Assault R
82 Victory! C
83 Leave Nothing Alive R
84 Banner of Fortitude U
85 Cache of Scrolls R
86 Lucas Volkmann, Middenheim Spy R
87 Maximillion Gluttonfist U
88 Ward of Wisdom C
89 Brotherhood of Grimnir C
90 Grimjaw's Feral Hammers U
91 Guildmaster Burlock Damminson (foil)
92 Ironbrow's Digger Company U
93 Ironfist's Disciples R
94 Ironfist's Doomseekers R
95 Makaisson's Belly of Fire C
96 Malakai Makaisson's Goblin-hewer R
97 Ambassador Kasper Von Velten R
98 Boris Todbringer (foil)
99 Bremen's Knights Panther C
100 Emperor Karl Franz (foil)
101 Heralds of Sigmar's Blood C
102 Kirenwulf Jasenland R
103 Lietdorf's Blood-Oathed C
104 Middenland Battalion U
105 Rein Volkhard R
106 Piotr's Gryphon Legion U
107 Swords of the Rieksguard U
108 The Black Raiders of Middenland U
109 Ambassador of the Empire R
110 Ludwig Scharzelm R
111 Archers of the Weeping Skies U
112 Aveldan's Sea Rangers C
113 Elduranel's Brilliant Lancers R
114 Glory's Fading U
115 Indomril's Sea Rangers R
116 Lindanel's Seeking Blades U
117 Sorrow's Song C
118 Yrlis Bluestorm (foil)
119 Anyone but Them! R
120 Helm of Dominion C

2004 WarCry Paths of Glory

1 Ni'nnanuam the Afflicted (foil)
2 Bilerot Plagueflesh U
3 Bileth's Marauders C
4 Festerheart's Plagueswords U
5 Feytor R
6 Gibbering Hordes C
7 Maggotkin R
8 Tallymen of Plagues U
9 Sa'har's Ashen Riders (foil)
10 Morbeth's Corsairs R
11 Morbeth's Dread Knights U
12 Morbeth's Hellblades U
13 Rikhaine's Black Legion C
14 T'aelira Morbeth C
15 Gorgut's Ladz U
16 Moggit's Savage Wazboyz R
17 Kaltorg Skinripper (foil)
18 Pigstikkas C
19 Rotfang's Brawlerz U
20 Skraggi's Wolf Riders C
21 Skullgrinder's Pigkart R
22 Wazzi's Night Raiderz C
23 Sniktnit's Warp Cannon (foil)
24 Screaming Bell of Clan Scryre R
25 Snikluk Fellpest U
26 Vermintide C
27 Giants of Albion R
28 Kreuger's Cursed Company R
29 A Taste of Their Own Tactics R
30 Arrows from the Hills C
31 Back Them Up U
32 Battlefield Spies C
33 Bring them to Us C
34 Chain Lightning C
35 Cunning Plan R
36 Diversity of Arms C
37 Empowered Strike U
38 Everwatch Technique U
39 Feed the Earth U
40 Feint East, Strike West C
41 Fire as They Come R
42 Flanking Charge R
43 For the Fallen! U
44 Force the Skirmish C
45 Forest Cover U
46 Frost Covered Hills U
47 Glory Favors the Brave R
48 Gausser's Return U
49 He's Mine R
50 High Winds U
51 Intervention R
52 Into the Heart of the Enemy C
53 Know the Terrain C
54 Last Ditch Effort U
55 Let Them Come R
56 Level the Field U
57 Look Them in the Eyes C
58 Make Something from Nothing U
59 Make Their Strengths Yours R
60 Marsh Land U
61 Norse Tactics C
62 Not Without a Fight U
63 Planned Diversion U
64 Prepare for the Worst U
65 Rear Charge R
66 Reinforced Supply Lines C
67 Research R
68 Scout the Terrain R
69 Scramble for a Solution R
70 See Through the Diversion U
71 Snow Burdened Hill R
72 Spectral Divination R
73 Strike As They Are Falling C
74 Suffer not the Witch R
75 The Charge of 1000 Horses R
76 Tides of Battle C
77 To the Teeth C
78 Trapping Attack U
79 Unexpected Strike C
80 Unity of Arms C
81 Until You Have Nothing Left U
82 Warrior's Rage R
83 We Claim this Territory R
84 We Have Nothing to Fear C
85 When Its All You've Got C
86 Wipe Them Out U
87 Word of Pain R
88 You'll Be Dead Before You Bleed C
89 Hilt of the Norn Sword (foil)
90 Ring of Stealth R
91 Scribe U
92 Standard of Faith C
93 The Green Knight (foil)
94 The Damsel's Guard U
95 Theolind Adaltrud R
96 Trebuchet C
97 Thorgrim's Trollslayers (foil)
98 Forest Stalkers U
99 Greybeard Thunderers U
100 Thagrund the Greybeard R
101 Thagrund's Gold Miners C
102 Thagrund's Longbeards R
103 Thagrund's Stone Thrower U
104 Thagrund's War Cannon C
105 Valten, Champion of Sigmar (foil)
106 Ophelia Grundheim R
107 Ratai's Frost Riders U
108 Ratai's Horse Archers C
109 Tamislav Ratai U
110 Tzarina Katarin the Ice Queen R
111 White Plain Kossars C
112 Korhil, Captain of the White Lions (foil)
113 Alarielle's Maidenguard R
114 Eataine's Coastal Protectors C
115 Ellerion's Ghost Blades U
116 Keepers of the Flame R
117 Luril Ellerion C
118 Luril's Guardians U
119 Rhyian's Emerald Company C
120 Zarahadron, Hydra of War R

2004 WarCry Siege of Middenheim

1 Archaon's Judgment (foil)
2 Bloodcrushers U
3 Changebringers U
4 Chaos Furies U
5 D'aggorn the Exalted – Veteran of Chaos R
6 Bile Rot, Daemonic Herald R
7 Flayerkin U
8 Kordel Shogaar, Standard Bearer of the Swords of Chaos R
9 Sorrowbringers U
10 Plagueriders U
11 Pleasureseekers U
12 Regiment of Khorne C
13 Siege Tower U
14 Siryk Silver Tongue - Greater Daemon (foil)
15 Narsin's Black Guard C
16 Death Dealer C
17 Blacktear's Brigands C
18 The Serrated C
19 Black Riders C
20 The Gates of Karond Kar R
21 Coven of Sorrows C
22 Loukhane Nightblade (foil)
23 Ardug the Unbreakable (foil)
24 Facebeata's Big'Uns C
25 Facebeata's Dark Boyz C
26 Skinripper's Horde of Greenies C
27 Facebeata's Ard House U
28 Farell Bloodfist U
29 Skinripper's Hoppin' Boyz R
30 Taugrek the Throttler R
31 Blood for the Blood God R
32 Last Waaagh! R
33 Standard of Darkness U
34 Watch Tower C
35 Join the Fray C
36 Reliable Support C
37 Deadly Attrition U
38 Awakening R
39 Blind Fury R
40 Clinch C
41 Close Support C
42 Crush the Weak C
43 Twister R
44 Danger to the Wind U
45 Desperate Gamble R
46 Destiny Now R
47 Destruction U
48 Dirty Fighting U
49 Divine Guidance R
50 Equipment Master U
51 Calm before the Storm C
52 Fast Strike C
53 Fate's Hand C
54 Another Day R
55 For the Greater Glory R
56 Hail of Fire U
57 Karma C
58 Last Chance C
59 Lasting Sting U
60 Great Leadership U
61 Look to the Sky U
62 Battlefield Presence C
63 Magnetism U
64 Measure your Opponent C
65 Phalanx R
66 Purity of Arms C
67 Ration U
68 Reinforcements! C
69 Ready and Willing U
70 Resistance R
71 Rush the Flank U
72 Rust R
73 Second Wind U
74 Sink Hole R
75 Siphon Strength U
76 Spy's Lament R
77 Steel Rain C
78 Stunning Blast U
79 Siege U
80 Supporting Fire R
81 The Time is Not Right R
82 Unfortunate News C
83 Veteran U
84 Winter's Chill U
85 Maps R
86 The Fey Enchantress (foil)
87 Drong's Slayer Pirates R
88 Gates of Karaz-a-Karak R
89 Grimjaw's Greying Veterans C
90 Thunderhead's Air Cavalry R
91 Grimjaw's Personal Bodyguard C
92 Grimjaw's Excavators R
93 Runesmith Morangrin U
94 The Spirit of Grungni (foil)
95 Prophets of Doom R
96 The Great Cannon of Middenheim R
97 Grand Theogonist Volkmar (foil)
98 Black Hand Pistoliers U
99 Ar-Ulric's Teutogen Guard R
100 Hunt Master Ethlich R
101 Knights of the Twin Tailed Comet U
102 Jasenland's Imperial Defenders R
103 High Priest Udo Latnehr U
104 Senechal Valdric Gathowe R
105 Vorn Thugenheim, Standard Bearer of Middenheim R
106 Warriors of Ulric C
107 Wolf Kin Skirmishers U
108 Archers of Nightfall C
109 Vanguard of the Silver Lord (foil)
110 Riders of the Golden Star C
111 The Fair Maiden of Uthuan U
112 Sea Guard of the Northern Ports C
113 Spearmen of the Golden Star C
114 Sword Maidens of Hoeth R
115 Ward Tower U
116 Defend the Walls R
117 Nerves of Steel R
118 For the Empire! C
119 Stand your Ground C
120 Standard of Light U

2005 WarCry Bearers of Redemption

1 Vayj-Naz, Lord of Change VR
2 Tzadiqel's Screamers U
3 Tzadiqel's Horrors U
4 Tzadiqel's Enchanted Warriors C
5 Tzadiqel's Screaming Chariot U
6 Iyar, Lord of Tzeentch R
7 Tzadiqel's Marauder Horsemen C
8 Requiel, Exalted of Tzeentch R
9 Tzadiqel, Prince of Change R
10 Tyamal Dancer VR
11 Fera Ebonheart C
12 Twilight Daughters of the Blade R
13 Ha'asek's Twilight Cauldron R
14 The Mothers of Twilight U
15 Lillet Nightwind U
16 Twilight Sisters of Khaine C
17 Kor'rin Blackheart R
18 Ha'asek's Feral Daughters C
19 Togurg The Filthy VR
20 Bartog's Savage Rippas C
21 Bartog's Boyz of the Bloody Fang C
22 Black Orcs of the Conqueror U
23 Bartog's Savage Boar Boyz C
24 The Conqueror's Smashin' Boyz C
25 Razalt Skineater R
26 Blagark the Colossal U
27 Bartog the Conqueror R
28 Rise from the Ashes R
29 Conscripts C
30 Pirazzo's Lost Legion R
31 Mercenary General Madinlich R
32 You're Next! VR
33 It Can't End That Way VR
34 Keep them Under Fire C
35 Gausser's Camouflage U
36 Second Wave Charge C
37 Knowing the Field of Battle U
38 Command Decisions U
39 Divine Intervention C
40 Tactics of Fright U
41 Ancient Knowledge C
42 News from the Front C
43 The Unseen Advantage U
44 Test of Resolve U
45 Rally Against the Unjust C
46 Fate's Cyclical Wheel C
47 Trump U
48 Take Control U
49 Everything Has a Price U
50 Back to basics R
51 Risky Proposition R
52 Making a Name... R

53 Preparations U
54 Bait and Strike R
55 Suicide Mission C
56 Experience of the Veteran C
57 Inflation R
58 Stand Against the Giants C
59 Jasenland's Justice R
60 The Iron Hand R
61 Use the Terrain to Your Advantage R
62 Deadly Gamble C
63 Test of Strength U
64 A Wall of Arrows R
65 Devious Tactics U
66 On Your Own R
67 I Live! U
68 Heroic Example C
69 All I Have C
70 Fate's Fortune C
71 Thieves' Tactics C
72 Overextended U
73 Gausser's Gambit R
74 Give it Your Best U
75 Inner Conflict R
76 The Sun Sets R
77 Dueling Master R
78 Sustained Assault R
79 Caught in the Bog U
80 StUNk in the Bog C
81 Trapped in the Bog C
82 Mired in the Bog R
83 Unsurpassed Strength R
84 Unsurpassed Loyalty R
85 Confined in the Bog U
86 Virtue of the Small C
87 Hidden Reserves U
88 The Horror R
89 Treasured Armour C
90 Witch Hunter U
91 Unity Stone R
92 Shadow Cloak R
93 Enchanted Spear U
94 Dumin Rockbrow VR
95 Uroken's Slayers of Skaven U
96 Halrig Bloodstone R
97 Stoneheart's Doomseekers R
98 Droken Stoneheart U
99 Grimjaw's Volunteer Corp C
100 Gnollen Stoneheart R
101 Stoneheart's Slayers of the Cursed U
102 Skollan Stoneheart R
103 The Implacable VR
104 Gausser's Huntsmen of the North U
105 Inner Circle of the Knights Panther C
106 Gausser's Huntsmen of the South U
107 Knights of the Bared Fang C
108 Leon Trolmann R
109 Knights of the Panther's Claw C
110 Knights of the Savage Cat U
111 Grand Master Denhaus of the Knights Panther R
112 Whitestar's Thundering Hooves VR
113 Whitestar's Shooting Star U
114 Whitestar's Whirling Blades C
115 Whitestar's Silvertips U
116 Bilgarim's Archers of Nightfall C
117 Calamir Truedance R
118 Ryndaire Goldenleaf U
119 Bilgarim's Silvercrests C
120 Whitestar's Protectorate R

2005 WarCry Bringers of Darkness

1 Anelia, Harridan of Slaneesh R
2 Brotherhood of Carnage C
3 Itmon, The Mountain That Breathes (foil)
4 Styrkaar's Bearers of Enigma U
5 Styrkaar's Blissful Spawn C
6 Styrkaar's Blood Sisters C
7 Styrkaar's Chariot of Sisters R
8 Styrkaar's Daughters of Bloodlust C
9 Xaphen Kell, Keeper of Secrets R
10 Ha'asek's Shadow Assassins (foil)
11 Lukhdror Fastdoom U
12 Ryneys Sharpwing R
13 The Black Hand of Twilight U
14 The Black Sky of Twilight C
15 The Dread Knights of Twilight R
16 The Silent Brothers of Twilight C
17 Twilight's Mistresses of Murder U
18 Yrleth Soaringvale R
19 Gotti Skullcrusher C
20 Grubbi's High Boys U
21 Grubbi's Net Tossers U
22 Grubbi's Savage Riders U
23 Grubbi's Wolf Raiders R
24 Manmangler's Black Orcs (foil)
25 Ozzi Batchewer R
26 Ozzi's Night Guard C
27 Rokki Blood Spitter U
28 Grunson's Marauders R
29 Voland's Venators R
30 Animosity C
31 Best Laid Plans U
32 Bitterness U
33 Blessings of Steel R
34 Brilliant Intellect C
35 Cautious Advance C
36 Choosing a General R
37 Command R
38 Confusion in Command R
39 Countrymen Stand Together U
40 Crushing Tactics R
41 Cunning Tactics U
42 Darkness Falls R
43 Deadly Games R
44 Death Mark R
45 Death of a Hero U
46 Departing the Field of Battle R
47 Detestation R
48 Divine the Future C
49 Established Dominance U
50 Falsified Orders R
51 Fight As One U
52 Guarded Coffers R
53 Heavy Rains U
54 Hide Your Strength U
55 Matter of Honor C
56 Might Wins the Skirmish U
57 Mirror Tactics R
58 Only One Shall Fall R
59 Overpower C
60 Point Blank Shot C
61 Possession U
62 Relent or We Both Die! U
63 Resourceful Management R
64 Restrained Power U
65 Rivalry R
66 Scheme With an Empty Castle (foil)
67 Steal a Sheep In Passing (foil)
68 Stomach for the Fight U
69 Sunrise U
70 Superior Strategies R
71 Surge of Power R
72 The Ties that Bind R
73 To The Last Man U
74 Unexpected Turn of Events U
75 Unity C
76 Victory has a Price C
77 When It's All You Have U
78 When You Stand With Your Brother R
79 Winds of Attrition C
80 Winds of Destruction C
81 Winds of Destiny C
82 Winds of Domination C
83 Winds of Luck C
84 Winds of Power C
85 Winds of Salvation C
86 Winds of Suffering C
87 Winds of War C
88 Ancestral Tablet C
89 Cavalry Banner U
90 Enchanted Halberd C
91 General's Standard U
92 Shadow Guide R
93 The Seventh Spear of the Fallen R
94 Alrik's Hunting Rangers C
95 Barak's Iron Wall U
96 Barak's Pipers C
97 Ganulf's Crack Shots U
98 Ganulf's Forest Walkers U
99 Ganulf's Ironworkers C
100 Grimjaw's Flying Hammers R
101 Hargum Ganulf R
102 Logtok Gimragson (foil)
103 Barthelm's Harriers C
104 Carroburg Swordguard U
105 Fandelhoch's Huntsmen U
106 Gausser's Foresters U
107 Gausser's Lead Breather R
108 Gunter Braunschaft R
109 Harman Barthelm R
110 Old Reliable (foil)
111 Theodoric's Sharp Shooters C
112 Bearers of the Sacred Flame C
113 Korrim's Grey Avengers U
114 Lord Korrim Swifteagle R
115 Luril's Seafarers C
116 Spears of the Fallen Tree U
117 Talaefanil Peacebringer (foil)
118 Tormeclis Keensight C
119 Warriors of the Fallen Tree R
120 Whitestar's Guardians R

2005 WarCry Death and Honor Imperial Vampire Hunters vs. Vampire Counts

1 Black Hand of Death U
2 Curse of the Immortal C
3 Curse of Years C
4 From Hell's Heart C
5 Gaze of Nagash C
6 Hand of Dust C
7 Hellish Vigor U
8 Invocation of Nehek C
9 That Which Does Not Die C
10 Vanhel's Danse Macabre U
11 Fandelhoch's Folly U
12 Ire of the Magus U
13 Strength of Forethought R
14 Carstein Ring U
15 Vial of Unicorn Blood U
16 Banner of Terror U
17 Adolphus Krieger U
18 Banshees of Nightfall U
19 Carstein's Black Hand C
20 Carstein's Black Knights C
21 Carstein's Flesh Eaters C
22 Carstein's Grave Guard C
23 Carstein's Wights C
24 Gothard, The Undying Knight C
25 Manfred Von Carstein U
26 A Good Death to Save Another C
27 Blood Precedes Glory U
28 Death Comes to All U
29 Devotion to a Cause C
30 Freedom is not Free C
31 That Which Does Not Kill Us... C
32 The Battle Goes to the Vigilant C
33 The Enemy is Ours U
34 Valor and Vigilance C
35 War is Cruelty C
36 Nobody Lives Forever! R
37 Grand Theogonist Kurt III U
38 Standard of Faith C
39 Sword of Striking C
40 Axelbrand, Archelector of Taal C
41 Knights of the Divine Sword C
42 Martin, Elector of Stirland U
43 Martin's War Hounds U
44 Ostermark Vampire Hunters C
45 Priests of Taal C
46 Stirland Crossbowmen of the Stake C
47 Woeful Flagellents U
48 Zealots of Taal C

2005 WarCry Harbingers of War

1 Bull Lords of Pain C
2 Korvin, Champion of Khorne (foil)
3 Korvin's Raging Centigors C
4 Pahadiel, The Mammoth Drawn Fortress R
5 Servants of Itmon R
6 Urmas, Champion of the Khorngor R
7 Ha'asek, The Archon of Twilight (foil)
8 Ha'asek's Black Arrows R
9 Ha'asek's Black Riders U
10 Ha'asek's Bolt Slinger U
11 Ha'asek's Devil Brides C
12 Ha'asek's Hands of Retribution C
13 Ha'asek's Knights of Terror U
14 Ha'asek's Standing Guard C
15 Ha'aseks Personal Guard R
16 Ha'aseks Wild Ones C
17 Ha'asek's Witch Elves R
18 Grubbi's Fast Fast Kart C
19 Manmangler's Armoured Orcs U
20 Manmangler's Big Chukka U
21 Manmangler's Boarboyz R
22 Manmangler's Brute Boyz R
23 Manmangler's Flailing Gobbos U
24 Manmangler's Hench Boyz R
25 Manmangler's River Trolls U
26 Manmangler's Savage Killaz U
27 Nazall the Nasty C
28 Urguck Manmangler, Orc Overlord (foil)
29 Anelia, Mistress of Slaanesh U
30 A Dangerous Game U
31 A Deadly Game U
32 A Fortunate Wind R
33 A Shift in Morale R
34 Act Foolish, Be Smart U
35 Aerial Suppport C
36 Attack the Neighbor with Impunity R
37 Beat the Grass to Startle the Snakes C
38 Calculated Reserves R
39 Catch the Leader to Nab the Bandits U
40 Charge under a Blackened Sky C
41 Costly Tactics C
42 Counter Spell C
43 Counter-Attack R
44 Dawn of a New Day R
45 Dawn Raid R
46 Drive them to the Skies C
47 Dwarven Victory R
48 Elven Victory R
49 End Game Maneuvers C
50 Enough! C
51 Face the Weary in a Condition of Ease C
52 Feint One Way, Strike Another C
53 Final Wave R
54 Force a Change in Fate C
55 Fortune Favours the Brave U
56 Hide a Sword in a Smile C
57 High and Low Charge C
58 High Pressure Tactics U
59 Hold Nothing Back R
60 Homeland Victories U
61 Imperial Victory R
62 Kill With A Borrowed Sword U
63 Lock the Gates to Catch the Bandits R
64 Magical Overload R
65 Make Allies at a Distance, Attack Nearby C
66 Dogged Determination U
67 Offer a Brick in Exchange for Gold U
68 One Defeat Follows Another C
69 One Tree Falls for Another U
70 Path of the Arrow C
71 Pick a Fight in the Enemy's Home U
72 Point at One to Scold Another U
73 Rally Up R
74 Replace Beams with Pillars U
75 Rob a Burning House R
76 Run Far Away C
77 Save Something for Later R
78 Scheme With Beauties (foil)
79 Scheme with Double Agents R
80 Scheme with Self Inflicted Wounds C
81 Take and Hold U
82 Take the Firewood from Under the Pot U
83 The Fall of the Mighty U
84 The Silver Serpent Sheds its Skin (foil)
85 The Weak Fall, The Strong Stand R
86 To the Bone U
87 Victory at Any Cost R
88 Amulet of the Southern Hand C
89 Banner of Warding U
90 Flying Mounts C
91 Standard of the Harbinger R
92 Barak Grimjaw, Hammer of the Dwarfs (foil)
93 Grimjaw's Dwarfs of Vigilance C
94 Grimjaw's Enchanted Bolt Thrower C
95 Grimjaw's Honour Guard U
96 Grimjaw's Iron Lords R
97 Grimjaw's Loners R
98 Grimjaw's Stouthearts C
99 Grimjaw's Undying Slayers U
100 Grimjaw's Valorous Veterans U
101 Grimjaw's Woodland Rangers R
102 Gausser's Veterans R
103 Gausser's Hellblaster R
104 Gausser's Young Guns R
105 Lifeguard of Frote C
106 Theodoric Gausser, Guardian of the Empire (foil)
107 Xavier, Transcriber of Wind U
108 Bilgarim Whitestar, Elven Lord (foil)
109 Whitestar's Archers of the White Pillar C
110 Whitestar's Coastal Guardians R
111 Whitestar's Guardians C
112 Whitestar's Guardians of the Sky C
113 Whitestar's Old Spears C
114 Whitestar's Order of the Black Rose U
115 Whitestar's Silverhelms R
116 Whitestar's White Lions U
117 Whitestar's White Reavers U
118 Whitestar's Youngheart Spearmen R
119 Doramin Gimragson R
120 Otwin Salenholt U

2005 WarCry Swords of Retribution

1 Zevael, Greater Daemon of Khorne VR
2 Bilerot's Marauders R
3 C'ulvan The Decayed R
4 C'ulvan's Chosen U
5 C'ulvans Pestilence Swarm U
6 Plague Bearers U
7 Tai'ir The Putrid U
8 Kurlon The Rotten, Trumpeter of Decay C
9 Plague Banner R
10 Khron Nightglade VR
11 Blackspear's Sacrificers R
12 Death Reapers C
13 Death Swords C
14 Ha'asek's Blackswords U
15 Nordhil Blackspear R
16 Ryna Bloodraven R
17 Hydra Banner R
18 Khardil, Herald of Naggaroth C
19 Vorott the Masher VR
20 Grimgore's Spider Riders U
21 Grubbi's Goblin Elfsnappers C
22 Urguck's 'eadloppas U
23 Urguck's Manstompas C
24 Urguck's Sneaky Shootaz U
25 Vagar Dwarfstomper R
26 Conductor of the Waaagh C
27 Raggedy Banner R
28 War Banner R
29 All We Have to Give C
30 Altered Orders U
31 Altered Strategies R
32 I'm Coming for You! VR
33 Last Ditch Effort VR
34 Altered Tactics C
35 Applied Knowledge U
36 Change in the Currents C
37 Changes in the Plan of Attack R
38 Clarity of the Veteran U
39 Empowerment U
40 End Game Maneuvering U
41 Extended to your Limits R
42 Quick Strike R
43 Fill the Gaps in the Line U
44 Forest C
45 Fortune on the Winds U
46 Full Pull and Release C
47 Get it Right This Time C
48 Herd of Wild Horses U
49 Herd of Wild Pegasi R
50 Influence Fate C
51 Ingrained Tactics C
52 Jasenland's Probing Tactics R
53 Lead by Example U
54 Lessons Learned C
55 Master of the Battlefield R
56 Maximize Resources U
57 Misguided Tactics C
58 Moving On U
59 Never Stop C
60 Nothing Left R
61 Nothing Saved C
62 Plan Twice, Attack Once R
63 Power Drain R
64 Rally to the Banner C
65 Recon Reports R
66 Redistribution C
67 Sacred Ground U
68 Shift in Power C
69 Stand Together as One U
70 Strategies of Sacrifice R
71 Supply Line Confusion U
72 Sweeping Flank U
73 Take Their Place R
74 Test of Faith R
75 Test of Will R
76 Testing Fate C
77 The Face of Horror C
78 The Price has Been Paid R
79 Tightened Ranks U
80 Troubles Come not Single Spies C
81 Unexpected Backlash R
82 Unexpected Tactics U
83 Watch and Learn U
84 Weaken their Ranks R
85 When We Need It The most R
86 You Get What You Invest In R
87 Abandoned Fort U
88 Dark Emissary C
89 Earthworks C
90 Ebonfang R
91 Furgut U
92 Morrigan's Mercenaries R
93 Truthsayer C
94 Varadin Redbeard VR
95 Barak's Ironbeards C
96 Dokkenrok Whitebeard R
97 Grimjaw's Drillers U
98 Grimjaw's Flying Cannons R
99 Grimjaw's Grudgebearers U
100 Makaisson's Bellows C
101 Bolok Rocksmasher, Drummer of Karaz A Karak C
102 Standard of Taunting R
103 Axelbrand Rainultz VR
104 Boris Mikhail C
105 Boris's Griffon Legion U
106 Katarin, Bringer of Winter R
107 Katarin's Kossars U
108 Katarin's Lancers U
109 Tzar Brodski U
110 Banner of Ursun R
111 Mikhail Alekhsko C
112 Glorenlil Suregrace VR
113 Aethrilmar, Prince of Ulthuan R
114 Eldorion Brightwood U
115 Swiftstrike U
116 Whitestar's Defenders C
117 Whitestar's Skirmishers C
118 Whitestar's Swordmasters R
119 Banner of the World Dragon R
120 Tylith Puresong C

2005 WarCry Valor and Treachery Wood Elves vs. Skaven

1 Clickclick Bangbang U
2 Headtaker's Censer Bearers C
3 Headtaker's Ratmen U
4 Queek's Foul Monks C
5 Queek's Vile Ratkin C
6 Skaven Tunnels U
7 Swarm of Skavenblight C
8 Warlock Quiksnak U
9 Warlord Queek Headtaker U
10 Cloak of Shadows U
11 Packmaster Teekteek C
12 Weeping Blade C
13 Death Frenzy U
14 Expendable C
15 He Who Runs Away... C
16 Lead from the Rear C
17 Make Them Fear Us C
18 Plague C
19 Skavenblight U
20 Swarm Them! C
21 Warpstone Mutation C
22 Buy Me Some Time R
23 Command the Heights R
24 Death From Afar C
25 Get Back Here! R
26 Glory Favors the Brave U
27 Life is Cheap U
28 Stare Into the Face of Death R
29 Athel Loren's Eternal Guard C
30 Callaen Strongblade C
31 Forest Lookout U
32 Naieth The Prophetess U
33 Orion U
34 Orion's Forest Guard C
35 Treekin of Athel Loren C
36 Warhawks of Kurnous C
37 Wild Riders of Kurnous U
38 Winter Guard U
39 A Murder of Spites C
40 Bow of Loren U
41 Athel Loren Territories U
42 Point Blank Fighting C
43 Rally Behind the Arrows C
44 Seize the Battle U
45 Strength in the Bow C
46 Strength in the Woods C
47 Taking Aim from on High C
48 Tighten the Ranks U
49 Woodlands C

2006 WarCry Hand of Fate

1 Blood Reavers R
2 Blood Scythes U
3 Kurt Virhoch, Chosen Of The Blood God R
4 Life Drinkers U
5 The Blood Sworn R
6 The Blooded U
7 The Skull Taker U
8 Virhoch's Blood Riders U
9 Virhoch's Blood Trackers C
10 Virhoch's Hounds C
11 Ebonkin's Line Breaker R
12 Hag Queen Hellebron (foil)
13 Hellebron's Witches C
14 Khaine's Will C
15 Lolisithi Coldwind U
16 Makdhaine's Corsairs R
17 Reapers Of Khaine C
18 Shadow Wind R
19 Makdhaine Ebonkin U
20 Rynsethryn Cruelheart U
21 Azraz Humiesplitter R
22 Azraz's Bashers R
23 Azraz's Boyz C
24 Azraz's Savage Manglers C
25 Dargur The Insane (foil)
26 Humiesplitter's Hackers R
27 Humiesplitters Big Uns U
28 The Impaler C
29 Kogkog The Dangerous U
30 Zagzog Gobbothrottler U
31 Druchii Ascendancy R
32 Gorks Warpath (foil)
33 Insidious Insinuation R
34 Khorne's Blessing R
35 Malicious Intent C
36 Baleful Sorcery U
37 Berzerker Fury (foil)
38 Bestial Rage C
39 Blackened Skies C
40 Blind Faith U

41 Devotional Sorcery U
42 Disarmament R
43 Done Deal R
44 Echoes Of The Distant Past R
45 Erode Their Position C
46 Extensive Preparation U
47 Forewarning U
48 Fortitude U
49 Glorious Charge C
50 Here Be Dragons U
51 I Give You This Sword C
52 Inspiring Leadership (foil)
53 Iron Constitution U
54 It's Good To Be King C
55 Kick 'Em While They're Down C
56 Lap Around! C
57 Lightning Reflexes U
58 Make The Most Of What You Have R
59 Making Sure C
60 Never Again U
61 Never Say Die C
62 One Shall Fall C
63 One Shall Stand U
64 Opening Their Guard U
65 Overwhelming Horror U
66 Petty Reprisal C
67 Price Of War R
68 Regimental Tactics C
69 Riposte U
70 Ruthless Expenditure U
71 See How It Feels C
72 Sigmar Protects U
73 Stack The Deck R
74 Stampede R
75 Stand Firm C
76 Steadfast C
77 Tactical Denial U
78 Tactics Of Intimidation U
79 ...There Is A Way U
80 To Me! R
81 To The Victor Go The Spoils R
82 To The Wire R
83 Trick Shot C
84 Undermine R
85 Unreliable C
86 Where There Is A Will... U
87 Tunnel Fighter U
88 Dorgan Darkeye U
89 Dorgan's Digger Crew R
90 Dorgan's Disgraced C
91 Dorgan's Hammers Of Spite R
92 Dorgan's Iron Guard R
93 Dorgan's Iron Warriors U
94 Dorgan's Rangers C
95 Throndil Starhammerer (foil)
96 Sons Of Grungni U
97 Black Knights Of Morr R
98 Fabian Techlich C
99 Fandelhoch's Halberdiers C
100 Fandelhoch's New Machine C
101 Fandelhoch's Outriders C
102 Fandelhoch's Riders U
103 Ivan Fandelhoch R
104 The Hunters Of Hochland U
105 Erwin Fandelhoch U
106 Toby Rutzpold U
107 Aetholbrin Eldenstar R
108 Aislinn's Sea Guard C
109 Aislinn's Sea Rangers C
110 Cython Menlui R
111 Eothrilion True Eye C
112 Kyrlranlaer Silvershore C
113 Sea Lord Aislinn (foil)
114 Ships Company Of The Pernicious C
115 Gaensofir Swiftfoot U
116 Loremaster U
117 Detachment Training R
118 Dwarfen Pride R
119 Pure Of Heart R
120 Unshakable Resolve (foil)

2006 WarCry War of Attrition

1 Archaon (foil)
2 Archaon's Vanguard C
3 Azymeth's Skullreavers C
4 Bilerot Plagueflesh U
5 Bilith's Madmen C
6 Bloodcrushers U
7 Bull Lords of Pain C
8 Crom's Chosen U
9 D'aggorn the Exalted – Veteran of Chaos R
10 D'aggorn's Deathblades C
11 Daemonettes of Slaanesh R
12 Feytor R
13 Gibbering Hordes C
14 Haargoth's Bloodletters U
15 Herd of Skulkkoth C
16 Kordel Shogaar, Standard Bearer R
17 Korvin, Champion of Khorne (foil)
18 Melekh the Changer R
19 Melekh's Horrors U
20 Rack of the Damned C
21 Regiment of Khorne C
22 Skulkkoth the Defiler R
23 Styrkaar's Bearers of Enigma U
24 Styrkaar's Chariot of Sisters R
25 The Skull Pack U
26 Tzeentch Screamers R
27 Xaphen Kell, Keeper of Secrets R
28 Anelia, Mistress of Slaanesh U
29 Raaghra the Culler U
30 Archers of Nightbreeze R
31 Black Rose Coven C
32 Cauldron of Blood (foil)
33 Dhargethen's Duskreavers R
34 Fell Sisters of Clar Karond R
35 Ganethia Blacksoul U
36 Ha'asek, The Archon of Twilight (foil)
37 Ha'asek's Black Riders U
38 Ha'asek's Bolt Slinger U
39 Ha'asek's Hands of Retribution C
40 Ha'asek's Knights of Terror U
41 Ha'asek's Standing Guard C
42 Ha'aseks Personal Guard R
43 Keth Zarene U
44 Korhadril's Nighthaunters C
45 Lukhdror Fastdoom U
46 Menghil's Mankillers R
47 Morathi, the Hag Sorceress (foil)
48 Morbeth's Hellblades U
49 Raven's Scythe C
50 Rikhaine's Black Legion C
51 Sa'har's Ashen Wraiths U
52 Saerith the Bladed R
53 Spirithaunters of Hag Graef C
54 The Dread Knights of Twilight R
55 The Silent Brothers of Twilight C
56 The Twilight Company R
57 Yrleth Soaringvale R
58 Zelekendel, Blade of Khaine U
59 Zelekendel's Blackblades C
60 Borgut Facebeata (foil)
61 Facebeata's Big'Uns C
62 Facebeata's Dark Boyz C
63 Gitnob's Gitz C
64 Gobbo Elfchasers C
65 Grubbi Hookblade R
66 Grubbi's High Boys U
67 Grubbi's Skullcracker C
68 Grubbi's Wolf Raiders R
69 Jezzi Poisonbite (foil)
70 Kurgrot's Doom Divers C
71 Manmangler's Armoured Orcs U
72 Manmangler's Brute Boyz R
73 Manmangler's Flailing Gobbos U
74 Manmangler's River Trolls U
75 Nhaga's Ladz U
76 Ogdrag's 'Arrer Boyz U
77 Ozol's Netterboyz U
78 Ozol's Squig Chasers C
79 Ozzi Batchewer R
80 Ozzi's Night Guard C
81 Roklog's Tuskas R
82 Rotfang's Brawlerz U
83 Skinripper's Hoppin' Boyz R
84 Skinripper's Horde of Greenies C
85 Warboss Urguck Man-mangler R
86 Wazzi Moonscowler U
87 Wazzi's Lunatic Gitz R
88 Borgokk Bonecaster R
89 Curse of Years C
90 From Hell's Heart C
91 Gaze of Nagash C
92 Hellish Vigor U
93 The Hordes of Darkness C
94 Vanhel's Danse Macabre U
95 Vial of Unicorn Blood U
96 Black Fire Bandits R
97 Carmen's Maiden Knights (foil)
98 Karkov's Winged Lancers U
99 Sengupta's Cobra Cult C
100 The Crowmaster (foil)
101 Black Raven's Lurkers R
102 Grunsom's Marauders R
103 Voland's Venators R
104 Watch Tower C
105 Accurate and Precise U
106 Animosity C
107 Attack the Neighbor with Impunity R
108 Back Them Up U
109 Battle Hardened (foil)
110 Battle Omens U
111 Battlefield Instinct U
112 Best Laid Plans U
113 Blessing R
114 Bogged Down C
115 Borgokk's Fog of War U
116 Borrowed Power (foil)
117 Break for Winter R
118 Brilliant Intellect C
119 Calculated Reserves R
120 Calm before the Storm C
121 Chain Lightning C
122 Change of Plan U
123 Channel Your Power C
124 Choosing a General R
125 Command the Heights C
126 Contingency Plan C
127 Counter Spell C
128 Critical Strike U
129 Crush the Weak C
130 Crushing Tactics R
131 Cunning Raid C
132 Danger to the Wind U
133 Deadly Games R
134 Death From Afar C
135 Death of a Hero U
136 Defense of the Empire C
137 Destiny Now R
138 Devil's Bargain R
139 Dissipate Magic R
140 Diversion C
141 Diversity of Arms C
142 Duplicate (foil)
143 Earthquake R
144 Enervation C
145 Enough! C
146 Epic Duel R
147 Fading Winds U
148 Faithful Devotion C
149 Fandelhoch's Folly U
150 Fast March C
151 Feint R
152 Fiery Blast C
153 Fight As One U
154 Fight Until Dawn R
155 Fire as They Come R
156 Fire on them Both U
157 Flanking Charge R
158 For the Greater Glory R
159 Fortune Favours the Brave U
160 Full Charge C
161 Furious Charge R
162 Get Back Here! R
163 Glory Favors the Brave R
164 Great Leadership U
165 Grim Resolution U
166 Ha'asek's Grief R
167 Hail of Doom R
168 Hail of Fire U
169 Heart of Darkness R
170 Heavy Cavalry Charge R
171 Heavy Rains U
172 Heroic Resolve C
173 Hex C
174 High Winds U
175 Hold Nothing Back R
176 Increased Supplies U
177 Inner Strength R
178 Inspirational Victory R
179 Intervention R
180 Lasting Sting U
181 Lay of the Land U
182 Leitdorf Maneuver R
183 Leitdorf's Plan C
184 Level the Field U
185 Look Out, Sir! U
186 Look Them in the Eyes C
187 Look to the Sky U
188 Low Morale R
189 Luck C
190 Magnify Terror R
191 Make Something from Nothing U
192 March of the Damned C
193 Marsh of Morr U
194 Mass Confusion R
195 Master of the Field C
196 Matter of Honor C
197 Melkior's Gambit C
198 Mettle C
199 Might of Heroes U
200 No Quarter! R
201 Nobody Lives Forever! R
202 Not Without a Plan C
203 One Defeat Follows Another C
204 One Last Charge C
205 One Tree Falls for Another U
206 Only One Shall Fall R
207 Onward! R
208 Open Field U
209 Out Think R
210 Outflank U
211 Overload U
212 Pick a Fight in the Enemy's Home U
213 Plotting Revenge C
214 Point Blank Shot C
215 Possession U
216 Prepare for the Worst U
217 Prepare Yourselves! C
218 Press the Advantage U
219 Proven Tactics R
220 Raise the Dead R
221 Rallying Cry R
222 Reap the Rewards C
223 Reckless Assault U
224 Relent or We Both Die! U
225 Relentless Advance R
226 Relentless March R
227 Reliable Support C
228 Renewal of Power C
229 Rivalry R
230 Rob a Burning House R
231 Rush the Flank U
232 Sacrifice R
233 Scatter the Ranks C
234 Scheme With an Empty Castle (foil)
235 Scheme With Beauties (foil)
236 Scheme with Self Inflicted Wounds C
237 See Through the Diversion U
238 Shield Wall R
239 Show of Force C
240 Siphon Strength U
241 Stare Into the Face of Death C
242 Steal a Sheep In Passing (foil)
243 Stomach for the Fight U
244 Stout of Heart U
245 Strategems R
246 Strategic Withdrawal U
247 Strength of Forethought R
248 Strength of Iron R
249 Strike As They Are Falling C
250 Stunning Blast U
251 Sudden Attack C
252 Sunrise U
253 Supporting Fire R
254 Surge of Power R
255 Sweeping Flank Maneuver U
256 Take the Firewood from Under the Pot U
257 Take Up the Charge C
258 The Conscripts Arrive R
259 The Silver Serpent Sheds its Skin (foil)
260 The Time is Not Right R
261 The Triumph of Huss R
262 The Weak Fall, The Strong Stand R
263 Threaten R
264 Tighten the Noose R
265 To Our Last Man R
266 To the Bone U
267 To The Last Man U
268 Triumphant Celebration U
269 Underhanded Tricks U
270 Unexpected Turn of Events U
271 Unfortunate News C
272 Unity C
273 Veteran U
274 Warrior's Rage R
275 Weapons Master C
276 When You Need It the Most C
277 Wind of Death (foil)
278 Winds of Fate (foil)
279 Wings of the Harpy R
280 Winter's Chill U
281 Banner of Terror U
282 Cache of Scrolls R
283 Enchanted Armor C
284 Enchanted Shield C
285 Lance of Piercing U
286 Maps R
287 Maximillion Gluttonfist U
288 Mighty Warhorn U
289 Musician U
290 Standard of Faith C
291 Steelheart Shield C
292 Talisman of Strength R
293 Ward of Wisdom C
294 Alrik's Hunting Rangers C
295 Barak Grimjaw, Hammer of the Dwarfs (foil)
296 Dorgan's Ironshields C
297 Drong's Slayer Pirates R
298 Ganulf's Crack Shots U
299 Ganulf's Forest Walkers U
300 Ganulf's Ironworkers C
301 Ganulf's Youngbeards R
302 Greyfathers of Karak-Hirn C
303 Grimjaw's Dwarfs of Vigilance C
304 Grimjaw's Flying Hammers R
305 Grimjaw's Greying Veterans C
306 Grimjaw's Stouthearts C
307 Grimjaw's Undying Slayers U
308 Grimjaw's Woodland Rangers R
309 Izzembard's Old Growlers U
310 Izzumbard Endrinkuli R
311 Makaisson's Belly of Fire C
312 Malakai Makaisson's Goblin-hewer R
313 Rockgrinder (foil)
314 Runesmith Gottri Grimsson U
315 Runesmith Morangrin U
316 Thagrund's War Cannon C
317 Thorgrim's Steel Hammers U
318 Thunderhead's Air Cavalry R
319 Ulfrik's Axe-bearers R
320 Boldur Runestriker R
321 Malakai Makaisson U
322 Snorri Nosebiter U
323 Ar-Ulric's Teutogen Guard R
324 Barthelm's Harriers C
325 Black Hand Pistoliers U
326 Dieter Menschaff U
327 Fandelhoch's Huntsmen U
328 Gausser's Lead Breather R
329 Gausser's Veterans R
330 Grand Master Hans Leitdorf (foil)
331 Gunther's Carroburgers C
332 Heralds of Sigmar's Blood C
333 High Priest Udo Latnehr U
334 Kirenwulf Jasenland R
335 Knight General Mikael Kobernecht R
336 Lector Wilhelm Faustus R
337 Lietdorf's Blood-Oathed C
338 Lifeguard of Frote C
339 Middenland Battalion U
340 Middenland Swordsmen U
341 Old Reliable (foil)
342 Pfanelholt's Swordsmen C
343 Piotr's Gryphon Legion U
344 Ratai's Horse Archers C
345 The Black Raiders of Middenland U
346 The Penitents of Altdorf R
347 Theodoric Gausser, Guardian of the Empire (foil)
348 Theodoric's Sharp Shooters C
349 Tzarina Katarin the Ice Queen R
350 White Plain Kossars C
351 Wolf Kin Skirmishers U
352 Gerhart Brennend, Bright Wizard R
353 Alarielle, the Everqueen R
354 Alarielle's Maidenguard R
355 Alith's Ghost Bows U
356 Archers of Nightfall C
357 Archers of the Weeping Skies U
358 Aveldan's Sea Rangers C
359 Bearers of the Sacred Flame C
360 Bilgarim Whitestar, Elven Lord (foil)
361 Calath's Sentinels C
362 Elduranel's Brilliant Lancers R
363 Galathel's Greycloaks U
364 Glory's Fading U
365 Imrik, Dragon Prince of Caledor (foil)
366 Keepers of the Flame R
367 Korrim's Grey Avengers U
368 Lindanel's Seeking Blades U
369 Lord Korrim Swifteagle R
370 Rhyian Dawnrider U
371 Spearmen of the Golden Star C
372 The Fair Maiden of Ulthuan U
373 Tyrion's Silver Riders C
374 Warriors of the Fallen Tree R
375 Whitestar's Archers of the White Pillar C
376 Whitestar's Coastal Guardians R
377 Whitestar's Guardians C
378 Whitestar's Guardians of the Sky C
379 Whitestar's Silverhelms R
380 Whitestar's White Lions U
381 Lady Ellaneil the Dawnbringer R
382 Blood Precedes Glory U
383 Devotion to a Cause C
384 Freedom is not Free C
385 The Enemy is Ours U
386 The Grand Alliance C
387 Valor and Vigilance C
388 War is Cruelty C

2007 WarCry Veterans of Battle

1 Fandar Warptouched C
2 Korvin, Khorne's Chosen VR
3 Korvin's Chosen Knights R
4 Korvin's Northern Warriors C
5 Morghur, Master Of Skulls R
6 Morghur's Horde U
7 Morghur's Ogres U
8 Raaghra's Wild Herd C
9 Mark Of The Chosen U
10 Arrows of Twilight R
11 Kyleth's Fellstalkers C
12 Kyleth's Reavers U
13 Nightbolt U
14 The Archon's Black Riders C
15 Twilight's Harbinger VR
16 Twilight's Steeds R
17 Tz'arthi, Beast Of Har Ganeth C
18 Kyleth The Cruel U
19 Da Overlord's Black Orcs U
20 Manmangler's Wild Boar Boyz R
21 Urguck's Arrer Boyz C
22 Urguck's Boyz U
23 Urguck's Sneaky Gits C
24 Warboss Man-Mangler VR
25 Wuzzag's Arrer Boyz R
26 Wuzzag's Gobbo Mob C
27 Whirly Skinripper U
28 Aura Of Fear C
29 Strength In Deception VR
30 Hunters Of The Eyebiter Tribe R
31 Armor Of Deflection C
32 Arrows Of Seeking U
33 Power Stone C
34 Staff Of Sorcery U
35 Sword of Battle R
36 Armored Protection C
37 Ashes Of The Fallen R
38 Back Up Your Brothers C
39 Battle Scream C
40 Behind The Scenes U
41 Brute Force U
42 Choose Your Allies Well R
43 Confidence C
44 Embark On A Quest VR
45 Examine Your Strategy U
46 Experience Has Its Rewards R
47 Explosion of Power VR
48 Feigned Weakness C
49 Fleet Of Foot R
50 Force Their Hand R
51 Gigantic Weakness C
52 Give And Take C
53 Gutsy Move U
54 Hasty Move R
55 Hidden Arms R
56 Hold Your Aim U
57 Holding Ground C
58 Immediate Weakness U
59 Integrity U
60 Keep Pace C
61 Know Their Formations C
62 Make Them Cow Before You C
63 Manipulation R
64 Money equals Power R
65 No Rest For The Weary U
66 On The Line R
67 Past Knowledge C
68 Poison The Well C
69 Power Over Those Who Fear U
70 Predict Their Moves R
71 Recycling your Decisions R
72 Resolute C
73 Stalwart C
74 Stand Alone U
75 Stay On Target U
76 Sling Of The Sword C
77 Strength From The Line U
78 Strength In Your Faith U
79 Strength On The Winds C
80 Strike Before They Do R
81 Strike With Your Sword R
82 The Knowledge Of Your Allies U
83 The Weak Stand Up U
84 The Tide Comes In U
85 Use Their Weapons Against Them R
86 Utilize Your Resources U
87 Variety Of Options U
88 Wait For It C
89 Well-Rested U
90 Barak Grimjaw, Harbinger of Pride VR
91 Barak's Ironbreakers U
92 Cannons of Silverspear R
93 Defender Of Karak-Kadrin C
94 Grimjaw's Falmethrower U
95 Grimjaw's Longbeards C
96 Grimjaw's Stonethrower R
97 Grimjaw's Thunderers C
98 Damakrin Giantbreaker U
99 Averland Halberdiers C
100 Count Theodric Gausser VR
101 Edwin Oftmeir U
102 Friedrich Ruerhart C
103 Gausser's Protector's R
104 Halberdiers Of Norland R
105 Marienburg Swordsmen C

106 Wissenburg Greatswords U
107 Anton Lutrecht U
108 Bilgarim's Silverhelms U
109 Eagles Of Ulthuan C
110 Helms Of Caladai U
111 Lathain's Phoenix Guard C
112 Lord Whitestar, Mage of Ulthuan VR
113 Sarathai, Dragon Of Caledor R
114 Whitestar's Shadow Warriors C
115 Whitestar's Truespear R
116 Kourdhir Brazenlight U
117 Bugman's Brew VR
118 Impressive Might R
119 Strength Versus The Weak U
120 Virtue Of Heroism C

2012 Warhammer Invasion The Accursed Dead

41 The Liber Mortis
42 Kurt Helborg
43 Reckless Engineer
44 Ancient Vengeance
45 Lion Standard
46 Purged By Flame
47 War Boar
48 Valley of Many Eyes
49 Roaming Shaman
50 Red Arrow Coach
51 Stricken Warrior
52 Rift of Battle
53 Treasure Thieves
54 Jealous Eyes
55 Bladesinger
56 Drakenhof Castle
57 Arcane Power
58 Rebuild the Hold
59 Hidden Operative
60 Beastman Incursion

2012 Warhammer Invasion City of Winter

81 Burlock's Ingenuity
82 Fists of Mork
83 Pigeon Bombs
84 Convocation of Eagles
85 Soporific Musk
86 Barbed Snares
87 Bannerman of the Crag
88 Egathrond
89 The Ebonblades
90 Anlec Lookout
91 Hag Queen
92 Promenade of Malice
93 Harpy Aerie
94 Court of the Witch King
95 Call of the Kraken
96 Kindred of Laith-Kourn
97 Pageant of Shrikes
98 Ratling Gun
99 Desertion
100 Raiding Ships

2012 Warhammer Invasion Days of Blood

1 Crone Hellebron
2 Capture Slaves
3 Bride of Khaine
4 Chill Sea Watchtower
5 Veteran Thunderers
6 Doors of Karak Hirn
7 Ludwig Schwarzheim
8 Middenheim Lookout
9 Midden Moors Watchtower
10 Great Fire Dragon
11 Shadowlands Hunter
12 Magic Ward
13 'Idden Boy
14 Banna Bearer
15 Warboss Banna
16 Norse Marauders
17 Ghorgon
18 Reckless Attack
19 Bordertown
20 Muster for War

2012 Warhammer Invasion The Imperial Throne

101 Clan Armoury
102 Baby Squig
103 Imperial Drummer
104 Werner Ludenhof
105 Devotee of Chamon
106 Priests of Sigmar
107 Stirland Deathjacks
108 Winged Riders of Kislev
109 The Imperial Zoo
110 Boiling Oil
111 Cathedral of Sigmar
112 Doubling of the Guard
113 Mage of the White Tower
114 Daemon Prince
115 Sacrificial Pyre
116 Warlock Engineer
117 Gaze of Nagash
118 A Promise of War
119 Captured Gunpowder
120 Recruiting for War

2012 Warhammer Invasion Oaths of Vengeance

21 Alith Anar
22 Rescue Prisoners
23 Outlying Tower
24 Nagarythe Archer
25 Karak Hirn Warrior
26 Band Together
27 Wealth of the Hold
28 Maid of Sigmar
29 Distribute the Spoils
30 Wolf Chariot
31 Goblin Raiders
32 Get Outta My Way!
33 Shaggoth Champion
34 Summons of Chaos
35 Vaedra Bloodsworn
36 Hag Graef Knights
37 Cavalry Raid
38 Stealthy Skink
39 Skaven Packmaster
40 All Out War

2012 Warhammer Invasion Portent of Doom

81 Eye of Sheerian
82 Skarbrand
83 Spirit Slayer
84 Strollaz's Banner
85 Roving Goblins
86 Progress in Numbers
87 Carroburg Cutthroats
88 The Sealed Vaults
89 Prince Althran
90 Mage of Loec
91 Fleeting Shade
92 Possess Mind
93 Murderlust
94 Swords of Chaos
95 Northern Forge
96 Council of Thirteen
97 Ghostly Apparition
98 Shield of the Gods
99 Unstable Flux
100 Border Patrol

2012 Warhammer Invasion Rising Dawn

1 Dawnstar Sword
2 Eltharion the Grim
3 Stone Vengeance
4 Calling the Council
5 Orc Bully
6 The Unending Horde
7 Emperor's Chosen
8 Rage of the Bear
9 Lothern Sea Master
10 Gathering the Winds
11 Helm of Fortune
12 Mounted Marauders
13 Boon of Tzeentch
14 Maranith
15 Tower of Oblivion
16 Blessed Enchantress
17 Hidden Sorceress
18 New Trade Route
19 Enslave the World
20 Heroic Task

2012 Warhammer Invasion Shield of the Gods

101 Shield of Aeons
102 Anethra Helbane
103 Dwarf Adventurer
104 Hospitable Cave
105 Mangler Squigs
106 Creature Pen
107 Steel Standard
108 Temple of Ulric
109 Ellyrian Elite
110 Valour of Ages
111 Slaanesh Cultist
112 Necrodomo's Prophecy
113 Black Guards
114 Naggarond Forge
115 Trinkets of Gold
116 Death in the Shadows
117 Talismanic Tatoos
118 Winter Campaign
119 Through All of Time
120 Guardians of the Gods

2012 Warhammer Invasion Vessel of the Winds

61 Windcatcher Prism
62 Gorbad Ironclaw
63 Brom Longbellow
64 Ale Hall
65 Honouring the Ancestors
66 Da Immortulz
67 Morglor the Mangler
68 Master Engineer
69 Runefang of Drakwald
70 Learned Mage
71 Echoes of Magic
72 Xirat'p
73 P'tarix
74 Elkana
75 Temple of Spite
76 Mage-Priest of Itza
77 Clan Eshin Mutant
78 Gathering the Horde
79 Pleasure Cults
80 Secret Crypts

2012 Warhammer Invasionn Fragments of Power

21 Star Crown Fragments
22 Ungrim Baragor
23 Master of Maps
24 Blood Vengeance
25 Arachnarok Spider
26 Da Great Leader
27 Averheim Soldiers
28 Higher Learning
29 Ellyrian Patron
30 Tor Elyr
31 Sworn of Khorne
32 Stolen Skin
33 Agent of Malekith
34 Swift-moving Storm
35 Arkayne Vampire
36 Descendant of Gods
37 Dance to Loec
38 Snotling Invasion
39 Summon the Reserves
40 We Hates Them All

2013 Warhammer Invasion Battle for the Old World

41 Wurrzag
42 Da Great Waaagh!
43 Mob 0' Hutz
44 Ded Scary Boy
45 Iron Defenders
46 Dead-Eye Cannon Crew
47 Reiksguard Elite
48 Devoted to Taal
49 Chapterhouse Stables
50 Lilea
51 Nagarythe Warrior
52 Hidden Outpost
53 Norse Clansman
54 Power of Chaos
55 Summoning Tower
56 Slave Hunter
57 Captured Mind
58 Hag Graef Mine
59 Pegasus Knight
60 Bonegrinder Giant

2013 Warhammer Invasion Cataclysm

2 Hammersmith
3 Grudge Keeper
5 Ancestral Engravings
6 Hall of Heroes
9 Makka Greenfist
13 Big Guns
19 Holy Defender
20 Fervent Disciple
21 Luminark of Hysh
22 Garrisoned
25 Lirdir
26 Iron-talon Eagle
27 Bearer of Eight
28 Arcane Purifier
29 Infused Parapet
32 Arcane Instinct
33 Lord of Khorne
34 Bloodcrusher
39 Chosen of the Gods
41 Lord of Ironfrost
42 Crimson Brides
43 Brave Volunteers
44 Atharti Night Maiden
45 Corsair Tower
46 Dark Covenant
49 Fickle Sellswords
52 Arcane Orrery
54 Dreadfire Portal
55 Witchfate Tor
56 Balewind Vortex
57 Lair of the Astromancer
58 The Eternity Stair
59 Magewrath Throne

2013 Warhammer Invasion Faith and Steel

101 Balthasar Gelt
102 Recon in Force
103 The Emperor's Statue
104 Celestial Wizard Acolyte
105 Vengeful Slayer
106 Doom-Seeker
107 Fearless in Battle
108 Warding Mage
109 Strike from the Shadows
110 Saphery Waystone
111 Gobbo Big Boss
112 Orc Warning Post
113 Skulltaker
114 Daemon Summoner
115 Nurgle's Reach
116 Spawn of Sulekh
117 Vigilant Druchii
118 Sacred Cauldron
119 Plunderer
120 End Times

2013 Warhammer Invasion Glory of Days Past

61 Thorek Ironbrow
62 Recover Mithril Lode
63 Mine Engineers
64 Karak Hirn Mine
65 Ostland Greatswords
66 Fulminating Cage
67 Master of Qhaysh
68 Guarding Boon
69 White Lion Master
70 Borgut Facebeater
71 Boar Rider
72 Get 'Em Ladz!
73 Chaos Dragon
74 Wasting Disease
75 Painful Mutation
76 Outlaw Sorcerer
77 Ghrond Errand Riders
78 Marked for Death
79 Rogue Warrior
80 Strength of Emperors

2013 Warhammer Invasion The Ruinous Hordes

81 Sigvald the Magnificent
82 Dominion of Chaos
83 Northern Wastes
84 Norse Charger
85 Steel Behemoth
86 Panther Champion
87 Pyromancy
88 King Alrik
89 Horn Hold Defender
90 Open the Armoury
91 Avelorn Sojourner
92 Sally Forth
93 Orc Warboss
94 Wolf Gobbos
95 Ded 'Ard
96 Cold One Champion
97 Test of Will
98 Spellweaver
99 Restless Corpse
100 Lying in Wait

2007 Warlord Fourth Edition

1 Alexa Genecourt U
2 Black Sun Knight U
3 Brymin of the Marches
4 Caleb the Shifter U
5 Castus the Burning U
6 Dahlia Genecourt R
7 Darius U
8 Genecourt Initiate C
9 Ghed Lionel R
10 Gustave C
11 Inquisitor Chroneus C
12 Layamon U
13 Lord Argen d'Ilchant R
14 Lord Miracus U
15 Magellan U
16 Mariah Blackthorn R
17 Sir Edgard Rellion R
18 Sir Magnus Arcadis R
19 Sister Megaria C
20 Squire Arrigan C
21 Squire Fastus C
22 Squire Fendric U
23 Takson the Intricate R
24 Thallen C
25 The Beast Knight R
26 Yavlo the Kindled
27 Arla Favorsight U
28 Atone U
29 Brawl R
30 Chant C
31 Crystalline Gargoyle U
32 Defiance C
33 Demand U
34 Edge U
35 Guardian C
36 Helt Royalwarden R
37 King Alaric
38 Kohn Peacehand R
39 Linnea Warsong C
40 Magma Gargoyle R
41 Magnite Gargoyle C
42 Mentor R
43 Profit C
44 Rust Gargoyle U
45 Shadowstone Gargoyle U
46 Sky U
47 Slate Gargoyle R
48 Stonefist R
49 Thekk Rockbender
50 Vex Duntan R
51 Wall U
52 Watcher C
53 Achilleus U
54 Amatria Tansiq C
55 Artheon U
56 Betwys R
57 Bone Fiend R
58 Bone Golem C
59 Corinth's Refuse U
60 Freia C
61 Jevae R
62 Jigoral C
63 Kaimir R
64 Kilis of Flesh R
65 Kinnell C
66 Maxt Stormcrow U
67 Mistress Allandra U
68 Morghen the Unliving
69 Nekrast R
70 Rotale Dythanus C
71 Severed of Bone U
72 Severed of Spirit R
73 Shadith Glyn U
74 Sileth Elestra R
75 Skyyrek U
76 The Lady of Pain
77 Vanthorine C
78 Zombie C
79 Aida C
80 Angus Hammerfall U
81 Anyah C
82 Arve Yscar R
83 Barrett Yscar R
84 Brogan R
85 Corten Lye U
86 Dame Martha U
87 Dreiga C
88 Enkida R
89 Graham Heyward R
90 Iam Hotelen U
91 Kiras Yscar U
92 Kylia Smythe C
93 Logan Ebonwoulfe
94 Martin Treek C
95 Niobe
96 Percy Dorn C
97 Selai Yscar U
98 Sergeant Fulford U
99 Sipho Hamisi R
100 Sir Erik Kaisen U
101 Sister Amanda R
102 Stanley C
103 Ursala Yscar R
104 Za'beth Candlebane C
105 Ballista Crew C
106 Bokos R
107 Disabling Unit U
108 Flamespitter R
109 Goza R
110 Grudurk C
111 Gunda C
112 Hagunk U
113 Hellbringer's Engine R
114 Hrunting U
115 Krenthor Gouge
116 Kul of Clan Tergoth R
117 Lorik C
118 Machine of Lukkot U
119 Muddflek C
120 Nath'rak R
121 Rress C
122 Rrok R
123 Scyrax
124 Six'La U
125 Skisk Foulfire C
126 Sohadze R
127 Strak U
128 Temb'w'bam U
129 Trugg C
130 Yemat U
131 Aimonos R
132 Atiratu
133 Besh-Kar U
134 Britomar C
135 Duanna C
136 Enhe C
137 Galgalax C
138 Getraxos R
139 Master Asrapi R
140 Master Mardu R
141 Master Naxagoras R
142 Master Tir-Koltis R
143 Naram-Sin
144 Nish-Bakr U
145 Pagophoros R
146 Redu Bir U
147 Redu Diran U
148 Shalta C
149 Shulgi C
150 The Earth U
151 The Harvest U
152 The Plentiful C
153 The Seed U
154 The Vessel U
155 The Wheat C
156 Ashreign R
157 Babbling Mouther R
158 Blackwind R
159 Brine Fiend C
160 Dragon's Lair U
161 Dragonkin R
162 Ivaas R
163 Keridwen U
164 King Dukault R
165 Markappal Ivy C
166 Minor Dragonkin C
167 Mourn Imp C
168 Pyrothraxas R
169 Sarakian Ettin U
170 Sedayah Rowan U
171 Stirges C
172 Thunic Hydra U
173 Thunic Wyvern U
174 Titan R
175 Validan R
176 Aegis R
177 Aura of Protection C
178 Banish the Wound U
179 Blessing of Swiftness U
180 Cause Serious Wounds R
181 Chosen U
182 Cure Lethal Wounds R
183 Divine Barrier U
184 Divine Guidance R
185 Forest's Hunger R
186 Holy Might U
187 Kor's Patience C
188 Lift Up Your Voices R
189 Mud Slick U
190 Quick Shielding C
191 Quick Strength C
192 Revigorate R
193 Sacrifice C
194 Withering Gaze C
195 Battle Plans R
196 Bear's Soul R
197 Bloodthirsty U
198 Bull Rush U
199 Call Verdatha U
200 Close Ranks C
201 Commit the Reserves R
202 Crush C
203 Cry Havoc R
204 Great Cleave R
205 I Have Your Back C
206 Instructed by Rren'the U
207 One with the Blade U
208 Outmatched C
209 Thrust C
210 Alert C
211 Backstab U

212 Coup de Grace R
213 Cunning Shot C
214 Fire at Will C
215 Leap of the Clouds U
216 Leg Sweep U
217 Misear Diplomacy R
218 Mobility R
219 Out of the Shadows U
220 Sneak R
221 Sniper Shot U
222 Springblade U
223 Steady Aim C
224 Swift C
225 To Fight Another Day C
226 Too Fast to See R
227 Zaina's Treachery R
228 Arc Lightning U
229 Ball Lightning C
230 Blink U
231 Call the Abyss C
232 Chain Lightning R
233 Curse of Heartless Lies C
234 Disintegrate U
235 Fireball U
236 Flame Arrows U
237 I Call Forth Valor U
238 Illusory Form C
239 Incinerate R
240 Jump C
241 Lightning Bolt U
242 Lordly Might R
243 Magic Missiles C
244 Magic Shifting C
245 Meteor Swarm R
246 Phantasmal Killer R
247 Phantom Steed U
248 Power Word Kill R
249 Teleport R
250 Thrice-Fell Horrors R
251 Distrust C
252 Leveled C
253 Meet at the Inn C
254 Rowan's Duty U
255 Thwarted U
256 Balian's Helm C
257 Blasphemous Sign C
258 Blessed Vestments U
259 Bloodoak Staff R
260 Chirurgery Kit R
261 Dallen's Blood R
262 Divining Cards C
263 Healing Potion C
264 Helm of Kor C
265 Hod's Legacy R
266 Lightning's Iron R
267 Loyal Nag U
268 Niobe's Leaf U
269 Rondoran's Staff U
270 Shield of the Simurgh R
271 Spirits' Blessings U
272 Staff C
273 Teufeltiger's Lies U
274 Axe of Tergoth U
275 Black Sun Helm C
276 Breastplate of Power R
277 Bruntor's Helm U
278 Celestial Flame C
279 Double Bladed Sword C
280 Dragon Buckler R
281 Dueling Saber U
282 Full Plate R
283 Griffon of Misear U
284 Krenthor's Maw R
285 Nothrog S'sike C
286 Scale Mail U
287 Tanning Knife C
288 The King's Lady R
289 Tower Shield U
290 Verdatha Mount R
291 War Horse C
292 Weapon Breaker C
293 Wyvern Gem U
294 Wyvernsteed R
295 Altus' Cloak R
296 Blacksand Trap U
297 Blade and Chain U
298 Bola C
299 Bow of Farsight R
300 Chained Claw R
301 Cloudracer U
302 Collapsing Bow C
303 Garrotte C
304 Gloves of Mischief R
305 Hashashin Blade R
306 Offhand Dagger C
307 Open Contract R
308 Scout Pony C
309 Shade Lion U
310 Shadow Token U
311 Springing Spear Trap C
312 Viper's Tongue U
313 Bracers of Deflection C
314 Darkwood Staff R
315 Doombringer R
316 Dythanus' Essence
317 Golden Circlet U
318 Ironcloth Bracer U
319 Ivory Scepter C
320 Living History C
321 Mirage Potion C
322 Ring of Vorn U
323 Shroud of Lost Souls R
324 Smoke Imp R
325 Spell Book U
326 Teufeltiger's Mask C
327 Wyvernskin Robe R
328 Blue Wyrm Helm R
329 Camel U
330 Skull of Great Omgah U
331 Squire's Banner U
332 Squire's Sash U
333 Troas' Pawn C
334 Xantin's Ward C
335 Xiathe's Touch C
336 Xienar's Guard C

2007 Warlord Light and Shadow

1 Clarion U
2 Zenith U
3 Halcyon U
4 Nadir U
5 Embrace Death C
6 Luminous Cure R
7 Sustaining Aura U
8 Armor of Devotion C
9 Entangle R
10 Thrust C
11 Inner Light R
12 Ways of War U
13 Refuse to Yield C
14 Close Combat U
15 Neutralize C
16 Fascinate R
17 Subvert U
18 Brilliant Bound R
19 Wheels within Wheels U
20 Evoke Crisis C
21 Dazzling Aptitude R
22 Curse of Broken Spire U
23 Rattle the Bones C
24 Sir Kolden Aedroud R
25 Lord Tuathal C
26 Madriga
27 Prioress Sophique R
28 Bishop Ambros U
29 Acolyte Chaston C
30 Sir Francis DeGraves R
31 Theodore d'Ilchant R
32 Vauxgen C
33 Danielle U
34 Kalten the Bleak
35 Dame Olivia C
36 Alynna the Fervent U
37 Sidor the Avenged C
38 Aridun of the Stone
39 Danres U
40 Icesecret Gargoyle C
41 Madnessfire Gargoyle U
42 Spiteful R
43 Lambaste C
44 Destruction U
45 Rouse R
46 Berlian the Stout
47 Quest C
48 Temper R
49 Faceless C
50 Fleshstone Gargoyle R
51 Stockpile U
52 Twisted Shade U
53 Serolia Calix
54 Valdania Calix U
55 Aellano Sessaran C
56 Pravian R
57 Flaming Spirit C
58 Zevil Adinerach
59 Cheadlon R
60 Nildrach R
61 Edoral Rowan U
62 Scetis C
63 Idrol C
64 Terbero R
65 Spectre of Madness U
66 Shadan Alder R
67 Yscarite Sentry U
68 Gladys Tynron U
69 Sadina Gleson C
70 Hex Starsmore C
71 Robert Mason R
72 Kara Wadreth
73 Arve Yscar R
74 Naro Yscar U
75 Haden Rhys C
76 Vermin Swarm C
77 Beastmaster Eladric
78 Feral Yscarite R
79 Loren U
80 Kevrosh Dathar
81 Nadion Dathar U
82 Bran Segula R
83 Lightspawn C
84 Shadowlurkers U
85 Lessari R
86 Belinda C
87 Turgan R
88 Nemtok R
89 Ker'zath R
90 Carg'rag C
91 Krasin C
92 Egrart C
93 Ar'bruz U
94 Skrim Spindlespleen
95 FirRal R
96 Baxod Firedancer U
97 Dorril U
98 Ar'tol C
99 Ga'dok U
100 DerRist
101 Isle of Madness U
102 Isle of Sorrow U
103 The Bastion of Bascaron R
104 Isle of Wind C
105 Isle of Secrets C
106 Isle of Ice R
107 Isle of Fire R
108 Symbol of Unity C
109 Ruby Staff of Selection R
110 The Cohorts' Ark U
111 Gossamer Mantle C
112 Calamity's Steel R
113 Aithon R
114 Mercy's Edge R
115 Balios C
116 Phantasmal Panther C
117 Frozen Servant C
118 Nostrum's Whisper U
119 Crown of the Isles R
120 Clandestine Crest C

2007 Warlord Plane of Secrets

1 Off the Beaten Path C
2 Devious Illusions C
3 Subdue C
4 Torment C
5 Rush to Battle C
6 Grasp of Vengeance R
7 Power of the Ancients C
8 Final Blessing U
9 Revitalize U
10 Nature's Corrosion U
11 Anointed by the Storm C
12 Deceitful Aid R
13 Soothing Aura R
14 Secrets of the Storm R
15 Inspiring Strike R
16 Overwhelm U
17 Backswing C
18 Powerful Swing U
19 Defy the Chains U
20 Slow March R
21 Reckless Abandon R
22 Secrets of the Suns R
23 Vengeful Strike R
24 Persecute U
25 Facing the Demons C
26 Undermine C
27 Clearing the Mark C
28 Focused Shot U
29 Will to Survive U
30 Hunting for Sport R
31 Passing the Knives R
32 Secrets of the Guild R
33 Astral Blast R
34 Combat Casting C
35 Chaotic Flames U
36 Summon Planar C
37 Grave Robbing U
38 Disintegrate U
39 Raze R
40 Kaballite Defiance R
41 Secrets of the Trials R
42 Dallen Stormlost
43 Ghed Brehm C
44 Sister Megaria C
45 Brother Vallerand R
46 Roman Aedroud C
47 Ghed Bodmin U
48 Ghed Trussen U
49 Ghed Vengir R
50 Laela U
51 Talib al-Sirr
52 Mozbach the Devious C
53 Mina the Disturbing U
54 Grigori the Spineless R
55 Grace Hearthpride
56 Battle C
57 Nilrem U
58 Justice R
59 Endure C
60 Rancor C
61 Brass Gargoyle U
62 Grit U
63 Eamon Geist U
64 Traveler R
65 Preen C
66 Militia R
67 Rockhome
68 Fevered Shade C
69 Skeletal Archer C
70 Averisk Glyn
71 Selye U
72 Tenanye C
73 Vanden U
74 Fiore R
75 Ophinuchus
76 Coblyn C
77 Ashling R
78 Orne U
79 Tisiphone U
80 Maes R
81 Dawes C
82 Eleora C
83 Thayes Ainsworth U
84 Aron U
85 Sestian U
86 Natalja Wynard C
87 Heath Stafford U
88 Kieran R
89 Nora Tristram R
90 Fernon Wynard C
91 Geraint the Grin R
92 Ferris Bachman
93 Arden Tide
94 Dorath Sa'dul
95 Jautya Syne R
96 Shadowblaze R
97 Riad Blight C
98 Richard Key U
99 Enigmist U
100 Belan C
101 Actelli U
102 Wanderetch R
103 Amoudasi's Candle C
104 Amoudasi's Blaze U
105 Isa the Tabernacle C
106 Amoudasi's Inferno R
107 Steam Ram U
108 Rathra Dak
109 Kinnag C
110 Fo'ttr'ak'ka
111 Shikhad R
112 Mammoth's Tusks U
113 Rhelok R
114 Sluagh C
115 Kulhen U
116 Sohadze R
117 Huldra C
118 Rangok C
119 Vaeghen U
120 Hall of Legends C
121 Malrog's Lair R
122 Reches' Labyrinth R
123 Nexus of Secrets U
124 Xienar's Guard C
125 Troas' Pawn C
126 Xiathe's Touch C
127 Xantin's Ward C
128 Symbiote R
129 Bag of Treasures R
130 Gacheru R
131 Glimmering Mail U
132 Shield of the Meek R
133 Blighted Tokens U
134 Colichemarde U
135 Tranquility R
136 Absolver U
137 Mizgo C
138 Devious Gauntlets U
139 Lifedrainer R
140 Tome of Memory C
141 Master's Trinkets R
142 Howling Guard U

2007 Warlord Stolen Destiny

1 Ginerva of the Moon
2 Sir Argen Undying
3 Baudwyn, Banished Poet
4 Sword-Dancer Kohn
5 Taltos Rellion
6 Lady Drac
7 Stonefist Gargoyle
8 Nolen, King's Guardian
9 Quartermaster Dirge
10 Time Lightprophet
11 Caldor Willful
12 Edge, Fiendblight
13 Hymn of Kor
14 Thekem Netheryn
15 Kapix the Cursed
16 Zelakin
17 Rafkin the Impure
18 Alessa
19 Eva Farstrider
20 Treyik Netheryn
21 Iam Unsullied
22 Martin Exemplar
23 Xiantha, Centaur Soldier
24 Novice Ruth
25 Quiltan the Apprentice
26 Jirar Huntsman
27 Patroness Kerro
28 Kayle, King Rowan
29 Mourn Jackals
30 Master of the Forge
31 Horror of the Brine
32 Essila, Wild Raven
33 Stasia
34 Ssithiss, Sutek King
35 Tactician Muddflek
36 B'haya, the Fiend
37 Calf Kar'Tal
38 Nightmaster Rress
39 Dev'irga
40 Orazhuk of Scarab
41 Warmistress Gurlda
42 Apprentice Ramah
43 Fires of Fate
44 Knights Repose
45 Cheat Death
46 Reflect
47 Pouncing Lunge
48 Taunting Blow
49 Gimme That
50 Spidersilk Trap
51 Phoenix Fire
52 Soul Siphon
53 Incite Courage
54 Taking a Stance
55 Tavern Brawl
56 Conjure Doom
57 Stolen Destiny
58 Paralysis Ward
59 Yawning Expanse
60 Ensnare
61 Elemental Barrage
62 Tome of the Adept
63 Ring of Piercing
64 Ring of Mending
65 Ring of Guile
66 Ring of Blasting
67 Neus' Helm
68 Lunatic's Genius
69 Phantom Blades
70 Ritual Circle
71 Ishara's Tidal Mace
72 Atlas of Vision
73 Silverwind
74 War Mace
75 Persecutor's Emblem
76 Frozen Tears
77 Howling Vardog
78 Binder's Staff

2008 Warlord Shattered Empires

1 Aureliane C
2 Bataar U
3 Cardinal Scelus R
4 Daufien U
5 Flavien Genecourt U
6 Ghed Nuri C
7 Ghed Romus U
8 Guillaume Rellion R
9 Inquisitor Dmitir
10 Liliane C
11 Lord Aurelius Rellion R
12 Squire Cambrie C
13 Thibaud Rellion R
14 Blunder C
15 Fancy U
16 Focus U
17 Grimur R
18 Hallur R
19 Hallvardur R
20 Hurl R
21 Ice Gargoyle U
22 Noose C
23 Salvage U
24 Sandscoured Gargoyle C
25 Sigurdur
26 Valdimar C
27 Atheris R
28 Crypt Guardian C
29 Cyrus Netheryn U
30 Dark Monolith R
31 Eldoreth R
32 Fayed Dythanus U
33 Ghast C
34 Kornell Calix U
35 Naala C
36 Raclesis
37 Remorna U
38 Suul R
39 Wythien C
40 Alanna C
41 Banyon R
42 Brigid R
43 Devlin Cormac U
44 Grace Heyward C
45 Jethro U
46 Lady Winifred U
47 Lasco Cormac C
48 Lyconos R
49 Moira Dunbar R
50 Pehtu Mennanakh U
51 Talin Tzin
52 Valeria Tremayne C
53 Ac'vuk C
54 Ar'dak R
55 Gee'ch C
56 Hovrakk R
57 Jistik U
58 Kast U
59 Korvos U
60 Rid'ar'rak C
61 Scyrax' Spear Streamer U
62 Sel'rokh
63 Snegrob R
64 Ter'til C
65 Vels of Clan Manaka R
66 Amand d'Ilchant C
67 As'sa R
68 Bar'rax U
69 Flayer of Dreams R
70 Forest People C
71 Lilith U
72 Mistress Sanai R
73 Nemrah U
74 Redu Tam R
75 Sanga-Kish
76 Shirti C
77 Shonta U
78 The Giving C
79 Alaya C
80 Azam R
81 Azelot il Dawud U
82 Bog Fiend C
83 Burrowing Basilisk U
84 Causticus R
85 Ebonscourge R
86 Jacob Windrider U
87 Lady Tornhawk U
88 Landshark R
89 Nyla Silvertongue U
90 Queen Yahia
91 Scaly Sycophant C
92 Twisted Hyenas C
93 Calm C
94 Decompose U
95 Final Blessing C
96 Fire Seeds R
97 Incessant Waves U
98 Lead by Example C
99 Rapid Regeneration R
100 Replenish U
101 Speed of the Falcon R
102 Accelerated Attack R
103 Beyond the Grave U
104 Improved Bull Rush R
105 Once Again R
106 Phalanx C

107 Sudden Reversal U
108 Valhala's Shout U
109 Wedge C
110 Backflip U
111 Choke Hold C
112 Desecration U
113 Double Shot U
114 Flank Attack C
115 From the Shadows C
116 Now I Am Not R
117 Set for the Charge R
118 The Slightest Cut R
119 Blood Price C
120 Create Golem R
121 Icy Surge U
122 Shards R
123 Sunder C
124 Teleport Object U
125 Uncertain Path U
126 Venom Vines R
127 Viper Whip C
128 Winter's Shadow C
129 Bribe U
130 Improvisation C
131 Beacon of Salvation U
132 Caliphate Mail R
133 Dayaa C
134 Dunewalker's Staff R
135 Imperial Chariot R
136 Potion of Strength C
137 Potion of Vigor U
138 Storm Stela C
139 Tears of the Storm U
140 Belt of Bear C
141 Havat-lahn Stance U
142 Krenthor's Club R
143 Rellion Truebred R
144 Sandbox U
145 Scimitar U
146 Spear C
147 Spiked Spaulders C
148 Uthanak's Ring R
149 Wildman's Mail C
150 Dirk C
151 Dragon Pipes R
152 Dreamsand C
153 Heartstrings U
154 Poison Arrows R
155 Swordman's Cape R
156 Thorns of Anger C
157 Tiger Trap U
158 Whirling Swamp Spear U
159 Castux C
160 Dark Heart of Kylnion U
161 Flying Carpet R
162 Gravity Rod U
163 Green Dragon Essence C
164 Heart of Embers R
165 Incendiary Glove R
166 Staff of Storage U
167 Cuirass of the Elements R
168 Mask of Command C

2009 Warlord Crimson Coast

1 Commander Kaiten
2 Count Brutan C
3 Gorlen the Pitiless R
4 Inquisitor Slayne U
5 Mistress Edrea U
6 Mother Delane R
7 Sir Chretien Rellion U
8 Sir Treguard U
9 Sister Wanda C
10 Squire Marie C
11 Temur R
12 Tybert the Worthy R
13 Amber Gargoyle C
14 Barb U
15 Coral Gargoyle U
16 Darkness C
17 Fortress R
18 Fridgeir R
19 Isolfur R
20 Mend U
21 Pendulum C
22 Pinion
23 Quicksilver Gargoyle R
24 Snare U
25 Ardanaalis U
26 Ayaaba Waverunner R
27 Calliopea U
28 Ciane C
29 Diirena Ebb R
30 Ebal C
31 Flesh-Feeder R
32 Hydriel C
33 Leelu U
34 Thalaasa
35 The Moon and the Sea R
36 Undead Sahuagin U
37 Captain Alera
38 Eloise U
39 Ersten Cormac C
40 Llyr Veterans U
41 Maddock Yscar U
42 Reese R
43 Reynold R
44 Rolando U
45 Selkie C
46 Shannon the Daring R
47 Snuff Garrett C
48 Tabisia R
49 Angry Crew U
50 Dor of Clan Manaka U
51 El'can the Wily U
52 Grilt Fenstalker
53 Grukth C
54 Kel'suk R
55 Mollo R
56 Ra'Zul R
57 Re'Tal U
58 Sappers C
59 Verusk R
60 Zen'tis C
61 Bal-Benoth R
62 Blood Cauldron U
63 Garowl U
64 Hastari C
65 Master Ezdeha R
66 Master Fabas R
67 Mistress Tamine R
68 Nin-Gula
69 Pazu-Gara U
70 The Devoted C
71 The Promised U
72 Winti C
73 Bosun Blacknose U
74 Dragon Turtle R
75 Drasek Berenj
76 Dryad C
77 Fylgia U
78 Green Hag R
79 Lady Ersane U
80 Leviathan R
81 Sahuagin Shaman U
82 SS-Slik C
83 Udar R
84 Zendik C
85 Call to War U
86 Debilitating Venom U
87 Decay C
88 Distribution U
89 Fervor C
90 Just a Little Scratch C
91 Precognition R
92 Putrescence R
93 Song of Strength C
94 White Squall R
95 Ardent R
96 Desperate Grab U
97 Faith in Steel U
98 Glory of the Black Sun R
99 Keep Up the Pace C
100 New Orders C
101 Out of Breath U
102 Savage Strike C
103 Shelter the Weak R
104 Death from Below U
105 Essence of Eban-Tarsis R
106 Hide in Shadows C
107 Lure U
108 Pick Pockets U
109 Ranging Shot C
110 Sling of the Lionfish C
111 Stormfront C
112 Submerge R
113 Uninvited R
114 Churning Wrath C
115 Confound C
116 Dancing Lights C
117 Death for Death C
118 Elemental Bolt U
119 Hallucination R
120 Hoarfrost R
121 Life is Magic C
122 Ride the Wave U
123 Tidal Mastery U
124 Tsunami R
125 Blind Vengeance C
126 Punitive Strike U
127 Armor of Pearl U
128 Chariot of Shell U
129 Corystes U
130 Dallen's Eye C
131 Fountain of Tears R
132 Healer's Pact C
133 Mace C
134 Mollusk Helm R
135 Quake Hammer R
136 Sanguine Shield C
137 Bardiche C
138 Collar of Damnation C
139 Gilded Chariot U
140 Great White R
141 Helm of the Deep C
142 Leviathan Hide R
143 Repeating Crossbow R
144 Shell Armor C
145 Tortoise Shield C
146 Tortoise Stance U
147 Tulwar U
148 Bared Heart R
149 Burning Arrow C
150 Conch Horn U
151 Jewel Spider Web C
152 Rustled Mount C
153 Serpentlash U
154 Shifts and Gears U
155 Skyfire R
156 Sugvira the Scamp R
157 Weighted Net C
158 Black Pearl U
159 Cloak of the Leech C
160 Extension Scroll U
161 Golem Manual R
162 Ivory Ring C
163 Living Statue C
164 Necklace of Spell Storing R
165 Orb of Mud U
166 Ring of Ice R
167 Giant Turtle R
168 Trident U

2009 Warlord Learn 2 Play

1 Amatria Tansiq C
2 Bone Fiend R
3 Freia C
4 Jigoral C
5 Kaimir R
6 Kinnell C
7 Maxt Stormcrow U
8 Mistress Allandra U
9 Raak
10 Rotale Dythanus C
11 Sedwin Elfhunter
12 Shadith Glyn U
13 Wythien C
14 Yvaalis
15 Babbling Mouther R
16 Brine Fiend C
17 Burrowing Basilisk U
18 Keridwen U
19 Landshark R
20 Minor Dragonkin C
21 Mourn Imp C
22 Shah'syss
23 Sta'ash
24 Stirges C
25 Su-tatra
26 Thunic Hydra U
27 Thunic Wyvern U
28 Twisted Hyenas C
29 Validan R
30 Bear's Soul R
31 Bloodthirsty U
32 Bull Rush U
33 Cry Havoc R
34 I Have Your Back C
35 Outmatched C
36 Stubborn
37 Backstab U
38 Double Shot U
39 Flurry of Knives
40 Leap of the Clouds U
41 Steady Aim C
42 Too Fast to See R
43 Leveled C
44 Rowan's Duty U
45 Ancient Scimitar
46 Axe of Tergoth U
47 Belt of Bear C
48 Breastplate
49 Griffon of Misear U
50 Handaxe
51 Scale Mail U
52 Scimitar U
53 Bola C
54 Cloudracer U
55 Collapsing Bow C
56 Gloves of Mischief R
57 Long Bow
58 Shade Lion U
59 Sharkbone Bow
60 Camel U

2009 Warlord Treasure Chest

1 Genecourt Initiate C
2 Okull the Defiant R
3 The Beast Knight R
4 Profit C
5 Sky U
6 Surge R
7 Amatria Tansiq C
8 Remorna U
9 Tyyphera R
10 Barrett Yscar R
11 Han of the Ferry R
12 Stanley C
13 Ballista Crew C
14 Gunda C
15 Mo'can R
16 Master Naxagoras R
17 Oloidynatos R
18 Pagophoros R
19 The Seed U
20 Azam R
21 Brine Fiend C
22 Judge Aeacus R
23 Ka-Nissus R
24 Aegis R
25 Kor's Patience C
26 Minor Miracle R
27 Revigorate R
28 Massacre R
29 Once Again R
30 Outmatched C
31 Sudden Reversal U
32 Backstab U
33 Slash and Lunge R
34 The Slightest Cut R
35 Zaina's Treachery R
36 Conjure Storm R
37 Disintegrate U
38 Icy Surge U
39 Incinerate R
40 Blind Vengeance C
41 Meet at the Inn C
42 Thwarted U
43 Healing Potion C
44 Hod's Legacy R
45 Ring of the Savant R
46 Axe of Fury R
47 Celestial Flame C
48 Griffon of Misear U
49 Blacksand Trap U
50 Cloudracer U
51 Nightmare Blade R
52 Chime of the Aerie R
53 Ring of Vorn U
54 Shroud of Lost Souls R
55 Camel U

2010 Warlord City of Gold

1 Black Sun Shieldman C
2 Brother Neris R
3 Corinne Drac U
4 Count Vyacheslav R
5 Evon Myerdeth U
6 Father Jourdain R
7 Ghed Headrix U
8 Ghed Symion R
9 Iphigenia R
10 Squire Packard C
11 Stanchion C
12 Tempest Guard C
13 Xaros the Mist U
14 Aguas R
15 Bem Kaundodo R
16 Demon of Kvar U
17 Dreadfang R
18 Dwarf-Eater U
19 Harun Qadir R
20 Menhetiri R
21 Meri-es-anch C
22 Narutep C
23 Swamp Hydra U
24 Vengeful Spirit U
25 Whizzwhir C
26 Wogh C
27 Call Lightning R
28 Cauterize R
29 Ferocious U
30 Hammer into Anvil U
31 Quicksand C
32 Soothing Waters R
33 Precise Strike C
34 Reckon the Sea R
35 Disorient C
36 Heaven's Wrath R
37 Kiss of the Mummy U
38 Rite of Power C
39 Stolen Substance C
40 Sunder the Soul C
41 Waking Terrors U
42 Burial Shroud C
43 Golden Tablet U
44 Inquisitor's Mask U
45 Totem Crawler R
46 War Eagle C
47 Mischievous Sprite R
48 Undead Steed C
49 Whirlwind Ring U
50 Consort's Crown R
51 Sumptuous Feast R
52 Amends U
53 Bastion U
54 Clockwork Scarab U
55 Gudleifur R
56 Limestone Gargoyle U
57 Pilfer R
58 Respite R
59 Savvy R
60 Scale U
61 Sharkskin Gargoyle R
62 Soil U
63 Wrath R
64 Yoke U
65 B'alam Nak R
66 Bithkrid U
67 Chaltak R
68 Dal'kir R
69 Durga U
70 Kar Longblade U
71 Skozt U
72 Sphlyrix U
73 Tacus Fylde U
74 The Retiarius R
75 Vannod U
76 Velk U
77 Witchwood Catapault U
78 Take a Rest R
79 Advance R
80 Countershot U
81 Coup d'arret U
82 Defy the Chains U
83 Fire and Steel R
84 Goodwife's Parry U
85 Onslaught R
86 Pikes Set U
87 Pillage R
88 Shoulder Charge U
89 Taking Trophies R
90 Veteran Training U
92 Cobbler's Lane R
93 Empty Racks U
94 Faerie Bolt R
95 Find the Seam U
96 On Silent Wings R
97 Precious R
98 Reconnaissance R
99 The Sweetest Death U
100 Thimblerig U
101 Volley U
102 Rabble Rousing R
103 Risk's Reward U
104 Backbiter U
105 Blazing Medallion R
106 Cobalt Land Dragon U
107 Commanding Presence R
108 Common Blade U
109 Engraved Plate U
110 Greaves U
111 Gris' Double Bit Axe R
112 Pyre U
113 Cloak of the Wisp U
114 Feathered Gauntlets R
115 Glyn Quiver U
116 Hawthorne's Arrows U
117 Nightfall Mask U
118 Norn's Stinger R
119 Scorpion Stance R
120 Tempest Arrow R
121 Frosttalon R
122 Radiant Symbol R
123 Red Steel Gauntlets R
124 War Plans R
125 Acanothropis R
126 Ayloch Glyn U
127 Flesh Gorger U
128 Indariel R
129 Knight of Falun R
130 Loncah Tansiq U
131 Menketh Adinerach R
132 Pridayn Glyn R
133 Rethriel U
134 Serket U
135 Tresven U
136 Treyik U
137 Agnieszka R
138 Bradley U
139 Clerimonde U
140 Elissa Yscar U
141 Felens Rowan U
142 Kinyon Yscar R
143 Lady Isabelle U
144 Leon Yscar U
145 Mairead R
146 Ragnell R
147 Raimi Mennanakh R
148 Serif Al Havoc R
149 Victoria R
150 Kallh U
151 Master Ashtaroth R
152 Mistress Alhana U
153 Mitrasz U
154 Redu Carr R
155 Redu Firam R
156 Redu Zayd U
157 Rhomel'zard R
158 Ruash-Shan R
159 Split-Tongue U
160 Tri-Claw U
161 Void Stalker R
162 Yeg-Igryll's Altar U
163 Bandage U
164 Defiant R
165 Draw the Essence R
166 Incentives R
167 Innocence R
168 Invoke Entropy U
169 Nature's Noose R
170 Show of Strength U
171 Spectral Guardian R
172 Bellicose U
173 Blindside Tackle U
174 Code of Chivalry R
175 Cold Iron U
176 Cut a Path R
177 Grapple U
178 Heart of the Warrior R
179 Sword Master R
180 Twist the Blade U
181 Drops of Drowsiness R
182 Easy Target U
183 False Haven R
184 Nightshade U
185 Plague Bomb R
186 Prey on the Hunter R
187 Spring the Trap U
188 To My Side R
189 Wigglewort Poison U
190 Cataract U
191 Crevice R
192 Entomb U
193 From Dust to Dust U
194 Tether R
195 Embrace the Eternal U
196 Eternal Champion U
197 Flame Blade R
198 Bascaron's Blessing R
199 Appeasement R
200 Blessed Bangle U
201 Brilliant Scales U
202 Cerberus U
203 Daemon Bile U
204 Helm of Swiftness R
205 Blood God's Basinet R
206 Command Post U
207 Invision R
208 Jirar Heirloom R
209 Savage Blade R
210 Skittish Charger R
211 Skull Mace U
212 Thessyrian War Chariot R
213 Boots of Stupendous Speed R
214 Coils of Cobra R
215 Dank Cloak U
216 Diadem of Contagion U
217 Dragonbone Cuirass R
218 Keen Dagger U
219 Riding Dog U
220 Sandtiger's Fang R
221 Dusty Shelves R
222 Orb of Light U
223 Phantasmal Steed U
224 Rod of Power R

225 Staff of War U
226 Thunderclap Bracers U
227 Armor of Absolution R
228 Aspis R
229 Bloodstone Rose R
230 Boomstick R
231 Fields of Sorrow R

2010 Warlord Sands of Oblivion

1 Ancestral Wraiths U
2 Dhamir il Maliq R
3 Ghed Kazouf R
4 Herick the Venomous U
5 Markhan C
6 Master Anandale U
7 Nu'man il Maliq R
8 Rellion Pikeman C
9 Sir Pelimere R
10 Squire Fenric U
11 Tegus Herders C
12 The Sable Knight R
13 Bludgeon U
14 Brom Frostbeard R
15 Vachir C
16 Dress C
17 Dust Gargoyle R
18 Glorgrim R
19 Linnea Warsong C
20 Pinion's Vise U
21 Rimefang R
22 Rumbling Gargoyle U
23 Sentinel Gargoyle R
24 Tumble C
25 Wall C
26 Warden U
27 Amon-Ka R
28 Austerion U
29 Baracuuda C
30 Forest of Bone C
31 Jigoral C
32 Khilkhameth R
33 Mormaenion R
34 Nothiel Elestra R
35 Orlanon U
36 Sachiel R
37 Shadith Glyn U
38 Soulless Scavenger C
39 Thrinnas Glyn U
40 Aida C
41 Alfred U
42 Carmag Hammerfall U
43 Darian Windson U
44 Dune Wolves R
45 Hamadryagh R
46 Keziah Firehair R
47 Leonora C
48 Nephela U
49 Pierce Devon R
50 Ryan Mornington C
51 Scarlett C
52 Xeanara R
53 Dar'rak R
54 D'nath U
55 G'rath Firefist R
56 Gush C
57 Lorik C
58 Mel'crah R
59 Pelanth U
60 Qar'Dak Stonerender R
61 Scyrax' Spear Streamer U
62 Sir'kan C
63 Tass'daesh C
64 Tra'kelt U
65 Zul'Tan Bloodletter R
66 Bixvrexe R
67 Dala C
68 Darkspawn C
69 Forest People C
70 Galam-Reth R
71 Harem Guard U
72 Master Kelkrys U
73 Raging Hungerer R
74 Sharru C
75 Shonta U
76 Wailing Scrambler U
77 Yil-Grayl R
78 Ygrassyne R
79 Amr Qadir R
80 Burning Basilisk U
81 Dragon's Lair U
82 Fesoof C
83 Fire Bats U
84 Giant Scorpion R
85 Gnoll Archer C
86 Haseeka C
87 Keridwen U
88 Mad Mel Reyvilo R
89 Magma Elemental C
90 Verdigris R
91 Zara R
92 Banish the Wound U
93 Blessing of Swiftness U
94 Dominate R
95 Guilt-Ridden R
96 Mud Slick U
97 Purify C
98 Return to Us R
99 Teshur's Thunderfist U
100 Back into the Fray C
101 Blood for Blood C
102 Bloodthirsty U
103 Coordinated Assault R
104 Hunter's Quarry U
105 Measured Blow U
106 Obliterate R
107 Outmatched C
108 Seek Out Thine Enemy R
109 Seize the Moment U
110 Whirling Blades R
111 Backstab U
112 Battle Tunes C
113 Choke Hold C
114 Fancy Footwork R
115 Leap of the Clouds U
116 Market Day R
117 Merciless Strike R
118 Mischief R
119 Tainted Wine U
120 Unbalanced C
121 Unerring Shot R
122 Blink U
123 Counterspell U
124 Detonate R
125 Dimensional Rift C
126 Disintegrate U
127 Fire Odem R
128 Hungry Spirits R
129 Jump C
130 Lightning Bolt U
131 Power Word Pain R
132 Puppet Mastery C
133 Soul Transfer C
134 Summon Stone C
135 Wither and Bloom U
136 Blessed Vestments U
137 Cowl of Knowledge U
138 Earth Mephit U
139 Gnarled Club C
140 Healing Potion C
141 Loyal Nag U
142 Maul of Justice R
143 Nabu's Necklace U
144 Scepter of Life R
145 Baraxton Courage C
146 Bruntor's Helm U
147 Dancing Scimitar R
148 Fists of Kor U
149 Frostscale U
150 Griffon of Misear U
151 Iridescent Armor R
152 Scale Mail U
153 Sky Splitter C
154 Stormwolf R
155 The Dark Horse C
156 War Horse C
157 Blowgun C
158 Face Kit R
159 Garrotte C
160 Giant Toad U
161 Gloves of the Fang R
162 Log Trap C
163 Mask of Past Lives R
164 Scourge of Fangs C
165 Shade Lion U
166 Shadow Token U
167 Spiritrender R
168 Troglodyte Egg U
169 Tzin's Blades C
170 Venomward C
171 Bracers of Deflection C
172 Eternity Gate R
173 Fire Dance C
174 Flamecaster R
175 Smoke Imp U
176 Symbiotic Bracers U
177 Spitting Cobra U
178 Teufeltiger's Mask C
179 Tome of Oblivion R

2011 Warlord Ancient Lore

1 Ghed Invictus R
2 Nepheline Gargoyle R
3 Revenant R
4 Aristaios R
5 Karn of Clan Manaka R
6 Shan-Kassyn R
7 Kardak-Vash R
8 Vash-Arrosh R
9 Embolden R
10 False God's Council R
11 Spiked Ale U
12 Champion of the Faith U
13 Order of Battle R
14 Superior Armament R
15 A Single Motion U
16 Dreadnaught U
17 Anticipate R
18 Finishing Move R
19 Lucky Shot U
20 Prince Among Thieves U
21 Harness the Storm R
22 Mind Over Body R
23 One Last Time R
24 Archmage U
25 Dragon Throne Crown R
26 Corvus R
27 Canticle U
28 Blight U
29 Crimson Dragon Shield R
30 Fiendish Plate R
31 Panthera U
32 Ghoststeel Gauntlets U
33 Shadowborn Harness R
34 Blood Hawk R
35 Perpetual Pouch U
36 Firewisp Orb U
37 Infinity Codex R
38 Cloak of Thousand Eyes R
39 Curious Mephit U
40 Great Wyrm Potion U

2014 WIXOSS SP-01 Ruko Kominato

SP01001 Tama, Full Moon Miko SP
SP01002 Tama, Waxing Gibbous Moon Miko SP
SP01003 Tama, Half Moon Miko SP
SP01004 Tama, Waxing Crescent Moon Miko SP
SP01005 Tama, New Moon Miko SP
SP01006 Rococo Boundary SP
SP01007 Avon SP
SP01008 Baroque Defense SP
SP01009 Spirit Salvage SP
SP01010 Modern Boundary SP
SP01011 Romail, Helmet Armor SP
SP01012 Caliburn, Greatsword SP
SP01013 Tourette, Gauntlet SP
SP01014 Flamber, Medium Sword SP
SP01015 Kukri, Small Sword SP
SP01016 Bonya, Small Bow SP
SP01017 Get Bible SP
SP01018 Servant D SP
SP01019 Servant O SP
SP01020 Jetting Knowledge SP

2014 WIXOSS SP-02 Hitoe Uemura

SP02001 Yuzuki-Four SP
SP02002 Yuzuki-Three SP
SP02003 Yuzuki-Two SP
SP02004 Yuzuki-One SP
SP02005 Yuzuki-Zero SP
SP02006 Firefly Sparks SP
SP02007 Back Against the Flame SP
SP02008 Burning Stone Flame SP
SP02009 One Rule, Two Birds SP
SP02010 See Through the Fiery Ambition SP
SP02011 Volcano, Natural Stone SP
SP02012 Silvan, Natural Stone SP
SP02013 Garnet, Natural Stone SP
SP02014 Bronda, Natural Stone SP
SP02015 Iron, Natural Stone SP
SP02016 Amethyst, Natural Stone SP
SP02017 Roaring Fire Pillar SP
SP02018 Servant D SP
SP02019 Servant O SP
SP02020 Jetting Knowledge SP

2014 WIXOSS SP-03 Iona Urazoe

SP03001 Ulith, Jailer Enma SP
SP03002 Ulith, Enma of Eternal Hell SP
SP03003 Ulith, Enma of Crushing Hell SP
SP03004 Ulith, Burning Eye Enma SP
SP03005 Ulith, Enma SP
SP03006 Moment Punish SP
SP03007 Eternal Punish SP
SP03008 Grave Out SP
SP03009 Grave Gut SP
SP03010 Thousand Punish SP
SP03011 Metsum, Fallen Cannon Girl SP
SP03012 Belze, Symbol of Wasteful Evil SP
SP03013 Carry, Fallen Cannon Girl SP
SP03014 Cosmo, Symbol of Immorality SP
SP03015 Kooni, Symbol of Lesser Sin SP
SP03016 Succu, Fallen Cannon Girl SP
SP03017 Servant D SP
SP03018 Servant O SP
SP03019 Hole Dark SP
SP03020 Recalled Blessing SP

2014 WIXOSS WX-01 Served Selector

WX01001 Tamayorihime, Sun Miko PR
WX01002 Tamayorihime, Dawn Miko LR
WX01003 Hanayo-Four, Hundred-Fire Profusion LR
WX01004 Hanayo-Two Remodeled, Roaring Flame LR
WX01005 Code Piruruku Omega LR
WX01006 Midoriko, War Empress Type Four LR
WX01007 Tamayorihime, Lunar Eclipse Miko LC
WX01008 Tamayorihime, Shooting Star Miko LC
WX01009 Tamayorihime, Nova Miko LC
WX01010 Xenogate LC
WX01011 Hanayo-Three, Blazing Flame Dance LC
WX01012 Hanayo-Two, Hard Flame LC
WX01013 Hanayo-One, the Flame LC
WX01014 Dominating Fury LC
WX01015 Code Piruruku Gamma LC
WX01016 Code Piruruku Beta LC
WX01017 Code Piruruku Alpha LC
WX01018 Anti-Spell LC
WX01019 Midoriko, Shining Empress Girl Type Four LC
WX01020 Midoriko, Feminine Girl Type Three LC
WX01021 Midoriko, Bridal Combat Girl Type Two LC
WX01022 Midoriko, Dancing Combat Girl Type One LC
WX01023 Big Bang LC
WX01024 Giant LC
WX01025 Salvage LC
WX01026 Charging LC
WX01027 Energe, Original Spear SR
WX01028 Arc Aura SR
WX01029 Adamasphere, Alluring Pyroxene SR
WX01030 Fires of Atonement SR
WX01031 Code Heart VAC SR
WX01032 SNATCHER SR
WX01033 Osaki, Phantom Beast Deity SR
WX01034 Repair SR
WX01035 Athena, Goddess of Blessing R
WX01036 Catapaul, Large Bow R
WX01037 Valkyrie, Unforgettable Fantasy R
WX01038 Get Dantalian R
WX01039 Cannon, Ballista R
WX01040 Orichalc, Alluring Stone R
WX01041 Ordnance, Roaring Gun R
WX01042 Fissure of Condemnation R
WX01043 Araial, Water Phantom R
WX01044 Code Art PZL R
WX01045 Shark Lance, Water Phantom R
WX01046 BAD CONDITION R
WX01047 Mandore, Alluring Plant R
WX01048 Bigtatt, Phantom Beast R
WX01049 Baromet, Alluring Plant R
WX01050 Enlarge R
WX01051 Servant Q R
WX01052 Encompassing Knowledge R
WX01053 God Eater, Ultimate Sword C
WX01054 Egis, Ultimate Shield C
WX01055 Riot, Large Shield C
WX01056 Square, Medium Shield C
WX01057 Sephiram, Shooting Bow C
WX01058 Michael, Voice of Reconciliation C
WX01059 Bow, Shooting Bow C
WX01060 Round, Small Shield C
WX01061 Haniel, Thoughts of Seeking C
WX01062 Get Open C
WX01063 Get Ready C
WX01064 Metallica, Alluring Stone C
WX01065 Emeralda, Alluring Stone C
WX01066 Rubyl, Alluring Stone C
WX01067 Rin, Alluring Stone C
WX01068 Amber, Alluring Stone C
WX01069 Ranchan, Explosive Gun C
WX01070 Macury, Alluring Stone C
WX01071 Sapphi, Alluring Stone C
WX01072 Dragunov, Small Gun C
WX01073 Flame Ball, Falling Star C
WX01074 Prismatic Fire Pillar C
WX01075 Code Art ASM C
WX01076 Code Art IDOL C
WX01077 Code Art ADB C
WX01078 Code Art STG C
WX01079 Code Art WTC C
WX01080 Shakotan, Water Phantom C
WX01081 Code Art TV C
WX01082 Code Art FAN C
WX01083 Kumanomin, Water Phantom C
WX01084 THREE OUT C
WX01085 FREEZE C
WX01086 Eagle, Phantom Beast C
WX01087 Cait Sith, Phantom Beast C
WX01088 Owl, Phantom Beast C
WX01089 Kuro, Phantom Beast C
WX01090 Sparrow, Phantom Beast C
WX01091 Koalan, Phantom Beast C
WX01092 Shiro, Phantom Beast C
WX01093 Dandelion, Alluring Plant C
WX01094 Swallow, Phantom Beast C
WX01095 Pandan, Phantom Beast C
WX01096 Mi-Ke, Phantom Beast C
WX01097 Salvia, Alluring Plant C
WX01098 Germinate C
WX01099 Reverse Summon C
WX01100 Servant T C
WX01101 Servant D C
WX01102 Servant O C
WX01103 Jetting Knowledge C
WX01104 Tamayorihime, Full Moon Miko SCR
WX01105 Tamayorihime, Sun Miko SCR
WX01106 Hanayo-Two Remodeled, Roaring Flame SCR
WX01107 Hanayo-Four, Hundred-Fire Profusion SCR
WX01108 Energe, Original Spear SCR
WX01109 Adamasphere, Alluring Pyroxene SCR
WX01110 Code Heart VAC SCR
WX01111 Osaki, Phantom Beast Deity SCR
WX01112 Tama C

2014 WIXOSS WX-02 Stirred Selector

WX02001 Tamayorihime, Sweet Olive Miko LR
WX02002 Yuzuki-Four, Fire of Nature LR
WX02003 Eldora×Mark IV LR
WX02004 Ulith, Infinite Enma LR
WX02005 White Hope LR
WX02006 Black Desire LR
WX02007 Yuzuki-Three, Roaring Flame Sin LC
WX02008 Yuzuki-Two, Regretful Flame LC
WX02009 Yuzuki-One, the Flame LC
WX02010 Eldora×Mark III LC
WX02011 Eldora×Mark II LC
WX02012 Eldora×Mark I LC
WX02013 Ulith, Enma of Screaming Hell LC
WX02014 Ulith, Enma of Black Rope Hell LC
WX02015 Ulith, Enma of Reviving Hell LC
WX02016 Gothic Boundary LC
WX02017 Vigorous Flame Aura LC
WX02018 Fiery Spring Landscape LC
WX02019 Cross Life Cloth LC
WX02020 Bloody Slash LC
WX02021 Arcgain, Archangel of Pioneering SR
WX02022 Gun Snipe, Ballista SR
WX02023 Spiral Carmilla, Water Phantom Princess SR
WX02024 Gauche Agnes, Silk Plant Princess SR
WX02025 Anna Mirage, Devil Princess SR
WX02026 Wish Crisis SR
WX02027 Price of Scorched Earth SR
WX02028 Enigma Aura SR
WX02029 Mitsurugi, Treasure Tool R
WX02030 Mikagami, Treasure Tool R
WX02031 Get Bound R
WX02032 Opalal, Silk Stone R
WX02033 Carnelian, Silk Stone R
WX02034 Unwanted Impulse R
WX02035 Code Art CPU R
WX02036 Code Art GRB R
WX02037 SPRASH R
WX02038 Pheasant, Phantom Beast R
WX02039 Hachi, Phantom Beast R
WX02040 Plant Wear R
WX02041 Heavy Loss R
WX02042 Code Anti Palbek R
WX02043 Code Anti Kythera R
WX02044 Baal, Reason of the Mortal Sin R
WX02045 Sacrifice Slash R
WX02046 Kiuael, Smile of Sacrifice C
WX02047 Ciel, Love of Fiction C
WX02048 Magatama, Treasure Tool C
WX02049 Saniel, Focus of Philanthropy C
WX02050 Sword Ability C
WX02051 Launchergear, Roaring Gun C
WX02052 MP5, Explosive Gun C
WX02053 Jade, Silk Stone C
WX02054 Smith, Small Gun C
WX02055 Sword of Shining Desire C
WX02056 Octo, Water Phantom C
WX02057 Pearl, Water Phantom C
WX02058 Code Art MMR C
WX02059 Kozame, Water Phantom C
WX02060 SEARCHER C
WX02061 BLUEGAIN C
WX02062 Mizuaoi, Silk Plant C
WX02063 Lotus, Silk Plant C
WX02064 Monkey, Phantom Beast C
WX02065 Suberia, Silk Plant C
WX02066 Abundance C
WX02067 Lilith, Recurring Nightmare C
WX02068 Morriga, Devil's Bravery C
WX02069 Code Anti Nebra C
WX02070 Anima, Reaper of Truth C
WX02071 Code Anti Delhi C
WX02072 Code Anti Machupi C
WX02073 Code Anti Texahammer C
WX02074 Grim, Melancholy of Small Evil C
WX02075 Grave Maker C
WX02076 Servant Q2 C
WX02077 Servant T2 C
WX02078 Servant D2 C
WX02079 Servant O2 C
WX02080 Recalled Blessing C
WX02081 Eldora×Mark IV LR
WX02082 Ulith, Infinite Enma LR
WX02083 Arcgain, Archangel of Pioneering SR
WX02084 Gun Snipe, Ballista SR
WX02085 Spiral Carmilla, Water Phantom Princess SR
WX02086 Gauche Agnes, Silk Plant Princess SR
WX02087 Anna Mirage, Devil Princess SR

2014 WIXOSS WX-03 Spread Selector

WX03P1 Midoriko SCR
WX03P2 Piruruku SCR
WX03001 Umuru=Fyra, Wielder of the Key of Creation LR
WX03002 Holy Act LR
WX03003 Gorgeous Hellfire LR
WX03004 Two Dust LR
WX03005 Restructure LR
WX03006 Tamayorihime, Sky Miko LC
WX03007 Hanayo-Pure Four LC
WX03008 Code Piruruku Sigma LC
WX03009 Midoriko, Type Four LC
WX03010 Ulith, Black Sand Enma LC
WX03011 Umuru=Tre, Wielder of the Key of Creation LC
WX03012 Umuru=Två, Wielder of the Key of Creation LC
WX03013 Umuru=Ett, Wielder of the Key of Creation LC
WX03014 Dead Splash LC
WX03015 Death Colossao LC
WX03016 Rabiel, Protector of Holy Arts SR
WX03017 Pencilrocket, Explosive Gun SR
WX03018 Kareira, Water Phantom SR
WX03019 Marigold, Alluring Plant SR
WX03020 Code Anti Partheno SR
WX03021 Lost Technology SR
WX03022 Samidare, Ultimate Sword R
WX03023 Kakumaru, Hand Sword R
WX03024 Get Grow R
WX03025 Shizuku, Alluring Stone R
WX03026 Ayabon, Hand Grenade R
WX03027 End of Eternity R
WX03028 Code Art RGN R
WX03029 Code Art CVY R
WX03030 PICK UP R
WX03031 Beiar, Phantom Beast R
WX03032 Kano, Alluring Plant R
WX03033 Super Loss R
WX03034 Code Anti Costaric R
WX03035 Code Anti Megatron R
WX03036 Overflowing Knowledge R
WX03037 Archold, Gospel of the Future C
WX03038 Zantetsu, Kunai C
WX03039 Claymore, Trap Gun C
WX03040 Corundum, Alluring Stone C
WX03041 Hiramena, Water Phantom C
WX03042 Code Art KEY C
WX03043 ICE BREAK C
WX03044 Glamis, Alluring Plant C
WX03045 Komaris, Phantom Beast C
WX03046 Strike Impact C
WX03047 Code Anti Aztec C
WX03048 Code Anti Cryskull C
WX03049 Self Slash C
WX03050 Lives Gut C
WX03051 Code Piruruku SCR
WX03052 Kakumaru, Hand Sword SCR
WX03053 Ayabon, Hand Grenade SCR
WX03054 Kano, Alluring Plant SCR
WX03055 Overflowing Knowledge SCR
WX03056 Umuru=Fyra, Wielder of the Key of Creation SCR

2014 WIXOSS WX-04 Infected Selector

WX04001 Tamayorihime, Vermilion Miko LR
WX04002 Yuzuki-Fourth Warning LR
WX04003 Mirurun Yocto LR
WX04004 Anne=Fourth, Melody of Horror LR
WX04005 Iona, Ultima/Maiden LR
WX04006 Ulith, Vermilion Enma LR
WX04007 Tamayorihime, Sixteenth Night Miko LC
WX04008 Fafnir LC
WX04009 Yuzuki-Three Armament LC
WX04010 Rekindling Effort LC
WX04011 Code Piruluk E LC
WX04012 Mirurun Femto LC
WX04013 Mirurun Pico LC
WX04014 Mirurun Nano LC
WX04015 Mind Mines LC
WX04016 Midoriko, Abundant Girl Type Three LC
WX04017 Anne=Third, Trusting Oracle LC
WX04018 Anne=Second, Value of Excess Knowledge LC
WX04019 Anne=First, Creation of the Imagination LC
WX04020 Golden Opportunity LC

WX04021 Ulith, Enma of Suffering LC
WX04022 Iona, Pluto/Maiden LC
WX04023 Iona, Uranus/Maiden LC
WX04024 Iona, Nepto/Maiden LC
WX04025 Dark Matter LC
WX04026 Oversalvage LC
WX04027 Doping LC
WX04028 Banishing LC
WX04029 Code Labyrinth Quinn SR
WX04030 Tri Signal SR
WX04031 Orochi, Phantom Dragon Princess SR
WX04032 Expelling Flames of the Dragon Phoenix SR
WX04033 Neon, Natural Source Princess SR
WX04034 SHORT SR
WX04035 Contempora, Inexplicable Superboast SR
WX04036 Rebirth SR
WX04037 Vier=Rikabuto SR
WX04038 Violence Splash SR
WX04039 Gabrie, Future of the Archangel R
WX04040 Hammer, Ultimate Breaker R
WX04041 Code Maze Skyju R
WX04042 Stinger, Ballista R
WX04043 Obsidian, Natural Stone R
WX04044 Tyranno, Phantom Dragon R
WX04045 Ouika, Water Phantom R
WX04046 Code Art ACG R
WX04047 Helium, Natural Source R
WX04048 Utsuboka, Natural Plant R
WX04049 Shienko, Phantom Beast R
WX04050 Cubi, Distorted Reality R
WX04051 Code Anti Ouroboros R
WX04052 Paimon, Fallen Nihilism R
WX04053 Drei=Capsule R
WX04054 Servant X R
WX04055 Rafae, From Your Tomorrow C
WX04056 Axe, Large Breaker C
WX04057 Urie, Sudden Ruination C
WX04058 Code Maze Tajmaha C
WX04059 Mornin, Medium Breaker C
WX04060 Sarie, Improvement of Historical Fact C
WX04061 Code Maze Towerb C
WX04062 Stick, Small Breaker C
WX04063 Get Gate C
WX04064 No Gain C
WX04065 Drasto, Roaring Gun C
WX04066 Tanza, Natural Stone C
WX04067 Nineteen, Explosive Gun C
WX04068 Wyvern, Phantom Dragon C
WX04069 Turquo, Natural Stone C
WX04070 Derrin, Small Gun C
WX04071 Topaz, Natural Stone C
WX04072 Echidna, Phantom Dragon C
WX04073 Twisted Dance of Flame Destruction C
WX04074 Doubting Lament C
WX04075 Kurage, Water Phantom C
WX04076 Code Art DEF C
WX04077 Hitode, Water Phantom C
WX04078 Code Art RPG C
WX04079 Fluorine, Natural Source C
WX04080 Clione, Water Phantom C
WX04081 Chlorine, Natural Source C
WX04082 Code Art SML C
WX04083 PRECIOUS C
WX04084 ATTRACTION C
WX04085 Droso, Natural Plant C
WX04086 Tosa, Phantom Beast C
WX04087 Haetori, Natural Plant C
WX04088 Beagle, Phantom Beast C
WX04089 Surrelis, Unresolved Deviation C
WX04090 Mousen, Natural Plant C
WX04091 Chihuahuan, Phantom Beast C
WX04092 Puri, Innocuous Match C
WX04093 Inactivity C
WX04094 Angry Roar C
WX04095 Code Anti Nazca C
WX04096 Oriens, Fallen Transgression C
WX04097 Code Anti Ashoka C
WX04098 Maimon, Fallen Confession C
WX04099 Zwei=Sarina C
WX04100 Code Anti Henge C
WX04101 Ein=Dagger C
WX04102 Ariton, Fallen Annihilation C
WX04103 Evil's Soul C
WX04104 End Slash C
WX04105 Growing Future C
WX04106 Mirurun Yocto LR
WX04107 Anne=Fourth, Melody of Horror LR
WX04108 Iona, Ultima/Maiden LR
WX04109 Code Labyrinth Quinn SR
WX04110 Orochi, Phantom Dragon Princess SR
WX04111 Neon, Natural Source Princess SR
WX04112 Contempora, Inexplicable Superboast SR
WX04113 Vier=Rikabuto SR
WX04000a Eldora C
WX04000b Iona C

2014 WIXOSS WX-05 Beginning Selector

WX05000 Hanayo (card) C
WX05001 Mayu, Genesis Miko LR
WX05002 Hanayo-Five LR
WX05003 Code Piruluk ACRO LR
WX05004 Midoriko, Type Five LR
WX05005 Tamayorihime, Sunspot Miko LR
WX05006 Ulith, Enma of Nihilism LR
WX05007 Last Select LC
WX05008 Yuzuki-Five LC
WX05009 Lit Situation LC
WX05010 Eldora=Mark V LC
WX05011 Mirurun Tico LC
WX05012 Fortune Five LC
WX05013 Anne Fifth, Violating God Seal LC
WX05014 Different Strokes LC
WX05015 Hate Impress LC
WX05016 End Hole LC
WX05017 Lucky Guard LC
WX05018 Arc Energe, Original Spear SR
WX05019 Code Labyrinth Louvre SR
WX05020 Diabride, Natural Pyroxene SR
WX05021 Muš?ušsu, Phantom Dragon Princess SR
WX05022 Code Love Heart CMR SR
WX05023 Uranium, Natural Source SR
WX05024 Lion, Phantom Beast Deity SR
WX05025 Suiboku, Single Stroke Worthy of Nobility SR
WX05026 Code Ancients Necronomico SR
WX05027 Lucifer, Fallen Talented Woman SR
WX05028 Aphrodite, Flower Bloom of Late Beginnings R
WX05029 Gaevolg, Ultimate Spear R
WX05030 Get Grimoire R
WX05031 Goddra, Phantom Dragon R
WX05032 Avenger, Ballista R
WX05033 Peridot, Natural Stone R
WX05034 Most Treasured Fragment R
WX05035 Radon, Natural Source R
WX05036 Jinbei, Water Phantom R
WX05037 Code Art SPK R
WX05038 SPIRAL R
WX05039 Dot, Limited Expression R
WX05040 Sakura, Natural Plant R
WX05041 Rhino, Phantom Beast R
WX05042 Increasing Force R
WX05043 Vier=Vial R
WX05044 Code Anti Marsface R
WX05045 Final Destruction R
WX05046 Code Maze Sagfami C
WX05047 Lævateinn, Greatsword C
WX05048 Code Maze Metron C
WX05049 Brionac, Medium Spear C
WX05050 Code Maze Michel C
WX05051 Engetsu, Small Sword C
WX05052 Get Almandal C
WX05053 Eingana, Phantom Dragon C
WX05054 Linfwurm, Phantom Dragon C
WX05055 Kannya, Phantom Dragon C
WX05056 Komodo, Phantom Dragon C
WX05057 Cuélep, Phantom Dragon C
WX05058 Tokage, Phantom Dragon C
WX05059 Life Extending Selection C
WX05060 Manganese, Natural Source C
WX05061 Thorium, Natural Source C
WX05062 Titanium, Natural Source C
WX05063 Actinium, Natural Source C
WX05064 Sulfur, Natural Source C
WX05065 Chromium, Natural Source C
WX05066 RAINY C
WX05067 Maki-e, Approximation of Tradition C
WX05068 Colla, Opposing Methodology C
WX05069 Pop, Vividly Famous Party C
WX05070 Ameco, Generous Light and Dark C
WX05071 Origami, Uniform Requirements C
WX05072 Crayon, Endorsement of Graffiti C
WX05073 Howl C
WX05074 Drei=Spore C
WX05075 Code Anti Arahabaki C
WX05076 Loki, Bewitching Magic C
WX05077 Zwei=Cobra C
WX05078 Ahriman, Fallen Glance C
WX05079 Ein=Gas C
WX05080 Hecate, Sloth of Mission C
WX05081 Revive Flare C
WX05082 Mayu, Genesis Miko SCR
WX05083 Ulith, Enma of Nihilism SCR
WX05084 Yuzuki-Five SCR
WX05085 Code Piruluk ACRO SCR
WX05086 Eldora=Mark V SCR
WX05087 Mirurun Tico SCR
WX05088 Anne Fifth, Violating God Seal SCR
WX05000b Yuzuki (card) C

2014 WIXOSS WXD-01 White Hope

WD01001 Tamayorihime, Full Moon Miko
WD01002 Tamayorihime, Waxing Gibbous Moon Miko
WD01003 Tamayorihime, Half Moon Miko
WD01004 Tamayorihime, Waxing Crescent Moon Miko
WD01005 Tamayorihime, New Moon Miko
WD01006 Rococo Boundary
WD01007 Avon
WD01008 Baroque Defense
WD01009 Romail, Helmet Armor
WD01010 Caliburn, Greatsword
WD01011 Tourette, Gauntlet
WD01012 Flamber, Medium Sword
WD01013 Kukri, Small Sword
WD01014 Bonya, Small Bow
WD01015 Get Bible
WD01016 Servant D
WD01017 Servant O
WD01018 Knowledge Jet

2014 WIXOSS WXD-02 Red Ambition

WD02001 Hanayo-Four
WD02002 Hanayo-Three
WD02003 Hanayo-Two
WD02004 Hanayo-One
WD02005 Hanayo-Zero
WD02006 Summer Insect Flying Flames
WD02007 Back Flame Formation
WD02008 Burning Stone Flame
WD02009 Volcano, Silk Stone
WD02010 Silvan, Silk Stone
WD02011 Garnet, Silk Stone
WD02012 Bronda, Silk Stone
WD02013 Iron, Silk Stone
WD02014 Amethyst, Silk Stone
WD02015 Roaring Fire Pillar
WD02016 Servant D
WD02017 Servant O
WD02018 Knowledge Jet

2014 WIXOSS WXD-03 Blue Appli

WD03001 Code Piruruku T
WD03002 Code Piruruku G
WD03003 Code Piruruku M
WD03004 Code Piruruku K
WD03005 Code Piruruku
WD03006 Peeping Analyze
WD03007 Don't Move
WD03008 Draw Two
WD03009 Code Art RMN
WD03010 Code Art DRS
WD03011 Code Art SMP
WD03012 Code Art JV
WD03013 Code Art SC
WD03014 Code Art RFR
WD03015 TOO BAD
WD03016 Servant D
WD03017 Servant O
WD03018 Knowledge Jet

2014 WIXOSS WXD-04 Green Wanna

WD04001 Midoriko, Fourth Girl
WD04002 Midoriko, Third Girl
WD04003 Midoriko, Second Girl
WD04004 Midoriko, First Girl
WD04005 Midoriko, Combat Girl
WD04006 All Yell
WD04007 Wake Up
WD04008 Big Wave
WD04009 Seiryu, Phantom Beast
WD04010 Misuzaku, Phantom Beast
WD04011 Bigtatt, Phantom Beast
WD04012 Koalan, Phantom Beast
WD04013 Kogenbu, Phantom Beast
WD04014 Pandan, Phantom Beast
WD04015 Hyakko, Phantom Beast
WD04016 Servant Q2
WD04017 Servant O2
WD04018 Fallen

2014 WIXOSS WXD-05 Black Desire

WD05001 Ulith, Jailer Enma
WD05002 Ulith, Enma of Eternal Hell
WD05003 Ulith, Enma of Crushing Hell
WD05004 Ulith, Burning Eye Enma
WD05005 Ulith, Enma
WD05006 Moment Punish
WD05007 Eternal Banish
WD05008 Grave Out
WD05009 Metsum, Fallen Cannon Girl
WD05010 Belze, Symbol of Wasteful Evil
WD05011 Carry, Fallen Cannon Girl
WD05012 Cosmo, Symbol of Immorality
WD05013 Kooni, Symbol of Lesser Sin
WD05014 Succu, Fallen Cannon Girl
WD05015 Servant D
WD05016 Servant O
WD05017 Hole Dark
WD05018 Recalled Blessing

2014 WIXOSS WXD-06 Blue Request

WD06001 Eldora=Mark IV'
WD06002 Eldora=Mark III'
WD06003 Eldora=Mark II'
WD06004 Eldora=Mark I'
WD06005 Eldora=Mark 0
WD06006 Cloth Crush Flash
WD06007 Surprise With Me
WD06008 But Any Other
WD06009 Shiira, Water Phantom
WD06010 Octo, Water Phantom
WD06011 Ryuuguu, Water Phantom
WD06012 Pearl, Water Phantom
WD06013 Chouan, Water Phantom
WD06014 Kozame, Water Phantom
WD06015 Una, Water Phantom
WD06016 Servant Q
WD06017 Servant O
WD06018 PLUS RUSH

2014 WIXOSS WXD-07 Black Crave

WD07001 Iona, Full/Maiden
WD07002 Iona, Pale/Maiden
WD07003 Iona, Half/Maiden
WD07004 Iona, Crescent/Maiden
WD07005 Iona, Zero/Maiden
WD07006 Grave Night
WD07007 Black Crisis
WD07008 Death Beam
WD07009 Code Maze Pyramid
WD07010 Code Maze Babel
WD07011 Code Maze Triumph
WD07012 Code Anti Vimana SR
WD07013 Code Anti Iron
WD07014 Code Anti Moa
WD07015 Code Anti Clay
WD07016 Servant Q2
WD07017 Servant O2
WD07018 Slash Miracle

2015 WIXOSS SP-06 Akira Aoi

SP06-001 Mirurun Zepto
SP06-002 Mirurun Femto
SP06-003 Mirurun Pico
SP06-004 Mirurun Nano
SP06-005 Mirurun Nought
SP06-006 Don't Move
SP06-007 Fortune Five
SP06-008 Mind Mines
SP06-009 Chemical Flash
SP06-010 Welcome Draw
SP06-011 Nickel, Natural Source
SP06-012 Manganese, Natural Source
SP06-013 Thorium, Natural Source
SP06-014 Titanium, Natural Source
SP06-015 Fluorine, Natural Source
SP06-016 Sulfur, Natural Source
SP06-017 Chlorine, Natural Source
SP06-018 Servant Q
SP06-019 Servant O2
SP06-020 Encompassing Knowledge

2015 WIXOSS SP-07 Fumio Futase

SP07-001 ?Anne=Fourth, Blessing of Revelation
SP07-002 Anne=Third, Trusting Oracle
SP07-003 Anne=Second, Value of Excess Knowledge
SP07-004 Anne=First, Creation of the Imagination
SP07-005 Anne, Locus of Miracles
SP07-006 Follow Blindly
SP07-007 Golden Opportunity
SP07-008 Different Strokes
SP07-009 Divine Grace
SP07-010 Swift Divine Punishment
SP07-011 Marche, Mysterious Fairytale
SP07-012 Maki-e, Approximation of Tradition
SP07-013 Colla, Opposing Methodology
SP07-014 Ameco, Generous Light and Dark
SP07-015 Surrelis, Unresolved Deviation
SP07-016 Origami, Uniform Requirements
SP07-017 Puri, Innocuous Match
SP07-018 Servant D
SP07-019 Servant O2
SP07-020 Encompassing Knowledge

2015 WIXOSS WX-01 Served Selector Chinese

WX01001 Tamayorihime, Sun Miko PR
WX01002 Tamayorihime, Dawn Miko LR
WX01003 Hanayo-Four, Hundred-Fire Profusion LR
WX01004 Hanayo-Two Remodeled, Roaring Flame LR
WX01005 Code Piruruku Omega LR
WX01006 Midoriko, War Empress Type Four LR
WX01007 Tamayorihime, Lunar Eclipse Miko LC
WX01008 Tamayorihime, Shooting Star Miko LC
WX01009 Tamayorihime, Nova Miko LC
WX01010 Xenogate LC
WX01011 Hanayo-Three, Blazing Flame Dance LC
WX01012 Hanayo-Two, Hard Flame LC
WX01013 Hanayo-One, the Flame LC
WX01014 Dominating Fury LC
WX01015 Code Piruruku Gamma LC
WX01016 Code Piruruku Beta LC
WX01017 Code Piruruku Alpha LC
WX01018 Anti-Spell LC
WX01019 Midoriko, Shining Empress Girl Type Four LC
WX01020 Midoriko, Feminine Girl Type Three LC
WX01021 Midoriko, Bridal Combat Girl Type Two LC
WX01022 Midoriko, Dancing Combat Girl Type One LC
WX01023 Big Bang LC
WX01024 Giant LC
WX01025 Salvage LC
WX01026 Charging LC
WX01027 Energe, Original Spear SR
WX01028 Arc Aura SR
WX01029 Adamasphere, Alluring Pyroxene SR
WX01030 Fires of Atonement SR
WX01031 Code Heart VAC SR
WX01032 SNATCHER SR
WX01033 Osaki, Phantom Beast Deity SR
WX01034 Repair SR
WX01035 Athena, Goddess of Blessing R
WX01036 Catapaul, Large Bow R
WX01037 Valkyrie, Unforgettable Fantasy R
WX01038 Get Dantalian R
WX01039 Cannon, Ballista R
WX01040 Orichalc, Alluring Stone R
WX01041 Ordnance, Roaring Gun R
WX01042 Fissure of Condemnation R
WX01043 Araial, Water Phantom R
WX01044 Code Art PZL R
WX01045 Shark Lance, Water Phantom R
WX01046 BAD CONDITION R
WX01047 Mandore, Alluring Plant R
WX01048 Bigtatt, Phantom Beast R
WX01049 Baromet, Alluring Plant R
WX01050 Enlarge R
WX01051 Servant Q R
WX01052 Encompassing Knowledge R
WX01053 God Eater, Ultimate Sword C
WX01054 Egis, Ultimate Shield C
WX01055 Riot, Large Shield C
WX01056 Square, Medium Shield C
WX01057 Sephiram, Shooting Bow C
WX01058 Michael, Voice of Reconciliation C
WX01059 Bow, Shooting Bow C
WX01060 Round, Small Shield C
WX01061 Haniel, Thoughts of Seeking C
WX01062 Get Open C
WX01063 Get Ready C
WX01064 Metallica, Alluring Stone C
WX01065 Emeralda, Alluring Stone C
WX01066 Rubyl, Alluring Stone C
WX01067 Rin, Alluring Stone C
WX01068 Amber, Alluring Stone C
WX01069 Ranchan, Explosive Gun C
WX01070 Macury, Alluring Stone C
WX01071 Sapphi, Alluring Stone C
WX01072 Dragunov, Small Gun C
WX01073 Flame Ball, Falling Star C
WX01074 Prismatic Fire Pillar C
WX01075 Code Art ASM C
WX01076 Code Art IDOL C
WX01077 Code Art ADB C
WX01078 Code Art STG C
WX01079 Code Art WTC C
WX01080 Shakotan, Water Phantom C
WX01081 Code Art TV C
WX01082 Code Art FAN C
WX01083 Kumanomin, Water Phantom C
WX01084 THREE OUT C
WX01085 FREEZE C
WX01086 Eagle, Phantom Beast C
WX01087 Cait Sith, Phantom Beast C
WX01088 Owl, Phantom Beast C
WX01089 Kuro, Phantom Beast C
WX01090 Sparrow, Phantom Beast C
WX01091 Koalan, Phantom Beast C
WX01092 Shiro, Phantom Beast C
WX01093 Dandelion, Alluring Plant C
WX01094 Swallow, Phantom Beast C
WX01095 Pandan, Phantom Beast C
WX01096 Mi-Ke, Phantom Beast C
WX01097 Salvia, Alluring Plant C
WX01098 Germinate C
WX01099 Reverse Summon C
WX01100 Servant T C
WX01101 Servant D C
WX01102 Servant O C
WX01103 Jetting Knowledge C
WX01104 Tamayorihime, Full Moon Miko SCR
WX01105 Tamayorihime, Sun Miko SCR
WX01106 Hanayo-Two Remodeled, Roaring Flame SCR
WX01107 Hanayo-Four, Hundred-Fire Profusion SCR
WX01108 Energe, Original Spear SCR
WX01109 Adamasphere, Alluring Pyroxene SCR
WX01110 Code Heart VAC SCR
WX01111 Osaki, Phantom Beast Deity SCR
WX01112 Tama C

2015 WIXOSS WX-06 Fortune Selector

WX06-CB01 Cyua, Natural Stone R
WX06-CB02 Code Art TAP R
WX06-CB03 Kayappa, Natural Plant R
WX06-CB04 Code Anti Doronjo R
WX06-CB01P Cyua, Natural Stone SCR
WX06-CB02P Code Art TAP SCR
WX06-CB03P Kayappa, Natural Plant SCR
WX06-001 Tawil=Fyra, Prolonged of Life LR
WX06-002 Pinch Defense LR
WX06-003 Interwoven Fire and Fortune LR
WX06-004 Don't Escape LR
WX06-005 Vanish Like Mist LR
WX06-006 Ancient Gate LR
WX06-007 Tawil=Tre, Prolonged of Life LC
WX06-008 Tawil=Två, Prolonged of Life LC
WX06-009 Tawil=Ett, Prolonged of Life LC
WX06-010 Tawil=Noll, Prolonged of Life LC
WX06-011 Soap Summon LC
WX06-012 Mirurun Alto LC
WX06-013 Anne=Third, Public Repentance LC
WX06-014 Umr=Fem, Wielder of the Key of Creation LC
WX06-015 Spell Salvage LC
WX06-016 Munkarun, Elder Sister Deity of the Holy Tomb SR
WX06-017 Nyarobu, Ultimate Fist SR
WX06-018 Colonel Flathro, Crossbow Flame SR
WX06-019 Shironakuji, Water Phantom SR
WX06-020 Rafflele, Natural Plant SR
WX06-021 Vier=Dio Princess SR
WX06-022 Tride, Greatspear R
WX06-023 Nakirun, Younger Sister Deity of the Holy Tomb R
WX06-024 Soap Sudden R
WX06-025 Lucky Three R
WX06-026 Kakusen, Natural Stone R
WX06-027 Brazaus, Phantom Dragon R
WX06-028 Gear of the Flame Machine R
WX06-029 Code Art OSS R
WX06-030 Argon, Natural Source R
WX06-031 TRICK OR TREAT R
WX06-032 Kuronyan, Phantom Beast R
WX06-033 Grid, Repeating Originality R
WX06-034 One Throw R
WX06-035 Cerberun, Three-Headed Barrage R
WX06-036 Code Anti Golspe R
WX06-037 Inhaling Hole R
WX06-038 Merisa, Large Fist C
WX06-039 Glova, Medium Fist C
WX06-040 Fingu, Small Fist C
WX06-041 Kakouga, Natural Stone C
WX06-042 Serikuga, Natural Stone C
WX06-043 Hareiga, Natural Stone C
WX06-044 Code Art ACD C
WX06-045 Code Art HMF C
WX06-046 Code Art DMF C
WX06-047 Kanruru, Phantom Beast C
WX06-048 Komorig, Phantom Beast C
WX06-049 Womba, Phantom Beast C
WX06-050 Saleos, Devil Rider C
WX06-051 Saros, Devil Rider C
WX06-052 Zaebos, Devil Rider C
WX06-053 Tawil=Fyra, Prolonged of Life LR
WX06-054 Umr=Fem, Wielder of the Key of Creation LC
WX06-055 Umr SCR
WX06-056 Mirurun SCR
WX06-057 Anne SCR

2015 WIXOSS WX-07 Next Selector

WX07-001 Sashe Pleine, Benevolent Messenger LR
WX07-002 Four of Tamayorihime, Strangely United Flames LR
WX07-003 Mirurun Union LR
WX07-004 Midoriko, Fourth Connecting Beast Girl LR
WX07-005 Ulith, Enma of the Sin Gate LR
WX07-006 Saturn, White Natural Star LR
WX07-007 Sashe Moitié, Benevolent Messenger LC
WX07-008 Res Hope LC
WX07-009 Jupiter, White Natural Star LC
WX07-010 Three of Tamayorihime, Cross Flame LC
WX07-011 Flaming Stubbornness LC
WX07-012 Explosive Solidarity LC
WX07-013 Mirurun Micro LC
WX07-014 Cross Scramble LC
WX07-015 Peeping Choice LC
WX07-016 Midoriko, Supportive Girl Type Three LC
WX07-017 Calm After the Typhoon LC
WX07-018 One Time, One Meeting LC
WX07-019 Ulith, Enma of Purgatory LC
WX07-020 Blood Dance LC
WX07-021 Attrac Punish LC
WX07-022 Exclude LC
WX07-023 Milky Way, Natural Star Princess SR
WX07-024 Meteo Advantage SR
WX07-025 Firerage, Ballista SR
WX07-026 Fissure of Conflagration SR
WX07-027 Hydrogen, Natural Source SR
WX07-028 JACKPOT SR

WX07-029 Usa, Phantom Beast SR
WX07-030 Perforation SR
WX07-031 Ungyou, Right Image of Destruction SR
WX07-032 Death Parade SR
WX07-033 Alphard, Natural Star R
WX07-034 Alphecca, Natural Star R
WX07-035 Mimosa, Natural Star R
WX07-036 Major Flathro, Crossbow Flame R
WX07-037 Musketta, Roaring Gun R
WX07-038 Gunsword, Explosive Gun R
WX07-039 Ununoctium, Natural Source R
WX07-040 Oxygen, Natural Source R
WX07-041 Nitrogen, Natural Source R
WX07-042 Rakuda, Phantom Beast R
WX07-043 Kame, Phantom Beast R
WX07-044 Cheetah, Phantom Beast R
WX07-045 Daewa, Flickering Sinful Elegance R
WX07-046 Agyou, Left Image of Transgression R
WX07-047 Faust, Fallen Left Sin R
WX07-048 Almach, Natural Star C
WX07-049 Regulus, Natural Star C
WX07-050 Alhena, Natural Star C
WX07-051 Arcturus, Natural Star C
WX07-052 Hadar, Natural Star C
WX07-053 Spica, Natural Star C
WX07-054 Antares, Natural Star C
WX07-055 Get Out C
WX07-056 Kalaniko, Roaring Gun C
WX07-057 Uzi, Explosive Gun C
WX07-058 Shield Missile, Shield Gun C
WX07-059 Glock, Small Gun C
WX07-060 Absolute Flame War C
WX07-061 Ununseptium, Natural Source C
WX07-062 Ununpentium, Natural Source C
WX07-063 Carbon, Natural Source C
WX07-064 Ununtrium, Natural Source C
WX07-065 FREEZE THROUGH C
WX07-066 CROSS RUSH C
WX07-067 Hyena, Phantom Beast C
WX07-068 Hagetaka, Phantom Beast C
WX07-069 Hyou, Phantom Beast C
WX07-070 Harinezu, Phantom Beast C
WX07-071 Unification C
WX07-072 Explosive Strike C
WX07-073 Druj, Abundant Woman of Collapse C
WX07-074 Apaosha, Dream Woman of Collapse C
WX07-075 Pheles, Fallen Right Sin C
WX07-076 Azidaha, Designation of Failure C
WX07-077 Death Like Death C
WX07-078 Dead Cross C
WX07-079 Servant Q C
WX07-080 Servant T C
WX07-081 Servant D C
WX07-082 Servant O C
WX07-083 Sashe Pleine, Benevolent Messenger SCR
WX07-084 Four of Tamayorihime, Strangely United Flames SCR
WX07-085 Mirurun Union SCR
WX07-086 Midoriko, Fourth Connecting Beast Girl SCR
WX07-087 Ulith, Enma of the Sin Gate SCR
WX07-088 Saturn, White Natural Star SCR
WX07-089 Spirit Salvage SCR
WX07-090 Modern Boundary SCR
WX07-091 Sashe SCR

2015 WIXOSS WX-08 Incubate Selector

WX08-001 Hanayo-Four, Golden Orchid Pledge LR
WX08-002 Code Piruluk Zeta LR
WX08-003 Anne=Fourth, Connected Integrity LR
WX08-004 Myuu=Flap LR
WX08-005 Uranus, White Natural Star LR
WX08-006 Arachne Pider, Black Phantom Insect LR
WX08-007 Reverse Mode LC
WX08-008 Mars, White Natural Star LC
WX08-009 Hanayo-Three, Combined Flaming Elegance LC
WX08-010 Tenacity LC
WX08-011 Fiery Harmony LC
WX08-012 Code Piruluk Theta LC
WX08-013 Rob Move LC
WX08-014 Don't Grow LC
WX08-015 Hammer Chance LC
WX08-016 Anne=Third, Converging Exercise LC
WX08-017 Rapid Advance LC
WX08-018 Most Humbly Pleased LC
WX08-019 Myuu=Ysalis LC
WX08-020 Grave Curse LC
WX08-021 Sasoris, Black Phantom Insect LC
WX08-022 Pay Charging LC
WX08-023 Fout, Natural Star Princess SR
WX08-024 Sunst, Natural Stone SR
WX08-025 Timebomb, Trap Gun SR
WX08-026 Gorgeous Fissure SR
WX08-027 Code Art HI SR
WX08-028 RECKLESS SR
WX08-029 To'on, Right Rhythm of the Scale SR
WX08-030 Destruction Spirit SR
WX08-031 Herakabuto, Great Phantom Insect SR
WX08-032 Worm Hole SR
WX08-033 Capella, Natural Star R
WX08-034 Diadem, Natural Star R
WX08-035 Torpedo, Ballista R
WX08-036 Spinel, Natural Stone R
WX08-037 Moonst, Natural Stone R
WX08-038 Tieye, Natural Stone R
WX08-039 Code Art MM R
WX08-040 Code Art DY R
WX08-041 Code Art FM R
WX08-042 Contra, Beautiful Symphony R
WX08-043 Heon, Left Technique of the Scale R
WX08-044 Flute, Left Sound of the Musical Performance R
WX08-045 Nokokuwa, Phantom Insect R
WX08-046 Tamamushi, Phantom Insect R
WX08-047 Kogane, Phantom Insect R
WX08-048 Gruid, Natural Star C
WX08-049 Cor Caro, Natural Star C
WX08-050 Sadalme, Natural Star C
WX08-051 Alscha, Natural Star C
WX08-052 Sulocin, Natural Star C
WX08-053 White Out C
WX08-054 Chrysoco, Natural Stone C
WX08-055 Plasbomb, Roaring Gun C
WX08-056 Chrysobe, Natural Stone C
WX08-057 Mine, Explosive Gun C
WX08-058 Chrysop, Natural Stone C
WX08-059 Cateye, Natural Stone C
WX08-060 Tuning of Mutual Love C
WX08-061 Twin Attack of the Revolving Storm C
WX08-062 Code Art MX C
WX08-063 Code Art SZ C
WX08-064 Code Art WS C
WX08-065 Code Art DP C
WX08-066 BEAUTIFUL C
WX08-067 PEEPING DECIDE C
WX08-068 Radabura, Suspicion of the String Scale C
WX08-069 Viola, Temptation of the String Scale C
WX08-070 Violi, Captivation of the String Scale C
WX08-071 Clarine, Right Sound of the Musical Performance C
WX08-072 Resolution C
WX08-073 Rush C
WX08-074 Queen Ant, Phantom Insect C
WX08-075 Tonosama, Phantom Insect C
WX08-076 Kumaze, Phantom Insect C
WX08-077 Kurumaba, Phantom Insect C
WX08-078 Minmin, Phantom Insect C
WX08-079 Shouryou, Phantom Insect C
WX08-080 Tsukutsuku, Phantom Insect C
WX08-081 Dead Make C
WX08-082 Servant Q2 C
WX08-083 Servant T2 C
WX08-084 Servant D2 C
WX08-085 Servant O2 C
WX08-086 Hanayo-Four, Golden Orchid Pledge SCR
WX08-087 Code Piruluk Zeta SCR
WX08-088 Anne=Fourth, Connected Integrity SCR
WX08-089 Myuu=Flap SCR
WX08-090 Uranus, White Natural Star SCR
WX08-091 Arachne Pider, Black Phantom Insect SCR
WX08-092 One Rule, Two Birds SCR
WX08-093 See Through the Fiery Ambition SCR
WX08-094 Myuu SCR

2015 WIXOSS WXD-01 White Hope Chinese

WD01001 Tamayorihime, Full Moon Miko
WD01002 Tamayorihime, Waxing Gibbous Moon Miko
WD01003 Tamayorihime, Half Moon Miko
WD01004 Tamayorihime, Waxing Crescent Moon Miko
WD01005 Tamayorihime, New Moon Miko
WD01006 Rococo Boundary
WD01007 Avon
WD01008 Baroque Defense
WD01009 Romail, Helmet Armor
WD01010 Caliburn, Greatsword
WD01011 Tourette, Gauntlet
WD01012 Flamber, Medium Sword
WD01013 Kukri, Small Sword
WD01014 Bonya, Small Bow
WD01015 Get Bible
WD01016 Servant D
WD01017 Servant O
WD01018 Knowledge Jet

2015 WIXOSS WXD-02 Red Ambition Chinese

WD02001 Hanayo-Four
WD02002 Hanayo-Three
WD02003 Hanayo-Two
WD02004 Hanayo-One
WD02005 Hanayo-Zero
WD02006 Summer Insect Flying Flames
WD02007 Back Flame Formation
WD02008 Burning Stone Flame
WD02009 Volcano, Silk Stone
WD02010 Silvan, Silk Stone
WD02011 Garnet, Silk Stone
WD02012 Bronda, Silk Stone
WD02013 Iron, Silk Stone
WD02014 Amethyst, Silk Stone
WD02015 Roaring Fire Pillar
WD02016 Servant D
WD02017 Servant O
WD02018 Knowledge Jet

2015 WIXOSS WXD-03 Blue Appli Chinese

WD03001 Code Piruruku T
WD03002 Code Piruruku G
WD03003 Code Piruruku M
WD03004 Code Piruruku K
WD03005 Code Piruruku
WD03006 Peeping Analyze
WD03007 Don't Move
WD03008 Draw Two
WD03009 Code Art RMN
WD03010 Code Art DRS
WD03011 Code Art SMP
WD03012 Code Art JV
WD03013 Code Art SC
WD03014 Code Art RFR
WD03015 TOO BAD
WD03016 Servant D
WD03017 Servant O
WD03018 Knowledge Jet

2015 WIXOSS WXD-08 Black Will

WD08-001 Umr=Fyra, Wielder of the Key of Chaos
WD08-002 Umr=Tre, Wielder of the Key of Chaos
WD08-003 Umr=Tva, Wielder of the Key of Chaos
WD08-004 Umr=Ett, Wielder of the Key of Chaos
WD08-005 Umr=Noll, Wielder of the Key of Chaos
WD08-006 Ancient Surprise
WD08-007 Ancient Digger
WD08-008 Ancient Return
WD08-009 Code Anti Nessie
WD08-010 Code Anti Nebra
WD08-011 Code Anti Ashiren
WD08-012 Code Anti Aztec
WD08-013 Code Anti Cabrera
WD08-014 Code Anti Texahammer
WD08-015 Code Anti Voyni
WD08-016 Servant T
WD08-017 Servant D
WD08-018 Grave Pain

2015 WIXOSS WXD-09 White Pray

WD09-001 Sashe Pleine, Eternal Messenger
WD09-002 Sashe Moitié, Eternal Messenger
WD09-003 Sashe Quartier, Eternal Messenger
WD09-004 Sashe Crois, Eternal Messenger
WD09-005 Sashe Nouvelle, Eternal Messenger
WD09-006 Romane Defense
WD09-007 Mercury, White Natural Star
WD09-008 Venus, White Natural Star
WD09-009 Vega, Natural Star
WD09-010 Betelgeuse, Natural Star
WD09-011 Altair, Natural Star
WD09-012 Sirius, Natural Star
WD09-013 Deneb, Natural Star
WD09-014 Procyon, Natural Star
WD09-015 Polaris, Natural Star
WD09-016 Servant D
WD09-017 Servant O
WD09-018 Get Twinkle

2015 WIXOSS WXD-10 Red Hope

WD10-001 Four of Tamayorihime, Brave and Bold
WD10-002 Three of Tamayorihime, Bullet's Final Sound
WD10-003 Two of Tamayorihime, the Roaring
WD10-004 One of Tamayorihime, the Flame
WD10-005 Zero of Tamayorihime
WD10-006 Dust-Free in All Directions
WD10-007 Eternal Karma
WD10-008 Crossroad
WD10-009 Heckler, Ballista
WD10-010 Drasto, Roaring Gun
WD10-011 Koch, Roaring Gun
WD10-012 Nineteen, Explosive Gun
WD10-013 Stun, Explosive Gun
WD10-014 Derrin, Small Gun
WD10-015 Grenade, Small Gun
WD10-016 Servant D
WD10-017 Servant O
WD10-018 Overlap of Fate

2015 WIXOSS WXD-11 Black Need

WD11-001 Myuu=Imago
WD11-002 Myuu=Emerge
WD11-003 Myuu=Pupa
WD11-004 Myuu=Larva
WD11-005 Myuu=Hatch
WD11-006 Macaron Bugs
WD11-007 Mukadesu, Black Phantom Insect
WD11-008 Yasudesu, Black Phantom Insect
WD11-009 Kuroha, Phantom Insect
WD11-010 Soldier Ant, Phantom Insect
WD11-011 Kiaha, Phantom Insect
WD11-012 Work Ant, Phantom Insect
WD11-013 Monchou, Phantom Insect
WD11-014 Child Ant, Phantom Insect
WD11-015 Monshiro, Phantom Insect
WD11-016 Servant D
WD11-017 Servant O
WD11-018 Get Insect

2008 World of Warcraft Drums of War

COMPLETE SET (268)	100.00	180.00
BOOSTER BOX (24 PACKS)	80.00	100.00
BOOSTER PACK (19 CARDS)	3.00	4.00
RELEASED IN NOVEMBER 2008		
1 Grand Marshall Goldensword U	.20	.50
2 Lord Benjamin Tremendouson U	.20	.50
3 Martiana the Mindwrench U	.20	.50
4 Oakenclaw U	.20	.50
5 Pidge Filthfinder U	.20	.50
6 Shaii, Strategist Supreme U	.20	.50
7 Spellweaver Jihan U	.20	.50
8 Umbrage U	.20	.50
9 Zorin of the Thunderhead U	.20	.50
10 Boarguts the Impaler U	.20	.50
11 Justice Blindburn U	.20	.50
12 The Longeye U	.20	.50
13 Maleo the Blur U	.20	.50
14 Shalu Stormshatter U	.20	.50
15 Sinthya Flabberghast U	.20	.50
16 Spiritualist Sunshroud U	.20	.50
17 Turane Soulpact U	.20	.50
18 Velindra Sepulchre U	.20	.50
19 Aquatic Form R	.50	1.00
20 Celestial Communion U	.20	.50
21 Cower U	.20	.50
22 Feral Charge R	2.00	4.00
23 Hibernate C	.10	.20
24 Life of the Land R	.50	1.00
25 Master Instinct C	.10	.20
26 Moonflare U	.20	.50
27 Empty the Stables R	.50	1.00
28 Hissy R	.50	1.00
29 Hunter's Mark U	.20	.50
30 Resourcefulness R	.50	1.00
31 Snipe C	.10	.20
32 Sudden Shot U	.20	.50
33 Turn the Blade C	.10	.20
34 Zip U	.20	.50
35 Conjured Cinnamon Roll U	.20	.50
36 Ice Lance C	.10	.20
37 Mystic Denial R	3.00	6.00
38 Presence of Mind R	.50	1.00
39 Pyroclastic Consumption R	.50	1.00
40 Spell Suppression C	.10	.20
41 Temporary Dissipation U	.20	.50
42 Transfigure U	.20	.50
43 Aura of Accuracy R	.50	1.00
44 Blessing of Trials U	.20	.50
45 Crusader Strike R	.50	1.00
46 Inspiring Light C	.10	.20
47 Penance R	.50	1.00
48 Reprisal U	.20	.50
49 Seal of Justice U	.20	.50
50 Seal of Righteousness C	.10	.20
51 Dawn's Grace U	.20	.50
52 Equalize R	3.00	6.00
53 Exasperate U	.20	.50
54 Misery R	2.00	4.00
55 Precognition R	.50	1.00
56 Shadow Word: Anguish C	.10	.20
57 Sublimate U	.20	.50
58 Vampiric Tendrils C	.10	.20
59 Deathblow U	.20	.50
60 Detect Traps R	2.00	4.00
61 Gang Up C	.10	.20
62 Nerves of Steel R	1.00	2.00
63 Pernicious Poison U	.20	.50
64 Ransack R	.50	1.00
65 Slay the Feeble C	.10	.20
66 Surge of Adrenaline U	.20	.50
67 Energized C	.10	.20
68 Greater Chain Lightning R	.50	1.00
69 Grounding Totem U	.20	.50
70 Lightning Overload R	.50	1.00
71 Natural Conduit C	.10	.20
72 Primal Totem U	.20	.50
73 Water Breathing R	.50	1.00
74 Winterstorm Totem U	.20	.50
75 Curse of Fatigue U	.20	.50
76 Drain Will C	.10	.20
77 Enslaved Abyssal R	.50	1.00
78 Gakmat U	.20	.50
79 Rain of Shadow U	.20	.50
80 Suspended Curse C	.10	.20
81 Unending Breath R	.50	1.00
82 Unholy Power R	.50	1.00
83 Absolute Poise U	.20	.50
84 Battle Tactics R	.50	1.00
85 Behead C	.10	.20
86 Enduring Shout U	.20	.50
87 Menace C	.10	.20
88 Taunt U	.20	.50
89 War of Attrition R	.50	1.00
90 Weapon Mastery R	.50	1.00
91 Arcane Spikes C	.10	.20
92 Bloody Ritual C	.10	.20
93 Courageous Defense C	.10	.20
94 Creeping Shadow C	.10	.20
95 Demolish C	.10	.20
96 Eagle Sight C	.10	.20
97 Engulfing Blaze C	.10	.20
98 Fire and Ice C	.10	.20
99 Immobilize C	.10	.20
100 Lose Control C	.10	.20
101 Natural Disaster C	.10	.20
102 Nature Unleashed C	.10	.20
103 Revitalize C	.10	.20
104 Revival Stone C	.10	.20
105 Spell Ricochet C	.10	.20
106 Sphere of Divinity C	.10	.20
107 Thud C	.10	.20
108 Topple C	.10	.20
109 Owned R	.50	1.00
110 Pandamonium R	.50	1.00
111 Slashdance U	.20	.50
112 Al'lanora U	.20	.50
113 Angur Frostbeard C	.10	.20
114 Braeden Highblade C	.10	.20
115 Brelnor Mindbender U	.20	.50
116 Catarina Clark C	.10	.20
117 Chief Researcher Kartos R	.50	1.00
118 Consul Rhys Lorgrand R	2.00	4.00
119 Cymbre Shadowdrifter C	.10	.20
120 Daniel Soortan C	.10	.20
121 Durgrin Ironedge C	.10	.20
122 Elementalist Psyrin C	.10	.20
123 Envoy Aiden LeNoir C	.10	.20
124 Envoy Samantha Dillon C	.10	.20
125 Errzig Cogflicker C	.10	.20
126 Falcore C	.10	.20
127 Gryth Thurden, Gryphon Master U	.20	.50
128 The Hammerhand Brothers C	.10	.20
129 Helena Demonfire R	.50	1.00
130 High Tinker Mekkatorque E	3.00	6.00
131 Keward Rocksalt C	.10	.20
132 Kinivus C	.10	.20
133 Lanthus of the Forest C	.10	.20
134 Lolly the Unsuspecting R	.50	1.00
135 Loraala C	.10	.20
136 Magnus Longbarrel C	.10	.20
137 Meganna Callaghan C	.10	.20
138 Mollie Brightheart C	.10	.20
139 Ninoo of the Light C	.10	.20
140 Rayne Savageboon C	.10	.20
141 Ryno the Short C	.10	.20
142 Swordsmith Hanso C	.10	.20
143 Tinker Art Seaclock C	.10	.20
144 Tinker Bixy Blue C	.10	.20
145 Tinker Burnfizzle C	.10	.20
146 Tinker Casey Springlock C	.10	.20
147 Tonks the Tenacious C	.10	.20
148 Treewarden Tolven C	.10	.20
149 Tully Fiddlewit U	.20	.50
150 Virkaltor C	.10	.20
151 Weldon Barov E	12.00	20.00
152 Woodsie Leafsong C	.10	.20
153 Wyler Surestrike C	.10	.20
154 Zempre, Grace of Elune R	2.00	4.00
155 Zophos C	.10	.20
156 Alamo R	.50	1.00
157 Alexi Barov E	4.00	8.00
158 Boum Headshot C	.10	.20
159 Cairne Bloodhoof E	4.00	8.00
160 Centurion Addisyn C	.10	.20
161 Chief Researcher Amereldine R	.50	1.00
162 Cromarius Blackfist C	.10	.20
163 Darbun Steppeheart C	.10	.20
164 Defender Kaniya C	.10	.20
165 Doomsayer Din'ju R	.50	1.00
166 Elizabeth Crowley C	.10	.20
167 Erindae Firestrider C	.10	.20
168 Gatlin Clouds-the-Sky C	.10	.20
169 Geoffrey Kimble C	.10	.20
170 Himul Longstrider C	.10	.20
171 Horkin Figluster C	.10	.20
172 Jack Coor C	.10	.20
173 Jee'zee C	.10	.20
174 Jil'ti U	.20	.50
175 Johnny Rotten U	.20	.50
176 Kileana Darkblaze C	.10	.20
177 Kirga Earthguard C	.10	.20
178 Kray'zin Firetusk R	.50	1.00
179 Lifemender Dorn C	.10	.20
180 Logor Blackfist C	.10	.20
181 Malicious Mallina U	.20	.50
182 Michael Garrett, Bat Handler U	.20	.50
183 Mistress Naila Flameburst C	.10	.20
184 Mortok C	.10	.20
185 Munkin Blackfist C	.10	.20
186 Nok'tal the Savage C	.10	.20
187 Orion C	.10	.20
188 Quakelord Razek Warhoof R	2.00	4.00
189 Rensarth Shadowsun C	.10	.20
190 Roktar Blackfist C	.10	.20
191 Rula Blackfist C	.10	.20
192 Sanva C	.10	.20
193 Sarn Earthtrembler C	.10	.20
194 Sepirion U	.20	.50
195 Skumm Bag'go C	.10	.20
196 Sorga the Swift C	.10	.20
197 Tormentor Emek C	.10	.20
198 Zari'zari C	.10	.20
199 Zi'mo C	.10	.20
200 Dagg'um Ty'gor U	.20	.50
201 The Red Bearon R	1.00	2.00
202 Vixton Pinchwhistle E	3.00	6.00
203 Amani Mask of Death R	.50	1.00
204 Blue Suede Shoes U	.20	.50
205 Boots of the Resilient U	.20	.50
206 Cloak of Subjugated Power R	.50	1.00
207 Forest Stalker's Bracers U	.20	.50
208 Girdle of the Blasted Reaches U	.20	.50
209 Gladiator's Regalia E	4.00	7.00
210 Masquerade Gown R	.50	1.00
211 Merciless Gladiator's Battlegear E	3.00	6.00
212 Mok'Nathal Wildercloak U	.20	.50
213 Nyn'jah's Tabi Boots R	.50	1.00
214 Scaled Breastplate of Carnage R	.50	1.00
215 Vengeful Gladiator's Vestments E	4.00	8.00
216 Arcanite Dragonling U	.20	.50
217 Rune of Metamorphosis U	.20	.50
218 Veteran's Pendant R	.50	1.00
219 Medallion of the Alliance U	.20	.50
220 Medallion of the Horde U	.20	.50
221 Black Amnesty R	2.00	4.00
222 Bloodseeker R	.50	1.00
223 Blue Diamond Witchwand U	.20	.50
224 Cold Forged Hammer R	.50	1.00
225 Continuum Blade R	.50	1.00
226 Frostguard U	.20	.50
227 Gladiator's Spellblade R	.50	1.00
228 Ice Barbed Spear R	.50	1.00
229 Light's Justice U	.20	.50
230 Lohn'goron, Bow of the Torn-heart U	.20	.50
231 Merciless Gladiator's Greatsword R	.50	1.00
232 Netherbane U	.20	.50
233 The Oathkeeper E	3.00	6.00
234 The Staff of Twin Worlds E	4.00	8.00
235 Vengeful Gladiator's Bonecracker R	.50	1.00
236 Wand of Biting Cold U	.20	.50
237 Electrified Dagger U	.20	.50
238 Glacial Blade U	.20	.50
239 Establishing New Outposts C	.10	.20
240 In Defense of Halaa C	.10	.20
241 Order Must Be Restored C	.10	.20
242 Bolstering Our Defenses C	.10	.20
243 Enemies, Old and New C	.10	.20
244 The Final Message to the Wildhammer C	.10	.20
245 Arena Master C	.10	.20
246 Corruption of Earth and Seed C	.10	.20
247 The Last Barov C	.10	.20
248 Oshu'gun Crystal Powder C	.10	.20
249 Outland Sucks C	.10	.20
250 A Rare Bean C	.10	.20
251 Revenge is Tasty C	.10	.20
252 Scouring the Desert C	.10	.20
253 Someone Else's Hard Work Pays Off R	.50	1.00
254 Soup for the Soul C	.10	.20
255 Spirits of Auchindoun C	.10	.20
256 Super Hot Stew C	.10	.20
257 Darnassus R	.50	1.00
258 Southshore U	.20	.50
259 Stormwind City R	3.00	6.00
260 Sen'jin Village R	.50	1.00
261 Tarren Mill U	.20	.50
262 Thunder Bluff R	.50	1.00
263 Auchindoun Spirit Towers U	.20	.50
264 Halaa U	.20	.50
265 Hellfire Citadel C	.10	.20
266 Silithus R	.50	1.00
267 Towers of Eastern Plaguelands C	.10	.20
268 Twin Spire Ruins C	.10	.20

2008 World of Warcraft Drums of War Loot

1 Slashdance	2.00	4.00
2 Owned	30.00	60.00
3 The Red Bearon	100.00	200.00

2008 World of Warcraft Hunt for Illidan

COMPLETE SET (252) 120.00 200.00
BOOSTER BOX (24 PACKS) 50.00 100.00
BOOSTER PACK (19 CARDS) 3.00 4.00
RELEASED IN JULY 2008
1 Black Ice Fizzlefreeze U .20 .50
2 Blaine Roberts U .20 .50
3 Durga Gravestone U .20 .50
4 Elumeria Wildershot U .20 .50
5 Eriun Moonglow U .20 .50
6 Kamboozle, Bringer of Doom U .20 .50
7 Marta Spires U .20 .50
8 Vakeron U .20 .50
9 Zaritha U .20 .50
10 Grindel Hellbringer U .20 .50
11 Joren the Martyr U .20 .50
12 Koth, Caller of the Hunt U .20 .50
13 Phosphus the Everburning U .20 .50
14 Ravenna U .20 .50
15 Ringleader Kuma U .20 .50
16 Tahanu Brinkrunner U .10 .20
17 Valterus U .20 .50
18 Warmaster Bo'jo U .20 .50
19 Kurzon the False U .20 .50
20 Famish the Binder U .20 .50
21 Imp Lord Pinprik U .20 .50
22 Mother Misery U .20 .50
23 Obliveron U .20 .50
24 Xia, Queen of Suffering U .20 .50
25 Brace or Mace U .20 .50
26 Energize C .10 .20
27 Feral Energy R .50 1.00
28 Ferociousness C .10 .20
29 Furor R .50 1.00
30 Insect Swarm R 2.00 5.00
31 Rebirth U .20 .50
32 Rotten to the Spore R .50 1.00
33 Stormfire C .10 .20
34 Typhoon U .20 .50
35 Bait the Trap U .20 .50
36 The Beast Within R .10 .20
37 Ice Trap C .10 .20
38 Patient Shot C .10 .20
39 Shadow C .10 .20
40 Stable Master U .20 .50
41 Trueshot Aura R 2.00 4.00
42 Viper Sting R .50 1.00
43 Webster R .50 1.00
44 Wipe or Snipe U .20 .50
45 Arcane Research C .10 .20
46 Astral Grief C .10 .20
47 Blast Wave R 5.00 10.00
48 Brain Lock C .10 .20
49 Flickers from the Past R .50 1.00
50 Mage Armor U .20 .50
51 The More, the Scarier R .50 1.00
52 Smoke or Croak U .20 .50
53 Supernova U .20 .50
54 Water Elemental R 7.00 15.00
55 Blessing of Salvation U .20 5.00
56 Blessing of Sanctuary R 1.50 3.00
57 Crusader's Sweep C .10 .20
58 Divine Plea R .50 1.00
59 Exemplar's Shield U .20 .50
60 Full Circle R .50 1.00
61 Holy Shock R 5.00 10.00
62 Righteousness Aura C .10 .20
63 Seal of Retribution C .10 .20
64 Shield or Wield U .20 .50
65 Circle of Healing R .50 1.00
66 Divine Spirit R 2.00 5.00
67 Equal Opportunity C .10 .20
68 Faces from the Past R 1.00 2.00
69 Lesser Heal C .10 .20
70 Levitate C .10 .20
71 Mana Burst U .20 .50
72 Mindflip R 1.50 3.00
73 Shadow Word: Agony U .20 .50
74 Woe or Grow U .20 .50
75 Dirty Work R 1.00 2.00
76 Disassemble C .10 .20
77 Feint C .10 .20
78 Fight or Blight U .20 .50
79 Knock Out U .20 .50
80 Massacre U .20 .50
81 Overkill R .50 1.00
82 Sap C .10 .20
83 Shadowstep R .50 1.00
84 Vigor R 2.00 4.00
85 Crackling Purge U .20 5.00
86 Exemplar's Blades U .20 .50
87 Far Sight C .10 .20
88 Gifts from the Past R .50 1.00
89 Lightning Arc C .10 .20
90 Magma Totem C .10 .20
91 Mend or End U .20 .50
92 Raise from the Ashes R .50 1.00
93 Spirit Weapons R .50 1.00
94 Totemic Mastery R .50 1.00
95 Aftermath R .50 1.00
96 Clinging Curse C .10 .20
97 Crush Soul C .10 .20
98 Curse of Exhaustion R .50 1.00
99 Demon Armor U .20 .50
100 Enslave Demon U .20 .50
101 Rain or Pain U .20 .50
102 Sarlia R .50 1.00
103 Velnoth C .10 .20
104 Vicious Circle R 1.50 3.00
105 Disarm C .10 .20
106 Duty Bound U .20 .50
107 Finishing Shout U .20 .50
108 Infuriate R .50 1.00
109 Pummel R 2.00 5.00
110 Slay or Stay U .20 .50
111 Sweeping Strikes R .20 .50
112 Taste for Blood C .10 .20
113 Taunting Blows C .10 .20
114 Vitality R .50 1.00
115 Disco Inferno R 1.00 2.00
116 The Footsteps of Illidan U .10 .20
117 Acolyte Kemistra U .20 .50
118 Alamira Grovetender C .10 .20
119 Bimble Blackout U .20 .50
120 Brodien U .20 .50
121 Dashel Stonefist U .20 .50
122 Defender Nagalaas C .10 .20
123 Elaar R .50 1.00
124 First Responder Avaressa C .10 .20
125 First Responder Margan C .10 .20
126 Harnum Firebelly C .10 .20
127 High Inspector Campbell R 1.50 3.00
128 Kathia the Quick C .10 .20
129 Kindara Mindflayer C .10 .20
130 Kurdran Wildhammer E 1.50 3.00
131 Liandra Rustshadow C .10 .20
132 Lord Cindervein C .10 .20
133 Luumon C .10 .20
134 Madison Alters U .20 .50
135 Master Marksman McGee R .50 1.00
136 Ol' Stonewall C .10 .20
137 Raena the Unpredictable C .10 .20
138 Ripley Spellfizzle C .10 .20
139 Scrapper Ironbane C .10 .20
140 Spirit of Stormrage E 3.00 6.00
141 Talian Bladebender C .10 .20
142 Wildwatcher Elandra C .10 .20
143 Wimbly Tinkerton U .20 .50
144 Zorus the Judicator R .50 1.00
145 Alecia Hall C .10 .20
146 Blood Guard Gulmok E 1.50 3.00
147 Blood Knight Kyria C .10 .20
148 Brok Bloodcaller U .20 .50
149 Chief Apothecary Hildagard E 2.00 4.00
150 Dawn Ravensdale C .10 .20
151 Deathgrip Jones C .10 .20
152 Elder Huntsman Swiftshot R .50 1.00
153 Eyeball Jones U .20 .50
154 Flame Bender Ta'jin U .20 .50
155 Forager Cloudbloom U .20 .50
156 Forager Hoofbeat C .10 .20
157 Illia the Bitter C .10 .20
158 Kaelos Sunscream C .10 .20
159 Kam'pah C .10 .20
160 Lu'ka de Wall C .10 .20
161 Natasha Hutchins C .10 .20
162 Offender Gora U .20 .50
163 Overlord Or'barokh R .50 1.00
164 The Painsaw C 1.50 3.00
165 Ra'waza Stonetusk C .10 .20
166 Roger Mortis C .10 .20
167 Roon Plainswalker C .10 .20
168 Skronk Skullseeker C .10 .20
169 The Soul Conductor R .10 .20
170 Tusk U .20 .50
171 Xela the Tormentor R .50 1.00
172 Ya'za the Vandal C .10 .20
173 Anchorite Ceyla R .50 1.00
174 Anchorite Kilandra C .10 .20
175 Exarch Onaala E 4.00 8.00
176 Instructor Giralo C .10 .20
177 Thief Catcher Norun C .10 .20
178 Vindicator Aluumen R .50 1.00
179 Vindicator Falaan R .50 1.00
180 Vindicator Javlo C .10 .20
181 Vindicator Kentho U .20 .50
182 Vindicator Lorin U .20 .50
183 Vindicator Vasha U .20 .50
184 Arcanist Bartis C .10 .20
185 Arcanist Renaan C .10 .20
186 Arcanist Thelis R .50 1.00
187 Battlemage Vyara R .50 1.00
188 Historian Firana C .10 .20
189 Magistrix Valthin U .20 .50
190 Retainer Alashon R .50 1.00
191 Retainer Faryn U .20 .50
192 Retainer Kai C .10 .20
193 Retainer Marcus U .10 .20
194 Varen the Reclaimer E 1.50 3.00
195 Akama E 5.00 10.00
196 Ambassador Jerrikar R .50 1.00
197 Azaloth E 5.00 10.00
198 Collidus the Warp-Watcher E 3.00 6.00
199 Doomwalker E 3.00 6.00
200 Edward the Odd E 2.00 4.00
201 Ethereal Plunderer R 1.00 2.00
202 Maiev Shadowsong E 6.00 12.00
203 Xi'ri E 3.00 6.00
204 Akama's Sash R .50 1.00
205 Ar'tor's Mainstay R .50 1.00
206 Borak's Belt of Bravery U .20 .50
207 Coif of the Wicked R .50 1.00
208 Doomplate Shoulderguards U .20 .50
209 Gloves of the High Magus E 5.00 10.00
210 Greaves of Desolation R .50 1.00
211 The Hands of Fate R .20 .50
212 Hauberk of Karabor R .50 1.00
213 Mana-Etched Spaulders U .20 .50
214 Naaru Belt of Precision R .50 1.00
215 Netherwing Protector's Shield U .20 .50
216 Pauldrons of Desolation R .50 1.00
217 Wastewalker Shoulderpads U .20 .50
218 Band of the Inevitable R 3.00 6.00
219 Lightwarden's Band R 2.00 4.00
220 Medallion of the Lightbearer U .20 .50
221 Scryer's Bloodgem U .20 .50
222 Seer's Signet R .50 1.00
223 Ashtongue Blade U .20 .50
224 Bloodwarder's Rifle R .50 1.00
225 Felstel Whisper Knives R 1.50 3.00
226 Hammer of the Naaru E 6.00 12.00
227 Illidari-Bane Mageblade U .20 .50
228 Lucky Strike Axe R .50 1.00
229 Staff of the Ashtongue Deathsworn R .50 1.00
230 Tirisfal Wand of Ascendancy U .20 .50
231 Vindicator's Brand R 2.00 4.00
232 Retainer's Blade R 4.00 8.00
233 Return to the Aldor C .10 .20
234 Return to the Scryers C .10 .20
235 Against the Illidari C .10 .20
236 Akama's Promise C .10 .20
237 Bane of the Illidari C .10 .20
238 Battle of the Crimson Watch C .10 .20
239 The Cipher of Damnation C .50 1.00
240 The Deathforge U .10 .20
241 The Fel and the Furious C .20 .50
242 I Was a Lot of Things C .10 .20
243 The Lexicon Demonica R .50 1.00
244 Minions of the Shadow Council R 3.00 6.00
245 The Path of Conquest C .10 .20
246 Reclaiming Holy Grounds U .20 .50
247 The Secret Compromised C .10 .20
248 Skywing R .50 1.00
249 The Summoning Chamber U .50 1.00
250 Tabards of the Illidari C .50 1.00
251 Teron Gorefiend, I Am C .10 .20
252 What Illidan Wants, Illidan Gets U .20 .50

2008 World of Warcraft Hunt for Illidan Loot

1 The Footsteps of Illidan 3.00 6.00
2 Disco Inferno 30.00 60.00
3 Ethereal Plunderer 150.00 300.00

2008 World of Warcraft Servants of the Betrayer

COMPLETE SET (264) 100.00 150.00
BOOSTER BOX (24 PACKS) 40.00 80.00
BOOSTER PACK (19 CARDS) 2.00 3.00
RELEASED IN APRIL 2008
1 Commander Michael Goodchilde U .20 .50
2 Fallingstar U .20 .50
3 Ixamos the Redeemed U .20 .50
4 Marlowe Christophers U .20 .50
5 Mythen of the Wild U .20 .50
6 Obora the Wise U .20 .50
7 Ressa Shadeshine U .20 .50
8 Sharpshooter Nally U .20 .50
9 Sister Remba U .20 .50
10 Crusader Michael Goodchilde U .20 .50
11 Fallenstar U .20 .50
12 Ixamos the Corrupted U .20 .50
13 Marlowe the Felsworn U .20 .50
14 Mythen of the Fang U .20 .50
15 Obora the Mad U .20 .50
16 Ressa the Leper Queen U .20 .50
17 Seadog Nally U .20 .50
18 Remba, Abbess of Ash U .20 .50
19 Jonas White U .20 .50
20 Kil'zin of the Darkspear U .20 .50
21 Lelora Sunlancer U .20 .50
22 Lionar, Unbound U .20 .50
23 Morn Walks-the-Path U .20 .50
24 Plague Fleshbane U .20 .50
25 Runetusk U .20 .50
26 Vor'na the Disciplined U .20 .50
27 Warden Stormclaw U .20 .50
28 Jonas the Red U .20 .50
29 Kil'zin of the Bloodscalp U .20 .50
30 Lelora the Dawnslayer U .20 .50
31 Lionar the Blood Cursed U .20 .50
32 Morn Salts-the-Land U .20 .50
33 Plague Demonsoul U .20 .50
34 Bloodtusk U .20 .50
35 Vor'na the Wretched U .20 .50
36 Desecrator Stormclaw U .20 .50
37 Chew Toy U .20 .50
38 Earth Mother's Blessing C .10 .20
39 Form of the Serpent R 5.00 10.00
40 Gift of Nature R .50 1.00
41 King of the Jungle R .50 1.00
42 Lacerate C .10 .20
43 The Natural Order C .10 .20
44 Savage Fury R .50 1.00
45 Tainted Earth U .20 .50
46 Tranquility U .20 .50
47 Bogspike C .10 .20
48 Death Trap R .50 1.00
49 Feeding Frenzy U .20 .50
50 Feign Death R 3.00 6.00
51 King Khan U .20 .50
52 Rain of Arrows C .10 .20
53 Ranged Weapon Specialization R 1.50 3.00
54 Run to Ground C .10 .20
55 Snake Trap U .20 .50
56 Survival Instincts R 1.00 2.00
57 Arcane Focus R .50 1.00
58 Blaze C .10 .20
59 Frost Armor U .20 .50
60 Frostbite R .50 1.00
61 Invisibility U .20 .50
62 Invocation R 1.00 2.00
63 Living Pyre C .10 .20
64 Metalmorph C .10 .20
65 Murderous Torment U .20 .50
66 Tomb of Ice R .50 1.00
67 Aura of Fanaticism U .20 .50
68 Avenging Wrath U .20 .50
69 Blessed Life R 1.00 2.00
70 Blessing of the Martyr C .10 .20
71 Crusade R .50 1.00
72 Divine Riposte U .20 .50
73 Flash of Light C .10 .20
74 Seal of Betrayal R 1.50 3.00
75 Seal of Redemption C .10 .20
76 Wrath of Turalyon R .50 1.00
77 Castigate U .20 .50
78 Darkness R .50 1.00
79 Eclipse U .20 .50
80 Enlightenment R .50 1.00
81 Fade U .20 .50
82 Melt Face C .10 .20
83 Prayer of Mending C .10 .20
84 Salvation C .10 .20
85 Shadow Silhouettes R .50 1.00
86 Spiritual Domination R 1.50 3.00
87 Blade Twisting R .50 1.00
88 Cloak of Shadows C .10 .20
89 Cut to the Chase U .20 .50
90 Diversion C .10 .20
91 Evasion R .50 1.00
92 Find Weakness R .50 1.00
93 Gut Shot R .50 1.00
94 Pilfer U .20 .50
95 Sacrificial Poison U .20 .50
96 Unbalance C .10 .20
97 Death Shock U .20 .50
98 Elemental Precision R .50 1.00
99 Life Cycle C .10 .20
100 Maelstrom Weapon C .10 .20
101 Shamanistic Dual Wield R 1.00 2.00
102 Stoneskin Totem U .20 .50
103 Storm Shock C .10 .20
104 Totemic Recovery R .50 1.00
105 Totem of Decay R .50 1.00
106 Water Shield U .20 .50
107 Apocanon U .20 .50
108 Banish to the Nether C .10 .20
109 Curse of Frenzy U .20 .50
110 Demonic Knowledge R .50 1.00
111 Dread Infernal R 2.00 4.00
112 Fel Fire C .10 .20
113 Gobloz C .10 .20
114 Ripped through the Portal R 4.00 8.00
115 Ritual of Souls U .20 .50
116 Shadow and Flame R .50 1.00
117 Armed to the Teeth C .10 .20
118 Bloodbath R .50 1.00
119 Champion Stance C .10 .20
120 Deafening Shout R .50 1.00
121 Shield Slam R .50 1.00
122 Smash C .20 .50
123 Sudden Death U .20 .50
124 Titan's Grip U .20 .50
125 Unbridled Wrath R .50 1.00
126 Whirlwind U .20 .50
127 Papa Hummel's .20 .50
Old-Fashioned Pet Biscuit U
128 Personal Weather Maker R .50 1.00
129 Angelista C .10 .20
130 Antikron the Unyielding U .20 .50
131 Barous the Storm Baron R 1.00 2.00
132 Bearlady Brala R .50 1.00
133 Breen Toestubber C .10 .20
134 Domona the Ever-Watchful U .20 .50
135 Falana of the Glen C .10 .20
136 Highlord Bolvar Fordragon E 2.50 5.00
137 Horace Shadowfall R .50 1.00
138 Inventor Dorbin Callus E 2.50 5.00
139 Jezbella of Karabor C .10 .20
140 Justicar Brace U .20 .50
141 Kronore R .50 1.00
142 Llyras Keeneye C .10 .20
143 Lunen the Moon Baron R .50 1.00
144 Miner Steelwhiskers C .10 .20
145 Myriam Starcaller C .10 .20
146 Narthadus C .10 .20
147 Orderkeeper Calister C .10 .20
148 Orderkeeper Henley C .10 .20
149 Orderkeeper Vesra U .20 .50
150 Quigley Slipshade C .10 .20
151 Rames the Purifier C .10 .20
152 Razak Ironsides E 4.00 8.00
153 Roke the Ice Baron R .50 1.00
154 Rysa the Earthcaller C .10 .20
155 Sampron the Banisher R .50 1.00
156 Stella Forgebane C .10 .20
157 Aesadonna Al'mere R .50 1.00
158 Alchemist Norrin'thal C .10 .20
159 Cerrik Blooddawn C .10 .20
160 David Smythe C .10 .20
161 Delrach the Vile C .10 .20
162 Gok Stormhammer R .50 1.00
163 Hulok Trailblazer C .10 .20
164 Icemistress Gal'ha R .50 1.00
165 Jae'va the Relentless C .10 .20
166 Jessup Smythe C .10 .20
167 Leoroxx E 3.00 6.00
168 Lifemistress Tanagra R .50 1.00
169 Lilith Smythe C .10 .20
170 Matalo Trailfinder U .20 .50
171 Mojo Doctor Zin'tar U .20 .50
172 Ras'fari Bloodfrenzy U .20 .50
173 Roena Trailmaker C .10 .20
174 Rogg Dreadnock U .20 .50
175 Saurfang the Younger E 1.50 3.00
176 Scholar Krosiss C .10 .20
177 Sek Grimlash R .50 1.00
178 Sha'kar C .50 1.00
179 Skymistress Taranna R .50 1.00
180 Tarn Darkwalker C .10 .20
181 Tatulla the Reclaimer C .10 .20
182 Ulrac Bloodshadow R .50 1.00
183 Vexmaster Nar'jo C .10 .20
184 Anchorite Fareena U .20 .50
185 Anchorite Karja E 1.00 2.00
186 Anchorite Onkoth U .20 .50
187 Alani of the Watch C .15 .20
188 Bulvai of the Watch C .10 .20
189 Exarch Orelis E 2.00 4.00
190 Marksman Eowan U .20 .50
191 Marksman Glous R 12.00 20.00
192 Niyore of the Watch R 2.50 5.00
193 Vindicator Agran C .10 .20
194 Vindicator Ostakron C .10 .20
195 Xanata the Lightsworn U .20 .50
196 Arcanist Alathana U .20 .50
197 Arcanist Atikan R .50 1.00
198 Arcanist Dayvana U .20 .50
199 Arcanist Lyronia C .10 .20
200 Magistrix Dianas C .10 .20
201 Magistrix Larynna E 2.50 5.00
202 Retainer Athan U .20 .50
203 Retainer Cara C .10 .20
204 Retainer Eteron R .50 1.00
205 Retainer Ryn U .20 .50
206 Retainer Zian C .10 .20
207 Spymaster Thalodien E 3.00 6.00
208 Coilfang Myrmidon C .10 .20
209 Lady Katrana Prestor E 2.00 4.00
210 Lady Vashj E 5.00 10.00
211 Millhouse Manastorm E 1.50 3.00
212 Pathaleon the Calculator R .50 1.00
213 Prince Kael'thas Sunstrider E 6.00 12.00
214 Sunseeker Astromage C .10 .20
215 Warlord Kalithresh R .50 1.00
216 X-51 Nether-Rocket R .50 1.00
217 Arcanium Signet Bands U .20 .50
218 Armwraps of Disdain U .20 .50
219 Azure-Shield of Coldarra R .50 1.00
220 Barbaric Legstraps U .20 .50
221 Doomplate Warhelm U .20 .50
222 Fanblade Pauldrons U .20 .50
223 Helm of Desolation U .20 .50
224 Legguards of the Shattered Hand R .50 1.00
225 Mana-Etched Crown R .50 1.00
226 Mana-Sphere Shoulderguards R .50 1.00
227 Wastewalker Helm U .20 .50
228 Wastewalker Leggings R 1.50 3.00
229 Choker of Vile Intent R .50 1.00
230 Hourglass of the Unraveller R .50 1.00
231 Quagmirran's Eye R 1.50 3.00
232 Ring of the Shadow Deeps U .20 .50
233 Ring of the Silver Hand R .50 1.00
234 Blade of Wizardry E 5.00 10.00
235 Bloodskull Destroyer U .20 .40
236 Essence Gatherer U .20 .50
237 Plasma Rat's Hyper-Scythe U .20 .50
238 Quantum Blade E 2.50 5.00
239 Reflex Blades U .20 .50
240 Terokk's Shadowstaff R 1.00 2.00
241 Vileblade of the Betrayer R .50 1.00
242 Voidfire Wand R 6.00 12.00
243 Wand of the Seer R .50 1.00
244 Wrathtide Longbow U .20 .50
245 Marks of Kil'jaeden C .10 .20
246 Sunfury Briefings C .10 .20
247 Firewing Signets C .10 .20
248 Manaforge B'naar C .50 1.00
249 Deep Sea Salvage C .10 .20
250 Dr. Boom C .10 .20
251 An Improper Burial C .10 .20
252 Information Gathering C .10 .20
253 Kim'jael Indeed U .20 .50
254 Leader of the Darkcrest C .10 .20
255 Meeting with the Master C .10 .20
256 Needs More Cowbell R 1.00 2.00
257 Orders From Lady Vashj C .10 .20
258 Potential Energy Source U .20 .50
259 Preparing for War C .10 .20
260 Shutting Down Manaforge Ara C .10 .20
261 The Sigil of Krasus C .10 .20
262 The Unending Invasion C .10 .20
263 A Warm Welcome R 1.00 2.00
264 You, Robot U .20 .50

2008 World of Warcraft Servants of the Betrayer Loot

1 Papa Hummel's Old-Fashioned Pet Biscuit 5.00 10.00
2 Personal Weather Maker 50.00 100.00
3 X-51 Nether-Rocket 250.00 350.00

2009 World of Warcraft Blood of Gladiators

COMPLETE SET (208) 50.00 100.00
BOOSTER BOX (24 PACKS) 30.00 60.00
BOOSTER PACK (19 CARDS) 1.50 3.00
RELEASED IN MARCH 2009
1 Bronson Greatwhisker U .20 .50
2 Chloe Mithrilbolt U .20 .50
3 Feera Quickshot U .20 .50
4 Gwon Strongbark U .20 .50
5 Gyro of the Ring U .20 .50
6 Kalatine Carmichael U .20 .50
7 Kristoff Manchester U .20 .50
8 Nicholas Merrick U .20 .50
9 Statia the Preserver U .20 .50
10 Andarius the Damned U .20 .50
11 Bonewall Simms U .20 .50
12 Brahu Starsear U .20 .50
13 Cerripha Sunstreak U .20 .50
14 Savitir Skullsmasher U .20 .50
15 Sharpeye Yan'ja U .20 .50
16 Thoros the Savior U .20 .50
17 Tribemother Torra U .20 .50
18 Witch Doctor Koo'zar U .20 .50
19 Friends in High Places C .10 .20
20 Nature's Reach R .60 1.50
21 Reforestation U .20 .50
22 The Sowing of Seeds U .20 .50
23 Starshot C .10 .20
24 Tiger's Fury R .40 1.00
25 Utopia R .40 1.00
26 The Aim of Eagles U .20 .50
27 Bolton U .20 .50
28 Clutch Shot C .10 .20
29 Improvised Weaponry R .40 1.00
30 Quickdraw C .10 .20

31 Scatter Shot R .60 1.50
32 Volley R .60 1.50
33 Blizzard R .40 1.00
34 Combustion R .40 1.00
35 Heartburn C .10 .20
36 Mana Ruby R .40 1.00
37 Meltdown U .20 .50
38 Sear C .10 .20
39 The Taste of Arcana U .20 .50
40 Atonement C .10 .20
41 Divine Favor R .60 1.50
42 Divine Justice C .10 .20
43 Glimmer of Hope U .20 .50
44 Reckoning of the Light R .60 1.50
45 The Rewards of Faith U .20 .50
46 Sacred Moment R .60 1.50
47 Darkest Before the Light R .40 1.00
48 Disperse Magic C .10 .20
49 Focused Will R .40 1.00
50 Horrify C .10 .20
51 The Omens of Terror U .20 .50
52 Power Word: Restore U .20 .50
53 Splinter Mind R .40 1.00
54 Deadliness R .40 1.00
55 The Depth of Shadows U .20 .50
56 Intuition C .10 .20
57 Slash and Dash C .10 .20
58 Stab in the Dark U .20 .50
59 Surgical Strikes R .40 1.00
60 Yoink! R .60 1.50
61 The Crash of Tides U .20 .50
62 Echo Totem R .40 1.00
63 Fork Lightning C .10 .20
64 Greater Chain Heal U .20 .50
65 Strength of Earth Totem C .10 .20
66 Tidal Mastery R .60 1.50
67 Tremor Shock R 1.25 3.00
68 Curse of Endless Suffering C .10 .20
69 Curse of Midnight U .20 .50
70 Dark Justice C .10 .20
71 Grim Reach R .75 2.00
72 Kreedom R .60 1.50
73 The Promises of Darkness U .20 .50
74 Ritual of Summoning R .40 1.00
75 The Benefits of Practice U .20 .50
76 Cowering Shout C .10 .20
77 Defiance R .40 1.00
78 A Final Sacrifice C .10 .20
79 A Flawless Advance R .40 1.00
80 Pulverize U .20 .50
81 Shield Wall R .60 1.50
82 Blessing of the Heavens C .10 .20
83 Burly Bellow C .10 .20
84 Disappear C .10 .20
85 Double Time C .10 .20
86 Optimize C .10 .20
87 Phase Hound C .10 .20
88 Poof! C .10 .20
89 Recall from the Brink C .10 .20
90 Victimize C .10 .20
91 Center of Attention R .40 1.00
92 Foam Sword Rack R .40 1.00
93 Anduin Wrynn E 1.25 3.00
94 Chillhands Spigotgulp U .20 .50
95 Cracklehands Spigotgulp C .10 .20
96 Elder Achillia C .10 .20
97 Elder Tomas C .10 .20
98 Elder Valdar of the Exodar C .10 .20
99 Elder Zeez C .10 .20
100 Gladiator Katianna C .10 .20
101 Gladiator Keward C .10 .20
102 Gladiator Kinivus C .10 .20
103 Gladiator Lanthus C .10 .20
104 Gladiator Loraala C .10 .20
105 Gladiator Magnus C .10 .20
106 Gladiator Meganna C .10 .20
107 Gladiator Ryno C .10 .20
108 Gladiator Zophos C .10 .20
109 Huntress Xenia C .10 .20
110 Kristina Soulcinder C .10 .20
111 Kurdoc Greybeard U .20 .50
112 Mikael the Blunt U .20 .50
113 Miranda McMiserson R .40 1.00
114 Ossus the Ancient R 1.50 4.00
115 Pappy Ironbane U .20 .50
116 Quickhands Spigotgulp C .10 .20
117 Trakas C .10 .20
118 Tyrus Lionheart C .10 .20
119 Wynnd the Spry C .10 .20
120 Aknot Whetstone C .10 .20
121 Canissa the Shadow C .10 .20
122 Edward Hack Robinson C .10 .20
123 Furious Kalla U .20 .50
124 Gladiator Addisyn C .10 .20
125 Gladiator Boum C .10 .20
126 Gladiator Dorn C .10 .20
127 Gladiator Emek C .10 .20
128 Gladiator Kaniya C .10 .20
129 Gladiator Kileana C .10 .20
130 Gladiator Sepirion C .10 .20
131 Gladiator Skumm C .10 .20
132 Gladiator Zi'mo C .10 .20
133 Grismare U .20 .50
134 Hex Doctor No'jin C .10 .20
135 Karina of Silvermoon C .10 .20
136 Karta Foultongue C .10 .20
137 Kazamon Steelskin R 5.00 10.00
138 Kino the Cold C .10 .20
139 Melissa Gerrard C .10 .20
140 Naliss the Silencer R .60 1.50
141 Nea Sunmark C .10 .20
142 Rorga Trueshot C .10 .20
143 Thomas Slash Robinson C .10 .20
144 Tor'gor Darkfire U .20 .50
145 Vol'jin E .75 2.00
146 Voltrinnia U .20 .50
147 Broll Bearmantle E .75 2.00
148 Lo'Gosh E 1.00 2.50
149 Rehgar Earthfury E 5.00 10.00
150 Valeera Sanguinar E 1.00 2.50
151 Krixel Pinchwhistle R .40 1.00
152 Mogor R .60 1.50
153 Sandbox Tiger U .20 .50
154 Short John Mithril R .60 1.50
155 Skarr the Unbreakable R .40 1.00
156 Amice of Brilliant Light U .20 .50
157 Antonidas's Aegis of Rapt Concentration R 2.00 5.00
158 Bloodsea Brigand's Vest U .20 .50
159 Cloak of the Shrouded Mists R .40 1.00
160 Cowl of the Guiltless U .20 .50
161 Cuffs of Devastation U .20 .50
162 Fists of Mukoa U .20 .50
163 Gladiator's Aegis E .75 2.00
164 Merciless Gladiator's Pursuit E .75 2.00
165 Quickstrider Moccasins R .40 1.00
166 Slayer's Waistguard U .20 .50
167 Vengeful Gladiator's Felshroud E 2.50 6.00
168 Band of Vile Aggression R .40 1.00
169 The Seal of Danzalar R .60 1.50
170 Talisman of the Alliance U .20 .50
171 Talisman of the Horde U .20 .50
172 Battle Mage's Baton R .60 1.50
173 Boggspine Knuckles U .20 .50
174 Boundless Agony R .40 1.00
175 The Decapitator R .60 1.50
176 Emerald Ripper R .60 1.50
177 Gladiator's Salvation R .60 1.50
178 Gorehowl E 2.00 5.00
179 King's Defender U .20 .50
180 Merciless Gladiator's Crossbow of the Phoenix R.40 1.00
181 Mogor's Anointing Club R .40 1.00
182 Nethershard R .60 1.50
183 Seth's Graphite Fishing Pole R .40 1.00
184 Shuriken of Negation R 1.00 2.50
185 Tempest of Chaos R .60 1.50
186 Twinblade of the Phoenix R 2.00 5.00
187 Vengeful Gladiator's Piercing Touch R .40 1.00
188 Wand of the Forgotten Star U .20 .50
189 World Breaker R .60 1.50
190 Arena Grandmaster C .10 .20
191 The Challenge C .10 .20
192 Mark V Is Alive! R .40 1.00
193 A Question of Gluttony C .10 .20
194 The Ring of Blood: The Blue Brothers C .10 .20
195 The Ring of Blood: Brokentoe C .10 .20
196 The Ring of Blood: The Final Challenge C .10 .20
197 The Ring of Blood: Rokdar the Sundered Lord C.10 .20
198 The Ring of Blood: Skra'gath C .10 .20
199 The Ring of Blood: The Warmaul Champion C.10 .20
200 Uncatalogued Species C .10 .20
201 Gurubashi Arena U .20 .50
202 The Ring of Blood U .20 .50
203 The Circle of Blood C .10 .20
204 Ring of Trials C .10 .20
205 The Ruins of Lordaeron C .10 .20
206 The Exodar R .40 1.00
207 Orgrimmar R 5.00 10.00
208 Silvermoon City R 2.50 6.00

2009 World of Warcraft Blood of Gladiators Loot

1 Sandbox Tiger 2.00 5.00
2 Center of Attention 25.00 50.00
3 Foam Sword Rack 40.00 80.00

2009 World of Warcraft Fields of Honor

COMPLETE SET (208) 50.00 100.00
BOOSTER BOX (24 PACKS) 40.00 80.00
BOOSTER PACK (19 CARDS) 2.00 4.00
RELEASED IN JUNE 2009
1 Katianna the Shrouded U .20 .50
2 Keward the Ravager U .20 .50
3 Kinivus the Focused U .20 .50
4 Lanthus the Restorer U .20 .50
5 Loraala the Frigid U .20 .50
6 Magnus the Depriver U .20 .50
7 Meganna the Stalker U .20 .50
8 Ryno the Wicked U .20 .50
9 Zophos the Vengeful U .20 .50
10 Addisyn the Untouchable U .20 .50
11 Boum the Bloodseeker U .20 .50
12 Dorn the Tranquil U .20 .50
13 Emek the Equalizer U .20 .50
14 Kaniya the Steadfast U .20 .50
15 Kileana the Inferno U .20 .50
16 Sepirion the Poised U .20 .50
17 Skumm the Pillager U .20 .50
18 Zi'mo the Empowered U .20 .50
19 Celestial Shard U .20 .50
20 Convocation R .40 1.00
21 Grizzly Defender R .40 1.00
22 Omen of Clarity R .40 1.00
23 Pack Tactics U .20 .50
24 Regrowth C .10 .20
25 Tanglevine C .10 .20
26 Crusty C .10 .20
27 Dundee R .40 1.00
28 Explosive Trap U .20 .50
29 Intimidation R .40 1.00
30 Planned Assault R .40 1.00
31 Reload U .20 .50
32 Track Hidden C .10 .20
33 Brittilize C .10 .20
34 Everlasting Cold C .10 .20
35 Ice Barbs R .40 1.00
36 Icy Veins R .40 1.00
37 Nether Fissure U .20 .50
38 Roaring Blaze U .20 .50
39 Set Ablaze R .40 1.00
40 Blessed Defense C .10 .20
41 Blessing of Kings R .40 1.00
42 Concentration Aura U .20 .50
43 Convert U .20 .50
44 Holy Strike C .10 .20
45 Resolute Aura R .40 1.00
46 Uplifting Prayer R .40 1.00
47 Blind Faith R .40 1.00
48 Mist of Corrosion C .10 .20
49 Searing Light R .40 1.00
50 A Taste of Divinity R .40 1.00
51 Tithe U .20 .50
52 United Front C .10 .20
53 Vampiric Dominance U .20 .50
54 Burgle R .40 1.00
55 Carnage U .20 .50
56 Hidden Weaponry C .10 .20
57 Kidney Shot R .40 1.00
58 Lead Astray C .10 .20
59 Rupture U .20 .50
60 Ruthlessness R .40 1.00
61 Chain Purge U .20 .50
62 Earthen Flurry C .10 .20
63 Elemental Weapons R .40 1.00
64 Hatchet Totem R .40 1.00
65 Spark U .20 .50
66 Wavestorm Totem C .10 .20
67 Windfury Infusion R .40 1.00
68 Backlash R .40 1.00
69 Cremate C .10 .20
70 Curse of the Elements R .40 1.00
71 Curse of Weakness C .10 .20
72 Dominate U .20 .50
73 Hesriana E 5.00 10.00
74 Soulstone U .20 .50
75 Bleed C .10 .20
76 Blood Frenzy R .40 1.00
77 Collateral Damage U .20 .50
78 Keys to the Armory R .40 1.00
79 Overpower R .40 1.00
80 Reckless Abandon U .20 .50
81 Split Open C .10 .20
82 Arcane Warding C .10 .20
83 Celerity C .10 .20
84 Essence of Mending C .10 .20
85 Fortifying Shout C .10 .20
86 Frigid Winds C .10 .20
87 No Man's Land C .10 .20
88 Pin C .10 .20
89 Sacrificial Vengeance C .10 .20
90 Screeching Shot C .10 .20
91 Path of Cenarius U .20 .50
92 Adam Eternum R .40 1.00
93 Baelgond Soulgrace U .20 .50
94 Bladehands Spigotgulp C .10 .20
95 Corvus Promaethon C .10 .20
96 Darok Steelstrike C .10 .20
97 Dimzer the Prestidigitator R .40 1.00
98 Durgle Wizzledab C .10 .20
99 Endina the Hunted C .10 .20
100 Gromble the Apt U .20 .50
101 Grudum, Trove Guardian C .10 .20
102 Illiyana Moonblaze E .75 2.00
103 Iravar U .20 .50
104 Jonas Targan C .10 .20
105 Lairin the Grounded C .10 .20
106 Larrington Zarus R .40 1.00
107 Maeryl Leafstrike C .10 .20
108 Marundal the Kindred R .40 1.00
109 Mayla Finkspotter C .10 .20
110 Modric Sternbeard C .10 .20
111 Naan the Selfless C .10 .20
112 Noxel Shroudhaggle C .10 .20
113 Orlund C .10 .20
114 Quenlan Lifeboon C .10 .20
115 Royal Guardian Jameson R .40 1.00
116 Skaduzzle C .10 .20
117 Spelunker Maddocks R .40 1.00
118 Vanndar Stormpike E 2.00 5.00
119 Vurkeran C .10 .20
120 Zumbly Fiddlespark C .10 .20
121 Blood Knight Haeleth C .10 .20
122 Bloodwatcher Denissa C .10 .20
123 Charkov C .10 .20
124 Dannon Spellsurge C .10 .20
125 Dark Archon Farrum U .20 .50
126 Deathstalker Leanna C .10 .20
127 Dethvir The Malignant R .40 1.00
128 Drek'Thar E 1.50 4.00
129 Elder Narando C .10 .20
130 Grugthar Sharpblade C .10 .20
131 Iku'tak C .10 .20
132 Keldor the Lost R .40 1.00
133 Kelm Hargunth E 1.25 3.00
134 Mojo Masher Shakko C .10 .20
135 Mojo Masher Ven'dango C .10 .20
136 Morkad Sharptooth C .10 .20
137 Nathaniel Voran C .10 .20
138 Nazguk Sharptongue R .40 1.00
139 Plainsrunner Marun C .10 .20
140 Plainswatcher Taro R .40 1.00
141 Rakasa Mournewind C .10 .20
142 Samuel Harrison C .10 .20
143 Scout Kurgo C .10 .20
144 Sergeant Pugg U .20 .50
145 Siaranna the Fickle R .40 1.00
146 Sivandra Darklust C .10 .20
147 Windstriker Larun R .40 1.00
148 Yula the Fair U .20 .50
149 Zalan Ragewind C .10 .20
150 Backstab Bindo E 1.50 4.00
151 El Pollo Grande R .40 1.00
152 Treebole E 1.25 3.00
153 Berserker Bracers R .40 1.00
154 Bonefist Gauntlets U .20 .50
155 Bulwark of the Amani Empire R .40 1.00
156 Don Alejandro's Money Belt R .40 1.00
157 Dryad's Wrist Bindings U .20 .50
158 Gladiator's Sanctuary E 1.25 3.00
159 Grips of Damnation U .20 .50
160 Marksman's Legguards U .20 .50
161 Merciless Gladiator's Raiment E 1.50 4.00
162 Vengeful Gladiator's Earthshaker E 1.25 3.00
163 Veteran's Dreadweave Belt R .40 1.00
164 Windtalker's Wristguards R .40 1.00
165 Bangle of Endless R .40 1.00
166 Pinata R .40 1.00
167 Stormpike Insignia U .20 .50
168 Frostwolf Insignia U .20 .50
169 Apostle of Argus U .20 .50
170 Arcanite Steam-Pistol U .20 .50
171 Blackout Truncheon R .40 1.00
172 Firemaul of Destruction U .20 .50
173 Gladiator's Maul R .40 1.00
174 Heartless U .20 .50
175 Heartrazor U .20 .50
176 Hope Ender R .40 1.00
177 Jin'rohk, The Great Apocalypse E 7.50 15.00
178 Merciless Gladiator's Gavel R .40 1.00
179 Steelhawk Crossbow R .40 1.00
180 Vengeful Gladiator's Cleaver R .40 1.00
181 Wand of Prismatic Focus U .20 .50
182 Wub's Cursed Hexblade R .40 1.00
183 Crackling Staff U .20 .50
184 Hellforged Halberd R .40 1.00
185 Blackened Spear R .40 1.00
186 Whiteout Staff U .20 .50
187 Call to Arms: Alterac Valley C .10 .20
188 Call to Arms: Arathi Basin C .10 .20
189 Call to Arms: Eye of the Storm C .10 .20
190 Call to Arms: Warsong Gulch C .10 .20
191 Capture a Mine C .10 .20
192 Defusing the Threat C .10 .20
193 The Eye of Command C .10 .20
194 In Nightmares U .20 .50
195 Legendary Heroes C .10 .20
196 Proving Grounds C .10 .20
197 Rise and Be Recognized C .10 .20
198 Showdown R .40 1.00
199 Towers and Bunkers C .10 .20
200 Concerted Efforts C .10 .20
201 For Great Honor C .10 .20
202 Alterac Valley C .10 .20
203 Arathi Basin C .10 .20
204 Eye of the Storm C .10 .20
205 Warsong Gulch C .10 .20
206 Gnomeregan R .40 1.00
207 Ironforge R .40 1.00
208 Undercity R .40 1.00

2009 World of Warcraft Fields of Honor Loot

1 Path of Cenarius 2.50 6.00
2 Pinata 20.00 40.00
3 El Pollo Grande 150.00 250.00

2009 World of Warcraft Scourgewar

COMPLETE SET (270) 80.00 120.00
BOOSTER BOX (24 PACKS) 50.00 100.00
BOOSTER PACK (19 CARDS) 3.00 5.00
RELEASED IN NOVEMBER 2009
1 Auryna the Lightsworn U .20 .50
2 Bordrak Barrelblast U .20 .50
3 Erondra Frostmoon U .20 .50
4 Felbender Lara U .20 .50
5 Ivan, Bladewind Brute U .20 .50
6 Nylaith, Guardian of the Wild U .20 .50
7 Prometha U .20 .50
8 Riley Sizzleswitch U .20 .50
9 Rordag the Sly U .20 .50
10 Xerandaal, Shade Servitor U .20 .50
11 Blythe the Pyromaniac U .20 .50
12 Emerson Zantides U .20 .50
13 Kaerie, Defender of the Sunwell U .20 .50
14 Levander of the Sanguine Shot U .20 .50
15 Maloduri U .20 .50
16 Souldrinker Bogmara U .20 .50
17 Teina Cloudstalker U .20 .50
18 Triton the Sacrilegious U .20 .50
19 Zagrun Wolfeye U .20 .50
20 Zorak'tul U .20 .50
21 Kel'Thuzad E 5.00 10.00
22 Army of the Dead R 1.25 4.00
23 Corpse Explosion R 1.25 3.00
24 Death and Decay U .20 .50
25 Deathcharger R 1.25 3.00
26 Death Pact U .20 .50
27 Icy Torment C .10 .20
28 Obliterate C .10 .20
29 Suffocating Grip C .10 .20
30 Unholy Presence C .10 .20
31 Unholy Rune C .10 .20
32 Berserk R .40 1.00
33 Blessing of Cenarius C .10 .20
34 Call of the Grove U .20 .50
35 Feline Grace C .10 .20
36 Hurricane R 2.00 5.00
37 Natural Repossession U .20 .50
38 Nature's Focus C .10 .20
39 Nourish R .75 2.00
40 Ursoc's Fury C .10 .20
41 Bombard R .75 2.00
42 Buzz U .20 .50
43 Chimera Shot R .40 1.00
44 Conflagration Trap C .10 .20
45 Fang C .10 .20
46 Master's Call U .20 .50
47 Raptor Strike C .10 .20
48 Scorpid Sting C .10 .20
49 Spoils of the Hunt R .40 1.00
50 Arcane Burst C .10 .20
51 Arcane Tactics C .10 .20
52 Astral Denial U .20 .50
53 Freeze U .20 .50
54 Living Bomb R .40 1.00
55 Mana Sapphire R .60 1.50
56 Mirror Image R .40 1.00
57 Polymorph: Penguin C .10 .20
58 Smoldering Blast C .10 .20
59 Blessing of Liberty U .20 .50
60 Boon of Light C .10 .20
61 Divine Storm R .40 1.00
62 Hammer of the Divine R .60 1.50
63 Seal of Divinity R .40 1.00
64 Shadow Resistance Aura C .10 .20
65 Stifling Decree C .10 .20
66 Vengeance of the Light U .20 .50
67 Vindictive Strike C .10 .20
68 Dark Penance C .10 .20
69 Delusions of Grandeur C .10 .20
70 Devouring Plague R .60 1.50
71 Dispersion R .60 1.50
72 Gathering of Wits R .40 1.00
73 Power Word: Sanctuary U .20 .50
74 Power Word: Vigor C .10 .20
75 Prayer of Shadow Protection U .20 .50
76 Shadow Word: Chaos C .10 .20
77 Aggressive Infiltration C .10 .20
78 Belligerence U .20 .50
79 Dead Weight C .10 .20
80 Deadly Throw R .40 1.00
81 Disarm Trap C .10 .20
82 Enveloping Shadows R .40 1.00
83 Perforation Poison C .10 .20
84 Plunder R .40 1.00
85 Sinister Set-up C .10 .20
86 Feral Spirit R 2.00 5.00
87 Incendiary Totem U .20 .50
88 Mass Purge C .10 .20
89 Soothing Wave C .10 .20
90 Squall Totem R 2.50 6.00
91 Surge of Lightning C .10 .20
92 Tidal Infusion C .10 .20
93 Water Walking U .20 .50
94 Wind Shear R 1.25 3.00
95 Detonate Soul R .60 1.50
96 Dreadsteed R 1.25 3.00
97 Haunt R 1.25 3.00
98 Jek'kresh U .20 .50
99 Offering to the Nether C .10 .20
100 Rhuunom C .10 .20
101 Shadow Burst C .10 .20
102 Shadow Ward C .10 .20
103 Terrifying Visage C .10 .20
104 Death Wish R 1.00 2.50
105 Debilitating Shout U .20 .50
106 Gushing Wound C .10 .20
107 Human Shield C .10 .20
108 Provoke C .10 .20
109 Recklessness R .40 1.00
110 Reconstruct R .75 2.00
111 Ruination C .10 .20
112 Shield Block C .10 .20
113 Tuskarr Kite U .20 .50
114 Bloody Grip U .20 .50
115 Crippling Strike U .20 .50
116 Frost Burst U .20 .50
117 Galvanize U .20 .50
118 Putrefying Poison U .20 .50
119 Shadows of Death U .20 .50
120 Shield of Distortion U .20 .50
121 Staunch Reprisal U .20 .50
122 Word of Blight U .20 .50
123 Next Stop, Menethil Harbor! C .10 .20
124 All Aboard for Undercity! C .10 .20
125 Anarchist Bladewalker U .20 .50
126 Anduros Silversong C .10 .20
127 Archduke Franklin Pearce C .10 .20
128 Corruptor Mimi Whippleshade U .20 .50
129 Danyssa Stillheart C .10 .20
130 Earthshaper Javuun C .10 .20
131 Ferandus Duskfall C .10 .20
132 Field Commander Foggo C .10 .20
133 Flint Shadowmore E 3.00 8.00
134 Great Elekk R .60 1.50
135 Gregory Flamewaker C .10 .20
136 High Magus Euli C .10 .20
137 Horatio Plaguetouch C .10 .20
138 Hulstom, Servant of the Light C .10 .20
139 Justicar Andaer Ragepaw U .20 .50
140 Justicar Broxlo Frostnuggle U .20 .50
141 Justicar Gavin Shadesticker U .20 .50
142 Justicar Maxwell Forthright U .20 .50
143 Kaale C .10 .20
144 King Varian Wrynn E 2.50 6.00
145 Mardun Valorhearth C .10 .20
146 Mioma Shadowflint C .10 .20
147 Mooncaller Jynalla Nightpath U .20 .50
148 Myrodan Silversong C .10 .20
149 Nakistis, Exodar Armorer C .10 .20
150 Olaf Steelbreaker C .10 .20
151 Petreus Roffe C .10 .20
152 Plasu C .10 .20
153 Skaala of the Somber Watch C .10 .20
154 Soulseeker Huulo C .10 .20
155 Starfi C .10 .20
156 Swift Nightsaber R .40 1.00
157 Swift Ram R .40 1.00
158 Trixie Boltclunker C .10 .20
159 Varah, Fury of the Stars C .10 .20
160 Vesperia Silversong C .10 .20
161 Voidmaven Christie Noone U .20 .50
162 Zealot Kalinox R .40 1.00
163 Azamoth Deathfang C .10 .20
164 Besora Galefeather C .10 .20
165 Broderick Langforth R 10.00 20.00
166 Claemora Amberglare C .10 .20
167 Conqueror Gurzom U .20 .50
168 Conqueror Jarano U .20 .50

169 Conqueror Neusuada U .20 .50
170 Conqueror Yun'zon U .20 .50
171 Drandus the Deathcaller U .20 .50
172 Emelia Darkhand C .10 .20
173 Farander Shadesurge C .10 .20
174 Firewarden Wyland Kaslinth C .10 .20
175 Garrosh Hellscream E 1.50 4.00
176 Ginza Darktusk C .10 .20
177 Great Kodo R .40 1.00
178 Grovemender Ash'lon C .10 .20
179 Haranto Darkstrider C .10 .20
180 Huro'shal Gutwrench C .10 .20
181 Huzrula C .10 .20
182 Jaroth Lightguard C .10 .20
183 Kurao Stormheart C .10 .20
184 Makta the Rumbler U .20 .50
185 Mojo Mistress Zurania C .10 .20
186 Nathanos Blightcaller E 5.00 10.00
187 Raztu'jor C .10 .20
188 Rukdara Dreadhand C .10 .20
189 Sindo'zur the Toxifier U .20 .50
190 Swift Raptor R 1.00 2.50
191 Tanzuri C .10 .20
192 Teresa Voidheart C .10 .20
193 Thag Big Bounty Cragshot C .10 .20
194 Thurgood Steelwall C .10 .20
195 Twilight Vanquisher Knolan R .60 1.50
196 Verzuk Bloodfist C .10 .20
197 Vindron the Impure U .20 .50
198 Whitney Gravecaller C .10 .20
199 Winston Duskhaven C .10 .20
200 Alard Schmied R .40 1.00
201 Azjol-anak Acidslinger C .10 .20
202 Azjol-anak Acidspewer C .10 .20
203 Azjol-anak Battleguard C .10 .20
204 Azjol-anak Broodguard C .10 .20
205 Azjol-anak Webspinner C .10 .20
206 Azjol-anak Webweaver C .10 .20
207 Charles Worth R .40 1.00
208 Diane Cannings R .40 1.00
209 Kilix the Unraveler R .40 1.00
210 Klannoc Macleod E .60 1.50
211 Lord Darion Mograine E .60 1.50
212 Lord Jorach Ravenholdt E 1.00 2.50
213 Mor'zul Bloodbringer E .60 1.50
214 Spectral Kitten R .75 2.00
215 Tiny U .20 .50
216 Bloodbane's Fall C .10 .20
217 Boots of the Whirling Mist R .40 1.00
218 Breastplate of Undeath U .20 .50
219 The Darkspeaker's Footpads C .10 .20
220 Greaves of Ancient Evil R .60 1.50
221 Incursion Vestments R .40 1.00
222 King Dred's Helm R .40 1.00
223 Riot Shield U .20 .50
224 Shoulderpads of Fleshwerks C .10 .20
225 Spaulders of Lost Secrets C .10 .20
226 Vengeance Wrap U .20 .50
227 Oracle Talisman of Ablution U .20 .50
228 Dragonflight Great-Ring E .75 2.00
229 Extract of Necromantic Power R 1.25 3.00
230 Mighty Shadow Protection Potion C .10 .20
231 Arm Blade of Augelmir U .20 .50
232 Blade of the Empty Void R .40 1.00
233 Crimson Cranium Crusher R .40 1.00
234 Dagger of Betrayal R .40 1.00
235 Edge of Oblivion R .75 2.00
236 Encrusted Zombie Finger R .40 1.00
237 Fleshwerk Throwing Glaive R .40 1.00
238 Gavel of the Fleshcrafter U .20 .50
239 Life-Staff of the Web Lair R .40 1.00
240 Netherbreath Spellblade R .60 1.50
241 Reanimator's Hacker U .20 .50
242 Reaper of Dark Souls U .20 .50
243 Saliva Corroded Pike U .20 .50
244 Staff of Sinister Claws U .20 .50
245 Touch of Unlife U .20 .50
246 Trapper's Rifle R .40 1.00
247 Trophy Gatherer U .20 .50
248 Unearthed Broadsword C .10 .20
249 Death to the Traitor King C .10 .20
250 A Voice in the Dark C .10 .20
251 Brothers in Death U .20 .50
252 Culling the Damned C .10 .20
253 Dark Horizon C .10 .20
254 Death's Gaze C .10 .20
255 Defiling the Defilers C .10 .20
256 Dreadsteed of Xoroth U .20 .50
257 Junkboxes Needed U .20 .50
258 Pure Evil C .10 .20
259 Sacrifices Must Be Made C .10 .20
260 Scourge Tactics C .10 .20
261 Tales of Destruction C .10 .20
262 The Overseer's Shadow C .10 .20
263 The Restless Dead C .10 .20
264 Under the Shadow C .10 .20
265 Unfit for Death C .10 .20
266 Whirlwind Weapon U .20 .50
267 World of Shadows C .10 .20
268 Legendary Leathers, Dalaran R .40 1.00
269 Talismanic Textiles, Dalaran R .40 1.00
270 Tanks for Everything, Dalaran R .40 1.00

2009 World of Warcraft Scourgewar Loot

1 Tiny 3.00 8.00
2 Tuskarr Kite 50.00 100.00
3 Spectral Kitten 100.00 175.00

2010 World of Warcraft Scourgewar Icecrown

COMPLETE SET (220) 50.00 100.00
BOOSTER BOX (24 PACKS) 50.00 100.00
BOOSTER PACK (19 CARDS) 3.00 5.00
RELEASED IN SEPTEMBER 2010
1 Arch Druid Lilliandra U .20 .50
2 Argent Confessor Paletress U .20 .50
3 Eadric the Pure U .20 .50
4 Rimblat Earthshatter U .20 .50
5 Dalronn the Controller U .20 .50
6 General Lightsbane U .20 .50
7 Overseer Savryn U .20 .50
8 Queen Angerboda U .20 .50
9 Syreian the Bonecarver U .20 .50
10 Thane Ufrang the Mighty U .20 .50
11 Turov the Risen U .20 .50
12 Askalti Darksteel U .20 .50
13 Blood Lord Vorath U .20 .50
14 Deathseer Zuk'raj U .20 .50
15 Kjaran the Callous U .20 .50
16 Lich King, The E 4.00 10.00
17 Arctic Blast C .10 .25
18 Blood Plague C .10 .25
19 Death Gate R .40 1.00
20 Entomb C .10 .25
21 Frost Rune U .20 .50
22 Frost Strike R .40 1.00
23 Mark of Undeath U .20 .50
24 Rune Strike C .10 .25
25 Feral Dominance U .20 .50
26 Gale Winds R .40 1.00
27 Mark of Life C .10 .25
28 Natural Reclamation R .40 1.00
29 Predatory Sense C .10 .25
30 Ravage C .10 .25
31 Savage Roar U .20 .50
32 Bestial Resurgence U .20 .50
33 Cold Bones C .10 .25
34 Deuce R 1.50 4.00
35 Freezing Arrow C .10 .25
36 Penetrating Shots R .40 1.00
37 Primal Focus U .20 .50
38 Sharp Eye C .10 .25
39 Arcane Binding R .40 1.00
40 Arcane Essence U .20 .50
41 Cone of Cold C .10 .25
42 Fingers of Frost R .40 1.00
43 Flame Burst C .10 .25
44 Frost Ward C .10 .25
45 Whiteout U .20 .50
46 Blessing of the Templar R .40 1.00
47 Deliberate Heal C .10 .25
48 Deliberate Vengeance C .10 .25
49 Frost Resistance Aura C .10 .25
50 Reckoning R .40 1.00
51 Restitution U .20 .50
52 Seal of Purity U .20 .50
53 Desperate Condemnation C .10 .25
54 Desperate Plea C .10 .25
55 Mind Sear U .20 .50
56 Power Infusion R .40 1.00
57 Prayer of Spirit U .20 .50
58 Prayer of Vitality C .10 .25
59 Psychic Shriek R .40 1.00
60 Butcher U .20 .50
61 Close Quarters Combat R .40 1.00
62 Divert C .10 .25
63 Fan of Knives R .60 1.50
64 Instant Poison C .10 .25
65 Paralyze U .20 .50
66 Poach C .10 .25
67 Colossal Totem U .20 .50
68 Elemental Shield C .10 .25
69 Frost Resistance Totem U .20 .50
70 Hex C .10 .25
71 Lava Burst C .10 .25
72 Spiritual Awakening R .40 1.00
73 Thunderstorm R .60 1.50
74 Demonic Accord C .10 .25
75 Embrace of the Nether C .10 .25
76 Fel Fury U .20 .50
77 Fel Infernal U .20 .50
78 Jaktip C .10 .25
79 Metamorphosis R .40 1.00
80 Nether Rift R .40 1.00
81 Command Decision C .10 .25
82 Conquering Shout C .10 .25
83 Fit of Rage R .40 1.00
84 Heroic Throw U .20 .50
85 Payment of Blood U .20 .50
86 Pierce C .10 .25
87 Warbringer R .40 1.00
88 Bloody Slaughter U .20 .50
89 Boundless Concentration U .20 .50
90 Embolism U .20 .50
91 Fortify U .20 .50
92 Frost Surge U .20 .50
93 Inner Rage U .20 .50
94 Necessary Sacrifice U .20 .50
95 Primal Taming U .20 .50
96 Torment of Shadows U .20 .50
97 Paint Bomb U .20 .50
98 Akiko the Alert U .20 .50
99 Ashnaar, Frost Herald R 2.00 5.00
100 Bronwyn Lightborn C .10 .25
101 Cynthia Masters C .10 .25
102 Darktwister Kern C .10 .25
103 Hazlow Mudshuggle C .10 .25
104 Jaina, Lady of Theramore E 5.00 12.00
105 Justicar Andra Goldblast U .20 .50
106 Justicar Johanna Rastol U .20 .50
107 Justicar Nordar Stonegrave U .20 .50
108 Kylanda the Harmonious U .20 .50
109 Kysa Shadowstalker C .10 .25
110 Lissie Spizfrat C .10 .25
111 Madrea Bluntbrew C .10 .25
112 Pathfinder Fansal R .40 1.00
113 Phantrich C .10 .25
114 Rhyllor of the Glade C .10 .25
115 Sparkington the Abrupt U .20 .50
116 Swift Palomino R .40 1.00
117 Tani Bixtix C .10 .25
118 Thassarian R .40 1.00
119 Vanora Moonshot C .10 .25
120 Vishala C .10 .25
121 Vylar Whitepaw C .10 .25
122 Wesley Shadowsworn C .10 .25
123 Adenda Lighthaven C .10 .25
124 Bradford the Frozen U .20 .50
125 Burna Sharpstride C .10 .25
126 Conqueror Edge U .20 .50
127 Conqueror Nairi U .20 .50
128 Conqueror Tristos U .20 .50
129 Deathlord Jones R .40 1.00
130 Doom C .10 .25
131 Frostweaver Dakar'sith R .40 1.00
132 Hansi Wildcoat C .10 .25
133 Indauma Bloodfire C .10 .25
134 Jasmine von Ludrow C .10 .25
135 Koltira Deathweaver R .40 1.00
136 Kozik Skullcracker C .10 .25
137 Kuz'vun C .10 .25
138 Loate Grimtusk C .10 .25
139 Savuka the Acute U .20 .50
140 Skeletal Warhorse R .40 1.00
141 Stephen Hathrow C .10 .25
142 Thrall, Warchief E 6.00 15.00
143 Torashu Stronghoof C .10 .25
144 Treewatcher Kursha U .20 .50
145 Uh'gali the Elementalist U .20 .50
146 Vukora Netherflame C .10 .25
147 Zaduru C .10 .25
148 Banshee Soulclaimer C .10 .25
149 Crypt Fiend C .10 .25
150 Hulking Abomination U .20 .50
151 King Ymiron R .40 1.00
152 Malefic Necromancer C .10 .25
153 Marauding Geist C .10 .25
154 Orbaz Bloodbane R .40 1.00
155 Overlord Drakuru R .40 1.00
156 Plague Eruptor U .20 .50
157 Shade of Arugal R .40 1.00
158 Sindragosa, Frost Queen E 1.25 3.00
159 Stonespine Gargoyle C .10 .25
160 Underking Talonox R .40 1.00
161 Ymirheim Chosen Warrior C .10 .25
162 Azjol-anak Deathwatcher R .40 1.00
163 Azjol-anak Skirmisher U .20 .50
164 Alchemist Finklestein U .20 .50
165 Babagahnoosh, Grumpy E 1.50 4.00
166 Bath'rah the Windwatcher E .75 2.00
167 Hemet Nesingwary E 3.00 8.00
168 Rhonin E .60 1.50
169 Wooly White Rhino R .40 1.00
170 Bitter Cold Armguards C .10 .25
171 Frost-bound Chain Bracers R .40 1.00
172 Gloves of the Frozen Glade R .40 1.00
173 Hero's Surrender R .60 1.50
174 Iceshear Mantle C .10 .25
175 Icy Scale Chestguard C .10 .25
176 Legplates of the Endless Void R .40 1.00
177 Shawl of Haunted R .40 1.00
178 Winter's Icy Embrace C .10 .25
179 Flare of the Heavens R .40 1.00
180 Frostbridge Orb R .40 1.00
181 Frostweave Bandage U .20 .50
182 Glacial Bag R .40 1.00
183 Portal Stone R .40 1.00
184 Sigil of the Vengeful Heart R .40 1.00
185 Soul of the Dead R .40 1.00
186 Super Simian Sphere R .40 1.00
187 Titan-forged Rune R .40 1.00
188 Totem of Splintering R .40 1.00
189 Avalanche R .40 1.00
190 Black Ice U .20 .50
191 Chilly Slobberknocker R .40 1.00
192 Hailstorm R .40 1.00
193 Iceshrieker's Touch U .20 .50
194 Journey's End R .40 1.00
195 Kel'Thuzad's Reach E .60 1.50
196 Kingsbane R .40 1.00
197 Nesingwary 4000 U .20 .50
198 Spinning Fate R .40 1.00
199 Stormstrike Mace R .40 1.00
200 Stormtip R .40 1.00
201 Val'anyr, Hammer of Ancient E 1.00 2.50
202 Voldrethar, Dark Blade R .40 1.00
203 Proper String, A U .20 .50
204 Rituals of Power U .20 .50
205 Spirit Totem U .20 .50
206 Army of the Damned C .10 .25
207 All Things in Good Time U .20 .50
208 Tirion's Gambit U .20 .50
209 Boon of A'dal, The C .10 .25
210 Boon of Alexstrasza, The C .10 .25
211 Boon of Remulos, The C .10 .25
212 Cold Hearted C .10 .25
213 Everfrost C .10 .25
214 Hero's Burden, A C .10 .25
215 Last Line of Defense, The C .10 .25
216 Rider of Frost, The C .10 .25
217 Storm King's Vengeance, The C .10 .25
218 That's Abominable! C .10 .25
219 Orgrim's Hammer R .40 1.00
220 Skybreaker, The R .40 1.00

2010 World of Warcraft Scourgewar Icecrown Loot

1 Paint Bomb 1.00 2.50
2 Portal Stone 20.00 50.00
3 Wooly White Rhino 75.00 150.00

2010 World of Warcraft Scourgewar Wrathgate

Complete Set (220) 50.00 100.00
Booster Box (24 Packs) 50.00 100.00
Booster Pack (19 Cards) 3.00 5.00
RELEASED IN MAY 2010
1 Archmage Barstow U .20 .50
2 Durzion, Champion of A'dal U .20 .50
3 Earthmender Vaaki U .20 .50
4 Esonea U .20 .50
5 Gramm Thunderjaw U .20 .50
6 Krunkle Deadspark U .20 .50
7 Lunira Swiftbreath U .20 .50
8 Rinni Gloomtrik U .20 .50
9 Sarina the Immaculate U .20 .50
10 Tysandri Duskstrike U .20 .50
11 Crusader Farisa U .20 .50
12 Harona Proudmane U .20 .50
13 Jeremiah Karvok U .20 .50
14 Krog the Deathfist U .20 .50
15 Kungen the Thunderer U .20 .50
16 Mojo Master Zandum U .20 .50
17 Nuvon Dawnfury U .20 .50
18 Spiritwalker Kavi'je U .20 .50
19 Sunstalker Andora U .20 .50
20 Thaka Deadeye U .20 .50
21 Highlord Tirion Fordring E 3.00 8.00
22 Anti-Magic Shell U .20 .50
23 Blood Rune U .20 .50
24 Dark Command C .10 .25
25 Frost Fever C .10 .25
26 Hysteria R .40 1.00
27 Lesson of the Grave C .10 .25
28 Pestilence R .40 1.00
29 Surge of Blood C .10 .25
30 Blustering Winds C .10 .25
31 Dire Bear Form U .20 .50
32 Gift of the Earthmother R 1.00 2.50
33 Lesson of the Wild C .10 .25
34 Nature's Vengeance R .40 1.00
35 Scent of Nature C .10 .25
36 Stranglevine U .20 .50
37 Banzai U .20 .50
38 Explosive Shot R .40 1.00
39 Eyes of the Beast U .20 .50
40 Hail of Arrows R .40 1.00
41 Lesson of the Beast C .10 .25
42 Mongoose Bite C .10 .25
43 Mothra C .10 .25
44 Explosive Flames C .10 .25
45 Flash of Brilliance R .40 1.00
46 Frozen Solid U .20 .50
47 Ice Nova U .20 .50
48 Lesson of the Arcane C .10 .25
49 Netherwind Presence R .40 1.00
50 Scald C .10 .25
51 Charger R .40 1.00
52 Holy Fury C .10 .25
53 Lesson of the Divine C .10 .25
54 Presence of the Divine U .20 .50
55 Seal of Sanctity U .20 .50
56 Shelter C .10 .25
57 Unyielding Faith R .40 1.00
58 Dementia U .20 .50
59 Fright C .10 .25
60 Holy Guardian R .40 1.00
61 Lesson of the Light C .10 .25
62 Power Word: Faith C .10 .25
63 Sacred Circle U .20 .50
64 Spirit of Redemption R .40 1.00
65 Flesh Eating Poison U .20 .50
66 Annihilate U .20 .50
67 Lesson of the Shadow C .10 .25
68 Master Poisoner R .40 1.00
69 Pick Lock C .10 .25
70 Raze R .40 1.00
71 Weakening Poison U .20 .50
72 Ancestral Awakening R .40 1.00
73 Astral Recall R .40 1.00
74 Fusion Totem U .20 .50
75 Gushing Totem U .20 .50
76 Infusion of Earth C .10 .25
77 Lesson of the Elements C .10 .25
78 Surge of Life C .10 .25
79 Curse of Doom U .20 .50
80 Devastation R .40 1.00
81 Drain Essence C .10 .25
82 Dread Doomguard R .40 1.00
83 Lesson of the Nether C .10 .25
84 Lynxia U .20 .50
85 Void Pact C .10 .25
86 Expertise of Steel R .40 1.00
87 Flawless Defense U .20 .50
88 Impede U .20 .50
89 Lesson of the Call C .10 .25
90 Mortal Slash C .10 .25
91 Requite C .10 .25
92 Wrecking Crew R .40 1.00
93 Bestial Rage U .20 .50
94 Feast of Flame U .20 .50
95 Gift of the Pious U .20 .50
96 Hit and Run U .20 .50
97 Holy Barrier U .20 .50
98 Kick Thinking U .20 .50
99 Master's Stable U .20 .50
100 Nurturing Spirit U .20 .50
101 Strength of Battle U .20 .50
102 Landro's Gift U .20 .50
103 Tubs Klankbopple C .10 .25
104 Antyr C .10 .25
105 Arlen the Untamed U .20 .50
106 Armored Snowy Gryphon R .40 1.00
107 Ayluro Nightwind C .10 .25
108 Baritham, Jadefist Apprentice C .10 .25
109 Blazemistress Lindsey C .10 .25
110 Bolvar, Highlord E .60 1.50
111 Bronthea the Resolute U .20 .50
112 Burly Berta R 3.00 8.00
113 Devona Berkshire R .40 1.00
114 Grumdur Bladebane C .10 .25
115 High Commander Halford E .60 1.50
116 Hurdan the Everlasting U .20 .50
117 Ixiya the Attuned C .10 .25
118 Justicar Drathnea U .20 .50
119 Justicar Nimzi Banedrizzle U .20 .50
120 Justicar Ularu U .20 .50
121 Kaelyn Vineminder C .10 .25
122 Lady Bancroft C .10 .25
123 Lyshala Ravenshot C .10 .25
124 Mithran the Sniper C .10 .25
125 Nethermaven Donna Chastain C .10 .25
126 Nurgle Tinkfrost C .10 .25
127 Swift Mechanostrider R .40 1.00
128 Wyndarr Shadefist C .10 .25
129 Armored Blue Wind Rider R .40 1.00
130 Astani Dawngrace C .10 .25
131 Bluffstalker Honovi C .10 .25
132 Cedric Darwin C .10 .25
133 Conqueror Hashkon U .20 .50
134 Conqueror Vun'jin U .20 .50
135 Conqueror Zaala U .20 .50
136 Daralis the Sanctifier U .20 .50
137 Dhoros Ravestrike C .10 .25
138 Dorzok Shadowhand C .10 .25
139 Goru Thornmane C .10 .25
140 Hanthal Lightward C .10 .25
141 Katoka Dreadblade R .40 1.00
142 Murphy Watson C .10 .25
143 Muruna the Savage U .20 .50
144 Roanauk Icemist E .60 1.50
145 Roshen the Oathsworn U .20 .50
146 Saurfang the Younger E 4.00 10.00
147 Soram Wildbark C .10 .25
148 Sullivan Holmes C .10 .25
149 Sunguard Cersie C .10 .25
150 Swift Hawkstrider R .40 1.00
151 Swift Timber Wolf R .40 1.00
152 Tuskmender Jan'zu C .10 .25
153 Uruka the Cutthroat R 1.00 2.50
154 Vuz'din C .10 .25
155 Zugna, Windseer Apprentice C .10 .25
156 Blazing Hippogryph R .40 1.00
157 Brother Keltan U .20 .50
158 Commander Falstaav C .10 .25
159 Crusade Commander Entari R .40 1.00
160 Crusade Engineer Spitzpatrick C .10 .25
161 Crusader Lord Dalfors C .10 .25
162 Eltrigg E .60 1.50
163 Father Gustav C .10 .25
164 Sister Colleen Tulley C .10 .25
165 Veteran Crusader Aliocha Segard C .10 .25
166 Azjol-anak Champion R 1.00 2.50
167 Aurius E .60 1.50
168 Eris Havenfire E .60 1.50
169 Keeper Remulos E .60 1.50
170 Boots of the Renewed Flight U .20 .50
171 Cloak of the Shadowed Sun R .40 1.00
172 Gloves of Token Respect R .40 1.00
173 Helm of Vital Protection R .40 1.00
174 Hood of the Exodus R .40 1.00
175 Leggings of the Honored U .20 .50
176 Protective Barricade of the Light R .40 1.00
177 Sun-Emblazoned Chestplate R .40 1.00
178 Sympathy U .20 .50
179 Upstanding Spaulders R .40 1.00
180 Gigantique Bag R .40 1.00
181 Idol of the Shooting Star R .40 1.00
182 Libram of Radiance R .40 1.00
183 Life-Binder's Locket R .40 1.00
184 Platinum Disks of Swiftness R .40 1.00
185 Statue Generator R .40 1.00
186 Angry Dread C .10 .25
187 Colossal Skull-Clad Cleaver U .20 .50
188 Fading Glow C .10 .25
189 Final Voyage R .40 1.00
190 Fist of the Deity R .40 1.00
191 Haunting Call R .40 1.00
192 Life and Death R .40 1.00
193 Lifeblade of Belgaristrasz R .40 1.00
194 Nerubian Conqueror R .40 1.00
195 Silent Crusader R .40 1.00
196 Spire of Sunset R .40 1.00
197 Staff of Trickery C .10 .25
198 Sword of Justice R .40 1.00
199 Torch of Holy Fire R .40 1.00
200 Wraith Spear R .40 1.00
201 No Mere Dream U .20 .50
202 Paladin Training U .20 .50
203 The Ichor of Undeath U .20 .50
204 The Call of the Crusade C .10 .25
205 Apply This Twice Daily C .10 .25
206 Conversing With the Depths C .10 .25
207 Cycle of Life C .10 .25
208 I'm Not Dead Yet! R .40 1.00
209 Light Within the Darkness C .10 .25
210 No One to Save You C .10 .25
211 On Ruby Wings R .40 1.00
212 Planning for the Future C .10 .25
213 Really Big Worm C .10 .25
214 Return to Angrathar C .10 .25
215 Seeds of the Lashers C .10 .25
216 A Tale of Valor C .10 .25
217 Wanton Warlord C .10 .25
218 Fordragon Hold R .40 1.00
219 Kor'kron Vanguard R 1.00 2.50
220 Angrathar the Wrathgate E .60 1.50

2010 World of Warcraft Scourgewar Wrathgate Loot

1 Landro's Gift 8.00 20.00
2 Statue Generator 20.00 40.00
3 Blazing Hippogryph 150.00 250.00

2010 World of Warcraft Worldbreaker

COMPLETE SET (270) 50.00 100.00
BOOSTER BOX (24 PACKS) 40.00 80.00
BOOSTER PACK (19 CARDS) 3.00 4.00
RELEASED IN DECEMBER 2010
1 Amaria Kelsur U .20 .50
2 Arturius Hathrow U .20 .50

3 Bragvi Stormstein U .20 .50
4 Caleb Pavish U .20 .50
5 Haedis U .20 .50
6 Jaenel U .20 .50
7 Kadus Frosthand U .20 .50
8 Peter Hottelet U .20 .50
9 Tilly Fiddlelight U .20 .50
10 Victor Baltus U .20 .50
11 Ayaka Winterhoof U .20 .50
12 Grizlik Sparkhex U .20 .50
13 Jai Dawnsteel U .20 .50
14 Jumo'zin U .20 .50
15 Malaxia Wizwhirl U .20 .50
16 Rekwa Proudhorn U .20 .50
17 Suvok Frozeneye U .20 .50
18 Valerie Worfield U .20 .50
19 Vorix Zorbuzz U .20 .50
20 Yuna Sunridge U .20 .50
21 Alexstrasza the Life-Binder E 5.00 12.00
22 Ysera the Dreamer E 1.00 2.50
23 Black Blood C .10 .25
24 Blood Chill C .10 .25
25 Chains of Ice R .40 1.00
26 Dancing Rune Weapon R .40 1.00
27 Frenzy U .20 .50
28 Grip of the Damned C .10 .25
29 Path of Frost C .10 .25
30 Strangulate U .20 .50
31 Unholy Ground R .40 1.00
32 Withering Decay U .20 .50
33 Earth and Moon R .40 1.00
34 Entangling Growth C .10 .25
35 Faerie Fire U .20 .50
36 Flourish U .20 .50
37 Mark of the Untamed U .20 .50
38 Nature's Fury R .40 1.00
39 Reawakening R .40 1.00
40 Rejuvenation C .10 .25
41 Savage Bear Form C .10 .25
42 Wrath C .10 .25
43 Aspect of the Wild R .40 1.00
44 Blast Trap U .20 .50
45 Boomer R 1.25 3.00
46 Detect Prey U .20 .50
47 Flare C .10 .25
48 Steady Shot U .20 .50
49 Tesla C .10 .25
50 Track Dragonkin C .10 .25
51 Wing Clip C .10 .25
52 Wyvern Sting R .40 1.00
53 Enduring Winter R .40 1.00
54 Extinguish U .20 .50
55 Fire Blast C .10 .25
56 Frost Wave C .10 .25
57 Frostfire Bolt U .20 .50
58 Frozen Nerves C .10 .25
59 Mana Diamond R .40 1.00
60 Mana Shift R .40 1.00
61 Ripple U .20 .50
62 Unstable Infusion C .10 .25
63 Blessing of Defense C .10 .25
64 Blessing of the Kindred R .40 1.00
65 Blessing of Virtue U .20 .50
66 Censure C .10 .25
67 Divine Cleansing U .20 .50
68 Holy Light C .10 .25
69 Repentance R .40 1.00
70 Sacred Shield U .20 .50
71 Seal of Wrath R .40 1.00
72 Stasis C .10 .25
73 Dark Extortion R .40 1.00
74 Divine Fury R .40 1.00
75 Divine Hymn U .20 .50
76 Flash Heal C .10 .25
77 Oppress C .10 .25
78 Power Word: Preservation C .10 .25
79 Power Word: Shelter U .20 .50
80 Psychic Wail U .20 .50
81 Seeping Shadows R .40 1.00
82 Spiritual Harmony C .10 .25
83 Aggressive Exploitation C .10 .25
84 Bully C .10 .25
85 Contagious Poison R .40 1.00
86 Daze U .20 .50
87 Draining Poison U .20 .50
88 Excessive Force C .10 .25
89 Gouge C .10 .25
90 Incapacitate U .20 .50
91 Seal Fate R .40 1.00
92 Steal Steel R .40 1.00
93 Ancestral Purge C .10 .25
94 Breath of the Elements R .40 1.00
95 Earthen Blast U .20 .50
96 Earthen Embrace C .10 .25
97 Elemental Vision C .10 .25
98 Lightning Bolt C .10 .25
99 Nature Resistance Totem U .20 .50
100 Rolling Thunder R .40 1.00
101 Spiritual Return R .40 1.00
102 Thunderstrike Weapon U .20 .50
103 Demonic Reclamation U .20 .50
104 Demonic Soulstone C .10 .25
105 Fear C .10 .25
106 Fel Blaze U .20 .50
107 Jhuunash R .40 1.00
108 Muddle U .20 .50
109 Nether Inversion C .10 .25
110 Sardok C .10 .25
111 Searing Pain R .40 1.00
112 Summoning Portal R .40 1.00
113 Chaotic Rush U .20 .50
114 Crushing Strike C .10 .25
115 Defender's Vigil C .10 .25
116 Execute C .10 .25
117 Heroic Impulse C .10 .25
118 Juggernaut R .40 1.00
119 Onslaught R .40 1.00
120 Raging Shout U .20 .50
121 Stance Mastery R .40 1.00
122 Thunderous Challenge U .20 .50
123 Avatar of the Wild E 4.00 10.00
124 Vigil of the Light E 1.00 2.50
125 Viciousness U .20 .50
126 Rocket Barrage U .20 .50
127 Adrienne the Inspiring U .20 .50
128 Aileen the Thunderblessed R .40 1.00
129 Alador Stonebrew C .10 .25
130 Allister Cooper C .10 .25
131 Andrew Ulric C .10 .25
132 Aresha Thorncaller U .20 .50
133 Arisa Sarum U .20 .50
134 Bayner Cogbertson C .10 .25
135 Bella Wilder C .10 .25
136 Fenton Guardmont C .10 .25
137 Furan Rookbane C .10 .25
138 Garet Vice C .10 .25
139 Gerana Sparkfist C .10 .25
140 Hira C .10 .25
141 Jarrod Gravon U .20 .50
142 Jinie Swizzleshade C .10 .25
143 Kalek Deepearth C .10 .25
144 Kentro Slade R .40 1.00
145 King Genn Greymane E 1.00 2.50
146 Kirjen Fizzgar C .10 .25
147 Koeus C .10 .25
148 Laenthor Shademoon C .10 .25
149 Loriam Argos C .10 .25
150 Magni, the Mountain King E 1.25 3.00
151 Marcus Dominar C .10 .25
152 Marius Jator U .20 .50
153 Nami Dabpox C .10 .25
154 Nightstalker Austen C .10 .25
155 Pixia Darkmist C .10 .25
156 Pyromancer Davins R .40 1.00
157 Rolan Phoenix R .60 1.50
158 Savis Cindur C .10 .25
159 Shanis Bladefall C .10 .25
160 Terina Calin C .10 .25
161 Varandas Silverleaf U .20 .50
162 Watchman Visi C .10 .25
163 Wazix Blonktop C .10 .25
164 Zuur C .10 .25
165 Boki Earthgaze C .10 .25
166 Cadon Thundershade C .10 .25
167 Cairne, Earthmother's E 5.00 12.00
168 Ceraka U .20 .50
169 Dorladris Spellfire C .10 .25
170 Drizzie Steelslam C .10 .25
171 Exxi the Windshaper R .40 1.00
172 Frek Snipelix U .20 .50
173 Gispax the Mixologist R .40 1.00
174 Gorz Blazefist C .10 .25
175 Grazzle Grubhook C .10 .25
176 Guardian Steelhoof C .10 .25
177 Huruk Lightvow C .10 .25
178 Jezziki Shinebog C .10 .25
179 Kerzok Plixboom U .20 .50
180 Kistix Shockvat C .10 .25
181 Kloxx Dedrix C .10 .25
182 Landon Dunavin C .10 .25
183 Mahna Lightsky U .20 .50
184 Neboz Tombwex U .20 .50
185 Onnekra Bloodfang C .10 .25
186 Orkahn of Orgrimmar U .20 .50
187 Oruk Starstorm C .10 .25
188 Rosalyne von Erantor U .20 .50
189 Ruon Wildhoof C .10 .25
190 Sava'gin the Reckless R .40 1.00
191 Sura Lightningheart C .10 .25
192 Telor Sunsurge C .10 .25
193 Thrandis the Venomous R .40 1.00
194 Toz'jun C .10 .25
195 Trade Prince Gallywix E 1.00 2.50
196 Traxel Emberklik C .10 .25
197 Vala Carville C .10 .25
198 Veline Bladestar C .10 .25
199 Zakis Trickstab C .10 .25
200 Zerzu C .10 .25
201 Zulanji C .10 .25
202 Zulbraka C .10 .25
203 Emerald Acidspewer C .10 .25
204 Emerald Captain C .10 .25
205 Emerald Emissary U .20 .50
206 Emerald Lifewarden U .20 .50
207 Emerald Soldier C .10 .25
208 Emerald Tree Warder C .10 .25
209 Emerald Wanderer C .10 .25
210 Eranikus R .40 1.00
211 Korialstrasz R .40 1.00
212 Ruby Blazewing U .20 .50
213 Ruby Emissary U .20 .50
214 Ruby Enforcer C .10 .25
215 Ruby Flameblade C .10 .25
216 Ruby Protector C .10 .25
217 Ruby Skyrazor C .10 .25
218 Ruby Stalker C .10 .25
219 Mottled Drake E .75 2.00
220 Landro's Lil' XT U .20 .50
221 Etched Dragonbone Girdle U .20 .50
222 Polished Breastplate of Valor R .40 1.00
223 Prized Beastmaster's Mantle R .40 1.00
224 Robe of the Waking Nightmare U .20 .50
225 Skinned Whelp Shoulders U .20 .50
226 Stained Shadowcraft Tunic R .40 1.00
227 Tattered Dreadmist Mantle R .40 1.00
228 Wyrmwing Treads U .20 .50
229 Discerning Eye of the Beast U .20 .50
230 Dread Pirate Ring U .20 .50
231 Grim Campfire R .40 1.00
232 Swift Hand of Justice U .20 .50
233 Abomination Knuckles C .10 .25
234 Abracadaver R .40 1.00
235 Balanced Heartseeker R .40 1.00
236 Bloodied Arcanite Reaper R .40 1.00
237 Charmed Ancient Bone Bow R .40 1.00
238 Citadel Enforcer's Claymore C .10 .25
239 Devout Aurastone Hammer R .40 1.00
240 Dignified Headmaster's Charge R .40 1.00
241 Gutbuster R .40 1.00
242 Hersir's Greatspear U .20 .50
243 Lockjaw U .20 .50
244 Ramaladni's Blade of Culling R .40 1.00
245 Repurposed Lava Dredger R .40 1.00
246 Stakethrower U .20 .50
247 Troggbane, Axe King E .60 1.50
248 Venerable Mass of McGowan R .40 1.00
249 Wand of Ruby Claret C .10 .25
250 Warmace of Menethil R .40 1.00
251 Leader of the Pack R .40 1.00
252 Warchief's Revenge R .40 1.00
253 Challenge to the Black Flight C .10 .25
254 Cleansing Witch Hill C .10 .25
255 Corrosion Prevention C .10 .25
256 Counting Out Time C .10 .25
257 Crystals of Power C .10 .25
258 Essence of Enmity, The C .10 .25
259 Finding the Source C .10 .25
260 Grimtotem Weapon, The C .10 .25
261 Key to Freedom, The C .10 .25
262 Locked Away C .10 .25
263 Matter of Time, A C .10 .25
264 Mighty U'cha, The C .10 .25
265 Mystery Goo C .10 .25
266 Torch of Retribution, The C .10 .25
267 What's Haunting Witch Hill? C .10 .25
268 Witch's Bane, The C .10 .25
269 Gilneas R .40 1.00
270 Lost Isles R .40 1.00

2010 World of Warcraft Worldbreaker Loot

1 Landro's Lil' XT 5.00 12.00
2 Grim Campfire 15.00 40.00
3 Mottled Drake 125.00 200.00

2011 World of Warcraft Throne of the Tides

COMPLETE SET (263) 80.00 120.00
BOOSTER BOX (36 PACKS) 50.00 100.00
BOOSTER PACK (16 CARDS) 3.00 4.00
RELEASED IN OCTOBER 2011
1 Anaka the Light's Bulwark U .20 .50
2 Barathex, Undeath's Hand U .20 .50
3 High Magus Olvek U .20 .50
4 Janvaru the Thunderspeaker U .20 .50
5 Master Sniper Simon McKey U .20 .50
6 Sana the Black Blade U .20 .50
7 Skodis the Nethertwister C .10 .25
8 Steelguard Adamson U .20 .50
9 Tinker Priest Cassie U .20 .50
10 Wildseer Varel U .20 .50
11 Drazul the Molten U .20 .50
12 Fama'sin the Lifeseer U .20 .50
13 Gaxtro, Bilgewater Marksman U .20 .50
14 Ghoulmaster Kalisa U .20 .50
15 High Priestess Neeri U .20 .50
16 Jak the Bilgewater Bruiser U .20 .50
17 Joleera U .20 .50
18 Rohashu, Zealot of the Sun U .20 .50
19 Samaku, Hand of the Tempest U .20 .50
20 Voidbringer Jindal'an U .20 .50
21 Deathbringer Kor'ush C .10 .25
22 Grglmrgl U .20 .50
23 Lady Sira'kess U .20 .50
24 Rawrbrgle U .20 .50
25 Neptulon E 1.00 2.50
26 Brittle Bones R .40 1.00
27 Claws of the Dead U .20 .50
28 Death's Duo R .60 1.50
29 Infestation U .20 .50
30 Monstrous Essence R .40 1.00
31 Plagued Mind U .20 .50
32 Skullchewer U .20 .50
33 Boundless Wild R .75 2.00
34 Fungal Growth R .60 1.50
35 Mark of Goldrinn C .10 .25
36 Stalwart Bear Form U .20 .50
37 Verdant Boon U .20 .50
38 Wild Roots U .20 .50
39 Bestial Revival R .40 1.00
40 Chompers U .20 .50
41 Clamps C .10 .25
42 Concussive Barrage R 1.00 2.50
43 Monstrous Mark R .40 1.00
44 Roar of the Beast U .20 .50
45 Track Enemy U .20 .50
46 Char R .60 1.50
47 Focus Magic R .75 2.00
48 Glacial Tomb C .10 .25
49 Molten Scorch U .20 .50
50 Monstrous Frostbolt Volley R .40 1.00
51 Touch of Brilliance U .20 .50
52 Vortex U .20 .50
53 Blessing of the Light C .10 .25
54 Blessing of the Righteous U .20 .50
55 Boundless Might R .60 1.50
56 Grand Crusader R 2.00 5.00
57 Hammer of the Zealot U .20 .50
58 Righteous Cleanse U .20 .50
59 Boundless Shadows R .40 1.00
60 Chakra R .75 2.00
61 Power Word: Purity C .10 .25
62 Power Word: Vitality U .20 .50
63 Psychic Screech U .20 .50
64 Tendrils of Darkness U .20 .50
65 Disorienting Blow U .20 .50
66 Distraction Technique U .20 .50
67 Poison Bomb R .60 1.50
68 Sleeping Poison R .60 1.50
69 Vendetta R .60 1.50
70 Boundless Life R .40 1.00
71 Earthen Might C .10 .25
72 Lava Shock U .20 .50
73 Shock of the Elements C .10 .25
74 Spark of Life R .40 1.00
75 Windguard Totem U .20 .50
76 Fel Summon U .20 .50
77 Grimnar U .20 .50
78 Hellisa C .10 .25
79 Nether Balance R .60 1.50
80 Soul Cleave U .20 .50
81 Soul Swap R .75 2.00
82 Armsman U .20 .50
83 Augment Steel R .40 1.00
84 Bloodsurge R .60 1.50
85 Furious Strike U .20 .50
86 Monstrous Cleave U .20 .50
87 Rallying Swarm R .60 1.50
88 Monstrous Strike C .10 .25
89 Monstrous Upheaval C .10 .25
90 RwlRwlRwlRwl! U .20 .50
91 Unleash the Swarm! U .20 .50
92 Face of Fear C .10 .25
93 Rallying Cry of the Dragonslayer C .10 .25
94 Strength of Will C .10 .25
95 Surge of Power R .75 2.00
96 Arcanomage Misti R .75 2.00
97 Ardon Almastor C .10 .25
98 Balrak Stoutstone C .10 .25
99 Braeo Darkpaw C .10 .25
100 Burdok Brewshot C .10 .25
101 Corin Stallnorth C .10 .25
102 Dastrin Bowman C .10 .25
103 Davius, Herald of Nature U .20 .50
104 Dradam Chillblade C .10 .25
105 Dulvar, Hand of the Light E .60 1.50
106 Evaax, Herald of Death U .20 .50
107 Faenis the Tranquil R .40 1.00
108 Faithseer Jasmina R .40 1.00
109 Fumdol Mountainfrost C .10 .25
110 Funken Fusemissile C .10 .25
111 Grumdak, Herald of the Hunt U .20 .50
112 Hadrack the Devoted R .60 1.50
113 Hunrik Blackiron C .10 .25
114 Jaema, Herald of the Light R .60 1.50
115 Kaelon, Herald of the Flame U .20 .50
116 Kara Vesstal C .10 .25
117 Kieron the Loaner R .60 1.50
118 Laetho Moonbranch C .10 .25
119 Larrisa Valorshield C .10 .25
120 Lodur, Herald of the Elements U .20 .50
121 Malar Silverfrost U .20 .50
122 Maloc, Herald of Trickery C .10 .25
123 Mekkatorque, King E .75 2.00
124 Militia Commander Balor R .60 1.50
125 Sebastian Malak C .10 .25
126 Shanla, Herald of Faith C .10 .25
127 Shaylith Swiftblade U .20 .50
128 Tallie Sprinklelight C .10 .25
129 Trista, Herald of the Fel U .20 .50
130 Vaakia C .10 .25
131 Valak the Vortex R .40 1.00
132 Vandos, Herald of War U .20 .50
133 Vindicator Saaris R .60 1.50
134 Wuzlo Grindergear C .10 .25
135 Xuurvis C .10 .25
136 Zintix the Frostbringer R .75 2.00
137 Akasi, Herald of Nature U .20 .50
138 Alana the Woebringer R .40 1.00
139 Alethia Brightsong C .10 .25
140 Amano, Herald of the Sun U .20 .50
141 Anastina, Herald of the Fel U .20 .50
142 Asoren Darksnout C .10 .25
143 Baxtan, Herald of the Flame U .20 .50
144 Daroka Venomfist C .10 .25
145 Deatheater Stroud U .20 .50
146 Draga'zal C .10 .25
147 Eralysa Sunshot C .10 .25
148 Hagtrix the Mindsifter R .60 1.50
149 Hesawa Stormwalker C .10 .25
150 Izzy Quizfiz C .10 .25
151 Jagrok, Herald of Trickery U .20 .50
152 Jaron, Herald of the Hunt U .20 .50
153 Jex'ali C .10 .25
154 Jumahko Thundersky C .10 .25
155 Kalam'ti R .40 1.00
156 Kazbaz C .10 .25
157 Kelena Ashford C .10 .25
158 Kinza, Mistress R .75 2.00
159 Krezza the Explosive R .60 1.50
160 Kromdar, Herald of War U .20 .50
161 Lordann the Bloodreaver R .75 2.00
162 Mazu'kon E 3.00 8.00
163 Moro Wildmesa C .10 .25
164 Nazuk Darkblood C .10 .25
165 Parexia, Herald of the Shadows U .20 .50
166 Prazo Whiptrick C .10 .25
167 Runzik Shrapnelwhiz C .10 .25
168 Samantha Galvington C .10 .25
169 Shala'zum R .60 1.50
170 Treespeaker Onaha R .75 2.00
171 Vol'jin, Darkspear Chieftain E .60 1.50
172 Vuza'jin C .10 .25
173 Yana'mi C .10 .25
174 Zarixx, Herald of Death U .20 .50
175 Zizzlix Drizzledrill C .10 .25
176 Zudzo, Herald of the Elements U .20 .50
177 Gilblin Bully C .10 .25
178 Gilblin Deathscrounger R .40 1.00
179 Gilblin Hoarder U .20 .50
180 Gilblin Plunderer U .20 .50
181 Gilblin Trickster U .20 .50
182 Bobbler U .20 .50
183 Brighteye C .10 .25
184 Bubblegil U .20 .50
185 Chumly U .20 .50
186 Crabbyfin U .20 .50
187 Gobbler R .40 1.00
188 Murloc Coastrunner C .10 .25
189 Nibbler C .10 .25
190 Slippyfist R .60 1.50
191 Snurky C .10 .25
192 Swarmtooth U .20 .50
193 Buldrug C .10 .25
194 Drugush the Crusher C .10 .25
195 Neph'lahim R .60 1.50
196 Tar'gak the Felcrazed U .20 .50
197 Thrug the Hurler U .20 .50
198 Zor'chal the Shadowseer U .20 .50
199 Commander Ulthok E 3.00 8.00
200 Faceless Sapper C .10 .25
201 Faceless Watcher R .40 1.00
202 Deep Subjugator U .20 .50
203 Mindbender Ghur'sha R .40 1.00
204 Idra'kess Enchantress U .20 .50
205 Idra'kess Mistress U .20 .50
206 Lady Naz'jar E .60 1.50
207 Naz'jar Harpooner C .10 .25
208 Naz'jar Myrmidon C .10 .25
209 Naz'jar Sorceress C .10 .25
210 Sira'kess Tide Priestess U .20 .50
211 Abyssal Seahorse R .60 1.50
212 Gnash R .75 2.00
213 Kolorath E .60 1.50
214 Nespirah R .60 1.50
215 Ozumat E 1.00 2.50
216 Revenant of Neptulon U .20 .50
217 Servant of Neptulon U .20 .50
218 Unstable Corruption R .40 1.00
219 Wasteland Tallstrider E .60 1.50
220 Bloat the Bubble Fish U .20 .50
221 Erunak Stonespeaker R .40 1.00
222 Toshe Chaosrender R .75 2.00
223 Periwinkle Cloak U .20 .50
224 Shroud of Cooperation U .20 .50
225 Triton Legplates R .75 2.00
226 Wentletrap Vest C .10 .25
227 Big Cauldron of Battle R .60 1.50
228 Blessing of the Old God C .10 .25
229 Bottled Cunning C .10 .25
230 Bottled Death C .10 .25
231 Bottled Elements C .10 .25
232 Bottled Knowledge C .10 .25
233 Bottled Life C .10 .25
234 Bottled Light C .10 .25
235 Bottled Mind C .10 .25
236 Bottled Rage C .10 .25
237 Bottled Spite C .10 .25
238 Bottled Void C .10 .25
239 Bottled Wild C .10 .25
240 Nautilus Ring U .20 .50
241 Ring of the Great Whale U .20 .50
242 Severed Visionary Tentacle U .20 .50
243 Throwing Starfish R .75 2.00
244 Breathstone-Infused Longbow U .20 .50
245 Cerith Spire Staff R .75 2.00
246 Dawnblaze Blade U .20 .50
247 Dirk's Command C .10 .25
248 Downfall Hammer U .20 .50
249 Eel Cutter C .10 .25
250 Lightning Whelk Axe C .10 .25
251 Potentate's Letter Opener U .20 .50
252 Sorrow's End R .40 1.00
253 Throat Slasher C .10 .25
254 The Culmination of Our Efforts C .10 .25
255 The Last Living Lorekeeper C .10 .25
256 Reoccupation U .20 .50
257 Rescue the Earthspeaker! C .10 .25
258 Seeds of Their Demise C .10 .25
259 Setting an Example C .10 .25
260 Wake of Destruction U .20 .50
261 Waking the Beast C .10 .25
262 Waters of Elune C .10 .25
263 Throne of the Tides R .60 1.50

2011 World of Warcraft Throne of the Tides Loot

1 Bloat the Bubble Fish 4.00 10.00
2 Throwing Starfish 5.00 12.00
3 Wasteland Tallstrider 50.00 100.00

2011 World of Warcraft Twilight of the Dragons

COMPLETE SET (220) 100.00 150.00
BOOSTER BOX (24 PACKS) 40.00 80.00
BOOSTER PACK (19 CARDS) 3.00 4.00
RELEASED IN JULY 2011
1 Auralyn the Light of Dawn U .20 .50
2 Bladesinger Alyssa U .20 .50
3 Deragor the Earthsworn U .20 .50
4 Jasmia, Nature's Chosen U .20 .50
5 Kavar the Bloodthirsty U .20 .50
6 Nomak the Blazingclaw U .20 .50
7 Soul-Eater Morgania U .20 .50
8 Trilik the Light's Spark U .20 .50
9 Vad of the Four Winds U .20 .50
10 Zane the Sniper U .20 .50
11 Amah the Sun's Grace U .20 .50
12 Amaxi the Cruel U .20 .50
13 Dar'thael the Bloodsworn U .20 .50
14 Dragonslayer Drux U .20 .50
15 Earthseer Nakza U .20 .50
16 Flame Keeper Rizzli U .20 .50
17 Samael the Bloodpoint U .20 .50
18 Sumi'jin, Guardian of Cenarius U .20 .50
19 Suncaller Haruh U .20 .50
20 Zazel the Greedy U .20 .50
21 Deathwing the Destroyer E 10.00 25.00
22 Black Death U .20 .50
23 Dark Simulacrum R .40 1.00

24 Favor of Undeath C .10 .25
25 Frozen Core C .10 .25
26 Glacial Strike C .10 .25
27 Hungering Cold R .60 1.50
28 Necrotic Strike U .20 .50
29 Twisted Death Pact U .20 .50
30 Favor of Nature C .10 .25
31 Fierce Cat Form U .20 .50
32 Living Roots C .10 .25
33 Rebirth U .20 .50
34 Tears of Aessina C .10 .25
35 Twisted Wrath U .20 .50
36 Wild Growth R .40 1.00
37 Wild Mushroom R .40 1.00
38 Camouflage R .40 1.00
39 Cinder C .10 .25
40 Disengage C .10 .25
41 Explosive Hunt U .20 .50
42 Favor of the Hunt C .10 .25
43 Immolation Trap U .20 .50
44 Master Marksman R .60 1.50
45 Nag the Twisted U .20 .50
46 Blazing Debris C .10 .25
47 Favor of the Arcane C .10 .25
48 Fireball U .20 .50
49 Flame Orb R .60 1.50
50 Glaciate C .10 .25
51 Pyromaniac R .75 2.00
52 Ring of Frost U .20 .50
53 Twisted Arcana U .20 .50
54 Beacon of Light R 1.00 2.50
55 Blessing of Might U .20 .50
56 Favor of the Light C .10 .25
57 Guardian of Ancient Kings R 2.00 5.00
58 Hammer of Retribution C .10 .25
59 Hand of Protection C .10 .25
60 Twisted Light U .20 .50
61 Word of Glory U .20 .50
62 Favor of Spirit C .10 .25
63 Heal U .20 .50
64 Holy Blaze U .20 .50
65 Inner Will R .40 1.00
66 Power Word: Absorb C .10 .25
67 Power Word: Barrier R .75 2.00
68 Psychic Melt C .10 .25
69 Twisted Mind Spike U .20 .50
70 Break Steel C .10 .25
71 Favor of Mischief C .10 .25
72 Mind-Numbing Poison U .20 .50
73 Revealing Strike R 1.00 2.50
74 Smoke Bomb R .75 2.00
75 Swindle U .20 .50
76 Twisted Massacre U .20 .50
77 Vicious Strike C .10 .25
78 Burning Winds R .40 1.00
79 Cleanse Spirit C .10 .25
80 Favor of the Elements C .10 .25
81 Flametongue Weapon U .20 .50
82 Inferno Totem U .20 .50
83 Primal Strike C .10 .25
84 Riptide R 1.00 2.50
85 Twisted Fire Nova U .20 .50
86 Chaos Bolt R 1.50 4.00
87 Demonic Corruption R 2.50 6.00
88 Favor of the Nether C .10 .25
89 Fel Immolation C .10 .25
90 Incinerate U .20 .50
91 Selora C .10 .25
92 Twisted Infernal U .20 .50
93 Void Rip U .20 .50
94 Colossus Smash R .40 1.00
95 Demoralizing Strike C .10 .25
96 Executioner's Mark C .10 .25
97 Favor of Steel C .10 .25
98 Heroic Leap U .20 .50
99 Shockwave R .60 1.50
100 Slam U .20 .50
101 Twisted Rampage U .20 .50
102 Frozen Frenzy E 2.00 5.00
103 Council of Three Hammers E 2.50 6.00
104 Fool's Gold R .60 1.50
105 Abbie Whizzleblade C .10 .25
106 Alrak Stonecrack C .10 .25
107 Brel Blazebeard C .10 .25
108 Chandra Marlight C .10 .25
109 Frizzle Stumbleshade C .10 .25
110 Gardos Gravefang U .20 .50
111 Haratha Hammerflame C .10 .25
112 Javeer C .10 .25
113 Jerrak Krandle U .20 .50
114 Jessa the Lifebound U .20 .50
115 Kalan Howland C .10 .25
116 Kelsa Wildfire C .10 .25
117 Knight Karia C .10 .25
118 Lord Darius Crowley U .20 .50
119 Lyrana of Eldre'Thalas R .40 1.00
120 Maurice Steelson U .20 .50
121 Prince Anduin Wrynn E 2.50 6.00
122 Roger Ulric C .10 .25
123 Stacia Markton U .20 .50
124 Stargazer Ronal C .10 .25
125 Tania Falan U .20 .50
126 Vakus the Inferno R 6.00 15.00
127 Windspeaker Nuvu C .10 .25
128 Abysswalker Rakax U .20 .50
129 Azami'tal the Flamebender R .60 1.50
130 Azizi Daggerflick C .10 .25
131 Banok Sunrock C .10 .25
132 Blood Knight Adrenna U .20 .50
133 Commander Molotov R .40 1.00
134 Dagax the Butcher R 5.00 12.00
135 Falixia Frizzleblast C .10 .25
136 Flamebringer Gaxix U .20 .50
137 Gavin Haverston C .10 .25
138 Gerwixicks C .10 .25
139 Gollom Skybang C .10 .25
140 Gordash Firetooth C .10 .25
141 High Chieftain Baine E 2.00 5.00
142 High Guard Braxx C .10 .25
143 Jaga'zul the Wild's Fury R .75 2.00
144 Kraxos Chizzlecoin U .20 .50
145 Kyroth Steelspite C .10 .25
146 Rakala Deathsmash C .10 .25
147 Sahama Brighthorn C .10 .25
148 Shade Emissary Vaxxod U .20 .50
149 Warchief Garrosh E 4.00 10.00
150 Wildweaver Masa'zun C .10 .25
151 Yazli Earthspark C .10 .25
152 Zor'dul Deathbinder C .10 .25
153 Nefarian U .20 .50
154 Obsidia R .40 1.00
155 Obsidian Drakonid C .10 .25
156 Obsidian Drudge C .10 .25
157 Obsidian Enforcer C .10 .25
158 Obsidian Pyrewing C .10 .25
159 Obsidian Skyterror C .10 .25
160 Sinestra R 2.00 5.00
161 Twilight Corruptor U .20 .50
162 Twilight Drake U .20 .50
163 Twilight Emissary U .20 .50
164 Twilight Shadowdrake U .20 .50
165 Twilight Wyrmkiller U .20 .50
166 Caelestrasz R 1.50 4.00
167 Merithra R .40 1.00
168 Arygos R 1.00 2.50
169 Anachronos R .40 1.00
170 Ignacious R .40 1.00
171 Feludius R .40 1.00
172 Arion R .60 1.50
173 Terrastra R .40 1.00
174 Cho'gall E 1.50 4.00
175 Amani Dragonhawk E 2.50 6.00
176 Nightsaber Cub U .20 .50
177 Thrall, Guardian E 3.00 8.00
178 Battleplate of the Apocalypse U .20 .50
179 Double Attack Handguards U .20 .50
180 Flame Pillar Leggings C .10 .25
181 Polished Helm of Valor R .60 1.50
182 Proto-Handler's Gauntlets C .10 .25
183 Stained Shadowcraft Cap R .75 2.00
184 Tarnished Raging Helm R .60 1.50
185 Tattered Dreadmist Mask R .60 1.50
186 Corrupted Egg Shell U .20 .50
187 Darkmoon Card: Hurricane R .75 2.00
188 Akirus the Worm-Breaker R 2.00 5.00
189 Axe of the Eclipse U .20 .50
190 Blade of the Burning Sun R .40 1.00
191 Blade of the Witching Hour C .10 .25
192 Chelley's Staff of Mending R .75 2.00
193 Claws of Torment C .10 .25
194 Cookie's Stirring Rod R .40 1.00
195 Crul'korak, the Lightning R 2.50 6.00
196 Darklight Torch U .20 .50
197 Dragonheart Piercer U .20 .50
198 Elementium Poleaxe U .20 .50
199 Lava Spine U .20 .50
200 Obsidium Executioner C .10 .25
201 Organic Lifeform Inverter U .20 .50
202 Shalug'doom, the Axe E 3.00 8.00
203 Twilight's Hammer R 1.50 4.00
204 Volatile Thunderstick U .20 .50
205 Battle of Life and Death C .10 .25
206 Blackout U .20 .50
207 The Crucible of Carnage: The Twilight Terror C .10 .25
208 Devoured C .10 .25
209 Enter the Dragon Queen C .10 .25
210 Far from the Nest C .10 .25
211 Fire the Cannon C .10 .25
212 A Fiery Reunion C .10 .25
213 Last of Her Kind C .10 .25
214 The Maw of Iso'rath C .10 .25
215 Mercy for the Bound C .10 .25
216 Mr. Goldmine's Wild Ride C .10 .25
217 Twilight Extermination C .10 .25
218 Unbinding C .10 .25
219 The Worldbreaker R .75 2.00
220 Twilight Citadel R 20.00 40.00

2011 World of Warcraft Twilight of the Dragons Loot

1 Nightsaber Cub 6.00 15.00
2 Fool's Gold 10.00 25.00
3 Amani Dragonhawk 125.00 200.00

2011 World of Warcraft War of the Elements

COMPLETE SET (220) 100.00 150.00
BOOSTER BOX (24 PACKS) 40.00 80.00
BOOSTER PACK (19 CARDS) 3.00 4.00
RELEASED IN APRIL 2011
1 Almia Moonwhisper U .20 .50
2 Aric Stonejack U .20 .50
3 Edwin Blademark U .20 .50
4 Grayson Steelworth U .20 .50
5 Gundek Hammerguard U .20 .50
6 Huntsman Gorwal U .20 .50
7 Merissa Firebrew U .20 .50
8 Olivia Demascas U .20 .50
9 Thira Anvilash U .20 .50
10 Vanira Raventhorne U .20 .50
11 Baxxel Geartooth U .20 .50
12 Fraznak the Furious U .20 .50
13 Jinxy Blastwheel U .20 .50
14 Kanga the Primal U .20 .50
15 Mindtwister Quimtrix U .20 .50
16 Sunwalker Nahano U .20 .50
17 Tazrik Crankrust U .20 .50
18 Uzak'zim U .20 .50
19 Zimzi the Trickster U .20 .50
20 Zin'sul U .20 .50
21 Kalecgos E 6.00 15.00
22 Nozdormu the Timeless E 4.00 10.00
23 Blight Bringers C .10 .20
24 Command of Undeath C .10 .20
25 Death Strike U .20 .50
26 Frozen Blight U .20 .50
27 Gargoyle R 6.00 15.00
28 Horn of Winter C .10 .20
29 Outbreak R .40 1.00
30 Sanguine Presence R .40 1.00
31 Brutal Bear Form U .20 .50
32 Celestial Moonfire R 1.50 4.00
33 Healing Touch U .20 .50
34 Maim C .10 .20
35 Moonshard C .10 .20
36 Rend and Tear R .75 2.00
37 Savage Cat Form C .10 .20
38 Starburst R 2.00 5.00
39 Arcane Shot C .10 .20
40 Cobra Shot R .75 2.00
41 Donatello C .10 .20
42 Loque R 2.00 5.00
43 Noxious Trap R .75 2.00
44 Warning Shot C .10 .20
45 Widow Venom U .20 .50
46 Wild Fervor U .20 .50
47 Arcane Barrage R 4.00 10.00
48 Arcane Foresight C .10 .20
49 Arcane Inferno R .40 1.00
50 Arcane Missiles C .10 .20
51 Draconic Flames U .20 .50
52 Flash Freeze C .10 .20
53 Mystical Refreshment R .40 1.00
54 Tidal Elemental U .20 .50
55 Blessing of Faith U .20 .50
56 Flash of Light C .10 .20
57 Holy Vengeance R .40 1.00
58 Holy Wrath R .40 1.00
59 Inquisition C .10 .20
60 Light of Reckoning C .10 .20
61 Shield of the Righteous R .40 1.00
62 Vengeful Crusader Strike U .20 .50
63 Dark Embrace R .40 1.00
64 Expel C .10 .20
65 Focused Dispel C .10 .20
66 Hymn of Hope U .20 .50
67 Leap of Faith R 3.00 8.00
68 Mind Melt R 1.50 4.00
69 Power Word: Endurance U .20 .50
70 Shadow Word: Death C .10 .20
71 Agonizing Poison U .20 .50
72 Coated Blades R .40 1.00
73 Infiltrate C .10 .20
74 Invigorate U .20 .50
75 Sap C .10 .20
76 Shadow Dance R 2.00 5.00
77 Tormenting Gouge C .10 .20
78 Tricksters Gambit R 2.00 5.00
79 Ancestral Recovery C .10 .20
80 Blazing Elemental Totem U .20 .50
81 Chain Heal C .10 .20
82 Elemental Flames C .10 .20
83 Primal Dexterity U .20 .50
84 Tempest Totem R 1.00 2.50
85 Totemic Vigor R .40 1.00
86 Unleash Elements R 2.00 5.00
87 Dread Touch C .10 .20
88 Everlasting Affliction R 1.50 4.00
89 Fel Covenant C .10 .20
90 Fel Flame R 1.50 4.00
91 Grimdron U .20 .50
92 Grim Harvest R .40 1.00
93 Mazzhum C .10 .20
94 Seed of Corruption U .20 .50
95 Burning Rage R .40 1.00
96 Dauntless Defender C .10 .20
97 Enraged Regeneration R .40 1.00
98 Intercept C .10 .20
99 Merciless Strikes U .20 .50
100 Peerless Guard C .10 .20
101 Shattering Throw U .20 .50
102 Intensify E 3.00 8.00
103 To Arms! E 4.00 10.00
104 Firelord's Gift, The U .20 .50
105 Stonemother's Gift, The U .20 .50
106 Tidehunter's Gift, The U .20 .50
107 Windlord's Gift, The U .20 .50
108 Arvos Jadestone C .10 .20
109 Axar C .10 .20
110 Brimi Tinkerblade C .10 .20
111 Cadric Talworth C .10 .20
112 Dagin Bootzap C .10 .20
113 Dominic Kandor C .10 .20
114 Elmira Moonsurge R .40 1.00
115 Erama C .10 .20
116 Gully Rustinax C .10 .20
117 Jenina Prescott C .10 .20
118 Jerrick Valder C .10 .20
119 Kane the Arcanist U .20 .50
120 Nathar Wilderson C .10 .20
121 Nessera Gildenrose C .10 .20
122 Patricia Potter C .10 .20
123 Rufus Claybourne R 4.00 10.00
124 Shadowseer Calista U .20 .50
125 Shaytha Lumenira U .20 .50
126 Stewrona Forgemender R .75 2.00
127 Tidus the Relentless R 2.00 5.00
128 Vincent Brayden C .10 .20
129 Xeris C .10 .20
130 Zooti Fizzlefury U .20 .50
131 Burom Bladeseer C .10 .20
132 Caera Sunforge C .10 .20
133 Drax Felfuse C .10 .20
134 Hanu Skyhorn U .20 .50
135 Kark Baneblood C .10 .20
136 Kizzli Grinderstub C .10 .20
137 Korlix Grimvik C .10 .20
138 Kuatha Mornhoof C .10 .20
139 Lena Naville C .10 .20
140 Maxie the Blaster R .40 1.00
141 Nikka Blastbor C .10 .20
142 Rakzi the Earthgraced R .75 2.00
143 Razo'jun U .20 .50
144 Rumu Moonhaze C .10 .20
145 Shaera Strikewing C .10 .20
146 Talaan Solaras C .10 .20
147 Timriv the Enforcer C .10 .20
148 Tharuk Foulblade U .20 .50
149 Tol'zin R 2.00 5.00
150 Valytha Colton C .10 .20
151 Yoza'tsu C .10 .20
152 Zarvix the Tormentor R .40 1.00
153 Zeni'vun U .20 .50
154 Azure Captain C .10 .20
155 Azure Drake C .10 .20
156 Azure Emissary U .20 .50
157 Azure Enforcer C .10 .20
158 Azure Magus C .10 .20
159 Azure Skyrazor U .20 .50
160 Tyrygosa R 1.50 4.00
161 Bronze Drake C .10 .20
162 Bronze Drakonid U .20 .50
163 Bronze Emissary U .20 .50
164 Bronze Guardian C .10 .20
165 Bronze Skyrazor C .10 .20
166 Bronze Warden C .10 .20
167 Soridormi R 1.50 4.00
168 Al'Akir the Windlord E 3.00 8.00
169 Bound Vortex U .20 .50
170 Bound Rumbler U .20 .50
171 Therazane Stonemother E 2.50 6.00
172 Bound Inferno U .20 .50
173 Ragnaros the Firelord E 2.50 6.00
174 Bound Torrent U .20 .50
175 Neptulon the Tidehunter E 2.50 6.00
176 Landro's Lichling U .20 .50
177 Malfurion Stormrage E 4.00 10.00
178 Savage Raptor E 2.50 6.00
179 Champions Dthdlr Brstplte R .75 2.00
180 Crown of Chelonian Freedom U .20 .50
181 God Grinding Grips U .20 .50
182 Helm of Terrorizing Fangs R .40 1.00
183 Leggings of the Vanquished Usurper U .20 .50
184 Polished Spaulders of Valor R .40 1.00
185 Stained Shadowcraft Spaulders R .40 1.00
186 Tattered Dreadmist Robe R .75 2.00
187 Wildlife Defender R .40 1.00
188 Darkmoon Card: Volcano R .40 1.00
189 Landros Hitching Post R .40 1.00
190 Axe of Grounded Flame R .40 1.00
191 Barnacle Coated Greataxe R .40 1.00
192 Blacksoul Polearm R .40 1.00
193 Crusher of Bonds C .10 .20
194 Fire Etched Dagger U .20 .50
195 Glyphtrace Ritual Knife R 1.50 4.00
196 Kickback 5000 R .40 1.00
197 Lightningflash U .20 .50
198 Lordbane Scepter R .40 1.00
199 Poisonfire Greatsword R .40 1.00
200 Perforator, The R .40 1.00
201 Wild Hammer R .40 1.00
202 Aessina's Miracle C .10 .20
203 All That Rises C .10 .20
204 Bird In Hand, A C .10 .20
205 Breaking the Bonds C .10 .20
206 Defending the Rift C .10 .20
207 Dragon, Unchained C .10 .20
208 Elemental Energy C .10 .20
209 End of the Supply Line C .10 .20
210 Entrenched C .10 .20
211 Forged of Shadow and Flame C .10 .20
212 Head Full of Wind, A U .20 .50
213 Lightning in a Bottle C .10 .20
214 Putting the Pieces Together U .20 .50
215 Sea Legs U .20 .50
216 Something That Burns U .20 .50
217 Abyssal Maw R 1.50 4.00
218 Deepholm R .75 2.00
219 Firelands R 2.00 5.00
220 Skywall R 1.00 2.50

2011 World of Warcraft War of the Elements Loot

1 Landro's Lichling 3.00 8.00
2 War Party Hitching Post 15.00 40.00
3 Savage Raptor 125.00 200.00

2012 World of Warcraft Crown of the Heavens

COMPLETE SET (202) 120.00 200.00
BOOSTER BOX (36 PACKS) 60.00 90.00
BOOSTER PACK (16 CARDS) 2.00 3.00
RELEASED IN JUNE 2012
1 Arisella, Daughter of Cenarius U .20 .50
2 Iso'rath U .20 .50
3 Tyrus Blackhorn U .20 .50
4 Warlord Grok'thol U .20 .50
5A Cenarius, Lord of the Forest E 2.00 5.00
5B Cenarius, Lord (Ext. Art) 4.00 10.00
6 Crimson Guard C .10 .25
7 Dark Transformation R .60 1.50
8 Despair of Undeath U .20 .50
9 Leeching Fever U .20 .50
10 Vampiric Siphon R .60 1.50
11 Ferocious Cat Form U .20 .50
12 Malfurion's Gift R .60 1.50
13 Mark of Elderlimb U .20 .50
14 Mark of the Ancients C .10 .25
15 Monstrous Boon R 1.50 4.00
16 Wild Cascade R .40 1.00
17 McCloud the Fox C .10 .25
18 Quick Trap U .20 .50
19 Sniper Training R 1.00 2.50
20 Yertle R 4.00 10.00
21 Flame Lance C .10 .25
22 Frost Blast U .20 .50
23 Ice Barrier R 4.00 10.00
24 Overload U .20 .50
25 Shroud of the Archmage R 2.00 5.00
26 The Art of War R .40 1.00
27 Blessing of the Devoted C .10 .25
28 Divine Bulwark R .40 1.00
29 Light of the Naaru U .20 .50
30 Vindicator's Shock U .20 .50
31 Borrowed Time R 1.50 4.00
32 Faithful Heal U .20 .50
33 Shadow Word: Despair U .20 .50
34 Shroud of the High Priest R .40 1.00
35 Spiritual Imbalance C .10 .25
36 Assassin's Strike C .10 .25
37 Boundless Thievery R 1.00 2.50
38 Hemorrhage R .40 1.00
39 Poison the Well U .20 .50
40 Earthquake R .40 1.00
41 Frost Arc C .10 .25
42 Monstrous Totem R 1.00 2.50
43 Rage of the Elements U .20 .50
44 Tidal Totem U .20 .50
45 Unleash Inferno R 1.25 3.00
46 Banish Soul U .20 .50
47 Fire and Brimstone R 1.00 2.50
48 Gakuri U .20 .50
49 Monstrous Void R 1.25 3.00
50 Shaalun C .10 .25
51 Shroud of the Nethermancer R .60 1.50
52 Bladestorm R 3.00 8.00
53 Boundless Rage R 1.00 2.50
54 Brutal Strike C .10 .25
55 Destructive Disarm U .20 .50
56 Infectious Brutality U .20 .50
57 Hexamorph U .20 .50
58 The Light's Gaze U .20 .50
59 Master's Embrace U .20 .50
60 Overwhelm U .20 .50
61 Paralyzing Strike U .20 .50
62 Essence of Aggression U .20 .50
63 Essence of Defense U .20 .50
64 Essence of Focus U .20 .50
65 Essence of Light U .20 .50
66 Essence of Rage U .20 .50
67 Essence of War U .20 .50
68 Bark and Bite R .60 1.50
69 Bash and Slash R 1.25 3.00
70 Fear and Loathing R .40 1.00
71 Preserve and Protect R 1.50 4.00
72 Rime and Freezin' R 1.50 4.00
73 Aeshia Moonstreak C .10 .25
74 Aleksei Brandal U .20 .50
75 Anathel the Eagle-Eye R 1.25 3.00
76 Andrews the Just C .10 .25
77 Archdruid Malfurion E 2.50 6.00
78 Bromor the Shadowblade R .40 1.00
79 Dar the Beastmaster C .10 .25
80 Emree U .20 .50
81 Esala U .20 .50
82 Father Charles C .10 .25
83 Flamesinger Zara C .10 .25
84 Frimzy Fuzzbum U .20 .50
85 Gerrunge the Sadist R .40 1.00
86 Graddis Battlebeard R .40 1.00
87 Grovewarden Daviak U .20 .50
88 Jeishal U .40 1.00
89 Kalam Blacksteel C .10 .25
90 Kaldric Stoutwhisker U .20 .50
91 Lucy Elizabeth C .10 .25
92 Shalyssa Groveshaper C .10 .25
93 Targus Roughblade C .10 .25
94 Thadrus, Shield of Teldrassil R 3.00 8.00
95 Tharal Wildbreeze C .10 .25
96 Tommi Spazzratchet C .10 .25
97 Tyrande, High Priestess E 4.00 10.00
98 Velkin Gray U .20 .50
99 Wendy Anne C .10 .25
100 Zazzo Dizzleflame R 1.00 2.50
101 Abasha Windstorm U .20 .50
102 Alyna Sunshower C .10 .25
103 Baru Gravehorn U .20 .50
104 Drotara the Bloodpoint C .10 .25
105 Elderguard Brennan U .20 .50
106 Grak Foulblade C .10 .25
107 Gravelord Adams R 1.00 2.50
108 Hamuul Runetotem E 1.00 2.50
109 Horngrim U .20 .50
110 Ian Lanstrick U .20 .50
111 Icaros the Sunward C .10 .25
112 Kraznix Smolderpain C .10 .25
113 Lazarus Marrowbane C .10 .25
114 Moharu the Skyseer R .40 1.00
115 Muluno Sunbreath U .20 .50
116 Nox the Lifedrainer R .40 1.00
117 Raezi C .10 .25
118 Soulde the Earthshaker R 1.25 3.00
119 Sylvanas, Queen E 2.00 5.00
120 Thespius Bloodblaze C .10 .25
121 Thunderpetal U .20 .50
122 Tor Earthwalker C .10 .25
123 Tristani the Sunblade R .40 1.00
124 Vazu'jin C .10 .25
125 Vizo Arctwister C .10 .25
126 Vor'zun C .10 .25
127 Witch Doctor Ka'booma R 3.00 8.00
128 Zaza'jun U .20 .50
129 Brogre U .20 .50
130 Deathsmasher Mogdar C .10 .25
131 Drak'narr C .10 .25
132 Dro'gash R .40 1.00
133 Grag'tok C .10 .25
134 Grug the Bonecrusher C .10 .25
135 High Warlord Zogar E 2.50 6.00

136 Krogar the Colossal R 3.00 8.00
137 Krum'shal U .20 .50
138 Throk the Conqueror C .10 .25
139 Torr'nag U .20 .50
140 Trag'ush C .10 .25
141 Jadefire Felsworn U .20 .50
142 Jadefire Hellcaller C .10 .25
143 Jadefire Rogue U .20 .50
144 Jadefire Satyr C .10 .25
145 Jadefire Scout C .10 .25
146 Jadefire Trickster C .10 .25
147 Prince Xavalis E 5.00 12.00
148 Vylokx R 2.50 6.00
149 Baby Murloc U 1.00 2.50
150 Bubblesmash C .10 .25
151 Guffin C .10 .25
152 King Bagurgle, Terror E 3.00 8.00
153 Splashtooth C .10 .25
154 Keeper Alinar C .10 .25
155 Keeper Balos C .10 .25
156 Keeper Sharus R 4.00 10.00
157 Remulos, Son of Cenarius R 2.50 6.00
158 Ashroot, Ancient of Lore U .20 .50
159 Stonebranch, Ancient of War U .20 .50
160 High Prophet Barim R .40 1.00
161 Neferset Darkcaster C .10 .25
162 Aessina R .40 1.00
163 Gronn Skullcracker R 2.50 6.00
164 Harpy Matriarch C .10 .25
165 Vicious Grell U .20 .50
166 Corrupted Hippogryph E 1.00 2.50
167 Farseer Nobundo R .40 1.00
168 Hyjal Stag C .10 .25
169 Muln Earthfury R 1.50 4.00
170 Belt of Absolute Zero C .10 .25
171 Crown of the Ogre King R 2.00 5.00
172 Gravitational Pull R 1.50 4.00
173 Power Generator Hood C .10 .25
174 Spaulders of the Scarred Lady U .20 .50
175 Magical Ogre Idol R 1.50 4.00
176 Miniature Voodoo Mask R 5.00 12.00
177 Vial of Stolen Memories R 1.50 4.00
178 Brainsplinter U .20 .50
179 Branch of Nordrassil R .40 1.00
180 Dragonwrath, Tarecgosa's Rest E 1.50 4.00
181 Gurubashi Punisher U .20 .50
182 Irontree Knives U .20 .50
183 Legacy of Arlokk U .20 .50
184 Lumbering Ogre Axe C .10 .25
185 Maimgor's Bite R 1.50 4.00
186 Mandible of Beth'tilac C .10 .25
187 Mandokir's Tribute U .20 .50
188 Reclaimed Ashkandi R 1.50 4.00
189 Skullstealer Greataxe C .10 .25
190 Sulfuras, Extinguished R 1.25 3.00
191 An Ancient Awakens C .10 .25
192 As Hyjal Burns C .10 .25
193 The Battle Is Won, the War Goes On C .10 .25
194 Black Heart of Flame C .10 .25
195 Cleaning House C .10 .25
196 If You're Not Against Us... C .10 .25
197 Signed in Blood C .10 .25
198 Nordrassil, the World Tree R 1.50 4.00

2012 World of Warcraft Crown of the Heavens Loot

1 Vicious Grell 5.00 12.00
2 Magical Ogre Idol 15.00 40.00
3 Corrupted Hippogryph 100.00 200.00

2012 World of Warcraft Tomb of the Forgotten

COMPLETE SET (202) 50.00 100.00
BOOSTER BOX (36 PACKS) 50.00 80.00
BOOSTER PACK (16 CARDS) 2.00 3.00
RELEASED IN JUNE 2012
1 Dark Pharaoh Tekahn U .20 .50
2 The Forgotten U .20 .50
3 Nexus-Thief Asar U .20 .50
4 Augh U .20 .50
5 High Guardian Malosun U .20 .50
6 Jasani, Shrine Keeper U .20 .50
7 Mistress Nesala U .20 .50
8 Mogdar the Frozenheart U .20 .50
9 Thrall the Earth-Warder E 4.00 10.00
9EA Thrall the Earth-Warder EA
10 Blood Parasite R .40 1.00
11 Boundless Winter R .40 1.00
12 Frozen Strength U .20 .50
13 Raise the Dead C .10 .25
14 Siphon of Undeath U .20 .50
15 Mark of Restoration U .20 .50
16 Natural Purification R .40 1.00
17 Primal Madness R .40 1.00
18 Wild Rejuvenation U .20 .50
19 Wild Wrath C .10 .25
20 Cobra Sting R .40 1.00
21 Hunter's Focus C .10 .25
22 Interfering Shot U .20 .50
23 Obliterating Trap U .20 .50
24 Uberserc R .40 1.00
25 Boundless Magic R .40 1.00
26 Firestarter R .40 1.00
27 Polymorph: Pig U .20 .50
28 Spark of Brilliance C .10 .25
29 Wildfire U .20 .50
30 Blessing of Resolution U .20 .50
31 Divine Redemption R .40 1.00
32 Hammer of Vengeance U .20 .50
33 Hand of Devotion U .20 .50
34 Monstrous Vengeance R .40 1.00
35 Tower of Radiance R .40 1.00
36 Faithful Dispel U .20 .50
37 Mind Shatter C .10 .25
38 Monstrous Intervention R .40 1.00
39 Power Word: Resurrection R .40 1.00
40 Shadow Word: Corruption U .20 .50
41 Shadowy Apparition R .75 2.00
42 Decisive Strike C .10 .25
43 Extortion U .20 .50
44 Monstrous Rush R .40 1.00
45 Restless Blades R .75 2.00
46 Slaughter R .40 1.00
47 Trickster's Reflex U .20 .50
48 Ancestral Revival R .40 1.00
49 Arc Heal U .20 .50
50 Call of Lightning U .20 .50
51 Force of Earth C .10 .25
52 Unleashed Rage R .40 1.00
53 Boundless Hellfire R 1.50 4.00
54 Dark Intent U .20 .50
55 Drain Soul C .10 .25
56 Frenzied Doomguard U .20 .50
57 Hand of Gul'dan R .40 1.00
58 Champion's Shout R .40 1.00
59 Concussion Blow R .40 1.00
60 Fearless Strike U .20 .50
61 Guardian's Endurance U .20 .50
62 Terrifying Shout C .10 .25
63 Thrall's Desire R .40 1.00
64 Thrall's Doubt R .40 1.00
65 Thrall's Fury R .40 1.00
66 Thrall's Patience R .40 1.00
67 Courage C .10 .25
68 Monstrous Heal C .10 .25
69 Monstrous Regeneration C .10 .25
70 Monstrous Strength C .10 .25
71 Power C .10 .25
72 Wisdom C .10 .25
73 Aaron Goodchilde R .40 1.00
74 Alaria the Huntress C .10 .25
75 Ashton Barstow C .10 .25
76 Baradis Darkstone C .10 .25
77 Bishop Ketodo C .10 .25
78 Crankston Deathspark C .10 .25
79 Darkstalker Soran E .75 2.00
80 Earthseer Dambrak R .40 1.00
81 Elementalist Arax U .20 .50
82 Goetia C .10 .25
83 Gretta Grindstone U .20 .50
84 Jaelen the Ripper R .75 2.00
85 Jarius Blackwood U .20 .50
86 Kalaan C .10 .25
87 Kedan Burstbeard C .10 .25
88 Kraven the Gravebound U .20 .50
89 Naasi C .10 .25
90 Philosopher Kirlenko U .20 .50
91 Renzo Soulfang R .40 1.00
92 Sergeant Corsetti C .10 .25
93 Shadowseer Thraner U .20 .50
94 Taliax the Ironjaw R .40 1.00
95 Velen, Prophet of the Naaru E .60 1.50
96 Zalabar the Dark Tinkerer R .40 1.00
97 Amara Kells C .10 .25
98 Brulu Breaks-the-Land U .20 .50
99 Daedak the Graveborne R 2.00 5.00
100 Dakturak C .10 .25
101 Deathguard Ashleigh R .40 1.00
102 Galvano the Beast Lord E .60 1.50
103 Grok Goreblade C .10 .25
104 Harudu Cloudshot C .10 .25
105 Ishael Bloodlight C .10 .25
106 Kaelzin C .10 .25
107 Lor'themar Theron, Regent Lord E .75 2.00
108 Nadina the Red R .75 2.00
109 Raso'jin U .20 .50
110 Seraxa Brightmix R .40 1.00
111 Sludgelauncher Krillzix R .40 1.00
112 Soulstealer Adams U .20 .50
113 Sunstalker Maelan C .10 .25
114 Thanu Sunhorn U .20 .50
115 Trickster Tesslah C .10 .25
116 Veliana Felblood U .20 .50
117 Wrex C .10 .25
118 Yunzo the Hexer U .20 .50
119 Zanrix Steelboot C .10 .25
120 Zindalan R .40 1.00
121 General Husam E 3.00 8.00
122 Harbinger Sefu R .40 1.00
123 High Oracle Naseem R .40 1.00
124 Neferset Bladelord C .10 .25
125 Neferset Champion C .10 .25
126 Neferset Darkcaster C .10 .25
127 Neferset Frostbringer C .10 .25
128 Neferset Runecaster C .10 .25
129 Neferset Scorpid Keeper C .10 .25
130 Neferset Sentry U .20 .50
131 Neferset Shadowlancer C .10 .25
132 Neferset Shadowstalker U .20 .50
133 Neferset Shieldguard U .20 .50
134 Okumet, Herald of the Light U .20 .50
135 Taluret, Herald of Faith U .20 .50
136 Dun'zarg C .10 .25
137 Gorlash, Herald of the Elements U .20 .50
138 Korbash the Devastator R .40 1.00
139 Mok'drul U .20 .50
140 Zog, Herald of Death U .20 .50
141 Zores, Herald of War U .20 .50
142 Zuglisch C .10 .25
143 Frizzlight C .10 .25
144 Nargle, Fang of the Swarm E .60 1.50
145 Ragespike C .10 .25
146 Shiverspine U .20 .50
147 Slimefin U .20 .50
148 Swifteye R .40 1.00
149 Kresss, Herald of the Hunt U .20 .50
150 Pythisss, Herald of Frost U .20 .50
151 Araxian, Herald of Trickery U .20 .50
152 Bazul, Herald of the Fel U .20 .50
153 Akhet R .40 1.00
154 Lockmaw R .40 1.00
155 Obsidian Colossus R .40 1.00
156 Pygmy Firebreather C .10 .25
157 Pygmy Pyramid E 6.00 15.00
158 Renshol, Herald of Nature U .20 .50
159 Siamat, Lord of the South Wind E .60 1.50
160 Sand Scarab U .20 .50
161 Aggra R 2.00 5.00
162 Harrison Jones R .40 1.00
163 White Camel E .60 1.50
164 Anraphet's Regalia C .10 .25
165 Bulwark of the Primordial Mound U .20 .50
166 Flickering Cowl U .20 .50
167 Flickering Shoulders C .10 .25
168 Gloves of Dissolving Smoke U .20 .50
169 Helm of Blazing Glory R .40 1.00
170 Helm of Setesh U .20 .50
171 Mantle of Master Cho U .20 .50
172 Pauldrons of Roaring Flame C .10 .25
173 Poison Fang Bracers U .20 .50
174 Scalp of the Bandit Prince R .40 1.00
175 Ammunae, Construct of Life R .40 1.00
176 Isiset, Construct of Magic R .40 1.00
177 Rajh, Construct of the Sun R .40 1.00
178 Setesh, Construct of Destruction R .40 1.00
179 Apparatus of Khaz'goroth C .10 .25
180 Rune of Zeth C .10 .25
181 Spurious Sarcophagus R .40 1.00
182 Variable Pulse Lightning Capacitor R .40 1.00
183 Barim's Main Cauche U .20 .50
184 Biting Wind U .20 .50
185 Fandral's Flamescythe C .10 .25
186 Feeding Frenzy R .40 1.00
187 Hammer of Sparks U .20 .50
188 Ko'gun, Hammer of the Firelord R .40 1.00
189 Lava Bolt Crossbow U .20 .50
190 Obsidim Cleaver C .10 .25
191 Overpowered Chicken Splitter C .10 .25
192 Ruthless Gladiator's Decapitator R .40 1.00
193 Scepter of Power U .20 .50
194 Spire of Scarlet Pain U .20 .50
195 Zoid's Firelit Greatsword U .20 .50
196 The Defense of Nahom C .10 .25
197 The Fall of Neferst City C .10 .25
198 Gnomebliteration C .10 .25
199 Tailgunner C .10 .25
200 Thieving Little Pluckers C .10 .25
201 Traitors! C .10 .25
202 Uldum R .40 1.00

2012 World of Warcraft Tomb of the Forgotten Loot

1 Sand Scarab 3.00 8.00
2 Spurious Sarcophagus 5.00 12.00
3 White Camel 50.00 100.00

2012 World of Warcraft War of the Ancients

COMPLETE SET (240) 100.00 150.00
Booster Box (36 packs) 50.00 80.00
BOOSTER PACK (15 CARDS) 2.00 3.00
RELEASED IN OCTOBER 2012
1EA Malorne the White Stag (Ext.Art) 1.50 4.00
1 Malorne the White Stag E 1.50 4.00
2 Beyond the Grave R .60 1.50
3 Crushing Death U .20 .50
4 Death's Decree U .20 .50
5 Despair of Winter R .40 1.00
6 Ebon Plague R .40 1.00
7 Festering Disease U .20 .50
8 Frigid Frailty C .10 .25
9 Ancient Bear Form U .20 .50
10 Euphoria R .60 1.50
11 Lions, Tigers, and Bears R .60 1.50
12 Mark of Growth U .20 .50
13 Mark of Malorne C .10 .25
14 Wild Attunement R .60 1.50
15 Wild Seeds U .20 .50
16 Arrowstorm C .10 .25
17 Bear Trap U .20 .50
18 Beast Mastery R .40 1.00
19 Endure R .60 1.50
20 Furious George U .20 .50
21 Skitter R .60 1.50
22 Arcane Potency R .75 2.00
23 Arcane Unraveling U .20 .50
24 Conjure Elementals R .60 1.50
25 Firestorm U .20 .50
26 Ice Prison C .10 .25
27 Manaflow R .60 1.50
28 Reckless Fireball U .20 .50
29 Blessing of Vigilance U .20 .50
30 Crusader's Might R .60 1.50
31 Divinity R .60 1.50
32 Guardian of the Light R .40 1.00
33 Hammer of Sanctity U .20 .50
34 Holy Ground U .20 .50
35 Shield of Light C .10 .25
36 Gifted Heal U .20 .50
37 Guardian Spirit R .60 1.50
38 Mind Crush U .20 .50
39 Power Word: Tenacity R .60 1.50
40 Redeeming Dispel C .10 .25
41 Shadow Word: Devour R .60 1.50
42 Spirit Shield U .20 .50
43 Devious Dismantle U .20 .50
44 Guise of the Stalker U .20 .50
45 Hands of Deceit R .40 1.00
46 Hidden Strike C .10 .25
47 Kiss of Death R .40 1.00
48 Opportunity R .60 1.50
49 Volatile Poison U .20 .50
50 Elemental Echo R .60 1.50
51 Elemental Purge U .20 .50
52 Gale Force C .10 .25
53 Lava Strike U .20 .50
54 Scalding Totem U .20 .50
55 Spark of Rage R .60 1.50
56 Spirit Link Totem R .60 1.50
57 Call the Void U .20 .50
58 Demonic Infusion U .20 .50
59 Gaktai C .10 .25
60 Netherpocalypse R .40 1.00
61 Nightfall R .40 1.00
62 Nimanda R .60 1.50
63 Soul Trap U .20 .50
64 Blind Rage U .20 .50
65 Bloodthirsty Shout C .10 .25
66 Combat Stance R .40 1.00
67 Decimate U .20 .50
68 Raging Blow R .60 1.50
69 Ruthless Execution U .20 .50
70 Strife R .40 1.00
71 Blitz C .10 .25
72 Focused Heal C .10 .25
73 Legacy of Stormrage E .60 1.50
74 Legacy of the Legion E 4.00 10.00
75 Vigilant Guard C .10 .25
76 Glory to the Alliance! C .10 .25
77 Blood and Thunder! C .10 .25
78 Burn Away C .10 .25
79 Elune's Blessing C .10 .25
80 Shattering Blow C .10 .25
81 Strike C .10 .25
82 Alpha Prime R .60 1.50
83 Ansem, Timewalker Deathblade R .40 1.00
84 Bolin Moonflare U .20 .50
85 Darkshire Deathsworn C .10 .25
86 Darlon Blacksoul U .20 .50
87 Darnassus Mooncaller C .10 .25
88 Darnassus Shadowblade C .10 .25
89 Darnassus Warrior C .10 .25
90 Delinar Silvershot U .20 .50
91 Eldre'Thalas Sorceress C .10 .25
92 Elysa Lockewood U .20 .50
93 Fimlet Sparklight U .20 .50
94 Hugh Mann U .20 .50
95 Ian Barus U .20 .50
96 Jaal U .20 .50
97 Jarod Shadowsong R .40 1.00
98 Lady Bancroft C .10 .25
99 Lara, Timewalker Commander R .60 1.50
100 Lexie Silverblade U .20 .50
101 Lord Kur'talos Ravencrest E 6.00 15.00
101EA Lord Kur'talos (Ext.Art) 12.00 30.00
102 Nalisa Nightbreeze U .20 .50
103 Northshire Cleric C .10 .25
104 Northshire Crusader C .10 .25
105 Nyala Shadefury U .20 .50
106 Rhonin the Time-Lost E .75 2.00
107 Shadowglen Stalker C .10 .25
108 Shandris Feathermoon R .40 1.00
109 SI:7 Assassin C .10 .25
110 Stella Bellamy U .20 .50
111 Stormwind Summoner C .10 .25
112 Tarwila Gladespring C .10 .25
113 Teldrassil Tracker C .10 .25
114 Teldrassil Wildguard C .10 .25
115 Tessa Black E 1.25 3.00
116 Timewalker Guard C .10 .25
117 Timewalker Lightsworn C .10 .25
118 Timewalker Sentinel C .10 .25
119 Toraan, Eye of O'ros R .60 1.50
120 Virgil, Timewalker Marshal R .60 1.50
121 Ahul Moonspeaker U .20 .50
122 Baine, Son of Cairne E .60 1.50
123 Belmaril, Timewalker Bloodmage R .60 1.50
124 Bhenn Checks-the-Sky C .10 .25
125 Bloodsoul C .10 .25
126 Dawnhoof Brightcaller C .10 .25
127 Drom'kor, Timewalker Necrolyte R .60 1.50
128 Durotar Flamecaster C .10 .25
129 Durotar Frostblade C .10 .25
130 Ellen Burroughs U .20 .50
131 Garrosh, Son of Grom E 2.00 5.00
131EA Garrosh, Son (Ext.Art) 12.00 30.00
132 Garyk Stormcrier U .20 .50
133 Jevan Grimtotem R .60 1.50
134 Kahul the Sunseer R 1.25 3.00
135 Klandark U .20 .50
136 Mulgore Deathwalker C .10 .25
137 Mulgore Guardian C .10 .25
138 Orgrimmar Heartstriker C .10 .25
139 Orgrimmar Killblade C .10 .25
140 Orgrimmar Marksman C .10 .25
141 Orox Darkhorn U .20 .50
142 Razor Hill Assassin C .10 .25
143 Razor Hill Spiritseer C .10 .25
144 Ror Tramplehoof U .20 .50
145 Shaka Deadmark U .20 .50
146 Soulrender Keldah U .20 .50
147 Stafa'jul U .20 .50
148 Takara, Timewalker Warlord R 1.25 3.00
149 Thunder Bluff Spiritwalker C .10 .25
150 Thunder Bluff Steelsnout C .10 .25
151 Thunder Bluff Sunwalker C .10 .25
152 Thunder Bluff Wildheart C .10 .25
153 Tilu Plainstalker U .20 .50
154 Timewalker Grunt C .10 .25
155 Timewalker Sunguard C .10 .25
156 Toho Bloomhorn U .20 .50
157 Torzuk Soulfang E 1.25 3.00
158 Vorgo, Timewalker Stormlord R .40 1.00
159 Xarantaur R .60 1.50
160 Zarim Redskull U .20 .50
161 Agamaggan R .60 1.50
162 Aviana the Reborn R .60 1.50
163 Azgalor the Pit Lord E 1.25 3.00
164 Azzinoth R .60 1.50
165 Blazing Infernal C .10 .25
166 Child of Agamaggan C .10 .25
167 Child of Aviana C .10 .25
168 Child of Goldrinn C .10 .25
169 Child of Tortolla C .10 .25
170 Child of Ursoc C .10 .25
171 Child of Ursol C .10 .25
172 Corrupted Furbolg U .20 .50
173 Eye of the Legion C .10 .25
174 Feldrake R .40 1.00
175 Felguard Marauder C .10 .25
176 Frenzied Felhound C .10 .25
177 Frenzyfin U .20 .50
178 Furbolg Avenger C .10 .25
179 Furbolg Chieftain U .20 .50
180 Furbolg Firecaller C .10 .25
181 Goldrinn R .40 1.00
182 Hulking Helboar C .10 .25
183 Jadefire Netherseer U .20 .50
184 Jadefire Soulstealer U .20 .50
185 Keening Shivarra U .20 .50
186 Keeper Yarashal C .10 .25
187 Leafbeard, Ancient of Lore U .20 .50
188 Legion Fel Reaver U .20 .50
189 Mo'arg Doomsmith U .20 .50
190 Monstrous Terrorguard U .20 .50
191 Mossbark, Ancient of War C .10 .25
192 Neltharion the Earth-Warder E .60 1.50
193 Peroth'arn R .60 1.50
194 Rampaging Furbolg C .10 .25
195 Scheming Dreadlord C .10 .25
196 Sinister Watcher C .10 .25
197 Strongroot, Ancient of War U .20 .50
198 Tortolla R .40 1.00
199 Trogg Earthrager C .10 .25
200 Unstoppable Abyssal C .10 .25
201 Ursoc the Mighty R .60 1.50
202 Ursol the Wise R .60 1.50
203 Void Terror C .10 .25
204 Volatile Terrorfiend U .20 .50
205 Warmaul Ogre C .10 .25
206 Dungard Ironcutter R .60 1.50
207 Earthen Crusher C .10 .25
208 Girdle of the Queen's Champion C .10 .25
209 Helm of Thorns C .10 .25
210 Historian's Sash U .20 .50
211 Legguards of the Legion R .40 1.00
212 Spaulders of Eternity C .10 .25
213 Darnassus Tabard U .20 .50
214 Demon Hunter's Aspect U .20 .50
215 Grand Marshal's Tome of Power U .20 .50
216 Orgrimmar Tabard U .20 .50
217 Signet of the Timewalker U .20 .50
218 Stormwind Tabard U .20 .50
219 Tabard of the Legion U .20 .50
220 Thunder Bluff Tabard U .20 .50
221 Arathar, the Eye of Flame U .20 .50
222 Axe of Cenarius E 2.00 5.00
223 Axe of the Tauren Chieftains C .10 .25
224 Crescent Wand R .60 1.50
225 Gavel of Peroth'arn R .60 1.50
226 High Warlord's Cleaver U .20 .50
227 Pit Lord's Destroyer C .10 .25
228 Scepter of Azshara R .60 1.50
229 Stalk of Corruption U .20 .50
230 Trickster's Edge R .60 1.50
231 Wand of the Demonsoul C .10 .25
232 Archival Purposes C .10 .25
233 The Caverns of Time U .20 .50
234 Documenting the Timeways C .10 .25
235 The End Time U .20 .50
236 In Unending Numbers U .20 .50
237 The Path to the Dragon Soul C .10 .25
238 The Vainglorious C .10 .25
239 The Well of Eternity C .10 .25
240 Zin-Azshari R .60 1.50
T1 Human Warrior TOKEN .10 .25
T2 Orc Warrior TOKEN .10 .25

2012 World of Warcraft War of the Ancients Loot

1 Eye of the Legion 3.00 8.00
2 Demon Hunter's Aspect 12.00 30.00
3 Feldrake 150.00 250.00

2013 World of Warcraft Betrayal of the Guardian

COMPLETE SET (202) 50.00 100.00
BOOSTER BOX (36 PACKS) 50.00 80.00
BOOSTER PACK (16 CARDS) 1.50 2.50
RELEASED IN FEBRUARY 2013
1 Aegwynn, Guardian of Tirisfal E .60 1.50
1EA Aegwynn, Guardian (Ext.Art) 10.00 25.00
2 Bone Shield R .60 1.50
3 Corruption of the Ages R .40 1.00
4 Grim Touch R .40 1.00
5 Hand of Dread C .10 .25
6 Soul Pox U .20 .50
7 Timeless Undeath U .20 .50
8 Ancient Moonkin Form R .40 1.00
9 Feral Prowess C .10 .25
10 Living Seed R .50 1.25
11 Roar of the Ages R .40 1.00
12 Thorns of Nordrassil U .20 .50
13 Timeless Bounty U .20 .50
14 Bitey C .10 .25
15 Gahz'rilla E .75 2.00
16 Intervening Shot U .20 .50
17 Piercing Shots R .40 1.00
18 Timeless Aim U .20 .50
19 Wrath of the Ages R .50 1.25
20 Arcane Shock U .20 .50
21 Critical Mass R .40 1.00
22 Flame Volley C .10 .25
23 Frost Stasis R .40 1.00
24 Secrets of the Ages R .50 1.25
25 Timeless Arcana U .20 .50
26 Blessing of the Pure C .10 .25
27 Crusade of Kings R .40 1.00
28 Guardian of the Ages R .60 1.50
29 Light of Dawn R .40 1.00
30 Light's Vengeance U .20 .50

31 Timeless Light U .20 .50
32 Dark Deliverance C .10 .25
33 Holy Word: Hope U .20 .50
34 Power Word: Spirit R .40 1.00
35 Prayer of the Ages R .50 1.25
36 Psychic Horror R .40 1.00
37 Timeless Agony U .20 .50
38 Fast-Acting Poison U .20 .50
39 No Mercy R .40 1.00
40 Timeless Deception U .20 .50
41 Venomous Wounds R .40 1.00
42 Cloudburst R .50 1.25
43 Freezing Rain Totem U .20 .50
44 Magma Blast C .10 .25
45 Static Shock R .40 1.00
46 Storm of the Ages R .50 1.25
47 Timeless Winds U .20 .50
48 Curse of the Fel R .40 1.00
49 Demonic Rebirth R .60 1.50
50 Fel Inversion C .10 .25
51 Ritual of the Ages R .50 1.25
52 Thoglos U .20 .50
53 Timeless Shadow U .20 .50
54 Bastion of Defense R .40 1.00
55 Brutal Steel R .50 1.25
56 Fortified Defenses U .20 .50
57 Fury of the Ages R .40 1.00
58 Timeless Resilience U .20 .50
59 Legacy of Betrayal E 8.00 20.00
60 More Work? C .10 .25
61 Sigil of the Legion C .10 .25
62 Archdruid Fandral Staghelm R 1.50 4.00
63 Belthira the Black Thorn E 2.00 5.00
64 Danath Trollbane R .40 1.00
65 Darris Leafshade U .20 .50
66 Dwarf Demolitionist U .20 .50
67 Elistari Silverwind U .20 .50
68 General Turalyon E .60 1.50
69 Gnomish Flying Machine U .20 .50
70 Human Darkweaver C .10 .25
71 Human Footman C .10 .25
72 Human Knight C .10 .25
73 Human Operative C .10 .25
74 Human Peasant C .10 .25
75 Human Sniper C .10 .25
76 Khadgar R .40 1.00
77 Lady Voltaire R .40 1.00
78 Loremaster Pooth R .50 1.25
79 Myro Lumastis U .20 .50
80 Night Elf Arcanist C .10 .25
81 Night Elf Bladedancer C .10 .25
82 Night Elf Grovewalker C .10 .25
83 Night Elf Moon Priestess C .10 .25
84 Night Elf Ranger C .10 .25
85 Night Elf Swiftblade C .10 .25
86 Thane Kurdran Wildhammer R .40 1.00
87 Virendra Moonglow U .20 .50
88 Xander Blackcrow U .20 .50
89 Blood Knight Lynesta R .40 1.00
90 Chora Cloudspeaker U .20 .50
91 Dohna Darksky U .20 .50
92 Draka R .40 1.00
93 Durotan R .50 1.25
94 Farseer Horgath R .40 1.00
95 Goblin Sapper U .20 .50
96 Korah Icefang U .20 .50
97 Korgen Skullcleaver U .20 .50
98 Magatha Grimtotem R .40 1.00
99 Makuna Halada E 1.25 3.00
100 Orc Blackblade C .10 .25
101 Orc Flamecaller C .10 .25
102 Orc Grunt C .10 .25
103 Orc Necrolyte C .10 .25
104 Orc Peon C .10 .25
105 Orgrim Doomhammer E .60 1.50
106 Tauren Deathwalker C .10 .25
107 Tauren Lightcaller C .10 .25
108 Tauren Mystic C .10 .25
109 Tauren Plainstrider C .10 .25
110 Tauren Sunhoof C .10 .25
111 Tauren Tracker C .10 .25
112 Tauren Wildmender C .10 .25
113 Troll Axethrower U .20 .50
114 Zafira Ragebolt U .20 .50
115 Zul'jin R .40 1.00
116 Bianca, Timewalker Mage U .20 .50
117 Enabrin, Timewalker Druid U .20 .50
118 Lyra, Timewalker Embermage U .20 .50
119 Moro, Timewalker Druid U .20 .50
120 Nazzik, Timewalker Trickster R .40 1.00
121 Nehru, Timewalker Hunter U .20 .50
122 Timewalker Juggernaut C .10 .25
123 Timewalker Shadowseer C .10 .25
124 Timewalker Smasher C .10 .25
125 Timewalker Vanguard C .10 .25
126 Watsun, Timewalker Lightshield R .40 1.00
127 Zor'ka, Timewalker Shaman U .20 .50
128 Arcane Anomaly C .10 .25
129 Arcane Protector U .20 .50
130 The Big Bad Wolf R .60 1.50
131 Bigbelly, Furbolg Chieftain R .40 1.00
132 Blackfang Tarantula C .10 .25
133 Darkwater Crocolisk C .10 .25
134 Doom Commander Zaakuul E 5.00 12.00
135 Doomguard Soldier C .10 .25
136 Durnholde Tracking Hound C .10 .25
137 Enslaved Red Dragon U .20 .50
138 Eredar Deathbringer C .10 .25
139 Ethereal Spellfilcher U .20 .50
140 Ethereal Thief U .20 .50
141 Felguard Annihilator C .10 .25
142 Frostwolf C .10 .25
143 Furbolg Shaman C .10 .25
144 Ghostly Charger R .50 1.25
145 Greater Fleshbeast C .10 .25
146 Highland Lion C .10 .25
147 Karazhan Concubine C .10 .25
148 Kil'rek R .40 1.00
149 Moroes R .60 1.50
150 Nightbane E .60 1.50
151 Prince Malchezaar E .75 2.00
152 Ravenous Furbolg C .10 .25
153 Servant of Terestian C .10 .25
154 Shade of Aran R .60 1.50
155 Shadowmoon Mage C .10 .25
156 Shivarra Deathspeaker C .10 .25
157 Snappyfin R .50 1.25
158 Spawn of Hyakiss U .20 .50
159 Spawn of Rokad U .20 .50
160 Spawn of Shadikith U .20 .50
161 Terestian Illhoof R .40 1.00
162 Vile Watcher C .10 .25
163 Voidshrieker C .10 .25
164 Wildhammer Gryphon U .20 .50
165 Wrathguard Defender C .10 .25
166 Floating Spellbook C .10 .25
167 Don Carlos' Famous Hat U .20 .50
168 Durotan's Battle Harness U .20 .50
169 Gauntlets of the Ancient Frostwolf U .20 .50
170 Khadgar's Kilt of Abjuration U .20 .50
171 Mantle of Abrahmis R .40 1.00
172 Royal Crest of Lordaeron R .40 1.00
173 VanCleef's Boots R .40 1.00
174 Dark Portal Hearthstone U .20 .50
175 Time-Bending Gem C .10 .25
176 Moroes' Lucky Pocket Watch U .20 .50
177 Atiesh, Greatstaff of the Guardian E .60 1.50
178 Bloodfire Greatstaff C .10 .25
179 Despair R .40 1.00
180 Fool's Bane R .40 1.00
181 Hellscream Slicer U .20 .50
182 Lothar's Edge U .20 .50
183 Millennium Blade C .10 .25
184 Quel'Serrar C .10 .25
185 Riftmaker R .40 1.00
186 Shard of the Virtuous U .20 .50
187 Staff of Infinite Mysteries R .40 1.00
188 Time-Shifted Dagger C .10 .25
189 Vagaries of Time C .10 .25
190 Warglaive of Azzinoth E 4.00 10.00
191 Windrunner's Bow R .40 1.00
192 Assault on Blackrock Spire U .20 .50
193 The Fall of Lordaeron U .20 .50
194 The Black Morass C .10 .25
195 A Demonic Presence U .20 .50
196 Escape from Durnholde C .10 .25
197 The Master's Touch C .10 .25
198 Medivh's Journal C .10 .25
199 The Opening of the Dark Portal C .10 .25
200 Taretha's Diversion C .10 .25
201 Capital City, Lordaeron R .40 1.00
202 Blackrock Spire R .40 1.00

2013 World of Warcraft Betrayal of the Guardian Loot

1 Floating Spellbook 4.00 10.00
2 Dark Portal Hearthstone 15.00 40.00
3 Ghostly Charger 100.00 200.00

2013 World of Warcraft Reign of Fire

COMPLETE SET (197) 80.00 120.00
BOOSTER BOX (36 PACKS) 100.00 150.00
BOOSTER PACK (16 CARDS) 3.00 5.00
RELEASED IN JULY 2013
1 Medivh the Prophet E 3.00 8.00
1EA Medivh the Prophet EA 6.00 15.00
2 Kil'jaeden the Deceiver E 2.00 5.00
3 Gravebound C .10 .25
4 Howling Blast R 2.50 6.00
5 Numbing Cold U .15 .40
6 Rune of Vengeance R .30 .75
7 Vilegut R 1.50 4.00
8 Will from Beyond U .15 .40
9 Agile Cat Form U .15 .40
10 Blood in the Water R .40 1.00
11 Lunar Barrage R .75 2.00
12 Nurture R .60 1.50
13 Snare from Beyond U .15 .40
14 Wild Harmony C .10 .25
15 Counterattack R .40 1.00
16 Dakota R 1.00 2.50
17 Disrupting Shot U .15 .40
18 Ravenous Frenzy C .10 .25
19 Track from Beyond U .15 .40
20 Unleash the Beasts R .30 .75
21 Arcane Breach U .15 .40
22 Flames from Beyond U .15 .40
23 Mass Teleport R .30 .75
24 Permafrost R .30 .75
25 Phoenix R 1.50 4.00
26 Temporal Shift C .10 .25
27 Blaze of Light C .10 .25
28 Blessing from Beyond U .15 .40
29 Blinding Word R 2.00 5.00
30 Heroic Bulwark U .15 .40
31 Mass Redemption R .30 .75
32 Zealotry R .40 1.00
33 Lightlance U .15 .40
34 Power Word: Bravery R .30 .75
35 Shadows from Beyond U .15 .40
36 Soul Warding R .60 1.50
37 Splintered Thought R .75 2.00
38 Spook C .10 .25
39 Bounty Hunt C .10 .25
40 Malice From Beyond U .15 .40
41 Savage Combat R .60 1.50
42 Smoke Screen U .15 .40
43 Torturous Poison R .30 .75
44 Ancestral Renewal R .30 .75
45 Feedback R .40 1.00
46 Lust for Battle C .10 .25
47 Magnetic Totem R .75 2.00
48 Tempest Elemental U .15 .40
49 Totem from Beyond U .25 .60
50 Curse from Beyond U .15 .40
51 Havoc R .40 1.00
52 Life Drain C .10 .25
53 Nether Rip R 1.00 2.50
54 Soulbond U .15 .40
55 Zhar'doom R 1.00 2.50
56 Bladewhirl R .40 1.00
57 Blade Strike U .15 .40
58 Howl from Beyond C .10 .25
59 Impale R .30 .75
60 Tactical Mastery R .30 .75
61 Thundercrash C .10 .25
62 Call of C'Thun R .30 .75
63 Call of Yogg-Saron R .30 .75
64 Dodge C .10 .25
65 Legacy of the Horde E 3.00 8.00
66 Legacy of Lordaeron E 1.50 4.00
67 Savage Beatdown C .10 .25
68 Alana the Hopebringer E 1.50 4.00
69 Alethar the Blightspreader R 1.00 2.50
70 Ashenvale Acolyte C .10 .25
71 Ashenvale Archer C .10 .25
72 Ashenvale Illusionist C .10 .25
73 Daniel Darkheart U .15 .40
74 Disciple of the Light C .10 .25
75 Druid of the Talon U .15 .40
76 Elwynn Burglar C .10 .25
77 Elwynn Huntsman C .10 .25
78 Emora Delwin U .15 .40
79 Felwood Grovestalker C .10 .25
80 Goran, Timewalker Lavacaller U .15 .40
81 Grand Admiral Daelin Proudmoore R .50 1.25
82 Huntress C .10 .25
83 Jaina, Apprentice of Antonidas R .75 2.00
84 Johnny B. Goode U .15 .40
85 Komma, Timewalker Graveguard U .15 .40
86 Ky'lai Darkblood U .15 .40
87 Lunaris Silverfrost U .15 .40
88 Mias the Fair C .10 .25
89 Muradin, Bronzebeard Adventurer R .75 2.00
90 Naisha R 3.00 8.00
91 Stormwind Recruit C .10 .25
92 Warden Maiev E 4.00 10.00
93 The Widow Deadsie R .40 1.00
94 Adoral Brokenhoof U .15 .40
95 Blackrock Shooter C .10 .25
96 Blurg Firekin U .15 .40
97 Bor Breakfist U .15 .40
98 Dawnstrider Sunward C .10 .25
99 Drek'Thar, Frostwolf General R .30 .75
100 Grom Hellscream R .40 1.00
101 Haro Setting-Sun U .15 .40
102 High Chieftain Cairne Bloodhoof E 1.25 3.00
103 High Warlord Gorebelly E 4.00 10.00
104 Joru the Blinding Light R 1.50 4.00
105 Kurala Deadshot U .15 .40
106 Nuada Windwaker U .15 .40
107 Orc Raider C .10 .25
108 Orc Shaman C .10 .25
109 Rokhan R .50 1.25
110 Roza the Star-Mother R .30 .75
111 Runetotem Guardian C .10 .25
112 Seres, Timewalker Assassin U .15 .40
113 Shattered Hand Cutthroat C .10 .25
114 Sixto the Earth-Blessed R 1.50 4.00
115 Sunwalker Lighthorn C .10 .25
116 Thunderhorn Windwalker C .10 .25
117 Valik, Timewalker Sharpshooter U .15 .40
118 Warsong Deadblade C .10 .25
119 Winterhoof Frostheart C .10 .25
120 Abomination U .15 .40
121 Anub'arak, The Traitor King E 4.00 10.00
122 Banshee U .15 .40
123 Blackhorn Fearmonger C .10 .25
124 Bleakheart Hellcaller C .10 .25
125 Brood Mother R .30 .75
126 Cult Master Kel'Thuzad R .75 2.00
127 Cunning Crypt Fiend C .10 .25
128 Darkflame Dreadlord C .10 .25
129 Doomguard Invader C .10 .25
130 Dreadhound C .10 .25
131 Eredar Chaosbringer U .15 .40
132 Eredar Strategist U .25 .60
133 Fel Imp U .15 .40
134 Felguard Basher C .10 .25
135 Frost Wyrm R .40 1.00
136 Furbolg Champion U .15 .40
137 Furbolg Spiritbinder C .10 .25
138 Hateful Darkweaver U .15 .40
139 Hateful Fiend U .15 .40
140 Hateful Infernal U .15 .40
141 Hateful Seductress U .15 .40
142 Hungry Ghoul C .10 .25
143 Mal'Ganis E 2.00 5.00
144 Mo'arg Punisher C .10 .25
145 Naga Royal Guard U .15 .40
146 Naga Siren U .15 .40
147 Necromancer U .15 .40
148 Priestess of Horror C .10 .25
149 Priestess of Ruin C .10 .25
150 Quillbeast C .10 .25
151 Savage Wrathguard C .10 .25
152 Scheming Watcher C .10 .25
153 Sister of Seduction C .10 .25
154 Sogoridon the Savage R .40 1.00
155 Terror Hound C .10 .25
156 Terrorguard Detonator C .10 .25
157 Thunder Hawk C .10 .25
158 Torrid Abyssal C .10 .25
159 Varimathras, Dreadlord Insurgent R 2.00 5.00
160 Void Brute C .10 .25
161 Zalekor the Ferocious R .60 1.50
162 Bloodmage Kael'thas R .30 .75
163 Goblin Tinkerer R .50 1.25
164 Pandaren Brewmaster R .75 2.00
165 Rexxar the Wanderer R 1.25 3.00
166 Belt of Giant Strength R .40 1.00
167 Boots of Quel'Thalas U .15 .40
168 Boots of Speed U .15 .40
169 Circlet of Nobility C .10 .25
170 Cloak of Flames U .15 .40
171 Mask of Death U .15 .40
172 Robe of the Magi R .30 .75
173 Amulet of Spell Shield U .15 .40
174 Anti-magic Potion C .10 .25
175 Glyph of Omniscience C .10 .25
176 Healing Wards U .15 .40
177 Health Stone C .10 .25
178 Orb of Darkness U .15 .40
179 Ring of Protection C .10 .25
180 Scroll of Town Portal C .10 .25
181 Claws of Attack R .30 .75
182 Corrupted Ashbringer R .40 1.00
183 Doomhammer E 1.25 3.00
184 Frostmourne E 2.50 6.00
185 Kelen's Dagger of Escape C .10 .25
186 Rod of Necromancy R .30 .75
187 Staff of Silence U .15 .40
188 Wand of Mana Stealing U .15 .40
189 Eternity's End U .15 .40
190 The Founding of Durotar U .15 .40
191 The Invasion of Kalimdor C .10 .25
192 Legacy of the Damned C .10 .25
193 Path of the Damned C .10 .25
194 The Scourge of Lordaeron C .10 .25
195 Terror of the Tides C .10 .25
196 Ashenvale R 5.00 12.00
197 Mulgore R .30 .75

1996 The X-Files Premiere Edition

COMPLETE SET (354) 120.00 250.00
BOOSTER BOX (36 PACKS) 30.00 40.00
BOOSTER PACK (15 CARDS) .75 1.25
XF960001v1 Aura Of Invulnerability U .25 .60
XF960002v1 First Aid C .12 .30
XF960003v1 Face-off U .25 .60
XF960004v1 Rending Claws U .25 .60
XF960005v1 Fast Strike R .40 1.00
XF960006v1 Sneak Attack R .40 1.00
XF960007v1 Ambush C .12 .30
XF960008v1 Kick C .12 .30
XF960009v1 Gun Jammed C .12 .30
XF960010v1 Hide C .12 .30
XF960011v1 Dodge U .25 .60
XF960012v1 Nerve Strike R .40 1.00
XF960013v1 Webbed R .40 1.00
XF960014v1 Vicious Fangs U .25 .60
XF960015v1 Spin Kick R .40 1.00
XF960016v1 Mind Control R .40 1.00
XF960017v1 Alien Stealth Technology U .25 .60
XF960018v1 Block And Attack R .40 1.00
XF960019v1 Block U .25 .60
XF960020v1 Body Armor U .25 .60
XF960021v1 Disarm R .40 1.00
XF960022v1 Running Gun Battle U .25 .60
XF960023v1 Fascination U .25 .60
XF960024v1 Internal Bleeding U .25 .60
XF960025v1 Covering Fire U .25 .60
XF960026v1 No Way Out U .25 .60
XF960027v1 Hard Punch C .12 .30
XF960028v1 Choke Hold R .40 1.00
XF960029v1 Fast Draw R .40 1.00
XF960030v1 Watch Out! U .25 .60
XF960031v1 Hit And Run U .25 .60
XF960032v1 Handcuff R .40 1.00
XF960033v1 Illusionary Foe R .40 1.00
XF960034v1 Run For It! U .25 .60
XF960035v1 Terminal Damage R .75 2.00
XF960036v1 Flaming Wall U .25 .60
XF960037v1 Massive Internal Damage U .25 .60
XF960038v1 Semi-jacketed Hollow Points U .25 .60
XF960039v1 Stunning Blow U .25 .60
XF960040v1 Take Cover! U .25 .60
XF960041v1 Energy Strike R .75 2.00
XF960042v1 Gibsonton, FL C .12 .30
XF960043v1 Excelsius Dei Convalescent Home, Worcester, MA U .25 .60
XF960044v1 Broad Street, Philadelphia, PA R .40 1.00
XF960045v1 Ellens Air Base, ID R .40 1.00
XF960046v1 Coastal Northwest Oregon C .12 .30
XF960047v1 Olympic National Forest, WA C .15 .40
XF960048v1 Arlington, VA C .12 .30
XF960049v1 Lake Okobogee, Campsite #53, Sioux City, IA C .12 .30
XF960050v1 Newark, NJ C .15 .40
XF960051v1 Central Prison, Raleigh, NC U .25 .60
XF960052v1 Genetics Clinic, Marin County, CA C .12 .30
XF960053v1 Cumberland Prison, VA C .12 .30
XF960054v1 Mt. Avalon, WA C .12 .30
XF960055v1 Northeast Georgetown Medical Center, Washington, DC R .40 1.00
XF960056v1 Nasa Mission Control, Houston, TX U .25 .60
XF960057v1 New York City, NY R .40 1.00
XF960058v1 Fairfield Zoo, Fairfield, ID C .12 .30
XF960059v1 Deadhorse, AK R .40 1.00
XF960060v1 Containment Facility, Georgetown, MD C .12 .30
XF960061v1 University Of Maryland, Baltimore, MD C .15 .40
XF960062v1 Chaco House, Dudley, AR U .25 .60
XF960063v1 Aubrey, MO C .12 .30
XF960064v1 Cape Cod, MA C .12 .30
XF960065v1 Icy Cap, AK .15 .40
XF960066v1 Farmington, NM U .25 .60
XF960067v1 U.f.o. Wreckage, Townsend, WI R .40 1.00
XF960068v1 Mattawa, WA C .12 .30
XF960069v1 Mahan Propulsion Laboratory, Colson, WA C .12 .30
XF960070v1 Church Of The Red Museum, Delta Glen, WI R .40 1.00
XF960071v1 Psychiatric Hospital, Richmond, VA C .12 .30
XF960072v1 Washington Monument, Washington, DC U .25 .60
XF960073v1 Marion, VA C .12 .30
XF960074v1 Arecibo, Puerto Rico U .25 .60
XF960075v1 Sea Off Tildeskan, Norway C .12 .30
XF960076v1 Aleister Crowley High School, Milford Haven, NH R .40 1.00
XF960077v1 Los Angeles, CA U .25 .60
XF960078v1 Minneapolis, MN U .25 .60
XF960079v1 Franklin, PA .15 .40
XF960080v1 Eurisko Building, Crystal City, VA U .25 .60
XF960081v1 Folkstone, NC U .25 .60
XF960082v1 Outskirts Of Atlantic City, NJ U .25 .60
XF960083v1 Browning, MT .15 .40
XF960084v1 Steveston, MA R .40 1.00
XF960085v1 Skyland Mountain, VA R .40 1.00
XF960086v1 Baltimore, MD U .25 .60
XF960087v1 Detective Kelly Ryan C .12 .30
XF960088v1 Sinus Cavity Implant U .25 .60
XF960089v1 Peter Tanaka U .25 .60
XF960090v1 Section Chief Joseph Mcgrath R 1.25 3.00
XF960091v1 Cigarette Butts C .12 .30
XF960092v1 Sheriff Daniels U .25 .60
XF960093v1 Dr. Berube C .12 .30
XF960094v1 The Overcoat Man C .12 .30
XF960095v1 You've Got A Tail C .12 .30
XF960096v1 Pete Calcagni U .25 .60
XF960097v1 Holtzman, D.s.a. C .12 .30
XF960098v1 Claude Peterson C .12 .30
XF960099v1 The Conundrum U .25 .60
XF960100v1 Paul Mossinger C .12 .30
XF960101v1 Intruder Counter-measures Program U .25 .60
XF960102v1 Dr. Aaron Monte C .12 .30
XF960103v1 Poisonous Gases C .12 .30
XF960104v1 Laser Barrier R .40 1.00
XF960105v1 Nasty Surprise U .25 .60
XF960106v1 Sleep Deprivation R .40 1.00
XF960107v1 Radioactve Area U .25 .60
XF960108v1 Ghost In The Machine C .12 .30
XF960109v1 Unnatural Aging U .25 .60
XF960110v1 Car Troubles .15 .40
XF960111v1 Puzzles Within Puzzles U .25 .60
XF960112v1 Government Cover-up C .12 .30
XF960113v1 Hazardous Sample C .12 .30
XF960114v1 Henry Trondheim U .25 .60
XF960115v1 Detective Miles U .25 .60
XF960116v1 Detective Thompson U .25 .60
XF960117v1 Harry Cokely C .12 .30
XF960118v1 Detective Tony Fiore U .25 .60
XF960119v1 B.j. Morrow, Genetic Trait Recipient .40 1.00
XF960120v1 Augustus Cole, A.k.a. The Preacher .40 1.00
XF960121v1 The Cigarette-smoking Man C .40 1.00
XF960122v1 Duane Barry .40 1.00
XF960123v1 The Jersey Devil C .40 1.00
XF960124v1 The Host .40 1.00
XF960125v1 Lucas Henry, Serial Killer .40 1.00
XF960126v1 Arthur Grable C .40 1.00
XF960127v1 Warren James Dupré, The Lazarus Man .40 1.00
XF960128v1 Colonel Wharton, Zombie Master C .40 1.00
XF960129v1 Alien Dna Steroid Program (project Purity Control) C .40 1.00
XF960130v1 The Gregors C .40 1.00
XF960131v1 Sheriff Tom Arens, Cannibal C .40 1.00
XF960132v1 The Vampire, A.k.a. The Unholy Spirit C .40 1.00
XF960133v1 Central Operating System, Artificial Intelligence .40 1.00
XF960134v1 Volcanic Spore C .40 1.00
XF960135v1 Michael Holvey, The Evil One .40 1.00
XF960136v1 Eugene Victor Tooms C .40 1.00
XF960137v1 Howard Graves, The Poltergeist C .40 1.00
XF960138v1 Dr. Banton And His Shadow C .40 1.00
XF960139v1 Alien Listeners C .40 1.00
XF960140v1 Commander Colin Henderson C .40 1.00
XF960141v1 Arctic Worm C .40 1.00
XF960142v1 The Manitou C .40 1.00
XF960143v1 Leonard Vance C .40 1.00
XF960144v1 Ancestor Spirits C .40 1.00
XF960145v1 Ed Funsch, Postal Worker C .40 1.00
XF960146v1 Mrs. Paddock, A.k.a. The Dark Angel C .40 1.00
XF960147v1 Dod Kalm C .40 1.00
XF960148v1 John Barnett .40 1.00
XF960149v1 Alien Conservationist C .40 1.00
XF960150v1 Faciphaga Emasculata C .40 1.00
XF960151v1 Donnie Pfaster, Death Fetishist .40 1.00
XF960152v1 Brother Martin, Rogue Kindred C .40 1.00
XF960153v1 Alien Abductors C .40 1.00
XF960154v1 Eve C .40 1.00
XF960155v1 Alien Experimenters C .40 1.00
XF960156v1 Reverse Engineers C .40 1.00
XF960157v1 The Swarm C .40 1.00
XF960158v1 Leonard, Detachable Congenital Twin C .40 1.00
XF960159v1 Cecil L'ively C .40 1.00
XF960160v1 Section Chief Scott Blevins 1.25 3.00
XF960161v1 Albert Hosteen .60 1.50
XF960162v1 Agent Alex Krycek UR 8.00 20.00
XF960163v1 Agent Fox Mulder UR 10.00 25.00
XF960164v1 Lt. Brian Tillman, Aubrey Police Department .50 1.25
XF960165v1 Agent Rich .50 1.25
XF960166v1 Agent Lucy Kazdin .50 1.25
XF960167v1 Agent Jack Willis .50 1.25
XF960168v1 Inspector Phoebe Green .50 1.25
XF960169v1 Agent Fox Mulder 1.00 2.50
XF960170v1 Agent Alex Krycek 1.00 2.50
XF960171v1 Agent Nancy Spiller .50 1.25
XF960172v1 Agent Dana Scully UR 10.00 25.00
XF960173v1 Agent Dana Scully 1.00 2.50
XF960174v1 Assistant Director Walter Skinner UR 8.00 20.00
XF960175v1 Dr. Charles Burk .50 1.25
XF960176v1 Agent Tom Colton .50 1.25
XF960177v1 Agent Janus, Trained Medic .50 1.25
XF960178v1 Agent Moe Bocks .50 1.25

Card	Low	High
XF960179v1 Agent Reggie Purdue	.50	1.25
XF960180v1 Assistant Director Walter Skinner	1.00	2.50
XF960181v1 Agent Weiss	.75	2.00
XF960182v1 Agent Jerry Lamana	.50	1.25
XF960183v1 Agent Karen Kosseff, Counselor	.50	1.25
XF960184v1 Sheriff Spencer C	.12	.30
XF960185v1 Dr. Blockhead R	.40	1.00
XF960186v1 The Thinker R	.40	1.00
XF960187v1 Byers	.15	.40
XF960188v1 Emil And Zoe U	.25	.60
XF960189v1 Dr. Davey U	.25	.60
XF960190v1 Billy Miles C	.12	.30
XF960191v1 Dr. Diamond R	.40	1.00
XF960192v1 Detective Frank Briggs U	.25	.60
XF960193v1 Dr. Grissom R	.40	1.00
XF960194v1 Kevin Morris, A.k.a. The Conduit R	.75	2.00
XF960195v1 Detective Sharon Lazard U	.25	.60
XF960196v1 Dr. Lakos U	.25	.60
XF960197v1 The Calusari R	.75	2.00
XF960198v1 Bill Mulder R	.75	2.00
XF960199v1 Charley Tskany R	.40	1.00
XF960200v1 Dr. Osborne R	.40	1.00
XF960201v1 Michelle Generoo R	.40	1.00
XF960202v1 Sir Malcolm Marsden C	.12	.30
XF960203v1 Samantha Mulder R	.40	1.00
XF960204v1 Max Fenig R	.40	1.00
XF960205v1 Dr. Hodge C	.12	.30
XF960206v1 Doug Spinney C	.12	.30
XF960207v1 Dr. Sheila Braun U	.25	.60
XF960208v1 U.s. Marshall Tapia	.15	.40
XF960209v1 Brad Wilczek U	.25	.60
XF960210v1 Dr. Nollette R	.40	1.00
XF960211v1 Ish--tribal Elder U	.25	.60
XF960212v1 Sheriff Mazeroski R	.40	1.00
XF960213v1 Lt. Colonel Marcus Aurelius Belt R	.40	1.00
XF960214v1 Gung Bituen R	.40	1.00
XF960215v1 Kristen Kilar R	.40	1.00
XF960216v1 Gerd Thomas	.15	.40
XF960217v1 Dr. Daniel Trepkos R	.40	1.00
XF960218v1 Maggie Holvey	.15	.40
XF960219v1 Luther Lee Boggs R	.40	1.00
XF960220v1 Senator Richard Matheson R	.40	1.00
XF960221v1 Successful Diagnosis U	.25	.60
XF960222v1 Deep Throat UR	10.00	25.00
XF960223v1 Shutting Down The X-files R	.40	1.00
XF960224v1 Reporters At The Crime Scene U	.25	.60
XF960225v1 I Want To Believe C	.12	.30
XF960226v1 Road Trip R	.40	1.00
XF960227v1 Hidden Transmitter U	.25	.60
XF960228v1 Medical Treatment C	.12	.30
XF960229v1 Agent Weiss Killed By Unknown Toxin R	.40	1.00
XF960230v1 The Cigarette-smoking Man Strikes R	.40	1.00
XF960231v1 Eve 7 R	.40	1.00
XF960232v1 Street Contacts U	.25	.60
XF960233v1 Government Arrests Suspects C	.12	.30
XF960234v1 Red Tape R	.40	1.00
XF960235v1 S.w.a.t. Training C	.12	.30
XF960236v1 Fingerprints U	.25	.60
XF960237v1 Back Tracking Program U	.25	.60
XF960238v1 Agent Lamana Dies In Fatal Elevator Accident R	.40	1.00
XF960239v1 Evidence Destroyed U	.25	.60
XF960240v1 Surfing The Net R	.40	1.00
XF960241v1 Government Sanctioned Pheromone Experiments R	.40	1.00
XF960242v1 Thorough Documentation R	.40	1.00
XF960243v1 Skinner Chooses A Side UR	5.00	12.00
XF960244v1 Overwhelming Force R	.40	1.00
XF960245v1 Warning From The Loa R	.40	1.00
XF960246v1 Evidence Overlooked C	.12	.30
XF960247v1 Message From The Stars R	.40	1.00
XF960248v1 Dana Scully, Abducted UR	5.00	12.00
XF960249v1 Reading The Signs U	.25	.60
XF960250v1 Agent Jack Willis Shot To Death In Bank Robbery R	.40	1.00
XF960251v1 Skinner Adopts The Company Line R	.40	1.00
XF960252v1 Safe House R	.40	1.00
XF960253v1 Crop Circles C	.12	.30
XF960254v1 Langly C	.12	.30
XF960255v1 Expedite Request For Resources U	.25	.60
XF960256v1 Paperwork U	.25	.60
XF960257v1 Unexplainable Time Loss R	.40	1.00
XF960258v1 Clone U	.25	.60
XF960259v1 Suspect Description U	.25	.60
XF960260v1 Smoke Screen U	.25	.60
XF960261v1 Dark Forces Align R	.40	1.00
XF960262v1 Computer Access Denied R	.40	1.00
XF960263v1 Improved Channels U	.25	.60
XF960264v1 The Erlenmeyer Flask R	1.25	3.00
XF960265v1 Krycek, The Double Agent R	.40	1.00
XF960266v1 Spying Mission U	.25	.60
XF960267v1 Authorized Access Only R	.40	1.00
XF960268v1 Equipment Malfunction U	.25	.60
XF960269v1 The Local Law Enforcement Are Uncooperative U	.25	.60
XF960270v1 The Lone Gunmen UR	10.00	25.00
XF960271v1 Alien Discretion R	.40	1.00
XF960272v1 Fingernail Scrapings C	.12	.30
XF960273v1 Trust No One R	.40	1.00
XF960274v1 Lula Phillips R	.40	1.00
XF960275v1 No Place Is Safe R	.40	1.00
XF960276v1 Blackmail R	.40	1.00
XF960277v1 Dissection U	.25	.60
XF960278v1 Hack Into Government Files R	.40	1.00
XF960279v1 Application For Fbi Resources Approved R	.40	1.00
XF960280v1 Expert Briefing C	.12	.30
XF960281v1 Access Personnel Files C	.12	.30
XF960282v1 Hard Evidence C	.12	.30
XF960283v1 Relentless Pursuit C	.12	.30
XF960284v1 Counterintelligence Measures UR	8.00	20.00
XF960285v1 Deductive Reasoning R	.40	1.00
XF960286v1 Grid Pattern Search R	.40	1.00
XF960287v1 Driving U	.25	.60
XF960288v1 In-service Training C	.12	.30
XF960289v1 Rejuvenating Caves U	.25	.60
XF960290v1 Alien Experimentation R	.40	1.00
XF960291v1 Hidden Grave U	.25	.60
XF960292v1 Trap U	.25	.60
XF960293v1 X UR	5.00	12.00
XF960294v1 Assigned To The X-files R	.40	1.00
XF960295v1 Plague Of Locusts R	.40	1.00
XF960296v1 X-files Research C	.12	.30
XF960297v1 A Friend In The Fbi R	.40	1.00
XF960298v1 Written Report C	.12	.30
XF960299v1 Government Mindwipe Serum U	.25	.60
XF960300v1 Travel Arrangements C	.12	.30
XF960301v1 Decoy U	.25	.60
XF960302v1 Autopsy U	.25	.60
XF960303v1 Evasive Maneuvers R	.40	1.00
XF960304v1 Frohike R	.40	1.00
XF960305v1 Agent Reggie Purdue Found Strangled R	.40	1.00
XF960306v1 Road Hazard U	.25	.60
XF960307v1 Core Training C	.12	.30
XF960308v1 Samuel Hartley R	.40	1.00
XF960309v1 True Grit R	.40	1.00
XF960310v1 Decreased Workload U	.25	.60
XF960311v1 Laptop Computer U	.25	.60
XF960312v1 Gas Chromatograph C	.12	.30
XF960313v1 Wire-tap C	.12	.30
XF960314v1 Binoculars C	.12	.30
XF960315v1 Medi-kit R	.40	1.00
XF960316v1 Kevlar Vest U	.25	.60
XF960317v1 Glock 19 Semi-automatic Pistol U	.25	.60
XF960318v1 High Resolution Camera C	.12	.30
XF960319v1 High-powered Flashlight U	.25	.60
XF960320v1 Government Car C	.12	.30
XF960321v1 Knife C	.12	.30
XF960322v1 Taped Intelligence R	.40	1.00
XF960323v1 Walther Ppk 7.65 Hold Out Weapon U	.25	.60
XF960324v1 Geiger Counter U	.25	.60
XF960325v1 Hospital Crash Cart R	.40	1.00
XF960326v1 Cellular Phone R	2.00	5.00
XF960327v1 Symbol Of Faith R	.50	1.25
XF960328v1 Electron Emission Microscope C	.12	.30
XF960329v1 Shotgun R	.50	1.25
XF960330v1 Mini-14 Assault Rifle U	.25	.60
XF960331v1 Mojo Bag U	.25	.60
XF960332v1 Lie Detector C	.12	.30
XF960333v1 Slithers In The Night	.15	.40
XF960334v1 Alien Harvester R	.50	1.25
XF960335v1 Hunter In The Dark	.15	.40
XF960336v1 Crew-cut Man U	.25	.60
XF960337v1 Alien Bounty Hunter R	.50	1.25
XF960338v1 The Host Attacks R	.50	1.25
XF960339v1 Pvt. Mcalpin, Zombie	.15	.40
XF960340v1 Good People, Good Food U	.25	.60
XF960341v1 The Sandman U	.25	.60
XF960342v1 Abduction R	.50	1.25
XF960343v1 Squeeze U	.25	.60
XF960344v1 The Psychotic Attack	.15	.40
XF960345v1 The Mechanic U	.25	.60
XF960346v1 Darkness Falls U	.25	.60
XF960347v1 Suppressed Fury	.15	.40
XF960348v1 Living Machine U	.25	.60
XF960349v1 Operation Falcon Blue Berets R	.50	1.25
XF960350v1 Pheromone-induced Psychosis U	.25	.60
XF960351v1 Deadly Blur U	.25	.60
XF960352v1 The Manitou Stalks His Prey R	.50	1.25
XF960353v1 Poltergeist Attack	.15	.40
XF960354v1 Kiss Of The Vampire R	.50	1.25

1997 The X-Files 101361

Card	Low	High
COMPLETE SET (125)	50.00	100.00
BOOSTER BOX (36 PACKS)	30.00	40.00
BOOSTER PACK (15 CARDS)	.75	1.25
XF970385x1 2shy C	.12	.30
XF970386x1 Darin Peter Oswald R	.75	2.00
XF970387x1 John Mostow C	.12	.30
XF970388x1 Margi Kleinjan U	.25	.60
XF970389x1 Puppet C	.12	.30
XF970390x1 Red-haired Man R	.75	2.00
XF970391x1 Simon Gates a.k.a. Ferreau U	.25	.60
XF970392x1 Terri Roberts U	.25	.60
XF970393x1 The List R	.75	2.00
XF970394x1 The Walk U	.25	.60
XF970395x1 Joseph Patnik U	.25	.60
XF970396x1 Agent Bill Patterson R	1.25	3.00
XF970397x1 Agent Danny Pendrell R	1.25	3.00
XF970398x1 Agent Fred Nemhauser C	.25	.60
XF970399x1 Agent Kreski C	.25	.60
XF970400x1 Clyde Bruckman R	1.25	3.00
XF970401x1 Detective Angela White C	.25	.60
XF970402x1 Detective Manners C	.25	.60
XF970403x1 Angry Townspeople C	.12	.30
XF970404x1 Big Blue C	.12	.30
XF970405x1 Philosophical Question C	.12	.30
XF970406x1 Cerulean Blue R	.40	1.00
XF970407x1 Darkened Forest C	.12	.30
XF970408x1 Dissolving Evidence C	.12	.30
XF970409x1 Deceiving The Flock C	.12	.30
XF970410x1 Festival Of The Hungry Ghosts R	.40	1.00
XF970411x1 Flesh Sculpting R	.40	1.00
XF970412x1 Veracity In Question C	.12	.30
XF970413x1 Heads Up C	.12	.30
XF970414x1 Mass Grave C	.12	.30
XF970415x1 Final Repose C	.12	.30
XF970416x1 No One Believes You R	.40	1.00
XF970417x1 Oubliette R	1.50	4.00
XF970418x1 Stoner, Chick, And Dude C	.25	.60
XF970419x1 The Mailman R	1.50	4.00
XF970420x1 This Is Not Happening C	.12	.30
XF970421x1 Visions Of A Madman R	.75	2.00
XF970422x1 You're A Dead Man R	1.00	2.50
XF970423x1 Two Lux Video Camera R	.75	2.00
XF970424x1 Alien Autopsy Video U	.25	.60
XF970425x1 Ambulance U	.25	.60
XF970426x1 M.R.I. U	.25	.60
XF970427x1 Classified Photos U	.25	.60
XF970428x1 Dental X-ray Plate U	.25	.60
XF970429x1 Desktop Computer U	.25	.60
XF970430x1 Dried Frog C	.12	.30
XF970431x1 Decomposing Victim U	.25	.60
XF970432x1 Garrote U	.25	.60
XF970433x1 Helicopter Spotter U	.25	.60
XF970434x1 Laser Targeter U	.25	.60
XF970435x1 Murder Weapon U	.25	.60
XF970436x1 Stationery U	.25	.60
XF970437x1 Queequeg R	1.00	2.50
XF970438x1 Satellite Photos U	.25	.60
XF970439x1 Secret Government Files U	.25	.60
XF970440x1 Secret Passage U	.25	.60
XF970441x1 Allen Stiletto UR	6.00	15.00
XF970442x1 Tape Recorder U	.25	.60
XF970443x1 Classified Ad U	.25	.60
XF970444x1 Foo Fighter R	.75	2.00
XF970445x1 Amaru Urn R	.40	1.00
XF970446x1 Avatar R	.60	1.50
XF970447x1 Captive Hybrid C	.12	.30
XF970448x1 Circuit Board Implant R	.60	1.50
XF970449x1 Disbelief C	.12	.30
XF970450x1 Eliminating The Source R	.40	1.00
XF970451x1 A Near Death Experience UR	6.00	15.00
XF970452x1 Hell Money R	.40	1.00
XF970453x1 Jose Chung's "from Outer Space" R	.60	1.50
XF970454x1 Krycek Possessed UR	6.00	15.00
XF970455x1 Mostow's Sketches R	1.25	3.00
XF970456x1 Ceremony R	.40	1.00
XF970457x1 Skinner Intervenes C	.12	.30
XF970458x1 Skinner's Wedding Ring C	.12	.30
XF970459x1 Men In Black UR	8.00	20.00
XF970460x1 The Video Trap C	.12	.30
XF970461x1 Tong Lottery Jar R	1.25	3.00
XF970462x1 Visit From The First Elder R	.75	2.00
XF970463x1 War Of The Coprophages R	.75	2.00
XF970464x1 White Buffalo R	.75	2.00
XF970465x1 Unexpected Call UR	6.00	15.00
XF970466x1 Work A Deal C	.12	.30
XF970467x1 Mostow's Studio, Washington, D.C. U	.25	.60
XF970468x1 Braddock Heights, Maryland C	.12	.30
XF970469x1 Chinatown, San Francisco, CA U	.25	.60
XF970470x1 Jerusalem, Ohio U	.25	.60
XF970471x1 Miller's Grove, Massachusetts U	.25	.60
XF970472x1 Positron Emission Tomography Lab, Allentown, Pennsylvania U	.25	.60
XF970473x1 Strikers Cove, Heuvalman's Lake, Blue Ridge Mountains, Georgia C	.12	.30
XF970474x1 Strughold Mining Company, Rural West Virginia U	.25	.60
XF970475x1 Tesos Dos Bichos Excavation, Equadorian Highlands, South America U	.25	.60
XF970476x1 Virgil Incanto's Apartment, Cleveland, Ohio C	.12	.30
XF970477x1 Agent Dan Kazanjian R	.40	1.00
XF970478x1 Carina Maywald R	.40	1.00
XF970479x1 Coast Guard Lieutenant C	.12	.30
XF970480x1 Detective Alan Cross U	.25	.60
XF970481x1 Detective Cline C	.12	.30
XF970482x1 Detective Havez C	.12	.30
XF970483x1 Detective Walter Eubanks R	.40	1.00
XF970484x1 Dr. Alexander Ivanov R	.40	1.00
XF970485x1 Dr. Bambi Berenbaum U	.25	.60
XF970486x1 Dr. Bugger U	.25	.60
XF970487x1 Dr. Jeff Eckerle U	.25	.60
XF970488x1 Dr. Rick Newton C	.12	.30
XF970489x1 Ellen Kaminski U	.25	.60
XF970490x1 Eric Hosteen U	.25	.60
XF970491x1 Escalante C	.12	.30
XF970492x1 General Thomas Callahan R	.40	1.00
XF970493x1 Jim Ullrich C	.12	.30
XF970494x1 Lottie Holoway R	.40	1.00
XF970495x1 Lt. Colonel Victor Stans C	.12	.30
XF970496x1 Lucy Householder R	.60	1.50
XF970497x1 Michael Kryder C	.12	.30
XF970498x1 Navajo Elder U	.25	.60
XF970499x1 Owen Jarvis R	.60	1.50
XF970500x1 Parmelly C	.12	.30
XF970501x1 Penny Northern C	.12	.30
XF970502x1 Sammon Roque U	.25	.60
XF970503x1 Sharon Kiveat C	.12	.30
XF970504x1 Sharon Skinner R	.75	2.00
XF970505x1 Sheriff John Teller U	.25	.60
XF970506x1 Stan Buxton U	.25	.60
XF970507x1 The Stupendous Yappi R	.40	1.00
XF970508x1 Victor Klemper R	.40	1.00
XF970509x1 Warden Leo Brodeur U	.25	.60

1997 The X-Files The Truth Is Out There

COMPLETE SET (353)
BOOSTER BOX ()
BOOSTER PACK ()
RELEASED ON
XF970001v2 Aura Of Invulnerability U
XF970002v2 First Aid C
XF970003v2 Face-off U
XF970004v2 Rending Claws U
XF970005v2 Fast Strike R
XF970006v2 Sneak Attack R
XF970007v2 Ambush C
XF970008v2 Kick C
XF970009v2 Gun Jammed C
XF970010v2 Hide C
XF970011v2 Dodge U
XF970012v2 Nerve Strike R
XF970013v2 Webbed R
XF970014v2 Vicious Fangs U
XF970015v2 Spin Kick R
XF970016v2 Mind Control R
XF970017v2 Alien Stealth Technology U
XF970018v2 Block And Attack R
XF970019v2 Block U
XF970020v2 Body Armor U
XF970021v2 Disarm R
XF970022v2 Running Gun Battle U
XF970023v2 Fascination U
XF970024v2 Internal Bleeding U
XF970025v2 Covering Fire U
XF970026v2 No Way Out U
XF970027v2 Hard Punch C
XF970028v2 Choke Hold R
XF970029v2 Fast Draw R
XF970030v2 Watch Out! U
XF970031v2 Hit And Run U
XF970032v2 Handcuff R
XF970033v2 Illusionary Foe R
XF970034v2 Run For It! U
XF970035v2 Terminal Damage R
XF970036v2 Flaming Wall U
XF970037v2 Massive Internal Damage U
XF970038v2 Semi-jacketed Hollow Points U
XF970039v2 Stunning Blow U
XF970040v2 Take Cover! U
XF970041v2 Energy Strike R
XF970042v2 Gibsonton, FL
XF970043v2 Excelsius Dei Convalescent Home, Worcester, MA U
XF970044v2 Broad Street, Philadelphia, PA C
XF970045v2 Ellens Air Base, ID U
XF970046v2 Coastal Northwest Oregon C
XF970047v2 Olympic National Forest, WA C
XF970048v2 Arlington, VA
XF970049v2 Lake Okobogee, Campsite #53, Sioux City, IA
XF970050v2 Newark, NJ
XF970051v2 Central Prison, Raleigh, NC U
XF970052v2 Genetics Clinic, Marin County, CA
XF970053v2 Cumberland Prison, VA
XF970054v2 Mt. Avalon, WA C
XF970055v2 Northeast Georgetown Medical Center, Washington, DC R
XF970056v2 Nasa Mission Control, Houston, TX R
XF970057v2 New York City, NY R
XF970058v2 Fairfield Zoo, Fairfield, ID
XF970059v2 Deadhorse, AK R
XF970060v2 Containment Facility, Georgetown, MD C
XF970061v2 University Of Maryland, Baltimore, MD
XF970062v2 Chaco House, Dudley, AR U
XF970063v2 Aubrey, MO
XF970064v2 Cape Cod, MA C
XF970065v2 Icy Cape, AK
XF970066v2 Farmington, NM U
XF970067v2 U.f.o. Wreckage, Townsend, WI R
XF970068v2 Mattawa, WA C
XF970069v2 Mahan Propulsion Laboratory, Colson, WA C
XF970070v2 Church Of The Red Museum, Delta Glen, WI R
XF970071v2 Psychiatric Hospital, Richmond, VA C
XF970072v2 Washington Monument, Washington, DC R
XF970073v2 Marion, VA
XF970074v2 Arecibo, Puerto Rico R
XF970075v2 Sea Off Tildeskan, Norway U
XF970076v2 Aleister Crowley High School, Milford Haven, NH R
XF970077v2 Los Angeles, CA R
XF970078v2 Minneapolis, MN U
XF970079v2 Franklin, PA
XF970080v2 Eurisko Building, Crystal City, VA U
XF970081v2 Folkstone, NC U
XF970082v2 Outskirts Of Atlantic City, NJ U
XF970083v2 Browning, MT
XF970084v2 Steveston, MA U
XF970085v2 Skyland Mountain, VA U
XF970086v2 Baltimore, MD U
XF970087v2 Detective Kelly Ryan C
XF970088v2 Sinus Cavity Implant U
XF970089v2 Peter Tanaka U
XF970090v2 Cigarette Butts C
XF970091v2 Cigarette Butts C
XF970092v2 Sheriff Daniels U
XF970093v2 Dr. Berube C
XF970094v2 The Overcoat Man C
XF970095v2 You've Got A Tail C
XF970096v2 Pete Calcagni U
XF970097v2 Holtzman, D.S.A. C
XF970098v2 Claude Peterson C
XF970099v2 The Conundrum U
XF970100v2 Paul Mossinger C
XF970101v2 Intruder Counter-measures Program U
XF970102v2 Dr. Aaron Monte C
XF970103v2 Poisonous Gases C
XF970104v2 Laser Barrier R
XF970105v2 Nasty Surprise U
XF970107v2 Radioactve Area U
XF970108v2 Ghost In The Machine
XF970109v2 Unnatural Aging U
XF970110v2 Car Troubles C
XF970111v2 Puzzles Within Puzzles U
XF970112v2 Government Cover-up C
XF970113v2 Hazardous Sample C
XF970114v2 Henry Trondheim U
XF970115v2 Detective Miles U
XF970116v2 Detective Thompson U
XF970117v2 Harry Cokely C
XF970118v2 Detective Tony Fiore U
XF970119v2 B.j. Morrow, Genetic Trait Recipient
XF970120v2 Augustus Cole, a.k.a. The Preacher
XF970121v2 The Cigarette-smoking Man
XF970122v2 Duane Barry
XF970123v2 The Jersey Devil
XF970124v2 The Host
XF970125v2 Lucas Henry, Serial Killer
XF970126v2 Arthur Grable
XF970127v2 Warren James Dupré, The Lazarus Man
XF970128v2 Colonel Wharton, Zombie Master
XF970129v2 Alien Dna Steroid Program (project Purity Control)
XF970131v2 Sheriff Tom Arens, Cannibal
XF970132v2 The Vampire, A.k.a. The Unholy Spirit
XF970133v2 Central Operating System, Artificial Intelligence
XF970134v2 Volcanic Spore
XF970135v2 Michael Holvey, The Evil One
XF970136v2 Eugene Victor Tooms
XF970137v2 Howard Graves, The Poltergeist
XF970138v2 Dr. Banton And His Shadow
XF970139v2 Alien Listeners
XF970140v2 Commander Colin Henderson
XF970141v2 Arctic Worm
XF970142v2 The Manitou
XF970143v2 Leonard Vance
XF970144v2 Ancestor Spirits
XF970145v2 Ed Funsch, Postal Worker
XF970146v2 Mrs. Paddock, a.k.a. The Dark Angel
XF970147v2 Dod Kalm
XF970148v2 John Barnett
XF970149v2 Alien Conservationist
XF970150v2 Faciphaga Emasculata
XF970151v2 Donnie Pfaster, Death Fetishist
XF970152v2 Brother Martin, Rogue Kindred
XF970153v2 Alien Abductors
XF970154v2 Eve
XF970155v2 Alien Experimenters
XF970156v2 Reverse Engineers
XF970157v2 The Swarm
XF970158v2 Leonard, Detachable Congenital Twin
XF970159v2 Cecil L'ively
XF970160v2 Section Chief Scott Blevins
XF970161v2 Albert Hosteen
XF970164v2 Lt. Brian Tillman, Aubrey Police Department
XF970165v2 Agent Rich
XF970166v2 Agent Lucy Kazdin
XF970167v2 Agent Jack Willis
XF970168v2 Inspector Phoebe Green
XF970169v2 Agent Fox Mulder
XF970170v2 Agent Alex Krycek
XF970171v2 Agent Nancy Spiller
XF970173v2 Agent Dana Scully
XF970175v2 Dr. Charles Burk
XF970176v2 Agent Tom Colton
XF970177v2 Agent Janus, Trained Medic
XF970178v2 Agent Moe Bocks
XF970179v2 Agent Reggie Purdue
XF970180v2 Assistant Director Walter Skinner
XF970181v2 Agent Weiss
XF970182v2 Agent Jerry Lamana
XF970183v2 Agent Karen Kosseff, Counselor
XF970184v2 Sheriff Spencer
XF970185v2 Dr. Blockhead R
XF970186v2 The Thinker R
XF970187v2 Byers C
XF970188v2 Emil And Zoe U
XF970189v2 Dr. Davey U
XF970190v2 Billy Miles
XF970191v2 Dr. Diamond R
XF970192v2 Detective Frank Briggs U
XF970195v2 Detective Sharon Lazard U
XF970196v2 Dr. Lakos U
XF970197v2 The Calusari R
XF970198v2 Bill Mulder R
XF970202v2 Sir Malcolm Marsden C
XF970203v2 Samantha Mulder R
XF970204v2 Max Fenig R
XF970205v2 Dr. Hodge
XF970206v2 Doug Spinney C
XF970207v2 Dr. Sheila Braun U
XF970208v2 U.s. Marshall Tapia
XF970209v2 Brad Wilczek U
XF970211v2 Ish--tribal Elder U
XF970212v2 Sheriff Mazeroski R
XF970213v2 Lt. Colonel Marcus Aurelius Belt R
XF970214v2 Gung Bituen R
XF970216v2 Gerd Thomas C
XF970217v2 Dr. Daniel Trepkos R
XF970218v2 Maggie Holvey C
XF970219v2 Luther Lee Boggs R
XF970220v2 Senator Richard Matheson R
XF970221v2 Successful Diagnosis U
XF970223v2 Shutting Down The X-files R
XF970224v2 Reporters At The Crime Scene U
XF970225v2 I Want To Believe C
XF970226v2 Road Trip R
XF970227v2 Hidden Transmitter U
XF970228v2 Medical Treatment C
XF970230v2 The Cigarette-smoking Man Strikes R
XF970231v2 Eve 7 R
XF970232v2 Street Contacts U
XF970233v2 Government Arrests Suspects
XF970234v2 Red Tape R
XF970235v2 S.w.a.t. Training C
XF970236v2 Fingerprints U
XF970237v2 Back Tracking Program
XF970239v2 Evidence Destroyed
XF970240v2 Surfing The Net R
XF970241v2 Government Sanctioned Pheromone Experiments R
XF970242v2 Thorough Documentation R
XF970246v2 Evidence Overlooked C
XF970249v2 Reading The Signs U
XF970251v2 Skinner Adopts The Company Line R
XF970252v2 Safe House R
XF970253v2 Crop Circles
XF970254v2 Langly U
XF970255v2 Expedite Request For Resources U
XF970256v2 Paperwork
XF970257v2 Unexplainable Time Loss R
XF970258v2 Clone
XF970259v2 Suspect Description C
XF970260v2 Smoke Screen U
XF970261v2 Dark Forces Align R
XF970262v2 Computer Access Denied R
XF970263v2 Improved Channels U
XF970265v2 Krycek, The Double Agent R
XF970266v2 Spying Mission U
XF970267v2 Authorized Access Only R
XF970268v2 Equipment Malfunction U
XF970269v2 The Local Law Enforcement Are Uncooperative U
XF970271v2 Alien Discretion R
XF970272v2 Fingernail Scrapings
XF970273v2 Trust No One R
XF970274v2 Lula Phillips R
XF970275v2 No Place Is Safe R
XF970276v2 Blackmail R
XF970277v2 Dissection U

XF970279v2 Application For Fbi Resources Approved R
XF970280v2 Expert Briefing C
XF970281v2 Access Personnel Files C
XF970282v2 Hard Evidence C
XF970283v2 Relentless Pursuit C
XF970285v2 Deductive Reasoning R
XF970286v2 Grid Pattern Search R
XF970287v2 Driving U
XF970288v2 In-service Training C
XF970289v2 Rejuvenating Caves U
XF970290v2 Alien Experimentation R
XF970291v2 Hidden Grave U
XF970292v2 Trap U
XF970294v2 Assigned To The X-files R
XF970296v2 X-files Research C
XF970297v2 A Friend In The FBI R
XF970298v2 Written Report C
XF970299v2 Government Mindwipe Serum U
XF970300v2 Travel Arrangements C
XF970301v2 Decoy U
XF970302v2 Autopsy U
XF970303v2 Evasive Maneuvers R
XF970304v2 Frohike R
XF970306v2 Road Hazard
XF970307v2 Core Training C
XF970308v2 Samuel Hartley R
XF970309v2 True Grit R
XF970310v2 Decreased Workload U
XF970311v2 Laptop Computer U
XF970312v2 Gas Chromatograph C
XF970313v2 Wire-tap
XF970314v2 Binoculars
XF970315v2 Medi-kit R
XF970316v2 Kevlar Vest U
XF970317v2 Glock 19 Semi-automatic Pistol U
XF970318v2 High Resolution Camera C
XF970319v2 High-powered Flashlight U
XF970320v2 Government Car
XF970321v2 Knife C
XF970322v2 Taped Intelligence R
XF970323v2 Walther Ppk 7.65 Hold Out Weapon U
XF970324v2 Geiger Counter U
XF970325v2 Hospital Crash Cart R
XF970326v2 Cellular Phone R
XF970327v2 Symbol Of Faith R
XF970328v2 Electron Emission Microscope C
XF970329v2 Shotgun R
XF970330v2 M-16 Assault Rifle U
XF970331v2 Mojo Bag U
XF970332v2 Lie Detector C
XF970333v2 Slithers In The Night C
XF970335v2 Hunter In The Dark C
XF970336v2 Crew-cut Man U
XF970337v2 Alien Bounty Hunter R
XF970338v2 The Host Attacks R
XF970339v2 Pvt. Mcalpin, Zombie C
XF970340v2 Good People, Good Food U
XF970341v2 The Sandman U
XF970342v2 Abduction R
XF970343v2 Squeeze U
XF970344v2 The Psychotic Attack C
XF970345v2 The Mechanic U
XF970346v2 Darkness Falls U
XF970347v2 Suppressed Fury C
XF970348v2 Living Machine U
XF970349v2 Operation Falcon Blue Berets R
XF970350v2 Pheromone-induced Psychosis U
XF970351v2 Deadly Blur U
XF970352v2 The Manitou Stalks His Prey R
XF970353v2 Poltergeist Attack
XF970354v2 Kiss Of The Vampire R
XF970355v2 John Barnett Links You To Mulder R
XF970356v2 Brother Martin Is Attracted To You R
XF970357v2 Leonard R
XF970358v2 F. Emasculata Outbreak R
XF970359v2 The Evil One R
XF970360v2 Spirit Of The Amaru UR
XF970361v2 Limited Choices UR
XF970362v2 Too Close To The Truth UR
XF970363v2 Injured Relative R
XF970364v2 Explosion R
XF970365v2 Lock Pick R
XF970366v2 U.s.g.s. Quadrant Map R
XF970367v2 Nurse Owens UR
XF970368v2 One Breath UR
XF970369v2 Taking Chances R
XF970370v2 A Friend In The Lab R
XF970371v2 A False Leads R
XF970372v2 Witness Intimidated R
XF970373v2 Assassinated R
XF970374v2 Security Clearance R
XF970375v2 Dr. Joe Ridley R
XF970376v2 Colonel Kissell R
XF970377v2 Meet Brother Andrew R
XF970378v2 Misclassified Case UR
XF970379v2 Additional Resources UR
XF970380v2 Women's Health Clinic, Richville, MD R
XF970381v2 Tracking The Killer R
XF970382v2 Mrs. Mulder UR
XF970383v2 Margaret Scully UR
XF970384v2 Melissa Scully UR

1999 Young Jedi Menace of Darth Maul

COMPLETE SET (140) 10.00 25.00
BOOSTER BOX (30 PACKS) 30.00 50.00
BOOSTER PACK (11 CARDS) 1.00 2.00
RELEASED ON MAY 12, 1999
1 Obi-Wan Kenobi, Young Jedi R 2.00 5.00
2 Qui-Gon Jinn, Jedi Master R 1.50 4.00
3 Jar Jar Binks, Gungan Chuba Thief R 1.00 2.50
4 Anakin Skywalker, Podracer Pilot R .75 2.00
5 Padme Naberrie, Handmaiden R 1.25 3.00
6 Captain Panaka, Protector of the Queen R .75 2.00
7 Mace Windu, Jedi Master R 1.00 2.50
8 Queen Amidala, Ruler of Naboo R 1.25 3.00
9 Queen Amidala, Royal Leader R 1.25 3.00
10 Yoda, Jedi Master R 1.25 3.00
11 R2-D2, Astromech Droid R 1.00 2.50
12 C-3PO, Anakin's Creation R 1.00 2.50
13 Boss Nass, Leader of the Gungans U .30 .75
14 Ric Olie, Ace Pilot U .30 .75
15 Captain Tarpals, Gungan Guard U .30 .75
16 Rabe, Handmaiden U .30 .75
17 Rep Been, Gungan U .30 .75
18 Mas Amedda, Vice Chancellor U .30 .75
19 Naboo Officer, Battle Planner U .30 .75
20 Naboo Security, Guard C .10 .25
21 Bravo Pilot, Veteran Flyer C .10 .25
22 Gungan Official, Bureaucrat C .10 .25
23 Gungan Soldier, Scout C .10 .25
24 Gungan Guard C .10 .25
25 Gungan Warrior, Infantry C .10 .25
26 Gungan Soldier, Veteran C .10 .25
27 Ishi Tib, Warrior C .10 .25
28 Ithorian, Merchant C .10 .25
29 Jawa, Thief C .10 .25
30 Jawa, Bargainer S .10 .25
31 Royal Guard, Leader C .10 .25
32 Royal Guard, Veteran C .10 .25
33 Obi-Wan Kenobi, Jedi Padawan S .10 .25
34 Obi-Wan Kenobi's Lightsaber R 1.00 2.50
35 Jedi Lightsaber .30 .75
Constructed by Ki-Adi-Mundi U
36 Anakin Skywalker's Podracer R .75 2.00
37 Captain Panaka's Blaster C .10 .25
38 Jar Jar Binks' Electropole U .30 .75
39 Electropole C .10 .25
40 Eopie C .10 .25
41 Kaadu C .10 .25
42 Flash Speeder C .10 .25
43 Jawa Ion Blaster C .10 .25
44 Naboo Blaster C .10 .25
45 Blaster C .10 .25
46 Blaster Rifle C .10 .25
47 Anakin Skywalker .30 .75
Meet Obi-Wan Kenobi U
48 Are You An Angel? U .30 .75
49 Cha Skrunee Da Pat, Sleemo C .10 .25
50 Counterparts U .30 .75
51 Da Beings Hereabouts Cawazy C .10 .25
52 Enough Of This Pretense U .30 .75
53 Fear Attracts The Fearful U .30 .75
54 Gungan Curiosity C .10 .25
55 He Was Meant To Help You U .30 .75
56 I Have A Bad Feeling About This U .30 .75
57 I've Been Trained In Defense U .30 .75
58 Security Volunteers C .10 .25
59 Shmi's Pride U .30 .75
60 The Federation Has Gone Too Far C .10 .25
61 The Negotiations Were Short C .10 .25
62 The Queen's Plan C .10 .25
63 We're Not In Trouble Yet U .30 .75
64 Yousa Guys Bombad! R .60 1.50
65 Tatooine Podrace Arena S .10 .25
66 Coruscant Capital City S .10 .25
67 Naboo Theed Palace S .10 .25
68 Bravo 1, Naboo Starfighter U .30 .75
69 Naboo Starfighter C .10 .25
70 Republic Cruiser, Transport C .10 .25
71 Darth Maul, Sith Apprentice R 2.50 6.00
72 Darth Sidious, Sith Master R 1.50 4.00
73 Sebulba, Bad-Tempered Dug R 1.00 2.50
74 Watto, Slave Owner R .75 2.00
75 Aurra Sing, Bounty Hunter R 1.25 3.00
76 Jabba the Hutt, Vile Crime Lord R 1.00 2.50
77 Gardulla the Hutt, Crime Lord U .30 .75
78 Destroyer Droid Squad .60 1.50
Security Division R
79 Battle Droid Squad, Assault Unit R .75 2.00
80 Ben Quadinaros, Podracer Pilot U .30 .75
81 Gasgano, Podracer Pilot U .30 .75
82 Mawhonic, Podracer Pilot U .30 .75
83 Teemto Pagalies, Podracer Pilot U .30 .75
84 Bib Fortuna, Twi'lek Advisor U .30 .75
85 Ann and Tann Gella .30 .75
Sebulba's Attendants U
86 Gragra, Chuba Peddler C .10 .25
87 Passel Argente, Senator C .10 .25
88 Trade Federation Tank .75 2.00
Armored Division R
89 Destroyer Droid, Wheel Droid C .10 .25
90 Destroyer Droid, Defense Droid C .10 .25
91 Sith Probe Droid, Spy Drone C .10 .25
92 Pit Droid, Engineer C .10 .25
93 Pit Droid, Heavy Lifter C .10 .25
94 Pit Droid, Mechanic C .10 .25
95 Tusken Raider, Nomad C .10 .25
96 Tusken Raider, Marksman C .10 .25
97 Battle Droid: Pilot, MTT Division C .10 .25
98 Battle Droid: Security, MTT Division C .10 .25
99 Battle Droid: Infantry, MTT Division C .10 .25
100 Battle Droid: Officer, MTT Division C .10 .25
101 Battle Droid: Pilot, AAT Division C .10 .25
102 Battle Droid: Security, AAT Division C .10 .25
103 Battle Droid: Infantry, AAT Division C .10 .25
104 Battle Droid: Officer, AAT Division C .10 .25
105 Neimoidian, Trade Federation Pilot S .10 .25
106 Darth Maul, Sith Lord S .40 1.00
107 Sith Lightsaber R .75 2.00
108 Aurra Sing's Blaster Rifle R .60 1.50
109 Sebulba's Podracer R .60 1.50
110 Ben Quadinaros' Podracer U .30 .75
111 Gasgano's Podracer U .30 .75
112 Mawhonic's Podracer U .30 .75
113 Teemto Pagalies' Podracer U .30 .75
114 Trade Federation Tank Laser Cannon U .30 .75
115 Multi Troop Transport U .30 .75
116 STAP U .30 .75
117 Tatooine Thunder Rifle C .10 .25
118 Battle Droid Blaster Rifle C .10 .25
119 Blaster C .10 .25
120 Blaster Rifle C .10 .25
121 At Last We Will Have Revenge R .60 1.50
122 Begin Landing Your Troops C .10 .25
123 Boonta Eve Podrace U .30 .75
124 Grueling Contest U .30 .75
125 In Complete Control C .10 .25
126 Kaa Bazza Kundee Hodrudda! U .30 .75
127 Opee Sea Killer C .10 .25
128 Podrace Preparation U .30 .75
129 Sandstorm C .10 .25
130 Sniper C .10 .25
131 The Invasion Is On Schedule C .10 .25
132 Vile Gangsters U .30 .75
133 Watto's Wager U .30 .75
134 You Have Been Well Trained R .60 1.50
135 Tatooine Desert Landing Site S .10 .25
136 Coruscant Jedi Council Chamber S .10 .25
137 Naboo Gungan Swamp S .10 .25
138 Darth Maul's Starfighter 1.00 2.50
Sith Infiltrator R
139 Droid Starfighter C .10 .25
140 Battleship .10 .25
Trade Federation Transport C

1999 Young Jedi Menace of Darth Maul Foil

COMPLETE SET (18) 6.00 15.00
F1 Obi-Wan Kenobi, Young Jedi R 2.50 6.00
F2 Jar-Jar Binks, Gungan Chuba Thief R 1.25 3.00
F3 Mace Windu, Jedi Master U 1.25 3.00
F4 Queen Amidala, Ruler of Naboo U 2.00 5.00
F5 C-3PO, Anakin's Creation U 1.25 3.00
F6 Obi-Wan Kenobi's Lightsaber C 1.00 2.50
F7 Anakin Skywalker's Podracer C .75 2.00
F8 Bravo 1, Naboo Starfighter C .40 1.00
F9 Republic Cruiser, Transport C .40 1.00
F10 Darth Maul, Sith Apprentice R 3.00 8.00
F11 Darth Sidious, Sith Master R 2.00 5.00
F12 Destroyer Droid Squad .60 1.50
Security Division U
F13 Battle Droid Squad, Assault Unit U .60 1.50
F14 Sebulba's Podracer U .60 1.50
F15 Ben Quadinaros' Podracer C .40 1.00
F16 Gasgano's Podracer C .40 1.00
F17 Mawhonic's Podracer C .40 1.00
F18 Teemto Pagalies' Podracer C .40 1.00

1999 Young Jedi The Jedi Council

COMPLETE SET (140) 8.00 20.00
BOOSTER BOX (30 PACKS) 20.00 30.00
BOOSTER BOX (11 CARDS) .75 1.25
RELEASED ON OCTOBER 27, 1999
1 Obi-Wan Kenobi, Jedi Apprentice R 1.50 4.00
2 Qui-Gon Jinn, Jedi Protector R 1.25 3.00
3 Jar Jar Binks, Gungan Outcast R .75 2.00
4 Anakin Skywalker, Child of Prophecy R .75 2.00
5 Padme Naberrie, Queen's Handmaiden R 1.00 2.50
6 Captain Panaka, Amidala's Bodyguard R .60 1.50
7 Mace Windu .75 2.00
Senior Jedi Council Member R
8 Queen Amidala, Representative of Naboo R 1.00 2.50
9 Queen Amidala, Voice of Her People R 1.00 2.50
10 Yoda, Jedi Council Member R 1.00 2.50
11 R2-D2, Loyal Droid R .75 2.00
12 Ki-Adi-Mundi, Cerean Jedi Knight R .75 2.00
13 Adi Gallia, Corellian Jedi Master U .30 .75
14 Depa Billaba, Jedi Master U .30 .75
15 Eeth Koth, Zabrak Jedi Master U .30 .75
16 Even Piell, Lannik Jedi Master U .30 .75
17 Oppo Rancisis, Jedi Master U .30 .75
18 Plo Koon, Jedi Master U .30 .75
19 Saesee Tiin, Iktotchi Jedi Master U .30 .75
20 Yaddle, Jedi Master U .30 .75
21 Yarael Poof, Quermian Jedi Master U .30 .75
22 Boss Nass, Gungan Leader U .30 .75
23 Ric Olié, Chief Pilot U .30 .75
24 Captain Tarpals, Gungan Battle Leader U .30 .75
25 Eirtae, Handmaiden U .30 .75
26 Valorum, Supreme Chancellor C .10 .25
27 Sci Taria, Chancellor's Aide C .10 .25
28 Naboo Officer, Liberator C .10 .25
29 Bravo Pilot, Naboo Volunteer C .10 .25
30 Naboo Security, Amidala's Guard C .10 .25
31 Republic Captain, Officer C .10 .25
32 Republic Pilot, Veteran C .10 .25
33 Coruscant Guard .10 .25
Coruscant Detachment C
34 Coruscant Guard, Peacekeeper C .10 .25
35 Coruscant Guard, Officer C .10 .25
36 Coruscant Guard, Chancellor's Guard C .10 .25
37 Wookiee Senator, Representative C .10 .25
38 Galactic Senator, Delegate S .10 .25
39 Obi-Wan Kenobi, Jedi Warrior S .10 .25
40 Qui-Gon Jinn's Lightsaber R .60 1.50
41 Amidala's Blaster R .60 1.50
42 Adi Gallia's Lightsaber U .30 .75
43 Coruscant Guard Blaster Rifle U .30 .75
44 Ascension Gun C .10 .25
45 Electropole C .10 .25
46 Kaadu C .10 .25
47 Flash Speeder C .10 .25
48 Gian Speeder C .10 .25
49 Naboo Blaster C .10 .25
50 Blaster C .10 .25
51 Blaster Rifle C .10 .25
52 Balance To The Force U .30 .75
53 Brave Little Droid U .30 .75
54 Dos Mackineeks No Comen Here! C .10 .25
55 Galactic Chancellor C .10 .25
56 Hate Leads To Suffering U .30 .75
57 I Will Not Cooperate U .30 .75
58 Invasion! C .10 .25
59 May The Force Be With You C .10 .25
60 Senator Palpatine C .10 .25
61 The Might Of The Republic C .10 .25
62 We Don't Have Time For This C .10 .25
63 We Wish To Board At Once C .10 .25
64 Wisdom Of The Council R .60 1.50
65 Tatooine Mos Espa S .10 .25
66 Coruscant Jedi Council Chamber S .10 .25
67 Naboo Gungan Swamp S .10 .25
68 Bravo 2, Naboo Starfighter U .30 .75
69 Naboo Starfighter C .10 .25
70 Radiant VII, Republic Cruiser Transport C .10 .25
71 Darth Maul, Master of Evil R 2.00 5.00
72 Darth Sidious, Lord of the Sith R 1.25 3.00
73 Sebulba, Podracer Pilot R .75 2.00
74 Watto, Junk Merchant R .60 1.50
75 Jabba the Hutt, Gangster R .75 2.00
76 Nute Gunray, Neimoidian Viceroy R .60 1.50
77 Rune Haako, Neimoidian Advisor R .60 1.50
78 Destroyer Droid Squad, Defense Division R .60 1.50
79 Battle Droid Squad, Escort Unit R .60 1.50
80 Trade Federation Tank, Assault Division R .60 1.50
81 Lott Dod, Neimoidian Senator R .60 1.50
82 Fode and Beed, Podrace Announcer R .60 1.50
83 Clegg Holdfast, Podracer Pilot U .30 .75
84 Dud Bolt, Podracer Pilot U .30 .75
85 Mars Guo, Podracer Pilot U .30 .75
86 Ody Mandrell, Podracer Pilot U .30 .75
87 Ratts Tyerell, Podracer Pilot U .30 .75
88 Aks Moe, Senator C .10 .25
89 Horox Ryyder, Senator C .10 .25
90 Edcel Bar Gane, Roona Senator C .10 .25
91 Galactic Delegate, Representative C .10 .25
92 Destroyer Droid, Assault Droid C .10 .25
93 Destroyer Droid, Battleship Security C .10 .25
94 Sith Probe Droid, Hunter Droid C .10 .25
95 Rodian, Mercenary C .10 .25
96 Battle Droid: Pilot, Assault Division C .10 .25
97 Battle Droid: Security, Assault Division C .10 .25
98 Battle Droid: Infantry, Assault Division C .10 .25
99 Battle Droid: Officer, Assault Division C .10 .25
100 Battle Droid: Pilot, Guard Division C .10 .25
101 Battle Droid: Security, Guard Division C .10 .25
102 Battle Droid: Infantry, Guard Division C .10 .25
103 Battle Droid: Officer, Guard Division C .10 .25
104 Neimoidian Aide .10 .25
Trade Federation Delegate S
105 Darth Maul, Sith Warrior S .10 .25
106 Darth Maul's Lightsaber R .60 1.50
107 Darth Maul's Sith Speeder R .60 1.50
108 Clegg Holdfast's Podracer U .30 .75
109 Dud Bolt's Podracer U .30 .75
110 Mars Guo's Podracer U .30 .75
111 Ody Mandrell's Podracer U .30 .75
112 Ratts Tyerell's Podracer U .30 .75
113 Trade Federation Tank Laser Cannon U .30 .75
114 Multi Troop Transport U .30 .75
115 STAP U .30 .75
116 Thermal Detonator U .30 .75
117 Battle Droid Blaster Rifle C .10 .25
118 Blaster C .10 .25
119 Blaster Rifle C .10 .25
120 I Object! C .10 .25
121 I Will Deal With Them Myself C .10 .25
122 Let Them Make The First Move R .60 1.50
123 Move Against The Jedi First C .10 .25
124 Open Fire! U .30 .75
125 Seal Off The Bridge U .30 .75
126 Start Your Engines! U .30 .75
127 Switch To Bio C .10 .25
128 Take Them To Camp Four C .10 .25
129 Very Unusual C .10 .25
130 Vote Of No Confidence C .10 .25
131 We Are Meeting No Resistance C .10 .25
132 We Have Them On The Run U .30 .75
133 Yoka To Bantha Poodoo C .10 .25
134 Your Little Insurrection Is At An End U .30 .75
135 Tatooine Podrace Arena S .10 .25
136 Coruscant Galactic Senate S .10 .25
137 Naboo Battle Plains S .10 .25
138 Sith Infiltrator, Starfighter U .30 .75
139 Droid Starfighter C .10 .25
140 Battleship, Trade Federation Transport C .10 .25

1999 Young Jedi The Jedi Council Foil

COMPLETE SET (18) 4.00 10.00
F1 Obi-Wan Kenobi, Jedi Apprentice UR 2.00 5.00
F2 Qui-Gon Jinn, Jedi Protector SR .75 2.00
F3 Padmé Naberrie .75 2.00
Queen's Handmaiden SR
F4 Captain Panaka .60 1.50
Amidala's Bodyguard SR
F5 Mace Windu 1.00 2.50
Senior Jedi Council Member SR
F6 Queen Amidala 1.25 3.00
Representative of Naboo VR
F7 R2-D2, Loyal Droid VR 1.25 3.00
F8 Qui-Gon Jinn's Lightsaber VR .40 1.00
F9 Amidala's Blaster VR .40 1.00
F10 Darth Maul, Master of Evil UR 2.00 5.00
F11 Darth Sidious, Lord of the Sith UR 1.25 3.00
F12 Watto, Junk Merchant SR .60 1.50
F13 Jabba the Hutt, Gangster SR .60 1.50
F14 Nute Gunray, Neimoidian Viceroy SR .60 1.50
F15 Rune Haako, Neimoidian Advisor VR .40 1.00
F16 Lott Dod, Neimoidian Senator VR .40 1.00
F17 Darth Maul's Lightsaber VR .40 1.00
F18 Darth Maul's Sith Speeder VR .40 1.00

2000 Young Jedi Battle of Naboo

COMPLETE SET (140) 8.00 20.00
BOOSTER BOX (30 PACKS) 15.00 30.00
BOOSTER PACK (11 CARDS) .75 1.25
RELEASED ON APRIL 5, 2000
1 Obi-Wan Kenobi, Jedi Knight R 1.50 4.00
2 Qui-Gon Jinn, Jedi Ambassador R 1.25 3.00
3 Jar Jar Binks, Bombad Gungan General R .75 2.00
4 Anakin Skywalker, Padawan R .75 2.00
5 Padme Naberrie, Amidala's Handmaiden R 1.00 2.50
6 Captain Panaka, Veteran Leader R .60 1.50
7 Mace Windu, Jedi Speaker R .75 2.00
8 Queen Amidala, Resolute Negotiator R 1.00 2.50
9 Queen Amidala, Keeper of the Peace R 1.00 2.50
10 Yoda, Jedi Elder R 1.00 2.50
11 R2-D2, The Queen's Hero R .75 2.00
12 Boss Nass, Gungan Chief U .30 .75
13 Ric Olie, Bravo Leader U .30 .75
14 Captain Tarpals, Gungan Officer U .30 .75
15 Sio Bibble, Governor of Naboo U .30 .75
16 Sabe, Handmaiden Decoy Queen U .30 .75
17 Sache, Handmaiden U .30 .75
18 Yane, Handmaiden U .30 .75
19 Naboo Officer, Squad Leader U .30 .75
20 Naboo Officer, Commander C .10 .25
21 Naboo Bureaucrat, Official C .10 .25
22 Naboo Security, Trooper C .10 .25
23 Naboo Security, Defender C .10 .25
24 Bravo Pilot, Ace Flyer C .10 .25
25 Coruscant Guard, Chancellor's Escort C .10 .25
26 Alderaan Diplomat, Senator C .10 .25
27 Council Member, Naboo Governor C .10 .25
28 Gungan Warrior, Veteran C .10 .25
29 Gungan Guard, Lookout C .10 .25
30 Gungan General, Army Leader C .10 .25
31 Gungan Soldier, Infantry C .10 .25
32 Rep Officer, Gungan Diplomat S .10 .25
33 Obi-Wan Kenobi, Jedi Negotiator S .10 .25
34 Mace Windu's Lightsaber R .60 1.50
35 Eeth Koth's Lightsaber U .30 .75
36 Captain Tarpals' Electropole U .30 .75
37 Planetary Shuttle C .10 .25
38 Fambaa C .10 .25
39 Electropole C .10 .25
40 Kaadu C .10 .25
41 Flash Speeder C .10 .25
42 Blaster C .10 .25
43 Heavy Blaster C .10 .25
44 Capture The Viceroy C .10 .25
45 Celebration C .10 .25
46 Guardians Of The Queen U .30 .75
47 Gunga City C .10 .25
48 Gungan Battle Cry U .30 .75
49 How Wude! U .30 .75
50 I Will Take Back What Is Ours C .10 .25
51 Jedi Force Push U .30 .75
52 Meeeesa Lika Dis! C .10 .25
53 NOOOOOOOOOO! R .60 1.50
54 Thanks, Artoo! U .30 .75
55 The Chancellor's Ambassador U .30 .75
56 The Will Of The Force R .60 1.50
57 Young Skywalker U .30 .75
58 Your Occupation Here Has Ended C .10 .25
59 Bombad General U .30 .75
60 Kiss Your Trade Franchise Goodbye U .30 .75
61 There's Always A Bigger Fish C .10 .25
62 Uh-Oh! C .10 .25
63 We Wish To Form An Alliance C .10 .25
64 Tatooine Desert Landing Site S .10 .25
65 Coruscant Galactic Senate S .10 .25
66 Naboo Battle Plains S .10 .25
67 Amidala's Starship, Royal Transport R .60 1.50
68 Bravo 3, Naboo Starfighter U .30 .75
69 Naboo Starfighter C .10 .25
70 Republic Cruiser, Transport C .10 .25
71 Darth Maul, Dark Lord of the Sith R 2.00 5.00
72 Darth Sidious, Sith Manipulator R 1.25 3.00
73 Sebulba, Dangerous Podracer Pilot R .60 1.50
74 Watto, Toydarian Gambler R .60 1.50
75 Aurra Sing, Mercenary R .75 2.00
76 Jabba The Hutt, Crime Lord R .60 1.50
77 Nute Gunray, Neimoidian Despot R .60 1.50
78 Rune Haako, Neimoidian Deputy R .60 1.50
79 Destroyer Droid Squad, Guard Division R .60 1.50
80 Battle Droid Squad, Guard Unit R .60 1.50
81 Trade Federation Tank, Guard Division R .60 1.50
82 Trade Federation Tank, Patrol Division R .60 1.50
83 P-59, Destroyer Droid Commander U .30 .75
84 OOM-9, Battle Droid Commander U .30 .75
85 Daultay Dofine, Neimoidian Attendant U .30 .75
86 Diva Shaliqua, Singer U .30 .75
87 Diva Funquita, Dancer U .30 .75
88 Bith, Musician U .30 .75
89 Quarren, Smuggler U .30 .75
90 Toonbuck Toora, Senator U .30 .75
91 Aqualish, Galactic Senator C .10 .25
92 Twi'lek Diplomat, Senator C .10 .25
93 Weequay, Enforcer C .10 .25
94 Nikto, Slave C .10 .25
95 Pacithhip, Prospector C .10 .25
96 Destroyer Droid, Vanguard Droid C .10 .25
97 Destroyer Droid, MTT Infantry C .10 .25
98 Sith Probe Droid, Remote Tracker C .10 .25
99 Battle Droid: Pilot, Patrol Division C .10 .25
100 Battle Droid: Security, Patrol Division C .10 .25
101 Battle Droid: Infantry, Patrol Division C .10 .25
102 Battle Droid: Officer, Patrol Division C .10 .25
103 Battle Droid: Pilot, Defense Division C .10 .25
104 Battle Droid: Security, Defense Division C .10 .25
105 Battle Droid: Infantry, Defense Division C .10 .25
106 Battle Droid: Officer, Defense Division C .10 .25
107 Neimoidian Advisor, Bureaucrat C .10 .25
108 Darth Maul, Evil Sith Lord S .10 .25
109 Darth Maul's Lightsaber R .75 2.00
110 Sith Lightsaber R .60 1.50
111 Darth Maul's Electrobinoculars U .30 .75
112 Trade Federation Tank Laser Cannon U .30 .75
113 Multi Troop Transport U .30 .75
114 STAP U .30 .75
115 Battle Droid Blaster Rifle C .10 .25
116 Blaster C .10 .25
117 Blaster Rifle C .10 .25
118 A Thousand Terrible Things C .10 .25
119 Armored Assault C .10 .25
120 Death From Above C .10 .25
121 Don't Spect A Werm Welcome C .10 .25
122 I Will Make It Legal C .10 .25

123 Not For A Sith R .60 1.50
124 Now There Are Two Of Them U .30 .75
125 Sith Force Push U .30 .75
126 The Phantom Menace U .30 .75
127 They Win This Round C .10 .25
128 We Are Sending All Troops C .10 .25
129 After Her! C .10 .25
130 Da Dug Chaaa! U .30 .75
131 Sando Aqua Monster C .10 .25
132 They Will Not Stay Hidden For Long C .10 .25
133 This Is Too Close! U .30 .75
134 Tatooine Mos Espa S .10 .25
135 Coruscant Capital City S .10 .25
136 Naboo Theed Palace S .10 .25
137 Droid Control Ship .30 .75
Trade Federation Transport U
138 Sith Infiltrator, Starfighter U .30 .75
139 Droid Starfighter C .10 .25
140 Battleship, Trade Federation Transport C .10 .25

2000 Young Jedi Battle of Naboo Foil

COMPLETE SET (18) 4.00 10.00
F1 Obi-Wan Kenobi, Jedi Knight UR 1.50 4.00
F2 Qui-Gon Jinn, Jedi Ambassador UR .75 2.00
F3 Queen Amidala, Keeper of the Peace SR .75 2.00
F4 Yoda, Jedi Elder SR .75 2.00
F5 R2-D2, The Queen's Hero SR .75 2.00
F6 Queen Amidala, Resolute Negotiator VR .60 1.50
F7 Mace Windu's Lightsaber VR .40 1.00
F8 The Will Of The Force VR .40 1.00
F9 Amidala's Starship, Royal Transport VR .40 1.00
F10 Darth Maul, Dark Lord of the Sith UR 1.50 4.00
F11 Aurra Sing, Mercenary UR .75 2.00
F12 Nute Gunray .60 1.50
Neimoidian Despot SR
F13 Destroyer Droid Squad .60 1.50
Guard Division SR
F14 Trade Federation Tank .60 1.50
Guard Division SR
F15 Battle Droid Squad, Guard Unit VR .40 1.00
F16 Trade Federation Tank .40 1.00
Patrol Division VR
F17 Darth Maul's Lightsaber VR .40 1.00
F18 Not For A Sith VR .40 1.00

2000 Young Jedi Duel of the Fates

COMPLETE SET (60) 5.00 12.00
BOOSTER BOX (30 PACKS) 30.00 40.00
BOOSTER PACK (11 CARDS) 1.00 1.50
RELEASED ON NOVEMBER 8, 2000
1 Obi-Wan Kenobi, Jedi Student R 1.50 4.00
2 Qui-Gon Jinn, Jedi Mentor UR 1.25 3.00
3 Anakin Skywalker, Rookie Pilot R .75 2.00
4 Captain Panaka, Security Commander R .60 1.50
5 Mace Windu, Jedi Councilor R .75 2.00
6 Queen Amidala, Young Leader R 1.00 2.50
7 Yoda, Jedi Philosopher R 1.00 2.50
8 R2-D2, Repair Droid R .75 2.00
9 Ric Olie, Starship Pilot R .60 1.50
10 Bravo Pilot, Flyer C .10 .25
11 Valorum, Leader of the Senate C .10 .25
12 Qui-Gon Jinn's Lightsaber .60 1.50
Wielded by Obi-Wan Kenobi R
13 Booma U .30 .75
14 A Powerful Opponent C .10 .25
15 Come On, Move! U .30 .75
16 Critical Confrontation C .10 .25
17 Gungan Mounted Troops U .30 .75
18 Naboo Fighter Attack C .10 .25
19 Qui-Gon's Final Stand C .10 .25
20 Run The Blockade C .10 .25
21 Twist Of Fate C .10 .25
22 You Are Strong With The Force U .30 .75
23 Gungan Energy Shield U .30 .75
24 He Can See Things Before They Happen U .30 .75
25 Jedi Meditation U .30 .75
26 Jedi Training U .30 .75
27 Naboo Royal Security Forces U .30 .75
28 Pounded Unto Death C .10 .25
29 Senate Guard C .10 .25
30 Naboo Starfighter C .10 .25
31 Darth Maul, Student of the Dark Side UR 1.50 4.00
32 Darth Sidious, Master of the Dark Side R 1.00 2.50
33 Aurra Sing, Trophy Collector R .75 2.00
34 Tey How, Neimoidian Command Officer R .60 1.50
35 OWO-1, Battle Droid Command Officer R .60 1.50
36 Rayno Vaca, Taxi Driver R .60 1.50
37 Baskol Yeesrim, Gran Senator R .60 1.50
38 Starfighter Droid, DFS-327 R .60 1.50
39 Starfighter Droid, DFS-1104 R .60 1.50
40 Starfighter Droid, DFS-1138 R .60 1.50
41 Jedi Lightsaber, Stolen by Aurra Sing U .30 .75
42 Coruscant Taxi U .30 .75
43 Neimoidian Viewscreen C .10 .25
44 Battle Droid Patrol U .30 .75
45 Change In Tactics C .10 .25
46 Dangerous Encounter C .10 .25
47 Darth Maul Defiant C .10 .25
48 Impossible! C .10 .25
49 It's A Standoff! U .30 .75
50 Mobile Assassin U .30 .75
51 Power Of The Sith C .10 .25
52 Starfighter Screen C .10 .25
53 To The Death C .10 .25
54 Use Caution U .30 .75
55 Blockade U .30 .75
56 End This Pointless Debate U .30 .75
57 The Duel Begins U .30 .75
58 The Jedi Are Involved U .30 .75
59 Where Are Those Droidekas? U .30 .75
60 Droid Starfighter C .10 .25

2000 Young Jedi Enhanced Menace of Darth Maul

P1 Qui-Gon Jinn, Jedi Protector 2.00 5.00
P2 Mace Windu, Jedi Warrior 1.25 3.00
P3 Queen Amidala, Cunning Warrior 4.00 10.00
P4 Darth Maul, Sith Assassin 2.00 5.00
P5 Sebulba, Champion Podracer Pilot 4.00 10.00
P6 Trade Federation Tank, Assault Leader 2.50 6.00

2001 Young Jedi Boonta Eve Podrace

COMPLETE SET (63) 4.00 10.00
BOOSTER BOX (30 PACKS) 30.00 40.00
BOOSTER PACK (11 CARDS) 1.00 1.50
RELEASED ON SEPTEMBER 5, 2001
1 Anakin Skywalker, Boonta Eve Podracer Pilot UR .75 2.00
2 Yoda, Jedi Instructor R 1.00 2.50
3 C-3PO, Human-Cyborg Relations Droid R .75 2.00
4 Jira, Pallie Vendor R .60 1.50
5 Kitster, Anakin's Friend R .60 1.50
6 Wald, Anakin's Friend R .60 1.50
7 Seek, Anakin's Friend U .30 .75
8 Amee, Anakin's Friend U .30 .75
9 Melee, Anakin's Friend U .30 .75
10 Captain Tarpals, Gungan Leader R .60 1.50
11 Boles Roor, Podracer Pilot U .30 .75
12 Elan Mak, Podracer Pilot U .30 .75
13 Neva Kee, Podracer Pilot U .30 .75
14 Wan Sandage, Podracer Pilot U .30 .75
15 Shmi Skywalker, Anakin's Mother R .60 1.50
16 Boles Roor's Podracer U .30 .75
17 Elan Mak's Podracer U .30 .75
18 Neva Kee's Podracer U .30 .75
19 Wan Sandage's Podracer U .30 .75
20 Comlink C .10 .25
21 Hold-Out Blaster C .10 .25
22 Dis Is Nutsen C .10 .25
23 Masquerade C .10 .25
24 No Giben Up, General Jar Jar C .10 .25
25 What Does Your Heart Tell You? C .10 .25
26 All-Out Defense U .30 .75
27 Bravo Squadron C .10 .25
28 Hologram Projector C .10 .25
29 Boonta Eve Classic R .60 1.50
30 Amidala's Starship R .60 1.50
31 Sebulba, Dug Podracer Pilot UR .60 1.50
32 Watto, Podrace Sponsor R .60 1.50
33 Aurra Sing, Formidable Adversary R .75 2.00
34 Jabba The Hutt, O Grandio Lust R .60 1.50
35 TC-14, Protocol Droid R .60 1.50
36 Orr'UrRuuR'R, Tusken Raider Leader Rare R .60 1.50
37 UrrOr'RuuR, Tusken Raider Warrior U .30 .75
38 RuuR'Ur, Tusken Raider Sniper C .10 .25
39 Sil Unch, Neimoidian Comm Officer U .30 .75
40 Graxol Kelvyyn and Shakka U .30 .75
41 Corix Venne, Bith Musician C .10 .25
42 Reike Th'san, Arms Smuggler R .60 1.50
43 Meddun, Nikto Mercenary U .30 .75
44 Rum Sleg, Bounty Hunter R .60 1.50
45 Aehrrley Rue, Freelance Pilot U .30 .75
46 Jedwar Seelah, Explorer Scout U .30 .75
47 Chokk, Klatooinian Explosives Expert C .10 .25
48 Tatooine Backpack C .10 .25
49 Gaderffii Stick C .10 .25
50 Hold-Out Blaster C .10 .25
51 Watto's Datapad U .30 .75
52 Colo Claw Fish C .10 .25
53 He Always Wins! C .10 .25
54 Bounty Hunter C .10 .25
55 Two-Pronged Attack C .10 .25
56 All-Out Attack U .30 .75
57 Eventually You'll Lose U .30 .75
58 Gangster's Paradise U .30 .75
59 Boonta Eve Classic R .60 1.50
60 Viceroy's Battleship R .60 1.50
R1 Rule Card 1 .08 .20
R2 Rule Card 2 .08 .20
R3 Rule Card 3 .08 .20

2001 Young Jedi Enhanced Battle of Naboo

COMPLETE SET (12) 30.00 80.00
RELEASED ON
P8 Obi-Wan Kenobi, Jedi Avenger 4.00 10.00
P9 Anakin Skywalker, Tested By The Jedi Council 10.00 25.00
P10 Padmé Naberrie, Loyal Handmaiden 12.00 30.00
P11 Captain Panaka, Royal Defender 2.00 5.00
P12 Yoda, Wise Jedi 4.00 10.00
P13 R2-D2, Starship Maintenance Droid 5.00 12.00
P14 Darth Sidious, The Phantom Menace 2.00 5.00
P15 Watto, Risk Taker 4.00 10.00
P16 Aurra Sing, Scoundrel 4.00 10.00
P17 Jabba The Hutt 4.00 10.00
P18 Nute Gunray, Neimoidean Bureaucrat 2.50 6.00
P19 Rune Haako, Neimoidean Lieutenant 5.00 12.00

2001 Young Jedi Reflections

COMPLETE SET (106) 200.00 350.00
RELEASED ON JULY 18, 2001
A1 Jar Jar Binks, Bombad Gungan General 1.25 3.00
Jar Jar Binks' Electropole
A2 Boss Nass, Gungan Chief 2.00 5.00
Fambaa
A3 Adi Gallia, Corellian Jedi Master 1.50 4.00
Adi Gallia's Lightsaber
A4 Eeth Koth, Zabrak Jedi Master 2.00 5.00
Eeth Koth's Lightsaber
A5 Ki-Adi-Mundi, Cerean Jedi Knight 2.00 5.00
Jedi Lightsaber, Constructed by Ki-Adi-Mundi
A6 Valorum, Supreme Chancellor 1.25 3.00
Planetary Shuttle
A7 Aurra Sing, Trophy Collector 2.00 5.00
Jedi Lightsaber, Stolen by Aurra Sing
A8 Nute Gunray, Neimoidian Viceroy 1.50 4.00
Neimoidian Viewscreen
A9 OOM-9, Battle Droid Commander 1.50 4.00
Battle Droid Blaster Rifle
A10 OWO-1, Battle Droid Command Officer 2.00 5.00
STAP
A11 P-59, Destroyer Droid Commander 1.50 4.00
Multi Troop Transport
A12 Toonbuck Toora, Senator 2.00 5.00
Coruscant Taxi
C1 Are You An Angel? .75 2.00
I've Been Trained In Defense
C2 Brave Little Droid .60 1.50
Counterparts
C3 Celebration .75 2.00
Gungan Mounted Trooops
C4 Enough Of This Pretense .60 1.50
I Will Not Cooperate
C5 Fear Attracts The Fearful .75 2.00
How Wude!
C6 I Have A Bad Feeling About This .75 2.00
NOOOOOOOOOO!
C7 Jedi Force Push .75 2.00
We're Not In Trouble Yet
C8 Dos Mackineeks No Comen Here! .75 2.00
Bombad General
C9 At last we will have revenge .40 1.00
Sith force push
C10 The Queen's Plan .75 2.00
Naboo Royal Security Forces
C11 The Might Of The Republic .75 2.00
Senate Guard
C12 The Negotiations Were Short .75 2.00
Qui-Gon's Final Stand
C13 Wisdom Of The Council .75 2.00
Jedi Training
C14 Yousa Guys Bombad! .75 2.00
Uh-Oh!
C15 A Thousand Terrible Things & .60 1.50
We Are Sending All Troops
C16 Battle Droid Patrol & In Complete Control .60 1.50
C17 Boonta Eve Podrace & .60 1.50
Kaa Bazza Kundee Hodrudda!
C18 Podrace Preparation & Yoka To Bantha Poodoo .75 2.00
C19 Switch To Bio & Your Little .40 1.00
Insurrection Is At An End
C20 The Phantom Menace & Use Caution .75 2.00
D1 Dos Mackineeks No Comen Here! .75 2.00
Bombad General
D2 Gunga City .75 2.00
Gungan Energy Shield
D3 The Queen's Plan .75 2.00
Naboo Royal Security Forces
D4 The Might Of The Republic .75 2.00
Senate Guard
D5 The Negotiations Were Short .75 2.00
Qui-Gon's Final Stand
D6 Wisdom Of The Council .75 2.00
Jedi Training
D7 Yousa Guys Bombad! .75 2.00
Uh-Oh!
D8 Grueling Contest .75 2.00
Da Dug Chaaa!
D9 Let Them Make The First Move .40 1.00
Very Unusual
D10 Now There Are Two Of Them .60 1.50
The Duel Begins
D11 Opee Sea Killer .75 2.00
To The Death
D12 Starfighter Screen .75 2.00
Blockade
D13 We Have Them On The Run .75 2.00
Where Are Those Droidekas?
D14 You Have Been Well Trained .44 1.00
After Her!
2BEP Yoda, Jedi Instructor (foil) 2.50 6.00
2MDM Qui-Gon Jinn, Jedi Master (foil) 10.00 25.00
3BEP C-3PO, Human-Cyborg Relations Droid (foil) 2.50 6.00
4BEP Jira, Pallie Vendor (foil) 1.25 3.00
4BON Anakin Skywalker, Padawan (foil) 3.00 8.00
4TJC Anakin Skywalker, Child of Prophecy (foil) 6.00 15.00
5BEP Kitster, Anakin's Friend (foil) 2.00 5.00
6BEP Wald, Anakin's Friend (foil) 1.50 4.00
7BON Mace Windu, Jedi Speaker (foil) 10.00 25.00
9MDM Queen Amidala, Royal Leader (foil) 3.00 8.00
9TJC Queen Amidala, Voice of Her People (foil) 4.00 10.00
10MDM Yoda, Jedi Master (foil) 2.00 5.00
1DOTF Obi-Wan Kenobi, Jedi Student (foil) 6.00 15.00
2DOTF Qui-Gon Jinn, Jedi Mentor (foil) 3.00 8.00
30BEP Amidala's Starship, Queen's Transport (foil) 2.00 5.00
32BEP Watto, Podrace Sponsor (foil) 2.00 5.00
33BEP Aurra Sing, Formidable Adversary (foil) 4.00 10.00
34BEP Jabba The Hutt, O Grandio Lust (foil) 2.00 5.00
35BEP TC-14, Protocol Droid (foil) 2.00 5.00
36BEP Orr'UrRuuR'R, Tusken Raider Leader (foil) 2.00 5.00
3DOTF Anakin Skywalker, Rookie Pilot (foil) 3.00 8.00
4DOTF Captain Panaka, Security Commander (foil) 2.00 5.00
5DOTF Mace Windu, Jedi Councilor (foil) 2.50 6.00
60BEP Viceroy's Battleship, 1.50 4.00
Trade Federation Transport (foil)
6DOTF Queen Amidala, Young Leader (foil) 3.00 8.00
72BON Darth Sidious, Sith Manipulator (foil) 3.00 8.00
73BON Sebulba, Dangerous Podracer Pilot (foil) 8.00 20.00
73TJC Sebulba, Podracer Pilot (foil) 1.50 4.00
74BON Watto, Toydarian Gambler (foil) 1.00 2.50
74MDM Watto, Slave Owner (foil) 2.00 5.00
75MDM Aurra Sing, Bounty Hunter (foil) 4.00 10.00
76BON Jabba The Hutt, Crime Lord (foil) 2.00 5.00
78BON Rune Haako, Neimoidian Deputy (foil) 2.00 5.00
78TJC Destroyer Droid Squad, Defense Division (foil) 3.00 8.00
79TJC Battle Droid Squad, Escort Unit (foil) 2.00 5.00
7DOTF Yoda, Jedi Philosopher (foil) 4.00 10.00
80TJC Trade Federation Tank, Assault Division (foil) 6.00 15.00
88MDM Trade Federation Tank, 2.00 5.00
Armored Division (foil)
31DOTF Darth Maul, Student of the Dark Side (foil) 3.00 8.00
32DOTF Darth Sidious, Master of the Dark Side (foil) 10.00 25.00
33DOTF Aurra Sing, Trophy Collector (foil) 1.50 4.00
P1EMDM Qui-Gon Jinn, Jedi Protector (foil) 4.00 10.00
P2EMDM Mace Windu, Jedi Warrior (foil) 4.00 10.00
P3EMDM Queen Amidala, Cunning Warrior (foil) 8.00 20.00
P4EMDM Darth Maul, Sith Assassin (foil) 8.00 20.00
P5EMDM Sebulba, Champion Podracer Pilot (foil) 2.00 5.00
P6EMDM Trade Federation Tank, Assault Leader (foil) 1.50 4.00
P7PREM Shmi Skywalker, Anakin's Mother (foil) 1.50 4.00
P8EBON Obi-Wan Kenobi, Jedi Avenger (foil) 3.00 8.00
P9EBON Anakin Skywalker, 3.00 8.00
Tested by the Jedi Council (foil)
P10EBON Padmé Naberrie, Loyal Handmaiden (foil) 2.00 5.00
P11EBON Captain Panaka, Royal Defender (foil) 2.00 5.00
P12EBON Yoda, Wise Jedi (foil) 4.00 10.00
P13EBON R2-D2, Starship Maintenance Droid (foil) 3.00 8.00
P14EBON Darth Sidious, The Phantom Menace (foil) 3.00 8.00
P15EBON Watto, Risk Taker (foil) 2.00 5.00
P16EBON Aurra Sing, Scoundrel (foil) 1.50 4.00
P17EBON Jabba The Hutt, Tatooine Tyrant (foil) 2.00 5.00
P18EBON Nute Gunray, Neimoidian Bureaucrat (foil) 1.50 4.00
P19EBON Rune Haako, Neimoidian Lieutenant (foil) 2.00 5.00

2003 Yu Yu Hakusho Dark Tournament

1 Wind Shinobi G
2 Yoko, the Spirit Fox G
3 Together Until the End of Time G
4 Forlorn Hope G
5 Hiei, the Stern U
6 Yukina, Ice Princess U
7 Allied Forces U
8 King Yama's Wrath U
9 The Dark Angel's Presence U
10 Botan's Tool Box U
11 Spiked Club U
12 Chu, Drunken Master S
13 Dr. Ichigaki, the Demon S
14 Genkai, the Mentor S
15 Koenma, Disguised S
16 Onji, the Experienced Fighter S
17 Earth Shinobi S
18 Suzaku, the Fierce S
19 Younger Toguro, Transformed S
20 Yusuke, the Student S
21 Yusuke, Unleashed S
22 Zeru, the Phoenix S
23 Botan, the Assistant R
24 Genbu, Master of Stone R
25 Ancient Tactics R
26 Calling the Spirits R
27 Empowered Emotions R
28 Final Gift R
29 Flashback R
30 Hiei's Secret R
31 Ooops! R
32 Surprise Attack R
33 Stand Off R
34 Cape of No Return R
35 Captured Souls R
36 Death Seed R
37 Dragon Pen R
38 Friends Forever R
39 Inter-Dimensional Breach R
40 Megiru Seal R
41 Sakyo's Lighter R
42 Walking Stick R
43 Desperate Assault R
44 Rainbow Cyclone R
45 Yuu Kaitou's Territory R
46 Asato Kido, Shadow Master C
47 Bui, Tormented Soul C
48 Elder Toguro, Puppet Master C
49 Juri, the First Timer C
50 Kayko, the Class President C
51 Kurama, the Tactician C
52 Karasu, Mad Bomber C
53 Kuro Momotaro, the Ape C
54 Kuwabara, Yukina's Champion C
55 M1, Blade Master C
56 M2, Javelin Master C
57 Makintaro, Furious Fighter C
58 Mitsunari Yanagisawa, the Copy Master C
59 Murugu, the Pestering C
60 Puu, Teddy Bear with a Beak C
61 Rinku, Yo-Yo Master C
62 Ruka, the Malicious C
63 Sakyo, the High Roller C
64 Seiryu, Cold Hearted C
65 Ura Urashima, Demon in Disguise C
66 Advantage Team Urameshi C
67 And the Winner is! C
68 Baiting the Dragon C
69 Botan's Calling C
70 Dark Glare C
71 Dark Shadows C
72 Defiant Stance C
73 Demonic Anger C
74 Determination C
75 Driven by Animosity C
76 Entrapment C
77 Face of Death C
78 Falling Apart C
79 Fighter in Training C
80 Freak Show C
81 Kuwabara's Inspiration C
82 Living the Nightmare C
83 Outnumbered C
84 Painful Memories C
85 Reliving the Past C
86 Retaliate C
87 Rokuyukai Challenge C
88 Showdown C
89 Spirit Phoenix C
90 Surprise! C
91 Suzaku's Multiform C
92 X-Treme Defense C
93 Yusuke's Sacrifice C
94 Zenith of Fear C
95 A Safe Place C
96 Ace of Spades C
97 Genkai's Hat C
98 Key C
99 Koenma's Gavel C
G0 The Dark One G
L1 Botan, the Lovely L
L2 Hiei, Unpredictable Warrior L
L3 Kayko, the Cute L
L4 Koenma, Noble Leader L
L5 Kuwabara, Honorable Friend L
L6 Kurama, Caring Fighter L
L7 Yusuke, Resourceful Apprentice L
L8 Binding Shinobi L
L9 Substitute L
P1 Mist Shinobi P
P2 Kurama's Last Stand P
P3 Power Strike P
R1 Burst of Power R
T1 Halt! TG
T2 Epic Showdown TU
T3 I'm Calling You Out! TU
T4 Ice Shinobi TS
T5 Yuu Kaitou, Taboo Master TS
T6 Flee the Arena TS
T7 Genkai, Young Fighter TR
T8 Display of Power TR
T9 Persevere TR
100 Microphone C
101 Mystic Whistle C
102 Red Rose C
103 Sun Glasses C
104 The Light in your Eye C
105 Villainous Talons C
106 Asato Kido's Territory C
107 Backstab C
108 Chorus of a Thousand Souls C
109 Death Tree C
110 Demonic Backbreaker C
111 Inspirational Slash C
112 Kurama's Whip Deception C
113 Kuwabara's Spirit Push C
114 Mitsunari Yanagisawa's Territory C
115 One, Two Setup C
116 Power Smack C
117 Quick Blow C
118 Rush C
119 Spirit Reflection Blast C
120 Spirit Shield C
121 Spirit Sphere C
G0b The Dark One (reprint) G
L10 Whip Slam L
T10 Precise Evasion TR
T11 Trial Sword TR
T12 Acid Blast TR
T13 Koto, the Experienced TC
T14 Confrontation TC
T15 Dark Power TC
T16 Heroic Stand TC
T17 Hiei's Essence TC
T18 Broom Stick TC
T19 Souls TC
T20 Watch TC
T21 Dark Sphere of No Return TC
T22 Double Barrel Blast TC
T23 Tornado Fist Double TC
TP1 Gotcha! TP

2003 Yu Yu Hakusho Gateway

1 Bull's-Eye GR 8.00 20.00
2 Darkness Approaches GR 1.00 2.50
3 Faces of Sensui GR 12.00 30.00
4 Sinning Tree GR 2.50 6.00
5 Apocalypse UBR 1.50 4.00
6 Bang! UBR .75 2.00
7 Gateway UBR 3.00 8.00
8 Spectacular Battle UBR 1.00 2.50
9 Surprised UBR 1.00 2.50
10 Sayaka, the Investigator UBR 1.00 2.50
11 Doushi, Raizen's Messenger U 1.25 3.00
12 Big Brother SPR 1.00 2.50
13 Blade Storm SPR 2.00 5.00
14 Contemplate SPR 2.00 5.00
15 Dark Ritual SPR 4.00 10.00
16 Distractions SPR 4.00 10.00
17 Double Block SPR 1.00 2.50
18 Sorrow SPR 1.00 2.50
19 Torture SPR 1.00 2.50
20 What Friends Are For SPR 1.00 2.50
21 Decoy SPR 1.00 2.50
22 Koenma's Pacifier SPR 2.00 5.00
23 Champion Driver R .20 .50
24 Clash of Champions R .20 .50
25 Heroic Sacrifice R .20 .50
26 Madness R .20 .50
27 Malice R .20 .50
28 Metamorphose R .20 .50
29 Mini Game, Action Battle R .20 .50
30 Morbid R .20 .50
31 Sensui's Energy Sphere R .20 .50
32 Test of Champions R .20 .50
33 Botan, Pilot of the River Styx R .20 .50
34 Younger Itsuki, Detective's Assistant R .20 .50
35 Hostage R .20 .50
36 Rubber Slam R .20 .50
37 Tracking Device R .20 .50
38 Genkai, Resurrected R .20 .50
39 Koenma, Disguised Leader R .20 .50
40 Yusuke, Entranced R .20 .50
41 Sensui, Dark Detective R .20 .50
42 Spirit Tornado R .20 .50
43 M4, Spineless Demon R .20 .50
44 Mitrai, The Seaman R .20 .50
45 Imposing Evil R .20 .50
46 Abduction C .10 .25
47 Cruel Punishment C .10 .25
48 Dark Encounter C .10 .25
49 Dark Gambit C .10 .25
50 Dazed and Confused C .10 .25
51 Exterminate C .10 .25
52 Genkai's Healing C .10 .25
53 Going to Megallica C .10 .25
54 Guardians of the Human World C .10 .25

55 Hiei's Peaceful Stance C .10 .25
56 Huh??? C .10 .25
57 Intensive Discipline C .10 .25
58 Invasion C .10 .25
59 Kurama's Determination C .10 .25
60 Liquid Drill C .10 .25
61 Liquid Rush C .10 .25
62 Malevolent Glare C .10 .25
63 Panic C .10 .25
64 Sinister Trap C .10 .25
65 Smoke Screen Catalyst C .10 .25
66 Stop it! C .10 .25
67 Taking Aim C .10 .25
68 Team Sensui Appears C .10 .25
69 The Arrival C .10 .25
70 Viral Demon Insects C .10 .25
71 Wicked Grin C .10 .25
72 Ayame, Koenma's Assistant C .10 .25
73 Botan, Wise Scholar? C .10 .25
74 Hiei, Enraged Demon C .10 .25
75 Jorge Satome, Blue Ogre C .10 .25
76 Kenko, Cute Healer C .10 .25
77 King Yama C .10 .25
78 Koenma, the Determined C .10 .25
79 Koorime, Guilty Conscience C .10 .25
80 Kurama, Entrapped Demon C .10 .25
81 M2, Ryo C .10 .25
82 M3, Kai C .10 .25
83 Mitamura, the Master C .10 .25
84 Murota, Mind Reader C .10 .25
85 Sasuga, Enchantress C .10 .25
86 Yuu, Bookworm C .10 .25
87 Butterfly Knife C .10 .25
88 Colorful Weapons C .10 .25
89 Deadly Dice C .10 .25
90 Framed Memories C .10 .25
91 Kazuya's Pistol C .10 .25
92 Koenma's Cloud? C .10 .25
93 Lamp Weed C .10 .25
94 The Chapter Black C .10 .25
95 Weapon of Destruction C .10 .25
96 Wet Shirt C .10 .25
97 Koenma, Young Ruler C 1.50 4.00
98 Kuwabara, Righteous Warrior C 1.50 4.00
99 Sensui, Kazuya's Personality C 2.50 6.00
L1 Yusuke, Noble Fighter L
L2 Yusuke's Tainted Glare L
L3 Hiei, Dark Fighter L
L4 Hiei's Tainted Glare L
L5 Kurama, Legendary Fighter L
L6 Kurama's Tainted Glare L
L7 Kuwabara, Emotional Fighter L
L8 Kuwabara's Tainted Glare L
L9 Tag Team L
P1 Hiei, Determined Warrior P
P2 Crazy World P
P3 Head-On Assault P
R2 Counter Strike R
S1 Yusuke, Raizen's Successor ST
T1 I Got Something For You! TG
T2 Gathering of Villains TU
T3 Protecting The Innocent TU
T4 Concealed Blade TS
T5 Kurama, Skilled Assassin TS
T6 Energy Release TS
T7 Game Battler TR
T8 Mini Game, Flight Shooter TR
T9 Mini Game, Master Quiz TR
X0 Kuwabara, Noble Champion X
X1 Ura-Otoko X
100 Consumer C .10 .25
101 Sinister Slash C .10 .25
102 Devastating Combination C .10 .25
103 Discharge C .10 .25
104 Hagiri's Territory C .10 .25
105 Heroic Strike C .10 .25
106 Kamiya's Territory C .10 .25
107 Liquid Guardian C .10 .25
108 Mafuuken C .10 .25
109 Palm Block C .10 .25
110 Tiny Guardian C .10 .25
111 Amanuma, the Gamer C .10 .25
112 Elder Toguro, the Indestructible C .10 .25
113 Gatasubal, Killing Machine C .10 .25
114 Hagiri, the Sniper C .10 .25
115 Itsuki, Demon in Love C .10 .25
116 Kamiya, the Malicious C .10 .25
117 Makihara, Gourmet C .10 .25
118 Mitarai, Misguided C .10 .25
119 Kuwabara, Righteous Warrior C 2.00 5.00
120 Aggression C .10 .25
121 Humans on the Hunt C .10 .25
L10 Mad Bomb L
T10 Mini Game, Tennis TR
T11 Recall TR
T12 Sensui, Spirit Detective TR
T13 Allure TC
T14 Full Tilt TC
T15 Natural Reaction TC
T16 Possessed TC
T17 Virus Carriers TC
T18 Demonic Strike TC
T19 Splinter-Resshuuken TC
T20 Tough Love TC
T21 Whip Mastery TC
T22 Hagiri, The Hunter TC
T23 Kamiya, The Doctor TC
TP2 Meditation TP

2003 Yu Yu Hakusho Ghost Files

10 Epic Tales G
13 Genkai P
14 Singing Potential V
23 Sacrifice of Life P
24 Perfect Balance V
33 Verruca P
34 Under Pressure V
44 Life Threads V
122 Bakken TC
222 Genbu TC
322 Gouki TC
422 Makintaro TC
522 Seiryu TC
622 Batting Practice TC
722 Befriend TC
822 Shinobi of the Spirit World TC
922 Unconscious TC
1022 Prism Storm of Torment TC
1122 Slice, Dice, and Incise TC
1176 Risho C
1222 Byakko TR
1322 Kurama, Reformed Demon TR
1422 The White Mist TR
1522 Death of a Hero TR
1622 Lost TR
1722 Rose Whip Thorn Wheel TR
1822 Grand Victory TS
1922 Headband of Love TS
2022 Angel Blades TS
2122 Ice Blade TU
2176 Suzaku C
2222 Katana TU
2322 Orb of Baast TG
3176 Suzuka R
4176 Risho, Butajiri's Henchman R
5176 Yusuke, Resurrected R
6176 Chu ST
7176 Dr. Ichigaki ST
8176 Younger Toguro ST
9176 Yusuke ST
10176 Chu, the Team Captain U
11176 Suzaku, Makai Master U
12176 Chinpoh, the Wanderer C
13176 Gama C
14176 Imajin C
15176 Gatasubal C
16176 Gokumonki C
17176 Hirue C
18176 Inmaki C
19176 Jyaki C
20176 Kazamaru C
21176 Kibano C
22176 Kuroda, Contract Killer C
23176 Miyuki C
24176 Mushashi C
25176 Rugby C
26176 Shishi Wakamaru C
27176 Shorin C
28176 Spider Demon C
29176 The Minotaur C
30176 Touya C
31176 Ura Urashima C
32176 Hiei, the Swordsman R
33176 Jin R
34176 Kuro Momotaru R
35176 Kuwabara, Street Fighter R
36176 Rando R
37176 Bui ST
38176 Elder Toguro ST
39176 Hiei ST
40176 Karasu ST
41176 Kurama ST
42176 Kuwabara ST
43176 M1 ST
44176 M2 ST
45176 M3 ST
46176 Rinku ST
47176 Roto ST
48176 Zeru ST
49176 Genkai, The Young S
50176 Shishi Wakamaru, Soul Stealer S
51176 Touya, the Ice Master S
52176 Abnormal Endurance C
53176 Alley Fight for Eikichi C
54176 Climactic Finish C
55176 Deadly Attack C
56176 Defensive Posture C
57176 Efflux C
58176 Evil Tendencies C
59176 Fervor of Fury C
60176 Flurry of Blows C
61176 Overpowered C
62176 Guru of Engagement C
63176 Heroic Team C
64176 Hiei's Sword Mastery C
65176 Improvised Weapon C
66176 Kidnapping C
67176 Zombies on the Hunt C
68176 Maze Castle C
69176 Mistaken Fatality C
70176 Shinobi Disguise C
71176 Overexertion C
72176 Physical Intensification C
73176 Protective Restraint C
74176 Rokuyukai Advantage C
75176 Sabotage C
76176 Spirit Dump C
77176 Spiritual Safeguard C
78176 Teamwork C
79176 Tears of Blood C
80176 The Best Defense is... C
81176 Theft in the Dark C
82176 Time Out C
83176 Weapons Master C
84176 All For One and One For All R
85176 Dr. Ichigaki's Control R
86176 Kitty Love R
87176 Lucky Winners R
88176 Masterful Speed R
89176 Overwhelming Kill R
90176 Rash Brawling R
91176 Signature Moves R
92176 Transcendent Might R
93176 Ultimate Test R
94176 A Man's Promise ST
95176 Botan's Healing ST
96176 Desperate Decision ST
97176 Feast of Souls ST
98176 Good Ref ST
99176 Investigation ST
100176 Koenma's Opening ST
101176 No Mercy ST
102176 Rando Appears ST
103176 Stunned ST
104176 Busted S
105176 Kayko's Promise S
106176 Party Time S
107176 The Genkai Bunch S
108176 Demonic Tricks U
109176 Double Teaming U
110176 Power Strike U
111176 Recuperation U
112176 Substitute U
113176 Backyard Dummy C
114176 Combat Knives C
115176 Idunn Box C
116176 Communication Mirror/Pocket Communicator C
117176 Demon Compass C
118176 Psychic Spyglass C
119176 Deadly Ninja Throwing Stars C
120176 Tape of the Mission C
121176 Trace-Eyes R
122176 Hospital Bed R
123176 Makai Whistle R
124176 Shadow Sword R
125176 Spirit Beast Egg R
126176 Spirit Cuffs R
127176 Steaming Sphere R
128176 Baseball Bat ST
129176 Botan's Oar ST
130176 Fishing Pole ST
131176 Bamboo ST
132176 Power Serum ST
133176 Really Big Axe ST
134176 Rose Whip ST
135176 Senseless Helmet ST
136176 Serpent Yo-Yos ST
137176 Spirit Ring ST
138176 Armor of Clay S
139176 School Girl Outfit S
140176 Banshee Shriek U
141176 Ogre Killer U
142176 Armor of the Ape C
143176 Axe-Blade Fist C
144176 Desperate Temper C
145176 Grizzly Claw C
146176 Headbutt C
147176 Ice Dragon C
148176 Jagan Eye C
149176 Make-up of Chains C
150176 Prism of Seven C
151176 Reduction C
152176 Rose Whiplash C
153176 Shotgun C
154176 Spirit Gun Double C
155176 Spirit Gun Focus C
156176 Storm of Torment C
157176 Banzai Missile R
158176 Fists of the Mortal Flame R
159176 Meteor Charge R
160176 Renkinyoujutsu R
161176 Reversal R
162176 Spirit Sword Double R
163176 Spirit Wave R
164176 Tornado Fists R
165176 Armor of the Hyena ST
166176 Power Slam ST
167176 Circles of Inferno ST
168176 Power of Love ST
169176 Shards of Winter ST
170176 Shibattou Shining Sword ST
171176 Spirit Fist ST
172176 Spirit Palm Blast ST
173176 Spirit Sword Monster Beast Donut ST
174176 Dragon of the Darkness Flame S
175176 Death Plant U
176176 Sword of the Darkness Flame U
177176 Younger Toguro, Latent Warrior G
178176 Burst of Power G
179176 Halt! G
180176 I'm Callin' You Out! G

2004 Yu Yu Hakusho Alliance

1 Raizen, Thunder God (Top Left) G
2 NO! G
3 Replay G
4 Solitaire G
5 Raizen, Thunder God (Top Right) U
6 Raizen, Thunder God (Bottom Left) U
7 Shishi Wakamaru, Summoner of a Thousand Souls U
8 The Legacy of One U
9 Winner U
10 Game Cartridge U
11 Sensui's TV U
12 Chu, Rugged Assailant S
13 Murugu, The Cunning S
14 Raizen, Thunder God (Bottom Right) S
15 Ruka, The Captivating S
16 Yomi, the Reformed S
17 Yusuke, Champion of the People S
18 Audience Participation S
19 Darkness Within S
20 Kaitou's Rules S
21 Mourning S
22 Joystick S
23 Juri, The Impartial R
24 Miyuki, of the Triad R
25 Touya R
26 Yukina, Ice Apparition R
27 Yusuke, Human World's Hero R
28 Can I Draw On Him R
29 Chant of Recollection R
30 Devastation R
31 Excitement R
32 Heroes United R
33 Hope Lost R
34 Influence R
35 Innocence R
36 Interrogation R
37 Koenma's Protection R
38 Quick Freeze R
39 Regression R
40 Resurrection R
41 Self-Preservation R
42 The Game is Afoot! R
43 Wait! R
44 Pairing Dice R
45 Psychic Scapel R
46 Botan, Detective's Assistant C
47 Enki, The Champion C
48 Genkai, Wise Master C
49 Hiei, The Demon World's Protector C
50 Hiei, Fearless Hero C
51 Jin, Carefree Spirit C
52 Jorge, The Narrator C
53 Kayko, The Independent C
54 Kokuo, The Broken Hearted C
55 Kujoo C
56 Kurama, Devoted Hero C
57 Kurama, The Uniting C
58 Kuwabara, Honarable Hero C
59 Mukuro, Fugitive Thrall C
60 Natsume, The Fearless C
61 Raizen, Fasting Devourer C
62 Rinku, Acrobatic Fighter C
63 Saizou C
64 Shu C
65 Souketsu C
66 Suzuka C
67 Tetsuzam C
68 Younger Toguro, Soul Taker C
69 110 percent C
70 Ambush C
71 Devastating Blow C
72 Extortion C
73 Force Field C
74 Gale Force C
75 Manipulate C
76 Morbid Beauty C
77 Nightmare C
78 Recruit C
79 Shrouded Evil C
80 Snatch C
81 Soul Extraction C
82 Squash C
83 Submission C
84 Truce C
85 Upsurge C
86 Vulnerable C
87 Armor of Containment C
88 Blue Seal C
89 Desu Button C
90 Double-Bladed Knives C
91 Event Ticket C
92 Kekkai Barrier C
93 Koenmatron 5000 C
94 Manacles C
95 Mask of Restriction C
96 Molotov Cocktail C
97 Paintbrush C
98 Pit Trap C
99 Red Seal C
100 Scythe C
101 Tanker Truck C
102 Tasty Beverages C
103 Tombstone C
104 Yellow Seal C
105 Body Manipulation C
106 Death Plant Efflorescence C
107 Finger Extension C
108 Hair Whip C
109 Left Pivot Kick C
110 Murota's Territory C
111 Pinkie String of Love C
112 Shadow Control C
113 Smelly Foot C
114 Spirit Orb C
115 Spirit Wave Orb C
116 Stomp C
117 Sword Extension C
118 Thumb Block C
119 Tiger Breath C
120 Twin Energy Punch C
121 Two-Fingered Poke C

2004 Yu Yu Hakusho Betrayal

1 Yomi, Sightless God (Lower Left) G
2 Acceptable Losses G
3 Ultimate Sacrifice G
4 Yusuke's Fury G
5 Yomi, Sightless God (Upper Left) U
6 Yomi, Sightless God (Upper Right) U
7 Puu U
8 Human World's Protectors U
9 Recuperation U
10 Reincarnation U
11 Spirit Detective Briefcase U
12 Roto, Malicious Shapeshifter S
13 Yusuke, Ma-Zoku S
14 Daunting Inferno S
15 Destined Greatness S
16 Grudge Match S
17 Haunted by the Past S
18 Insatiable S
19 Life Energy Transfer S
20 Stern Teachings S
21 Body Armor S
22 Joker S
23 Hiei, Mukuro's General R
24 Jorge Satome, Superhero R
25 Kazuma, Kuwabara R
26 Kokou, Repressed Lover R
27 Kurama, Calm Cruelty R
28 Raizen, Bloodthirsty Pacifist R
29 Seiryu, Blue Dragon R
30 Shura, Mischievous Prince R
31 Yusuke, Demonic Heir R
32 All For One and One For All R
33 Circumvention R
34 Demoralize R
35 Icy Glare R
36 Inhuman Potential R
37 Materialize R
38 Mischief R
39 Overwhelming Kill R
40 Overwhelming Odds R
41 Provocation R
42 Retaliation R
43 Trident R
44 Battle Aura R
45 Tornado Fists R
46 Binding Shinobi, Incapacitation Master C
47 Dr. Ichigaki, Corrupted Geneticist C
48 Earth Shinobi, Shrouded Leader C
49 Genwaku Kyoushu, Assassin C
50 Gunsotsu C
51 Hiei, Cursed Child C
52 Itsuki, Yaminate C
53 Karasu, Methodical Tactician C
54 Kirin, Demonic Arts Guru C
55 Kiseichu, Parasite Demon C
56 Kiyoshi Mitarai C
57 Komada C
58 Kurama, Strategic Leader C
59 Mukuro, Tortured Sovereign C
60 Natsume, Resilient Warrior C
61 Okubo C
62 Risho, Earthen Master C
63 Sasuga, Paramour C
64 Seitei C
65 Shachi, Unseated Commander C
66 Shigure, Surgeon of the Damned C
67 Shougo Satou, Sympathetic Psychic C
68 Soruja C
69 Touou C
70 Ura Urashima C
71 Yoko, Systematic Larcenist C
72 Yomi, Reckless Thief C
73 Apocalyptic Prevention C
74 Bond of Friends C
75 Cunning Bandits C
76 Defiance of Authority C
77 Domination C
78 Friendly Fire C
79 Heroic Aspirations C
80 Human Enhancements C
81 Humanity Returned C
82 Impeded Progress C
83 Imprisonment C
84 Overextend C
85 Overloaded C
86 Preemptive Strike C
87 Raizen Supremacy C
88 Reality Shift C
89 Renewed Kinship C
90 Ruler's Regard C
91 Shinobis Unmasked C
92 Spirit Siphon C
93 Struggle for Parity C
94 Taunt C
95 Bandages C
96 Demon Compass C
97 Fire Extinguisher C
98 Makeup C
99 Suzaku's Orb C
P1 Serenity P
P2 Point Blank P
P3 Mukuro's Spirit of Words P
P4 Sanctuary P
T1 Yomi, Sightless God (Lower Right) TG
T2 Twilight TU
T3 Gaming System TU
T4 Jin, the Wind Master TS
T5 Soul Exchange TS
T6 Demon Energy Scanner TS
T7 Koto, the MC TR
T8 Youda, Veteran Advisor TR
T9 Bicycle TR
100 Shoe C
101 Switchblade C
102 Yomi's Spirit of Words C
103 Ability Theft C
104 Acid Splash C
105 Aura Vortex C
106 Bone Scythe C
107 Claw Extension C
108 Demon Spiral C
109 Demonic Absorption Wall C
110 Demonic Kremastos C
111 Flesh Puppet C
112 Flyby C
113 Handstand Kick C
114 Icy Battlefield C
115 Identity Theft C
116 Lightning Absorption C
117 Space Tornado Hand C
118 Sphere of Protection C
119 Sword of Second Energy C

120 Tactical Advantage C
121 Tornado Attack C
T10 Mother's Tear TR
T11 Rurimaru Stones TR
T12 Yukina's Gift TR
T13 Atsuko, Inebriated Matron TC
T14 Hokushin, Paranormal Taoist TC
T15 Miyamoto TC
T16 Nankai TC
T17 no description TC
T18 Exterminated TC
T19 Final Sacrifice TC
T20 The Past Resolved TC
T21 Demonic Inhibitor TC
T22 Double Bladed Axe TC
T23 Spirit Blast TC
TP4 Hajime! TP
TX1 Grim Determination TX

2004 Yu Yu Hakusho Exile

1 Horrified GR 3.00 8.00
2 In Shadow GR 10.00 25.00
3 Meow GR 6.00 15.00
4 Yusuke, The Raver (Upper Left) GR 6.00 15.00
5 Powerful Demons GR 3.00 8.00
6 Regeneration GR 2.50 6.00
7 Villionaire Wages GR 2.00 5.00
8 Yusuke's Altar GR 3.00 8.00
9 Mukuro, Enslaved Soul (Upper Right) GR 6.00 15.00
10 Yusuke, The Raver (Upper Right) GR 6.00 15.00
11 All You Need is the Ground UBR 1.50 4.00
12 Flee UBR 1.25 3.00
13 Gloom UBR 2.00 5.00
14 Grand Entrance UBR 1.25 3.00
15 Reckless Charge UBR 2.50 6.00
16 Unknown Allies UBR 1.25 3.00
17 Yukina's Tears UBR 1.25 3.00
18 Mukuro, Enslaved Soul (Lower Left) UBR 2.50 6.00
19 Mukuro, Enslaved Soul (Lower Right) UBR 2.00 5.00
20 Yusuke, The Raver (Lower Left) UBR 4.00 10.00
21 Yusuke, The Raver (Lower Right) UBR 4.00 10.00
22 Hasty Slash UBR 1.25 3.00
23 Spin Kick UBR 1.25 3.00
24 Spirit Dragon UBR 1.25 3.00
25 Angelic Embrace SPR 1.00 2.50
26 Awaken SPR 1.00 2.50
27 Breaking Point SPR 1.00 2.50
28 Bui's Final Strike SPR 1.00 2.50
29 Carnage SPR 1.00 2.50
30 Challenge of Wills SPR 1.25 3.00
31 Congregate SPR 1.25 3.00
32 Crucial Encounter SPR 1.25 3.00
33 Delude SPR 3.00 8.00
34 Demonic Presence SPR 1.25 3.00
35 Destructive Lust SPR 1.25 3.00
36 Intensive Training SPR 1.50 4.00
37 Intimidate SPR 1.00 2.50
38 Later SPR 2.00 5.00
39 Malevolent Influence SPR 1.25 3.00
40 Mukuro's Unforgiving Glare SPR 2.00 5.00
41 Perfect Timing SPR 1.00 2.50
42 Rose Petal Shower SPR 1.25 3.00
43 Spirit Force Emerges SPR 1.00 2.50
44 Spirit Force Starter SPR .75 2.00
45 Time Freeze! SPR 3.00 8.00
46 Yusuke's Alliance SPR 1.00 2.50
47 Bu-Wha-Ha-Ha-Ha! R .20 .50
48 Continue? R .20 .50
49 Demon Gene R .20 .50
50 Kiss of Legend R .20 .50
51 Surrender R .20 .50
52 Team Genkai's Support R .20 .50
53 Team Ichigaki's Devastation R .20 .50
54 Team Koenma's Support R .20 .50
55 Team Kurama's Support R .20 .50
56 Team Masho's Overwhelming Power R .20 .50
57 Team Raizen's Support R .20 .50
58 Team Rokuyukai's Hidden Power R .20 .50
59 Team Saint Beasts Advantage R .20 .50
60 Team Toguro's Surprise R .20 .50
61 Team Urameshi's Support R .20 .50
62 Team Uraotogi on the Hunt R .20 .50
63 Ayame, King Yama's Messenger R .20 .50
64 Kaisei Satou R .20 .50
65 Shunjun R .20 .50
66 Yukina, Welcoming Child R .20 .50
67 Gama, Devoted Artist R .20 .50
68 Genkai, Fighter in Love R .20 .50
69 Yoko, Legendary Bandit R .20 .50
70 Yusuke, Tribal Fighter R .20 .50
71 Lu, Brute Mercenary R .20 .50
72 Shishi, Cute Devil R .20 .50
73 Suzaku, Lightning Master R .20 .50
74 Abide C .10 .25
75 Amidst C .10 .25
76 Bizarre! C .10 .25
77 Bui's Fighting Stance C .10 .25
78 Concealed Spirit Energy C .10 .25
79 Counterparts C .10 .25
80 Dark Artifacts C .10 .25
81 Demon Unleashed C .10 .25
82 Demonic Clash C .10 .25
83 Demonic Resurrection C .10 .25
84 Denied! C .10 .25
85 Destined Gathering C .10 .25
86 Disintegrate C .10 .25
87 Double Slash C .10 .25
88 Evolution Stage 1 C .10 .25
89 Evolution Stage 2 C .10 .25
90 Feeding Frenzy C .10 .25
91 Final Charge C .10 .25
92 Glaring Evil C .10 .25
93 Good Times C .10 .25
94 Hiei's Emotional Slash C .10 .25
95 Insect Invasion C .10 .25
96 Kazuya's Malevolent Glare C .10 .25
97 King's Conflict C .10 .25
98 Kuroko's Power Strike C .10 .25
99 Kuwabara's Emotional Slash C .10 .25
L1 Code L
L2 Remembrance L
L3 Villainous Energy L
L4 Hiei, Arrogant Demon L
L5 Koenma, Loyal Friend L
L6 Kurama, Gloomy Shadow L
L7 Kuwabara, Old Rival L
L8 Mr. Yukimura, Friendly Chef L
L9 Energy Spiral L
P1 Malefic Grenade P
P2 Hatred P
P3 Banished P
P4 Peek! P
P5 Coalition P
T1 Mukuro, Enslaved Soul (Upper Left) TG
T2 Concealed Darkness TU
T3 Rejected! TU
T4 Demoralized TS
T5 Dragon's Victory TS
T6 Purgatory TS
T7 An Old Demon Rises TR
T8 Awestruck TR
T9 Chaos TR
100 Making the News C .10 .25
101 Malevolent Apprentice C .10 .25
102 Malevolent Strike C .10 .25
103 Malicious Children C .10 .25
104 Meltdown C .10 .25
105 Misguided Bandits C .10 .25
106 Mock C .10 .25
107 Mourn C .10 .25
108 Narrow Escape C .10 .25
109 Nausea C .10 .25
110 Raise Your Team IQ C .10 .25
111 Renounce C .10 .25
112 Rinku's Rush C .10 .25
113 Spirit Absorption C .10 .25
114 Stalk C .10 .25
115 Swift Moves C .10 .25
116 Take Me! C .10 .25
117 Test of Endurance C .10 .25
118 Uncontrollable Power C .10 .25
119 Unity C .10 .25
120 Very Bizarre! C .10 .25
121 Wicked Influence C .10 .25
122 Amanuma, Resurrected C .10 .25
123 Fubuki Satou C .10 .25
124 Kurama, Prepared Fighter C .10 .25
125 Kuwabara, Young Friend C .10 .25
126 Minori Kamiya, Body Shifter C .10 .25
127 Rinbai C .10 .25
128 Ryuuhi C .10 .25
129 Sourai C .10 .25
130 Shizuru, Gifted Seer C .10 .25
131 Shougo Satou, Palm Reader C .10 .25
132 Younger Toguro, Tormented Sensei C .10 .25
133 Yukina, Happy Girl C .10 .25
134 Yusuke, Young Punk C .10 .25
135 Botan's Orb C .10 .25
136 Deleterious Bomb C .10 .25
137 Emotional Shackles C .10 .25
138 Magical Drink C .10 .25
139 Invincible Bombs C .10 .25
140 Nekotama, Fierce Tiger C .10 .25
141 Ookii Kouckuu, Indestructible Goliath C .10 .25
142 Hiei, Charming Goth C .10 .25
143 Sensui, Resshuuken Armor C .10 .25
144 Aerial Kick C .10 .25
145 Arm Blast C .10 .25
146 Cataclysmic Slam C .10 .25
147 Choke Hold C .10 .25
148 Demonic Spirit Gun C .10 .25
149 Devastating Slash C .10 .25
150 Fatal Blow C .10 .25
151 Fist of Fury C .10 .25
152 Flames of Power C .10 .25
153 Flying Kick C .10 .25
154 Improvised Attack C .10 .25
155 Improvised Defense C .10 .25
156 Sensui's Spirit Sphere C .10 .25
157 Vine Thrust C .10 .25
158 Baldok, Winged Fiend C .10 .25
159 Hiei, Villain Demon C .10 .25
160 Himatsubushi, Evil Spirit C .10 .25
161 Itsuki, Distressed Lover C .10 .25
162 Kirin, Loyal Sentinal C .10 .25
163 Rando, Demonic Spirit C .10 .25
164 Sakyo, Sadistic Creature C .10 .25
165 Shigure, Skilled Slayer C .10 .25
166 Shigure, Cool Mercenary C .10 .25
167 Shoutenki, Green Demon C .10 .25
168 Fire Seal ST .15 .40
169 Fruit of the Previous Life ST .15 .40
170 Ootake, Captain ST .15 .40
171 Kuwabara, Charming Lackey ST .15 .40
172 Yoko, Charming Fox ST .15 .40
173 Yusuke, Charming Devil ST .15 .40
174 Chu, 13th Fighter ST .15 .40
175 Genkai, Spirit Guide ST .15 .40
176 Kayko, Mature Beauty ST .15 .40
177 Hiei, the Vanquisher ST .15 .40
178 Sensui, Sacred Armor ST .15 .40
179 Shura, Loving Son ST .15 .40
180 Black Inferno ST .15 .40
181 Stone Toss ST .15 .40
L10 Piercing Beam L
T10 Consumed TR
T11 Remember Us? TR
T12 Kurama, Loving Friend TR
T13 Resurgence of Power TC
T14 Game Machine TC
T15 Rose Petals TC
T16 Shackles TC
T17 Kuroko, Former Spirit Detective TC
T18 Double Finger Block TC
T19 Scatter Shot TC
T20 Spirit Flare TC
T21 Byakko, Feline Warrior TC
TP3 The End TP

2012 Z/X Zillions of Enemy X Encounter with the Parallel Worlds

B01001 Hound of Fate, Lailaps R :R:
B01002 Sword Craftsman, Ittou C :R:
B01003 Heat Generating Coal, Coal Armadillo C :R:
B01004 Shining Gold, Gold Peacock R :R:
B01005 Queen of Desert, Cleopatra R :R:
B01006 Goddess of Hunting, Artemis R :R:
B01007 Divine Messenger of Sun, Yatagarasu C :R:
B01008 Forging Blacksmith, Forge C :R:
B01009 Black Horse of Conquest, Bucephalus R :R:
B01010 Unrivaled Plan, Ishida Mitsunari SR :R:
B01011 Tender Glass, Glass Elephant U :R:
B01012 Nine Great Heroes, Alexander SR :R:
B01013 Flat-out Run Iron Cavalry, Tank Heart U :R:
B01014 Heavy Stone, Stone Turtle U :R:
B01015 Dignified Divine Emperor, Augustus U :R:
B01016 Indomitable Steel, Steel Leopard U :R:
B01017 Imperator Judge C :R:
B01018 Champion's Tremor Spear R :R:
B01019 Exploding Coal U :R:
B01020 Main Armament, Fire! C :R:
B01021 Steel Castle, Astatine C :C:
B01022 Erasure Machine, Erase C :C:
B01023 Cymbal Player, Strauss R :C:
B01024 Steel Castle, Technetium C :C:
B01025 City Guard, Phecda C :C:
B01026 Erasure Machine, Void R :C:
B01027 Meteor Sword, Spica R :C:
B01028 ?-S02 Alioth R :C:
B01029 Steel Castle, Europium U :C:
B01030 Erasure Machine, Delete U :C:
B01031 Calm Evening Diva, Smetina R :C:
B01032 Electronic Appliance Union, Tantalum U :C:
B01033 Performer Voice, Vival R :C:
B01034 Sword Sniper, Rigel SR :C:
B01035 t-A03 Aspidiske U :C:
B01036 Castle of the Speed of Sound, Darmstadtium SR :C:
B01037 Scientific Development C :C:
B01038 Comet Shoot C :C:
B01039 Soaring Racing Shoot R :C:
B01040 Sonata of Return U :C:
B01041 Lawbringer, Distaghil C :W:
B01042 Part of Fate Revolution, Lilliel Saotome R :W:
B01043 Holy Beast, Aura Pegasus C :W:
B01044 Pot Selling Siamese C :W:
B01045 Absconding Maine Coon R :W:
B01046 Lawbringer, Dhaulagiri R :W:
B01047 Lien the Bonds R :W:
B01048 Holy Beast, Aura Phoenix U :W:
B01049 Cheerful Burmese U :W:
B01050 Lawbringer, Shishapangma U :W:
B01051 Sagesse the Wisdom U :W:
B01052 Holy Beast, Aura Byakko C :W:
B01053 Lawbringer, Batura SR :W:
B01054 Admiration the Longing U :W:
B01055 Lawbringer, Ushba R :W:
B01056 Fierte the Pride SR :W:
B01057 Arrogant Light Wall C :W:
B01058 Angelic Light Attack U :W:
B01059 Revenge Force C :W:
B01060 Dazzling Saint Aura R :W:
B01061 Demon of Seduction, Luscious C :K:
B01062 Wandering Head Crusher C :K:
B01063 Fanged Bone Dog, Bone Keeper R :K:
B01064 Chain of Death, Kette C :K:
B01065 Demon of Lament, Maeror R :K:
B01066 Demon of Misfortune, Miseria R :K:
B01067 Merry-Go-Round Horse C :K:
B01068 Powerful Swing, Sting Beat U :K:
B01069 Flaying Iron Maiden R :K:
B01070 Quadruped Victor, Sieger SR :K:
B01071 Sure-kill Arrow, Pfeil U :K:
B01072 Demon of Hatred, Odium SR :K:
B01073 Bone Shark, Skeletal Shark U :K:
B01074 Conjugated Hollow Giant, Huge Corpse R :K:
B01075 Demon of Despair, Desperatio U :K:
B01076 Dark Bishop, Skeletal Bishop U :K:
B01077 Dark Moon C :K:
B01078 Curse Diffusion C :K:
B01079 Awakening of Demon U :K:
B01080 Moonlight Funeral Fang R :K:
B01081 Cherry Blossom Butterfly, Full Blossom C :G:
B01082 Beastman, Were-Bear R :G:
B01083 Caretaking Flax C :G:
B01084 Rose Helmet, Wild Rose R :G:
B01085 Wild Sickle and Chain, Housenka R :G:
B01086 Expert of Future, Tanpopo C :G:
B01087 Beastman, Were-Koala U :G:
B01088 Easygoing Rurijissa U :G:
B01089 King of Beasts, Were-Lion R :G:
B01090 Tidy Lemon Balm U :G:
B01091 Beastman, Were-Antler C :G:
B01092 Graceful Naginata, Ayame SR :G:
B01093 Morning Glory Mantis, Glory Scythe U :G:
B01094 Sword Warrior, Rindou SR :G:
B01095 Powerful Pike, Kakitsubata U :G:
B01096 Giant Beast, Were-Rhino R :G:
B01097 Military Emperor's Sword Flash Attack R :G:
B01098 Unify Earth C :G:
B01099 Good Night C :G:
B01100 Green Erosion U :G:
B01101 Hero of World Destruction, Oda Nobunaga Z/XR :R:
B01102 Seraph of Arrival, Michael Z/XR :W:
B01103 Fallen Angel of Grief, Lucifer Z/XR :K:

2012 Z/X Zillions of Enemy X Extra Pack 1 Heroic Feast

E01001 Queen of Land of the Rising Sun, Himiko SR :R:
E01002 Style of Seigan, Okita Souji R :R:
E01003 Respected Divine General, Hannibal Barca R :R:
E01004 Holy Emperor, Kan'u Unchou R :R:
E01005 Laser Scythe, Avior R :B:
E01006 Administrator Denebola R :B:
E01007 Biblioblade, Fomalhaut SR :B:
E01008 Circular Drill, Girtab R :B:
E01009 Ciel the Sky R :W:
E01010 Regle the Law R :W:
E01011 Priere the Prayer R :W:
E01012 Eclair the Flash SR :W:
E01013 Demon of Solitude, Solitus R :K:
E01014 Demon of Cruelty, Saevum R :K:
E01015 Demon of Madness, Lunatics SR :K:
E01016 Demon of Savagery, Barbarus R :K:
E01017 Concealed Shuriken, Otogirisou R :G:
E01018 Bow of Temperance, Satsuki R :G:
E01019 Vajra of Nobility, Mokuren R :G:
E01020 Cross Spear of Refinement, Ibuki Toranoo SR :G:
E01021 Kurosaki Mikado IGR :R:
E01022 Kagamihara Azumi IGR :B:
E01023 Tennoji Asuka IGR :W:
E01024 Kamiyugi Ayase IGR :K:
E01025 Aoba Chitose IGR :G:

2012 Z/X Zillions of Enemy X Feast of Darkness and Festival of the Holy Light

F00001 Kido Arato
F01008 Kurosaki Mikado :R:
F02008 Kamiyugi Ayase :K:
F03008 Aoba Chitose :G:
F04008 Kagamihara Azumi :B:
F04008 Tennoji Asuka :W:
F06001 Wandering Head Crusher :K:
F06002 Chain of Death, Kette :K:
F06003 Demon of Misfortune, Miseria :K:
F06004 Powerful Swing, Sting Beat :K:
F06005 Bone Shark, Skeletal Shark :K:
F06006 Demon of Savagery, Barbarus :K:
F06007 Holy Beast, Aura Pegasus :W:
F06008 Pot Selling Siamese :W:
F06009 Absconding Maine Coon :W:
F06010 Lawbringer, Dhaulagiri :W:
F06011 Lien the Bonds :W:
F06012 Priere the Prayer :W:
F06013 Revenge Force :W:

2012 Z/X Zillions of Enemy X Free Set 1-1 Crimson Hero and Jet-Black Demon

F01001 Sword Craftsman, Ittou :R:
F01002 Queen of Desert, Cleopatra :R:
F01003 Divine Messenger of Sun, Yatagarasu :R:
F01004 Tender Glass, Glass Elephant :R:
F01005 Heavy Stone, Stone Turtle :R:
F01006 Dignified Divine Emperor, Augustus :R:
F01007 Imperator Judge :R:
F01008 Kurosaki Mikado :R:
F02001 Demon of Seduction, Luscious :K:
F02002 Fanged Bone Dog, Bone Keeper :K:
F02003 Merry-Go-Round Horse :K:
F02004 Powerful Swing, Sting Beat :K:
F02005 Sure-kill Arrow, Pfeil :K:
F02006 Demon of Despair, Desperatio :K:
F02007 Curse Diffusion :K:
F02008 Kamiyugi Ayase :K:

2012 Z/X Zillions of Enemy X Free Set 1-2 Dark Green Tree People and Pure White Angel

F03001 Beastman, Were-Bear :G:
F03002 Rose Helmet, Wild Rose :G:
F03003 Expert of Future, Tanpopo :G:
F03004 Easygoing Rurijissa :G:
F03005 Beastman, Were-Antler :G:
F03006 Powerful Pike, Kakitsubata :G:
F03007 Good Night :G:
F03008 Aoba Chitose :G:
F04001 Lawbringer, Distaghil :W:
F04002 Holy Beast, Aura Pegasus :W:
F04003 Pot Selling Siamese :W:
F04004 Lawbringer, Shishapangma :W:
F04005 Sagesse the Wisdom :W:
F04006 Admiration the Longing :W:
F04007 Arrogant Light Wall :W:
F04008 Tennoji Asuka :W:

2012 Z/X Zillions of Enemy X Free Set 1-3 Azure Mechanical Soldier

F05001 Erasure Machine, Erase :B:
F05002 Steel Castle, Technetium :B:
F05003 City Guard, Phecda :B:
F05004 Steel Castle, Europium :B:
F05005 Performer Voice, Vival :B:
F05006 t-A03 Aspidiske :B:
F05007 Comet Shoot :B:
F05008 Kagamihara Azumi :B:

2012 Z/X Zillions of Enemy X Free Set 2 Crimson Pyroxene and Strategy of Blue Sky

F01008 Kurosaki Mikado :R:
F05008 Kagamihara Azumi :B:
F07001 Flower of Warring States, Mori Ranmaru :R:
F07002 Goddess of Love and Beauty, Aphrodite :R:
F07003 Swift Tourmaline, Tourmaline Hawk :R:
F07004 Armor Blacksmith, Reinforce :R:
F07005 Thousand Li per Day, Sekitoba :R:
F07006 Sharp Obsidian, Obsidian Alligator :R:
F07007 Critical Strike :R:
F07008 Ambush Machine, Raid :B:
F07009 String Performer, Sariel :B:
F07010 Heavy Arms, Alpheratz :B:
F07011 Great Sky Tree, Rhenium :B:
F07012 Light Whip, Atria :B:
F07013 Castle of Science, Bismuth :B:
F07014 Million Rain :B:

2012 Z/X Zillions of Enemy X Invitation to Struggle

F01002 Queen of Desert, Cleopatra :R:
F01003 Divine Messenger of Sun, Yatagarasu :R:
F01004 Tender Glass, Glass Elephant :R:
F01005 Heavy Stone, Stone Turtle :R:
F01006 Dignified Divine Emperor, Augustus :R:
F02002 Fanged Bone Dog, Bone Keeper :K:
F02004 Powerful Swing, Sting Beat :K:
F02005 Sure-kill Arrow, Pfeil :K:
F02007 Curse Diffusion :K:
F02009 Mascot Character, Rincle :K:
F03001 Beastman, Were-Bear :G:
F03002 Rose Helmet, Wild Rose :G:
F03003 Expert of Future, Tanpopo :G:
F03004 Easygoing Rurijissa :G:
F03005 Beastman, Were-Antler :G:
F03006 Powerful Pike, Kakitsubata :G:

2012 Z/X Zillions of Enemy X Roar of the Titans

B02001 Flower of Warring States, Mori Ranmaru R :R:
B02002 Sagacious Silver, Silver Fox C :R:
B02003 Demonic Wolf, Fenrir R :R:
B02004 Goddess of Love and Beauty, Aphrodite C :R:
B02005 Handgun Craftsman, Quick Draw R :R:
B02006 Gold Winged Bird, Garuda R :R:
B02007 Swift Tourmaline, Tourmaline Hawk U :R:
B02008 Armor Blacksmith, Reinforce C :R:
B02009 Nine Great Heroes, Jeanne d'Arc SR :R:
B02010 Large Sword Workshop, Claymore U :R:
B02011 Graceful Crystal, Crystal Swan C :R:
B02012 Thousand Li per Day, Sekitoba C :R:
B02013 Sharp Obsidian, Obsidian Alligator U :R:
B02014 Cheerful Sun God, Apollon Agana Belea R :R:
B02015 Hero of Restoration, Sakamoto Ryouma U :R:
B02016 Ultimate Overdragon, Orichalcum Tyranno SR :R:
B02017 Critical Strike U :R:
B02018 Steel Impact U :R:
B02019 Tyrant Parade U :R:
B02020 Dual Fire R :R:
B02021 Ambush Machine, Raid C :B:
B02022 Cross Sniper, Scheat R :B:
B02023 String Performer, Sariel C :B:
B02024 Thunderbolt, Deneb U :B:
B02025 Transformed Windmill, Fermium R :B:
B02026 Heavy Arms, Alpheratz R :B:
B02027 Destruction Machine, Ruin C :B:
B02028 Thinker, Velte U :B:
B02029 Great Sky Tree, Rhenium C :B:
B02030 Light Whip, Atria U :B:
B02031 Captivating Performer, Puccini U :B:
B02032 Dust Hammer, Algol C :B:
B02033 Looting Machine, Plunder R :B:
B02034 Castle of Science, Bismuth R :B:
B02035 Supreme Commander, Meitnerium SR :B:
B02036 Super Steel Regalia, Lawrencium SR :B:
B02037 Shut Down U :B:
B02038 Million Rain C :B:
B02039 Boy Meets Justice R :B:
B02040 Wait, Now Go! U :B:
B02041 Aube the Dawn U :W:
B02042 Holy Beast, Aura Komainu C :W:
B02043 Writing Abyssinian C :W:
B02044 Holy Beast, Aura Sphinx C :W:
B02045 Etoile the Star R :W:
B02046 Lawbringer, Carstensz R :W:
B02047 Lawbringer, Santa Cruz R :W:
B02048 Cleaning Bobtail U :W:
B02049 Creation the Genesis SR :W:
B02050 Lawbringer, Aconcagua R :W:
B02051 Accessory Selling Short-Hair R :W:
B02052 Volonte the Will U :W:
B02053 Holy Beast, Aura Narasimha U :W:
B02054 Lawbringer, Trivor C :W:
B02055 Coucher the Sunset U :W:
B02056 Apex of Order, Sir Garmatha SR :W:
B02057 Cat Sith Market C :W:
B02058 Maximum Mace C :W:
B02059 Rebellion of Guardian R :W:
B02060 Chain Bind U :W:
B02061 Demon of Punishment, Poena C :K:
B02062 Falling Spear, Speer R :K:
B02063 Three Headed Mercenary, Drei Soldner C :K:
B02064 Assassin Dagger of Abyss, Flame Corpse U :K:
B02065 Enthusiastic Electric Chair C :K:
B02066 Demon of Vengeance, Ultio R :K:
B02067 Bone Knight, Skeletal Knight R :K:
B02068 Demon of Domination, Imperium C :K:
B02069 Cavalry Assault, Kavallerist R :K:
B02070 Revenant, Black Arts U :K:
B02071 Demon of Arrogance, Arrogans C :K:
B02072 Black Sword, Cursed Soul SR :K:
B02073 Flapping Guillotine U :K:
B02074 Warming Blazen Bull U :K:
B02075 Demon of Evening, Crepus SR :K:
B02076 Undying King, Immortal King R :K:
B02077 Black Union C :K:
B02078 Fang Crush C :K:
B02079 Invitation to Embrace R :K:
B02080 Corrupted Aura U :K:
B02081 Quiet Rosemary C :G:
B02082 Rabbit Girl, Were-Rabbit R :G:
B02083 Homely Sage U :G:
B02084 Petal Ant, Petal Soldier C :G:
B02085 Transforming Triple Staff, Yamabuki R :G:
B02086 Cooking Beastman, Were-Hamster C :G:
B02087 Bamboo Breaking War Fan, Kinmokusei U :G:
B02088 Colour Changing Lizard, Apple Chameleon U :G:
B02089 Dignified Hairpin, Kuroyuri C :G:

2012 Z/X Zillions of Enemy X Roar of the Titans

B02090 Thorned Bug, Thorn Crest U :G:
B02091 Hunting Pheasant, Pheasant R :G:
B02092 Alluring Seven-Branched Sword, Gekkakou SR :G:
B02093 Dog Girl, Were-Dog R :G:
B02094 Courageous Fennel R :G:
B02095 Vivid Japanese Umbrella, Cosmos C :G:
B02096 Maiden of Forest, Feuille SR :G:
B02097 Daddy, Help! C :G:
B02098 Verdure Meditation R :G:
B02099 Horizontal Halberd Strike C :G:
B02100 Feuille is Always Energetic! U :G:
B02101 The Most Evil on Earth, Ryofu Housen Z/XR :R:
B02102 Magical Fencer, Elnath Z/XR :B:
B02103 Splendorous Kunai, Botan Z/XR :G:
B02104 Dragon Maiden IGR :M:

2012 Z/X Zillions of Enemy X Starter Deck 1 Angel's Charity

C01001 Tennoji Asuka SR :W:
C01002 Incorruptible Feelings, Fierte SR :W:
C01003 Crimson Fang, Ruby Howl PR :R:
C01004 Queen of Desert, Cleopatra R :R:
C01005 Armor Blacksmith, Reinforce C :R:
C01006 Graceful Crystal, Crystal Swan C :R:
C01007 Courageous Bear Warrior, Sakata Kintoki U :R:
C01008 Dignified Divine Emperor, Augustus U :R:
C01009 Exploding Coal U :R:
C01010 Holy Beast, Aura Komainu C :W:
C01011 Ciel the Sky R :W:
C01012 Lawbringer, Dhaulagiri R :W:
C01013 Sleeping Snow White U :W:
C01014 Volonte the Will U :W:
C01015 Sagesse the Wisdom U :W:
C01016 Holy Beast, Aura Narasimha U :W:
C01017 Arrogant Light Wall C :W:

2012 Z/X Zillions of Enemy X Starter Deck 1 Angel's Charity Hologram Rare Exclusive

C01004 Queen of Desert, Cleopatra R :R:

2012 Z/X Zillions of Enemy X Starter Deck 1 Battle Blade of the Black Beast

C02001 Kamiyugi Ayase SR :K:
C02002 Jet-Black Blade, Sieger SR :K:
C02003 Cymbal Player, Strauss R :B:
C02004 String Performer, Sariel C :B:
C02005 Erasure Machine, Void R :B:
C02006 Great Sky Tree, Rhenium C :B:
C02007 Captivating Performer, Puccini U :B:
C02008 Ogre Slayer, Momotarou U :B:
C02009 Electronic Appliance Union, Tantalum U :B:
C02010 Million Rain C :B:
C02011 Demon of Punishment, Poena C :K:
C02012 Bone Snake, Skeletal Viper PR :K:
C02013 Demon of Solitude, Solitus R :K:
C02014 Demon of Domination, Imperium C :K:
C02015 Demonic Princess of Moonlight, Queen Kaguya U :K:
C02016 Dark Bishop, Skeletal Bishop U :K:
C02017 Fang Crush C :K:

2012 Z/X Zillions of Enemy X Starter Deck 1 Battle Blade of the Black Beast Hologram Rare Exclusive

C02003 Cymbal Player, Strauss R :B:

2013 Z/X Zillions of Enemy X Advent of the Five Dragon Emperors

B03001 Castle-toppling Beauty, Chousen C :R:
B03002 Beautiful Quartz, Quartz Crab C :R:
B03003 Majestic Luvulite, Luvulite Elephant C :R:
B03004 Ornament Craftsman, Tiara R :R:
B03005 Flying Malachite, Malachite Bat R :R:
B03006 Goddess of Strategy, Athena R :R:
B03007 Ferocious Tiger's Eye Gem, Tiger's Eye U :R:
B03008 One-Eyed Giant, Cyclops C :R:
B03009 Nine Great Heroes, Lancelot SR :R:
B03010 Country Eating Manticore C :R:
B03011 Courageous Bear Warrior, Sakata Kintoki U :R:
B03012 Outfitting Craftsman, Hindenburg U :R:
B03013 Root of Evil, Azi Dahaka R :R:
B03014 Tough Carnelian, Carnelian Bear U :R:
B03015 Lionheart King, Richard I R :R:
B03016 Iron Shoe Craftsman, Greave U :R:
B03017 Tyrant Dragon, Cardinal Blade SR :R:
B03018 Sunset Intercept R :R:
B03019 Nobunaga's Gun U :R:
B03020 Holy Sword That Waits To Be Awakened C :R:
B03021 Pole Performer, Lavery C :B:
B03022 Steel Castle, Osmium C :B:
B03023 Evaporation Machine, Evaporation U :B:
B03024 Transformed Two Wheels, Flerovium R :B:
B03025 Laser Blade, Benetnasch C :B:
B03026 Extreme Performer, Horatio C :B:
B03027 Amusement Union, Platinum Aurum C :B:
B03028 Ogre Slayer, Momotarou U :B:
B03029 Duel Machine, Duel R :B:
B03030 Drill Machine, Boring C :B:
B03031 Barrette Rider, Schedar R :B:
B03032 Space Fortress, Strontium U :B:
B03033 Permanent Hidden Character, Asagi R :B:
B03034 Original XIII Type.X "Mb29Ve" SR :B:
B03035 Dazzling Keyboard, Wagner U :B:
B03036 Gigantic Clock, Berkelium U :B:
B03037 Mechanical Dragon, Drive Pinion SR :B:
B03038 First Combat Deployment U :B:
B03039 Atria's Holiday R :B:
B03040 Crimson Invasion R :B:
B03041 Ceramic Making Singapura C :W:
B03042 Pur the Pure C :W:
B03043 Holy Beast, Aura Tapir R :W:
B03044 Puissance the Power R :W:
B03045 Lawbringer, Grandes Jorasses C :W:
B03046 Illusion the Fantasy R :W:
B03047 Holy Beast, Aura Unicorn R :W:
B03048 Sleeping Snow White U :W:
B03049 Inept Detective, Russian Blue C :W:
B03050 Lawbringer, Ararat U :W:
B03051 Twelve Apostles - Aquarius Gambiel SR :W:
B03052 Lawbringer, Annapurna U :W:
B03053 Lawbringer, Fitz Roy C :W:
B03054 Charismatic Persia R :W:
B03055 Holy Beast, Aura Coatl U :W:
B03056 Lawbringer, Tirich Mir R :W:
B03057 Celestial Dragon, Holy Sky SR :W:
B03058 Phantom Shoot U :W:
B03059 Avenger of Tears C :W:
B03060 Bobtail Cleaning Technique U :W:
B03061 Black Robber, Rauber C :K:
B03062 Blade Strike, Klinge R :K:
B03063 Jack-o'-Lantern the Pumpkin Ghost C :K:
B03064 Revenant, Twilight Ash R :K:
B03065 Wandering Bone, Bone Ship C :K:
B03066 Running Around Painful Wheel C :K:
B03067 Girl of Illusion Path, Alice R :K:
B03068 Ominous Traveler, Reisender R :K:
B03069 Demon of Taciturn, Tacitus U :K:
B03070 Headless Tank, Dullahan U :K:
B03071 Demonic Princess of Moonlight, Queen Kaguya U :K:
B03072 Snipping Pretty U :K:
B03073 Jump in Car's Car's R :K:
B03074 Demon of Duel, Monomachia C :K:
B03075 Kick Away Break Striker U :K:
B03076 Seven Deadly Sins - Demon of Lust, Luxuria SR :K:
B03077 Ruin-Hell Dragon, Destiny Vein SR :K:
B03078 Midnight Emperor C :K:
B03079 Disaster Blade U :K:
B03080 The Abyss R :K:
B03081 Laundry Beastman, Were-Racoon C :G:
B03082 Walking Stevia C :G:
B03083 Beastman, Were-Hedgehog R :G:
B03084 Flower Patterned Ladybug, Floral Bug C :G:
B03085 Sheep Girl, Were-Sheep U :G:
B03086 Fearless Tonfa, Shakuyaku R :G:
B03087 Handicrafting Oregano C :G:
B03088 Squirrel Girl, Were-Squirrel R :G:
B03089 Grasshopper King, King Hopper C :G:
B03090 Beastman, Were-Hound U :G:
B03091 Stern Hand Claws, Hyakujitsukou R :G:
B03092 Strong Horn, Great Hercules U :G:
B03093 Honest Nodachi, Hanazuou R :G:
B03094 Caraway of the Sleeping Forest U :G:
B03095 Eight Great Dragon Kings, Utpalaka SR :G:
B03096 Small Sword of Blinking Speed, Issun-Boshi U :G:
B03097 Flower Dragon, Ivy Wing SR :G:
B03098 Thorn Prison U :G:
B03099 Timber Force C :G:
B03100 Little Guardian R :G:
B03101 Super Transformed Gear, KHD-8000 Z/XR :B:
B03102 Demon of Mind, Animus Z/XR :K:
B03103 Noble Queen, Laurier Z/XR :G:
B03104 Kurosaki Mikado IGR :R:
B03105 Kagamihara Azumi IGR :B:
B03106 Tennoji Asuka IGR :W:
B03107 Kamiyugi Ayase IGR :K:
B03108 Aoba Chitose IGR :G:

2013 Z/X Zillions of Enemy X Assault of the Black Knight Deity

B04001 Sky Soaring Warhorse, Sleipnir R :R:
B04002 Goddess of Fortune, Lakshmi C :R:
B04003 Tank Craftsman, Cannon Shell R :R:
B04004 Flying Amethyst, Amethyst Swallow U :R:
B04005 Master of Labyrinth, Minotaur C :R:
B04006 Noisy Garnet, Garnet Ultan U :R:
B04007 Faithful Warrior Woman, Tomoe Gozen R :R:
B04008 Battle Axe Workshop, Bardiche C :R:
B04009 Ruthless Fluorite, Fluorite Lynx C :R:
B04010 Bizarre Coral, Coral Lizard U :R:
B04011 Musketeer of Oath, D'Artagnan U :R:
B04012 Stabbing Spinel, Spinel Penguin R :R:
B04013 Serpent of Chaos, Yamata no Orochi SR :R:
B04014 Unlucky Earth God, Hades Aidoneus U :R:
B04015 Arms Craftsman, Spark Launcher R :R:
B04016 Nine Great Heroes, Shakespeare SR :R:
B04017 Tokyo Recapture Operation U :R:
B04018 Tyrant Blade, Dragonic Flare R :R:
B04019 Strongest Bear Determination Match C :R:
B04020 Skinship C :R:
B04021 Cannon Tamer, Mimosa U :B:
B04022 Transformed Golden Shachi, Nagoyan U :B:
B04023 Cyber Rapier, Alphard R :B:
B04024 Throwing Machine, Throwing C :B:
B04025 Bombarding Machine, Bombardment C :B:
B04026 Apprentice Voice, Vilde C :B:
B04027 Conductor, Amadius R :B:
B04028 Battle Hero, Markab C :B:
B04029 Shock Machine, Shock R :B:
B04030 Drop Sound, Fiore U :B:
B04031 Star Shooter, Capella C :B:
B04032 Invincible Haniwa, Honey-One R :B:
B04033 Transformed Church, Hafnium R :B:
B04034 Playground Union, Polonium R :B:
B04035 Administrator Vega SR :B:
B04036 Sword Emperor Regalia, Cyclotron SR :B:
B04037 Royal Straight Flush U :B:
B04038 Mechanical Cannon, Dragonic Cannon U :B:
B04039 Sword Revolution C :B:
B04040 Jet-Black Lawrencium U :B:
B04041 Destinee the Fate R :W:
B04042 Evilbane, Mont Blanc C :W:
B04043 Reigning Mike U :W:
B04044 Holy Beast, Aura Kirin C :W:
B04045 Ame the Soul C :W:
B04046 Errer the Wander R :W:
B04047 Evilbane, Elbrus U :W:
B04048 Holy Beast, Aura Centaur C :W:
B04049 Escaping Pixie-bob R :W:
B04050 Evilbane, Damavand R :W:
B04051 Evilbane, Massif U :W:
B04052 Holy Beast, Aura Genbu U :W:
B04053 Sterk the Strength R :W:
B04054 Twelve Apostles - Leo Verchiel SR :W:
B04055 Caring Siberian U :W:
B04056 Evilbane, K-Two SR :W:
B04057 Guardian Heart C :W:
B04058 Shining Angel U :W:
B04059 Celestial Ray, Gem Shine U :W:
B04060 Extermination Flow R :W:
B04061 Bone Soldier, Skeletal Fighter U :K:
B04062 Revenant, Dusk Axe R :K:
B04063 Playful Road Roller R :K:
B04064 Demon of Forfeiture, Perdere U :K:
B04065 Demon of Boredom, Inertia C :K:
B04066 Demon of Blade, Lamina C :K:
B04067 Demon of Shadow, Umbra U :K:
B04068 Executioner Sickle, Scharfrichter C :K:
B04069 Aiming to Hit Snap Shooter U :K:
B04070 Chewing Vise U :K:
B04071 Ominous King, Konig C :K:
B04072 Skeletal Hollow Giant, Huge Golem U :K:
B04073 Fang Hunter, Jager R :K:
B04074 Dancing Skeleton, Skeletal Dancer R :K:
B04075 Cutting Charm SR :K:
B04076 Seven Deadly Sins - Demon of Greed, Avaritia SR :K:
B04077 Charm Spell C :K:
B04078 Mystic Adventure R :K:
B04079 Lunatic Sickle C :K:
B04080 Ruin-Hell Wave, Doom Blast R :K:
B04081 Glorious Baking Stone, Himawari U :G:
B04082 Plain Octagonal Pole, Natsume C :G:
B04083 Beastman, Were-Capybara R :G:
B04084 Medical Care Marshmallow R :G:
B04085 Agricultural Birdman, Were-Lark C :G:
B04086 Shell Mushroom, Mush Snail U :G:
B04087 Cherry Blossom Crest, Cherry Beetle C :G:
B04088 Linden's Own Pace U :G:
B04089 Wise Elder, Were-Owl U :G:
B04090 Beastman, Were-Ursus R :G:
B04091 Beastman, Were-Leopard R :G:
B04092 Thorn Spider, Needle Spider C :G:
B04093 Eight Great Dragon Kings, Taksaka SR :G:
B04094 Merciless Crimson Spear, Hagoromosou C :G:
B04095 Raging Jasmine R :G:
B04096 Iron Claw of Green Sky, Misohagi SR :G:
B04097 Girls' Talk U :G:
B04098 Taksaka's Divine Power R :G:
B04099 Happiness Time C :G:
B04100 Flower Wind, Life Storm U :G:
B04101 Mischievous Nine-Tails, Dakki Z/XR :R:
B04102 Original XIII Type.I "A-Z" Z/XR :B:
B04103 Four Archangels - Uriel A.T. Z/XR :W:
B04104 Kurashiki Sera IGR :R:
B04105 Sento Reia IGR :B:
B04106 Yuzuriha Misaki IGR :W:
B04107 Tennoji Yamato IGR :K:
B04108 Kenbuchi Soma IGR :G:
B04109 Aoba Chitose CVR :G:
B04110 Kenbuchi Soma CVR :G:

2013 Z/X Zillions of Enemy X Extra Pack 2 Nippon Ichi Software

E02001 Raging Laharl C :R:
E02002 Laughing Aloud, Laharl R :R:
E02003 Taking a Rest, Laharl C :R:
E02004 Raiding Laharl U :R:
E02005 Receiving Challenge, Laharl R :R:
E02006 Provoking Laharl U :R:
E02007 Selfish Laharl R :R:
E02008 Feinting Laharl U :R:
E02009 Awakening Laharl R :R:
E02010 Attacking Laharl R :R:
E02011 Laharl's Supreme Rule C :R:
E02012 Evilest Overlord, Laharl SR :R:
E02013 Aim to be Hero, Mao R :R:
E02014 Brain with 1.8 Million Evil Quotient, Mao U :R:
E02015 Delinquent Girl, Raspberyl SR :R:
E02016 Raspberyl's Volunteering Hobby C :R:
E02017 Mao's Rival, Raspberyl C :R:
E02018 Enjoying Victory, Mid-Boss U :R:
E02019 Narcissistic Mid-Boss C :R:
E02020 Overlord That Connect Two Worlds U :R:
E02021 High Spirited Asagi R :B:
E02022 Dozing Off Asagi C :B:
E02023 Cheerful Asagi U :B:
E02024 Uniform Asagi R :B:
E02025 Pajama Asagi C :B:
E02026 Floating Asagi R :B:
E02027 Asagi's War Preparation U :B:
E02028 Holding a Bread, Asagi C :B:
E02029 Vow to Become Protagonist, Asagi C :B:
E02030 Expressionless Asagi R :B:
E02031 Aim to Shoot, Asagi U :B:
E02032 Beach Asagi SR :B:
E02033 Vow to Overthrow Zenon, Adell U :B:
E02034 Protecting Rozalin, Adell U :B:
E02035 Overlord's Only Daughter, Rozalin SR :B:
E02036 Together with Adell, Rozalin C :B:
E02037 Steamy Rozalin U :B:
E02038 Axel the A-Virus Hazard R :B:
E02039 Netherworld's Famous Person? Axel C :B:
E02040 Watermelon Splitting R :B:
E02041 Flonne the Love Freak U :W:
E02042 Upset Flonne C :W:
E02043 Sexy Flonne R :W:
E02044 Sprawling Flonne R :W:
E02045 Burning Flash Flonne C :W:
E02046 Enthusiastic Flonne U :W:
E02047 Play in the Beach, Flonne U :W:
E02048 Flonne the Fallen Angel C :W:
E02049 Flonne the Ditz R :W:
E02050 Giving Peace Sign, Flonne U :W:
E02051 Go for It, Flonne SR :W:
E02052 Awakening Angel, Pure Flonne SR :W:
E02053 God's Personal Angel, Lilliel C :W:
E02054 Novice Angel, Lilliel C :W:
E02055 Lilliel's Powerful Support! R :W:
E02056 Angel of Avarice, Artina R :W:
E02057 Dazzling Artina U :W:
E02058 Hand-to-Hand Combat Specialist, Priere C :W:
E02059 Overlord Priere U :W:
E02060 Love Preaching Fallen Angel R :W:
E02061 Angry Etna C :K:
E02062 Rough Prinny User, Etna R :K:
E02063 Eating Ice Cream, Etna U :K:
E02064 Free Heroine, Etna R :K:
E02065 Etna the Sharp Tsukkomi R :K:
E02066 Cruel Etna U :K:
E02067 Resting Etna C :K:
E02068 Throw a Prinny, Etna C :K:
E02069 Etna the Cutting Board C :K:
E02070 Unforgiving Demon, Etna SR :K:
E02071 Looking Back, Etna C :K:
E02072 Strongest Demon in the World, Etna SR :K:
E02073 Sardine Loving Valvatorez U :K:
E02074 Keep an Oath, Valvatorez R :K:
E02075 Yearn for Fuka, Desco U :K:
E02076 Final Boss In Training, Desco U :K:
E02077 Fuka the Hat-Only Prinny R :K:
E02078 Middle School Girl, Fuka C :K:
E02079 Aiming for Home Run, Fuka R :K:
E02080 20 Hour Work, Without Welfare Program U :K:
E02081 Getting Things Done, Prinny C :G:
E02082 Go for It, Prinny R :G:
E02083 1000 Prinny Squad C :G:
E02084 Resting Prinny C :G:
E02085 Adventuring Prinny U :G:
E02086 Historical Weakest! Hero Prinny R :G:
E02087 Stubborn Prinny, Asagi U :G:
E02088 Unidentified? Big Sis Prinny U :G:
E02089 Dandy Prinny, Kurtis C :G:
E02090 Arrogant Prinny, Laharl R :G:
E02091 Do the Best, Marona U :G:
E02092 Tender-Hearted Ash C :G:
E02093 User of Water Dragon's Power, Ash R :G:
E02094 Metallia the Atrocious Freedom SR :G:
E02095 Master Metallia U :G:
E02096 Master of the Hundred Knight, Metallia SR :G:
E02097 Genius Witch, Metallia R :G:
E02098 Legendary Deity, The Hundred Knight C :G:
E02099 Inquisitor, Vesco U :G:
E02100 Overthrow the Forest Witch! R :G:
E02101 Aim to be Protagonist! Asagi Z/XR :B:
E02102 Everyone's Best Friend, Flonne Z/XR :W:
E02103 Prinny Master, Etna Z/XR :K:
E02104 Laharl IGR :R:
E02105 Asagi IGR :B:
E02106 Flonne IGR :W:
E02107 Etna IGR :K:
E02108 Metallia IGR :G:

2013 Z/X Zillions of Enemy X Extra Pack 2 Nippon Ichi Software Promos

E02P01 Aim to be Protagonist! Asagi :B:
E02P02 Everyone's Best Friend, Flonne :W:
E02P03 Prinny Master, Etna :K:
E02P04 Laharl :R:
E02P05 Asagi :B:
E02P06 Flonne :W:
E02P07 Etna :K:
E02P08 Metallia :G:
E02P09 Idol Overlord, Laharl-chan :R:
E02P10 Pram the Oracle :W:
E02P11 Ivy Tower Manager, Ms. Dungeon :G:

2013 Z/X Zillions of Enemy X Free Set 3 Round Dance of Dark Night and Melody of Sunshine

F02008 Kamiyugi Ayase :K:
F03008 Aoba Chitose :G:
F08001 Blade Strike, Klinge :K:
F08002 Revenant, Twillight Ash :K:
F08003 Running Around Painful Wheel :K:
F08004 Girl of Illusion Path, Alice :K:
F08005 Demon of Duel, Monomachia :K:
F08006 Kick Away Break Striker :K:
F08007 Midnight Emperor :K:
F08008 Laundry Beastman, Were-Racoon :G:
F08009 Walking Stevia :G:
F08010 Flower Patterned Ladybug, Floral Bug :G:
F08011 Sheep Girl, Were-Sheep :G:
F08012 Fearless Tonfa, Shakuyaku :G:
F08013 Small Sword of Blinking Speed, Issun-Boshi :G:
F08014 Timber Force :G:

2013 Z/X Zillions of Enemy X Free Set 4 Blue Sky Lion and Silver Guardian

F04009 Yuzuriha Misaki :W:
F05010 Sento Reia :B:
F09001 Transformed Golden Shachihoko, Nagoyan :B:
F09002 Cyber Rapier, Alphard :B:
F09003 Apprentice Voice, Vilde :B:
F09004 Battle Hero, Markab :B:
F09005 Shock Machine, Shock :B:
F09006 Invincible Haniwa, Honey-One :B:
F09007 Sword Revolution :B:
F09008 Destinee the Fate :W:
F09009 Evilbane, Mont Blanc :W:
F09010 Holy Beast, Aura Kirin :W:
F09011 Errer the Wander :W:
F09012 Evilbane, Elbrus :W:
F09013 Caring Siberian :W:
F09014 Guardian Heart :W:

2013 Z/X Zillions of Enemy X Free Set 5 Maiden of Crusade and Great Tree of Paradise

F10001 Pluie the Rain :W:
F10002 Evilbane, Eiger :W:
F10003 Evilbane, Kula Kangri :W:
F10004 Holy Beast, Aura Roc :W:
F10005 Korat the Painter :W:
F10006 Esprit the Wit :W:
F10007 Confront Order :W:
F10008 Sweet Honeybee, Queen Bee :G:
F10009 Fickle Marjoram :G:
F10010 Beastman Parent and Child, Were-Kangaroo :G:
F10011 Tempering Kick, Karin :G:
F10012 Bewitching Blue Dragon Sword, Mizubashou :G:
F10013 Beastman, Were-Panda :G:
F10014 Queen's Entertainment :G:
F10014 Aoba Chitose :G:
F10015 Tennoji Asuka :W:

2013 Z/X Zillions of Enemy X Free Set 6 Magical Beast of Prominance and Revenant of Darkness

F11001 Calm Silver Steel, Metal Hound :R:
F11002 Petrifying Glare, Cockatrice :R:
F11003 Apprentice Blacksmith, Kodachi :R:
F11004 Frivolous Three Musketeers, Porthos :R:
F11005 Shiver Emerald, Emerald Stag :R:
F11006 Goddess of Wisdom, Minerva :R:
F11007 Main Armament, Fire! :R:
F11008 Demon of Jewel, Lapis :K:
F11009 Hand of Conviction, Spion :K:
F11010 Wailing Girl, Banshee :K:
F11011 Licking Mimic :K:
F11012 Skeleton Captain, Hook :K:
F11013 Executor, Excuor :K:
F11014 Dead End Darts :K:
F11015 Kurashiki Sera :R:
F11016 Tennoji Yamato :K:

2013 Z/X Zillions of Enemy X Quick Start Deck Lapis Lazuli Forest

B01081 Cherry Blossom Butterfly, Full Blossom C :G:
B01087 Beastman, Were-Koala UC :G:
B01088 Easygoing Rurijissa UC :G:
B01091 Beastman, Were-Antler C :G:
B01097 Military Emperor's Sword Flash Attack UC :G:
B02023 String Performer, Sariel C :B:
B02034 Castle of Science, Bismuth R :B:
B02038 Million Rain C :B:
B02083 Homely Sage UC :G:
B02084 Petal Ant, Petal Soldier C :G:
B02095 Vivid Japanese Umbrella, Cosmos UC :G:
B02100 Feuille is Always Energetic! UC :G:
B03021 Pole Performer, Lavery C :B:
B03085 Sheep Girl, Were-Sheep UC :G:
B04026 Apprentice Voice, Vilde C :B:
B04028 Battle Hero, Markab C :B:
F05001 Erasure Machine, Erase F :B:
F09006 Invincible Haniwa, Honey-One F :B:
P02007 Steel Castle, Selenium PR :B:
P03013 Flower Dwelling Clary Sage PR :G:
Q02001 Destruction Machine, Ruin F :B:
Q02002 Flower Patterned Ladybug, Floral Bug F :G:

2013 Z/X Zillions of Enemy X Quick Start Deck Secret Stone of Black Flame

B01019 Exploding Coal U :R:
B01064 Chain of Death, Kette C :K:
B01073 Bone Shark, Skeletal Shark U :K:
B01074 Conjugated Hollow Giant, Huge Corpse R :K:
B01076 Dark Bishop, Skeletal Bishop U :K:
B01080 Moonlight Funeral Fang R :K:
B02002 Sagacious Silver, Silver Fox C :R:
B02007 Swift Tourmaline, Tourmaline Hawk U :R:
B02013 Sharp Obsidian, Obsidian Alligator U :R:
B02061 Demon of Punishment, Poena C :K:
B02068 Demon of Domination, Imperium C :K:
B02078 Fang Crush C :K:
B03003 Majestic Luvulite, Luvulite Elephant C :R:
B03007 Ferocious Tiger's Eye Gem, Tiger's Eye U :R:
B03014 Tough Carnelian, Carnelian Bear U :R:
B03063 Jack-o'-Lantern the Pumpkin Ghost C :K:
B04004 Flying Amethyst, Amethyst Swallow U :R:
F02001 Demon of Seduction, Luscious F :K:
P01009 Crimson Fang, Ruby Howl PR :R:
P03010 Squeaking Cool Beauty PR :K:
Q01001 Beautiful Quartz, Quartz Crab F :R:
Q01001 Wandering Bone, Bone Ship F :K:

2013 Z/X Zillions of Enemy X Starter Deck 2 Dual Blade of the Green Dragon

C04001 Aoba Chitose SR :G:
C04002 Will of Dual Sword, Rindou SR :G:
C04003 Castle-toppling Beauty, Chousen C :R:
C04004 Goddess of Love and Beauty, Aphrodite C :R:
C04005 Goddess of Hunting, Artemis R :R:
C04006 Divine Messenger of Sun, Yatagarasu C :R:
C04007 One-Eyed Giant, Cyclops C :R:
C04008 Two Wheels Craftsman, Twin Wheel PR :R:
C04009 Bizarre Coral, Coral Lizard U :R:
C04010 Dignified Divine Emperor, Augustus U :R:
C04011 Iron Shoe Craftsman, Greave U :R:
C04012 Main Armament, Fire! C :R:
C04013 Quiet Rosemary C :G:
C04014 Concealed Shuriken, Otogirisou R :D:
C04015 Homely Sage U :M:
C04016 Expert of Future, Tanpopo C :W:
C04017 Easygoing Rurijissa U :B:
C04018 Dignified Hairpin, Kuroyuri C :K:
C04019 Thorned Bug, Thorn Crest U :R:
C04020 Grasshopper King, King Hopper C :G:
C04021 Thorn Prison U :D:

2013 Z/X Zillions of Enemy X Starter Deck 2 Dual Blade of the Green Dragon Hologram Rare Exclusives

C04005 Goddess of Hunting, Artemis R :R:
C04017 Easygoing Rurijissa U :B:

2013 Z/X Zillions of Enemy X Starter Deck 2 Sword Princess of the Blue Star

C03001 Kagamihara Azumi SR :B:
C03002 Sword Liberator, Rigel SR :B:
C03003 Steel Castle, Astatine C :B:
C03004 City Guard, Phecda U :B:
C03005 Laser Scythe, Avior R :B:
C03006 Laser Blade, Benetnasch C :B:
C03007 Erasure Machine, Delete U :B:
C03008 Light Whip, Atria U :B:
C03009 Electronic Appliance Union, Tantalum U :B:
C03010 Performer Voice, Vival U :B:
C03011 Wait, Now Go! U :B:
C03012 Ceramic Making Singapura C :W:
C03013 Holy Beast, Aura Pegasus C :W:
C03014 Etoile the Star R :W:
C03015 Inept Detective, Russian Blue C :W:
C03016 Sagesse the Wisdom U :W:
C03017 Lawbringer, Fitz Roy C :W:
C03018 Neige the Snow PR :W:
C03019 Coucher the Sunset U :W:
C03020 Revenge Force C :W:
C03021 Chain Bind U :W:

2013 Z/X Zillions of Enemy X Starter Deck 2 Sword Princess of the Blue Star Hologram Rare Exclusives

C03011 Wait, Now Go! U :B:
C03014 Etoile the Star R :W:

2013 Z/X Zillions of Enemy X Starter Deck 3 Asuka and Ayase

C05001 Tennoji Asuka SR :W:
C05002 Kamiyugi Ayase SR :K:
C05003 Point of Ruin, Sleger SR :K:
C05003 Aurora Crown, Fierte SR :W:
C05005 Lawbringer, Distaghil C :W:
C05006 Pur the Pure C :W:
C05007 Ciel the Sky R :W:
C05008 Ame the Soul C :W:
C05009 Etoile the Star R :W:
C05010 Holy Beast, Aura Roc U :W:
C05011 Lawbringer, Yerupaja U :W:
C05012 Heroic Courage PR :W:
C05013 Holy Beast, Aura Sebek U :W:
C05014 Angel of Quest, Admiration R :W:
C05015 Punishment Cross C :W:
C05016 Chain Bind U :W:
C05017 Wandering Head Crusher C :K:
C05018 Bone Snake, Skeletal Viper PR :K:
C05019 Demon of Solitude, Solitus R :K:
C05020 Three Headed Mercenary, Drei Soldner C :K:
C05021 Enthusiastic Electric Chair C :K:
C05022 Rampaging Berserk Bike R :K:
C05023 Cavalry Assault, Kavallerist R :K:
C05024 Twenty Pair of Swords, Schwert PR :K:
C05025 Business Skeleton, Skeletal Sales U :K:
C05026 Skeleton Captain, Hook C :K:
C05027 Non-Stopping Jet Coaster U :K:
C05028 Black Union C :K:

2013 Z/X Zillions of Enemy X Starter Deck 3 Asuka and Ayase Hologram Rare Exclusive

C05022 Rampaging Berserk Bike R :K:

2013 Z/X Zillions of Enemy X Starter Deck 3 Azumi and Sera

C07001 Kagamihara Azumi SR :B:
C07002 Kurashiki Sera SR :R:
C07003 Quantum Shooter, Rigel SR :B:
C07004 Avatar of Destruction, Orichalcum Tyranno SR :R:
C07005 Ambush Machine, Raid C :B:
C07006 Steel Castle, Technetium C :B:
C07007 City Guard, Phecda C :B:
C07008 Evaporation Machine, Evaporation U :B:
C07009 Erasure Machine, Void R :B:
C07010 Laser Scythe, Avior R :B:
C07011 ?-S02 Alioth R :B:
C07012 Extreme Performer, Horatio C :B:
C07013 Transformed Gladius, Molybdenum U :B:
C07014 Steel Castle, Promethium PR :B:
C07015 Rapid Performer, Fitznell U :B:
C07016 Million Rain C :B:
C07017 Sagacious Silver, Silver Fox C :R:
C07018 Shining Gold, Gold Peacock R :R:
C07019 Goddess of Hunting, Artemis R :R:
C07020 Forging Blacksmith, Forge C :R:
C07021 Flying Amethyst, Amethyst Swallow U :R:
C07022 Armor Blacksmith, Reinforce C :R:
C07023 Bewitching Gorgon, Lamia R :R:
C07024 Tender Glass, Glass Elephant U :R:
C07025 Ferocious Black Stone, Jet Lion PR :R:
C07026 Unparalleled Diamond, Diamond Giganoto U :R:
C07027 Indomitable Steel, Steel Leopard U :R:
C07028 Tokyo Recapture Operation U :R:

2013 Z/X Zillions of Enemy X Starter Deck 3 Azumi and Sera Hologram Rare Exclusive

C07023 Bewitching Gorgon, Lamia R :R:

2013 Z/X Zillions of Enemy X Starter Deck 3 Mikado and Chitose

C06001 Kurosaki Mikado SR :R:
C06002 Aoba Chitose SR :G:
C06003 Brilliant War Hero, Alexander SR :R:
C06004 Green Samurai, Rindou SR :G:
C06005 Sword Craftsman, Ittou C :R:
C06006 Goddess of Love and Beauty, Aphrodite C :R:
C06007 Crimson Fang, Ruby Howl PR :R:
C06008 Goddess of Fortune, Lakshmi C :R:
C06009 Goddess of Hunting, Artemis R :R:
C06010 Iron Pyrite, Pyrite Tortoise U :R:
C06011 Battle Axe Workshop, Bardiche C :R:
C06012 Crimson Spinning Arm, Salamander PR :R:
C06013 Cheerful Sun God, Apollon Agana Belea R :R:
C06014 Valiant Mithril, Mithril Lion U :R:
C06015 Giant Beast of Riot, Behemoth U :R:
C06016 Main Armament, Fire! C :R:
C06017 Laundry Beastman, Were-Racoon C :G:
C06018 Walking Stevia C :G:
C06019 Concealed Shuriken, Otogirisou R :G:
C06020 Plain Octagonal Pole, Natsume C :G:
C06021 Merry Dandelion R :G:
C06022 Beastman, Were-Koala U :G:
C06023 Easygoing Rurijissa U :G:
C06024 Ninja Birdman, Were-Eagle PR :G:
C06025 Malicious Iron Whip, Kaede C :G:
C06026 Bamboo Shoot Beetle, Bamboo Horn U :G:
C06027 Giant Beast, Were-Rhino R :G:
C06028 Feuille is Always Energetic! U :G:

2013 Z/X Zillions of Enemy X Starter Deck 3 Mikado and Chitose Hologram Rare Exclusive

C06021 Merry Dandelion R :G:

2013 Z/X Zillions of Enemy X Victory Song of the Overlord

B05001 Goddess of Fate, Verdandi U :R:
B05002 Moving Sculpture, Gargoyle R :R:
B05003 Queen of Warrior, Zenobia R :R:
B05004 Gloves Craftsman, Gauntlet R :R:
B05005 Beautiful Opal, Opal Fox C :R:
B05006 Stubborn Iron, Iron Rhino C :R:
B05007 Great Man of Three Kingdoms, Ryuubi Gentoku U :R:
B05008 Sword Blacksmith, Gladius C :R:
B05009 Moment of Rest, Mori Ranmaru R :R:
B05010 Unparalleled Diamond, Diamond Giganoto U :R:
B05011 Valiant Mithril, Mithril Lion U :R:
B05012 Sly Topaz, Topaz Falcon R :R:
B05013 Excavation Craftsman, Mattock C :R:
B05014 Giant Beast of Riot, Behemoth U :R:
B05015 Covetous Evil Bird, Harpuia SR :R:
B05016 Devil King of the Sixth Realm, Oda Nobunaga SR :R:
B05017 Shard Burst U :R:
B05018 Tank Touring C :R:
B05019 Lightning Thrust C :R:
B05020 Crimson Roar R :R:
B05021 Plague Machine, Pox U :B:
B05022 Lovely Weibel R :B:
B05023 First-Aid Union, Curium C :B:
B05024 Plasma Saw, Hadar C :B:
B05025 Academic Institution Union, Nobelium U :B:
B05026 Crushing Machine, Crush U :B:
B05027 Gigantic Art, Francium R :B:
B05028 Sonic Gunner, Sirius C :B:
B05029 Battle Hero, Gruid R :B:
B05030 Invulnerable Man, Technetium R :B:
B05031 Calamity Machine, Calamity C :B:
B05032 Rapid Performer, Fitznell U :B:
B05033 Wings of Blue Sky, Xenon R :B:
B05034 Megaton Fist, Mizar U :B:
B05035 Divine Voice, Menote SR :B:
B05036 Blue Guardian, Phecda SR :B:
B05037 Jam Session U :B:
B05038 Defeat of Justice C :B:
B05039 Overbearing Bit C :B:
B05040 The Cat Returns R :B:
B05041 King of the Underworld, Curl R :W:
B05042 Evilbane, Eiger R :W:
B05043 Evilbane, Manaslu C :W:
B05044 Holy Beast, Aura Heget R :W:
B05045 Pluie the Rain C :W:
B05046 Evilbane, Kula Kangri C :W:
B05047 Holy Beast, Aura Roc U :W:
B05048 Evilbane, Shivling C :W:
B05049 Korat the Painter C :W:
B05050 Vent the Wind R :W:
B05051 Esprit the Wit U :W:
B05052 Holy Beast, Aura Hippogriff C :W:
B05053 Evilbane, Weisshorn U :W:
B05054 Soul Binding Angel, Lien SR :W:
B05055 Imperial Guard Captain, Somali SR :W:
B05056 Angel of Quest, Admiration R :W:
B05057 Confront Order R :W:
B05058 The First Maiden War U :W:
B05059 Punishment Cross C :W:
B05060 Hey, Wait! U :W:
B05061 Demon of Memory, Memoria U :K:
B05062 Prickling Cute U :K:
B05063 Demon of Delicacy, Epulum R :K:
B05064 Bone Elephant C :K:
B05065 Wandering Solitus R :K:
B05066 Fang of Fresh Blood, Soldat R :K:
B05067 Business Skeleton, Skeletal Sales U :K:
B05068 Demon of Fear, Metus U :K:
B05069 Passionate Cauldron C :K:
B05070 Vessel of Gluttony, Gezant C :K:
B05071 Fighting Strong Wrestler R :K:
B05072 Non-Stopping Jet Coaster U :K:
B05073 Demon of Box, Feles R :K:
B05074 Revenant, Ebony Clown U :K:
B05075 Black Knight of Nothingness, Cursed Soul SR :K:
B05076 Demonic Wolf Champion, Hoelscher SR :K:
B05077 Deathsmith Firm Exhibition C :K:
B05078 Heaven Tower C :K:
B05079 Mind Desire C :K:
B05080 Craving R :K:
B05081 Sweet Honeybee, Queen Bee U :G:
B05082 Fickle Marjoram C :G:
B05083 Beastman Parent and Child, Were-Kangaroo R :G:
B05084 Tempering Kick, Karin U :G:
B05085 Bewitching Blue Dragon Sword, Mizubashou R :G:
B05086 Beastman, Were-Ferret R :G:
B05087 Bashful Wijnruit C :G:
B05088 Dog Girl, Were-Poodle R :G:
B05089 Sleep Scale, Sleep Papillon U :G:
B05090 Invisible Iron-Cutting Sword, Kikyou C :G:
B05091 Malicious Iron Whip, Kaede C :G:
B05092 Beastman, Were-Panda C :G:
B05093 Preaching Anise U :G:
B05094 Bamboo Shoot Beetle, Bamboo Horn U :G:
B05095 Verdant Beauty, Ayame SR :G:
B05096 Golden Leader, Were-Tiger SR :G:
B05097 Joint Training C :G:
B05098 Delicious Present R :G:
B05099 Mask Abuser Gathering R :G:
B05100 Queen's Entertainment U :G:
B05101 Four Archangels - Michael S.K. Z/XR :W:
B05102 Seven Deadly Sins - Demon of Envy, Invidia Z/XR :K:
B05103 Unwavering Resolve, Were-Antler Z/XR :G:
B05104 Kurashiki Sera IGR :R:
B05105 Kagamihara Azumi IGR :B:
B05106 Yuzuriha Misaki IGR :W:
B05107 Kamiyugi Ayase IGR :K:
B05108 Aoba Chitose IGR :G:
B05109 Tennoji Asuka CVR :W:
B05110 Yuzuriha Misaki CVR :W:
B05111 Queen of Land of the Rising Sun, Himiko SR :R:
B05112 Respected Divine General, Hannibal Barca R :R:
B05113 Laser Scythe, Avior R :B:
B05114 Administrator Denebola R :B:
B05115 Ciel the Sky R :W:
B05116 Priere the Prayer R :W:
B05117 Demon of Cruelty, Saevum R :K:
B05118 Demon of Savagery, Barbarus R :K:
B05119 Bow of Temperance, Satsuki R :G:
B05120 Vajra of Nobility, Mokuren R :G:

2014 Z/X Zillions of Enemy X Fated Rivalry

B07001 Divine Shield Craftsman, Aigis R :R:
B07002 One Horned Rabbit, Almiraj R :R:
B07003 Timid Platinum, Platina Hamster R :R:
B07004 Talented Beauty, Kou Getsuei U :R:
B07005 Transforming Crystal, Prism Chameleon U :R:
B07006 Iron Pyrite, Pyrite Tortoise U :R:
B07007 Temple Bake-danuki, Bunbuku Chagama C :R:
B07008 Daughter of Thunder God, Tachibana Ginchiyo R :R:
B07009 Magical Beast of the Country of Mirror, Jabberwocky R :R:
B07010 Noble-minded Three Musketeers, Athos C :R:
B07011 Short Tempered Sulfur, Sulfur Boar U :R:
B07012 Roaming God, Zeus C :R:
B07013 Vagrant Swordsmith, Nagamitsu R :R:
B07014 Great Crimson Horn, Ruby Tricera C :R:
B07015 Clothing Craftsman, Lacquery SR :R:
B07016 Goddess of Justice, Astraea SR :R:
B07017 Oath of the Peach Garden U :R:
B07018 Nine-Tails' Fire Dance C :R:
B07019 Feathers Dyed Crimson C :R:
B07020 The Three Musketeers' Hatsumode U :R:
B07021 Play Stream, Float R :B:
B07022 Mobile Passenger Boat, Gallium U :B:
B07023 Conquest Machine, Conqueror R :B:
B07024 Armed Dogu, D-GU C :B:
B07025 Mirage Dagger, Bellatrix R :B:
B07026 Valiant Collider, Castor C :B:
B07027 Sharp Slicer, Enif R :B:
B07028 String Princess of Ancient Moon, Lucia R :B:
B07029 Storm Machine, Cyclone U :B:
B07030 Atomic Pile, Wezen C :B:
B07031 Battery Machine, Battery R :B:
B07032 Transformed Gladius, Molybdenum U :B:
B07033 Bell Sound, Sciarrino C :B:
B07034 Original XIII Type.IX "Rt23Ar" SR :B:
B07035 Heavy Machinery Union, Bohrium C :B:
B07036 Blue Star Regalia, Lawrencium SR :B:
B07037 Clash of the Blue and Red U :B:
B07038 Secret Plan U :B:
B07039 Heartless Eliminate U :B:
B07040 Versus Chaser C :B:
B07041 Parfum the Fragrance R :W:
B07042 Evilbane, Shankar U :W:
B07043 Scoop Chasing Munchkin R :W:
B07044 Holy Beast, Aura Frost R :W:
B07045 Bengal the Sculptor U :W:
B07046 Scintillement the Spark C :W:
B07047 Livre the Book C :W:
B07048 Lawbringer, Yerupaja U :W:
B07049 Lawbringer, Chamlang C :W:
B07050 Evilbane, McKinley U :W:
B07051 Victoire the Victory C :W:
B07052 Rebel of Faith, Sir Garmatha SR :W:
B07053 Sage of Blazing Light, Fausseflamme SR :W:
B07054 Curl's Number 2 Henchman, Bombay U :W:
B07055 Zephyr the Breeze R :W:
B07056 Holy Beast, Aura Kraken R :W:
B07057 Cats Running Around in Yard C :W:
B07058 Atonement Lamb R :W:
B07059 Refugee from Parallel World C :W:
B07060 Separated Pair U :W:
B07061 Slashing Cookie U :K:
B07062 Puppeteer Girl, Puella U :K:
B07063 Loitering Corpse, Jiangshi U :K:
B07064 Calamity Headpiece, Lanze R :K:
B07065 Transient Jaw, Bajonett C :K:
B07066 Demon of Ark, Arcae U :K:
B07067 Chopping Vorpal Scythe C :K:
B07068 Black Moon of Abyss, Almathar SR :K:
B07069 Captive Hollow Giant, Huge Gigas R :K:
B07070 Skeleton Samurai, Skeletal Bushido R :K:
B07071 Aloof Wendy R :K:
B07072 Demon of Dark Night, Nox C :K:
B07073 Demon of Darkness, Niger R :K:
B07074 Wings of Stars, Crepus SR :K:
B07075 Ferryman of Hades, Charon C :K:
B07076 Seeker of Abyss, Lich U :K:
B07077 Negative Wave C :K:
B07078 Bay Bridge's Desperate Struggle R :K:
B07079 Sera Loves Castella C :K:
B07080 First Three Days of the New Year U :K:
B07081 Fruit Loving Heartsease R :G:
B07082 Overseer Elder C :G:
B07083 Bird Girl, Were-Parrot R :G:
B07084 Violent Bullet, Kunugi R :G:
B07085 Lacework Sorrel U :G:
B07086 Beastman, Were-Armadillo U :G:
B07087 Beautiful Folding Fan, Renge C :G:
B07088 Grape Bagworm, Grape Cocoon C :G:
B07089 Beastman, Were-Shepherd R :G:
B07090 Eight Great Dragon Kings, Sagara SR :G:
B07091 Fantasy Butterfly, Swallowtail R :G:
B07092 Eight Way Meteor of Lunar Mansion, Kimikagesou U :G:
B07093 Green Hunter, Feuille SR :G:
B07094 Beastman, Were-Monkey C :G:
B07095 Faithful Dual Sword, Enoki R :G:
B07096 Lily Sickle, Lyrical Sickle U :G:
B07097 Seal of Sky Abyss U :G:
B07098 !! (Bakon!) U :G:
B07099 Midnight Escape Drama C :G:
B07100 Sagara's Request C :G:
B07101 Ambitious Skilled General, Kuroda Kanbei Z/XR :R:
B07102 Twelve Apostles - Gemini Ambriel Z/XR :W:
B07103 Illusion in the Deep Green, Benihime Z/XR :G:
B07104 Sento Reia IGR :B:
B07105 Yuzuriha Misaki IGR :W:
B07106 Tennoji Yamato IGR :K:
B07107 Kenbuchi Soma IGR :G:
B07108 Kamiyugi Sakura IGR :W:
B07109 Kamiyugi Yachiyo IGR :K:
B07110 Kagamihara Azumi CVR :B:
B07111 Sento Reia CVR :B:

2014 Z/X Zillions of Enemy X Free Set 7 Oath of Blue Waters and Gorgeous Flower Dance

F12001 Conquest Machine, Conqueror :B:
F12002 Armed Dogu, D-GU :B:
F12003 Mirage Dagger, Bellatrix :B:
F12004 Valiant Collider, Castor :B:
F12005 Bell Sound, Sciarrino :B:
F12006 Heavy Machinery Union, Bohrium :B:
F12007 Secret Plan :B:
F12008 Fruit Loving Heartsease :G:
F12009 Bird Girl, Were-Parrot :G:
F12010 Tyrant Bullet, Kunugi :G:
F12011 Beautiful Folding Fan, Renge :G:
F12012 Beastman, Were-Monkey :G:
F12013 Lily Sickle, Lyrical Sickle :G:
F12014 Seal of Sky Abyss :G:
F12015 Kagamihara Azumi :B:
F12016 Kenbuchi Soma :G:

2014 Z/X Zillions of Enemy X Free Set 8 War God's Embrace and Celestial Light Hammer

F13001 Mischievous Fairy, Pixie :R:
F13002 Goddess of Battle, Morrigan :R:
F13003 Hyacinth Ore, Zircon Horse :R:
F13004 Explosive Workshop, Grenade :R:
F13005 Incandescent Reef, Magma Ankylo :R:
F13006 Hero of Imperial Capital, Musashibou Benkei :R:
F13007 Lovely Hug :R:
F13008 Aiding Ringtail :W:
F13009 Lawbringer, Chhish :W:
F13010 World Chronicler, Registre :W:
F13011 Jewel Beast, Aura Carbuncle :W:
F13012 Evilbane, Kommunizm :W:
F13013 Marteau the Light Hammer :W:
F13014 Grace Perfume :W:
F13015 Kurosaki Mikado :R:
F13016 Tennoji Asuka :W:

2014 Z/X Zillions of Enemy X Quickening of the Divine Progenitor

B08001 Mischievous Fairy, Pixie R :R:
B08002 Flawless Three Musketeers, Aramis U :R:
B08003 Goddess of Battle, Morrigan R :R:
B08004 Silent Bronze, Bronze Lobster U :R:
B08005 Explosive Workshop, Grenade U :R:
B08006 Steam Mechanical Hand, Steam Hands C :R:
B08007 Phantom Floating Island, Aspidochelone R :R:
B08008 Airfight Workshop, Zero R :R:
B08009 Incandescent Reef, Magma Ankylo C :R:
B08010 Rend Bloodstone, Blood Raven C :R:
B08011 Nine Great Heroes, Arthur SR :R:
B08012 Hero of Imperial Capital, Musashibou Benkei U :R:
B08013 Astrologer, Nostradamus R :R:
B08014 Great Sage Equal of Heaven, Son Goku U :R:
B08015 Hyacinth Ore, Zircon Horse R :R:
B08016 Dawn of Ten Heavens, Tahrir Hajes SR :R:
B08017 Double Crime U :R:
B08018 Emperor Dragon VS Radiant Dragon C :R:
B08019 Treasure Discovery Meow! C :R:
B08020 Lovely Hug C :R:
B08021 Slash Claw, Durbe U :B:
B08022 Pollution Machine, Infect U :B:
B08023 Shooting Star, Alhena U :B:
B08024 Leisure Performer, Curti R :B:
B08025 Transformed Burst Runner, Palladium C :B:
B08026 Pierce Machine, Penetrate R :B:
B08027 Mobile Police, Argon C :B:
B08028 Echo Drum, Vella R :B:
B08029 Transformed Government Office, Iridium R :B:
B08030 Assault Shooter, Procyon R :B:
B08031 Original XIII Type.II "Sd03Ve" SR :B:
B08032 Transformed Pyramid, Trigold R :B:
B08033 Blue Drum and Fife Player, Ludwig SR :B:
B08034 Ignition Machine, Pyro U :B:
B08035 Transportation Union, Nickel C :B:
B08036 Battle Hero, Gemma C :B:
B08037 Mirage Rule C :B:
B08038 Do or Die Defensive Battle U :B:
B08039 Justice Dekopin C :B:
B08040 Turbine Bit U :B:
B08041 Holy Beast, Aura Barong U :W:
B08042 Aiding Ringtail U :W:
B08043 Dormir the Tranquil C :W:
B08044 Lawbringer, Chhish R :W:
B08045 Evilbane, Disteghil C :W:
B08046 World Chronicler, Registre R :W:
B08047 Jewel Beast, Aura Carbuncle C :W:
B08048 Lawbringer, Rimo U :W:
B08049 Evilbane, Kommunizm C :W:
B08050 Veteran Police Inspector, Cymric R :W:
B08051 Avenir the Future R :W:
B08052 Lumiere the Radiance U :W:
B08053 Great Phantom Thief of the Century, Wire SR :W:
B08054 Holy Beast, Aura Garuda R :W:
B08055 Marteau the Light Hammer U :W:
B08056 Successor of Harmony, K-Two SR :W:
B08057 Grace Perfume C :W:
B08058 Happiness Bloom R :W:
B08059 Nemesis Zero C :W:
B08060 Somali's Military Drill U :W:
B08061 Demon of Abyss, Abysso U :K:
B08062 Spire of Steel, Rakete R :K:
B08063 Gate of Despair, Bone Gate C :K:
B08064 Jumping Sprinter R :K:
B08065 Crimson Fang Emperor, Kaiser R :K:
B08066 Noisy Poltergeist C :K:
B08067 Skeleton General, Skeletal Officer R :K:
B08068 Chopping Flying Scissors C :K:
B08069 Demon of Faith, Fides R :K:
B08070 Seven Deadly Sins - Demon of Sloth, Acedia SR :K:
B08071 Demon of Stigma, Stigma C :K:
B08072 Pierced Straw Doll C :K:
B08073 Windshear Wings, Axt U :K:
B08074 Silent Knight, Criminal Chain U :K:
B08075 Demon of Ruins, Ruina U :K:
B08076 Rustling Anko SR :K:
B08077 Fly High U :K:
B08078 Black Gale U :K:
B08079 Dolls' Meeting for Reviewing C :K:
B08080 Ayase and Yachiyo R :K:
B08081 Dotanuki of Purifying Moon, Hinagiku U :G:
B08082 Great Beetle, Dudleya Grandis R :G:
B08083 Scout Beastman, Were-Suricate U :G:
B08084 Stinger Bug, Death Needle R :G:
B08085 Heavenly Kogarasu of Parhelion, Gogyou R :G:
B08086 Pillage Beastman, Were-Hyena C :G:
B08087 Birdman Lady, Were-Flamingo C :G:
B08088 Playing in Water, Mitsuba R :G:
B08089 Distant Shigeto Bow, Yukiyanagi U :G:
B08090 Beastman, Were-Buffalo C :G:
B08091 Fishing Sanzashi C :G:
B08092 Aim to be Idol, Verbena U :G:
B08093 Beastman, Were-Husky R :G:
B08094 Beetle Queen, Hell Thorn SR :G:
B08095 Long-bladed Spear of Spring Thunder, Seri R :G:
B08096 Eight Great Dragon Kings, Nanda SR :G:
B08097 Maintenance Time C :G:
B08098 Dragon Tail C :G:
B08099 Illusion Noise U :G:
B08100 Searching for Truth U :G:
B08101 Administrator Polaris Z/XR :B:
B08102 Four Archangels - Raphael A.K. Z/XR :W:
B08103 Great Calamities, Satan Z/XR :K:
B08104 Kurosaki Mikado IGR :R:
B08105 Kagamihara Azumi IGR :B:
B08106 Tennoji Asuka IGR :W:
B08107 Kamiyugi Ayase IGR :K:
B08108 Aoba Chitose IGR :G:
B08109 Raichou Suguru IGR :B:
B08110 Kurosaki Mikado CVR :R:
B08111 Kurashiki Sera CVR :R:

2014 Z/X Zillions of Enemy X Starter Deck 4 Advances of the Hero King

C08001 Kurosaki Mikado SR :R:
C08002 Great Hero of Blazing Sun, Alexander SR :R:
C08003 Original XIII Type.VII "Ju17Ca" SR :B:
C08004 Goddess of Fate, Verdandi U :R:
C08005 Flower of Warring States, Mori Ranmaru R :R:
C08006 Handgun Craftsman, Quick Draw R :R:
C08007 Goddess of Fortune, Lakshmi C :R:
C08008 Talented Beauty, Kou Getsuei U :R:
C08009 Swift Tourmaline, Tourmaline Hawk U :R:
C08010 Shipbuilding Engineer, Jemina R :R:
C08011 Graceful Crystal, Crystal Swan C :R:
C08012 Musketeer of Oath, D'Artagnan U :R:
C08013 Goddess of Wisdom, Minerva U :R:
C08014 Plague Machine, Pox U :B:
C08015 Evaporation Machine, Evaporation U :B:
C08016 Erasure Machine, Void R :B:
C08017 Transformed Gladius, Molybdenum U :B:
C08018 Bell Sound, Sciarrino C :B:
C08019 Rapid Performer, Fitznell U :B:
C08020 Space Station, Hassium R :B:
C08021 Transformed Locomotive, Lanthanum PR :B:
C08022 Secret Plan U :B:
C08023 The Cat Returns R :B:

2014 Z/X Zillions of Enemy X Starter Deck 4 Bewitching Magic

C09001 Tennoji Yamato SR :K:
C09002 Sword Maiden of Midnight, Crepus SR :K:
C09003 Eight Great Dragon Kings, Anavatapta SR :G:
C09004 Demon of Abyss, Abysso U :K:
C09005 Jack-o'-Lantern the Pumpkin Ghost C :K:
C09006 Demon of Vengeance, Ultio R :K:
C09007 Bone Knight, Skeletal Knight R :K:
C09008 Demon of Blade, Lamina C :K:
C09009 Chief Clerk, Skeletal Sales R :K:
C09010 Demon of Domination, Imperium C :K:
C09011 Chopping Vorpal Scythe C :K:
C09012 Non-Stopping Jet Coaster U :K:
C09013 Dark Bishop, Skeletal Bishop U :K:
C09014 Sweet Honeybee, Queen Bee U :G:
C09015 Rabbit Girl, Were-Rabbit R :G:
C09016 Rose Helmet, Wild Rose R :G:
C09017 Lacework Sorrel U :G:
C09018 Beastman, Were-Cheetah PR :G:
C09019 Graceful Birdman, Were-Kuina R :G:
C09020 Invisible Iron-Cutting Sword, Kikyou C :G:
C09021 Eight Way Meteor of Lunar Mansion, Kimikagesou U :G:
C09022 Seal of Sky Abyss U :G:
C09023 Feuille is Always Energetic! U :G:

Figurines

HOW TO USE

`What's Listed

Products listed in the Price Guide typically: 1) are produced by licensed manufacturers, 2) are widely available and 3) have market activity on single items.

What the Columns Mean

The LO and HI columns reflect current retail selling ranges. The HI column on the right generally represents the full retail selling price. The LO column on the left generally represents the lowest price one would expect to find with extensive shopping.

Grading

All cards in the Price Guide are based on NrMint to Mint condition. Damaged cards are generally sold for 25 to 75 percent of Mint value. Toy prices are based on mint condition. Toys that are loose (out of package), are generally sold for 50 percent of the listed price.

Currency

This Price Guide is intended to reflect the entire North American market. All listed prices are in U.S. dollars.

Legend

C – Common figurine

CH – Chase figurine

E – Experienced figurine

LE – Limited Edition figurine

R – Rare or rookie figurine

SR – Super rare figurine

U – Uncommon figurine

V – Veteran figurine

Attention Dealers: If you would like to be a Price Guide Contributor for this almanac, please e-mail your name and phone number to: nonsports@beckett.com

2003 Dungeons and Dragons Dragoneye

COMPLETE SET (60)
BOOSTER BOX ()
BOOSTER PACK ()
RELEASED ON DECEMBER 19, 2003

1 Cleric of Moradin U	1.00	2.00
2 Dwarven Defender R	7.50	15.00
3 Gnome Fighter C	.50	1.00
4 Gold Champion (Half-Dragon) R	7.50	15.00
5 Human Crossbowman C	.50	1.00
6 Lion Falcon Monk R	7.50	15.00
7 Purple Dragon Knight R	7.50	15.00
8 Stalwart Paladin U	1.00	2.00
9 Stonechild C	.50	1.00
10 Dwarven Werebear (Hybrid Form) U	1.00	2.00
11 Dire Lion R	7.50	15.00
12 Regdar, Human Fighter U	1.00	2.00
13 Bladesinger R	7.50	15.00
14 Brass Dragon (Young) R	10.00	20.00
15 Copper Samurai U	1.00	2.00
16 Daring Rogue U	1.00	2.00
17 Drunken Master U	1.00	2.00
18 Dwarf Barbarian C	.50	1.00
19 Elf Spearguard C	.50	1.00
20 Half-Elf Sorcerer U	1.00	2.00
21 Halfling Outrider R	7.50	15.00
22 Kerwyn, Human Rogue U	1.00	2.00
23 Medium Air Elemental U	1.00	2.00
24 Silver Sorcerer (Half-Dragon) R	12.50	25.00
25 Barbarian Mercenary C	.50	1.00
26 Dire Ape R	10.00	20.00
27 Druid of Obad-Hai U	1.00	2.00
28 Baaz Draconian C	.50	1.00
29 Blue Wyrmling U	1.00	2.00
30 Cleric of Nerull U	1.00	2.00
31 Goblin Skirmisher C	.50	1.00
32 Goblin Warrior C	.50	1.00
33 Hobgoblin Warrior C	.50	1.00
34 Kapak Draconian U	1.00	2.00
35 Kobold Skirmisher C	.50	1.00
36 Medium Water Elemental U	1.00	2.00
37 Salamander R	7.50	15.00
38 Thayan Knight R	7.50	15.00
39 Urthok the Vicious U	1.00	2.00
40 Wererat (Hybrid Form) U	1.00	2.00
41 Carrion Crawler R	7.50	15.00
42 Grimlock C	.50	1.00
43 Abyssal Maw C	.50	1.00
44 Black Dragon (Young) R	10.00	20.00
45 Bright Naga R	7.50	15.00
46 Bugbear C	.50	1.00
47 Chitine U	1.00	2.00
48 Dretch C	.50	1.00
49 Drow Warrior U	1.00	2.00
50 Drow Wizard U	1.00	2.00
51 Eye of Gruumsh R	10.00	20.00
52 Gargoyle U	1.00	2.00
53 Harpy U	1.00	2.00
54 Large Monstrous Spider R	15.00	30.00
55 Large Red Dragon Young R	15.00	30.00
56 Ogre Ravager R	12.50	25.00
57 Orc Druid R	7.50	15.00
58 Red Samurai U	1.00	2.00
59 Small White Dragon (Very Young) U	1.00	2.00
60 Troglodyte C	.50	1.00

2003 Dungeons and Dragons Harbinger

COMPLETE SET (80)
BOOSTER BOX ()
BOOSTER PACK ()
RELEASED ON SEPTEMBER 26, 2003

1 Cleric of Order U	1.00	2.00
2 Cleric of Yondalla U	1.00	2.00
3 Dwarf Axefighter C	.50	1.00
4 Ember, Human Monk U	1.00	2.00
5 Evoker's Apprentice U	1.00	2.00
6 Halfling Veteran U	1.00	2.00
7 Hound Archon R	15.00	30.00
8 Human Commoner C	.50	1.00
9 Large Earth Elemental R	10.00	20.00
10 Man-at-Arms C	.50	1.00
11 Sun Soul Initiate U	1.00	2.00
12 Sword of Heironeous R	15.00	30.00
13 Tordek, Dwarf Fighter U	1.00	2.00
14 Jozan, Cleric of Pelor U	1.00	2.00
15 Arcane Archer R	10.00	20.00
16 Axe Sister U	1.00	2.00
17 Centaur R	10.00	20.00
18 Cleric of Corellon Larethian R	15.00	30.00
19 Crested Felldrake C	.50	1.00
20 Devis, Half-Elf Bard U	1.00	2.00
21 Elf Archer C	.50	1.00
22 Elf Pyromancer R	15.00	30.00
23 Elf Ranger U	1.00	2.00
24 Gnome Recruit C	.50	1.00
25 Human Wanderer U	1.00	2.00
26 Krusk, Half-Orc Barbarian U	1.00	2.00
27 Lidda, Halfling Rogue U	1.00	2.00
28 Nebin, Gnome Illusionist U	1.00	2.00
29 Vadania, Half-Elf Druid R	15.00	30.00
30 Wild Elf Barbarian U	1.00	2.00
31 Wood Elf Skirmisher U	1.00	2.00
32 Azer Raider U	1.00	2.00
33 Half-Orc Monk U	1.00	2.00
34 Dire Boar R	15.00	30.00
35 Lizardfolk U	1.00	2.00
36 Shambling Mound R	15.00	30.00
37 Wolf C	.50	1.00
38 Thri-Kreen Ranger R	10.00	20.00
39 Barghest R	10.00	20.00
40 Bearded Devil R	25.00	40.00
41 Displacer Beast R	15.00	30.00
42 Goblin Sneak C	.50	1.00
43 Half-Orc Fighter C	.50	1.00
44 Hell Hound C	.50	1.00
45 Human Blackguard R	15.00	30.00
46 Human Executioner U	1.00	2.00
47 Human Thug U	1.00	2.00
48 Kobold Warrior C	.50	1.00
49 Medusa R	10.00	20.00
50 Mind Flayer R	15.00	30.00
51 Mummy R	10.00	20.00
52 Wight U	1.00	2.00
53 Wraith R	15.00	30.00
54 Owlbear R	15.00	30.00
55 Skeleton C	.50	1.00
56 Troglodyte Zombie U	1.00	2.00
57 Wolf Skeleton C	.50	1.00
58 Zombie C	.50	1.00
59 Cleric of Gruumsh R	15.00	30.00
60 Drow Archer U	1.00	2.00
61 Drow Cleric of Lolth R	25.00	40.00
62 Drow Fighter U	1.00	2.00
63 Ghoul C	.50	1.00
64 Gnoll U	1.00	2.00
65 Half-Orc Assassin U	1.00	2.00
66 Human Bandit C	.50	1.00
67 Hyena C	.50	1.00
68 Kuo-Toa C	.50	1.00
69 Large Fire Elemental R	15.00	30.00
70 Minotaur R	15.00	30.00
71 Ogre R	15.00	30.00
72 Orc Archer U	1.00	2.00
73 Orc Berserker U	1.00	2.00
74 Orc Spearfighter C	.50	1.00
75 Orc Warrior C	.50	1.00
76 Tiefling Captain U	1.00	2.00
77 Troll R	15.00	30.00
78 Umber Hulk R	15.00	30.00
79 Werewolf U	1.00	2.00
80 Worg U	1.00	2.00

2004 Dungeons and Dragons Aberrations

1 Alusair Obarskyr R	7.50	15.00
2 Anvil of Thunder U	1.00	2.00
3 Celestial Black Bear C	.50	1.00
4 Cleric of St. Cuthbert U	1.00	2.00
5 Dragon Samurai R	7.50	15.00
6 Exorcist of the Silver Flame R	7.50	15.00
7 Hill Dwarf Warrior C	.50	1.00
8 Man-at-Arms C	.50	1.00
9 Rhek U	1.00	2.00
10 Warforged Hero R	7.50	15.00
11 Aasimar Favored Soul U	1.00	2.00
12 Adventuring Wizard R	7.50	15.00
13 Bariaur Ranger U	1.00	2.00
14 Cleric of Garl Glittergold U	1.00	2.00
15 Crow Shaman R	10.00	20.00
16 Elf Warrior C	.50	1.00
17 Frenzied Berserker R	7.50	15.00
18 Half-Elf Bow Initiate R	7.50	15.00
19 Longtooth Barbarian U	1.00	2.00
20 Sharn Cutthroat (Changeling) U	1.00	2.00
21 Valenar Commander R	7.50	15.00
22 Formian Warrior U	1.00	2.00
23 Ethereal Filcher U	1.00	2.00
24 Ryld Argith (Drow) R	10.00	20.00
25 Wyvern R	7.50	15.00
26 Achaierai R	7.50	15.00
27 Bladebearer Hobgoblin U	1.00	2.00
28 Dekanter Goblin C	.50	1.00
29 Destrachan U	1.00	2.00
30 Emerald Claw Soldier C	.50	1.00
31 Fiendish Dire Weasel C	.50	1.00
32 Green Dragon (very young) R	10.00	20.00
33 Half-Elf Hexblade U	1.00	2.00
34 Half-Illithid Lizardfolk U	1.00	2.00
35 Hook Horror R	7.50	15.00
36 Iron Cobra U	1.00	2.00
37 Kobold Champion C	.50	1.00
38 Kobold Sorcerer U	1.00	2.00
39 Mind Flayer Telepath R	10.00	20.00
40 Mongrelfolk C	.50	1.00
41 Myconid Guard C	.50	1.00
42 Sahuagin Ranger U	1.00	2.00
43 Silent Wolf Goblin C	.50	1.00
44 Skullsplitter R	6.00	12.00
45 Flesh Golem R	7.50	15.00
46 Carrion Tribe Barbarian C	.50	1.00
47 Choker U	1.00	2.00
48 Chuul R	7.50	15.00
49 Fiendish Giant Praying Mantis R	7.50	15.00
50 Gibbering Mouther R	7.50	15.00
51 Gnoll C	.50	1.00
52 Gnoll Skeleton C	.50	1.00
53 Ice Troll R	7.50	15.00
54 Mad Slasher U	1.00	2.00
55 Mountain Orc C	.50	1.00
56 Ogre Zombie R	7.50	15.00
57 Orc Sergeant U	1.00	2.00
58 Taer C	.50	1.00
59 Yuan-Ti Abomination R	7.50	15.00
60 Yuan-Ti Halfblood U	1.00	2.00

2004 Dungeons and Dragons Archfiends

COMPLETE SET (60)
BOOSTER BOX ()
BOOSTER PACK ()
RELEASED ON MARCH 25, 2004

1 Cleric of Lathander U	1.00	2.00
2 Dalelands Militia C	.50	1.00
3 Gold Dwarf Fighter U	1.00	2.00
4 Human Dragonslayer U	1.00	2.00
5 Large Silver Dragon R	25.00	40.00
6 Medium Earth Elemental U	1.00	2.00
7 Paladin of Torm R	10.00	20.00
8 Soldier of Cormyr C	.50	1.00
9 Healer U	1.00	2.00
10 Mialee, Elf Wizard U	1.00	2.00
11 Catfolk C	.50	1.00
12 Champion of Eilistraee R	15.00	30.00
13 Cleric of Kord U	1.00	2.00
14 Drizzt, Drow Ranger R	30.00	50.00
15 Evermeet Wizard U	1.00	2.00
16 Graycloak Ranger C	.50	1.00
17 Halfling Ranger U	1.00	2.00
18 Halfling Wizard U	1.00	2.00
19 Ialdabode, Human Psion U	1.00	2.00
20 Moon Elf Fighter U	1.00	2.00
21 Ragnara, Psychic Warrior U	1.00	2.00
22 Unicorn R	12.50	25.00
23 Githzerai C	.50	1.00
24 Sage C	.50	1.00
25 Clay Golem R	12.50	25.00
26 Half-Orc Barbarian U	1.00	2.00
27 Wereboar U	1.00	2.00
28 Aspect of Bane R	10.00	20.00
29 Bone Devil R	10.00	20.00

30 Dark Moon Monk U 1.00 2.00
31 Dread Guard C .50 1.00
32 Duergar Warrior C .50 1.00
33 Erinyes R 10.00 20.00
34 Gauth R 12.50 25.00
35 Human Cleric of Bane R 10.00 20.00
36 Nothic U 1.00 2.00
37 Red Wizard R 12.50 25.00
38 Snig the Axe C .50 1.00
39 Xill U 1.00 2.00
40 Zhentarim Fighter C .50 1.00
41 Gravehound C .50 1.00
42 Ochre Jelly R 12.50 25.00
43 Warrior Skeleton C .50 1.00
44 Abyssal Eviscerator U 1.00 2.00
45 Aspect of Demogorgon R 12.50 25.00
46 Aspect of Lolth R 15.00 30.00
47 Aspect of Orcus R 12.50 25.00
48 Cultist of the Dragon C .50 1.00
49 Cursed Spirit C .50 1.00
50 Drow Sergeant U 1.00 2.00
51 Githyanki Fighter U 1.00 2.00
52 Gnoll Archer C .50 1.00
53 Hill Giant R 12.50 25.00
54 Medium Fire Elemental U 1.00 2.00
55 Orc Champion R 12.50 25.00
56 Orc Raider C .50 1.00
57 Vampire Aristocrat R 12.50 25.00
58 Vrock R 12.50 25.00
59 Young Minotaur U 1.00 2.00
60 Yuan-Ti Pureblood U 1.00 2.00

2004 Dungeons and Dragons Giants of Legend

COMPLETE SET (72)
BOOSTER BOX ()
BOOSTER PACK ()
RELEASED ON JUNE 18, 2004
1 Bronze Wyrmling U 1.00 2.00
2 Dwarf Sergeant U 1.00 2.00
3 Standardbearer U 1.00 2.00
4 Stone Golem R 10.00 20.00
5 Sword of Glory U 1.00 2.00
6 Warforged Fighter U 1.00 2.00
7 Warmage U 1.00 2.00
8 Young Master R 7.50 15.00
9 Aramil, Adventurer U 1.00 2.00
10 Eberk, Adventurer U 1.00 2.00
11 Protectar U 1.00 2.00
12 Regdar, Adventurer U 1.00 2.00
13 Basilisk U 1.00 2.00
14 Deepshadow Elf C .50 1.00
15 Fire Genasi Dervish R 7.50 15.00
16 Githyanki Renegade R 7.50 15.00
17 Half-Giant Psychic Warrior R 7.50 15.00
18 Inspiring Marshal R 7.50 15.00
19 Lidda, Adventurer U 1.00 2.00
20 Medium Astral Construct C .50 1.00
21 War Chanter R 7.50 15.00
22 Xeph Soulknife U 1.00 2.00
23 City Guard C .50 1.00
24 Crucian U 1.00 2.00
25 Dire Wolf R 7.50 15.00
26 Mordenkainen the Mage R 12.50 25.00
27 Otyugh R 7.50 15.00
28 Bladeling Fighter C .50 1.00
29 Blue C .50 1.00
30 Dire Rat C .50 1.00
31 Fire Giant R 12.50 25.00
32 Hobgoblin Sergeant C .50 1.00
33 King Snurre R 10.00 20.00
34 Lemure C .50 1.00
35 Lizardfolk Rogue C .50 1.00
36 Lord Soth R 15.00 30.00
37 Manticore R 7.50 15.00
38 Rakshasa R 10.00 20.00
39 Scarlet Brotherhood Monk U 1.00 2.00
40 Zombie C .50 1.00
41 Blue Slaad R 10.00 20.00
42 Bugbear Footpad C .50 1.00
43 Displacer Serpent C .50 1.00
44 Drider Sorcerer R 10.00 20.00
45 Drow Fighter U 1.00 2.00
46 Drow Rogue U 1.00 2.00
47 Ettercap C .50 1.00
48 Frost Giant R 12.50 25.00
49 Ghast C .50 1.00
50 Gnoll Sergeant U 1.00 2.00
51 Grick C .50 1.00
52 Lareth the Beautiful R 7.50 15.00
53 Lich Necromancer R 12.50 25.00
54 Minotaur R 10.00 20.00
55 Minotaur Skeleton R 7.50 15.00
56 Orc Brute C .50 1.00
57 Quasit U 1.00 2.00
58 Red Wyrmling R 7.50 15.00
59 Tanarukk C .50 1.00
60 Werewolf U 1.00 2.00
61 Huge Gold Dragon R .50
62 Cloud Giant U 1.00 2.00
63 Storm Giant R 12.50 25.00
64 Treant U 1.00 2.00
65 Warforged Titan R 15.00 30.00
66 Behir R 15.00 30.00
67 Bulette U 1.00 2.00
68 Fiendish Tyrannosaurus U 1.00 2.00
69 Fomorian U 1.00 2.00
70 Glabrezu R 20.00 35.00
71 Huge Red Dragon R 35.00 60.00
72 Nightwalker U 1.00 2.00

2005 Dungeons and Dragons Angelfire

COMPLETE SET (60)
BOOSTER BOX ()
BOOSTER PACK ()
RELEASED ON JULY 21, 2005
1 Caravan Guard C .50 1.00
2 Cleric of Dol Arrah U 1.00 2.00
3 Dwarf Raider C .50 1.00
4 Dwarf Wizard U 1.00 2.00
5 Justice Archon U 1.00 2.00
6 Mounted Paladin R 10.00 20.00
7 Spiker Champion U 1.00 2.00
8 Stone Giant R 7.50 15.00
9 Sword Archon R 6.00 12.00
10 Trumpet Archon R 6.00 12.00
11 Ulmo Lightbringer R 6.00 12.00
12 Village Priest U 1.00 2.00
13 Werebear U 1.00 2.00
14 Archmage R 7.50 15.00
15 Celestial Pegasus R 6.00 12.00
16 Divine Crusader of Corellon R 6.00 12.00
17 Djinni R 7.50 15.00
18 Elf Swashbuckler U 1.00 2.00
19 Ghaele Eladrin R 6.00 12.00
20 Large Air Elemental U 1.00 2.00
21 Large Copper Dragon R 10.00 20.00
22 Longstrider Ranger U 1.00 2.00
23 Phoelarch R 6.00 12.00
24 Talenta Halfling U 1.00 2.00
25 Thorn U 1.00 2.00
26 Thri-Kreen Barbarian R 7.50 15.00
27 Wand Expert U 1.00 2.00
28 Weretiger U 1.00 2.00
29 Wild Elf Raider C .50 1.00
30 Xeph Warrior C .50 1.00
31 Dwarf Mercenary C .50 1.00
32 Blackscale Lizardfolk U 1.00 2.00
33 Red Slaad R 7.50 15.00
34 Scorpion Clan Drow Fighter U 1.00 2.00
35 Barbed Devil R 6.00 12.00
36 Chain Devil R 7.50 15.00
37 Chraal U 1.00 2.00
38 Direguard C .50 1.00
39 Efreeti R 7.50 15.00
40 Flamebrother Salamander U 1.00 2.00
41 Ghostly Consort R 6.00 12.00
42 Hobgoblin Impaler C .50 1.00
43 Imp U 1.00 2.00
44 Kobold Soldier C .50 1.00
45 Mina, Dark Cleric R 7.50 15.00
46 Ogre Mage R 6.00 12.00
47 Orog Warlord R 6.00 12.00
48 Steel Predator R 6.00 12.00
49 Vargouille U 1.00 2.00
50 Skeletal Archer C .50 1.00
51 Abyssal Skulker C .50 1.00
52 Bugbear Champion of Erythnul U 1.00 2.00
53 Feral Minotaur U 1.00 2.00
54 Fiendish Dire Wolverine U 1.00 2.00
55 Hezrou R 7.50 15.00
56 Magmin U 1.00 2.00
57 Ophidian C .50 1.00
58 Orc Wolf Shaman R 6.00 12.00
59 Troll Slasher U 1.00 2.00
60 Wrackspawn C .50 1.00

2005 Dungeons and Dragons Deathknell

COMPLETE SET (60)
BOOSTER BOX ()
BOOSTER PACK ()
RELEASED ON MARCH 24, 2005
1 Champion of Yondalla R 7.50 15.00
2 Couatl R 10.00 20.00
3 Dwarf Artificer U 1.00 2.00
4 Dwarf Caver U 1.00 2.00
5 Dwarf Phalanx Soldier U 1.00 2.00
6 Dwarf Samurai R 7.50 15.00
7 Gold Dragon R 10.00 20.00
8 Skullclan Hunter U 1.00 2.00
9 Soldier of Thrane U 1.00 2.00
10 Valorous Prince R 7.50 15.00
11 Warforged Wizard U 1.00 2.00
12 Whirling Steel Monk U 1.00 2.00
13 Celestial Dire Badger C .50 1.00
14 Catfolk Wilder U 1.00 2.00
15 Centaur Hero R 7.50 15.00
16 Dark Traveler U 1.00 2.00
17 Dragonblade Ninja U 1.00 2.00
18 Goliath Barbarian R 7.50 15.00
19 Greenfang Druid R 7.50 15.00
20 Griffon R 7.50 15.00
21 Ibixian C .50 1.00
22 Rask, Half-Orc Chainfighter R 7.50 15.00
23 Renegade Warlock U 1.00 2.00
24 Undying Soldier U 1.00 2.00
25 Voice of Battle U 1.00 2.00
26 Dire Bear U 1.00 2.00
27 Timber Wolf C .50 1.00
28 Giant Frog C .50 1.00
29 Wood Woad U 1.00 2.00
30 Ambush Drake R 7.50 15.00
31 Aspect of Nerull R 10.00 20.00
32 Beholder R 25.00 40.00
33 Death Knight R 7.50 15.00
34 Goblin Adept C .50 1.00
35 Grell U 1.00 2.00
36 Grim Necromancer U 1.00 2.00
37 Kruthik Hatchling C .50 1.00
38 Large Blue Dragon R 10.00 20.00
39 Mummy Lord R 7.50 15.00
40 Skeletal Dwarf C .50 1.00
41 Skullcrusher Ogre U 1.00 2.00
42 Spectre R 7.50 15.00
43 Spellstitched Hobgoblin Zombie C .50 1.00
44 Thaskor R 7.50 15.00
45 Warpriest of Hextor R 7.50 15.00
46 Bloodhulk Fighter U 1.00 2.00
47 Boneclaw R 7.50 15.00
48 Bullywug Thug C .50 1.00
49 Burning Skeleton U 1.00 2.00
50 Deathlock C .50 1.00
51 Dolgrim U 1.00 2.00
52 Eltin Skirmisher R 7.50 15.00
53 Fiendish Monstrous Scorpion R 7.50 15.00
54 Flind Captain U 1.00 2.00
55 Forest Troll U 1.00 2.00
56 Kenku Sneak C .50 1.00
57 Orc Savage C .50 1.00
58 Ravenous Vampire R 7.50 15.00
59 Vampire Spawn U 1.00 2.00
60 Zombie White Dragon R 12.50 25.00

2005 Dungeons and Dragons Underdark

COMPLETE SET (69)
BOOSTER BOX ()
BOOSTER PACK ()
RELEASED ON NOVEMBER 3, 2005
1 Battle Plate Marshal R 6.00 12.00
2 Dwarf Ancestor R 6.00 12.00
3 Earth Shugenja U 1.00 2.00
4 Githzerai Monk U 1.00 2.00
5 Gold Dwarf Soldier C .50 1.00
6 Half-Orc Paladin U 1.00 2.00
7 Lantern Bearer U 1.00 2.00
8 Loyal Earth Elemental U 1.00 2.00
9 Epic Marut R 7.50 15.00
9 Marut R 6.00 12.00
10 Medium Silver Dragon R 12.50 25.00
11 Royal Guard C .50 1.00
12 Slayer of Domiel R 6.00 12.00
13A Aspect of Kord R 6.00 12.00
13B Epic Aspect of Kord R 6.00 12.00
14 Dromite Wilder R 6.00 12.00
15 Elf Stalker U 1.00 2.00
16A Elminster of Shadowdale R 12.50 25.00
16B Epic Elminster of Shadowdale R 6.00 12.00
17 Guenhwyvar U 1.00 2.00
18 Half-Ogre Barbarian U 1.00 2.00
19 Halfling Sneak C .50 1.00
20 Nentyar Hunter U 1.00 2.00
21A Epic Rikka, Angelic Avenger R 6.00 12.00
21B Rikka, Angelic Avenger R 7.50 15.00
22 Satyr U 1.00 2.00
23 Spirit Folk Fighter C .50 1.00
24 Wizard Tactician U 1.00 2.00
25A Epic Iron Golem R 6.00 12.00
25B Iron Golem R 7.50 15.00
26A Epic Justicator R 6.00 12.00
26B Justicator R 6.00 12.00
27 Mercenary Sergeant C .50 1.00
28 Xorn U 1.00 2.00
29 Monitor Lizard C .50 1.00
30 Ankheg U 1.00 2.00
31 Xen'drik Champion R 6.00 12.00
32A Artemis Entreri R 10.00 20.00
32B Epic Artemis Entreri R 6.00 12.00
33 Dark Naga U 1.00 2.00
34 Dolgaunt Monk U 1.00 2.00
35 Duergar Champion U 1.00 2.00
36 Half-Orc Executioner U 1.00 2.00
37 Helmed Horror R 6.00 12.00
38 Kobold Miner C .50 1.00
39 Skeletal Equiceph U 1.00 2.00
40 Troglodyte Captain U 1.00 2.00
41A Balor R 15.00 30.00
41B Epic Balor R 6.00 12.00
42 Dark Creeper C .50 1.00
43A Death Slaad R 6.00 12.00
43B Epic Death Slaad R 6.00 12.00
44 Dire Bat U 1.00 2.00
45 Draegloth R 6.00 12.00
46 Drow Arachnomancer R 7.50 15.00
47 Drow Arcane Guard U 1.00 2.00
48 Gray Render R 6.00 12.00
49 Grimlock Barbarian U 1.00 2.00
50 Half-Fiend Ogre R 6.00 12.00
51 Hunched Giant R 6.00 12.00
52 Large Deep Dragon R 10.00 20.00
53 Lolth's Sting C .50 1.00
54 Mounted Drow Patrol R 7.50 15.00
55 Orc Skeleton C .50 1.00
56 Roper R 6.00 12.00
57 Spider of Lolth C .50 1.00
58 Swarm of Spiders U 1.00 2.00
59 Troglodyte Barbarian C .50 1.00
60 Winter Wolf U 1.00 2.00

2006 Dungeons and Dragons Blood War

COMPLETE SET (60)
BOOSTER BOX ()
BOOSTER PACK ()
RELEASED ON NOVEMBER 6, 2006
1 Arcadian Hippogriff R 6.00 12.00
2 Celestial Giant Stag Beetle U 1.00 2.00
3 Dwarf Sniper U 1.00 2.00
4 Elf Dragonkith R 6.00 12.00
5 Elf Warmage U 1.00 2.00
6 Half-Orc Spy U 1.00 2.00
7 Hammerer C .50 1.00
8 Harmonium Guard C .50 1.00
9 Kolyarut R 6.00 12.00
10 Solar R 7.50 15.00
11 Soldier of Bytopia C .50 1.00
12 Thundertusk Cavalry R 6.00 12.00
13 Air Genasi Swashbuckler R 6.00 12.00
14 Bralani Eladrin R 6.00 12.00
15 Centaur War Hulk R 6.00 12.00
16 Free League Ranger C .50 1.00
17 Gnome Trickster U 1.00 2.00
18 Hero of Valhalla C .50 1.00
19 Lillend R 6.00 12.00
20 Medium Copper Dragon U 1.00 2.00
21 Phoera U 1.00 2.00
22 Shadowdancer U 1.00 2.00
23 Storm Silverhand R 7.50 15.00
24 Valenar Nomad Charger R 6.00 12.00
25 Dragonmark Heir of Deneith U 1.00 2.00
26 Maug U 1.00 2.00
27 Living Flaming Sphere U 1.00 2.00
28 Acheron Goblin C .50 1.00
29 Blood of Vol Cultist C .50 1.00
30 Bluespawn Stormlizard U 1.00 2.00
31 Fire Giant Forgepriest R 7.50 15.00
32 Greenspawn Sneak C .50 1.00
33 Hellcat R 6.00 12.00
34 Horned Devil R 10.00 20.00
35 Ice Devil R 7.50 15.00
36 Karsite Fighter U 1.00 2.00
37 Kobold Monk C .50 1.00
38 Large Water Elemental U 1.00 2.00
39 Lord of Blades R 6.00 12.00
40 Mercykiller U 1.00 2.00
41 Mezzoloth U 1.00 2.00
42 Pit Fiend R 10.00 20.00
43 Red Hand War Sorcerer U 1.00 2.00
44 Soulknife Infiltrator U 1.00 2.00
45 Chasme R 6.00 12.00
46 Demonic Gnoll Priestess U 6.00 12.00
47 Doomguard C .50 1.00
48 Earth Element Gargoyle U 1.00 2.00
49 Ethereal Marauder U 1.00 2.00
50 Fiendish Snake C .50 1.00
51 Githyanki Dragon Knight R 6.00 12.00
52 Gnoll Barbarian U 1.00 2.00
53 Green Slaad U 1.00 2.00
54 Howler R 6.00 12.00
55 Marilith R 7.50 15.00
56 Orc Wizard U 1.00 2.00
57 Owlbear Rager R 6.00 12.00
58 Skeletal Reaper C .50 1.00
59 Succubus R 6.00 12.00
60 Vlaakith the Lich Queen R 7.50 15.00

2006 Dungeons and Dragons War Drums

COMPLETE SET (60)
BOOSTER BOX ()
BOOSTER PACK ()
RELEASED ON MARCH 3, 2006
1 Arcane Ballista R 6.00 12.00
2 Arcanix Guard C .50 1.00
3 Aspect of Moradin R 7.50 15.00
4 Axe Soldier C .50 1.00
5 Combat Medic U 1.00 2.00
6 Elemental Wall U 1.00 2.00
7 Large Bronze Dragon R 10.00 20.00
8 Sacred Watcher U 1.00 2.00
9 Sand Giant R 6.00 12.00
10 Shieldwall Soldier C .50 1.00
11 Warforged Bodyguard U 1.00 2.00
12 Warforged Captain U 1.00 2.00
13 Warforged Scout U 1.00 2.00
14 Warpriest of Moradin U 1.00 2.00
15 Brass Samurai U 1.00 2.00
16 Dragon Totem Hero R 6.00 12.00
17 Dragonne R 6.00 12.00
18 Halfling Slinger C .50 1.00
19 Hunting Cougar C .50 1.00
20 Lion of Talisid U 1.00 2.00
21 Mephling Pyromancer U 1.00 2.00
22 Steelheart Archer U 1.00 2.00
23 Warbound Impaler R 6.00 12.00
24 Warforged Barbarian R 6.00 12.00
25 Wemic Barbarian R 6.00 12.00
26 Wood Elf Ranger C .50 1.00
27 Gulgar R 6.00 12.00
28 Aspect of Hextor R 7.50 15.00
29 Flameskull U 1.00 2.00
30 Goblin Blackblade C .50 1.00
31 Goblin Underboss U 1.00 2.00
32 Hobgoblin Archer C .50 1.00
33 Inspired Lieutenant U 1.00 2.00
34 Karrnathi Zombie U 1.00 2.00
35 Khumat R 6.00 12.00
36 Large Duergar U 1.00 2.00
37 Night Hag R 6.00 12.00
38 Shuluth, Archvillain R 6.00 12.00
39 Skeletal Legionnaire C .50 1.00
40 Snig, Worg Rider R 6.00 12.00
41 Terror Wight C .50 1.00
42 War Troll R 7.50 15.00
43 Zakya Rakshasa R 6.00 12.00
44 Blood Ghost Berserker U 1.00 2.00
45 Chimera R 6.00 12.00
46 Derro C .50 1.00
47 Fiendish Girallon U 1.00 2.00
48 Frost Dwarf U 1.00 2.00
49 Hill Giant Barbarian U 1.00 2.00
50 Hill Giant Chieftain R 6.00 12.00
51 Horde Zombie C .50 1.00
52 Howling Orc C .50 1.00
53 King Obould Many-Arrows R 6.00 12.00
54 Ogre War Hulk R 6.00 12.00
55 Orc Mauler C .50 1.00
56 Orc Wardrummer R 6.00 12.00
57 Quaggoth Slave C .50 1.00
58 Tiefling Blademaster U 1.00 2.00
59 Troglodyte Thug C .50 1.00
60 Warduke R 7.50 15.00

2006 Dungeons and Dragons War of the Dragon Queen

COMPLETE SET (64)
BOOSTER BOX ()
BOOSTER PACK ()
RELEASED ON JULY 7, 2006
1 Aasimar Fighter C .50 1.00
2 Epic Aspect of Bahamut R 12.50 25.00
3 Cleric of Syreth U 1.00 2.00
4 Dragonborn Fighter R 5.00 10.00
5 Golden Protector R 5.00 10.00
6 Meepo, Dragonlord R 5.00 10.00
7A Epic Slaughterstone Eviscerator R 5.00 10.00
7B Slaughterstone Eviscerator R 5.00 10.00
8A Epic Tordek, Dwarf Champion R 5.00 10.00
8B Tordek, Dwarf Champion R 5.00 10.00
9 War Weaver R 5.00 10.00
10 Bonded Fire Summoner U 1.00 2.00
11 Clawfoot Rider R 5.00 10.00
12 Goliath Cleric of Kavaki R 5.00 10.00
13A Epic Griffon Cavalry R 5.00 10.00
13B Griffon Cavalry R 7.50 15.00
14 Small Copper Dragon U 1.00 2.00
15 Spellscale Sorcerer R 5.00 10.00
16 Storm Archer U 1.00 2.00
17 Tavern Brawler C .50 1.00
18 Warden of the Wood U 1.00 2.00
19 Azer Fighter C .50 1.00
20 Epic Huge Fire Elemental U 1.00 2.00
21 Epic Purple Worm U 1.00 2.00
22 War Ape C .50 1.00
23 Wizened Elder Watcher R 5.00 10.00
24 Epic Aspect of Tiamat R 15.00 30.00
25A Blackguard on Nightmare R 7.50 15.00
25B Epic Blackguard on Nightmare R 5.00 10.00
26 Epic Bluespawn Godslayer U 1.00 2.00
27 Cadaver Collector R 7.50 15.00
28 Diseased Dire Rat C .50 1.00
29 Epic Displacer Beast Pack Lord U 1.00 2.00
30 Doom Fist Monk C .50 1.00
31 Epic Dracolich R 12.50 25.00
32 Dragonwrought Kobold U 1.00 2.00
33 Dread Warrior C .50 1.00
34 Epic Eldritch Giant R 6.00 12.00
35 Greenspawn Razorfiend U 1.00 2.00
36 Hobgoblin Talon of Tiamat R 5.00 10.00
37 Kobold Zombie C .50 1.00
38 Large Green Dragon R 10.00 20.00
39 Wererat Rogue U 1.00 2.00
40 Poison Dusk Lizardfolk U 1.00 2.00
41 Witchknife C .50 1.00

Card	Low	High
42 Blackspawn Exterminator U	1.00	2.00
43 Cleric of Laogzed C	.50	1.00
44 Cloudreaver C	.50	1.00
45 Demonic Gnoll Archer U	1.00	2.00
46 Epic Huge Fiendish Spider U	1.00	2.00
47 Hunting Hyena C	.50	1.00
48 Large Fang Dragon R	7.50	15.00
49 Magma Hurler R	5.00	10.00
50 Epic Mountain Troll U	1.00	2.00
51 Ogre Skirmisher U	1.00	2.00
52 Redspawn Firebelcher R	5.00	10.00
53 Small Black Dragon U	1.00	2.00
54 Small Fire Elemental U	1.00	2.00
55 Epic Sorcerer on Black Dragon R	10.00	20.00
56 Stirge U	1.00	2.00
57 Epic Tundra Scout R	7.50	15.00
58 Twig Blight C	.50	1.00
59 Whitespawn Hordeling C	.50	1.00
60 Yuan-Ti Halfblood Sorcerer U	1.00	2.00

2007 Dungeons and Dragons Desert of Desolation

Card	Low	High
COMPLETE SET (60)		
BOOSTER BOX ()		
BOOSTER PACK ()		
RELEASED ON OCTOBER 26, 2007		
1 Angel of Vengeance R	7.50	15.00
2 Animated Statue C	.50	1.00
3 Dwarf Brawler U	1.00	2.00
4 Dwarf Maulfighter U	1.00	2.00
5 Human Cleric of Bahamut U	1.00	2.00
6 Macetail Behemoth R	7.50	15.00
7 Militia Archer C	.50	1.00
8 Sphinx R	7.50	15.00
9 Thundertusk Boar U	1.00	2.00
10 Bruenor Battlehammer R	7.50	15.00
11 Farmer C	.50	1.00
12 Merchant Guard C	.50	1.00
13 Warhorse U	1.00	2.00
14 Black Woods Dryad C	.50	1.00
15 Cliffwalk Archer U	1.00	2.00
16 Elf Conjurer R	7.50	15.00
17 Eternal Blade U	1.00	2.00
18 Halfling Enchanter U	1.00	2.00
19 Halfling Rogue U	1.00	2.00
20 Gelatinous Cube R	7.50	15.00
21 Mercenary General R	7.50	15.00
22 Visejaw Crocodile U	1.00	2.00
23 Capricious Copper Dragon R	12.50	25.00
24 Tiefling Cleric U	1.00	2.00
25 Tiefling Rogue U	1.00	2.00
26 Astral Stalker U	1.00	2.00
27 Blood of Vol Fanatic C	.50	1.00
28 Guardian Mummy U	1.00	2.00
29 Manticore Sniper R	7.50	15.00
30 Nightmare R	7.50	15.00
31 Osyluth R	7.50	15.00
32 Rot Scarab Swarm C	.50	1.00
33 Sahuagin U	1.00	2.00
34 Sahuagin Baron R	7.50	15.00
35 Shakar-Kai Assassin U	1.00	2.00
36 Shadow Mastiff U	1.00	2.00
37 Spined Devil U	1.00	2.00
38 Blade Spider R	7.50	15.00
39 Boneshard Skeleton C	.50	1.00
40 Cyclops R	7.50	15.00
41 Demonweb Swarm C	.50	1.00
42 Flame Snake C	.50	1.00
43 Naga R	7.50	15.00
44 Bar-Lgura R	7.50	15.00
45 Drider R	10.00	20.00
46 Drow Blademaster C	.50	1.00
47 Drow Spider Priestess U	1.00	2.00
48 Ettercap Webspinner U	1.00	2.00
49 Feral Troll R	7.50	15.00
50 Fire Archon R	7.50	15.00
51 Large Fire Elemental U	1.00	2.00
52 Ogre Brute R	7.50	15.00
53 Rage Drake R	7.50	15.00
54 Ravenous Ghoul U	1.00	2.00
55 Shrieking Harpy U	1.00	2.00
56 Snaketongue Cultist C	.50	1.00
57 Umber Hulk Delver R	10.00	20.00
58 Werewolf Champion R	7.50	15.00
59 Yuan-Ti Champion of Zehir R	7.50	15.00
60 Yuan-Ti Malison U	1.00	2.00

2007 Dungeons and Dragons Night Below

Card	Low	High
COMPLETE SET (62)		
BOOSTER BOX ()		
BOOSTER PACK ()		
RELEASED ON JULY 6, 2007		
1 Arcadian Avenger U	1.00	2.00
2 Brass Golem U	1.00	2.00
3 Champion of Dol Dorn U	1.00	2.00
4 Deep Legionnaire C	.50	1.00
5 Delver Sergeant C	.50	1.00
6 Earth Mephit U	1.00	2.00
7 Guard of Mithral Hall C	.50	1.00
8 Guardian Naga R	7.50	15.00
9 Kalashtar Bodyguard U	1.00	2.00
10A Epic Large Gold Dragon R	7.50	15.00
10B Large Gold Dragon R	10.00	20.00
11 Shadowbane Inquisitor U	1.00	2.00
12 Valiant Cavalry R	7.50	15.00
13 Greyhawk City Militia Sergeant C	.50	1.00
14 Raistlin Majere R	12.50	25.00
15 Darkmantle C	.50	1.00
16 Digester U	1.00	2.00
17 Dire Tiger R	7.50	15.00
18 Giant Eagle U	1.00	2.00
19 Greater Basilisk R	7.50	15.00
20 Halfling Tombseeker U	1.00	2.00
21 Hierophant of the Seventh Wind R	7.50	15.00
22 Verdant of the Reaver U	1.00	2.00
23 Warpriest of Vandria U	1.00	2.00
24 Wild Mage U	1.00	2.00
25 Epic Wulfgar R	7.50	15.00
25 Wulfgar R	7.50	15.00
26 Aspect of Loviatar R	7.50	15.00
27 Assassin R	7.50	15.00
28 Bluespawn Ambusher C	.50	1.00
29 Dread Wraith R	7.50	15.00
30 Exarch of Tyranny R	7.50	15.00
31 Greater Barghest R	7.50	15.00
32 Greenspawn Zealot U	1.00	2.00
33 Hobgoblin Marshal C	.50	1.00
34 Ice Mephit U	1.00	2.00
35 Kobold Trapmaker C	.50	1.00
36 Lady Vol R	7.50	15.00
37 Medusa Archer U	1.00	2.00
38 Mind Flayer Lich R	7.50	15.00
39 Noble Salamander R	7.50	15.00
40 Prisoner C	.50	1.00
41 Skeletal Courser R	7.50	15.00
42 Trained Carrion Crawler U	1.00	2.00
43 Krenshar U	1.00	2.00
44 Lifeleech Otyugh R	7.50	15.00
45 Babau U	1.00	2.00
46 Berserk Flesh Golem R	7.50	15.00
47 Carnage Demon C	.50	1.00
48 Cerebrilith U	1.00	2.00
49 Clawborn Scorrow R	7.50	15.00
50 Dracotaur Rager R	7.50	15.00
51 Drow Enforcer U	1.00	2.00
52 Frost Giant Jarl R	7.50	15.00
53 Gnoll Claw Fighter C	.50	1.00
54 Kuo-Toa Hunter C	.50	1.00
55 Kuo-Toa Whip U	1.00	2.00
56 Large Chaos Beast U	1.00	2.00
57 Large Shadow Dragon R	10.00	20.00
58 Large White Dragon R	10.00	20.00
59 Orc Banebreak Rider R	7.50	15.00
60 Shadow U	1.00	2.00

2008 Dungeons and Dragons Against the Giants

Card	Low	High
COMPLETE SET (60)		
BOOSTER BOX ()		
BOOSTER PACK ()		
RELEASED ON JULY 12, 2008		
1 Shocktroop Devil R	7.50	15.00
2 Voracious Ice Devil R	7.50	15.00
3 Deathpriest of Orcus U	1.00	2.00
4 Degenerate Cultist of Orcus C	.50	1.00
5 Gnaw Demon C	.50	1.00
6 Efreeti Flamestrider R	7.50	15.00
7 Visceral Devourer U	1.00	2.00
8 Doresain, the Ghoul King R	6.00	12.00
9 Thunderblast Cyclone U	1.00	2.00
10 Yuan-Ti Anathema R	7.50	15.00
11 Elder Red Dragon R	15.00	30.00
12 Fire Titan R	10.00	20.00
13 Armored Guulvorg U	1.00	2.00
14 Bugbear Lancebreaker U	1.00	2.00
15 Dragonborn Defender R	7.50	15.00
16 Dragonborn Myrmidon R	6.00	12.00
17 Dwarf Warsword U	1.00	2.00
18 Feybound Halfling U	1.00	2.00
19 Fire Giant Raider R	7.50	15.00
20 Fist of Moradin U	1.00	2.00
21 Goblin Runner C	.50	1.00
22 Hobgoblin Guard C	.50	1.00
23 Mighty Blademaster R	6.00	12.00
24 Skullcleave Warrior R	6.00	12.00
25 Tiefling Gladiator R	6.00	12.00
26 Fire Bat U	1.00	2.00
27 Orc Zombie C	.50	1.00
28 Plaguechanged Ghoul U	1.00	2.00
29 Shadow Hulk R	10.00	20.00
30 Xorn Ravager U	1.00	2.00
31 Cave Bear U	1.00	2.00
32 Cockatrice U	1.00	2.00
33 Earth Titan U	1.00	2.00
34 Flamescorched Kobold C	.50	1.00
35 Furious Owlbear R	6.00	12.00
36 Galeb Duhr C	.50	1.00
37 Lizardfolk Raider U	1.00	2.00
38 Shifter Claw Adept U	1.00	2.00
39 Storm Giant Thunderer R	7.50	15.00
40 Angel of Retribution R	6.00	12.00
41 Captain of the Watch U	1.00	2.00
42 Chain Golem U	1.00	2.00
43 Cloaktrick Rogue R	6.00	12.00
44 Half-Elf Assassin U	1.00	2.00
45 Eladrin Pyromancer U	1.00	2.00
46 Golden Wyvern Initiate U	1.00	2.00
47 Tomebound Arcanist R	6.00	12.00
48 Blazing Skeleton U	1.00	2.00
49 Boneclaw Impaler R	6.00	12.00
50 Death Titan R	10.00	20.00
51 Lurking Wraith U	1.00	2.00
52 Young Adamantine Dragon R	7.50	15.00
53 Blackroot Treant U	1.00	2.00
54 Enormous Carrion Crawler U	1.00	2.00
55 Hellwasp U	1.00	2.00
56 Ochre Jelly C	.50	1.00
57 Ravenous Dire Rat C	.50	1.00
58 Roper R	6.00	12.00
59 Elder White Dragon R	15.00	30.00
60 Elf Arcane Archer U	1.00	2.00

2008 Dungeons and Dragons Dungeons of Dread

Card	Low	High
COMPLETE SET (60)		
BOOSTER BOX ()		
BOOSTER PACK ()		
RELEASED ON MARCH 28, 2008		
1 Dwarf Warlord U	1.00	2.00
2 Angel of Valor R	6.00	12.00
3 Cleric of Pelor U	1.00	2.00
4 Halfling Paladin U	1.00	2.00
5 Young Silver Dragon R	10.00	20.00
6 Elf Archer C	.50	1.00
7 Death Knight R	7.50	15.00
8 Orc Raider C	.50	1.00
9 Young Red Dragon R	10.00	20.00
10 Gargoyle U	1.00	2.00
11 Oni R	6.00	12.00
12 Chillborn C	.50	1.00
13 Drow Spiderguard U	1.00	2.00
14 Eye of Flame R	10.00	20.00
15 Immolith R	6.00	12.00
16 Shadow Demon U	1.00	2.00
17 Warrior Wight U	1.00	2.00
18 Howling Hag U	1.00	2.00
19 Magma Brute U	1.00	2.00
20 Vrock R	6.00	12.00
21 Ascendant Hellsword R	6.00	12.00
22 Rakshasa Baron R	6.00	12.00
23 Vampire Spawn C	.50	1.00
24 Champion of Baphomet R	6.00	12.00
25 Balhannoth R	6.00	12.00
26 Mind Flayer Scourge R	7.50	15.00
27 Troglodyte Bonecrusher C	.50	1.00
28 Vampire Vizier R	7.50	15.00
29 Ice Archon U	1.00	2.00
30 Lamia R	6.00	12.00
31 Gnoll Marauder U	1.00	2.00
32 Bugbear Headreaver U	1.00	2.00
33 Dwarf Shieldmaiden U	1.00	2.00
34 Goblin Picador C	.50	1.00
35 Human Fighter U	1.00	2.00
36 Iron Defender C	.50	1.00
37 Dire Wolf U	1.00	2.00
38 Ettin Jack-of-Irons R	6.00	12.00
39 Everfrost Ranger U	1.00	2.00
40 Griffon R	6.00	12.00
41 Kobold Archer C	.50	1.00
42 Wyvern R	7.50	15.00
43 Defiant Rake U	1.00	2.00
44 Emerald Orb Wizard R	6.00	12.00
45 Grick C	.50	1.00
46 Spectral Magelord R	6.00	12.00
47 Tiefling Warlock U	1.00	2.00
48 Warforged Infiltrator U	1.00	2.00
49 Runecarved Eidolon R	6.00	12.00
50 Drow Wand Mage U	1.00	2.00
51 Shade Knight U	1.00	2.00
52 Skeletal Tomb Guardian R	6.00	12.00
53 Bulette U	1.00	2.00
54 Deathjump Spider C	.50	1.00
55 Fen Hydra R	7.50	15.00
56 Giant Centipede C	.50	1.00
57 Hook Horror U	1.00	2.00
58 Shadowhunter Bat U	1.00	2.00
59 Spectral Panther U	1.00	2.00
60 Bralani R	6.00	12.00

2003 DC Heroclix Cosmic Justice

Card	Low	High
COMPLETE SET (96)	150.00	225.00
BOOSTER PACK	5.00	7.00
RELEASED ON JUNE 1, 2003.		
1 Easy Company Soldier R	.25	.50
2 Easy Company Soldier E	.50	.75
3 Easy Company Soldier V	.75	1.00
4 Easy Company Medic R	.25	.50
5 Easy Company Medic E	.50	.75
6 Easy Company Medic V	.75	1.00
7 Parademon Scout R	.25	.50
8 Parademon Scout E	.50	.75
9 Parademon Scout V	.75	1.00
10 Parademon Warrior R	.25	.50
11 Parademon Warrior E	.50	.75
12 Parademon Warrior V	.75	1.00
13 Lex Corp. Security R	.25	.50
14 Lex Corp. Security E	.50	.75
15 Lex Corp. Security V	.75	1.00
16 Lex Corp. Battlesuit R	.25	.50
17 Lex Corp. Battlesuit E	.50	.75
18 Lex Corp. Battlesuit V	.75	1.00
19 Sgt. Rock R	.25	.50
20 Sgt. Rock E	.50	.75
21 Sgt. Rock V	1.00	2.00
22 Penguin R	.50	1.00
23 Penguin E	1.00	2.00
24 Penguin V	2.00	3.00
25 Manhunter R	.25	.50
26 Manhunter E	.50	.75
27 Manhunter V	.75	1.00
28 Fury R	.25	.50
29 Fury E	.50	.75
30 Fury V	1.00	2.00
31 Poison Ivy R	.50	.75
32 Poison Ivy E	.75	1.00
33 Poison Ivy V	1.00	2.00
34 Black Canary R	.25	.50
35 Black Canary E	.50	.75
36 Black Canary V	.75	1.00
37 Green Arrow R	.75	1.50
38 Green Arrow E	1.00	3.00
39 Green Arrow V	5.00	8.00
40 Troia R	.25	.50
41 Troia E	.50	.75
42 Troia V	.75	1.00
43 Cosmic Boy R	.25	.50
44 Cosmic Boy E	.50	.75
45 Cosmic Boy V	.75	1.00
46 Live Wire R	.25	.50
47 Live Wire E	.50	.75
48 Live Wire V	1.00	2.00
49 Saturn Girl R	.25	.50
50 Saturn Girl E	.50	.75
51 Saturn Girl V	.75	1.00
52 Fatality R	.25	.50
53 Fatality E	.50	.75
54 Fatality V	1.00	2.00
55 Zatanna R	.25	.50
56 Zatanna E	.50	.75
57 Zatanna V	1.00	2.00
58 Lady Shiva R	.25	.50
59 Lady Shiva E	.50	.75
60 Lady Shiva V	1.00	2.00
61 Starfire R	.75	2.00
62 Starfire E	2.00	4.00
63 Starfire V	3.00	6.00
64 Starman R	.75	2.00
65 Starman E	2.00	4.00
66 Starman V	3.00	6.00
67 Firestorm R	2.00	4.00
68 Firestorm E	3.00	6.00
69 Firestorm V	5.00	8.00
70 Cheetah R	.70	1.00
71 Cheetah E	1.00	3.00
72 Cheetah V	2.00	4.00
73 Deathstroke R	.50	1.00
74 Deathstroke E	1.00	3.00
75 Deathstroke V	2.00	4.00
76 Wonder Woman R	.50	1.00
77 Wonder Woman E	2.00	3.00
78 Wonder Woman V	3.00	6.00
79 Circe R	.50	1.00
80 Circe E	1.00	3.00
81 Circe V	3.00	5.00
82 Green Lantern R	1.00	2.00
83 Green Lantern E	2.00	4.00
84 Green Lantern V	3.00	7.00
85 Martian Manhunter U	30.00	45.00
86 Bizarro U	18.00	30.00
87 Brother Blood U	9.00	12.00
88 Amazo U	20.00	35.00
89 Lex Luthor U	15.00	20.00
90 Eclipso U	15.00	20.00
91 Despero U	15.00	20.00
92 Modru U	15.00	20.00
93 Catgirl U	7.00	13.00
94 Batgirl U	15.00	20.00
95 Batman U	15.00	22.00
96 Superman U	30.00	45.00
201 Easy Co. (Little Sure Shot) LE	6.00	10.00
202 Easy Co. Medic (Four Eyes) LE	2.00	5.00
203 Parademon Scout (Pharzoof) LE	4.00	10.00
204 Parademon Warrior (Valinus) LE	4.00	7.00
205 Lex Corp. Security (Hope) LE	4.00	7.00
206 Lex Corp. Battlesuit (Eddie Carlin) LE	4.00	7.00
207 Sgt. Rock (General Frank Rock) LE	3.00	6.00
208 Penguin (Oswald Cobblepot) LE	5.00	10.00
209 Manhunter (Manhunter 2.0) LE	4.00	8.00
210 Fury (Hippolyta Trevor-Hall) LE	3.00	6.00
211 Poison Ivy (Pamela Isley) LE	3.00	7.00
212 Black Canary (Dinah Lance) LE	2.00	5.00
213 Green Arrow (Oliver Queen) LE	8.00	15.00
214 Troia (Donna Troy) LE	3.00	6.00
215 Live Wire (Garth Ranzz) LE	3.00	5.00
216 Cosmic Boy (Rokk Krinn) LE	5.00	10.00
217 Satrun Girl (Irma Ardeen) LE	4.00	7.00
218 Fatality (Yrra Cynril) LE	12.00	20.00
219 Zatanna Zatara LE	7.00	12.00
220 Lady Shiva (Sandra Wu-San) LE	3.00	7.00
221 Green Lantern (Phasing) LE	8.00	12.00
222 Atom LE	15.00	25.00
223 Plastic Man (Mailbox) LE	15.00	20.00

2004 DC Heroclix Unleashed

Card	Low	High
COMPLETE SET (97)	175.00	250.00
BOOSTER PACK	5.00	7.00
RELEASED ON MARCH 1, 2004		
1 DEO Agent R	.50	.75
2 DEO Agent E	.75	1.00
3 DEO Agent V	1.00	1.50
4 HDC Trooper R	.50	.75
5 HDC Trooper E	.75	1.00
6 HDC Trooper V	1.00	1.50
7 Gotham Undercover R	.50	.75
8 Gotham Undercover E	.75	1.00
9 Gotham Undercover V	1.00	1.50
10 Science Police R	.50	.75
11 Science Police E	.75	1.00
12 Science Police V	1.00	1.50
13 Kobra Fanatic R	.50	.75
14 Kobra Fanatic E	.75	1.00
15 Kobra Fanatic V	1.00	1.50
16 Hawkgirl R	.50	.75
17 Hawkgirl E	.75	1.00
18 Hawkgirl V	1.00	1.50
19 Brainiac 5 R	.50	.75
20 Brainiac 5 E	.75	1.00
21 Brainiac 5 V	1.00	1.50
22 Scarecrow R	.50	.75
23 Scarecrow E	.75	1.00
24 Scarecrow V	1.00	1.50
25 Deadshot R	.50	.75
26 Deadshot E	.75	1.00
27 Deadshot V	1.00	1.50
28 Two-Face R	.50	.75
29 Two-Face E	.75	1.00
30 Two-Face V	1.00	2.00
31 Cheshire R	.50	.75
32 Cheshire E	.75	1.00
33 Cheshire V	1.00	1.50
34 Rocket Red R	.50	.75
35 Rocket Red E	.75	1.00
36 Rocket Red V	1.00	1.50
37 Chameleon R	.50	.75
38 Chameleon E	.75	1.00
39 Chameleon V	1.00	2.00
40 Kobra R	.50	.75
41 Kobra E	.75	1.00
42 Kobra V	1.00	1.50
43 Killer Croc R	.50	.75
44 Killer Croc E	.75	1.00
45 Killer Croc V	1.00	2.00
46 Killer Frost R	.50	.75
47 Killer Frost E	.75	1.00
48 Killer Frost V	1.00	1.50
49 Batgirl R	.50	.75
50 Batgirl E	.75	1.00
51 Batgirl V	2.00	4.00
52 Cyborg R	.50	.75
53 Cyborg E	.75	1.00
54 Cyborg V	1.00	1.50
55 Queen Bee R	.50	.75
56 Queen Bee E	.75	1.00
57 Queen Bee V	1.00	1.50
58 Big Barda R	.50	.75
59 Big Barda E	.75	1.00
60 Big Barda V	1.00	1.50
61 Shade R	.50	1.00
62 Shade E	1.00	2.00
63 Shade V	2.00	3.00
64 Raven R	.50	.75
65 Raven E	1.00	2.00
66 Raven V	2.00	3.00
67 Jesse Quick R	.50	.75
68 Jesse Quick E	.75	1.00
69 Jesse Quick V	1.00	1.50
70 Dr. Fate R	.50	1.00
71 Dr. Fate E	1.00	2.00
72 Dr. Fate V	4.00	8.00
73 Maxima R	.50	1.00
74 Maxima E	1.00	2.00
75 Maxima V	2.00	4.00
76 Supergirl R	1.00	1.50
77 Supergirl E	2.00	3.00
78 Supergirl V	3.00	4.00
79 Black Adam R	1.00	2.00
80 Black Adam E	2.00	3.00
81 Black Adam V	4.00	8.00
82 Green Lantern R	2.00	4.00
83 Green Lantern E	3.00	6.00
84 Green Lantern V	6.00	12.00
85 Metallo U	18.00	22.00
86 The General U	15.00	18.00

Card	Low	High
87 Kilowog U	20.00	25.00
88 Shazam! U	25.00	35.00
89 Ultrahumanite U	6.00	12.00
90 Silver Swan U	10.00	18.00
91 Nu'bia U	5.00	12.00
92 Mr. Bones U	10.00	15.00
93 Wonder Woman U	22.00	30.00
94 Batman U	25.00	40.00
95 Superman U	40.00	60.00
96 Magog U	20.00	30.00
97 Bat Sentry U	20.00	30.00
201 DEO Agent (Cameron Chase) LE	6.00	10.00
202 HDC Trooper (Montgomery Kelley) LE	6.00	10.00
203 Gotham Undercover (Matches Malone) LE	3.00	7.00
204 Science Police (Shvaugh Erin) LE	3.00	7.00
205 Kobra (Jason Burr) LE	5.00	10.00
206 Hawkgirl (Kendra Saunders) LE	10.00	16.00
207 Brainiac 5 (Querl Dox) LE	10.00	16.00
208 Scarecrow (Jonathan Crane) LE	10.00	20.00
210 Two-Face (Harvey Dent) LE	10.00	20.00
211 Cheshire (Jade) LE	10.00	16.00
212 Rocket Red (Dmitri Pushkin) LE	10.00	20.00
215 Jesse Quick (Jesse Chambers) LE	12.00	25.00
216 Dr. Fate (Hector Hall) LE	12.00	20.00
217 Maxima (Maxima of Almerac) LE	10.00	18.00
218 Supergirl (Kara Zor-El) LE	10.00	18.00
219 Black Adam (Teth-Adam) LE	6.00	12.00
220 Green Lantern (Hal Jordan) LE	30.00	55.00
221 Shazam! (Kingdom Come) LE	12.00	20.00
222 Catwoman LE	15.00	25.00

2005 DC Heroclix Hypertime

Card	Low	High
COMPLETE SET (130)	175.00	235.00
BOOSTER PACK	4.00	7.00
STARTER SET	8.00	15.00
RELEASED ON SEPTEMBER 1, 2002		
1 Gotham Policeman R	.25	.35
2 Gotham Policeman E	.50	.75
3 Gotham Policeman V	1.00	1.50
4 Metropolis S.C.U R	.25	.35
5 Metropolis S.C.U E	.50	.75
6 Metropolis S.C.U V	1.00	1.50
7 Checkmate Agent R	.25	.35
8 Checkmate Agent E	.50	.75
9 Checkmate Agent V	1.00	2.00
10 Checkmate Medic R	.25	.35
11 Checkmate Medic E	.50	.75
12 Checkmate Medic V	1.00	1.50
13 Intergang Agent R	.25	.35
14 Intergang Agent E	.50	.75
15 Intergang Agent V	1.00	2.00
16 Intergang Medic R	.25	.35
17 Intergang Medic E	.50	.75
18 Intergang Medic V	1.00	2.00
19 Lackey R	.25	.35
20 Lackey E	.50	.75
21 Lackey V	1.00	2.50
22 Criminal R	.25	.35
23 Criminal E	.50	.75
24 Criminal V	.75	1.00
25 Huntress R	.25	.35
26 Huntress E	.50	.75
27 Huntress V	.75	1.00
28 Robin R	.25	.35
29 Robin E	.50	.75
30 Robin V	1.00	2.00
31 Hawkman R	.25	.35
32 Hawkman E	.50	.75
33 Hawkman V	1.00	2.00
34 Harley Quinn R	.75	1.50
35 Harley Quinn E	1.00	2.00
36 Harley Quinn V	2.00	4.00
37 Catwoman R	.25	.50
38 Catwoman E	.75	1.00
39 Catwoman V	1.00	2.00
40 Man-Bat R	.25	.35
41 Man-Bat E	.50	.75
42 Man-Bat V	.75	1.00
43 Riddler R	.50	1.00
44 Riddler E	1.00	2.00
45 Riddler V	2.00	4.00
46 Mad Hatter R	.25	.35
47 Mad Hatter E	.50	.75
48 Mad Hatter V	1.00	1.50
49 T.O. Morrow R	.25	.35
50 T.O. Morrow E	.50	.75
51 T.O. Morrow V	1.00	1.50
52 Aquaman R	1.00	1.50
53 Aquaman E	1.50	2.50
54 Aquaman V	2.00	4.00
55 Blue Beetle R	.25	.35
56 Blue Beetle E	.50	.75
57 Blue Beetle V	1.00	1.50
58 Booster Gold R	.25	.35
59 Booster Gold E	.50	.75
60 Booster Gold V	1.00	1.50
61 Nightwing R	.75	1.00
62 Nightwing E	1.00	2.00
63 Nightwing V	3.00	5.00
64 Changeling R	.25	.35
65 Changeling E	.50	.75
66 Changeling V	1.00	1.50
67 Steel R	.30	.50
68 Steel E	1.00	2.00
69 Steel V	2.00	3.00
70 Gorilla Grodd R	.50	1.00
71 Gorilla Grodd E	1.00	2.00
72 Gorilla Grodd V	2.00	4.00
73 Soloman Grundy R	.50	1.00
74 Soloman Grundy E	1.00	2.00
75 Soloman Grundy V	2.00	4.00
76 Black Manta R	.50	1.00
77 Black Manta E	1.00	2.00
78 Black Manta V	2.00	4.00
79 Weather Wizard R	.50	1.00
80 Weather Wizard E	1.00	2.00
81 Weather Wizard V	2.00	4.00
82 Clayface III R	.50	1.00
83 Clayface III E	1.00	2.00
84 Clayface III V	2.00	4.00
85 Hawk R	.50	1.00
86 Hawk E	1.00	2.00
87 Hawk V	2.00	4.00
88 Dove R	1.00	2.00
89 Dove E	2.00	5.00
90 Dove V	5.00	8.00
91 Bane R	1.00	2.00
92 Bane E	2.00	3.00
93 Bane V	3.00	5.00
94 Doomsday R	.50	1.50
95 Doomsday E	1.00	2.00
96 Doomsday V	2.00	4.00
97 Joker R	1.00	2.00
98 Joker E	2.00	4.00
99 Joker V	5.00	8.00
100 Plastic Man R	.50	1.00
101 Plastic Man E	1.00	2.00
102 Plastic Man V	3.00	5.00
103 Flash R	1.00	2.00
104 Flash E	3.00	5.00
105 Flash V	4.00	8.00
106 Batman R	.75	1.50
107 Batman E	1.00	2.50
108 Batman V	6.00	11.00
109 Superman R	1.00	2.00
110 Superman E	2.00	3.00
111 Superman V	4.00	6.00
112 Arcane R	1.00	2.00
113 Arcane E	2.00	4.00
114 Arcane V	3.00	6.00
115 Swamp Thing R	1.00	2.00
116 Swamp Thing E	2.00	4.00
117 Swamp Thing V	3.00	7.00
118 Braniac 13 R	.50	1.00
119 Braniac 13 E	1.00	2.00
120 Braniac 13 V	2.00	4.00
121 Parasite U	4.00	8.00
122 Desaad U	8.00	15.00
123 Darkseid U	10.00	18.00
124 Commissioner Gordon U	8.00	12.00
125 The Key U	4.00	8.00
126 Joker U	8.00	20.00
127 Catwoman U	10.00	20.00
128 Flash U	15.00	20.00
129 Batman U	20.00	30.00
130 Superman U	15.00	25.00
131 Hawkman (Carter Hall) LE	8.00	10.00
132 Harley Quinn (Harleen Quinzel) LE	6.00	8.00
133 Catwoman (Selina Kyle) LE	10.00	15.00
134 Man-Bat (Kirk Langstrom) LE	5.00	7.00
135 Riddler (Eddie Nashton) LE	5.00	8.00
136 Mad Hatter (Jervis Tetch) LE	3.00	5.00
137 T.O. Morrow (TO Morrow) LE	3.00	5.00
138 Aquaman (Arthur Curry) LE	7.00	12.00
139 Blue Beetle (Ted Kord) LE	6.00	12.00
140 Booster Gold (Michael Jon Carter) LE	8.00	12.00
141 Superman (OWAW) LE	12.00	20.00

2005 DC Heroclix Icons

Card	Low	High
COMPLETE SET (64)		
BOOSTER PACK	6.00	8.00
BYSTANDER CARDS (B1-B6)	.50	1.00
INFILTRATION CARDS (IBF1-IBF9)	.50	1.00
ROOKIE	.25	.50
EXPERIENCED	.50	1.00
VETERAN	1.00	2.00
RELEASED ON SEPTEMBER 1, 2005		
1 Batman E	1.00	2.00
2 Robin E	.50	1.00
3 Hawkgirl E	.25	.50
4 The Joker E	1.00	2.00
5 Harley Quinn E	.30	1.00
6 Man-Bat E	.25	.50
7 Scarecrow R	.25	.50
8 Scarecrow E	.50	1.00
9 Scarecrow V	1.00	2.00
10 Beast Boy R	.25	.50
11 Changeling E	.50	1.00
12 Beast Boy V	1.00	2.00
13 Robin R	.50	1.00
14 Robin E	1.00	2.00
15 Robin V	2.00	4.00
16 Cheetah R	.25	.50
17 Cheetah E	.50	1.00
18 Cheetah V	1.00	2.00
19 Blackfire R	.25	.50
20 Blackfire E	.50	1.00
21 Blackfire V	1.00	2.00
22 Starfire R	.25	.50
23 Starfire E	.50	1.00
24 Starfire V	1.00	2.00
25 Aquaman R	.50	1.00
26 Aquaman E	1.00	2.00
27 Aquaman V	2.00	4.00
28 Raven R	.25	.50
29 Raven E	.50	1.00
30 Raven V	1.00	2.00
31 Wonder Woman R	.50	1.00
32 Wonder Woman E	1.00	2.00
33 Wonder Woman V	2.00	4.00
34 Bizarro R	.50	1.00
35 Bizarro E	1.00	2.00
36 Bizarro V	2.00	4.00
37 The Joker R	.50	1.00
38 The Joker E	1.00	2.00
39 The Joker V	3.00	5.00
40 Batman R	.50	1.00
41 Batman E	1.00	2.00
42 Batman V	3.00	5.00
43 Darkseid R	.25	.50
44 Darkseid E	.50	1.00
45 Darkseid V	1.00	2.00
46 Superman R	.50	1.00
47 Superman E	1.00	2.00
48 Superman V	3.00	5.00
49 Ra's al-Ghul U	10.00	15.00
50 Brainiac U	20.00	30.00
51 Lex Luthor U	15.00	25.00
52 Terra U	12.00	18.00
53 Cyborg U	12.00	16.00
54 The Flash U	15.00	25.00
201 Dr. Jonathan Crane U	3.00	5.00
202 Gar Logan U	15.00	20.00
203 Tim Drake U	15.00	20.00
204 Barbara Ann Minerva U	15.00	20.00
205 Princess Komand'r U	15.00	20.00
206 Princess Koriand'r U	15.00	20.00
207 Dark Knight Detective U	15.00	20.00
208 Batman E (Promo)	1.00	1.00
209 Professor Zoom U	15.00	20.00
B7 Speed Saunders U	15.00	20.00

2005 DC Heroclix Legacy

Card	Low	High
COMPLETE SET (97)	250.00	350.00
BOOSTER PACK	6.00	8.00
FEATS CARDS (F1-F8)	1.00	2.00
BATTLEFIELD CARDS (BF1-BF6)	.50	1.00
TOKENS (B1-B7)	.50	1.00
RELEASED ON MARCH 1, 2005		
1 Spoiler R	.50	.75
2 Spoiler E	.75	1.50
3 Spoiler V	1.00	2.00
4 Hyena R	.50	.75
5 Hyena E	.75	1.50
6 Hyena V	1.00	2.00
7 Enchantress R	.50	.75
8 Enchantress E	.75	1.50
9 Enchantress V	1.00	2.00
10 Talia R	.50	.75
11 Talia E	.75	1.50
12 Talia V	1.00	2.00
13 Hourman R	.50	.75
14 Hourman E	.75	1.50
15 Hourman V	1.00	2.00
16 Mr. Terrific R	.50	.75
17 Mr. Terrific E	.75	1.50
18 Mr. Terrific V	1.00	2.00
19 Star-Spangled Kid R	.50	.75
20 Star-Spangled Kid E	.75	1.50
21 Stargirl V	1.00	2.00
22 Ravager R	.50	.75
23 Ravager E	.75	1.50
24 Ravager V	1.00	2.00
25 Power Girl R	.50	.75
26 Power Girl E	.75	1.50
27 Power Girl V	1.00	2.00
28 Impulse R	.50	.75
29 Impulse E	.75	1.50
30 Kid Flash V	2.00	4.00
31 Kid Quantum R	.50	.75
32 Kid Quantum E	.75	1.50
33 Kid Quantum V	1.00	2.00
34 Jinx R	.50	.75
35 Jinx E	.75	1.50
36 Jinx V	1.00	2.00
37 Mr. Freeze R	1.00	2.00
38 Mr. Freeze E	2.00	4.00
39 Mr. Freeze V	3.00	6.00
40 Speedy R	.50	.75
41 Arsenal E	.75	1.50
42 Arsenal V	1.00	2.00
43 Wildfire R	.50	.75
44 Wildfire E	.75	1.50
45 Wildfire V	1.00	2.00
46 Superwoman R	.50	.75
47 Superwoman E	.75	1.50
48 Superwoman V	1.00	2.00
49 The Demon R	.50	.75
50 The Demon E	.75	1.50
51 The Demon V	2.00	4.00
52 Obsidian R	.50	.75
53 Obsidian E	.75	1.50
54 Obsidian V	1.00	2.00
55 Jade R	.50	.75
56 Jade E	.75	1.50
57 Jade V	2.00	4.00
58 Sinestro R	1.00	2.00
59 Sinestro E	2.00	4.00
60 Sinestro V	4.00	8.00
61 Blockbuster R	.50	.75
62 Blockbuster E	.75	1.50
63 Blockbuster V	1.00	2.00
64 Superboy R	1.00	2.00
65 Superboy E	2.00	4.00
66 Superboy V	3.00	6.00
67 Persuader R	.50	.75
68 Persuader E	.75	1.50
69 Persuader V	1.00	2.00
70 Captain Atom R	.50	.75
71 Captain Atom E	.75	1.50
72 Captain Atom V	1.00	2.00
73 Major Force R	.50	.75
74 Major Force E	.75	1.50
75 Major Force V	1.00	2.00
76 Ra's al-Ghul R	.50	.75
77 Ra's al-Ghul E	.75	1.50
78 Ra's al-Ghul V	1.00	2.00
79 The Joker R	2.00	3.00
80 The Joker E	3.00	5.00
81 The Joker V	4.00	8.00
82 Batman R	2.00	3.00
83 Batman E	3.00	5.00
84 Batman V	4.00	8.00
85 Oracle U	15.00	25.00
86 Hush U	12.00	18.00
87 Wonder Woman U	20.00	30.00
88 Ares U	10.00	12.00
89 Ultraman U	12.00	15.00
90 General Zod U	12.00	15.00
91 Prometheus U	8.00	10.00
92 Mongul U	8.00	10.00
93 Hawkman U	8.00	10.00
94 Red Robin U	15.00	20.00
95 Flash U	20.00	25.00
96 Green Lantern U	40.00	60.00
97 Steel E	15.00	20.00
201 Victor Fries U	12.00	18.00
202 Roy Harper, Jr. U	10.00	18.00
203 Drake Burroughs U	10.00	18.00
204 Lois Lane U	12.00	20.00
205 Etrigan U	10.00	18.00
206 Todd Rice U	10.00	18.00
207 Jennifer-Lynn Hayden U	10.00	18.00
208 Sinestro of Korugar U	12.00	20.00
209 Roland Desmond U	10.00	18.00
210 Connor Kent U	12.00	20.00
211 Nyeun Chun Ti U	10.00	18.00
212 Capt. Nathaniel Adam U	12.00	20.00
213 Clifford Zmeck U	10.00	18.00
214 The Demon's Head U	10.00	18.00
215 The Red Hood U	10.00	18.00
216 Bruce Wayne U	20.00	30.00
221 Mr. Freeze U	12.00	18.00

2006 DC Heroclix Collateral Damage

COMPLETE SET (96)
RELEASED ON FEBRUARY 1, 2006
1 HIVE Trooper R
2 HIVE Trooper E
3 HIVE Trooper V
4 Ragman R
5 Ragman E
6 Ragman V
7 Vixen R
8 Vixen E
9 Vixen V
10 Black Mask R
11 Black Mask E
12 Black Mask V
13 Trickster R
14 Trickster E
15 Trickster V
16 Azrael R
17 Azrael E
18 Azrael V
19 Katana R
20 Katana E
21 Katana V
22 Dr. Mid-Nite R
23 Dr. Mid-Nite E
24 Dr. Mid-Nite V
25 Green Flame R
26 Fire E
27 Fire V
28 Icemaiden R
29 Ice E
30 Ice V
31 Speedy R
32 Speedy E
33 Speedy V
34 Shadow Lass R
35 Umbra E
36 Shadow Lass V
37 Captain Cold R
38 Captain Cold E
39 Captain Cold V
40 Elongated Man R
41 Elongated Man E
42 Elongated Man V
43 Blue Devil R
44 Blue Devil E
45 Blue Devil V
46 Black Lightning R
47 Black Lightning E
48 Black Lightning V
49 Green Lantern R
50 Green Lantern E
51 Green Lantern V
52 Manhunter R
53 Manhunter E
54 Manhunter V
55 Clayface R
56 Clayface E
57 Clayface V
58 Metamorpho R
59 Metamorpho E
60 Metamorpho V
61 Emerald Empress R
62 Emerald Empress E
63 Emerald Empress V
64 Dr. Light R
65 Dr. Light E
66 Dr. Light V
67 Superman Blue R
68 Superman Red E
69 Superman V
70 Red Tornado R
71 Red Tornado E
72 Red Tornado V
73 Geo-Force R
74 Geo-Force E
75 Geo-Force V
76 OMAC R
77 OMAC E
78 OMAC V
79 Mary Marvel R
80 Mary Marvel E
81 Mary Marvel V
82 Monsieur Mallah R
83 The Brain E
84 Monsieur Mallah & the Brain V
85 Felix Faust U
86 Guardian U
87 Crimson Avenger U
88 Ambush Bug U
89 Dr. Psycho U
90 Orion U
91 Jonah Hex U
92 Eclipso U
93 Captain Boomerang U
94 Owlman U
95 Kalibak U
96 Adam Strange U
201 Len Snart U
202 Ralph Dibny U
203 Dan Cassidy U
204 Jefferson Pierce U
205 Kyle Rayner U
206 Kate Spencer U
207 Basil Karlo U
208 Rex Mason U
209 Emerald Eye of Ekron U
210 Arthur Light U
211 Clark Kent U
212 Tornado Tyrant U
213 Prince Brion Markov U
214 OMAC 5674 U
215 Captain Marvel U
216 GeneGrafted Brain U
217 Krypto U
218 Superman U
219 Parallax U
220 Ultimate Clayface U
221 Superman Robot U
222 The Man of Steel U
223 The Dark Knight U

2006 DC Heroclix Giants

COMPLETE SET (7)
RELEASED ON MARCH 1, 2006
1 Atom Smasher E
2 Validus E
3 Colossal Boy E
4 Rita Farr E
5 Giganta E

6 Alloy E
7 Chemo E

2006 DC Heroclix Green Lantern Corps

COMPLETE (7)
RELEASED ON AUGUST 1, 2006
1 G'nort R
2 Ch'p E
3 Abin Sur U
4 Arisia V
5 Katma Tui E
6 Ganthet U
7 Tomar Re E

2007 DC Heroclix Justice League

COMPLETE SET (60)
RELEASED ON SEPTEMBER 1, 2007

1 Batman V	4.00	10.00
2 Aquaman R	.20	.50
3 Creeper E	.40	1.00
4 Firehawk E	.40	1.00
5 Mento V	2.00	5.00
6 Heat Wave E	.40	1.00
7 Icicle R	.20	.50
8 Lex Luthor V	2.00	5.00
9 The Joker U	4.00	10.00
10 Bulleteer R	.20	.50
11 Black Canary E	.40	1.00
12 Crimson Fox R	.20	.50
13 Doctor Light E	.40	1.00
14 Green Arrow E	.40	1.00
15 Gypsy E	.40	1.00
16 Bouncing Boy E	.40	1.00
17 Parasite U	4.00	10.00
18 Firestorm R	.20	.50
19 Merlyn E	.40	1.00
20 Black Hand E	.40	1.00
21 King Shark E	.40	1.00
22 Professor Ivo V	2.00	5.00
23 Toyman R	.20	.50
24 Chronos V	2.00	5.00
25 Dr. Alchemy E	.40	1.00
26 Captain Boomerang V	2.00	5.00
27 The Flash U	4.00	10.00
28 Zatanna E	.40	1.00
29 Zauriel R	.20	.50
30 Plastic Man V	2.00	5.00
31 Tharok E	.40	1.00
32 Bronze Tiger E	.40	1.00
33 Vigilante R	.20	.50
34 August General in Iron R	.20	.50
35 Deadman U	4.00	10.00
36 Granny Goodness U	4.00	10.00
37 Wonder Woman E	.40	1.00
38 Batman and Robin U	4.00	10.00
39 Batzarro R	.20	.50
40 Hector Hammond E	.40	1.00
41 Mr. Mxyzptlk U	4.00	10.00
42 Abra Kadabra V	2.00	5.00
43 Dr. Polaris V	2.00	5.00
44 Major Disaster V	2.00	5.00
45 Aztek R	.20	.50
46 Superman E	.40	1.00
47 Hourman R	.20	.50
48 Dream Girl R	.20	.50
49 Shining Knight R	.20	.50
50 Power Ring U	4.00	10.00
51 Lobo U	15.00	30.00
52 Amazo U	4.00	10.00
53 Big Barda and Mr. Miracle U	4.00	10.00
54 Doomsday U	15.00	30.00
55 Green Lantern V	2.00	5.00
56 Time Trapper E	.40	1.00
57 The Flash E	.40	1.00
58 Batman V	2.00	5.00
59 Wonder Woman E	.40	1.00
60 Superman V	2.00	5.00
61 Phantom Stranger U	4.00	10.00

2007 DC Heroclix Legion of Superheroes

COMPLETE SET (8)
RELEASED JUNE 1, 2007

1 Lightning Lad E	.75	2.00
2 Saturn Girl E	.75	2.00
3 Cosmic Boy E	.75	2.00
4 Timber Wolf E	.75	2.00
5 Phantom Girl R	.75	2.00
6 Ultra Boy R	.75	2.00
7 Young Superman R	.75	2.00
8 Shrinking Violet E	.75	2.00

2007 DC Heroclix Origins

COMPLETE SET (96)
RELEASED ON FEBRUARY 1, 2007
1 Blackhawks R
2 Blackhawks E
3 Blackhawks V
4 Phantom Lady R
5 Phantom Lady E
6 Phantom Lady V
7 Robotman R
8 Robotman E
9 Robotman V
10 Ray R
11 Ray E
12 Ray V
13 Wildcat R
14 Wildcat E
15 Wildcat V
16 Damage R
17 Damage E
18 Damage V
19 Halo R
20 Halo E
21 Halo V
22 Mano R
23 Mano E
24 Mano V
25 Shadow Thief R
26 Shadow Thief E
27 Shadow Thief V
28 Knockout R
29 Knockout E
30 Knockout V
31 Copperhead R
32 Copperhead E
33 Copperhead V
34 Question R
35 Question E
36 Question V
37 Animal Man R
38 Animal Man E
39 Animal Man V
40 Cat-Man R
41 Cat-Man E
42 Cat-Man V
43 Booster Gold R
44 Booster Gold E
45 Booster Gold V
46 The All-New Atom R
47 Atom E
48 Atom V
49 Mirror Master R
50 Mirror Master E
51 Mirror Master V
52 Triplicate Girl R
53 Triplicate Girl E
54 Triplicate Girl V
55 Supergirl R
56 Supergirl E
57 Supergirl V
58 Hawkman R
59 Hawkman E
60 Hawkman V
61 Wonder Girl R
62 Wonder Girl E
63 Wonder Girl V
64 Cyborg Superman R
65 Cyborg Superman E
66 Cyborg Superman V
67 Steel R
68 Steel E
69 Steel V
70 Mister Miracle R
71 Mister Miracle E
72 Mister Miracle V
73 Mon-El R
74 Valor E
75 M'Onel V
76 Green Lantern R
77 Sentinel E
78 Green Lantern V
79 Shazam R
80 Shazam E
81 Shazam V
82 Martian Manhunter R
83 Martian Manhunter E
84 Martian Manhunter V
85 Starman U
86 Sandman U
87 Blue Beetle U
88 Mister Mind U
89 Jakeem Thunder U
90 Gentleman Ghost U
91 Vandal Savage U
92 Johnny Quick U
93 Negative Woman U
94 STRIPE U
95 Batman U
96 Superman U
201 Animal Master U
202 Michael Carter U
203 Ray Palmer U
204 Duo Damsel U
205 Supergirl U
206 Carter Hall U
207 Cassie Sandsmark U
208 Alan Scott U
209 Guardian of Eternity U
210 Detective John Jones U
211 Wonder Woman U
212 Dr. Fate U
213 Johnny Thunder U
214 Alfred Pennyworth U

2008 DC Heroclix Arkham Asylum

COMPLETE SET (60)
RELEASED ON OCTOBER 23, 2008

1 White Martian V	3.00	8.00
2 Manhunter R	.20	.50
3 Multiplex E	.40	1.00
4 The Question R	.20	.50
5 Floronic Man E	.40	1.00
6 Gotham City Detective V	3.00	8.00
7 Two-Face V	3.00	8.00
8 Street Thug R	.20	.50
9 Kid Devil R	.20	.50
10 Gorilla Grodd V	3.00	8.00
11 The Riddler V	3.00	8.00
12 Amanda Waller R	.20	.50
13 Human Bomb R	.20	.50
14 Scandal Savage E	.40	1.00
15 Plasmus R	.20	.50
16 Batman R	.20	.50
17 Man-Bat Assassin R	.20	.50
18 Solomon Grundy E	.40	1.00
19 Lashina U	8.00	20.00
20 Anarky E	.40	1.00
21 Miss Martian R	.20	.50
22 Hitman V	3.00	8.00
23 Wonder Woman V	3.00	8.00
24 Count Vertigo V	3.00	8.00
25 Johnny Sorrow U	8.00	20.00
26 Nightshade E	.40	1.00
27 Firefly E	.40	1.00
28 Arkillo E	.40	1.00
29 Per Degation U	8.00	20.00
30 Amon Sur R	.20	.50
31 Captain Gordon E	.40	1.00
32 Lightning Lord V	3.00	8.00
33 Thinker U	8.00	20.00
34 Robin V	3.00	8.00
35 Ghost Fox Killer E	.40	1.00
36 Zoom U	8.00	20.00
37 Element Lad R	.20	.50
38 The Penguin V	3.00	8.00
39 Cosmic King V	3.00	8.00
40 Doctor Destiny U	8.00	20.00
41 Frankenstein V	3.00	8.00
42 Ventriloquist E	.40	1.00
43 Calculator U	8.00	20.00
44 Yellow Lantern R	.20	.50
45 Circe U	8.00	20.00
46 Lyssa Drak E	.40	1.00
47 Ultra-Humanite V	3.00	8.00
48 Bizarro #1 V	3.00	8.00
49 Black Manta V	3.00	8.00
50 Metron U	8.00	20.00
51 Mad Hatter V	3.00	8.00
52 Batgirl E	.40	1.00
53 The Top V	3.00	8.00
54 Despero U	8.00	20.00
55 Sabbac R	.20	.50
56 The Flash U	8.00	20.00
57 Saturn Queen V	3.00	8.00
58 Chang Tzu U	8.00	20.00
59 The Joker U	8.00	20.00
60 Superman Prime U	20.00	40.00
61 Clown Prince of Crime U	20.00	40.00
99 Batman U	75.00	100.00
100 Batman U	75.00	100.00
101 Crispus Allen U	8.00	20.00
102 Harvey Dent U	6.00	15.00
103 Henchman U	6.00	15.00
104 Grodd E	.40	1.00
105 Edward Nigma U	6.00	15.00

2008 DC Heroclix Batman Alpha

COMPLETE SET (30)
RELEASED ON JUNE 4, 2008

1 Batman SE	8.00	20.00
2 The Caped Crusader SE	8.00	20.00
3 The Masked Manhunter SE	8.00	20.00
4 Batman SE	8.00	20.00
5 Robin C	.20	.50
6 Harley Quinn C	.20	.50
7 Penguin C	.20	.50
8 Poison Ivy C	.20	.50
9 Clayface C	.20	.50
10 Scarecrow C	.20	.50
11 Huntress C	.20	.50
12 Bane C	.20	.50
13 Mad Hatter C	.20	.50
14 Alfred C	.20	.50
15 Gotham City P.D. C	.20	.50
16 Riddler C	.20	.50
17 Killer Croc C	.20	.50
18 Talia C	.20	.50
19 Joker U	.40	1.00
20 Commissioner Gordon U	.40	1.00
21 Two-Face U	.40	1.00
22 Ra's Al Ghul U	.40	1.00
23 Mr. Freeze U	.40	1.00
24 Batgirl U	.40	1.00
25 Oracle U	.40	1.00
26 Catwoman U	.40	1.00
27 Clown Prince of Crime R	3.00	8.00
28 Boy Wonder R	3.00	8.00
29 Nightwing R	3.00	8.00
30 Dynamic Duo R	3.00	8.00
31 Batman SE	8.00	20.00

2008 DC Heroclix Crisis

COMPLETE SET (60)
RELEASED ON FEBRUARY 1, 2008

1 Robin R	.20	.50
2 Kid Flash R	.20	.50
3 Wonder Girl R	.20	.50
4 Aqualad R	.20	.50
5 Speedy R	.20	.50
6 Shimmer E	.40	1.00
7 Jericho E	.40	1.00
8 Mercury E	.40	1.00
9 Gold E	.40	1.00
10 Liberty Belle V	3.00	8.00
11 Klarion R	.20	.50
12 Supernova E	.40	1.00
13 Robin V	3.00	8.00
14 Batgirl E	.40	1.00
15 Iron E	.40	1.00
16 Ace R	.20	.50
17 Red Hood E	.40	1.00
18 Red Arrow V	3.00	8.00
19 Batwoman R	.20	.50
20 Dr. Sivana U	8.00	20.00
21 Rip Hunter U	8.00	20.00
22 Dawnstar E	.40	1.00
23 Green Lantern V	3.00	8.00
24 Karate Kid V	3.00	8.00
25 Jack and Ten R	.20	.50
26 Green Arrow V	3.00	8.00
27 Trickster and Pied Piper V	3.00	8.00
28 Deathstroke U	8.00	20.00
29 Nightwing V	3.00	8.00
30 Blue Beetle V	3.00	8.00
31 Mammoth E	.40	1.00
32 Hawk and Dove R	.20	.50
33 Psimon E	.40	1.00
34 Lead and Tin E	.40	1.00
35 Uncle Sam U	8.00	20.00
36 The Chief R	.20	.50
37 Kyle Rayner V	3.00	8.00
38 Wonder Girl V	3.00	8.00
39 Harbinger R	.20	.50
40 Forerunner E	.40	1.00
41 Mary Marvel V	3.00	8.00
42 Mordru U	8.00	20.00
43 Monarch E	.40	1.00
44 Accomplished Perfect Physician R	.20	.50
45 Trigon U	8.00	20.00
46 Star Sapphire V	3.00	8.00
47 Tempest V	3.00	8.00
48 Darkseid V	6.00	15.00
49 Will Magnus and Platinum E	.40	1.00
50 Captain Marvel, Jr. E	.40	1.00
51 King and Queen R	.20	.50
52 Psycho-Pirate V	3.00	8.00
53 Black Adam U	15.00	30.00
54 Alex Luthor U	8.00	20.00
55 Sinestro V	30.00	60.00
56 Supergirl V	8.00	20.00
57 The Flash U	15.00	30.00
58 Nightwing and Starfire E	.40	1.00
59 The Spectre U	15.00	30.00
60 Monitor V	3.00	8.00
61 World's Finest U	8.00	20.00
100 Superman U	8.00	20.00
105 Superman U	8.00	20.00

2010 DC Heroclix Blackest Night

COMPLETE SET	10.00	25.00
1 Mera	2.00	5.00
2 Lex Luthor	2.00	5.00
3 Scarecrow	2.00	5.00
4 Green Lantern	2.00	5.00
5 Flash	2.00	5.00
6 Atom	2.00	5.00
7 Wonder Woman	2.00	5.00

2010 DC Heroclix Brightest Day Action Pack

COMPLETE SET	10.00	25.00
1 Martian Manhunter	2.00	5.00
2 Firestorm	2.00	5.00
3 Hawkgirl	2.00	5.00
4 Captain Boomerang	2.00	5.00
5 Captain Boomerang	2.00	5.00
6 Aquaman	2.00	5.00
7 Osiris	2.00	5.00

2010 DC Heroclix Brave and the Bold

1 Bruce Wayne C	.20	.50
2 Clark Kent C	.20	.50
3 Diana Prince C	.20	.50
4 League Assassin C	.20	.50
5 Amazon C	.20	.50
6 Checkmate Pawn (W) C	.20	.50
7 Checkmate Knight (W) C	.20	.50
8 Parademon Grunt C	.20	.50
9 The Atom and Hawkman C	.20	.50
10 Jason Blood C	.20	.50
11 League Elite C	.20	.50
12 Amazon of Bana-Mighdall C	.20	.50
13 Checkmate Pawn (B) C	.20	.50
14 Checkmate Knight (B) C	.20	.50
15 Parademon Drill Sergeant C	.20	.50
16 Batman U U	.50	1.00
17 Superman U	.50	1.00
18 Wonder Woman U	.50	1.00
19 Talia U	.50	1.00
20 Damian Wayne U	.50	1.00
21 The Holiday Killer U	.50	1.00
22 Cave Carson U	.50	1.00
23 Max Mercury U	.50	1.00
24 Mikron O'Jeneus U	.50	1.00
25 Goodness and Mercy U	.50	1.00
26 The Sensei U	.50	1.00
27 Phillipus U	.50	1.00
28 Pawn 502 U	.50	1.00
29 Mademoiselle Marie U	.50	1.00
30 The Parademon U	.50	1.00
31 Brainiac R	2.00	5.00
32 Kryptonite Man R	2.00	5.00
33 Metallo R	2.00	5.00
34 Ra's Al Ghul R	2.00	5.00
35 Power Girl R	2.00	5.00
36 Martian Manhunter R	2.00	5.00
37 Extant R	2.00	5.00
38 Inertia R	2.00	5.00
39 Etrigan R	2.00	5.00
40 Lex Luthor and Brainiac R	2.00	5.00
41 Talia al Ghul R	2.00	5.00
42 Robin R	2.00	5.00
43 Kid Zoom R	2.00	5.00
44 Black Flash R	2.00	5.00
45 The Wizard Shazam! R	2.00	5.00
46 Batman and Green Arrow SR	8.00	20.00
47 The Flashes SR	8.00	20.00
48 Flash and Green Lantern SR	8.00	20.00
49 Superman and the Flash SR	8.00	20.00
50 Fire and Ice SR	8.00	20.00
51 Green Lantern and Green Arrow SR	8.00	20.00
52 Blue Beetle and Booster Gold SR	8.00	20.00
53 Poison Ivy and Harley Quinn SR	8.00	20.00
54 Mister Miracle and Oberon SR	8.00	20.00
55 Shazam and Black Adam SR	10.00	25.00
56 Black Hand CH	50.00	75.00
57 Martian Manhunter CH	50.00	75.00
58 Kal-L CH	75.00	125.00
59 Nekron CH	50.00	75.00
100 Batman and Catwoman LE	15.00	30.00
101 Bruce Wayne LE	15.00	30.00
102 Clark Kent LE	15.00	30.00
103 Diana Prince LE	15.00	30.00

2010 DC Heroclix Jonah Hex Battle Pack

1 Jonah Hex	1.00	2.50
2 Quentin Turnbull	1.00	2.50
3 Lilah	1.00	2.50

2010 DC Heroclix 75th Anniversary

1 Easy Company Soldier C	.20	.50
2 Zamaron C	.20	.50
3 Dominator C	.20	.50
4 Gorilla City Warrior C	.20	.50
5 Deadshot C	.20	.50
6 Donna Troy C	.20	.50
7 Ice C	.20	.50
8 Crimson Avenger C	.20	.50
9 Bart Allen C	.20	.50
10 Johnny Quick C	.20	.50
11 Mr. Terrific C	.20	.50
12 The Atom C	.20	.50
13 Green Arrow C	.20	.50
14 Beast Boy C	.20	.50
15 Beast Boy (Bear) C	.20	.50
16 Beast Boy (Cheetah) C	.20	.50
17 Sgt. Rock U	.40	1.00
18 Queen Aga'po U	.40	1.00
19 Ruling Caste Dominator U	.40	1.00
20 Solovar U	.40	1.00
21 Warlord U	.40	1.00
22 Nightmaster U	.40	1.00
23 Osiris U	.40	1.00
24 Detective Chimp U	.40	1.00
25 Sargon the Sorcerer U	.40	1.00
26 Superboy U	.40	1.00
27 Ocean Master U	.40	1.00
28 Mera U	.40	1.00
29 Aquaman U	.40	1.00
30 Wonder Woman U	.40	1.00
31 Batman U	.40	1.00
32 Superman U	.40	1.00
33 Isis R	2.00	5.00

34 Black Alice R	2.00	5.00
35 Ragdoll R	2.00	5.00
36 Animal Man R	2.00	5.00
37 Captain Comet R	2.00	5.00
38 Kyle Rayner R	2.00	5.00
39 Guy Gardner R	2.00	5.00
40 Saint Walker R	2.00	5.00
41 Inigo - 1 R	2.00	5.00
42 Atrocitus R	2.00	5.00
43 Larfleeze R	2.00	5.00
44 Mongul R	2.00	5.00
45 Scar R	2.00	5.00
46 John Stewart R	2.00	5.00
47 Carol Ferris R	2.00	5.00
48 Ganthet R	2.00	5.00
49 Green Lantern SR	15.00	30.00
50 Superman SR	10.00	25.00
51 Wonder Woman SR	10.00	25.00
52 Batman SR	10.00	25.00
53 Hal Jordan SR	15.00	30.00
54 Barry Allen SR	10.00	25.00
55 Beast Boy (T-Rex) SR	10.00	25.00
56 Doomsday SR	10.00	25.00
57 Bane SR	20.00	40.00
58 Ares SR	10.00	25.00
59 Wonder Twins SR	10.00	25.00
60 Sinestro SR	25.00	50.00
100 Sinestro	25.00	50.00
101 Grodd LE	5.00	12.00
102 Gleek LE	6.00	15.00
103 Troia LE	4.00	10.00
104 Impulse LE	4.00	10.00
105 Ice Maiden LE	5.00	12.00
200 Green Lantern (FCBD) LE	2.00	5.00
201 Wonder Woman (Conv) LE	75.00	150.00
W-1 Ice CH	25.00	50.00
W-2 Bart Allen CH	25.00	50.00
W-3 Donna Troy CH	30.00	60.00
W-4 Hal Jordan CH	60.00	120.00
W-5 Animal Man CH	30.00	60.00
W-6 Superman CH	40.00	80.00
W-7 Flash CH	50.00	100.00
W-8 Wonder Woman CH	30.00	60.00
W-9 Superboy CH	25.00	50.00
W-10 Green Arrow CH	40.00	80.00

2010 DC Heroclix Watchmen

1 Rorschach	6.00	15.00
2 Silk Spectre	6.00	15.00
3 Nite Owl	6.00	15.00
4 Ozymandias	6.00	15.00
5 Dr. Manhattan	6.00	15.00
6 The Comedian	1.50	4.00
7 Hooded Justice	1.50	4.00
8 Captain Metropolis	1.50	4.00
9 The Comedian	1.50	4.00
10 Silk Spectre	1.50	4.00
11 Dr. Manhattan	1.50	4.00
12 Nite Owl	1.50	4.00
13 Walter Kovacs	1.50	4.00
14 Mask-Killer	1.50	4.00
15 Bubastis	1.50	4.00
16 Knot Top Leader	1.50	4.00
17 Knot Top	1.50	4.00
18 Moloch the Mystic	1.50	4.00
19 Big Figure	1.50	4.00
20 Larry and Mike	1.50	4.00
21 The Comedian and Nite Owl	1.50	4.00
22 Silk Spectre and Dr. Manhattan	1.50	4.00
23 Ozymandias and Bubastis	1.50	4.00
24 Nite Owl and Rorschach	1.50	4.00
25 Dr. Manhattan	1.50	4.00
NNO Dr. Manhattan (SDCC promo)	70.00	100.00

2011 DC Heroclix Green Lantern Fast Forces

Complete Set	8.00	20.00
1 Green Lantern	.60	1.50
2 Kilowog	.60	1.50
3 Tomar Re	.40	1.00
4 Sinestro	.75	2.00
5 Guardian of the Universe	3.00	8.00
6 Abin Sur	.75	2.00

2011 DC Heroclix Green Lantern Gravity Feed

1 Green Lantern	.75	2.00
2 Hal Jordan	.60	1.50
3 Kilowog	1.25	3.00
4 Tomar Re	.40	1.00
5 Sinestro	.75	2.00
6 Ganthet	1.50	4.00
7 Abin Sur	.75	2.00
8 R'Amey Holl	1.00	2.50
9 Salaak	2.50	6.00
10 Boodikka	1.00	2.50

2011 DC Heroclix Superman

1 Superman C	1.50	4.00
2 Kryptonian Soldier C	.20	.50
3 Kryptonian Infiltrator C	.20	.50
4 Intergang Underboss C	.20	.50
5 Seven Deadly Brothers C	.60	1.50
6 All-Star Bizarro C	.20	.50
7 Starboy C	.20	.50
8 Brainiac 5 C	.20	.50
9 Lois Lane, Superwoman C	.20	.50
10 Supergirl C	.75	2.00
11 Gangbuster C	.20	.50
12 Livewire C	.20	.50
13 Maxwell Lord C	.20	.50
14 Mercy Graves C	.20	.50
15 Lex Luthor C	.20	.50
16 Element Woman C	.20	.50
17 Superboy U	.40	1.00
18 Steel U	.50	1.25
19 Magog U	.40	1.00
20 Bruno Mannheim U	.40	1.00
21 Human Target U	.40	1.00
22 Sun Boy U	.40	1.00
23 Earth Man U	.40	1.00
24 Invisible Kid U	.40	1.00
25 Matter-Eater Lad U	.40	1.00
26 Lucy Lane, Superwoman U	.50	1.25
27 Parasite U	.40	1.00
28 Manchester Black U	.40	1.00
29 Silver Banshee U	.60	1.50
30 Hope Taya U	.40	1.00
31 Non U	.50	1.25
32 Project: Superman U	.40	1.00
33 Eradicator R	2.50	6.00
34 Cyborg Superman R	1.50	4.00
35 Magog KC R	.40	1.00
36 Composite Superman R	.75	2.00
37 Libra R	.40	1.00
38 Princess Projectra R	.40	1.00
39 Wildfire R	.40	1.00
40 Maxwell Lord R	.40	1.00
41 Starman R	.40	1.00
42 Lobo R	2.00	5.00
43 Doomsday R	1.00	2.50
44 Ursa R	.60	1.50
45 Wonder Woman SR	3.00	8.00
46 The Bat-Man (Batman) SR	3.00	8.00
47 The Flash SR	4.00	10.00
48 Aquaman SR	4.00	10.00
49 Queen of Fables SR	2.50	6.00
50 Imperiex SR	3.00	8.00
51 Swamp Thing SR	3.00	8.00
52 Darkseid SR	8.00	20.00
53 Zod SR	3.00	8.00
54 Black Adam SR	10.00	25.00
55 Superman (Earth One) CH	8.00	20.00
56 Superman (Son of Darkseid) CH	12.00	30.00
57 Superman CH	8.00	20.00
58 Kal CH	5.00	12.00
101 Commander El	1.50	4.00
102 Manhunter Grandmaster	3.00	8.00
103 Bizarro-Girl	2.50	6.00
104 Zibarro	1.50	4.00
105 Superman Beyond	4.00	10.00

2011 DC Heroclix Superman Fast Forces Battle For Smallville

1 Superman	6.00	15.00
2 Supergirl	2.50	6.00
3 Steel	.75	2.00
4 Lex Luthor	1.50	4.00
5 Kryptonian Renegade	3.00	8.00
6 Bizarro	1.50	4.00

2012 DC Heroclix 10th Anniversary

1 Batman C	1.25	3.00
2 Wonder Woman C	.40	1.00
3 John Jones C	.40	1.00
4 Green Lantern C	1.25	3.00
5 Brainiac C	.40	1.00
6 Batgirl C	.75	2.00
7 Nightwing C	2.50	6.00
8 Catwoman C	.40	1.00
9 Blue Beetle C	2.00	5.00
10 The Flash U	2.50	6.00
11 Green Lantern U	1.25	3.00
12 Brainiac U	2.00	5.00
13 Lex Luthor U	.40	1.00
14 Robin U	.40	1.00
15 Catwoman U	1.50	4.00
16 Blue Beetle U	1.00	2.50
17 Oracle R	6.00	15.00
18 The Flash R	3.00	8.00
19 Martian Manhunter R	3.00	8.00
20 Lex Luthor R	6.00	15.00
21 Superman R	5.00	12.00
22 Black Lantern Wonder Woman CH	10.00	25.00
23 Black Lantern Batman CH	12.00	30.00
24 Black Lantern Superman CH	12.00	30.00

2012 DC Heroclix Batman

1 Batman C	.60	1.50
2 Bruce Wayne C	.40	1.00
3 Arkham Asylum Guard C	.60	1.50
4 The Joker Thug C	.60	1.50
5 Beast Boy C	.40	1.00
6 Hired Henchman C	.60	1.50
7a Catwoman C	.40	1.00
7b Selina Kyle C	2.50	6.00
8 Nightwing C	.40	1.00
9 Red Robin C	.40	1.00
10 Blackbat C	.40	1.00
11 Katana C	.40	1.00
12 Grifter C	.40	1.00
13 The Joker C	.40	1.00
14 Harley Quinn C	.50	1.25
15 Nightrunner C	.40	1.00
16 Batgirl C	.40	1.00
17 Robin U	.40	1.00
18 Aaron Cash U	.40	1.00
19 Beast Boy U	.40	1.00
20 KGBeast U	.40	1.00
21 Thunder U	.40	1.00
22 Two-Face U	.40	1.00
23a Sasha Bordeaux U	.40	1.00
23b Black Queen U	2.00	5.00
24 Maul U	.40	1.00
25 Batgirl U	.50	1.25
26 Roy Raymond, Jr. U	.40	1.00
27 Dick Grayson U	.40	1.00
28 Zealot U	.40	1.00
29 Godiva U	.40	1.00
30 El Gaucho U	.40	1.00
31 Alfred Pennyworth U	.75	2.00
32 Big Barda R	2.50	6.00
33 Bad Samaritan R	.40	1.00
34 Poison Ivy R	.75	2.00
35 Rocket Red R	.40	1.00
36 Batwoman R	.50	1.25
37a Hush R	1.50	4.00
37b Bruce Wayne R	8.00	20.00
38 August General in Iron R	.40	1.00
39 Hugo Strange R	.60	1.50
40 Halo R	.40	1.00
41 Lucius Fox R	.40	1.00
42 Batwing R	.40	1.00
43 Warblade R	.60	1.50
44 Mr. Unknown R	.40	1.00
45 Black Lightning SR	2.50	6.00
46 Geo-Force SR	2.50	6.00
47 Doctor Phosphorus SR	2.00	5.00
48 Mr. Freeze SR	6.00	15.00
49 Socialist Red Guardsman SR	1.50	4.00
50 Remac SR	1.50	4.00
51 Rex Mason SR	2.00	5.00
52 Booster Gold SR	4.00	10.00
53a Batman SR	6.00	15.00
53b The Caped Crusader SR	30.00	60.00
54 Voodoo SR	5.00	12.00
55 The Insider CH	6.00	15.00
56 Batman CH	8.00	20.00
57 Omega Batman CH	10.00	25.00
58 Batman CH	25.00	50.00
59 Batman CH	8.00	20.00
99a Flock of Bats (Black) C	1.25	3.00
99b Flock of Bats (Brown) C	2.50	6.00
99c Flock of Bats (Grey) C	4.00	10.00
100 Nightwing and Batgirl M	.40	1.00
V001 Batmobile SR	12.00	30.00
V002 Batwing SR	6.00	15.00
V003 Invisible Jet SR	6.00	15.00
V004 GCPD Cruiser SR	10.00	25.00
V005 Military Tank SR	6.00	15.00
V006 Haunted Tank SR	12.00	30.00
V007 The Bug SR	30.00	60.00

2012 DC Heroclix Batman Fast Forces

COMPLETE SET (6)
RELEASED ON NOVEMBER 14, 2012

1 Batman	2.00	5.00
2 Damian Wayne	.75	2.00
3 Nightwing	2.50	6.00
4 Red Robin	1.00	2.50
5 Alfred Pennyworth	2.50	6.00
6 Batgirl	1.25	3.00

2012 DC Heroclix Batman Gravity Feed

COMPLETE SET (10)
RELEASED ON NOVEMBER 14, 2012

201 Batman	1.50	4.00
202 Bruce Wayne	2.00	5.00
203 Hired Goon	1.50	4.00
204 Catwoman	2.00	5.00
205 Nightwing	.40	1.00
206 Red Robin	.40	1.00
207 The Joker	1.50	4.00
208 Harley Quinn	2.00	5.00
209 Batgirl	2.00	5.00
210 Two-Face	.60	1.50

2012 DC Heroclix Batman Streets of Gotham

COMPLETE SET (49)
RELEASED ON DECEMBER 19, 2012

1 GCPD Officer C	1.50	4.00
2 Lady Blackhawk C	.40	1.00
3 Black Canary C	.40	1.00
4 GCPD Detective C	1.00	2.50
5 GCPD Sergeant C	1.25	3.00
6 Blue Beetle C	.40	1.00
7 False Facer C	.40	1.00
8 Fire C	.50	1.25
9 Dove C	.50	1.25
10 Black Glove Demon C	.75	2.00
11 Dr. Hurt C	.40	1.00
12 Robin C	.40	1.00
13 Batman C	1.25	3.00
14 Huntress U	1.00	2.50
15a Renee Montoya U	1.50	4.00
15b The Question U	6.00	15.00
16 Harvey Bullock U	.75	2.00
17 Ice U	1.25	3.00
18 Hawk U	.40	1.00
19 Red Hood U	3.00	8.00
20 Calendar Man U	1.25	3.00
21 Killer Croc U	2.50	6.00
22 Harvey Dent U	.40	1.00
23 Scarecrow U	2.00	5.00
24 Mr. Zsasz R	3.00	8.00
25 Omac R	2.00	5.00
26 Commissioner Gordon R	2.50	6.00
27 Guy Gardner R	8.00	20.00
28 Vixen R	2.50	6.00
29 Onomatopoeia R	2.50	6.00
30 Black Mask R	2.50	6.00
31 The Architect R	1.25	3.00
32 Batman SR	2.00	5.00
33 Superman SR	3.00	8.00
34 Wonder Woman SR	2.00	5.00
35 Void SR	6.00	15.00
36 Spartan Warrior Spirit SR	3.00	8.00
37 Emp SR	2.50	6.00
38 David Cain SR	3.00	8.00
39 Lady Shiva SR	4.00	10.00
40 Deathstroke SR	6.00	15.00
41 Black Canary SR	1.50	4.00
42 Starling SR	2.00	5.00
43 Katana SR	2.00	5.00
44 Starfire SR	5.00	12.00
45 Arsenal SR	2.00	5.00
46 Crux SR	1.25	3.00
47 Batman SR	2.00	5.00
48 Robin SR	.75	2.00
49 GCPD Motor Officer SR	2.00	5.00
50 Batman CH	10.00	25.00
51 Batman CH	10.00	25.00
52 Batman CH	12.00	30.00
100 Batman of the Future LE	2.00	5.00
V001 Batcycle SR	8.00	20.00
V002 Robincycle SR	2.50	6.00
V003 GCPD Motorcycle SR	4.00	10.00

2012 DC Heroclix Batman Streets of Gotham Fast Forces

COMPLETE SET (6)
RELEASED ON DECEMBER 19, 2012

1 Oracle	4.00	10.00
2 Lady Blackhawk	.40	1.00
3 Huntress	1.25	3.00
4 Black Canary	.75	2.00
5 Hawk	.60	1.50
6 Dove	.40	1.00

2012 DC Heroclix Justice League New 52

COMPLETE SET (21)
RELEASED ON AUGUST 15, 2012

1 Superman C	3.00	8.00
2 Batman C	2.00	5.00
3 Wonder Woman C	2.00	5.00
4 Green Lantern C	1.50	4.00
5 Aquaman C	2.00	5.00
6 Cyborg C	1.25	3.00
7 Green Arrow C	5.00	12.00
8 Mera C	.50	1.25
9 Firestorm C	.75	2.00
10 Firestorm C	.60	1.50
11 Hawkman U	3.00	8.00
12 Shade the Changing Man U	.50	1.25
13 Deadman U	1.25	3.00
14 Zatanna U	2.50	6.00
15 Mindwarp U	.75	2.00
16 Enchantress U	8.00	20.00
17 The Flash R	4.00	10.00
18 Madame Xanadu R	4.00	10.00
19 John Constantine R	10.00	25.00
20 Deathstroke R	8.00	20.00
21 Fury R	3.00	8.00

2012 DC Heroclix Justice League New 52 Fast Forces

COMPLETE SET (6)
RELEASED ON AUGUST 15, 2012

1 Cyborg	.75	2.00
2 Superman	2.50	6.00
3 Batman	2.00	5.00
4 Wonder Woman	4.00	10.00
5 The Flash	5.00	12.00
6 Green Lantern	1.50	4.00

2012 DC Heroclix The Dark Knight Rises

COMPLETE SET (36)
RELEASED ON JUNE 6, 2012

1 The Dark Knight C	2.00	5.00
2 Shadow Assassin C	2.00	5.00
3 Bruce Wayne C	.75	2.00
4 Arkham Asylum Inmate C	1.25	3.00
5 GCPD Officer C	2.00	5.00
6 Catwoman C	.75	2.00
7 The Joker's Henchman C	.75	2.00
8 Mercenary C	1.50	4.00
9 Two-Face C	.40	1.00
10 Falcone Bodyguard C	1.25	3.00
11 GCPD Riot Officer C	2.00	5.00
12 Miranda Tate U	.60	1.50
13 Alfred Pennyworth U	2.50	6.00
14 Bane U	2.00	5.00
15 Master Bruce Wayne U	.75	2.00
16 Salvatore Maroni U	.75	2.00
17 Harvey Dent U	2.00	5.00
18 Rachel Dawes U	1.25	3.00
19 The Joker's Henchman U	3.00	8.00
20 The Joker as Sgt. U	1.25	3.00
21 Lt. Gordon U	6.00	15.00
22 Ra's Al Ghul R	3.00	8.00
23 Henri Ducard R	5.00	12.00
24 Carmine Falcone R	1.50	4.00
25 Scarecrow R	5.00	12.00
26 Lucius Fox R	4.00	10.00
27 Commissioner Gordon R	5.00	12.00
28 The Joker R	10.00	25.00
29 The Batman R	6.00	15.00
100 Batman LE	1.50	4.00
101 Batman F	1.50	4.00
102 Catwoman F	.60	1.50
103 Bane F	4.00	10.00
104 The Joker F	4.00	10.00
105 Harvey Two-Face F	.40	1.00
106 Sgt. Gordon F	1.00	2.50

2012 DC Heroclix The Dark Knight Rises Gravity Feed

COMPLETE SET (10)
RELEASED ON JUNE 6, 2012

201 Batman	2.50	6.00
202 Bruce Wayne	.60	1.50
203 Catwoman	1.50	4.00
204 Bane	1.25	3.00
205 Rachel Dawes	1.25	3.00
206 John Blake	6.00	15.00
207 The Joker's Henchman #3	3.00	8.00
208 The Joker's Henchman #4	4.00	10.00
209 The Joker	4.00	10.00
210 Arkham Asylum Escapee	1.50	4.00

2014 DC Heroclix Justice League Strategy Game

1 Superman
2 Batman
3 Wonder Woman
4 Cyborg
5 Darkseid
001r Superman
002r Batman
003r Wonder Woman
005e Darkseid
B001 Parademon

2014 DC Heroclix Superman and the Legion of Superheroes

1 Cosmic Boy C	1.50	4.00
2 Saturn Girl C	2.00	5.00
3 Lightning Lad C	1.50	4.00
4 Science Police Officer C	2.00	5.00
6 Triplicate Girl C	1.50	4.00
7 Shrinking Violet C	.40	1.00
8 Phantom Girl C	1.50	4.00
9 Blight C	1.25	3.00
10 Polar Boy C	1.25	3.00
11 Sensor Girl C	1.50	4.00
12 Tyroc C	.40	1.00
13 Ladytron C	1.50	4.00
14 Daemonite C	1.50	4.00
15 Timber Wolf C	1.25	3.00
16 Giganta C	1.25	3.00
18 Ultra Boy U	1.25	3.00
19 Amethyst U	1.25	3.00
20 Blok U	1.25	3.00
21 Wildfire U	1.25	3.00
22 Gates U	1.25	3.00
23 Mr. Majestic U	1.50	4.00
24 Lex Luthor U	1.50	4.00
25 Mano U	1.50	4.00
26 Mister Miracle U	1.50	4.00
27 Kalibak U	1.50	4.00
28 Lightray U	1.25	3.00
29 Tharok U	1.00	2.50
30 Dawnstar U	1.25	3.00
31 Chameleon Girl U	1.25	3.00
32 Colossal Boy U	2.00	5.00
33 Stargirl R	1.50	4.00

34 Starman (Jack Knight) R 1.25 3.00
35 Shadow Lass R 1.25 3.00
36 Glorith R 1.50 4.00
38 Black Manta R 1.50 4.00
39 Bizarro R 3.00 8.00
40 Emerald Empress R 2.50 6.00
41 Universo R 1.25 3.00
42 Helspont R 2.00 5.00
43 Orion R 1.50 4.00
44 Darkseid R 10.00
45 Computo R 1.25 3.00
46 Superboy SR 5.00 12.00
48 Tellus SR 3.00 8.00
49 Solomon Grundy SR 6.00 15.00
50 Toyman SR 4.00 10.00
51 Takion SR 2.50 6.00
52 Hightather SR 2.50 6.00
53 Big Barda and Mr. Miracle SR 4.00 10.00
54 Persuader SR 2.50 6.00
55 Validus SR 6.00 15.00
56 Mordru SR 2.50 6.00
57 Lydea Mallor CH 15.00 40.00
58 Kalibak CH 10.00 25.00
59 Guardian CH 6.00 15.00
5a Daxamite C 1.00 2.50
5b Mon-El C 5.00 12.00
60 Orion CH 8.00 20.00
61 Superman CH 15.00 40.00
17a Cheetah (Priscilla Rich) U 1.25 3.00
17b Cheetah (Barbara Ann Minerva) U 4.00 10.00
37a Riddler R 4.00 10.00
37b Edward Nigma R 6.00 15.00
47a White Witch SR 5.00 12.00
47b Black Witch SR 12.00 30.00

2014 DC Heroclix Superman and the Legion of Superheroes Fast Forces

1 Lex Luthor .40 1.00
2 Bizarro .75 2.00
3 Cheetah .40 1.00
4 Black Manta .60 1.50
5 Solomon Grundy 2.50 6.00
6 Giganta .75 2.00

2014 DC Heroclix Superman and the Legion of Superheroes Gravity Feed

201 Cosmic Boy C 2.00 5.00
202 Saturn Girl C 1.25 3.00
203 Lightning Lad C 1.25 3.00
204 Ultra-Boy C .40 1.00
205 Amethyst C 1.25 3.00
206 Triplicate Girl C 2.00 5.00
207 Shrinking Violet C 1.50 4.00
208 Phantom Girl C 1.25 3.00
209 Science Police Officer C 1.25 3.00
210 Daxamite C 1.50 4.00

2014 DC Heroclix Superman and the Legion of Superheroes Op Kit

101 Mordru 6.00 15.00
102 Mon-El (Green Lantern) 8.00 20.00
103 Shrinking Violet 1.25 3.00
99e Superman Action Figure 2.00 5.00
S0101 Legion Flight Ring 2.00 5.00
S0102 Mother Box 1.50 4.00

2014 DC Heroclix Superman and the Legion of Superheroes Toyman Drones

99a Airplane
99b Race Car
99c Cymbal-Banging Monkey
99d Teddy Bear 3.00 8.00

2014 DC Heroclix War of Light

1 Orange Lantern Construct
2 Red Lantern Recruit
3 Sinestro Corps Recruit
4 Indigo Tribe Recruit
5 Green Lantern Recruit
6 Star Sapphire Recruit
7 Blue Lantern Recruit
8 Black Lantern Reanimate
9 Controller Construct
10 Controller
14 Rankorr
15 Arisia
16 Soranik Natu
17 Boodikka
18 Munk
18 Munk
19 Bedovian
21 Lyssa Drak
22 Katma Tui
23 Mongul
24 Saarek
25 The Weaponer of Qward
26 Sodam Yat
27 Graf Toren
28 Kilowog
29 Brother Hymn
32 Miri Riam
33 Sister Sercy
34 Aquaman
36 Bleez
37 Karu-Sil
38 Dex-Starr
39 Kryb
40 Salaak
41 Parallax (Hal Jordan)
43 Hannu
44 Fatality
45 Brother Warth
47 Ganthet
48 Firestorm
49 First Lantern
51 Krona
52 Hal Jordan and Sinestro
53 Swamp Thing
54 Morro
55 Parallax (Kyle Rayner)
56 Sinestro (Indigo Tribe)
58 Galius Zed (Black Lantern)
60 Black Hand
61 Entity
62 Ion
63 Ophidian
64 Proselyte
65 Parallax
66 Butcher
67 Adara
68 Predator
99 Despotellis
101 Sinestro
102 Hal Jordan (Green Lantern)
103 Rond Vidar
104 Guy Gardner (Green Lantern)
105 John Stewart
106 Jade
109 Larfleeze
110 Arkillo
111 Saint Walker
112 Atrocitus
113 Indigo-1
114 Star Sapphire
115 Nekron
011a Hal Jordan (Orange Lantern)
011b Hal Jordan (Blue Lantern)
012a Hal Jordan (Red Lantern)
012b Hal Jordan (Black Lantern)
013a Romat-Ru
013b Tomar Tu
020a Laira (Red Lantern)
020b Laira (Green Lantern)
025e The Weaponer of Qward
026e Sodam Yat
030a Guy Gardner (Star Sapphires)
030b Guy Gardner (Red Lantern)
031a Kyle Rayner (Blue Lantern)
031b Kyle Rayner (White Lantern)
035a Sayd (Orange Lantern)
035b Sayd (Blue Lantern)
042a John Stewart (Black Lantern)
042b John Stewart (Indigo Tribe)
044r Fatality
046a Abin Sur (Black Lantern)
046b Abin Sur (Green Lantern)
050a Spectre (Red Lantern)
050b Spectre (Black Lantern)
051e Krona
052r Hal Jordan and Sinestro
057a Superboy Prime (Sinestro Corps)
057b Superboy Prime (Red Lantern)
059a Zilius Zox
059b Galius Zed (Green Lantern)
060p Black Hand
061p Entity
062p Ion
063p Ophidian
063p Ophidian
064p Proselyte
065p Parallax
066p Butcher
067p Adara
068p Predator
101r Sinestro
104r Guy Gardner (Green Lantern)
105r John Stewart
110r Arkillo
115a Nekron (Darkness Incarnate)
115b Nekron (Lord of the Unliving)
115c Nekron (The Void Before Time)
115d Nekron (The Death That Walks)
034bt Undead Shark
037bt The Pack
050ae Spectre (Red Lantern)
057ar Superboy Prime (Sinestro Corps)
B001 Cowgirl
B002 Rocket Man
B003 Thomas Kalmaku
H001 Orange Lantern Absorbed
H002 Black Lantern Risen
H003 Yellow Lantern Initiate
H004 Green Lantern Initiate
H005 Daxamite
H006 Manhunter Alpha
H007 Zamaron Trainee
R100 Power Battery (Green Lantern Corps)
R101 Power Battery (White Lantern Corps)
R102 Power Battery (Red Lantern Corps)
R103 Power Battery (Orange Lantern Corps)
R104 Power Battery (Indigo Tribe)
R105 Power Battery (Sinestro Corps)
R106 Power Battery (Star Sapphires)
R107 Power Battery (Blue Lantern Corps)
R108 Power Battery (Black Lantern Corps)
R200 Shield (Green)
R300 Green Lantern Ring
R301 White Lantern Ring
R302 Red Lantern Ring
R303 Orange Lantern Ring
R304 Indigo Tribe Ring
R305 Sinestro Corps Ring
R306 Star Sapphire Ring
R307 Blue Lantern Ring
R308 Black Lantern Ring
S300 Green Lantern Ring
S301 White Lantern Ring
S302 Red Lantern Ring
S303 Orange Lantern Ring
S304 Indigo Tribe Ring
S305 Sinestro Corps Ring
S306 Star Sapphire Ring
S307 Blue Lantern Ring
S308 Black Lantern Ring
115de Nekron (The Death That Walks)
R200.01 Net (Green)
R200.02 Axe (Green)
R200.03 Mallet (Green)
R200.04 Wall (Green)
R200.05 Crossbow (Green)
R200.06 Decoy (Green)
R200.07 Catapult (Green)
R200.08 Scissors (Green)
R200.09 Nurse (Green)
R200.10 Boxing Glove (Green)
R201.05 Crossbow (White)
R201.06 Decoy (White)
R201.07 Catapult (White)
R201.08 Scissors (White)
R201.09 Nurse (White)
R201.10 Boxing Glove (White)
R201.14 Sniper Rifle (White)
R208.01 Net (Black)
R208.05 Crossbow (Black)
R208.06 Decoy (Black)
R208.07 Catapult (Black)
R208.08 Scissors (Black)
R208.09 Nurse (Black)
R208.10 Boxing Glove (Black)

2003 Indy Heroclix

COMPLETE SET (120) 100.00 175.00
BOOSTER PACK 5.00 7.00
RELEASED ON OCTOBER 1, 2003
1 Ashleigh R .30 .50
2 Ashleigh E .50 1.00
3 Ashleigh V 1.00 2.00
4 Tomoe R .30 .50
5 Tomoe E .50 1.00
6 Tomoe V 1.00 2.00
7 Saurian Trooper R .30 .50
8 Saurian Trooper E .50 1.00
9 Saurian Trooper V 1.00 2.00
10 Scarab R .30 .50
11 Scarab E .50 1.00
12 Scarab V 1.00 2.00
13 Tiger Lilly R .30 .50
14 Tiger Lilly E .50 1.00
15 Tiger Lilly V 1.00 2.00
16 Sydney Savage R .30 .50
17 Sydney Savage E .50 1.00
18 Sydney Savage V 1.00 2.00
19 Johnny Alpha R .30 .50
20 Johnny Alpha E .50 1.00
21 Johnny Alpha V 1.00 2.00
22 Judge Hershey R .30 .50
23 Judge Hershey E .50 1.00
24 Judge Hershey V 1.00 2.00
25 Aphrodite IX R .30 .50
26 Aphrodite IX E .50 1.00
27 Aphrodite IX V 1.00 2.00
28 Magdalena R .30 .50
29 Magdalena E .50 1.00
30 Magdalena V 1.00 2.00
31 Arashi R .30 .50
32 Arashi E .50 1.00
33 Arashi V 1.00 2.00
34 Lobster Johnson R .30 .50
35 Lobster Johnson E .50 1.00
36 Lobster Johnson V 1.00 2.00
37 Arwyn R .30 .50
38 Arwyn E .50 1.00
39 Arwyn V 1.00 2.00
40 Boon R .30 .50
41 Boon E .50 1.00
42 Boon V 1.00 2.00
43 Ian Nottingham R .30 .50
44 Ian Nottingham E .50 1.00
45 Ian Nottingham V 1.00 2.00
46 The Darkness R .30 .50
47 The Darkness E .50 1.00
48 The Darkness V 1.00 2.00
49 Natalia Kassle R .30 .50
50 Natalia Kassle E .50 1.00
51 Natalia Kassle V 1.00 2.00
52 Major Maxim R .30 .50
53 Major Maxim E .50 1.00
54 Major Maxim V 1.00 2.00
55 Bron R .30 .50
56 Bron E .50 1.00
57 Bron V 1.00 2.00
58 Shi R .30 .50
59 Shi E .50 1.00
60 Shi V 1.00 2.00
61 Yukio R .30 .50
62 Yukio E .50 1.00
63 Yukio V 1.00 2.00
64 Witchblade R .30 .50
65 Witchblade E .50 1.00
66 Witchblade V 1.00 2.00
67 Hellboy R .50 1.00
68 Hellboy E 1.00 2.00
69 Hellboy V 3.00 5.00
70 Judge Dredd R .30 .50
71 Judge Dredd E .50 1.00
72 Judge Dredd V 1.00 2.00
73 Abbey Chase R .30 .50
74 Abbey Chase E .50 1.00
75 Abbey Chase V 1.00 2.00
76 Kabuki R .30 .50
77 Kabuki E .50 1.00
78 Kabuki V 1.00 2.00
79 Death Demon R .30 .50
80 Death Demon E .50 1.00
81 Death Demon V 1.00 2.00
82 Rasputin R .30 .50
83 Rasputin E .50 1.00
84 Rasputin V 1.00 2.00
85 Samandhal Rey U 8.00 12.00
86 Arwyn U 10.00 15.00
87 Hellboy U 20.00 30.00
88 Hecate U 10.00 15.00
89 Shi U 10.00 15.00
90 Abbey Chase U 10.00 15.00
91 Judge Anderson U 10.00 18.00
92 Judge Death U 10.00 18.00
93 Witchblade U 10.00 18.00
94 Angelus U 10.00 15.00
95 Siamese U 8.00 12.00
96 Cyblade U 8.00 12.00
97 Brit City Judge R .30 .50
98 Brit City Judge E .50 1.00
99 Brit City Judge V 1.00 2.00
100 Stix R .30 .50
101 Stix E .50 1.00
102 Stix V 1.00 2.00
103 Wulf Sternhammer R .30 .50
104 Wulf Sternhammer E .50 1.00
105 Wulf Sternhammer V 1.00 2.00
106 Torquemada R .30 .50
107 Torquemada E .50 1.00
108 Torquemada V 1.00 2.00
109 Nemesis R .30 .50
110 Nemesis E .50 1.00
111 Nemesis V 1.00 2.00
112 Judge Fire R .30 .50
113 Judge Fire E .50 1.00
114 Judge Fire V 1.00 2.00
115 Judge Mortis R .30 .50
116 Judge Mortis E .50 1.00
117 Judge Mortis V 1.00 2.00
118 Judge Fear R .30 .50
119 Judge Fear E .50 1.00
120 Judge Fear V 1.00 2.00
201 Ashleigh (Princess Ashleigh) LE 10.00 15.00
202 Tomoe (Tomoe Gozan) LE 8.00 12.00
203 Saurian Trooper (Bajounte-Ka) LE 8.00 12.00
204 Scarab (Keiko) LE 8.00 12.00
205 Tiger Lilly (Akemi) LE 8.00 12.00
206 Sydney Savage (Spec Ops Savage) LE 8.00 12.00
207 Johnny Alpha (Search/Destroy Agent Alpha) LE 8.00 15.00
208 Judge Hershey (Barbara Hershey) LE 12.00 18.00
209 Aphrodite IX (Aphrodite) LE 8.00 12.00
210 Magdalena (Sister Magdalena) LE 8.00 12.00
211 Arashi (Masahiro Arashi) LE 8.00 12.00
212 Lobster Johnson (Lobster Johnson) LE 8.00 12.00
221 Witchblade (Scrye) LE 12.00 20.00
222 Boon (Inquest) LE 8.00 12.00
223 Arwyn 8.00 12.00
P1 Johnny Alpha PROMO

2011 Indy HeroClix Gears of War

COMPLETE SET 30.00 60.00
1 Marcus Fenix 3.00 8.00
2 Dominic Santiago 3.00 8.00
3 Augustus Cole 3.00 8.00
4 Damon Baird 3.00 8.00
5 Anya Stroud 3.00 8.00
6 Mauler 3.00 8.00
7 Locust Drone 3.00 8.00
8 Kantus 3.00 8.00
9 General RAAM 3.00 8.00
10 Skorge 3.00 8.00

2011 Indy Heroclix Street Fighter

BOOSTER BOX 4.00 8.00
1 Ken C 3.00 6.00
2 Ryu C 3.00 6.00
3 Blanka C .50 1.00
3B Blanka CH 25.00 40.00
4 Dhalsim C .50 1.00
5 Zangief C 1.00 2.00
5B Zangief CH 20.00 30.00
6 E. Honda C 1.00 2.00
7 Guile C 1.00 2.00
8 Chun-Li C .50 1.00
8B Chun-Li CH 25.00 40.00
9 Cammy C 1.00 2.00
9B Cammy CH 30.00 50.00
10 Dee Jay C 1.00 2.00
11 Fei Long U 3.00 8.00
12 T. Hawk U 2.00 5.00
13 Balrog U 3.00 8.00
14 Vega U 6.00 15.00
15 Sagat U 3.00 8.00
16 Ken U 5.00 10.00
17 Dhalsim U 2.00 5.00
18 Guile U 5.00 10.00
19 M. Bison R 15.00 30.00
20 Ryu R 10.00 20.00
21 Ken R 10.00 20.00
22 Akuma R 15.00 30.00
23 Evil Ryu R 10.00 20.00
101 Ryu F 3.00 6.00
102 Blanka F 3.00 6.00
103 Dhalsim F 3.00 6.00
104 Chun-Li F 3.00 6.00
105 Guile F 3.00 6.00
106 Ken F 3.00 6.00

2002 Marvel Heroclix Clobberin Time

COMPLETE SET (96) 200.00 275.00
BOOSTER PACK 8.00 12.00
RELEASED ON NOVEMBER 1, 2002
1 S.H.I.E.L.D. Trooper R .30 .50
2 S.H.I.E.L.D. Trooper E .50 .75
3 S.H.I.E.L.D. Trooper V 1.00 2.00
4 S.H.I.E.L.D. Sniper R .30 .50
5 S.H.I.E.L.D. Sniper E .50 .75
6 S.H.I.E.L.D. Sniper V 1.00 2.00
7 Mandroid Armor R .30 .50
8 Mandroid Armor E .50 .75
9 Mandroid Armor V 1.00 2.00
10 A.I.M. Agent R .30 .50
11 A.I.M. Agent E .50 .75
12 A.I.M. Agent V 1.00 2.00
13 A.I.M. Medic R .30 .50
14 A.I.M. Medic E .50 .75
15 A.I.M. Medic V 1.00 2.00
16 Skrull Commando R .30 .50
17 Skrull Commando E .50 .75
18 Skrull Commando V 1.00 2.00
19 Vampire Lackey R .30 .50
20 Vampire Lackey E .50 .75
21 Vampire Lackey V 1.00 2.00
22 Black Cat R .30 .50
23 Black Cat E .50 .75
24 Black Cat V 1.00 2.00
25 Yellowjacket R .30 .50
26 Yellowjacket E .50 .75
27 Yellowjacket V 1.00 2.00
28 Doombot R 1.00 2.00
29 Doombot E 2.00 3.00
30 Doombot V 4.00 6.00
31 Avalanche R .30 .50
32 Avalanche E .50 .75
33 Avalanche V 1.00 2.00
34 Blob R .30 .50
35 Blob E .50 .75
36 Blob V 1.00 2.00
37 Toad R .30 .50
38 Toad E .50 .75
39 Toad V 1.00 2.00
40 Elektra R .30 .50
41 Elektra E .50 .75
42 Elektra V 1.00 2.00
43 Invisible Girl R 5.00 10.00
44 Invisible Girl E 10.00 15.00
45 Invisible Woman V 15.00 25.00
46 Thing R 4.00 7.00
47 Thing E 5.00 10.00
48 Thing V 10.00 20.00
49 Human Torch R 4.00 7.00
50 Human Torch E 5.00 10.00
51 Human Torch V 15.00 20.00
52 Hawkeye R .30 .50

53 Hawkeye E	.50	.75
54 Hawkeye V	1.00	2.00
55 Black Widow R	.30	.50
56 Black Widow E	.50	.75
57 Black Widow V	1.00	2.00
58 Blastaar R	.30	.50
59 Blastaar E	.50	.75
60 Blastaar V	1.00	2.00
61 Thor R	6.00	10.00
62 Thor E	10.00	15.00
63 Thor V	15.00	25.00
64 Sandman R	.30	.50
65 Sandman E	.50	.75
66 Sandman V	1.00	2.00
67 Logan R	1.00	2.00
68 Logan E	3.00	5.00
69 Logan V	6.00	10.00
70 Mr. Fantastic R	4.00	8.00
71 Mr. Fantastic E	8.00	12.00
72 Mr. Fantastic V	10.00	20.00
73 Dr. Doom R	6.00	10.00
74 Dr. Doom E	10.00	20.00
75 Dr. Doom V	20.00	35.00
76 Dr. Octopus R	3.00	6.00
77 Dr. Octopus E	4.00	8.00
78 Dr. Octopus V	7.00	12.00
79 White Queen R	3.00	5.00
80 White Queen E	4.00	8.00
81 White Queen V	7.00	12.00
82 She-Hulk R	1.00	2.00
83 She-Hulk E	3.00	5.00
84 She-Hulk V	5.00	10.00
85 Nightcrawler U	55.00	90.00
86 Nick Fury U	25.00	40.00
87 Moondragon U	15.00	30.00
88 Spider-Man U	20.00	30.00
89 Mojo U	18.00	30.00
90 Super Skrull U	18.00	30.00
91 Red Skull U	20.00	30.00
92 Spiral U	20.00	40.00
93 Titania U	15.00	25.00
94 Mr. Fix-It U	18.00	30.00
95 Medusa U	15.00	25.00
96 Enchantress U	15.00	25.00
101 S.H.I.E.L.D. Trooper (Clay Quartermain) LE	10.00	15.00
102 S.H.I.E.L.D. Sniper (Laura Brown) LE	12.00	18.00
103 Mandroid Armor (Agent Beaulieu) LE	12.00	18.00
104 AIM Agent (George Tarleton) LE	10.00	15.00
105 AIM Agent (Scientist Supreme) LE	12.00	18.00
106 Skrull Commando (Paibok) LE	8.00	15.00
107 Vampire Lackey (Rachel Van Helsing) LE	12.00	18.00
108 Black Cat (Felicia Hardy) LE	12.00	18.00
109 Yellowjacket (Rita DeMara) LE	15.00	25.00
110 Dr. Doom (Dr. Doom) LE	25.00	35.00
111 Avalanche (Dominic Petros) LE	10.00	15.00
112 Blob (Fred J. Dukes) LE	15.00	22.00
113 Toad (Mortimer Toynbee) LE	12.00	18.00
114 Elektra (Elektra Natchios) LE	10.00	15.00
115 Invisible Woman (Sue Storm) LE	20.00	25.00
116 Thing (Benjamin J. Grimm) LE	20.00	30.00
117 Human Torch (Johnny Storm) LE	20.00	30.00
118 Hawkeye (Clint Barton) LE	18.00	25.00
119 Black Widow (Natasha Romanov) LE	60.00	90.00
120 Blastaar (Blastaar of Baluur) LE	20.00	40.00

2002 Marvel Heroclix Infinity Challenge

COMPLETE SET (150)	125.00	200.00
BOOSTER PACK	3.00	5.00
RELEASED ON MAY 1, 2002		
1 S.H.I.E.L.D. Agent R	.25	.40
2 S.H.I.E.L.D. Agent E	.30	.60
3 S.H.I.E.L.D. Agent V	1.00	1.50
4 S.H.I.E.L.D. Medic R	.25	.40
5 S.H.I.E.L.D. Medic E	.30	.60
6 S.H.I.E.L.D. Medic V	1.00	2.00
7 Hydra Operative R	.25	.40
8 Hydra Operative E	.30	.60
9 Hydra Operative V	1.00	1.50
10 Hydra Medic R	.25	.40
11 Hydra Medic E	.30	.60
12 Hydra Medic V	1.00	1.50
13 Thug R	.25	.40
14 Thug E	.30	.60
15 Thug V	1.00	1.50
16 Henchman R	.25	.40
17 Henchman E	.30	.60
18 Henchman V	1.00	1.50
19 Skrull Agent R	.25	.40
20 Skrull Agent E	.30	.60
21 Skrull Agent V	1.00	3.00
22 Skrull Warrior R	.25	.40
23 Skrull Warrior E	.30	.60
24 Skrull Warrior V	1.00	3.00
25 Blade R	.25	.40
26 Blade E	.30	.60
27 Blade V	1.50	2.00
28 Wolfsbane R	.25	.40
29 Wolfsbane E	.30	.60
30 Wolfsbane V	1.50	2.00
31 Elektra R	.25	.40
32 Elektra E	.30	.60
33 Elektra V	1.50	2.00
34 Wasp R	.25	.40
35 Wasp E	.30	.60
36 Wasp V	1.00	1.50
37 Constrictor R	.25	.40
38 Constrictor E	.30	.60
39 Constrictor V	1.00	1.50
40 Boomerang R	.25	.40
41 Boomerang E	.30	.60
42 Boomerang V	1.00	1.50
43 Kingpin R	.25	.50
44 Kingpin E	.40	.75
45 Kingpin V	1.00	2.00
46 Vulture R	.50	.75
47 Vulture E	1.00	1.50
48 Vulture V	1.50	2.00
49 Jean Grey R	1.00	1.50
50 Jean Grey E	2.00	3.00
51 Jean Grey V	3.00	4.00
52 Hobgoblin R	.50	.75
53 Hobgoblin E	.75	1.00
54 Hobgoblin V	1.00	2.50
55 Sabretooth R	.50	.75
56 Sabretooth E	.75	1.00
57 Sabretooth V	2.00	3.00
58 Hulk R	1.00	1.50
59 Hulk E	2.00	3.00
60 Hulk V	5.00	8.00
61 Puppet Master R	.25	.40
62 Puppet Master E	.30	.60
63 Puppet Master V	1.00	1.50
64 Annihilus R	.25	.40
65 Annihilus E	.30	.60
66 Annihilus V	1.00	3.00
67 Captain America R	2.00	3.00
68 Captain America E	3.00	5.00
69 Captain America V	5.00	7.00
70 Spider-Man R	2.00	2.50
71 Spider-Man E	3.00	4.00
72 Spider-Man V	5.00	6.00
73 Wolverine R	3.00	4.00
74 Wolverine E	4.00	5.00
75 Wolverine V	5.00	8.00
76 Professor Xavier R	1.00	1.50
77 Professor Xavier E	2.00	2.50
78 Professor Xavier V	3.00	5.00
79 Juggernaut R	1.00	2.00
80 Juggernaut E	2.00	3.00
81 Juggernaut V	4.00	6.00
82 Cyclops R	1.00	1.50
83 Cyclops E	2.00	3.00
84 Cyclops V	3.00	5.00
85 Black Panther R	1.00	2.00
86 Black Panther E	2.00	2.50
87 Black Panther V	3.00	5.00
88 Blizzard R	.25	.40
89 Blizzard E	.30	.60
90 Blizzard V	1.00	2.00
91 Pyro R	.50	1.00
92 Pyro E	1.00	2.00
93 Pyro V	3.00	4.00
94 Whirlwind R	.25	.40
95 Whirlwind E	.30	.60
96 Whirlwind V	1.00	1.50
97 Daredevil R	.50	.75
98 Daredevil E	1.00	1.50
99 Daredevil V	2.00	3.00
100 Bullseye R	.75	1.00
101 Bullseye E	1.00	2.00
102 Bullseye V	3.00	5.00
103 Scarlet Witch R	1.00	1.50
104 Scarlet Witch E	1.50	2.00
105 Scarlet Witch V	3.00	4.00
106 Quicksilver R	1.00	1.50
107 Quicksilver E	1.50	2.00
108 Quicksilver V	3.00	5.00
109 Mr. Hyde R	.25	.40
110 Mr. Hyde E	.30	.60
111 Mr. Hyde V	1.00	1.50
112 Klaw R	.25	.40
113 Klaw E	.30	.60
114 Klaw V	1.00	2.00
115 Controller R	.25	.40
116 Controller E	.30	.60
117 Controller V	2.00	3.00
118 Hercules R	.50	.75
119 Hercules E	1.00	1.50
120 Hercules V	3.00	4.00
121 Rogue R	1.00	2.00
122 Rogue E	2.00	3.00
123 Rogue V	5.00	8.00
124 Dr. Strange R	1.00	2.00
125 Dr. Strange E	2.00	3.50
126 Dr. Strange V	4.00	7.00
127 Magneto R	2.00	3.00
128 Magneto E	4.00	6.00
129 Magneto V	7.00	12.00
130 Kang R	.75	1.00
131 Kang E	1.00	2.00
132 Kang V	2.00	3.00
133 Ultron R	1.00	1.50
134 Ultron E	2.00	3.00
135 Ultron V	3.00	5.00
136 Firelord R	1.00	2.00
137 Firelord E	2.00	3.00
138 Firelord V	4.00	6.00
139 Vision U	15.00	20.00
140 Quasar U	9.00	15.00
141 Thanos U	15.00	20.00
142 Nightmare U	10.00	15.00
143 Wasp U	8.00	12.00
144 Elektra U	8.00	12.00
145 Professor Xavier U	10.00	15.00
146 Juggernaut U	10.00	15.00
147 Cyclops U	8.00	12.00
148 Captain America U	10.00	15.00
149 Wolverine U	10.00	20.00
150 Spider-Man U	12.00	20.00
151 S.H.I.E.L.D. Agent (Gabriel Jones) LE	10.00	14.00
152 S.H.I.E.L.D. Medic (Tia Senyaka) LE	10.00	18.00
153 Hydra Operative (Operative #128) LE	7.00	12.00
154 Hydra Medic (Medic #519) LE	7.00	12.00
155 Thug (Knuckles) LE	7.00	12.00
156 Thug (Joey the Snake) LE	7.00	12.00
157 Skrull Agent (Nenora) LE	10.00	12.00
158 Skrull Warrior (Raksor) LE	9.00	15.00
159 Blade (Blade) LE	9.00	15.00
160 Wolfsbane (Rahne Sinclair) LE	8.00	12.00
161 Constrictor (Frank Schlichting) LE	8.00	12.00
162 Boomerang (Fred Myers) LE	15.00	20.00
163 Kingpin (Wilson Fisk) LE	10.00	15.00
164 Vulture (Adrian Toomes) LE	10.00	15.00
165 Jean Grey LE	15.00	30.00
166 Hobgoblin (Ned Leeds) LE	15.00	25.00
167 Sabretooth (Victor Creed) LE	30.00	60.00
168 Hulk (Bruce Banner) LE	30.00	50.00
169 Puppet Master (Phillip Masters) LE	10.00	18.00
170 Annihilus LE	30.00	60.00
171 Wolverine (Bezerker) LE	10.00	20.00
172 Yellowjacket LE	15.00	20.00
173 Ant-Man LE	20.00	25.00
199 Hulk (Playstation) LE	25.00	35.00
BF1 Sentinel (Big Figure)	25.00	40.00
PR Spider-man (Promo)	5.00	10.00

2003 Marvel Heroclix Critical Mass

COMPLETE SET (96)	175.00	275.00
BOOSTER PACK	5.00	8.00
RELEASED ON NOVEMBER 1, 2003		
1 Moloid R	.30	.50
2 Moloid E	.50	.75
3 Moloid V	1.00	2.00
4 Brood Warrior R	.30	.50
5 Brood Warrior E	.50	.75
6 Brood Warrior V	1.00	2.00
7 Kree Warrior R	.30	.50
8 Kree Warrior E	.50	.75
9 Kree Warrior V	1.00	2.00
10 SWAT Heavy Weapons R	.30	.50
11 SWAT Heavy Weapons E	.50	.75
12 SWAT Heavy Weapons V	1.00	2.00
13 Dreadnought R	.30	.50
14 Dreadnought E	.50	.75
15 Dreadnought V	1.00	2.00
16 Hepzibah R	.30	.50
17 Hepzibah E	.50	.75
18 Hepzibah V	1.00	2.00
19 Marrow R	.30	.50
20 Marrow E	.50	.75
21 Marrow V	1.00	2.00
22 Corsair R	.30	.50
23 Corsair E	.50	.75
24 Corsair V	1.00	2.00
25 Moon Knight R	.30	.50
26 Moon Knight E	.50	1.00
27 Moon Knight V	1.00	3.00
28 Calypso R	.30	.50
29 Calypso E	.50	.75
30 Calypso V	1.00	2.00
31 Elektra R	.50	1.00
32 Elektra E	1.00	2.00
33 Elektra V	2.00	4.00
34 Daredevil R	1.00	2.00
35 Daredevil E	2.00	3.00
36 Daredevil V	3.00	5.00
37 Magick R	.30	.50
38 Magick E	.50	.75
39 Magick V	1.00	2.00
40 Archangel R	.30	.50
41 Archangel E	.50	.75
42 Archangel V	3.00	5.00
43 Kraven R	.30	.50
44 Kraven E	.50	.75
45 Kraven V	1.00	2.00
46 Rhino R	.30	.50
47 Rhino E	.50	.75
48 Rhino V	1.00	2.00
49 Mole Man R	.30	.50
50 Mole Man E	.50	.75
51 Mole Man V	1.00	2.00
52 Nebula R	.30	.50
53 Nebula E	.50	.75
54 Nebula V	1.00	2.00
55 Moonstone R	.30	.50
56 Meteorite E	.50	.75
57 Meteorite V	1.00	2.00
58 Brood Queen R	.30	.50
59 Brood Queen E	.50	.75
60 Brood Queen V	1.00	2.00
61 Patch R	.30	.50
62 Patch E	.50	.75
63 Patch V	1.00	2.00
64 Diablo R	.30	.50
65 Diablo E	.50	.75
66 Diablo V	1.00	2.00
67 Spider-Man R	1.00	2.00
68 Spider-Man E	2.00	3.00
69 Spider-Man V	3.00	6.00
70 Venom R	1.00	2.00
71 Venom E	2.00	4.00
72 Venom V	3.00	6.00
73 Ulik R	.30	.50
74 Ulik E	.50	.75
75 Ulik V	1.00	2.00
76 Umar R	.30	.50
77 Umar E	.50	.75
78 Umar V	1.00	2.00
79 Black Queen R	.30	.50
80 Selene E	.50	.75
81 Selene V	1.00	2.00
82 Absorbing Man R	1.00	2.00
83 Absorbing Man E	2.00	3.00
84 Absorbing Man V	3.00	6.00
85 Warbird U	8.00	12.00
86 Captain Marvel U	8.00	12.00
87 Adam Warlock U	10.00	18.00
88 Ronan the Accuser U	8.00	15.00
89 Sersi U	8.00	12.00
90 Morgan Le Fay U	8.00	12.00
91 Terrax U	15.00	20.00
92 Dormammu U	8.00	12.00
93 Nova U	10.00	15.00
94 Beta Ray Bill U	10.00	15.00
95 Hulk U	20.00	30.00
96 Silver Surfer U	30.00	40.00
201 Moloid (Val-Or) LE	15.00	25.00
202 Brood Warrior (Dive Bomber) LE	10.00	15.00
203 Kree Warrior (Captain Mar-vell) LE	12.00	18.00
204 SWAT Heavy Arms (Roger Falcone) LE	10.00	15.00
206 Hepzibah (Hepzibah) LE	10.00	15.00
207 Marrow (Sarah) LE	10.00	15.00
208 Corsair (Major Christopher Summers) LE	10.00	18.00
209 Moon Knight (Marc Spector) LE	12.00	15.00
210 Calypso (Calypso Ezili) LE	7.00	15.00
211 Elektra (Elektra Natchios) LE	10.00	15.00
212 Daredevil (Matt Murdock) LE	15.00	25.00
214 Archangel (Warren Worthington III) LE	25.00	40.00
215 Kraven (Sergei Kravinov) LE	10.00	15.00
216 Rhino (Alex O'Hirn) LE	15.00	25.00
217 Mole Man (Rupert) LE	20.00	30.00
218 Nebula (Nebula) LE	10.00	15.00
219 Meteorite (Dr. Karla Sofen) LE	20.00	30.00
220 Brood Queen (Professor Xavier) LE	15.00	20.00
221 Silver Surfer (Chromed) LE	25.00	40.00
222 Invisible Woman (Dial Only) LE	20.00	30.00
G1 Galactus (Big Figure)	125.00	200.00

2003 Marvel Heroclix Xplosion

COMPLETE SET (96)	175.00	225.00
BOOSTER PACK	4.00	6.00
RELEASED ON MARCH 1, 2003		
1 Con Artist R	.30	.50
2 Con Artist E	.50	.75
3 Con Artist V	1.00	2.00
4 Hand Ninja Katana R	.30	.50
5 Hand Ninja Katana E	.50	.75
6 Hand Ninja Katana V	1.00	2.00
7 Hand Ninja Nunchuks R	.30	.50
8 Hand Ninja Nunchuks E	.50	.75
9 Hand Ninja Nunchuks V	1.00	2.00
10 SWAT Officer R	.30	.50
11 SWAT Officer E	.50	.75
12 SWAT Officer V	1.00	2.00
13 SWAT Specialist R	.30	.50
14 SWAT Specialist E	.50	.75
15 SWAT Specialist V	1.00	2.00
16 Paramedic R	.30	.50
17 Paramedic E	.50	.75
18 Paramedic V	1.00	2.00
19 Typhoid Mary R	.30	.50
20 Typhoid Mary E	.50	.75
21 Typhoid Mary V	1.00	2.00
22 Destiny R	.30	.50
23 Destiny E	.50	.75
24 Destiny V	1.00	2.00
25 Boom Boom R	.30	.50
26 Boom Boom E	.50	.75
27 Meltdown V	1.00	2.00
28 Mystique R	.30	.50
29 Mystique E	.50	.75
30 Mystique V	1.00	2.00
31 Viper R	.30	.50
32 Viper E	.50	.75
33 Viper V	1.00	2.00
34 Shadowcat R	.30	.50
35 Shadowcat E	.50	.75
36 Shadowcat V	1.00	2.00
37 Iceman R	.30	.50
38 Iceman E	.50	.75
39 Iceman V	1.00	2.00
40 Madame Masque R	.30	.50
41 Madame Masque E	.50	.75
42 Madame Masque V	1.00	2.00
43 Doc Samson R	.30	.50
44 Doc Samson E	.50	.75
45 Doc Samson V	1.00	2.00
46 Scorpion R	.30	.50
47 Scorpion E	.50	.75
48 Scorpion V	1.00	2.00
49 Abomination R	.30	.50
50 Abomination E	.50	.75
51 Abomination V	2.00	4.00
52 Crimson Dynamo R	.30	.50
53 Crimson Dynamo E	.50	.75
54 Crimson Dynamo V	1.00	2.00
55 Beast R	.50	1.00
56 Beast E	1.00	2.00
57 Beast V	2.00	3.00
58 Psylocke R	.30	.50
59 Psylocke E	.50	.75
60 Psylocke V	1.00	2.00
61 Daredevil R	.50	1.00
62 Daredevil E	2.00	3.00
63 Daredevil V	3.00	5.00
64 Taskmaster R	.30	.50
65 Taskmaster E	.50	.75
66 Taskmaster V	1.00	2.00
67 Silver Samurai R	.30	.50
68 Silver Samurai E	.50	.75
69 Silver Samurai V	1.00	2.00
70 Gambit R	.50	1.00
71 Gambit E	1.00	2.00
72 Gambit V	2.00	3.00
73 Mandarin R	.30	.50
74 Mandarin E	.50	.75
75 Mandarin V	1.00	2.00
76 Iron Man R	1.00	2.00
77 Iron Man E	2.00	4.00
78 Iron Man V	3.00	6.00
79 Colossus R	.30	.50
80 Colossus E	.50	.75
81 Colossus V	1.00	2.00
82 Storm R	.50	1.00
83 Storm E	1.00	2.00
84 Storm V	2.00	3.00
85 Shadowcat U	10.00	15.00
86 Elektra U	15.00	20.00
87 Deathbird U	10.00	15.00
88 Apocalypse U	15.00	25.00
89 Green Goblin U	20.00	30.00
90 The Leader U	12.00	18.00
91 Sauron U	12.00	18.00
92 Lady Deathstrike U	15.00	20.00
93 Spider-Man U	25.00	35.00
94 Hulk (Savage) U	20.00	30.00
95 Phoenix U	20.00	25.00
96 Weapon X U	18.00	25.00
201 Con Artist (Sarah St. John) LE	10.00	18.00
202 Hand Ninja (Kirigi) LE	10.00	15.00
203 Hand Ninja (Elektra) LE	15.00	20.00
204 SWAT Specialist (Sammy Liebman) LE	12.00	15.00
205 SWAT Officer (Frank Gunzer) LE	12.00	15.00
206 Paramedic (Jane Foster) LE	40.00	60.00
207 Typhoid Mary (Mary Walker) LE	10.00	15.00
208 Destiny (Irene Adler) LE	40.00	65.00
209 Boom-Boom (Tabitha Smith) LE	10.00	15.00
210 Mystique (Raven Darkholme) LE	12.00	18.00
211 Viper (Madame Hydra) LE	10.00	15.00
212 Shadowcat (Kitty Pryde) LE	15.00	25.00
213 Iceman (Bobby Drake) LE	20.00	30.00
214 Madame Masque (Whitney Frost) LE	12.00	15.00
215 Doc Samson (Leonard Samson) LE	18.00	25.00
216 Scorpion (Mac Gargan) LE	15.00	25.00
217 Abomination (Emil Blonsky) LE	12.00	18.00
218 Crimson Dynamo (Dimitri Bukharin) LE	15.00	30.00
219 Beast (Hank McCoy) LE	20.00	30.00
220 Psylocke (Betsy Braddock) LE	18.00	25.00

2004 Marvel Heroclix Mutant Mayhem

COMPLETE SET (97)	150.00	200.00
BOOSTER PACK	4.00	7.00
RELEASED ON NOVEMBER 1, 2004		
1 U-Men R	.30	.50
2 U-Men E	.50	.75
3 U-Men V	1.00	2.00
4 Vanisher R	.30	.50
5 Vanisher E	.50	.75
6 Vanisher V	1.00	2.00
7 Skullbuster R	.30	.50
8 Skullbuster E	.50	.75
9 Skullbuster V	1.00	2.00
10 Harpoon R	.30	.50

11 Harpoon E .50 .75
12 Harpoon V 1.00 2.00
13 Vertigo R .30 .50
14 Vertigo E .50 .75
15 Vertigo V 1.00 2.00
16 Arclight R .30 .50
17 Arclight E .50 .75
18 Arclight V 1.00 2.00
19 Wild Child R .30 .50
20 Wildheart E .50 .75
21 Wild Child V 1.00 2.00
22 Blade R .50 1.00
23 Blade E 1.00 2.00
24 Blade V 2.00 4.00
25 Puck R .30 .50
26 Puck E .50 .75
27 Puck V 1.00 2.00
28 Domino R .30 .50
29 Domino E .50 .75
30 Domino V 1.00 2.00
31 Polaris R .30 .50
32 Polaris E .50 .75
33 Polaris V 1.00 2.00
34 Silver Sable R .30 .50
35 Silver Sable E .50 .75
36 Silver Sable V 1.00 2.00
37 Havok R .30 .50
38 Havok E .50 .75
39 Havok V 1.00 2.00
40 Wonder Man R .30 .50
41 Wonder Man E .50 .75
42 Wonder Man V 1.00 2.00
43 Firestar R .30 .50
44 Firestar E .50 .75
45 Firestar V 1.00 2.00
46 Cloak R .30 .50
47 Cloak E .50 .75
48 Cloak V 1.00 2.00
49 Dagger R .30 .50
50 Dagger E .50 .75
51 Dagger V 1.00 2.00
52 Bishop R .50 1.00
53 Bishop E 1.00 2.00
54 Bishop V 2.00 4.00
55 Blink R .30 .50
56 Blink E .50 .75
57 Blink V 1.00 2.00
58 Spider-Man R 1.00 2.00
59 Spider-Man E 2.00 3.00
60 Spider-Man V 4.00 6.00
61 Man-Thing R .30 .50
62 Man-Thing E .50 .75
63 Man-Thing V 1.00 2.00
64 Snowbird R .30 .50
65 Snowbird E .50 .75
66 Snowbird V 3.00 5.00
67 Northstar R .30 .50
68 Northstar E .50 .75
69 Northstar V 1.00 2.00
70 Sasquatch R .30 .50
71 Sasquatch E .50 .75
72 Tanaraq V 1.00 2.00
73 Cable R .30 .50
74 Cable E .50 .75
75 Soldier X V 3.00 5.00
76 Deadpool R .30 .50
77 Deadpool E .50 .75
78 Deadpool V 1.00 3.00
79 Wolverine R 1.00 2.00
80 Wolverine E 2.00 3.00
81 Wolverine V 4.00 7.00
82 Hulk R 1.00 2.00
83 Hulk E 2.00 3.00
84 Hulk V 3.00 6.00
85 Longshot U 10.00 15.00
86 Mimic U 10.00 15.00
87 Fantomex U 10.00 15.00
88 Donald Pierce U 10.00 15.00
89 Bastion U 9.00 12.00
90 M.O.D.O.K. U 10.00 15.00
91 Gladiator U 12.00 18.00
92 Black Queen U 9.00 12.00
93 Shadow King U 10.00 15.00
94 N'astirh U 10.00 15.00
95 Count Nefaria U 10.00 18.00
96 Loki U 10.00 18.00
97 Giant-Man E 18.00 25.00
201 Alex Summers U 10.00 15.00
202 Simon Williams U 10.00 15.00
203 Angelica Jones U 10.00 15.00
204 Tyrone Johnson U 10.00 15.00
205 Tandy Bowen U 10.00 15.00
206 Bishop of XSE U 10.00 15.00
207 Clarice Ferguson U 10.00 15.00
208 Peter Parker U 18.00 25.00
209 Ted Sallis U 10.00 15.00
210 Narya U 10.00 15.00
211 Jean-Paul Beaubier U 10.00 15.00
212 Walter Langkowski U 10.00 15.00
213 Nathaniel Summers U 10.00 15.00
214 Wade Wilson U 10.00 15.00
215 Logan U 12.00 20.00
216 Dr. Bruce Banner U 12.00 20.00
217 Polaris U 10.00 15.00
218 Hulk U 20.00 25.00
220 Dark Phoenix V 35.00 65.00
220 Dark Phoenix E 35.00 65.00
220 Dark Phoenix R 35.00 60.00
221 Nova U 20.00 30.00
222 Hulk U 20.00 25.00

2004 Marvel Heroclix Ultimates

COMPLETE SET (96) 200.00 275.00
BOOSTER PACK 5.00 8.00
RELEASED ON JUNE 1, 2004
1 Morlock R .30 .50
2 Morlock E .50 .75
3 Morlock V 1.00 2.00
4 Hellfire Guard R .30 .50
5 Hellfire Guard E .50 .75
6 Hellfire Guard V 1.00 2.00
7 Scourge R .30 .50
8 Scourge E .50 .75
9 Scourge V 1.00 2.00
10 Sentinel Trooper R .30 .50
11 Sentinel Trooper E .50 .75
12 Sentinel Trooper V 1.00 2.00
13 Lizard R .30 .50
14 Lizard E .50 .75
15 Lizard V 1.00 2.00
16 Princess Python R .30 .50
17 Princess Python E .50 .75
18 Princess Python V 1.00 2.00
19 Calisto R .30 .50
20 Calisto E .50 .75
21 Calisto V 1.00 2.00
22 Sidewinder R .30 .50
23 Sidewinder E .50 .75
24 Sidewinder V 1.00 2.00
25 Black Widow R .30 .50
26 Black Widow E .50 .75
27 Black Widow V 1.00 2.00
28 Storm R .50 1.00
29 Storm E 1.00 2.00
30 Storm V 2.00 4.00
31 Anaconda R .30 .50
32 Anaconda E .50 .75
33 Anaconda V 1.00 2.00
34 Hawkeye R .30 .50
35 Hawkeye E .50 .75
36 Hawkeye V 1.00 2.00
37 Hellcat R .30 .50
38 Hellcat E .50 .75
39 Hellcat V 1.00 2.00
40 Spider-Man R 1.00 2.00
41 Spider-Man E 2.00 3.00
42 Spider-Man V 3.00 5.00
43 Beast R .50 1.00
44 Beast E 1.00 2.00
45 Beast V 2.00 4.00
46 Wolverine R 1.00 2.00
47 Wolverine E 2.00 4.00
48 Wolverine V 4.00 8.00
49 Mysterio R .30 .50
50 Mysterio E .50 .75
51 Mysterio V 1.00 2.00
52 Punisher R .50 1.00
53 Punisher E 1.00 2.00
54 Punisher V 2.00 4.00
55 Electro R .30 .50
56 Electro E .50 .75
57 Electro V 1.00 2.00
58 Ghost Rider R 1.00 2.00
59 Ghost Rider E 2.00 3.00
60 Ghost Rider V 3.00 5.00
61 Cyclops R 1.00 2.00
62 Cyclops E 2.00 3.00
63 Cyclops V 3.00 5.00
64 Captain America R 1.00 2.00
65 Captain America E 2.00 3.00
66 Captain America V 4.00 7.00
67 Sabretooth R 1.00 2.00
68 Sabretooth E 2.00 3.00
69 Sabretooth V 3.00 5.00
70 Doctor Octopus R 1.00 2.00
71 Doctor Octopus E 2.00 3.00
72 Doctor Octopus V 4.00 6.00
73 Colossus R 1.00 2.00
74 Colossus E 2.00 3.00
75 Colossus V 3.00 5.00
76 Marvel Girl R .30 .50
77 Marvel Girl E .50 .75
78 Marvel Girl V 1.00 2.00
79 Wrecker R .30 .50
80 Wrecker E .50 .75
81 Wrecker V 1.00 2.00
82 Captain Britain R .30 .50
83 Captain Britain E .50 .75
84 Captain Britain V 3.00 5.00
85 Xorn U 15.00 20.00
86 Baron Zemo U 10.00 15.00
87 Carnage U 20.00 28.00
88 Vindicator U 10.00 15.00
89 Iron Man U 20.00 30.00
90 Mr. Sinister U 12.00 20.00
91 Crimson Cowl U 10.00 15.00
92 Magneto U 15.00 22.00
93 Phoenix U 15.00 25.00
94 Goblin Queen U 10.00 18.00
95 Hulk U 20.00 30.00
96 Thor U 25.00 45.00
200 Magneto LE 20.00 30.00
201 Morlock (Jonny Ell) LE 12.00 20.00
202 Hellfire Guard (Wade Cole) LE 12.00 20.00
203 Scourge (Justice is Served) LE 10.00 15.00
204 Sentinel Trooper (Sentinel Captain LE 10.00 15.00
205 Dr. Curtis Connors LE 10.00 18.00
206 Princess Python (Zelda Dubois) LE 10.00 15.00
207 Morlock Leader LE 10.00 18.00
208 Seth Voelker LE 10.00 18.00
209 Natasha Romanova LE 10.00 18.00
210 Ororo Munroe LE 10.00 18.00
211 Blanche Sitznski LE 10.00 18.00
212 Clint Barton LE 10.00 18.00
213 Hellcat (Patsy Walker) LE 10.00 15.00
214 Peter Parker (Spider-Man) LE 18.00 25.00
215 Beast (Hank McCoy) LE 12.00 18.00
216 Wolverine (James Howlett) LE 12.00 20.00
217 Electro (Quentin Beck) LE 10.00 15.00
218 Punisher (Frank Castle) LE 10.00 15.00
219 Electro (Maxwell Dillon) LE 10.00 18.00
220 Ghost Rider (Danny Ketch) LE 12.00 20.00
221 Doc Ock (Dr.Otto Octavius) 20.00 25.00

2004 Marvel Heroclix Universe

COMPLETE SET (126) 300.00 400.00
BOOSTER PACK 2.50 4.00
RELEASED ON MAY 1, 2004
1 Spider-Man E 1.00 2.00
2 Wolverine E 1.00 2.00
3 Wasp E .50 .75
4 Hobgoblin E 1.00 2.00
5 Sabretooth E 1.00 2.00
6 Elektra E 1.00 2.00
7 Con Artist R .30 .50
8 Con Artist E .50 .75
9 Con Artist V 1.00 2.00
10 Hand Ninja Katana R .30 .50
11 Hand Ninja Katana E .50 .75
12 Hand Ninja Katana V 1.00 2.00
13 Hand Ninja Nunchuks R .30 .50
14 Hand Ninja Nunchuks E .50 .75
15 Hand Ninja Nunchuks V 1.00 2.00
16 SWAT Officer R .30 .50
17 SWAT Officer E .50 .75
18 SWAT Officer V 1.00 2.00
19 SWAT Specialist R .30 .50
20 SWAT Specialist E .50 .75
21 SWAT Specialist V 1.00 2.00
22 Paramedic R .30 .50
23 Paramedic E .50 .75
24 Paramedic V 1.00 2.00
25 Typhoid Mary R .30 .50
26 Typhoid Mary E .50 .75
27 Typhoid Mary V 1.00 2.00
28 Destiny R .30 .50
29 Destiny E .50 .75
30 Destiny V 1.00 2.00
31 Boom Boom R .30 .50
32 Boom Boom E .50 .75
33 Meltdown V 1.00 2.00
34 Mystique R .30 .50
35 Mystique E .50 .75
36 Mystique V 2.00 4.00
37 Viper R .30 .50
38 Viper E .50 .75
39 Viper V 1.00 2.00
40 Shadowcat R .30 .50
41 Shadowcat E .50 .75
42 Shadowcat V 1.00 2.00
43 Daredevil R .50 1.00
44 Daredevil E 1.00 2.00
45 Daredevil V 2.00 4.00
46 Taskmaster R .30 .50
47 Taskmaster E .50 .75
48 Taskmaster V 1.00 2.00
49 Silver Samurai R .30 .50
50 Silver Samurai E .50 .75
51 Silver Samurai V 1.00 2.00
52 Gambit R 1.00 2.00
53 Gambit E 2.00 3.00
54 Gambit V 3.00 5.00
55 Mandarin R .30 .50
56 Mandarin E .50 .75
57 Mandarin V 1.00 2.00
58 Iron Man R 1.00 2.00
59 Iron Man E 2.00 4.00
60 Iron Man V 4.00 7.00
61 Colossus R 1.00 2.00
62 Colossus E 2.00 3.00
63 Colossus V 3.00 5.00
64 Storm R 1.00 2.00
65 Storm E 2.00 3.00
66 Storm V 3.00 5.00
67 Kingpin R .30 .50
68 Kingpin E .50 .75
69 Kingpin V 1.00 2.00
70 Vulture R .30 .50
71 Vulture E .50 .75
72 Vulture V 2.00 4.00
73 Jean Grey R .50 1.00
74 Jean Grey E 1.00 2.00
75 Jean Grey V 2.00 4.00
76 Hobgoblin R .30 .50
77 Hobgoblin E .50 .75
78 Hobgoblin V 1.00 2.00
79 Sabretooth R .50 1.00
80 Sabretooth E 1.00 2.00
81 Sabretooth V 2.00 4.00
82 Hulk R .50 1.00
83 Hulk E 1.00 2.00
84 Hulk V 2.00 4.00
85 Puppet Master R .30 .50
86 Puppet Master E .50 .75
87 Puppet Master V 1.00 2.00
88 Annihilus R .30 .50
89 Annihilus E .50 .75
90 Annihilus V 1.00 2.00
91 Captain America R 1.00 2.00
92 Captain America E 2.00 3.00
93 Captain America V 3.00 5.00
94 Spider-Man R 1.00 2.00
95 Spider-Man E 2.00 3.00
96 Spider-Man V 3.00 6.00
97 Wolverine R 1.00 2.00
98 Wolverine E 2.00 4.00
99 Wolverine V 4.00 7.00
100 Professor Xavier R .50 1.00
101 Professor Xavier E 1.00 2.00
102 Professor Xavier V 2.00 4.00
103 Cyclops R 1.00 2.00
104 Cyclops E 2.00 3.00
105 Cyclops V 3.00 5.00
106 Black Panther R .30 .50
107 Black Panther E .50 .75
108 Black Panther V 1.00 2.00
109 Pyro R .30 .50
110 Pyro E .50 .75
111 Pyro V 1.00 2.00
112 Bullseye R .30 .50
113 Bullseye E .50 .75
114 Bullseye V 1.00 2.00
115 Vision U 8.00 12.00
116 Quasar U 8.00 10.00
117 Thanos U 12.00 20.00
118 Nightmare U 10.00 12.00
119 Wasp U 10.00 12.00
120 Elektra U 8.00 10.00
121 Professor Xavier U 8.00 12.00
122 Juggernaut U 8.00 10.00
123 Cyclops U 8.00 10.00
124 Captain America U 10.00 12.00
125 Wolverine U 15.00 18.00
126 Spider-Man U 15.00 20.00

2005 Marvel Heroclix Armor Wars

COMPLETE SET (96)
RELEASED ON NOVEMBER 1, 2005
1 Firebrand R .20 .50
2 Firebrand E .40 1.00
3 Firebrand V .75 2.00
4 Paladin R .20 .50
5 Paladin E .40 1.00
6 Paladin V 1.00
7 Lorelei R .20 .50
8 Lorelei E .40 1.00
9 Lorelei V 1.00
10 Diamond Lil R .20 .50
11 Diamond Lil E .40 1.00
12 Diamond Lil V .75 2.00
13 Echo R .20 .50
14 Echo E .40 1.00
15 Echo V 1.00
16 Killer Shrike R .20 .50
17 Killer Shrike E .40 1.00
18 Killer Shrike V .75 2.00
19 Thunderbird R .20 .50
20 Thunderbird E .40 1.00
21 Warpath V .75 2.00
22 Banshee R .20 .50
23 Banshee E .40 1.00
24 Banshee V .75 2.00
25 Spymaster R .20 .50
26 Spymaster E .40 1.00
27 Spymaster V .75 2.00
28 Ghost R .20 .50
29 Ghost E .40 1.00
30 Ghost V .75 2.00
31 Magma R .20 .50
32 Magma E .40 1.00
33 Magma V .75 2.00
34 Marrina R .20 .50
35 Marrina E .40 1.00
36 Marrina V .75 2.00
37 Thunderball R .20 .50
38 Thunderball E .40 1.00
39 Thunderball V .75 2.00
40 Aurora R .20 .50
41 Aurora E .40 1.00
42 Aurora V .75 2.00
43 Cannonball R .20 .50
44 Cannonball E .40 1.00
45 Cannonball V .75 2.00
46 Wendigo R .20 .50
47 Wendigo E .40 1.00
48 Wendigo V .75 2.00
49 Shaman R .20 .50
50 Shaman E .40 1.00
51 Shaman V .75 2.00
52 Quicksilver R .20 .50
53 Quicksilver E .40 1.00
54 Quicksilver V .75 2.00
55 Psylocke R .20 .50
56 Psylocke E .40 1.00
57 Psylocke V .75 2.00
58 Sunrise R .20 .50
59 Sunrise E .40 1.00
60 Sunrise V .75 2.00
61 Dazzler R .20 .50
62 Dazzler E .40 1.00
63 Dazzler V .75 2.00
64 Executioner R .20 .50
65 Executioner E .40 1.00
66 Executioner V .75 2.00
67 War Machine R .20 .50
68 War Machine E .40 1.00
69 War Machine V .75 2.00
70 Crimson Dynamo R .20 .50
71 Crimson Dynamo E .40 1.00
72 Crimson Dynamo V .75 2.00
73 Titanium Man R .20 .50
74 Titanium Man E .40 1.00
75 Titanium Man V .75 2.00
76 Iron Man R .20 .50
77 Iron Man E .40 1.00
78 Iron Man V .75 2.00
79 Captain America R .20 .50
80 Captain America E .40 1.00
81 Captain America V 2.00 5.00
82 Ultron-5 R .20 .50
83 Ultron-11 E .40 1.00
84 Ultron-16 V .75 2.00
85 Crystal U 3.00 8.00
86 Shathra U 3.00 8.00
87 Jocasta U 3.00 8.00
88 Iron Man U 3.00 8.00
89 Black King U 3.00 8.00
90 Iron Monger U 3.00 8.00
91 Sentry U 3.00 8.00
92 Spider-Woman U 3.00 8.00
93 Spider-Man U 3.00 8.00
94 Mystique U 3.00 8.00
95 Wolverine U 3.00 8.00
96 Magneto U 3.00 8.00
201 Eliot Franklin LE 6.00 15.00
202 Jeanne-Marie Beaubier LE 6.00 15.00
203 Sam Guthrie LE 6.00 15.00
204 Georges Baptiste LE 6.00 15.00
205 Talisman LE 6.00 15.00
206 Sir Pietro Maximoff LE 6.00 15.00
207 Captain Britain LE 6.00 15.00
208 Shiro Yoshida LE 6.00 15.00
209 Ali Blair LE 6.00 15.00
210 Skurge LE 6.00 15.00
211 James Rhodes LE 6.00 15.00
212 Gennady Gavrilov LE 6.00 15.00
213 The Gremlin LE 6.00 15.00
214 Tony Stark LE 6.00 15.00
215 John Walker LE 6.00 15.00
216 Ultron-13 LE 6.00 15.00
217 Jessica Drew LE 6.00 15.00
218 Anthony Stark LE 6.00 15.00

2005 Marvel Heroclix Fantastic Forces

COMPLETE SET (96) 250.00 300.00
BOOSTER PACK 5.00 7.00
BATTLEFIELD CARDS (BF1-BF6) .50 1.00
FEATS CARDS (F1-F8) 1.00 2.00
TOKEN CARDS (B1-B6) .50 1.00
RELEASED ON JUNE 1, 2005
1 Lockjaw R .30 .50
2 Lockjaw E .50 .75
3 Lockjaw V 1.00 2.00
4 Black Knight R .30 .50
5 Black Knight E .50 .75
6 Black Knight V 1.00 2.00
7 Mirage R .30 .50
8 Moonstar E .50 .75
9 Moonstar V 1.00 2.00
10 Hawkeye R .30 .50
11 Hawkeye E .50 .75
12 Hawkeye V 1.00 2.00
13 Awesome Android R .30 .50

14 Awesome Android E	.50	.75
15 Awesome Andy V	1.00	2.00
16 Goliath R	.30	.50
17 Atlas E	.50	.75
18 Atlas V	1.00	2.00
19 Yellowjacket R	.30	.50
20 Yellowjacket E	.50	.75
21 Yellowjacket V	2.00	3.00
22 Ghost Rider R	.50	1.00
23 Ghost Rider E	1.00	2.00
24 Ghost Rider V	2.00	3.00
25 Asp R	.30	.50
26 Asp E	.50	.75
27 Asp V	1.00	2.00
28 Shocker R	.30	.50
29 Shocker E	.50	.75
30 Shocker V	2.00	4.00
31 Tigra R	.30	.50
32 Tigra E	.50	.75
33 Tigra V	2.00	4.00
34 Jolt R	.30	.50
35 Jolt E	.50	.75
36 Jolt V	1.00	2.00
37 Karma R	.30	.50
38 Karma E	.50	.75
39 Karma V	1.00	2.00
40 Vulture R	.30	.50
41 Vulture E	.50	.75
42 Vulture V	3.00	5.00
43 Songbird R	.30	.50
44 Songbird E	.50	.75
45 Songbird V	1.00	2.00
46 Iron Fist R	.30	.50
47 Iron Fist E	1.00	2.00
48 Iron Fist V	3.00	5.00
49 Power Man R	.30	.50
50 Power Man E	1.00	2.00
51 Cage V	2.00	3.00
52 Scarlet Witch R	.30	.50
53 Scarlet Witch E	1.00	2.00
54 Scarlet Witch V	2.00	4.00
55 Rogue R	.30	.50
56 Rogue E	.50	.75
57 Rogue V	1.00	2.00
58 Dr. Strange R	.50	1.00
59 Dr. Strange E	1.00	2.00
60 Dr. Strange V	3.00	5.00
61 Green Goblin R	1.00	2.00
62 Green Goblin E	2.00	3.00
63 Green Goblin V	3.00	5.00
64 Juggernaut R	1.00	2.00
65 Juggernaut E	2.00	3.00
66 Juggernaut V	4.00	6.00
67 Sub-Mariner R	2.00	3.00
68 Sub-Mariner E	3.00	4.00
69 Sub-Mariner V	4.00	6.00
70 Human Torch R	1.00	2.00
71 Human Torch E	2.00	3.00
72 Human Torch V	3.00	5.00
73 Invisible Woman R	1.00	2.00
74 Invisible Woman E	2.00	3.00
75 Invisible Woman V	4.00	7.00
76 The Thing R	1.00	2.00
77 The Thing E	2.00	3.00
78 The Thing V	3.00	6.00
79 Mr. Fantastic R	1.00	2.00
80 Mr. Fantastic E	2.00	3.00
81 Mr. Fantastic V	3.00	6.00
82 Nightcrawler R	1.00	2.00
83 Nightcrawler E	2.00	3.00
84 Nightcrawler V	3.00	6.00
85 Volcana U	10.00	15.00
86 Mad Thinker U	12.00	18.00
87 Arnim Zola U	10.00	15.00
88 Baron Mordo U	10.00	15.00
89 Baron Blood U	10.00	15.00
90 Nimrod U	20.00	40.00
91 Orphan U	10.00	15.00
92 Wolverine U	12.00	20.00
93 Warlock U	12.00	20.00
94 Professor Xavier U	18.00	25.00
95 Dr. Doom U	10.00	18.00
96 Spider-Man U	20.00	30.00
201 Norman Osborn U	15.00	25.00
202 Cain Marko U	20.00	25.00
203 Namor U	15.00	25.00
204 Johnny Storm U	15.00	20.00

2006 Marvel Heroclix 2099

COMPLETE SET (7)
RELEASED ON DECEMBER 1, 2006

1 Hulk U	8.00	20.00
2 Ravage E	4.00	10.00
3 Punisher V	4.00	10.00
4 Ghost Rider E	6.00	15.00
5 Meanstreak E	4.00	10.00
6 Junkpile V	4.00	10.00
7 Doom U	6.00	15.00

2006 Marvel Heroclix Danger Room

COMPLETE SET (6)
RELEASED ON JUNE 1, 2006

1 Cyclops V	1.00	2.50
2 Colossus V	1.00	2.50
3 Angel V	3.00	8.00
4 Jean Grey V	1.00	2.50
5 Beast V	1.00	2.50
6 Storm V	1.00	2.50

2006 Marvel Heroclix Sinister

COMPLETE SET (96)
RELEASED ON JUNE 1, 2006

1 HYDRA Footsoldier R	.20	.50
2 HYDRA Technician E	.40	1.00
3 HYDRA Officer V	2.00	5.00
4 SHIELD Trooper R	.20	.50
5 SHIELD Sniper E	.40	1.00
6 SHIELD Agent V	2.00	5.00
7 Swordsman R	.20	.50
8 Swordsman E	.40	1.00
9 Swordsman V	2.00	5.00
10 Hydro Man R	.20	.50
11 Hydro Man E	.40	1.00
12 Hydro Man V	2.00	5.00
13 Paste Pot Pete R	.20	.50
14 Trapster E	.40	1.00
15 Trapster V	2.00	5.00
16 Mockingbird R	.20	.50
17 Mockingbird E	.40	1.00
18 Mockingbird V	2.00	5.00
19 Jewel R	.20	.50
20 Jessica Jones E	.40	1.00
21 Jessica Jones V	2.00	5.00
22 Beetle R	.20	.50
23 Beetle E	.40	1.00
24 Beetle V	2.00	5.00
25 Wingless Wizard R	.20	.50
26 Wizard E	.40	1.00
27 Wizard V	2.00	5.00
28 Electro R	.20	.50
29 Electro E	.40	1.00
30 Electro V	2.00	5.00
31 Fixer R	.20	.50
32 Techno E	.40	1.00
33 Fixer V	2.00	5.00
34 Jack O'Lantern R	.20	.50
35 Jack O'Lantern E	.40	1.00
36 Jack O'Lantern V	2.00	5.00
37 Sprite R	.20	.50
38 Shadowcat E	.40	1.00
39 Shadowcat V	2.00	5.00
40 MACH-1 R	.20	.50
41 MACH-3 E	.40	1.00
42 MACH-4 V	2.00	5.00
43 Nighthawk R	.20	.50
44 Nighthawk E	.40	1.00
45 Nighthawk V	2.00	5.00
46 Valkyrie R	.20	.50
47 Valkyrie E	.40	1.00
48 Valkyrie V	2.00	5.00
49 Multiple Man R	.20	.50
50 Multiple Man E	.40	1.00
51 Madrox V	2.00	5.00
52 Deathlok R	.20	.50
53 Deathlok E	.40	1.00
54 Deathlok V	2.00	5.00
55 Falcon R	.20	.50
56 Falcon E	.40	1.00
57 Falcon V	2.00	5.00
58 Spider-Man R	.20	.50
59 Spider-Man E	.40	1.00
60 Spider-Man V	2.00	5.00
61 Radioactive Man R	.20	.50
62 Radioactive Man E	.40	1.00
63 Radioactive Man V	2.00	5.00
64 Captain Marvel R	.20	.50
65 Photon E	.40	1.00
66 Pulsar V	2.00	5.00
67 Rhino R	.20	.50
68 Rhino E	.40	1.00
69 Rhino V	2.00	5.00
70 Whizzer R	.20	.50
71 Speed Demon E	.40	1.00
72 Speed Demon V	2.00	5.00
73 Daredevil R	.20	.50
74 Daredevil E	.40	1.00
75 Daredevil V	2.00	5.00
76 Meggan R	.20	.50
77 Meggan E	.40	1.00
78 Meggan V	2.00	5.00
79 Bullseye R	.20	.50
80 Bullseye E	.40	1.00
81 Bullseye V	4.00	10.00
82 Kraven R	.20	.50
83 Kraven E	.40	1.00
84 Kraven V	2.00	5.00
85 Forge U	4.00	10.00
86 Purple Man U	4.00	10.00
87 Maximus U	4.00	10.00
88 Baron Strucker U	4.00	10.00
89 Charcoal U	4.00	10.00
90 Wolverine U	15.00	30.00
91 Nick Fury U	4.00	10.00
92 Arkon U	4.00	10.00
93 Ka-Zar U	4.00	10.00
94 Scarlet Spider U	4.00	10.00
95 Stilt Man U	6.00	15.00
96 Black Bolt U	15.00	30.00
201 Soulsword Wielder U	4.00	10.00
202 Abner Jenkins U	4.00	10.00
203 Kyle Richmond U	4.00	10.00
204 Brunnhilde U	4.00	10.00
205 James Madrox U	4.00	10.00
206 Michael Roth U	4.00	10.00
207 Sam Wilson U	4.00	10.00
208 Symbiote U	4.00	10.00
209 Dr. Chen Lu U	4.00	10.00
210 Monica Rambeau U	4.00	10.00
211 Aleksei Mikhailovich U	4.00	10.00
212 James Sanders U	4.00	10.00
213 Kingpin of Hell's Kitchen U	4.00	10.00
214 Goblin Princess U	4.00	10.00
215 Lester U	4.00	10.00
216 Kraven the Spider U	4.00	10.00
217 Spider-Man U	4.00	10.00
218 Venom U	15.00	30.00
219 Snap Wilson U	4.00	10.00

2006 Marvel Heroclix Supernova

COMPLETE SET (96)
RELEASED ON NOVEMBER 1, 2006

1 Kree Warrior R	.20	.50
2 Kree Captain E	.40	1.00
3 Kree Colonel V	2.00	5.00
4 Skrull Infiltrator R	.20	.50
5 Skrull Warrior E	.40	1.00
6 Skrull General V	2.00	5.00
7 Shi'ar Warrior R	.20	.50
8 Shi'ar Borderer E	.40	1.00
9 Shi'ar Admiral V	2.00	5.00
10 Badoon Warrior R	.20	.50
11 Badoon Guard E	.40	1.00
12 Badoon Commander V	2.00	5.00
13 Night Thrasher R	.20	.50
14 Night Thrasher E	.40	1.00
15 Night Thrasher V	2.00	5.00
16 Jubilee R	.20	.50
17 Jubilee E	.40	1.00
18 Jubilee V	2.00	5.00
19 Super-Apes: Igor R	.20	.50
20 Super-Apes: Mikhlo E	.40	1.00
21 Super-Apes: Peotor V	2.00	5.00
22 Raza R	.20	.50
23 Raza E	.40	1.00
24 Raza V	2.00	5.00
25 Sunspot R	.20	.50
26 Sunspot E	.40	1.00
27 Sunspot V	2.00	5.00
28 Marvel Boy R	.20	.50
29 Justice E	.40	1.00
30 Justice V	2.00	5.00
31 Tessa R	.20	.50
32 Sage E	.40	1.00
33 Sage V	2.00	5.00
34 Nocturne R	.20	.50
35 Nocturne E	.40	1.00
36 Nocturne V	2.00	5.00
37 Nova R	.20	.50
38 Kid Nova E	.40	1.00
39 Nova V	2.00	5.00
40 Bulldozer R	.20	.50
41 Bulldozer E	.40	1.00
42 Bulldozer V	2.00	5.00
43 Aleta R	.20	.50
44 Aleta E	.40	1.00
45 Starhawk V	2.00	5.00
46 Kang R	.20	.50
47 Kang E	.40	1.00
48 Kang the Conqueror V	2.00	5.00
49 Ant-Man R	.20	.50
50 Ant-Man E	.40	1.00
51 Ant-Man V	2.00	5.00
52 Weapon Alpha R	.20	.50
53 Guardian E	.40	1.00
54 Vindicator V	2.00	5.00
55 She-Hulk R	.20	.50
56 She-Hulk E	.40	1.00
57 She-Hulk V	2.00	5.00
58 Vance Astro R	.20	.50
59 Vance Astro E	.40	1.00
60 Major Victory V	2.00	5.00
61 Vision R	.20	.50
62 Vision E	.40	1.00
63 Vision V	2.00	5.00
64 Drax the Destroyer R	.20	.50
65 Drax the Destroyer E	.40	1.00
66 Drax V	2.00	5.00
67 Mantis R	.20	.50
68 Mantis E	.40	1.00
69 Mantis V	2.00	5.00
70 Doctor Spectrum R	.20	.50
71 Doctor Spectrum E	.40	1.00
72 Doctor Spectrum V	2.00	5.00
73 Hyperion R	.20	.50
74 Hyperion E	.40	1.00
75 Hyperion V	2.00	5.00
76 Silver Surfer R	.20	.50
77 Silver Surfer E	.40	1.00
78 Silver Surfer V	6.00	15.00
79 Legacy R	.20	.50
80 Captain Marvel E	.40	1.00
81 Photon V	4.00	10.00
82 Thor R	.20	.50
83 Thor E	.40	1.00
84 Thor V	2.00	5.00
85 Majestrix Lilandra U	4.00	10.00
86 Red Ghost U	4.00	10.00
87 Machine Man U	4.00	10.00
88 Karnak U	4.00	10.00
89 Power Princess U	4.00	10.00
90 Jack of Hearts U	4.00	10.00
91 Super Skrull U	4.00	10.00
92 Korvac U	4.00	10.00
93 Captain Mar-Vell U	4.00	10.00
94 Binary U	4.00	10.00
95 Graviton U	4.00	10.00
96 Thanos U	6.00	15.00
201 Super-Nova U	4.00	10.00
202 Henry Camp U	4.00	10.00
203 One-Who-Knows U	4.00	10.00
204 Nathaniel Richards U	4.00	10.00
205 Dr. Hank Pym U	4.00	10.00
206 James MacDonald Hudson U	4.00	10.00
207 Jennifer Walters, Esq. U	4.00	10.00
208 Vance Astrovik U	4.00	10.00
209 Victor Shade U	4.00	10.00
210 Arthur Douglas U	4.00	10.00
211 Celestial Madonna U	4.00	10.00
212 Joe Ledger U	4.00	10.00
213 King Hyperion U	4.00	10.00
214 Norrin Radd U	6.00	15.00
215 Genis-Vell U	4.00	10.00
216 Dr. Donald Blake U	4.00	10.00
217 Iron Man U	4.00	10.00
218 Doom U	6.00	15.00
219 Skymax U	4.00	10.00
220 Spider-Man U	4.00	10.00
221 Colonel America U	4.00	10.00
222 Wolverine U	4.00	10.00
223 Hulk U	4.00	10.00
224 The Mighty Thor U	4.00	10.00

2007 Marvel Heroclix Avengers

COMPLETE SET (60)
RELEASED ON JUNE 1, 2007

1 Captain America R	.20	.50
2 Iron Man U	8.00	20.00
3 Captain Britain R	.20	.50
4 Gargoyle V	4.00	10.00
5 Guardsman V	4.00	10.00
6 Moon Knight V	4.00	10.00
7 Crossbones E	.40	1.00
8 Wonder Man V	4.00	10.00
9 Hulkling R	.20	.50
10 Patriot R	.20	.50
11 Stature R	.20	.50
12 Shang-Chi E	.40	1.00
13 Piledriver E	.40	1.00
14 Stingray R	.20	.50
15 US Agent V	4.00	10.00
16 Luke Cage V	4.00	10.00
17 Living Laser V	4.00	10.00
18 Blazing Skull V	4.00	10.00
19 Darkhawk R	.20	.50
20 Dragon Man E	.40	1.00
21 Toro R	.20	.50
22 Iron Widow E	.40	1.00
23 Lionheart R	.20	.50
24 Black Panther R	.20	.50
25 Quicksilver R	.20	.50
26 Scarlet Witch R	.20	.50
27 Vision R	.20	.50
28 Wasp E	.40	1.00
29 Taskmaster U	8.00	20.00
30 Iron Lad R	.20	.50
31 Ronin R	.20	.50
32 Red Skull U	8.00	20.00
33 Abomination R	.20	.50
34 Baron Zemo V	4.00	10.00
35 Bucky R	.20	.50
36 Falcon E	.40	1.00
37 Thin Man V	4.00	10.00
38 Giant Man R	.20	.50
39 Spitfire V	4.00	10.00
40 Namor U	8.00	20.00
41 Union Jack E	.40	1.00
42 Starfox E	.40	1.00
43 Molecule Man U	8.00	20.00
44 Grim Reaper V	4.00	10.00
45 Thunderstrike R	.20	.50
46 Namorita E	.40	1.00
47 Wiccan R	.20	.50
48 Yondu V	4.00	10.00
49 Two-Gun Kid V	4.00	10.00
50 Winter Soldier V	4.00	10.00
51 Spider-Man V	8.00	20.00
52 Citizen V V	4.00	10.00
53 The Colonel R	.20	.50
54 Ares U	8.00	20.00
55 Hulk U	8.00	20.00
56 Hawkeye U	8.00	20.00
57 Scarlet Witch R	.20	.50
58 Quicksilver R	.20	.50
59 Wasp R	.20	.50
60 Cap and Bucky U	8.00	20.00
61 Mandarin U	8.00	20.00
100 Silver Surfer U	8.00	20.00
101 Terrax the Tamer U	8.00	20.00
102 Firelord U	8.00	20.00
103 Stardust U	8.00	20.00

2007 Marvel Heroclix Mutations and Monsters

COMPLETE SET (60)
RELEASED ON NOVEMBER 1, 2007

1 Marvel Girl C	.20	.50
2 Cyclops C	.20	.50
3 Beast C	.20	.50
4 Iceman C	.20	.50
5 Strong Guy C	.20	.50
6 Pete Wisdom C	.20	.50
7 Brood C	.20	.50
8 Box C	.20	.50
9 Cuckoo C	.20	.50
10 Maverick C	.20	.50
11 Dazzler C	.20	.50
12 Colossus C	.20	.50
13 Agent Brand C	.20	.50
14 Bishop C	.20	.50
15 The Hood C	.20	.50
16 Miek C	.20	.50
17 Hulk U	.40	1.00
18 Korg U	.40	1.00
19 Absorbing Man U	.40	1.00
20 Morph U	.40	1.00
21 Mimic U	.40	1.00
22 Gorgon U	.40	1.00
23 Cyclops U	.40	1.00
24 Shatterstar U	.40	1.00
25 Zzzax U	.40	1.00
26 Chamber U	.40	1.00
27 Beast U	.40	1.00
28 Giant-Man U	.40	1.00
29 Iceman U	.40	1.00
30 X-23 U	.40	1.00
31 Professor X U	.40	1.00
32 Gambit U	.40	1.00
33 Green Scar R	6.00	15.00
34 Archangel R	4.00	10.00
35 Ahab R	4.00	10.00
36 Fabian Cortez R	4.00	10.00
37 Jean Grey R	4.00	10.00
38 Omegaed R	4.00	10.00
39 Danger R	4.00	10.00
40 Devil Dinosaur & Moon Boy R	4.00	10.00
41 Spider-Man R	4.00	10.00
42 Unus thentouchable R	4.00	10.00
43 Black Tom Cassidy R	4.00	10.00
44 The Leader R	4.00	10.00
45 High Evolutionary R	4.00	10.00
46 Arcade R	4.00	10.00
47 Super-Adaptoid R	4.00	10.00
48 Wrecker R	4.00	10.00
49 Cassandra Nova SR	6.00	15.00
50 Hulkbuster SR	15.00	30.00
51 Silver Savage SR	6.00	15.00
52 Mastermind SR	6.00	15.00
53 Emma Frost SR	15.00	30.00
54 Living Monolith SR	6.00	15.00
55 Iron Man SR	6.00	15.00
56 Wolverine SR	8.00	20.00
57 Storm SR	6.00	15.00
58 Warskrull SR	6.00	15.00
59 Apocalypse SR	15.00	30.00
60 Maestro SR	6.00	15.00
61 Dark Beast LE	8.00	20.00
62 Rampaging Hulk LE	8.00	20.00
101 Esme Cuckoo LE	8.00	20.00
102 Incredible Hulk LE	8.00	20.00
103 Proteus LE	8.00	20.00
104 Charles Xavier LE	10.00	25.00

2007 Marvel Heroclix Secret Invasion

COMPLETE SET (60)
RELEASED ON JULY 24, 2008

1 Spider-Man C	.20	.50
2 Moloid C	.20	.50
3 Tombstone C	.20	.50
4 Iron Fist C	.20	.50
5 Sharon Carter C	.20	.50
6 Yellowjacket C	.20	.50
7 Atlantean Warrior C	.20	.50
8 Ms. Marvel C	.20	.50

9 Gravity C	.20	.50
10 Grey Gargoyle C	.20	.50
11 Arachne C	.20	.50
12 Gee C	.20	.50
13 Lightspeed C	.20	.50
14 Massmaster C	.20	.50
15 Energizer C	.20	.50
16 Hercules C	.20	.50
17 Human Torch U	.40	1.00
18 Clea U	.40	1.00
19 Captain America U	.40	1.00
20 Immortus U	.40	1.00
21 Iron Man U	.40	1.00
22 Goliath U	.40	1.00
23 Hawkeye U	.40	1.00
24 Spider-Slayer U	.40	1.00
25 She-Thing U	.40	1.00
26 Kristoff U	.40	1.00
27 Tarantula U	.40	1.00
28 Altuma U	.40	1.00
29 Morbius U	.40	1.00
30 Punisher U	.40	1.00
31 Mole Man U	.40	1.00
32 Dum Dum Dugan U	.40	1.00
33 Dr. Strange R	2.00	5.00
34 Dr. Octopus R	2.00	5.00
35 Howard the Duck R	2.00	5.00
36 Malice R	2.00	5.00
37 Triton R	2.00	5.00
38 Speedball R	2.00	5.00
39 Cloak and Dagger R	2.00	5.00
40 Doom R	2.00	5.00
41 Spider-Girl R	2.00	5.00
42 Captain Mar-Vell R	2.00	5.00
43 Psycho-Man R	2.00	5.00
44 Super-Skrull: X-Men R	2.00	5.00
45 Namor R	2.00	5.00
46 Thor Girl R	2.00	5.00
47 Adam Warlock R	2.00	5.00
48 Elektra R	2.00	5.00
49 Ringmaster SR	8.00	20.00
50 Magus SR	8.00	20.00
51 Nick Fury SR	8.00	20.00
52 Impossible Man SR	8.00	20.00
53 Skrull Emperor SR	8.00	20.00
54 Gamora SR	8.00	20.00
55 Mephisto SR	8.00	20.00
56 Annihilus SR	8.00	20.00
57 Jarvis SR	8.00	20.00
58 Power Man and Iron Fist SR	8.00	20.00
59 Sentry SR	8.00	20.00
60 Super-Skrull: Avengers SR	8.00	20.00
100 Spider-Woman CH	30.00	60.00
199 Susan Richards CH	25.00	50.00

2009 Marvel Heroclix Hammer of Thor

COMPLETE SET (60)
RELEASED ON NOVEMBER 18, 2009

1 Bug C	.20	.50
2 Kingpin C	.20	.50
3 Hand Ninja C	.20	.50
4 Rock Troll C	.20	.50
5 Jimmy Woo C	.20	.50
6 Pip the Troll C	.20	.50
7 Marvel Boy C	.20	.50
8 Phalanx Soldier C	.20	.50
9 Malakith C	.20	.50
10 M-11 C	.20	.50
11 Enchantress C	.20	.50
12 Valkyrie C	.20	.50
13 Bi-Beast C	.20	.50
14 Asguardian Warrior C	.20	.50
15 Fire Demon C	.20	.50
16 Thor C	.20	.50
17 Balder U	.40	1.00
18 Fandril U	.40	1.00
19 Chase Stein U	.40	1.00
20 Karnilla U	.40	1.00
21 Ulik U	.40	1.00
22 Moonstone U	.40	1.00
23 Beta Ray Bill U	.40	1.00
24 Namora U	.40	1.00
25 Starlord U	.40	1.00
26 Pluto U	.40	1.00
27 Moondragon U	.40	1.00
28 Rocket Raccoon U	.40	1.00
29 Gorilla Man U	.40	1.00
30 Owl U	.40	1.00
31 Ronan the Accuser U	.40	1.00
32 Daredevil U	.40	1.00
33 Sif R	4.00	10.00
34 Hogun R	4.00	10.00
35 Loki R	15.00	30.00
36 Heimdall R	4.00	10.00
37 Songbird R	4.00	10.00
38 Venom R	4.00	10.00
39 Destroyer R	4.00	10.00
40 Captain America R	15.00	30.00
41 Molly Hayes R	4.00	10.00
42 Phyl-vell R	4.00	10.00
43 Penance R	4.00	10.00
44 Air-Walker R	4.00	10.00
45 Karolina R	4.00	10.00
46 Fenris Wolf R	4.00	10.00
47 Nico Minoru R	4.00	10.00
48 Spider-Man R	8.00	20.00
49 Ultron SR	20.00	40.00
50 Hela SR	4.00	10.00
51 Odin SR	8.00	20.00
52 Venus SR	4.00	10.00
53 Seth SR	4.00	10.00
54 Loki SR	8.00	20.00
55 Valkyrie SR	15.00	30.00
56 Surtur SR	4.00	10.00
57 Thor and Loki SR	15.00	30.00
58 Gertrude Yorkes and Old Lace SR	8.00	20.00
59 Volstagg SR	20.00	40.00
60 Kurse SR	8.00	20.00
61 Thor's Mighty Chariot CH	15.00	30.00
99 Thorbuster CH	30.00	60.00
100 Thor, Frog of Thunder LE	30.00	60.00
101 Samantha Parrington LE	15.00	30.00
102 Skill-Brother LE	15.00	30.00
103 Gharskygt LE	15.00	30.00
104 Son of Surtur LE	15.00	30.00
105 Thor, the Reigning LE	15.00	30.00
201 Ragnarok Surtur CH	15.00	30.00

2010 Marvel Heroclix Web of Spider-Man

1 H.A.M.M.E.R. Agent C	.20	.50
2 Symbiote C	.20	.50
3 Reseacher C	.20	.50
4 Nurse C	.20	.50
5 Code: Blue Officer C	.20	.50
6 Mugger C	.20	.50
7 Spider-Man C	.20	.50
8 Peter Parker C	.20	.50
9 Venom C	.20	.50
10 Eddie Brock C	.20	.50
11 Prowler C	.20	.50
12 Puma C	.20	.50
13 Will-O'-the-Wisp C	.20	.50
14 Iron Man C	.20	.50
15 Molten Man C	.20	.50
16 Ironclad C	.20	.50
17 H.A.M.M.E.R. Elite U	.40	1.00
18 Carnage U	.40	1.00
19 Chameleon U	.40	1.00
20 Firestar U	.40	1.00
21 Lt. Marcus Stone U	.40	1.00
22 Spider-Man U	.40	1.00
23 Norman Osborn U	.40	1.00
24 Ben Rielly U	.40	1.00
25 Anti-Venom U	.40	1.00
26 Black Cat U	.40	1.00
27 X-23 U	.40	1.00
28 Warpath U	.40	1.00
29 Wolfsbane U	.40	1.00
30 Mary Jane Watson U	.40	1.00
31 Daken U	.40	1.00
32 Vector U	.40	1.00
33 Menace R	4.00	10.00
34 Victor Mancha R	4.00	10.00
35 J. Jonah Jameson R	4.00	10.00
36 Vermin R	4.00	10.00
37 Scorpion R	4.00	10.00
38 Noh-Varr R	4.00	10.00
39 Iron Patriot R	4.00	10.00
40 Scarlet Spider R	4.00	10.00
41 Cardiac R	4.00	10.00
42 Bullseye R	4.00	10.00
43 Wolverine R	4.00	10.00
44 Rocket Racer R	4.00	10.00
45 Solo R	4.00	10.00
46 Jackal R	4.00	10.00
47 Nightcrawler R	6.00	15.00
48 X-Ray R	4.00	10.00
49 Groot SR	6.00	15.00
50 Red Hulk SR	25.00	50.00
51 The Spot SR	6.00	15.00
52 Morlun SR	6.00	15.00
53 Red She-Hulk SR	8.00	20.00
54 Doctor Octopus SR	6.00	15.00
55 Sandman SR	6.00	15.00
56 Mysterio SR	6.00	15.00
57 Deadpool SR	25.00	50.00
58 Green Goblin SR	10.00	25.00
59 Iron Man/War Machine SR	20.00	40.00
60 Vapor SR	6.00	15.00
61 Spider-Hulk SR	10.00	25.00
62 Doppleganger CH	15.00	30.00
63 Bombastic Bag-Man CH	15.00	30.00
64 Cosmic Spider-Man LE	25.00	50.00
100 Spider-Man LE	8.00	20.00
101 Venom LE	8.00	20.00
102 Night Nurse LE	8.00	20.00
103 Toxin LE	8.00	20.00
104 Daken LE	8.00	20.00
105 The Burglar LE	8.00	20.00

2011 Marvel Heroclix Captain America

1 Captain America C	.40	1.00
2 Howling Commando C	.40	1.00
3 Hydra Agent C	.75	2.00
4 S.H.E.I.L.D. Specialist C	.40	1.00
5 S.H.E.I.L.D. Agent C	.40	1.00
6 Black Widow C	.20	.50
7 Adaptoid C	.20	.50
8 Stonewall C	.20	.50
9 Slingshot C	.20	.50
10 Mentallo C	.20	.50
11 Jack Flag C	.20	.50
12 Diamondback C	.20	.50
13 Mister Hyde C	.20	.50
14 Luke Cage C	.20	.50
15 Red Guardian C	.20	.50
16 Nomad C	.20	.50
17 Richard Fisk U	.20	.50
18 Maria Hill U	.20	.50
19 Yelena Belova U	.20	.50
20 Super-Adaptoid U	.20	.50
21 Phobos U	.20	.50
22 Hardball U	.20	.50
23 Nick Fury U	.40	1.00
24 Doorman U	.30	.75
25 Sin U	.20	.50
26 Viper U	.40	1.00
27 Nightshade U	.20	.50
28 Batroc U	.30	.75
29 Klaw U	.20	.50
30 Falcon U	.30	.75
31 Steve Rogers U	.40	1.00
32 Scorpion U	.20	.50
33 Scientist Supreme R	.30	.75
34 Quake R	.40	1.00
35 Hellfire R	.20	.50
36 Armadillo R	.40	1.00
37 Black Panther R	1.25	3.00
38 Cobra R	.40	1.00
39 Eel R	.40	1.00
40 Captain America R	3.00	8.00
41 Mr. Immortal R	.30	.75
42 Crimson Dynamo R	.75	2.00
43 Darkstar R	1.00	2.50
44 Ursa Major R	.60	1.50
45 Fixer R	.50	1.25
46 Gorgon R	.75	2.00
47 Dirk Anger R	.40	1.00
48 Quasar SR	4.00	10.00
49 Maelstorm SR	3.00	8.00
50 MODOK SR	10.00	25.00
51 Scorpio SR	2.50	6.00
52 Red Skull SR	4.00	10.00
53 Baron Strucker SR	3.00	8.00
54 Baron Zemo SR	3.00	8.00
55 Kitty Pryde SR	4.00	10.00
56 Squirrel Girl SR	6.00	15.00
57 Invisible Woman SR	8.00	20.00
58 Human Torch SR	8.00	20.00
59 Weapon X CH	20.00	40.00
60 Captain America CH	15.00	30.00
61 Capwolf CH	20.00	40.00
62 The Captain CH	25.00	50.00
63 Rojhaz CH	6.00	15.00
100 Life Model Decoy LMD	3.00	6.00
101 Red Guardian LE	.75	2.00
102 Bob, Agent of Hydra LE	2.50	6.00
103 Gabe Jones LE	1.00	2.50
104 Successful Dirk Anger LE	1.25	3.00
105 Madame Hydra LE	2.50	6.00
201 Howling Commando	3.00	8.00
202 Hydra Officer	2.00	5.00
203 S.H.I.E.L.D. Field Agent	2.00	5.00
204 S.H.I.E.L.D. Sentry	1.50	4.00
205 Captain America	1.25	3.00
206 Black Widow	.60	1.50
207 Nick Fury	.75	2.00
208 Red Skull	2.50	6.00
209 Sin	1.25	3.00
210 Klaw	2.00	5.00

2011 Marvel Heroclix Giant Size X-Men

1 Madrox C	1.50	4.00
2 Purifier C	.20	.50
3 Omega Prime Sentinel C	1.00	2.50
4 Hellfire Club Guard C	1.25	3.00
5 Mindless One C	2.50	6.00
6 Skullbuster C	.20	.50
7 Pretty Boy C	.20	.50
8 Cyclops C	2.50	6.00
9 Wolverine C	3.00	8.00
10 Beast C	.60	1.50
11 Emma Frost C	.75	2.00
12 Cypher C	.60	1.50
13 Empath C	.20	.50
14 Roullette C	.40	1.00
15 Tabitha Smith C	.20	.50
16 Aaron Stack C	.20	.50
17 Domino C	1.50	4.00
18 Caliban U	.30	.75
19 William Stryker U	.30	.75
20 Harry Leland U	.30	.75
21 Tarot U	.40	1.00
22 Cannonball U	.20	.50
23 Psylocke U	3.00	8.00
24 Gideon U	.30	.75
25 Elixir U	.40	1.00
26 Leech U	.60	1.50
27 Siryn U	.30	.75
28 Elsa Bloodstone U	1.00	2.50
29 Monica Rambeau U	.30	.75
30 Rogue U	2.00	5.00
31 Angel U	1.25	3.00
32 Ch'od U	.20	.50
33 Blob U	1.50	4.00
34 Pyro R	3.00	8.00
35 Mystique R	4.00	10.00
36 Professor X R	8.00	20.00
37 Gatecrasher R	.20	.50
38 Iceman R	2.00	5.00
39 Lockheed R	4.00	10.00
40 Sabretooth R	6.00	15.00
41 Stryfe R	1.25	3.00
42 Predator X R	2.50	6.00
43 Trevor Fitzroy R	.75	2.00
44 Bonebreaker R	.75	2.00
45 Vulcan R	2.00	5.00
46 Juggernaut SR	25.00	50.00
47 Phoenix SR	20.00	40.00
48 Storm SR	15.00	30.00
49 Archangel SR	10.00	25.00
50 Armor SR	6.00	15.00
51 Hulk SR	10.00	25.00
52 Wolverine SR	8.00	20.00
53 Magneto SR	40.00	75.00
54 The Captain SR	4.00	10.00
55 Cable & Deadpool CH	15.00	30.00
56 Colossus & Wolverine CH	15.00	30.00
57 Cyclops & Phoenix CH	10.00	20.00
58 Gambit & Rogue CH	8.00	20.00
100 Jamie Madrox	.75	2.00
101 Psylocke LE	2.50	6.00
102 Cable LE	15.00	30.00
103 Deadpool LE	20.00	40.00
104 Archangel LE	15.00	30.00
105 Karima LE	1.50	4.00
201 Pestilence LE	20.00	40.00
202 War LE	25.00	50.00
203 Famine LE	3.00	6.00
G01 Sentinel Mark II	10.00	25.00
G02 Sentinel Mark V	8.00	20.00
G03 Apocalypse	15.00	30.00
G04 Onslaught	25.00	50.00
G05 Nemesis	8.00	20.00
G06 Frost Giant	10.00	25.00
G07 Apocalypse	15.00	30.00
G08 Sentinel Mark II	15.00	30.00
G09 Sentinel Mark V	8.00	20.00
M001 Moonstone LE		

2011 Marvel Heroclix Hammer of Thor Fast Forces

COMPLETE SET (6)	10.00	20.00
1 Fandral	2.00	5.00
2 Hogun	2.00	5.00
3 Volstagg	2.00	5.00
4 Asguardian Brawler	2.00	5.00
5 Thor	5.00	10.00
6 Loki	5.00	10.00

2012 Marvel Heroclix The Incredible Hulk

1 Hulk C	.60	1.50
2 Bruce Banner C	.20	.50
3 A.I.M. AIM Agent C	.60	1.50
4 Hulkbuster Soldier C	.40	1.00
5 Humanoid C	.40	1.00
6 Hulk Robot C	.20	.50
7 She-Hulk C	.40	1.00
8 John Jameson C	.20	.50
9 Man-Wolf C	.20	.50
10 Punisher C	.20	.50
11 Punisher C	.30	.75
12 Thundra C	.20	.50
13 Abomination C	.20	.50
14 The Leader C	.20	.50
15 Skaar U	.40	1.00
16 Lyra U	.20	.50
17 A.I.M. Renegade U	.60	1.50
18 A.I. Marine U	.40	1.00
19 Black Tarantula U	.40	1.00
20 White Tiger U	.20	.50
21 Daredevil U	.20	.50
22 Matt Murdock U	.20	.50
23 Punisher U	.20	.50
24 Jigsaw U	.20	.50
25 Rick Jones U	.20	.50
26 Hercules U	.40	1.00
27 Amadeus Cho R	.75	2.00
28 Red Hulk R	2.00	5.00
29 General Thunderbolt Ross R	.20	.50
30 Doc Samson R	.20	.50
31 Daredevil R	.50	1.25
32 Shanna R	.20	.50
33 Tiger Shark R	.60	1.50
34 Man-Beast R	.20	.50
35 Wolverine R	.40	1.00
36 Joe Fixit R	.40	1.00
37 Ghost Rider SR	6.00	15.00
38 Spider-Man SR	4.00	10.00
39 Caiera SR	4.00	10.00
40 A-Bomb SR	2.50	6.00
41 Ka-Zar SR	2.00	5.00
42 Black Bolt SR	8.00	20.00
43 Hulk SR	5.00	12.00
44 Red King SR	3.00	8.00
45 Cosmic Hulk SR	5.00	12.00
46 Winter Hulk CH	10.00	25.00
47 Hulklops CH	8.00	20.00
48 Icehulk CH	8.00	20.00
49 Hulkmariner CH	6.00	15.00
50 Mighty Thorr CH	10.00	25.00
51 Wolverine CH	10.00	25.00
100 A.I. Marine Hulk LE	.75	2.00
101 Bruce Banner LE	1.50	4.00
102 Major Glenn Talbot LE	1.25	3.00
103 Daredevil LE	1.50	4.00
104 Black Bolt LE	3.00	8.00
S101 Gamma Bomb	5.00	12.00
S102 Globe of Ultimate Knowledge	.75	2.00

2012 Marvel Heroclix The Incredible Hulk Fast Forces

1 Hulk	.75	2.00
2 Hulkbuster Wrangler	1.00	2.50
3 She-Hulk	1.50	4.00
4 Abomination	.60	1.50
5 General Thunderbolt Ross	.40	1.00
6 The Leader	.40	1.00

2012 Marvel Heroclix The Incredible Hulk Gravity Feed

201 Hulk	1.25	3.00
202 Bruce Banner	.40	1.00
203 Hulkbuster Squad Leader	.75	2.00
204 She-Hulk	1.50	4.00
205 Punisher	2.00	5.00
206 Abomination	.75	2.00
207 Skaar	.75	2.00
208 General Thunderbolt Ross	1.00	2.50
209 The Leader	.40	1.00
210 Red Hulk	3.00	8.00

2012 Marvel Heroclix 10th Anniversary

COMPLETE SET (24)
RELEASED ON SEPTEMBER 12, 2012

1 Captain America C	.75	2.00
2 Hulk C	.75	2.00
3 Thing C	.75	2.00
4 Green Goblin C	1.25	3.00
5 Thor C	2.00	5.00
6 Marvel Girl C	1.25	3.00
7 Storm C	1.50	4.00
8 White Queen C	1.25	3.00
9 Iron Man C	4.00	10.00
10 Weapon X U	1.00	2.50
11 Thing U	.75	2.00
12 Iron Man U	1.25	3.00
13 Hulk U	8.00	20.00
14 Emma Frost U	3.00	8.00
15 Magneto U	1.50	4.00
16 Thor U	2.50	6.00
17 Spider-Man U	6.00	15.00
18 Green Goblin R	8.00	20.00
19 Magneto R	12.00	30.00
20 Storm R	8.00	20.00
21 Dark Phoenix R	25.00	50.00
22 Skrull Wolverine CH	12.00	30.00
23 Skrull Captain America CH	10.00	25.00
24 Skrull Spider-Man CH	12.00	30.00

2012 Marvel Heroclix Avengers Movie

COMPLETE SET (42)
RELEASED ON APRIL 18, 2012

1 Captain America C	1.25	3.00
2 Hydra Soldier C	1.50	4.00
3 Agent of S.H.I.E.L.D. C	.75	2.00
4 Thor C	1.50	4.00
5 Frost Giant C	2.00	5.00
6 Iron Man C	1.50	4.00
7 Black Widow C	1.25	3.00
8 Skrull Commando C	1.25	3.00
9 Hawkeye C	1.50	4.00
10 S.H.I.E.L.D. Commando C	1.25	3.00
11 Maria Hill U	.75	2.00
12 Sif U	.75	2.00
13 Bruce Banner U	.40	1.00
14 Hulk U	1.50	4.00
15 Loki U	2.50	6.00
16 Red Skull U	1.25	3.00
17 Bucky Barnes U	.75	2.00
18 Captain America R	2.50	6.00

19 Iron Man R 1.50 4.00
20 Thor R 2.00 5.00
21 Howard Stark R 1.25 3.00
22 Destroyer R 6.00 15.00
23 Volstagg SR 1.25 3.00
24 Hogun SR 1.25 3.00
25 Fandral SR 1.25 3.00
26 Dum Dum Dugan SR 2.50 6.00
27 Gabe Jones SR 1.25 3.00
28 Captain America SR 3.00 8.00
29 Loki SR 3.00 8.00
30 Laufey SR 4.00 10.00
31 Frost Giant Champion SR 3.00 8.00
32 Skrull General SR 2.50 6.00
33 Skrull Saboteur SR 1.50 4.00
34 Skrull Warrior SR 2.00 5.00
35 Nick Fury SR 3.00 8.00
36 Black Widow SR 2.00 5.00
37 S.H.I.E.L.D. Enforcer SR 2.50 6.00
38 Johann Schmidt SR .75 2.00
39 Hydra Footsoldier SR 2.50 6.00
40 Hydra Technician SR 5.00 12.00
41 Red Skull CH 6.00 15.00
42 Odin CH 8.00 20.00

2012 Marvel Heroclix Avengers Movie Gravity Feed

COMPLETE SET (11)
RELEASED ON APRIL 18, 2012
201 Thor 2.50 6.00
202 Hulk 12.00 30.00
203 Nick Fury 2.00 5.00
204 Captain America 3.00 8.00
205 Iron Man 2.00 5.00
206 Agent Coulson 8.00 20.00
207 Skrull Infiltrator 3.00 8.00
208 Hawkeye 3.00 8.00
209 Tony Stark 2.00 5.00
210 Heimdall 3.00 8.00
211 Loki 15.00 40.00

2012 Marvel Heroclix Avengers Movie Starter Set

COMPLETE SET (6)
RELEASED ON APRIL 18, 2012
1 The Mighty Avenger 1.00 2.50
2 The First Avenger 2.00 5.00
3 The Armored Avenger .60 1.50
4 The Covert Avenger .75 2.00
5 The Sharpshooting Avenger 2.00 5.00
6 The Incredible Avenger 1.25 3.00

2012 Marvel Heroclix Chaos War

COMPLETE SET (60)
RELEASED ON JULY 11, 2012
1 Captain America C .20 .50
2 Iron Man Drone C .75 2.00
3 Ultron Drone C .40 1.00
4 Egghead C .20 .50
5 Sentinel C 1.25 3.00
6 Space Phantom C .20 .50
7 Masque Duplicate C .20 .50
8 Lava Man C .20 .50
9 Shadow Council Soldier C .40 1.00
10 Donald Blake C .40 1.00
11 Tony Stark C .20 .50
12 Dinah Soar C .20 .50
13 Vision C .20 .50
14 Hank Pym C .20 .50
15 Ant-Man C .30 .75
16 Wasp U .20 .50
17 Madame Masque U .20 .50
18 Jinku U .20 .50
19 Max Fury U .20 .50
20 Black Knight U .20 .50
21 Speed U .20 .50
22 Sharon Carter U .20 .50
23 Ms. Marvel U .40 1.00
24 Iron Man U .75 2.00
25 Nitro U .20 .50
26 Ant-Man U .20 .50
27 Genis-Vell U .30 .75
28 Wonder Man U .20 .50
29 Wolverine U 1.25 3.00
30 Wasp R 1.25 3.00
31 Black Knight R .60 1.50
32 Quicksilver R .75 2.00
33 Victoria Hand R .40 1.00
34 Ares R .75 2.00
35 Sentry R 1.00 2.50
36 Tigra R .40 1.00
37 Spider-Woman R .40 1.00
38 Thor R 1.25 3.00
39 Hawkeye R 4.00 10.00
40 Nick Fury R .60 1.50
41 Baron Zemo R .75 2.00
42 Loki SR 3.00 8.00
43 Binary SR 2.50 6.00
44 Crystal SR 5.00 12.00
45 Void SR 6.00 15.00
46 The Unspoken SR 3.00 8.00
47 Mr. Sinister SR 10.00 25.00
48 Taskmaster SR 8.00 20.00
49 Morgan Le Fay SR 6.00 15.00
50 Kang SR 6.00 15.00
51 Chaos King SR 6.00 15.00
52 Lockjaw and Hairball SR 2.50 6.00
53 Ant-Man and Wasp CH 10.00 25.00
54 Hawkeye and Mockingbird CH 8.00 20.00
55 Vision and Scarlet Witch CH 6.00 15.00
56 Scarlet Witch and Wonder Man CH 6.00 15.00
57 Sentry and Void CH 35.00 70.00
58 Dr. Doom and Kang CH 12.00 30.00
59 Thor and Hercules CH 10.00 25.00
60 Avengers Prime CH 35.00 70.00
100 Vision LE 2.50 6.00
101 Mr. Fantastic LE 3.00 8.00
102 Invisible Woman LE 4.00 10.00
103 Thing LE 2.50 6.00
104 Spider-Man LE 5.00 12.00

2012 Marvel Heroclix Chaos War Fast Forces

COMPLETE SET (6)
RELEASED ON JULY 11, 2012
1 Iron Man 1.25 3.00
2 Thor 1.25 3.00
3 Captain America 1.25 3.00
4 Wasp 1.25 3.00
5 Mockingbird 4.00 10.00
6 Scarlet Witch 30.00 60.00

2012 Marvel Heroclix Galactic Guardians

COMPLETE SET (49)
RELEASED ON APRIL 11, 2012
1 Nova Prime C .40 1.00
2 Nova Corps Recruit C .40 1.00
3 Cardinal of the UCT C .40 1.00
4 Skrull Rebel C .20 .50
5 Annihilation Seeker C .20 .50
6 Doombot C .75 2.00
7 Blood Brother C .20 .50
8 Nebula C .20 .50
9 Namor C .20 .50
10 Adam Warlock C .20 .50
11 Drax C .20 .50
12 Charlie-27 C .20 .50
13 Hollywood C .20 .50
14 Astral Dr. Strange U 2.00 5.00
15 Nova Corps Centurion U .30 .75
16 Cardinal Raker U .20 .50
17 Lyja the Laserfist U .20 .50
18 Ravenous U .20 .50
19 Dr. Doom U 1.25 3.00
20 Magus U .30 .75
21 Red Shift U .20 .50
22 Xavin U .20 .50
23 Blastaar U .20 .50
24 Nikki U .20 .50
25 Martinex U .20 .50
26 Mole Man U 1.25 3.00
27 Hulk R .75 2.00
28 Dr. Strange R 1.25 3.00
29 Morg R .75 2.00
30 Fallen One R .40 1.00
31 Captain Marvel R 1.00 2.50
32 Adam Warlock R .60 1.50
33 Gamora R .40 1.00
34 Super-Skrull R .50 1.25
35 Replica R .30 .75
36 Silver Surfer R 2.00 5.00
37 Mr. Fantastic SR 4.00 10.00
38 The Thing SR 5.00 12.00
39 Cosmo SR 6.00 15.00
40 Gladiator SR 3.00 8.00
41 Lord Mar-Vell SR 3.00 8.00
42 Medusa SR 4.00 10.00
43 Stranger SR 2.50 6.00
44 Mistress Death SR 8.00 20.00
45 Thanos SR 10.00 25.00
46 Dr. Doom CH 12.00 30.00
47 Mr. Fantastic CH 8.00 20.00
48 Keeper CH 8.00 20.00
49 Thanos CH 40.00 80.00
100 Super Nova LE 1.25 3.00
101 Iron Man LE 5.00 12.00
102 Hulk LE 2.00 5.00
103 Wolverine LE 5.00 12.00
104 Spider-Man LE 4.00 10.00
S101 Nova Helmet .75 2.00
S102 Cosmic Cube 2.00 5.00

2012 Marvel Heroclix Galactic Guardians Fast Forces

COMPLETE SET (6)
RELEASED ON APRIL 11, 2012
1 Nova C 1.25 3.00
2 Silver Surfer C 2.50 6.00
3 Gladiator C 2.50 6.00
4 Quasar C 3.00 8.00
5 Beta Ray Bill C 6.00 15.00
6 Ronan the Accuser C 3.00 8.00

2012 Marvel Heroclix Galactic Guardians Giant

COMPLETE SET (6)
RELEASED ON APRIL 11, 2012
G1 Galactus SR 40.00 80.00
G2 Ziran the Tester SR 12.00 30.00
G3 Master Gold SR 15.00 40.00
G4 Giganto, The Mole Monster SR 12.00 30.00
G5 Uatu, The Watcher SR 15.00 40.00
G6 Dormammu SR 25.00 50.00

2012 Marvel Heroclix Galactic Guardians Gravity Feed

COMPLETE SET (10)
RELEASED ON APRIL 11, 2012
201 Nova C .40 1.00
202 Skrull Assassin C .75 2.00
203 Namor C .60 1.50
204 Drax C .40 1.00
205 Dr. Doom C 2.00 5.00
206 Dr. Strange C 3.00 8.00
207 Hulk C 1.25 3.00
208 Super Skrull C .75 2.00
209 Silver Surfer C 2.00 5.00
210 Nova Corps Denarian C 1.25 3.00

2014 Marvel Heroclix Captain America The Winter Soldier

1 Captain America C 2.00 5.00
2 S.H.I.E.L.D. Soldier C 1.50 4.00
3 Black Widow C 3.00 8.00
4 Batroc C 1.50 4.00
5 S.H.I.E.L.D. Agent C 1.50 4.00
6 Falcon C 2.50 6.00
7 S.H.I.E.L.D. Commander C .75 2.00
8 Winter Soldier C 2.50 6.00
9 Steve Rogers R .75 2.00
10 Brock Rumlow R 1.50 4.00
11 Maria Hill R 2.00 5.00
12 Captain America R 2.50 6.00
13 Agent 13 LE 6.00 15.00
14 Agent Sitwell LE 3.00 8.00
15 Nick Fury LE 5.00 12.00
16 Winter Soldier LE 4.00 10.00
17 Captain America and Black Widow CH 6.00 15.00
18 Captain America and Bucky CH 6.00 15.00

2014 Marvel Heroclix Captain America The Winter Soldier Team Pack

H1 S.H.I.E.L.D. Support
H2 S.H.I.E.L.D. Trooper
H3 Batroc's Brigade
H4 KGB Agent
H5 Mercenary
H6 KGB Spy
101 Captain America (TWS FF) 1.25 3.00
102 Black Widow (TWS FF) 1.00 2.50
103 Falcon (TWS FF) .75 2.00
104 Batroc (TWS FF) .75 2.00
105 Winter Soldier (TWS FF) 2.50 6.00
106 S.H.I.E.L.D. Agent (TWS FF) 1.25 3.00

2014 Marvel Heroclix Deadpool

1 Agent X C 1.00 2.50
2 Headpool C 1.25 3.00
3 Dogpool C 1.25 3.00
4 Secret Empire Agent C .40 1.00
5 ULTIMATUM Soldier C 1.25 3.00
6 Hand Ninja C 1.50 4.00
7a Weapon X Scientist C 1.25 3.00
7b The Professor C 2.00 5.00
8 Colleen Wing C 1.25 3.00
9 Misty Knight C 2.00 5.00
10 Humbug C 1.25 3.00
11 Silver Sable C 1.25 3.00
12 Weapon X C 1.25 3.00
12bt Rocket Hand C
13 Anaconda C 1.50 4.00
14 Hammerhead C 1.25 3.00
15 Daredevil C 1.25 3.00
16 Animus C 1.50 4.00
17 Vamp C 1.50 4.00
18 Blind Al C 1.00 2.50
19a Deadpool C 4.00 10.00
019b Evil Deadpool C 8.00 20.00
019ae Deadpool C 4.00 10.00
20 Weasel C 1.25 3.00
21 Outlaw C 1.50 4.00
22 Kidpool C 1.25 3.00
23 Black Cat C 1.25 3.00
24 Number One C 1.25 3.00
25 Flag-Smasher C 1.25 3.00
26 Agent Zero C 1.00 2.50
27 Domino C 1.25 3.00
28 Siryn C 1.00 2.50
29 Lady Bullseye C 1.25 3.00
30 Paladin C 1.25 3.00
31 Elektra C 1.25 3.00
32 Punisher C 1.50 4.00
33 Red Hulk R 2.50 6.00
34 Venom R 4.00 10.00
35 Mercy R 2.00 5.00
36 Bullseye R 4.00 10.00
37 Lady Deadpool R 3.00 8.00
38 Copycat R 1.50 4.00
39 Constrictor R 1.25 3.00
40 Doctor Bong R 1.25 3.00
41 GW Bridge R 1.00 2.50
42 Grasshopper R 1.00 2.50
43 Black Talon R 1.25 3.00
44 Black Tom Cassidy R 1.50 4.00
45 Genesis R 1.50 4.00
46 Shroud R 2.00 5.00
47a Shang-Chi R 3.00 8.00
47b Cat R 8.00 20.00
48 Blink R 4.00 10.00
49 Deadpool and Bob SR 8.00 20.00
50 Wolverine and X-23 SR 8.00 20.00
51 Banshee SR 8.00 20.00
52 Cable SR 10.00 25.00
53a Speed Demon SR 8.00 20.00
53b Whizzer SR 15.00 40.00
54 Arnim Zola SR 2.50 6.00
54bt Gwen Stacy Clone SR
55 Deadpool SR 6.00 15.00
56 T-Ray SR 2.50 6.00
57 Tiamat SR 4.00 10.00
58a Typhoid Mary SR 2.50 6.00
58b Bloody Mary SR 2.50 6.00
59 Kingpin SR 4.00 10.00
60 Superior Spider-Man SR 8.00 20.00
61 Kingpin CH 25.00 60.00
62 Rhino CH 25.00 60.00
63 Green Goblin CH 30.00 80.00
64 Electro CH 30.00 80.00
65 Doctor Octopus CH 25.00 60.00
66 Venom CH 25.00 60.00
67 Sabretooth CH 20.00 50.00
68 Juggernaut CH 25.00 60.00

2014 Marvel Heroclix Deadpool Gravity Feed

201 Deadpool 6.00 15.00
202 Daredevil 2.50 6.00
203 Black Cat 2.00 5.00
204 Secret Empire Number 9 1.50 4.00
205 ULTIMATUM Major
206 Snakeroot Clan Ninja 3.00 8.00
207 Adamantium Specialist 2.00 5.00
208 Silver Sable 1.25 3.00
209 Domino 2.50 6.00
210 Hammerhead 1.50 4.00

2014 Marvel Heroclix Deadpool Special Objects

S101 Omega Drive 2.00 5.00
S102 Straightjacket 2.00 5.00

2014 Marvel Heroclix Deadpool Spider-Bots

99a Spider-Bot (Mark 1) 2.00 5.00
99b Spider-Bot (Mark 2) 2.50 6.00

2014 Marvel Heroclix Guardians of the Galaxy Movie

1 Star-Lord 2.50 6.00
2 Gamora 1.50 4.00
3 Nova Corpsman 2.00 5.00
4 Nova Corps Officer 1.50 4.00
5 Rocket Raccoon 4.00 10.00
6 Sakaaran Soldier 1.50 4.00
7 Sakaaran Commander 1.25 3.00
8 Ronan the Accuser 2.00 5.00
008e Ronan the Accuser
008r Ronan the Accuser
9 Groot 4.00 10.00
009r Groot
10 Nebula 2.00 5.00
11 Irani Rael 2.50 6.00
12 Yondu 1.50 4.00
13 Drax the Destroyer 6.00 15.00
14 Rhomann Dey 3.00 8.00
15 Korath the Pursuer 5.00 12.00
015e Korath the Pursuer
16 The Collector 5.00 12.00
17 Star-Lord 6.00 15.00
18 Rocket Raccoon 8.00 20.00
101 Star-Lord 4.00 10.00
102 Rocket Raccoon 5.00 12.00
103 Gamora 2.50 6.00
103r Gamora
104 Drax the Destroyer 5.00 12.00
105 Groot 6.00 15.00
105r Groot
106 Ronan 3.00 8.00
106e Ronan
106r Ronan

2014 Marvel Heroclix X-Men Days of Future Past

1 Sentinel C 3.00 8.00
1e Sentinel C
1r Sentinel C
2 Ariel C 1.25 3.00
3 Colossus C 1.25 3.00
3r Colossus C
4 Avalanche C 1.25 3.00
5 Angel C 3.00 8.00
6 Pyro C 1.25 3.00
6bt Flame Construct C
7 Franklin Richards C 1.25 3.00
8 Senator Robert Kelly C 1.25 3.00
9 Nightcrawler U 6.00 15.00
10 Rachel Summers U 1.50 4.00
11 Destiny U 1.50 4.00
12 Storm U 2.00 5.00
13 Wolverine U 4.00 10.00
14 Colossus U 1.25 3.00
15 Blob U 2.00 5.00
16 Moira MacTaggert U 2.50 6.00
17 Magneto R 4.00 10.00
18 Mystique R 4.00 10.00
19 Wolverine R 6.00 15.00
20 Sprite R 4.00 10.00
21 Storm R 3.00 8.00
22 Professor X R 3.00 8.00
23 Sentinel Alpha 3 R 8.00 20.00
23e Sentinel Alpha 3 R
23r Sentinel Alpha 3 R
24 Nimrod CH 20.00 50.00
24e Nimrod CH
24r Nimrod CH 25.00 60.00
H001 Sentinel (Hunter)
H002 Sentinel Sentry
H003 Human Protestor
H004 Mutant Protestor

2014 Marvel Heroclix X-Men Days of Future Past Scenario Pack

G001 Alpha Class Sentinel (attack)
G002 Alpha Class Sentinel (defense)
G001e Alpha Class Sentinel (attack)
G001r Alpha Class Sentinel (attack)
G002e Alpha Class Sentinel (defense)
G002r Alpha Class Sentinel (defense)

2008 World of Warcraft Miniatures

1 Aleyah Dawnborn C 1.00 2.00
2 Amalar Ironhoof R 2.50 6.00
3 Amon Darkheart C 1.00 2.00
4 Archmage Arugal E 12.50 25.00
5 Azarak Wolfsblood R 2.00 5.00
6 Bleakheart Hellcaller R 2.00 5.00
7 Blindlight Murloc C 1.00 2.00
8 Bloodscale Wavecaller R 2.00 5.00
9 Bog Elemental C 1.00 2.00
10 Boris Brightbeard C 1.00 2.00
11 Boulderfist Warrior C 1.00 2.00
12 Celenias Firemane C 1.00 2.00
13 Chen Stormstout R 2.50 6.00
14 Crushridge Ogre R 2.00 5.00
15 Daelas Firewing R 2.00 5.00
16 Delyn Darksun C 1.00 2.00
17 Dizdemona R 2.50 6.00
18 Dralor R 2.00 5.00
19 Elendril C 1.00 2.00
20 Enraged Fire Spirit R 2.50 6.00
21 Fillet Kneecapper Extraordinaire R 2.50 6.00
22 Frostmane Troll R 2.00 5.00
23 Frostsaber Prowler C 1.00 2.00
24 Goblin Shredder R 3.00 8.00
25 Gorebelly C 1.25 3.00
26 Graccus C 1.00 2.00
27 Grumpherys R 2.00 5.00
28 Haruka Skycaller R 3.00 8.00
29 Harvest Golem C 1.00 2.00
30 Helwen C 1.25 3.00
31 High Priestess Tyrande Whisperwind E 15.00 30.00
32 Highlord Bolvar Fordragon E 12.50 25.00
33 Irana R 2.50 6.00
34 Ji'lan C 1.00 2.00
35 Kayleitha C 1.00 2.00
36 Leeroy Jenkins R 3.00 8.00
37 Litori Frostburn C 1.00 2.00
38 Loriai Risingmoon C 1.00 2.00
39 Lotherin C 1.00 2.50
40 Magistrix Kiala R 2.50 6.00
41 Marsh Murloc R 2.50 6.00
42 Mojo Mender Ja'nah C 1.00 2.00
43 Mojo Shaper Ojo'mon C 1.00 2.00
44 Moonshadow C 1.00 2.50
45 Morganis Blackvein C 1.00 2.00
46 Namrah R 3.00 8.00
47 Nathressa Darkstrider R 3.00 8.00
48 Omedus the Punisher R 2.00 5.00
49 Ona Skyshot R 2.50 6.00
50 Phadalus the Enlightened C 1.00 2.00
51 Radak Doombringer C 1.00 2.00
52 Ras Frostwhisper E 12.50 25.00
53 Rethilgore C 1.00 2.00
54 Roria R 2.00 5.00
55 Ruby Gemsparkle C 1.00 2.50
56 Sarmoth C 1.25 3.00
57 Savin Lightguard R 2.50 6.00
58 Skeletal Priest R 3.00 8.00
59 Slitherblade Tidehunter C 1.00 2.00

2004 Star Wars Rebel Storm Miniatures

COMPLETE SET (60) 120.00 250.00
RELEASED ON SEPTEMBER 3, 2004
1 4-LOM R 5.00 10.00
2 Bespin Guard C .30 .75
3 Boba Fett VR 15.00 40.00
4 Bossk R 5.00 10.00
5 Bothan Spy U .60 1.50
6 C-3PO R 5.00 10.00
7 Chewbacca R 6.00 12.00
8 Commando on Speeder Bike VR 15.00 25.00
9 Darth Vader, Dark Jedi R 6.00 12.00
10 Darth Vader, Sith Lord VR 12.50 25.00
11 Dengar R 5.00 10.00
12 Duros Mercenary U .60 1.50
13 Elite Hoth Trooper U .60 1.50
14 Elite Rebel Trooper C .30 .75
15 Elite Snowtrooper U .60 1.50
16 Elite Stormtrooper U .60 1.50
17 Emperor Palpatine VR 15.00 30.00
18 Ewok C .30 .75
19 Gamorrean Guard U .60 1.50
20 General Veers R 5.00 10.00
21 Grand Moff Tarkin R 5.00 10.00
22 Greedo R 5.00 10.00
23 Han Solo R 5.00 10.00
24 Heavy Stormtrooper U .60 1.50
25 Hoth Trooper C .30 .75
26 IG-88 R 5.00 10.00
27 Imperial Officer U .60 1.50
28 Ithorian Scout U .60 1.50
29 Jabba the Hutt VR 12.50 25.00
30 Jawa C .30 .75
31 Lando Calrissian R 5.00 10.00
32 Luke Skywalker, Jedi Knight VR 18.00 30.00
33 Luke Skywalker, Rebel R 6.00 12.00
34 Mara Jade Emperor's Hand R 5.00 10.00
35 Mon Calamari Mercenary C .30 .75
36 Obi-Wan Kenobi VR 12.50 25.00
37 Princess Leia, Captive VR 12.50 25.00
38 Princess Leia, Senator R 6.00 12.00
39 Probe Droid VR 10.00 20.00
40 Quarren Assassin U .60 1.50
41 R2-D2 R 6.00 12.00
42 Rebel Commando U .60 1.50
43 Rebel Officer U .60 1.50
44 Rebel Pilot C .30 .75
45 Rebel Trooper C .30 .75
46 Rebel Trooper C .30 .75
47 Royal Guard U .60 1.50
48 Sandtrooper on Dewback VR 10.00 20.00
49 Scout Trooper on Bike VR 10.00 20.00
50 Scout Trooper U .60 1.50
51 Snowtrooper C .30 .75
52 Stormtrooper C .30 .75
53 Stormtrooper C .30 .75
54 Stormtrooper C .30 .75
55 Stormtrooper Officer U .60 1.50
56 Tusken Raider C .30 .75
57 Twi'lek Bodyguard U .60 1.50
58 Twi'lek Scoundrel C .30 .75
59 Wampa VR 10.00 20.00
60 Wookiee Soldier C .30 .75

2004 Star Wars Clone Strike Miniatures

COMPLETE SET (60) 150.00 300.00
RELEASED ON DECEMBER 13, 2004
1 48 Super Battle Droid U .60 1.50
2 Aayla Secura VR 12.00 20.00
3 Aerial Clone Trooper Captain R 6.00 12.00
4 Agen Kolar R 6.00 12.00
5 Anakin Skywalker VR 15.00 25.00
6 Aqualish Spy C .30 .75
7 ARC Trooper U .60 1.50
8 Asajj Ventress R 6.00 12.00
9 Aurra Sing VR 20.00 35.00
10 Battle Droid C .30 .75
11 Battle Droid C .30 .75
12 Battle Droid C .30 .75
13 Battle Droid Officer U .60 1.50
14 Battle Droid on STAP R 6.00 12.00
15 Captain Typho R 6.00 12.00
16 Clone Trooper C .30 .75
17 Clone Trooper C .30 .75
18 Clone Trooper Commander U .60 1.50
19 Clone Trooper Grenadier C .30 .75
20 Clone Trooper Sergeant C .30 .75
21 Count Dooku VR 15.00 25.00
22 Dark Side Acolyte U .60 1.50
23 Darth Maul VR 18.00 30.00
24 Darth Sidious VR 15.00 25.00
25 Destroyer Droid R 6.00 12.00
26 Devaronian Bounty Hunter C .30 .75
27 Durge R 6.00 12.00
28 Dwarf Spider Droid R 6.00 12.00
29 General Grievous VR 18.00 30.00
30 General Kenobi R 6.00 12.00
31 Geonosian Drone C .30 .75
32 Geonosian Overseer U .60 1.50
33 Geonosian Picador on Orray R 6.00 12.00
34 Geonosian Soldier U .60 1.50
35 Gran Raider C .30 .75
36 Gungan Cavalry on Kaadu R 6.00 12.00
37 Gungan Infantry C .30 .75
38 Ishi Tib Scout U .60 1.50
39 Jango Fett R 6.00 12.00
40 Jedi Guardian U .60 1.50
41 Ki-Adi-Mundi R 6.00 12.00
42 Kit Fisto R 6.00 12.00
43 Klatooinian Enforcer C .30 .75
44 Luminara Unduli R 6.00 12.00
45 Mace Windu VR 15.00 25.00
46 Naboo Soldier U .60 1.50
47 Nikto Soldier C .30 .75
48 Padme Amidala VR 12.00 20.00
49 Plo Koon R 6.00 12.00
50 Quarren Raider U .60 1.50
51 Qui-Gon Jinn VR 12.00 20.00
52 Quinlan Vos VR 12.00 20.00
53 Rodian Mercenary U .60 1.50
54 Saesee Tiin R 6.00 12.00
55 Security Battle Droid C .30 .75
56 Super Battle Droid U .60 1.50
57 Weequay Mercenary C .30 .75
58 Wookiee Commando U .60 1.50
59 Yoda VR 18.00 30.00
60 Zam Wesell R 6.00 12.00

2005 Star Wars Revenge of the Sith Miniatures

COMPLETE SET (61) 120.00 250.00
RELEASED ON APRIL 2, 2005
1 49 Nautolan Soldier C .30 .75
2 Agen Kolar, Jedi Master R 6.00 12.00
3 Alderaan Trooper U .75 1.50
4 Anakin Skywalker, Jedi Knight R 6.00 12.00
5 Anakin Skywalker Sith Apprentice VR 15.00 25.00
6 AT-RT VR 15.00 25.00
7 Bail Organa VR 10.00 20.00
8 Battle Droid C .30 .75
9 Battle Droid C .30 .75
10 Boba Fett, Young Mercenary R 6.00 12.00
11 Bodyguard Droid U .75 1.50
12 Bodyguard Droid U .75 1.50
13 Captain Antilles R 6.00 12.00
14 Chagrian Mercenary Commander U .75 1.50
15 Chewbacca of Kashyyk VR 15.00 25.00
16 Clone Trooper C .30 .75
17 Clone Trooper C .30 .75
18 Clone Trooper Commander U .75 1.50
19 Clone Trooper Gunner C .30 .75
20 Dark Side Adept U .75 1.50
21 Darth Tyranus R 6.00 12.00
22 Darth Vader VR 18.00 30.00
23 Destroyer Droid R 6.00 12.00
24 Devaronian Soldier C .30 .75
25 Emperor Palpatine, Sith Lord VR 18.00 30.00
26 General Grievous, Jedi Hunter VR 18.00 30.00
27 General Grievous, Supreme Commander R 6.00 12.00
28 Gotal Fringer U .75 1.50
29 Grievous Wheel Bike VR 15.00 25.00
30 Human Mercenary U .75 1.50
31 Iktotchi Tech Specialist U .75 1.50
32 Jedi Knight U .75 1.50
33 Mace Windu, Jedi Master VR 18.00 30.00
34 Medical Droid R 6.00 12.00
35 Mon Mothma VR 10.00 20.00
36 Muun Guard U .75 1.50
37 Neimoidian Soldier U .75 1.50
38 Neimoidian Soldier U .75 1.50
39 Obi-Wan Kenobi, Jedi Master R 6.00 12.00
40 Polis Massa Medic C .30 .75
41 R2-D2, Astromech Droid VR 15.00 25.00
42 Royal Guard U .75 1.50
43 San Hill R 6.00 12.00
44 Senate Guard U .75 1.50
45 Separatist Commando C .30 .75
46 Shaak Ti R 6.00 12.00
47 Sly Moore R 6.00 12.00
48 Stass Allie R 6.00 12.00
49 Super Battle Droid C .30 .75
50 Super Battle Droid C .30 .75
51 Tarfful R 6.00 12.00
52 Tion Medon R 6.00 12.00
53 Utapaun Soldier C .30 .75
54 Utapaun Soldier C .30 .75
55 Utapaun Soldier C .30 .75
56 Wat Tambor R 6.00 12.00
57 Wookiee Berserker C .30 .75
58 Wookiee Scout U .75 1.50
59 Yoda, Jedi Master R 7.50 15.00
60 Yuzzem C .30 .75
61 Zabrak Fringer C .30 .75

2005 Star Wars Universe Miniatures

COMPLETE SET (61) 150.00 300.00
RELEASED ON AUGUST 19, 2005
1 Abyssin Black Sun Thug C .30 .75
2 Acklay U .75 1.50
3 Admiral Ackbar VR 10.00 20.00
4 ASP-7 U .75 1.50
5 AT-ST R 7.50 15.00
6 B'omarr Monk R 7.50 15.00
7 Baron Fel VR 18.00 30.00
8 Battle Droid U .75 1.50
9 Battle Droid U .75 1.50
10 Bith Rebel C .30 .75
11 Chewbacca, Rebel Hero R 7.50 15.00
12 Clone Trooper C .30 .75
13 Clone Trooper on BARC Speeder R 10.00 20.00
14 Dark Side Marauder U .75 1.50
15 Dark Trooper Phase III U .75 1.50
16 Darth Maul on Speeder VR 12.50 25.00
17 Darth Vader, Jedi Hunter R 7.50 15.00
18 Dash Rendar R 7.50 15.00
19 Dr. Evazan VR 10.00 20.00
20 Dressellian Commando C .30 .75
21 Elite Clone Trooper U .75 1.50
22 Flash Speeder U .75 1.50
23 Gonk Power Droid C .30 .75
24 Grand Admiral Thrawn VR 18.00 30.00
25 Guri R 7.50 15.00
26 Hailfire Droid U .75 1.50
27 Han Solo, Rebel Hero R 7.50 15.00
28 Kaminoan Ascetic C .30 .75
29 Kyle Katarn VR 10.00 20.00
30 Lando Calrissian, Hero of Taanab R 7.50 15.00
31 Lobot R 6.00 12.00
32 Luke Skywalker on Tauntaun R 10.00 20.00
33 Luke Skywalker, Jedi Master VR 18.00 30.00
34 New Republic Commander U .75 1.50
35 New Republic Trooper C .30 .75
36 Nexu U .75 1.50
37 Nien Nunb R 6.00 12.00
38 Nightsister Sith Witch U .75 1.50
39 Noghri U .75 1.50
40 Nom Anor R 7.50 15.00
41 Nute Gunray R 6.00 12.00
42 Obi-Wan on Boga VR 12.50 25.00
43 Ponda Baba R 6.00 12.00
44 Prince Xizor VR 10.00 20.00
45 Princess Leia, Rebel Hero VR 10.00 20.00
46 Rancor VR 20.00 35.00
47 Reek U .75 1.50
48 Rodian Black Sun Vigo U .75 1.50
49 Shistavanen Pilot U .75 1.50
50 Stormtrooper C .30 .75
51 Stormtrooper Commander U .75 1.50
52 Super Battle Droid C .30 .75
53 Super Battle Droid Commander U .75 1.50
54 Tusken Raider on Bantha U .75 1.50
55 Vornskr C .30 .75
56 Warmaster Tsavong Lah VR 15.00 25.00
57 Wedge Antilles R 7.50 15.00
58 X-1 Viper Droid U .75 1.50
59 Young Jedi Knight C .30 .75
60 Yuuzhan Vong Subaltern U .75 1.50
61 Yuuzhan Vong Warrior C .30 .75

2006 Star Wars Champions of the Force Miniatures

COMPLETE SET (61) 120.00 250.00
RELEASED ON JUNE 6, 2006
1 Arcona Smuggler C .30 .75
2 Barriss Offee R 6.00 12.00
3 Bastila Shan VR 10.00 20.00
5 Clone Commander Bacara R 6.00 12.00
6 Clone Commander Cody R 7.50 15.00
7 Clone Commander Gree R 6.00 12.00
8 Corran Horn R 6.00 12.00
9 Coruscant Guard C .30 .75
10 Crab Droid U .60 1.50
11 Dark Jedi U .60 1.50
12 Dark Jedi Master U .60 1.50
13 Dark Side Enforcer U .60 1.50
14 Dark Trooper Phase I C .30 .75
15 Dark Trooper Phase II U .60 1.50
16 Dark Trooper Phase II VR 10.00 20.00
17 Darth Bane VR 12.50 25.00
18 Darth Malak VR 12.50 25.00
19 Darth Maul, Champion of the Sith R 7.50 15.00
20 Darth Nihilus VR 10.00 20.00
21 Darth Sidious, Dark Lord of the Sith R 6.00 12.00
22 Depa Billaba R 6.00 12.00
23 Even Piell R 6.00 12.00
24 Exar Kun VR 12.50 25.00
25 General Windu R 6.00 12.00
26 Gundark Fringe U .60 1.50
27 HK-47 VR 10.00 20.00
28 Hoth Trooper with Algar Cannon R 6.00 12.00
29 Jacen Solo VR 10.00 20.00
30 Jaina Solo VR 10.00 20.00
31 Jedi Consular U .60 1.50
32 Jedi Guardian U .60 1.50
33 Jedi Padawan U .60 1.50
34 Jedi Sentinel U .60 1.50
35 Jedi Weapon Master C .30 .75
36 Kashyyyk Trooper C .30 .75
37 Luke Skywalker, Young Jedi VR 12.50 25.00
38 Mas Amedda R 7.50 15.00
39 Massassi Sith Mutant U .60 1.50
41 Octuparra Droid R 6.00 12.00
42 Old Republic Commander U .60 1.50
43 Old Republic Trooper U .60 1.50
44 Old Republic Trooper C .30 .75
45 Queen Amidala R 6.00 12.00
46 Qui-Gon Jinn, Jedi Master R 7.50 15.00
47 R5 Astromech Droid C .30 .75
48 Republic Commando Boss U .60 1.50
49 Republic Commando Fixer C .30 .75
50 Republic Commando Scorch C .30 .75
51 Republic Commando Sev C .30 .75
52 Saleucami Trooper C .30 .75
53 Sandtrooper C .30 .75
54 Sith Assault Droid U .60 1.50
55 Sith Trooper C .30 .75
56 Sith Trooper C .30 .75
57 Sith Trooper Commander U .60 1.50
58 Snowtrooper with E-Web Blaster R 6.00 12.00
59 Ugnaught Demolitionist C .30 .75
60 Ulic Qel-Droma VR 7.50 15.00
61 Utapau Trooper C .30 .75
62 Varactyl Wrangler C .30 .75
63 Yoda of Dagobah VR 12.50 25.00

2006 Star Wars Bounty Hunters Miniatures

COMPLETE SET (60) 150.00 300.00
RELEASED ON SEPTEMBER 23, 2006
1 4-LOM, Bounty Hunter R 6.00 12.00
2 Aqualish Assassin C .30 .75
3 Ayy Vida R 6.00 12.00
4 Basilisk War Droid U .60 1.50
5 Bib Fortuna R 6.00 12.00
6 Bith Black Sun Vigo U .60 1.50
7 Boba Fett, Bounty Hunter VR 15.00 40.00
8 BoShek R 6.00 12.00
9 Bossk, Bounty Hunter R 7.50 15.00
10 Boushh R 6.00 12.00
11 Calo Nord R 6.00 12.00
12 Chewbacca w/C-3PO VR 10.00 18.00
13 Commerce Guild Homing Spider Droid U .60 1.50
14 Corellian Pirate U .60 1.50
15 Corporate Alliance Tank Droid U .60 1.50
16 Dannik Jerriko VR 7.50 15.00
17 Dark Hellion Marauder on Swoop Bike U .60 1.50
18 Dark Hellion Swoop Gang Member C .30 .75
19 Defel Spy C .30 .75
20 Dengar, Bounty Hunter R 7.50 15.00
21 Djas Puhr R 6.00 12.00
22 Droid Starfighter in Walking Mode R 7.50 15.00
23 E522 Assassin Droid U .60 1.50
24 Gamorrean Thug C .30 .75
25 Garindan R 6.00 12.00
26 Han Solo, Scoundrel VR 7.50 15.00
27 Huge Crab Droid U .60 1.50
28 Human Blaster-for-Hire C .30 .75
29 IG-88, Bounty Hunter VR 15.00 25.00
30 ISP Speeder R 6.00 12.00
31 Jango Fett, Bounty Hunter VR 15.00 30.00
32 Klatooinian Hunter C .30 .75
33 Komari Vosa R 7.50 15.00
34 Lord Vader VR 10.00 20.00
35 Luke Skywalker of Dagobah R 7.50 15.00
36 Mandalore the Indomitable VR 12.50 25.00
37 Mandalorian Blademaster U .60 1.50
38 Mandalorian Commander U .60 1.50
39 Mandalorian Soldier C .30 .75
40 Mandalorian Supercommando C .30 .75
41 Mandalorian Warrior C .30 .75
42 Mistryl Shadow Guard U .60 1.50
43 Mustafarian Flea Rider R 6.00 12.00
44 Mustafarian Soldier C .30 .75
45 Nikto Gunner on Desert Skiff VR 10.00 20.00
46 Nym VR 7.50 15.00
47 Princess Leia, Hoth Commander R 7.50 15.00
48 Quarren Bounty Hunter C .30 .75
49 Rebel Captain U .60 1.50
50 Rebel Heavy Trooper U .60 1.50
51 Rebel Snowspeeder U .60 1.50
52 Rodian Hunt Master U .60 1.50
53 Talon Karrde VR 7.50 15.00
54 Tamtel Skreej VR 7.50 15.00
55 Tusken Raider Sniper C .30 .75
56 Utapaun on Dactillion VR 7.50 15.00
57 Weequay Leader U .60 1.50
58 Weequay Thug C .30 .75
59 Young Krayt Dragon VR 10.00 20.00
60 Zuckuss R 7.50 15.00

2007 Star Wars Alliance and Empire Miniatures

COMPLETE SET (60) 100.00 200.00
BOOSTER BOX ()
BOOSTER PACK ()
RELEASED IN MAY 2007
1 Admiral Piett R 5.00 10.00
2 Advance Agent, Officer U .60 1.50
3 Advance Scout C .30 .75
4 Aurra Sing, Jedi Hunter VR 10.00 20.00
5 Biggs Darklighter VR 7.50 15.00
6 Boba Fett, Enforcer VR 12.50 25.00
7 C-3PO and R2-D2 R 5.00 10.00
8 Chadra-Fan Pickpocket U .60 1.50
9 Chewbacca, Enraged Wookiee R 5.00 10.00
10 Darth Vader, Imperial Commander VR 12.50 25.00
11 Death Star Gunner U .60 1.50
12 Death Star Trooper C .30 .75
13 Duros Explorer C .30 .75
14 Elite Hoth Trooper C .30 .75
15 Ephant Mon VR 7.50 15.00
16 Ewok Hang Glider R 5.00 10.00
17 Ewok Warrior C .30 .75
18 Gamorrean Guard C .30 .75
19 Han Solo in Stormtrooper Armor R 5.00 10.00
20 Han Solo on Tauntaun VR 10.00 20.00
21 Han Solo Rogue R 5.00 10.00
22 Heavy Stormtrooper U .60 1.50
23 Human Force Adept C .30 .75
24 Imperial Governor Tarkin R 5.00 10.00
25 Imperial Officer U .60 1.50
26 Ithorian Commander U .60 1.50
27 Jabba, Crime Lord VR 7.50 15.00
28 Jawa on Ronto VR 7.50 15.00
29 Jawa Trader U .60 1.50
30 Lando Calrissian, Dashing Scoundrel R 5.00 10.00
31 Luke Skywalker, Champion of the Force VR 12.50 25.00
32 Luke Skywalker, Hero of Yavin R 5.00 10.00
33 Luke's Landspeeder VR 7.50 15.00
34 Mara Jade, Jedi R 5.00 10.00
35 Mon Calamari Tech Specialist C .30 .75
36 Nikto Soldier C .30 .75
37 Obi-Wan Kenobi, Force Spirit VR 7.50 15.00
38 Princess Leia R 5.00 10.00
39 Quinlan Vos, Infiltrator VR 10.00 20.00
40 Rampaging Wampa VR 7.50 15.00
41 Rebel Commando C .30 .75
42 Rebel Commando Strike Leader U .60 1.50
43 Rebel Leader U .60 1.50
44 Rebel Pilot C .30 .75
45 Rebel Trooper U .60 1.50
46 Rodian Scoundrel U .60 1.50
47 Scout Trooper U .60 1.50
48 Snivvian Fringer C .30 .75
49 Snowtrooper C .30 .75
50 Storm Commando R 5.00 10.00
51 Stormtrooper C .30 .75
52 Stormtrooper Officer U .60 1.50
53 Stormtrooper on Repulsor Sled VR 10.00 20.00
54 Talz Spy Fringe U .60 1.50
55 Trandoshan Mercenary U .60 1.50
56 Tusken Raider C .30 .75
57 Twi'lek Rebel Agent U .60 1.50
58 Wicket R 5.00 10.00
59 Wookiee Freedom Fighter C .30 .75
60 Yomin Carr R 6.00 12.00

2009 World of Warcraft Spoils of War Miniatures

1 Anchorite Cristia R 2.00 5.00
2 Beren Embersbane C 1.00 2.00
3 Bogstrok Razorclaw R 2.00 5.00
4 Cairne Bloodhoof E 15.00 30.00
5 Champion Shadowsun R 2.00 5.00
6 Chancellor Velora C 1.00 2.00
7 Conqueror Aluna R 2.00 5.00
8 Crashing Wave-Spirit C 1.00 2.00
9 Dagg'um Ty'gor R 2.00 5.00
10 Daspien Bladedancer R 2.00 5.00
11 Daxin Firesworn C 1.00 2.00
12 Deathwhisperer R 2.00 5.00
13 Drokkar of the Four Boars C 1.00 2.00
14 Elanna Starbreeze C 1.00 2.00
15 Elizabetha Cairnwillow R 2.00 5.00
16 Ethereal Crypt Raider C 1.00 2.00
17 Ethereal Priest C 1.00 2.00
18 Felguard Legionnaire C 1.00 2.00
19 Grimdron R 2.00 5.00
20 Harnum Firebelly C 1.00 2.00
21 Hulok Trailblazer C 1.00 2.00
22 Illiana Sunshield R 2.50 6.00
23 Ironfur Bear C 1.00 2.00
24 Ixamos the Redeemed R 2.50 6.00
25 Lady Jaina Proudmoore E 12.50 25.00
26 Lady Vashj E 20.00 40.00
27 Magdeline Prideheart R 2.00 5.00
28 Magistrix Enaria R 2.00 5.00
29 Marlowe Christophers C 1.00 2.00
30 Morova of the Sands R 2.50 6.00
31 Najan Spiritbinder C 1.00 2.00
32 Parvink R 2.00 5.00
33 Prince Kael'thas Sunstrider E 12.50 25.00
34 Prophet Velen E 12.50 25.00
35 Razaani Nexus Stalker R 2.00 5.00
36 Rexxar E 12.50 25.00
37 Ryno the Short R 3.00 8.00
38 Sethekk Talon Lord C 2.00
39 Sha'do R 2.00 5.00
40 Shienor Sorcerer R 2.00 5.00
41 Sidian Morningblade C 1.00 2.00